PrincetonReview.com

THE COMPLETE
BOOK OF COLLEGES

WITHDRAWN

2018 EDITION

| Penguin
Random
House

The Princeton Review
555 West 18th Street
New York, NY 10011
editorialsupport@review.com

Published in the United States by Penguin Random
House LLC, New York, and in Canada by Random
House of Canada, a division of Penguin Random
House Ltd.,Toronto. This is a revised edition of a
book first published in 1989.

ISBN: 978-0-451-48773-5
ISSN: 1088-8594

Production: Best Content Solutions, LLC
Production Editor: Melissa Duclos

Printed in the United States of America.

9 8 7 6 5 4 3 2 1

2018 Edition

Editorial
Robert Franek, Editor-in-Chief

David Soto, Director of Content Development

Kristen O'Toole, Editorial Director

Stephen Koch, Student Survey Manager

Pia Aliperti, Editor

Penguin Random House Publishing Team
Tom Russell, VP, Publisher

Alison Stoltzfus, Publishing Director

Ellen L. Reed, Production Manager

Jake Eldred, Associate Managing Editor

Suzanne Lee, Designer

ACKNOWLEDGMENTS

Each year we assemble an awe-inspiringly talented group of colleagues who work together to produce our guidebooks; this year is no exception. Everyone involved in this effort—authors, editors, data collectors, production specialists, and designers—gives so much more than is required to make *The Complete Book of Colleges* an exceptional student resource guide.

My sincere thanks go to the many who contributed to this tremendous project. Very special thanks go to Kristen O'Toole for her editorial commitment and vision. A warm and special thank you goes to our Student Survey expert, Stephen Koch, who continues to work in partnership with school administrators and students alike. My continued thanks go to our data collection pro, David Soto, for his successful efforts in collecting and accurately representing the statistical data that appear with each college profile and to Melissa Duclos for her dedication to reading through the massive amounts of data. The enormousness of this project and its deadline constraints could not have been realized without the calm presence of our production partner, Scott Harris. Scott's many years of dedication and focus continue to delight and remind me of what a pleasure it is to work together on this project each year. Special thanks also go to Jeanne Krier, our Random House publicist, for the dedicated work she continues to do on this book and the overall series since its inception. Jeanne continues to be my trusted colleague, media advisor, and friend. I would also like to make special mention of Tom Russell and Alison Stoltzfus, our Random House publishing team, for their continuous investment and faith in our ideas. Last, I thank my Princeton Review Partner Team, Kate Walker, Amy Calhoun, Stacy Caldwell, Casey Cornelius, and Vincent Jungels, for their confidence in me and my content team and for their commitment to providing students the resources they need to find the right fit school for them. Again, to all who contributed so much to this publication, thank you for your efforts; they do not go unnoticed.

Robert Franek
Editor-in-Chief

CONTENTS

CONTENTS

FOREWORD

Welcome. You have found the best place to begin, fine-tune, and execute the search for your perfect college. With the understanding that choosing a school wisely is a top priority for each prospective student, we have provided a significant breadth of information in this text to help you navigate the exciting, amazing, and sometimes confusing process of choosing the right college.

The design of this guidebook will allow you to narrow your search of colleges from 1,357 to a few dozen. Here you'll find all the individual college statistics you'll need to make informed choices about the competitiveness, size, location, and academic offerings of the schools available to you. In addition, you can find even more information about individual schools at The Princeton Review's website, PrincetonReview.com. The site includes college search features, college profiles, college discussion boards, a college majors search engine, and much more.

By using this book, you can search for, choose, and apply to colleges with the confidence of a pro—or at the very least a well-informed undergraduate hopeful! We supply the information and guidance, and you ultimately make your own decision.

The college selection, application, and interview processes can be overwhelming at times. They can also be rewarding experiences. For most, choosing a college is the first major life decision. I know it was mine. Remember that your college decision is yours alone, so arm yourself with the best available information. Badger teachers, friends, high school and college admissions counselors, brothers, sisters, and parents; ask them how they chose their colleges and why. The more you know when beginning the process, the more in control of the situation you'll feel.

Whatever it is that you choose as your path in life, your college selection will forever be your first step in that direction. The friends you make, the professors you meet, and the classes you take are all springboards to the next phase of your life.

I wish you much luck and success at whichever college you decide to attend. My sincere hope is that this publication and other Princeton Review tools will be helpful in the process.

Robert Franek
Editor-in-Chief

INTRODUCTION

Before you dive into *The Complete Book of Colleges*, we want to give you some tips for your college search—especially on how to get the most out of this book and what to do once you've made your choices and are ready to apply. Since the most important thing for you to do now is to start your search, we want to start right off by revealing the secret to getting admitted to the college of your choice.

A crucial, and often overlooked, element to getting into college is matchmaking: that is, finding colleges that have the educational and social environments you're looking for, where you are well-suited academically, and have something the college is looking for in return. You have a lot more control over where you end up going to college than you might think.

Matchmaking is a two-step process. You should begin with a thorough self-examination or personal inventory. Your personal inventory is best structured in the form of a chart, so that when you begin to consider your options, you can check off those colleges that satisfy the various needs or wants you've identified. In this way, your best college choices will gradually begin to identify themselves.

Divide your inventory into two sections. One section should be biographical, including your high school course selection, GPA, SAT or ACT scores, class rank, and personal information like extracurricular activities—especially those you plan to continue in college. This will help you to assess how you stack up against each college's admissions standards and student body. The second section is a listing of the characteristics you need or want in the college you'll choose to attend. This list should include anything and everything you consider important, such as location, size of the student body, availability of scholarships, dormitory options, clubs and activities, even school colors if you want. This part of your inventory should grow continuously as you become more and more aware of what is important to you in your choice of colleges.

Armed with your personal inventory, you can begin to take advantage of the numerous resources available to help you narrow your choices of where to apply. There are five sources for information and advice that have become standard for most college-bound students:

1. College websites, Facebook pages, videos, brochures, catalogs...

If you are a junior or senior in high school, you probably know more about the information these materials should include than the people who are responsible for designing and writing them. College marketing material will give you an overview of the academic offerings and the basic admissions requirements. You will never see anything but the most appealing architecture and the best-looking students on campus, nor will you hear about the recent tuition increases that were greater than the rate of inflation. Look these materials over, but don't make any decisions based solely on what you read or see.

2. Your friends

The experts on specific colleges and universities are the students who currently attend them. Seek out any and all of your friends, offspring of your parents' friends, and recent graduates of your high school who attend colleges that you are considering. Talk to them when they come home. Arrange to stay with them when you visit their colleges. Pick their brains for everything they know. It doesn't get any more direct and honest than this.

3. Books and college guides

There are two types of books that can be helpful to you in your search: those that discuss specific aspects of going to college and college guides. A great narrative guide that stresses students' own opinions of colleges is our own annual *Best Colleges* guide. In addition, look at other guides for good second opinions. As for comprehensive guides—those that emphasize data over narrative content—you're holding the most up-to-date and useful one in your hands.

4. The Internet

Beyond a college's own website and social media presence, there are many publications and communities online dedicated to college admissions. Our site, PrincetonReview.com, provides a wide range of resources to help you research colleges, prepare for standarized tests, raise your grades, and complete your college application.

5. Your counselor

Since it's *critically* important, we'll say it again: Once you've developed some ideas about your personal inventory and college options, schedule a meeting with your guidance counselor. The more research you've done before you get together, the more help you're likely to get. Good advice comes out of thoughtful discussion, not from the expectation that your counselor will do your work. When it comes time to file applications, look over the materials and requirements together, and allow plenty of time to put forth your best.

USING COLLEGE INFORMATION IN THE COMPLETE BOOK OF COLLEGES AND ELSEWHERE

Throughout the course of your college search, you'll confront an amazing array of statistics and other data related to every college you consider. In order for all of this information to be helpful, you need to have some sense of how to interpret it. We've included a detailed key to the college entries in this book a few pages deeper into this introduction. Almost all the statistics we've compiled are self-explanatory, but there are a few that will be more useful with some elaboration.

Let's start with **student/teacher ratio**. Don't use it to assess average class size; they are not interchangeable terms. At almost every college, the average class size is larger than its student/teacher ratio. At many big universities, it is considerably larger. What is useful about the ratio is that it can give you an idea of how accessible your professors will be outside of the classroom. Once you are in college, you'll grow to realize just how important this is.

In the same way, the **percentage of faculty that holds PhDs** is useful information. When you're paying thousands of dollars in tuition each year, there's something comforting about knowing that your professors have a considerably broader and deeper grasp of what you're studying than you do. In contrast, teaching assistants (TAs) may often be just one or two steps ahead of you.

Another interesting group of statistics deals with the **percentage of students who go on to graduate or professional school**. Never allow yourself to be swayed by such statistics, unless you've taken the time to ponder their meaning and visited the college in question. High percentages almost always mean one of two things: that the college is an intellectual enclave that inspires students onward to further their education, or that it is a pre-professional bastion of aggressive careerists. There isn't anything inherently wrong with either scenario, but neither has universal appeal to prospective students. Colleges that are exceptions to this rule are rare and precious. The most misleading figures provided to prospective students are those for medical school acceptance rates. Virtually every college in the country can boast of high acceptance rates to medical school for its graduates; pre-med programs are designed to weed out those who will not be strong candidates before they even get to apply! If you're thinking about medical school, ask colleges how many of their students apply to medical school each year. Also, try to get a sense of the attrition rate within the pre-med program.

One final piece of advice about statistics relates to the **college's acceptance rate**. Simply knowing the percentage of applicants who are admitted each year is helpful, but it is even more helpful if you also know how many applied. When you compare these figures to the freshman profile, you have the most accurate picture of just how tough it is to get in. An 80 percent acceptance rate doesn't mean there's an open door if you don't match up well to the academic achievements of the college's typical freshman. Beyond this, keep an eye out for colleges that have relatively self-selecting applicant pools. In these cases, high acceptance rates may be misleading. When evaluating highly selective public colleges as an out-of-state applicant, remember that you will likely face a more selective evaluation than state residents.

A Few Final Thoughts

Once you've narrowed down your options and decided where to apply, find the applications on PrincetonReview.com and get to work filling them out. The admissions process is stressful enough without putting extra pressure on yourself by waiting until the last minute. The first thing you should do when you receive the necessary forms is go over them with your guidance counselor. Immediately remove the recommendation forms (if they are required) and give them to the teachers and counselor(s) who will be completing them for you. They'll have a better opportunity to write a thorough and supportive recommendation if you give them enough time to complete them. This is also the time to make your request for official transcripts. Again, it takes time to do these things. Plan ahead.

As for completing the applications, organize yourself and all the materials. Keep everything in folders (physically; on your computer; or in the cloud) and accessible in case you need to speak with an admissions officer over the telephone. When essays and information on your extracurricular activities are required, do some outlining and rough draft-writing before you commit yourself to the actual forms or online tools, and make sure you ask someone you trust to proofread your work.

Paying for college requires some work on your part, too. While this book is not dedicated to the subject, it's very important that you get to work on your financial circumstances right away. Keep in mind that while college is expensive, few people pay the full "sticker price." You have to have your finances in order before you can get the most financial aid possible. Visit fafsa.gov for the latest on the Free Application for Federal Student Aid. You can also find the most exhaustive strategies for financing your education in our book *Paying for College Without Going Broke*.

Last but not least, **don't take it easy during your senior year!** Colleges routinely request mid-year grades, and they expect you to continue taking challenging academic courses and keep your grades up throughout your high school career. Doing so takes you one step closer to getting good news. On behalf of The Princeton Review, have a good time, and good luck. See you on campus!

Nota Bene

The data reported in this book, unless otherwise noted, was collected from the profiled colleges from the fall of 2016 through the spring of 2017. In some cases, we were unable to publish the most recent data because schools did not report the necessary statistics to us in time, despite our repeated outreach efforts. Because enrollment and financial statistics as well as application and financial aid deadlines fluctuate from one year to another, we recommend that you check to make sure you have the most current information before applying. Best of luck!

HOW THE COMPLETE BOOK OF COLLEGES *IS ORGANIZED*

There are two types of profiles in this book. Not every school listed will have both. All of the 1,357 colleges and universities included in this book have their own informational profiles, and each entry follows the same basic format. Many of the institutions also have special two-page portraits located at the back of the book. These are written by the colleges and universities that wanted to present detailed descriptions of their campuses and programs.

Unless noted in the descriptions below, the Admissions Services Division of The Princeton Review collected all of the data presented in the informational profiles. As is customary with college guides, all data reflect figures for the academic year prior to publication, unless otherwise indicated. Since college offerings and demographics vary significantly from one institution to another and some colleges report data more thoroughly than others, few entries will include all of the individual data points described below.

The Heading
This section includes school name, address, telephone number, fax number, e-mail address, website, financial aid telephone number, and college code numbers for both the College Board (CEEB) and the American College Testing Program (ACT) when applicable. All website addresses were accurate and functioning at the time of publication. Check PrincetonReview.com for the most up-to-date links to colleges.

The Icons
The icons are a feature we hope will make using *The Complete Book of Colleges* easier. Icons appear under the school name for schools that are profiled in *The Best Colleges*.

The Blurb
Describes the college or university. Includes all available data that relate to the date of founding of the school, religious affiliation, whether the school is public or private, and campus size.

Ratings

This section includes the school's Fire Safety Rating, its Admissions Selectivity Rating, and its Green Rating.

Admissions Selectivity Rating

This rating measures how competitive admissions are at the school. This rating is determined by several institutionally reported factors, including: the class rank, standardized test scores, and high school GPA of entering freshmen; the percentage of students who hail from out-of-state; and the percentage of applicants accepted and those deciding to enroll. This rating is given on a scale of 60–99 . Please note that if a school has an Admissions Selectivity Rating of 60* (sixty with an asterisk), it means that the school did not report to us enough of the statistics that go into the rating in order for us to accurately measure its admissions selectivity.

Fire Safety

We asked all the schools from which we collect data annually to answer several questions about their efforts to ensure fire safety for campus residents. Each school's responses to nine of those questions were considered when calculating its Fire Safety Rating. The questions were developed in consultation with the Center for Campus Fire Safety (www.campusfire.org), and they cover: 1) The percentage of student housing sleeping rooms protected by an automatic fire sprinkler system with a fire sprinkler head located in the individual sleeping rooms; 2) The percentage of student housing sleeping rooms equipped with a smoke detector connected to a supervised fire alarm system; 3) The number of malicious fire alarms that occur in student housing per year; 4) The number of unwanted fire alarms that occur in student housing per year; 5) The banning of certain hazardous items and activities in residence halls, like candles, smoking, halogen lamps, etc.; 6) The percentage of student housing building fire alarm systems that, if activated, result in a signal being transmitted to a monitored location on campus or the fire department.

Schools that did not report answers to any of the above questions receive a Fire Safety Rating of 60*. The schools have an opportunity to update their fire safety data every year and will have their fire safety ratings re-calculated and published annually.

Each individual rating places a college on a continuum for purposes of comparing all colleges within this academic year only. Though similar, these ratings are not intended to be compared directly to those that appeared on PrincetonReview.com in any prior academic year or within any Princeton Review print publication, except for *The Best Colleges, 2017 Edition*. Our ratings computations are refined and change annually.

Green

This rating, on a scale of 60–99, provides a comprehensive measure of a school's performance as an environmentally aware and prepared institution. Specifically, it includes 1) whether students have a campus quality of life that is both healthy and sustainable, 2) how well a school is preparing students for employment in the clean-energy economy of the 21st century as well as for citizenship in a world now defined by environmental concerns and opportunities and 3) how environmentally responsible a school's policies are. Colleges that did not supply answers to a sufficient number of the questions for us to fairly compare them to other schools received a Green Rating of 60*.

Students & Faculty

Enrollment

The total number of full-time undergraduates.

Student Body

The percentage of male, female, out-of-state, and international students, and the number of foreign countries represented.

Ethnic Representation

By percentage according to ethnic group. Figures may not add up to 100 percent, as student reporting of ethnicity is voluntary by law.

Retention and Graduation

The percentage of freshmen who return for sophomore year. The percentage of last year's seniors who entered as freshmen and graduated in four years. The percentage of graduates who pursue further study within one year. The percentage of graduates who pursue further study at law school. The percentage of graduates who pursue further study at business school. The percentage of graduates who pursue further study at medical school.

Faculty

The ratio of undergraduates to full-time faculty. The number of full-time instructional faculty. The percentage of faculty who hold PhDs. The percentage of faculty members who teach undergraduates.

Academics

Degrees
The types of degrees awarded to students.

Academic Requirements
Areas in which all or most students are required to complete some course work prior to graduation. Can include general education (nonspecific), arts/fine arts, computer literacy, philosophy, foreign languages, history, humanities, mathematics, English (including composition), sciences (biological or physical), social sciences, and other requirements as specified by each school.

Classes
Number of students in an average regular class and an average lab/discussion section.

Majors with Highest Enrollment
The most popular majors.

Special Study Options
May include accelerated programs, cross registration, cooperative (work-study) program, distance learning, double majors, dual enrollment, English as a Second Language, student exchange programs (domestic), external degree programs, honors programs, independent study, internships, liberal arts/career combinations, student-designed majors, study abroad, teacher certification programs, weekend college, and other options as specified by each school.

Facilities

Housing
Types of school-owned or affiliated housing available. May include coed dorms, women's dorms, men's dorms, apartments for married students, apartments for single students, special housing for disabled students, special housing for international students, fraternity/sorority housing, cooperative housing, and other options as specified by the school. The availability of assistance in finding off-campus housing. Any housing requirements that may exist, such as required on-campus residence for freshmen.

Special Academic Facilities/Equipment

Other facilities and equipment of note (e.g., nuclear reactor, on-campus elementary school for student teachers, scanning electron microscopes, and so forth).

Campus Life

Activities

Standard activities available. May include campus ministries, choral groups, concert band, dance, drama/theater, international student organization, jazz band, literary magazine, Model UN, musical ensembles, musical theater, opera, pep band, radio station, student film society, student government, student newspaper, symphony orchestra, television station, and yearbook.

Organizations

Total number of registered organizations, honor societies, religious organizations, fraternities, sororities.

Athletics

Intercollegiate athletics available, listed by sex.

Admissions

Freshman Academic Profile

Average high school GPA. Class rank distribution. The percentage from public high schools. Average SAT (Math, Critical Reading, and Writing sections) and/or ACT composite scores. Median range of SAT (Math, Critical Reading, and Writing sections) and/or ACT composite scores. Test of English as a Foreign Language (TOEFL) requirements for international students.

An Important Note About SAT Scores Published in The Complete Book of Colleges 2018 Edition:

The SAT underwent major changes in March 2016. The admission data reported in this book reflects the entering class of fall 2016, a population that submitted applications in fall 2015 prior to the test redesign. You can find the SAT score range for the middle 50% of first year students that enrolled in fall 2016 on each school profile under Reported SAT (pre-2016 redesign).

To provide rising juniors and seniors in high school with predictive models of target score ranges, we have used the old SAT scores reported by each school and concordance information published by the College Board to provide Concordant SAT scores. The College Board's SAT concordance methodology and tools are available at: https://collegereadiness.collegeboard.org/educators/higher-ed/scoring-changes/concordance. We generated Evidence-Based Reading and Writing scores using Table 11 and New Math scores using Table 12 from for the 25th and 75th percentiles.

Basis for Candidate Selection
The criteria considered by the admissions committee in evaluating candidates. May include secondary school record, class rank, recommendations, standardized test scores, essay, interview, extracurricular activities, talent/ability, character/personal qualities, alumni/-ae relations, geographic residence, state residency, religious affiliation/commitment, minority status, volunteer work, work experience.

Freshman Admission Requirements
High school diploma/GED requirements. The number of academic units required or recommended in total and by academic subject. (Individual subject totals may not equal the complete sum of academic units required; in most cases, the difference is made up with electives. Check with the admissions office for any additional requirements.)

Freshman Admissions Statistics
The number of students who applied, the percentage of applicants who were accepted, and the percentage of those accepted who ultimately enrolled.

Transfer Admissions Requirements
Application requirements (may include high school transcript, college transcript, essay, interview, standardized tests, statement of good standing from prior school). Minimum high school GPA required. Minimum college GPA required. Lowest course grade transferable.

General Admissions Information
Application fee. Application deadlines. Admission notification date. "Rolling" indicates that decisions are sent to candidates as they are made, rather than held for a common notification date. Registration policy for terms other than the fall term. Common Application participation. Credit policies for College Entrance Examination Board Advanced Placement tests. Deferred admission policy.

Costs and Financial Aid

Tuition, room & board, fees, and books.

Required Forms and Deadlines

Forms that applicants for financial aid must file and their respective deadlines. May include FAFSA, institution's own financial aid form, CSS/Financial Aid PROFILE, business/farm supplement, state aid form, noncustodial (divorced/separated) parent statement, and other forms specified by the school. Deadlines for filing financial aid forms.

Notification of Awards

The date that notification of financial aid awards occurs. "Rolling" indicates that notification is ongoing—the sooner you complete all of your required financial aid paperwork, the sooner you'll hear about your package.

Types of Aid

Need-based scholarships and grants may include Federal Pell, SEOG, state scholarships/grants, private scholarships, college/university gift aid from institutional funds, United Negro College Fund, Federal Nursing Scholarship, and other resources as specified by the school. Loans may include Direct Subsidized Stafford Loans, Direct Unsubsidized Stafford Loans, Direct PLUS Loans, Federal Perkins Loans, Federal Nursing Loans, state loans, college/university loans from institutional funds, and other resources as specified by the school.

Student Employment

Availability of Federal Work-Study, a federal program that is need-based and part of most financial aid packages. Availability of part-time jobs direct from the college that are not based on need. The college's own assessment of part-time employment opportunities off campus.

Financial Aid Statistics

The percentage of freshmen who received some form of need-based financial aid. The percentage of undergraduates who received some form of need-based financial aid. The number of freshmen and undergrads who received an athletic scholarship or grant. The average amount of freshman scholarships and grants. The average amount of freshman loans. The average income from an on-campus job.

The Best Colleges Icon

 Indicates whether the school can be found in our annual book, *The Best Colleges*. In that book, each school has a detailed profile that includes the results of our surveys regarding student opinion about many aspects of their schools and their educations.

COLLEGE DIRECTORY

ABILENE CHRISTIAN UNIVERSITY

ACU Box 29000, Abilene, TX 79699
Phone: 325-674-2650 • **Financial Aid Phone:** 325-674-2300
E-mail: info@admissions.acu.edu • **CEEB Code:** 6001
Fax: 325-674-2130 • **Website:** www.acu.edu • **ACT Code:** 4050

This private school, affiliated with the Church of Christ Church, was founded in 1906. It has a 208-acre campus.

RATINGS
Admissions Selectivity Rating: 85   **Fire Safety Rating:** 76   **Green Rating:** 65

STUDENTS AND FACULTY
Enrollment: 3,719. **Student Body:** 59% female, 41% male, 13% out-of-state, 4% international (41 countries represented). Asian 1%, African American 9%, Caucasian 64%, Hispanic 16%, Native American <1%, Pacific Islander <1%, Two or more races 5%, Race unknown <1%.
Retention and Graduation: 76% freshmen return for sophomore year. 48% freshmen graduate within 4 years. 62% freshmen graduate within 6 years. 35% grads go on to further study within 1 year. 12% grads pursue arts and sciences degrees. 1% grads pursue law degrees. 5% grads pursue business degrees. 3% grads pursue medical degrees. **Faculty:** Student/faculty ratio 14:1. 253 full-time faculty, 79% hold PhDs, 13% are are members of minority groups, 40% are women. 1% of classes are taught by teaching assistants.

ACADEMICS
Degrees: associate, bachelor's, certificate, master's, postbachelor's certificate, post-master's certificate. **Classes:** Most classes have 20-29 students. Most lab/discussion sessions have 10-19 students. **Most popular majors:** Registered Nursing/Registered Nurse; Accounting; Psychology. **Special Study Options:** cross-registration, distance learning, double major, dual enrollment, English as a Second Language (ESL), honors program, independent study, internships, student-designed major, study abroad, teacher certification program. **Honors Programs:** The Honors College offers highly motivated students extra stimulation and recognition in their course work, opportunities to work with selected faculty members and the chance to do independent projects in their major field. Ten percent of the ACU students participate. To graduate with University Honors will require 30 hours of Honors Courses. **Disability Services:** Special programs offered to physically disabled students, including note-taking services, reader services, tape recorders. **Career Services:** Alumni network, Alumni services, Career/job search classes, Career assessment, Internships. Body and Soul Pre-med program. College of Business Administration Leadership Development.

FACILITIES
Housing: special housing for disabled students, men's dorms, special housing for international students, women's dorms. 95% of campus accessible to physically diasbled. **Special Academic Facilities/Equipment:** Museum of university's history, biblical restoration studies center, voice institute, demonstration farm and ranch, observatory. **Computers:** 100% of classrooms, 100% of dorms, 100% of libraries, 100% of dining areas, 100% of student union, 87% of common outdoor areas have wireless network access. Students can register for classes online. Administrative functions (other than registration) can be performed online.

CAMPUS LIFE
Environment: City. **Activities:** Choral groups, concert band, drama/theater, jazz band, literary magazine, marching band, music ensembles, musical theater, opera, radio station, student government, student newspaper, symphony orchestra, television station, yearbook, Campus Ministries, Student Organization. 108 registered organizations, 14 honor societies, 16 religious organizations. 4 fraternities, 7 sororities. **Athletics (Intercollegiate):** *Men:* baseball, basketball, cross-country, football, tennis, track/field (outdoor), track/field (indoor). *Women:* basketball, cross-country, soccer, softball, tennis, track/field (outdoor), track/field (indoor), volleyball. **On-Campus Highlights:** Learning Commons in Brown Library, Jacob's Dream Sculpture, World Famous Bean in McGlothlin Campus Cntr., Hunter Welcome Center, Williams Performing Arts Building, Abilene Christian University remains proud to be one of the first to catch the vision of the learning commons nationwide. The Learning Commons combines group work space with computers and Starbucks coffee inside the Library. **Environmental Initiatives:** Cenergistic Energy Program.

ADMISSIONS
Freshman Academic Profile: Average high school GPA 3.6. 21% in top 10% of high school class, 56% in top 25% of high school class, 84% in top 50% of high school class. 67% from public high schools. **Reported SAT (pre-2016 redesign) scores:** SAT Math middle 50% range 470-580. SAT Critical Reading middle 50% range 460-580. SAT Writing middle 50% range 440-560. **Concordant SAT scores:** SAT EBRW middle 50% 500–630. SAT Math middle 50% range 510–600. ACT middle 50% range 21-27. Minimum internet-based TOEFL 80. Minimum paper TOEFL 525. **Basis for Candidate Selection:** *Very important factors considered include:* rigor of secondary school record, class rank, academic GPA, standardized test scores. *Important factors considered include:* talent/ability, character/personal qualities. *Other factors considered include:* application essay, recommendation(s), extracurricular activities, first generation, alumni/ae relation, volunteer work, work experience, level of applicant's interest. **Freshman Admission Requirements:** High school diploma is required and GED is accepted. *Academic units recommended:* 4 English, 3 math, 3 science, 2 science labs, 2 foreign language, 1 history, and 1 unit from above areas or other academic areas. **Freshman Admission Statistics:** 10,252 applied, 50.89% admitted, 20% enrolled. **Transfer Admission Requirements:** High school transcript, college transcript(s), interview, Minimum college GPA of 2.0 required. Lowest grade transferable 2. **General Admission Information:** Application fee $50. Regular application deadline 2/15. Regular notification 2/15. Nonfall registration accepted.

COSTS AND FINANCIAL AID
Annual tuition $32,020. Room and board $9,730. Required fees $50. Average book expense $1,250. **Required Forms and Deadlines:** FAFSA. **Notification of Awards:** Applicants will be notified of awards on a rolling basis beginning 4/1. **Types of Aid:** *Need-based scholarships/grants:* Federal Pell, FSEOG, State scholarships/grants, Private scholarships, College/university scholarship or grant aid from institutional funds. *Loans:* Direct Subsidized Stafford Loans, Direct Unsubsidized Stafford Loans, Direct PLUS loans, Federal Perkins Loans, State Loans. *Student Employment:* Federal Work-Study Program available. Institutional employment available. **Financial Aid Statistics:** 100% needy freshmen, 100% needy undergrads receive need-based scholarship or grant aid. 100% freshmen, 99% undergrads receive non-need-based scholarship or grant aid. 68% freshmen, 67% undergrads receive need-based self-help aid. 5% freshmen, 6% undergrads receive athletic scholarships. 100% freshmen, 94% undergrads receive any aid. **Criteria for awarding aid:** *Non-need-based:* Academics, Art, Athletics, Leadership, Minority status, Music/drama, Religious affiliation, State/district residency.

ACADEMY OF ART UNIVERSITY

79 New Montgomery St, San Francisco, CA 94105
Phone: 415-274-2222 • **Financial Aid Phone:** 800-544-2787
E-mail: info@academyart.edu
Fax: 415-618-6287 • **Website:** www.academyart.edu • **ACT Code:** 155

This proprietary school was founded in 1929. It has a 20-acre campus.

RATINGS
Admissions Selectivity Rating: 62   **Fire Safety Rating:** 91   **Green Rating:** 60*

STUDENTS AND FACULTY
Enrollment: 8,182. **Student Body:** 57% female, 43% male, 41% out-of-state, 29% international (100 countries represented). Asian 7%, African American 7%, Caucasian 20%, Hispanic 12%, Native American <1%, Pacific Islander 1%, Two or more races 3%, Race unknown 22%.
Retention and Graduation: 71% freshmen return for sophomore year. 5% freshmen graduate within 4 years. **Faculty:** Student/faculty ratio 14:1. 270 full-time faculty, 17% hold PhDs, 5% are are members of minority groups, 40% are women. 0% of classes are taught by teaching assistants.

ACADEMICS
Degrees: associate, bachelor's, certificate, master's. **Classes:** Most classes have 10-19 students. **Most popular majors:** Animation, Interactive Technology, Video Graphics and Special Effects; Fashion/Apparel Design; Illustration. **Special Study Options:** Accelerated program, cooperative education program, distance learning, English as a Second Language (ESL), independent study, internships, weekend college, Portfolio Development, Personal Enrichment program. **Disability Services:** Special programs offered to physically disabled students, including note-taking services, reader services, tape recorders, tutors. **Career Services:** Alumni network, Alumni services, Career/job search classes, Career assessment, Internships, Regional alumni, On-campus interviews. Career driven online workshops available to students and alumni anytime, anywhere. One on one assistance with resume writing and launching a job or internship search. Maintaining an active job board and coordinating professionals to visit and recruit.

FACILITIES
Housing: Coed dorms, men's dorms, women's dorms, apartments for married students, apartments for single students. 80% of campus accessible to physically diasbled. **Special Academic Facilities/Equipment:** 3 Art galleries (public) for

display of student work. **Computers:** Students can register for classes online. Administrative functions (other than registration) can be performed online.

CAMPUS LIFE

Environment: Metropolis. **Activities:** dance, drama/theater, musical theater, student newspaper, student-run film society, student organization. 27 registered organizations. **Athletics (Intercollegiate):** *Men:* baseball, basketball, cross-country, golf, soccer, tennis, track/field (outdoor). *Women:* basketball, cross-country, golf, soccer, softball, tennis, track/field (outdoor), volleyball.

ADMISSIONS

Freshman Admission Requirements: High school diploma is required and GED is accepted. **Freshman Admission Statistics:** 2,761 applied, 100.00% admitted, 39% enrolled. **Transfer Admission Requirements:** High school transcript, college transcript(s), Minimum college GPA of 2.0 required. Lowest grade transferable C. **General Admission Information:** Application fee $100. Nonfall registration accepted. Admission may be deferred for a maximum of 24 months.

COSTS AND FINANCIAL AID

Annual tuition $26,190. Room and board $15,792. Required fees $300. Average book expense $1,854. **Required Forms and Deadlines:** FAFSA, Institution's own financial aid form. **Notification of Awards:** Applicants will be notified of awards on a rolling basis beginning 3/15. **Types of Aid:** *Need-based scholarships/grants:* Federal Pell, FSEOG, State scholarships/grants, Private scholarships, College/university scholarship or grant aid from institutional funds. *Loans:* Direct Subsidized Stafford Loans, Direct Unsubsidized Stafford Loans, Direct PLUS loans. *Student Employment:* Federal Work-Study Program available. **Financial Aid Statistics:** 70% needy freshmen, 72% needy undergrads receive need-based scholarship or grant aid. 7% freshmen, 6% undergrads receive non-need-based scholarship or grant aid. 87% freshmen, 86% undergrads receive need-based self-help aid. 3% freshmen, 2% undergrads receive athletic scholarships. 52% freshmen, 61% undergrads receive any aid. 63% undergrads borrow to pay for school. Average cumulative indebtedness $27,020. **Criteria for awarding aid:** *Non-need-based:* Academics, Art, Athletics.

ACADIA UNIVERSITY

Admissions Office, Wolfville, NS B4P 2R6
Phone: 1-902-585-1446 • **Financial Aid Phone:** 902-585-1016
E-mail: pam.dimock@acadiau.ca
Fax: 902-585-1092 • **Website:** www.acadiau.ca

This public school was founded in 1838. It has a 200-acre campus.

RATINGS

Admissions Selectivity Rating: 71   **Fire Safety Rating:** 60*   **Green Rating:** 60*

STUDENTS AND FACULTY

Student Body: 55% female, 45% male, 42% out-of-state.
Retention and Graduation: 83% freshmen return for sophomore year.
Faculty: Student/faculty ratio 10:1. 243 full-time faculty, 0% hold PhDs, 0% are are members of minority groups, 36% are women. 0% of classes are taught by teaching assistants.

ACADEMICS

Degrees: bachelor's, certificate, diploma, master's. **Special Study Options:** cooperative education program, distance learning, double major, English as a Second Language (ESL), exchange student program (domestic), honors program, independent study, internships, study abroad. **Career Services:** Career/job search classes, Career assessment, Internships.

FACILITIES

Housing: Coed dorms, special housing for disabled students, men's dorms, women's dorms, apartments for single students. **Computers:** Students can register for classes online. Administrative functions (other than registration) can be performed online.

CAMPUS LIFE

Environment: Rural. **Activities:** Choral groups, concert band, dance, drama/theater, jazz band, literary magazine, music ensembles, musical theater, opera, pep band, radio station, student government, student newspaper, symphony orchestra, yearbook, Campus Ministries, Student Organization. 60 registered organizations, 3 religious organizations. **Athletics (Intercollegiate):** *Men:* basketball, cheerleading, cross-country, football, ice hockey, rugby, soccer, track/field (outdoor), volleyball. *Women:* basketball, cheerleading, cross-country, ice hockey, rugby, soccer, track/field (outdoor), volleyball. **On-Campus Highlights:** KC Irving Environmental Science Centre, The Sheldon L. Fountain Learning Commons.

ADMISSIONS

Freshman Academic Profile: 80% from public high schools. Minimum paper TOEFL 550. **Basis for Candidate Selection:** *Very important factors considered include:* rigor of secondary school record, academic GPA. *Important factors considered include:* recommendation(s), talent/ability. *Other factors considered include:* class rank, standardized test scores, extracurricular activities, character/personal qualities, geographical residence, volunteer work, work experience. **Freshman Admission Requirements:** High school diploma is required and GED is not accepted. *Academic units required:* 1 English, 1 math. *Academic units recommended:* 1 English, 2 math, 1 science, 1 foreign language, 1 social studies, 1 history, 2 academic electives. **Freshman Admission Statistics:** 1,600 applied, 49.44% admitted, 68% enrolled. **Transfer Admission Requirements:** college transcript(s). **General Admission Information:** Application fee $25. Priority deadline 3/15. Nonfall registration accepted. Admission may be deferred.

COSTS AND FINANCIAL AID

Annual in-state tuition $8,062. Annual out-of-state tuition $8,062. Room and board $8,284. Required fees $180. Average book expense $1,200. **Notification of Awards:** Applicants will be notified of awards on or about 4/15. **Types of Aid:** *Loans:* Direct Subsidized Stafford Loans, Direct Unsubsidized Stafford Loans, Direct PLUS loans. **Criteria for awarding aid:** *Need-based:* Leadership. *Non-need-based:* Academics, Leadership, Music/drama, State/district residency.

ADAMS STATE UNIVERSITY

208 Edgemont Blvd, Alamosa, CO 81102
Phone: 719-587-7712 • **Financial Aid Phone:** 719-587-7306
E-mail: ascadmit@adams.edu • **CEEB Code:** 4001
Fax: 719-587-7522 • **ACT Code:** 496

This public school was founded in 1921. It has a 90-acre campus.

RATINGS

Admissions Selectivity Rating: 86   **Fire Safety Rating:** 74   **Green Rating:** 60*

STUDENTS AND FACULTY

Enrollment: 2,169. **Student Body:** 47% female, 53% male, 33% out-of-state, <1% international (10 countries represented). Asian 1%, African American 7%, Caucasian 50%, Hispanic 32%, Native American 1%, Pacific Islander <1%, Two or more races 4%, Race unknown 4%.
Retention and Graduation: 58% freshmen return for sophomore year. 11% freshmen graduate within 4 years. 29% freshmen graduate within 6 years. 0% grads go on to further study within 1 year. **Faculty:** Student/faculty ratio 15:1. 113 full-time faculty, 63% hold PhDs, 23% are are members of minority groups, 42% are women. 0% of classes are taught by teaching assistants.

ACADEMICS

Degrees: associate, bachelor's, master's. **Classes:** Most classes have fewer than 10 students. Most lab/discussion sessions have 10-19 students. **Most popular majors:** Teacher Education, Multiple Levels; Business Administration and Management; Kinesiology and Exercise Science. **Special Study Options:** Accelerated program, distance learning, double major, independent study, internships, study abroad, teacher certification program, weekend college, High School dual enrollment. **Disability Services:** Special programs offered to physically disabled students, including note-taking services, reader services, tutors. **Career Services:** Alumni network, Career/job search classes, Career assessment, Internships, On-Campus Interviews, Career Fair, Career Counseling Services.

FACILITIES

Housing: Coed dorms, men's dorms, women's dorms, apartments for married students, apartments for single students, Learning Community. 95% of campus accessible to physically disabled. **Special Academic Facilities/Equipment:** Luther Bean Museum, Hatfield Gallery, Gallery 114, Leon Memorial Music Hall, Zacheis Planetarium, Ryan Geology Museum. **Computers:** 10% of classrooms, 100% of dorms, 100% of libraries, 100% of dining areas, 99% of student union, have wireless network access. Students can register for classes online. Administrative functions (other than registration) can be performed online.

CAMPUS LIFE

Environment: Village. **Activities:** Choral groups, concert band, dance, drama/theater, jazz band, literary magazine, marching band, music ensembles, musical theater, pep band, radio station, student government, student newspaper, Campus Ministries, Model UN. 23 registered organizations, 2 religious organizations. **Athletics (Intercollegiate):** *Men:* basketball, cross-country, football, golf, soccer, track/field (outdoor), track/field (indoor), wrestling. *Women:* basketball, cross-country, golf, soccer, softball, swimming, track/field (outdoor), track/field (indoor), volleyball. **On-Campus Highlights:** Leon Memorial Concert Hall, Zacheis Planetarium, Nielson Library, Plachy Hall, Rex Activity Center, Student Union Building (SUB). **Environmental Initiatives:** Establishment of EARTH (Environmental Action for Resources, Transportation, & Health) group on campus.

ADMISSIONS

Freshman Academic Profile: Average high school GPA 3.1. 6% in top 10% of high school class, 25% in top 25% of high school class, 58% in top 50% of high school class. **Reported SAT (pre-2016 redesign) scores:** SAT Math middle 50% range 470-530. SAT Critical Reading middle 50% range 430-530. **Concordant SAT scores:** SAT Math middle 50% range 510–560. ACT middle 50% range 17-22. Minimum internet-based TOEFL 79. Minimum paper TOEFL 550. **Basis for Candidate Selection:** *Very important factors considered include:* rigor of secondary school record, standardized test scores. *Important factors considered include:* academic GPA. *Other factors considered include:* class rank, application essay, recommendation(s), interview, extracurricular activities, character/personal qualities, geographical residence, state residency. **Freshman Admission Requirements:** High school diploma is required and GED is accepted. *Academic units recommended:* 4 English, 4 math, 3 science, 2 science labs, 1 foreign language, 2 social studies, 1 history, 2 academic electives. **Freshman Admission Statistics:** 2,531 applied, 18.85% admitted, 92% enrolled. **Transfer Admission Requirements:** college transcript(s), Minimum college GPA of 2.0 required. Lowest grade transferable D. **General Admission Information:** Application fee $30. Priority deadline 8/1. Nonfall registration accepted. Admission may be deferred for a maximum of 2 years.

COSTS AND FINANCIAL AID

Required Forms and Deadlines: FAFSA. **Notification of Awards:** Applicants will be notified of awards on a rolling basis beginning 3/1. **Types of Aid:** *Need-based scholarships/grants:* Federal Pell, FSEOG, State scholarships/grants, Private scholarships, College/university scholarship or grant aid from institutional funds. *Loans:* Direct Subsidized Stafford Loans, Direct Unsubsidized Stafford Loans, Direct PLUS loans, Federal Perkins Loans. *Student Employment:* Federal Work-Study Program available. Institutional employment available. **Financial Aid Statistics:** 97% needy freshmen, 92% needy undergrads receive need-based scholarship or grant aid. 0% undergrads receive non-need-based scholarship or grant aid. 66% freshmen, 76% undergrads receive need-based self-help aid. 0% freshmen, 0% undergrads receive athletic scholarships. 95% freshmen, 94% undergrads receive any aid. **Criteria for awarding aid:** *Need-based:* Academics, Alumni affiliation, Art, Athletics, Leadership, Minority status, Music/drama. *Non-need-based:* Academics, Alumni affiliation, Art, Athletics, Leadership, Minority status, Music/drama, State/district residency.

ADELPHI UNIVERSITY

Nexus Building, Room 111, Garden City, NY 11530
Phone: 516-877-3050 • **Financial Aid Phone:** 516-877-3080
E-mail: admissions@adelphi.edu • **CEEB Code:** 2003
Fax: 516-877-3039 • **Website:** www.adelphi.edu • **ACT Code:** 2664

This private school was founded in 1896. It has a 75-acre campus.

RATINGS

Admissions Selectivity Rating: 84   **Fire Safety Rating:** 95   **Green Rating:** 78

STUDENTS AND FACULTY

Enrollment: 5,135. **Student Body:** 69% female, 31% male, 7% out-of-state, 3% international (48 countries represented). Asian 10%, African American 10%, Caucasian 52%, Hispanic 16%, Native American <1%, Pacific Islander 0%, Two or more races 2%, Race unknown 6%.
Retention and Graduation: 83% freshmen return for sophomore year. 57% freshmen graduate within 4 years. 68% freshmen graduate within 6 years. 31% grads go on to further study within 1 year. 1% grads pursue law degrees. 2% grads pursue business degrees. 3% grads pursue medical degrees. **Faculty:** Student/faculty ratio 12:1. 320 full-time faculty, 89% hold PhDs, 24% are are members of minority groups, 53% are women. 0% of classes are taught by teaching assistants.

ACADEMICS

Degrees: associate, bachelor's, doctoral/professional, doctoral/research, master's, postbachelor's certificate, post-master's certificate. **Classes:** Most classes have 10-19 students. Most lab/discussion sessions have 10-19 students. **Most popular majors:** Business/Commerce; Registered Nursing/Registered Nurse; Biology/Biological Sciences. **Special Study Options:** Accelerated

program, cross-registration, distance learning, double major, dual enrollment, English as a Second Language (ESL), honors program, independent study, internships, liberal arts/career combination, student-designed major, study abroad, teacher certification program, weekend college, Joint Degrees, Learning Disabilities Program. Distance Learning Program is being restructured. **Honors Programs:** The Honors College seeks to prepare highly talented and motivated students to face the 21st century by providing them with the intellectual perspectives and critical skills necessary to exercise responsible leadership. It involves an intense curricular and extracurricular program that asks students to view themselves and their work with integrity, passion, and seriousness. Combined degree programs: BA/JD, BA/MA, BA/DDS, BA/MEng, Optometry, Dentistry, Physical therapy, Law, Environment Studies, Osteopathic. **Disability Services:** Special programs offered to physically disabled students, including note-taking services, reader services, tape recorders, tutors. **Career Services:** Alumni network, Alumni services, Career/job search classes, Career assessment, Internships, Regional alumni.

FACILITIES

Housing: Coed dorms, special housing for disabled students, Theme Housing, Honors students live in the same residence hall; EXCEL mentoring program. 95% of campus accessible to physically diasbled. **Special Academic Facilities/Equipment:** Art gallery, sculpture and ceramics studios, bronze-casting foundry, theatre, language labs. **Computers:** 90% of dorms, 99% of libraries, 99% of dining areas, 90% of student union, 75% of common outdoor areas have wireless network access. Students can register for classes online. Administrative functions (other than registration) can be performed online.

CAMPUS LIFE

Environment: Metropolis. **Activities:** Choral groups, concert band, dance, drama/theater, jazz band, literary magazine, music ensembles, musical theater, opera, radio station, student government, student newspaper, student-run film society, symphony orchestra, yearbook, Campus Ministries, Student Organization, Model UN. 80 registered organizations, 21 honor societies, 5 religious organizations. 3 fraternities, 7 sororities. **Athletics (Intercollegiate):** *Men:* baseball, basketball, cross-country, golf, lacrosse, soccer, swimming, tennis, track/field (outdoor), track/field (indoor). *Women:* basketball, bowling, cross-country, field hockey, lacrosse, soccer, softball, swimming, tennis, track/field (outdoor), track/field (indoor), volleyball. **On-Campus Highlights:** Ruth S. Harley University Center, UnderGround Cafe, Swirbul Library, New Fine Arts Building, New Recreational Center. **Environmental Initiatives:** LEED silver rating for the CSPA project.

ADMISSIONS

Freshman Academic Profile: Average high school GPA 3.6. 31% in top 10% of high school class, 64% in top 25% of high school class, 89% in top 50% of high school class. 67% from public high schools. **Reported SAT (pre-2016 redesign) scores:** SAT Math middle 50% range 510-610. SAT Critical Reading middle 50% range 500-600. SAT Writing middle 50% range 500-600. **Concordant SAT scores:** SAT EBRW middle 50% 560–650. SAT Math middle 50% range 540–630. ACT middle 50% range 22-27. Minimum internet-based TOEFL 80. Minimum paper TOEFL 550. **Basis for Candidate Selection:** *Very important factors considered include:* rigor of secondary school record. *Important factors considered include:* class rank, academic GPA, standardized test scores, application essay, recommendation(s), extracurricular activities, talent/ability, character/personal qualities, volunteer work. *Other factors considered include:* interview, first generation, alumni/ae relation, work experience, level of applicant's interest. **Freshman Admission Requirements:** High school diploma is required and GED is accepted. *Academic units recommended:* 4 English, 3 math, 3 science, 2 foreign language, and 4 units from above areas or other academic areas. **Freshman Admission Statistics:** 11,863 applied, 70.29% admitted, 15% enrolled. **Transfer Admission Requirements:** college transcript(s), essay or personal statement, Minimum college GPA of 2.3 required. **General Admission Information:** Application fee $40. Nonfall registration accepted. Admission may be deferred.

COSTS AND FINANCIAL AID

Annual tuition $34,000. Room and board $14,052. Required fees $1,740. Average book expense $1,020. **Required Forms and Deadlines:** FAFSA, State aid form. **Notification of Awards:** Applicants will be notified of awards on a rolling basis beginning 3/1. **Types of Aid:** *Need-based scholarships/grants:* Federal Pell, FSEOG, State scholarships/grants, Private scholarships, College/university scholarship or grant aid from institutional funds, United Negro College Fund. *Loans:* Direct Subsidized Stafford Loans, Direct Unsubsidized Stafford Loans, Direct PLUS loans, Federal Perkins Loans, Federal Nursing Loans. *Student Employment:* Federal Work-Study Program available. Institutional employment available. **Financial Aid Statistics:** 65% needy freshmen, 97% needy undergrads receive need-based scholarship or grant aid. 85% freshmen, 86% undergrads receive non-need-based scholarship or grant aid. 87% freshmen, 87% undergrads receive need-based self-help aid. 2% freshmen, 2% undergrads receive athletic scholarships. 96% freshmen, 91% undergrads receive any aid. 64% undergrads borrow to pay for school. Average cumulative indebtedness $32,558. **Criteria for awarding aid:** *Need-*

based: Job skills. *Non-need-based:* Academics, Alumni affiliation, Art, Athletics, Leadership, Minority status, Music/drama, Religious affiliation, State/district residency.

ADRIAN COLLEGE

110 South Madison Street, Adrian, MI 49221
Phone: 517-265-5161 • **Financial Aid Phone:** 517-265-5161
E-mail: admissions@adrian.edu • **CEEB Code:** 1001
Fax: 517-264-3331 • **Website:** www.adrian.edu • **ACT Code:** 1954

This private school, affiliated with the Methodist Church, was founded in 1859. It has a 100-acre campus.

RATINGS
Admissions Selectivity Rating: 81   **Fire Safety Rating:** 69   **Green Rating:** 60*

STUDENTS AND FACULTY
Enrollment: 1,308. **Student Body:** 47% female, 53% male, 24% out-of-state, 4% international (6 countries represented). Asian 1%, African American 4%, Caucasian 77%, Hispanic 2%, Native American <1%, Pacific Islander 0%, Two or more races 0%, Race unknown 12%.
Retention and Graduation: 73% freshmen return for sophomore year. 40% freshmen graduate within 4 years. 50% freshmen graduate within 6 years. 25% grads go on to further study within 1 year. 51% grads pursue arts and sciences degrees. 9% grads pursue law degrees. 9% grads pursue business degrees. 22% grads pursue medical degrees. **Faculty:** Student/faculty ratio 12:1. 78 full-time faculty, 82% hold PhDs, 9% are are members of minority groups, 41% are women. 0% of classes are taught by teaching assistants.

ACADEMICS
Degrees: associate, bachelor's, transfer. **Classes:** Most classes have 10-19 students. Most lab/discussion sessions have 10-19 students. **Most popular majors:** Business/Commerce; English Language and Literature; Kinesiology and Exercise Science. **Special Study Options:** double major, dual enrollment, honors program, independent study, internships, student-designed major, study abroad, teacher certification program. Combined degree programs: BA/MEng. **Disability Services:** Special programs offered to physically disabled students, including note-taking services, reader services, tape recorders, tutors. **Career Services:** Alumni network, Alumni services, Career assessment, Internships, Regional alumni, Internships.

FACILITIES
Housing: Coed dorms, men's dorms, women's dorms, fraternity/sorority housing, apartments for single students, special-interest houses. 50% of campus accessible to physically diasbled. **Special Academic Facilities/Equipment:** Art gallery, studio theatre, arboretum, education resource center, language lab, observatory, planetarium, solar greenhouse, nuclear magnetic resonance spectrometer, differential scanning calorimeter. **Computers:** 100% of classrooms, 100% of dorms, 100% of libraries, 100% of dining areas, 100% of student union, 100% of common outdoor areas have wireless network access. Students can register for classes online. Administrative functions (other than registration) can be performed online.

CAMPUS LIFE
Environment: Town. **Activities:** Choral groups, concert band, dance, drama/theater, jazz band, literary magazine, marching band, music ensembles, musical theater, pep band, radio station, student government, student newspaper, symphony orchestra, yearbook, Campus Ministries, Student Organization. 68 registered organizations, 13 honor societies, 8 religious organizations. 4 fraternities, 3 sororities. **Athletics (Intercollegiate):** *Men:* baseball, basketball, cross-country, football, golf, ice hockey, lacrosse, soccer, tennis, track/field (outdoor). *Women:* basketball, bowling, cross-country, golf, ice hockey, lacrosse, soccer, softball, tennis, track/field (outdoor), volleyball. **On-Campus Highlights:** Caine Student Center, Shipman Library, Merillat Sport and Fitness Center.

ADMISSIONS
Freshman Academic Profile: Average high school GPA 3.3. 17% in top 10% of high school class, 46% in top 25% of high school class, 81% in top 50% of high school class. **Reported SAT (pre-2016 redesign) scores:** SAT Math middle 50% range 410-535. SAT Critical Reading middle 50% range 430-515. **Concordant SAT scores:** SAT Math middle 50% range 450–570. ACT middle 50% range 20-25. Minimum paper TOEFL 500. **Basis for Candidate Selection:** *Very important factors considered include:* rigor of secondary school record, class rank. *Important factors considered include:* academic GPA, standardized test scores, talent/ability. *Other factors considered include:* interview, extracurricular activities, character/personal qualities, alumni/ae relation, volunteer work, work experience, level of applicant's interest. **Freshman Admission Requirements:** High school diploma is required and

GED is accepted. *Academic units recommended:* 4 English, 3 math, 2 science, 1 science lab, 2 foreign language, 1 social studies, 1 history, 2 academic electives. **Freshman Admission Statistics:** 3,709 applied, 63.98% admitted, 21% enrolled. **Transfer Admission Requirements:** High school transcript, college transcript(s), Minimum college GPA of 2.7 required. Lowest grade transferable C. **General Admission Information:** Priority deadline 3/15. Nonfall registration not accepted. Admission may be deferred for a maximum of 1 year.

COSTS AND FINANCIAL AID
Annual tuition $23,090. Room and board $7,600. Required fees $300. Average book expense $400. **Required Forms and Deadlines:** FAFSA. **Notification of Awards:** Applicants will be notified of awards on a rolling basis beginning 3/15. **Types of Aid:** *Need-based scholarships/grants:* Federal Pell, FSEOG, State scholarships/grants, Private scholarships, College/university scholarship or grant aid from institutional funds. *Loans:* Federal Perkins Loans. *Student Employment:* Federal Work-Study Program available. Institutional employment available. **Financial Aid Statistics:** 87% needy freshmen, 86% needy undergrads receive need-based scholarship or grant aid. 88% freshmen, 86% undergrads receive non-need-based scholarship or grant aid. 89% freshmen, 88% undergrads receive need-based self-help aid. 0% freshmen, 0% undergrads receive athletic scholarships. 98% freshmen, 92% undergrads receive any aid. **Criteria for awarding aid:** *Non-need-based:* Academics, Alumni affiliation, Art, Leadership, Music/drama, Religious affiliation.

AGNES SCOTT COLLEGE

141 E. College Ave., Decatur, GA 30030-3770
Phone: 404-471-6285 • **Financial Aid Phone:** 404-471-6395
E-mail: https://agnesscott.edu/admission/index.h • **CEEB Code:** 5002
Fax: 404-471-6414 • **Website:** www.agnesscott.edu • **ACT Code:** 780

This private school, affiliated with the Presbyterian Church, was founded in 1889. It has a 100-acre campus.

RATINGS
Admissions Selectivity Rating: 89   **Fire Safety Rating:** 96   **Green Rating:** 91

STUDENTS AND FACULTY
Enrollment: 886. **Student Body:** 100% female, 0% male, 52% out-of-state, 9% international (32 countries represented). Asian 8%, African American 30%, Caucasian 35%, Hispanic 10%, Native American <1%, Pacific Islander <1%, Two or more races 6%, Race unknown 2%.
Retention and Graduation: 84% freshmen return for sophomore year. 67% freshmen graduate within 4 years. 70% freshmen graduate within 6 years. 20% grads go on to further study within 1 year. **Faculty:** Student/faculty ratio 10:1. 78 full-time faculty, 100% hold PhDs, 21% are are members of minority groups, 67% are women. 0% of classes are taught by teaching assistants.

ACADEMICS
Degrees: bachelor's. **Classes:** Most classes have 10-19 students. Most lab/discussion sessions have 10-19 students. **Most popular majors:** Psychology; Creative Writing; Business Administration and Management. **Special Study Options:** Accelerated program, cross-registration, double major, dual enrollment, exchange student program (domestic), external degree program, independent study, internships, student-designed major, study abroad, teacher certification program, Woodruff Scholars program for women beyond traditional college age; exchange program with Mills College; Atlanta Semester. Combined degree programs: BA/BSN w/Emory, BA/BS in computer science from Emory. **Disability Services:** Special programs offered to physically disabled students, including note-taking services, reader services, tape recorders, tutors. **Career Services:** Alumni network, Alumni services, Career/job search classes, Career assessment, Internships, Regional alumni. All incoming first-year students will work with a four-person Board of Advisors as part of Agnes Scott's Summit. Students will consult with board members, one of which who is a Career Mentor, to make informed decisions about how best to cultivate the leadership skills, global perspective and breadth of knowledge necessary to move through the world with confidence.

FACILITIES
Housing: women's dorms, apartments for single students, Theme Housing. 90% of campus accessible to physically diasbled. **Special Academic Facilities/Equipment:** Art galleries,state-of the art science building opened in January 2003, collaborative learning centers, language lab, electron microscope, observatory, 30-inch Beck telescope, planetarium, interactive learning center,

multimedia presentation classrooms, instructional technology center, multi-media production facility. **Computers:** 50% of classrooms, 100% of libraries, 100% of student union, 10% of common outdoor areas have wireless network access. Students can register for classes online. Administrative functions (other than registration) can be performed online.

CAMPUS LIFE

Environment: Metropolis. **Activities:** Choral groups, dance, drama/theater, literary magazine, marching band, music ensembles, musical theater, pep band, student government, student newspaper, symphony orchestra, television station, yearbook, Campus Ministries, Student Organization, Model UN. 80 registered organizations, 12 honor societies, 12 religious organizations. **Athletics (Intercollegiate):** *Women:* basketball, lacrosse, soccer, softball, tennis, volleyball. **On-Campus Highlights:** New $36.5 million Science Center, Alston Campus Center, Newly renovated Bradley Observatory, McCain Library, Several residence halls are on the National Register. **Environmental Initiatives:** Converted to campus-wide single stream recycling and composting. Agnes Scott is committed to Zero Waste and has already achieved a 62% waste diversion rate.

ADMISSIONS

Freshman Academic Profile: Average high school GPA 3.8. 43% in top 10% of high school class, 72% in top 25% of high school class, 92% in top 50% of high school class. 74% from public high schools. **Reported SAT (pre-2016 redesign) scores:** SAT Math middle 50% range 520-630. SAT Critical Reading middle 50% range 560-680. SAT Writing middle 50% range 540-650. **Concordant SAT scores:** SAT EBRW middle 50% 610–710. SAT Math middle 50% range 550–650. ACT middle 50% range 24-30. Minimum internet-based TOEFL 80. **Basis for Candidate Selection:** *Very important factors considered include:* rigor of secondary school record, academic GPA, talent/ability, character/personal qualities. *Important factors considered include:* standardized test scores, application essay, recommendation(s), extracurricular activities, volunteer work. *Other factors considered include:* class rank, interview, first generation, alumni/ae relation, geographical residence, state residency, work experience, level of applicant's interest. **Freshman Admission Requirements:** High school diploma is required and GED is accepted. *Academic units recommended:* 4 English, 3 math, 2 science, 2 science labs, 2 foreign language, 2 social studies. **Freshman Admission Statistics:** 1,399 applied, 64.69% admitted, 30% enrolled. **Transfer Admission Requirements:** High school transcript, college transcript(s), essay or personal statement, statement of good standing from prior institution(s). Minimum college GPA of 3.0 required. Lowest grade transferable C. **General Admission Information:** Priority deadline 1/15. Regular application deadline 3/15. Regular notification 4/15. Nonfall registration not accepted. Admission may be deferred for a maximum of 1 year.

COSTS AND FINANCIAL AID

Annual tuition $39,720. Room and board $11,970. Required fees $240. Average book expense $1,000. **Required Forms and Deadlines:** FAFSA. **Notification of Awards:** Applicants will be notified of awards on a rolling basis beginning 3/1. **Types of Aid:** *Need-based scholarships/grants:* Federal Pell, FSEOG, State scholarships/grants, Private scholarships, College/university scholarship or grant aid from institutional funds. *Loans:* Direct Subsidized Stafford Loans, Direct Unsubsidized Stafford Loans, Direct PLUS loans. *Student Employment:* Federal Work-Study Program available. Institutional employment available. **Financial Aid Statistics:** 100% needy freshmen, 100% needy undergrads receive need-based scholarship or grant aid. 30% freshmen, 25% undergrads receive non-need-based scholarship or grant aid. 73% freshmen, 82% undergrads receive need-based self-help aid. 0% freshmen, 0% undergrads receive athletic scholarships. 100% freshmen, 99% undergrads receive any aid. 75% undergrads borrow to pay for school. Average cumulative indebtedness $34,022. **Criteria for awarding aid:** *Non-need-based:* Academics, Leadership, Minority status, Music/drama, Religious affiliation.

ALABAMA A&M UNIVERSITY

P.O. Box 908, Normal, AL 35762
Phone: 256-851-5245
E-mail: juan.alexander@aamu.edu • **CEEB Code:** 1003
Fax: 256-851-5249 • **ACT Code:** 2

This public school was founded in 1875. It has a 880-acre campus.

RATINGS

Admissions Selectivity Rating: 75   **Fire Safety Rating:** 60*   **Green Rating:** 60*

STUDENTS AND FACULTY

Enrollment: 3,270. **Student Body:** 52% female, 48% male, 31% out-of-state, 1% international (42 countries represented). Asian 0%, African American 96%,

Caucasian 2%, Hispanic <1%, Native American <1%, Pacific Islander 0%, Two or more races 0%, Race unknown <1%.
Retention and Graduation: 77% grads go on to further study within 1 year. 40% grads pursue arts and sciences degrees. 2% grads pursue law degrees. 45% grads pursue business degrees. 11% grads pursue medical degrees. **Faculty:** Student/faculty ratio 14:1. 314 full-time faculty, 45% hold PhDs, 55% are members of minority groups, 39% are women. 1% of classes are taught by teaching assistants.

ACADEMICS

Degrees: bachelor's, master's, post-master's certificate. **Classes:** Most classes have fewer than 10 students. Most lab/discussion sessions have 20-29 students. **Most popular majors:** Elementary Education and Teaching; Mechanical Engineering Related Technologies/Technicians; Biology/Biological Sciences. **Special Study Options:** Accelerated program, cooperative education program, distance learning, double major, dual enrollment, exchange student program (domestic), honors program, independent study, internships, study abroad, teacher certification program, weekend college. **Disability Services:** Special programs offered to physically disabled students, including note-taking services, reader services, tape recorders, tutors. **Career Services:** Career/job search classes, Career assessment, Internships, Regional alumni.

FACILITIES

Housing: men's dorms, women's dorms, apartments for single students. 65% of campus accessible to physically diasbled. **Special Academic Facilities/Equipment:** State Black Archives **Computers:** Students can register for classes online.

CAMPUS LIFE

Environment: City. **Activities:** Choral groups, concert band, dance, drama/theater, jazz band, literary magazine, marching band, music ensembles, pep band, radio station, student government, student newspaper, symphony orchestra, television station, yearbook, Campus Ministries, Student Organization. 76 registered organizations, 14 honor societies, 3 religious organizations. 4 fraternities, 4 sororities. **Athletics (Intercollegiate):** *Men:* baseball, basketball, cross-country, football, golf, soccer, track/field (outdoor). *Women:* basketball, cross-country, soccer, softball, track/field (outdoor), volleyball. **On-Campus Highlights:** Engineering Building, Cafeteria, Gym, Business School, Dawson Building.

ADMISSIONS

Freshman Academic Profile: 90% from public high schools. **Reported SAT (pre-2016 redesign) scores:** SAT Math middle 50% range 380-470. SAT Critical Reading middle 50% range 400-470. SAT Writing middle 50% range 380-460. **Concordant SAT scores:** SAT EBRW middle 50% 440–520. SAT Math middle 50% range 420–510. ACT middle 50% range 16-19. Minimum paper TOEFL 550. **Basis for Candidate Selection:** *Very important factors considered include:* standardized test scores, alumni/ae relation, geographical residence, state residency. *Important factors considered include:* racial/ethnic status. *Other factors considered include:* class rank, recommendation(s). **Freshman Admission Requirements:** High school diploma is required and GED is accepted. *Academic units required:* 4 English, 4 math, 4 science, 2 science labs, 4 social studies, 4 history. **Freshman Admission Statistics:** 5,697 applied, 47.32% admitted, 39% enrolled. **Transfer Admission Requirements:** High school transcript, college transcript(s), standardized test scores, statement of good standing from prior institution(s). Minimum college GPA of 2.5 required. Lowest grade transferable C. **General Admission Information:** Application fee $10. Priority deadline 4/1. Regular application deadline 7/1. Nonfall registration accepted. Admission may be deferred for a maximum of 12 months.

COSTS AND FINANCIAL AID

Annual in-state tuition $3,948. Annual out-of-state tuition $7,896. Room and board $5,350. Required fees $744. **Required Forms and Deadlines:** FAFSA, Institution's own financial aid form. **Types of Aid:** *Need-based scholarships/grants:* Federal Pell, FSEOG, State scholarships/grants, Private scholarships, College/university scholarship or grant aid from institutional funds, United Negro College Fund. *Loans:* Direct Subsidized Stafford Loans, Direct Unsubsidized Stafford Loans, Direct PLUS loans, Federal Perkins Loans, State Loans, College/university loans from institutional funds. *Student Employment:* Federal Work-Study Program available. Institutional employment available.

ALASKA PACIFIC UNIVERSITY

4101 University Drive, Anchorage, AK 99508-4625
Phone: 907-564-8248 • **Financial Aid Phone:** 907-564-8341
E-mail: admissions@alaskapacific.edu • **CEEB Code:** 4201
Fax: 907-564-8317 • **Website:** http://www.alaskapacific.edu • **ACT Code:** 62

This private school was founded in 1957. It has a 170-acre campus.

RATINGS
Admissions Selectivity Rating: 84   **Fire Safety Rating:** 91   **Green Rating:** 60*

STUDENTS AND FACULTY
Enrollment: 455. **Student Body:** 65% female, 35% male, 32% out-of-state, <1% international (3 countries represented). Asian 2%, African American 3%, Caucasian 58%, Hispanic 3%, Native American 15%, Pacific Islander <1%, Two or more races 0%, Race unknown 18%.
Retention and Graduation: 67% freshmen return for sophomore year. 20% freshmen graduate within 4 years. 27% freshmen graduate within 6 years.
Faculty: Student/faculty ratio 10:1. 50 full-time faculty, 64% hold PhDs, 4% are are members of minority groups, 58% are women. 0% of classes are taught by teaching assistants.

ACADEMICS
Degrees: associate, bachelor's, certificate, doctoral/professional, master's, postbachelor's certificate, terminal. **Classes:** Most classes have fewer than 10 students. Most lab/discussion sessions have fewer than 10 students. **Most popular majors:** Marine Biology and Biological Oceanography; Elementary Education and Teaching; Business Administration and Management. **Special Study Options:** distance learning, double major, exchange student program (domestic), independent study, internships, student-designed major, study abroad, teacher certification program, Degree Completion program for adult students and a distance education program for Rural Alaskan Native Adults. **Disability Services:** Special programs offered to physically disabled students, including note-taking services, tape recorders, tutors. **Career Services:** Career/job search classes, Career assessment, Internships.

FACILITIES
Housing: Coed dorms, cooperative housing, several theme houses—example "Nordic Skiers House" for ski team members. 75% of campus accessible to physically diasbled. **Special Academic Facilities/Equipment:** Alaskana collection GIS lab gym with pool Student Center with weight room and indoor climbing wall Outdoor recreation center with classes and rental equipment Lake for canoeing and kayaking trails for running, skiing, hiking, biking, etc., connected to city's trail system **Computers:** 100% of classrooms, 100% of dorms, 100% of libraries, 100% of dining areas, 100% of student union, 100% of common outdoor areas have wireless network access. Students can register for classes online. Administrative functions (other than registration) can be performed online.

CAMPUS LIFE
Environment: City. **Activities:** drama/theater, literary magazine, music ensembles, student government, student newspaper, yearbook. 15 registered organizations, 1 religious organization. **On-Campus Highlights:** Student Center, Climbing wall and weight room, Pool, lounges in Grant Hall and in Carr Gottst. **Environmental Initiatives:** Kellogg Farm dedicated to organic and sustainable enterprises.

ADMISSIONS
Freshman Academic Profile: Average high school GPA 3.3. 17% in top 10% of high school class, 31% in top 25% of high school class, 72% in top 50% of high school class. 95% from public high schools. **Reported SAT (pre-2016 redesign) scores:** SAT Math middle 50% range 470-560. SAT Critical Reading middle 50% range 490-600. SAT Writing middle 50% range 460-610. **Concordant SAT scores:** SAT EBRW middle 50% 530–660. SAT Math middle 50% range 510–580. ACT middle 50% range 21-27. Minimum internet-based TOEFL 79. Minimum paper TOEFL 550. **Basis for Candidate Selection:** *Very important factors considered include:* rigor of secondary school record, academic GPA, application essay. *Important factors considered include:* standardized test scores, recommendation(s), alumni/ae relation, level of applicant's interest. *Other factors considered include:* extracurricular activities, talent/ability, volunteer work, work experience. **Freshman Admission Requirements:** High school diploma is required and GED is accepted. *Academic units recommended:* 4 English, 3 math, 2 science, 1 science lab, 2 foreign language, 1 social studies, 1 history. **Freshman Admission Statistics:** 245 applied, 48.16% admitted, 43% enrolled. **Transfer Admission Requirements:** college transcript(s), essay or personal statement, statement of good standing from prior institution(s). Minimum college GPA of 2.0 required. Lowest grade transferable C. **General Admission Information:** Application fee $25. Priority deadline 12/1. Regular application deadline 8/15. Nonfall registration accepted. Admission may be deferred for a maximum of 12 months.

COSTS AND FINANCIAL AID
Annual tuition $26,250. Room and board $9,300. Required fees $110. Average book expense $1,000. **Required Forms and Deadlines:** FAFSA. **Notification of Awards:** Applicants will be notified of awards on a rolling basis beginning 2/1. **Types of Aid:** *Need-based scholarships/grants:* Federal Pell, FSEOG, State scholarships/grants, Private scholarships, College/university scholarship or grant aid from institutional funds. *Loans:* Direct Subsidized Stafford Loans, Direct Unsubsidized Stafford Loans, Direct PLUS loans, State Loans. *Student Employment:* Federal Work-Study Program available. Institutional employment available. **Financial Aid Statistics:** 47% needy freshmen, 55% needy undergrads receive need-based scholarship or grant aid. 100% freshmen, 48% undergrads receive non-need-based scholarship or grant aid. 68% freshmen, 42% undergrads receive need-based self-help aid. 0% freshmen, 0% undergrads receive athletic scholarships. 88% freshmen, 92% undergrads receive any aid. **Criteria for awarding aid:** *Need-based:* Academics, Alumni affiliation, Leadership, Minority status, Religious affiliation. *Non-need-based:* Academics, Alumni affiliation, Leadership, Religious affiliation, State/district residency.

ALBANY COLLEGE OF PHARMACY

106 New Scotland Avenue, Albany, NY 12208
Phone: 518-694-7221 • **Financial Aid Phone:** 518-694-7256
E-mail: admissions@acp.edu • **CEEB Code:** 2013
Fax: 518-694-7322 • **Website:** www.acp.edu • **ACT Code:** 2672

This private school was founded in 1881. It has a 21-acre campus.

RATINGS
Admissions Selectivity Rating: 89   **Fire Safety Rating:** 70   **Green Rating:** 60*

STUDENTS AND FACULTY
Enrollment: 1,015. **Student Body:** 58% female, 42% male, 10% out-of-state, 8% international (6 countries represented). Asian 13%, African American 2%, Caucasian 73%, Hispanic 1%, Native American <1%, Pacific Islander 0%, Two or more races 0%, Race unknown 3%.
Retention and Graduation: 79% freshmen return for sophomore year.
Faculty: Student/faculty ratio 16:1. 82 full-time faculty, 74% hold PhDs, 12% are are members of minority groups, 49% are women. 0% of classes are taught by teaching assistants.

ACADEMICS
Degrees: bachelor's, certificate. **Classes:** Most classes have 20-29 students. Most lab/discussion sessions have 20-29 students. **Most popular majors:** Pharmacy. **Special Study Options:** Accelerated program, cross-registration. Combined degree programs: BA/JD, Pharm.D./MS, Pharm.D./MBA, BS/Phy Asst. **Disability Services:** Special programs offered to physically disabled students, including tutors. **Career Services:** Career/job search classes, Career assessment.

FACILITIES
Housing: Coed dorms, apartments for single students. 100% of campus accessible to physically diasbled. **Special Academic Facilities/Equipment:** Throop Pharmaceutical Museum. **Computers:** Students can register for classes online. Administrative functions (other than registration) can be performed online. Undergraduates are required to own a computer.

CAMPUS LIFE
Environment: City. **Activities:** Choral groups, concert band, dance, literary magazine, student government, student newspaper, yearbook, Student Organization. 2 honor societies, 1 religious organization. **Athletics (Intercollegiate):** *Men:* basketball, soccer. *Women:* basketball, soccer. **On-Campus Highlights:** NEW—ACP Student Center.

ADMISSIONS
Freshman Academic Profile: Average high school GPA 92.0. 47% in top 10% of high school class, 86% in top 25% of high school class, 99% in top 50% of high school class. **Reported SAT (pre-2016 redesign) scores:** SAT Math middle 50% range 570-650. SAT Critical Reading middle 50% range 530-620. SAT Writing middle 50% range 510-600. **Concordant SAT scores:** SAT EBRW middle 50% 580–660. SAT Math middle 50% range 590–670. ACT middle 50% range 23-28. Minimum paper TOEFL 600. **Basis for Candidate Selection:** *Very important factors considered include:* academic GPA, standardized test scores. *Important factors considered include:* rigor of secondary school record, class rank. *Other factors considered include:* application essay, recommendation(s), extracurricular activities, talent/ability, character/personal qualities, alumni/ae relation, geographical residence, volunteer work, work experience, level of applicant's interest. **Freshman Admission Requirements:** High school diploma is required and GED is accepted. *Academic units required:* 4 English, 4 math, 3 science, 3 science

labs, 4 social studies. *Academic units recommended:* 4 science, 4 science labs, 4 foreign language. **Freshman Admission Statistics:** 1,049 applied, 61.30% admitted, 41% enrolled. **Transfer Admission Requirements:** college transcript(s), essay or personal statement, statement of good standing from prior institution(s). Minimum college GPA of 3.2 required. Lowest grade transferable B. **General Admission Information:** Application fee $75. Priority deadline 2/1. Regular application deadline 3/1. Regular notification 3/15. Nonfall registration not accepted. Admission may be deferred for a maximum of 1 year.

COSTS AND FINANCIAL AID

Required Forms and Deadlines: FAFSA. **Notification of Awards:** Applicants will be notified of awards on a rolling basis beginning 3/25. **Types of Aid:** *Need-based scholarships/grants:* Federal Pell, FSEOG, State scholarships/grants, Private scholarships, College/university scholarship or grant aid from institutional funds. *Loans:* Federal Perkins Loans. *Student Employment:* Federal Work-Study Program available. Institutional employment available. **Financial Aid Statistics:** 92% needy freshmen, 80% needy undergrads receive need-based scholarship or grant aid. 12% freshmen, 6% undergrads receive non-need-based scholarship or grant aid. 84% freshmen, 92% undergrads receive need-based self-help aid. 0% freshmen, 0% undergrads receive athletic scholarships. **Criteria for awarding aid:** *Need-based:* Academics, Alumni affiliation, Leadership. *Non-need-based:* Academics, Alumni affiliation, Leadership.

ALBANY STATE UNIVERSITY

504 College Drive, Albany, GA 31705
Phone: 229-430-4646 • **Financial Aid Phone:** 229-430-4650
E-mail: enrollmentservices@asurams.edu • **CEEB Code:** 5004
Fax: 229-430-4105 • **Website:** http://www.asurams.edu • **ACT Code:** 782

This public school was founded in 1903. It has a 232-acre campus.

RATINGS

Admissions Selectivity Rating: 82　　**Fire Safety Rating:** 90　　**Green Rating:** 60*

STUDENTS AND FACULTY

Enrollment: 4,173. **Student Body:** 66% female, 34% male, 4% out-of-state, <1% international (22 countries represented). Asian 0%, African American 83%, Caucasian 4%, Hispanic 1%, Native American <1%, Pacific Islander <1%, Two or more races <1%, Race unknown 11%.
Retention and Graduation: 65% freshmen return for sophomore year. 41% freshmen graduate within 6 years. **Faculty:** Student/faculty ratio 21:1. 164 full-time faculty, 77% hold PhDs, 78% are are members of minority groups, 45% are women. 0% of classes are taught by teaching assistants.

ACADEMICS

Degrees: bachelor's, master's, post-master's certificate. **Classes:** Most classes have 20-29 students. **Most popular majors:** Business Administration and Management; Early Childhood Education and Teaching; Criminal Justice/Safety Studies. **Special Study Options:** cooperative education program, cross-registration, distance learning, double major, dual enrollment, honors program, independent study, internships, liberal arts/career combination, study abroad, teacher certification program, weekend college, 3+2 & 2+2 engineering program with GA Tech. Pre-med, pre-med technology, pre-pharmacy study options. Online degree programs. **Honors Programs:** The Velma Fudge Grant Honors Program represents a commitment made by Albany State University (ASU) to broaden and enrich educational experiences of bright, highly motivated and creative students. Honors Program students are provided opportunities for scholarships, access to special extracurricular programs, a chance to pursue independent projects and research interests, professional experience through internship programs and special service options. Through its specially designed curriculum, the University provides the opportunity for faculty to teach academically talented students in inventive, interdisciplinary, small class settings designed to fulfill core curriculum requirements, as well as in advanced or intensive classes in particular disciplines. The Honors Program is specifically designed for academic scholarship recipients, academically talented students and entering freshman and transfer students with a proven dedication to academic excellence and scholarship. The Honors Program student must reach beyond good grades for success and have the courage to demonstrate superior ethical leadership in his/her chosen field of study. Combined degree programs: BA/MEng. **Disability Services:** Special programs offered to physically disabled students, including note-taking services, reader services, tape recorders, tutors. **Career Services:** Alumni network, Alumni services, Career assessment, Internships, Regional alumni. All opportunities are welcomed to provide experiential learning experiences for ASU students, especially those that result in employment opportunities.

FACILITIES

Housing: Coed dorms, men's dorms, women's dorms, apartments for single students, Upper classmen and graduate halls. 98% of campus accessible to physically diasbled. **Computers:** 67% of dorms, have wireless network access.

CAMPUS LIFE

Environment: City. **Activities:** Choral groups, concert band, dance, drama/theater, jazz band, marching band, opera, radio station, student government, student newspaper, television station, Campus Ministries, Student Organization, Model UN. 70 registered organizations, 10 honor societies, 6 fraternities, 4 sororities. **Athletics (Intercollegiate):** *Men:* baseball, basketball, cross-country, football, track/field (outdoor). *Women:* basketball, cross-country, softball, tennis, track/field (outdoor), volleyball. **On-Campus Highlights:** Student Affairs Building, Gymnasium, Housing, Stadium **Environmental Initiatives:** 1. Hazardous Waste Labels, 2. Paint shops and carpentry, 3. Universal Waste.

ADMISSIONS

Freshman Academic Profile: 10% in top 10% of high school class, 30% in top 25% of high school class, 67% in top 50% of high school class. **Reported SAT (pre-2016 redesign) scores:** SAT Math middle 50% range 390-460. SAT Critical Reading middle 50% range 390-450. **Concordant SAT scores:** SAT Math middle 50% range 430–500. ACT middle 50% range 16-19. Minimum paper TOEFL 523. **Basis for Candidate Selection:** *Very important factors considered include:* academic GPA, standardized test scores. *Other factors considered include:* rigor of secondary school record, class rank, application essay, recommendation(s). **Freshman Admission Requirements:** *Academic units required:* 4 English, 4 math, 3 science, 2 science labs, 2 foreign language, 3 social studies. **Freshman Admission Statistics:** 6,554 applied, 28.65% admitted, 57% enrolled. **Transfer Admission Requirements:** college transcript(s), Minimum college GPA of 2.0 required. Lowest grade transferable D. **General Admission Information:** Application fee $20. Priority deadline 5/1. Regular application deadline 6/1. Nonfall registration accepted. Admission may be deferred for a maximum of one year.

COSTS AND FINANCIAL AID

Required Forms and Deadlines: FAFSA, State aid form. **Notification of Awards:** Applicants will be notified of awards on a rolling basis beginning 1/7. *Student Employment:* Federal Work-Study Program available. Institutional employment available. **Criteria for awarding aid:** *Non-need-based:* Academics, Alumni affiliation, Art, Athletics.

ALBERTA COLLEGE OF ART + DESIGN

1407 14 Avenue NW, Calgary, AB T2N 4R3
Phone: 403-284-7617 • **Financial Aid Phone:** 403-284-7600
E-mail: admissions@acad.ca
Fax: 403-284-7644 • **Website:** www.acad.ca

This public school was founded in 1926.

RATINGS

Admissions Selectivity Rating: 70　　**Fire Safety Rating:** 60*　　**Green Rating:** 60*

STUDENTS AND FACULTY

Enrollment: 1,155. **Student Body:** 73% female, 27% male, 11% out-of-state, 5% international (49 countries represented). Asian 0%, African American 0%, Caucasian 0%, Hispanic 0%, Native American 0%, Pacific Islander 0%, Two or more races 0%, Race unknown 95%.
Retention and Graduation: 64% freshmen return for sophomore year. 38% freshmen graduate within 4 years. 1% freshmen graduate within 6 years. **Faculty:** Student/faculty ratio 15:1. 46 full-time faculty, 0% hold PhDs, 0% are are members of minority groups, 0% are women.

ACADEMICS

Degrees: bachelor's. **Most popular majors:** Drawing; Painting; Sculpture. **Special Study Options:** cross-registration, exchange student program (domestic), internships, study abroad, Mobility and Exchange. **Disability Services:** Special programs offered to physically disabled students, including reader services, tutors. **Career Services:** On-campus interviews.

FACILITIES

Housing: Coed dorms, Assisted off-campus housing search. 100% of campus accessible to physically diasbled. **Special Academic Facilities/Equipment:** 2 Art Galleries **Computers:** 100% of classrooms, have wireless network access. Students can register for classes online. Administrative functions (other than registration) can be performed online.

CAMPUS LIFE

Environment: Metropolis. **Activities:** student government. **Athletics (Intercollegiate):** *Men:* basketball, ice hockey, volleyball. *Women:* basketball, volleyball. **On-Campus Highlights:** Facilities, Glass Department, Graffitt Stairwell, Residence.

ADMISSIONS

Freshman Academic Profile: 91% from public high schools. Minimum internet-based TOEFL 83. Minimum paper TOEFL 560. **Basis for Candidate Selection:** *Very important factors considered include:* academic GPA, application essay, talent/ability, level of applicant's interest. *Other factors considered include:* standardized test scores, recommendation(s), extracurricular activities, character/personal qualities, work experience. **Freshman Admission Requirements:** High school diploma is required and GED is not accepted. *Academic units required:* 4 English. **Freshman Admission Statistics:** 576 applied, 65.45% admitted, 74% enrolled. **Transfer Admission Requirements:** college transcript(s), essay or personal statement. **General Admission Information:** Application fee $85. Regular application deadline 4/1. Regular notification 5/15. Nonfall registration accepted.

COSTS AND FINANCIAL AID

Annual in-state tuition $4,435. Annual out-of-state tuition $4,435. Required fees $831. Average book expense $3,150. **Required Forms and Deadlines:** FAFSA. **Criteria for awarding aid:** *Need-based:* Academics, Art. *Non-need-based:* Academics, Art.

ALBERTUS MAGNUS COLLEGE

700 Prospect Street, New Haven, CT 6511
Phone: 203-773-8501 • **Financial Aid Phone:** 203-773-8508
E-mail: admissions@albertus.edu • **CEEB Code:** 3001
Fax: 203-773-5248 • **Website:** www.albertus.edu • **ACT Code:** 549

This private school, affiliated with the Roman Catholic Church, was founded in 1925. It has a 50-acre campus.

RATINGS

Admissions Selectivity Rating: 74   **Fire Safety Rating:** 85   **Green Rating:** 60*

STUDENTS AND FACULTY

Enrollment: 1,682. **Student Body:** 68% female, 32% male, 15% out-of-state, <1% international. Asian 1%, African American 27%, Caucasian 55%, Hispanic 10%, Native American <1%, Pacific Islander 0%, Two or more races 0%, Race unknown 7%.
Retention and Graduation: 78% freshmen return for sophomore year. 49% freshmen graduate within 4 years. 62% freshmen graduate within 6 years.
Faculty: Student/faculty ratio 13:1. 42 full-time faculty, 79% hold PhDs, 0% are are members of minority groups, 43% are women. 0% of classes are taught by teaching assistants.

ACADEMICS

Degrees: associate, bachelor's, certificate, master's. **Classes:** Most classes have 10-19 students. **Most popular majors:** Psychology; Business/Commerce; Education. **Special Study Options:** Accelerated program, double major, honors program, independent study, internships, student-designed major, teacher certification program. **Honors Programs:** Students may apply to follow the Honors Program, which involves work in special courses designated each semester as honors courses and the development of individual projects designed in consultation with faculty mentors. Entering qualified students are assigned to special honors courses and returning students interested in such a program should consult, by the spring of their sophomore year or earlier, with their advisor and the Director of the Honors Program. **Disability Services:** Special programs offered to physically disabled students, including note-taking services, reader services, tape recorders, tutors. **Career Services:** Alumni network, Career/job search classes, Career assessment, Internships.

FACILITIES

Housing: Coed dorms, women's dorms, Mansion style residence halls. Substance free and quiet halls. 70% of campus accessible to physically diasbled. **Special Academic Facilities/Equipment:** Margart McDonough Art Gallery

CAMPUS LIFE

Environment: City. **Activities:** Choral groups, dance, drama/theater, literary magazine, musical theater, student government, yearbook, Campus Ministries. 1 honor society, 1 religious organization. **Athletics (Intercollegiate):** *Men:* baseball, basketball, cross-country, lacrosse, soccer, tennis, volleyball. *Women:* basketball, cross-country, lacrosse, soccer, softball, tennis, volleyball. **On-Campus Highlights:** Center for Science, Art and Technology, Athletic Center, Library, Campus Center, Art Gallery.

ADMISSIONS

Freshman Academic Profile: Average high school GPA 3.0. 10% in top 10% of high school class, 29% in top 25% of high school class, 68% in top 50%

of high school class. 70% from public high schools. **Reported SAT (pre-2016 redesign) scores:** SAT Math middle 50% range 470-500. SAT Critical Reading middle 50% range 490-560. SAT Writing middle 50% range 430-560. **Concordant SAT scores:** SAT EBRW middle 50% 510–620. SAT Math middle 50% range 510–530. Minimum paper TOEFL 550. **Basis for Candidate Selection:** *Very important factors considered include:* rigor of secondary school record, academic GPA. *Important factors considered include:* standardized test scores, recommendation(s). *Other factors considered include:* class rank, application essay, interview, extracurricular activities, talent/ability, character/personal qualities, first generation, alumni/ae relation, volunteer work, work experience, level of applicant's interest. **Freshman Admission Requirements:** High school diploma is required and GED is accepted. *Academic units required:* 4 English, 2 math, 2 science, 2 foreign language, 2 social studies, 2 history, 2 academic electives. *Academic units recommended:* 3 math, 3 science, 1 science lab, 3 foreign language, 1 social studies, 2 history. **Freshman Admission Statistics:** 556 applied, 84.17% admitted, 26% enrolled. **Transfer Admission Requirements:** college transcript(s), Minimum college GPA of 2.0 required. Lowest grade transferable C. **General Admission Information:** Application fee $35. Nonfall registration accepted. Admission may be deferred.

COSTS AND FINANCIAL AID

Annual tuition $20,166. Room and board $8,907. Required fees $908. Average book expense $920. **Required Forms and Deadlines:** FAFSA, Institution's own financial aid form. **Notification of Awards:** Applicants will be notified of awards on a rolling basis beginning 3/1. **Types of Aid:** *Need-based scholarships/grants:* Federal Pell, FSEOG, State scholarships/grants, College/university scholarship or grant aid from institutional funds. *Loans:* Direct Subsidized Stafford Loans, Direct Unsubsidized Stafford Loans, Direct PLUS loans, Federal Perkins Loans. *Student Employment:* Federal Work-Study Program available. Institutional employment available. **Financial Aid Statistics:** 89% needy freshmen, 93% needy undergrads receive need-based scholarship or grant aid. 60% freshmen, 65% undergrads receive non-need-based scholarship or grant aid. 37% freshmen, 39% undergrads receive need-based self-help aid. 87% freshmen, 75% undergrads receive any aid. **Criteria for awarding aid:** *Need-based:* Academics. *Non-need-based:* Academics, Leadership, Religious affiliation.

ALBION COLLEGE

611 East Porter, Albion, MI 49224
Phone: 517-629-0321 • **Financial Aid Phone:** 517-629-0440
E-mail: admission@albion.edu • **CEEB Code:** 1007
Fax: 517-629-0569 • **Website:** www.albion.edu • **ACT Code:** 1956

This private school, affiliated with the Methodist Church, was founded in 1835. It has a 585-acre campus.

RATINGS

Admissions Selectivity Rating: 81   **Fire Safety Rating:** 88   **Green Rating:** 73

STUDENTS AND FACULTY

Enrollment: 1,393. **Student Body:** 52% female, 48% male, 17% out-of-state, 2% international (15 countries represented). Asian 3%, African American 9%, Caucasian 71%, Hispanic 7%, Native American <1%, Pacific Islander <1%, Two or more races 3%, Race unknown 6%.
Retention and Graduation: 82% freshmen return for sophomore year. 61% freshmen graduate within 4 years. 70% freshmen graduate within 6 years. 29% grads go on to further study within 1 year. 44% grads pursue arts and sciences degrees. 5% grads pursue law degrees. 4% grads pursue business degrees. 9% grads pursue medical degrees. **Faculty:** Student/faculty ratio 12:1. 104 full-time faculty, 94% hold PhDs, 11% are are members of minority groups, 49% are women. 0% of classes are taught by teaching assistants.

ACADEMICS

Degrees: bachelor's. **Classes:** Most classes have 10-19 students. Most lab/discussion sessions have 10-19 students. **Most popular majors:** Biology/Biological Sciences; Economics; Psychology. **Special Study Options:** double major, dual enrollment, honors program, independent study, internships, liberal arts/career combination, student-designed major, study abroad, teacher certification program, Environmental Institute, Ford Institute for Public Service, Gerstacker Liberal Arts Program in Professional Management. **Honors Programs:** The Honors Program at Albion was founded in 1976, and in August of 2004 it was renamed The Prentiss M. Brown Honors Institute. We provide an exciting and unique variety of academic experiences for highly motivated and talented students. The Institute's mix of small discussion classes, independent research, academic rigor, and personal attention provides Honors students with special challenges and opportunities for growth. Many of the College's finest teachers and scholars regularly contribute to the Institute's curriculum. Combined degree programs: BA/MEng. **Disability Services:** Special programs offered to physically disabled students, including note-taking services, reader services, tape recorders, tutors. **Career Services:** Alumni network, Alumni services, Career/job search classes, Career assessment, Internships, Regional alumni. Our Programs of Distinction: Professional Management, Environmental, Education, Public Policy & Service, Honors and Pre-Health. All incorporate internships or experiential learning into the curriculum.

FACILITIES

Housing: Coed dorms, special housing for disabled students, women's dorms, fraternity/sorority housing, apartments for married students, cooperative housing, apartments for single students, Special interest annexes available. 95% of campus accessible to physically diasbled. **Special Academic Facilities/Equipment:** Visual arts museum, nature center, science complex museum, shark aquarium, greenhouse, geographic information systems/computer-aided mapping lab, observatory. **Computers:** 95% of classrooms, 100% of dorms, 100% of libraries, 100% of dining areas, 100% of student union, 25% of common outdoor areas have wireless network access. Students can register for classes online. Administrative functions (other than registration) can be performed online.

CAMPUS LIFE

Environment: Village. **Activities:** Choral groups, concert band, dance, drama/theater, jazz band, literary magazine, marching band, music ensembles, musical theater, pep band, radio station, student government, symphony orchestra, yearbook, Campus Ministries, Student Organization, Model UN. 122 registered organizations, 17 honor societies, 11 religious organizations. 6 fraternities, 7 sororities. **Athletics (Intercollegiate):** *Men:* baseball, basketball, cross-country, diving, equestrian sports, football, golf, soccer, swimming, tennis, track/field (outdoor), track/field (indoor). *Women:* basketball, cross-country, diving, equestrian sports, golf, soccer, softball, swimming, tennis, track/field (outdoor), track/field (indoor), volleyball. **On-Campus Highlights:** Kellogg Center- Student Center, Dow Recreation Center- Athletic Facility, Quad- Lawn in the center of campus, Baldwin- Dining Hall, Science Center Atrium, Albion is often lauded for the amount of student space available. Whether it's lounge areas, computer classrooms, meeting spaces, or the myriad rooms in the Kellogg Center, Albion students find many areas to congregate socially and academically. **Environmental Initiatives:** Sustainability was chosen as a key theme in Albion's new strategic plan. Sustainability was showcased in the inaugural edition of our Theme Year initiative in 2010-11. The Sustainability Theme Year encompassed facilities management and a variety of campus activities including a common reading, named lectures, a film series, career fairs, dining hall meals, and an ongoing lifestyle challenge. We are currently in our second year (2013-14) of this initiative.

ADMISSIONS

Freshman Academic Profile: Average high school GPA 3.4. ACT middle 50% range 20-26. Minimum internet-based TOEFL 79. Minimum paper TOEFL 550. **Basis for Candidate Selection:** *Very important factors considered include:* rigor of secondary school record, academic GPA, standardized test scores. *Important factors considered include:* class rank. *Other factors considered include:* application essay, recommendation(s), interview, extracurricular activities, talent/ability, character/personal qualities, alumni/ae relation, geographical residence, state residency, racial/ethnic status, volunteer work, work experience. **Freshman Admission Requirements:** High school diploma is required and GED is accepted. *Academic units recommended:* 4 English, 4 math, 3 science, 2 science labs, 2 foreign language, 2 social studies. **Freshman Admission Statistics:** 3,338 applied, 72.26% admitted, 17% enrolled. **Transfer Admission Requirements:** High school transcript, college transcript(s), essay or personal statement, interview, standardized test scores, statement of good standing from prior institution(s). Minimum college GPA of 2.5 required. Lowest grade transferable C. **General Admission Information:** Nonfall registration accepted. Admission may be deferred for a maximum of 1 year.

COSTS AND FINANCIAL AID

Annual tuition $40,570. Room and board $11,610. Required fees $470. Average book expense $700. **Required Forms and Deadlines:** FAFSA. **Notification of Awards:** Applicants will be notified of awards on a rolling basis beginning 3/15. **Types of Aid:** *Need-based scholarships/grants:* Federal Pell, FSEOG, State scholarships/grants, Private scholarships, College/university scholarship or grant aid from institutional funds. *Loans:* Direct Subsidized Stafford Loans, Direct Unsubsidized Stafford Loans, Direct PLUS loans, Federal Perkins Loans. *Student Employment:* Federal Work-Study Program available. Institutional employment available. **Financial Aid Statistics:** 100% needy freshmen, 100% needy undergrads receive need-based scholarship or grant aid. 99% freshmen, 98% undergrads receive non-need-based scholarship or grant aid. 85% freshmen, 84% undergrads receive need-based self-help aid.

0% freshmen, 0% undergrads receive athletic scholarships. 100% freshmen, 99% undergrads receive any aid. 68% undergrads borrow to pay for school. Average cumulative indebtedness $38,356. **Criteria for awarding aid:** *Need-based:* Academics, Alumni affiliation, Art, Leadership, Music/drama, Religious affiliation. *Non-need-based:* Academics, Alumni affiliation, Art, Leadership, Music/drama.

ALBRIGHT COLLEGE

PO Box 15234, Reading, PA 19612-5234
Phone: 610-921-7799 • **Financial Aid Phone:** 610-921-7264
E-mail: admission@albright.edu • **CEEB Code:** 2004
Fax: 610-921-7729 • **Website:** www.albright.edu • **ACT Code:** 2004

This private school, affiliated with the Methodist Church, was founded in 1856. It has a 118-acre campus.

RATINGS

Admissions Selectivity Rating: 84   **Fire Safety Rating:** 61   **Green Rating:** 60*

STUDENTS AND FACULTY

Enrollment: 2,291. **Student Body:** 60% female, 40% male, 41% out-of-state, 2% international (18 countries represented). Asian 2%, African American 20%, Caucasian 49%, Hispanic 10%, Native American 1%, Pacific Islander 0%, Two or more races 1%, Race unknown 14%.
Retention and Graduation: 71% freshmen return for sophomore year. 47% freshmen graduate within 4 years. 54% freshmen graduate within 6 years. 17% grads go on to further study within 1 year. **Faculty:** Student/faculty ratio 14:1. 110 full-time faculty, 84% hold PhDs, 18% are are members of minority groups, 47% are women.

ACADEMICS

Degrees: bachelor's, certificate, master's. **Classes:** Most classes have 10-19 students. Most lab/discussion sessions have 10-19 students. **Most popular majors:** Sociology; Business/Commerce. **Special Study Options:** Accelerated program, cross-registration, dual enrollment, English as a Second Language (ESL), exchange student program (domestic), honors program, independent study, internships, liberal arts/career combination, student-designed major, study abroad, teacher certification program, Interdisciplinary. **Career Services:** Alumni network, Alumni services, Career/job search classes, Career assessment, Internships, Regional alumni.

FACILITIES

Housing: Coed dorms, men's dorms, women's dorms, apartments for single students, Honors, Special Interest, Freshmen Floors vs Dorms. **Special Academic Facilities/Equipment:** Freedman Art Gallery

CAMPUS LIFE

Environment: City. **Activities:** Choral groups, concert band, dance, drama/theater, jazz band, literary magazine, music ensembles, musical theater, pep band, radio station, student government, student newspaper, television station, yearbook. 84 registered organizations, 10 honor societies, 3 religious organizations. 4 fraternities, 3 sororities. **Athletics (Intercollegiate):** *Men:* baseball, basketball, cheerleading, cross-country, football, golf, soccer, swimming, tennis, track/field (outdoor), track/field (indoor), wrestling. *Women:* badminton, basketball, cheerleading, cross-country, field hockey, soccer, softball, swimming, tennis, track/field (outdoor), track/field (indoor), volleyball. **On-Campus Highlights:** Student Center, Jake's Place, Wachovia Theatre, Sports Center, Natatorium.

ADMISSIONS

Freshman Academic Profile: Average high school GPA 3.4. 19% in top 10% of high school class, 44% in top 25% of high school class, 76% in top 50% of high school class. 77% from public high schools. **Reported SAT (pre-2016 redesign) scores:** SAT Math middle 50% range 470-570. SAT Critical Reading middle 50% range 480-573. **Concordant SAT scores:** SAT Math middle 50% range 510–590. ACT middle 50% range 20-24. **Basis for Candidate Selection:** *Very important factors considered include:* rigor of secondary school record, academic GPA. *Important factors considered include:* class rank, character/personal qualities. *Other factors considered include:* standardized test scores, application essay, recommendation(s), interview, extracurricular activities, talent/ability, alumni/ae relation, volunteer work, work experience, level of applicant's interest. **Freshman Admission Requirements:** High school diploma is required and GED is accepted. *Academic units required:* 4 English, 3 math, 3 science, 1 science lab, 2 foreign language, 2 social studies, 1 history. *Academic units recommended:* 4 English, 3 math, 4 science, 2 science labs, 3 foreign language, 2 social studies, 1 academic elective. **Freshman Admission Statistics:** 8,832 applied, 51.11% admitted, 13% enrolled. **Transfer Admission Requirements:** college transcript(s), essay or personal statement,

statement of good standing from prior institution(s). Minimum college GPA of 2.0 required. Lowest grade transferable C-. **General Admission Information:** Application fee $35. Priority deadline 9/1. Nonfall registration accepted. Admission may be deferred.

COSTS AND FINANCIAL AID

Annual tuition $42,404. Room and board $11,606. Required fees $900. Average book expense $1,000. **Required Forms and Deadlines:** FAFSA. **Notification of Awards:** Applicants will be notified of awards on a rolling basis beginning 11/20. **Types of Aid:** *Need-based scholarships/grants:* Federal Pell, FSEOG, State scholarships/grants, Private scholarships, College/university scholarship or grant aid from institutional funds, United Negro College Fund. *Loans:* Direct Subsidized Stafford Loans, Direct Unsubsidized Stafford Loans, Direct PLUS loans, Federal Perkins Loans. *Student Employment:* Federal Work-Study Program available. Institutional employment available. **Financial Aid Statistics:** 100% needy freshmen, 100% needy undergrads receive need-based scholarship or grant aid. 8% freshmen, 8% undergrads receive non-need-based scholarship or grant aid. 88% freshmen, 89% undergrads receive need-based self-help aid. 0% freshmen, 0% undergrads receive athletic scholarships. 89% undergrads borrow to pay for school. Average cumulative indebtedness $38,196. **Criteria for awarding aid:** *Non-need-based:* Academics, Art, Music/drama, Religious affiliation, State/district residency.

ALCORN STATE UNIVERSITY

1000 ASU Drive #300, Lorman, MS 39096
Phone: 601-877-6147
E-mail: ksampson@alcorn.edu • **CEEB Code:** 1008
Fax: 601-877-6347 • **Website:** www.alcorn.edu • **ACT Code:** 2176

This public school was founded in 1871. It has a 1756-acre campus.

RATINGS

Admissions Selectivity Rating: 72   **Fire Safety Rating:** 60*   **Green Rating:** 60*

STUDENTS AND FACULTY

Enrollment: 3,006. **Student Body:** 64% female, 36% male, 13% out-of-state, 1% international (14 countries represented). Asian 0%, African American 94%, Caucasian 2%, Hispanic <1%, Native American <1%, Pacific Islander <1%, Two or more races 2%, Race unknown 0%.
Retention and Graduation: 76% freshmen return for sophomore year. 20% freshmen graduate within 4 years. 40% freshmen graduate within 6 years. 38% grads go on to further study within 1 year. **Faculty:** Student/faculty ratio 17:1. 163 full-time faculty, 66% hold PhDs, 80% are are members of minority groups, 45% are women.

ACADEMICS

Degrees: associate, bachelor's, master's, post-master's certificate. **Classes:** Most classes have 20-29 students. Most lab/discussion sessions have fewer than 10 students. **Most popular majors:** Elementary Education and Teaching; Liberal Arts and Sciences/Liberal Studies. **Special Study Options:** Accelerated program, cooperative education program, distance learning, double major, dual enrollment, honors program, independent study, internships, liberal arts/career combination, study abroad, teacher certification program, Undergrads may take grad level classes (restrictions apply). Combined degree programs: Cooperative physics program with Howard U. **Career Services:** Internships.

FACILITIES

Housing: men's dorms, women's dorms, Honor's Dorm. 0% of campus accessible to physically diasbled. **Special Academic Facilities/Equipment:** Honor's Resident Hall **Computers:** Students can register for classes online. Administrative functions (other than registration) can be performed online.

CAMPUS LIFE

Environment: Rural. **Activities:** Choral groups, concert band, dance, drama/theater, jazz band, marching band, music ensembles, radio station, student government, student newspaper, television station, yearbook. 120 registered organizations, 10 honor societies, 8 religious organizations. 8 fraternities, 7 sororities. **Athletics (Intercollegiate):** *Men:* baseball, basketball, cross-country, football, golf, tennis, track/field (outdoor). *Women:* basketball, cross-country, golf, soccer, softball, tennis, track/field (outdoor), volleyball.

ADMISSIONS

Freshman Academic Profile: Average high school GPA 3.0. 68% in top 50% of high school class. 99% from public high schools. **Reported SAT (pre-2016 redesign) scores:** SAT Math middle 50% range 405-500. SAT Critical Reading middle 50% range 390-485. **Concordant SAT scores:** SAT Math middle 50% range 450–530. ACT middle 50% range 16-20. Minimum paper TOEFL 525. **Basis for Candidate Selection:** *Very important factors considered include:*

rigor of secondary school record, class rank, academic GPA. *Important factors considered include:* standardized test scores. *Other factors considered include:* recommendation(s), interview. **Freshman Admission Requirements:** High school diploma is required and GED is accepted. *Academic units required:* 4 English, 3 math, 3 science, 2 science labs, 1 foreign language, 3 social studies, 1 academic elective. *Academic units recommended:* 4 English, 4 math, 4 science, 2 science labs, 1 foreign language, 4 social studies, 1 academic elective, 1 visual/performing arts. **Freshman Admission Statistics:** 2,078 applied, 78.44% admitted, 32% enrolled. **Transfer Admission Requirements:** college transcript(s), statement of good standing from prior institution(s). Minimum college GPA of 2.0 required. Lowest grade transferable C. **General Admission Information:** Nonfall registration accepted. Admission may be deferred.

COSTS AND FINANCIAL AID

Required Forms and Deadlines: FAFSA, Institution's own financial aid form. **Notification of Awards:** Applicants will be notified of awards on a rolling basis beginning 4/1. **Types of Aid:** *Need-based scholarships/grants:* Federal Pell, FSEOG, State scholarships/grants, Private scholarships, College/university scholarship or grant aid from institutional funds. *Loans:* Direct Subsidized Stafford Loans, Direct Unsubsidized Stafford Loans, Direct PLUS loans. *Student Employment:* Federal Work-Study Program available. Institutional employment available. **Financial Aid Statistics:** 95% needy freshmen, 93% needy undergrads receive need-based scholarship or grant aid. 33% freshmen, 24% undergrads receive non-need-based scholarship or grant aid. 75% freshmen, 84% undergrads receive need-based self-help aid. 10% freshmen, 8% undergrads receive athletic scholarships. **Criteria for awarding aid:** *Need-based:* Academics, Alumni affiliation, Athletics, Leadership, Minority status, Music/drama. *Non-need-based:* Academics, Athletics, Leadership.

ALDERSON BROADDUS UNIVERSITY

101 College Hill Drive, Philippi, WV 26416
Phone: 800-263-1549 • **Financial Aid Phone:** 304-457-6354
E-mail: admissions@ab.edu • **CEEB Code:** 5005
Fax: 304-457-6239 • **Website:** www.ab.edu • **ACT Code:** 4508

This private school, affiliated with the American Baptist Church, was founded in 1871. It has a 170-acre campus.

RATINGS

Admissions Selectivity Rating: 81   **Fire Safety Rating:** 83   **Green Rating:** 60*

STUDENTS AND FACULTY

Enrollment: 1,066. **Student Body:** 46% female, 54% male, 63% out-of-state, 5% international (11 countries represented). Asian 1%, African American 16%, Caucasian 73%, Hispanic 4%, Native American <1%, Pacific Islander <1%, Two or more races 1%, Race unknown 0%.
Retention and Graduation: 55% freshmen return for sophomore year. 27% freshmen graduate within 4 years. 38% freshmen graduate within 6 years. 7% grads go on to further study within 1 year. 19% grads pursue arts and sciences degrees. 4% grads pursue law degrees. 7% grads pursue business degrees. 11% grads pursue medical degrees. **Faculty:** Student/faculty ratio 17:1. 62 full-time faculty, 47% hold PhDs, 6% are are members of minority groups, 55% are women. 0% of classes are taught by teaching assistants.

ACADEMICS

Degrees: associate, bachelor's, master's. **Classes:** Most classes have fewer than 10 students. Most lab/discussion sessions have 10-19 students. **Most popular majors:** Registered Nursing/Registered Nurse; Biology/Biological Sciences; Athletic Training/Trainer. **Special Study Options:** double major, honors program, independent study, internships, liberal arts/career combination, study abroad, teacher certification program, Business Department offers on-line certificate program. **Disability Services:** Special programs offered to physically disabled students, including note-taking services, reader services, tape recorders, tutors. **Career Services:** Alumni network, Career/job search classes, Career assessment, Internships, On-campus interviews.

FACILITIES

Housing: Coed dorms, special housing for disabled students, women's dorms, apartments for married students, apartments for single students, Wellness Housing. 70% of campus accessible to physically diasbled. **Special Academic Facilities/Equipment:** Art Gallery in Burbick Hall, Campbell School House. **Computers:** 75% of classrooms, 100% of dorms, 90% of libraries, 100% of dining areas, 100% of student union, have wireless network access. Administrative functions (other than registration) can be performed online.

CAMPUS LIFE

Environment: Rural. **Activities:** Choral groups, concert band, drama/theater, jazz band, literary magazine, music ensembles, musical theater, radio station, student government, student newspaper, television station, yearbook, Campus Ministries. 49 registered organizations, 2 honor societies, 2 religious organizations. 2 fraternities, 3 sororities. **Athletics (Intercollegiate):** *Men:* baseball, basketball, cross-country, soccer, track/field (outdoor), track/field (indoor). *Women:* basketball, cross-country, soccer, softball, track/field (outdoor), track/field (indoor), volleyball. **On-Campus Highlights:** Cave, Burbick Hall, Rex Pyles Arena, Wilcox Chapel. **Environmental Initiatives:** recycling efforts.

ADMISSIONS

Freshman Academic Profile: Average high school GPA 3.2. 11% in top 10% of high school class, 31% in top 25% of high school class, 69% in top 50% of high school class. 97% from public high schools. **Reported SAT (pre-2016 redesign) scores:** SAT Math middle 50% range 450-530. SAT Critical Reading middle 50% range 440-510. SAT Writing middle 50% range 410-490. **Concordant SAT scores:** SAT EBRW middle 50% 480–560. SAT Math middle 50% range 490–560. ACT middle 50% range 19-23. Minimum paper TOEFL 500. **Basis for Candidate Selection:** *Very important factors considered include:* rigor of secondary school record, academic GPA, standardized test scores. *Important factors considered include:* application essay. *Other factors considered include:* recommendation(s), interview, talent/ability, first generation, alumni/ae relation, level of applicant's interest. **Freshman Admission Requirements:** High school diploma is required and GED is accepted. *Academic units required:* 4 English, 3 math, 3 science, 1 science lab, 1 social studies. *Academic units recommended:* 3 science labs, 1 foreign language, 3 social studies. **Freshman Admission Statistics:** 4,206 applied, 53.69% admitted, 15% enrolled. **Transfer Admission Requirements:** High school transcript, college transcript(s), statement of good standing from prior institution(s). Minimum college GPA of 2.0 required. Lowest grade transferable C. **General Admission Information:** Nonfall registration accepted. Admission may be deferred for a maximum of 1 year.

COSTS AND FINANCIAL AID

Annual tuition $23,930. Room and board $7,606. Required fees $210. Average book expense $800. **Required Forms and Deadlines:** FAFSA, State aid form. **Notification of Awards:** Applicants will be notified of awards on a rolling basis beginning 3/1. **Types of Aid:** *Need-based scholarships/grants:* Federal Pell, FSEOG, State scholarships/grants, Private scholarships, College/university scholarship or grant aid from institutional funds, Federal Nursing Scholarships. *Loans:* Direct Subsidized Stafford Loans, Direct Unsubsidized Stafford Loans, Direct PLUS loans, Federal Perkins Loans, Federal Nursing Loans. *Student Employment:* Federal Work-Study Program available. **Financial Aid Statistics:** 100% needy freshmen, 99% needy undergrads receive need-based scholarship or grant aid. 10% freshmen, 13% undergrads receive non-need-based scholarship or grant aid. 96% freshmen, 84% undergrads receive need-based self-help aid. 5% freshmen, 5% undergrads receive athletic scholarships. 100% freshmen, 99% undergrads receive any aid. 88% undergrads borrow to pay for school. Average cumulative indebtedness $23,715. **Criteria for awarding aid:** *Need-based:* Academics, Athletics, Music/drama, Religious affiliation. *Non-need-based:* Academics, Athletics, Music/drama.

ALFRED UNIVERSITY

Alumni Hall, Alfred, NY 14802-1205
Phone: 607-871-2115 • **Financial Aid Phone:** 607-871-2159
E-mail: admissions@alfred.edu • **CEEB Code:** 2005
Fax: 607-871-2198 • **Website:** www.alfred.edu • **ACT Code:** 2666

This private school was founded in 1836. It has a 600-acre campus.

RATINGS

Admissions Selectivity Rating: 84   **Fire Safety Rating:** 88   **Green Rating:** 60*

STUDENTS AND FACULTY

Enrollment: 1,929. **Student Body:** 51% female, 49% male, 24% out-of-state, 3% international (4 countries represented). Asian 2%, African American 8%, Caucasian 67%, Hispanic 7%, Native American <1%, Pacific Islander 0%, Two or more races 3%, Race unknown 11%.
Retention and Graduation: 75% freshmen return for sophomore year. 44% freshmen graduate within 4 years. 62% freshmen graduate within 6 years. 30% grads go on to further study within 1 year. **Faculty:** Student/faculty ratio 12:1. 159 full-time faculty, 0% hold PhDs, 0% are are members of minority groups, 45% are women. 0% of classes are taught by teaching assistants.

ACADEMICS

Degrees: bachelor's, doctoral/research, master's, post-master's certificate. **Classes:** Most classes have 10-19 students. Most lab/discussion sessions have 10-19 students. **Most popular majors:** Business/Commerce; Ceramic Arts and Ceramics; Psychology. **Special Study Options:** cooperative education program, cross-registration, double major, English as a Second Language (ESL), exchange student program (domestic), honors program, independent study, internships, liberal arts/career combination, student-designed major, study abroad, teacher certification program. **Honors Programs:** The Alfred University Honors Program is designed to enrich the lives of exceptional students. It has two components: an honors seminar—meets one evening a week and the senior thesis. Combined degree programs: 4+1 MBA program for bus, liberal arts and sciences. **Disability Services:** Special programs offered to physically disabled students, including note-taking services, tape recorders, tutors. **Career Services:** Alumni network, Alumni services, Career assessment, Internships. We are extremely proud of all of the services offered by the staff at the Robert R. McComsey Career Development Center.

FACILITIES

Housing: Coed dorms, apartments for single students, Theme housing (i.e. Environmental Studies House, Language House, etc.). 50% of campus accessible to physically diasbled. **Special Academic Facilities/Equipment:** Art museums, carillon, language labs, electron microscope, observatory, extensive engineering equipment, performing arts center. **Computers:** 90% of classrooms, 100% of dorms, 100% of libraries, 100% of student union, have wireless network access. Students can register for classes online. Administrative functions (other than registration) can be performed online.

CAMPUS LIFE

Environment: Rural. **Activities:** Choral groups, concert band, dance, drama/theater, literary magazine, music ensembles, musical theater, pep band, radio station, student government, student newspaper, student-run film society, television station, yearbook, Campus Ministries, Student Organization. 90 registered organizations, 13 honor societies, 3 religious organizations. **Athletics (Intercollegiate):** *Men:* basketball, cross-country, diving, equestrian sports, football, lacrosse, skiing (downhill/alpine), soccer, swimming, tennis, track/field (outdoor), track/field (indoor). *Women:* basketball, cross-country, diving, equestrian sports, lacrosse, skiing (downhill/alpine), soccer, softball, swimming, tennis, track/field (outdoor), track/field (indoor), volleyball. **On-Campus Highlights:** Powell Campus Center, Binns Merrill Hall, Schein-Joseph International Museum of Ceramic Art, John L. Stull Observatory, Robert Turner Student Art Gallery. **Environmental Initiatives:** Campus-wide recycling program (paper, glass, plastic, electronics, printer/toner cartridges).

ADMISSIONS

Freshman Academic Profile: Average high school GPA 3.2. 16% in top 10% of high school class, 43% in top 25% of high school class, 84% in top 50% of high school class. **Reported SAT (pre-2016 redesign) scores:** SAT Math middle 50% range 510-610. SAT Critical Reading middle 50% range 490-590. SAT Writing middle 50% range 460-570. **Concordant SAT scores:** SAT EBRW middle 50% 530–640. SAT Math middle 50% range 540–630. ACT middle 50% range 22-27. Minimum internet-based TOEFL 80. Minimum paper TOEFL 550. **Basis for Candidate Selection:** *Very important factors considered include:* rigor of secondary school record, class rank, academic GPA, extracurricular activities, character/personal qualities. *Important factors considered include:* standardized test scores, application essay, recommendation(s), volunteer work, work experience. *Other factors considered include:* interview, talent/ability, first generation, racial/ethnic status, level of applicant's interest. **Freshman Admission Requirements:** High school diploma is required and GED is accepted. *Academic units required:* 4 English. *Academic units recommended:* 4 English, 4 math, 3 science, 3 science labs, 1 foreign language, 3 social studies. **Freshman Admission Statistics:** 3,417 applied, 69.80% admitted, 22% enrolled. **Transfer Admission Requirements:** college transcript(s), statement of good standing from prior institution(s). Minimum college GPA of 2.5 required. Lowest grade transferable C. **General Admission Information:** Application fee $50. Priority deadline 2/1. Regular application deadline 8/1. Nonfall registration accepted. Admission may be deferred for a maximum of 1 year.

COSTS AND FINANCIAL AID

Annual tuition $27,824. Room and board $11,618. Required fees $950. Average book expense $1,150. **Required Forms and Deadlines:** FAFSA, Institution's own financial aid form, State aid form, Noncustodial PROFILE, Business/Farm Supplement. **Notification of Awards:** Applicants will be notified of awards on a rolling basis beginning 2/15. **Types of Aid:** *Need-based scholarships/grants:* Federal Pell, FSEOG, State scholarships/grants, Private scholarships, College/university scholarship or grant aid from institutional funds. *Loans:* Direct Subsidized Stafford Loans, Direct Unsubsidized Stafford Loans, Direct PLUS loans, Federal Perkins Loans, College/university loans from institutional funds. *Student Employment:* Federal Work-Study Program available. Institutional employment available. **Financial Aid Statistics:** 100% needy freshmen, 99%

needy undergrads receive need-based scholarship or grant aid. 78% freshmen, 62% undergrads receive non-need-based scholarship or grant aid. 90% freshmen, 89% undergrads receive need-based self-help aid. 0% freshmen, 0% undergrads receive athletic scholarships. 96% freshmen, 92% undergrads receive any aid. **Criteria for awarding aid:** *Need-based:* Academics, Art. *Non-need-based:* Academics, Art, Leadership, Music/drama.

ALICE LLOYD COLLEGE

100 Purpose Road, Pippa Passes, KY 41844
Phone: 606-368-6036
E-mail: admissions@alc.edu • **CEEB Code:** 1098
Fax: 606-368-6215 • **Website:** www.alc.edu • **ACT Code:** 1502

This private school was founded in 1923. It has a 225-acre campus.

RATINGS
Admissions Selectivity Rating: 85   **Fire Safety Rating:** 93   **Green Rating:** 60*

STUDENTS AND FACULTY
Enrollment: 607. **Student Body:** 51% female, 49% male, 13% out-of-state, <1% international (1 countries represented). Asian 0%, African American 1%, Caucasian 99%, Hispanic 0%, Native American 0%, Pacific Islander 0%, Two or more races 0%, Race unknown 0%.
Retention and Graduation: 63% freshmen return for sophomore year. 25% freshmen graduate within 4 years. 33% freshmen graduate within 6 years. 55% grads go on to further study within 1 year. 35% grads pursue arts and sciences degrees. 5% grads pursue law degrees. 10% grads pursue business degrees. 5% grads pursue medical degrees. **Faculty:** Student/faculty ratio 18:1. 29 full-time faculty, 59% hold PhDs, 10% are are members of minority groups, 41% are women. 0% of classes are taught by teaching assistants.

ACADEMICS
Degrees: bachelor's. **Classes:** Most classes have 20-29 students. **Most popular majors:** Business/Commerce; Education; Biology/Biological Sciences. **Special Study Options:** cooperative education program, double major, honors program, independent study, internships, liberal arts/career combination, study abroad, teacher certification program. **Disability Services:** Special programs offered to physically disabled students, including reader services, tutors. **Career Services:** Alumni network, Alumni services, Career assessment, Internships, Regional alumni.

FACILITIES
Housing: men's dorms, women's dorms. 90% of campus accessible to physically disabled. **Special Academic Facilities/Equipment:** Photographic archives, oral history museum, Appalachian collection, on-campus day care center, kindergarten, elementary, and secondary school. **Computers:** 100% of classrooms, 50% of dorms, 100% of libraries, 100% of dining areas, 75% of common outdoor areas have wireless network access.

CAMPUS LIFE
Environment: Rural. **Activities:** Choral groups, drama/theater, music ensembles, musical theater, pep band, radio station, student government, student newspaper, yearbook. 19 registered organizations, 2 honor societies, 1 religious organization. **Athletics (Intercollegiate):** *Men:* baseball, basketball, cheerleading, cross-country, golf, tennis. *Women:* basketball, cheerleading, cross-country, golf, softball, tennis. **On-Campus Highlights:** Jerry Davis Student Center, Historical Tour, Grady Nutt Athletic Center, Campbell Arts Center, Cushing Hall.

ADMISSIONS
Freshman Academic Profile: Average high school GPA 3.4. 30% in top 10% of high school class, 58% in top 25% of high school class, 86% in top 50% of high school class. 90% from public high schools. **Reported SAT (pre-2016 redesign) scores:** SAT Math middle 50% range 480-570. SAT Critical Reading middle 50% range 440-590. SAT Writing middle 50% range 430-520. **Concordant SAT scores:** SAT EBRW middle 50% 490–610. SAT Math middle 50% range 510–590. ACT middle 50% range 17-23. Minimum paper TOEFL 550. **Basis for Candidate Selection:** *Very important factors considered include:* rigor of secondary school record, standardized test scores, character/personal qualities, geographical residence. *Important factors considered include:* class rank, recommendation(s), alumni/ae relation, state residency. *Other factors considered include:* application essay, interview, extracurricular activities, talent/ability, volunteer work, work experience. **Freshman Admission Requirements:** High school diploma is required and GED is accepted. *Academic units required:* 4 English, 3 math, 2 science, 2 social studies, 1 history *Academic units recommended:* 4 English, 3 math, 2 science, 2 foreign language, 2 social studies. **Freshman Admission Statistics:** 994 applied, 55.94% admitted, 35% enrolled. **Transfer Admission Requirements:**

High school transcript, college transcript(s), standardized test scores, statement of good standing from prior institution(s). Minimum college GPA of 2.0 required. Lowest grade transferable C. **General Admission Information:** Priority deadline 6/1. Regular application deadline 5/1. Nonfall registration accepted.

COSTS AND FINANCIAL AID
Room and board $4,250. Required fees $1,300. Average book expense $850. **Required Forms and Deadlines:** FAFSA. **Notification of Awards:** Applicants will be notified of awards on a rolling basis beginning 4/1. **Types of Aid:** *Need-based scholarships/grants:* Federal Pell, FSEOG, State scholarships/grants, Private scholarships, College/university scholarship or grant aid from institutional funds. *Loans:* College/university loans from institutional funds. *Student Employment:* Federal Work-Study Program available. Institutional employment available. **Financial Aid Statistics:** 99% needy freshmen, 99% needy undergrads receive need-based scholarship or grant aid. 11% freshmen, 16% undergrads receive non-need-based scholarship or grant aid. 89% freshmen, 84% undergrads receive need-based self-help aid. 7% freshmen, 5% undergrads receive athletic scholarships. 100% freshmen, 100% undergrads receive any aid. **Criteria for awarding aid:** *Non-need-based:* Athletics, Minority status, State/district residency.

ALLEGHENY COLLEGE

Best Colleges

Allegheny College, Meadville, PA 16335
Phone: 814-332-4351 • **Financial Aid Phone:** 800-835-7780
E-mail: admissions@allegheny.edu • **CEEB Code:** 2006
Fax: 814-337-0431 • **Website:** www.allegheny.edu • **ACT Code:** 3520

This private school was founded in 1815. It has a 565-acre campus.

RATINGS
Admissions Selectivity Rating: 87   **Fire Safety Rating:** 86   **Green Rating:** 88

STUDENTS AND FACULTY
Enrollment: 1,884. **Student Body:** 52% female, 48% male, 49% out-of-state, 3% international (51 countries represented). Asian 2%, African American 7%, Caucasian 73%, Hispanic 8%, Native American <1%, Pacific Islander <1%, Two or more races 4%, Race unknown 2%.
Retention and Graduation: 83% freshmen return for sophomore year. 70% freshmen graduate within 4 years. 76% freshmen graduate within 6 years. 29% grads go on to further study within 1 year. 10% grads pursue arts and sciences degrees. 1% grads pursue law degrees. 1% grads pursue business degrees. 9% grads pursue medical degrees. **Faculty:** Student/faculty ratio 11:1. 167 full-time faculty, 92% hold PhDs, 17% are are members of minority groups, 49% are women. 0% of classes are taught by teaching assistants.

ACADEMICS
Degrees: bachelor's. **Classes:** Most classes have 10-19 students. Most lab/discussion sessions have 10-19 students. **Most popular majors:** Psychology; Biology/Biological Sciences; Economics. **Special Study Options:** double major, dual enrollment, English as a Second Language (ESL), exchange student program (domestic), independent study, internships, student-designed major, study abroad, Pre-professional programs, teacher preparation partnerships, combined degree programs,experiential learning terms (summer study program), marine biology study program, Washington Semester, medical school partnerships, graduate school partnerships, double minor, domestic off campus semester away study programs, accelerated masters and doctorate degree programs. Combined degree programs: BA/MA, BA/MEng, Arts Management,Public Policy & Mgmt,Nursing,Occupational Therapy,Physcian Asst, Health Care Policy & Mgmt, Information Systems Mgmt. **Disability Services:** Special programs offered to physically disabled students, including note-taking services, tape recorders, tutors. **Career Services:** Alumni network, Alumni services, Career/job search classes, Career assessment, Internships, Regional alumni. Employers rank a student's internship experience as one of the top three criteria used in evaluating a candidate. Nearly 75% of all employers prefer to hire students who have had relevant work experience. (NACE, Job Outlook) However, nationally, only 55% of college graduates complete an internship prior to graduation. Over the past five years, 75-89% of Allegheny College graduates completed one or more internships prior to graduation. Furthermore, 50% of our on-campus recruiters have an alumni connection. This is relevant as one of the top factors in school selection from the employer's perspective is success of a school's alumni in the organization (NACE Journal, April 2011).

FACILITIES

Housing: Coed dorms, special housing for disabled students, men's dorms, women's dorms, fraternity/sorority housing, apartments for single students, Wellness Housing, Theme Housing, quiet study floors; townhouses-environmentally-sensitive, low fume material, LEED certified. 50% of campus accessible to physically diasbled. **Special Academic Facilities/Equipment:** New Center For Communication Arts with a trap stage and green and blue screen room; radio and television stations; state-of-the-art, nationally acclaimed science complex; videoconference facilities; planetarium; observatory; GIS lab; state-of-the-art language-learning center; smart classrooms; renovated dance and art studios and performance spaces; art galleries; world's largest solid-volume glass sculpture grouping; 283-acre Environmental Research Reserve; 80-acre protected forest; new alumni center; comprehensive sports and fitness center, seismographic network station, Center for Political Participation, Center for Economic and Environmental Development, environmental roof garden. **Computers:** 50% of classrooms, 100% of dorms, 100% of libraries, 100% of dining areas, 100% of student union, 100% of common outdoor areas have wireless network access. Students can register for classes online. Administrative functions (other than registration) can be performed online.

CAMPUS LIFE

Environment: Town. **Activities:** Choral groups, concert band, dance, drama/theater, jazz band, literary magazine, music ensembles, musical theater, radio station, student government, student newspaper, symphony orchestra, television station, yearbook, Campus Ministries, Student Organization, Model UN. 113 registered organizations, 15 honor societies, 8 religious organizations. 5 fraternities, 5 sororities. **Athletics (Intercollegiate):** *Men:* baseball, basketball, cross-country, diving, football, golf, soccer, swimming, tennis, track/field (outdoor), track/field (indoor). *Women:* basketball, cross-country, diving, golf, lacrosse, soccer, softball, swimming, tennis, track/field (outdoor), track/field (indoor), volleyball. **On-Campus Highlights:** Rustic Bridge, Wise Sport and Fitness Center, Henderson Campus Center, Pelletier Library, World's largest solid-volume glass sculpture group, State-of-the-art, nationally acclaimed science complex dedicated to biology, chemistry and environmental science; Patricia Bush Tippie Alumni Center; seismographic network station; Center for Political Participation; Center for Economic & Environmental Development; radio and TV stations, Grounds For Change Coffeehouse, Vukovich Communication Arts Building Environmental Roof Garden; Robertson athletic fields and recreation area. **Environmental Initiatives:** Climate action plan.

ADMISSIONS

Freshman Academic Profile: Average high school GPA 3.7. 37% in top 10% of high school class, 66% in top 25% of high school class, 89% in top 50% of high school class. 84% from public high schools. **Reported SAT (pre-2016 redesign) scores:** SAT Math middle 50% range 540-640. SAT Critical Reading middle 50% range 530-650. SAT Writing middle 50% range 500-630. **Concordant SAT scores:** SAT EBRW middle 50% 570–690. SAT Math middle 50% range 570–660. ACT middle 50% range 24-29. Minimum internet-based TOEFL 80. Minimum paper TOEFL 550. **Basis for Candidate Selection:** *Very important factors considered include:* rigor of secondary school record, class rank, academic GPA. *Important factors considered include:* recommendation(s), interview, extracurricular activities, character/personal qualities, level of applicant's interest. *Other factors considered include:* standardized test scores, application essay, talent/ability, first generation, alumni/ae relation, geographical residence, racial/ethnic status, volunteer work, work experience. **Freshman Admission Requirements:** High school diploma is required and GED is accepted. *Academic units required:* 4 English, 3 math, 3 science, 2 foreign language, 3 social studies, 1 academic elective. **Freshman Admission Statistics:** 4,724 applied, 67.76% admitted, 17% enrolled. **Transfer Admission Requirements:** High school transcript, college transcript(s), essay or personal statement, standardized test scores, Minimum college GPA of 2.5 required. Lowest grade transferable C. **General Admission Information:** Regular application deadline 2/15. Regular notification 4/1. Nonfall registration accepted. Admission may be deferred for a maximum of 1 year.

COSTS AND FINANCIAL AID

Annual tuition $45,470. Room and board $11,650. Required fees $500. Average book expense $1,000. **Required Forms and Deadlines:** FAFSA. **Notification of Awards:** Applicants will be notified of awards on a rolling basis beginning 3/1. **Types of Aid:** *Need-based scholarships/grants:* Federal Pell, FSEOG, State scholarships/grants, Private scholarships, College/university scholarship or grant aid from institutional funds. *Loans:* Direct Subsidized Stafford Loans, Direct Unsubsidized Stafford Loans, Direct PLUS loans, Federal Perkins Loans. *Student Employment:* Federal Work-Study Program available. Institutional employment available. **Financial Aid Statistics:** 100% needy freshmen, 100% needy undergrads receive need-based scholarship or grant aid. 15% freshmen, 17% undergrads receive non-need-based scholarship or grant aid. 85% freshmen, 84% undergrads receive need-based self-help aid. 0% freshmen, 0% undergrads receive athletic scholarships. 99% freshmen, 99% undergrads receive any aid. **Criteria for awarding aid:** *Need-based:* Academics, Minority

status. *Non-need-based:* Academics, Leadership, Minority status, State/district residency.

See page 904.

ALLEN COLLEGE

1825 Logan Avenue, Waterloo, IA 50703
Phone: 319-226-2000 • **Financial Aid Phone:** 319-226-2000
E-mail: Admissions@AllenCollege.edu
Fax: 319-226-2051 • **Website:** www.allencollege.edu • **ACT Code:** 30691

This private school was founded in 1989.

RATINGS

Admissions Selectivity Rating: 61   **Fire Safety Rating:** 63   **Green Rating:** 60*

STUDENTS AND FACULTY

Enrollment: 358. **Student Body:** 92% female, 8% male, 4% out-of-state, 0% international (2 countries represented). Asian 1%, African American 2%, Caucasian 88%, Hispanic 0%, Native American <1%, Pacific Islander 1%, Two or more races 1%, Race unknown 7%.
Retention and Graduation: 10% grads go on to further study within 1 year.
Faculty: Student/faculty ratio 46:1. 42 full-time faculty, 36% hold PhDs, 2% are are members of minority groups, 93% are women. 0% of classes are taught by teaching assistants.

ACADEMICS

Degrees: associate, bachelor's, certificate, doctoral, master's, post-master's certificate. **Classes:** Most classes have fewer than 10 students. Most lab/discussion sessions have fewer than 10 students. **Most popular majors:** Health Services/Allied Health/Health Sciences; Registered Nursing/Registered Nurse. **Special Study Options:** Accelerated program, cooperative education program, distance learning, honors program, independent study, internships. **Disability Services:** Special programs offered to physically disabled students, including tutors. **Career Services:** On-campus interviews.

FACILITIES

Housing: Coed dorms, Housing also available at a cooperating institution. 100% of campus accessible to physically diasbled. **Computers:** 100% of classrooms, 100% of dorms, 100% of libraries, 100% of student union, 100% of common outdoor areas have wireless network access. Administrative functions (other than registration) can be performed online.

CAMPUS LIFE

Environment: City. **Activities:** Choral groups, student government, student newspaper, yearbook. 4 registered organizations, 1 honor society, 1 religious organization.

ADMISSIONS

Freshman Academic Profile: 0% from public high schools. **Basis for Candidate Selection:** *Important factors considered include:* rigor of secondary school record, class rank, academic GPA, standardized test scores, application essay, recommendation(s), extracurricular activities, character/personal qualities. *Other factors considered include:* interview, talent/ability, first generation, alumni/ae relation, racial/ethnic status, volunteer work, work experience, level of applicant's interest. **Freshman Admission Requirements:** High school diploma is required and GED is accepted. *Academic units required:* 8 English, 6 math, 6 science, 6 social studies. **Transfer Admission Requirements:** High school transcript, college transcript(s), essay or personal statement, standardized test scores, Minimum college GPA of 2.7 required. Lowest grade transferable C. **General Admission Information:** Application fee $50. Priority deadline 2/1. Nonfall registration accepted.

COSTS AND FINANCIAL AID

Annual tuition $16,876. Room and board $7,425. Required fees $1,338. Average book expense $1,200. **Required Forms and Deadlines:** FAFSA, Institution's own financial aid form. **Notification of Awards:** Applicants will be notified of awards on a rolling basis beginning 4/1. **Types of Aid:** *Need-based scholarships/grants:* Federal Pell, FSEOG, State subsidops/grants, Private scholarships, College/university scholarship or grant aid from institutional funds, Federal Nursing Scholarships. *Loans:* Direct Subsidized Stafford Loans, Direct Unsubsidized Stafford Loans, Direct PLUS loans, Federal Perkins Loans, Federal Nursing Loans, College/university loans from institutional funds. *Student Employment:* Federal Work-Study Program available. **Financial Aid Statistics:** 100% needy freshmen, 88% needy undergrads receive need-based scholarship or grant aid. 15% undergrads receive non-need-based scholarship or grant aid. 100% freshmen, 87% undergrads receive need-based self-help aid. 0% freshmen, 0% undergrads receive athletic scholarships. 100% freshmen, 99% undergrads receive any aid. 0% undergrads borrow to pay for school.

Average cumulative indebtedness $0. **Criteria for awarding aid:** *Need-based:* Academics, Alumni affiliation, Leadership, Minority status. *Non-need-based:* Academics, Alumni affiliation, Leadership, Minority status, State/district residency.

ALMA COLLEGE

614 West Superior Street, Alma, MI 48801-1599
Phone: 989-463-7139 • **Financial Aid Phone:** 989-463-7347
E-mail: admissions@alma.edu • **CEEB Code:** 1010
Fax: 989-463-7057 • **Website:** www.alma.edu • **ACT Code:** 1958

This private school, affiliated with the Presbyterian Church, was founded in 1886. It has a 125-acre campus.

RATINGS

Admissions Selectivity Rating: 79   **Fire Safety Rating:** 72   **Green Rating:** 60*

STUDENTS AND FACULTY

Enrollment: 1,414. **Student Body:** 57% female, 43% male, 8% out-of-state, 1% international (9 countries represented). Asian 1%, African American 4%, Caucasian 78%, Hispanic 5%, Native American <1%, Pacific Islander <1%, Two or more races 2%, Race unknown 8%. **Retention and Graduation:** 80% freshmen return for sophomore year. 56% freshmen graduate within 4 years. 67% freshmen graduate within 6 years. 20% grads go on to further study within 1 year. **Faculty:** Student/faculty ratio 12:1. 99 full-time faculty, 82% hold PhDs, 14% are are members of minority groups, 45% are women. 0% of classes are taught by teaching assistants.

ACADEMICS

Degrees: bachelor's. **Classes:** Most classes have 10-19 students. Most lab/discussion sessions have 10-19 students. **Most popular majors:** Business Administration and Management; Health and Wellness; Education. **Special Study Options:** double major, dual enrollment, exchange student program (domestic), honors program, independent study, internships, student-designed major, study abroad, teacher certification program. **Honors Programs:** Students in the Honors Program participate in special seminar opportunities and enroll in courses designed for honors scholars. Combined degree programs: 3-2 occupational therapy. **Disability Services:** Special programs offered to physically disabled students, including note-taking services, reader services, tape recorders, tutors. **Career Services:** Alumni services, Career assessment, Internships. The Center for Student Opportunity offers services for career services, internships, diversity support, academic support, financial counseling, disability support and first generation student support.

FACILITIES

Housing: Coed dorms, fraternity/sorority housing, Theme Housing. 75% of campus accessible to physically disabled. **Special Academic Facilities/Equipment:** Music and arts centers, science lab, planetarium, a DNA synthesizer and sequencer, and a multinuclear magnetic resonance spectrometer. **Computers:** 60% of classrooms, 100% of libraries, 100% of dining areas, 100% of student union, have wireless network access. Students can register for classes online.

CAMPUS LIFE

Environment: Village. **Activities:** Choral groups, concert band, dance, drama/theater, jazz band, marching band, music ensembles, radio station, student government, student newspaper, symphony orchestra, yearbook, Campus Ministries, Student Organization, Model UN. 75 registered organizations, 20 honor societies, 4 religious organizations. 6 fraternities, 5 sororities. **Athletics (Intercollegiate):** *Men:* baseball, basketball, cross-country, diving, football, golf, soccer, swimming, tennis, track/field (outdoor). *Women:* basketball, cross-country, diving, golf, soccer, softball, swimming, tennis, track/field (outdoor), volleyball. **On-Campus Highlights:** Joe's Place, Stone Center for Recreation, Library, Remick Heritage Center, Wright Hall (residence hall). **Environmental Initiatives:** Alma green residence hall, Wright Hall, was completed in January 2005. The modern, 60-bed apartment-style hall features a number of environmentally friendly features, including geothermal heating and cooling, recycled-content ceiling tiles and carpeting, energy-efficient windows, rooftop solar heating panels, energy-efficient showers and washing machines, and a computerized energy monitoring system.

ADMISSIONS

Freshman Academic Profile: Average high school GPA 3.5. 18% in top 10% of high school class, 25% in top 25% of high school class, 84% in top 50% of high school class. 92% from public high schools. **Reported SAT (pre-2016 redesign) scores:** SAT Math middle 50% range 460-593. SAT Critical Reading middle 50% range 420-590. SAT Writing middle 50% range 403-620. **Concordant SAT scores:** SAT EBRW middle 50% 460-660. SAT Math middle

50% range 500-610. ACT middle 50% range 21-26. Minimum internet-based TOEFL 79. Minimum paper TOEFL 550. **Basis for Candidate Selection:** *Very important factors considered include:* academic GPA, standardized test scores, application essay. *Important factors considered include:* rigor of secondary school record, character/personal qualities. *Other factors considered include:* class rank, recommendation(s), interview, extracurricular activities, talent/ability, alumni/ae relation, volunteer work, work experience, level of applicant's interest. **Freshman Admission Requirements:** High school diploma is required and GED is accepted. *Academic units required:* 4 English, 3 math, 3 science, 3 social studies. *Academic units recommended:* 2 foreign language. **Freshman Admission Statistics:** 4,695 applied, 67.82% admitted, 14% enrolled. **Transfer Admission Requirements:** High school transcript, college transcript(s), statement of good standing from prior institution(s). Minimum college GPA of 3.0 required. Lowest grade transferable C. **General Admission Information:** Application fee $25. Nonfall registration accepted. Admission may be deferred for a maximum of 1 year.

COSTS AND FINANCIAL AID

Annual tuition $36,890. Room and board $10,238. Required fees $420. Average book expense $800. **Required Forms and Deadlines:** FAFSA. **Notification of Awards:** Applicants will be notified of awards on a rolling basis beginning 3/1. **Types of Aid:** *Need-based scholarships/grants:* Federal Pell, FSEOG, State scholarships/grants, Private scholarships, College/university scholarship or grant aid from institutional funds. *Loans:* Direct Subsidized Stafford Loans, Direct Unsubsidized Stafford Loans, Direct PLUS loans, Federal Perkins Loans, College/university loans from institutional funds. *Student Employment:* Federal Work-Study Program available. Institutional employment available. **Financial Aid Statistics:** 100% needy freshmen, 99% needy undergrads receive need-based scholarship or grant aid. 12% freshmen, 12% undergrads receive non-need-based scholarship or grant aid. 85% freshmen, 81% undergrads receive need-based self-help aid. 0% freshmen, 0% undergrads receive athletic scholarships. 99% freshmen, 99% undergrads receive any aid. 83% undergrads borrow to pay for school. Average cumulative indebtedness $36,046. **Criteria for awarding aid:** *Non-need-based:* Academics, Alumni affiliation, Art, Minority status, Music/drama, Religious affiliation.

ALVERNO COLLEGE

3400 South 43rd Street, Milwaukee, WI 53234-3922
Phone: 414-382-6101 • **Financial Aid Phone:** 414-382-6046
E-mail: admissions@alverno.edu • **CEEB Code:** 1012
Fax: 414-382-6055 • **Website:** www.alverno.edu • **ACT Code:** 4558

This private school, affiliated with the Roman Catholic Church, was founded in 1887. It has a 47-acre campus.

RATINGS

Admissions Selectivity Rating: 72   **Fire Safety Rating:** 84   **Green Rating:** 69

STUDENTS AND FACULTY

Enrollment: 1,380. **Student Body:** 100% female, 0% male, 6% out-of-state, <1% international (13 countries represented). Asian 5%, African American 13%, Caucasian 53%, Hispanic 23%, Native American 1%, Pacific Islander <1%, Two or more races 4%, Race unknown 0%. **Retention and Graduation:** 72% freshmen return for sophomore year. 11% freshmen graduate within 4 years. 42% freshmen graduate within 6 years. **Faculty:** Student/faculty ratio 10:1. 94 full-time faculty, 88% hold PhDs, 9% are are members of minority groups, 79% are women. 0% of classes are taught by teaching assistants.

ACADEMICS

Degrees: associate, bachelor's, master's, postbachelor's certificate, post-master's certificate. **Classes:** Most classes have 20-29 students. Most lab/discussion sessions have 20-29 students. **Most popular majors:** Business Administration and Management; Registered Nursing/Registered Nurse; Education. **Special Study Options:** double major, independent study, internships, student-designed major, study abroad, teacher certification program, weekend college. **Disability Services:** Special programs offered to physically disabled students, including note-taking services, reader services, tape recorders, tutors. **Career Services:** Alumni services, Career/job search classes, Career assessment, On-campus interviews. We are proudest of our integration into the Alverno curriculum. Counselors design and teach 3 courses that are required by various disciplines (one at the first-year level and two at the senior level), as well as teach segments in several additional courses. The result is that virtually every student has done in-class work with a career counselor prior to graduation.

FACILITIES

Housing: women's dorms. 95% of campus accessible to physically disabled. **Special Academic Facilities/Equipment:** Art & Culture Gallery, Career Center, Fitness center, Reiman Gymnasium, Nursing Skills Lab, Student centered multi-media production facility, Diagnostic Digital Portfolio, computer center, science labs, theatre venue. **Computers:** 35% of classrooms, 100% of dorms, 100% of libraries, 100% of dining areas, 100% of student union, have wireless network access. Students can register for classes online. Administrative functions (other than registration) can be performed online.

CAMPUS LIFE

Environment: Metropolis. **Activities:** Choral groups, dance, drama/theater, literary magazine, music ensembles, student government, student newspaper, Campus Ministries, Student Organization. 37 registered organizations, 1 honor society, 1 religious organization. 2 sororities. **Athletics (Intercollegiate):** *Women:* basketball, cross-country, soccer, softball, tennis, volleyball. **On-Campus Highlights:** Teaching, Learning and Technology Center, The Mug Coffee House, Fitness Center, The Pipeline—Activity Center, Reiman Gymnasium. **Environmental Initiatives:** Renovated and new construction totaling 13,000 sq ft utilizing LED lighting throughout project.

ADMISSIONS

Freshman Academic Profile: Average high school GPA 3.1. 86% from public high schools. ACT middle 50% range 18-22. Minimum internet-based TOEFL 68. Minimum paper TOEFL 520. **Basis for Candidate Selection:** *Very important factors considered include:* academic GPA, standardized test scores. *Important factors considered include:* rigor of secondary school record. *Other factors considered include:* application essay, recommendation(s), interview, extracurricular activities, talent/ability, character/personal qualities, volunteer work, work experience, level of applicant's interest. **Freshman Admission Requirements:** High school diploma is required and GED is accepted. *Academic units required:* 4 English, 3 math, 3 science, 3 social studies, 4 academic electives. *Academic units recommended:* 2 foreign language. **Freshman Admission Statistics:** 698 applied, 73.93% admitted, 33% enrolled. **Transfer Admission Requirements:** High school transcript, college transcript(s), essay or personal statement, Minimum college GPA of 2.0 required. Lowest grade transferable C. **General Admission Information:** Nonfall registration accepted. Admission may be deferred for a maximum of 1 year.

COSTS AND FINANCIAL AID

Average book expense $625. **Required Forms and Deadlines:** FAFSA. **Notification of Awards:** Applicants will be notified of awards on a rolling basis beginning 3/1. **Types of Aid:** *Need-based scholarships/grants:* Federal Pell, FSEOG, State scholarships/grants, Private scholarships, College/university scholarship or grant aid from institutional funds. *Loans:* Direct Subsidized Stafford Loans, Direct Unsubsidized Stafford Loans, Direct PLUS loans, State Loans. *Student Employment:* Federal Work-Study Program available. Institutional employment available. **Financial Aid Statistics:** 100% needy freshmen, 99% needy undergrads receive need-based scholarship or grant aid. 90% freshmen, 88% undergrads receive non-need-based scholarship or grant aid. 96% freshmen, 89% undergrads receive need-based self-help aid. 0% freshmen, 0% undergrads receive athletic scholarships. 99% freshmen, 94% undergrads receive any aid. 88% undergrads borrow to pay for school. Average cumulative indebtedness $41,044. **Criteria for awarding aid:** *Non-need-based:* Academics, Alumni affiliation.

AMERICAN INTERNATIONAL COLLEGE

1000 State Street, Springfield, MA 01109-3184
Phone: 413-205-3201 • **Financial Aid Phone:** 413-205-3259
E-mail: inquiry@aic.edu • **CEEB Code:** 3002
Fax: 413-205-3051 • **Website:** www.aic.edu • **ACT Code:** 1772

This private school was founded in 1885. It has a 58-acre campus.

RATINGS

Admissions Selectivity Rating: 72   **Fire Safety Rating:** 85   **Green Rating:** 60*

STUDENTS AND FACULTY

Enrollment: 1,478. **Student Body:** 60% female, 40% male, 39% out-of-state, 3% international (27 countries represented). Asian 1%, African American 25%, Caucasian 39%, Hispanic 14%, Native American <1%, Pacific Islander <1%, Two or more races 3%, Race unknown 14%.
Retention and Graduation: 72% freshmen return for sophomore year. 25% freshmen graduate within 4 years. 38% freshmen graduate within 6 years. 34% grads go on to further study within 1 year. **Faculty:** Student/faculty ratio 14:1. 74 full-time faculty, 64% hold PhDs, 16% are are members of minority groups, 58% are women. 0% of classes are taught by teaching assistants.

ACADEMICS

Degrees: associate, bachelor's, doctoral/professional, doctoral/research, master's, postbachelor's certificate, post-master's certificate, terminal. **Classes:** Most classes have 10-19 students. Most lab/discussion sessions have 10-19

students. **Most popular majors:** Psychology; Registered Nursing/Registered Nurse; Criminal Justice and Corrections. **Special Study Options:** Accelerated program, cross-registration, distance learning, double major, dual enrollment, English as a Second Language (ESL), honors program, independent study, internships, liberal arts/career combination, study abroad, teacher certification program, weekend college, Off-campus study in Washington, DC; upper division undergrads may take grad level courses. **Honors Programs:** Four Year Honors program open to students in any major with appropriate credentials. Combined degree programs: BA/MA, 4+1 bachelor's/M.B.A. program. 4+1 bachelor's/MEd. **Disability Services:** Special programs offered to physically disabled students, including note-taking services, reader services, tape recorders, tutors. **Career Services:** Alumni services, Career/job search classes, Career assessment, Internships.

FACILITIES

Housing: Coed dorms, women's dorms, Wellness Housing. 90% of campus accessible to physically diasbled. **Special Academic Facilities/Equipment:** Centers for child development, cultural arts, and human technology. **Computers:** 100% of classrooms, 90% of dorms, 100% of libraries, 100% of dining areas, 100% of student union, 100% of common outdoor areas have wireless network access. Students can register for classes online. Administrative functions (other than registration) can be performed online.

CAMPUS LIFE

Environment: City. **Activities:** Choral groups, dance, drama/theater, literary magazine, musical theater, pep band, radio station, student government, student newspaper, yearbook, Campus Ministries, Student Organization. 45 registered organizations, 5 honor societies, 3 religious organizations. 4 fraternities, 5 sororities. **Athletics (Intercollegiate):** *Men:* baseball, basketball, cheerleading, cross-country, football, golf, ice hockey, lacrosse, soccer, tennis, track/field (outdoor), track/field (indoor), wrestling. *Women:* basketball, cheerleading, cross-country, field hockey, lacrosse, soccer, softball, tennis, track/field (outdoor), track/field (indoor), volleyball. **On-Campus Highlights:** Courniotes Hall—Health Sciences, Karen Sprague Cultural Arts Center, Butova & Metcalf Gymnasiums, WAIC-FM (Radio Station).

ADMISSIONS

Freshman Academic Profile: Average high school GPA 2.8. **Reported SAT (pre-2016 redesign) scores:** SAT Math middle 50% range 400-500. SAT Critical Reading middle 50% range 390-480. SAT Writing middle 50% range 380-480. **Concordant SAT scores:** SAT EBRW middle 50% 430–540. SAT Math middle 50% range 440–530. ACT middle 50% range 16-23. Minimum internet-based TOEFL 80. Minimum paper TOEFL 550. **Basis for Candidate Selection:** *Very important factors considered include:* academic GPA, standardized test scores. *Important factors considered include:* rigor of secondary school record. *Other factors considered include:* application essay, recommendation(s), extracurricular activities, talent/ability, character/personal qualities, first generation, alumni/ae relation, volunteer work, work experience, level of applicant's interest. **Freshman Admission Requirements:** High school diploma is required and GED is accepted. *Academic units recommended:* 4 English, 3 math, 2 science, 2 science labs, 1 foreign language, 2 social studies, 4 academic electives. **Freshman Admission Statistics:** 1,522 applied, 86.40% admitted, 26% enrolled. **Transfer Admission Requirements:** High school transcript, college transcript(s), Minimum college GPA of 2.0 required. Lowest grade transferable C. **General Admission Information:** Regular notification 9/2. Nonfall registration accepted. Admission may be deferred for a maximum of 1 year.

COSTS AND FINANCIAL AID

Annual tuition $33,140. Room and board $13,590. Required fees $60. Average book expense $1,235. **Required Forms and Deadlines:** FAFSA. **Notification of Awards:** Applicants will be notified of awards on a rolling basis beginning 3/1. **Types of Aid:** *Need-based scholarships/grants:* Federal Pell, FSEOG, State scholarships/grants, Private scholarships, College/university scholarship or grant aid from institutional funds, Federal Nursing Scholarships. *Loans:* Direct Subsidized Stafford Loans, Direct Unsubsidized Stafford Loans, Direct PLUS loans. *Student Employment:* Federal Work-Study Program available. Institutional employment available. **Financial Aid Statistics:** 100% needy freshmen, 100% needy undergrads receive need-based scholarship or grant aid. 10% freshmen, 10% undergrads receive non-need-based scholarship or grant aid. 89% freshmen, 89% undergrads receive need-based self-help aid. 7% freshmen, 9% undergrads receive athletic scholarships. 100% freshmen, 85% undergrads receive any aid. 91% undergrads borrow to pay for school. Average cumulative indebtedness $22,976. **Criteria for awarding aid:** *Non-need-based:* Academics, Athletics.

AMERICAN JEWISH UNIVERSITY

15600 Mulholland Drive, Familian Campus, Bel Air, CA 90077
Phone: 310-440-1247 • **Financial Aid Phone:** 310-440-1252
E-mail: admissions@ajula.edu • **CEEB Code:** 4876
Fax: 310-471-3657 • **Website:** www.ajula.edu • **ACT Code:** 462

This private school, affiliated with the Jewish Church, was founded in 1947. It has a 28-acre campus.

RATINGS
Admissions Selectivity Rating: 73   **Fire Safety Rating:** 76   **Green Rating:** 60*

STUDENTS AND FACULTY
Enrollment: 128. **Student Body:** 49% female, 51% male, 15% out-of-state, 5% international (6 countries represented). Asian 2%, African American 2%, Caucasian 48%, Hispanic 3%, Native American 2%, Pacific Islander 0%, Two or more races 0%, Race unknown 37%.
Retention and Graduation: 58% freshmen return for sophomore year. 36% freshmen graduate within 6 years. **Faculty:** Student/faculty ratio 7:1. 8 full-time faculty, 88% hold PhDs, 0% are are members of minority groups, 38% are women. 0% of classes are taught by teaching assistants.

ACADEMICS
Degrees: bachelor's, master's. **Classes:** Most classes have fewer than 10 students. Most lab/discussion sessions have fewer than 10 students. **Most popular majors:** Political Science and Government; Business/Commerce; Bioethics/Medical Ethics. **Special Study Options:** cross-registration, double major, independent study, internships, student-designed major, study abroad. Combined degree programs: BA/MBA, BA/MAEd. **Career Services:** Alumni network, Alumni services, Career/job search classes, Career assessment, Internships, On-campus interviews. Mentor Program: Provide support for students as they plan their futures; Foster relationships between the students and the community members; Explore career development concerns and the issues that arise as students anticipate life after graduation.

FACILITIES
Housing: Coed dorms, special housing for disabled students, apartments for married students, apartments for single students. 90% of campus accessible to physically disabled. **Special Academic Facilities/Equipment:** Art Gallery, Ostrow Library. **Computers:** 100% of dorms, 100% of libraries, 100% of student union, 50% of common outdoor areas have wireless network access. Administrative functions (other than registration) can be performed online.

CAMPUS LIFE
Environment: Metropolis. **Activities:** Choral groups, drama/theater, literary magazine, student government, student newspaper, Model UN. 17 registered organizations, 1 religious organization. **On-Campus Highlights:** Residence Halls, Auerbach Student Union, The Berg, our kosher dining hall, Sculpture Garden, Ostrow Library. **Environmental Initiatives:** Energy Management

ADMISSIONS
Freshman Academic Profile: Average high school GPA 3.1. 0% in top 10% of high school class, 33% in top 25% of high school class, 67% in top 50% of high school class. 36% from public high schools. **Reported SAT (pre-2016 redesign) scores:** SAT Math middle 50% range 500-570. SAT Critical Reading middle 50% range 490-520. SAT Writing middle 50% range 500-560. **Concordant SAT scores:** SAT EBRW middle 50% 550–600. SAT Math middle 50% range 530–590. ACT middle 50% range 17-22. Minimum internet-based TOEFL 75. Minimum paper TOEFL 530. **Basis for Candidate Selection:** *Very important factors considered include:* application essay, recommendation(s), interview, extracurricular activities, talent/ability, character/personal qualities, volunteer work. *Important factors considered include:* academic GPA, standardized test scores, level of applicant's interest. *Other factors considered include:* rigor of secondary school record, class rank, alumni/ae relation, geographical residence, state residency, religious affiliation/commitment, work experience. **Freshman Admission Requirements:** High school diploma is required and GED is accepted. **Freshman Admission Statistics:** 28 applied, 96.43% admitted, 48% enrolled. **Transfer Admission Requirements:** college transcript(s), essay or personal statement, Minimum college GPA of N/A required. Lowest grade transferable C. **General Admission Information:** Application fee $35. Regular application deadline 5/31. Nonfall registration accepted. Admission may be deferred for a maximum of 1 year.

COSTS AND FINANCIAL AID
Annual tuition $26,784. Room and board $14,082. Required fees $1,712. Average book expense $1,710. **Required Forms and Deadlines:** FAFSA, Institution's own financial aid form. **Notification of Awards:** Applicants will be notified of awards on a rolling basis beginning 1/1. **Types of Aid:** *Need-based scholarships/grants:* Federal Pell, FSEOG, State scholarships/grants, Private scholarships, College/university scholarship or grant aid from institutional funds. *Loans:* Direct Subsidized Stafford Loans, Direct Unsubsidized Stafford Loans, Direct PLUS loans. *Student Employment:* Federal Work-Study Program available. Institutional employment available. **Financial Aid Statistics:** 27% needy freshmen, 51% needy undergrads receive need-based scholarship or grant aid. 35% freshmen, 54% undergrads receive non-need-based scholarship or grant aid. 13% freshmen, 34% undergrads receive need-based self-help aid. 0% freshmen, 0% undergrads receive athletic scholarships. **Criteria for awarding aid:** *Need-based:* Academics. *Non-need-based:* Leadership, Minority status, Music/drama, State/district residency.

AMERICAN PUBLIC UNIVERSITY SYSTEM

111 W. Congress St., Charles Town, WV 25414
Phone: 877-777-9081 • **Financial Aid Phone:** 877-468-6268
E-mail: info@apus.edu
Website: www.apus.edu

RATINGS
Admissions Selectivity Rating: 60*   **Fire Safety Rating:** 60*   **Green Rating:** 74

STUDENTS AND FACULTY
Enrollment: 37,826. **Student Body:** 36% female, 64% male, 1% international (47 countries represented). Asian 2%, African American 17%, Caucasian 57%, Hispanic 11%, Native American 1%, Pacific Islander 1%, Two or more races 4%, Race unknown 6%.
Faculty: Student/faculty ratio 19:1. 404 full-time faculty, 54% hold PhDs, 15% are are members of minority groups, 57% are women. 0% of classes are taught by teaching assistants.

ACADEMICS
Degrees: associate, bachelor's, certificate, master's, postbachelor's certificate. **Most popular majors:** Business Administration and Management; International/Global Studies; General Studies. **Career Services:** Alumni network, Alumni services, Career assessment, On-campus interviews.

CAMPUS LIFE
Environmental Initiatives: Green building practices (all new construction built to at least USGBC LEED Silver standards and extensive adaptive reuse practices for existing [often historic] buildings on campus).

ADMISSIONS
Minimum paper TOEFL 520. **General Admission Information:** Nonfall registration accepted. Admission may be deferred for a maximum of 12 months.

COSTS AND FINANCIAL AID
Required Forms and Deadlines: FAFSA, Institution's own financial aid form. **Notification of Awards:** Applicants will be notified of awards on or about 3/1. **Types of Aid:** *Need-based scholarships/grants:* Federal Pell, Private scholarships, College/university scholarship or grant aid from institutional funds. *Loans:* Direct Subsidized Stafford Loans, Direct Unsubsidized Stafford Loans, Direct PLUS loans. **Financial Aid Statistics:** 91% needy freshmen, 84% needy undergrads receive need-based scholarship or grant aid. 19% freshmen, 34% undergrads receive non-need-based scholarship or grant aid. 91% freshmen, 78% undergrads receive need-based self-help aid. 0% freshmen, 0% undergrads receive athletic scholarships. 33% undergrads borrow to pay for school. Average cumulative indebtedness $34,395.

AMERICAN UNIVERSITY

4400 Massachusetts Ave, NW, Washington, DC 20016-8001
Phone: 202-885-6000 • **Financial Aid Phone:** 202-885-6500
E-mail: admissions@american.edu • **CEEB Code:** 5007
Fax: 202-885-1025 • **Website:** www.american.edu • **ACT Code:** 648

This private school, affiliated with the Methodist Church, was founded in 1893. It has a 84-acre campus.

RATINGS

Admissions Selectivity Rating: 94   **Fire Safety Rating:** 84   **Green Rating:** 98

STUDENTS AND FACULTY

Enrollment: 7,277. **Student Body:** 63% female, 37% male, 82% out-of-state, 7% international (94 countries represented). Asian 7%, African American 7%, Caucasian 59%, Hispanic 13%, Native American <1%, Pacific Islander <1%, Two or more races 5%, Race unknown 3%.
Retention and Graduation: 88% freshmen return for sophomore year. 76% freshmen graduate within 4 years. 81% freshmen graduate within 6 years.
Faculty: Student/faculty ratio 12:1. 787 full-time faculty, 94% hold PhDs, 19% are are members of minority groups, 50% are women. 0% of classes are taught by teaching assistants.

ACADEMICS

Degrees: associate, bachelor's, certificate, doctoral/professional, doctoral/research, master's, postbachelor's certificate. **Classes:** Most classes have 10-19 students. **Most popular majors:** International Relations and Affairs; Business/Commerce; Political Science and Government. **Special Study Options:** Accelerated program, cooperative education program, cross-registration, double major, exchange student program (domestic), honors program, independent study, internships, student-designed major, study abroad, teacher certification program, weekend college, AU Abroad offers more than 100 study Abroad programs in 33 geographic locations around the world. Earn college credit, learn a foreign language, pursue and internship and gain international experience and contacts. One-semester, full year, alternative spring break, and language immersion options are available. With AU Abroad partner universities in Canada, Mexico, England, Scotland, Ireland, Argentina, Australia, Egypt,the United Arab Emirates and numerous other countries around the world, you have the ability to go almost anywhere. **Honors Programs:** The University Honors Program is designed to promote a continuous learning environment, making optimum use of AU"s outstanding faculty, campus facilities and the numerous resources available in the Washington, D.C. area and abroad. Students enjoy small classes, proven instructors, cultural events, a wide range of social activities and the option of living in Honors housing. Members of the University Honors Program can major in any discipline at the university and can also participate in multidisciplinary Honors Colloquia. Combined degree programs: BA/MA, BS/MS, BA/MPA, BA/MA. **Disability Services:** Special programs offered to physically disabled students, including note-taking services, reader services, tape recorders, tutors. **Career Services:** Alumni network, Alumni services, Career/job search classes, Career assessment, Internships, Regional alumni.

FACILITIES

Housing: Coed dorms, special housing for disabled students, special housing for international students, apartments for married students, apartments for single students. 95% of campus accessible to physically diasbled. **Special Academic Facilities/Equipment:** Student-run Radio and TV Facilities, Watkins Art Gallery, Katzen Arts Center, Experimental Theatre, Greenberg Theatre, Friedheim Journalism Center, William I Jacobs Fitness Center, Language Resource Center, Multimedia Center, Audiotechnology Lab, UNIX and Oracle Labs, Kay Spiritual Life Center(interdenominational). **Computers:** 100% of classrooms, 100% of dorms, 100% of libraries, 100% of dining areas, 100% of student union, 100% of common outdoor areas have wireless network access. Students can register for classes online. Administrative functions (other than registration) can be performed online.

CAMPUS LIFE

Environment: Metropolis. **Activities:** Choral groups, dance, drama/theater, jazz band, literary magazine, music ensembles, musical theater, opera, pep band, radio station, student government, student newspaper, student-run film society, symphony orchestra, television station, yearbook, Student Organization. 180 registered organizations, 15 honor societies, 15 religious organizations. 11 fraternities, 12 sororities. **Athletics (Intercollegiate):** Men: basketball, cross-country, diving, soccer, swimming, track/field (outdoor), track/field (indoor), wrestling. Women: basketball, cross-country, diving, field hockey, lacrosse, soccer, swimming, track/field (outdoor), track/field (indoor), volleyball. **On-Campus Highlights:** Mary Graydon Center, Sports Center Complex and Jacobs Fitness, Katzen Arts Center, The Quad, Terrace Dining Room. **Environmental Initiatives:** A Climate Action Plan which calls for achieving carbon neutrality by 2020.

ADMISSIONS

Reported SAT (pre-2016 redesign) scores: SAT Math middle 50% range 560-650. SAT Critical Reading middle 50% range 590-690. SAT Writing middle 50% range 570-670. **Concordant SAT scores:** SAT EBRW middle 50% 640–720. SAT Math middle 50% 580–670. ACT middle 50% range 26-31. Minimum internet-based TOEFL 80. Minimum paper TOEFL 550. **Basis for Candidate Selection:** *Very important factors considered include:* rigor of secondary school record, academic GPA, level of applicant's interest. *Important factors considered include:* application essay, recommendation(s), extracurricular activities, talent/ability, character/personal qualities, volunteer work. *Other factors considered include:* standardized test scores, first generation, alumni/ae relation, geographical residence, racial/ethnic status, work experience. **Freshman Admission Requirements:** High school diploma is required and GED is accepted. *Academic units required:* 4 English, 3 math, 3 science, 2 science labs, 2 foreign language, 2 social studies, 3 academic electives. *Academic units recommended:* 4 English, 4 math, 4 science, 3 foreign language, 4 social studies, 4 academic electives. **Freshman Admission Statistics:** 19,325 applied, 25.91% admitted, 34% enrolled. **Transfer Admission Requirements:** college transcript(s), essay or personal statement, Minimum college GPA of 2.5 required. Lowest grade transferable C. **General Admission Information:** Application fee $70. Regular application deadline 1/15. Regular notification 4/1. Nonfall registration accepted. Admission may be deferred for a maximum of 1 year.

COSTS AND FINANCIAL AID

Annual tuition $44,046. Room and board $14,526. Required fees $807. Average book expense $800. **Required Forms and Deadlines:** FAFSA, CSS/Financial Aid PROFILE. **Notification of Awards:** Applicants will be notified of awards on or about 4/1. **Types of Aid:** *Need-based scholarships/grants:* Federal Pell, FSEOG, Private scholarships, College/university scholarship or grant aid from institutional funds. *Loans:* Direct Subsidized Stafford Loans, Direct Unsubsidized Stafford Loans, Direct PLUS loans, Federal Perkins Loans, College/university loans from institutional funds. *Student Employment:* Federal Work-Study Program available. Institutional employment available. **Financial Aid Statistics:** 84% needy undergrads receive need-based scholarship or grant aid. 27% freshmen, 31% undergrads receive non-need-based scholarship or grant aid. 94% freshmen, 93% undergrads receive need-based self-help aid. 2% freshmen, 2% undergrads receive athletic scholarships. 89% freshmen, 71% undergrads receive any aid. 65% undergrads borrow to pay for school. Average cumulative indebtedness $32,394. **Criteria for awarding aid:** *Need-based:* Academics, Leadership. *Non-need-based:* Academics, Alumni affiliation, Athletics, Leadership, Minority status, Music/drama, Religious affiliation, State/district residency.

AMERICAN UNIVERSITY IN CAIRO

AUC Avenue, P.O. Box 74 New Cairo 11835,
Phone: 20.2.26151459 • **Financial Aid Phone:** 2.02.2615-3865
E-mail: enrolauc@aucegypt.edu
Website: www.aucegypt.edu

This private school was founded in 1919. It has a 260-acre campus.

RATINGS

Admissions Selectivity Rating: 79   **Fire Safety Rating:** 87   **Green Rating:** 86

STUDENTS AND FACULTY

Student Body: 54% female, 46% male, (38 countries represented). **Retention and Graduation:** 91% freshmen return for sophomore year. 37% freshmen graduate within 4 years. 73% freshmen graduate within 6 years. **Faculty:** Student/faculty ratio 13:1. 401 full-time faculty, 74% hold PhDs, 0% are are members of minority groups, 50% are women. 0% of classes are taught by teaching assistants.

ACADEMICS

Degrees: bachelor's, diploma, doctoral, master's. **Classes:** Most classes have 10-19 students. Most lab/discussion sessions have 10-19 students. **Most popular majors:** Mechanical Engineering; Business Administration, Management and Operations; Construction Engineering. **Special Study Options:** double major, English as a Second Language (ESL), independent study, internships, liberal arts/career combination, study abroad. Combined degree programs: BA/MA, BSc/MPA. **Career Services:** Alumni network, Alumni services, Career/job search classes, Career assessment, Internships, Regional alumni. Job shadwoing and internships to help students explore career options. Online recruitment and Employment Fairs generate employment opportunities.(We are proud of the University's Employment Fairs that are held in the Spring and Fall of each year. The fairs are professionally set up, are highly regarded by employers and attract a wide talent pool of around 1800 students and alumni in each event. Information on participating companies and details on announced career opportunities are included in a special event's publication that is published in conjunction with the employment fair.)

FACILITIES

Housing: men's dorms, women's dorms, apartments for married students, apartments for single students. 100% of campus accessible to physically diasbled. **Computers:** 100% of classrooms, 100% of dorms, 100% of libraries, 100% of dining areas, 100% of student union, 100% of common outdoor areas have wireless network access. Students can register for classes online. Administrative functions (other than registration) can be performed online.

CAMPUS LIFE

Environment: Metropolis. **Activities:** Choral groups, dance, drama/theater, literary magazine, music ensembles, radio station, student government, student newspaper, student-run film society, yearbook, Student Organization, Model UN. 62 registered organizations. **Athletics (Intercollegiate):** *Men:* basketball, boxing, fencing, football, gymnastics, handball, rugby, soccer, squash, swimming, table tennis, tennis, track/field (outdoor), volleyball, water polo, wrestling. *Women:* basketball, fencing, football, gymnastics, handball, soccer, squash, swimming, table tennis, tennis, track/field (outdoor), volleyball. **On-Campus Highlights:** Athletic Facility, Food Court, Library, Student Center **Environmental Initiatives:** AUC Publishes Carbon Footprint Report.

ADMISSIONS

Reported SAT (pre-2016 redesign) scores: SAT Math middle 50% range 560-660. SAT Critical Reading middle 50% range 450-530. SAT Writing middle 50% range 560-640. **Concordant SAT scores:** SAT EBRW middle 50% 560–640. SAT Math middle 50% range 580–690. Minimum internet-based TOEFL 48. Minimum paper TOEFL 460. **Basis for Candidate Selection:** *Very important factors considered include:* academic GPA, standardized test scores. *Important factors considered include:* recommendation(s), alumni/ae relation, geographical residence, state residency. *Other factors considered include:* extracurricular activities, talent/ability, character/personal qualities, volunteer work, work experience. **Freshman Admission Requirements:** High school diploma is required and GED is accepted. *Academic units recommended:* 3 English, 3 math, 2 science, 2 foreign language, 3 social studies. **Freshman Admission Statistics:** 2,948 applied, 47.66% admitted, 67% enrolled. **Transfer Admission Requirements:** High school transcript, college transcript(s), essay or personal statement, standardized test scores, statement of good standing from prior institution(s). Minimum college GPA of 2.0 required. Lowest grade transferable C. **General Admission Information:** Application fee $50. Priority deadline 3/1. Regular application deadline 5/15. Nonfall registration accepted. Admission may be deferred for a maximum of One semester.

COSTS AND FINANCIAL AID

Required Forms and Deadlines: Institution's own financial aid form. **Types of Aid:** *Need-based scholarships/grants:* Federal Pell, FSEOG, State scholarships/grants, College/university scholarship or grant aid from institutional funds. *Loans:* Direct Subsidized Stafford Loans, Direct Unsubsidized Stafford Loans, Direct PLUS loans, Federal Perkins Loans, State Loans. **Financial Aid Statistics:** 16% freshmen, 56% undergrads receive non-need-based scholarship or grant aid. 2% freshmen, 0% undergrads receive need-based self-help aid. 1% freshmen, 2% undergrads receive athletic scholarships. 63% freshmen, 62% undergrads receive any aid. **Criteria for awarding aid:** *Need-based:* Academics, Leadership. *Non-need-based:* Academics, Athletics, Music/drama.

THE AMERICAN UNIVERSITY OF ROME

Via Pietro Roselli 4, Rome, 153
Phone: +39.06.5833.0919
E-mail: admissions@aur.edu
Website: http://www.aur.edu/

RATINGS

Admissions Selectivity Rating: 60*   **Fire Safety Rating:** 60*   **Green Rating:** 60*

STUDENTS AND FACULTY

Student Body: (40 countries represented).
Retention and Graduation: 47% grads go on to further study within 1 year.
Faculty: 0% of classes are taught by teaching assistants.

ACADEMICS

Degrees: associate, bachelor's, master's. **Most popular majors:** Business Administration and Management; International Relations and Affairs. **Career Services:** Alumni network, Alumni services, Career/job search classes, Internships, On-campus interviews.

ADMISSIONS

Basis for Candidate Selection: *Important factors considered include:* academic GPA, standardized test scores, application essay, recommendation(s), interview, level of applicant's interest. *Other factors considered include:* rigor of secondary school record, class rank, extracurricular activities, talent/ability, character/personal qualities, alumni/ae relation, volunteer work, work experience. **General Admission Information:** Priority deadline 3/31. Nonfall registration accepted. Admission may be deferred.

COSTS AND FINANCIAL AID

Student Employment: Federal Work-Study Program available. Institutional employment available.

AMHERST COLLEGE

220 South Pleasant Street, Amherst, MA 1002
Phone: 413-542-2328 • **Financial Aid Phone:** 413-542-2296
E-mail: admission@amherst.edu • **CEEB Code:** 3003
Fax: 413-542-2040 • **Website:** www.amherst.edu • **ACT Code:** 1774

This private school was founded in 1821. It has a 999-acre campus.

RATINGS

Admissions Selectivity Rating: 98   **Fire Safety Rating:** 97   **Green Rating:** 81

STUDENTS AND FACULTY

Enrollment: 1,849. **Student Body:** 50% female, 50% male, 87% out-of-state, 9% international (54 countries represented). Asian 14%, African American 12%, Caucasian 43%, Hispanic 14%, Native American <1%, Pacific Islander 0%, Two or more races 5%, Race unknown 3%.
Retention and Graduation: 96% freshmen return for sophomore year. 86% freshmen graduate within 4 years. 93% freshmen graduate within 6 years. **Faculty:** Student/faculty ratio 8:1. 209 full-time faculty, 91% hold PhDs, 21% are are members of minority groups, 49% are women. 0% of classes are taught by teaching assistants.

ACADEMICS

Degrees: bachelor's, certificate. **Classes:** Most classes have 10-19 students. Most lab/discussion sessions have 10-19 students. **Most popular majors:** Economics; English Language and Literature; Psychology. **Special Study Options:** cross-registration, double major, exchange student program (domestic), honors program, independent study, student-designed major, study abroad, teacher certification program. **Honors Programs:** Senior Honors Thesis-an opportunity to engage in extensive research with a professor as the student's advisor. **Disability Services:** Special programs offered to physically disabled students, including note-taking services, reader services, tape recorders, tutors. **Career Services:** Alumni network, Alumni services, Career/job search classes, Career assessment, Internships, Regional alumni.

FACILITIES

Housing: Coed dorms, cooperative housing, French/Spanish language house, German/Russian language house, Latino culture house, African American culture house, Health and Wellness house, Arts house, Food Cooperative house and single sex floors for men and women within specific dorms. **Special Academic Facilities/Equipment:** Art, natural history, geology museums, language labs, observatory,planetarium, The Amherst Center for Russian Culture, The Dickinson Homestead. **Computers:** Administrative functions (other than registration) can be performed online.

CAMPUS LIFE

Environment: Town. **Activities:** Choral groups, concert band, dance, drama/theater, jazz band, literary magazine, music ensembles, musical theater, opera, radio station, student government, student newspaper, student-run film society, symphony orchestra, yearbook, Student Organization, Model UN. 100 registered organizations, 2 honor societies, 7 religious organizations. **Athletics (Intercollegiate):** *Men:* baseball, basketball, cross-country, diving, football, golf, ice hockey, lacrosse, soccer, squash, swimming, tennis, track/field (outdoor), track/field (indoor). *Women:* basketball, cross-country, diving, field hockey, golf, ice hockey, lacrosse, soccer, softball, squash, swimming, tennis, track/field (outdoor), track/field (indoor), volleyball. **On-Campus Highlights:** Mead Art Museum, Pratt Museum of Natural History, Russian Cultural Center, Japanese Peace Garden, Observatory. **Environmental Initiatives:** One of the first schools to install an on-campus co-generation plant that operates primarily on Natural Gas

ADMISSIONS

Freshman Academic Profile: 87% in top 10% of high school class, 96% in top 25% of high school class, 99% in top 50% of high school class. 59% from public high schools. **Reported SAT (pre-2016 redesign) scores:** SAT Math middle 50% range 680-780. SAT Critical Reading middle 50% range 680-780. SAT Writing middle 50% range 680-780. **Concordant SAT scores:** SAT EBRW middle 50% 720–790. SAT Math middle 50% range 710–790. ACT middle 50% range 31-34. Minimum internet-based TOEFL 100. **Basis for Candidate Selection:** *Very important factors considered include:* rigor of secondary school record, academic GPA, standardized test scores, application essay, recommendation(s), extracurricular activities, talent/ability, character/personal qualities, first generation. *Important factors considered include:* class rank, volunteer work. *Other factors considered include:* alumni/ae relation, geographical residence, racial/ethnic status, work experience. **Freshman Admission Requirements:** High school diploma or equivalent is not required. *Academic units recommended:* 4 English, 4 math, 3 science, 1 science lab, 2 social studies, 2 history. **Freshman Admission Statistics:** 8,406 applied, 13.81% admitted, 41% enrolled. **Transfer Admission Requirements:** High school transcript, college transcript(s), essay or personal statement, statement of good standing from prior institution(s). Minimum college GPA of 3.5 required. Lowest grade transferable C. **General Admission Information:** Application fee $60. Regular application deadline 1/1. Regular notification 4/1. Nonfall registration not accepted. Admission may be deferred for a maximum of 2 years.

COSTS AND FINANCIAL AID

Annual tuition $51,620. Room and board $13,710. Required fees $856. Average book expense $1,000. **Required Forms and Deadlines:** FAFSA, CSS/Financial Aid PROFILE, Noncustodial PROFILE, Business/Farm Supplement. **Notification of Awards:** Applicants will be notified of awards on or about 4/1. **Types of Aid:** *Need-based scholarships/grants:* Federal Pell, FSEOG, State scholarships/grants, Private scholarships, College/university scholarship or grant aid from institutional funds. *Loans:* Direct Subsidized Stafford Loans, Direct Unsubsidized Stafford Loans, Direct PLUS loans, Federal Perkins Loans, College/university loans from institutional funds. *Student Employment:* Federal Work-Study Program available. Institutional employment available. **Financial Aid Statistics:** 100% needy freshmen, 100% needy undergrads receive need-based scholarship or grant aid. 0% undergrads receive non-need-based scholarship or grant aid. 78% freshmen, 86% undergrads receive need-based self-help aid. 0% freshmen, 0% undergrads receive athletic scholarships. 54% freshmen, 58% undergrads receive any aid. 22% undergrads borrow to pay for school. Average cumulative indebtedness $18,662.

ANDERSON UNIVERSITY (IN)

1100 East Fifth Street, Anderson, IN 46012-3495
Phone: 765-641-4080 • **Financial Aid Phone:** 765-641-4180
E-mail: info@anderson.edu • **CEEB Code:** 1016
Fax: 765-641-4091 • **Website:** www.anderson.edu • **ACT Code:** 1174

This private school, affiliated with the Church of God Church, was founded in 1917. It has a 100-acre campus.

RATINGS

Admissions Selectivity Rating: 82	Fire Safety Rating: 85	Green Rating: 69

STUDENTS AND FACULTY

Enrollment: 1,702. **Student Body:** 59% female, 41% male, 24% out-of-state, 2% international (19 countries represented). Asian 2%, African American 9%, Caucasian 80%, Hispanic 2%, Native American 1%, Pacific Islander <1%, Two or more races <1%, Race unknown 3%.
Retention and Graduation: 78% freshmen return for sophomore year. 49% freshmen graduate within 4 years. 58% freshmen graduate within 6 years. **Faculty:** Student/faculty ratio 12:1. 116 full-time faculty, 67% hold PhDs, 11% are are members of minority groups, 38% are women. 0% of classes are taught by teaching assistants.

ACADEMICS

Degrees: associate, bachelor's, doctoral, master's. **Classes:** Most classes have 10-19 students. Most lab/discussion sessions have 10-19 students. **Most popular majors:** Registered Nursing/Registered Nurse; Marketing/Marketing Management; Elementary Education and Teaching. **Special Study Options:** Accelerated program, cross-registration, double major, honors program, independent study, internships, student-designed major, study abroad, teacher

certification program, Summer over seas service program. **Honors Programs:** The Honors Program at Anderson University is devoted to fostering within its honors scholars a passionate dedication to intellectual inquiry and spiritual development so that they may serve as vibrant leaders in their professions and in their communities. **Disability Services:** Special programs offered to physically disabled students, including note-taking services, reader services, tape recorders, tutors. **Career Services:** Alumni network, Alumni services, Career/job search classes, Career assessment, Internships. We are please to be able to help students as they navigate their vocation/calling by providing assessments and counseling to help students make informed decisions about their future.

FACILITIES

Housing: Coed dorms, men's dorms, women's dorms, apartments for married students, apartments for single students, one house. 95% of campus accessible to physically diasbled. **Special Academic Facilities/Equipment:** Gustav Jeeninga Museum of Bible and Near Eastern Studies, Wilson Galleries, Archives of the Church of God **Computers:** Students can register for classes online. Administrative functions (other than registration) can be performed online.

CAMPUS LIFE

Environment: Town. **Activities:** Choral groups, concert band, dance, drama/theater, jazz band, literary magazine, music ensembles, musical theater, opera, pep band, radio station, student government, student newspaper, symphony orchestra, yearbook. 33 registered organizations, 12 honor societies, 15 religious organizations. **Athletics (Intercollegiate):** *Men:* baseball, basketball, cheerleading, cross-country, football, golf, soccer, tennis, track/field (outdoor). *Women:* basketball, cheerleading, cross-country, golf, soccer, softball, tennis, track/field (outdoor), volleyball. **On-Campus Highlights:** Kardatzke Wellness Center, Mocha Joe's in the Olt Student Center, Decker Commons and Cafe Ole, Reardon Auditorium **Environmental Initiatives:** Recycling.

ADMISSIONS

Freshman Academic Profile: Average high school GPA 3.4. 20% in top 10% of high school class, 50% in top 25% of high school class, 74% in top 50% of high school class. 95% from public high schools. **Reported SAT (pre-2016 redesign) scores:** SAT Math middle 50% range 460-560. SAT Critical Reading middle 50% range 450-550. **Concordant SAT scores:** SAT Math middle 50% range 500–580. ACT middle 50% range 19-25. Minimum internet-based TOEFL 78. Minimum paper TOEFL 547. **Basis for Candidate Selection:** *Very important factors considered include:* rigor of secondary school record, recommendation(s), religious affiliation/commitment. *Important factors considered include:* class rank, academic GPA, standardized test scores, interview, extracurricular activities, character/personal qualities, volunteer work. *Other factors considered include:* application essay, talent/ability, first generation, alumni/ae relation, racial/ethnic status, level of applicant's interest. **Freshman Admission Requirements:** High school diploma is required and GED is not accepted. *Academic units required:* 4 English, 3 math, 3 science, 3 science labs, 2 foreign language, 1 social studies, 1 history. *Academic units recommended:* 4 English, 4 math, 4 science, 4 science labs, 3 foreign language, 2 social studies, 2 history, 5 academic electives, 1 computer science, 1 visual/performing arts. **Freshman Admission Statistics:** 2,650 applied, 66.42% admitted, 24% enrolled. **Transfer Admission Requirements:** High school transcript, college transcript(s), standardized test scores, statement of good standing from prior institution(s). Minimum college GPA of 2.0 required. Lowest grade transferable C-. **General Admission Information:** Application fee $25. Priority deadline 1/1. Regular application deadline 7/1. Nonfall registration accepted. Admission may be deferred for a maximum of 1 year.

COSTS AND FINANCIAL AID

Annual tuition $27,520. Required fees $80. Average book expense $1,200. **Required Forms and Deadlines:** FAFSA. **Notification of Awards:** Applicants will be notified of awards on a rolling basis beginning 2/15. **Types of Aid:** *Need-based scholarships/grants:* Federal Pell, FSEOG, State scholarships/grants, Private scholarships, College/university scholarship or grant aid from institutional funds. *Loans:* Federal Perkins Loans, College/university loans from institutional funds. *Student Employment:* Federal Work-Study Program available. Institutional employment available. **Financial Aid Statistics:** 100% needy freshmen, 100% needy undergrads receive need-based scholarship or grant aid. 73% freshmen, 63% undergrads receive non-need-based scholarship or grant aid. 99% freshmen, 99% undergrads receive need-based self-help aid. 0% freshmen, 0% undergrads receive athletic scholarships. **Criteria for awarding aid:** *Need-based:* Religious affiliation. *Non-need-based:* Academics.

ANDERSON UNIVERSITY (SC)

316 Boulevard, Anderson, SC 29621
Phone: 864-231-2030 • **Financial Aid Phone:** 864-231-2070
E-mail: admission@andersonuniversity.edu • **CEEB Code:** 5008
Fax: 864-231-2033 • **Website:** www.andersonuniversity.edu • **ACT Code:** 3832

This private school, affiliated with the Southern Baptist Church, affiliated with the South Carolina Baptist Convention Church, was founded in 1911. It has a 56-acre campus.

RATINGS
Admissions Selectivity Rating: 87   **Fire Safety Rating:** 84   **Green Rating:** 60*

STUDENTS AND FACULTY
Enrollment: 2,176. **Student Body:** 67% female, 33% male, 19% out-of-state, 1% international (29 countries represented). Asian 1%, African American 9%, Caucasian 80%, Hispanic 3%, Native American 1%, Pacific Islander 1%, Two or more races 0%, Race unknown <1%.
Retention and Graduation: 74% freshmen return for sophomore year. 1% freshmen graduate within 4 years. 48% freshmen graduate within 6 years. 40% grads go on to further study within 1 year. 13% grads pursue arts and sciences degrees. 1% grads pursue law degrees. 9% grads pursue business degrees. 3% grads pursue medical degrees. **Faculty:** Student/faculty ratio 14:1. 128 full-time faculty, 63% hold PhDs, 5% are are members of minority groups, 54% are women. 0% of classes are taught by teaching assistants.

ACADEMICS
Degrees: bachelor's, doctoral/professional, master's. **Classes:** Most classes have 20-29 students. Most lab/discussion sessions have 20-29 students. **Most popular majors:** Kinesiology and Exercise Science; Business Administration and Management; Elementary Education and Teaching. **Special Study Options:** Accelerated program, cooperative education program, distance learning, double major, dual enrollment, honors program, independent study, internships, liberal arts/career combination, study abroad, teacher certification program, Washington Semester. **Disability Services:** Special programs offered to physically disabled students, including note-taking services, reader services, tape recorders, tutors. **Career Services:** Alumni services, Career assessment, Internships, Regional alumni.

FACILITIES
Housing: men's dorms, women's dorms. **Special Academic Facilities/Equipment:** Electronic classroom, Art galleries, Recording studio. **Computers:** Students can register for classes online. Administrative functions (other than registration) can be performed online.

CAMPUS LIFE
Environment: Town. **Activities:** Choral groups, concert band, dance, drama/theater, jazz band, literary magazine, music ensembles, musical theater, student government, student newspaper, symphony orchestra, yearbook, Campus Ministries. 27 registered organizations, 1 honor society, 6 religious organizations. **Athletics (Intercollegiate):** *Men:* baseball, basketball, cross-country, equestrian sports, golf, soccer, tennis, track/field (outdoor), wrestling. *Women:* basketball, cheerleading, cross-country, equestrian sports, golf, soccer, softball, tennis, track/field (outdoor), volleyball. **On-Campus Highlights:** Java City, Student Center, Bunton Computer Lab, Thrift Libary, Fitness Center.

ADMISSIONS
Freshman Academic Profile: Average high school GPA 3.7. 37% in top 10% of high school class, 62% in top 25% of high school class, 87% in top 50% of high school class. **Reported SAT (pre-2016 redesign) scores:** SAT Math middle 50% range 470-590. SAT Critical Reading middle 50% range 480-593. SAT Writing middle 50% range 470-590. **Concordant SAT scores:** SAT EBRW middle 50% 530–650. SAT Math middle 50% range 510–610. ACT middle 50% range 21-26. Minimum paper TOEFL 550. **Basis for Candidate Selection:** *Very important factors considered include:* rigor of secondary school record. *Important factors considered include:* class rank, academic GPA, standardized test scores, character/personal qualities. *Other factors considered include:* application essay, recommendation(s), extracurricular activities, talent/ability, volunteer work. **Freshman Admission Requirements:** High school diploma is required and GED is accepted. *Academic units required:* 4 English, 3 math, 3 science, 2 science labs, 2 foreign language. **Freshman Admission Statistics:** 3,322 applied, 54.94% admitted, 36% enrolled. **Transfer Admission Requirements:** college transcript(s), Minimum college GPA of 2.0 required. Lowest grade transferable C. **General Admission Information:** Application fee $25. Regular application deadline 8/1. Regular notification 9/1. Nonfall registration accepted. Admission may be deferred for a maximum of 1 year.

COSTS AND FINANCIAL AID
Annual tuition $22,570. Room and board $8,860. Required fees $2,290. Average book expense $2,000. **Required Forms and Deadlines:** FAFSA, State aid form. **Notification of Awards:** Applicants will be notified of awards on a rolling basis beginning 3/15. **Types of Aid:** *Need-based scholarships/grants:* Federal Pell, FSEOG, State scholarships/grants, Private scholarships, College/university scholarship or grant aid from institutional funds. *Loans:* Direct Subsidized Stafford Loans, Direct Unsubsidized Stafford Loans, Direct PLUS loans, Federal Perkins Loans, State Loans, College/university loans from institutional funds. *Student Employment:* Federal Work-Study Program available. Institutional employment available. **Financial Aid Statistics:** 63% needy freshmen, 71% needy undergrads receive need-based scholarship or grant aid. 100% freshmen, 100% undergrads receive non-need-based scholarship or grant aid. 73% freshmen, 72% undergrads receive need-based self-help aid. 5% freshmen, 4% undergrads receive athletic scholarships. **Criteria for awarding aid:** *Need-based:* Academics, Art, Leadership, Minority status, Music/drama. *Non-need-based:* Academics, Art, Athletics, Leadership, Minority status, Music/drama, Religious affiliation, State/district residency.

ANGELO STATE UNIVERSITY

ASU Station #11014, San Angelo, TX 76909-1014
Phone: 325-942-2041 • **Financial Aid Phone:** 325-942-2246
E-mail: admissions@angelo.edu • **CEEB Code:** 6644
Fax: 325-942-2078 • **Website:** www.angelo.edu • **ACT Code:** 4164

This public school was founded in 1928. It has a 268-acre campus.

RATINGS
Admissions Selectivity Rating: 81   **Fire Safety Rating:** 96   **Green Rating:** 82

STUDENTS AND FACULTY
Enrollment: 5,404. **Student Body:** 55% female, 45% male, 3% out-of-state, 4% international (24 countries represented). Asian 1%, African American 8%, Caucasian 52%, Hispanic 32%, Native American <1%, Pacific Islander <1%, Two or more races 3%, Race unknown <1%.
Retention and Graduation: 63% freshmen return for sophomore year. 17% freshmen graduate within 4 years. 31% freshmen graduate within 6 years. 15% grads go on to further study within 1 year. **Faculty:** Student/faculty ratio 23:1. 263 full-time faculty, 81% hold PhDs, 17% are are members of minority groups, 44% are women. 3% of classes are taught by teaching assistants.

ACADEMICS
Degrees: bachelor's, doctoral/professional, master's. **Classes:** Most classes have 20-29 students. Most lab/discussion sessions have 10-19 students. **Most popular majors:** Multi-/Interdisciplinary Studies; Registered Nursing/Registered Nurse; Psychology. **Special Study Options:** distance learning, double major, dual enrollment, honors program, independent study, internships, study abroad, teacher certification program, 4+1 programs in various disciplines allowing students to complete a bachelor's degree in four years and a master's degree in a related field in one year at Texas Tech University. Also, 3+2 physics/pre-engineering program allowing three years of study in applied physics and two years at an affiliated university for an engineering degree. **Honors Programs:** http://www.angelo.edu/dept/honors/index.htm Combined degree programs: BA/MA, BBA/MBA, BS/MBA. **Disability Services:** Special programs offered to physically disabled students, including note-taking services, tutors. **Career Services:** Alumni services, Career assessment, Internships. The Career Development Office offers a vast array of tools and resources to assist students and alumni with the career exploration process. All of the services are free to ASU students and alumni. ASU's multiple internship programs have provided exceptional work-life experiences for undergraduates with students interning in positions at institutions as prestigious as the Los Alamos National Labs to Washington, D.C., news services.

FACILITIES
Housing: Coed dorms, women's dorms, apartments for single students, Theme Housing, Rooms for disabled and Honors students. 99% of campus accessible to physically diasbled. **Special Academic Facilities/Equipment:** Planetarium; West Texas Collection; Management, Instruction, and Research (Agricultural) Center; Food Safety and Product Development Lab. **Computers:** 100% of classrooms, 100% of dorms, 100% of libraries, 100% of dining areas, 100% of student union, 100% of common outdoor areas have wireless network access. Students can register for classes online. Administrative functions (other than registration) can be performed online.

CAMPUS LIFE

Environment: City. **Activities:** Choral groups, concert band, dance, drama/theater, jazz band, literary magazine, marching band, music ensembles, musical theater, pep band, radio station, student government, student newspaper, student-run film society, television station, Campus Ministries, Student Organization. 76 registered organizations, 11 honor societies, 9 religious organizations. 4 fraternities, 2 sororities. **Athletics (Intercollegiate):** *Men:* baseball, basketball, cross-country, football, track/field (outdoor). *Women:* basketball, cross-country, golf, soccer, softball, track/field (outdoor), volleyball. **On-Campus Highlights:** Houston Harte University Center, Junell Center/Stephens Arena, ASU Planetarium, ASU Lake House, West Texas Collection, ASU Mall and Student Gathering Areas Porter Henderson Library. **Environmental Initiatives:** LEED Certification initiataives in all new buildings.

ADMISSIONS

Freshman Academic Profile: 14% in top 10% of high school class, 31% in top 25% of high school class, 73% in top 50% of high school class. 96% from public high schools. **Reported SAT (pre-2016 redesign) scores:** SAT Math middle 50% range 430-530. SAT Critical Reading middle 50% range 420-520. SAT Writing middle 50% range 400-491. **Concordant SAT scores:** SAT EBRW middle 50% 460–560. SAT Math middle 50% range 470–560. ACT middle 50% range 18-23. Minimum internet-based TOEFL 79. Minimum paper TOEFL 550. **Basis for Candidate Selection:** *Very important factors considered include:* class rank, standardized test scores. *Important factors considered include:* rigor of secondary school record. *Other factors considered include:* academic GPA. **Freshman Admission Requirements:** High school diploma is required and GED is accepted. *Academic units recommended:* 4 English, 4 math, 4 science, 2 foreign language, 1 visual/performing arts, and 2 units from above areas or other academic areas. **Freshman Admission Statistics:** 3,822 applied, 76.77% admitted, 46% enrolled. **Transfer Admission Requirements:** college transcript(s), statement of good standing from prior institution(s). Minimum college GPA of 2.0 required. Lowest grade transferable D. **General Admission Information:** Application fee $35. Regular application deadline 8/27. Nonfall registration accepted. Admission may be deferred for a maximum of 1 year.

COSTS AND FINANCIAL AID

Annual in-state tuition $4,860. Annual out-of-state tuition $16,560. Room and board $7,702. Required fees $3,004. Average book expense $1,200. **Required Forms and Deadlines:** FAFSA. **Notification of Awards:** Applicants will be notified of awards on a rolling basis beginning 4/1. **Types of Aid:** *Need-based scholarships/grants:* Federal Pell, FSEOG, State scholarships/grants, Private scholarships, College/university scholarship or grant aid from institutional funds, Federal Nursing Scholarships. *Loans:* Direct Subsidized Stafford Loans, Direct Unsubsidized Stafford Loans, Direct PLUS loans, Federal Perkins Loans, Federal Nursing Loans, State Loans, College/university loans from institutional funds. *Student Employment:* Federal Work-Study Program available. Institutional employment available. **Financial Aid Statistics:** 79% needy freshmen, 82% needy undergrads receive need-based scholarship or grant aid. 67% freshmen, 38% undergrads receive non-need-based scholarship or grant aid. 75% freshmen, 76% undergrads receive need-based self-help aid. 6% freshmen, 6% undergrads receive athletic scholarships. 87% freshmen, 81% undergrads receive any aid. 61% undergrads borrow to pay for school. Average cumulative indebtedness $26,033. **Criteria for awarding aid:** *Need-based:* Academics. *Non-need-based:* Academics, Art, Athletics, Leadership, Music/drama, State/district residency.

ANNA MARIA COLLEGE

50 Sunset Lane, Paxton, MA 01612-1198
Phone: 508-849-3360 • **Financial Aid Phone:** 508-849-3366
E-mail: admission@annamaria.edu • **CEEB Code:** 3005
Fax: 508-849-3362 • **Website:** www.annamaria.edu • **ACT Code:** 3232

This private school, affiliated with the Roman Catholic Church, was founded in 1946. It has a 190-acre campus.

RATINGS

Admissions Selectivity Rating: 72   **Fire Safety Rating:** 83   **Green Rating:** 60*

STUDENTS AND FACULTY

Enrollment: 978. **Student Body:** 56% female, 44% male, 12% out-of-state, 1% international. Asian 1%, African American 6%, Caucasian 73%, Hispanic 5%, Native American <1%, Pacific Islander 0%, Two or more races 0%, Race unknown 14%.
Retention and Graduation: 70% freshmen return for sophomore year. 50% freshmen graduate within 4 years. 59% freshmen graduate within 6 years. 47%

grads go on to further study within 1 year. 19% grads pursue arts and sciences degrees. 2% grads pursue law degrees. 1% grads pursue business degrees. **Faculty:** Student/faculty ratio 10:1. 50 full-time faculty, 72% hold PhDs, 0% are members of minority groups, 66% are women. 0% of classes are taught by teaching assistants.

ACADEMICS

Degrees: associate, bachelor's, certificate, master's, postbachelor's certificate, post-master's certificate. **Classes:** Most classes have 10-19 students. Most lab/discussion sessions have fewer than 10 students. **Most popular majors:** Fire Science/Fire; Criminal Justice/Safety Studies; Business Administration and Management. **Special Study Options:** Accelerated program, cooperative education program, cross-registration, double major, independent study, internships, liberal arts/career combination, student-designed major, study abroad, teacher certification program. **Honors Programs:** The Honors Program at Anna Maria College is designed to intellectually challenge highly motivated scholastic achievers. The Program is now a member of "National Collegiate Honors Programs," the national association of Honors Programs. Each Honors Program participant will have the opportunity to engage directly in foreign culture through interesting study abroad programs, such as a semester abroad experience,or a focused Urban Seminar that meets in a city like Paris, Vienna, Rome or Berlin that is sponsored by the College and supervised by a professor who oversees the program. Combined degree programs: BA/MA. **Disability Services:** Special programs offered to physically disabled students, including note-taking services, reader services, tape recorders, tutors. **Career Services:** Alumni services, Career assessment, Internships, On-campus interviews.

FACILITIES

Housing: Coed dorms, special housing for disabled students, Wellness Housing. **Special Academic Facilities/Equipment:** The Mondor-Eagan Library houses Anna Maria College"s volumes, stacks, periodicals, study rooms, computer center, resource centers, and language laboratory. Classrooms are located in Trinity Hall, Cardinal Cushing Hall, and Foundress Hall. Foundress Hall houses the Zecco Performing Arts Center. Trinity Hall also houses the learning center. Among the other buildings are Madore Chapel, St. Joseph's Hall for sciences and Miriam Hall for music, performance, and art. **Computers:** 100% of classrooms, 100% of dorms, 100% of libraries, 100% of dining areas, 100% of student union, 100% of common outdoor areas have wireless network access. Administrative functions (other than registration) can be performed online.

CAMPUS LIFE

Environment: Rural. **Activities:** Choral groups, dance, drama/theater, jazz band, pep band, student government, student newspaper, yearbook, Campus Ministries. 17 registered organizations, 5 honor societies, 1 religious organization. **Athletics (Intercollegiate):** *Men:* baseball, basketball, cross-country, football, golf, lacrosse, soccer, tennis. *Women:* basketball, field hockey, lacrosse, soccer, softball, tennis, volleyball. **On-Campus Highlights:** New Residence Hall, New Exercise / Weight Room, New Art Building w/ art gallery, Snack bar / Lounge, Student Center. **Environmental Initiatives:** There is a "Green Committee" that meets regularly to discuss environmental issues and ways that the college can be be more sustainable.

ADMISSIONS

Freshman Academic Profile: Average high school GPA 2.6. 2% in top 10% of high school class, 13% in top 25% of high school class, 41% in top 50% of high school class. **Reported SAT (pre-2016 redesign) scores:** SAT Math middle 50% range 378-480. SAT Critical Reading middle 50% range 378-490. **Concordant SAT scores:** SAT Math middle 50% range 420–510. ACT middle 50% range 18-21. Minimum paper TOEFL 500. **Basis for Candidate Selection:** *Very important factors considered include:* academic GPA, standardized test scores. *Other factors considered include:* rigor of secondary school record, application essay, recommendation(s), extracurricular activities, volunteer work, work experience, level of applicant's interest. **Freshman Admission Requirements:** High school diploma is required and GED is accepted. *Academic units required:* 4 English, 3 math, 3 science, 1 science lab, 2 foreign language, 2 social studies, 2 history, 4 academic electives. **Freshman Admission Statistics:** 712 applied, 87.22% admitted, 41% enrolled. **Transfer Admission Requirements:** High school transcript, college transcript(s), essay or personal statement, statement of good standing from prior institution(s). Minimum college GPA of 2.0 required. Lowest grade transferable C. **General Admission Information:** Application fee $40. Priority deadline 3/1. Nonfall registration accepted. Admission may be deferred for a maximum of 1 year.

COSTS AND FINANCIAL AID

Annual tuition $23,500. Room and board $9,350. Required fees $2,350. Average book expense $800. **Required Forms and Deadlines:** FAFSA, State aid form. **Notification of Awards:** Applicants will be notified of awards on a rolling basis beginning 4/1. **Types of Aid:** *Need-based scholarships/grants:* Federal Pell, FSEOG, State scholarships/grants, Private scholarships, College/university scholarship or grant aid from institutional funds, United Negro College Fund. *Loans:* Federal Perkins Loans, College/university loans from institutional funds.

Student Employment: Federal Work-Study Program available. **Financial Aid Statistics:** 99% needy freshmen, 98% needy undergrads receive need-based scholarship or grant aid. 99% freshmen, 98% undergrads receive non-need-based scholarship or grant aid. 92% freshmen, 92% undergrads receive need-based self-help aid. 0% freshmen, 0% undergrads receive athletic scholarships. 98% freshmen, 95% undergrads receive any aid. **Criteria for awarding aid:** *Non-need-based:* Academics, Alumni affiliation, Music/drama, Religious affiliation, State/district residency.

ANTIOCH COLLEGE

1 Morgan Place, Yellow Springs, OH 45387
Phone: 937-319-6082 • **Financial Aid Phone:** 937-319-6016
E-mail: admission@antiochcollege.edu
Fax: 937-319-6085 • **Website:** www.antiochcollege.edu • **ACT Code:** 3232

This private school was founded in 1852. It has a 100-acre campus.

RATINGS
Admissions Selectivity Rating: 70 **Fire Safety Rating:** 91 **Green Rating:** 92

STUDENTS AND FACULTY
Enrollment: 217. **Student Body:** 60% female, 40% male, 70% out-of-state, 0% international (10 countries represented). Asian 4%, African American 8%, Caucasian 65%, Hispanic 9%, Native American 2%, Pacific Islander <1%, Two or more races 8%, Race unknown 5%.
Retention and Graduation: 59% freshmen return for sophomore year.
Faculty: Student/faculty ratio 6:1. 34 full-time faculty, 79% hold PhDs, 32% are are members of minority groups, 53% are women. 0% of classes are taught by teaching assistants.

ACADEMICS
Degrees: bachelor's. **Classes:** Most classes have fewer than 10 students. **Most popular majors:** Psychology; Liberal Arts and Sciences Studies and Humanities; Political Economy. **Special Study Options:** cooperative education program, cross-registration, dual enrollment, independent study, internships, liberal arts/career combination, student-designed major, study abroad. **Disability Services:** Special programs offered to physically disabled students, including note-taking services, reader services, tape recorders, tutors. **Career Services:** Alumni network, Alumni services, Career/job search classes, Career assessment, Internships, Regional alumni. Antioch College is the only non-profit liberal arts institution in the nation to require a comprehensive off-campus cooperative work program of all its students.

FACILITIES
Housing: Coed dorms, special housing for disabled students, special housing for international students, Gender specific floors. 86% of campus accessible to physically diasbled. **Special Academic Facilities/Equipment:** 1,000-acre nature preserve.

CAMPUS LIFE
Environment: Rural. **Activities:** Choral groups, dance, drama/theater, literary magazine, music ensembles, musical theater, radio station, student government, student newspaper. 16 registered organizations. **On-Campus Highlights:** Herndon Gallery, Glen Hellen Nature Preserve, Japanese Tea Garden, Community Bike Shop, Alternative Library. **Environmental Initiatives:** Antioch College is committed to sustainable energy and building design and demonstrates this commitment in a variety of ways. Antioch College has an on-campus, five-acre solar farm of 3,300 solar panels that produces 1.2 million kilowatt hours of energy annually. This solar array provides enough power to offset the electrical consumption of the College's Central Geothermal Plant. The Central Geothermal Plant, which heats and cools campus buildings, offsets 2,900 tons of CO2 when compared with traditional heating and cooling methods. The College tracks and monitors all energy consumption at 66% of campus buildings and provides real-time updates of that energy consumption through online data dashboards.

ADMISSIONS
Freshman Academic Profile: Average high school GPA 2.9. **Basis for Candidate Selection:** *Very important factors considered include:* application essay, recommendation(s), interview, character/personal qualities, level of applicant's interest. *Important factors considered include:* rigor of secondary school record, class rank, academic GPA, extracurricular activities, volunteer work, work experience. *Other factors considered include:* standardized test scores, talent/ability, first generation, alumni/ae relation, geographical residence, state residency, racial/ethnic status. **Freshman Admission Requirements:** High school diploma is required and GED is accepted. *Academic units*

recommended: 4 English, 4 math, 4 science, 4 foreign language, 4 social studies, 4 history, 4 academic electives. **Freshman Admission Statistics:** 94 applied, 73.40% admitted, 64% enrolled. **Transfer Admission Requirements:** High school transcript, college transcript(s), essay or personal statement, statement of good standing from prior institution(s). **General Admission Information:** Priority deadline 12/1. Regular application deadline 2/15. Nonfall registration not accepted. Admission may be deferred for a maximum of 1 year.

COSTS AND FINANCIAL AID
Annual tuition $34,568. Room and board $11,364. Required fees $1,000. Average book expense $1,200. **Required Forms and Deadlines:** Institution's own financial aid form. **Notification of Awards:** Applicants will be notified of awards on a rolling basis beginning 4/1. **Types of Aid:** *Need-based scholarships/ grants:* Federal Pell, Private scholarships, College/university scholarship or grant aid from institutional funds. *Loans:* Direct Subsidized Stafford Loans, Direct Unsubsidized Stafford Loans, Direct PLUS loans. *Student Employment:* Institutional employment available. **Financial Aid Statistics:** 100% needy freshmen, 100% needy undergrads receive need-based scholarship or grant aid. 100% freshmen, 100% undergrads receive non-need-based scholarship or grant aid. 100% freshmen, 100% undergrads receive need-based self-help aid. 0% freshmen, 0% undergrads receive athletic scholarships. 100% freshmen, 100% undergrads receive any aid. **Criteria for awarding aid:** *Need-based:* Academics, Minority status. *Non-need-based:* Academics.

ANTIOCH UNIVERSITY SANTA BARBARA

801 Garden Street, Santa Barbara, CA 93101
Phone: 805-962-8179 • **Financial Aid Phone:** 805-962-8179
E-mail: admissions@antiochsb.edu
Fax: 805-962-4786 • **Website:** www.antiochsb.edu

This private school was founded in 1852.

RATINGS
Admissions Selectivity Rating: 60* **Fire Safety Rating:** 60* **Green Rating:** 60*

STUDENTS AND FACULTY
Student Body: 75% female, 25% male, (11 countries represented).
Faculty: 16 full-time faculty, 0% hold PhDs, 0% are are members of minority groups, 69% are women.

ACADEMICS
Degrees: bachelor's, master's. **Special Study Options:** cross-registration, double major, independent study, internships, liberal arts/career combination, study abroad, teacher certification program, weekend college.

FACILITIES
Computers: Students can register for classes online. Administrative functions (other than registration) can be performed online.

CAMPUS LIFE
Environment: City.

ADMISSIONS
Freshman Admission Requirements: High school diploma is required and GED is accepted. **Transfer Admission Requirements:** High school transcript, college transcript(s), essay or personal statement, interview, statement of good standing from prior institution(s). Minimum college GPA of 2.0 required. Lowest grade transferable C. **General Admission Information:** Application fee $60. Nonfall registration not accepted.

COSTS AND FINANCIAL AID
Annual tuition $15,375. Required fees $26. **Required Forms and Deadlines:** FAFSA, Institution's own financial aid form. **Types of Aid:** *Need-based scholarships/grants:* Federal Pell, FSEOG, State scholarships/grants, Private scholarships, College/university scholarship or grant aid from institutional funds. *Loans:* Federal Perkins Loans. *Student Employment:* Federal Work-Study Program available. Institutional employment available. **Financial Aid Statistics:** 54% needy undergrads receive need-based scholarship or grant aid. 0% undergrads receive non-need-based scholarship or grant aid. 54% undergrads receive need-based self-help aid. **Criteria for awarding aid:** *Need-based:* Minority status.

APPALACHIAN STATE UNIVERSITY

Office of Admissions, Boone, NC 28608-2004
Phone: 828-262-2120 • **Financial Aid Phone:** 828-262-2190
E-mail: admissions@appstate.edu • **CEEB Code:** 5010
Fax: 828-262-3296 • **Website:** www.appstate.edu • **ACT Code:** 3062

This public school was founded in 1899. It has a 1300-acre campus.

RATINGS
Admissions Selectivity Rating: 85   **Fire Safety Rating:** 95   **Green Rating:** 98

STUDENTS AND FACULTY
Enrollment: 16,442. **Student Body:** 55% female, 45% male, 8% out-of-state, <1% international (39 countries represented). Asian 2%, African American 4%, Caucasian 84%, Hispanic 5%, Native American <1%, Pacific Islander <1%, Two or more races 3%, Race unknown 1%.
Retention and Graduation: 87% freshmen return for sophomore year. 49% freshmen graduate within 4 years. 72% freshmen graduate within 6 years.
Faculty: Student/faculty ratio 16:1. 952 full-time faculty, 99% hold PhDs, 7% are are members of minority groups, 47% are women. 1% of classes are taught by teaching assistants.

ACADEMICS
Degrees: bachelor's, doctoral/research, master's, postbachelor's certificate, post-master's certificate. **Classes:** Most classes have 20-29 students. Most lab/discussion sessions have 20-29 students. **Most popular majors:** Psychology; Kinesiology and Exercise Science; Business Administration and Management. **Special Study Options:** distance learning, double major, dual enrollment, English as a Second Language (ESL), exchange student program (domestic), honors program, independent study, internships, liberal arts/career combination, student-designed major, study abroad, teacher certification program. **Honors Programs:** Heltzer Honors Program offers promising and highly motivated students opportunities by providing honors classes in many fields. Combined degree programs: Accelerated bachelor's/MBA for Honors students. **Disability Services:** Special programs offered to physically disabled students, including note-taking services, reader services, tape recorders, tutors. **Career Services:** Alumni network, Alumni services, Career/job search classes, Career assessment, Internships, Regional alumni.

FACILITIES
Housing: Coed dorms, special housing for disabled students, men's dorms, special housing for international students, women's dorms, apartments for married students, apartments for single students, Wellness Housing, Theme Housing, Sorority housing. 100% of campus accessible to physically diasbled. **Special Academic Facilities/Equipment:** Language lab, Dark Sky Observatory http://www.dancaton.physics.appstate.edu/Observatories/DSO/index.htm, meteorological reporting station, art gallery, Living Learning Center, geology museum and rock garden http://www.geology.appstate.edu/museum/museum.htm, wind research site http://www.wind.appstate.edu/swiwind/smallwindrdsite.php, library Special Collections http://www.library.appstate.edu/collections/sc/index.html **Computers:** 95% of classrooms, 70% of dorms, 90% of libraries, 90% of dining areas, 85% of student union, 5% of common outdoor areas have wireless network access. Students can register for classes online. Administrative functions (other than registration) can be performed online.

CAMPUS LIFE
Environment: Village. **Activities:** Choral groups, concert band, dance, drama/theater, jazz band, literary magazine, marching band, music ensembles, musical theater, opera, pep band, radio station, student government, student newspaper, student-run film society, symphony orchestra, Campus Ministries, Student Organization, Model UN. 270 registered organizations, 20 honor societies, 25 religious organizations. 18 fraternities, 11 sororities. **Athletics (Intercollegiate):** *Men:* baseball, basketball, cross-country, football, golf, soccer, tennis, track/field (outdoor), track/field (indoor), wrestling. *Women:* basketball, cross-country, field hockey, golf, soccer, softball, tennis, track/field (outdoor), track/field (indoor), volleyball. **On-Campus Highlights:** Student Union, Central Dining Hall, Belk Library, Student Recreation Center, Holmes Convocation Center. **Environmental Initiatives:** Signatory of the American College and University Presidents Climate Commitment. On track with the target requirements. Climate Action Plan completed 2010. Climate neutrality date of 2050.

ADMISSIONS
Freshman Academic Profile: Average high school GPA 4.2. 19% in top 10% of high school class, 57% in top 25% of high school class, 92% in top 50% of high school class. 92% from public high schools. **Reported SAT (pre-2016 redesign) scores:** SAT Math middle 50% range 520-620. SAT Critical Reading middle 50% range 510-620. SAT Writing middle 50% range 490-590. **Concordant SAT scores:** SAT EBRW middle 50% 560–660. SAT Math middle 50% range 550–640. ACT middle 50% range 23-27. Minimum internet-based

TOEFL 75. Minimum paper TOEFL 525. **Basis for Candidate Selection:** *Very important factors considered include:* rigor of secondary school record, class rank, academic GPA, standardized test scores. *Other factors considered include:* application essay, recommendation(s), extracurricular activities, talent/ability, character/personal qualities, first generation, alumni/ae relation, racial/ethnic status, volunteer work, work experience. **Freshman Admission Requirements:** High school diploma is required and GED is not accepted. *Academic units required:* 4 English, 4 math, 3 science, 1 science lab, 2 foreign language, 1 social studies, 1 history. **Freshman Admission Statistics:** 13,202 applied, 68.32% admitted, 35% enrolled. **Transfer Admission Requirements:** High school transcript, college transcript(s), Minimum college GPA of 2.0 required. Lowest grade transferable C. **General Admission Information:** Application fee $55. Priority deadline 11/15. Regular application deadline 3/15. Nonfall registration accepted. Admission may be deferred.

COSTS AND FINANCIAL AID
Annual in-state tuition $4,159. Annual out-of-state tuition $18,675. Room and board $4,340. Required fees $8,100. Average book expense $700. **Required Forms and Deadlines:** FAFSA. **Notification of Awards:** Applicants will be notified of awards on a rolling basis beginning 4/1. **Types of Aid:** *Need-based scholarships/grants:* Federal Pell, FSEOG, State scholarships/grants, Private scholarships, College/university scholarship or grant aid from institutional funds. *Loans:* Direct Subsidized Stafford Loans, Direct Unsubsidized Stafford Loans, Direct PLUS loans, Federal Perkins Loans. *Student Employment:* Federal Work-Study Program available. Institutional employment available. **Financial Aid Statistics:** 67% needy freshmen, 74% needy undergrads receive need-based scholarship or grant aid. 5% freshmen, 3% undergrads receive non-need-based scholarship or grant aid. 77% freshmen, 78% undergrads receive need-based self-help aid. 1% freshmen, 1% undergrads receive athletic scholarships. 69% freshmen, 66% undergrads receive any aid. 56% undergrads borrow to pay for school. Average cumulative indebtedness $22,696. **Criteria for awarding aid:** *Non-need-based:* Academics, Alumni affiliation, Art, Athletics, Job skills, Leadership, Minority status, Music/drama, Religious affiliation, State/district residency.

AQUINAS COLLEGE

1607 Robinson Road SE, Grand Rapids, MI 49506-1799
Phone: 616-632-2900 • **Financial Aid Phone:** 616-632-2893
E-mail: admissions@aquinas.edu • **CEEB Code:** 1018
Fax: 616-732-4469 • **Website:** www.aquinas.edu • **ACT Code:** 1962

This private school was founded in 1886. It has a 107-acre campus.

RATINGS
Admissions Selectivity Rating: 75   **Fire Safety Rating:** 97   **Green Rating:** 91

STUDENTS AND FACULTY
Enrollment: 1,845. **Student Body:** 62% female, 38% male, 6% out-of-state, 1% international (8 countries represented). Asian 1%, African American 3%, Caucasian 85%, Hispanic 5%, Native American <1%, Pacific Islander 0%, Two or more races 2%, Race unknown 3%.
Retention and Graduation: 76% freshmen return for sophomore year. 33% freshmen graduate within 4 years. 17% grads go on to further study within 1 year. 7% grads pursue arts and sciences degrees. 3% grads pursue law degrees. 3% grads pursue business degrees. 2% grads pursue medical degrees. **Faculty:** 86 full-time faculty, 78% hold PhDs, 9% are are members of minority groups, 44% are women.

ACADEMICS
Degrees: associate, bachelor's, master's. **Classes:** Most classes have 20-29 students. **Most popular majors:** Liberal Arts and Sciences/Liberal Studies. **Special Study Options:** Accelerated program, cooperative education program, cross-registration, distance learning, double major, dual enrollment, exchange student program (domestic), honors program, independent study, internships, liberal arts/career combination, student-designed major, study abroad, teacher certification program, Service learning experiences in Peru, Haiti, Mexico. Semester abroad in Costa Rica, France, Germany, Spain,Italy, Japan and Ireland. Domestic exchange in California, Florida and Chicago. **Honors Programs:** Insignis Honors Program. **Disability Services:** Special programs offered to physically disabled students, including note-taking services, reader services, tape recorders, tutors. **Career Services:** Alumni network, Alumni services, Career/job search classes, Career assessment, Internships.

FACILITIES
Housing: Coed dorms, women's dorms, apartments for single students, Theme Housing. 95% of campus accessible to physically diasbled. **Special Academic Facilities/Equipment:** Observatory and Jarecki Center for Advanced Learning featuring high-speed, two-way interactive video conferencing for courses and

a virtual connection for external experts to interact with classes (sound, video, graphics) using a laptop computer equipped with a camera that is housed in a self-contained briefcase. The package includes all the technology needed to accomplish the connection through a standard phone jack. This "virtual faculty briefcase" can be shipped to a guest lecturer at another location anywhere in the world and they are able to conduct an interactive lecture or discussion with an Aquinas classroom. **Computers:** 100% of classrooms, 100% of dorms, 100% of libraries, 100% of dining areas, 100% of student union, 80% of common outdoor areas have wireless network access. Administrative functions (other than registration) can be performed online.

CAMPUS LIFE

Environment: Metropolis. **Activities:** Choral groups, concert band, dance, drama/theater, jazz band, literary magazine, music ensembles, radio station, student government, student newspaper, Campus Ministries, Model UN. 71 registered organizations, 4 honor societies, 2 religious organizations. **Athletics (Intercollegiate):** *Men:* baseball, basketball, cheerleading, cross-country, golf, lacrosse, soccer, tennis, track/field (outdoor), track/field (indoor). *Women:* basketball, cheerleading, cross-country, golf, lacrosse, soccer, softball, tennis, track/field (outdoor), track/field (indoor), volleyball. **On-Campus Highlights:** Physical Education Building, Jarecki Center, Moose Cafe, Wege Student Center, Performing Arts Center, The new, state-of-the-art, Grace Hauenstein Library located in the Jarecki Center opened in August 2006. With ample parking, many meeting rooms, and the latest technology, it is now the most popular meeting place on the campus. **Environmental Initiatives:** Sustainable Business practices restore environmental quality, promote stable and healthy communities, and increase long-term profitability. The Aquinas Sustainable Business Degree program fosters ecological and social intelligence in all business decisions and is the only undergraduate program of its kind in Michigan and possibly the United States. Aquinas also offers a Master of Sustainable Business.

ADMISSIONS

Freshman Academic Profile: Average high school GPA 3.5. 19% in top 10% of high school class, 45% in top 25% of high school class, 77% in top 50% of high school class. 80% from public high schools. ACT middle 50% range 21-26. Minimum paper TOEFL 550. **Basis for Candidate Selection:** *Very important factors considered include:* rigor of secondary school record, academic GPA, standardized test scores. *Other factors considered include:* class rank, application essay, recommendation(s), interview, extracurricular activities, talent/ability, character/personal qualities, first generation, volunteer work, work experience, level of applicant's interest. **Freshman Admission Requirements:** High school diploma is required and GED is not accepted. *Academic units recommended:* 4 English, 4 math, 3 science, 2 foreign language, 3 social studies. **Freshman Admission Statistics:** 1,842 applied, admitted, 21% enrolled. **Transfer Admission Requirements:** High school transcript, college transcript(s), Minimum college GPA of 2.0 required. Lowest grade transferable D. **General Admission Information:** Priority deadline 5/1. Nonfall registration accepted. Admission may be deferred for a maximum of one year.

COSTS AND FINANCIAL AID

Annual tuition $27,332. Room and board $8,350. Required fees $394. Average book expense $800. **Required Forms and Deadlines:** FAFSA. **Notification of Awards:** Applicants will be notified of awards on a rolling basis beginning 3/1. **Types of Aid:** *Need-based scholarships/grants:* Federal Pell, FSEOG, State scholarships/grants, Private scholarships, College/university scholarship or grant aid from institutional funds. *Loans:* Direct Subsidized Stafford Loans, Direct Unsubsidized Stafford Loans, Direct PLUS loans. *Student Employment:* Federal Work-Study Program available. Institutional employment available. **Financial Aid Statistics:** 100% needy freshmen, 100% needy undergrads receive need-based scholarship or grant aid. 74% freshmen, 69% undergrads receive non-need-based scholarship or grant aid. 100% freshmen, 100% undergrads receive need-based self-help aid. 2% freshmen, 6% undergrads receive athletic scholarships. 95% freshmen, 90% undergrads receive any aid. **Criteria for awarding aid:** *Non-need-based:* Academics, Alumni affiliation, Art, Athletics, Leadership, Music/drama.

ARCADIA UNIVERSITY

450 South Easton Road, Glenside, PA 19038
Phone: 215-572-2910 • **Financial Aid Phone:** 215-572-2980
E-mail: admiss@arcadia.edu • **CEEB Code:** 2039
Fax: 215-572-4049 • **Website:** www.arcadia.edu

This private school, affiliated with the Presbyterian Church, was founded in 1853. It has a 60-acre campus.

RATINGS

Admissions Selectivity Rating: 87   **Fire Safety Rating:** 60*   **Green Rating:** 60*

STUDENTS AND FACULTY

Enrollment: 2,151. **Student Body:** 71% female, 29% male, 38% out-of-state, 1% international (28 countries represented). Asian 4%, African American 7%, Caucasian 67%, Hispanic 5%, Native American <1%, Pacific Islander <1%, Two or more races 3%, Race unknown 12%.
Retention and Graduation: 78% freshmen return for sophomore year. 52% freshmen graduate within 4 years. 61% freshmen graduate within 6 years. 28% grads go on to further study within 1 year. 24% grads pursue arts and sciences degrees. 2% grads pursue law degrees. 2% grads pursue business degrees. 2% grads pursue medical degrees. **Faculty:** Student/faculty ratio 11:1. 161 full-time faculty, 0% hold PhDs, 0% are are members of minority groups, 0% are women. 0% of classes are taught by teaching assistants.

ACADEMICS

Degrees: bachelor's, doctoral/professional, master's, postbachelor's certificate, post-master's certificate. **Classes:** Most classes have 10-19 students. Most lab/discussion sessions have 10-19 students. **Most popular majors:** Biology/Biological Sciences; Psychology; English Language and Literature. **Special Study Options:** cooperative education program, cross-registration, double major, exchange student program (domestic), honors program, independent study, internships, liberal arts/career combination, student-designed major, study abroad, teacher certification program, Arcadia also offers programs in Washington DC and a Philadelphia Urban Semester. Undergraduate students may also take gradutate courses. The university also offers evening and some weekend classes. **Honors Programs:** Honors program for invited students Combined degree programs: BA/MA, 4-2 1/2 PT;4+2 PA, 4+2, FS, 7-yr optometry. **Disability Services:** Special programs offered to physically disabled students, including reader services, tape recorders, tutors. **Career Services:** Alumni network, Alumni services, Career/job search classes, Career assessment, Internships.

FACILITIES

Housing: Coed dorms, special housing for disabled students, women's dorms, apartments for single students, Living Learning Communities. 99% of campus accessible to physically diasbled. **Special Academic Facilities/Equipment:** Art gallery, language lab, observatory. **Computers:** Students can register for classes online. Administrative functions (other than registration) can be performed online.

CAMPUS LIFE

Environment: Town. **Activities:** Choral groups, dance, drama/theater, literary magazine, music ensembles, musical theater, radio station, student government, student newspaper, television station, yearbook. 40 registered organizations, 8 honor societies, 3 religious organizations. **Athletics (Intercollegiate):** *Men:* baseball, basketball, cheerleading, golf, soccer, swimming, tennis. *Women:* basketball, cheerleading, field hockey, lacrosse, soccer, softball, swimming, tennis, volleyball. **On-Campus Highlights:** Grey Towers Castle, Kuch Center, The Chat, Walk of Pride, Landman Library.

ADMISSIONS

Freshman Academic Profile: Average high school GPA 3.6. 30% in top 10% of high school class, 62% in top 25% of high school class, 90% in top 50% of high school class. 72% from public high schools. **Reported SAT (pre-2016 redesign) scores:** SAT Math middle 50% range 510-600. SAT Critical Reading middle 50% range 510-600. SAT Writing middle 50% range 500-600. **Concordant SAT scores:** SAT EBRW middle 50% 560–650. SAT Math middle 50% range 540–620. ACT middle 50% range 22-27. Minimum internet-based TOEFL 90. Minimum paper TOEFL 530. **Basis for Candidate Selection:** *Very important factors considered include:* rigor of secondary school record, class rank, academic GPA, standardized test scores, recommendation(s). *Important factors considered include:* application essay, extracurricular activities, alumni/ae relation, level of applicant's interest. *Other factors considered include:* interview, talent/ability, character/personal qualities, volunteer work, work experience. **Freshman Admission Requirements:** High school diploma is required and GED is accepted. *Academic units required:* 4 English, 3 math, 3 science, 2 science labs, 2 foreign language, 4 social studies. **Freshman Admission Statistics:** 7,673 applied, 53.54% admitted, 25% enrolled. **Transfer Admission Requirements:** college transcript(s), essay or personal statement, Minimum college GPA of 2.5 required. Lowest grade transferable C-. **General Admission Information:** Application fee $30. Priority deadline 1/15. Regular application deadline 3/1. Nonfall registration accepted. Admission may be deferred for a maximum of 12 months.

COSTS AND FINANCIAL AID

Annual tuition $33,490. Room and board $11,640. Required fees $660. Average book expense $1,400. **Required Forms and Deadlines:** FAFSA, Institution's own financial aid form. **Notification of Awards:** Applicants will be notified of awards on a rolling basis beginning 2/1. **Types of Aid:** *Need-based scholarships/ grants:* Federal Pell, FSEOG, State scholarships/grants, Private scholarships, College/university scholarship or grant aid from institutional funds. *Loans:* Direct Subsidized Stafford Loans, Direct Unsubsidized Stafford Loans, Direct PLUS loans, Federal Perkins Loans. *Student Employment:* Federal Work-Study Program available. Institutional employment available. **Financial Aid Statistics:** 90% needy freshmen, 99% needy undergrads receive need-based scholarship or grant aid. 12% freshmen, 10% undergrads receive non-need-based scholarship or grant aid. 86% freshmen, 88% undergrads receive need-based self-help aid. 0% freshmen, 0% undergrads receive athletic scholarships. 97% freshmen receive any aid. **Criteria for awarding aid:** *Non-need-based:* Academics, Alumni affiliation, Art, Leadership, Music/drama.

ARIZONA CHRISTIAN UNIVERSITY

2625 East Cactus Road, Phoenix, AZ 85032
Phone: 602-386-4100 • **Financial Aid Phone:** 602-386-4106
E-mail: admissions@arizonachristian.edu
Fax: 602-404-2159 • **Website:** www.arizonachristian.edu

This private school, affiliated with the Baptist Church, was founded in 1960. It has a 17-acre campus.

RATINGS

Admissions Selectivity Rating: 74   **Fire Safety Rating:** 85   **Green Rating:** 60*

STUDENTS AND FACULTY

Enrollment: 292. **Student Body:** 57% female, 43% male, 27% out-of-state, 2% international. Asian 2%, African American 8%, Caucasian 79%, Hispanic 8%, Native American 1%, Pacific Islander 0%, Two or more races 0%, Race unknown <1%. **Retention and Graduation:** 56% freshmen return for sophomore year. 70% freshmen graduate within 4 years. 70% freshmen graduate within 6 years. **Faculty:** Student/faculty ratio 16:1. 13 full-time faculty, 69% hold PhDs, 0% are are members of minority groups, 0% are women.

ACADEMICS

Degrees: associate, bachelor's. **Career Services:** On-campus interviews.

FACILITIES

Housing: men's dorms, women's dorms, apartments for single students.

CAMPUS LIFE

Environment: Village. **Activities:** Choral groups, drama/theater, music ensembles, student government, student newspaper, yearbook. **Athletics (Intercollegiate):** *Men:* basketball. *Women:* basketball, volleyball.

ADMISSIONS

Freshman Academic Profile: 72% from public high schools. **Reported SAT (pre-2016 redesign) scores:** SAT Math middle 50% range 450-560. SAT Critical Reading middle 50% range 460-570. **Concordant SAT scores:** SAT Math middle 50% range 490–580. ACT middle 50% range 19-24. Minimum internet-based TOEFL 61. Minimum paper TOEFL 500. **Basis for Candidate Selection:** *Very important factors considered include:* rigor of secondary school record, academic GPA, standardized test scores, application essay, recommendation(s), religious affiliation/commitment. *Important factors considered include:* class rank, character/personal qualities, level of applicant's interest. *Other factors considered include:* interview, extracurricular activities, talent/ability. **Freshman Admission Requirements:** High school diploma is required and GED is accepted. **Freshman Admission Statistics:** 223 applied, 74.44% admitted, 61% enrolled. **Transfer Admission Requirements:** High school transcript, college transcript(s), essay or personal statement, statement of good standing from prior institution(s). Minimum college GPA of 2.0 required. Lowest grade transferable C. **General Admission Information:** Application fee $30. Priority deadline 3/1. Nonfall registration accepted. Admission may be deferred for a maximum of 1 semester.

COSTS AND FINANCIAL AID

Annual tuition $17,982. Room and board $7,374. Required fees $986. Average book expense $1,600. **Required Forms and Deadlines:** FAFSA, Institution's own financial aid form. **Notification of Awards:** Applicants will be notified of

awards on a rolling basis beginning 5/1. **Types of Aid:** *Need-based scholarships/ grants:* Federal Pell, FSEOG, State scholarships/grants, Private scholarships, College/university scholarship or grant aid from institutional funds. *Loans:* Direct Subsidized Stafford Loans, Direct Unsubsidized Stafford Loans, Direct PLUS loans. *Student Employment:* Federal Work-Study Program available. Institutional employment available. **Financial Aid Statistics:** 0% freshmen, 0% undergrads receive athletic scholarships. **Criteria for awarding aid:** *Need-based:* Minority status. *Non-need-based:* Academics, Alumni affiliation, Athletics, Leadership, Music/drama, Religious affiliation.

ARIZONA STATE UNIVERSITY AT THE DOWNTOWN PHOENIX CAMPUS

Admissions Services, Tempe, AZ 85287-0112
Phone: 480-965-7788 • **Financial Aid Phone:** 480-965-1127
E-mail: admissions@asu.edu
Fax: 480-965-3610 • **Website:** https://campus.asu.edu/downtown/

RATINGS

Admissions Selectivity Rating: 83   **Fire Safety Rating:** 92   **Green Rating:** 98

STUDENTS AND FACULTY

Enrollment: 9,232. **Student Body:** 27% out-of-state, 2% international (35 countries represented). Asian 5%, African American 6%, Caucasian 50%, Hispanic 29%, Native American 2%, Pacific Islander <1%, Two or more races 4%, Race unknown 1%. **Retention and Graduation:** 84% freshmen return for sophomore year. 53% freshmen graduate within 4 years. 67% freshmen graduate within 6 years. 9% grads go on to further study within 1 year. 10% grads pursue arts and sciences degrees.

ACADEMICS

Degrees: bachelor's, certificate, doctoral/research, master's, postbachelor's certificate. **Most popular majors:** Criminal Justice/Law Enforcement Administration; Journalism; Registered Nursing/Registered Nurse. Combined degree programs: BS/MA; BS/MS; BA/MMC; BS/MPA, BS/MAS, BA/MMC. **Career Services:** Alumni network, Alumni services, Career/job search classes, Career assessment, Internships, Regional alumni. Over the last year, Career and Professional Development Services has implemented a revised model of working with Students, Alumni and Employers titled Career Interest Areas. Our team is phasing out the conversation with those we provide career counseling too regarding your major equals X career. Now the conversation aims to connect those to a career interest area which allows them to take into account their personality, abilities, educational experiences and passions and identify an interest area where they feel most they can best contribute their skills. Career Advisors now provide students with tailored counseling conversations around their career interests along with targeted events, workshops and connections to employers. Employers are now able to better identify the kinds of students they would like to recruit by matching their postings to an appropriate interest area. Instead of searching through hundreds of majors they are able to easily choose from the 9 career interest areas. This has allowed Career and Professional Development Services to better design a personalized plan that will leverage the skills and experiences of those we counsel to better achieve their goals.

FACILITIES

Housing: 99% of campus accessible to physically diasbled.

ADMISSIONS

Freshman Academic Profile: Average high school GPA 3.5. 28% in top 10% of high school class, 64% in top 25% of high school class, 93% in top 50% of high school class. **Reported SAT (pre-2016 redesign) scores:** SAT Math middle 50% range 480-590. SAT Critical Reading middle 50% range 480-590. **Concordant SAT scores:** SAT Math middle 50% range 510–610. ACT middle 50% range 21-26. Minimum internet-based TOEFL 61. Minimum paper TOEFL 500. **Basis for Candidate Selection:** *Very important factors considered include:* class rank, academic GPA, standardized test scores. *Important factors considered include:* rigor of secondary school record. *Other factors considered include:* state residency. **Freshman Admission Requirements:** *Academic units required:* 4 English, 4 math, 3 science, 3 science labs, 2 foreign language, 1 social studies, 1 history, and 1 unit from above areas or other academic areas. **Freshman Admission Statistics:** 5,224 applied, 76.70% admitted, 32% enrolled. **General Admission Information:** Application fee $50. Priority deadline 2/1. Nonfall registration accepted.

COSTS AND FINANCIAL AID

Annual in-state tuition $9,684. Annual out-of-state tuition $25,784. Room and board $13,310. Required fees $686. Average book expense $1,103. **Required Forms and Deadlines:** FAFSA. **Notification of Awards:** Applicants will be notified of awards on a rolling basis beginning 3/1. **Types of Aid:** *Need-based scholarships/grants:* Federal Pell, FSEOG, State scholarships/grants, Private scholarships, College/university scholarship or grant aid from institutional funds, United Negro College Fund, Federal Nursing Scholarships. *Loans:* Direct Subsidized Stafford Loans, Direct Unsubsidized Stafford Loans, Direct PLUS loans, Federal Perkins Loans, Federal Nursing Loans, State Loans. *Student Employment:* Federal Work-Study Program available. Institutional employment available. **Financial Aid Statistics:** 97% needy freshmen, 90% needy undergrads receive need-based scholarship or grant aid. 12% freshmen, 6% undergrads receive non-need-based scholarship or grant aid. 59% freshmen, 72% undergrads receive need-based self-help aid. 0% freshmen, 1% undergrads receive athletic scholarships. 972% freshmen, 89% undergrads receive any aid. 61% undergrads borrow to pay for school. Average cumulative indebtedness $25,342. **Criteria for awarding aid:** *Need-based:* Academics. *Non-need-based:* Academics, Athletics, Leadership, State/district residency.

ARIZONA STATE UNIVERSITY AT THE POLYTECHNIC CAMPUS

Admissions Services, Tempe, AZ 85287-0112
Phone: 480-965-7788 • **Financial Aid Phone:** 480-965-1127
E-mail: admissions@asu.edu • **CEEB Code:** 4007
Fax: 480-965-3610 • **Website:** https://campus.asu.edu/polytechnic
ACT Code: 88

RATINGS
Admissions Selectivity Rating: 83 **Fire Safety Rating:** 92 **Green Rating:** 98

STUDENTS AND FACULTY
Enrollment: 3,861. **Student Body:** 22% out-of-state, 8% international (43 countries represented). Asian 6%, African American 4%, Caucasian 55%, Hispanic 20%, Native American 1%, Pacific Islander <1%, Two or more races 4%, Race unknown 1%.
Retention and Graduation: 85% freshmen return for sophomore year. 36% freshmen graduate within 4 years. 61% freshmen graduate within 6 years. 9% grads go on to further study within 1 year. 9% grads pursue arts and sciences degrees. 2% grads pursue business degrees. 2% grads pursue medical degrees.

ACADEMICS
Degrees: bachelor's, certificate, doctoral/research, master's. **Classes:** Most classes have 10-19 students **Most popular majors:** Engineering; Biology/ Biological Sciences; Business, Management, Marketing, and Related Support Services. Combined degree programs: BAS/MSTech, BAE/MA, BS/MSTech (Graphic Info). **Career Services:** Alumni network, Alumni services, Career/ job search classes, Career assessment, Internships, Regional alumni. Over the last year, Career and Professional Development Services has implemented a revised model of working with Students, Alumni and Employers titled Career Interest Areas. Our team is phasing out the conversation with those we provide career counseling too regarding your major equals X career. Now the conversation aims to connect those to a career interest area which allows them to take into account their personality, abilities, educational experiences and passions and identify an interest area where they feel most they can best contribute their skills. Career Advisors now provide students with tailored counseling conversations around their career interests along with targeted events, workshops and connections to employers.' Employers are now able to better identify the kinds of students they would like to recruit by matching their postings to an appropriate interest area. Instead of searching through hundreds of majors they are able to easily choose from the 9 career interest areas.' This has allowed Career and Professional Development Services to better design a personalized plan that will leverage the skills and experiences of those we counsel to better achieve their goals.

FACILITIES
Housing: 99% of campus accessible to physically diasbled.

ADMISSIONS
Freshman Academic Profile: Average high school GPA 3.4. 28% in top 10% of high school class, 59% in top 25% of high school class, 86% in top 50% of high school class. **Reported SAT (pre-2016 redesign) scores:** SAT Math middle 50% range 520-640. SAT Critical Reading middle 50% range 490-610. **Concordant SAT scores:** SAT Math middle 50% range 550–660. ACT middle 50% range 22-28. Minimum internet-based TOEFL 61. Minimum paper TOEFL 500. **Basis for Candidate Selection:** *Very important factors considered include:* class rank, academic GPA, standardized test scores. *Important factors considered include:* rigor of secondary school record. *Other factors considered include:* state residency. **Freshman Admission Requirements:** *Academic units required:* 4 English, 4 math, 3 science, 3

science labs, 2 foreign language, 1 social studies, 1 history, and 1 unit from above areas or other academic areas. **Freshman Admission Statistics:** 1,974 applied, 76.09% admitted, 33% enrolled. **General Admission Information:** Application fee $50. Priority deadline 2/1. Nonfall registration accepted.

COSTS AND FINANCIAL AID
Annual in-state tuition $9,200. Annual out-of-state tuition $24,495. Room and board $11,474. Required fees $686. Average book expense $1,103. **Required Forms and Deadlines:** FAFSA. **Notification of Awards:** Applicants will be notified of awards on a rolling basis beginning 3/1. **Types of Aid:** *Need-based scholarships/grants:* Federal Pell, FSEOG, State scholarships/grants, Private scholarships, College/university scholarship or grant aid from institutional funds, United Negro College Fund. *Loans:* Direct Subsidized Stafford Loans, Direct Unsubsidized Stafford Loans, Direct PLUS loans, Federal Perkins Loans, State Loans. *Student Employment:* Federal Work-Study Program available. Institutional employment available. **Financial Aid Statistics:** 97% needy freshmen, 91% needy undergrads receive need-based scholarship or grant aid. 10% freshmen, 7% undergrads receive non-need-based scholarship or grant aid. 58% freshmen, 74% undergrads receive need-based self-help aid. 0% freshmen, 0% undergrads receive athletic scholarships. 94% freshmen, 86% undergrads receive any aid. 59% undergrads borrow to pay for school. Average cumulative indebtedness $26,925. **Criteria for awarding aid:** *Need-based:* Academics. *Non-need-based:* Academics, Athletics, Leadership, State/district residency.

ARIZONA STATE UNIVERSITY AT THE TEMPE CAMPUS

PO Box 870112, Tempe, AZ 85287-0112
Phone: 480-965-7788 • **Financial Aid Phone:** 480-965-1127
E-mail: admissions@asu.edu • **CEEB Code:** 4007
Fax: 480-965-3610 • **Website:** www.asu.edu • **ACT Code:** 88

This public school was founded in 1885. It has a 1963.73-acre campus.

RATINGS
Admissions Selectivity Rating: 83 **Fire Safety Rating:** 92 **Green Rating:** 98

STUDENTS AND FACULTY
Enrollment: 42,224. **Student Body:** 43% female, 57% male, 26% out-of-state, 13% international (108 countries represented). Asian 7%, African American 4%, Caucasian 51%, Hispanic 20%, Native American 1%, Pacific Islander <1%, Two or more races 4%, Race unknown 1%.
Retention and Graduation: 86% freshmen return for sophomore year. 49% freshmen graduate within 4 years. 67% freshmen graduate within 6 years. 20% grads go on to further study within 1 year. 13% grads pursue arts and sciences degrees. 1% grads pursue law degrees. 2% grads pursue business degrees. 1% grads pursue medical degrees.

ACADEMICS
Degrees: bachelor's, certificate, doctoral/professional, doctoral/research, master's, postbachelor's certifiate, post-master's certificate. **Classes:** Most classes have 10-19 students. Most lab/discussion sessions have 20-29 students. **Most popular majors:** Business, Management, Marketing, and Related Support Services; Biology/Biological Sciences; Psychology. **Special Study Options:** Accelerated program, cooperative education program, distance learning, double major, exchange student program (domestic), honors program, independent study, internships, study abroad, teacher certification program, ASU offers internships in many disciplines, study abroad in 60 countries, work-study programs, accelerated degree programs and a variety of interdisciplinary undergraduate programs. Students may participate in educational programs supported by several institutes and centers. Also available are continuing education programs and a summer programs for high school students. **Honors Programs:** The Honors College at ASU, Barrett, is a selective, residential college that educates academically outstanding undergraduates from across the nation. Students enrolled in Barrett are part of both the honors college community and an ASU disciplinary college of their choice. They may major in any field offered at any one of ASU's four campuses. Honors courses are taught by honors faculty within the college and within a variety of departments and programs. Combined degree programs: BA/MA, BS/MS; BS/M.Acc; BS/M.Tax; BS/MA ; BSP/MUEP, BA/MSTP, BS/PSM, BA/MTESOL, BSE/ PSM, BA/MAE, BS/MSTP, BA/MS. **Disability Services:** Special programs offered to physically disabled students, including note-taking services, reader services, tape recorders, tutors. **Career Services:** Alumni network, Alumni

services, Career/job search classes, Career assessment, Internships, Regional alumni. Over the last year, Career and Professional Development Services has implemented a revised model of working with Students, Alumni and Employers titled Career Interest Areas. Our team is phasing out the conversation with those we provide career counseling too regarding your major equals X career. Now the conversation aims to connect those to a career interest area which allows them to take into account their personality, abilities, educational experiences and passions and identify an interest area where they feel most they can best contribute their skills. Career Advisors now provide students with tailored counseling conversations around their career interests along with targeted events, workshops and connections to employers. Employers are now able to better identify the kinds of students they would like to recruit by matching their postings to an appropriate interest area. Instead of searching through hundreds of majors they are able to easily choose from the 9 career interest areas. This has allowed Career and Professional Development Services to better design a personalized plan that will leverage the skills and experiences of those we counsel to better achieve their goals.

FACILITIES

Housing: Coed dorms, fraternity/sorority housing, apartments for married students, apartments for single students, Freshmen Housing. Please visit—http://www.asu.edu/housing. 99% of campus accessible to physically diasbled. **Special Academic Facilities/Equipment:** Art, anthropology, geology, history, and sports museums, early childhood development lab, herbarium, robotics lab, semiconductor clean room, high-resolution electron microscope facility, gamma cell irradiation chamber, solar research facilities, nuclear reactor, biodesign institute, thermal emission imaging system, melikian center, KAET (public television station), KASR 1260 AM, Phoenix urban research laboratory, Arizona biomedical collaborative, altitude chamber, simulator building, planetarium **Computers:** 100% of classrooms, 100% of dorms, 100% of libraries, 100% of dining areas, 100% of student union, 70% of common outdoor areas have wireless network access. Students can register for classes online. Administrative functions (other than registration) can be performed online.

CAMPUS LIFE

Environment: Metropolis. **Activities:** Choral groups, concert band, dance, drama/theater, jazz band, literary magazine, marching band, music ensembles, musical theater, opera, pep band, radio station, student government, student newspaper, student-run film society, symphony orchestra, television station, Campus Ministries, Student Organization, Model UN. 675 registered organizations, 16 honor societies, 51 religious organizations. 32 fraternities, 22 sororities. **Athletics (Intercollegiate):** *Men:* baseball, basketball, cross-country, diving, football, golf, swimming, track/field (outdoor), wrestling. *Women:* basketball, cross-country, diving, golf, gymnastics, soccer, softball, swimming, tennis, track/field (outdoor), volleyball, water polo. **On-Campus Highlights:** ASU Memorial Union—Tempe campus, Grady Gammage Auditorium—Tempe campus, Barrett Honors Complex—Tempe campus, Fletcher Library—West campus, Union—Polytechnic campus, Hayden Library—Tempe campus, Walter Cronkite School of Journalism and Mass Communication—Downtown Phoenix campus, Academic Complex—Polytechnic campus, Las Casas Residence Hall—West campus, Taylor Place—Downtown Phoenix campus.

ADMISSIONS

Freshman Academic Profile: Average high school GPA 3.5. 30% in top 10% of high school class, 60% in top 25% of high school class, 88% in top 50% of high school class. **Reported SAT (pre-2016 redesign) scores:** SAT Math middle 50% range 520-650. SAT Critical Reading middle 50% range 500-630. **Concordant SAT scores:** SAT Math middle 50% range 550–670. ACT middle 50% range 22-28. Minimum internet-based TOEFL 61. Minimum paper TOEFL 500. **Basis for Candidate Selection:** *Very important factors considered include:* class rank, academic GPA, standardized test scores. *Important factors considered include:* rigor of secondary school record. *Other factors considered include:* state residency. **Freshman Admission Requirements:** High school diploma is required and GED is accepted. *Academic units required:* 4 English, 4 math, 3 science, 3 science labs, 2 foreign language, 1 social studies, 1 history, and 1 unit from above areas or other academic areas. **Freshman Admission Statistics:** 24,764 applied, 82.50% admitted, 40% enrolled. **Transfer Admission Requirements:** college transcript(s), standardized test scores, Minimum college GPA of 2.0 required. Lowest grade transferable C. **General Admission Information:** Application fee $50. Priority deadline 2/1. Nonfall registration accepted.

COSTS AND FINANCIAL AID

Annual in-state tuition $9,684. Annual out-of-state tuition $25,784. Room and board $11,386. Required fees $686. Average book expense $1,103. **Required Forms and Deadlines:** FAFSA. **Notification of Awards:** Applicants will be notified of awards on a rolling basis beginning 3/1. **Types of Aid:** *Need-based scholarships/grants:* Federal Pell, FSEOG, State scholarships/grants, Private scholarships, College/university scholarship or grant aid from institutional funds, United Negro College Fund. *Loans:* Direct Subsidized Stafford Loans, Direct Unsubsidized Stafford Loans, Direct PLUS loans, Federal Perkins Loans, State Loans. *Student Employment:* Federal Work-Study Program available. Institutional employment available. **Financial Aid Statistics:** 99%

needy freshmen, 93% needy undergrads receive need-based scholarship or grant aid. 13% freshmen, 9% undergrads receive non-need-based scholarship or grant aid. 56% freshmen, 68% undergrads receive need-based self-help aid. 1% freshmen, 1% undergrads receive athletic scholarships. 90% freshmen, 83% undergrads receive any aid. 49% undergrads borrow to pay for school. Average cumulative indebtedness $22,903. **Criteria for awarding aid:** *Need-based:* Academics. *Non-need-based:* Academics, Art, Athletics, Leadership, Music/drama, State/district residency.

ARIZONA STATE UNIVERSITY AT THE WEST CAMPUS

Admissions Services, Tempe, AZ 85287-0112
Phone: 480-965-7788 • **Financial Aid Phone:** 480-965-1127
E-mail: admissions@asu.edu • **CEEB Code:** 4007
Fax: 480-965-3610 • **Website:** https://campus.asu.edu/west • **ACT Code:** 880

RATINGS

Admissions Selectivity Rating: 83   **Fire Safety Rating:** 92   **Green Rating:** 98

STUDENTS AND FACULTY

Enrollment: 3,201. **Student Body:** 15% out-of-state, 4% international (22 countries represented). Asian 5%, African American 6%, Caucasian 47%, Hispanic 31%, Native American 1%, Pacific Islander <1%, Two or more races 4%, Race unknown 1%.
Retention and Graduation: 87% freshmen return for sophomore year. 45% freshmen graduate within 4 years. 66% freshmen graduate within 6 years. 20% grads go on to further study within 1 year. 3% grads pursue arts and sciences degrees. 2% grads pursue law degrees. 3% grads pursue business degrees. 3% grads pursue medical degrees.

ACADEMICS

Degrees: bachelor's, certificate, doctoral/research, master's, postbachelor's certificate. **Most popular majors:** Psychology; Business, Management, Marketing, and Related Support Services; Speech Communication and Rhetoric. Combined degree programs: BA/MA, BS/MA, BS/MTax, BAS/MA, BAE/MA. **Career Services:** Alumni network, Alumni services, Career/job search classes, Career assessment, Internships, Regional alumni. Over the last year, Career and Professional Development Services has implemented a revised model of working with Students, Alumni and Employers titled Career Interest Areas. Our team is phasing out the conversation with those we provide career counseling too regarding your major equals X career. Now the conversation aims to connect those to a career interest area which allows them to take into account their personality, abilities, educational experiences and passions and identify an interest area where they feel most they can best contribute their skills. Career Advisors now provide students with tailored counseling conversations around their career interests along with targeted events, workshops and connections to employers. Employers are now able to better identify the kinds of students they would like to recruit by matching their postings to an appropriate interest area. Instead of searching through hundreds of majors they are able to easily choose from the 9 career interest areas. This has allowed Career and Professional Development Services to better design a personalized plan that will leverage the skills and experiences of those we counsel to better achieve their goals.

FACILITIES

Housing: 99% of campus accessible to physically diasbled.

ADMISSIONS

Freshman Academic Profile: Average high school GPA 3.5. 33% in top 10% of high school class, 67% in top 25% of high school class, 95% in top 50% of high school class. **Reported SAT (pre-2016 redesign) scores:** SAT Math middle 50% range 480-580. SAT Critical Reading middle 50% range 480-590. **Concordant SAT scores:** SAT Math middle 50% range 510–600. ACT middle 50% range 21-26. Minimum internet-based TOEFL 61. Minimum paper TOEFL 500. **Basis for Candidate Selection:** *Very important factors considered include:* class rank, academic GPA, standardized test scores. *Important factors considered include:* rigor of secondary school record. *Other factors considered include:* state residency. **Freshman Admission Requirements:** *Academic units required:* 4 English, 4 math, 3 science, 3 science labs, 2 foreign language, 1 social studies, 1 history, and 1 unit from above areas or other academic areas. **Freshman Admission Statistics:** 1,504 applied, 77.86% admitted, 33% enrolled. **General Admission Information:** Application fee $50. Priority deadline 2/1. Nonfall registration accepted.

COSTS AND FINANCIAL AID

Annual in-state tuition $9,200. Annual out-of-state tuition $24,495. Room and board $10,754. Required fees $686. Average book expense $1,103. **Required Forms and Deadlines:** FAFSA. **Notification of Awards:** Applicants will be notified of awards on a rolling basis beginning 3/1. **Types of Aid:** *Need-based scholarships/grants:* Federal Pell, FSEOG, State scholarships/grants, Private scholarships, College/university scholarship or grant aid from institutional funds, United Negro College Fund. *Loans:* Direct Subsidized Stafford Loans, Direct Unsubsidized Stafford Loans, Direct PLUS loans, Federal Perkins Loans, State Loans. *Student Employment:* Federal Work-Study Program available. Institutional employment available. **Financial Aid Statistics:** 96% needy freshmen, 92% needy undergrads receive need-based scholarship or grant aid. 5% undergrads receive non-need-based scholarship or grant aid. 72% undergrads receive need-based self-help aid. 0% freshmen, 0% undergrads receive athletic scholarships. 94% freshmen, 88% undergrads receive any aid. 56% undergrads borrow to pay for school. Average cumulative indebtedness $22,251. **Criteria for awarding aid:** *Need-based:* Academics. *Non-need-based:* Academics, Athletics, Leadership, State/district residency.

ARKANSAS STATE UNIVERSITY

PO Box 1570, State University, AR 72467
Phone: 870-972-3024 • **Financial Aid Phone:** 870-972-2310
E-mail: admissions@astate.edu • **CEEB Code:** 6011
Fax: 870-972-3406 • **Website:** www.astate.edu • **ACT Code:** 116

This public school was founded in 1909. It has a 941-acre campus.

RATINGS
Admissions Selectivity Rating: 83   **Fire Safety Rating:** 90   **Green Rating:** 60*

STUDENTS AND FACULTY
Enrollment: 8,909. **Student Body:** 57% female, 43% male, 11% out-of-state, 6% international (50 countries represented). Asian 1%, African American 14%, Caucasian 74%, Hispanic 2%, Native American <1%, Pacific Islander <1%, Two or more races 2%, Race unknown 1%.
Retention and Graduation: 76% freshmen return for sophomore year. 21% freshmen graduate within 4 years. 39% freshmen graduate within 6 years. 22% grads go on to further study within 1 year. 15% grads pursue arts and sciences degrees. 1% grads pursue law degrees. 20% grads pursue business degrees. 24% grads pursue medical degrees. **Faculty:** Student/faculty ratio 17:1. 505 full-time faculty, 69% hold PhDs, 16% are are members of minority groups, 53% are women. 4% of classes are taught by teaching assistants.

ACADEMICS
Degrees: associate, bachelor's, doctoral/professional, doctoral/research, master's, postbachelor's certificate, post-master's certificate. **Classes:** Most classes have 20-29 students. Most lab/discussion sessions have fewer than 10 students. **Most popular majors:** General Studies; Registered Nursing/ Registered Nurse; Early Childhood Education and Teaching. **Special Study Options:** Accelerated program, cooperative education program, distance learning, double major, dual enrollment, English as a Second Language (ESL), exchange student program (domestic), honors program, independent study, internships, study abroad, teacher certification program. **Disability Services:** Special programs offered to physically disabled students, including note-taking services, reader services, tape recorders, tutors. **Career Services:** Alumni services, Career/job search classes, Career assessment, Internships.

FACILITIES
Housing: men's dorms, women's dorms, fraternity/sorority housing, apartments for married students, apartments for single students, Married and graduate student housing. 90% of campus accessible to physically diasbled. **Special Academic Facilities/Equipment:** Art gallery, museum of Native American cultures and Arkansas artifacts. Ecotoxicology research facility, electron microscope facility, geographic information system facility. Equine center. **Computers:** Students can register for classes online. Administrative functions (other than registration) can be performed online.

CAMPUS LIFE
Environment: Town. **Activities:** Choral groups, concert band, dance, drama/ theater, jazz band, marching band, music ensembles, musical theater, opera, pep band, radio station, student government, student newspaper, symphony orchestra, television station, yearbook. 192 registered organizations, 42 honor societies, 16 religious organizations. 12 fraternities, 9 sororities. **Athletics (Intercollegiate):** *Men:* baseball, basketball, cross-country, football, golf, track/field (outdoor), track/field (indoor). *Women:* basketball, cross-country, golf, soccer, tennis, track/field (outdoor), track/field (indoor), volleyball. **On-Campus Highlights:** New Student Union, Fowler Center for Performing Arts, ASU Convocation Center, Outdoor theatre, ASU Museum. **Environmental Initiatives:** Recycling.

ADMISSIONS
Freshman Academic Profile: Average high school GPA 3.5. 27% in top 10% of high school class, 49% in top 25% of high school class, 74% in top 50%

of high school class. 93% from public high schools. **Reported SAT (pre-2016 redesign) scores:** SAT Math middle 50% range 470-540. SAT Critical Reading middle 50% range 400-540. SAT Writing middle 50% range 420-480. **Concordant SAT scores:** SAT EBRW middle 50% 460–570. SAT Math middle 50% range 510–570. ACT middle 50% range 21-26. Minimum internet-based TOEFL 61. Minimum paper TOEFL 500. **Basis for Candidate Selection:** *Very important factors considered include:* rigor of secondary school record, standardized test scores. *Important factors considered include:* class rank. *Other factors considered include:* recommendation(s), talent/ability. **Freshman Admission Requirements:** High school diploma is required and GED is accepted. *Academic units required:* 4 English, 4 math, 3 science, 3 science labs, 1 social studies, 2 history. *Academic units recommended:* 2 foreign language. **Freshman Admission Statistics:** 5,346 applied, 70.24% admitted, 42% enrolled. **Transfer Admission Requirements:** college transcript(s), Minimum college GPA of 2.0 required. Lowest grade transferable C. **General Admission Information:** Application fee $15. Regular application deadline 8/24. Nonfall registration accepted. Admission may be deferred.

COSTS AND FINANCIAL AID
Annual in-state tuition $6,060. Annual out-of-state tuition $12,120. Room and board $8,540. Required fees $2,140. Average book expense $1,000. **Required Forms and Deadlines:** FAFSA, Institution's own financial aid form. **Notification of Awards:** Applicants will be notified of awards on a rolling basis beginning 6/1. **Types of Aid:** *Need-based scholarships/grants:* Federal Pell, FSEOG, State scholarships/grants, Private scholarships, College/university scholarship or grant aid from institutional funds. *Loans:* Direct Subsidized Stafford Loans, Direct Unsubsidized Stafford Loans, Direct PLUS loans, Federal Perkins Loans. *Student Employment:* Federal Work-Study Program available. Institutional employment available. **Financial Aid Statistics:** 98% needy freshmen, 96% needy undergrads receive need-based scholarship or grant aid. 46% undergrads, 55% undergrads receive non-need-based scholarship or grant aid. 53% freshmen, 65% undergrads receive need-based self-help aid. 5% freshmen, 4% undergrads receive athletic scholarships. 92% freshmen, 79% undergrads receive any aid. 67% undergrads borrow to pay for school. Average cumulative indebtedness $27,400. **Criteria for awarding aid:** *Need-based:* Academics. *Non-need-based:* Academics, Alumni affiliation, Art, Athletics, Leadership, Minority status, Music/drama, State/district residency.

See page 908.

ARKANSAS TECH UNIVERSITY

Doc Bryan; 1605 Coliseum Dr, Russellville, AR 72801
Phone: 479-968-0343 • **Financial Aid Phone:** 479-968-0399
E-mail: tech.enroll@atu.edu • **CEEB Code:** 6010
Fax: 479-964-0522 • **Website:** http://www.atu.edu/ • **ACT Code:** 114

This public school was founded in 1909. It has a 541-acre campus.

RATINGS
Admissions Selectivity Rating: 75   **Fire Safety Rating:** 91   **Green Rating:** 60*

STUDENTS AND FACULTY
Enrollment: 8,799. **Student Body:** 55% female, 45% male, 4% out-of-state, 4% international (36 countries represented). Asian 1%, African American 10%, Caucasian 76%, Hispanic 6%, Native American 1%, Pacific Islander <1%, Two or more races 3%, Race unknown 0%.
Retention and Graduation: 71% freshmen return for sophomore year. 28% freshmen graduate within 4 years. 47% freshmen graduate within 6 years. **Faculty:** Student/faculty ratio 19:1. 349 full-time faculty, 62% hold PhDs, 9% are are members of minority groups, 50% are women. 1% of classes are taught by teaching assistants.

ACADEMICS
Degrees: associate, bachelor's, certificate, master's, post-master's certificate, terminal. **Classes:** Most classes have 20-29 students. Most lab/discussion sessions have 10-19 students. **Special Study Options:** distance learning, double major, dual enrollment, English as a Second Language (ESL), honors program, independent study, internships, study abroad, teacher certification program. **Disability Services:** Special programs offered to physically disabled students, including note-taking services, reader services, tape recorders, tutors. **Career Services:** Career/job search classes, Career assessment, Internships.

FACILITIES
Housing: Coed dorms, special housing for disabled students, men's dorms, women's dorms, fraternity/sorority housing, apartments for single students. 100% of campus accessible to physically diasbled. **Special Academic Facilities/Equipment:** 1. Arkansas Center for Energy, Natural Resources, and Environmental Studies. 2. Crabaugh Communications Center. 3. Museum of Prehistory and History. 4. Technology Center. **Computers:** Students can

register for classes online. Administrative functions (other than registration) can be performed online.

CAMPUS LIFE
Environment: Town. **Activities:** Choral groups, concert band, dance, drama/theater, jazz band, literary magazine, marching band, music ensembles, musical theater, pep band, radio station, student government, student newspaper, television station, Campus Ministries, Student Organization. 130 registered organizations, 14 honor societies, 13 religious organizations. 6 fraternities, 4 sororities. **Athletics (Intercollegiate):** *Men:* baseball, basketball, cheerleading, football, golf. *Women:* basketball, cheerleading, cross-country, golf, softball, tennis, volleyball. **On-Campus Highlights:** Ross Pendergraft Library and Technology Center, Tech Fit, Doc's Place, Summit Hall, Tucker Coliseum.

ADMISSIONS
Freshman Academic Profile: Average high school GPA 3.2. 13% in top 10% of high school class, 34% in top 25% of high school class, 65% in top 50% of high school class. **Reported SAT (pre-2016 redesign) scores:** SAT Math middle 50% range 440-590. SAT Critical Reading middle 50% range 440-530. **Concordant SAT scores:** SAT Math middle 50% range 480–610. ACT middle 50% range 18-25. Minimum internet-based TOEFL 61. Minimum paper TOEFL 500. **Basis for Candidate Selection:** *Very important factors considered include:* academic GPA, standardized test scores. *Important factors considered include:* rigor of secondary school record. *Other factors considered include:* class rank. **Freshman Admission Requirements:** High school diploma is required and GED is accepted. *Academic units required:* 4 English, 4 math, 3 science, 3 science labs, 2 foreign language, 3 social studies, 1 history, and 2 units from above areas or other academic areas. **Freshman Admission Statistics:** 4,619 applied, 89.11% admitted, 49% enrolled. **Transfer Admission Requirements:** college transcript(s), Minimum college GPA of 2.0 required. Lowest grade transferable D. **General Admission Information:** Nonfall registration accepted. Admission may be deferred for a maximum of 1 semester.

COSTS AND FINANCIAL AID
Annual in-state tuition $6,450. Annual out-of-state tuition $12,900. Room and board $7,098. Required fees $1,290. Average book expense $1,410. **Required Forms and Deadlines:** FAFSA, Institution's own financial aid form. **Notification of Awards:** Applicants will be notified of awards on a rolling basis beginning 3/15. **Types of Aid:** *Need-based scholarships/grants:* Federal Pell, FSEOG, State scholarships/grants, Private scholarships. *Loans:* Direct Subsidized Stafford Loans, Direct Unsubsidized Stafford Loans, Direct PLUS loans, Federal Perkins Loans. *Student Employment:* Federal Work-Study Program available. Institutional employment available. **Financial Aid Statistics:** 84% needy freshmen, 82% needy undergrads receive need-based scholarship or grant aid. 71% freshmen, 49% undergrads receive non-need-based scholarship or grant aid. 63% freshmen, 70% undergrads receive need-based self-help aid. 4% freshmen, 3% undergrads receive athletic scholarships. **Criteria for awarding aid:** *Non-need-based:* Academics, Athletics, Leadership, Music/drama, State/district residency.

ARLINGTON BAPTIST COLLEGE

Admissions Office, Arlington, TX 76012
Phone: 817-461-8741 • **Financial Aid Phone:** 817-461-8741, ext 110
E-mail: jtaylor@arlingtonbaptistcollege.edu
Fax: 817-274-1138 • **Website:** www.arlingtonbaptistcollege.edu • **ACT Code:** 4163

This private school, affiliated with the Baptist Church, was founded in 1939. It has a 35-acre campus.

RATINGS
Admissions Selectivity Rating: 64   **Fire Safety Rating:** 94   **Green Rating:** 60*

STUDENTS AND FACULTY
Enrollment: 220. **Student Body:** 45% female, 55% male, 17% out-of-state, 1% international (1 countries represented). Asian 0%, African American 18%, Caucasian 71%, Hispanic 8%, Native American 2%, Pacific Islander 0%, Two or more races 0%, Race unknown 0%. **Retention and Graduation:** 51% freshmen return for sophomore year. 19% freshmen graduate within 4 years. 41% freshmen graduate within 6 years. 15% grads go on to further study within 1 year. **Faculty:** Student/faculty ratio 16:1. 12 full-time faculty, 17% hold PhDs, 0% are are members of minority groups, 25% are women.

ACADEMICS
Degrees: bachelor's, certificate, diploma, master's. **Classes:** Most classes have fewer than 10 students. Most lab/discussion sessions have 10-19 students. **Most popular majors:** Religious Education; Theological and Ministerial Studies; Pastoral Studies/Counseling. **Special Study Options:** distance learning, double major, dual enrollment, external degree program, teacher certification program.

FACILITIES
Housing: men's dorms, women's dorms, Wellness Housing. **Special Academic Facilities/Equipment:** Heritage Collection **Computers:** 100% of classrooms, 100% of dorms, 100% of libraries, have wireless network access.

CAMPUS LIFE
Environment: Metropolis. **Activities:** Choral groups, student government, yearbook, Campus Ministries. 5 religious organizations. **Athletics (Intercollegiate):** *Men:* baseball, basketball. *Women:* basketball, cheerleading, volleyball. **On-Campus Highlights:** Student Union Building, Library, Heritage Collection

ADMISSIONS
Freshman Academic Profile: Average high school GPA 2.9. 2% in top 10% of high school class, 21% in top 25% of high school class, 47% in top 50% of high school class. 80% from public high schools. Minimum paper TOEFL 550. **Basis for Candidate Selection:** *Very important factors considered include:* application essay, recommendation(s), religious affiliation/commitment. *Important factors considered include:* interview, level of applicant's interest. *Other factors considered include:* character/personal qualities. **Freshman Admission Requirements:** High school diploma is required and GED is accepted. *Academic units required:* 3 English, 2 math, 1 science, 2 social studies. **Freshman Admission Statistics:** 86 applied, 100.00% admitted, 63% enrolled. **Transfer Admission Requirements:** High school transcript, college transcript(s), essay or personal statement, Lowest grade transferable C. **General Admission Information:** Application fee $15. Priority deadline 8/1. Nonfall registration accepted. Admission may be deferred.

COSTS AND FINANCIAL AID
Annual tuition $7,100. Room and board $4,800. Required fees $740. Average book expense $750. **Required Forms and Deadlines:** FAFSA. **Notification of Awards:** Applicants will be notified of awards on a rolling basis beginning 12/1. **Types of Aid:** *Need-based scholarships/grants:* Federal Pell, Private scholarships, College/university scholarship or grant aid from institutional funds. *Loans:* Direct Subsidized Stafford Loans, Direct Unsubsidized Stafford Loans, Direct PLUS loans. *Student Employment:* Institutional employment available. **Financial Aid Statistics:** 100% needy freshmen, 100% needy undergrads receive need-based scholarship or grant aid. 0% undergrads receive non-need-based scholarship or grant aid. 0% freshmen, 0% undergrads receive need-based self-help aid. 0% freshmen, 0% undergrads receive athletic scholarships. 80% freshmen, 80% undergrads receive any aid. **Criteria for awarding aid:** *Need-based:* Academics, Alumni affiliation, Leadership, Religious affiliation. *Non-need-based:* Academics, Leadership, Religious affiliation.

ART ACADEMY OF CINCINNATI

1212 Jackson Street, Cincinnati, OH 45202
Phone: 513-562-8740 • **Financial Aid Phone:** 513-562-8751
E-mail: admissions@artacademy.edu
Fax: 513-562-8778 • **Website:** www.artacademy.edu • **ACT Code:** 3011

This private school was founded in 1887.

RATINGS
Admissions Selectivity Rating: 75   **Fire Safety Rating:** 60*   **Green Rating:** 60*

STUDENTS AND FACULTY
Enrollment: 159. **Student Body:** 64% female, 36% male, 1% international (2 countries represented). Asian 1%, African American 4%, Caucasian 90%, Hispanic 1%, Native American 0%, Pacific Islander 0%, Two or more races 0%, Race unknown 2%.
Faculty: Student/faculty ratio 6:1. 14 full-time faculty, 100% hold PhDs, 7% are are members of minority groups, 57% are women. 0% of classes are taught by teaching assistants.

ACADEMICS
Degrees: associate, bachelor's, master's. **Most popular majors:** Graphic Design; Illustration; Painting. **Special Study Options:** cooperative education program, cross-registration, double major, internships. **Disability Services:** Special programs offered to physically disabled students, including note-taking services, tape recorders, tutors. **Career Services:** On-campus interviews.

FACILITIES
Housing: Coed dorms.

CAMPUS LIFE
Environment: Metropolis. **Activities:** literary magazine, student government, student-run film society, yearbook. **On-Campus Highlights:** New Building, Dorms, Student Studios, Student Commons, Three Art Galleries. **Environmental Initiatives:** Received Leadership in Energy and

Environmental Design (LEED) Green Building certification by the United States Green Building Council.

ADMISSIONS

Reported SAT (pre-2016 redesign) scores: SAT Math middle 50% range 420-570. SAT Critical Reading middle 50% range 480-600. **Concordant SAT scores:** SAT Math middle 50% range 460–590. ACT middle 50% range 18-24. Minimum internet-based TOEFL 80. Minimum paper TOEFL 550. **Basis for Candidate Selection:** *Very important factors considered include:* rigor of secondary school record, interview, talent/ability. *Important factors considered include:* academic GPA, application essay. *Other factors considered include:* standardized test scores, recommendation(s), extracurricular activities, character/personal qualities. **Freshman Admission Requirements:** High school diploma is required and GED is accepted. *Academic units recommended:* 4 English, 3 math, 2 science, 1 social studies. **Freshman Admission Statistics:** 192 applied, 56.77% admitted, 45% enrolled. **Transfer Admission Requirements:** High school transcript, college transcript(s), essay or personal statement, interview, Minimum college GPA of 2.0 required. Lowest grade transferable C. **General Admission Information:** Priority deadline 3/1. Regular application deadline 6/30. Nonfall registration accepted. Admission may be deferred for a maximum of one year.

COSTS AND FINANCIAL AID

Annual tuition $21,500. Required fees $380. Average book expense $1,200. **Required Forms and Deadlines:** FAFSA, State aid form. **Notification of Awards:** Applicants will be notified of awards on a rolling basis beginning 3/1. **Types of Aid:** *Need-based scholarships/grants:* Federal Pell, FSEOG, State scholarships/grants, Private scholarships, College/university scholarship or grant aid from institutional funds. *Loans:* Direct Subsidized Stafford Loans, Direct Unsubsidized Stafford Loans, Direct PLUS loans, Federal Perkins Loans. *Student Employment:* Federal Work-Study Program available. Institutional employment available. **Financial Aid Statistics:** 95% undergrads receive any aid. **Criteria for awarding aid:** *Non-need-based:* Academics, Art.

ART CENTER COLLEGE OF DESIGN

1700 Lida Street, Pasadena, CA 91103-1999
Phone: 626-396-2373 • **Financial Aid Phone:** 626-396-2215
E-mail: admissions@artcenter.edu • **CEEB Code:** 4009
Fax: 626-795-0578 • **Website:** www.artcenter.edu • **ACT Code:** 164

This private school was founded in 1930. It has a 175-acre campus.

RATINGS

Admissions Selectivity Rating: 60*   **Fire Safety Rating:** 60*   **Green Rating:** 87

STUDENTS AND FACULTY

Enrollment: 1,890. **Student Body:** 50% female, 50% male, 27% international (43 countries represented). Asian 36%, African American 1%, Caucasian 18%, Hispanic 12%, Native American <1%, Pacific Islander <1%, Two or more races 4%, Race unknown 1%.
Retention and Graduation: 76% freshmen return for sophomore year. 68% freshmen graduate within 6 years. **Faculty:** Student/faculty ratio 9 are women. 0% of classes are taught by teaching assistants.

ACADEMICS

Degrees: bachelor's, master's. **Classes:** Most classes have 10-19 students. **Most popular majors:** Engineering; Graphic Design; Illustration. **Special Study Options:** cooperative education program, independent study, internships. **Disability Services:** Special programs offered to physically disabled students, including note-taking services, tape recorders, tutors. **Career Services:** Alumni network, Alumni services, Career/job search classes, Career assessment, Internships, Regional alumni. The internship program and on-campus recruiting connects students with creative professionals. The Office of Career and Professional Development at Art Center has an extensive list of corporate and community partners in order to assist our students with their career aspirations.

FACILITIES

Housing: 98% of campus accessible to physically diasbled. **Special Academic Facilities/Equipment:** 2 art galleries. **Computers:** Administrative functions (other than registration) can be performed online.

CAMPUS LIFE

Environment: City. **Activities:** student government 12 registered organizations. **On-Campus Highlights:** Student Gallery **Environmental Initiatives:** Replaced all non-recyclable disposables in cafeteria with compostable items and established recycling area in cafeteria.

ADMISSIONS

Minimum internet-based TOEFL 80. **Basis for Candidate Selection:** *Very important factors considered include:* rigor of secondary school record, application essay, talent/ability. *Important factors considered include:* class rank, academic GPA, standardized test scores, character/personal qualities. *Other factors considered include:* recommendation(s), extracurricular activities, first generation, geographical residence, volunteer work, work experience. **Freshman Admission Requirements:** High school diploma is required and GED is accepted. **Transfer Admission Requirements:** college transcript(s), essay or personal statement, Lowest grade transferable c. **General Admission Information:** Application fee $50. Priority deadline 2/15. Nonfall registration accepted. Admission may be deferred for a maximum of 1 term.

COSTS AND FINANCIAL AID

Annual tuition $40,046. Required fees $550. **Required Forms and Deadlines:** FAFSA. **Types of Aid:** *Need-based scholarships/grants:* Federal Pell, FSEOG, State scholarships/grants, Private scholarships, College/university scholarship or grant aid from institutional funds. *Loans:* Direct Subsidized Stafford Loans, Direct Unsubsidized Stafford Loans, Direct PLUS loans, Federal Perkins Loans, College/university loans from institutional funds. *Student Employment:* Federal Work-Study Program available. Institutional employment available. **Criteria for awarding aid:** *Need-based:* Art. *Non-need-based:* Art.

THE ART INSTITUTE OF ATLANTA

6600 Peachtree Dunwoody Road, Atlanta, GA 30328
Phone: 770-394-8300 • **Financial Aid Phone:** 770-689-4824
E-mail: aia-admis@aii.edu
Fax: 770-394-0008 • **Website:** http://www.artinstitutes.edu/atlanta/
ACT Code: 859

This proprietary school was founded in 1949. It has a 7-acre campus.

RATINGS

Admissions Selectivity Rating: 60*   **Fire Safety Rating:** 60*   **Green Rating:** 60*

STUDENTS AND FACULTY

Enrollment: 2,413. **Student Body:** 44% female, 56% male, <1% international (33 countries represented). Asian 1%, African American 36%, Caucasian 30%, Hispanic 3%, Native American <1%, Pacific Islander 0%, Two or more races 0%, Race unknown 30%.
Faculty: Student/faculty ratio 21:1. 131 full-time faculty, 48% hold PhDs, 21% are are members of minority groups, 45% are women.

ACADEMICS

Degrees: associate, bachelor's, certificate, diploma. **Classes:** Most classes have 10-19 students. **Most popular majors:** Culinary Arts/Chef Training; Commercial and Advertising Art; Interior Design. **Special Study Options:** Accelerated program, distance learning, dual enrollment, honors program, independent study, internships, study abroad, weekend college. **Honors Programs:** Design Honors Studio for graphic design students: students work with clients in the community. **Disability Services:** Special programs offered to physically disabled students, including note-taking services, reader services, tape recorders, tutors. **Career Services:** Alumni network, Alumni services, Career/job search classes, Internships.

FACILITIES

Housing: Coed dorms. 100% of campus accessible to physically diasbled. **Special Academic Facilities/Equipment:** Art gallery, multi-camera video studio with digital and non-linear video editing suites, and an audio studio and control room featuring Protools stations. Professional photography studios with traditional and digital darkroom facilities containing high-end professional equipment such as the Imacon scanner, Cone Piezograph BandW printers, Epson 5500 printer, and Epson 10000 printer. Photographic video editing stations consist of Dual Processor G4s with cinema displays that are color managed with Greytag MacBeth equipment. Culinary facilities with five teaching kitchens and a dining lab. **Computers:** Students can register for classes online.

CAMPUS LIFE

Environment: Metropolis. **Activities:** student government, Student Organization. 16 registered organizations. **On-Campus Highlights:** Gallery, Supply Store, Coffee Bar, Snack Bar, Creations Dining Lab, Entertainers perform in the coffee bar and reduced-price tickets are often available for events in Atlanta. The student affairs department also coordinates college community service programs and quarterly blood drives. Besides being enjoyable, student activities provide opportunities for making new friends and trying new experiences, as well as offering a great way to gain leadership experience.

ADMISSIONS

Freshman Academic Profile: 97% from public high schools. Minimum paper TOEFL 550. **Basis for Candidate Selection:** *Very important factors considered include:* academic GPA, standardized test scores, application essay, recommendation(s). *Important factors considered include:* interview. **Freshman Admission Requirements:** High school diploma is required and GED is accepted. **Transfer Admission Requirements:** High school transcript, college transcript(s), essay or personal statement, interview, standardized test scores, statement of good standing from prior institution(s). Lowest grade transferable C. **General Admission Information:** Application fee $50. Nonfall registration accepted. Admission may be deferred for a maximum of 4 quarters.

COSTS AND FINANCIAL AID

Annual tuition $23,535. Average book expense $1,700. **Required Forms and Deadlines:** FAFSA, State aid form. **Notification of Awards:** Applicants will be notified of awards on a rolling basis beginning 3/15. **Types of Aid:** *Need-based scholarships/grants:* Federal Pell, FSEOG, State scholarships/grants, Private scholarships, College/university scholarship or grant aid from institutional funds. *Loans:* Direct Subsidized Stafford Loans, Direct Unsubsidized Stafford Loans, Direct PLUS loans, Federal Perkins Loans. *Student Employment:* Federal Work-Study Program available. Institutional employment available. **Financial Aid Statistics:** 52% needy freshmen, 72% needy undergrads receive need-based scholarship or grant aid. 39% freshmen, 8% undergrads receive non-need-based scholarship or grant aid. 100% freshmen, 100% undergrads receive need-based self-help aid. 0% freshmen, 0% undergrads receive athletic scholarships. 19% freshmen, 81% undergrads receive any aid. **Criteria for awarding aid:** *Non-need-based:* Academics, Art, State/district residency.

THE ART INSTITUTE OF BOSTON
AT LESLEY UNIVERSITY

700 Beacon Street, Boston, MA 02215-2598
Phone: 617-585-6710 • **Financial Aid Phone:** 617-349-8710
E-mail: admissions@aiboston.edu • **CEEB Code:** 3777
Fax: 617-585-6720 • **Website:** aiboston.edu • **ACT Code:** 1850

This private school was founded in 1912. It has a 1-acre campus.

RATINGS

Admissions Selectivity Rating: 80   **Fire Safety Rating:** 89   **Green Rating:** 60*

STUDENTS AND FACULTY

Enrollment: 1,261. **Student Body:** 75% female, 25% male, 44% out-of-state, 3% international (15 countries represented). Asian 3%, African American 4%, Caucasian 63%, Hispanic 5%, Native American <1%, Pacific Islander 0%, Two or more races 0%, Race unknown 21%.
Retention and Graduation: 66% freshmen return for sophomore year. 37% freshmen graduate within 4 years. 49% freshmen graduate within 6 years.
Faculty: Student/faculty ratio 10:1. 73 full-time faculty, 68% hold PhDs, 12% are are members of minority groups, 55% are women. 0% of classes are taught by teaching assistants.

ACADEMICS

Degrees: associate, bachelor's, master's, post-master's certificate. **Classes:** Most classes have 10-19 students. **Most popular majors:** Graphic Design; Illustration; Photography. **Special Study Options:** Accelerated program, cross-registration, distance learning, double major, dual enrollment, exchange student program (domestic), honors program, independent study, internships, liberal arts/career combination, student-designed major, study abroad, teacher certification program, Studio Courses. **Honors Programs:** First year foundation students are eligible for advanced placement, foundation studio exemptions, and enrolling in Honors Studio and Honors English. Combined degree programs: BFA/M.Ed. **Disability Services:** Special programs offered to physically disabled students, including note-taking services, reader services, tape recorders, tutors. **Career Services:** Alumni network, Alumni services, Career/job search classes, Career assessment, Internships, Regional alumni. We are proud of the wide range of services available to our students and alumni through our new online system, Lesley Career Connection, which includes job listings, internships, career fairs, career center workshops, employer directory and more.

FACILITIES

Housing: Coed dorms, women's dorms, Special Interest and themed housing. 90% of campus accessible to physically diasbled. **Special Academic Facilities/Equipment:** Art Gallery with regular shows of prominant artists; art library; applied art facilities, including state of the art photo and computer labs,

animmation studio, ceramics studio, wood shop, metals studio, and printmaking studio **Computers:** 100% of classrooms, 10% of dorms, 100% of libraries, 100% of dining areas, 100% of student union, 25% of common outdoor areas have wireless network access. Students can register for classes online. Administrative functions (other than registration) can be performed online.

CAMPUS LIFE

Environment: Metropolis. **Activities:** Choral groups, dance, drama/theater, literary magazine, musical theater, student government, student newspaper, Campus Ministries, Student Organization. 25 registered organizations, 2 honor societies, 2 religious organizations. **Athletics (Intercollegiate):** *Men:* basketball, cross-country, soccer, tennis, volleyball. *Women:* basketball, crew/rowing, cross-country, soccer, softball, tennis, volleyball. **On-Campus Highlights:** Gallery, Computer Labs, Animation Studio, Photo Labs, Student Lounge. **Environmental Initiatives:** Continual enhancement of recycling, waste management and composting programs on campus.

ADMISSIONS

Freshman Academic Profile: Average high school GPA 3.0. 12% in top 10% of high school class, 38% in top 25% of high school class, 70% in top 50% of high school class. 84% from public high schools. **Reported SAT (pre-2016 redesign) scores:** SAT Math middle 50% range 460-560. SAT Critical Reading middle 50% range 490-600. SAT Writing middle 50% range 490-590. **Concordant SAT scores:** SAT EBRW middle 50% 550–650. SAT Math middle 50% range 500–580. ACT middle 50% range 19-26. Minimum internet-based TOEFL 61. Minimum paper TOEFL 500. **Basis for Candidate Selection:** *Very important factors considered include:* rigor of secondary school record, academic GPA. *Important factors considered include:* class rank, standardized test scores, application essay, recommendation(s), interview, extracurricular activities, talent/ability, character/personal qualities. *Other factors considered include:* first generation, alumni/ae relation, geographical residence, racial/ethnic status, volunteer work, work experience, level of applicant's interest. **Freshman Admission Requirements:** High school diploma is required and GED is accepted. *Academic units required:* 4 English. *Academic units recommended:* 4 English, 1 math, 1 science, 1 foreign language, 2 social studies, 2 history, 2 academic electives, and 2 units from above areas or other academic areas. **Freshman Admission Statistics:** 2,523 applied, 64.96% admitted, 20% enrolled. **Transfer Admission Requirements:** High school transcript, college transcript(s), essay or personal statement, interview, statement of good standing from prior institution(s). Minimum college GPA of 2.0 required. Lowest grade transferable C. **General Admission Information:** Application fee $50. Priority deadline 2/15. Nonfall registration accepted. Admission may be deferred for a maximum of 1 year.

COSTS AND FINANCIAL AID

Annual tuition $28,000. Room and board $13,250. Required fees $750. Average book expense $1,575. **Required Forms and Deadlines:** FAFSA. **Notification of Awards:** Applicants will be notified of awards on a rolling basis beginning 2/15. **Types of Aid:** *Need-based scholarships/grants:* Federal Pell, FSEOG, State scholarships/grants, Private scholarships, College/university scholarship or grant aid from institutional funds. *Loans:* Direct Subsidized Stafford Loans, Direct Unsubsidized Stafford Loans, Direct PLUS loans, Federal Perkins Loans, State Loans. *Student Employment:* Federal Work-Study Program available. Institutional employment available. **Financial Aid Statistics:** 98% needy freshmen, 96% needy undergrads receive need-based scholarship or grant aid. 19% freshmen, 38% undergrads receive non-need-based scholarship or grant aid. 73% freshmen, 70% undergrads receive need-based self-help aid. 0% freshmen, 0% undergrads receive athletic scholarships. 70% freshmen, 70% undergrads receive any aid. **Criteria for awarding aid:** *Need-based:* Academics, Art, Minority status. *Non-need-based:* Academics, Art, Leadership, Minority status, State/district residency.

THE ART INSTITUTE OF LAS VEGAS

Phone: 702-369-9944
E-mail: ailvadm@aii.edu
Fax: 702-992-8458 • **Website:** http://www.artinstitutes.edu/lasvegas/

This is a proprietary school. It has a 1.5-acre campus.

RATINGS

Admissions Selectivity Rating: 70   **Fire Safety Rating:** 71   **Green Rating:** 60*

STUDENTS AND FACULTY

Enrollment: 1,301. **Student Body:** 48% female, 52% male, 0% international. Asian 12%, African American 9%, Caucasian 35%, Hispanic 14%, Native American 1%, Pacific Islander 0%, Two or more races 0%, Race unknown 28%.
Retention and Graduation: 54% freshmen return for sophomore year.
Faculty: Student/faculty ratio 17:1. 27 full-time faculty, 7% hold PhDs, 0% are

are members of minority groups, 22% are women. 0% of classes are taught by teaching assistants.

ACADEMICS

Degrees: associate, bachelor's. **Classes:** Most classes have 10-19 students. **Most popular majors:** Digital Communication and Media/Multimedia; Culinary Arts/Chef Training. **Special Study Options:** distance learning, independent study, internships, study abroad. **Disability Services:** Special programs offered to physically disabled students, including note-taking services, reader services, tape recorders, tutors. **Career Services:** Alumni network, Alumni services, Career/job search classes, Career assessment, Internships, Regional alumni, On-campus interviews.

FACILITIES

Housing: apartments for single students, Wellness Housing.

CAMPUS LIFE

Environment: City. **Activities:** student-run film society. **On-Campus Highlights:** Student Lounge.

ADMISSIONS

Freshman Academic Profile: Average high school GPA 2.6. Minimum paper TOEFL 500. **Basis for Candidate Selection:** *Very important factors considered include:* application essay, interview. *Important factors considered include:* talent/ability, level of applicant's interest. *Other factors considered include:* academic GPA, standardized test scores, character/personal qualities. **Freshman Admission Requirements:** High school diploma is required and GED is accepted. **Freshman Admission Statistics:** 436 applied, 67.89% admitted, 78% enrolled. **Transfer Admission Requirements:** High school transcript, college transcript(s), essay or personal statement, interview, statement of good standing from prior institution(s). Minimum college GPA of 2.0 required. Lowest grade transferable 2. **General Admission Information:** Application fee $150. Nonfall registration accepted. Admission may be deferred.

COSTS AND FINANCIAL AID

Annual tuition $21,552. Required fees $450. *Student Employment:* Federal Work-Study Program available.

THE ART INSTITUTES INTERNATIONAL MINNESOTA

15 South 9th Street, Minneapolis, mn 55402
Phone: 612-332-3361 • **Financial Aid Phone:** 612-332-3361
E-mail: aimadm@aii.edu
Fax: 612-332-3934 • **Website:** www.artinstitutes.edu/minneapolis

This proprietary school was founded in 1997.

RATINGS

Admissions Selectivity Rating: 61   **Fire Safety Rating:** 85   **Green Rating:** 60*

STUDENTS AND FACULTY

Student Body: 61% female, 39% male, 20% out-of-state.
Retention and Graduation: 60% freshmen return for sophomore year.
Faculty: Student/faculty ratio 20:1. 56 full-time faculty, 0% hold PhDs, 0% are are members of minority groups, 36% are women.

ACADEMICS

Degrees: associate, bachelor's, certificate. **Special Study Options:** distance learning, independent study, internships, study abroad, Evening & Weekend. **Disability Services:** Special programs offered to physically disabled students, including note-taking services, tape recorders, tutors. **Career Services:** Alumni network, Alumni services, Career/job search classes, Internships, Regional alumni.

FACILITIES

Housing: apartments for single students. 100% of campus accessible to physically diasbled. **Computers:** 100% of classrooms, 100% of dorms, 100% of libraries, 100% of dining areas, 100% of student union, have wireless network access. Students can register for classes online. Administrative functions (other than registration) can be performed online.

CAMPUS LIFE

Environment: Metropolis. **Activities:** literary magazine, student newspaper, Campus Ministries, Student Organization. 16 registered organizations, 1 honor society. **On-Campus Highlights:** School dining lab, Art galleries, Connection to the city's skyway system, New second campus.

ADMISSIONS

Basis for Candidate Selection: *Very important factors considered include:* application essay, interview. *Important factors considered include:* talent/ability. *Other factors considered include:* academic GPA, standardized test scores, extracurricular activities, character/personal qualities, level of applicant's interest. **Transfer Admission Requirements:** High school transcript, college transcript(s). **General Admission Information:** Application fee $50. Nonfall registration accepted.

COSTS AND FINANCIAL AID

Annual tuition $22,416. **Required Forms and Deadlines:** FAFSA. **Types of Aid:** *Need-based scholarships/grants:* Federal Pell, FSEOG, State scholarships/grants, Private scholarships, College/university scholarship or grant aid from institutional funds, United Negro College Fund. *Loans:* Direct Subsidized Stafford Loans, Direct Unsubsidized Stafford Loans, Direct PLUS loans, State Loans, College/university loans from institutional funds. *Student Employment:* Federal Work-Study Program available. Institutional employment available. **Criteria for awarding aid:** *Need-based:* Academics.

ASHLAND UNIVERSITY

401 College Ave, Ashland, OH 44805
Phone: 419-289-5052 • **Financial Aid Phone:** 419-289-5002
E-mail: enrollme@ashland.edu • **CEEB Code:** 1021
Fax: 419-289-5999 • **Website:** www.ashland.edu • **ACT Code:** 3234

This private school, affiliated with the Church of Brethren Church, was founded in 1878. It has a 12-acre campus.

RATINGS

Admissions Selectivity Rating: 81   **Fire Safety Rating:** 73   **Green Rating:** 60*

STUDENTS AND FACULTY

Enrollment: 3,232. **Student Body:** 51% female, 49% male, 15% out-of-state, 2% international (16 countries represented). Asian 0%, African American 13%, Caucasian 78%, Hispanic 3%, Native American <1%, Pacific Islander <1%, Two or more races 1%, Race unknown 2%.
Retention and Graduation: 77% freshmen return for sophomore year. 43% freshmen graduate within 4 years. 59% freshmen graduate within 6 years. 13% grads go on to further study within 1 year. 2% grads pursue arts and sciences degrees. 1% grads pursue law degrees. 1% grads pursue business degrees. 1% grads pursue medical degrees. **Faculty:** Student/faculty ratio 13:1. 251 full-time faculty, 78% hold PhDs, 0% are are members of minority groups, 0% are women. 0% of classes are taught by teaching assistants.

ACADEMICS

Degrees: associate, bachelor's, certificate, diploma, doctoral, master's, terminal, transfer. **Classes:** Most classes have 10-19 students. Most lab/discussion sessions have 10-19 students. **Most popular majors:** Education; Business/Commerce. **Special Study Options:** double major, English as a Second Language (ESL), honors program, independent study, internships, student-designed major, study abroad, teacher certification program, weekend college, Ashbrook Center for Public Affairs. **Honors Programs:** Ashland University Honors Program. **Disability Services:** Special programs offered to physically disabled students, including note-taking services, reader services, tape recorders, tutors. **Career Services:** Alumni network, Alumni services, Career/job search classes, Career assessment, Internships.

FACILITIES

Housing: Coed dorms, special housing for disabled students, men's dorms, women's dorms, fraternity/sorority housing, apartments for single students, Theme Housing. 70% of campus accessible to physically diasbled. **Special Academic Facilities/Equipment:** Neumismatic Center, Patterson Technology Center, Coburn Art Gallery, Hugo Young Theatre, Studio Theatre, 33 room Radio/Television Condex, Media Center, Pre-Columbian Art Exhibit, Ashbrook Center. **Computers:** 90% of classrooms, 50% of dorms, 100% of libraries, 50% of dining areas, 100% of student union, 50% of common outdoor areas have wireless network access. Students can register for classes online. Administrative functions (other than registration) can be performed online.

CAMPUS LIFE

Environment: Town. **Activities:** Choral groups, concert band, dance, drama/theater, jazz band, literary magazine, marching band, music ensembles, musical theater, pep band, radio station, student government, student newspaper, symphony orchestra, television station, yearbook, Campus Ministries, Student Organization. 102 registered organizations, 18 honor societies, 9 religious organizations. 4 fraternities, 5 sororities. **Athletics (Intercollegiate):** *Men:* baseball, basketball, cross-country, diving, football, golf, soccer, swimming, track/field (outdoor), track/field (indoor), wrestling. *Women:* basketball, cheerleading, cross-country, diving, golf, soccer, softball, swimming, tennis, track/field (outdoor), track/field (indoor), volleyball. **On-Campus Highlights:** Kettering Science Center, Recreation and Sport Sciences Center, Schar College of Education, Dauch College of Business and Economics, National ranked food service, NCAA Division II Athletics 2009-2010 New football stadium, new soccer complex, new track and field complex.

ADMISSIONS

Freshman Academic Profile: Average high school GPA 3.4. 22% in top 10% of high school class, 49% in top 25% of high school class, 80% in top 50% of high school class. 89% from public high schools. **Reported SAT (pre-2016 redesign) scores:** SAT Math middle 50% range 490-580. SAT Critical Reading middle 50% range 460-560. **Concordant SAT scores:** SAT Math middle 50% range 520–600. ACT middle 50% range 20-25. Minimum internet-based TOEFL 65. Minimum paper TOEFL 500. **Basis for Candidate Selection:** *Very important factors considered include:* rigor of secondary school record, academic GPA, standardized test scores. *Important factors considered include:* class rank, extracurricular activities, level of applicant's interest. *Other factors considered include:* application essay, recommendation(s), talent/ability, character/personal qualities, first generation, alumni/ae relation, religious affiliation/commitment, volunteer work, work experience. **Freshman Admission Requirements:** High school diploma is required and GED is accepted. *Academic units required:* 3 English, 3 math, 3 science, 2 social studies, 1 history. *Academic units recommended:* 4 English, 4 math, 4 science, 2 foreign language, 3 social studies, 3 history, 1 academic elective, 1 computer science. **Freshman Admission Statistics:** 3,184 applied, 71.86% admitted, 26% enrolled. **Transfer Admission Requirements:** college transcript(s), essay or personal statement, Minimum college GPA of 2.5 required. Lowest grade transferable C-. **General Admission Information:** Priority deadline 1/1. Nonfall registration accepted. Admission may be deferred for a maximum of 1 Semester.

COSTS AND FINANCIAL AID

Annual tuition $29,844. Room and board $9,602. Required fees $944. Average book expense $800. **Required Forms and Deadlines:** FAFSA. **Notification of Awards:** Applicants will be notified of awards on a rolling basis beginning 3/1. **Types of Aid:** *Need-based scholarships/grants:* Federal Pell, FSEOG, State scholarships/grants, Private scholarships, College/university scholarship or grant aid from institutional funds. *Loans:* Direct Subsidized Stafford Loans, Direct Unsubsidized Stafford Loans, Direct PLUS loans, Federal Perkins Loans, Federal Nursing Loans, State Loans, College/university loans from institutional funds. *Student Employment:* Federal Work-Study Program available. Institutional employment available. **Financial Aid Statistics:** 95% needy freshmen, 91% needy undergrads receive need-based scholarship or grant aid. 0% undergrads receive non-need-based scholarship or grant aid. 95% freshmen, 91% undergrads receive need-based self-help aid. 4% freshmen, 4% undergrads receive athletic scholarships. 99% freshmen, 98% undergrads receive any aid. **Criteria for awarding aid:** *Need-based:* Academics, Job skills, Minority status. *Non-need-based:* Academics, Alumni affiliation, Art, Athletics, Job skills, Leadership, Minority status, Music/drama, Religious affiliation.

ASSUMPTION COLLEGE

500 Salisbury Street, Worcester, MA 01609-1296
Phone: 508-767-7285 • **Financial Aid Phone:** 508-767-7158
E-mail: admiss@assumption.edu • **CEEB Code:** 3009
Fax: 508-799-4412 • **Website:** www.assumption.edu • **ACT Code:** 1782

This private school, affiliated with the Roman Catholic Church, was founded in 1904. It has a 180-acre campus.

RATINGS

Admissions Selectivity Rating: 81   **Fire Safety Rating:** 82   **Green Rating:** 60*

STUDENTS AND FACULTY

Enrollment: 1,979. **Student Body:** 59% female, 41% male, 35% out-of-state, 2% international (23 countries represented). Asian 2%, African American 6%, Caucasian 75%, Hispanic 7%, Native American <1%, Pacific Islander <1%, Two or more races 2%, Race unknown 6%.
Retention and Graduation: 83% freshmen return for sophomore year. 70% freshmen graduate within 4 years. 73% freshmen graduate within 6 years. 25% grads go on to further study within 1 year. 15% grads pursue arts and sciences degrees. 2% grads pursue law degrees. 3% grads pursue business degrees. 1%

grads pursue medical degrees. **Faculty:** Student/faculty ratio 12:1. 144 full-time faculty, 92% hold PhDs, 6% are are members of minority groups, 43% are women. 0% of classes are taught by teaching assistants.

ACADEMICS

Degrees: bachelor's, master's, post-master's certificate. **Classes:** Most classes have 20-29 students. Most lab/discussion sessions have 10-19 students. **Most popular majors:** Rehabilitation and Therapeutic Professions; Psychology; Accounting. **Special Study Options:** cross-registration, double major, honors program, independent study, internships, student-designed major, study abroad, teacher certification program. **Honors Programs:** The Assumption College Honors Program is a selective program designed to foster academic engagement inside and outside the classroom. The program promotes intellectual friendship and discourse while providing a common, intensive learning experience in small seminar classes. Combined degree programs: BA/MA, BA/MAs SP ED, Rehab Couns, School Couns; BA/MBA. **Disability Services:** Special programs offered to physically disabled students, including note-taking services, reader services, tape recorders, tutors. **Career Services:** Alumni network, Career/job search classes, Career assessment, Internships, Regional alumni.

FACILITIES

Housing: Coed dorms, special housing for disabled students, women's dorms, Wellness Housing, Theme Housing, Freshmen dorms. 71% of campus accessible to physically diasbled. **Special Academic Facilities/Equipment:** French Institute museum, Institute for Social and Rehabilitation Services, language lab, media center, Living/Learning Center, Testa Science Center, Information Technology Center. **Computers:** 100% of classrooms, 100% of libraries, 50% of dining areas, 100% of student union, 25% of common outdoor areas have wireless network access. Students can register for classes online. Administrative functions (other than registration) can be performed online.

CAMPUS LIFE

Environment: City. **Activities:** Choral groups, concert band, drama/theater, literary magazine, musical theater, pep band, student government, student newspaper, student-run film society, television station, yearbook, Campus Ministries. 50 registered organizations, 12 honor societies, 1 religious organization. **Athletics (Intercollegiate):** *Men:* baseball, basketball, cross-country, football, golf, ice hockey, lacrosse, soccer, tennis, track/field (outdoor), track/field (indoor). *Women:* basketball, crew/rowing, cross-country, field hockey, lacrosse, soccer, softball, swimming, tennis, track/field (outdoor), track/field (indoor), volleyball. **On-Campus Highlights:** Testa Science Center, Living Learning Center, Plourde Recreation Center, Charlie's Cafe, D'Alzon Library.

ADMISSIONS

Freshman Academic Profile: Average high school GPA 3.4. 12% in top 10% of high school class, 43% in top 25% of high school class, 81% in top 50% of high school class. 68% from public high schools. **Reported SAT (pre-2016 redesign) scores:** SAT Math middle 50% range 510-600. SAT Critical Reading middle 50% range 510-600. **Concordant SAT scores:** SAT Math middle 50% range 540–620. ACT middle 50% range 23-26. Minimum internet-based TOEFL 80. Minimum paper TOEFL 550. **Basis for Candidate Selection:** *Very important factors considered include:* academic GPA, application essay. *Important factors considered include:* rigor of secondary school record, recommendation(s), interview, volunteer work, level of applicant's interest. *Other factors considered include:* class rank, standardized test scores, extracurricular activities, talent/ability, character/personal qualities, first generation, alumni/ae relation, racial/ethnic status. **Freshman Admission Requirements:** High school diploma is required and GED is accepted. *Academic units required:* 4 English, 3 math, 2 science, 2 foreign language, 2 history, 5 academic electives. **Freshman Admission Statistics:** 4,769 applied, 75.78% admitted, 16% enrolled. **Transfer Admission Requirements:** High school transcript, college transcript(s), essay or personal statement, statement of good standing from prior institution(s). Minimum college GPA of 2.5 required. Lowest grade transferable C. **General Admission Information:** Application fee $50. Regular application deadline 2/15. Nonfall registration accepted. Admission may be deferred for a maximum of 1 year.

COSTS AND FINANCIAL AID

Annual tuition $35,510. Required fees $750. Average book expense $1,000. **Required Forms and Deadlines:** FAFSA. **Notification of Awards:** Applicants will be notified of awards on a rolling basis beginning 2/16. **Types of Aid:** *Need-based scholarships/grants:* Federal Pell, FSEOG, State scholarships/grants, Private scholarships, College/university scholarship or grant aid from institutional funds. *Loans:* Direct Subsidized Stafford Loans, Direct Unsubsidized Stafford Loans, Direct PLUS loans, Federal Perkins Loans, State Loans. *Student Employment:* Federal Work-Study Program available. Institutional employment available. **Financial Aid Statistics:** 100% needy freshmen, 100% needy undergrads receive need-based scholarship or grant aid. 22% freshmen, 16% undergrads receive non-need-based scholarship or grant aid. 75% freshmen, 81% undergrads receive need-based self-help aid. 4% freshmen, 4% undergrads receive athletic scholarships. 98% freshmen,

98% undergrads receive any aid. **Criteria for awarding aid:** *Need-based:* Academics, Athletics. *Non-need-based:* Academics, Athletics, Music/drama.

See page 910.

ATHABASCA UNIVERSITY

1 University Drive, Athabasca, AB T9S 3A3
Phone: 800-788-9041 • **Financial Aid Phone:** 780-675-6147
Fax: 780-675-6145 • **Website:** www.athabascau.ca

This public school was founded in 1970.

RATINGS
Admissions Selectivity Rating: 64   **Fire Safety Rating:** 60*   **Green Rating:** 60*

STUDENTS AND FACULTY
Student Body: 61% out-of-state, (90 countries represented).

ACADEMICS
Degrees: bachelor's, certificate, diploma, doctoral, master's, postbachelor's certificate, post-master's certificate. **Most popular majors:** Elementary Education and Teaching; Criminal Justice/Safety Studies. **Special Study Options:** Accelerated program, cross-registration, distance learning, English as a Second Language (ESL), external degree program. **Disability Services:** Special programs offered to physically disabled students, including tape recorders, tutors.

FACILITIES
Housing: Coed dorms. **Computers:** Students can register for classes online. Administrative functions (other than registration) can be performed online.

CAMPUS LIFE
Environment: Rural. **Activities:** student government, yearbook.

ADMISSIONS
Freshman Admission Statistics: 38,876 applied, 100.00% admitted, 100% enrolled. **Transfer Admission Requirements:** High school transcript, college transcript(s). **General Admission Information:** Application fee $100. Nonfall registration accepted. Admission may be deferred for a maximum of 1 year.

COSTS AND FINANCIAL AID
Annual in-state tuition $657. Annual out-of-state tuition $762. *Student Employment:* Federal Work-Study Program available. Institutional employment available.

AUBURN UNIVERSITY

The Quad Center, Auburn, AL 36849-5149
Phone: 334-844-6425 • **Financial Aid Phone:** 334-844-4634
E-mail: admissions@auburn.edu • **CEEB Code:** 1005
Fax: 334-844-6436 • **Website:** www.auburn.edu • **ACT Code:** 11

This public school was founded in 1856. It has a 1875-acre campus.

RATINGS
Admissions Selectivity Rating: 85   **Fire Safety Rating:** 89   **Green Rating:** 86

STUDENTS AND FACULTY
Enrollment: 22,095. **Student Body:** 49% female, 51% male, 34% out-of-state, 2% international (58 countries represented). Asian 3%, African American 7%, Caucasian 83%, Hispanic 3%, Native American 1%, Pacific Islander <1%, Two or more races 1%, Race unknown 1%.
Retention and Graduation: 91% freshmen return for sophomore year. 47% freshmen graduate within 4 years. 75% freshmen graduate within 6 years. 42% grads go on to further study within 1 year. 6% grads pursue arts and sciences degrees. 5% grads pursue law degrees. 17% grads pursue business degrees. 29% grads pursue medical degrees. **Faculty:** Student/faculty ratio 19:1. 1,260 full-time faculty, 92% hold PhDs, 18% are are members of minority groups, 39% are women.

ACADEMICS
Degrees: bachelor's, doctoral/professional, doctoral/research, doctoral, master's, postbachelor's certificate, post-master's certificate. **Classes:** Most classes have 20-29 students. Most lab/discussion sessions have 10-19 students. **Most popular majors:** Mechanical Engineering; Business Administration and Management; Secondary Education and Teaching. **Special Study Options:** Accelerated program, cooperative education program, distance learning, double major, dual enrollment, English as a Second Language (ESL), honors program, independent study, internships, liberal arts/career combination, study abroad, teacher certification program. **Honors Programs:** The Auburn University's Honors College offers qualified students a unique academic experience, designed to provide many of the advantages of a small college in the midst of the many diverse opportunities available at a large university. It is designed for students capable of academic excellence. The program selects 200 entering freshmen each year, who may be enrolled in any College or School of the University which has undergraduate programs or offerings. Students already enrolled at Auburn can also qualify for the Honors College. Combined degree programs: w/ Liberal Arts or Agriculture. **Disability Services:** Special programs offered to physically disabled students, including note-taking services, reader services, tape recorders, tutors. **Career Services:** Alumni network, Alumni services, Career/job search classes, Career assessment, Internships. Handshake—a platform for student and employer connections.

FACILITIES
Housing: Coed dorms, special housing for disabled students, men's dorms, women's dorms, fraternity/sorority housing, apartments for married students, apartments for single students, Housing for students enrolled in Honors College and academic-themed learning communities (i.e. Agriculture Pre-Vet, AT&T Minority Engineering Program, Conservation Biology). 100% of campus accessible to physically diasbled. **Special Academic Facilities/Equipment:** Nuclear Science Center; Hybridoma Facility; Freeman Herbarium; Jule Collins Smith Art Museum; Hypervelocity Impact Facility; Advanced Microscopy & Imaging Laboratory; Alabama Microelectronics Science & Technology Center; Alabama Water Resources Research Institute; AU Airport with single/multi-engine aircraft and flight simulators; Center for Forest Sustainability; Center for Governmental Services; Center for Pharmacy Operations & Designs; Drug Information & Learning Resources Center; Economic & Community Development Institute; Fish Molecular Genetics & Biotechnology Laboratory; Forest Policy Center; Forest Products Development Center; Fusion Lab; Harris Early Learning Center; Dept of Psychology Health Behavior Assessment Center; Highway Research Center; Marriage & Family Therapy Center; Microfibrous Materials Manufacturing Center; Dept of Kinesiology Biomechanics Lab, and Motor Behavior Center; Plasma Sciences Lab; Veterinary Medicine Radiology Clinic, Scott-Ritchey Research Center, Southeastern Raptor Rehabilitation Center, Small & Large Animal Health Clinics **Computers:** 35% of classrooms, 100% of dorms, 95% of libraries, 50% of dining areas, 100% of student union, 30% of common outdoor areas have wireless network access. Students can register for classes online. Administrative functions (other than registration) can be performed online.

CAMPUS LIFE
Environment: Town. **Activities:** Choral groups, concert band, dance, drama/theater, jazz band, literary magazine, marching band, music ensembles, musical theater, opera, pep band, radio station, student government, student newspaper, student-run film society, symphony orchestra, television station, yearbook, Student Organization. 300 registered organizations, 56 honor societies, 15 religious organizations. 30 fraternities, 19 sororities. **Athletics (Intercollegiate):** *Men:* baseball, basketball, cheerleading, cross-country, diving, football, golf, swimming, tennis, track/field (outdoor), track/field (indoor). *Women:* basketball, cheerleading, cross-country, diving, equestrian sports, golf, gymnastics, soccer, softball, swimming, tennis, track/field (outdoor), track/field (indoor), volleyball. **On-Campus Highlights:** Telfair B. Peet Theatre, Student Activity Center, Haley Center Concourse, Library Coffee Shop, War Eagle Dining, Student Center; Arboretum; Agricultural Heritage Park; Forest Ecology Preserve. **Environmental Initiatives:** Incorporation of sustainability initiatives into university curricula, including one of the first truly interdisciplinary sustainability minors in the country.

ADMISSIONS
Freshman Academic Profile: Average high school GPA 3.9. 30% in top 10% of high school class, 62% in top 25% of high school class, 90% in top 50% of high school class. 86% from public high schools. **Reported SAT (pre-2016 redesign) scores:** SAT Math middle 50% range 530-640. SAT Critical Reading middle 50% range 530-620. SAT Writing middle 50% range 510-610. **Concordant SAT scores:** SAT EBRW middle 50% 580–670. SAT Math middle 50% range 560–660. ACT middle 50% range 24-30. Minimum internet-based TOEFL 79. Minimum paper TOEFL 550. **Basis for Candidate Selection:** *Very important factors considered include:* academic GPA, standardized test scores, application essay. *Important factors considered include:* rigor of secondary school record, extracurricular activities, talent/ability, character/personal qualities, first generation, alumni/ae relation, geographical residence,

state residency, volunteer work, work experience, level of applicant's interest. *Other factors considered include:* recommendation(s). **Freshman Admission Requirements:** High school diploma is required and GED is accepted. *Academic units required:* 4 English, 3 math, 2 science, 1 science lab, 3 social studies. *Academic units recommended:* 2 science labs, 1 foreign language, 4 social studies. **Freshman Admission Statistics:** 18,256 applied, 80.54% admitted, 31% enrolled. **Transfer Admission Requirements:** college transcript(s), Minimum college GPA of 2.5 required. Lowest grade transferable C. **General Admission Information:** Application fee $50. Priority deadline 2/1. Regular application deadline 6/1. Regular notification 2/15. Nonfall registration accepted. Admission may be deferred for a maximum of 1 year.

COSTS AND FINANCIAL AID

Annual in-state tuition $9,072. Annual out-of-state tuition $27,216. Room and board $12,898. Required fees $1,624. Average book expense $1,200. **Required Forms and Deadlines:** FAFSA. **Notification of Awards:** Applicants will be notified of awards on a rolling basis beginning 10/2. **Types of Aid:** *Need-based scholarships/grants:* Federal Pell, FSEOG, State scholarships/grants, Private scholarships, College/university scholarship or grant aid from institutional funds. *Loans:* Direct Subsidized Stafford Loans, Direct Unsubsidized Stafford Loans, Direct PLUS loans, Federal Perkins Loans, Federal Nursing Loans, College/university loans from institutional funds. *Student Employment:* Federal Work-Study Program available. Institutional employment available. **Financial Aid Statistics:** 81% needy freshmen, 72% needy undergrads receive need-based scholarship or grant aid. 14% freshmen, 9% undergrads receive non-need-based scholarship or grant aid. 64% freshmen, 77% undergrads receive need-based self-help aid. 2% freshmen, 2% undergrads receive athletic scholarships. 50% freshmen, 44% undergrads receive any aid. 41% undergrads borrow to pay for school. Average cumulative indebtedness $28,170.

AUBURN UNIVERSITY AT MONTGOMERY

P.O. Box 244023, Montgomery, AL 36124-4023
Phone: 334-244-3615 • **Financial Aid Phone:** 334-244-3571
E-mail: admissions@aum.edu
Fax: 334-244-3795 • **Website:** www.aum.edu • **ACT Code:** 57

This public school was founded in 1967. It has a 500-acre campus.

RATINGS

Admissions Selectivity Rating: 77   **Fire Safety Rating:** 89   **Green Rating:** 60*

STUDENTS AND FACULTY

Enrollment: 4,179. **Student Body:** 64% female, 36% male, 6% out-of-state, 4% international (31 countries represented). Asian 2%, African American 36%, Caucasian 51%, Hispanic 1%, Native American 1%, Pacific Islander <1%, Two or more races 3%, Race unknown 1%.
Retention and Graduation: 7% freshmen graduate within 4 years. **Faculty:** Student/faculty ratio 16:1. 191 full-time faculty, 0% hold PhDs, 19% are are members of minority groups, 43% are women. 3% of classes are taught by teaching assistants.

ACADEMICS

Degrees: bachelor's, master's, post-master's certificate. **Classes:** Most classes have 20-29 students. Most lab/discussion sessions have 20-29 students. **Most popular majors:** Elementary Education and Teaching; Business/Commerce; Registered Nursing/Registered Nurse. **Special Study Options:** Accelerated program, cooperative education program, cross-registration, distance learning, double major, dual enrollment, English as a Second Language (ESL), honors program, independent study, internships, liberal arts/career combination, study abroad, teacher certification program, weekend college, Joint Ph.D.in public administration with Auburn University; Ed.D. in cooperation with Auburn University. **Disability Services:** Special programs offered to physically disabled students, including note-taking services, reader services, tape recorders, tutors. **Career Services:** Alumni services, Career/job search classes, Career assessment, Internships, On-campus interviews.

FACILITIES

Housing: Coed dorms, special housing for disabled students, apartments for married students, apartments for single students. 100% of campus accessible to physically diasbled. **Computers:** Students can register for classes online. Administrative functions (other than registration) can be performed online.

CAMPUS LIFE

Environment: City. **Activities:** Choral groups, dance, drama/theater, musical theater, student government, student newspaper, student-run film society, Campus Ministries, Student Organization. 50 registered organizations, 10 honor societies, 7 religious organizations. 3 fraternities, 6 sororities. **Athletics (Intercollegiate):** *Men:* baseball, basketball, cheerleading, soccer, tennis.

Women: basketball, cheerleading, soccer, softball, tennis. **On-Campus Highlights:** Senator's Cafe, Computer Labs, Taylor Center/Student Union, Residence Hall, Athletic Facility. **Environmental Initiatives:** Recycling.

ADMISSIONS

Freshman Academic Profile: Average high school GPA 3.3. 16% in top 10% of high school class, 44% in top 25% of high school class, 80% in top 50% of high school class. **Reported SAT (pre-2016 redesign) scores:** SAT Math middle 50% range 445-495. SAT Critical Reading middle 50% range 435-495. **Concordant SAT scores:** SAT Math middle 50% range 490–530. ACT middle 50% range 19-24. Minimum internet-based TOEFL 61. Minimum paper TOEFL 500. **Basis for Candidate Selection:** *Very important factors considered include:* rigor of secondary school record, academic GPA, standardized test scores. **Freshman Admission Requirements:** High school diploma is required and GED is accepted. *Academic units recommended:* 3 English, 3 math, 2 science, 2 science labs, 2 foreign language, 2 social studies, 2 history, 2 academic electives. **Freshman Admission Statistics:** 2,905 applied, 76.59% admitted, 27% enrolled. **Transfer Admission Requirements:** college transcript(s), Minimum college GPA of 2.0 required. Lowest grade transferable D. **General Admission Information:** Regular application deadline 8/15. Nonfall registration accepted.

COSTS AND FINANCIAL AID

Annual in-state tuition $8,880. Annual out-of-state tuition $19,950. Room and board $5,650. Required fees $760. Average book expense $1,100. **Required Forms and Deadlines:** FAFSA. **Notification of Awards:** Applicants will be notified of awards on a rolling basis beginning 4/15. **Types of Aid:** *Need-based scholarships/grants:* Federal Pell, FSEOG, State scholarships/grants, College/university scholarship or grant aid from institutional funds. *Loans:* Direct Subsidized Stafford Loans, Direct Unsubsidized Stafford Loans, Direct PLUS loans, Federal Perkins Loans. *Student Employment:* Federal Work-Study Program available. Institutional employment available. **Financial Aid Statistics:** 72% needy freshmen, 74% needy undergrads receive need-based scholarship or grant aid. 35% freshmen, 23% undergrads receive non-need-based scholarship or grant aid. 97% freshmen, 96% undergrads receive need-based self-help aid. 0% freshmen, 0% undergrads receive athletic scholarships. 77% freshmen, 63% undergrads receive any aid. 69% undergrads borrow to pay for school. Average cumulative indebtedness $30,454.

AUGSBURG COLLEGE

2211 Riverside Avenue South, Minneapolis, MN 55454
Phone: 612-330-1001 • **Financial Aid Phone:** 612-330-1046
E-mail: admissions@augsburg.edu • **CEEB Code:** 6014
Fax: 612-330-1590 • **Website:** www.augsburg.edu • **ACT Code:** 2080

This private school, affiliated with the Lutheran Church, was founded in 1869. It has a 23-acre campus.

RATINGS

Admissions Selectivity Rating: 83   **Fire Safety Rating:** 83   **Green Rating:** 60*

STUDENTS AND FACULTY

Enrollment: 3,014. **Student Body:** 55% female, 45% male, 13% out-of-state, 2% international (24 countries represented). Asian 7%, African American 9%, Caucasian 68%, Hispanic 3%, Native American 2%, Pacific Islander <1%, Two or more races 2%, Race unknown 6%.
Retention and Graduation: 83% freshmen return for sophomore year. 41% freshmen graduate within 4 years. 62% freshmen graduate within 6 years. 27% grads go on to further study within 1 year. 15% grads pursue arts and sciences degrees. 2% grads pursue law degrees. 4% grads pursue business degrees. 5% grads pursue medical degrees. **Faculty:** Student/faculty ratio 16:1. 195 full-time faculty, 75% hold PhDs, 8% are are members of minority groups, 51% are women. 0% of classes are taught by teaching assistants.

ACADEMICS

Degrees: bachelor's, certificate, doctoral/professional, master's. **Classes:** Most classes have 10-19 students. Most lab/discussion sessions have 10-19 students. **Most popular majors:** Education; Business/Commerce. **Special Study Options:** cooperative education program, cross-registration, double major, dual enrollment, honors program, independent study, internships, liberal arts/career combination, student-designed major, study abroad, teacher certification program, weekend college. **Honors Programs:** First, the Honors Signature Courses, based on the medieval divisions of knowledge, automatically satisfy all of the College's general education requirements (except health/physical education and modern language) in a simple sequence of challenging courses, created just for Honors students. Second, Student-Created Courses allow students to design their own courses'—as either a replacement or supplement to the established Honors courses. Students can learn through one-on-one tutoring, small reading groups, or out-of-classroom experiences. Third, Honors Leadership Activities give Honors students access to the The Augsburg Review, Honors Debate League, Faculty/Student Research Collaboration, and the Honors Houses. Through these activities, students can engage in travel abroad, service-learning, social justice activities, political activism, leadership, research, and social gatherings with their friends. **Disability Services:** Special programs offered to physically disabled students, including note-taking services, reader services, tape recorders, tutors. **Career Services:** Alumni network, Career/job search classes, Internships, Regional alumni.

FACILITIES

Housing: Coed dorms, special housing for disabled students, Special housing for Step-Up program students (i.e. Sober student program). 99% of campus accessible to physically diasbled. **Special Academic Facilities/Equipment:** Electron microscope, center for atmospheric science research, theatre, pipe organ. **Computers:** Students can register for classes online. Administrative functions (other than registration) can be performed online.

CAMPUS LIFE

Environment: Metropolis. **Activities:** Choral groups, concert band, dance, drama/theater, jazz band, literary magazine, music ensembles, opera, radio station, student government, student newspaper, yearbook, Campus Ministries, Student Organization. 35 registered organizations, 1 honor society, 1 religious organization. **Athletics (Intercollegiate). Men:** baseball, basketball, cross-country, football, golf, ice hockey, soccer, tennis, track/field (outdoor), track/field (indoor), wrestling. *Women:* basketball, cheerleading, cross-country, golf, ice hockey, soccer, softball, swimming, tennis, track/field (outdoor), track/field (indoor), volleyball. **On-Campus Highlights:** Christensen Center/Starbucks Coffee Shop, Si Melby Athletic Fieldhouse, Lindell Library, Foss Center/Atrium, Gateway Center.

ADMISSIONS

Freshman Academic Profile: Average high school GPA 3.3. 11% in top 10% of high school class, 37% in top 25% of high school class, 69% in top 50% of high school class. **Reported SAT (pre-2016 redesign) scores:** SAT Math middle 50% range 500-640. SAT Critical Reading middle 50% range 510-640. SAT Writing middle 50% range 480-600. **Concordant SAT scores:** SAT EBRW middle 50% 550–670. SAT Math middle 50% range 530–660. ACT middle 50% range 19-25. Minimum paper TOEFL 550. **Basis for Candidate Selection:** *Very important factors considered include:* rigor of secondary school record, class rank, academic GPA, application essay, recommendation(s). *Important factors considered include:* standardized test scores, extracurricular activities, alumni/ae relation, level of applicant's interest. *Other factors considered include:* interview, talent/ability, first generation, volunteer work, work experience. **Freshman Admission Requirements:** High school diploma is required and GED is accepted. *Academic units required:* 4 English, 3 math, 3 science, 2 foreign language, 2 social studies. *Academic units recommended:* 4 social studies, 2 history. **Freshman Admission Statistics:** 2,192 applied, 54.15% admitted, 35% enrolled. **Transfer Admission Requirements:** college transcript(s), statement of good standing from prior institution(s). Minimum college GPA of 2.5 required. Lowest grade transferable B. **General Admission Information:** Application fee $25. Priority deadline 5/1. Regular application deadline 8/15. Nonfall registration accepted. Admission may be deferred for a maximum of 24 months.

COSTS AND FINANCIAL AID

Annual tuition $29,794. Room and board $8,072. Required fees $624. Average book expense $1,000. **Required Forms and Deadlines:** FAFSA. **Notification of Awards:** Applicants will be notified of awards on a rolling basis beginning 3/1. **Types of Aid:** *Need-based scholarships/grants:* Federal Pell, FSEOG, State scholarships/grants, Private scholarships, College/university scholarship or grant aid from institutional funds. *Loans:* Direct Subsidized Stafford Loans, Direct Unsubsidized Stafford Loans, Direct PLUS loans, Federal Perkins Loans, Federal Nursing Loans, State Loans. *Student Employment:* Federal Work-Study Program available. Institutional employment available. **Financial Aid Statistics:** 99% needy freshmen, 91% needy undergrads receive need-based scholarship or grant aid. 19% freshmen, 17% undergrads receive non-need-based scholarship or grant aid. 94% freshmen, 92% undergrads receive need-based self-help aid. 0% freshmen, 0% undergrads receive athletic scholarships. 93% freshmen, 86% undergrads receive any aid. **Criteria for awarding aid:** *Need-based:* Academics, Minority status. *Non-need-based:* Academics, Alumni affiliation, Art, Leadership, Minority status, Music/drama, Religious affiliation.

AUGUSTANA COLLEGE (IL)

639 38th Street, Rock Island, IL 61201-2296
Phone: 309-794-7341 • **Financial Aid Phone:** 309-794-7207
E-mail: admissions@augustana.edu • **CEEB Code:** 1025
Fax: 309-794-7422 • **Website:** www.augustana.edu • **ACT Code:** 946

This private school, affiliated with the Lutheran Church, was founded in 1860. It has a 115-acre campus.

RATINGS

Admissions Selectivity Rating: 86   **Fire Safety Rating:** 93   **Green Rating:** 60*

STUDENTS AND FACULTY

Enrollment: 2,522. **Student Body:** 57% female, 43% male, 15% out-of-state, 5% international (29 countries represented). Asian 2%, African American 4%, Caucasian 75%, Hispanic 10%, Native American <1%, Pacific Islander <1%, Two or more races 3%, Race unknown 1%.
Retention and Graduation: 89% freshmen return for sophomore year. 71% freshmen graduate within 4 years. 38% grads go on to further study within 1 year. 12% grads pursue arts and sciences degrees. 1% grads pursue law degrees. 6% grads pursue business degrees. 9% grads pursue medical degrees. **Faculty:** 174 full-time faculty, 0% hold PhDs, 0% are are members of minority groups, 0% are women. 0% of classes are taught by teaching assistants.

ACADEMICS

Degrees: bachelor's. **Classes:** Most classes have 10-19 students. **Most popular majors:** Biology/Biological Sciences; Business Administration and Management; Psychology. **Special Study Options:** Accelerated program, double major, honors program, independent study, internships, liberal arts/career combination, student-designed major, study abroad, teacher certification program. **Honors Programs:** Augustana has two tracks in first-year honors studies, Foundations and Logos. The Foundations program is a challenging interdisciplinary honors curriculum offering an intensive examination of the basic questions that have perplexed humans for centuries, and focuses on integrated learning and the development of critical thinking and writing skills. Logos is a challenging interdisciplinary honors curriculum with a special focus on how science has evolved across the centuries, how science has been used and viewed at particular historical moments, and how we live with the fruits of science today. Combined degree programs: Env. Mgt., Forestry, Occ. Therapy, Landscape Arch. **Disability Services:** Special programs offered to physically disabled students, including reader services, tape recorders, tutors. **Career Services:** Alumni network, Alumni services, Career/job search classes, Career assessment, Internships. Our Augie Choice program gives $2,000 to every student to support a qualifying hands-on learning experience. Augie Choice programs are found in CORE (Careers-Opportunities-Research-Exploration) which helps students connect the three major parts of the Augustana residential liberal arts experience: academics (classes, majors), experiential learning (study away, research) and community (volunteering, service). Students work with multiple advisors and counselors who will get them where they want to be. "Our goal in launching CORE was to ensure that all students have the opportunity to participate in learning experiences that help them discover their purpose and passions, and connect them to their career aspirations. We want our students to explore the possibilities and engage in meaningful experiences from the day they step on campus so that in four years they will be fully prepared to take the next step in their life's journey."
Dr. Pareena Lawrence, provost and dean of the college

FACILITIES

Housing: Coed dorms, men's dorms, women's dorms, apartments for single students. **Special Academic Facilities/Equipment:** Educational technology building, art gallery, black culture house, Hispanic culture house, geology museum, on-campus preschool, immigration research center, scanning and transmission electron microscopes, nuclear magnetic resonance, atomic absorption, and diode array mass spectrophotometers, planetarium, observatory with celestron telescope, environmental field stations. **Computers:** 50% of classrooms, 30% of dorms, 100% of libraries, 100% of dining areas, 90% of student union, 25% of common outdoor areas have wireless network access. Students can register for classes online. Administrative functions (other than registration) can be performed online.

CAMPUS LIFE

Environment: City. **Activities:** Choral groups, concert band, dance, drama/theater, jazz band, literary magazine, music ensembles, musical theater, opera, pep band, radio station, student government, student newspaper, symphony orchestra, yearbook, Campus Ministries, Student Organization, Model UN. 128 registered organizations, 15 honor societies, 5 religious organizations. 7 fraternities, 6 sororities. **Athletics (Intercollegiate):** *Men:* baseball, basketball, cross-country, diving, football, golf, soccer, swimming, tennis, track/field (outdoor), track/field (indoor), wrestling. *Women:* basketball, cross-country, diving, golf, lacrosse, soccer, softball, swimming, tennis, track/field (outdoor), track/field (indoor), volleyball. **On-Campus Highlights:** Thomas Tredway Library, Pepsico Recreation Center, Java 101-Coffee shop, F.W. Olin Center for Educational Technology, College Center. **Environmental Initiatives:** Recycling Program.

ADMISSIONS

Freshman Academic Profile: Average high school GPA 3.3. 29% in top 10% of high school class, 62% in top 25% of high school class, 90% in top 50% of high school class. ACT middle 50% range 23-28. Minimum internet-based TOEFL 80. Minimum paper TOEFL 550. **Basis for Candidate Selection:** *Very important factors considered include:* rigor of secondary school record, class rank, academic GPA. *Important factors considered include:* standardized test scores, application essay, recommendation(s), interview, extracurricular activities, talent/ability, character/personal qualities, level of applicant's interest. *Other factors considered include:* alumni/ae relation, geographical residence, religious affiliation/commitment, racial/ethnic status, volunteer work, work experience. **Freshman Admission Requirements:** High school diploma is required and GED is accepted. *Academic units required:* 3 English, 3 math, 3 science, 2 science labs, 1 foreign language, 1 social studies, 1 history. *Academic units recommended:* 4 English, 4 math, 4 science, 2 science labs, 2 foreign language, 2 social studies, 1 history, 4 academic electives. **Freshman Admission Statistics:** 6,587 applied, 51.62% admitted, 21% enrolled. **Transfer Admission Requirements:** High school transcript, college transcript(s), statement of good standing from prior institution(s). Minimum college GPA of 2.0 required. Lowest grade transferable D. **General Admission Information:** Priority deadline 2/1. Nonfall registration accepted. Admission may be deferred.

COSTS AND FINANCIAL AID

Annual tuition $40,908. Room and board $10,314. Average book expense $1,000. **Required Forms and Deadlines:** FAFSA, Institution's own financial aid form. **Notification of Awards:** Applicants will be notified of awards on a rolling basis beginning 3/1. **Types of Aid:** *Need-based scholarships/grants:* Federal Pell, FSEOG, State scholarships/grants, Private scholarships, College/university scholarship or grant aid from institutional funds. *Loans:* Direct Subsidized Stafford Loans, Direct Unsubsidized Stafford Loans, Direct PLUS loans, Federal Perkins Loans. *Student Employment:* Federal Work-Study Program available. Institutional employment available. **Financial Aid Statistics:** 98% needy freshmen receive need-based scholarship or grant aid. 99% freshmen, 99% undergrads receive any aid. **Criteria for awarding aid:** *Need-based:* Minority status. *Non-need-based:* Academics, Alumni affiliation, Art, Leadership, Music/drama, Religious affiliation.

AUGUSTANA UNIVERSITY

2001 South Summit Avenue, Sioux Falls, SD 57197
Phone: 605-274-5516 • **Financial Aid Phone:** 605-274-5216
E-mail: admission@augie.edu • **CEEB Code:** 6015
Fax: 605-274-5518 • **Website:** www.augie.edu • **ACT Code:** 3902

This private school, affiliated with the Lutheran Church, was founded in 1860. It has a 100-acre campus.

RATINGS

Admissions Selectivity Rating: 86   **Fire Safety Rating:** 94   **Green Rating:** 80

STUDENTS AND FACULTY

Enrollment: 1,886. **Student Body:** 60% female, 40% male, 50% out-of-state, 7% international (39 countries represented). Asian 1%, African American 2%, Caucasian 85%, Hispanic 3%, Native American <1%, Pacific Islander 0%, Two or more races 2%, Race unknown <1%.
Retention and Graduation: 84% freshmen return for sophomore year. 54% freshmen graduate within 4 years. 71% freshmen graduate within 6 years. 21% grads go on to further study within 1 year. 10% grads pursue arts and sciences degrees. 2% grads pursue law degrees. 10% grads pursue business degrees. 6% grads pursue medical degrees. **Faculty:** Student/faculty ratio 11:1. 131 full-time faculty, 86% hold PhDs, 8% are are members of minority groups, 51% are women. 0% of classes are taught by teaching assistants.

ACADEMICS

Degrees: bachelor's, master's. **Classes:** Most classes have 10-19 students. Most lab/discussion sessions have fewer than 10 students. **Most popular majors:** Business Administration, Management and Operations; Registered Nursing/Registered Nurse; Education. **Special Study Options:** cooperative education program, cross-registration, double major, dual enrollment, exchange student program (domestic), external degree program, honors program, independent study, internships, liberal arts/career combination, study abroad, teacher certification program, Metro-Urban Studies through HECUA. January Abroad program through UMAIE. Washington, D.C. Semesters. Study Australia

through EAN. Dual Degree Program in Engineering. Service-Learning Spring Breaks trips; Faculty-led Spring Breaks Abroad; Honors Courses in Western Civilization, Chemistry, and Religion. Civitas honors program for students with 27 ACT and 3.5 GPA. **Honors Programs:** Our campus-wide, interdisciplinary Honors program is called Civitas (citizenship). Specific majors also offer departmental honors programs for students willing to accept academic challenges that go well beyond those required for graduation. Combined degree programs: BA/MEng. **Disability Services:** Special programs offered to physically disabled students, including note-taking services, reader services, tape recorders, tutors. **Career Services:** Alumni network, Alumni services, Career/job search classes, Career assessment, Internships, Regional alumni. The city of Sioux Falls (170,000) along with a network of Augustana Alumni provide excellent opportunities for internships, research, and employment. Sioux Falls is a thriving, real-world "laboratory" for our students.

FACILITIES

Housing: Coed dorms, special housing for disabled students, apartments for married students, apartments for single students, Theme Housing, Housing is available for students with children. 85% of campus accessible to physically diasbled. **Special Academic Facilities/Equipment:** Center for Western Studies, Archeology Lab, Eide/Dalrymple Gallery, Center for Liturgical Art **Computers:** 25% of classrooms, 25% of dorms, 100% of libraries, 100% of dining areas, 75% of student union, have wireless network access. Students can register for classes online. Administrative functions (other than registration) can be performed online.

CAMPUS LIFE

Environment: City. **Activities:** Choral groups, concert band, dance, drama/theater, jazz band, literary magazine, music ensembles, musical theater, opera, pep band, student government, student newspaper, student-run film society, symphony orchestra, yearbook, Campus Ministries, Student Organization. 92 registered organizations, 13 honor societies, 9 religious organizations. **Athletics (Intercollegiate):** *Men:* baseball, basketball, cross-country, football, golf, tennis, track/field (outdoor), track/field (indoor), wrestling. *Women:* basketball, cheerleading, cross-country, golf, soccer, softball, tennis, track/field (outdoor), track/field (indoor), volleyball. **On-Campus Highlights:** Morrison Commons, The Huddle, Mikkelson Library, Elmen Center, Center for Visual Arts, The Madsen Center, home to our social science programs, is also a popular place for students to gather and study, or use the computer lab. With newly renovated and refurbished lounges, our resident halls also serve as gathering areas for students to converse, watch TV, play ping pong or pool. **Environmental Initiatives:** Recent program to measure utilities used by certain student housing and incentives provided to reduce consumption.

ADMISSIONS

Freshman Academic Profile: Average high school GPA 3.8. 30% in top 10% of high school class, 53% in top 25% of high school class, 73% in top 50% of high school class. 85% from public high schools. ACT middle 50% range 23-29. Minimum internet-based TOEFL 79. Minimum paper TOEFL 550. **Basis for Candidate Selection:** *Important factors considered include:* rigor of secondary school record, academic GPA, standardized test scores, application essay, recommendation(s). *Other factors considered include:* class rank, interview, extracurricular activities, character/personal qualities, alumni/ae relation, volunteer work, work experience, level of applicant's interest. **Freshman Admission Requirements:** High school diploma is required and GED is accepted. *Academic units recommended:* 4 English, 4 math, 4 science, 2 foreign language, 3 social studies, 3 visual/performing arts. **Freshman Admission Statistics:** 1,464 applied, 69.13% admitted, 42% enrolled. **Transfer Admission Requirements:** High school transcript, college transcript(s), essay or personal statement, Minimum college GPA of 2.2 required. Lowest grade transferable C-. **General Admission Information:** Priority deadline 1/15. Nonfall registration accepted. Admission may be deferred for a maximum of 1 year.

COSTS AND FINANCIAL AID

Annual tuition $30,454. Room and board $7,774. Required fees $490. Average book expense $1,000. **Required Forms and Deadlines:** FAFSA. **Notification of Awards:** Applicants will be notified of awards on a rolling basis beginning 4/1. **Types of Aid:** *Need-based scholarships/grants:* Federal Pell, FSEOG, State scholarships/grants, Private scholarships, College/university scholarship or grant aid from institutional funds. *Loans:* Direct Subsidized Stafford Loans, Direct Unsubsidized Stafford Loans, Direct PLUS loans, Federal Perkins Loans, Federal Nursing Loans, College/university loans from institutional funds. *Student Employment:* Federal Work-Study Program available. Institutional employment available. **Financial Aid Statistics:** 100% needy freshmen, 99% needy undergrads receive need-based scholarship or grant aid. 98% freshmen, 96% undergrads receive non-need-based scholarship or grant aid. 64% freshmen, 71% undergrads receive need-based self-help aid. 22% freshmen, 19% undergrads receive athletic scholarships. 99% freshmen, 99% undergrads receive any aid. 67% undergrads borrow to pay for school. Average cumulative indebtedness $36,950. **Criteria for awarding aid:** *Need-based:* Academics, Athletics, Leadership, Minority status, Music/drama, Religious affiliation. *Non-need-based:* Academics, Alumni affiliation, Art, Athletics, Leadership, Minority status, Music/drama, Religious affiliation, State/district residency.

AUGUSTA STATE UNIVERSITY

2500 Walton Way, Augusta, GA 30904-2200
Phone: 706-737-1632 • **Financial Aid Phone:** 706-737-1431
E-mail: admissio@aug.edu • **CEEB Code:** 5336
Fax: 706-667-4355 • **ACT Code:** 796

This public school was founded in 1925. It has a 76-acre campus.

RATINGS
Admissions Selectivity Rating: 78   **Fire Safety Rating:** 73   **Green Rating:** 60*

STUDENTS AND FACULTY
Enrollment: 5,394. **Student Body:** 64% female, 36% male, 9% out-of-state, 1% international (60 countries represented). Asian 3%, African American 28%, Caucasian 59%, Hispanic 3%, Native American <1%, Pacific Islander 0%, Two or more races 0%, Race unknown 5%.
Retention and Graduation: 69% freshmen return for sophomore year. 4% freshmen graduate within 4 years. 21% freshmen graduate within 6 years. **Faculty:** Student/faculty ratio 18:1. 236 full-time faculty, 64% hold PhDs, 16% are members of minority groups, 51% are women. 0% of classes are taught by teaching assistants.

ACADEMICS
Degrees: associate, bachelor's, master's, post-master's certificate, terminal, transfer. **Classes:** Most classes have 20-29 students. Most lab/discussion sessions have 20-29 students. **Most popular majors:** Elementary Education and Teaching; Biology/Biological Sciences; Psychology. **Special Study Options:** cooperative education program, cross-registration, distance learning, double major, dual enrollment, English as a Second Language (ESL), honors program, independent study, internships, study abroad, teacher certification program, Paralegal Certification. **Honors Programs:** Augusta State University's Honors Program provides about 100 of our best students with special sections of classes in the core curriculum. Those classes are usually smaller, involve much closer interaction with the professor, and encourage more independent and collaborative work than non-honors sections of these courses. In their Junior and Senior years, Honors students take two interdisciplinary courses, prepare, write, and defend a thesis, and conclude their undergraduate program with a Capstone course. **Disability Services:** Special programs offered to physically disabled students, including note-taking services, reader services, tape recorders, tutors. **Career Services:** Alumni services. Our outreach to students via the classrooms and appointments for individualized help.

FACILITIES
Housing: apartments for single students. 90% of campus accessible to physically diasbled. **Special Academic Facilities/Equipment:** Performing Arts Theatre, Christenberry Field House, Forest Hill Golf Course **Computers:** 95% of classrooms, 5% of dorms, 100% of libraries, 100% of dining areas, 100% of student union, have wireless network access. Students can register for classes online. Administrative functions (other than registration) can be performed online.

CAMPUS LIFE
Environment: City. **Activities:** Choral groups, concert band, drama/theater, jazz band, literary magazine, pep band, radio station, student government, student newspaper. 60 registered organizations, 5 honor societies, 5 religious organizations. 3 fraternities, 3 sororities. **Athletics (Intercollegiate):** *Men:* baseball, basketball, golf, tennis. *Women:* basketball, golf, softball, tennis, volleyball. **On-Campus Highlights:** Allgood Hall, Christenberry Field House, University Hall, Jaguar Student Activities Center, Maxwell Performing Arts Theater.

ADMISSIONS
Freshman Academic Profile: Average high school GPA 2.9. 95% from public high schools. **Reported SAT (pre-2016 redesign) scores:** SAT Math middle 50% range 430-540. SAT Critical Reading middle 50% range 440-540. **Concordant SAT scores:** SAT Math middle 50% range 470–570. ACT middle 50% range 17-21. Minimum paper TOEFL 500. **Basis for Candidate Selection:** *Important factors considered include:* rigor of secondary school record, academic GPA, standardized test scores. **Freshman Admission Requirements:** High school diploma is required and GED is accepted. *Academic units required:* 4 English, 4 math, 3 science, 2 foreign language, 3 social studies. **Freshman Admission Statistics:** 2,401 applied, 52.02% admitted, 76% enrolled. **Transfer Admission Requirements:** college transcript(s), Minimum college GPA of 2.0 required. Lowest grade transferable D. **General Admission Information:** Application fee $20. Priority deadline 7/1. Nonfall registration accepted. Admission may be deferred.

COSTS AND FINANCIAL AID
Average book expense $1,000. **Required Forms and Deadlines:** FAFSA, State aid form. **Notification of Awards:** Applicants will be notified of awards on or about 6/1. **Types of Aid:** *Need-based scholarships/grants:* Federal Pell, FSEOG, State scholarships/grants, Private scholarships, College/university scholarship or grant aid from institutional funds. *Loans:* Federal Perkins Loans, State Loans, College/university loans from institutional funds. *Student Employment:* Federal Work-Study Program available. Institutional employment available. **Financial Aid Statistics:** 73% needy freshmen, 67% needy undergrads receive need-based scholarship or grant aid. 27% freshmen, 31% undergrads receive non-need-based scholarship or grant aid. 73% freshmen, 70% undergrads receive need-based self-help aid. 0% freshmen, 2% undergrads receive athletic scholarships. **Criteria for awarding aid:** *Need-based:* Academics, Art, Leadership, Music/drama. *Non-need-based:* Academics, Alumni affiliation, Art, Athletics, Job skills, Leadership, Minority status, Music/drama, State/district residency.

AURORA UNIVERSITY

347 South Gladstone Ave, Aurora, IL 60506
Phone: 630-844-5533 • **Financial Aid Phone:** 630-844-6190
E-mail: admission@aurora.edu • **CEEB Code:** 1027
Fax: 630-844-5535 • **Website:** www.aurora.edu • **ACT Code:** 950

This private school was founded in 1893. It has a 30-acre campus.

RATINGS
Admissions Selectivity Rating: 72   **Fire Safety Rating:** 88   **Green Rating:** 60*

STUDENTS AND FACULTY
Enrollment: 3,784. **Student Body:** 65% female, 35% male, 12% out-of-state, <1% international (2 countries represented). Asian 2%, African American 8%, Caucasian 54%, Hispanic 27%, Native American <1%, Pacific Islander <1%, Two or more races 3%, Race unknown 5%.
Retention and Graduation: 67% freshmen return for sophomore year. 41% freshmen graduate within 4 years. 58% freshmen graduate within 6 years. **Faculty:** Student/faculty ratio 17:1. 154 full-time faculty, 0% hold PhDs, 12% are are members of minority groups, 54% are women. 0% of classes are taught by teaching assistants.

ACADEMICS
Degrees: bachelor's, doctoral/research, master's, postbachelor's certifiate, post-master's certificate. **Classes:** Most classes have 10-19 students. Most lab/discussion sessions have 10-19 students. **Most popular majors:** Elementary Education and Teaching Business Administration and Management. **Special Study Options:** Accelerated program, cross-registration, double major, honors program, independent study, internships, liberal arts/career combination, student-designed major, study abroad, teacher certification program. **Honors Programs:** Honors Program including honors seminars, honors section of some general education courses and a senior honors project. **Disability Services:** Special programs offered to physically disabled students, including note-taking services, reader services, tape recorders, tutors. **Career Services:** Alumni network, Alumni services, Career/job search classes, Career assessment, Internships.

FACILITIES
Housing: Coed dorms. 95% of campus accessible to physically diasbled. **Special Academic Facilities/Equipment:** Schingoethe Center for Native American Culture Downstairs Dunham Gallery Center For Faith And Action Perry Theatre in the Aurora Foundation Center for Community Education **Computers:** 100% of classrooms, 80% of dorms, 100% of libraries, 100% of dining areas, 100% of student union, 90% of common outdoor areas have wireless network access. Administrative functions (other than registration) can be performed online.

CAMPUS LIFE
Environment: City. **Activities:** Choral groups, drama/theater, literary magazine, pep band, radio station, student government, student newspaper, Campus Ministries, Model UN. 49 registered organizations, 2 honor societies, 1 religious organization. 1 fraternity, 4 sororities. **Athletics (Intercollegiate):** *Men:* baseball, basketball, cross-country, football, golf, soccer, tennis, track/field (outdoor), track/field (indoor). *Women:* basketball, cross-country, golf, soccer, softball, tennis, track/field (outdoor), track/field (indoor), volleyball. **On-Campus Highlights:** The Spartan Spot, Fitness Center, The Learning Center, Computer Labs, Vago Stadium. **Environmental Initiatives:** Campus-wide Recycling.

ADMISSIONS
Freshman Academic Profile: Average high school GPA 3.3. 92% from public high schools. **Reported SAT (pre-2016 redesign) scores:** SAT Math middle 50% range 430-530. SAT Critical Reading middle 50% range 420-520. **Concordant SAT scores:** SAT Math middle 50% range 470–560. ACT

middle 50% range 19-24. Minimum internet-based TOEFL 79. Minimum paper TOEFL 550. **Basis for Candidate Selection:** *Very important factors considered include:* rigor of secondary school record, class rank, academic GPA, standardized test scores, interview. *Important factors considered include:* extracurricular activities, character/personal qualities, alumni/ae relation. *Other factors considered include:* application essay, recommendation(s), talent/ability, first generation, volunteer work, work experience, level of applicant's interest. **Freshman Admission Requirements:** High school diploma is required and GED is accepted. *Academic units required:* 4 English, 3 math, 3 science, 3 social studies, 3 academic electives. **Freshman Admission Statistics:** 2,615 applied, 87.72% admitted, 29% enrolled. **Transfer Admission Requirements:** college transcript(s), statement of good standing from prior institution(s). Minimum college GPA of 2.0 required. Lowest grade transferable C. **General Admission Information:** Application fee $25. Regular application deadline 5/1. Nonfall registration accepted. Admission may be deferred.

COSTS AND FINANCIAL AID

Annual tuition $23,260. Room and board $11,470. Required fees $260. Average book expense $1,000. **Required Forms and Deadlines:** FAFSA. **Notification of Awards:** Applicants will be notified of awards on a rolling basis beginning 3/1. **Types of Aid:** *Need-based scholarships/grants:* Federal Pell, FSEOG, State scholarships/grants, Private scholarships, College/university scholarship or grant aid from institutional funds. *Loans:* Direct Subsidized Stafford Loans, Direct Unsubsidized Stafford Loans, Direct PLUS loans, Federal Perkins Loans, College/university loans from institutional funds. *Student Employment:* Federal Work-Study Program available. Institutional employment available. **Financial Aid Statistics:** 78% needy freshmen, 91% needy undergrads receive need-based scholarship or grant aid. 18% freshmen, 17% undergrads receive non-need-based scholarship or grant aid. 88% freshmen, 89% undergrads receive need-based self-help aid. 0% freshmen, 0% undergrads receive athletic scholarships. 100% freshmen, 98% undergrads receive any aid. 83% undergrads borrow to pay for school. Average cumulative indebtedness $27,578. **Criteria for awarding aid:** *Need-based:* Leadership, Religious affiliation. *Non-need-based:* Academics, Alumni affiliation, Art, Music/drama, Religious affiliation, State/district residency.

AUSTIN COLLEGE

900 N. Grand Avenue, Sherman, TX 75090
Phone: 903-813-3000 • **Financial Aid Phone:** 903-813-2900
E-mail: admission@austincollege.edu • **CEEB Code:** 6016
Fax: 903-813-3198 • **Website:** 900 N. Grand Avenue • **ACT Code:** 4058

This private school, affiliated with the Presbyterian Church, was founded in 1849. It has a 70-acre campus.

RATINGS
Admissions Selectivity Rating: 88   **Fire Safety Rating:** 84   **Green Rating:** 80

STUDENTS AND FACULTY

Enrollment: 1,250. **Student Body:** 52% female, 48% male, 9% out-of-state, 3% international (15 countries represented). Asian 13%, African American 7%, Caucasian 53%, Hispanic 19%, Native American 1%, Pacific Islander <1%, Two or more races 1%, Race unknown 3%.
Retention and Graduation: 83% freshmen return for sophomore year. 71% freshmen graduate within 4 years. 73 35% grads go on to further study within 1 year. 3% grads pursue law degrees. 9% grads pursue medical degrees. **Faculty:** Student/faculty ratio 13:1. 91 full-time faculty, 98% hold PhDs, 11% are are members of minority groups, 29% are women. 0% of classes are taught by teaching assistants.

ACADEMICS

Degrees: bachelor's, master's. **Classes:** Most classes have fewer than 10 students. Most lab/discussion sessions have 10-19 students. **Most popular majors:** Biology/Biological Sciences; Business/Commerce; Psychology. **Special Study Options:** double major, exchange student program (domestic), honors program, independent study, internships, student-designed major, study abroad, teacher certification program, Phi Beta Kappa. Combined degree programs: 3-2 Program in Engineeri with UT, Dal and Wash Univ. **Disability Services:** Special programs offered to physically disabled students, including tutors. **Career Services:** Alumni network, Alumni services, Career/job search classes, Career assessment, Internships.

FACILITIES

Housing: Coed dorms, special housing for disabled students, men's dorms, women's dorms, apartments for single students, Jordan Family Language House. 99% of campus accessible to physically diasbled. **Special Academic Facilities/Equipment:** Tissue culture facility, high-performance numerics and graphics computing facility. **Computers:** 30% of classrooms, 100% of dorms, 100% of libraries, 100% of dining areas, 100% of student union, 30% of common outdoor areas have wireless network access. Students can register for classes online. Administrative functions (other than registration) can be performed online.

CAMPUS LIFE

Environment: Town. **Activities:** Choral groups, dance, drama/theater, jazz band, literary magazine, music ensembles, musical theater, pep band, student government, student newspaper, symphony orchestra, yearbook, Campus Ministries, Student Organization, Model UN. 52 registered organizations, 15 honor societies, 6 religious organizations. 6 fraternities, 6 sororities. **Athletics (Intercollegiate):** *Men:* baseball, basketball, football, soccer, swimming, tennis. *Women:* basketball, soccer, softball, swimming, tennis, volleyball. **On-Campus Highlights:** Wright Campus Center, Jordan Family Language House, Verde Dickey Fitness Pavilion, Abell Library, Residence hall facilities, Roo Suites, a suite-style residence facility for upperclass students is the favored residential experience. **Environmental Initiatives:** Board approval of Climate Action Plan to reduce emissions to 0 and well established Center for Envronmental Studies that offers a major and minor.

ADMISSIONS

Freshman Academic Profile: Average high school GPA 3.5. 36% in top 10% of high school class, 71% in top 25% of high school class, 93% in top 50% of high school class. 77% from public high schools. **Reported SAT (pre-2016 redesign) scores:** SAT Math middle 50% range 540-640. SAT Critical Reading middle 50% range 540-650. SAT Writing middle 50% range 500-630. **Concordant SAT scores:** SAT EBRW middle 50% 580–690. SAT Math middle 50% range 570–660. ACT middle 50% range 22-28. Minimum paper TOEFL 550. **Basis for Candidate Selection:** *Very important factors considered include:* rigor of secondary school record, academic GPA. *Important factors considered include:* standardized test scores, application essay, recommendation(s), character/personal qualities. *Other factors considered include:* class rank, interview, extracurricular activities, talent/ability, geographical residence, state residency, religious affiliation/commitment, volunteer work, work experience, level of applicant's interest. **Freshman Admission Requirements:** High school diploma is required and GED is accepted. *Academic units required:* 4 English, 3 math, 3 science, 1 science lab, 2 foreign language, 2 social studies, 1 visual/performing arts. *Academic units recommended:* 4 English, 3 math, 4 science, 2 science labs, 2 visual/performing arts. **Freshman Admission Statistics:** 3,357 applied, 54.10% admitted, 20% enrolled. **Transfer Admission Requirements:** college transcript(s), essay or personal statement, statement of good standing from prior institution(s). Minimum college GPA of 3.0 required. Lowest grade transferable C. **General Admission Information:** Priority deadline 3/1. Regular notification 11/15. Nonfall registration not accepted. Admission may be deferred for a maximum of 1 Year.

COSTS AND FINANCIAL AID

Annual tuition $36,415. Room and board $12,082. Required fees $185. Average book expense $1,250. **Required Forms and Deadlines:** FAFSA. **Notification of Awards:** Applicants will be notified of awards on a rolling basis beginning 2/15. **Types of Aid:** *Need-based scholarships/grants:* Federal Pell, FSEOG, State scholarships/grants, Private scholarships, College/university scholarship or grant aid from institutional funds. *Loans:* Direct Subsidized Stafford Loans, Direct Unsubsidized Stafford Loans, Direct PLUS loans, Federal Perkins Loans, State Loans. *Student Employment:* Federal Work-Study Program available. Institutional employment available. **Financial Aid Statistics:** 100% needy freshmen, 100% needy undergrads receive need-based scholarship or grant aid. 55% freshmen, 19% undergrads receive non-need-based scholarship or grant aid. 69% freshmen, 72% undergrads receive need-based self-help aid. 0% freshmen, 0% undergrads receive athletic scholarships. 97% freshmen, 98% undergrads receive any aid. **Criteria for awarding aid:** *Non-need-based:* Academics, Alumni affiliation, Art, Leadership, Music/drama, Religious affiliation.

AUSTIN PEAY STATE UNIVERSITY

P.O. Box 4548, Clarksville, TN 37044
Phone: 931-221-7661
E-mail: admissions@apsu.edu • **CEEB Code:** 1028
Fax: 931-221-6168 • **Website:** www.apsu.edu • **ACT Code:** 3944

This public school was founded in 1927. It has a 210-acre campus.

RATINGS

Admissions Selectivity Rating: 75   **Fire Safety Rating:** 60*   **Green Rating:** 60*

STUDENTS AND FACULTY

Enrollment: 9,116. **Student Body:** 58% female, 42% male, 10% out-of-state, <1% international (13 countries represented). Asian 2%, African American 21%, Caucasian 61%, Hispanic 7%, Native American <1%, Pacific Islander <1%, Two or more races 6%, Race unknown 2%.
Retention and Graduation: 66% freshmen return for sophomore year. 19% freshmen graduate within 4 years. 40% freshmen graduate within 6 years. **Faculty:** Student/faculty ratio 18:1. 370 full-time faculty, 0% hold PhDs, 14% are members of minority groups, 49% are women. 0% of classes are taught by teaching assistants.

ACADEMICS

Degrees: associate, bachelor's, master's, postbachelor's certificate, post-master's certificate, terminal, transfer. **Classes:** Most classes have 20-29 students. Most lab/discussion sessions have 20-29 students. **Special Study Options:** Accelerated program, cooperative education program, distance learning, double major, dual enrollment, English as a Second Language (ESL), honors program, independent study, internships, study abroad, teacher certification program, Servicemembers Opportunity College (SOC) for associate and bachelor's degrees. **Disability Services:** Special programs offered to physically disabled students, including note-taking services, reader services, tutors. **Career Services:** Career/job search classes, Career assessment, Internships.

FACILITIES

Housing: Coed dorms, special housing for disabled students, men's dorms, women's dorms, fraternity/sorority housing, apartments for married students, apartments for single students, For faculty/staff. 100% of campus accessible to physically diasbled. **Special Academic Facilities/Equipment:** Art museum, biology museum, language lab, demonstration farm, 21st century classroom.

CAMPUS LIFE

Environment: Village. **Activities:** Choral groups, concert band, dance, drama/theater, jazz band, literary magazine, marching band, music ensembles, musical theater, opera, pep band, radio station, student government, student newspaper, student-run film society, symphony orchestra, television station, yearbook, Campus Ministries, Student Organization. 50 registered organizations, 13 honor societies, 10 religious organizations. 8 fraternities, 6 sororities. **Athletics (Intercollegiate):** *Men:* baseball, basketball, cheerleading, cross-country, football, golf, tennis. *Women:* basketball, cheerleading, cross-country, golf, riflery, soccer, softball, tennis, track/field (outdoor), volleyball. **On-Campus Highlights:** University Center, Sundquist Science Complex, Hand Village, Dunn Center.

ADMISSIONS

Freshman Academic Profile: Average high school GPA 3.2. 14% in top 10% of high school class, 37% in top 25% of high school class, 71% in top 50% of high school class. 95% from public high schools. **Reported SAT (pre-2016 redesign) scores:** SAT Math middle 50% range 463-563. SAT Critical Reading middle 50% range 470-561. **Concordant SAT scores:** SAT Math middle 50% range 500–580. ACT middle 50% range 19-24. Minimum paper TOEFL 500. **Basis for Candidate Selection:** *Very important factors considered include:* academic GPA, standardized test scores. *Other factors considered include:* rigor of secondary school record. **Freshman Admission Requirements:** High school diploma is required and GED is accepted. *Academic units required:* 4 English, 3 math, 2 science, 1 science lab, 2 foreign language, 1 social studies, 1 history, 1 visual/performing arts. **Freshman Admission Statistics:** 6,272 applied, 88.81% admitted, 35% enrolled. **Transfer Admission Requirements:** college transcript(s), Lowest grade transferable D. **General Admission Information:** Application fee $15. Regular application deadline 8/3. Nonfall registration accepted. Admission may be deferred for a maximum of 12 months.

COSTS AND FINANCIAL AID

Annual in-state tuition $6,522. Annual out-of-state tuition $22,518. Required fees $1,473. Average book expense $1,550. **Required Forms and Deadlines:** FAFSA. **Notification of Awards:** Applicants will be notified of awards on a rolling basis beginning 4/15. **Types of Aid:** *Need-based scholarships/grants:* Federal Pell, FSEOG, State scholarships/grants, Private scholarships, College/university scholarship or grant aid from institutional funds. *Loans:* Direct Subsidized Stafford Loans, Direct Unsubsidized Stafford Loans, Direct

PLUS loans, Federal Perkins Loans. *Student Employment:* Federal Work-Study Program available. Institutional employment available. **Financial Aid Statistics:** 80% needy freshmen, 86% needy undergrads receive need-based scholarship or grant aid. 82% freshmen, 60% undergrads receive non-need-based scholarship or grant aid. 62% freshmen, 68% undergrads receive need-based self-help aid. 2% freshmen, 1% undergrads receive athletic scholarships. 69% undergrads borrow to pay for school. Average cumulative indebtedness $23,808. **Criteria for awarding aid:** *Non-need-based:* Academics, Alumni affiliation, Art, Athletics, Leadership, Music/drama, State/district residency.

AVERETT UNIVERSITY

420 West Main Street, Danville, VA 24541
Phone: 434-791-5600 • **Financial Aid Phone:** 434-791-5890 • **CEEB Code:** 5017
Fax: 434-797-2784 • **Website:** www.averett.edu • **ACT Code:** 4338

This private school was founded in 1859. It has a 19-acre campus.

RATINGS

Admissions Selectivity Rating: 78   **Fire Safety Rating:** 97   **Green Rating:** 65

STUDENTS AND FACULTY

Enrollment: 849. **Student Body:** 49% female, 51% male, 36% out-of-state, 5% international (16 countries represented). Asian 1%, African American 32%, Caucasian 58%, Hispanic 3%, Native American 1%, Pacific Islander <1%, Two or more races 0%, Race unknown 0%.
Retention and Graduation: 55% freshmen return for sophomore year. 34% freshmen graduate within 4 years. 41% freshmen graduate within 6 years. 40% grads go on to further study within 1 year. **Faculty:** Student/faculty ratio 11:1. 62 full-time faculty, 66% hold PhDs, 10% are members of minority groups, 53% are women. 0% of classes are taught by teaching assistants.

ACADEMICS

Degrees: associate, bachelor's, master's. **Classes:** Most classes have 10-19 students. Most lab/discussion sessions have 10-19 students. **Most popular majors:** Pre-Medicine/Pre-Medical Studies; Nursing Science; Criminal Justice/Law Enforcement Administration. **Special Study Options:** Accelerated program, cooperative education program, cross-registration, distance learning, double major, dual enrollment, exchange student program (domestic), honors program, independent study, internships, student-designed major, study abroad, teacher certification program, Also offered: Interdisciplinary studies and Leadership studies. Undergraduates may take grad level classes. Some online courses available. **Honors Programs:** Averett's Honors Program gives students the opportunity to go a step beyond regular classroom study. Honors students explore, in-depth, selected areas of academics. Participation in the Honors Program demonstrates a commitment to scholarship and will give students an edge in graduate study or in the job market. To earn the honors distinction, approximately 20% of all coursework completed must carry honors credit. The program culminates with a senior honors project. Honors Program students may also participate in the Honors Association and attend conferences, social activities and cultural performances. **Disability Services:** Special programs offered to physically disabled students, including note-taking services, reader services, tape recorders, tutors. **Career Services:** Alumni network, Alumni services, Career/job search classes, Career assessment, Internships, Regional alumni, On-campus interviews. In July 2014, Averett University established the Center for Community Engagement and Career Competitiveness. Career Services is now housed within the Center, and collaborates with community partners to provide leadership and direction for comprehensive career planning to Averett University students and alumni. Through dynamic programming, these initiatives provide support, resources, counseling, and networking opportunities to develop students as young professionals.

FACILITIES

Housing: Coed dorms, men's dorms, women's dorms, apartments for single students. 73% of campus accessible to physically diasbled. **Special Academic Facilities/Equipment:** Averett's Flight Center located 4 miles from the main campus at Danville Regional Airport has two runways (one with ILS approach), automated weather system, and UNICOM service. Averett's facility houses aircraft, areas for ground instruction, simulator rooms, technology center. Averett's 100-acre Equestrian Center is a 15-minute drive from the main campus. It houses an indoor ring, 40 stalls with removable partitions, 3 tack rooms, wash room for horses and equipment, breeding area, offices, and a laboratory. The outdoor facilities include a round pen, riding ring, jumping area, pastures, and cross-country trails. **Computers:** 100% of libraries, 100% of dining areas, 100% of student union, have wireless network access. Students can register for classes online. Administrative functions (other than registration) can be performed online.

CAMPUS LIFE

Environment: Town. **Activities:** Choral groups, drama/theater, literary magazine, musical theater, student government, student newspaper, Student Organization. 30 registered organizations, 4 honor societies, 4 religious organizations. 1 fraternity, 1 sorority. **Athletics (Intercollegiate):** *Men:* baseball, basketball, cheerleading, cross-country, equestrian sports, football, golf, soccer, tennis. *Women:* basketball, cheerleading, cross-country, equestrian sports, soccer, softball, tennis, volleyball. **On-Campus Highlights:** Student Center, Grant Athletic Center (North Campus), Equestrian Center, Airport Facilities, Jut's Cafe.

ADMISSIONS

Freshman Academic Profile: Average high school GPA 3.2. 6% in top 10% of high school class, 23% in top 25% of high school class, 56% in top 50% of high school class. 94% from public high schools. **Reported SAT (pre-2016 redesign) scores:** SAT Math middle 50% range 400-510. SAT Critical Reading middle 50% range 410-500. SAT Writing middle 50% range 380-480. **Concordant SAT scores:** SAT EBRW middle 50% 440–550. SAT Math middle 50% range 440–540. ACT middle 50% range 17-21. Minimum internet-based TOEFL 61. Minimum paper TOEFL 500. **Basis for Candidate Selection:** *Very important factors considered include:* rigor of secondary school record, class rank, academic GPA, standardized test scores. *Other factors considered include:* application essay, recommendation(s), interview, extracurricular activities, character/personal qualities, alumni/ae relation, volunteer work, work experience, level of applicant's interest. **Freshman Admission Requirements:** High school diploma is required and GED is accepted. *Academic units required:* 4 English, 3 math, 3 science, 2 science labs, 3 social studies, 3 history. *Academic units recommended:* 2 foreign language. **Freshman Admission Statistics:** 2,247 applied, 54.78% admitted, 19% enrolled. **Transfer Admission Requirements:** college transcript(s), statement of good standing from prior institution(s). Minimum college GPA of 2.0 required. Lowest grade transferable C. **General Admission Information:** Nonfall registration accepted. Admission may be deferred for a maximum of 2 years.

COSTS AND FINANCIAL AID

Annual tuition $31,980. Average book expense $1,000. **Required Forms and Deadlines:** FAFSA, State aid form. **Types of Aid:** *Need-based scholarships/grants:* Federal Pell, FSEOG, State scholarships/grants, Private scholarships, College/university scholarship or grant aid from institutional funds. *Loans:* Direct Subsidized Stafford Loans, Direct Unsubsidized Stafford Loans, Direct PLUS loans, Federal Perkins Loans, State Loans, College/university loans from institutional funds. *Student Employment:* Federal Work-Study Program available. Institutional employment available. **Financial Aid Statistics:** 100% needy freshmen, 100% needy undergrads receive need-based scholarship or grant aid. 11% freshmen, 12% undergrads receive non-need-based scholarship or grant aid. 84% freshmen, 82% undergrads receive need-based self-help aid. 0% freshmen, 0% undergrads receive athletic scholarships. 99% freshmen, 99% undergrads receive any aid. 81% undergrads borrow to pay for school. Average cumulative indebtedness $35,659. **Criteria for awarding aid:** *Need-based:* Academics, Art, Job skills, Leadership, Minority status, Music/drama, Religious affiliation. *Non-need-based:* Academics, Alumni affiliation, Art, Job skills, Leadership, Minority status, Music/drama, Religious affiliation, State/district residency.

AZUSA PACIFIC UNIVERSITY

PO Box 7000, Azusa, CA 91702-7000
Phone: 626-812-3016 • **Financial Aid Phone:** 626-815-2020
E-mail: admissions@apu.edu • **CEEB Code:** 4596
Fax: 626-812-3096 • **Website:** www.apu.edu • **ACT Code:** 166

This private school, affiliated with the Christian (Nondenominational) Church, was founded in 1899. It has a 103-acre campus.

RATINGS

Admissions Selectivity Rating: 73   **Fire Safety Rating:** 64   **Green Rating:** 60*

STUDENTS AND FACULTY

Enrollment: 5,762. **Student Body:** 66% female, 34% male, 19% out-of-state, 3% international. Asian 9%, African American 5%, Caucasian 41%, Hispanic 31%, Native American <1%, Pacific Islander 1%, Two or more races 8%, Race unknown 2%.
Retention and Graduation: 86% freshmen return for sophomore year. 51% freshmen graduate within 4 years. 70% freshmen graduate within 6 years.
Faculty: Student/faculty ratio 12:1. 458 full-time faculty, 63% hold PhDs, 28% are are members of minority groups, 52% are women.

ACADEMICS

Degrees: bachelor's, certificate, doctoral/professional, doctoral/research, master's, postbachelor's certificate, post-master's certificate. **Classes:** Most classes have 10-19 students. Most lab/discussion sessions have 10-19 students. **Most popular majors:** Business, Management, Marketing, and Related Support Services; Psychology. **Special Study Options:** Accelerated program, cooperative education program, distance learning, double major, English as a Second Language (ESL), exchange student program (domestic), honors program, independent study, internships, study abroad, teacher certification program. Combined degree programs: BA/MA, Millennial MBA, Young Executive MBA, Young Executive MBM, Master of Professional Accountancy. **Career Services:** Alumni services, Career/job search classes, Career assessment, Internships.

FACILITIES

Housing: Coed dorms, men's dorms, women's dorms, apartments for single students. 100% of campus accessible to physically diasbled. **Special Academic Facilities/Equipment:** Electron microscope. **Computers:** 100% of classrooms, 100% of dorms, 100% of libraries, 100% of dining areas, 100% of student union, 100% of common outdoor areas have wireless network access. Students can register for classes online. Administrative functions (other than registration) can be performed online.

CAMPUS LIFE

Environment: Town. **Activities:** Choral groups, concert band, drama/theater, jazz band, marching band, music ensembles, musical theater, opera, pep band, radio station, student government, student newspaper, symphony orchestra, television station, yearbook. 30 registered organizations, 7 honor societies. **Athletics (Intercollegiate):** *Men:* baseball, basketball, cross-country, football, soccer, tennis, track/field (outdoor), volleyball. *Women:* basketball, cheerleading, cross-country, diving, soccer, softball, swimming, tennis, track/field (outdoor), volleyball, water polo. **On-Campus Highlights:** Coffee Shops, Cougars' Den (Dining Facility), An Athletic Facility, Darling Library, Cougar Dome.

ADMISSIONS

Freshman Academic Profile: Average high school GPA 3.7. **Reported SAT (pre-2016 redesign) scores:** SAT Math middle 50% range 460-580. SAT Critical Reading middle 50% range 470-580. **Concordant SAT scores:** SAT Math middle 50% range 500–600. ACT middle 50% range 21-26. Minimum internet-based TOEFL 68. **Basis for Candidate Selection:** *Very important factors considered include:* class rank, academic GPA, standardized test scores, application essay, character/personal qualities. *Important factors considered include:* recommendation(s), religious affiliation/commitment. *Other factors considered include:* rigor of secondary school record, interview, extracurricular activities, talent/ability, first generation, alumni/ae relation, racial/ethnic status, volunteer work, level of applicant's interest. **Freshman Admission Requirements:** High school diploma is required and GED is accepted. *Academic units recommended:* 4 English, 3 math, 2 science, 3 foreign language, 1 social studies, 2 history. **Freshman Admission Statistics:** 6,605 applied, 83.53% admitted, 21% enrolled. **Transfer Admission Requirements:** college transcript(s), essay or personal statement, statement of good standing from prior institution(s). Minimum college GPA of 2.2 required. Lowest grade transferable C. **General Admission Information:** Application fee $45. Priority deadline 2/15. Regular application deadline 6/1. Regular notification 4/1. Nonfall registration not accepted.

COSTS AND FINANCIAL AID

Annual tuition $35,540. Required fees $580. Average book expense $1,792. *Student Employment:* Federal Work-Study Program available. Institutional employment available. **Financial Aid Statistics:** 92% needy freshmen, 98% needy undergrads receive need-based scholarship or grant aid. 10% freshmen, 7% undergrads receive non-need-based scholarship or grant aid. 71% freshmen, 78% undergrads receive need-based self-help aid. 5% freshmen, 5% undergrads receive athletic scholarships. 35% freshmen, 38% undergrads receive any aid. Average cumulative indebtedness $24,338.

BABSON COLLEGE

Lunder Hall, Babson Park, MA 2457
Phone: 781-239-5522 • **Financial Aid Phone:** 781-239-4015
E-mail: ugradadmission@babson.edu • **CEEB Code:** 2121
Fax: 781-239-4006 • **Website:** www.babson.edu • **ACT Code:** 1780

This private school was founded in 1919. It has a 370-acre campus.

RATINGS
Admissions Selectivity Rating: 94   **Fire Safety Rating:** 95   **Green Rating:** 92

STUDENTS AND FACULTY
Enrollment: 2,283. **Student Body:** 48% female, 52% male, 72% out-of-state, 27% international (77 countries represented). Asian 12%, African American 5%, Caucasian 38%, Hispanic 10%, Native American <1%, Pacific Islander <1%, Two or more races 2%, Race unknown 5%.
Retention and Graduation: 95% freshmen return for sophomore year. 88% freshmen graduate within 4 years. 91% freshmen graduate within 6 years. 5% grads go on to further study within 1 year. **Faculty:** Student/faculty ratio 12:1. 177 full-time faculty, 89% hold PhDs, 19% are are members of minority groups, 37% are women. 0% of classes are taught by teaching assistants.

ACADEMICS
Degrees: bachelor's, master's, postbachelor's certificate. **Classes:** Most classes have 30-39 students. **Most popular majors:** Business Administration and Management. **Special Study Options:** cross-registration, exchange student program (domestic), honors program, independent study, internships, liberal arts/career combination, study abroad, We offer 26 concentrations which provide groupings of courses that help students choose a coherent set of courses for academic and external recognition. **Honors Programs:** The Honors Program consists of three components in which participants add to their academic and cocurricular development. These include honors courses, an honors project and an international experience. **Disability Services:** Special programs offered to physically disabled students, including note-taking services, reader services, tape recorders. **Career Services:** Alumni network, Alumni services, Career/job search classes, Career assessment, Internships, Regional alumni. The Management Consulting Field Experience (MCFE) offers students the opportunity to gain practical industry experience while working with professionals in the business community. The MCFE program connects organizations with talented Babson students who work as consultants to address a current business challenge. Students gain valuable experience while providing creativity, insights, and results to partner organizations.

FACILITIES
Housing: Coed dorms, special housing for disabled students, fraternity/sorority housing, substance free, special interest housing. 50% of campus accessible to physically diasbled. **Special Academic Facilities/Equipment:** The Babson World Globe, Roger Babson Museum, Isaac Newton Museum, Arthur M. Blank Center for Entrepreneurship **Computers:** 100% of classrooms, 100% of dorms, 100% of libraries, 100% of dining areas, 100% of student union, 100% of common outdoor areas have wireless network access. Students can register for classes online. Administrative functions (other than registration) can be performed online. Undergraduates are required to own a computer.

CAMPUS LIFE
Environment: Village. **Activities:** dance, drama/theater, jazz band, literary magazine, musical theater, radio station, student government, student newspaper, yearbook. 78 registered organizations, 3 religious organizations. 4 fraternities, 3 sororities. **Athletics (Intercollegiate):** *Men:* baseball, basketball, cross-country, diving, golf, ice hockey, lacrosse, skiing (downhill/alpine), soccer, swimming, tennis, track/field (outdoor), track/field (indoor). *Women:* basketball, cross-country, diving, field hockey, lacrosse, skiing (downhill/alpine), soccer, softball, swimming, tennis, track/field (outdoor), track/field (indoor), volleyball. **On-Campus Highlights:** Sorenson Arts Center, Blank Center for Entrepeneurship, Glavin Family Chapel, Reynolds Student Center, Webster Athletic Center. **Environmental Initiatives:** Babson joined the American College & University Presidents' Climate Commitment and wrote a Sustainability and Climate Action Plan. To implement its commitments, Babson engages GreenerU, Inc.—an innovative, higher education-focused energy and sustainability services company—to operate our dedicated Sustainability Office.

ADMISSIONS
Reported SAT (pre-2016 redesign) scores: SAT Math middle 50% range 610-720. SAT Critical Reading middle 50% range 560-650. SAT Writing middle 50% range 580-680. **Concordant SAT scores:** SAT EBRW middle 50%

630–710. SAT Math middle 50% range 630–750. ACT middle 50% range 27-31. Minimum internet-based TOEFL 100. Minimum paper TOEFL 600. **Basis for Candidate Selection:** *Very important factors considered include:* rigor of secondary school record, class rank, academic GPA, standardized test scores, application essay, recommendation(s), extracurricular activities, character/personal qualities. *Other factors considered include:* interview, talent/ability, first generation, alumni/ae relation, geographical residence, state residency, racial/ethnic status, volunteer work, work experience, level of applicant's interest. **Freshman Admission Requirements:** High school diploma is required and GED is accepted. *Academic units required:* 4 English, 4 math, 3 science, 4 foreign language, 4 social studies. **Freshman Admission Statistics:** 7,648 applied, 24.59% admitted, 31% enrolled. **Transfer Admission Requirements:** High school transcript, college transcript(s), essay or personal statement, statement of good standing from prior institution(s). Lowest grade transferable C. **General Admission Information:** Application fee $75. Priority deadline 11/1. Regular application deadline 1/1. Regular notification 4/1. Nonfall registration accepted. Admission may be deferred for a maximum of 2 years.

COSTS AND FINANCIAL AID
Annual tuition $48,288. Room and board $15,376. Required fees $0. Average book expense $1,050. **Required Forms and Deadlines:** FAFSA, CSS/Financial Aid PROFILE, Noncustodial PROFILE. **Notification of Awards:** Applicants will be notified of awards on or about 4/1. **Types of Aid:** *Need-based scholarships/grants:* Federal Pell, FSEOG, State scholarships/grants, Private scholarships, College/university scholarship or grant aid from institutional funds. *Loans:* Direct Subsidized Stafford Loans, Direct Unsubsidized Stafford Loans, Direct PLUS loans, State Loans. *Student Employment:* Federal Work-Study Program available. Institutional employment available. **Financial Aid Statistics:** 89% needy freshmen, 95% needy undergrads receive need-based scholarship or grant aid. 12% freshmen, 18% undergrads receive non-need-based scholarship or grant aid. 88% freshmen, 81% undergrads receive need-based self-help aid. 0% freshmen, 0% undergrads receive athletic scholarships. 53% freshmen, 50% undergrads receive any aid. 44% undergrads borrow to pay for school. Average cumulative indebtedness $36,556. **Criteria for awarding aid:** *Non-need-based:* Academics, Leadership.

See page 912.

BAKER UNIVERSITY

P.O. Box 65, Baldwin City, KS 66006
Phone: 785-594-8325 • **Financial Aid Phone:** 785-594-4595
E-mail: admissions@bakeru.edu • **CEEB Code:** 6031
Fax: 785-594-8353 • **Website:** www.bakerU.edu • **ACT Code:** 1386

This private school, affiliated with the Methodist Church, was founded in 1858. It has a 36-acre campus.

RATINGS
Admissions Selectivity Rating: 83   **Fire Safety Rating:** 83   **Green Rating:** 60*

STUDENTS AND FACULTY
Enrollment: 858. **Student Body:** 48% female, 52% male, 35% out-of-state, 2% international (15 countries represented). Asian 0%, African American 11%, Caucasian 69%, Hispanic 8%, Native American 2%, Pacific Islander 1%, Two or more races 3%, Race unknown 3%.
Retention and Graduation: 80% freshmen return for sophomore year. 41% freshmen graduate within 4 years. 55% freshmen graduate within 6 years. 20% grads go on to further study within 1 year. 17% grads pursue arts and sciences degrees. 2% grads pursue law degrees. 4% grads pursue business degrees. 1% grads pursue medical degrees. **Faculty:** Student/faculty ratio 13:1. 57 full-time faculty, 82% hold PhDs, 4% are members of minority groups, 49% are women. 0% of classes are taught by teaching assistants.

ACADEMICS
Degrees: bachelor's. **Classes:** Most classes have 10-19 students. Most lab/discussion sessions have fewer than 10 students. **Most popular majors:** Business/Commerce; Kinesiology and Exercise Science; Elementary Education and Teaching. **Special Study Options:** Accelerated program, double major, honors program, independent study, internships, liberal arts/career combination, student-designed major, study abroad, teacher certification program, Students can transfer to the School of Nursing (located in a clinical setting in Topeka, KS) after completing their first two years of general education and pre-nursing course work. Baker also offers an Interterm program (3 weeks in January), during which students can take classes on campus, pursue travel courses, or work in internships. **Honors Programs:** Honors Program, Bronston Fellows Program. **Disability Services:** Special programs offered to physically disabled students, including note-taking services, reader services, tape recorders, tutors. **Career Services:** Alumni services, Career/job search

classes, Career assessment, Internships. Professional project-based practicum experiences sponsored by local businesses and organizations.

FACILITIES

Housing: Coed dorms, special housing for disabled students, men's dorms, women's dorms, fraternity/sorority housing, apartments for single students. 85% of campus accessible to physically diasbled. **Special Academic Facilities/Equipment:** Old Castle Museum, Quayle Bible Collection **Computers:** 95% of classrooms, 100% of dorms, 100% of libraries, 100% of dining areas, 100% of student union, have wireless network access. Students can register for classes online. Administrative functions (other than registration) can be performed online.

CAMPUS LIFE

Environment: Rural. **Activities:** Choral groups, concert band, dance, drama/theater, jazz band, literary magazine, music ensembles, pep band, radio station, student government, student newspaper, television station, yearbook, Student Organization. 60 registered organizations, 18 honor societies, 2 religious organizations. 5 fraternities, 5 sororities. **Athletics (Intercollegiate):** *Men:* baseball, basketball, cheerleading, cross-country, football, golf, soccer, tennis, track/field (outdoor), track/field (indoor), wrestling. *Women:* basketball, bowling, cheerleading, cross-country, golf, soccer, softball, tennis, track/field (outdoor), track/field (indoor), volleyball. **On-Campus Highlights:** Library, Wildcat Cafe, Osborne Chapel, Fitness Center, Living Learning Center.

ADMISSIONS

Freshman Academic Profile: Average high school GPA 3.4. 12% in top 10% of high school class, 40% in top 25% of high school class, 76% in top 50% of high school class. 90% from public high schools. ACT middle 50% range 20-25. Minimum internet-based TOEFL 69. Minimum paper TOEFL 525. **Basis for Candidate Selection:** *Very important factors considered include:* rigor of secondary school record, academic GPA, standardized test scores, recommendation(s), level of applicant's interest. *Important factors considered include:* class rank. *Other factors considered include:* application essay, interview, extracurricular activities, talent/ability, character/personal qualities, alumni/ae relation, geographical residence, volunteer work, work experience. **Freshman Admission Requirements:** High school diploma is required and GED is accepted. *Academic units recommended:* 4 English, 3 math, 3 science, 1 science lab, 2 foreign language, 3 social studies, 1 computer science, 1 visual/performing arts. **Freshman Admission Statistics:** 1,403 applied, 49.82% admitted, 34% enrolled. **Transfer Admission Requirements:** High school transcript, college transcript(s), standardized test scores, Minimum college GPA of 2.3 required. Lowest grade transferable C. **General Admission Information:** Nonfall registration accepted. Admission may be deferred for a maximum of 1 year.

COSTS AND FINANCIAL AID

Annual tuition $27,600. Room and board $8,230. Required fees $355. Average book expense $1,200. **Required Forms and Deadlines:** FAFSA. **Notification of Awards:** Applicants will be notified of awards on a rolling basis beginning 3/1. **Types of Aid:** *Need-based scholarships/grants:* Federal Pell, FSEOG, State scholarships/grants, Private scholarships, College/university scholarship or grant aid from institutional funds. *Loans:* Direct Subsidized Stafford Loans, Direct Unsubsidized Stafford Loans, Direct PLUS loans, Federal Perkins Loans. *Student Employment:* Federal Work-Study Program available. Institutional employment available. **Financial Aid Statistics:** 100% needy freshmen, 91% needy undergrads receive need-based scholarship or grant aid. 100% freshmen, 100% undergrads receive non-need-based scholarship or grant aid. 98% freshmen, 77% undergrads receive need-based self-help aid. 84% freshmen, 66% undergrads receive athletic scholarships. 70% undergrads borrow to pay for school. Average cumulative indebtedness $27,627. **Criteria for awarding aid:** *Need-based:* Minority status. *Non-need-based:* Academics, Alumni affiliation, Art, Athletics, Music/drama, Religious affiliation.

BALDWIN WALLACE UNIVERSITY

275 Eastland Rd, Berea, OH 44017
Phone: 440-826-2222 • **Financial Aid Phone:** 440-826-2108
E-mail: admission@bw.edu • **CEEB Code:** 1050
Fax: 440-826-3830 • **Website:** www.bw.edu • **ACT Code:** 3236

This private school was founded in 1845. It has a 100-acre campus.

RATINGS

Admissions Selectivity Rating: 84   **Fire Safety Rating:** 85   **Green Rating:** 77

STUDENTS AND FACULTY

Enrollment: 3,245. **Student Body:** 54% female, 46% male, 22% out-of-state, 1% international (16 countries represented). Asian 2%, African American 10%,

Caucasian 78%, Hispanic 5%, Native American <1%, Pacific Islander <1%, Two or more races 5%, Race unknown <1%.
Retention and Graduation: 80% freshmen return for sophomore year. 54% freshmen graduate within 4 years. 67% freshmen graduate within 6 years. 10% grads go on to further study within 1 year. 7% grads pursue arts and sciences degrees. 1% grads pursue law degrees. **Faculty:** Student/faculty ratio 12:1. 207 full-time faculty, 77% hold PhDs, 10% are are members of minority groups, 49% are women. 0% of classes are taught by teaching assistants.

ACADEMICS

Degrees: bachelor's, certificate, master's. **Classes:** Most classes have 10-19 students. Most lab/discussion sessions have 20-29 students. **Most popular majors:** Business Administration and Management; Accounting; Psychology. **Special Study Options:** Accelerated program, cross-registration, distance learning, double major, dual enrollment, English as a Second Language (ESL), exchange student program (domestic), honors program, independent study, internships, liberal arts/career combination, student-designed major, study abroad, teacher certification program, weekend college, 3-2 in Engineering with Case Western Reserve University and Columbia University; 3-2 in Social Work with Case Western Reserve University; 3/2 Accounting MBA, 3/2 Human Resources MBA and 3/2 Computer Science/Info. Systems MBA Programs. **Honors Programs:** Liberal Arts Program Combined degree programs: BA/MBA Acct,BA/MBA HR, BS-CompSci/MBA,BS-CompInfoSyst/MBA,BA/MSSASocialWork. **Disability Services:** Special programs offered to physically disabled students, including note-taking services, reader services, tutors. **Career Services:** Alumni network, Alumni services, Career/job search classes, Career assessment, Internships. The beauty of our services is that they are comprehensive (serve students/alumni along the full spectrum of their career needs) and individualized (tailored to the unique needs of the user). We specialize in career advising, job search skill development, and connecting students/alumni to desired opportunities.

FACILITIES

Housing: Coed dorms, special housing for disabled students, special housing for international students, women's dorms, fraternity/sorority housing, apartments for single students, ThemeHousingCarmel Living Learning Center (Education-based), Student-Directed Learning Communities (Sustainability, Art, Women's Christian, Men's Christian), Themed Housing (STEM, Language, Conservatory, SPROUT-for single mothers and children). 80% of campus accessible to physically diasbled. **Special Academic Facilities/Equipment:** Art gallery, electron microscope, observatory. **Computers:** 100% of classrooms, 100% of dorms, 100% of libraries, 100% of dining areas, 100% of student union, 100% of common outdoor areas have wireless network access. Students can register for classes online. Administrative functions (other than registration) can be performed online.

CAMPUS LIFE

Environment: Village. **Activities:** Choral groups, concert band, dance, drama/theater, jazz band, literary magazine, marching band, music ensembles, musical theater, opera, pep band, radio station, student government, student newspaper, student-run film society, symphony orchestra, television station, yearbook, Campus Ministries, Student Organization, Model UN. 136 registered organizations, 25 honor societies, 7 religious organizations. 5 fraternities, 5 sororities. **Athletics (Intercollegiate):** *Men:* baseball, basketball, cross-country, diving, football, golf, soccer, swimming, tennis, track/field (outdoor), track/field (indoor), wrestling. *Women:* basketball, cross-country, diving, golf, soccer, softball, swimming, tennis, track/field (outdoor), track/field (indoor), volleyball. **On-Campus Highlights:** CyberCafe, The Hive, The S.A.C. (Student Activities Center), Conservatory/Theatre performances, Recreation Center, The new Lou Higgins Recreation Center features a Fitness Center, Weight Room, Dance Studio, multipurpose basketball, volleyball, badminton courts and racquetball courts, swimming pool, indoor batting cage and second-floor computer lab. The Student Activities Center provides a club-like atmosphere for entertainment programming on campus. It features a pulsating sound and dance light system, a 10' x 12' video screen, neon lights and snack bar. Comedians, live bands, disc jockeys, multi-media capabilities and special snack foods attracting students to all-campus events. **Environmental Initiatives:** Commitment to geo-thermal energy with all new buildings and major renovations

ADMISSIONS

Freshman Academic Profile: Average high school GPA 3.5. 21% in top 10% of high school class, 47% in top 25% of high school class, 81% in top 50% of high school class. 86% from public high schools. **Reported SAT (pre-2016 redesign) scores:** SAT Math middle 50% range 470-580. SAT Critical Reading middle 50% range 480-590. SAT Writing middle 50% range 460-570. **Concordant SAT scores:** SAT EBRW middle 50% 530–640. SAT Math middle 50% range 510–600. ACT middle 50% range 21-27. Minimum internet-based TOEFL 79. Minimum paper TOEFL 550. **Freshman Admission Requirements:** High school diploma is required and GED is accepted. *Academic units required:* 4 English, 4 math, 3 science, 2 science labs, 1 foreign language, 2 social studies, 1 history. *Academic units recommended:* 4 English, 4 math, 4 science, 2 science labs, 2 foreign language, 3 social studies, 1 history, 3 academic electives. **Freshman Admission Statistics:** 4,515 applied, 59.73% admitted, 26% enrolled. **Transfer Admission Requirements:** High school transcript, college transcript(s), statement of good standing from prior institution(s). Minimum college GPA of 2.5 required. Lowest grade transferable C. **General Admission Information:** Application fee $25. Priority deadline 3/1. Nonfall registration accepted. Admission may be deferred for a maximum of 1 year.

COSTS AND FINANCIAL AID
Annual tuition $31,668. Room and board $9,142. Average book expense $1,654. **Required Forms and Deadlines:** FAFSA. **Notification of Awards:** Applicants will be notified of awards on a rolling basis beginning 2/15. **Types of Aid:** *Need-based scholarships/grants:* Federal Pell, FSEOG, State scholarships/grants, Private scholarships, College/university scholarship or grant aid from institutional funds. *Loans:* Direct Subsidized Stafford Loans, Direct Unsubsidized Stafford Loans, Direct PLUS loans, Federal Perkins Loans. *Student Employment:* Federal Work-Study Program available. Institutional employment available. **Financial Aid Statistics:** 100% needy freshmen, 100% needy undergrads receive need-based scholarship or grant aid. 19% freshmen, 43% undergrads receive non-need-based scholarship or grant aid. 88% freshmen, 89% undergrads receive need-based self-help aid. 0% freshmen, 0% undergrads receive athletic scholarships. 100% freshmen, 98% undergrads receive any aid. 80% undergrads borrow to pay for school. Average cumulative indebtedness $34,423. **Criteria for awarding aid:** *Need-based:* Academics, Minority status, Music/drama, Religious affiliation. *Non-need-based:* Academics, Alumni affiliation, Art, Minority status, Music/drama, Religious affiliation, State/district residency.

BALL STATE UNIVERSITY

Admissions Office, Ball State University, Muncie, IN 47306-0855
Phone: 765-285-8300 • **Financial Aid Phone:** 765-285-5600
E-mail: askus@bsu.edu • **CEEB Code:** 1051
Fax: 765-285-1632 • **Website:** www.bsu.edu • **ACT Code:** 1176

This public school was founded in 1918. It has a 1035-acre campus.

RATINGS
Admissions Selectivity Rating: 83   **Fire Safety Rating:** 89   **Green Rating:** 99

STUDENTS AND FACULTY
Enrollment: 16,602. **Student Body:** 59% female, 41% male, 13% out-of-state, 2% international (44 countries represented). Asian 1%, African American 7%, Caucasian 80%, Hispanic 4%, Native American <1%, Pacific Islander <1%, Two or more races 3%, Race unknown 2%.
Retention and Graduation: 82% freshmen return for sophomore year. 41% freshmen graduate within 4 years. **Faculty:** Student/faculty ratio 14:1. 1,017 full-time faculty, 74% hold PhDs, 7% are are members of minority groups, 47% are women.

ACADEMICS
Degrees: associate, bachelor's, doctoral/professional, doctoral/research, doctoral, master's, postbachelor's certificate, post-master's certificate. **Classes:** Most classes have 20-29 students. **Most popular majors:** General Studies; Elementary Education and Teaching; Radio and Television. **Special Study Options:** Accelerated program, distance learning, double major, dual enrollment, English as a Second Language (ESL), exchange student program (domestic), external degree program, honors program, independent study, internships, student-designed major, study abroad, teacher certification program. **Honors Programs:** BSU offers an Honors College which has its own curriculum, undergraduate research fellowships and study abroad programs. **Disability Services:** Special programs offered to physically disabled students, including note-taking services, reader services, tape recorders, tutors. **Career Services:** Alumni services, Career/job search classes, Career assessment, Internships, Regional alumni. KEY Careers is an intentional intervention with the incoming freshman class. The goals of the program are to: Help students choose a major earlier in their college career, Decrease the frequency of major changes, Encourage students to begin the career exploration process at an earlier point in their college career, Begin introducing them and engaging them with resources available to them on campus, and Educate students about the current state and future labor market. Through an pre- and post-test assessment using My Vocational Situation (MVS), we are able to offer feedback and programming to freshmen through the KEY Careers workshop. We had 3659 students complete the initial MVS at student orientation. 1604 students participated in the KEY Careers workshop held in November 2011. The second MVS survey distribution resulted in 1021 completed post-surveys. We were able to see that there was a significant change in the in the low and average VI scores

from the pre-test to the post-test. Low scores increased by 4 points, Average scores increased by 1 point and High scores stayed at the same level. Regression analysis most importantly showed that the Key Career workshop significantly accounted for the change in VI scores.

FACILITIES
Housing: Coed dorms, special housing for disabled students, men's dorms, special housing for international students, women's dorms, fraternity/sorority housing, apartments for married students, apartments for single students, Wellness Housing, Theme Housing, Living/Learning Communities. 95% of campus accessible to physically disabled. **Special Academic Facilities/Equipment:** Art gallery, museum, on-campus school (K-12), learning center, weather station, physical therapy lab, human performance lab, planetarium/observatory, wildlife and nature preserve. **Computers:** 100% of classrooms, 100% of dorms, 100% of libraries, 100% of dining areas, 100% of student union, 100% of common outdoor areas have wireless network access. Students can register for classes online. Administrative functions (other than registration) can be performed online. Undergraduates are required to own a computer.

CAMPUS LIFE
Environment: City. **Activities:** Choral groups, concert band, dance, drama/theater, jazz band, literary magazine, marching band, music ensembles, musical theater, opera, pep band, radio station, student government, student newspaper, student-run film society, symphony orchestra, television station, Campus Ministries. 355 registered organizations, 31 honor societies, 32 religious organizations. 15 fraternities, 12 sororities. **Athletics (Intercollegiate):** *Men:* baseball, basketball, cheerleading, cross-country, diving, football, golf, swimming, tennis, volleyball. *Women:* basketball, cheerleading, cross-country, diving, field hockey, golf, gymnastics, soccer, softball, swimming, tennis, track/field (outdoor), volleyball. **On-Campus Highlights:** Museum of Art, Worthen Arena, Emens Auditorium, Atrium, Letterman Communication & Media Bldg, Emens Auditorium, Music Building/Sursa Hall, Bracken Library. **Environmental Initiatives:** Installing a district-scale ground-source heating and cooling system to serve all 45 campus buildings and eliminate four coal-fired boilers and reduce our GHG emissions by nearly 50%.

ADMISSIONS
Freshman Academic Profile: Average high school GPA 3.5. 19% in top 10% of high school class, 50% in top 25% of high school class, 90% in top 50% of high school class. 93% from public high schools. **Reported SAT (pre-2016 redesign) scores:** SAT Math middle 50% range 500-590. SAT Critical Reading middle 50% range 510-600. SAT Writing middle 50% range 490-580. **Concordant SAT scores:** SAT EBRW middle 50% 560-650. SAT Math middle 50% range 530-610. ACT middle 50% range 20-24. Minimum internet-based TOEFL 79. Minimum paper TOEFL 550. **Basis for Candidate Selection:** *Very important factors considered include:* rigor of secondary school record, academic GPA, standardized test scores. *Other factors considered include:* application essay, recommendation(s), extracurricular activities, talent/ability, volunteer work, work experience. **Freshman Admission Requirements:** High school diploma is required and GED is accepted. *Academic units required:* 4 English, 3 math, 3 science, 2 science labs, 2 social studies, 2 history. *Academic units recommended:* 4 math, 3 foreign language. **Freshman Admission Statistics:** 22,147 applied, 60.50% admitted, 26% enrolled. **Transfer Admission Requirements:** college transcript(s), Minimum college GPA of 2.0 required. Lowest grade transferable C. **General Admission Information:** Application fee $55. Priority deadline 3/1. Regular application deadline 8/15. Nonfall registration accepted. Admission may be deferred.

COSTS AND FINANCIAL AID
Annual in-state tuition $8,992. Annual out-of-state tuition $24,766. Room and board $9,936. Required fees $602. Average book expense $1,320. **Required Forms and Deadlines:** FAFSA. **Notification of Awards:** Applicants will be notified of awards on a rolling basis beginning 4/1. **Types of Aid:** *Need-based scholarships/grants:* Federal Pell, FSEOG, State scholarships/grants, Private scholarships, College/university scholarship or grant aid from institutional funds. *Loans:* Direct Subsidized Stafford Loans, Direct Unsubsidized Stafford Loans, Direct PLUS loans, Federal Perkins Loans. *Student Employment:* Federal Work-Study Program available. Institutional employment available. **Financial Aid Statistics:** 63% needy freshmen, 60% needy undergrads receive need-based scholarship or grant aid. 71% freshmen, 54% undergrads receive non-need-based scholarship or grant aid. 92% freshmen, 91% undergrads receive need-based self-help aid. 2% freshmen, 2% undergrads receive athletic scholarships. 82% freshmen, 78% undergrads receive any aid. 72% undergrads borrow to pay for school. Average cumulative indebtedness $27,732. **Criteria for awarding aid:** *Need-based:* Academics, Alumni affiliation, Art, Leadership, Minority status, Music/drama. *Non-need-based:* Academics, Athletics, Leadership, Minority status, Music/drama, State/district residency.

BAPTIST COLLEGE OF FLORIDA

5400 College Drive, Graceville, FL 32440-1898
Phone: 850-263-3261 • **Financial Aid Phone:** 1-800-328-2660 ext. 461
E-mail: admissions@baptistcollege.edu
Fax: 850-263-9026 • **Website:** www.baptistcollege.edu • **ACT Code:** 6870

This private school, affiliated with the Southern Baptist Church, was founded in 1943. It has a 217-acre campus.

RATINGS
Admissions Selectivity Rating: 74　　**Fire Safety Rating:** 81　　**Green Rating:** 60*

STUDENTS AND FACULTY
Enrollment: 434. **Student Body:** 34% female, 66% male, 30% out-of-state, 0% international (1 countries represented). Asian 0%, African American 8%, Caucasian 80%, Hispanic 3%, Native American <1%, Pacific Islander <1%, Two or more races 3%, Race unknown 5%.
Retention and Graduation: 74% freshmen return for sophomore year. 28% freshmen graduate within 4 years. 53% freshmen graduate within 6 years. 50% grads go on to further study within 1 year. 84% grads pursue arts and sciences degrees. 2% grads pursue law degrees. 4% grads pursue business degrees.
Faculty: Student/faculty ratio 10:1. 25 full-time faculty, 68% hold PhDs, 0% are are members of minority groups, 20% are women. 0% of classes are taught by teaching assistants.

ACADEMICS
Degrees: associate, bachelor's, certificate, master's. **Classes:** Most classes have fewer than 10 students. Most lab/discussion sessions have 10-19 students. **Most popular majors:** Religious Education; Theology/Theological Studies; Pastoral Studies/Counseling. **Special Study Options:** distance learning, double major, independent study, internships, teacher certification program, -Academic Remediation -Advanced Placement Credit -Learning Disabilities Services.
Disability Services: Special programs offered to physically disabled students, including note-taking services, reader services, tape recorders, tutors. **Career Services:** Alumni services, Internships.

FACILITIES
Housing: special housing for disabled students, men's dorms, women's dorms, apartments for married students. 100% of campus accessible to physically diasbled. **Special Academic Facilities/Equipment:** Florida Baptist Historical Society; Heritage Village; Weight Rooms in Assembly Center. **Computers:** 100% of classrooms, 100% of dorms, 100% of libraries, 100% of dining areas, 100% of student union, 100% of common outdoor areas have wireless network access. Students can register for classes online. Administrative functions (other than registration) can be performed online.

CAMPUS LIFE
Environment: Rural. **Activities:** Choral groups, concert band, drama/theater, jazz band, music ensembles, radio station, Campus Ministries. 3 registered organizations, 2 religious organizations. **Athletics (Intercollegiate):** *Men:* golf. *Women:* volleyball. **On-Campus Highlights:** Athletic Center, Coffee Shop, Courtyard, Student Center, Chapel.

ADMISSIONS
Freshman Academic Profile: 90% from public high schools. **Reported SAT (pre-2016 redesign) scores:** SAT Math middle 50% range 400-430. SAT Critical Reading middle 50% range 430-440. **Concordant SAT scores:** SAT Math middle 50% range 440–470. ACT middle 50% range 17-22. Minimum paper TOEFL 500. **Basis for Candidate Selection:** *Very important factors considered include:* recommendation(s), character/personal qualities, religious affiliation/commitment, level of applicant's interest. *Important factors considered include:* academic GPA, talent/ability, alumni/ae relation. *Other factors considered include:* rigor of secondary school record, standardized test scores, interview, extracurricular activities, volunteer work. **Freshman Admission Requirements:** High school diploma is required and GED is accepted. *Academic units recommended:* 4 English, 4 math, 3 science, 1 social studies, 2 history. **Freshman Admission Statistics:** 119 applied, 59.66% admitted, 56% enrolled. **Transfer Admission Requirements:** High school transcript, college transcript(s), essay or personal statement, Minimum college GPA of 2.0 required. Lowest grade transferable C. **General Admission Information:** Application fee $25. Regular application deadline 8/15. Nonfall registration accepted. Admission may be deferred for a maximum of 2 semesters.

COSTS AND FINANCIAL AID
Annual tuition $10,200. Room and board $4,138. Required fees $900. Average book expense $950. **Required Forms and Deadlines:** FAFSA, Institution's own financial aid form, State aid form, Business/Farm Supplement. **Notification of Awards:** Applicants will be notified of awards on a rolling basis beginning 6/15. **Types of Aid:** *Need-based scholarships/grants:* Federal Pell, FSEOG, State scholarships/grants, Private scholarships, College/university

scholarship or grant aid from institutional funds. *Loans:* College/university loans from institutional funds. *Student Employment:* Federal Work-Study Program available. Institutional employment available. **Financial Aid Statistics:** 61% needy freshmen, 84% needy undergrads receive need-based scholarship or grant aid. 1% undergrads receive non-need-based scholarship or grant aid. 44% freshmen, 66% undergrads receive need-based self-help aid. 0% freshmen, 0% undergrads receive athletic scholarships. 86% freshmen, 97% undergrads receive any aid. 66% undergrads borrow to pay for school. Average cumulative indebtedness $17,485. **Criteria for awarding aid:** *Need-based:* Academics, Minority status, Music/drama, Religious affiliation. *Non-need-based:* Academics, Minority status, Music/drama, Religious affiliation.

BARD COLLEGE

Office of Admissions, Annandale-on-Hudson, NY 12504
Phone: 845-758-7472 • **Financial Aid Phone:** 845-758-7526
E-mail: admissions@bard.edu • **CEEB Code:** 2037
Fax: 845-758-5208 • **Website:** www.bard.edu • **ACT Code:** 2674

This private school was founded in 1860. It has a 600-acre campus.

RATINGS
Admissions Selectivity Rating: 92　　**Fire Safety Rating:** 97　　**Green Rating:** 91

STUDENTS AND FACULTY
Enrollment: 1,962. **Student Body:** 55% female, 45% male, 66% out-of-state, 10% international (57 countries represented). Asian 6%, African American 8%, Caucasian 63%, Hispanic 1%, Native American 1%, Pacific Islander 0%, Two or more races 0%, Race unknown 11%.
Retention and Graduation: 85% freshmen return for sophomore year. 69% freshmen graduate within 4 years. 78% freshmen graduate within 6 years.
Faculty: Student/faculty ratio 10:1. 152 full-time faculty, 96% hold PhDs, 16% are are members of minority groups, 43% are women. 0% of classes are taught by teaching assistants.

ACADEMICS
Degrees: associate, bachelor's, doctoral/research, master's. **Classes:** Most classes have 10-19 students. **Most popular majors:** English Language and Literature; Social Sciences; Visual and Performing Arts. **Special Study Options:** cross-registration, double major, dual enrollment, English as a Second Language (ESL), independent study, internships, student-designed major, study abroad, Intensive language studies in Italy, Germany, France, Mexico, Russia, China, program in International Education (Central and Eastern Europe and Southern Africa). Combined degree programs: BA/MA, BA/MEng, http://www.bard.edu/catalogue/index.php?aid=11506&sid=669479.
Disability Services: Special programs offered to physically disabled students, including note-taking services, reader services, tape recorders, tutors. **Career Services:** Alumni network, Alumni services, Career/job search classes, Career assessment, Internships, Regional alumni. The Career Office offers over 60 career information workshops a year and makes a concerted effort to include alumni/ae on career panels and events. The career office has a strong working relationship with the Alumni/ae Affairs office to foster networking opportunities for the broad Bard network.

FACILITIES
Housing: Coed dorms, women's dorms, cooperative housing, Wellness Housing, Theme Housing. 70% of campus accessible to physically diasbled. **Special Academic Facilities/Equipment:** Performing arts center, gallery, art museum, collection of contemporary art, center for curatorial studies, language lab, nursery school, ecology field station, archaeology field school, economics institute. **Computers:** 5% of classrooms, 50% of dorms, 100% of libraries, 100% of dining areas, 100% of student union, have wireless network access. Students can register for classes online. Administrative functions (other than registration) can be performed online.

CAMPUS LIFE
Environment: Rural. **Activities:** Choral groups, concert band, dance, drama/theater, jazz band, literary magazine, music ensembles, musical theater, opera, radio station, student government, student newspaper, student-run film society, symphony orchestra, Campus Ministries, Student Organization, Model UN. 120 registered organizations, 5 religious organizations. **Athletics (Intercollegiate):** *Men:* basketball, cross-country, soccer, squash, tennis, track/field (outdoor), volleyball. *Women:* basketball, cross-country, soccer, tennis,

track/field (outdoor), volleyball. **On-Campus Highlights:** Richard B Fisher Center for the Performing Arts, Stevenson Library, Bertelsmann Campus Center, Museum @ Center for Curatorial Studies, Levy Economics Institute—Blithewood Mansion, A new Center for Science and Computation designed by the renowned firm Rafael Vinoly Architects opened in the fall of 2007. **Environmental Initiatives:** 40% of the total building square footages utilizes geothermal heat-exchange for space heating and cooling.

ADMISSIONS

Freshman Academic Profile: 49% in top 10% of high school class, 76% in top 25% of high school class, 96% in top 50% of high school class. 58% from public high schools. **Reported SAT (pre-2016 redesign) scores:** SAT Math 50% range 570-680. SAT Critical Reading middle 50% range 590-690. **Concordant SAT scores:** SAT Math middle 50% range 590–710. Minimum internet-based TOEFL 100. Minimum paper TOEFL 600. **Basis for Candidate Selection:** *Very important factors considered include:* rigor of secondary school record, academic GPA, application essay, recommendation(s), extracurricular activities, talent/ability, character/personal qualities. *Important factors considered include:* volunteer work, work experience. *Other factors considered include:* class rank, standardized test scores, interview, first generation, alumni/ae relation, geographical residence, state residency, religious affiliation/commitment, racial/ethnic status, level of applicant's interest. **Freshman Admission Requirements:** High school diploma is required and GED is accepted. *Academic units recommended:* 4 English, 4 math, 4 science, 3 science labs, 4 foreign language, 4 social studies, 4 history. **Freshman Admission Statistics:** 7,044 applied, 32.17% admitted, 20% enrolled. **Transfer Admission Requirements:** college transcript(s), essay or personal statement, statement of good standing from prior institution(s). Minimum college GPA of 3.0 required. Lowest grade transferable C. **General Admission Information:** Application fee $50. Regular application deadline 1/1. Nonfall registration not accepted. Admission may be deferred for a maximum of 1 year.

COSTS AND FINANCIAL AID

Annual tuition $50,704. Room and board $14,540. Required fees $680. Average book expense $950. **Required Forms and Deadlines:** FAFSA, CSS/Financial Aid PROFILE, State aid form, Noncustodial PROFILE. **Notification of Awards:** Applicants will be notified of awards on or about 4/1. **Types of Aid:** *Need-based scholarships/grants:* Federal Pell, FSEOG, State scholarships/grants, Private scholarships, College/university scholarship or grant aid from institutional funds. *Loans:* Direct Subsidized Stafford Loans, Direct Unsubsidized Stafford Loans, Direct PLUS loans, Federal Perkins Loans, College/university loans from institutional funds. *Student Employment:* Federal Work-Study Program available. Institutional employment available. **Financial Aid Statistics:** 98% needy freshmen, 97% needy undergrads receive need-based scholarship or grant aid. 0% undergrads receive non-need-based scholarship or grant aid. 85% freshmen, 82% undergrads receive need-based self-help aid. 0% freshmen, 0% undergrads receive athletic scholarships. 70% freshmen, 72% undergrads receive any aid. 54% undergrads borrow to pay for school. Average cumulative indebtedness $28,261. **Criteria for awarding aid:** *Need-based:* Academics. *Non-need-based:* Academics.

BARD COLLEGE AT SIMON'S ROCK

84 Alford Road, Great Barrington, MA 1230
Financial Aid Phone: 413-528-7297
E-mail: admit@simons-rock.edu • **CEEB Code:** 3795
Fax: 413-541-0081 • **Website:** www.simons-rock.edu • **ACT Code:** 1893

This private school was founded in 1964. It has a 275-acre campus.

RATINGS

Admissions Selectivity Rating: 89   **Fire Safety Rating:** 95   **Green Rating:** 60*

STUDENTS AND FACULTY

Enrollment: 359. **Student Body:** 61% female, 39% male, 88% out-of-state, 14% international (15 countries represented). Asian 11%, African American 4%, Caucasian 56%, Hispanic 3%, Native American 1%, Pacific Islander 0%, Two or more races 3%, Race unknown 8%.
Retention and Graduation: 75% freshmen return for sophomore year. 29% freshmen graduate within 4 years. 35% freshmen graduate within 6 years.
Faculty: Student/faculty ratio 7:1. 51 full-time faculty, 90% hold PhDs, 16% are members of minority groups, 49% are women. 0% of classes are taught by teaching assistants.

ACADEMICS

Degrees: associate, bachelor's. **Classes:** Most classes have fewer than 10 students. Most lab/discussion sessions have 10-19 students. **Most popular majors:** Political Science and Government; Biology/Biological Sciences; Visual and Performing Arts. **Special Study Options:** Accelerated program, cooperative education program, cross-registration, dual enrollment, exchange student program (domestic), independent study, internships, student-designed major, study abroad, Study Abroad Program(s)within in the last two years: In Hondorus, Spain, England, Germany, Thailand, South Africa, Japan, China. Combined degree programs: BA/MS Environ. Sciences with Bard College. **Disability Services:** Special programs offered to physically disabled students, including tape recorders, tutors. **Career Services:** Alumni network, Alumni services, Career/job search classes, Career assessment, Internships, Regional alumni, On-campus interviews. Bard College at Simon's Rock provides multiple opportunities for students to network with a supportive community of alumni. The most popular networking program happens each semester, when alumni in a variety of professional fields visit campus in-person, virtually, and by telephone to hold one-on-one "office hours" sessions with students. Students may sign up for multiple meetings with alumni in their fields of interest during the event, and they gather advice and connections on internships, graduate school, and career paths through these individualized sessions. The program began in 2013, and has received positive reviews from students and alumni alike.

FACILITIES

Housing: Coed dorms, men's dorms, women's dorms, apartments for single students. If students propose a plan for cooperative housing it will be considered by Dean of Student Life. 75% of campus accessible to physically diasbled. **Special Academic Facilities/Equipment:** Daniel Arts Center, Fisher Science and Academic Center. **Computers:** Administrative functions (other than registration) can be performed online.

CAMPUS LIFE

Environment: Village. **Activities:** Choral groups, dance, drama/theater, jazz band, literary magazine, music ensembles, radio station, student government, student newspaper, student-run film society, yearbook. 21 registered organizations, 3 religious organizations. **Athletics (Intercollegiate):** *Men:* basketball, soccer, swimming, tennis. *Women:* basketball, soccer, swimming, tennis. **On-Campus Highlights:** Fisher Science and Academic Center, Daniel Arts Center, Alumni Library, Kellogg Music Center, Kilpatrick Athletic Center, New building coming on line in 2005: Livingston Hall Student Union.

ADMISSIONS

Freshman Academic Profile: Average high school GPA 3.5. 52% in top 10% of high school class, 22% in top 25% of high school class, 18% in top 50% of high school class. 71% from public high schools. **Reported SAT (pre-2016 redesign) scores:** SAT Math middle 50% range 610-650. SAT Critical Reading middle 50% range 640-750. SAT Writing middle 50% range 610-700. **Concordant SAT scores:** SAT EBRW middle 50% 680–750. SAT Math middle 50% range 630–670. ACT middle 50% range 28-30. Minimum internet-based TOEFL 100. Minimum paper TOEFL 600. **Basis for Candidate Selection:** *Very important factors considered include:* rigor of secondary school record, academic GPA, application essay, interview, talent/ability. *Important factors considered include:* recommendation(s), character/personal qualities. *Other factors considered include:* class rank, standardized test scores, extracurricular activities, first generation, alumni/ae relation, volunteer work, work experience, level of applicant's interest. **Freshman Admission Requirements:** High school diploma or equivalent is not required. **Freshman Admission Statistics:** 387 applied, 67.70% admitted, 56% enrolled. **Transfer Admission Requirements:** college transcript(s), essay or personal statement, interview, Minimum college GPA of 2.0 required. Lowest grade transferable C. **General Admission Information:** Nonfall registration accepted.

COSTS AND FINANCIAL AID

Annual tuition $50,600. Room and board $14,060. Required fees $1,135. Average book expense $1,000. **Required Forms and Deadlines:** FAFSA, CSS/Financial Aid PROFILE, State aid form, Noncustodial PROFILE. **Notification of Awards:** Applicants will be notified of awards on a rolling basis beginning 1/2. **Types of Aid:** *Need-based scholarships/grants:* Federal Pell, FSEOG, State scholarships/grants, Private scholarships, College/university scholarship or grant aid from institutional funds. *Loans:* Direct Subsidized Stafford Loans, Direct Unsubsidized Stafford Loans, Direct PLUS loans, Federal Perkins Loans. *Student Employment:* Federal Work-Study Program available. Institutional employment available. **Financial Aid Statistics:** 97% needy freshmen, 99% needy undergrads receive need-based scholarship or grant aid. 0% undergrads receive non-need-based scholarship or grant aid. 69% freshmen, 71% undergrads receive need-based self-help aid. 0% freshmen, 0% undergrads receive athletic scholarships. 90% freshmen, 86% undergrads receive any aid. 61% undergrads borrow to pay for school. Average cumulative indebtedness $24,098. **Criteria for awarding aid:** *Need-based:* Academics, Minority status. *Non-need-based:* Academics, Alumni affiliation, Minority status, State/district residency.

BARNARD COLLEGE

3009 Broadway, New York, NY 10027
Phone: 212-854-2014 • **Financial Aid Phone:** 212-854-2154
E-mail: admissions@barnard.edu • **CEEB Code:** 2038
Fax: 212-854-6220 • **Website:** www.barnard.edu • **ACT Code:** 2718

This private school was founded in 1889. It has a 4-acre campus.

RATINGS

Admissions Selectivity Rating: 98 **Fire Safety Rating:** 79 **Green Rating:** 74

STUDENTS AND FACULTY

Enrollment: 2,536. **Student Body:** 100% female, 0% male, 74% out-of-state, 8% international (51 countries represented). Asian 14%, African American 7%, Caucasian 53%, Hispanic 12%, Native American <1%, Pacific Islander <1%, Two or more races 6%, Race unknown 1%.
Retention and Graduation: 95% freshmen return for sophomore year. 85% freshmen graduate within 4 years. 91% freshmen graduate within 6 years. 29% grads go on to further study within 1 year. 15% grads pursue law degrees. 17% grads pursue medical degrees. **Faculty:** Student/faculty ratio 10:1. 214 full-time faculty, 92% hold PhDs, 23% are are members of minority groups, 62% are women. 0% of classes are taught by teaching assistants.

ACADEMICS

Degrees: bachelor's. **Classes:** Most classes have 10-19 students. Most lab/discussion sessions have 10-19 students. **Most popular majors:** Psychology; English Language and Literature; Economics. **Special Study Options:** Accelerated program, cross-registration, double major, dual enrollment, exchange student program (domestic), honors program, independent study, internships, liberal arts/career combination, student-designed major, study abroad, teacher certification program, independant scholars program, BA/BS in engineering and applied science. **Honors Programs:** The Barnard Centennial Scholars Program, established in 1984, offers selected students the opportunity to pursue courses of independent study early in their college careers. Working closely with mentors of their choice over a period of several semesters, these young women undertake investigations in areas of personal interest that culminate in projects presented to faculty and peers. The Athena Center for Leadership Studies was launched in September of 2009 and offers a range of academic courses that examines all aspects of women's leadership, sponsored lectures, mentoring and leadership opportunities and a lab which offers a wide range of workshops designed to teach practical elements of leadership to students, alums and other leaders in New York. Combined degree programs: BA/JD, BA/MA, BA/DDS, BA/MIA or BA/MPA Columbia School of International and Public Affairs, AB/BA Jewish Theological Seminary. **Disability Services:** Special programs offered to physically disabled students, including note-taking services, reader services, tape recorders, tutors. **Career Services:** Alumni network, Alumni services, Career/job search classes, Career assessment, Internships, Regional alumni. Because of our urban setting, our students are exposed to extremely wide range of internship opportunities. Barnard also offers funding for some unpaid internships.

FACILITIES

Housing: Coed dorms, special housing for disabled students, women's dorms, apartments for single students. 100% of campus accessible to physically diasbled. **Special Academic Facilities/Equipment:** Black Box theater, infant-toddler center, greenhouse, academic computer center, advanced architecture labs. **Computers:** 60% of classrooms, 80% of dorms, 80% of libraries, 100% of dining areas, 100% of student union, 100% of common outdoor areas have wireless network access. Students can register for classes online. Administrative functions (other than registration) can be performed online.

CAMPUS LIFE

Environment: Metropolis. **Activities:** Choral groups, concert band, dance, drama/theater, jazz band, literary magazine, marching band, music ensembles, musical theater, opera, pep band, radio station, student government, student newspaper, student-run film society, symphony orchestra, television station, yearbook, Campus Ministries. 100 registered organizations, 1 honor society. **Athletics (Intercollegiate):** *Women:* archery, basketball, crew/rowing, cross-country, diving, fencing, field hockey, golf, lacrosse, soccer, softball, swimming, tennis, track/field (outdoor), volleyball. **On-Campus Highlights:** Diana Center, Arthur Ross Greenhouse, Held Auditorium, Smart Media Classrooms, Liz's Place Cafe. **Environmental Initiatives:** Barnard has mandated LEED certification for new buildings. The newest addition to Barnard's campus, The Diana Center, is a LEED Gold building.

ADMISSIONS

Freshman Academic Profile: Average high school GPA 3.9. 81% in top 10% of high school class, 94% in top 25% of high school class, 99% in top 50% of high school class. 55% from public high schools. **Reported SAT (pre-2016 redesign) scores:** SAT Math middle 50% range 620-720. SAT Critical Reading middle 50% range 640-730. SAT Writing middle 50% range 650-740. **Concordant SAT scores:** SAT EBRW middle 50% 690–760. SAT Math middle 50% range 640–750. ACT middle 50% range 29-32. Minimum internet-based TOEFL 100. Minimum paper TOEFL 600. **Basis for Candidate Selection:** *Very important factors considered include:* rigor of secondary school record, academic GPA, application essay, recommendation(s), character/personal qualities. *Important factors considered include:* class rank, standardized test scores, extracurricular activities, talent/ability, volunteer work, work experience. *Other factors considered include:* interview, first generation, alumni/ae relation, geographical residence, racial/ethnic status, level of applicant's interest. **Freshman Admission Requirements:** High school diploma or equivalent is not required. *Academic units recommended:* 4 English, 3 math, 3 science, 3 foreign language, 3 history. **Freshman Admission Statistics:** 6,655 applied, 19.62% admitted, 49% enrolled. **Transfer Admission Requirements:** High school transcript, college transcript(s), essay or personal statement, standardized test scores, statement of good standing from prior institution(s). Lowest grade transferable C-. **General Admission Information:** Application fee $75. Regular application deadline 1/1. Regular notification 4/1. Nonfall registration not accepted. Admission may be deferred for a maximum of 1 year.

COSTS AND FINANCIAL AID

Annual tuition $48,614. Room and board $15,598. Required fees $1,780. **Required Forms and Deadlines:** FAFSA, CSS/Financial Aid PROFILE, State aid form, Noncustodial PROFILE. **Notification of Awards:** Applicants will be notified of awards on or about 3/31. **Types of Aid:** *Need-based scholarships/grants:* Federal Pell, FSEOG, State scholarships/grants, Private scholarships, College/university scholarship or grant aid from institutional funds. *Loans:* Direct Subsidized Stafford Loans, Direct Unsubsidized Stafford Loans, Direct PLUS loans, Federal Perkins Loans. *Student Employment:* Federal Work-Study Program available. Institutional employment available. **Financial Aid Statistics:** 98% needy freshmen, 98% needy undergrads receive need-based scholarship or grant aid. 0% undergrads receive non-need-based scholarship or grant aid. 100% freshmen, 100% undergrads receive need-based self-help aid. 0% freshmen, 0% undergrads receive athletic scholarships. 53% freshmen, 48% undergrads receive any aid. 44% undergrads borrow to pay for school. Average cumulative indebtedness $20,008.

See page 914.

BARRY UNIVERSITY

11300 NE 2nd Avenue, Miami Shores, FL 33161-6695
Phone: 305-899-3100 • **Financial Aid Phone:** 305-899-3673
E-mail: dmissions@barry.edu • **CEEB Code:** 5053
Fax: 305-899-2971 • **Website:** www.barry.edu • **ACT Code:** 718

This private school, affiliated with the Roman Catholic Church, was founded in 1940. It has a 122-acre campus.

RATINGS

Admissions Selectivity Rating: 74 **Fire Safety Rating:** 60* **Green Rating:** 60*

STUDENTS AND FACULTY

Enrollment: 3,461. **Student Body:** 61% female, 39% male, 21% out-of-state, 8% international (101 countries represented). Asian 1%, African American 29%, Caucasian 19%, Hispanic 31%, Native American <1%, Pacific Islander <1%, Two or more races 2%, Race unknown 9%.
Retention and Graduation: 65% freshmen return for sophomore year. 16% freshmen graduate within 4 years.

ACADEMICS

Degrees: bachelor's, master's, postbachelor's certificate, post-master's certificate. **Classes:** Most classes have 10-19 students. **Most popular majors:** Information Science/Studies; Elementary Education and Teaching; Business/Commerce. **Special Study Options:** Accelerated program, double major, English as a Second Language (ESL), honors program, internships, study abroad, teacher certification program. Combined degree programs: DPM/MBA; JD/MBA; MSN/MBA. **Disability Services:** Special programs offered to physically disabled students, including note-taking services, reader services, tape recorders, tutors. **Career Services:** Alumni services, On-campus interviews.

FACILITIES

Housing: Coed dorms, special housing for disabled students, men's dorms, women's dorms. 82% of campus accessible to physically diasbled. **Special

Academic Facilities/Equipment: Human performance lab, broadcasting studio, radio station, athletic training room, cell biology/biotechnology labs, Classroom of Tomorrow, Biomechanics lab,Photogrpahy lab, darkroom, and studio, Language lab, athletic training room. **Computers:** Students can register for classes online. Administrative functions (other than registration) can be performed online.

CAMPUS LIFE

Environment: Village. **Activities:** Choral groups, dance, drama/theater, literary magazine, music ensembles, musical theater, radio station, student government, student newspaper, television station, Campus Ministries, Student Organization. 67 registered organizations, 20 honor societies, 5 religious organizations. 2 fraternities, 2 sororities. **Athletics (Intercollegiate):** *Men:* baseball, basketball, golf, soccer, tennis. *Women:* basketball, crew/rowing, golf, soccer, softball, tennis, volleyball. **On-Campus Highlights:** Thompson Hall-Student Center, Human Performance Leisure Sciences-Athletic Complex, Penaport Pool, Residence Halls, Library.

ADMISSIONS

Freshman Academic Profile: Average high school GPA 3.2. **Reported SAT (pre-2016 redesign) scores:** SAT Math middle 50% range 420-500. SAT Critical Reading middle 50% range 430-510. **Concordant SAT scores:** SAT Math middle 50% range 460–530. ACT middle 50% range 18-21. Minimum internet-based TOEFL 61. **Basis for Candidate Selection:** *Very important factors considered include:* academic GPA, standardized test scores. *Important factors considered include:* interview, talent/ability, character/personal qualities. *Other factors considered include:* rigor of secondary school record, class rank, application essay, recommendation(s), extracurricular activities, volunteer work, work experience. **Freshman Admission Requirements:** High school diploma is required and GED is accepted. *Academic units recommended:* 4 English, 3 math, 3 science, 3 social studies. **Freshman Admission Statistics:** 4,982 applied, 61.62% admitted, 16% enrolled. **Transfer Admission Requirements:** college transcript(s), Minimum college GPA of 2.0 required. Lowest grade transferable C. **General Admission Information:** Nonfall registration accepted. Admission may be deferred for a maximum of 1 year.

COSTS AND FINANCIAL AID

Annual tuition $28,800. Room and board $10,800. Average book expense $1,500. **Required Forms and Deadlines:** FAFSA. **Notification of Awards:** Applicants will be notified of awards on a rolling basis beginning 1/25. **Types of Aid:** *Need-based scholarships/grants:* Federal Pell, FSEOG, State scholarships/ grants, Private scholarships, College/university scholarship or grant aid from institutional funds, Federal Nursing Scholarships. *Loans:* Direct Subsidized Stafford Loans, Direct Unsubsidized Stafford Loans, Direct PLUS loans, Federal Perkins Loans, Federal Nursing Loans, College/university loans from institutional funds. *Student Employment:* Federal Work-Study Program available. Institutional employment available. **Financial Aid Statistics:** 83% needy freshmen, 79% needy undergrads receive need-based scholarship or grant aid. 93% freshmen, 93% undergrads receive non-need-based scholarship or grant aid. 80% freshmen, 82% undergrads receive need-based self-help aid. 5% freshmen, 5% undergrads receive athletic scholarships. 98% freshmen, 85% undergrads receive any aid. 68% undergrads borrow to pay for school. Average cumulative indebtedness $39,248. **Criteria for awarding aid:** *Non-need-based:* Academics, Art, Athletics, Music/drama.

BARTON COLLEGE

Box 5000, Wilson, NC 27893-7000
Phone: 252-399-6317 • **Financial Aid Phone:** 252-399-6316
E-mail: enroll@barton.edu • **CEEB Code:** 5016
Fax: 252-399-6572 • **Website:** www.barton.edu • **ACT Code:** 3066

This private school, affiliated with the Disciples of Christ Church, was founded in 1902. It has a 76-acre campus.

RATINGS

Admissions Selectivity Rating: 80   **Fire Safety Rating:** 88   **Green Rating:** 60*

STUDENTS AND FACULTY

Enrollment: 1,069. **Student Body:** 69% female, 31% male, 11% out-of-state, 3% international (8 countries represented). Asian 1%, African American 27%, Caucasian 59%, Hispanic 3%, Native American 1%, Pacific Islander <1%, Two or more races 4%, Race unknown 2%.
Retention and Graduation: 71% freshmen return for sophomore year. 35% freshmen graduate within 4 years. 47% freshmen graduate within 6 years.
Faculty: Student/faculty ratio 12:1. 69 full-time faculty, 68% hold PhDs, 13% are are members of minority groups, 49% are women. 0% of classes are taught by teaching assistants.

ACADEMICS

Degrees: bachelor's, master's. **Classes:** Most classes have 10-19 students. Most lab/discussion sessions have fewer than 10 students. **Most popular majors:** Elementary Education and Teaching Business Administration and Management. **Special Study Options:** cooperative education program, double major, honors program, independent study, internships, liberal arts/career combination, study abroad, teacher certification program, weekend college. **Honors Programs:** Three competitive international travel scholarships awarded to entering honors students. **Disability Services:** Special programs offered to physically disabled students, including note-taking services, reader services, tape recorders, tutors. **Career Services:** Alumni services, Career/job search classes, Career assessment, Internships.

FACILITIES

Housing: Coed dorms, special housing for disabled students, women's dorms, fraternity/sorority housing. 90% of campus accessible to physically diasbled. **Special Academic Facilities/Equipment:** tv station, art museum, music recording studio, greenhouse. **Computers:** 90% of libraries, 90% of dining areas, have wireless network access. Administrative functions (other than registration) can be performed online.

CAMPUS LIFE

Environment: Town. **Activities:** Choral groups, dance, drama/theater, musical theater, pep band, student government, student newspaper, symphony orchestra, Campus Ministries. 51 registered organizations, 7 honor societies, 4 religious organizations. 3 fraternities, 3 sororities. **Athletics (Intercollegiate):** *Men:* baseball, basketball, cross-country, golf, soccer, tennis. *Women:* basketball, cross-country, soccer, softball, tennis, volleyball. **On-Campus Highlights:** Hamlin Student Center, Sam and Marjorie Ragan Writing Center, Kennedy Recreation and Intramural Center, Hackney Library, Barton Art Museum.

ADMISSIONS

Freshman Academic Profile: Average high school GPA 3.0. 12% in top 10% of high school class, 35% in top 25% of high school class, 73% in top 50% of high school class. 87% from public high schools. **Reported SAT (pre-2016 redesign) scores:** SAT Math middle 50% range 430-540. SAT Critical Reading middle 50% range 420-520. **Concordant SAT scores:** SAT Math middle 50% range 470–570. Minimum paper TOEFL 525. **Basis for Candidate Selection:** *Very important factors considered include:* academic GPA, standardized test scores. *Other factors considered include:* rigor of secondary school record, class rank, recommendation(s), interview, extracurricular activities, volunteer work, work experience. **Freshman Admission Requirements:** High school diploma is required and GED is accepted. *Academic units required:* 4 English, 3 math, 2 science, 1 science lab, 1 academic elective. *Academic units recommended:* 2 foreign language, and 2 units from above areas or other academic areas. **Freshman Admission Statistics:** 3,017 applied, 44.41% admitted, 15% enrolled. **Transfer Admission Requirements:** college transcript(s), statement of good standing from prior institution(s). Minimum college GPA of 2.0 required. Lowest grade transferable C. **General Admission Information:** Application fee $25. Nonfall registration accepted. Admission may be deferred for a maximum of 1 year.

COSTS AND FINANCIAL AID

Annual tuition $22,278. Room and board $7,940. Required fees $1,902. Average book expense $1,200. **Required Forms and Deadlines:** FAFSA. **Notification of Awards:** Applicants will be notified of awards on a rolling basis beginning 2/29. **Types of Aid:** *Need-based scholarships/grants:* Federal Pell, FSEOG, State scholarships/grants, Private scholarships, College/university scholarship or grant aid from institutional funds. *Loans:* Federal Perkins Loans. *Student Employment:* Federal Work-Study Program available. Institutional employment available. **Financial Aid Statistics:** 99% needy freshmen, 96% needy undergrads receive need-based scholarship or grant aid. 10% freshmen, 6% undergrads receive non-need-based scholarship or grant aid. 87% freshmen, 87% undergrads receive need-based self-help aid. 9% freshmen, 6% undergrads receive athletic scholarships. 98% freshmen, 93% undergrads receive any aid. **Criteria for awarding aid:** *Need-based:* Minority status, Religious affiliation. *Non-need-based:* Academics, Alumni affiliation, Art, Athletics, Leadership, Minority status, Music/drama, Religious affiliation, State/district residency.

BASTYR UNIVERSITY

14500 Juanita Drive NE, Kenmore, WA 98028
Phone: 425-602-3330 • **Financial Aid Phone:** 425-602-3083
E-mail: admissions@bastyr.edu
Fax: 425-602-3090 • **Website:** www.bastyr.edu

This private school was founded in 1978. It has a 51-acre campus.

RATINGS
Admissions Selectivity Rating: 61   **Fire Safety Rating:** 88   **Green Rating:** 60*

STUDENTS AND FACULTY
Enrollment: 227. **Student Body:** 87% female, 13% male, 5% out-of-state, 3% international (31 countries represented). Asian 8%, African American 4%, Caucasian 71%, Hispanic 5%, Native American 2%, Pacific Islander 1%, Two or more races 4%, Race unknown 3%.
Faculty: 43 full-time faculty, 0% hold PhDs, 19% are are members of minority groups, 63% are women. 0% of classes are taught by teaching assistants.

ACADEMICS
Degrees: bachelor's, certificate, doctoral/professional, master's, post-master's certificate. **Most popular majors:** Acupuncture and Oriental Medicine; Nutrition Sciences; Herbalism/Herbalist. **Special Study Options:** double major, internships, selected tracks within major. Combined degree programs: naturopathic medicine and acupuncture. **Career Services:** Alumni services, Career/job search classes, Career assessment, Internships, On-campus interviews. Bastyr University Venture Grants fund unique and innovative student travel projects of high merit that encourage student's personal and professional development, offer a return benefit to the Bastyr community, and create a vital force in the improvement of the health and well-being of humanity. The program offers support for Bastyr students to explore the vision of this University throughout the world on domestic or international trips.

FACILITIES
Housing: Coed dorms, Wellness Housing. 100% of campus accessible to physically diasbled.

CAMPUS LIFE
Environment: Town. **Activities:** Choral groups, student government. **On-Campus Highlights:** Vegetarian cafeteria, Medicinal herb garden, Spacious campus grounds and playfields, Adjacent state park, Bookstore. **Environmental Initiatives:** Our 11-building Student Village has earned LEED Platinum-certification (the first student housing project on the West Coast to receive this honor) and the U.S. Green Building Council's (USGBC) Outstanding Multifamily Project in the 2010 LEED for Homes Awards. The buildings feature "butterfly" roofs to capture rainwater, high efficiency water heaters and gas boilers, energy-efficient appliances and light fixtures, low-flow plumbing, natural ventilation, radiant-heat flooring made of finished concrete, sustainable landscaping, and bicycle storage.

ADMISSIONS
Minimum internet-based TOEFL 79. Minimum paper TOEFL 550. **Transfer Admission Requirements:** college transcript(s), essay or personal statement, Minimum college GPA of 2.25 required. Lowest grade transferable 2. **General Admission Information:** Application fee $75. Regular application deadline 3/15. Admission may be deferred.

COSTS AND FINANCIAL AID
Annual tuition $24,273. Average book expense $2,250. **Required Forms and Deadlines:** FAFSA, Institution's own financial aid form. **Notification of Awards:** Applicants will be notified of awards on a rolling basis beginning 2/1. **Types of Aid:** *Need-based scholarships/grants:* Federal Pell, FSEOG, State scholarships/grants, Private scholarships, College/university scholarship or grant aid from institutional funds. *Loans:* Direct Subsidized Stafford Loans, Direct Unsubsidized Stafford Loans, Direct PLUS loans, Federal Perkins Loans. *Student Employment:* Federal Work-Study Program available. Institutional employment available. **Financial Aid Statistics:** 91% needy undergrads receive need-based scholarship or grant aid. 2% undergrads receive non-need-based scholarship or grant aid. 0% undergrads receive athletic scholarships. 87% undergrads receive any aid. **Criteria for awarding aid:** *Need-based:* Academics, Alumni affiliation, Job skills, Leadership. *Non-need-based:* Academics, Alumni affiliation, Job skills, Leadership.

BATES COLLEGE

23 Campus Avenue, Lewiston, ME 4240
Phone: 207-786-6000 • **Financial Aid Phone:** 207-786-6096
E-mail: admission@bates.edu • **CEEB Code:** 3076
Fax: 207-786-6025 • **Website:** www.bates.edu • **ACT Code:** 1634

This private school was founded in 1855. It has a 109-acre campus.

RATINGS
Admissions Selectivity Rating: 95   **Fire Safety Rating:** 98   **Green Rating:** 60*

STUDENTS AND FACULTY
Enrollment: 1,780. **Student Body:** 51% female, 49% male, 7% international (71 countries represented). Asian 4%, African American 6%, Caucasian 70%, Hispanic 9%, Native American <1%, Pacific Islander 0%, Two or more races 4%, Race unknown <1%.
Retention and Graduation: 95% freshmen return for sophomore year. 84% freshmen graduate within 4 years. **Faculty:** Student/faculty ratio 10:1. 169 full-time faculty, 96% hold PhDs, 16% are are members of minority groups, 51% are women. 0% of classes are taught by teaching assistants.

ACADEMICS
Degrees: bachelor's. **Classes:** Most classes have 10-19 students. Most lab/discussion sessions have 10-19 students. **Most popular majors:** Political Science and Government; Psychology; History. **Special Study Options:** Accelerated program, cooperative education program, double major, honors program, independent study, internships, liberal arts/career combination, student-designed major, study abroad, teacher certification program. **Honors Programs:** The Honors Program. **Disability Services:** Special programs offered to physically disabled students, including note-taking services, reader services, tape recorders, tutors. **Career Services:** Alumni network, Alumni services, Career/job search classes, Career assessment, Internships, Regional alumni. The Bates Career Development Center incorporates a multi-pronged strategy that provides a variety of touch points for students to engage and explore in career-related activities. From targeted programs by class year designed to engage students early in their career development to programming aimed at specific fields and industries (i.e., finance/banking, medicine, public health, law, education), the BCDC crafts and delivers programs that meet students (both individually and in groups) where they are in their exploration.

FACILITIES
Housing: Coed dorms, men's dorms, women's dorms, Theme houses, quiet/study houses and halls, chem-free and low chem houses and halls. 60% of campus accessible to physically diasbled. **Special Academic Facilities/Equipment:** Art gallery, Edmund S. Muskie Archives, language labs, planetarium, 600-acre conservation area on seacoast for environmental studies, scanning electron microscope, Imaging Center. **Computers:** 40% of classrooms, 100% of dorms, 100% of libraries, 100% of dining areas, 100% of student union, 10% of common outdoor areas have wireless network access. Students can register for classes online. Administrative functions (other than registration) can be performed online.

CAMPUS LIFE
Environment: Town. **Activities:** Choral groups, dance, drama/theater, jazz band, literary magazine, music ensembles, pep band, radio station, student government, student newspaper, student-run film society, symphony orchestra, yearbook, Campus Ministries, Student Organization. 99 registered organizations, 3 honor societies, 9 religious organizations. **Athletics (Intercollegiate):** *Men:* baseball, basketball, crew/rowing, cross-country, diving, football, golf, lacrosse, skiing (downhill/alpine), skiing (nordic/cross-country), soccer, squash, swimming, tennis, track/field (outdoor), track/field (indoor). *Women:* basketball, crew/rowing, cross-country, diving, field hockey, golf, lacrosse, skiing (downhill/alpine), skiing (nordic/cross-country), soccer, softball, squash, swimming, tennis, track/field (outdoor), track/field (indoor), volleyball. **On-Campus Highlights:** Pettengill Hall, Bates College Museum of Art, Dining Commons, The George and Helen Ladd Library, Merrill Gymnasium/Underhill Arena. **Environmental Initiatives:** Developing sustainable building guidelines and campus energy goals.

ADMISSIONS
Freshman Academic Profile: 58% in top 10% of high school class. 53% from public high schools. **Reported SAT (pre-2016 redesign) scores:** SAT Math middle 50% range 580-700. SAT Critical Reading middle 50% range 570-690. SAT Writing middle 50% range 580-690. **Concordant SAT scores:** SAT EBRW middle 50% 630–730. SAT Math middle 50% range 600–730.

ACT middle 50% range 27-32. **Basis for Candidate Selection:** *Very important factors considered include:* rigor of secondary school record, class rank, academic GPA, application essay, recommendation(s), extracurricular activities, talent/ability, character/personal qualities, level of applicant's interest. *Important factors considered include:* interview, first generation, geographical residence. *Other factors considered include:* standardized test scores, alumni/ae relation, state residency, racial/ethnic status, volunteer work, work experience. **Freshman Admission Requirements:** High school diploma is required and GED is not accepted. *Academic units required:* 4 English, 3 math, 3 science, 2 science labs, 2 foreign language, 3 social studies, 3 history. *Academic units recommended:* 4 English, 4 math, 4 science, 3 science labs, 4 foreign language, 4 social studies, 4 history. **Freshman Admission Statistics:** 5,356 applied, 22.65% admitted, 40% enrolled. **Transfer Admission Requirements:** High school transcript, college transcript(s), essay or personal statement, statement of good standing from prior institution(s). Lowest grade transferable C. **General Admission Information:** Application fee $60. Regular application deadline 1/1. Regular notification 4/1. Nonfall registration accepted. Admission may be deferred for a maximum of 1 year.

COSTS AND FINANCIAL AID

Annual tuition $50,310. Room and board $14,190. Average book expense $800. **Required Forms and Deadlines:** FAFSA, CSS/Financial Aid PROFILE, Noncustodial PROFILE. **Notification of Awards:** Applicants will be notified of awards on or about 4/1. **Types of Aid:** *Need-based scholarships/grants:* Federal Pell, FSEOG, State scholarships/grants, Private scholarships, College/university scholarship or grant aid from institutional funds. *Loans:* Direct Subsidized Stafford Loans, Direct Unsubsidized Stafford Loans, Direct PLUS loans, Federal Perkins Loans. *Student Employment:* Federal Work-Study Program available. Institutional employment available. **Financial Aid Statistics:** 100% needy freshmen, 100% needy undergrads receive need-based scholarship or grant aid. 0% undergrads receive non-need-based scholarship or grant aid. 98% freshmen, 99% undergrads receive need-based self-help aid. 0% freshmen, 0% undergrads receive athletic scholarships. 42% freshmen, 42% undergrads receive any aid. 34% undergrads borrow to pay for school. Average cumulative indebtedness $22,845.

BAY PATH UNIVERSITY

588 Longmeadow Street, Longmeadow, MA 01106-2292
Phone: 413-565-1331 • **Financial Aid Phone:** 413-565-1345
E-mail: admiss@baypath.edu • **CEEB Code:** 2122
Fax: 413-565-1105 • **Website:** www.baypath.edu • **ACT Code:** 1785

This private school was founded in 1897. It has a 48-acre campus.

RATINGS

Admissions Selectivity Rating: 81   **Fire Safety Rating:** 99   **Green Rating:** 60*

STUDENTS AND FACULTY

Enrollment: 1,886. **Student Body:** 100% female, 0% male, 42% out-of-state, 1% international (5 countries represented). Asian 2%, African American 13%, Caucasian 57%, Hispanic 19%, Native American <1%, Pacific Islander <1%, Two or more races 3%, Race unknown 5%.
Retention and Graduation: 72% freshmen return for sophomore year. 53% freshmen graduate within 4 years. 60% freshmen graduate within 6 years.
Faculty: Student/faculty ratio 11:1. 62 full-time faculty, 61% hold PhDs, 11% are are members of minority groups, 74% are women. 0% of classes are taught by teaching assistants.

ACADEMICS

Degrees: associate, bachelor's, certificate, master's, postbachelor's certificate, post-master's certificate. **Classes:** Most classes have 10-19 students. Most lab/discussion sessions have 10-19 students. **Most popular majors:** Psychology; Business Administration, Management and Operations; Liberal Arts and Sciences/Liberal Studies. **Special Study Options:** Accelerated program, cooperative education program, cross-registration, distance learning, double major, English as a Second Language (ESL), exchange student program (domestic), honors program, independent study, internships, student-designed major, study abroad, teacher certification program, weekend college, Directed study program. **Honors Programs:** The Bay Path Honors Program offers unique learning experiences to the most qualified undergraduate students through honors courses, service projects, on and off campus events and participation in and development of the Bay Path College Honors Program community. The Honors Program at Bay Path provides academically talented and motivated students with uniquely challenging and intellectually stimulating educational opportunities. In the first two years, Honors students take team-taught, interdisciplinary seminars on specific topics, such as Darwin Across the Disciplines. This innovative approach broadens exposure to areas outside the major and provides connections with other Honors students. In the last two years, under the guidance of a faculty mentor, students are immersed in their field of study, and are urged to explore new areas of knowledge with an Honors thesis or creative project. Combined degree programs: BA/MOT. **Disability Services:** Special programs offered to physically disabled students, including tutors. **Career Services:** Alumni network, Alumni services, Career/job search classes, Career assessment, Internships, Regional alumni, On-campus interviews. We have a very strong internship program, with all students required in each respective major to perform fieldwork, an internship, student teaching, or experiential learning. Internships are listed in the top 3 important experiences employers wish to see on a college student's resume, aside from major and degree achieved.

FACILITIES

Housing: women's dorms. 50% of campus accessible to physically diasbled. **Special Academic Facilities/Equipment:** Blake Student Commons, Bashevkin Academic Development Center, Breck Fitness Center, occupational therapy laboratory, and D'Amour Hall for Business, Communications and Technology. **Computers:** 100% of libraries, 100% of dining areas, 100% of student union, 25% of common outdoor areas have wireless network access. Students can register for classes online. Administrative functions (other than registration) can be performed online.

CAMPUS LIFE

Environment: Village. **Activities:** Choral groups, dance, drama/theater, literary magazine, musical theater, student government, student newspaper, Student Organization, Model UN. 42 registered organizations, 3 honor societies, 1 religious organization. **Athletics (Intercollegiate):** *Women:* basketball, cross-country, field hockey, soccer, softball, tennis, volleyball. **On-Campus Highlights:** Carpe Diem Cafe, Toner/Helliwell Hearth and Lounge, Game Room, Breck Fitness Center, D'Amour Hall for Business, Communications and Tech. **Environmental Initiatives:** Recycling program.

ADMISSIONS

Freshman Academic Profile: Average high school GPA 3.3. 15% in top 10% of high school class, 44% in top 25% of high school class, 76% in top 50% of high school class. **Reported SAT (pre-2016 redesign) scores:** SAT Math middle 50% range 420-515. SAT Critical Reading middle 50% range 425-550. SAT Writing middle 50% range 420-540. **Concordant SAT scores:** SAT EBRW middle 50% 480-600. SAT Math middle 50% range 460-550. ACT middle 50% range 19-25. Minimum internet-based TOEFL 76. **Basis for Candidate Selection:** *Very important factors considered include:* rigor of secondary school record, academic GPA, application essay, recommendation(s), interview. *Important factors considered include:* extracurricular activities, talent/ability, level of applicant's interest. *Other factors considered include:* class rank, standardized test scores, character/personal qualities, first generation, alumni/ae relation, geographical residence, volunteer work, work experience. **Freshman Admission Requirements:** High school diploma is required and GED is accepted. *Academic units required:* 4 English, 3 math, 2 science, 2 science labs, 2 social studies, 1 history. *Academic units recommended:* 3 science, 3 science labs, 2 foreign language. **Freshman Admission Statistics:** 1,542 applied, 59.92% admitted, 17% enrolled. **Transfer Admission Requirements:** college transcript(s), Minimum college GPA of 2.0 required. Lowest grade transferable c-. **General Admission Information:** Application fee $25. Priority deadline 12/15. Regular application deadline 8/1. Nonfall registration accepted. Admission may be deferred for a maximum of 1 year.

COSTS AND FINANCIAL AID

Annual tuition $32,739. Room and board $12,610. Average book expense $1,100. **Required Forms and Deadlines:** FAFSA. **Notification of Awards:** Applicants will be notified of awards on a rolling basis beginning 3/1. **Types of Aid:** *Need-based scholarships/grants:* Federal Pell, FSEOG, State scholarships/grants, Private scholarships, College/university scholarship or grant aid from institutional funds. *Loans:* Direct Subsidized Stafford Loans, Direct Unsubsidized Stafford Loans, Direct PLUS loans, Federal Perkins Loans. *Student Employment:* Federal Work-Study Program available. Institutional employment available. **Financial Aid Statistics:** 100% needy freshmen, 100% needy undergrads receive need-based scholarship or grant aid. 4% freshmen, 6% undergrads receive non-need-based scholarship or grant aid. 95% freshmen, 92% undergrads receive need-based self-help aid. 0% freshmen, 0% undergrads receive athletic scholarships. 97% freshmen, 90% undergrads receive any aid. **Criteria for awarding aid:** *Non-need-based:* Academics.

BAYLOR UNIVERSITY

One Bear Place #97056, Waco, TX 76798-7056
Phone: 254-710-3435 • **Financial Aid Phone:** 254-710-2611
E-mail: admissions@baylor.edu • **CEEB Code:** 6032
Fax: 254-710-3436 • **Website:** www.baylor.edu • **ACT Code:** 4062

This private school was founded in 1845. It has a 508-acre campus.

RATINGS
Admissions Selectivity Rating: 91   **Fire Safety Rating:** 98   **Green Rating:** 83

STUDENTS AND FACULTY
Enrollment: 14,309. **Student Body:** 42% female, 58% male, 29% out-of-state, 3% international (79 countries represented). Asian 6%, African American 7%, Caucasian 64%, Hispanic 15%, Native American <1%, Pacific Islander <1%, Two or more races 5%, Race unknown <1%.
Retention and Graduation: 89% freshmen return for sophomore year. 58% freshmen graduate within 4 years. 74% freshmen graduate within 6 years.
Faculty: Student/faculty ratio 15:1. 1,023 full-time faculty, 83% hold PhDs, 14% are are members of minority groups, 41% are women.

ACADEMICS
Degrees: bachelor's, doctoral/professional, doctoral/research, master's, post-master's certificate. **Classes:** Most classes have 10-19 students. Most lab/discussion sessions have 10-19 students. **Most popular majors:** Registered Nursing/Registered Nurse; Biology/Biological Sciences; Accounting. **Special Study Options:** Accelerated program, double major, honors program, internships, student-designed major, study abroad, teacher certification program. **Honors Programs:** Honors Program, University Scholars Program, Great Texts Program Combined degree programs: BBA/MAccounting, BBA/MTax, BSN/MSNursing, BBA/MBA, BSE/MSBE, BSE/ME, ETC. **Disability Services:** Special programs offered to physically disabled students, including note-taking services, reader services. **Career Services:** Alumni network, Alumni services, Career/job search classes, Career assessment, Internships.

FACILITIES
Housing: special housing for disabled students, men's dorms, special housing for international students, women's dorms, apartments for married students, apartments for single students, Theme Housing, Living-Learning centers. 98% of campus accessible to physically diasbled. **Special Academic Facilities/Equipment:** Language and environmental studies labs, natural science museum, high definition television, Armstrong Browning library, Texas Collection Library, Strecker Museum/Bill and Vara Daniel Historical Village, TV Station, Radio Station **Computers:** 98% of classrooms, 10% of dorms, 95% of libraries, 95% of dining areas, 95% of student union, 50% of common outdoor areas have wireless network access. Students can register for classes online. Administrative functions (other than registration) can be performed online.

CAMPUS LIFE
Environment: City. **Activities:** Choral groups, concert band, dance, drama/theater, jazz band, literary magazine, marching band, music ensembles, musical theater, opera, pep band, radio station, student government, student newspaper, student-run film society, symphony orchestra, television station, yearbook, Campus Ministries, Student Organization, Model UN. 222 registered organizations, 32 honor societies, 11 religious organizations. 22 fraternities, 20 sororities. **Athletics (Intercollegiate):** *Men:* baseball, basketball, cheerleading, cross-country, football, golf, tennis, track/field (outdoor), track/field (indoor). *Women:* basketball, cheerleading, cross-country, equestrian sports, golf, soccer, softball, tennis, track/field (outdoor), track/field (indoor), volleyball. **On-Campus Highlights:** Mayborn Museum Complex, Armstrong Browning Library, Baylor Sciences Building, Student Life Center, Chili's Too – 1st on a University Campus. **Environmental Initiatives:** Campus wide recycling, with over 700 locations on campus to recycle in which to recycle and collaboration with Athletics Department to recycle at all university sporting events.

ADMISSIONS
Freshman Academic Profile: 41% in top 10% of high school class, 75% in top 25% of high school class, 97% in top 50% of high school class. **Reported SAT (pre-2016 redesign) scores:** SAT Math middle 50% range 570-660. SAT Critical Reading middle 50% range 550-650. SAT Writing middle 50% range 530-630. **Concordant SAT scores:** SAT EBRW middle 50% 600-690. SAT Math middle 50% range 590-690. ACT middle 50% range 26-30. Minimum internet-based TOEFL 76. Minimum paper TOEFL 540. **Basis for Candidate Selection:** *Very important factors considered include:* rigor of secondary

school record, class rank, standardized test scores. *Important factors considered include:* academic GPA, application essay, recommendation(s), extracurricular activities, talent/ability, character/personal qualities, level of applicant's interest. *Other factors considered include:* interview, alumni/ae relation, religious affiliation/commitment, volunteer work, work experience. **Freshman Admission Requirements:** High school diploma is required and GED is accepted. *Academic units required:* 4 English, 4 math, 4 science, 2 science labs, 2 foreign language, 2 social studies, 1 history. **Freshman Admission Statistics:** 34,636 applied, 39.72% admitted, 25% enrolled. **Transfer Admission Requirements:** college transcript(s), Minimum college GPA of 2.5 required. Lowest grade transferable C. **General Admission Information:** Regular application deadline 2/1. Nonfall registration accepted.

COSTS AND FINANCIAL AID
Annual tuition $39,610. Room and board $13,013. Required fees $4,180. Average book expense $1,200. **Required Forms and Deadlines:** FAFSA. **Notification of Awards:** Applicants will be notified of awards on a rolling basis beginning 3/15. **Types of Aid:** *Need-based scholarships/grants:* Federal Pell, FSEOG, State scholarships/grants, Private scholarships, College/university scholarship or grant aid from institutional funds. *Loans:* Direct Subsidized Stafford Loans, Direct Unsubsidized Stafford Loans, Direct PLUS loans, Federal Perkins Loans, Federal Nursing Loans, State Loans. *Student Employment:* Federal Work-Study Program available. Institutional employment available. **Financial Aid Statistics:** 100% needy freshmen, 97% needy undergrads receive need-based scholarship or grant aid. 99% freshmen, 93% undergrads receive non-need-based scholarship or grant aid. 79% freshmen, 80% undergrads receive need-based self-help aid. 2% freshmen, 2% undergrads receive athletic scholarships. 98% freshmen, 93% undergrads receive any aid. 53% undergrads borrow to pay for school. Average cumulative indebtedness $44,540. **Criteria for awarding aid:** *Need-based:* Academics, Art, Athletics, Leadership, Music/drama, Religious affiliation. *Non-need-based:* Academics, Art, Athletics, Leadership, Music/drama, Religious affiliation.

BEACON COLLEGE

105 E. Main Street, Leesburg, FL 34748
Phone: 352-638-9731 • **Financial Aid Phone:** 352-787-6306
E-mail: admissions@beaconcollege.edu
Fax: 352-787-0721 • **Website:** www.beaconcollege.edu • **ACT Code:** 704

This private school was founded in 1989.

RATINGS
Admissions Selectivity Rating: 64   **Fire Safety Rating:** 94   **Green Rating:** 60*

STUDENTS AND FACULTY
Enrollment: 128. **Student Body:** 38% female, 63% male, 80% out-of-state, 0% international (2 countries represented). Asian 2%, African American 10%, Caucasian 85%, Hispanic 3%, Native American 0%, Pacific Islander 0%, Two or more races 0%, Race unknown 0%.
Retention and Graduation: 73% freshmen return for sophomore year. 50% freshmen graduate within 4 years. **Faculty:** 17 full-time faculty, 65% hold PhDs, 6% are are members of minority groups, 59% are women. 0% of classes are taught by teaching assistants.

ACADEMICS
Degrees: associate, bachelor's. **Classes:** Most classes have 10-19 students. **Special Study Options:** cooperative education program, independent study, internships, study abroad. **Honors Programs:** Psi Tau Omega is the academic honor society at Beacon College. **Disability Services:** Special programs offered to physically disabled students, including note-taking services, reader services, tape recorders, tutors.

FACILITIES
Housing: special housing for disabled students, apartments for single students, Students enjoy 1, 2, and 3 bedroom apartment style living accommodations. **Computers:** 100% of classrooms, have wireless network access.

CAMPUS LIFE
Environment: Village. **Activities:** Choral groups, drama/theater, literary magazine, student government, student newspaper, yearbook. 13 registered organizations, 1 honor society, 1 fraternity, 1 sorority. **On-Campus Highlights:** New Resident Apartment Complex, Student Center, Stoer Building—Office of Student Services, Beacon College Library, Administration Building.

ADMISSIONS
Freshman Academic Profile: Average high school GPA 2.8. Minimum paper TOEFL 525. **Basis for Candidate Selection:** *Very important factors considered include:* recommendation(s). *Important factors considered include:* rigor of secondary school record, standardized test scores, application essay,

talent/ability, character/personal qualities. *Other factors considered include:* class rank, academic GPA, interview, extracurricular activities, volunteer work, work experience. **Freshman Admission Requirements:** High school diploma is required and GED is accepted. *Academic units required:* 4 English, 1 math, 1 science, 1 social studies, 2 history, 3 academic electives. **Freshman Admission Statistics:** 53 applied, 92.45% admitted, 59% enrolled. **Transfer Admission Requirements:** High school transcript, college transcript(s), essay or personal statement, interview, Lowest grade transferable C. **General Admission Information:** Application fee $50. Priority deadline 6/1. Regular application deadline 8/1. Nonfall registration accepted.

COSTS AND FINANCIAL AID

Annual tuition $27,000. Room and board $8,150. Required fees $700. Average book expense $900. **Required Forms and Deadlines:** FAFSA, Institution's own financial aid form, State aid form. **Notification of Awards:** Applicants will be notified of awards on or about 2/1. *Types of Aid: Need-based scholarships/grants:* Federal Pell, FSEOG, State scholarships/grants, Private scholarships, College/university scholarship or grant aid from institutional funds. *Student Employment:* Federal Work-Study Program available. Institutional employment available. **Financial Aid Statistics:** 60% needy freshmen, 22% needy undergrads receive need-based scholarship or grant aid. 0% undergrads receive non-need-based scholarship or grant aid. 60% freshmen, 22% undergrads receive need-based self-help aid. 0% freshmen, 0% undergrads receive athletic scholarships.

BECKER COLLEGE

61 Sever Street, Worcester, MA 1609
Phone: 508-373-9400 • **Financial Aid Phone:** 508-373-9440
E-mail: admissions@becker.edu • **CEEB Code:** 3079
Fax: 508-890-1500 • **Website:** www.becker.edu • **ACT Code:** 1784

RATINGS

Admissions Selectivity Rating: 83   Fire Safety Rating: 88   Green Rating: 60*

STUDENTS AND FACULTY

Enrollment: 1,951. **Student Body:** 59% female, 41% male, 47% out-of-state, 1% international (23 countries represented). Asian 2%, African American 8%, Caucasian 71%, Hispanic 9%, Native American <1%, Pacific Islander <1%, Two or more races 3%, Race unknown 7%.
Retention and Graduation: 68% freshmen return for sophomore year. 25% freshmen graduate within 4 years. 37% freshmen graduate within 6 years.
Faculty: Student/faculty ratio 17:1. 44 full-time faculty, 68% hold PhDs, 9% are are members of minority groups, 66% are women. 0% of classes are taught by teaching assistants.

ACADEMICS

Degrees: associate, bachelor's, certificate, master's. **Classes:** Most classes have 20-29 students. Most lab/discussion sessions have 10-19 students. **Most popular majors:** Game and Interactive Media Design; Pre-Veterinary Studies; Business Administration and Management. **Special Study Options:** Accelerated program, cooperative education program, cross-registration, distance learning, double major, dual enrollment, independent study, internships, study abroad, teacher certification program. **Career Services:** Alumni network, Alumni services, Career/job search classes, Career assessment, Internships, Regional alumni. Career/job search. Becker has a job site/database where store the information of 1200 active employers

FACILITIES

Housing: 8% of campus accessible to physically diasbled.

CAMPUS LIFE

Environment: City.

ADMISSIONS

Freshman Academic Profile: Average high school GPA 3.2. 65% from public high schools. **Reported SAT (pre-2016 redesign) scores:** SAT Math middle 50% range 460-560. SAT Critical Reading middle 50% range 460-570. SAT Writing middle 50% range 440-540. **Concordant SAT scores:** SAT EBRW middle 50% 500–610. SAT Math middle 50% range 500–580. ACT middle 50% range 21-26. Minimum paper TOEFL 550. **Basis for Candidate Selection:** *Very important factors considered:* rigor of secondary school record, academic GPA, standardized test scores. *Important factors considered include:* class rank, recommendation(s). *Other factors considered include:*

application essay, interview, extracurricular activities, alumni/ae relation, volunteer work, work experience, level of applicant's interest. **Freshman Admission Requirements:** High school diploma is required and GED is accepted. *Academic units recommended:* 4 English, 3 math, 3 science, 2 science labs, 2 foreign language, 2 social studies, 2 history. **Freshman Admission Statistics:** 4,458 applied, 65.34% admitted, 14% enrolled. **Transfer Admission Requirements:** college transcript(s), Minimum college GPA of 2.00 required. Lowest grade transferable C. **General Admission Information:** Nonfall registration accepted. Admission may be deferred.

COSTS AND FINANCIAL AID

Annual tuition $34,650. Room and board $13,300. Required fees $3,600. Average book expense $960. **Required Forms and Deadlines:** FAFSA. **Notification of Awards:** Applicants will be notified of awards on a rolling basis beginning 3/15. *Types of Aid: Need-based scholarships/grants:* Federal Pell, FSEOG, State scholarships/grants, Private scholarships, College/university scholarship or grant aid from institutional funds. *Loans:* Direct Subsidized Stafford Loans, Direct Unsubsidized Stafford Loans, Direct PLUS loans, State Loans. *Student Employment:* Federal Work-Study Program available. Institutional employment available. **Financial Aid Statistics:** 75% needy freshmen, 68% needy undergrads receive need-based scholarship or grant aid. 98% freshmen, 94% undergrads receive non-need-based scholarship or grant aid. 93% freshmen, 93% undergrads receive need-based self-help aid. 0% freshmen, 0% undergrads receive athletic scholarships. 100% freshmen, 88% undergrads receive any aid. **Criteria for awarding aid:** *Non-need-based:* Academics, State/district residency.

See page 916.

BELHAVEN UNIVERSITY

1500 Peachtree Street, Jackson, MS 39202
Phone: 601-968-5940 • **Financial Aid Phone:** 601-968-5920
E-mail: admission@belhaven.edu • **CEEB Code:** 1055
Fax: 601-968-8946 • **Website:** www.belhaven.edu • **ACT Code:** 2180

This private school, affiliated with the Presbyterian Church, was founded in 1883. It has a 42-acre campus.

RATINGS

Admissions Selectivity Rating: 80   Fire Safety Rating: 60*   Green Rating: 60*

STUDENTS AND FACULTY

Enrollment: 2,329. **Student Body:** 65% female, 35% male, 28% out-of-state, 2% international (21 countries represented). Asian 1%, African American 49%, Caucasian 35%, Hispanic 5%, Native American 1%, Pacific Islander <1%, Two or more races 2%, Race unknown 7%.
Retention and Graduation: 66% freshmen return for sophomore year. 28% freshmen graduate within 4 years. 36% freshmen graduate within 6 years.
Faculty: Student/faculty ratio 11:1. 101 full-time faculty, 73% hold PhDs, 0% are are members of minority groups, 44% are women. 0% of classes are taught by teaching assistants.

ACADEMICS

Degrees: associate, bachelor's, certificate, master's. **Classes:** Most classes have fewer than 10 students. Most lab/discussion sessions have fewer than 10 students. **Most popular majors:** Social Sciences; Dance; Business/Commerce. **Special Study Options:** Accelerated program, distance learning, double major, dual enrollment, English as a Second Language (ESL), honors program, independent study, internships, student-designed major, study abroad, teacher certification program. **Honors Programs:** Honors Program: The Honors College at Belhaven College gives academically advanced, highly motivated students a forum in which to deepen and expand their college education, both intellectually and spiritually. Enrollment in the Honors College is limited to students who demonstrate a past record of academic achievement, seriousness about their calling, and enthusiasm for challenging dialogue with students and scholars from a variety of fields. **Career Services:** Internships, On-campus interviews.

FACILITIES

Housing: men's dorms, women's dorms. **Special Academic Facilities/ Equipment:** Bitsy Irby art gallery **Computers:** 100% of dorms, 100% of libraries, 100% of student union, have wireless network access. Students can register for classes online. Administrative functions (other than registration) can be performed online.

CAMPUS LIFE

Environment: City. **Activities:** Choral groups, dance, drama/theater, jazz band, literary magazine, marching band, music ensembles, pep band, student government, student newspaper, yearbook, Student Organization. 29 registered organizations, 5 religious organizations. **Athletics (Intercollegiate):** *Men:* baseball, basketball, cheerleading, cross-country, football, golf, soccer, tennis.

Women: basketball, cheerleading, cross-country, golf, soccer, softball, tennis, volleyball.

ADMISSIONS

Freshman Academic Profile: Average high school GPA 3.4. **Reported SAT (pre-2016 redesign) scores:** SAT Math middle 50% range 450-580. SAT Critical Reading middle 50% range 440-610. **Concordant SAT scores:** SAT Math middle 50% range 490–600. ACT middle 50% range 20-23. Minimum internet-based TOEFL 61. Minimum paper TOEFL 500. **Basis for Candidate Selection:** *Very important factors considered include:* academic GPA, standardized test scores. *Other factors considered include:* rigor of secondary school record, application essay, recommendation(s), interview, extracurricular activities, talent/ability, character/personal qualities, alumni/ae relation, level of applicant's interest. **Freshman Admission Requirements:** High school diploma is required and GED is accepted. *Academic units required:* 4 English, 2 math, 1 science, 1 history, 8 academic electives. *Academic units recommended:* 1 computer science. **Freshman Admission Statistics:** 2,474 applied, 42.56% admitted, 23% enrolled. **Transfer Admission Requirements:** college transcript(s), Minimum college GPA of 2.0 required. Lowest grade transferable D. **General Admission Information:** Application fee $25. Nonfall registration accepted. Admission may be deferred.

COSTS AND FINANCIAL AID

Annual tuition $21,626. Room and board $8,000. Required fees $190. Average book expense $1,250. **Required Forms and Deadlines:** FAFSA. **Notification of Awards:** Applicants will be notified of awards on a rolling basis beginning 2/1. **Types of Aid:** *Need-based scholarships/grants:* Federal Pell, FSEOG, State scholarships/grants, Private scholarships, College/university scholarship or grant aid from institutional funds. *Loans:* Federal Perkins Loans. *Student Employment:* Federal Work-Study Program available. **Financial Aid Statistics:** 100% needy freshmen receive need-based scholarship or grant aid. **Criteria for awarding aid:** *Non-need-based:* Academics, Alumni affiliation, Art, Music/drama.

BELLARMINE UNIVERSITY

2001 Newburg Road, Louisville, KY 40205
Phone: 502-272-8131 • **Financial Aid Phone:** 502-272-8124
E-mail: admissions@bellarmine.edu • **CEEB Code:** 1056
Fax: 502-272-8002 • **Website:** www.bellarmine.edu • **ACT Code:** 1490

This private school, affiliated with the Roman Catholic Church, was founded in 1950. It has a 135-acre campus.

RATINGS

Admissions Selectivity Rating: 81   **Fire Safety Rating:** 96   **Green Rating:** 60*

STUDENTS AND FACULTY

Enrollment: 2,584. **Student Body:** 65% female, 35% male, 33% out-of-state, 1% international (14 countries represented). Asian 2%, African American 4%, Caucasian 85%, Hispanic 3%, Native American <1%, Pacific Islander <1%, Two or more races 3%, Race unknown 2%.
Retention and Graduation: 81% freshmen return for sophomore year. 51% freshmen graduate within 4 years. 67% freshmen graduate within 6 years. 26% grads go on to further study within 1 year. **Faculty:** Student/faculty ratio 12:1. 167 full-time faculty, 83% hold PhDs, 10% are are members of minority groups, 54% are women. 0% of classes are taught by teaching assistants.

ACADEMICS

Degrees: bachelor's, doctoral/professional, doctoral/research, master's, postbachelor's certificate. **Classes:** Most classes have 10-19 students. Most lab/discussion sessions have 10-19 students. **Most popular majors:** Psychology; Registered Nursing/Registered Nurse; Kinesiology and Exercise Science. **Special Study Options:** Accelerated program, cross-registration, double major, dual enrollment, honors program, independent study, internships, liberal arts/career combination, student-designed major, study abroad, teacher certification program. **Honors Programs:** Bellarmine Honors Program Bellarmine Brown Scholars Program Combined degree programs: Accounting BA and MBA. **Disability Services:** Special programs offered to physically disabled students, including note-taking services, reader services, tutors. **Career Services:** Alumni network, Alumni services, Career/job search classes, Career assessment, Internships, Regional alumni. The Career Development Center and Alumni Relations have successfully partnered for several years to sponsor

the Alumni Mentor Program. This collaborative effort aims to pair current BU undergraduates with Bellarmine alumni in the students' field of interest. These mentoring relationships are fostered through structured events by the university, as well as more organic conversation and rapport building initiated by the alumni/student pair. In previous years, the Alumni Mentor Program has helped student participants to make decisions within their career path, gain advice relevant to their field, as well as land internships and even jobs. The 2015 year was the largest to date for the program, with 244 student participants from majors across the university.

FACILITIES

Housing: Coed dorms, special housing for disabled students, men's dorms, women's dorms, 4 bedroom or 2 bedroom suites. **Special Academic Facilities/Equipment:** McGrath Art Gallery; Thomas Merton Center. **Computers:** 50% of classrooms, 100% of dorms, 100% of libraries, 25% of dining areas, 100% of student union, 25% of common outdoor areas have wireless network access. Students can register for classes online. Administrative functions (other than registration) can be performed online.

CAMPUS LIFE

Environment: Metropolis. **Activities:** Choral groups, concert band, dance, drama/theater, jazz band, literary magazine, music ensembles, musical theater, pep band, radio station, student government, student newspaper, yearbook, Campus Ministries, Student Organization. 70 registered organizations, 3 honor societies, 6 religious organizations. 1 fraternity, 1 sorority. **Athletics (Intercollegiate):** *Men:* baseball, basketball, bowling, cross-country, golf, lacrosse, soccer, tennis, track/field (outdoor). *Women:* basketball, bowling, cheerleading, cross-country, field hockey, golf, soccer, softball, tennis, track/field (outdoor), volleyball. **On-Campus Highlights:** Norton Health Science Center, Our Lady of the Woods Chapel, Siena Halls, Owsley B. Frazier Stadium, The Thomas Merton Center. The $5.1 million Owsley B. Frazier Stadium has taken approximately 18 months to build and will be the new home for Bellarmine's soccer, field hockey, lacrosse, and track teams. The new facility has several outstanding features which are outlined below: • Artificial Turf – The artificial turf product, called "24/7," was produced and installed by the Motz Group. It has permanent markings for soccer, field hockey, and lacrosse and has an exceptional drainage system to allow for extensive play in all weather conditions. • Lighting – Lighting has been installed at the field to allow for night play. The Musco Lighting system features redirected lighting which bends spill lighting back on to the field, drastically reducing the amount of light which will fall outside the stadium's perimeter. • Track Surface – The track is an eight-lane, 400-meter track, featuring three long jump pits, two pole vault areas, a high jump pit, and a steeplechase water jump pit. The surface is a dual-durometer, polyurethane poured surface provided by Beynon Sport Surfaces, the same company which has installed tracks at other top college facilities over the past three years including Illinois, Maryland, and Purdue. • Capacity – Chairback bench seating is available for 2,000 spectators. • Scoreboard – A Daktronics scoreboard featuring a 17' x 3' scrolling message board is installed on the three-story clock tower at the south end of the stadium. • Press Box – The fully enclosed press box features seating for 14 people and wireless internet access. The stadium also has a concession stand, public address system, officials' locker rooms, storage areas, and public restrooms. **Environmental Initiatives:** Development of an on-campus fruit/vegetable garden.

ADMISSIONS

Freshman Academic Profile: Average high school GPA 3.5. 25% in top 10% of high school class, 59% in top 25% of high school class, 85% in top 50% of high school class. 74% from public high schools. **Reported SAT (pre-2016 redesign) scores:** SAT Math middle 50% range 500-610. SAT Critical Reading middle 50% range 495-590. **Concordant SAT scores:** SAT Math middle 50% range 530–630. ACT middle 50% range 22-27. Minimum internet-based TOEFL 80. Minimum paper TOEFL 550. **Basis for Candidate Selection:** *Very important factors considered include:* rigor of secondary school record, academic GPA, standardized test scores, recommendation(s), character/personal qualities, level of applicant's interest. *Important factors considered include:* class rank, extracurricular activities. *Other factors considered include:* application essay, interview, talent/ability, first generation, alumni/ae relation, geographical residence, state residency, racial/ethnic status, volunteer work, work experience. **Freshman Admission Requirements:** High school diploma is required and GED is accepted. *Academic units required:* 4 English, 3 math, 3 science, 2 science labs, 2 foreign language, 2 social studies, 1 history, 5 academic electives. *Academic units recommended:* 4 English, 4 math, 4 science, 2 science labs, 2 foreign language, 3 social studies, 2 history, 7 academic electives. **Freshman Admission Statistics:** 5,885 applied, 83.94% admitted, 14% enrolled. **Transfer Admission Requirements:** college transcript(s), Minimum college GPA of 2.0 required. Lowest grade transferable D. **General Admission Information:** Application fee $25. Priority deadline 2/1. Regular application deadline 8/15. Nonfall registration accepted. Admission may be deferred for a maximum of 12 months.

COSTS AND FINANCIAL AID

Annual tuition $37,850. Room and board $11,870. Required fees $1,500. Average book expense $792. **Required Forms and Deadlines:** FAFSA. **Notification of Awards:** Applicants will be notified of awards on a rolling basis beginning 3/15. **Types of Aid:** *Need-based scholarships/grants:* Federal Pell, FSEOG, State scholarships/grants, Private scholarships, College/university scholarship or grant aid from institutional funds. *Loans:* Direct Subsidized Stafford Loans, Direct Unsubsidized Stafford Loans, Direct PLUS loans, Federal Perkins Loans, College/university loans from institutional funds. *Student Employment:* Federal Work-Study Program available. Institutional employment available. **Financial Aid Statistics:** 100% needy freshmen, 98% needy undergrads receive need-based scholarship or grant aid. 35% freshmen, 33% undergrads receive non-need-based scholarship or grant aid. 66% freshmen, 67% undergrads receive need-based self-help aid. 5% freshmen, 7% undergrads receive athletic scholarships. 100% freshmen, 91% undergrads receive any aid. Average cumulative indebtedness $30,110. **Criteria for awarding aid:** *Non-need-based:* Academics, Alumni affiliation, Art, Athletics, Leadership, Minority status, Music/drama, Religious affiliation, State/district residency.

BELMONT ABBEY COLLEGE

100 Belmont-Mount Holly Road, Belmont, NC 28012
Financial Aid Phone: 704-461-6718
E-mail: admissions@bac.edu • **CEEB Code:** 5055
Website: www.belmontabbeycollege.edu • **ACT Code:** 3070

This private school, affiliated with the Roman Catholic Church, was founded in 1876. It has a 650-acre campus.

RATINGS

Admissions Selectivity Rating: 75   **Fire Safety Rating:** 83   **Green Rating:** 60*

STUDENTS AND FACULTY

Enrollment: 1,545. **Student Body:** 57% female, 43% male, 28% out-of-state, 1% international (13 countries represented). Asian 1%, African American 25%, Caucasian 41%, Hispanic 1%, Native American <1%, Pacific Islander 0%, Two or more races <1%, Race unknown 30%.
Retention and Graduation: 63% freshmen return for sophomore year. 33% freshmen graduate within 4 years. 38% freshmen graduate within 6 years.
Faculty: Student/faculty ratio 17:1. 75 full-time faculty, 69% hold PhDs, 5% are are members of minority groups, 47% are women. 0% of classes are taught by teaching assistants.

ACADEMICS

Degrees: bachelor's. **Classes:** Most classes have 10-19 students. **Most popular majors:** Education; Business Administration and Management; Elementary Education and Teaching. **Special Study Options:** Accelerated program, cooperative education program, double major, dual enrollment, external degree program, honors program, independent study, internships, liberal arts/career combination, study abroad, teacher certification program, weekend college. **Honors Programs:** Anne Horne Little Honors Program Hintemeyer Scholars Program. **Disability Services:** Special programs offered to physically disabled students, including tutors. **Career Services:** Alumni services, Career/job search classes, Career assessment, Internships, Regional alumni. The Office of Career Services & Internships manages both the required and optional internship programs for all majors on campus. The office maintains an online database of all available internships, and will assist students in searching for and locating opportunities locally, regionally, nationally, and internationally.

FACILITIES

Housing: Coed dorms, men's dorms, women's dorms, apartments for single students. 85% of campus accessible to physically diasbled. **Special Academic Facilities/Equipment:** Museum with rare book collection. **Computers:** 10% of classrooms, 100% of libraries, 100% of dining areas, 100% of student union, have wireless network access.

CAMPUS LIFE

Environment: Village. **Activities:** Choral groups, drama/theater, literary magazine, musical theater, student government, student newspaper, Campus Ministries, Student Organization. 21 registered organizations, 5 honor societies, 3 religious organizations. 5 fraternities, 4 sororities. **Athletics (Intercollegiate):** *Men:* baseball, basketball, cross-country, golf, soccer, tennis, wrestling. *Women:* basketball, cross-country, soccer, softball, tennis, volleyball. **On-Campus Highlights:** Church/Basillica, Weeler Center Athletic Center, Dining hall, Holy Grounds Coffee Shop

ADMISSIONS

Freshman Academic Profile: Average high school GPA 3.1. 5% in top 10% of high school class, 15% in top 25% of high school class, 61% in top

---

50% of high school class. **Reported SAT (pre-2016 redesign) scores:** SAT Math middle 50% range 450-570. SAT Critical Reading middle 50% range 440-550. **Concordant SAT scores:** SAT Math middle 50% range 490–590. ACT middle 50% range 18-24. Minimum internet-based TOEFL 79. Minimum paper TOEFL 550. **Basis for Candidate Selection:** *Very important factors considered include:* rigor of secondary school record, academic GPA, standardized test scores. *Important factors considered include:* class rank, interview. *Other factors considered include:* application essay, recommendation(s), extracurricular activities, talent/ability, volunteer work, work experience, level of applicant's interest. **Freshman Admission Requirements:** High school diploma is required and GED is accepted. *Academic units required:* 4 English, 3 math, 2 science, 2 foreign language, 1 social studies, 1 history, 3 academic electives. *Academic units recommended:* 4 math, 3 foreign language. **Freshman Admission Statistics:** 1,950 applied, 69.23% admitted, 22% enrolled. **Transfer Admission Requirements:** college transcript(s), Minimum college GPA of 2.0 required. Lowest grade transferable C. **General Admission Information:** Application fee $35. Regular application deadline 8/1. Nonfall registration accepted. Admission may be deferred for a maximum of 2 semesters.

COSTS AND FINANCIAL AID

Annual tuition $18,500. Room and board $10,094. Average book expense $1,200. **Required Forms and Deadlines:** FAFSA. **Notification of Awards:** Applicants will be notified of awards on a rolling basis beginning 3/15. **Types of Aid:** *Need-based scholarships/grants:* Federal Pell, FSEOG, State scholarships/ grants, College/university scholarship or grant aid from institutional funds. *Loans:* Direct Subsidized Stafford Loans, Direct Unsubsidized Stafford Loans, Direct PLUS loans. *Student Employment:* Federal Work-Study Program available. Institutional employment available. **Financial Aid Statistics:** 99% needy freshmen, 95% needy undergrads receive need-based scholarship or grant aid. 11% freshmen, 5% undergrads receive non-need-based scholarship or grant aid. 87% freshmen, 95% undergrads receive need-based self-help aid. 13% freshmen, 7% undergrads receive athletic scholarships. 98% freshmen, 90% undergrads receive any aid. **Criteria for awarding aid:** *Need-based:* Religious affiliation. *Non-need-based:* Academics, Athletics, Religious affiliation, State/district residency.

BELMONT UNIVERSITY

mary.lucus@belmont.edu, Tennessee, TN Tennessee
Phone: 615-460-6785 • **Financial Aid Phone:** 615-460-6403
E-mail: admissions@belmont.edu • **CEEB Code:** 1058
Fax: 615-460-5434 • **Website:** 1900 Belmont Blvd • **ACT Code:** 3946

This private school, affiliated with the Christian (Nondenominational) Church, was founded in 1860. It has a 66-acre campus.

RATINGS

Admissions Selectivity Rating: 84   **Fire Safety Rating:** 98   **Green Rating:** 80

STUDENTS AND FACULTY

Enrollment: 6,232. **Student Body:** 63% female, 37% male, 70% out-of-state, 1% international (30 countries represented). Asian 2%, African American 5%, Caucasian 80%, Hispanic 5%, Native American <1%, Pacific Islander <1%, Two or more races 4%, Race unknown 3%.
Retention and Graduation: 83% freshmen return for sophomore year. 59% freshmen graduate within 4 years. 70% freshmen graduate within 6 years. 17% grads go on to further study within 1 year. **Faculty:** Student/faculty ratio 13:1. 344 full-time faculty, 89% hold PhDs, 11% are are members of minority groups, 48% are women.

ACADEMICS

Degrees: bachelor's, doctoral/professional, master's. **Classes:** Most classes have 10-19 students. Most lab/discussion sessions have 10-19 students. **Most popular majors:** Music Management; Registered Nursing/Registered Nurse; Music. **Special Study Options:** Accelerated program, cooperative education program, distance learning, double major, honors program, independent study, internships, liberal arts/career combination, student-designed major, study abroad, teacher certification program. **Career Services:** Alumni network, Alumni services, Career/job search classes, Career assessment, Internships. We are extremely proud of our campus-based business program. Our undergraduate students run six campus-based businesses that are collaborations with other programs on campus. This offers experiential learning for students who do not yet have a business of their own. Three of these businesses are retail oriented—located in 3,400 square feet of prime retail space in our student life building facing the edge of campus, and the other three are service business. These programs involve as many as 60 students from all across campus at any given time.

Businesses remain as long as they are financially sound and able to cover costs. When this is no longer an option, we send out a request for proposals to all students to generate ideas and begin the process of filling the spot with a business that benefits the student body and our Nashville neighbors. We provide more detail on this program later in our submission.

FACILITIES

Housing: men's dorms, women's dorms, apartments for single students. 98% of campus accessible to physically diasbled. **Special Academic Facilities/Equipment:** Language lab, recording studio, the Belmont Mansion, Little Theatre **Computers:** 100% of classrooms, 100% of dorms, 100% of libraries, 100% of dining areas, 100% of student union, 100% of common outdoor areas have wireless network access. Students can register for classes online. Administrative functions (other than registration) can be performed online.

CAMPUS LIFE

Environment: Metropolis. **Activities:** Choral groups, concert band, dance, drama/theater, jazz band, literary magazine, marching band, music ensembles, musical theater, opera, pep band, radio station, student government, student newspaper, symphony orchestra, television station, Campus Ministries, Student Organization. 80 registered organizations, 17 honor societies, 12 religious organizations. 3 fraternities, 4 sororities. **Athletics (Intercollegiate):** *Men:* baseball, basketball, cross-country, golf, soccer, tennis, track/field (outdoor). *Women:* basketball, cross-country, golf, soccer, softball, tennis, track/field (outdoor), volleyball. **On-Campus Highlights:** Beaman Student Life Center, Curb Event Center, Belmont Mansion, Center for Music Business Recording Studios, Massey Courtyard. **Environmental Initiatives:** Recycle.

ADMISSIONS

Freshman Academic Profile: Average high school GPA 3.7. 27% in top 10% of high school class, 60% in top 25% of high school class, 88% in top 50% of high school class. **Reported SAT (pre-2016 redesign) scores:** SAT Math middle 50% range 510-620. SAT Critical Reading middle 50% range 530-630. **Concordant SAT scores:** SAT Math middle 50% range 540–640. ACT middle 50% range 24-29. Minimum paper TOEFL 550. **Basis for Candidate Selection:** *Very important factors considered include:* rigor of secondary school record, academic GPA, standardized test scores. *Important factors considered include:* application essay, recommendation(s). *Other factors considered include:* class rank, extracurricular activities, talent/ability, character/personal qualities, first generation, alumni/ae relation, religious affiliation/commitment, racial/ethnic status, volunteer work, work experience. **Freshman Admission Requirements:** High school diploma is required and GED is accepted. *Academic units required:* 4 English, 3 math, 3 science, 2 foreign language, 3 social studies, 3 academic electives. *Academic units recommended:* 4 English, 4 math, 4 science, 2 foreign language, 3 social studies, 3 academic electives. **Freshman Admission Statistics:** 6,765 applied, 87.01% admitted, 27% enrolled. **Transfer Admission Requirements:** High school transcript, college transcript(s), essay or personal statement, standardized test scores, Minimum college GPA of 2.0 required. Lowest grade transferable C. **General Admission Information:** Application fee $50. Priority deadline 12/1. Regular application deadline 8/1. Nonfall registration accepted. Admission may be deferred for a maximum of 1 year.

COSTS AND FINANCIAL AID

Annual tuition $31,300. Room and board $11,680. Required fees $1,520. Average book expense $1,400. **Required Forms and Deadlines:** FAFSA. **Notification of Awards:** Applicants will be notified of awards on a rolling basis beginning 3/15. **Types of Aid:** *Need-based scholarships/grants:* Federal Pell, FSEOG, State scholarships/grants, Private scholarships, College/university scholarship or grant aid from institutional funds. *Loans:* Direct Subsidized Stafford Loans, Direct Unsubsidized Stafford Loans, Direct PLUS loans, Federal Perkins Loans. *Student Employment:* Federal Work-Study Program available. **Financial Aid Statistics:** 89% needy freshmen, 88% needy undergrads receive need-based scholarship or grant aid. 13% freshmen, 10% undergrads receive non-need-based scholarship or grant aid. 81% freshmen, 84% undergrads receive need-based self-help aid. 1% freshmen, 3% undergrads receive athletic scholarships. 53% undergrads borrow to pay for school. Average cumulative indebtedness $31,020. **Criteria for awarding aid:** *Non-need-based:* Academics, Art, Athletics, Leadership, Music/drama, Religious affiliation, State/district residency.

See page 918.

See page 918.

BELOIT COLLEGE

700 College St., Beloit, WI 53511
Phone: 608-363-2500 • **Financial Aid Phone:** 608-363-2663
E-mail: admiss@beloit.edu • **CEEB Code:** 1059
Fax: 608-363-2075 • **Website:** www.beloit.edu • **ACT Code:** 4564

This private school was founded in 1846. It has a 75-acre campus.

RATINGS

Admissions Selectivity Rating: 87   **Fire Safety Rating:** 84   **Green Rating:** 78

STUDENTS AND FACULTY

Enrollment: 1,315. **Student Body:** 53% female, 47% male, 83% out-of-state, 13% international (28 countries represented). Asian 3%, African American 5%, Caucasian 62%, Hispanic 9%, Native American <1%, Pacific Islander <1%, Two or more races 3%, Race unknown 4%.
Retention and Graduation: 86% freshmen return for sophomore year. 64% freshmen graduate within 4 years. 73% freshmen graduate within 6 years.
Faculty: 0% of classes are taught by teaching assistants.

ACADEMICS

Degrees: bachelor's. **Classes:** Most classes have 10-19 students. **Most popular majors:** Psychology; Science, Technology and Society; Anthropology. **Special Study Options:** double major, English as a Second Language (ESL), exchange student program (domestic), independent study, internships, liberal arts/career combination, student-designed major, study abroad, teacher certification program, 3-2 Programs in Engineering and Forestry. Over half of our graduates earn credit off-campus for at least a semester through our comprehensive study abroad and "field term" programs. Combined degree programs: BA/MEng. **Disability Services:** Special programs offered to physically disabled students, including note-taking services, tape recorders, tutors. **Career Services:** Alumni network, Alumni services, Career/job search classes, Career assessment, Internships, Regional alumni. Beloit College offers career development opportunities at every stage of a student's college career, from introducing resume creation in the First Year Initiatives seminars to providing job shadow opportunities for sophomores and juniors and providing seniors with the tools for a successful job search. We believe that all of the opportunities at our residential, liberal arts setting, both in the curriculum and co-curriculum, help Beloit College students to grow into future professionals.

FACILITIES

Housing: Coed dorms, women's dorms, fraternity/sorority housing, cooperative housing, apartments for single students, Theme Housing, Wide variety of special-interest housing, particularly for languages. See Beloit College's web site for a current list of special-interest housing. 50% of campus accessible to physically diasbled. **Special Academic Facilities/Equipment:** Wright Museum of Art Logan Museum of Anthropology Center for Language Study Student Run Market Research Company (BELMARK) Alfred S. Thompson Observatory Center for Entrepreneurial Leadership (CELEB) **Computers:** 80% of classrooms, 10% of dorms, 100% of libraries, 100% of dining areas, 80% of student union, 4% of common outdoor areas have wireless network access. Administrative functions (other than registration) can be performed online.

CAMPUS LIFE

Environment: Town. **Activities:** Choral groups, dance, drama/theater, jazz band, literary magazine, music ensembles, musical theater, radio station, student government, student newspaper, student-run film society, symphony orchestra, television station, yearbook, Student Organization. 95 registered organizations, 6 honor societies, 3 religious organizations. 3 fraternities, 3 sororities. **Athletics (Intercollegiate):** *Men:* baseball, basketball, cross-country, football, golf, soccer, swimming, tennis, track/field (outdoor), track/field (indoor). *Women:* basketball, cross-country, soccer, softball, swimming, tennis, track/field (outdoor), track/field (indoor), volleyball. **On-Campus Highlights:** Logan Museum of Anthropology, Wright Museum of Art, Center for the Sciences, Alfred S. Thompson Observatory, Laura H. Idrich Neese Theatre Complex, Other popular spaces include the Poetry Garden, the Java Joint, Morse Library, Sports Center, and Pearsons Hall. **Environmental Initiatives:** New Science Center has been platinum-level LEED certified, one of only three such buildings in the state.

ADMISSIONS

Freshman Academic Profile: Average high school GPA 3.3. 31% in top 10% of high school class, 62% in top 25% of high school class, 86% in top 50% of high school class. 75% from public high schools. **Reported SAT (pre-2016 redesign) scores:** SAT Math middle 50% range 545-690. SAT Critical Reading middle 50% range 520-680. **Concordant SAT scores:** SAT Math middle 50% range 570–720. ACT middle 50% range 24-30. Minimum internet-based TOEFL 80. Minimum paper TOEFL 550. **Basis for Candidate Selection:** *Very important factors considered include:* rigor of secondary school record, academic GPA, application essay, recommendation(s). *Important factors considered include:* class rank, extracurricular activities, talent/ability. *Other factors considered include:* standardized test scores, interview, character/personal qualities, first generation, alumni/ae relation, volunteer work, work experience, level of applicant's interest. **Freshman Admission Requirements:** High school diploma is required and GED is accepted. *Academic units recommended:* 4 English, 3 math, 3 science, 3 science labs, 3 foreign language, 4 social studies. **Freshman Admission Statistics:** 3,855 applied, 69.86% admitted, 14% enrolled. **Transfer Admission Requirements:** college transcript(s), essay or personal statement, statement of good standing from prior institution(s). Minimum college GPA of 3.00 required. Lowest grade transferable C. **General Admission Information:** Priority deadline 1/15. Nonfall registration accepted. Admission may be deferred for a maximum of 12 months.

COSTS AND FINANCIAL AID

Annual tuition $48,237. Room and board $8,435. Required fees $470. Average book expense $1,000. **Required Forms and Deadlines:** FAFSA. **Notification of Awards:** Applicants will be notified of awards on a rolling basis beginning 3/1. **Types of Aid:** *Need-based scholarships/grants:* Federal Pell, FSEOG, State scholarships/grants, Private scholarships, College/university scholarship or grant aid from institutional funds. *Loans:* Direct Subsidized Stafford Loans, Direct Unsubsidized Stafford Loans, Direct PLUS loans, Federal Perkins Loans, College/university loans from institutional funds. *Student Employment:* Federal Work-Study Program available. Institutional employment available. **Financial Aid Statistics:** 99% needy freshmen receive need-based scholarship or grant aid. 99% freshmen, 99% undergrads receive any aid. **Criteria for awarding aid:** *Need-based:* Academics. *Non-need-based:* Academics, Leadership, Minority status, Music/drama.

BEMIDJI STATE UNIVERSITY

1500 Birchmont Dr. NE, Bemidji, MN 56601
Phone: 218-755-2040 • **Financial Aid Phone:** 218-755-2034
E-mail: admissions@bemidjistate.edu • **CEEB Code:** 6676
Fax: 218-755-2390 • **Website:** http://www.bemidjistate.edu/ • **ACT Code:** 2084

This public school was founded in 1919. It has a 90-acre campus.

RATINGS

Admissions Selectivity Rating: 72   **Fire Safety Rating:** 72   **Green Rating:** 80

STUDENTS AND FACULTY

Enrollment: 4,393. **Student Body:** 57% female, 43% male, 10% out-of-state, 2% international (35 countries represented). Asian 1%, African American 2%, Caucasian 85%, Hispanic 2%, Native American 3%, Pacific Islander 0%, Two or more races 3%, Race unknown 2%.
Retention and Graduation: 66% freshmen return for sophomore year. 26% freshmen graduate within 4 years. 45% freshmen graduate within 6 years. **Faculty:** Student/faculty ratio 19:1. 174 full-time faculty, 68% hold PhDs, 9% are are members of minority groups, 44% are women. 5% of classes are taught by teaching assistants.

ACADEMICS

Degrees: associate, bachelor's, certificate, master's, postbachelor's certificate. **Classes:** Most classes have 10-19 students. Most lab/discussion sessions have 20-29 students. **Most popular majors:** Education; Industrial Production Technologies/Technicians; Business/Commerce. **Special Study Options:** Accelerated program, cooperative education program, distance learning, double major, dual enrollment, English as a Second Language (ESL), exchange student program (domestic), external degree program, honors program, independent study, internships, liberal arts/career combination, study abroad, teacher certification program, Eurospring Semester, Sino-Summer, Exchange program with other Minnesota state universities; other study-travel. **Disability Services:** Special programs offered to physically disabled students, including note-taking services, reader services, tutors. **Career Services:** Alumni services, Career/job search classes, Career assessment, Internships, Regional alumni. We are working with the Neilson Foundation in Bemidji and they are sponsoring up to 17 internships per year in which they pay half of the intern's salary and the private employer pays the other half, up to $2,500

FACILITIES

Housing: Coed dorms, men's dorms, special housing for international students, women's dorms, apartments for married students, cooperative housing, apartments for single students, Two floors for SOTA (Students Older Than

Average age.)Cooperative housing for international students. 95% of campus accessible to physically diasbled. **Special Academic Facilities/Equipment:** Aquatics lab. Waterfront. C.V. Hobson Forest. Center for Research and Innovation (CRI). **Computers:** 90% of classrooms, 90% of dorms, 100% of libraries, 100% of student union, have wireless network access. Students can register for classes online. Administrative functions (other than registration) can be performed online.

CAMPUS LIFE

Environment: Village. **Activities:** Choral groups, concert band, dance, drama/theater, jazz band, literary magazine, music ensembles, musical theater, opera, pep band, radio station, student government, student newspaper, student-run film society, symphony orchestra, television station, Campus Ministries, Student Organization, Model UN. 83 registered organizations, 1 honor society, 8 religious organizations. 2 fraternities, 1 sorority. **Athletics (Intercollegiate):** *Men:* baseball, basketball, cross-country, football, golf, ice hockey, soccer, softball, tennis, track/field (outdoor), track/field (indoor), volleyball. *Women:* basketball, cross-country, golf, ice hockey, soccer, softball, tennis, track/field (outdoor), track/field (indoor), volleyball. **On-Campus Highlights:** Recreation Center, Student Union, Library, Dormitories, Computer labs. **Environmental Initiatives:** Signature theme of Environmental Stewardship.

ADMISSIONS

Freshman Academic Profile: Average high school GPA 3.1. 7% in top 10% of high school class, 23% in top 25% of high school class, 56% in top 50% of high school class. 95% from public high schools. ACT middle 50% range 19-24. Minimum internet-based TOEFL 61. Minimum paper TOEFL 500. **Basis for Candidate Selection:** *Very important factors considered include:* class rank, standardized test scores. *Important factors considered include:* rigor of secondary school record. *Other factors considered include:* academic GPA, application essay, recommendation(s), extracurricular activities, first generation. **Freshman Admission Requirements:** High school diploma is required and GED is accepted. *Academic units required:* 4 English, 3 math, 3 science, 2 foreign language, 3 social studies, 1 academic elective. **Freshman Admission Statistics:** 2,566 applied, 93.80% admitted, 31% enrolled. Minimum college GPA of 2.0 required. Lowest grade transferable C. **General Admission Information:** Application fee $20. Priority deadline 2/1. Nonfall registration accepted. Admission may be deferred for a maximum of 1 year.

COSTS AND FINANCIAL AID

Annual in-state tuition $7,360. Annual out-of-state tuition $7,360. Room and board $8,500. Required fees $950. **Required Forms and Deadlines:** FAFSA, Institution's own financial aid form. **Notification of Awards:** Applicants will be notified of awards on or about 3/15. **Types of Aid:** *Need-based scholarships/grants:* Federal Pell, FSEOG, State scholarships/grants, Private scholarships, College/university scholarship or grant aid from institutional funds. *Loans:* Direct Subsidized Stafford Loans, Direct Unsubsidized Stafford Loans, Direct PLUS loans, Federal Perkins Loans, State Loans. *Student Employment:* Federal Work-Study Program available. Institutional employment available. **Financial Aid Statistics:** 70% needy freshmen, 72% needy undergrads receive need-based scholarship or grant aid. 80% freshmen, 76% undergrads receive non-need-based scholarship or grant aid. 83% freshmen, 82% undergrads receive need-based self-help aid. 6% freshmen, 6% undergrads receive athletic scholarships. 62% freshmen, 65% undergrads receive any aid. **Criteria for awarding aid:** *Non-need-based:* Academics, Alumni affiliation, Art, Athletics, Job skills, Leadership, Minority status, Music/drama, Religious affiliation.

BENEDICT COLLEGE

1600 Harden St, Columbia, SC 29204
Phone: 803-705-4491
E-mail: thompso@benedict.edu
Fax: 803-253-5167 • **Website:** www.benedict.edu

This private school, affiliated with the Baptist Church, was founded in 1870. It has a 110-acre campus.

RATINGS

Admissions Selectivity Rating: 71   **Fire Safety Rating:** 60*   **Green Rating:** 60*

STUDENTS AND FACULTY

Enrollment: 2,641. **Student Body:** 51% female, 49% male, 40% out-of-state, 0% international. Asian 0%, African American 99%, Caucasian <1%, Hispanic 1%, Native American <1%, Pacific Islander 0%, Two or more races 0%, Race unknown <1%.
Retention and Graduation: 53% freshmen return for sophomore year. 11% freshmen graduate within 4 years. 26% freshmen graduate within 6 years. **Faculty:** Student/faculty ratio 19:1. 117 full-time faculty, 65% hold PhDs, 95% are are members of minority groups, 58% are women.

ACADEMICS

Degrees: bachelor's. **Classes:** Most classes have fewer than 10 students. Most lab/discussion sessions have fewer than 10 students. **Special Study Options:** Accelerated program, double major, dual enrollment, external degree program, honors program, internships, teacher certification program, weekend college.

FACILITIES

Housing: men's dorms, women's dorms.

CAMPUS LIFE

Environment: City. **Activities:** Choral groups, concert band, marching band, student government, student newspaper, Campus Ministries, Student Organization.

ADMISSIONS

Freshman Academic Profile: Average high school GPA 2.5. 5% in top 10% of high school class, 15% in top 25% of high school class, 39% in top 50% of high school class. 74% from public high schools. **Reported SAT (pre-2016 redesign) scores:** SAT Math middle 50% range 320-430. SAT Critical Reading middle 50% range 320-430. **Concordant SAT scores:** SAT Math middle 50% range 360–470. ACT middle 50% range 13-17. Minimum internet-based TOEFL 80. Minimum paper TOEFL 550. **Freshman Admission Requirements:** High school diploma is required and GED is accepted. *Academic units recommended:* 4 English, 3 math, 2 science, 3 social studies. **Freshman Admission Statistics:** 4,624 applied, 82.89% admitted, 17% enrolled. **Transfer Admission Requirements:** High school transcript, college transcript(s), statement of good standing from prior institution(s). Minimum college GPA of 2.0 required. Lowest grade transferable C. **General Admission Information:** Application fee $25. Nonfall registration accepted. Admission may be deferred.

COSTS AND FINANCIAL AID

Annual tuition $12,516. Room and board $6,444. Required fees $1,494. Average book expense $1,000. **Required Forms and Deadlines:** FAFSA. **Types of Aid:** *Need-based scholarships/grants:* Federal Pell, FSEOG, State scholarships/grants, Private scholarships, College/university scholarship or grant aid from institutional funds, United Negro College Fund. *Loans:* Direct Subsidized Stafford Loans, Direct Unsubsidized Stafford Loans, Direct PLUS loans. *Student Employment:* Federal Work-Study Program available. Institutional employment available. **Criteria for awarding aid:** *Need-based:* Academics, Alumni affiliation, Athletics, Music/drama, Religious affiliation.

BENEDICTINE COLLEGE

1020 North Second Street, Atchison, KS 66002
Phone: 800-467-5340 • **Financial Aid Phone:** 913-360-7480
E-mail: bcadmiss@benedictine.edu • **CEEB Code:** 6056
Fax: 913-367-5462 • **Website:** www.benedictine.edu • **ACT Code:** 1444

This private school, affiliated with the Roman Catholic Church, was founded in 1859. It has a 225-acre campus.

RATINGS

Admissions Selectivity Rating: 79   **Fire Safety Rating:** 64   **Green Rating:** 60*

STUDENTS AND FACULTY

Enrollment: 1,922. **Student Body:** 54% female, 46% male, 77% out-of-state, 2% international (12 countries represented). Asian 1%, African American 3%, Caucasian 78%, Hispanic 6%, Native American <1%, Pacific Islander <1%, Two or more races <1%, Race unknown 9%.
Retention and Graduation: 80% freshmen return for sophomore year. 49% freshmen graduate within 4 years. 63% freshmen graduate within 6 years. 12% grads go on to further study within 1 year. **Faculty:** Student/faculty ratio 14:1. 110 full-time faculty, 75% hold PhDs, 7% are are members of minority groups, 31% are women. 0% of classes are taught by teaching assistants.

ACADEMICS

Degrees: bachelor's, master's. **Classes:** Most classes have 20-29 students. Most lab/discussion sessions have 10-19 students. **Most popular majors:** Elementary Education and Teaching; Business Administration and Management; Theological and Ministerial Studies. **Special Study Options:** cooperative education program, double major, dual enrollment, English as a Second Language (ESL), independent study, internships, liberal arts/career combination, student-designed major, study abroad, teacher certification program. **Disability Services:** Special programs offered to physically disabled students, including tutors. **Career Services:** Alumni network, Career/job search classes, Career assessment, Internships.

FACILITIES

Housing: Coed dorms, men's dorms, women's dorms, Off-campus college-owned housing. 95% of campus accessible to physically diasbled. **Special Academic Facilities/Equipment:** Language and special education labs, high tech classroom, stadium, student union. **Computers:** 60% of classrooms, 100% of dorms, 100% of libraries, 100% of dining areas, 100% of student union, 75% of common outdoor areas have wireless network access. Administrative functions (other than registration) can be performed online.

CAMPUS LIFE

Environment: Town. **Activities:** Choral groups, concert band, dance, drama/theater, jazz band, literary magazine, music ensembles, musical theater, pep band, student government, student newspaper, symphony orchestra, yearbook. 38 registered organizations, 14 honor societies, 4 religious organizations. **Athletics (Intercollegiate):** *Men:* baseball, basketball, cheerleading, cross-country, football, golf, soccer, tennis, track/field (outdoor), track/field (indoor). *Women:* basketball, cheerleading, cross-country, golf, soccer, softball, tennis, track/field (outdoor), track/field (indoor), volleyball. **On-Campus Highlights:** Raven Roost, Ferrell Hall, Student Union, Abbey Church, River Lookout.

ADMISSIONS

Freshman Academic Profile: Average high school GPA 3.4. 19% in top 10% of high school class, 42% in top 25% of high school class, 67% in top 50% of high school class. 43% from public high schools. **Reported SAT (pre-2016 redesign) scores:** SAT Math middle 50% range 470-630. SAT Critical Reading middle 50% range 500-670. **Concordant SAT scores:** SAT Math middle 50% range 510–650. ACT middle 50% range 21-28. **Basis for Candidate Selection:** *Very important factors considered include:* rigor of secondary school record, academic GPA. *Important factors considered include:* class rank, standardized test scores. *Other factors considered include:* recommendation(s), interview, extracurricular activities, talent/ability, character/personal qualities, first generation, volunteer work, work experience. **Freshman Admission Requirements:** High school diploma is required and GED is accepted. *Academic units recommended:* 4 English, 2 social studies, 1 history. **Freshman Admission Statistics:** 2,182 applied, 97.71% admitted, 24% enrolled. **Transfer Admission Requirements:** college transcript(s), Minimum college GPA of 2.0 required. Lowest grade transferable C. **General Admission Information:** Application fee $50. Nonfall registration accepted. Admission may be deferred for a maximum of 1 year.

COSTS AND FINANCIAL AID

Required Forms and Deadlines: FAFSA. **Notification of Awards:** Applicants will be notified of awards on a rolling basis beginning 2/1. **Types of Aid:** *Need-based scholarships/grants:* Federal Pell, FSEOG, State scholarships/grants, Private scholarships, College/university scholarship or grant aid from institutional funds. *Loans:* Direct Subsidized Stafford Loans, Direct Unsubsidized Stafford Loans, Direct PLUS loans, Federal Perkins Loans. *Student Employment:* Federal Work-Study Program available. Institutional employment available. **Financial Aid Statistics:** 100% needy freshmen, 100% needy undergrads receive need-based scholarship or grant aid. 18% freshmen, 16% undergrads receive non-need-based scholarship or grant aid. 76% freshmen, 77% undergrads receive need-based self-help aid. 9% freshmen, 9% undergrads receive athletic scholarships. 73% undergrads borrow to pay for school. Average cumulative indebtedness $29,602. **Criteria for awarding aid:** *Need-based:* Minority status, Religious affiliation. *Non-need-based:* Academics, Alumni affiliation, Art, Athletics, Job skills, Leadership, Minority status, Music/drama, Religious affiliation, State/district residency.

BENEDICTINE UNIVERSITY

5700 College Road, Lisle, IL 60532-0900
Phone: 630-829-6300 • **Financial Aid Phone:** 630-829-6100
E-mail: admissions@ben.edu • **CEEB Code:** 1707
Fax: 630-829-6301 • **Website:** www.ben.edu • **ACT Code:** 1132

This private school, affiliated with the Roman Catholic Church, was founded in 1887. It has a 108-acre campus.

RATINGS

Admissions Selectivity Rating: 81   **Fire Safety Rating:** 96   **Green Rating:** 60*

STUDENTS AND FACULTY

Enrollment: 2,903. **Student Body:** 58% female, 42% male, 8% out-of-state, 1% international (17 countries represented). Asian 18%, African American 8%, Caucasian 44%, Hispanic 10%, Native American <1%, Pacific Islander <1%, Two or more races 0%, Race unknown 19%.
Retention and Graduation: 74% freshmen return for sophomore year. 38% freshmen graduate within 4 years. 52% freshmen graduate within 6 years.

Faculty: Student/faculty ratio 18:1. 128 full-time faculty, 88% hold PhDs, 16% are are members of minority groups, 48% are women. 0% of classes are taught by teaching assistants.

ACADEMICS
Degrees: associate, bachelor's, certificate, doctoral/research, master's, postbachelor's certificate, transfer. **Classes:** Most classes have 10-19 students. **Most popular majors:** Psychology; Biology/Biological Sciences; Organizational Behavior Studies. **Special Study Options:** Accelerated program, cross-registration, distance learning, double major, dual enrollment, English as a Second Language (ESL), honors program, independent study, internships, study abroad, teacher certification program, weekend college, Engineering degree program with Illinois Institute of Technology. **Honors Programs:** University Scholars Program. **Disability Services:** Special programs offered to physically disabled students, including note-taking services, reader services, tape recorders, tutors. **Career Services:** Alumni network, Alumni services, Career/job search classes, Career assessment, Internships. Internship program.

FACILITIES
Housing: Coed dorms, men's dorms, women's dorms, apartments for married students, apartments for single students, Wellness Housing. 100% of campus accessible to physically diasbled. **Special Academic Facilities/Equipment:** Natural science and history museums,http://www.ben.edu/museum/ Exercise physiology lab. **Computers:** 100% of dorms, 100% of libraries, 100% of student union, have wireless network access. Students can register for classes online. Administrative functions (other than registration) can be performed online.

CAMPUS LIFE
Environment: Town. **Activities:** Choral groups, concert band, dance, drama/theater, jazz band, literary magazine, music ensembles, pep band, student government, student newspaper, student-run film society, symphony orchestra, television station, Campus Ministries, Student Organization, Model UN. 40 registered organizations, 3 religious organizations. **Athletics (Intercollegiate):** *Men:* baseball, basketball, cross-country, football, golf, soccer, track/field (outdoor), track/field (indoor). *Women:* basketball, cross-country, golf, soccer, softball, tennis, track/field (outdoor), track/field (indoor), volleyball. **On-Campus Highlights:** Jurica Nature Museum, Kindlon Hall and Benedictine Library, Birck Hall of Science, Krasa Center: Chapel, cafeteria, snack bar, The Sports Complex, Coal Ben. **Environmental Initiatives:** Energy reduction.

ADMISSIONS
Freshman Academic Profile: Average high school GPA 3.4. 21% in top 10% of high school class, 48% in top 25% of high school class, 79% in top 50% of high school class. 85% from public high schools. ACT middle 50% range 20-26. Minimum internet-based TOEFL 79. Minimum paper TOEFL 550. **Basis for Candidate Selection:** *Very important factors considered include:* rigor of secondary school record, class rank, academic GPA, standardized test scores. *Other factors considered include:* application essay, recommendation(s), interview, extracurricular activities. **Freshman Admission Requirements:** High school diploma is required and GED is accepted. *Academic units required:* 4 English, 3 math, 2 science, 1 science lab, 2 foreign language, 3 social studies, 1 history. *Academic units recommended:* 4 math, 3 science, 2 science labs. **Freshman Admission Statistics:** 2,108 applied, 69.50% admitted, 32% enrolled. **Transfer Admission Requirements:** college transcript(s), statement of good standing from prior institution(s). Minimum college GPA of 2.0 required. Lowest grade transferable D. **General Admission Information:** Application fee $40. Regular application deadline 8/30. Nonfall registration accepted. Admission may be deferred.

COSTS AND FINANCIAL AID
Annual tuition $25,950. Room and board $8,280. Required fees $1,000. Average book expense $1,450. **Required Forms and Deadlines:** FAFSA. **Notification of Awards:** Applicants will be notified of awards on a rolling basis beginning 2/1. **Types of Aid:** *Need-based scholarships/grants:* Federal Pell, FSEOG, State scholarships/grants, Private scholarships, College/university scholarship or grant aid from institutional funds. *Loans:* Direct Subsidized Stafford Loans, Direct Unsubsidized Stafford Loans, Direct PLUS loans, Federal Perkins Loans. *Student Employment:* Federal Work-Study Program available. Institutional employment available. **Financial Aid Statistics:** 63% needy freshmen, 62% needy undergrads receive need-based scholarship or grant aid. 98% freshmen, 85% undergrads receive non-need-based scholarship or grant aid. 76% freshmen, 90% undergrads receive need-based self-help aid. 0% freshmen, 0% undergrads receive athletic scholarships. 98% freshmen, 89% undergrads receive any aid. **Criteria for awarding aid:** *Non-need-based:* Academics, Alumni affiliation, Leadership, Music/drama, State/district residency.

BENNETT COLLEGE

900 East Washington Street, Greensboro, NC 27401
Phone: 336-370-8624 • **Financial Aid Phone:** 336-517-2220
E-mail: admiss@bennett.edu • **CEEB Code:** 5058
Fax: 336-370-8653 • **Website:** www.bennett.edu • **ACT Code:** 3072

This private school, affiliated with the Methodist Church, was founded in 1873. It has a 55-acre campus.

RATINGS
Admissions Selectivity Rating: 74   **Fire Safety Rating:** 80   **Green Rating:** 60*

STUDENTS AND FACULTY
Enrollment: 651. **Student Body:** 100% female, 0% male, 62% out-of-state, <1% international (2 countries represented). Asian 0%, African American 94%, Caucasian <1%, Hispanic 2%, Native American <1%, Pacific Islander 0%, Two or more races 2%, Race unknown 2%.
Retention and Graduation: 58% freshmen return for sophomore year. 20% freshmen graduate within 4 years. 34% freshmen graduate within 6 years.
Faculty: Student/faculty ratio 10:1. 61 full-time faculty, 64% hold PhDs, 70% are are members of minority groups, 77% are women. 0% of classes are taught by teaching assistants.

ACADEMICS
Degrees: bachelor's. **Classes:** Most classes have fewer than 10 students. Most lab/discussion sessions have 30-39 students. **Most popular majors:** Communication and Media Studies; Psychology; Biological and Physical Sciences. **Special Study Options:** Accelerated program, cooperative education program, cross-registration, double major, dual enrollment, honors program, independent study, internships, student-designed major, study abroad, teacher certification program, Collaborative degree program with Howard University in Nursing (2x2). **Disability Services:** Special programs offered to physically disabled students, including tape recorders, tutors. **Career Services:** Alumni network, Alumni services, Career/job search classes, Internships, Regional alumni.

FACILITIES
Housing: women's dorms, Wellness Housing. **Special Academic Facilities/Equipment:** Children's House, Constance Maiteena collection, college archives, telecommunications satellite dish. **Computers:** Students can register for classes online.

CAMPUS LIFE
Environment: City. **Activities:** Choral groups, dance, drama/theater, literary magazine, music ensembles, student government, student newspaper, Campus Ministries, Student Organization. 34 registered organizations, 5 honor societies, 1 religious organization. 4 sororities. **Athletics (Intercollegiate):** *Women:* basketball, cheerleading, cross-country, softball, swimming, tennis, track/field (outdoor), volleyball. **On-Campus Highlights:** Student Union, Chapel, Little Theathre, Holgate Library, Lda Goode Gym.

ADMISSIONS
Freshman Academic Profile: 8% in top 10% of high school class, 12% in top 25% of high school class, 50% in top 50% of high school class. **Reported SAT (pre-2016 redesign) scores:** SAT Math middle 50% range 350-420. SAT Critical Reading middle 50% range 350-430. **Concordant SAT scores:** SAT Math middle 50% range 390–460. **Basis for Candidate Selection:** *Very important factors considered include:* rigor of secondary school record, academic GPA, recommendation(s), talent/ability. *Important factors considered include:* class rank, application essay. *Other factors considered include:* standardized test scores, interview, extracurricular activities, character/personal qualities, first generation, alumni/ae relation, geographical residence, state residency, religious affiliation/commitment, racial/ethnic status, volunteer work, work experience, level of applicant's interest. **Freshman Admission Requirements:** High school diploma is required and GED is accepted. *Academic units required:* 4 English, 3 math, 2 science, 2 foreign language, 2 social studies, 5 academic electives. **Freshman Admission Statistics:** 1,433 applied, 62.81% admitted, 18% enrolled. **Transfer Admission Requirements:** college transcript(s), essay or personal statement, Minimum college GPA of 2.0 required. Lowest grade transferable C. **General Admission Information:** Application fee $35. Nonfall registration accepted. Admission may be deferred for a maximum of 1 year.

COSTS AND FINANCIAL AID
Annual tuition $14,614. Room and board $7,428. Required fees $2,180. Average book expense $1,500. **Required Forms and Deadlines:** FAFSA, Institution's own financial aid form. **Notification of Awards:** Applicants will be notified of awards on or about 7/15. **Types of Aid:** *Need-based scholarships/grants:* Federal Pell, FSEOG, State scholarships/grants, Private scholarships, College/

university scholarship or grant aid from institutional funds, United Negro College Fund, Federal Nursing Scholarships. *Loans:* Direct Subsidized Stafford Loans, Direct Unsubsidized Stafford Loans, Federal Perkins Loans. *Student Employment:* Federal Work-Study Program available. **Financial Aid Statistics:** 96% needy freshmen, 93% needy undergrads receive need-based scholarship or grant aid. 1% freshmen, 2% undergrads receive non-need-based scholarship or grant aid. 96% freshmen, 94% undergrads receive need-based self-help aid. 0% freshmen, 0% undergrads receive athletic scholarships. **Criteria for awarding aid:** *Need-based:* Academics, Alumni affiliation, Leadership, Minority status, Religious affiliation. *Non-need-based:* Academics, Alumni affiliation, Leadership, Minority status, Religious affiliation, State/district residency.

BENNINGTON COLLEGE

One College Drive, Bennington, VT 5201
Phone: 802-440-4312 • **Financial Aid Phone:** 800-833-6845
E-mail: admissions@bennington.edu • **CEEB Code:** 3080
Fax: 802-440-4320 • **Website:** www.bennington.edu • **ACT Code:** 4296

This private school was founded in 1932. It has a 470-acre campus.

RATINGS
Admissions Selectivity Rating: 88   **Fire Safety Rating:** 96   **Green Rating:** 82

STUDENTS AND FACULTY
Enrollment: 701. **Student Body:** 65% female, 35% male, 98% out-of-state, 15% international (35 countries represented). Asian 2%, African American 3%, Caucasian 60%, Hispanic 9%, Native American 1%, Pacific Islander 0%, Two or more races 5%, Race unknown 5%.
Retention and Graduation: 80% freshmen return for sophomore year. 65% freshmen graduate within 4 years. 70 10% grads go on to further study within 1 year. 10% grads pursue arts and sciences degrees. **Faculty:** Student/faculty ratio 9:1. 61 full-time faculty, 79% hold PhDs, 8% are are members of minority groups, 48% are women. 1% of classes are taught by teaching assistants.

ACADEMICS
Degrees: bachelor's, master's, postbachelor's certificate. **Classes:** Most classes have 10-19 students. **Most popular majors:** English Language and Literature; Visual and Performing Arts; Social Sciences. **Special Study Options:** Accelerated program, cross-registration, double major, English as a Second Language (ESL), independent study, internships, student-designed major, study abroad, teacher certification program, Postbaccalaureate program in preparation for Medical or Allied Health School Grad Programs. **Disability Services:** Special programs offered to physically disabled students, including note-taking services, reader services, tape recorders. **Career Services:** Alumni network, Alumni services, Career/job search classes, Career assessment, Internships. Each academic year at Bennington College includes a seven-week winter term of field work off campus. During Field Work Term (FWT), students take their interests to the world beyond the College, where they work at jobs or internships in fields that complement their studies, clarify their interests, and open possibilities for their future. After spending four terms at work in the world, each student graduates with a resume as well as a diploma.

FACILITIES
Housing: Coed dorms, cooperative housing, Theme Housing, Off-campus. 75% of campus accessible to physically diasbled. **Special Academic Facilities/ Equipment:** Observatory; greenhouse; digital arts lab; architecture, drawing, painting, printmaking, and sculpture studios; ceramics studio and kilns; color and black-and-white photography darkrooms; film and video editing studio; fully equipped professional theaters; scripts library; dance studios and archives; electronic music and sound recording studios; music practice rooms and music library **Computers:** 100% of classrooms, 100% of dorms, 100% of libraries, 100% of dining areas, 100% of student union, 75% of common outdoor areas have wireless network access. Administrative functions (other than registration) can be performed online.

CAMPUS LIFE
Environment: Town. **Activities:** Choral groups, dance, drama/theater, literary magazine, music ensembles, musical theater, radio station, student government, student newspaper, Student Organization. 21 registered organizations. **On-Campus Highlights:** Edward Clark Crossett Library, Visual and Performing Arts Center, Student Center, Commons Dining Hall and Lounge, Meyer Recreation Barn, Opening in 2011, the Center for the Advancement of Public

Action (CAPA), is a $20-million, state-of-the-art, green, academic facility for Bennington's new citizenship curriculum. It morphs the studio of the artist, the laboratory of a scientist, the workshop of a craftsman, and the think tank of policy work. **Environmental Initiatives:** Converting to a campus-wide biomass heating system

ADMISSIONS
Freshman Academic Profile: 42% from public high schools. **Reported SAT (pre-2016 redesign) scores:** SAT Math middle 50% range 570-668. SAT Critical Reading middle 50% range 620-710. SAT Writing middle 50% range 583-690. **Concordant SAT scores:** SAT EBRW middle 50% 650–730. SAT Math middle 50% range 590–700. ACT middle 50% range 26-31. Minimum paper TOEFL 577. **Basis for Candidate Selection:** *Very important factors considered include:* rigor of secondary school record, academic GPA, application essay, recommendation(s), interview, talent/ability, character/personal qualities. *Other factors considered include:* class rank, standardized test scores, extracurricular activities, volunteer work, work experience. **Freshman Admission Requirements:** High school diploma is required and GED is accepted. **Freshman Admission Statistics:** 1,236 applied, 59.95% admitted, 29% enrolled. **Transfer Admission Requirements:** High school transcript, college transcript(s), essay or personal statement, statement of good standing from prior institution(s). Lowest grade transferable C. **General Admission Information:** Regular application deadline 1/3. Regular notification 4/1. Nonfall registration accepted. Admission may be deferred for a maximum of one year.

COSTS AND FINANCIAL AID
Annual tuition $51,240. Room and board $15,040. Required fees $1,180. Average book expense $1,000. **Required Forms and Deadlines:** FAFSA, Institution's own financial aid form, CSS/Financial Aid PROFILE, Noncustodial PROFILE. **Notification of Awards:** Applicants will be notified of awards on or about 3/26. **Types of Aid:** *Need-based scholarships/grants:* Federal Pell, FSEOG, State scholarships/grants, Private scholarships, College/university scholarship or grant aid from institutional funds. *Loans:* Direct Subsidized Stafford Loans, Direct Unsubsidized Stafford Loans, Direct PLUS loans. *Student Employment:* Federal Work-Study Program available. Institutional employment available. **Financial Aid Statistics:** 98% needy freshmen, 99% needy undergrads receive need-based scholarship or grant aid. 8% freshmen, 8% undergrads receive non-need-based scholarship or grant aid. 89% freshmen, 89% undergrads receive need-based self-help aid. 0% freshmen, 0% undergrads receive athletic scholarships. 52% undergrads borrow to pay for school. Average cumulative indebtedness $28,648. **Criteria for awarding aid:** *Need-based:* Academics, Alumni affiliation, Art, Leadership, Minority status, Music/drama. *Non-need-based:* Academics, Alumni affiliation, Art, Leadership, Minority status, Music/drama, State/district residency.

BENTLEY UNIVERSITY

175 Forest Street, Waltham, MA 2452
Phone: 781-891-2244 • **Financial Aid Phone:** 781-891-3441
E-mail: ugadmission@bentley.edu • **CEEB Code:** 3096
Fax: 781-891-3414 • **Website:** www.bentley.edu • **ACT Code:** 1783

This private school was founded in 1917. It has a 163-acre campus.

RATINGS
Admissions Selectivity Rating: 90   **Fire Safety Rating:** 99   **Green Rating:** 97

STUDENTS AND FACULTY
Enrollment: 4,152. **Student Body:** 41% female, 59% male, 57% out-of-state, 14% international (101 countries represented). Asian 8%, African American 3%, Caucasian 62%, Hispanic 8%, Native American 0%, Pacific Islander <1%, Two or more races 2%, Race unknown 4%.
Retention and Graduation: 94% freshmen return for sophomore year. 83% freshmen graduate within 4 years. 89% freshmen graduate within 6 years.
Faculty: Student/faculty ratio 12:1. 284 full-time faculty, 84% hold PhDs, 17% are are members of minority groups, 39% are women. 0% of classes are taught by teaching assistants.

ACADEMICS
Degrees: bachelor's, doctoral/research, master's, postbachelor's certificate, post-master's certificate. **Classes:** Most classes have 20-29 students. **Most popular majors:** Marketing/Marketing Management; Finance; Business, Management,

Marketing, and Related Support Services. **Special Study Options:** Accelerated program, cross-registration, double major, honors program, independent study, internships, liberal arts/career combination, student-designed major, study abroad, 5 year Bachelors/Masters program in Business Administration, Accountancy, Finance, Marketing, Analytics, Info Technology, Financial Planning, Taxation. **Honors Programs:** The Honors Program is a four-year journey that provides special challenge and fulfillment to select Bentley students. Students in approximately the top ten percent of the entering class are invited to participate in this four-year program. **Disability Services:** Special programs offered to physically disabled students, including note-taking services, reader services, tape recorders, tutors. **Career Services:** Alumni network, Alumni services, Career/job search classes, Career assessment, Internships, Regional alumni. In 2013, Bentley launched Career Development Introduction 101 (CDI 101) to equip first year students with a comprehensive career toolkit and the ability to understand and 'tell their story'. The course is the first step in a four year Hire Education program designed to support our belief that competence, confidence, and community lead to meaningful careers and lives.

FACILITIES

Housing: Coed dorms, special housing for disabled students, apartments for single students, Wellness Housing, Theme Housing, Three Wellness Houses with an overall health and wellness theme are available. Global living floors with a focus on connecting international and US students are available to residents. 80% of campus accessible to physically diasbled. **Special Academic Facilities/Equipment:** Academic Technology Center, Alliance for Ethics and Social Responsibility, Center for Business Ethics, Center for International Students and Scholars, Center for Quantitative Analysis, Art Gallery, Center for Marketing Technology, Center for Languages and International Collaboration, ESOL Center, Math Learning Center, Writing Center, Financial Trading Room, Design and Usability Center, Service Learning Center, Cronin International Center, Cyberlaw Center, Enterprise Risk Management Program, Hughey Center for Financial Services, Library, Media & Culture labs and studio, Valente Center for Arts and Sciences, Winer Accounting Center, Women"s Leadership Institute, Academic Technology Center, Spiritual Life Center. **Computers:** 100% of classrooms, 100% of dorms, 100% of libraries, 100% of dining areas, 100% of student union, 100% of common outdoor areas have wireless network access. Students can register for classes online. Administrative functions (other than registration) can be performed online. Undergraduates are required to own a computer.

CAMPUS LIFE

Environment: Town. **Activities:** Choral groups, dance, drama/theater, jazz band, literary magazine, music ensembles, pep band, radio station, student government, student newspaper, television station, Campus Ministries, Student Organization, Model UN. 101 registered organizations, 3 honor societies, 4 religious organizations. 5 fraternities, 4 sororities. **Athletics (Intercollegiate):** *Men:* baseball, basketball, cross-country, diving, football, golf, ice hockey, lacrosse, soccer, swimming, tennis, track/field (outdoor), track/field (indoor). *Women:* basketball, cross-country, diving, field hockey, lacrosse, soccer, softball, swimming, tennis, track/field (outdoor), track/field (indoor), volleyball. **On-Campus Highlights:** Student Center, Dana Athletic Center, Currito Burrito, Einstein's Coffee Shop, Library. **Environmental Initiatives:** Bentley University is committed to the following carbon footprint reduction targets (compared to a 2008 baseline): 50% by 2015, 70% by 2020 and 100% by 2030. As of January 1, 2016 we have achieved a 50% reduction in our carbon footprint.

ADMISSIONS

Freshman Academic Profile: 32% in top 10% of high school class, 72% in top 25% of high school class, 96% in top 50% of high school class. 67% of public high schools. **Reported SAT (pre-2016 redesign) scores:** SAT Math middle 50% range 600-690. SAT Critical Reading middle 50% range 550-630. SAT Writing middle 50% range 560-650. **Concordant SAT scores:** SAT EBRW middle 50% 610–690. SAT Math middle 50% range 620–720. ACT middle 50% range 26-30. Minimum internet-based TOEFL 90. Minimum paper TOEFL 577. **Basis for Candidate Selection:** *Very important factors considered include:* rigor of secondary school record, academic GPA, standardized test scores. *Important factors considered include:* application essay, recommendation(s), extracurricular activities, talent/ability, character/personal qualities, volunteer work, work experience. *Other factors considered include:* class rank, interview, first generation, alumni/ae relation, geographical residence, state residency, racial/ethnic status, level of applicant's interest. **Freshman Admission Requirements:** High school diploma is required and GED is accepted. *Academic units required:* 4 English, 4 math, 3 science, 2 science labs, 3 foreign language, 3 social studies. *Academic units recommended:* 4 English, 4 math, 4 science, 3 science labs, 4 foreign language, 4 social studies, and 2 units from above areas or other academic areas. **Freshman Admission Statistics:** 8,281 applied, 46.32% admitted, 27% enrolled. **Transfer Admission Requirements:** High school transcript, college transcript(s), essay or personal statement, statement of good standing from prior institution(s). Lowest grade transferable C. **General Admission Information:** Application fee $50. Regular application deadline 1/7. Nonfall registration accepted. Admission may be deferred for a maximum of One year.

COSTS AND FINANCIAL AID

Annual tuition $44,210. Room and board $15,130. Required fees $1,550. Average book expense $1,260. **Required Forms and Deadlines:** FAFSA, CSS/Financial Aid PROFILE, Noncustodial PROFILE, Business/Farm Supplement. **Notification of Awards:** Applicants will be notified of awards on or about 3/31. **Types of Aid:** *Need-based scholarships/grants:* Federal Pell, FSEOG, State scholarships/grants, Private scholarships, College/university scholarship or grant aid from institutional funds. *Loans:* Direct Subsidized Stafford Loans, Direct Unsubsidized Stafford Loans, Direct PLUS loans, State Loans. *Student Employment:* Federal Work-Study Program available. Institutional employment available. **Financial Aid Statistics:** 98% needy freshmen, 98% needy undergrads receive need-based scholarship or grant aid. 25% freshmen, 15% undergrads receive non-need-based scholarship or grant aid. 94% freshmen, 96% undergrads receive need-based self-help aid. 1% freshmen, 2% undergrads receive athletic scholarships. 73% freshmen, 66% undergrads receive any aid. 54% undergrads borrow to pay for school. Average cumulative indebtedness $29,547. **Criteria for awarding aid:** *Need-based:* Academics, Athletics, Minority status. *Non-need-based:* Academics, Athletics, Leadership, Minority status.

See page 920.

BEREA COLLEGE

CPO 2220, Berea, KY 40404
Phone: 859-985-3500 • **Financial Aid Phone:** 859-985-3310
E-mail: admissions@berea.edu • **CEEB Code:** 1060
Fax: 859-985-3512 • **Website:** www.berea.edu • **ACT Code:** 1492

This private school was founded in 1855. It has a 140-acre campus.

RATINGS

Admissions Selectivity Rating: 94   **Fire Safety Rating:** 96   **Green Rating:** 91

STUDENTS AND FACULTY

Enrollment: 1,612. **Student Body:** 57% female, 43% male, 53% out-of-state, 8% international (70 countries represented). Asian 2%, African American 15%, Caucasian 59%, Hispanic 9%, Native American <1%, Pacific Islander <1%, Two or more races 6%, Race unknown 1%.
Retention and Graduation: 84% freshmen return for sophomore year. 48% freshmen graduate within 4 years. 63% freshmen graduate within 6 years. **Faculty:** Student/faculty ratio 11:1. 137 full-time faculty, 91% hold PhDs, 15% are are members of minority groups, 47% are women. 0% of classes are taught by teaching assistants.

ACADEMICS

Degrees: bachelor's. **Classes:** Most classes have 10-19 students. **Most popular majors:** Business/Commerce; Family and Consumer Sciences/Human Sciences; Biology/Biological Sciences. **Special Study Options:** double major, English as a Second Language (ESL), exchange student program (domestic), honors program, independent study, internships, student-designed major, study abroad, teacher certification program, 3-2 engineering program with Washington University, St. Louis, and University of Kentucky. Combined degree programs: at University of Kentucky resulting in BS. **Disability Services:** Special programs offered to physically disabled students, including note-taking services, reader services, tape recorders. **Career Services:** Alumni network, Alumni services, Career/job search classes, Career assessment, Internships, On-campus interviews.

FACILITIES

Housing: men's dorms, women's dorms, apartments for married students, Apartments for single parents and married students at our Ecovillage (see the following site for more information: http://www.berea.edu/sens/ecovillage/). 75% of campus accessible to physically diasbled. **Special Academic Facilities/Equipment:** Appalachian Gallery, Special Collections and Sound Archives in the Hutchins Library, Planetarium and Observatory, Geology Museum, The Ecovillage, the Child Development Laboratory, extensive acreage of farmland and forestland, and the Monty Saulmon Early Technology Lab. **Computers:** 33% of classrooms, 100% of libraries, 100% of dining areas, 100% of student union, 33% of common outdoor areas have wireless network access. Students can register for classes online. Administrative functions (other than registration) can be performed online. Undergraduates are required to own a computer.

CAMPUS LIFE

Environment: Village. **Activities:** Choral groups, dance, drama/theater, jazz band, literary magazine, music ensembles, pep band, student government, student newspaper, yearbook, Campus Ministries, Student Organization. 75 registered organizations, 14 honor societies, 5 religious organizations. **Athletics (Intercollegiate):** *Men:* baseball, basketball, cross-country, golf, soccer, swimming, tennis, track/field (outdoor). *Women:* basketball, cross-country, soccer, softball, swimming, tennis, track/field (outdoor), volleyball. **On-Campus Highlights:** Carillon (in Draper building tower), EcoVillage (married and single parent housing), Alumni Building (cafeteria, lounge, gameroom), Woods-Penn Complex (post office, cafe, etc), Seabury Center (gym).

ADMISSIONS

Freshman Academic Profile: Average high school GPA 3.5. 23% in top 10% of high school class, 66% in top 25% of high school class, 96% in top 50% of high school class. **Reported SAT (pre-2016 redesign) scores:** SAT Math middle 50% range 510-620. SAT Critical Reading middle 50% range 490-600. SAT Writing middle 50% range 500-620. **Concordant SAT scores:** SAT EBRW middle 50% 550–660. SAT Math middle 50% range 540–640. ACT middle 50% range 22-27. Minimum internet-based TOEFL 68. Minimum paper TOEFL 520. **Basis for Candidate Selection:** *Very important factors considered include:* interview. *Important factors considered include:* rigor of secondary school record, class rank, academic GPA, standardized test scores, application essay, character/personal qualities. *Other factors considered include:* recommendation(s), extracurricular activities, talent/ability, first generation, geographical residence, state residency, racial/ethnic status, volunteer work, work experience, level of applicant's interest. **Freshman Admission Requirements:** High school diploma is required and GED is accepted. *Academic units recommended:* 4 English, 3 math, 2 science, 2 science labs, 2 foreign language, 2 social studies. **Freshman Admission Statistics:** 1,744 applied, 32.80% admitted, 77% enrolled. **Transfer Admission Requirements:** High school transcript, college transcript(s), interview, Minimum college GPA of 2.0 required. Lowest grade transferable C. **General Admission Information:** Regular application deadline 4/30. Nonfall registration not accepted.

COSTS AND FINANCIAL AID

Annual tuition $0. Room and board $6,472. Required fees $570. Average book expense $700. **Required Forms and Deadlines:** FAFSA. **Notification of Awards:** Applicants will be notified of awards on a rolling basis beginning 11/1. **Types of Aid:** *Need-based scholarships/grants:* Federal Pell, FSEOG, State scholarships/grants, Private scholarships, College/university scholarship or grant aid from institutional funds. *Loans:* Direct Subsidized Stafford Loans, Direct Unsubsidized Stafford Loans, Direct PLUS loans, College/university loans from institutional funds. *Student Employment:* Federal Work-Study Program available. Institutional employment available. **Financial Aid Statistics:** 100% needy freshmen, 100% needy undergrads receive need-based scholarship or grant aid. 0% undergrads receive non-need-based scholarship or grant aid. 100% freshmen, 100% undergrads receive need-based self-help aid. 0% freshmen, 0% undergrads receive athletic scholarships. 100% freshmen, 100% undergrads receive any aid. 65% undergrads borrow to pay for school. Average cumulative indebtedness $7,062.

BERKELEY COLLEGE

44 Rifle Camp Road, Woodland Park, NJ 7424
Phone: 1-800-446-5400 xG26
E-mail: info@berkeleycollege.edu • **CEEB Code:** 2061
ACT Code: 2576

This proprietary school was founded in 1931. It has a 25-acre campus.

RATINGS

Admissions Selectivity Rating: 61   **Fire Safety Rating:** 60*   **Green Rating:** 60*

STUDENTS AND FACULTY

Enrollment: 3,806. **Student Body:** 73% female, 27% male, 4% out-of-state, <1% international. Asian 2%, African American 21%, Caucasian 15%, Hispanic 34%, Native American <1%, Pacific Islander <1%, Two or more races 0%, Race unknown 26%.
Retention and Graduation: 68% freshmen return for sophomore year.
Faculty: Student/faculty ratio 17:1. 137 full-time faculty, 0% hold PhDs, 47% are are members of minority groups, 0% are women.

ACADEMICS

Degrees: associate, bachelor's, certificate, terminal, transfer. **Most popular majors:** Business Administration and Management; Accounting; Fashion Merchandising. **Special Study Options:** Accelerated program, distance

---

learning, internships, study abroad, Academic remediation, Off-campus study at Berkeley College, New York City; Berkeley College, White Plains. **Disability Services:** Special programs offered to physically disabled students, including tutors.

FACILITIES

Housing: Coed dorms. **Computers:** Administrative functions (other than registration) can be performed online.

CAMPUS LIFE

Environment: City. **Activities:** Choral groups, literary magazine, student government, student newspaper. 8 registered organizations, 1 honor society.

ADMISSIONS

Minimum paper TOEFL 500. **Basis for Candidate Selection:** *Very important factors considered include:* rigor of secondary school record, interview. *Important factors considered include:* standardized test scores. *Other factors considered include:* class rank, academic GPA, recommendation(s), extracurricular activities, talent/ability, character/personal qualities, volunteer work, work experience. **Freshman Admission Requirements:** High school diploma is required and GED is accepted. **Transfer Admission Requirements:** college transcript(s), Lowest grade transferable C. **General Admission Information:** Application fee $50. Nonfall registration accepted. Admission may be deferred.

COSTS AND FINANCIAL AID

Annual tuition $17,400. Room and board $12,500. Required fees $750. Average book expense $1,200. **Required Forms and Deadlines:** FAFSA. **Notification of Awards:** Applicants will be notified of awards on a rolling basis beginning 3/1. **Types of Aid:** *Need-based scholarships/grants:* Federal Pell, FSEOG, State scholarships/grants, Private scholarships, College/university scholarship or grant aid from institutional funds. *Loans:* State Loans. *Student Employment:* Federal Work-Study Program available. Institutional employment available. **Financial Aid Statistics:** 85% freshmen receive any aid. **Criteria for awarding aid:** *Non-need-based:* Academics, Alumni affiliation.

BERKLEE COLLEGE OF MUSIC

1140 Boylston Street, Boston, MA 02215-3693
Phone: 617-747-2222 • **Financial Aid Phone:** 617-747-2274
E-mail: admissions@berklee.edu • **CEEB Code:** 3107
Fax: 617-747-2047 • **Website:** www.berklee.edu • **ACT Code:** 1789

This private school was founded in 1945.

RATINGS

Admissions Selectivity Rating: 73   **Fire Safety Rating:** 60*   **Green Rating:** 60*

STUDENTS AND FACULTY

Enrollment: 3,846. **Student Body:** 31% female, 69% male, 84% out-of-state, 25% international (70 countries represented). Asian 3%, African American 6%, Caucasian 45%, Hispanic 10%, Native American <1%, Pacific Islander <1%, Two or more races 3%, Race unknown 8%.
Retention and Graduation: 79% freshmen return for sophomore year.
Faculty: Student/faculty ratio 13:1. 240 full-time faculty, 15% hold PhDs, 0% are are members of minority groups, 23% are women.

ACADEMICS

Degrees: bachelor's, diploma, master's. **Classes:** Most classes have fewer than 10 students. **Most popular majors:** Music Performance; Music. **Special Study Options:** cooperative education program, cross-registration, distance learning, double major, dual enrollment, English as a Second Language (ESL), independent study, internships, student-designed major, study abroad, teacher certification program, Berkleemusic.com is the online continuing education division of Berklee College of Music. Study is online with Berklee's renowned faculty in areas that include Music Business, Music Production, Guitar, Theory, Harmony & Ear Training, and Songwriting. **Disability Services:** Special programs offered to physically disabled students, including reader services, tape recorders, tutors. **Career Services:** Alumni services, Career/job search classes, Internships, On-campus interviews.

FACILITIES

Housing: Coed dorms. 80% of campus accessible to physically disabled. **Special Academic Facilities/Equipment:** Ensemble library, 10 professional recording studios, film scoring and editing studio, analog and digital music synthesis labs, 1,200-seat performance center, learning center.

CAMPUS LIFE

Environment: Metropolis. **Activities:** Choral groups, concert band, dance, jazz band, literary magazine, music ensembles, musical theater, radio station, student government, student newspaper, student-run film society, Student Organization. 47 registered organizations, 2 honor societies, 4 religious organizations. **On-Campus Highlights:** Student Activities Center, Berklee Performance Center, Practice Rooms, Stan Getz Media Center.

ADMISSIONS
Minimum paper TOEFL 500. **Basis for Candidate Selection:** *Very important factors considered include:* interview, talent/ability. *Important factors considered include:* rigor of secondary school record, academic GPA, character/personal qualities, level of applicant's interest. *Other factors considered include:* class rank, standardized test scores, application essay, recommendation(s), extracurricular activities, first generation, geographical residence, volunteer work, work experience. **Freshman Admission Requirements:** High school diploma is required and GED is accepted. **Freshman Admission Statistics:** 5,538 applied, 19.16% admitted, 84% enrolled. **Transfer Admission Requirements:** High school transcript, college transcript, essay or personal statement, interview, Lowest grade transferable C. **General Admission Information:** Application fee $150. Priority deadline 11/1. Regular application deadline 1/15. Regular notification 3/31. Nonfall registration accepted. Admission may be deferred for a maximum of 1 year.

COSTS AND FINANCIAL AID
Room and board $17,200. Required fees $3,032. Average book expense $474. *Student Employment:* Federal Work-Study Program available. **Financial Aid Statistics:** 50% needy freshmen, 50% needy undergrads receive need-based scholarship or grant aid. 48% freshmen, 50% undergrads receive non-need-based scholarship or grant aid. 98% freshmen, 98% undergrads receive need-based self-help aid. 0% freshmen, 0% undergrads receive athletic scholarships. 57% freshmen, 38% undergrads receive any aid.

BERRY COLLEGE

P.O. Box 490159, Mount Berry, GA 30149-0159
Phone: 706-236-2215 • **Financial Aid Phone:** 706-236-1714
E-mail: admissions@berry.edu • **CEEB Code:** 5059
Fax: 706-290-2178 • **Website:** www.berry.edu • **ACT Code:** 798

This private school was founded in 1902. It has a 26000-acre campus.

RATINGS
Admissions Selectivity Rating: 87   **Fire Safety Rating:** 94   **Green Rating:** 77

STUDENTS AND FACULTY
Enrollment: 2,055. **Student Body:** 60% female, 40% male, 33% out-of-state, <1% international (11 countries represented). Asian 1%, African American 4%, Caucasian 81%, Hispanic 7%, Native American <1%, Pacific Islander 0%, Two or more races 3%, Race unknown 3%.
Retention and Graduation: 85% freshmen return for sophomore year. 59% freshmen graduate within 4 years. 66% freshmen graduate within 6 years. 24% grads go on to further study within 1 year. **Faculty:** Student/faculty ratio 12:1. 167 full-time faculty, 89% hold PhDs, 6% are are members of minority groups, 48% are women.

ACADEMICS
Degrees: bachelor's, master's. **Classes:** Most classes have 10-19 students. Most lab/discussion sessions have 20-29 students. **Most popular majors:** Zoology/Animal Biology; Psychology; Communication, Journalism, and Related Programs. **Special Study Options:** cooperative education program, cross-registration, double major, dual enrollment, honors program, independent study, internships, student-designed major, study abroad, teacher certification program, 3-2 nursing with Emory University, 3-2 engineering with Georgia Institute of Technology. **Honors Programs:** The Berry College Honors Program provides students with an opportunity to learn within an intellectually challenging community of peers and instructors. Honors courses familiarize students with works that have been central to our past and contemporary intellectual traditions, while encouraging them to examine issues or themes from multiple and conflicting perspectives. All Honors courses are taught as seminars that provide an ideal environment for the development of effective communication and critical-thinking skills. As part of the Honors program the Oxbridge Lecture Series uses the English model of instruction with public lectures and private tutorials. Students enrolled benefit from small group, intensive student-faculty interaction, and exploratory assignments that stimulate inquiry and intellectual growth. Additionally, the Berry College Honors Program now offers a unique education abroad opportunity in conjunction

with the University of Glasgow in Scotland and Berry College International Programs. Combined degree programs: 3-2 Nursing with Emory University. **Disability Services:** Special programs offered to physically disabled students, including note-taking services, reader services, tape recorders, tutors. **Career Services:** Alumni network, Alumni services, Career/job search classes, Career assessment, Internships, Regional alumni.

FACILITIES
Housing: Coed dorms, men's dorms, women's dorms, apartments for single students, Wellness Housing. Traditional residence halls are single sex; apartments and townhouses are co-ed by site or apartment. Special-interest houses for Women in Math and Science (primarily first-year students). 80% of campus accessible to physically diasbled. **Special Academic Facilities/Equipment:** The 131,000-square-foot Steven J. Cage Athletic and Recreation Center, National Historic Site containing Oak Hill and The Martha Berry Museum, 34-foot overshot waterwheel, Georgia wildlife management area and refuge, equine center, dairy and beef cattle research center, on-campus elementary and middle schools, child development center, science center featuring 60-foot Foucault pendulum. **Computers:** 100% of classrooms, 100% of dorms, 100% of libraries, 100% of dining areas, 100% of student union, 10% of common outdoor areas have wireless network access. Students can register for classes online. Administrative functions (other than registration) can be performed online.

CAMPUS LIFE
Environment: Town. **Activities:** Choral groups, concert band, dance, drama/theater, jazz band, literary magazine, music ensembles, musical theater, student government, student newspaper, symphony orchestra, television station, yearbook, Campus Ministries, Student Organization, Model UN. 75 registered organizations, 15 honor societies, 11 religious organizations. **Athletics (Intercollegiate):** *Men:* baseball, basketball, cross-country, diving, golf, lacrosse, soccer, swimming, tennis. *Women:* basketball, cross-country, diving, equestrian sports, golf, lacrosse, soccer, softball, swimming, tennis, volleyball. **On-Campus Highlights:** Steven J. Cage Athletic & Recreation Ctr, Ford Complex, Science Center, Gunby Equestrian Center (Mountain Campus), The Old Mill (Mountain Campus), The 131,000 square foot Steven J. Cage Athletic and Recreation Center houses an indoor swimming pool, three basketball courts, two racquetball courts, one multi-purpose court and a jogging track. Berry Beanery (Starbucks) in Krannert Student Center. **Environmental Initiatives:** Tree Campus USA award last year.

ADMISSIONS
Freshman Academic Profile: Average high school GPA 3.7. 33% in top 10% of high school class, 69% in top 25% of high school class, 93% in top 50% of high school class. 66% from public high schools. **Reported SAT (pre-2016 redesign) scores:** SAT Math middle 50% range 530-610. SAT Critical Reading middle 50% range 530-630. SAT Writing middle 50% range 510-610. **Concordant SAT scores:** SAT EBRW middle 50% 580-670. SAT Math middle 50% range 560-630. ACT middle 50% range 24-29. Minimum internet-based TOEFL 80. Minimum paper TOEFL 550. **Basis for Candidate Selection:** *Very important factors considered:* rigor of secondary school record, academic GPA, standardized test scores. *Important factors considered include:* extracurricular activities. *Other factors considered include:* application essay, recommendation(s), interview, volunteer work, work experience. **Freshman Admission Requirements:** High school diploma is required and GED is accepted. *Academic units required:* 4 English, 4 math, 3 science, 2 foreign language, 3 social studies, 4 academic electives. **Freshman Admission Statistics:** 3,477 applied, 62.09% admitted, 25% enrolled. **Transfer Admission Requirements:** college transcript(s), statement of good standing from prior institution(s). Minimum college GPA of 2.5 required. Lowest grade transferable C. **General Admission Information:** Application fee $50. Priority deadline 2/1. Regular application deadline 7/22. Nonfall registration accepted.

COSTS AND FINANCIAL AID
Annual tuition $31,770. Room and board $11,190. Required fees $226. Average book expense $1,000. **Required Forms and Deadlines:** FAFSA. **Notification of Awards:** Applicants will be notified of awards on a rolling basis beginning 2/15. **Types of Aid:** *Need-based scholarships/grants:* Federal Pell, FSEOG, College/university scholarship or grant aid from institutional funds. *Loans:* Direct Subsidized Stafford Loans, Direct Unsubsidized Stafford Loans, Direct PLUS loans, Federal Perkins Loans, State Loans, College/university loans from institutional funds. *Student Employment:* Federal Work-Study Program available. Institutional employment available. **Financial Aid Statistics:** 100% needy freshmen, 100% needy undergrads receive need-based scholarship or grant aid. 24% freshmen, 20% undergrads receive non-need-based scholarship or grant aid. 75% freshmen, 79% undergrads receive need-based self-help aid. 0% freshmen, 0% undergrads receive athletic scholarships. 100% freshmen, 99% undergrads receive any aid. 71% undergrads borrow to pay for school. Average cumulative indebtedness $26,449. **Criteria for awarding aid:** *Need-based:* Academics, Job skills, Leadership, Minority status, Music/drama. *Non-need-based:* Academics, Art, Leadership, Minority status, Music/drama, Religious affiliation.

BETHANY COLLEGE (KS)

335 E Swensson, Lindsborg, KS 67456-1897
Phone: 785-227-3311 • **Financial Aid Phone:** 785-227-3311
E-mail: admissions@bethanylb.edu • **CEEB Code:** 6034
Fax: 785-227-8993 • **Website:** www.bethanylb.edu • **ACT Code:** 1388

This private school, affiliated with the Lutheran Church, was founded in 1881. It has a 62-acre campus.

RATINGS

Admissions Selectivity Rating: 80 **Fire Safety Rating:** 96 **Green Rating:** 60*

STUDENTS AND FACULTY

Enrollment: 569. **Student Body:** 48% female, 52% male, 49% out-of-state, 6% international (29 countries represented). Asian 1%, African American 11%, Caucasian 71%, Hispanic 7%, Native American 1%, Pacific Islander 0%, Two or more races 0%, Race unknown 4%.
Retention and Graduation: 61% freshmen return for sophomore year. 32% freshmen graduate within 4 years. 40% freshmen graduate within 6 years. 20% grads go on to further study within 1 year. 1% grads pursue law degrees. 3% grads pursue medical degrees. **Faculty:** Student/faculty ratio 9:1. 44 full-time faculty, 57% hold PhDs, 5% are are members of minority groups, 36% are women. 0% of classes are taught by teaching assistants.

ACADEMICS

Degrees: bachelor's. **Classes:** Most classes have fewer than 10 students. Most lab/discussion sessions have fewer than 10 students. **Most popular majors:** Elementary Education and Teaching; Biology/Biological Sciences; Business Administration and Management. **Special Study Options:** Accelerated program, cross-registration, double major, dual enrollment, exchange student program (domestic), honors program, independent study, internships, liberal arts/career combination, student-designed major, study abroad, teacher certification program. **Honors Programs:** Honors program offered Combined degree programs: BA/MEng. **Disability Services:** Special programs offered to physically disabled students, including note-taking services, reader services, tape recorders, tutors. **Career Services:** Alumni network, Alumni services, Career/job search classes, Career assessment, Internships, Regional alumni, Experienced Based Education.

FACILITIES

Housing: Coed dorms, women's dorms, apartments for single students, special interest housing- bid on by student groups, community service and house improvements. 80% of campus accessible to physically diasbled. **Special Academic Facilities/Equipment:** Mingenback Gallery, Bethany College Archives, Plym Gallery, Sandzen Gallery.

CAMPUS LIFE

Environment: Rural. **Activities:** Choral groups, concert band, dance, drama/theater, jazz band, music ensembles, musical theater, pep band, student government, student newspaper, symphony orchestra, yearbook, Campus Ministries, Student Organization. 49 registered organizations, 8 honor societies, 9 religious organizations. 3 fraternities, 3 sororities. **Athletics (Intercollegiate):** *Men:* baseball, basketball, cheerleading, cross-country, football, golf, soccer, tennis, track/field (outdoor), track/field (indoor). *Women:* basketball, cheerleading, cross-country, golf, soccer, softball, tennis, track/field (outdoor), track/field (indoor), volleyball. **On-Campus Highlights:** Student Union, Walderstadt Library, Mingenback Art Gallery, Residence Halls, Athletic Fields.

ADMISSIONS

Freshman Academic Profile: Average high school GPA 3.3. 15% in top 10% of high school class, 42% in top 25% of high school class, 76% in top 50% of high school class. 97% from public high schools. **Reported SAT (pre-2016 redesign) scores:** SAT Math middle 50% range 420-560. SAT Critical Reading middle 50% range 370-500. SAT Writing middle 50% range 380-490. **Concordant SAT scores:** SAT EBRW middle 50% 420–550. SAT Math middle 50% range 460–580. ACT middle 50% range 19-24. Minimum internet-based TOEFL 71. Minimum paper TOEFL 525. **Basis for Candidate Selection:** *Very important factors considered include:* rigor of secondary school record, academic GPA, standardized test scores. *Other factors considered include:* application essay, recommendation(s), extracurricular activities, talent/ability, character/personal qualities, racial/ethnic status, volunteer work. **Freshman Admission Requirements:** High school diploma is required and GED is accepted. *Academic units recommended:* 4 English, 3 math, 3 science, 2 science labs, 2 foreign language, 3 social studies. **Freshman Admission Statistics:** 811 applied, 65.35% admitted, 34% enrolled. **Transfer Admission Requirements:** college transcript(s), statement of good standing from prior institution(s). Minimum college GPA of 2.3 required. Lowest grade transferable D. **General Admission Information:** Application fee $20. Priority deadline 2/1. Regular application deadline 7/1. Nonfall registration accepted.

COSTS AND FINANCIAL AID

Annual tuition $17,824. Room and board $5,650. Required fees $300. Average book expense $1,000. **Required Forms and Deadlines:** FAFSA. **Notification of Awards:** Applicants will be notified of awards on a rolling basis beginning 3/1. **Types of Aid:** *Need-based scholarships/grants:* Federal Pell, FSEOG, State scholarships/grants, Private scholarships, College/university scholarship or grant aid from institutional funds. *Loans:* Federal Perkins Loans. *Student Employment:* Federal Work-Study Program available. Institutional employment available. **Financial Aid Statistics:** 85% needy freshmen, 84% needy undergrads receive need-based scholarship or grant aid. 40% freshmen, 32% undergrads receive non-need-based scholarship or grant aid. 76% freshmen, 78% undergrads receive need-based self-help aid. 0% freshmen, 7% undergrads receive athletic scholarships. 100% freshmen, 98% undergrads receive any aid. **Criteria for awarding aid:** *Non-need-based:* Academics, Alumni affiliation, Art, Athletics, Leadership, Music/drama, Religious affiliation.

BETHANY COLLEGE (WV)

31 E Campus Dr, Bethany, WV 26032
Phone: 304-829-7611 • **Financial Aid Phone:** 304-829-7611
E-mail: enrollment@bethanyww.edu • **CEEB Code:** 5060
Fax: 304-829-7142 • **Website:** www.bethanywv.edu • **ACT Code:** 4512

This private school, affiliated with the Disciples of Christ Church, was founded in 1840. It has a 400-acre campus.

RATINGS

Admissions Selectivity Rating: 78 **Fire Safety Rating:** 88 **Green Rating:** 60*

STUDENTS AND FACULTY

Enrollment: 716. **Student Body:** 41% female, 59% male, 68% out-of-state, 2% international (11 countries represented). Asian 0%, African American 20%, Caucasian 54%, Hispanic 4%, Native American 1%, Pacific Islander <1%, Two or more races 3%, Race unknown 16%.
Retention and Graduation: 70% freshmen return for sophomore year. **Faculty:** Student/faculty ratio 12:1. 48 full-time faculty, 79% hold PhDs, 4% are are members of minority groups, 44% are women. 0% of classes are taught by teaching assistants.

ACADEMICS

Degrees: bachelor's, master's. **Classes:** Most classes have 10-19 students. Most lab/discussion sessions have 10-19 students. **Most popular majors:** Psychology; Speech Communication and Rhetoric; Elementary Education and Teaching. **Special Study Options:** double major, exchange student program (domestic), independent study, internships, liberal arts/career combination, student-designed major, study abroad, teacher certification program, Off Campus Study: Washington, DC. Combined degree programs: BA/JD, BA/MA, BA/JD with Duquesne, BA/MA with Carnegie Mellon. **Disability Services:** Special programs offered to physically disabled students, including note-taking services, reader services, tape recorders, tutors. **Career Services:** Alumni network, Alumni services, Career assessment, Internships, Regional alumni, On-campus interviews. Bethany hosts career and graduate school fairs throughout the year. Bethany also offers a "Career Closet" program that helps students dress for interview success.

FACILITIES

Housing: Coed dorms, special housing for disabled students, men's dorms, women's dorms, fraternity/sorority housing, apartments for married students, apartments for single students. **Computers:** Administrative functions (other than registration) can be performed online.

CAMPUS LIFE

Environment: Rural. **Activities:** Choral groups, concert band, drama/theater, jazz band, literary magazine, music ensembles, musical theater, pep band, radio station, student government, student newspaper, student-run film society, television station, yearbook. 38 registered organizations, 16 honor societies, 3 religious organizations. 6 fraternities, 3 sororities. **Athletics (Intercollegiate):** *Men:* baseball, basketball, cross-country, diving, football, golf, soccer, swimming, tennis, track/field (outdoor), track/field (indoor). *Women:* basketball, cross-country, diving, golf, soccer, softball, swimming, tennis, track/field (outdoor), track/field (indoor), volleyball. **On-Campus Highlights:** Old Main, Bethany House, Athletic Facilities, Campbell Village, Campbell Mansion.

ADMISSIONS

Freshman Academic Profile: Average high school GPA 2.9. 6% in top 10% of high school class, 20% in top 25% of high school class, 49% in top 50% of high school class. 90% from public high schools. **Reported SAT (pre-2016 redesign) scores:** SAT Math middle 50% range 390-490. SAT Critical Reading middle 50% range 370-500. SAT Writing middle 50% range 360-470.

Concordant SAT scores: SAT EBRW middle 50% 410–540. SAT Math middle 50% range 430–520. ACT middle 50% range 17-23. Minimum internet-based TOEFL 90. Minimum paper TOEFL 500. **Basis for Candidate Selection:** *Very important factors considered include:* rigor of secondary school record, academic GPA, standardized test scores, application essay, recommendation(s), character/personal qualities. *Important factors considered include:* class rank, level of applicant's interest. *Other factors considered include:* interview, extracurricular activities, talent/ability, alumni/ae relation, volunteer work, work experience. **Freshman Admission Requirements:** High school diploma is required and GED is accepted. *Academic units recommended:* 4 English, 3 math, 3 science, 2 foreign language, 3 social studies. **Freshman Admission Statistics:** 1,394 applied, 62.05% admitted, 28% enrolled. **Transfer Admission Requirements:** college transcript(s), essay or personal statement, statement of good standing from prior institution(s). Minimum college GPA of 2.0 required. Lowest grade transferable D°. **General Admission Information:** Priority deadline 3/1. Nonfall registration accepted. Admission may be deferred for a maximum of 1 year.

COSTS AND FINANCIAL AID

Annual tuition $24,836. Room and board $9,636. Required fees $900. Average book expense $1,200. **Required Forms and Deadlines:** FAFSA. **Notification of Awards:** Applicants will be notified of awards on a rolling basis beginning 2/15. **Types of Aid:** *Need-based scholarships/grants:* Federal Pell, FSEOG, State scholarships/grants, Private scholarships, College/university scholarship or grant aid from institutional funds. *Loans:* Direct Subsidized Stafford Loans, Direct Unsubsidized Stafford Loans, Direct PLUS loans, Federal Perkins Loans. *Student Employment:* Federal Work-Study Program available. Institutional employment available. **Financial Aid Statistics:** 80% needy freshmen, 79% needy undergrads receive need-based scholarship or grant aid. 100% freshmen, 99% undergrads receive non-need-based scholarship or grant aid. 77% freshmen, 79% undergrads receive need-based self-help aid. 0% freshmen, 0% undergrads receive athletic scholarships. 99% freshmen, 99% undergrads receive any aid. **Criteria for awarding aid:** *Need-based:* Academics, Alumni affiliation, Leadership, Music/drama, Religious affiliation. *Non-need-based:* Academics, Alumni affiliation, Leadership, Music/drama, Religious affiliation, State/district residency.

See page 922.

BETHEL COLLEGE (IN)

1001 Bethel Circle, Mishawaka, IN 46545
Phone: 574-807-7600 • **Financial Aid Phone:** 574-257-3316
E-mail: admissions@bethelcollege.edu • **CEEB Code:** 1079
Fax: 574-807-7650 • **Website:** www.bethelcollege.edu • **ACT Code:** 1178

This private school was founded in 1947. It has a 75-acre campus.

RATINGS

Admissions Selectivity Rating: 76   **Fire Safety Rating:** 81   **Green Rating:** 60*

STUDENTS AND FACULTY

Enrollment: 1,335. **Student Body:** 64% female, 36% male, 28% out-of-state, 1% international (18 countries represented). Asian 2%, African American 11%, Caucasian 73%, Hispanic 7%, Native American <1%, Pacific Islander 0%, Two or more races 5%, Race unknown 1%.
Retention and Graduation: 76% freshmen return for sophomore year. 54% freshmen graduate within 4 years. 66% freshmen graduate within 6 years.
Faculty: Student/faculty ratio 12:1. 71 full-time faculty, 58% hold PhDs, 13% are are members of minority groups, 45% are women. 0% of classes are taught by teaching assistants.

ACADEMICS

Degrees: associate, bachelor's, master's. **Classes:** Most classes have 10-19 students. Most lab/discussion sessions have fewer than 10 students.
Most popular majors: Elementary Education and Teaching; Business Administration and Management; Registered Nursing/Registered Nurse.
Special Study Options: Accelerated program, cross-registration, double major, English as a Second Language (ESL), exchange student program (domestic), independent study, internships, student-designed major, study abroad, teacher certification program. **Disability Services:** Special programs offered to physically disabled students, including note-taking services, reader services, tape recorders, tutors. **Career Services:** Alumni services, Career/job search classes, Career assessment, Internships. Reputation of Career Service Office—student usage is up and more employers are recruiting on campus.

FACILITIES

Housing: special housing for disabled students, men's dorms, women's dorms. 90% of campus accessible to physically diasbled. **Special Academic Facilities/**

Equipment: Bowen Museum Weaver Gallery **Computers:** 25% of classrooms, 100% of dorms, 100% of libraries, 100% of dining areas, 100% of student union, 25% of common outdoor areas have wireless network access. Administrative functions (other than registration) can be performed online.

CAMPUS LIFE

Environment: City. **Activities:** Choral groups, concert band, dance, drama/theater, jazz band, literary magazine, music ensembles, musical theater, pep band, radio station, student government, student newspaper, yearbook. 18 registered organizations, 1 honor society, 5 religious organizations. **Athletics (Intercollegiate):** *Men:* baseball, basketball, cheerleading, cross-country, golf, soccer, tennis, track/field (outdoor), track/field (indoor). *Women:* basketball, cheerleading, cross-country, golf, soccer, softball, tennis, track/field (outdoor), track/field (indoor), volleyball. **On-Campus Highlights:** Acorn Student Center, Everst Rohrer Chapel, Sufficient Grounds Coffee House, Wiekamp Athletic Center, Dining Commons, workout and weight rooms. **Environmental Initiatives:** Recycle trash

ADMISSIONS

Freshman Academic Profile: Average high school GPA 3.5. 21% in top 10% of high school class, 47% in top 25% of high school class, 76% in top 50% of high school class. 82% from public high schools. **Reported SAT (pre-2016 redesign) scores:** SAT Math middle 50% range 470-590. SAT Critical Reading middle 50% range 440-560. SAT Writing middle 50% range 430-540. **Concordant SAT scores:** SAT EBRW middle 50% 490–610. SAT Math middle 50% range 510–610. ACT middle 50% range 20-25. Minimum internet-based TOEFL 76. Minimum paper TOEFL 540. **Basis for Candidate Selection:** *Very important factors considered include:* standardized test scores. *Important factors considered include:* rigor of secondary school record, class rank, academic GPA, extracurricular activities, character/personal qualities, volunteer work. *Other factors considered include:* recommendation(s), interview, racial/ethnic status, work experience. **Freshman Admission Requirements:** High school diploma is required and GED is accepted. *Academic units recommended:* 4 English, 3 math, 1 science, 1 science lab, 2 foreign language, 1 social studies, 2 history, 3 academic electives. **Freshman Admission Statistics:** 1,168 applied, 97.77% admitted, 21% enrolled. **Transfer Admission Requirements:** High school transcript, college transcript(s), essay or personal statement, standardized test scores, statement of good standing from prior institution(s). Minimum college GPA of 2.0 required. Lowest grade transferable C-. **General Admission Information:** Priority deadline 12/1. Regular application deadline 8/15. Nonfall registration accepted. Admission may be deferred for a maximum of 1 year.

COSTS AND FINANCIAL AID

Annual tuition $27,580. Room and board $8,800. Required fees $350. Average book expense $1,200. **Required Forms and Deadlines:** FAFSA, Institution's own financial aid form. **Notification of Awards:** Applicants will be notified of awards on a rolling basis beginning 3/1. **Types of Aid:** *Need-based scholarships/grants:* Federal Pell, FSEOG, State scholarships/grants, Private scholarships, College/university scholarship or grant aid from institutional funds, Federal Nursing Scholarships. *Loans:* Direct Subsidized Stafford Loans, Direct Unsubsidized Stafford Loans, Direct PLUS loans, Federal Perkins Loans, Federal Nursing Loans. *Student Employment:* Federal Work-Study Program available. Institutional employment available. **Financial Aid Statistics:** 76% freshmen, 73% undergrads receive any aid. 70% undergrads borrow to pay for school. Average cumulative indebtedness $34,148. **Criteria for awarding aid:** *Non-need-based:* Academics, Art, Athletics, Leadership, Minority status, Music/drama, Religious affiliation.

BETHEL COLLEGE (KS)

300 E 27th Street, North Newton, KS 67117
Phone: 316-284-5230 • **Financial Aid Phone:** 316-284-5232
E-mail: admissions@bethelks.edu • **CEEB Code:** 6037
Fax: 316-284-5870 • **Website:** www.bethelks.edu • **ACT Code:** 1390

This private school was founded in 1887. It has a 60-acre campus.

RATINGS

Admissions Selectivity Rating: 83   **Fire Safety Rating:** 82   **Green Rating:** 60*

STUDENTS AND FACULTY

Enrollment: 483. **Student Body:** 51% female, 49% male, 38% out-of-state, 2% international (13 countries represented). Asian 0%, African American 15%, Caucasian 71%, Hispanic 10%, Native American <1%, Pacific Islander 0%, Two or more races 2%, Race unknown 0%.
Retention and Graduation: 63% freshmen return for sophomore year. 42% freshmen graduate within 4 years. **Faculty:** Student/faculty ratio 10:1. 38 full-

time faculty, 66% hold PhDs, 5% are are members of minority groups, 55% are women. 0% of classes are taught by teaching assistants.

ACADEMICS

Degrees: bachelor's, certificate. **Classes:** Most classes have 10-19 students. Most lab/discussion sessions have 10-19 students. **Most popular majors:** Business/Commerce Biology/Biological Sciences. **Special Study Options:** cross-registration, double major, dual enrollment, independent study, internships, liberal arts/career combination, study abroad, teacher certification program. Combined degree programs: BA/MEng. **Disability Services:** Special programs offered to physically disabled students, including note-taking services, reader services, tape recorders, tutors. **Career Services:** Alumni network, Career/job search classes, Career assessment, On-campus interviews. The liberal arts program provides students with a foundational, broad understanding of the social and natural world. Focused study in a major field equips students with the intellectual achievement vital to vocational success. Internships are thus an additional, integrated component of a larger academic program that fosters in students a powerful sense of purpose. The skills developed in a liberal education—the ability to speak, read and write correctly, clearly and cogently—are the skills needed in employment. Internship experiences help students understand the relationship of their educational experience to potential careers.

FACILITIES

Housing: Coed dorms, special housing for disabled students, apartments for married students, apartments for single students. 75% of campus accessible to physically disabled. **Special Academic Facilities/Equipment:** Art gallery, natural history and midwestern/Kansas history museums, 80 acre natural history field laboratory for biological studies, Mennonite Historical Library and Archives, Institute for Peace and Conflict Resolution, observatory **Computers:** 25% of classrooms, 75% of libraries, 100% of dining areas, 100% of student union, 50% of common outdoor areas have wireless network access. Administrative functions (other than registration) can be performed online.

CAMPUS LIFE

Environment: Village. **Activities:** Choral groups, concert band, dance, drama/theater, jazz band, literary magazine, music ensembles, musical theater, opera, radio station, student government, student newspaper, symphony orchestra, television station, yearbook, Campus Ministries, Student Organization. 50 registered organizations, 2 religious organizations. **Athletics (Intercollegiate):** *Men:* basketball, cross-country, football, golf, soccer, tennis, track/field (outdoor), track/field (indoor). *Women:* basketball, cross-country, golf, soccer, tennis, track/field (outdoor), track/field (indoor), volleyball. **On-Campus Highlights:** Student Center, Krehbiel Science Center, Athletic Complex, The Green, Warkentine Court.

ADMISSIONS

Freshman Academic Profile: Average high school GPA 3.4. 17% in top 10% of high school class, 38% in top 25% of high school class, 73% in top 50% of high school class, 97% from public high schools. **Reported SAT (pre-2016 redesign) scores:** SAT Math middle 50% range 425-475. SAT Critical Reading middle 50% range 380-435. SAT Writing middle 50% range 340-440. **Concordant SAT scores:** SAT EBRW middle 50% 410–490. SAT Math middle 50% range 470–510. ACT middle 50% range 19-25. Minimum internet-based TOEFL 76. Minimum paper TOEFL 540. **Basis for Candidate Selection:** *Very important factors considered include:* academic GPA, standardized test scores, level of applicant's interest. *Important factors considered include:* class rank, extracurricular activities, character/personal qualities, alumni/ae relation. *Other factors considered include:* rigor of secondary school record, recommendation(s). **Freshman Admission Requirements:** High school diploma is required and GED is accepted. *Academic units recommended:* 4 English, 4 math, 3 science, 2 foreign language, 3 social studies. **Freshman Admission Statistics:** 833 applied, 49.10% admitted, 27% enrolled. **Transfer Admission Requirements:** High school transcript, college transcript(s), statement of good standing from prior institution(s). Lowest grade transferable D-. **General Admission Information:** Application fee $20. Regular application deadline 8/1. Nonfall registration accepted. Admission may be deferred for a maximum of 1 year.

COSTS AND FINANCIAL AID

Annual tuition $23,500. Room and board $7,980. Average book expense $900. **Required Forms and Deadlines:** FAFSA. **Notification of Awards:** Applicants will be notified of awards on a rolling basis beginning 2/1. **Types of Aid:** *Need-based scholarships/grants:* Federal Pell, FSEOG, State scholarships/grants, Private scholarships, College/university scholarship or grant aid from institutional funds, Federal Nursing Scholarships. *Loans:* Direct Subsidized Stafford Loans, Direct Unsubsidized Stafford Loans, Direct PLUS loans, Federal Perkins Loans. *Student Employment:* Federal Work-Study Program available. Institutional employment available. **Financial Aid Statistics:** 88% needy freshmen, 85% needy undergrads receive need-based scholarship or grant aid. 100% freshmen, 100% undergrads receive non-need-based scholarship or grant aid. 89% freshmen, 90% undergrads receive need-based self-help aid. 66% freshmen, 48% undergrads receive athletic scholarships.

100% freshmen, 94% undergrads receive any aid. **Criteria for awarding aid:** *Non-need-based:* Academics, Alumni affiliation, Art, Athletics, Minority status, Music/drama, Religious affiliation, State/district residency.

BETHEL UNIVERSITY

Office of Admissions–CAS, Saint Paul, MN 55112
Phone: 651-638-6242 • **Financial Aid Phone:** 651-638-6241
E-mail: undergrad-admissions@bethel.edu • **CEEB Code:** 6038
Fax: 651-635-1490 • **Website:** www.bethel.edu • **ACT Code:** 2088

This private school was founded in 1871. It has a 247-acre campus.

RATINGS

Admissions Selectivity Rating: 82   **Fire Safety Rating:** 69   **Green Rating:** 65

STUDENTS AND FACULTY

Enrollment: 2,846. **Student Body:** 61% female, 39% male, 20% out-of-state, <1% international (11 countries represented). Asian 3%, African American 4%, Caucasian 72%, Hispanic 5%, Native American <1%, Pacific Islander <1%, Two or more races 3%, Race unknown 13%.
Retention and Graduation: 88% freshmen return for sophomore year. 66% freshmen graduate within 4 years. 74% freshmen graduate within 6 years. 24% grads go on to further study within 1 year. 6% grads pursue arts and sciences degrees. 1% grads pursue law degrees. 2% grads pursue business degrees. 6% grads pursue medical degrees. **Faculty:** Student/faculty ratio 11:1. 220 full-time faculty, 79% hold PhDs, 11% are are members of minority groups, 48% are women. 0% of classes are taught by teaching assistants.

ACADEMICS

Degrees: associate, bachelor's, doctoral/professional, doctoral/research, doctoral, master's, postbachelor's certificate, post-master's certificate. **Classes:** Most classes have 10-19 students. Most lab/discussion sessions have 10-19 students. **Most popular majors:** Business Administration and Management; Education; Registered Nursing/Registered Nurse. **Special Study Options:** double major, exchange student program (domestic), honors program, independent study, internships, student-designed major, study abroad, teacher certification program. **Honors Programs:** The program consists of two honors courses in the freshman year, one in the sophomore year and one in the junior year. In their senior year the student will complete an Honors Senior Project. The two courses in the sophomore year and junior year, as well as the Honors Senior Project are geared toward a discipline of the students choosing. This program also consists of other Honors classes and Honors Forums throughout all four years. **Disability Services:** Special programs offered to physically disabled students, including note-taking services, reader services, tape recorders, tutors. **Career Services:** Alumni services, Career/job search classes, Career assessment, Internships. We have a very collaborative network of colleagues around the state and provide high quality job fairs through our joint effort.

FACILITIES

Housing: Coed dorms, special housing for disabled students, apartments for single students. 99% of campus accessible to physically disabled. **Special Academic Facilities/Equipment:** Two Art galleries, media center, closed circuit TV, television studio, and radio station, cadaver lab **Computers:** 100% of classrooms, 50% of dorms, 100% of libraries, 100% of dining areas, 100% of student union, 50% of common outdoor areas have wireless network access. Students can register for classes online. Administrative functions (other than registration) can be performed online.

CAMPUS LIFE

Environment: Metropolis. **Activities:** Choral groups, concert band, dance, drama/theater, jazz band, literary magazine, music ensembles, musical theater, radio station, student government, student newspaper, student-run film society, symphony orchestra, Campus Ministries, Student Organization. 55 registered organizations, 5 honor societies, 20 religious organizations. **Athletics (Intercollegiate):** *Men:* baseball, basketball, cross-country, football, golf, ice hockey, soccer, tennis, track/field (outdoor), track/field (indoor). *Women:* basketball, cross-country, golf, ice hockey, soccer, softball, tennis, track/field (outdoor), track/field (indoor), volleyball. **On-Campus Highlights:** Brushaber Commons (new student facility), SRC-Student Recreation Center, Market Square/Dining Center, Lissner Hall-New Dorm/ Lounges, Ona Orth Athletic Complex, Brushaber Commons: all new student facility. Great Hall: seats 1600 people; location of Chapel services, Vespers, concerts, musicals and large on-campus events. **Environmental Initiatives:** Green Roof and Permeable Pavers for Brushaber Commons.

ADMISSIONS

Freshman Academic Profile: Average high school GPA 3.5. 29% in top 10% of high school class, 53% in top 25% of high school class, 84% in top

50% of high school class. 81% from public high schools. ACT middle 50% range 21-28. Minimum internet-based TOEFL 70. Minimum paper TOEFL 525. **Basis for Candidate Selection:** *Very important factors considered include:* rigor of secondary school record, academic GPA, standardized test scores, character/personal qualities, alumni/ae relation, religious affiliation/commitment. *Important factors considered include:* application essay, volunteer work, level of applicant's interest. *Other factors considered include:* class rank, recommendation(s), interview, extracurricular activities, talent/ability, first generation, racial/ethnic status. **Freshman Admission Requirements:** High school diploma is required and GED is accepted. *Academic units required:* 4 English, 3 math, 3 science, 2 science labs, 4 social studies. *Academic units recommended:* 2 foreign language, 2 history, 1 computer science, 1 visual/performing arts. **Freshman Admission Statistics:** 1,798 applied, 82.37% admitted, 38% enrolled. **Transfer Admission Requirements:** college transcript(s), essay or personal statement, Minimum college GPA of 2.5 required. Lowest grade transferable C. **General Admission Information:** Priority deadline 12/1. Nonfall registration accepted.

COSTS AND FINANCIAL AID

Annual tuition $36,060. Room and board $10,340. Required fees $150. Average book expense $1,214. **Required Forms and Deadlines:** FAFSA. **Notification of Awards:** Applicants will be notified of awards on a rolling basis beginning 3/1. **Types of Aid:** *Need-based scholarships/grants:* Federal Pell, FSEOG, State scholarships/grants, Private scholarships, College/university scholarship or grant aid from institutional funds. *Loans:* Direct Subsidized Stafford Loans, Direct Unsubsidized Stafford Loans, Direct PLUS loans, State Loans. *Student Employment:* Federal Work-Study Program available. Institutional employment available. **Financial Aid Statistics:** 100% needy freshmen, 100% needy undergrads receive need-based scholarship or grant aid. 13% freshmen, 13% undergrads receive non-need-based scholarship or grant aid. 84% freshmen, 85% undergrads receive need-based self-help aid. 0% freshmen, 0% undergrads receive athletic scholarships. 100% freshmen, 94% undergrads receive any aid. 77% undergrads borrow to pay for school. Average cumulative indebtedness $36,132. **Criteria for awarding aid:** *Need-based:* Minority status. *Non-need-based:* Academics, Alumni affiliation, Art, Leadership, Music/drama, State/district residency.

BIOLA UNIVERSITY

13800 Biola Avenue, La Mirada, CA 90639
Phone: 1-800-OK-BIOLA • **Financial Aid Phone:** 562-903-4752
E-mail: admissions@biola.edu • **CEEB Code:** 4017
Fax: 562-903-4709 • **Website:** www.biola.edu • **ACT Code:** 172

This private school, affiliated with the Christian (Nondenominational) Church, was founded in 1908. It has a 95-acre campus.

RATINGS

Admissions Selectivity Rating: 83 Fire Safety Rating: 85 Green Rating: 72

STUDENTS AND FACULTY

Enrollment: 4,370. **Student Body:** 63% female, 37% male, 22% out-of-state, 3% international (40 countries represented). Asian 16%, African American 2%, Caucasian 52%, Hispanic 18%, Native American <1%, Pacific Islander <1%, Two or more races 6%, Race unknown 2%.
Retention and Graduation: 87% freshmen return for sophomore year. 53% freshmen graduate within 4 years. **Faculty:** Student/faculty ratio 16:1. 259 full-time faculty, 82% hold PhDs, 19% are are members of minority groups, 34% are women. 0% of classes are taught by teaching assistants.

ACADEMICS

Degrees: bachelor's, certificate, doctoral/professional, doctoral/research, doctoral, master's, postbachelor's certificate, post-master's certificate. **Classes:** Most classes have 10-19 students. Most lab/discussion sessions have 10-19 students. **Most popular majors:** Elementary Education and Teaching; Psychology; Business/Commerce. **Special Study Options:** double major, English as a Second Language (ESL), exchange student program (domestic), honors program, internships, study abroad, teacher certification program. **Disability Services:** Special programs offered to physically disabled students, including note-taking services, reader services, tape recorders, tutors. **Career Services:** Alumni network, Alumni services, Career/job search classes, Career assessment, Internships, Regional alumni. Biola University provides internships applicable to a student's major allowing them to gain academic credit and career development.

FACILITIES

Housing: Coed dorms, special housing for disabled students, men's dorms, women's dorms, apartments for married students, apartments for single

students, Flex style dorms—separate floors and wings for specific genders Off Campus Apartments On Campus Apartments. 85% of campus accessible to physically diasbled. **Special Academic Facilities/Equipment:** Art gallery, electron microscope, TV production facility, film editing facility, media center, writing center, Student Ministry Union and tutoring services. **Computers:** 100% of dorms, 100% of libraries, 100% of student union, 75% of common outdoor areas have wireless network access. Students can register for classes online. Administrative functions (other than registration) can be performed online.

CAMPUS LIFE

Environment: Town. **Activities:** Choral groups, concert band, drama/theater, jazz band, music ensembles, musical theater, opera, radio station, student government, student newspaper, student-run film society, symphony orchestra, television station, yearbook. 33 registered organizations, 2 honor societies. **Athletics (Intercollegiate):** *Men:* baseball, basketball, cross-country, golf, soccer, swimming, tennis, track/field (outdoor). *Women:* basketball, cross-country, golf, soccer, softball, swimming, tennis, track/field (outdoor), volleyball. **On-Campus Highlights:** Common Grounds, The Eagle's Nest, Art Gallery, McNally Field, The Sub (Student Union Building). **Environmental Initiatives:** Cogen—We produce clean power on campus and use clean waste heat. A certain percentage of this is also used towards cooling purposes.

ADMISSIONS

Freshman Academic Profile: Average high school GPA 3.5. 30% in top 10% of high school class, 58% in top 25% of high school class, 88% in top 50% of high school class. 59% from public high schools. **Reported SAT (pre-2016 redesign) scores:** SAT Math middle 50% range 490-610. SAT Critical Reading middle 50% range 490-620. SAT Writing middle 50% range 490-610. **Concordant SAT scores:** SAT EBRW middle 50% 550-670. SAT Math middle 50% range 520-630. ACT middle 50% range 22-28. Minimum internet-based TOEFL 100. Minimum paper TOEFL 600. **Basis for Candidate Selection:** *Very important factors considered include:* academic GPA, standardized test scores, application essay, character/personal qualities, religious affiliation/commitment. *Important factors considered include:* rigor of secondary school record, recommendation(s), interview, extracurricular activities. *Other factors considered include:* class rank, talent/ability, first generation, alumni/ae relation, geographical residence, state residency, racial/ethnic status, volunteer work, work experience, level of applicant's interest. **Freshman Admission Requirements:** High school diploma is required and GED is accepted. *Academic units recommended:* 4 English, 3 math, 2 science, 1 science lab, 4 foreign language, 1 social studies, 1 history. **Freshman Admission Statistics:** 3,874 applied, 75.40% admitted, 32% enrolled. **Transfer Admission Requirements:** High school transcript, college transcript(s), essay or personal statement, statement of good standing from prior institution(s). Minimum college GPA of 2.0 required. Lowest grade transferable C. **General Admission Information:** Application fee $45. Priority deadline 3/1. Regular notification 1/15. Nonfall registration accepted. Admission may be deferred for a maximum of 2 yrs.

COSTS AND FINANCIAL AID

Annual tuition $33,322. Room and board $9,316. Required fees $0. Average book expense $1,746. **Required Forms and Deadlines:** FAFSA, Institution's own financial aid form, State aid form. **Notification of Awards:** Applicants will be notified of awards on a rolling basis beginning 3/1. **Types of Aid:** *Need-based scholarships/grants:* Federal Pell, FSEOG, State scholarships/grants, Private scholarships, College/university scholarship or grant aid from institutional funds. *Loans:* Direct Subsidized Stafford Loans, Direct Unsubsidized Stafford Loans, Direct PLUS loans, Federal Perkins Loans, Federal Nursing Loans, College/university loans from institutional funds. *Student Employment:* Federal Work-Study Program available. Institutional employment available. **Financial Aid Statistics:** 98% needy freshmen, 97% needy undergrads receive need-based scholarship or grant aid. 6% freshmen, 3% undergrads receive non-need-based scholarship or grant aid. 77% freshmen, 82% undergrads receive need-based self-help aid. 2% freshmen, 2% undergrads receive athletic scholarships. 87% freshmen, 91% undergrads receive any aid. **Criteria for awarding aid:** *Non-need-based:* Academics, Alumni affiliation, Art, Athletics, Leadership, Minority status, Music/drama.

BIRMINGHAM-SOUTHERN COLLEGE

Box 549008, Birmingham, AL 35254
Phone: 205-226-4696 • **Financial Aid Phone:** 205-226-4688
E-mail: admission@bsc.edu • **CEEB Code:** 1064
Fax: 205-226-3074 • **Website:** www.bsc.edu • **ACT Code:** 1012

This private school, affiliated with the Methodist Church, was founded in 1856. It has a 196-acre campus.

RATINGS

Admissions Selectivity Rating: 85   **Fire Safety Rating:** 87   **Green Rating:** 60*

STUDENTS AND FACULTY

Enrollment: 1,220. **Student Body:** 47% female, 53% male, 41% out-of-state, 0% international (12 countries represented). Asian 4%, African American 8%, Caucasian 84%, Hispanic 3%, Native American 1%, Pacific Islander 0%, Two or more races 0%, Race unknown 1%.
Retention and Graduation: 81% freshmen return for sophomore year. 65% freshmen graduate within 6 years. 42% grads go on to further study within 1 year. 27% grads pursue arts and sciences degrees. 17% grads pursue law degrees. 13% grads pursue business degrees. 24% grads pursue medical degrees. **Faculty:** Student/faculty ratio 13:1. 86 full-time faculty, 97% hold PhDs, 3% are are members of minority groups, 38% are women. 0% of classes are taught by teaching assistants.

ACADEMICS

Degrees: bachelor's. **Classes:** Most classes have 10-19 students. Most lab/discussion sessions have 10-19 students. **Most popular majors:** Business/Commerce; Psychology; Biology/Biological Sciences. **Special Study Options:** cooperative education program, cross-registration, double major, dual enrollment, exchange student program (domestic), honors program, independent study, internships, liberal arts/career combination, student-designed major, study abroad, teacher certification program. **Honors Programs:** The Honors Program at Birmingham-Southern is designed to engage students' intellectual curiosity, enhance their oral and written communications skills, and further develop their ability to think and study independently. The importance of viewing issues from interdisciplinary perspectives and of integrating—as well as analyzing—knowledge is a special focus of the program's courses and requirements. The program addresses its mission through small, interdisciplinary seminars developed specifically for Honors students and through upper-level courses with an interdisciplinary focus. The Honors Program serves as a complementary approach to fulfilling the requirements of the College's Foundations Plan for General Education. "… Honors students are open to new ideas, aware of expanding horizons, and willing to change their own ideas to make room for the knowledge that they gain. They incorporate, embrace, and encourage differences. 'Honors' is not synonymous with straight A's and valedictorians. Ideal Honors students would participate in the program even if it did not appear on their transcripts."—Excerpted from "The Ideal Student in the Honors Program" as adopted by the Honors Committee 2002. The Honors Program component of Honors student's general education consists of five units of Honors seminars and one unit of independent study, known as the Honors Project. The specific general education requirements met by Honors courses and those met by regular courses will vary from student to student, depending on which Honors courses the student elects to take. Students may take one January Interim Term Honors project which will count toward the five units of Honors seminars. Students who participate in study abroad programs that include interdisciplinary courses also may petition to count one such course toward their Honors requirements. Honors students' remaining general education coursework is completed in the regular curriculum of the College. The student's sixth unit in independent study is typically taken over two terms. One-half unit is taken while the project is being designed by the student, the program director, and a faculty sponsor. The project must be interdisciplinary in nature and outside the student's major. Once approved by the Honors Program Committee, the independent study is completed the next term, giving the second half-unit of credit. All Honors Senior, or independent study, projects are presented publicly as part of the program's requirements. Combined degree programs: BA/MEng, BS/MSN (with Vanderbilt University; BS/MF or BS/MEM (with Duke Univ.). **Career Services:** Alumni network, Alumni services, Career/job search classes, Career assessment, Internships, Regional alumni. The Mentor Program is a unique job shadowing program that matches students with local successful professionals in the student's field of interest.

FACILITIES

Housing: special housing for disabled students, men's dorms, special housing for international students, women's dorms, fraternity/sorority housing, apartments for married students, apartments for single students, Wellness Housing, Theme Housing, "Honors" floors in residence halls. 90% of campus accessible to physically diasbled. **Special Academic Facilities/Equipment:** Theatre planetarium Environmental Center Urban Environmental Park Kennedy Art Center Ropes Course for Leadership Training **Computers:** 100% of classrooms, 100% of dorms, 100% of libraries, 100% of dining areas, 100% of student union, 90% of common outdoor areas have wireless network access. Students can register for classes online. Administrative functions (other than registration) can be performed online.

CAMPUS LIFE

Environment: Metropolis. **Activities:** Choral groups, dance, drama/theater, jazz band, literary magazine, musical theater, opera, pep band, student government, student newspaper, yearbook, Campus Ministries, Student Organization. 70 registered organizations, 18 honor societies, 5 religious organizations. 6 fraternities, 6 sororities. **Athletics (Intercollegiate):** *Men:* baseball, basketball, cheerleading, cross-country, football, golf, lacrosse, soccer, tennis, track/field (outdoor), track/field (indoor). *Women:* basketball, cheerleading, cross-country, golf, lacrosse, riflery, soccer, softball, tennis, track/field (outdoor), track/field (indoor), volleyball. **On-Campus Highlights:** Urban Environmental Park, Striplin Physical Fitness Center, The Cellar—Coffee House, The Court **Environmental Initiatives:** 10 compressed natural gas operations vehicles will come on line this spring. Campus police vehicles are hybrids.

ADMISSIONS

Freshman Academic Profile: Average high school GPA 3.5. 29% in top 10% of high school class, 61% in top 25% of high school class, 82% in top 50% of high school class. 65% from public high schools. **Reported SAT (pre-2016 redesign) scores:** SAT Math middle 50% range 510-610. SAT Critical Reading middle 50% range 500-610. SAT Writing middle 50% range 490-583. **Concordant SAT scores:** SAT EBRW middle 50% 550–650. SAT Math middle 50% range 540–630. ACT middle 50% range 23-29. Minimum internet-based TOEFL 61. Minimum paper TOEFL 500. **Basis for Candidate Selection:** *Very important factors considered include:* academic GPA, standardized test scores, application essay, recommendation(s). *Important factors considered include:* rigor of secondary school record, class rank, extracurricular activities, character/personal qualities. *Other factors considered include:* interview, talent/ability, work experience. **Freshman Admission Requirements:** High school diploma is required and GED is accepted. *Academic units required:* 4 English. *Academic units recommended:* 2 math, 2 science, 1 science lab, 2 foreign language, 2 social studies, 2 history, 2 academic electives. **Freshman Admission Statistics:** 1,846 applied, 65.11% admitted, 27% enrolled. **Transfer Admission Requirements:** High school transcript, college transcript(s), essay or personal statement, standardized test scores, statement of good standing from prior institution(s). Minimum college GPA of 2.0 required. Lowest grade transferable D. **General Admission Information:** Application fee $40. Regular application deadline 2/1. Nonfall registration accepted. Admission may be deferred for a maximum of 1 year.

COSTS AND FINANCIAL AID

Annual tuition $31,954. Room and board $11,350. Required fees $1,174. Average book expense $1,300. **Required Forms and Deadlines:** FAFSA, State aid form. **Notification of Awards:** Applicants will be notified of awards on a rolling basis beginning 3/1. **Types of Aid:** *Need-based scholarships/grants:* Federal Pell, FSEOG, State scholarships/grants, Private scholarships, College/university scholarship or grant aid from institutional funds. *Loans:* Direct Subsidized Stafford Loans, Direct Unsubsidized Stafford Loans, Direct PLUS loans, Federal Perkins Loans, College/university loans from institutional funds. *Student Employment:* Federal Work-Study Program available. Institutional employment available. **Financial Aid Statistics:** 76% needy freshmen, 82% needy undergrads receive need-based scholarship or grant aid. 92% freshmen, 89% undergrads receive non-need-based scholarship or grant aid. 99% freshmen, 82% undergrads receive need-based self-help aid. 0% freshmen, 0% undergrads receive athletic scholarships. 99% freshmen, 98% undergrads receive any aid. **Criteria for awarding aid:** *Non-need-based:* Academics, Alumni affiliation, Art, Leadership, Music/drama, Religious affiliation, State/district residency.

BLACKBURN COLLEGE

700 College Ave., Carlinville, il 62626
Phone: 217-854-3231
E-mail: admit@blackburn.edu
Fax: 217-854-3713 • **Website:** www.blackburn.edu • **ACT Code:** 958

This private school, affiliated with the Presbyterian Church, was founded in 1837. It has a 80-acre campus.

RATINGS

Admissions Selectivity Rating: 71   **Fire Safety Rating:** 60*   **Green Rating:** 60*

STUDENTS AND FACULTY

Student Body: 59% female, 41% male, (0 countries represented).
Faculty: Student/faculty ratio 17:1. 31 full-time faculty, 0% hold PhDs, 6% are are members of minority groups, 35% are women.

ACADEMICS

Degrees: bachelor's. **Special Study Options:** double major, exchange student program (domestic), honors program, independent study, internships, liberal arts/career combination, student-designed major, study abroad, teacher certification program.

FACILITIES

Housing: Coed dorms, men's dorms, women's dorms, Theme Housing.

CAMPUS LIFE

Environment: Village. **Activities:** Choral groups, dance, drama/theater, jazz band, literary magazine, music ensembles, musical theater, radio station, student government, student newspaper, student-run film society, yearbook, Campus Ministries, Student Organization.

ADMISSIONS

Freshman Academic Profile: Average high school GPA 3.5. 16% in top 10% of high school class, 22% in top 25% of high school class, 37% in top 50% of high school class. 81% from public high schools. Minimum internet-based TOEFL 70. Minimum paper TOEFL 525. **Basis for Candidate Selection:** *Very important factors considered include:* rigor of secondary school record, academic GPA, standardized test scores. *Important factors considered include:* class rank, level of applicant's interest. *Other factors considered include:* application essay, recommendation(s), extracurricular activities, talent/ability, character/personal qualities, alumni/ae relation, volunteer work, work experience. **Freshman Admission Requirements:** High school diploma is required and GED is accepted. *Academic units recommended:* 4 English, 3 math, 3 science, 2 foreign language, 3 social studies. **Freshman Admission Statistics:** 893 applied, 63.94% admitted, 26% enrolled. **Transfer Admission Requirements:** High school transcript, college transcript(s), standardized test scores, Minimum college GPA of 2.0 required. Lowest grade transferable C. **General Admission Information:** Nonfall registration accepted. Admission may be deferred.

COSTS AND FINANCIAL AID

Average book expense $1,000. *Student Employment:* Federal Work-Study Program available. Institutional employment available.

BLOOMFIELD COLLEGE

One Park Place, Bloomfield, NJ 7003
Phone: 973-748-9000 (x1230) • **Financial Aid Phone:** 973-748-9000 x1213
E-mail: admission@bloomfield.edu • **CEEB Code:** 2044
Fax: 973-748-0916 • **Website:** www.bloomfield.edu • **ACT Code:** 2540

This private school, affiliated with the Presbyterian Church, was founded in 1868. It has a 12.5-acre campus.

RATINGS

Admissions Selectivity Rating: 74   **Fire Safety Rating:** 98   **Green Rating:** 68

STUDENTS AND FACULTY

Enrollment: 1,937. **Student Body:** 64% female, 36% male, 5% out-of-state, 4% international (18 countries represented). Asian 3%, African American 50%, Caucasian 10%, Hispanic 26%, Native American <1%, Pacific Islander <1%, Two or more races 1%, Race unknown 4%.
Retention and Graduation: 70% freshmen return for sophomore year. 7% freshmen graduate within 4 years. 14% grads go on to further study within 1 year. **Faculty:** Student/faculty ratio 15:1. 73 full-time faculty, 75% hold PhDs, 26% are are members of minority groups, 62% are women. 0% of classes are taught by teaching assistants.

ACADEMICS

Degrees: bachelor's, certificate, master's, postbachelor's certificate. **Classes:** Most classes have 10-19 students. Most lab/discussion sessions have 10-19 students. **Most popular majors:** Visual and Performing Arts; Sociology; Registered Nursing/Registered Nurse. **Special Study Options:** Accelerated program, distance learning, double major, dual enrollment, English as a Second Language (ESL), honors program, independent study, internships, liberal arts/career combination, student-designed major, study abroad, teacher certification program, Four-year clinical laboratory science program and allied health technologies major offered in conjunction with University of Medicine and Dentistry of New Jersey. Joint BS/MS in computer information systems program offered with NJIT. Special programs offered by the Institute of Technology and Professional Studies. **Honors Programs:** Honors program

open to new and enrolled students consisting of interdisciplinary courses, honors seminars in the arts and sciences, special courses, and honors projects. Combined degree programs: BA/MA, Joint BS/MS Comp Inform Sys Dgr with NJ Inst Tech. **Disability Services:** Special programs offered to physically disabled students, including note-taking services, reader services, tape recorders, tutors. **Career Services:** Alumni network, Alumni services, Career/job search classes, Career assessment, Internships, Regional alumni. Personalized career counseling to identify individual skills and abilities as the relate to career options and internship opportunities.

FACILITIES

Housing: Coed dorms, Theme Housing. 78% of campus accessible to physically diasbled. **Special Academic Facilities/Equipment:**—Westminster Theatre—Art Gallery—State-of-the-Art Library **Computers:** 20% of classrooms, 100% of dorms, 100% of libraries, 100% of dining areas, 100% of student union, have wireless network access. Administrative functions (other than registration) can be performed online.

CAMPUS LIFE

Environment: Town. **Activities:** dance, drama/theater, radio station, student government, Campus Ministries, Student Organization. 40 registered organizations, 4 honor societies, 1 religious organization. 6 fraternities, 6 sororities. **Athletics (Intercollegiate):** *Men:* baseball, basketball, cross-country, soccer, tennis. *Women:* basketball, cross-country, soccer, softball, volleyball. **On-Campus Highlights:** Library, Art Gallery, College Center, Deacons Den, Gymnasium, Quad. **Environmental Initiatives:** Campus-wide recycling program.

ADMISSIONS

Freshman Academic Profile: Average high school GPA 2.7. 3% in top 10% of high school class, 14% in top 25% of high school class, 42% in top 50% of high school class. 77% from public high schools. **Reported SAT (pre-2016 redesign) scores:** SAT Math middle 50% range 390-480. SAT Critical Reading middle 50% range 380-470. **Concordant SAT scores:** SAT Math middle 50% range 430–510. ACT middle 50% range 15-19. Minimum internet-based TOEFL 79. Minimum paper TOEFL 550. **Basis for Candidate Selection:** *Very important factors considered include:* rigor of secondary school record, academic GPA, standardized test scores, recommendation(s). *Important factors considered include:* class rank, application essay, interview, extracurricular activities. *Other factors considered include:* talent/ability, character/personal qualities, first generation, alumni/ae relation, geographical residence, state residency, volunteer work, work experience, level of applicant's interest. **Freshman Admission Statistics:** 3,027 applied, 59.70% admitted, 24% enrolled. **Transfer Admission Requirements:** college transcript(s), Minimum college GPA of 2.0 required. Lowest grade transferable 2. **General Admission Information:** Application fee $40. Priority deadline 3/14. Regular application deadline 8/1. Nonfall registration accepted. Admission may be deferred for a maximum of 1 year.

COSTS AND FINANCIAL AID

Annual tuition $28,600. Room and board $11,500. Required fees $0. **Required Forms and Deadlines:** FAFSA. **Notification of Awards:** Applicants will be notified of awards on a rolling basis beginning 3/15. *Types of Aid: Need-based scholarships/grants:* Federal Pell, FSEOG, State scholarships/grants, Private scholarships, College/university scholarship or grant aid from institutional funds. *Loans:* Direct Subsidized Stafford Loans, Direct Unsubsidized Stafford Loans, Direct PLUS loans. *Student Employment:* Federal Work-Study Program available. Institutional employment available. **Financial Aid Statistics:** 100% needy freshmen, 97% needy undergrads receive need-based scholarship or grant aid. 49% freshmen, 43% undergrads receive non-need-based scholarship or grant aid. 39% freshmen, 38% undergrads receive need-based self-help aid. 6% freshmen, 8% undergrads receive athletic scholarships. 98% freshmen, 94% undergrads receive any aid. 95% undergrads borrow to pay for school. Average cumulative indebtedness $46,574. **Criteria for awarding aid:** *Need-based:* Academics, Alumni affiliation, Religious affiliation. *Non-need-based:* Academics, Alumni affiliation, Athletics, Leadership.

BLOOMSBURG UNIVERSITY OF PENNSYLVANIA

104 Student Services Center, Bloomsburg, PA 17815
Phone: 570-389-4316 • **Financial Aid Phone:** 570-389-4279
E-mail: www.bloomu.edu/admissions • **CEEB Code:** 2646
Fax: 570-389-4741 • **Website:** www.bloomu.edu • **ACT Code:** 3692

This public school was founded in 1839. It has a 282-acre campus.

RATINGS

Admissions Selectivity Rating: 74   **Fire Safety Rating:** 97   **Green Rating:** 60*

STUDENTS AND FACULTY

Enrollment: 8,734. **Student Body:** 56% female, 44% male, 9% out-of-state, <1% international (31 countries represented). Asian 1%, African American 9%, Caucasian 79%, Hispanic 7%, Native American <1%, Pacific Islander <1%, Two or more races 3%, Race unknown 1%.

Retention and Graduation: 76% freshmen return for sophomore year. 38% freshmen graduate within 4 years. 62% freshmen graduate within 6 years. 21% grads go on to further study within 1 year. **Faculty:** Student/faculty ratio 20:1. 410 full-time faculty, 84% hold PhDs, 12% are are members of minority groups, 42% are women. 0% of classes are taught by teaching assistants.

ACADEMICS

Degrees: bachelor's, doctoral/professional, master's, postbachelor's certificate. **Classes:** Most classes have 20-29 students. Most lab/discussion sessions have 10-19 students. **Most popular majors:** Business Administration and Management; Psychology; Organizational Communication. **Special Study Options:** cooperative education program, cross-registration, distance learning, double major, dual enrollment, English as a Second Language (ESL), exchange student program (domestic), honors program, independent study, internships, liberal arts/career combination, study abroad, teacher certification program. **Honors Programs:** The Honors Program's goals are: to challenge students to perform at the highest level of excellence to encourage independent thinking and learning; to create a supportive environment that encourages the aspirations and achievements of students and fosters their dignity, self esteem and sense of initiative; to encourage creativity, intellectual independence, analytical thinking and problem solving and the growth of communication skills through a strong emphasis on reading, writing and research; to provide opportunities for students to develop a broader perspective on national and global issues; to provide forums for symposia, experiential learning and independent study; to create a meaningful learning community; to develop students' leadership potential; to enable students to engage in a rigorous, coherent, integrated academic experience with a high degree of student-faculty interaction. **Disability Services:** Special programs offered to physically disabled students, including note-taking services, reader services, tape recorders, tutors. **Career Services:** Alumni network, Career/job search classes, Career assessment, Internships. Bloomsburg University offers students multiple opportunities to obtain professional experience and build a career network while pursuing a degree.

FACILITIES

Housing: Coed dorms, apartments for single students, Affiliated off-campus apartments operated by the Community Government Association. 100% of campus accessible to physically diasbled. **Special Academic Facilities/ Equipment:** Art gallery, language lab, TV studio, radio station. **Computers:** 100% of classrooms, 100% of libraries, 100% of student union, 50% of common outdoor areas have wireless network access. Students can register for classes online. Administrative functions (other than registration) can be performed online.

CAMPUS LIFE

Environment: Village. **Activities:** Choral groups, concert band, dance, drama/theater, literary magazine, marching band, music ensembles, pep band, radio station, student government, student newspaper, television station, yearbook, Campus Ministries, Student Organization, Model UN. 195 registered organizations, 19 honor societies, 8 religious organizations. 15 fraternities, 13 sororities. **Athletics (Intercollegiate):** *Men:* baseball, basketball, cheerleading, cross-country, football, soccer, swimming, tennis, track/field (outdoor), track/field (indoor), wrestling. *Women:* basketball, cheerleading, cross-country, field hockey, lacrosse, soccer, softball, swimming, tennis, track/field (outdoor), track/field (indoor). **On-Campus Highlights:** Kehr Student Union, Dining Hall/Food Court, Climbing Wall, Recreation Center, Redman Stadium, Starbucks. **Environmental Initiatives:** Biofuel bus: One of Bloomsburg's shuttle buses uses carbon neutral B100 fuel processed from dining services' used cooking oil during fall and spring.

ADMISSIONS

Freshman Academic Profile: Average high school GPA 3.3. 7% in top 10% of high school class, 27% in top 25% of high school class, 61% in top 50% of high school class. 86% from public high schools. **Reported SAT (pre-2016 redesign) scores:** SAT Math middle 50% range 440-540. SAT Critical Reading middle 50% range 430-530. SAT Writing middle 50% range 410-510. **Concordant SAT scores:** SAT EBRW middle 50% 470–580. SAT Math middle 50% range 480–570. ACT middle 50% range 18-23. Minimum paper TOEFL 550. **Basis for Candidate Selection:** *Very important factors considered include:* rigor of secondary school record, class rank, academic GPA, standardized test scores. *Other factors considered include:* application essay, recommendation(s), interview, extracurricular activities, talent/ability, character/personal qualities, geographical residence, state residency, volunteer work, work experience, level of applicant's interest. **Freshman Admission Requirements:** High school diploma is required and GED is accepted. *Academic units required:* 4 English, 3 math, 3 science, 2 social studies, 2 history, 2 academic electives. *Academic units recommended:* 4 English, 4 math, 4 science, 2 foreign language, 2 social studies, 2 history, 2 academic electives, 1 computer science.

Freshman Admission Statistics: 9,330 applied, 77.56% admitted, 26% enrolled. **Transfer Admission Requirements:** High school transcript, college transcript(s), Minimum college GPA of 2.0 required. Lowest grade transferable C. **General Admission Information:** Application fee $35. Priority deadline 12/1. Nonfall registration accepted. Admission may be deferred for a maximum of 1 year.

COSTS AND FINANCIAL AID

Annual in-state tuition $7,238. Annual out-of-state tuition $18,096. Room and board $8,912. Required fees $2,916. Average book expense $1,200. **Required Forms and Deadlines:** FAFSA. **Notification of Awards:** Applicants will be notified of awards on a rolling basis beginning 4/1. **Types of Aid:** *Need-based scholarships/grants:* Federal Pell, FSEOG, State scholarships/grants, Private scholarships, College/university scholarship or grant aid from institutional funds. *Loans:* Direct Subsidized Stafford Loans, Direct Unsubsidized Stafford Loans, Direct PLUS loans, Federal Perkins Loans, State Loans. *Student Employment:* Federal Work-Study Program available. Institutional employment available. **Financial Aid Statistics:** 63% needy freshmen, 64% needy undergrads receive need-based scholarship or grant aid. 27% freshmen, 20% undergrads receive non-need-based scholarship or grant aid. 92% freshmen, 92% undergrads receive need-based self-help aid. 3% freshmen, 2% undergrads receive athletic scholarships. 84% undergrads receive any aid. **Criteria for awarding aid:** *Need-based:* Academics, Alumni affiliation, Leadership, Minority status. *Non-need-based:* Academics, Art, Athletics, Job skills, Leadership, Minority status, Music/drama, State/district residency.

BLUE MOUNTAIN COLLEGE

PO Box 160, Blue Mountain, MS 38610
Phone: 662-685-4771 • **Financial Aid Phone:** 662-685-4771
E-mail: admissions@bmc.edu
Fax: 662-685-4776 • **Website:** bmc.edu

This private school, affiliated with the Baptist Church, was founded in 1873. It has a 44-acre campus.

RATINGS

Admissions Selectivity Rating: 85   **Fire Safety Rating:** 71   **Green Rating:** 60*

STUDENTS AND FACULTY

Enrollment: 406. **Student Body:** 64% female, 36% male, 12% out-of-state, <1% international (1 countries represented). Asian 0%, African American 12%, Caucasian 87%, Hispanic <1%, Native American 0%, Pacific Islander 0%, Two or more races 0%, Race unknown 0%.

Retention and Graduation: 72% freshmen return for sophomore year. 31% freshmen graduate within 4 years. 58% freshmen graduate within 6 years. 14% grads go on to further study within 1 year. 14% grads pursue arts and sciences degrees. 1% grads pursue business degrees. 2% grads pursue medical degrees. **Faculty:** Student/faculty ratio 13:1. 24 full-time faculty, 67% hold PhDs, 0% are are members of minority groups, 54% are women. 0% of classes are taught by teaching assistants.

ACADEMICS

Degrees: bachelor's, master's. **Classes:** Most classes have 10-19 students. Most lab/discussion sessions have 10-19 students. **Most popular majors:** Elementary Education and Teaching; Bible/Biblical Studies; Psychology. **Special Study Options:** double major, honors program, internships, teacher certification program. **Honors Programs:** Academic Honors Program. **Disability Services:** Special programs offered to physically disabled students, including note-taking services, tutors.

FACILITIES

Housing: men's dorms, women's dorms. 50% of campus accessible to physically diasbled.

CAMPUS LIFE

Environment: Rural. **Activities:** Choral groups, drama/theater, literary magazine, musical theater, student government, yearbook. 28 registered organizations, 4 honor societies, 2 religious organizations. **Athletics (Intercollegiate):** *Women:* basketball, tennis. **On-Campus Highlights:** Johnnie Armstrong Gal-ry, Student Union Building, Tyler Gymnasium, Broach Hall, Fisher-Washburn Hall.

ADMISSIONS

Freshman Academic Profile: Average high school GPA 3.3. 19% in top 10% of high school class, 50% in top 25% of high school class, 86% in top 50% of high school class. 73% from public high schools. ACT middle 50% range 18-23. Minimum paper TOEFL 500. **Basis for Candidate Selection:**

Important factors considered include: rigor of secondary school record, class rank, academic GPA, standardized test scores. *Other factors considered include:* recommendation(s), character/personal qualities, alumni/ae relation. **Freshman Admission Requirements:** High school diploma is required and GED is accepted. *Academic units required:* 4 English, 3 math, 3 science, 2 science labs, 2 foreign language, 1 social studies, 2 history. *Academic units recommended:* 4 English, 3 math, 3 science, 2 science labs, 2 foreign language, 1 social studies, 2 history. **Freshman Admission Statistics:** 146 applied, 46.58% admitted, 87% enrolled. **Transfer Admission Requirements:** college transcript(s), Lowest grade transferable C. **General Admission Information:** Application fee $10. Nonfall registration accepted. Admission may be deferred.

COSTS AND FINANCIAL AID

Annual tuition $6,900. Room and board $3,766. Required fees $540. Average book expense $650. **Required Forms and Deadlines:** FAFSA, Institution's own financial aid form. **Notification of Awards:** Applicants will be notified of awards on a rolling basis beginning 4/1. **Types of Aid:** *Need-based scholarships/ grants:* Federal Pell, FSEOG, State scholarships/grants, Private scholarships. *Loans:* Federal Perkins Loans. *Student Employment:* Federal Work-Study Program available. Institutional employment available. **Financial Aid Statistics:** 81% needy freshmen, 64% needy undergrads receive need-based scholarship or grant aid. 81% freshmen, 100% undergrads receive non-need-based scholarship or grant aid. 62% freshmen, 18% undergrads receive need-based self-help aid. 8% freshmen, 6% undergrads receive athletic scholarships. 95% freshmen, 96% undergrads receive any aid. **Criteria for awarding aid:** *Need-based:* Alumni affiliation. *Non-need-based:* Academics, Alumni affiliation, Athletics, Religious affiliation, State/district residency.

BLUFFTON UNIVERSITY

Office of Admissions, Bluffton, OH 45817
Phone: 419-358-3257 • **Financial Aid Phone:** 419-358-3409
E-mail: admissions@bluffton.edu • **CEEB Code:** 1067
Fax: 419-358-3081 • **Website:** www.bluffton.edu • **ACT Code:** 3238

This private school, affiliated with the Mennonite Church, was founded in 1899. It has a 65-acre campus.

RATINGS

Admissions Selectivity Rating: 79   **Fire Safety Rating:** 60*   **Green Rating:** 60*

STUDENTS AND FACULTY

Enrollment: 833. **Student Body:** 51% female, 49% male, 12% out-of-state, <1% international. Asian 0%, African American 6%, Caucasian 85%, Hispanic 4%, Native American 0%, Pacific Islander 0%, Two or more races 3%, Race unknown 2%.
Retention and Graduation: 72% freshmen return for sophomore year. 41% freshmen graduate within 4 years. 46% freshmen graduate within 6 years. **Faculty:** Student/faculty ratio 12:1. 56 full-time faculty, 80% hold PhDs, 2% are are members of minority groups, 39% are women. 0% of classes are taught by teaching assistants.

ACADEMICS

Degrees: bachelor's, master's, postbachelor's certificate. **Classes:** Most classes have 10-19 students. Most lab/discussion sessions have 10-19 students. **Most popular majors:** Business Administration and Management; Early Childhood Education and Teaching; Social Work. **Special Study Options:** distance learning, double major, dual enrollment, English as a Second Language (ESL), honors program, independent study, internships, student-designed major, study abroad, teacher certification program. **Disability Services:** Special programs offered to physically disabled students, including reader services, tape recorders, tutors. **Career Services:** Alumni services, Career/job search classes.

FACILITIES

Housing: Coed dorms, men's dorms, women's dorms, Theme Housing. 99% of campus accessible to physically diasbled. **Special Academic Facilities/ Equipment:** Mennonite historical library, peace arts center, nature preserve.

CAMPUS LIFE

Environment: Rural. **Activities:** Choral groups, concert band, dance, drama/ theater, jazz band, literary magazine, music ensembles, musical theater, pep band, radio station, student government, Campus Ministries, Student Organization. 50 registered organizations, 19 honor societies, 10 religious organizations. **Athletics (Intercollegiate):** *Men:* baseball, basketball, cheerleading, cross-country, football, golf, soccer, tennis, track/field (outdoor), track/field (indoor). *Women:* basketball, cheerleading, cross-country, golf, soccer, softball, tennis, track/field (outdoor), track/field (indoor), volleyball. **On-Campus Highlights:** Centennial Hall-academic center, Marbeck Center-

student union, College Hall-administrative/classroom building, Salzman Stadium-Football Stadium, Founders Hall-gymnasium.

ADMISSIONS

Freshman Academic Profile: Average high school GPA 3.2. 12% in top 10% of high school class, 25% in top 25% of high school class, 67% in top 50% of high school class. 98% from public high schools. **Reported SAT (pre-2016 redesign) scores:** SAT Math middle 50% range 430-560. SAT Critical Reading middle 50% range 410-580. SAT Writing middle 50% range 420-550. **Concordant SAT scores:** SAT EBRW middle 50% 460–620. SAT Math middle 50% range 470–580. ACT middle 50% range 18-23. Minimum paper TOEFL 500. **Basis for Candidate Selection:** *Very important factors considered include:* class rank, academic GPA, standardized test scores. *Other factors considered include:* interview, extracurricular activities, talent/ability, character/ personal qualities. **Freshman Admission Requirements:** High school diploma is required and GED is accepted. *Academic units recommended:* 4 English, 3 math, 3 science, 3 foreign language, 3 social studies. **Freshman Admission Statistics:** 1,652 applied, 53.57% admitted, 25% enrolled. **Transfer Admission Requirements:** High school transcript, college transcript(s), statement of good standing from prior institution(s). Minimum college GPA of 2.0 required. Lowest grade transferable C-. **General Admission Information:** Application fee $20. Nonfall registration accepted. Admission may be deferred.

COSTS AND FINANCIAL AID

Required Forms and Deadlines: FAFSA. **Notification of Awards:** Applicants will be notified of awards on a rolling basis beginning 3/1. **Types of Aid:** *Need-based scholarships/grants:* Federal Pell, FSEOG, State scholarships/ grants, Private scholarships. *Loans:* Direct Subsidized Stafford Loans, Direct Unsubsidized Stafford Loans, Direct PLUS loans, Federal Perkins Loans. *Student Employment:* Federal Work-Study Program available. Institutional employment available. **Financial Aid Statistics:** 99% needy freshmen, 99% needy undergrads receive need-based scholarship or grant aid. 11% freshmen, 11% undergrads receive non-need-based scholarship or grant aid. 91% freshmen, 90% undergrads receive need-based self-help aid. 0% freshmen, 0% undergrads receive athletic scholarships. **Criteria for awarding aid:** *Need-based:* Job skills. *Non-need-based:* Academics, Art, Job skills, Minority status, Music/drama, Religious affiliation, State/district residency.

BOB JONES UNIVERSITY

1700 Wade Hampton Blvd, Greenville, SC 29614
Phone: 800-252-6363 • **Financial Aid Phone:** 864-242-5100 Ext 3040
E-mail: admission@bju.edu • **CEEB Code:** 5065
Fax: 800-232-9258 • **Website:** www.bju.edu • **ACT Code:** 3836

This proprietary school was founded in 1927. It has a 225-acre campus.

RATINGS

Admissions Selectivity Rating: 80   **Fire Safety Rating:** 87   **Green Rating:** 60*

STUDENTS AND FACULTY

Enrollment: 2,552. **Student Body:** 56% female, 44% male, 67% out-of-state, 6% international (47 countries represented). Asian 2%, African American 1%, Caucasian 77%, Hispanic 6%, Native American <1%, Pacific Islander <1%, Two or more races 3%, Race unknown 4%.
Retention and Graduation: 81% freshmen return for sophomore year. 59% freshmen graduate within 4 years. 72% freshmen graduate within 6 years. **Faculty:** Student/faculty ratio 14:1. 190 full-time faculty, 56% hold PhDs, 3% are are members of minority groups, 38% are women.

ACADEMICS

Degrees: associate, bachelor's, doctoral, master's. **Classes:** Most classes have fewer than 10 students. Most lab/discussion sessions have fewer than 10 students. **Most popular majors:** Registered Nursing/Registered Nurse; Accounting; Business Administration and Management. **Special Study Options:** Accelerated program, distance learning, English as a Second Language (ESL), internships, teacher certification program. **Disability Services:** Special programs offered to physically disabled students, including note-taking services, reader services, tape recorders, tutors. **Career Services:** Alumni services, Career/job search classes, Career assessment.

FACILITIES

Housing: special housing for disabled students, men's dorms, women's dorms, apartments for married students, apartments for single students. 90% of campus accessible to physically diasbled. **Special Academic Facilities/Equipment:** Museum & Gallery Davis Field House Rodeheaver Auditorium Bob Jones Jr. Memorial Seminary & Evangelism Center **Computers:** 85% of classrooms, 100% of dorms, 100% of libraries, 20% of dining areas, 100% of student union,

70% of common outdoor areas have wireless network access. Students can register for classes online. Administrative functions (other than registration) can be performed online.

CAMPUS LIFE

Environment: City. **Activities:** Choral groups, concert band, drama/theater, music ensembles, opera, radio station, student government, student newspaper, symphony orchestra, television station, yearbook, Campus Ministries. 31 registered organizations, 18 religious organizations. **On-Campus Highlights:** University Student Center, Davis Field House, Cuppa Jones coffee shop, Fast Break lunch area, BJU Museum & Gallery.

ADMISSIONS

Freshman Academic Profile: Average high school GPA 3.4. 12% in top 10% of high school class, 35% in top 25% of high school class, 62% in top 50% of high school class. 5% from public high schools. ACT middle 50% range 20-26. Minimum internet-based TOEFL 61. Minimum paper TOEFL 500. **Basis for Candidate Selection:** *Very important factors considered include:* academic GPA, recommendation(s), character/personal qualities, religious affiliation/commitment, level of applicant's interest. *Important factors considered include:* rigor of secondary school record, application essay. *Other factors considered include:* class rank, standardized test scores, extracurricular activities, talent/ability, first generation, alumni/ae relation, volunteer work, work experience. **Freshman Admission Requirements:** High school diploma is required and GED is accepted. *Academic units recommended:* 3 English, 2 math, 1 science, 2 foreign language, 2 social studies, 6 academic electives. **Freshman Admission Statistics:** 1,049 applied, 80.93% admitted, 72% enrolled. **Transfer Admission Requirements:** college transcript(s), Minimum college GPA of 2.0 required. Lowest grade transferable D-. **General Admission Information:** Application fee $45. Regular application deadline 8/1. Nonfall registration accepted. Admission may be deferred for a maximum of 1 year.

COSTS AND FINANCIAL AID

Annual tuition $13,570. Room and board $6,090. Required fees $650. Average book expense $1,200. **Required Forms and Deadlines:** FAFSA. **Notification of Awards:** Applicants will be notified of awards on a rolling basis beginning 4/1. **Types of Aid:** *Need-based scholarships/grants:* Federal Pell, FSEOG, State scholarships/grants, Private scholarships, College/university scholarship or grant aid from institutional funds, United Negro College Fund. *Loans:* Direct Subsidized Stafford Loans, Direct Unsubsidized Stafford Loans, Direct PLUS loans, College/university loans from institutional funds. *Student Employment:* Federal Work-Study Program available. Institutional employment available. **Financial Aid Statistics:** 100% needy undergrads receive need-based scholarship or grant aid. 39% undergrads receive non-need-based scholarship or grant aid. 58% undergrads receive need-based self-help aid. 0% undergrads receive athletic scholarships. 60% freshmen, 61% undergrads receive any aid. **Criteria for awarding aid:** *Need-based:* Academics, Alumni affiliation, Leadership. *Non-need-based:* State/district residency.

BOISE STATE UNIVERSITY

1910 University Drive, Boise, ID 83725
Phone: 208-426-1156 • **Financial Aid Phone:** 208-426-1664
E-mail: bsuinfo@boisestate.edu • **CEEB Code:** 4018
Fax: 208-426-3765 • **ACT Code:** 914

This public school was founded in 1932. It has a 150-acre campus.

RATINGS

Admissions Selectivity Rating: 78   **Fire Safety Rating:** 81   **Green Rating:** 66

STUDENTS AND FACULTY

Enrollment: 15,959. **Student Body:** 53% female, 47% male, 24% out-of-state, 5% international (73 countries represented). Asian 2%, African American 2%, Caucasian 74%, Hispanic 11%, Native American 1%, Pacific Islander <1%, Two or more races 4%, Race unknown 2%.
Retention and Graduation: 76% freshmen return for sophomore year. 15% freshmen graduate within 4 years. 38% freshmen graduate within 6 years. 15% grads go on to further study within 1 year. 4% grads pursue arts and sciences degrees. 1% grads pursue law degrees. 2% grads pursue business degrees. 1% grads pursue medical degrees. **Faculty:** Student/faculty ratio 18:1. 713 full-time faculty, 69% hold PhDs, 11% are are members of minority groups, 48% are women. 1% of classes are taught by teaching assistants.

ACADEMICS

Degrees: associate, bachelor's, doctoral/research, master's, postbachelor's certificate, terminal. **Classes:** Most classes have 20-29 students. Most lab/discussion sessions have 20-29 students. **Most popular majors:** Speech Communication and Rhetoric; Registered Nursing/Registered Nurse; Business/

Commerce. **Special Study Options:** cooperative education program, distance learning, double major, dual enrollment, English as a Second Language (ESL), exchange student program (domestic), honors program, independent study, internships, liberal arts/career combination, study abroad, teacher certification program, weekend college. **Disability Services:** Special programs offered to physically disabled students, including note-taking services, reader services, tape recorders, tutors. **Career Services:** Alumni network, Alumni services, Career assessment, Internships.

FACILITIES

Housing: Coed dorms, special housing for disabled students, men's dorms, women's dorms, fraternity/sorority housing, apartments for married students, apartments for single students. 95% of campus accessible to physically diasbled. **Computers:** Students can register for classes online. Administrative functions (other than registration) can be performed online.

CAMPUS LIFE

Environment: City. **Activities:** Choral groups, drama/theater, literary magazine, marching band, music ensembles, musical theater, pep band, radio station, student government, student newspaper, student-run film society, Student Organization. 180 registered organizations, 4 fraternities, 3 sororities. **Athletics (Intercollegiate):** *Men:* basketball, cheerleading, cross-country, football, golf, tennis, track/field (outdoor), track/field (indoor), wrestling. *Women:* basketball, cheerleading, cross-country, golf, gymnastics, skiing (downhill/alpine), soccer, tennis, track/field (outdoor), track/field (indoor), volleyball.

ADMISSIONS

Freshman Academic Profile: Average high school GPA 3.4. 15% in top 10% of high school class, 40% in top 25% of high school class, 75% in top 50% of high school class. 89% from public high schools. **Reported SAT (pre-2016 redesign) scores:** SAT Math middle 50% range 460-570. SAT Critical Reading middle 50% range 460-570. SAT Writing middle 50% range 440-550. **Concordant SAT scores:** SAT EBRW middle 50% 500–620. SAT Math middle 50% range 500–590. ACT middle 50% range 20-26. Minimum paper TOEFL 500. **Basis for Candidate Selection:** *Other factors considered include:* academic GPA, standardized test scores. **Freshman Admission Requirements:** High school diploma is required and GED is accepted. *Academic units recommended:* 8 English, 6 math, 6 science, 2 science labs, 2 foreign language, 5 social studies, and 3 units from above areas or other academic areas. **Freshman Admission Statistics:** 8,155 applied, 79.57% admitted, 34% enrolled. **Transfer Admission Requirements:** college transcript(s), Minimum college GPA of 2.0 required. Lowest grade transferable c. **General Admission Information:** Application fee $50. Regular application deadline 5/15. Nonfall registration accepted. Admission may be deferred.

COSTS AND FINANCIAL AID

Required Forms and Deadlines: FAFSA. **Notification of Awards:** Applicants will be notified of awards on a rolling basis beginning 3/15. **Types of Aid:** *Need-based scholarships/grants:* Federal Pell, FSEOG, State scholarships/grants, Private scholarships, College/university scholarship or grant aid from institutional funds, Federal Nursing Scholarships. *Loans:* Direct Subsidized Stafford Loans, Direct Unsubsidized Stafford Loans, Direct PLUS loans, Federal Perkins Loans, Federal Nursing Loans, College/university loans from institutional funds. *Student Employment:* Federal Work-Study Program available. Institutional employment available. **Financial Aid Statistics:** 73% needy freshmen, 75% needy undergrads receive need-based scholarship or grant aid. 7% freshmen, 3% undergrads receive non-need-based scholarship or grant aid. 72% freshmen, 82% undergrads receive need-based self-help aid. 1% freshmen, 1% undergrads receive athletic scholarships. 70% freshmen, 80% undergrads receive any aid. 79% undergrads borrow to pay for school. Average cumulative indebtedness $26,772. **Criteria for awarding aid:** *Need-based:* Athletics, Music/drama. *Non-need-based:* Academics, Alumni affiliation, Art, Athletics, Music/drama.

BOSTON COLLEGE

140 Commonwealth Avenue, Chestnut Hill, MA 02467-3809
Phone: 617-552-3100 • **Financial Aid Phone:** 617-552-3300 • **CEEB Code:** 3083
Fax: 617-552-0798 • **Website:** www.bc.edu • **ACT Code:** 1788

This private school, affiliated with the Roman Catholic Church, was founded in 1863. It has a 386.1-acre campus.

RATINGS
Admissions Selectivity Rating: 96   **Fire Safety Rating:** 98   **Green Rating:** 77

STUDENTS AND FACULTY
Enrollment: 9,309. **Student Body:** 54% female, 46% male, 74% out-of-state, 7% international (68 countries represented). Asian 10%, African American 4%, Caucasian 63%, Hispanic 10%, Native American <1%, Pacific Islander <1%, Two or more races 3%, Race unknown 4%.
Retention and Graduation: 95% freshmen return for sophomore year. 89% freshmen graduate within 4 years. 92% freshmen graduate within 6 years. 19% grads go on to further study within 1 year. 8% grads pursue arts and sciences degrees. 5% grads pursue law degrees. 1% grads pursue business degrees. 3% grads pursue medical degrees. **Faculty:** Student/faculty ratio 12:1. 805 full-time faculty, 95% hold PhDs, 17% are are members of minority groups, 41% are women.

ACADEMICS
Degrees: bachelor's, doctoral/professional, doctoral/research, doctoral, master's, post-master's certificate. **Classes:** Most classes have 10-19 students. **Most popular majors:** Communication and Media Studies; Finance; Economics. **Special Study Options:** Accelerated program, cross-registration, distance learning, double major, English as a Second Language (ESL), exchange student program (domestic), honors program, independent study, internships, liberal arts/career combination, student-designed major, study abroad, teacher certification program. **Honors Programs:** Multiple Honors Programs in various Schools and Departments, along with a Presidential Scholars Program Combined degree programs: BA/MD, BA/MA, MD with Tufts Medical School. **Disability Services:** Special programs offered to physically disabled students, including note-taking services, reader services, tape recorders, tutors. **Career Services:** Alumni network, Alumni services, Career/job search classes, Career assessment, Internships, Regional alumni.

FACILITIES
Housing: Coed dorms, special housing for disabled students, women's dorms, Greycliff Honors House, multicultural and intercultural floors, a quiet floor, social justice floor, a community living floor, and a leadership house. Also apartment style housing and Townhouse apartments. 95% of campus accessible to physically disabled. **Special Academic Facilities/Equipment:** Art museum, theatre arts center, on-campus school for multihandicapped students, athletic facility, state-of-the-art science facilities. **Computers:** 100% of classrooms, 100% of dorms, 100% of libraries, 100% of dining areas, 100% of student union, 100% of common outdoor areas have wireless network access. Students can register for classes online. Administrative functions (other than registration) can be performed online.

CAMPUS LIFE
Environment: City. **Activities:** Choral groups, concert band, dance, drama/theater, jazz band, literary magazine, marching band, music ensembles, musical theater, pep band, radio station, student government, student newspaper, student-run film society, symphony orchestra, television station, yearbook, Campus Ministries, Student Organization. 225 registered organizations, 12 honor societies, 14 religious organizations. **Athletics (Intercollegiate):** *Men:* baseball, basketball, cross-country, diving, fencing, football, golf, ice hockey, lacrosse, sailing, skiing (downhill/alpine), soccer, swimming, tennis, track/field (outdoor), track/field (indoor). *Women:* basketball, crew/rowing, cross-country, diving, fencing, field hockey, golf, ice hockey, lacrosse, sailing, skiing (downhill/alpine), soccer, softball, swimming, tennis, track/field (outdoor), track/field (indoor), volleyball. **On-Campus Highlights:** McMullen Museum of Art, Alumni Stadium/Conte Forum, Robsham Theater, Bapst Library, McElroy Commons/Bookstore. **Environmental Initiatives:** Green Building Commitment—New Buildings to be LEED Silver, minimum.

ADMISSIONS
Freshman Academic Profile: 80% in top 10% of high school class, 95% in top 25% of high school class, 99% in top 50% of high school class. 48% from public high schools. **Reported SAT (pre-2016 redesign) scores:** SAT Math middle 50% range 640-740. SAT Critical Reading middle 50% range 620-720. SAT

Writing middle 50% range 640-730. **Concordant SAT scores:** SAT EBRW middle 50% 680–750. SAT Math middle 50% range 660–760. ACT middle 50% range 30-33. Minimum internet-based TOEFL 100. Minimum paper TOEFL 600. **Basis for Candidate Selection:** *Very important factors considered include:* rigor of secondary school record, academic GPA, standardized test scores. *Important factors considered include:* class rank, application essay, recommendation(s), extracurricular activities, talent/ability, character/personal qualities, alumni/ae relation, religious affiliation/commitment, volunteer work. *Other factors considered include:* first generation, racial/ethnic status, work experience. **Freshman Admission Requirements:** High school diploma is required and GED is accepted. *Academic units recommended:* 4 English, 4 math, 4 science, 4 science labs, 4 foreign language, 4 social studies, 4 history. **Freshman Admission Statistics:** 28,956 applied, 31.14% admitted, 26% enrolled. **Transfer Admission Requirements:** High school transcript, college transcript(s), essay or personal statement, standardized test scores, statement of good standing from prior institution(s). Minimum college GPA of 3.0 required. Lowest grade transferable C. **General Admission Information:** Application fee $75. Regular application deadline 1/1. Regular notification 4/15. Nonfall registration accepted. Admission may be deferred for a maximum of 2 years.

COSTS AND FINANCIAL AID
Annual tuition $50,480. Room and board $13,818. Required fees $816. Average book expense $1,250. **Required Forms and Deadlines:** FAFSA, CSS/Financial Aid PROFILE, Noncustodial PROFILE, Business/Farm Supplement. **Notification of Awards:** Applicants will be notified of awards on or about 4/1. **Types of Aid:** *Need-based scholarships/grants:* Federal Pell, FSEOG, State scholarships/grants, Private scholarships, College/university scholarship or grant aid from institutional funds. *Loans:* Direct Subsidized Stafford Loans, Direct Unsubsidized Stafford Loans, Direct PLUS loans, Federal Perkins Loans, Federal Nursing Loans, State Loans. *Student Employment:* Federal Work-Study Program available. Institutional employment available. **Financial Aid Statistics:** 88% needy freshmen, 88% needy undergrads receive need-based scholarship or grant aid. 3% freshmen, 2% undergrads receive non-need-based scholarship or grant aid. 92% freshmen, 92% undergrads receive need-based self-help aid. 3% freshmen, 3% undergrads receive athletic scholarships. 63% freshmen, 66% undergrads receive any aid. 49% undergrads borrow to pay for school. Average cumulative indebtedness $20,849. **Criteria for awarding aid:** *Need-based:* Academics. *Non-need-based:* Academics, Athletics, Leadership.

BOSTON CONSERVATORY

8 The Fenway, Boston, MA 2215
Phone: 617-912-9153
E-mail: admissions@bostonconservatory.edu • **CEEB Code:** 3084
Fax: 617-247-3159 • **Website:** www.bostonconservatory.edu • **ACT Code:** 1790

This private school was founded in 1867.

RATINGS
Admissions Selectivity Rating: 71   **Fire Safety Rating:** 60*   **Green Rating:** 60*

STUDENTS AND FACULTY
Enrollment: 561. **Student Body:** 63% female, 37% male, 60% out-of-state, 9% international (26 countries represented). Asian 2%, African American 4%, Caucasian 50%, Hispanic 9%, Native American 0%, Pacific Islander 0%, Two or more races 2%, Race unknown 25%.
Faculty: Student/faculty ratio 4:1. 74 full-time faculty, 0% hold PhDs, 0% are are members of minority groups, 0% are women. 0% of classes are taught by teaching assistants.

ACADEMICS
Degrees: bachelor's, master's, postbachelor's certificate, post-master's certificate. **Classes:** Most classes have fewer than 10 students. **Special Study Options:** cross-registration, double major, English as a Second Language (ESL), independent study, teacher certification program. **Career Services:** Alumni services, Career/job search classes, Career assessment, Internships, On-campus interviews.

FACILITIES
Housing: Coed dorms, women's dorms, Graduate house.

CAMPUS LIFE
Activities: literary magazine, student government, student newspaper. 11 registered organizations, 1 honor society, 1 religious organization.

ADMISSIONS
Freshman Academic Profile: 90% from public high schools. ACT middle 50% range 0-0. **Basis for Candidate Selection:** *Very important factors considered include:* recommendation(s), talent/ability, character/personal qualities. *Important factors considered include:* rigor of secondary school

record, class rank, academic GPA, application essay, level of applicant's interest. *Other factors considered include:* interview, extracurricular activities. **Freshman Admission Requirements:** High school diploma is required and GED is accepted. *Academic units required:* 4 English, 3 math, 2 science, 2 foreign language, 2 social studies, 2 history. **Freshman Admission Statistics:** 1,216 applied, 45.89% admitted, 33% enrolled. **Transfer Admission Requirements:** High school transcript, college transcript(s), essay or personal statement, Minimum college GPA of 2.5 required. Lowest grade transferable C. **General Admission Information:** Application fee $110. Priority deadline 12/15. Regular notification 4/1. Nonfall registration accepted. Admission may be deferred.

COSTS AND FINANCIAL AID
Average book expense $0. **Required Forms and Deadlines:** FAFSA. **Notification of Awards:** Applicants will be notified of awards on or about 4/1. **Types of Aid:** *Need-based scholarships/grants:* Federal Pell, FSEOG, State scholarships/grants, Private scholarships, College/university scholarship or grant aid from institutional funds. *Loans:* Direct Subsidized Stafford Loans, Direct Unsubsidized Stafford Loans, Direct PLUS loans, State Loans, College/university loans from institutional funds. *Student Employment:* Federal Work-Study Program available. Institutional employment available. **Financial Aid Statistics:** 75% needy freshmen, 90% needy undergrads receive need-based scholarship or grant aid. 10% freshmen, 7% undergrads receive non-need-based scholarship or grant aid. 90% freshmen, 78% undergrads receive need-based self-help aid. 0% freshmen, 0% undergrads receive athletic scholarships. 61% undergrads borrow to pay for school. Average cumulative indebtedness $49,000. **Criteria for awarding aid:** *Need-based:* Music/drama. *Non-need-based:* Music/drama.

BOSTON UNIVERSITY

233 Bay State Road, Boston, MA 2215
Phone: 617-353-2300 • **Financial Aid Phone:** 617-353-4176
E-mail: admissions@bu.edu; intadmis@bu.edu • **CEEB Code:** 3087
Fax: 617-353-9695 • **Website:** www.bu.edu • **ACT Code:** 1794

This private school was founded in 1839. It has a 132-acre campus.

RATINGS
Admissions Selectivity Rating: 95   **Fire Safety Rating:** 93   **Green Rating:** 92

STUDENTS AND FACULTY
Enrollment: 16,511. **Student Body:** 61% female, 39% male, 80% out-of-state, 22% international (106 countries represented). Asian 14%, African American 4%, Caucasian 41%, Hispanic 11%, Native American <1%, Pacific Islander <1%, Two or more races 4%, Race unknown 4%.
Retention and Graduation: 93% freshmen return for sophomore year. 81% freshmen graduate within 4 years. 87% freshmen graduate within 6 years. 10% grads go on to further study within 1 year. **Faculty:** Student/faculty ratio 12:1. 1,798 full-time faculty, 90% hold PhDs, 14% are are members of minority groups, 42% are women. 6% of classes are taught by teaching assistants.

ACADEMICS
Degrees: bachelor's, certificate, doctoral/professional, doctoral/research, master's, postbachelor's certifiate, post-master's certificate. **Classes:** Most classes have 10-19 students. Most lab/discussion sessions have 20-29 students. **Most popular majors:** Business Administration and Management; Communication; Psychology. **Special Study Options:** Accelerated program, cooperative education program, cross-registration, distance learning, double major, dual enrollment, English as a Second Language (ESL), honors program, independent study, internships, liberal arts/career combination, student-designed major, study abroad, teacher certification program, weekend college, Field study in Marine Science at the Woods Hole Institute and in Environmental/Ecological Science in Ecuador at the Biodiversity Station in the tropical rain forest. The Photonics Center. **Honors Programs:** Honors Programs are offered in the College of Arts and Sciences and the School of Management Combined degree programs: BA/MD, BA/MA, BA/DMD, BS/MS, BA/MD,BS/MSOT,BS/DPT,BA/BS,BS/MS,BS/PhD,MS/MD,MS/MB. **Disability Services:** Special programs offered to physically disabled students, including note-taking services, reader services, tape recorders, tutors. **Career Services:** Career/job search classes, Career assessment, Internships. The Boston University Center for Career Development offers two Funded Internship Programs: the Santander Sophomore Internship Program and the

Yawkey Nonprofit Internship Program. These selective programs are designed to expand opportunities for BU students to engage in meaningful workplace experiences through qualified unpaid internships at nonprofits, NGOs, government agencies, and small/medium-sized entrepreneurial organizations. The programs enable students to access these opportunities by providing living allowance stipends. In addition, the programs' required components and educational framework help students to plan for, engage in, and reflect upon their internships.

FACILITIES
Housing: Coed dorms, special housing for disabled students, women's dorms, apartments for married students, cooperative housing, apartments for single students, Specialty dorms/floors for groups of students with a common interest or academic major. 95% of campus accessible to physically diasbled. **Special Academic Facilities/Equipment:** Center for Computational Science, Center for Advanced Biotechnology, Center for Photonics Research, art galleries, planetarium, commercial TV station, National Public Radio station, 20th century archives, professional theatre and theatre company, Center for Remote Sensing, Geddes Language Labratory, speech, language and hearing clinic, Culinary Center, Metcalf Center for Science and Engineering, Tsai Performance Center, and College of Communication Multimedia Lab. **Computers:** Students can register for classes online. Administrative functions (other than registration) can be performed online.

CAMPUS LIFE
Environment: Metropolis. **Activities:** Choral groups, concert band, dance, drama/theater, jazz band, literary magazine, marching band, music ensembles, musical theater, opera, radio station, student government, student newspaper, student-run film society, symphony orchestra, yearbook, Student Organization. 400 registered organizations, 11 honor societies, 26 religious organizations. 9 fraternities, 9 sororities. **Athletics (Intercollegiate):** *Men:* basketball, crew/rowing, cross-country, diving, golf, ice hockey, soccer, swimming, tennis, track/field (outdoor), track/field (indoor), wrestling. *Women:* basketball, crew/rowing, cross-country, diving, field hockey, golf, ice hockey, lacrosse, soccer, softball, swimming, tennis, track/field (outdoor), track/field (indoor). **On-Campus Highlights:** Marsh Chapel Plaza, Mugar Memorial Library, special collections, DeWolfe Boathouse, George Sherman Student Union, The Photonics Center. **Environmental Initiatives:** Energy Efficiency Retrofits http://www.bu.edu/facilities/what-we-do/energy/

ADMISSIONS
Freshman Academic Profile: Average high school GPA 3.6. 63% in top 10% of high school class, 91% in top 25% of high school class, 99% in top 50% of high school class. 64% from public high schools. **Reported SAT (pre-2016 redesign) scores:** SAT Math middle 50% range 630-740. SAT Critical Reading middle 50% range 590-680. SAT Writing middle 50% range 610-700. **Concordant SAT scores:** SAT EBRW middle 50% 650–730. SAT Math middle 50% range 650–760. ACT middle 50% range 28-32. **Basis for Candidate Selection:** *Very important factors considered include:* rigor of secondary school record. *Important factors considered include:* class rank, academic GPA, standardized test scores, application essay, recommendation(s), level of applicant's interest. *Other factors considered include:* extracurricular activities, character/personal qualities, first generation, alumni/ae relation, geographical residence, state residency, racial/ethnic status, volunteer work, work experience. **Freshman Admission Requirements:** High school diploma is required and GED is accepted. *Academic units required:* 4 English, 3 math, 3 science, 3 science labs, 2 foreign language, 3 social studies, 3 history. *Academic units recommended:* 4 English, 4 math, 4 science, 4 science labs, 4 foreign language, 4 social studies, 4 history. **Freshman Admission Statistics:** 57,441 applied, 29.43% admitted, 21% enrolled. **Transfer Admission Requirements:** High school transcript, college transcript(s), essay or personal statement, standardized test scores, statement of good standing from prior institution(s). Minimum college GPA of 3.5 required. Lowest grade transferable C. **General Admission Information:** Application fee $80. Priority deadline 11/1. Regular application deadline 1/3. Regular notification 4/1. Nonfall registration accepted. Admission may be deferred for a maximum of 1 year.

COSTS AND FINANCIAL AID
Annual tuition $49,176. Room and board $14,870. Required fees $1,064. Average book expense $1,000. **Required Forms and Deadlines:** FAFSA, CSS/Financial Aid PROFILE, Noncustodial PROFILE. **Notification of Awards:** Applicants will be notified of awards on a rolling basis beginning 4/1. **Types of Aid:** *Need-based scholarships/grants:* Federal Pell, FSEOG, State scholarships/grants, Private scholarships, College/university scholarship or grant aid from institutional funds. *Loans:* Direct Subsidized Stafford Loans, Direct Unsubsidized Stafford Loans, Direct PLUS loans, Federal Perkins Loans, State Loans. *Student Employment:* Federal Work-Study Program available. Institutional employment available. **Financial Aid Statistics:** 100% needy freshmen, 99% needy undergrads receive need-based scholarship or grant aid. 11% freshmen, 7% undergrads receive non-need-based scholarship or grant aid. 88% freshmen, 89% undergrads receive need-based self-help aid. 2% freshmen, 2% undergrads receive athletic scholarships. 54% freshmen, 54% undergrads

receive any aid. 51% undergrads borrow to pay for school. Average cumulative indebtedness $41,098. **Criteria for awarding aid:** *Need-based:* Academics, Alumni affiliation, Art, Leadership, Minority status, Music/drama, Religious affiliation. *Non-need-based:* Academics, Alumni affiliation, Art, Athletics, Leadership, Music/drama, Religious affiliation, State/district residency.

See page 924.

BOWDOIN COLLEGE

5000 College Station, Brunswick, ME 04011-8441
Phone: 207-725-3100 • **Financial Aid Phone:** 207-725-3146
E-mail: admissions@bowdoin.edu • **CEEB Code:** 3089
Fax: 207-725-3101 • **Website:** www.bowdoin.edu • **ACT Code:** 1636

This private school was founded in 1794. It has a 205-acre campus.

RATINGS

Admissions Selectivity Rating: 97   **Fire Safety Rating:** 95   **Green Rating:** 91

STUDENTS AND FACULTY

Enrollment: 1,799. **Student Body:** 50% female, 50% male, 90% out-of-state, 5% international (32 countries represented). Asian 6%, African American 6%, Caucasian 64%, Hispanic 11%, Native American <1%, Pacific Islander <1%, Two or more races 7%, Race unknown <1%.
Retention and Graduation: 94% freshmen return for sophomore year. 89% freshmen graduate within 4 years. 94% freshmen graduate within 6 years. 19% grads go on to further study within 1 year. 12% grads pursue arts and sciences degrees. 1% grads pursue law degrees. 1% grads pursue business degrees. 3% grads pursue medical degrees. **Faculty:** Student/faculty ratio 9:1. 195 full-time faculty, 100% hold PhDs, 14% are are members of minority groups, 51% are women. 0% of classes are taught by teaching assistants.

ACADEMICS

Degrees: bachelor's. **Classes:** Most classes have 10-19 students. Most lab/discussion sessions have 10-19 students. **Most popular majors:** Political Science and Government; Economics; Mathematics. **Special Study Options:** Accelerated program, double major, exchange student program (domestic), independent study, liberal arts/career combination, student-designed major, study abroad, teacher certification program, 3-2 or 4-2 Engineering Degree Programs with Dartmouth College, California Institute of Technology, Columbia University and the University of Maine; and 3-3 Legal Studies Degree Program with Columbia University Law School. Pass/Fail grading options are available. Combined degree programs: BA/JD, BA/MEng, 3-3 Law—Columbia University Law. **Disability Services:** Special programs offered to physically disabled students, including note-taking services, reader services, tape recorders, tutors. **Career Services:** Alumni network, Alumni services, Career/job search classes, Career assessment, Internships, Regional alumni. Through the generosity of alumni and parent donors, competitive grants are available to support unpaid internship experiences. Many of these internships serve the needs of underserved and disadvantaged populations.

FACILITIES

Housing: Coed dorms, special housing for disabled students, apartments for single students, Wellness Housing, Three small college houses and 8 college house system houses. 72% of campus accessible to physically diasbled. **Special Academic Facilities/Equipment:** Art Museum; Arctic Museum; Arctic Studies Center; coastal marine biology and ornithology research facility on Orr's Island; scientific station on Kent Island; black box theater; Pickard Theater; Baldwin Center for Learning and Teaching; Outdoor Leadership Center; Visual Arts Center; Crafts Center; 8 specialized libraries, including the Language Media Center; Coleman Farm; Quantitative Skills Program; The Writing Project; Gibson Hall of Music; Recital Hall; Educational Technology Center; Environmental Studies Center; Russwurm African-American Center; Women's Resource Center; Off-Campus Study Office; Office of Health Professions Advising; Pre-Law Advising Office; Career Planning Center; Community Service Resource Center; Electronic Classroom; Recording Studio; and a state-of-the-art science facility. **Computers:** 100% of classrooms, 100% of dorms, 100% of libraries, 100% of dining areas, 100% of student union, 100% of common outdoor areas have wireless network access. Administrative functions (other than registration) can be performed online.

CAMPUS LIFE

Environment: Village. **Activities:** Choral groups, concert band, dance, drama/theater, jazz band, literary magazine, music ensembles, musical theater, radio station, student government, student newspaper, student-run film society, symphony orchestra, television station, yearbook, Student Organization. 109 registered organizations, 1 honor society, 4 religious organizations. **Athletics (Intercollegiate): Men:** baseball, basketball, cross-country, diving, football, golf, ice hockey, lacrosse, sailing, skiing (nordic/cross-country), soccer, squash, swimming, tennis, track/field (outdoor), track/field (indoor). *Women:* basketball, cross-country, diving, field hockey, golf, ice hockey, lacrosse, rugby, sailing, skiing (nordic/cross-country), soccer, softball, squash, swimming, tennis, track/field (outdoor), track/field (indoor), volleyball. **On-Campus Highlights:** Bowdoin College Museum of Art, Druckenmiller Science Building, Studzinski Recital Hall, Schwartz Outdoor Leadership Center, Wish / Pickard Theater, Peary MacMillan Arctic Museum; Visual Arts Center and McLellan art studios; Hawthorne-Longfellow Library; Smith Student Union; Thorne Dining Hall; top of Coles Tower (for birds-eye view); athletic facilities and playing fields/trails; walk the Bowdoin Quad and the Bowdoin Pines. **Environmental Initiatives:** Bowdoin has committed to becoming a carbon-neutral campus by 2020 and provided a detailed Climate Action Plan to help achieve the goal. As part of this plan, Bowdoin installed a co-generation system at its campus steam plant, along with a 1,920-square-foot solar hot water system, and most recently Bowdoin installed a 1.2 megawatt solar power complex that went live in fall 2014 and includes approximately 4,420 solar panels roof mounted on three major athletic buildings, along with a 654-kW ground-mount installation on three acres owned by the college at the former Naval Air Station Brunswick. The Co-Gen system produced 1,076,000 kWhs or roughly 6% of Bowdoin electricity in FY12-13, its first full year of operation. It is anticipated that the new solar PV system will produce roughly 8% of Bowdoin annual electricity usage in its first full year of operation.

ADMISSIONS

Freshman Academic Profile: 80% in top 10% of high school class, 97% in top 25% of high school class, 100% in top 50% of high school class. 48% from public high schools. **Reported SAT (pre-2016 redesign) scores:** SAT Math middle 50% range 640-760. SAT Critical Reading middle 50% range 650-750. SAT Writing middle 50% range 650-760. **Concordant SAT scores:** SAT EBRW middle 50% 700–770. SAT Math middle 50% range 660–780. ACT middle 50% range 30-34. Minimum internet-based TOEFL 100. Minimum paper TOEFL 600. **Basis for Candidate Selection:** *Very important factors considered include:* rigor of secondary school record, class rank, academic GPA, application essay, recommendation(s), extracurricular activities, talent/ability, character/personal qualities. *Important factors considered include:* standardized test scores, first generation, alumni/ae relation. *Other factors considered include:* interview, geographical residence, state residency, racial/ethnic status. **Freshman Admission Requirements:** High school diploma is required and GED is not accepted. *Academic units recommended:* 4 English, 4 math, 4 science, 3 science labs, 4 foreign language, 4 social studies. **Freshman Admission Statistics:** 6,799 applied, 14.84% admitted, 50% enrolled. **Transfer Admission Requirements:** High school transcript, college transcript(s), essay or personal statement, statement of good standing from prior institution(s). Minimum college GPA of 3.0 required. Lowest grade transferable C-. **General Admission Information:** Application fee $60. Regular application deadline 1/1. Regular notification 4/5. Nonfall registration not accepted. Admission may be deferred for a maximum of 12 months.

COSTS AND FINANCIAL AID

Annual tuition $49,416. Room and board $13,600. Required fees $484. Average book expense $840. **Required Forms and Deadlines:** FAFSA, CSS/Financial Aid PROFILE, Noncustodial PROFILE, Business/Farm Supplement. **Notification of Awards:** Applicants will be notified of awards on or about 4/5. **Types of Aid:** *Need-based scholarships/grants:* Federal Pell, FSEOG, State scholarships/grants, Private scholarships, College/university scholarship or grant aid from institutional funds. *Loans:* Direct Subsidized Stafford Loans, Direct Unsubsidized Stafford Loans, Federal Perkins Loans, State Loans. *Student Employment:* Federal Work-Study Program available. Institutional employment available. **Financial Aid Statistics:** 100% needy freshmen, 100% needy undergrads receive need-based scholarship or grant aid. 0% undergrads receive non-need-based scholarship or grant aid. 95% freshmen, 96% undergrads receive need-based self-help aid. 0% freshmen, 0% undergrads receive athletic scholarships. 49% freshmen, 48% undergrads receive any aid. 27% undergrads borrow to pay for school. Average cumulative indebtedness $23,120. **Criteria for awarding aid:** *Non-need-based:* Academics, Leadership.

BOWLING GREEN STATE UNIVERSITY

110 McFall Center, Bowling Green, OH 43403-0085
Phone: 419-372-BGSU • **Financial Aid Phone:** 419-372-2651
E-mail: choosebgsu@bgsu.edu • **CEEB Code:** 1069
Fax: 419-372-6955 • **Website:** http://www.bgsu.edu • **ACT Code:** 3240

This public school was founded in 1910. It has a 1250-acre campus.

RATINGS

Admissions Selectivity Rating: 78 **Fire Safety Rating:** 91 **Green Rating:** 95

STUDENTS AND FACULTY

Enrollment: 13,901. **Student Body:** 57% female, 43% male, 12% out-of-state, 2% international (42 countries represented). Asian 1%, African American 10%, Caucasian 78%, Hispanic 4%, Native American <1%, Pacific Islander <1%, Two or more races 3%, Race unknown 2%.
Retention and Graduation: 78% freshmen return for sophomore year. 34% freshmen graduate within 4 years. 56% freshmen graduate within 6 years.
Faculty: Student/faculty ratio 19:1. 679 full-time faculty, 81% hold PhDs, 13% are are members of minority groups, 48% are women.

ACADEMICS

Degrees: bachelor's, doctoral, master's, postbachelor's certificate, post-master's certificate. **Classes:** Most classes have 20-29 students. **Most popular majors:** Biology/Biological Sciences; Education/Teaching of Individuals in Early Childhood Special Education Programs; Teacher Education, Multiple Levels. **Special Study Options:** Accelerated program, cooperative education program, cross-registration, distance learning, double major, dual enrollment, English as a Second Language (ESL), exchange student program (domestic), honors program, independent study, internships, liberal arts/career combination, student-designed major, study abroad, teacher certification program. **Honors Programs:** http://www.bgsu.edu/offices/honors/. **Disability Services:** Special programs offered to physically disabled students, including note-taking services, reader services, tape recorders, tutors. **Career Services:** Alumni network, Alumni services, Career/job search classes, Career assessment, Internships, Regional alumni.

FACILITIES

Housing: Coed dorms, fraternity/sorority housing, Wellness Housing, Theme Housing, residental learning communities (including Wellness Community), no-alcohol wings. **Special Academic Facilities/Equipment:** http://go2.bgsu.edu/choose/campus/tour/ http://www.bgsu.edu/map/buildings/ **Computers:** 99% of classrooms, 64% of dorms, 100% of libraries, 100% of dining areas, 100% of student union, 40% of common outdoor areas have wireless network access. Students can register for classes online. Administrative functions (other than registration) can be performed online.

CAMPUS LIFE

Environment: Town. **Activities:** Choral groups, concert band, dance, drama/theater, jazz band, literary magazine, marching band, music ensembles, musical theater, radio station, student government, student newspaper, student-run film society, symphony orchestra, television station, yearbook, Student Organization. 20 honor societies, 24 fraternities, 19 sororities. **Athletics (Intercollegiate):** *Men:* baseball, basketball, cross-country, football, golf, ice hockey, soccer. *Women:* basketball, cross-country, golf, gymnastics, soccer, softball, swimming, tennis, track/field (outdoor), track/field (indoor), volleyball. **On-Campus Highlights:** Bowen Thompson Student Union, Jerome Library, McFall Center, College of Business Administration, Residence Halls, http://go2.bgsu.edu/choose/campus/tour/. **Environmental Initiatives:** Completion of the Climate Action Plan by the ACUPCC Working Group, under the leadership of the Office of Campus Sustainability in 2013-14.

ADMISSIONS

Freshman Academic Profile: Average high school GPA 3.3. 12% in top 10% of high school class, 36% in top 25% of high school class, 71% in top 50% of high school class. 89% from public high schools. **Reported SAT (pre-2016 redesign) scores:** SAT Math middle 50% range 460-580. SAT Critical Reading middle 50% range 460-580. SAT Writing middle 50% range 420-550. **Concordant SAT scores:** SAT EBRW middle 50% range 490–620. SAT Math middle 50% range 500–600. ACT middle 50% range 20-25. Minimum internet-based TOEFL 71. Minimum paper TOEFL 530. **Basis for Candidate Selection:** *Very important factors considered include:* rigor of secondary school record, academic GPA, standardized test scores. *Important factors considered include:* class rank, talent/ability. *Other factors considered include:* application essay, recommendation(s), interview, extracurricular activities, character/personal qualities, first generation, alumni/ae relation, racial/ethnic status, volunteer work, work experience, level of applicant's interest. **Freshman Admission Requirements:** High school diploma is required and GED is accepted. *Academic units recommended:* 4 English, 3 math, 3 science, 2 science labs, 2 foreign language, 3 social studies, 1 visual/performing arts. **Freshman**

Admission Statistics: 14,887 applied, 75.50% admitted, 30% enrolled. Minimum college GPA of 2.5 required. Lowest grade transferable C. **General Admission Information:** Application fee $45. Priority deadline 2/1. Regular application deadline 7/15. Nonfall registration accepted. Admission may be deferred.

COSTS AND FINANCIAL AID

Annual in-state tuition $9,096. Annual out-of-state tuition $16,632. Required fees $1,700. Average book expense $1,020. **Required Forms and Deadlines:** FAFSA. **Notification of Awards:** Applicants will be notified of awards on a rolling basis beginning 4/15. *Student Employment:* Federal Work-Study Program available. Institutional employment available. **Financial Aid Statistics:** 90% needy freshmen, 82% needy undergrads receive need-based scholarship or grant aid. 10% freshmen, 8% undergrads receive non-need-based scholarship or grant aid. 80% freshmen, 85% undergrads receive need-based self-help aid. 3% freshmen, 3% undergrads receive athletic scholarships. 95% freshmen, 87% undergrads receive any aid. 78% undergrads borrow to pay for school. Average cumulative indebtedness $31,746. **Criteria for awarding aid:** *Need-based:* Academics, Minority status. *Non-need-based:* Academics, Alumni affiliation, Art, Athletics, Leadership, Minority status, Music/drama, State/district residency.

BRADLEY UNIVERSITY

1501 W. Bradley Avenue, Peoria, IL 61625
Phone: 309-677-1000 • **Financial Aid Phone:** 309-677-3089
E-mail: admissions@bradley.edu • **CEEB Code:** 1070
Fax: 309-677-2797 • **Website:** www.bradley.edu • **ACT Code:** 960

This private school was founded in 1897. It has a 85-acre campus.

RATINGS

Admissions Selectivity Rating: 84 **Fire Safety Rating:** 91 **Green Rating:** 71

STUDENTS AND FACULTY

Enrollment: 4,464. **Student Body:** 51% female, 49% male, 17% out-of-state, 1% international (33 countries represented). Asian 3%, African American 5%, Caucasian 57%, Hispanic 7%, Native American <1%, Pacific Islander <1%, Two or more races 2%, Race unknown 25%.
Retention and Graduation: 87% freshmen return for sophomore year. 54% freshmen graduate within 4 years. 74% freshmen graduate within 6 years. 19% grads go on to further study within 1 year. 15% grads pursue arts and sciences degrees. 1% grads pursue medical degrees. **Faculty:** Student/faculty ratio 12:1. 345 full-time faculty, 83% hold PhDs, 19% are are members of minority groups, 41% are women. 0% of classes are taught by teaching assistants.

ACADEMICS

Degrees: bachelor's, master's, postbachelor's certificate, post-master's certificate. **Classes:** Most classes have 10-19 students. **Most popular majors:** Business, Management, Marketing, and Related Support Services; Engineering; Health Professions and Related Clinical Sciences. **Special Study Options:** Accelerated program, cooperative education program, distance learning, double major, honors program, independent study, internships, liberal arts/career combination, student-designed major, study abroad, teacher certification program, Limited distance learning courses available. Collaborative classes with other institutions taught through Internet2. **Honors Programs:** The Honors Program is structured so that students majoring in any department are eligible to participate. The programs builds progressively through a student's four years, beginning with special honors sections of General Education courses and leading to interdisciplinary seminars and possibilities for independent research. Combined degree programs: BS/MSA, BSN/MSN, BS/MS-FIN, BS/MS-BIO, BS/MS-CHEM. **Disability Services:** Special programs offered to physically disabled students, including tutors. **Career Services:** Alumni network, Alumni services, Career/job search classes, Career assessment, Internships, Regional alumni. Bradley's Springer Center for Internships provides opportunities for students to gain career-related experience, encourages more student participation in the cooperative education and internship programs, increases awareness of international internship opportunities, enhances activities that assist students in conducting their job searches and prepares students for on-the-job success, as well as provides continuous evaluation and improvement of the cooperative education and internship program policies and procedures.

FACILITIES

Housing: Coed dorms, fraternity/sorority housing, apartments for single students, Wellness Housing, Service and leadership floor. 75% of campus accessible to physically diasbled. **Special Academic Facilities/Equipment:** Caterpillar Global Communication Center, two art galleries on campus. **Computers:** 95% of classrooms, 5% of dorms, 100% of libraries, 80% of dining areas, 100% of student union, 30% of common outdoor areas have wireless network access. Students can register for classes online. Administrative functions (other than registration) can be performed online.

CAMPUS LIFE

Environment: City. **Activities:** Choral groups, concert band, dance, drama/theater, jazz band, literary magazine, music ensembles, musical theater, pep band, radio station, student government, student newspaper, student-run film society, symphony orchestra, television station, yearbook, Campus Ministries, Student Organization, Model UN. 220 registered organizations, 31 honor societies, 17 religious organizations. 16 fraternities, 11 sororities. **Athletics (Intercollegiate):** *Men:* baseball, basketball, cross-country, golf, soccer, tennis. *Women:* basketball, cross-country, golf, softball, tennis, track/field (outdoor), track/field (indoor), volleyball. **On-Campus Highlights:** Markin Family Student Recreation Center, Caterpillar Global Communications Center, Olin Hall of Science, Michel Student Center, Cullom-Davis Library, Bradley's 85-acre campus, is the heart of a residential neighborhood just 1 mile from downtown. Peoria is the largest metropolitan area in Illinois south of Chicago.

ADMISSIONS

Freshman Academic Profile: Average high school GPA 3.7. 27% in top 10% of high school class, 61% in top 25% of high school class, 90% in top 50% of high school class. 82% from public high schools. **Reported SAT (pre-2016 redesign) scores:** SAT Math middle 50% range 480-620. SAT Critical Reading middle 50% range 480-620. SAT Writing middle 50% range 470-580. **Concordant SAT scores:** SAT EBRW middle 50% 530–650. SAT Math middle 50% range 510–640. ACT middle 50% range 22-28. Minimum internet-based TOEFL 79. Minimum paper TOEFL 550. **Basis for Candidate Selection:** *Very important factors considered include:* rigor of secondary school record, academic GPA. *Important factors considered include:* class rank, standardized test scores. *Other factors considered include:* application essay, recommendation(s), interview, extracurricular activities, talent/ability, character/personal qualities, first generation, alumni/ae relation, geographical residence, racial/ethnic status, volunteer work, work experience, level of applicant's interest. **Freshman Admission Requirements:** High school diploma is required and GED is accepted. *Academic units required:* 4 English, 3 math, 2 science, 2 science labs, 2 social studies. *Academic units recommended:* 5 English, 4 math, 3 science, 3 science labs, 2 foreign language, 3 social studies, 2 history. **Freshman Admission Statistics:** 9,786 applied, 69.81% admitted, 16% enrolled. **Transfer Admission Requirements:** college transcript(s), statement of good standing from prior institution(s). Minimum college GPA of 2.0 required. Lowest grade transferable C. **General Admission Information:** Application fee $35. Priority deadline 2/1. Nonfall registration accepted. Admission may be deferred for a maximum of 12 months.

COSTS AND FINANCIAL AID

Annual tuition $31,740. Room and board $10,010. Required fees $380. Average book expense $1,200. **Required Forms and Deadlines:** FAFSA. **Notification of Awards:** Applicants will be notified of awards on a rolling basis beginning 3/1. **Types of Aid:** *Need-based scholarships/grants:* Federal Pell, FSEOG, State scholarships/grants, Private scholarships, College/university scholarship or grant aid from institutional funds. *Loans:* Direct Subsidized Stafford Loans, Direct Unsubsidized Stafford Loans, Direct PLUS loans, Federal Perkins Loans, Federal Nursing Loans. *Student Employment:* Federal Work-Study Program available. Institutional employment available. **Financial Aid Statistics:** 99% needy freshmen, 96% needy undergrads receive need-based scholarship or grant aid. 14% freshmen, 11% undergrads receive non-need-based scholarship or grant aid. 77% freshmen, 81% undergrads receive need-based self-help aid. 4% freshmen, 3% undergrads receive athletic scholarships. 95% freshmen, 88% undergrads receive any aid. **Criteria for awarding aid:** *Need-based:* Academics. *Non-need-based:* Academics, Alumni affiliation, Art, Athletics, Leadership, Minority status, Music/drama.

BRANDEIS UNIVERSITY

415 South St., Waltham, MA 02454-9110
Phone: 781-736-3500 • **Financial Aid Phone:** 781-736-3700
E-mail: admissions@brandeis.edu • **CEEB Code:** 3092
Fax: 781-736-3536 • **Website:** http://www.brandeis.edu/ • **ACT Code:** 1802

This private school was founded in 1948. It has a 235-acre campus.

RATINGS

Admissions Selectivity Rating: 96   **Fire Safety Rating:** 97   **Green Rating:** 85

STUDENTS AND FACULTY

Enrollment: 3,597. **Student Body:** 58% female, 42% male, 72% out-of-state, 21% international (54 countries represented). Asian 13%, African American 5%, Caucasian 46%, Hispanic 8%, Native American <1%, Pacific Islander <1%, Two or more races 3%, Race unknown 4%.

Retention and Graduation: 93% freshmen return for sophomore year. 83% freshmen graduate within 4 years. 90% freshmen graduate within 6 years. 20% grads go on to further study within 1 year. 11% grads pursue arts and sciences degrees. 1% grads pursue business degrees. **Faculty:** Student/faculty ratio 10:1. 360 full-time faculty, 95% hold PhDs, 13% are are members of minority groups, 43% are women.

ACADEMICS

Degrees: bachelor's, doctoral, master's, postbachelor's certifiate, post-master's certificate. **Classes:** Most classes have 10-19 students. **Most popular majors:** Biology/Biological Sciences; Economics; Psychology. **Special Study Options:** cross-registration, double major, independent study, internships, student-designed major, study abroad. Combined degree programs: BA/MA, Early admission to Mt. Sinai;Tufts medical schools. **Disability Services:** Special programs offered to physically disabled students, including note-taking services, tape recorders. **Career Services:** Alumni network, Alumni services, Career/job search classes, Career assessment, Internships, Regional alumni. Brandeis University offers students and faculty a wide range of hands-on learning and teaching opportunities including: independent research, experiential learning courses, internships, community-engaged projects, studio and art work and study abroad programs. The Experiential Learning program was developed to expand on some of the vibrant aspects of the Brandeis mission, particularly preparing students to fully participate in a changing society. In addition to academic experiential learning, Brandeis has an array of not-for-credit opportunities for student leadership and volunteer projects which encompass the learning by doing. Many projects take students beyond campus by partnering with community groups, or conducting research at a museum in Boston, or serving as an intern for a semester, or through study abroad.

FACILITIES

Housing: Coed dorms, men's dorms, women's dorms, apartments for single students, Thematic Learning Communities. 78% of campus accessible to physically diasbled. **Special Academic Facilities/Equipment:** Art museum, multicultural library, intercultural center, theater arts complex, language lab, spatial orientation lab, research centers on aging, basic medical sciences, complex systems, family/children's policy, health policy, mental retardation, public policy, study of European Jewry, student leadership Development Room. **Computers:** 100% of classrooms, 100% of dorms, 100% of libraries, 100% of dining areas, 100% of student union, 100% of common outdoor areas have wireless network access. Students can register for classes online. Administrative functions (other than registration) can be performed online.

CAMPUS LIFE

Environment: City. **Activities:** Choral groups, concert band, dance, drama/theater, jazz band, literary magazine, music ensembles, musical theater, radio station, student government, student newspaper, student-run film society, symphony orchestra, television station, yearbook, Campus Ministries, Student Organization. 253 registered organizations, 4 honor societies, 19 religious organizations. **Athletics (Intercollegiate):** *Men:* baseball, basketball, cross-country, diving, fencing, soccer, tennis, track/field (outdoor), track/field (indoor), wrestling. *Women:* basketball, cheerleading, cross-country, diving, fencing, soccer, softball, tennis, track/field (outdoor), track/field (indoor), volleyball, wrestling. **On-Campus Highlights:** Shapiro Science Center, Spingold Theater, Usen Castle, Shapiro Campus Center, Rapaporte Treasure Hall. **Environmental Initiatives:** The Brandeis University Climate Action Plan was completed in Fall of 2009. This plan sets aggressive goals for future energy and climate impact reductions. Brandeis has invested significantly since 2005 in energy reduction efforts- realizing an over 10% drop in campus energy use. The

Climate Action Plan builds on these past successes to further reduce cost and environmental impact.

ADMISSIONS

Freshman Academic Profile: Average high school GPA 3.9. 72% in top 10% of high school class, 95% in top 25% of high school class, 100% in top 50% of high school class. 62% from public high schools. **Reported SAT (pre-2016 redesign) scores:** SAT Math middle 50% range 660-770. SAT Critical Reading middle 50% range 610-710. SAT Writing middle 50% range 640-720. **Concordant SAT scores:** SAT EBRW middle 50% 680–740. SAT Math middle 50% range 690–780. ACT middle 50% range 29-33. Minimum internet-based TOEFL 100. Minimum paper TOEFL 600. **Basis for Candidate Selection:** *Very important factors considered include:* rigor of secondary school record, class rank, academic GPA, character/personal qualities. *Important factors considered include:* application essay, recommendation(s), extracurricular activities, talent/ability, volunteer work, work experience, level of applicant's interest. *Other factors considered include:* standardized test scores, interview, first generation, alumni/ae relation, geographical residence, state residency, racial/ethnic status. **Freshman Admission Requirements:** High school diploma is required and GED is accepted. *Academic units recommended:* 4 English, 4 math, 4 science, 2 science labs, 4 foreign language, 4 social studies. **Freshman Admission Statistics:** 11,351 applied, 33.44% admitted, 22% enrolled. **Transfer Admission Requirements:** High school transcript, college transcript(s), essay or personal statement, standardized test scores, statement of good standing from prior institution(s). Minimum college GPA of 3.20 required. Lowest grade transferable C-. **General Admission Information:** Application fee $75. Regular application deadline 1/1. Regular notification 4/1. Nonfall registration accepted. Admission may be deferred for a maximum of 1 year.

COSTS AND FINANCIAL AID

Annual tuition $49,586. Room and board $14,380. Required fees $1,659. Average book expense $1,000. **Required Forms and Deadlines:** FAFSA, CSS/Financial Aid PROFILE, Noncustodial PROFILE. **Notification of Awards:** Applicants will be notified of awards on or about 4/1. **Types of Aid:** *Need-based scholarships/grants:* Federal Pell, FSEOG, State scholarships/grants, Private scholarships, College/university scholarship or grant aid from institutional funds. *Loans:* Direct Subsidized Stafford Loans, Direct Unsubsidized Stafford Loans, Direct PLUS loans, Federal Perkins Loans, State Loans, College/university loans from institutional funds. *Student Employment:* Federal Work-Study Program available. Institutional employment available. **Financial Aid Statistics:** 97% needy freshmen, 94% needy undergrads receive need-based scholarship or grant aid. 7% freshmen, 5% undergrads receive non-need-based scholarship or grant aid. 88% freshmen, 93% undergrads receive need-based self-help aid. 0% freshmen, 0% undergrads receive athletic scholarships. 63% freshmen, 65% undergrads receive any aid. 55% undergrads borrow to pay for school. Average cumulative indebtedness $32,922. **Criteria for awarding aid:** *Non-need-based:* Academics.

BRENAU UNIVERSITY

500 Washington St SE, Gainesville, GA 30501
Phone: 770-534-6100 • **Financial Aid Phone:** 770-534-6152
E-mail: admissions@brenau.edu • **CEEB Code:** 5066
Fax: 770-538-4306 • **Website:** www.brenau.edu • **ACT Code:** 800

This private school was founded in 1878. It has a 56-acre campus.

RATINGS

Admissions Selectivity Rating: 78   **Fire Safety Rating:** 98   **Green Rating:** 60*

STUDENTS AND FACULTY

Enrollment: 1,638. **Student Body:** 90% female, 10% male, 5% out-of-state, 3% international. Asian 2%, African American 33%, Caucasian 48%, Hispanic 9%, Native American <1%, Pacific Islander <1%, Two or more races 3%, Race unknown 2%. **Retention and Graduation:** 71% freshmen return for sophomore year. 37% freshmen graduate within 4 years. 43 **Faculty:** Student/faculty ratio 10:1. 122 full-time faculty, 80% hold PhDs, 16% are are members of minority groups, 73% are women. 0% of classes are taught by teaching assistants.

ACADEMICS

Degrees: associate, bachelor's, doctoral/professional, master's. **Classes:** Most classes have 10-19 students. Most lab/discussion sessions have 10-19 students. **Most popular majors:** Nursing Practice; Health Services/Allied Health/Health Sciences; Business/Commerce. **Special Study Options:** cross-registration, distance learning, double major, dual enrollment, English as a Second Language (ESL), honors program, independent study, internships, student-designed major, study abroad, teacher certification program, weekend college. **Honors Programs:** The Honors Program at the Women's College of Brenau University

begins in the freshman year and is followed throughout the student's entire college career at Brenau. Special classes reserved for honors students are taught in an enriched manner, affording these students an approach to their general education courses which enables them to study these subjects at an advanced level. Combined degree programs: BS/MS in Occupational Therapy. **Disability Services:** Special programs offered to physically disabled students, including note-taking services, tape recorders, tutors. **Career Services:** Alumni network, Alumni services, Career/job search classes, Career assessment, Internships.

FACILITIES

Housing: special housing for disabled students, special housing for international students, women's dorms, fraternity/sorority housing, cooperative housing, apartments for single students. 90% of campus accessible to physically diasbled. **Special Academic Facilities/Equipment:** Simmons Art Gallery, Wages House, Whitepath House, Natatorium Physical Fitness Center, Leo Castelli Art Gallery **Computers:** Students can register for classes online. Administrative functions (other than registration) can be performed online.

CAMPUS LIFE

Environment: Town. **Activities:** Choral groups, dance, drama/theater, literary magazine, music ensembles, musical theater, radio station, student government, student newspaper, television station, yearbook, Campus Ministries, Student Organization. 54 registered organizations, 12 honor societies, 2 religious organizations. 8 sororities. **Athletics (Intercollegiate):** *Women:* basketball, cross-country, soccer, softball, swimming, tennis, volleyball. **On-Campus Highlights:** Pearce Auditorium, Burd Center for Performing Arts, Fitness Center, Dining Hall and Tea Room, Northeast Georgia History Center.

ADMISSIONS

Reported SAT (pre-2016 redesign) scores: SAT Math middle 50% range 420-500. SAT Critical Reading middle 50% range 450-540. **Concordant SAT scores:** SAT Math middle 50% range 460–530. ACT middle 50% range 19-24. Minimum internet-based TOEFL 61. Minimum paper TOEFL 500. **Basis for Candidate Selection:** *Very important factors considered include:* academic GPA. *Important factors considered include:* rigor of secondary school record, standardized test scores. *Other factors considered include:* class rank, application essay, recommendation(s), interview, extracurricular activities, talent/ability, character/personal qualities, first generation, alumni/ae relation, volunteer work, work experience. **Freshman Admission Requirements:** High school diploma is required and GED is accepted. *Academic units required:* 4 English, 4 math, 3 science, 2 foreign language, 3 social studies. **Freshman Admission Statistics:** 1,975 applied, 35.65% admitted, 30% enrolled. **Transfer Admission Requirements:** college transcript(s), Minimum college GPA of 2.0 required. Lowest grade transferable C. **General Admission Information:** Application fee $35. Priority deadline 1/15. Nonfall registration accepted. Admission may be deferred for a maximum of 1 year.

COSTS AND FINANCIAL AID

Annual tuition $25,478. Room and board $11,998. Required fees $400. Average book expense $1,300. **Required Forms and Deadlines:** FAFSA, Noncustodial PROFILE. **Notification of Awards:** Applicants will be notified of awards on a rolling basis beginning 3/1. **Types of Aid:** *Need-based scholarships/grants:* Federal Pell, FSEOG, Private scholarships, College/university scholarship or grant aid from institutional funds. *Loans:* Direct Subsidized Stafford Loans, Direct Unsubsidized Stafford Loans, Direct PLUS loans, Federal Perkins Loans, State Loans. *Student Employment:* Federal Work-Study Program available. **Financial Aid Statistics:** 99% needy freshmen, 0% needy undergrads receive need-based scholarship or grant aid. 0% undergrads receive non-need-based scholarship or grant aid. 0% freshmen, 0% undergrads receive need-based self-help aid. 0% freshmen, 0% undergrads receive athletic scholarships. **Criteria for awarding aid:** *Need-based:* Minority status. *Non-need-based:* Academics, Art, Athletics, Leadership, Music/drama.

BRESCIA UNIVERSITY

717 Frederica Street, Owensboro, KY 42301-3023
Phone: 270-686-4241 • **Financial Aid Phone:** 1-877-BRESCIA
E-mail: admissions@brescia.edu • **CEEB Code:** 1071
Fax: 270-686-4314 • **Website:** www.brescia.edu • **ACT Code:** 14980

This private school, affiliated with the Roman Catholic Church, was founded in 1950. It has a 9-acre campus.

RATINGS

Admissions Selectivity Rating: 76   **Fire Safety Rating:** 94   **Green Rating:** 60*

STUDENTS AND FACULTY

Enrollment: 958. **Student Body:** 74% female, 26% male, 29% out-of-state, 1% international (17 countries represented). Asian 0%, African American 13%,

Caucasian 69%, Hispanic 3%, Native American 1%, Pacific Islander 1%, Two or more races 0%, Race unknown 12%.
Retention and Graduation: 64% freshmen return for sophomore year.
Faculty: Student/faculty ratio 13:1. 37 full-time faculty, 70% hold PhDs, 16% are members of minority groups, 51% are women. 0% of classes are taught by teaching assistants.

ACADEMICS

Degrees: associate, bachelor's, master's, postbachelor's certificate. **Classes:** Most classes have fewer than 10 students. Most lab/discussion sessions have fewer than 10 students. **Most popular majors:** Elementary Education and Teaching; General Studies; Social Work. **Special Study Options:** Accelerated program, cross-registration, distance learning, double major, English as a Second Language (ESL), exchange student program (domestic), honors program, independent study, internships, liberal arts/career combination, student-designed major, teacher certification program, weekend college. **Disability Services:** Special programs offered to physically disabled students, including note-taking services, tape recorders, tutors. **Career Services:** Alumni services, Career/job search classes, Career assessment, Internships, On-campus interviews.

FACILITIES

Housing: Coed dorms, special housing for disabled students, men's dorms, women's dorms, apartments for single students, Theme Housing. **Special Academic Facilities/Equipment:** Art Gallery, computer labs, campus center, greenhouse, observatory,science building. **Computers:** 100% of classrooms, 100% of dorms, 100% of libraries, 100% of dining areas, 100% of common outdoor areas have wireless network access. Administrative functions (other than registration) can be performed online.

CAMPUS LIFE

Environment: City. **Activities:** Choral groups, dance, drama/theater, literary magazine, pep band, student government, student newspaper, Campus Ministries, Student Organization. 22 registered organizations, 3 honor societies, 2 religious organizations. **Athletics (Intercollegiate):** *Men:* baseball, basketball, cross-country, golf, soccer, tennis, track/field (outdoor). *Women:* basketball, cross-country, golf, soccer, softball, tennis, track/field (outdoor), volleyball. **Environmental Initiatives:** Recycling.

ADMISSIONS

Freshman Academic Profile: Average high school GPA 3.3. 61% from public high schools. **Reported SAT (pre-2016 redesign) scores:** SAT Math middle 50% range 400-580. SAT Critical Reading middle 50% range 440-480. **Concordant SAT scores:** SAT Math middle 50% range 440–600. ACT middle 50% range 20-25. Minimum paper TOEFL 550. **Basis for Candidate Selection:** *Very important factors considered include:* academic GPA, standardized test scores. **Freshman Admission Requirements:** High school diploma is required and GED is accepted. *Academic units recommended:* 4 English, 3 math, 2 science, 2 foreign language, 2 social studies, 2 history, 2 academic electives. **Freshman Admission Statistics:** 3,757 applied, 49.27% admitted, 9% enrolled. **Transfer Admission Requirements:** High school transcript, college transcript(s), Minimum college GPA of 2.0 required. Lowest grade transferable C. **General Admission Information:** Application fee $25. Nonfall registration accepted. Admission may be deferred for a maximum of 1 year.

COSTS AND FINANCIAL AID

Annual tuition $19,500, Room and board $8,000. Required fees $490. **Required Forms and Deadlines:** FAFSA. **Notification of Awards:** Applicants will be notified of awards on a rolling basis beginning 3/1. **Types of Aid:** *Need-based scholarships/grants:* Federal Pell, FSEOG, State scholarships/grants, Private scholarships, College/university scholarship or grant aid from institutional funds. *Loans:* Direct Subsidized Stafford Loans, Direct Unsubsidized Stafford Loans, Direct PLUS loans, Federal Perkins Loans, College/university loans from institutional funds. *Student Employment:* Federal Work-Study Program available. Institutional employment available. **Financial Aid Statistics:** 0% freshmen, 0% undergrads receive athletic scholarships. 99% freshmen, 98% undergrads receive any aid. **Criteria for awarding aid:** *Non-need-based:* Academics, Alumni affiliation, Art, Athletics, Minority status, Music/drama, Religious affiliation, State/district residency.

BREVARD COLLEGE

One Brevard College Drive, Brevard, NC 28712
Phone: 828-884-8300 • **Financial Aid Phone:** 828-884-8261
E-mail: admissions@brevard.edu • **CEEB Code:** 5067
Fax: 828-884-3790 • **ACT Code:** 3074

This private school, affiliated with the Methodist Church, was founded in 1853. It has a 120-acre campus.

RATINGS

Admissions Selectivity Rating: 80   **Fire Safety Rating:** 81   **Green Rating:** 60*

STUDENTS AND FACULTY

Enrollment: 696. **Student Body:** 42% female, 58% male, 42% out-of-state, 6% international (17 countries represented). Asian 1%, African American 10%, Caucasian 71%, Hispanic 2%, Native American 1%, Pacific Islander <1%, Two or more races 3%, Race unknown 6%.
Retention and Graduation: 59% freshmen return for sophomore year. 36% freshmen graduate within 4 years. 43% freshmen graduate within 6 years.
Faculty: Student/faculty ratio 11:1. 51 full-time faculty, 84% hold PhDs, 0% are are members of minority groups, 47% are women. 0% of classes are taught by teaching assistants.

ACADEMICS

Degrees: bachelor's. **Classes:** Most classes have 10-19 students. Most lab/discussion sessions have 10-19 students. **Most popular majors:** Business Administration and Management; Parks, Recreation and Leisure Studies; Multi-/Interdisciplinary Studies. **Special Study Options:** double major, dual enrollment, honors program, independent study, internships, student-designed major, study abroad, teacher certification program. **Honors Programs:** To complete the Honors Program, students must take a minimum of 19 s.h. in honors courses during the typical 4-year period of their enrollment at Brevard College. These hours include honors enrichment seminar courses, honors-designated sections of courses, and a senior project. The only coursework of these 19 hours that is not directly attributable to core or major requirements is 4 s.h. of ENR (Enrichment) seminars. **Disability Services:** Special programs offered to physically disabled students, including note-taking services, reader services, tape recorders, tutors. **Career Services:** Career/job search classes, Career assessment, Internships, On-campus interviews.

FACILITIES

Housing: Coed dorms, special housing for disabled students, men's dorms, women's dorms, Coed upper classperson dorm. 100% of campus accessible to physically diasbled. **Special Academic Facilities/Equipment:** Porter Center for Performing Arts; Sims Art Center; Morrison Playhouse; Fitness Appraisal Laboratory; Academic Enrichment Center; Center for Career, Service, and Learning; Medical Services Building; Stamey Counseling Center; 24-hour computer lab; Library with wireless connection; Moore Science Annex Building **Computers:** 25% of dorms, 100% of libraries, 100% of dining areas, 100% of student union, have wireless network access. Administrative functions (other than registration) can be performed online.

CAMPUS LIFE

Environment: Village. **Activities:** Choral groups, concert band, dance, drama/theater, jazz band, literary magazine, music ensembles, musical theater, opera, pep band, student government, student newspaper, yearbook, Campus Ministries. 32 registered organizations, 3 honor societies, 1 religious organization. **Athletics (Intercollegiate):** *Men:* baseball, basketball, cheerleading, cross-country, cycling, football, golf, soccer, tennis, track/field (outdoor). *Women:* basketball, cheerleading, cross-country, cycling, golf, soccer, softball, tennis, track/field (outdoor), volleyball. **On-Campus Highlights:** Food Court & Dining Hall, Porter Center for Performing Arts, The Village, MG Super Lab, Moore Science Annex Building, Academic Enrichment Center. **Environmental Initiatives:** Campus-wide recycling program.

ADMISSIONS

Freshman Academic Profile: Average high school GPA 3.1. 6% in top 10% of high school class, 24% in top 25% of high school class, 62% in top 50% of high school class. 82% from public high schools. **Reported SAT (pre-2016 redesign) scores:** SAT Math middle 50% range 420-530. SAT Critical Reading middle 50% range 420-520. **Concordant SAT scores:** SAT Math middle 50% range 460–560. ACT middle 50% range 17-22. Minimum paper TOEFL 537. **Basis for Candidate Selection:** *Very important factors considered include:* rigor of secondary school record, academic GPA, level of applicant's interest. *Important factors considered include:* class rank, application essay, interview, extracurricular activities, talent/ability, character/personal qualities, volunteer work. *Other factors considered include:* standardized test scores, recommendation(s), alumni/ae relation, work experience. **Freshman Admission Requirements:** High school diploma is required and GED is accepted. *Academic units recommended:* 4 English, 3 math, 3 science, 1 science lab, 2 foreign language, 4 social studies, 1 history, 4 academic electives. **Freshman Admission Statistics:** 2,858 applied, 43.21% admitted, 18% enrolled. **Transfer Admission Requirements:** High school transcript, college transcript(s), essay or personal statement, standardized test scores, statement of good standing from prior institution(s). Minimum college GPA of 2.0 required. Lowest grade transferable C-. **General Admission Information:** Nonfall registration accepted. Admission may be deferred for a maximum of one semester.

COSTS AND FINANCIAL AID

Required Forms and Deadlines: FAFSA. **Notification of Awards:** Applicants will be notified of awards on a rolling basis beginning 2/1. **Types of Aid:** *Need-based scholarships/grants:* Federal Pell, FSEOG, State scholarships/grants, Private scholarships, College/university scholarship or grant aid from institutional funds. *Loans:* Direct Subsidized Stafford Loans, Direct Unsubsidized Stafford Loans, Direct PLUS loans, Federal Perkins Loans, State Loans. *Student Employment:* Federal Work-Study Program available. Institutional employment available. **Financial Aid Statistics:** 82% needy freshmen, 80% needy undergrads receive need-based scholarship or grant aid. 100% freshmen, 60% undergrads receive non-need-based scholarship or grant aid. 82% freshmen, 80% undergrads receive need-based self-help aid. 7% freshmen, 7% undergrads receive athletic scholarships. **Criteria for awarding aid:** *Non-need-based:* Academics, Art, Athletics, Leadership, Music/drama, Religious affiliation, State/district residency.

BRIAR CLIFF UNIVERSITY

3303 Rebecca Street, Sioux City, IA 51104
Phone: 712-279-5200 • **Financial Aid Phone:** 712-279-5239
E-mail: admissions@briarcliff.edu • **CEEB Code:** 1846
Fax: 712-279-1632 • **Website:** www.briarcliff.edu • **ACT Code:** 1276

This private school, affiliated with the Roman Catholic Church, was founded in 1930. It has a 70-acre campus.

RATINGS
Admissions Selectivity Rating: 79   **Fire Safety Rating:** 88   **Green Rating:** 71

STUDENTS AND FACULTY
Enrollment: 972. **Student Body:** 55% female, 45% male, 40% out-of-state, 5% international (11 countries represented). Asian 1%, African American 9%, Caucasian 66%, Hispanic 15%, Native American 2%, Pacific Islander 1%, Two or more races 1%, Race unknown 0%.
Retention and Graduation: 79% freshmen return for sophomore year. 37% freshmen graduate within 4 years. 44% freshmen graduate within 6 years. 21% grads go on to further study within 1 year. 3% grads pursue arts and sciences degrees. 3% grads pursue law degrees. 4% grads pursue business degrees. 11% grads pursue medical degrees. **Faculty:** Student/faculty ratio 13:1. 66 full-time faculty, 71% hold PhDs, 8% are are members of minority groups, 48% are women. 0% of classes are taught by teaching assistants.

ACADEMICS
Degrees: associate, bachelor's, master's, postbachelor's certificate, post-master's certificate. **Classes:** Most classes have 10-19 students. Most lab/discussion sessions have fewer than 10 students. **Most popular majors:** Business Administration and Management; Registered Nursing/Registered Nurse; Biology/Biological Sciences. **Special Study Options:** Accelerated program, cross-registration, distance learning, double major, dual enrollment, honors program, independent study, internships, liberal arts/career combination, student-designed major, study abroad, teacher certification program, weekend college. **Honors Programs:** Briar Cliffs Honor Program involves elements of leadership, service and character as well as academics, and is led by the Student Honors Executive Board. In addition to talking Honors courses with small enrollments, Honors students perform individual research work with faculty at the upper levels. Combined degree programs: BA/MA. **Disability Services:** Special programs offered to physically disabled students, including note-taking services, reader services, tape recorders, tutors. **Career Services:** Alumni services, Career/job search classes, Career assessment, Internships. The Chicago Semester allows students from any major field of study to work, study, and live in Chicago for a semester.

FACILITIES
Housing: Coed dorms, men's dorms, women's dorms, apartments for single students. 90% of campus accessible to physically diasbled. **Special Academic Facilities/Equipment:** Nursing Simulation Lab Integrated Multimedia Center Human Anatomy Lab Clausen Art Gallery **Computers:** 100% of classrooms, 100% of libraries, 100% of dining areas, 100% of student union, have wireless network access. Administrative functions (other than registration) can be performed online.

CAMPUS LIFE
Environment: City. **Activities:** Choral groups, drama/theater, jazz band, literary magazine, music ensembles, musical theater, opera, radio station, student government, student newspaper, Campus Ministries. 36 registered organizations, 2 honor societies, 3 religious organizations. **Athletics (Intercollegiate):** *Men:* baseball, basketball, cross-country, football, golf, soccer, tennis, track/field (outdoor), track/field (indoor), wrestling. *Women:* basketball, cross-country, golf, soccer, softball, tennis, track/field (outdoor), track/field (indoor), volleyball. **On-Campus Highlights:** Java City, Stark Student Center, Newman Flanagan Athletic Center, Game Room, tunnels, The McCoy Arnold Athletic Facility was completed in 2004. This multi-use athletic facility provides additional facilities for students to work on personal training and fitness. **Environmental Initiatives:** Recycling.

ADMISSIONS
Freshman Academic Profile: Average high school GPA 3.2. 11% in top 10% of high school class, 25% in top 25% of high school class, 72% in top 50% of high school class. 86% from public high schools. **Reported SAT (pre-2016 redesign) scores:** SAT Math middle 50% range 440-540. SAT Critical Reading middle 50% range 420-490. **Concordant SAT scores:** SAT Math middle 50% range 480–570. ACT middle 50% range 18-24. Minimum internet-based TOEFL 70. Minimum paper TOEFL 525. **Basis for Candidate Selection:** *Very important factors considered include:* rigor of secondary school record, academic GPA, standardized test scores. *Other factors considered include:* class rank, application essay, recommendation(s), interview, extracurricular activities, talent/ability, character/personal qualities, first generation, alumni/ae relation. **Freshman Admission Requirements:** High school diploma is required and GED is accepted. *Academic units recommended:* 4 English, 3 math, 3 science, 2 foreign language, 3 social studies, 1 academic elective. **Freshman Admission Statistics:** 1,491 applied, 59.83% admitted, 24% enrolled. **Transfer Admission Requirements:** High school transcript, college transcript(s), statement of good standing from prior institution(s). Minimum college GPA of 2.0 required. Lowest grade transferable D. **General Admission Information:** Application fee $20. Priority deadline 4/1. Nonfall registration accepted. Admission may be deferred for a maximum of 1 year.

COSTS AND FINANCIAL AID
Annual tuition $28,650. Room and board $9,086. Required fees $1,136. Average book expense $1,339. **Required Forms and Deadlines:** FAFSA. **Types of Aid:** *Need-based scholarships/grants:* Federal Pell, FSEOG, State scholarships/grants, Private scholarships, College/university scholarship or grant aid from institutional funds. *Loans:* Federal Perkins Loans, State Loans. *Student Employment:* Federal Work-Study Program available. Institutional employment available. **Financial Aid Statistics:** 100% needy freshmen, 99% needy undergrads receive need-based scholarship or grant aid. 24% freshmen, 24% undergrads receive non-need-based scholarship or grant aid. 82% freshmen, 86% undergrads receive need-based self-help aid. 75% freshmen, 57% undergrads receive athletic scholarships. 100% freshmen, 97% undergrads receive any aid. 92% undergrads borrow to pay for school. Average cumulative indebtedness $29,484. **Criteria for awarding aid:** *Need-based:* Academics, Minority status. *Non-need-based:* Academics, Alumni affiliation, Art, Athletics, Leadership, Music/drama, Religious affiliation, State/district residency.

See page 926.

BRIDGEWATER COLLEGE

402 East College Street, Bridgewater, VA 22812-1599
Phone: 540-828-5375 • **Financial Aid Phone:** 540-828-5376
E-mail: admissions@bridgewater.edu • **CEEB Code:** 5069
Fax: 540-828-5481 • **Website:** www.bridgewater.edu • **ACT Code:** 4342

This private school, affiliated with the Church of Brethren Church, was founded in 1880. It has a 190-acre campus.

RATINGS
Admissions Selectivity Rating: 82   **Fire Safety Rating:** 91   **Green Rating:** 60*

STUDENTS AND FACULTY
Enrollment: 1,871. **Student Body:** 54% female, 46% male, 27% out-of-state, 1% international (12 countries represented). Asian 1%, African American 13%, Caucasian 68%, Hispanic 6%, Native American <1%, Pacific Islander <1%, Two or more races 6%, Race unknown 4%.
Retention and Graduation: 78% freshmen return for sophomore year. 58% freshmen graduate within 4 years. 66% freshmen graduate within 6 years. **Faculty:** Student/faculty ratio 14:1. 115 full-time faculty, 80% hold PhDs, 9% are are members of minority groups, 48% are women. 0% of classes are taught by teaching assistants.

ACADEMICS

Degrees: bachelor's. **Classes:** Most classes have 10-19 students. Most lab/discussion sessions have 10-19 students. **Most popular majors:** Business Administration and Management; Biology/Biological Sciences; Health and Physical Education/Fitness. **Special Study Options:** double major, honors program, independent study, internships, liberal arts/career combination, study abroad, teacher certification program, Dual Degree Programs: 3-2 Engineering Program with George Washington University(BA/BA) 3-2 Engineering Program with Virginia Tech (BA/BA) 3-2 Nursing Program with Vanderbilt University (BA/MN) 3-4 Veterinary Science Program with Virginia Tech (BA/DVM) 3-4 Physical Therapy Program with Shenandoah University (BA/DPT) Pre Professional Programs in Dentistry, Engineering, Law, Medicine, Ministry, Nursing, Occupational Therapy, Pharmacy, Physical Therapy, and Veterinary Science. **Honors Programs:** The Honors Program is designed to provide additional challenges and opportunities for outstanding students. Honors courses are taught as smaller classes and provide opportunities for different types of student learning and faculty teaching–greater independence, research, and discussion formats. An Honors Project is one in which a student researches a subject, by examination of relevant literature or by experimentation or both; the student reports the results in an accurately documented and well-written paper or appropriate representation of the work. Combined degree programs: BA/MA, 3-4 Physical Therapy with Shenandoah Univ (BA/DPT), 3-2 Nursing with Vanderbilt Univ (BA/MN); 3-4 Veterinary Medicine with Virginia Tech (BA/DVM). **Disability Services:** Special programs offered to physically disabled students, including note-taking services, reader services, tape recorders, tutors. **Career Services:** Alumni services, Career/job search classes, Career assessment, Internships, Regional alumni. Career Exploration Day where alumni and students interface for conversations regarding transitioning from college to career

FACILITIES

Housing: Coed dorms, special housing for disabled students, men's dorms, women's dorms, apartments for single students, Wellness Housing, Theme Housing, Honor Housing. 95% of campus accessible to physically disabled. **Special Academic Facilities/Equipment:** Museum of Shenandoah region and Brethren history. **Computers:** 5% of classrooms, 10% of dorms, 75% of libraries, 100% of dining areas, 100% of student union, have wireless network access. Students can register for classes online. Administrative functions (other than registration) can be performed online.

CAMPUS LIFE

Environment: Village. **Activities:** Choral groups, concert band, dance, drama/theater, jazz band, literary magazine, music ensembles, musical theater, pep band, radio station, student government, student newspaper, yearbook, Campus Ministries, Student Organization. 74 registered organizations, 8 honor societies, 9 religious organizations. **Athletics (Intercollegiate):** *Men:* baseball, basketball, cross-country, equestrian sports, football, golf, soccer, tennis, track/field (outdoor), track/field (indoor). *Women:* basketball, cross-country, equestrian sports, field hockey, lacrosse, soccer, softball, swimming, tennis, track/field (outdoor), track/field (indoor), volleyball. **On-Campus Highlights:** McKinney Center for Science and Mathematics, Kline Campus Center, Funkhouser Center for Health and Wellness, Carter Center for Worship and Music, Eagle's Nest (snack shop). **Environmental Initiatives:** Energy and water conservation.

ADMISSIONS

Freshman Academic Profile: Average high school GPA 3.5. 15% in top 10% of high school class, 42% in top 25% of high school class, 78% in top 50% of high school class. 92% from public high schools. **Reported SAT (pre-2016 redesign) scores:** SAT Math middle 50% range 450-550. SAT Critical Reading middle 50% range 460-560. SAT Writing middle 50% range 430-530. **Concordant SAT scores:** SAT EBRW middle 50% 500–600. SAT Math middle 50% range 490–570. ACT middle 50% range 20-26. Minimum internet-based TOEFL 79. Minimum paper TOEFL 550. **Basis for Candidate Selection:** *Very important factors considered include:* rigor of secondary school record, academic GPA, standardized test scores. *Important factors considered include:* class rank, recommendation(s), interview, extracurricular activities, talent/ability, character/personal qualities. *Other factors considered include:* geographical residence, state residency, volunteer work, work experience, level of applicant's interest. **Freshman Admission Requirements:** High school diploma is required and GED is accepted. *Academic units required:* 4 English, 3 math, 3 science, 3 science labs, 4 academic electives, and 3 units from above areas or other academic areas. *Academic units recommended:* 4 English, 3 math, 3 science, 3 science labs, 2 foreign language, 4 academic electives, and 3 units from above areas or other academic areas. **Freshman Admission Statistics:** 7,486 applied, 52.75% admitted, 15% enrolled. **Transfer Admission Requirements:** High school transcript, college transcript(s), standardized test scores, statement of good standing from prior institution(s). Minimum college GPA of 2.2 required. Lowest grade transferable C. **General Admission Information:** Regular application deadline 5/1. Nonfall registration accepted. Admission may be deferred for a maximum of 1 year.

COSTS AND FINANCIAL AID

Annual tuition $33,000. Room and board $12,440. Required fees $820. Average book expense $1,150. **Required Forms and Deadlines:** FAFSA, State aid form. **Notification of Awards:** Applicants will be notified of awards on a rolling basis beginning 3/15. **Types of Aid:** *Need-based scholarships/grants:* Federal Pell, FSEOG, State scholarships/grants, Private scholarships, College/university scholarship or grant aid from institutional funds. *Loans:* Direct Subsidized Stafford Loans, Direct Unsubsidized Stafford Loans, Direct PLUS loans, Federal Perkins Loans. *Student Employment:* Federal Work-Study Program available. Institutional employment available. **Financial Aid Statistics:** 100% needy freshmen, 100% needy undergrads receive need-based scholarship or grant aid. 100% freshmen, 100% undergrads receive non-need-based scholarship or grant aid. 74% freshmen, 73% undergrads receive need-based self-help aid. 0% freshmen, 0% undergrads receive athletic scholarships. 100% freshmen, 99% undergrads receive any aid. 75% undergrads borrow to pay for school. Average cumulative indebtedness $34,035. **Criteria for awarding aid:** *Non-need-based:* Academics, Minority status, Music/drama, Religious affiliation, State/district residency.

BRIDGEWATER STATE COLLEGE

Gates House, Bridgewater State College, Bridgewater, MA 2325
Phone: 508-531-1237 • **Financial Aid Phone:** 508-531-1341
E-mail: admission@bridgew.edu • **CEEB Code:** 3517
Fax: 508-531-1746 • **Website:** www.bridgew.edu • **ACT Code:** 1900

This public school was founded in 1840. It has a 235-acre campus.

RATINGS

Admissions Selectivity Rating: 77   **Fire Safety Rating:** 60*   **Green Rating:** 60*

STUDENTS AND FACULTY

Enrollment: 8,310. **Student Body:** 60% female, 40% male, 5% out-of-state, 1% international (52 countries represented). Asian 2%, African American 6%, Caucasian 81%, Hispanic 2%, Native American <1%, Pacific Islander 0%, Two or more races 0%, Race unknown 8%.
Retention and Graduation: 80% freshmen return for sophomore year. 22% freshmen graduate within 4 years. 51% freshmen graduate within 6 years. 16% grads go on to further study within 1 year. 2% grads pursue law degrees. 1% grads pursue business degrees. **Faculty:** Student/faculty ratio 19:1. 306 full-time faculty, 90% hold PhDs, 11% are are members of minority groups, 48% are women. 0% of classes are taught by teaching assistants.

ACADEMICS

Degrees: bachelor's, master's, postbachelor's certificate, post-master's certificate. **Classes:** Most classes have 20-29 students. Most lab/discussion sessions have 10-19 students. **Most popular majors:** Elementary Education and Teaching; Psychology; Business/Commerce. **Special Study Options:** Accelerated program, cross-registration, distance learning, double major, dual enrollment, English as a Second Language (ESL), exchange student program (domestic), honors program, independent study, internships, study abroad, teacher certification program. Combined degree programs: BS/MSM in Management, BSE/M.Ed in Elem/Spec. Ed. **Disability Services:** Special programs offered to physically disabled students, including note-taking services, reader services, tape recorders, tutors. **Career Services:** Alumni services, Career/job search classes, Career assessment, Internships.

FACILITIES

Housing: Coed dorms, special housing for disabled students, apartments for single students, break housing for athletes, student teachers, students, visiting lecturers. 95% of campus accessible to physically disabled. **Special Academic Facilities/Equipment:** On-campus school, children's physical development clinic, human performance lab, TV studio, observatory, flight simulators, electron microscope, Moakley Technology Center **Computers:** Students can register for classes online. Administrative functions (other than registration) can be performed online. Undergraduates are required to own a computer.

CAMPUS LIFE

Environment: Village. **Activities:** Choral groups, concert band, dance, drama/theater, jazz band, literary magazine, marching band, music ensembles, musical theater, radio station, student government, student newspaper, yearbook, Campus Ministries, Student Organization. 67 registered organizations, 11 honor societies, 1 religious organization. **Athletics (Intercollegiate):** *Men:* baseball, basketball, cross-country, football, soccer, swimming, tennis, track/field (outdoor), wrestling. *Women:* basketball, cross-country, field hockey, lacrosse, soccer, softball, swimming, tennis, track/field (outdoor), volleyball.

ADMISSIONS

Freshman Academic Profile: Average high school GPA 3.0. 8% in top 10% of high school class, 32% in top 25% of high school class, 77% in top 50% of high school class. **Reported SAT (pre-2016 redesign) scores:** SAT Math middle 50% range 470-560. SAT Critical Reading middle 50% range 460-560. **Concordant SAT scores:** SAT Math middle 50% range 510–580. ACT middle 50% range 19-23. Minimum paper TOEFL 500. **Basis for Candidate Selection:** *Very important factors considered include:* rigor of secondary school record, academic GPA. *Important factors considered include:* class rank, standardized test scores. *Other factors considered include:* application essay, recommendation(s), extracurricular activities, talent/ability, character/personal qualities, alumni/ae relation, racial/ethnic status, volunteer work, work experience. **Freshman Admission Requirements:** High school diploma is required and GED is accepted. *Academic units required:* 4 English, 3 math, 3 science, 2 science labs, 2 foreign language, 1 social studies, 1 history, 2 academic electives. *Academic units recommended:* 4 English, 3 math, 3 science, 2 science labs, 2 foreign language, 1 social studies, 1 history, 2 academic electives. **Freshman Admission Statistics:** 6,532 applied, 71.03% admitted, 32% enrolled. **Transfer Admission Requirements:** college transcript(s), essay or personal statement, Minimum college GPA of 2.0 required. Lowest grade transferable C-. **General Admission Information:** Nonfall registration accepted. Admission may be deferred.

COSTS AND FINANCIAL AID

Annual in-state tuition $910. Annual out-of-state tuition $7,050. Room and board $6,852. Required fees $5,327. Average book expense $1,000. **Required Forms and Deadlines:** FAFSA. **Types of Aid:** *Need-based scholarships/ grants:* Federal Pell, FSEOG, State scholarships/grants, Private scholarships, College/university scholarship or grant aid from institutional funds. *Loans:* Direct Subsidized Stafford Loans, Direct Unsubsidized Stafford Loans, Direct PLUS loans, Federal Perkins Loans, State Loans. *Student Employment:* Federal Work-Study Program available. Institutional employment available. **Financial Aid Statistics:** 83% needy freshmen, 83% needy undergrads receive need-based scholarship or grant aid. 24% freshmen, 10% undergrads receive non-need-based scholarship or grant aid. 97% freshmen, 100% undergrads receive need-based self-help aid. **Criteria for awarding aid:** *Non-need-based:* Academics, Leadership, Minority status, State/district residency.

BRIERCREST COLLEGE AND SEMINARY

510 College Drive, Caronport, SK S0H 0S0
Phone: 1-800-667-5199
E-mail: admissions@briercrest.ca
Fax: 800-667-5500 • **Website:** www.briercrest.ca

This private school was founded in 1935. It has a 160-acre campus.

RATINGS

Admissions Selectivity Rating: 61   **Fire Safety Rating:** 60*   **Green Rating:** 60*

STUDENTS AND FACULTY

Student Body: 4% out-of-state.
Faculty: Student/faculty ratio 18:1. 31 full-time faculty, 0% hold PhDs, 0% are are members of minority groups.

ACADEMICS

Degrees: associate, bachelor's, certificate, master's, postbachelor's certificate. **Special Study Options:** distance learning, double major, English as a Second Language (ESL), independent study, internships, study abroad. **Career Services:** Alumni services, Career assessment.

FACILITIES

Housing: Coed dorms, special housing for disabled students, Suite, corridor, singles, smoke-free, over 21 yrs, over 24 yrs, wellness living, quiet study, same curriculum housing, baccalaureate, single room options, and computer life style New upperclassmen apartment suite complex. **Computers:** Students can register for classes online.

CAMPUS LIFE

Environment: Rural. **Activities:** Choral groups, concert band, drama/theater, jazz band, literary magazine, music ensembles, musical theater, radio station, student government, student newspaper, symphony orchestra, yearbook. **Athletics (Intercollegiate):** *Men:* basketball, ice hockey, volleyball. *Women:* basketball, volleyball.

ADMISSIONS

Basis for Candidate Selection: *Very important factors considered include:* academic GPA, application essay, recommendation(s), character/personal qualities, religious affiliation/commitment, level of applicant's interest. *Other*

---

factors considered include: standardized test scores, interview, volunteer work. **Transfer Admission Requirements:** High school transcript, college transcript(s), essay or personal statement. **General Admission Information:** Application fee $50. Priority deadline 4/1. Nonfall registration accepted. Admission may be deferred for a maximum of 1 year.

COSTS AND FINANCIAL AID

Annual tuition $7,470. Room and board $2,515. Required fees $250. Average book expense $500. **Required Forms and Deadlines:** Institution's own financial aid form, State aid form. **Types of Aid:** *Need-based scholarships/ grants:* Private scholarships, College/university scholarship or grant aid from institutional funds. *Student Employment:* Federal Work-Study Program available. Institutional employment available.

BRIGHAM YOUNG UNIVERSITY—HAWAII

BYU- Hawaii # 1973, Laie, HI 96762
Phone: 808-675- 3738 • **Financial Aid Phone:** 808-293-3530
E-mail: admissions@byuh.edu • **CEEB Code:** 4106
Fax: 808-675-3741 • **ACT Code:** 899

This private school, affiliated with the Church of Jesus Christ of Latt Church, was founded in 1955. It has a 60-acre campus.

RATINGS

Admissions Selectivity Rating: 86   **Fire Safety Rating:** 73   **Green Rating:** 60*

STUDENTS AND FACULTY

Enrollment: 2,312. **Student Body:** 56% female, 44% male, 68% out-of-state, 44% international (67 countries represented). Asian 22%, African American 1%, Caucasian 29%, Hispanic 2%, Native American 1%, Pacific Islander 0%, Two or more races 0%, Race unknown 1%.
Retention and Graduation: 57% freshmen return for sophomore year. 25% freshmen graduate within 4 years. 39% freshmen graduate within 6 years. **Faculty:** Student/faculty ratio 14:1. 122 full-time faculty, 80% hold PhDs, 23% are are members of minority groups, 21% are women. 0% of classes are taught by teaching assistants.

ACADEMICS

Degrees: bachelor's. **Classes:** Most classes have 10-19 students. Most lab/ discussion sessions have 10-19 students. **Most popular majors:** Information Science/Studies; Intercultural/Multicultural and Diversity Studies; International Business/Trade/Commerce. **Special Study Options:** Accelerated program, cooperative education program, distance learning, English as a Second Language (ESL), exchange student program (domestic), honors program, independent study, internships, student-designed major, teacher certification program. **Honors Programs:** The University Honors Program is open to all interested students who feel they are capable of accepting the challenge of an Honors Education. You will have the opportunity to participate in a stimulating class environment with other top students and the best professors. **Disability Services:** Special programs offered to physically disabled students, including note-taking services, reader services, tape recorders, tutors.

FACILITIES

Housing: men's dorms, women's dorms, apartments for married students. 90% of campus accessible to physically diasbled. **Special Academic Facilities/ Equipment:** Museum of Natural History Media Lab **Computers:** 100% of classrooms, 100% of libraries, 100% of dining areas, 100% of student union, 100% of common outdoor areas have wireless network access. Students can register for classes online. Administrative functions (other than registration) can be performed online.

CAMPUS LIFE

Environment: Village. **Activities:** Choral groups, concert band, dance, jazz band, literary magazine, music ensembles, pep band, student government, student newspaper, student-run film society 52 registered organizations, 3 honor societies. **Athletics (Intercollegiate):** *Men:* basketball, cross-country, golf, soccer, tennis. *Women:* basketball, cross-country, soccer, softball, tennis, volleyball. **On-Campus Highlights:** Joseph F. Smith Library, Cannon Activities Center, The Club Cafe, The Seasider Snackbar, Aloha Center.

ADMISSIONS

Freshman Academic Profile: Average high school GPA 3.4. **Reported SAT (pre-2016 redesign) scores:** SAT Math middle 50% range 480-600. SAT Critical Reading middle 50% range 460-580. **Concordant SAT scores:** SAT Math middle 50% range 510–620. ACT middle 50% range 20-27. Minimum paper TOEFL 475. **Basis for Candidate Selection:** *Very important factors considered include:* rigor of secondary school record, standardized test scores, application essay, recommendation(s), interview, extracurricular activities, character/personal qualities, geographical residence, religious affiliation/ commitment. *Important factors considered include:* class rank, talent/ability, alumni/ae relation, volunteer work, work experience. *Other factors considered include:* state residency. **Freshman Admission Requirements:** High school diploma is required and GED is not accepted. *Academic units recommended:* 4 English, 2 math, 2 science, 2 science labs, 2 foreign language, 2 history. **Freshman Admission Statistics:** 2,078 applied, 18.86% admitted, 76% enrolled. **Transfer Admission Requirements:** college transcript(s), essay or personal statement, statement of good standing from prior institution(s). Minimum college GPA of 3.0 required. Lowest grade transferable C-. **General Admission Information:** Application fee $30. Regular application deadline 2/15. Regular notification 4/1. Nonfall registration accepted. Admission may be deferred for a maximum of 1 semester.

COSTS AND FINANCIAL AID

Annual tuition $3,600. Room and board $5,568. Required fees $0. Average book expense $900. **Required Forms and Deadlines:** FAFSA, Institution's own financial aid form. **Notification of Awards:** Applicants will be notified of awards on or about 6/30. **Types of Aid:** *Need-based scholarships/grants:* Federal Pell, Private scholarships, College/university scholarship or grant aid from institutional funds. *Loans:* College/university loans from institutional funds. *Student Employment:* Institutional employment available. **Financial Aid Statistics:** 88% needy freshmen, 64% needy undergrads receive need-based scholarship or grant aid. 24% freshmen, 45% undergrads receive non-need-based scholarship or grant aid. 73% freshmen, 45% undergrads receive need-based self-help aid. 13% freshmen, 7% undergrads receive athletic scholarships. 70% freshmen, 72% undergrads receive any aid. **Criteria for awarding aid:** *Non-need-based:* Academics, Art, Athletics, Leadership, Music/drama, State/ district residency.

BRIGHAM YOUNG UNIVERSITY (UT)

Best Colleges

A-153 ASB, Provo, UT 84602-1110
Phone: 801-422-2507 • **Financial Aid Phone:** 801-378-4104
E-mail: admissions@byu.edu • **CEEB Code:** 4019
Fax: 801-422-0005 • **Website:** www.byu.edu • **ACT Code:** 4266

This private school, affiliated with the Church of Jesus Christ of Latt Church, was founded in 1875. It has a 557-acre campus.

RATINGS

Admissions Selectivity Rating: 94 **Fire Safety Rating:** 75 **Green Rating:** 60*

STUDENTS AND FACULTY

Enrollment: 25,733. **Student Body:** 48% female, 52% male, 66% out-of-state, 3% international (121 countries represented). Asian 1%, African American <1%, Caucasian 2%, Hispanic 6%, Native American 1%, Pacific Islander 82%, Two or more races 4%, Race unknown <1%. **Retention and Graduation:** 90% freshmen return for sophomore year. 29% freshmen graduate within 4 years. 83% freshmen graduate within 6 years. **Faculty:** Student/faculty ratio 21:1. 1,257 full-time faculty, 92% hold PhDs, 6% are are members of minority groups, 20% are women.

ACADEMICS

Degrees: bachelor's, doctoral/professional, doctoral/research, master's, postbachelor's certificate, post-master's certificate. **Classes:** Most classes have 10-19 students. **Most popular majors:** Business/Commerce; Exercise Physiology; Elementary Education and Teaching. **Special Study Options:** Accelerated program, cooperative education program, cross-registration, distance learning, double major, English as a Second Language (ESL), external degree program, honors program, independent study, internships, liberal arts/ career combination, study abroad, teacher certification program. **Honors Programs:** The Honors Program, participation in which is open to all BYU students, complements the university's expansive educational agenda by providing the benefits of a small liberal arts learning community. These benefits include offering small classes with high-quality teaching and learning that challenge students to reach their highest potential; fostering a spirit of ongoing inquiry that includes undergraduate research in a mentored environment; and underscoring the importance of combining personal excellence, faithful discipleship, and meaningful service. Combined degree programs: BA/JD, BA/MA, BA/Macc, BS/MS. **Disability Services:** Special programs offered to physically disabled students, including note-taking services, reader services, tape recorders, tutors.

FACILITIES

Housing: special housing for disabled students, men's dorms, women's dorms, apartments for married students, apartments for single students, Language houses are available. 97% of campus accessible to physically diasbled. **Special Academic Facilities/Equipment:** Art, peoples/cultures, life science, and earth science museums, film studio, on-campus nursery school, language research center, seismography equipment, electron microscope. **Computers:** 10% of classrooms, 100% of libraries, 100% of dining areas, 100% of student union, have wireless network access. Students can register for classes online. Administrative functions (other than registration) can be performed online.

CAMPUS LIFE

Environment: City. **Activities:** Choral groups, concert band, dance, drama/ theater, jazz band, literary magazine, marching band, music ensembles, musical theater, opera, pep band, radio station, student government, student newspaper, student-run film society, symphony orchestra, television station 390 registered organizations, 22 honor societies, 25 religious organizations. **Athletics (Intercollegiate):** *Men:* baseball, basketball, cheerleading, cross-country, diving, football, golf, swimming, tennis, track/field (outdoor), track/ field (indoor), volleyball. *Women:* basketball, cheerleading, cross-country, diving, golf, gymnastics, soccer, softball, swimming, tennis, track/field (outdoor), track/field (indoor), volleyball. **On-Campus Highlights:** Monte L. Bean Life Science Museum, The Museum of Art, Gordon B. Hinckley Alumni & Visitors Cen, Harold B. Lee Library, Wilkinson Student Center, Some of the popular places on campus are the HFAC theatres and music halls, the Creamery on 9th, and the Marriott Center (where weekly devotionals and forums as well as sports events are held). Campus highlights also include BYU's new Student Athlete Building houses the impressive Legacy Hall (BYU sports Hall of Fame) and the popular Legends Grille, the very large (athletic teams')Indoor Practice Facility is completed, the newly remodeled Brimhall Building is housing the Communications Department, and the new Joseph F. Smith Building (which replaced the Smith Family Living Center) has been completed and now houses the College of Family, Home and Social Sciences.

ADMISSIONS

Freshman Academic Profile: Average high school GPA 3.8. 55% in top 10% of high school class, 86% in top 25% of high school class, 98% in top 50% of high school class. **Reported SAT (pre-2016 redesign) scores:** SAT Math middle 50% range 580-690. SAT Critical Reading middle 50% range 580-690. SAT Writing middle 50% range 560-660. **Concordant SAT scores:** SAT EBRW middle 50% 630-710. SAT Math middle 50% range 600-720. ACT middle 50% range 27-31. Minimum paper TOEFL 500. **Basis for Candidate Selection:** *Very important factors considered include:* rigor of secondary school record, academic GPA, standardized test scores, interview, character/personal qualities, religious affiliation/commitment. *Important factors considered include:* application essay, recommendation(s), extracurricular activities, racial/ ethnic status, volunteer work. *Other factors considered include:* talent/ability, first generation, geographical residence, state residency, work experience, level of applicant's interest. **Freshman Admission Requirements:** High school diploma is required and GED is accepted. *Academic units recommended:* 4 English, 4 math, 3 science, 2 foreign language, 2 history. **Freshman Admission Statistics:** 12,739 applied, 51.18% admitted, 80% enrolled. **Transfer Admission Requirements:** college transcript(s), essay or personal statement, interview, Minimum college GPA of 3.0 required. Lowest grade transferable C-. **General Admission Information:** Application fee $35. Priority deadline 12/1. Regular application deadline 2/1. Regular notification 2/28. Nonfall registration accepted. Admission may be deferred for a maximum of 2 years.

COSTS AND FINANCIAL AID

Annual tuition $5,300. Room and board $7,448. Required fees $0. Average book expense $812. **Required Forms and Deadlines:** FAFSA. **Types of Aid:** *Need-based scholarships/grants:* Federal Pell, Private scholarships, College/university scholarship or grant aid from institutional funds. *Loans:* Direct Subsidized Stafford Loans, Direct Unsubsidized Stafford Loans, Direct PLUS loans. *Student Employment:* Federal Work-Study Program available. Institutional employment available. **Financial Aid Statistics:** 57% needy freshmen, 80% needy undergrads receive need-based scholarship or grant aid. 68% freshmen, 47% undergrads receive non-need-based scholarship or grant aid. 28% freshmen, 30% undergrads receive need-based self-help aid. 3% freshmen, 2% undergrads receive athletic scholarships. 53% freshmen, 64% undergrads receive any aid. 26% undergrads borrow to pay for school. Average cumulative indebtedness $15,158. **Criteria for awarding aid:** *Need-based:* Academics, Alumni affiliation, Minority status, Religious affiliation. *Non-need-based:* Academics, Art, Athletics, Leadership, Minority status, Music/drama, Religious affiliation, State/district residency.

BROCK UNIVERSITY

500 Glenridge Avenue, St. Catharines, ON L2S 3A1
Phone: 905-688-5550
E-mail: admissns@brocku.ca
Fax: 905-988-5488 • **Website:** www.brocku.ca

This public school was founded in 1964. It has a 457-acre campus.

RATINGS
Admissions Selectivity Rating: 61   **Fire Safety Rating:** 85   **Green Rating:** 60*

STUDENTS AND FACULTY
Student Body: 8% out-of-state, (80 countries represented).
Retention and Graduation: 52% freshmen graduate within 4 years. **Faculty:** Student/faculty ratio 27:1. 577 full-time faculty, 0% hold PhDs, 0% are are members of minority groups, 43% are women, 0% of classes are taught by teaching assistants.

ACADEMICS
Degrees: bachelor's, certificate, master's. **Most popular majors:** Education; Health Professions and Related Clinical Sciences; Business/Commerce. **Special Study Options:** cooperative education program, double major, English as a Second Language (ESL), exchange student program (domestic), honors program, internships, liberal arts/career combination, student-designed major, study abroad, teacher certification program, Liberal arts/career combination: Students may choose from 7 Concurrent Education programs, combining their undergraduate degree and Bachelor of Education degree. Combined degree programs: BA/BEd; BSc/BEd; BPHEd/BEd. **Disability Services:** Special programs offered to physically disabled students, including note-taking services, reader services, tape recorders, tutors. **Career Services:** Career/job search classes, Internships. Brock offers the third largest selection of Co-op programs in Ontario. A variety of additional experiential learning opportunities are built into virtually all of our programs.

FACILITIES
Housing: Coed dorms, special housing for disabled students, women's dorms, Village Residence and Quarry View Residence (Townhouses). 100% of campus accessible to physically diasbled. **Special Academic Facilities/Equipment:** Cool Climate Oenology and Viticulture Institute Map Library Intructional Resource Centre Rodman Hall Arts Centre Cypriote Museum **Computers:** 100% of classrooms, 100% of libraries, 100% of student union, have wireless network access. Students can register for classes online. Administrative functions (other than registration) can be performed online.

CAMPUS LIFE
Environment: City. **Activities:** Choral groups, concert band, dance, drama/theater, literary magazine, music ensembles, musical theater, radio station, student government, student newspaper, student-run film society, symphony orchestra, television station, yearbook, Campus Ministries. 40 registered organizations, 6 religious organizations. **Athletics (Intercollegiate):** *Men:* baseball, basketball, cheerleading, crew/rowing, cross-country, curling, fencing, ice hockey, lacrosse, rugby, soccer, squash, swimming, wrestling. *Women:* basketball, cheerleading, crew/rowing, cross-country, curling, fencing, ice hockey, rugby, soccer, swimming, volleyball, wrestling. **On-Campus Highlights:** Residences, Walker Complex—athletic facility, Computer Commons, Isaacs, Plaza Building. **Environmental Initiatives:** Our newest building earned LEED Silver Certification. The energy cost performance is almost 43 per cent better than the Model National Energy Code.

ADMISSIONS
Minimum internet-based TOEFL 88. **Basis for Candidate Selection:** *Very important factors considered include:* rigor of secondary school record, academic GPA. *Important factors considered include:* standardized test scores. *Other factors considered include:* class rank, recommendation(s), talent/ability. **Freshman Admission Requirements:** High school diploma is required and GED is accepted. **Freshman Admission Statistics:** 16,870 applied, admitted. **Transfer Admission Requirements:** High school transcript, college transcript(s). **General Admission Information:** Application fee $155. Regular application deadline 4/1. Nonfall registration not accepted.

COSTS AND FINANCIAL AID
Annual in-state tuition $4,852. Room and board $8,215. Required fees $0. Average book expense $900. **Required Forms and Deadlines:** Institution's own financial aid form. **Types of Aid:** *Need-based scholarships/grants:* College/university scholarship or grant aid from institutional funds. *Student Employment:* Federal Work-Study Program available. Institutional employment available. **Financial Aid Statistics:** 29% needy undergrads receive need-based scholarship or grant aid. 0% undergrads receive non-need-based scholarship or grant aid. 0% undergrads receive need-based self-help aid. 0% undergrads receive athletic scholarships. 39% undergrads receive any aid. **Criteria for**

awarding aid: *Need-based:* Academics, Athletics, Leadership. *Non-need-based:* Academics, Athletics, Leadership.

BROWN UNIVERSITY

Box 1876, Providence, RI 2912
Phone: 401-863-2378 • **Financial Aid Phone:** 401-863-2721
E-mail: admission@brown.edu • **CEEB Code:** 3094
Fax: 401-863-9300 • **Website:** www.brown.edu • **ACT Code:** 3800

This private school was founded in 1764. It has a 146-acre campus.

RATINGS
Admissions Selectivity Rating: 98   **Fire Safety Rating:** 91   **Green Rating:** 93

STUDENTS AND FACULTY
Enrollment: 6,580. **Student Body:** 52% female, 48% male, 95% out-of-state, 11% international (111 countries represented). Asian 14%, African American 7%, Caucasian 43%, Hispanic 12%, Native American <1%, Pacific Islander <1%, Two or more races 6%, Race unknown 6%.
Retention and Graduation: 98% freshmen return for sophomore year. 84% freshmen graduate within 4 years. 96% freshmen graduate within 6 years. 20% grads go on to further study within 1 year. 11% grads pursue arts and sciences degrees. 2% grads pursue law degrees. 1% grads pursue business degrees. 6% grads pursue medical degrees. **Faculty:** Student/faculty ratio 7:1. 770 full-time faculty, 95% hold PhDs, 20% are are members of minority groups, 35% are women.

ACADEMICS
Degrees: bachelor's, doctoral/professional, doctoral/research, master's. **Classes:** Most classes have 10-19 students. **Most popular majors:** Economics; Biology/Biological Sciences; Computer and Information Sciences. **Special Study Options:** cross-registration, double major, exchange student program (domestic), honors program, independent study, internships, student-designed major, study abroad, teacher certification program, 8-Year medical program (AB or SCB plus MD) 5-year degree program (AB and SCB). Combined degree programs: BA/MD, BA/MA, BA/BS, BS/MS, BA/MS, BS/MA, BS/MD. **Disability Services:** Special programs offered to physically disabled students, including note-taking services, reader services, tape recorders, tutors. **Career Services:** Alumni network, Career/job search classes, Career assessment, Internships, Regional alumni. Each year, hundreds of Brown students receive funding to pursue independent research, internships, projects, or faculty collaborations to deepen and connect their learning and experience. BrownConnect, an exciting campus initiative, enables students to follow their own paths beyond the classroom. With this new program, students have access to an extensive network of Brown alumni, parents, and friends as well as diverse internship opportunities. BrownConnect provides "one-stop shopping" for internships and research opportunities in a wide range of fields and geographic locations.

FACILITIES
Housing: Coed dorms, special housing for disabled students, fraternity/sorority housing, cooperative housing, apartments for single students, Wellness Housing, Theme Housing. **Special Academic Facilities/Equipment:** Art gallery, anthropology museum, language lab, information technology center, NASA research center, center for modern culture/media. **Computers:** 50% of classrooms, 100% of dorms, 100% of libraries, 100% of dining areas, 100% of student union, 50% of common outdoor areas have wireless network access. Students can register for classes online. Administrative functions (other than registration) can be performed online.

CAMPUS LIFE
Environment: City. **Activities:** Choral groups, concert band, dance, drama/theater, jazz band, literary magazine, marching band, music ensembles, musical theater, opera, pep band, radio station, student government, student newspaper, student-run film society, symphony orchestra, television station, yearbook, Campus Ministries, Student Organization, Model UN. 400 registered organizations, 3 honor societies, 20 religious organizations. 8 fraternities, 2 sororities. **Athletics (Intercollegiate):** *Men:* baseball, basketball, crew/rowing, cross-country, diving, fencing, football, golf, ice hockey, lacrosse, soccer, squash, swimming, tennis, track/field (outdoor), track/field (indoor), water polo, wrestling. *Women:* basketball, crew/rowing, cross-country, diving, equestrian sports, fencing, field hockey, golf, gymnastics, ice hockey, lacrosse,

skiing (downhill/alpine), soccer, softball, squash, swimming, tennis, track/field (outdoor), track/field (indoor), volleyball, water polo. **On-Campus Highlights:** The College Green, Bell Gallery, Libraries—Jon Hay, John Carter Brown, Watson Institute, Lyman Hall & Dill Center. **Environmental Initiatives:** Reduce GHG emissions to 42% (15% below 1990) below 2007 for existing buildings by 2020

ADMISSIONS

Freshman Academic Profile: 92% in top 10% of high school class, 99% in top 25% of high school class, 100% in top 50% of high school class. 58% from public high schools. **Reported SAT (pre-2016 redesign) scores:** SAT Math middle 50% range 690-790. SAT Critical Reading middle 50% range 680-780. SAT Writing middle 50% range 690-780. **Concordant SAT scores:** SAT EBRW middle 50% 720–790. SAT Math middle 50% range 720–800. ACT middle 50% range 31-34. Minimum internet-based TOEFL 100. Minimum paper TOEFL 600. **Basis for Candidate Selection:** *Very important factors considered include:* rigor of secondary school record, class rank, academic GPA, standardized test scores, application essay, recommendation(s), talent/ability, character/personal qualities. *Important factors considered include:* extracurricular activities. *Other factors considered include:* interview, first generation, alumni/ae relation, geographical residence, state residency, racial/ethnic status, volunteer work, work experience. **Freshman Admission Requirements:** High school diploma is required and GED is not accepted. *Academic units required:* 4 English, 3 math, 3 science, 2 science labs, 3 foreign language, 2 history, 1 academic elective. *Academic units recommended:* 4 English, 4 math, 4 science, 3 science labs, 4 foreign language, 1 social studies, 2 history, 1 academic elective, 1 computer science, 1 visual/performing arts. **Freshman Admission Statistics:** 32,390 applied, 9.31% admitted, 56% enrolled. **Transfer Admission Requirements:** High school transcript, college transcript(s), essay or personal statement, standardized test scores, statement of good standing from prior institution(s). Lowest grade transferable C. **General Admission Information:** Application fee $75. Regular application deadline 1/1. Nonfall registration not accepted. Admission may be deferred for a maximum of 1 year.

COSTS AND FINANCIAL AID

Annual tuition $50,224. Room and board $13,200. Required fees $1,142. Average book expense $1,540. **Required Forms and Deadlines:** FAFSA, CSS/Financial Aid PROFILE, Noncustodial PROFILE. **Notification of Awards:** Applicants will be notified of awards on or about 4/1. **Types of Aid:** *Need-based scholarships/grants:* Federal Pell, FSEOG, State scholarships/grants, Private scholarships, College/university scholarship or grant aid from institutional funds. *Loans:* Direct Subsidized Stafford Loans, Direct Unsubsidized Stafford Loans, Direct PLUS loans, Federal Perkins Loans, College/university loans from institutional funds. *Student Employment:* Federal Work-Study Program available. Institutional employment available. **Financial Aid Statistics:** 96% needy freshmen, 94% needy undergrads receive need-based scholarship or grant aid. 0% undergrads receive non-need-based scholarship or grant aid. 81% freshmen, 87% undergrads receive need-based self-help aid. 0% freshmen, 0% undergrads receive athletic scholarships. 55% freshmen, 57% undergrads receive any aid. 37% undergrads borrow to pay for school. Average cumulative indebtedness $23,810.

BRYAN COLLEGE

Bryan College Office of Admissions, Dayton, TN 37321
Phone: 423-775-7158 • **Financial Aid Phone:** 423-775-7339
E-mail: admissions@bryan.edu • **CEEB Code:** 1908
Fax: 423-775-7199 • **Website:** www.bryan.edu • **ACT Code:** 4038

This private school was founded in 1930. It has a 125-acre campus.

RATINGS

Admissions Selectivity Rating: 86   **Fire Safety Rating:** 97   **Green Rating:** 60*

STUDENTS AND FACULTY

Enrollment: 605. **Student Body:** 53% female, 47% male, 66% out-of-state, 5% international (22 countries represented). Asian 0%, African American 3%, Caucasian 87%, Hispanic 3%, Native American 0%, Pacific Islander 0%, Two or more races 3%, Race unknown 0%.
Retention and Graduation: 60% freshmen return for sophomore year. 45% freshmen graduate within 4 years. 54% freshmen graduate within 6 years. **Faculty:** Student/faculty ratio 15:1. 36 full-time faculty, 64% hold PhDs, 0% are are members of minority groups, 28% are women. 0% of classes are taught by teaching assistants.

ACADEMICS

Degrees: associate, bachelor's, master's. **Classes:** Most classes have 10-19 students. **Most popular majors:** Business Administration and Management;

Health and Physical Education/Fitness; Communication, Journalism, and Related Programs. **Special Study Options:** distance learning, dual enrollment, honors program, independent study, internships, study abroad. **Disability Services:** Special programs offered to physically disabled students, including note-taking services, reader services, tape recorders, tutors. **Career Services:** Alumni network, Alumni services, Career/job search classes, Career assessment, Internships, On-campus interviews. Internships, Mock Interviews, Networking/job search workshops

FACILITIES

Housing: men's dorms, women's dorms, apartments for married students, apartments for single students. **Special Academic Facilities/Equipment:** Willard Henning Natural History Museum **Computers:** 100% of classrooms, 100% of dorms, 100% of libraries, 100% of dining areas, 100% of student union, 80% of common outdoor areas have wireless network access. Administrative functions (other than registration) can be performed online.

CAMPUS LIFE

Environment: Town. **Activities:** Choral groups, drama/theater, musical theater, radio station, student government, student newspaper, yearbook, Campus Ministries. **Athletics (Intercollegiate):** *Men:* baseball, basketball, cross-country, golf, soccer, track/field (outdoor), track/field (indoor). *Women:* basketball, cross-country, golf, soccer, softball, track/field (outdoor), track/field (indoor). **On-Campus Highlights:** Student Center, Library, The "Grassy Bowl", The Commons

ADMISSIONS

Freshman Academic Profile: Average high school GPA 3.6. 16% in top 10% of high school class, 48% in top 25% of high school class, 76% in top 50% of high school class. 55% from public high schools. **Reported SAT (pre-2016 redesign) scores:** SAT Math middle 50% range 450-580. SAT Critical Reading middle 50% range 450-600. SAT Writing middle 50% range 440-590. **Concordant SAT scores:** SAT EBRW middle 50% 500–650. SAT Math middle 50% range 490–600. ACT middle 50% range 20-26. Minimum internet-based TOEFL 75. **Basis for Candidate Selection:** *Very important factors considered include:* rigor of secondary school record, academic GPA, standardized test scores, application essay. *Important factors considered include:* recommendation(s), interview, character/personal qualities, religious affiliation/commitment, level of applicant's interest. *Other factors considered include:* class rank, extracurricular activities, talent/ability, alumni/ae relation, volunteer work. **Freshman Admission Requirements:** High school diploma is required and GED is accepted. *Academic units recommended:* 4 English, 3 math, 3 science, 2 foreign language, 3 social studies. **Freshman Admission Statistics:** 760 applied, 48.42% admitted, 50% enrolled. **Transfer Admission Requirements:** college transcript(s), essay or personal statement, standardized test scores, Minimum college GPA of 2.75 required. Lowest grade transferable 2. **General Admission Information:** Application fee $35. Nonfall registration accepted. Admission may be deferred.

COSTS AND FINANCIAL AID

Annual tuition $22,200. Room and board $6,550. Average book expense $1,250. **Required Forms and Deadlines:** FAFSA. **Types of Aid:** *Need-based scholarships/grants:* Federal Pell, FSEOG, State scholarships/grants, Private scholarships, College/university scholarship or grant aid from institutional funds. *Loans:* Direct Subsidized Stafford Loans, Direct Unsubsidized Stafford Loans, Direct PLUS loans, Federal Perkins Loans, College/university loans from institutional funds. *Student Employment:* Federal Work-Study Program available. Institutional employment available. **Financial Aid Statistics:** 0% freshmen, 2% undergrads receive athletic scholarships. 100% freshmen, 98% undergrads receive any aid. **Criteria for awarding aid:** *Need-based:* Academics, Minority status. *Non-need-based:* Academics, Alumni affiliation, Athletics, Leadership, Minority status, Music/drama, State/district residency.

BRYANT UNIVERSITY

Office of Admission; 1150 Douglas Pike, Smithfield, RI 02917-1291
Phone: 401-232-6100 • **Financial Aid Phone:** 401-232-6020
E-mail: http://www.bryant.edu/admissions/request • **CEEB Code:** 3095
Fax: 401-232-6731 • **Website:** http://www.bryant.edu/ • **ACT Code:** 3802

This private school was founded in 1863. It has a 420-acre campus.

RATINGS

Admissions Selectivity Rating: 85   **Fire Safety Rating:** 89   **Green Rating:** 81

STUDENTS AND FACULTY

Enrollment: 3,430. **Student Body:** 41% female, 59% male, 88% out-of-state, 8% international (72 countries represented). Asian 5%, African American 4%, Caucasian 73%, Hispanic 7%, Native American <1%, Pacific Islander <1%, Two or more races 1%, Race unknown 2%.

Retention and Graduation: 90% freshmen return for sophomore year. 76% freshmen graduate within 4 years. 80 21% grads go on to further study within 1 year. 2% grads pursue arts and sciences degrees. 2% grads pursue law degrees. 17% grads pursue business degrees. **Faculty:** Student/faculty ratio 13:1. 166 full-time faculty, 80% hold PhDs, 16% are are members of minority groups, 43% are women. 0% of classes are taught by teaching assistants.

ACADEMICS

Degrees: bachelor's, master's. **Classes:** Most classes have 30-39 students. Most lab/discussion sessions have fewer than 10 students. **Most popular majors:** Accounting; Finance; Marketing/Marketing Management. **Special Study Options:** double major, English as a Second Language (ESL), honors program, independent study, internships, study abroad. **Honors Programs:** The Bryant University Honors Program offers its members a personalized, distinctive experience that enriches their academic, social, cultural and professional talents in a mentor-oriented environment. The Program offers its members a different experience to develop the unique talents of exceptionally prepared and focused individuals. Designated courses in the Honors Program are organized to encourage in-depth classroom discussions and application of business and liberal arts disciplines with reduced class sizes. **Disability Services:** Special programs offered to physically disabled students, including note-taking services, tape recorders, tutors. **Career Services:** Alumni network, Alumni services, Career/job search classes, Career assessment, Internships, Regional alumni. Career planning is a lifelong process that is best started early. Our nationally recognized Amica Center for Career Education helps connect students, alumni mentors and potential employers, and helps you connect your interests and goals to a path toward success by offering you comprehensive career development, academic internship programs, corporate recruiting, workshops, career fairs, and other events.

FACILITIES

Housing: Coed dorms, special housing for disabled students, women's dorms, apartments for single students, Honors, Business. 90% of campus accessible to physically diasbled. **Special Academic Facilities/Equipment:** George E. Bello Center for Information and Technology, Koffler Technology Center and Communications Complex, John H. Chafee Center for International Business, Koffler Television Studio, C.V. Starr Financial Markets Center, Learning and Language Lab. **Computers:** 100% of classrooms, 100% of dorms, 100% of libraries, 100% of dining areas, 100% of student union, 100% of common outdoor areas have wireless network access. Students can register for classes online. Administrative functions (other than registration) can be performed online. Undergraduates are required to own a computer.

CAMPUS LIFE

Environment: Village. **Activities:** Choral groups, dance, drama/theater, jazz band, literary magazine, music ensembles, musical theater, pep band, radio station, student government, student newspaper, television station, yearbook, Campus Ministries, Student Organization. 87 registered organizations, 6 honor societies, 5 religious organizations. 6 fraternities, 2 sororities. **Athletics (Intercollegiate):** *Men:* baseball, basketball, cross-country, football, golf, lacrosse, soccer, swimming, tennis, track/field (outdoor), track/field (indoor). *Women:* basketball, cross-country, field hockey, lacrosse, soccer, softball, swimming, tennis, track/field (outdoor), track/field (indoor), volleyball. **On-Campus Highlights:** Bello Center for Information andTechnolo, Chase Athletics and Wellness Center, Unistructure Rotunda, Koffler Technology and Communications Co, Bryant Center, The Bello Center for Information & Technology houses the Douglas & Judith Krupp Library, the Stepan Grand Hall, and the C.V. Starr Financial Markets Center (FMC) featuring real-time stock market data and Reuters 3000. The Wellness Center features a fitness center modeled after private health clubs and a six-lane, 25-yard swimming pool. The Bryant Center houses offices for student organizations around campus including The Archway, the student newspaper, as well as dining options including Subway, South Side Deli, the Scoop, South Cafe, and the Sky Ranch Grill. The Rotunda is a hub of student activity located in the main classroom building, the Unistructure. The Communication Complex houses the all-digital television studio and radio station, WJMF, as well as advanced multimedia editing rooms for use with AVID software. WJMF streams live over the internet and offers podcasts on its website, http://www.wjmf887.com. **Environmental Initiatives:** Recycling Program.

ADMISSIONS

Freshman Academic Profile: Average high school GPA 3.4. 24% in top 10% of high school class, 58% in top 25% of high school class, 90% in top 50% of high school class. 71% from public high schools. **Reported SAT (pre-2016 redesign) scores:** SAT Math middle 50% range 560-640. SAT Critical Reading middle 50% range 530-610. SAT Writing middle 50% range 510-610. **Concordant SAT scores:** SAT EBRW middle 50% 580–660. SAT Math middle 50% range 580–660. ACT middle 50% range 23-27. Minimum internet-based

TOEFL 80. Minimum paper TOEFL 550. **Basis for Candidate Selection:** *Very important factors considered include:* rigor of secondary school record, academic GPA. *Important factors considered include:* class rank, standardized test scores, application essay, recommendation(s). *Other factors considered include:* interview, extracurricular activities, talent/ability, character/personal qualities, first generation, alumni/ae relation, geographical residence, state residency, racial/ethnic status, volunteer work, work experience, level of applicant's interest. **Freshman Admission Requirements:** High school diploma is required and GED is accepted. *Academic units required:* 4 English, 4 math, 2 science, 2 science labs, 2 foreign language, 2 history. *Academic units recommended:* 4 English, 4 math, 3 science, 2 science labs, 2 foreign language, 3 history. **Freshman Admission Statistics:** 6,705 applied, 72.32% admitted, 19% enrolled. **Transfer Admission Requirements:** High school transcript, college transcript(s), essay or personal statement, Minimum college GPA of 2.5 required. Lowest grade transferable C. **General Admission Information:** Application fee $50. Regular application deadline 2/1. Regular notification 3/15. Nonfall registration accepted. Admission may be deferred for a maximum of 1 year.

COSTS AND FINANCIAL AID

Annual tuition $40,564. Room and board $14,975. Required fees $398. Average book expense $1,300. **Required Forms and Deadlines:** FAFSA. **Notification of Awards:** Applicants will be notified of awards on or about 3/24. **Types of Aid:** *Need-based scholarships/grants:* Federal Pell, FSEOG, State scholarships/grants, Private scholarships, College/university scholarship or grant aid from institutional funds. *Loans:* Direct Subsidized Stafford Loans, Direct Unsubsidized Stafford Loans, Direct PLUS loans, Federal Perkins Loans. *Student Employment:* Federal Work-Study Program available. Institutional employment available. **Financial Aid Statistics:** 71% needy freshmen, 70% needy undergrads receive need-based scholarship or grant aid. 82% freshmen, 75% undergrads receive non-need-based scholarship or grant aid. 91% freshmen, 94% undergrads receive need-based self-help aid. 4% freshmen, 5% undergrads receive athletic scholarships. 79% freshmen, 87% undergrads receive any aid. 71% undergrads borrow to pay for school. Average cumulative indebtedness $44,384. **Criteria for awarding aid:** *Need-based:* Minority status. *Non-need-based:* Academics, Athletics, Minority status.

See page 928.

BRYN ATHYN COLLEGE OF THE NEW CHURCH

P.O. Box 462, Bryn Athyn, PA 19009
Phone: 267-502-6000 • **Financial Aid Phone:** 267-502-6034
E-mail: admissions@brynathyn.edu • **CEEB Code:** 2002
Fax: 267-502-2593 • **Website:** www.brynathyn.edu • **ACT Code:** 3228

This private school was founded in 1877. It has a 130-acre campus.

RATINGS

Admissions Selectivity Rating: 79 **Fire Safety Rating:** 95 **Green Rating:** 60*

STUDENTS AND FACULTY

Enrollment: 273. **Student Body:** 47% female, 53% male, 41% out-of-state, 4% international (8 countries represented). Asian 3%, African American 20%, Caucasian 62%, Hispanic 10%, Native American 0%, Pacific Islander <1%, Two or more races <1%, Race unknown 1%.

Retention and Graduation: 64% freshmen return for sophomore year. 57% freshmen graduate within 4 years. 77% freshmen graduate within 6 years. 5% grads go on to further study within 1 year. 5% grads pursue arts and sciences degrees. 5% grads pursue business degrees. 10% grads pursue medical degrees. **Faculty:** Student/faculty ratio 8:1. 28 full-time faculty, 61% hold PhDs, 4% are are members of minority groups, 39% are women. 0% of classes are taught by teaching assistants.

ACADEMICS

Degrees: associate, bachelor's, master's. **Classes:** Most classes have 10-19 students. **Most popular majors:** Multi-/Interdisciplinary Studies; Psychology; Business/Commerce. **Special Study Options:** Accelerated program, cooperative education program, cross-registration, distance learning, English as a Second Language (ESL), independent study, internships, student-designed major, study abroad, teacher certification program. Combined degree programs: **Disability Services:** Special programs offered to physically disabled students, including tape recorders, tutors. **Career Services:** Alumni network, Alumni services, Career assessment, Internships, Regional alumni, On-campus interviews. Internships at Bryn Athyn College are developed on an individual basis, and occur in places around the world. Opportunities can be arranged as early as the first year, founded on the belief that this applied learning can help new first-year students chart their academic programs of study.

FACILITIES

Housing: men's dorms, women's dorms, On-campus cottages for upperclassmen. 70% of campus accessible to physically diasbled. **Special Academic Facilities/Equipment:** Glencairn Museum Swedenborg Library Swedenborgiana Academy of the New Church Archives John Pitcairn Archives Raymond and Mildred Pitcairn Archives **Computers:** 100% of classrooms, 100% of dorms, 100% of libraries, 75% of common outdoor areas have wireless network access.

CAMPUS LIFE

Environment: Village. **Activities:** Choral groups, concert band, dance, drama/theater, music ensembles, student government, student newspaper, Student Organization. 15 registered organizations. **On-Campus Highlights:** College Grounds Cafe, Swedenborg Library, Brickman Center for Student Life, Asplundh Field House, Glencairn Museum. **Environmental Initiatives:** Chemical purchase, storage and disposal plan, Recycling program for glass and paper in all buildings.

ADMISSIONS

Freshman Academic Profile: Average high school GPA 3.1. **Reported SAT (pre-2016 redesign) scores:** SAT Math middle 50% range 395-550. SAT Critical Reading middle 50% range 390-555. SAT Writing middle 50% range 388-530. **Concordant SAT scores:** SAT EBRW middle 50% 440–600. SAT Math middle 50% range 440–570. ACT middle 50% range 17.5-23. Minimum internet-based TOEFL 70. Minimum paper TOEFL 520. **Basis for Candidate Selection:** *Very important factors considered include:* rigor of secondary school record, academic GPA, standardized test scores, application essay, recommendation(s). *Important factors considered include:* character/personal qualities. *Other factors considered include:* interview, extracurricular activities, talent/ability, alumni/ae relation, religious affiliation/commitment, racial/ethnic status, volunteer work, work experience, level of applicant's interest. **Freshman Admission Requirements:** High school diploma is required and GED is accepted. *Academic units required:* 4 English, 3 math, 3 science, 2 foreign language, 3 social studies, 3 history. *Academic units recommended:* 3 science labs. **Freshman Admission Statistics:** 439 applied, 42.14% admitted, 42% enrolled. **Transfer Admission Requirements:** High school transcript, college transcript(s), essay or personal statement, Minimum college GPA of 2.0 required. Lowest grade transferable C. **General Admission Information:** Nonfall registration accepted. Admission may be deferred for a maximum of 1 year.

COSTS AND FINANCIAL AID

Annual tuition $18,558. Room and board $11,538. Required fees $1,324. Average book expense $750. **Required Forms and Deadlines:** FAFSA, State aid form. **Notification of Awards:** Applicants will be notified of awards on a rolling basis beginning 3/1. **Types of Aid:** *Need-based scholarships/grants:* Federal Pell, FSEOG, State scholarships/grants, Private scholarships, College/university scholarship or grant aid from institutional funds. *Loans:* Direct Subsidized Stafford Loans, Direct Unsubsidized Stafford Loans, Direct PLUS loans, College/university loans from institutional funds. *Student Employment:* Federal Work-Study Program available. Institutional employment available. **Financial Aid Statistics:** 88% needy freshmen, 85% needy undergrads receive need-based scholarship or grant aid. 48% freshmen, 51% undergrads receive non-need-based scholarship or grant aid. 78% freshmen, 79% undergrads receive need-based self-help aid. 0% freshmen, 0% undergrads receive athletic scholarships. 71% freshmen, 65% undergrads receive any aid. 77% undergrads borrow to pay for school. Average cumulative indebtedness $23,625. **Criteria for awarding aid:** *Non-need-based:* Academics, Religious affiliation.

BRYN MAWR COLLEGE

Best Colleges

101 North Merion Avenue, Bryn Mawr, PA 19010-2859
Phone: 610-526-5152 • **Financial Aid Phone:** 610-526-5245
E-mail: admissions@brynmawr.edu • **CEEB Code:** 2049
Fax: 610-526-7471 • **Website:** www.brynmawr.edu • **ACT Code:** 3526

This private school was founded in 1885. It has a 135-acre campus.

RATINGS

Admissions Selectivity Rating: 94   **Fire Safety Rating:** 87   **Green Rating:** 82

STUDENTS AND FACULTY

Enrollment: 1,371. **Student Body:** 100% female, 0% male, 84% out-of-state, 23% international (60 countries represented). Asian 12%, African American 6%, Caucasian 36%, Hispanic 9%, Native American <1%, Pacific Islander <1%, Two or more races 6%, Race unknown 8%.

Retention and Graduation: 94% freshmen return for sophomore year. 78% freshmen graduate within 4 years. 83% freshmen graduate within 6 years. 24% grads go on to further study within 1 year. 9% grads pursue arts and sciences degrees. 1% grads pursue law degrees. 1% grads pursue business degrees. 1% grads pursue medical degrees. **Faculty:** Student/faculty ratio 8:1. 152 full-time faculty, 97% hold PhDs, 17% are are members of minority groups, 57% are women. 0% of classes are taught by teaching assistants.

ACADEMICS

Degrees: bachelor's, doctoral/research, master's, postbachelor's certificate. **Classes:** Most classes have 10-19 students. **Most popular majors:** Biology/Biological Sciences; Psychology; English Language and Literature. **Special Study Options:** Accelerated program, cross-registration, double major, dual enrollment, exchange student program (domestic), independent study, internships, liberal arts/career combination, student-designed major, study abroad, teacher certification program, A.B./M.A. City Planning 3-2 Program in City and Regional Planning offered with the University of Pennsylvania. A.B./B.S. 3-2 engineering programs with Cal Tech. Combined degree programs: BA/MA, 3-2 progam in city planning w/U Penn. **Disability Services:** Special programs offered to physically disabled students, including note-taking services, reader services, tape recorders, tutors. **Career Services:** Alumni network, Alumni services, Career assessment, Internships, Regional alumni. Praxis I for 3 hours per week, Praxis II for 6—8 hours per week and Praxis III as a supervised independent study involving 10—12 hours per week in the field. These are courses for full credit.

FACILITIES

Housing: Coed dorms, women's dorms, cooperative housing, apartments for single students, Students may live at Haverford. Foreign language houses available to students studying Chinese, French, German, Hebrew, Italian, Russsian or Spanish. Coed housing is available. Special housing available for non-traditional-aged students. Co-ops, such as Vegan House, are available as well. **Special Academic Facilities/Equipment:** Museum of classical and Near Eastern archaeology, mineral collection, Child Study Institute, on-campus nursery school, Newfeld Collection of African Art, Language Learning Center. **Computers:** 60% of classrooms, 10% of dorms, 25% of libraries, 10% of dining areas, 100% of student union, 10% of common outdoor areas have wireless network access. Students can register for classes online. Administrative functions (other than registration) can be performed online.

CAMPUS LIFE

Environment: Metropolis. **Activities:** Choral groups, dance, drama/theater, jazz band, literary magazine, marching band, music ensembles, musical theater, radio station, student government, student newspaper, student-run film society, yearbook. 94 registered organizations, 10 religious organizations. **Athletics (Intercollegiate):** *Women:* badminton, basketball, crew/rowing, cross-country, field hockey, lacrosse, soccer, swimming, tennis, track/field (outdoor), track/field (indoor), volleyball. **On-Campus Highlights:** Thomas Hall (on National Historic Landma, Erdman Hall (designed by famed architect, The Cloister and Great Hall, Taft Garden, Rhys Carpenter Library, Goodhart Theater. **Environmental Initiatives:** We have received two Pennsylvania Growing Greener Grants for watershed improvements under the Environmental improvement and Watershed Protection Act. We are committed to being good steward's of the waterway that pass through our campus.

ADMISSIONS

Freshman Academic Profile: 66% in top 10% of high school class, 90% in top 25% of high school class, 96% in top 50% of high school class. 62% from public high schools. **Reported SAT (pre-2016 redesign) scores:** SAT Math middle 50% range 610-720. SAT Critical Reading middle 50% range 610-730. SAT Writing middle 50% range 630-720. **Concordant SAT scores:** SAT EBRW middle 50% 670–750. SAT Math middle 50% range 630–750. ACT middle 50% range 28-32. Minimum internet-based TOEFL 100. Minimum paper TOEFL 600. **Basis for Candidate Selection:** *Very important factors considered include:* rigor of secondary school record, recommendation(s). *Important factors considered include:* academic GPA, application essay, extracurricular activities, character/personal qualities. *Other factors considered include:* class rank, standardized test scores, interview, talent/ability, first generation, alumni/ae relation, geographical residence, state residency, racial/ethnic status, volunteer work, work experience. **Freshman Admission Requirements:** High school diploma is required and GED is accepted. *Academic units recommended:* 4 English, 3 math, 2 science, 1 science lab, 3 foreign language, 2 social studies, 2 history, 2 academic electives. **Freshman Admission Statistics:** 3,012 applied, 39.94% admitted, 34% enrolled. **Transfer Admission Requirements:** High school transcript, college transcript(s), essay or personal statement, standardized test scores, statement of good standing from prior institution(s). Lowest grade transferable C. **General Admission Information:** Application fee $50. Regular application deadline 1/15. Regular notification 4/1. Nonfall registration not accepted. Admission may be deferred for a maximum of 12 months.

COSTS AND FINANCIAL AID

Required Forms and Deadlines: FAFSA, CSS/Financial Aid PROFILE. **Types of Aid:** *Need-based scholarships/grants:* Federal Pell, FSEOG, State scholarships/grants, College/university scholarship or grant aid from institutional funds. *Loans:* Direct Subsidized Stafford Loans, Direct Unsubsidized Stafford Loans, Direct PLUS loans, Federal Perkins Loans. *Student Employment:* Federal Work-Study Program available. Institutional employment available. **Financial Aid Statistics:** 100% needy freshmen, 98% needy undergrads receive need-based scholarship or grant aid. 6% freshmen, 5% undergrads receive non-need-based scholarship or grant aid. 94% freshmen, 94% undergrads receive need-based self-help aid. 0% freshmen, 0% undergrads receive athletic scholarships. 74% freshmen, 74% undergrads receive any aid. 52% undergrads borrow to pay for school. Average cumulative indebtedness $23,081. **Criteria for awarding aid:** *Non-need-based:* Academics, Leadership.

BUCKNELL UNIVERSITY

Office of Admissions, 1 Dent Drive, Lewisburg, PA 17837
Phone: 570-577-3000 • **Financial Aid Phone:** 570-577-1331
E-mail: admissions@bucknell.edu • **CEEB Code:** 2050
Fax: 570-577-3538 • **Website:** www.bucknell.edu • **ACT Code:** 3528

This private school was founded in 1846. It has a 446-acre campus.

RATINGS

Admissions Selectivity Rating: 94   **Fire Safety Rating:** 94   **Green Rating:** 96

STUDENTS AND FACULTY

Enrollment: 3,531. **Student Body:** 51% female, 49% male, 78% out-of-state, 6% international (51 countries represented). Asian 5%, African American 3%, Caucasian 75%, Hispanic 6%, Native American <1%, Pacific Islander 0%, Two or more races 4%, Race unknown <1%.
Retention and Graduation: 92% freshmen return for sophomore year. 84% freshmen graduate within 4 years. 88% freshmen graduate within 6 years. 20% grads go on to further study within 1 year. 8% grads pursue arts and sciences degrees. 1% grads pursue law degrees. 1% grads pursue business degrees. 4% grads pursue medical degrees. **Faculty:** Student/faculty ratio 9:1. 378 full-time faculty, 97% hold PhDs, 17% are are members of minority groups, 41% are women. 0% of classes are taught by teaching assistants.

ACADEMICS

Degrees: bachelor's, master's. **Classes:** Most classes have 10-19 students. Most lab/discussion sessions have 10-19 students. **Most popular majors:** Economics; Biology; Psychology. **Special Study Options:** double major, dual enrollment, honors program, independent study, internships, liberal arts/career combination, student-designed major, study abroad, teacher certification program. Combined degree programs: BS/MS 5-yr. program in biology, chem, math, eng. **Disability Services:** Special programs offered to physically disabled students, including tape recorders, tutors. **Career Services:** Alumni network, Alumni services, Career/job search classes, Career assessment, Internships, Regional alumni. Bucknell's Institute for Leadership in Technology and Management (ILTM) was founded in 1993 to offer Bucknell students a unique learning experience that bridges the disciplines of engineering and management. Consisting of a two-summer sequence of programs, the ILTM brings together in the first summer 18 of the best and most highly motivated rising juniors in engineering and management to engage in an extremely intensive, six-week, on-campus program that focuses on globalization, ethics, communication skills, critical thinking, teamwork, and leadership.

FACILITIES

Housing: Coed dorms, special housing for disabled students, men's dorms, special housing for international students, women's dorms, fraternity/sorority housing, cooperative housing, apartments for single students, Wellness Housing, Theme Housing. 80% of campus accessible to physically disabled. **Special Academic Facilities/Equipment:** Art gallery, center for performing arts, poetry center, photography lab, observatory, 63-acre nature site, greenhouse, primate facility, gas chromatograph/mass spectrometer, electron microscope, herbarium, crafts center, engineering structural test lab, nuclear magnetic resonance spectrometer, 18-hole golf course, conference center, high ropes course **Computers:** 100% of classrooms, 100% of dorms, 100% of libraries, 100% of dining areas, 100% of student union, 95% of common outdoor areas have wireless network access. Students can register for classes online. Administrative functions (other than registration) can be performed online.

CAMPUS LIFE

Environment: Village. **Activities:** Choral groups, concert band, dance, drama/theater, jazz band, literary magazine, music ensembles, musical theater, opera, pep band, radio station, student government, student newspaper, student-run film society, symphony orchestra, yearbook, Campus Ministries, Student Organization, Model UN. 150 registered organizations, 23 honor societies, 13 religious organizations. 12 fraternities, 8 sororities. **Athletics (Intercollegiate):** *Men:* baseball, basketball, cross-country, diving, football, golf, lacrosse, soccer, swimming, tennis, track/field (outdoor), track/field (indoor), water polo, wrestling. *Women:* basketball, crew/rowing, cross-country, diving, field hockey, golf, lacrosse, soccer, softball, swimming, tennis, track/field (outdoor), track/field (indoor), volleyball, water polo. **On-Campus Highlights:** Weis Center for the Performing Arts, Outdoor Primate Facilities, Uptown Night Club, Stadler Poetry Center, Library with Technology and Media Commons, Bertrand Library, Seventh Street Cafe, Elaine Langone Center (student center), Bucknell Observatory, Environmental Center, Samek Art Gallery. **Environmental Initiatives:** In May 2009, the Bucknell University Environmental Center (BUEC) completed a campus-wide environmental assessment of the university's operations, involving over 70 faculty, students, staff, and community members in a highly educational and collaborative project. Teams conducted research on ten indicators of sustainability, including administration/policy, education, energy, water, solid waste, hazardous materials, purchasing, dining, built environment, and landscape. The full report is available at http:www.bucknell.edu/x45647.xml.

ADMISSIONS

Freshman Academic Profile: Average high school GPA 3.5. 59% in top 10% of high school class, 84% in top 25% of high school class, 98% in top 50% of high school class. 64% from public high schools. **Reported SAT (pre-2016 redesign) scores:** SAT Math middle 50% range 610-710. SAT Critical Reading middle 50% range 590-670. SAT Writing middle 50% range 590-690. **Concordant SAT scores:** SAT EBRW middle 50% 650–720. SAT Math middle 50% range 630–740. ACT middle 50% range 28-32. Minimum internet-based TOEFL 100. Minimum paper TOEFL 600. **Basis for Candidate Selection:** *Very important factors considered include:* rigor of secondary school record, academic GPA, standardized test scores, application essay, talent/ability, character/personal qualities. *Important factors considered include:* recommendation(s), extracurricular activities, volunteer work, work experience. *Other factors considered include:* class rank, first generation, alumni/ae relation, geographical residence, religious affiliation/commitment, racial/ethnic status. **Freshman Admission Requirements:** High school diploma is required and GED is accepted. *Academic units required:* 4 English, 3 math, 2 science, 2 foreign language, 2 social studies, 2 history, 1 academic elective. *Academic units recommended:* 4 English, 4 math, 2 science, 2 science labs, 4 foreign language, 2 social studies, 2 history, 1 academic elective. **Freshman Admission Statistics:** 10,487 applied, 29.92% admitted, 30% enrolled. **Transfer Admission Requirements:** High school transcript, college transcript(s), essay or personal statement, standardized test scores, statement of good standing from prior institution(s). Minimum college GPA of 2.5 required. Lowest grade transferable C. **General Admission Information:** Application fee $40. Regular application deadline 1/15. Regular notification 4/1. Nonfall registration not accepted. Admission may be deferred for a maximum of 2 years.

COSTS AND FINANCIAL AID

Annual tuition $51,676. Room and board $12,656. Required fees $284. Average book expense $900. **Required Forms and Deadlines:** FAFSA, CSS/Financial Aid PROFILE. **Notification of Awards:** Applicants will be notified of awards on or about 4/1. **Types of Aid:** *Need-based scholarships/grants:* Federal Pell, FSEOG, State scholarships/grants, Private scholarships, College/university scholarship or grant aid from institutional funds. *Loans:* Direct Subsidized Stafford Loans, Direct Unsubsidized Stafford Loans, Direct PLUS loans, Federal Perkins Loans. *Student Employment:* Federal Work-Study Program available. Institutional employment available. **Financial Aid Statistics:** 89% needy freshmen, 95% needy undergrads receive need-based scholarship or grant aid. 27% freshmen, 23% undergrads receive non-need-based scholarship or grant aid. 100% freshmen, 100% undergrads receive need-based self-help aid. 4% freshmen, 5% undergrads receive athletic scholarships. 62% freshmen, 62% undergrads receive any aid. Average cumulative indebtedness $22,600. **Criteria for awarding aid:** *Need-based:* Academics, Athletics, Minority status. *Non-need-based:* Academics, Art, Athletics, Leadership, Music/drama.

See page 930.

BUENA VISTA UNIVERSITY

610 West Fourth Street, Storm Lake, IA 50588-1798
Phone: 712-749-2235 • **Financial Aid Phone:** 712-749-2164
E-mail: admissions@bvu.edu • **CEEB Code:** 6047
Fax: 712-749-2035 • **Website:** www.bvu.edu • **ACT Code:** 1278

This private school, affiliated with the Presbyterian Church, was founded in 1891. It has a 60-acre campus.

RATINGS
Admissions Selectivity Rating: 80   **Fire Safety Rating:** 62   **Green Rating:** 60*

STUDENTS AND FACULTY
Enrollment: 781. **Student Body:** 51% female, 49% male, 21% out-of-state, 5% international (16 countries represented). Asian 2%, African American 3%, Caucasian 75%, Hispanic 7%, Native American 0%, Pacific Islander <1%, Two or more races 4%, Race unknown 4%.
Retention and Graduation: 73% freshmen return for sophomore year. 44% freshmen graduate within 4 years. 53% freshmen graduate within 6 years. 13% grads go on to further study within 1 year. **Faculty:** Student/faculty ratio 9:1. 82 full-time faculty, 77% hold PhDs, 9% are are members of minority groups, 55% are women. 0% of classes are taught by teaching assistants.

ACADEMICS
Degrees: bachelor's, master's. **Classes:** Most classes have 10-19 students. Most lab/discussion sessions have 10-19 students. **Most popular majors:** Biology/Biological Sciences; Elementary Education and Teaching; Business/Commerce. **Special Study Options:** distance learning, double major, dual enrollment, English as a Second Language (ESL), external degree program, honors program, independent study, internships, student-designed major, study abroad, teacher certification program, Off-Campus Study:Other semester-away programs available. Academic and cultural events series brings national and world leaders and performers to campus; students earn credits for attendance. **Disability Services:** Special programs offered to physically disabled students, including note-taking services, reader services, tape recorders, tutors. **Career Services:** Alumni network, Alumni services, Career/job search classes, Career assessment, Internships.

FACILITIES
Housing: Coed dorms, men's dorms, women's dorms. **Special Academic Facilities/Equipment:** Art gallery, language lab, television station, radio station, satellite telecommunications system, computer labs/centers, electron microscope. **Computers:** 100% of classrooms, 100% of dorms, 100% of libraries, 100% of dining areas, 100% of common outdoor areas have wireless network access. Students can register for classes online. Administrative functions (other than registration) can be performed online.

CAMPUS LIFE
Environment: Village. **Activities:** Choral groups, concert band, dance, drama/theater, jazz band, music ensembles, musical theater, pep band, radio station, student government, student newspaper, television station, Campus Ministries, Student Organization. 65 registered organizations, 5 honor societies, 3 religious organizations. **Athletics (Intercollegiate):** *Men:* baseball, basketball, cross-country, football, golf, soccer, tennis, track/field (outdoor), track/field (indoor), wrestling. *Women:* basketball, cross-country, golf, soccer, softball, tennis, track/field (outdoor), track/field (indoor), volleyball. **On-Campus Highlights:** Recreation Center, Harold Walter Siebens Forum, Centennial Room, Suites are the biggest dorms on campus.

ADMISSIONS
Freshman Academic Profile: Average high school GPA 3.4. 16% in top 10% of high school class, 40% in top 25% of high school class, 79% in top 50% of high school class. 85% from public high schools. ACT middle 50% range 19-26. Minimum internet-based TOEFL 59. Minimum paper TOEFL 500. **Basis for Candidate Selection:** *Very important factors considered include:* class rank, academic GPA, standardized test scores. *Important factors considered include:* extracurricular activities, character/personal qualities. *Other factors considered include:* rigor of secondary school record, application essay, recommendation(s), interview, talent/ability, alumni/ae relation, volunteer work, work experience. **Freshman Admission Requirements:** High school diploma is required and GED is accepted. *Academic units recommended:* 4 English, 4 math, 3 science, 1 science lab, 3 social studies. **Freshman Admission Statistics:** 1,256 applied, 63.69% admitted, 23% enrolled. **Transfer Admission Requirements:** college transcript(s), statement of good standing from prior institution(s). Minimum college GPA of 2.0 required. Lowest grade transferable D. **General Admission Information:** Nonfall registration accepted. Admission may be deferred for a maximum of 1 year.

COSTS AND FINANCIAL AID
Annual tuition $32,854. Room and board $9,490. Average book expense $999. **Required Forms and Deadlines:** FAFSA. **Types of Aid:** *Need-based*

scholarships/grants: Federal Pell, FSEOG, State scholarships/grants, Private scholarships, College/university scholarship or grant aid from institutional funds. *Loans:* Direct Subsidized Stafford Loans, Direct Unsubsidized Stafford Loans, Direct PLUS loans, Federal Perkins Loans, College/university loans from institutional funds. *Student Employment:* Federal Work-Study Program available. Institutional employment available. **Financial Aid Statistics:** 98% needy freshmen, 99% needy undergrads receive need-based scholarship or grant aid. 15% freshmen, 17% undergrads receive non-need-based scholarship or grant aid. 90% freshmen, 90% undergrads receive need-based self-help aid. 0% freshmen, 0% undergrads receive athletic scholarships. 99% freshmen, 98% undergrads receive any aid. 86% undergrads borrow to pay for school. Average cumulative indebtedness $33,559. **Criteria for awarding aid:** *Non-need-based:* Academics, Art, Minority status, Music/drama.

BURLINGTON COLLEGE

351 North Ave, Burlington, VT 5401
Phone: 802-862-9616 x104 • **Financial Aid Phone:** 802-862-9616 ext 110
E-mail: admissions@burlington.edu • **CEEB Code:** 1119
Fax: 802-660-4331 • **Website:** www.burlington.edu • **ACT Code:** 4329

This private school was founded in 1972. It has a 1-acre campus.

RATINGS
Admissions Selectivity Rating: 73   **Fire Safety Rating:** 70   **Green Rating:** 60*

STUDENTS AND FACULTY
Enrollment: 178. **Student Body:** 48% female, 52% male, 46% out-of-state, 2% international (5 countries represented). Asian 1%, African American 1%, Caucasian 83%, Hispanic 2%, Native American 1%, Pacific Islander 0%, Two or more races 1%, Race unknown 11%.
Retention and Graduation: 40% freshmen return for sophomore year. 16% grads go on to further study within 1 year. 10% grads pursue arts and sciences degrees. 5% grads pursue law degrees. **Faculty:** Student/faculty ratio 6:1. 5 full-time faculty, 60% hold PhDs, 0% are are members of minority groups, 60% are women. 0% of classes are taught by teaching assistants.

ACADEMICS
Degrees: associate, bachelor's, certificate, master's. **Classes:** Most classes have fewer than 10 students. **Most popular majors:** Multi-/Interdisciplinary Studies; Cinematography and Film/Video Production; English Language and Literature/Letters. **Special Study Options:** cross-registration, distance learning, double major, dual enrollment, external degree program, independent study, internships, liberal arts/career combination, student-designed major, study abroad, Flexible, self-designed degree program, independent study option. **Honors Programs:** A capstone Degree Project, equivalent to a graduate thesis, is required of all BA candidates. **Disability Services:** Special programs offered to physically disabled students, including note-taking services, reader services, tape recorders, tutors. **Career Services:** Career/job search classes, Internships, On-campus interviews. Action Learning/Internship. There is an internship requirement for each major carrying a minimum of 3 academic credits (96 on-site hours). For each credit, the student must complete 32 hrs of field-supervised, hands-on experience and attend a concurrent seminar which provides guidance and support.

FACILITIES
Housing: cooperative housing, apartments for single students. 100% of campus accessible to physically diasbled. **Special Academic Facilities/Equipment:** The main campus houses classrooms, film and video editing labs, a photography darkroom, a college-operated gallery and a community garden. We are within walking distance from the ECHO lake aquarium and science center, the Waterfront Blackbox Theatre and Cinema, the Community Sailing Center, the YMCA, and the Flynn Theatre. As Burlington's College, our downtown location also allows us to utilize multiple local art galleries and music venues for showcasing students arts and talents. **Computers:** 100% of classrooms, 100% of dorms, 100% of libraries, 100% of student union, have wireless network access.

CAMPUS LIFE
Environment: Town. **Activities:** literary magazine, student government, student-run film society 1 registered organization. **On-Campus Highlights:** Burlington College Community Gallery, Miller Studio, Photography Darkroom. **Environmental Initiatives:** New lighting with motion sensors.

ADMISSIONS
Freshman Academic Profile: Average high school GPA 2.9. 5% in top 10% of high school class, 19% in top 25% of high school class, 38% in top 50% of high school class. 72% from public high schools. **Reported SAT (pre-2016 redesign) scores:** SAT Math middle 50% range 425-530. SAT Critical Reading middle 50% range 440-575. SAT Writing middle 50% range 420-565.

Concordant SAT scores: SAT EBRW middle 50% 480–630. SAT Math middle 50% range 470–560. ACT middle 50% range 18-26. Minimum internet-based TOEFL 79. Minimum paper TOEFL 550. **Basis for Candidate Selection:** *Very important factors considered include:* application essay, interview, character/personal qualities. *Important factors considered include:* academic GPA, recommendation(s), talent/ability, volunteer work, level of applicant's interest. *Other factors considered include:* rigor of secondary school record, class rank, standardized test scores, extracurricular activities, first generation, alumni/ae relation, work experience. **Freshman Admission Requirements:** High school diploma is required and GED is accepted. *Academic units recommended:* 4 English, 3 math, 2 science, 2 science labs, 2 foreign language, 4 social studies, 3 history, 4 academic electives. **Freshman Admission Statistics:** 180 applied, 85.56% admitted, 25% enrolled. **Transfer Admission Requirements:** High school transcript, college transcript(s), essay or personal statement, Lowest grade transferable C. **General Admission Information:** Application fee $50. Regular application deadline 8/15. Nonfall registration accepted. Admission may be deferred for a maximum of 1 year.

COSTS AND FINANCIAL AID

Annual tuition $22,410. Required fees $135. Average book expense $1,064. **Required Forms and Deadlines:** FAFSA. **Notification of Awards:** Applicants will be notified of awards on a rolling basis beginning 2/15. **Types of Aid:** *Need-based scholarships/grants:* Federal Pell, FSEOG, State scholarships/grants, Private scholarships, College/university scholarship or grant aid from institutional funds. *Loans:* Direct Subsidized Stafford Loans, Direct Unsubsidized Stafford Loans, Direct PLUS loans, Federal Perkins Loans. *Student Employment:* Federal Work-Study Program available. **Financial Aid Statistics:** 100% needy freshmen, 95% needy undergrads receive need-based scholarship or grant aid. 0% undergrads receive non-need-based scholarship or grant aid. 86% freshmen, 96% undergrads receive need-based self-help aid. 0% freshmen, 0% undergrads receive athletic scholarships. 75% freshmen, 76% undergrads receive any aid. **Criteria for awarding aid:** *Need-based:* Academics, Leadership. *Non-need-based:* Academics, Leadership.

BUTLER UNIVERSITY

Robertson Hall, 4600 Sunset Avenue, Indianapolis, IN 46208
Phone: 317-940-8100 • **Financial Aid Phone:** 317-940-8200
E-mail: admission@butler.edu • **CEEB Code:** 1073
Fax: 317-940-8150 • **Website:** www.butler.edu • **ACT Code:** 1180

This private school was founded in 1855. It has a 290-acre campus.

RATINGS

Admissions Selectivity Rating: 88   **Fire Safety Rating:** 77   **Green Rating:** 60*

STUDENTS AND FACULTY

Enrollment: 4,236. **Student Body:** 60% female, 40% male, 55% out-of-state, 1% international (56 countries represented). Asian 3%, African American 4%, Caucasian 82%, Hispanic 4%, Native American <1%, Pacific Islander <1%, Two or more races 3%, Race unknown 3%.
Retention and Graduation: 92% freshmen return for sophomore year. 57% freshmen graduate within 4 years. 74% freshmen graduate within 6 years. 18% grads go on to further study within 1 year. 24% grads pursue arts and sciences degrees. 5% grads pursue law degrees. 5% grads pursue business degrees. 30% grads pursue medical degrees. **Faculty:** Student/faculty ratio 11:1. 359 full-time faculty, 80% hold PhDs, 11% are are members of minority groups, 50% are women. 0% of classes are taught by teaching assistants.

ACADEMICS

Degrees: bachelor's, certificate, doctoral/professional, master's. **Classes:** Most classes have 10-19 students. Most lab/discussion sessions have 20-29 students. **Most popular majors:** Marketing/Marketing Management; Pharmacy; Biology/Biological Sciences. **Special Study Options:** cross-registration, double major, dual enrollment, exchange student program (domestic), honors program, independent study, internships, student-designed major, study abroad, teacher certification program, Cooperative program in Business only. **Honors Programs:** The Butler University Honors Program exists to meet the expectations of academically outstanding students in all colleges and majors who wish to develop their talents and potential to the fullest. Through a combination of honors courses, cultural events, independent study, creative activity and research, it is designed to foster a diverse and challenging intellectual environment for honors students and to enhance our academic community by adding a distinctive note of innovative thinking and interdisciplinary dialogue. Combined degree programs: Dual-degree engineering program. **Disability Services:** Special programs offered to physically disabled students, including note-taking services, reader services. **Career Services:** Alumni network, Alumni services, Career/job search classes, Career assessment, Internships,

Regional alumni. Butler has a successful experiential learning program for its pharmacy doctoral candidates. Each student completes 10 rotations in a variety of areas including retail pharmacy, hospital, research, and clinical pharmacy. These rotations prepare pharmacists for a variety of career options.

FACILITIES

Housing: Coed dorms, women's dorms, fraternity/sorority housing, apartments for single students. 100% of campus accessible to physically diasbled. **Special Academic Facilities/Equipment:** Holcomb Observatory, Clowes Memorial Hall (performing arts theatre) **Computers:** 100% of classrooms, 100% of dorms, 100% of libraries, 100% of dining areas, 100% of student union, have wireless network access. Students can register for classes online. Administrative functions (other than registration) can be performed online.

CAMPUS LIFE

Environment: Metropolis. **Activities:** Choral groups, concert band, dance, drama/theater, jazz band, literary magazine, marching band, music ensembles, musical theater, opera, pep band, student government, student newspaper, symphony orchestra, television station, yearbook, Campus Ministries, Student Organization, Model UN. 135 registered organizations, 8 honor societies, 6 religious organizations. 7 fraternities, 9 sororities. **Athletics (Intercollegiate):** *Men:* baseball, basketball, cross-country, football, golf, soccer, tennis, track/field (outdoor), track/field (indoor). *Women:* basketball, cross-country, golf, soccer, softball, swimming, tennis, track/field (outdoor), track/field (indoor), volleyball. **On-Campus Highlights:** Starbucks in the Union, Carillon on Lake Road, Holcomb Gardens, Fairbanks Center, Lilly Music Hall (newly renovated). **Environmental Initiatives:** College of Pharmacy and Health Sciences building will be "Leed Certified-Silver."

ADMISSIONS

Freshman Academic Profile: Average high school GPA 3.8. 46% in top 10% of high school class, 76% in top 25% of high school class, 95% in top 50% of high school class. **Reported SAT (pre-2016 redesign) scores:** SAT Math middle 50% range 530-638. SAT Critical Reading middle 50% range 530-630. SAT Writing middle 50% range 510-610. **Concordant SAT scores:** SAT EBRW middle 50% 580–670. SAT Math middle 50% range 560–660. ACT middle 50% range 25-30. Minimum internet-based TOEFL 79. Minimum paper TOEFL 550. **Basis for Candidate Selection:** *Very important factors considered include:* rigor of secondary school record, academic GPA, extracurricular activities, character/personal qualities. *Important factors considered include:* application essay, recommendation(s), talent/ability, level of applicant's interest. *Other factors considered include:* class rank, first generation, alumni/ae relation, geographical residence, racial/ethnic status, volunteer work, work experience. **Freshman Admission Requirements:** High school diploma is required and GED is accepted. *Academic units required:* 4 English, 3 math, 3 science, 3 science labs, 2 foreign language, 2 social studies, 2 history. *Academic units recommended:* 4 math, 4 science. **Freshman Admission Statistics:** 12,937 applied, 72.71% admitted, 13% enrolled. **Transfer Admission Requirements:** college transcript(s), essay or personal statement, statement of good standing from prior institution(s). Minimum college GPA of 2.0 required. Lowest grade transferable C. **General Admission Information:** Priority deadline 11/1. Nonfall registration accepted. Admission may be deferred.

COSTS AND FINANCIAL AID

Annual tuition $37,400. Room and board $13,830. Required fees $960. Average book expense $1,000. **Required Forms and Deadlines:** FAFSA. **Notification of Awards:** Applicants will be notified of awards on a rolling basis beginning 3/15. **Types of Aid:** *Need-based scholarships/grants:* Federal Pell, FSEOG, State scholarships/grants, Private scholarships, College/university scholarship or grant aid from institutional funds. *Loans:* Direct Subsidized Stafford Loans, Direct Unsubsidized Stafford Loans, Direct PLUS loans, Federal Perkins Loans. *Student Employment:* Federal Work-Study Program available. Institutional employment available. **Financial Aid Statistics:** 100% needy freshmen, 98% needy undergrads receive need-based scholarship or grant aid. 17% freshmen, 13% undergrads receive non-need-based scholarship or grant aid. 73% freshmen, 76% undergrads receive need-based self-help aid. 2% freshmen, 2% undergrads receive athletic scholarships. 90% freshmen, 90% undergrads receive any aid. 63% undergrads borrow to pay for school. Average cumulative indebtedness $35,730. **Criteria for awarding aid:** *Non-need-based:* Academics, Alumni affiliation, Athletics, Leadership, Music/drama.

CABRINI COLLEGE

610 King of Prussia Road, Radnor, PA 19087-3698
Phone: 610-902-8552 • **Financial Aid Phone:** 610-902-8420
E-mail: admit@cabrini.edu • **CEEB Code:** 2071
Fax: 610-902-8508 • **Website:** www.cabrini.edu • **ACT Code:** 3532

This private school, affiliated with the Roman Catholic Church, was founded in 1957. It has a 112-acre campus.

RATINGS
Admissions Selectivity Rating: 73   **Fire Safety Rating:** 96   **Green Rating:** 60*

STUDENTS AND FACULTY
Enrollment: 1,820. **Student Body:** 66% female, 34% male, 34% out-of-state, 1% international (34 countries represented). Asian 2%, African American 6%, Caucasian 83%, Hispanic 3%, Native American <1%, Pacific Islander 0%, Two or more races 0%, Race unknown 6%.
Retention and Graduation: 66% freshmen return for sophomore year. 46% freshmen graduate within 4 years. 59% freshmen graduate within 6 years. 21% grads go on to further study within 1 year. 16% grads pursue arts and sciences degrees. 1% grads pursue law degrees. 3% grads pursue business degrees. 1% grads pursue medical degrees. **Faculty:** Student/faculty ratio 16:1. 64 full-time faculty, 80% hold PhDs, 5% are are members of minority groups, 55% are women. 0% of classes are taught by teaching assistants.

ACADEMICS
Degrees: bachelor's, certificate, master's, postbachelor's certificate. **Classes:** Most classes have 20-29 students. Most lab/discussion sessions have 10-19 students. **Most popular majors:** Elementary Education and Teaching; Business, Management, Marketing, and Related Support Services. **Special Study Options:** Accelerated program, cooperative education program, cross-registration, double major, honors program, independent study, internships, liberal arts/career combination, student-designed major, study abroad, teacher certification program. **Honors Programs:** Cabrini College Honors Program; Honors in the major. **Disability Services:** Special programs offered to physically disabled students, including note-taking services, reader services, tape recorders, tutors. **Career Services:** Alumni network, Alumni services, Career/job search classes, Career assessment, Internships. Parallel cooperative education program semester to semester.

FACILITIES
Housing: Coed dorms, special housing for disabled students, women's dorms, Special Interest Housing is available. 97% of campus accessible to physically diasbled. **Special Academic Facilities/Equipment:** Exercise Science Lab, Communications center (includes a graphic design lab, radio station, newsroom, and television studio.) Science Education and Technology building with state-of-the-art biology, chemistry, and physics labs, Instructional Technology labs, and research space. **Computers:** 100% of classrooms, 95% of dorms, 100% of libraries, 100% of dining areas, 100% of student union, 95% of common outdoor areas have wireless network access. Students can register for classes online. Administrative functions (other than registration) can be performed online.

CAMPUS LIFE
Environment: Town. **Activities:** Choral groups, dance, drama/theater, literary magazine, radio station, student government, student newspaper, student-run film society, television station, yearbook, Campus Ministries, Student Organization. 32 registered organizations, 18 honor societies, 1 religious organization. **Athletics (Intercollegiate):** *Men:* basketball, cross-country, golf, lacrosse, soccer, swimming, tennis, track/field (outdoor). *Women:* basketball, cross-country, field hockey, lacrosse, soccer, softball, swimming, tennis, track/field (outdoor), volleyball. **On-Campus Highlights:** Dixon Center- Athletic/Recreation facility, Jazzman's Cafe, Holy Spirit Library, Mansion, Science Technology Education Building, The College also has a Communications Center with a radio station, newsroom, graphic design lab, and a television studio.

ADMISSIONS
Freshman Academic Profile: Average high school GPA 3.1. 6% in top 10% of high school class, 20% in top 25% of high school class, 49% in top 50% of high school class. 56% from public high schools. **Reported SAT (pre-2016 redesign) scores:** SAT Math middle 50% range 430-520. SAT Critical Reading middle 50% range 440-530. **Concordant SAT scores:** SAT Math middle 50% range 470–550. Minimum paper TOEFL 500. **Basis for Candidate Selection:** *Very important factors considered include:* academic GPA, standardized test scores. *Important factors considered include:* level of applicant's interest. *Other factors considered include:* rigor of secondary school record, class rank, application essay, recommendation(s), interview, extracurricular activities, talent/ability, character/personal qualities, alumni/ae relation, volunteer work, work experience. **Freshman Admission Requirements:** High school diploma is required and GED is accepted. *Academic units required:* 4 English, 3 math, 3 science, 2 foreign language, 3 social studies, 3 history. *Academic units recommended:* 4 English, 4 math, 3 science, 2 foreign language, 3 social studies, 3 history, 2 academic electives. **Freshman Admission Statistics:** 2,374 applied, 87.41% admitted, 26% enrolled. **Transfer Admission Requirements:** college transcript(s), Minimum college GPA of 2.2 required. Lowest grade transferable C-. **General Admission Information:** Application fee $35. Priority deadline 5/1. Nonfall registration accepted. Admission may be deferred for a maximum of 1 year.

COSTS AND FINANCIAL AID
Average book expense $960. **Required Forms and Deadlines:** FAFSA. **Notification of Awards:** Applicants will be notified of awards on a rolling basis beginning 2/20. **Types of Aid:** *Need-based scholarships/grants:* Federal Pell, FSEOG, State scholarships/grants, Private scholarships, College/university scholarship or grant aid from institutional funds. *Loans:* Federal Perkins Loans. *Student Employment:* Federal Work-Study Program available. Institutional employment available. **Financial Aid Statistics:** 81% needy freshmen, 78% needy undergrads receive need-based scholarship or grant aid. 92% freshmen, 94% undergrads receive non-need-based scholarship or grant aid. 80% freshmen, 84% undergrads receive need-based self-help aid. 0% freshmen, 0% undergrads receive athletic scholarships. 98% freshmen, 97% undergrads receive any aid. **Criteria for awarding aid:** *Non-need-based:* Academics, Alumni affiliation.

See page 932.

CAIRN UNIVERSITY

200 Manor Avenue, Langhorne, PA 19047
Phone: 215-702-4235 • **Financial Aid Phone:** 215-702-4246
E-mail: admissions@cairn.edu
Fax: 215-702-4248 • **Website:** www.cairn.edu • **ACT Code:** 3658

This private school, affiliated with the Protestant Church, was founded in 1913. It has a 114-acre campus.

RATINGS
Admissions Selectivity Rating: 81   **Fire Safety Rating:** 82   **Green Rating:** 60*

STUDENTS AND FACULTY
Enrollment: 937. **Student Body:** 53% female, 47% male, 44% out-of-state, 2% international (31 countries represented). Asian 4%, African American 14%, Caucasian 72%, Hispanic 5%, Native American 1%, Pacific Islander 0%, Two or more races 2%, Race unknown 1%.
Retention and Graduation: 78% freshmen return for sophomore year. 20% freshmen graduate within 4 years. 40% grads go on to further study within 1 year. **Faculty:** Student/faculty ratio 13:1. 50 full-time faculty, 70% hold PhDs, 18% are are members of minority groups, 30% are women. 0% of classes are taught by teaching assistants.

ACADEMICS
Degrees: bachelor's, certificate, master's, postbachelor's certificate. **Classes:** Most classes have 10-19 students. **Most popular majors:** Elementary Education and Teaching; Bible/Biblical Studies; Social Work. **Special Study Options:** Accelerated program, double major, honors program, internships, study abroad, teacher certification program. Combined degree programs: BS in Bible+ MS in Chr Counseling or MS in Education or MS in Org. Leader. **Disability Services:** Special programs offered to physically disabled students, including reader services, tutors. **Career Services:** Alumni network, Alumni services, Career/job search classes, Career assessment, Internships.

FACILITIES
Housing: special housing for disabled students, men's dorms, special housing for international students, women's dorms, apartments for married students, apartments for single students. 99% of campus accessible to physically diasbled. **Special Academic Facilities/Equipment:** Biblical Learning Center Museum area **Computers:** 59% of classrooms, 62% of dorms, 90% of libraries, 100% of dining areas, 100% of student union, 15% of common outdoor areas have wireless network access. Students can register for classes online. Administrative functions (other than registration) can be performed online.

CAMPUS LIFE
Environment: Village. **Activities:** Choral groups, concert band, drama/theater, music ensembles, musical theater, opera, student government, student newspaper, symphony orchestra, yearbook, Campus Ministries, Student Organization. 25 registered organizations, 4 honor societies, 3 religious organizations. **Athletics (Intercollegiate):** *Men:* baseball, basketball, cross-country, golf, soccer, volleyball. *Women:* basketball, cross-country, soccer, softball, tennis, volleyball. **On-Campus Highlights:** Eagle's Nest grill & cafe, Student Lounge, Campus Walkway, Sports Fields, Heritage Hall Lounge.

ADMISSIONS

Freshman Academic Profile: Average high school GPA 3.3. 18% in top 10% of high school class, 39% in top 25% of high school class, 17% in top 50% of high school class. 60% from public high schools. **Reported SAT (pre-2016 redesign) scores:** SAT Math middle 50% range 450-580. SAT Critical Reading middle 50% range 470-590. **Concordant SAT scores:** SAT Math middle 50% range 490–600. ACT middle 50% range 17-24.3. Minimum paper TOEFL 520. **Basis for Candidate Selection:** *Very important factors considered include:* academic GPA, standardized test scores, interview, character/personal qualities, religious affiliation/commitment, level of applicant's interest. *Important factors considered include:* rigor of secondary school record, application essay. *Other factors considered include:* class rank, recommendation(s), extracurricular activities. **Freshman Admission Requirements:** High school diploma is required and GED is accepted. *Academic units recommended:* 4 English, 1 math, 2 science, 2 foreign language, 3 social studies. **Freshman Admission Statistics:** 482 applied, 74.27% admitted, 41% enrolled. **Transfer Admission Requirements:** college transcript(s), essay or personal statement, interview, Minimum college GPA of 2.2 required. Lowest grade transferable C. **General Admission Information:** Application fee $25. Nonfall registration accepted. Admission may be deferred for a maximum of 1 year.

COSTS AND FINANCIAL AID

Annual tuition $21,500. Room and board $8,525. Required fees $205. Average book expense $1,200. **Required Forms and Deadlines:** FAFSA. **Notification of Awards:** Applicants will be notified of awards on a rolling basis beginning 2/15. **Types of Aid:** *Need-based scholarships/grants:* Federal Pell, FSEOG, State scholarships/grants, Private scholarships, College/university scholarship or grant aid from institutional funds. *Loans:* Direct Subsidized Stafford Loans, Direct Unsubsidized Stafford Loans, Direct PLUS loans. *Student Employment:* Federal Work-Study Program available. Institutional employment available. **Financial Aid Statistics:** 99% needy freshmen, 96% needy undergrads receive need-based scholarship or grant aid. 6% freshmen, 6% undergrads receive non-need-based scholarship or grant aid. 98% freshmen, 96% undergrads receive need-based self-help aid. 0% freshmen, 0% undergrads receive athletic scholarships. 84% freshmen, 82% undergrads receive any aid. **Criteria for awarding aid:** *Non-need-based:* Academics, Leadership, Music/drama.

CALIFORNIA BAPTIST UNIVERSITY

8432 Magnolia Ave, Riverside, CA 92504
Phone: 951-343-4212 • **Financial Aid Phone:** 951-343-4236
E-mail: admissions@calbaptist.edu • **CEEB Code:** 4094
Fax: 951-343-4525 • **Website:** www.calbaptist.edu • **ACT Code:** 4094

This private school, affiliated with the Southern Baptist Church, was founded in 1950. It has a 103-acre campus.

RATINGS

Admissions Selectivity Rating: 80   **Fire Safety Rating:** 64   **Green Rating:** 60*

STUDENTS AND FACULTY

Enrollment: 6,904. **Student Body:** 63% female, 37% male, 7% out-of-state, 2% international (27 countries represented). Asian 5%, African American 8%, Caucasian 38%, Hispanic 36%, Native American 1%, Pacific Islander 1%, Two or more races 6%, Race unknown 4%.
Retention and Graduation: 75% freshmen return for sophomore year. 42% freshmen graduate within 4 years. 60% freshmen graduate within 6 years. **Faculty:** 315 full-time faculty, 75% hold PhDs, 29% are are members of minority groups, 47% are women. 0% of classes are taught by teaching assistants.

ACADEMICS

Degrees: bachelor's, doctoral/research, master's. **Classes:** Most classes have 10-19 students. Most lab/discussion sessions have 10-19 students. **Most popular majors:** Registered Nursing/Registered Nurse; Psychology; Business/Commerce. **Special Study Options:** Accelerated program, distance learning, double major, English as a Second Language (ESL), exchange student program (domestic), honors program, internships, liberal arts/career combination, study abroad, teacher certification program, weekend college. **Honors Programs:** The Honors program offers students from all major areas of study the opportunity to participate in rigorous study, requiring diligence in reading primary sources and writing original essays thorough 8 intensive seminars. Honors students progressively investigate a single generative idea using primary texts, drawing upon the expertise of leading faculty. These seminars may be used to fulfill elective unit requirements and specially selected general education requirements. Successful completion of the Honors Program will be posted on the academic transcript and students will be designated as Honors Program graduates at commencement. Combined degree programs: BA/MArch. **Disability Services:** Special programs offered to physically disabled

students, including note-taking services, tutors. **Career Services:** Alumni network, Alumni services, Career/job search classes, Career assessment, Internships. Internship elective credit is available for students in most academic disciplines. In addition, a RE-FOCUS program is available which seeks to prepare students in their transition from the academic culture of the university to a professional culture. The program is designed for Juniors and Seniors and offers interactive workshops such as mock interviews hosted by a national employer, business etiquette dinners, resume and interview skills workshops and graduate school information sessions.

FACILITIES

Housing: men's dorms, women's dorms, cooperative housing, apartments for single students. 95% of campus accessible to physically diasbled. **Special Academic Facilities/Equipment:** Metcalf Art Gallery, Annie Gabriel Library, Wallace Theater, P. Boyd Smith Hymnology Collection, School of Music Performance and Recording Studios, Nie Wieder! Collection, Lancer Sports Complex and Aquatic Center **Computers:** 40% of classrooms, 10% of dorms, 100% of libraries, 100% of dining areas, 100% of student union, 25% of common outdoor areas have wireless network access. Students can register for classes online. Administrative functions (other than registration) can be performed online.

CAMPUS LIFE

Environment: City. **Activities:** Choral groups, concert band, drama/theater, jazz band, music ensembles, musical theater, pep band, student government, student newspaper, symphony orchestra, yearbook, Campus Ministries, Student Organization. 30 registered organizations, 2 honor societies, 6 religious organizations. **Athletics (Intercollegiate):** *Men:* baseball, basketball, cheerleading, cross-country, diving, golf, soccer, swimming, volleyball, water polo, wrestling. *Women:* basketball, cheerleading, cross-country, diving, golf, soccer, softball, swimming, volleyball, water polo. **On-Campus Highlights:** Alumni Dining Commons, Student Activity Center, Wanda's (Coffee Shop), Van Dyne Gymnasium, Aquatic Center. **Environmental Initiatives:** Energy Efficient Lighting.

ADMISSIONS

Freshman Academic Profile: Average high school GPA 3.4. 15% in top 10% of high school class, 41% in top 25% of high school class, 76% in top 50% of high school class. 77% from public high schools. **Reported SAT (pre-2016 redesign) scores:** SAT Math middle 50% range 420-550. SAT Critical Reading middle 50% range 430-550. SAT Writing middle 50% range 420-530. **Concordant SAT scores:** SAT EBRW middle 50% 480–600. SAT Math middle 50% range 460–570. ACT middle 50% range 19-24. Minimum internet-based TOEFL 71. Minimum paper TOEFL 527. **Basis for Candidate Selection:** *Very important factors considered include:* rigor of secondary school record, academic GPA, standardized test scores, application essay, recommendation(s), character/personal qualities. *Important factors considered include:* level of applicant's interest. *Other factors considered include:* class rank, extracurricular activities, talent/ability, volunteer work. **Freshman Admission Requirements:** High school diploma is required and GED is accepted. *Academic units required:* 4 English, 3 math, 2 science, 2 science labs, 2 foreign language, 2 social studies, 2 history. *Academic units recommended:* 4 English, 4 math, 3 science, 3 science labs, 3 foreign language, 2 social studies, 2 history, 3 academic electives, 1 visual/performing arts, and 2 units from above areas or other academic areas. **Freshman Admission Statistics:** 4,971 applied, 63.99% admitted, 36% enrolled. **Transfer Admission Requirements:** college transcript(s), essay or personal statement, statement of good standing from prior institution(s). Minimum college GPA of 2.0 required. Lowest grade transferable C. **General Admission Information:** Application fee $45. Nonfall registration accepted. Admission may be deferred for a maximum of 1 year.

COSTS AND FINANCIAL AID

Annual tuition $30,446. Room and board $11,540. Required fees $2,120. Average book expense $1,790. **Required Forms and Deadlines:** FAFSA, State aid form. **Notification of Awards:** Applicants will be notified of awards on a rolling basis beginning 3/2. **Types of Aid:** *Need-based scholarships/grants:* Federal Pell, FSEOG, State scholarships/grants, Private scholarships, College/university scholarship or grant aid from institutional funds, Federal Nursing Scholarships. *Loans:* Direct Subsidized Stafford Loans, Direct Unsubsidized Stafford Loans, Direct PLUS loans, Federal Perkins Loans. *Student Employment:* Federal Work-Study Program available. Institutional employment available. **Financial Aid Statistics:** 90% needy freshmen, 75% needy undergrads receive need-based scholarship or grant aid. 85% freshmen, 61% undergrads receive non-need-based scholarship or grant aid. 64% freshmen, 63% undergrads receive need-based self-help aid. 5% freshmen, 4% undergrads receive athletic scholarships. 90% freshmen, 90% undergrads receive any aid. 77% undergrads borrow to pay for school. Average cumulative indebtedness $20,693. **Criteria for awarding aid:** *Need-based:* Academics, Art, Athletics, Music/drama, Religious affiliation. *Non-need-based:* Academics, Art, Athletics, Music/drama, Religious affiliation.

CALIFORNIA COLLEGE OF THE ARTS

1111 Eighth Street, San Francisco, CA 94107
Phone: 415-703-9523 • **Financial Aid Phone:** 415-703-9528
E-mail: enroll@cca.edu • **CEEB Code:** 4031
Fax: 415-703-9539 • **Website:** www.cca.edu • **ACT Code:** 176

This private school was founded in 1907. It has a 4-acre campus.

RATINGS

Admissions Selectivity Rating: 73 **Fire Safety Rating:** 94 **Green Rating:** 87

STUDENTS AND FACULTY

Enrollment: 1,515. **Student Body:** 64% female, 36% male, 35% out-of-state, 35% international (54 countries represented). Asian 18%, African American 6%, Caucasian 23%, Hispanic 12%, Native American <1%, Pacific Islander 1%, Two or more races 0%, Race unknown 6%.
Retention and Graduation: 82% freshmen return for sophomore year. 40% freshmen graduate within 4 years. 58% freshmen graduate within 6 years. **Faculty:** 100 full-time faculty, 64% hold PhDs, 32% are are members of minority groups, 48% are women. 0% of classes are taught by teaching assistants.

ACADEMICS

Degrees: bachelor's, master's. **Classes:** Most classes have 10-19 students. **Most popular majors:** Graphic Design; Illustration; Industrial and Product Design. **Special Study Options:** cross-registration, double major, English as a Second Language (ESL), exchange student program (domestic), independent study, internships, student-designed major, study abroad, Sponsored studios and project-based learning with community engagement courses integrated in the curriculum. Learning disability services also offered. **Disability Services:** Special programs offered to physically disabled students, including note-taking services, reader services, tape recorders, tutors. **Career Services:** Alumni services, Career/job search classes, Career assessment, Internships. Internships are required in some majors but recommended for all.

FACILITIES

Housing: Coed dorms, special housing for disabled students, apartments for single students, Theme Housing, Themed communities and living-learning communities. 95% of campus accessible to physically diasbled. **Special Academic Facilities/Equipment:** Logan Gallery on the San Francisco Campus, Wattis Institute for Contemporary Art **Computers:** 100% of classrooms, 60% of dorms, 100% of libraries, 100% of dining areas, 90% of common outdoor areas have wireless network access. Students can register for classes online. Administrative functions (other than registration) can be performed online.

CAMPUS LIFE

Environment: Metropolis. **Activities:** literary magazine, student government, student-run film society, Student Organization. 10 registered organizations,1 fraternity. **On-Campus Highlights:** The Nave- San Francisco campus, The Foundry—Oakland campus, Individualized Painting Studios—SF, North/South Student Galleries—Oakland, Wattis Institute for Contemporary Art, Students learn from individuals, the inter-cultural community, and the myriad events and activities sponsored by the Center for Art and Public Life, the CCA Wattis Institute, and the Student Affairs Office. Activities range from social events, yoga classes, exhibition receptions, workshops, and topical forums to programs designed to engage the public and the academic community in a dialogue about the nature of arts and culture. Readings, lectures, performances, issue-based symposia, and panel discussions on the arts, architecture, design, and humanities are offered throughout the year. **Environmental Initiatives:** Largest solar heated facility in San Francisco, named Top Ten Green Building on Earth Day 2001.

ADMISSIONS

Freshman Academic Profile: Average high school GPA 3.3. **Reported SAT (pre-2016 redesign) scores:** SAT Math middle 50% range 450-620. SAT Critical Reading middle 50% range 445-580. SAT Writing middle 50% range 440-580. **Concordant SAT scores:** SAT EBRW middle 50% 500–640. SAT Math middle 50% range 490–640. ACT middle 50% range 20-27. Minimum internet-based TOEFL 80. Minimum paper TOEFL 550. **Basis for Candidate Selection:** *Very important factors considered include:* academic GPA, application essay, talent/ability. *Important factors considered include:* recommendation(s). *Other factors considered include:* rigor of secondary school record, standardized test scores, interview, extracurricular activities, character/personal qualities, first generation, alumni/ae relation, racial/ethnic status, volunteer work, work experience, level of applicant's interest. **Freshman Admission Requirements:** High school diploma is required and GED is accepted. **Freshman Admission Statistics:** 1,896 applied, 80.75% admitted, 17% enrolled. **Transfer Admission Requirements:** college transcript(s), essay or personal statement, Minimum college GPA of 2.0 required. Lowest

grade transferable C. **General Admission Information:** Application fee $60. Priority deadline 2/1. Nonfall registration accepted. Admission may be deferred for a maximum of one semester.

COSTS AND FINANCIAL AID

Annual tuition $44,976. Required fees $460. Average book expense $1,500. **Required Forms and Deadlines:** FAFSA, State aid form. **Notification of Awards:** Applicants will be notified of awards on a rolling basis beginning 3/15. **Types of Aid:** *Need-based scholarships/grants:* Federal Pell, FSEOG, State scholarships/grants, Private scholarships, College/university scholarship or grant aid from institutional funds. *Loans:* Direct Subsidized Stafford Loans, Direct Unsubsidized Stafford Loans, Direct PLUS loans, Federal Perkins Loans. *Student Employment:* Federal Work-Study Program available. Institutional employment available. **Financial Aid Statistics:** 100% needy freshmen, 100% needy undergrads receive need-based scholarship or grant aid. 88% freshmen, 61% undergrads receive non-need-based scholarship or grant aid. 95% freshmen, 96% undergrads receive need-based self-help aid. 0% freshmen, 0% undergrads receive athletic scholarships. **Criteria for awarding aid:** *Non-need-based:* Academics, Art.

CALIFORNIA INSTITUTE OF THE ARTS

24700 McBean Parkway, Valencia, CA 91355
Phone: 661-255-1050 • **Financial Aid Phone:** 661-253-7869
E-mail: admissions@calarts.edu • **CEEB Code:** 4049
Fax: 661-253-7710 • **Website:** www.calarts.edu • **ACT Code:** 121

This private school was founded in 1961. It has a 60-acre campus.

RATINGS

Admissions Selectivity Rating: 71 **Fire Safety Rating:** 75 **Green Rating:** 60*

STUDENTS AND FACULTY

Enrollment: 888. **Student Body:** 49% female, 51% male, 49% out-of-state, 8% international (34 countries represented). Asian 12%, African American 8%, Caucasian 58%, Hispanic 12%, Native American 1%, Pacific Islander 0%, Two or more races 0%, Race unknown 1%.
Retention and Graduation: 75% freshmen return for sophomore year. 57% freshmen graduate within 6 years. **Faculty:** Student/faculty ratio 7:1. 160 full-time faculty, 100% hold PhDs, 18% are are members of minority groups, 44% are women. 0% of classes are taught by teaching assistants.

ACADEMICS

Degrees: bachelor's, certificate, doctoral, master's, postbachelor's certificate. **Classes:** Most classes have fewer than 10 students. **Most popular majors:** Music Performance. **Special Study Options:** independent study, internships, student-designed major, study abroad. **Disability Services:** Special programs offered to physically disabled students, including note-taking services, reader services, tape recorders, tutors. **Career Services:** Career/job search classes, Career assessment, Internships. The new career mentoship program "Arts In The world Coaching."

FACILITIES

Housing: Coed dorms, special housing for disabled students, apartments for single students. 98% of campus accessible to physically diasbled. **Special Academic Facilities/Equipment:** 7 Art galleries, TV studio, Walt Disney Theater, Roy Disney Music Hall, Sharon Disney Lund Dance Theater, Bijou Film Theater **Computers:** 20% of classrooms, 100% of libraries, 100% of dining areas, 20% of common outdoor areas have wireless network access. Students can register for classes online. Administrative functions (other than registration) can be performed online.

CAMPUS LIFE

Environment: City. **Activities:** Choral groups, dance, drama/theater, jazz band, literary magazine, music ensembles, opera, radio station, student government, student newspaper, student-run film society, symphony orchestra, television station 5 registered organizations. **On-Campus Highlights:** Modular Theater, Permanent Set, Gamelan Room, Main Gallery, Lund Dance Theater, Roy O. Disney Music Hall, Bijou Theater. **Environmental Initiatives:** Recycling Program.

ADMISSIONS

Minimum internet-based TOEFL 80. Minimum paper TOEFL 550. **Basis for Candidate Selection:** *Very important factors considered include:* application essay, talent/ability. *Important factors considered include:* recommendation(s), extracurricular activities. *Other factors considered include:* rigor of secondary school record, academic GPA, interview, character/personal qualities, level of applicant's interest. **Freshman Admission Requirements:** High school diploma is required and GED is accepted. *Academic units recommended:* 4 English, 3 math, 3 science, 2 foreign language, 3 social studies, 2 academic electives, 1 computer science. **Freshman Admission Statistics:** 1,186 applied, 33.47% admitted, 40% enrolled. **Transfer Admission Requirements:** High school transcript, college transcript(s), essay or personal statement, Lowest grade transferable C. **General Admission Information:** Application fee $70. Priority deadline 12/1. Regular application deadline 1/5. Nonfall registration accepted.

COSTS AND FINANCIAL AID

Annual tuition $36,166. Room and board $9,293. Required fees $576. Average book expense $1,500. **Required Forms and Deadlines:** FAFSA. **Notification of Awards:** Applicants will be notified of awards on a rolling basis beginning 4/1. **Types of Aid:** *Need-based scholarships/grants:* Federal Pell, FSEOG, State scholarships/grants, Private scholarships, College/university scholarship or grant aid from institutional funds. *Loans:* Federal Perkins Loans, College/university loans from institutional funds. *Student Employment:* Federal Work-Study Program available. Institutional employment available. **Financial Aid Statistics:** 92% needy freshmen, 93% needy undergrads receive need-based scholarship or grant aid. 0% undergrads receive non-need-based scholarship or grant aid. 88% freshmen, 91% undergrads receive need-based self-help aid. 0% freshmen, 0% undergrads receive athletic scholarships. 71% freshmen, 77% undergrads receive any aid. **Criteria for awarding aid:** *Need-based:* Art, Minority status, Music/drama. *Non-need-based:* Art, Minority status, Music/drama.

CALIFORNIA INSTITUTE OF TECHNOLOGY

Best Colleges

Caltech Office of Undergrad Admissions, Pasadena, CA 91125
Phone: 626-395-6341 • **Financial Aid Phone:** 626-395-6280
E-mail: ugadmissions@caltech.edu • **CEEB Code:** 4034
Fax: 626-683-3026 • **Website:** www.caltech.edu • **ACT Code:** 182

This private school was founded in 1891. It has a 124-acre campus.

RATINGS

Admissions Selectivity Rating: 99   **Fire Safety Rating:** 89   **Green Rating:** 60*

STUDENTS AND FACULTY

Enrollment: 979. **Student Body:** 41% female, 59% male, 66% out-of-state, 9% international (32 countries represented). Asian 43%, African American 1%, Caucasian 29%, Hispanic 12%, Native American 0%, Pacific Islander 0%, Two or more races 6%, Race unknown 0%.
Retention and Graduation: 98% freshmen return for sophomore year. 81% freshmen graduate within 4 years. 94% freshmen graduate within 6 years. 48% grads go on to further study within 1 year. **Faculty:** Student/faculty ratio 3:1. 336 full-time faculty, 99% hold PhDs, 19% are are members of minority groups, 21% are women. 0% of classes are taught by teaching assistants.

ACADEMICS

Degrees: bachelor's, doctoral/research, doctoral, master's, post-master's certificate. **Classes:** Most classes have 10-19 students. Most lab/discussion sessions have 10-19 students. **Most popular majors:** Mechanical Engineering; Physics; Computer and Information Sciences. **Special Study Options:** cooperative education program, cross-registration, double major, English as a Second Language (ESL), exchange student program (domestic), independent study, liberal arts/career combination, student-designed major, study abroad, "Remedial services" are not formally offered. However, remediation is available for students who are deficient in basic scientific knowledge or technical skills. Combined degree programs: Caltech-UCSD Medical Scholars Program. **Disability Services:** Special programs offered to physically disabled students, including note-taking services, reader services, tape recorders, tutors.

FACILITIES

Housing: Coed dorms, special housing for disabled students, apartments for married students, single-unit houses. 95% of campus accessible to physically diasbled. **Special Academic Facilities/Equipment:** Jet Propulsion Laboratory, Palomar Observatory, Seismological Laboratory, Beckman Institute for Fundamental Research in Biology and Chemistry, Mead Chemistry Laboratory, Moore Laboratory. **Computers:** 50% of classrooms, 50% of dorms, 100% of libraries, 50% of dining areas, 100% of student union, 50% of common outdoor areas have wireless network access. Students can register for classes online. Administrative functions (other than registration) can be performed online.

CAMPUS LIFE

Environment: Metropolis. **Activities:** Choral groups, concert band, dance, drama/theater, jazz band, literary magazine, music ensembles, musical theater, opera, pep band, student government, student newspaper, student-run film society, symphony orchestra, yearbook. 148 registered organizations, 2 honor societies, 6 religious organizations. **Athletics (Intercollegiate):** *Men:* baseball, basketball, cross-country, diving, fencing, soccer, swimming, tennis, track/field (outdoor), water polo. *Women:* basketball, cross-country, diving, fencing, swimming, tennis, track/field (outdoor), volleyball, water polo. **On-Campus Highlights:** Caltech Bookstore, Moore Laboratory, Mead Chemistry Laboratory, Broad Center for the Biological Sciences, Red Door Cafe. **Environmental Initiatives:** Energy efficiency and retro-commissioning programs finances through the use of a green revolving loan fund (http://sustainability.caltech.edu/energy/CECIP).

ADMISSIONS

Freshman Academic Profile: 97% in top 10% of high school class, 100% in top 25% of high school class, 100% in top 50% of high school class. 70% from public high schools. **Reported SAT (pre-2016 redesign) scores:** SAT Math middle 50% range 770-800. SAT Critical Reading middle 50% range 740-800. SAT Writing middle 50% range 730-800. **Concordant SAT scores:** SAT EBRW middle 50% 760–800. SAT Math middle 50% range 780–800. ACT middle 50% range 34-36. Minimum internet-based TOEFL 110. **Basis for Candidate Selection:** *Very important factors considered include:* rigor of secondary school record, standardized test scores, application essay, recommendation(s), character/personal qualities. *Important factors considered include:* class rank, academic GPA, extracurricular activities. *Other factors considered include:* talent/ability, first generation, alumni/ae relation, racial/ethnic status, volunteer work, work experience. **Freshman Admission Requirements:** High school diploma or equivalent is not required. *Academic units required:* 3 English, 4 math, 2 science, 1 science lab, 1 social studies, 1 history. *Academic units recommended:* 4 English, 4 science, 3 foreign language, 3 social studies, 1 history. **Freshman Admission Statistics:** 6,855 applied, 8.07% admitted, 42% enrolled. **Transfer Admission Requirements:** High school transcript, college transcript(s), essay or personal statement, statement of good standing from prior institution(s). **General Admission Information:** Application fee $75. Regular application deadline 1/3. Regular notification 4/1. Nonfall registration not accepted. Admission may be deferred for a maximum of 2 years.

COSTS AND FINANCIAL AID

Annual tuition $43,710. Room and board $13,371. Required fees $1,680. Average book expense $1,323. **Required Forms and Deadlines:** FAFSA, Institution's own financial aid form, CSS/Financial Aid PROFILE, State aid form, Noncustodial PROFILE, Business/Farm Supplement. **Notification of Awards:** Applicants will be notified of awards on a rolling basis beginning 4/15. **Types of Aid:** *Need-based scholarships/grants:* Federal Pell, FSEOG, State scholarships/grants, Private scholarships, College/university scholarship or grant aid from institutional funds. *Loans:* Direct Subsidized Stafford Loans, Direct Unsubsidized Stafford Loans, Direct PLUS loans, Federal Perkins Loans, College/university loans from institutional funds. *Student Employment:* Federal Work-Study Program available. Institutional employment available. **Financial Aid Statistics:** 100% needy freshmen, 100% needy undergrads receive need-based scholarship or grant aid. 1% undergrads receive non-need-based scholarship or grant aid. 62% freshmen, 68% undergrads receive need-based self-help aid. 0% freshmen, 0% undergrads receive athletic scholarships. 75% freshmen, 60% undergrads receive any aid. 33% undergrads borrow to pay for school. Average cumulative indebtedness $18,219. **Criteria for awarding aid:** *Need-based:* Academics, Leadership.

CALIFORNIA LUTHERAN UNIVERSITY

60 West Olsen Road, Thousand Oaks, CA 91360
Phone: 805-493-3135 • **Financial Aid Phone:** 805-493-3115
E-mail: admissions@callutheran.edu • **CEEB Code:** 4088
Fax: 805-493-3645 • **Website:** www.callutheran.edu • **ACT Code:** 183

This private school, affiliated with the Lutheran Church, was founded in 1959. It has a 290-acre campus.

RATINGS

Admissions Selectivity Rating: 86   **Fire Safety Rating:** 90   **Green Rating:** 60*

STUDENTS AND FACULTY

Enrollment: 2,802. **Student Body:** 57% female, 43% male, 13% out-of-state, 3% international (52 countries represented). Asian 6%, African American 4%, Caucasian 49%, Hispanic 27%, Native American 1%, Pacific Islander 1%, Two or more races 6%, Race unknown 4%.

Retention and Graduation: 84% freshmen return for sophomore year. 60% freshmen graduate within 4 years. 28% grads go on to further study within 1 year. 35% grads pursue arts and sciences degrees. 3% grads pursue law degrees. 7% grads pursue business degrees. 4% grads pursue medical degrees. **Faculty:** Student/faculty ratio 15:1. 193 full-time faculty, 85% hold PhDs, 17% are are members of minority groups, 48% are women. 0% of classes are taught by teaching assistants.

ACADEMICS

Degrees: bachelor's, doctoral/professional, master's, postbachelor's certificate, post-master's certificate. **Classes:** Most classes have 20-29 students. Most lab/discussion sessions have 10-19 students. **Most popular majors:** Liberal Arts and Sciences/Liberal Studies; Business/Commerce; Psychology. **Special Study Options:** Accelerated program, cooperative education program, double major, dual enrollment, exchange student program (domestic), honors program, independent study, internships, student-designed major, study abroad, teacher certification program. **Honors Programs:** Honors Program. **Disability Services:** Special programs offered to physically disabled students, including note-taking services, reader services, tape recorders, tutors. **Career Services:** Alumni network, Alumni services, Career/job search classes, Career assessment, Internships, Regional alumni, 4 A Cause NonProfit Internship Program. The '4A Cause' Experiential Learning Internship Program gives students the opportunity to work with a nonprofit organization that they feel passionate about helping. Organizations in many areas participate including: social justice, animal rights, public policy, environmental or social issues, education, and more. There are over 20 "Cause" areas. This program will provide students with new skills essential to career development, along with a new understanding of community efforts going on in the "real world". Students receive a mandatory initial training called Boot Camp on how to be effective in the workplace, and an awards ceremony takes place at the conclusion of the program. Students build their resumes with experience while learning more about advocacy in the surrounding community. In addition, studies confirm experiential learning internships can lead to other assignments and future work or projects for the student.

FACILITIES

Housing: Coed dorms, special housing for disabled students, apartments for single students. 95% of campus accessible to physically diasbled. **Special Academic Facilities/Equipment:** On-campus pre-school, hypermedia lab, multimedia center and program, film studio, Kwan Fong Art Gallary, Scandinavian Center, Educational Technology Center. **Computers:** Students can register for classes online. Administrative functions (other than registration) can be performed online.

CAMPUS LIFE

Environment: Town. **Activities:** Choral groups, concert band, dance, drama/theater, jazz band, literary magazine, music ensembles, musical theater, pep band, radio station, student government, student newspaper, symphony orchestra, television station, yearbook. 75 registered organizations, 11 honor societies, 3 religious organizations. **Athletics (Intercollegiate):** *Men:* baseball, basketball, cheerleading, cross-country, diving, football, golf, soccer, swimming, tennis, track/field (outdoor), water polo. *Women:* basketball, cheerleading, cross-country, diving, soccer, softball, swimming, tennis, track/field (outdoor), volleyball, water polo. **On-Campus Highlights:** Education and Technology Building, Soland Humanities Center, The Apartments, Kingsmen Park, Samuelson Chapel, new athletics complex and lab facilities for sports medicine.

ADMISSIONS

Freshman Academic Profile: Average high school GPA 3.7. 30% in top 10% of high school class, 72% in top 25% of high school class, 93% in top 50% of high school class. 75% from public high schools. **Reported SAT (pre-2016 redesign) scores:** SAT Math middle 50% range 500-600. SAT Critical Reading middle 50% range 500-600. **Concordant SAT scores:** SAT Math middle 50% range 530–620. ACT middle 50% range 22-27. Minimum internet-based TOEFL 79. Minimum paper TOEFL 550. **Basis for Candidate Selection:** *Very important factors considered include:* rigor of secondary school record, academic GPA, standardized test scores, application essay, recommendation(s). *Important factors considered include:* class rank, extracurricular activities, talent/ability, alumni/ae relation. *Other factors considered include:* interview, character/personal qualities, first generation, geographical residence, state residency, religious affiliation/commitment, racial/ethnic status, volunteer work, work experience. **Freshman Admission Requirements:** High school diploma is required and GED is accepted. *Academic units required:* 4 English, 3 math, 3 science, 2 science labs, 2 foreign language, 2 social studies. *Academic units recommended:* 4 English, 4 math, 3 science. **Freshman Admission Statistics:** 6,569 applied, 61.56% admitted, 15% enrolled. **Transfer Admission Requirements:** college transcript(s), essay or personal statement, statement of good standing from prior institution(s). Minimum college GPA of 2.8 required. Lowest grade transferable D. **General Admission Information:** Application fee $25. Priority deadline 11/1. Regular application deadline 1/1. Nonfall registration accepted. Admission may be deferred for a maximum of 1 year.

COSTS AND FINANCIAL AID

Annual tuition $39,310. Room and board $12,740. Required fees $450. Average book expense $1,764. **Required Forms and Deadlines:** FAFSA, State aid form. **Notification of Awards:** Applicants will be notified of awards on a rolling basis beginning 2/15. **Types of Aid:** *Need-based scholarships/grants:* Federal Pell, FSEOG, State scholarships/grants, Private scholarships, College/university scholarship or grant aid from institutional funds, United Negro College Fund. *Loans:* Direct Subsidized Stafford Loans, Direct Unsubsidized Stafford Loans, Direct PLUS loans, Federal Perkins Loans. *Student Employment:* Federal Work-Study Program available. Institutional employment available. **Financial Aid Statistics:** 100% needy freshmen, 100% needy undergrads receive need-based scholarship or grant aid. 38% freshmen, 49% undergrads receive non-need-based scholarship or grant aid. 77% freshmen, 76% undergrads receive need-based self-help aid. 0% freshmen, 0% undergrads receive athletic scholarships. 96% freshmen, 95% undergrads receive any aid. 62% undergrads borrow to pay for school. Average cumulative indebtedness $28,186. **Criteria for awarding aid:** *Need-based:* Academics, Alumni affiliation, Art, Leadership, Minority status, Music/drama, Religious affiliation. *Non-need-based:* Academics, Alumni affiliation, Art, Leadership, Minority status, Music/drama, Religious affiliation, State/district residency.

CALIFORNIA POLYTECHNIC STATE UNIVERSITY

Admissions Office, San Luis Obispo, CA 93407-0031
Phone: 805-756-2311 • **Financial Aid Phone:** 805-756-2927
E-mail: admissions@calpoly.edu • **CEEB Code:** 4038
Fax: 805-756-5400 • **Website:** www.calpoly.edu • **ACT Code:** 188

This public school was founded in 1901. It has a 9678-acre campus.

RATINGS

Admissions Selectivity Rating: 93   **Fire Safety Rating:** 65   **Green Rating:** 98

STUDENTS AND FACULTY

Enrollment: 20,367. **Student Body:** 47% female, 53% male, 2% international. Asian 13%, African American 1%, Caucasian 57%, Hispanic 16%, Native American <1%, Pacific Islander <1%, Two or more races 7%, Race unknown 5%.
Retention and Graduation: 95% freshmen return for sophomore year. 48% freshmen graduate within 4 years. 83% freshmen graduate within 6 years. **Faculty:** Student/faculty ratio 19:1. 907 full-time faculty, 76% hold PhDs, 0% are are members of minority groups, 36% are women.

ACADEMICS

Degrees: bachelor's, master's. **Classes:** Most classes have 20-29 students. Most lab/discussion sessions have 20-29 students. **Special Study Options:** cooperative education program, distance learning, double major, English as a Second Language (ESL), exchange student program (domestic), honors program, internships, liberal arts/career combination, study abroad, teacher certification program. Combined degree programs: BS/MS. **Disability Services:** Special programs offered to physically disabled students, including note-taking services, reader services, tape recorders, tutors. **Career Services:** Alumni network, Alumni services, Career/job search classes, Career assessment, Internships, Regional alumni. Cooperative Education Program.

FACILITIES

Housing: Coed dorms, special housing for disabled students, special housing for international students, apartments for single students, Theme Housing. **Special Academic Facilities/Equipment:** Dairy, veterinary clinic, printing museum, art gallery **Computers:** 100% of classrooms, 5% of dorms, 100% of libraries, 100% of dining areas, 100% of student union, 5% of common outdoor areas have wireless network access. Students can register for classes online. Administrative functions (other than registration) can be performed online.

CAMPUS LIFE

Environment: Town. **Activities:** Choral groups, concert band, dance, drama/theater, jazz band, literary magazine, marching band, music ensembles, musical theater, opera, pep band, radio station, student government, student newspaper, symphony orchestra, television station, Campus Ministries, Student Organization, Model UN. 400 registered organizations, 14 religious organizations. 25 fraternities, 14 sororities. **Athletics (Intercollegiate):** *Men:* baseball, basketball, cross-country, football, golf, soccer, swimming, tennis, track/field (outdoor), wrestling. *Women:* basketball, cross-country, golf, soccer, softball, swimming, tennis, track/field (outdoor), track/field (indoor), volleyball. **On-Campus Highlights:** Performing Arts Center, Recreation Center, Julian's Coffee Shop, Spanos Stadium, University Union, El Corral Bookstore.

ADMISSIONS

Freshman Academic Profile: Average high school GPA 3.9. 56% in top 10% of high school class, 88% in top 25% of high school class, 99% in top 50% of high school class. **Reported SAT (pre-2016 redesign) scores:** SAT Math middle 50% range 590-700. SAT Critical Reading middle 50% range 560-660. **Concordant SAT scores:** SAT Math middle 50% range 610–730. ACT middle 50% range 26-31. Minimum internet-based TOEFL 80. Minimum paper TOEFL 550. **Basis for Candidate Selection:** *Very important factors considered include:* rigor of secondary school record, academic GPA, standardized test scores. *Other factors considered include:* extracurricular activities, talent/ability, first generation, geographical residence, volunteer work, work experience. **Freshman Admission Requirements:** High school diploma is required and GED is accepted. *Academic units required:* 4 English, 3 math, 2 science, 2 science labs, 2 foreign language, 1 social studies, 1 history, 1 academic elective, 1 visual/performing arts. *Academic units recommended:* 4 science, 2 science labs, 4 foreign language, 1 social studies, 1 history, 1 academic elective, 2 visual/performing arts. **Freshman Admission Statistics:** 48,162 applied, 29.49% admitted, 31% enrolled. **Transfer Admission Requirements:** college transcript(s), Minimum college GPA of 2.0 required. Lowest grade transferable D. **General Admission Information:** Application fee $55. Regular application deadline 11/30. Regular notification 4/1. Nonfall registration not accepted.

COSTS AND FINANCIAL AID

Annual in-state tuition $5,472. Room and board $12,507. Required fees $3,603. Average book expense $1,848. **Required Forms and Deadlines:** FAFSA. **Notification of Awards:** Applicants will be notified of awards on a rolling basis beginning 4/1. **Types of Aid:** *Need-based scholarships/grants:* Federal Pell, FSEOG, State scholarships/grants, Private scholarships, College/university scholarship or grant aid from institutional funds. *Loans:* Direct Subsidized Stafford Loans, Direct Unsubsidized Stafford Loans, Direct PLUS loans, Federal Perkins Loans, College/university loans from institutional funds. *Student Employment:* Federal Work-Study Program available. Institutional employment available. **Financial Aid Statistics:** 92% needy freshmen, 88% needy undergrads receive need-based scholarship or grant aid. 4% freshmen, 3% undergrads receive non-need-based scholarship or grant aid. 69% freshmen, 67% undergrads receive need-based self-help aid. 2% freshmen, 2% undergrads receive athletic scholarships. 40% undergrads borrow to pay for school. Average cumulative indebtedness $22,413. **Criteria for awarding aid:** *Need-based:* Academics, Art, Job skills, Leadership, Music/drama. *Non-need-based:* Academics, Alumni affiliation, Art, Athletics, Job skills, Leadership, Music/drama, State/district residency.

CALIFORNIA STATE POLYTECHNIC UNIVERSITY, POMONA

3801 W Temple Ave, Pomona, CA 91768
Phone: 909-869-5299 • **Financial Aid Phone:** 909-869-3700
E-mail: admissions@cpp.edu • **CEEB Code:** 4082
Fax: 909-869-4529 • **Website:** www.cpp.edu • **ACT Code:** 4048

This public school was founded in 1938. It has a 1437-acre campus.

RATINGS

Admissions Selectivity Rating: 76 **Fire Safety Rating:** 92 **Green Rating:** 93

STUDENTS AND FACULTY

Enrollment: 23,611. **Student Body:** 45% female, 55% male, 1% out-of-state, 6% international (100 countries represented). Asian 23%, African American 3%, Caucasian 18%, Hispanic 42%, Native American <1%, Pacific Islander <1%, Two or more races 4%, Race unknown 4%.
Retention and Graduation: 89% freshmen return for sophomore year. 18% freshmen graduate within 4 years. 69% freshmen graduate within 6 years. **Faculty:** Student/faculty ratio 23:1. 611 full-time faculty, 80% hold PhDs, 40% are are members of minority groups, 42% are women. 3% of classes are taught by teaching assistants.

ACADEMICS

Degrees: bachelor's, doctoral/professional, master's. **Classes:** Most classes have 30-39 students. Most lab/discussion sessions have 20-29 students. **Most popular majors:** Business Administration and Management; Hospitality Administration/Management; Mechanical Engineering. **Special Study Options:** cooperative education program, cross-registration, distance learning, double major, dual enrollment, English as a Second Language (ESL), exchange student program (domestic), external degree program, honors program, internships, study abroad, teacher certification program, Ocean Studies Institute Desert Studies Consortium. **Honors Programs:** See web site for complete information about The Kellogg Honors College: http://www.

csupomona.edu/~honorscollege/. **Disability Services:** Special programs offered to physically disabled students, including note-taking services, reader services, tutors. **Career Services:** Alumni network, Alumni services, Career/job search classes, Career assessment, Internships, Regional alumni. Career Development/Counseling: The Career Center assists all students in selecting or changing their major, as well as, what students can do with their major. Students are offered a number of career assessment inventories to assist with career development. The Career Center at Cal Poly Pomona has one of the largest number of organizations recruiting Cal Poly Pomona students in the State of California.

FACILITIES

Housing: Coed dorms, apartments for single students. 95% of campus accessible to physically disabled. **Special Academic Facilities/Equipment:** Center for hospitality management, art gallery, center for regenerative studies, citrus-packing house, meat-processing building, poultry plant, feed mill, beef, sheep, swine, Arabian horse units, horse show arena, and aerospace wind tunnel. **Computers:** 10% of classrooms, 10% of dorms, 100% of libraries, 100% of dining areas, 100% of student union, 60% of common outdoor areas have wireless network access. Students can register for classes online. Administrative functions (other than registration) can be performed online.

CAMPUS LIFE

Environment: City. **Activities:** Choral groups, concert band, dance, drama/theater, jazz band, literary magazine, music ensembles, musical theater, opera, pep band, student government, student newspaper, symphony orchestra, yearbook, Campus Ministries, Student Organization. 280 registered organizations, 26 honor societies, 10 religious organizations. 12 fraternities, 8 sororities. **Athletics (Intercollegiate):** *Men:* baseball, basketball, cheerleading, cross-country, soccer, tennis, track/field (outdoor). *Women:* basketball, cheerleading, cross-country, soccer, tennis, track/field (outdoor), volleyball. **On-Campus Highlights:** The Farmstore at Kellogg Ranch, The Rain Bird Aquatic, Ethnobotony & Rainforest Learning Centers, W. K. Kellogg Arabian Horse Center, Kellogg House Pomona, John T. Lyle Center for Regenerative Studies. Cal Poly Pomona is located on the eastern edge of Southern California's San Gabriel Valley. The University's 1,400-acre campus features lush rolling hills; flowers, plants and trees from all seven continents; a rose garden personally built by W.K. Kellogg; and a beautifully landscaped Japanese garden. The university's aesthetic qualities are one of its best kept secrets. Some of the world's finest architects and landscape architects designed and built the ranch—a hybrid of architecture, which combined the formal courtyards, gardens and elements of Spanish, Italian and Islamic architecture with the informality of a growing nouveau-riche society. Pasadena architect Myron Hunt (Rose Bowl, Huntington Library) designed W.K. Kellogg's main house. Charles Gibbs Adams whose work included the Hearst Castle Gardens in San Simeon, California was selected to landscape the grounds. Later, the landscape was completed by Florence Yoch and Lucile Council, widely recognized as two of the finest garden designers and landscape architects in California. More recently, Antoine Predock designed the University's administration building with a desert theme. **Environmental Initiatives:** Completed baseline inventory and updated GHG inventory for 2009.

ADMISSIONS

Freshman Academic Profile: Average high school GPA 3.5. 87% from public high schools. **Reported SAT (pre-2016 redesign) scores:** SAT Math middle 50% range 460-600. SAT Critical Reading middle 50% range 440-560. **Concordant SAT scores:** SAT Math middle 50% range 500–620. ACT middle 50% range 20-27. Minimum paper TOEFL 525. **Basis for Candidate Selection:** *Very important factors considered include:* rigor of secondary school record, academic GPA, standardized test scores. **Freshman Admission Requirements:** High school diploma is required and GED is accepted. *Academic units required:* 4 English, 3 math, 2 science, 2 science labs, 2 foreign language, 1 social studies, 1 history, 1 academic elective, 1 visual/performing arts. *Academic units recommended:* 4 math. **Freshman Admission Statistics:** 32,917 applied, 59.16% admitted, 22% enrolled. **Transfer Admission Requirements:** college transcript(s), statement of good standing from prior institution(s). Minimum college GPA of 2.0 required. **General Admission Information:** Application fee $55. Priority deadline 11/30. Regular application deadline 11/30. Nonfall registration not accepted.

COSTS AND FINANCIAL AID

Annual in-state tuition $5,472. Annual out-of-state tuition $16,632. Room and board $14,514. Required fees $1,555. Average book expense $1,650. **Required Forms and Deadlines:** FAFSA. **Notification of Awards:** Applicants will be notified of awards on a rolling basis beginning 4/1. **Types of Aid:** *Need-based scholarships/grants:* Federal Pell, FSEOG, State scholarships/grants, Private scholarships, College/university scholarship or grant aid from institutional funds. *Loans:* Direct Subsidized Stafford Loans, Direct Unsubsidized Stafford Loans, Direct PLUS loans, Federal Perkins Loans, College/university loans from institutional funds. *Student Employment:* Federal Work-Study Program available. Institutional employment available. **Financial Aid Statistics:** 74% needy freshmen, 73% needy undergrads receive need-based scholarship or grant aid. 9% freshmen, 6% undergrads receive non-need-based scholarship or grant aid. 47% freshmen, 49% undergrads receive need-based self-help aid. 0% freshmen, 0% undergrads receive athletic scholarships. 74% freshmen, 72% undergrads receive any aid. 53% undergrads borrow to pay for school. Average cumulative indebtedness $22,235. **Criteria for awarding aid:** *Need-based:* Academics. *Non-need-based:* Academics, Alumni affiliation, Athletics, Leadership, State/district residency.

CALIFORNIA STATE UNIVERSITY, CHICO

400 West First Street, Chico, CA 95929-0722
Phone: 530-898-4428 • **Financial Aid Phone:** 530-898-6451
E-mail: info@csuchico.edu • **CEEB Code:** 4048
Fax: 530-898-6456 • **Website:** www.csuchico.edu • **ACT Code:** 212

This public school was founded in 1887. It has a 130-acre campus.

RATINGS
Admissions Selectivity Rating: 84   Fire Safety Rating: 74   Green Rating: 90

STUDENTS AND FACULTY
Enrollment: 16,471. **Student Body:** 53% female, 47% male, 1% out-of-state, 4% international (46 countries represented). Asian 6%, African American 2%, Caucasian 44%, Hispanic 31%, Native American 1%, Pacific Islander <1%, Two or more races 5%, Race unknown 8%.
Retention and Graduation: 85% freshmen return for sophomore year.
Faculty: Student/faculty ratio 24:1. 507 full-time faculty, 85% hold PhDs, 17% are are members of minority groups, 47% are women. 1% of classes are taught by teaching assistants.

ACADEMICS
Degrees: bachelor's, certificate, master's, postbachelor's certificate, post-master's certificate. **Classes:** Most classes have 20-29 students. Most lab/discussion sessions have 20-29 students. **Most popular majors:** Business Administration and Management; Education; Engineering. **Special Study Options:** cooperative education program, cross-registration, distance learning, double major, dual enrollment, English as a Second Language (ESL), exchange student program (domestic), external degree program, honors program, independent study, internships, student-designed major, study abroad, teacher certification program. **Honors Programs:** Honors in General Education (HGE) Honors in the Major (HIM) Combined degree programs: We currently offer BA or BS combined with a post-bac credential. **Disability Services:** Special programs offered to physically disabled students, including note-taking services, reader services, tape recorders, tutors. **Career Services:** Alumni network, Alumni services, Career assessment, Internships.

FACILITIES
Housing: Coed dorms, special housing for disabled students, special housing for international students, fraternity/sorority housing, apartments for single students, Thematic housing for honors, engineering, minorities in engineering and science, business, and math. Theme floors include community service, recreational sports, leadership, and Adventure Outings. 95% of campus accessible to physically diasbled. **Special Academic Facilities/Equipment:** Anthropology museum, center for intercultural studies, satellite communication dishes, biological field station, university farm, electron microscope. **Computers:** 100% of classrooms, 100% of dorms, 100% of libraries, 100% of dining areas, 100% of student union, 25% of common outdoor areas have wireless network access. Students can register for classes online. Administrative functions (other than registration) can be performed online.

CAMPUS LIFE
Environment: City. **Activities:** Choral groups, concert band, dance, drama/theater, jazz band, literary magazine, music ensembles, musical theater, opera, pep band, radio station, student government, student newspaper, student-run film society, symphony orchestra, yearbook. 192 registered organizations, 18 honor societies, 12 religious organizations. 15 fraternities, 14 sororities. **Athletics (Intercollegiate):** *Men:* baseball, basketball, cross-country, golf, soccer, track/field (outdoor). *Women:* basketball, cross-country, golf, soccer, softball, track/field (outdoor), volleyball. **On-Campus Highlights:** Bell Memorial Union, Meriam Library, Turner Print Museum, Humanities Gallery/University Gallery, Wildcat Recreation Center, Nettleton Stadium; on-campus housing facilities; athletic facilities; recording arts studio. **Environmental Initiatives:** This Way to Sustainability Conference

ADMISSIONS
Freshman Academic Profile: Average high school GPA 3.3. 35% in top 10% of high school class, 76% in top 25% of high school class, 100% in top 50% of high school class. 93% from public high schools. **Reported SAT (pre-2016 redesign) scores:** SAT Math middle 50% range 440-550. SAT Critical Reading

middle 50% range 440-550. **Concordant SAT scores:** SAT Math middle 50% range 480–570. ACT middle 50% range 19-24. Minimum internet-based TOEFL 79. Minimum paper TOEFL 500. **Basis for Candidate Selection:** *Very important factors considered include:* academic GPA, standardized test scores. *Important factors considered include:* geographical residence, state residency. **Freshman Admission Requirements:** High school diploma is required and GED is accepted. *Academic units required:* 4 English, 3 math, 2 science, 2 science labs, 2 foreign language, 2 social studies, 1 academic elective, 1 visual/performing arts. **Freshman Admission Statistics:** 23,124 applied, 66.57% admitted, 18% enrolled. **Transfer Admission Requirements:** college transcript(s), statement of good standing from prior institution(s). Minimum college GPA of 2.0 required. Lowest grade transferable D. **General Admission Information:** Application fee $55. Priority deadline 10/1. Regular application deadline 11/30. Nonfall registration not accepted. Admission may be deferred for a maximum of 1 year.

COSTS AND FINANCIAL AID
Annual in-state tuition $7,044. Annual out-of-state tuition $18,204. Room and board $12,824. Required fees $1,572. Average book expense $1,719. **Required Forms and Deadlines:** FAFSA. **Notification of Awards:** Applicants will be notified of awards on a rolling basis beginning 3/2. **Types of Aid:** *Need-based scholarships/grants:* Federal Pell, FSEOG, State scholarships/grants, Private scholarships, College/university scholarship or grant aid from institutional funds. *Loans:* Direct Subsidized Stafford Loans, Direct Unsubsidized Stafford Loans, Direct PLUS loans, Federal Perkins Loans, College/university loans from institutional funds. *Student Employment:* Federal Work-Study Program available. Institutional employment available. **Financial Aid Statistics:** 75% needy freshmen, 78% needy undergrads receive need-based scholarship or grant aid. 23% freshmen, 13% undergrads receive non-need-based scholarship or grant aid. 67% freshmen, 67% undergrads receive need-based self-help aid. 66% freshmen, 63% undergrads receive any aid. **Criteria for awarding aid:** *Need-based:* Academics, Minority status. *Non-need-based:* Academics, Art, Athletics, Leadership, Minority status, Music/drama, Religious affiliation.

CALIFORNIA STATE UNIVERSITY— DOMINGUEZ HILLS

100 East Victoria Street, Carson, CA 90747
Phone: 310-243-3645 • **Financial Aid Phone:** 310-243-3691
E-mail: info@csudh.edu • **CEEB Code:** 4098
Fax: 310-516-3609 • **Website:** www.csudh.edu • **ACT Code:** 203

This public school was founded in 1960. It has a 346-acre campus.

RATINGS
Admissions Selectivity Rating: 71   Fire Safety Rating: 72   Green Rating: 70

STUDENTS AND FACULTY
Enrollment: 12,613. **Student Body:** 63% female, 37% male, 0% out-of-state, 4% international (37 countries represented). Asian 10%, African American 13%, Caucasian 7%, Hispanic 60%, Native American <1%, Pacific Islander <1%, Two or more races 3%, Race unknown 3%.
Retention and Graduation: 82% freshmen return for sophomore year. 5% freshmen graduate within 4 years. **Faculty:** Student/faculty ratio 21:1. 277 full-time faculty, 73% hold PhDs, 41% are are members of minority groups, 56% are women. 0% of classes are taught by teaching assistants.

ACADEMICS
Degrees: bachelor's, master's, postbachelor's certificate, post-master's certificate. **Classes:** Most classes have 20-29 students. Most lab/discussion sessions have 20-29 students. **Most popular majors:** Psychology; Business Administration and Management; Criminal Justice/Safety Studies. **Special Study Options:** cooperative education program, cross-registration, distance learning, double major, dual enrollment, external degree program, honors program, independent study, internships, study abroad, teacher certification program, weekend college. **Disability Services:** Special programs offered to physically disabled students, including note-taking services, reader services, tape recorders, tutors. **Career Services:** Alumni services, Career/job search classes, Career assessment, Internships. We have a full complement of internship services for students which include thousands of internship postings annually with area employers and have bi-annual internship job fairs as well as other employer internship opportunities for our students.

FACILITIES
Housing: apartments for married students, apartments for single students. 100% of campus accessible to physically diasbled. **Special Academic Facilities/Equipment:** University Art Gallery. Olympic Velodrome University Theater

CAMPUS LIFE

Environment: City. **Activities:** Choral groups, concert band, dance, drama/theater, jazz band, music ensembles, student government, student newspaper, symphony orchestra 65 registered organizations, 6 honor societies, 3 religious organizations. 4 fraternities, 4 sororities. **Athletics (Intercollegiate):** *Men:* baseball, basketball, golf, soccer. *Women:* basketball, cross-country, soccer, softball, tennis, track/field (outdoor), volleyball. **On-Campus Highlights:** Welch Hall, Student Union, Library, Athletic Fields/Home Depot Center, Sculpture Garden.

ADMISSIONS

Freshman Academic Profile: Average high school GPA 3.1. 93% from public high schools. **Reported SAT (pre-2016 redesign) scores:** SAT Math middle 50% range 380-470. SAT Critical Reading middle 50% range 380-470. SAT Writing middle 50% range 380-460. **Concordant SAT scores:** SAT EBRW middle 50% 430–520. SAT Math middle 50% range 420–510. ACT middle 50% range 15-19. Minimum internet-based TOEFL 61. Minimum paper TOEFL 500. **Basis for Candidate Selection:** *Other factors considered include:* academic GPA, standardized test scores. **Freshman Admission Requirements:** High school diploma is required and GED is accepted. *Academic units required:* 4 English, 3 math, 2 science, 2 science labs, 2 foreign language, 1 social studies, 1 history, 1 academic elective, 1 visual/performing arts. **Freshman Admission Statistics:** 10,615 applied, 75.12% admitted, 16% enrolled. **Transfer Admission Requirements:** High school transcript, college transcript(s), Minimum college GPA of 2.0 required. Lowest grade transferable c. **General Admission Information:** Application fee $55. Nonfall registration accepted.

COSTS AND FINANCIAL AID

Annual in-state tuition $5,472. Annual out-of-state tuition $16,632. Required fees $950. Average book expense $1,850. **Required Forms and Deadlines:** FAFSA. **Notification of Awards:** Applicants will be notified of awards on a rolling basis beginning 4/1. **Types of Aid:** *Need-based scholarships/grants:* Federal Pell, FSEOG, State scholarships/grants, Private scholarships, College/university scholarship or grant aid from institutional funds. *Loans:* Direct Subsidized Stafford Loans, Direct Unsubsidized Stafford Loans, Direct PLUS loans, Federal Perkins Loans, College/university loans from institutional funds. *Student Employment:* Federal Work-Study Program available. Institutional employment available. **Financial Aid Statistics:** 89% needy freshmen, 86% needy undergrads receive need-based scholarship or grant aid. 17% freshmen, 25% undergrads receive non-need-based scholarship or grant aid. 1% freshmen, 2% undergrads receive need-based self-help aid. 0% freshmen, 0% undergrads receive athletic scholarships. 87% freshmen, 81% undergrads receive any aid. 58% undergrads borrow to pay for school. Average cumulative indebtedness $16,370. **Criteria for awarding aid:** *Need-based:* Academics, Athletics. *Non-need-based:* Academics, Alumni affiliation, Art, Athletics, Leadership, Music/drama.

CALIFORNIA STATE UNIVERSITY—EAST BAY

25800 Carlos Bee Blvd., Hayward, CA 94542-3035
Phone: 510-885-2784 • **Financial Aid Phone:** 510-885-2784
E-mail: admissions@csueastbay.edu • **CEEB Code:** 4011
Fax: 510-885-3505 • **Website:** www.csueastbay.edu • **ACT Code:** 154

This public school was founded in 1957. It has a 342-acre campus.

RATINGS

Admissions Selectivity Rating: 77   **Fire Safety Rating:** 75   **Green Rating:** 60*

STUDENTS AND FACULTY

Enrollment: 9,788. **Student Body:** 60% female, 40% male, 1% out-of-state, 8% international (86 countries represented). Asian 20%, African American 10%, Caucasian 22%, Hispanic 19%, Native American <1%, Pacific Islander 3%, Two or more races 3%, Race unknown 14%.
Retention and Graduation: 76% freshmen return for sophomore year. 16% freshmen graduate within 4 years. 43% freshmen graduate within 6 years.
Faculty: Student/faculty ratio 26:1. 322 full-time faculty, 0% hold PhDs, 34% are are members of minority groups, 49% are women. 5% of classes are taught by teaching assistants.

ACADEMICS

Degrees: bachelor's, certificate, doctoral, master's, postbachelor's certificate, post-master's certificate. **Special Study Options:** cooperative education program, cross-registration, distance learning, double major, dual enrollment, English as a Second Language (ESL), exchange student program (domestic), external degree program, honors program, independent study, internships, liberal arts/career combination, student-designed major, study abroad, teacher certification program, weekend college, Year round operation with state

supported summer quarter. Joint Master's Degree in Marine Science offered at Moss Landing Marine Lab. Joint MFA in Creative Writing in summer. Overseas MBA programs in Hong Kong, Moscow, Singapore, and Vienna. **Disability Services:** Special programs offered to physically disabled students, including note-taking services, reader services, tape recorders, tutors. **Career Services:** Alumni services, Career/job search classes, Career assessment, Internships.

FACILITIES

Housing: apartments for single students, 95% of campus accessible to physically diasbled. **Special Academic Facilities/Equipment:** Anthropology museum, art gallery, scanning electron microsope facility, marine lab, ecological field station, geology summer camp. **Computers:** Students can register for classes online. Administrative functions (other than registration) can be performed online.

CAMPUS LIFE

Environment: City. **Activities:** Choral groups, concert band, dance, drama/theater, jazz band, literary magazine, music ensembles, musical theater, opera, pep band, radio station, student government, student newspaper, symphony orchestra, television station 100 registered organizations, 2 honor societies, 2 religious organizations. 7 fraternities, 7 sororities. **Athletics (Intercollegiate):** *Men:* baseball, basketball, cross-country, golf, soccer. *Women:* basketball, cross-country, golf, soccer, softball, swimming, volleyball, water polo. **On-Campus Highlights:** University Union, Gymnasium/Pools, Warren Hall /Administration, University Theatre, University Art Gallery.

ADMISSIONS

Freshman Academic Profile: Average high school GPA 3.1. **Reported SAT (pre-2016 redesign) scores:** SAT Math middle 50% range 400-510. SAT Critical Reading middle 50% range 400-500. SAT Writing middle 50% range 410-500. **Concordant SAT scores:** SAT EBRW middle 50% 450–560. SAT Math middle 50% range 440–540. ACT middle 50% range 16-21. Minimum paper TOEFL 525. **Basis for Candidate Selection:** *Very important factors considered include:* rigor of secondary school record, academic GPA, standardized test scores. *Other factors considered include:* recommendation(s), state residency. **Freshman Admission Requirements:** High school diploma is required and GED is accepted. *Academic units required:* 4 English, 3 math, 2 science, 2 science labs, 2 foreign language, 1 social studies, 1 history, 1 academic elective, and 1 unit from above areas or other academic areas. **Freshman Admission Statistics:** 10,778 applied, 35.63% admitted, 32% enrolled. **Transfer Admission Requirements:** college transcript(s), statement of good standing from prior institution(s). Minimum college GPA of 2.0 required. Lowest grade transferable D. **General Admission Information:** Application fee $55. Priority deadline 11/30. Regular application deadline 6/30. Nonfall registration accepted. Admission may be deferred for a maximum of 2 quarters.

COSTS AND FINANCIAL AID

Annual in-state tuition $5,091. Annual out-of-state tuition $14,019. Room and board $11,042. Average book expense $1,734. **Required Forms and Deadlines:** FAFSA. **Notification of Awards:** Applicants will be notified of awards on a rolling basis beginning 3/15. **Types of Aid:** *Need-based scholarships/grants:* Federal Pell, FSEOG, State scholarships/grants, Private scholarships, College/university scholarship or grant aid from institutional funds. *Loans:* Federal Perkins Loans. *Student Employment:* Federal Work-Study Program available. Institutional employment available. **Financial Aid Statistics:** 83% needy freshmen, 83% needy undergrads receive need-based scholarship or grant aid. 0% undergrads receive non-need-based scholarship or grant aid. 63% freshmen, 62% undergrads receive need-based self-help aid. 0% freshmen, 0% undergrads receive athletic scholarships. 43% freshmen, 42% undergrads receive any aid. **Criteria for awarding aid:** *Need-based:* Academics. *Non-need-based:* Academics.

CALIFORNIA STATE UNIVERSITY, FRESNO

5150 North Maple Ave. M/S JA 57, Fresno, CA 93740-8026
Phone: 559-278-2261 • **Financial Aid Phone:** 559-278-2182
E-mail: admissions@csufresno.edu • **CEEB Code:** 4312
Fax: 559-278-4812 • **Website:** www.csufresno.edu • **ACT Code:** 266

This public school was founded in 1911. It has a 388-acre campus.

RATINGS

Admissions Selectivity Rating: 83   **Fire Safety Rating:** 78   **Green Rating:** 60*

STUDENTS AND FACULTY

Enrollment: 18,784. **Student Body:** 57% female, 43% male, 0% out-of-state, 3% international (116 countries represented). Asian 15%, African American 5%, Caucasian 30%, Hispanic 38%, Native American 1%, Pacific Islander <1%, Two or more races 3%, Race unknown 6%.

Retention and Graduation: 86% freshmen return for sophomore year. 14% freshmen graduate within 4 years. 49% freshmen graduate within 6 years. **Faculty:** Student/faculty ratio 22:1. 624 full-time faculty, 95% hold PhDs, 29% are are members of minority groups, 42% are women. 8% of classes are taught by teaching assistants.

ACADEMICS

Degrees: bachelor's, doctoral/research, master's, postbachelor's certificate, post-master's certificate. **Classes:** Most classes have 20-29 students. Most lab/discussion sessions have 20-29 students. **Most popular majors:** Liberal Arts and Sciences/Liberal Studies; Psychology; Health Services/Allied Health/Health Sciences. **Special Study Options:** Accelerated program, cooperative education program, cross-registration, distance learning, double major, dual enrollment, English as a Second Language (ESL), exchange student program (domestic), honors program, independent study, internships, student-designed major, study abroad, teacher certification program. **Disability Services:** Special programs offered to physically disabled students, including note-taking services, reader services, tape recorders, tutors.

FACILITIES

Housing: Coed dorms, men's dorms, women's dorms, fraternity/sorority housing. 100% of campus accessible to physically disabled. **Special Academic Facilities/Equipment:** Marine lab, Downing Planeterium. **Computers:** 100% of classrooms, 100% of dorms, 100% of libraries, 100% of dining areas, 100% of student union, 20% of common outdoor areas have wireless network access. Students can register for classes online. Administrative functions (other than registration) can be performed online. Undergraduates are required to own a computer.

CAMPUS LIFE

Environment: Metropolis. **Activities:** Choral groups, concert band, dance, drama/theater, jazz band, marching band, music ensembles, musical theater, radio station, student government, student newspaper, symphony orchestra, television station, Student Organization. 250 registered organizations, 21 honor societies, 11 religious organizations. 19 fraternities, 13 sororities. **Athletics (Intercollegiate):** *Men:* baseball, basketball, cheerleading, cross-country, football, golf, tennis, track/field (outdoor). *Women:* basketball, cheerleading, cross-country, diving, equestrian sports, golf, lacrosse, light weight football, soccer, softball, swimming, tennis, track/field (outdoor), volleyball. **On-Campus Highlights:** Savemart Events Center, Downing Planetarium, Kennel Bookstore, New Ciminology Center, Henry Madden Library, Please check out our website for more inforamtion: www.gotofresnostate.com. **Environmental Initiatives:** Solar Photovoltaic Canopy Parking Structure (Lot V) This structure is a 1.1 megawatt solar system, making it the largest photovoltaic paneled parting installation at a U.S. university. Completed in the fall of 2007, the structure was estimated to provide 20% of the core campus power. The system offsets approximately 950 metric tons of carbon monoxide emissions—that is equivalent to planting over 24,300 trees or eliminating from our road systems over 200 vehicles a year!

ADMISSIONS

Freshman Academic Profile: Average high school GPA 3.3. 15% in top 10% of high school class, 80% in top 25% of high school class, 100% in top 50% of high school class. 99% from public high schools. **Reported SAT (pre-2016 redesign) scores:** SAT Math middle 50% range 410-530. SAT Critical Reading middle 50% range 400-510. SAT Writing middle 50% range 400-510. **Concordant SAT scores:** SAT EBRW middle 50% 450–570. SAT Math middle 50% range 450–560. ACT middle 50% range 16-22. Minimum internet-based TOEFL 61. Minimum paper TOEFL 500. **Basis for Candidate Selection:** *Very important factors considered include:* rigor of secondary school record, academic GPA, standardized test scores. **Freshman Admission Requirements:** High school diploma is required and GED is accepted. *Academic units required:* 4 English, 3 math, 1 science, 1 science lab, 2 foreign language, 1 social studies, 1 history, 1 academic elective, 1 visual/performing arts. **Freshman Admission Statistics:** 15,482 applied, 60.41% admitted, 31% enrolled. **Transfer Admission Requirements:** college transcript(s), Minimum college GPA of 2.4 required. Lowest grade transferable D. **General Admission Information:** Application fee $55. Regular application deadline 11/30. Nonfall registration not accepted.

COSTS AND FINANCIAL AID

Annual in-state tuition $0. Annual out-of-state tuition $11,160. Room and board $10,550. Required fees $790. Average book expense $1,256. **Required Forms and Deadlines:** FAFSA. **Notification of Awards:** Applicants will be notified of awards on a rolling basis beginning 4/1. **Types of Aid:** *Need-based scholarships/grants:* Federal Pell, FSEOG, State scholarships/grants, Private scholarships, College/university scholarship or grant aid from institutional funds. *Loans:* Direct Subsidized Stafford Loans, Direct Unsubsidized Stafford Loans, Direct PLUS loans, Federal Perkins Loans, Federal Nursing Loans. *Student Employment:* Federal Work-Study Program available. Institutional employment available. **Financial Aid Statistics:** 83% needy freshmen, 80% needy undergrads receive need-based scholarship or grant aid. 2% freshmen,

9% undergrads receive non-need-based scholarship or grant aid. 69% freshmen, 82% undergrads receive need-based self-help aid. 3% freshmen, 2% undergrads receive athletic scholarships. 76% freshmen, 78% undergrads receive any aid. **Criteria for awarding aid:** *Need-based:* Academics, Athletics. *Non-need-based:* Academics, Art, Athletics, Leadership, Music/drama, State/district residency.

CALIFORNIA STATE UNIVERSITY, FULLERTON

P.O.Box 6900, Fullerton, CA 92834-6900
Phone: 657-278-7788 • **Financial Aid Phone:** 657-278-3125
E-mail: admissions@fullerton.edu • **CEEB Code:** 4589
Fax: 657-278-7699 • **Website:** www.fullerton.edu • **ACT Code:** 355

This public school was founded in 1957. It has a 225-acre campus.

RATINGS

Admissions Selectivity Rating: 85   **Fire Safety Rating:** 84   **Green Rating:** 91

STUDENTS AND FACULTY

Enrollment: 34,416. **Student Body:** 56% female, 44% male, 1% out-of-state, 6% international (77 countries represented). Asian 21%, African American 2%, Caucasian 20%, Hispanic 42%, Native American <1%, Pacific Islander <1%, Two or more races 4%, Race unknown 4%.
Retention and Graduation: 89% freshmen return for sophomore year. 18% freshmen graduate within 4 years. 62% freshmen graduate within 6 years. **Faculty:** Student/faculty ratio 27:1. 981 full-time faculty, 0% hold PhDs, 8% are are members of minority groups, 50% are women. 0% of classes are taught by teaching assistants.

ACADEMICS

Degrees: bachelor's, doctoral/professional, doctoral/research, master's. **Classes:** Most classes have 20-29 students. Most lab/discussion sessions have 20-29 students. **Most popular majors:** Business Administration and Management; Psychology; Accounting. **Special Study Options:** cooperative education program, double major, honors program, independent study, internships, student-designed major, study abroad. **Disability Services:** Special programs offered to physically disabled students, including note-taking services, reader services, tape recorders, tutors. **Career Services:** Alumni network, Alumni services, Career/job search classes, Career assessment, Internships, Regional alumni. CSUF Entrepreneurship conducts over 110 student consulting projects annually with small and medium sized firms. The typical student project team has 5-6 students who collectively put in 300-400 hours of work on the project. Our client satisfaction surveys find that our clients are overwhelmingly satisfied with the projects' results and most clients report that the students far exceeded their expectations. As for the students, most students report that this applied learning process is the highlight of their college experience. Our students created the first ever national fraternity for Entrepreneurship: Epsilon Nu Tau.

FACILITIES

Housing: fraternity/sorority housing, apartments for single students. 100% of campus accessible to physically disabled. **Computers:** Students can register for classes online. Administrative functions (other than registration) can be performed online.

CAMPUS LIFE

Activities: Choral groups, concert band, dance, drama/theater, jazz band, music ensembles, musical theater, radio station, student government, student newspaper. **Athletics (Intercollegiate):** *Men:* baseball, basketball, cross-country, fencing, soccer, track/field (outdoor), wrestling. *Women:* basketball, cross-country, fencing, gymnastics, soccer, softball, tennis, track/field (outdoor), volleyball. **On-Campus Highlights:** Fullerton Arboretum, 5 Starbucks Coffee shops, Titan Student Union Underground.

ADMISSIONS

Freshman Academic Profile: Average high school GPA 3.6. 20% in top 10% of high school class, 68% in top 25% of high school class, 97% in top 50% of high school class. 89% from public high schools. **Reported SAT (pre-2016 redesign) scores:** SAT Math middle 50% range 470-570. SAT Critical Reading middle 50% range 450-550. **Concordant SAT scores:** SAT Math middle 50% range 510–590. ACT middle 50% range 19-24. Minimum internet-based TOEFL 61. Minimum paper TOEFL 500. **Basis for Candidate Selection:** *Very important factors considered include:* academic GPA, standardized test scores, geographical residence, state residency. **Freshman Admission Requirements:** High school diploma is required and GED is accepted. *Academic units required:* 4 English, 3 math, 2 science, 2 science labs, 2 foreign language, 1 social studies, 1 history, 1 academic elective, 1 visual/performing arts. *Academic units recommended:* 4 English, 3 math, 2 science, 2 science labs, 3 foreign language, 1 social studies, 1 history, 1 academic elective, 1 visual/performing arts. **Freshman Admission Statistics:** 44,493 applied, 48.23% admitted, 21% enrolled. **Transfer Admission Requirements:** college transcript(s), statement of good standing from prior institution(s). Minimum college GPA of 2.0 required. Lowest grade transferable C. **General Admission Information:** Application fee $55. Priority deadline 10/30. Regular application deadline 11/30. Nonfall registration not accepted.

COSTS AND FINANCIAL AID
Annual in-state tuition $5,472. Annual out-of-state tuition $16,632. Room and board $13,510. Required fees $964. Average book expense $1,898. **Required Forms and Deadlines:** FAFSA. **Types of Aid:** *Need-based scholarships/ grants:* Federal Pell, FSEOG, State scholarships/grants, Private scholarships, College/university scholarship or grant aid from institutional funds, Federal Nursing Scholarships. *Loans:* Direct Subsidized Stafford Loans, Direct Unsubsidized Stafford Loans, Direct PLUS loans, Federal Perkins Loans, College/university loans from institutional funds. *Student Employment:* Federal Work-Study Program available. Institutional employment available. **Financial Aid Statistics:** 80% needy freshmen, 76% needy undergrads receive need-based scholarship or grant aid. 14% freshmen, 9% undergrads receive non-need-based scholarship or grant aid. 28% freshmen, 33% undergrads receive need-based self-help aid. 1% freshmen, 0% undergrads receive athletic scholarships. 67% freshmen, 54% undergrads receive any aid. **Criteria for awarding aid:** *Need-based:* Academics, Art, Athletics, Music/drama. *Non-need-based:* Academics, Art, Athletics, Leadership, Music/drama.

CALIFORNIA STATE UNIVERSITY—LONG BEACH

1250 Bellflower Boulevard, Long Beach, CA 90840
Phone: 562-985-5471
E-mail: eslb@csulb.edu • **CEEB Code:** 4389
Fax: 562-985-4973 • **Website:** www.csulb.edu

This public school was founded in 1949. It has a 322-acre campus.

RATINGS
Admissions Selectivity Rating: 80   **Fire Safety Rating:** 67   **Green Rating:** 60*

STUDENTS AND FACULTY
Enrollment: 31,523. **Student Body:** 56% female, 44% male, 1% out-of-state, 6% international. Asian 23%, African American 4%, Caucasian 20%, Hispanic 38%, Native American <1%, Pacific Islander <1%, Two or more races 5%, Race unknown 4%.
Retention and Graduation: 90% freshmen return for sophomore year. 14% freshmen graduate within 4 years. 65% freshmen graduate within 6 years.
Faculty: Student/faculty ratio 24:1. 941 full-time faculty, 86% hold PhDs, 33% are are members of minority groups, 46% are women. 8% of classes are taught by teaching assistants.

ACADEMICS
Degrees: bachelor's, doctoral, master's, postbachelor's certificate. **Classes:** Most classes have 20-29 students. Most lab/discussion sessions have 20-29 students. **Most popular majors:** Psychology; Corrections and Criminal Justice; Management Information Systems. **Special Study Options:** Accelerated program, cross-registration, distance learning, double major, dual enrollment, English as a Second Language (ESL), honors program, independent study, internships, student-designed major, study abroad, teacher certification program. **Disability Services:** Special programs offered to physically disabled students, including note-taking services, reader services. **Career Services:** Alumni services, Career assessment, Internships.

FACILITIES
Housing: Coed dorms, special housing for international students 98% of campus accessible to physically disabled. **Special Academic Facilities/ Equipment:** Art and science museums, Japanese garden, special events arena with meeting facilities.

CAMPUS LIFE
Activities: Choral groups, concert band, dance, drama/theater, jazz band, literary magazine, music ensembles, musical theater, opera, radio station, student government, student newspaper, student-run film society, symphony orchestra, television station, yearbook. 300 registered organizations, 25 honor societies, 20 religious organizations. 16 fraternities, 15 sororities. **Athletics (Intercollegiate):** *Men:* baseball, basketball, cross-country, golf, track/field (outdoor), volleyball, water polo. *Women:* basketball, cross-country, golf, soccer, softball, tennis, track/field (outdoor), volleyball, water polo.

ADMISSIONS
Freshman Academic Profile: Average high school GPA 3.5. 0% in top 25% of high school class, 0% in top 50% of high school class. 82% from public high

schools. **Reported SAT (pre-2016 redesign) scores:** SAT Math middle 50% range 480-600. SAT Critical Reading middle 50% range 460-570. **Concordant SAT scores:** SAT Math middle 50% range 510–620. ACT middle 50% range 20-25. Minimum paper TOEFL 525. **Basis for Candidate Selection:** *Very important factors considered include:* academic GPA, standardized test scores, geographical residence, state residency. *Important factors considered include:* talent/ability. *Other factors considered include:* rigor of secondary school record, application essay, recommendation(s), extracurricular activities, character/ personal qualities, volunteer work, work experience. **Freshman Admission Requirements:** High school diploma is required and GED is accepted. *Academic units required:* 4 English, 3 math, 2 science, 2 science labs, 2 foreign language, 1 social studies, 1 history, 1 academic elective, and 1 unit from above areas or other academic areas. **Freshman Admission Statistics:** 56,357 applied, 36.07% admitted, 21% enrolled. **Transfer Admission Requirements:** college transcript(s), Minimum college GPA of 2.0 required. Lowest grade transferable C. **General Admission Information:** Application fee $55. Regular application deadline 11/30. Nonfall registration not accepted.

COSTS AND FINANCIAL AID
Annual in-state tuition $5,472. Annual out-of-state tuition $11,160. Room and board $11,880. Required fees $980. Average book expense $1,828. **Required Forms and Deadlines:** FAFSA. **Notification of Awards:** Applicants will be notified of awards on a rolling basis beginning 4/1. **Types of Aid:** *Need-based scholarships/grants:* Federal Pell, FSEOG, State scholarships/grants, Private scholarships, College/university scholarship or grant aid from institutional funds. *Loans:* Direct Subsidized Stafford Loans, Direct Unsubsidized Stafford Loans, Direct PLUS loans, Federal Perkins Loans. *Student Employment:* Federal Work-Study Program available. Institutional employment available. **Financial Aid Statistics:** 80% needy freshmen, 80% needy undergrads receive need-based scholarship or grant aid. 25% freshmen, 26% undergrads receive non-need-based scholarship or grant aid. 72% freshmen, 83% undergrads receive need-based self-help aid. 2% freshmen, 1% undergrads receive athletic scholarships. **Criteria for awarding aid:** *Need-based:* Academics, Art. *Non-need-based:* Academics, Art, Athletics, Job skills, Leadership, Music/drama, State/district residency.

CALIFORNIA STATE UNIVERSITY— LOS ANGELES

5151 State University Drive, Los Angeles, CA 90032
Phone: 323-343-3901 • **Financial Aid Phone:** 323-343-6260
E-mail: admission@calstatela.edu • **CEEB Code:** 4399
Fax: 323-343-6306 • **ACT Code:** 320

This public school was founded in 1947. It has a 175-acre campus.

RATINGS
Admissions Selectivity Rating: 72   **Fire Safety Rating:** 77   **Green Rating:** 60*

STUDENTS AND FACULTY
Enrollment: 18,074. **Student Body:** 59% female, 41% male, 0% out-of-state, 4% international (121 countries represented). Asian 17%, African American 5%, Caucasian 8%, Hispanic 58%, Native American <1%, Pacific Islander <1%, Two or more races 2%, Race unknown 6%.
Retention and Graduation: 81% freshmen return for sophomore year. 7% freshmen graduate within 4 years. 37% freshmen graduate within 6 years.
Faculty: Student/faculty ratio 25:1. 533 full-time faculty, 46% hold PhDs, 44% are are members of minority groups, 47% are women. 14% of classes are taught by teaching assistants.

ACADEMICS
Degrees: bachelor's, certificate, master's, postbachelor's certificate. **Classes:** Most classes have 20-29 students. **Most popular majors:** Psychology; Criminal Justice/Law Enforcement Administration; Business Administration and Management. **Special Study Options:** Accelerated program, cooperative education program, cross-registration, distance learning, double major, dual enrollment, English as a Second Language (ESL), exchange student program (domestic), honors program, independent study, internships, student-designed major, study abroad, teacher certification program. **Disability Services:** Special programs offered to physically disabled students, including note-taking services, reader services. **Career Services:** Career/job search classes, Internships.

FACILITIES
Housing: Coed dorms, special housing for international students, fraternity/ sorority housing, apartments for single students, Wellness Housing, ThemeHousing(Special Interest Housing) First Year House Quite House ACLP/International House The Neighborhood Wellness/Substance Free

House The Village Quiet House. 99% of campus accessible to physically diasbled. **Special Academic Facilities/Equipment:** Baroque pipe organ, bilingual center, entrepreneurship and small business institutes, center for study of armament and disarmament, Van de Graaff accelerator. **Computers:** Administrative functions (other than registration) can be performed online.

CAMPUS LIFE

Environment: Metropolis. **Activities:** Choral groups, dance, drama/theater, jazz band, literary magazine, music ensembles, musical theater, opera, radio station, student government, student newspaper, symphony orchestra, yearbook. 130 registered organizations, 3 religious organizations. 7 fraternities, 4 sororities. **Athletics (Intercollegiate):** *Men:* baseball, basketball, cross-country, soccer, track/field (outdoor). *Women:* basketball, cross-country, soccer, tennis, track/field (outdoor), volleyball.

ADMISSIONS

Freshman Academic Profile: Average high school GPA 3.2. **Reported SAT (pre-2016 redesign) scores:** SAT Math middle 50% range 390-510. SAT Critical Reading middle 50% range 380-480. **Concordant SAT scores:** SAT Math middle 50% range 430–540. ACT middle 50% range 15-20. Minimum paper TOEFL 550. **Basis for Candidate Selection:** *Very important factors considered include:* rigor of secondary school record, academic GPA, standardized test scores. *Other factors considered include:* state residency. **Freshman Admission Requirements:** High school diploma is required and GED is accepted. *Academic units required:* 4 English, 3 math, 2 science, 2 science labs, 2 foreign language, 1 social studies, 1 history, 1 academic elective, 1 visual/performing arts. *Academic units recommended:* 4 English, 3 math, 2 science, 2 science labs, 2 foreign language, 1 social studies, 1 history, 1 academic elective, 1 visual/performing arts. **Freshman Admission Statistics:** 24,218 applied, 69.42% admitted, 17% enrolled. **Transfer Admission Requirements:** college transcript(s), Minimum college GPA of 2.0 required. Lowest grade transferable C. **General Admission Information:** Application fee $55. Regular application deadline 11/30. Nonfall registration accepted.

COSTS AND FINANCIAL AID

Annual in-state tuition $6,101. Annual out-of-state tuition $17,759. Room and board $9,728. Average book expense $1,665. **Required Forms and Deadlines:** FAFSA. **Notification of Awards:** Applicants will be notified of awards on or about 4/1. **Types of Aid:** *Need-based scholarships/grants:* Federal Pell, FSEOG, State scholarships/grants, Private scholarships, College/university scholarship or grant aid from institutional funds. *Loans:* Direct Subsidized Stafford Loans, Direct Unsubsidized Stafford Loans, Federal Perkins Loans, Federal Nursing Loans. *Student Employment:* Federal Work-Study Program available. Institutional employment available. **Financial Aid Statistics:** 88% needy freshmen, 88% needy undergrads receive need-based scholarship or grant aid. 0% undergrads receive non-need-based scholarship or grant aid. 66% freshmen, 81% undergrads receive need-based self-help aid. 0% freshmen, 0% undergrads receive athletic scholarships. 76% freshmen, 77% undergrads receive any aid.

2-month training cruise around the pacific rim over the summer on The GOLDEN BEAR. **Disability Services:** Special programs offered to physically disabled students, including tutors. **Career Services:** Alumni services, Career/job search classes, Internships.

FACILITIES

Housing: Coed dorms. 70% of campus accessible to physically diasbled. **Special Academic Facilities/Equipment:** Bookstore, Library, Gym, Swimming Pool.

CAMPUS LIFE

Activities: student government 16 registered organizations. **Athletics (Intercollegiate):** *Men:* basketball, crew/rowing, golf, sailing, soccer, water polo. *Women:* crew/rowing, sailing, volleyball.

ADMISSIONS

Freshman Academic Profile: Average high school GPA 3.3. 80% from public high schools. **Reported SAT (pre-2016 redesign) scores:** SAT Math middle 50% range 510-610. SAT Critical Reading middle 50% range 490-600. SAT Writing middle 50% range 470-570. **Concordant SAT scores:** SAT EBRW middle 50% 540–640. SAT Math middle 50% range 540–630. ACT middle 50% range 21-27. Minimum paper TOEFL 550. **Basis for Candidate Selection:** *Very important factors considered include:* academic GPA, standardized test scores. *Other factors considered include:* rigor of secondary school record, application essay, extracurricular activities, talent/ability, character/personal qualities, alumni/ae relation, geographical residence, state residency. **Freshman Admission Requirements:** High school diploma is required and GED is accepted. *Academic units required:* 4 English, 3 math, 2 science, 2 science labs, 2 foreign language, 1 social studies, 1 history, 1 academic elective, 1 visual/performing arts. **Freshman Admission Statistics:** 1,206 applied, 81.51% admitted, 23% enrolled. **Transfer Admission Requirements:** college transcript(s), statement of good standing from prior institution(s). Minimum college GPA of 2.0 required. Lowest grade transferable C. **General Admission Information:** Application fee $55. Priority deadline 11/30. Nonfall registration not accepted.

COSTS AND FINANCIAL AID

Annual in-state tuition $9,960. Room and board $10,544. Required fees $1,314. Average book expense $1,336. **Required Forms and Deadlines:** FAFSA. **Notification of Awards:** Applicants will be notified of awards on a rolling basis beginning 4/15. **Types of Aid:** *Need-based scholarships/grants:* Federal Pell, FSEOG, State scholarships/grants, Private scholarships, College/university scholarship or grant aid from institutional funds. *Loans:* Federal Perkins Loans. *Student Employment:* Federal Work-Study Program available. Institutional employment available. **Financial Aid Statistics:** 84% needy undergrads receive need-based scholarship or grant aid. 0% undergrads receive non-need-based scholarship or grant aid. 80% freshmen, 17% undergrads receive need-based self-help aid. 0% freshmen, 0% undergrads receive athletic scholarships. **Criteria for awarding aid:** *Need-based:* Academics, Leadership.

CALIFORNIA STATE UNIVERSITY MARITIME ACADEMY

200 Maritime Academy, Vallejo, CA 94590-0644
Phone: 707-654-1330 • **Financial Aid Phone:** 707-654-1276
E-mail: admission@csum.edu • **CEEB Code:** 4035
Fax: 707-654-1336 • **Website:** www.csum.edu • **ACT Code:** 184

This public school was founded in 1929. It has a 67-acre campus.

RATINGS

Admissions Selectivity Rating: 73   **Fire Safety Rating:** 60*   **Green Rating:** 60*

STUDENTS AND FACULTY

Enrollment: 1,072. **Student Body:** 15% female, 85% male, 1% international. Asian 10%, African American 2%, Caucasian 53%, Hispanic 17%, Native American <1%, Pacific Islander <1%, Two or more races 11%, Race unknown 6%.
Retention and Graduation: 82% freshmen return for sophomore year. **Faculty:** Student/faculty ratio 15 64 full-time faculty, 63% hold PhDs, 6% are are members of minority groups, 20% are women. 0% of classes are taught by teaching assistants.

ACADEMICS

Degrees: bachelor's, master's. **Most popular majors:** Mechanical Engineering; Marine Science/Merchant Marine Officer; International Relations and Affairs. **Special Study Options:** cooperative education program, distance learning, double major, internships, all students participate in at least one

---

CALIFORNIA STATE UNIVERSITY, MONTEREY BAY

100 Campus Center, Seaside, CA 93955
Phone: 831-582-3738 • **Financial Aid Phone:** 831-582-5100
E-mail: admissions@csumb.edu • **CEEB Code:** 1945
Fax: 831-582-3783 • **Website:** http://www.csumb.edu • **ACT Code:** 321

This public school was founded in 1994. It has a 1387-acre campus.

RATINGS

Admissions Selectivity Rating: 82   **Fire Safety Rating:** 87   **Green Rating:** 93

STUDENTS AND FACULTY

Enrollment: 6,657. **Student Body:** 62% female, 38% male, 2% out-of-state, 4% international (20 countries represented). Asian 6%, African American 7%, Caucasian 34%, Hispanic 36%, Native American 1%, Pacific Islander 1%, Two or more races 7%, Race unknown 4%.
Retention and Graduation: 82% freshmen return for sophomore year. 21% freshmen graduate within 4 years. **Faculty:** Student/faculty ratio 25:1. 152 full-time faculty, 91% hold PhDs, 44% are are members of minority groups, 50% are women. 0% of classes are taught by teaching assistants.

ACADEMICS

Degrees: bachelor's, master's. **Classes:** Most classes have 20-29 students. Most lab/discussion sessions have 20-29 students. **Most popular majors:** Business Administration and Management; Psychology; Health and Physical Education/Fitness. **Special Study Options:** cross-registration, distance learning, double major, exchange student program (domestic), independent study, internships, student-designed major, study abroad, teacher certification program, service learning. **Disability Services:** Special programs offered to physically disabled students, including note-taking services, reader services, tape recorders. **Career Services:** Alumni services, Career/job search classes, Career assessment, Internships.

FACILITIES

Housing: Coed dorms, special housing for disabled students, special housing for international students, apartments for married students, apartments for single students, Wellness Housing, Theme Housing, six-person suite-style living with living areas and kitchenette; substance-free residence hall. 85% of campus accessible to physically diasbled. **Special Academic Facilities/Equipment:** Panetta Institute, Tanimura & Antle Family Memorial Library **Computers:** 100% of classrooms, 100% of dorms, 100% of libraries, 100% of dining areas, 100% of student union, 25% of common outdoor areas have wireless network access. Students can register for classes online. Administrative functions (other than registration) can be performed online.

CAMPUS LIFE

Environment: Village. **Activities:** Choral groups, concert band, dance, drama/theater, jazz band, music ensembles, radio station, student government, student newspaper, Campus Ministries, Student Organization, Model UN. 71 registered organizations, 4 religious organizations. 5 fraternities, 8 sororities. **Athletics (Intercollegiate):** *Men:* baseball, basketball, cross-country, golf, sailing, soccer. *Women:* basketball, cross-country, golf, sailing, soccer, softball, volleyball, water polo. **On-Campus Highlights:** Black Box Cabaret, University Center, Student Center, Tanimura & Antle Library, Chapman Science Academic Center. **Environmental Initiatives:** We are an early signatory to the Presidents Climate Commitment

ADMISSIONS

Freshman Academic Profile: Average high school GPA 3.3. 15% in top 10% of high school class, 51% in top 25% of high school class, 88% in top 50% of high school class. 89% from public high schools. **Reported SAT (pre-2016 redesign) scores:** SAT Math middle 50% range 423-550. SAT Critical Reading middle 50% range 430-550. SAT Writing middle 50% range 420-530. **Concordant SAT scores:** SAT EBRW middle 50% 480–600. SAT Math middle 50% range 460–570. ACT middle 50% range 17-23. Minimum internet-based TOEFL 61. Minimum paper TOEFL 500. **Basis for Candidate Selection:** *Important factors considered include:* rigor of secondary school record, academic GPA, standardized test scores. *Other factors considered include:* recommendation(s), state residency. **Freshman Admission Requirements:** High school diploma is required and GED is accepted. *Academic units required:* 4 English, 3 math, 2 science, 2 science labs, 2 foreign language, 1 social studies, 1 history, 1 academic elective, 1 visual/performing arts. **Freshman Admission Statistics:** 15,561 applied, 48.69% admitted, 14% enrolled. **Transfer Admission Requirements:** High school transcript, essay or personal statement, standardized test scores, Minimum college GPA of 2.5 required. Lowest grade transferable C. **General Admission Information:** Application fee $55. Priority deadline 11/30. Regular application deadline 11/30. Nonfall registration accepted. Admission may be deferred.

COSTS AND FINANCIAL AID

Annual in-state tuition $0. Annual out-of-state tuition $11,160. Room and board $10,542. Required fees $6,119. Average book expense $1,311. **Required Forms and Deadlines:** FAFSA, State aid form. **Notification of Awards:** Applicants will be notified of awards on or about 4/1. **Types of Aid:** *Need-based scholarships/grants:* Federal Pell, FSEOG, State scholarships/grants, Private scholarships, College/university scholarship or grant aid from institutional funds. *Loans:* Direct Subsidized Stafford Loans, Direct Unsubsidized Stafford Loans, Direct PLUS loans, Federal Perkins Loans. *Student Employment:* Federal Work-Study Program available. Institutional employment available. **Financial Aid Statistics:** 74% needy freshmen, 75% needy undergrads receive need-based scholarship or grant aid. 14% freshmen, 8% undergrads receive non-need-based scholarship or grant aid. 70% freshmen, 64% undergrads receive need-based self-help aid. 4% freshmen, 2% undergrads receive athletic scholarships. 49% freshmen, 59% undergrads receive any aid. 64% undergrads borrow to pay for school. Average cumulative indebtedness $20,806. **Criteria for awarding aid:** *Non-need-based:* Academics, Athletics, Leadership, State/district residency.

CALIFORNIA STATE UNIVERSITY, NORTHRIDGE

Admissions and Records, CSU Northridge, Northridge, CA 91330-8207
Phone: 818-677-3700 • **Financial Aid Phone:** 818-677-4085
E-mail: admissions.records@csun.edu • **CEEB Code:** 4707
Fax: 818-677-3766 • **Website:** www.csun.edu • **ACT Code:** 400

This public school was founded in 1956. It has a 350-acre campus.

RATINGS
Admissions Selectivity Rating: 71   **Fire Safety Rating:** 60*   **Green Rating:** 95

STUDENTS AND FACULTY
Enrollment: 36,908. **Student Body:** 54% female, 46% male, 1% out-of-state, 6% international. Asian 12%, African American 5%, Caucasian 23%, Hispanic 46%, Native American <1%, Pacific Islander <1%, Two or more races 3%, Race unknown 5%.
Retention and Graduation: 78% freshmen return for sophomore year. 4% freshmen graduate within 4 years. 28% freshmen graduate within 6 years. **Faculty:** 917 full-time faculty, 0% hold PhDs, 0% are are members of minority groups, 0% are women.

ACADEMICS
Degrees: bachelor's, doctoral/professional, master's. **Most popular majors:** Psychology; Sociology. **Special Study Options:** Accelerated program, English as a Second Language (ESL), honors program, student-designed major, study abroad. **Disability Services:** Special programs offered to physically disabled students, including note-taking services, reader services, tape recorders, tutors. **Career Services:** Alumni network, Alumni services, Career/job search classes.

FACILITIES
Housing: Coed dorms, special housing for international students, fraternity/sorority housing, apartments for married students, apartments for single students. **Special Academic Facilities/Equipment:** Anthropology museum, art galleries, deafness center, urban archives, map library, cancer research/developmental biology center, planetarium, observatory.

CAMPUS LIFE
Activities: Choral groups, concert band, drama/theater, jazz band, literary magazine, marching band, music ensembles, musical theater, radio station, student government, student newspaper, yearbook. 267 registered organizations, 18 honor societies, 13 religious organizations. 24 fraternities, 12 sororities. **Athletics (Intercollegiate):** *Men:* baseball, basketball, cross-country, diving, football, golf, soccer, swimming, track/field (outdoor), track/field (indoor), volleyball. *Women:* basketball, cross-country, diving, football, golf, soccer, softball, swimming, tennis, track/field (outdoor), track/field (indoor), volleyball.

ADMISSIONS
Minimum paper TOEFL 500. **Basis for Candidate Selection:** *Very important factors considered include:* standardized test scores. **Freshman Admission Requirements:** High school diploma is required and GED is accepted. High school diploma is required and GED is not accepted. *Academic units required:* 4 English, 3 math, 1 science, 2 science labs, 2 foreign language, 2 history, 1 academic elective, and 1 unit from above areas or other academic areas. **Freshman Admission Statistics:** 32,743 applied, 28.49% admitted. Lowest grade transferable D. **General Admission Information:** Application fee $55. Nonfall registration accepted.

COSTS AND FINANCIAL AID
Annual in-state tuition $6,564. Annual out-of-state tuition $11,028. Room and board $9,962. Average book expense $1,860. **Required Forms and Deadlines:** FAFSA. **Types of Aid:** *Need-based scholarships/grants:* Federal Pell, FSEOG, State scholarships/grants, Private scholarships, College/university scholarship or grant aid from institutional funds, Federal Nursing Scholarships. *Loans:* Federal Perkins Loans, Federal Nursing Loans, College/university loans from institutional funds. *Student Employment:* Federal Work-Study Program available. Institutional employment available.

CALIFORNIA STATE UNIVERSITY— SACRAMENTO

6000 J Street, Sacramento, CA 95819-2694
Phone: 916-278-7766 • **Financial Aid Phone:** 916-278-6554
E-mail: outreach@csus.edu • **CEEB Code:** 4671
Fax: 916-278-5603 • **Website:** www.csus.edu • **ACT Code:** 382

This public school was founded in 1947. It has a 300-acre campus.

RATINGS

Admissions Selectivity Rating: 73   **Fire Safety Rating:** 73   **Green Rating:** 99

STUDENTS AND FACULTY

Enrollment: 25,457. **Student Body:** 57% female, 43% male, 1% out-of-state, 1% international (122 countries represented). Asian 21%, African American 6%, Caucasian 39%, Hispanic 19%, Native American 1%, Pacific Islander 1%, Two or more races 4%, Race unknown 7%.
Retention and Graduation: 81% freshmen return for sophomore year. 10% freshmen graduate within 4 years. 41% freshmen graduate within 6 years.
Faculty: Student/faculty ratio 28:1. 558 full-time faculty, 87% hold PhDs, 31% are are members of minority groups, 47% are women. 0% of classes are taught by teaching assistants.

ACADEMICS

Degrees: bachelor's, doctoral/research, master's. **Classes:** Most classes have 20-29 students. Most lab/discussion sessions have 10-19 students. **Most popular majors:** Criminal Justice/Law Enforcement Administration Business/Commerce. **Special Study Options:** Accelerated program, cooperative education program, cross-registration, distance learning, double major, dual enrollment, English as a Second Language (ESL), honors program, independent study, internships, student-designed major, study abroad, teacher certification program. Combined degree programs: BA/MA. **Disability Services:** Special programs offered to physically disabled students, including note-taking services, reader services, tape recorders, tutors. **Career Services:** Alumni network, Alumni services, Career assessment, Internships, Regional alumni.

FACILITIES

Housing: Coed dorms. 95% of campus accessible to physically diasbled. **Special Academic Facilities/Equipment:** CSUS Museum of Anthropology University Library Gallery (Art) Else Gallery (Art) Witt Gallery (Art) **Computers:** Students can register for classes online. Administrative functions (other than registration) can be performed online.

CAMPUS LIFE

Environment: Metropolis. **Activities:** Choral groups, concert band, dance, drama/theater, jazz band, marching band, music ensembles, musical theater, opera, pep band, radio station, student government, student newspaper, symphony orchestra 222 registered organizations, 7 honor societies, 13 religious organizations. 19 fraternities, 20 sororities. **Athletics (Intercollegiate):** *Men:* baseball, basketball, cheerleading, cross-country, football, golf, soccer, tennis, track/field (outdoor). *Women:* basketball, cheerleading, crew/rowing, cross-country, golf, gymnastics, soccer, softball, tennis, track/field (outdoor), volleyball. **On-Campus Highlights:** University Union, River Front Center, Guy West Bridge, Mariposa Hall, Hornet Stadium.

ADMISSIONS

Freshman Academic Profile: Average high school GPA 3.3. 100% in top 50% of high school class. 89% from public high schools. **Reported SAT (pre-2016 redesign) scores:** SAT Math middle 50% range 430-540. SAT Critical Reading middle 50% range 410-520. **Concordant SAT scores:** SAT Math middle 50% range 470–570. ACT middle 50% range 17-22. Minimum paper TOEFL 510. **Basis for Candidate Selection:** *Very important factors considered include:* academic GPA, standardized test scores. *Other factors considered include:* recommendation(s), state residency. **Freshman Admission Requirements:** High school diploma is required and GED is accepted. *Academic units required:* 4 English, 3 math, 2 science, 2 science labs, 2 foreign language, 2 history, 1 academic elective, 1 visual/performing arts. **Freshman Admission Statistics:** 19,702 applied, 69.68% admitted, 23% enrolled. **Transfer Admission Requirements:** college transcript(s), statement of good standing from prior institution(s). Minimum college GPA of 2.0 required. Lowest grade transferable D. **General Admission Information:** Application fee $55. Regular application deadline 11/30. Regular notification 3/1. Nonfall registration accepted. Admission may be deferred for a maximum of one semester.

COSTS AND FINANCIAL AID

Annual in-state tuition $5,472. Annual out-of-state tuition $16,632. Required fees $1,130. Average book expense $1,754. **Required Forms and Deadlines:**

FAFSA. **Notification of Awards:** Applicants will be notified of awards on a rolling basis beginning 4/27. **Types of Aid:** *Need-based scholarships/grants:* Federal Pell, FSEOG, State scholarships/grants, Private scholarships, Federal Nursing Scholarships. *Loans:* Direct Subsidized Stafford Loans, Direct Unsubsidized Stafford Loans, Direct PLUS loans, Federal Perkins Loans, Federal Nursing Loans, College/university loans from institutional funds. *Student Employment:* Federal Work-Study Program available. Institutional employment available. **Financial Aid Statistics:** 77% needy freshmen, 78% needy undergrads receive need-based scholarship or grant aid. 16% freshmen, 7% undergrads receive non-need-based scholarship or grant aid. 100% freshmen, 99% undergrads receive need-based self-help aid. 0% freshmen, 0% undergrads receive athletic scholarships. 50% undergrads receive any aid.

CALIFORNIA STATE UNIVERSITY– SAN BERNARDINO

5500 University Parkway, San Bernardino, CA 92407-2397
Phone: 909-537-5188 • **Financial Aid Phone:** 909-537-5227
E-mail: moreinfo@mail.csusb.edu • **CEEB Code:** 4099
Fax: 909-537-7034 • **Website:** www.csusb.edu • **ACT Code:** 205

This public school was founded in 1965. It has a 430-acre campus.

RATINGS

Admissions Selectivity Rating: 74   **Fire Safety Rating:** 60*   **Green Rating:** 60*

STUDENTS AND FACULTY

Enrollment: 18,453. **Student Body:** 60% female, 40% male, 0% out-of-state, 7% international (78 countries represented). Asian 6%, African American 6%, Caucasian 13%, Hispanic 63%, Native American <1%, Pacific Islander <1%, Two or more races 3%, Race unknown 4%.
Retention and Graduation: 85% freshmen return for sophomore year. 12% freshmen graduate within 4 years. 55% freshmen graduate within 6 years.
Faculty: Student/faculty ratio 28:1. 458 full-time faculty, 78% hold PhDs, 33% are are members of minority groups, 47% are women.

ACADEMICS

Degrees: bachelor's, certificate, doctoral, master's, postbachelor's certificate. **Classes:** Most classes have 20-29 students. Most lab/discussion sessions have 20-29 students. **Most popular majors:** Business Administration and Management; Psychology; Social Sciences. **Special Study Options:** Accelerated program, cooperative education program, cross-registration, distance learning, double major, dual enrollment, exchange student program (domestic), honors program, independent study, internships, study abroad, teacher certification program, School of Social and Behavioral Sciences offers Master's in National Security Studies. **Disability Services:** Special programs offered to physically disabled students, including note-taking services, reader services, tape recorders. **Career Services:** Alumni services, Career/job search classes, Career assessment, Internships.

FACILITIES

Housing: Coed dorms, women's dorms, apartments for single students, Wellness Housing. **Special Academic Facilities/Equipment:** Simulation labs, electronic music studios, language lab, desert studies center. Robert V. Fullerton Art Museum. Anthropology Museum **Computers:** Students can register for classes online. Administrative functions (other than registration) can be performed online.

CAMPUS LIFE

Environment: City. **Activities:** Choral groups, dance, drama/theater, jazz band, music ensembles, musical theater, radio station, student government, student newspaper, television station, Campus Ministries, Student Organization, Model UN. 97 registered organizations, 3 religious organizations. 9 fraternities, 6 sororities. **Athletics (Intercollegiate):** *Men:* baseball, basketball, golf, soccer, swimming, water polo. *Women:* basketball, cross-country, soccer, softball, swimming, tennis, volleyball, water polo. **On-Campus Highlights:** Coussoulis Arena, Robert V. Fullerton Art Museum, Social and Behavorial Sciences Building, Santos Manuel Student Union, Pfau Library.

ADMISSIONS

Freshman Academic Profile: Average high school GPA 3.3. 95% from public high schools. **Reported SAT (pre-2016 redesign) scores:** SAT Math middle 50% range 390-490. SAT Critical Reading middle 50% range 390-490. SAT Writing middle 50% range 390-480. **Concordant SAT scores:** SAT EBRW middle 50% 440–540. SAT Math middle 50% range 430–520. ACT middle 50% range 16-20. Minimum internet-based TOEFL 61. Minimum paper TOEFL 500. **Basis for Candidate Selection:** *Very important factors considered include:* academic GPA, standardized test scores. *Important factors considered include:* geographical residence. **Freshman Admission Requirements:** High school diploma is required and GED is accepted. *Academic units required:* 4 English, 3 math, 2 science, 2 science labs, 2 foreign language, 1 social studies, 1 history, 1 academic elective, 1 visual/performing arts. **Freshman Admission Statistics:** 15,740 applied, 58.14% admitted, 30% enrolled. **Transfer Admission Requirements:** college transcript(s), Minimum college GPA of 2.0 required. Lowest grade transferable C. **General Admission Information:** Application fee $55. Nonfall registration accepted.

COSTS AND FINANCIAL AID

Annual in-state tuition $5,472. Annual out-of-state tuition $11,160. Room and board $12,966. Required fees $1,129. Average book expense $1,791. **Required Forms and Deadlines:** FAFSA, State aid form. **Notification of Awards:** Applicants will be notified of awards on a rolling basis beginning 4/1. **Types of Aid:** *Need-based scholarships/grants:* Federal Pell, FSEOG, State scholarships/grants, Private scholarships, College/university scholarship or grant aid from institutional funds. *Loans:* Direct Subsidized Stafford Loans, Direct Unsubsidized Stafford Loans, Direct PLUS loans, Federal Perkins Loans, College/university loans from institutional funds. *Student Employment:* Federal Work-Study Program available. Institutional employment available. **Financial Aid Statistics:** 96% needy freshmen, 89% needy undergrads receive need-based scholarship or grant aid. 75% freshmen, 52% undergrads receive non-need-based scholarship or grant aid. 32% freshmen, 38% undergrads receive need-based self-help aid. 0% freshmen, 0% undergrads receive athletic scholarships. 66% undergrads borrow to pay for school. Average cumulative indebtedness $22,452. **Criteria for awarding aid:** *Need-based:* Academics, Alumni affiliation, Art, Athletics, Job skills, Leadership, Minority status, Music/drama, Religious affiliation.

CALIFORNIA STATE UNIVERSITY— SAN MARCOS

Office of Admission, San Marcos, CA 92096-0001
Phone: 760-750-4848 • **Financial Aid Phone:** 760-750-4850
E-mail: apply@csusm.edu • **CEEB Code:** 5677
Fax: 760-750-3248 • **Website:** www.csusm.edu

This public school was founded in 1989. It has a 304-acre campus.

RATINGS
Admissions Selectivity Rating: 73   **Fire Safety Rating:** 60*   **Green Rating:** 60*

STUDENTS AND FACULTY
Enrollment: 12,096. **Student Body:** 61% female, 39% male, 1% out-of-state, 2% international. Asian 10%, African American 3%, Caucasian 30%, Hispanic 42%, Native American <1%, Pacific Islander <1%, Two or more races 6%, Race unknown 5%.
Retention and Graduation: 82% freshmen return for sophomore year. 15% freshmen graduate within 4 years. 53% freshmen graduate within 6 years. **Faculty:** Student/faculty ratio 25:1. 254 full-time faculty, 0% hold PhDs, 32% are are members of minority groups, 50% are women.

ACADEMICS
Degrees: bachelor's, master's. **Classes:** Most classes have 30-39 students. **Special Study Options:** Accelerated program, cross-registration, distance learning, double major, dual enrollment, English as a Second Language (ESL), independent study, internships, student-designed major, study abroad, teacher certification program, weekend college, Evening degree program, Program for Adult College Education (PACE), Saturday classes, Air Force ROTC, extended studies, open university, special sessions, including winter. **Disability Services:** Special programs offered to physically disabled students, including note-taking services, reader services, tape recorders, tutors. **Career Services:** Alumni services, Career assessment, Internships.

FACILITIES
Housing: special housing for disabled students, special housing for international students, apartments for single students, Our housing is privatized and operated by Allen and O'Hara. **Computers:** Students can register for classes online.

CAMPUS LIFE
Environment: Town. **Activities:** Choral groups, drama/theater, music ensembles, student newspaper. 70 registered organizations, 5 honor societies, 2 religious organizations. 2 fraternities, 2 sororities. **Athletics (Intercollegiate):** *Men:* baseball, cross-country, golf, soccer, track/field (outdoor). *Women:* cross-country, golf, soccer, softball, track/field (outdoor).

ADMISSIONS
Freshman Academic Profile: Average high school GPA 3.3. **Reported SAT (pre-2016 redesign) scores:** SAT Math middle 50% range 430-530. SAT

Critical Reading middle 50% range 420-520. **Concordant SAT scores:** SAT Math middle 50% range 470–560. Minimum paper TOEFL 550. **Basis for Candidate Selection:** *Very important factors considered include:* academic GPA, standardized test scores. *Other factors considered include:* geographical residence, state residency. **Freshman Admission Requirements:** High school diploma is required and GED is accepted. *Academic units required:* 4 English, 3 math, 2 science, 2 science labs, 2 foreign language, 1 social studies, 1 history, 1 academic elective, 1 visual/performing arts. *Academic units recommended:* 4 English, 4 math, 2 science, 2 foreign language, 1 social studies, 1 history, 1 academic elective, 1 visual/performing arts. **Freshman Admission Statistics:** 11,560 applied, 67.01% admitted, 28% enrolled. **Transfer Admission Requirements:** college transcript(s), Minimum college GPA of 2.0 required. Lowest grade transferable C. **General Admission Information:** Application fee $55. Regular application deadline 11/30. Nonfall registration not accepted.

COSTS AND FINANCIAL AID
Annual in-state tuition $5,472. Annual out-of-state tuition $14,400. Room and board $13,240. Required fees $1,792. Average book expense $1,764. **Required Forms and Deadlines:** FAFSA. **Notification of Awards:** Applicants will be notified of awards on or about 4/15. **Types of Aid:** *Need-based scholarships/grants:* Federal Pell, FSEOG, State scholarships/grants, Private scholarships, College/university scholarship or grant aid from institutional funds. *Loans:* Direct Subsidized Stafford Loans, Direct Unsubsidized Stafford Loans, Direct PLUS loans, Federal Perkins Loans, College/university loans from institutional funds. *Student Employment:* Federal Work-Study Program available. Institutional employment available. **Criteria for awarding aid:** *Need-based:* Academics, Athletics, Leadership. *Non-need-based:* Academics, Athletics, Leadership, State/district residency.

CALIFORNIA STATE UNIVERSITY, STANISLAUS

One University Circle, Turlock, CA 95382
Phone: 209-667-3070 • **Financial Aid Phone:** 209-667-3336
E-mail: Outreach_Help_Desk@csustan.edu • **CEEB Code:** 4713
Fax: 209-667-3788 • **Website:** www.csustan.edu • **ACT Code:** 435

This public school was founded in 1957. It has a 228-acre campus.

RATINGS
Admissions Selectivity Rating: 79   **Fire Safety Rating:** 97   **Green Rating:** 70

STUDENTS AND FACULTY
Enrollment: 8,610. **Student Body:** 65% female, 35% male, 0% out-of-state, 4% international (22 countries represented). Asian 10%, African American 2%, Caucasian 23%, Hispanic 51%, Native American <1%, Pacific Islander 1%, Two or more races 4%, Race unknown 5%.
Retention and Graduation: 85% freshmen return for sophomore year. 16% freshmen graduate within 4 years. 57 **Faculty:** Student/faculty ratio 21:1. 292 full-time faculty, 86% hold PhDs, 31% are are members of minority groups, 45% are women.

ACADEMICS
Degrees: bachelor's, master's, postbachelor's certificate, post-master's certificate. **Classes:** Most classes have 20-29 students. Most lab/discussion sessions have 20-29 students. **Most popular majors:** Business/Commerce; Psychology; Criminal Justice/Safety Studies. **Special Study Options:** cooperative education program, distance learning, double major, dual enrollment, English as a Second Language (ESL), exchange student program (domestic), honors program, independent study, internships, liberal arts/career combination, student-designed major, study abroad, teacher certification program. **Honors Programs:** University Honors Program. **Disability Services:** Special programs offered to physically disabled students, including note-taking services, reader services, tape recorders, tutors. **Career Services:** Alumni network, Alumni services, Career/job search classes, Career assessment, Internships, Regional alumni. Our Internship Program is exceptional. We work with employers to develop internship and co-op opportunities, post information online for students to help them connect with their college department internship coordinator for course credit, and post internship information in the Career Services Center to help students identify appropriate opportunities related to their major course of study.

FACILITIES
Housing: Coed dorms, apartments for single students, Housing available in the summer months. ADA compliant units available. 99% of campus accessible

to physically diasbled. **Special Academic Facilities/Equipment:** Marine sciences station, laser lab, greenhouse, art gallery, mainstage theatre, recital hall, observatory, science building, art complex, distance learning studios, BioAg Eco building. **Computers:** 100% of classrooms, 100% of dorms, 100% of libraries, 100% of dining areas, 100% of student union, 10% of common outdoor areas have wireless network access. Students can register for classes online. Administrative functions (other than registration) can be performed online.

CAMPUS LIFE

Environment: Town. **Activities:** Choral groups, concert band, dance, drama/theater, jazz band, music ensembles, musical theater, opera, radio station, student government, student newspaper, symphony orchestra, television station, Student Organization. 76 registered organizations, 11 honor societies, 4 religious organizations. 7 fraternities, 9 sororities. **Athletics (Intercollegiate):** *Men:* baseball, basketball, cross-country, golf, soccer, track/field (outdoor), track/field (indoor). *Women:* basketball, cross-country, soccer, softball, tennis, track/field (outdoor), track/field (indoor), volleyball. **On-Campus Highlights:** Naraghi Hall of Science, MSR Educational Services Gateway Buildin, JFR Faculty Development Center, CSU Stanislaus University Art Gallery, Cafeteria and adjoining room, Student Union recently renovated; game room. **Environmental Initiatives:** The campus has replaced ten building air handler units in three major buildings. These new air handler units are more energy efficient and have also improved the air quality of the conditioned spaces. Project cost $1.6 million.

ADMISSIONS

Freshman Academic Profile: Average high school GPA 3.3. 96% from public high schools. **Reported SAT (pre-2016 redesign) scores:** SAT Math middle 50% range 400-500. SAT Critical Reading middle 50% range 390-500. SAT Writing middle 50% range 390-480. **Concordant SAT scores:** SAT EBRW middle 50% 440–550. SAT Math middle 50% range 440–530. ACT middle 50% range 16-21. Minimum internet-based TOEFL 61. Minimum paper TOEFL 500. **Basis for Candidate Selection:** *Very important factors considered include:* rigor of secondary school record, academic GPA, standardized test scores. *Important factors considered include:* class rank. **Freshman Admission Requirements:** High school diploma is required and GED is accepted. *Academic units required:* 4 English, 3 math, 2 science, 2 science labs, 2 foreign language, 1 social studies, 1 history, 1 academic elective, 1 visual/performing arts. *Academic units recommended:* 4 English, 3 math, 2 science, 2 science labs, 2 foreign language, 1 social studies, 1 history, 1 academic elective, 1 visual/performing arts. **Freshman Admission Statistics:** 7,618 applied, 74.34% admitted, 25% enrolled. **Transfer Admission Requirements:** college transcript(s), statement of good standing from prior institution(s). Minimum college GPA of 2.0 required. Lowest grade transferable D. **General Admission Information:** Application fee $55. Priority deadline 11/30. Regular application deadline 11/30. Nonfall registration not accepted.

COSTS AND FINANCIAL AID

Annual in-state tuition $5,472. Annual out-of-state tuition $16,632. Room and board $8,567. Required fees $1,256. Average book expense $1,500. **Required Forms and Deadlines:** FAFSA, State aid form. **Notification of Awards:** Applicants will be notified of awards on a rolling basis beginning 4/1. **Types of Aid:** *Need-based scholarships/grants:* Federal Pell, FSEOG, State scholarships/grants, Private scholarships, College/university scholarship or grant aid from institutional funds. *Loans:* Direct Subsidized Stafford Loans, Direct Unsubsidized Stafford Loans, Direct PLUS loans, Federal Perkins Loans. *Student Employment:* Federal Work-Study Program available. Institutional employment available. **Financial Aid Statistics:** 90% freshmen, 81% undergrads receive any aid. **Criteria for awarding aid:** *Need-based:* Academics, Alumni affiliation, Art, Leadership, Music/drama. *Non-need-based:* Academics, Alumni affiliation, Art, Athletics, Leadership, Music/drama, State/district residency.

CALIFORNIA UNIVERSITY OF PENNSYLVANIA

250 University Avenue, California, PA 15419
Phone: 724-938-4404 • **Financial Aid Phone:** 724-938-4415
E-mail: inquiry@cup.edu • **CEEB Code:** 2647
Fax: 724-938-4564 • **Website:** www.calu.edu • **ACT Code:** 3694

This public school was founded in 1852. It has a 188-acre campus.

RATINGS

Admissions Selectivity Rating: 72   **Fire Safety Rating:** 97   **Green Rating:** 73

STUDENTS AND FACULTY

Enrollment: 5,426. **Student Body:** 54% female, 46% male, 11% out-of-state, 1% international (29 countries represented). Asian 1%, African American 13%, Caucasian 77%, Hispanic 3%, Native American <1%, Pacific Islander <1%, Two or more races 4%, Race unknown 2%.

Retention and Graduation: 72% freshmen return for sophomore year. 37% freshmen graduate within 4 years. 10% grads go on to further study within 1 year. **Faculty:** Student/faculty ratio 19:1. 256 full-time faculty, 86% hold PhDs, 14% are are members of minority groups, 51% are women. 0% of classes are taught by teaching assistants.

ACADEMICS

Degrees: associate, bachelor's, certificate, master's, postbachelor's certifiate, post-master's certificate. **Classes:** Most classes have 20-29 students. Most lab/discussion sessions have 20-29 students. **Most popular majors:** Sport and Fitness Administration/Management; Business Administration and Management; Junior High/Intermediate/Middle School Education and Teaching. **Special Study Options:** Accelerated program, cooperative education program, distance learning, double major, dual enrollment, exchange student program (domestic), honors program, independent study, internships, liberal arts/career combination, student-designed major, study abroad, teacher certification program, weekend college, Undergrads may take grad classes. **Disability Services:** Special programs offered to physically disabled students, including note-taking services, reader services, tape recorders, tutors. **Career Services:** Alumni network, Alumni services, Career/job search classes, Career assessment, Internships, Regional alumni. Extensive programs in Internships and training

FACILITIES

Housing: Coed dorms, special housing for disabled students, men's dorms, special housing for international students, women's dorms, fraternity/sorority housing, cooperative housing, Wellness Housing, ThemeHousingJefferson Apartments, Garden style with outdoor pool/sandlot volleyball court and extensive gym. 90% of campus accessible to physically diasbled. **Special Academic Facilities/Equipment:** Manderino Gallery of Fine Arts, hosts top 40 corporate art collection sin the world **Computers:** Students can register for classes online. Administrative functions (other than registration) can be performed online.

CAMPUS LIFE

Environment: Village. **Activities:** Choral groups, concert band, dance, drama/theater, jazz band, literary magazine, marching band, music ensembles, musical theater, opera, pep band, radio station, student government, student newspaper, symphony orchestra, television station, yearbook, Campus Ministries, Student Organization. 25 honor societies, 1 religious organization. 6 fraternities, 7 sororities. **Athletics (Intercollegiate):** *Men:* baseball, basketball, cheerleading, cross-country, football, golf, rugby, soccer, softball, track/field (outdoor), track/field (indoor), volleyball. *Women:* basketball, cheerleading, cross-country, diving, golf, rugby, soccer, softball, swimming, tennis, track/field (outdoor), track/field (indoor), volleyball. **On-Campus Highlights:** Residence Halls, Student Union, Classrooms, Herron Rec Center, Library. **Environmental Initiatives:** Multimillion Dollar Geothermal project plus replacing ALL residence halls in less than 5 years with Green buildings.

ADMISSIONS

Freshman Academic Profile: Average high school GPA 3.1. 8% in top 10% of high school class, 23% in top 25% of high school class, 53% in top 50% of high school class. 90% from public high schools. **Reported SAT (pre-2016 redesign) scores:** SAT Math middle 50% range 400-510. SAT Critical Reading middle 50% range 410-520. SAT Writing middle 50% range 380-490. **Concordant SAT scores:** SAT EBRW middle 50% 440–560. SAT Math middle 50% range 440–540. ACT middle 50% range 16-22. Minimum paper TOEFL 450. **Basis for Candidate Selection:** *Very important factors considered include:* rigor of secondary school record, class rank, academic GPA, standardized test scores. *Important factors considered include:* application essay, recommendation(s), extracurricular activities, talent/ability, character/personal qualities. *Other factors considered include:* interview, volunteer work, work experience, level of applicant's interest. **Freshman Admission Requirements:** High school diploma is required and GED is accepted. *Academic units required:* 1 unit from above areas or other academic areas. *Academic units recommended:* 1 unit from above areas or other academic areas. **Freshman Admission Statistics:** 3,202 applied, 93.50% admitted, 30% enrolled. **Transfer Admission Requirements:** High school transcript, college transcript(s), statement of good standing from prior institution(s). Minimum college GPA of 2.3 required. Lowest grade transferable C. **General Admission Information:** Application fee $25. Priority deadline 8/22. Nonfall registration accepted. Admission may be deferred for a maximum of 3 years.

COSTS AND FINANCIAL AID

Annual in-state tuition $7,238. Annual out-of-state tuition $10,858. Room and board $10,086. Required fees $3,101. Average book expense $1,000. **Required Forms and Deadlines:** FAFSA. **Notification of Awards:** Applicants will be notified of awards on a rolling basis beginning 4/1. **Types of Aid:** *Need-based scholarships/grants:* Federal Pell, FSEOG, State scholarships/grants, Private scholarships, College/university scholarship or grant aid from institutional funds. *Loans:* Direct Subsidized Stafford Loans, Direct Unsubsidized Stafford Loans, Direct PLUS loans, Federal Perkins Loans. *Student Employment:* Federal Work-Study Program available. Institutional employment available. **Financial Aid Statistics:** 79% needy freshmen, 83% needy undergrads receive need-based scholarship or grant aid. 34% freshmen, 22% undergrads receive non-need-based scholarship or grant aid. 94% freshmen, 93% undergrads receive need-based self-help aid. 2% freshmen, 1% undergrads receive athletic scholarships. 90% freshmen receive any aid. 88% undergrads borrow to pay for school. Average cumulative indebtedness $25,683. **Criteria for awarding aid:** *Need-based:* Academics, Leadership, Minority status, Music/drama. *Non-need-based:* Academics, Athletics, Leadership, Minority status, Music/drama, State/district residency.

CALVARY BIBLE COLLEGE AND THEOLOGICAL SEMINARY

15800 Calvary Rd., Kansas City, MO 64147
Phone: 816-322-3960 • **Financial Aid Phone:** 816-322-0110
E-mail: admissions@calvary.edu
Fax: 816-331-4474 • **Website:** http://www.college.calvary.edu/ • **ACT Code:** 2312

This private school was founded in 1961. It has a 55-acre campus.

RATINGS

Admissions Selectivity Rating: 73 **Fire Safety Rating:** 83 **Green Rating:** 61

STUDENTS AND FACULTY

Enrollment: 226. **Student Body:** 50% female, 50% male, 65% out-of-state, 0% international (1 countries represented). Asian 2%, African American 11%, Caucasian 80%, Hispanic 3%, Native American 1%, Pacific Islander 0%, Two or more races 3%, Race unknown 0%.
Retention and Graduation: 69% freshmen return for sophomore year. 32% freshmen graduate within 4 years. **Faculty:** Student/faculty ratio 7:1. 17 full-time faculty, 71% hold PhDs, 12% are are members of minority groups, 41% are women. 0% of classes are taught by teaching assistants.

ACADEMICS

Degrees: associate, bachelor's, certificate, master's. **Most popular majors:** Bible/Biblical Studies; Pastoral Studies/Counseling; Music. **Special Study Options:** cooperative education program, double major, independent study, internships, student-designed major, teacher certification program. **Career Services:** On-campus interviews.

FACILITIES

Housing: men's dorms, women's dorms, apartments for married students, apartments for single students, Single students required to live in college housing unless living with parents or at least 23 years of age. Duplexes available for married students. 50% of campus accessible to physically diasbled. **Computers:** 100% of dorms, 100% of libraries, 100% of student union, have wireless network access. Students can register for classes online.

CAMPUS LIFE

Environment: Village. **Activities:** Choral groups, drama/theater, music ensembles, musical theater, pep band, radio station, student government, yearbook. **Athletics (Intercollegiate):** *Men:* basketball, soccer. *Women:* basketball, volleyball. **On-Campus Highlights:** Student Lounge, The Point, Gymnasium.

ADMISSIONS

Freshman Academic Profile: Average high school GPA 3.4. **Reported SAT (pre-2016 redesign) scores:** SAT Math middle 50% range 497.5-517.5. SAT Critical Reading middle 50% range 445-517.5. **Concordant SAT scores:** SAT Math middle 50% range 530–550. ACT middle 50% range 19-24. Minimum paper TOEFL 525. **Basis for Candidate Selection:** *Very important factors considered include:* academic GPA, application essay, recommendation(s), character/personal qualities, religious affiliation/commitment, level of applicant's interest. *Important factors considered include:* standardized test scores. *Other factors considered include:* class rank, interview, extracurricular activities, talent/ability, alumni/ae relation, volunteer work, work experience. **Freshman Admission Requirements:** High school diploma is required and GED is accepted. **Freshman Admission Statistics:** 52 applied, 94.23% admitted, 67% enrolled. **Transfer Admission Requirements:** college transcript(s), essay or personal statement, Minimum college GPA of 2.0 required. Lowest grade transferable C-. **General Admission Information:** Nonfall registration accepted. Admission may be deferred for a maximum of One Year.

COSTS AND FINANCIAL AID

Average book expense $794. **Required Forms and Deadlines:** FAFSA. **Types of Aid:** *Need-based scholarships/grants:* Federal Pell, FSEOG, College/university scholarship or grant aid from institutional funds. *Loans:* Direct Subsidized Stafford Loans, Direct Unsubsidized Stafford Loans, Direct PLUS loans. *Student Employment:* Federal Work-Study Program available.

Institutional employment available. **Financial Aid Statistics:** 100% needy freshmen, 91% needy undergrads receive need-based scholarship or grant aid. 19% freshmen, 10% undergrads receive non-need-based scholarship or grant aid. 100% freshmen, 88% undergrads receive need-based self-help aid. 0% freshmen, 0% undergrads receive athletic scholarships. 75% freshmen, 76% undergrads receive any aid. Average cumulative indebtedness $15,498. **Criteria for awarding aid:** *Non-need-based:* Academics, Alumni affiliation, Music/drama, Religious affiliation.

CALVIN COLLEGE

3201 Burton Street S.E., Grand Rapids, MI 49546
Phone: 616-526-6106 • **Financial Aid Phone:** 800-688-0122
E-mail: admissions@calvin.edu • **CEEB Code:** 1095
Fax: 616-526-6777 • **Website:** www.calvin.edu • **ACT Code:** 1968

This private school, affiliated with the Christian Reformed Church, was founded in 1876. It has a 400-acre campus.

RATINGS

Admissions Selectivity Rating: 86 **Fire Safety Rating:** 82 **Green Rating:** 82

STUDENTS AND FACULTY

Enrollment: 3,722. **Student Body:** 54% female, 46% male, 44% out-of-state, 11% international (62 countries represented). Asian 4%, African American 3%, Caucasian 73%, Hispanic 4%, Native American <1%, Pacific Islander 0%, Two or more races 4%, Race unknown 2%.
Retention and Graduation: 85% freshmen return for sophomore year. 61% freshmen graduate within 4 years. 76% freshmen graduate within 6 years. 25% grads go on to further study within 1 year. 19% grads pursue arts and sciences degrees. 1% grads pursue law degrees. 1% grads pursue business degrees. 3% grads pursue medical degrees. **Faculty:** Student/faculty ratio 13:1. 252 full-time faculty, 90% hold PhDs, 10% are are members of minority groups, 36% are women. 0% of classes are taught by teaching assistants.

ACADEMICS

Degrees: bachelor's, certificate, master's. **Classes:** Most classes have 20-29 students. Most lab/discussion sessions have 10-19 students. **Most popular majors:** Business/Commerce; Engineering; Registered Nursing/Registered Nurse. **Special Study Options:** Accelerated program, double major, dual enrollment, honors program, independent study, internships, student-designed major, study abroad, teacher certification program, Academically-based Service-learning. **Honors Programs:** For almost forty years Calvin College has challenged its best students with a campus-wide Honors Program–part of our overall mission to encourage academic excellence in a Christ-centered environment. The McGregor Sophomore Scholars Program develops targeted programming for sophomores in the Honors Program, such as one-on-one mentoring with faculty and program leaders and special events. **Disability Services:** Special programs offered to physically disabled students, including note-taking services, reader services, tape recorders, tutors. **Career Services:** Alumni network, Alumni services, Career/job search classes, Career assessment, Internships, Regional alumni. Thanks to a grant by the McGregor Foundation, Calvin College created the Comenius (pronounced kuh-mee-nee-uhs) Scholars Program, a paid, for-credit internship program for liberal arts students to work in non-profit organizations.

FACILITIES

Housing: men's dorms, women's dorms, apartments for single students, Theme Housing, Project Neighborhood Houses. 95% of campus accessible to physically diasbled. **Special Academic Facilities/Equipment:** Art gallery, observatory, ecosystem preserve, electron microscope, seismograph lab. **Computers:** 40% of classrooms, 100% of dorms, 100% of libraries, 75% of dining areas, 20% of student union, 10% of common outdoor areas have wireless network access. Students can register for classes online. Administrative functions (other than registration) can be performed online.

CAMPUS LIFE

Environment: City. **Activities:** Choral groups, concert band, dance, drama/theater, jazz band, literary magazine, music ensembles, musical theater, pep band, student government, student newspaper, student-run film society, symphony orchestra, yearbook, Campus Ministries, Student Organization, Model UN. 60 registered organizations, 6 honor societies, 5 religious organizations. **Athletics (Intercollegiate):** *Men:* baseball, basketball, cross-country, diving, golf, soccer, swimming, tennis, track/field (outdoor). *Women:* basketball, cross-country, diving, golf, soccer, softball, swimming, tennis, track/field (outdoor), volleyball. **On-Campus Highlights:** Field House, Johnny's Cafe, Heckman Library, DeVos Communications Building, Engineering Projects and Design Building. **Environmental Initiatives:** The Calvin Energy Recovery Fund, a green revolving fund(http://www.calvin.edu/admin/development/cerf).

ADMISSIONS

Freshman Academic Profile: Average high school GPA 3.7. 32% in top 10% of high school class, 57% in top 25% of high school class, 84% in top 50% of high school class. 47% from public high schools. **Reported SAT (pre-2016 redesign) scores:** SAT Math middle 50% range 530-650. SAT Critical Reading middle 50% range 520-635. **Concordant SAT scores:** SAT Math middle 50% range 560–670. ACT middle 50% range 23-29. Minimum internet-based TOEFL 80. Minimum paper TOEFL 550. **Basis for Candidate Selection:** *Very important factors considered include:* rigor of secondary school record, academic GPA, standardized test scores, religious affiliation/commitment. *Important factors considered include:* application essay, recommendation(s), extracurricular activities, character/personal qualities. *Other factors considered include:* class rank, volunteer work, work experience, level of applicant's interest. **Freshman Admission Requirements:** High school diploma is required and GED is accepted. *Academic units required:* 3 English, 3 math, 2 science, 2 social studies, 3 academic electives. *Academic units recommended:* 4 English, 3 math, 2 science, 1 science lab, 2 foreign language, 3 social studies, 3 academic electives. **Freshman Admission Statistics:** 3,981 applied, 74.60% admitted, 31% enrolled. **Transfer Admission Requirements:** High school transcript, college transcript(s), essay or personal statement, statement of good standing from prior institution(s). Minimum college GPA of 2.5 required. Lowest grade transferable C. **General Admission Information:** Application fee $35. Regular application deadline 8/15. Nonfall registration accepted. Admission may be deferred for a maximum of 1 year.

COSTS AND FINANCIAL AID

Annual tuition $31,730. Room and board $9,840. Average book expense $1,100. **Required Forms and Deadlines:** FAFSA. **Notification of Awards:** Applicants will be notified of awards on a rolling basis beginning 3/15. **Types of Aid:** *Need-based scholarships/grants:* Federal Pell, FSEOG, State scholarships/grants, Private scholarships, College/university scholarship or grant aid from institutional funds. *Loans:* Direct Subsidized Stafford Loans, Direct Unsubsidized Stafford Loans, Direct PLUS loans, Federal Perkins Loans, State Loans, College/university loans from institutional funds. *Student Employment:* Federal Work-Study Program available. Institutional employment available. **Financial Aid Statistics:** 100% needy freshmen, 99% needy undergrads receive need-based scholarship or grant aid. 15% freshmen, 12% undergrads receive non-need-based scholarship or grant aid. 83% freshmen, 87% undergrads receive need-based self-help aid. 0% freshmen, 0% undergrads receive athletic scholarships. 99% freshmen, 95% undergrads receive any aid. 60% undergrads borrow to pay for school. Average cumulative indebtedness $30,998. **Criteria for awarding aid:** *Need-based:* Academics, Alumni affiliation, Leadership, Minority status. *Non-need-based:* Academics, Alumni affiliation, Art, Leadership, Minority status, Music/drama, Religious affiliation, State/district residency.

CAMBRIDGE COLLEGE

1000 Massachusetts Avenue, Cambridge, MA 02138-5304
Phone: 617-868-1000 • **Financial Aid Phone:** 800-877-4723 ext. 1440
E-mail: admit@cambridgecollege.edu
Fax: 617-349-3561 • **Website:** www.cambridgecollege.edu

This is a private school.

RATINGS

Admissions Selectivity Rating: 61   **Fire Safety Rating:** 60*   **Green Rating:** 60*

STUDENTS AND FACULTY

Enrollment: 1,002. **Student Body:** 75% female, 25% male, 18% out-of-state, 9% international. Asian 3%, African American 30%, Caucasian 18%, Hispanic 22%, Native American <1%, Pacific Islander <1%, Two or more races 1%, Race unknown 16%.
Retention and Graduation: 21% freshmen return for sophomore year. **Faculty:** Student/faculty ratio 16:1. 19 full-time faculty, 68% hold PhDs, 26% are are members of minority groups, 47% are women.

ACADEMICS

Degrees: bachelor's, certificate, doctoral/research, master's, postbachelor's certificate, post-master's certificate. **Classes:** Most classes have 10-19 students. **Career Services:** On-campus interviews.

ADMISSIONS

Minimum paper TOEFL 550. **Basis for Candidate Selection:** *Other factors considered include:* class rank, academic GPA, application essay, recommendation(s), interview, character/personal qualities, work experience, level of applicant's interest. **General Admission Information:** Nonfall registration accepted. Admission may be deferred for a maximum of 1 Year.

COSTS AND FINANCIAL AID

Annual tuition $13,140. Required fees $140. **Required Forms and Deadlines:** FAFSA, Institution's own financial aid form. **Types of Aid:** *Need-based scholarships/grants:* Federal Pell, FSEOG, State scholarships/grants, Private scholarships, College/university scholarship or grant aid from institutional funds. *Loans:* Direct Subsidized Stafford Loans, Direct PLUS loans, Federal Perkins Loans. *Student Employment:* Federal Work-Study Program available. Institutional employment available. **Financial Aid Statistics:** 1% needy undergrads receive need-based scholarship or grant aid. 0% undergrads receive non-need-based scholarship or grant aid. 0% freshmen, 0% undergrads receive need-based self-help aid. 0% freshmen, 0% undergrads receive athletic scholarships. **Criteria for awarding aid:** *Need-based:* Academics, Religious affiliation.

CAMPBELLSVILLE UNIVERSITY

1 University Drive, Campbellsville, KY 42718-2799
Phone: 270-789-5220 • **Financial Aid Phone:** 270-789-5013
E-mail: admissions@campbellsville.edu • **CEEB Code:** 1097
Fax: 270-789-5071 • **ACT Code:** 1500

This private school, affiliated with the Baptist Church, was founded in 1906. It has a 90-acre campus.

RATINGS

Admissions Selectivity Rating: 80   **Fire Safety Rating:** 75   **Green Rating:** 60*

STUDENTS AND FACULTY

Enrollment: 2,250. **Student Body:** 58% female, 42% male, 12% out-of-state, 7% international. Asian 0%, African American 15%, Caucasian 74%, Hispanic 1%, Native American <1%, Pacific Islander <1%, Two or more races 1%, Race unknown 2%.
Retention and Graduation: 65% freshmen return for sophomore year. 26% freshmen graduate within 4 years. 41% freshmen graduate within 6 years. 20% grads go on to further study within 1 year. 25% grads pursue arts and sciences degrees. 1% grads pursue law degrees. 15% grads pursue business degrees. 1% grads pursue medical degrees. **Faculty:** Student/faculty ratio 13:1. 146 full-time faculty, 62% hold PhDs, 10% are are members of minority groups, 49% are women. 0% of classes are taught by teaching assistants.

ACADEMICS

Degrees: associate, bachelor's, certificate, master's. **Classes:** Most classes have fewer than 10 students. **Most popular majors:** Business, Management, Marketing, and Related Support Services; Junior High/Intermediate/Middle School Education and Teaching; Registered Nursing/Registered Nurse. **Special Study Options:** cooperative education program, distance learning, double major, dual enrollment, English as a Second Language (ESL), honors program, independent study, internships, liberal arts/career combination, study abroad, teacher certification program, weekend college. **Disability Services:** Special programs offered to physically disabled students, including tutors. **Career Services:** Alumni services, Career assessment, Internships.

FACILITIES

Housing: men's dorms, women's dorms, apartments for married students, apartments for single students. 70% of campus accessible to physically diasbled. **Special Academic Facilities/Equipment:** Computer labs: Technology lab **Computers:** Students can register for classes online. Administrative functions (other than registration) can be performed online.

CAMPUS LIFE

Environment: Rural. **Activities:** Choral groups, concert band, dance, drama/theater, jazz band, literary magazine, marching band, music ensembles, musical theater, pep band, radio station, student government, student newspaper, television station, yearbook, Campus Ministries, Student Organization. 49 registered organizations, 1 honor society, 7 religious organizations. **Athletics (Intercollegiate):** *Men:* baseball, basketball, bowling, cheerleading, cross-country, football, golf, soccer, tennis, track/field (outdoor), wrestling. *Women:* basketball, bowling, cheerleading, cross-country, golf, soccer, softball, swimming, tennis, track/field (outdoor), volleyball. **On-Campus Highlights:** Technology Center, Athletic Center, New Resident Village, Library, Fine Arts Center.

ADMISSIONS

Freshman Academic Profile: Average high school GPA 3.2. 17% in top 10% of high school class, 38% in top 25% of high school class, 69% in top 50% of high school class. 90% from public high schools. **Reported SAT (pre-2016 redesign) scores:** SAT Math middle 50% range 430-580. SAT Critical Reading middle 50% range 420-590. SAT Writing middle 50% range 410-540. **Concordant SAT scores:** SAT EBRW middle 50% 460–620. SAT Math middle 50% range 470–600. ACT middle 50% range 18-23. Minimum paper TOEFL 500. **Basis for Candidate Selection:** *Very important factors considered include:* rigor of secondary school record. *Important factors considered include:* class rank, standardized test scores, recommendation(s), interview, character/personal qualities. *Other factors considered include:* application essay, extracurricular activities, talent/ability, alumni/ae relation, religious affiliation/commitment, volunteer work, work experience. **Freshman Admission Requirements:** High school diploma is required and GED is accepted. *Academic units recommended:* 4 English, 3 math, 3 science, 1 science lab, 2 social studies, 1 history, 6 academic electives, and 1 unit from above areas or other academic areas. **Freshman Admission Statistics:** 2,477 applied, 66.65% admitted, 35% enrolled. **Transfer Admission Requirements:** college transcript(s), Lowest grade transferable C. **General Admission Information:** Application fee $20. Priority deadline 4/15. Regular application deadline 8/15. Nonfall registration accepted. Admission may be deferred.

COSTS AND FINANCIAL AID

Annual tuition $21,100. Room and board $7,120. Required fees $500. Average book expense $1,000. **Required Forms and Deadlines:** FAFSA. **Notification of Awards:** Applicants will be notified of awards on a rolling basis beginning 2/15. **Types of Aid:** *Need-based scholarships/grants:* Federal Pell, FSEOG, State scholarships/grants, Private scholarships, College/university scholarship or grant aid from institutional funds. *Loans:* Federal Perkins Loans, College/university loans from institutional funds. *Student Employment:* Federal Work-Study Program available. Institutional employment available. **Financial Aid Statistics:** 100% needy freshmen, 97% needy undergrads receive need-based scholarship or grant aid. 14% freshmen, 11% undergrads receive non-need-based scholarship or grant aid. 74% freshmen, 78% undergrads receive need-based self-help aid. 5% freshmen, 6% undergrads receive athletic scholarships. 95% freshmen, 92% undergrads receive any aid. **Criteria for awarding aid:** *Need-based:* Academics, Art, Athletics, Leadership, Minority status, Music/drama, Religious affiliation. *Non-need-based:* Academics, Art, Athletics, Leadership, Minority status, Music/drama, Religious affiliation, State/district residency.

CAMPBELL UNIVERSITY

Post Office Box 546, Buies Creek, NC 27506
Phone: 910-893-1200
E-mail: admissions@campbell.edu • **CEEB Code:** 5100
Website: www.campbell.edu • **ACT Code:** 3076

This private school, affiliated with the Southern Baptist Church, was founded in 1887. It has a 850-acre campus.

RATINGS

Admissions Selectivity Rating: 76   **Fire Safety Rating:** 75   **Green Rating:** 60*

STUDENTS AND FACULTY

Enrollment: 4,236. **Student Body:** 52% female, 48% male, 22% out-of-state, 2% international. Asian 2%, African American 18%, Caucasian 57%, Hispanic 7%, Native American 1%, Pacific Islander <1%, Two or more races 2%, Race unknown 11%.
Retention and Graduation: 72% freshmen return for sophomore year. 37% freshmen graduate within 4 years. 23% grads go on to further study within 1 year. 5% grads pursue arts and sciences degrees. 4% grads pursue law degrees. 7% grads pursue business degrees. **Faculty:** Student/faculty ratio 14:1. 196 full-time faculty, 91% hold PhDs, 0% are are members of minority groups, 33% are women. 0% of classes are taught by teaching assistants.

ACADEMICS

Degrees: bachelor's, doctoral/professional, doctoral/research, master's, postbachelor's certificate. **Classes:** Most classes have fewer than 10 students. **Special Study Options:** Accelerated program, cooperative education program, distance learning, double major, dual enrollment, exchange student program (domestic), honors program, independent study, internships, liberal arts/career combination, study abroad, teacher certification program. Combined degree programs: BA/JD, BA/MA, BA/MBA PHD/MBA. **Disability Services:** Special programs offered to physically disabled students, including note-taking services, tape recorders. **Career Services:** Career/job search classes, Career assessment, Internships.

FACILITIES

Housing: special housing for disabled students, men's dorms, women's dorms, apartments for married students, apartments for single students, Student apartments and suites for sophomores, juniors and seniors; also graduate apartments. All off-campus housing must be approved by the Office of Residence Life. 75% of campus accessible to physically diasbled. **Special Academic Facilities/Equipment:** Taylor Bott-Rogers Fine Arts Bldg. Lundy-Fetterman School of Business museum and exhibit hall School of Pharmacy Clinical Research Facility

CAMPUS LIFE

Environment: Rural. **Activities:** Choral groups, concert band, drama/theater, jazz band, literary magazine, music ensembles, musical theater, pep band, radio station, student government, student newspaper, yearbook, Campus Ministries, Student Organization. 44 registered organizations, 14 honor societies, 20 religious organizations. **Athletics (Intercollegiate):** *Men:* baseball, basketball, cross-country, golf, soccer, tennis, track/field (outdoor), wrestling. *Women:* basketball, cheerleading, cross-country, golf, soccer, softball, swimming, tennis, track/field (outdoor), volleyball. **On-Campus Highlights:** Lundy-Fetterman School of Business, Wallace Student Center/Oasis Grill/Starbucks, Keith Hills Country Club and Golf Course, Eakes Sports Complex, D. Rich Memorial Hall, Saylor Park.

ADMISSIONS

Freshman Academic Profile: Average high school GPA 3.4. 38% in top 10% of high school class, 80% in top 25% of high school class, 92% in top 50% of high school class. 85% from public high schools. Minimum paper TOEFL 500. **Basis for Candidate Selection:** *Very important factors considered include:* rigor of secondary school record, academic GPA, standardized test scores. *Important factors considered include:* class rank, interview, talent/ability. *Other factors considered include:* application essay, recommendation(s), extracurricular activities, character/personal qualities, alumni/ae relation, volunteer work, work experience, level of applicant's interest. **Freshman Admission Requirements:** High school diploma is required and GED is accepted. *Academic units required:* 4 English, 3 math, 2 science, 1 science lab, 2 foreign language, and 2 units from above areas or other academic areas. **Freshman Admission Statistics:** 3,014 applied, 59.72% admitted, 50% enrolled. **Transfer Admission Requirements:** High school transcript, college transcript(s), standardized test scores, statement of good standing from prior institution(s). Minimum college GPA of 2.5 required. Lowest grade transferable C. **General Admission Information:** Application fee $35. Regular application deadline 8/19. Nonfall registration accepted. Admission may be deferred.

COSTS AND FINANCIAL AID

Annual tuition $19,650. Room and board $6,830. Required fees $700. Average book expense $1,100. **Required Forms and Deadlines:** FAFSA. **Notification of Awards:** Applicants will be notified of awards on a rolling basis beginning 2/1. **Types of Aid:** *Need-based scholarships/grants:* Federal Pell, FSEOG, State scholarships/grants, Private scholarships, College/university scholarship or grant aid from institutional funds. *Loans:* Direct Subsidized Stafford Loans, Direct Unsubsidized Stafford Loans, Direct PLUS loans, Federal Perkins Loans, State Loans. *Student Employment:* Federal Work-Study Program available. Institutional employment available. **Financial Aid Statistics:** 69% needy freshmen, 73% needy undergrads receive need-based scholarship or grant aid. 95% freshmen, 77% undergrads receive non-need-based scholarship or grant aid. 87% freshmen, 88% undergrads receive need-based self-help aid. 4% freshmen, 3% undergrads receive athletic scholarships. 97% freshmen, 92% undergrads receive any aid. **Criteria for awarding aid:** *Non-need-based:* Academics, Athletics, Music/drama, Religious affiliation, State/district residency.

CANISIUS COLLEGE

2001 Main Street, Buffalo, NY 14208
Phone: 716-888-2200 • **Financial Aid Phone:** 716-888-2300
E-mail: admissions@canisius.edu • **CEEB Code:** 2073
Fax: 716-888-3230 • **Website:** http://www.canisius.edu • **ACT Code:** 2690

This private school, affiliated with the Roman Catholic-Jesuit Church, was founded in 1870. It has a 32-acre campus.

RATINGS

Admissions Selectivity Rating: 81   **Fire Safety Rating:** 89   **Green Rating:** 69

STUDENTS AND FACULTY

Enrollment: 2,488. **Student Body:** 52% female, 48% male, 10% out-of-state, 4% international (21 countries represented). Asian 2%, African American 8%, Caucasian 73%, Hispanic 7%, Native American <1%, Pacific Islander <1%, Two or more races 2%, Race unknown 4%.

Retention and Graduation: 83% freshmen return for sophomore year. 61% freshmen graduate within 4 years. 71% freshmen graduate within 6 years. **Faculty:** Student/faculty ratio 11:1. 182 full-time faculty, 98% hold PhDs, 9% are are members of minority groups, 42% are women. 0% of classes are taught by teaching assistants.

ACADEMICS

Degrees: associate, bachelor's, master's, postbachelor's certificate, post-master's certificate. **Classes:** Most classes have 20-29 students. Most lab/discussion sessions have 20-29 students. **Most popular majors:** Biology/Biological Sciences; Psychology; Business Administration and Management. **Special Study Options:** cooperative education program, cross-registration, distance learning, double major, dual enrollment, English as a Second Language (ESL), exchange student program (domestic), honors program, independent study, internships, study abroad, teacher certification program, 4 + 1 BS/MBA 3 + 4 BS/DD (Bio and Dentistry)-Early Assurance guaranteed Medical School Admission). **Honors Programs:** The All College Honors Program offers outstanding students the opportunity for a highly demanding and rewarding experience of the core curriculum. Students study under the college's most distinguished faculty, participate in educational travel, write a senior thesis and compete for special awards and honors. Combined degree programs: BA/BS-MBA, BA/BS-MBAPA. **Disability Services:** Special programs offered to physically disabled students, including note-taking services, reader services, tape recorders, tutors. **Career Services:** Alumni network, Alumni services, Career/job search classes, Career assessment, Internships, Regional alumni. The strength of the Canisius alumni network isn't just that it's 40,000 strong; the strength of our alumni network is that they stay connected. They don't forget Canisius after they graduate. They subscribe to The Griffin. They stop by to visit former professors. They volunteer on Community Day. When we battle Niagara, you'll see business executives and entrepreneurs decked out in blue and gold, respected community leaders and esteemed academics cheering as loudly as undergraduates.

FACILITIES

Housing: Coed dorms, special housing for disabled students, special housing for international students, apartments for single students, Honors Student Housing. All college owned housing is handicapped accessible. 95% of campus accessible to physically disabled. **Special Academic Facilities/Equipment:** TV studio, electron microscope, seismograph, language lab, digital lab, human performance lab, molecular biology and physics labs, mini-planetarium. **Computers:** 100% of classrooms, 100% of dorms, 100% of libraries, 100% of dining areas, 100% of student union, 100% of common outdoor areas have wireless network access. Students can register for classes online. Administrative functions (other than registration) can be performed online.

CAMPUS LIFE

Environment: Metropolis. **Activities:** Choral groups, concert band, dance, drama/theater, jazz band, literary magazine, music ensembles, musical theater, pep band, radio station, student government, student newspaper, student-run film society, television station, yearbook, Campus Ministries, Student Organization, Model UN. 102 registered organizations, 16 honor societies, 2 religious organizations. 1 fraternity, 1 sorority. **Athletics (Intercollegiate):** *Men:* baseball, basketball, cross-country, diving, golf, ice hockey, lacrosse, soccer, swimming. *Women:* basketball, cross-country, diving, lacrosse, soccer, softball, swimming, synchronized swimming, volleyball. **On-Campus Highlights:** Montante Cultural Center, Delavan Townhouses, Palisano Pavillion, Koessler Athletic Center, Richard E. Winter Student Center, Canisius College sponsors a variety of on-campus entertainment to keep students busy throughout the year. Our highly popular Java Jams is a weekly coffee-style event offering entertainment in the Palisano Pavilion. **Environmental Initiatives:** Canisius College is deeply committed to utility conservation and the sustainability of our natural resources. This is accomplished in part through our development of policies and practices which are designed to promote sound energy management, and the economic, social and environmental well-being of our students and staff. Canisius College is working with Ecology and Environment, Inc. (E & E) to develop and implement an energy conservation program. The overall goal of the program is to reduce the college annual electric consumption by five percent, based on historical consumption during the last three academic years. A web page is being designed to explain how Canisius College conserves and supports sustainable use of our natural resources.

ADMISSIONS

Freshman Academic Profile: Average high school GPA 3.6. 24% in top 10% of high school class, 53% in top 25% of high school class, 85% in top 50% of high school class. 71% from public high schools. **Reported SAT (pre-2016 redesign) scores:** SAT Math middle 50% range 490-600. SAT Critical Reading middle 50% range 480-590. **Concordant SAT scores:** SAT Math middle 50% range 520–620. ACT middle 50% range 22-28. Minimum internet-based TOEFL 79. Minimum paper TOEFL 550. **Basis for Candidate Selection:** *Very important factors considered:* rigor of secondary school record, academic GPA, standardized test scores. *Important factors considered:*

application essay, recommendation(s), extracurricular activities, volunteer work. *Other factors considered include:* class rank, interview, talent/ability, character/personal qualities, first generation, alumni/ae relation, work experience, level of applicant's interest. **Freshman Admission Requirements:** High school diploma is required and GED is accepted. *Academic units required:* 4 English, 3 math, 3 science, 2 science labs, 2 foreign language, 4 social studies. *Academic units recommended:* 4 English, 4 math, 4 science, 2 science labs, 4 foreign language, 4 social studies, 4 academic electives. **Freshman Admission Statistics:** 4,620 applied, 77.86% admitted, 17% enrolled. **Transfer Admission Requirements:** college transcript(s), statement of good standing from prior institution(s). Minimum college GPA of 2.0 required. Lowest grade transferable C. **General Admission Information:** Application fee $40. Priority deadline 3/1. Regular application deadline 5/1. Nonfall registration accepted. Admission may be deferred for a maximum of 1 year.

COSTS AND FINANCIAL AID

Annual tuition $33,948. Room and board $13,022. Required fees $1,476. Average book expense $1,000. **Required Forms and Deadlines:** FAFSA, State aid form. **Notification of Awards:** Applicants will be notified of awards on a rolling basis beginning 3/1. **Types of Aid:** *Need-based scholarships/grants:* Federal Pell, FSEOG, State scholarships/grants, Private scholarships, College/university scholarship or grant aid from institutional funds. *Loans:* Direct Subsidized Stafford Loans, Direct Unsubsidized Stafford Loans, Direct PLUS loans, Federal Perkins Loans. *Student Employment:* Federal Work-Study Program available. Institutional employment available. **Financial Aid Statistics:** 100% needy freshmen, 99% needy undergrads receive need-based scholarship or grant aid. 26% freshmen, 23% undergrads receive non-need-based scholarship or grant aid. 74% freshmen, 76% undergrads receive need-based self-help aid. 4% freshmen, 5% undergrads receive athletic scholarships. 98% freshmen, 97% undergrads receive any aid. 74% undergrads borrow to pay for school. Average cumulative indebtedness $33,973. **Criteria for awarding aid:** *Non-need-based:* Academics, Alumni affiliation, Art, Athletics, Job skills, Music/drama.

CAPITAL UNIVERSITY

Admission Office, Columbus, OH 43209
Phone: 614-236-6101 • **Financial Aid Phone:** 614-236-6511
E-mail: admission@capital.edu • **CEEB Code:** 1099
Fax: 614-236-6926 • **Website:** www.capital.edu • **ACT Code:** 3242

This private school, affiliated with the Lutheran Church, was founded in 1830. It has a 48-acre campus.

RATINGS

Admissions Selectivity Rating: 81   **Fire Safety Rating:** 66   **Green Rating:** 60*

STUDENTS AND FACULTY

Enrollment: 2,654. **Student Body:** 58% female, 42% male, 10% out-of-state, 2% international (18 countries represented). Asian 1%, African American 10%, Caucasian 75%, Hispanic 4%, Native American <1%, Pacific Islander 0%, Two or more races 5%, Race unknown 3%.
Retention and Graduation: 76% freshmen return for sophomore year. 56% freshmen graduate within 4 years. 63% freshmen graduate within 6 years.
Faculty: Student/faculty ratio 12:1. 159 full-time faculty, 77% hold PhDs, 9% are are members of minority groups, 49% are women. 0% of classes are taught by teaching assistants.

ACADEMICS

Degrees: bachelor's, doctoral/professional, master's, postbachelor's certificate. **Classes:** Most classes have 10-19 students. Most lab/discussion sessions have 20-29 students. **Most popular majors:** Education; Registered Nursing/Registered Nurse; Business Administration and Management. **Special Study Options:** Accelerated program, cooperative education program, cross-registration, double major, English as a Second Language (ESL), exchange student program (domestic), honors program, independent study, internships, liberal arts/career combination, student-designed major, study abroad, teacher certification program. **Honors Programs:** Capital University Honors Program Combined degree programs: MSN/JD, MSN/MBA, MSN/Master's of Lay Ministry. **Disability Services:** Special programs offered to physically disabled students, including tape recorders, tutors. **Career Services:** Alumni network, Alumni services, Career/job search classes, Career assessment, Internships.

FACILITIES

Housing: Coed dorms, special housing for disabled students, special housing for international students, fraternity/sorority housing, apartments for single students, Student organization and special interest housing. 100% of campus accessible to physically disabled. **Special Academic Facilities/Equipment:** Art gallery, Conservatory of Music **Computers:** Students can register for classes online. Administrative functions (other than registration) can be performed online.

CAMPUS LIFE
Environment: Metropolis. **Activities:** Choral groups, concert band, dance, drama/theater, jazz band, literary magazine, music ensembles, musical theater, radio station, student government, student newspaper, symphony orchestra, television station, yearbook, Campus Ministries, Student Organization. 63 registered organizations, 16 honor societies, 5 religious organizations. 5 fraternities, 5 sororities. **Athletics (Intercollegiate):** *Men:* baseball, basketball, cross-country, football, golf, soccer, tennis, track/field (outdoor), track/field (indoor). *Women:* basketball, cross-country, golf, soccer, softball, tennis, track/field (outdoor), track/field (indoor), volleyball. **On-Campus Highlights:** Capital Center, College Avenue Residence Hall, Schumacher Gallery. **Environmental Initiatives:** Energy management.

ADMISSIONS
Freshman Academic Profile: Average high school GPA 3.5. 16% in top 10% of high school class, 47% in top 25% of high school class, 81% in top 50% of high school class. 92% from public high schools. **Reported SAT (pre-2016 redesign) scores:** SAT Math middle 50% range 480-580. SAT Critical Reading middle 50% range 480-610. SAT Writing middle 50% range 460-590. **Concordant SAT scores:** SAT EBRW middle 50% 530–650. SAT Math middle 50% range 510–600. ACT middle 50% range 22-28. Minimum paper TOEFL 500. **Basis for Candidate Selection:** *Very important factors considered include:* academic GPA, standardized test scores, talent/ability. *Other factors considered include:* rigor of secondary school record, recommendation(s), interview, extracurricular activities, alumni/ae relation, geographical residence, state residency, religious affiliation/commitment, racial/ethnic status, level of applicant's interest. **Freshman Admission Requirements:** High school diploma is required and GED is accepted. *Academic units recommended:* 4 English, 3 math, 3 science, 2 science labs, 2 foreign language, 3 social studies, 1 visual/performing arts. **Freshman Admission Statistics:** 3,718 applied, 72.22% admitted, 25% enrolled. **Transfer Admission Requirements:** college transcript(s), Minimum college GPA of 2.5 required. Lowest grade transferable C-. **General Admission Information:** Application fee $25. Priority deadline 12/1. Regular application deadline 5/1. Nonfall registration accepted. Admission may be deferred for a maximum of 1 year.

COSTS AND FINANCIAL AID
Annual tuition $32,630. Room and board $9,250. Required fees $200. Average book expense $1,550. **Required Forms and Deadlines:** FAFSA. **Notification of Awards:** Applicants will be notified of awards on a rolling basis beginning 3/15. **Types of Aid:** *Need-based scholarships/grants:* Federal Pell, FSEOG, State scholarships/grants, Private scholarships, College/university scholarship or grant aid from institutional funds. *Loans:* Direct Subsidized Stafford Loans, Direct Unsubsidized Stafford Loans, Direct PLUS loans, Federal Perkins Loans, Federal Nursing Loans, College/university loans from institutional funds. *Student Employment:* Federal Work-Study Program available. Institutional employment available. **Financial Aid Statistics:** 99% needy freshmen, 95% needy undergrads receive need-based scholarship or grant aid. 98% freshmen, 93% undergrads receive non-need-based scholarship or grant aid. 75% freshmen, 78% undergrads receive need-based self-help aid. 0% freshmen, 0% undergrads receive athletic scholarships. 99% freshmen receive any aid. 82% undergrads borrow to pay for school. Average cumulative indebtedness $31,563. **Criteria for awarding aid:** *Non-need-based:* Academics, Alumni affiliation, Art, Leadership, Minority status, Music/drama, Religious affiliation, State/district residency.

CARLETON COLLEGE

100 South College Street, Northfield, MN 55057
Phone: 507-222-4190 • **Financial Aid Phone:** 507-222-4138
E-mail: admissions@carleton.edu • **CEEB Code:** 6081
Fax: 507-222-4526 • **Website:** www.carleton.edu • **ACT Code:** 2092

This private school was founded in 1866. It has a 955-acre campus.

RATINGS
Admissions Selectivity Rating: 96   **Fire Safety Rating:** 79   **Green Rating:** 93

STUDENTS AND FACULTY
Enrollment: 2,045. **Student Body:** 50% female, 50% male, 83% out-of-state, 10% international (37 countries represented). Asian 9%, African American 4%, Caucasian 62%, Hispanic 7%, Native American <1%, Pacific Islander <1%, Two or more races 6%, Race unknown 2%.
Retention and Graduation: 96% freshmen return for sophomore year. 88% freshmen graduate within 4 years. 92% freshmen graduate within 6 years. 17% grads go on to further study within 1 year. **Faculty:** Student/faculty ratio 9:1. 209 full-time faculty, 98% hold PhDs, 27% are are members of minority groups, 46% are women. 0% of classes are taught by teaching assistants.

ACADEMICS
Degrees: bachelor's. **Classes:** Most classes have 10-19 students. Most lab/discussion sessions have 10-19 students. **Most popular majors:** Biology/Biological Sciences; Economics; Computer and Information Sciences. **Special Study Options:** Accelerated program, cross-registration, double major, dual enrollment, independent study, internships, student-designed major, study abroad, teacher certification program. Combined degree programs: BA/JD, 3-3 Law at Columbia University. **Disability Services:** Special programs offered to physically disabled students, including note-taking services, reader services, tape recorders, tutors. **Career Services:** Alumni network, Alumni services, Career/job search classes, Career assessment, Internships, Regional alumni. Carleton provides significant financial support for students undertaking unpaid or low-paying internships in many different fields and in locations throughout the world. Carleton's Externship Program provides 1-4 week-long "mini-internships" during Carleton's December break. In 2016, more than 200 students participated in this program at sites across the country, in fields including healthcare, advertising, finance, science research, education, social service, publishing, and more. Carleton's online Student and Alumni Profiles and Career Guides program allows students and alumni to connect based on a variety of interests and goals, and enables students to quickly and easily access the powerful Carleton alumni network for informational interviews and career advice.

FACILITIES
Housing: Coed dorms, special housing for disabled students, apartments for single students, 25 college-owned houses within 2 blocks of campus with varying meal plan options. Some are designated as special interest houses (ex: Green House, Culinary House). 39% of campus accessible to physically diasbled. **Special Academic Facilities/Equipment:** Arboretum, greenhouse, observatory, scanning and transmission electron microscopes, refractor and reflector telescopes, nuclear magnetic resonance spectrometer, art gallery. **Computers:** 45% of classrooms, 15% of dorms, 85% of libraries, 50% of dining areas, 100% of student union, 15% of common outdoor areas have wireless network access. Students can register for classes online.

CAMPUS LIFE
Environment: Village. **Activities:** Choral groups, concert band, dance, drama/theater, jazz band, literary magazine, music ensembles, musical theater, radio station, student government, student newspaper, student-run film society, symphony orchestra, yearbook, Campus Ministries, Student Organization, Model UN. 132 registered organizations, 3 honor societies, 17 religious organizations. **Athletics (Intercollegiate):** *Men:* baseball, basketball, cross-country, diving, football, golf, soccer, swimming, tennis, track/field (outdoor), track/field (indoor). *Women:* basketball, cross-country, diving, golf, soccer, softball, swimming, synchronized swimming, tennis, track/field (outdoor), track/field (indoor), volleyball. **On-Campus Highlights:** Cowling Arboretum, Art Gallery, Historic Goodsell Observatory, Japanese Garden, Recreation Center, Sayles Campus Center, Library. **Environmental Initiatives:** 2nd Wind Turbine provided power directly to the campus grid

ADMISSIONS
Freshman Academic Profile: 75% in top 10% of high school class, 93% in top 25% of high school class, 100% in top 50% of high school class. 60% from public high schools. **Reported SAT (pre-2016 redesign) scores:** SAT Math middle 50% range 660-770. SAT Critical Reading middle 50% range 660-770. SAT Writing middle 50% range 650-750. **Concordant SAT scores:** SAT EBRW middle 50% 700–770. SAT Math middle 50% range 690–780. ACT middle 50% range 30-33. Minimum paper TOEFL 600. **Basis for Candidate Selection:** *Very important factors considered include:* rigor of secondary school record, class rank, academic GPA. *Important factors considered include:* standardized test scores, application essay, recommendation(s), extracurricular activities, talent/ability, character/personal qualities, alumni/ae relation, racial/ethnic status, volunteer work, work experience. *Other factors considered include:* interview, first generation, geographical residence, state residency. **Freshman Admission Requirements:** High school diploma is required and GED is accepted. *Academic units recommended:* 4 English, 3 math, 3 science, 1 science lab, 3 foreign language, 3 social studies. **Freshman Admission Statistics:** 6,485 applied, 22.62% admitted, 39% enrolled. **Transfer Admission Requirements:** High school transcript, college transcript(s), essay or personal statement, standardized test scores, statement of good standing from prior institution(s). Minimum college GPA of 2.0 required. Lowest grade transferable C-. **General Admission Information:** Application fee $30. Regular application deadline 1/15. Regular notification 3/31. Nonfall registration not accepted. Admission may be deferred for a maximum of 1 year.

COSTS AND FINANCIAL AID

Required Forms and Deadlines: FAFSA, CSS/Financial Aid PROFILE, Noncustodial PROFILE. **Notification of Awards:** Applicants will be notified of awards on or about 4/1. **Types of Aid:** *Need-based scholarships/grants:* Federal Pell, FSEOG, State scholarships/grants, Private scholarships, College/university scholarship or grant aid from institutional funds. *Loans:* Direct Subsidized Stafford Loans, Direct Unsubsidized Stafford Loans, Direct PLUS loans, Federal Perkins Loans, State Loans, College/university loans from institutional funds. *Student Employment:* Federal Work-Study Program available. Institutional employment available. **Financial Aid Statistics:** 100% needy freshmen, 100% needy undergrads receive need-based scholarship or grant aid. 14% freshmen, 16% undergrads receive non-need-based scholarship or grant aid. 98% freshmen, 99% undergrads receive need-based self-help aid. 0% freshmen, 0% undergrads receive athletic scholarships. 54% freshmen, 56% undergrads receive any aid. 41% undergrads borrow to pay for school. Average cumulative indebtedness $22,641. **Criteria for awarding aid:** *Non-need-based:* Academics.

CARLOW UNIVERSITY

3333 Fifth Avenue, Pittsburgh, PA 15213-3165
Phone: 412-578-6059
E-mail: admissions@carlow.edu • **CEEB Code:** 2421
Fax: 412-578-6321 • **Website:** www.carlow.edu • **ACT Code:** 2421

This private school, affiliated with the Roman Catholic Church, was founded in 1929. It has a 15-acre campus.

RATINGS

Admissions Selectivity Rating: 76   **Fire Safety Rating:** 72   **Green Rating:** 60*

STUDENTS AND FACULTY

Enrollment: 1,175. **Student Body:** 86% female, 14% male, 5% out-of-state, <1% international (2 countries represented). Asian 1%, African American 20%, Caucasian 63%, Hispanic 3%, Native American <1%, Pacific Islander <1%, Two or more races 5%, Race unknown 7%.
Retention and Graduation: 74% freshmen return for sophomore year. 40% freshmen graduate within 4 years. 57% freshmen graduate within 6 years.
Faculty: Student/faculty ratio 12:1. 97 full-time faculty, 72% hold PhDs, 5% are are members of minority groups, 73% are women. 0% of classes are taught by teaching assistants.

ACADEMICS

Degrees: bachelor's, doctoral/professional, master's, postbachelor's certificate, post-master's certificate. **Classes:** Most classes have 10-19 students. **Most popular majors:** Registered Nursing/Registered Nurse; Biology/Biological Sciences; Psychology. **Special Study Options:** Accelerated program, cross-registration, distance learning, double major, dual enrollment, honors program, independent study, internships, liberal arts/career combination, student-designed major, study abroad, teacher certification program, weekend college, 3/2 programs with Carnegie Mellon for Chem. Engineering, Environmental Engineering, Mechanical Engineering. Other programs with Duquesne U. in Environmental Science and Mgt.(3/2), several programs with Art Institute of Pittsburgh. **Career Services:** Alumni network, Career/job search classes, Career assessment, Internships, Regional alumni.

FACILITIES

Housing: women's dorms. **Special Academic Facilities/Equipment:** The A.J. Palumbo Hall of Science and Technology. features research labs, as well as a greenhouse, darkroom, biochamber, an on-site reference library and specially designed study and work zones on every floor to encourage team research. The building incorporates more than 1000 outlets for internet access. Also,on-campus preschool and elementary school. **Computers:** 100% of classrooms, 100% of dorms, 100% of libraries, 100% of dining areas, 100% of student union, have wireless network access. Students can register for classes online.

CAMPUS LIFE

Environment: City. **Activities:** Choral groups, drama/theater, literary magazine, student government, student newspaper, yearbook, Campus Ministries, Student Organization. 28 registered organizations, 5 honor societies, 1 religious organization. **Athletics (Intercollegiate):** *Women:* basketball, soccer, softball, tennis, volleyball.

ADMISSIONS

Freshman Academic Profile: Average high school GPA 3.4. 16% in top 10% of high school class, 40% in top 25% of high school class, 68% in top 50% of high school class. **Reported SAT (pre-2016 redesign) scores:** SAT Math middle 50% range 430-530. SAT Critical Reading middle 50% range 440-540. **Concordant SAT scores:** SAT Math middle 50% range 470–560. ACT middle 50% range 19-24. **Basis for Candidate Selection:** *Very important*

factors considered include: rigor of secondary school record, academic GPA, standardized test scores. *Important factors considered include:* class rank. *Other factors considered include:* application essay, recommendation(s), interview, extracurricular activities, talent/ability, character/personal qualities, first generation, alumni/ae relation, volunteer work, work experience, level of applicant's interest. **Freshman Admission Requirements:** High school diploma is required and GED is accepted. *Academic units required:* 4 English, 3 math, 3 science, 2 social studies, 2 history, 4 academic electives. *Academic units recommended:* 4 math, 4 science, 2 science labs. **Freshman Admission Statistics:** 806 applied, 86.35% admitted, 31% enrolled. **Transfer Admission Requirements:** college transcript(s), Minimum college GPA of 2.0 required. Lowest grade transferable C. **General Admission Information:** Application fee $20. Nonfall registration accepted. Admission may be deferred for a maximum of 1 year.

COSTS AND FINANCIAL AID

Required Forms and Deadlines: FAFSA, State aid form. **Notification of Awards:** Applicants will be notified of awards on a rolling basis beginning 2/15. **Types of Aid:** *Need-based scholarships/grants:* Federal Pell, FSEOG, State scholarships/grants, Private scholarships, College/university scholarship or grant aid from institutional funds. *Loans:* Direct Subsidized Stafford Loans, Direct Unsubsidized Stafford Loans, Direct PLUS loans, Federal Perkins Loans, Federal Nursing Loans. *Student Employment:* Federal Work-Study Program available. Institutional employment available. **Financial Aid Statistics:** 100% needy freshmen, 81% needy undergrads receive need-based scholarship or grant aid. 92% freshmen, 77% undergrads receive non-need-based scholarship or grant aid. 76% freshmen, 89% undergrads receive need-based self-help aid. 17% freshmen, 12% undergrads receive athletic scholarships. **Criteria for awarding aid:** *Non-need-based:* Academics, Alumni affiliation, Art, Athletics, Job skills, State/district residency.

CARNEGIE MELLON UNIVERSITY

5000 Forbes Avenue, Pittsburgh, PA 15213
Phone: 412-268-2082 • **Financial Aid Phone:** 412-268-8186
E-mail: undergraduate-admissions@andrew.cmu.edu • **CEEB Code:** 2074
Fax: 412-268-7838 • **Website:** www.cmu.edu • **ACT Code:** 3534

This private school was founded in 1900. It has a 136-acre campus.

RATINGS

Admissions Selectivity Rating: 98   **Fire Safety Rating:** 89   **Green Rating:** 98

STUDENTS AND FACULTY

Enrollment: 6,574. **Student Body:** 47% female, 53% male, 85% out-of-state, 23% international (60 countries represented). Asian 28%, African American 4%, Caucasian 28%, Hispanic 8%, Native American <1%, Pacific Islander <1%, Two or more races 4%, Race unknown 5%.
Retention and Graduation: 96% freshmen return for sophomore year. 75% freshmen graduate within 4 years. 90% freshmen graduate within 6 years. 22% grads go on to further study within 1 year. 14% grads pursue arts and sciences degrees. 1% grads pursue law degrees. 1% grads pursue business degrees. 1% grads pursue medical degrees. **Faculty:** Student/faculty ratio 13 995 full-time faculty, 93% hold PhDs, 18% are are members of minority groups, 27% are women.

ACADEMICS

Degrees: bachelor's, doctoral/research, master's. **Classes:** Most classes have 10-19 students. Most lab/discussion sessions have 20-29 students. **Most popular majors:** Computer Science; Electrical and Electronics Engineering; Mechanical Engineering. **Special Study Options:** cooperative education program, cross-registration, distance learning, double major, dual enrollment, exchange student program (domestic), independent study, internships, liberal arts/career combination, student-designed major, study abroad, teacher certification program. Combined degree programs: BA/MA, BA/MEng, BS/MBA Industrial Admin. **Disability Services:** Special programs offered to physically disabled students, including note-taking services, reader services, tape recorders, tutors. **Career Services:** Alumni network, Alumni services, Career/job search classes, Career assessment, Internships, Regional alumni. Our mission:
*Students who value experiential learning and who have participated in internships; campus, summer, part-time employment; and/or community service opportunities.

*An energized and expanding employer base (artistic, corporate, public, service, campus) committed to long term relationships with Carnegie Mellon (and the Career Center) founded on the continual enhancement and development of employer relationships.
Internship Development and Placement Programs:
- Student Employment-Experiential and Professional Development
- Summer Internship Funding: multiple funds designed to defray the expenses for students completing low paid or unpaid internships
- Variety of general and industry specific recruiting events
- On-Campus Recruiting
- Networking Events-New York, DC, Boston, Chicago, Silicon Valley, Pittsburgh, Baltimore
- Internship Search Workshop Series

FACILITIES

Housing: Coed dorms, special housing for disabled students, men's dorms, women's dorms, fraternity/sorority housing, apartments for single students, Special interest housing. 95% of campus accessible to physically diasbled. **Special Academic Facilities/Equipment:** Rare books collection, Entertainment Technology Center, Art galleries, Theatres, Botanical Institute, Extensive lab facilities and equipment, Recording studio, Robotics Institute, Design studios, Photo shoot studio and darkrooms, Radio station, Collaborative Innovation Center, LEED-certified green residence hall, Campo Garden, Observatory, Wood shops **Computers:** 100% of classrooms, 100% of dorms, 100% of libraries, 100% of dining areas, 100% of student union, 100% of common outdoor areas have wireless network access. Students can register for classes online. Administrative functions (other than registration) can be performed online.

CAMPUS LIFE

Environment: Metropolis. **Activities:** Choral groups, concert band, dance, drama/theater, literary magazine, marching band, music ensembles, musical theater, pep band, radio station, student government, student newspaper, student-run film society, symphony orchestra, television station, yearbook, Campus Ministries, Student Organization. 225 registered organizations, 18 religious organizations. 16 fraternities, 7 sororities. **Athletics (Intercollegiate):** *Men:* basketball, cheerleading, cross-country, diving, football, golf, soccer, swimming, tennis, track/field (outdoor). *Women:* basketball, cheerleading, cross-country, diving, soccer, swimming, tennis, track/field (outdoor), volleyball. **On-Campus Highlights:** Hunt Library, Skibo Coffee House, The Cut, The Underground, University Center Building—Student Center. **Environmental Initiatives:** PRACTICE: Bellfield Boiler Plant now using Natural Gas instead of Coal as fuel to produce steam, the purchase of 100% renewable electricity for campus electricity needs and, at minimum, USGBC LEED Silver guidelines required for all building projects and most renovations.

ADMISSIONS

Freshman Academic Profile: Average high school GPA 3.8. 75% in top 10% of high school class, 95% in top 25% of high school class, 99% in top 50% of high school class. **Reported SAT (pre-2016 redesign) scores:** SAT Math middle 50% range 720-800. SAT Critical Reading middle 50% range 660-750. SAT Writing middle 50% range 670-760. **Concordant SAT scores:** SAT EBRW middle 50% 710–770. SAT Math middle 50% range 750–800. ACT middle 50% range 31-34. Minimum internet-based TOEFL 102. **Basis for Candidate Selection:** *Very important factors considered include:* rigor of secondary school record, class rank, academic GPA, standardized test scores. *Important factors considered include:* application essay, recommendation(s), interview, extracurricular activities, talent/ability, character/personal qualities, first generation, alumni/ae relation, racial/ethnic status, volunteer work, work experience, level of applicant's interest. **Freshman Admission Requirements:** High school diploma is required and GED is accepted. *Academic units required:* 4 English, 4 math, 3 science, 3 science labs, 2 foreign language, 3 academic electives. *Academic units recommended:* 4 English, 4 math, 3 science, 3 science labs, 2 foreign language, 3 academic electives. **Freshman Admission Statistics:** 21,189 applied, 21.71% admitted, 34% enrolled. **Transfer Admission Requirements:** High school transcript, college transcript(s), essay or personal statement, standardized test scores, statement of good standing from prior institution(s). **General Admission Information:** Application fee $75. Regular application deadline 1/1. Regular notification 4/15. Nonfall registration not accepted. Admission may be deferred for a maximum of 1 year.

COSTS AND FINANCIAL AID

Annual tuition $52,732. Room and board $13,474. Required fees $888. Average book expense $2,400. **Required Forms and Deadlines:** FAFSA, Institution's own financial aid form, CSS/Financial Aid PROFILE, Noncustodial PROFILE. **Notification of Awards:** Applicants will be notified of awards on or about 4/15. **Types of Aid:** *Need-based scholarships/grants:* Federal Pell, FSEOG, State scholarships/grants, Private scholarships, College/university scholarship or grant aid from institutional funds. *Loans:* Direct Subsidized Stafford Loans, Direct Unsubsidized Stafford Loans, Direct PLUS loans, Federal Perkins Loans. *Student Employment:* Federal Work-Study Program available. Institutional employment available. **Financial Aid Statistics:** 96% needy freshmen, 95%

needy undergrads receive need-based scholarship or grant aid. 9% freshmen, 9% undergrads receive non-need-based scholarship or grant aid. 87% freshmen, 87% undergrads receive need-based self-help aid. 0% freshmen, 0% undergrads receive athletic scholarships. 51% undergrads borrow to pay for school. Average cumulative indebtedness $30,866. **Criteria for awarding aid:** *Need-based:* Academics, Art, Music/drama. *Non-need-based:* Academics, Art, Leadership, Minority status, Music/drama, State/district residency.

CARROLL COLLEGE (MT)

1601 North Benton Avenue, Helena, MT 59625
Phone: 406-447-4384 • **Financial Aid Phone:** 406-447-5423
E-mail: admission@carroll.edu • **CEEB Code:** 4041
Fax: 406-447-4533 • **Website:** www.carroll.edu • **ACT Code:** 2408

This private school, affiliated with the Roman Catholic Church, was founded in 1909. It has a 63-acre campus.

RATINGS

Admissions Selectivity Rating: 80   **Fire Safety Rating:** 68   **Green Rating:** 60*

STUDENTS AND FACULTY

Enrollment: 1,376. **Student Body:** 58% female, 42% male, 54% out-of-state, 1% international (15 countries represented). Asian 1%, African American 1%, Caucasian 81%, Hispanic 4%, Native American 1%, Pacific Islander <1%, Two or more races 1%, Race unknown 8%.
Retention and Graduation: 81% freshmen return for sophomore year. 50% freshmen graduate within 4 years. 67% freshmen graduate within 6 years. 22% grads go on to further study within 1 year. **Faculty:** Student/faculty ratio 13:1. 80 full-time faculty, 70% hold PhDs, 3% are are members of minority groups, 36% are women. 0% of classes are taught by teaching assistants.

ACADEMICS

Degrees: associate, bachelor's, certificate, transfer. **Classes:** Most classes have 10-19 students. Most lab/discussion sessions have 20-29 students. **Most popular majors:** Registered Nursing, Nursing Administration, Nursing Research and Clinical Nursing; Biology/Biological Sciences; Psychology. **Special Study Options:** Accelerated program, cooperative education program, double major, dual enrollment, English as a Second Language (ESL), exchange student program (domestic), honors program, independent study, internships, liberal arts/career combination, student-designed major, study abroad, teacher certification program. **Disability Services:** Special programs offered to physically disabled students, including tutors. **Career Services:** Career/job search classes, Career assessment, Internships.

FACILITIES

Housing: Coed dorms, apartments for single students, Theme Housing. 75% of campus accessible to physically diasbled. **Special Academic Facilities/Equipment:** Arts lab, observatory, seismograph station, engineering lab.

CAMPUS LIFE

Environment: Village. **Activities:** Choral groups, dance, drama/theater, literary magazine, music ensembles, musical theater, pep band, radio station, student government, student newspaper, student-run film society, yearbook, Campus Ministries, Student Organization. 34 registered organizations, 10 honor societies, 4 religious organizations. **Athletics (Intercollegiate):** *Men:* basketball, cheerleading, football, golf. *Women:* basketball, cheerleading, golf, soccer, volleyball. **On-Campus Highlights:** Science and Technology Center, Nelson Stadium, Campus Center, St. Charles Chapel, Fitness Center.

ADMISSIONS

Freshman Academic Profile: Average high school GPA 3.5. 25% in top 10% of high school class, 61% in top 25% of high school class, 90% in top 50% of high school class. 75% from public high schools. **Reported SAT (pre-2016 redesign) scores:** SAT Math middle 50% range 510-610. SAT Critical Reading middle 50% range 490-620. SAT Writing middle 50% range 490-590. **Concordant SAT scores:** SAT EBRW middle 50% 550–660. SAT Math middle 50% range 540–630. ACT middle 50% range 22-27. **Basis for Candidate Selection:** *Very important factors considered include:* rigor of secondary school record, academic GPA. *Important factors considered include:* standardized test scores, talent/ability, character/personal qualities. *Other factors considered include:* class rank, application essay, recommendation(s), interview, extracurricular activities, first generation, volunteer work, work experience, level of applicant's interest. **Freshman Admission Requirements:** High school diploma is required and GED is accepted. *Academic units recommended:* 4 English, 3 math, 2 science, 1 science lab, 2 social studies, 2 history, 2 academic electives, 1 visual/performing arts. **Freshman Admission Statistics:** 13 applied, admitted, 18% enrolled. **Transfer Admission Requirements:** college transcript(s), essay or personal statement, statement of good standing from prior institution(s). Minimum college GPA of 2.5 required. Lowest grade transferable C. **General Admission Information:** Application fee $35. Priority deadline 3/1. Regular application deadline 6/1. Nonfall registration accepted. Admission may be deferred for a maximum of 1 year.

COSTS AND FINANCIAL AID

Annual tuition $27,303. Room and board $8,668. Required fees $610. Average book expense $1,000. **Required Forms and Deadlines:** FAFSA. **Notification of Awards:** Applicants will be notified of awards on a rolling basis beginning 3/1. **Types of Aid:** *Need-based scholarships/grants:* Federal Pell, FSEOG, State scholarships/grants, Private scholarships, College/university scholarship or grant aid from institutional funds. *Loans:* Federal Perkins Loans. *Student Employment:* Federal Work-Study Program available. Institutional employment available. **Financial Aid Statistics:** 99% needy freshmen, 99% needy undergrads receive need-based scholarship or grant aid. 17% freshmen, 14% undergrads receive non-need-based scholarship or grant aid. 81% freshmen, 85% undergrads receive need-based self-help aid. 20% freshmen, 19% undergrads receive athletic scholarships. 98% freshmen, 98% undergrads receive any aid. **Criteria for awarding aid:** *Need-based:* Academics, Art, Athletics, Minority status, Religious affiliation. *Non-need-based:* Academics, Art, Athletics, Leadership, Minority status, Music/drama, Religious affiliation.

CARROLL UNIVERSITY

100 North East Avenue, Waukesha, WI 53186
Phone: 262-524-7220 • **Financial Aid Phone:** 262-524-7297 • **CEEB Code:** 1101
Fax: 262-951-3037 • **Website:** www.carrollu.edu • **ACT Code:** 4570

This private school, affiliated with the Presbyterian Church, was founded in 1846. It has a 52-acre campus.

RATINGS

Admissions Selectivity Rating: 82   **Fire Safety Rating:** 72   **Green Rating:** 60*

STUDENTS AND FACULTY

Enrollment: 2,925. **Student Body:** 31% out-of-state, 2% international (39 countries represented). Asian 1%, African American 2%, Caucasian 87%, Hispanic 3%, Native American <1%, Pacific Islander 0%, Two or more races 0%, Race unknown 4%.
Retention and Graduation: 41% freshmen graduate within 4 years. 53% freshmen graduate within 6 years. 13% grads go on to further study within 1 year. **Faculty:** Student/faculty ratio 14:1. 139 full-time faculty, 0% hold PhDs, 0% are are members of minority groups, 0% 0% of classes are taught by teaching assistants.

ACADEMICS

Degrees: bachelor's, master's, postbachelor's certificate. **Classes:** Most classes have 10-19 students. Most lab/discussion sessions have 10-19 students. **Most popular majors:** Business Administration and Management; Psychology; Biology/Biological Sciences. **Special Study Options:** distance learning, double major, exchange student program (domestic), honors program, independent study, internships, liberal arts/career combination, student-designed major, study abroad, teacher certification program. **Disability Services:** Special programs offered to physically disabled students, including note-taking services, tape recorders, tutors. **Career Services:** Alumni network, Career/job search classes, Career assessment, Internships.

FACILITIES

Housing: Coed dorms, women's dorms, apartments for single students. 50% of campus accessible to physically disabled. **Special Academic Facilities/ Equipment:** A 60 acre scientific study and conservancy area with a class 1 trout stream and associated wetland and upland habitats. **Computers:** 80% of classrooms, 100% of dorms, 100% of libraries, 100% of dining areas, 100% of student union, 90% of common outdoor areas have wireless network access. Students can register for classes online. Administrative functions (other than registration) can be performed online.

CAMPUS LIFE

Environment: Town. **Activities:** Choral groups, concert band, dance, drama/theater, jazz band, literary magazine, music ensembles, pep band, radio station, student government, student newspaper, Student Organization. 40 registered organizations, 2 religious organizations. 2 fraternities, 4 sororities. **Athletics (Intercollegiate):** *Men:* baseball, basketball, cross-country, football, golf, soccer, swimming, tennis, track/field (outdoor), track/field (indoor). *Women:* basketball, cross-country, golf, soccer, softball, swimming, tennis, track/field (outdoor), track/field (indoor), volleyball. **On-Campus Highlights:** Main Hall, Van Male Fieldhouse, Campus Center, Shattuck, Physical Therapy Building.

ADMISSIONS

Freshman Academic Profile: 38% in top 10% of high school class, 62% in top 25% of high school class, 83% in top 50% of high school class. 87% from public

high schools. ACT middle 50% range 21-26. Minimum paper TOEFL 550. **Basis for Candidate Selection:** *Very important factors considered include:* rigor of secondary school record, class rank, academic GPA. *Important factors considered include:* standardized test scores. *Other factors considered include:* application essay, recommendation(s), interview, extracurricular activities, talent/ability, character/personal qualities, alumni/ae relation, geographical residence, state residency, racial/ethnic status, work experience. **Freshman Admission Requirements:** High school diploma is required and GED is accepted. *Academic units recommended:* 4 English, 4 math, 3 science, 2 science labs, 3 social studies, 3 history. **Freshman Admission Statistics:** 2,868 applied, 82.98% admitted. **Transfer Admission Requirements:** High school transcript, college transcript(s), Minimum college GPA of 2.0 required. Lowest grade transferable C. **General Admission Information:** Nonfall registration accepted. Admission may be deferred.

COSTS AND FINANCIAL AID

Annual tuition $27,850. Room and board $8,513. Required fees $430. **Required Forms and Deadlines:** FAFSA. **Notification of Awards:** Applicants will be notified of awards on a rolling basis beginning 2/15. **Types of Aid:** *Need-based scholarships/grants:* Federal Pell, FSEOG, State scholarships/grants, Private scholarships, College/university scholarship or grant aid from institutional funds, Federal Nursing Scholarships. *Loans:* Federal Perkins Loans, State Loans. *Student Employment:* Federal Work-Study Program available. Institutional employment available. **Financial Aid Statistics:** 100% needy freshmen, 100% needy undergrads receive need-based scholarship or grant aid. 91% freshmen, 91% undergrads receive non-need-based scholarship or grant aid. 73% freshmen, 79% undergrads receive need-based self-help aid. 0% freshmen, 0% undergrads receive athletic scholarships. 98% freshmen, 98% undergrads receive any aid. **Criteria for awarding aid:** *Need-based:* Academics, Art, Leadership, Religious affiliation. *Non-need-based:* Academics, Alumni affiliation, Art, Leadership, Minority status, Religious affiliation.

CARSON-NEWMAN UNIVERSITY

1646 Russell Avenue, Jefferson City, TN 37760
Phone: 865-471-3223
E-mail: admitme@.cn.edu • **CEEB Code:** 1102
Fax: 865-471-4817 • **Website:** www.cn.edu • **ACT Code:** 3950

This private school, affiliated with the Baptist Church, was founded in 1851. It has a 90-acre campus.

RATINGS

Admissions Selectivity Rating: 75   **Fire Safety Rating:** 78   **Green Rating:** 60*

STUDENTS AND FACULTY

Enrollment: 1,748. **Student Body:** 58% female, 42% male, 20% out-of-state, 3% international. Asian 1%, African American 8%, Caucasian 82%, Hispanic 3%, Native American 1%, Pacific Islander 0%, Two or more races 2%, Race unknown 1%.
Retention and Graduation: 70% freshmen return for sophomore year. 42% freshmen graduate within 4 years. 49% freshmen graduate within 6 years. 25% grads go on to further study within 1 year. 20% grads pursue arts and sciences degrees. 3% grads pursue law degrees. 1% grads pursue business degrees. 2% grads pursue medical degrees. **Faculty:** Student/faculty ratio 13:1. 122 full-time faculty, 78% hold PhDs, 4% are are members of minority groups, 56% are women. 0% of classes are taught by teaching assistants.

ACADEMICS

Degrees: associate, bachelor's, doctoral/research, master's, postbachelor's certificate. **Classes:** Most classes have 10-19 students. Most lab/discussion sessions have 10-19 students. **Most popular majors:** Business Administration and Management; Registered Nursing/Registered Nurse; Educational, Instructional, and Curriculum Supervision. **Special Study Options:** cooperative education program, double major, dual enrollment, English as a Second Language (ESL), honors program, independent study, internships, student-designed major, study abroad, teacher certification program. Combined degree programs: MSC/EDS. **Disability Services:** Special programs offered to physically disabled students, including note-taking services, reader services, tape recorders, tutors. **Career Services:** Alumni network, Alumni services, Career/job search classes, Career assessment, Internships, Regional alumni. Of the various areas of need met by Career Services, at this point, our most complete service is meeting the need of career assessment due to the capacity and tools available. The office offers career counseling and access to tools such as Focus 2 and the MBTI, accompanied by a certified practitioner to interpret results for students and alums. These services among others are also offered to interested students in the form of a 1 hour course on Major and Career Exploration taught by the Career Services staff. These capabilities and resources result in yielding one of the office's most effective services to our students and alum.

FACILITIES

Housing: men's dorms, women's dorms, apartments for married students, apartments for single students. 80% of campus accessible to physically diasbled. **Special Academic Facilities/Equipment:** Art galleries, Appalachian history museum, home management house, language lab.

CAMPUS LIFE

Environment: Rural. **Activities:** Choral groups, concert band, dance, drama/theater, jazz band, literary magazine, marching band, music ensembles, musical theater, opera, pep band, student government, student newspaper, television station, yearbook. 45 registered organizations, 10 honor societies, 5 religious organizations. 2 fraternities, 2 sororities. **Athletics (Intercollegiate):** *Men:* baseball, basketball, cheerleading, cross-country, football, golf, soccer, tennis, track/field (outdoor), wrestling. *Women:* basketball, cheerleading, cross-country, soccer, softball, tennis, track/field (outdoor), volleyball. **On-Campus Highlights:** Maddox Student Activities Center, Coffee House (in MSAC) and TV lounge, Workout/Weight Rooms (in MSAC), Cafeteria, Swann Field (Intramurals).

ADMISSIONS

Freshman Academic Profile: Average high school GPA 3.5. **Reported SAT (pre-2016 redesign) scores:** SAT Math middle 50% range 440-560. SAT Critical Reading middle 50% range 400-560. **Concordant SAT scores:** SAT Math middle 50% range 480–580. ACT middle 50% range 20-26. Minimum paper TOEFL 550. **Basis for Candidate Selection:** *Very important factors considered include:* academic GPA, standardized test scores, character/personal qualities. *Important factors considered include:* rigor of secondary school record, class rank, extracurricular activities. *Other factors considered include:* application essay, recommendation(s), interview, talent/ability, work experience. **Freshman Admission Requirements:** High school diploma is required and GED is accepted. *Academic units required:* 4 English, 3 math, 3 science, 2 social studies, 1 history, 6 academic electives, and 1 unit from above areas or other academic areas. *Academic units recommended:* 2 foreign language. **Freshman Admission Statistics:** 6,496 applied, 63.29% admitted, 12% enrolled. **Transfer Admission Requirements:** college transcript(s), Minimum college GPA of 2.0 required. Lowest grade transferable d. **General Admission Information:** Nonfall registration accepted. Admission may be deferred for a maximum of 1 year.

COSTS AND FINANCIAL AID

Annual tuition $26,200. Room and board $8,630. Required fees $1,200. Average book expense $1,600. **Required Forms and Deadlines:** FAFSA. **Notification of Awards:** Applicants will be notified of awards on a rolling basis beginning 2/1. **Types of Aid:** *Need-based scholarships/grants:* Federal Pell, FSEOG, State scholarships/grants, Private scholarships, College/university scholarship or grant aid from institutional funds, Federal Nursing Scholarships. *Loans:* Direct Subsidized Stafford Loans, Direct Unsubsidized Stafford Loans, Direct PLUS loans, Federal Perkins Loans, State Loans. *Student Employment:* Federal Work-Study Program available. Institutional employment available. **Financial Aid Statistics:** 99% needy freshmen, 98% needy undergrads receive need-based scholarship or grant aid. 16% freshmen, 19% undergrads receive non-need-based scholarship or grant aid. 75% freshmen, 76% undergrads receive need-based self-help aid. 6% freshmen, 6% undergrads receive athletic scholarships. 73% undergrads borrow to pay for school. Average cumulative indebtedness $27,418. **Criteria for awarding aid:** *Need-based:* Art, Music/drama, Religious affiliation. *Non-need-based:* Academics, Art, Athletics, Leadership, Music/drama, Religious affiliation, State/district residency.

CARTHAGE COLLEGE

2001 Alford Park Drive, Kenosha, WI 53140
Phone: 262-551-6000 • **Financial Aid Phone:** 262-551-6001
E-mail: admissions@carthage.edu • **CEEB Code:** 1103
Fax: 262-551-5762 • **Website:** www.carthage.edu • **ACT Code:** 4571

This private school, affiliated with the Lutheran Church, was founded in 1847. It has a 95-acre campus.

RATINGS

Admissions Selectivity Rating: 83   **Fire Safety Rating:** 80   **Green Rating:** 60*

STUDENTS AND FACULTY

Enrollment: 2,823. **Student Body:** 54% female, 46% male, 68% out-of-state, <1% international (16 countries represented). Asian 1%, African American 5%, Caucasian 77%, Hispanic 4%, Native American <1%, Pacific Islander <1%, Two or more races 2%, Race unknown 10%.

Retention and Graduation: 78% freshmen return for sophomore year. 54% freshmen graduate within 4 years. 16% grads go on to further study within 1 year. 4% grads pursue arts and sciences degrees. 2% grads pursue law degrees. 1% grads pursue business degrees. 1% grads pursue medical degrees. **Faculty:** Student/faculty ratio 8:1. 149 full-time faculty, 91% hold PhDs, 7% are are members of minority groups, 40% are women. 0% of classes are taught by teaching assistants.

ACADEMICS

Degrees: bachelor's, master's. **Classes:** Most classes have 20-29 students. **Most popular majors:** Elementary Education and Teaching; Biology/Biological Sciences; Business Administration and Management. **Special Study Options:** Accelerated program, cross-registration, double major, honors program, independent study, internships, student-designed major, study abroad, teacher certification program. **Honors Programs:** We offer All College Honors as well as Honors in the Major. Combined degree programs: BA/MA, Occupational Therapy at Wash Univ—St. Louis. **Disability Services:** Special programs offered to physically disabled students, including note-taking services, reader services, tape recorders, tutors. **Career Services:** Career/job search classes, Career assessment, Internships.

FACILITIES

Housing: Coed dorms, men's dorms, women's dorms, fraternity/sorority housing, Best Western Harborside through Carthage. 99% of campus accessible to physically diasbled. **Special Academic Facilities/Equipment:** H.F. Johnson Art Gallery, Center for CHildren's Literature, planetarium, undergraduate science research lab, graphic design lab, greenhouse, computer/math research lab, physics research lab, ScienceWorks lab, A.W. Clausen Center Boardroom **Computers:** Students can register for classes online. Administrative functions (other than registration) can be performed online.

CAMPUS LIFE

Environment: City. **Activities:** Choral groups, concert band, dance, drama/theater, jazz band, literary magazine, music ensembles, musical theater, opera, pep band, radio station, student government, student newspaper, student-run film society, symphony orchestra, yearbook. 90 registered organizations, 20 honor societies, 7 religious organizations. 8 fraternities, 7 sororities. **Athletics (Intercollegiate):** *Men:* baseball, basketball, cross-country, football, golf, soccer, swimming, tennis, track/field (outdoor), track/field (indoor), volleyball. *Women:* basketball, cross-country, golf, soccer, softball, swimming, tennis, track/field (outdoor), track/field (indoor), volleyball, water polo. **On-Campus Highlights:** Tarble Athletic and Recreation Center, Hedberg Library, A.W. Clausen Center for World Business, Oaks Residence Halls, Lake Michigan, Located midway between Chicago and Milwaukee, Carthage is easily accessibe by car, airplane and train. Our 95 acre, park-like campus is on the shore of Lake Michigan.

ADMISSIONS

Freshman Academic Profile: Average high school GPA 3.3. 21% in top 10% of high school class, 44% in top 25% of high school class, 75% in top 50% of high school class. 91% from public high schools. **Reported SAT (pre-2016 redesign) scores:** SAT Math middle 50% range 490-620. SAT Critical Reading middle 50% range 480-610. **Concordant SAT scores:** SAT Math middle 50% range 520–640. ACT middle 50% range 21-27. Minimum paper TOEFL 500. **Basis for Candidate Selection:** *Very important factors considered include:* rigor of secondary school record, academic GPA, standardized test scores. *Other factors considered include:* class rank, application essay, recommendation(s), interview, extracurricular activities, talent/ability, character/personal qualities, volunteer work, work experience. **Freshman Admission Requirements:** High school diploma is required and GED is accepted. *Academic units recommended:* 4 English, 3 math, 3 science, 2 foreign language, 3 social studies, 3 academic electives. **Freshman Admission Statistics:** 7,174 applied, 70.31% admitted, 14% enrolled. **Transfer Admission Requirements:** college transcript(s), statement of good standing from prior institution(s). Minimum college GPA of 2.0 required. Lowest grade transferable C-. **General Admission Information:** Application fee $35. Nonfall registration accepted. Admission may be deferred for a maximum of one year.

COSTS AND FINANCIAL AID

Annual tuition $36,570. Room and board $9,970. Required fees $0. Average book expense $1,600. **Required Forms and Deadlines:** FAFSA. **Notification of Awards:** Applicants will be notified of awards on a rolling basis beginning 2/1. **Types of Aid:** *Need-based scholarships/grants:* Federal Pell, FSEOG, State scholarships/grants, Private scholarships, College/university scholarship or grant aid from institutional funds. *Loans:* Direct Subsidized Stafford Loans, Direct Unsubsidized Stafford Loans, Direct PLUS loans, Federal Perkins Loans, College/university loans from institutional funds. *Student Employment:* Federal Work-Study Program available. Institutional employment available. **Financial Aid Statistics:** 100% needy freshmen, 100% needy undergrads receive need-based scholarship or grant aid. 13% freshmen, 11% undergrads receive non-need-based scholarship or grant aid. 83% freshmen, 84% undergrads receive need-based self-help aid. 0% freshmen, 0% undergrads receive athletic scholarships. 97% freshmen, 97% undergrads receive any aid.

Criteria for awarding aid: *Need-based:* Academics, Alumni affiliation, Art, Leadership, Music/drama, Religious affiliation. *Non-need-based:* Academics, Alumni affiliation, Art, Leadership, Music/drama, Religious affiliation, State/district residency.

CASCADE COLLEGE

9101 East Burnside Street, Portland, OR 97216-1515
Phone: 503-257-1202 • **Financial Aid Phone:** 503-257-1241
E-mail: admissions@cascade.edu
Fax: 503-257-1222 • **Website:** www.cascade.edu • **ACT Code:** 3459

This private school, affiliated with the Church of Christ Church, was founded in 1993. It has a 12-acre campus.

RATINGS
Admissions Selectivity Rating: 71   **Fire Safety Rating:** 70   **Green Rating:** 60*

STUDENTS AND FACULTY
Enrollment: 107. **Student Body:** 59% female, 41% male, 64% out-of-state, 2% international (8 countries represented). Asian 7%, African American 11%, Caucasian 64%, Hispanic 12%, Native American 1%, Pacific Islander 0%, Two or more races 0%, Race unknown 3%.
Retention and Graduation: 46% freshmen return for sophomore year. 23% freshmen graduate within 4 years. 30% freshmen graduate within 6 years. 15% grads go on to further study within 1 year. 10% grads pursue arts and sciences degrees. 2% grads pursue law degrees. 1% grads pursue business degrees.
Faculty: Student/faculty ratio 12:1. 15 full-time faculty, 60% hold PhDs, 13% are are members of minority groups, 27% are women. 0% of classes are taught by teaching assistants.

ACADEMICS
Degrees: bachelor's. **Classes:** Most classes have 10-19 students. Most lab/discussion sessions have fewer than 10 students. **Most popular majors:** Teacher Education, Multiple Levels; Psychology; Business/Commerce. **Special Study Options:** double major, dual enrollment, independent study, internships, student-designed major, study abroad, teacher certification program. **Disability Services:** Special programs offered to physically disabled students, including note-taking services, reader services, tutors. **Career Services:** Most majors provide an opportunity for students to participate in an internship or practicum in the area of the major giving most graduates hand-on experience and an opportunity to experience a career in the major.

FACILITIES
Housing: special housing for disabled students, men's dorms, women's dorms, apartments for married students. 70% of campus accessible to physically diasbled. **Computers:** 100% of classrooms, 100% of dorms, 100% of libraries, 100% of dining areas, 100% of student union, 100% of common outdoor areas have wireless network access. Administrative functions (other than registration) can be performed online.

CAMPUS LIFE
Environment: Metropolis. **Activities:** Choral groups, drama/theater, jazz band, literary magazine, music ensembles, musical theater, student government, yearbook. 16 registered organizations, 2 honor societies. **Athletics (Intercollegiate):** *Men:* basketball, cross-country, soccer, track/field (outdoor), track/field (indoor). *Women:* basketball, cross-country, soccer, track/field (outdoor), track/field (indoor), volleyball. **On-Campus Highlights:** Classrooms, Student Center, The Cabin (coffee shop), Weight room, Womack and Hamstreet Fountains.

ADMISSIONS
Freshman Academic Profile: Average high school GPA 3.0. 85% from public high schools. Minimum paper TOEFL 500. **Basis for Candidate Selection:** *Other factors considered include:* academic GPA, standardized test scores, recommendation(s). **Freshman Admission Requirements:** High school diploma is required and GED is accepted. *Academic units recommended:* 4 English, 3 math, 2 science, 1 science lab, 2 foreign language, 4 social studies, 2 history, 1 computer science. **Freshman Admission Statistics:** 204 applied, 56.86% admitted, 57% enrolled. **Transfer Admission Requirements:** High school transcript, college transcript(s), Minimum college GPA of 2.0 required. Lowest grade transferable D. **General Admission Information:** Application fee $25. Nonfall registration accepted. Admission may be deferred for a maximum of 1 year.

COSTS AND FINANCIAL AID
Average book expense $900. **Required Forms and Deadlines:** FAFSA, Institution's own financial aid form. **Notification of Awards:** Applicants will be notified of awards on a rolling basis beginning 2/15. **Types of Aid:** *Need-based scholarships/grants:* Federal Pell, FSEOG, Private scholarships,

College/university scholarship or grant aid from institutional funds. *Student Employment:* Federal Work-Study Program available. Institutional employment available. **Financial Aid Statistics:** 100% needy freshmen, 63% needy undergrads receive need-based scholarship or grant aid. 19% freshmen, 92% undergrads receive non-need-based scholarship or grant aid. 87% freshmen, 84% undergrads receive need-based self-help aid. 48% freshmen, 36% undergrads receive athletic scholarships. 100% freshmen, 99% undergrads receive any aid. **Criteria for awarding aid:** *Need-based:* Leadership. *Non-need-based:* Academics, Athletics, Leadership, Music/drama, Religious affiliation, State/district residency.

CASE WESTERN RESERVE UNIVERSITY

Wolstein Hall, Cleveland, OH 44106-7055
Phone: 216-368-4450 • **Financial Aid Phone:** 216-368-4530
E-mail: admission@case.edu • **CEEB Code:** 1105
Fax: 216-368-5111 • **Website:** www.case.edu • **ACT Code:** 3244

This private school was founded in 1826. It has a 155-acre campus.

RATINGS
Admissions Selectivity Rating: 94   **Fire Safety Rating:** 88   **Green Rating:** 95

STUDENTS AND FACULTY
Enrollment: 5,048. **Student Body:** 45% female, 55% male, 68% out-of-state, 12% international (35 countries represented). Asian 20%, African American 4%, Caucasian 50%, Hispanic 6%, Native American <1%, Pacific Islander <1%, Two or more races 5%, Race unknown 2%.
Retention and Graduation: 92% freshmen return for sophomore year. 64% freshmen graduate within 4 years. 82% freshmen graduate within 6 years. 36% grads go on to further study within 1 year. 2% grads pursue law degrees. 16% grads pursue medical degrees. **Faculty:** Student/faculty ratio 11:1. 771 full-time faculty, 91% hold PhDs, 18% are are members of minority groups, 44% are women. 5% of classes are taught by teaching assistants.

ACADEMICS
Degrees: bachelor's, doctoral/professional, doctoral/research, doctoral, master's, postbachelor's certificate, post-master's certificate. **Classes:** Most classes have 10-19 students. Most lab/discussion sessions have fewer than 10 students. **Most popular majors:** Mechanical Engineering; Biology/Biological Sciences; Bioengineering and Biomedical Engineering. **Special Study Options:** Accelerated program, cooperative education program, cross-registration, double major, dual enrollment, English as a Second Language (ESL), exchange student program (domestic), honors program, independent study, internships, liberal arts/career combination, student-designed major, study abroad, teacher certification program, Washington Semester. **Honors Programs:** The College Scholars Program is a three-year honors program for a small group of students interested in exploring how academic learning can address larger world concerns. Combined degree programs: BA/MA, BA/DDS, BS/MEng, BA/MS, BS/MS, BS/MBA, BS/MAcc, BA/MPH, Sr Yr Prof Studies. **Disability Services:** Special programs offered to physically disabled students, including note-taking services, reader services, tape recorders, tutors. **Career Services:** Alumni network, Alumni services, Career/job search classes, Career assessment, Internships, Regional alumni. CWRU's experiential learning options come in many forms. More than 99% of our undergraduate students participate in opportunities for research, cultural immersion through study abroad programs, clinical work in nursing, and internship and co-op programs, or garner valuable leadership experiences through campus, club, and community interactions.

FACILITIES
Housing: Coed dorms, fraternity/sorority housing, apartments for single students, Wellness Housing, Secured women-only floor available. Special-interest housing available. Residential Colleges for first-year students. 90% of campus accessible to physically diasbled. **Special Academic Facilities/Equipment:** Art, natural history, and auto-aviation museums, historical society, botanical garden, biology field stations, observatory. **Computers:** 100% of classrooms, 100% of dorms, 100% of libraries, 100% of dining areas, 100% of student union, 100% of common outdoor areas have wireless network access. Students can register for classes online. Administrative functions (other than registration) can be performed online.

CAMPUS LIFE

Environment: Metropolis. **Activities:** Choral groups, concert band, dance, drama/theater, jazz band, literary magazine, marching band, music ensembles, musical theater, pep band, radio station, student government, student newspaper, student-run film society, symphony orchestra, yearbook, Campus Ministries, Student Organization, Model UN. 150 registered organizations, 8 honor societies, 4 religious organizations. 16 fraternities, 8 sororities. **Athletics (Intercollegiate):** *Men:* baseball, basketball, cross-country, football, soccer, swimming, tennis, track/field (outdoor), track/field (indoor), wrestling. *Women:* basketball, cross-country, soccer, softball, swimming, tennis, track/field (outdoor), track/field (indoor), volleyball. **On-Campus Highlights:** North Residential Village, Peter B. Lewis Building, Kelvin Smith Library, Veale Convocation and Athletic Center, Turning Point Sculpture Garden. **Environmental Initiatives:** In 2008 President Barbara Snyder signed the American and College and University President Climate Commitment, which is a public declaration that CWRU will aim to be a carbon neutral campus by 2050. The commitment requires public reporting of CWRU greenhouse gas inventory and other sustainability metrics. CWRU is proud to be a community steward and leader on this vital topic and works with the City of Cleveland and other entries to share strategies and best practices.

ADMISSIONS

Freshman Academic Profile: 71% in top 10% of high school class, 94% in top 25% of high school class, 100% in top 50% of high school class. 70% from public high schools. **Reported SAT (pre-2016 redesign) scores:** SAT Math middle 50% range 680-770. SAT Critical Reading middle 50% range 600-720. SAT Writing middle 50% range 620-720. **Concordant SAT scores:** SAT EBRW middle 50% 660–750. SAT Math middle 50% range 710–780. ACT middle 50% range 30-34. Minimum internet-based TOEFL 90. Minimum paper TOEFL 577. **Basis for Candidate Selection:** *Very important factors considered include:* rigor of secondary school record, class rank, academic GPA, standardized test scores, extracurricular activities. *Important factors considered include:* application essay, recommendation(s), interview, talent/ability, character/personal qualities, volunteer work, work experience, level of applicant's interest. *Other factors considered include:* first generation, alumni/ae relation, racial/ethnic status. **Freshman Admission Requirements:** High school diploma is required and GED is accepted. *Academic units required:* 4 English, 3 math, 3 science, 2 science labs, 2 foreign language, 3 social studies. *Academic units recommended:* 4 math, 3 science labs, 3 foreign language, 4 social studies. **Freshman Admission Statistics:** 23,115 applied, 35.44% admitted, 15% enrolled. **Transfer Admission Requirements:** High school transcript, college transcript(s), essay or personal statement, statement of good standing from prior institution(s). Minimum college GPA of 3.2 required. Lowest grade transferable C. **General Admission Information:** Regular application deadline 1/15. Regular notification 3/20. Nonfall registration accepted. Admission may be deferred for a maximum of 1 year.

COSTS AND FINANCIAL AID

Annual tuition $45,592. Room and board $14,298. Required fees $414. Average book expense $1,200. **Required Forms and Deadlines:** FAFSA, Institution's own financial aid form, CSS/Financial Aid PROFILE, Noncustodial PROFILE. **Notification of Awards:** Applicants will be notified of awards on a rolling basis beginning 3/15. **Types of Aid:** *Need-based scholarships/grants:* Federal Pell, FSEOG, State scholarships/grants, Private scholarships, College/university scholarship or grant aid from institutional funds. *Loans:* Direct Subsidized Stafford Loans, Direct Unsubsidized Stafford Loans, Direct PLUS loans, Federal Perkins Loans, College/university loans from institutional funds. *Student Employment:* Federal Work-Study Program available. Institutional employment available. **Financial Aid Statistics:** 97% needy freshmen, 97% needy undergrads receive need-based scholarship or grant aid. 30% freshmen, 14% undergrads receive non-need-based scholarship or grant aid. 69% freshmen, 81% undergrads receive need-based self-help aid. 0% freshmen, 0% undergrads receive athletic scholarships. 83% freshmen, 87% undergrads receive any aid. 51% undergrads borrow to pay for school. Average cumulative indebtedness $30,561. **Criteria for awarding aid:** *Non-need-based:* Academics, Alumni affiliation, Art, Leadership, Music/drama.

CASTLETON STATE COLLEGE

Office of Admissions, Castleton, VT 5735
Phone: 802-468-1213 • **Financial Aid Phone:** 802-468-6070
E-mail: info@castleton.edu • **CEEB Code:** 3765
Fax: 802-468-1476 • **Website:** www.castleton.edu • **ACT Code:** 4314

This public school was founded in 1787. It has a 165-acre campus.

RATINGS

Admissions Selectivity Rating: 75 **Fire Safety Rating:** 86 **Green Rating:** 60*

STUDENTS AND FACULTY

Enrollment: 1,890. **Student Body:** 52% female, 48% male, 30% out-of-state, 2% international (16 countries represented). Asian 1%, African American 2%, Caucasian 85%, Hispanic 2%, Native American <1%, Pacific Islander 0%, Two or more races 2%, Race unknown 6%.
Retention and Graduation: 70% freshmen return for sophomore year. 37% freshmen graduate within 4 years. 50% freshmen graduate within 6 years. **Faculty:** Student/faculty ratio 10:1. 102 full-time faculty, 93% hold PhDs, 6% are are members of minority groups, 51% are women. 0% of classes are taught by teaching assistants.

ACADEMICS

Degrees: associate, bachelor's, master's, post-master's certificate. **Classes:** Most classes have 10-19 students. Most lab/discussion sessions have 10-19 students. **Most popular majors:** Psychology; Business/Commerce. **Special Study Options:** cooperative education program, double major, dual enrollment, honors program, independent study, internships, liberal arts/career combination, student-designed major, study abroad, teacher certification program. Combined degree programs: BA/MA, 4+1 Accounting; 4+1 M.B.A.; 4+3 Phys. Therapy; 4+2 Occupational Therapy. **Disability Services:** Special programs offered to physically disabled students, including note-taking services, reader services, tape recorders, tutors. **Career Services:** Alumni network, Career assessment, Internships.

FACILITIES

Housing: Coed dorms. 100% of campus accessible to physically diasbled. **Special Academic Facilities/Equipment:** Historical/medical museum **Computers:** 25% of classrooms, 100% of dorms, 100% of libraries, 100% of dining areas, 100% of student union, have wireless network access.

CAMPUS LIFE

Environment: Rural. **Activities:** Choral groups, dance, drama/theater, jazz band, literary magazine, music ensembles, musical theater, radio station, student government, student newspaper, student-run film society, television station, yearbook. 40 registered organizations, 7 honor societies, 1 religious organization. **Athletics (Intercollegiate):** *Men:* baseball, basketball, cross-country, football, ice hockey, lacrosse, skiing (downhill/alpine), soccer, tennis. *Women:* basketball, cross-country, field hockey, ice hockey, lacrosse, skiing (downhill/alpine), soccer, softball, tennis. **On-Campus Highlights:** Fireside Cafe, Coffee Cottage, Fitness center, Library **Environmental Initiatives:** Student-driven recycling effort.

ADMISSIONS

Freshman Academic Profile: Average high school GPA 3.0. 6% in top 10% of high school class, 29% in top 25% of high school class, 61% in top 50% of high school class. **Reported SAT (pre-2016 redesign) scores:** SAT Math middle 50% range 430-540. SAT Critical Reading middle 50% range 420-530. SAT Writing middle 50% range 420-520. **Concordant SAT scores:** SAT EBRW middle 50% 470–580. SAT Math middle 50% range 470–570. ACT middle 50% range 18-22. Minimum internet-based TOEFL 80. Minimum paper TOEFL 500. **Basis for Candidate Selection:** *Very important factors considered include:* rigor of secondary school record, class rank, academic GPA, application essay, recommendation(s), character/personal qualities. *Other factors considered include:* standardized test scores, interview, extracurricular activities, volunteer work, level of applicant's interest. **Freshman Admission Requirements:** High school diploma is required and GED is accepted. *Academic units required:* 4 English, 3 math, 3 science, 2 science labs, 3 social studies, 3 history. *Academic units recommended:* 2 foreign language. **Freshman Admission Statistics:** 2,397 applied, 77.93% admitted, 20% enrolled. **Transfer Admission Requirements:** college transcript(s), essay or personal statement, Minimum college GPA of 2.0 required. Lowest grade transferable C-. **General Admission Information:** Application fee $40. Priority deadline 5/1. Nonfall registration accepted. Admission may be deferred for a maximum of 1 year.

COSTS AND FINANCIAL AID

Annual in-state tuition $9,768. Annual out-of-state tuition $24,432. Room and board $9,414. Required fees $1,004. Average book expense $1,000. **Required Forms and Deadlines:** FAFSA. **Notification of Awards:** Applicants will be notified of awards on a rolling basis beginning 2/15. **Types of Aid:** *Need-based scholarships/grants:* Federal Pell, FSEOG, State scholarships/grants, Private scholarships, College/university scholarship or grant aid from institutional funds. *Loans:* Direct Subsidized Stafford Loans, Direct Unsubsidized Stafford Loans, Direct PLUS loans, Federal Perkins Loans, Federal Nursing Loans. *Student Employment:* Federal Work-Study Program available. Institutional employment available. **Criteria for awarding aid:** *Need-based:* Academics, Music/drama. *Non-need-based:* Academics, Alumni affiliation, Music/drama, State/district residency.

CATAWBA COLLEGE

2300 West Innes Street, Salisbury, NC 28144
Phone: 704-637-4402 • **Financial Aid Phone:** 704-637-4416
E-mail: admission@catawba.edu • **CEEB Code:** 5103
Fax: 704-637-4222 • **Website:** www.catawba.edu • **ACT Code:** 3080

This private school, affiliated with the United Church of Christ Church, was founded in 1851. It has a 276-acre campus.

RATINGS
Admissions Selectivity Rating: 89   **Fire Safety Rating:** 89   **Green Rating:** 94

STUDENTS AND FACULTY
Enrollment: 1,276. **Student Body:** 53% female, 47% male, 21% out-of-state, 2% international (15 countries represented). Asian 1%, African American 19%, Caucasian 67%, Hispanic 7%, Native American <1%, Pacific Islander <1%, Two or more races 3%, Race unknown <1%.
Retention and Graduation: 72% freshmen return for sophomore year. 39% freshmen graduate within 4 years. 52 **Faculty:** Student/faculty ratio 13:1. 80 full-time faculty, 80% hold PhDs, 16% are are members of minority groups, 49% are women. 0% of classes are taught by teaching assistants.

ACADEMICS
Degrees: bachelor's, master's. **Classes:** Most classes have 10-19 students. **Most popular majors:** Business Administration and Management; Sport and Fitness Administration/Management; Kindergarten/Preschool Education and Teaching. **Special Study Options:** cross-registration, double major, dual enrollment, honors program, independent study, internships, liberal arts/career combination, student-designed major, study abroad, teacher certification program. **Disability Services:** Special programs offered to physically disabled students, including note-taking services, tape recorders, tutors. **Career Services:** Alumni network, Career/job search classes, Career assessment, Internships. Quality Enhancement Plan (QEP) Catawba College's mission statement articulates our commitment to providing students an education rich in personal attention that blends the knowledge and competencies of liberal studies with career preparation. In conjunction with our mission, the QEP will improve the career awareness of students to more effectively prepare them to pursue graduate studies or to enter the workforce. As an approach to improving the career awareness of students at Catawba College, the QEP committee developed a program identified as Catawba to Career (C2C). As an institution grounded in the tradition of liberal education, we place a high value on our students exploring, understanding, and applying a broad range of knowledge. As we blend the knowledge and competencies of liberal studies with career preparation, we recognize that students must embrace a major area of study fairly early in their college career in order to be eligible to graduate within four years. C2C should equip students with information they need to make informed decisions about how their aptitudes and values align with specific career paths.

FACILITIES
Housing: Coed dorms, men's dorms, women's dorms, Substance free housing. 95% of campus accessible to physically disabled. **Special Academic Facilities/ Equipment:** Ecology preserve (183 acres). Wildlife preserve (300 acres) **Computers:** 90% of classrooms, 95% of dorms, 100% of libraries, 25% of dining areas, 80% of student union, 10% of common outdoor areas have wireless network access. Administrative functions (other than registration) can be performed online.

CAMPUS LIFE
Environment: Town. **Activities:** Choral groups, concert band, dance, drama/theater, jazz band, literary magazine, music ensembles, musical theater, pep band, student government, student newspaper, symphony orchestra, yearbook, Campus Ministries. 38 registered organizations, 9 honor societies, 4 religious organizations. **Athletics (Intercollegiate):** *Men:* baseball, basketball, cheerleading, cross-country, football, golf, lacrosse, soccer, swimming, tennis. *Women:* basketball, cheerleading, cross-country, golf, soccer, softball, swimming, tennis, volleyball. **On-Campus Highlights:** Center for the Environment, Cannon Field House, Robertson College Community Center, Ketner Hall, Cannon Student Center. **Environmental Initiatives:** Center for the Environment, along with its national, regional, and community environmental outreach.The Center for the Environment at Catawba College sets us apart from other environmental programs. We offer value-added education that goes well beyond classroom teaching, providing many real-world opportunities for our students. See: http://catawba.edu/academics/schools/arts-sciences/environmental-science-studies/ The Center for the Environment

at Catawba College has assumed the leadership of the N.C. Green Schools program, a nonprofit organization that promotes sustainability in the state's schools from pre-kindergarten through 12th grade.

ADMISSIONS
Freshman Academic Profile: Average high school GPA 3.7. 11% in top 10% of high school class, 39% in top 25% of high school class, 77% in top 50% of high school class. 88% from public high schools. Minimum internet-based TOEFL 69. **Basis for Candidate Selection:** *Very important factors considered include:* academic GPA, talent/ability, character/personal qualities, geographical residence. *Important factors considered include:* rigor of secondary school record, standardized test scores, extracurricular activities, volunteer work, work experience. *Other factors considered include:* class rank, application essay, interview, first generation, alumni/ae relation, state residency, religious affiliation/commitment, racial/ethnic status, level of applicant's interest. **Freshman Admission Requirements:** High school diploma is required and GED is accepted. *Academic units required:* 4 English, 3 math, 3 science, 3 social studies. *Academic units recommended:* 2 foreign language. **Freshman Admission Statistics:** 2,528 applied, 47.07% admitted, 29% enrolled. **Transfer Admission Requirements:** High school transcript, college transcript(s), essay or personal statement, statement of good standing from prior institution(s). Minimum college GPA of 2.0 required. Lowest grade transferable C. **General Admission Information:** Priority deadline 3/1. Admission may be deferred for a maximum of 1 Year.

COSTS AND FINANCIAL AID
Annual tuition $29,920. Room and board $10,488. Required fees $0. Average book expense $1,400. **Required Forms and Deadlines:** FAFSA. **Notification of Awards:** Applicants will be notified of awards on a rolling basis beginning 3/1. **Types of Aid:** *Need-based scholarships/grants:* Federal Pell, FSEOG, State scholarships/grants, Private scholarships, College/university scholarship or grant aid from institutional funds. *Loans:* Direct Subsidized Stafford Loans, Direct Unsubsidized Stafford Loans, Direct PLUS loans, Federal Perkins Loans, State Loans, College/university loans from institutional funds. *Student Employment:* Federal Work-Study Program available. Institutional employment available. **Financial Aid Statistics:** 72% needy freshmen, 78% needy undergrads receive need-based scholarship or grant aid. 99% freshmen, 86% undergrads receive non-need-based scholarship or grant aid. 81% freshmen, 78% undergrads receive need-based self-help aid. 25% freshmen, 25% undergrads receive athletic scholarships. 99% freshmen, 99% undergrads receive any aid. 77% undergrads borrow to pay for school. Average cumulative indebtedness $30,490. **Criteria for awarding aid:** *Non-need-based:* Academics, Athletics, Leadership, Music/drama, Religious affiliation, State/district residency.

THE CATHOLIC UNIVERSITY OF AMERICA

Office of Undergraduate Admissions, Washington, DC 20064
Phone: 202-319-5305 • **Financial Aid Phone:** 202-319-5307
E-mail: cua-admissions@cua.edu • **CEEB Code:** 5104
Fax: 202-319-6533 • **Website:** www.cua.edu • **ACT Code:** 654

This private school, affiliated with the Roman Catholic Church, was founded in 1887. It has a 193-acre campus.

RATINGS
Admissions Selectivity Rating: 81   **Fire Safety Rating:** 93   **Green Rating:** 78

STUDENTS AND FACULTY
Enrollment: 2,497. **Student Body:** 55% female, 45% male, 96% out-of-state, 6% international (78 countries represented). Asian 4%, African American 6%, Caucasian 63%, Hispanic 13%, Native American <1%, Pacific Islander <1%, Two or more races 5%, Race unknown 3%.
Retention and Graduation: 84% freshmen return for sophomore year. 62% freshmen graduate within 4 years. 19% grads go on to further study within 1 year. 4% grads pursue law degrees. **Faculty:** Student/faculty ratio 7:1. 413 full-time faculty, 92% hold PhDs, 13% are are members of minority groups, 38% are women. 8% of classes are taught by teaching assistants.

ACADEMICS
Degrees: associate, bachelor's, certificate, doctoral/professional, doctoral/research, doctoral, master's, postbachelor's certificate, post-master's certificate. **Classes:** Most classes have 10-19 students. Most lab/discussion sessions have 10-19 students. **Most popular majors:** Architecture; Political Science and

Government; Registered Nursing/Registered Nurse. **Special Study Options:** Accelerated program, cross-registration, distance learning, double major, dual enrollment, English as a Second Language (ESL), honors program, independent study, internships, study abroad, teacher certification program. **Honors Programs:** The University Honors Program offers classes in the classical liberal arts and contemporary social and environmental sciences to compliment students' major studies. Students take small, rigorous, discussion-based courses from offerings in philosophy, theology, history and literature, social science, environmental science, and media studies. Students completing any of these six tracks receive distinction at graduation; students completing three tracks and a senior seminar are designated University Scholars. Special lectures, symposia, social events, and trips are organized for students in the program. Combined degree programs: BA/MA; BS/MS; BA/MS; BS/MA. **Disability Services:** Special programs offered to physically disabled students, including note-taking services, reader services, tape recorders, tutors. **Career Services:** Alumni network, Alumni services, Career assessment, Internships, Regional alumni. Through Cardinal Connection (Jobs and Internships Online), we share with students the amazing variety and quality of experiential opportunities available to them. Each year hundreds of organizations in the Washington, D.C. area and nationwide list internships and jobs that give students a chance to become involved in a range of responsibilities in politics, research, marketing, accounting, finance, public relations, computer science, engineering, architecture and arts management, to name a few. These experiences not only complement students' classroom education, they often lead to offers of full-time employment upon graduation from CUA.

FACILITIES

Housing: Coed dorms, special housing for disabled students, men's dorms, women's dorms, apartments for single students, Wellness Housing, Theme Housing, Residential college, honors community, politics and current events community, living as leaders community and social justice community. 75% of campus accessible to physically disabled. **Special Academic Facilities/ Equipment:** Facilities available on the university campus include an art department gallery; the John K. Mullen of Denver Memorial Library, which features a rare book collection containing 65,000 volumes that range from medieval documents to first editions of 20th-century authors; the university archives, which has nearly 9,000 feet of records and manuscripts; the Vitreous State Laboratory, which engages some of the world"s leading glass scientists to help research and develop methods for safe containment of disposed radioactive materials, primarily by converting nuclear waste into solid glass using vitrification techniques. In 2008, the university dedicated Opus Hall, the first LEED (Leadership in Energy and Environmental Design)-compliant residence hall among colleges and universities in Washington, D.C. The Edward J. Pryzbyla University Center includes nine meeting spaces, two separate dining facilities, a convenience store, the campus bookstore, offices, various atrium and lounge spaces and a 7,500-square-foot great room, where Pope Benedict XVI delivered a speech in April 2008. Adjacent to the campus is the Roman Catholic Basilica of the National Shrine of the Immaculate Conception, the largest church in the Western hemisphere. University Masses and commencement are held every year at the National Shrine. Directly across the street from the university is the Pope John Paul II Cultural Center, a major Catholic museum. **Computers:** 40% of classrooms, 90% of dorms, 100% of libraries, 100% of dining areas, 100% of student union, 20% of common outdoor areas have wireless network access. Students can register for classes online. Administrative functions (other than registration) can be performed online.

CAMPUS LIFE

Environment: Metropolis. **Activities:** Choral groups, dance, drama/theater, jazz band, literary magazine, music ensembles, musical theater, opera, radio station, student government, student newspaper, student-run film society, symphony orchestra, yearbook, Campus Ministries, Student Organization. 87 registered organizations, 16 honor societies, 4 religious organizations. 1 fraternity, 1 sorority. **Athletics (Intercollegiate):** *Men:* baseball, basketball, cross-country, football, lacrosse, soccer, swimming, tennis, track/field (outdoor), track/field (indoor). *Women:* basketball, cross-country, field hockey, lacrosse, soccer, softball, swimming, tennis, track/field (outdoor), track/field (indoor), volleyball. **On-Campus Highlights:** Edward J. Pryzbyla University Center, Eugene I. Kane Fitness Center, St. Vincent de Paul Chapel, Raymond A. Dufour (athletic) Center, John K. Mullen of Denver Memorial Library, Catholic University's 193 acre campus is the largest among universities in Washington, D.C. Its spacious campus setting is adjacent to a Washington Metrorail and has several campus malls for frisbee, football, softball, picnicking and sunning. **Environmental Initiatives:** LEED-NC Certified, 402 Bed Student Dormitory LEED-Silver (anticipated) Administrative Building—major renovation

ADMISSIONS

Freshman Academic Profile: Average high school GPA 3.4. 37% from public high schools. **Reported SAT (pre-2016 redesign) scores:** SAT Math middle 50% range 520-620. SAT Critical Reading middle 50% range 520-630. **Concordant SAT scores:** SAT Math middle 50% range 550–640. ACT middle 50% range 23-29. Minimum internet-based TOEFL 80. Minimum paper TOEFL 550. **Basis for Candidate Selection:** *Very important*

factors considered include: rigor of secondary school record, academic GPA, recommendation(s), character/personal qualities. *Important factors considered include:* application essay, extracurricular activities, talent/ability, first generation, volunteer work. *Other factors considered include:* class rank, standardized test scores, interview, alumni/ae relation, geographical residence, racial/ethnic status, work experience, level of applicant's interest. **Freshman Admission Requirements:** High school diploma is required and GED is accepted. *Academic units recommended:* 4 English, 3 math, 3 science, 1 science lab, 3 foreign language, 4 social studies, and 1 unit from above areas or other academic areas. **Freshman Admission Statistics:** 5,926 applied, 79.55% admitted, 15% enrolled. **Transfer Admission Requirements:** High school transcript, college transcript(s), essay or personal statement, standardized test scores, Minimum college GPA of 2.8 required. Lowest grade transferable C. **General Admission Information:** Application fee $55. Regular application deadline 1/15. Nonfall registration accepted. Admission may be deferred for a maximum of 1 year.

COSTS AND FINANCIAL AID

Annual tuition $41,800. Room and board $13,820. Required fees $736. Average book expense $838. **Required Forms and Deadlines:** FAFSA, CSS/Financial Aid PROFILE, Noncustodial PROFILE. **Notification of Awards:** Applicants will be notified of awards on a rolling basis beginning 3/20. **Types of Aid:** *Need-based scholarships/grants:* Federal Pell, FSEOG, State scholarships/grants, Private scholarships, College/university scholarship or grant aid from institutional funds. *Loans:* Direct Subsidized Stafford Loans, Direct Unsubsidized Stafford Loans, Direct PLUS loans, Federal Nursing Loans. *Student Employment:* Federal Work-Study Program available. Institutional employment available. **Financial Aid Statistics:** 98% needy freshmen, 98% needy undergrads receive need-based scholarship or grant aid. 0% undergrads receive non-need-based scholarship or grant aid. 83% freshmen, 86% undergrads receive need-based self-help aid. 0% freshmen, 0% undergrads receive athletic scholarships. 94% freshmen, 89% undergrads receive any aid. 70% undergrads borrow to pay for school. Average cumulative indebtedness $46,779. **Criteria for awarding aid:** *Need-based:* Academics. *Non-need-based:* Academics, Alumni affiliation, Music/drama, Religious affiliation.

CAZENOVIA COLLEGE

3 Sullivan Street, Cazenovia, NY 13035
Phone: 315-655-7208 • **Financial Aid Phone:** 315-655-7887
E-mail: admission@cazenovia.edu
Fax: 315-655-4860 • **Website:** www.cazenovia.edu

This private school was founded in 1824.

RATINGS

Admissions Selectivity Rating: 77   Fire Safety Rating: 99   Green Rating: 60*

STUDENTS AND FACULTY

Enrollment: 1,067. **Student Body:** 72% female, 28% male, 15% out-of-state, 0% international (3 countries represented). Asian 1%, African American 7%, Caucasian 67%, Hispanic 6%, Native American 1%, Pacific Islander <1%, Two or more races 4%, Race unknown 14%. **Retention and Graduation:** 73% freshmen return for sophomore year. 55% freshmen graduate within 4 years. 58% freshmen graduate within 6 years. 20% grads go on to further study within 1 year. **Faculty:** Student/faculty ratio 12:1. 57 full-time faculty, 77% hold PhDs, 0% are are members of minority groups, 68% are women. 0% of classes are taught by teaching assistants.

ACADEMICS

Degrees: associate, bachelor's, certificate. **Classes:** Most classes have 10-19 students. **Most popular majors:** Interior Design; Fine/Studio Arts; Business Administration, Management and Operations. **Special Study Options:** Accelerated program, double major, exchange student program (domestic), honors program, independent study, internships, student-designed major, study abroad, teacher certification program. **Honors Programs:** The All-College Honors Program at Cazenovia College offers to outstanding students in all majors (in the liberal arts and in the professional studies) a stimulating learning environment beyond that found in standard classroom coursework, and fosters their exceptional academic talents and intellectual curiosity. Demanding curriculum, independent research opportunities and co-curricular activities challenge students to achieve their full educational potential not only through encouraging academic excellence but also through promoting social responsibilities in the global community. An honors degree certifies that students have produced academic work that meets the highest standards of academic rigor in both general education and in their career field. **Disability Services:** Special programs offered to physically disabled students, including note-taking services, reader services, tape recorders, tutors. **Career Services:**

Alumni network, Alumni services, Career/job search classes, Career assessment, Internships, Regional alumni. The College's academic programs provide students the opportunity to participate in off-campus internships, often as a graduation requirement. Internships generally provide students with one of three types of experience:

° A continuation of work in a familiar field to increase student knowledge by performing tasks beyond those already mastered in this career area

° An experience intended to broaden student expertise within a career area by working in an area of that profession not previously experienced; and

° A shadowing or observational experience of a professional in a specific career field as a means of exploring a possible new career interest. Regardless of the type of experience, internships make valuable connections between the world of work and the student's academic study. Each academic program has specific eligibility requirements for internships that can be checked in the College Catalog or by contacting either the Program Director or the Director of Career Services.

FACILITIES

Housing: Coed dorms, special housing for disabled students, women's dorms, Single room suites. **Special Academic Facilities/Equipment:** Reisman Hall is a state-of-the-art Art and Design facility and gallery; 243-acre Equine Education Center; historic Catherine Cummings Theatre. **Computers:** Administrative functions (other than registration) can be performed online.

CAMPUS LIFE

Environment: Rural. **Activities:** Choral groups, dance, drama/theater, jazz band, musical theater, radio station, student government, student newspaper, student-run film society, yearbook, Campus Ministries. 54 registered organizations, 5 honor societies, 1 religious organization. **Athletics (Intercollegiate):** *Men:* baseball, basketball, cheerleading, crew/rowing, cross-country, equestrian sports, golf, horseback riding, lacrosse, soccer, swimming. *Women:* basketball, cheerleading, crew/rowing, cross-country, equestrian sports, horseback riding, lacrosse, soccer, softball, swimming, volleyball. **On-Campus Highlights:** Residence Halls, Academic Facilities—Art and Design Building, Equestrian Center, Athletic Facilities / Pool, Dining Hall. **Environmental Initiatives:** Environmental Studies education programs; Look Again program—sustainability in fashion.

ADMISSIONS

Freshman Academic Profile: Average high school GPA 3.3. 14% in top 10% of high school class, 40% in top 25% of high school class, 78% in top 50% of high school class. 90% from public high schools. **Reported SAT (pre-2016 redesign) scores:** SAT Math middle 50% range 430-530. SAT Critical Reading middle 50% range 430-540. **Concordant SAT scores:** SAT Math middle 50% range 470–560. ACT middle 50% range 19-24. Minimum paper TOEFL 550. **Basis for Candidate Selection:** *Very important factors considered include:* rigor of secondary school record, talent/ability. *Important factors considered include:* class rank, academic GPA, standardized test scores, recommendation(s), interview, extracurricular activities. *Other factors considered include:* application essay, character/personal qualities, alumni/ae relation, volunteer work, work experience, level of applicant's interest. **Freshman Admission Requirements:** High school diploma is required and GED is accepted. *Academic units recommended:* 4 English, 2 math, 2 science, 4 social studies. **Freshman Admission Statistics:** 2,382 applied, 76.20% admitted, 19% enrolled. **Transfer Admission Requirements:** High school transcript, college transcript(s), Minimum college GPA of 2.0 required. Lowest grade transferable C. **General Admission Information:** Application fee $30. Priority deadline 3/1. Nonfall registration accepted. Admission may be deferred for a maximum of 1 year.

COSTS AND FINANCIAL AID

Annual tuition $30,028. Room and board $11,880. Required fees $532. **Required Forms and Deadlines:** FAFSA, State aid form. **Notification of Awards:** Applicants will be notified of awards on a rolling basis beginning 11/1. **Types of Aid:** *Need-based scholarships/grants:* Federal Pell, FSEOG, State scholarships/grants, Private scholarships, College/university scholarship or grant aid from institutional funds. *Loans:* Direct Subsidized Stafford Loans, Direct Unsubsidized Stafford Loans, Direct PLUS loans. *Student Employment:* Federal Work-Study Program available. **Financial Aid Statistics:** 100% needy freshmen, 96% needy undergrads receive need-based scholarship or grant aid. 9% freshmen, 12% undergrads receive non-need-based scholarship or grant aid. 100% freshmen, 96% undergrads receive need-based self-help aid. 0% freshmen, 0% undergrads receive athletic scholarships. 92% freshmen, 91% undergrads receive any aid. **Criteria for awarding aid:** *Need-based:* Academics, Leadership. *Non-need-based:* Academics, Leadership.

CEDAR CREST COLLEGE

100 College Drive, Allentown, PA 18104
Phone: 610-740-3780 • **Financial Aid Phone:** 610-606-4602
E-mail: admissions@cedarcrest.edu • **CEEB Code:** 2079
Fax: 610-606-4647 • **Website:** http://www.cedarcrest.edu • **ACT Code:** 3536

This private school was founded in 1867. It has a 84-acre campus.

RATINGS

Admissions Selectivity Rating: 81   **Fire Safety Rating:** 81   **Green Rating:** 60*

STUDENTS AND FACULTY

Enrollment: 1,397. **Student Body:** 87% female, 13% male, 18% out-of-state, 10% international (22 countries represented). Asian 3%, African American 9%, Caucasian 58%, Hispanic 14%, Native American <1%, Pacific Islander <1%, Two or more races 1%, Race unknown 3%.
Retention and Graduation: 79% freshmen return for sophomore year. 40% freshmen graduate within 4 years. 56% freshmen graduate within 6 years. 65% grads go on to further study within 1 year. 55% grads pursue arts and sciences degrees. 1% grads pursue law degrees. 2% grads pursue business degrees. 3% grads pursue medical degrees. **Faculty:** Student/faculty ratio 10:1. 74 full-time faculty, 72% hold PhDs, 0% are are members of minority groups, 0% are women. 0% of classes are taught by teaching assistants.

ACADEMICS

Degrees: bachelor's, certificate, master's, postbachelor's certificate. **Classes:** Most classes have 10-19 students. Most lab/discussion sessions have 10-19 students. **Most popular majors:** Registered Nursing/Registered Nurse; Social Work; Foods, Nutrition, and Wellness Studies. **Special Study Options:** cross-registration, distance learning, double major, honors program, independent study, internships, liberal arts/career combination, student-designed major, study abroad, teacher certification program, Ethics. **Honors Programs:** Special courses reserved for Honors Students, undergraduate research opportunities, including Honors Thesis. **Disability Services:** Special programs offered to physically disabled students, including note-taking services, reader services, tape recorders, tutors. **Career Services:** Alumni network, Alumni services, Career/job search classes, Career assessment, Internships, Regional alumni. The Career Planning Center assists all departments with developing new internship/experiential education opportunities. Each freshman student is involved in an informational interview to learn more about her chosen career field. Alumnae engagement is utilized in this area to connect current students with alumnae who are in their field of interest.

FACILITIES

Housing: special housing for disabled students, women's dorms. 90% of campus accessible to physically diasbled. **Special Academic Facilities/Equipment:** Alumnae Museum **Computers:** 75% of classrooms, 85% of dorms, 100% of libraries, 85% of dining areas, 85% of student union, 50% of common outdoor areas have wireless network access. Students can register for classes online. Administrative functions (other than registration) can be performed online.

CAMPUS LIFE

Environment: City. **Activities:** Choral groups, dance, drama/theater, literary magazine, music ensembles, musical theater, radio station, student government, student newspaper, yearbook, Campus Ministries, Student Organization. 18 honor societies, 4 religious organizations. **Athletics (Intercollegiate):** *Women:* basketball, cross-country, field hockey, lacrosse, soccer, softball, tennis, volleyball. **On-Campus Highlights:** Bistro, College Center, Fitness Center, Rodale Aquatic Center **Environmental Initiatives:** Recycling: participating in national Recyclemania

ADMISSIONS

Freshman Academic Profile: Average high school GPA 3.4. 18% in top 10% of high school class, 55% in top 25% of high school class, 77% in top 50% of high school class. 84% from public high schools. **Reported SAT (pre-2016 redesign) scores:** SAT Math middle 50% range 440-540. SAT Critical Reading middle 50% range 440-550. SAT Writing middle 50% range 420-530. **Concordant SAT scores:** SAT EBRW middle 50% 480–600. SAT Math middle 50% range 480–570. ACT middle 50% range 18.75-24. Minimum internet-based TOEFL 61. Minimum paper TOEFL 500. **Basis for Candidate Selection:** *Very important factors considered include:* rigor of secondary school record, class rank, academic GPA, standardized test scores, application essay, recommendation(s). *Other factors considered include:* interview, extracurricular activities, alumni/ae relation, volunteer work, work experience. **Freshman Admission Requirements:** High school diploma is required and GED is accepted. *Academic units required:* 4 English, 3 math, 2 science, 2 science labs, 2 foreign language, 3 social studies, 3 history, 3 academic electives. **Freshman Admission Statistics:** 1,193 applied, 66.47% admitted, 23% enrolled. **Transfer Admission Requirements:** High school transcript, college transcript(s),

Minimum college GPA of 2.00 required. Lowest grade transferable C. **General Admission Information:** Application fee $30. Nonfall registration accepted.

COSTS AND FINANCIAL AID

Annual tuition $37,492. Room and board $11,208. Required fees $600. Average book expense $2,000. **Required Forms and Deadlines:** FAFSA. **Notification of Awards:** Applicants will be notified of awards on a rolling basis beginning 9/15. **Types of Aid:** *Need-based scholarships/grants:* Federal Pell, FSEOG, State scholarships/grants, Private scholarships, College/university scholarship or grant aid from institutional funds. *Loans:* Direct Subsidized Stafford Loans, Direct Unsubsidized Stafford Loans, Direct PLUS loans, Federal Perkins Loans, Federal Nursing Loans. *Student Employment:* Federal Work-Study Program available. Institutional employment available. **Financial Aid Statistics:** 100% needy freshmen, 100% needy undergrads receive need-based scholarship or grant aid. 12% freshmen, 9% undergrads receive non-need-based scholarship or grant aid. 85% freshmen, 87% undergrads receive need-based self-help aid. 0% freshmen, 0% undergrads receive athletic scholarships. 97% freshmen, 99% undergrads receive any aid. 94% undergrads borrow to pay for school. Average cumulative indebtedness $38,726. **Criteria for awarding aid:** *Non-need-based:* Academics, Alumni affiliation, Art, Music/drama.

CEDARVILLE UNIVERSITY

251 N.Main Street, Cedarville, OH 45314
Phone: 937-766-7700 • **Financial Aid Phone:** 937-766-7866
E-mail: admiss@cedarville.edu
Fax: 937-766-7575 • **Website:** www.cedarville.edu • **ACT Code:** 3245

This private school, affiliated with the Baptist Church, was founded in 1887. It has a 400-acre campus.

RATINGS

Admissions Selectivity Rating: 87   **Fire Safety Rating:** 95   **Green Rating:** 60*

STUDENTS AND FACULTY

Enrollment: 3,063. **Student Body:** 51% female, 49% male, 63% out-of-state, 2% international (35 countries represented). Asian 2%, African American 1%, Caucasian 87%, Hispanic 3%, Native American <1%, Pacific Islander 0%, Two or more races 3%, Race unknown 1%.
Retention and Graduation: 85% freshmen return for sophomore year. 59% freshmen graduate within 4 years. 72% freshmen graduate within 6 years. 18% grads go on to further study within 1 year. **Faculty:** Student/faculty ratio 13:1. 190 full-time faculty, 68% hold PhDs, 8% are are members of minority groups, 36% are women. 0% of classes are taught by teaching assistants.

ACADEMICS

Degrees: bachelor's, certificate, doctoral/professional, master's, postbachelor's certificate, post-master's certificate. **Classes:** Most classes have 10-19 students. Most lab/discussion sessions have 10-19 students. **Most popular majors:** Registered Nursing/Registered Nurse; Mechanical Engineering; Early Childhood Education and Teaching. **Special Study Options:** Accelerated program, distance learning, double major, dual enrollment, honors program, independent study, internships, student-designed major, study abroad, teacher certification program. Combined degree programs: M.B.A./Pharm.D. **Disability Services:** Special programs offered to physically disabled students, including reader services, tape recorders, tutors. **Career Services:** Alumni network, Alumni services, Career/job search classes, Career assessment, Internships, Regional alumni.

FACILITIES

Housing: men's dorms, women's dorms, apartments for married students. 85% of campus accessible to physically disabled. **Computers:** 100% of classrooms, 100% of dorms, 100% of libraries, 100% of dining areas, 100% of student union, 80% of common outdoor areas have wireless network access. Students can register for classes online. Administrative functions (other than registration) can be performed online.

CAMPUS LIFE

Environment: Rural. **Activities:** Choral groups, concert band, drama/theater, jazz band, music ensembles, musical theater, pep band, radio station, student government, student newspaper, symphony orchestra, yearbook. 74 registered organizations, 4 honor societies. **Athletics (Intercollegiate):** *Men:* baseball, basketball, cheerleading, cross-country, golf, soccer, tennis, track/field (outdoor), track/field (indoor). *Women:* basketball, cheerleading, cross-country, soccer, softball, tennis, track/field (outdoor), track/field (indoor), volleyball. **On-Campus Highlights:** Fitness and Recreation Center, The Hive—student snack shop, Dixon Ministry Center—daily chapel and concerts, Chucks—student cafeteria (popular hangout), Callan Athletic Center.

ADMISSIONS

Freshman Academic Profile: Average high school GPA 3.7. 36% in top 10% of high school class, 68% in top 25% of high school class, 90% in top 50% of high school class. 49% from public high schools. **Reported SAT (pre-2016 redesign) scores:** SAT Math middle 50% range 540-650. SAT Critical Reading middle 50% range 540-660. SAT Writing middle 50% range 520-620. **Concordant SAT scores:** SAT EBRW middle 50% 590–690. SAT Math middle 50% range 570–670. ACT middle 50% range 23-29. Minimum internet-based TOEFL 80. Minimum paper TOEFL 550. **Basis for Candidate Selection:** *Very important factors considered include:* rigor of secondary school record, academic GPA, standardized test scores, recommendation(s), character/personal qualities. *Important factors considered include:* class rank, application essay, alumni/ae relation, religious affiliation/commitment, racial/ethnic status, level of applicant's interest. *Other factors considered include:* extracurricular activities, talent/ability, first generation, geographical residence, state residency, volunteer work, work experience. **Freshman Admission Requirements:** High school diploma is required and GED is accepted. *Academic units recommended:* 4 English, 2 science labs, 3 foreign language, 2 social studies, 2 history. **Freshman Admission Statistics:** 4,092 applied, 69.06% admitted, 27% enrolled. **Transfer Admission Requirements:** High school transcript, college transcript(s), essay or personal statement, statement of good standing from prior institution(s). Minimum college GPA of 3.0 required. Lowest grade transferable C-. **General Admission Information:** Application fee $30. Priority deadline 11/1. Regular application deadline 8/1. Nonfall registration accepted. Admission may be deferred for a maximum of 1 year.

COSTS AND FINANCIAL AID

Annual tuition $28,956. Room and board $7,088. Required fees $200. Average book expense $1,220. **Required Forms and Deadlines:** FAFSA. **Notification of Awards:** Applicants will be notified of awards on a rolling basis beginning 3/1. **Types of Aid:** *Need-based scholarships/grants:* Federal Pell, FSEOG, State scholarships/grants, Private scholarships, College/university scholarship or grant aid from institutional funds, Federal Nursing Scholarships. *Loans:* Direct Subsidized Stafford Loans, Direct Unsubsidized Stafford Loans, Direct PLUS loans, Federal Perkins Loans, Federal Nursing Loans, College/university loans from institutional funds. *Student Employment:* Federal Work-Study Program available. Institutional employment available. **Financial Aid Statistics:** 86% needy freshmen, 85% needy undergrads receive need-based scholarship or grant aid. 94% freshmen, 91% undergrads receive non-need-based scholarship or grant aid. 86% freshmen, 89% undergrads receive need-based self-help aid. 7% freshmen, 7% undergrads receive athletic scholarships. 100% freshmen, 100% undergrads receive any aid. 61% undergrads borrow to pay for school. Average cumulative indebtedness $29,454. **Criteria for awarding aid:** *Need-based:* Academics. *Non-need-based:* Academics, Athletics, Minority status, Music/drama.

CENTENARY COLLEGE

400 Jefferson Street, Hackettstown, NJ 7840
Phone: 800-236-8679 • **Financial Aid Phone:** 1-800-236-8679
E-mail: admissions@centenarycollege.edu • **CEEB Code:** 2080
Fax: 908-852-3454 • **Website:** www.centenarycollege.edu • **ACT Code:** 2544

This private school, affiliated with the Methodist Church, was founded in 1867. It has a 42-acre campus.

RATINGS

Admissions Selectivity Rating: 73   **Fire Safety Rating:** 60*   **Green Rating:** 60*

STUDENTS AND FACULTY

Enrollment: 1,199. **Student Body:** 60% female, 40% male, 20% out-of-state, 5% international (17 countries represented). Asian 1%, African American 10%, Caucasian 60%, Hispanic 9%, Native American 1%, Pacific Islander 0%, Two or more races 1%, Race unknown 13%.
Retention and Graduation: 71% freshmen return for sophomore year. 56% freshmen graduate within 4 years. 57% freshmen graduate within 6 years. 18% grads go on to further study within 1 year. 8% grads pursue arts and sciences degrees. 8% grads pursue business degrees. **Faculty:** Student/faculty ratio 17:1. 79 full-time faculty, 62% hold PhDs, 8% are are members of minority groups, 54% are women. 0% of classes are taught by teaching assistants.

ACADEMICS

Degrees: associate, bachelor's, master's, postbachelor's certificate, terminal, transfer. **Classes:** Most classes have 10-19 students. Most lab/discussion sessions have 10-19 students. **Most popular majors:** Elementary Education and Teaching; Business Administration and Management; Criminal Justice/Police Science. **Special Study Options:** Accelerated program, cross-registration, distance learning, double major, dual enrollment, English as a Second Language (ESL), exchange student program (domestic), honors program, independent study, internships, liberal arts/career combination, student-designed major, study abroad, teacher certification program, weekend college. **Disability Services:** Special programs offered to physically disabled students, including note-taking services, reader services, tutors. **Career Services:** Alumni network, Alumni services, Career/job search classes, Career assessment, Internships, Regional alumni.

FACILITIES

Housing: Coed dorms, apartments for single students. 70% of campus accessible to physically diasbled. **Special Academic Facilities/Equipment:** Art gallery, radio station WNTI 91.9FM, equity-status theater, equestrian center. **Computers:** 100% of classrooms, 100% of dorms, 100% of libraries, 100% of dining areas, 100% of student union, 100% of common outdoor areas have wireless network access. Students can register for classes online. Administrative functions (other than registration) can be performed online. Undergraduates are required to own a computer.

CAMPUS LIFE

Environment: Town. **Activities:** Choral groups, dance, drama/theater, literary magazine, music ensembles, musical theater, radio station, student government, student newspaper, student-run film society, television station, yearbook, Campus Ministries, Student Organization, Model UN. 30 registered organizations, 2 honor societies, 2 fraternities, 3 sororities. **Athletics (Intercollegiate):** *Men:* baseball, basketball, cross-country, golf, lacrosse, soccer, wrestling. *Women:* basketball, cross-country, golf, lacrosse, soccer, softball, volleyball. **On-Campus Highlights:** Reeves Athletic Facility, Bennett Smith Dormitory, Tilly's Cafe, Library, Cyber Cafe.

ADMISSIONS

Freshman Academic Profile: Average high school GPA 3.0. 11% in top 10% of high school class, 28% in top 25% of high school class, 55% in top 50% of high school class. 85% from public high schools. **Reported SAT (pre-2016 redesign) scores:** SAT Math middle 50% range 410-550. SAT Critical Reading middle 50% range 410-540. SAT Writing middle 50% range 400-540. **Concordant SAT scores:** SAT EBRW middle 50% 450–600. SAT Math middle 50% range 450–570. ACT middle 50% range 18-23. Minimum paper TOEFL 450. **Basis for Candidate Selection:** *Very important factors considered include:* rigor of secondary school record, academic GPA, standardized test scores. *Important factors considered include:* application essay, recommendation(s), interview, extracurricular activities. *Other factors considered include:* class rank, talent/ability, character/personal qualities, alumni/ae relation, religious affiliation/commitment, volunteer work, work experience, level of applicant's interest. **Freshman Admission Requirements:** High school diploma is required and GED is accepted. *Academic units required:* 4 English, 3 math, 2 science, 1 science lab. *Academic units recommended:* 4 English, 4 math, 3 science, 1 science lab, 2 foreign language, 4 social studies. **Freshman Admission Statistics:** 1,038 applied, 90.94% admitted, 22% enrolled. **Transfer Admission Requirements:** High school transcript, college transcript(s), essay or personal statement, Minimum college GPA of 2.0 required. Lowest grade transferable C-. **General Admission Information:** Application fee $30. Priority deadline 3/1. Nonfall registration accepted. Admission may be deferred for a maximum of 1 semester.

COSTS AND FINANCIAL AID

Annual tuition $15,700. Room and board $6,850. Required fees $1,100. Average book expense $666. **Required Forms and Deadlines:** FAFSA. **Notification of Awards:** Applicants will be notified of awards on a rolling basis beginning 3/15. **Types of Aid:** *Need-based scholarships/grants:* Federal Pell, FSEOG, State scholarships/grants, Private scholarships, College/university scholarship or grant aid from institutional funds. *Loans:* Federal Perkins Loans, State Loans. *Student Employment:* Federal Work-Study Program available. Institutional employment available. **Financial Aid Statistics:** 100% needy freshmen, 99% needy undergrads receive need-based scholarship or grant aid. 10% freshmen, 7% undergrads receive non-need-based scholarship or grant aid. 90% freshmen, 92% undergrads receive need-based self-help aid. 0% freshmen, 0% undergrads receive athletic scholarships. 98% freshmen receive any aid. **Criteria for awarding aid:** *Non-need-based:* Academics, Alumni affiliation, Art, Leadership, Minority status, Music/drama, Religious affiliation, State/district residency.

CENTENARY COLLEGE OF LOUISIANA

P.O. Box 41188, Shreveport, LA 71134-1188
Phone: 318-869-5131 • **Financial Aid Phone:** 318-869-5137
E-mail: admissions@centenary.edu
Fax: 318-869-5005 • **Website:** www.centenary.edu • **ACT Code:** 1576

This private school, affiliated with the Methodist Church, was founded in 1825. It has a 68-acre campus.

RATINGS
Admissions Selectivity Rating: 85   **Fire Safety Rating:** 78   **Green Rating:** 60*

STUDENTS AND FACULTY

Enrollment: 520. **Student Body:** 56% female, 44% male, 42% out-of-state, 2% international (5 countries represented). Asian 3%, African American 35%, Caucasian 48%, Hispanic 6%, Native American 1%, Pacific Islander <1%, Two or more races 5%, Race unknown 0%.
Retention and Graduation: 74% freshmen return for sophomore year. 46% freshmen graduate within 4 years. 55% freshmen graduate within 6 years.
Faculty: Student/faculty ratio 8:1. 57 full-time faculty, 96% hold PhDs, 9% are are members of minority groups, 37% are women. 0% of classes are taught by teaching assistants.

ACADEMICS

Degrees: bachelor's, master's. **Classes:** Most classes have 10-19 students. Most lab/discussion sessions have 10-19 students. **Most popular majors:** Biology/Biological Sciences; Psychology; Business Administration and Management. **Special Study Options:** cross-registration, double major, dual enrollment, exchange student program (domestic), honors program, independent study, internships, liberal arts/career combination, student-designed major, study abroad, teacher certification program, weekend college, 3/2 Dual Degree (Liberal Arts/Engineering) program in cooperation with Case Western Reserve University, Columbia University, Texas A and M University, University of Southern California, and Washington University in St. Louis; Mathematics/Computer Science double degree program with Southern Methodist University; Semester in Washington D.C.; British Studies at Oxford summer program. **Disability Services:** Special programs offered to physically disabled students, including note-taking services, reader services, tape recorders, tutors. **Career Services:** Alumni services, Career/job search classes, Career assessment, Internships. Both Service Learning and Intercultural Experience expose students to people and places quite different from their own and help them appreciate and understand human diversity.

FACILITIES

Housing: Coed dorms, women's dorms, fraternity/sorority housing. 95% of campus accessible to physically diasbled. **Special Academic Facilities/Equipment:** Art museum, Art Center, art studios, theatre, performance and practice organs, piano lab, language lab, School of Music recording studio, Science Hall multimedia auditorium **Computers:** 50% of classrooms, 25% of dorms, 50% of libraries, 100% of dining areas, 50% of student union, 10% of common outdoor areas have wireless network access. Students can register for classes online. Administrative functions (other than registration) can be performed online.

CAMPUS LIFE

Environment: Metropolis. **Activities:** Choral groups, concert band, dance, drama/theater, jazz band, literary magazine, music ensembles, musical theater, opera, radio station, student government, student newspaper, student-run film society, yearbook, Campus Ministries, Student Organization. 58 registered organizations, 15 honor societies, 8 religious organizations. 5 fraternities, 2 sororities. **Athletics (Intercollegiate):** *Men:* baseball, basketball, cross-country, golf, soccer, swimming, tennis. *Women:* basketball, cross-country, golf, gymnastics, soccer, softball, swimming, tennis, volleyball. **On-Campus Highlights:** Fitness Center, Jones-Rice Field, Student Union Building, Anderson Choral Building, Gold Dome, Peavy Climbing Tower, Anderson Choral Building, Crumley Gardens Aboretum, Feazel Instrumental Hall.

ADMISSIONS

Freshman Academic Profile: Average high school GPA 3.5. **Reported SAT (pre-2016 redesign) scores:** SAT Math middle 50% range 490-610. SAT Critical Reading middle 50% range 490-590. **Concordant SAT scores:** SAT Math middle 50% range 520–630. ACT middle 50% range 21-28. Minimum paper TOEFL 550. **Basis for Candidate Selection:** *Very important* factors considered include: rigor of secondary school record, academic GPA, standardized test scores, application essay. *Important factors considered include:* class rank, recommendation(s), extracurricular activities, volunteer work. *Other factors considered include:* interview, talent/ability, character/personal qualities, alumni/ae relation, work experience. **Freshman Admission Requirements:** High school diploma is required and GED is accepted. *Academic units recommended:* 4 English, 3 math, 3 science, 2 foreign language, 3 social studies. **Freshman Admission Statistics:** 747 applied, 67.07% admitted, 31% enrolled. **Transfer Admission Requirements:** High school transcript, college transcript(s), essay or personal statement, statement of good standing from prior institution(s). Minimum college GPA of 2.0 required. Lowest grade transferable C. **General Admission Information:** Priority deadline 2/15. Regular application deadline 8/1. Regular notification 4/1. Nonfall registration accepted.

COSTS AND FINANCIAL AID
Annual tuition $35,430. Required fees $100. Average book expense $1,200. **Required Forms and Deadlines:** FAFSA. **Notification of Awards:** Applicants will be notified of awards on a rolling basis beginning 3/15. **Types of Aid:** *Need-based scholarships/grants:* Federal Pell, FSEOG, State scholarships/grants, Private scholarships, College/university scholarship or grant aid from institutional funds. *Loans:* Direct Subsidized Stafford Loans, Direct Unsubsidized Stafford Loans, Direct PLUS loans, Federal Perkins Loans. *Student Employment:* Federal Work-Study Program available. Institutional employment available. **Financial Aid Statistics:** 100% needy freshmen, 100% needy undergrads receive need-based scholarship or grant aid. 70% freshmen, 74% undergrads receive non-need-based scholarship or grant aid. 63% freshmen, 71% undergrads receive need-based self-help aid. 0% freshmen, 0% undergrads receive athletic scholarships. 100% freshmen, 99% undergrads receive any aid. 68% undergrads borrow to pay for school. Average cumulative indebtedness $25,770. **Criteria for awarding aid:** *Non-need-based:* Academics, Alumni affiliation, Art, Music/drama, Religious affiliation, State/district residency.

CENTRAL COLLEGE

812 University Street, Pella, IA 50219-1999
Phone: 641-628-5286 • **Financial Aid Phone:** 641-628-5336
E-mail: admission@central.edu • **CEEB Code:** 6087
Fax: 641-628-5983 • **Website:** www.central.edu • **ACT Code:** 1284

This private school, affiliated with the Reformed Church Church, was founded in 1853. It has a 133-acre campus.

RATINGS
Admissions Selectivity Rating: 83   **Fire Safety Rating:** 89   **Green Rating:** 60*

STUDENTS AND FACULTY
Enrollment: 1,225. **Student Body:** 52% female, 48% male, 21% out-of-state, <1% international (6 countries represented). Asian 1%, African American 2%, Caucasian 87%, Hispanic 4%, Native American <1%, Pacific Islander <1%, Two or more races 1%, Race unknown 3%.
Retention and Graduation: 78% freshmen return for sophomore year. 60% freshmen graduate within 4 years. 67% freshmen graduate within 6 years. 27% grads go on to further study within 1 year. 17% grads pursue arts and sciences degrees. 2% grads pursue law degrees. 2% grads pursue business degrees. 4% grads pursue medical degrees. **Faculty:** Student/faculty ratio 12:1. 100 full-time faculty, 88% hold PhDs, 12% are are members of minority groups, 45% are women. 0% of classes are taught by teaching assistants.

ACADEMICS
Degrees: bachelor's. **Classes:** Most classes have 10-19 students. Most lab/discussion sessions have 10-19 students. **Most popular majors:** Business/Commerce; Biology/Biological Sciences; Exercise Physiology. **Special Study Options:** double major, English as a Second Language (ESL), honors program, independent study, internships, liberal arts/career combination, student-designed major, study abroad, teacher certification program, Off-Campus Study: Washington, DC,Chicago Metro Program. Study abroad in nine countries. Exploring Student Program encourages two years of multidisciplinary study before selecting a major. **Honors Programs:** The entire 4-year Honors program is outstanding Combined degree programs: Nursing and Chiropractic. **Disability Services:** Special programs offered to physically disabled students, including note-taking services, reader services, tape recorders, tutors. **Career Services:** Alumni network, Alumni services, Career/job search classes, Career assessment, Internships, Regional alumni. Experiential learning. Central College has been named to the President's Higher Education Community Service Honor Roll With Distinction for four consecutive years, the only school in Iowa to do so.

FACILITIES
Housing: Coed dorms, special housing for disabled students, men's dorms, special housing for international students, women's dorms, fraternity/sorority housing, apartments for married students, apartments for single students. 95% of campus accessible to physically diasbled. **Special Academic Facilities/Equipment:** Art gallery, center for communication and theatre, music center, language lab, glass-blowing studio. **Computers:** Students can register for classes online. Administrative functions (other than registration) can be performed online.

CAMPUS LIFE
Environment: Village. **Activities:** Choral groups, concert band, drama/theater, jazz band, literary magazine, music ensembles, musical theater, radio station, student government, student newspaper, symphony orchestra, yearbook. 50 registered organizations, 4 religious organizations. 4 fraternities, 2 sororities. **Athletics (Intercollegiate):** *Men:* baseball, basketball, football, golf, soccer, tennis, track/field (outdoor), track/field (indoor), wrestling. *Women:* basketball, cross-country, golf, softball, tennis, track/field (outdoor), track/field (indoor), volleyball.

ADMISSIONS
Freshman Academic Profile: Average high school GPA 3.6. 23% in top 10% of high school class, 54% in top 25% of high school class, 85% in top 50% of high school class. 95% from public high schools. **Reported SAT (pre-2016 redesign) scores:** SAT Math middle 50% range 470-600. SAT Critical Reading middle 50% range 410-560. **Concordant SAT scores:** SAT Math middle 50% range 510–620. ACT middle 50% range 20-26. Minimum internet-based TOEFL 71. Minimum paper TOEFL 530. **Basis for Candidate Selection:** *Very important factors considered include:* rigor of secondary school record, academic GPA, standardized test scores. *Important factors considered include:* class rank. *Other factors considered include:* application essay, recommendation(s), interview, extracurricular activities, talent/ability, character/personal qualities, first generation, alumni/ae relation, volunteer work, work experience, level of applicant's interest. **Freshman Admission Requirements:** High school diploma is required and GED is accepted. *Academic units recommended:* 4 English, 2 math, 2 science, 2 science labs, 2 foreign language, 3 social studies. **Freshman Admission Statistics:** 3,071 applied, 64.28% admitted, 16% enrolled. **Transfer Admission Requirements:** High school transcript, college transcript(s), standardized test scores, statement of good standing from prior institution(s). Minimum college GPA of 2.5 required. Lowest grade transferable C-. **General Admission Information:** Application fee $25. Regular application deadline 8/15. Nonfall registration accepted. Admission may be deferred for a maximum of 1 year.

COSTS AND FINANCIAL AID
Required Forms and Deadlines: FAFSA. **Notification of Awards:** Applicants will be notified of awards on a rolling basis beginning 3/1. **Types of Aid:** *Need-based scholarships/grants:* Federal Pell, FSEOG, State scholarships/grants, Private scholarships, College/university scholarship or grant aid from institutional funds. *Loans:* Direct Subsidized Stafford Loans, Direct Unsubsidized Stafford Loans, Direct PLUS loans, Federal Perkins Loans, College/university loans from institutional funds. *Student Employment:* Federal Work-Study Program available. Institutional employment available. **Financial Aid Statistics:** 100% needy freshmen, 100% needy undergrads receive need-based scholarship or grant aid. 83% freshmen, 12% undergrads receive non-need-based scholarship or grant aid. 100% freshmen, 89% undergrads receive need-based self-help aid. 0% freshmen, 0% undergrads receive athletic scholarships. 100% freshmen, 99% undergrads receive any aid. 78% undergrads borrow to pay for school. Average cumulative indebtedness $37,169. **Criteria for awarding aid:** *Need-based:* Academics, Minority status, Music/drama. *Non-need-based:* Academics, Alumni affiliation, Art, Minority status, Music/drama, Religious affiliation, State/district residency.

CENTRAL CONNECTICUT STATE UNIVERSITY

1615 Stanley Street, New Britain, CT 6050
Phone: 860-832-2278 • **Financial Aid Phone:** 860-832-2200
E-mail: admissions@ccsu.edu • **CEEB Code:** 3898
Fax: 862-832-2295 • **Website:** www.ccsu.edu • **ACT Code:** 596

This public school was founded in 1849. It has a 294-acre campus.

RATINGS
Admissions Selectivity Rating: 78   **Fire Safety Rating:** 92   **Green Rating:** 81

STUDENTS AND FACULTY
Enrollment: 9,269. **Student Body:** 46% female, 54% male, 4% out-of-state, 2% international (16 countries represented). Asian 4%, African American 12%,

Caucasian 63%, Hispanic 14%, Native American <1%, Pacific Islander <1%, Two or more races 3%, Race unknown 3%.
Retention and Graduation: 78% freshmen return for sophomore year. 21% freshmen graduate within 4 years. 54% freshmen graduate within 6 years. **Faculty:** Student/faculty ratio 15:1. 446 full-time faculty, 87% hold PhDs, 22% are are members of minority groups, 42% are women. 0% of classes are taught by teaching assistants.

ACADEMICS
Degrees: bachelor's, certificate, doctoral/research, master's, postbachelor's certificate, post-master's certificate. **Classes:** Most classes have 20-29 students. Most lab/discussion sessions have fewer than 10 students. **Most popular majors:** Accounting; Psychology; Criminology. **Special Study Options:** cooperative education program, cross-registration, distance learning, double major, dual enrollment, English as a Second Language (ESL), exchange student program (domestic), honors program, independent study, internships, student-designed major, study abroad, teacher certification program, Undergrads may take grad classes. Co-Op programs: Arts, Business, Computer Science, Education, Humanities, Natural Science, Social/Behavioral Science, Technologies. **Honors Programs:** Interdisciplinary writing/reading program for undergraduates with strong academic skills. Areas of study: Western Culture, Science and Society, and World Culture, capstone honors thesis in junior year. Scholarship available. **Disability Services:** Special programs offered to physically disabled students, including note-taking services, reader services, tape recorders, tutors. **Career Services:** Alumni services, Career/job search classes, Career assessment, Internships. Cooperative learning in the form of cooperative education

FACILITIES
Housing: Coed dorms, women's dorms. 95% of campus accessible to physically diasbled. **Special Academic Facilities/Equipment:** Art gallery, language lab, childhood center, planetarium and space science center, center for economic education, TV studio. **Computers:** 50% of classrooms, 100% of libraries, 100% of dining areas, 100% of student union, 50% of common outdoor areas have wireless network access. Students can register for classes online. Administrative functions (other than registration) can be performed online.

CAMPUS LIFE
Environment: Town. **Activities:** Choral groups, concert band, dance, drama/theater, jazz band, literary magazine, music ensembles, musical theater, radio station, student government, student newspaper, student-run film society, television station, yearbook, Student Organization. 101 registered organizations, 18 honor societies, 5 religious organizations. 1 sororities. **Athletics (Intercollegiate):** *Men:* baseball, basketball, cross-country, football, golf, soccer, track/field (outdoor), track/field (indoor). *Women:* basketball, cross-country, diving, golf, lacrosse, soccer, softball, swimming, track/field (outdoor), track/field (indoor), volleyball. **On-Campus Highlights:** Student Center, Cafeteria, Memorial Hall, Torp Theatre, Davidson Hall, Vance Academic Center, Vance Hall, James Hall (Residence Hall), Semesters, Student Center. **Environmental Initiatives:** Fuel cell Class schedule for carpool ease Building use in summer

ADMISSIONS
Freshman Academic Profile: Average high school GPA 3.1. 9% in top 10% of high school class, 32% in top 25% of high school class, 69% in top 50% of high school class. 95% from public high schools. **Reported SAT (pre-2016 redesign) scores:** SAT Math middle 50% range 450-550. SAT Critical Reading middle 50% range 450-550. SAT Writing middle 50% range 450-550. **Concordant SAT scores:** SAT EBRW middle 50% 500–610. SAT Math middle 50% range 490–570. ACT middle 50% range 19-24. Minimum paper TOEFL 500. **Basis for Candidate Selection:** *Very important factors considered include:* rigor of secondary school record, class rank, academic GPA, standardized test scores, recommendation(s). *Other factors considered include:* application essay, interview, extracurricular activities, talent/ability, first generation, alumni/ae relation, geographical residence, state residency, racial/ethnic status, level of applicant's interest. **Freshman Admission Requirements:** High school diploma is required and GED is accepted. *Academic units required:* 4 English, 3 math, 2 science, 1 science lab, 2 social studies, 1 history. *Academic units recommended:* 3 foreign language. **Freshman Admission Statistics:** 7,810 applied, 60.01% admitted, 27% enrolled. **Transfer Admission Requirements:** High school transcript, college transcript(s), statement of good standing from prior institution(s). Minimum college GPA of 2.0 required. Lowest grade transferable C. **General Admission Information:** Application fee $50. Priority deadline 10/15. Regular application deadline 6/1. Nonfall registration accepted. Admission may be deferred.

COSTS AND FINANCIAL AID
Annual in-state tuition $5,216. Annual out-of-state tuition $16,882. Room and board $11,462. Required fees $4,525. Average book expense $1,300. **Required Forms and Deadlines:** FAFSA. **Notification of Awards:** Applicants will be notified of awards on a rolling basis beginning 3/30. **Types of Aid:** *Need-based scholarships/grants:* Federal Pell, FSEOG, State scholarships/grants, College/university scholarship or grant aid from institutional funds. *Loans:*

Direct Subsidized Stafford Loans, Direct Unsubsidized Stafford Loans, Direct PLUS loans, Federal Perkins Loans. *Student Employment:* Federal Work-Study Program available. Institutional employment available. **Financial Aid Statistics:** 75% needy freshmen, 65% needy undergrads receive need-based scholarship or grant aid. 14% freshmen, 15% undergrads receive non-need-based scholarship or grant aid. 74% freshmen, 78% undergrads receive need-based self-help aid. 2% freshmen, 4% undergrads receive athletic scholarships. 64% freshmen, 65% undergrads receive any aid. 74% undergrads borrow to pay for school. Average cumulative indebtedness $28,016. **Criteria for awarding aid:** *Non-need-based:* Academics, Alumni affiliation, Athletics.

See page 934.

CENTRAL MICHIGAN UNIVERSITY

102 Warriner Hall, Mount Pleasant, MI 48859
Phone: 989-774-3076 • **Financial Aid Phone:** 888-392-0007
E-mail: cmuadmit@cmich.edu • **CEEB Code:** 1106
Fax: 989-774-7267 • **Website:** www.cmich.edu • **ACT Code:** 1972

This public school was founded in 1892. It has a 854-acre campus.

RATINGS
Admissions Selectivity Rating: 78 | **Fire Safety Rating:** 93 | **Green Rating:** 91

STUDENTS AND FACULTY
Enrollment: 19,551. **Student Body:** 56% female, 44% male, 5% out-of-state, 2% international (56 countries represented). Asian 1%, African American 9%, Caucasian 78%, Hispanic 4%, Native American 1%, Pacific Islander <1%, Two or more races 4%, Race unknown 2%.
Retention and Graduation: 77% freshmen return for sophomore year. 22% freshmen graduate within 4 years. 57% freshmen graduate within 6 years. 16% grads go on to further study within 1 year. 26% grads pursue arts and sciences degrees. 5% grads pursue business degrees. **Faculty:** Student/faculty ratio 22:1. 608 full-time faculty, 96% hold PhDs, 23% are are members of minority groups, 42% are women. 5% of classes are taught by teaching assistants.

ACADEMICS
Degrees: bachelor's, doctoral/professional, doctoral/research, doctoral, master's, postbachelor's certificate, post-master's certificate. **Classes:** Most classes have 20-29 students. Most lab/discussion sessions have 10-19 students. **Most popular majors:** Kinesiology and Exercise Science; Psychology; Marketing/Marketing Management. **Special Study Options:** Accelerated program, distance learning, double major, dual enrollment, English as a Second Language (ESL), honors program, independent study, internships, student-designed major, study abroad, teacher certification program, Leadership Institute: The Central Michigan University Leadership Institute, which features a four-year leadership development program, an academic minor, and a scholarship cohort that includes a residential experience, s the premier center for leadership education, training, and development in the Midwest. **Honors Programs:** The Honors Program, Centralis Program Combined degree programs: BA/MA, 8 Accelerated Masters Degree Programs. **Disability Services:** Special programs offered to physically disabled students, including note-taking services, reader services, tape recorders, tutors. **Career Services:** Alumni network, Alumni services, Career/job search classes, Career assessment, Internships, Regional alumni. 85% of undergraduates complete Internships.

FACILITIES
Housing: Coed dorms, special housing for disabled students, men's dorms, special housing for international students, women's dorms, fraternity/sorority housing, apartments for married students, apartments for single students, Theme Housing, Residential Colleges: areas of residence halls designated for students with the same majors or academic interests. 99% of campus accessible to physically diasbled. **Special Academic Facilities/Equipment:** Clarke Historical Library, Central Michigan University Museum of Cultural and Natural History, Gerald L. Poor School Museum, Brooks Astronomical Observatory, University Art Gallery, University Theater, Public Broadcasting, Student Activity Center, Charles V. Park Library, body scanner **Computers:** 100% of classrooms, 100% of dorms, 100% of libraries, 100% of dining areas, 100% of student union, have wireless network access. Students can register for classes online. Administrative functions (other than registration) can be performed online.

CAMPUS LIFE
Environment: Town. **Activities:** Choral groups, concert band, dance, drama/theater, jazz band, literary magazine, marching band, music ensembles, musical theater, pep band, radio station, student government, student newspaper, student-run film society, television station, yearbook, Campus Ministries, Student Organization. 150 registered organizations, 6 honor

societies, 12 religious organizations. 15 fraternities, 15 sororities. **Athletics (Intercollegiate):** *Men:* baseball, basketball, cross-country, football, track/field (outdoor), track/field (indoor), wrestling. *Women:* basketball, cross-country, field hockey, gymnastics, soccer, softball, track/field (outdoor), track/field (indoor), volleyball. **On-Campus Highlights:** Education Building (2009), Student Activity Center, Bovee University Center, Park Library, Academic Buildings. **Environmental Initiatives:** Campus Sustainability Advisory Committee.

ADMISSIONS

Freshman Academic Profile: Average high school GPA 3.4. 14% in top 10% of high school class, 39% in top 25% of high school class, 74% in top 50% of high school class. 92% from public high schools. **Reported SAT (pre-2016 redesign) scores:** SAT Math middle 50% range 440-570. SAT Critical Reading middle 50% range 450-570. SAT Writing middle 50% range 460-560. **Concordant SAT scores:** SAT EBRW middle 50% 510–620. SAT Math middle 50% range 480–590. ACT middle 50% range 20-25. **Basis for Candidate Selection:** *Very important factors considered include:* rigor of secondary school record, academic GPA, standardized test scores. *Important factors considered include:* class rank, talent/ability. *Other factors considered include:* application essay, recommendation(s), interview, extracurricular activities, character/personal qualities, alumni/ae relation, geographical residence, volunteer work, work experience, level of applicant's interest. **Freshman Admission Requirements:** High school diploma is required and GED is accepted. *Academic units recommended:* 4 English, 4 math, 4 science, 1 science lab, 2 foreign language, 2 social studies, 2 history, 1 computer science, 2 visual/performing arts. **Freshman Admission Statistics:** 18,875 applied, 72.02% admitted, 25% enrolled. **Transfer Admission Requirements:** college transcript(s), statement of good standing from prior institution(s). Minimum college GPA of 2.00 required. Lowest grade transferable C-. **General Admission Information:** Application fee $35. Priority deadline 10/1. Regular application deadline 7/1. Nonfall registration accepted. Admission may be deferred for a maximum of 1 year.

COSTS AND FINANCIAL AID

Annual in-state tuition $12,150. Annual out-of-state tuition $23,670. Room and board $9,406. Required fees $0. Average book expense $1,000. **Required Forms and Deadlines:** FAFSA. **Notification of Awards:** Applicants will be notified of awards on a rolling basis beginning 3/31. **Types of Aid:** *Need-based scholarships/grants:* Federal Pell, FSEOG, State scholarships/grants, Private scholarships, College/university scholarship or grant aid from institutional funds. *Loans:* Direct Subsidized Stafford Loans, Direct Unsubsidized Stafford Loans, Direct PLUS loans, Federal Perkins Loans, College/university loans from institutional funds. *Student Employment:* Federal Work-Study Program available. Institutional employment available. **Financial Aid Statistics:** 88% needy freshmen, 77% needy undergrads receive need-based scholarship or grant aid. 10% freshmen, 6% undergrads receive non-need-based scholarship or grant aid. 76% freshmen, 85% undergrads receive need-based self-help aid. 1% freshmen, 1% undergrads receive athletic scholarships. 89% freshmen, 84% undergrads receive any aid. 70% undergrads borrow to pay for school. Average cumulative indebtedness $33,480. **Criteria for awarding aid:** *Need-based:* Leadership. *Non-need-based:* Academics, Alumni affiliation, Art, Athletics, Leadership, Minority status, Music/drama, State/district residency.

CENTRAL OHIO TECHNICAL COLLEGE

1179 University Drive, Newark, OH 43055
Phone: 740-366-9494
E-mail: cotcadmissions@cotc.edu
Fax: 740-366-9290 • **Website:** www.cotc.edu

RATINGS

Admissions Selectivity Rating: 60*   **Fire Safety Rating:** 60*   **Green Rating:** 60*

STUDENTS AND FACULTY

Enrollment: 3,513. **Student Body:** 71% female, 29% male, 1% out-of-state, 0% international. Asian 1%, African American 9%, Caucasian 82%, Hispanic 1%, Native American <1%, Pacific Islander <1%, Two or more races 2%, Race unknown 4%.

ACADEMICS

Degrees: associate, certificate.

ADMISSIONS

General Admission Information: Application fee $20. Nonfall registration accepted.

COSTS AND FINANCIAL AID

Annual in-state tuition $4,200. Annual out-of-state tuition $6,960. Average book expense $1,800. *Student Employment:* Federal Work-Study Program available. Institutional employment available.

CENTRAL STATE UNIVERSITY

PO Box 1004, Wilberforce, OH 45384
Phone: 937-376-6348
E-mail: admissions@centralstate.edu • **CEEB Code:** 1107
Fax: 937-376-6648 • **Website:** www.centralstate.edu • **ACT Code:** 3246

This public school was founded in 1887. It has a 60-acre campus.

RATINGS

Admissions Selectivity Rating: 78   **Fire Safety Rating:** 60*   **Green Rating:** 60*

STUDENTS AND FACULTY

Enrollment: 1,701. **Student Body:** 55% female, 45% male, 45% out-of-state, 1% international. Asian 0%, African American 94%, Caucasian 1%, Hispanic 1%, Native American <1%, Pacific Islander 0%, Two or more races 1%, Race unknown 2%.
Retention and Graduation: 40% freshmen return for sophomore year. 9% freshmen graduate within 4 years. 26% freshmen graduate within 6 years. 32% grads go on to further study within 1 year. 50% grads pursue arts and sciences degrees. 7% grads pursue law degrees. 29% grads pursue business degrees. **Faculty:** Student/faculty ratio 13:1. 97 full-time faculty, 74% hold PhDs, 78% are are members of minority groups, 36% are women.

ACADEMICS

Degrees: bachelor's, master's. **Classes:** Most classes have 20-29 students. Most lab/discussion sessions have 10-19 students. **Special Study Options:** cooperative education program, cross-registration, double major, honors program, independent study, internships, study abroad, teacher certification program. **Disability Services:** Special programs offered to physically disabled students, including note-taking services, reader services, tape recorders, tutors. **Career Services:** Alumni services, Career/job search classes, Career assessment, Internships, Regional alumni.

FACILITIES

Housing: Coed dorms, men's dorms, women's dorms. 1% of campus accessible to physically diasbled. **Special Academic Facilities/Equipment:** National Afro-American Museum and Cultural Center; CJ McLin International Center for Water Resources Management; Center for Integrated Manufacturing Protocols Architectures and Logistics Laboratory; Biology Technique Laboratory; Electrochemistry Research Laboratory; Cosby Mass Communication Center; Paul Robeson Cultural and Performing Arts Center **Computers:** Administrative functions (other than registration) can be performed online.

CAMPUS LIFE

Environment: Rural. **Activities:** Choral groups, concert band, dance, drama/theater, jazz band, marching band, music ensembles, pep band, radio station, student government, student newspaper, television station, Campus Ministries. 30 registered organizations, 3 honor societies, 4 religious organizations. 1 fraternity, 3 sororities. **Athletics (Intercollegiate):** *Men:* basketball, cheerleading, cross-country, golf, track/field (outdoor). *Women:* basketball, cheerleading, cross-country, golf, track/field (outdoor), volleyball.

ADMISSIONS

Freshman Academic Profile: Average high school GPA 2.5. 5% in top 10% of high school class, 20% in top 25% of high school class, 49% in top 50% of high school class. **Reported SAT (pre-2016 redesign) scores:** SAT Math middle 50% range 340-430. SAT Critical Reading middle 50% range 340-430. **Concordant SAT scores:** SAT Math middle 50% range 380–470. ACT middle 50% range 15-18. Minimum paper TOEFL 500. **Basis for Candidate Selection:** *Very important factors considered include:* rigor of secondary school record, academic GPA, standardized test scores. *Important factors considered include:* class rank, application essay, character/personal qualities, geographical residence, state residency. *Other factors considered include:* recommendation(s), interview, extracurricular activities, talent/ability. **Freshman Admission Requirements:** High school diploma is required and GED is accepted. *Academic units recommended:* 4 English, 3 math, 3 science, 2 foreign language, 3 social studies, and 1 unit from above areas or other academic areas. **Freshman Admission Statistics:** 7,669 applied, 42.01% admitted, 20% enrolled. **Transfer Admission Requirements:** college transcript(s), statement of good standing from prior institution(s). Minimum college GPA of 2.0 required. Lowest grade transferable D. **General Admission Information:** Application fee $20. Nonfall registration accepted. Admission may be deferred.

COSTS AND FINANCIAL AID

Annual in-state tuition $3,926. Annual out-of-state tuition $5,776. Room and board $9,934. Required fees $2,320. Average book expense $1,200. **Required Forms and Deadlines:** FAFSA. **Notification of Awards:** Applicants will be notified of awards on a rolling basis beginning 4/15. **Types of Aid:** *Need-based* *scholarships/grants:* Federal Pell, FSEOG, State scholarships/grants, Private scholarships, College/university scholarship or grant aid from institutional funds. *Loans:* Direct Subsidized Stafford Loans, Direct Unsubsidized Stafford Loans, Direct PLUS loans. *Student Employment:* Federal Work-Study Program available. Institutional employment available. **Financial Aid Statistics:** 100% needy freshmen, 100% needy undergrads receive need-based scholarship or grant aid. 0% undergrads receive non-need-based scholarship or grant aid. 0% freshmen, 0% undergrads receive need-based self-help aid. 0% freshmen, 0% undergrads receive athletic scholarships. **Criteria for awarding aid:** *Need-based:* Academics. *Non-need-based:* Academics, Alumni affiliation, Art, Athletics, Leadership, Music/drama.

CENTRAL WASHINGTON UNIVERSITY

Admissions Office, Ellensburg, WA 98926-7463
Phone: 509-963-1211 • **Financial Aid Phone:** 509-963-1611
E-mail: cwuadmis@cwu.edu • **CEEB Code:** 4044
Fax: 509-963-3022 • **Website:** www.cwu.edu • **ACT Code:** 4444

This public school was founded in 1891. It has a 350-acre campus.

RATINGS

Admissions Selectivity Rating: 74   Fire Safety Rating: 75   Green Rating: 60*

STUDENTS AND FACULTY

Enrollment: 9,688. **Student Body:** 51% female, 49% male, 2% out-of-state, 2% international (60 countries represented). Asian 7%, African American 3%, Caucasian 75%, Hispanic 8%, Native American 3%, Pacific Islander 0%, Two or more races 0%, Race unknown 3%.
Retention and Graduation: 75% freshmen return for sophomore year. 26% freshmen graduate within 4 years. 55% freshmen graduate within 6 years.
Faculty: Student/faculty ratio 20:1. 432 full-time faculty, 0% hold PhDs, 12% are are members of minority groups, 39% are women. 3% of classes are taught by teaching assistants.

ACADEMICS

Degrees: bachelor's, master's, postbachelor's certificate. **Classes:** Most classes have 20-29 students. Most lab/discussion sessions have 10-19 students. **Most popular majors:** Business/Commerce; Elementary Education and Teaching; Social Sciences. **Special Study Options:** cooperative education program, distance learning, double major, dual enrollment, English as a Second Language (ESL), exchange student program (domestic), honors program, independent study, internships, liberal arts/career combination, student-designed major, study abroad, teacher certification program. **Honors Programs:** The Douglas Honors College student is expected to maintain a grade point average above 3.0. A student will be placed on probation if the grade point average falls below 3.0, and will be dismissed from the Douglas Honors College if the cumulative grade point average is below 3.0 for two consecutive quarters. This policy does not affect academic standing as a student of Central Washington University. **Disability Services:** Special programs offered to physically disabled students, including note-taking services, reader services, tape recorders, tutors. **Career Services:** Alumni network, Alumni services, Career/job search classes, Career assessment, Internships, Regional alumni.

FACILITIES

Housing: Coed dorms, special housing for disabled students, special housing for international students, women's dorms, apartments for married students, apartments for single students, Theme Housing, Upperclassmen and 21 years and older. 100% of campus accessible to physically diasbled. **Special Academic Facilities/Equipment:** Chimpanzee and Human Communication Institute, Geodesy Laboratory—a data analysis facility of the Pacific Northwest Geodetic Array, Educational Technology Center, Museum collection of NW Native Amer and Circum-Pacific artifacts for teaching and research, regional site of the National Consortium for Rural Geospatial Innovations, Sarah Spugeon Art Gallery, Science Facility Building. **Computers:** 100% of libraries, 100% of dining areas, 100% of student union, 100% of common outdoor areas have wireless network access. Students can register for classes online. Administrative functions (other than registration) can be performed online.

CAMPUS LIFE

Environment: Village. **Activities:** Choral groups, concert band, dance, drama/theater, jazz band, literary magazine, marching band, music ensembles, musical theater, opera, pep band, radio station, student government, student newspaper, student-run film society, symphony orchestra, television station, Campus Ministries, Student Organization. 96 registered organizations, 3 honor societies, 9 religious organizations. **Athletics (Intercollegiate):** *Men:* baseball, basketball, cheerleading, cross-country, football, track/field (outdoor), track/field (indoor). *Women:* basketball, cheerleading, cross-country, soccer, softball, track/field (outdoor), track/field (indoor), volleyball. **On-Campus Highlights:**

Award-winning Student Union Recreation Center, Japanese Garden, Nicholson Pavilion Athletic Facilities, Chimpanzee and Human Communication Institute, Performing Arts Center, Presidential Speaker Series. **Environmental Initiatives:** Carbon Reduction.

ADMISSIONS

Freshman Academic Profile: Average high school GPA 3.2. 4% in top 10% of high school class, 23% in top 25% of high school class, 65% in top 50% of high school class. **Reported SAT (pre-2016 redesign) scores:** SAT Math middle 50% range 440-550. SAT Critical Reading middle 50% range 440-540. **Concordant SAT scores:** SAT Math middle 50% range 480–570. ACT middle 50% range 18-23. Minimum paper TOEFL 525. **Basis for Candidate Selection:** *Very important factors considered include:* rigor of secondary school record, academic GPA. *Important factors considered include:* standardized test scores, application essay. *Other factors considered include:* class rank, recommendation(s), interview, extracurricular activities, talent/ability, character/personal qualities, first generation, volunteer work, work experience, level of applicant's interest. **Freshman Admission Requirements:** High school diploma is required and GED is accepted. *Academic units required:* 4 English, 3 math, 2 science, 1 science lab, 2 foreign language, 3 social studies. *Academic units recommended:* 4 English, 4 math, 3 science, 2 science labs, 2 foreign language, 3 social studies. **Freshman Admission Statistics:** 5,013 applied, 79.15% admitted, 40% enrolled. **Transfer Admission Requirements:** college transcript(s), statement of good standing from prior institution(s). Minimum college GPA of 2.5 required. Lowest grade transferable D-. **General Admission Information:** Application fee $55. Regular application deadline 4/1. Nonfall registration accepted.

COSTS AND FINANCIAL AID

Annual in-state tuition $4,842. Annual out-of-state tuition $14,013. Room and board $8,052. Required fees $882. Average book expense $924. **Required Forms and Deadlines:** FAFSA. **Notification of Awards:** Applicants will be notified of awards on a rolling basis beginning 4/15. **Types of Aid:** *Need-based scholarships/grants:* Federal Pell, FSEOG, State scholarships/grants, Private scholarships, College/university scholarship or grant aid from institutional funds. *Loans:* Direct Subsidized Stafford Loans, Direct Unsubsidized Stafford Loans, Direct PLUS loans, Federal Perkins Loans, State Loans, College/university loans from institutional funds. *Student Employment:* Federal Work-Study Program available. Institutional employment available. **Financial Aid Statistics:** 68% freshmen, 68% undergrads receive any aid. **Criteria for awarding aid:** *Need-based:* Academics. *Non-need-based:* Academics, Alumni affiliation, Art, Athletics, Job skills, Leadership, Minority status, Music/drama, Religious affiliation, State/district residency.

CENTRAL WYOMING COLLEGE

2660 Peck Avenue, Riverton, WY 82501
Phone: 307-855-2000 • **Financial Aid Phone:** 307-855-2150
E-mail: admit@cwc.edu • **CEEB Code:** 4115
Fax: 307-855-2065 • **Website:** www.cwc.edu • **ACT Code:** 514999

This public school was founded in 1966. It has a 200-acre campus.

RATINGS

Admissions Selectivity Rating: 72   Fire Safety Rating: 84   Green Rating: 60*

STUDENTS AND FACULTY

Enrollment: 1,045. **Student Body:** 60% female, 40% male, 13% out-of-state, <1% international (6 countries represented). Asian 1%, African American 2%, Caucasian 71%, Hispanic 10%, Native American 11%, Pacific Islander <1%, Two or more races 4%, Race unknown 1%.
Retention and Graduation: 52% freshmen return for sophomore year.
Faculty: Student/faculty ratio 12:1. 58 full-time faculty, 78% hold PhDs, 5% are are members of minority groups, 55% are women. 0% of classes are taught by teaching assistants.

ACADEMICS

Degrees: associate, certificate, diploma, terminal, transfer. **Classes:** Most classes have fewer than 10 students. **Most popular majors:** General Studies; Parks, Recreation and Leisure Facilities Management. **Special Study Options:** cooperative education program, cross-registration, distance learning, double major, dual enrollment, external degree program, honors program, independent study, student-designed major, teacher certification program. **Disability Services:** Special programs offered to physically disabled students, including note-taking services, reader services, tape recorders, tutors. **Career Services:** Career/job search classes, Career assessment, Internships, Experiential Learning.

FACILITIES

Housing: Coed dorms, apartments for married students, apartments for single students. 100% of campus accessible to physically disabled. **Special Academic Facilities/Equipment:** Fine Arts Center, Microsoft training lab, Cisco training lab, Wyoming Public Television Station and Radio station, Stewart Collection (Native American Artifacts), Sinks Canyon Center, Rodeo Arena, Library, Arts Gallery. **Computers:** Students can register for classes online. Administrative functions (other than registration) can be performed online.

CAMPUS LIFE

Environment: Village. **Activities:** Choral groups, concert band, dance, drama/theater, jazz band, music ensembles, musical theater, radio station, student government, television station, Student Organization. 16 registered organizations, 2 honor societies, 2 religious organizations. **Athletics (Intercollegiate):** *Men:* basketball, rodeo. *Women:* basketball, rodeo, volleyball. **On-Campus Highlights:** Arts Center, Stewart Collection, Student Center, Food Court, The Underground, Others depend on the students interests. For instance, if they are interested in our equine program we would take them to our equine facilities.

ADMISSIONS

Freshman Academic Profile: Average high school GPA 3.1. 5% in top 10% of high school class, 17% in top 25% of high school class, 45% in top 50% of high school class. 89% from public high schools. **Reported SAT (pre-2016 redesign) scores:** SAT Math middle 50% range 400-490. SAT Critical Reading middle 50% range 400-620. **Concordant SAT scores:** SAT Math middle 50% range 440–520. ACT middle 50% range 17-22. Minimum internet-based TOEFL 60. Minimum paper TOEFL 500. **Freshman Admission Requirements:** High school diploma is required and GED is accepted. **Freshman Admission Statistics:** 516 applied, 100.00% admitted, 53% enrolled. **General Admission Information:** Nonfall registration accepted. Admission may be deferred.

COSTS AND FINANCIAL AID

Annual in-state tuition $1,992. Annual out-of-state tuition $5,976. Required fees $720. Average book expense $1,200. **Required Forms and Deadlines:** FAFSA, Institution's own financial aid form. **Notification of Awards:** Applicants will be notified of awards on a rolling basis beginning 5/1. **Types of Aid:** *Need-based scholarships/grants:* Federal Pell, FSEOG, State scholarships/grants, Private scholarships, College/university scholarship or grant aid from institutional funds. *Loans:* Direct Subsidized Stafford Loans, Direct Unsubsidized Stafford Loans, Direct PLUS loans, State Loans. *Student Employment:* Federal Work-Study Program available. Institutional employment available. **Financial Aid Statistics:** 77% needy freshmen, 75% needy undergrads receive need-based scholarship or grant aid. 89% freshmen, 84% undergrads receive non-need-based scholarship or grant aid. 37% freshmen, 42% undergrads receive need-based self-help aid. 0% freshmen, 0% undergrads receive athletic scholarships. 34% freshmen, 43% undergrads receive any aid. **Criteria for awarding aid:** *Non-need-based:* Academics, Alumni affiliation, Art, Athletics, Leadership, Minority status, Music/drama, State/district residency.

CENTRE COLLEGE

600 West Walnut Street, Danville, KY 40422
Phone: 859-238-5350 • **Financial Aid Phone:** 800-423-6236
E-mail: admission@centre.edu • **CEEB Code:** 1109
Fax: 859-238-5373 • **Website:** www.centre.edu • **ACT Code:** 1506

This private school, affiliated with the Presbyterian Church, was founded in 1819. It has a 115-acre campus.

RATINGS

Admissions Selectivity Rating: 90   **Fire Safety Rating:** 76   **Green Rating:** 78

STUDENTS AND FACULTY

Enrollment: 1,422. **Student Body:** 51% female, 49% male, 43% out-of-state, 7% international (13 countries represented). Asian 5%, African American 5%, Caucasian 76%, Hispanic 4%, Native American <1%, Pacific Islander <1%, Two or more races 3%, Race unknown 1%.
Retention and Graduation: 93% freshmen return for sophomore year. 85% freshmen graduate within 4 years. 86% freshmen graduate within 6 years. 28% grads go on to further study within 1 year. 10% grads pursue arts and sciences degrees. 13% grads pursue law degrees. 10% grads pursue business degrees. 15% grads pursue medical degrees. **Faculty:** Student/faculty ratio 10:1. 129 full-time faculty, 98% hold PhDs, 8% are are members of minority groups, 43% are women. 0% of classes are taught by teaching assistants.

ACADEMICS

Degrees: bachelor's. **Classes:** Most classes have 10-19 students. Most lab/discussion sessions have 10-19 students. **Most popular majors:** Economics; Economics; Biology/Biological Sciences. **Special Study Options:** cross-registration, double major, honors program, independent study, internships, student-designed major, study abroad, teacher certification program. **Disability Services:** Special programs offered to physically disabled students, including note-taking services, reader services, tape recorders, tutors. **Career Services:** Alumni network, Alumni services, Career/job search classes, Career assessment, Internships, Regional alumni. We provide a college-wide comprehensive internship program. We also provide a "Career Roadmap" to assist students with helping to discern and advance their career path during each year of their undergraduate career.

FACILITIES

Housing: Coed dorms, special housing for disabled students, men's dorms, fraternity/sorority housing, apartments for single students, Wellness Housing, Theme Housing. 80% of campus accessible to physically disabled. **Special Academic Facilities/Equipment:** Arts center, physical science and math facility, electron microscope, visible and infrared mass spectroscopy equipment, visual arts center. **Computers:** Administrative functions (other than registration) can be performed online.

CAMPUS LIFE

Environment: Village. **Activities:** Choral groups, dance, drama/theater, jazz band, literary magazine, music ensembles, musical theater, opera, pep band, radio station, student government, student newspaper, symphony orchestra, television station, Campus Ministries, Student Organization. 70 registered organizations, 12 honor societies, 6 religious organizations. 4 fraternities, 4 sororities. **Athletics (Intercollegiate):** *Men:* baseball, basketball, cheerleading, cross-country, diving, football, golf, soccer, swimming, tennis, track/field (outdoor). *Women:* basketball, cheerleading, cross-country, diving, field hockey, golf, soccer, softball, swimming, tennis, track/field (outdoor), volleyball. **On-Campus Highlights:** Norton Center for the Arts, College Centre, athletic and library, Combs Center, student center, 21 campus buildings on National Register, Jazzman's Cafe. **Environmental Initiatives:** All new buildings and major renovations will be designed and built to conserve energy and enhance the human environment as evaluated by LEED silver standards or equivalent. Certification through U.S.G.B.C. will be pursued as appropriate.

ADMISSIONS

Freshman Academic Profile: Average high school GPA 3.6. 62% in top 10% of high school class, 88% in top 25% of high school class, 97% in top 50% of high school class. 64% from public high schools. **Reported SAT (pre-2016 redesign) scores:** SAT Math middle 50% range 560-690. SAT Critical Reading middle 50% range 520-650. SAT Writing middle 50% range 540-660. **Concordant SAT scores:** SAT EBRW middle 50% 590–700. SAT Math middle 50% range 580–720. ACT middle 50% range 26-31. Minimum internet-based TOEFL 90. Minimum paper TOEFL 580. **Basis for Candidate Selection:** *Very important factors considered include:* rigor of secondary school record, academic GPA. *Important factors considered include:* class rank, standardized test scores, application essay, recommendation(s). *Other factors considered include:* interview, extracurricular activities, talent/ability, character/personal qualities, first generation, alumni/ae relation, geographical residence, racial/ethnic status, volunteer work, work experience. **Freshman Admission Requirements:** High school diploma or equivalent is not required. *Academic units required:* 4 English, 3 math, 2 science, 2 science labs, 2 foreign language, 2 history. *Academic units recommended:* 4 math, 4 science, 4 foreign language, 2 social studies, 2 history, 1 visual/performing arts. **Freshman Admission Statistics:** 2,595 applied, 74.26% admitted, 21% enrolled. **Transfer Admission Requirements:** High school transcript, college transcript(s), essay or personal statement, standardized test scores, statement of good standing from prior institution(s). Lowest grade transferable C. **General Admission Information:** Regular application deadline 1/15. Regular notification 3/15. Nonfall registration not accepted. Admission may be deferred for a maximum of 1 year.

COSTS AND FINANCIAL AID

Annual tuition $39,300. Room and board $9,950. Average book expense $1,500. **Required Forms and Deadlines:** FAFSA, Institution's own financial aid form. **Notification of Awards:** Applicants will be notified of awards on a rolling basis beginning 3/19. **Types of Aid:** *Need-based scholarships/grants:* Federal Pell, FSEOG, State scholarships/grants, Private scholarships, College/university scholarship or grant aid from institutional funds. *Loans:* Direct Subsidized Stafford Loans, Direct Unsubsidized Stafford Loans, Direct PLUS loans, Federal Perkins Loans, College/university loans from institutional funds. *Student Employment:* Federal Work-Study Program available. Institutional employment available. **Financial Aid Statistics:** 100% needy freshmen,

99% needy undergrads receive need-based scholarship or grant aid. 0% undergrads receive non-need-based scholarship or grant aid. 60% freshmen, 65% undergrads receive need-based self-help aid. 0% freshmen, 0% undergrads receive athletic scholarships. 97% freshmen, 96% undergrads receive any aid. 48% undergrads borrow to pay for school. Average cumulative indebtedness $26,740. **Criteria for awarding aid:** *Need-based:* Academics, Leadership. *Non-need-based:* Academics, Alumni affiliation, Art, Leadership, Music/drama.

CHAMINADE UNIVERSITY OF HONOLULU

3140 Waialae Avenue, Honolulu, HI 96816-1578
Phone: 808-735-4735 • **Financial Aid Phone:** 808-735-4780
E-mail: admissions@chaminade.edu • **CEEB Code:** 4105
Fax: 808-739-4647 • **Website:** www.chaminade.edu • **ACT Code:** 898

This private school, affiliated with the Roman Catholic Church, was founded in 1955. It has a 67-acre campus.

RATINGS

Admissions Selectivity Rating: 78   **Fire Safety Rating:** 62   **Green Rating:** 60*

STUDENTS AND FACULTY

Enrollment: 1,167. **Student Body:** 72% female, 28% male, 30% out-of-state, 1% international (18 countries represented). Asian 39%, African American 3%, Caucasian 13%, Hispanic 5%, Native American 1%, Pacific Islander 21%, Two or more races 13%, Race unknown 4%.
Retention and Graduation: 74% freshmen return for sophomore year. 35% freshmen graduate within 4 years. 56% freshmen graduate within 6 years.
Faculty: Student/faculty ratio 11:1. 93 full-time faculty, 0% hold PhDs, 28% are are members of minority groups, 44% are women. 0% of classes are taught by teaching assistants.

ACADEMICS

Degrees: associate, bachelor's, master's, postbachelor's certificate. **Classes:** Most classes have 10-19 students. Most lab/discussion sessions have 10-19 students. **Most popular majors:** Criminal Justice/Safety Studies; Psychology; Registered Nursing, Nursing Administration, Nursing Research and Clinical Nursing. **Special Study Options:** Accelerated program, distance learning, double major, exchange student program (domestic), independent study, internships, student-designed major, study abroad, teacher certification program. **Disability Services:** Special programs offered to physically disabled students, including note-taking services, reader services, tape recorders. **Career Services:** Alumni network, Career/job search classes, Career assessment, Internships.

FACILITIES

Housing: Coed dorms, women's dorms, apartments for single students. 100% of campus accessible to physically diasbled. **Special Academic Facilities/Equipment:** Montessori lab school, observatory, black box theatre. **Computers:** Students can register for classes online. Administrative functions (other than registration) can be performed online.

CAMPUS LIFE

Environment: Metropolis. **Activities:** Choral groups, drama/theater, literary magazine, musical theater, student government, student newspaper, symphony orchestra, yearbook, Campus Ministries. 38 registered organizations, 7 honor societies, 1 religious organization. **Athletics (Intercollegiate):** *Men:* basketball, cross-country, golf, tennis, water polo. *Women:* cross-country, golf, softball, tennis, volleyball. **On-Campus Highlights:** Jean E. Rolles Sculoture Center, Henry Hall Courtyard Cafe, Brother's Brew Cafe, Weigand Observatory, Vi and Paul Loo Student Center.

ADMISSIONS

Freshman Academic Profile: Average high school GPA 3.4. 23% in top 10% of high school class, 48% in top 25% of high school class, 81% in top 50% of high school class. **Reported SAT (pre-2016 redesign) scores:** SAT Math middle 50% range 440-540. SAT Critical Reading middle 50% range 430-520. **Concordant SAT scores:** SAT Math middle 50% range 480-570. ACT middle 50% range 19-23. Minimum internet-based TOEFL 79. Minimum paper TOEFL 550. **Basis for Candidate Selection:** *Very important factors considered include:* academic GPA, standardized test scores, application essay. *Important factors considered include:* rigor of secondary school record, recommendation(s). *Other factors considered include:* extracurricular activities, talent/ability, character/personal qualities, volunteer work, work experience. **Freshman Admission Requirements:** High school diploma is required and GED is accepted. *Academic units required:* 4 English, 3 math, 2 science, 3 social studies, and 4 units from above areas or other academic areas. *Academic units recommended:* 4 math, 4 science. **Freshman Admission Statistics:** 842 applied, 91.33% admitted, 33% enrolled. **Transfer Admission Requirements:** college transcript(s), essay or personal statement, statement of good standing

from prior institution(s). Minimum college GPA of 2.0 required. Lowest grade transferable C. **General Admission Information:** Application fee $50. Nonfall registration accepted. Admission may be deferred for a maximum of 1 year.

COSTS AND FINANCIAL AID

Average book expense $1,600. **Required Forms and Deadlines:** FAFSA. **Types of Aid:** *Need-based scholarships/grants:* Federal Pell, FSEOG, Private scholarships, College/university scholarship or grant aid from institutional funds. *Loans:* Direct Subsidized Stafford Loans, Direct Unsubsidized Stafford Loans, Direct PLUS loans. *Student Employment:* Federal Work-Study Program available. Institutional employment available. **Financial Aid Statistics:** 98% needy freshmen, 93% needy undergrads receive need-based scholarship or grant aid. 99% freshmen, 97% undergrads receive non-need-based scholarship or grant aid. 86% freshmen, 87% undergrads receive need-based self-help aid. 4% freshmen, 4% undergrads receive athletic scholarships. 100% freshmen, 97% undergrads receive any aid. 64% undergrads borrow to pay for school. Average cumulative indebtedness $31,145. **Criteria for awarding aid:** *Need-based:* Academics. *Non-need-based:* Academics, Athletics, Minority status, Religious affiliation, State/district residency.

CHAMPLAIN COLLEGE

Best Colleges

163 South Willard Street Box 670, Burlington, VT 05402-0670
Phone: 802-860-2727 • **Financial Aid Phone:** 802-860-2730
E-mail: admission@champlain.edu • **CEEB Code:** 3291
Fax: 802-860-2767 • **Website:** www.champlain.edu/ • **ACT Code:** 3291

This private school was founded in 1878. It has a 19-acre campus.

RATINGS

Admissions Selectivity Rating: 85   **Fire Safety Rating:** 98   **Green Rating:** 96

STUDENTS AND FACULTY

Enrollment: 3,249. **Student Body:** 42% female, 58% male, 78% out-of-state, 1% international (27 countries represented). Asian 2%, African American 5%, Caucasian 70%, Hispanic 5%, Native American <1%, Pacific Islander <1%, Two or more races 3%, Race unknown 14%.
Retention and Graduation: 79% freshmen return for sophomore year. 48% freshmen graduate within 4 years. 58% freshmen graduate within 6 years.
Faculty: Student/faculty ratio 13:1. 113 full-time faculty, 68% hold PhDs, 0% are are members of minority groups, 38% are women. 0% of classes are taught by teaching assistants.

ACADEMICS

Degrees: associate, bachelor's, master's, postbachelor's certificate. **Classes:** Most classes have 10-19 students. Most lab/discussion sessions have 10-19 students. **Most popular majors:** Game and Interactive Media Design; Business/Commerce; Graphic Design. **Special Study Options:** Accelerated program, cross-registration, distance learning, double major, honors program, independent study, internships, liberal arts/career combination, study abroad, teacher certification program. **Honors Programs:** Honors Program invitation based on high school gpa and SAT/ACT scores. **Disability Services:** Special programs offered to physically disabled students, including note-taking services, reader services, tape recorders, tutors. **Career Services:** Alumni network, Alumni services, Career/job search classes, Career assessment, Internships. We are very proud of our model which aligns members of the Career Services team with specific academic divisions. We are also proud of our partnership with LEAD through which students think about lifelong career management at the start of their academic career.

FACILITIES

Housing: Coed dorms, special housing for international students, women's dorms, Wellness, Performing Arts, dorm. Suites style singles with common living room and kitchenette (for selected sophomores, juniors and seniors. 79% of campus accessible to physically diasbled. **Computers:** Students can register for classes online. Administrative functions (other than registration) can be performed online.

CAMPUS LIFE

Environment: Town. **Activities:** Choral groups, dance, drama/theater, literary magazine, musical theater, radio station, student government, student newspaper, television station 40 registered organizations, 2 honor societies, 1 religious organization. **On-Campus Highlights:** Center for Global Technology,

The View, Hauke Family Center, Student Life Center, Main Street Suites, Miller Information Commons. **Environmental Initiatives:** Green Buildings (Master Plan).

ADMISSIONS

Freshman Academic Profile: Average high school GPA 3.2. 10% in top 10% of high school class, 34% in top 25% of high school class, 77% in top 50% of high school class. **Reported SAT (pre-2016 redesign) scores:** SAT Math middle 50% range 510-630. SAT Critical Reading middle 50% range 520-630. SAT Writing middle 50% range 490-600. **Concordant SAT scores:** SAT EBRW middle 50% 560–670. SAT Math middle 50% range 540–650. ACT middle 50% range 23-29. Minimum internet-based TOEFL 79. **Basis for Candidate Selection:** *Very important factors considered include:* rigor of secondary school record, academic GPA, talent/ability. *Important factors considered include:* class rank, standardized test scores, application essay, recommendation(s), extracurricular activities, character/personal qualities, first generation, racial/ethnic status. *Other factors considered include:* alumni/ae relation, volunteer work, work experience. **Freshman Admission Requirements:** High school diploma is required and GED is accepted. *Academic units required:* 4 English, 3 math, 3 science, 3 science labs, 2 foreign language, 4 history, 4 academic electives. *Academic units recommended:* 4 math, 4 science, 4 foreign language. **Freshman Admission Statistics:** 5,587 applied, 66.17% admitted, 15% enrolled. **Transfer Admission Requirements:** High school transcript, college transcript(s), essay or personal statement, Minimum college GPA of 2.0 required. Lowest grade transferable C. **General Admission Information:** Nonfall registration accepted. Admission may be deferred for a maximum of 1 year.

COSTS AND FINANCIAL AID

Annual tuition $38,560. Room and board $14,472. Required fees $100. Average book expense $1,000. **Required Forms and Deadlines:** FAFSA. **Notification of Awards:** Applicants will be notified of awards on a rolling basis beginning 3/1. **Types of Aid:** *Need-based scholarships/grants:* Federal Pell, FSEOG, State scholarships/grants, Private scholarships, College/university scholarship or grant aid from institutional funds. *Loans:* Direct Subsidized Stafford Loans, Direct Unsubsidized Stafford Loans, Direct PLUS loans, Federal Perkins Loans. *Student Employment:* Federal Work-Study Program available. Institutional employment available. **Financial Aid Statistics:** 99% needy freshmen, 98% needy undergrads receive need-based scholarship or grant aid. 11% freshmen, 10% undergrads receive non-need-based scholarship or grant aid. 86% freshmen, 84% undergrads receive need-based self-help aid. 0% freshmen, 0% undergrads receive athletic scholarships. 90% freshmen, 83% undergrads receive any aid. 73% undergrads borrow to pay for school. Average cumulative indebtedness $33,236. **Criteria for awarding aid:** *Need-based:* Academics, Leadership, Minority status. *Non-need-based:* Academics, Alumni affiliation, Leadership, Minority status.

CHAPMAN UNIVERSITY

One University Drive, Orange, CA 92866
Phone: 714-997-6711 • **Financial Aid Phone:** 714-997-6741
E-mail: admit@chapman.edu • **CEEB Code:** 4047
Fax: 714-997-6713 • **Website:** www.chapman.edu • **ACT Code:** 210

This private school, affiliated with the Disciples of Christ Church, was founded in 1861. It has a 75-acre campus.

RATINGS

Admissions Selectivity Rating: 89   **Fire Safety Rating:** 86   **Green Rating:** 60*

STUDENTS AND FACULTY

Enrollment: 6,338. **Student Body:** 61% female, 39% male, 32% out-of-state, 4% international (83 countries represented). Asian 11%, African American 2%, Caucasian 57%, Hispanic 15%, Native American <1%, Pacific Islander <1%, Two or more races 7%, Race unknown 4%.
Retention and Graduation: 89% freshmen return for sophomore year. 65% freshmen graduate within 4 years. 79% freshmen graduate within 6 years.
Faculty: Student/faculty ratio 14:1. 459 full-time faculty, 85% hold PhDs, 0% are are members of minority groups, 41% are women.

ACADEMICS

Degrees: bachelor's, doctoral/professional, doctoral/research, master's.
Classes: Most classes have 10-19 students. Most lab/discussion sessions have 10-19 students. **Most popular majors:** Business Administration and Management; Cinematography and Film/Video Production; Public Relations/Image Management. **Special Study Options:** distance learning, double major, English as a Second Language (ESL), honors program, independent study, internships, liberal arts/career combination, student-designed major, study abroad, teacher certification program. **Honors Programs:** University Honors Program. **Disability Services:** Special programs offered to physically disabled students, including note-taking services, reader services, tape recorders, tutors. **Career Services:** Alumni network, Alumni services, Career/job search classes, Career assessment, Internships. We are very proud of our venture capital and startup internship programs. Our Students have access to Tech Coast Angels (TCA), the largest angel group in the world. TCA has invested over $110 million in startup companies, which have attracted over $1 billion of follow-on financing. Chapman hosts on-campus screenings to allow students to observe and participate in the screening process of entrepreneurs seeking startup capital. In addition, there are several internship opportunities for students at start-up companies and TCA, such as screening activities, due diligence, and the overall investment process.

FACILITIES

Housing: Coed dorms, special housing for disabled students, apartments for married students, apartments for single students, Houses for married, single, and students with dependents. **Special Academic Facilities/Equipment:** Anderson Center for Economic Research, Leatherby Center for Entrepreneurship and Business Ethics, Schmid Center for International Business, Law and organizational Economics Center, Center for Cold War Studies, Henley Social Science Research Laboratory, Guggenhiem Art gallery, TV studio, film and television production and digital editing studios, Waltmer Theatre, Albert Schweitzer Collection **Computers:** 100% of classrooms, 100% of dorms, 100% of libraries, 100% of dining areas, 100% of common outdoor areas have wireless network access. Students can register for classes online. Administrative functions (other than registration) can be performed online.

CAMPUS LIFE

Environment: Metropolis. **Activities:** Choral groups, concert band, dance, drama/theater, jazz band, literary magazine, music ensembles, musical theater, opera, pep band, radio station, student government, student newspaper, student-run film society, symphony orchestra, yearbook, Campus Ministries, Student Organization, Model UN. 84 registered organizations, 8 honor societies, 8 religious organizations. 6 fraternities, 6 sororities. **Athletics (Intercollegiate):** *Men:* baseball, basketball, cross-country, football, golf, soccer, tennis, water polo. *Women:* basketball, crew/rowing, cross-country, soccer, softball, swimming, tennis, track/field (outdoor), volleyball, water polo. **On-Campus Highlights:** Marion Knott Film Studios, Leatherby Libraries, Liberty Plaza, Beckman Hall, All-Faiths Chapel. **Environmental Initiatives:** Adoption of LEED standards in new building projects.

ADMISSIONS

Freshman Academic Profile: Average high school GPA 3.7. 38% in top 10% of high school class, 81% in top 25% of high school class, 96% in top 50% of high school class. **Reported SAT (pre-2016 redesign) scores:** SAT Math middle 50% range 560-650. SAT Critical Reading middle 50% range 550-650. SAT Writing middle 50% range 560-660. **Concordant SAT scores:** SAT EBRW middle 50% 610–700. SAT Math middle 50% range 580–670. ACT middle 50% range 25-30. Minimum paper TOEFL 550. **Basis for Candidate Selection:** *Very important factors considered include:* rigor of secondary school record, class rank, academic GPA, standardized test scores, application essay, character/personal qualities. *Important factors considered include:* extracurricular activities, talent/ability, volunteer work. *Other factors considered include:* recommendation(s), interview, first generation, alumni/ae relation, geographical residence, state residency, racial/ethnic status, work experience. **Freshman Admission Requirements:** High school diploma is required and GED is accepted. *Academic units required:* 2 English, 2 math, 2 science, 1 science lab, 2 foreign language, 3 social studies. *Academic units recommended:* 4 English, 4 math, 4 science, 2 science labs, 4 foreign language, 4 social studies. **Freshman Admission Statistics:** 12,821 applied, 54.03% admitted, 22% enrolled. **Transfer Admission Requirements:** college transcript(s), essay or personal statement, Minimum college GPA of 2.5 required. Lowest grade transferable C-. **General Admission Information:** Application fee $65. Regular application deadline 1/15. Nonfall registration accepted.

COSTS AND FINANCIAL AID

Annual tuition $50,210. Room and board $14,910. Required fees $384. Average book expense $1,560. **Required Forms and Deadlines:** FAFSA, State aid form. **Notification of Awards:** Applicants will be notified of awards on a rolling basis beginning 3/15. **Types of Aid:** *Need-based scholarships/grants:* Federal Pell, FSEOG, State scholarships/grants, Private scholarships, College/university scholarship or grant aid from institutional funds. *Loans:* Direct Subsidized Stafford Loans, Direct Unsubsidized Stafford Loans, Federal Perkins Loans. *Student Employment:* Federal Work-Study Program available. Institutional employment available. **Financial Aid Statistics:** 86% needy freshmen, 90% needy undergrads receive need-based scholarship or grant aid. 75% freshmen,

66% undergrads receive non-need-based scholarship or grant aid. 78% freshmen, 89% undergrads receive need-based self-help aid. 0% freshmen, 0% undergrads receive athletic scholarships. 54% undergrads borrow to pay for school. Average cumulative indebtedness $25,959. **Criteria for awarding aid:** *Non-need-based:* Academics, Alumni affiliation, Art, Music/drama, Religious affiliation.

CHARTER OAK STATE COLLEGE

55 Paul Manafort Drive, New Britain, CT 6053
Phone: 860-515-3701 • **Financial Aid Phone:** 860-515-3703
E-mail: admissions@charteroak.edu
Website: www.charteroak.edu

This public school was founded in 1973.

RATINGS
Admissions Selectivity Rating: 61   **Fire Safety Rating:** 60*   **Green Rating:** 60*

STUDENTS AND FACULTY
Enrollment: 1,459. **Student Body:** 68% female, 32% male, 20% out-of-state, 1% international. Asian 1%, African American 17%, Caucasian 58%, Hispanic 15%, Native American 1%, Pacific Islander <1%, Two or more races 2%, Race unknown 4%.
Faculty: Student/faculty ratio 12:1.

ACADEMICS
Degrees: associate, bachelor's, certificate. **Special Study Options:** distance learning, external degree program, independent study, liberal arts/career combination, student-designed major.

FACILITIES
Housing: 100% of campus accessible to physically diasbled. **Computers:** Students can register for classes online. Administrative functions (other than registration) can be performed online.

CAMPUS LIFE
Environment: Village.

ADMISSIONS
Freshman Admission Requirements: High school diploma is required and GED is accepted. **Transfer Admission Requirements:** college transcript(s), Lowest grade transferable D. **General Admission Information:** Application fee $75. Priority deadline 7/1. Nonfall registration accepted. Admission may be deferred for a maximum of 12 months.

COSTS AND FINANCIAL AID
Required Forms and Deadlines: FAFSA. **Types of Aid:** *Need-based scholarships/grants:* Federal Pell, FSEOG, State scholarships/grants, Private scholarships, College/university scholarship or grant aid from institutional funds. *Loans:* Direct Subsidized Stafford Loans, Direct Unsubsidized Stafford Loans, Direct PLUS loans, State Loans. *Student Employment:* Institutional employment available.

CHATHAM UNIVERSITY

Woodland Road, Pittsburgh, PA 15232
Phone: 412-365-1825 • **Financial Aid Phone:** 412-365-2797
E-mail: admission@chatham.edu • **CEEB Code:** 2081
Fax: 412-365-1609 • **Website:** www.chatham.edu • **ACT Code:** 3538

This private school was founded in 1869. It has a 39388-acre campus.

RATINGS
Admissions Selectivity Rating: 85   **Fire Safety Rating:** 84   **Green Rating:** 99

STUDENTS AND FACULTY
Enrollment: 786. **Student Body:** 81% female, 19% male, 19% out-of-state, 3% international (16 countries represented). Asian 3%, African American 10%, Caucasian 74%, Hispanic 4%, Native American 1%, Pacific Islander <1%, Two or more races 2%, Race unknown 4%.
Retention and Graduation: 81% freshmen return for sophomore year. 48% freshmen graduate within 4 years. 52% freshmen graduate within 6 years. 17% grads go on to further study within 1 year. 23% grads pursue arts and sciences degrees. 6% grads pursue medical degrees. **Faculty:** Student/faculty ratio 10:1. 111 full-time faculty, 93% hold PhDs, 9% are are members of minority groups, 67% are women. 0% of classes are taught by teaching assistants.

ACADEMICS
Degrees: bachelor's, certificate, doctoral/professional, master's, postbachelor's certificate. **Classes:** Most classes have 10-19 students. Most lab/discussion sessions have 10-19 students. **Most popular majors:** Registered Nursing, Nursing Administration, Nursing Research and Clinical Nursing; Biology/Biological Sciences; Business Administration and Management. **Special Study Options:** Accelerated program, cooperative education program, cross-registration, distance learning, double major, dual enrollment, English as a Second Language (ESL), exchange student program (domestic), honors program, independent study, internships, liberal arts/career combination, student-designed major, study abroad, teacher certification program, Five-year bachelors/masters programs; five-year bachelors/masters programs also available with Carnegie Mellon (e.g. engineering, public policy) and other institutions. **Honors Programs:** The Chatham Scholars Program offers students a challenging, integrated curriculum with special opportunities for enrichment, mentoring, and networking. Combined degree programs: BA/MA, 3-2 b/m in 9 fields and 4-2 b/doctorate in Phys Ther. **Disability Services:** Special programs offered to physically disabled students, including note-taking services, reader services, tape recorders, tutors. **Career Services:** Alumni network, Alumni services, Career/job search classes, Career assessment, Internships. The Chatham Plan—an integrated curricular approach to marrying skills acquired in a liberal arts setting with application to a students' career. Students begin in their first year with a common professional development course. They continue with a 3 credit internship and also participate in 3 credits of course work in their major focused on skills and competencies needed for field specific success.

FACILITIES
Housing: women's dorms, apartments for married students, apartments for single students, Theme Housing. 75% of campus accessible to physically diasbled. **Special Academic Facilities/Equipment:** Athletic and Fitness Center; Art and Design Center; broadcast studio; art gallery, classroom space, and coffee shop; campus arboretum and greenhouse; proscenium theater. **Computers:** 100% of classrooms, 20% of dorms, 100% of libraries, 100% of dining areas, 100% of student union, 75% of common outdoor areas have wireless network access. Students can register for classes online. Administrative functions (other than registration) can be performed online. Undergraduates are required to own a computer.

CAMPUS LIFE
Environment: Metropolis. **Activities:** Choral groups, dance, drama/theater, literary magazine, music ensembles, musical theater, student government, student newspaper, yearbook. 25 registered organizations, 10 honor societies, 6 religious organizations. **Athletics (Intercollegiate):** *Women:* basketball, cross-country, ice hockey, soccer, softball, swimming, tennis, volleyball, water polo. **On-Campus Highlights:** New coffee shop and art gallery (2005), Athletic and Fitness Center (2004), Art and Design Center (2004), Science Complex (2001), Campus Arboretum, Many of the campus residence halls are renovated historic mansions. The campus also features an outdoor meditation labyrinth, the largest in Pittsburgh. The Shadyside Campus on Woodland Road is a registered arboretum, with over 120 distinct tree species. **Environmental Initiatives:** The creation of the Falk School of Sustainability and the Environment. The Falk School provides innovative, interdisciplinary education and research opportunities for undergraduate, graduate and professional students to better prepare them to identify and solve challenges related to the environment and sustainability. The school is located at Eden Hall Campus, on a 300-acre farm with forest. Phases 1A and B of the Master Plan are constructed, and our first group of residents is in place at Orchard Hall. The Eden Hall campus is designed to be a net-zero energy campus upon completion.

ADMISSIONS
Freshman Academic Profile: Average high school GPA 3.7. 26% in top 10% of high school class, 55% in top 25% of high school class, 88% in top 50% of high school class. **Reported SAT (pre-2016 redesign) scores:** SAT Math middle 50% range 480-570. SAT Critical Reading middle 50% range 470-600. SAT Writing middle 50% range 460-570. **Concordant SAT scores:** SAT EBRW middle 50% 520–640. SAT Math middle 50% range 510–590. ACT middle 50% range 21-27. Minimum internet-based TOEFL 60. Minimum paper TOEFL 500. **Basis for Candidate Selection:** *Very important factors considered include:* rigor of secondary school record. *Important factors considered include:* academic GPA, application essay. *Other factors considered include:* class rank, standardized test scores, recommendation(s), interview, extracurricular activities, talent/ability, character/personal qualities, alumni/ae relation, volunteer work, work experience, level of applicant's interest. **Freshman Admission Requirements:** High school diploma is required and GED is accepted. *Academic units required:* 4 English, 2 math, 2 science, and 3 units from above areas or other academic areas. *Academic units recommended:* 4 English, 3 math, 3 science, 2 foreign language, 3 social studies. **Freshman Admission Statistics:** 1,916 applied, 52.97% admitted, 19% enrolled. **Transfer Admission Requirements:** college transcript(s), essay or personal statement, Minimum college GPA of 2.0 required. Lowest grade transferable C-. **General Admission Information:** Application fee $35. Priority deadline 3/15. Regular application deadline 8/1. Nonfall registration accepted. Admission may be deferred for a maximum of 1 year.

COSTS AND FINANCIAL AID

Annual tuition $34,195. Room and board $11,042. Required fees $1,280. Average book expense $1,000. **Required Forms and Deadlines:** FAFSA. **Notification of Awards:** Applicants will be notified of awards on a rolling basis beginning 3/1. **Types of Aid:** *Need-based scholarships/grants:* Federal Pell, FSEOG, State scholarships/grants, Private scholarships, College/university scholarship or grant aid from institutional funds. *Loans:* Direct Subsidized Stafford Loans, Direct Unsubsidized Stafford Loans, Direct PLUS loans, Federal Perkins Loans. *Student Employment:* Federal Work-Study Program available. Institutional employment available. **Financial Aid Statistics:** 88% needy freshmen, 87% needy undergrads receive need-based scholarship or grant aid. 100% freshmen, 87% undergrads receive non-need-based scholarship or grant aid. 98% freshmen, 87% undergrads receive need-based self-help aid. 0% freshmen, 0% undergrads receive athletic scholarships. 100% freshmen, 95% undergrads receive any aid. 83% undergrads borrow to pay for school. Average cumulative indebtedness $37,734. **Criteria for awarding aid:** *Need-based:* Academics. *Non-need-based:* Academics, Alumni affiliation, Art, Music/drama.

See page 936.

CHESTNUT HILL COLLEGE

9601 Germantown Avenue, Philadelphia, PA 19118-2693
Phone: 215-248-7100 • **Financial Aid Phone:** 215-248-7182
E-mail: chcapply@chc.edu • **CEEB Code:** 2082
Fax: 215-248-7082 • **Website:** www.chc.edu • **ACT Code:** 3540

This private school, affiliated with the Roman Catholic Church, was founded in 1924. It has a 75-acre campus.

RATINGS

Admissions Selectivity Rating: 73   **Fire Safety Rating:** 87   **Green Rating:** 60*

STUDENTS AND FACULTY

Enrollment: 1,364. **Student Body:** 65% female, 35% male, 37% out-of-state, 2% international (39 countries represented). Asian 2%, African American 35%, Caucasian 39%, Hispanic 9%, Native American <1%, Pacific Islander <1%, Two or more races 4%, Race unknown 8%.
Retention and Graduation: 79% freshmen return for sophomore year. 37% freshmen graduate within 4 years. 48% freshmen graduate within 6 years. 19% grads go on to further study within 1 year. 8% grads pursue arts and sciences degrees. 1% grads pursue law degrees. 5% grads pursue business degrees. 1% grads pursue medical degrees. **Faculty:** Student/faculty ratio 10:1. 87 full-time faculty, 85% hold PhDs, 9% are are members of minority groups, 66% are women. 0% of classes are taught by teaching assistants.

ACADEMICS

Degrees: associate, bachelor's, certificate, doctoral/professional, master's, postbachelor's certifiate, post-master's certificate, transfer. **Classes:** Most classes have 10-19 students. Most lab/discussion sessions have 10-19 students. **Most popular majors:** Human Services; Criminal Justice/Law Enforcement Administration; Elementary Education and Teaching. **Special Study Options:** cooperative education program, cross-registration, double major, dual enrollment, English as a Second Language (ESL), exchange student program (domestic), honors program, independent study, internships, student-designed major, study abroad, teacher certification program, Upperclass undergraduates may take graduate classes. **Honors Programs:** Interdisciplinary Honors Program for outstanding incoming first year students offers team-taught interdisciplinary seminars emphasizing discussion and writing which satisfy general education requirements. Departmental Honors challenges students in the junior and senior year to complete an independent research project in their major field. Combined degree programs: BA/MA, BS/MEd, MA/PsyD, BS/BS, BS/MS. **Disability Services:** Special programs offered to physically disabled students, including reader services, tutors. **Career Services:** Alumni network, Career/job search classes, Career assessment, Internships, On-campus interviews. Chestnut Hill College encourages all students to participate in some form of experiential learning. Internships are available in a large number of majors and work areas. Many majors require an internship.

FACILITIES

Housing: Coed dormsOn-campus housing includes singles, doubles, suites, and apartment-like units. A new main campus residence hall opened in Fall 2006 and a renovated building opened as a residence hall on the SugarLoaf Hill campus in 2008. 80% of campus accessible to physically diasbled. **Special Academic Facilities/Equipment:** Rare book collection, Irish literature collection, observatory, planetarium. **Computers:** 40% of classrooms, 100% of dorms, 100% of libraries, have wireless network access. Students can register for classes online. Undergraduates are required to own a computer.

CAMPUS LIFE

Environment: Metropolis. **Activities:** Choral groups, drama/theater, jazz band, literary magazine, music ensembles, musical theater, opera, student government, student newspaper, symphony orchestra, television station, yearbook, Campus Ministries, Student Organization. 19 registered organizations, 14 honor societies, 1 religious organization. **Athletics (Intercollegiate):** *Men:* baseball, basketball, cross-country, golf, lacrosse, soccer, tennis. *Women:* basketball, cross-country, golf, lacrosse, soccer, softball, tennis, volleyball. **On-Campus Highlights:** Martino Hall (smart classrooms, gym), Griffin's Den, Fitzsimmons Hall (new residence hall), Dining Hall, Rotunda of Saint Joseph Hall, SugarLoaf Hill, a 32-acre recent addition to campus, will soon provide additional space for many campus activities. **Environmental Initiatives:** Recycling program.

ADMISSIONS

Freshman Academic Profile: Average high school GPA 3.2. 6% in top 10% of high school class, 26% in top 25% of high school class, 62% in top 50% of high school class. 60% from public high schools. **Reported SAT (pre-2016 redesign) scores:** SAT Math middle 50% range 420-530. SAT Critical Reading middle 50% range 420-540. SAT Writing middle 50% range 410-520. **Concordant SAT scores:** SAT EBRW middle 50% 460–590. SAT Math middle 50% range 460–560. ACT middle 50% range 17-21. Minimum internet-based TOEFL 79. Minimum paper TOEFL 550. **Basis for Candidate Selection:** *Very important factors considered include:* academic GPA, standardized test scores. *Important factors considered include:* character/personal qualities, geographical residence, state residency, volunteer work. *Other factors considered include:* rigor of secondary school record, class rank, application essay, recommendation(s), interview, extracurricular activities, talent/ability, first generation, alumni/ae relation, level of applicant's interest. **Freshman Admission Requirements:** High school diploma is required and GED is accepted. *Academic units recommended:* 4 English, 3 math, 3 science, 2 foreign language, 4 social studies, 4 history. **Freshman Admission Statistics:** 1,242 applied, 93.80% admitted, 21% enrolled. **Transfer Admission Requirements:** college transcript(s), essay or personal statement, Minimum college GPA of 2.0 required. Lowest grade transferable C. **General Admission Information:** Application fee $35. Nonfall registration accepted. Admission may be deferred for a maximum of 1 year.

COSTS AND FINANCIAL AID

Annual tuition $34,950. Room and board $10,400. Average book expense $1,150. **Required Forms and Deadlines:** FAFSA. **Notification of Awards:** Applicants will be notified of awards on a rolling basis beginning 2/16. **Types of Aid:** *Need-based scholarships/grants:* Federal Pell, FSEOG, State scholarships/grants, Private scholarships, College/university scholarship or grant aid from institutional funds. *Loans:* Direct Subsidized Stafford Loans, Direct Unsubsidized Stafford Loans, Direct PLUS loans, Federal Perkins Loans. *Student Employment:* Federal Work-Study Program available. Institutional employment available. **Financial Aid Statistics:** 100% needy freshmen, 96% needy undergrads receive need-based scholarship or grant aid. 8% freshmen, 5% undergrads receive non-need-based scholarship or grant aid. 92% freshmen, 94% undergrads receive need-based self-help aid. 7% freshmen, 6% undergrads receive athletic scholarships. 83% freshmen, 84% undergrads receive any aid. 87% undergrads borrow to pay for school. Average cumulative indebtedness $42,058. **Criteria for awarding aid:** *Non-need-based:* Academics, Alumni affiliation, Athletics, Leadership, Music/drama.

CHEYNEY UNIVERSITY OF PENNSYLVANIA

1837 University Circle, Cheyney, PA 19319
Phone: 610-399-2275 • **Financial Aid Phone:** 610-399-2302
E-mail: abrown@cheyney.edu • **CEEB Code:** 2648
Fax: 610-399-2099 • **Website:** www.cheyney.edu

This public school was founded in 1837. It has a 275-acre campus.

RATINGS

Admissions Selectivity Rating: 76   **Fire Safety Rating:** 98   **Green Rating:** 60*

STUDENTS AND FACULTY

Enrollment: 1,339. **Student Body:** 53% female, 47% male, 22% out-of-state, <1% international (4 countries represented). Asian 0%, African American 92%, Caucasian 1%, Hispanic 1%, Native American <1%, Pacific Islander 0%, Two or more races 0%, Race unknown 6%.
Retention and Graduation: 60% freshmen return for sophomore year.
Faculty: Student/faculty ratio 15:1. 75 full-time faculty, 0% hold PhDs, 79% are are members of minority groups, 48% are women. 0% of classes are taught by teaching assistants.

ACADEMICS

Degrees: associate, bachelor's, master's, postbachelor's certificate. **Most popular majors:** Speech Communication and Rhetoric; Social Sciences; Business Administration and Management. **Special Study Options:** cooperative education program, cross-registration, distance learning, double major, honors program, independent study, internships, study abroad, teacher certification program. **Honors Programs:** Keystone Honors Program. **Disability Services:** Special programs offered to physically disabled students, including note-taking services, tape recorders, tutors. **Career Services:** Alumni services, Career/job search classes, Internships.

FACILITIES

Housing: Coed dorms, men's dorms, women's dorms, Honors dorm. 60% of campus accessible to physically diasbled. **Special Academic Facilities/ Equipment:** Afro-American history/culture collection, planetarium, weather station, satellite communication network. **Computers:** 60% of classrooms, 100% of libraries, 100% of student union, 20% of common outdoor areas have wireless network access. Students can register for classes online. Administrative functions (other than registration) can be performed online.

CAMPUS LIFE

Environment: Village. **Activities:** Choral groups, drama/theater, jazz band, marching band, music ensembles, radio station, student government, student newspaper, student-run film society, television station, yearbook. 30 registered organizations, 12 honor societies, 1 religious organization. 5 fraternities, 4 sororities. **Athletics (Intercollegiate):** *Men:* basketball, cross-country, football, tennis, track/field (outdoor), wrestling. *Women:* basketball, bowling, cross-country, tennis, track/field (outdoor), volleyball. **On-Campus Highlights:** Athletics, Culinary Arts, Communication Arts, Dorms, Bookstore. **Environmental Initiatives:** Re-cycling.

ADMISSIONS

Freshman Academic Profile: Average high school GPA 2.4. 6% in top 10% of high school class, 15% in top 25% of high school class, 46% in top 50% of high school class. **Reported SAT (pre-2016 redesign) scores:** SAT Math middle 50% range 320-410. SAT Critical Reading middle 50% range 330-420. SAT Writing middle 50% range 320-405. **Concordant SAT scores:** SAT EBRW middle 50% 370–460. SAT Math middle 50% range 360–450. ACT middle 50% range 14-21. Minimum paper TOEFL 500. **Basis for Candidate Selection:** *Very important factors considered include:* rigor of secondary school record, recommendation(s). *Important factors considered include:* class rank, standardized test scores, application essay, interview, extracurricular activities, state residency. *Other factors considered include:* talent/ability, racial/ethnic status. **Freshman Admission Requirements:** High school diploma is required and GED is accepted. *Academic units required:* 4 English, 3 math, 2 science, 2 foreign language, 2 history. **Freshman Admission Statistics:** 3,298 applied, 49.64% admitted, 37% enrolled. **Transfer Admission Requirements:** college transcript(s), interview, statement of good standing from prior institution(s). Minimum college GPA of 2.0 required. Lowest grade transferable C. **General Admission Information:** Application fee $20. Priority deadline 6/15. Regular application deadline 3/31. Nonfall registration accepted. Admission may be deferred for a maximum of 1 year.

COSTS AND FINANCIAL AID

Required Forms and Deadlines: FAFSA. **Notification of Awards:** Applicants will be notified of awards on a rolling basis beginning 3/15. **Types of Aid:** *Need-based scholarships/grants:* Federal Pell, FSEOG, State scholarships/ grants, Private scholarships, College/university scholarship or grant aid from institutional funds. *Loans:* Federal Perkins Loans. *Student Employment:* Federal Work-Study Program available. Institutional employment available. **Financial Aid Statistics:** 82% needy freshmen, 94% needy undergrads receive need-based scholarship or grant aid. 32% freshmen, 39% undergrads receive non-need-based scholarship or grant aid. 84% freshmen, 99% undergrads receive need-based self-help aid. 0% freshmen, 0% undergrads receive athletic scholarships. **Criteria for awarding aid:** *Need-based:* Academics, Alumni affiliation, Athletics, Minority status. *Non-need-based:* Academics, Alumni affiliation, Athletics, Minority status.

CHRISTENDOM COLLEGE

134 Christendom Drive, Front Royal, VA 22630
Phone: 540-636-2900 • **Financial Aid Phone:** 800-877-5456
E-mail: admissions@christendom.edu • **CEEB Code:** 5691
Fax: 540-636-1655 • **Website:** www.christendom.edu • **ACT Code:** 4339

This private school, affiliated with the Roman Catholic Church, was founded in 1977. It has a 100-acre campus.

RATINGS

Admissions Selectivity Rating: 78   **Fire Safety Rating:** 62   **Green Rating:** 60*

STUDENTS AND FACULTY

Student Body: 57% female, 43% male, 75% out-of-state, (3 countries represented).
Retention and Graduation: 84% freshmen return for sophomore year. 63% freshmen graduate within 6 years. 25% grads go on to further study within 1 year. 15% grads pursue arts and sciences degrees. 5% grads pursue law degrees. 5% grads pursue business degrees. **Faculty:** Student/faculty ratio 14:1. 26 full-time faculty, 0% hold PhDs, 0% are are members of minority groups, 12% are women. 0% of classes are taught by teaching assistants.

ACADEMICS

Degrees: associate, bachelor's, master's. **Classes:** Most classes have 10-19 students. **Most popular majors:** Philosophy; Political Science and Government; History. **Special Study Options:** double major, honors program, independent study, internships, study abroad, Semester in Rome.

FACILITIES

Housing: men's dorms, women's dorms.

CAMPUS LIFE

Environment: Rural. **Activities:** Choral groups, dance, drama/theater, literary magazine, musical theater, student government, student newspaper, student-run film society, yearbook. 5 registered organizations, 4 religious organizations. **Athletics (Intercollegiate):** *Men:* baseball, basketball, soccer. *Women:* basketball, soccer, softball, volleyball. **On-Campus Highlights:** St. John the Evangelist Library, Chapel of Christ the King, Regina Coeli Building, John Paul II Student Center.

ADMISSIONS

Freshman Academic Profile: Average high school GPA 3.5. 0% in top 50% of high school class. 8% from public high schools. **Reported SAT (pre-2016 redesign) scores:** SAT Math middle 50% range 510-620. SAT Critical Reading middle 50% range 550-700. SAT Writing middle 50% range 530-650. **Concordant SAT scores:** SAT EBRW middle 50% 600–710. SAT Math middle 50% range 540–640. ACT middle 50% range 23-31. Minimum paper TOEFL 550. **Basis for Candidate Selection:** *Very important factors considered include:* standardized test scores, application essay, character/ personal qualities, religious affiliation/commitment, level of applicant's interest. *Important factors considered include:* rigor of secondary school record, recommendation(s), interview. *Other factors considered include:* class rank, academic GPA, extracurricular activities, talent/ability, first generation, alumni/ae relation, volunteer work, work experience. **Freshman Admission Requirements:** High school diploma or equivalent is not required. *Academic units recommended:* 4 English, 2 math, 2 science, 2 foreign language, 1 social studies, 2 history, 1 academic elective. **Freshman Admission Statistics:** 323 applied, 87.00% admitted, 42% enrolled. **Transfer Admission Requirements:** college transcript(s), essay or personal statement, Minimum college GPA of 2.8 required. Lowest grade transferable C. **General Admission Information:** Application fee $25. Priority deadline 3/1. Regular application deadline 3/1. Regular notification 4/1. Nonfall registration not accepted.

COSTS AND FINANCIAL AID

Annual tuition $24,710. Room and board $9,976. Required fees $870. Average book expense $450. **Required Forms and Deadlines:** Institution's own financial aid form. **Notification of Awards:** Applicants will be notified of awards on a rolling basis beginning 2/1. **Types of Aid:** *Need-based scholarships/ grants:* Private scholarships, College/university scholarship or grant aid from institutional funds. *Loans:* College/university loans from institutional funds. *Student Employment:* Institutional employment available. **Financial Aid Statistics:** 95% needy freshmen, 100% needy undergrads receive need-based scholarship or grant aid. 3% freshmen, 3% undergrads receive non-need-based scholarship or grant aid. 96% freshmen, 96% undergrads receive need-based self-help aid. 0% freshmen, 0% undergrads receive athletic scholarships. 80% freshmen, 65% undergrads receive any aid. 69% undergrads borrow to pay for school. Average cumulative indebtedness $27,005. **Criteria for awarding aid:** *Non-need-based:* Academics.

CHRISTIAN BROTHERS UNIVERSITY

Admissions, Box T-6, Memphis, TN 38104-5519
Phone: 901-321-3205 • **Financial Aid Phone:** 901-321-3306
E-mail: admissions@cbu.edu • **CEEB Code:** 1121
Fax: 901-321-3202 • **Website:** www.cbu.edu • **ACT Code:** 3952

This private school, affiliated with the Roman Catholic Church, was founded in 1871. It has a 75-acre campus.

RATINGS

Admissions Selectivity Rating: 87   **Fire Safety Rating:** 63   **Green Rating:** 71

STUDENTS AND FACULTY

Enrollment: 1,295. **Student Body:** 55% female, 45% male, 20% out-of-state, 3% international (22 countries represented). Asian 5%, African American 32%, Caucasian 45%, Hispanic 7%, Native American <1%, Pacific Islander <1%, Two or more races 2%, Race unknown 5%.
Retention and Graduation: 83% freshmen return for sophomore year. 33% freshmen graduate within 4 years. 55% freshmen graduate within 6 years. 23% grads go on to further study within 1 year. 5% grads pursue arts and sciences degrees. 4% grads pursue law degrees. 5% grads pursue business degrees. 6% grads pursue medical degrees. **Faculty:** Student/faculty ratio 10:1. 104 full-time faculty, 88% hold PhDs, 12% are are members of minority groups, 38% are women. 0% of classes are taught by teaching assistants.

ACADEMICS

Degrees: associate, bachelor's, master's, postbachelor's certificate. **Classes:** Most classes have 10-19 students. **Most popular majors:** Psychology; Accounting and Related Services; Biology/Biological Sciences. **Special Study Options:** Accelerated program, distance learning, double major, dual enrollment, honors program, independent study, internships, liberal arts/career combination, study abroad, teacher certification program. **Honors Programs:** The Honors Program at Christian Brothers University is designed to serve the capacities and needs of students with proven academic abilities who seek a more intensive and challenging educational experience. Students accepted into the Honors Program will be allowed each semester to take at least one special-topics course offered only to a limited number of Honors students by an instructor carefully chosen for his or her teaching expertise. These Honors courses will explore important topics in depth, often through a multi-disciplinary approach, and while the pace and the workload will demand self-motivated students, the small size of each Honors class will insure ample group discussion and individual interaction with the instructor. Besides taking honors classes, members of the Honors Program will participate in various extra-curricular activities, including outings to cultural events and regional honors conferences. **Disability Services:** Special programs offered to physically disabled students, including note-taking services, reader services, tape recorders, tutors. **Career Services:** Alumni network, Alumni services, Career/job search classes, Career assessment, Internships, On-campus interviews.

FACILITIES

Housing: men's dorms, women's dorms, apartments for single students, ThemeHousingJuniors and seniors may live in on-campus apartments. All freshmen and sophomores whose permanent address is beyond a 30 mile radius are required to to live on campus. Some houses are available. A private quiet study facility is available. **Special Academic Facilities/Equipment:** Art exhibits, audiovisual lab, MAC graphics lab, engineering graphics lab, Ghandi institute for nonviolence, Facing History. **Computers:** 90% of classrooms, 100% of libraries, 100% of dining areas, 25% of common outdoor areas have wireless network access. Students can register for classes online. Administrative functions (other than registration) can be performed online.

CAMPUS LIFE

Environment: Metropolis. **Activities:** Choral groups, drama/theater, literary magazine, radio station, student government, yearbook, Campus Ministries. 37 registered organizations, 10 honor societies, 3 religious organizations. 5 fraternities, 6 sororities. **Athletics (Intercollegiate):** *Men:* baseball, basketball, cross-country, golf, soccer, tennis. *Women:* basketball, cross-country, golf, soccer, softball, tennis, volleyball. **On-Campus Highlights:** Thomas Center (cafeteria, coffee shop/grill gather, Canale Arena Gymnasium, Computer Center, Canale Outdoor Pool, Art Gallery in library. **Environmental Initiatives:** Building a new "green" dorm that has 90+ beds

ADMISSIONS

Freshman Academic Profile: Average high school GPA 3.7. 28% in top 10% of high school class, 60% in top 25% of high school class, 93% in top 50% of high school class. 69% from public high schools. ACT middle 50% range 21-27. Minimum internet-based TOEFL 68. Minimum paper TOEFL 520. **Basis for Candidate Selection:** *Very important factors considered include:* rigor of secondary school record, academic GPA, standardized test scores. *Important factors considered include:* class rank, application essay, recommendation(s),

interview, extracurricular activities, talent/ability, alumni/ae relation, volunteer work, work experience. **Freshman Admission Requirements:** High school diploma is required and GED is accepted. *Academic units recommended:* 4 English, 4 math, 4 science. **Freshman Admission Statistics:** 2,229 applied, 49.71% admitted, 32% enrolled. **Transfer Admission Requirements:** college transcript(s), Minimum college GPA of 2.5 required. Lowest grade transferable C. **General Admission Information:** Application fee $25. Priority deadline 12/1. Nonfall registration accepted. Admission may be deferred for a maximum of 1 year.

COSTS AND FINANCIAL AID

Annual tuition $29,316. Room and board $7,000. Required fees $790. Average book expense $1,000. **Required Forms and Deadlines:** FAFSA. **Notification of Awards:** Applicants will be notified of awards on a rolling basis beginning 3/1. **Types of Aid:** *Need-based scholarships/grants:* Federal Pell, FSEOG, State scholarships/grants, Private scholarships, College/university scholarship or grant aid from institutional funds. *Loans:* Direct Subsidized Stafford Loans, Direct Unsubsidized Stafford Loans, Direct PLUS loans, Federal Perkins Loans, State Loans, College/university loans from institutional funds. *Student Employment:* Federal Work-Study Program available. Institutional employment available. **Financial Aid Statistics:** 100% needy freshmen, 98% needy undergrads receive need-based scholarship or grant aid. 17% freshmen, 15% undergrads receive non-need-based scholarship or grant aid. 70% freshmen, 75% undergrads receive need-based self-help aid. 17% freshmen, 11% undergrads receive athletic scholarships. **Criteria for awarding aid:** *Need-based:* Minority status. *Non-need-based:* Academics, Alumni affiliation, Athletics, Leadership, Music/drama, State/district residency.

CHRISTOPHER NEWPORT UNIVERSITY

1 Avenue of the Arts, Newport News, VA 23606-3072
Phone: 757-594-7015 • **Financial Aid Phone:** 757-594-7170
E-mail: admit@cnu.edu • **CEEB Code:** 5128
Fax: 757-594-7333 • **Website:** www.cnu.edu • **ACT Code:** 4345

This public school was founded in 1960. It has a 260-acre campus.

RATINGS

Admissions Selectivity Rating: 86   **Fire Safety Rating:** 96   **Green Rating:** 60*

STUDENTS AND FACULTY

Enrollment: 4,921. **Student Body:** 57% female, 43% male, 8% out-of-state, <1% international (32 countries represented). Asian 3%, African American 8%, Caucasian 75%, Hispanic 5%, Native American <1%, Pacific Islander <1%, Two or more races 5%, Race unknown 5%.
Retention and Graduation: 86% freshmen return for sophomore year. 63% freshmen graduate within 4 years. 75% freshmen graduate within 6 years. 30% grads go on to further study within 1 year. 11% grads pursue arts and sciences degrees. 5% grads pursue law degrees. 7% grads pursue business degrees. 5% grads pursue medical degrees. **Faculty:** Student/faculty ratio 15:1. 278 full-time faculty, 87% hold PhDs, 14% are are members of minority groups, 45% are women. 0% of classes are taught by teaching assistants.

ACADEMICS

Degrees: bachelor's, master's. **Classes:** Most classes have 10-19 students. **Most popular majors:** Psychology; Biology/Biological Sciences; Speech Communication and Rhetoric. **Special Study Options:** cross-registration, double major, dual enrollment, honors program, independent study, internships, student-designed major, study abroad, Member of the Virginia Tidewater Consortium, Freshman Learning Communities. **Honors Programs:** CNU Honors Program provides enriched educational experience for academically talented students motivated to participate in challenging courses and cultural and intellectual activities. **Disability Services:** Special programs offered to physically disabled students, including note-taking services, tape recorders. **Career Services:** Alumni network, Alumni services, Career/job search classes, Career assessment, Internships.

FACILITIES

Housing: Coed dorms, fraternity/sorority housing, apartments for single students, Theme Housing. 96% of campus accessible to physically diasbled. **Special Academic Facilities/Equipment:** Falk Art Gallery, The Freeman Center, The Ferguson Center for the Arts, Trible Library houses the Mariners Museum Collection. **Computers:** 10% of classrooms, 10% of dorms, 100% of libraries, 100% of dining areas, 100% of student union, 100% of common outdoor areas have wireless network access. Students can register for classes online. Administrative functions (other than registration) can be performed online.

CAMPUS LIFE

Environment: City. **Activities:** Choral groups, concert band, dance, drama/theater, jazz band, literary magazine, marching band, music ensembles, musical theater, opera, pep band, radio station, student government, student newspaper, student-run film society, symphony orchestra, television station, Campus Ministries, Student Organization, Model UN. 139 registered organizations, 23 honor societies, 12 religious organizations. 7 fraternities, 7 sororities. **Athletics (Intercollegiate):** *Men:* baseball, basketball, cheerleading, cross-country, football, golf, lacrosse, sailing, soccer, tennis, track/field (outdoor), track/field (indoor). *Women:* basketball, cheerleading, cross-country, field hockey, lacrosse, sailing, soccer, softball, tennis, track/field (outdoor), track/field (indoor), volleyball. **On-Campus Highlights:** Trible Library, Freeman Athletic Center, Ferguson Center for the Arts, McMurran Classroom Building, David Student Union, CNU Village for upper class students.

ADMISSIONS

Freshman Academic Profile: Average high school GPA 3.8. 19% in top 10% of high school class, 53% in top 25% of high school class, 87% in top 50% of high school class. 70% from public high schools. **Reported SAT (pre-2016 redesign) scores:** SAT Math middle 50% range 530-620. SAT Critical Reading middle 50% range 530-630. **Concordant SAT scores:** SAT Math middle 50% range 560–640. ACT middle 50% range 23-28. Minimum internet-based TOEFL 71. Minimum paper TOEFL 530. **Basis for Candidate Selection:** *Very important factors considered include:* rigor of secondary school record, academic GPA. *Important factors considered include:* class rank, standardized test scores, application essay, recommendation(s), interview, extracurricular activities, talent/ability, character/personal qualities, level of applicant's interest. *Other factors considered include:* first generation, alumni/ae relation, geographical residence, state residency, volunteer work, work experience. **Freshman Admission Requirements:** High school diploma is required and GED is accepted. *Academic units required:* 4 English, 4 math, 4 science, 3 foreign language, 4 social studies, 2 academic electives, 1 visual/performing arts, and 4 units from above areas or other academic areas. *Academic units recommended:* 4 English, 4 math, 4 science, 3 science labs, 3 foreign language, 4 social studies, 2 academic electives, 1 visual/performing arts, and 4 units from above areas or other academic areas. **Freshman Admission Statistics:** 7,532 applied, 62.16% admitted, 26% enrolled. **Transfer Admission Requirements:** High school transcript, college transcript(s), statement of good standing from prior institution(s). Minimum college GPA of 3.0 required. Lowest grade transferable C. **General Admission Information:** Application fee $50. Priority deadline 11/15. Regular application deadline 2/1. Regular notification 3/15. Nonfall registration accepted. Admission may be deferred for a maximum of 12 Months.

COSTS AND FINANCIAL AID

Required Forms and Deadlines: FAFSA. **Notification of Awards:** Applicants will be notified of awards on a rolling basis beginning 3/1. **Types of Aid:** *Need-based scholarships/grants:* Federal Pell, FSEOG, State scholarships/grants, Private scholarships, College/university scholarship or grant aid from institutional funds. *Loans:* Direct Subsidized Stafford Loans, Direct Unsubsidized Stafford Loans, Direct PLUS loans. *Student Employment:* Federal Work-Study Program available. Institutional employment available. **Financial Aid Statistics:** 66% needy freshmen, 65% needy undergrads receive need-based scholarship or grant aid. 49% freshmen, 33% undergrads receive non-need-based scholarship or grant aid. 74% freshmen, 83% undergrads receive need-based self-help aid. 0% freshmen, 0% undergrads receive athletic scholarships. 71% freshmen, 59% undergrads receive any aid. 60% undergrads borrow to pay for school. Average cumulative indebtedness $30,451. **Criteria for awarding aid:** *Need-based:* Academics, Leadership. *Non-need-based:* Academics, Alumni affiliation, Art, Leadership, Music/drama, State/district residency.

See page 938.

THE CITADEL, THE MILITARY COLLEGE OF SOUTH CAROLINA

171 Moultrie Street, Charleston, SC 29409
Phone: 843-953-5230 • **Financial Aid Phone:** 843-953-5187
E-mail: admissions@citadel.edu • **CEEB Code:** 5108
Fax: 843-953-7036 • **Website:** www.citadel.edu • **ACT Code:** 3838

This public school was founded in 1842. It has a 300-acre campus.

RATINGS

Admissions Selectivity Rating: 78   **Fire Safety Rating:** 97   **Green Rating:** 69

STUDENTS AND FACULTY

Enrollment: 2,693. **Student Body:** 9% female, 91% male, 35% out-of-state, 1% international (11 countries represented). Asian 2%, African American 9%, Caucasian 76%, Hispanic 7%, Native American 1%, Pacific Islander <1%, Two or more races 4%, Race unknown <1%.
Retention and Graduation: 85% freshmen return for sophomore year. **Faculty:** Student/faculty ratio 12:1. 193 full-time faculty, 94% hold PhDs, 15% are are members of minority groups, 35% are women. 0% of classes are taught by teaching assistants.

ACADEMICS

Degrees: bachelor's, master's, postbachelor's certificate, post-master's certificate. **Classes:** Most classes have 20-29 students. Most lab/discussion sessions have 10-19 students. **Most popular majors:** Business Administration and Management; Criminal Justice/Law Enforcement Administration; Political Science and Government. **Special Study Options:** cooperative education program, distance learning, double major, English as a Second Language (ESL), honors program, independent study, internships, study abroad, teacher certification program. **Honors Programs:** The Citadel's Honors Program is a specially designed educational experience meeting the needs of students with an outstanding record of academic achievement and a sense of intellectual adventure. While pursuing any one of seventeen degree programs offered by The Citadel, Honors Students take a series of Core Curriculum Honors courses–for example, studies based in literature and writing, history, and mathematics, concentrated in their first two years, and an occasional Honors Seminar in their third and fourth years. For the qualified student, advantages of the Honors Program are clear: special program of pre-professional counseling, small classes, discussion-style teaching, tutorial session, special curriculum, fellow honors students, student advisory committee, honors faculty, special diploma seal and transcript, and emphasis on leadership. **Career Services:** Alumni network, Alumni services, Career/job search classes, Career assessment, Internships.

FACILITIES

Housing: Coed dorms. **Special Academic Facilities/Equipment:** Archives and Museum **Computers:** 5% of classrooms, 20% of dorms, 100% of libraries, 75% of student union, 10% of common outdoor areas have wireless network access. Students can register for classes online. Administrative functions (other than registration) can be performed online.

CAMPUS LIFE

Environment: City. **Activities:** Choral groups, concert band, jazz band, literary magazine, marching band, pep band, student government, student newspaper, yearbook, Campus Ministries. 79 registered organizations, 12 honor societies, 16 religious organizations. **Athletics (Intercollegiate):** *Men:* baseball, basketball, cross-country, football, riflery, tennis, track/field (outdoor), track/field (indoor), wrestling. *Women:* cross-country, golf, riflery, soccer, track/field (outdoor), track/field (indoor), volleyball. **On-Campus Highlights:** Summerall Chapel, Mark Clark Hall, Daniel Library, Citadel Museum, McAlister Field House. **Environmental Initiatives:** $5 Million Energy Performance Contract

ADMISSIONS

Freshman Academic Profile: Average high school GPA 3.6. 9% in top 10% of high school class, 30% in top 25% of high school class, 65% in top 50% of high school class. **Reported SAT (pre-2016 redesign) scores:** SAT Math middle 50% range 480-580. SAT Critical Reading middle 50% range 470-580. **Concordant SAT scores:** SAT Math middle 50% range 510–600. ACT middle 50% range 20-25. Minimum internet-based TOEFL 79. Minimum paper TOEFL 550. **Basis for Candidate Selection:** *Very important factors considered include:* rigor of secondary school record, academic GPA, standardized test scores, level of applicant's interest. *Important factors considered include:* extracurricular activities, talent/ability, character/personal qualities, state residency. *Other factors considered include:* class rank, recommendation(s), interview, first generation, alumni/ae relation, geographical residence, volunteer work. **Freshman Admission Requirements:** High school diploma is required and GED is accepted. *Academic units required:* 4 English, 4 math, 3 science, 3 science labs, 2 foreign language, 2 social studies,

1 history, 1 academic elective, 1 visual/performing arts, and 1 unit from above areas or other academic areas. **Freshman Admission Statistics:** 2,620 applied, 82.29% admitted, 34% enrolled. **Transfer Admission Requirements:** High school transcript, college transcript(s), standardized test scores, statement of good standing from prior institution(s). Minimum college GPA of 2.0 required. Lowest grade transferable C. **General Admission Information:** Application fee $40. Nonfall registration not accepted.

COSTS AND FINANCIAL AID

Average book expense $7,700. **Required Forms and Deadlines:** FAFSA. **Notification of Awards:** Applicants will be notified of awards on a rolling basis beginning 4/1. **Types of Aid:** *Need-based scholarships/grants:* Federal Pell, FSEOG, State scholarships/grants, Private scholarships, College/university scholarship or grant aid from institutional funds. *Loans:* Direct Subsidized Stafford Loans, Direct Unsubsidized Stafford Loans, Direct PLUS loans, Federal Perkins Loans. *Student Employment:* Federal Work-Study Program available. Institutional employment available. **Financial Aid Statistics:** 79% needy freshmen, 79% needy undergrads receive need-based scholarship or grant aid. 16% freshmen, 19% undergrads receive non-need-based scholarship or grant aid. 77% freshmen, 76% undergrads receive need-based self-help aid. 8% freshmen, 10% undergrads receive athletic scholarships. 78% freshmen, 81% undergrads receive any aid. 59% undergrads borrow to pay for school. Average cumulative indebtedness $27,872. **Criteria for awarding aid:** *Need-based:* Academics, Alumni affiliation, Leadership, Minority status, Religious affiliation. *Non-need-based:* Academics, Alumni affiliation, Athletics, Leadership, Minority status, Music/drama, Religious affiliation, State/district residency.

CITY UNIVERSITY OF NEW YORK— BARUCH COLLEGE

One Bernard Baruch Way, New York, NY 10010
Phone: 646-312-1400 • **Financial Aid Phone:** 646-312-1390
E-mail: admissions@baruch.cuny.edu • **CEEB Code:** 2034
Fax: 646-312-1361 • **Website:** www.baruch.cuny.edu

This public school was founded in 1968.

RATINGS

Admissions Selectivity Rating: 92   **Fire Safety Rating:** 60*   **Green Rating:** 60*

STUDENTS AND FACULTY

Enrollment: 14,858. **Student Body:** 51% female, 49% male, 3% out-of-state, 11% international (168 countries represented). Asian 32%, African American 9%, Caucasian 21%, Hispanic 25%, Native American <1%, Pacific Islander <1%, Two or more races 1%, Race unknown 0%.
Retention and Graduation: 91% freshmen return for sophomore year. 38% freshmen graduate within 4 years. 66 **Faculty:** Student/faculty ratio 17:1. 513 full-time faculty, 95% hold PhDs, 29% are are members of minority groups, 39% are women. 1% of classes are taught by teaching assistants.

ACADEMICS

Degrees: bachelor's, master's, post-master's certificate. **Classes:** Most classes have 20-29 students. Most lab/discussion sessions have 20-29 students. **Most popular majors:** Accounting; Finance. **Special Study Options:** Accelerated program, cross-registration, distance learning, double major, English as a Second Language (ESL), exchange student program (domestic), honors program, independent study, internships, liberal arts/career combination, student-designed major, study abroad. **Honors Programs:** CUNY Honors Program Combined degree programs: BA/MA. **Disability Services:** Special programs offered to physically disabled students, including note-taking services, reader services, tape recorders, tutors. **Career Services:** Alumni network, Alumni services, Career/job search classes, Career assessment, Internships. The Lawrence N. Field Center for Entrepreneurship is the jewel of our programs. The Field Center is a model of entrepreneurship education built around the collaboration of an institution of higher education, government, and the private sector. Faculty and students from Baruch's Zicklin School of Business, Baruch's Small Business Development Center (SBDC) Business Advisors, alumni and volunteers are brought together to support the entrepreneurial endeavors of start-up and established businesses and the college's constituents.
The Field Center recently celebrated its 17 year anniversary which comes at the heel of the continuing generosity of Lawrence N. Field ('52) and his family. In

2008 the Eris and Larry Field Foundation endowed the Field Center with a $10 million gift (previously Larry Field endowed the Center with a $3 million gift).

FACILITIES

Housing: 100% of campus accessible to physically diasbled. **Special Academic Facilities/Equipment:** Art gallery, Subotnik Financial Services Center and Wasserman Trading Floor **Computers:** 25% of classrooms, 100% of libraries, 100% of dining areas, 100% of student union, 100% of common outdoor areas have wireless network access. Students can register for classes online. Administrative functions (other than registration) can be performed online.

CAMPUS LIFE

Environment: Metropolis. **Activities:** Choral groups, dance, drama/theater, literary magazine, musical theater, radio station, student government, student newspaper, yearbook, Campus Ministries, Model UN. 172 registered organizations, 9 honor societies, 7 religious organizations. 9 fraternities, 7 sororities. **Athletics (Intercollegiate):** *Men:* baseball, basketball, cross-country, soccer, swimming, tennis, volleyball. *Women:* basketball, cheerleading, cross-country, softball, swimming, tennis, volleyball. **On-Campus Highlights:** Student Club Area- Vertical Campus Build, NewMan Library, Lobby- 23 St. Building, Food Court- Vertical Campus Building, College Fitness Center-Vertical Campus.

ADMISSIONS

Freshman Academic Profile: Average high school GPA 3.3. 47% in top 10% of high school class, 76% in top 25% of high school class, 93% in top 50% of high school class. 87% from public high schools. **Reported SAT (pre-2016 redesign) scores:** SAT Math middle 50% range 570-680. SAT Critical Reading middle 50% range 520-630. **Concordant SAT scores:** SAT Math middle 50% range 590–710. Minimum internet-based TOEFL 80. Minimum paper TOEFL 550. **Basis for Candidate Selection:** *Very important factors considered include:* rigor of secondary school record, academic GPA, standardized test scores. *Important factors considered include:* application essay, recommendation(s). *Other factors considered include:* interview, extracurricular activities, talent/ability, character/personal qualities, work experience. **Freshman Admission Requirements:** High school diploma is required and GED is accepted. *Academic units required:* 4 English, 3 math, 2 science, 2 science labs, 2 foreign language, 4 social studies. *Academic units recommended:* 2 foreign language, 1 academic elective. **Freshman Admission Statistics:** 20,789 applied, 30.67% admitted, 22% enrolled. **Transfer Admission Requirements:** High school transcript, college transcript(s), statement of good standing from prior institution(s). Minimum college GPA of 2.7 required. Lowest grade transferable C. **General Admission Information:** Application fee $65. Priority deadline 12/1. Regular application deadline 2/1. Regular notification 5/1. Nonfall registration accepted. Admission may be deferred.

COSTS AND FINANCIAL AID

Annual in-state tuition $6,330. Annual out-of-state tuition $16,800. Required fees $531. Average book expense $1,364. **Required Forms and Deadlines:** FAFSA, State aid form. **Notification of Awards:** Applicants will be notified of awards on a rolling basis beginning 4/15. **Types of Aid:** *Need-based scholarships/grants:* Federal Pell, FSEOG, State scholarships/grants, Private scholarships, College/university scholarship or grant aid from institutional funds. *Loans:* Direct Subsidized Stafford Loans, Direct Unsubsidized Stafford Loans, Direct PLUS loans, Federal Perkins Loans. *Student Employment:* Federal Work-Study Program available. Institutional employment available. **Financial Aid Statistics:** 99% needy freshmen, 100% needy undergrads receive need-based scholarship or grant aid. 6% freshmen, 2% undergrads receive non-need-based scholarship or grant aid. 15% freshmen, 27% undergrads receive need-based self-help aid. 0% freshmen, 0% undergrads receive athletic scholarships. 67% freshmen, 53% undergrads receive any aid. 30% undergrads borrow to pay for school. Average cumulative indebtedness $7,915. **Criteria for awarding aid:** *Need-based:* Academics. *Non-need-based:* Academics, State/district residency.

CITY UNIVERSITY OF NEW YORK— BROOKLYN COLLEGE

2900 Bedford Avenue, Brooklyn, NY 11210
Phone: 718-951-5001 • **Financial Aid Phone:** 718-951-51
Fax: 718-951-4506 • **Website:** www.brooklyn.cuny.edu • **ACT Code:** 20169

This public school was founded in 1930. It has a 26-acre campus.

RATINGS
Admissions Selectivity Rating: 89   **Fire Safety Rating:** 60*   **Green Rating:** 60*

STUDENTS AND FACULTY
Enrollment: 13,380. **Student Body:** 58% female, 42% male, 2% out-of-state, 3% international. Asian 19%, African American 21%, Caucasian 31%, Hispanic 23%, Native American <1%, Pacific Islander <1%, Two or more races 2%, Race unknown 0%.
Retention and Graduation: 82% freshmen return for sophomore year. 25% freshmen graduate within 4 years. 51% freshmen graduate within 6 years. **Faculty:** Student/faculty ratio 17:1. 544 full-time faculty, 92% hold PhDs, 24% are are members of minority groups, 47% are women.

ACADEMICS
Degrees: bachelor's, certificate, master's, postbachelor's certificate, post-master's certificate. **Classes:** Most classes have 20-29 students. **Most popular majors:** Accounting; Psychology; Computer and Information Sciences. **Special Study Options:** distance learning, double major, dual enrollment, English as a Second Language (ESL), honors program, independent study, internships, study abroad, teacher certification program, weekend college. **Honors Programs:** See the URL below for more information: http://www.brooklyn.cuny.edu/pub/1654.htm Combined degree programs: BA/MD. **Disability Services:** Special programs offered to physically disabled students, including note-taking services, reader services, tutors. **Career Services:** Alumni network, Alumni services, Career/job search classes, Career assessment, Internships. Magner Center for Career Development and Internships has enabled our students to explore their career options, network within top firms and companies and gain valuable experience–and often job offers–before they graduate.

FACILITIES
Housing: 100% of campus accessible to physically diasbled. **Special Academic Facilities/Equipment:** Art museum. language lab, TV studios, speech clinic, research centers and institutes, paricle accelerator. **Computers:** 2% of classrooms, 90% of libraries, 100% of dining areas, 75% of student union, 75% of common outdoor areas have wireless network access. Students can register for classes online. Administrative functions (other than registration) can be performed online.

CAMPUS LIFE
Environment: Metropolis. **Activities:** dance, drama/theater, literary magazine, music ensembles, musical theater, radio station, student government, student newspaper, television station, yearbook, Student Organization. 171 registered organizations, 7 honor societies, 7 fraternities, 9 sororities. **Athletics (Intercollegiate):** *Men:* basketball, cross-country, soccer, tennis, track/field (outdoor), track/field (indoor), volleyball. *Women:* basketball, cross-country, softball, tennis, track/field (outdoor), track/field (indoor), volleyball. **On-Campus Highlights:** Library, Student Center, Lily Pond, Library Cafe, Cafeteria, Dining Hall, Magner Center, James Hall. **Environmental Initiatives:** Reduce material consumption/waste.

ADMISSIONS
Freshman Academic Profile: Average high school GPA 3.3. 17% in top 10% of high school class, 49% in top 25% of high school class, 79% in top 50% of high school class. **Reported SAT (pre-2016 redesign) scores:** SAT Math middle 50% range 500-610. SAT Critical Reading middle 50% range 470-570. **Concordant SAT scores:** SAT Math middle 50% range 530–630. Minimum paper TOEFL 500. **Basis for Candidate Selection:** *Very important factors considered include:* rigor of secondary school record, academic GPA, standardized test scores. **Freshman Admission Requirements:** High school diploma is required and GED is accepted. *Academic units recommended:* 4 English, 3 math, 3 science, 3 foreign language, 4 social studies, 4 academic electives. **Freshman Admission Statistics:** 20,608 applied, 37.49% admitted, 17% enrolled. **Transfer Admission Requirements:** college transcript(s), Minimum college GPA of 2.3 required. Lowest grade transferable C-. **General Admission Information:** Application fee $65. Priority deadline 2/1. Nonfall registration accepted.

COSTS AND FINANCIAL AID
Annual in-state tuition $6,330. Required fees $508. **Required Forms and Deadlines:** FAFSA. **Notification of Awards:** Applicants will be notified of awards on a rolling basis beginning 5/1. **Types of Aid:** *Need-based scholarships/grants:* Federal Pell, FSEOG, State scholarships/grants, Private scholarships, College/university scholarship or grant aid from institutional funds. *Loans:* Direct Subsidized Stafford Loans, Direct Unsubsidized Stafford Loans, Direct PLUS loans, Federal Perkins Loans. *Student Employment:* Federal Work-Study Program available. Institutional employment available. **Financial Aid Statistics:** 64% needy freshmen, 82% needy undergrads receive need-based scholarship or grant aid. 26% freshmen, 27% undergrads receive non-need-based scholarship or grant aid. 77% freshmen, 89% undergrads receive need-based self-help aid. 0% freshmen, 0% undergrads receive athletic scholarships. **Criteria for awarding aid:** *Non-need-based:* Academics, Art, Leadership, Music/drama, State/district residency.

CITY UNIVERSITY OF NEW YORK— CITY COLLEGE

160 Convent Avenue, Wille Admin. Bldg., New York, NY 10031
Phone: 212 650 6977 • **Financial Aid Phone:** 212 650 5824
E-mail: admissions@ccny.cuny.edu • **CEEB Code:** 2083
Fax: 212 650 6417 • **Website:** www.ccny.cuny.edu • **ACT Code:** 2950

This public school was founded in 1847. It has a 36-acre campus.

RATINGS
Admissions Selectivity Rating: 90   **Fire Safety Rating:** 97   **Green Rating:** 94

STUDENTS AND FACULTY
Enrollment: 12,614. **Student Body:** 50% female, 50% male, 1% out-of-state, 6% international (100 countries represented). Asian 25%, African American 16%, Caucasian 14%, Hispanic 36%, Native American <1%, Pacific Islander <1%, Two or more races 2%, Race unknown 0%.
Retention and Graduation: 92% freshmen return for sophomore year. 47% freshmen graduate within 6 years. 18% grads go on to further study within 1 year. 1% grads pursue law degrees. 2% grads pursue business degrees. 27% grads pursue medical degrees. **Faculty:** Student/faculty ratio 15:1. 515 full-time faculty, 77% hold PhDs, 17% are are members of minority groups, 37% are women.

ACADEMICS
Degrees: bachelor's, doctoral/research, master's, post-master's certificate. **Classes:** Most classes have 20-29 students. Most lab/discussion sessions have 20-29 students. **Most popular majors:** Communication and Media Studies; Mechanical Engineering/Mechanical Technology/Technician; Psychology. **Special Study Options:** Accelerated program, cross-registration, double major, English as a Second Language (ESL), honors program, independent study, internships, study abroad, teacher certification program, Adult program called The Center for Worker Education which offers a evening and weekend program in liberal arts. **Honors Programs:** CUNY Macauley College and City College Honors Program. Combined degree programs: BA/MD, BA/MA. **Disability Services:** Special programs offered to physically disabled students, including note-taking services, reader services, tape recorders, tutors. **Career Services:** Alumni network, Alumni services, Career/job search classes, Career assessment, Internships.

FACILITIES
Housing: The Towers new residence hall with apartment style quarter. **Special Academic Facilities/Equipment:** Planetarium, NYC Structural Biological Center, Aaron Davis Hall/Harlem Stage Gatehouse, Landmarked Gothic orignaial campus buildings. **Computers:** 100% of classrooms, 100% of libraries, 100% of dining areas, 100% of common outdoor areas have wireless network access. Students can register for classes online. Administrative functions (other than registration) can be performed online.

CAMPUS LIFE
Environment: Metropolis. **Activities:** Choral groups, concert band, dance, drama/theater, jazz band, literary magazine, radio station, student government, student newspaper, student-run film society, yearbook, Student Organization, Model UN. 145 registered organizations, 8 religious organizations. 2 fraternities, 1 sorority. **Athletics (Intercollegiate):** *Men:* baseball, basketball, cross-country, soccer, tennis, track/field (outdoor), track/field (indoor), volleyball.

Women: basketball, fencing, soccer, tennis, track/field (outdoor), track/field (indoor), volleyball. **On-Campus Highlights:** NAC Rotunda and Plaza, Spitzer School of Archtiecture, Wingate Hall Athletic Center, North Campus Quad in warm weather, The Towers -Residence Hall. **Environmental Initiatives:** Signed on to ACUPCC and NYC Mayor's Campus 30in10 Challenge to reduce GHG emissions

ADMISSIONS

Freshman Academic Profile: 85% from public high schools. **Reported SAT (pre-2016 redesign) scores:** SAT Math middle 50% range 510-640. SAT Critical Reading middle 50% range 525-580. SAT Writing middle 50% range 450-570. **Concordant SAT scores:** SAT EBRW middle 50% 550–630. SAT Math middle 50% range 540–660. Minimum internet-based TOEFL 61. Minimum paper TOEFL 500. **Basis for Candidate Selection:** *Very important factors considered include:* rigor of secondary school record, academic GPA. *Important factors considered include:* standardized test scores. *Other factors considered include:* application essay, recommendation(s). **Freshman Admission Requirements:** High school diploma is required and GED is accepted. *Academic units recommended:* 4 English, 3 math, 2 science, 2 science labs, 3 foreign language, 4 social studies, 1 visual/performing arts. **Freshman Admission Statistics:** 23,285 applied, 37.87% admitted, 21% enrolled. **Transfer Admission Requirements:** college transcript(s), Minimum college GPA of 2.0 required. Lowest grade transferable C. **General Admission Information:** Application fee $65. Priority deadline 2/1. Nonfall registration accepted. Admission may be deferred for a maximum of 1 year.

COSTS AND FINANCIAL AID

Annual in-state tuition $6,330. Annual out-of-state tuition $16,800. Required fees $410. Average book expense $1,364. **Required Forms and Deadlines:** FAFSA, State aid form. **Notification of Awards:** Applicants will be notified of awards on a rolling basis beginning 4/1. **Types of Aid:** *Need-based scholarships/ grants:* Federal Pell, FSEOG, State scholarships/grants, College/university scholarship or grant aid from institutional funds. *Loans:* Direct Subsidized Stafford Loans, Direct Unsubsidized Stafford Loans, Direct PLUS loans. *Student Employment:* Federal Work-Study Program available. Institutional employment available. **Financial Aid Statistics:** 91% needy freshmen, 96% needy undergrads receive need-based scholarship or grant aid. 54% freshmen, 61% undergrads receive non-need-based scholarship or grant aid. 45% freshmen, 63% undergrads receive need-based self-help aid. 0% freshmen, 0% undergrads receive athletic scholarships. 80% freshmen, 79% undergrads receive any aid. **Criteria for awarding aid:** *Need-based:* Academics, Alumni affiliation, Art, Leadership, Minority status. *Non-need-based:* Academics, Alumni affiliation, Art, Leadership, Minority status, Music/drama.

CITY UNIVERSITY OF NEW YORK— COLLEGE OF STATEN ISLAND

2800 Victory Boulevard, Staten Island, NY 10314
Phone: 718-982-2010 • **Financial Aid Phone:** 718-982-2030
E-mail: admissions@csi.cuny.edu • **CEEB Code:** 2778
Fax: 718-982-2500 • **Website:** www.csi.cuny.edu • **ACT Code:** 2950

This public school was founded in 1955. It has a 204-acre campus.

RATINGS

Admissions Selectivity Rating: 71   **Fire Safety Rating:** 90   **Green Rating:** 60*

STUDENTS AND FACULTY

Enrollment: 12,139. **Student Body:** 56% female, 44% male, 1% out-of-state, 3% international (114 countries represented). Asian 13%, African American 16%, Caucasian 50%, Hispanic 18%, Native American <1%, Pacific Islander 0%, Two or more races 0%, Race unknown <1%.
Retention and Graduation: 81% freshmen return for sophomore year. 21% freshmen graduate within 4 years. 39% freshmen graduate within 6 years.
Faculty: Student/faculty ratio 18:1. 344 full-time faculty, 83% hold PhDs, 29% are are members of minority groups, 47% are women.

ACADEMICS

Degrees: associate, bachelor's, certificate, doctoral/professional, doctoral, master's, postbachelor's certifiate, post-master's certificate, terminal, transfer. **Classes:** Most classes have 30-39 students. Most lab/discussion sessions have 30-39 students. **Most popular majors:** Psychology; Business/Commerce; Registered Nursing/Registered Nurse. **Special Study Options:** Accelerated program, cooperative education program, cross-registration, distance learning, double major, dual enrollment, English as a Second Language (ESL), exchange student program (domestic), honors program, independent study, internships, liberal arts/career combination, study abroad, teacher certification program, weekend college. **Honors Programs:** CSI is one of seven campuses within

CUNY that participates in the William E. Macaulay Honors College. **Disability Services:** Special programs offered to physically disabled students, including note-taking services, reader services, tape recorders, tutors. **Career Services:** Alumni network, Alumni services, Career/job search classes, Career assessment, Internships, Regional alumni, CUNY Service Corps.

FACILITIES

Housing: 100% of campus accessible to physically diasbled. **Special Academic Facilities/Equipment:** Astrophysical Observatory, Archives and Special Collections, Center for the Arts, Center for Engineered Polymeric Materials, Center for Environmental Science, Center for Developmental Neuroscience and Developmental Disabilities, and the CSI Art Gallery **Computers:** 97% of classrooms, 100% of libraries, 100% of dining areas, 100% of student union, 100% of common outdoor areas have wireless network access. Students can register for classes online. Administrative functions (other than registration) can be performed online.

CAMPUS LIFE

Environment: Metropolis. **Activities:** Choral groups, dance, drama/ theater, jazz band, literary magazine, music ensembles, radio station, student government, student newspaper, student-run film society, yearbook, Campus Ministries, Student Organization. 47 registered organizations, 2 honor societies, 4 religious organizations. **Athletics (Intercollegiate):** *Men:* baseball, basketball, cross-country, diving, soccer, swimming, tennis. *Women:* basketball, cross-country, diving, soccer, softball, swimming, tennis, volleyball. **On- Campus Highlights:** Campus Center Rotunda, Center for the Performing Arts, Library, Sports and Recreation Center, Campus Center Game Room, The Student Lounges are also a popular site on campus for students.

ADMISSIONS

Freshman Academic Profile: Average high school GPA 3.1. 81% from public high schools. **Reported SAT (pre-2016 redesign) scores:** SAT Math middle 50% range 460-560. SAT Critical Reading middle 50% range 440-540. SAT Writing middle 50% range 430-530. **Concordant SAT scores:** SAT EBRW middle 50% 490–590. SAT Math middle 50% range 500–580. Minimum internet-based TOEFL 45. Minimum paper TOEFL 450. **Basis for Candidate Selection:** *Very important factors considered include:* rigor of secondary school record. *Important factors considered include:* academic GPA, standardized test scores. *Other factors considered include:* class rank, application essay, recommendation(s), interview, extracurricular activities, volunteer work, level of applicant's interest. **Freshman Admission Requirements:** High school diploma is required and GED is accepted. *Academic units required:* 4 English, 2 math, 2 science, 2 foreign language, 4 social studies. *Academic units recommended:* 3 math, 3 science, 3 foreign language. **Freshman Admission Statistics:** 14,018 applied, 100.00% admitted, 19% enrolled. **Transfer Admission Requirements:** college transcript(s), Minimum college GPA of 2.0 required. Lowest grade transferable C. **General Admission Information:** Application fee $65. Priority deadline 2/1. Nonfall registration accepted. Admission may be deferred for a maximum of 1 year.

COSTS AND FINANCIAL AID

Required Forms and Deadlines: FAFSA, State aid form. **Notification of Awards:** Applicants will be notified of awards on a rolling basis beginning 6/1. **Types of Aid:** *Need-based scholarships/grants:* Federal Pell, FSEOG, State scholarships/grants, Private scholarships, College/university scholarship or grant aid from institutional funds, United Negro College Fund, Federal Nursing Scholarships. *Loans:* Direct Subsidized Stafford Loans, Direct Unsubsidized Stafford Loans, Direct PLUS loans, Federal Perkins Loans. *Student Employment:* Federal Work-Study Program available. Institutional employment available. **Financial Aid Statistics:** 63% needy freshmen, 78% needy undergrads receive need-based scholarship or grant aid. 76% freshmen, 77% undergrads receive non-need-based scholarship or grant aid. 34% freshmen, 31% undergrads receive need-based self-help aid. 0% freshmen, 0% undergrads receive athletic scholarships. **Criteria for awarding aid:** *Need-based:* Academics, Alumni affiliation, Art, Leadership, Minority status, Music/drama. *Non-need-based:* Academics, Alumni affiliation, Art, Leadership, Minority status, Music/drama, State/district residency.

CITY UNIVERSITY OF NEW YORK— HUNTER COLLEGE

695 Park Ave, Room N203, New York, NY 10065
Phone: 212-772-4490 • **Financial Aid Phone:** 212-772-4820
E-mail: admissions@hunter.cuny.edu • **CEEB Code:** 2301
Fax: 212-650-3472 • **Website:** www.hunter.cuny.edu

This public school was founded in 1870.

RATINGS

Admissions Selectivity Rating: 90 **Fire Safety Rating:** 97 **Green Rating:** 92

STUDENTS AND FACULTY

Enrollment: 15,632. **Student Body:** 64% female, 36% male, 3% out-of-state, 6% international (151 countries represented). Asian 29%, African American 12%, Caucasian 32%, Hispanic 21%, Native American <1%, Pacific Islander 0%, Two or more races 0%, Race unknown 0%.
Retention and Graduation: 85% freshmen return for sophomore year. 24% freshmen graduate within 4 years. 53% freshmen graduate within 6 years.
Faculty: Student/faculty ratio 14:1. 677 full-time faculty, 83% hold PhDs, 19% are are members of minority groups, 51% are women.

ACADEMICS

Degrees: bachelor's, doctoral, master's, postbachelor's certificate, post-master's certificate. **Classes:** Most classes have 20-29 students. **Most popular majors:** Psychology; English Language and Literature; Chemistry. **Special Study Options:** Accelerated program, cross-registration, distance learning, double major, dual enrollment, exchange student program (domestic), honors program, independent study, internships, liberal arts/career combination, student-designed major, study abroad, teacher certification program. Combined degree programs: BA/MA, BA/MS. **Disability Services:** Special programs offered to physically disabled students, including note-taking services, reader services, tape recorders, tutors. **Career Services:** Alumni network, Alumni services, Career/job search classes, Internships.

FACILITIES

Housing: Coed dorms. 100% of campus accessible to physically diasbled.
Special Academic Facilities/Equipment: Art Gallery, theatre, geology club, on-campus elementary and secondary schools. **Computers:** 70% of classrooms, have wireless network access. Students can register for classes online.

CAMPUS LIFE

Environment: Metropolis. **Activities:** Choral groups, concert band, dance, drama/theater, jazz band, literary magazine, music ensembles, musical theater, radio station, student government, student newspaper, student-run film society, symphony orchestra, television station, yearbook. 150 registered organizations, 20 honor societies, 2 fraternities, 2 sororities. **Athletics (Intercollegiate):** *Men:* basketball, cross-country, fencing, soccer, tennis, track/field (outdoor), track/field (indoor), volleyball, wrestling. *Women:* basketball, cross-country, diving, fencing, softball, swimming, tennis, track/field (outdoor), track/field (indoor), volleyball. **On-Campus Highlights:** Over 100 Campus Clubs, CARSI Geography Lab, Television Studio, Learning Center and Computer Lab, Sports Complex. **Environmental Initiatives:** Hunter has an extensive program for recycling paper, metal, glass, plastic, e-waste, and household batteries. This program is continuously being expanded.

ADMISSIONS

Freshman Academic Profile: Average high school GPA 3.3. 70% from public high schools. **Reported SAT (pre-2016 redesign) scores:** SAT Math middle 50% range 580-640. SAT Critical Reading middle 50% range 560-610. **Concordant SAT scores:** SAT Math middle 50% range 600–660. Minimum paper TOEFL 500. **Basis for Candidate Selection:** *Very important factors considered include:* rigor of secondary school record, academic GPA, standardized test scores, application essay. **Freshman Admission Requirements:** High school diploma is required and GED is accepted. *Academic units required:* 2 English, 2 math, 1 science, 1 science lab. *Academic units recommended:* 4 English, 3 math, 2 science, 2 foreign language, 4 social studies, 1 academic elective, 1 visual/performing arts. **Freshman Admission Statistics:** 28,510 applied, 38.53% admitted, 20% enrolled. **Transfer Admission Requirements:** college transcript(s), Minimum college GPA of 2.3 required. Lowest grade transferable C. **General Admission Information:** Application fee $65. Regular application deadline 3/15. Nonfall registration accepted.

COSTS AND FINANCIAL AID

Annual in-state tuition $6,330. Annual out-of-state tuition $16,800. Room and board $8,655. Required fees $450. **Required Forms and Deadlines:** FAFSA, State aid form. **Notification of Awards:** Applicants will be notified of awards on a rolling basis beginning 5/15. **Types of Aid:** *Need-based scholarships/ grants:* Federal Pell, State scholarships/grants, College/university scholarship or grant aid from institutional funds. *Loans:* Direct Subsidized Stafford Loans, Direct Unsubsidized Stafford Loans, Direct PLUS loans, Federal Perkins Loans, State Loans, College/university loans from institutional funds. *Student Employment:* Federal Work-Study Program available. Institutional employment available. **Financial Aid Statistics:** 89% needy freshmen, 86% needy undergrads receive need-based scholarship or grant aid. 84% freshmen, 39% undergrads receive non-need-based scholarship or grant aid. 8% freshmen, 17% undergrads receive need-based self-help aid. 0% freshmen, 0% undergrads receive athletic scholarships. 91% freshmen, 94% undergrads receive any aid. **Criteria for awarding aid:** *Need-based:* Academics. *Non-need-based:* Academics.

CITY UNIVERSITY OF NEW YORK— KINGSBOROUGH COMMUNITY COLLEGE

2001 Oriental Blvd., Brooklyn, NY 11235
Phone: 718-368-4600 • **Financial Aid Phone:** 718-368-4644
E-mail: info@kbcc.cuny.edu
Fax: 718-368-5356

This is a public school.

RATINGS

Admissions Selectivity Rating: 60* **Fire Safety Rating:** 60* **Green Rating:** 60*

STUDENTS AND FACULTY

Enrollment: 14,997. **Student Body:** 56% female, 44% male, 4% international (137 countries represented). Asian 12%, African American 35%, Caucasian 33%, Hispanic 16%, Native American <1%, Pacific Islander 0%, Two or more races 0%, Race unknown 0%.
Retention and Graduation: 66% freshmen return for sophomore year.
Faculty: Student/faculty ratio 23:1. 354 full-time faculty, 54% hold PhDs, 26% are are members of minority groups, 52% are women. 0% of classes are taught by teaching assistants.

ACADEMICS

Degrees: associate, certificate, terminal, transfer. **Classes:** Most classes have 20-29 students. **Most popular majors:** Liberal Arts and Sciences/Liberal Studies; Business/Commerce; Biology/Biological Sciences. **Special Study Options:** Accelerated program, cross-registration, dual enrollment, English as a Second Language (ESL), honors program, independent study, internships, My Turn Program for senior citizens. New Start Program for students academically dismissed from 4-year institutions.

ADMISSIONS

Minimum paper TOEFL 475. **Freshman Admission Requirements:** High school diploma or equivalent is not required. *Academic units recommended:* 4 English, 3 math, 2 science, 2 foreign language, 4 social studies, and 1 unit from above areas or other academic areas. **Transfer Admission Requirements:** college transcript(s), essay or personal statement, interview, Lowest grade transferable C. **General Admission Information:** Application fee $65. Priority deadline 7/15. Regular application deadline 8/15. Nonfall registration accepted.

COSTS AND FINANCIAL AID

Annual in-state tuition $3,610. Annual out-of-state tuition $7,200. Required fees $350. *Student Employment:* Federal Work-Study Program available. Institutional employment available.

CITY UNIVERSITY OF NEW YORK— LEHMAN COLLEGE

250 Bedford Park Boulevard West, Bronx, NY 10468
Phone: 718-960-8000 • **Financial Aid Phone:** 718-960-8545
E-mail: wilkes@alpha.lehman.cuny.edu • **CEEB Code:** 2950
Fax: 718-960-8712

This public school was founded in 1968. It has a 38-acre campus.

RATINGS
Admissions Selectivity Rating: 79   **Fire Safety Rating:** 60*   **Green Rating:** 60*

STUDENTS AND FACULTY
Enrollment: 8,236. **Student Body:** 71% female, 29% male, 1% out-of-state, 5% international (123 countries represented). Asian 4%, African American 32%, Caucasian 10%, Hispanic 49%, Native American <1%, Pacific Islander 0%, Two or more races 0%, Race unknown 0%.
Retention and Graduation: 77% freshmen return for sophomore year. 12% freshmen graduate within 4 years. 33% freshmen graduate within 6 years.
Faculty: Student/faculty ratio 15:1. 368 full-time faculty, 75% hold PhDs, 27% are are members of minority groups, 52% are women.

ACADEMICS
Degrees: bachelor's, certificate, diploma, master's. **Classes:** Most classes have 20-29 students. **Most popular majors:** Social Work; Sociology. **Special Study Options:** Accelerated program, cooperative education program, cross-registration, distance learning, double major, dual enrollment, English as a Second Language (ESL), exchange student program (domestic), honors program, independent study, internships, student-designed major, study abroad, teacher certification program, weekend college, bilingual liberal arts (first 2 years may be taken in Spanish), professional writing concentration, 3-2 engineering program with City College. **Honors Programs:** Lehman Scholars Program. Students receive full tuition, stipends, an expense account to use for academically enriching experiences and a laptop computer. Combined degree programs: BA/MA. **Disability Services:** Special programs offered to physically disabled students, including note-taking services, reader services, tape recorders, tutors.

FACILITIES
Housing: n/a. 80% of campus accessible to physically diasbled. **Special Academic Facilities/Equipment:** Art gallery, concert hall, sports complex. **Computers:** Students can register for classes online. Administrative functions (other than registration) can be performed online.

CAMPUS LIFE
Environment: Metropolis. **Activities:** Choral groups, concert band, dance, drama/theater, jazz band, literary magazine, music ensembles, musical theater, opera, radio station, student government, student newspaper, student-run film society, symphony orchestra, television station, yearbook, Student Organization. 3 honor societies, 1 religious organization. 1 fraternity, 1 sorority. **Athletics (Intercollegiate):** *Men:* badminton, baseball, basketball, cross-country, diving, swimming, tennis, track/field (outdoor), volleyball. *Women:* badminton, basketball, cross-country, diving, softball, swimming, tennis, track/field (outdoor), volleyball. **On-Campus Highlights:** APEX athletic facility, Cyber Cafe, Art Gallery, Concert Hall, Information Technology Center.

ADMISSIONS
Freshman Academic Profile: Average high school GPA 2.7. 74% from public high schools. **Reported SAT (pre-2016 redesign) scores:** SAT Math middle 50% range 400-500. SAT Critical Reading middle 50% range 400-490. **Concordant SAT scores:** SAT Math middle 50% range 440–530. Minimum paper TOEFL 500. **Basis for Candidate Selection:** *Very important factors considered include:* rigor of secondary school record, standardized test scores. *Important factors considered include:* academic GPA. *Other factors considered include:* application essay, recommendation(s), interview, extracurricular activities, talent/ability. **Freshman Admission Requirements:** High school diploma is required and GED is accepted. *Academic units required:* 4 English, 2 math, 2 science, 1 science lab, 2 foreign language, 1 social studies, 1 history. *Academic units recommended:* 4 English, 3 math, 3 science, 2 foreign language, 2 social studies, 2 history, 1 visual/performing arts. **Freshman Admission Statistics:** 14,155 applied, 31.61% admitted, 58% enrolled. **Transfer Admission Requirements:** college transcript(s), Minimum college GPA of 2 required. Lowest grade transferable C. **General Admission Information:** Application fee $65. Priority deadline 1/15. Regular application deadline 8/15. Nonfall registration accepted. Admission may be deferred for a maximum of 1 semester.

COSTS AND FINANCIAL AID
Annual in-state tuition $4,000. Annual out-of-state tuition $10,800. Required fees $290. Average book expense $938. **Required Forms and Deadlines:**

FAFSA, State aid form. **Notification of Awards:** Applicants will be notified of awards on a rolling basis beginning 3/1. **Types of Aid:** *Need-based scholarships/grants:* Federal Pell, FSEOG, State scholarships/grants, Private scholarships, College/university scholarship or grant aid from institutional funds. *Loans:* Direct Subsidized Stafford Loans, Direct Unsubsidized Stafford Loans, Direct PLUS loans, Federal Perkins Loans, State Loans, College/university loans from institutional funds. *Student Employment:* Federal Work-Study Program available. Institutional employment available. **Financial Aid Statistics:** 88% needy freshmen, 90% needy undergrads receive need-based scholarship or grant aid. 42% freshmen, 15% undergrads receive non-need-based scholarship or grant aid. 19% freshmen, 44% undergrads receive need-based self-help aid. 0% freshmen, 0% undergrads receive athletic scholarships. 83% freshmen, 80% undergrads receive any aid. **Criteria for awarding aid:** *Need-based:* Academics. *Non-need-based:* Academics.

CITY UNIVERSITY OF NEW YORK— MEDGAR EVERS COLLEGE

1665 Bedford Avenue, Brooklyn, NY 11225
Phone: 718-270-6024 • **Financial Aid Phone:** 718-270-6133
E-mail: applytomec@mec.cuny.edu
Fax: 718-270-6411

This public school was founded in 1969. It has a 7-acre campus.

RATINGS
Admissions Selectivity Rating: 71   **Fire Safety Rating:** 60*   **Green Rating:** 60*

STUDENTS AND FACULTY
Enrollment: 6,257. **Student Body:** 73% female, 27% male, 0% out-of-state, 1% international. Asian 2%, African American 67%, Caucasian 1%, Hispanic 13%, Native American 1%, Pacific Islander 0%, Two or more races 0%, Race unknown 15%.
Retention and Graduation: 65% freshmen return for sophomore year. 7% freshmen graduate within 4 years. 19% freshmen graduate within 6 years.
Faculty: 180 full-time faculty, 63% hold PhDs, 0% are are members of minority groups, 46% are women. 0% of classes are taught by teaching assistants.

ACADEMICS
Degrees: associate, bachelor's, certificate. **Classes:** Most classes have 30-39 students. Most lab/discussion sessions have 10-19 students. **Most popular majors:** Liberal Arts and Sciences/Liberal Studies; Business Administration and Management; Biology/Biological Sciences. **Special Study Options:** cross-registration, distance learning, English as a Second Language (ESL), honors program, independent study, internships, study abroad, teacher certification program. **Disability Services:** Special programs offered to physically disabled students, including note-taking services, reader services, tape recorders, tutors. **Career Services:** Alumni services, Career/job search classes, Career assessment, Internships. Career Job Search classes, Business Etiquette Series, Interviewing Skills.

FACILITIES
Housing: 100% of campus accessible to physically diasbled. **Computers:** 90% of classrooms, 100% of libraries, have wireless network access. Students can register for classes online. Administrative functions (other than registration) can be performed online.

CAMPUS LIFE
Environment: Metropolis. **Activities:** Choral groups, dance, drama/theater, jazz band, literary magazine, musical theater, radio station, student government, student newspaper, television station, yearbook, Student Organization. 32 registered organizations, 4 honor societies, 2 religious organizations. **Athletics (Intercollegiate):** *Men:* basketball, cross-country, soccer, swimming, track/field (outdoor), track/field (indoor), volleyball. *Women:* basketball, cheerleading, cross-country, soccer, softball, swimming, tennis, track/field (outdoor), track/field (indoor), volleyball. **On-Campus Highlights:** Amphitheater, NASA Space Center Lab, Library, Departments, New Building.

ADMISSIONS
Reported SAT (pre-2016 redesign) scores: SAT Math middle 50% range 340-430. SAT Critical Reading middle 50% range 350-430. SAT Writing middle 50% range 350-430. **Concordant SAT scores:** SAT EBRW middle 50% 400–480. SAT Math middle 50% range 380–470. Minimum paper TOEFL 475. **Basis for Candidate Selection:** *Other factors considered include:* rigor of secondary school record, academic GPA, standardized test scores. **Freshman Admission Requirements:** High school diploma is required and GED is accepted. *Academic units recommended:* 4 English, 3 math, 2 science, 2 foreign language, 4 social studies, 2 academic electives. **Freshman Admission**

Statistics: 1,092 applied, 100.00% admitted, 100% enrolled. **Transfer Admission Requirements:** college transcript(s), Minimum college GPA of 2.0 required. Lowest grade transferable C. **General Admission Information:** Application fee $65. Nonfall registration accepted. Admission may be deferred for a maximum of one semester.

COSTS AND FINANCIAL AID
Annual in-state tuition $3,630. Annual out-of-state tuition $16,800. Required fees $125. Average book expense $1,364. **Required Forms and Deadlines:** FAFSA, State aid form. **Notification of Awards:** Applicants will be notified of awards on a rolling basis beginning 5/1. **Types of Aid:** *Need-based scholarships/ grants:* Federal Pell, FSEOG, State scholarships/grants. *Loans:* Direct Subsidized Stafford Loans, Direct Unsubsidized Stafford Loans, Direct PLUS loans, Federal Perkins Loans. *Student Employment:* Federal Work-Study Program available. Institutional employment available. **Criteria for awarding aid:** *Non-need-based:* Academics, Leadership.

CITY UNIVERSITY OF NEW YORK— NEW YORK CITY COLLEGE OF TECHNOLOGY

300 Jay Street, Brooklyn, NY 11201
Phone: 718-260-5500 • **Financial Aid Phone:** 718-260-5700
E-mail: admissions@citytech.cuny.edu • **CEEB Code:** 2550
Fax: 718-260-5504 • **Website:** http://www.citytech.cuny.edu/ • **ACT Code:** 2950

This public school was founded in 1946. It has a 3-acre campus.

RATINGS
Admissions Selectivity Rating: 64   **Fire Safety Rating:** 60*   **Green Rating:** 60*

STUDENTS AND FACULTY
Enrollment: 15,917. **Student Body:** 44% female, 56% male, 1% out-of-state, 5% international (106 countries represented). Asian 18%, African American 32%, Caucasian 13%, Hispanic 31%, Native American <1%, Pacific Islander <1%, Two or more races 1%, Race unknown 0%.
Retention and Graduation: 77% freshmen return for sophomore year. 3% freshmen graduate within 4 years. 24% freshmen graduate within 6 years. **Faculty:** Student/faculty ratio 17:1. 433 full-time faculty, 63% hold PhDs, 45% are are members of minority groups, 48% are women. 0% of classes are taught by teaching assistants.

ACADEMICS
Degrees: associate, bachelor's, certificate. **Classes:** Most classes have 20-29 students. Most lab/discussion sessions have 20-29 students. **Most popular majors:** Information Science/Studies; Design and Visual Communications; Hospitality Administration/Management. **Special Study Options:** distance learning, dual enrollment, English as a Second Language (ESL), honors program, independent study, internships, study abroad, teacher certification program, Bridge programs to higher education or careers in engineering technology, alternate format program for those out of high school 5 years with or without diploma. **Disability Services:** Special programs offered to physically disabled students, including note-taking services, reader services, tape recorders, tutors. **Career Services:** Alumni network, Alumni services, Career/ job search classes, Career assessment, Internships.

FACILITIES
Housing: Some housing avilable at nearby university. 100% of campus accessible to physically diasbled. **Computers:** Students can register for classes online. Administrative functions (other than registration) can be performed online.

CAMPUS LIFE
Environment: Metropolis. **Activities:** dance, drama/theater, musical theater, student government, student newspaper. 60 registered organizations. **Athletics (Intercollegiate):** *Men:* basketball, tennis, track/field (outdoor). *Women:* basketball, tennis, track/field (outdoor). **Environmental Initiatives:** reducing the amount of waste produced by our purchasing and procurement system

ADMISSIONS
Minimum internet-based TOEFL 61. Minimum paper TOEFL 500. **Basis for Candidate Selection:** *Important factors considered include:* rigor of secondary school record, academic GPA. *Other factors considered include:* class rank, standardized test scores, application essay, recommendation(s). **Freshman Admission Requirements:** High school diploma is required and GED is accepted. *Academic units required:* 4 English, 3 math, 2 science, 2 science labs, 2 foreign language, 3 social studies, 1 visual/performing arts. *Academic units recommended:* 4 English, 4 math, 3 science, 3 science labs, 2 foreign language, 4 social studies, 1 visual/performing arts. **Freshman Admission Statistics:** 17,465 applied, 70.58% admitted, 27% enrolled. **Transfer Admission**

Requirements: High school transcript, college transcript(s), statement of good standing from prior institution(s). Minimum college GPA of 2.0 required. Lowest grade transferable C. **General Admission Information:** Application fee $65. Priority deadline 2/1. Regular application deadline 2/1. Nonfall registration accepted. Admission may be deferred for a maximum of 1 semester.

COSTS AND FINANCIAL AID
Annual in-state tuition $5,730. Annual out-of-state tuition $15,300. Required fees $339. **Required Forms and Deadlines:** FAFSA, State aid form. **Types of Aid:** *Need-based scholarships/grants:* Federal Pell, FSEOG, State scholarships/grants, Federal Nursing Scholarships. *Loans:* Direct Subsidized Stafford Loans, Direct Unsubsidized Stafford Loans, Direct PLUS loans, Federal Perkins Loans. *Student Employment:* Federal Work-Study Program available. Institutional employment available. **Criteria for awarding aid:** *Need-based:* Academics. *Non-need-based:* State/district residency.

CITY UNIVERSITY OF NEW YORK— QUEENS COLLEGE

6530 Kissena Blvd, Queens, NY 11367
Phone: 718-997-5600 • **Financial Aid Phone:** 718-997-5123
E-mail: vincent.angrisani@qc.cuny.edu • **CEEB Code:** 2750
Fax: 718-997-5617 • **Website:** www.qc.cuny.edu • **ACT Code:** 20173

This public school was founded in 1937. It has a 76-acre campus.

RATINGS
Admissions Selectivity Rating: 89   **Fire Safety Rating:** 97   **Green Rating:** 87

STUDENTS AND FACULTY
Enrollment: 15,426. **Student Body:** 55% female, 45% male, 1% out-of-state, 5% international (176 countries represented). Asian 30%, African American 11%, Caucasian 33%, Hispanic 21%, Native American <1%, Pacific Islander 0%, Two or more races 0%, Race unknown 0%.
Retention and Graduation: 84% freshmen return for sophomore year. 31% freshmen graduate within 4 years. 35% grads go on to further study within 1 year. 10% grads pursue arts and sciences degrees. 2% grads pursue law degrees. 1% grads pursue business degrees. 1% grads pursue medical degrees. **Faculty:** Student/faculty ratio 14:1. 611 full-time faculty, 87% hold PhDs, 22% are are members of minority groups, 46% are women. 1% of classes are taught by teaching assistants.

ACADEMICS
Degrees: bachelor's, master's, postbachelor's certificate, post-master's certificate. **Classes:** Most classes have 20-29 students. **Most popular majors:** Accounting; Psychology; Economics. **Special Study Options:** Accelerated program, cross-registration, double major, dual enrollment, English as a Second Language (ESL), honors program, independent study, internships, liberal arts/career combination, student-designed major, study abroad, teacher certification program, weekend college, Courses offered through Blackboard. **Honors Programs:** Queens College participates in the CUNY Honors College—a highly selective program that offers a challenging curriculum and a full tuition scholarship plus other financial support. The program accepts first-time freshmen in the fall semester only. Combined degree programs: BA/ MA. **Disability Services:** Special programs offered to physically disabled students, including note-taking services, reader services, tape recorders, tutors. **Career Services:** Alumni network, Alumni services, Career/job search classes, Career assessment, Internships. Career Fair—over 70 employers from various fields (Accounting, Banking, Finance, Human Services, Publishing, Media, Government, Technology, etc) come to the campus to interview and meet with students.

FACILITIES
Housing: Coed dorms. 100% of campus accessible to physically diasbled. **Special Academic Facilities/Equipment:** Godwin-Ternbach Museum, Louis Armstrong House Museum & Archieves, Colden Auditorium, Kupferberg Center for the Performing Arts, Art Library **Computers:** 100% of classrooms, 100% of dorms, 100% of libraries, 100% of dining areas, 100% of student union, 100% of common outdoor areas have wireless network access. Students can register for classes online. Administrative functions (other than registration) can be performed online.

CAMPUS LIFE

Environment: Metropolis. **Activities:** Choral groups, concert band, dance, drama/theater, jazz band, literary magazine, music ensembles, musical theater, radio station, student government, student newspaper, student-run film society, symphony orchestra, television station, yearbook, Student Organization. 114 registered organizations, 5 honor societies, 12 religious organizations. 4 fraternities, 3 sororities. **Athletics (Intercollegiate):** *Men:* baseball, basketball, cross-country, diving, soccer, swimming, tennis, track/field (outdoor), water polo. *Women:* basketball, cross-country, diving, fencing, lacrosse, soccer, softball, swimming, tennis, track/field (outdoor), volleyball, water polo. **On-Campus Highlights:** Rosenthal Library, Student Union, Athletic Center, Dining Hall, Classrooms and Laboratory Facilities, Cafes around campus. **Environmental Initiatives:** Retrofit and completion of mechanical upgrade 27M for the new Science Building that will significantly reduce energy consumption.

ADMISSIONS

Freshman Academic Profile: 75% from public high schools. **Reported SAT (pre-2016 redesign) scores:** SAT Math middle 50% range 520-610. SAT Critical Reading middle 50% range 480-570. SAT Writing middle 50% range 460-555. **Concordant SAT scores:** SAT EBRW middle 50% 530–620. SAT Math middle 50% range 550–630. Minimum internet-based TOEFL 62. Minimum paper TOEFL 500. **Basis for Candidate Selection:** *Very important factors considered include:* rigor of secondary school record, academic GPA, standardized test scores. **Freshman Admission Requirements:** High school diploma is required and GED is accepted. *Academic units required:* 4 English, 3 math, 2 science, 2 science labs, 3 foreign language, 4 social studies. *Academic units recommended:* 3 science, 3 science labs. **Freshman Admission Statistics:** 18,142 applied, 41.34% admitted, 20% enrolled. **Transfer Admission Requirements:** High school transcript, college transcript(s), standardized test scores, Minimum college GPA of 2.25 required. Lowest grade transferable 2. **General Admission Information:** Application fee $65. Priority deadline 2/1. Nonfall registration accepted. Admission may be deferred for a maximum of 1 semester.

COSTS AND FINANCIAL AID

Annual in-state tuition $6,330. Annual out-of-state tuition $16,800. Required fees $608. Average book expense $1,364. **Required Forms and Deadlines:** FAFSA, Institution's own financial aid form, State aid form. **Notification of Awards:** Applicants will be notified of awards on a rolling basis beginning 3/1. **Types of Aid:** *Need-based scholarships/grants:* Federal Pell, FSEOG, State scholarships/grants, Private scholarships, College/university scholarship or grant aid from institutional funds. *Loans:* Direct Subsidized Stafford Loans, Direct Unsubsidized Stafford Loans, Direct PLUS loans, Federal Perkins Loans. *Student Employment:* Federal Work-Study Program available. Institutional employment available. **Financial Aid Statistics:** 86% needy freshmen, 84% needy undergrads receive need-based scholarship or grant aid. 3% freshmen, 3% undergrads receive non-need-based scholarship or grant aid. 15% freshmen, 35% undergrads receive need-based self-help aid. 2% freshmen, 1% undergrads receive athletic scholarships. 85% freshmen, 53% undergrads receive any aid. 15% undergrads borrow to pay for school. Average cumulative indebtedness $15,000. **Criteria for awarding aid:** *Non-need-based:* Academics, Athletics.

CLAFLIN UNIVERSITY

400 Magnolia Street, Orangeburg, SC 29115
Phone: 803-535-5340 • **Financial Aid Phone:** 803-535-5720
E-mail: admissions@claflin.edu • **CEEB Code:** 5109
Fax: 803-535-5387 • **ACT Code:** 3840

This private school, affiliated with the Methodist Church, was founded in 1869. It has a 43-acre campus.

RATINGS

Admissions Selectivity Rating: 78 **Fire Safety Rating:** 88 **Green Rating:** 90

STUDENTS AND FACULTY

Enrollment: 1,803. **Student Body:** 65% female, 35% male, 19% out-of-state, 3% international (15 countries represented). Asian 1%, African American 92%, Caucasian 1%, Hispanic 2%, Native American 1%, Pacific Islander 0%, Two or more races <1%, Race unknown 0%.
Retention and Graduation: 73% freshmen return for sophomore year. 32% freshmen graduate within 4 years. 49% freshmen graduate within 6 years.
Faculty: Student/faculty ratio 13:1. 119 full-time faculty, 84% hold PhDs, 76% are are members of minority groups, 43% are women.

ACADEMICS

Degrees: bachelor's, master's. **Classes:** Most classes have 20-29 students. Most lab/discussion sessions have 10-19 students. **Most popular majors:**

Business Administration and Management; Sociology; Biology/Biological Sciences. **Special Study Options:** Accelerated program, cooperative education program, cross-registration, double major, dual enrollment, English as a Second Language (ESL), honors program, independent study, internships, study abroad, teacher certification program, weekend college, (3+2) BS Mathematics(Applied Mathematics Track)/Claflin + BS Engineering/Clemson (3+2) BS Mathematics(Applied Mathematics Track)/Claflin + BS Engineering Technology/South Carolina State University (2+2) Associates Degree/Orangeburg-Calhoun Technical College + BS Biotechnology/Claflin University. **Honors Programs:** The Alice Carson Tisdale Honors College Combined degree programs: Dual-degree(2+2) in Biotechnology. **Disability Services:** Special programs offered to physically disabled students, including note-taking services. **Career Services:** Career/job search classes, Career assessment, Internships.

FACILITIES

Housing: men's dorms, women's dorms. 90% of campus accessible to physically diasbled. **Special Academic Facilities/Equipment:** T.V. studio, NMR Wilbur R. Gregg collection, Aruther Rose Museum. **Computers:** 33% of classrooms, 100% of libraries, 100% of dining areas, have wireless network access. Students can register for classes online. Administrative functions (other than registration) can be performed online.

CAMPUS LIFE

Environment: Village. **Activities:** Choral groups, concert band, dance, drama/theater, jazz band, literary magazine, music ensembles, radio station, student government, student newspaper, student-run film society, television station, yearbook, Student Organization. 3 honor societies, 4 fraternities, 4 sororities. **Athletics (Intercollegiate):** *Men:* baseball, basketball, cross-country, track/field (outdoor), track/field (indoor). *Women:* basketball, cross-country, softball, track/field (outdoor), track/field (indoor), volleyball. **On-Campus Highlights:** Student Life Center, Computer Labs, SOAR Center, Center for Vocational Reflections, Arthur Rose Museum, Jonas T. Kennedy Health And Physical Education Center. **Environmental Initiatives:** Recycling Program.

ADMISSIONS

Freshman Academic Profile: Average high school GPA 2.7. 10% in top 10% of high school class, 26% in top 25% of high school class, 63% in top 50% of high school class. **Reported SAT (pre-2016 redesign) scores:** SAT Math middle 50% range 350-440. SAT Critical Reading middle 50% range 350-440. **Concordant SAT scores:** SAT Math middle 50% range 390–480. ACT middle 50% range 15-19. **Basis for Candidate Selection:** *Very important factors considered include:* rigor of secondary school record, class rank, academic GPA, standardized test scores, character/personal qualities, first generation. *Important factors considered include:* application essay, extracurricular activities, talent/ability, alumni/ae relation, level of applicant's interest. *Other factors considered include:* recommendation(s), state residency, volunteer work, work experience. **Freshman Admission Requirements:** High school diploma is required and GED is accepted. *Academic units required:* 4 English, 3 math, 3 science, 1 foreign language, 1 social studies, 1 history, 7 academic electives, 1 computer science, and 2 units from above areas or other academic areas. **Freshman Admission Statistics:** 5,237 applied, 43.77% admitted, 17% enrolled. **Transfer Admission Requirements:** college transcript(s), statement of good standing from prior institution(s). Minimum college GPA of 2.0 required. Lowest grade transferable C. **General Admission Information:** Application fee $30. Priority deadline 1/15. Regular application deadline 8/1. Nonfall registration accepted. Admission may be deferred.

COSTS AND FINANCIAL AID

Annual tuition $14,640. Room and board $8,420. Required fees $370. Average book expense $1,750. **Required Forms and Deadlines:** FAFSA, Institution's own financial aid form. **Notification of Awards:** Applicants will be notified of awards on a rolling basis beginning 5/3. **Types of Aid:** *Need-based scholarships/grants:* Federal Pell, FSEOG, State scholarships/grants, Private scholarships, College/university scholarship or grant aid from institutional funds, United Negro College Fund. *Loans:* Federal Perkins Loans. *Student Employment:* Federal Work-Study Program available. Institutional employment available. **Financial Aid Statistics:** 88% needy freshmen, 95% needy undergrads receive need-based scholarship or grant aid. 7% freshmen, 6% undergrads receive non-need-based scholarship or grant aid. 75% freshmen, undergrads receive need-based self-help aid. 0% freshmen, 0% undergrads receive athletic scholarships. **Criteria for awarding aid:** *Need-based:* Academics, Alumni affiliation, Art, Athletics, Leadership, Music/drama, Religious affiliation.

CLAREMONT MCKENNA COLLEGE

888 Columbia Avenue, Claremont, CA 91711
Phone: 909-621-8088 • **Financial Aid Phone:** 909-621-8356
E-mail: admission@cmc.edu • **CEEB Code:** 4054
Fax: 909-621-8516 • **Website:** www.claremontmckenna.edu • **ACT Code:** 224

This private school was founded in 1946. It has a 56-acre campus.

RATINGS

Admissions Selectivity Rating: 98   **Fire Safety Rating:** 88   **Green Rating:** 79

STUDENTS AND FACULTY

Enrollment: 1,344. **Student Body:** 49% female, 51% male, 56% out-of-state, 17% international (31 countries represented). Asian 10%, African American 5%, Caucasian 42%, Hispanic 14%, Native American <1%, Pacific Islander <1%, Two or more races 6%, Race unknown 6%.
Retention and Graduation: 93% freshmen return for sophomore year. 86% freshmen graduate within 4 years. 93 12% grads go on to further study within 1 year. **Faculty:** Student/faculty ratio 9:1. 142 full-time faculty, 99% hold PhDs, 15% are are members of minority groups, 36% are women.

ACADEMICS

Degrees: bachelor's, master's. **Classes:** Most classes have 10-19 students. **Most popular majors:** Economics; Political Science and Government; Psychology. **Special Study Options:** cross-registration, double major, English as a Second Language (ESL), exchange student program (domestic), independent study, internships, student-designed major, study abroad. Combined degree programs: BA/MA, BA/MBA. **Disability Services:** Special programs offered to physically disabled students, including note-taking services, reader services, tape recorders, tutors. **Career Services:** Alumni network, Alumni services, Career/job search classes, Career assessment, Internships, Regional alumni. Our Sponsored Internship Program provides significant funding for students to pursue unpaid internships anywhere in the world.

FACILITIES

Housing: Coed dorms, special housing for disabled students, apartments for single students. **Special Academic Facilities/Equipment:** Art galleries, athenaeum complex, centers for Black and Chicano studies, computer lab, leadership lab, science center. **Computers:** 100% of classrooms, 100% of dorms, 100% of libraries, 100% of dining areas, 100% of student union, 100% of common outdoor areas have wireless network access. Administrative functions (other than registration) can be performed online.

CAMPUS LIFE

Environment: Town. **Activities:** Choral groups, dance, drama/theater, music ensembles, pep band, radio station, student government, student newspaper, symphony orchestra, yearbook, Campus Ministries, Student Organization, Model UN. 280 registered organizations, 7 honor societies, 5 religious organizations. **Athletics (Intercollegiate):** *Men:* baseball, basketball, cross-country, diving, football, golf, soccer, swimming, tennis, track/field (outdoor), water polo. *Women:* basketball, cross-country, diving, golf, lacrosse, soccer, softball, swimming, tennis, track/field (outdoor), volleyball, water polo. **On-Campus Highlights:** Marian Miner Cook Athenaeum, Athletic/Aquatics Center, Emett Student Center/The Hub, The Research Institutes, Keck Science Center, 11 of our 13 dorms have either been recently built or remodelled. Our newest dorm, Claremont Hall, finished construction last summer and is LEED certified Silver.

ADMISSIONS

Freshman Academic Profile: 68% in top 10% of high school class, 100% in top 25% of high school class, 100% in top 50% of high school class. **Reported SAT (pre-2016 redesign) scores:** SAT Math middle 50% range 670-750. SAT Critical Reading middle 50% range 650-740. SAT Writing middle 50% range 670-750. **Concordant SAT scores:** SAT EBRW middle 50% 700–760. SAT Math middle 50% range 700–770. ACT middle 50% range 31-33. Minimum internet-based TOEFL 100. Minimum paper TOEFL 600. **Basis for Candidate Selection:** *Very important factors considered include:* rigor of secondary school record, class rank, academic GPA, standardized test scores, recommendation(s), extracurricular activities, character/personal qualities. *Important factors considered include:* application essay, talent/ability. *Other factors considered include:* interview, first generation, alumni/ae relation, geographical residence, racial/ethnic status, volunteer work, work experience. **Freshman Admission Requirements:** High school diploma is required and GED is accepted. *Academic units required:* 4 English, 3 math, 2 science, 2 science labs, 3 foreign language, 1 social studies, 1 history. *Academic units*

recommended: 4 English, 4 math, 3 science, 3 science labs, 3 foreign language, 1 social studies, 1 history. **Freshman Admission Statistics:** 6,342 applied, 9.44% admitted, 54% enrolled. **Transfer Admission Requirements:** High school transcript, college transcript(s), essay or personal statement, statement of good standing from prior institution(s). Lowest grade transferable C. **General Admission Information:** Application fee $60. Regular application deadline 1/1. Regular notification 4/1. Nonfall registration not accepted. Admission may be deferred for a maximum of 2 years.

COSTS AND FINANCIAL AID

Annual tuition $50,700. Room and board $15,740. Required fees $245. **Required Forms and Deadlines:** FAFSA, CSS/Financial Aid PROFILE, State aid form, Noncustodial PROFILE, Business/Farm Supplement. **Notification of Awards:** Applicants will be notified of awards on or about 4/1. **Types of Aid:** *Need-based scholarships/grants:* Federal Pell, FSEOG, State scholarships/grants, Private scholarships, College/university scholarship or grant aid from institutional funds. *Loans:* Direct Subsidized Stafford Loans, Direct Unsubsidized Stafford Loans, Direct PLUS loans, Federal Perkins Loans, College/university loans from institutional funds. *Student Employment:* Federal Work-Study Program available. Institutional employment available. **Financial Aid Statistics:** 97% needy freshmen, 98% needy undergrads receive need-based scholarship or grant aid. 56% freshmen, 55% undergrads receive non-need-based scholarship or grant aid. 92% freshmen, 92% undergrads receive need-based self-help aid. 0% freshmen, 0% undergrads receive athletic scholarships. 43% freshmen, 45% undergrads receive any aid. 27% undergrads borrow to pay for school. Average cumulative indebtedness $23,375. **Criteria for awarding aid:** *Need-based:* Academics. *Non-need-based:* Academics, Leadership.

CLARION UNIVERSITY OF PA

Admissions Office, Clarion, PA 16214
Phone: 814-393-2306 • **Financial Aid Phone:** 814-393-2315
E-mail: admissions@clarion.edu • **CEEB Code:** 2649
Fax: 814-393-2030 • **Website:** www.clarion.edu • **ACT Code:** 3698

This public school was founded in 1867. It has a 192-acre campus.

RATINGS

Admissions Selectivity Rating: 72   **Fire Safety Rating:** 93   **Green Rating:** 60*

STUDENTS AND FACULTY

Enrollment: 5,046. **Student Body:** 62% female, 38% male, 10% out-of-state, 1% international (35 countries represented). Asian 0%, African American 7%, Caucasian 88%, Hispanic 1%, Native American <1%, Pacific Islander <1%, Two or more races 2%, Race unknown 2%.
Retention and Graduation: 33% freshmen graduate within 4 years. **Faculty:** Student/faculty ratio 20:1. 222 full-time faculty, 87% hold PhDs, 14% are are members of minority groups, 49% are women. 0% of classes are taught by teaching assistants.

ACADEMICS

Degrees: associate, bachelor's, certificate, master's, postbachelor's certificate, post-master's certificate. **Classes:** Most classes have 20-29 students. Most lab/discussion sessions have 10-19 students. **Most popular majors:** Elementary Education and Teaching; Business Administration and Management. **Special Study Options:** Accelerated program, cooperative education program, distance learning, double major, dual enrollment, honors program, independent study, internships, liberal arts/career combination, student-designed major, study abroad, teacher certification program, weekend college. **Honors Programs:** Clarion University's Honors Program is a close-knit group of talented students preparing for the future. Honors courses satisfy general educational requirements and include field experiences. The 21-credit curriculum promotes development of essential life skills targeted for successful career outcomes. The Honors experience extends beyond the walls of the traditional classroom. Students may spend time with archaeologists in Italy, with anthropologists at a primate center, with large corporate firms and in small businesses, and with molecular biologists in laboratories. Studies have included 20th-century music, learning the art of problem solving, and pondered the ethical implications of research. Co-curricular themes prepare Honors Program students to assume leadership roles. The Honors Program is not for all students–only those individuals who desire professional success, demand academic excellence, and expect to create the future. Each year 50 freshmen are selected for the Honors Program. Courses are taught as special topics and faculty instructors are recruited for their scholarly expertise. Honors students major in every department within the university and receive pre-professional advisement. Students take a six-credit linked English and Speech class and a three-credit Humanities course in the Freshman year. In the sophomore year, students take a three-credit mathematics or science class and a three-credit social sciences course. As juniors, students take a Junior Seminar that culminates in a project prospectus for the capstone experience. Honors 450 is the Senior Presentation delivered in a university-wide presentation. The following program standards must be maintained at the end of each academic year: Freshman Year 3.0 QPA 9 program credits Sophomore Year 3.25 QPA 15 program credits Junior Year 3.4 QPA 18 program credits Senior Year 3.4 QPA 21 program credits To be considered for Honors Program admission, entering freshman must have a minimum SAT score of 1150 or equivalent ACT scores, graduate in the top 15 percent of high school class, and successful completion of an interview. Undergraduate students already enrolled or transfer students may also apply. If a student should fail to residence at Clarion University. Candidates for graduation with an associate degree must complete a minimum of 30 credit hours in residence at the Venango Campus in Oil City, Pennsylvania. maintain the required QPA and course progression, the student will be placed on probation and have one semester to meet the requirements. A student who fails to achieve the required QPA and course progression by the end of the probationary semester will not be allowed to continue in the Honors Program or to continue to receive an Honors scholarship. **Disability Services:** Special programs offered to physically disabled students, including note-taking services, reader services, tape recorders, tutors. **Career Services:** Career/job search classes, Career assessment, Internships.

FACILITIES

Housing: Coed dorms, men's dorms, women's dorms, fraternity/sorority housing, apartments for single students, Sororities occupy single floors of residence halls. 98% of campus accessible to physically diasbled. **Special Academic Facilities/Equipment:** Planetarium. Art Gallery. **Computers:** 40% of classrooms, 100% of libraries, 50% of dining areas, 90% of student union, 10% of common outdoor areas have wireless network access. Students can register for classes online. Administrative functions (other than registration) can be performed online.

CAMPUS LIFE

Environment: Village. **Activities:** Choral groups, concert band, dance, drama/theater, jazz band, literary magazine, marching band, music ensembles, musical theater, pep band, radio station, student government, student newspaper, television station, Campus Ministries, Student Organization. 150 registered organizations, 17 honor societies, 4 religious organizations. 5 fraternities, 8 sororities. **Athletics (Intercollegiate):** *Men:* baseball, basketball, diving, football, golf, swimming, wrestling. *Women:* basketball, cross-country, diving, soccer, softball, swimming, tennis, track/field (outdoor), volleyball. **On-Campus Highlights:** Recreation Center, Carlson Library/Art Gallery, Student Center, Athletic Field, Tippin Gymnasium.

ADMISSIONS

Freshman Academic Profile: Average high school GPA 3.2. 2% in top 10% of high school class, 9% in top 25% of high school class, 39% in top 50% of high school class. 87% from public high schools. **Reported SAT (pre-2016 redesign) scores:** SAT Math middle 50% range 420-520. SAT Critical Reading middle 50% range 420-510. SAT Writing middle 50% range 400-490. **Concordant SAT scores:** SAT EBRW middle 50% 460–560. SAT Math middle 50% range 460–550. ACT middle 50% range 17-22. Minimum paper TOEFL 500. **Basis for Candidate Selection:** *Very important factors considered include:* rigor of secondary school record, academic GPA, standardized test scores. *Important factors considered include:* class rank, application essay, recommendation(s). *Other factors considered include:* interview, extracurricular activities, talent/ability, character/personal qualities, first generation, racial/ethnic status, volunteer work, work experience, level of applicant's interest. **Freshman Admission Requirements:** High school diploma is required and GED is accepted. *Academic units required:* 4 English, 3 math, 3 science, 3 social studies. *Academic units recommended:* 4 English, 4 math, 4 science, 1 science lab, 2 foreign language, 4 social studies, 1 history. **Freshman Admission Statistics:** 2,071 applied, 93.48% admitted, 55% enrolled. **Transfer Admission Requirements:** High school transcript, college transcript(s), statement of good standing from prior institution(s). Minimum college GPA of 2.0 required. Lowest grade transferable C. **General Admission Information:** Priority deadline 2/15. Regular application deadline 8/1. Nonfall registration accepted. Admission may be deferred.

COSTS AND FINANCIAL AID

Annual in-state tuition $5,554. Annual out-of-state tuition $11,108. Room and board $6,390. Required fees $1,826. Average book expense $900. **Required Forms and Deadlines:** FAFSA, State aid form. **Notification of Awards:** Applicants will be notified of awards on a rolling basis beginning 3/30. **Types of Aid:** *Need-based scholarships/grants:* Federal Pell, FSEOG, State scholarships/grants, Private scholarships, College/university scholarship or grant aid from institutional funds, United Negro College Fund. *Loans:* Direct Subsidized Stafford Loans, Direct Unsubsidized Stafford Loans, Direct PLUS loans, Federal Perkins Loans. *Student Employment:* Federal Work-Study Program available. Institutional employment available. **Financial Aid Statistics:** 78% needy freshmen, 75% needy undergrads receive need-based scholarship or

grant aid. 39% freshmen, 26% undergrads receive non-need-based scholarship or grant aid. 91% freshmen, 61% undergrads receive need-based self-help aid. 4% freshmen, 3% undergrads receive athletic scholarships. 78% freshmen, 75% undergrads receive any aid. **Criteria for awarding aid:** *Need-based:* Academics, Alumni affiliation, Art, Leadership, Minority status, Music/drama. *Non-need-based:* Academics, Alumni affiliation, Art, Athletics, Job skills, Leadership, Minority status, Music/drama, State/district residency.

CLARK ATLANTA UNIVERSITY

223 James P. Brawley Dr., SW, Atlanta, GA 30314-4391
Phone: 404-880-8784 • **Financial Aid Phone:** 404-880-8992
E-mail: cauadmissions@cau.edu • **CEEB Code:** 5110
Fax: 404-880-6605 • **Website:** www.cau.edu • **ACT Code:** 804

This private school, affiliated with the Methodist Church, was founded in 1988. It has a 126-acre campus.

RATINGS
Admissions Selectivity Rating: 77   **Fire Safety Rating:** 97   **Green Rating:** 60*

STUDENTS AND FACULTY
Enrollment: 3,093. **Student Body:** 71% female, 29% male, 65% out-of-state, 4% international (10 countries represented). Asian 0%, African American 83%, Caucasian <1%, Hispanic <1%, Native American <1%, Pacific Islander 0%, Two or more races 0%, Race unknown 12%.
Retention and Graduation: 67% freshmen return for sophomore year. 23% freshmen graduate within 4 years. 38% freshmen graduate within 6 years. 27% grads go on to further study within 1 year. 24% grads pursue arts and sciences degrees. 2% grads pursue business degrees. **Faculty:** Student/faculty ratio 19:1. 176 full-time faculty, 85% hold PhDs, 90% are are members of minority groups, 43% are women. 0% of classes are taught by teaching assistants.

ACADEMICS
Degrees: bachelor's, doctoral/research, master's, postbachelor's certificate, post-master's certificate. **Classes:** Most classes have 20-29 students. Most lab/discussion sessions have fewer than 10 students. **Most popular majors:** Business Administration and Management; Radio, Television, and Digital Communication; Biology/Biological Sciences. **Special Study Options:** Accelerated program, cooperative education program, cross-registration, double major, dual enrollment, exchange student program (domestic), honors program, independent study, internships, study abroad, teacher certification program, weekend college. Combined degree programs: BA/MA. **Disability Services:** Special programs offered to physically disabled students, including note-taking services, reader services, tape recorders, tutors. **Career Services:** Career/job search classes, Career assessment, Internships, On-campus interviews.

FACILITIES
Housing: Coed dorms, men's dorms, women's dorms, apartments for single students. 80% of campus accessible to physically diasbled. **Computers:** 100% of classrooms, 5% of dorms, 100% of libraries, 100% of dining areas, 100% of student union, 80% of common outdoor areas have wireless network access. Students can register for classes online. Administrative functions (other than registration) can be performed online.

CAMPUS LIFE
Environment: Metropolis. **Activities:** Choral groups, concert band, dance, drama/theater, marching band, music ensembles, musical theater, opera, pep band, radio station, student government, student newspaper, student-run film society, symphony orchestra, television station, yearbook, Campus Ministries, Student Organization. 80 registered organizations, 12 honor societies, 5 religious organizations. 4 fraternities, 4 sororities. **Athletics (Intercollegiate):** *Men:* baseball, basketball, cross-country, football, track/field (outdoor). *Women:* basketball, cross-country, softball, tennis, track/field (outdoor), volleyball. **On-Campus Highlights:** Robert W. Woodruff Library, CAU Radio & Television Station, CAU Art Galleries, Heritage Commons Residence Hall, Henderson Student Center.

ADMISSIONS
Freshman Academic Profile: Average high school GPA 3.2. 9% in top 10% of high school class, 30% in top 25% of high school class, 69% in top 50% of high school class. 90% from public high schools. **Reported SAT (pre-2016 redesign) scores:** SAT Math middle 50% range 400-480. SAT Critical Reading middle 50% range 420-490. **Concordant SAT scores:** SAT Math middle 50% range 440–510. ACT middle 50% range 18-21. Minimum paper TOEFL 500. **Basis for Candidate Selection:** *Very important factors considered include:* rigor of secondary school record, academic GPA, standardized test scores, character/personal qualities. *Important factors considered include:* application essay, recommendation(s), talent/ability. *Other factors considered include:*

alumni/ae relation, work experience, level of applicant's interest. **Freshman Admission Requirements:** High school diploma is required and GED is accepted. *Academic units required:* 4 English, 3 math, 3 science, 1 science lab, 2 foreign language, 3 social studies, 3 academic electives. **Freshman Admission Statistics:** 10,733 applied, 71.84% admitted, 13% enrolled. **Transfer Admission Requirements:** college transcript(s), statement of good standing from prior institution(s). Minimum college GPA of 2.5 required. Lowest grade transferable C. **General Admission Information:** Application fee $35. Priority deadline 3/1. Regular application deadline 6/1. Nonfall registration accepted. Admission may be deferred for a maximum of 1 year.

COSTS AND FINANCIAL AID

Annual tuition $19,880. Room and board $10,800. Required fees $2,516. Average book expense $1,500. **Required Forms and Deadlines:** FAFSA, State aid form. **Notification of Awards:** Applicants will be notified of awards on a rolling basis beginning 4/1. **Types of Aid:** *Need-based scholarships/grants:* Federal Pell, FSEOG, State scholarships/grants, Private scholarships, College/university scholarship or grant aid from institutional funds, United Negro College Fund. *Loans:* Direct Subsidized Stafford Loans, Direct Unsubsidized Stafford Loans, Direct PLUS loans, Federal Perkins Loans. *Student Employment:* Federal Work-Study Program available. Institutional employment available. **Financial Aid Statistics:** 93% needy freshmen, 90% needy undergrads receive need-based scholarship or grant aid. 17% freshmen, 15% undergrads receive non-need-based scholarship or grant aid. 96% freshmen, 95% undergrads receive need-based self-help aid. 0% freshmen, 0% undergrads receive athletic scholarships. 92% freshmen, 94% undergrads receive any aid. 91% undergrads borrow to pay for school. Average cumulative indebtedness $40,393. **Criteria for awarding aid:** *Non-need-based:* Academics, Art, Athletics, Leadership, Minority status, Music/drama, Religious affiliation, State/district residency.

CLARK UNIVERSITY

950 Main Street, Worcester, MA 01610-1477
Phone: 508-793-7431 • **Financial Aid Phone:** 508-793-7478
E-mail: admissions@clarku.edu • **CEEB Code:** 3279
Fax: 508-793-8821 • **Website:** www.clarku.edu • **ACT Code:** 1808

This private school was founded in 1887. It has a 50-acre campus.

RATINGS

Admissions Selectivity Rating: 90   **Fire Safety Rating:** 98   **Green Rating:** 89

STUDENTS AND FACULTY

Enrollment: 2,247. **Student Body:** 61% female, 39% male, 62% out-of-state, 14% international (64 countries represented). Asian 7%, African American 4%, Caucasian 57%, Hispanic 7%, Native American <1%, Pacific Islander 0%, Two or more races 2%, Race unknown 7%.
Retention and Graduation: 88% freshmen return for sophomore year. 72% freshmen graduate within 4 years. 78 42% grads go on to further study within 1 year. 25% grads pursue arts and sciences degrees. 1% grads pursue law degrees. 5% grads pursue business degrees. 1% grads pursue medical degrees. **Faculty:** Student/faculty ratio 9:1. 206 full-time faculty, 93% hold PhDs, 21% are members of minority groups, 44% are women. 1% of classes are taught by teaching assistants.

ACADEMICS

Degrees: bachelor's, certificate, doctoral/research, doctoral, master's, postbachelor's certificate, post-master's certificate. **Classes:** Most classes have 10-19 students. Most lab/discussion sessions have 10-19 students.
Most popular majors: Biology/Biological Sciences; Political Science and Government; Psychology. **Special Study Options:** cross-registration, double major, English as a Second Language (ESL), independent study, internships, liberal arts/career combination, student-designed major, study abroad, teacher certification program. Combined degree programs: BA/MA, BA/MA BA/MAT BA/MBA BA/MSF BA/MSPC. **Disability Services:** Special programs offered to physically disabled students, including note-taking services, tutors.
Career Services: Alumni network, Alumni services, Career/job search classes, Career assessment, Internships, Regional alumni. Liberal Education and Effective Practice (LEEP) is Clark's bold effort to advance liberal education. It intentionally links a deep and integrated undergraduate curriculum with opportunities to put knowledge into practice in order to prepare our students for remarkable careers and purposeful, accomplished lives.

FACILITIES

Housing: Coed dorms, special housing for disabled students, women's dorms, apartments for single students, Wellness Housing. **Special Academic Facilities/Equipment:** Galleries, theatres, Robert H. Goddard historical exhibition, rare book room, craft center, music center, map library, arboretum, herbarium, extensive darkroom facilities, satellite dish for international program reception, electron microscope, nuclear magnetic resonance spectrometer.
Computers: 100% of classrooms, 15% of dorms, 100% of libraries, 100% of dining areas, 100% of student union, 15% of common outdoor areas have wireless network access. Students can register for classes online. Administrative functions (other than registration) can be performed online.

CAMPUS LIFE

Environment: City. **Activities:** Choral groups, concert band, dance, drama/theater, jazz band, literary magazine, marching band, music ensembles, musical theater, pep band, radio station, student government, student newspaper, student-run film society, symphony orchestra, television station, yearbook, Campus Ministries, Student Organization, Model UN. 110 registered organizations, 10 honor societies, 7 religious organizations. **Athletics (Intercollegiate):** *Men:* baseball, basketball, crew/rowing, cross-country, diving, lacrosse, soccer, swimming, tennis. *Women:* basketball, crew/rowing, cross-country, diving, field hockey, soccer, softball, swimming, tennis, volleyball.
On-Campus Highlights: Larger than life statue of Freud, Rare book room, Goddard Library, Traina Center for the Arts, New: Dolan Field House and updated fields, The Green on a warm spring day. **Environmental Initiatives:** Becoming Climate Neutral—Zero Emissions—by 2030.

ADMISSIONS

Freshman Academic Profile: Average high school GPA 3.7. 36% in top 10% of high school class, 74% in top 25% of high school class, 96% in top 50% of high school class. 75% from public high schools. **Reported SAT (pre-2016 redesign) scores:** SAT Math middle 50% range 550-660. SAT Critical Reading middle 50% range 560-665. SAT Writing middle 50% range 560-650. **Concordant SAT scores:** SAT EBRW middle 50% 620–700. SAT Math middle 50% range 570–690. ACT middle 50% range 27-31. Minimum paper TOEFL 550. **Basis for Candidate Selection:** *Very important factors considered include:* rigor of secondary school record, academic GPA, recommendation(s). *Important factors considered include:* application essay, extracurricular activities, talent/ability, character/personal qualities, volunteer work. *Other factors considered include:* class rank, standardized test scores, interview, first generation, alumni/ae relation, geographical residence, racial/ethnic status, work experience, level of applicant's interest. **Freshman Admission Requirements:** High school diploma is required and GED is accepted. *Academic units recommended:* 4 English, 3 math, 3 science, 2 science labs, 2 foreign language, 2 social studies, 2 history. **Freshman Admission Statistics:** 7,914 applied, 54.73% admitted, 13% enrolled. **Transfer Admission Requirements:** High school transcript, college transcript(s), essay or personal statement, standardized test scores, statement of good standing from prior institution(s). Minimum college GPA of 2.8 required. **General Admission Information:** Application fee $60. Regular application deadline 1/15. Regular notification 4/1. Nonfall registration accepted. Admission may be deferred for a maximum of 1 year.

COSTS AND FINANCIAL AID

Annual tuition $42,800. Room and board $8,450. Required fees $350. Average book expense $800. **Required Forms and Deadlines:** FAFSA, CSS/Financial Aid PROFILE, Noncustodial PROFILE. **Notification of Awards:** Applicants will be notified of awards on or about 3/31. **Types of Aid:** *Need-based scholarships/grants:* Federal Pell, FSEOG, State scholarships/grants, College/university scholarship or grant aid from institutional funds. *Loans:* Direct Subsidized Stafford Loans, Direct Unsubsidized Stafford Loans, Direct PLUS loans, Federal Perkins Loans, State Loans. *Student Employment:* Federal Work-Study Program available. Institutional employment available. **Financial Aid Statistics:** 98% needy freshmen, 97% needy undergrads receive need-based scholarship or grant aid. 20% freshmen, 18% undergrads receive non-need-based scholarship or grant aid. 72% freshmen, 73% undergrads receive need-based self-help aid. 0% freshmen, 0% undergrads receive athletic scholarships. 91% freshmen, 89% undergrads receive any aid. 90% undergrads borrow to pay for school. Average cumulative indebtedness $26,870. **Criteria for awarding aid:** *Non-need-based:* Academics, Leadership.

CLARKE UNIVERSITY

1550 Clarke Drive, Dubuque, IA 52001-3198
Phone: 563-588-6316
E-mail: admissions@clarke.edu • **CEEB Code:** 6099
Fax: 563-588-6789 • **Website:** www.clarke.edu • **ACT Code:** 1290

This private school, affiliated with the Roman Catholic Church, was founded in 1843. It has a 55-acre campus.

RATINGS
Admissions Selectivity Rating: 81   **Fire Safety Rating:** 60*   **Green Rating:** 60*

STUDENTS AND FACULTY
Enrollment: 933. **Student Body:** 69% female, 31% male, 38% out-of-state, 1% international (8 countries represented). Asian 1%, African American 4%, Caucasian 89%, Hispanic 5%, Native American <1%, Pacific Islander 0%, Two or more races <1%, Race unknown 0%.
Retention and Graduation: 73% freshmen return for sophomore year. 49% freshmen graduate within 4 years. 68% freshmen graduate within 6 years. 25% grads go on to further study within 1 year. 23% grads pursue arts and sciences degrees. 2% grads pursue business degrees. **Faculty:** Student/faculty ratio 10:1. 89 full-time faculty, 67% hold PhDs, 3% are are members of minority groups, 67% are women. 0% of classes are taught by teaching assistants.

ACADEMICS
Degrees: associate, bachelor's, doctoral/professional, master's. **Classes:** Most classes have fewer than 10 students. Most lab/discussion sessions have fewer than 10 students. **Most popular majors:** Psychology Business/Commerce. **Special Study Options:** Accelerated program, cross-registration, distance learning, double major, honors program, independent study, internships, student-designed major, study abroad, teacher certification program. Combined degree programs: BS/MS in Physical Therapy. **Disability Services:** Special programs offered to physically disabled students, including note-taking services, reader services, tape recorders, tutors. **Career Services:** Alumni services, Career/job search classes, Career assessment, Internships. Clarke College created a Professional Development School (PDS) model for its elementary education program in 1999. In Clarke's version of the PDS model, the professional-sequence, junior-year teaching methods students take a block of courses that are offered in K-5 schools. The classroom assigned for these courses is literally in the K-5 school, so students are in the school at least three hours-a-day, five days-a-week. Having the courses meet in elementary schools allows for a much closer relationship with the school, teachers, and elementary students. There are two college instructors at the school with the college students daily to teach methods, guide lesson planning, observe the students teach, and provide immediate feedback on their teaching. Elementary education majors spend one semester at a private, parochial elementary school, and one semester at a public elementary school. Students working toward an endorsement in special education spend an additional semester in a third elementary school, serving children identified for special education. Music education majors take their elementary music methods course in an elementary PDS as well.

FACILITIES
Housing: Coed dorms, men's dorms, women's dorms, apartments for single students. 90% of campus accessible to physically diasbled. **Special Academic Facilities/Equipment:** Art gallery, computer classrooms for math, biology, and computer science, computer-interfaced chemistry lab, human gross anatomy and nursing labs, electron microscope, music performance hall, foreign language lab, distance learning classroom **Computers:** Students can register for classes online. Administrative functions (other than registration) can be performed online.

CAMPUS LIFE
Environment: Town. **Activities:** Choral groups, concert band, dance, drama/theater, jazz band, literary magazine, music ensembles, musical theater, radio station, student government, student newspaper, yearbook. 48 registered organizations, 5 honor societies, 1 religious organization. **Athletics (Intercollegiate):** *Men:* baseball, basketball, cheerleading, cross-country, golf, soccer, tennis, volleyball. *Women:* basketball, cheerleading, cross-country, golf, soccer, softball, tennis, volleyball.

ADMISSIONS
Freshman Academic Profile: Average high school GPA 3.5. 13% in top 10% of high school class, 55% in top 25% of high school class, 84% in top 50% of high school class. 81% from public high schools. **Reported SAT (pre-2016 redesign) scores:** SAT Math middle 50% range 475-550. SAT Critical Reading middle 50% range 470-530. **Concordant SAT scores:** SAT Math middle 50% range 510–570. ACT middle 50% range 20-24. Minimum paper TOEFL 527. **Basis for Candidate Selection:** *Very important factors considered include:*

rigor of secondary school record, academic GPA, standardized test scores, talent/ability. *Important factors considered include:* class rank. *Other factors considered include:* interview, extracurricular activities, racial/ethnic status, volunteer work. **Freshman Admission Requirements:** High school diploma is required and GED is accepted. *Academic units required:* 4 English, 3 math, 3 science, 2 science labs, 2 foreign language, 2 social studies, 4 academic electives. *Academic units recommended:* 4 math, 4 science. **Freshman Admission Statistics:** 1,359 applied, 70.49% admitted, 19% enrolled. **Transfer Admission Requirements:** High school transcript, college transcript(s), standardized test scores, statement of good standing from prior institution(s). Minimum college GPA of 2.0 required. Lowest grade transferable C. **General Admission Information:** Application fee $25. Nonfall registration accepted. Admission may be deferred for a maximum of 12 months.

COSTS AND FINANCIAL AID
Annual tuition $28,000. Room and board $8,400. Required fees $900. Average book expense $1,160. **Notification of Awards:** Applicants will be notified of awards on a rolling basis beginning 3/15. **Types of Aid:** *Need-based scholarships/grants:* Federal Pell, FSEOG, State scholarships/grants, Private scholarships, College/university scholarship or grant aid from institutional funds, Federal Nursing Scholarships. *Loans:* Direct Subsidized Stafford Loans, Direct Unsubsidized Stafford Loans, Direct PLUS loans, Federal Perkins Loans, Federal Nursing Loans, College/university loans from institutional funds. *Student Employment:* Federal Work-Study Program available. Institutional employment available. **Financial Aid Statistics:** 100% needy freshmen, 100% needy undergrads receive need-based scholarship or grant aid. 99% freshmen, 95% undergrads receive non-need-based scholarship or grant aid. 90% freshmen, 89% undergrads receive need-based self-help aid. 41% freshmen, 33% undergrads receive athletic scholarships. **Criteria for awarding aid:** *Need-based:* Academics. *Non-need-based:* Academics, Art, Athletics, Leadership, Music/drama.

CLARKSON UNIVERSITY

8 Clarkson Ave, Box 5605, Potsdam, NY 13699
Phone: 315-268-6480 • **Financial Aid Phone:** 315-268-6480
E-mail: admission@clarkson.edu • **CEEB Code:** 2084
Fax: 315-268-7647 • **Website:** www.clarkson.edu

This private school was founded in 1896. It has a 640-acre campus.

RATINGS
Admissions Selectivity Rating: 87   **Fire Safety Rating:** 96   **Green Rating:** 86

STUDENTS AND FACULTY
Enrollment: 3,176. **Student Body:** 30% female, 70% male, 27% out-of-state, 2% international (22 countries represented). Asian 3%, African American 2%, Caucasian 83%, Hispanic 5%, Native American <1%, Pacific Islander <1%, Two or more races 3%, Race unknown 2%.
Retention and Graduation: 89% freshmen return for sophomore year. 57% freshmen graduate within 4 years. 72% freshmen graduate within 6 years. 17% grads go on to further study within 1 year. 7% grads pursue arts and sciences degrees. 1% grads pursue business degrees. **Faculty:** Student/faculty ratio 14:1. 251 full-time faculty, 88% hold PhDs, 23% are are members of minority groups, 29% are women. 0% of classes are taught by teaching assistants.

ACADEMICS
Degrees: bachelor's, doctoral/professional, doctoral/research, master's, postbachelor's certificate. **Classes:** Most classes have 10-19 students. Most lab/discussion sessions have 20-29 students. **Most popular majors:** Civil Engineering; Mechanical Engineering; Engineering/Industrial Management. **Special Study Options:** Accelerated program, cooperative education program, cross-registration, distance learning, double major, dual enrollment, English as a Second Language (ESL), honors program, independent study, liberal arts/career combination, student-designed major, study abroad, Women In Science and Engineering (WISE) Living/Learning Community; interdisciplinary degree programs that combine Engineering and Business, Business and Liberal Arts, and Environmental Science and Policy; a large number of 3+2 and 2+2 articulation agreements that facilitate transfer to Clarkson from community colleges and other baccalaureate institutions; business students experience a unique introduction to entrepreneurship through working with the Shipley Center for Innovation, the Clarkson Entrepreneurs Organization (CEO) and the Clarkson Center for Global Competitiveness. **Honors Programs:** Built upon current and emerging problems in science, technology and society, the

Clarkson University Honors Program offers unique academic challenges and opportunities for Clarkson's most promising students. The program is a gateway to a multitude of opportunities that include internships, research experience, fellowships, graduate schools, study abroad, and jobs. Combined degree programs: Combined BS Business/Liberal Arts; Liberal Arts/Communication. **Disability Services:** Special programs offered to physically disabled students, including note-taking services, reader services, tape recorders, tutors. **Career Services:** Alumni network, Alumni services, Career/job search classes, Career assessment, Internships, Regional alumni. The Clarkson University School of Business houses the Reh Center for Entrepreneurship. The Reh Center immerses students of all majors in experiential entrepreneurship programs designed to create skillsets and mindsets that are transferrable to students' future careers. Incoming students currently operating a business or working on an innovation have an opportunity to pitch their venture in a unique tuition for equity competition (see website for details).

FACILITIES

Housing: Coed dorms, special housing for disabled students, men's dorms, special housing for international students, women's dorms, fraternity/sorority housing, apartments for single students, Wellness Housing, Theme Housing. 85% of campus accessible to physically diasbled. **Special Academic Facilities/ Equipment:** The Center for Advanced Materials Processing (CAMP) is dedicated to developing innovations in advanced materials processing and to transfer this technology to business and industry, and is built on Clarkson's recognized expertise in colloid and surface science and fine particle technology. The Center for the Environment facilitates the development, promotion and operation of environmental activities within the University and among its partners. The Center for Rehabilitative Science and Technology (CREST) **Computers:** 100% of classrooms, 100% of libraries, 100% of dining areas, 100% of student union, 20% of common outdoor areas have wireless network access. Students can register for classes online. Administrative functions (other than registration) can be performed online.

CAMPUS LIFE

Environment: Village. **Activities:** Choral groups, drama/theater, jazz band, literary magazine, musical theater, pep band, radio station, student government, student newspaper, symphony orchestra, television station, yearbook, Student Organization. 117 registered organizations, 7 honor societies, 3 religious organizations. 11 fraternities, 3 sororities. **Athletics (Intercollegiate):** *Men:* baseball, basketball, cross-country, diving, golf, ice hockey, lacrosse, skiing (downhill/alpine), skiing (nordic/cross-country), soccer, swimming. *Women:* basketball, cross-country, diving, ice hockey, lacrosse, skiing (downhill/ alpine), skiing (nordic/cross-country), soccer, swimming, volleyball. **On-Campus Highlights:** Snell Hall Shipley Center for Innovation, Adirondack Lodge, Cheel Campus Center Club 99, CAMP Building SPEED Labs, Java City/Library, Fitness Center. **Environmental Initiatives:** Our campus has undertaken many activities to integrate sustainability into facilities and campus life. For example, as part of a significant renovation of the Woodstock Village Apartments to increase its energy efficiency, four of the buildings were modified to create our campus' Smart Housing Project. These buildings have a high density of water, electricity and air quality sensors that are used for building energy modeling, advanced building automation and feedback to students about their utility use. Research is on-going to determine how to best use messaging and feedback to motivate students to conserve their utility use.

ADMISSIONS

Freshman Academic Profile: Average high school GPA 3.6. 38% in top 10% of high school class, 74% in top 25% of high school class, 95% in top 50% of high school class. 87% from public high schools. **Reported SAT (pre-2016 redesign) scores:** SAT Math middle 50% range 560-663. SAT Critical Reading middle 50% range 520-620. SAT Writing middle 50% range 480-590. **Concordant SAT scores:** SAT EBRW middle 50% 560–660. SAT Math middle 50% range 580–690. ACT middle 50% range 24-29. Minimum internet-based TOEFL 80. Minimum paper TOEFL 550. **Basis for Candidate Selection:** *Very important factors considered include:* rigor of secondary school record, academic GPA. *Important factors considered include:* class rank, standardized test scores, recommendation(s), extracurricular activities, volunteer work. *Other factors considered include:* application essay, talent/ability, character/ personal qualities, first generation, alumni/ae relation, work experience, level of applicant's interest. **Freshman Admission Requirements:** High school diploma is required and GED is accepted. *Academic units required:* 4 English, 3 math, 1 science, and 4 units from above areas or other academic areas. *Academic units recommended:* 4 math, 4 science. **Freshman Admission Statistics:** 7,066 applied, 68.21% admitted, 17% enrolled. **Transfer Admission Requirements:** college transcript(s), Minimum college GPA of 2.75 required. Lowest grade transferable 2. **General Admission Information:** Application fee $50. Regular application deadline 1/15. Nonfall registration accepted. Admission may be deferred for a maximum of 12 Months.

COSTS AND FINANCIAL AID

Required Forms and Deadlines: FAFSA, State aid form. **Notification of Awards:** Applicants will be notified of awards on a rolling basis beginning 3/14. **Types of Aid:** *Need-based scholarships/grants:* Federal Pell, FSEOG,

State scholarships/grants, Private scholarships, College/university scholarship or grant aid from institutional funds. *Loans:* Direct Subsidized Stafford Loans, Direct Unsubsidized Stafford Loans, Direct PLUS loans, Federal Perkins Loans, College/university loans from institutional funds. *Student Employment:* Federal Work-Study Program available. Institutional employment available. **Financial Aid Statistics:** 99% needy freshmen, 99% needy undergrads receive need-based scholarship or grant aid. 14% freshmen, 14% undergrads receive non-need-based scholarship or grant aid. 79% freshmen, 81% undergrads receive need-based self-help aid. 1% freshmen, 1% undergrads receive athletic scholarships. 97% freshmen, 97% undergrads receive any aid. 85% undergrads borrow to pay for school. Average cumulative indebtedness $23,500. **Criteria for awarding aid:** *Need-based:* Academics, Minority status. *Non-need-based:* Academics, Alumni affiliation, Leadership, Minority status.

CLAYTON STATE UNIVERSITY

2000 Clayton State Blvd., Morrow, GA 30206-0285
Phone: 678-466-4115
E-mail: ccsu-info@mail.clayton.edu
Fax: 678-466-4149 • **Website:** www.clayton.edu

This is a public school.

RATINGS

Admissions Selectivity Rating: 73   **Fire Safety Rating:** 60*   **Green Rating:** 60*

STUDENTS AND FACULTY

Enrollment: 5,661. **Student Body:** 69% female, 31% male, 5% out-of-state, 2% international. Asian 4%, African American 48%, Caucasian 43%, Hispanic 3%, Native American 1%, Pacific Islander 0%, Two or more races 0%, Race unknown 0%.
Retention and Graduation: 61% freshmen return for sophomore year.
Faculty: Student/faculty ratio 28:1. 157 full-time faculty, 57% hold PhDs, 15% are are members of minority groups, 59% are women.

ACADEMICS

Degrees: associate, bachelor's, certificate, master's, terminal, transfer. **Classes:** Most classes have 20-29 students. Most lab/discussion sessions have fewer than 10 students. **Special Study Options:** cooperative education program, cross-registration, distance learning, double major, dual enrollment, exchange student program (domestic), honors program, independent study, internships, liberal arts/career combination, study abroad, teacher certification program. **Career Services:** On-campus interviews.

FACILITIES

Housing: apartments for single students, Local Private Apartment Living.

CAMPUS LIFE

Activities: Choral groups, drama/theater, jazz band, literary magazine, music ensembles, musical theater, opera, pep band, student government, student newspaper.

ADMISSIONS

Freshman Academic Profile: Average high school GPA 2.9. **Reported SAT (pre-2016 redesign) scores:** SAT Math middle 50% range 440-550. SAT Critical Reading middle 50% range 450-550. **Concordant SAT scores:** SAT Math middle 50% range 480–570. ACT middle 50% range 17-21. **Basis for Candidate Selection:** *Very important factors considered include:* rigor of secondary school record, academic GPA, standardized test scores. *Other factors considered include:* class rank, extracurricular activities, talent/ability. **Freshman Admission Requirements:** High school diploma is required and GED is not accepted. *Academic units required:* 4 English, 4 math, 3 science, 2 foreign language, 3 social studies. **Freshman Admission Statistics:** 2,920 applied, 70.99% admitted, 63% enrolled. **Transfer Admission Requirements:** college transcript(s), statement of good standing from prior institution(s). Minimum college GPA of 2.0 required. Lowest grade transferable D. **General Admission Information:** Application fee $40. Priority deadline 2/1. Regular application deadline 7/1. Nonfall registration accepted. Admission may be deferred.

COSTS AND FINANCIAL AID

Annual in-state tuition $2,212. Annual out-of-state tuition $8,848. Average book expense $1,000. **Required Forms and Deadlines:** FAFSA, State aid form. **Types of Aid:** *Need-based scholarships/grants:* Federal Pell, FSEOG, State scholarships/grants, Private scholarships, College/university scholarship or grant aid from institutional funds, Federal Nursing Scholarships. *Loans:* State Loans. **Financial Aid Statistics:** 65% needy freshmen, 67% needy undergrads receive need-based scholarship or grant aid. 76% freshmen, 45% undergrads receive non-need-based scholarship or grant aid. 45% freshmen, 64% undergrads receive need-based self-help aid. 1% freshmen, 3% undergrads receive athletic scholarships. **Criteria for awarding aid:** *Need-based:* Academics. *Non-need-based:* Academics.

CLEAR CREEK BAPTIST BIBLE COLLEGE

300 Clear Creek Road, Pineville, KY 40977-9754
Phone: 606-337-3196 • **Financial Aid Phone:** 606-337-1457
E-mail: ccbbc@ccbbc.edu
Fax: 606-337-2372 • **Website:** www.ccbbc.edu

This private school, affiliated with the Southern Baptist Church, was founded in 1926. It has a 700-acre campus.

RATINGS
Admissions Selectivity Rating: 64   **Fire Safety Rating:** 72   **Green Rating:** 60*

STUDENTS AND FACULTY
Enrollment: 173. **Student Body:** 22% female, 78% male, 60% out-of-state, 0% international (0 countries represented). Asian 1%, African American 1%, Caucasian 95%, Hispanic 2%, Native American 0%, Pacific Islander 0%, Two or more races 0%, Race unknown 1%.
Retention and Graduation: 93% freshmen return for sophomore year. 25% freshmen graduate within 4 years. 30% grads go on to further study within 1 year. **Faculty:** Student/faculty ratio 10:1. 6 full-time faculty, 83% hold PhDs, 0% are are members of minority groups, 0% are women.

ACADEMICS
Degrees: associate, bachelor's, certificate. **Classes:** Most classes have 10-19 students. Most lab/discussion sessions have 10-19 students. **Most popular majors:** Bible/Biblical Studies. **Special Study Options:** distance learning, double major, independent study, internships. **Career Services:** Alumni network.

FACILITIES
Housing: men's dorms, women's dorms, apartments for married students, apartments for single students, Wellness Housing. 95% of campus accessible to physically disabled. **Special Academic Facilities/Equipment:** Jerusalem model **Computers:** 10% of dorms, 100% of libraries, 5% of common outdoor areas have wireless network access. Students can register for classes online.

CAMPUS LIFE
Environment: Rural. **Activities:** Choral groups, music ensembles, radio station, student government, student newspaper, Campus Ministries. **On-Campus Highlights:** Kelly Hall, Jerusalem model, Family Life Center, Creek and walking trails, Carolyn Boatman Brooks Memorial Library.

ADMISSIONS
Freshman Academic Profile: 95% from public high schools. Minimum paper TOEFL 550. **Basis for Candidate Selection:** *Very important factors considered include:* application essay, recommendation(s), character/personal qualities, religious affiliation/commitment. *Important factors considered include:* interview. *Other factors considered include:* talent/ability, alumni/ae relation, level of applicant's interest. **Freshman Admission Requirements:** High school diploma is required and GED is accepted. **Freshman Admission Statistics:** 14 applied, 92.86% admitted, 85% enrolled. **Transfer Admission Requirements:** High school transcript, college transcript(s), essay or personal statement, interview, Minimum college GPA of 2.0 required. Lowest grade transferable C. **General Admission Information:** Application fee $40. Priority deadline 7/15. Regular application deadline 8/2. Nonfall registration accepted. Admission may be deferred for a maximum of 2 years.

COSTS AND FINANCIAL AID
Annual tuition $5,482. Room and board $3,470. Required fees $400. Average book expense $1,200. **Required Forms and Deadlines:** FAFSA, Institution's own financial aid form. **Notification of Awards:** Applicants will be notified of awards on a rolling basis beginning 5/1. **Types of Aid:** *Need-based scholarships/grants:* Federal Pell, FSEOG, Private scholarships, College/university scholarship or grant aid from institutional funds. *Student Employment:* Federal Work-Study Program available. Institutional employment available. **Financial Aid Statistics:** 100% needy freshmen, 100% needy undergrads receive need-based scholarship or grant aid. 22% freshmen, 42% undergrads receive non-need-based scholarship or grant aid. 33% freshmen, 37% undergrads receive need-based self-help aid. 0% freshmen, 0% undergrads receive athletic scholarships. 81% freshmen, 75% undergrads receive any aid. **Criteria for awarding aid:** *Need-based:* Academics, Alumni affiliation, Leadership, Religious affiliation. *Non-need-based:* Academics, Leadership, Religious affiliation, State/district residency.

CLEARWATER CHRISTIAN COLLEGE

3400 Gulf-to-Bay Boulevard, Clearwater, FL 33759-4595
Phone: 727-726-1153 • **Financial Aid Phone:** 727-726-1153
E-mail: admissions@clearwater.edu
Fax: 727-726-8597 • **Website:** www.clearwater.edu • **ACT Code:** 715

This private school, affiliated with the Christian (Nondenominational) Church, was founded in 1966. It has a 138-acre campus.

RATINGS
Admissions Selectivity Rating: 74   **Fire Safety Rating:** 96   **Green Rating:** 60*

STUDENTS AND FACULTY
Enrollment: 546. **Student Body:** 50% female, 50% male, 52% out-of-state, <1% international (2 countries represented). Asian 1%, African American 5%, Caucasian 82%, Hispanic 4%, Native American <1%, Pacific Islander 0%, Two or more races 0%, Race unknown 8%.
Retention and Graduation: 70% freshmen return for sophomore year. 34% freshmen graduate within 4 years. 42% freshmen graduate within 6 years. 26% grads go on to further study within 1 year. 16% grads pursue arts and sciences degrees. 1% grads pursue law degrees. 2% grads pursue business degrees. 4% grads pursue medical degrees. **Faculty:** Student/faculty ratio 175:1. 28 full-time faculty, 68% hold PhDs, 4% are members of minority groups, 32% are women. 0% of classes are taught by teaching assistants.

ACADEMICS
Degrees: associate, bachelor's, certificate, master's. **Classes:** Most classes have fewer than 10 students. **Most popular majors:** Business Administration and Management; Elementary Education and Teaching; Kinesiology and Exercise Science. **Special Study Options:** cooperative education program, distance learning, double major, dual enrollment, honors program, independent study, internships, liberal arts/career combination, student-designed major, study abroad, teacher certification program, Semester in Washington, DC. **Honors Programs:** Interdisciplinary Studies, a self-designed multidisciplinary program for students with exceptional ability and focus. **Disability Services:** Special programs offered to physically disabled students, including tape recorders, tutors. **Career Services:** Alumni services, Career/job search classes, Internships. During an education student's last semester, the director of clinical field experiences places the student in Hillsborough and Pinellas County public and private schools for a 14-week teaching internship.

FACILITIES
Housing: men's dorms, women's dorms. **Computers:** 100% of classrooms, 100% of dorms, 100% of libraries, 100% of dining areas, have wireless network access. Administrative functions (other than registration) can be performed online.

CAMPUS LIFE
Environment: City. **Activities:** Choral groups, concert band, drama/theater, music ensembles, pep band, student government, student newspaper, student-run film society, symphony orchestra, yearbook, Campus Ministries. 17 registered organizations, 1 honor society, 1 religious organization. 5 fraternities, 6 sororities. **Athletics (Intercollegiate):** *Men:* baseball, basketball, golf, soccer. *Women:* basketball, golf, soccer, softball, volleyball. **On-Campus Highlights:** Centre Court Cafe, Gymnasium, Cathcart Hall Cafeteria, Easter Library

ADMISSIONS
Freshman Academic Profile: 30% from public high schools. **Reported SAT (pre-2016 redesign) scores:** SAT Math middle 50% range 450-530. SAT Critical Reading middle 50% range 470-560. **Concordant SAT scores:** SAT Math middle 50% range 490–560. ACT middle 50% range 21-23. Minimum internet-based TOEFL 84. Minimum paper TOEFL 500. **Basis for Candidate Selection:** *Very important factors considered include:* standardized test scores, application essay, recommendation(s), character/personal qualities, religious affiliation/commitment. *Important factors considered include:* rigor of secondary school record, academic GPA, interview. *Other factors considered include:* alumni/ae relation, volunteer work, level of applicant's interest. **Freshman Admission Requirements:** High school diploma is required and GED is accepted. *Academic units required:* 4 English, 3 math, 3 science, 2 foreign language, 3 social studies. **Freshman Admission Statistics:** 341 applied, 73.90% admitted, 56% enrolled. **Transfer Admission Requirements:** High school transcript, college transcript(s), essay or personal statement, standardized test scores, statement of good standing from prior institution(s). Minimum college GPA of 2.0 required. Lowest grade transferable C-. **General Admission Information:** Application fee $35. Regular application deadline 8/1. Nonfall registration not accepted. Admission may be deferred for a maximum of 1 year.

COSTS AND FINANCIAL AID

Annual tuition $16,250. Required fees $95. Average book expense $1,000. **Required Forms and Deadlines:** FAFSA, Institution's own financial aid form, State aid form. **Notification of Awards:** Applicants will be notified of awards on a rolling basis beginning 3/15. **Types of Aid:** *Need-based scholarships/grants:* Federal Pell, FSEOG, State scholarships/grants, Private scholarships, College/university scholarship or grant aid from institutional funds. *Loans:* Direct Subsidized Stafford Loans, Direct Unsubsidized Stafford Loans, Direct PLUS loans, State Loans. *Student Employment:* Federal Work-Study Program available. Institutional employment available. **Financial Aid Statistics:** 100% needy freshmen, 99% needy undergrads receive need-based scholarship or grant aid. 9% freshmen, 9% undergrads receive non-need-based scholarship or grant aid. 63% freshmen, 64% undergrads receive need-based self-help aid. 0% freshmen, 0% undergrads receive athletic scholarships. 97% freshmen, 94% undergrads receive any aid. **Criteria for awarding aid:** *Need-based:* Academics, Alumni affiliation, Music/drama, Religious affiliation. *Non-need-based:* Academics, Alumni affiliation, Leadership, Music/drama, Religious affiliation.

CLEMSON UNIVERSITY

105 Sikes Hall, Clemson, SC 29634-5124
Phone: 864-656-2287 • **Financial Aid Phone:** 864-656-2280
E-mail: cuadmissions@clemson.edu • **CEEB Code:** 5111
Fax: 864-656-2464 • **Website:** www.clemson.edu • **ACT Code:** 3842

This public school was founded in 1889.

RATINGS

Admissions Selectivity Rating: 92   **Fire Safety Rating:** 96   **Green Rating:** 60*

STUDENTS AND FACULTY

Enrollment: 17,740. **Student Body:** 47% female, 53% male, 35% out-of-state, 1% international (84 countries represented). Asian 2%, African American 7%, Caucasian 83%, Hispanic 3%, Native American <1%, Pacific Islander <1%, Two or more races 3%, Race unknown 1%.
Retention and Graduation: 93% freshmen return for sophomore year. 61% freshmen graduate within 4 years. 82% freshmen graduate within 6 years. 28% grads go on to further study within 1 year. 25% grads pursue arts and sciences degrees. 5% grads pursue law degrees. 21% grads pursue business degrees. 8% grads pursue medical degrees. **Faculty:** Student/faculty ratio 18:1. 1,134 full-time faculty, 87% hold PhDs, 19% are are members of minority groups, 36% are women. 7% of classes are taught by teaching assistants.

ACADEMICS

Degrees: bachelor's, doctoral, master's, postbachelor's certificate, post-master's certificate. **Classes:** Most classes have 10-19 students. Most lab/discussion sessions have 20-29 students. **Most popular majors:** Engineering; Business/Commerce; Biology/Biological Sciences. **Special Study Options:** cooperative education program, distance learning, double major, exchange student program (domestic), honors program, independent study, internships, study abroad, teacher certification program, We have an RN to BSN program located in Greenville, SC. This is an off-campus degree program for students that have a 2 year degree in Nursing and an RN. **Honors Programs:** The National Scholars Program. Please visit: http://www.clemson.edu/national_scholars/ Combined degree programs: BA/MEng, Rn to BSN program. **Disability Services:** Special programs offered to physically disabled students, including note-taking services, reader services, tape recorders, tutors. **Career Services:** Alumni network, Alumni services, Career/job search classes, Career assessment, Internships, Regional alumni. Our alumni network has grown in both strength and number over the past few years. Current alumni recognize that today's Clemson graduates are significantly better prepared to enter the job market, if they choose to delay graduate school. Assisting other members of the "Clemson Family" is a natural bond ingrained as one prepares to leave the campus—as hard as that may be!

FACILITIES

Housing: Coed dorms, men's dorms, special housing for international students, women's dorms, fraternity/sorority housing, apartments for single students, Wellness Housing, Theme Housing, Learning-living communities. **Special Academic Facilities/Equipment:** The South Carolina Botanical Gardens, the Campbell Geology Museum, the Brooks Center for the Performing Arts, the Rudolph Lee Art Gallery, The Garrison Livestock Arena, The John C. Calhoun Home **Computers:** 75% of classrooms, 25% of dorms, 100% of libraries, 100% of dining areas, 100% of student union, 40% of common outdoor areas have wireless network access. Students can register for classes online. Administrative functions (other than registration) can be performed online. Undergraduates are required to own a computer.

CAMPUS LIFE

Environment: Village. **Activities:** Choral groups, concert band, dance, drama/theater, jazz band, literary magazine, marching band, music ensembles, pep band, radio station, student government, student newspaper, television station, yearbook. 292 registered organizations, 23 honor societies, 24 religious organizations. 26 fraternities, 17 sororities. **Athletics (Intercollegiate):** *Men:* baseball, basketball, cheerleading, cross-country, diving, football, golf, soccer, swimming, tennis, track/field (outdoor), track/field (indoor). *Women:* basketball, cheerleading, crew/rowing, cross-country, diving, soccer, swimming, tennis, track/field (outdoor), track/field (indoor), volleyball. **On-Campus Highlights:** SC Botanical Garden/ Discovery Center/Geology Muse, Hendrix Student Center—Clemson Ice Cream, Conference Center and Inn at Clemson/Walker Golf C, Fort Hill—John C. Calhoun House, Lee Art Gallery, Please visit: http://www.clemson.edu/visitors/index.html. **Environmental Initiatives:** LEED.

ADMISSIONS

Freshman Academic Profile: Average high school GPA 4.0. 56% in top 10% of high school class, 86% in top 25% of high school class, 98% in top 50% of high school class. 89% from public high schools. **Reported SAT (pre-2016 redesign) scores:** SAT Math middle 50% range 590-690. SAT Critical Reading middle 50% range 560-660. **Concordant SAT scores:** SAT Math middle 50% range 610–720. ACT middle 50% range 27-31. Minimum paper TOEFL 550. **Basis for Candidate Selection:** *Very important factors considered include:* rigor of secondary school record, class rank, academic GPA, standardized test scores, state residency. *Important factors considered include:* alumni/ae relation. *Other factors considered include:* application essay, recommendation(s), extracurricular activities, talent/ability. **Freshman Admission Requirements:** High school diploma is required and GED is accepted. *Academic units required:* 4 English, 3 math, 3 science, 3 science labs, 2 foreign language, 1 social studies, 1 history, 2 academic electives, 1 computer science, 1 visual/performing arts, and 1 unit from above areas or other academic areas. *Academic units recommended:* 4 math, 4 science labs, 3 foreign language. **Freshman Admission Statistics:** 22,396 applied, 51.27% admitted, 30% enrolled. **Transfer Admission Requirements:** college transcript(s), Minimum college GPA of 2.5 required. Lowest grade transferable C. **General Admission Information:** Application fee $70. Priority deadline 12/1. Regular application deadline 5/1. Nonfall registration accepted.

COSTS AND FINANCIAL AID

Annual in-state tuition $13,186. Annual out-of-state tuition $32,738. Required fees $1,132. Average book expense $1,308. **Required Forms and Deadlines:** FAFSA. **Notification of Awards:** Applicants will be notified of awards on a rolling basis beginning 4/1. **Types of Aid:** *Need-based scholarships/grants:* Federal Pell, FSEOG, State scholarships/grants, Private scholarships, College/university scholarship or grant aid from institutional funds, Federal Nursing Scholarships. *Loans:* Direct Subsidized Stafford Loans, Direct Unsubsidized Stafford Loans, Direct PLUS loans, Federal Perkins Loans, State Loans, College/university loans from institutional funds. *Student Employment:* Federal Work-Study Program available. Institutional employment available. **Financial Aid Statistics:** 92% needy freshmen, 81% needy undergrads receive need-based scholarship or grant aid. 71% freshmen, 52% undergrads receive non-need-based scholarship or grant aid. 69% freshmen, 78% undergrads receive need-based self-help aid. 3% freshmen, 3% undergrads receive athletic scholarships. 87% freshmen, 71% undergrads receive any aid. 49% undergrads borrow to pay for school. Average cumulative indebtedness $30,270. **Criteria for awarding aid:** *Need-based:* Academics, Leadership, Minority status, Music/drama. *Non-need-based:* Academics, Art, Athletics, Leadership, Minority status, Music/drama, State/district residency.

See page 940.

THE CLEVELAND INSTITUTE OF ART

11610 Euclid Avenue, Cleveland, OH 44106
Phone: 216-421-7418 • **Financial Aid Phone:** 216-421-7425
E-mail: admissions@cia.edu • **CEEB Code:** 1152
Fax: 216-754-3634 • **Website:** www.cia.edu • **ACT Code:** 3243

This private school was founded in 1882. It has a 488-acre campus.

RATINGS

Admissions Selectivity Rating: 83   **Fire Safety Rating:** 95   **Green Rating:** 67

STUDENTS AND FACULTY

Enrollment: 614. **Student Body:** 60% female, 40% male, 36% out-of-state, 9% international (8 countries represented). Asian 4%, African American 9%, Caucasian 69%, Hispanic 5%, Native American <1%, Pacific Islander 0%, Two or more races 3%, Race unknown 0%.

Retention and Graduation: 82% freshmen return for sophomore year. 58% freshmen graduate within 4 years. 65% freshmen graduate within 6 years. 3% grads go on to further study within 1 year. 3% grads pursue arts and sciences degrees. **Faculty:** Student/faculty ratio 9:1. 49 full-time faculty, 61% hold PhDs, 12% are are members of minority groups, 31% are women. 0% of classes are taught by teaching assistants.

ACADEMICS

Degrees: bachelor's. **Classes:** Most classes have 10-19 students. Most lab/discussion sessions have 10-19 students. **Most popular majors:** Illustration; Industrial and Product Design; Animation, Interactive Technology, Video Graphics and Special Effects. **Special Study Options:** cooperative education program, cross-registration, exchange student program (domestic), honors program, independent study, internships, study abroad, Study for up to 2 semesters at an Alliance of Independent Colleges of Art and Design. **Disability Services:** Special programs offered to physically disabled students, including note-taking services, tape recorders, tutors. **Career Services:** Alumni network, Alumni services, Career/job search classes, Career assessment, Internships. The Business and Professional Practices mandatory curriculum emphasizes three important tracks for students in a small classroom setting and lecture series from professionals in the community.
- Studio and Exhibitions: Learn to set up a professional studio, write grants, develop exhibitions, communicate through artist talks and statements, and approach dealers, curators, and collectors.
- Entrepreneurship: Learn how to establish your own business by exploring business finance, sales and marketing, taxes, insurance, copyright and contracts, professional writing, and more.
- Industry: Learn how to thrive in a business organization by discussing presentation and interview skills, ethics and conflict resolution, business plans, communication etiquette, professional associations and more.

FACILITIES

Housing: Coed dorms, fraternity/sorority housing, apartments for single students. 100% of campus accessible to physically diasbled. **Special Academic Facilities/Equipment:** The Reinberger Galleries **Computers:** 40% of classrooms, 100% of dorms, 100% of libraries, have wireless network access. Students can register for classes online. Administrative functions (other than registration) can be performed online.

CAMPUS LIFE

Environment: Metropolis. **Activities:** marching band, student government, student newspaper, student-run film society, Campus Ministries. 7 registered organizations, 2 religious organizations. **On-Campus Highlights:** Arabica Coffee Shop, Frank Gehry and Peter B. Lewis Building, Live music at Barking Spider, Cleveland Museum of Art, Reinberger Galleries. **Environmental Initiatives:** Recycling.

ADMISSIONS

Freshman Academic Profile: Average high school GPA 3.4. 19% in top 10% of high school class, 38% in top 25% of high school class, 67% in top 50% of high school class. **Reported SAT (pre-2016 redesign) scores:** SAT Math middle 50% range 490-600. SAT Critical Reading middle 50% range 520-620. SAT Writing middle 50% range 490-580. **Concordant SAT scores:** SAT EBRW middle 50% 560–650. SAT Math middle 50% range 520–620. ACT middle 50% range 20-26. Minimum internet-based TOEFL 79. Minimum paper TOEFL 550. **Basis for Candidate Selection:** *Very important factors considered include:* talent/ability. *Important factors considered include:* rigor of secondary school record, academic GPA, standardized test scores, application essay, recommendation(s), interview, character/personal qualities. *Other factors considered include:* extracurricular activities, level of applicant's interest. **Freshman Admission Requirements:** High school diploma is required and GED is accepted. *Academic units recommended:* 4 English, 3 math, 3 science, 3 social studies, 6 academic electives, and 3 units from above areas or other academic areas. **Freshman Admission Statistics:** 864 applied, 61.57% admitted, 30% enrolled. **Transfer Admission Requirements:** college transcript(s), essay or personal statement, Minimum college GPA of 2.0 required. Lowest grade transferable C. **General Admission Information:** Application fee $40. Priority deadline 7/1. Nonfall registration not accepted. Admission may be deferred for a maximum of 1 year.

COSTS AND FINANCIAL AID

Annual tuition $37,980. Required fees $2,565. Average book expense $2,190. **Required Forms and Deadlines:** FAFSA, Institution's own financial aid form. **Notification of Awards:** Applicants will be notified of awards on a rolling basis beginning 3/15. **Types of Aid:** *Need-based scholarships/grants:* Federal Pell, FSEOG, State scholarships/grants, Private scholarships, College/university scholarship or grant aid from institutional funds. *Loans:* Direct Subsidized Stafford Loans, Direct Unsubsidized Stafford Loans, Direct PLUS loans,

Federal Perkins Loans. *Student Employment:* Federal Work-Study Program available. Institutional employment available. **Financial Aid Statistics:** 96% needy freshmen, 100% needy undergrads receive need-based scholarship or grant aid. 5% freshmen, 5% undergrads receive non-need-based scholarship or grant aid. 95% freshmen, 95% undergrads receive need-based self-help aid. 0% freshmen, 0% undergrads receive athletic scholarships. 80% freshmen, 95% undergrads receive any aid. 88% undergrads borrow to pay for school. Average cumulative indebtedness $35,136. **Criteria for awarding aid:** *Need-based:* Academics, Art. *Non-need-based:* Academics, Art.

See page 942.

CLEVELAND STATE UNIVERSITY

2121 Euclid Avenue, Cleveland, OH 44115-2214
Phone: 216-523-7416 • **Financial Aid Phone:** 216-687-5594
E-mail: admissions@csuohio.edu • **CEEB Code:** 3032
Fax: 216-687-5501 • **Website:** www.csuohio.edu • **ACT Code:** 1221

This public school was founded in 1964. It has a 82-acre campus.

RATINGS

Admissions Selectivity Rating: 75   **Fire Safety Rating:** 60*   **Green Rating:** 60*

STUDENTS AND FACULTY

Enrollment: 11,669. **Student Body:** 53% female, 47% male, 4% out-of-state, 5% international (85 countries represented). Asian 3%, African American 17%, Caucasian 64%, Hispanic 5%, Native American <1%, Pacific Islander <1%, Two or more races 3%, Race unknown 2%.

Retention and Graduation: 71% freshmen return for sophomore year. **Faculty:** Student/faculty ratio 24:1. 524 full-time faculty, 89% hold PhDs, 14% are are members of minority groups, 43% are women. 1% of classes are taught by teaching assistants.

ACADEMICS

Degrees: bachelor's, doctoral/professional, doctoral/research, doctoral, master's, postbachelor's certificate, post-master's certificate. **Classes:** Most classes have 20-29 students. **Most popular majors:** Psychology; Accounting; Business Administration, Management and Operations. **Special Study Options:** Accelerated program, cooperative education program, cross-registration, distance learning, double major, dual enrollment, English as a Second Language (ESL), exchange student program (domestic), honors program, independent study, internships, liberal arts/career combination, student-designed major, study abroad, teacher certification program, weekend college. **Honors Programs:** CSU's Honors Program was established in 2004 to serve the needs of academically talented students. Each year, it accepts approximately 40 first-year students and 20-25 juniors who have demonstrated superior academic achievement through their coursework and results on tests such as the ACT and SAT. Honors students at CSU receive a scholarship that covers full tuition as well as all academic fees and the cost of books required for their classes. Honors students in good standing receive this support throughout their four-year undergraduate academic career. Combined degree programs: JD/MBA. **Disability Services:** Special programs offered to physically disabled students, including note-taking services, reader services, tape recorders, tutors. **Career Services:** Alumni services, Career/job search classes, Career assessment, Internships.

FACILITIES

Housing: Coed dorms, special housing for disabled students, fraternity/sorority housing. 90% of campus accessible to physically diasbled. **Computers:** Students can register for classes online. Administrative functions (other than registration) can be performed online.

CAMPUS LIFE

Environment: Metropolis. **Activities:** Choral groups, concert band, dance, drama/theater, jazz band, literary magazine, musical theater, opera, pep band, radio station, student government, student newspaper, student-run film society, symphony orchestra, Student Organization. 10 religious organizations. 8 fraternities, 7 sororities. **Athletics (Intercollegiate):** *Men:* baseball, basketball, fencing, golf, soccer, swimming, wrestling. *Women:* basketball, cross-country, fencing, softball, swimming, tennis, track/field (outdoor), track/field (indoor), volleyball. **On-Campus Highlights:** Recreation Center, Main Classroom Atrium, Michael Schwartz Library, The Green Room, Farmer's Market.

ADMISSIONS

Freshman Academic Profile: Average high school GPA 3.3. 15% in top 10% of high school class, 39% in top 25% of high school class, 71% in top 50% of high school class. **Reported SAT (pre-2016 redesign) scores:** SAT Math middle 50% range 450-570. SAT Critical Reading middle 50% range 440-570. **Concordant SAT scores:** SAT Math middle 50% range 490–590. ACT middle 50% range 19-25. Minimum internet-based TOEFL 78. Minimum paper TOEFL 550. **Basis for Candidate Selection:** *Very important factors considered include:* rigor of secondary school record, academic GPA, standardized test scores. *Important factors considered include:* class rank. **Freshman Admission Requirements:** High school diploma is required and GED is accepted. *Academic units required:* 4 English, 3 math, 3 science, 3 social studies. *Academic units recommended:* 2 foreign language, 1 visual/performing arts. **Freshman Admission Statistics:** 7,544 applied, 91.15% admitted, 28% enrolled. **Transfer Admission Requirements:** college transcript(s), Minimum college GPA of 2.0 required. Lowest grade transferable D. **General Admission Information:** Application fee $30. Priority deadline 7/15. Regular application deadline 8/15. Nonfall registration accepted. Admission may be deferred for a maximum of 1 year.

COSTS AND FINANCIAL AID

Annual in-state tuition $9,636. Annual out-of-state tuition $12,878. Room and board $12,500. Average book expense $800. **Required Forms and Deadlines:** FAFSA. **Notification of Awards:** Applicants will be notified of awards on a rolling basis beginning 3/15. *Types of Aid: Need-based scholarships/grants:* Federal Pell, FSEOG, State scholarships/grants, Private scholarships, College/university scholarship or grant aid from institutional funds. *Loans:* Direct Subsidized Stafford Loans, Direct Unsubsidized Stafford Loans, Direct PLUS loans, Federal Perkins Loans, State Loans. *Student Employment:* Federal Work-Study Program available. Institutional employment available. **Financial Aid Statistics:** 80% needy freshmen, 75% needy undergrads receive need-based scholarship or grant aid. 5% freshmen, 3% undergrads receive non-need-based scholarship or grant aid. 74% freshmen, 81% undergrads receive need-based self-help aid. 2% freshmen, 2% undergrads receive athletic scholarships. **Criteria for awarding aid:** *Non-need-based:* Academics, Alumni affiliation, Art, Athletics, Leadership, Music/drama.

COASTAL CAROLINA UNIVERSITY

PO Box 261954, Conway, SC 29528-6054
Phone: 843-349-2170 • **Financial Aid Phone:** 843-349-2313
E-mail: admissions@coastal.edu • **CEEB Code:** 5837
Fax: 843-349-2127 • **Website:** www.coastal.edu • **ACT Code:** 3843

This public school was founded in 1954. It has a 302-acre campus.

RATINGS

Admissions Selectivity Rating: 80　　**Fire Safety Rating:** 92　　**Green Rating:** 80

STUDENTS AND FACULTY

Enrollment: 9,460. **Student Body:** 53% female, 47% male, 50% out-of-state, 1% international (55 countries represented). Asian 1%, African American 20%, Caucasian 67%, Hispanic 4%, Native American <1%, Pacific Islander <1%, Two or more races 5%, Race unknown 1%.
Retention and Graduation: 69% freshmen return for sophomore year. 27% freshmen graduate within 4 years. 42% freshmen graduate within 6 years.
Faculty: Student/faculty ratio 17:1. 448 full-time faculty, 76% hold PhDs, 11% are are members of minority groups, 44% are women. 0% of classes are taught by teaching assistants.

ACADEMICS

Degrees: bachelor's, certificate, doctoral/research, master's, postbachelor's certificate, post-master's certificate. **Classes:** Most classes have 20-29 students. Most lab/discussion sessions have 10-19 students. **Most popular majors:** Marine Biology and Biological Oceanography; Business Administration and Management; Kinesiology and Exercise Science. **Special Study Options:** Accelerated program, cooperative education program, distance learning, double major, dual enrollment, honors program, independent study, internships, student-designed major, study abroad, teacher certification program. **Disability Services:** Special programs offered to physically disabled students, including note-taking services, reader services, tape recorders, tutors. **Career Services:** Alumni network, Alumni services, Career/job search classes, Career assessment, Internships, Regional alumni. Career Assessment Program which is an integral part of University 110 and is required of all freshmen.

FACILITIES

Housing: Coed dorms, special housing for disabled students. 98% of campus accessible to physically diasbled. **Computers:** 100% of classrooms, 100% of libraries, 100% of dining areas, 100% of student union, 83% of common outdoor areas have wireless network access. Students can register for classes online. Administrative functions (other than registration) can be performed online.

CAMPUS LIFE

Environment: Town. **Activities:** Choral groups, concert band, dance, drama/theater, jazz band, literary magazine, marching band, music ensembles, musical theater, pep band, radio station, student government, student newspaper, Campus Ministries, Student Organization. 91 registered organizations, 32 honor societies, 13 religious organizations. 9 fraternities, 7 sororities. **Athletics (Intercollegiate):** *Men:* baseball, basketball, cheerleading, cross-country, football, golf, soccer, tennis, track/field (outdoor). *Women:* basketball, cheerleading, cross-country, golf, soccer, softball, tennis, track/field (outdoor), volleyball. **On-Campus Highlights:** Humanities and Fine Arts Building, Brooks Stadium, CINO Grille / Student Center, Recreation Center, Java City Cafe. **Environmental Initiatives:** Sustainable Transportation including: Zip Car, 330 in the bike sharing fleet, 2 bike fix stations, shuttles and EV stations

ADMISSIONS

Freshman Academic Profile: Average high school GPA 3.5. 9% in top 10% of high school class, 33% in top 25% of high school class, 69% in top 50% of high school class. 92% from public high schools. **Reported SAT (pre-2016 redesign) scores:** SAT Math middle 50% range 470-550. SAT Critical Reading middle 50% range 460-540. **Concordant SAT scores:** SAT Math middle 50% range 510–570. ACT middle 50% range 20-25. Minimum internet-based TOEFL 71. Minimum paper TOEFL 527. **Basis for Candidate Selection:** *Very important factors considered include:* rigor of secondary school record, academic GPA. *Important factors considered include:* class rank, standardized test scores. *Other factors considered include:* application essay, recommendation(s), extracurricular activities, talent/ability, character/personal qualities, first generation, alumni/ae relation, geographical residence, state residency. **Freshman Admission Requirements:** High school diploma is required and GED is accepted. *Academic units required:* 4 English, 4 math, 3 science, 3 science labs, 2 foreign language, 2 social studies, 1 history, 1 academic elective, 1 visual/performing arts, and 1 unit from above areas or other academic areas. *Academic units recommended:* 1 computer science. **Freshman Admission Statistics:** 17,768 applied, 61.18% admitted, 21% enrolled. **Transfer Admission Requirements:** college transcript(s), statement of good standing from prior institution(s). Minimum college GPA of 2.0 required. Lowest grade transferable C-. **General Admission Information:** Application fee $45. Priority deadline 12/1. Regular application deadline 8/1. Nonfall registration accepted. Admission may be deferred for a maximum of 1 year.

COSTS AND FINANCIAL AID

Annual in-state tuition $10,696. Annual out-of-state tuition $24,940. Room and board $8,890. Required fees $180. Average book expense $1,160. **Required Forms and Deadlines:** FAFSA. **Notification of Awards:** Applicants will be notified of awards on a rolling basis beginning 3/1. *Types of Aid: Need-based scholarships/grants:* Federal Pell, FSEOG, State scholarships/grants, Private scholarships, College/university scholarship or grant aid from institutional funds. *Loans:* Direct Subsidized Stafford Loans, Direct Unsubsidized Stafford Loans, Direct PLUS loans, Federal Perkins Loans, State Loans. *Student Employment:* Federal Work-Study Program available. Institutional employment available. **Financial Aid Statistics:** 53% needy freshmen, 54% needy undergrads receive need-based scholarship or grant aid. 45% freshmen, 31% undergrads receive non-need-based scholarship or grant aid. 93% freshmen, 93% undergrads receive need-based self-help aid. 4% freshmen, 4% undergrads receive athletic scholarships. 86% freshmen, 92% undergrads receive any aid. 77% undergrads borrow to pay for school. Average cumulative indebtedness $38,897. **Criteria for awarding aid:** *Non-need-based:* Academics, Art, Athletics, Leadership.

COE COLLEGE

1220 First Avenue NE, Cedar Rapids, IA 52402
Phone: 319-399-8500 • **Financial Aid Phone:** 319-399-8540
E-mail: admission@coe.edu • **CEEB Code:** 6101
Fax: 319-399-8816 • **Website:** www.coe.edu • **ACT Code:** 1294

This private school, affiliated with the Presbyterian Church, was founded in 1851. It has a 53-acre campus.

RATINGS

Admissions Selectivity Rating: 88　　**Fire Safety Rating:** 88　　**Green Rating:** 81

STUDENTS AND FACULTY

Enrollment: 1,323. **Student Body:** 57% female, 43% male, 53% out-of-state, 3% international (16 countries represented). Asian 2%, African American 7%,

Caucasian 73%, Hispanic 9%, Native American <1%, Pacific Islander <1%, Two or more races 3%, Race unknown 3%.

Retention and Graduation: 75% freshmen return for sophomore year. 62% freshmen graduate within 4 years. 67% freshmen graduate within 6 years. 19% grads go on to further study within 1 year. **Faculty:** Student/faculty ratio 11:1. 96 full-time faculty, 91% hold PhDs, 7% are are members of minority groups, 40% are women. 0% of classes are taught by teaching assistants.

ACADEMICS

Degrees: bachelor's. **Classes:** Most classes have fewer than 10 students. Most lab/discussion sessions have 10-19 students. **Most popular majors:** Biology/ Biological Sciences; Business Administration and Management; Psychology. **Special Study Options:** Accelerated program, cross-registration, double major, dual enrollment, English as a Second Language (ESL), exchange student program (domestic), honors program, independent study, internships, student-designed major, study abroad, teacher certification program. **Honors Programs:** College honors program consisting of five honors seminars and an honors project or thesis. Combined degree programs: BA/JD, BA/MEng, Master of Public Health with University of Iowa. **Disability Services:** Special programs offered to physically disabled students, including note-taking services, tape recorders, tutors. **Career Services:** Alumni network, Alumni services, Career/job search classes, Career assessment, Internships, Regional alumni. The Coe Plan requires all students to complete an internship, research, study abroad, or other "out of the classroom" experience during their junior or senior year.

FACILITIES

Housing: Coed dorms, men's dorms, women's dorms, fraternity/sorority housing, apartments for single students, Wellness Housing, Theme Housing. 70% of campus accessible to physically disabled. **Special Academic Facilities/ Equipment:** Ornithological museum, writing lab, theatre. **Computers:** 70% of classrooms, 10% of dorms, 100% of libraries, 100% of dining areas, 100% of student union, 80% of common outdoor areas have wireless network access. Students can register for classes online.

CAMPUS LIFE

Environment: City. **Activities:** Choral groups, concert band, dance, drama/theater, jazz band, literary magazine, music ensembles, musical theater, pep band, radio station, student government, student newspaper, symphony orchestra, television station, yearbook, Campus Ministries, Student Organization. 60 registered organizations, 8 honor societies, 4 religious organizations. 5 fraternities, 3 sororities. **Athletics (Intercollegiate):** *Men:* baseball, basketball, cross-country, diving, football, golf, soccer, swimming, tennis, track/field (outdoor), track/field (indoor), wrestling. *Women:* basketball, cheerleading, cross-country, diving, golf, soccer, softball, swimming, tennis, track/field (outdoor), track/field (indoor), volleyball. **On-Campus Highlights:** Student Union/Coffee Shop, Dows Theatre, Library/Art Galleries, Fitness Center, Racquet Center. **Environmental Initiatives:** Coe College is embarking on a $3.45m major energy reduction program that will decrease the institution's electricity use by 25 percent and natural gas consumption by almost 50 percent, and deliver approximately $220,000 in guaranteed energy and operational savings each year.

ADMISSIONS

Freshman Academic Profile: Average high school GPA 3.6. 30% in top 10% of high school class, 65% in top 25% of high school class, 89% in top 50% of high school class. **Reported SAT (pre-2016 redesign) scores:** SAT Math middle 50% range 510-650. SAT Critical Reading middle 50% range 510-620. SAT Writing middle 50% range 480-620. **Concordant SAT scores:** SAT EBRW middle 50% 550–670. SAT Math middle 50% range 540–670. ACT middle 50% range 22-28. Minimum internet-based TOEFL 68. Minimum paper TOEFL 520. **Basis for Candidate Selection:** *Very important factors considered include:* academic GPA, standardized test scores. *Important factors considered include:* class rank. *Other factors considered include:* rigor of secondary school record, application essay, recommendation(s), interview, extracurricular activities, talent/ability, character/personal qualities, first generation, alumni/ae relation, racial/ethnic status, volunteer work, level of applicant's interest. **Freshman Admission Requirements:** High school diploma is required and GED is accepted. *Academic units recommended:* 4 English, 3 math, 3 science, 1 science lab, 2 foreign language, 3 social studies, 2 academic electives. **Freshman Admission Statistics:** 6,725 applied, 49.95% admitted, 11% enrolled. **Transfer Admission Requirements:** High school transcript, college transcript(s), essay or personal statement, statement of good standing from prior institution(s). Minimum college GPA of 2.5 required. Lowest grade transferable C. **General Admission Information:** Application fee $30. Priority deadline 12/10. Regular application deadline 3/1. Nonfall registration accepted. Admission may be deferred for a maximum of 2 years.

COSTS AND FINANCIAL AID

Annual tuition $42,090. Room and board $9,140. Required fees $340. Average book expense $1,000. **Required Forms and Deadlines:** FAFSA. **Notification of Awards:** Applicants will be notified of awards on a rolling basis beginning 3/15. **Types of Aid:** *Need-based scholarships/grants:* Federal Pell, FSEOG,

State scholarships/grants, Private scholarships, College/university scholarship or grant aid from institutional funds. *Loans:* Direct Subsidized Stafford Loans, Direct Unsubsidized Stafford Loans, Direct PLUS loans, Federal Perkins Loans, College/university loans from institutional funds. *Student Employment:* Federal Work-Study Program available. Institutional employment available. **Financial Aid Statistics:** 100% needy freshmen, 100% needy undergrads receive need-based scholarship or grant aid. 14% freshmen, 14% undergrads receive non-need-based scholarship or grant aid. 85% freshmen, 82% undergrads receive need-based self-help aid. 0% freshmen, 0% undergrads receive athletic scholarships. 99% freshmen, 99% undergrads receive any aid. 82% undergrads borrow to pay for school. Average cumulative indebtedness $35,782. **Criteria for awarding aid:** *Non-need-based:* Academics, Alumni affiliation, Art, Minority status, Music/drama, State/district residency.

COGSWELL COLLEGE

191 Baypointe Parkway, San Jose, CA 95134
Phone: 408-498-5160 • **Financial Aid Phone:** 408-498-5145
E-mail: admissions@cogswell.edu • **CEEB Code:** 1177
Fax: 408-747-0764 • **ACT Code:** 1177

This private school was founded in 1887. It has a 5-acre campus.

RATINGS

Admissions Selectivity Rating: 73   **Fire Safety Rating:** 96   **Green Rating:** 65

STUDENTS AND FACULTY

Enrollment: 653. **Student Body:** 29% female, 71% male, 7% out-of-state, <1% international (13 countries represented). Asian 20%, African American 5%, Caucasian 36%, Hispanic 21%, Native American 1%, Pacific Islander 1%, Two or more races 9%, Race unknown 7%.

Retention and Graduation: 77% freshmen return for sophomore year. 10% freshmen graduate within 4 years. 19% freshmen graduate within 6 years. 1% grads pursue business degrees. **Faculty:** Student/faculty ratio 14:1. 16 full-time faculty, 25% hold PhDs, 0% are are members of minority groups, 38% are women. 0% of classes are taught by teaching assistants.

ACADEMICS

Degrees: bachelor's, master's. **Classes:** Most classes have fewer than 10 students. **Most popular majors:** Animation, Interactive Technology, Video Graphics and Special Effects; Game and Interactive Media Design; Music Technology. **Special Study Options:** cooperative education program, distance learning, double major, exchange student program (domestic), internships, student-designed major, study abroad. Combined degree programs: Digital Art and Animation, Game Design Art, Digital Audio Technology. **Career Services:** Alumni network, Alumni services, Career/job search classes, Internships.

FACILITIES

Housing: apartments for single students. 100% of campus accessible to physically disabled. **Special Academic Facilities/Equipment:** The Gallery at Cogswell **Computers:** 100% of classrooms, 100% of libraries, 100% of dining areas, 100% of student union, have wireless network access. Students can register for classes online. Administrative functions (other than registration) can be performed online. Undergraduates are required to own a computer.

CAMPUS LIFE

Environment: Village. **Activities:** drama/theater, radio station, student government 5 registered organizations. **On-Campus Highlights:** Gallery, Library, Smart Lab, Dragon's Den, Audio Recording Studio. **Environmental Initiatives:** saving energy.

ADMISSIONS

Reported SAT (pre-2016 redesign) scores: SAT Math middle 50% range 480-585. SAT Critical Reading middle 50% range 490-592. SAT Writing middle 50% range 440-572. **Concordant SAT scores:** SAT EBRW middle 50% 520–640. SAT Math middle 50% range 510–610. ACT middle 50% range 20-24. Minimum internet-based TOEFL 69. Minimum paper TOEFL 525. **Basis for Candidate Selection:** *Very important factors considered include:* academic GPA, talent/ability, level of applicant's interest. *Important factors considered include:* rigor of secondary school record, application essay, recommendation(s), interview. *Other factors considered include:* class rank, standardized test scores, extracurricular activities, character/personal qualities, volunteer work, work experience. **Freshman Admission Requirements:** High school diploma is required and GED is accepted. *Academic units required:* 3 English, 3 math, 1 science, 1 science lab. *Academic units recommended:* 1 computer science, 1 visual/performing arts. **Freshman Admission Statistics:** 281 applied, 82.56% admitted, 69% enrolled. **Transfer Admission Requirements:** High school transcript, college transcript(s), essay or personal statement, Minimum college GPA of 2.5 required. Lowest grade transferable C. **General Admission**

Information: Regular application deadline 8/15. Nonfall registration accepted. Admission may be deferred for a maximum of 1 year.

COSTS AND FINANCIAL AID
Annual tuition $18,096. Required fees $1,000. Average book expense $1,791. **Required Forms and Deadlines:** FAFSA, State aid form. **Notification of Awards:** Applicants will be notified of awards on a rolling basis beginning 4/1. **Types of Aid:** *Need-based scholarships/grants:* Federal Pell, FSEOG, State scholarships/grants, Private scholarships, College/university scholarship or grant aid from institutional funds. *Loans:* Direct Subsidized Stafford Loans, Direct Unsubsidized Stafford Loans, Direct PLUS loans. *Student Employment:* Federal Work-Study Program available. Institutional employment available. **Criteria for awarding aid:** *Need-based:* Academics, Alumni affiliation, Music/drama. *Non-need-based:* Academics, Alumni affiliation, Art, Music/drama.

COKER COLLEGE

300 East College Avenue, Hartsville, SC 29550
Phone: 843-383-8050
E-mail: admissions@coker.edu
Fax: 843-383-8056 • **Website:** www.coker.edu

This is a private school.

RATINGS
Admissions Selectivity Rating: 79   **Fire Safety Rating:** 60*   **Green Rating:** 60*

STUDENTS AND FACULTY
Enrollment: 674. **Student Body:** 63% female, 37% male, 19% out-of-state, 3% international. Asian 0%, African American 27%, Caucasian 67%, Hispanic 2%, Native American 1%, Pacific Islander <1%, Two or more races 0%, Race unknown <1%.
Retention and Graduation: 71% freshmen return for sophomore year. 48% freshmen graduate within 4 years. 60% freshmen graduate within 6 years.
Faculty: Student/faculty ratio 10:1. 58 full-time faculty, 81% hold PhDs, 12% are are members of minority groups, 47% are women. 0% of classes are taught by teaching assistants.

ACADEMICS
Degrees: bachelor's. **Classes:** Most classes have 10-19 students. Most lab/discussion sessions have 10-19 students. **Most popular majors:** Psychology; Graphic Design; Business/Commerce. **Special Study Options:** double major, dual enrollment, honors program, independent study, internships, student-designed major, study abroad, teacher certification program. **Disability Services:** Special programs offered to physically disabled students, including tape recorders, tutors. **Career Services:** Career/job search classes, Career assessment, Internships, On-campus interviews. With our internships students have the opportunity to receive hands-on experience in their field, which gives them a competitive edge in today's job market.

FACILITIES
Housing: Coed dorms, special housing for international students 80% of campus accessible to physically diasbled. **Special Academic Facilities/Equipment:** Art gallery, state-of-the-art performing arts center, dark rooms, botanical gardens, graduate-level science equipment. **Computers:** Administrative functions (other than registration) can be performed online.

CAMPUS LIFE
Activities: Choral groups, dance, drama/theater, literary magazine, music ensembles, musical theater, student government, student newspaper, Campus Ministries, Student Organization. 27 registered organizations, 4 honor societies, 2 religious organizations. **Athletics (Intercollegiate):** *Men:* baseball, basketball, cheerleading, cross-country, golf, soccer, tennis. *Women:* basketball, cheerleading, cross-country, soccer, softball, tennis, volleyball. **On-Campus Highlights:** The Cobra Den, The Cobra Caf, The Student Center, The Performing Arts Center, Outdoor Volleyball Courts, The Cobra Den includes a coffee area, dance floor, and a game room.

ADMISSIONS
Freshman Academic Profile: Average high school GPA 3.4. 1% in top 10% of high school class, 28% in top 25% of high school class, 70% in top 50% of high school class. **Reported SAT (pre-2016 redesign) scores:** SAT Math middle 50% range 440-570. SAT Critical Reading middle 50% range 420-570. **Concordant SAT scores:** SAT Math middle 50% range 480–590. ACT middle 50% range 17-22. Minimum paper TOEFL 500. **Basis for Candidate Selection:** *Very important factors considered include:* standardized test scores. *Important factors considered include:* rigor of secondary school record, class rank, level of applicant's interest. *Other factors considered include:* application essay, recommendation(s), interview, extracurricular activities, talent/ability,

character/personal qualities, alumni/ae relation, volunteer work, work experience. **Freshman Admission Requirements:** High school diploma is required and GED is accepted. *Academic units required:* 4 English, 3 math, 3 science, 1 science lab, 2 foreign language, 3 social studies. **Freshman Admission Statistics:** 1,112 applied, 55.76% admitted, 25% enrolled. **Transfer Admission Requirements:** High school transcript, college transcript(s), statement of good standing from prior institution(s). Minimum college GPA of 2.0 required. Lowest grade transferable C. **General Admission Information:** Application fee $15. Priority deadline 5/1. Regular application deadline 8/1. Nonfall registration accepted. Admission may be deferred for a maximum of 1 year.

COSTS AND FINANCIAL AID
Annual tuition $22,200. Room and board $6,950. Average book expense $1,500. **Required Forms and Deadlines:** FAFSA. **Notification of Awards:** Applicants will be notified of awards on a rolling basis beginning 3/1. **Types of Aid:** *Need-based scholarships/grants:* Federal Pell, FSEOG, State scholarships/grants, Private scholarships, College/university scholarship or grant aid from institutional funds. *Loans:* Direct Subsidized Stafford Loans, Direct Unsubsidized Stafford Loans, Direct PLUS loans, Federal Perkins Loans, State Loans. *Student Employment:* Federal Work-Study Program available. Institutional employment available. **Financial Aid Statistics:** 96% needy freshmen, 96% needy undergrads receive need-based scholarship or grant aid. 100% freshmen, 93% undergrads receive non-need-based scholarship or grant aid. 78% freshmen, 80% undergrads receive need-based self-help aid. 5% freshmen, 6% undergrads receive athletic scholarships. 100% freshmen, 100% undergrads receive any aid. **Criteria for awarding aid:** *Need-based:* Academics, Job skills, Minority status, Music/drama, Religious affiliation. *Non-need-based:* Academics, Alumni affiliation, Art, Athletics, Job skills, Leadership, Minority status, Music/drama, Religious affiliation, State/district residency.

COLBY COLLEGE

4800 Mayflower Hill, Waterville, ME 4901
Phone: 207-859-4828 • **Financial Aid Phone:** 207-859-4814
E-mail: admissions@colby.edu • **CEEB Code:** 3280
Fax: 207-859-4828 • **Website:** www.colby.edu • **ACT Code:** 1638

This private school was founded in 1813. It has a 714-acre campus.

RATINGS
Admissions Selectivity Rating: 95   **Fire Safety Rating:** 97   **Green Rating:** 99

STUDENTS AND FACULTY
Enrollment: 1,879. **Student Body:** 52% female, 48% male, 86% out-of-state, 11% international (74 countries represented). Asian 6%, African American 4%, Caucasian 62%, Hispanic 7%, Native American <1%, Pacific Islander <1%, Two or more races 5%, Race unknown 5%.
Retention and Graduation: 93% freshmen return for sophomore year. 84% freshmen graduate within 4 years. 89 29% grads go on to further study within 1 year. 20% grads pursue arts and sciences degrees. 3% grads pursue law degrees. 3% grads pursue medical degrees. **Faculty:** Student/faculty ratio 9:1. 191 full-time faculty, 97% hold PhDs, 15% are are members of minority groups, 46% are women. 0% of classes are taught by teaching assistants.

ACADEMICS
Degrees: bachelor's. **Classes:** Most classes have 10-19 students. Most lab/discussion sessions have 10-19 students. **Most popular majors:** Biology/Biological Sciences; Economics; English Language and Literature. **Special Study Options:** cross-registration, double major, exchange student program (domestic), honors program, independent study, internships, student-designed major, study abroad, teacher certification program, Summer research assistantships; Colby has coordinated 3-2 engineering programs with Dartmouth; Colby offers junior-year abroad programs in France, Spain, and Russia. **Disability Services:** Special programs offered to physically disabled students, including note-taking services, reader services, tape recorders, tutors. **Career Services:** Alumni network, Alumni services, Career/job search classes, Career assessment, Internships, Regional alumni. Colby Connect is a four-year career development curriculum that inspires success through a sequence of practical workshops, information sessions, and related programming. Colby Connect embraces students by connecting them to fellowships, internships, job shadowing, Jan Plan, and employment opportunities, and graduate studies. Colby Connect integrates alumni, parents, faculty, and recruiters into Career

Center programming. Colby has dozens of funds that offer financial grants so students can take unpaid or low-paying internship opportunities that they couldn't afford otherwise.

FACILITIES

Housing: Coed dorms, Wellness Housing, Theme Housing, quiet halls, chem-free halls, apartments for seniors only, student interest halls. 88% of campus accessible to physically diasbled. **Special Academic Facilities/Equipment:** 28,000 square foot art museum, completely renovated student center (Pulver Pavilion), arboretum, electronic microscopes, greenhouse, astronomical observatory, writer's center, cross-country ski trails, Goldfarb Center for Public Affairs and Civic Engagement, multicultural center, rare books and archives library, computer research classroom, language lab. **Computers:** 100% of classrooms, 100% of dorms, 100% of libraries, 100% of dining areas, 100% of student union, 10% of common outdoor areas have wireless network access. Students can register for classes online. Administrative functions (other than registration) can be performed online.

CAMPUS LIFE

Environment: Village. **Activities:** Choral groups, concert band, dance, drama/theater, jazz band, literary magazine, music ensembles, musical theater, radio station, student government, student newspaper, student-run film society, symphony orchestra, yearbook, Student Organization. 91 registered organizations, 9 honor societies, 6 religious organizations. **Athletics (Intercollegiate):** *Men:* baseball, basketball, crew/rowing, cross-country, diving, football, golf, ice hockey, lacrosse, skiing (downhill/alpine), skiing (nordic/cross-country), soccer, squash, swimming, tennis, track/field (outdoor), track/field (indoor). *Women:* basketball, crew/rowing, cross-country, diving, field hockey, golf, ice hockey, lacrosse, skiing (downhill/alpine), skiing (nordic/cross-country), soccer, softball, squash, swimming, tennis, track/field (outdoor), track/field (indoor), volleyball. **On-Campus Highlights:** Pulver Pavillion, Colby College Museum of Art, Johnson Pond, Perkins Arboretum trails (running, cross-country). **Environmental Initiatives:** In April 2013, Colby College became the fourth institution of higher education in the world to achieve carbon neutrality.

ADMISSIONS

Freshman Academic Profile: 63% in top 10% of high school class, 93% in top 25% of high school class, 97% in top 50% of high school class. 52% from public high schools. **Reported SAT (pre-2016 redesign) scores:** SAT Math middle 50% range 640-740. SAT Critical Reading middle 50% range 630-720. SAT Writing middle 50% range 630-730. **Concordant SAT scores:** SAT EBRW middle 50% 680–750. SAT Math middle 50% range 660–760. ACT middle 50% range 29-32. Minimum internet-based TOEFL 100. **Basis for Candidate Selection:** *Very important factors considered include:* rigor of secondary school record, academic GPA, recommendation(s), character/personal qualities. *Important factors considered include:* class rank, standardized test scores, application essay, extracurricular activities, talent/ability, racial/ethnic status. *Other factors considered include:* interview, first generation, alumni/ae relation, geographical residence, state residency, volunteer work, work experience, level of applicant's interest. **Freshman Admission Requirements:** High school diploma or equivalent is not required. *Academic units recommended:* 4 English, 3 math, 2 science, 2 science labs, 3 foreign language, 2 social studies. **Freshman Admission Statistics:** 7,593 applied, 22.52% admitted, 30% enrolled. **Transfer Admission Requirements:** High school transcript, college transcript(s), essay or personal statement, standardized test scores, statement of good standing from prior institution(s). Minimum college GPA of 3.0 required. Lowest grade transferable C. **General Admission Information:** Regular application deadline 1/1. Regular notification 4/1. Nonfall registration accepted. Admission may be deferred for a maximum of 1 yr usually.

COSTS AND FINANCIAL AID

Annual tuition $48,820. Room and board $13,100. Required fees $2,140. Average book expense $732. **Required Forms and Deadlines:** FAFSA, CSS/Financial Aid PROFILE, Business/Farm Supplement. **Notification of Awards:** Applicants will be notified of awards on or about 4/1. **Types of Aid:** *Need-based scholarships/grants:* Federal Pell, FSEOG, State scholarships/grants, Private scholarships, College/university scholarship or grant aid from institutional funds. *Loans:* Direct Subsidized Stafford Loans, Direct Unsubsidized Stafford Loans, Direct PLUS loans, Federal Perkins Loans, State Loans. *Student Employment:* Federal Work-Study Program available. Institutional employment available. **Financial Aid Statistics:** 100% needy freshmen, 99% needy undergrads receive need-based scholarship or grant aid. 2% freshmen, 1% undergrads receive non-need-based scholarship or grant aid. 65% freshmen, 72% undergrads receive need-based self-help aid. 0% freshmen, 0% undergrads receive athletic scholarships. 41% freshmen, 43% undergrads receive any aid. Average cumulative indebtedness $23,343.

541 Main Street, New London, NH 03257-7835
Phone: 603-526-3700 • **Financial Aid Phone:** 603-526-3717
E-mail: admissions@colbysawyer.edu • **CEEB Code:** 3281
Fax: 603-526-3452 • **Website:** www.colby-sawyer.edu • **ACT Code:** 2506

This private school was founded in 1837. It has a 200-acre campus.

RATINGS

Admissions Selectivity Rating: 72   **Fire Safety Rating:** 75   **Green Rating:** 60*

STUDENTS AND FACULTY

Enrollment: 942. **Student Body:** 65% female, 35% male, 68% out-of-state, 1% international (11 countries represented). Asian 1%, African American 1%, Caucasian 90%, Hispanic 1%, Native American <1%, Pacific Islander 0%, Two or more races 0%, Race unknown 5%.
Retention and Graduation: 71% freshmen return for sophomore year. 51% freshmen graduate within 4 years. 60% freshmen graduate within 6 years.
Faculty: Student/faculty ratio 11:1. 60 full-time faculty, 73% hold PhDs, 2% are are members of minority groups, 52% are women. 0% of classes are taught by teaching assistants.

ACADEMICS

Degrees: associate, bachelor's, transfer. **Classes:** Most classes have 10-19 students. Most lab/discussion sessions have 10-19 students. **Most popular majors:** Business Administration and Management Sport and Fitness Administration/Management. **Special Study Options:** Accelerated program, cross-registration, double major, dual enrollment, English as a Second Language (ESL), exchange student program (domestic), honors program, independent study, internships, student-designed major, study abroad, teacher certification program. **Honors Programs:** The Wesson Honors Program is designed to provide highly motivated students with an optional intensive experience in the liberal arts. By creating academic, cultural, and social opportunities for integrative and interdisciplinary intellectual discovery, the program challenges students not only to widen their own avenues of intellectual exploration, but to take leadership in a community of scholars and participate as catalysts for inquiry and discussion across the college. **Disability Services:** Special programs offered to physically disabled students, including tape recorders, tutors.

FACILITIES

Housing: Coed dorms, special housing for disabled students, women's dorms, Substance-free Residence Hall. 50% of campus accessible to physically diasbled. **Special Academic Facilities/Equipment:** Sawyer Fine Arts Center, Windy Hill School (pre-school- grade 3 laboratory school), Ivey Science Center, Hogan Sports Center, Video Studio and Editing Room, Radio Station (WSCS 90.9 FM)

CAMPUS LIFE

Environment: Rural. **Activities:** Choral groups, dance, drama/theater, literary magazine, musical theater, radio station, student government, student newspaper, yearbook. 40 registered organizations, 5 honor societies, 1 religious organization. **Athletics (Intercollegiate):** *Men:* baseball, basketball, diving, equestrian sports, skiing (downhill/alpine), soccer, swimming, tennis, track/field (outdoor). *Women:* basketball, diving, equestrian sports, lacrosse, skiing (downhill/alpine), soccer, swimming, tennis, track/field (outdoor), volleyball. **On-Campus Highlights:** Dan and Kathleen Hogan Sports Center, Susan Colgate Cleveland Library/Learning Center, Lethbridge Lodge, Thornton Livingroom, Rooke Hall.

ADMISSIONS

Freshman Academic Profile: Average high school GPA 3.0. 83% from public high schools. **Reported SAT (pre-2016 redesign) scores:** SAT Math middle 50% range 440-530. SAT Critical Reading middle 50% range 440-540. **Concordant SAT scores:** SAT Math middle 50% range 480–560. ACT middle 50% range 18-22. Minimum paper TOEFL 500. **Basis for Candidate Selection:** *Very important factors considered include:* rigor of secondary school record, academic GPA, interview. *Important factors considered include:* class rank, standardized test scores, application essay, recommendation(s), extracurricular activities, talent/ability, alumni/ae relation, volunteer work, work experience, level of applicant's interest. *Other factors considered include:* first generation, geographical residence, state residency. **Freshman Admission Requirements:** High school diploma is required and GED is accepted. *Academic units recommended:* 4 English, 3 math, 3 science, 3 science labs, 2 foreign language, 3 social studies. **Freshman Admission Statistics:** 1,402 applied, 87.52% admitted, 29% enrolled. **Transfer Admission Requirements:** college transcript(s), essay or personal statement, Minimum college GPA of 2.0 required. Lowest grade transferable C. **General Admission Information:** Application fee $45. Regular application deadline 4/1. Nonfall registration accepted. Admission may be deferred for a maximum of 1 year.

COSTS AND FINANCIAL AID

Annual tuition $29,620. Room and board $10,340. Required fees $0. Average book expense $750. **Required Forms and Deadlines:** FAFSA. **Notification of Awards:** Applicants will be notified of awards on a rolling basis beginning 3/1. **Types of Aid:** *Need-based scholarships/grants:* Federal Pell, FSEOG, State scholarships/grants, Private scholarships, College/university scholarship or grant aid from institutional funds. *Loans:* Federal Perkins Loans, State Loans, College/university loans from institutional funds. *Student Employment:* Federal Work-Study Program available. Institutional employment available. **Financial Aid Statistics:** 100% needy freshmen, 95% needy undergrads receive need-based scholarship or grant aid. 4% freshmen, 6% undergrads receive non-need-based scholarship or grant aid. 93% freshmen, 99% undergrads receive need-based self-help aid. 0% freshmen, 0% undergrads receive athletic scholarships. 83% freshmen, 83% undergrads receive any aid. **Criteria for awarding aid:** *Need-based:* Academics. *Non-need-based:* Academics, Alumni affiliation, Art, Leadership, Music/drama.

COLGATE UNIVERSITY

13 Oak Drive, Hamilton, NY 13346
Phone: 315-228-7401 • **Financial Aid Phone:** 315-228-7431
E-mail: admission@colgate.edu • **CEEB Code:** 2086
Fax: 315-228-7524 • **Website:** www.colgate.edu • **ACT Code:** 2702

This private school was founded in 1819. It has a 515-acre campus.

RATINGS

Admissions Selectivity Rating: 97   **Fire Safety Rating:** 95   **Green Rating:** 95

STUDENTS AND FACULTY

Enrollment: 2,865. **Student Body:** 55% female, 45% male, 73% out-of-state, 9% international (47 countries represented). Asian 4%, African American 5%, Caucasian 66%, Hispanic 9%, Native American <1%, Pacific Islander 0%, Two or more races 4%, Race unknown 4%.
Retention and Graduation: 94% freshmen return for sophomore year. 85% freshmen graduate within 4 years. 90 14% grads go on to further study within 1 year. 10% grads pursue arts and sciences degrees. 4% grads pursue law degrees. 1% grads pursue business degrees. 3% grads pursue medical degrees. **Faculty:** Student/faculty ratio 9:1. 297 full-time faculty, 99% hold PhDs, 25% are are members of minority groups, 44% are women.

ACADEMICS

Degrees: bachelor's, master's. **Classes:** Most classes have 10-19 students. Most lab/discussion sessions have 10-19 students. **Most popular majors:** English Language and Literature; Economics; Political Science and Government. **Special Study Options:** cross-registration, double major, honors program, independent study, internships, liberal arts/career combination, student-designed major, study abroad, teacher certification program, Extended study program allows students to further academic work with a 3-5 week off campus experience during the winter or summer break. Recent trips have travelled to 13 locations around the world including South Africa, Ireland, and China. **Honors Programs:** Each year, Colgate honors its top (approximately) 200 accepted students as Alumni Memorial Scholars. This recognition is the highest honor within the admission process, and an indication of an excellent match, both academically and personally, with Colgate. **Disability Services:** Special programs offered to physically disabled students, including note-taking services, reader services, tape recorders, tutors. **Career Services:** Alumni network, Alumni services, Career/job search classes, Career assessment, Internships. Career Services' Summer Funding provides grants to students to pursue unpaid or underpaid internships, research, long-term service, and independent projects. Grants are 100% alumni and parent donor funded. Since the inception of this program in spring 2012, Career Services has funded over 600 students for over $2.3MM.

FACILITIES

Housing: Coed dorms, special housing for disabled students, fraternity/sorority housing, cooperative housing, apartments for single students, Wellness Housing, Theme **Housing:** Peace Studies, La Casa Pan Latina, Harlem Reniassance Center, French-Italian House, etc. Accomodations for students with special needs. Townhouses for small groups of students. **Special Academic Facilities/ Equipment:** Art galleries, anthropology museum, language lab, cable TV station, life sciences complex, geology/fossil collection, observatory, electron microscopes, laser lab, weather lab. **Computers:** Students can register for classes online. Administrative functions (other than registration) can be performed online.

CAMPUS LIFE

Environment: Rural. **Activities:** Choral groups, concert band, dance, drama/ theater, jazz band, literary magazine, music ensembles, musical theater, pep band, radio station, student government, student newspaper, student-run film society, symphony orchestra, television station, yearbook, Campus Ministries, Student Organization, Model UN. 160 registered organizations, 4 honor societies, 8 religious organizations. 6 fraternities, 3 sororities **Athletics (Intercollegiate):** *Men:* basketball, crew/rowing, cross-country, diving, football, golf, ice hockey, lacrosse, soccer, swimming, tennis, track/field (outdoor). *Women:* basketball, crew/rowing, cross-country, diving, field hockey, ice hockey, lacrosse, soccer, softball, swimming, tennis, track/field (outdoor), volleyball. **On-Campus Highlights:** Picker Art Gallery, Case-Geyer Library, ALANA Culture Center, Ho Science Center, O'Connor Campus Center (The Coop), Two recently completed building projects: $52 million renovation to the Case Library and The Robert H.N. Ho Science Center. **Environmental Initiatives:** All electricity used on campus is hydroelectric, with some supplemental nuclear power. Colgate wood-chip-burning heating plant utilizes a renewable energy source to provide about 70 percent of our total requirement.

ADMISSIONS

Freshman Academic Profile: Average high school GPA 3.7. 72% in top 10% of high school class, 93% in top 25% of high school class, 98% in top 50% of high school class. 58% from public high schools. **Reported SAT (pre-2016 redesign) scores:** SAT Math middle 50% range 650-740. SAT Critical Reading middle 50% range 640-720. **Concordant SAT scores:** SAT Math middle 50% range 670–760. ACT middle 50% range 30-33. **Basis for Candidate Selection:** *Very important factors considered include:* rigor of secondary school record, class rank, academic GPA. *Important factors considered include:* standardized test scores, application essay, recommendation(s), extracurricular activities, talent/ability, character/personal qualities. *Other factors considered include:* first generation, alumni/ae relation, geographical residence, racial/ ethnic status, volunteer work, work experience. **Freshman Admission Requirements:** High school diploma is required and GED is accepted. *Academic units required:* 4 English, 3 math, 3 science, 2 science labs, 3 foreign language, 3 social studies. *Academic units recommended:* 4 English, 4 math, 4 science, 4 science labs, 4 foreign language, 4 social studies. **Freshman Admission Statistics:** 8,394 applied, 28.78% admitted, 32% enrolled. **Transfer Admission Requirements:** High school transcript, college transcript(s), essay or personal statement, standardized test scores, statement of good standing from prior institution(s). Minimum college GPA of 3.00 required. Lowest grade transferable C. **General Admission Information:** Application fee $60. Regular application deadline 1/15. Regular notification 4/1. Nonfall registration not accepted. Admission may be deferred for a maximum of 1 year.

COSTS AND FINANCIAL AID

Annual tuition $51,635. Room and board $13,075. Required fees $320. Average book expense $2,260. **Required Forms and Deadlines:** CSS/Financial Aid PROFILE, Noncustodial PROFILE. **Notification of Awards:** Applicants will be notified of awards on or about 3/26. **Types of Aid:** *Need-based scholarships/ grants:* Federal Pell, FSEOG. *Loans:* Direct Subsidized Stafford Loans, Direct Unsubsidized Stafford Loans, Direct PLUS loans, Federal Perkins Loans. *Student Employment:* Federal Work-Study Program available. Institutional employment available. **Financial Aid Statistics:** 100% needy freshmen, 99% needy undergrads receive need-based scholarship or grant aid. 0% undergrads receive non-need-based scholarship or grant aid. 77% freshmen, 81% undergrads receive need-based self-help aid. 10% freshmen, 10% undergrads receive athletic scholarships. 41% freshmen, 42% undergrads receive any aid. 34% undergrads borrow to pay for school. Average cumulative indebtedness $21,427. **Criteria for awarding aid:** *Non-need-based:* Athletics.

COLLEGE FOR CREATIVE STUDIES

201 East Kirby, Detroit, MI 48202
Phone: 313-664-7425 • **Financial Aid Phone:** 313-664-7495
E-mail: admissions@collegeforcreativestudies.edu • **CEEB Code:** 1035
Fax: 313-872-2739 • **Website:** www.collegeforcreativestudies.edu • **ACT Code:** 1989

This private school was founded in 1906. It has a 11-acre campus.

RATINGS

Admissions Selectivity Rating: 78   **Fire Safety Rating:** 87   **Green Rating:** 60*

STUDENTS AND FACULTY

Enrollment: 1,307. **Student Body:** 17% out-of-state, 4% international (15 countries represented). Asian 4%, African American 6%, Caucasian 71%,

Hispanic 5%, Native American 1%, Pacific Islander 0%, Two or more races 0%, Race unknown 10%.
Retention and Graduation: 73% freshmen return for sophomore year.
Faculty: Student/faculty ratio 8:1. 51 full-time faculty, 61% hold PhDs, 14% are are members of minority groups, 31% 0% of classes are taught by teaching assistants.

ACADEMICS
Degrees: bachelor's, master's, postbachelor's certificate. **Most popular majors:** Commercial and Advertising Art; Industrial and Product Design; Film/Video and Photographic Arts. **Special Study Options:** cooperative education program, double major, dual enrollment, English as a Second Language (ESL), exchange student program (domestic), independent study, internships, study abroad, teacher certification program. **Disability Services:** Special programs offered to physically disabled students, including reader services, tape recorders, tutors. **Career Services:** Alumni network, Alumni services, Career/job search classes, Career assessment, Internships, Regional alumni. All seniors take part in a practicum class that allows students to work with and for outside companies, such as Ford Motor Company, Pixar, DaimlerChrysler and various other companies.

FACILITIES
Housing: Coed dorms. 95% of campus accessible to physically diasbled.
Special Academic Facilities/Equipment: Top-of-the-line technology for design, animation and audiovisual editing. Wood and Metal shops, hot glass studio, gallery, private studios.

CAMPUS LIFE
Environment: Metropolis. **Activities:** student government 5 registered organizations. **On-Campus Highlights:** Center Galleries, U245 Student Art Gallery, Jazzman's Cafe

ADMISSIONS
ACT middle 50% range 18-23. Minimum paper TOEFL 525. **Basis for Candidate Selection:** *Very important factors considered include:* talent/ability. *Important factors considered include:* academic GPA, standardized test scores. *Other factors considered include:* level of applicant's interest. **Freshman Admission Requirements:** High school diploma is required and GED is accepted. **Freshman Admission Statistics:** 1,260 applied, 38.73% admitted, 51% enrolled. **Transfer Admission Requirements:** High school transcript, college transcript(s), Minimum college GPA of 2.0 required. Lowest grade transferable C. **General Admission Information:** Application fee $35. Priority deadline 3/1. Regular application deadline 8/1. Nonfall registration accepted. Admission may be deferred for a maximum of 4 semesters.

COSTS AND FINANCIAL AID
Annual tuition $27,090. Required fees $1,185. Average book expense $2,500.
Required Forms and Deadlines: FAFSA. **Notification of Awards:** Applicants will be notified of awards on a rolling basis beginning 3/15. **Types of Aid:** *Need-based scholarships/grants:* Federal Pell, FSEOG, State scholarships/grants, Private scholarships, College/university scholarship or grant aid from institutional funds. *Student Employment:* Federal Work-Study Program available. Institutional employment available. **Criteria for awarding aid:** *Non-need-based:* Academics, Art, Minority status.

COLLEGE OF THE ATLANTIC

105 Eden Street, Bar Harbor, ME 4609
Phone: 207-288-5015 • **Financial Aid Phone:** 207-801-5645
E-mail: inquiry@coa.edu • **CEEB Code:** 3305
Fax: 207-288-4126 • **Website:** www.coa.edu • **ACT Code:** 1637

This private school was founded in 1969. It has a 35-acre campus.

RATINGS
Admissions Selectivity Rating: 86   **Fire Safety Rating:** 97   **Green Rating:** 99

STUDENTS AND FACULTY
Enrollment: 333. **Student Body:** 70% female, 30% male, 78% out-of-state, 17% international (40 countries represented). Asian 3%, African American 1%, Caucasian 72%, Hispanic 5%, Native American 0%, Pacific Islander 0%, Two or more races 2%, Race unknown 1%.
Retention and Graduation: 80% freshmen return for sophomore year. 59% freshmen graduate within 4 years. 70% freshmen graduate within 6 years. 16% grads go on to further study within 1 year. 8% grads pursue arts and sciences

degrees. 4% grads pursue law degrees. 2% grads pursue medical degrees.
Faculty: Student/faculty ratio 10:1. 26 full-time faculty, 96% hold PhDs, 8% are are members of minority groups, 42% are women. 0% of classes are taught by teaching assistants.

ACADEMICS
Degrees: bachelor's, master's. **Classes:** Most classes have 10-19 students. Most lab/discussion sessions have fewer than 10 students. **Most popular majors:** Ecology; Humanities/Humanistic Studies; Multi-/Interdisciplinary Studies. **Special Study Options:** cross-registration, exchange student program (domestic), independent study, internships, liberal arts/career combination, student-designed major, study abroad, teacher certification program, Winter term program in Yucatan, Mexico. EcoLeague—consortium agreement with five other colleges for student exchanges (Alaska Pacific University, Antioch College, Green Mountain College, Northland College, Prescott College. Exchange program with Olin College of Engineering and University of Maine at Orono. **Honors Programs:** We consider all our students to be capable of honors work, which is why all students finish their time at COA with a term-long capstone, or senior project. **Disability Services:** Special programs offered to physically disabled students, including note-taking services, reader services, tape recorders, tutors. **Career Services:** Alumni network, Alumni services, Career assessment, Internships, Regional alumni. Internships are required for graduation and allow students to apply their classroom knowledge to the world of work over ten weeks and 400 hours. Students have found permanent jobs through their internships, modified their projected career focus—or changed course altogether from the process. We consider all the outcomes to be quite positive, including the last one—better to discover what you like and don't like in college, rather than 10 years down the line!

FACILITIES
Housing: Coed dorms, special housing for disabled students, Substance-free housing; green (environmentally conscious)housing. 70% of campus accessible to physically diasbled. **Special Academic Facilities/Equipment:** Natural history museum, pottery studio, greenhouse, Geographic Information Systems lab, Green Graphics Studio Deering Common Campus Center, organic community garden, Blum Gallery, outdoor equipment, two boats: Indigo and Borealis, off-site organic farm and two island research stations **Computers:** 100% of classrooms, 100% of dorms, 100% of libraries, 100% of dining areas, 100% of student union, 25% of common outdoor areas have wireless network access. Students can register for classes online. Administrative functions (other than registration) can be performed online.

CAMPUS LIFE
Environment: Rural. **Activities:** Choral groups, dance, drama/theater, jazz band, literary magazine, music ensembles, student government, student newspaper, yearbook. **On-Campus Highlights:** George B. Dorr Museum of Natural History, Blum Art Gallery, The pier, Turrets, Take-A-Break, College of the Atlantic has recently completed state-of-the-art sustainable dorms and a creative restoration of an historic building into a similarly sustainable campus center. These are also very popular places to visit. **Environmental Initiatives:** Energy Framework: In March of 2013 the college adopted an Energy Framework that seeks to make the college fossil fuel-free by 2050. The framework includes interim goals for 2015 and 2020 that the college is working on now to achieve. The framework focuses on reducing fossil fuel use and pursuing renewable sources of energy on campus and at our two nearby farms. Integral to the policy is the requirement that our students be involved in creating a fossil fuel-free campus through our hands-on curriculum. We have purchased an electric van and lease an electric Ford Focus for student transportation and have established three solar/electric charging stations for them on campus and at our two farms. These will also be used for additional electric vehicles we expect to bring into service.

ADMISSIONS
Freshman Academic Profile: Average high school GPA 3.6. 26% in top 10% of high school class, 47% in top 25% of high school class, 95% in top 50% of high school class. 56% from public high schools. **Reported SAT (pre-2016 redesign) scores:** SAT Math middle 50% range 540-630. SAT Critical Reading middle 50% range 590-680. SAT Writing middle 50% range 580-670. **Concordant SAT scores:** SAT EBRW middle 50% range 640–710. SAT Math middle 50% range 570–650. ACT middle 50% range 28-32. Minimum internet-based TOEFL 86. Minimum paper TOEFL 567. **Basis for Candidate Selection:** *Very important factors considered include:* rigor of secondary school record, application essay, recommendation(s). *Important factors considered include:* class rank, academic GPA, interview, extracurricular activities, talent/ability, character/personal qualities, volunteer work, work experience. *Other factors considered include:* standardized test scores, first generation, alumni/ae relation, geographical residence, state residency, racial/ethnic status, level of applicant's interest. **Freshman Admission Requirements:** High school diploma is required and GED is accepted. *Academic units required:* 4 English, 3 math, 2 science, 2 science labs, 2 social studies. *Academic units recommended:* 4 math, 3 science, 2 foreign language, 2 history, 1 academic elective. **Freshman Admission Statistics:** 400 applied, 75.50% admitted, 27% enrolled. **Transfer Admission Requirements:** High school transcript, college transcript(s),

essay or personal statement, Minimum college GPA of 3.0 required. Lowest grade transferable C. **General Admission Information:** Application fee $50. Regular application deadline 2/15. Regular notification 4/1. Nonfall registration accepted. Admission may be deferred for a maximum of 1 year.

COSTS AND FINANCIAL AID

Annual tuition $42,993. Room and board $9,747. Required fees $549. Average book expense $600. **Required Forms and Deadlines:** FAFSA, Institution's own financial aid form, Noncustodial PROFILE, Business/Farm Supplement. **Notification of Awards:** Applicants will be notified of awards on or about 4/1. **Types of Aid:** *Need-based scholarships/grants:* Federal Pell, FSEOG, State scholarships/grants, Private scholarships, College/university scholarship or grant aid from institutional funds. *Loans:* Direct Subsidized Stafford Loans, Direct Unsubsidized Stafford Loans, Direct PLUS loans, Federal Perkins Loans. *Student Employment:* Federal Work-Study Program available. **Financial Aid Statistics:** 100% needy freshmen, 99% needy undergrads receive need-based scholarship or grant aid. 1% freshmen, 1% undergrads receive non-need-based scholarship or grant aid. 96% freshmen, 99% undergrads receive need-based self-help aid. 0% freshmen, 0% undergrads receive athletic scholarships. 98% freshmen, 97% undergrads receive any aid. 57% undergrads borrow to pay for school. Average cumulative indebtedness $23,002. **Criteria for awarding aid:** *Need-based:* Academics, Art, Leadership, Music/drama. *Non-need-based:* Academics, Art, Leadership, Music/drama.

COLLEGE OF CHARLESTON

66 George Street, Charleston, SC 29424
Phone: 843-953-5670 • **Financial Aid Phone:** 843-953-5540
E-mail: admissions@cofc.edu • **CEEB Code:** 5113
Fax: 843-953-6322 • **Website:** http://cofc.edu • **ACT Code:** 3846

This public school was founded in 1770. It has a 52-acre campus.

RATINGS

Admissions Selectivity Rating: 81   **Fire Safety Rating:** 97   **Green Rating:** 86

STUDENTS AND FACULTY

Enrollment: 10,033. **Student Body:** 64% female, 36% male, 33% out-of-state, 1% international (60 countries represented). Asian 2%, African American 8%, Caucasian 79%, Hispanic 5%, Native American <1%, Pacific Islander <1%, Two or more races 4%, Race unknown 1%.
Retention and Graduation: 79% freshmen return for sophomore year. 58% freshmen graduate within 4 years. 69% freshmen graduate within 6 years. 38% grads go on to further study within 1 year. 4% grads pursue law degrees. 7% grads pursue medical degrees. **Faculty:** Student/faculty ratio 15:1. 553 full-time faculty, 91% hold PhDs, 15% are are members of minority groups, 45% are women. 0% of classes are taught by teaching assistants.

ACADEMICS

Degrees: bachelor's, master's, postbachelor's certificate, post-master's certificate. **Classes:** Most classes have 20-29 students. Most lab/discussion sessions have 20-29 students. **Most popular majors:** Business Administration and Management; Biology/Biological Sciences; Psychology. **Special Study Options:** Accelerated program, cooperative education program, cross-registration, distance learning, double major, dual enrollment, English as a Second Language (ESL), exchange student program (domestic), honors program, independent study, internships, liberal arts/career combination, study abroad, teacher certification program, Semester at Sea. **Honors Programs:** The Honors College at the College of Charleston began as an Honors Program in 1978 to provide a program and a community for talented and motivated students who enjoy active participation in small stimulating classes and want to be involved in a meaningful way in undergraduate research. In order to better serve the needs of the students, it became an Honors College in 2005, with new positions to provide academic advising and assistance in applying for postgraduate fellowships and additional funding to support its mission. The Honors College is dedicated to providing these students with a place where they can flourish and grow, a true learning community of teachers and students. In addition to receiving exciting and unique educational experiences, students can participate with their fellow Honors students in social, cultural, and intellectual events on the campus and in historic Charleston, SC. The Honors College challenges intellectually talented students to make the most of the opportunities available to them, to become actively involved in their own education, and to prepare themselves to excel in graduate programs, medical or law school, or in whatever

comes after they complete their undergraduate education. In Honors classes, students take responsibility for their own learning through class discussions, through interaction with faculty and fellow students, and through independent research. Honors students are advised by a full time Honors academic advisor and specially chosen faculty mentors, receive priority registration, and have the opportunity to room with other Honors students in special Honors residence halls. Classes, seminars, and student gatherings are held in the Honors Center, the historic William Aiken House built by Governor William Aiken in 1839. **Disability Services:** Special programs offered to physically disabled students, including note-taking services, reader services, tape recorders, tutors. **Career Services:** Alumni network, Alumni services, Career/job search classes, Career assessment, Internships, Regional alumni, Internships. Most academic departments offer internships for credit and the career center offers a certificate/no-credit option. A large number of students do these each year.

FACILITIES

Housing: Coed dorms, men's dorms, women's dorms, fraternity/sorority housing, apartments for single students, ThemeHousingRestored old Charleston houses used as residence halls, some with kitchen facilities in suites. 70% of campus accessible to physically diasbled. **Special Academic Facilities/ Equipment:** Halsey Institute of Contemporary Art, sculpture facility, Rivers Communications Museum, Miles Early Childhood Development Center, Avery Institute for African-American History and Culture, physics and astronomy observatory, Grice Marine Laboratory, Patriots Point Athletics Complex (includes softball, baseball, tennis, soccer and sailing) **Computers:** 75% of classrooms, 100% of dorms, 100% of libraries, 100% of dining areas, 100% of student union, 80% of common outdoor areas have wireless network access. Students can register for classes online. Administrative functions (other than registration) can be performed online.

CAMPUS LIFE

Environment: City. **Activities:** Choral groups, dance, drama/theater, jazz band, literary magazine, music ensembles, musical theater, pep band, radio station, student government, student newspaper, symphony orchestra, yearbook, Campus Ministries, Student Organization. 120 registered organizations, 19 honor societies, 16 religious organizations. 13 fraternities, 12 sororities. **Athletics (Intercollegiate):** *Men:* baseball, basketball, cross-country, diving, golf, sailing, soccer, swimming, tennis. *Women:* basketball, cross-country, diving, equestrian sports, golf, sailing, soccer, softball, swimming, tennis, track/field (outdoor), track/field (indoor), volleyball. **On-Campus Highlights:** The Cistern Yard, Carolina First Arena, Fresh Food Company, Addlestone Library, Cougar Plaza, The College opened two new facilities in January 2010: The The Marion and Wayland H. Cato Jr. Center for the Arts and a second building for the School of Sciences and Mathematics. Their completion is part of a significant transformation of the College's facilities, providing students with the best and most effective learning and recreational opportunities. Six new facilities were completed in 2007, and several others were finished in 2008. Patriots Point Athletics Complex is located just across the Ravenel Bridge in Mt. Pleasant. Recently renovated, this 35-acre complex is home to baseball, soccer, softball, sailing and tennis.

ADMISSIONS

Freshman Academic Profile: Average high school GPA 3.9. 20% in top 10% of high school class, 52% in top 25% of high school class, 87% in top 50% of high school class. 75% from public high schools. **Reported SAT (pre-2016 redesign) scores:** SAT Math middle 50% range 500-590. SAT Critical Reading middle 50% range 500-600. **Concordant SAT scores:** SAT Math middle 50% range 530–610. ACT middle 50% range 22-27. Minimum internet-based TOEFL 80. Minimum paper TOEFL 570. **Basis for Candidate Selection:** *Very important factors considered include:* rigor of secondary school record, academic GPA, standardized test scores. *Important factors considered include:* class rank, talent/ability, character/personal qualities, first generation, state residency. *Other factors considered include:* application essay, recommendation(s), extracurricular activities, alumni/ae relation, geographical residence, racial/ethnic status, volunteer work, work experience, level of applicant's interest. **Freshman Admission Requirements:** High school diploma is required and GED is accepted. *Academic units required:* 4 English, 4 math, 3 science, 3 science labs, 3 foreign language, 2 social studies, 1 history, 3 academic electives, 1 visual/performing arts, and 1 unit from above areas or other academic areas. *Academic units recommended:* 4 English, 4 math, 2 history, 1 computer science. **Freshman Admission Statistics:** 10,828 applied, 84.13% admitted, 26% enrolled. **Transfer Admission Requirements:** college transcript(s), Minimum college GPA of 2.6 required. Lowest grade transferable C. **General Admission Information:** Application fee $50. Priority deadline 2/1. Regular application deadline 4/1. Nonfall registration accepted. Admission may be deferred for a maximum of 1 or 2 semesters.

COSTS AND FINANCIAL AID

Annual in-state tuition $11,386. Annual out-of-state tuition $29,544. Required fees $460. Average book expense $1,159. **Required Forms and Deadlines:** FAFSA. **Notification of Awards:** Applicants will be notified of awards on a rolling basis beginning 4/10. **Types of Aid:** *Need-based scholarships/grants:* Federal Pell, FSEOG, State scholarships/grants, Private scholarships, College/

university scholarship or grant aid from institutional funds. *Loans:* Direct Subsidized Stafford Loans, Direct Unsubsidized Stafford Loans, Direct PLUS loans, Federal Perkins Loans. *Student Employment:* Federal Work-Study Program available. Institutional employment available. **Financial Aid Statistics:** 71% needy freshmen, 69% needy undergrads receive need-based scholarship or grant aid. 77% freshmen, 49% undergrads receive non-need-based scholarship or grant aid. 70% freshmen, 78% undergrads receive need-based self-help aid. 1% freshmen, 1% undergrads receive athletic scholarships. 53% freshmen, 47% undergrads receive any aid. 51% undergrads borrow to pay for school. Average cumulative indebtedness $26,586. **Criteria for awarding aid:** *Non-need-based:* Academics, Alumni affiliation, Art, Athletics, Music/drama.

COLLEGE OF THE HOLY CROSS

1 College Street, Worcester, MA 01610-2395
Phone: 508-793-2443 • **Financial Aid Phone:** 508-793-2265
E-mail: admissions@holycross.edu • **CEEB Code:** 3282
Fax: 508-793-3888 • **Website:** www.holycross.edu • **ACT Code:** 1810

This private school, affiliated with the Roman Catholic Church, was founded in 1843. It has a 174-acre campus.

RATINGS
Admissions Selectivity Rating: 93   **Fire Safety Rating:** 97   **Green Rating:** 84

STUDENTS AND FACULTY
Enrollment: 2,910. **Student Body:** 51% female, 49% male, 60% out-of-state, 3% international (15 countries represented). Asian 5%, African American 4%, Caucasian 70%, Hispanic 10%, Native American <1%, Pacific Islander <1%, Two or more races 3%, Race unknown 5%.
Retention and Graduation: 96% freshmen return for sophomore year. 89% freshmen graduate within 4 years. 92% freshmen graduate within 6 years. 17% grads go on to further study within 1 year. 9% grads pursue arts and sciences degrees. 2% grads pursue law degrees. 1% grads pursue business degrees. 1% grads pursue medical degrees. **Faculty:** Student/faculty ratio 10:1. 279 full-time faculty, 93% hold PhDs, 13% are are members of minority groups, 44% are women. 0% of classes are taught by teaching assistants.

ACADEMICS
Degrees: bachelor's. **Classes:** Most classes have 10-19 students. Most lab/discussion sessions have fewer than 10 students. **Most popular majors:** Economics; Psychology; Political Science and Government. **Special Study Options:** Accelerated program, cross-registration, double major, dual enrollment, exchange student program (domestic), honors program, independent study, internships, liberal arts/career combination, student-designed major, study abroad, teacher certification program, First-year integrated living and learning program ("Montserrat"). **Honors Programs:** Fenwick Scholar Program. **Disability Services:** Special programs offered to physically disabled students, including note-taking services, reader services, tutors. **Career Services:** Alumni network, Alumni services, Career/job search classes, Career assessment, Internships, Regional alumni, Crusader Internship Fund.

FACILITIES
Housing: Coed dorms, special housing for disabled students, apartments for single students, Suites on campus available for juniors and seniors. Substance-free housing also available. 85% of campus accessible to physically diasbled. **Special Academic Facilities/Equipment:** Art gallery, Concert Hall, Taylor and Boody tracker organ, O'Callahan Science Library, Rehm Library, Multimedia Resource Center, Wellness Center; scientific equipment on par with the best research universities. **Computers:** 100% of classrooms, 100% of dorms, 100% of libraries, 100% of dining areas, 100% of student union, 60% of common outdoor areas have wireless network access. Students can register for classes online. Administrative functions (other than registration) can be performed online.

CAMPUS LIFE
Environment: City. **Activities:** Choral groups, concert band, dance, drama/theater, jazz band, literary magazine, marching band, music ensembles, musical theater, pep band, radio station, student government, student newspaper, yearbook, Campus Ministries, Student Organization. 105 registered organizations, 20 honor societies, 4 religious organizations. **Athletics (Intercollegiate):** *Men:* baseball, basketball, crew/rowing, cross-country,

diving, football, golf, ice hockey, lacrosse, soccer, swimming, tennis, track/field (outdoor), track/field (indoor). *Women:* basketball, crew/rowing, cross-country, diving, field hockey, golf, ice hockey, lacrosse, soccer, softball, swimming, tennis, track/field (outdoor), track/field (indoor), volleyball. **On-Campus Highlights:** Library, Smith Hall, St. Joseph Chapel, Hart Recreation Center, Hogan Campus Center. **Environmental Initiatives:** College exceeded the 20% carbon reduction by 2015 and Carbon Neutrality however the College has already achieved a 47% reduction in carbon emissions.

ADMISSIONS
Freshman Academic Profile: 61% in top 10% of high school class, 87% in top 25% of high school class, 100% in top 50% of high school class. 50% from public high schools. **Reported SAT (pre-2016 redesign) scores:** SAT Math middle 50% range 620-690. SAT Critical Reading middle 50% range 600-680. SAT Writing middle 50% range 600-700. **Concordant SAT scores:** SAT EBRW middle 50% 650–730. SAT Math middle 50% range 640–720. ACT middle 50% range 28-31. Minimum internet-based TOEFL 100. Minimum paper TOEFL 600. **Basis for Candidate Selection:** *Very important factors considered include:* rigor of secondary school record, academic GPA, recommendation(s), interview. *Important factors considered include:* class rank, application essay, extracurricular activities, character/personal qualities. *Other factors considered include:* standardized test scores, talent/ability, first generation, alumni/ae relation, geographical residence, state residency, religious affiliation/commitment, racial/ethnic status, volunteer work, work experience, level of applicant's interest. **Freshman Admission Requirements:** High school diploma is required and GED is accepted. *Academic units recommended:* 4 English, 4 math, 4 science, 2 science labs, 4 foreign language, 2 social studies, 2 history. **Freshman Admission Statistics:** 6,693 applied, 38.46% admitted, 30% enrolled. **Transfer Admission Requirements:** High school transcript, college transcript(s), essay or personal statement, statement of good standing from prior institution(s). Lowest grade transferable C. **General Admission Information:** Application fee $60. Regular application deadline 1/15. Nonfall registration not accepted. Admission may be deferred for a maximum of 12 months.

COSTS AND FINANCIAL AID
Annual tuition $48,295. Room and board $13,225. Required fees $645. Average book expense $1,000. **Required Forms and Deadlines:** FAFSA, CSS/Financial Aid PROFILE, Noncustodial PROFILE, Business/Farm Supplement. **Notification of Awards:** Applicants will be notified of awards on or about 4/1. **Types of Aid:** *Need-based scholarships/grants:* Federal Pell, FSEOG, State scholarships/grants, Private scholarships, College/university scholarship or grant aid from institutional funds. *Loans:* Direct Subsidized Stafford Loans, Direct Unsubsidized Stafford Loans, Direct PLUS loans, Federal Perkins Loans. *Student Employment:* Federal Work-Study Program available. Institutional employment available. **Financial Aid Statistics:** 85% needy freshmen, 82% needy undergrads receive need-based scholarship or grant aid. 3% freshmen, 3% undergrads receive non-need-based scholarship or grant aid. 92% freshmen, 94% undergrads receive need-based self-help aid. 8% freshmen, 6% undergrads receive athletic scholarships. 61% freshmen, 56% undergrads receive any aid. 62% undergrads borrow to pay for school. Average cumulative indebtedness $25,446. **Criteria for awarding aid:** *Need-based:* Athletics. *Non-need-based:* Academics, Athletics, Music/drama, State/district residency.

COLLEGE OF IDAHO

2112 Cleveland Blvd, Caldwell, ID 83605-4432
Phone: 208-459-5305 • **Financial Aid Phone:** 208-459-5307
E-mail: admissions@collegeofidaho.edu • **CEEB Code:** 4060
Fax: 208-459-5757 • **Website:** www.collegeofidaho.edu • **ACT Code:** 916

This private school was founded in 1891. It has a 50-acre campus.

RATINGS
Admissions Selectivity Rating: 80   **Fire Safety Rating:** 88   **Green Rating:** 71

STUDENTS AND FACULTY
Enrollment: 953. **Student Body:** 50% female, 50% male, 71% out-of-state, 7% international (46 countries represented). Asian 2%, African American 2%, Caucasian 66%, Hispanic 13%, Native American 1%, Pacific Islander 1%, Two or more races 4%, Race unknown 5%.
Retention and Graduation: 70% freshmen return for sophomore year. 45% freshmen graduate within 4 years. 57% freshmen graduate within 6 years. 34% grads go on to further study within 1 year. 19% grads pursue arts and sciences

degrees. 4% grads pursue law degrees. 6% grads pursue medical degrees. **Faculty:** Student/faculty ratio 9:1. 87 full-time faculty, 82% hold PhDs, 7% are are members of minority groups, 39% are women. 0% of classes are taught by teaching assistants.

ACADEMICS

Degrees: bachelor's, master's. **Classes:** Most classes have 10-19 students. Most lab/discussion sessions have 10-19 students. **Most popular majors:** Biology/Biological Sciences; Business Administration and Management; Psychology. **Special Study Options:** cross-registration, double major, dual enrollment, exchange student program (domestic), honors program, independent study, internships, liberal arts/career combination, student-designed major, study abroad, teacher certification program. **Honors Programs:** Heritage Scholars Program, Gipson Honors Program; Kathryn Albertson Scholars Program; Davis United World Scholars Combined degree programs: Pharmacy; Nursing; Speech-Language Path & Audio; Med Lab Science; Occupational Therapy; Public Health. **Disability Services:** Special programs offered to physically disabled students, including note-taking services, reader services, tape recorders. **Career Services:** Alumni network, Alumni services, Career/job search classes, Career assessment, Internships, Regional alumni. Programming that helps students to developmentally prepare strong application materials.

FACILITIES

Housing: Coed dorms, special housing for disabled students, fraternity/sorority housing, apartments for single students, College owned houses; dorms for Healthy/Quiet Lifestyle, Academic Honor, First Year Community, Honor Code. 95% of campus accessible to physically diasbled. **Special Academic Facilities/Equipment:** Art and natural history museums, gem and mineral collections, observatory, planetarium, nuclear magnetic resonance spectrometer, gas chromatograph, gamma camera, graphic computer, art gallery, Robert E. Smylie Archives. **Computers:** 100% of classrooms, 100% of dorms, 100% of libraries, 100% of dining areas, 100% of student union, 100% of common outdoor areas have wireless network access. Administrative functions (other than registration) can be performed online.

CAMPUS LIFE

Environment: Town. **Activities:** Choral groups, concert band, dance, drama/theater, jazz band, literary magazine, music ensembles, musical theater, opera, pep band, radio station, student government, student newspaper, student-run film society, symphony orchestra, yearbook, Campus Ministries, Student Organization, Model UN. 55 registered organizations, 4 honor societies, 3 religious organizations. 3 fraternities, 4 sororities. **Athletics (Intercollegiate):** *Men:* baseball, cheerleading, cross-country, golf, skiing (downhill/alpine), skiing (nordic/cross-country), snowboarding, soccer, swimming, tennis, track/field (outdoor). *Women:* basketball, cheerleading, cross-country, golf, skiing (downhill/alpine), skiing (nordic/cross-country), snowboarding, soccer, softball, swimming, tennis, track/field (outdoor), volleyball. **On-Campus Highlights:** J.A. Albertson Activity Center, McCain Student Center, Langroise Center for Performing and Fine Arts, Centennial Amphitheater, Dorms. **Environmental Initiatives:** Student Sustainability Steward Position.

ADMISSIONS

Freshman Academic Profile: Average high school GPA 3.6. 23% in top 10% of high school class, 27% in top 25% of high school class, 25% in top 50% of high school class. **Reported SAT (pre-2016 redesign) scores:** SAT Math middle 50% range 460-580. SAT Critical Reading middle 50% range 460-570. SAT Writing middle 50% range 440-560. **Concordant SAT scores:** SAT EBRW middle 50% 500–620. SAT Math middle 50% range 500–600. ACT middle 50% range 21-27. Minimum internet-based TOEFL 79. Minimum paper TOEFL 550. **Basis for Candidate Selection:** *Very important factors considered include:* academic GPA. *Important factors considered include:* rigor of secondary school record, standardized test scores, application essay, recommendation(s), character/personal qualities, alumni/ae relation. *Other factors considered include:* class rank, interview, extracurricular activities, talent/ability, first generation, volunteer work, work experience, level of applicant's interest. **Freshman Admission Requirements:** High school diploma is required and GED is accepted. *Academic units recommended:* 4 English, 3 math, 2 science, 2 foreign language, 2 social studies, 2 history, 4 academic electives. **Freshman Admission Statistics:** 975 applied, 84.82% admitted, 29% enrolled. **Transfer Admission Requirements:** college transcript(s), essay or personal statement, Minimum college GPA of 2.2 required. Lowest grade transferable D-. **General Admission Information:** Priority deadline 11/15. Regular application deadline 2/16. Nonfall registration accepted. Admission may be deferred.

COSTS AND FINANCIAL AID

Room and board $9,334. Required fees $755. Average book expense $1,200. **Required Forms and Deadlines:** FAFSA. **Notification of Awards:** Applicants will be notified of awards on or about 3/15. **Types of Aid:** *Need-based scholarships/grants:* Federal Pell, FSEOG, State scholarships/grants, Private scholarships, College/university scholarship or grant aid from institutional funds. *Loans:* Direct Subsidized Stafford Loans, Direct Unsubsidized Stafford Loans, Direct PLUS loans, Federal Perkins Loans.

Student Employment: Federal Work-Study Program available. Institutional employment available. **Financial Aid Statistics:** 100% needy freshmen, 86% needy undergrads receive need-based scholarship or grant aid. 100% freshmen, 100% undergrads receive non-need-based scholarship or grant aid. 82% freshmen, 82% undergrads receive need-based self-help aid. 45% freshmen, 34% undergrads receive athletic scholarships. 99% freshmen, 100% undergrads receive any aid. 59% undergrads borrow to pay for school. Average cumulative indebtedness $7,270. **Criteria for awarding aid:** *Need-based:* Art, Athletics, Job skills, Leadership, Minority status, Music/drama, Religious affiliation. *Non-need-based:* Academics, Alumni affiliation, Athletics, Job skills.

COLLEGE OF MOUNT SAINT VINCENT

6301 Riverdale Avenue, Riverdale, NY 10471
Phone: 718-405-3267 • **Financial Aid Phone:** 718-405-3349
E-mail: admissions@mountsaintvincent.edu • **CEEB Code:** 2088
Fax: 718-549-7945 • **Website:** www.mountsaintvincent.edu

This private school, affiliated with the Roman Catholic Church, was founded in 1847. It has a 70-acre campus.

RATINGS

Admissions Selectivity Rating: 72   **Fire Safety Rating:** 90   **Green Rating:** 60*

STUDENTS AND FACULTY

Enrollment: 1,594. **Student Body:** 69% female, 31% male, 14% out-of-state, 2% international (4 countries represented). Asian 10%, African American 15%, Caucasian 27%, Hispanic 38%, Native American <1%, Pacific Islander 0%, Two or more races 5%, Race unknown 4%.
Retention and Graduation: 78% freshmen return for sophomore year. 34% freshmen graduate within 4 years. 53% freshmen graduate within 6 years. **Faculty:** Student/faculty ratio 14:1. 79 full-time faculty, 87% hold PhDs, 18% are are members of minority groups, 58% are women. 0% of classes are taught by teaching assistants.

ACADEMICS

Degrees: associate, bachelor's, master's, post-master's certificate. **Classes:** Most classes have 20-29 students. Most lab/discussion sessions have 10-19 students. **Most popular majors:** Business/Commerce; Registered Nursing/Registered Nurse; Communication and Media Studies. **Special Study Options:** Accelerated program, double major, honors program, independent study, internships, liberal arts/career combination, study abroad, teacher certification program. **Honors Programs:** At present, the Honors Program reflects several distinctive dimensions and provides gifted students with the opportunity to develop critical thinking skills, an affirmative acknowledgement of the human dignity of self and others, and a commitment to realize one's intellectual potential, through participation in enhanced learning experiences both in and out of the classroom. Freshman and sophomore honors students are required to complete six of eight paired Honors Sections of the college's Core Curriculum courses. Specifically, in freshman year, literature is paired with psychology and fine arts with history; sociology is paired with economics and philosophy with religious studies in sophomore year. Juniors and seniors are challenged to enrich themselves through involvement in research projects that are faculty-mentored and through engaging themselves in reflective extra-curricular events (e.g., attending lectures, conferences, or cultural event) with faculty assistance and support. At the same time, the college has initiated a process to further develop and restructure the honors experience by the development of courses that are more inter-disciplinary in nature, utilize more diversified pedagogical styles, and, consistent with the college's mission, provide the opportunity for community service and learning. Through its honors program, the college seeks to develop informed, critically reflective, and value-oriented young men and women who will successfully pursue higher educational opportunities and make meaningful contributions to society both professionally and in their personal lives. **Disability Services:** Special programs offered to physically disabled students, including note-taking services, tape recorders, tutors. **Career Services:** Career/job search classes, Career assessment, Internships, Regional alumni.

FACILITIES

Housing: Coed dorms, special housing for disabled students, women's dorms. 90% of campus accessible to physically diasbled. **Special Academic Facilities/Equipment:** Newly renovated Maryvale Hall,with newly constructed wing, for Communications and Fine Arts Departments; Nursing lab,TV studio, radio station, Elizabeth Seton Travelling Museum, Forensic Laboratory equipment **Computers:** Students can register for classes online. Administrative functions (other than registration) can be performed online.

CAMPUS LIFE

Environment: Metropolis. **Activities:** dance, drama/theater, literary magazine, musical theater, radio station, student government, student newspaper, television station, yearbook, Campus Ministries. 30 registered organizations, 15 honor societies, 2 religious organizations. **Athletics (Intercollegiate):** *Men:* baseball, basketball, cross-country, lacrosse, soccer, swimming, tennis, volleyball. *Women:* basketball, cross-country, lacrosse, soccer, softball, swimming, tennis, track/field (outdoor), volleyball. **On-Campus Highlights:** Crossroads (Student Lounge), Maryvale (new Communication/Art building), Fitness Center (includes swimming pool), Benedict's Cafe. **Environmental Initiatives:** Recycling.

ADMISSIONS

Freshman Academic Profile: Average high school GPA 3.0. 5% in top 10% of high school class, 19% in top 25% of high school class, 64% in top 50% of high school class. 58% from public high schools. **Reported SAT (pre-2016 redesign) scores:** SAT Math middle 50% range 400-490. SAT Critical Reading middle 50% range 410-500. SAT Writing middle 50% range 410-490. **Concordant SAT scores:** SAT EBRW middle 50% 460–550. SAT Math middle 50% range 440–520. ACT middle 50% range 18-22. Minimum paper TOEFL 550. **Basis for Candidate Selection:** *Very important factors considered include:* rigor of secondary school record, academic GPA. *Important factors considered include:* standardized test scores, application essay, recommendation(s), interview, extracurricular activities, character/personal qualities. *Other factors considered include:* class rank, alumni/ae relation, geographical residence, state residency, volunteer work, work experience, level of applicant's interest. **Freshman Admission Requirements:** High school diploma is required and GED is accepted. *Academic units required:* 4 English, 3 math, 2 science, 2 science labs, 2 foreign language, 3 social studies, 2 academic electives. *Academic units recommended:* 4 English, 4 math, 3 science, 3 science labs, 3 foreign language, 4 social studies, 3 academic electives. **Freshman Admission Statistics:** 2,734 applied, 86.06% admitted, 14% enrolled. **Transfer Admission Requirements:** college transcript(s), essay or personal statement, Minimum college GPA of 2.0 required. Lowest grade transferable C. **General Admission Information:** Application fee $35. Priority deadline 3/1. Nonfall registration accepted. Admission may be deferred for a maximum of 1 year.

COSTS AND FINANCIAL AID

Annual tuition $28,980. Room and board $12,060. Required fees $1,310. Average book expense $1,185. **Required Forms and Deadlines:** FAFSA, State aid form. **Notification of Awards:** Applicants will be notified of awards on a rolling basis beginning 3/1. **Types of Aid:** *Need-based scholarships/grants:* Federal Pell, FSEOG, State scholarships/grants, Private scholarships, College/university scholarship or grant aid from institutional funds. *Loans:* Federal Perkins Loans. *Student Employment:* Federal Work-Study Program available. Institutional employment available. **Financial Aid Statistics:** 100% needy freshmen, 100% needy undergrads receive need-based scholarship or grant aid. 0% undergrads receive non-need-based scholarship or grant aid. 100% freshmen, 100% undergrads receive need-based self-help aid. 0% freshmen, 0% undergrads receive athletic scholarships. 87% freshmen, 86% undergrads receive any aid. **Criteria for awarding aid:** *Non-need-based:* Academics, Alumni affiliation, Leadership.

THE COLLEGE OF NEW JERSEY

PO Box 7718, Ewing, NJ 08628-0718
Phone: 609-771-2131 • **Financial Aid Phone:** 609-771-2211
E-mail: tcnjinfo@tcnj.edu • **CEEB Code:** 2519
Fax: 609-637-5174 • **Website:** www.tcnj.edu • **ACT Code:** 2614

This public school was founded in 1855. It has a 289-acre campus.

RATINGS

Admissions Selectivity Rating: 89   **Fire Safety Rating:** 98   **Green Rating:** 83

STUDENTS AND FACULTY

Enrollment: 6,666. **Student Body:** 58% female, 42% male, 6% out-of-state, <1% international (32 countries represented). Asian 11%, African American 6%, Caucasian 66%, Hispanic 13%, Native American <1%, Pacific Islander <1%, Two or more races <1%, Race unknown 3%.
Retention and Graduation: 94% freshmen return for sophomore year. 75% freshmen graduate within 4 years. 87% freshmen graduate within 6 years. 25%

grads go on to further study within 1 year. 16% grads pursue arts and sciences degrees. 3% grads pursue law degrees. 3% grads pursue medical degrees. **Faculty:** Student/faculty ratio 13:1. 355 full-time faculty, 90% hold PhDs, 23% are are members of minority groups, 53% are women. 0% of classes are taught by teaching assistants.

ACADEMICS

Degrees: bachelor's, master's, postbachelor's certificate, post-master's certificate. **Classes:** Most classes have 20-29 students. Most lab/discussion sessions have 10-19 students. **Most popular majors:** Education; Marketing; Psychology. **Special Study Options:** Accelerated program, double major, dual enrollment, exchange student program (domestic), honors program, independent study, internships, liberal arts/career combination, student-designed major, study abroad, teacher certification program, 7 year medical program with UMDNJ, 7 year BS/OD program with SUNY, Mentored undergraduate summer research program. Combined degree programs: BA/MD, BS/OD, BS/MAT, BABME/MD, BS/MD. **Disability Services:** Special programs offered to physically disabled students, including note-taking services, reader services, tape recorders, tutors. **Career Services:** Alumni services, Career/job search classes, Career assessment, Internships, Education Interview Days Each Spring TCNJ hosts up to 150 school district interview visits. The districts send administrators to conduct 30 minute interviews on-campus. Over the four days the visits are scheduled more than 1500 first-round interviews are conducted. Though the school districts are primarily from New Jersey and the surrounding area, we attract school districts from throughout the nation, including as far away as Hawaii. Students and employers both report that this is a highly successful program for meeting their recruitment needs.

FACILITIES

Housing: Coed dorms, special housing for disabled students, special housing for international students, women's dorms, apartments for single students, Wellness Housing. Faculty and students have the opportunity to develop their own special interest learning communities on campus. 90% of campus accessible to physically diasbled. **Special Academic Facilities/Equipment:** Art gallery, concert hall, greenhouse, observatory, planetarium, nuclear magnetic resonance lab, optical spectroscopy lab, scanning and transmission electron microscopes. **Computers:** 22% of classrooms, 5% of dorms, 100% of libraries, 85% of dining areas, 70% of student union, 5% of common outdoor areas have wireless network access. Students can register for classes online. Administrative functions (other than registration) can be performed online.

CAMPUS LIFE

Environment: Village. **Activities:** Choral groups, concert band, dance, drama/theater, jazz band, literary magazine, music ensembles, musical theater, opera, pep band, radio station, student government, student newspaper, symphony orchestra, television station, yearbook, Campus Ministries, Student Organization, Model UN. 205 registered organizations, 16 honor societies, 11 religious organizations. 12 fraternities, 16 sororities. **Athletics (Intercollegiate):** *Men:* baseball, basketball, cross-country, diving, football, soccer, swimming, tennis, track/field (outdoor), track/field (indoor). *Women:* basketball, cross-country, diving, field hockey, lacrosse, soccer, softball, swimming, tennis, track/field (outdoor), track/field (indoor). **On-Campus Highlights:** New Library, New Science Complex, New Arts and Multimedia Building, Student Center, Athletic Center. **Environmental Initiatives:** Commitment to sustainability being incorporated into the curriculum at TCNJ. This may include Freshman seminars, liberal learning programs, research and possible new minor or major degrees. The College's Municipal Land Use Center is authoring the State's sustainabilty and climate neutrality plans.

ADMISSIONS

Freshman Academic Profile: 40% in top 10% of high school class, 76% in top 25% of high school class, 98% in top 50% of high school class. 70% from public high schools. **Reported SAT (pre-2016 redesign) scores:** SAT Math middle 50% range 560-660. SAT Critical Reading middle 50% range 540-640. SAT Writing middle 50% range 540-650. **Concordant SAT scores:** SAT EBRW middle 50% 600–690. SAT Math middle 50% range 580–690. ACT middle 50% range 25-30. Minimum internet-based TOEFL 90. Minimum paper TOEFL 550. **Basis for Candidate Selection:** *Very important factors considered include:* rigor of secondary school record, class rank, standardized test scores, extracurricular activities, volunteer work. *Important factors considered include:* application essay, recommendation(s), talent/ability, character/personal qualities, geographical residence, state residency. *Other factors considered include:* academic GPA, first generation, alumni/ae relation, racial/ethnic status, work experience, level of applicant's interest. **Freshman Admission Requirements:** High school diploma is required and GED is accepted. *Academic units required:* 4 English, 4 math, 4 science, 2 science labs, 2 foreign language, 2 social studies. **Freshman Admission Statistics:** 11,825 applied, 48.86% admitted, 25% enrolled. **Transfer Admission Requirements:** High school transcript, college transcript(s), essay or personal statement, standardized test scores, statement of good standing from prior institution(s). Minimum college GPA of 2.5 required. Lowest grade transferable C. **General Admission Information:** Application fee $75. Priority deadline 11/1. Regular application deadline 2/1. Nonfall registration accepted. Admission may be deferred for a maximum of 2 semesters.

COSTS AND FINANCIAL AID
Annual in-state tuition $11,124. Annual out-of-state tuition $22,301. Room and board $12,881. Required fees $4,670. Average book expense $1,200. **Required Forms and Deadlines:** FAFSA, CSS/Financial Aid PROFILE. **Notification of Awards:** Applicants will be notified of awards on a rolling basis beginning 6/1. **Types of Aid:** *Need-based scholarships/grants:* Federal Pell, FSEOG, State scholarships/grants, Private scholarships, College/university scholarship or grant aid from institutional funds, Federal Nursing Scholarships. *Loans:* Direct Subsidized Stafford Loans, Direct Unsubsidized Stafford Loans, Direct PLUS loans, Federal Perkins Loans, Federal Nursing Loans. *Student Employment:* Federal Work-Study Program available. Institutional employment available. **Financial Aid Statistics:** 37% needy freshmen, 39% needy undergrads receive need-based scholarship or grant aid. 32% freshmen, 26% undergrads receive non-need-based scholarship or grant aid. 72% freshmen, 81% undergrads receive need-based self-help aid. 0% freshmen, 0% undergrads receive athletic scholarships. 70% freshmen, 62% undergrads receive any aid. Average cumulative indebtedness $36,994. **Criteria for awarding aid:** *Need-based:* Academics. *Non-need-based:* Academics, Art, Music/drama.

See page 944.

COLLEGE OF THE OZARKS

Office of Admissions, Point Lookout, MO 65726
Phone: 417-690-2636 • **Financial Aid Phone:** 417-690-3292
E-mail: admiss4@cofo.edu • **CEEB Code:** 6713
Fax: 417-690-2635 • **Website:** www.cofo.edu • **ACT Code:** 2364

This private school was founded in 1906. It has a 1000-acre campus.

RATINGS
Admissions Selectivity Rating: 97   **Fire Safety Rating:** 89   **Green Rating:** 70

STUDENTS AND FACULTY
Enrollment: 1,512. **Student Body:** 55% female, 45% male, 22% out-of-state, 1% international (16 countries represented). Asian 1%, African American 1%, Caucasian 92%, Hispanic 2%, Native American <1%, Pacific Islander <1%, Two or more races 2%, Race unknown <1%.
Retention and Graduation: 75% freshmen return for sophomore year. 54% freshmen graduate within 4 years. 69% freshmen graduate within 6 years. 6% grads go on to further study within 1 year. 7% grads pursue arts and sciences degrees. 1% grads pursue law degrees. 1% grads pursue business degrees.
Faculty: Student/faculty ratio 14:1. 89 full-time faculty, 61% hold PhDs, 1% are are members of minority groups, 46% are women. 0% of classes are taught by teaching assistants.

ACADEMICS
Degrees: bachelor's. **Classes:** Most classes have 10-19 students. Most lab/discussion sessions have 10-19 students. **Most popular majors:** Business Administration and Management; Elementary Education and Teaching; Health Services/Allied Health/Health Sciences. **Special Study Options:** Accelerated program, double major, dual enrollment, independent study, internships, student-designed major, teacher certification program. Combined degree programs: BA/JD, BA/MEng. **Disability Services:** Special programs offered to physically disabled students, including note-taking services, reader services, tape recorders, tutors. **Career Services:** Career/job search classes, Career assessment, Internships. Outstanding internships that offer graduates opportunities for phenomenal careers.

FACILITIES
Housing: men's dorms, women's dorms, Wellness Housing. All full-time students must live in residence halls unless they meet one of the following criteria: 21 years of age or older, married, living with parents, or veteran of the armed forces. 80% of campus accessible to physically diasbled. **Special Academic Facilities/Equipment:** Ralph Foster Museum, Edwards Mill, The Keeter Center, Fruitcake and Jelly Kitchen, Greenhouses. **Computers:** 100% of dorms, 100% of libraries, 100% of dining areas, 100% of student union, have wireless network access. Students can register for classes online. Administrative functions (other than registration) can be performed online.

CAMPUS LIFE
Environment: Rural. **Activities:** Choral groups, concert band, drama/theater, jazz band, literary magazine, music ensembles, musical theater, pep band, radio station, student government, student newspaper, student-run film society, yearbook, Campus Ministries. 45 registered organizations, 6 honor societies, 10 religious organizations. **Athletics (Intercollegiate):** *Men:* baseball, basketball, cheerleading. *Women:* basketball, cheerleading, volleyball. **On-Campus Highlights:** Memorial Fieldhouse and Keeter Gymnasium, Ralph Foster Museum, Williams Memorial Chapel, The Keeter Center, Agriculture, Edwards Mill, Fruitcake and Jelly Kitchen. **Environmental Initiatives:** 1. The College ensures proper management of hazardous, special and universal waste. There is campus-wide recycling: plastic bottles, corrugated cardboard, aluminum cans, tin cans, batteries, tires, light bulbs and electronic products. Light bulb reclamation (recycle of bulbs) and energy efficient lights

ADMISSIONS
Freshman Academic Profile: Average high school GPA 3.7. 28% in top 10% of high school class, 66% in top 25% of high school class, 94% in top 50% of high school class. 78% from public high schools. **Reported SAT (pre-2016 redesign) scores:** SAT Math middle 50% range 500-592. SAT Critical Reading middle 50% range 525-630. SAT Writing middle 50% range 492-620. **Concordant SAT scores:** SAT EBRW middle 50% 570–680. SAT Math middle 50% range 530–610. ACT middle 50% range 21-25. Minimum internet-based TOEFL 79. Minimum paper TOEFL 550. **Basis for Candidate Selection:** *Very important factors considered include:* rigor of secondary school record, class rank, interview, character/personal qualities. *Important factors considered include:* academic GPA, standardized test scores, recommendation(s), geographical residence, volunteer work, work experience, level of applicant's interest. *Other factors considered include:* extracurricular activities, talent/ability, first generation, alumni/ae relation, state residency, religious affiliation/commitment. **Freshman Admission Requirements:** High school diploma is required and GED is accepted. *Academic units required:* 4 English, 3 math, 2 science, 1 science lab, 3 history. *Academic units recommended:* 2 foreign language, 3 social studies. **Freshman Admission Statistics:** 2,896 applied, 14.26% admitted, 94% enrolled. **Transfer Admission Requirements:** college transcript(s), interview, statement of good standing from prior institution(s). Minimum college GPA of 3.0 required. Lowest grade transferable D-. **General Admission Information:** Priority deadline 2/15. Nonfall registration not accepted.

COSTS AND FINANCIAL AID
Annual tuition $0. Room and board $7,100. Required fees $430. Average book expense $1,000. **Required Forms and Deadlines:** FAFSA. **Notification of Awards:** Applicants will be notified of awards on or about 7/1. **Types of Aid:** *Need-based scholarships/grants:* Federal Pell, FSEOG, State scholarships/grants, Private scholarships, College/university scholarship or grant aid from institutional funds. *Student Employment:* Federal Work-Study Program available. Institutional employment available. **Financial Aid Statistics:** 100% needy freshmen, 100% needy undergrads receive need-based scholarship or grant aid. 7% freshmen, 13% undergrads receive non-need-based scholarship or grant aid. 93% freshmen, 87% undergrads receive need-based self-help aid. 2% freshmen, 2% undergrads receive athletic scholarships. 100% freshmen, 100% undergrads receive any aid. 0% undergrads borrow to pay for school. Average cumulative indebtedness $0. **Criteria for awarding aid:** *Need-based:* Academics, Alumni affiliation, Leadership, Minority status. *Non-need-based:* Academics, Art, Athletics, Leadership, Music/drama, State/district residency.

COLLEGE OF PERFORMING ARTS

72 Fifth Avenue, New York, NY 10003
Phone: 212-580-5150 • **Financial Aid Phone:** 212-229-8930
E-mail: admission@newschool.edu • **CEEB Code:** 2398, 6153, 7336
Website: http://www.newschool.edu • **ACT Code:** 2828

This private school was founded in 1916.

RATINGS
Admissions Selectivity Rating: 81   **Fire Safety Rating:** 89   **Green Rating:** 90

STUDENTS AND FACULTY
Enrollment: 516. **Student Body:** 40% female, 60% male, 76% out-of-state, 29% international (31 countries represented). Asian 4%, African American 6%, Caucasian 43%, Hispanic 12%, Native American 0%, Pacific Islander 0%, Two or more races 3%, Race unknown 3%.
Retention and Graduation: 71% freshmen return for sophomore year. 53% freshmen graduate within 4 years. 64% freshmen graduate within 6 years. 22% grads go on to further study within 1 year. **Faculty:** Student/faculty ratio 5:1. 20 full-time faculty, 25% hold PhDs, 15% are are members of minority groups, 55% are women. 0% of classes are taught by teaching assistants.

ACADEMICS

Degrees: bachelor's, diploma, master's. **Classes:** Most classes have fewer than 10 students. **Special Study Options:** Accelerated program, double major, English as a Second Language (ESL), independent study, internships. Combined degree programs: BABFA. **Disability Services:** Special programs offered to physically disabled students, including note-taking services, reader services, tape recorders. **Career Services:** Alumni network, Alumni services, Career/job search classes, Career assessment, Internships, Regional alumni. Both programs provide students with unique opportunities to explore future career paths, to learn new skills and to build strong communities.

FACILITIES

Housing: Coed dorms, special housing for disabled students, apartments for single students. 99% of campus accessible to physically diasbled. **Special Academic Facilities/Equipment:** Art gallery, photography gallery, extensive collections of contemporary art, concert hall, public lectures, conferences, cultural and intellectual events. **Computers:** 95% of classrooms, 100% of libraries, 100% of dining areas, 100% of common outdoor areas have wireless network access. Students can register for classes online. Administrative functions (other than registration) can be performed online.

CAMPUS LIFE

Environment: Metropolis. **Activities:** Choral groups, dance, drama/theater, jazz band, literary magazine, music ensembles, opera, radio station, student government, student newspaper, symphony orchestra, Student Organization. 39 registered organizations. **On-Campus Highlights:** Mannes Concert Hall **Environmental Initiatives:** Lighting Retrofits: 2W 13th St. and 66 5th Ave are in the midst of an ongoing replacement of all non-LED fixtures. The majority of the building's T8 fluorescent bulbs are being replaced with LED, stairwells are being replaced with dimming-occupancy based bi-level fixtures, and all rooms will be equiped with vacancy sensors. The main lobby and gallery spaces will also recieve significant upgrades as well. These same upgrades are being applied to 2 other large buildings, with a goal of completing the entire campus by early 2017.

ADMISSIONS

Freshman Academic Profile: Average high school GPA 3.1. 6% in top 10% of high school class, 17% in top 25% of high school class, 31% in top 50% of high school class. 72% from public high schools. **Reported SAT (pre-2016 redesign) scores:** SAT Math middle 50% range 500-630. SAT Critical Reading middle 50% range 500-620. SAT Writing middle 50% range 500-620. **Concordant SAT scores:** SAT EBRW middle 50% 560–670. SAT Math middle 50% range 530–650. Minimum internet-based TOEFL 79. **Basis for Candidate Selection:** *Very important factors considered include:* academic GPA, application essay, extracurricular activities. *Important factors considered include:* rigor of secondary school record, recommendation(s), character/personal qualities. *Other factors considered include:* class rank, standardized test scores, interview, talent/ability, volunteer work, work experience, level of applicant's interest. **Freshman Admission Requirements:** High school diploma is required and GED is accepted. *Academic units required:* 4 English. *Academic units recommended:* 4 math, 4 science, 4 foreign language, 4 social studies, 4 history. **Freshman Admission Statistics:** 901 applied, 58.93% admitted, 24% enrolled. **Transfer Admission Requirements:** college transcript(s), essay or personal statement, Minimum college GPA of 2.0 required. Lowest grade transferable C. **General Admission Information:** Application fee $50. Priority deadline 1/15. Regular application deadline 8/1. Nonfall registration accepted. Admission may be deferred for a maximum of 1 year.

COSTS AND FINANCIAL AID

Annual tuition $42,080. Room and board $18,930. Required fees $926. Average book expense $920. **Required Forms and Deadlines:** FAFSA, State aid form. **Types of Aid:** *Need-based scholarships/grants:* Federal Pell, FSEOG, State scholarships/grants, Private scholarships, College/university scholarship or grant aid from institutional funds. *Loans:* Direct Subsidized Stafford Loans, Direct Unsubsidized Stafford Loans, Direct PLUS loans, Federal Perkins Loans. *Student Employment:* Federal Work-Study Program available. Institutional employment available. **Financial Aid Statistics:** 80% needy freshmen, 81% needy undergrads receive need-based scholarship or grant aid. 51% freshmen, 52% undergrads receive non-need-based scholarship or grant aid. 86% freshmen, 85% undergrads receive need-based self-help aid. 0% freshmen, 0% undergrads receive athletic scholarships. 64% freshmen, 44% undergrads receive any aid. 68% undergrads borrow to pay for school. Average cumulative indebtedness $20,736. **Criteria for awarding aid:** *Need-based:* Academics, Art, Leadership, Minority status, Music/drama. *Non-need-based:* Academics, Art, Leadership, Minority status, Music/drama, State/district residency.

COLLEGE OF SAINT BENEDICT/ SAINT JOHN'S UNIVERSITY

PO Box 7155, Collegeville, MN 56321-7155
Phone: 320-363-5060 • **Financial Aid Phone:** 320-363-5388
E-mail: admissions@csbsju.edu • **CEEB Code:** 6624
Fax: 320-363-5650 • **Website:** www.csbsju.edu • **ACT Code:** 2140

This private school, affiliated with the Roman Catholic Church, was founded in 1857. It has a 2400-acre campus.

RATINGS

Admissions Selectivity Rating: 81   **Fire Safety Rating:** 97   **Green Rating:** 81

STUDENTS AND FACULTY

Enrollment: 3,712. **Student Body:** 53% female, 47% male, 19% out-of-state, 4% international (27 countries represented). Asian 4%, African American 4%, Caucasian 79%, Hispanic 7%, Native American 1%, Pacific Islander <1%, Two or more races 1%, Race unknown 0%.
Retention and Graduation: 86% freshmen return for sophomore year. 76% freshmen graduate within 4 years. 82% freshmen graduate within 6 years. 16% grads go on to further study within 1 year. **Faculty:** Student/faculty ratio 12:1. 286 full-time faculty, 92% hold PhDs, 10% are are members of minority groups, 51% are women. 0% of classes are taught by teaching assistants.

ACADEMICS

Degrees: bachelor's, master's. **Classes:** Most classes have 10-19 students. Most lab/discussion sessions have 10-19 students. **Most popular majors:** Business Administration and Management; Biology/Biological Sciences; Accounting and Finance. **Special Study Options:** cross-registration, double major, dual enrollment, English as a Second Language (ESL), exchange student program (domestic), honors program, independent study, internships, student-designed major, study abroad, teacher certification program. **Honors Programs:** All departments may contribute courses to our honors program. Students in all majors may participate in the Honors Program and receive honors distinction inside the major. **Disability Services:** Special programs offered to physically disabled students, including note-taking services, tape recorders, tutors. **Career Services:** Alumni network, Alumni services, Career assessment, Internships, Regional alumni. The CSB\SJU Office of Experiential Learning & Community Engagement provides students with access to hands-on experiences that compliment and accompany ideas, theories, practices, and methods taught in the classroom. Housing programs that existed individually in the past at CSB|SJU, the Office now administers the Bonner Leader, Internship, CSB Marie and Robert Jackson Fellows, Service-Learning, and Undergraduate Research programs.
$10 million gift to the College of Saint Benedict to create Center for Ethical Leadership in Action. The gift, from an anonymous donor, will create a permanent endowment fund, which will fund the operations of the Center, including the support of experiential learning as well as a mentoring program and speaker series.

FACILITIES

Housing: special housing for disabled students, men's dorms, special housing for international students, women's dorms, apartments for single students, Health and Wellness floor, Global Initiative Group house, ROTC housing. 90% of campus accessible to physically diasbled. **Special Academic Facilities/Equipment:** Hill Museum and Manuscript Library, art galleries, natural science museum, arboretum, Benedicta Arts Center, Sommers Digital Lab **Computers:** 100% of classrooms, 20% of dorms, 100% of libraries, 100% of dining areas, 100% of student union, 100% of common outdoor areas have wireless network access. Students can register for classes online. Administrative functions (other than registration) can be performed online.

CAMPUS LIFE

Environment: Village. **Activities:** Choral groups, concert band, dance, drama/theater, jazz band, literary magazine, music ensembles, musical theater, opera, pep band, radio station, student government, student newspaper, symphony orchestra, Campus Ministries, Student Organization, Model UN. 85 registered organizations, 3 honor societies, 4 religious organizations. **Athletics (Intercollegiate):** *Men:* baseball, basketball, cross-country, diving, football, golf, ice hockey, skiing (nordic/cross-country), soccer, swimming, tennis, track/field (outdoor), track/field (indoor), wrestling. *Women:* basketball, cross-country, diving, golf, ice hockey, skiing (nordic/cross-country), soccer, softball, swimming, tennis, track/field (outdoor), track/field (indoor), volleyball. **On-Campus Highlights:** Gorecki Dining Center, Benedicta Ars Center,

Warner Palaestra/Clemens Field House, Lake Sagatagan/Stell Maris Chapel, Brother Willie's Pub/O'Connell's Coffee, Abbey Church/Sacred Heart Chapel; Hill Museum and Manuscript Library; 15 KM hiking trails. **Environmental Initiatives:** Renewable Energy/Carbon neutrality.

ADMISSIONS

Freshman Academic Profile: Average high school GPA 3.6. 29% in top 10% of high school class, 58% in top 25% of high school class, 88% in top 50% of high school class. 73% from public high schools. **Reported SAT (pre-2016 redesign) scores:** SAT Math middle 50% range 440-570. SAT Critical Reading middle 50% range 470-560. SAT Writing middle 50% range 460-560. **Concordant SAT scores:** SAT EBRW middle 50% 520–620. SAT Math middle 50% range 480–590. ACT middle 50% range 22-28. Minimum internet-based TOEFL 80. Minimum paper TOEFL 550. **Basis for Candidate Selection:** *Very important factors considered include:* rigor of secondary school record, academic GPA, standardized test scores, extracurricular activities. *Important factors considered include:* class rank, application essay, recommendation(s), alumni/ae relation. *Other factors considered include:* interview, talent/ability, character/personal qualities, first generation, geographical residence, volunteer work, work experience. **Freshman Admission Requirements:** High school diploma is required and GED is accepted. *Academic units required:* 4 English, 3 math, 2 science, 2 science labs, 2 social studies, 4 academic electives. *Academic units recommended:* 2 foreign language. **Freshman Admission Statistics:** 3,316 applied, 87.76% admitted, 33% enrolled. **Transfer Admission Requirements:** High school transcript, college transcript(s), essay or personal statement, statement of good standing from prior institution(s). Minimum college GPA of 2.75 required. Lowest grade transferable C. **General Admission Information:** Priority deadline 11/15. Regular notification 4/1. Nonfall registration accepted. Admission may be deferred for a maximum of one year.

COSTS AND FINANCIAL AID

Annual tuition $41,245. Room and board $10,535. Required fees $1,026. Average book expense $1,000. **Required Forms and Deadlines:** FAFSA, Institution's own financial aid form. **Notification of Awards:** Applicants will be notified of awards on a rolling basis beginning 3/15. **Types of Aid:** *Need-based scholarships/grants:* Federal Pell, FSEOG, State scholarships/grants, College/university scholarship or grant aid from institutional funds. *Loans:* Direct Subsidized Stafford Loans, Direct Unsubsidized Stafford Loans, Direct PLUS loans, Federal Perkins Loans, State Loans. *Student Employment:* Federal Work-Study Program available. Institutional employment available. **Financial Aid Statistics:** 98% needy freshmen, 88% needy undergrads receive need-based scholarship or grant aid. 96% freshmen, 96% undergrads receive non-need-based scholarship or grant aid. 97% freshmen, 97% undergrads receive need-based self-help aid. 0% freshmen, 0% undergrads receive athletic scholarships. 95% freshmen, 94% undergrads receive any aid. 69% undergrads borrow to pay for school. Average cumulative indebtedness $39,904. **Criteria for awarding aid:** *Non-need-based:* Academics, Alumni affiliation, Art, Leadership, Music/drama.

COLLEGE OF SAINT ELIZABETH

Admissions Office, Morristown, NJ 07960-6989
Phone: 973-290-4700 • **Financial Aid Phone:** 973-290-4432
E-mail: apply@cse.edu • **CEEB Code:** 2090
Fax: 973-290-4710

This private school, affiliated with the Roman Catholic Church, was founded in 1899. It has a 200-acre campus.

RATINGS
Admissions Selectivity Rating: 74　　**Fire Safety Rating:** 96　　**Green Rating:** 60*

STUDENTS AND FACULTY
Enrollment: 468. **Student Body:** 94% female, 6% male, 4% out-of-state, 4% international (8 countries represented). Asian 2%, African American 41%, Caucasian 26%, Hispanic 20%, Native American 1%, Pacific Islander 0%, Two or more races 2%, Race unknown 4%.
Retention and Graduation: 69% freshmen return for sophomore year. 39% freshmen graduate within 4 years. 50% freshmen graduate within 6 years.
Faculty: Student/faculty ratio 12:1. 52 full-time faculty, 83% hold PhDs, 8% are are members of minority groups, 65% are women. 0% of classes are taught by teaching assistants.

ACADEMICS
Degrees: bachelor's, certificate, doctoral, master's, postbachelor's certificate, post-master's certificate. **Classes:** Most classes have 10-19 students. **Most popular majors:** Registered Nursing/Registered Nurse; Psychology; Criminal

Justice/Safety Studies. **Special Study Options:** Accelerated program, cross-registration, distance learning, double major, dual enrollment, English as a Second Language (ESL), exchange student program (domestic), honors program, independent study, internships, student-designed major, study abroad, teacher certification program, weekend college. Combined degree programs: BA/MA, BS/MS. **Disability Services:** Special programs offered to physically disabled students, including note-taking services, reader services, tape recorders, tutors. **Career Services:** Alumni network, Career/job search classes, Career assessment, Internships. Partnerships with employers such as American Red Cross, MEDCO Solutions, Verizon Wireless & the Department of Human Services have fortified our students with practical opportunities for development. An example of this is a collaborative venture between Career Services, the Communications and Business departments and the Business Club. Students are scheduled to spend a half day at Verizon, experiencing corporate culture and attend workshops lead by Verizon Human Resources staff on topics such as 'Group Interviewing'.

FACILITIES
Housing: women's dorms. 85% of campus accessible to physically diasbled. **Computers:** 100% of classrooms, 100% of dorms, 100% of libraries, 100% of dining areas, 100% of student union, 5% of common outdoor areas have wireless network access.

CAMPUS LIFE
Environment: Village. **Activities:** Choral groups, dance, drama/theater, literary magazine, music ensembles, student government, student newspaper, yearbook, Campus Ministries, Student Organization. 28 registered organizations, 9 honor societies, 1 religious organization. **Athletics (Intercollegiate):** *Women:* basketball, equestrian sports, soccer, softball, swimming, tennis. **On-Campus Highlights:** St. Joesph's Hall-Student Center, Henderson Hall-Classroom Building, O'Connor Hall-Residence Hall, Santa Rita Hall-Administration Building, Mahoney Library. **Environmental Initiatives:** Hazardous Waste Management process exists.

ADMISSIONS
Freshman Academic Profile: 81% from public high schools. **Reported SAT (pre-2016 redesign) scores:** SAT Math middle 50% range 370-465. SAT Critical Reading middle 50% range 380-470. SAT Writing middle 50% range 380-488. **Concordant SAT scores:** SAT EBRW middle 50% 430–540. SAT Math middle 50% range 410–510. Minimum internet-based TOEFL 61. Minimum paper TOEFL 500. **Basis for Candidate Selection:** *Very important factors considered include:* rigor of secondary school record, class rank, academic GPA, standardized test scores, recommendation(s). *Important factors considered include:* application essay, character/personal qualities. *Other factors considered include:* interview, extracurricular activities, talent/ability, first generation, alumni/ae relation, geographical residence, volunteer work, work experience, level of applicant's interest. **Freshman Admission Requirements:** High school diploma is required and GED is accepted. *Academic units required:* 3 English, 2 math, 1 science, 1 science lab, 2 foreign language, 1 history, 7 academic electives. *Academic units recommended:* 3 English, 3 math, 1 science, 2 science labs, 1 history, 8 academic electives. **Freshman Admission Statistics:** 2,496 applied, 48.36% admitted, 10% enrolled. **Transfer Admission Requirements:** college transcript(s), essay or personal statement, Minimum college GPA of 2.0 required. Lowest grade transferable C. **General Admission Information:** Application fee $35. Priority deadline 3/1. Regular application deadline 8/15. Nonfall registration accepted. Admission may be deferred for a maximum of 1 year.

COSTS AND FINANCIAL AID
Annual tuition $29,148. Room and board $12,744. Required fees $1,947. Average book expense $1,300. **Required Forms and Deadlines:** FAFSA. **Notification of Awards:** Applicants will be notified of awards on a rolling basis beginning 11/15. **Types of Aid:** *Need-based scholarships/grants:* Federal Pell, FSEOG, State scholarships/grants, Private scholarships, College/university scholarship or grant aid from institutional funds. *Loans:* Direct Subsidized Stafford Loans, Direct Unsubsidized Stafford Loans, Direct PLUS loans, Federal Perkins Loans, State Loans, College/university loans from institutional funds. *Student Employment:* Federal Work-Study Program available. Institutional employment available. **Financial Aid Statistics:** 89% needy freshmen, 81% needy undergrads receive need-based scholarship or grant aid. 100% freshmen, 88% undergrads receive non-need-based scholarship or grant aid. 93% freshmen, 91% undergrads receive need-based self-help aid. 0% freshmen, 0% undergrads receive athletic scholarships. 87% freshmen, 98% undergrads receive any aid. **Criteria for awarding aid:** *Need-based:* Academics, Minority status. *Non-need-based:* Academics, Alumni affiliation, Art, Leadership, Religious affiliation, State/district residency.

COLLEGE OF SAINT MARY

7000 Mercy Rd., Omaha, NE 68106
Phone: 402-399-2355 • **Financial Aid Phone:** 402-399-2415
E-mail: enroll@csm.edu • **CEEB Code:** 6106
Fax: 402-399-2412 • **Website:** www.csm.edu • **ACT Code:** 2440

This private school, affiliated with the Roman Catholic Church, was founded in 1923. It has a 25-acre campus.

RATINGS
Admissions Selectivity Rating: 85   **Fire Safety Rating:** 97   **Green Rating:** 73

STUDENTS AND FACULTY
Enrollment: 691. **Student Body:** 100% female, 0% male, 20% out-of-state, 1% international (7 countries represented). Asian 1%, African American 6%, Caucasian 78%, Hispanic 11%, Native American <1%, Pacific Islander 0%, Two or more races 2%, Race unknown 0%.
Retention and Graduation: 79% freshmen return for sophomore year. 28% freshmen graduate within 4 years. 40% freshmen graduate within 6 years. 51% grads go on to further study within 1 year. **Faculty:** Student/faculty ratio 9:1. 61 full-time faculty, 66% hold PhDs, 11% are are members of minority groups, 77% are women. 0% of classes are taught by teaching assistants.

ACADEMICS
Degrees: associate, bachelor's, certificate, doctoral/research, master's, postbachelor's certificate, terminal. **Classes:** Most classes have fewer than 10 students. Most lab/discussion sessions have fewer than 10 students. **Most popular majors:** Registered Nursing/Registered Nurse; Biology; Business Administration and Management. **Special Study Options:** Accelerated program, cooperative education program, distance learning, double major, dual enrollment, honors program, independent study, internships, study abroad, teacher certification program, weekend college. **Honors Programs:** Honors Program. **Disability Services:** Special programs offered to physically disabled students, including note-taking services, reader services, tape recorders, tutors. **Career Services:** Alumni services, Career/job search classes, Career assessment, Internships. Cooperative learning projects are an integral part of classes.

FACILITIES
Housing: special housing for disabled students, women's dorms, Women with children housing. 100% of campus accessible to physically diasbled. **Special Academic Facilities/Equipment:** Hillmer Art Gallery Gross Auditorium **Computers:** 100% of classrooms, 100% of dorms, 100% of libraries, 100% of dining areas, 100% of student union, 100% of common outdoor areas have wireless network access. Students can register for classes online. Administrative functions (other than registration) can be performed online.

CAMPUS LIFE
Environment: Metropolis. **Activities:** Choral groups, music ensembles, student government, Campus Ministries. 20 registered organizations, 2 honor societies, 1 religious organization. **Athletics (Intercollegiate):** *Women:* basketball, cross-country, soccer, softball, swimming, volleyball. **On-Campus Highlights:** Hillmer Art Gallery—Year round exhibits, Gross Theater, Hixson-Lied Commons—Student Center, Library, Lied Fitness Center—gym, weight rm, pool, tennis, Our Lady of Mercy Chapel—Daily Mass offered, Our residence halls include computer labs, lounge areas, a prayer and reflection room, and study area/small group meeting rooms. **Environmental Initiatives:** Reuseable to-go containers in dining hall.

ADMISSIONS
Freshman Academic Profile: Average high school GPA 3.6. 28% in top 10% of high school class, 51% in top 25% of high school class, 87% in top 50% of high school class. 80% from public high schools. ACT middle 50% range 20-26. Minimum internet-based TOEFL 80. **Basis for Candidate Selection:** *Very important factors considered include:* academic GPA, standardized test scores. *Important factors considered include:* class rank. *Other factors considered include:* recommendation(s), extracurricular activities. **Freshman Admission Requirements:** High school diploma is required and GED is accepted. *Academic units required:* 4 English, 2 math, 2 science, 2 social studies. *Academic units recommended:* 3 math, 3 science. **Freshman Admission Statistics:** 347 applied, 54.47% admitted, 47% enrolled. **Transfer Admission Requirements:** High school transcript, college transcript(s), Minimum college GPA of 2.0 required. Lowest grade transferable C. **General Admission Information:** Application fee $30. Nonfall registration accepted. Admission may be deferred for a maximum of 12 months.

COSTS AND FINANCIAL AID
Annual tuition $24,830. Room and board $6,800. Required fees $480. Average book expense $1,280. **Required Forms and Deadlines:** FAFSA. **Notification of Awards:** Applicants will be notified of awards on a rolling basis beginning 3/1. **Types of Aid:** *Need-based scholarships/grants:* Federal Pell, FSEOG,

State scholarships/grants, Private scholarships, College/university scholarship or grant aid from institutional funds, Federal Nursing Scholarships. *Loans:* Direct Subsidized Stafford Loans, Direct Unsubsidized Stafford Loans, Direct PLUS loans, Federal Perkins Loans, Federal Nursing Loans. *Student Employment:* Federal Work-Study Program available. Institutional employment available. **Financial Aid Statistics:** 100% needy freshmen, 97% needy undergrads receive need-based scholarship or grant aid. 26% freshmen, 8% undergrads receive non-need-based scholarship or grant aid. 69% freshmen, 89% undergrads receive need-based self-help aid. 15% freshmen, 7% undergrads receive athletic scholarships. 94% freshmen, 92% undergrads receive any aid. **Criteria for awarding aid:** *Non-need-based:* Academics, Athletics.

THE COLLEGE OF SAINT ROSE

432 Western Avenue, Albany, NY 12203
Phone: 518-454-5150 • **Financial Aid Phone:** 518-458-5464
E-mail: admit@strose.edu • **CEEB Code:** 2091
Fax: 518-454-2013 • **Website:** www.strose.edu • **ACT Code:** 2714

This private school, affiliated with the Roman Catholic Church, was founded in 1920. It has a 28-acre campus.

RATINGS
Admissions Selectivity Rating: 77   **Fire Safety Rating:** 95   **Green Rating:** 60*

STUDENTS AND FACULTY
Enrollment: 2,626. **Student Body:** 66% female, 34% male, 12% out-of-state, 2% international (40 countries represented). Asian 2%, African American 10%, Caucasian 67%, Hispanic 6%, Native American <1%, Pacific Islander <1%, Two or more races 7%, Race unknown 5%.
Retention and Graduation: 79% freshmen return for sophomore year. 46% freshmen graduate within 4 years. 61% freshmen graduate within 6 years. **Faculty:** Student/faculty ratio 14:1. 204 full-time faculty, 93% hold PhDs, 12% are are members of minority groups, 54% are women. 0% of classes are taught by teaching assistants.

ACADEMICS
Degrees: bachelor's, certificate, master's, postbachelor's certificate, post-master's certificate. **Classes:** Most classes have 20-29 students. Most lab/discussion sessions have 10-19 students. **Most popular majors:** Business Administration and Management; Elementary Education and Teaching; Communication and Media Studies. **Special Study Options:** Accelerated program, cross-registration, double major, exchange student program (domestic), independent study, internships, liberal arts/career combination, student-designed major, study abroad, teacher certification program. Combined degree programs: BA/JD, BA/MA, MBA/JD graduate degree; BS/MS Clinical Lab Sciences; BS/Certified Medical Technologist. **Disability Services:** Special programs offered to physically disabled students, including note-taking services, reader services, tape recorders, tutors. **Career Services:** Alumni network, Alumni services, Career/job search classes, Career assessment, Internships, Regional alumni.

FACILITIES
Housing: Coed dorms, men's dorms, women's dorms, apartments for single students. 90% of campus accessible to physically diasbled. **Special Academic Facilities/Equipment:** The Center for Art and Design houses the Saint Rose Art Gallery, the venue for student art shows and exhibits by acclaimed visiting artists, in addition to one of the largest screen printing facilities in the state of New York. The College's full-scale television studio is where communications students produce three 30-minute weekly television shows aired on Time Warner Cable. The Music Center features the Saints and Sinners Sound Studio, a 16-track professional recording studio, in addition to a music library. Athletic Facilities include the College's new Fitness Center, competition-size pool, weight room, and regulation NCAA basketball court. The Hubbard Interfaith Sanctuary is home to Campus Ministry and hosts a variety of interfaith lectures, concerts and poetry readings. With private meditation rooms and an indoor garden, this interreligious space provides a place to escape for a few minutes of quiet prayer. The Center for Cultural Diversity provides academic, social, and cultural support in an effort to enhance the quality of experiences for our diverse student population. **Computers:** 98% of classrooms, 90% of dorms, 100% of libraries, 100% of dining areas, 100% of student union, 80% of common outdoor areas have wireless network access. Students can register for classes online. Administrative functions (other than registration) can be performed online.

CAMPUS LIFE
Environment: City. **Activities:** Choral groups, concert band, dance, drama/theater, jazz band, literary magazine, music ensembles, musical theater, radio station, student government, student newspaper, symphony orchestra, television station, yearbook, Campus Ministries, Student Organization. 38

registered organizations, 6 honor societies, 2 religious organizations. **Athletics (Intercollegiate):** *Men:* baseball, basketball, cross-country, golf, soccer, swimming, track/field (outdoor). *Women:* basketball, cross-country, soccer, softball, swimming, tennis, track/field (outdoor), volleyball. **On-Campus Highlights:** Lally School of Education, Massry Center for the Fine Arts/Center for Art and D, Events and Athletic Center, Quiznos and Starbucks, Student Solution Center, Completely renovated (all) classrooms.

ADMISSIONS

Freshman Academic Profile: Average high school GPA 89.2. 14% in top 10% of high school class, 40% in top 25% of high school class, 73% in top 50% of high school class. **Reported SAT (pre-2016 redesign) scores:** SAT Math middle 50% range 470-560. SAT Critical Reading middle 50% range 480-570. **Concordant SAT scores:** SAT Math middle 50% range 510–580. ACT middle 50% range 20-25. Minimum internet-based TOEFL 80. Minimum paper TOEFL 550. **Basis for Candidate Selection:** *Very important factors considered include:* rigor of secondary school record, academic GPA. *Important factors considered include:* recommendation(s), extracurricular activities, talent/ability, character/personal qualities, first generation, volunteer work, level of applicant's interest. *Other factors considered include:* standardized test scores, application essay, interview, alumni/ae relation, work experience. **Freshman Admission Requirements:** High school diploma is required and GED is accepted. *Academic units required:* 4 English, 3 math, 3 science, 2 science labs, 1 foreign language, 4 social studies, 4 history. *Academic units recommended:* 4 English, 4 math, 4 science, 2 science labs, 2 foreign language, 4 social studies, 4 history, 4 academic electives. **Freshman Admission Statistics:** 5,599 applied, 81.76% admitted, 14% enrolled. **Transfer Admission Requirements:** High school transcript, college transcript(s), statement of good standing from prior institution(s). Minimum college GPA of 2.5 required. Lowest grade transferable C-. **General Admission Information:** Priority deadline 12/1. Regular application deadline 5/1. Regular notification 5/1. Nonfall registration accepted. Admission may be deferred for a maximum of 1 semester.

COSTS AND FINANCIAL AID

Required Forms and Deadlines: FAFSA. **Notification of Awards:** Applicants will be notified of awards on a rolling basis beginning 3/1. **Types of Aid:** *Need-based scholarships/grants:* Federal Pell, FSEOG, State scholarships/grants, Private scholarships, College/university scholarship or grant aid from institutional funds. *Loans:* Direct Subsidized Stafford Loans, Direct Unsubsidized Stafford Loans, Direct PLUS loans, Federal Perkins Loans. *Student Employment:* Federal Work-Study Program available. Institutional employment available. **Financial Aid Statistics:** 90% needy freshmen, 86% needy undergrads receive need-based scholarship or grant aid. 85% undergrads receive non-need-based scholarship or grant aid. 2% freshmen, 2% undergrads receive athletic scholarships. 99% freshmen, 89% undergrads receive any aid. 88% undergrads borrow to pay for school. Average cumulative indebtedness $36,432. **Criteria for awarding aid:** *Need-based:* Academics. *Non-need-based:* Academics, Alumni affiliation, Art, Athletics, Music/drama.

THE COLLEGE OF SAINT SCHOLASTICA

1200 Kenwood Avenue, Duluth, MN 55811-4199
Phone: 218-723-6046 • **Financial Aid Phone:** 218-723-6047
E-mail: admissions@css.edu • **CEEB Code:** 6107
Fax: 218-723-5991 • **Website:** www.css.edu • **ACT Code:** 2098

This private school, affiliated with the Roman Catholic Church, was founded in 1912. It has a 186-acre campus.

RATINGS

Admissions Selectivity Rating: 83   **Fire Safety Rating:** 79   **Green Rating:** 60*

STUDENTS AND FACULTY

Enrollment: 2,792. **Student Body:** 72% female, 28% male, 15% out-of-state, 3% international (34 countries represented). Asian 2%, African American 3%, Caucasian 83%, Hispanic 3%, Native American 1%, Pacific Islander <1%, Two or more races 3%, Race unknown <1%.
Retention and Graduation: 81% freshmen return for sophomore year. 57% freshmen graduate within 4 years. 66% freshmen graduate within 6 years. 29% grads go on to further study within 1 year. **Faculty:** Student/faculty ratio 15:1. 190 full-time faculty, 61% hold PhDs, 10% are members of minority groups, 69% are women. 0% of classes are taught by teaching assistants.

ACADEMICS

Degrees: bachelor's, certificate, doctoral/professional, master's, postbachelor's certificate, post-master's certificate. **Classes:** Most classes have 20-29 students. Most lab/discussion sessions have 20-29 students. **Most popular majors:** Computer and Information Sciences; Business Administration and Management; Registered Nursing/Registered Nurse. **Special Study Options:**

Accelerated program, cross-registration, distance learning, double major, dual enrollment, external degree program, honors program, independent study, internships, liberal arts/career combination, student-designed major, study abroad, teacher certification program. **Honors Programs:** The Honors Program at The College of St. Scholastica was created to give honors students enriched learning experiences and to provide a community of support for learners devoted to a vigorous life of the mind. Combined degree programs: BA/MA, BA/Doctor of Physical Therapy. **Disability Services:** Special programs offered to physically disabled students, including note-taking services, reader services, tape recorders, tutors. **Career Services:** Alumni network, Alumni services, Career/job search classes, Career assessment, Internships, Regional alumni. Career Services hosts an etiquette dinner called "No Jobs for Slobs." Each year approximately 100 students participate in this 5 course meal with instructions on how to conduct oneself during networking events, interviews that include a shared meal and business dinners.

FACILITIES

Housing: Coed dorms, special housing for disabled students, special housing for international students, apartments for single students, Wellness Housing, Apartments for students with dependent children. Quiet or study wings available. 95% of campus accessible to physically diasbled. **Computers:** Students can register for classes online. Administrative functions (other than registration) can be performed online.

CAMPUS LIFE

Environment: City. **Activities:** Choral groups, concert band, dance, drama/theater, jazz band, literary magazine, music ensembles, pep band, student government, student newspaper, television station, Campus Ministries, Student Organization. 67 registered organizations, 2 honor societies, 7 religious organizations. **Athletics (Intercollegiate):** *Men:* baseball, basketball, cross-country, ice hockey, skiing (nordic/cross-country), soccer, tennis, track/field (outdoor), track/field (indoor). *Women:* basketball, cross-country, skiing (nordic/cross-country), soccer, softball, tennis, track/field (outdoor), track/field (indoor), volleyball. **On-Campus Highlights:** Wellness Center, Student Union, Storm's Den, Cedar Hall

ADMISSIONS

Freshman Academic Profile: Average high school GPA 3.5. 22% in top 10% of high school class, 52% in top 25% of high school class, 77% in top 50% of high school class. **Reported SAT (pre-2016 redesign) scores:** SAT Math middle 50% range 460-570. SAT Critical Reading middle 50% range 430-550. SAT Writing middle 50% range 410-560. **Concordant SAT scores:** SAT EBRW middle 50% 470–610. SAT Math middle 50% range 500–590. ACT middle 50% range 21-26. Minimum internet-based TOEFL 79. Minimum paper TOEFL 550. **Basis for Candidate Selection:** *Very important factors considered include:* academic GPA, standardized test scores. *Important factors considered include:* rigor of secondary school record, class rank. *Other factors considered include:* application essay, recommendation(s), interview. **Freshman Admission Requirements:** High school diploma is required and GED is accepted. *Academic units recommended:* 4 English, 2 math, 3 science, 3 foreign language, 3 social studies, 3 history. **Freshman Admission Statistics:** 3,232 applied, 63.71% admitted, 22% enrolled. **Transfer Admission Requirements:** college transcript(s), Minimum college GPA of 1.5 required. Lowest grade transferable C. **General Admission Information:** Nonfall registration accepted. Admission may be deferred for a maximum of 1 year.

COSTS AND FINANCIAL AID

Annual tuition $34,764. Room and board $9,314. Required fees $562. Average book expense $1,150. **Required Forms and Deadlines:** FAFSA. **Notification of Awards:** Applicants will be notified of awards on a rolling basis beginning 3/1. **Types of Aid:** *Need-based scholarships/grants:* Federal Pell, FSEOG, State scholarships/grants, Private scholarships, College/university scholarship or grant aid from institutional funds. *Loans:* Direct Subsidized Stafford Loans, Direct Unsubsidized Stafford Loans, Direct PLUS loans, Federal Perkins Loans, Federal Nursing Loans, State Loans. *Student Employment:* Federal Work-Study Program available. Institutional employment available. **Financial Aid Statistics:** 76% needy freshmen, 74% needy undergrads receive need-based scholarship or grant aid. 100% freshmen, 80% undergrads receive non-need-based scholarship or grant aid. 75% freshmen, 76% undergrads receive need-based self-help aid. 0% freshmen, 0% undergrads receive athletic scholarships. 75% freshmen, 98% undergrads receive any aid. 77% undergrads borrow to pay for school. Average cumulative indebtedness $40,774. **Criteria for awarding aid:** *Non-need-based:* Academics, Alumni affiliation, Music/drama, Religious affiliation, State/district residency.

COLLEGE OF ST. JOSEPH IN VERMONT

71 Clement Road, Rutland, VT 5701
Phone: 802-776-5286 • **Financial Aid Phone:** 802-776-5218
E-mail: admissions@csj.edu • **CEEB Code:** 3297
Fax: 802-776-5258 • **Website:** www.csj.edu

This private school, affiliated with the Roman Catholic Church, was founded in 1956. It has a 116-acre campus.

RATINGS

Admissions Selectivity Rating: 71   **Fire Safety Rating:** 76   **Green Rating:** 60*

STUDENTS AND FACULTY

Enrollment: 208. **Student Body:** 55% female, 45% male, 42% out-of-state, 0% international (6 countries represented). Asian 1%, African American 4%, Caucasian 89%, Hispanic 5%, Native American 1%, Pacific Islander 0%, Two or more races 0%, Race unknown 0%.
Retention and Graduation: 83% freshmen return for sophomore year. 40% freshmen graduate within 4 years. 45% freshmen graduate within 6 years. **Faculty:** Student/faculty ratio 11:1. 15 full-time faculty, 47% hold PhDs, 0% are are members of minority groups, 40% are women. 0% of classes are taught by teaching assistants.

ACADEMICS

Degrees: associate, bachelor's, master's. **Classes:** Most classes have fewer than 10 students. **Most popular majors:** Business, Management, Marketing, and Related Support Services; Psychology; Elementary Education and Teaching. **Special Study Options:** Accelerated program, double major, dual enrollment, independent study, internships, liberal arts/career combination, teacher certification program. **Disability Services:** Special programs offered to physically disabled students, including note-taking services, reader services, tape recorders, tutors. **Career Services:** Alumni services, Career/job search classes, Career assessment, Internships, On-campus interviews. Variety of internships available.

FACILITIES

Housing: men's dorms, women's dorms. 100% of campus accessible to physically diasbled. **Special Academic Facilities/Equipment:** Theater and Athletic Center. **Computers:** 100% of libraries, have wireless network access.

CAMPUS LIFE

Environment: Village. **Activities:** Choral groups, drama/theater, literary magazine, student government, Campus Ministries. 20 registered organizations, 6 honor societies, 1 religious organization. **Athletics (Intercollegiate):** *Men:* baseball, basketball, soccer. *Women:* basketball, soccer, softball. **On-Campus Highlights:** Tuttle Hall-Student Center, Athletic Center, Theater, Giorgetti Library, St. Joseph Hall.

ADMISSIONS

Freshman Academic Profile: Average high school GPA 2.6. 0% in top 10% of high school class, 3% in top 25% of high school class, 36% in top 50% of high school class. 75% from public high schools. **Reported SAT (pre-2016 redesign) scores:** SAT Math middle 50% range 390-490. SAT Critical Reading middle 50% range 410-530. **Concordant SAT scores:** SAT Math middle 50% range 430–520. ACT middle 50% range 17-23. Minimum internet-based TOEFL 79. Minimum paper TOEFL 550. **Basis for Candidate Selection:** *Very important factors considered include:* rigor of secondary school record, academic GPA, recommendation(s). *Important factors considered include:* standardized test scores, application essay, interview, character/personal qualities. *Other factors considered include:* class rank, extracurricular activities, talent/ability, alumni/ae relation, volunteer work, level of applicant's interest. **Freshman Admission Requirements:** High school diploma is required and GED is not accepted. *Academic units required:* 4 English, 3 math, 2 science, 2 social studies, 2 history, 5 academic electives. *Academic units recommended:* 2 foreign language. **Freshman Admission Statistics:** 127 applied, 89.76% admitted, 35% enrolled. **Transfer Admission Requirements:** High school transcript, college transcript(s), essay or personal statement, Minimum college GPA of 2.0 required. Lowest grade transferable C. **General Admission Information:** Application fee $25. Priority deadline 5/1. Nonfall registration accepted. Admission may be deferred for a maximum of 1 year.

COSTS AND FINANCIAL AID

Annual tuition $15,500. Room and board $7,600. Required fees $260. Average book expense $1,000. **Required Forms and Deadlines:** FAFSA, Institution's own financial aid form. **Notification of Awards:** Applicants will be notified of awards on a rolling basis beginning 3/15. **Types of Aid:** *Need-based scholarships/grants:* Federal Pell, FSEOG, State scholarships/grants, Private scholarships, College/university scholarship or grant aid from institutional funds. *Loans:* Federal Perkins Loans. *Student Employment:* Federal Work-Study Program available. Institutional employment available. **Financial Aid Statistics:** 100% needy freshmen, 98% needy undergrads receive need-based scholarship or grant aid. 3% undergrads receive non-need-based scholarship or grant aid. 96% freshmen, 94% undergrads receive need-based self-help aid. 0% freshmen, 0% undergrads receive athletic scholarships. 91% freshmen, 88% undergrads receive any aid. **Criteria for awarding aid:** *Need-based:* Academics, Alumni affiliation, Leadership, Religious affiliation. *Non-need-based:* Academics, Music/drama.

COLLEGE OF WILLIAM AND MARY

Best Colleges

Office of Admissions, P.O. Box 8795, Williamsburg, VA 23187-8795
Phone: 757-221-4223 • **Financial Aid Phone:** 757-221-2420
E-mail: admission@wm.edu • **CEEB Code:** 5115
Fax: 757-221-1242 • **Website:** www.wm.edu • **ACT Code:** 4344

This public school was founded in 1693. It has a 1200-acre campus.

RATINGS

Admissions Selectivity Rating: 96   **Fire Safety Rating:** 91   **Green Rating:** 83

STUDENTS AND FACULTY

Enrollment: 6,245. **Student Body:** 58% female, 42% male, 30% out-of-state, 6% international (46 countries represented). Asian 8%, African American 7%, Caucasian 59%, Hispanic 9%, Native American <1%, Pacific Islander <1%, Two or more races 5%, Race unknown 6%.
Retention and Graduation: 95% freshmen return for sophomore year. 90% freshmen graduate within 6 years. **Faculty:** 0% of classes are taught by teaching assistants.

ACADEMICS

Degrees: bachelor's, doctoral/professional, doctoral/research, doctoral, master's, postbachelor's certificate, post-master's certificate. **Most popular majors:** Business Administration and Management; Biology/Biological Sciences; Political Science and Government. **Special Study Options:** Accelerated program, double major, dual enrollment, honors program, independent study, internships, student-designed major, study abroad, teacher certification program. **Honors Programs:** Monroe Scholars; Sharpe Scholars; Murray Scholars; William and Mary Scholar Award; Alpha Lambda Delta and Phi Eta Sigma Honor Societies for Freshman Combined degree programs: BA/MA, BS / MS Degrees in Chemistry. **Disability Services:** Special programs offered to physically disabled students, including note-taking services, reader services, tape recorders, tutors. **Career Services:** Alumni network, Alumni services, Career/job search classes, Career assessment, Internships. The Alumni Mentoring Program provides valuable and searchable information for students and alumni alike to connect for the purposes of seeking career advice, support, and referral. The synergy of this networking program simultaneously strengthens the College community.

FACILITIES

Housing: Coed dorms, special housing for disabled students, special housing for international students, fraternity/sorority housing, apartments for single students, Wellness Housing, ThemeHousingInternational Studies hall, Eco-House, Community Scholars House, Africana House, Multicultural Unit, and 8 language houses (Arabic, Chinese, French, German, Italian, Japanese, Russian, Spanish). 95% of campus accessible to physically diasbled. **Special Academic Facilities/Equipment:** observatory, continuous beam accelerator, 3 interdisciplinary centers in humanities, studies, writing resources, marine science institute, materials processes research center,public policy research center. **Computers:** 100% of classrooms, 100% of dorms, 100% of libraries, 100% of dining areas, 100% of student union, 33% of common outdoor areas have wireless network access. Students can register for classes online. Administrative functions (other than registration) can be performed online. Undergraduates are required to own a computer.

CAMPUS LIFE

Environment: Village. **Activities:** Choral groups, concert band, dance, drama/theater, jazz band, literary magazine, music ensembles, musical theater, opera, pep band, radio station, student government, student newspaper, student-run film society, symphony orchestra, television station, yearbook, Campus Ministries, Student Organization, Model UN. 375 registered organizations, 32 honor societies, 32 religious organizations. 18 fraternities, 11 sororities. **Athletics (Intercollegiate):** *Men:* baseball, basketball, cheerleading, cross-country, diving, football, golf, gymnastics, soccer, swimming, tennis, track/field (outdoor), track/field (indoor). *Women:* basketball, cheerleading, cross-country, diving, field hockey, golf, gymnastics, lacrosse, soccer, swimming, tennis, track/

field (outdoor), track/field (indoor), volleyball. **On-Campus Highlights:** Wren Building (oldest academic building), Muscarelle Museum of Art, Lake Matoaka/College Woods, Crim Dell Bridge, Sunken Garden. **Environmental Initiatives:** Adhere to LEED construction guidelines in all new construction and renovations. Three buildings have been LEED certified to date and two are in progress.

ADMISSIONS

Freshman Academic Profile: Average high school GPA 4.2. 78% in top 10% of high school class, 96% in top 25% of high school class, 99% in top 50% of high school class. 77% from public high schools. **Reported SAT (pre-2016 redesign) scores:** SAT Math middle 50% range 620-740. SAT Critical Reading middle 50% range 630-730. SAT Writing middle 50% range 620-720. **Concordant SAT scores:** SAT EBRW middle 50% 680–750. SAT Math middle 50% range 640–760. ACT middle 50% range 28-33. Minimum internet-based TOEFL 100. Minimum paper TOEFL 600. **Basis for Candidate Selection:** *Very important factors considered include:* rigor of secondary school record, class rank, academic GPA, standardized test scores, application essay, recommendation(s), extracurricular activities, talent/ability, character/personal qualities, state residency, volunteer work, work experience. *Other factors considered include:* interview, first generation, alumni/ae relation, geographical residence, racial/ethnic status. **Freshman Admission Requirements:** High school diploma or equivalent is not required. *Academic units recommended:* 4 English, 4 math, 4 science, 3 science labs, 4 foreign language, 4 social studies. **Freshman Admission Statistics:** 14,382 applied, 36.52% admitted, 29% enrolled. **Transfer Admission Requirements:** High school transcript, college transcript(s), essay or personal statement, statement of good standing from prior institution(s). Minimum college GPA of 3.00 required. Lowest grade transferable C. **General Admission Information:** Application fee $70. Regular application deadline 1/1. Regular notification 4/1. Nonfall registration not accepted. Admission may be deferred for a maximum of 1 year.

COSTS AND FINANCIAL AID

Required Forms and Deadlines: FAFSA, CSS/Financial Aid PROFILE. **Types of Aid:** *Need-based scholarships/grants:* Federal Pell, FSEOG, State scholarships/grants, Private scholarships, College/university scholarship or grant aid from institutional funds. *Loans:* Direct Subsidized Stafford Loans, Direct Unsubsidized Stafford Loans, Direct PLUS loans, Federal Perkins Loans. *Student Employment:* Federal Work-Study Program available. Institutional employment available. **Financial Aid Statistics:** 86% needy undergrads receive need-based scholarship or grant aid. 0% undergrads receive non-need-based scholarship or grant aid. 0% freshmen, 0% undergrads receive need-based self-help aid. 0% freshmen, 0% undergrads receive athletic scholarships. 54% freshmen, 53% undergrads receive any aid. **Criteria for awarding aid:** *Need-based:* Academics, Alumni affiliation, Athletics, Music/drama. *Non-need-based:* Academics, Art, Athletics, Music/drama.

THE COLLEGE OF WOOSTER

847 College Avenue, Wooster, OH 44691
Phone: 330-263-2322 • **Financial Aid Phone:** 800-877-3688
E-mail: admissions@wooster.edu • **CEEB Code:** 1134
Fax: 330-263-2621 • **Website:** www.wooster.edu • **ACT Code:** 3260

This private school was founded in 1866. It has a 240-acre campus.

RATINGS

Admissions Selectivity Rating: 88   **Fire Safety Rating:** 86   **Green Rating:** 79

STUDENTS AND FACULTY

Enrollment: 1,980. **Student Body:** 54% female, 46% male, 61% out-of-state, 11% international (35 countries represented). Asian 5%, African American 8%, Caucasian 67%, Hispanic 5%, Native American 1%, Pacific Islander <1%, Two or more races 0%, Race unknown 2%.
Retention and Graduation: 87% freshmen return for sophomore year. 71% freshmen graduate within 4 years. 76% freshmen graduate within 6 years. 23% grads go on to further study within 1 year. 44% grads pursue arts and sciences degrees. 9% grads pursue law degrees. 9% grads pursue medical degrees.
Faculty: Student/faculty ratio 11:1. 164 full-time faculty, 95% hold PhDs, 16% are are members of minority groups, 48% are women. 0% of classes are taught by teaching assistants.

ACADEMICS

Degrees: bachelor's. **Classes:** Most classes have fewer than 10 students. Most lab/discussion sessions have 10-19 students. **Most popular majors:** History; Psychology; English Language and Literature. **Special Study Options:** cooperative education program, double major, dual enrollment, exchange student program (domestic), independent study, internships, student-designed major, study abroad, teacher certification program. Combined degree programs: BA/MA, BA/DDS, BA/MEng, many combined programs with other institutions. **Disability Services:** Special programs offered to physically disabled students, including note-taking services, reader services, tape recorders, tutors. **Career Services:** Alumni network, Alumni services, Career/job search classes, Career assessment, Internships, Regional alumni. APEX (Advising, Planning and Experiential Learning) Center provides academic advising, career planning, the Entrepreneurship Office, Experiential Learning Office, and support centers such as the Writing Center and Math Center, in one location.

FACILITIES

Housing: Coed dorms, special housing for international students, women's dorms, fraternity/sorority housing, apartments for single students, Theme Housing, Special housing for students participating in volunteer programs. 95% of campus accessible to physically diasbled. **Special Academic Facilities/Equipment:** Art museum, language lab, on-campus nursery school, science library. **Computers:** 100% of classrooms, 95% of dorms, 100% of libraries, 100% of dining areas, 100% of student union, 50% of common outdoor areas have wireless network access. Students can register for classes online. Administrative functions (other than registration) can be performed online.

CAMPUS LIFE

Environment: Town. **Activities:** Choral groups, concert band, dance, drama/theater, jazz band, literary magazine, marching band, music ensembles, musical theater, pep band, radio station, student government, student newspaper, student-run film society, symphony orchestra, yearbook, Campus Ministries, Student Organization, Model UN. 100 registered organizations, 6 honor societies, 9 religious organizations. 5 fraternities, 6 sororities. **Athletics (Intercollegiate):** *Men:* baseball, basketball, cross-country, diving, football, golf, lacrosse, soccer, swimming, tennis, track/field (outdoor), track/field (indoor). *Women:* basketball, cross-country, diving, field hockey, lacrosse, soccer, softball, swimming, tennis, track/field (outdoor), track/field (indoor), volleyball. **On-Campus Highlights:** Kauke Hall, Severance Hall Chemistry Bldg., Timken Science Library, Ebert Art Center, Burton D. Morgan Hall, Gault Manor (residence hall). **Environmental Initiatives:** Completed $5M Energy Performance Contract that reduced the College's carbon footprint by 36% through lighting and water conservation, building automation system upgrades, and the installation of two new electric chillers and a steam condensor at the Power Plant.

ADMISSIONS

Freshman Academic Profile: Average high school GPA 3.7. 45% in top 10% of high school class, 69% in top 25% of high school class. 69% from public high schools. **Reported SAT (pre-2016 redesign) scores:** SAT Math middle 50% range 550-680. SAT Critical Reading middle 50% range 520-670. SAT Writing middle 50% range 520-660. **Concordant SAT scores:** SAT EBRW middle 50% 580–710. SAT Math middle 50% range 570–710. ACT middle 50% range 24-30. Minimum internet-based TOEFL 81. **Basis for Candidate Selection:** *Very important factors considered include:* rigor of secondary school record, academic GPA. *Important factors considered include:* class rank, standardized test scores, application essay, recommendation(s), interview, extracurricular activities, character/personal qualities, level of applicant's interest. *Other factors considered include:* talent/ability, first generation, alumni/ae relation, geographical residence, state residency, racial/ethnic status, volunteer work, work experience. **Freshman Admission Requirements:** High school diploma is required and GED is accepted. *Academic units required:* 4 English, 3 math, 3 science, 2 science labs, 2 foreign language, 3 social studies, 1 academic elective. **Freshman Admission Statistics:** 5,667 applied, 58.16% admitted, 17% enrolled. **Transfer Admission Requirements:** High school transcript, college transcript(s), essay or personal statement, standardized test scores, statement of good standing from prior institution(s). Minimum college GPA of 2.5 required. Lowest grade transferable C. **General Admission Information:** Application fee $45. Regular application deadline 2/15. Regular notification 4/1. Nonfall registration accepted. Admission may be deferred for a maximum of 1 year.

COSTS AND FINANCIAL AID

Annual tuition $46,430. Room and board $11,040. Required fees $430. Average book expense $1,000. **Required Forms and Deadlines:** FAFSA, Institution's own financial aid form, CSS/Financial Aid PROFILE. **Notification of Awards:** Applicants will be notified of awards on a rolling basis beginning 3/15. **Types of Aid:** *Need-based scholarships/grants:* Federal Pell, FSEOG, State scholarships/grants, Private scholarships, College/university scholarship or grant aid from institutional funds, United Negro College Fund. *Loans:* Direct Subsidized Stafford Loans, Direct Unsubsidized Stafford Loans, Direct PLUS loans, Federal Perkins Loans. *Student Employment:* Federal Work-Study Program available. Institutional employment available. **Financial Aid Statistics:** 97% needy freshmen, 97% needy undergrads receive need-based scholarship or grant aid. 18% freshmen, 13% undergrads receive non-need-based scholarship or grant aid. 80% freshmen, 83% undergrads receive need-based self-help aid. 0% freshmen receive athletic scholarships. 99% freshmen, 99% undergrads receive any aid. 61% undergrads borrow to pay for school. Average cumulative indebtedness $29,650. **Criteria for awarding aid:** *Need-based:* Academics, Minority status. *Non-need-based:* Academics, Minority status, Music/drama, Religious affiliation.

COLORADO CHRISTIAN UNIVERSITY

8787 W. Alameda Ave., Lakewood, CO 80226
Phone: 303-963-3200 • **Financial Aid Phone:** 303-963-3233
E-mail: ccuadmissions@ccu.edu • **CEEB Code:** 4659
Fax: 303-963-3201 • **Website:** www.ccu.edu • **ACT Code:** 523

This private school, affiliated with the Christian (Nondenominational) Church, was founded in 1914. It has a 26-acre campus.

RATINGS
Admissions Selectivity Rating: 82   **Fire Safety Rating:** 61   **Green Rating:** 60*

STUDENTS AND FACULTY
Enrollment: 1,661. **Student Body:** 60% female, 40% male, 56% out-of-state, 1% international. Asian 1%, African American 4%, Caucasian 76%, Hispanic 9%, Native American 1%, Pacific Islander 0%, Two or more races 0%, Race unknown 8%.
Retention and Graduation: 86% freshmen return for sophomore year. 34% freshmen graduate within 4 years. 44% freshmen graduate within 6 years.
Faculty: Student/faculty ratio 21:1. 41 full-time faculty, 68% hold PhDs, 5% are are members of minority groups, 46% are women. 0% of classes are taught by teaching assistants.

ACADEMICS
Degrees: associate, bachelor's, master's. **Classes:** Most classes have fewer than 10 students. Most lab/discussion sessions have 10-19 students. **Most popular majors:** Computer/Information Technology Services Administration and Management; Liberal Arts and Sciences/Liberal Studies; Management Information Systems. **Special Study Options:** Accelerated program, cooperative education program, distance learning, double major, honors program, independent study, internships, student-designed major, study abroad, teacher certification program, weekend college, American Studies Program (Washington DC); Host University for Institute for Family Studies; China Studies Program (various sites in China); Latin American Studies Program (Costa Rica); Los Angeles Film Studies Center; Middle East Studies (Cairo, Egypt); Oxford Honors Program (University of Oxford, England); Russian Studies Program (various sites in Russia); Summer Institute of Journalism (Washington DC). **Disability Services:** Special programs offered to physically disabled students, including tutors. **Career Services:** Alumni services, Career/job search classes, Career assessment, Internships.

FACILITIES
Housing: Coed dorms, special housing for disabled students, men's dorms, women's dorms, apartments for single students, Theme Housing. 85% of campus accessible to physically diasbled. **Special Academic Facilities/Equipment:** Music recording studio, electron microscope. **Computers:** 100% of classrooms, 100% of dorms, 100% of student union, have wireless network access. Students can register for classes online. Administrative functions (other than registration) can be performed online.

CAMPUS LIFE
Activities: Choral groups, concert band, drama/theater, jazz band, literary magazine, music ensembles, musical theater, student government, student newspaper, symphony orchestra 21 registered organizations, 3 honor societies, 14 religious organizations. **Athletics (Intercollegiate):** *Men:* basketball, cross-country, golf, soccer, tennis. *Women:* basketball, cross-country, soccer, tennis, volleyball.

ADMISSIONS
Freshman Academic Profile: Average high school GPA 3.4. 22% in top 10% of high school class, 46% in top 25% of high school class, 79% in top 50% of high school class. **Reported SAT (pre-2016 redesign) scores:** SAT Math middle 50% range 480-590. SAT Critical Reading middle 50% range 510-630. **Concordant SAT scores:** SAT Math middle 50% range 510-610. ACT middle 50% range 20-26. Minimum paper TOEFL 500. **Basis for Candidate Selection:** *Very important factors considered include:* rigor of secondary school record, standardized test scores, application essay, talent/ability, character/personal qualities, first generation, religious affiliation/commitment. *Important factors considered include:* class rank, academic GPA, recommendation(s), extracurricular activities, racial/ethnic status, volunteer work, level of applicant's

interest. *Other factors considered include:* interview, alumni/ae relation, work experience. **Freshman Admission Requirements:** High school diploma is required and GED is accepted. *Academic units recommended:* 4 English, 3 math, 3 science, 2 science labs, 3 foreign language, 1 social studies, 2 history, and 1 unit from above areas or other academic areas. **Freshman Admission Statistics:** 946 applied, 77.06% admitted, 33% enrolled. **Transfer Admission Requirements:** college transcript(s), essay or personal statement, statement of good standing from prior institution(s). Minimum college GPA of 2.0 required. Lowest grade transferable C. **General Admission Information:** Application fee $50. Priority deadline 3/1. Regular application deadline 8/21. Nonfall registration accepted. Admission may be deferred for a maximum of 1 year.

COSTS AND FINANCIAL AID
Annual tuition $18,850. Room and board $6,682. Required fees $150. Average book expense $1,188. **Required Forms and Deadlines:** FAFSA. **Notification of Awards:** Applicants will be notified of awards on a rolling basis beginning 4/1. **Types of Aid:** *Need-based scholarships/grants:* Federal Pell, FSEOG, Private scholarships, College/university scholarship or grant aid from institutional funds. *Loans:* Federal Perkins Loans. *Student Employment:* Federal Work-Study Program available. Institutional employment available. **Financial Aid Statistics:** 97% needy freshmen, 88% needy undergrads receive need-based scholarship or grant aid. 88% freshmen, 82% undergrads receive non-need-based scholarship or grant aid. 100% freshmen, 100% undergrads receive need-based self-help aid. 14% freshmen, 7% undergrads receive athletic scholarships. **Criteria for awarding aid:** *Non-need-based:* Academics, Athletics, Leadership, Minority status.

COLORADO COLLEGE

14 East Cache la Poudre Street, Colorado Springs, CO 80903
Phone: 719-389-6344 • **Financial Aid Phone:** 719-389-6651
E-mail: admission@coloradocollege.edu • **CEEB Code:** 4072
Fax: 719-389-6816 • **Website:** www.coloradocollege.edu • **ACT Code:** 498

This private school was founded in 1874. It has a 90-acre campus.

RATINGS
Admissions Selectivity Rating: 97   **Fire Safety Rating:** 95   **Green Rating:** 91

STUDENTS AND FACULTY
Enrollment: 2,084. **Student Body:** 54% female, 46% male, 83% out-of-state, 8% international (69 countries represented). Asian 4%, African American 3%, Caucasian 66%, Hispanic 9%, Native American 1%, Pacific Islander 0%, Two or more races 9%, Race unknown 1%.
Retention and Graduation: 96% freshmen return for sophomore year. 82% freshmen graduate within 4 years. 87% freshmen graduate within 6 years.
Faculty: Student/faculty ratio 10:1. 186 full-time faculty, 99% hold PhDs, 25% are are members of minority groups, 48% are women. 0% of classes are taught by teaching assistants.

ACADEMICS
Degrees: bachelor's, master's, postbachelor's certificate. **Classes:** Most classes have 10-19 students. **Most popular majors:** Economics; Sociology; Political Science and Government. **Special Study Options:** double major, English as a Second Language (ESL), independent study, internships, liberal arts/career combination, student-designed major, study abroad, Teacher licensure program; Cooperative 3/2 program. Combined degree programs: BA/MEng. **Disability Services:** Special programs offered to physically disabled students, including note-taking services, tutors. **Career Services:** Alumni network, Alumni services, Career/job search classes, Career assessment, Internships, Regional alumni, On-campus interviews.

FACILITIES
Housing: Coed dorms, men's dorms, women's dorms, fraternity/sorority housing, apartments for single students, Theme Housing. **Special Academic Facilities/Equipment:** Electronic music studio, telescope dome, multimedia computer laboratory, Balinese orchestras, The Colorado Electronic music studio, Observatory, Extensive herbarium collection 4 greenhouses Environmental Science van equipped for field research Fourier transform nuclear magnetic resonance spectrometer Packard Hall, 300 seat concert/lecture hall Photography darkrooms Drama/Dance: Armstrong Theatre, 740 seat proscenium theatre Armstrong 32, 100 seat experimental theatre 4 dance studios w/Marley, variable speed cd players Drama computer lab Geology: Petrographic microscopes X-ray diffractometer Sedimentology lab

El Pomar Sports Center: Metabolic Equipment (COSMED Quark PFT Ergo) Hydrostatic Weighing Equipment Cadaver study in Sports Science Biology: Scanning electron microscope Transmission electron microscope **Computers:** 100% of classrooms, 100% of dorms, 100% of libraries, 100% of dining areas, 100% of student union, 80% of common outdoor areas have wireless network access. Students can register for classes online. Administrative functions (other than registration) can be performed online.

CAMPUS LIFE

Environment: Metropolis. **Activities:** Choral groups, concert band, dance, drama/theater, jazz band, literary magazine, music ensembles, musical theater, radio station, student government, student newspaper, student-run film society, yearbook, Campus Ministries, Student Organization. 147 registered organizations, 13 honor societies, 20 religious organizations. 1 fraternity, 3 sororities. **Athletics (Intercollegiate):** *Men:* basketball, cross-country, ice hockey, lacrosse, soccer, swimming, tennis, track/field (outdoor). *Women:* basketball, cross-country, lacrosse, soccer, swimming, tennis, track/field (outdoor), track/field (indoor), volleyball. **On-Campus Highlights:** Worner Student Center, Palmer Hall, Shove Chapel, Cutler Hall—Admission, View of Pikes Peak. **Environmental Initiatives:** The College is committed to achieving carbon neutrality by 2020. The plan includes an efficiency target in all campus buildings that will reduce energy intensity by 30%, along with a 20% reduction target through behavior change and conservation, and a strategy to derive 100% of electricity from renewable sources.

ADMISSIONS

Freshman Academic Profile: 69% in top 10% of high school class, 90% in top 25% of high school class, 100% in top 50% of high school class. **Reported SAT (pre-2016 redesign) scores:** SAT Math middle 50% range 620-720. SAT Critical Reading middle 50% range 610-730. SAT Writing middle 50% range 620-710. **Concordant SAT scores:** SAT EBRW middle 50% 670–750. SAT Math middle 50% range 640–750. ACT middle 50% range 28-32. **Basis for Candidate Selection:** *Very important factors considered include:* rigor of secondary school record. *Important factors considered include:* class rank, academic GPA, standardized test scores, application essay, recommendation(s), interview, extracurricular activities. *Other factors considered include:* talent/ability, character/personal qualities, first generation, alumni/ae relation, religious affiliation/commitment, racial/ethnic status, volunteer work, work experience, level of applicant's interest. **Freshman Admission Requirements:** High school diploma or equivalent is not required. *Academic units required:* 4 English. *Academic units recommended:* 4 English. **Freshman Admission Statistics:** 7,894 applied, 15.99% admitted, 42% enrolled. **Transfer Admission Requirements:** High school transcript, college transcript(s), essay or personal statement, standardized test scores, statement of good standing from prior institution(s). Lowest grade transferable C. **General Admission Information:** Application fee $60. Priority deadline 1/15. Regular application deadline 1/15. Regular notification 4/1. Nonfall registration accepted. Admission may be deferred for a maximum of 1 year.

COSTS AND FINANCIAL AID

Annual tuition $50,472. Required fees $420. Average book expense $1,248. **Required Forms and Deadlines:** FAFSA, CSS/Financial Aid PROFILE, Noncustodial PROFILE. **Notification of Awards:** Applicants will be notified of awards on or about 3/15. **Types of Aid:** *Need-based scholarships/grants:* Federal Pell, FSEOG, State scholarships/grants, Private scholarships, College/university scholarship or grant aid from institutional funds. *Loans:* Direct Subsidized Stafford Loans, Direct Unsubsidized Stafford Loans, Direct PLUS loans, Federal Perkins Loans. *Student Employment:* Federal Work-Study Program available. Institutional employment available. **Financial Aid Statistics:** 97% needy freshmen, 95% needy undergrads receive need-based scholarship or grant aid. 27% freshmen, 18% undergrads receive non-need-based scholarship or grant aid. 74% freshmen, 76% undergrads receive need-based self-help aid. 2% freshmen, 2% undergrads receive athletic scholarships. 57% freshmen, 54% undergrads receive any aid. 41% undergrads borrow to pay for school. Average cumulative indebtedness $20,742. **Criteria for awarding aid:** *Non-need-based:* Academics, Athletics, Leadership.

COLORADO SCHOOL OF MINES

1812 Illinois Street, Golden, CO 80401
Phone: 303-273-3220 • **Financial Aid Phone:** 303-273-3220
E-mail: admissions@mines.edu • **CEEB Code:** 4073
Fax: 303-273-3509 • **Website:** www.mines.edu • **ACT Code:** 500

This public school was founded in 1874. It has a 373-acre campus.

RATINGS

Admissions Selectivity Rating: 93   **Fire Safety Rating:** 88   **Green Rating:** 70

STUDENTS AND FACULTY

Enrollment: 4,566. **Student Body:** 28% female, 72% male, 38% out-of-state, 6% international (79 countries represented). Asian 5%, African American 1%, Caucasian 74%, Hispanic 7%, Native American <1%, Pacific Islander <1%, Two or more races 5%, Race unknown 1%.
Retention and Graduation: 92% freshmen return for sophomore year. 52% freshmen graduate within 4 years. 75% freshmen graduate within 6 years. 14% grads go on to further study within 1 year. 4% grads pursue arts and sciences degrees. 1% grads pursue law degrees. 2% grads pursue business degrees. 1% grads pursue medical degrees. **Faculty:** Student/faculty ratio 15:1. 285 full-time faculty, 88% hold PhDs, 18% are members of minority groups, 28% are women. 3% of classes are taught by teaching assistants.

ACADEMICS

Degrees: bachelor's, doctoral/research, master's, post-master's certificate. **Classes:** Most classes have 10-19 students. Most lab/discussion sessions have 20-29 students. **Most popular majors:** Mechanical Engineering; Chemical Engineering; Petroleum Engineering. **Special Study Options:** Accelerated program, cooperative education program, double major, dual enrollment, English as a Second Language (ESL), exchange student program (domestic), honors program, independent study, internships, study abroad. **Honors Programs:** McBride Honors Program—The McBride Honors Program, instituted in 1978 through a grant from the National Endowment for the Humanities, is a 24 semester-hour program of seminars and off-campus activities that has as its primary goal: To provide a select community of CSM students the enhanced opportunity to explore the interfaces between their areas of technical expertise and the humanities and social sciences; to gain the sensitivity to project and test the moral and social implications of their future professional judgments and activities; and to foster their leadership abilities in preparation for managing change and promoting the general welfare in an evolving technological and global context. To achieve this goal, the program seeks to bring themes from the humanities and the social sciences into the engineering curriculum that will encourage in students the habits of thought necessary for effective management and enlightened leadership. Combined degree programs: BS/MS. **Disability Services:** Special programs offered to physically disabled students, including note-taking services, reader services, tape recorders, tutors. **Career Services:** Alumni services, Career/job search classes, Career assessment, Internships. Internship opportunities are vast. More than 80% of undergraduates have an internship (usually in the summer) related to major area of study. One of the newest opportunities is through the Renewable Energy Materials Research Science and Engineering Center: The Center focuses on preparing undergraduate and graduate students to embark on careers in renewable fields by providing a multitude of research and classroom experiences in renewable energy. REMRSEC offers a coordinated approach from K to gray in renewable energy education, outreach, and work force development founded on research proven best practices.

FACILITIES

Housing: Coed dorms, fraternity/sorority housing, apartments for married students, apartments for single students. 95% of campus accessible to physically diasbled. **Special Academic Facilities/Equipment:** Geology Museum, US Geological Survey & Earthquake Center, Edgar Experimental Mine, Graduate Research Laboratory (GRL), Center for Technology & Learning Media which houses supercomputer "'Ra,'"—high performance computing (HPC) cluster that aims to be a national hub for computational inquiries aimed at the discovery of new ways to meet the world''s energy demands. Estimated peak performance will be approximately 20 teraflops'—This places the machine well within the top-100 fastest computers in the world. The new facility, administered by the Golden Energy Computing Organization (GECO), is dedicated to advancing energy-related science. **Computers:** 100% of classrooms, 100% of dorms, 100% of libraries, 100% of dining areas, 100% of student union, 80% of common outdoor areas have wireless network access. Students can register for classes online. Administrative functions (other than registration) can be performed online.

CAMPUS LIFE

Environment: Metropolis. **Activities:** Choral groups, concert band, dance, drama/theater, jazz band, literary magazine, marching band, music ensembles, musical theater, pep band, radio station, student government, student newspaper, symphony orchestra, yearbook, Campus Ministries, Student Organization. 148 registered organizations, 9 honor societies, 7 religious organizations. 7 fraternities, 3 sororities. **Athletics (Intercollegiate):** *Men:* baseball, basketball, cross-country, diving, football, golf, soccer, swimming, track/field (outdoor), track/field (indoor), wrestling. *Women:* basketball, cross-country, diving, soccer, softball, swimming, track/field (outdoor), track/field (indoor), volleyball. **On-Campus Highlights:** Student Recreation Center, Outdoor Recreation Center, Geology Museum, National Earthquake Center, Computer Commons at the CTLM.

ADMISSIONS

Freshman Academic Profile: Average high school GPA 3.8. 56% in top 10% of high school class, 90% in top 25% of high school class, 99% in top

50% of high school class. 81% from public high schools. **Reported SAT (pre-2016 redesign) scores:** SAT Math middle 50% range 650-730. SAT Critical Reading middle 50% range 600-690. SAT Writing middle 50% range 560-650. **Concordant SAT scores:** SAT EBRW middle 50% 640–710. SAT Math middle 50% range 670–760. ACT middle 50% range 29-32. Minimum internet-based TOEFL 79. Minimum paper TOEFL 550. **Basis for Candidate Selection:** *Very important factors considered include:* rigor of secondary school record, class rank, academic GPA, standardized test scores. *Other factors considered include:* application essay, recommendation(s), interview, extracurricular activities, talent/ability, character/personal qualities, alumni/ae relation, geographical residence, state residency, level of applicant's interest. **Freshman Admission Requirements:** High school diploma is required and GED is accepted. *Academic units required:* 4 English, 4 math, 3 science, 3 science labs, 1 foreign language, 3 social studies, 2 academic electives. **Freshman Admission Statistics:** 12,284 applied, 40.35% admitted, 20% enrolled. **Transfer Admission Requirements:** High school transcript, college transcript(s), statement of good standing from prior institution(s). Minimum college GPA of 2.75 required. Lowest grade transferable C. **General Admission Information:** Application fee $45. Priority deadline 4/1. Regular application deadline 5/1. Nonfall registration accepted. Admission may be deferred for a maximum of 12 months.

COSTS AND FINANCIAL AID

Annual in-state tuition $15,690. Annual out-of-state tuition $34,020. Room and board $11,477. Required fees $2,152. Average book expense $1,500. **Required Forms and Deadlines:** FAFSA. **Notification of Awards:** Applicants will be notified of awards on a rolling basis beginning 3/15. **Types of Aid:** *Need-based scholarships/grants:* Federal Pell, FSEOG, State scholarships/grants, Private scholarships, College/university scholarship or grant aid from institutional funds. *Loans:* Direct Subsidized Stafford Loans, Direct Unsubsidized Stafford Loans, Direct PLUS loans, Federal Perkins Loans, College/university loans from institutional funds. *Student Employment:* Federal Work-Study Program available. Institutional employment available. **Financial Aid Statistics:** 52% needy freshmen, 56% needy undergrads receive need-based scholarship or grant aid. 87% freshmen, 67% undergrads receive non-need-based scholarship or grant aid. 86% freshmen, 91% undergrads receive need-based self-help aid. 2% freshmen, 8% undergrads receive athletic scholarships. 89% freshmen, 80% undergrads receive any aid. 58% undergrads borrow to pay for school. Average cumulative indebtedness $32,901. **Criteria for awarding aid:** *Need-based:* Academics, Alumni affiliation. *Non-need-based:* Academics, Alumni affiliation, Athletics, Music/drama.

COLORADO STATE UNIVERSITY

1062 Campus Delivery, Fort Collins, CO 80523-1062
Phone: 970-491-6909 • **Financial Aid Phone:** 970-491-6321
E-mail: admissions@colostate.edu • **CEEB Code:** 4075
Fax: 970-491-7799 • **Website:** www.colostate.edu/ • **ACT Code:** 504

This public school was founded in 1870. It has a 582-acre campus.

RATINGS

Admissions Selectivity Rating: 83   **Fire Safety Rating:** 89   **Green Rating:** 99

STUDENTS AND FACULTY

Enrollment: 23,768. **Student Body:** 51% female, 49% male, 23% out-of-state, 4% international (66 countries represented). Asian 3%, African American 2%, Caucasian 72%, Hispanic 12%, Native American <1%, Pacific Islander <1%, Two or more races 3%, Race unknown 3%.
Retention and Graduation: 86% freshmen return for sophomore year. 42% freshmen graduate within 4 years. 67% freshmen graduate within 6 years. 24% grads go on to further study within 1 year. **Faculty:** Student/faculty ratio 18:1. 1,026 full-time faculty, 100% hold PhDs, 18% are are members of minority groups, 37% are women. 8% of classes are taught by teaching assistants.

ACADEMICS

Degrees: bachelor's, doctoral/professional, doctoral/research, doctoral, master's, postbachelor's certificate. **Classes:** Most classes have 10-19 students. Most lab/discussion sessions have 20-29 students. **Most popular majors:** Human Development and Family Studies; Human Development and Family Studies; Speech Communication and Rhetoric. **Special Study Options:** Accelerated program, cooperative education program, cross-registration, distance learning, double major, dual enrollment, English as a Second Language

(ESL), exchange student program (domestic), honors program, independent study, internships, liberal arts/career combination, study abroad, teacher certification program. **Honors Programs:** University Honors Program. Combined degree programs: MS/DVM. MBA/DVM, PhD/DVM, MS of Public Health/DVM, BS/MS, DVM/MST, MSW/MPH. **Disability Services:** Special programs offered to physically disabled students, including note-taking services, reader services, tape recorders, tutors. **Career Services:** Alumni network, Alumni services, Career/job search classes, Career assessment, Internships, Regional alumni. Career Communities are fifteen career-interest area communities that provide an exclusive opportunity for students, employers, alumni and faculty/staff to connect both online and in-person about common job interests.

FACILITIES

Housing: Coed dorms, special housing for disabled students, apartments for married students, apartments for single students, Wellness Housing, Theme Housing, Non college-owned fraternity/sorority housing. is available. Also available are Living-Learning Communities, and special interest floors. 98% of campus accessible to physically diasbled. **Special Academic Facilities/ Equipment:** International Poster collection, Gustafson Gallery–historic clothing, Curfman Gallery– Art, Student Recreation Center, Ropes Course, University Center for the Arts (performance hall, thrust theater, art museum), Avenir Museum of Design and Merchandising (Costumes, Textiles, Interior Artifacts). **Computers:** 100% of classrooms, 100% of dorms, 100% of libraries, 100% of dining areas, 100% of student union, 60% of common outdoor areas have wireless network access. Students can register for classes online. Administrative functions (other than registration) can be performed online.

CAMPUS LIFE

Environment: City. **Activities:** Choral groups, concert band, dance, drama/ theater, jazz band, literary magazine, marching band, music ensembles, musical theater, opera, pep band, radio station, student government, student newspaper, symphony orchestra, television station, Campus Ministries, Student Organization. 350 registered organizations, 35 honor societies, 28 religious organizations. 21 fraternities, 14 sororities. **Athletics (Intercollegiate):** *Men:* basketball, cross-country, football, golf, track/field (outdoor), track/field (indoor). *Women:* basketball, cross-country, diving, golf, softball, swimming, tennis, track/field (outdoor), track/field (indoor), volleyball, water polo.
On-Campus Highlights: Lory Student Center, Student Recreation Center, Library, University Center For the Arts, Moby Arena, The University Center for the Arts is complete, featuring the newly-constructed University Art Museum. Also housed at the UCA is the Griffin Concert Hall, Bohemian Complex with 317 seat thrust theatre, Casavant Organ Recital Hall, and other world-class student resources. **Environmental Initiatives:** Several renewable energy sources went live in the year 2010 including: a second phase of a large solar array that now totals 5,300 kilowatts on the Foothills Campus, an 18.9 kW solar array on the roof of the Engineering building, and a 12.6 kW solar array at the Academic Village residence hall, 133 kW solar array on the roof of the Lake Street Parking Garage, a 15.8 kW on the Behavioral Sciences Building and a 54 kW solar array at the Research Innovation Center. The five smaller arrays are owned and operated by the University, the larger array is owned by a third party and Colorado State serves as a site host and purchases the power produced by the panels. In addition to solar power, CSU Foothills Campus is also home to a biomass heating plant on the Foothills Campus. This plant burns wood chips to produce hot water for building heat and displaces natural gas use.

ADMISSIONS

Freshman Academic Profile: Average high school GPA 3.6. 21% in top 10% of high school class, 48% in top 25% of high school class, 83% in top 50% of high school class. **Reported SAT (pre-2016 redesign) scores:** SAT Math middle 50% range 510-630. SAT Critical Reading middle 50% range 510-620. **Concordant SAT scores:** SAT Math middle 50% range 540–650. ACT middle 50% range 23-28. Minimum internet-based TOEFL 79. Minimum paper TOEFL 550. **Basis for Candidate Selection:** *Very important factors considered include:* rigor of secondary school record, academic GPA. *Important factors considered include:* class rank, standardized test scores, application essay, recommendation(s). *Other factors considered include:* extracurricular activities, talent/ability, character/personal qualities, first generation, alumni/ae relation, geographical residence, volunteer work, work experience. **Freshman Admission Requirements:** High school diploma is required and GED is accepted. *Academic units required:* 4 English, 4 math, 3 science, 2 science labs, 1 foreign language, 2 social studies, 1 history, 2 academic electives. *Academic units recommended:* 4 English, 4 math, 3 science, 2 science labs, 2 foreign language, 2 social studies, 1 history, 2 academic electives. **Freshman Admission Statistics:** 21,759 applied, 77.96% admitted, 29% enrolled. **Transfer Admission Requirements:** college transcript(s), essay or personal statement, Minimum college GPA of 2.0 required. Lowest grade transferable C-. **General Admission Information:** Application fee $50. Regular application deadline 2/1. Nonfall registration accepted. Admission may be deferred for a maximum of 1 year.

COSTS AND FINANCIAL AID

Annual in-state tuition $8,716. Annual out-of-state tuition $26,010. Room and board $11,110. Required fees $2,336. Average book expense $1,200. **Required Forms and Deadlines:** FAFSA, CSS/Financial Aid PROFILE, Noncustodial PROFILE. **Notification of Awards:** Applicants will be notified of awards on a rolling basis beginning 3/1. **Types of Aid:** *Need-based scholarships/ grants:* Federal Pell, FSEOG, State scholarships/grants, Private scholarships, College/university scholarship or grant aid from institutional funds. *Loans:* Direct Subsidized Stafford Loans, Direct Unsubsidized Stafford Loans, Direct PLUS loans, Federal Perkins Loans. *Student Employment:* Federal Work-Study Program available. Institutional employment available. **Financial Aid Statistics:** 75% needy freshmen, 68% needy undergrads receive need-based scholarship or grant aid. 28% freshmen, 12% undergrads receive non-need-based scholarship or grant aid. 76% freshmen, 80% undergrads receive need-based self-help aid. 0% freshmen, 1% undergrads receive athletic scholarships. 76% freshmen, 67% undergrads receive any aid. 54% undergrads borrow to pay for school. Average cumulative indebtedness $25,155. **Criteria for awarding aid:** *Need-based:* Academics. *Non-need-based:* Academics, Alumni affiliation, Art, Athletics, Leadership, Music/drama, State/district residency.

COLORADO STATE UNIVERSITY—PUEBLO

Admissions, Pueblo, CO 81001
Phone: 719-549-2461 • **Financial Aid Phone:** 719-549-2178
E-mail: info@colostate-pueblo.edu • **CEEB Code:** 4611
Fax: 719-549-2419 • **Website:** www.colostate-pueblo.edu • **ACT Code:** 524

This public school was founded in 1933. It has a 275-acre campus.

RATINGS

Admissions Selectivity Rating: 71   **Fire Safety Rating:** 79   **Green Rating:** 60*

STUDENTS AND FACULTY

Enrollment: 3,947. **Student Body:** 57% female, 43% male, 7% out-of-state, 2% international (27 countries represented). Asian 3%, African American 6%, Caucasian 55%, Hispanic 25%, Native American 2%, Pacific Islander 0%, Two or more races 0%, Race unknown 6%.
Retention and Graduation: 63% freshmen return for sophomore year. **Faculty:** Student/faculty ratio 17:1. 155 full-time faculty, 0% hold PhDs, 17% are are members of minority groups, 47% are women. 0% of classes are taught by teaching assistants.

ACADEMICS

Degrees: bachelor's, master's. **Classes:** Most classes have 10-19 students. Most lab/discussion sessions have 10-19 students. **Most popular majors:** Mass Communication/Media Studies; Liberal Arts and Sciences/Liberal Studies; Biology/Biological Sciences. **Special Study Options:** Accelerated program, cooperative education program, distance learning, double major, dual enrollment, English as a Second Language (ESL), external degree program, independent study, internships, liberal arts/career combination, study abroad, teacher certification program, weekend college. **Honors Programs:** We do not have an Honor Program, however, we offer several undergraduate honor courses. Combined degree programs: BSBA/MBA, BS/MS. **Disability Services:** Special programs offered to physically disabled students, including note-taking services, reader services, tape recorders, tutors.

FACILITIES

Housing: Coed dorms, special housing for disabled students, apartments for single students. 100% of campus accessible to physically diasbled. **Special Academic Facilities/Equipment:** Recital hall, public television and radio station. **Computers:** Students can register for classes online. Administrative functions (other than registration) can be performed online.

CAMPUS LIFE

Environment: City. **Activities:** Choral groups, concert band, dance, jazz band, literary magazine, music ensembles, pep band, student government, student newspaper, symphony orchestra, television station 24 registered organizations, 6 honor societies, 4 religious organizations. 2 fraternities, 1 sorority. **Athletics (Intercollegiate):** *Men:* baseball, basketball, golf, soccer, tennis. *Women:* basketball, cross-country, golf, soccer, softball, tennis, volleyball. **On-Campus Highlights:** University Library, Occhiato University Center—La Cantina, Occhiato University Center—The Underground, The Pavillion, The Wall.

ADMISSIONS

Freshman Academic Profile: Average high school GPA 3.1. 2% in top 10% of high school class, 8% in top 25% of high school class, 36% in top 50% of high school class. 85% from public high schools. **Reported SAT (pre-2016 redesign) scores:** SAT Math middle 50% range 420-550. SAT Critical Reading middle 50% range 420-530. **Concordant SAT scores:** SAT Math middle

50% range 460–570. ACT middle 50% range 18–22. Minimum paper TOEFL 500. **Basis for Candidate Selection:** *Very important factors considered include:* rigor of secondary school record, academic GPA, standardized test scores. *Important factors considered include:* class rank. *Other factors considered include:* application essay, recommendation(s), interview, talent/ ability, character/personal qualities, volunteer work, work experience, level of applicant's interest. **Freshman Admission Requirements:** High school diploma is required and GED is accepted. *Academic units required:* 4 English, 3 math, 3 science, 2 science labs, 2 foreign language, 2 social studies, 1 history. *Academic units recommended:* 4 English, 3 math, 3 science, 2 science labs, 2 foreign language, 2 social studies, 1 history. **Freshman Admission Statistics:** 1,698 applied, 96.11% admitted, 41% enrolled. **Transfer Admission Requirements:** college transcript(s), Minimum college GPA of 2.3 required. Lowest grade transferable C-. **General Admission Information:** Application fee $25. Regular application deadline 8/1. Nonfall registration accepted. Admission may be deferred for a maximum of 1 semester.

COSTS AND FINANCIAL AID

Annual in-state tuition $3,422. Annual out-of-state tuition $13,543. Room and board $6,300. Required fees $996. Average book expense $1,698. **Required Forms and Deadlines:** FAFSA, Institution's own financial aid form. **Notification of Awards:** Applicants will be notified of awards on a rolling basis beginning 3/15. **Types of Aid:** *Need-based scholarships/grants:* Federal Pell, FSEOG, State scholarships/grants, Private scholarships, College/university scholarship or grant aid from institutional funds. *Loans:* Federal Perkins Loans. *Student Employment:* Federal Work-Study Program available. Institutional employment available. **Financial Aid Statistics:** 81% needy freshmen, 80% needy undergrads receive need-based scholarship or grant aid. 7% freshmen, 4% undergrads receive non-need-based scholarship or grant aid. 78% freshmen, 87% undergrads receive need-based self-help aid. 3% freshmen, 4% undergrads receive athletic scholarships. 81% freshmen, 86% undergrads receive any aid. **Criteria for awarding aid:** *Need-based:* Academics, Alumni affiliation, Minority status. *Non-need-based:* Academics, Alumni affiliation, Art, Athletics, Leadership, Minority status, Music/drama, State/district residency.

COLORADO TECHNICAL UNIVERSITY

4435 North Chestnut Street, Colorado Springs, CO 80907-3740
Phone: 719-598-0200
E-mail: cosadmissions@coloradotech.edu
Website: http://www.coloradotech.edu/

This is a proprietary school.

RATINGS

Admissions Selectivity Rating: 60*   **Fire Safety Rating:** 60*   **Green Rating:** 60*

STUDENTS AND FACULTY

Enrollment: 1,261. **Student Body:** 1% international. Asian 4%, African American 8%, Caucasian 73%, Hispanic 6%, Native American <1%, Pacific Islander 0%, Two or more races 0%, Race unknown 9%.
Faculty: Student/faculty ratio 25:1. 31 full-time faculty, 52% hold PhDs, 13% are are members of minority groups, 35%

ACADEMICS

Degrees: associate, bachelor's, certificate, master's, transfer. **Classes:** Most classes have 10-19 students. **Special Study Options:** Accelerated program, double major, independent study, internships, weekend college, Sixteen and 1/2 month M.S. degree programs and 2-year doctoral programs.

CAMPUS LIFE

Activities: student government.

ADMISSIONS

Basis for Candidate Selection: *Other factors considered include:* rigor of secondary school record, class rank, standardized test scores, recommendation(s), interview, character/personal qualities, alumni/ae relation, work experience. **Freshman Admission Requirements:** *Academic units required:* 1 English, 1 math, 1 science, 1 science lab. *Academic units recommended:* 2 English, 2 math, 2 science, 1 science lab. **Transfer Admission Requirements:** college transcript(s), statement of good standing from prior institution(s). Lowest grade transferable C. **General Admission Information:** Application fee $50. Regular application deadline 10/2. Nonfall registration accepted.

COSTS AND FINANCIAL AID

Required fees $171. Average book expense $1,000. **Required Forms and Deadlines:** FAFSA, Institution's own financial aid form, State aid form. **Notification of Awards:** Applicants will be notified of awards on a rolling basis beginning 2/1. **Types of Aid:** *Loans:* Federal Perkins Loans. *Student Employment:* Federal Work-Study Program available. Institutional employment available.

COLUMBIA COLLEGE CHICAGO (IL)

600 South Michigan Avenue, Chicago, IL 60605-1996
Phone: 1-312-369-7130 • **Financial Aid Phone:** 312-369-7831
E-mail: admissions@colum.edu • **CEEB Code:** 1135
Fax: 312-369-8024 • **Website:** www.colum.edu • **ACT Code:** 1002

This private school was founded in 1890.

RATINGS
Admissions Selectivity Rating: 77   **Fire Safety Rating:** 81   **Green Rating:** 60*

STUDENTS AND FACULTY
Enrollment: 8,929. **Student Body:** 56% female, 44% male, 40% out-of-state, 3% international (48 countries represented). Asian 3%, African American 16%, Caucasian 57%, Hispanic 10%, Native American <1%, Pacific Islander <1%, Two or more races 5%, Race unknown 6%.
Retention and Graduation: 71% freshmen return for sophomore year. 30% freshmen graduate within 4 years. 9% grads go on to further study within 1 year. 10% grads pursue arts and sciences degrees. **Faculty:** Student/faculty ratio 11:1. 374 full-time faculty, 51% hold PhDs, 17% are are members of minority groups, 47% are women. 0% of classes are taught by teaching assistants.

ACADEMICS
Degrees: bachelor's, master's. **Classes:** Most classes have 10-19 students. **Most popular majors:** Cinematography and Film/Video Production; Drama and Dramatics/Theatre Arts; Photography. **Special Study Options:** cross-registration, exchange student program (domestic), honors program, independent study, internships, student-designed major, study abroad, teacher certification program. **Disability Services:** Special programs offered to physically disabled students, including note-taking services, reader services, tape recorders, tutors. **Career Services:** Alumni network, Alumni services, Internships.

FACILITIES
Housing: Coed dorms, apartments for single students. 90% of campus accessible to physically diasbled. **Special Academic Facilities/Equipment:** Art galleries, center for black music research, contemporary photography museum, dance center. **Computers:** Students can register for classes online. Administrative functions (other than registration) can be performed online.

CAMPUS LIFE
Environment: Metropolis. **Activities:** Choral groups, concert band, dance, drama/theater, jazz band, literary magazine, music ensembles, musical theater, opera, radio station, student government, student newspaper, student-run film society, television station, Campus Ministries, Student Organization. 64 registered organizations. **On-Campus Highlights:** Museum of Contemporary Photography, Center for Black Music Research, Hokin Annex and Gallery **Environmental Initiatives:** Campus-wide recycling of paper, plastic, glass, techno.

ADMISSIONS
Freshman Academic Profile: Average high school GPA 3.3. 8% in top 10% of high school class, 29% in top 25% of high school class, 63% in top 50% of high school class. **Reported SAT (pre-2016 redesign) scores:** SAT Math middle 50% range 440-570. SAT Critical Reading middle 50% range 485-605. SAT Writing middle 50% range 470-590. **Concordant SAT scores:** SAT EBRW middle 50% 540–650. SAT Math middle 50% range 480–590. ACT middle 50% range 19-25. Minimum internet-based TOEFL 80. Minimum paper TOEFL 533. **Basis for Candidate Selection:** *Very important factors considered include:* application essay. *Important factors considered include:* academic GPA, recommendation(s), character/personal qualities, level of applicant's interest. *Other factors considered include:* rigor of secondary school record, class rank, standardized test scores, extracurricular activities, talent/ability, volunteer work, work experience. **Freshman Admission Requirements:** High school diploma is required and GED is accepted. **Freshman Admission Statistics:** 8,953 applied, 82.32% admitted, 25% enrolled. **Transfer Admission Requirements:** High school transcript, college transcript(s), essay or personal statement, Lowest grade transferable C. **General Admission Information:** Application fee $35. Priority deadline 5/1. Nonfall registration accepted. Admission may be deferred for a maximum of 1 year.

COSTS AND FINANCIAL AID
Annual tuition $22,884. Room and board $12,450. Required fees $660. Average book expense $1,708. **Required Forms and Deadlines:** FAFSA, Institution's own financial aid form. **Types of Aid:** *Need-based scholarships/grants:* Federal Pell, FSEOG, State scholarships/grants, Private scholarships, College/university scholarship or grant aid from institutional funds. *Loans:* Direct Subsidized Stafford Loans, Direct Unsubsidized Stafford Loans, Direct PLUS loans. *Student Employment:* Federal Work-Study Program available. Institutional employment available. **Financial Aid Statistics:** 90% needy freshmen, 82% needy undergrads receive need-based scholarship or grant aid. 0% undergrads receive non-need-based scholarship or grant aid. 0% freshmen, 1% undergrads receive need-based self-help aid. 0% freshmen, 0% undergrads receive athletic scholarships. 73% freshmen, 71% undergrads receive any aid. **Criteria for awarding aid:** *Need-based:* Academics, Art, Leadership, Music/drama. *Non-need-based:* Academics, Art, Leadership, Music/drama, State/district residency.

COLUMBIA COLLEGE (MO)

1001 Rogers St., Columbia, MO 65211
Phone: 573-875-7352 • **Financial Aid Phone:** 573-875-7390
E-mail: admissions@ccis.edu • **CEEB Code:** 6095
Fax: 573-875-7506 • **Website:** http://www.ccis.edu • **ACT Code:** 2276

This private school, affiliated with the Disciples of Christ Church, was founded in 1851. It has a 33-acre campus.

RATINGS
Admissions Selectivity Rating: 85   **Fire Safety Rating:** 90   **Green Rating:** 69

STUDENTS AND FACULTY
Enrollment: 896. **Student Body:** 59% female, 41% male, 12% out-of-state, 9% international (36 countries represented). Asian 1%, African American 3%, Caucasian 76%, Hispanic 2%, Native American 1%, Pacific Islander 0%, Two or more races 5%, Race unknown 3%.
Retention and Graduation: 73% freshmen return for sophomore year. 41% freshmen graduate within 4 years. 52% freshmen graduate within 6 years. 21% grads go on to further study within 1 year. 2% grads pursue arts and sciences degrees. 26% grads pursue law degrees. 2% grads pursue business degrees. 2% grads pursue medical degrees. **Faculty:** Student/faculty ratio 12:1. 68 full-time faculty, 81% hold PhDs, 9% are are members of minority groups, 47% are women. 0% of classes are taught by teaching assistants.

ACADEMICS
Degrees: associate, bachelor's, certificate, master's. **Classes:** Most classes have 10-19 students. Most lab/discussion sessions have 10-19 students. **Most popular majors:** Business Administration and Management; Psychology; Criminal Justice/Law Enforcement Administration. **Special Study Options:** cross-registration, distance learning, double major, dual enrollment, English as a Second Language (ESL), honors program, independent study, internships, student-designed major, study abroad, teacher certification program. **Honors Programs:** The Honors Program is designed for high achieving students who are philosophers in the literal sense, i.e., lovers of wisdom. The goal of the program is to promote genuine inquiry and collaborative learning, emphasizing the dialogic nature of academic work and intellectual discovery. Combined degree programs: MAT/DAYSTAR. **Disability Services:** Special programs offered to physically disabled students, including note-taking services, tutors. **Career Services:** Alumni network, Alumni services, Career/job search classes, Career assessment, Internships, Regional alumni. All of our Career Services that are offered to our regular students are offered to Alumni and they are FREE.

FACILITIES
Housing: Coed dorms, special housing for disabled students, special housing for international students, women's dorms, apartments for single students, Wellness Housing. 100% of campus accessible to physically diasbled. **Special Academic Facilities/Equipment:** Most classrooms are multimedia with SmartBoards, new student commons building, arts center, Larson Gallery, Jane Froman Archive **Computers:** 100% of classrooms, 100% of dorms, 100% of libraries, 100% of dining areas, 100% of student union, have wireless network access. Students can register for classes online. Administrative functions (other than registration) can be performed online.

CAMPUS LIFE
Environment: City. **Activities:** Choral groups, dance, drama/theater, literary magazine, music ensembles, musical theater, student government, student newspaper, Campus Ministries, Student Organization, Model UN. 42 registered organizations, 16 honor societies, 2 religious organizations. **Athletics (Intercollegiate):** *Men:* basketball, soccer. *Women:* basketball, softball, volleyball. **On-Campus Highlights:** Larson Art Gallery, The newly expanded Southwell Athletic Complex, New Atkins-Holman Student Commons building, Stafford Library **Environmental Initiatives:** 77% of campus building square footage is on highly efficient ground source water heat pump system.

ADMISSIONS

Freshman Academic Profile: Average high school GPA 3.5. 52% in top 10% of high school class, 19% in top 25% of high school class, 71% in top 50% of high school class. **Reported SAT (pre-2016 redesign) scores:** SAT Math middle 50% range 490-585. SAT Critical Reading middle 50% range 445-595. **Concordant SAT scores:** SAT Math middle 50% range 520–610. ACT middle 50% range 21-26. Minimum internet-based TOEFL 61. Minimum paper TOEFL 500. **Basis for Candidate Selection:** *Very important factors considered include:* class rank, academic GPA, standardized test scores. *Other factors considered include:* rigor of secondary school record, application essay, recommendation(s), interview. **Freshman Admission Requirements:** High school diploma is required and GED is accepted. *Academic units recommended:* 4 English. **Freshman Admission Statistics:** 1,580 applied, 50.70% admitted, 25% enrolled. **Transfer Admission Requirements:** college transcript(s), statement of good standing from prior institution(s). Minimum college GPA of 2.0 required. Lowest grade transferable 2. **General Admission Information:** Application fee $35. Nonfall registration accepted. Admission may be deferred for a maximum of 1 year.

COSTS AND FINANCIAL AID

Required Forms and Deadlines: FAFSA. **Notification of Awards:** Applicants will be notified of awards on a rolling basis beginning 5/1. **Types of Aid:** *Need-based scholarships/grants:* Federal Pell, FSEOG, State scholarships/grants, Private scholarships, College/university scholarship or grant aid from institutional funds. *Loans:* Direct Subsidized Stafford Loans, Direct Unsubsidized Stafford Loans, Direct PLUS loans. *Student Employment:* Federal Work-Study Program available. Institutional employment available. **Financial Aid Statistics:** 73% needy freshmen, 74% needy undergrads receive need-based scholarship or grant aid. 100% freshmen, 85% undergrads receive non-need-based scholarship or grant aid. 72% freshmen, 71% undergrads receive need-based self-help aid. 24% freshmen, 20% undergrads receive athletic scholarships. 62% freshmen, 56% undergrads receive any aid. Average cumulative indebtedness $21,934. **Criteria for awarding aid:** *Need-based:* Academics, Art. *Non-need-based:* Academics, Alumni affiliation, Art, Athletics, Job skills, Leadership, Minority status, Music/drama, Religious affiliation, State/district residency.

COLUMBIA COLLEGE (SC)

1301 Columbia College Drive, Columbia, SC 29203
Phone: 803-786-3871 • **Financial Aid Phone:** 803-786-3612
E-mail: admissions@columbiasc.edu • **CEEB Code:** 5117
Fax: 803-786-3674 • **Website:** www.columbiacollegesc.edu • **ACT Code:** 3850

This private school, affiliated with the Methodist Church, was founded in 1854. It has a 33-acre campus.

RATINGS

Admissions Selectivity Rating: 77   **Fire Safety Rating:** 86   **Green Rating:** 60*

STUDENTS AND FACULTY

Student Body: 78% female, 22% male, 7% out-of-state, (14 countries represented).
Retention and Graduation: 62% freshmen return for sophomore year. 48% freshmen graduate within 6 years. **Faculty:** Student/faculty ratio 3:1. 79 full-time faculty, 77% hold PhDs, 18% are are members of minority groups, 68% are women. 0% of classes are taught by teaching assistants.

ACADEMICS

Degrees: bachelor's, master's, postbachelor's certificate. **Classes:** Most classes have 10-19 students. **Most popular majors:** Business Administration and Management; Human Development, Family Studies, and Related Services; Elementary Education and Teaching. **Special Study Options:** distance learning, double major, dual enrollment, honors program, independent study, internships, student-designed major, study abroad, teacher certification program. **Honors Programs:** The Columbia College Honors Program provides enriched academic and co-curricular experiences for outstanding, motivated students committed to excellence. Offering a variety of opportunities for superior, engaged learning both within and outside the classroom, honors challenges students to reach their highest potential as scholars, individual thinkers, and leaders by emphasizing rigorous intellectual standards, risk, creativity, integrity, and dedication to service and leadership. The program is deeply active in the National Collegiate Honors Council and its regional association, regularly sponsoring numerous faculty and students at annual conferences and in executive leadership positions; honors has also earned special recognition through national and regional awards for honors faculty and students. To complete honors, students take 24 semester hours across disciplines in honors courses, including the 3 hour interdisciplinary senior

seminar and the 3—4 hour mentored independent project. Students must maintain at least a 3.4 cumulative GPA to remain in honors. **Career Services:** Career/job search classes, Career assessment, Internships.

FACILITIES

Housing: women's dorms, Special programs: Leadership; Honors Program. 75% of campus accessible to physically disabled. **Special Academic Facilities/Equipment:** Language lab, Alumnae Hall, Barbara Bush Center for Science and Technology, Breed Leadership Center for Women. **Computers:** 50% of libraries, 100% of dining areas, 100% of student union, 30% of common outdoor areas have wireless network access. Students can register for classes online. Administrative functions (other than registration) can be performed online.

CAMPUS LIFE

Environment: Metropolis. **Activities:** Choral groups, concert band, dance, drama/theater, literary magazine, music ensembles, musical theater, opera, student government, student newspaper, yearbook, Campus Ministries, Student Organization. 53 registered organizations, 10 honor societies, 7 religious organizations. **Athletics (Intercollegiate):** *Women:* basketball, soccer, softball, tennis, volleyball. **On-Campus Highlights:** Leadership Center, Terrace Cafe, Student Union, Cottingham Performance Theatre, Bush Science Center. **Environmental Initiatives:** Student-sponsored and initiated recycling program.

ADMISSIONS

Freshman Academic Profile: Average high school GPA 3.7. 15% in top 10% of high school class, 47% in top 25% of high school class, 78% in top 50% of high school class. **Reported SAT (pre-2016 redesign) scores:** SAT Math middle 50% range 410-520. SAT Critical Reading middle 50% range 430-550. SAT Writing middle 50% range 410-530. **Concordant SAT scores:** SAT EBRW middle 50% 470–600. SAT Math middle 50% range 450–550. ACT middle 50% range 18-24. Minimum paper TOEFL 550. **Basis for Candidate Selection:** *Very important factors considered include:* rigor of secondary school record, standardized test scores, recommendation(s). *Important factors considered include:* class rank, character/personal qualities. *Other factors considered include:* application essay, extracurricular activities, talent/ability, alumni/ae relation, volunteer work. **Freshman Admission Requirements:** High school diploma is required and GED is accepted. *Academic units recommended:* 4 English, 3 math, 2 science, 2 science labs, 2 foreign language, 2 social studies, 1 history, 2 academic electives. **Freshman Admission Statistics:** 506 applied, 88.93% admitted, 41% enrolled. **Transfer Admission Requirements:** High school transcript, college transcript(s), standardized test scores, statement of good standing from prior institution(s). Minimum college GPA of 2.0 required. Lowest grade transferable C. **General Admission Information:** Application fee $25. Regular application deadline 8/1. Nonfall registration accepted. Admission may be deferred for a maximum of 1 year.

COSTS AND FINANCIAL AID

Annual tuition $28,100. Room and board $7,400. Average book expense $850. **Required Forms and Deadlines:** FAFSA. **Notification of Awards:** Applicants will be notified of awards on a rolling basis beginning 3/1. **Types of Aid:** *Need-based scholarships/grants:* Federal Pell, FSEOG, State scholarships/grants, Private scholarships, College/university scholarship or grant aid from institutional funds, United Negro College Fund. *Loans:* Federal Perkins Loans, State Loans. *Student Employment:* Federal Work-Study Program available. Institutional employment available. **Financial Aid Statistics:** 82% needy freshmen, 94% needy undergrads receive need-based scholarship or grant aid. 18% freshmen, 15% undergrads receive non-need-based scholarship or grant aid. 76% freshmen, 78% undergrads receive need-based self-help aid. 6% freshmen, 5% undergrads receive athletic scholarships. 99% freshmen, 92% undergrads receive any aid. 90% undergrads borrow to pay for school. Average cumulative indebtedness $29,407. **Criteria for awarding aid:** *Need-based:* Academics, Alumni affiliation, Religious affiliation. *Non-need-based:* Academics, Alumni affiliation, Art, Athletics, Leadership, Music/drama.

COLUMBIA INTERNATIONAL UNIVERSITY

PO Box 3122, Columbia, SC 29230-3122
Phone: 803-754-4100
E-mail: yesciu@ciu.edu
Fax: 803-786-4041 • **Website:** www.ciu.edu • **ACT Code:** 5016

This private school was founded in 1923. It has a 400-acre campus.

RATINGS

Admissions Selectivity Rating: 80   **Fire Safety Rating:** 60*   **Green Rating:** 60*

STUDENTS AND FACULTY

Enrollment: 580. **Student Body:** 54% female, 46% male, 56% out-of-state, 0% international. Asian 0%, African American 0%, Caucasian 0%, Hispanic 0%, Native American 0%, Pacific Islander 0%, Two or more races 0%, Race unknown 0%. **Retention and Graduation:** 77% freshmen return for sophomore year. 35% freshmen graduate within 4 years. **Faculty:** Student/faculty ratio 19:1. 19 full-time faculty, 58% hold PhDs, 11% are are members of minority groups, 21% are women.

ACADEMICS

Degrees: associate, bachelor's, certificate, doctoral/professional, doctoral, master's, postbachelor's certificate, terminal, transfer. **Special Study Options:** cross-registration, distance learning, double major, dual enrollment, English as a Second Language (ESL), independent study, internships, liberal arts/career combination, study abroad, Cooperative studies with Midlands Technical College. **Disability Services:** Special programs offered to physically disabled students, including note-taking services, reader services, tape recorders, tutors. **Career Services:** Alumni services, On-campus interviews.

FACILITIES

Housing: men's dorms, women's dorms, apartments for single students, mobile home park for married students.

CAMPUS LIFE

Environment: Village. **Activities:** Choral groups, concert band, drama/theater, music ensembles, student government, symphony orchestra, yearbook. 4 religious organizations.

ADMISSIONS

Freshman Academic Profile: Average high school GPA 3.9. 27% in top 10% of high school class, 47% in top 25% of high school class, 75% in top 50% of high school class. **Reported SAT (pre-2016 redesign) scores:** SAT Math middle 50% range 490-580. SAT Critical Reading middle 50% range 530-630. SAT Writing middle 50% range 490-600. **Concordant SAT scores:** SAT EBRW middle 50% 570–670. SAT Math middle 50% range 520–600. ACT middle 50% range 20-26. Minimum paper TOEFL 525. **Basis for Candidate Selection:** *Very important factors considered include:* academic GPA, standardized test scores, application essay, recommendation(s), character/personal qualities, religious affiliation/commitment. *Important factors considered include:* class rank, extracurricular activities, volunteer work, level of applicant's interest. *Other factors considered include:* rigor of secondary school record, interview, talent/ability, alumni/ae relation, work experience. **Freshman Admission Requirements:** High school diploma is required and GED is accepted. *Academic units recommended:* 4 English, 2 math, 1 science, 2 foreign language, 2 history. **Freshman Admission Statistics:** 163 applied, 98.77% admitted, 52% enrolled. **Transfer Admission Requirements:** college transcript(s), essay or personal statement, statement of good standing from prior institution(s). Minimum college GPA of 2.0 required. Lowest grade transferable C. **General Admission Information:** Application fee $45. Priority deadline 2/28. Regular application deadline 8/1. Nonfall registration accepted. Admission may be deferred for a maximum of 1 year.

COSTS AND FINANCIAL AID

Annual tuition $8,980. Room and board $4,520. Required fees $160. Average book expense $800. **Required Forms and Deadlines:** FAFSA. **Types of Aid:** *Need-based scholarships/grants:* Federal Pell, FSEOG, State scholarships/grants, Private scholarships, College/university scholarship or grant aid from institutional funds. *Loans:* College/university loans from institutional funds. *Student Employment:* Federal Work-Study Program available. **Financial Aid Statistics:** 75% needy freshmen, 78% needy undergrads receive need-based scholarship or grant aid. 0% freshmen, 0% undergrads receive athletic scholarships. **Criteria for awarding aid:** *Need-based:* Academics, Leadership, Minority status, Music/drama.

COLUMBIA UNIVERSITY—COLUMBIA COLLEGE AND FU FOUNDATION SCHOOL OF ENGINEERING

212 Hamilton Hall MC 2807, New York, NY 10027
Phone: 212-854-2522
E-mail: ugrad-ask@columbia.edu • **CEEB Code:** 2116
Fax: 212-894-1209 • **Website:** www.columbia.edu • **ACT Code:** 2717

This private school was founded in 1754. It has a 36-acre campus.

RATINGS

| Admissions Selectivity Rating: 99 | Fire Safety Rating: 85 | Green Rating: 95 |

STUDENTS AND FACULTY

Enrollment: 6,158. **Student Body:** 48% female, 52% male, 77% out-of-state, 15% international (87 countries represented). Asian 23%, African American 11%, Caucasian 34%, Hispanic 12%, Native American 2%, Pacific Islander 0%, Two or more races 0%, Race unknown 3%. **Retention and Graduation:** 99% freshmen return for sophomore year. 96% freshmen graduate within 6 years. **Faculty:** Student/faculty ratio 6:1. 1,446 full-time faculty, 0% hold PhDs, 24% are are members of minority groups, 34% are women. 0% of classes are taught by teaching assistants.

ACADEMICS

Degrees: bachelor's, doctoral, master's. **Classes:** Most classes have 10-19 students. **Most popular majors:** Political Science and Government; English Language and Literature; Engineering. **Special Study Options:** Accelerated program, cooperative education program, cross-registration, double major, dual enrollment, English as a Second Language (ESL), exchange student program (domestic), independent study, internships, liberal arts/career combination, student-designed major, study abroad, teacher certification program, Combined 3-2 program. Combined degree programs: BA/JD, BA/MIA and BA/MPA (programs with SIPA). **Disability Services:** Special programs offered to physically disabled students, including note-taking services, reader services, tape recorders, tutors. **Career Services:** Alumni network, Alumni services, Career/job search classes, Career assessment, Internships.

FACILITIES

Housing: Coed dorms, special housing for disabled students, fraternity/sorority housing, Special Interest **Housing:** Single-Sex First-Year Floor available. 95% of campus accessible to physically diasbled. **Special Academic Facilities/Equipment:** Art and Architecture Galleries; Theatres, Cinema, Observatory **Computers:** Students can register for classes online. Administrative functions (other than registration) can be performed online.

CAMPUS LIFE

Environment: Metropolis. **Activities:** Choral groups, concert band, dance, drama/theater, jazz band, literary magazine, marching band, music ensembles, musical theater, opera, pep band, radio station, student government, student newspaper, student-run film society, symphony orchestra, television station, yearbook, Campus Ministries, Student Organization, Model UN. 300 registered organizations, 17 religious organizations. 17 fraternities, 11 sororities. **Athletics (Intercollegiate):** *Men:* baseball, basketball, crew/rowing, cross-country, diving, fencing, football, golf, soccer, swimming, tennis, track/field (outdoor), track/field (indoor), wrestling. *Women:* archery, basketball, crew/rowing, cross-country, diving, fencing, field hockey, golf, lacrosse, soccer, softball, swimming, tennis, track/field (outdoor), track/field (indoor), volleyball. **On-Campus Highlights:** Low Library and Plaza, Butler Library, Postcrypt Coffee House, Ferris Booth Commons, Levian Gym, www.studentaffairs.columbia.edu/admissions/virtualvisit/. **Environmental Initiatives:** Greenhouse gas reduction program targeted to meet a 30% reduction by 2017 and clean heat initiative to improve air quality and asthma rates by phasing out the use of heavy heating oils to cleaner fuels like natural gas and low-sulfur #2 oil. Columbia has also converted its entire 14 car public safety fleet to hybrid vehicles. As part of our energy efficiency initiatives, 45% of all food purchased is local and/ororganic. All honey and apples are purchased through vendors at the on-campus green market from NY farmers. Annually Dining Services contracts with a local NY farmer and canner to make all the salsa and strawberry jam for the year. In addition all milk is local and hormone free. Liquid eggs are certified humane. All coffee is roasted locally and is fair-trade, organic, shade grown and bird friendly. Tomatoes are also fair trade. All bakery items and grab and go sandwiches are purchased from local vendors. 50% of daily meals served in the dining halls are vegetarian and Meatless Mondays are run every Monday.

ADMISSIONS

Freshman Academic Profile: 56% from public high schools. **Reported SAT (pre-2016 redesign) scores:** SAT Math middle 50% range 720-800. SAT Critical Reading middle 50% range 710-800. SAT Writing middle 50% range 710-790. **Concordant SAT scores:** SAT EBRW middle 50% 740–800. SAT Math middle 50% range 750–800. ACT middle 50% range 32-35. Minimum paper TOEFL 600. **Basis for Candidate Selection:** *Very important factors considered include:* rigor of secondary school record, class rank, academic GPA, standardized test scores, application essay, recommendation(s), character/personal qualities. *Important factors considered include:* extracurricular activities, talent/ability. *Other factors considered include:* interview, alumni/ae relation, geographical residence, racial/ethnic status, volunteer work, work experience. **Freshman Admission Requirements:** High school diploma is required and GED is accepted. *Academic units recommended:* 4 English, 4 math, 4 science, 4 science labs, 4 foreign language, 4 history, 4 academic electives. **Freshman Admission Statistics:** 36,292 applied, 6.28% admitted, 62% enrolled. **Transfer Admission Requirements:** High school transcript, college transcript(s), essay or personal statement, standardized test scores, statement of good standing from prior institution(s). Lowest grade transferable C. **General Admission Information:** Application fee $85. Regular application deadline 1/1. Regular notification 4/1. Nonfall registration not accepted. Admission may be deferred for a maximum of 2 years.

COSTS AND FINANCIAL AID
Annual tuition $52,478. Room and board $13,244. Required fees $2,578. Average book expense $1,223. **Required Forms and Deadlines:** FAFSA, CSS/Financial Aid PROFILE, Noncustodial PROFILE. **Notification of Awards:** Applicants will be notified of awards on or about 4/1. **Types of Aid:** *Need-based scholarships/grants:* Federal Pell, FSEOG, State scholarships/grants, Private scholarships, College/university scholarship or grant aid from institutional funds. *Loans:* Direct Subsidized Stafford Loans, Direct Unsubsidized Stafford Loans, Direct PLUS loans, Federal Perkins Loans, College/university loans from institutional funds. *Student Employment:* Federal Work-Study Program available. Institutional employment available. **Financial Aid Statistics:** 96% needy freshmen, 97% needy undergrads receive need-based scholarship or grant aid. 1% freshmen, 1% undergrads receive non-need-based scholarship or grant aid. 78% freshmen, 86% undergrads receive need-based self-help aid. 0% freshmen, 0% undergrads receive athletic scholarships. 55% freshmen, 60% undergrads receive any aid. 27% undergrads borrow to pay for school. Average cumulative indebtedness $25,167. **Criteria for awarding aid:**

COLUMBIA UNIVERSITY SCHOOL OF GENERAL STUDIES

408 Lewisohn Hall, Mail Code 4101, New York, NY 10027
Phone: 2012-854-2772 • **Financial Aid Phone:** 202-854-5410
E-mail: gsdegree@columbia.edu • **CEEB Code:** 2095
Fax: 212-854-6316 • **Website:** www.gs.columbia.edu • **ACT Code:** 2716

This private school was founded in 1947. It has a 36-acre campus.

RATINGS
Admissions Selectivity Rating: 87   **Fire Safety Rating:** 88   **Green Rating:** 95

STUDENTS AND FACULTY
Enrollment: 2,005. **Student Body:** 41% female, 59% male, 56% out-of-state, 18% international (62 countries represented). Asian 8%, African American 5%, Caucasian 49%, Hispanic 10%, Native American <1%, Pacific Islander <1%, Two or more races <1%, Race unknown 9%.

ACADEMICS
Degrees: bachelor's, postbachelor's certificate. **Most popular majors:** Economics; Political Science and Government; English Language and Literature. **Special Study Options:** Accelerated program, cross-registration, double major, dual enrollment, exchange student program (domestic), honors program, independent study, internships, student-designed major, study abroad, teacher certification program. **Honors Programs:** Honor Society of School of General Studies Combined degree programs: BA/JD, BA/MA, BA/DDS, BA/MEng, Joint Programs. **Disability Services:** Special programs offered to physically disabled students, including note-taking services, reader services, tape recorders, tutors. **Career Services:** Alumni network, Alumni services, Career/job search classes, Career assessment, Internships, Regional alumni.

FACILITIES
Housing: Coed dorms, special housing for international students, fraternity/sorority housing, apartments for married students, cooperative housing, apartments for single students, Theme Housing. 100% of campus accessible to physically diasbled. **Special Academic Facilities/Equipment:** Earth Institute, Lamont-Doherty Earth Observatory University Art Collection Miller Theatre Low Memorial Library Rotunda LeRoy Neiman Center for Print Studies Music at St. Paul's Postcrypt Coffeehouse Miriam and Ira D. Wallach Art Gallery Language Houses **Computers:** 50% of classrooms, 10% of dorms, 64% of libraries, 50% of dining areas, 90% of student union, 25% of common outdoor areas have wireless network access. Students can register for classes online. Administrative functions (other than registration) can be performed online.

CAMPUS LIFE
Environment: Metropolis. **Activities:** Choral groups, concert band, dance, drama/theater, jazz band, literary magazine, marching band, music ensembles, musical theater, opera, radio station, student government, student newspaper, student-run film society, symphony orchestra, television station, yearbook, Campus Ministries, Student Organization, Model UN. 250 registered

organizations, 2 honor societies, 21 religious organizations. **Athletics (Intercollegiate):** *Men:* baseball, basketball, crew/rowing, cross-country, diving, fencing, football, golf, soccer, swimming, track/field (outdoor), track/field (indoor). *Women:* archery, basketball, crew/rowing, cross-country, diving, fencing, field hockey, golf, lacrosse, soccer, softball, swimming, track/field (outdoor), track/field (indoor), volleyball. **On-Campus Highlights:** Low Library, Lerner Hall, Butler Library, Miller Theater, College Walk, Low Plaza. **Environmental Initiatives:** Greenhouse gas reduction program targeted to meet a 30% reduction by 2017 and clean heat initiative to improve air quality and asthma rates by phasing out the use of heavy heating oils to cleaner fuels like natural gas and low-sulfur #2 oil. Columbia has also converted its entire 14 car public safety fleet to hybrid vehicles. As part of our energy efficiency initiatives, 45% of all food purchased is local and/ororganic. All honey and apples are purchased through vendors at the on-campus green market from NY farmers. Annually Dining Services contracts with a local NY farmer and canner to make all the salsa and strawberry jam for the year. In addition all milk is local and hormone free. Liquid eggs are certified humane. All coffee is roasted locally and is fair-trade, organic, shade grown and bird friendly. Tomatoes are also fair trade. All bakery items and grab and go sandwiches are purchased from local vendors. 50% of daily meals served in the dining halls are vegetarian and Meatless Mondays are run every Monday.

ADMISSIONS
Freshman Academic Profile: Average high school GPA 3.7. **Reported SAT (pre-2016 redesign) scores:** SAT Math middle 50% range 630-740. SAT Critical Reading 'middle 50% range 630-750. SAT Writing middle 50% range 640-750. **Concordant SAT scores:** SAT EBRW middle 50% 680–770. SAT Math middle 50% range 650–760. ACT middle 50% range 29-32. Minimum paper TOEFL 600. **Basis for Candidate Selection:** *Very important factors considered include:* rigor of secondary school record, academic GPA, standardized test scores, application essay, interview, character/personal qualities, first generation, work experience, level of applicant's interest. *Important factors considered include:* class rank, recommendation(s), extracurricular activities, talent/ability, racial/ethnic status. *Other factors considered include:* alumni/ae relation, geographical residence, state residency, volunteer work. **Freshman Admission Requirements:** High school diploma is required and GED is accepted. **Freshman Admission Statistics:** 661 applied, 32.98% admitted, 59% enrolled. **Transfer Admission Requirements:** High school transcript, college transcript(s), Lowest grade transferable C. **General Admission Information:** Application fee $80. Priority deadline 3/1. Regular application deadline 6/1. Regular notification 7/15. Nonfall registration accepted. Admission may be deferred for a maximum of 2 semesters.

COSTS AND FINANCIAL AID
Annual tuition $48,900. Room and board $10,356. Required fees $2,214. Average book expense $1,400. **Required Forms and Deadlines:** FAFSA, Institution's own financial aid form. **Types of Aid:** *Need-based scholarships/grants:* Federal Pell, FSEOG, State scholarships/grants, Private scholarships, College/university scholarship or grant aid from institutional funds. *Loans:* Direct Subsidized Stafford Loans, Direct Unsubsidized Stafford Loans, Direct PLUS loans, Federal Perkins Loans, College/university loans from institutional funds. *Student Employment:* Federal Work-Study Program available. Institutional employment available. **Financial Aid Statistics:** 93% needy freshmen, 98% needy undergrads receive need-based scholarship or grant aid. 2% undergrads receive non-need-based scholarship or grant aid. 85% freshmen, 87% undergrads receive need-based self-help aid. 0% freshmen, 0% undergrads receive athletic scholarships. 70% undergrads receive any aid. **Criteria for awarding aid:** *Need-based:* Academics. *Non-need-based:* Academics.

COLUMBUS COLLEGE OF ART AND DESIGN

Admissions, Columbus, OH 43215-3875
Phone: 614-222-3261 • **Financial Aid Phone:** 614-222-3295
E-mail: admissions@ccad.edu • **CEEB Code:** 1085
Fax: 614-232-8344 • **Website:** www.ccad.edu • **ACT Code:** 3281

This private school was founded in 1879. It has a 17-acre campus.

RATINGS
Admissions Selectivity Rating: 74   **Fire Safety Rating:** 91   **Green Rating:** 60*

STUDENTS AND FACULTY
Enrollment: 1,262. **Student Body:** 62% female, 38% male, 27% out-of-state, 8% international (35 countries represented). Asian 3%, African American 8%, Caucasian 68%, Hispanic 5%, Native American <1%, Pacific Islander 0%, Two or more races 4%, Race unknown 3%.
Retention and Graduation: 78% freshmen return for sophomore year. 47% freshmen graduate within 4 years. 8% grads go on to further study within 1 year.

7% grads pursue arts and sciences degrees. 1% grads pursue medical degrees. **Faculty:** Student/faculty ratio 11:1. 72 full-time faculty, 69% hold PhDs, 7% are are members of minority groups, 38% are women. 0% of classes are taught by teaching assistants.

ACADEMICS

Degrees: bachelor's, master's. **Most popular majors:** Graphic Design; Illustration. **Special Study Options:** cooperative education program, cross-registration, internships, study abroad, Undergrads may take grad level classes. Other Special Programs: Evening classes for credit. Saturday School (ages 6-18). **Career Services:** Alumni services, Career/job search classes, Career assessment, Internships.

FACILITIES

Housing: Coed dorms. **Special Academic Facilities/Equipment:** Student art exhibition hall, gallery, auditorium, recreation center.

CAMPUS LIFE

Activities: literary magazine, student government, student newspaper. 2 registered organizations, 1 religious organization.

ADMISSIONS

Freshman Academic Profile: Average high school GPA 3.2. 6% in top 10% of high school class, 18% in top 25% of high school class, 59% in top 50% of high school class. **Reported SAT (pre-2016 redesign) scores:** SAT Math middle 50% range 450-570. SAT Critical Reading middle 50% range 470-610. SAT Writing middle 50% range 460-580. **Concordant SAT scores:** SAT EBRW middle 50% 520–650. SAT Math middle 50% range 490–590. ACT middle 50% range 19-25. Minimum internet-based TOEFL 173. Minimum paper TOEFL 500. **Basis for Candidate Selection:** *Very important factors considered include:* academic GPA, standardized test scores, application essay, recommendation(s), talent/ability. *Important factors considered include:* level of applicant's interest. *Other factors considered include:* rigor of secondary school record, interview, extracurricular activities, character/personal qualities, first generation, alumni/ae relation, geographical residence, state residency, volunteer work, work experience. **Freshman Admission Requirements:** High school diploma is required and GED is accepted. *Academic units recommended:* 4 English, 2 math, 2 science, 2 foreign language. **Freshman Admission Statistics:** 666 applied, 87.39% admitted, 40% enrolled. **Transfer Admission Requirements:** High school transcript, college transcript(s), essay or personal statement, Minimum college GPA of 2.0 required. Lowest grade transferable C. **General Admission Information:** Application fee $40. Priority deadline 2/15. Regular application deadline 8/22. Nonfall registration accepted. Admission may be deferred.

COSTS AND FINANCIAL AID

Annual tuition $28,872. Room and board $7,740. Average book expense $4,000. **Required Forms and Deadlines:** FAFSA. **Notification of Awards:** Applicants will be notified of awards on a rolling basis beginning 3/15. **Types of Aid:** *Need-based scholarships/grants:* Federal Pell, FSEOG, State scholarships/grants, College/university scholarship or grant aid from institutional funds. *Loans:* Direct Subsidized Stafford Loans, Direct Unsubsidized Stafford Loans, Direct PLUS loans, Federal Perkins Loans. *Student Employment:* Federal Work-Study Program available. Institutional employment available. **Financial Aid Statistics:** 100% needy freshmen, 98% needy undergrads receive need-based scholarship or grant aid. 4% freshmen, 3% undergrads receive non-need-based scholarship or grant aid. 84% freshmen, 84% undergrads receive need-based self-help aid. 0% freshmen, 0% undergrads receive athletic scholarships. 74% freshmen, 81% undergrads receive any aid. **Criteria for awarding aid:** *Non-need-based:* Academics, Art.

COLUMBUS STATE UNIVERSITY

4225 University Avenue, Columbus, GA 31907-5645
Phone: 706-568-2035 • **Financial Aid Phone:** 706-507-8800
E-mail: admissions@colstate.edu
Fax: 706-568-5091 • **Website:** www.columbusstate.edu

This public school was founded in 1958. It has a 150-acre campus.

RATINGS

Admissions Selectivity Rating: 75　　**Fire Safety Rating:** 87　　**Green Rating:** 60*

STUDENTS AND FACULTY

Enrollment: 6,890. **Student Body:** 60% female, 40% male, 14% out-of-state, 1% international (67 countries represented). Asian 2%, African American 35%, Caucasian 55%, Hispanic 4%, Native American 1%, Pacific Islander <1%, Two or more races 2%, Race unknown 0%.
Retention and Graduation: 69% freshmen return for sophomore year. 12% freshmen graduate within 4 years. **Faculty:** Student/faculty ratio 18:1. 279 full-time faculty, 78% hold PhDs, 23% are are members of minority groups, 43% are women. 0% of classes are taught by teaching assistants.

ACADEMICS

Degrees: bachelor's, certificate, doctoral/research, doctoral, master's, post-master's certificate, terminal, transfer. **Classes:** Most classes have 20-29 students. Most lab/discussion sessions have 10-19 students. **Special Study Options:** Accelerated program, cooperative education program, distance learning, double major, dual enrollment, English as a Second Language (ESL), honors program, independent study, internships, liberal arts/career combination, study abroad, teacher certification program. **Honors Programs:** Honors Program Servant Leadership Program. **Disability Services:** Special programs offered to physically disabled students, including note-taking services, reader services, tape recorders, tutors. **Career Services:** Alumni network, Alumni services, Career/job search classes, Career assessment, Internships, Regional alumni. Internships and experiential learning via volunteer placements in the community.

FACILITIES

Housing: special housing for disabled students, special housing for international students, apartments for married students, apartments for single students, Theme Housing. 100% of campus accessible to physically diasbled. **Computers:** 80% of classrooms, 100% of libraries, 100% of dining areas, 100% of student union, 25% of common outdoor areas have wireless network access. Students can register for classes online. Administrative functions (other than registration) can be performed online.

CAMPUS LIFE

Environment: City. **Activities:** Choral groups, concert band, dance, drama/theater, jazz band, literary magazine, music ensembles, musical theater, pep band, student government, student newspaper, symphony orchestra, Campus Ministries, Student Organization, Model UN. 90 registered organizations, 22 honor societies, 10 religious organizations. 7 fraternities, 6 sororities. **Athletics (Intercollegiate):** *Men:* baseball, basketball, cheerleading, cross-country, golf, riflery, tennis. *Women:* basketball, cheerleading, cross-country, golf, riflery, soccer, softball, tennis. **On-Campus Highlights:** Einstein Bos. Bagels, RiverPark Campus, Davidson Student Center, Lumpkin Center, Coca Cola Space Science Center. **Environmental Initiatives:** Green Seal Cleaning Products.

ADMISSIONS

Freshman Academic Profile: Average high school GPA 3.0. **Reported SAT (pre-2016 redesign) scores:** SAT Math middle 50% range 420-540. SAT Critical Reading middle 50% range 430-550. SAT Writing middle 50% range 420-530. **Concordant SAT scores:** SAT EBRW middle 50% 480–600. SAT Math middle 50% range 460–570. ACT middle 50% range 17-22. Minimum internet-based TOEFL 79. Minimum paper TOEFL 550. **Basis for Candidate Selection:** *Very important factors considered include:* rigor of secondary school record. *Important factors considered include:* academic GPA, standardized test scores. *Other factors considered include:* interview, extracurricular activities, talent/ability, geographical residence. **Freshman Admission Requirements:** High school diploma is required and GED is not accepted. *Academic units required:* 4 English, 4 math, 3 science, 2 science labs, 2 foreign language, 3 social studies. **Freshman Admission Statistics:** 3,454 applied, 60.08% admitted, 60% enrolled. **Transfer Admission Requirements:** college transcript(s), statement of good standing from prior institution(s). Minimum college GPA of 2.00 required. Lowest grade transferable D. **General Admission Information:** Application fee $30. Priority deadline 5/15. Regular application deadline 6/30. Nonfall registration accepted. Admission may be deferred for a maximum of 1 year.

COSTS AND FINANCIAL AID

Annual in-state tuition $3,281. Annual out-of-state tuition $12,669. Room and board $7,280. Required fees $1,300. Average book expense $1,072. **Required Forms and Deadlines:** FAFSA. **Notification of Awards:** Applicants will be notified of awards on a rolling basis beginning 5/15. **Types of Aid:** *Need-based scholarships/grants:* Federal Pell, FSEOG, State scholarships/grants, Private scholarships, College/university scholarship or grant aid from institutional funds. *Loans:* Direct Subsidized Stafford Loans, Direct Unsubsidized Stafford Loans, Direct PLUS loans, Federal Perkins Loans, Federal Nursing Loans, State Loans, College/university loans from institutional funds. *Student Employment:* Federal Work-Study Program available. Institutional employment available. **Financial Aid Statistics:** 71% needy freshmen, 72% needy undergrads receive need-based scholarship or grant aid. 51% freshmen, 34% undergrads receive non-need-based scholarship or grant aid. 66% freshmen, 73% undergrads receive need-based self-help aid. 4% freshmen, 4% undergrads receive athletic scholarships. 87% freshmen, 78% undergrads receive any aid. **Criteria for awarding aid:** *Need-based:* Academics, Alumni affiliation, Art, Athletics, Job skills, Leadership, Minority status, Music/drama. *Non-need-based:* Academics, Alumni affiliation, Art, Athletics, Job skills, Leadership, Minority status, Music/drama.

CONCORD UNIVERSITY

1000 Vermillion Street, Athens, WV 24712
Phone: 304-384-5248 • **Financial Aid Phone:** 304-384-6069
E-mail: admissions@concord.edu • **CEEB Code:** 5120
Fax: 304-384-9044 • **Website:** www.concord.edu • **ACT Code:** 3810

This public school was founded in 1872. It has a 123-acre campus.

RATINGS
Admissions Selectivity Rating: 81   **Fire Safety Rating:** 91   **Green Rating:** 60*

STUDENTS AND FACULTY
Enrollment: 2,857. **Student Body:** 55% female, 45% male, 18% out-of-state, 0% international (16 countries represented). Asian 2%, African American 6%, Caucasian 91%, Hispanic 1%, Native American <1%, Pacific Islander 0%, Two or more races 0%, Race unknown 0%.
Retention and Graduation: 65% freshmen return for sophomore year. 15% freshmen graduate within 4 years. 39% freshmen graduate within 6 years. 33% grads go on to further study within 1 year. 8% grads pursue arts and sciences degrees. 2% grads pursue law degrees. 10% grads pursue business degrees. 3% grads pursue medical degrees. **Faculty:** Student/faculty ratio 23:1. 121 full-time faculty, 64% hold PhDs, 3% are are members of minority groups, 41% are women.

ACADEMICS
Degrees: associate, bachelor's, master's, terminal. **Classes:** Most classes have fewer than 10 students. Most lab/discussion sessions have 10-19 students. **Most popular majors:** Education; Business Administration and Management; Social Sciences. **Special Study Options:** cooperative education program, double major, dual enrollment, English as a Second Language (ESL), honors program, student-designed major, teacher certification program. **Career Services:** Alumni services, Career/job search classes, Career assessment, Internships.

FACILITIES
Housing: Coed dorms, special housing for disabled students, men's dorms, special housing for international students, women's dorms, apartments for married students. 100% of campus accessible to physically diasbled. **Computers:** 50% of classrooms, 20% of dorms, 100% of libraries, 100% of dining areas, 100% of student union, 50% of common outdoor areas have wireless network access. Students can register for classes online. Administrative functions (other than registration) can be performed online.

CAMPUS LIFE
Environment: Rural. **Activities:** Choral groups, concert band, drama/theater, jazz band, pep band, radio station, student government, student newspaper, student-run film society, television station, yearbook. 57 registered organizations, 1 honor society, 2 religious organizations. 6 fraternities, 4 sororities. **Athletics (Intercollegiate): Men:** baseball, basketball, cheerleading, cross-country, football, golf, soccer, tennis, track/field (outdoor). **Women:** basketball, cheerleading, cross-country, golf, soccer, softball, tennis, track/field (outdoor), volleyball. **On-Campus Highlights:** Rahall Technology Ctr, 48 Bell Carillon, University Point, Beasley Student Ctr., Callaghan Stadium.

ADMISSIONS
Freshman Academic Profile: Average high school GPA 3.2. 18% in top 10% of high school class, 45% in top 25% of high school class, 73% in top 50% of high school class. 95% from public high schools. **Reported SAT (pre-2016 redesign) scores:** SAT Math middle 50% range 420-520. SAT Critical Reading middle 50% range 420-540. **Concordant SAT scores:** SAT Math middle 50% range 460–550. ACT middle 50% range 17-25. Minimum paper TOEFL 500. **Basis for Candidate Selection:** *Very important factors considered include:* rigor of secondary school record. *Important factors considered include:* class rank, standardized test scores, extracurricular activities. *Other factors considered include:* application essay, recommendation(s), interview, talent/ability, character/personal qualities, alumni/ae relation, geographical residence, racial/ethnic status, volunteer work, work experience. **Freshman Admission Requirements:** High school diploma is required and GED is accepted. *Academic units required:* 4 English, 4 math, 3 science, 3 science labs, 2 foreign language, 2 social studies, 1 history, 1 visual/performing arts. **Freshman Admission Statistics:** 2,290 applied, 60.61% admitted, 41% enrolled. **Transfer Admission Requirements:** college transcript(s), Lowest grade transferable D. **General Admission Information:** Nonfall registration accepted. Admission may be deferred for a maximum of 1 YEAR.

COSTS AND FINANCIAL AID
Annual in-state tuition $4,974. Annual out-of-state tuition $11,050. Room and board $6,962. Required fees $85. Average book expense $1,100. **Required Forms and Deadlines:** FAFSA, Institution's own financial aid form. **Notification of Awards:** Applicants will be notified of awards on a rolling basis beginning 4/15. **Types of Aid:** *Need-based scholarships/grants:* Federal Pell, FSEOG, State scholarships/grants, Private scholarships, College/university

scholarship or grant aid from institutional funds. *Loans:* Direct Subsidized Stafford Loans, Direct Unsubsidized Stafford Loans, Direct PLUS loans, Federal Perkins Loans. *Student Employment:* Federal Work-Study Program available. Institutional employment available. **Financial Aid Statistics:** 84% needy freshmen, 83% needy undergrads receive need-based scholarship or grant aid. 52% freshmen, 36% undergrads receive non-need-based scholarship or grant aid. 74% freshmen, 75% undergrads receive need-based self-help aid. 5% freshmen, 4% undergrads receive athletic scholarships. 90% freshmen, 77% undergrads receive any aid. **Criteria for awarding aid:** *Non-need-based:* Academics, Alumni affiliation, Art, Athletics, Job skills, Leadership, Minority status, Music/drama, State/district residency.

CONCORDIA COLLEGE (MOORHEAD, MN)

901 8th Street South, Moorhead, MN 56562
Phone: 218-299-3004 • **Financial Aid Phone:** 218-299-3010
E-mail: admissions@cord.edu • **CEEB Code:** 6113
Fax: 218-299-4720 • **Website:** https://www.concordiacollege.edu
ACT Code: 2104

This private school, affiliated with the Lutheran Church, was founded in 1891. It has a 120-acre campus.

RATINGS
Admissions Selectivity Rating: 85   **Fire Safety Rating:** 85   **Green Rating:** 60*

STUDENTS AND FACULTY
Enrollment: 2,035. **Student Body:** 58% female, 42% male, 30% out-of-state, 3% international (42 countries represented). Asian 1%, African American 2%, Caucasian 84%, Hispanic 2%, Native American 1%, Pacific Islander <1%, Two or more races 2%, Race unknown 5%.
Retention and Graduation: 84% freshmen return for sophomore year. 70% freshmen graduate within 4 years. 74% freshmen graduate within 6 years. 24% grads go on to further study within 1 year. 5% grads pursue arts and sciences degrees. 4% grads pursue law degrees. 3% grads pursue business degrees. 4% grads pursue medical degrees. **Faculty:** Student/faculty ratio 11:1. 167 full-time faculty, 84% hold PhDs, 7% are are members of minority groups, 49% are women. 0% of classes are taught by teaching assistants.

ACADEMICS
Degrees: bachelor's, master's. **Classes:** Most classes have 20-29 students. **Most popular majors:** Business Administration and Management; Biology/Biological Sciences; Education. **Special Study Options:** cooperative education program, double major, exchange student program (domestic), honors program, independent study, internships, liberal arts/career combination, study abroad, teacher certification program. Combined degree programs: BA/BS Engineering NOSU, U of Minnesota Institute. **Disability Services:** Special programs offered to physically disabled students, including note-taking services, reader services, tape recorders, tutors. **Career Services:** Alumni network, Alumni services, Career/job search classes, Career assessment, Internships.

FACILITIES
Housing: Coed dorms, special housing for disabled students, men's dorms, women's dorms, apartments for single students, French, German, and Spanish language houses. 95% of campus accessible to physically diasbled. **Special Academic Facilities/Equipment:** Cyrus M. Running Gallery. **Computers:** Administrative functions (other than registration) can be performed online.

CAMPUS LIFE
Environment: City. **Activities:** Choral groups, concert band, dance, drama/theater, jazz band, literary magazine, music ensembles, musical theater, pep band, radio station, student government, student newspaper, symphony orchestra, television station, yearbook. 80 registered organizations, 22 honor societies, 12 religious organizations. 2 fraternities, 2 sororities. **Athletics (Intercollegiate): Men:** baseball, basketball, cross-country, football, golf, ice hockey, soccer, tennis, track/field (outdoor), track/field (indoor), wrestling. **Women:** basketball, cross-country, diving, golf, ice hockey, soccer, softball, swimming, tennis, track/field (outdoor), track/field (indoor), volleyball.

ADMISSIONS
Freshman Academic Profile: Average high school GPA 3.5. 27% in top 10% of high school class, 55% in top 25% of high school class, 82% in top 50% of high school class. ACT middle 50% range 22-28. Minimum paper TOEFL 550. **Basis for Candidate Selection:** *Very important factors considered include:* rigor of secondary school record. *Important factors considered include:* academic GPA, standardized test scores, recommendation(s). *Other factors considered include:* class rank, application essay, interview, extracurricular activities, talent/ability, character/personal qualities, first generation, alumni/ae relation, religious affiliation/commitment, racial/ethnic status, volunteer work, work experience, level of applicant's interest. **Freshman Admission**

Requirements: High school diploma is required and GED is accepted. *Academic units recommended:* 4 English, 3 math, 3 science, 2 foreign language, 3 social studies, 1 computer science, 1 visual/performing arts. **Freshman Admission Statistics:** 3,754 applied, 65.02% admitted, 22% enrolled. **Transfer Admission Requirements:** college transcript(s), Minimum college GPA of 2.0 required. Lowest grade transferable C-. **General Admission Information:** Application fee $20. Nonfall registration accepted. Admission may be deferred for a maximum of 1 Year.

COSTS AND FINANCIAL AID

Annual tuition $36,650. Room and board $7,810. Required fees $228. Average book expense $1,000. **Required Forms and Deadlines:** FAFSA. **Notification of Awards:** Applicants will be notified of awards on a rolling basis beginning 3/15. **Types of Aid:** *Need-based scholarships/grants:* Federal Pell, FSEOG, State scholarships/grants, Private scholarships, College/university scholarship or grant aid from institutional funds. *Loans:* Direct Subsidized Stafford Loans, Direct Unsubsidized Stafford Loans, Direct PLUS loans, State Loans, College/university loans from institutional funds. *Student Employment:* Federal Work-Study Program available. Institutional employment available. **Financial Aid Statistics:** 98% needy freshmen, 98% needy undergrads receive need-based scholarship or grant aid. 17% freshmen, 16% undergrads receive non-need-based scholarship or grant aid. 81% freshmen, 82% undergrads receive need-based self-help aid. 0% freshmen, 0% undergrads receive athletic scholarships. 100% freshmen, 96% undergrads receive any aid. Average cumulative indebtedness $39,837. **Criteria for awarding aid:** *Need-based:* Academics, Minority status. *Non-need-based:* Academics, Art, Leadership, Minority status, Music/drama.

CONCORDIA COLLEGE (NY)

171 White Plains Road, Bronxville, NY 10708
Phone: 914-337-9300
E-mail: admission@concordia-ny.edu • **CEEB Code:** 2096
Fax: 914-395-4636 • **Website:** www.concordia-ny.edu • **ACT Code:** 2722

This private school, affiliated with the Lutheran Church, was founded in 1881. It has a 33-acre campus.

RATINGS

Admissions Selectivity Rating: 71   **Fire Safety Rating:** 60*   **Green Rating:** 60*

STUDENTS AND FACULTY

Student Body: 27% out-of-state, (36 countries represented).
Retention and Graduation: 69% freshmen return for sophomore year. 40% grads go on to further study within 1 year. 30% grads pursue arts and sciences degrees. 2% grads pursue law degrees. 30% grads pursue business degrees. 10% grads pursue medical degrees. **Faculty:** Student/faculty ratio 12:1. 54 full-time faculty, 0% hold PhDs, 0% are are members of minority groups, 0% of classes are taught by teaching assistants.

ACADEMICS

Degrees: associate, bachelor's, master's. **Classes:** Most classes have 10-19 students. Most lab/discussion sessions have 10-19 students. **Most popular majors:** Education; Social Sciences; Business/Commerce. **Special Study Options:** Accelerated program, cooperative education program, cross-registration, double major, English as a Second Language (ESL), exchange student program (domestic), honors program, independent study, internships, liberal arts/career combination, student-designed major, study abroad, teacher certification program. **Disability Services:** Special programs offered to physically disabled students, including reader services, tutors. **Career Services:** Career/job search classes, Career assessment, Internships.

FACILITIES

Housing: men's dorms, women's dorms. 50% of campus accessible to physically disabled. **Special Academic Facilities/Equipment:** Art gallery, center for worship and performing arts, English language center, distance learning classroom.

CAMPUS LIFE

Environment: Village. **Activities:** Choral groups, concert band, drama/theater, jazz band, literary magazine, music ensembles, musical theater, student government, student newspaper, yearbook. 35 registered organizations, 1 honor society, 3 religious organizations. **Athletics (Intercollegiate):** *Men:* baseball, basketball, soccer, tennis, volleyball. *Women:* basketball, soccer, softball, tennis, volleyball.

ADMISSIONS

Freshman Academic Profile: Average high school GPA 2.7. 60% from public high schools. **Reported SAT (pre-2016 redesign) scores:** SAT Math middle 50% range 415-505. SAT Critical Reading middle 50% range 420-500. SAT

Writing middle 50% range 415-480. **Concordant SAT scores:** SAT EBRW middle 50% 470–550. SAT Math middle 50% range 460–540. ACT middle 50% range 16-20. Minimum paper TOEFL 550. **Basis for Candidate Selection:** *Very important factors considered include:* rigor of secondary school record. *Important factors considered include:* class rank, standardized test scores, interview, character/personal qualities. *Other factors considered include:* application essay, recommendation(s), extracurricular activities, talent/ability, alumni/ae relation, religious affiliation/commitment, volunteer work, work experience. **Freshman Admission Requirements:** High school diploma is required and GED is accepted. **Transfer Admission Requirements:** High school transcript, college transcript(s), statement of good standing from prior institution(s). Minimum college GPA of 2.0 required. Lowest grade transferable C. **General Admission Information:** Application fee $50. Priority deadline 3/15. Regular application deadline 3/15. Nonfall registration accepted. Admission may be deferred.

COSTS AND FINANCIAL AID

Annual tuition $27,740. Room and board $10,265. Required fees $1,030. Average book expense $1,000. *Student Employment:* Federal Work-Study Program available. Institutional employment available.

CONCORDIA UNIVERSITY IRVINE

1530 Concordia West, Irvine, CA 92612-3299
Phone: 949-854-8002 • **Financial Aid Phone:** 949-854-8002
E-mail: admission@cui.edu
Fax: 949-854-6894 • **Website:** www.cui.edu • **ACT Code:** 227

This private school, affiliated with the Lutheran Church, was founded in 1976. It has a 70-acre campus.

RATINGS

Admissions Selectivity Rating: 82   **Fire Safety Rating:** 90   **Green Rating:** 60*

STUDENTS AND FACULTY

Enrollment: 1,203. **Student Body:** 61% female, 39% male, 17% out-of-state, 2% international (18 countries represented). Asian 4%, African American 4%, Caucasian 68%, Hispanic 13%, Native American 1%, Pacific Islander 0%, Two or more races 0%, Race unknown 7%.
Retention and Graduation: 73% freshmen return for sophomore year. 56% freshmen graduate within 4 years. 62% freshmen graduate within 6 years. **Faculty:** Student/faculty ratio 14:1. 91 full-time faculty, 67% hold PhDs, 0% are are members of minority groups, 37% are women. 0% of classes are taught by teaching assistants.

ACADEMICS

Degrees: associate, bachelor's, master's, postbachelor's certificate. **Classes:** Most classes have 10-19 students. **Most popular majors:** Liberal Arts and Sciences/Liberal Studies; Psychology; Business/Commerce. **Special Study Options:** Accelerated program, cross-registration, distance learning, double major, dual enrollment, English as a Second Language (ESL), exchange student program (domestic), honors program, independent study, internships, liberal arts/career combination, student-designed major, study abroad, teacher certification program. **Honors Programs:** General Education Honor Programs Combined degree programs: BA/MA. **Disability Services:** Special programs offered to physically disabled students, including tutors. **Career Services:** On-campus interviews. We are proud of all the programs offered by Concordia University.

FACILITIES

Housing: special housing for disabled students, men's dorms, women's dorms. 75% of campus accessible to physically disabled. **Special Academic Facilities/Equipment:** A hi-tech Educational/Business/Technology building, which was recently completed, houses also an art gallery. **Computers:** 60% of classrooms, 100% of dorms, 95% of libraries, 70% of dining areas, 100% of student union, 10% of common outdoor areas have wireless network access. Students can register for classes online.

CAMPUS LIFE

Environment: City. **Activities:** Choral groups, concert band, dance, drama/theater, literary magazine, music ensembles, musical theater, pep band, radio station, student government, student newspaper, student-run film society, yearbook, Campus Ministries. 18 registered organizations, 5 honor societies, 8 religious organizations. **Athletics (Intercollegiate):** *Men:* baseball, basketball, cross-country, golf, soccer, swimming, tennis, track/field (outdoor), water polo. *Women:* basketball, cross-country, golf, soccer, softball, swimming, tennis, track/field (outdoor), volleyball, water polo. **On-Campus Highlights:** The Gym, Student Life Center (Lounge and computer resource), Library, CU Center (Worship Center), Student Union (cafeteria).

ADMISSIONS

Freshman Academic Profile: Average high school GPA 3.5. 20% in top 10% of high school class, 54% in top 25% of high school class, 84% in top 50% of high school class. **Reported SAT (pre-2016 redesign) scores:** SAT Math middle 50% range 450-570. SAT Critical Reading middle 50% range 450-570. **Concordant SAT scores:** SAT Math middle 50% range 490–590. ACT middle 50% range 20-24. Minimum paper TOEFL 550. **Basis for Candidate Selection:** *Very important factors considered include:* rigor of secondary school record, class rank, academic GPA, standardized test scores, character/personal qualities. *Important factors considered include:* recommendation(s), religious affiliation/commitment. *Other factors considered include:* application essay, interview, extracurricular activities, talent/ability, alumni/ae relation, racial/ethnic status, volunteer work, work experience, level of applicant's interest. **Freshman Admission Requirements:** High school diploma is required and GED is accepted. *Academic units required:* 4 English, 3 math, 3 science, 2 foreign language, 2 social studies. **Freshman Admission Statistics:** 897 applied, 65.55% admitted, 42% enrolled. **Transfer Admission Requirements:** High school transcript, college transcript(s), statement of good standing from prior institution(s). Minimum college GPA of 2.3 required. Lowest grade transferable D. **General Admission Information:** Application fee $50. Priority deadline 3/2. Nonfall registration accepted. Admission may be deferred for a maximum of 12 months.

COSTS AND FINANCIAL AID

Annual tuition $23,400. Room and board $7,650. Required fees $300. **Required Forms and Deadlines:** FAFSA, Institution's own financial aid form, State aid form. **Notification of Awards:** Applicants will be notified of awards on a rolling basis beginning 2/1. **Types of Aid:** *Need-based scholarships/grants:* Federal Pell, FSEOG, State scholarships/grants, Private scholarships, College/university scholarship or grant aid from institutional funds. *Student Employment:* Federal Work-Study Program available. Institutional employment available. **Financial Aid Statistics:** 95% needy freshmen, 92% needy undergrads receive need-based scholarship or grant aid. 18% freshmen, 13% undergrads receive non-need-based scholarship or grant aid. 71% freshmen, 77% undergrads receive need-based self-help aid. 10% freshmen, 7% undergrads receive athletic scholarships. 74% freshmen, 71% undergrads receive any aid. **Criteria for awarding aid:** *Need-based:* Job skills. *Non-need-based:* Academics, Art, Athletics, Leadership, Music/drama, Religious affiliation.

CONCORDIA UNIVERSITY, NEBRASKA

800 North Columbia Avenue, Seward, NE 68434-1556
Phone: 800-535-5494 • **Financial Aid Phone:** 800-535-5494
E-mail: admiss@cune.edu • **CEEB Code:** 6116
Fax: 402-643-4073 • **Website:** www.cune.edu • **ACT Code:** 2442

This private school, affiliated with the Lutheran Church, was founded in 1894. It has a 120-acre campus.

RATINGS

Admissions Selectivity Rating: 81   **Fire Safety Rating:** 89   **Green Rating:** 60*

STUDENTS AND FACULTY

Enrollment: 1,233. **Student Body:** 52% female, 48% male, 54% out-of-state, 2% international (11 countries represented). Asian 1%, African American 4%, Caucasian 76%, Hispanic 6%, Native American <1%, Pacific Islander <1%, Two or more races <1%, Race unknown 10%.
Retention and Graduation: 74% freshmen return for sophomore year. 50% freshmen graduate within 4 years. 67% freshmen graduate within 6 years. 17% grads go on to further study within 1 year. 4% grads pursue arts and sciences degrees. 1% grads pursue law degrees. 1% grads pursue business degrees. 6% grads pursue medical degrees. **Faculty:** Student/faculty ratio 13:1. 63 full-time faculty, 71% hold PhDs, 3% are are members of minority groups, 35% are women. 0% of classes are taught by teaching assistants.

ACADEMICS

Degrees: bachelor's, master's. **Classes:** Most classes have 20-29 students. Most lab/discussion sessions have 10-19 students. **Most popular majors:** Business/Commerce; Elementary Education and Teaching; Secondary Education and Teaching. **Special Study Options:** Accelerated program, distance learning, double major, dual enrollment, English as a Second Language (ESL), exchange student program (domestic), independent study, internships, study abroad, teacher certification program, Undergradate students may take graduate level classes. **Disability Services:** Special programs offered to physically disabled students, including note-taking services, reader services, tape recorders, tutors. **Career Services:** Alumni network, Alumni services, Career/job search classes, Career assessment, Internships, Regional alumni. Intentional "4 year plan" to serve students prior to graduation.

FACILITIES

Housing: special housing for disabled students, men's dorms, women's dorms, apartments for married students, apartments for single students. 75% of campus accessible to physically disabled. **Special Academic Facilities/Equipment:** Art gallery, Bartels rock museum, observatory, arboretum **Computers:** 40% of classrooms, 100% of dorms, 100% of libraries, 100% of student union, have wireless network access. Students can register for classes online. Administrative functions (other than registration) can be performed online.

CAMPUS LIFE

Environment: Village. **Activities:** Choral groups, concert band, dance, drama/theater, jazz band, literary magazine, music ensembles, musical theater, pep band, student government, student newspaper, symphony orchestra, yearbook, Campus Ministries. 33 registered organizations, 1 honor society, 5 religious organizations. **Athletics (Intercollegiate):** *Men:* baseball, basketball, cross-country, football, golf, soccer, tennis, track/field (outdoor), track/field (indoor), wrestling. *Women:* basketball, cross-country, golf, soccer, softball, tennis, track/field (outdoor), track/field (indoor), volleyball. **On-Campus Highlights:** Student Center / Game Room, Coffee Shop, Marxhausen Art Gallery, Osten Observatory, Physical Education Building. **Environmental Initiatives:** The committee is charged with outlining short-term and long-term plans that will render the university carbon neutral as soon as is feasible and to report progress periodically. Specific plans have not yet been formulated.

ADMISSIONS

Freshman Academic Profile: Average high school GPA 3.5. 18% in top 10% of high school class, 41% in top 25% of high school class, 68% in top 50% of high school class. **Reported SAT (pre-2016 redesign) scores:** SAT Math middle 50% range 450-567.5. SAT Critical Reading middle 50% range 440-535. **Concordant SAT scores:** SAT Math middle 50% range 490–590. ACT middle 50% range 20-27. **Basis for Candidate Selection:** *Very important factors considered include:* academic GPA, standardized test scores. *Important factors considered include:* rigor of secondary school record, class rank, character/personal qualities. *Other factors considered include:* application essay, recommendation(s), interview, extracurricular activities, alumni/ae relation, religious affiliation/commitment. **Freshman Admission Requirements:** High school diploma is required and GED is accepted. *Academic units recommended:* 4 English, 3 math, 2 science, 1 foreign language, 3 social studies, 3 history, and 3 units from above areas or other academic areas. **Freshman Admission Statistics:** 1,396 applied, 73.28% admitted, 32% enrolled. **Transfer Admission Requirements:** High school transcript, college transcript(s), Minimum college GPA of 2.0 required. Lowest grade transferable D. **General Admission Information:** Priority deadline 7/1. Regular application deadline 8/1. Nonfall registration accepted. Admission may be deferred for a maximum of 1 year.

COSTS AND FINANCIAL AID

Annual tuition $30,400. Room and board $8,100. Required fees $600. Average book expense $1,000. **Required Forms and Deadlines:** FAFSA. **Notification of Awards:** Applicants will be notified of awards on a rolling basis beginning 3/1. **Types of Aid:** *Need-based scholarships/grants:* Federal Pell, FSEOG, State scholarships/grants, Private scholarships, College/university scholarship or grant aid from institutional funds. *Loans:* Direct Subsidized Stafford Loans, Direct Unsubsidized Stafford Loans, Direct PLUS loans, Federal Perkins Loans. *Student Employment:* Federal Work-Study Program available. Institutional employment available. **Financial Aid Statistics:** 100% needy freshmen, 100% needy undergrads receive need-based scholarship or grant aid. 27% freshmen, 21% undergrads receive non-need-based scholarship or grant aid. 64% freshmen, 69% undergrads receive need-based self-help aid. 14% freshmen, 14% undergrads receive athletic scholarships. 100% freshmen, 99% undergrads receive any aid. 73% undergrads borrow to pay for school. Average cumulative indebtedness $26,328. **Criteria for awarding aid:** *Need-based:* Minority status. *Non-need-based:* Academics, Alumni affiliation, Art, Athletics, Leadership, Music/drama, Religious affiliation.

CONCORDIA UNIVERSITY (OR)

2811 NE Holman St, Portland, OR 97211-6099
Phone: 503-280-8501 • **Financial Aid Phone:** 800-321-9371
E-mail: admissions@cu-portland.edu • **CEEB Code:** 4078
Fax: 503-280-8531 • **Website:** www.cu-portland.edu • **ACT Code:** 3458

This private school, affiliated with the Lutheran Church, was founded in 1905. It has a 12-acre campus.

RATINGS

Admissions Selectivity Rating: 83   **Fire Safety Rating:** 60*   **Green Rating:** 60*

STUDENTS AND FACULTY

Enrollment: 1,073. **Student Body:** 64% female, 36% male, 41% out-of-state, 1% international. Asian 6%, African American 7%, Caucasian 65%, Hispanic 6%, Native American 1%, Pacific Islander 0%, Two or more races 0%, Race unknown 14%.
Retention and Graduation: 74% freshmen return for sophomore year. 41% freshmen graduate within 6 years. **Faculty:** Student/faculty ratio 18:1. 52 full-time faculty, 67% hold PhDs, 4% are are members of minority groups, 48% are women. 0% of classes are taught by teaching assistants.

ACADEMICS

Degrees: bachelor's, certificate, master's, postbachelor's certifate, terminal. **Classes:** Most classes have 10-19 students. **Special Study Options:** Accelerated program, cross-registration, distance learning, dual enrollment, English as a Second Language (ESL), honors program, independent study, internships, study abroad, teacher certification program. **Honors Programs:** Honors program features limited enrollment to 25 students create greater intellectual opportunity. **Career Services:** Alumni services, Career assessment, Internships, Regional alumni, On-campus interviews. Concordia Committment offers students who complete the 4-year program partial tuition reimbursement if they are not employed in the field of their choice 6 months after graduation.

FACILITIES

Housing: Coed dorms, apartments for single students. **Computers:** Administrative functions (other than registration) can be performed online.

CAMPUS LIFE

Environment: Metropolis. **Activities:** Choral groups, drama/theater, literary magazine, music ensembles, student government, student newspaper, Campus Ministries, Student Organization. 10 registered organizations, 2 honor societies, 1 religious organization. **Athletics (Intercollegiate):** *Men:* baseball, basketball, cross-country, golf, soccer, track/field (outdoor), track/field (indoor). *Women:* basketball, cross-country, golf, soccer, softball, track/field (outdoor), track/field (indoor), volleyball.

ADMISSIONS

Freshman Academic Profile: Average high school GPA 3.4. 19% in top 10% of high school class, 45% in top 25% of high school class, 76% in top 50% of high school class. **Reported SAT (pre-2016 redesign) scores:** SAT Math middle 50% range 460-560. SAT Critical Reading middle 50% range 450-570. **Concordant SAT scores:** SAT Math middle 50% range 500–580. ACT middle 50% range 18-24. Minimum paper TOEFL 500. **Basis for Candidate Selection:** *Very important factors considered include:* rigor of secondary school record, standardized test scores, recommendation(s). *Other factors considered include:* class rank, academic GPA, application essay, interview, character/personal qualities. **Freshman Admission Requirements:** High school diploma is required and GED is accepted. *Academic units recommended:* 4 English, 3 math, 3 science, 2 foreign language, 3 social studies, 3 academic electives, and 1 unit from above areas or other academic areas. **Freshman Admission Statistics:** 1,002 applied, 59.48% admitted, 32% enrolled. **Transfer Admission Requirements:** college transcript(s), statement of good standing from prior institution(s). Minimum college GPA of 2.0 required. Lowest grade transferable D. **General Admission Information:** Application fee $20. Priority deadline 3/1. Regular application deadline 7/1. Nonfall registration accepted. Admission may be deferred.

COSTS AND FINANCIAL AID

Annual tuition $20,900. Room and board $6,270. Required fees $210. Average book expense $800. **Required Forms and Deadlines:** FAFSA. **Notification of Awards:** Applicants will be notified of awards on a rolling basis beginning 3/15. **Types of Aid:** *Need-based scholarships/grants:* Federal Pell, FSEOG, State scholarships/grants, College/university scholarship or grant aid from institutional funds. *Loans:* Federal Perkins Loans. *Student Employment:* Federal Work-Study Program available. Institutional employment available. **Financial Aid Statistics:** 83% needy freshmen, 81% needy undergrads receive need-based scholarship or grant aid. 91% freshmen, 88% undergrads receive non-need-based scholarship or grant aid. 77% freshmen, 78% undergrads receive need-based self-help aid. 28% freshmen, 27% undergrads receive athletic scholarships. 95% freshmen receive any aid. **Criteria for awarding aid:** *Need-based:* Academics. *Non-need-based:* Academics, Athletics, Leadership, Music/drama, Religious affiliation.

CONCORDIA UNIVERSITY—ST PAUL

1282 Concordia Avenue, Saint Paul, MN 55104-5494
Phone: 651-641-8230 • **Financial Aid Phone:** 651-603-6300
E-mail: admission@csp.edu • **CEEB Code:** 6114
Fax: 651-603-6320 • **ACT Code:** 2106

This private school, affiliated with the Lutheran Church, was founded in 1893. It has a 37-acre campus.

RATINGS

Admissions Selectivity Rating: 79   **Fire Safety Rating:** 80   **Green Rating:** 60*

STUDENTS AND FACULTY

Enrollment: 2,356. **Student Body:** 59% female, 41% male, 24% out-of-state, 5% international (11 countries represented). Asian 8%, African American 12%, Caucasian 65%, Hispanic 4%, Native American <1%, Pacific Islander <1%, Two or more races 4%, Race unknown 2%.
Retention and Graduation: 72% freshmen return for sophomore year. 37% freshmen graduate within 4 years. 50% freshmen graduate within 6 years. **Faculty:** Student/faculty ratio 17:1. 101 full-time faculty, 74% hold PhDs, 6% are are members of minority groups, 52% are women. 0% of classes are taught by teaching assistants.

ACADEMICS

Degrees: associate, bachelor's, certificate, doctoral/professional, master's, postbachelor's certifate, post-master's certificate. **Classes:** Most classes have 10-19 students. **Most popular majors:** Business/Commerce; Education; Kinesiology and Exercise Science. **Special Study Options:** Accelerated program, cross-registration, distance learning, double major, dual enrollment, exchange student program (domestic), honors program, independent study, internships, student-designed major, study abroad, teacher certification program. Combined degree programs: BA/MA, Excercise Science, Family Science, Sports Management. **Disability Services:** Special programs offered to physically disabled students, including note-taking services, reader services, tape recorders, tutors. **Career Services:** Career/job search classes, Career assessment, Internships.

FACILITIES

Housing: Coed dorms, men's dorms, women's dorms, apartments for married students, apartments for single students. 80% of campus accessible to physically diasbled. **Computers:** Students can register for classes online. Administrative functions (other than registration) can be performed online.

CAMPUS LIFE

Environment: Metropolis. **Activities:** Choral groups, concert band, drama/theater, jazz band, music ensembles, musical theater, student government, student newspaper, television station, Campus Ministries. **Athletics (Intercollegiate):** *Men:* baseball, basketball, cross-country, football, golf, track/field (outdoor), track/field (indoor). *Women:* basketball, cross-country, golf, soccer, softball, track/field (outdoor), track/field (indoor), volleyball. **On-Campus Highlights:** Residence Life Center, Library Technology Center, Graebner Memorial Chapel, Gangelhoff Athletic Center, Pearson Theater.

ADMISSIONS

Freshman Academic Profile: Average high school GPA 3.2. 12% in top 10% of high school class, 31% in top 25% of high school class, 66% in top 50% of high school class. 90% from public high schools. ACT middle 50% range 18-24. Minimum internet-based TOEFL 65. **Basis for Candidate Selection:** *Very important factors considered include:* academic GPA, standardized test scores, recommendation(s). *Important factors considered include:* rigor of secondary school record. *Other factors considered include:* class rank, application essay, extracurricular activities, talent/ability, volunteer work, work experience, level of applicant's interest. **Freshman Admission Requirements:** High school diploma is required and GED is accepted. *Academic units required:* 4 English, 2 math, 2 science, 2 science labs, 2 social studies, 2 history, 2 visual/performing arts, and 1 unit from above areas or other academic areas. *Academic units recommended:* 4 English, 3 math, 3 science, 1 foreign language, 2 social studies, 2 history, 2 visual/performing arts, and 1 unit from above areas or other academic areas. **Freshman Admission Statistics:** 1,704 applied, 55.69% admitted, 26% enrolled. **Transfer Admission Requirements:** college transcript(s), statement of good standing from prior institution(s). Minimum college GPA of 2.0 required. Lowest grade transferable D. **General Admission Information:** Application fee $30. Priority deadline 12/1. Regular application deadline 8/1. Nonfall registration accepted. Admission may be deferred for a maximum of 1 year.

COSTS AND FINANCIAL AID

Annual tuition $21,750. Room and board $8,750. Required fees $0. Average book expense $2,000. **Required Forms and Deadlines:** FAFSA, State aid form. **Notification of Awards:** Applicants will be notified of awards on a rolling basis beginning 3/1. **Types of Aid:** *Need-based scholarships/grants:* Federal Pell, FSEOG, State scholarships/grants, Private scholarships, College/university scholarship or grant aid from institutional funds. *Loans:* Direct Subsidized Stafford Loans, Direct Unsubsidized Stafford Loans, Direct PLUS loans, Federal Perkins Loans, State Loans. *Student Employment:* Federal Work-Study Program available. Institutional employment available. **Financial Aid Statistics:** 99% needy freshmen, 72% needy undergrads receive need-based scholarship or grant aid. 7% freshmen, 8% undergrads receive non-need-based scholarship or grant aid. 73% freshmen, 73% undergrads receive need-based self-help aid. 9% freshmen, 7% undergrads receive athletic scholarships. 92% freshmen, 73% undergrads receive any aid. 80% undergrads borrow to pay for school. Average cumulative indebtedness $33,183. **Criteria for awarding aid:** *Need-based:* Academics, Art, Athletics, Leadership, Music/drama, Religious affiliation. *Non-need-based:* Academics, Art, Athletics, Music/drama, Religious affiliation.

CONCORDIA UNIVERSITY WISCONSIN

12800 North Lake Shore Drive, Mequon, WI 53097-2418
Phone: 262-243-5700 • **Financial Aid Phone:** 262-243-4392
E-mail: admissions@cuw.edu • **CEEB Code:** 1139
Fax: (262) 243-4545 • **Website:** www.cuw.edu • **ACT Code:** 4574

This private school, affiliated with the Lutheran Church, was founded in 1881. It has a 192-acre campus.

RATINGS
Admissions Selectivity Rating: 79   **Fire Safety Rating:** 60*   **Green Rating:** 60*

STUDENTS AND FACULTY
Enrollment: 4,326. **Student Body:** 65% female, 35% male, 20% out-of-state, 1% international (23 countries represented). Asian 2%, African American 18%, Caucasian 67%, Hispanic 2%, Native American 1%, Pacific Islander <1%, Two or more races 2%, Race unknown 6%.
Retention and Graduation: 74% freshmen return for sophomore year. 35% freshmen graduate within 4 years. 28% grads go on to further study within 1 year. **Faculty:** Student/faculty ratio 14:1. 162 full-time faculty, 77% hold PhDs, 6% are are members of minority groups, 49% are women. 0% of classes are taught by teaching assistants.

ACADEMICS
Degrees: associate, bachelor's, certificate, doctoral/professional, doctoral, master's, post-master's certificate. **Classes:** Most classes have 10-19 students. Most lab/discussion sessions have 10-19 students. **Most popular majors:** Education; Health Services/Allied Health/Health Sciences; Business/Commerce. **Special Study Options:** Accelerated program, cross-registration, distance learning, double major, dual enrollment, English as a Second Language (ESL), exchange student program (domestic), independent study, internships, liberal arts/career combination, student-designed major, study abroad, teacher certification program, CUW offers cooperative programs with Cardinal Stritch University, Marquette University, Milwaukee Institute of Art and Design and Alverno College. Combined degree programs: 2-2 interior design program. **Disability Services:** Special programs offered to physically disabled students, including note-taking services, reader services, tape recorders, tutors. **Career Services:** Alumni network, Alumni services, Career/job search classes, Career assessment, Internships, Regional alumni.

FACILITIES
Housing: men's dorms, women's dorms.

CAMPUS LIFE
Environment: Village. **Activities:** Choral groups, concert band, dance, drama/theater, jazz band, music ensembles, musical theater, pep band, radio station, student government, student newspaper, Campus Ministries, Student Organization. **Athletics (Intercollegiate):** *Men:* baseball, basketball, cross-country, football, ice hockey, soccer, tennis, track/field (outdoor), volleyball, wrestling. *Women:* basketball, cross-country, ice hockey, soccer, softball, tennis, track/field (outdoor), volleyball. **On-Campus Highlights:** Coberg Residence Hall—new, Sports and Fitness Center, Field House **Environmental Initiatives:** Construction of environmental education center with LEED status.

ADMISSIONS
Freshman Academic Profile: Average high school GPA 3.3. 16% in top 10% of high school class, 40% in top 25% of high school class, 75% in top 50% of high school class. **Reported SAT (pre-2016 redesign) scores:** SAT Math middle 50% range 453-600. SAT Critical Reading middle 50% range 450-530. SAT Writing middle 50% range 437-520. **Concordant SAT scores:** SAT EBRW middle 50% 500–580. SAT Math middle 50% range 490–620. ACT middle 50% range 20-25. Minimum paper TOEFL 500. **Basis for**

Candidate Selection: *Very important factors considered include:* rigor of secondary school record, academic GPA, application essay. *Important factors considered include:* standardized test scores, character/personal qualities, work experience. *Other factors considered include:* class rank, recommendation(s), interview, extracurricular activities, talent/ability, alumni/ae relation, state residency, religious affiliation/commitment, racial/ethnic status, volunteer work. **Freshman Admission Requirements:** High school diploma is required and GED is accepted. *Academic units required:* 3 English, 2 math, 2 science, 2 social studies, 5 academic electives. *Academic units recommended:* 4 English, 3 math, 2 foreign language, 5 academic electives. **Freshman Admission Statistics:** 2,517 applied, 70.20% admitted, 35% enrolled. **Transfer Admission Requirements:** college transcript(s), statement of good standing from prior institution(s). Minimum college GPA of 2.0 required. Lowest grade transferable C. **General Admission Information:** Application fee $35. Regular application deadline 8/15.

COSTS AND FINANCIAL AID
Required Forms and Deadlines: FAFSA. **Notification of Awards:** Applicants will be notified of awards on a rolling basis beginning 2/1. **Types of Aid:** *Need-based scholarships/grants:* Federal Pell, FSEOG, State scholarships/grants, Private scholarships, College/university scholarship or grant aid from institutional funds. *Loans:* Direct Subsidized Stafford Loans, Direct Unsubsidized Stafford Loans, Direct PLUS loans. *Student Employment:* Federal Work-Study Program available. Institutional employment available. **Financial Aid Statistics:** 97% needy freshmen, 93% needy undergrads receive need-based scholarship or grant aid. 22% freshmen, 16% undergrads receive non-need-based scholarship or grant aid. 82% freshmen, 84% undergrads receive need-based self-help aid. 0% freshmen, 0% undergrads receive athletic scholarships. 95% freshmen receive any aid. **Criteria for awarding aid:** *Need-based:* Academics. *Non-need-based:* Academics, Art, Minority status, Music/drama.

CONNECTICUT COLLEGE

270 Mohegan Avenue, New London, CT 6320
Phone: 860-439-2200 • **Financial Aid Phone:** 860-439-2058
E-mail: admission@conncoll.edu • **CEEB Code:** 3284
Fax: 860-439-4301 • **Website:** www.conncoll.edu • **ACT Code:** 556

This private school was founded in 1911. It has a 750-acre campus.

RATINGS
Admissions Selectivity Rating: 93   **Fire Safety Rating:** 60*   **Green Rating:** 60*

STUDENTS AND FACULTY
Enrollment: 1,822. **Student Body:** 63% female, 37% male, 81% out-of-state, 7% international (43 countries represented). Asian 4%, African American 4%, Caucasian 70%, Hispanic 9%, Native American <1%, Pacific Islander <1%, Two or more races 3%, Race unknown 3%.
Retention and Graduation: 89% freshmen return for sophomore year. 81% freshmen graduate within 4 years. 84% freshmen graduate within 6 years. **Faculty:** Student/faculty ratio 9:1. 177 full-time faculty, 93% hold PhDs, 25% are are members of minority groups, 53% are women. 0% of classes are taught by teaching assistants.

ACADEMICS
Degrees: bachelor's, master's. **Classes:** Most classes have 10-19 students. Most lab/discussion sessions have 10-19 students. **Most popular majors:** Economics; Psychology; Biology/Biological Sciences. **Special Study Options:** cross-registration, double major, exchange student program (domestic), independent study, internships, student-designed major, study abroad, teacher certification program, Cross-registration with the U.S. Coast Guard Academy, Trinity College, and Wesleyan University; 3-2 Program with Washington University or Boston University for a five-year BA/BS degree; Exchange Student Program; 12 Exchanges. Combined degree programs: BA/MA. **Disability Services:** Special programs offered to physically disabled students, including note-taking services, reader services, tape recorders, tutors. **Career Services:** Alumni network, Alumni services, Career/job search classes, Career assessment, Internships, Regional alumni. Our Office of Career and Professional Development administers a program that facilitates College-funded internships for students who complete a series of preparatory seminars and workshops. Over 75% of graduates typically participate.

FACILITIES

Housing: Coed dorms, special housing for disabled students, Wellness Housing, Theme Housing, Thematic housing (environmentalism, foreign language, substance-free housing, etc.), men's floors, women's floors; living and learning arrangements. **Special Academic Facilities/Equipment:** Children's Program used as "lab school" for human development program, language lab, 750-acre arboretum, botanic garden, greenhouse, environment control labs, transmission and scanning electron microscope, ion accelerator, GIS lab, refracting telescope, observatory. **Computers:** 75% of classrooms, 100% of dorms, 100% of libraries, 100% of dining areas, 100% of student union, 70% of common outdoor areas have wireless network access. Students can register for classes online. Administrative functions (other than registration) can be performed online.

CAMPUS LIFE

Environment: Town. **Activities:** Choral groups, concert band, dance, drama/theater, jazz band, literary magazine, music ensembles, radio station, student government, student newspaper, student-run film society, symphony orchestra, yearbook, Campus Ministries, Student Organization. 60 registered organizations, 5 honor societies, 6 religious organizations. **Athletics (Intercollegiate):** *Men:* basketball, crew/rowing, cross-country, diving, ice hockey, lacrosse, sailing, soccer, squash, swimming, tennis, track/field (outdoor), track/field (indoor), water polo. *Women:* basketball, crew/rowing, cross-country, diving, field hockey, ice hockey, lacrosse, sailing, soccer, squash, swimming, tennis, track/field (outdoor), track/field (indoor), volleyball, water polo. **On-Campus Highlights:** College Center (Crozier-Williams), Connecticut College Arboretum, Blue Camel Cafe (in library), Athletics Center, Coffee Grounds.

ADMISSIONS

Freshman Academic Profile: 45% in top 10% of high school class, 79% in top 25% of high school class, 97% in top 50% of high school class. 50% from public high schools. **Reported SAT (pre-2016 redesign) scores:** SAT Math middle 50% range 620-700. SAT Critical Reading middle 50% range 610-698. SAT Writing middle 50% range 620-700. **Concordant SAT scores:** SAT EBRW middle 50% 670–730. SAT Math middle 50% range 640–730. ACT middle 50% range 29-32. **Basis for Candidate Selection:** *Very important factors considered include:* rigor of secondary school record, class rank, academic GPA, character/personal qualities. *Important factors considered include:* application essay, recommendation(s), interview, extracurricular activities, talent/ability, racial/ethnic status, volunteer work, work experience. *Other factors considered include:* standardized test scores, first generation, alumni/ae relation, geographical residence, state residency, religious affiliation/commitment, level of applicant's interest. **Freshman Admission Requirements:** High school diploma is required and GED is accepted. **Freshman Admission Statistics:** 5,879 applied, 35.13% admitted, 23% enrolled. **Transfer Admission Requirements:** High school transcript, college transcript(s), essay or personal statement, statement of good standing from prior institution(s). Lowest grade transferable C. **General Admission Information:** Application fee $60. Regular application deadline 1/1. Regular notification 3/31. Nonfall registration accepted. Admission may be deferred for a maximum of 1 year.

COSTS AND FINANCIAL AID

Required Forms and Deadlines: FAFSA, CSS/Financial Aid PROFILE, Noncustodial PROFILE. **Notification of Awards:** Applicants will be notified of awards on or about 4/1. **Types of Aid:** *Need-based scholarships/grants:* Federal Pell, FSEOG, State scholarships/grants. *Loans:* Direct Subsidized Stafford Loans, Direct Unsubsidized Stafford Loans, Direct PLUS loans, Federal Perkins Loans. *Student Employment:* Federal Work-Study Program available. Institutional employment available. **Financial Aid Statistics:** 96% needy freshmen, 94% needy undergrads receive need-based scholarship or grant aid. 0% undergrads receive non-need-based scholarship or grant aid. 89% freshmen, 90% undergrads receive need-based self-help aid. 0% freshmen, 0% undergrads receive athletic scholarships. 59% freshmen, 54% undergrads receive any aid. 49% undergrads borrow to pay for school. Average cumulative indebtedness $27,514. **Criteria for awarding aid:** *Need-based:* Academics, Alumni affiliation, Art, Athletics, Job skills, Leadership, Minority status, Music/drama, Religious affiliation.

CONVERSE COLLEGE

580 East Main Street, Spartanburg, SC 29302
Phone: 864-596-9040 • **Financial Aid Phone:** 864-596-9019
E-mail: admissions@converse.edu • **CEEB Code:** 5121
Fax: 864-596-9225 • **Website:** www.converse.edu • **ACT Code:** 3852

This private school was founded in 1889. It has a 70-acre campus.

RATINGS

Admissions Selectivity Rating: 85   Fire Safety Rating: 79   Green Rating: 60*

STUDENTS AND FACULTY

Enrollment: 687. **Student Body:** 100% female, 0% male, 23% out-of-state, 1% international. Asian 1%, African American 8%, Caucasian 46%, Hispanic 3%, Native American <1%, Pacific Islander <1%, Two or more races 3%, Race unknown 39%.
Retention and Graduation: 76% freshmen return for sophomore year. 56% freshmen graduate within 4 years. 57% freshmen graduate within 6 years. 37% grads go on to further study within 1 year. **Faculty:** Student/faculty ratio 11:1. 76 full-time faculty, 91% hold PhDs, 7% are are members of minority groups, 59% are women. 0% of classes are taught by teaching assistants.

ACADEMICS

Degrees: bachelor's, master's, post-master's certificate. **Classes:** Most classes have fewer than 10 students. Most lab/discussion sessions have fewer than 10 students. **Most popular majors:** Education; Psychology; Biology. **Special Study Options:** cross-registration, double major, English as a Second Language (ESL), honors program, independent study, internships, liberal arts/career combination, student-designed major, study abroad, teacher certification program, Undergrads may take grad level classes. **Honors Programs:** Nisbet Honors Program Combined degree programs: Nursing with Vanderbilt University. **Disability Services:** Special programs offered to physically disabled students, including note-taking services, tape recorders, tutors. **Career Services:** Alumni network, Alumni services, Career/job search classes, Career assessment, Internships, Regional alumni.

FACILITIES

Housing: women's dorms. **Special Academic Facilities/Equipment:** Language lab. Phifer Science Building, Blackman Auditorium (Music), DNA sequencer and lab. **Computers:** Students can register for classes online. Administrative functions (other than registration) can be performed online.

CAMPUS LIFE

Environment: City. **Activities:** Choral groups, concert band, dance, drama/theater, literary magazine, music ensembles, musical theater, opera, student government, student newspaper, symphony orchestra, yearbook. 60 registered organizations, 16 honor societies, 7 religious organizations. **Athletics (Intercollegiate):** *Women:* basketball, cross-country, lacrosse, soccer, swimming, tennis, volleyball. **On-Campus Highlights:** Montgomery Student Life Center, Weisiger Physical Activity Complex, Phifer Science Complex, Petrie School of Music- Twichell Auditorium, Outdoor Quad area for studying and relaxing. **Environmental Initiatives:** LEED Certified new construction.

ADMISSIONS

Freshman Academic Profile: 18% in top 10% of high school class, 43% in top 25% of high school class, 80% in top 50% of high school class. 80% from public high schools. **Reported SAT (pre-2016 redesign) scores:** SAT Math middle 50% range 460-570. SAT Critical Reading middle 50% range 470-600. **Concordant SAT scores:** SAT Math middle 50% range 500–590. ACT middle 50% range 20-26. Minimum internet-based TOEFL 79. Minimum paper TOEFL 550. **Basis for Candidate Selection:** *Very important factors considered include:* academic GPA, standardized test scores. *Important factors considered include:* rigor of secondary school record, class rank. *Other factors considered include:* application essay, recommendation(s), talent/ability, alumni/ae relation. **Freshman Admission Requirements:** High school diploma is required and GED is accepted. *Academic units recommended:* 4 English, 3 math, 3 science, 1 science lab, 2 foreign language, 2 social studies, 2 history, 8 academic electives. **Freshman Admission Statistics:** 1,383 applied, 51.34% admitted, 26% enrolled. **Transfer Admission Requirements:** college transcript(s), statement of good standing from prior institution(s). Minimum college GPA of 2.0 required. Lowest grade transferable C. **General Admission Information:** Priority deadline 3/1. Nonfall registration accepted. Admission may be deferred for a maximum of 1 year.

COSTS AND FINANCIAL AID

Annual tuition $27,276. Room and board $8,854. Required fees $1,000. Average book expense $1,000. **Required Forms and Deadlines:** FAFSA. **Notification of Awards:** Applicants will be notified of awards on a rolling basis beginning 3/1. **Types of Aid:** *Need-based scholarships/grants:* Federal Pell, FSEOG, State scholarships/grants, Private scholarships, College/university scholarship or grant aid from institutional funds. *Loans:* Direct Subsidized Stafford Loans, Direct Unsubsidized Stafford Loans, Direct PLUS loans, Federal Perkins Loans, State Loans. *Student Employment:* Federal Work-Study Program available. Institutional employment available. **Financial Aid Statistics:** 100% needy freshmen, 98% needy undergrads receive need-based scholarship or grant aid. 18% freshmen, 17% undergrads receive non-need-based scholarship or grant aid. 79% freshmen, 77% undergrads receive need-based self-help aid. 14% freshmen, 8% undergrads receive athletic scholarships. 95% freshmen, 93% undergrads receive any aid. **Criteria for awarding aid:** *Need-based:* Academics, Art, Athletics, Music/drama. *Non-need-based:* Academics, Art, Athletics, Music/drama.

THE COOPER UNION FOR THE ADVANCEMENT OF SCIENCE AND ART

30 Cooper Square, New York, NY 10003
Phone: 212-353-4120 • **Financial Aid Phone:** 212-353-4130
E-mail: admissions@cooper.edu • **CEEB Code:** 2097
Fax: 212-353-4342 • **Website:** cooper.edu • **ACT Code:** 2724

This private school was founded in 1859.

RATINGS

Admissions Selectivity Rating: 98   **Fire Safety Rating:** 97   **Green Rating:** 60*

STUDENTS AND FACULTY

Enrollment: 857. **Student Body:** 33% female, 67% male, 51% out-of-state, 18% international. Asian 20%, African American 3%, Caucasian 30%, Hispanic 10%, Native American 0%, Pacific Islander 0%, Two or more races 9%, Race unknown 10%.
Retention and Graduation: 95% freshmen return for sophomore year. 75% freshmen graduate within 4 years. 87% freshmen graduate within 6 years. 45% grads go on to further study within 1 year. 4% grads pursue arts and sciences degrees. 9% grads pursue medical degrees. **Faculty:** Student/faculty ratio 8:1. 57 full-time faculty, 91% hold PhDs, 18% are are members of minority groups, 26% are women. 0% of classes are taught by teaching assistants.

ACADEMICS

Degrees: bachelor's, certificate, master's. **Classes:** Most classes have 10-19 students. **Most popular majors:** Electrical and Electronics Engineering; Mechanical Engineering; Fine and Studio Arts. **Special Study Options:** cross-registration, exchange student program (domestic), independent study, internships, student-designed major, study abroad, Cooper Union is indeed an all-honors college. Research opportunities available. Students may take up to one year off during their studies with us to pursue other interests. **Honors Programs:** Cooper Union is an all-honors college Combined degree programs: MEng/MD. **Disability Services:** Special programs offered to physically disabled students, including reader services, tape recorders, tutors. **Career Services:** Alumni network, Alumni services, Career/job search classes, Career assessment, Internships, Regional alumni. on-campus interviews and presentations. Our recruiting activities build heavily on strong relationships with alumni who return year after year to hire Cooper students.

FACILITIES

Housing: Coed dorms. 75% of campus accessible to physically diasbled. The Great Hall; Houghton Gallery; The Brooks Lab, Prototyping Lab, Bio-Medical Engineering Lab, Tissue Engineering Lab, Center for Sustainable Design, Center for Infrastructure and Urban Systems, Center for Signal Processing Communications and Computer Engineering Research, **Computers:** 85% of classrooms, have wireless network access. Administrative functions (other than registration) can be performed online.

CAMPUS LIFE

Environment: Metropolis. **Activities:** Choral groups, concert band, dance, drama/theater, jazz band, literary magazine, music ensembles, student government, student newspaper, student-run film society, symphony orchestra, yearbook. 90 registered organizations, 18 honor societies, 8 religious organizations. 2 fraternities, 1 sorority. **Athletics (Intercollegiate):** *Men:* baseball, basketball, cross-country, soccer, tennis, volleyball. *Women:* basketball, cross-country, soccer, tennis, volleyball. **On-Campus Highlights:** Great Hall, 41 Cooper Square, Foundation Building, Houghton Gallery, 41 Cooper Square Gallery, 41 Cooper Square-our newest building, Opened in September of 2009 to critical acclaim. Designed by Pritzker Prize winning architect, Thom Mayne, this building has many green features and is targeted to earn Platinum LEED certification. **Environmental Initiatives:** 41 Cooper Square Building please see: cooper.edu.

ADMISSIONS

Freshman Academic Profile: Average high school GPA 3.6. 85% in top 10% of high school class, 90% in top 25% of high school class, 95% in top 50% of high school class. 65% from public high schools. **Reported SAT (pre-2016 redesign) scores:** SAT Math middle 50% range 640-780. SAT Critical Reading middle 50% range 600-720. SAT Writing middle 50% range 590-710. **Concordant SAT scores:** SAT EBRW middle 50% 650-740. SAT Math middle 50% range 660-790. ACT middle 50% range 30-34. Minimum internet-based TOEFL 100. Minimum paper TOEFL 600. **Basis for Candidate Selection:**

Very important factors considered include: rigor of secondary school record, academic GPA, standardized test scores, talent/ability, level of applicant's interest. *Important factors considered include:* application essay, extracurricular activities, character/personal qualities. *Other factors considered include:* class rank, recommendation(s), interview, first generation, racial/ethnic status, volunteer work, work experience. **Freshman Admission Requirements:** High school diploma is required and GED is accepted. *Academic units required:* 4 English, 1 math, 1 science, 1 social studies, 1 history, 8 academic electives. *Academic units recommended:* 4 English, 4 math, 4 science, 3 science labs, 2 foreign language, 4 social studies. **Freshman Admission Statistics:** 2,654 applied, 12.96% admitted, 70% enrolled. **Transfer Admission Requirements:** High school transcript, college transcript(s), essay or personal statement, standardized test scores, statement of good standing from prior institution(s). Minimum college GPA of 3.0 required. Lowest grade transferable B. **General Admission Information:** Application fee $75. Priority deadline 12/1. Regular application deadline 1/11. Regular notification 4/1. Nonfall registration not accepted. Admission may be deferred for a maximum of 1 year.

COSTS AND FINANCIAL AID

Annual tuition $43,250. Room and board $16,270. Required fees $1,850. Average book expense $1,650. **Required Forms and Deadlines:** FAFSA, CSS/Financial Aid PROFILE. **Notification of Awards:** Applicants will be notified of awards on a rolling basis beginning 12/20. **Types of Aid:** *Need-based scholarships/grants:* Federal Pell, FSEOG, State scholarships/grants, Private scholarships, College/university scholarship or grant aid from institutional funds. *Loans:* Direct Subsidized Stafford Loans, Direct Unsubsidized Stafford Loans, Direct PLUS loans, Federal Perkins Loans, College/university loans from institutional funds. *Student Employment:* Federal Work-Study Program available. Institutional employment available. **Financial Aid Statistics:** 84% needy freshmen, 100% needy undergrads receive need-based scholarship or grant aid. 100% freshmen, 100% undergrads receive non-need-based scholarship or grant aid. 39% freshmen, 37% undergrads receive need-based self-help aid. 0% freshmen, 0% undergrads receive athletic scholarships. 100% freshmen, 100% undergrads receive any aid. 22% undergrads borrow to pay for school. Average cumulative indebtedness $21,919. **Criteria for awarding aid:** *Need-based:* Academics. *Non-need-based:* Academics.

CORBAN UNIVERSITY

5000 Deer Park Drive SE, Salem, OR 97317
Phone: 503-375-7005 • **Financial Aid Phone:** 503-375-7030
E-mail: admissions@corban.edu
Fax: 503-585-4316 • **Website:** www.corban.edu • **ACT Code:** 477

This private school, affiliated with the Baptist Church, was founded in 1935. It has a 145-acre campus.

RATINGS

Admissions Selectivity Rating: 87   **Fire Safety Rating:** 85   **Green Rating:** 60*

STUDENTS AND FACULTY

Enrollment: 1,024. **Student Body:** 60% female, 40% male, 50% out-of-state, 2% international (7 countries represented). Asian 3%, African American 1%, Caucasian 78%, Hispanic 3%, Native American 1%, Pacific Islander 1%, Two or more races 6%, Race unknown 6%.
Retention and Graduation: 77% freshmen return for sophomore year. 50% freshmen graduate within 4 years. 56% freshmen graduate within 6 years. **Faculty:** Student/faculty ratio 14:1. 49 full-time faculty, 73% hold PhDs, 0% are are members of minority groups, 22% are women. 0% of classes are taught by teaching assistants.

ACADEMICS

Degrees: associate, bachelor's, master's. **Classes:** Most classes have 10-19 students. Most lab/discussion sessions have 10-19 students. **Most popular majors:** Education; Business Administration and Management; Pre-medical studies. **Special Study Options:** Accelerated program, cross-registration, distance learning, double major, dual enrollment, honors program, independent study, internships, liberal arts/career combination, study abroad, teacher certification program, weekend college. Combined degree programs: BA/MA. **Disability Services:** Special programs offered to physically disabled students, including note-taking services, reader services, tape recorders, tutors. **Career Services:** Career/job search classes, Career assessment, Internships, On-campus interviews. Corban Consulting Partners Program. Undergraduate students in the School of Business work in teams on real life consulting projects with local business and non-profit organizations.

FACILITIES

Housing: men's dorms, women's dorms, apartments for married students, apartments for single students. 80% of campus accessible to physically diasbled.

Special Academic Facilities/Equipment: Prewitt-Allen Archeological Museum, Psalms Performing Arts Center. **Computers:** Students can register for classes online.

CAMPUS LIFE

Environment: City. **Activities:** Choral groups, concert band, drama/theater, jazz band, music ensembles, student government, student newspaper, yearbook, Campus Ministries. 1 honor society, 10 religious organizations. **Athletics (Intercollegiate):** *Men:* baseball, basketball, cross-country, golf, soccer, track/field (outdoor). *Women:* basketball, cross-country, golf, soccer, softball, track/field (outdoor), volleyball. **On-Campus Highlights:** Common Grounds Coffee Shop, Dining Hall, Gymnasium and Athletic Fields, Computer Lab, Book Store, Archaeological Museum, Psalms Performing Arts Center.

ADMISSIONS

Freshman Academic Profile: Average high school GPA 3.6. 26% in top 10% of high school class, 58% in top 25% of high school class, 88% in top 50% of high school class. 60% from public high schools. **Reported SAT (pre-2016 redesign) scores:** SAT Math middle 50% range 440-560. SAT Critical Reading middle 50% range 455-580. SAT Writing middle 50% range 440-550. **Concordant SAT scores:** SAT EBRW middle 50% 500–620. SAT Math middle 50% range 480–580. ACT middle 50% range 18-25. Minimum paper TOEFL 500. **Basis for Candidate Selection:** *Very important factors considered include:* academic GPA, application essay, recommendation(s), religious affiliation/commitment. *Important factors considered include:* rigor of secondary school record, standardized test scores, character/personal qualities, level of applicant's interest. *Other factors considered include:* class rank, interview, extracurricular activities, alumni/ae relation. **Freshman Admission Requirements:** High school diploma is required and GED is accepted. *Academic units recommended:* 4 English, 3 math, 2 science, 2 foreign language, 3 social studies. **Freshman Admission Statistics:** 2,678 applied, 37.38% admitted, 22% enrolled. **Transfer Admission Requirements:** High school transcript, college transcript(s), essay or personal statement, Minimum college GPA of 2.00 required. Lowest grade transferable C-. **General Admission Information:** Application fee $40. Priority deadline 3/1. Regular application deadline 8/1. Nonfall registration accepted. Admission may be deferred.

COSTS AND FINANCIAL AID

Annual tuition $28,980. Room and board $9,240. Required fees $660. Average book expense $900. **Required Forms and Deadlines:** FAFSA. **Notification of Awards:** Applicants will be notified of awards on a rolling basis beginning 3/1. **Types of Aid:** *Need-based scholarships/grants:* Federal Pell, FSEOG, State scholarships/grants, Private scholarships, College/university scholarship or grant aid from institutional funds. *Loans:* Direct Subsidized Stafford Loans, Direct Unsubsidized Stafford Loans, Direct PLUS loans, Federal Perkins Loans. *Student Employment:* Federal Work-Study Program available. Institutional employment available. **Financial Aid Statistics:** 98% needy freshmen receive need-based scholarship or grant aid. 13% freshmen, 12% undergrads receive non-need-based scholarship or grant aid. 76% freshmen, 74% undergrads receive need-based self-help aid. 10% freshmen, 10% undergrads receive athletic scholarships. 97% freshmen, 97% undergrads receive any aid. **Criteria for awarding aid:** *Need-based:* Academics, Alumni affiliation, Athletics, Leadership.

CORCORAN COLLEGE OF ART + DESIGN

500 17th Street NW, Washington, DC 20006-4804
Phone: 202-639-1814 • **Financial Aid Phone:** 202-639-1851
E-mail: admissions@corcoran.org
Fax: 202-639-1830 • **Website:** www.corcoran.edu

This private school was founded in 1890. It has a 7-acre campus.

RATINGS

Admissions Selectivity Rating: 60*   **Fire Safety Rating:** 67   **Green Rating:** 60*

STUDENTS AND FACULTY

Faculty: Student/faculty ratio 15:1. 0% of classes are taught by teaching assistants.

ACADEMICS

Degrees: associate, bachelor's, certificate, master's. **Classes:** Most classes have fewer than 10 students. **Most popular majors:** Graphic Design; Photography; Fine/Studio Arts. **Special Study Options:** cross-registration, exchange student program (domestic), internships, study abroad. **Disability Services:** Special programs offered to physically disabled students, including note-taking services, reader services, tape recorders, tutors. **Career Services:** Alumni network, Alumni services, Career/job search classes, Internships.

FACILITIES

Housing: Corcoran Leased Apartments and assistance in finding area housing. **Special Academic Facilities/Equipment:** Art gallery. Student exhibition spaces **Computers:** Administrative functions (other than registration) can be performed online. Undergraduates are required to own a computer.

CAMPUS LIFE

Environment: Metropolis. **Activities:** student government, student-run film society. **On-Campus Highlights:** Corcoran Gallery, Corcoran Studios, Corcoran Cafe des Artistes.

ADMISSIONS

Minimum internet-based TOEFL 80. **Freshman Admission Requirements:** High school diploma is required and GED is accepted. **Transfer Admission Requirements:** High school transcript, college transcript(s), Minimum college GPA of 2.5 required. Lowest grade transferable C. **General Admission Information:** Application fee $45.

COSTS AND FINANCIAL AID

Annual tuition $30,930. *Student Employment:* Federal Work-Study Program available. Institutional employment available.

CORNELL COLLEGE

600 First Street South West, Mount Vernon, IA 52314-1098
Phone: 319-895-4161 • **Financial Aid Phone:** 319-895-4216
E-mail: admissions@cornellcollege.edu • **CEEB Code:** 6119
Fax: 319-895-4451 • **Website:** www.cornellcollege.edu • **ACT Code:** 1296

This private school, affiliated with the Methodist Church, was founded in 1853. It has a 129-acre campus.

RATINGS

Admissions Selectivity Rating: 84   **Fire Safety Rating:** 83   **Green Rating:** 60*

STUDENTS AND FACULTY

Enrollment: 974. **Student Body:** 50% female, 50% male, 81% out-of-state, 5% international (14 countries represented). Asian 3%, African American 5%, Caucasian 67%, Hispanic 12%, Native American 1%, Pacific Islander 0%, Two or more races 3%, Race unknown 5%.
Retention and Graduation: 78% freshmen return for sophomore year. 65% freshmen graduate within 4 years. 68% freshmen graduate within 6 years.
Faculty: Student/faculty ratio 10:1. 84 full-time faculty, 96% hold PhDs, 8% are are members of minority groups, 52% are women. 0% of classes are taught by teaching assistants.

ACADEMICS

Degrees: bachelor's. **Classes:** Most classes have 10-19 students. **Most popular majors:** Economics; Psychology; Biochemistry. **Special Study Options:** Accelerated program, double major, English as a Second Language (ESL), exchange student program (domestic), independent study, internships, liberal arts/career combination, student-designed major, study abroad, teacher certification program. Combined degree programs: BA/MA, Forestry and Environmental Management, Duke University. **Disability Services:** Special programs offered to physically disabled students, including tape recorders, tutors. **Career Services:** Alumni network, Alumni services, Career/job search classes, Career assessment, Internships, Regional alumni. Fellowships with premier internship programs. Externship Program, 3-5 day job shadowing opportunites.

FACILITIES

Housing: Coed dorms, men's dorms, women's dorms, apartments for single students, Our first year students live on first- year only floors and/or in first-year only residence halls. 51% of campus accessible to physically diasbled. **Special Academic Facilities/Equipment:** Geology center and museum, MNR machine in West Sc. Building, Luce Art Gallery. **Computers:** 100% of classrooms, 20% of dorms, 100% of libraries, 100% of dining areas, 100% of student union, 10% of common outdoor areas have wireless network access. Administrative functions (other than registration) can be performed online.

CAMPUS LIFE

Environment: Rural. **Activities:** Choral groups, concert band, dance, drama/theater, jazz band, literary magazine, music ensembles, musical theater, opera, radio station, student government, student newspaper, symphony orchestra, yearbook, Campus Ministries, Student Organization. 90 registered organizations, 11 honor societies, 11 religious organizations. 8 fraternities, 7 sororities. **Athletics (Intercollegiate):** *Men:* baseball, basketball, cross-country, football, golf, soccer, tennis, track/field (outdoor), track/field (indoor), wrestling. *Women:* basketball, cross-country, golf, soccer, softball, tennis, track/field (outdoor), track/field (indoor), volleyball. **On-Campus Highlights:** Commons—Orange Carpet—student center, Cole Library, Small Multi-Sports Center, Kimmel Theatre—new state of the art theatre, McWethy Hall—newly renovated art building, Most prodominant features on campus are our beautiful King Chapel. A newly renovated Armstrong Hall of Fine Arts. A new pedestrian mall [with outdoor ampitheatre]that connects the entire campus. **Environmental Initiatives:** Engineering study on costs of replacing current campus-side steam heat network, including specific costs and energy savings payback times for each building. Implementation of plan in two building remodels and designed into two upcoming remodel projects.

ADMISSIONS

Freshman Academic Profile: Average high school GPA 3.5. 19% in top 10% of high school class, 41% in top 25% of high school class, 76% in top 50% of high school class. **Reported SAT (pre-2016 redesign) scores:** SAT Math middle 50% range 495-620. SAT Critical Reading middle 50% range 475-655. **Concordant SAT scores:** SAT Math middle 50% range 530–640. ACT middle 50% range 23-29. Minimum internet-based TOEFL 79. Minimum paper TOEFL 550. **Basis for Candidate Selection:** *Very important factors considered include:* rigor of secondary school record, academic GPA, character/personal qualities. *Important factors considered include:* class rank, application essay, recommendation(s), extracurricular activities, talent/ability, volunteer work, work experience. *Other factors considered include:* standardized test scores, interview, first generation, alumni/ae relation, geographical residence, state residency, racial/ethnic status, level of applicant's interest. **Freshman Admission Requirements:** High school diploma is required and GED is accepted. *Academic units recommended:* 4 English, 3 math, 3 science, 2 foreign language, 3 social studies, 1 academic elective. **Freshman Admission Statistics:** 1,965 applied, 70.94% admitted, 21% enrolled. **Transfer Admission Requirements:** college transcript(s), essay or personal statement, statement of good standing from prior institution(s). Lowest grade transferable C. **General Admission Information:** Application fee $30. Priority deadline 12/1. Regular application deadline 2/1. Nonfall registration accepted. Admission may be deferred for a maximum of 1 year.

COSTS AND FINANCIAL AID

Annual tuition $39,675. Room and board $8,900. Required fees $225. Average book expense $1,253. **Required Forms and Deadlines:** FAFSA. **Notification of Awards:** Applicants will be notified of awards on a rolling basis beginning 3/1. **Types of Aid:** *Need-based scholarships/grants:* Federal Pell, FSEOG, State scholarships/grants, Private scholarships, College/university scholarship or grant aid from institutional funds. *Loans:* Direct Subsidized Stafford Loans, Direct Unsubsidized Stafford Loans, Direct PLUS loans, Federal Perkins Loans. *Student Employment:* Federal Work-Study Program available. Institutional employment available. **Financial Aid Statistics:** 100% needy freshmen, 100% needy undergrads receive need-based scholarship or grant aid. 11% freshmen, 11% undergrads receive non-need-based scholarship or grant aid. 84% freshmen, 84% undergrads receive need-based self-help aid. 0% freshmen, 0% undergrads receive athletic scholarships. 99% freshmen, 98% undergrads receive any aid. 75% undergrads borrow to pay for school. Average cumulative indebtedness $31,975. **Criteria for awarding aid:** *Non-need-based:* Academics, Alumni affiliation, Art, Leadership, Music/drama, Religious affiliation, State/district residency.

CORNELL UNIVERSITY

Ithaca, NY 14850
Phone: 607-255-5241 • **Financial Aid Phone:** 607-255-5145
E-mail: admissions@cornell.edu • **CEEB Code:** 2098
Fax: 607-255-0659 • **Website:** www.cornell.edu • **ACT Code:** 2726

This private school was founded in 1865. It has a 745-acre campus.

RATINGS

Admissions Selectivity Rating: 98   **Fire Safety Rating:** 90   **Green Rating:** 99

STUDENTS AND FACULTY

Enrollment: 14,471. **Student Body:** 52% female, 48% male, 66% out-of-state, 10% international (82 countries represented). Asian 18%, African American 6%,

Caucasian 40%, Hispanic 13%, Native American <1%, Pacific Islander <1%, Two or more races 5%, Race unknown 8%.
Retention and Graduation: 97% freshmen return for sophomore year. 87% freshmen graduate within 4 years. 94% freshmen graduate within 6 years. 24% grads go on to further study within 1 year. 16% grads pursue arts and sciences degrees. 2% grads pursue law degrees. 1% grads pursue business degrees. 3% grads pursue medical degrees.

ACADEMICS

Degrees: bachelor's, doctoral/professional, doctoral/research, master's. **Classes:** Most classes have 10-19 students. Most lab/discussion sessions have 10-19 students. **Most popular majors:** Biology/Biological Sciences; Hotel/Motel Administration/Management; Labor and Industrial Relations. **Special Study Options:** Accelerated program, cooperative education program, cross-registration, distance learning, double major, English as a Second Language (ESL), exchange student program (domestic), honors program, independent study, internships, liberal arts/career combination, student-designed major, study abroad, teacher certification program. Combined degree programs: BA/BS, BA/BArch, BA/BFA. **Disability Services:** Special programs offered to physically disabled students, including note-taking services, reader services, tape recorders, tutors. **Career Services:** Alumni network, Alumni services, Career/job search classes, Career assessment, Internships, Regional alumni. Cornell Career Services is increasing it outreach student services organizations on campus to increase awareness of NACE Career Readiness Competencies. Undergraduates also have the opportunity to shadow and work with alumni through our Alumni Connections Program. Students broaden their horizons by exploring unfamiliar career fields or deepen their knowledge of a career field through hands-on exposure. In addition, the programs build networking skills in students and foster positive alumni connections with the University.

FACILITIES

Housing: Coed dorms, special housing for disabled students, men's dorms, special housing for international students, women's dorms, fraternity/sorority housing, apartments for married students, cooperative housing, apartments for single students, Theme Housing, See http://www.campuslife.cornell.edu/campuslife/housing. **Special Academic Facilities/Equipment:** Biotechnology institute, a woods sanctuary, 4 designated national resource centers, 2 local optical observatories, Africana studies and research center, arboretum, particle accelerator, supercomputer, national research centers, performing arts center, art museum, lab of ornithology, vertebrates museum, living and learning communities, campus orchard, dairy pilot plant, mineralogical museum, animal teaching hospital, 2 agricultural experiment stations, and marine laboratory. **Computers:** 20% of classrooms, 100% of dorms, 100% of libraries, 100% of dining areas, 75% of student union, 20% of common outdoor areas have wireless network access. Students can register for classes online. Administrative functions (other than registration) can be performed online.

CAMPUS LIFE

Environment: Town. **Activities:** Choral groups, concert band, dance, drama/theater, jazz band, literary magazine, marching band, music ensembles, musical theater, pep band, radio station, student government, student newspaper, student-run film society, symphony orchestra, television station, yearbook, Campus Ministries, Student Organization, Model UN. 841 registered organizations, 22 honor societies, 61 religious organizations. 50 fraternities, 19 sororities. **Athletics (Intercollegiate):** *Men:* baseball, basketball, crew/rowing, cross-country, diving, football, golf, ice hockey, lacrosse, polo, soccer, squash, swimming, tennis, track/field (outdoor), track/field (indoor), wrestling. *Women:* basketball, crew/rowing, cross-country, diving, equestrian sports, fencing, field hockey, gymnastics, ice hockey, lacrosse, polo, soccer, softball, squash, swimming, tennis, track/field (outdoor), track/field (indoor), volleyball. **On-Campus Highlights:** Johnson Art Museum, Gorges and waterfalls bordering campus, Center for Theater Arts, Cornell Plantations, including Beebe Lak, Willard Straight Hall, http://explore.cornell.edu/. **Environmental Initiatives:** In acknowledgement of the pressing issue of climate change, Cornell has created a Senior Leaders Climate Action Group charged with directing Cornell pivotal role as an international leader and exemplar to the world in addressing climate change and promoting sustainability through research, education, engagement, and operations ?é?Çô using our own campus as a living laboratory. Cornell recently completed it second 2MW solar farm and has signed contracts to construct 6MW of additional solar PV in 2016. http://www.sustainablecampus.cornell.edu/blogs/news/posts/toward-a-sustainable-future

ADMISSIONS

Freshman Academic Profile: 90% in top 10% of high school class, 98% in top 25% of high school class, 100% in top 50% of high school class. **Reported SAT (pre-2016 redesign) scores:** SAT Math middle 50% range 680-780. SAT Critical Reading middle 50% range 650-750. **Concordant SAT scores:** SAT Math middle 50% range 710–790. ACT middle 50% range 31-34. Minimum internet-based TOEFL 100. Minimum paper TOEFL 600. **Basis for Candidate Selection:** *Very important factors considered include:* rigor of secondary school record, academic GPA, standardized test scores, application essay, recommendation(s), extracurricular activities, talent/ability, character/

personal qualities. *Important factors considered include:* class rank. *Other factors considered include:* interview, first generation, alumni/ae relation, geographical residence, state residency, racial/ethnic status, volunteer work, work experience. **Freshman Admission Requirements:** High school diploma or equivalent is not required. *Academic units required:* 4 English, 3 math. *Academic units recommended:* 3 science, 3 science labs, 3 foreign language, 3 social studies, 3 history. **Freshman Admission Statistics:** 44,965 applied, 14.09% admitted, 52% enrolled. **Transfer Admission Requirements:** High school transcript, college transcript(s), essay or personal statement, statement of good standing from prior institution(s). Lowest grade transferable C. **General Admission Information:** Application fee $80. Regular application deadline 1/2. Nonfall registration not accepted. Admission may be deferred.

COSTS AND FINANCIAL AID

Required Forms and Deadlines: FAFSA, CSS/Financial Aid PROFILE, Noncustodial PROFILE. **Notification of Awards:** Applicants will be notified of awards on or about 4/1. **Types of Aid:** *Need-based scholarships/grants:* Federal Pell, FSEOG, State scholarships/grants, Private scholarships, College/university scholarship or grant aid from institutional funds. *Loans:* Direct Subsidized Stafford Loans, Direct Unsubsidized Stafford Loans, Direct PLUS loans, Federal Perkins Loans, College/university loans from institutional funds. *Student Employment:* Federal Work-Study Program available. Institutional employment available. **Financial Aid Statistics:** 98% needy freshmen, 98% needy undergrads receive need-based scholarship or grant aid. 0% undergrads receive non-need-based scholarship or grant aid. 89% freshmen, 92% undergrads receive need-based self-help aid. 0% freshmen, 0% undergrads receive athletic scholarships. 60% freshmen, 57% undergrads receive any aid. 41% undergrads borrow to pay for school. Average cumulative indebtedness $23,389. **Criteria for awarding aid:** *Need-based:* Leadership.

CORNERSTONE UNIVERSITY

1001 East Beltline Avenue, NE, Grand Rapids, MI 49525-5897
Phone: 616-222-1418 • **Financial Aid Phone:** 616-949-5300
E-mail: admissions@cornerstone.edu
Fax: 616-222-1418 • **Website:** www.cornerstone.edu • **ACT Code:** 2002

This private school, affiliated with the Christian (Nondenominational) Church, was founded in 1941. It has a 130-acre campus.

RATINGS

Admissions Selectivity Rating: 74   **Fire Safety Rating:** 96   **Green Rating:** 60*

STUDENTS AND FACULTY

Enrollment: 1,741. **Student Body:** 59% female, 41% male, 16% out-of-state, 1% international (15 countries represented). Asian 1%, African American 11%, Caucasian 83%, Hispanic 4%, Native American <1%, Pacific Islander 0%, Two or more races 0%, Race unknown 0%.
Retention and Graduation: 69% freshmen return for sophomore year. 15% grads go on to further study within 1 year. 10% grads pursue arts and sciences degrees. 1% grads pursue law degrees. 3% grads pursue business degrees. 1% grads pursue medical degrees. **Faculty:** Student/faculty ratio 13:1. 62 full-time faculty, 50% hold PhDs, 5% are are members of minority groups, 32% are women. 0% of classes are taught by teaching assistants.

ACADEMICS

Degrees: associate, bachelor's, certificate, diploma, master's, terminal. **Classes:** Most classes have 10-19 students. **Most popular majors:** Youth Ministry; Elementary Education and Teaching; Mass Communication/Media Studies. **Special Study Options:** Accelerated program, distance learning, double major, dual enrollment, English as a Second Language (ESL), honors program, independent study, internships, liberal arts/career combination, study abroad, teacher certification program, weekend college. **Honors Programs:** Honors Program based on a "great books" curriculum. **Disability Services:** Special programs offered to physically disabled students, including note-taking services, reader services, tape recorders, tutors. **Career Services:** Career/job search classes, Career assessment, Internships. The required internship of all students as part of the graduation requirements.

FACILITIES

Housing: special housing for disabled students, men's dorms, women's dorms, apartments for married students, apartments for single students, Theme Housing. 100% of campus accessible to physically diasbled. **Computers:** 100% of classrooms, 100% of dorms, 100% of libraries, 100% of dining areas, 100% of student union, 100% of common outdoor areas have wireless network access. Students can register for classes online. Administrative functions (other than registration) can be performed online.

CAMPUS LIFE

Environment: City. **Activities:** Choral groups, concert band, dance, drama/theater, jazz band, literary magazine, music ensembles, musical theater, opera, pep band, radio station, student government, student newspaper, student-run film society, Campus Ministries, Student Organization. 11 registered organizations, 2 honor societies, 1 religious organization. **Athletics (Intercollegiate): Men:** basketball, cross-country, golf, soccer, track/field (outdoor), track/field (indoor). *Women:* basketball, cross-country, golf, soccer, softball, track/field (outdoor), track/field (indoor), volleyball. **On-Campus Highlights:** Corum Student Union, Bernice Hansen Athletic Center, Campus Bookstore Atrium, Faber Hall Seating Area, Gordon Music Hall. **Environmental Initiatives:** On campus dialogue and focus on sustainability issues.

ADMISSIONS

Freshman Academic Profile: Average high school GPA 3.3. 60% from public high schools. **Reported SAT (pre-2016 redesign) scores:** SAT Math middle 50% range 440-540. SAT Critical Reading middle 50% range 360-580. SAT Writing middle 50% range 480-500. **Concordant SAT scores:** SAT EBRW middle 50% 470–600. SAT Math middle 50% range 480–570. ACT middle 50% range 20-25. Minimum paper TOEFL 500. **Basis for Candidate Selection:** *Very important factors considered include:* academic GPA, standardized test scores, application essay, recommendation(s), character/personal qualities, religious affiliation/commitment. *Important factors considered include:* rigor of secondary school record, class rank. *Other factors considered include:* level of applicant's interest. **Freshman Admission Requirements:** High school diploma is required and GED is accepted. *Academic units recommended:* 4 English, 3 math, 2 science, 1 science lab, 2 foreign language, 3 social studies, 2 history, 4 academic electives. **Freshman Admission Statistics:** 1,109 applied, 72.86% admitted, 45% enrolled. **Transfer Admission Requirements:** High school transcript, college transcript(s), essay or personal statement, Minimum college GPA of 2.0 required. Lowest grade transferable C-. **General Admission Information:** Application fee $25. Priority deadline 7/1. Nonfall registration accepted.

COSTS AND FINANCIAL AID

Annual tuition $19,190. Room and board $6,500. Required fees $340. Average book expense $1,000. **Required Forms and Deadlines:** FAFSA. **Notification of Awards:** Applicants will be notified of awards on a rolling basis beginning 2/15. **Types of Aid:** *Need-based scholarships/grants:* Federal Pell, FSEOG, State scholarships/grants, Private scholarships, College/university scholarship or grant aid from institutional funds. *Loans:* Federal Perkins Loans. *Student Employment:* Federal Work-Study Program available. Institutional employment available. **Financial Aid Statistics:** 100% needy freshmen, 99% needy undergrads receive need-based scholarship or grant aid. 100% freshmen, 94% undergrads receive non-need-based scholarship or grant aid. 81% freshmen, 79% undergrads receive need-based self-help aid. 23% freshmen, 15% undergrads receive athletic scholarships. 100% freshmen, 98% undergrads receive any aid. **Criteria for awarding aid:** *Need-based:* Academics, Alumni affiliation, Minority status. *Non-need-based:* Academics, Athletics, Leadership, Music/drama, State/district residency.

CORNISH COLLEGE OF THE ARTS

1000 Lenora Street, Seattle, WA 98121
Phone: 206-726-5016 • **Financial Aid Phone:** 206-726-5013
E-mail: admissions@cornish.edu • **CEEB Code:** 58
Fax: 206-720-1011 • **Website:** www.cornish.edu • **ACT Code:** 4801

This private school was founded in 1914. It has a 4-acre campus.

RATINGS

Admissions Selectivity Rating: 64   **Fire Safety Rating:** 60*   **Green Rating:** 60*

STUDENTS AND FACULTY

Enrollment: 604. **Student Body:** 64% female, 36% male, 52% out-of-state, 4% international (25 countries represented). Asian 6%, African American 4%, Caucasian 63%, Hispanic 9%, Native American 1%, Pacific Islander <1%, Two or more races 7%, Race unknown 6%.
Retention and Graduation: 12% grads go on to further study within 1 year. 5% grads pursue arts and sciences degrees. **Faculty:** Student/faculty ratio 8:1.

ACADEMICS

Degrees: bachelor's, postbachelor's certificate. **Classes:** Most classes have 10-19 students. **Most popular majors:** Design and Visual Communications; Drama and Dramatics/Theatre Arts; Music Performance. **Special Study Options:** cooperative education program, independent study, internships, study abroad. **Disability Services:** Special programs offered to physically disabled students, including note-taking services, tape recorders. **Career Services:** Internships.

FACILITIES

Housing: 50% of campus accessible to physically diasbled. **Special Academic Facilities/Equipment:** Art galleries, extensive art studio space, theatres, electronic music studio, dance studio, concert hall.

CAMPUS LIFE

Environment: Metropolis. **Activities:** Choral groups, concert band, dance, drama/theater, jazz band, literary magazine, music ensembles, musical theater, opera, student government, student newspaper, student-run film society 18 registered organizations, 6 honor societies, 1 religious organization. **On-Campus Highlights:** Raisbeck Performance Hall, Cornsh Gallery, Nellie's Cafe.

ADMISSIONS

Freshman Academic Profile: Average high school GPA 3.2. 75% from public high schools. Minimum paper TOEFL 525. **Basis for Candidate Selection:** *Very important factors considered include:* talent/ability. *Important factors considered include:* rigor of secondary school record, application essay. *Other factors considered include:* academic GPA, standardized test scores, recommendation(s), interview, extracurricular activities. **Freshman Admission Requirements:** High school diploma is required and GED is accepted. *Academic units required:* 4 English, 2 math, 2 science, 1 science lab, 3 social studies. *Academic units recommended:* 4 math, 4 science, 2 foreign language. **Freshman Admission Statistics:** 1,134 applied, 85.54% admitted, 17% enrolled. **Transfer Admission Requirements:** High school transcript, college transcript(s), essay or personal statement, interview, Minimum college GPA of 2.0 required. Lowest grade transferable C. **General Admission Information:** Application fee $40. Priority deadline 2/1. Regular application deadline 8/15. Nonfall registration not accepted. Admission may be deferred for a maximum of 12 months.

COSTS AND FINANCIAL AID

Annual tuition $31,980. **Required Forms and Deadlines:** FAFSA, Institution's own financial aid form. **Notification of Awards:** Applicants will be notified of awards on or about 5/15. **Types of Aid:** *Need-based scholarships/grants:* Federal Pell, FSEOG, State scholarships/grants. *Loans:* Federal Perkins Loans. *Student Employment:* Federal Work-Study Program available. **Financial Aid Statistics:** 84% needy undergrads receive need-based scholarship or grant aid. 100% undergrads receive non-need-based scholarship or grant aid. 84% undergrads receive need-based self-help aid. 0% undergrads receive athletic scholarships. **Criteria for awarding aid:** *Need-based:* Academics, Art, Music/drama. *Non-need-based:* Academics, Art, Music/drama.

COVENANT COLLEGE

14049 Scenic Highway, Lookout Mtn., GA 30750
Phone: 706-820-2398 • **Financial Aid Phone:** 706-419-1126
E-mail: admissions@covenant.edu • **CEEB Code:** 6124
Fax: 706-820-0893 • **Website:** www.covenant.edu • **ACT Code:** 3951

This private school was founded in 1955. It has a 300-acre campus.

RATINGS

Admissions Selectivity Rating: 85   **Fire Safety Rating:** 88   **Green Rating:** 60*

STUDENTS AND FACULTY

Enrollment: 981. **Student Body:** 54% female, 46% male, 73% out-of-state, 3% international (21 countries represented). Asian 1%, African American 3%, Caucasian 86%, Hispanic 3%, Native American 0%, Pacific Islander <1%, Two or more races 3%, Race unknown <1%.
Retention and Graduation: 86% freshmen return for sophomore year. 59% freshmen graduate within 4 years. 67% freshmen graduate within 6 years. 28% grads go on to further study within 1 year. 10% grads pursue arts and sciences degrees. 1% grads pursue law degrees. 2% grads pursue business degrees. 1% grads pursue medical degrees. **Faculty:** Student/faculty ratio 13:1. 66 full-time faculty, 92% hold PhDs, 11% are are members of minority groups, 23% are women. 0% of classes are taught by teaching assistants.

ACADEMICS

Degrees: bachelor's, master's. **Classes:** Most classes have 10-19 students. Most lab/discussion sessions have 20-29 students. **Most popular majors:** Sociology; English Language and Literature; Elementary Education and Teaching. **Special Study Options:** double major, dual enrollment, exchange student program (domestic), independent study, internships, student-designed major, study abroad, teacher certification program, Dual-engineering degree with Georgia Tech; cooperative nursing program with Emory University and Chattanooga State; bridge program for MSN with Vanderbilt University. **Disability Services:** Special programs offered to physically disabled students, including note-taking services, tape recorders. **Career Services:** Alumni network, Alumni services, Career assessment, Internships.

FACILITIES

Housing: men's dorms, women's dorms, apartments for single students. 95% of campus accessible to physically diasbled. **Computers:** 100% of classrooms, 100% of dorms, 100% of libraries, 100% of dining areas, 100% of common outdoor areas have wireless network access. Students can register for classes online. Administrative functions (other than registration) can be performed online.

CAMPUS LIFE

Environment: City. **Activities:** Choral groups, concert band, drama/theater, jazz band, literary magazine, music ensembles, radio station, student government, student newspaper, yearbook. 40 registered organizations, 4 honor societies, 1 religious organization. **Athletics (Intercollegiate):** *Men:* baseball, basketball, cross-country, golf, soccer, tennis. *Women:* basketball, cross-country, golf, soccer, softball, tennis, volleyball. **On-Campus Highlights:** Probasco Visitor's Center, Carter Hall, The Overlook, The Chapel, Ashe Gym, The campus is located on top of Lookout Mountain in Georgia, providing a backdrop of scenic beauty.

ADMISSIONS

Freshman Academic Profile: Average high school GPA 3.7. 26% in top 10% of high school class, 85% in top 25% of high school class, 85% in top 50% of high school class. 55% from public high schools. **Reported SAT (pre-2016 redesign) scores:** SAT Math middle 50% range 510-630. SAT Critical Reading middle 50% range 540-670. SAT Writing middle 50% range 510-640. **Concordant SAT scores:** SAT EBRW middle 50% 580–700. SAT Math middle 50% range 540–650. ACT middle 50% range 24-29. Minimum internet-based TOEFL 75. **Basis for Candidate Selection:** *Very important factors considered include:* rigor of secondary school record, academic GPA, standardized test scores, application essay, recommendation(s), character/personal qualities, religious affiliation/commitment. *Important factors considered include:* interview. *Other factors considered include:* class rank, extracurricular activities, first generation, alumni/ae relation, racial/ethnic status, volunteer work, level of applicant's interest. **Freshman Admission Requirements:** High school diploma is required and GED is accepted. *Academic units required:* 4 English, 3 math, 2 science, 2 social studies, 3 academic electives. *Academic units recommended:* 4 English, 3 math, 2 science, 2 foreign language, 2 social studies, 3 academic electives. **Freshman Admission Statistics:** 612 applied, 96.24% admitted, 45% enrolled. **Transfer Admission Requirements:** High school transcript, college transcript(s), essay or personal statement, interview, standardized test scores, statement of good standing from prior institution(s). Minimum college GPA of 2.0 required. Lowest grade transferable C-. **General Admission Information:** Application fee $35. Priority deadline 3/1. Regular application deadline 8/15. Nonfall registration accepted. Admission may be deferred for a maximum of 1 year.

COSTS AND FINANCIAL AID

Annual tuition $31,320. Room and board $9,630. Required fees $910. Average book expense $1,170. **Required Forms and Deadlines:** FAFSA, State aid form. **Notification of Awards:** Applicants will be notified of awards on a rolling basis beginning 2/1. **Types of Aid:** *Need-based scholarships/grants:* Federal Pell, FSEOG, State scholarships/grants, Private scholarships, College/university scholarship or grant aid from institutional funds. *Loans:* Federal Perkins Loans, State Loans. *Student Employment:* Federal Work-Study Program available. Institutional employment available. **Financial Aid Statistics:** 99% needy freshmen, 99% needy undergrads receive need-based scholarship or grant aid. 17% freshmen, 16% undergrads receive non-need-based scholarship or grant aid. 85% freshmen, 89% undergrads receive need-based self-help aid. 0% freshmen, 0% undergrads receive athletic scholarships. 100% freshmen, 99% undergrads receive any aid. 64% undergrads borrow to pay for school. Average cumulative indebtedness $24,484. **Criteria for awarding aid:** *Need-based:* Academics, Alumni affiliation, Art, Job skills, Leadership, Minority status, Music/drama. *Non-need-based:* Academics, Alumni affiliation, Art, Job skills, Leadership, Minority status, Music/drama, Religious affiliation, State/district residency.

CRANDALL UNIVERSITY

Crandall Admissions Office, Moncton, NB E1C 9L7
Phone: 506-858-8970
E-mail: admissions@crandallu.ca
Fax: 506-858-9694 • **Website:** www.crandallu.ca

This is a private school.

RATINGS

Admissions Selectivity Rating: 63   **Fire Safety Rating:** 60*   **Green Rating:** 60*

STUDENTS AND FACULTY

Student Body: 11% out-of-state.

Retention and Graduation: 48% freshmen return for sophomore year. 33% freshmen graduate within 4 years. **Faculty:** Student/faculty ratio 14:1. 26 full-time faculty, 81% hold PhDs, 15% are are members of minority groups, 35% are women.

ACADEMICS

Degrees: bachelor's, certificate, postbachelor's certificate. **Special Study Options:** cooperative education program, double major, dual enrollment, English as a Second Language (ESL), honors program, independent study, internships, liberal arts/career combination, study abroad, teacher certification program.

FACILITIES

Housing: men's dorms, women's dorms.

CAMPUS LIFE

Activities: drama/theater, student government, student newspaper, yearbook, Campus Ministries, Student Organization.

ADMISSIONS

Basis for Candidate Selection: *Important factors considered include:* academic GPA. **Freshman Admission Statistics:** 149 applied, 93.29% admitted, 71% enrolled. **Transfer Admission Requirements:** college transcript(s), Lowest grade transferable C-. **General Admission Information:** Application fee $35. Priority deadline 3/1. Nonfall registration accepted. Admission may be deferred for a maximum of one year.

COSTS AND FINANCIAL AID

Average book expense $1,600. *Student Employment:* Federal Work-Study Program available. Institutional employment available.

CREIGHTON UNIVERSITY

Best Colleges

2500 California Plaza, Omaha, NE 68178
Phone: 402-280-2703 • **Financial Aid Phone:** 402-280-2731
E-mail: admissions@creighton.edu • **CEEB Code:** 6121
Fax: 402-280-2685 • **Website:** www.creighton.edu • **ACT Code:** 2444

This private school, affiliated with the Roman Catholic Church, was founded in 1878. It has a 130-acre campus.

RATINGS

Admissions Selectivity Rating: 87   **Fire Safety Rating:** 96   **Green Rating:** 82

STUDENTS AND FACULTY

Enrollment: 4,149. **Student Body:** 57% female, 43% male, 76% out-of-state, 3% international (33 countries represented). Asian 9%, African American 2%, Caucasian 70%, Hispanic 8%, Native American <1%, Pacific Islander <1%, Two or more races 4%, Race unknown 2%.
Retention and Graduation: 89% freshmen return for sophomore year. 72% freshmen graduate within 4 years. 79% freshmen graduate within 6 years. **Faculty:** Student/faculty ratio 10:1. 569 full-time faculty, 91% hold PhDs, 11% are are members of minority groups, 46% are women. 0% of classes are taught by teaching assistants.

ACADEMICS

Degrees: associate, bachelor's, certificate, doctoral/professional, doctoral/research, doctoral, master's, postbachelor's certificate, post-master's certificate. **Classes:** Most classes have 10-19 students. Most lab/discussion sessions have 10-19 students. **Most popular majors:** Registered Nursing/Registered Nurse; Biology/Biological Sciences; Psychology. **Special Study Options:** Accelerated program, cross-registration, distance learning, double major, dual enrollment, English as a Second Language (ESL), exchange student program (domestic), honors program, independent study, internships, liberal arts/career combination, study abroad, teacher certification program, 3-3 Engineering Program with University of Detroit Mercy; 3-3 Law Program within Creighton University. **Honors Programs:** Designed for talented, imaginative students desirous of participation in small, iscussion-oriented classes and in courses on interdisciplinary and topical issues. Combined degree programs: BA/JD. **Disability Services:** Special programs offered to physically disabled students, including note-taking services, reader services, tape recorders, tutors. **Career Services:** Alumni network, Alumni services, Career/job search classes, Career assessment, Internships, Regional alumni.

FACILITIES

Housing: Coed dorms, special housing for disabled students, women's dorms, apartments for married students, apartments for single students, Honors, Freshman Leadership. 87% of campus accessible to physically diasbled. **Special Academic Facilities/Equipment:** Fine arts/performing center, health science and research complex, hospital. **Computers:** 100% of classrooms, 100% of dorms, 100% of libraries, 100% of dining areas, 100% of student union, 100% of common outdoor areas have wireless network access. Students can register for classes online. Administrative functions (other than registration) can be performed online.

CAMPUS LIFE

Environment: Metropolis. **Activities:** Choral groups, concert band, dance, drama/theater, jazz band, literary magazine, music ensembles, musical theater, pep band, student government, student newspaper, symphony orchestra, television station, yearbook, Campus Ministries, Student Organization, Model UN. 182 registered organizations, 11 honor societies, 6 religious organizations. 5 fraternities, 8 sororities. **Athletics (Intercollegiate):** *Men:* baseball, basketball, cross-country, golf, soccer, tennis. *Women:* basketball, crew/rowing, cross-country, golf, soccer, softball, tennis, volleyball. **On-Campus Highlights:** Harper Living Learning Center, Campus Mall and green in front of Studen, Hixson-Lied Science Building, Morrison Soccer stadium, Jesuit Gardens, Ryan Athletics Center and D.J. Sokol Auditorium completed Fall 2009. **Environmental Initiatives:** Stewardship of the environment has become central to the mission of Creighton University and the wider Jesuit community. The Energy Technology Program has allowed the university to become more sustainable, with 120 kW of renewable energy generated on site, including the largest solar photovoltaic array in Nebraska. Not only have these technologies reduced Creighton environmental footprint, but they have also become the foundation for a hands-on educational platform, allowing students to work and conduct research on professional systems. The University has continued to expand renewable energy sources including solar photovoltaic and solar thermal panels, four wind turbines designed for urban environments, geothermal hearing, low voltage lighting, solar hot water, and a ground source heat pump. The presence of these technologies at Creighton exposes everyone in the community to them and concretely conveys Creighton commitment to environmental responsibility.

ADMISSIONS

Freshman Academic Profile: Average high school GPA 3.8. 35% in top 10% of high school class, 70% in top 25% of high school class, 91% in top 50% of high school class. 52% from public high schools. **Reported SAT (pre-2016 redesign) scores:** SAT Math middle 50% range 530-650. SAT Critical Reading middle 50% range 520-630. SAT Writing middle 50% range 510-610. **Concordant SAT scores:** SAT EBRW middle 50% 570–670. SAT Math middle 50% range 560–670. ACT middle 50% range 24-30. Minimum internet-based TOEFL 80. Minimum paper TOEFL 550. **Basis for Candidate Selection:** *Very important factors considered include:* rigor of secondary school record, academic GPA. *Important factors considered include:* standardized test scores, application essay. *Other factors considered include:* class rank, recommendation(s), extracurricular activities, talent/ability, character/personal qualities, first generation, racial/ethnic status, volunteer work, level of applicant's interest. **Freshman Admission Requirements:** High school diploma is required and GED is accepted. *Academic units required:* 4 English, 3 math, 2 science, 1 science lab, 2 foreign language, 2 social studies, 3 academic electives. *Academic units recommended:* 4 English, 4 math, 3 science, 2 science labs, 3 foreign language, 4 social studies, 3 academic electives. **Freshman Admission Statistics:** 10,352 applied, 70.66% admitted, 14% enrolled. **Transfer Admission Requirements:** High school transcript, college transcript(s), statement of good standing from prior institution(s). Minimum college GPA of 2.50 required. Lowest grade transferable C. **General Admission Information:** Application fee $40. Priority deadline 12/1. Regular application deadline 2/15. Nonfall registration accepted. Admission may be deferred for a maximum of 1 year.

COSTS AND FINANCIAL AID

Annual tuition $35,942. Room and board $10,600. Required fees $1,664. Average book expense $1,200. **Required Forms and Deadlines:** FAFSA, Institution's own financial aid form. **Notification of Awards:** Applicants will be notified of awards on a rolling basis beginning 3/15. *Types of Aid: Need-based scholarships/grants:* Federal Pell, FSEOG, State scholarships/grants, Private scholarships, College/university scholarship or grant aid from institutional funds. *Loans:* Direct Subsidized Stafford Loans, Direct Unsubsidized Stafford Loans, Direct PLUS loans, Federal Perkins Loans, Federal Nursing Loans. *Student Employment:* Federal Work-Study Program available. Institutional employment available. **Financial Aid Statistics:** 96% needy undergrads receive need-based scholarship or grant aid. 24% freshmen, 18% undergrads receive non-need-based scholarship or grant aid. 76% freshmen, 79% undergrads receive need-based self-help aid. 4% freshmen, 4% undergrads receive athletic scholarships. 61% undergrads borrow to pay for school. Average cumulative indebtedness $35,921. **Criteria for awarding aid:** *Need-based:* Academics, Leadership. *Non-need-based:* Academics, Alumni affiliation, Art, Athletics, Leadership, Minority status, Music/drama.

CROWN COLLEGE

8700 College View Drive, St. Bonifacius, MN 55375-9001
Phone: 952-446-4142 • **Financial Aid Phone:** 952-446-4175
E-mail: info@crown.edu
Fax: 952-446-4149 • **Website:** www.crown.edu • **ACT Code:** 2152

This private school, affiliated with the Christian & Missionary Allianc Church, was founded in 1916. It has a 215-acre campus.

RATINGS
Admissions Selectivity Rating: 80   **Fire Safety Rating:** 74   **Green Rating:** 60*

STUDENTS AND FACULTY
Enrollment: 1,017. **Student Body:** 57% female, 43% male, 31% out-of-state, 1% international (21 countries represented). Asian 7%, African American 4%, Caucasian 78%, Hispanic 2%, Native American 1%, Pacific Islander <1%, Two or more races 1%, Race unknown 7%.
Retention and Graduation: 63% freshmen return for sophomore year. 40% freshmen graduate within 4 years. 52% freshmen graduate within 6 years.
Faculty: Student/faculty ratio 14:1. 34 full-time faculty, 47% hold PhDs, 6% are are members of minority groups, 26% are women. 0% of classes are taught by teaching assistants.

ACADEMICS
Degrees: associate, bachelor's, certificate, master's, postbachelor's certificate.
Classes: Most classes have 10-19 students. Most lab/discussion sessions have 20-29 students. **Most popular majors:** Theology and Religious Vocations; Elementary Education and Teaching; Business Administration and Management. **Special Study Options:** Accelerated program, distance learning, double major, dual enrollment, English as a Second Language (ESL), honors program, independent study, internships, study abroad, teacher certification program, weekend college, 2-2 with non-accredited Bible colleges. **Honors Programs:** The Honors Program. **Disability Services:** Special programs offered to physically disabled students, including note-taking services, reader services, tape recorders, tutors. **Career Services:** Alumni services, Career/job search classes, Career assessment, Internships. We are very excited about the number of opportunities that students have to engage in practical hands-on learning activities through the SIFE and practicum programs.

FACILITIES
Housing: special housing for disabled students, men's dorms, women's dorms, apartments for married students, apartments for single studentsApartments for students with dependent children. 95% of campus accessible to physically diasbled. **Special Academic Facilities/Equipment:** Peter Watne Memorial Library **Computers:** 100% of classrooms, 20% of dorms, 100% of libraries, 100% of dining areas, 100% of student union, 10% of common outdoor areas have wireless network access. Administrative functions (other than registration) can be performed online.

CAMPUS LIFE
Environment: Rural. **Activities:** Choral groups, concert band, drama/theater, jazz band, literary magazine, music ensembles, musical theater, pep band, radio station, student government, student newspaper, student-run film society, yearbook, Campus Ministries, Student Organization. 19 registered organizations, 1 honor society, 6 religious organizations. **Athletics (Intercollegiate):** *Men:* baseball, basketball, cross-country, football, golf, soccer. *Women:* basketball, cross-country, golf, soccer, softball, volleyball. **On-Campus Highlights:** Student Center, Coffee Shoppe and Climbing Wall, Storm Cafe/student union, Wild Athletic Center/Weight Room, Life Fitness Center. **Environmental Initiatives:** The College recycles all cardboard and provides co-mingled recycling containers in all common areas, each classroom, and in each office. We post recycling program notes on our website from time to time and also posters throughout the building quarterly. Large amounts of metals, plastics, light bulbs, electronics, etc. are recycled each month by facilities mgmt.

ADMISSIONS
Freshman Academic Profile: Average high school GPA 3.4. 13% in top 10% of high school class, 38% in top 25% of high school class, 79% in top 50% of high school class. **Reported SAT (pre-2016 redesign) scores:** SAT Math middle 50% range 475-598. SAT Critical Reading middle 50% range 508-600. SAT Writing middle 50% range 533-618. **Concordant SAT scores:** SAT EBRW middle 50% 580–660. SAT Math middle 50% range 510–620. ACT middle 50% range 21-25. Minimum internet-based TOEFL 75. Minimum paper TOEFL 500. **Basis for Candidate Selection:** *Very important factors considered include:* academic GPA, standardized test scores, application essay, religious affiliation/commitment. *Other factors considered include:* rigor of secondary school record, recommendation(s). **Freshman Admission Requirements:** High school diploma is required and GED is accepted. *Academic units recommended:* 4 English, 3 math, 3 science, 2 foreign language, 3 social studies. **Freshman Admission Statistics:** 453 applied, 77.70% admitted, 45% enrolled. **Transfer Admission Requirements:** High school transcript, college transcript(s), essay or personal statement, Minimum college GPA of 2.0 required. Lowest grade transferable C. **General Admission Information:** Application fee $20. Regular application deadline 8/20. Nonfall registration accepted. Admission may be deferred for a maximum of 1 year.

COSTS AND FINANCIAL AID
Annual tuition $22,100. Room and board $7,480. Average book expense $1,140. **Required Forms and Deadlines:** FAFSA, Institution's own financial aid form. **Notification of Awards:** Applicants will be notified of awards on a rolling basis beginning 3/1. **Types of Aid:** *Need-based scholarships/grants:* Federal Pell, FSEOG, State scholarships/grants, Private scholarships, College/university scholarship or grant aid from institutional funds. *Loans:* Direct Subsidized Stafford Loans, Direct Unsubsidized Stafford Loans, Direct PLUS loans, Federal Perkins Loans, State Loans. *Student Employment:* Federal Work-Study Program available. **Financial Aid Statistics:** 84% freshmen, 83% undergrads receive any aid. **Criteria for awarding aid:** *Need-based:* Academics. *Non-need-based:* Academics, Alumni affiliation, Leadership, Minority status, Music/drama, Religious affiliation.

THE CULINARY INSTITUTE OF AMERICA

1946 Campus Drive, Hyde Park, NY 12538
Phone: 845-452-9430 • **Financial Aid Phone:** 845-451-1243
E-mail: admissions@culinary.edu • **CEEB Code:** 3301
Fax: 845-451-1068 • **Website:** www.ciachef.edu • **ACT Code:** 2728

RATINGS
Admissions Selectivity Rating: 75   **Fire Safety Rating:** 98   **Green Rating:** 60*

STUDENTS AND FACULTY
Student Body: 51% female, 49% male, 68% out-of-state, (37 countries represented).
Faculty: 0% of classes are taught by teaching assistants.

ACADEMICS
Degrees: associate, bachelor's, certificate, postbachelor's certificate. **Most popular majors:** Restaurant/Food Services Management; Culinary Science/Culinology; Multi-/Interdisciplinary Studies. **Career Services:** Alumni network, Career/job search classes, Career assessment, Internships. Our three annual Career Fairs bring top industry employers to campus. Our 2016 fairs averaged 143 companies attending at each of the three events.

ADMISSIONS
Freshman Academic Profile: Average high school GPA 3.1. 6% in top 10% of high school class, 24% in top 25% of high school class, 57% in top 50% of high school class. **Reported SAT (pre-2016 redesign) scores:** SAT Math middle 50% range 450-560. SAT Critical Reading middle 50% range 448-560. SAT Writing middle 50% range 410-540. **Concordant SAT scores:** SAT EBRW middle 50% 480–610. SAT Math middle 50% range 490–580. ACT middle 50% range 17-23. Minimum internet-based TOEFL 80. Minimum paper TOEFL 550. **Basis for Candidate Selection:** *Important factors considered include:* rigor of secondary school record, academic GPA. *Other factors considered include:* class rank, standardized test scores, application essay, recommendation(s), extracurricular activities, talent/ability, character/personal qualities, alumni/ae relation, volunteer work, work experience, level of applicant's interest. **Freshman Admission Requirements:** *Academic units required:* 4 English, 3 math, 3 science, 4 social studies. *Academic units recommended:* 4 English, 3 math, 3 science, 2 foreign language, 4 social studies. **Freshman Admission Statistics:** 989 applied, 94.44% admitted, 55% enrolled. **General Admission Information:** Application fee $50. Nonfall registration accepted. Admission may be deferred for a maximum of 1 year.

COSTS AND FINANCIAL AID
Annual tuition $29,380. Room and board $10,870. Required fees $2,236. Average book expense $800. **Required Forms and Deadlines:** FAFSA, State aid form. **Notification of Awards:** Applicants will be notified of awards on a rolling basis beginning 3/5. **Types of Aid:** *Need-based scholarships/grants:* Federal Pell, FSEOG, State scholarships/grants, Private scholarships, College/university scholarship or grant aid from institutional funds. *Loans:* Direct Subsidized Stafford Loans, Direct Unsubsidized Stafford Loans, Direct PLUS loans, Federal Perkins Loans. *Student Employment:* Federal Work-Study Program available. Institutional employment available. **Financial Aid Statistics:** 92% needy undergrads receive need-based scholarship or grant aid. 86% freshmen, 77% undergrads receive non-need-based scholarship or grant aid. 94% freshmen, 88% undergrads receive need-based self-help aid. 0% freshmen, 0% undergrads receive athletic scholarships. 94% freshmen, 90% undergrads receive any aid. 63% undergrads borrow to pay for school. Average cumulative indebtedness $51,200. **Criteria for awarding aid:** *Non-need-based:* Academics, Alumni affiliation, Job skills, Leadership.

CULVER-STOCKTON COLLEGE

One College Hill, Canton, MO 63435
Phone: 573-288-6331 • **Financial Aid Phone:** 573-288-6307
E-mail: admissions@culver.edu • **CEEB Code:** 6123
Fax: 573-288-6618 • **ACT Code:** 2290

This private school, affiliated with the Disciples of Christ Church, was founded in 1853. It has a 139-acre campus.

RATINGS
Admissions Selectivity Rating: 78   **Fire Safety Rating:** 74   **Green Rating:** 60*

STUDENTS AND FACULTY
Enrollment: 1,058. **Student Body:** 52% female, 48% male, 48% out-of-state, 6% international (11 countries represented). Asian 1%, African American 11%, Caucasian 74%, Hispanic 5%, Native American <1%, Pacific Islander <1%, Two or more races 2%, Race unknown 0%.
Retention and Graduation: 64% freshmen return for sophomore year. 40% freshmen graduate within 4 years. 47% freshmen graduate within 6 years. 16% grads go on to further study within 1 year. 6% grads pursue arts and sciences degrees. 2% grads pursue law degrees. 3% grads pursue business degrees. 1% grads pursue medical degrees. **Faculty:** Student/faculty ratio 15:1. 51 full-time faculty, 65% hold PhDs, 8% are are members of minority groups, 47% are women. 0% of classes are taught by teaching assistants.

ACADEMICS
Degrees: bachelor's, master's. **Classes:** Most classes have 10-19 students. Most lab/discussion sessions have 10-19 students. **Most popular majors:** Business Administration and Management; Criminal Justice/Law Enforcement Administration; Sport and Fitness Administration/Management. **Special Study Options:** Accelerated program, distance learning, double major, dual enrollment, honors program, independent study, internships, liberal arts/career combination, student-designed major, study abroad, teacher certification program. **Honors Programs:** Honors Scholars are expected to complete both an academic and enrichment requirement. Combined degree programs: Washington University-OT program. **Disability Services:** Special programs offered to physically disabled students, including note-taking services, reader services, tape recorders, tutors. **Career Services:** Alumni network, Alumni services, Career/job search classes, Career assessment, Internships, Regional alumni. All students have participated in experiential learning since fall 2008 as part of our curriculum.

FACILITIES
Housing: Coed dorms, fraternity/sorority housing. 40% of campus accessible to physically diasbled. **Special Academic Facilities/Equipment:** Art gallery, performing arts center. **Computers:** 100% of classrooms, 100% of dorms, 100% of libraries, 100% of dining areas, 100% of student union, 100% of common outdoor areas have wireless network access. Students can register for classes online. Administrative functions (other than registration) can be performed online.

CAMPUS LIFE
Environment: Rural. **Activities:** Choral groups, concert band, dance, drama/theater, jazz band, literary magazine, music ensembles, musical theater, pep band, radio station, student government, student newspaper, Campus Ministries, Student Organization, Model UN. 44 registered organizations, 11 honor societies, 4 religious organizations. 4 fraternities, 3 sororities. **Athletics (Intercollegiate):** *Men:* baseball, basketball, cheerleading, cross-country, football, golf, soccer, track/field (outdoor), track/field (indoor). *Women:* basketball, cheerleading, cross-country, golf, soccer, softball, track/field (outdoor), track/field (indoor), volleyball. **On-Campus Highlights:** Computer labs, Cat's 'Pause', Cafeteria, Joe Charles Field House, Activity & Recreation Center. **Environmental Initiatives:** Thermostat control.

ADMISSIONS
Freshman Academic Profile: Average high school GPA 3.2. 6% in top 10% of high school class, 24% in top 25% of high school class, 61% in top 50% of high school class. 95% from public high schools. **Reported SAT (pre-2016 redesign) scores:** SAT Math middle 50% range 430-510. SAT Critical Reading middle 50% range 420-490. **Concordant SAT scores:** SAT Math middle 50% range 470-540. ACT middle 50% range 18-23. Minimum internet-based TOEFL 79. Minimum paper TOEFL 550. **Basis for Candidate Selection:** *Very important factors considered include:* academic GPA, standardized test scores. *Important factors considered include:* rigor of secondary school record. *Other factors considered include:* class rank, application essay, recommendation(s), interview. **Freshman Admission Requirements:** High school diploma is required and GED is accepted. *Academic units recommended:* 4 English, 2 math, 2 science, 1 foreign language, 3 social studies, 3 history. **Freshman Admission Statistics:** 3,305 applied, 58.12% admitted, 14% enrolled. **Transfer Admission Requirements:** college transcript(s),

Minimum college GPA of 2.0 required. Lowest grade transferable C-.
General Admission Information: Regular application deadline 8/15. Nonfall registration accepted. Admission may be deferred for a maximum of 1 year.

COSTS AND FINANCIAL AID
Annual tuition $25,615. Room and board $8,310. Required fees $425. Average book expense $1,100. **Required Forms and Deadlines:** FAFSA. **Notification of Awards:** Applicants will be notified of awards on a rolling basis beginning 2/15. **Types of Aid:** *Need-based scholarships/grants:* Federal Pell, FSEOG, State scholarships/grants, Private scholarships, College/university scholarship or grant aid from institutional funds. *Loans:* Direct Subsidized Stafford Loans, Direct Unsubsidized Stafford Loans, Direct PLUS loans, Federal Perkins Loans, State Loans, College/university loans from institutional funds. *Student Employment:* Federal Work-Study Program available. Institutional employment available. **Financial Aid Statistics:** 100% needy freshmen, 99% needy undergrads receive need-based scholarship or grant aid. 15% freshmen, 12% undergrads receive non-need-based scholarship or grant aid. 82% freshmen, 87% undergrads receive need-based self-help aid. 15% freshmen, 17% undergrads receive athletic scholarships. 94% freshmen, 97% undergrads receive any aid. 85% undergrads borrow to pay for school. Average cumulative indebtedness $28,605. **Criteria for awarding aid:** *Need-based:* Academics, Art, Athletics, Music/drama, Religious affiliation. *Non-need-based:* Academics, Alumni affiliation, Art, Athletics, Leadership, Music/drama, Religious affiliation.

CURRY COLLEGE

1071 Blue Hill Avenue, Milton, MA 2186
Phone: 617-333-2210
E-mail: curryadm@curry.edu • **CEEB Code:** 3285
Fax: 617-333-2114 • **Website:** www.curry.edu • **ACT Code:** 1814

This private school was founded in 1879. It has a 137-acre campus.

RATINGS
Admissions Selectivity Rating: 72   **Fire Safety Rating:** 60*   **Green Rating:** 60*

STUDENTS AND FACULTY
Enrollment: 2,843. **Student Body:** 63% female, 37% male, 22% out-of-state, 1% international (20 countries represented). Asian 2%, African American 9%, Caucasian 69%, Hispanic 5%, Native American <1%, Pacific Islander 0%, Two or more races 2%, Race unknown 12%.
Retention and Graduation: 71% freshmen return for sophomore year. 36% freshmen graduate within 4 years. 45% freshmen graduate within 6 years. 17% grads go on to further study within 1 year. 10% grads pursue arts and sciences degrees. 1% grads pursue law degrees. 2% grads pursue business degrees. **Faculty:** Student/faculty ratio 11:1. 122 full-time faculty, 81% hold PhDs, 7% are are members of minority groups, 67% are women. 0% of classes are taught by teaching assistants.

ACADEMICS
Degrees: bachelor's, master's. **Special Study Options:** Accelerated program, double major, honors program, independent study, internships, liberal arts/career combination, student-designed major, study abroad, teacher certification program, weekend college. **Disability Services:** Special programs offered to physically disabled students, including tape recorders, tutors.

FACILITIES
Housing: Coed dorms, special housing for international students, women's dorms. **Special Academic Facilities/Equipment:** On-campus preschool, nursing lab, psychology lab. **Computers:** Students can register for classes online.

CAMPUS LIFE
Environment: Village. **Activities:** Choral groups, dance, drama/theater, literary magazine, music ensembles, radio station, student government, student newspaper, television station, yearbook. 1 honor society, 2 religious organizations. **Athletics (Intercollegiate):** *Men:* baseball, basketball, cheerleading, football, ice hockey, lacrosse, soccer, tennis. *Women:* basketball, cheerleading, cross-country, lacrosse, soccer, softball, tennis. **On-Campus Highlights:** Drapkin Student Center, Levin Library, WMLN Campus Radio Station, The Suites- New Residence Hall, Hafer Academic Center.

ADMISSIONS
Freshman Academic Profile: Average high school GPA 2.8. 5% in top 10% of high school class, 18% in top 25% of high school class, 53% in top 50% of high school class. 76% from public high schools. **Reported SAT (pre-2016 redesign) scores:** SAT Math middle 50% range 430-520. SAT Critical Reading middle 50% range 420-520. SAT Writing middle 50% range 420-520. **Concordant SAT scores:** SAT EBRW middle 50% 470-580. SAT Math middle 50% range 470-550. ACT middle 50% range 18-21. Minimum paper TOEFL

500. **Basis for Candidate Selection:** *Very important factors considered include:* rigor of secondary school record. *Important factors considered include:* academic GPA, standardized test scores, application essay, recommendation(s), interview, extracurricular activities, character/personal qualities. *Other factors considered include:* class rank, talent/ability, alumni/ae relation, volunteer work, work experience, level of applicant's interest. **Freshman Admission Requirements:** High school diploma is required and GED is accepted. *Academic units required:* 4 English, 3 math. *Academic units recommended:* 2 science, 1 science lab, 2 foreign language, 2 social studies, 2 history. **Freshman Admission Statistics:** 5,448 applied, 86.88% admitted, 14% enrolled. **Transfer Admission Requirements:** college transcript(s), essay or personal statement, Minimum college GPA of 2.0 required. Lowest grade transferable C-. **General Admission Information:** Application fee $50. Priority deadline 4/1. Nonfall registration accepted. Admission may be deferred.

COSTS AND FINANCIAL AID

Annual tuition $34,730. Room and board $13,900. Required fees $1,715. Average book expense $1,150. **Required Forms and Deadlines:** FAFSA. **Notification of Awards:** Applicants will be notified of awards on a rolling basis beginning 3/1. **Types of Aid:** *Need-based scholarships/grants:* Federal Pell, FSEOG, State scholarships/grants, Private scholarships, College/university scholarship or grant aid from institutional funds. *Loans:* Direct Subsidized Stafford Loans, Direct Unsubsidized Stafford Loans, Direct PLUS loans, Federal Perkins Loans, State Loans. *Student Employment:* Federal Work-Study Program available. Institutional employment available. **Financial Aid Statistics:** 79% needy freshmen, 85% needy undergrads receive need-based scholarship or grant aid. 8% freshmen, 6% undergrads receive non-need-based scholarship or grant aid. 86% freshmen, 89% undergrads receive need-based self-help aid. 0% freshmen, 0% undergrads receive athletic scholarships. **Criteria for awarding aid:** *Non-need-based:* Academics, Alumni affiliation, Leadership.

D'YOUVILLE COLLEGE

320 Porter Avenue, Buffalo, NY 14201
Phone: 716-829-7600 • **Financial Aid Phone:** 716-829-7500
E-mail: admissions@dyc.edu • **CEEB Code:** 2197
Fax: 716-829-7790 • **Website:** www.dyc.edu • **ACT Code:** 2732

This private school was founded in 1908. It has a 7-acre campus.

RATINGS

Admissions Selectivity Rating: 78   **Fire Safety Rating:** 82   **Green Rating:** 60*

STUDENTS AND FACULTY

Enrollment: 1,982. **Student Body:** 73% female, 27% male, 4% out-of-state, 7% international (55 countries represented). Asian 3%, African American 10%, Caucasian 70%, Hispanic 4%, Native American 1%, Pacific Islander 0%, Two or more races 1%, Race unknown 4%.
Retention and Graduation: 72% freshmen return for sophomore year. 32% freshmen graduate within 4 years. 52% freshmen graduate within 6 years.
Faculty: Student/faculty ratio 8:1. 180 full-time faculty, 76% hold PhDs, 8% are are members of minority groups, 61% are women. 0% of classes are taught by teaching assistants.

ACADEMICS

Degrees: bachelor's, doctoral/professional, doctoral/research, master's, postbachelor's certificate, post-master's certificate. **Classes:** Most classes have 10-19 students. Most lab/discussion sessions have 10-19 students. **Most popular majors:** Education Business/Commerce. **Special Study Options:** Accelerated program, cooperative education program, cross-registration, distance learning, double major, dual enrollment, exchange student program (domestic), independent study, internships, liberal arts/career combination, study abroad, teacher certification program, weekend college. Combined degree programs: BS/MS. **Disability Services:** Special programs offered to physically disabled students, including note-taking services, reader services, tape recorders, tutors.

FACILITIES

Housing: Coed dorms, special housing for disabled students, apartments for married students, apartments for single studentsQuiet floors for 3rd-5th year students. Separate male and female floors available. New apartment style housing opened 1/05. 100% of campus accessible to physically diasbled. **Special Academic Facilities/Equipment:** Kavinoky Theatre (professional theatre). **Computers:** Students can register for classes online. Administrative functions (other than registration) can be performed online.

CAMPUS LIFE

Environment: City. **Activities:** Choral groups, drama/theater, literary magazine, student government, student newspaper, yearbook. 25 registered

organizations, 3 honor societies, 1 religious organization. **Athletics (Intercollegiate):** *Men:* baseball, basketball, golf, soccer, volleyball. *Women:* basketball, crew/rowing, golf, soccer, softball, volleyball. **On-Campus Highlights:** New Academic Center, New Gym, Spot Spartian Cafe, Weight Room, Gross anatomy lab, New apartment style housing for junior level and up opening 1/05.

ADMISSIONS

Freshman Academic Profile: 18% in top 10% of high school class, 52% in top 25% of high school class, 87% in top 50% of high school class. 75% from public high schools. **Reported SAT (pre-2016 redesign) scores:** SAT Math middle 50% range 490-580. SAT Critical Reading middle 50% range 470-550. SAT Writing middle 50% range 450-540. **Concordant SAT scores:** SAT EBRW middle 50% 510–600. SAT Math middle 50% range 520–600. ACT middle 50% range 21-25. Minimum paper TOEFL 500. **Basis for Candidate Selection:** *Very important factors considered include:* rigor of secondary school record, academic GPA, standardized test scores. *Important factors considered include:* class rank. *Other factors considered include:* recommendation(s), interview, extracurricular activities, talent/ability, character/personal qualities, alumni/ae relation, volunteer work, work experience. **Freshman Admission Requirements:** High school diploma is required and GED is accepted. *Academic units recommended:* 4 English, 3 math, 3 science, 3 foreign language, 3 social studies. **Freshman Admission Statistics:** 1,023 applied, 80.35% admitted, 29% enrolled. **Transfer Admission Requirements:** High school transcript, college transcript(s), Minimum college GPA of 2.0 required. Lowest grade transferable C. **General Admission Information:** Application fee $25. Nonfall registration accepted. Admission may be deferred for a maximum of 12 months.

COSTS AND FINANCIAL AID

Annual tuition $21,930. Room and board $10,250. Required fees $310. Average book expense $1,200. **Required Forms and Deadlines:** FAFSA, State aid form. **Notification of Awards:** Applicants will be notified of awards on a rolling basis beginning 4/15. **Types of Aid:** *Need-based scholarships/grants:* Federal Pell, FSEOG, State scholarships/grants, Private scholarships, College/university scholarship or grant aid from institutional funds. *Loans:* Direct Subsidized Stafford Loans, Direct Unsubsidized Stafford Loans, Direct PLUS loans, Federal Perkins Loans, Federal Nursing Loans, State Loans. *Student Employment:* Federal Work-Study Program available. Institutional employment available. **Financial Aid Statistics:** 100% needy freshmen receive need-based scholarship or grant aid. 10% freshmen, 5% undergrads receive non-need-based scholarship or grant aid. 89% freshmen, 92% undergrads receive need-based self-help aid. 0% freshmen, 0% undergrads receive athletic scholarships. **Criteria for awarding aid:** *Need-based:* Academics, Alumni affiliation. *Non-need-based:* Academics, Leadership, Religious affiliation.

DAEMEN COLLEGE

4380 Main Street, Amherst, NY 14226-3592
Phone: 716-839-8225 • **Financial Aid Phone:** 716-839-8254
E-mail: admissions@daemen.edu • **CEEB Code:** 2762
Fax: 716-839-8229 • **Website:** www.daemen.edu • **ACT Code:** 2874

This private school was founded in 1947. It has a 35-acre campus.

RATINGS

Admissions Selectivity Rating: 86   **Fire Safety Rating:** 90   **Green Rating:** 60*

STUDENTS AND FACULTY

Enrollment: 1,884. **Student Body:** 70% female, 30% male, 5% out-of-state, 1% international (6 countries represented). Asian 2%, African American 11%, Caucasian 74%, Hispanic 7%, Native American <1%, Pacific Islander <1%, Two or more races 1%, Race unknown 2%.
Retention and Graduation: 79% freshmen return for sophomore year. 34% freshmen graduate within 4 years. 56% freshmen graduate within 6 years.
Faculty: Student/faculty ratio 16:1. 122 full-time faculty, 76% hold PhDs, 6% are are members of minority groups, 59% are women. 0% of classes are taught by teaching assistants.

ACADEMICS

Degrees: bachelor's, certificate, doctoral/professional, master's, postbachelor's certificate, post-master's certificate. **Classes:** Most classes have 10-19 students. Most lab/discussion sessions have 10-19 students. **Most popular majors:** Registered Nursing/Registered Nurse; Elementary Education and Teaching; Natural Sciences. **Special Study Options:** Accelerated program, cross-registration, distance learning, double major, dual enrollment, English as a Second Language (ESL), exchange student program (domestic), honors program, independent study, internships, liberal arts/career combination, student-designed major, study abroad, teacher certification program, weekend college, Washington semester through the Washington Internship Institute. Dual degree (BS/MS) awarded at the completion of the program in physician assistant studies and professional accountancy. **Honors Programs:** The Honors Program provides an enriched curriculum relying upon multiple perspectives and using primary sources rather than textbooks. Honors program students enjoy special residential accommodations, priority registration by class rank, opportunities for domestic and international travel, and unique offerings such as field trips, access to campus speakers, and research and publication opportunities. Combined degree programs: BS/MS Health Sci/Phys. Asst.; BS/MS Accountancy; BS/MS Athletic Training. **Disability Services:** Special programs offered to physically disabled students, including note-taking services, tape recorders, tutors. **Career Services:** Alumni network, Alumni services, Career/job search classes, Career assessment, Internships, Regional alumni. Two outstanding programs are: Physician Assistant Studies and the new Animation program.

FACILITIES

Housing: Coed dorms, Coed apartment-style residence halls for single students; some apartments are handicapped accessible. 99% of campus accessible to physically diasbled. **Special Academic Facilities/Equipment:** Teaching Resource Center; Franette Goldman/Carolyn Greenfield Art Gallery; Natural and Health Sciences Research Center; video conferencing center; Research & Information Commons (new). **Computers:** 60% of classrooms, 100% of dorms, 100% of libraries, 75% of dining areas, 50% of student union, 10% of common outdoor areas have wireless network access. Students can register for classes online. Administrative functions (other than registration) can be performed online.

CAMPUS LIFE

Environment: City. **Activities:** Choral groups, dance, drama/theater, literary magazine, student government, student newspaper, yearbook, Campus Ministries. 45 registered organizations, 8 honor societies, 1 fraternity, 4 sororities. **Athletics (Intercollegiate):** *Men:* basketball, cross-country, golf, soccer. *Women:* basketball, cross-country, soccer, volleyball. **On-Campus Highlights:** Research and Information Commons, Modern Apartment-Style Residence Halls, Wick Student Center, Academic Computing Facilities, Athletic Facilities. **Environmental Initiatives:** College has hosted conferences and symposia on campus: Annual Environmental Summit; Green Jobs Workshop; World on Your Plate Symposium, Focus the Nation Teach-In.

ADMISSIONS

Freshman Academic Profile: Average high school GPA 3.6. 28% in top 10% of high school class, 58% in top 25% of high school class, 89% in top 50% of high school class. **Reported SAT (pre-2016 redesign) scores:** SAT Math middle 50% range 470-590. SAT Critical Reading middle 50% range 450-570. SAT Writing middle 50% range 440-540. **Concordant SAT scores:** SAT EBRW middle 50% 500–610. SAT Math middle 50% range 510–610. ACT middle 50% range 21-27. Minimum internet-based TOEFL 61. Minimum paper TOEFL 500. **Basis for Candidate Selection:** *Very important factors considered include:* standardized test scores. *Important factors considered include:* rigor of secondary school record, class rank, academic GPA, application essay, recommendation(s), interview. *Other factors considered include:* extracurricular activities, talent/ability, character/personal qualities, alumni/ae relation, volunteer work, work experience, level of applicant's interest. **Freshman Admission Requirements:** High school diploma is required and GED is accepted. *Academic units recommended:* 4 English, 4 math, 4 science, 1 science lab, 4 social studies. **Freshman Admission Statistics:** 3,219 applied, 51.97% admitted, 23% enrolled. **Transfer Admission Requirements:** college transcript(s), statement of good standing from prior institution(s). Minimum college GPA of 2.0 required. Lowest grade transferable C. **General Admission Information:** Application fee $25. Nonfall registration accepted. Admission may be deferred for a maximum of 12 months.

COSTS AND FINANCIAL AID

Annual tuition $21,800. Room and board $10,840. Required fees $510. Average book expense $800. **Required Forms and Deadlines:** FAFSA, State aid form. **Notification of Awards:** Applicants will be notified of awards on a rolling basis beginning 2/15. **Types of Aid:** *Need-based scholarships/grants:* Federal Pell, FSEOG, State scholarships/grants, Private scholarships, College/university scholarship or grant aid from institutional funds. *Loans:* Direct Subsidized Stafford Loans, Direct Unsubsidized Stafford Loans, Direct PLUS loans, Federal Perkins Loans. *Student Employment:* Federal Work-Study Program available. Institutional employment available. **Financial Aid Statistics:** 92% needy freshmen, 94% needy undergrads receive need-based scholarship or grant aid. 96% freshmen, 96% undergrads receive non-need-based scholarship or grant aid. 91% freshmen, 93% undergrads receive need-based self-help aid. 5% freshmen, 5% undergrads receive athletic scholarships. 99% freshmen, 84% undergrads receive any aid. **Criteria for awarding aid:** *Need-based:* Academics. *Non-need-based:* Academics, Art, Athletics, Leadership.

See page 946.

DAKOTA STATE UNIVERSITY

820 North Washington Ave., Madison, SD 57042
Phone: 605-256-5139 • **Financial Aid Phone:** 605-256-5152
E-mail: admissions@dsu.edu • **CEEB Code:** 6247
Fax: 605-256-5020 • **Website:** www.dsu.edu • **ACT Code:** 3910

This public school was founded in 1881. It has a 20-acre campus.

RATINGS
Admissions Selectivity Rating: 75   **Fire Safety Rating:** 85   **Green Rating:** 61

STUDENTS AND FACULTY
Enrollment: 1,936. **Student Body:** 36% female, 64% male, 32% out-of-state, 1% international (14 countries represented). Asian 2%, African American 4%, Caucasian 83%, Hispanic 4%, Native American 1%, Pacific Islander <1%, Two or more races 4%, Race unknown 1%.
Retention and Graduation: 72% freshmen return for sophomore year. 21% freshmen graduate within 4 years. 37% freshmen graduate within 6 years.
Faculty: Student/faculty ratio 17:1. 100 full-time faculty, 66% hold PhDs, 13% are members of minority groups, 35% are women. 1% of classes are taught by teaching assistants.

ACADEMICS
Degrees: associate, bachelor's, certificate, doctoral/research, master's, postbachelor's certifiate. **Classes:** Most classes have 20-29 students. Most lab/discussion sessions have 10-19 students. **Most popular majors:** Computer and Information Systems Security/Information Assurance; Computer and Information Sciences; System, Networking, and LAN/WAN Management/Manager. **Special Study Options:** cooperative education program, cross-registration, distance learning, double major, dual enrollment, English as a Second Language (ESL), honors program, independent study, internships, teacher certification program. **Honors Programs:** Center of Excellence(CEX), Honors Combined degree programs: BS/MS. **Disability Services:** Special programs offered to physically disabled students, including note-taking services, reader services, tape recorders, tutors. **Career Services:** Alumni services, Career/job search classes, Career assessment, Internships. Interviewing opportunities (for internships and full-time positions) are available through the on-campus interview program, DSU Career Fair, BIG Job Fair, mock interviews and employer information sessions. We also have a very robust employer relations program in which relationships with local, state and regional employers are developed and fostered.

FACILITIES
Housing: Coed dorms, men's dorms, special housing for international students, women's dorms, apartments for single students. 80% of campus accessible to physically diasbled. **Special Academic Facilities/Equipment:** Smith Zimmerman Museum **Computers:** 100% of classrooms, 100% of dorms, 100% of libraries, 100% of dining areas, 100% of student union, 100% of common outdoor areas have wireless network access. Students can register for classes online. Administrative functions (other than registration) can be performed online. Undergraduates are required to own a computer.

CAMPUS LIFE
Environment: Rural. **Activities:** Choral groups, dance, drama/theater, literary magazine, music ensembles, musical theater, pep band, radio station, student government, student newspaper, Student Organization. 33 registered organizations, 3 honor societies, 2 religious organizations. **Athletics (Intercollegiate):** *Men:* baseball, basketball, cheerleading, cross-country, football, track/field (outdoor), track/field (indoor). *Women:* basketball, cheerleading, cross-country, softball, track/field (outdoor), track/field (indoor), volleyball. **On-Campus Highlights:** Tunhiem Classroom Building, Community Center, Trojan Center, Myxers Coffee Shop, The Marketplace. **Environmental Initiatives:** LEED Silver project in progress.

ADMISSIONS
Freshman Academic Profile: Average high school GPA 3.2. 7% in top 10% of high school class, 25% in top 25% of high school class, 55% in top 50% of high school class. **Reported SAT (pre-2016 redesign) scores:** SAT Math middle 50% range 430-585. SAT Critical Reading middle 50% range 430-580. **Concordant SAT scores:** SAT Math middle 50% range 470–610. ACT middle 50% range 19-25. Minimum internet-based TOEFL 79. Minimum paper TOEFL 550. **Basis for Candidate Selection:** *Important factors considered include:* rigor of secondary school record, class rank, academic GPA, standardized test scores. **Freshman Admission Requirements:** High school diploma is required and GED is accepted. *Academic units recommended:* 4 English, 3 math, 3 science, 3 science labs, 3 social studies, 1 visual/performing arts. **Freshman Admission Statistics:** 921 applied, 82.63% admitted, 43% enrolled. **Transfer Admission Requirements:** High school transcript, college transcript(s), Minimum college GPA of 2.0 required. Lowest grade transferable D. **General Admission Information:** Application fee $20. Nonfall registration accepted.

COSTS AND FINANCIAL AID

Annual in-state tuition $6,984. Annual out-of-state tuition $9,900. Room and board $6,411. Required fees $1,943. Average book expense $1,200. **Required Forms and Deadlines:** FAFSA. **Notification of Awards:** Applicants will be notified of awards on a rolling basis beginning 4/1. **Types of Aid:** *Need-based scholarships/grants:* Federal Pell, FSEOG, State scholarships/grants, Private scholarships, College/university scholarship or grant aid from institutional funds. *Loans:* Direct Subsidized Stafford Loans, Direct Unsubsidized Stafford Loans, Direct PLUS loans, Federal Perkins Loans. *Student Employment:* Federal Work-Study Program available. Institutional employment available. **Financial Aid Statistics:** 62% needy freshmen, 60% needy undergrads receive need-based scholarship or grant aid. 71% freshmen, 44% undergrads receive non-need-based scholarship or grant aid. 95% freshmen, 93% undergrads receive need-based self-help aid. 21% freshmen, 13% undergrads receive athletic scholarships. 75% freshmen, 75% undergrads receive any aid. 79% undergrads borrow to pay for school. Average cumulative indebtedness $24,444. **Criteria for awarding aid:** *Need-based:* Academics, Athletics, Minority status. *Non-need-based:* Academics, Alumni affiliation, Art, Athletics, Leadership, Minority status, Music/drama, State/district residency.

DALLAS BAPTIST UNIVERSITY

3000 Mountain Creek Parkway, Dallas, TX 75211-9299
Phone: 214-333-5360 • **Financial Aid Phone:** 214-333-5363
E-mail: admiss@dbu.edu • **CEEB Code:** 6159
Fax: 214-333-5447 • **Website:** http://www.dbu.edu/ • **ACT Code:** 4080

This private school, affiliated with the Baptist Church, was founded in 1898. It has a 293-acre campus.

RATINGS

Admissions Selectivity Rating: 86   **Fire Safety Rating:** 91   **Green Rating:** 60*

STUDENTS AND FACULTY

Enrollment: 3,109. **Student Body:** 59% female, 41% male, 8% out-of-state, 6% international (36 countries represented). Asian 2%, African American 14%, Caucasian 60%, Hispanic 16%, Native American 1%, Pacific Islander <1%, Two or more races 0%, Race unknown 0%.
Retention and Graduation: 77% freshmen return for sophomore year. 43% freshmen graduate within 4 years. 59% freshmen graduate within 6 years. **Faculty:** Student/faculty ratio 12:1. 128 full-time faculty, 83% hold PhDs, 9% are are members of minority groups, 40% are women. 0% of classes are taught by teaching assistants.

ACADEMICS

Degrees: associate, bachelor's, certificate, doctoral/research, master's, postbachelor's certificate, post-master's certificate, transfer. **Classes:** Most classes have 10-19 students. Most lab/discussion sessions have 10-19 students. **Most popular majors:** Multi-/Interdisciplinary Studies; Business Administration and Management; Psychology. **Special Study Options:** Accelerated program, distance learning, double major, dual enrollment, English as a Second Language (ESL), honors program, independent study, internships, study abroad, teacher certification program, weekend college. **Honors Programs:** www.dbu.edu/honors/ Combined degree programs: BA/MA, BS/MA, BAS/MA, BBS/MA, BBA/MA, BA/MBA, BS/MBA, BBA/MBA, BBS/MBA, BA/MS, BS/MS, BA/M, ED., BS/M.Ed. **Disability Services:** Special programs offered to physically disabled students, including note-taking services, reader services, tape recorders, tutors. **Career Services:** Alumni services, Career/job search classes, Career assessment, Internships, Regional alumni. The program we are most proud of is our Alumni services. All of our services: career counseling, resume critique, mock interviews, and job search through CareerBridge are extended to our alumni free of charge as long as it is needed.

FACILITIES

Housing: special housing for disabled students, men's dorms, women's dorms, apartments for married students, apartments for single students, Wellness Housing, Townhomes. 90% of campus accessible to physically disabled. **Special Academic Facilities/Equipment:** Corrie ten Boom Collection **Computers:** Students can register for classes online.

CAMPUS LIFE

Environment: Metropolis. **Activities:** Choral groups, dance, drama/theater, music ensembles, musical theater, opera, student government, yearbook, Campus Ministries, Student Organization. 36 registered organizations, 4 honor societies, 3 religious organizations. **Athletics (Intercollegiate):** *Men:* baseball, cross-country, golf, soccer, tennis, track/field (outdoor). *Women:* cross-country, golf, soccer, tennis, track/field (outdoor), volleyball. **On-Campus Highlights:** Mahler Student Center, Burg Center, Coffee House, Collins Learning Center, Crowley Co-Ed.

ADMISSIONS

Freshman Academic Profile: Average high school GPA 3.7. 19% in top 10% of high school class, 46% in top 25% of high school class, 75% in top 50% of high school class. 73% from public high schools. **Reported SAT (pre-2016 redesign) scores:** SAT Math middle 50% range 510-590. SAT Critical Reading middle 50% range 520-600. **Concordant SAT scores:** SAT Math middle 50% range 540-610. ACT middle 50% range 19-25. Minimum internet-based TOEFL 71. Minimum paper TOEFL 525. **Basis for Candidate Selection:** *Very important factors considered include:* rigor of secondary school record, class rank, academic GPA, standardized test scores, application essay, talent/ability, character/personal qualities, religious affiliation/commitment. *Important factors considered include:* interview, extracurricular activities. *Other factors considered include:* recommendation(s), alumni/ae relation, volunteer work, work experience, level of applicant's interest. **Freshman Admission Requirements:** High school diploma is required and GED is accepted. *Academic units recommended:* 4 English, 3 math, 2 science, 1 science lab, 2 foreign language, 3 social studies, 4 history. **Freshman Admission Statistics:** 3,259 applied, 43.11% admitted, 38% enrolled. **Transfer Admission Requirements:** college transcript(s), essay or personal statement, Minimum college GPA of 2.5 required. Lowest grade transferable C. **General Admission Information:** Application fee $25. Priority deadline 11/1. Nonfall registration accepted. Admission may be deferred for a maximum of 1 year.

COSTS AND FINANCIAL AID

Annual tuition $25,380. Room and board $7,533. Required fees $800. Average book expense $1,260. **Required Forms and Deadlines:** FAFSA, Institution's own financial aid form. **Notification of Awards:** Applicants will be notified of awards on a rolling basis beginning 2/1. **Types of Aid:** *Need-based scholarships/grants:* Federal Pell, FSEOG, State scholarships/grants, Private scholarships, College/university scholarship or grant aid from institutional funds. *Loans:* Direct Subsidized Stafford Loans, Direct Unsubsidized Stafford Loans, Direct PLUS loans, State Loans, College/university loans from institutional funds. *Student Employment:* Federal Work-Study Program available. Institutional employment available. **Financial Aid Statistics:** 63% needy freshmen, 63% needy undergrads receive need-based scholarship or grant aid. 95% freshmen, 89% undergrads receive non-need-based scholarship or grant aid. 81% freshmen, 79% undergrads receive need-based self-help aid. 5% freshmen, 4% undergrads receive athletic scholarships. 96% freshmen, 89% undergrads receive any aid. 79% undergrads borrow to pay for school. Average cumulative indebtedness $22,568. **Criteria for awarding aid:** *Non-need-based:* Academics, Athletics, Job skills, Leadership, Music/drama, Religious affiliation.

DARTMOUTH COLLEGE

6016 McNutt Hall, Hanover, NH 3755
Phone: 603-646-2875 • **Financial Aid Phone:** 800-443-3605
E-mail: admissions.office@dartmouth.edu • **CEEB Code:** 3351
Fax: 603-646-1216 • **Website:** www.dartmouth.edu • **ACT Code:** 2508

This private school was founded in 1769. It has a 265-acre campus.

RATINGS

Admissions Selectivity Rating: 98   **Fire Safety Rating:** 89   **Green Rating:** 89

STUDENTS AND FACULTY

Enrollment: 4,230. **Student Body:** 50% female, 50% male, 98% out-of-state, 8% international (70 countries represented). Asian 15%, African American 7%, Caucasian 50%, Hispanic 9%, Native American 2%, Pacific Islander <1%, Two or more races 5%, Race unknown 3%.
Retention and Graduation: 98% freshmen return for sophomore year. 88% freshmen graduate within 4 years. **Faculty:** Student/faculty ratio 7:1. 591 full-time faculty, 94% hold PhDs, 17% are are members of minority groups, 37% are women. 0% of classes are taught by teaching assistants.

ACADEMICS

Degrees: bachelor's, doctoral/professional, doctoral/research, doctoral, master's. **Classes:** Most classes have 10-19 students. **Most popular majors:** Economics; Psychology; Political Science and Government. **Special Study Options:** double major, exchange student program (domestic), honors program, independent study, internships, student-designed major, study abroad, teacher certification program. **Honors Programs:** Presidential Scholarship Research Program; Senior Honors Thesis; Senior Fellowship. **Disability Services:** Special programs offered to physically disabled students, including note-taking services, tape recorders, tutors. **Career Services:** Alumni network, Alumni services, Career/job search classes, Career assessment, Internships, Regional alumni. Unpaid internships are financially supported through the Rockefeller Center (public policy or political internships), the Dickey Center for International Understanding (overseas opportunities), the Tucker Foundation (religious or community service organizations), and through other sources on campus.

FACILITIES

Housing: Coed dorms, special housing for international students, fraternity/ sorority housing, apartments for married students, cooperative housing, apartments for single students, Theme Housing, Academic Affinity Housing, Faculty-In-Residence Programs, Sustainable Living Center, Interfaith Living, Special Interest Housing. 75% of campus accessible to physically disabled. **Special Academic Facilities/Equipment:** Hood Museum of Art, Hopkins Center for Performing Arts, Tucker Foundation for volunteer services, observatory, centers for humanities, social science, and science. **Computers:** 100% of classrooms, 100% of dorms, 100% of libraries, 100% of dining areas, 100% of student union, 100% of common outdoor areas have wireless network access. Students can register for classes online. Administrative functions (other than registration) can be performed online. Undergraduates are required to own a computer.

CAMPUS LIFE

Environment: Village. **Activities:** Choral groups, concert band, dance, drama/theater, jazz band, literary magazine, marching band, music ensembles, musical theater, opera, pep band, radio station, student government, student newspaper, student-run film society, symphony orchestra, television station, yearbook, Campus Ministries, Student Organization, Model UN. 330 registered organizations, 26 religious organizations. 14 fraternities, 6 sororities. **Athletics (Intercollegiate):** *Men:* baseball, basketball, crew/rowing, cross-country, diving, equestrian sports, fencing, football, golf, ice hockey, lacrosse, sailing, skiing (downhill/alpine), skiing (nordic/cross-country), soccer, squash, swimming, tennis, track/field (outdoor), track/field (indoor). *Women:* basketball, crew/rowing, cross-country, diving, equestrian sports, fencing, field hockey, golf, ice hockey, lacrosse, sailing, skiing (downhill/alpine), skiing (nordic/cross-country), soccer, softball, squash, swimming, tennis, track/field (outdoor), track/field (indoor), volleyball. **On-Campus Highlights:** Hopkins Center for Creative and Performing Arts, Hood Museum of Art, Murals by Jose Clemente Orozco, Ten library system, all open to visitors, Ledyard Canoe Club, oldest in the country. **Environmental Initiatives:** As part of our commitment to reduce greenhouse gas emissions, Dartmouth commissioned an energy audit for the buildings that collectively use 75% of the energy on campus. Based on the results of this audit, the Trustees invested $12.5 million in 250 energy conservation and efficiency projects in existing buildings, which are now underway.

ADMISSIONS

Freshman Academic Profile: 93% in top 10% of high school class, 99% in top 25% of high school class, 100% in top 50% of high school class. 55% from public high schools. **Reported SAT (pre-2016 redesign) scores:** SAT Math middle 50% range 680-780. SAT Critical Reading middle 50% range 670-780. SAT Writing middle 50% range 680-790. **Concordant SAT scores:** SAT EBRW middle 50% 710–790. SAT Math middle 50% range 710–790. ACT middle 50% range 30-34. Minimum internet-based TOEFL 250. Minimum paper TOEFL 600. **Basis for Candidate Selection:** *Very important factors considered include:* rigor of secondary school record, class rank, academic GPA, standardized test scores, application essay, recommendation(s), extracurricular activities, character/personal qualities. *Important factors considered include:* talent/ability, volunteer work. *Other factors considered include:* interview, first generation, alumni/ae relation, geographical residence, racial/ethnic status. **Freshman Admission Requirements:** High school diploma or equivalent is not required. *Academic units recommended:* 4 English, 4 math, 4 science, 4 foreign language, 4 social studies. **Freshman Admission Statistics:** 20,675 applied, 10.60% admitted, 51% enrolled. **Transfer Admission Requirements:** High school transcript, college transcript(s), essay or personal statement, standardized test scores, statement of good standing from prior institution(s). Lowest grade transferable B. **General Admission Information:** Application fee $80. Regular application deadline 1/1. Regular notification 4/10. Nonfall registration not accepted. Admission may be deferred for a maximum of 2 years.

COSTS AND FINANCIAL AID

Annual tuition $49,998. Room and board $14,736. Required fees $1,440. Average book expense $1,260. **Required Forms and Deadlines:** FAFSA, CSS/Financial Aid PROFILE, Noncustodial PROFILE, Business/Farm Supplement. **Notification of Awards:** Applicants will be notified of awards on or about 4/2. **Types of Aid:** *Need-based scholarships/grants:* Federal Pell, FSEOG, State scholarships/grants, Private scholarships, College/university scholarship or grant aid from institutional funds. *Loans:* Direct Subsidized Stafford Loans, Direct Unsubsidized Stafford Loans, Direct PLUS loans, Federal Perkins Loans, State Loans, College/university loans from institutional funds. *Student Employment:* Federal Work-Study Program available.

Institutional employment available. **Financial Aid Statistics:** 98% needy freshmen, 96% needy undergrads receive need-based scholarship or grant aid. 0% undergrads receive non-need-based scholarship or grant aid. 89% freshmen, 91% undergrads receive need-based self-help aid. 0% freshmen, 0% undergrads receive athletic scholarships. 58% freshmen, 54% undergrads receive any aid. Average cumulative indebtedness $17,849.

DAVIDSON COLLEGE

PO Box 7156, Davidson, NC 28035-7156
Phone: 704-894-2230
E-mail: admission@davidson.edu • **CEEB Code:** 5150
Fax: 704-894-2016 • **Website:** www.davidson.edu • **ACT Code:** 3086

This private school, affiliated with the Presbyterian Church, was founded in 1837. It has a 556-acre campus.

RATINGS

Admissions Selectivity Rating: 97   **Fire Safety Rating:** 60*   **Green Rating:** 67

STUDENTS AND FACULTY

Enrollment: 1,791. **Student Body:** 49% female, 51% male, 77% out-of-state, 7% international (42 countries represented). Asian 5%, African American 7%, Caucasian 67%, Hispanic 7%, Native American 1%, Pacific Islander 0%, Two or more races 4%, Race unknown 2%.
Retention and Graduation: 93% freshmen return for sophomore year. 90% freshmen graduate within 4 years. 93% freshmen graduate within 6 years. 21% grads go on to further study within 1 year. **Faculty:** Student/faculty ratio 10:1. 185 full-time faculty, 97% hold PhDs, 22% are are members of minority groups, 43% are women. 0% of classes are taught by teaching assistants.

ACADEMICS

Degrees: bachelor's. **Classes:** Most classes have 10-19 students. Most lab/ discussion sessions have 10-19 students. **Most popular majors:** Biology/ Biological Sciences; Political Science and Government; Psychology. **Special Study Options:** cross-registration, double major, exchange student program (domestic), honors program, independent study, student-designed major, study abroad, teacher certification program. **Disability Services:** Special programs offered to physically disabled students, including note-taking services, reader services, tape recorders, tutors. **Career Services:** Alumni network, Alumni services, Career/job search classes, Career assessment, Internships.

FACILITIES

Housing: Coed dorms, cooperative housing, apartments for single students, Wellness Housing, Theme Housing. 90% of campus accessible to physically disabled. **Special Academic Facilities/Equipment:** Art gallery, scanning electron microscopes, UV-visible spectrometer, laser systems, Baker sports complex, Visual Arts building. **Computers:** Students can register for classes online.

CAMPUS LIFE

Environment: Village. **Activities:** Choral groups, concert band, dance, drama/theater, jazz band, literary magazine, music ensembles, musical theater, pep band, radio station, student government, student newspaper, symphony orchestra, yearbook, Campus Ministries, Student Organization. 151 registered organizations, 15 honor societies, 16 religious organizations. 8 fraternities. **Athletics (Intercollegiate):** *Men:* baseball, basketball, cross-country, diving, football, golf, soccer, swimming, tennis, track/field (outdoor), wrestling. *Women:* basketball, cross-country, diving, field hockey, lacrosse, soccer, swimming, tennis, track/field (outdoor), volleyball. **On-Campus Highlights:** Belk Visual Arts Center, Baker-Watt Science Complex, Baker Sports Complex, Campus Center, Lake Campus. **Environmental Initiatives:** Solar PV and solar thermal array on Baker Sports Complex.

ADMISSIONS

Freshman Academic Profile: Average high school GPA 3.9. 77% in top 10% of high school class, 95% in top 25% of high school class, 99% in top 50% of high school class. 47% from public high schools. **Reported SAT (pre-2016 redesign) scores:** SAT Math middle 50% range 620-720. SAT Critical Reading middle 50% range 630-720. SAT Writing middle 50% range 620-730. **Concordant SAT scores:** SAT EBRW middle 50% 680–750. SAT Math middle 50% range 640–750. ACT middle 50% range 28-33. Minimum internet-based TOEFL 100. Minimum paper TOEFL 600. **Basis for Candidate Selection:**

Very important factors considered include: rigor of secondary school record, recommendation(s), character/personal qualities, volunteer work. Important factors considered include: standardized test scores, application essay, interview, extracurricular activities, talent/ability. Other factors considered include: class rank, academic GPA, alumni/ae relation. **Freshman Admission Requirements:** High school diploma is required and GED is not accepted. Academic units required: 4 English, 3 math, 2 science, 2 foreign language, and 2 units from above areas or other academic areas. Academic units recommended: 4 math, 4 science, 4 foreign language, and 4 units from above areas or other academic areas. **Freshman Admission Statistics:** 5,618 applied, 20.11% admitted, 45% enrolled. **Transfer Admission Requirements:** High school transcript, college transcript(s), essay or personal statement, standardized test scores, statement of good standing from prior institution(s). Minimum college GPA of 3.0 required. Lowest grade transferable C. **General Admission Information:** Application fee $50. Regular application deadline 1/2. Regular notification 4/1. Nonfall registration not accepted. Admission may be deferred for a maximum of 1 year.

COSTS AND FINANCIAL AID

Annual tuition $47,897. Room and board $13,547. Required fees $479. Average book expense $1,000. **Required Forms and Deadlines:** FAFSA, CSS/Financial Aid PROFILE, Noncustodial PROFILE, Business/Farm Supplement. **Notification of Awards:** Applicants will be notified of awards on or about 4/1. **Types of Aid:** Need-based scholarships/grants: Federal Pell, FSEOG, State scholarships/grants, Private scholarships, College/university scholarship or grant aid from institutional funds. Loans: Direct Subsidized Stafford Loans, Direct Unsubsidized Stafford Loans, Direct PLUS loans. Student Employment: Federal Work-Study Program available. Institutional employment available. **Financial Aid Statistics:** 99% needy freshmen, 98% needy undergrads receive need-based scholarship or grant aid. 34% freshmen, 27% undergrads receive non-need-based scholarship or grant aid. 63% freshmen, 66% undergrads receive need-based self-help aid. 5% freshmen, 7% undergrads receive athletic scholarships. 52% freshmen, 52% undergrads receive any aid. 26% undergrads borrow to pay for school. Average cumulative indebtedness $20,431. **Criteria for awarding aid:** Non-need-based: Academics, Alumni affiliation, Art, Athletics, Leadership, Minority status, Music/drama.

DE SALES UNIVERSITY

2755 Station Ave., Center Valley, PA 18034
Phone: 610-282-4443 • **Financial Aid Phone:** 610-282-4443
E-mail: admiss@desales.edu • **CEEB Code:** 2021
Fax: 610-282-0131 • **Website:** www.desales.edu • **ACT Code:** 3525

This private school, affiliated with the Roman Catholic Church, was founded in 1964. It has a 400-acre campus.

RATINGS

Admissions Selectivity Rating: 80 **Fire Safety Rating:** 88 **Green Rating:** 73

STUDENTS AND FACULTY

Enrollment: 2,291. **Student Body:** 60% female, 40% male, 28% out-of-state, 0% international (6 countries represented). Asian 2%, African American 4%, Caucasian 75%, Hispanic 12%, Native American 1%, Pacific Islander <1%, Two or more races 0%, Race unknown 6%.
Retention and Graduation: 79% freshmen return for sophomore year. 60% freshmen graduate within 4 years. 70% freshmen graduate within 6 years. **Faculty:** Student/faculty ratio 13:1. 125 full-time faculty, 87% hold PhDs, 10% are are members of minority groups, 50% are women. 0% of classes are taught by teaching assistants.

ACADEMICS

Degrees: bachelor's, certificate, doctoral/professional, master's, postbachelor's certificate, post-master's certificate. **Classes:** Most classes have 20-29 students. Most lab/discussion sessions have fewer than 10 students. **Special Study Options:** Accelerated program, cross-registration, distance learning, double major, dual enrollment, English as a Second Language (ESL), exchange student program (domestic), honors program, independent study, internships, liberal arts/career combination, student-designed major, study abroad, teacher certification program, weekend college, Online degrees. **Honors Programs:** Faith and Reason Honors Program is competive and is limited to fifteen (15) students in each academic class. Studnets can find a description of the program at: www4.desales.edu/SCFC/FRseminars. Combined degree programs: BS/MBA, BSMS/MSPAS, BA/MACJ, BS/DPT. **Disability Services:** Special programs offered to physically disabled students, including note-taking services, reader services, tape recorders, tutors. **Career Services:** Alumni network, Alumni services, Career/job search classes, Career assessment, Internships.

FACILITIES

Housing: men's dorms, women's dorms, cooperative housing, Theme Housing. 99% of campus accessible to physically diasbled. **Computers:** 100% of classrooms, 5% of dorms, 100% of libraries, 100% of dining areas, 5% of student union, 20% of common outdoor areas have wireless network access. Students can register for classes online. Administrative functions (other than registration) can be performed online.

CAMPUS LIFE

Environment: Town. **Activities:** Choral groups, dance, drama/theater, musical theater, pep band, radio station, student government, student newspaper, television station, yearbook, Campus Ministries, Student Organization, Model UN. 42 registered organizations, 12 honor societies, 1 religious organization. **Athletics (Intercollegiate):** Men: baseball, basketball, cross-country, golf, lacrosse, soccer, tennis, track/field (outdoor), track/field (indoor). Women: basketball, cross-country, field hockey, soccer, softball, tennis, track/field (outdoor), track/field (indoor), volleyball. **On-Campus Highlights:** Billera Athletics and Recreation Center, Hurd Science Center, Dog Pound in McShea Student Center, University Center, Labuda Center for the Performing Arts, Summer brings the Pennsylvania Shakespeare Festival to campus at the Labuda Center for the Performing Arts. **Environmental Initiatives:** Water reduction program—after adding one new residence hall we still reduced our water usage by 10% from 2008 to 2009.

ADMISSIONS

Freshman Academic Profile: Average high school GPA 3.3. 21% in top 10% of high school class, 47% in top 25% of high school class, 75% in top 50% of high school class. 62% from public high schools. **Reported SAT (pre-2016 redesign) scores:** SAT Math middle 50% range 440-590. SAT Critical Reading middle 50% range 450-590. SAT Writing middle 50% range 450-580. **Concordant SAT scores:** SAT EBRW middle 50% 500–640. SAT Math middle 50% range 480–610. ACT middle 50% range 21-28. Minimum paper TOEFL 550. **Basis for Candidate Selection:** Very important factors considered include: rigor of secondary school record, academic GPA, character/personal qualities. Important factors considered include: class rank, standardized test scores, application essay, recommendation(s), interview, level of applicant's interest. Other factors considered include: extracurricular activities, talent/ability, first generation, volunteer work, work experience. **Freshman Admission Requirements:** High school diploma is required and GED is accepted. Academic units required: 4 English, 3 math, 2 science, 2 science labs, 2 foreign language, 3 social studies. Academic units recommended: 4 English, 4 math, 3 science, 3 science labs, 4 foreign language, 3 social studies. **Freshman Admission Statistics:** 2,706 applied, 77.61% admitted, 20% enrolled. **Transfer Admission Requirements:** High school transcript, college transcript(s), statement of good standing from prior institution(s). Minimum college GPA of 2.00 required. Lowest grade transferable 2. **General Admission Information:** Priority deadline 3/1. Regular application deadline 8/1. Nonfall registration accepted. Admission may be deferred.

COSTS AND FINANCIAL AID

Annual tuition $32,000. Room and board $12,050. Required fees $1,550. Average book expense $992. **Required Forms and Deadlines:** FAFSA. **Notification of Awards:** Applicants will be notified of awards on a rolling basis beginning 2/15. **Types of Aid:** Need-based scholarships/grants: Federal Pell, FSEOG, State scholarships/grants, Private scholarships, College/university scholarship or grant aid from institutional funds. Loans: Direct Subsidized Stafford Loans, Direct Unsubsidized Stafford Loans, Direct PLUS loans, Federal Perkins Loans, Federal Nursing Loans, State Loans. Student Employment: Federal Work-Study Program available. Institutional employment available. **Financial Aid Statistics:** 100% needy freshmen, 95% needy undergrads receive need-based scholarship or grant aid. 93% freshmen, 83% undergrads receive non-need-based scholarship or grant aid. 76% freshmen, 81% undergrads receive need-based self-help aid. 0% freshmen, 0% undergrads receive athletic scholarships. 81% freshmen, 77% undergrads receive any aid. 81% undergrads borrow to pay for school. Average cumulative indebtedness $15,189,850. **Criteria for awarding aid:** Need-based: Academics, Alumni affiliation. Non-need-based: Academics, Alumni affiliation, Art, Leadership, Music/drama, Religious affiliation.

See page 948.

DEEP SPRINGS COLLEGE

Applications Committee, Dyer, NV 89010
Phone: 760-872-2000 • **Financial Aid Phone:** 760-872-2000
E-mail: apcom@deepsprings.edu • **CEEB Code:** 4281
Fax: 760-872-4466 • **Website:** www.deepsprings.edu

This private school was founded in 1917. It has a 30000-acre campus.

RATINGS
Admissions Selectivity Rating: 99   **Fire Safety Rating:** 88   **Green Rating:** 60*

STUDENTS AND FACULTY
Enrollment: 28. **Student Body:** 0% female, 100% male, 82% out-of-state, 14% international (3 countries represented). Asian 14%, African American 0%, Caucasian 64%, Hispanic 4%, Native American 0%, Pacific Islander 0%, Two or more races 4%, Race unknown 0%.
Retention and Graduation: 92% freshmen return for sophomore year. 96% grads go on to further study within 1 year. **Faculty:** Student/faculty ratio 4:1. 3 full-time faculty, 100% hold PhDs, 0% are are members of minority groups, 67% are women. 0% of classes are taught by teaching assistants.

ACADEMICS
Degrees: associate. **Classes:** Most classes have fewer than 10 students. **Most popular majors:** Liberal Arts and Sciences Studies and Humanities. **Special Study Options:** independent study, internships.

FACILITIES
Housing: men's dorms 100% of campus accessible to physically diasbled. **Special Academic Facilities/Equipment:** Ranch- 300 cattle, 20 horses, organic farm growing hay and produce; thousands of acres of wilderness surround the college

CAMPUS LIFE
Environment: Rural. **Activities:** student government 1 registered organization. **On-Campus Highlights:** Boarding House, Dairy Barn, Horse Stables, The Upper Reservoir, The Druid.

ADMISSIONS
Freshman Academic Profile: 100% in top 10% of high school class, 100% in top 25% of high school class, 100% in top 50% of high school class. 64% from public high schools. **Reported SAT (pre-2016 redesign) scores:** SAT Math middle 50% range 670-740. SAT Critical Reading middle 50% range 740-800. **Concordant SAT scores:** SAT Math middle 50% range 700-760. **Basis for Candidate Selection:** *Very important factors considered include:* application essay, interview, character/personal qualities, level of applicant's interest. *Important factors considered include:* rigor of secondary school record, academic GPA, extracurricular activities, volunteer work, work experience. *Other factors considered include:* class rank, standardized test scores, recommendation(s), talent/ability, first generation, racial/ethnic status. **Freshman Admission Requirements:** High school diploma or equivalent is not required. **Freshman Admission Statistics:** 200 applied, 9.50% admitted, 84% enrolled. **Transfer Admission Requirements:** High school transcript, college transcript(s), essay or personal statement, interview, standardized test scores. **General Admission Information:** Regular application deadline 11/7. Regular notification 4/15. Nonfall registration not accepted.

COSTS AND FINANCIAL AID
Annual tuition $0. Average book expense $1,200. **Financial Aid Statistics:** 0% freshmen, 0% undergrads receive athletic scholarships. 100% freshmen, 100% undergrads receive any aid. **Criteria for awarding aid:** *Non-need-based:* Academics, Art, Job skills, Leadership.

DEFIANCE COLLEGE

701 North Clinton Street, Defiance, OH 43512-1695
Phone: 419-783-2359 • **Financial Aid Phone:** 419-783-2458
E-mail: admissions@defiance.edu • **CEEB Code:** 1162
Fax: 419-783-2468 • **Website:** www.defiance.edu • **ACT Code:** 3264

This private school, affiliated with the United Church of Christ Church, was founded in 1850. It has a 150-acre campus.

RATINGS
Admissions Selectivity Rating: 77   **Fire Safety Rating:** 90   **Green Rating:** 68

STUDENTS AND FACULTY
Enrollment: 801. **Student Body:** 49% female, 51% male, 28% out-of-state, 2% international (2 countries represented). Asian 1%, African American 12%, Caucasian 77%, Hispanic 5%, Native American 1%, Pacific Islander 0%, Two or more races 1%, Race unknown 1%.
Retention and Graduation: 55% freshmen return for sophomore year. 42% freshmen graduate within 4 years. 49% freshmen graduate within 6 years. **Faculty:** Student/faculty ratio 12:1. 39 full-time faculty, 67% hold PhDs, 13% are are members of minority groups, 46% are women. 0% of classes are taught by teaching assistants.

ACADEMICS
Degrees: associate, bachelor's, certificate, master's. **Classes:** Most classes have 10-19 students. Most lab/discussion sessions have 10-19 students. **Most popular majors:** Education; Forensic Science and Technology; Criminal Justice and Corrections. **Special Study Options:** cooperative education program, distance learning, double major, dual enrollment, honors program, independent study, internships, student-designed major, study abroad, teacher certification program, weekend college. **Career Services:** Alumni network, Alumni services, Career/job search classes, Career assessment, Internships, Regional alumni, Partnership for Jobs.

FACILITIES
Housing: Coed dorms, apartments for single students. 100% of campus accessible to physically diasbled. **Special Academic Facilities/Equipment:** Art gallery, media center, Eisenhower archives room, curriculum resource center, Cultural Arts Center, Indian wars collection. **Computers:** 100% of classrooms, 30% of dorms, 100% of libraries, 100% of dining areas, 100% of student union, 100% of common outdoor areas have wireless network access.

CAMPUS LIFE
Environment: Rural. **Activities:** Choral groups, concert band, drama/ theater, literary magazine, musical theater, pep band, student government, student newspaper, yearbook, Campus Ministries. 30 registered organizations, 1 honor society, 2 religious organizations. 1 fraternity, 2 sororities. **Athletics (Intercollegiate):** *Men:* baseball, basketball, cross-country, football, golf, soccer, tennis, track/field (outdoor), track/field (indoor). *Women:* basketball, cross-country, golf, soccer, softball, tennis, track/field (outdoor), track/ field (indoor), volleyball. **On-Campus Highlights:** Smart Fitness Center, Tenzer Hall, Serrick Center, Hubbard Hall, Weaner/McMaster Center. **Environmental Initiatives:** Lowering Electrical, Gas, and Water Usage.

ADMISSIONS
Freshman Academic Profile: Average high school GPA 3.1. 12% in top 10% of high school class, 29% in top 25% of high school class, 57% in top 50% of high school class. 97% from public high schools. **Reported SAT (pre-2016 redesign) scores:** SAT Math middle 50% range 390-500. SAT Critical Reading middle 50% range 400-500. SAT Writing middle 50% range 350-480. **Concordant SAT scores:** SAT EBRW middle 50% range 420-550. SAT Math middle 50% range 430-530. ACT middle 50% range 18-23. Minimum internet-based TOEFL 79. Minimum paper TOEFL 550. **Basis for Candidate Selection:** *Very important factors considered include:* rigor of secondary school record, academic GPA, standardized test scores. *Other factors considered include:* class rank, application essay, recommendation(s), interview, extracurricular activities, character/personal qualities, volunteer work, work experience. **Freshman Admission Requirements:** High school diploma is required and GED is accepted. *Academic units recommended:* 4 English, 3 math, 3 science, 2 science labs, 2 foreign language, 2 social studies, 2 visual/performing arts, and 1 unit from above areas or other academic areas. **Freshman Admission Statistics:** 1,671 applied, 64.69% admitted, 22% enrolled. **Transfer Admission Requirements:** High school transcript, college transcript(s), essay or personal statement, statement of good standing from prior institution(s). Minimum college GPA of 2.0 required. Lowest grade transferable C. **General Admission Information:** Application fee $25. Nonfall registration accepted. Admission may be deferred for a maximum of one year.

COSTS AND FINANCIAL AID
Annual tuition $29,256. Room and board $9,522. Required fees $719. Average book expense $1,350. **Required Forms and Deadlines:** FAFSA. **Notification**

of Awards: Applicants will be notified of awards on a rolling basis beginning 2/1. **Types of Aid:** *Need-based scholarships/grants:* Federal Pell, FSEOG, State scholarships/grants, Private scholarships, College/university scholarship or grant aid from institutional funds. *Loans:* Direct Subsidized Stafford Loans, Direct Unsubsidized Stafford Loans, Direct PLUS loans, Federal Perkins Loans. *Student Employment:* Federal Work-Study Program available. Institutional employment available. **Financial Aid Statistics:** 86% needy freshmen, 83% needy undergrads receive need-based scholarship or grant aid. 100% freshmen, 97% undergrads receive non-need-based scholarship or grant aid. 93% freshmen, 92% undergrads receive need-based self-help aid. 0% freshmen, 0% undergrads receive athletic scholarships. 100% freshmen, 99% undergrads receive any aid. **Criteria for awarding aid:** *Need-based:* Alumni affiliation, Religious affiliation. *Non-need-based:* Academics, Leadership, Minority status, Music/drama.

DELAWARE VALLEY COLLEGE

700 East Butler Avenue, Doylestown, PA 18901-2697
Phone: 215-489-2211 • **Financial Aid Phone:** 215-489-2272
E-mail: ADMITME@delval.edu • **CEEB Code:** 2510
Fax: 215-230-2968 • **Website:** www.delval.edu • **ACT Code:** 3551

This private school was founded in 1896. It has a 600-acre campus.

RATINGS
Admissions Selectivity Rating: 83   **Fire Safety Rating:** 86   **Green Rating:** 60*

STUDENTS AND FACULTY
Enrollment: 1,877. **Student Body:** 58% female, 42% male, 39% out-of-state, <1% international (4 countries represented). Asian 1%, African American 4%, Caucasian 84%, Hispanic 2%, Native American <1%, Pacific Islander 0%, Two or more races 0%, Race unknown 9%.
Retention and Graduation: 76% freshmen return for sophomore year. 37% freshmen graduate within 4 years. 50% freshmen graduate within 6 years. 51% grads go on to further study within 1 year. 1% grads pursue law degrees. 9% grads pursue business degrees. 10% grads pursue medical degrees. **Faculty:** Student/faculty ratio 15:1. 82 full-time faculty, 57% hold PhDs, 10% are are members of minority groups, 41% are women. 0% of classes are taught by teaching assistants.

ACADEMICS
Degrees: associate, bachelor's, certificate, master's, terminal, transfer. **Classes:** Most classes have 10-19 students. Most lab/discussion sessions have 10-19 students. **Most popular majors:** Animal Sciences; Animal Sciences; Business Administration and Management. **Special Study Options:** Accelerated program, cross-registration, distance learning, double major, honors program, independent study, internships, study abroad, teacher certification program, weekend college. **Honors Programs:** The DVC Honors Program is an educational enrichment program designed to enhance the eductional opportunities and experiences of students admitted to the program. The programs consists of an Honors Colloquium followed by independent study programs in the 3rd and 4th years. It features guest lecturers, field trips and both faculty and student-led discussions. **Disability Services:** Special programs offered to physically disabled students, including note-taking services, reader services, tape recorders. **Career Services:** Alumni services, Career/job search classes, Career assessment, Internships. Our required employment program requires students to work 500 hours in their field before they graduate. Delaware Valley College's Employment Program, an experience-based graduation requirement, fosters the integration of theory and practice throughout the educational continuum, and helps students develop linkages with professionals in their fields of study. The Employment Program empowers students by equipping them with the skills and abilities necessary for success as they transition from college to career. Because of the college's commitment to career-oriented education, students graduate with a level of skill and experience that far exceeds that of the average entry-level candidate. Delaware Valley College is one of only 3% of colleges nationwide with a mandatory experiential-learning requirement, making it one of the most important and unique aspects of the DelVal educational experience.

FACILITIES
Housing: Coed dorms, women's dorms. **Special Academic Facilities/Equipment:** Dairy processing plant, greenhouse and nursery lab complex, small animal science labs, poultry diagnostic lab, arboretum, equine facilities, 500+-acre farm, tissue culture lab. **Computers:** 25% of classrooms, 100% of dorms, 100% of libraries, 80% of student union, 20% of common outdoor areas have wireless network access. Students can register for classes online. Administrative functions (other than registration) can be performed online.

CAMPUS LIFE
Environment: Village. **Activities:** Choral groups, concert band, drama/theater, literary magazine, music ensembles, radio station, student government, student newspaper, yearbook. 62 registered organizations, 2 honor societies, 2 religious organizations. 5 fraternities, 3 sororities. **Athletics (Intercollegiate):** *Men:* baseball, basketball, cross-country, football, golf, soccer, track/field (outdoor), track/field (indoor), wrestling. *Women:* basketball, cheerleading, cross-country, field hockey, soccer, softball, track/field (outdoor), track/field (indoor), volleyball. **On-Campus Highlights:** Smart Classroom, Small Animal Facility, Athletic Complex, Student Center, Equine center, The campus has many unique areas that are are of specific interest depending on a student's major field of study (i.e. dairy barn, equine center, etc.). **Environmental Initiatives:** Recycling.

ADMISSIONS
Freshman Academic Profile: Average high school GPA 3.5. 13% in top 10% of high school class, 73% in top 25% of high school class, 27% in top 50% of high school class. 85% from public high schools. **Reported SAT (pre-2016 redesign) scores:** SAT Math middle 50% range 460-560. SAT Critical Reading middle 50% range 450-550. SAT Writing middle 50% range 430-550. **Concordant SAT scores:** SAT EBRW middle 50% 490–610. SAT Math middle 50% range 500–580. ACT middle 50% range 20-25. Minimum paper TOEFL 500. **Basis for Candidate Selection:** *Very important factors considered include:* academic GPA, standardized test scores. *Important factors considered include:* rigor of secondary school record, class rank, interview. *Other factors considered include:* application essay, recommendation(s), extracurricular activities, talent/ability, character/personal qualities, alumni/ae relation, volunteer work, work experience, level of applicant's interest. **Freshman Admission Requirements:** High school diploma is required and GED is accepted. *Academic units required:* 3 English, 2 math, 2 science, 1 science lab, 2 social studies, 6 academic electives. **Freshman Admission Statistics:** 1,770 applied, 71.53% admitted, 36% enrolled. **Transfer Admission Requirements:** High school transcript, college transcript(s), statement of good standing from prior institution(s). Minimum college GPA of 2.0 required. Lowest grade transferable C. **General Admission Information:** Application fee $50. Priority deadline 5/1. Nonfall registration accepted. Admission may be deferred for a maximum of 12 months.

COSTS AND FINANCIAL AID
Annual tuition $28,596. Room and board $10,842. Required fees $2,050.
Required Forms and Deadlines: FAFSA, State aid form. **Notification of Awards:** Applicants will be notified of awards on a rolling basis beginning 2/15. **Types of Aid:** *Need-based scholarships/grants:* Federal Pell, FSEOG, State scholarships/grants, Private scholarships, College/university scholarship or grant aid from institutional funds. *Loans:* Direct Subsidized Stafford Loans, Direct Unsubsidized Stafford Loans, Direct PLUS loans, Federal Perkins Loans. *Student Employment:* Federal Work-Study Program available. Institutional employment available. **Financial Aid Statistics:** 99% needy freshmen, 99% needy undergrads receive need-based scholarship or grant aid. 9% freshmen, 8% undergrads receive non-need-based scholarship or grant aid. 83% freshmen, 80% undergrads receive need-based self-help aid. 0% freshmen, 0% undergrads receive athletic scholarships. 98% freshmen, 91% undergrads receive any aid. **Criteria for awarding aid:** *Non-need-based:* Academics, Alumni affiliation, Music/drama, State/district residency.

DENISON UNIVERSITY

100 West College Street, Granville, OH 43023
Phone: 740-587-6276 • **Financial Aid Phone:** 740-587-6279
E-mail: admissions@denison.edu • **CEEB Code:** 1164
Fax: 740-587-6306 • **Website:** denison.edu • **ACT Code:** 3266

This private school was founded in 1831. It has a 900-acre campus.

RATINGS
Admissions Selectivity Rating: 90   **Fire Safety Rating:** 96   **Green Rating:** 94

STUDENTS AND FACULTY
Enrollment: 2,255. **Student Body:** 57% female, 43% male, 72% out-of-state, 8% international (34 countries represented). Asian 4%, African American 7%, Caucasian 66%, Hispanic 10%, Native American <1%, Pacific Islander <1%, Two or more races 4%, Race unknown 2%.
Retention and Graduation: 89% freshmen return for sophomore year. 78% freshmen graduate within 4 years. 80% freshmen graduate within 6 years. 25%

grads go on to further study within 1 year. 15% grads pursue arts and sciences degrees. 3% grads pursue law degrees. 3% grads pursue business degrees. 3% grads pursue medical degrees. **Faculty:** Student/faculty ratio 10:1. 216 full-time faculty, 100% hold PhDs, 21% are are members of minority groups, 45% are women. 0% of classes are taught by teaching assistants.

ACADEMICS

Degrees: bachelor's. **Classes:** Most classes have 10-19 students. **Most popular majors:** Economics; Psychology; Biology. **Special Study Options:** double major, honors program, independent study, internships, student-designed major, study abroad, teacher certification program, 3-2 Duke U Environmental Management; 3-2 U. of Michigan Natural Resources, 3-4 Case Western Reserve Dental; 3-2 Rensselaer Poly., Washington U. (St. Louis), Case Western Reserve, Columbia U. Engineering; Washington U. (St. Louis) Occupational Therapy. **Disability Services:** Special programs offered to physically disabled students, including note-taking services, reader services, tape recorders, tutors. **Career Services:** Alumni network, Alumni services, Career assessment, Internships, Regional alumni. The Denison Internship Program is in it's 27th year providing opportunities to students across the country and abroad. In the past 10 years, 3,000 Denison University students secured internships in the arts, business, education, health, manufacturing, science, technology, government and the non-profit sectors.

FACILITIES

Housing: Coed dorms, men's dorms, women's dorms, cooperative housing, apartments for single students, Wellness Housing, Theme Housing. 72% of campus accessible to physically disabled. **Special Academic Facilities/Equipment:** Burmese art collection in the Denison Museum, language lab, research station in 350-acre biological reserve, observatory, high resolution spectrometer lab, nuclear magnetic resonance spectrometer, planetarium, Economics computer laboratories. **Computers:** 100% of classrooms, 100% of dorms, 100% of libraries, 100% of dining areas, 100% of student union, 100% of common outdoor areas have wireless network access. Administrative functions (other than registration) can be performed online.

CAMPUS LIFE

Environment: Village. **Activities:** Choral groups, dance, drama/theater, jazz band, music ensembles, musical theater, radio station, student government, student newspaper, student-run film society, television station, yearbook, Campus Ministries, Student Organization. 160 registered organizations, 15 honor societies, 7 religious organizations. 8 fraternities, 6 sororities. **Athletics (Intercollegiate): Men:** baseball, basketball, cross-country, diving, football, golf, lacrosse, soccer, swimming, tennis, track/field (outdoor), track/field (indoor). **Women:** basketball, cross-country, diving, field hockey, golf, lacrosse, soccer, softball, swimming, tennis, track/field (outdoor), track/field (indoor), volleyball. **On-Campus Highlights:** Samson Talbot Hall of Biological Science, Mitchell Recreation and Athletics Center, Swasey Chapel, Biological Reserve and Polly Anderson Fi, Burke Hall Art Gallery, Burton D. Morgan Center. **Environmental Initiatives:** The signing of the ACUPCC and the development of a standing Campus Sustainability Committee as part of the campus governance system.

ADMISSIONS

Freshman Academic Profile: Average high school GPA 3.6. 55% in top 10% of high school class, 23% in top 25% of high school class, 96% in top 50% of high school class. 66% from public high schools. **Reported SAT (pre-2016 redesign) scores:** SAT Math middle 50% range 580-680. SAT Critical Reading middle 50% range 580-680. **Concordant SAT scores:** SAT Math middle 50% range 600–710. ACT middle 50% range 26-31. Minimum paper TOEFL 599. **Basis for Candidate Selection:** *Very important factors considered include:* rigor of secondary school record, academic GPA, application essay, recommendation(s). *Important factors considered include:* interview, extracurricular activities, talent/ability, level of applicant's interest. *Other factors considered include:* class rank, standardized test scores, character/personal qualities, first generation, alumni/ae relation, geographical residence, state residency, racial/ethnic status, volunteer work, work experience. **Freshman Admission Requirements:** High school diploma is required and GED is accepted. *Academic units required:* 4 English, 4 math, 4 science, 3 foreign language, 2 social studies, 1 history, 1 academic elective. **Freshman Admission Statistics:** 6,110 applied, 47.99% admitted, 22% enrolled. **Transfer Admission Requirements:** High school transcript, college transcript(s), essay or personal statement, statement of good standing from prior institution(s). Minimum college GPA of 3.0 required. Lowest grade transferable C-. **General Admission Information:** Priority deadline 11/15. Regular application deadline 1/15. Regular notification 3/15. Nonfall registration accepted. Admission may be deferred for a maximum of 1 year.

COSTS AND FINANCIAL AID

Annual tuition $46,250. Room and board $11,570. Required fees $1,040. Average book expense $650. **Required Forms and Deadlines:** FAFSA. **Notification of Awards:** Applicants will be notified of awards on a rolling basis beginning 3/28. **Types of Aid:** *Need-based scholarships/grants:* Federal Pell,

FSEOG, State scholarships/grants, Private scholarships, College/university scholarship or grant aid from institutional funds. *Loans:* Direct Subsidized Stafford Loans, Direct Unsubsidized Stafford Loans, Direct PLUS loans, Federal Perkins Loans, College/university loans from institutional funds. *Student Employment:* Federal Work-Study Program available. Institutional employment available. **Financial Aid Statistics:** 100% needy freshmen, 100% needy undergrads receive need-based scholarship or grant aid. 93% freshmen, 93% undergrads receive non-need-based scholarship or grant aid. 78% freshmen, 77% undergrads receive need-based self-help aid. 0% freshmen, 0% undergrads receive athletic scholarships. 99% freshmen, 98% undergrads receive any aid. 50% undergrads borrow to pay for school. Average cumulative indebtedness $28,146. **Criteria for awarding aid:** *Need-based:* Academics, Alumni affiliation, Art, Leadership, Minority status, Music/drama. *Non-need-based:* Academics, Alumni affiliation, Art, Leadership, Minority status, Music/drama, State/district residency.

DEPAUL UNIVERSITY

1 East Jackson Boulevard, Chicago, IL 60604-2287
Phone: 312-362-8300 • **Financial Aid Phone:** 312-362-8091
E-mail: admission@depaul.edu • **CEEB Code:** 001671-00
Fax: 312-362-5749 • **Website:** www.depaul.edu • **ACT Code:** 1012

This private school, affiliated with the Roman Catholic Church, was founded in 1898. It has a 36-acre campus.

RATINGS

Admissions Selectivity Rating: 84   **Fire Safety Rating:** 99   **Green Rating:** 87

STUDENTS AND FACULTY

Enrollment: 15,683. **Student Body:** 53% female, 47% male, 23% out-of-state, 3% international (84 countries represented). Asian 8%, African American 8%, Caucasian 55%, Hispanic 18%, Native American <1%, Pacific Islander <1%, Two or more races 4%, Race unknown 4%. **Retention and Graduation:** 84% freshmen return for sophomore year. 73 **Faculty:** Student/faculty ratio 16:1. 914 full-time faculty, 86% hold PhDs, 20% are are members of minority groups, 46% are women. 3% of classes are taught by teaching assistants.

ACADEMICS

Degrees: bachelor's, certificate, doctoral/professional, doctoral/research, doctoral, master's, postbachelor's certifiate, post-master's certificate. **Classes:** Most classes have 20-29 students. Most lab/discussion sessions have 20-29 students. **Most popular majors:** Accounting; Public Relations, Advertising, and Applied Communication'; Psychology. **Special Study Options:** Accelerated program, cooperative education program, distance learning, double major, dual enrollment, English as a Second Language (ESL), honors program, independent study, internships, student-designed major, study abroad, teacher certification program, weekend college. **Honors Programs:** DePaul's honors program offers small classes organized in a seminar format and taught by faculty committed to academic excellence and the attainment of lifelong learning strategies. Benefits of our scholarly community include academic advising, an Honors Lounge, a student government, peer mentoring, student-faculty dinners, newsletters, cultural outings, service activities, and many other experiences that enrich the Honors community while extending the Honors experience beyond the classroom. Combined degree programs: BA/MA, BS/MS, BA/MA, BS/PharmD, BA/PharmD, BA/MED, BS/MED, BA/MS, BS/MA, BSB/MACC. **Disability Services:** Special programs offered to physically disabled students, including note-taking services, reader services, tape recorders, tutors. **Career Services:** Alumni network, Alumni services, Career/job search classes, Career assessment, Internships, Regional alumni. The Alumni Sharing Knowledge Program (ASK) is a network of 1200 alumni volunteers who serve as career mentors working with students one-on-one, in practice interviews and at job fairs, speaking at networking events and open houses throughout the university. Each alumnus provides unique insight into a myriad of degrees, industries and professions.

FACILITIES

Housing: Coed dorms, special housing for disabled students, special housing for international students, apartments for single students, Theme Housing. **Special Academic Facilities/Equipment:** Monsignor Andrew J. McGowan Environmental Science & Chemistry building (gold LEED-certified, 2009), Digital Cinema laboratory with motion-capture system, Green-screen studio, converged newsroom, Merle Reskin Theatre, Art Museum, William G. McGowan Biological & Environmental Science Building (1998), Ray Meyer Fitness & Recreational Center (1999), and Three-level student center (2002) **Computers:** 60% of classrooms, 100% of dorms, 100% of libraries, 100% of dining areas, 75% of student union, 25% of common outdoor areas have wireless network access. Students can register for classes online. Administrative functions (other than registration) can be performed online.

CAMPUS LIFE

Environment: Metropolis. **Activities:** Choral groups, concert band, dance, drama/theater, jazz band, literary magazine, marching band, music ensembles, musical theater, opera, pep band, radio station, student government, student newspaper, student-run film society, symphony orchestra, yearbook, Campus Ministries, Student Organization, Model UN. 311 registered organizations, 9 honor societies, 19 religious organizations. 9 fraternities, 13 sororities. **Athletics (Intercollegiate):** *Men:* basketball, cross-country, golf, soccer, tennis, track/field (outdoor), track/field (indoor). *Women:* basketball, cross-country, soccer, softball, tennis, track/field (outdoor), track/field (indoor), volleyball. **On-Campus Highlights:** Quad (outside center of campus), Ray Meyer Fitness Center, Student Center, Student Lounge in DePaul Center, The Bean Cafe in the Schmitt Acad. Cntr. **Environmental Initiatives:** The Sustainability Initiative Task Force (SITF) created an Institutional Sustainability Plan, which can be accessed at http://mission.depaul.edu/Programs/Sustainability/Documents/SUSTAINABILITYPLANFINAL.pdf. This plan is derived from the results of a comprehensive sustainability audit conducted by five SITF Working Groups: Curriculum, Operations, Administration and Planning, Research, and Engagement—and builds on SITF Report #4 (Sustainability at DePaul University: Recommendations to the Strategic Planning Task Force) which describes the Working Groups' recommendations and attendant actionable goals for making environmental, social and economic sustainability clearly articulated strategic priorities of the next University Strategic Plan. Each Working Group was responsible for conducting the wide-ranging Sustainability Tracking, Assessment, and Rating System TM (STARS) audit. This report also influenced Vision 2018, DePaul strategic plan, which can be accessed at the following link: http://offices.depaul.edu/president/strategic-directions/vision-2018/Pages/default.aspx.

ADMISSIONS

Freshman Academic Profile: Average high school GPA 3.6. 20% in top 10% of high school class, 54% in top 25% of high school class, 87% in top 50% of high school class. 77% from public high schools. **Reported SAT (pre-2016 redesign) scores:** SAT Math middle 50% range 490-610. SAT Critical Reading middle 50% range 520-620. **Concordant SAT scores:** SAT Math middle 50% range 520–630. ACT middle 50% range 22-28. Minimum internet-based TOEFL 80. Minimum paper TOEFL 550. **Basis for Candidate Selection:** *Very important factors considered include:* rigor of secondary school record, academic GPA, standardized test scores. *Important factors considered include:* class rank, recommendation(s), extracurricular activities, talent/ability, character/personal qualities, volunteer work, work experience, level of applicant's interest. *Other factors considered include:* application essay, interview, first generation, alumni/ae relation, geographical residence, state residency, religious affiliation/commitment, racial/ethnic status. **Freshman Admission Requirements:** High school diploma is required and GED is accepted. *Academic units required:* 4 English, 3 math, 3 science, 2 science labs, and 2 units from above areas or other academic areas. *Academic units recommended:* 4 English, 3 math, 3 science, 2 science labs, 2 foreign language, and 2 units from above areas or other academic areas. **Freshman Admission Statistics:** 19,628 applied, 71.98% admitted, 18% enrolled. **Transfer Admission Requirements:** college transcript(s), Minimum college GPA of 2.0 required. Lowest grade transferable D. **General Admission Information:** Priority deadline 11/15. Regular application deadline 2/1. Regular notification 3/15. Nonfall registration accepted. Admission may be deferred for a maximum of 1 year.

COSTS AND FINANCIAL AID

Annual tuition $37,020. Room and board $13,387. Required fees $606. Average book expense $1,104. **Required Forms and Deadlines:** FAFSA. **Notification of Awards:** Applicants will be notified of awards on a rolling basis beginning 3/15. **Types of Aid:** *Need-based scholarships/grants:* Federal Pell, FSEOG, State scholarships/grants, Private scholarships, College/university scholarship or grant aid from institutional funds. *Loans:* Direct Subsidized Stafford Loans, Direct Unsubsidized Stafford Loans, Direct PLUS loans, Federal Perkins Loans. *Student Employment:* Federal Work-Study Program available. Institutional employment available. **Financial Aid Statistics:** 90% needy freshmen, 85% needy undergrads receive need-based scholarship or grant aid. 86% freshmen, 67% undergrads receive non-need-based scholarship or grant aid. 73% freshmen, 78% undergrads receive need-based self-help aid. 2% freshmen, 2% undergrads receive athletic scholarships. 98% freshmen, 87% undergrads receive any aid. Average cumulative indebtedness $29,932. **Criteria for awarding aid:** *Non-need-based:* Academics, Art, Athletics, Leadership, Music/drama, State/district residency.

DEPAUW UNIVERSITY

204 E. Seminary Street, Greencastle, IN 46135
Phone: 765-658-4006 • **Financial Aid Phone:** 765-658-4030
E-mail: admission@depauw.edu • **CEEB Code:** 1166
Fax: 765-658-4007 • **Website:** www.depauw.edu • **ACT Code:** 1184

This private school, affiliated with the Methodist Church, was founded in 1837. It has a 1100-acre campus.

RATINGS
Admissions Selectivity Rating: 88   **Fire Safety Rating:** 73   **Green Rating:** 76

STUDENTS AND FACULTY
Enrollment: 2,181. **Student Body:** 53% female, 47% male, 60% out-of-state, 8% international (34 countries represented). Asian 3%, African American 6%, Caucasian 69%, Hispanic 5%, Native American <1%, Pacific Islander 0%, Two or more races 6%, Race unknown 2%.
Retention and Graduation: 92% freshmen return for sophomore year. 78% freshmen graduate within 4 years. 85 23% grads go on to further study within 1 year. 15% grads pursue arts and sciences degrees. 5% grads pursue law degrees. 1% grads pursue business degrees. 2% grads pursue medical degrees. **Faculty:** Student/faculty ratio 9:1. 229 full-time faculty, 98% hold PhDs, 22% are members of minority groups, 45% are women. 0% of classes are taught by teaching assistants.

ACADEMICS
Degrees: bachelor's. **Classes:** Most classes have 10-19 students. Most lab/discussion sessions have 10-19 students. **Most popular majors:** Economics; Speech Communication and Rhetoric. **Special Study Options:** double major, dual enrollment, exchange student program (domestic), honors program, independent study, internships, student-designed major, study abroad, teacher certification program. **Honors Programs:** Please visit the following website for information about DePauw's **Honors Programs:** http://www.depauw.edu/honors/index.asp. **Disability Services:** Special programs offered to physically disabled students, including note-taking services, reader services, tape recorders, tutors. **Career Services:** Alumni network, Alumni services, Career/job search classes, Career assessment, Internships, Regional alumni.

FACILITIES
Housing: Coed dorms, special housing for disabled students, special housing for international students, fraternity/sorority housing, apartments for single students. 85% of campus accessible to physically diasbled. **Special Academic Facilities/Equipment:** Recently opened Peeler Art Center housing gallery and studio space; Center for Contemporary Media; Performing Arts Center; Anthropology Museum; Shidzuo Iikudo Museum **Computers:** Students can register for classes online. Administrative functions (other than registration) can be performed online. Undergraduates are required to own a computer.

CAMPUS LIFE
Environment: Village. **Activities:** Choral groups, concert band, dance, drama/theater, jazz band, literary magazine, music ensembles, musical theater, opera, pep band, radio station, student government, student newspaper, student-run film society, symphony orchestra, television station, Campus Ministries, Student Organization. 119 registered organizations, 13 honor societies, 10 religious organizations. 13 fraternities, 11 sororities. **Athletics (Intercollegiate):** *Men:* baseball, basketball, cross-country, diving, football, golf, soccer, swimming, tennis, track/field (outdoor), track/field (indoor). *Women:* basketball, cross-country, diving, field hockey, golf, soccer, softball, swimming, tennis, track/field (outdoor), track/field (indoor), volleyball. **On-Campus Highlights:** DePauw University School of Music, Roy O. West Library, Music Library, and the Prevo Science Library, Cafe Roy coffee shop, Memorial Student Union, Bowman Park. **Environmental Initiatives:** LEED certified construction of the Janet Prindle Institute for Ethics.

ADMISSIONS
Freshman Academic Profile: Average high school GPA 3.8. 45% in top 10% of high school class, 75% in top 25% of high school class, 97% in top 50% of high school class. 83% from public high schools. **Reported SAT (pre-2016 redesign) scores:** SAT Math middle 50% range 530-660. SAT Critical Reading middle 50% range 510-620. SAT Writing middle 50% range 520-620. **Concordant SAT scores:** SAT EBRW middle 50% 570–670. SAT Math middle 50% range 560–690. ACT middle 50% range 24-29. Minimum paper TOEFL 560. **Basis for Candidate Selection:** *Very important factors considered include:* rigor of secondary school record, academic GPA, standardized test scores. *Important factors considered include:* class rank, application essay,

recommendation(s). *Other factors considered include:* interview, extracurricular activities, talent/ability, character/personal qualities, first generation, alumni/ae relation, geographical residence, state residency, volunteer work, work experience, level of applicant's interest. **Freshman Admission Requirements:** High school diploma is required and GED is accepted. *Academic units recommended:* 4 English, 4 math, 2 science labs. **Freshman Admission Statistics:** 4,845 applied, 65.37% admitted, 18% enrolled. **Transfer Admission Requirements:** High school transcript, college transcript(s), essay or personal statement, statement of good standing from prior institution(s). Minimum college GPA of 3.0 required. Lowest grade transferable C. **General Admission Information:** Application fee $40. Regular application deadline 2/1. Nonfall registration accepted. Admission may be deferred for a maximum of 1 year.

COSTS AND FINANCIAL AID

Annual tuition $45,660. Room and board $12,160. Required fees $788. Average book expense $900. **Required Forms and Deadlines:** FAFSA, CSS/Financial Aid PROFILE. **Notification of Awards:** Applicants will be notified of awards on a rolling basis beginning 3/10. **Types of Aid:** *Need-based scholarships/grants:* Federal Pell, FSEOG, State scholarships/grants, Private scholarships, College/university scholarship or grant aid from institutional funds. *Loans:* Direct Subsidized Stafford Loans, Direct Unsubsidized Stafford Loans, Direct PLUS loans, Federal Perkins Loans, College/university loans from institutional funds. *Student Employment:* Federal Work-Study Program available. Institutional employment available. **Financial Aid Statistics:** 100% needy freshmen, 100% needy undergrads receive need-based scholarship or grant aid. 24% freshmen, 20% undergrads receive non-need-based scholarship or grant aid. 75% freshmen, 79% undergrads receive need-based self-help aid. 0% freshmen, 0% undergrads receive athletic scholarships. Average cumulative indebtedness $25,990. **Criteria for awarding aid:** *Non-need-based:* Academics, Leadership, Music/drama.

DICKINSON COLLEGE

P.O. Box 1773, Carlisle, PA 17013-2896
Phone: 717-245-1231 • **Financial Aid Phone:** 717-245-1308
E-mail: admissions@dickinson.edu • **CEEB Code:** 2186
Fax: 717-245-1442 • **Website:** www.dickinson.edu/ • **ACT Code:** 3550

This private school was founded in 1783. It has a 308-acre campus.

RATINGS

Admissions Selectivity Rating: 91   **Fire Safety Rating:** 90   **Green Rating:** 99

STUDENTS AND FACULTY

Enrollment: 2,370. **Student Body:** 58% female, 42% male, 78% out-of-state, 10% international (46 countries represented). Asian 3%, African American 5%, Caucasian 69%, Hispanic 7%, Native American <1%, Pacific Islander <1%, Two or more races 4%, Race unknown 1%.
Retention and Graduation: 90% freshmen return for sophomore year. 81% freshmen graduate within 4 years. 84% freshmen graduate within 6 years. 54% grads go on to further study within 1 year. 18% grads pursue arts and sciences degrees. 1% grads pursue law degrees. 4% grads pursue business degrees. 5% grads pursue medical degrees. **Faculty:** Student/faculty ratio 9:1. 225 full-time faculty, 93% hold PhDs, 12% are are members of minority groups, 49% are women. 0% of classes are taught by teaching assistants.

ACADEMICS

Degrees: bachelor's. **Classes:** Most classes have 10-19 students. **Most popular majors:** International Business/Trade/Commerce; Psychology; Economics. **Special Study Options:** Accelerated program, cross-registration, double major, English as a Second Language (ESL), exchange student program (domestic), independent study, internships, liberal arts/career combination, student-designed major, study abroad, teacher certification program. Combined degree programs: BA/JD, BA/MEng, 3-3 Dickinson School of Law (Penn State); 3-2 Johns Hopkins U. Nursing. **Disability Services:** Special programs offered to physically disabled students, including note-taking services, reader services, tape recorders, tutors. **Career Services:** Alumni network, Alumni services, Career/job search classes, Career assessment, Internships, Regional alumni. Dickinson College believes in the power of experiential education. Our students have access to over 8,000 internships postings across the country and multiple majors require some kind of experiential learning as part of their curriculum. Students participate in internships throughout the fall and spring semesters and over the summer. We have a Dickinson in New York City

program and partner with The Washington Center in Washington, D.C. to provide students an opportunity to live and intern in these cities as part of their academic curriculum. Students participating in internships over the summer are eligible to apply for a Dickinson Internship Grant in order to assist with offsetting expenses incurred while participating in the internship. In addition to internships, students may participate in a short-term externship over the winter break. These experiences provide students with an opportunity to gain a better understanding of a particular career field over a short duration of time. For more information on what Dickinson students have done for internships please visit Life Beyond the Limestone.

FACILITIES

Housing: Coed dorms, special housing for disabled students, fraternity/sorority housing, apartments for single students, Theme Housing, Foreign languages, arts, environmental, multicultural, etc. 70% of campus accessible to physically diasbled. **Special Academic Facilities/Equipment:** Art gallery, center for the arts, planetarium, observatory, scanning electron microscope, archeology. **Computers:** 10% of classrooms, 100% of dorms, 100% of libraries, 100% of dining areas, 100% of student union, 5% of common outdoor areas have wireless network access. Students can register for classes online. Administrative functions (other than registration) can be performed online.

CAMPUS LIFE

Environment: City. **Activities:** Choral groups, concert band, dance, drama/theater, jazz band, literary magazine, music ensembles, musical theater, radio station, student government, student newspaper, student-run film society, symphony orchestra, yearbook, Student Organization, Model UN. 112 registered organizations, 15 honor societies, 11 religious organizations. 6 fraternities, 6 sororities. **Athletics (Intercollegiate):** *Men:* baseball, basketball, cross-country, football, golf, lacrosse, soccer, swimming, tennis, track/field (outdoor), track/field (indoor). *Women:* basketball, cross-country, field hockey, golf, lacrosse, soccer, softball, swimming, tennis, track/field (outdoor), track/field (indoor), volleyball. **On-Campus Highlights:** Old West, designed by Benjamin Latrobe, Rector Science Complex, Waidner Spahr Library, Stern Center for Global Education, Kline Athletic Center, The Quarry (coffee shop and late night party/gathering space), Weiss Center for the Arts, and the Trout Gallery. **Environmental Initiatives:** Integrating sustainability throughout the curriculum, supported by the Center for Sustainability Education.

ADMISSIONS

Freshman Academic Profile: 48% in top 10% of high school class, 82% in top 25% of high school class, 99% in top 50% of high school class. 57% from public high schools. **Reported SAT (pre-2016 redesign) scores:** SAT Math middle 50% range 610-705. SAT Critical Reading middle 50% range 590-680. SAT Writing middle 50% range 600-690. **Concordant SAT scores:** SAT EBRW middle 50% 650–720. SAT Math middle 50% range 630–740. ACT middle 50% range 28-31. Minimum internet-based TOEFL 90. **Basis for Candidate Selection:** *Very important factors considered include:* rigor of secondary school record, academic GPA, application essay, recommendation(s), extracurricular activities, talent/ability, character/personal qualities, volunteer work, level of applicant's interest. *Important factors considered include:* class rank, standardized test scores, interview, alumni/ae relation, geographical residence, state residency, racial/ethnic status, work experience. *Other factors considered include:* first generation. **Freshman Admission Requirements:** High school diploma is required and GED is accepted. *Academic units required:* 4 English, 3 math, 3 science, 2 science labs, 2 foreign language, 2 social studies, 2 academic electives. *Academic units recommended:* 3 foreign language. **Freshman Admission Statistics:** 6,172 applied, 43.21% admitted, 23% enrolled. **Transfer Admission Requirements:** High school transcript, college transcript(s), essay or personal statement, statement of good standing from prior institution(s). Minimum college GPA of 2 required. Lowest grade transferable C. **General Admission Information:** Application fee $65. Regular application deadline 2/1. Regular notification 3/20. Nonfall registration not accepted. Admission may be deferred for a maximum of 2 years.

COSTS AND FINANCIAL AID

Annual tuition $50,730. Room and board $12,794. Required fees $450. Average book expense $1,170. **Required Forms and Deadlines:** FAFSA, CSS/Financial Aid PROFILE, State aid form, Noncustodial PROFILE. **Notification of Awards:** Applicants will be notified of awards on or about 3/20. **Types of Aid:** *Need-based scholarships/grants:* Federal Pell, FSEOG, State scholarships/grants, Private scholarships, College/university scholarship or grant aid from institutional funds. *Loans:* Direct Subsidized Stafford Loans, Direct Unsubsidized Stafford Loans, Direct PLUS loans, Federal Perkins Loans, College/university loans from institutional funds. *Student Employment:* Federal Work-Study Program available. Institutional employment available. **Financial Aid Statistics:** 98% needy freshmen, 98% needy undergrads receive need-based scholarship or grant aid. 4% freshmen, 6% undergrads receive non-need-based scholarship or grant aid. 94% freshmen, 91% undergrads receive need-based self-help aid. 0% freshmen, 0% undergrads receive athletic scholarships. 81% freshmen, 76% undergrads receive any aid. 54% undergrads borrow to pay for school. Average cumulative indebtedness $26,908. **Criteria** for awarding aid: *Need-based:* Music/drama. *Non-need-based:* Academics, Leadership, Music/drama.

DICKINSON STATE UNIVERSITY

Office of Enrollment Services, Dickinson, ND 58601-4896
Phone: 701-483-2175 • **Financial Aid Phone:** 701-483-2371
E-mail: dsu.hawks@dsu.nodak.edu
Fax: 701-483-2409 • **Website:** www.dickinsonstate.com • **ACT Code:** 3210

This public school was founded in 1918. It has a 137-acre campus.

RATINGS
Admissions Selectivity Rating: 73   **Fire Safety Rating:** 60*   **Green Rating:** 60*

STUDENTS AND FACULTY
Enrollment: 2,670. **Student Body:** 59% female, 41% male, 34% out-of-state, 12% international (30 countries represented). Asian 0%, African American 1%, Caucasian 71%, Hispanic 1%, Native American 2%, Pacific Islander 0%, Two or more races 0%, Race unknown 12%.
Retention and Graduation: 60% freshmen return for sophomore year. 9% freshmen graduate within 4 years. 31% freshmen graduate within 6 years.
Faculty: Student/faculty ratio 19:1. 86 full-time faculty, 52% hold PhDs, 6% are are members of minority groups, 43% are women.

ACADEMICS
Degrees: associate, bachelor's, certificate, terminal, transfer. **Classes:** Most classes have 10-19 students. **Most popular majors:** Teacher Education, Multiple Levels Business/Commerce. **Special Study Options:** Accelerated program, distance learning, double major, dual enrollment, honors program, independent study, internships, liberal arts/career combination, student-designed major, study abroad, teacher certification program. **Career Services:** Alumni network, Alumni services, Career/job search classes, Career assessment, Internships.

FACILITIES
Housing: Coed dorms, special housing for disabled students, men's dorms, women's dorms, apartments for married students, apartments for single students, Apartments for upperclassmen; apartments for scholars. **Special Academic Facilities/Equipment:** Art gallery, smart classrooms **Computers:** Students can register for classes online.

CAMPUS LIFE
Environment: Rural. **Activities:** Choral groups, concert band, dance, drama/theater, jazz band, literary magazine, marching band, music ensembles, musical theater, pep band, student government, student newspaper, student-run film society, yearbook, Student Organization. 51 registered organizations, 7 honor societies, 6 religious organizations. **Athletics (Intercollegiate):** *Men:* baseball, basketball, cheerleading, cross-country, football, golf, rodeo, track/field (outdoor), track/field (indoor), wrestling. *Women:* basketball, cheerleading, cross-country, golf, rodeo, softball, track/field (outdoor), track/field (indoor), volleyball. **On-Campus Highlights:** Murphy Hall, Student Center, Common Grounds Coffee Shop, Whitney Stadium

ADMISSIONS
Freshman Academic Profile: Average high school GPA 3.2. 6% in top 10% of high school class, 19% in top 25% of high school class, 53% in top 50% of high school class. 98% from public high schools. **Reported SAT (pre-2016 redesign) scores:** SAT Math middle 50% range 470-590. SAT Critical Reading middle 50% range 430-530. **Concordant SAT scores:** SAT Math middle 50% range 510–610. ACT middle 50% range 18-23. Minimum paper TOEFL 525. **Freshman Admission Requirements:** High school diploma is required and GED is accepted. *Academic units required:* 4 English, 3 math, 3 science, and 3 units from above areas or other academic areas. **Freshman Admission Statistics:** 527 applied, 95.83% admitted, 75% enrolled. **Transfer Admission Requirements:** college transcript(s), Minimum college GPA of 2.0 required. Lowest grade transferable D. **General Admission Information:** Application fee $35. Nonfall registration accepted. Admission may be deferred.

COSTS AND FINANCIAL AID
Annual in-state tuition $3,828. Annual out-of-state tuition $10,222. Room and board $4,076. Required fees $945. Average book expense $900. **Required Forms and Deadlines:** FAFSA. **Notification of Awards:** Applicants will be notified of awards on a rolling basis beginning 4/30. **Types of Aid:** *Need-based scholarships/grants:* Federal Pell, FSEOG, State scholarships/grants, Private scholarships, College/university scholarship or grant aid from institutional funds. *Loans:* Federal Perkins Loans, Federal Nursing Loans. *Student Employment:* Federal Work-Study Program available. Institutional employment available. **Criteria for awarding aid:** *Need-based:* Academics, Job skills, Minority status. *Non-need-based:* Academics, Alumni affiliation, Art, Athletics, Job skills, Leadership, Minority status, Music/drama, State/district residency.

DIGIPEN INSTITUTE OF TECHNOLOGY

9931 Willows Road NE, Redmond, WA 98052
Phone: 425-629-5001 • **Financial Aid Phone:** 425-629-5002
E-mail: admissions@digipen.edu • **CEEB Code:** 37243
Fax: 425-558-0378 • **Website:** www.digipen.edu • **ACT Code:** 6659

This is a proprietary school.

RATINGS
Admissions Selectivity Rating: 80   **Fire Safety Rating:** 87   **Green Rating:** 65

STUDENTS AND FACULTY
Student Body: 45% out-of-state, (45 countries represented).
Retention and Graduation: 72% freshmen return for sophomore year.
Faculty: Student/faculty ratio 11:1. 65 full-time faculty, 42% hold PhDs, 0% are are members of minority groups, 23% 0% of classes are taught by teaching assistants.

ACADEMICS
Degrees: bachelor's, master's. **Most popular majors:** Animation, Interactive Technology, Video Graphics and Special Effects; Modeling, Virtual Environments and Simulation; Game and Interactive Media Design. Combined degree programs: BS/MS. **Career Services:** Alumni network, Alumni services, Career/job search classes, Internships. DIT's Career Services team provides a variety of resources for students to jumpstart their professional development before they graduate and seamlessly transition into the industry afterward. These resources include on-campus events for students to meet and interact with game industry professionals, online tools and on-campus facilities to help connect students with prospective employers, and both group and one-on-one training sessions covering resume and cover letter writing, interviewing, and other job search skills.
On-Campus Events: Career services organizes a variety of on-campus events for students. These include weekly Company Day presentations where recruiters meet with students, offer insight into their companies, review resumes and student work, and interview potential new hires; an annual Career Fair where representatives from dozens of companies visit booths run by our graduating students that showcase their best work; and guest lectures where students learn about their field from respected industry veterans.
During the 2011-2012 academic school year, DIT hosted 19 Company Day presentations by such major game development studios as ArenaNet, BioWare, Blizzard, Disney Interactive Media Group, Insomniac Games, LucasFilm, Microsoft Game Studios, Nintendo Software Technology, and PopCap Games. At these events, students learned about each company's products, development cycle, and culture, then had the opportunity to meet individually with the company's representatives and submit their resume face-to-face. In its ninth annual Career Fair last year, DIT over 100 representatives from 45 game companies from around the country. 120 graduating students showcased their games, designs, and portfolios to employers and recruiters, who demoed the projects and spoke directly with students about their work. Because there were more company representatives than students, students had great access and opportunity to connect with employers. Finally, Career Services worked closely with DIT faculty, many of whom are industry veterans themselves, to host guest lectures by renowned industry professionals. Recent lecturers include Karen Prell, a former Jim Henson Company puppeteer and current animator at Valve Software, and Walt Disney Animation Studios' Dave Goetz, Art Director for the animated film Tangled.

FACILITIES
Housing: 100% of campus accessible to physically diasbled.

ADMISSIONS
Freshman Academic Profile: Average high school GPA 3.3. **Reported SAT (pre-2016 redesign) scores:** SAT Math middle 50% range 545-680. SAT Critical Reading middle 50% range 550-660. SAT Writing middle 50% range 485-610. **Concordant SAT scores:** SAT EBRW middle 50% 580–680. SAT Math middle 50% range 570–710. ACT middle 50% range 26-31. Minimum internet-based TOEFL 80. Minimum paper TOEFL 550. **Basis for Candidate Selection:** *Important factors considered include:* rigor of secondary school record, academic GPA, standardized test scores, application essay, talent/ability, level of applicant's interest. *Other factors considered include:* recommendation(s), extracurricular activities, character/personal qualities, work experience. **Freshman Admission Requirements:** *Academic units recommended:* 4 English, 4 math, 4 science, 1 computer science, 1 visual/performing arts. **Freshman Admission Statistics:** 767 applied, 54.11% admitted, 55% enrolled. **General Admission Information:** Application fee $35. Priority deadline 2/1. Nonfall registration not accepted. Admission may be deferred for a maximum of 1 year.

COSTS AND FINANCIAL AID

Annual tuition $28,800. Required fees $200. **Required Forms and Deadlines:** FAFSA. **Notification of Awards:** Applicants will be notified of awards on a rolling basis beginning 1/1. **Types of Aid:** *Need-based scholarships/ grants:* Federal Pell, FSEOG, State scholarships/grants, Private scholarships, College/university scholarship or grant aid from institutional funds. *Loans:* Direct Subsidized Stafford Loans, Direct Unsubsidized Stafford Loans, Direct PLUS loans. *Student Employment:* Institutional employment available. **Financial Aid Statistics:** 43% needy freshmen, 52% needy undergrads receive need-based scholarship or grant aid. 41% freshmen, 25% undergrads receive non-need-based scholarship or grant aid. 3% freshmen, 13% undergrads receive need-based self-help aid. 0% freshmen, 0% undergrads receive athletic scholarships. Average cumulative indebtedness $32,513.

See page 950.

DIVINE WORD COLLEGE

Office of Admissions, Epworth, IA 52045
Phone: 563-876-3332
E-mail: svdvocations@dwci.edu • **CEEB Code:** 6174
Fax: 563-876-5515

This private school, affiliated with the Roman Catholic Church, was founded in 1964. It has a 30-acre campus.

RATINGS

Admissions Selectivity Rating: 70   **Fire Safety Rating:** 60*   **Green Rating:** 60*

STUDENTS AND FACULTY

Student Body: 100% out-of-state, (12 countries represented).
Faculty: Student/faculty ratio 3:1. 16 full-time faculty, 56% hold PhDs, 25% are are members of minority groups, 56% 0% of classes are taught by teaching assistants.

ACADEMICS

Degrees: associate, bachelor's. **Special Study Options:** double major, English as a Second Language (ESL), independent study, liberal arts/career combination. **Career Services:** On-campus interviews.

FACILITIES

Housing: men's dorms

CAMPUS LIFE

Environment: Rural. **Activities:** Choral groups, student government, yearbook, Campus Ministries, Student Organization. **Athletics (Intercollegiate):** *Men:* soccer.

ADMISSIONS

Freshman Academic Profile: 0% in top 25% of high school class. Minimum paper TOEFL 550. **Basis for Candidate Selection:** *Very important factors considered include:* interview, character/personal qualities, religious affiliation/ commitment, level of applicant's interest. *Important factors considered include:* academic GPA, application essay, recommendation(s). *Other factors considered include:* rigor of secondary school record, class rank, standardized test scores, extracurricular activities, talent/ability, geographical residence, volunteer work, work experience. **Freshman Admission Requirements:** High school diploma is required and GED is accepted. **Freshman Admission Statistics:** 3 applied, 66.67% admitted. **Transfer Admission Requirements:** High school transcript, college transcript(s), essay or personal statement, interview, statement of good standing from prior institution(s). **General Admission Information:** Application fee $25. Nonfall registration accepted. Admission may be deferred for a maximum of one semester.

COSTS AND FINANCIAL AID

Annual tuition $10,400. Room and board $2,700. Required fees $120. Average book expense $500. **Types of Aid:** *Need-based scholarships/grants:* Federal Pell, FSEOG, State scholarships/grants, Private scholarships, College/university scholarship or grant aid from institutional funds. *Loans:* Direct Subsidized Stafford Loans, Direct Unsubsidized Stafford Loans, Federal Perkins Loans, State Loans. *Student Employment:* Federal Work-Study Program available. **Criteria for awarding aid:** *Need-based:* Academics, Leadership.

DOANE COLLEGE

1014 Boswell Avenue, Crete, NE 68333
Phone: 402-826-8222 • **Financial Aid Phone:** 402-826-8260
E-mail: admissions@doane.edu • **CEEB Code:** 6165
Fax: 402-826-8600 • **Website:** www.doane.edu • **ACT Code:** 2448

This private school, affiliated with the United Church of Christ Church, was founded in 1872. It has a 300-acre campus.

RATINGS

Admissions Selectivity Rating: 78   **Fire Safety Rating:** 91   **Green Rating:** 60*

STUDENTS AND FACULTY

Enrollment: 1,633. **Student Body:** 55% female, 45% male, 23% out-of-state, 1% international (16 countries represented). Asian 1%, African American 4%, Caucasian 81%, Hispanic 7%, Native American 1%, Pacific Islander <1%, Two or more races 3%, Race unknown 2%.
Retention and Graduation: 71% freshmen return for sophomore year. 52% freshmen graduate within 4 years. 58% freshmen graduate within 6 years. 32% grads go on to further study within 1 year. 15% grads pursue arts and sciences degrees. 1% grads pursue law degrees. 1% grads pursue business degrees. 5% grads pursue medical degrees. **Faculty:** Student/faculty ratio 11:1. 84 full-time faculty, 81% hold PhDs, 1% are are members of minority groups, 50% are women. 0% of classes are taught by teaching assistants.

ACADEMICS

Degrees: bachelor's, doctoral, master's, post-master's certificate. **Classes:** Most classes have fewer than 10 students. Most lab/discussion sessions have fewer than 10 students. **Most popular majors:** Biological and Physical Sciences; Elementary Education and Teaching; Business Administration and Management. **Special Study Options:** double major, English as a Second Language (ESL), honors program, independent study, internships, student-designed major, study abroad, teacher certification program. **Honors Programs:** The Honors Program is designed to enrich, in a variety of ways, the educational experience of selected Doane students. Specialized, interdisciplinary, one-credit honors seminars form the intellectual core of the program. Another component is the study abroad experience undertaken during the junior or senior year. The culminating experience is a collaborative research project. Combined degree programs: BA/MEng. **Disability Services:** Special programs offered to physically disabled students, including tutors. **Career Services:** Alumni network, Career assessment, Internships. The intenship program at Doane offers students quality internship that build upon their academic coursework. up to 12 credit hours can apply toward graduation, giving students an edge in the job market and on graduate school acceptance.

FACILITIES

Housing: Coed dorms, men's dorms, women's dorms, Theme Housing. 60% of campus accessible to physically diasbled. **Special Academic Facilities/ Equipment:** Art gallery, language lab, communication studies facilities, electron microscope, observatory, outdoor challenge course. **Computers:** 90% of classrooms, 100% of dorms, 100% of libraries, 100% of dining areas, 100% of student union, 10% of common outdoor areas have wireless network access. Students can register for classes online. Administrative functions (other than registration) can be performed online.

CAMPUS LIFE

Environment: Rural. **Activities:** Choral groups, concert band, dance, drama/ theater, jazz band, literary magazine, marching band, music ensembles, musical theater, pep band, radio station, student government, student newspaper, television station, yearbook, Campus Ministries. 50 registered organizations, 8 honor societies, 2 religious organizations. 5 fraternities, 4 sororities. **Athletics (Intercollegiate):** *Men:* baseball, basketball, cross-country, football, golf, soccer, tennis, track/field (outdoor), track/field (indoor). *Women:* basketball, cheerleading, cross-country, golf, soccer, softball, tennis, track/field (outdoor), track/field (indoor), volleyball. **On-Campus Highlights:** Tiger Inn, Perkins Library, The Quads, Fuhrer Field House, Heckman Auditorium. **Environmental Initiatives:** Recycling.

ADMISSIONS

Freshman Academic Profile: Average high school GPA 3.6. 11% in top 10% of high school class, 44% in top 25% of high school class, 91% in top 50% of high school class. 90% from public high schools. ACT middle 50% range 20-26. Minimum paper TOEFL 525. **Basis for Candidate Selection:** *Very important factors considered include:* academic GPA, standardized test scores. *Important factors considered include:* rigor of secondary school record, character/ personal qualities, alumni/ae relation, level of applicant's interest. *Other factors considered include:* class rank, recommendation(s), interview, extracurricular activities, talent/ability, racial/ethnic status, volunteer work, work experience. **Freshman Admission Requirements:** High school diploma is required and GED is accepted. *Academic units recommended:* 4 English, 3 math, 3 science,

2 foreign language, 3 social studies. **Freshman Admission Statistics:** 1,972 applied, 75.86% admitted, 20% enrolled. **Transfer Admission Requirements:** High school transcript, college transcript(s), statement of good standing from prior institution(s). Minimum college GPA of 2.0 required. Lowest grade transferable C-. **General Admission Information:** Nonfall registration accepted. Admission may be deferred for a maximum of one year.

COSTS AND FINANCIAL AID

Annual tuition $29,720. Room and board $8,750. Required fees $714. Average book expense $1,000. **Required Forms and Deadlines:** FAFSA. **Notification of Awards:** Applicants will be notified of awards on a rolling basis beginning 3/15. **Types of Aid:** *Need-based scholarships/grants:* Federal Pell, FSEOG, State scholarships/grants, Private scholarships, College/university scholarship or grant aid from institutional funds. *Loans:* Direct Unsubsidized Stafford Loans, Federal Perkins Loans. *Student Employment:* Federal Work-Study Program available. Institutional employment available. **Financial Aid Statistics:** 100% needy freshmen, 100% needy undergrads receive need-based scholarship or grant aid. 22% freshmen, 17% undergrads receive non-need-based scholarship or grant aid. 77% freshmen, 82% undergrads receive need-based self-help aid. 11% freshmen, 14% undergrads receive athletic scholarships. 100% freshmen, 98% undergrads receive any aid. 78% undergrads borrow to pay for school. Average cumulative indebtedness $30,720. **Criteria for awarding aid:** *Non-need-based:* Academics, Alumni affiliation, Athletics, Leadership, Music/drama, Religious affiliation.

DOMINICAN COLLEGE

470 Western Highway, Orangeburg, NY 10962-1210
Phone: 845-848-7901 • **Financial Aid Phone:** 845-848-7818
E-mail: admissions@dc.edu • **CEEB Code:** 2190
Fax: 845-365-3150 • **Website:** http://www.dc.edu • **ACT Code:** 2730

This private school was founded in 1952. It has a 70-acre campus.

RATINGS
Admissions Selectivity Rating: 64   **Fire Safety Rating:** 93   **Green Rating:** 60*

STUDENTS AND FACULTY

Enrollment: 1,552. **Student Body:** 66% female, 34% male, 25% out-of-state, 1% international (15 countries represented). Asian 7%, African American 17%, Caucasian 32%, Hispanic 29%, Native American 0%, Pacific Islander <1%, Two or more races 3%, Race unknown 11%.
Retention and Graduation: 71% freshmen return for sophomore year. 26% freshmen graduate within 4 years. 46% freshmen graduate within 6 years.
Faculty: Student/faculty ratio 16:1. 73 full-time faculty, 68% hold PhDs, 15% are are members of minority groups, 70% are women. 0% of classes are taught by teaching assistants.

ACADEMICS

Degrees: associate, bachelor's, doctoral, master's. **Classes:** Most classes have 20-29 students. **Most popular majors:** Social Sciences; Business/Commerce. **Special Study Options:** Accelerated program, cooperative education program, distance learning, dual enrollment, honors program, independent study, internships, liberal arts/career combination, teacher certification program, weekend college, Independent study. Combined degree programs: BS/MS Occupational Therapy. **Disability Services:** Special programs offered to physically disabled students, including note-taking services, reader services, tutors. **Career Services:** Career/job search classes, Career assessment, Internships, Regional alumni.

FACILITIES

Housing: Coed dorms. 100% of campus accessible to physically diasbled. **Special Academic Facilities/Equipment:** New State of the Art Prusmack Center for Health Care Programs and Science Education. **Computers:** 100% of classrooms, 100% of dorms, 100% of libraries, 100% of dining areas, have wireless network access.

CAMPUS LIFE

Environment: Metropolis. **Activities:** Choral groups, dance, drama/theater, literary magazine, musical theater, student government, student newspaper, yearbook, Campus Ministries, Model UN. 26 registered organizations, 8 honor societies, 1 religious organization. **Athletics (Intercollegiate):** *Men:* baseball, basketball, golf, lacrosse, soccer. *Women:* basketball, cross-country, lacrosse, soccer, softball, track/field (outdoor), volleyball. **On-Campus Highlights:** Prusmack Center for Health and Science Education, Granito Center: Book Store, Health Services, Hennessy Athletic Center, Sullivan Library, Rosary Hall Lounge, Wild Onion Lounge/Cafeteria in Casey Hall. **Environmental Initiatives:** Geothermal HVAC system installed in most recently constructed academic building.

ADMISSIONS

Freshman Academic Profile: Average high school GPA 3.0. 69% from public high schools. Minimum paper TOEFL 550. **Basis for Candidate Selection:** *Important factors considered include:* academic GPA, standardized test scores, recommendation(s). *Other factors considered include:* rigor of secondary school record, application essay, interview, extracurricular activities, talent/ability, character/personal qualities, volunteer work, work experience, level of applicant's interest. **Freshman Admission Requirements:** High school diploma is required and GED is accepted. *Academic units required:* 4 English, 3 math, 3 science, 1 science lab, 1 foreign language, 3 social studies, 3 history, 2 academic electives. *Academic units recommended:* 4 English, 3 math, 3 science, 1 science lab, 2 foreign language, 4 social studies, 4 history, 2 academic electives. **Freshman Admission Statistics:** 1,959 applied, 71.47% admitted, 26% enrolled. **Transfer Admission Requirements:** college transcript(s), Minimum college GPA of 2.0 required. Lowest grade transferable C. **General Admission Information:** Application fee $35. Nonfall registration accepted. Admission may be deferred for a maximum of 1 year.

COSTS AND FINANCIAL AID

Annual tuition $26,578. Room and board $12,420. Required fees $860. Average book expense $1,350. **Required Forms and Deadlines:** FAFSA, State aid form. **Notification of Awards:** Applicants will be notified of awards on a rolling basis beginning 2/1. **Types of Aid:** *Need-based scholarships/grants:* Federal Pell, FSEOG, State scholarships/grants, Private scholarships, College/university scholarship or grant aid from institutional funds. *Loans:* Direct Subsidized Stafford Loans, Direct Unsubsidized Stafford Loans, Direct PLUS loans, Federal Perkins Loans, Federal Nursing Loans, State Loans, College/university loans from institutional funds. *Student Employment:* Federal Work-Study Program available. Institutional employment available. **Financial Aid Statistics:** 97% needy freshmen, 95% needy undergrads receive need-based scholarship or grant aid. 9% freshmen, 8% undergrads receive non-need-based scholarship or grant aid. 80% freshmen, 85% undergrads receive need-based self-help aid. 8% freshmen, 5% undergrads receive athletic scholarships. 98% freshmen, 97% undergrads receive any aid. **Criteria for awarding aid:** *Need-based:* Academics, Athletics. *Non-need-based:* Academics, Athletics.

DOMINICAN SCHOOL OF PHILOSOPHY AND THEOLOGY

2301 Vine Street, Berkeley, CA 94708
Phone: 510-883-2073
E-mail: admissions@dspt.edu
Fax: 510-849-1372 • **Website:** www.dspt.edu

This private school, affiliated with the Roman Catholic Church, was founded in 1932. It has a -1-acre campus.

RATINGS
Admissions Selectivity Rating: 60*   **Fire Safety Rating:** 60*   **Green Rating:** 60*

STUDENTS AND FACULTY

Enrollment: 5. **Student Body:** 40% female, 60% male, 0% international (6 countries represented). Asian 40%, African American 0%, Caucasian 20%, Hispanic 40%, Native American 0%, Pacific Islander 0%, Two or more races 0%, Race unknown 0%.
Retention and Graduation: 100% freshmen return for sophomore year. 50% grads go on to further study within 1 year. 60% grads pursue arts and sciences degrees. 10% grads pursue law degrees. 50% grads pursue medical degrees.
Faculty: Student/faculty ratio 4:1. 12 full-time faculty, 100% hold PhDs, 0% are are members of minority groups, 17% are women. 10% of classes are taught by teaching assistants.

ACADEMICS

Degrees: bachelor's, certificate, master's. **Classes:** Most classes have 10-19 students. **Special Study Options:** cross-registration, independent study, study abroad, Select graduate level courses available to undergradute students.

FACILITIES

Housing: men's dorms, women's dorms, apartments for married students, apartments for single students. 50% of campus accessible to physically diasbled. **Computers:** Administrative functions (other than registration) can be performed online.

CAMPUS LIFE

Environment: City. **Activities:** Choral groups, concert band, music ensembles, student government, yearbook.

ADMISSIONS

Minimum paper TOEFL 550. **Freshman Admission Requirements:** High school diploma is required and GED is accepted. **Transfer Admission Requirements:** college transcript(s), essay or personal statement, Minimum college GPA of 2.3 required. Lowest grade transferable C. **General Admission Information:** Application fee $40. Priority deadline 3/15. Nonfall registration not accepted. Admission may be deferred for a maximum of 1 year.

COSTS AND FINANCIAL AID

Annual tuition $11,880. Required fees $100. Average book expense $1,113. *Student Employment:* Federal Work-Study Program available. Institutional employment available.

DOMINICAN UNIVERSITY

7900 West Division, River Forest, IL 60305
Phone: 708-524-6800 • **Financial Aid Phone:** 708-524-6950
E-mail: domadmis@dom.edu • **CEEB Code:** 1667
Fax: 708-524-6864 • **Website:** www.dom.edu • **ACT Code:** 1126

This private school, affiliated with the Roman Catholic Church, was founded in 1901. It has a 37-acre campus.

RATINGS

Admissions Selectivity Rating: 84   **Fire Safety Rating:** 96   **Green Rating:** 75

STUDENTS AND FACULTY

Enrollment: 2,288. **Student Body:** 67% female, 33% male, 6% out-of-state, 3% international (11 countries represented). Asian 3%, African American 7%, Caucasian 35%, Hispanic 48%, Native American <1%, Pacific Islander <1%, Two or more races 1%, Race unknown 2%.

Retention and Graduation: 72% freshmen return for sophomore year. 51% freshmen graduate within 4 years. 62% freshmen graduate within 6 years. 32% grads go on to further study within 1 year. **Faculty:** Student/faculty ratio 11:1. 165 full-time faculty, 87% hold PhDs, 22% are are members of minority groups, 57% are women. 0% of classes are taught by teaching assistants.

ACADEMICS

Degrees: bachelor's, certificate, doctoral, master's, postbachelor's certificate, post-master's certificate. **Classes:** Most classes have 10-19 students. Most lab/discussion sessions have 10-19 students. **Most popular majors:** Business/Commerce; Psychology; Sociology. **Special Study Options:** Accelerated program, cross-registration, distance learning, double major, dual enrollment, English as a Second Language (ESL), honors program, independent study, internships, liberal arts/career combination, student-designed major, study abroad, teacher certification program. **Honors Programs:** Honors seminars for high ability students Combined degree programs: BA/MA, BA/MBA; BA/MSLIS; BA/MSSPED; 5 yr. pr. w/ Rush U. **Disability Services:** Special programs offered to physically disabled students, including note-taking services, reader services, tape recorders, tutors. **Career Services:** Alumni network, Alumni services, Career/job search classes, Career assessment, Internships, Regional alumni. We have an excellent Chicago internship program.

FACILITIES

Housing: Coed dorms, special housing for disabled students, co-ed by floor. 100% of campus accessible to physically diasbled. **Special Academic Facilities/Equipment:** Art gallery, Technology Center, language lab, Recital Hall **Computers:** 70% of classrooms, 100% of libraries, 75% of dining areas, 100% of student union, have wireless network access. Students can register for classes online. Administrative functions (other than registration) can be performed online.

CAMPUS LIFE

Environment: Metropolis. **Activities:** Choral groups, dance, drama/theater, literary magazine, musical theater, student government, student newspaper, Campus Ministries, Student Organization. 76 registered organizations, 14 honor societies, 2 religious organizations. **Athletics (Intercollegiate):** *Men:* baseball, basketball, cross-country, soccer, tennis. *Women:* basketball, cross-country, soccer, softball, tennis, volleyball. **On-Campus Highlights:** Cybercafe, New science building (Parmer Hall), Reading Room, Centennial Hall (residence hall), New parking pavillion. **Environmental Initiatives:** Over half the surface parking lots have permeable pavers

ADMISSIONS

Freshman Academic Profile: Average high school GPA 3.7. 26% in top 10% of high school class, 56% in top 25% of high school class, 85% in top 50% of high school class. 80% from public high schools. **Reported SAT (pre-2016 redesign) scores:** SAT Math middle 50% range 430-630. SAT Critical Reading middle 50% range 480-570. SAT Writing middle 50% range 440-540. **Concordant SAT scores:** SAT EBRW middle 50% 510–610. SAT Math middle

50% range 470–650. ACT middle 50% range 20-25. Minimum internet-based TOEFL 79. Minimum paper TOEFL 550. **Basis for Candidate Selection:** *Very important factors considered include:* rigor of secondary school record, class rank, academic GPA, standardized test scores. *Other factors considered include:* application essay, recommendation(s), interview, extracurricular activities, talent/ability, character/personal qualities, alumni/ae relation. **Freshman Admission Requirements:** High school diploma is required and GED is accepted. *Academic units recommended:* 4 English, 3 math, 3 science, 2 science labs, 2 foreign language, 1 social studies, 2 history, and 1 unit from above areas or other academic areas. **Freshman Admission Statistics:** 4,568 applied, 63.73% admitted, 17% enrolled. **Transfer Admission Requirements:** college transcript(s), essay or personal statement, Minimum college GPA of 2.5 required. Lowest grade transferable C-. **General Admission Information:** Application fee $25. Nonfall registration accepted. Admission may be deferred for a maximum of 1 semester.

COSTS AND FINANCIAL AID

Annual tuition $32,160. Room and board $9,942. Required fees $370. Average book expense $1,200. **Required Forms and Deadlines:** FAFSA. **Notification of Awards:** Applicants will be notified of awards on a rolling basis beginning 3/15. **Types of Aid:** *Need-based scholarships/grants:* Federal Pell, FSEOG, State scholarships/grants, Private scholarships, College/university scholarship or grant aid from institutional funds. *Loans:* Direct Subsidized Stafford Loans, Direct Unsubsidized Stafford Loans, Direct PLUS loans. *Student Employment:* Federal Work-Study Program available. Institutional employment available. **Financial Aid Statistics:** 100% needy freshmen, 99% needy undergrads receive need-based scholarship or grant aid. 6% freshmen, 8% undergrads receive non-need-based scholarship or grant aid. 91% freshmen, 90% undergrads receive need-based self-help aid. 0% freshmen, 0% undergrads receive athletic scholarships. 100% freshmen, 91% undergrads receive any aid. 88% undergrads borrow to pay for school. Average cumulative indebtedness $28,533. **Criteria for awarding aid:** *Need-based:* Academics, Alumni affiliation, Art, Minority status, Religious affiliation. *Non-need-based:* Academics, Alumni affiliation, Art, Minority status, Religious affiliation.

DOMINICAN UNIVERSITY OF CALIFORNIA

Admissions, San Rafael, CA 94901-2298
Phone: 415-485-3204 • **Financial Aid Phone:** 415-257-1302
E-mail: enroll@dominican.edu • **CEEB Code:** 4284
Website: www.dominican.edu

This private school was founded in 1890. It has a 80-acre campus.

RATINGS

Admissions Selectivity Rating: 80   **Fire Safety Rating:** 99   **Green Rating:** 60*

STUDENTS AND FACULTY

Enrollment: 1,374. **Student Body:** 73% female, 27% male, 9% out-of-state, 1% international (20 countries represented). Asian 23%, African American 5%, Caucasian 34%, Hispanic 20%, Native American 1%, Pacific Islander 1%, Two or more races 7%, Race unknown 7%.

Retention and Graduation: 87% freshmen return for sophomore year. 54% freshmen graduate within 4 years. 68 **Faculty:** Student/faculty ratio 9:1. 102 full-time faculty, 73% hold PhDs, 17% are members of minority groups, 58% are women. 0% of classes are taught by teaching assistants.

ACADEMICS

Degrees: bachelor's, master's, postbachelor's certificate. **Classes:** Most classes have 10-19 students. Most lab/discussion sessions have fewer than 10 students. **Special Study Options:** Accelerated program, cross-registration, distance learning, double major, dual enrollment, English as a Second Language (ESL), exchange student program (domestic), honors program, independent study, internships, study abroad, teacher certification program, weekend college. **Honors Programs:** Honors Program Scholar in the World. **Disability Services:** Special programs offered to physically disabled students, including note-taking services, reader services, tape recorders, tutors. **Career Services:** Alumni network, Alumni services, Career/job search classes, Career assessment, Internships, Regional alumni, On-campus interviews. **Internship Program:** Most programs at Dominican University of California require an internship of 45-135 hours, undertaken after completing some coursework in the major. The internship helps students clarify and test their career goals, obtain hands-on work experience related to their major, gain professional contacts, and develop self-confidence. In addition to the completion of the internship hours, students must maintain a journal, submit a paper or give an oral presentation, and evaluate the internship at midterm and upon completion.

FACILITIES

Housing: Coed dorms, Wellness Housing. 65% of campus accessible to physically diasbled. **Special Academic Facilities/Equipment:** Art Gallery, Science Lab, Computer Labs, Nursing Skills. Lab **Computers:** 10% of classrooms, 5% of dorms, 100% of libraries, 100% of dining areas, 100% of student union, have wireless network access. Administrative functions (other than registration) can be performed online.

CAMPUS LIFE

Environment: Town. **Activities:** Choral groups, dance, drama/theater, jazz band, literary magazine, music ensembles, musical theater, radio station, student government, student newspaper, yearbook, Campus Ministries. 19 registered organizations, 7 honor societies, 4 religious organizations. **Athletics (Intercollegiate):** *Men:* basketball, golf, lacrosse, soccer. *Women:* basketball, golf, soccer, softball, tennis, volleyball. **On-Campus Highlights:** Conlan Recreation Center, Caleruega Dining Hall, Guzman Lecture Hall, Alemany Library, Science Center. **Environmental Initiatives:** We established the Dominican Center for Sustainability. The Center serves as ground central for Dominican University's numerous green activities, including educational programs, scholarships, community outreach, and national and international partnerships. We created the Center to tap the wealth of intellectual capital in place at Dominican in order to support existing and emerging green programs. The Center identifies and promotes economically viable green business practices and serves as a think-tank for ongoing green projects on a community, regional, and global level.

ADMISSIONS

Freshman Academic Profile: Average high school GPA 3.5. 25% in top 10% of high school class, 57% in top 25% of high school class, 84% in top 50% of high school class. **Reported SAT (pre-2016 redesign) scores:** SAT Math middle 50% range 468-560. SAT Critical Reading middle 50% range 450-563. SAT Writing middle 50% range 460-560. **Concordant SAT scores:** SAT EBRW middle 50% 510–620. SAT Math middle 50% range 510–580. ACT middle 50% range 21-25. Minimum paper TOEFL 550. **Basis for Candidate Selection:** *Very important factors considered include:* rigor of secondary school record, academic GPA, standardized test scores, application essay, recommendation(s), character/personal qualities, first generation. *Important factors considered include:* class rank, interview, extracurricular activities, talent/ability, volunteer work, work experience. *Other factors considered include:* alumni/ae relation. **Freshman Admission Requirements:** High school diploma is required and GED is accepted. *Academic units required:* 4 English, 2 math, 2 foreign language, 1 history. *Academic units recommended:* 34 math, 2 history. **Freshman Admission Statistics:** 2,049 applied, 77.75% admitted, 17% enrolled. **Transfer Admission Requirements:** college transcript(s), essay or personal statement, Minimum college GPA of 2.0 required. Lowest grade transferable C. **General Admission Information:** Application fee $40. Priority deadline 2/1. Nonfall registration accepted. Admission may be deferred for a maximum of one term.

COSTS AND FINANCIAL AID

Annual tuition $42,950. Room and board $14,220. Required fees $450. Average book expense $1,790. **Required Forms and Deadlines:** FAFSA, Institution's own financial aid form. **Notification of Awards:** Applicants will be notified of awards on a rolling basis beginning 3/15. **Types of Aid:** *Need-based scholarships/grants:* Federal Pell, FSEOG, State scholarships/grants, Private scholarships, College/university scholarship or grant aid from institutional funds. *Loans:* Federal Perkins Loans. *Student Employment:* Federal Work-Study Program available. Institutional employment available. **Financial Aid Statistics:** 100% needy freshmen, 100% needy undergrads receive need-based scholarship or grant aid. 12% freshmen, 10% undergrads receive non-need-based scholarship or grant aid. 72% freshmen, 87% undergrads receive need-based self-help aid. 1% freshmen, 2% undergrads receive athletic scholarships. 98% freshmen, 84% undergrads receive any aid. 82% undergrads borrow to pay for school. Average cumulative indebtedness $35,369. **Criteria for awarding aid:** *Need-based:* Academics, Athletics, Leadership, Minority status, Music/drama. *Non-need-based:* Academics, Alumni affiliation, Athletics, Leadership, Minority status, Music/drama.

DORDT COLLEGE

498 4th Avenue Northeast, Sioux Center, IA 51250
Phone: 712-722-6080 • **Financial Aid Phone:** 712-722-6087
E-mail: admissions@dordt.edu • **CEEB Code:** 6171
Fax: 712-722-6035 • **Website:** www.dordt.edu • **ACT Code:** 1301

This private school was founded in 1955. It has a 150-acre campus.

RATINGS

Admissions Selectivity Rating: 83   **Fire Safety Rating:** 89   **Green Rating:** 60*

STUDENTS AND FACULTY

Enrollment: 1,194. **Student Body:** 45% female, 55% male, 57% out-of-state, 8% international (21 countries represented). Asian 1%, African American 1%, Caucasian 85%, Hispanic 1%, Native American <1%, Pacific Islander 0%, Two or more races 0%, Race unknown 4%.
Retention and Graduation: 80% freshmen return for sophomore year. 54% freshmen graduate within 4 years. 62% freshmen graduate within 6 years. 15% grads go on to further study within 1 year. 9% grads pursue arts and sciences degrees. 1% grads pursue law degrees. 3% grads pursue business degrees. 2% grads pursue medical degrees. **Faculty:** Student/faculty ratio 12:1. 81 full-time faculty, 68% hold PhDs, 1% are are members of minority groups, 15% are women. 0% of classes are taught by teaching assistants.

ACADEMICS

Degrees: associate, bachelor's, master's, terminal. **Classes:** Most classes have 10-19 students. Most lab/discussion sessions have 10-19 students. **Most popular majors:** Engineering; Education; Business/Commerce. **Special Study Options:** cooperative education program, double major, English as a Second Language (ESL), honors program, independent study, internships, liberal arts/career combination, student-designed major, study abroad, teacher certification program. **Disability Services:** Special programs offered to physically disabled students, including note-taking services, reader services, tape recorders, tutors. **Career Services:** Alumni network, Alumni services, Career/job search classes, Career assessment, Internships, Regional alumni.

FACILITIES

Housing: special housing for disabled students, men's dorms, women's dorms, apartments for married students, apartments for single students. 100% of campus accessible to physically diasbled. **Special Academic Facilities/Equipment:** observatories 160 acre research farm for Ag program, modern recreation facilities which include indoor track, swimming and ice arena **Computers:** 100% of classrooms, 100% of dorms, 100% of libraries, 100% of dining areas, 100% of student union, 100% of common outdoor areas have wireless network access. Students can register for classes online. Administrative functions (other than registration) can be performed online.

CAMPUS LIFE

Environment: Village. **Activities:** Choral groups, concert band, dance, drama/theater, jazz band, literary magazine, music ensembles, musical theater, opera, pep band, radio station, student government, student newspaper, student-run film society, symphony orchestra, yearbook, Campus Ministries, Student Organization. 40 registered organizations, 4 honor societies, 6 religious organizations. **Athletics (Intercollegiate):** *Men:* baseball, basketball, cross-country, football, golf, ice hockey, soccer, tennis, track/field (outdoor), track/field (indoor). *Women:* basketball, cross-country, soccer, softball, tennis, track/field (outdoor), track/field (indoor), volleyball. **On-Campus Highlights:** Campus Center, Recreation Center and De Wit Gymnasium, B J Haan Auditorium, Southview apartments, Covenant Hall.

ADMISSIONS

Freshman Academic Profile: Average high school GPA 3.5. 21% in top 10% of high school class, 44% in top 25% of high school class, 73% in top 50% of high school class. 30% from public high schools. **Reported SAT (pre-2016 redesign) scores:** SAT Math middle 50% range 500-630. SAT Critical Reading middle 50% range 450-610. SAT Writing middle 50% range 470-590. **Concordant SAT scores:** SAT EBRW middle 50% 510–650. SAT Math middle 50% range 530–650. ACT middle 50% range 21-28. Minimum internet-based TOEFL 80. Minimum paper TOEFL 550. **Basis for Candidate Selection:** *Very important factors considered include:* rigor of secondary school record, academic GPA, standardized test scores, religious affiliation/commitment. *Other factors considered include:* class rank, recommendation(s), extracurricular activities, talent/ability, character/personal qualities, first generation, alumni/ae relation, level of applicant's interest. **Freshman Admission Requirements:** High school diploma is required and GED is accepted. *Academic units required:* 3 English, 2 math, 2 science, 2 foreign language, 2 history, 6 academic electives. *Academic units recommended:* 4 English, 3 math, 4 science, 3 foreign language, 1 social studies. **Freshman Admission Statistics:** 1,356 applied,

75.00% admitted, 37% enrolled. **Transfer Admission Requirements:** High school transcript, college transcript(s), standardized test scores, Minimum college GPA of 2.0 required. Lowest grade transferable C. **General Admission Information:** Priority deadline 7/1. Regular application deadline 8/1. Nonfall registration accepted. Admission may be deferred for a maximum of 1 year.

COSTS AND FINANCIAL AID

Annual tuition $26,100. Room and board $7,620. Required fees $440. Average book expense $910. **Required Forms and Deadlines:** FAFSA, Institution's own financial aid form. **Notification of Awards:** Applicants will be notified of awards on a rolling basis beginning 3/1. **Types of Aid:** *Need-based scholarships/grants:* Federal Pell, FSEOG, State scholarships/grants, Private scholarships, College/university scholarship or grant aid from institutional funds. *Loans:* Direct Subsidized Stafford Loans, Direct Unsubsidized Stafford Loans, Direct PLUS loans, Federal Perkins Loans, College/university loans from institutional funds. *Student Employment:* Federal Work-Study Program available. Institutional employment available. **Financial Aid Statistics:** 100% needy freshmen, 100% needy undergrads receive need-based scholarship or grant aid. 14% freshmen, 14% undergrads receive non-need-based scholarship or grant aid. 99% freshmen, 100% undergrads receive need-based self-help aid. 8% freshmen, 7% undergrads receive athletic scholarships. 98% freshmen, 98% undergrads receive any aid. **Criteria for awarding aid:** *Need-based:* Academics, Alumni affiliation, Art, Athletics, Job skills, Leadership, Minority status, Music/drama, Religious affiliation. *Non-need-based:* Academics, Alumni affiliation, Art, Athletics, Job skills, Leadership, Minority status, Music/drama, Religious affiliation, State/district residency.

DOWLING COLLEGE

Idle Hour Boulevard, Oakdale, NY 11769-1999
Phone: 800-369-5464 • **Financial Aid Phone:** 631-244-3220
E-mail: admissions@dowling.edu • **CEEB Code:** 2011
Fax: 631-563-3827 • **Website:** www.dowling.edu • **ACT Code:** 2665

This private school was founded in 1959. It has a 157-acre campus.

RATINGS

Admissions Selectivity Rating: 74   **Fire Safety Rating:** 80   **Green Rating:** 60*

STUDENTS AND FACULTY

Enrollment: 1,152. **Student Body:** 51% female, 49% male, 10% out-of-state, 4% international (53 countries represented). Asian 1%, African American 11%, Caucasian 32%, Hispanic 9%, Native American <1%, Pacific Islander <1%, Two or more races 0%, Race unknown 42%.
Retention and Graduation: 68% freshmen return for sophomore year. 22% freshmen graduate within 4 years. 36% freshmen graduate within 6 years.
Faculty: Student/faculty ratio 16:1. 47 full-time faculty, 89% hold PhDs, 13% are are members of minority groups, 36% are women. 0% of classes are taught by teaching assistants.

ACADEMICS

Degrees: bachelor's, master's, postbachelor's certificate, post-master's certificate. **Classes:** Most classes have 10-19 students. **Most popular majors:** Special Education and Teaching; Business/Commerce; Psychology. **Special Study Options:** Accelerated program, double major, English as a Second Language (ESL), honors program, independent study, internships, liberal arts/career combination, student-designed major, study abroad, teacher certification program, weekend college. **Honors Programs:** The honor programs are for highly motivated, academically superior, and creative students. **Disability Services:** Special programs offered to physically disabled students, including note-taking services, reader services, tape recorders, tutors. **Career Services:** Alumni services, Career/job search classes, Internships, On-campus interviews.

FACILITIES

Housing: Coed dorms. 100% of campus accessible to physically disabled. **Special Academic Facilities/Equipment:** Art gallery, cultural study center, media center, human factors lab, meteorology lab. **Computers:** Students can register for classes online. Administrative functions (other than registration) can be performed online.

CAMPUS LIFE

Environment: Town. **Activities:** Choral groups, drama/theater, jazz band, literary magazine, music ensembles, musical theater, student government, student newspaper, symphony orchestra, yearbook. 29 registered organizations, 10 honor societies, 1 religious organization. **Athletics (Intercollegiate):** *Men:* baseball, basketball, crew/rowing, golf, lacrosse, soccer, tennis. *Women:* basketball, crew/rowing, cross-country, equestrian sports, soccer, softball, tennis, volleyball. **On-Campus Highlights:** Riverside Cafe, Giordano Gallery, Loft Theatre, Connetuot River, Henry Building Atrium.

ADMISSIONS

Freshman Academic Profile: Average high school GPA 2.8. 6% in top 10% of high school class, 19% in top 25% of high school class, 50% in top 50% of high school class. 89% from public high schools. **Reported SAT (pre-2016 redesign) scores:** SAT Math middle 50% range 410-520. SAT Critical Reading middle 50% range 410-520. **Concordant SAT scores:** SAT Math middle 50% range 450-550. **Basis for Candidate Selection:** *Very important factors considered include:* rigor of secondary school record. *Other factors considered include:* class rank, academic GPA, standardized test scores, application essay, recommendation(s), extracurricular activities, talent/ability, character/personal qualities, alumni/ae relation. **Freshman Admission Requirements:** High school diploma is required and GED is accepted. *Academic units recommended:* 4 English, 3 math, 2 science, 3 social studies, and 4 units from above areas or other academic areas. **Freshman Admission Statistics:** 1,864 applied, 74.79% admitted, 15% enrolled. **Transfer Admission Requirements:** college transcript(s), Minimum college GPA of 2.0 required. Lowest grade transferable C. **General Admission Information:** Application fee $25. Nonfall registration accepted. Admission may be deferred for a maximum of 1 year.

COSTS AND FINANCIAL AID

Annual tuition $29,100. Room and board $11,120. Required fees $0. Average book expense $1,000. **Required Forms and Deadlines:** FAFSA, State aid form. **Notification of Awards:** Applicants will be notified of awards on a rolling basis beginning 3/15. **Types of Aid:** *Need-based scholarships/grants:* Federal Pell, FSEOG, State scholarships/grants, Private scholarships, College/university scholarship or grant aid from institutional funds. *Loans:* Direct Subsidized Stafford Loans, Direct Unsubsidized Stafford Loans, Direct PLUS loans, Federal Perkins Loans. *Student Employment:* Federal Work-Study Program available. Institutional employment available. **Financial Aid Statistics:** 85% needy freshmen, 88% needy undergrads receive need-based scholarship or grant aid. 76% freshmen, 59% undergrads receive non-need-based scholarship or grant aid. 96% freshmen, 89% undergrads receive need-based self-help aid. 19% freshmen, 15% undergrads receive athletic scholarships. 82% freshmen, 77% undergrads receive any aid. 84% undergrads borrow to pay for school. Average cumulative indebtedness $39,540. **Criteria for awarding aid:** *Need-based:* Athletics. *Non-need-based:* Academics, Alumni affiliation, Athletics.

DRAKE UNIVERSITY

2507 University Avenue, Des Moines, IA 50311-4505
Phone: 515-271-3181 • **Financial Aid Phone:** 515-271-2905
E-mail: admission@drake.edu • **CEEB Code:** 6168
Fax: 515-271-2831 • **Website:** www.drake.edu • **ACT Code:** 1302

This private school was founded in 1881. It has a 150-acre campus.

RATINGS

Admissions Selectivity Rating: 88   **Fire Safety Rating:** 98   **Green Rating:** 60*

STUDENTS AND FACULTY

Enrollment: 3,196. **Student Body:** 57% female, 43% male, 69% out-of-state, 7% international (43 countries represented). Asian 3%, African American 4%, Caucasian 79%, Hispanic 4%, Native American <1%, Pacific Islander 0%, Two or more races 2%, Race unknown <1%.
Retention and Graduation: 88% freshmen return for sophomore year. 70% freshmen graduate within 4 years. 78% freshmen graduate within 6 years. 22% grads go on to further study within 1 year. 9% grads pursue arts and sciences degrees. 4% grads pursue law degrees. 3% grads pursue business degrees. 4% grads pursue medical degrees. **Faculty:** Student/faculty ratio 12:1. 301 full-time faculty, 92% hold PhDs, 15% are are members of minority groups, 47% are women. 0% of classes are taught by teaching assistants.

ACADEMICS

Degrees: bachelor's, doctoral/professional, doctoral/research, master's, postbachelor's certificate, post-master's certificate. **Classes:** Most classes have 10-19 students. Most lab/discussion sessions have 10-19 students. **Most popular majors:** Actuarial Science; Psychology; Pharmacy. **Special Study Options:** Accelerated program, cooperative education program, distance learning, double major, dual enrollment, English as a Second Language (ESL), honors program, independent study, internships, liberal arts/career combination, student-designed major, study abroad, teacher certification program. **Honors Programs:** The Honors Program is designed for motivated students who want to participate in challenging, discussion-based courses on interdisciplinary and topical issues. The program provides a unique opportunity for intellectual enrichment both in and out of the classroom. Combined degree programs: BA/JD, PharmD/MBA; PharmD/MPA; PharmD/J.D.; AandS/J.D. **Disability Services:** Special programs offered to physically disabled students, including note-taking services, reader services, tape recorders, tutors. **Career**

Services: Alumni network, Alumni services, Career/job search classes, Career assessment, Internships, Regional alumni. Our Professional and Career Development Services does exemplary programming that empowers students to pursue their professional objectives.

FACILITIES

Housing: Coed dorms, special housing for disabled students, fraternity/sorority housing, apartments for single students, ThemeHousingThere are a total of 261 undergrad students and 58 Grad students residing in DWV Drake Realty houses 152 undergraduates and 46 graduate students Greek Life 324 undergraduate students Residence Life 831 EFR and 1795 undergraduate students. 93% of campus accessible to physically diasbled. **Special Academic Facilities/Equipment:** Language lab, observatory, media service center, Anderson art gallery, Oreon E. Scott Chapel. **Computers:** 100% of classrooms, 100% of dorms, 100% of libraries, 100% of dining areas, 100% of student union, have wireless network access. Students can register for classes online. Administrative functions (other than registration) can be performed online.

CAMPUS LIFE

Environment: Metropolis. **Activities:** Choral groups, concert band, drama/theater, jazz band, literary magazine, marching band, music ensembles, musical theater, pep band, radio station, student government, student newspaper, symphony orchestra, Campus Ministries, Student Organization, Model UN. 160 registered organizations, 24 honor societies, 10 religious organizations. 7 fraternities, 6 sororities. **Athletics (Intercollegiate):** *Men:* basketball, cheerleading, cross-country, football, golf, soccer, tennis, track/field (outdoor), track/field (indoor). *Women:* basketball, cheerleading, crew/rowing, cross-country, golf, soccer, softball, tennis, track/field (outdoor), track/field (indoor), volleyball. **On-Campus Highlights:** Athletic Facilities, Olmsted Center, Anderson Gallery, Helmick Commons, Residence Halls / Residence Life. **Environmental Initiatives:** Sustainable building practices.

ADMISSIONS

Freshman Academic Profile: Average high school GPA 3.7. 37% in top 10% of high school class, 68% in top 25% of high school class, 95% in top 50% of high school class. **Reported SAT (pre-2016 redesign) scores:** SAT Math middle 50% range 540-690. SAT Critical Reading middle 50% range 510-650. **Concordant SAT scores:** SAT Math middle 50% range 570–720. ACT middle 50% range 25-30. Minimum internet-based TOEFL 71. Minimum paper TOEFL 530. **Basis for Candidate Selection:** *Very important factors considered include:* academic GPA, standardized test scores, application essay. *Important factors considered include:* rigor of secondary school record, recommendation(s), interview. *Other factors considered include:* class rank, extracurricular activities, talent/ability, character/personal qualities, volunteer work, work experience. **Freshman Admission Requirements:** High school diploma is required and GED is accepted. *Academic units recommended:* 4 English, 3 math, 2 science, 1 science lab, 2 foreign language, 4 social studies. **Freshman Admission Statistics:** 4,959 applied, 68.95% admitted, 22% enrolled. **Transfer Admission Requirements:** college transcript(s), Minimum college GPA of 2.0 required. Lowest grade transferable C. **General Admission Information:** Application fee $25. Priority deadline 3/1. Nonfall registration accepted. Admission may be deferred for a maximum of 12 months.

COSTS AND FINANCIAL AID

Annual tuition $35,060. Room and board $9,850. Required fees $146. Average book expense $1,100. **Required Forms and Deadlines:** FAFSA. **Notification of Awards:** Applicants will be notified of awards on a rolling basis beginning 3/1. **Types of Aid:** *Need-based scholarships/grants:* Federal Pell, FSEOG, State scholarships/grants, Private scholarships, College/university scholarship or grant aid from institutional funds. *Loans:* Direct Subsidized Stafford Loans, Direct Unsubsidized Stafford Loans, Direct PLUS loans, Federal Perkins Loans, College/university loans from institutional funds. *Student Employment:* Federal Work-Study Program available. Institutional employment available. **Financial Aid Statistics:** 99% needy freshmen, 98% needy undergrads receive need-based scholarship or grant aid. 24% freshmen, 18% undergrads receive non-need-based scholarship or grant aid. 79% freshmen, 85% undergrads receive need-based self-help aid. 3% freshmen, 4% undergrads receive athletic scholarships. 99% freshmen, 97% undergrads receive any aid. 63% undergrads borrow to pay for school. Average cumulative indebtedness $33,649. **Criteria for awarding aid:** *Need-based:* Academics. *Non-need-based:* Academics, Alumni affiliation, Art, Athletics, Music/drama, State/district residency.

See page 952.

DREW UNIVERSITY

Office of College Admissions, Madison, NJ 07940-1493
Phone: 973-408-3739 • **Financial Aid Phone:** 973-408-3112
E-mail: cadm@drew.edu • **CEEB Code:** 2193
Fax: 973-408-3068 • **Website:** www.drew.edu • **ACT Code:** 2550

This private school, affiliated with the Methodist Church, was founded in 1868. It has a 186-acre campus.

RATINGS

Admissions Selectivity Rating: 87   **Fire Safety Rating:** 92   **Green Rating:** 88

STUDENTS AND FACULTY

Enrollment: 1,407. **Student Body:** 61% female, 39% male, 33% out-of-state, 8% international (30 countries represented). Asian 6%, African American 9%, Caucasian 55%, Hispanic 11%, Native American 0%, Pacific Islander <1%, Two or more races 5%, Race unknown 7%.
Retention and Graduation: 87% freshmen return for sophomore year. 57% freshmen graduate within 4 years. 61% freshmen graduate within 6 years. 31% grads go on to further study within 1 year. 19% grads pursue arts and sciences degrees. 2% grads pursue law degrees. 1% grads pursue business degrees. 3% grads pursue medical degrees. **Faculty:** Student/faculty ratio 10:1. 150 full-time faculty, 98% hold PhDs, 17% are are members of minority groups, 50% are women. 0% of classes are taught by teaching assistants.

ACADEMICS

Degrees: bachelor's, doctoral/professional, doctoral/research, master's, postbachelor's certificate, post-master's certificate. **Classes:** Most classes have 10-19 students. Most lab/discussion sessions have 10-19 students. **Most popular majors:** Business Administration and Management; Psychology; Biology/Biological Sciences. **Special Study Options:** Accelerated program, cross-registration, double major, exchange student program (domestic), independent study, internships, student-designed major, study abroad, teacher certification program, Seven-year dual degree BA/MD program with UMDNJ-New Jersey Medical school. Five-year dual degree (B.A./B.S. or B.Eng.) programs in engineering and technologies with Columbia University, Stevens Institute of Technology, and Washington University. Five-year dual degree (B.A./Master of Forestry or Master of Environmental Management)program with Duke University. **Honors Programs:** Phi Beta Kappa; Beta Beta Beta (biology), Delta Phi Alpha (German), Omicron Delta Epsilon (economics), Phi Alpha Theta (history), Pi Sigma Alpha (political science), Psi Chi (psychology), Dobro Slovo (Russian), Sigma Delta Pi (Spanish), Sigma Pi Sigma (physics), Pi Mu Epsilon (mathematics), Pi Delta Phi (French), Alpha Kappa Delta (sociology), Pinnacle (nontraditional continuing education students), and Epsilon Omega Psi (Educational Opportunity Scholars). Specialized Honors. Combined degree programs: BA/MD, BA/JD, BA/MA. **Disability Services:** Special programs offered to physically disabled students, including note-taking services, tape recorders, tutors. **Career Services:** Alumni network, Alumni services, Career/job search classes, Career assessment, Internships, Regional alumni. Drew is located in the midst of one of the largest concentrations of corporate headquarters and research centers in the country, and only 30 miles from New York City. Because of our unique location, we can offer students unmatched opportunities for career discovery and development through internships for academic credit. Through this practical experience, students enrich the skills and theories learned in the classroom and see how they are applied in the workplace. Moreover, as a member of a consortium of prestigious liberal arts colleges, Drew students have access to a database of thousands of internships throughout the country. Internships frequently lead to full time jobs for Drew students, either at the location of the internship or with another company in a related field.

FACILITIES

Housing: Coed dorms, special housing for disabled students, Wellness Housing, Theme Housing. **Special Academic Facilities/Equipment:** Art gallery, photography gallery, multimedia language lab, child development center, research greenhouse, arboretum, observatory, laser holography lab, nuclear magnetic resonator, electron microscope, optical and radio telescopes, computer graphics laboratory, New Jersey Shakespeare Festival (professional acting company). **Computers:** 90% of classrooms, 20% of dorms, 100% of libraries, 100% of dining areas, 100% of student union, 25% of common outdoor areas have wireless network access. Students can register for classes online. Administrative functions (other than registration) can be performed online. Undergraduates are required to own a computer.

CAMPUS LIFE

Environment: Village. **Activities:** Choral groups, dance, drama/theater, literary magazine, music ensembles, radio station, student government, student newspaper, student-run film society, symphony orchestra, television station, yearbook, Campus Ministries. 80 registered organizations, 17 honor societies, 9 religious organizations. **Athletics (Intercollegiate):** *Men:* baseball, basketball, cross-country, fencing, lacrosse, soccer, swimming, tennis. *Women:* basketball, cross-country, fencing, field hockey, lacrosse, soccer, softball, swimming, tennis. **On-Campus Highlights:** Dorothy Young Center for the Arts, Simon Forum, Rose Memorial Library, University Center, Commons. **Environmental Initiatives:** New residence hall, McLendon Hall, meets USGBC Leadership in Energy and Environmental Design (LEED) Silver certification.

ADMISSIONS

Freshman Academic Profile: Average high school GPA 3.4. 27% in top 10% of high school class, 61% in top 25% of high school class, 85% in top 50% of high school class. 62% from public high schools. **Reported SAT (pre-2016 redesign) scores:** SAT Math middle 50% range 510-610. SAT Critical Reading middle 50% range 520-640. SAT Writing middle 50% range 500-620. **Concordant SAT scores:** SAT EBRW middle 50% 570–680. SAT Math middle 50% range 540–630. ACT middle 50% range 23-28. Minimum internet-based TOEFL 80. Minimum paper TOEFL 550. **Basis for Candidate Selection:** *Very important factors considered include:* rigor of secondary school record, academic GPA, interview. *Important factors considered include:* application essay, recommendation(s), extracurricular activities, talent/ability, character/personal qualities. *Other factors considered include:* class rank, standardized test scores, alumni/ae relation, racial/ethnic status, volunteer work, work experience, level of applicant's interest. **Freshman Admission Requirements:** High school diploma or equivalent is not required. *Academic units recommended:* 4 English, 3 math, 2 science, 2 foreign language, 2 social studies, 2 history, 3 academic electives. **Freshman Admission Statistics:** 3,494 applied, 57.16% admitted, 18% enrolled. **Transfer Admission Requirements:** High school transcript, college transcript(s), essay or personal statement, statement of good standing from prior institution(s). Lowest grade transferable C. **General Admission Information:** Application fee $60. Regular application deadline 2/15. Regular notification 3/25. Nonfall registration accepted. Admission may be deferred for a maximum of 1 year.

COSTS AND FINANCIAL AID

Annual tuition $46,920. Room and board $13,296. Required fees $832. Average book expense $1,200. **Required Forms and Deadlines:** FAFSA. **Notification of Awards:** Applicants will be notified of awards on or about 3/25. **Types of Aid:** *Need-based scholarships/grants:* Federal Pell, FSEOG, State scholarships/grants, Private scholarships, College/university scholarship or grant aid from institutional funds. *Loans:* Direct Subsidized Stafford Loans, Direct Unsubsidized Stafford Loans, Direct PLUS loans, Federal Perkins Loans. *Student Employment:* Federal Work-Study Program available. Institutional employment available. **Financial Aid Statistics:** 100% needy freshmen, 100% needy undergrads receive need-based scholarship or grant aid. 10% freshmen, 9% undergrads receive non-need-based scholarship or grant aid. 84% freshmen, 82% undergrads receive need-based self-help aid. 0% freshmen, 0% undergrads receive athletic scholarships. 98% freshmen, 95% undergrads receive any aid. 67% undergrads borrow to pay for school. Average cumulative indebtedness $24,964. **Criteria for awarding aid:** *Need-based:* Academics. *Non-need-based:* Academics, Art, Leadership, Minority status, Music/drama.

DREXEL UNIVERSITY

3141 Chestnut Street, Main Building, Philadelphia, PA 19104
Phone: 215-895-2400 • **Financial Aid Phone:** 215-895-2537
E-mail: enroll@drexel.edu • **CEEB Code:** 2194
Fax: 215-895-1285 • **Website:** www.drexel.edu • **ACT Code:** 3556

This private school was founded in 1891. It has a 40-acre campus.

RATINGS

Admissions Selectivity Rating: 86   **Fire Safety Rating:** 97   **Green Rating:** 88

STUDENTS AND FACULTY

Enrollment: 13,249. **Student Body:** 47% female, 53% male, 47% out-of-state, 14% international (104 countries represented). Asian 16%, African American 6%, Caucasian 52%, Hispanic 6%, Native American <1%, Pacific Islander 1%, Two or more races 4%, Race unknown 2%.

Retention and Graduation: 89% freshmen return for sophomore year. 70% freshmen graduate within 6 years. 13% grads go on to further study within 1 year. **Faculty:** Student/faculty ratio 1,172 full-time faculty, 86% hold PhDs, 19% are are members of minority groups, 46% are women.

ACADEMICS

Degrees: associate, bachelor's, certificate, doctoral/professional, doctoral/research, doctoral, master's, postbachelor's certificate, post-master's certificate. **Classes:** Most classes have 10-19 students. **Most popular majors:** Registered Nursing/Registered Nurse; Mechanical Engineering; Business/Commerce. **Special Study Options:** Accelerated program, cooperative education program, distance learning, double major, dual enrollment, English as a Second Language (ESL), honors program, independent study, internships, study abroad, teacher certification program, weekend college, 3-3 programs in engineering with Lincoln University, Indiana Univ. of Penn. **Honors Programs:** The Pennoni Honors College enriches the University experience for students from all majors with demonstrated academic achievement and broad intellectual interests. Consider the benefits: ° Individual attention paid to your academic progress. ° A variety of small group courses with Drexel's best faculty. ° The experience of being in a small college while enjoying the diverse academic opportunities offered by a major medical and technological research University. ° Opportunities to meet students from a variety of fields who share many of your interests. ° Preparation assistance for admission to graduate or professional school, and for fellowships to further your education at home or abroad. ° Social and cultural events. ° The option of taking part in a true living-learning community in the residence halls, which have locations set aside specifically for Honors students. Combined degree programs: BA/MD, BA/MA, BA/MEng, Engineering BS/PhD, BS/DPT, BSN/MSN, BS/MBA, BS/MS. **Disability Services:** Special programs offered to physically disabled students, including note-taking services, reader services, tape recorders, tutors. **Career Services:** Alumni services, Career/job search classes, Career assessment, Internships. A pioneer in co-operative education since 1919, Drexel operates one of the largest co-operative education programs in the nation (in students placed annually). Over 1,500 business, industrial, governmental, and other institutions located in 27 states and 12 foreign countries "cooperate" with Drexel in offering students the opportunity to acquire practical experience in employment related to college studies.

FACILITIES

Housing: Coed dorms, special housing for disabled students, special housing for international students, fraternity/sorority housing, apartments for single students, Freshmen required to live on campus unless living with parents. 98% of campus accessible to physically diasbled. **Special Academic Facilities/Equipment:** Art museum, theatre, audiovisual center, TV studio, recreational center, center for automation technology, engineering center. **Computers:** 100% of classrooms, 100% of dorms, 100% of libraries, 100% of dining areas, 100% of student union, 100% of common outdoor areas have wireless network access. Students can register for classes online. Administrative functions (other than registration) can be performed online. Undergraduates are required to own a computer.

CAMPUS LIFE

Environment: Metropolis. **Activities:** Choral groups, concert band, dance, drama/theater, jazz band, literary magazine, music ensembles, musical theater, pep band, radio station, student government, student newspaper, student-run film society, television station, yearbook, Campus Ministries. 136 registered organizations, 8 honor societies, 8 religious organizations. 12 fraternities, 11 sororities. **Athletics (Intercollegiate):** *Men:* basketball, cheerleading, crew/rowing, diving, golf, lacrosse, soccer, swimming, tennis, wrestling. *Women:* basketball, cheerleading, crew/rowing, diving, field hockey, lacrosse, soccer, softball, swimming, tennis, volleyball. **On-Campus Highlights:** Ross Commons, University Bookstore, Creese Caf, Crossroads at the Handschumacher Dining Hall, The Quad. **Environmental Initiatives:** Green Power: n 2002, Drexel became one of the first universities to purchase wind generated energy. In 2006, Drexel entered into a contract with PECO Wind, to purchase wind energy directly linked to the Exelon-Community Energy Wind Farms located in the PJM Interconnection, supplying Drexel with 4,000.8 MWH per year, which translated into approximately 7.92% of Drexel's total annual electric use. In 2008, Drexel entered into a contract with Community Energy, Inc. to purchase energy linked to the PJM Interconnection, which translated into 12.9% of Drexel total annual use; the University increased its purchase to 30% of its total annual electric usage the following year. In 2010, Drexel entered into a new agreement with Community Energy to purchase Renewable Energy Certificates equal to 100% of the University total energy use (84,268 MWH) starting in January 2011, making Drexel one of the top 50 purchasers of wind energy in the nation according to the EPA Green Power Partnership Rankings. In 2013, Drexel expanded its leadership with a renewed commitment to purchase 100% wind and solar energy from Community Energy.

ADMISSIONS

Freshman Academic Profile: Average high school GPA 3.6. 40% in top 10% of high school class, 69% in top 25% of high school class, 92% in top 50% of

high school class. **Reported SAT (pre-2016 redesign) scores:** SAT Math middle 50% range 560-670. SAT Critical Reading middle 50% range 520-630. **Concordant SAT scores:** SAT Math middle 50% range 580–700. ACT middle 50% range 25-30. Minimum paper TOEFL 550. **Basis for Candidate Selection:** *Very important factors considered include:* rigor of secondary school record, class rank, academic GPA, standardized test scores. *Important factors considered include:* application essay, recommendation(s), character/personal qualities. *Other factors considered include:* interview, extracurricular activities, talent/ability, first generation, alumni/ae relation, volunteer work, work experience, level of applicant's interest. **Freshman Admission Requirements:** High school diploma is required and GED is accepted. *Academic units required:* 3 math, 1 science, 1 science lab. *Academic units recommended:* 1 foreign language. **Freshman Admission Statistics:** 28,535 applied, 74.64% admitted, 11% enrolled. **Transfer Admission Requirements:** college transcript(s), Minimum college GPA of 2.5 required. Lowest grade transferable C. **General Admission Information:** Application fee $50. Regular application deadline 1/15. Nonfall registration accepted. Admission may be deferred for a maximum of 12 months.

COSTS AND FINANCIAL AID

Annual tuition $49,632. Room and board $13,890. Required fees $2,370. Average book expense $1,700. **Required Forms and Deadlines:** FAFSA, CSS/Financial Aid PROFILE. **Notification of Awards:** Applicants will be notified of awards on a rolling basis beginning 3/15. **Types of Aid:** *Need-based scholarships/grants:* Federal Pell, FSEOG, State scholarships/grants, Private scholarships, College/university scholarship or grant aid from institutional funds. *Loans:* Direct Subsidized Stafford Loans, Direct Unsubsidized Stafford Loans, Direct PLUS loans, Federal Perkins Loans, State Loans. *Student Employment:* Federal Work-Study Program available. Institutional employment available. **Financial Aid Statistics:** 100% needy freshmen, 95% needy undergrads receive need-based scholarship or grant aid. 16% freshmen, 9% undergrads receive non-need-based scholarship or grant aid. 71% freshmen, 80% undergrads receive need-based self-help aid. 2% freshmen, 1% undergrads receive athletic scholarships. **Criteria for awarding aid:** *Need-based:* Academics, Art, Athletics, Music/drama. *Non-need-based:* Academics, Art, Athletics, Music/drama, State/district residency.

DRURY UNIVERSITY

900 North Benton Avenue, Springfield, MO 65802-3712
Phone: 417-873-7205 • **Financial Aid Phone:** 417-873-7312
E-mail: druryad@drury.edu • **CEEB Code:** 6169
Fax: 417-866-3873 • **Website:** www.drury.edu • **ACT Code:** 2292

This private school was founded in 1873. It has a 84-acre campus.

RATINGS
Admissions Selectivity Rating: 82   **Fire Safety Rating:** 82   **Green Rating:** 78

STUDENTS AND FACULTY
Enrollment: 1,370. **Student Body:** 54% female, 46% male, 15% out-of-state, 10% international (41 countries represented). Asian 1%, African American 3%, Caucasian 78%, Hispanic 3%, Native American <1%, Pacific Islander <1%, Two or more races 3%, Race unknown 0%.
Retention and Graduation: 79% freshmen return for sophomore year. 48% freshmen graduate within 4 years. 70% freshmen graduate within 6 years. 35% grads go on to further study within 1 year. 5% grads pursue arts and sciences degrees. 5% grads pursue law degrees. 9% grads pursue business degrees. 15% grads pursue medical degrees. **Faculty:** Student/faculty ratio 12:1. 110 full-time faculty, 94% hold PhDs, 7% are are members of minority groups, 42% are women. 0% of classes are taught by teaching assistants.

ACADEMICS
Degrees: associate, bachelor's, master's. **Classes:** Most classes have 10-19 students. Most lab/discussion sessions have 20-29 students. **Most popular majors:** Business Administration and Management; Biology/Biological Sciences; Drama and Dramatics/Theatre Arts. **Special Study Options:** Accelerated program, cooperative education program, distance learning, double major, dual enrollment, English as a Second Language (ESL), honors program, independent study, internships, liberal arts/career combination, student-designed major, study abroad, teacher certification program, Drury Center in Volos, Greece; Living-Learning Communities; Washington Semester. **Honors Programs:** Drury Honors Program Combined degree programs: BA/MEng, 3+2 Occupational therapy with Washington Univ. **Disability Services:** Special programs offered to physically disabled students, including note-taking services, reader services, tape recorders, tutors. **Career Services:** Alumni network, Alumni services, Career/job search classes, Career assessment, Internships, Regional alumni. 70% of students complete at least one internship. Recent

...ions include National Public Radio in Washington, D.C.; state and federal ...ors' offices, McSweeney's magazine, San Francisco; Fleishman-Hillard ...re lations, numerous not-for-profit organizations. Myriad opportunities **FA...e** thanks to Drury's widespread alumni base.

Housing...
housing, a...orms, special housing for disabled students, fraternity/sorority Living-learn...s for married students, apartments for single students, accessible to p...unities; Leadership/community service. 97% of campus Science center w...diasbled. **Special Academic Facilities/Equipment:** art center with two...house and astronomical observaton station, new visual language lab, electron... TV studio, radio station, teleconference facility, 30% of dorms, 100% of... lab, laser lab. **Computers:** 100% of classrooms, 20% of common outdoor a... 100% of dining areas, 75% of student union, register for classes online. Ac...e wireless network access. Students can be performed online. ...ative functions (other than registration) can

CAMPUS LIFE
Environment: City. **Activities:** Cho... theater, jazz band, literary magazine, m...ps, concert band, dance, drama/ pep band, radio station, student governme...sembles, musical theater, opera, film society, symphony orchestra, television...dent newspaper, student-run Organization. 90 registered organizations, 11 h... Campus Ministries, Student organizations. 4 fraternities, 4 sororities. **Athletic...**societies, 7 religious baseball, basketball, cheerleading, cross-country, d...**ntercollegiate):** Men: swimming, tennis. *Women:* basketball, cheerleading, ...golf, soccer, softball, soccer, softball, swimming, tennis, volleyball. **On-Camp...**country, diving, golf, Science Center, Sunderland Hall (new student housing), C...**Highlights:** Trustee Art Center, College Park student housing, The Drury campu...Library, Pool maintained and is a registered tree farm; its overall appearance ...impeccably highlight of a tour. **Environmental Initiatives:** Energy Manage...the greatest on buildings upgrading lighting, HVAC systems). Bicycle rentals fo...**nt strategies** use for the semester for $25. ...udents to

ADMISSIONS
Freshman Academic Profile: Average high school GPA 3.8. 21% in top...% of high school class, 41% in top 25% of high school class, 89% in top 50% of high school class. 85% from public high schools. ACT middle 50% range 22-2... Minimum internet-based TOEFL 72. **Basis for Candidate Selection:** *Very important factors considered include:* academic GPA, standardized test scores, recommendation(s), character/personal qualities. *Important factors considered include:* rigor of secondary school record, application essay, extracurricular activities, talent/ability, level of applicant's interest. *Other factors considered include:* interview, alumni/ae relation, racial/ethnic status, volunteer work, work experience. **Freshman Admission Requirements:** High school diploma is required and GED is accepted. *Academic units required:* 4 English, 3 math, 3 science, 2 foreign language, 3 social studies. *Academic units recommended:* 4 English, 4 math, 4 science, 2 foreign language, 3 social studies. **Freshman Admission Statistics:** 1,563 applied, 69.61% admitted, 36% enrolled. **Transfer Admission Requirements:** High school transcript, college transcript(s), essay or personal statement, Minimum college GPA of 2.0 required. Lowest grade transferable C. **General Admission Information:** Application fee $50. Priority deadline 1/10. Regular application deadline 5/1. Nonfall registration accepted. Admission may be deferred for a maximum of 1 Year.

COSTS AND FINANCIAL AID
Annual tuition $25,850. Room and board $8,036. Required fees $1,005. Average book expense $1,200. **Required Forms and Deadlines:** FAFSA, Institution's own financial aid form. **Notification of Awards:** Applicants will be notified of awards on a rolling basis beginning 3/1. **Types of Aid:** *Need-based scholarships/grants:* Federal Pell, FSEOG, State scholarships/grants, Private scholarships, College/university scholarship or grant aid from institutional funds. *Loans:* Direct Subsidized Stafford Loans, Direct Unsubsidized Stafford Loans, Direct PLUS loans, Federal Perkins Loans. *Student Employment:* Federal Work-Study Program available. Institutional employment available. **Financial Aid Statistics:** 100% needy freshmen, 100% needy undergrads receive need-based scholarship or grant aid. 15% freshmen, 14% undergrads receive non-need-based scholarship or grant aid. 81% freshmen, 82% undergrads receive need-based self-help aid. 13% freshmen, 11% undergrads receive athletic scholarships. 81% freshmen, 94% undergrads receive any aid. 55% undergrads borrow to pay for school. Average cumulative indebtedness $31,011. **Criteria for awarding aid:** *Need-based:* Alumni affiliation, Job skills. *Non-need-based:* Academics, Alumni affiliation, Art, Athletics, Job skills, Leadership, Minority status, Music/drama, Religious affiliation.

DUKE UNIVERSITY

2138 Campus Drive, Durham, NC 27708-0586
Phone: 919-684-3214
E-mail: undergrad-admissions@duke.edu • **CEEB C.:** 3088
Fax: 9196681661 • **Website:** www.duke.edu •

This private school, affiliated with the M___st Church, was founded in 1838. It has a 8500-acre campus.

RATINGS
Admissions Selectivity Rating: 98   Safety Rating: 60*   **Green Rating:** 90

STUDENTS AND FACULTY:
Enrollment: 6,485. Students 49% female, 51% male, 87% out-of-state, 10% international (89 count represented). Asian 22%, African American 7%, Native American 1%, Pacific Islander <1%, 10%, Caucasian 46%, Hi unknown 2%.
Two or more races 2%ion: 97% freshmen return for sophomore year. 86%
Retention and Gra in 4 years. 95% freshmen graduate within 6 years. 38% freshmen graduate study within 1 year. 14% grads pursue arts and sciences grads go on to fu pursue law degrees. 1% grads pursue business degrees. degrees. 11% g medical degrees. **Faculty:** Student/faculty ratio 6:1. 1,462 12% grads pu y, 96% hold PhDs, 19% are are members of minority groups, full-time fa en. 4% of classes are taught by teaching assistants. 39% are w

ACADEMICS
Degr: bachelor's, doctoral/professional, doctoral/research, master's, pos bachelor's certificate. **Classes:** Most classes have 10-19 students. Most lab/ di ussion sessions have 10-19 students. **Most popular majors:** Psychology; ublic Policy Analysis; Economics. **Special Study Options:** Accelerated program, cross-registration, distance learning, double major, exchange student program (domestic), honors program, independent study, internships, student-designed major, study abroad, teacher certification program, Undergrads may take grad level classes. Off-Campus Study: New York Arts Program. Other Special Programs: Semester and summer programs in ecology, geology, oceanography, physiology, and zoology at marine laboratory in Beaufort. Combined degree programs: BA/MA, BA/MEng, 3-2 and 4-1 med-tech programs. **Disability Services:** Special programs offered to physically disabled students, including note-taking services, reader services, tape recorders, tutors. **Career Services:** Alumni services, Career/job search classes, Career assessment, Internships.

FACILITIES
Housing: Coed dorms, men's dorms, women's dorms, fraternity/sorority housing, apartments for single students, Theme houses. **Special Academic Facilities/Equipment:** Art museum, language lab, university forest, primate center, phytotron, electron laser, nuclear magnetic resonance machine, nuclear lab. **Computers:** Students can register for classes online.

CAMPUS LIFE
Environment: City. **Activities:** Choral groups, concert band, dance, drama/ theater, jazz band, literary magazine, marching band, music ensembles, musical theater, opera, pep band, radio station, student government, student newspaper, student-run film society, symphony orchestra, television station, yearbook. 200 registered organizations, 10 honor societies, 25 religious organizations. 21 fraternities, 14 sororities. **Athletics (Intercollegiate):** *Men:* baseball, basketball, cross-country, diving, fencing, football, golf, lacrosse, soccer, swimming, tennis, track/field (outdoor), track/field (indoor), volleyball, wrestling. *Women:* basketball, crew/rowing, cross-country, diving, fencing, field hockey, golf, lacrosse, soccer, swimming, tennis, track/field (outdoor), track/ field (indoor), volleyball. **On-Campus Highlights:** Duke Chapel, Primate Center, Sarah P. Duke Gardens, Duke Forest, Levine Science Research Center. **Environmental Initiatives:** Duke has signed the ACUPCC and made a commitment to make Duke a climate neutral institution.

ADMISSIONS
Freshman Academic Profile: 91% in top 10% of high school class, 98% in top 25% of high school class. 65% from public high schools. **Reported SAT (pre-2016 redesign) scores:** SAT Math middle 50% range 690-790. SAT Critical Reading middle 50% range 670-760. SAT Writing middle 50% range 690-780. **Concordant SAT scores:** SAT EBRW middle 50% 720–780. SAT Math middle 50% range 720–800. ACT middle 50% range 31-34. **Basis for Candidate Selection:** *Very important factors considered include:* rigor of secondary school record, class rank, academic GPA, standardized test scores, application

commendation(s), extracurricular activities, talent/ability, character/ essnal qualities. *Other factors considered include:* interview, first generation, lumni/ae relation, geographical residence, state residency, religious affiliation/ commitment, racial/ethnic status, volunteer work, work experience. **Freshman Admission Requirements:** High school diploma is required and GED is not accepted. *Academic units recommended:* 4 English, 3 math, 3 science, 3 foreign language, 3 social studies. **Freshman Admission Statistics:** 30,112 applied, 11.84% admitted, 49% enrolled. **Transfer Admission Requirements:** High school transcript, college transcript(s), essay or personal statement, standardized test scores, Lowest grade transferable C. **General Admission Information:** Application fee $85. Priority deadline 12/20. Regular application deadline 1/2. Regular notification 4/1. Nonfall registration not accepted. Admission may be deferred for a maximum of 1 year.

COSTS AND FINANCIAL AID
Annual tuition $49,575. Room and board $14,438. Required fees $1,690. Average book expense $1,260. **Required Forms and Deadlines:** FAFSA, CSS/Financial Aid PROFILE, Noncustodial PROFILE, Business/Farm Supplement. **Notification of Awards:** Applicants will be notified of awards on or about 4/1. **Types of Aid:** *Need-based scholarships/grants:* Federal Pell, FSEOG, State scholarships/grants, Private scholarships, College/university scholarship or grant aid from institutional funds. *Loans:* Direct Subsidized Stafford Loans, Direct Unsubsidized Stafford Loans, Direct PLUS loans, Federal Perkins Loans, College/university loans from institutional funds. *Student Employment:* Federal Work-Study Program available. Institutional employment available. **Financial Aid Statistics:** 85% needy freshmen, 94% needy undergrads receive need-based scholarship or grant aid. 13% freshmen, 10% undergrads receive non-need-based scholarship or grant aid. 83% freshmen, 87% undergrads receive need-based self-help aid. 0% freshmen, 0% undergrads receive athletic scholarships. 35% undergrads borrow to pay for school. Average cumulative indebtedness $19,104. **Criteria for awarding aid:** *Need-based:* Academics, Alumni affiliation, Leadership, Minority status, Music/ drama, Religious affiliation. *Non-need-based:* Academics, Alumni affiliation, Athletics, Leadership, Minority status, Music/drama, Religious affiliation, State/ district residency.

DUQUESNE UNIVERSITY

600 Forbes Avenue, Pittsburgh, PA 15282
Phone: 412-396-6222 • **Financial Aid Phone:** 412-396-6607
E-mail: admissions@duq.edu
Fax: 412-396-6223 • **Website:** www.duq.edu

This private school, affiliated with the Roman Catholic Church, was founded in 1878. It has a 49-acre campus.

RATINGS
Admissions Selectivity Rating: 85   **Fire Safety Rating:** 99   **Green Rating:** 82

STUDENTS AND FACULTY
Enrollment: 6,018. **Student Body:** 63% female, 37% male, 29% out-of-state, 4% international (47 countries represented). Asian 3%, African American 5%, Caucasian 80%, Hispanic 3%, Native American <1%, Pacific Islander <1%, Two or more races 3%, Race unknown 1%.
Retention and Graduation: 87% freshmen return for sophomore year. 68% freshmen graduate within 4 years. 77% freshmen graduate within 6 years. 31% grads go on to further study within 1 year. 19% grads pursue arts and sciences degrees. 6% grads pursue law degrees. 6% grads pursue business degrees. 3% grads pursue medical degrees. **Faculty:** Student/faculty ratio 14:1. 493 full-time faculty, 95% hold PhDs, 7% are are members of minority groups, 49% are women.

ACADEMICS
Degrees: bachelor's, doctoral/professional, doctoral/research, master's, postbachelor's certificate, post-master's certificate. **Classes:** Most classes have 10-19 students. Most lab/discussion sessions have 10-19 students. **Most popular majors:** Nursing Science; Pharmacy; Psychology. **Special Study Options:** Accelerated program, cross-registration, distance learning, double major, dual enrollment, English as a Second Language (ESL), exchange student program (domestic), external degree program, honors program, independent study, internships, liberal arts/career combination, student-designed major, study abroad, teacher certification program, weekend college, Students have the opportunity to study abroad on our Italian campus in Rome, Italy. **Honors**

Programs: Duquesne University offers it's most qualified and outstanding freshmen the opportunity to participate in the Honors College. This selective and intellectually challenging program is available by invitation only after review of the applicant's academic record. The Honors College combines liberal arts, with opportunities for professional studies while providing the thinking, writing, and speaking skill necessary for continuing success. The foundation of Duquesne's Honors College is the Integrated Honors Program, an enhanced track of the University Core Curriculum. Special honors sections of the core courses feature some of the University's most distinguished faculty. Integrated Honors Program courses focus on our essential human heritage and on the major ideas and issues forming the background and direction of modern life. They are taught in small class sections allowing for close interaction between students and teachers and encouraging individual initiative as well as collaborative learning. Combined degree programs: BA/JD, BA/MA. **Disability Services:** Special programs offered to physically disabled students, including note-taking services, reader services, tape recorders, tutors. **Career Services:** Alumni network, Alumni services, Career/job search classes, Career assessment, Internships, Regional alumni. Duquesne University's Internship Program is designed to provide students with professional, entry-level work experience as a valuable element of their academic curriculum. The Internship Program is open to all current students. Available internship positions are posted through the DuqCareerLink website on an on-going basis. In addition, companies seeking interns may participate in the On-Campus Recruiting Program. It is the responsibility of the student to apply for these positions according to the posted deadline dates. Students may also seek internship opportunities through other means, such as networking and the application process. The University grants credits for an internship when it meets the University's criteria for internship credit (a professional or pre-professional position) and when it fits into the student's curriculum. In addition, students must meet specific University requirements, such as GPA and student status standards, to qualify for internship credits. Many but not all students register for internship credits and oftentimes, students accept internship positions to gain valuable hands-on experience but not to earn credits.

FACILITIES

Housing: Coed dorms, special housing for disabled students, fraternity/sorority housing, apartments for married students, apartments for single students, Wellness Housing, Sorority and fraternity wings; club wings; international wings. **Special Academic Facilities/Equipment:** Student Art Gallery **Computers:** 10% of classrooms, 100% of libraries, 85% of dining areas, 100% of student union, 100% of common outdoor areas have wireless network access. Students can register for classes online. Administrative functions (other than registration) can be performed online.

CAMPUS LIFE

Environment: Metropolis. **Activities:** Choral groups, concert band, dance, drama/theater, jazz band, literary magazine, marching band, music ensembles, musical theater, opera, pep band, radio station, student government, student newspaper, student-run film society, symphony orchestra, television station, yearbook, Campus Ministries, Student Organization, Model UN. 160 registered organizations, 34 honor societies, 7 religious organizations. 10 fraternities, 7 sororities. **Athletics (Intercollegiate):** *Men:* basketball, cross-country, football, soccer, tennis, track/field (outdoor). *Women:* basketball, crew/rowing, cross-country, lacrosse, soccer, swimming, tennis, track/field (outdoor), track/field (indoor), volleyball. **On-Campus Highlights:** Power Recreation Center, Starbucks, The Red Ring, Academic Walk, The Night Spot, The Power Recreation Center is a newly opened recreation and fitness center. Starbucks is a popular coffeehouse located in the Duquesne Union. The Red Ring is a new, full service restaurant/bar with nightly musical entertainment. Academic Walk is the main walkway through campus where many activities are held. There is also a new quiet Study Lounge located on the second floor of the Union.

ADMISSIONS

Freshman Academic Profile: Average high school GPA 3.7. 25% in top 10% of high school class, 56% in top 25% of high school class, 87% in top 50% of high school class. **Reported SAT (pre-2016 redesign) scores:** SAT Math middle 50% range 530-620. SAT Critical Reading middle 50% range 525-610. SAT Writing middle 50% range 510-590. **Concordant SAT scores:** SAT EBRW middle 50% 580–650. SAT Math middle 50% range 560–640. ACT middle 50% range 24-29. Minimum internet-based TOEFL 90. Minimum paper TOEFL 575. **Basis for Candidate Selection:** *Very important factors considered include:* rigor of secondary school record, academic GPA. *Important factors considered include:* standardized test scores. *Other factors considered include:* class rank, application essay, recommendation(s), interview, extracurricular activities, talent/ability, character/personal qualities, first generation, alumni/ae relation, racial/ethnic status, volunteer work, work experience, level of applicant's interest. **Freshman Admission Requirements:** High school diploma is required and GED is accepted. *Academic units recommended:* 4 English, 2 math, 2 science, 2 foreign language, 2 social studies, 4 academic electives. **Freshman Admission Statistics:** 7,655 applied, 72.63% admitted, 28% enrolled. **Transfer Admission Requirements:** High school transcript, college transcript(s), essay or personal statement, statement of good

standing from prior institution(s). Minimum college GPA of 2.5 required. Lowest grade transferable C. **General Admission Information:** Application fee $50. Priority deadline 11/1. Regular application deadline 7/1. Nonfall registration accepted. Admission may be deferred for a maximum of One academic year.

COSTS AND FINANCIAL AID

Annual tuition $35,062. Room and board $11,760. Average book expense $1,400. **Required Forms and Deadlines:** FAFSA, Institution's own financial aid form. **Notification of Awards:** Applicants will be notified of awards on a rolling basis beginning 3/1. **Types of Aid:** *Need-based scholarships/grants:* Federal Pell, FSEOG, State scholarships/grants, Private scholarships, College/university scholarship or grant aid from institutional funds, United Negro College Fund. *Loans:* Direct Subsidized Stafford Loans, Direct Unsubsidized Stafford Loans, Direct PLUS loans, Federal Perkins Loans, Federal Nursing Loans. *Student Employment:* Federal Work-Study Program available. Institutional employment available. **Financial Aid Statistics:** 100% needy freshmen, 97% needy undergrads receive need-based scholarship or grant aid. 100% freshmen, 95% undergrads receive non-need-based scholarship or grant aid. 78% freshmen, 80% undergrads receive need-based self-help aid. 6% freshmen, 6% undergrads receive athletic scholarships. 99% freshmen, 96% undergrads receive any aid. 59% undergrads borrow to pay for school. Average cumulative indebtedness $41,272. **Criteria for awarding aid:** *Need-based:* Academics, Athletics, Minority status. *Non-need-based:* Academics, Athletics, Music/drama.

EARLHAM COLLEGE

801 National Road West, Richmond, IN 47374-4095
Phone: 765-983-1600 • **Financial Aid Phone:** 765-983-1217
E-mail: admissions@earlham.edu • **CEEB Code:** 1195
Fax: 765-983-1560 • **Website:** www.earlham.edu • **ACT Code:** 1186

This private school, affiliated with the Quaker Church, was founded in 1847. It has a 800-acre campus.

RATINGS

Admissions Selectivity Rating: 89   **Fire Safety Rating:** 93   **Green Rating:** 90

STUDENTS AND FACULTY

Enrollment: 994. **Student Body:** 55% female, 45% male, 79% out-of-state, 23% international (76 countries represented). Asian 6%, African American 12%, Caucasian 50%, Hispanic 7%, Native American 1%, Pacific Islander <1%, Two or more races <1%, Race unknown 2%.
Retention and Graduation: 80% freshmen return for sophomore year. 65% freshmen graduate within 4 years. 71% freshmen graduate within 6 years. 21% grads go on to further study within 1 year. **Faculty:** Student/faculty ratio 10:1. 101 full-time faculty, 97% hold PhDs, 12% are are members of minority groups, 50% are women. 0% of classes are taught by teaching assistants.

ACADEMICS

Degrees: bachelor's, master's. **Classes:** Most classes have 10-19 students. Most lab/discussion sessions have fewer than 10 students. **Most popular majors:** Biology/Biological Sciences; Psychology; Multi-/Interdisciplinary Studies. **Special Study Options:** Accelerated program, cross-registration, double major, dual enrollment, English as a Second Language (ESL), independent study, internships, student-designed major, study abroad, teacher certification program, Teacher certification at Master's Degree level only. **Disability Services:** Special programs offered to physically disabled students, including note-taking services, reader services, tape recorders, tutors. **Career Services:** Alumni network, Alumni services, Career/job search classes, Career assessment, Internships, Regional alumni. The Center for Career and Community Engagement is the hub for experiential learning including internships, research and opportunities in professional environments. These opportunities are located in the local community and far-flung places as part of an off-campus study program.

FACILITIES

Housing: Coed dorms, special housing for disabled students, men's dorms, special housing for international students, women's dorms, Wellness Housing, Theme Housing, Friendship houses. 80% of campus accessible to physically diasbled. **Special Academic Facilities/Equipment:** Major academic building Landrum Bolling Center for Interdisciplinary and Social Studies opened in 2002, natural history museum, cultural centers, language labs, greenhouse, observatory, planetarium. **Computers:** 95% of classrooms, have wireless network access. Administrative functions (other than registration) can be performed online.

CAMPUS LIFE

Environment: Town. **Activities:** Choral groups, concert band, dance, drama/theater, jazz band, literary magazine, music ensembles, radio station, student government, student newspaper, student-run film society, symphony orchestra, yearbook, Campus Ministries, Student Organization, Model UN. 70 registered organizations, 1 honor society, 15 religious organizations. **Athletics (Intercollegiate):** *Men:* baseball, basketball, cross-country, football, soccer, tennis, track/field (outdoor), track/field (indoor). *Women:* basketball, cross-country, field hockey, soccer, tennis, track/field (outdoor), track/field (indoor), volleyball. **On-Campus Highlights:** Landrum Bolling Center— Interdisciplinary Studies, Athletics and Wellness Center, Runyan Center, Natural History Museum, Coffee Shop. **Environmental Initiatives:** Earlham recently spent the 2011-12 year in a planning process leading to the Earlham Sustainability Plan, a comprehensive public document.

ADMISSIONS

Freshman Academic Profile: Average high school GPA 3.7. 36% in top 10% of high school class, 67% in top 25% of high school class, 93% in top 50% of high school class. 73% from public high schools. **Reported SAT (pre-2016 redesign) scores:** SAT Math middle 50% range 550-700. SAT Critical Reading middle 50% range 580-680. SAT Writing middle 50% range 550-670. **Concordant SAT scores:** SAT EBRW middle 50% 620–710. SAT Math middle 50% range 570–730. ACT middle 50% range 25-31. Minimum internet-based TOEFL 80. Minimum paper TOEFL 550. **Basis for Candidate Selection:** *Very important factors considered include:* rigor of secondary school record, academic GPA, application essay. *Important factors considered include:* recommendation(s), extracurricular activities, character/personal qualities. *Other factors considered include:* class rank, standardized test scores, interview, talent/ability, alumni/ae relation, racial/ethnic status, volunteer work, work experience. **Freshman Admission Requirements:** High school diploma is required and GED is accepted. *Academic units required:* 4 English, 3 math, 3 science, 2 science labs, 2 foreign language, 2 social studies, 2 history. *Academic units recommended:* 4 math, 4 science, 4 foreign language, 2 social studies, 2 history. **Freshman Admission Statistics:** 2,917 applied, 57.63% admitted, 21% enrolled. **Transfer Admission Requirements:** High school transcript, college transcript(s), essay or personal statement, standardized test scores, statement of good standing from prior institution(s). Minimum college GPA of 2.7 required. Lowest grade transferable C. **General Admission Information:** Priority deadline 12/1. Regular application deadline 2/15. Regular notification 4/1. Nonfall registration accepted. Admission may be deferred for a maximum of 2 years.

COSTS AND FINANCIAL AID

Annual tuition $44,370. Required fees $930. Average book expense $1,200. **Required Forms and Deadlines:** FAFSA. **Notification of Awards:** Applicants will be notified of awards on a rolling basis beginning 3/15. **Types of Aid:** *Need-based scholarships/grants:* Federal Pell, FSEOG, State scholarships/grants, Private scholarships, College/university scholarship or grant aid from institutional funds. *Loans:* Direct Subsidized Stafford Loans, Direct Unsubsidized Stafford Loans, Direct PLUS loans, Federal Perkins Loans, State Loans, College/university loans from institutional funds. *Student Employment:* Federal Work-Study Program available. Institutional employment available. **Financial Aid Statistics:** 97% needy freshmen, 100% needy undergrads receive need-based scholarship or grant aid. 32% freshmen, 39% undergrads receive non-need-based scholarship or grant aid. 87% freshmen, 87% undergrads receive need-based self-help aid. 0% freshmen, 0% undergrads receive athletic scholarships. 98% freshmen, 96% undergrads receive any aid. 60% undergrads borrow to pay for school. Average cumulative indebtedness $25,784. **Criteria for awarding aid:** *Non-need-based:* Academics, Leadership, Minority status, Religious affiliation.

EAST CAROLINA UNIVERSITY

Office of Undergraduate Admissions, Greenville, NC 27858-4353
Phone: 252-328-6640 • **Financial Aid Phone:** 252-328-4347
E-mail: admis@ecu.edu • **CEEB Code:** 5180
Fax: 252-328-6945 • **Website:** www.ecu.edu • **ACT Code:** 3094

This public school was founded in 1907. It has a 1379-acre campus.

RATINGS

Admissions Selectivity Rating: 81   **Fire Safety Rating:** 86   **Green Rating:** 87

STUDENTS AND FACULTY

Enrollment: 21,697. **Student Body:** 58% female, 42% male, 12% out-of-state, <1% international (41 countries represented). Asian 3%, African American 16%, Caucasian 69%, Hispanic 6%, Native American 1%, Pacific Islander <1%, Two or more races 3%, Race unknown 2%.
Retention and Graduation: 80% freshmen return for sophomore year. 33% freshmen graduate within 4 years. **Faculty:** Student/faculty ratio 18:1. 1,199 full-time faculty, 81% hold PhDs, 16% are are members of minority groups, 49% are women.

ACADEMICS

Degrees: bachelor's, certificate, doctoral/professional, doctoral/research, doctoral, master's, postbachelor's certificate, post-master's certificate. **Classes:** Most classes have fewer than 10 students. Most lab/discussion sessions have fewer than 10 students. **Most popular majors:** Elementary Education and Teaching; Speech Communication and Rhetoric; Business Administration and Management. **Special Study Options:** Accelerated program, cooperative education program, distance learning, double major, dual enrollment, exchange student program (domestic), honors program, independent study, internships, student-designed major, study abroad, teacher certification program. Combined degree programs: MA/CAS in School Psychology; AuD/PhD. **Disability Services:** Special programs offered to physically disabled students, including note-taking services, reader services, tape recorders, tutors. **Career Services:** Alumni network, Alumni services, Career/job search classes, Career assessment, Internships, Regional alumni.

FACILITIES

Housing: Coed dorms, men's dorms, women's dorms, fraternity/sorority housing, First-year students floor, leadership hall, extended quiet study hours floor, upper division, academic year residence halls, music student communities, service community, engineering. 95% of campus accessible to physically disabled. **Special Academic Facilities/Equipment:** Wellington B. Gray Gallery, Museum Without Walls, Ledonia Wright Cultural Center, A.J. Fletcher Recital Hall, Hendrix Theatre, Jenkins Fine Arts Center, McGinnis Theatre, and Mendenhall Student Center. **Computers:** 68% of classrooms, 20% of dorms, 100% of libraries, 100% of dining areas, 100% of student union, 25% of common outdoor areas have wireless network access. Students can register for classes online. Administrative functions (other than registration) can be performed online.

CAMPUS LIFE

Environment: Town. **Activities:** Choral groups, concert band, dance, drama/theater, jazz band, literary magazine, marching band, music ensembles, musical theater, radio station, student government, student newspaper, student-run film society, symphony orchestra, television station, yearbook, Campus Ministries, Student Organization, Model UN. 297 registered organizations, 11 honor societies, 27 religious organizations. 20 fraternities, 13 sororities. **Athletics (Intercollegiate):** *Men:* baseball, basketball, cheerleading, cross-country, diving, football, golf, swimming, tennis, track/field (outdoor). *Women:* basketball, cheerleading, cross-country, diving, golf, soccer, softball, swimming, tennis, track/field (outdoor), volleyball. **On-Campus Highlights:** Student Recreation Center, Wright Plaza, Mendenhall Student Center, Blounts Sports Complex, Science and Technology Building, Athletic facilities include: Dowdy-Ficklen Stadium, Williams Arena in Minges Coliseum and Harrington Field. **Environmental Initiatives:** Water conservation.

ADMISSIONS

Freshman Academic Profile: Average high school GPA 3.8. 16% in top 10% of high school class, 44% in top 25% of high school class, 80% in top 50% of high school class. **Reported SAT (pre-2016 redesign) scores:** SAT Math middle 50% range 490-560. SAT Critical Reading middle 50% range 470-550. SAT Writing middle 50% range 450-540. **Concordant SAT scores:** SAT EBRW middle 50% 510–600. SAT Math middle 50% range 520–580. ACT middle 50% range 20-24. Minimum internet-based TOEFL 80. Minimum paper TOEFL 500. **Basis for Candidate Selection:** *Very important factors considered include:* rigor of secondary school record, academic GPA, standardized test scores, state residency. *Important factors considered include:* class rank. *Other factors considered include:* application essay, extracurricular activities, talent/ability, character/personal qualities, first generation, alumni/ae relation, volunteer work, work experience, level of applicant's interest. **Freshman Admission Requirements:** High school diploma is required and GED is accepted. *Academic units required:* 4 English, 4 math, 3 science, 1 science lab, 2 foreign language, 2 social studies, 1 history. *Academic units recommended:* 4 English, 4 math, 3 science, 1 science lab, 2 foreign language, 2 social studies, 1 history, 1 visual/performing arts. **Freshman Admission Statistics:** 16,871 applied, 69.04% admitted, 37% enrolled. **Transfer Admission Requirements:** High school transcript, college transcript(s), Minimum college GPA of 2.0 required. Lowest grade transferable C. **General Admission Information:** Application fee $70. Regular application deadline 3/15. Nonfall registration accepted. Admission may be deferred for a maximum of 1 semester.

COSTS AND FINANCIAL AID

Annual in-state tuition $4,157. Annual out-of-state tuition $19,731. Room and board $9,319. Required fees $2,393. Average book expense $1,254. **Required Forms and Deadlines:** FAFSA. **Notification of Awards:** Applicants will be notified of awards on a rolling basis beginning 4/1. **Types of Aid:** *Need-based scholarships/grants:* Federal Pell, FSEOG, State scholarships/grants, Private scholarships, College/university scholarship or grant aid from institutional funds, Federal Nursing Scholarships. *Loans:* Direct Subsidized Stafford Loans, Direct Unsubsidized Stafford Loans, Direct PLUS loans, Federal Perkins Loans, Federal Nursing Loans, State Loans. *Student Employment:* Federal Work-Study Program available. Institutional employment available. **Financial Aid Statistics:** 67% needy freshmen, 73% needy undergrads receive need-based scholarship or grant aid. 25% freshmen, 17% undergrads receive non-need-based scholarship or grant aid. 86% freshmen, 84% undergrads receive need-based self-help aid. 2% freshmen, 2% undergrads receive athletic scholarships. 70% freshmen, 70% undergrads receive any aid. Average cumulative indebtedness $27,774. **Criteria for awarding aid:** *Need-based:* Academics. *Non-need-based:* Academics, Alumni affiliation, Art, Athletics, Music/drama.

EAST STROUDSBURG UNIVERSITY OF PENNSYLVANIA

East Stroudsburg University, East Stroudsburg, PA 18301-2999
Phone: 570-422-3542 • **Financial Aid Phone:** 570-422-2800
E-mail: undergrads@po-box.esu.edu • **CEEB Code:** 2650
Fax: 570-422-3933 • **Website:** www4.esu.edu • **ACT Code:** 3700

This public school was founded in 1893. It has a 213-acre campus.

RATINGS

Admissions Selectivity Rating: 77   **Fire Safety Rating:** 98   **Green Rating:** 60*

STUDENTS AND FACULTY

Enrollment: 6,274. **Student Body:** 55% female, 45% male, 25% out-of-state, 1% international (24 countries represented). Asian 1%, African American 7%, Caucasian 76%, Hispanic 7%, Native American <1%, Pacific Islander <1%, Two or more races <1%, Race unknown 8%.
Retention and Graduation: 78% freshmen return for sophomore year. 34% freshmen graduate within 4 years. **Faculty:** Student/faculty ratio 17:1. 330 full-time faculty, 74% hold PhDs, 16% are are members of minority groups, 51% are women. 0% of classes are taught by teaching assistants.

ACADEMICS

Degrees: associate, bachelor's, master's. **Classes:** Most classes have 20-29 students. Most lab/discussion sessions have 10-19 students. **Most popular majors:** Elementary Education and Teaching; Physical Education Teaching and Coaching; Business Administration and Management. **Special Study Options:** Accelerated program, cross-registration, distance learning, double major, dual enrollment, exchange student program (domestic), honors program, independent study, internships, student-designed major, study abroad, teacher certification program. **Honors Programs:** The Honors Program at ESU offers academically superior students an opportunity to challenge themselves intellectually both within and beyond the classroom setting. The focus of the Program was, and is, located in the area of the liberal arts general education curriculum. The goal of the program is to foster in the students an appreciation of the liberal arts perspective and a commitment to lifelong learning. **Disability Services:** Special programs offered to physically disabled students, including note-taking services, reader services, tape recorders, tutors. **Career Services:** Career assessment. We have had several interns placed at Sanofi Pasteur, a major Parmaceutical company. Our individual career counseling services are rated very highly.

FACILITIES

Housing: Coed dorms. 95% of campus accessible to physically diasbled. **Special Academic Facilities/Equipment:** Natural history museum, human performance lab, TV production studios, 119-acre student-owned/operated recreation area and wildlife sanctuary, observatory, electron microscopes. **Computers:** 50% of classrooms, 100% of dorms, 100% of libraries, 100% of student union, 10% of common outdoor areas have wireless network access. Students can register for classes online. Administrative functions (other than registration) can be performed online.

CAMPUS LIFE

Environment: Village. **Activities:** Choral groups, concert band, dance, drama/theater, jazz band, literary magazine, marching band, music ensembles, musical theater, pep band, radio station, student government, student newspaper, symphony orchestra, Campus Ministries, Student Organization. 110 registered organizations, 28 honor societies, 3 religious organizations. 5 fraternities, 5 sororities. **Athletics (Intercollegiate):** *Men:* baseball, basketball, cross-country, football, soccer, tennis, track/field (outdoor), track/field (indoor), wrestling. *Women:* basketball, cross-country, field hockey, golf, lacrosse, soccer, softball, swimming, tennis, track/field (outdoor), track/field (indoor), volleyball. **On-Campus Highlights:** Recreation Center, Java CIty, University Center, Stoney Acres, The Quad.

ADMISSIONS

Freshman Academic Profile: 7% in top 10% of high school class, 30% in top 25% of high school class, 72% in top 50% of high school class. 90% from public high schools. **Reported SAT (pre-2016 redesign) scores:** SAT Math middle 50% range 460-550. SAT Critical Reading middle 50% range 440-530. SAT Writing middle 50% range 440-530. **Concordant SAT scores:** SAT EBRW middle 50% 490–590. SAT Math middle 50% range 500–570. Minimum internet-based TOEFL 83. Minimum paper TOEFL 560. **Basis for Candidate Selection:** *Very important factors considered include:* rigor of secondary school record, class rank, academic GPA, standardized test scores. **Freshman Admission Requirements:** High school diploma is required and GED is accepted. *Academic units recommended:* 4 English, 4 math, 3 science, 2 science labs, 2 foreign language, 3 social studies. **Freshman Admission Statistics:** 7,258 applied, 62.83% admitted, 26% enrolled. **Transfer Admission Requirements:** college transcript(s), Minimum college GPA of 2.0 required. Lowest grade transferable C. **General Admission Information:** Application fee $35. Regular application deadline 4/1. Nonfall registration accepted.

COSTS AND FINANCIAL AID

Annual in-state tuition $5,804. Annual out-of-state tuition $14,510. Room and board $6,658. Required fees $1,974. Average book expense $1,200. **Required Forms and Deadlines:** FAFSA. **Notification of Awards:** Applicants will be notified of awards on or about 4/1. **Types of Aid:** *Need-based scholarships/grants:* Federal Pell, FSEOG, State scholarships/grants, Private scholarships, College/university scholarship or grant aid from institutional funds. *Loans:* Direct Subsidized Stafford Loans, Direct Unsubsidized Stafford Loans, Direct PLUS loans, Federal Perkins Loans. *Student Employment:* Federal Work-Study Program available. Institutional employment available. **Financial Aid Statistics:** 55% needy freshmen, 56% needy undergrads receive need-based scholarship or grant aid. 6% freshmen, 5% undergrads receive non-need-based scholarship or grant aid. 91% freshmen, 89% undergrads receive need-based self-help aid. 6% freshmen, 4% undergrads receive athletic scholarships. 75% freshmen, 84% undergrads receive any aid. **Criteria for awarding aid:** *Need-based:* Academics. *Non-need-based:* Academics, Alumni affiliation, Art, Athletics, Leadership, Minority status, Music/drama, Religious affiliation, State/district residency.

EAST TENNESSEE STATE UNIVERSITY

ETSU Box 70731, Johnson City, TN 37614
Phone: 423-439-4213 • **Financial Aid Phone:** 423-439-4300
E-mail: go2etsu@etsu.edu • **CEEB Code:** 1198
Fax: 423-439-4630 • **Website:** www.etsu.edu • **ACT Code:** 3958

This public school was founded in 1911. It has a 366-acre campus.

RATINGS

Admissions Selectivity Rating: 79   **Fire Safety Rating:** 60*   **Green Rating:** 60*

STUDENTS AND FACULTY

Enrollment: 10,960. **Student Body:** 56% female, 44% male, 14% out-of-state, 3% international (57 countries represented). Asian 1%, African American 7%, Caucasian 82%, Hispanic 2%, Native American <1%, Pacific Islander <1%, Two or more races 3%, Race unknown 1%.
Retention and Graduation: 71% freshmen return for sophomore year. 20% freshmen graduate within 4 years. 43% freshmen graduate within 6 years. **Faculty:** Student/faculty ratio 17:1. 575 full-time faculty, 0% hold PhDs, 11% are are members of minority groups, 47% are women.

ACADEMICS

Degrees: bachelor's, certificate, doctoral/professional, doctoral/research, doctoral, master's, postbachelor's certifiate, post-master's certificate. **Classes:** Most classes have 20-29 students. Most lab/discussion sessions have 20-29 students. **Most popular majors:** Business Administration and Management. **Special Study Options:** cooperative education program, distance learning, double major, dual enrollment, exchange student program (domestic), external degree program, honors program, independent study, internships, student-designed major, study abroad, teacher certification program. **Honors Programs:** University Honors Program Honors-in-Discipline Programs. **Disability Services:** Special programs offered to physically disabled students, including note-taking services, reader services, tape recorders, tutors. **Career Services:** Alumni network, Alumni services, Career/job search classes, Career assessment, Internships, Regional alumni.

FACILITIES

Housing: Coed dorms, special housing for disabled students, men's dorms, women's dorms, fraternity/sorority housing, apartments for married students, apartments for single students. 75% of campus accessible to physically diasbled. **Special Academic Facilities/Equipment:** Regional history museum, art gallery, archives of Appalachia, planetarium. **Computers:** Students can register for classes online. Administrative functions (other than registration) can be performed online.

CAMPUS LIFE

Environment: Town. **Activities:** Choral groups, concert band, drama/theater, jazz band, literary magazine, music ensembles, pep band, radio station, student government, student newspaper, television station, Campus Ministries, Student Organization. 200 registered organizations, 19 honor societies, 13 religious organizations. 9 fraternities, 7 sororities. **Athletics (Intercollegiate):** *Men:* baseball, basketball, cheerleading, cross-country, golf, soccer, tennis, track/field (outdoor), track/field (indoor). *Women:* basketball, cheerleading, cross-country, golf, soccer, softball, tennis, track/field (outdoor), track/field (indoor), volleyball. **On-Campus Highlights:** Memorial Center, New Sherrod Library, New Physical Activities Center, The Cave- a unique pizza pub located in the DP Culp Center. Built around a huge rock formation, indoors, Amphitheater-Natural stone + earth outdoor theater.

ADMISSIONS

Freshman Academic Profile: Average high school GPA 3.4. 20% in top 10% of high school class, 47% in top 25% of high school class, 75% in top 50% of high school class. 90% from public high schools. **Reported SAT (pre-2016 redesign) scores:** SAT Math middle 50% range 420-590. SAT Critical Reading middle 50% range 420-540. **Concordant SAT scores:** SAT Math middle 50% range 460–610. ACT middle 50% range 20-26. Minimum internet-based TOEFL 61. Minimum paper TOEFL 500. **Basis for Candidate Selection:** *Very important factors considered include:* rigor of secondary school record, academic GPA. *Important factors considered include:* standardized test scores. **Freshman Admission Requirements:** High school diploma is required and GED is accepted. *Academic units required:* 4 English, 3 math, 2 science, 1 science lab, 2 foreign language, 1 social studies, 1 history, 1 visual/performing arts. *Academic units recommended:* 4 English, 4 math, 3 science, 1 science lab, 2 foreign language, 1 social studies, 1 history, 1 visual/performing arts. **Freshman Admission Statistics:** 8,253 applied, 79.22% admitted, 31% enrolled. **Transfer Admission Requirements:** High school transcript, college transcript(s), Minimum college GPA of 2.0 required. Lowest grade transferable D. **General Admission Information:** Application fee $25. Priority deadline 2/1. Regular application deadline 8/15. Nonfall registration accepted.

COSTS AND FINANCIAL AID

Annual in-state tuition $7,002. Annual out-of-state tuition $25,098. Room and board $7,952. Required fees $1,669. Average book expense $1,090. **Required Forms and Deadlines:** FAFSA. **Notification of Awards:** Applicants will be notified of awards on a rolling basis beginning 3/15. **Types of Aid:** *Need-based scholarships/grants:* Federal Pell, FSEOG, State scholarships/grants, Private scholarships, College/university scholarship or grant aid from institutional funds, Federal Nursing Scholarships. *Loans:* Direct Subsidized Stafford Loans, Direct Unsubsidized Stafford Loans, Direct PLUS loans, Federal Perkins Loans, Federal Nursing Loans, State Loans, College/university loans from institutional funds. *Student Employment:* Federal Work-Study Program available. Institutional employment available. **Financial Aid Statistics:** 0% freshmen, 0% undergrads receive athletic scholarships. **Criteria for awarding aid:** *Need-based:* Academics, Alumni affiliation, Art, Athletics, Job skills, Leadership, Minority status, Music/drama, Religious affiliation. *Non-need-based:* Academics, Alumni affiliation, Art, Athletics, Leadership, Minority status, Music/drama, Religious affiliation, State/district residency.

EAST TEXAS BAPTIST UNIVERSITY

One Tiger Drive, Marshall, TX 75670-1498
Phone: 903-923-2000 • **Financial Aid Phone:** 903-923-2137
E-mail: admissions@etbu.edu • **CEEB Code:** 6187
Fax: 903-923-2001 • **Website:** https://www.etbu.edu • **ACT Code:** 4086

This private school, affiliated with the Baptist Church, was founded in 1912. It has a 200-acre campus.

RATINGS

Admissions Selectivity Rating: 82   **Fire Safety Rating:** 80   **Green Rating:** 60*

STUDENTS AND FACULTY

Enrollment: 1,218. **Student Body:** 51% female, 49% male, 10% out-of-state, 1% international (10 countries represented). Asian 0%, African American 19%, Caucasian 67%, Hispanic 8%, Native American <1%, Pacific Islander <1%, Two or more races 4%, Race unknown <1%.
Retention and Graduation: 68% freshmen return for sophomore year. 25% freshmen graduate within 4 years. 38% freshmen graduate within 6 years. 35% grads go on to further study within 1 year. **Faculty:** Student/faculty ratio 15:1. 68 full-time faculty, 87% hold PhDs, 10% are are members of minority groups, 35% are women. 0% of classes are taught by teaching assistants.

ACADEMICS

Degrees: bachelor's, certificate, master's. **Classes:** Most classes have 10-19 students. Most lab/discussion sessions have 10-19 students. **Most popular majors:** Elementary Education and Teaching; Registered Nursing/Registered Nurse; Multi-/Interdisciplinary Studies. **Special Study Options:** Accelerated program, cross-registration, distance learning, double major, dual enrollment, exchange student program (domestic), honors program, independent study, internships, liberal arts/career combination, student-designed major, study abroad, teacher certification program. **Disability Services:** Special programs offered to physically disabled students, including reader services, tutors. **Career Services:** Alumni services, Career/job search classes, Career assessment, Internships. The ETBU Career Fair provides an opportunity for students to visit with employers and graduate school recruiters in order to explore potential opportunities for their career path following graduation.

FACILITIES

Housing: men's dorms, women's dorms, apartments for married students, Campus houses for married students. 95% of campus accessible to physically diasbled. **Computers:** 100% of classrooms, 100% of dorms, 100% of libraries, 100% of dining areas, 100% of student union, 100% of common outdoor areas have wireless network access. Students can register for classes online. Administrative functions (other than registration) can be performed online.

CAMPUS LIFE

Environment: Village. **Activities:** Choral groups, concert band, drama/theater, jazz band, literary magazine, marching band, music ensembles, musical theater, pep band, radio station, student government, student newspaper, symphony orchestra, yearbook, Campus Ministries, Student Organization, Model UN. 38 registered organizations, 7 honor societies, 3 religious organizations. 2 fraternities, 2 sororities. **Athletics (Intercollegiate):** *Men:* baseball, basketball, cross-country, football, soccer. *Women:* basketball, cross-country, soccer, softball, volleyball. **On-Campus Highlights:** Scarborough Hall, The Quad, Bennett Student Center, Dean Healthplex, Tiger Grrill.

ADMISSIONS

Freshman Academic Profile: Average high school GPA 3.4. 14% in top 10% of high school class, 36% in top 25% of high school class, 74% in top 50% of high school class. 88% from public high schools. **Reported SAT (pre-2016 redesign) scores:** SAT Math middle 50% range 440-530. SAT Critical Reading middle 50% range 430-520. **Concordant SAT scores:** SAT Math middle 50% range 480–560. ACT middle 50% range 18-22. Minimum internet-based TOEFL 61. Minimum paper TOEFL 500. **Basis for Candidate Selection:** *Very important factors considered include:* class rank, standardized test scores. *Important factors considered include:* academic GPA. *Other factors considered include:* character/personal qualities. **Freshman Admission Requirements:** High school diploma is required and GED is accepted. **Freshman Admission Statistics:** 1,397 applied, 50.75% admitted, 49% enrolled. **Transfer Admission Requirements:** college transcript(s), statement of good standing from prior institution(s). Minimum college GPA of 2.00 required. Lowest grade transferable D. **General Admission Information:** Application fee $25. Regular application deadline 9/1. Nonfall registration accepted. Admission may be deferred for a maximum of 1 year.

COSTS AND FINANCIAL AID

Required Forms and Deadlines: FAFSA, Institution's own financial aid form. **Notification of Awards:** Applicants will be notified of awards on a rolling basis beginning 1/1. **Types of Aid:** *Need-based scholarships/grants:* Federal Pell, FSEOG, State scholarships/grants, Private scholarships, College/university scholarship or grant aid from institutional funds. *Loans:* Direct Subsidized Stafford Loans, Direct Unsubsidized Stafford Loans, Direct PLUS loans, Federal Perkins Loans, State Loans. *Student Employment:* Federal Work-Study Program available. Institutional employment available. **Financial Aid Statistics:** 76% needy freshmen, 76% needy undergrads receive need-based scholarship or grant aid. 99% freshmen, 99% undergrads receive non-need-based scholarship or grant aid. 78% freshmen, 80% undergrads receive need-based self-help aid. 0% freshmen, 0% undergrads receive athletic scholarships. 99% freshmen, 99% undergrads receive any aid. 82% undergrads borrow to pay for school. Average cumulative indebtedness $34,048. **Criteria for awarding aid:** *Non-need-based:* Academics, Alumni affiliation, Leadership, Music/drama, Religious affiliation, State/district residency.

EASTERN CONNECTICUT STATE UNIVERSITY

83 Windham Street, Willimantic, CT 6226
Phone: 860-465-5286 • **Financial Aid Phone:** 860-365-5205
E-mail: admissions@easternct.edu • **CEEB Code:** 3966
Fax: 860-465-5286 • **Website:** www.easternct.edu

This public school was founded in 1889. It has a 182-acre campus.

RATINGS
Admissions Selectivity Rating: 78   **Fire Safety Rating:** 95   **Green Rating:** 90

STUDENTS AND FACULTY
Enrollment: 5,035. **Student Body:** 53% female, 47% male, 7% out-of-state, 1% international (44 countries represented). Asian 2%, African American 7%, Caucasian 79%, Hispanic 7%, Native American <1%, Pacific Islander <1%, Two or more races 2%, Race unknown 2%.
Retention and Graduation: 77% freshmen return for sophomore year. 32% freshmen graduate within 4 years. 52% freshmen graduate within 6 years. 30% grads go on to further study within 1 year. **Faculty:** Student/faculty ratio 16:1. 198 full-time faculty, 96% hold PhDs, 22% are are members of minority groups, 44% are women. 0% of classes are taught by teaching assistants.

ACADEMICS
Degrees: associate, bachelor's, master's. **Classes:** Most classes have 20-29 students. Most lab/discussion sessions have 10-19 students. **Most popular majors:** Business/Commerce; Psychology; Communication and Media Studies. **Special Study Options:** Accelerated program, cooperative education program, cross-registration, distance learning, double major, dual enrollment, exchange student program (domestic), honors program, independent study, internships, student-designed major, study abroad, teacher certification program, weekend college. **Honors Programs:** University Honor Scholars Program offers interdisciplinary and independent study opportunities. **Disability Services:** Special programs offered to physically disabled students, including note-taking services, reader services, tape recorders, tutors. **Career Services:** Alumni network, Alumni services, Career/job search classes, Career assessment, Internships, Regional alumni. Internships that lead to permanent employment.

FACILITIES
Housing: Coed dorms, apartments for single students. 95% of campus accessible to physically diasbled. Art Gallery, Arboretum, Church Farm, Family/Child Development Center(2007), Green science bldg/labs(2008), electron microscope, planetarium, Media center with TV and radio station, Sports/Fitness Center and Studios, Center for Connecticut studies. **Computers:** 100% of libraries, 100% of dining areas, 100% of student union, 100% of common outdoor areas have wireless network access. Students can register for classes online. Administrative functions (other than registration) can be performed online.

CAMPUS LIFE
Environment: Village. **Activities:** Choral groups, concert band, dance, drama/theater, jazz band, literary magazine, music ensembles, musical theater, radio station, student government, student newspaper, television station, yearbook, Student Organization. 68 registered organizations, 17 honor societies, 3 religious organizations. **Athletics (Intercollegiate): Men:** baseball, basketball, cross-country, golf, lacrosse, soccer, track/field (outdoor), track/field (indoor). *Women:* basketball, cross-country, diving, field hockey, lacrosse, soccer, softball, swimming, track/field (outdoor), track/field (indoor), volleyball. **On-Campus Highlights:** Library, Student Center, Sports Center, Church Farm, Planetarium. **Environmental Initiatives:** Education Project http://www.ctenergyeducation.com/

ADMISSIONS
Freshman Academic Profile: Average high school GPA 3.0. 7% in top 10% of high school class, 25% in top 25% of high school class, 70% in top 50% of high school class. **Reported SAT (pre-2016 redesign) scores:** SAT Math middle 50% range 480-580. SAT Critical Reading middle 50% range 470-570. **Concordant SAT scores:** SAT Math middle 50% range 510–600. Minimum paper TOEFL 550. **Basis for Candidate Selection:** *Very important factors considered include:* class rank, standardized test scores, talent/ability. *Important factors considered include:* rigor of secondary school record, academic GPA, recommendation(s), level of applicant's interest. *Other factors considered include:* application essay, interview, extracurricular activities, character/personal qualities, volunteer work, work experience. **Freshman Admission Requirements:** High school diploma is required and GED is accepted. *Academic units required:* 4 English, 3 math, 2 science, 1 science lab, 2 foreign language, 2 social studies, 3 history. *Academic units recommended:* 4 math, 3 social studies. **Freshman Admission Statistics:** 3,493 applied, 64.50% admitted, 41% enrolled. **Transfer Admission Requirements:** High school transcript, college transcript(s), Minimum college GPA of 2.0 required. Lowest grade transferable C-. **General Admission Information:** Application fee $50. Priority deadline 5/1. Nonfall registration accepted. Admission may be deferred.

COSTS AND FINANCIAL AID
Annual in-state tuition $4,510. Annual out-of-state tuition $14,594. Required fees $4,866. Average book expense $1,554. **Required Forms and Deadlines:** FAFSA. **Types of Aid:** *Need-based scholarships/grants:* Federal Pell, FSEOG, State scholarships/grants, Private scholarships, College/university scholarship or grant aid from institutional funds. *Loans:* Federal Perkins Loans. *Student Employment:* Federal Work-Study Program available. Institutional employment available. **Financial Aid Statistics:** 68% needy freshmen, 66% needy undergrads receive need-based scholarship or grant aid. 4% freshmen, 1% undergrads receive non-need-based scholarship or grant aid. 92% freshmen, 93% undergrads receive need-based self-help aid. 0% freshmen, 0% undergrads receive athletic scholarships. 69% freshmen, 75% undergrads receive any aid. **Criteria for awarding aid:** *Need-based:* Academics. *Non-need-based:* Academics.

EASTERN ILLINOIS UNIVERSITY

600 Lincoln Avenue, Charleston, IL 61920
Phone: 217-581-2223 • **Financial Aid Phone:** 217-581-3713
E-mail: admissions@eiu.edu • **CEEB Code:** 1199
Fax: 217-581-7060 • **Website:** https://www.eiu.edu/ • **ACT Code:** 1016

This public school was founded in 1895. It has a 320-acre campus.

RATINGS
Admissions Selectivity Rating: 80   **Fire Safety Rating:** 97   **Green Rating:** 81

STUDENTS AND FACULTY
Enrollment: 4,981. **Student Body:** 60% female, 40% male, 6% out-of-state, 2% international (26 countries represented). Asian 1%, African American 18%, Caucasian 69%, Hispanic 6%, Native American <1%, Pacific Islander <1%, Two or more races 2%, Race unknown 2%.
Retention and Graduation: 71% freshmen return for sophomore year. 34% freshmen graduate within 4 years. 57% freshmen graduate within 6 years. **Faculty:** Student/faculty ratio 14:1. 419 full-time faculty, 79% hold PhDs, 15% are are members of minority groups, 46% are women. 3% of classes are taught by teaching assistants.

ACADEMICS
Degrees: bachelor's, master's, postbachelor's certificate, post-master's certificate. **Classes:** Most classes have 20-29 students. **Most popular majors:** Kinesiology and Exercise Science; Liberal Arts and Sciences/Liberal Studies; Communication. **Special Study Options:** distance learning, double major, dual enrollment, exchange student program (domestic), external degree program, honors program, independent study, internships, study abroad, teacher certification program. **Honors Programs:** Honors College Combined degree programs: Dual MBA & MS in Sustainable Energy. **Disability Services:** Special programs offered to physically disabled students, including note-taking services, reader services, tape recorders, tutors. **Career Services:** Alumni network, Alumni services, Career/job search classes, Career assessment, Internships, Regional alumni. Both of these programs go hand in hand with one another. We offer the students an opportunity to gain experience in their field by observing professionals and building relationships with mentors so that they can continue to work with them as they are progressing through their education.

FACILITIES
Housing: Coed dorms, special housing for disabled students, men's dorms, women's dorms, fraternity/sorority housing, apartments for married students, apartments for single students. 80% of campus accessible to physically diasbled. **Special Academic Facilities/Equipment:** Arts center, electron microscope. **Computers:** 100% of classrooms, 50% of dorms, 100% of libraries, 100% of dining areas, 100% of student union, have wireless network access. Students can register for classes online. Administrative functions (other than registration) can be performed online.

CAMPUS LIFE
Environment: Village. **Activities:** Choral groups, concert band, dance, drama/theater, jazz band, literary magazine, marching band, music ensembles, musical theater, opera, pep band, radio station, student government, student newspaper, symphony orchestra, television station, yearbook, Campus Ministries, Student Organization. 232 registered organizations, 19 honor societies, 16 religious organizations. 15 fraternities, 11 sororities. **Athletics (Intercollegiate):** *Men:* baseball, basketball, cross-country, football, golf, soccer, swimming, tennis, track/field (outdoor), track/field (indoor). *Women:* basketball, cross-country, golf, rugby, soccer, softball, swimming, tennis, track/field (outdoor), track/field (indoor), volleyball. **On-Campus Highlights:** Doudna Fine Arts Building,

Old Main, Martin Luther King Jr. University Union, Pemberton Hall, Student Recreation Center. **Environmental Initiatives:** Reduced campus water consumption by over 50%.

ADMISSIONS

Freshman Academic Profile: Average high school GPA 3:1. 13% in top 10% of high school class, 33% in top 25% of high school class, 69% in top 50% of high school class. ACT middle 50% range 18-24. Minimum internet-based TOEFL 61. Minimum paper TOEFL 500. **Basis for Candidate Selection:** *Very important factors considered include:* rigor of secondary school record, academic GPA, standardized test scores. *Other factors considered include:* class rank, application essay, recommendation(s), talent/ability, character/personal qualities. **Freshman Admission Requirements:** High school diploma is required and GED is accepted. *Academic units required:* 4 English, 3 math, 3 science, 3 science labs, 3 social studies, 2 academic electives. *Academic units recommended:* 2 foreign language. **Freshman Admission Statistics:** 8,420 applied, 46.88% admitted, 20% enrolled. **Transfer Admission Requirements:** High school transcript, college transcript(s), standardized test scores, Minimum college GPA of 2.0 required. **General Admission Information:** Application fee $30. Regular application deadline 8/15. Nonfall registration accepted. Admission may be deferred for a maximum of 1 year.

COSTS AND FINANCIAL AID

Annual in-state tuition $8,670. Annual out-of-state tuition $10,830. Room and board $9,546. Required fees $2,910. Average book expense $150. **Required Forms and Deadlines:** FAFSA. **Notification of Awards:** Applicants will be notified of awards on a rolling basis beginning 3/1. **Types of Aid:** *Need-based scholarships/grants:* Federal Pell, FSEOG, State scholarships/grants, Private scholarships, College/university scholarship or grant aid from institutional funds. *Loans:* Direct Subsidized Stafford Loans, Direct Unsubsidized Stafford Loans, Direct PLUS loans, Federal Perkins Loans. *Student Employment:* Federal Work-Study Program available. Institutional employment available. **Financial Aid Statistics:** 74% needy freshmen, 75% needy undergrads receive need-based scholarship or grant aid. 65% freshmen, 48% undergrads receive non-need-based scholarship or grant aid. 75% freshmen, 80% undergrads receive need-based self-help aid. 3% freshmen, 3% undergrads receive athletic scholarships. 73% freshmen, 68% undergrads receive any aid. 79% undergrads borrow to pay for school. Average cumulative indebtedness $31,382. **Criteria for awarding aid:** *Need-based:* Minority status. *Non-need-based:* Academics, Art, Athletics, Leadership, Music/drama.

EASTERN KENTUCKY UNIVERSITY

SSB CPO 54, Richmond, KY 40475
Phone: 859-622-2106 • **Financial Aid Phone:** 859-622-2361
E-mail: admissions@eku.edu • **CEEB Code:** 1200
Fax: 859-622-8024 • **Website:** www.eku.edu • **ACT Code:** 1512

This public school was founded in 1906. It has a 675-acre campus.

RATINGS

Admissions Selectivity Rating: 77   **Fire Safety Rating:** 90   **Green Rating:** 60*

STUDENTS AND FACULTY

Student Body: 56% female, 44% male, 13% out-of-state, (36 countries represented).
Retention and Graduation: 68% freshmen return for sophomore year.
Faculty: Student/faculty ratio 16:1. 697 full-time faculty, 68% hold PhDs, 10% are members of minority groups, 52% are women. 0% of classes are taught by teaching assistants.

ACADEMICS

Degrees: associate, bachelor's, certificate, doctoral/professional, master's, postbachelor's certificate. **Classes:** Most classes have 10-19 students. **Most popular majors:** Elementary Education and Teaching; Criminal Justice/Law Enforcement Administration. **Special Study Options:** cooperative education program, distance learning, double major, English as a Second Language (ESL), honors program, independent study, internships, study abroad, teacher certification program. **Honors Programs:** Honors Program: www.honors. eku.edu. **Disability Services:** Special programs offered to physically disabled students, including note-taking services, reader services, tape recorders, tutors. **Career Services:** Alumni network, Alumni services, Career/job search classes, Career assessment, Internships, Regional alumni.

FACILITIES

Housing: Coed dorms, men's dorms, special housing for international students, women's dorms, fraternity/sorority housing, apartments for married students. 90% of campus accessible to physically disabled. **Special Academic Facilities/ Equipment:** Hummel Planetarium, Giles Gallery. **Computers:** Students can

register for classes online. Administrative functions (other than registration) can be performed online.

CAMPUS LIFE

Environment: Town. **Activities:** Choral groups, concert band, dance, drama/theater, jazz band, literary magazine, marching band, music ensembles, musical theater, pep band, radio station, student government, student newspaper, symphony orchestra 178 registered organizations, 30 honor societies, 11 religious organizations. 16 fraternities, 13 sororities. **Athletics (Intercollegiate):** *Men:* baseball, basketball, cheerleading, cross-country, football, golf, tennis, track/field (outdoor), track/field (indoor). *Women:* basketball, cheerleading, cross-country, golf, soccer, softball, tennis, track/field (outdoor), track/field (indoor), volleyball. **On-Campus Highlights:** Student Wellness Center (New), Library Cafe (New), Student Services Building (New), First Weekend Events.

ADMISSIONS

Freshman Academic Profile: Average high school GPA 3.2. 13% in top 10% of high school class, 34% in top 25% of high school class, 66% in top 50% of high school class. ACT middle 50% range 19-24. Minimum paper TOEFL 500. **Basis for Candidate Selection:** *Very important factors considered include:* rigor of secondary school record, academic GPA, standardized test scores. **Freshman Admission Requirements:** High school diploma is required and GED is accepted. *Academic units required:* 4 English, 3 math, 3 science, 1 science lab, 2 foreign language, 3 social studies, 7 academic electives, and 2 units from above areas or other academic areas. **Freshman Admission Statistics:** 9,776 applied, 73.87% admitted, 38% enrolled. **Transfer Admission Requirements:** college transcript(s), Minimum college GPA of 2.0 required. Lowest grade transferable D. **General Admission Information:** Application fee $35. Regular application deadline 8/1. Nonfall registration accepted. Admission may be deferred for a maximum of 1 semester.

COSTS AND FINANCIAL AID

Annual in-state tuition $8,150. Annual out-of-state tuition $17,640. Room and board $8,188. Average book expense $1,000. **Required Forms and Deadlines:** FAFSA. **Notification of Awards:** Applicants will be notified of awards on a rolling basis beginning 4/1. **Types of Aid:** *Need-based scholarships/grants:* Federal Pell, FSEOG, State scholarships/grants, Private scholarships, College/university scholarship or grant aid from institutional funds. *Loans:* Direct Subsidized Stafford Loans, Direct Unsubsidized Stafford Loans, Direct PLUS loans, Federal Perkins Loans, College/university loans from institutional funds. *Student Employment:* Federal Work-Study Program available. Institutional employment available. **Financial Aid Statistics:** 66% needy freshmen, 66% needy undergrads receive need-based scholarship or grant aid. 91% freshmen, 61% undergrads receive non-need-based scholarship or grant aid. 81% freshmen, 83% undergrads receive need-based self-help aid. 2% freshmen, 3% undergrads receive athletic scholarships. 94% freshmen, 86% undergrads receive any aid. Average cumulative indebtedness $27,438. **Criteria for awarding aid:** *Non-need-based:* Academics, Alumni affiliation, Athletics, Leadership, Minority status, Music/drama.

EASTERN MICHIGAN UNIVERSITY

Eastern Michigan University, Ypsilanti, MI 48197
Phone: 734-487-3060 • **Financial Aid Phone:** 734-487-0455
E-mail: admissions@emich.edu • **CEEB Code:** 1201
Fax: 734-487-1484 • **Website:** www.emich.edu • **ACT Code:** 1990

This public school was founded in 1849. It has a 460-acre campus.

RATINGS

Admissions Selectivity Rating: 78   **Fire Safety Rating:** 86   **Green Rating:** 60*

STUDENTS AND FACULTY

Enrollment: 17,284. **Student Body:** 59% female, 41% male, 10% out-of-state, 2% international (80 countries represented). Asian 2%, African American 20%, Caucasian 65%, Hispanic 5%, Native American <1%, Pacific Islander <1%, Two or more races 4%, Race unknown 2%.
Retention and Graduation: 72% freshmen return for sophomore year. 13% freshmen graduate within 4 years. **Faculty:** Student/faculty ratio 17:1. 753 full-time faculty, 80% hold PhDs, 19% are members of minority groups, 52% are women. 3% of classes are taught by teaching assistants.

ACADEMICS

Degrees: bachelor's, doctoral/research, master's, postbachelor's certificate, post-master's certificate. **Classes:** Most classes have 20-29 students. Most lab/discussion sessions have 20-29 students. **Most popular majors:** Registered Nursing/Registered Nurse; Psychology; Social Work. **Special Study Options:** Accelerated program, cooperative education program, distance learning, double major, dual enrollment, English as a Second Language (ESL), external degree program, honors program, independent study, internships, student-designed major, study abroad, teacher certification program, weekend college, Dual enrollment note: high school students may enroll in college courses while still enrolled in high school, but are required to apply for admission to Eastern. Combined degree programs: BA/MA, BA/BBA, BA/MSA, BS/MA, BS/MOT. **Disability Services:** Special programs offered to physically disabled students, including note-taking services, reader services, tape recorders, tutors. **Career Services:** Alumni network, Alumni services, Career/job search classes, Career assessment, Internships, On-campus interviews. We connect with area businesses to provide hands-on learning opportunities for our students. All three of the programs above work hand-in-hand toward helping students gain experience in their field of study (number one attributes employers look for in job candidates).

FACILITIES

Housing: Coed dorms, special housing for disabled students, special housing for international students, fraternity/sorority housing, apartments for married students, cooperative housing, apartments for single students, Theme Housing, house rental to sorority house. 80% of campus accessible to physically diasbled. **Special Academic Facilities/Equipment:** Intermedia art gallery, paint research center, Sherzer observatory, Bruce T. Halle Library, Terrestial and Aquatics Ecology Research Facility, Coatings Research Institute, the John W. Porter Building housing the College of Education and the Marshall Building housing the College of Health and Human Services. **Computers:** 100% of classrooms, 25% of dorms, 100% of libraries, 100% of dining areas, 100% of student union, 15% of common outdoor areas have wireless network access. Students can register for classes online. Administrative functions (other than registration) can be performed online.

CAMPUS LIFE

Environment: City. **Activities:** Choral groups, concert band, dance, literary magazine, marching band, music ensembles, musical theater, pep band, radio station, student government, student newspaper, student-run film society, symphony orchestra, television station, Campus Ministries, Student Organization. 220 registered organizations, 14 honor societies, 24 religious organizations. 11 fraternities, 13 sororities. **Athletics (Intercollegiate):** *Men:* basketball, diving, football, golf, swimming, track/field (outdoor), track/field (indoor), wrestling. *Women:* basketball, crew/rowing, diving, golf, gymnastics, soccer, softball, swimming, tennis, track/field (outdoor), track/field (indoor), volleyball. **On-Campus Highlights:** New Student Center, Recreations and Intramurals Building, The Lakehouse, Halle Library, Athletic Campus. **Environmental Initiatives:** Energy performance contract.

ADMISSIONS

Freshman Academic Profile: Average high school GPA 3.3. 13% in top 10% of high school class, 39% in top 25% of high school class, 76% in top 50% of high school class. 85% from public high schools. **Reported SAT (pre-2016 redesign) scores:** SAT Math middle 50% range 450-590. SAT Critical Reading middle 50% range 440-593. SAT Writing middle 50% range 430-580. **Concordant SAT scores:** SAT EBRW middle 50% 490–640. SAT Math middle 50% range 490–610. ACT middle 50% range 19-25. Minimum paper TOEFL 500. **Basis for Candidate Selection:** *Very important factors considered include:* academic GPA, standardized test scores. *Important factors considered include:* rigor of secondary school record. *Other factors considered include:* application essay, recommendation(s). **Freshman Admission Requirements:** High school diploma is required and GED is accepted. *Academic units recommended:* 4 English, 4 math, 4 science, 1 science lab, 2 foreign language, 2 social studies, 1 history, 4 academic electives. **Freshman Admission Statistics:** 14,228 applied, 74.78% admitted, 27% enrolled. **Transfer Admission Requirements:** college transcript(s), Minimum college GPA of 2.0 required. Lowest grade transferable C. **General Admission Information:** Application fee $35. Nonfall registration accepted. Admission may be deferred for a maximum of 1 year.

COSTS AND FINANCIAL AID

Annual in-state tuition $8,888. Annual out-of-state tuition $26,183. Room and board $9,344. Required fees $1,529. Average book expense $1,000. **Required Forms and Deadlines:** FAFSA. **Notification of Awards:** Applicants will be notified of awards on a rolling basis beginning 3/1. **Types of Aid:** *Need-based scholarships/grants:* Federal Pell, FSEOG, State scholarships/grants, Private scholarships, College/university scholarship or grant aid from institutional funds, Federal Nursing Scholarships. *Student Employment:* Federal Work-Study Program available. Institutional employment available. **Financial Aid Statistics:** 71% needy freshmen, 74% needy undergrads receive need-based scholarship or grant aid. 77% freshmen, 47% undergrads receive non-need-based scholarship or grant aid. 72% freshmen, 78% undergrads receive need-based self-help aid. 3% freshmen, 3% undergrads receive athletic scholarships. 98% freshmen, 88% undergrads receive any aid. **Criteria for awarding aid:** *Non-need-based:* Academics, Alumni affiliation, Art, Athletics, Leadership, Music/drama.

EASTERN NEW MEXICO UNIVERSITY

Station #7, Portales, NM 88130
Phone: 575-562-2178 • **Financial Aid Phone:** 575-562-2194
E-mail: admissions@enmu.edu • **CEEB Code:** 4299
Fax: 575-562-2118 • **ACT Code:** 2636

This public school was founded in 1934. It has a 400-acre campus.

RATINGS

Admissions Selectivity Rating: 80   **Fire Safety Rating:** 92   **Green Rating:** 60*

STUDENTS AND FACULTY

Enrollment: 3,618. **Student Body:** 57% female, 43% male, 23% out-of-state, 3% international (23 countries represented). Asian 1%, African American 5%, Caucasian 54%, Hispanic 33%, Native American 3%, Pacific Islander <1%, Two or more races 2%, Race unknown 1%.
Retention and Graduation: 62% freshmen return for sophomore year. 11% freshmen graduate within 4 years. **Faculty:** Student/faculty ratio 17:1. 146 full-time faculty, 76% hold PhDs, 14% are are members of minority groups, 47% are women. 3% of classes are taught by teaching assistants.

ACADEMICS

Degrees: associate, bachelor's, master's, terminal, transfer. **Classes:** Most classes have 10-19 students. Most lab/discussion sessions have 10-19 students. **Most popular majors:** Business Administration and Management; Elementary Education and Teaching; General Studies. **Special Study Options:** Accelerated program, distance learning, double major, dual enrollment, English as a Second Language (ESL), exchange student program (domestic), independent study, internships, student-designed major, teacher certification program. **Disability Services:** Special programs offered to physically disabled students, including note-taking services, reader services, tape recorders, tutors. **Career Services:** Alumni network, Career assessment, Internships.

FACILITIES

Housing: Coed dorms, special housing for disabled students, women's dorms, fraternity/sorority housing, apartments for married students, apartments for single students. 100% of campus accessible to physically diasbled. **Special Academic Facilities/Equipment:** Natural history and historical museums, theatre, child development center, audiovisual center, electron microscopes, laser, KNEW Broadcast Center. **Computers:** Students can register for classes online. Administrative functions (other than registration) can be performed online.

CAMPUS LIFE

Environment: Village. **Activities:** Choral groups, concert band, dance, drama/theater, jazz band, literary magazine, marching band, music ensembles, radio station, student government, student newspaper, student-run film society, symphony orchestra, television station, Campus Ministries, Student Organization. 55 registered organizations, 2 honor societies, 4 religious organizations. 4 fraternities, 2 sororities. **Athletics (Intercollegiate):** *Men:* baseball, basketball, cross-country, football, rodeo, soccer, track/field (outdoor). *Women:* basketball, cross-country, rodeo, soccer, softball, track/field (outdoor), volleyball. **On-Campus Highlights:** New Science facilities/Natural History Museum, Campus Union Building, Communications-Broadcast Center, Library, University Theatre Center. **Environmental Initiatives:** Water savings project.

ADMISSIONS

Freshman Academic Profile: Average high school GPA 3.2. 11% in top 10% of high school class, 34% in top 25% of high school class, 68% in top 50% of high school class. 98% from public high schools. **Reported SAT (pre-2016 redesign) scores:** SAT Math middle 50% range 430-530. SAT Critical Reading middle 50% range 420-525. **Concordant SAT scores:** SAT Math middle 50% range 470–560. ACT middle 50% range 17-23. Minimum paper TOEFL 500. **Basis for Candidate Selection:** *Very important factors considered include:* academic GPA, standardized test scores. **Freshman Admission Requirements:** High school diploma is required and GED is accepted. *Academic units recommended:* 4 English, 4 math, 2 science, 2 social studies. **Freshman Admission Statistics:** 2,164 applied, 59.75% admitted, 48% enrolled. **Transfer Admission Requirements:** college transcript(s), statement of good standing from prior institution(s). Minimum college GPA of 2.0 required. Lowest grade transferable D. **General Admission Information:** Priority deadline 8/1. Nonfall registration accepted. Admission may be deferred for a maximum of 1 semester.

COSTS AND FINANCIAL AID

Annual in-state tuition $2,688. Annual out-of-state tuition $8,220. Room and board $5,612. Required fees $1,212. Average book expense $500. **Required Forms and Deadlines:** FAFSA. **Notification of Awards:** Applicants will be notified of awards on a rolling basis beginning 5/1. **Types of Aid:** *Need-based scholarships/grants:* Federal Pell, FSEOG, State scholarships/grants,

College/university scholarship or grant aid from institutional funds. *Loans:* Direct Subsidized Stafford Loans, Direct Unsubsidized Stafford Loans, Direct PLUS loans, Federal Perkins Loans. *Student Employment:* Federal Work-Study Program available. Institutional employment available. **Financial Aid Statistics:** 97% needy freshmen, 97% needy undergrads receive need-based scholarship or grant aid. 88% freshmen, 56% undergrads receive non-need-based scholarship or grant aid. 25% freshmen, 27% undergrads receive need-based self-help aid. 10% freshmen, 8% undergrads receive athletic scholarships. 99% freshmen, 91% undergrads receive any aid. **Criteria for awarding aid:** *Non-need-based:* Academics, Alumni affiliation, Art, Athletics, Leadership, Music/drama, State/district residency.

EASTERN OREGON UNIVERSITY

One University Blvd, La Grande, OR 97850
Phone: 1-541-962-3393 • **Financial Aid Phone:** 1-800-452-8639
E-mail: admissions@eou.edu • **CEEB Code:** 4300
Fax: 541-962-3418 • **Website:** www.eou.edu • **ACT Code:** 3460

This public school was founded in 1929. It has a 121-acre campus.

RATINGS

Admissions Selectivity Rating: 79   **Fire Safety Rating:** 89   **Green Rating:** 60*

STUDENTS AND FACULTY

Enrollment: 2,997. **Student Body:** 63% female, 37% male, 28% out-of-state, 2% international (20 countries represented). Asian 2%, African American 3%, Caucasian 76%, Hispanic 6%, Native American 3%, Pacific Islander 1%, Two or more races 2%, Race unknown 6%.
Retention and Graduation: 58% freshmen return for sophomore year.
Faculty: Student/faculty ratio 22:1. 106 full-time faculty, 75% hold PhDs, 8% are are members of minority groups, 42% are women.

ACADEMICS

Degrees: associate, bachelor's, certificate, master's. **Classes:** Most classes have 10-19 students. Most lab/discussion sessions have 10-19 students. **Most popular majors:** Business Administration, Management and Operations; Liberal Arts and Sciences/Liberal Studies; Education. **Special Study Options:** cooperative education program, cross-registration, distance learning, double major, dual enrollment, exchange student program (domestic), external degree program, honors program, independent study, internships, liberal arts/career combination, student-designed major, study abroad, teacher certification program, weekend college. **Disability Services:** Special programs offered to physically disabled students, including note-taking services, reader services, tape recorders, tutors. **Career Services:** Alumni services, Career/job search classes, Career assessment, Internships.

FACILITIES

Housing: Coed dorms, apartments for married students. 95% of campus accessible to physically diasbled. **Special Academic Facilities/Equipment:** Art gallery, archaeological museum **Computers:** 40% of classrooms, 80% of libraries, 90% of dining areas, 90% of student union, 50% of common outdoor areas have wireless network access. Students can register for classes online.

CAMPUS LIFE

Environment: Village. **Activities:** Choral groups, concert band, dance, drama/theater, jazz band, literary magazine, music ensembles, musical theater, radio station, student government, student newspaper, symphony orchestra 57 registered organizations, 2 honor societies, 4 religious organizations. **Athletics (Intercollegiate):** *Men:* basketball, cross-country, football, track/field (outdoor), track/field (indoor). *Women:* basketball, cross-country, soccer, softball, track/field (outdoor), track/field (indoor), volleyball. **On-Campus Highlights:** Loso Hall, Hoke Union, Community Stadium, Quinn Coliseum, Sports Practice Fields.

ADMISSIONS

Freshman Academic Profile: Average high school GPA 3.2. 9% in top 10% of high school class, 36% in top 25% of high school class, 74% in top 50% of high school class. **Reported SAT (pre-2016 redesign) scores:** SAT Math middle 50% range 410-520. SAT Critical Reading middle 50% range 410-530. SAT Writing middle 50% range 390-510. **Concordant SAT scores:** SAT EBRW middle 50% 450–580. SAT Math middle 50% range 450–550. ACT middle 50% range 18-24. Minimum paper TOEFL 520. **Basis for Candidate Selection:** *Very important factors considered include:* rigor of secondary school record, academic GPA. *Important factors considered include:* recommendation(s), talent/ability. *Other factors considered include:* class rank, standardized test scores, application essay, extracurricular activities, first generation, geographical residence, volunteer work, work experience, level of applicant's interest.
Freshman Admission Requirements: High school diploma is required and

GED is accepted. *Academic units required:* 4 English, 3 math, 3 science, 2 foreign language, 3 social studies. *Academic units recommended:* 1 science labs. **Freshman Admission Statistics:** 1,530 applied, 64.18% admitted, 32% enrolled. **Transfer Admission Requirements:** college transcript(s), Minimum college GPA of 2.2 required. Lowest grade transferable D-. **General Admission Information:** Priority deadline 2/1. Regular application deadline 9/1. Nonfall registration accepted. Admission may be deferred for a maximum of 1 year.

COSTS AND FINANCIAL AID

Annual in-state tuition $6,030. Annual out-of-state tuition $16,110. Room and board $9,642. Required fees $1,410. Average book expense $1,425. **Required Forms and Deadlines:** FAFSA. **Notification of Awards:** Applicants will be notified of awards on a rolling basis beginning 4/1. **Types of Aid:** *Need-based scholarships/grants:* Federal Pell, FSEOG, State scholarships/grants, Private scholarships, College/university scholarship or grant aid from institutional funds. *Loans:* Direct Subsidized Stafford Loans, Direct Unsubsidized Stafford Loans, Direct PLUS loans, Federal Perkins Loans. *Student Employment:* Federal Work-Study Program available. Institutional employment available. **Financial Aid Statistics:** 69% needy freshmen, 75% needy undergrads receive need-based scholarship or grant aid. 10% freshmen, 7% undergrads receive non-need-based scholarship or grant aid. 86% freshmen, 91% undergrads receive need-based self-help aid. 13% freshmen, 9% undergrads receive athletic scholarships. **Criteria for awarding aid:** *Need-based:* Academics. *Non-need-based:* Academics, Art, Leadership, Minority status, Music/drama, State/district residency.

EASTERN WASHINGTON UNIVERSITY

304 Sutton Hall, Cheney, WA 99004
Phone: 509-359-6692 • **Financial Aid Phone:** 509-359-2314
E-mail: admissions@ewu.edu • **CEEB Code:** 4301
Fax: 509-359-6692 • **Website:** www.ewu.edu • **ACT Code:** 4454

This public school was founded in 1882. It has a 335-acre campus.

RATINGS

Admissions Selectivity Rating: 71   **Fire Safety Rating:** 88   **Green Rating:** 93

STUDENTS AND FACULTY

Enrollment: 10,546. **Student Body:** 53% female, 47% male, 6% out-of-state, 5% international (64 countries represented). Asian 3%, African American 4%, Caucasian 64%, Hispanic 15%, Native American 1%, Pacific Islander <1%, Two or more races 6%, Race unknown 2%.
Retention and Graduation: 76% freshmen return for sophomore year. 21% freshmen graduate within 4 years. 46 44% grads go on to further study within 1 year. **Faculty:** Student/faculty ratio 21:1. 480 full-time faculty, 89% hold PhDs, 17% are are members of minority groups, 48% are women. 0% of classes are taught by teaching assistants.

ACADEMICS

Degrees: bachelor's, certificate, doctoral/professional, master's, postbachelor's certifiate, post-master's certificate. **Classes:** Most classes have 20-29 students. Most lab/discussion sessions have 20-29 students. **Most popular majors:** Business Administration and Management; Biology/Biological Sciences; Psychology. **Special Study Options:** distance learning, double major, English as a Second Language (ESL), honors program, independent study, internships, student-designed major, study abroad, teacher certification program. **Honors Programs:** EWU Honors Combined degree programs: BA/MA, MBA/MPA, Social Work/MPA. **Disability Services:** Special programs offered to physically disabled students, including note-taking services, reader services, tape recorders. **Career Services:** Alumni network, Alumni services, Career/job search classes, Career assessment, Internships, Regional alumni. EagleAXIS, the online career management system for EWU students and alumni that offers personalized career services.

FACILITIES

Housing: Coed dorms, special housing for disabled students, fraternity/sorority housing, apartments for married students, Wellness Housing, Theme Housing. 77% of campus accessible to physically diasbled. **Special Academic Facilities/Equipment:** Anthropology museum, on-campus elementary school, education lab, primate research center, marine biology lab, ecological studies lab, wildlife refuge, planetarium. **Computers:** Students can register for classes online. Administrative functions (other than registration) can be performed online.

CAMPUS LIFE

Environment: Town. **Activities:** Choral groups, concert band, dance, drama/theater, jazz band, literary magazine, marching band, music ensembles, musical theater, pep band, radio station, student government, student newspaper, student-run film society, symphony orchestra, Campus Ministries, Student Organization, Model UN. 100 registered organizations, 14 honor societies, 10 religious organizations. 5 fraternities, 5 sororities. **Athletics (Intercollegiate):** *Men:* basketball, cross-country, football, golf, tennis, track/field (outdoor), track/field (indoor). *Women:* basketball, cross-country, golf, soccer, tennis, track/field (outdoor), track/field (indoor), volleyball. **On-Campus Highlights:** Pence Union Building, CyberCafe, Phase Athletic Facilities, Woodward Stadium, Central campus mall, EWU Gallery of Art. **Environmental Initiatives:** Facilities Maintenance Energy Management Program: Limiting the greenhouse gas emission.

ADMISSIONS

Freshman Academic Profile: Average high school GPA 3.2. 95% from public high schools. **Reported SAT (pre-2016 redesign) scores:** SAT Math middle 50% range 430-540. SAT Critical Reading middle 50% range 420-540. SAT Writing middle 50% range 400-510. **Concordant SAT scores:** SAT EBRW middle 50% 460–580. SAT Math middle 50% range 470–570. ACT middle 50% range 17-23. Minimum internet-based TOEFL 71. Minimum paper TOEFL 525. **Basis for Candidate Selection:** *Very important factors considered include:* academic GPA, standardized test scores. *Important factors considered include:* rigor of secondary school record, application essay. *Other factors considered include:* recommendation(s), extracurricular activities, talent/ability, character/personal qualities, volunteer work, work experience. **Freshman Admission Requirements:** High school diploma or equivalent is not required. *Academic units required:* 4 English, 3 math, 2 science, 2 science labs, 2 foreign language, 3 social studies, 1 visual/performing arts, and 1 unit from above areas or other academic areas. **Freshman Admission Statistics:** 4,224 applied, 95.48% admitted, 42% enrolled. **Transfer Admission Requirements:** college transcript(s), essay or personal statement, Minimum college GPA of 2.0 required. Lowest grade transferable D-. **General Admission Information:** Application fee $50. Priority deadline 2/15. Nonfall registration accepted. Admission may be deferred for a maximum of 1 year.

COSTS AND FINANCIAL AID

Required Forms and Deadlines: FAFSA. **Notification of Awards:** Applicants will be notified of awards on a rolling basis beginning 4/1. **Types of Aid:** *Need-based scholarships/grants:* Federal Pell, FSEOG, State scholarships/grants, Private scholarships, College/university scholarship or grant aid from institutional funds. *Loans:* Direct Subsidized Stafford Loans, Direct Unsubsidized Stafford Loans, Direct PLUS loans, Federal Perkins Loans. *Student Employment:* Federal Work-Study Program available. Institutional employment available. **Financial Aid Statistics:** 77% needy freshmen, 74% needy undergrads receive need-based scholarship or grant aid. 54% freshmen, 28% undergrads receive non-need-based scholarship or grant aid. 69% freshmen, 80% undergrads receive need-based self-help aid. 2% freshmen, 2% undergrads receive athletic scholarships. 69% freshmen, 59% undergrads receive any aid. **Criteria for awarding aid:** *Need-based:* Academics, Alumni affiliation, Art, Athletics, Job skills, Music/drama. *Non-need-based:* Academics, Alumni affiliation, Art, Athletics, Job skills, Music/drama, State/district residency.

ECKERD COLLEGE

4200 54th Avenue South, St.Petersburg, FL 33711
Phone: 727-864-8331 • **Financial Aid Phone:** 727-864-8854
E-mail: admissions@eckerd.edu
Fax: 727-866-2304 • **Website:** www.eckerd.edu • **ACT Code:** 731

This private school, affiliated with the Presbyterian Church, was founded in 1958. It has a 188-acre campus.

RATINGS

Admissions Selectivity Rating: 81   **Fire Safety Rating:** 83   **Green Rating:** 83

STUDENTS AND FACULTY

Enrollment: 1,802. **Student Body:** 61% female, 39% male, 83% out-of-state, 4% international (39 countries represented). Asian 2%, African American 2%, Caucasian 80%, Hispanic 8%, Native American <1%, Pacific Islander <1%, Two or more races 3%, Race unknown 1%.
Retention and Graduation: 81% freshmen return for sophomore year. 59% freshmen graduate within 4 years. 65% freshmen graduate within 6 years.
Faculty: Student/faculty ratio 12:1. 114 full-time faculty, 95% hold PhDs, 11% are are members of minority groups, 39% are women. 0% of classes are taught by teaching assistants.

ACADEMICS

Degrees: bachelor's. **Classes:** Most classes have 20-29 students. Most lab/discussion sessions have 20-29 students. **Most popular majors:** Environmental Studies; Marine Biology and Biological Oceanography; Psychology. **Special Study Options:** Accelerated program, double major, honors program, independent study, internships, liberal arts/career combination, student-designed major, study abroad. **Honors Programs:** Ford Apprentice Scholar Program The Honors Program at Eckerd College Combined degree programs: BA/JD, Engineering dual degree (3-2) agreements with Columbia U & Washington U. **Disability Services:** Special programs offered to physically disabled students, including reader services, tape recorders, tutors. **Career Services:** Alumni network, Alumni services, Career/job search classes, Career assessment, Internships.

FACILITIES

Housing: Coed dorms, women's dorms, suite-style dorms wellness housing pet dorms community service dorms. 90% of campus accessible to physically diasbled. **Special Academic Facilities/Equipment:** Language lab, oral communications lab, marine science center. **Computers:** 100% of classrooms, 100% of dorms, 100% of libraries, 100% of dining areas, 100% of student union, 90% of common outdoor areas have wireless network access. Students can register for classes online. Administrative functions (other than registration) can be performed online.

CAMPUS LIFE

Environment: City. **Activities:** Choral groups, concert band, dance, drama/theater, literary magazine, music ensembles, radio station, student government, student newspaper, television station, Campus Ministries, Student Organization, Model UN. 74 registered organizations, 8 honor societies, 3 religious organizations. **Athletics (Intercollegiate):** *Men:* baseball, basketball, golf, sailing, soccer, tennis. *Women:* basketball, golf, sailing, soccer, softball, tennis, volleyball. **On-Campus Highlights:** Peter Armacost Library, Turley Athletic Complex, Gailbraith Marine Science Lab, Hough Campus Center/Campus Pub, Eckerd Waterfront/Wallace Boathouse, Awarded Phi Beta Kappa Chapter in Summer 2003. **Environmental Initiatives:** The yellow bike has in recent years become a new symbol of Eckerd College. The Yellow Bike Program started in the spring of 2004, and since then it has gained national recognition Students, faculty, staff, and even the College President can be spotted riding them. The goal of the program is to have less vehicle traffic which decreases greenhouse gas emissions and reduces our harm to the environment. The bikes on campus will help lead to a mostly walking campus, and an eco-friendly campus. The Yellow Bike Program was recognized in 2005 by the National Wildlife Federation, and it has gained local and national news attention.

ADMISSIONS

Freshman Academic Profile: Average high school GPA 3.4. **Reported SAT (pre-2016 redesign) scores:** SAT Math middle 50% range 500-610. SAT Critical Reading middle 50% range 510-630. **Concordant SAT scores:** SAT Math middle 50% range 530–630. ACT middle 50% range 23-29. Minimum internet-based TOEFL 79. Minimum paper TOEFL 550. **Basis for Candidate Selection:** *Very important factors considered include:* rigor of secondary school record, academic GPA. *Important factors considered include:* standardized test scores, application essay, recommendation(s), interview, extracurricular activities, talent/ability, character/personal qualities. *Other factors considered include:* class rank, first generation, alumni/ae relation, volunteer work, work experience, level of applicant's interest. **Freshman Admission Requirements:** High school diploma is required and GED is accepted. *Academic units recommended:* 4 English, 3 math, 3 science, 2 science labs, 2 foreign language, 2 social studies, 1 history, 3 academic electives. **Freshman Admission Statistics:** 2,498 applied, 84.39% admitted, 24% enrolled. **Transfer Admission Requirements:** college transcript(s), essay or personal statement, statement of good standing from prior institution(s). Minimum college GPA of 2.5 required. Lowest grade transferable C. **General Admission Information:** Application fee $40. Nonfall registration accepted. Admission may be deferred for a maximum of 1 year.

COSTS AND FINANCIAL AID

Annual tuition $41,192. Room and board $11,336. Required fees $346. Average book expense $1,200. **Required Forms and Deadlines:** FAFSA. **Notification of Awards:** Applicants will be notified of awards on a rolling basis beginning 2/20. **Types of Aid:** *Need-based scholarships/grants:* Federal Pell, FSEOG, State scholarships/grants, Private scholarships, College/university scholarship or grant aid from institutional funds. *Loans:* Direct Subsidized Stafford Loans, Direct Unsubsidized Stafford Loans, Direct PLUS loans, Federal Perkins Loans, College/university loans from institutional funds. *Student Employment:* Federal Work-Study Program available. Institutional employment available. **Financial Aid Statistics:** 100% needy freshmen, 100% needy undergrads receive need-based scholarship or grant aid. 0% undergrads receive non-need-based scholarship or grant aid. 82% freshmen, 87% undergrads receive need-based self-help aid. 3% freshmen, 3% undergrads receive athletic scholarships. 97% freshmen, 95% undergrads receive any aid. 60% undergrads borrow to pay for school. Average cumulative indebtedness $32,387. **Criteria for awarding** aid: *Need-based:* Religious affiliation. *Non-need-based:* Academics, Art, Athletics, Music/drama, State/district residency.

EDGEWOOD COLLEGE

1000 Edgewood College Drive, Madison, WI 53711-1997
Phone: 608-663-2294 • **Financial Aid Phone:** 608-663-4300
E-mail: admissions@edgewood.edu • **CEEB Code:** 1202
Fax: 608-663-2214 • **Website:** www.edgewood.edu • **ACT Code:** 4582

This private school, affiliated with the Roman Catholic Church, was founded in 1927. It has a 55-acre campus.

RATINGS
Admissions Selectivity Rating: 78   **Fire Safety Rating:** 86   **Green Rating:** 85

STUDENTS AND FACULTY
Enrollment: 1,615. **Student Body:** 72% female, 28% male, 8% out-of-state, 4% international (44 countries represented). Asian 3%, African American 3%, Caucasian 79%, Hispanic 6%, Native American <1%, Pacific Islander <1%, Two or more races 3%, Race unknown 3%.
Retention and Graduation: 78% freshmen return for sophomore year. 40% freshmen graduate within 4 years. 63% freshmen graduate within 6 years.
Faculty: Student/faculty ratio 10:1. 163 full-time faculty, 73% hold PhDs, 12% are are members of minority groups, 60% are women. 0% of classes are taught by teaching assistants.

ACADEMICS
Degrees: bachelor's, certificate, doctoral/professional, doctoral/research, master's, postbachelor's certificate, post-master's certificate. **Classes:** Most classes have 10-19 students. **Most popular majors:** Registered Nursing/Registered Nurse; Business/Commerce; Psychology. **Special Study Options:** Accelerated program, double major, dual enrollment, honors program, independent study, internships, liberal arts/career combination, student-designed major, study abroad, teacher certification program. **Honors Programs:** We have an Honors Program for undergraduates. **Disability Services:** Special programs offered to physically disabled students, including note-taking services, reader services, tape recorders, tutors. **Career Services:** Alumni network, Alumni services, Career/job search classes, Career assessment, Internships, Regional alumni.

FACILITIES
Housing: Coed dorms, special housing for disabled students, women's dorms, Theme Housing. 90% of campus accessible to physically diasbled. **Special Academic Facilities/Equipment:** DeRicci Art Gallery, and Science Exploration Center. **Computers:** 90% of classrooms, 100% of dorms, 100% of libraries, 100% of dining areas, 100% of student union, 80% of common outdoor areas have wireless network access. Students can register for classes online. Administrative functions (other than registration) can be performed online.

CAMPUS LIFE
Environment: City. **Activities:** Choral groups, concert band, dance, drama/theater, jazz band, literary magazine, marching band, music ensembles, musical theater, pep band, student government, student newspaper, symphony orchestra, Campus Ministries, Student Organization. 45 registered organizations, 4 honor societies, 1 religious organization. **Athletics (Intercollegiate):** *Men:* baseball, basketball, cross-country, golf, soccer, tennis, track/field (outdoor), track/field (indoor). *Women:* basketball, cross-country, golf, soccer, softball, tennis, track/field (outdoor), track/field (indoor), volleyball. **On-Campus Highlights:** Dominican Hall, Mazzuchelli Hall, Lake Wingra Boardwalk, Predolin Humanities Center, SondeRegger Science Center. **Environmental Initiatives:** The Campus Sustainability Coordinating Team has completed a Campus Sustainability Plan, components of which are incorporated into the College's Master Plan.

ADMISSIONS
Freshman Academic Profile: Average high school GPA 3.4. 15% in top 10% of high school class, 46% in top 25% of high school class, 77% in top 50% of high school class. 93% from public high schools. **Reported SAT (pre-2016 redesign) scores:** SAT Math middle 50% range 465-525. SAT Critical Reading middle 50% range 490-553. **Concordant SAT scores:** SAT Math middle 50% range 510–560. ACT middle 50% range 21-25. Minimum internet-based TOEFL 71. Minimum paper TOEFL 525. **Basis for Candidate Selection:** *Very important factors considered include:* class rank, academic GPA, standardized test scores. *Other factors considered include:* application essay, recommendation(s). **Freshman Admission Requirements:** High school diploma is required and GED is accepted. *Academic units required:* 4 English, 2 math, 2 science, 1 science lab, 2 foreign language, 2 social studies, 1

history. *Academic units recommended:* 4 English, 2 math, 2 science, 1 science lab, 2 foreign language, 2 social studies, 1 history. **Freshman Admission Statistics:** 1,035 applied, 78.07% admitted, 33% enrolled. **Transfer Admission Requirements:** High school transcript, college transcript(s), Minimum college GPA of 2.0 required. Lowest grade transferable C-. **General Admission Information:** Application fee $30. Priority deadline 3/1. Regular application deadline 8/15. Nonfall registration accepted. Admission may be deferred for a maximum of 12 months.

COSTS AND FINANCIAL AID
Annual tuition $27,530. Room and board $9,870. Average book expense $800. **Required Forms and Deadlines:** FAFSA. **Notification of Awards:** Applicants will be notified of awards on a rolling basis beginning 3/15. **Types of Aid:** *Need-based scholarships/grants:* Federal Pell, FSEOG, State scholarships/grants, Private scholarships, College/university scholarship or grant aid from institutional funds. *Loans:* Direct Subsidized Stafford Loans, Direct Unsubsidized Stafford Loans, Direct PLUS loans, Federal Perkins Loans, State Loans. *Student Employment:* Federal Work-Study Program available. Institutional employment available. **Financial Aid Statistics:** 99% needy freshmen, 98% needy undergrads receive need-based scholarship or grant aid. 7% freshmen, 7% undergrads receive non-need-based scholarship or grant aid. 93% freshmen, 92% undergrads receive need-based self-help aid. 0% freshmen, 0% undergrads receive athletic scholarships. 100% freshmen, 93% undergrads receive any aid. 80% undergrads borrow to pay for school. Average cumulative indebtedness $33,104. **Criteria for awarding aid:** *Need-based:* Academics, Alumni affiliation, Religious affiliation. *Non-need-based:* Academics, Alumni affiliation, Art, Leadership, Music/drama, Religious affiliation.

EDINBORO UNIVERSITY OF PENNSYLVANIA

200 East Normal Street, Edinboro, PA 16444
Phone: 814-732-2761 • **Financial Aid Phone:** 814-732-3500
E-mail: eup_admissions@edinboro.edu • **CEEB Code:** 2651
Fax: 814-732-2420 • **Website:** http://www.edinboro.edu/ • **ACT Code:** 3702

This public school was founded in 1857. It has a 585-acre campus.

RATINGS
Admissions Selectivity Rating: 74   **Fire Safety Rating:** 97   **Green Rating:** 68

STUDENTS AND FACULTY
Enrollment: 6,348. **Student Body:** 56% female, 44% male, 11% out-of-state, 1% international (31 countries represented). Asian 1%, African American 9%, Caucasian 86%, Hispanic 2%, Native American <1%, Pacific Islander 0%, Two or more races 0%, Race unknown 1%.
Retention and Graduation: 75% freshmen return for sophomore year. 24% freshmen graduate within 4 years. 47% freshmen graduate within 6 years.
Faculty: 346 full-time faculty, 0% hold PhDs, 7% are are members of minority groups, 46% are women. 0% of classes are taught by teaching assistants.

ACADEMICS
Degrees: associate, bachelor's, master's, postbachelor's certificate, post-master's certificate. **Classes:** Most classes have 20-29 students. **Most popular majors:** Fine/Studio Arts; Business Administration and Management; Criminal Justice/Safety Studies. **Special Study Options:** cooperative education program, cross-registration, distance learning, double major, dual enrollment, honors program, independent study, internships, liberal arts/career combination, student-designed major, study abroad, teacher certification program. **Honors Programs:** Admission to the Upper Division Honors Program, may be made by any full time EUP student who has completed 63 credit hours with an overall GPA of 3.4 or higher. They must also provide letters of support from two faculty members, secure approval of their academic advisor, and complete a proposal for the Senior Project in consultation with the Honors Director, Academic Advisor and and Faculty Member who will supervise the Senior Project. Combined degree programs: BA/MEng. **Disability Services:** Special programs offered to physically disabled students, including note-taking services, reader services, tape recorders, tutors. **Career Services:** Alumni services, Career/job search classes, Career assessment, Internships. The University offers numerous internships to students in all programs. In addition, there is a Community Outreach Center that offers numerous volunteer/experiential learning opportunities to students.

FACILITIES
Housing: Coed dorms, special housing for disabled students, Living-Learning and Suite Style housing. Choosing to become part of a living-learning community is a unique opportunity for any student to live on the same floor with others who share the same major, filed of study, or interest area. Participants will interact with faculty and staff outside of the classroom through programs, activities, and events. Residents are able to gain assistance

and ideas from peers who share their strong commitment to the living-learning experience. 98% of campus accessible to physically diasbled. **Special Academic Facilities/Equipment:** Planetarium, Solar Observatory, Governor George Leader Speech and Hearing Center, Bates Art Gallery, Bruce Gallery. **Computers:** 90% of classrooms, 30% of dorms, 100% of libraries, 100% of dining areas, 75% of student union, 40% of common outdoor areas have wireless network access. Students can register for classes online. Administrative functions (other than registration) can be performed online.

CAMPUS LIFE

Environment: Rural. **Activities:** Choral groups, dance, drama/theater, jazz band, literary magazine, marching band, music ensembles, opera, radio station, student government, student newspaper, student-run film society, television station, Campus Ministries, Student Organization. 157 registered organizations, 13 honor societies, 4 religious organizations. 10 fraternities, 7 sororities. **Athletics (Intercollegiate):** *Men:* basketball, cross-country, football, swimming, track/field (outdoor), track/field (indoor), wheel-chair basketball, wrestling. *Women:* basketball, cross-country, lacrosse, soccer, softball, swimming, track/field (outdoor), track/field (indoor), volleyball. **On-Campus Highlights:** Frank G. Pogue Student Center, Baron-Forness Library, R. Benjamin Wiley Arts & Sciences Center, Louis J. Cole Memorial Auditorium, McComb Fieldhouse, Planetarium.

ADMISSIONS

Freshman Academic Profile: Average high school GPA 3.2. 5% in top 10% of high school class, 20% in top 25% of high school class, 51% in top 50% of high school class. **Reported SAT (pre-2016 redesign) scores:** SAT Math middle 50% range 410-520. SAT Critical Reading middle 50% range 415-520. **Concordant SAT scores:** SAT Math middle 50% range 450–550. ACT middle 50% range 17-23. Minimum internet-based TOEFL 61. Minimum paper TOEFL 500. **Basis for Candidate Selection:** *Very important factors considered include:* rigor of secondary school record, class rank, academic GPA, standardized test scores. *Other factors considered include:* application essay, recommendation(s), interview, extracurricular activities, talent/ability, character/personal qualities, volunteer work, work experience. **Freshman Admission Requirements:** High school diploma is required and GED is accepted. *Academic units recommended:* 4 English, 3 math, 3 science, 2 foreign language, 4 social studies, 1 computer science. **Freshman Admission Statistics:** 4,411 applied, 73.41% admitted, 44% enrolled. **Transfer Admission Requirements:** High school transcript, college transcript(s), statement of good standing from prior institution(s). Minimum college GPA of 2.0 required. Lowest grade transferable C-. **General Admission Information:** Application fee $30. Nonfall registration accepted. Admission may be deferred for a maximum of 1 year.

COSTS AND FINANCIAL AID

Annual in-state tuition $5,554. Annual out-of-state tuition $8,332. Room and board $7,130. Average book expense $900. **Required Forms and Deadlines:** FAFSA. **Notification of Awards:** Applicants will be notified of awards on a rolling basis beginning 3/22. **Types of Aid:** *Need-based scholarships/grants:* Federal Pell, FSEOG, State scholarships/grants, Private scholarships, College/university scholarship or grant aid from institutional funds. *Loans:* Direct Subsidized Stafford Loans, Direct Unsubsidized Stafford Loans, Federal Perkins Loans, Federal Nursing Loans. *Student Employment:* Federal Work-Study Program available. Institutional employment available. **Financial Aid Statistics:** 90% needy freshmen, 92% needy undergrads receive need-based scholarship or grant aid. 97% freshmen, 96% undergrads receive non-need-based scholarship or grant aid. 85% freshmen, 88% undergrads receive need-based self-help aid. 3% freshmen, 2% undergrads receive athletic scholarships. 91% freshmen, 88% undergrads receive any aid. **Criteria for awarding aid:** *Need-based:* Academics, Alumni affiliation, Art, Athletics, Job skills, Leadership, Minority status, Music/drama, Religious affiliation. *Non-need-based:* Academics, Alumni affiliation, Art, Athletics, Job skills, Leadership, Minority status, Music/drama, Religious affiliation, State/district residency.

ELIZABETHTOWN COLLEGE

Leffler House, Elizabethtown, PA 17022-2298
Phone: 717-361-1400 • **Financial Aid Phone:** 717-361-1404
E-mail: admissions@etown.edu • **CEEB Code:** 2225
Fax: 717-361-1364 • **Website:** www.etown.edu • **ACT Code:** 3568

This private school, affiliated with the Church of Brethren Church, was founded in 1899. It has a 193-acre campus.

RATINGS

Admissions Selectivity Rating: 82   **Fire Safety Rating:** 62   **Green Rating:** 60*

STUDENTS AND FACULTY

Enrollment: 1,713. **Student Body:** 61% female, 39% male, 34% out-of-state, 3% international (17 countries represented). Asian 3%, African American 3%, Caucasian 85%, Hispanic 4%, Native American <1%, Pacific Islander <1%, Two or more races 2%, Race unknown 0%.
Retention and Graduation: 87% freshmen return for sophomore year. 69% freshmen graduate within 4 years. 74% freshmen graduate within 6 years. 20% grads go on to further study within 1 year. **Faculty:** Student/faculty ratio 12:1. 129 full-time faculty, 94% hold PhDs, 11% are are members of minority groups, 47% are women. 0% of classes are taught by teaching assistants.

ACADEMICS

Degrees: bachelor's, master's. **Classes:** Most classes have 10-19 students. Most lab/discussion sessions have 10-19 students. **Most popular majors:** Communication, Journalism, and Related Programs Business/Commerce.
Special Study Options: Accelerated program, cooperative education program, distance learning, double major, dual enrollment, English as a Second Language (ESL), exchange student program (domestic), honors program, independent study, internships, liberal arts/career combination, study abroad, teacher certification program, 2+2, 3+3 and 4+2 (PT docotorate) programs with Thomas Jefferson University in nursing, physical therapy, labratory sceinces, diagnostic imaging, 3+2 in engineering with Pennsylvania State University–University, 3+2 with Duke University in Forestry, 3+3 in physical therapy with Widener University and University of Maryland, Baltimore County, 3+1 in Invasive Cardiovascular Technology with Lancaster Institute for Health Education,articulation agreements with Lehigh Unversity, Rutgers Univesity, Loyola College (MD) and Pennsylvania State University–University, Harrisburg to satisfy 150-hour requirment in Accounting. Combined degree programs: BA/MD, BA/MA, 3+3 physical therapy with Thomas Jefferson Univers. **Disability Services:** Special programs offered to physically disabled students, including tape recorders, tutors.

FACILITIES

Housing: Coed dorms, special housing for disabled students, special housing for international students, women's dorms, apartments for single students, Off-campus houses for student service-learning groups. 75% of campus accessible to physically diasbled. **Special Academic Facilities/Equipment:** Art gallery, Meetinghouse/center for Anabaptist and Pietist studies, chapel/performance center, Fourier transform multinuclear NMR spectrometer, blood gas analyzer, scanning densitometer, PCR machine, radiometer/data logger, automated ion analyzer, computerized language lab **Computers:** Students can register for classes online. Administrative functions (other than registration) can be performed online.

CAMPUS LIFE

Environment: Village. **Activities:** Choral groups, concert band, dance, drama/theater, jazz band, literary magazine, music ensembles, musical theater, pep band, radio station, student government, student newspaper, student-run film society, symphony orchestra, television station, yearbook. 80 registered organizations, 16 honor societies, 6 religious organizations. **Athletics (Intercollegiate):** *Men:* baseball, basketball, cross-country, diving, golf, lacrosse, soccer, swimming, tennis, track/field (outdoor), track/field (indoor), wrestling. *Women:* basketball, cross-country, diving, field hockey, lacrosse, soccer, softball, swimming, tennis, track/field (outdoor), track/field (indoor), volleyball. **On-Campus Highlights:** Brossman Commons Students Center, The Jay's Nest Snack Bar, The Dell, The Blue Bean Cafe, The Ira R Herr Soccer Complex, During the academic year it is great to hang out in The Dell, located in the middle of campus, on a hot day for frisbee or just soaking up the sun. The Ira R Herr Soccer Complex is the place to be to see the Blue Jays men's or women's soccer team in action–either day or night–the stadium is one of the finest soccer venues in the East.

ADMISSIONS

Freshman Academic Profile: 30% in top 10% of high school class, 62% in top 25% of high school class, 86% in top 50% of high school class. 80% from public high schools. **Reported SAT (pre-2016 redesign) scores:** SAT Math middle 50% range 490-550. SAT Critical Reading middle 50% range 500-610. SAT Writing middle 50% range 480-590. **Concordant SAT scores:** SAT EBRW middle 50% range 550–650. SAT Math middle 50% range 520–570. ACT middle 50% range 21-28. Minimum paper TOEFL 525. **Basis for Candidate Selection:** *Very important factors considered include:* rigor of secondary school record. *Important factors considered include:* class rank, academic GPA, standardized test scores, recommendation(s), interview. *Other factors considered include:* application essay, extracurricular activities, talent/ability, character/personal qualities, first generation, alumni/ae relation, geographical residence, state residency, religious affiliation/commitment, racial/ethnic status, volunteer work, work experience, level of applicant's interest. **Freshman Admission Requirements:** High school diploma is required and GED is accepted. *Academic units required:* 4 English, 3 math, 2 science, 2 science labs, 2 foreign language, 2 social studies, 2 history. *Academic units recommended:* 4 English, 4 math, 4 science, 3 science labs, 2 foreign language, 2 social studies, 2 history, 2 academic electives. **Freshman Admission Statistics:** 2,904 applied, 73.48% admitted, 21% enrolled. **Transfer Admission Requirements:** High school transcript, college transcript(s), essay or personal statement, standardized test scores, statement of good standing from prior institution(s). Minimum college GPA of 2.5 required. Lowest grade transferable C. **General Admission Information:** Application fee $30. Priority deadline 3/1. Regular notification 4/1. Nonfall registration accepted. Admission may be deferred for a maximum of 1 year.

COSTS AND FINANCIAL AID

Annual tuition $43,490. Room and board $10,560. Required fees $0. Average book expense $1,100. **Required Forms and Deadlines:** FAFSA. **Notification of Awards:** Applicants will be notified of awards on a rolling basis beginning 3/1. **Types of Aid:** *Need-based scholarships/grants:* Federal Pell, FSEOG, State scholarships/grants, Private scholarships, College/university scholarship or grant aid from institutional funds. *Loans:* Direct Subsidized Stafford Loans, Direct Unsubsidized Stafford Loans, Direct PLUS loans, Federal Perkins Loans. *Student Employment:* Federal Work-Study Program available. Institutional employment available. **Financial Aid Statistics:** 100% needy freshmen, 100% needy undergrads receive need-based scholarship or grant aid. 22% freshmen, 18% undergrads receive non-need-based scholarship or grant aid. 75% freshmen, 79% undergrads receive need-based self-help aid. 0% freshmen, 0% undergrads receive athletic scholarships. 96% freshmen, 94% undergrads receive any aid. Average cumulative indebtedness $28,106. **Criteria for awarding aid:** *Need-based:* Academics, Alumni affiliation, Art, Minority status, Music/drama, Religious affiliation. *Non-need-based:* Academics, Alumni affiliation, Art, Music/drama, Religious affiliation.

ELMHURST COLLEGE

190 S Prospect Avenue, Elmhurst, IL 60126
Phone: 630-617-3400 • **Financial Aid Phone:** 630-617-3075
E-mail: admit@elmhurst.edu • **CEEB Code:** 1204
Fax: 630-617-5501 • **Website:** public.elmhurst.edu • **ACT Code:** 1020

This private school, affiliated with the United Church of Christ Church, was founded in 1871. It has a 38-acre campus.

RATINGS

Admissions Selectivity Rating: 73   **Fire Safety Rating:** 89   **Green Rating:** 60*

STUDENTS AND FACULTY

Enrollment: 2,763. **Student Body:** 59% female, 41% male, 10% out-of-state, 0% international (34 countries represented). Asian 6%, African American 6%, Caucasian 64%, Hispanic 19%, Native American <1%, Pacific Islander <1%, Two or more races 3%, Race unknown 2%.
Retention and Graduation: 84% freshmen return for sophomore year. 56% freshmen graduate within 4 years. 69% freshmen graduate within 6 years. 17% grads go on to further study within 1 year. 1% grads pursue law degrees. 8% grads pursue business degrees. 2% grads pursue medical degrees. **Faculty:** Student/faculty ratio 13:1. 159 full-time faculty, 81% hold PhDs, 13% are members of minority groups, 60% are women. 0% of classes are taught by teaching assistants.

ACADEMICS

Degrees: bachelor's, master's. **Classes:** Most classes have 20-29 students. **Most popular majors:** Elementary Education and Teaching; Business Administration and Management. **Special Study Options:** Accelerated program, double major, dual enrollment, honors program, independent study, internships, liberal arts/career combination, student-designed major, study abroad, teacher certification program. **Honors Programs:** The Elmhurst College Honors program provides a challenging set of educational experiences for the most academically students featuring small, stimulating seminar courses where class discussions are lively and engaging; opportunities to conduct and present professional-level research; private receptions with distinguished guest speakers; trips to theatre and dance performances, social events, and more. Combined degree programs: BA/MEng. **Disability Services:** Special programs offered to physically disabled students, including note-taking services, reader services, tape recorders, tutors. **Career Services:** Alumni network, Career/job search classes, Career assessment, Internships. Elmhurst College's Center for Professional Excellence provides a comprehensive suite of services to link students' academic expereinces with opportunities to explore career options and to prepare for future careers

FACILITIES

Housing: Coed dorms, apartments for single students. 95% of campus accessible to physically diasbled. **Special Academic Facilities/Equipment:** Accelerator/art space, language lab, recording studio, computer science/technology center, four electron microscopes. **Computers:** Students can register for classes online. Administrative functions (other than registration) can be performed online.

CAMPUS LIFE

Environment: Town. **Activities:** Choral groups, concert band, dance, drama/theater, jazz band, literary magazine, music ensembles, musical theater, radio station, student government, student newspaper, symphony orchestra, yearbook, Campus Ministries, Student Organization, Model UN. 106 registered organizations, 15 honor societies, 6 religious organizations. 3 fraternities, 6 sororities. **Athletics (Intercollegiate):** *Men:* baseball, basketball, cross-country, football, golf, soccer, tennis, track/field (outdoor), wrestling. *Women:* basketball, bowling, cross-country, golf, soccer, softball, tennis, track/field (outdoor), volleyball. **On-Campus Highlights:** Alumni Circle, Frick Center, Library, Tyrrell Fitness Center, Circle Hall. **Environmental Initiatives:** Development and execution of our Sustainability Plan. It is a living document that continues to expand as goals are achieved.

ADMISSIONS

Freshman Academic Profile: 92% from public high schools. **Reported SAT (pre-2016 redesign) scores:** SAT Math middle 50% range 450-630. SAT Critical Reading middle 50% range 460-600. SAT Writing middle 50% range 450-590. **Concordant SAT scores:** SAT EBRW middle 50% 510–650. SAT Math middle 50% range 490–650. ACT middle 50% range 21-26. Minimum paper TOEFL 550. **Basis for Candidate Selection:** *Very important factors considered include:* rigor of secondary school record, class rank, academic GPA, standardized test scores. *Important factors considered include:* application essay, recommendation(s), interview. *Other factors considered include:* extracurricular activities, talent/ability, character/personal qualities, alumni/ae relation. **Freshman Admission Requirements:** High school diploma is required and GED is accepted. *Academic units required:* 4 English, 2 math, 2 science, 2 science labs, 1 foreign language, 2 social studies, 1 history, 4 academic electives. *Academic units recommended:* 4 English, 3 math, 3 science, 3 science labs, 2 foreign language, 3 social studies, 2 history, 4 academic electives. **Freshman Admission Statistics:** 3,193 applied, 67.71% admitted, 24% enrolled. **Transfer Admission Requirements:** High school transcript, college transcript(s), statement of good standing from prior institution(s). Minimum college GPA of 2.6 required. Lowest grade transferable C. **General Admission Information:** Priority deadline 4/15. Nonfall registration accepted. Admission may be deferred for a maximum of 2 years.

COSTS AND FINANCIAL AID

Annual tuition $35,250. Room and board $9,928. Required fees $250. Average book expense $1,000. **Required Forms and Deadlines:** FAFSA. **Notification of Awards:** Applicants will be notified of awards on a rolling basis beginning 3/1. **Types of Aid:** *Need-based scholarships/grants:* Federal Pell, FSEOG, State scholarships/grants, Private scholarships, College/university scholarship or grant aid from institutional funds. *Loans:* Direct Subsidized Stafford Loans, Direct Unsubsidized Stafford Loans, Direct PLUS loans, Federal Perkins Loans. *Student Employment:* Federal Work-Study Program available. Institutional employment available. **Financial Aid Statistics:** 100% needy freshmen, 100% needy undergrads receive need-based scholarship or grant aid. 31% freshmen, 35% undergrads receive non-need-based scholarship or grant aid. 73% freshmen, 86% undergrads receive need-based self-help aid. 0% freshmen, 0% undergrads receive athletic scholarships. 95% freshmen, 87% undergrads receive any aid. 73% undergrads borrow to pay for school. Average cumulative indebtedness $28,383. **Criteria for awarding aid:** *Need-based:* Academics, Music/drama, Religious affiliation. *Non-need-based:* Academics, Alumni affiliation, Art, Minority status, Music/drama, Religious affiliation, State/district residency.

ELMIRA COLLEGE

One Park Place, Elmira, NY 14901
Phone: 607-735-1724 • **Financial Aid Phone:** 607-735-1728
E-mail: admissions@elmira.edu • **CEEB Code:** 2226
Fax: 607-735-1718 • **Website:** www.elmira.edu • **ACT Code:** 2736

This private school was founded in 1855. It has a 50-acre campus.

RATINGS

Admissions Selectivity Rating: 78   **Fire Safety Rating:** 88   **Green Rating:** 60*

STUDENTS AND FACULTY

Enrollment: 1,067. **Student Body:** 70% female, 30% male, 38% out-of-state, 4% international (20 countries represented). Asian 2%, African American 5%, Caucasian 78%, Hispanic 4%, Native American <1%, Pacific Islander 0%, Two or more races 2%, Race unknown 5%.
Retention and Graduation: 76% freshmen return for sophomore year. 56% freshmen graduate within 4 years. 60% freshmen graduate within 6 years. 4% grads pursue law degrees. 3% grads pursue business degrees. 3% grads pursue medical degrees. **Faculty:** Student/faculty ratio 11:1. 71 full-time faculty, 87%

hold PhDs, 17% are are members of minority groups, 56% are women. 0% of classes are taught by teaching assistants.

ACADEMICS

Degrees: associate, bachelor's, master's, postbachelor's certificate. **Classes:** Most classes have 10-19 students. Most lab/discussion sessions have 10-19 students. **Most popular majors:** Psychology; Education; Business Administration and Management. **Special Study Options:** Accelerated program, double major, English as a Second Language (ESL), exchange student program (domestic), independent study, internships, liberal arts/career combination, student-designed major, study abroad, teacher certification program. Combined degree programs: 4+1 MBA program with Alfred, Clarkson, RIT, or Union College. **Career Services:** Alumni network, Alumni services, Career assessment, Internships. In addition to the above services, we provide cover letter and resume critiques, practice interviews, workshops and events, and career/graduate school advising.

FACILITIES

Housing: Coed dorms, special housing for disabled students, women's dorms, apartments for single students. 25% of campus accessible to physically diasbled. **Special Academic Facilities/Equipment:** Center for Mark Twain studies, American studies center.

CAMPUS LIFE

Environment: Town. **Activities:** Choral groups, concert band, dance, drama/theater, literary magazine, music ensembles, musical theater, pep band, radio station, student government, student newspaper, yearbook. 85 registered organizations, 13 honor societies, 3 religious organizations. **Athletics (Intercollegiate):** *Men:* basketball, cheerleading, golf, ice hockey, lacrosse, soccer, tennis. *Women:* basketball, cheerleading, field hockey, golf, ice hockey, lacrosse, soccer, softball, tennis, volleyball. **On-Campus Highlights:** Emerson Hall, Mark Twain Study, Towers, Campus Center, The Puddle.

ADMISSIONS

Freshman Academic Profile: Average high school GPA 3.2. 20% in top 10% of high school class, 45% in top 25% of high school class, 69% in top 50% of high school class. **Reported SAT (pre-2016 redesign) scores:** SAT Math middle 50% range 490-580. SAT Critical Reading middle 50% range 470-570. **Concordant SAT scores:** SAT Math middle 50% range 520–600. ACT middle 50% range 22-25. Minimum internet-based TOEFL 64. Minimum paper TOEFL 500. **Basis for Candidate Selection:** *Very important factors considered include:* rigor of secondary school record, academic GPA, application essay, interview, character/personal qualities. *Important factors considered include:* class rank, standardized test scores, recommendation(s), extracurricular activities, level of applicant's interest. *Other factors considered include:* talent/ability, alumni/ae relation, geographical residence, racial/ethnic status, volunteer work, work experience. **Freshman Admission Requirements:** High school diploma is required and GED is accepted. *Academic units required:* 4 English, 3 math, 3 science, 2 science labs, 3 social studies, 1 history, 2 academic electives. *Academic units recommended:* 2 foreign language. **Freshman Admission Statistics:** 2,103 applied, 82.17% admitted, 12% enrolled. **Transfer Admission Requirements:** college transcript(s), essay or personal statement, statement of good standing from prior institution(s). Minimum college GPA of 2.0 required. Lowest grade transferable C-. **General Admission Information:** Application fee $50. Priority deadline 2/1. Nonfall registration accepted. Admission may be deferred for a maximum of 1 year.

COSTS AND FINANCIAL AID

Annual tuition $41,900. Room and board $12,000. Average book expense $600. **Required Forms and Deadlines:** FAFSA, State aid form. **Notification of Awards:** Applicants will be notified of awards on a rolling basis beginning 2/1. *Types of Aid: Need-based scholarships/grants:* Federal Pell, FSEOG, State scholarships/grants, Private scholarships, College/university scholarship or grant aid from institutional funds. *Loans:* Direct Subsidized Stafford Loans, Direct Unsubsidized Stafford Loans, Direct PLUS loans, Federal Perkins Loans. *Student Employment:* Federal Work-Study Program available. Institutional employment available. **Financial Aid Statistics:** 100% needy freshmen, 100% needy undergrads receive need-based scholarship or grant aid. 17% freshmen, 14% undergrads receive non-need-based scholarship or grant aid. 81% freshmen, 80% undergrads receive need-based self-help aid. 0% freshmen, 0% undergrads receive athletic scholarships. 98% freshmen, 98% undergrads receive any aid. Average cumulative indebtedness $27,757. **Criteria for awarding aid:** *Need-based:* Academics. *Non-need-based:* Academics, Leadership, State/district residency.

100 Campus Drive, Elon, NC 27244-2010
Phone: 336-278-3566 • **Financial Aid Phone:** 336-278-7640
E-mail: admissions@elon.edu • **CEEB Code:** 5183
Fax: 336-278-7699 • **Website:** www.elon.edu • **ACT Code:** 3096

This private school, affiliated with the United Church of Christ Church, was founded in 1889. It has a 575-acre campus.

RATINGS

Admissions Selectivity Rating: 88   **Fire Safety Rating:** 93   **Green Rating:** 93

STUDENTS AND FACULTY

Enrollment: 6,008. **Student Body:** 59% female, 41% male, 78% out-of-state, 2% international (49 countries represented). Asian 2%, African American 5%, Caucasian 81%, Hispanic 6%, Native American <1%, Pacific Islander <1%, Two or more races 3%, Race unknown <1%.
Retention and Graduation: 91% freshmen return for sophomore year. 76% freshmen graduate within 4 years. 82% freshmen graduate within 6 years. 26% grads go on to further study within 1 year. 8% grads pursue arts and sciences degrees. 2% grads pursue law degrees. 2% grads pursue business degrees. 4% grads pursue medical degrees. **Faculty:** Student/faculty ratio 12:1. 425 full-time faculty, 86% hold PhDs, 16% are are members of minority groups, 49% are women. 0% of classes are taught by teaching assistants.

ACADEMICS

Degrees: bachelor's, doctoral/professional, master's. **Classes:** Most classes have 10-19 students. Most lab/discussion sessions have 10-19 students. **Most popular majors:** Business Administration and Management; Communication; Psychology. **Special Study Options:** Accelerated program, cross-registration, distance learning, double major, dual enrollment, English as a Second Language (ESL), exchange student program (domestic), honors program, independent study, internships, liberal arts/career combination, student-designed major, study abroad, teacher certification program. **Honors Programs:** Forty freshmen are selected for the Honors Fellows program, which has benefits of specialized courses, $2,500-$10,000 scholarship renewable annually based on academic performance and participation in the program, $1,000 study abroad grant, development and presentation of their honors thesis, and housing options such as a living-learning community for Fellows. Combined degree programs: BS/BS (3-2) Engineering. **Disability Services:** Special programs offered to physically disabled students, including note-taking services, reader services, tape recorders, tutors. **Career Services:** Alumni network, Alumni services, Career/job search classes, Career assessment, Internships, Regional alumni. All students are required to particpate in two experiential learning experiences and most Elon students particpate in internship/coop (86%).

FACILITIES

Housing: Coed dorms, men's dorms, special housing for international students, women's dorms, fraternity/sorority housing, apartments for single students, Wellness Housing, Theme Housing. 85% of campus accessible to physically diasbled. **Special Academic Facilities/Equipment:** Resource center, fine arts center with recital hall, theatre, television studios, music rooms, campus center, athletic center, art gallery. **Computers:** 100% of classrooms, 100% of dorms, 100% of libraries, 100% of dining areas, 100% of student union, 25% of common outdoor areas have wireless network access. Students can register for classes online. Administrative functions (other than registration) can be performed online.

CAMPUS LIFE

Environment: Town. **Activities:** Choral groups, concert band, dance, drama/theater, jazz band, literary magazine, marching band, music ensembles, musical theater, pep band, radio station, student government, student newspaper, student-run film society, symphony orchestra, television station, yearbook, Campus Ministries, Student Organization, Model UN. 150 registered organizations, 27 honor societies, 10 religious organizations. 11 fraternities, 12 sororities. **Athletics (Intercollegiate):** *Men:* baseball, basketball, cheerleading, cross-country, football, golf, soccer, tennis. *Women:* basketball, cheerleading, cross-country, golf, soccer, softball, tennis, track/field (outdoor), track/field (indoor), volleyball. **On-Campus Highlights:** Belk Library, Rhodes Football Stadium, Koury Business Center, Moseley Student Center, Koury Athletic Center, Lindner Hall, Academic Village. **Environmental Initiatives:** Reducing greenhouse gas emissions.

ADMISSIONS

Freshman Academic Profile: Average high school GPA 4.0. 29% in top 10% of high school class, 62% in top 25% of high school class, 89% in top 50% of high school class. 58% from public high schools. **Reported SAT (pre-2016 redesign) scores:** SAT Math middle 50% range 550-640. SAT Critical Reading middle 50% range 550-640. SAT Writing middle 50% range 550-650. **Concordant SAT scores:** SAT EBRW middle 50% 610–690. SAT Math middle 50% range 570–660. ACT middle 50% range 25-29. Minimum internet-based TOEFL 79. Minimum paper TOEFL 550. **Basis for Candidate Selection:** *Very important factors considered include:* rigor of secondary school record, academic GPA, standardized test scores, application essay. *Important factors considered include:* recommendation(s), extracurricular activities, talent/ability, alumni/ae relation, volunteer work, work experience. *Other factors considered include:* class rank, character/personal qualities, first generation, geographical residence, state residency, racial/ethnic status, level of applicant's interest. **Freshman Admission Requirements:** High school diploma is required and GED is accepted. *Academic units required:* 4 English, 3 math, 3 science, 1 science lab, 2 foreign language, 1 social studies, 2 history. *Academic units recommended:* 4 English, 4 math, 3 science, 1 science lab, 3 foreign language, 1 social studies, 2 history. **Freshman Admission Statistics:** 10,098 applied, 60.44% admitted, 25% enrolled. **Transfer Admission Requirements:** High school transcript, college transcript(s), standardized test scores, statement of good standing from prior institution(s). Minimum college GPA of 2.7 required. Lowest grade transferable C-. **General Admission Information:** Application fee $50. Priority deadline 11/10. Regular application deadline 1/10. Regular notification 3/20. Nonfall registration accepted. Admission may be deferred for a maximum of 1 year.

COSTS AND FINANCIAL AID

Annual tuition $32,685. Required fees $419. Average book expense $900. **Required Forms and Deadlines:** FAFSA, Institution's own financial aid form, CSS/Financial Aid PROFILE. **Notification of Awards:** Applicants will be notified of awards on a rolling basis beginning 3/30. **Types of Aid:** *Need-based scholarships/grants:* Federal Pell, FSEOG, State scholarships/grants, Private scholarships, College/university scholarship or grant aid from institutional funds. *Loans:* Direct Subsidized Stafford Loans, Direct Unsubsidized Stafford Loans, Direct PLUS loans, Federal Perkins Loans. *Student Employment:* Federal Work-Study Program available. Institutional employment available. **Financial Aid Statistics:** 86% needy freshmen, 90% needy undergrads receive need-based scholarship or grant aid. 44% freshmen, 46% undergrads receive non-need-based scholarship or grant aid. 79% freshmen, 80% undergrads receive need-based self-help aid. 4% freshmen, 5% undergrads receive athletic scholarships. 63% freshmen, 61% undergrads receive any aid. 42% undergrads borrow to pay for school. Average cumulative indebtedness $30,170. **Criteria for awarding aid:** *Need-based:* Religious affiliation. *Non-need-based:* Academics, Alumni affiliation, Art, Athletics, Leadership, Music/drama, Religious affiliation.

EMBRY RIDDLE AERONAUTICAL UNIVERSITY (FL)

600 South Clyde Morris Boulevard, Daytona Beach, FL 32114-3900
Phone: 386-226-6100 • **Financial Aid Phone:** 800-226-6307
E-mail: dbadmit@erau.edu • **CEEB Code:** 5190
Fax: 386-226-7070 • **Website:** www.embryriddle.edu • **ACT Code:** 725

This private school was founded in 1926. It has a 185-acre campus.

RATINGS

Admissions Selectivity Rating: 85   **Fire Safety Rating:** 94   **Green Rating:** 60*

STUDENTS AND FACULTY

Enrollment: 5,247. **Student Body:** 19% female, 81% male, 63% out-of-state, 14% international (100 countries represented). Asian 4%, African American 6%, Caucasian 54%, Hispanic 4%, Native American <1%, Pacific Islander <1%, Two or more races 8%, Race unknown 9%.
Retention and Graduation: 77% freshmen return for sophomore year. 31% freshmen graduate within 4 years. 55% freshmen graduate within 6 years. 28% grads go on to further study within 1 year. 5% grads pursue business degrees.
Faculty: 0% of classes are taught by teaching assistants.

ACADEMICS

Degrees: associate, bachelor's, doctoral/research, master's. **Classes:** Most classes have 20-29 students. Most lab/discussion sessions have 10-19 students. **Most popular majors:** Aerospace, Aeronautical and Astronautical/ Space Engineering; Airline/Commercial/Professional Pilot and Flight Crew; Mechanical Engineering. **Special Study Options:** Accelerated

program, cooperative education program, distance learning, double major, dual enrollment, English as a Second Language (ESL), honors program, independent study, internships, student-designed major, study abroad. **Honors Programs:** The Embry-Riddle Honors Program is highly selective, offering its student members enriched educational experiences. Emphasizing Honors course work in General Education and in the majors, the Program involves selected faculty who develop innovative courses and establish mentoring relationships with students. The Program is designed to attract and retain top students and to develop their communicative, analytical, critical, and research skills, nurturing a love of life-long learning, leadership, and service. **Disability Services:** Special programs offered to physically disabled students, including reader services, tape recorders, tutors. **Career Services:** Alumni network, Alumni services, Career/job search classes, Career assessment, Internships. Cooperative Education/Internship Program: The Co-op/Internship program provides students with practical experience which reinforces the theoretical concepts learned in the classroom. The Co-op/Internship program aids in bridging the gap between student life and the world of work. This program combines students' academic and career interests with work experience in business, industry, government, or service organizations. Key elements of the Co-op/Internship program experience are: Professional level work assignments in areas related to the student's academic major. Supervision and evaluation of performance by professionals in a chosen career field. Completion of learning objectives designed to relate academic studies to the work world

FACILITIES

Housing: Coed dorms, apartments for married students, apartments for single students. 95% of campus accessible to physically diasbled. **Special Academic Facilities/Equipment:** Fully equipped aircraft, training simulators, airway science simulation lab, wind tunnel. **Computers:** 100% of classrooms, 100% of dorms, 100% of libraries, 100% of dining areas, 100% of student union, 15% of common outdoor areas have wireless network access. Students can register for classes online. Administrative functions (other than registration) can be performed online.

CAMPUS LIFE

Environment: Town. **Activities:** Choral groups, dance, drama/theater, music ensembles, pep band, radio station, student government, student newspaper, yearbook, Campus Ministries, Student Organization, Model UN. 140 registered organizations, 12 honor societies, 5 religious organizations. 12 fraternities, 4 sororities. **Athletics (Intercollegiate):** *Men:* baseball, basketball, cheerleading, cross-country, golf, soccer, softball, tennis, track/field (outdoor), volleyball. *Women:* basketball, cheerleading, cross-country, golf, soccer, softball, tennis, track/field (outdoor), volleyball. **On-Campus Highlights:** Lehman Engineering and Technology Center, College of Aviation, Simulator Building, ICI Center (fieldhouse), The Green Garage—EcoCAR Challenge, The College of Aviation tour is a brief look at the Air Traffic Management Laboratory and its Pseudo-Pilots' Lab, the Aircraft Performance Lab, the Computer Flight Simulation Lab, the College of Aviation Student Success Center (Tutor Lab), and the Flight Tutor Lab. The COA building also contains a Weather Center and two Meteorology Labs, Basic and Advanced. **Environmental Initiatives:** Embry-Riddle Opens ?é?Çÿ'Green Garage' Doors: EcoCAR Project Advances University Environmental Commitment Daytona Beach, Fla., Dec. 10, 2009 – Embry-Riddle Aeronautical University has opened the doors of a new green garage, where engineering students are using aerospace techniques to develop the car of tomorrow. The garage includes a rotary vehicle lift, dedicated high-voltage room, and integrated hardware-in-the-loop laboratory donated by National Instruments. It also showcases an environmental focus at Embry-Riddle College of Engineering. Every component in the lab was chosen to reduce environmental impact, including the floor covering, which is made from recycled tires. Interior design students from Daytona State College assisted in designing the new facility. http://givingto.erau.edu/givingnews/09releases/ecocar.html

ADMISSIONS

Freshman Academic Profile: Average high school GPA 3.7. 22% in top 10% of high school class, 53% in top 25% of high school class, 83% in top 50% of high school class. **Reported SAT (pre-2016 redesign) scores:** SAT Math middle 50% range 520-640. SAT Critical Reading middle 50% range 490-600. SAT Writing middle 50% range 470-580. **Concordant SAT scores:** SAT EBRW middle 50% 540–650. SAT Math middle 50% range 550–660. ACT middle 50% range 22-28. Minimum internet-based TOEFL 79. Minimum paper TOEFL 550. **Basis for Candidate Selection:** *Very important factors considered include:* standardized test scores. *Important factors considered include:* rigor of secondary school record, class rank, academic GPA, application essay, recommendation(s). *Other factors considered include:* interview, extracurricular activities, alumni/ae relation, work experience. **Freshman Admission Requirements:** High school diploma is required and GED is accepted. *Academic units required:* 4 English, 3 math, 2 science, 1 science lab, 3 social studies. *Academic units recommended:* 4 English, 4 math, 3 science, 1 science lab, 3 social studies. **Freshman Admission Statistics:** 4,588 applied, 68.88% admitted, 40% enrolled. **Transfer Admission Requirements:** college transcript(s), Minimum college GPA of 2.0 required. Lowest grade transferable

C. **General Admission Information:** Application fee $50. Priority deadline 3/1. Nonfall registration accepted. Admission may be deferred for a maximum of 1 year.

COSTS AND FINANCIAL AID
Annual tuition $32,592. Room and board $10,826. Required fees $1,294. Average book expense $1,400. **Required Forms and Deadlines:** FAFSA. **Types of Aid:** *Need-based scholarships/grants:* Federal Pell, FSEOG, State scholarships/grants, Private scholarships, College/university scholarship or grant aid from institutional funds. *Loans:* Direct Subsidized Stafford Loans, Direct Unsubsidized Stafford Loans, Direct PLUS loans, Federal Perkins Loans. *Student Employment:* Federal Work-Study Program available. Institutional employment available. **Criteria for awarding aid:** *Need-based:* Academics, Alumni affiliation, Athletics, Leadership.

EMBRY RIDDLE AERONAUTICAL UNIVERSITY— PRESCOTT

3700 Willow Creek, Prescott, AZ 86301
Phone: 928-777-6600 • **Financial Aid Phone:** 928-777-3765
E-mail: prescott@erau.edu • **CEEB Code:** 4305
Fax: 928-777-6606 • **Website:** www.embryriddle.edu • **ACT Code:** 725

This private school was founded in 1926. It has a 539-acre campus.

RATINGS
Admissions Selectivity Rating: 86   **Fire Safety Rating:** 76   **Green Rating:** 60*

STUDENTS AND FACULTY
Enrollment: 2,193. **Student Body:** 23% female, 77% male, 77% out-of-state, 10% international (31 countries represented). Asian 5%, African American 2%, Caucasian 59%, Hispanic 4%, Native American <1%, Pacific Islander 1%, Two or more races 10%, Race unknown 9%.
Retention and Graduation: 77% freshmen return for sophomore year. 39% freshmen graduate within 4 years. 59% freshmen graduate within 6 years. 21% grads go on to further study within 1 year. 3% grads pursue arts and sciences degrees. 3% grads pursue business degrees. **Faculty:** 0% of classes are taught by teaching assistants.

ACADEMICS
Degrees: bachelor's, certificate, master's. **Classes:** Most classes have 10-19 students. Most lab/discussion sessions have 10-19 students. **Most popular majors:** Aerospace, Aeronautical and Astronautical/Space Engineering; Airline/Commercial/Professional Pilot and Flight Crew; International Relations and Affairs. **Special Study Options:** Accelerated program, cooperative education program, distance learning, double major, dual enrollment, English as a Second Language (ESL), exchange student program (domestic), honors program, independent study, internships, Flight Training. **Disability Services:** Special programs offered to physically disabled students, including note-taking services, reader services, tape recorders, tutors. **Career Services:** Alumni network, Alumni services, Career/job search classes, Career assessment, Internships, Regional alumni.

FACILITIES
Housing: Coed dorms, apartments for single students. 80% of campus accessible to physically diasbled. **Computers:** 100% of classrooms, 100% of dorms, 100% of libraries, 100% of dining areas, 100% of student union, 80% of common outdoor areas have wireless network access. Administrative functions (other than registration) can be performed online.

CAMPUS LIFE
Environment: Town. **Activities:** dance, literary magazine, music ensembles, radio station, student government, student newspaper. 85 registered organizations, 5 honor societies, 2 religious organizations. 5 fraternities, 3 sororities. **Athletics (Intercollegiate):** *Men:* wrestling. **On-Campus Highlights:** Flight Line Facilities, Wind Tunnel Labs, Outdoor Pool and Racquetball, Tennis Area, The Hangar—Cafeteria, Two athletic facilities and weight room, Embry-Riddle Prescott is culturally diverse with students representing 49 states and 24 countries for a combined total of approximately 1700 students. Embry-Riddle Prescott is home to the Golden Eagles Flight Team, a nationally ranked flight team. In the last 22 years, the Golden Eagles are undefeated at the regional level, and the National Championship has been secured six times.

ADMISSIONS
Freshman Academic Profile: Average high school GPA 3.6. 28% in top 10% of high school class, 57% in top 25% of high school class, 85% in top 50% of high school class. **Reported SAT (pre-2016 redesign) scores:** SAT Math middle 50% range 520-640. SAT Critical Reading middle 50% range 490-610. SAT Writing middle 50% range 470-590. **Concordant SAT scores:** SAT EBRW middle 50% 540–650. SAT Math middle 50% range 550–660. ACT middle 50% range 23-28. Minimum internet-based TOEFL 79. Minimum paper TOEFL 550. **Basis for Candidate Selection:** *Very important factors considered include:* rigor of secondary school record, academic GPA. *Important factors considered include:* class rank, standardized test scores, recommendation(s). *Other factors considered include:* application essay, extracurricular activities, character/personal qualities, alumni/ae relation, volunteer work, work experience. **Freshman Admission Requirements:** *Academic units required:* 4 English, 3 math, 2 science, 1 science lab, 2 social studies. *Academic units recommended:* 4 English, 4 math, 3 science, 1 science lab, 2 social studies. **Freshman Admission Statistics:** 1,908 applied, 79.14% admitted, 84% enrolled. **Transfer Admission Requirements:** college transcript(s). **General Admission Information:** Application fee $50. Nonfall registration accepted. Admission may be deferred for a maximum of 1 year.

COSTS AND FINANCIAL AID
Annual tuition $32,592. Room and board $10,228. Required fees $1,234. Average book expense $1,400. **Required Forms and Deadlines:** FAFSA. **Notification of Awards:** Applicants will be notified of awards on a rolling basis beginning 3/1. **Types of Aid:** *Need-based scholarships/grants:* Federal Pell, FSEOG, State scholarships/grants, Private scholarships, College/university scholarship or grant aid from institutional funds. *Loans:* Direct Subsidized Stafford Loans, Direct Unsubsidized Stafford Loans, Direct PLUS loans. *Student Employment:* Federal Work-Study Program available. Institutional employment available. **Criteria for awarding aid:** *Need-based:* Academics, Athletics, Leadership.

EMERSON COLLEGE

120 Boylston Street, Boston, MA 02116-4624
Phone: 617-824-8600 • **Financial Aid Phone:** 617-824-8655
E-mail: admission@emerson.edu • **CEEB Code:** 3367
Fax: 617-824-8609 • **Website:** www.emerson.edu • **ACT Code:** 1820

This private school was founded in 1880. It has a 10-acre campus.

RATINGS
Admissions Selectivity Rating: 90   **Fire Safety Rating:** 94   **Green Rating:** 67

STUDENTS AND FACULTY
Enrollment: 3,757. **Student Body:** 61% female, 39% male, 76% out-of-state, 5% international (60 countries represented). Asian 4%, African American 3%, Caucasian 67%, Hispanic 10%, Native American <1%, Pacific Islander <1%, Two or more races 5%, Race unknown 6%.
Retention and Graduation: 89% freshmen return for sophomore year. 77% freshmen graduate within 4 years. 80% freshmen graduate within 6 years. 10% grads go on to further study within 1 year. **Faculty:** Student/faculty ratio 13:1. 197 full-time faculty, 73% hold PhDs, 19% are are members of minority groups, 45% are women. 3% of classes are taught by teaching assistants.

ACADEMICS
Degrees: bachelor's, master's. **Classes:** Most classes have 10-19 students. Most lab/discussion sessions have 10-19 students. **Most popular majors:** Cinematography and Film/Video Production; Theatre/Theater. **Special Study Options:** cross-registration, double major, honors program, independent study, internships, liberal arts/career combination, student-designed major, study abroad, teacher certification program. Combined degree programs: BS/MSSp in Communication Disorders. **Disability Services:** Special programs offered to physically disabled students, including note-taking services, reader services, tape recorders, tutors. **Career Services:** Alumni network, Alumni services, Career/job search classes, Career assessment, Internships, Regional alumni.

FACILITIES
Housing: Coed dorms, Optional Learning Communities, such as the Writers' Block, Film Immersion Community, and Digital Culture Floor. 80% of campus accessible to physically diasbled. **Special Academic Facilities/Equipment:** Emerson is home to the historic 1,200-seat Cutler Majestic Theatre and WERS-FM, Boston's oldest noncommercial broadcaster. The College has an 11-story performance and production center, housing rehearsal space, a costume shop, makeup lab, theatre design/tech center, and sound-treated TV studios. There are also digital and audio post-production labs, recording studios,

a film equipment distribution center, seven clinics/programs to observe speech and hearing therapy, an integrated digital newsroom, and marketing research suite. A new 14-story campus center and residence hall houses a gymnasium and space for student organizations. Current campus construction projects include new student residences in the renovated Colonial Building and a sound stage, scene shop, black box, and cinema in the refurbished Paramount Theatre complex. **Computers:** 100% of classrooms, 100% of dorms, 100% of libraries, 100% of dining areas, 100% of student union, 100% of common outdoor areas have wireless network access. Students can register for classes online. Administrative functions (other than registration) can be performed online.

CAMPUS LIFE

Environment: Metropolis. **Activities:** Choral groups, dance, drama/theater, literary magazine, music ensembles, musical theater, radio station, student government, student newspaper, student-run film society, television station, yearbook, Campus Ministries, Student Organization. 60 registered organizations, 4 honor societies, 4 religious organizations. 4 fraternities, 3 sororities. **Athletics (Intercollegiate):** *Men:* baseball, basketball, cross-country, golf, lacrosse, soccer, tennis, track/field (indoor), volleyball. *Women:* basketball, cross-country, golf, lacrosse, soccer, softball, tennis, track/field (indoor), volleyball. **On-Campus Highlights:** WERS-FM (Boston's oldest public radio), Historic Cutler Majestic Theatre, Tufte Performance and Production Center, Journalism's Integrated Digital Newsroom, Piano Row Residence Hall/College Center, Emerson is currently remodeling the Colonial Building into student residences and renovating the Paramount Theater complex to house a sound stage, scene shop, rehearsal space, and a student residence. **Environmental Initiatives:** 3 LEED certified buildings (Colonial Building, Piano Row, and Emerson Los Angeles).

ADMISSIONS

Freshman Academic Profile: Average high school GPA 3.7. 37% in top 10% of high school class, 73% in top 25% of high school class, 95% in top 50% of high school class. 68% from public high schools. **Reported SAT (pre-2016 redesign) scores:** SAT Math middle 50% range 560-650. SAT Critical Reading middle 50% range 580-680. SAT Writing middle 50% range 580-670. **Concordant SAT scores:** SAT EBRW middle 50% 640–710. SAT Math middle 50% range 580–670. ACT middle 50% range 26-30. Minimum internet-based TOEFL 80. Minimum paper TOEFL 550. **Basis for Candidate Selection:** *Very important factors considered include:* academic GPA, standardized test scores. *Important factors considered include:* rigor of secondary school record, class rank, application essay, recommendation(s), extracurricular activities, talent/ability, character/personal qualities. *Other factors considered include:* first generation, alumni/ae relation, geographical residence, racial/ethnic status, volunteer work, work experience. **Freshman Admission Requirements:** High school diploma is required and GED is accepted. *Academic units required:* 4 English, 3 math, 3 science, 3 foreign language, 3 social studies. *Academic units recommended:* 4 English, 3 math, 3 science, 3 foreign language, 3 social studies, 4 academic electives. **Freshman Admission Statistics:** 8,709 applied, 49.18% admitted, 20% enrolled. **Transfer Admission Requirements:** High school transcript, college transcript(s), essay or personal statement, statement of good standing from prior institution(s). Minimum college GPA of 3.0 required. Lowest grade transferable C. **General Admission Information:** Application fee $65. Regular application deadline 1/5. Regular notification 4/1. Nonfall registration accepted. Admission may be deferred for a maximum of 1 Year.

COSTS AND FINANCIAL AID

Annual tuition $38,304. Room and board $15,700. Required fees $732. Average book expense $1,000. **Required Forms and Deadlines:** FAFSA, CSS/Financial Aid PROFILE, Noncustodial PROFILE, Business/Farm Supplement. **Notification of Awards:** Applicants will be notified of awards on or about 4/1. **Types of Aid:** *Need-based scholarships/grants:* Federal Pell, FSEOG, State scholarships/grants, Private scholarships, College/university scholarship or grant aid from institutional funds. *Loans:* Direct Subsidized Stafford Loans, Direct Unsubsidized Stafford Loans, Direct PLUS loans, Federal Perkins Loans, State Loans. *Student Employment:* Federal Work-Study Program available. Institutional employment available. **Financial Aid Statistics:** 91% needy freshmen, 87% needy undergrads receive need-based scholarship or grant aid. 23% freshmen, 15% undergrads receive non-need-based scholarship or grant aid. 94% freshmen, 96% undergrads receive need-based self-help aid. 0% freshmen, 0% undergrads receive athletic scholarships. **Criteria for awarding aid:** *Need-based:* Academics, Music/drama. *Non-need-based:* Academics, Leadership, Music/drama, State/district residency.

See page 954.

EMILY CARR UNIVERSITY OF ART + DESIGN

1399 Johnston Street, Vancouver, BC V6H 3R9
Phone: 604-844-3897 • **Financial Aid Phone:** 1-604-844-3844
E-mail: admissions@ecuad.ca
Fax: 604-844-3089 • **Website:** www.ecuad.ca

This public school was founded in 1925. It has a 80-acre campus.

RATINGS
Admissions Selectivity Rating: 71   **Fire Safety Rating:** 60*   **Green Rating:** 60*

STUDENTS AND FACULTY
Student Body: 32% out-of-state, (53 countries represented).
Retention and Graduation: 85% freshmen return for sophomore year.
Faculty: 0% of classes are taught by teaching assistants.

ACADEMICS
Degrees: bachelor's, master's. **Most popular majors:** Design and Visual Communications; Industrial and Product Design; Fine and Studio Arts. **Special Study Options:** cooperative education program, cross-registration, distance learning, exchange student program (domestic), external degree program, independent study, internships, liberal arts/career combination, student-designed major, study abroad. **Disability Services:** Special programs offered to physically disabled students, including note-taking services, reader services, tape recorders, tutors. **Career Services:** Alumni network, Alumni services, Career/job search classes, Career assessment, Internships, Regional alumni.

FACILITIES
Housing: Off campus housing assistance. 100% of campus accessible to physically diasbled. **Special Academic Facilities/Equipment:** Two Galleries A Centre for Art and Technology

CAMPUS LIFE
Activities: student government, student newspaper, yearbook. 12 registered organizations.

ADMISSIONS
Freshman Academic Profile: 85% from public high schools. Minimum internet-based TOEFL 84. Minimum paper TOEFL 570. **Basis for Candidate Selection:** *Very important factors considered include:* talent/ability, character/personal qualities, level of applicant's interest. *Important factors considered include:* rigor of secondary school record, academic GPA. *Other factors considered include:* extracurricular activities, volunteer work, work experience. **Freshman Admission Requirements:** High school diploma is required and GED is not accepted. *Academic units required:* 3 English, 6 academic electives, 6 visual/performing arts. **Freshman Admission Statistics:** 1,112 applied, 57.28% admitted, 65% enrolled. **Transfer Admission Requirements:** college transcript(s), essay or personal statement, statement of good standing from prior institution(s). Minimum college GPA of 2.0 required. Lowest grade transferable C. **General Admission Information:** Application fee $70. Regular application deadline 2/1. Regular notification 4/1. Nonfall registration accepted. Admission may be deferred for a maximum of one year.

COSTS AND FINANCIAL AID
Annual in-state tuition $3,788. Required fees $935. Average book expense $3,000. *Student Employment:* Institutional employment available.

EMMANUEL COLLEGE

400 The Fenway, Boston, MA 2115
Phone: 617-735-9715 • **Financial Aid Phone:** 617-735-9938
E-mail: enroll@emmanuel.edu • **CEEB Code:** 3368
Fax: 617-735-9801 • **Website:** www.emmanuel.edu • **ACT Code:** 1822

This private school, affiliated with the Roman Catholic Church, was founded in 1919. It has a 17-acre campus.

RATINGS
Admissions Selectivity Rating: 76   **Fire Safety Rating:** 99   **Green Rating:** 76

STUDENTS AND FACULTY
Enrollment: 1,907. **Student Body:** 74% female, 26% male, 44% out-of-state, 2% international (52 countries represented). Asian 4%, African American 5%, Caucasian 71%, Hispanic 10%, Native American <1%, Pacific Islander <1%, Two or more races 3%, Race unknown 4%.

Retention and Graduation: 80% freshmen return for sophomore year. 60% freshmen graduate within 4 years. 67 **Faculty:** Student/faculty ratio 13:1. 94 full-time faculty, 87% hold PhDs, 16% are are members of minority groups, 62% are women. 0% of classes are taught by teaching assistants.

ACADEMICS

Degrees: bachelor's, master's, postbachelor's certificate. **Classes:** Most classes have 10-19 students. Most lab/discussion sessions have 10-19 students. **Most popular majors:** Biology/Biological Sciences; Business Administration and Management; Psychology. **Special Study Options:** Accelerated program, cross-registration, distance learning, double major, exchange student program (domestic), honors program, independent study, internships, liberal arts/career combination, student-designed major, study abroad, teacher certification program. **Honors Programs:** Emmanuel College's Honors Program is a four-year academic and co-curricular program that combines rigorous, discussion-based course work with special complementary opportunities such as cultural activities, faculty-directed research projects, and service in the community. The program begins with the yearlong Honors Colloquium, a forum for students to engage in an active and open dialogue with their peers and members of the College's faculty from across the disciplines. Students also participate in four interdisciplinary writing-intensive seminars over the course of their studies, as well as a research and presentation skills seminar in preparation for independent study as an upperclassman, and ultimately the opportunity to achieve Distinction in the Field. Combined degree programs: 4+1 BA MeD program. **Disability Services:** Special programs offered to physically disabled students, including note-taking services, reader services, tape recorders, tutors. **Career Services:** Alumni network, Alumni services, Career/job search classes, Career assessment, Internships. Nearly 90% of our students take part in at least one internship as part of their educational experience.

FACILITIES

Housing: Coed dorms, special housing for disabled students, Theme Housing. 100% of campus accessible to physically diasbled. **Special Academic Facilities/Equipment:** Academic Science Center, Lillian Immig Gallery, Academic Resource Center, Jean Yawkey Center **Computers:** Students can register for classes online. Administrative functions (other than registration) can be performed online.

CAMPUS LIFE

Environment: Metropolis. **Activities:** Choral groups, dance, drama/theater, jazz band, literary magazine, music ensembles, musical theater, pep band, radio station, student government, student newspaper, student-run film society, symphony orchestra, yearbook, Campus Ministries, Student Organization, Model UN. 48 registered organizations, 11 honor societies. **Athletics (Intercollegiate):** *Men:* basketball, cross-country, golf, soccer, track/field (outdoor), track/field (indoor), volleyball. *Women:* basketball, cross-country, lacrosse, soccer, softball, tennis, track/field (outdoor), track/field (indoor), volleyball. **On-Campus Highlights:** Jean Yawkey Center, Residence Halls, Academic Science Center, Chapel **Environmental Initiatives:** Continue to improve our diversion rate our single-stream recycling and composting programs.

ADMISSIONS

Freshman Academic Profile: Average high school GPA 3.7. 74% from public high schools. **Reported SAT (pre-2016 redesign) scores:** SAT Math middle 50% range 510-600. SAT Critical Reading middle 50% range 520-600. SAT Writing middle 50% range 500-600. **Concordant SAT scores:** SAT EBRW middle 50% 570–650. SAT Math middle 50% range 540–620. ACT middle 50% range 23-27. Minimum internet-based TOEFL 79. Minimum paper TOEFL 550. **Basis for Candidate Selection:** *Very important factors considered include:* rigor of secondary school record, academic GPA, application essay, recommendation(s). *Important factors considered include:* extracurricular activities, character/personal qualities, volunteer work, level of applicant's interest. *Other factors considered include:* class rank, standardized test scores, interview, talent/ability, first generation, alumni/ae relation, geographical residence, religious affiliation/commitment, work experience. **Freshman Admission Requirements:** High school diploma is required and GED is accepted. *Academic units required:* 4 English, 3 math, 3 science, 2 science labs, 3 foreign language, 3 social studies. **Freshman Admission Statistics:** 6,223 applied, 71.40% admitted, 13% enrolled. **Transfer Admission Requirements:** High school transcript, college transcript(s), essay or personal statement, standardized test scores, statement of good standing from prior institution(s). Minimum college GPA of n/a required. Lowest grade transferable C. **General Admission Information:** Application fee $60. Priority deadline 11/1. Regular application deadline 2/15. Nonfall registration accepted. Admission may be deferred for a maximum of one year.

COSTS AND FINANCIAL AID

Annual tuition $38,584. Room and board $14,628. Required fees $260. Average book expense $880. **Required Forms and Deadlines:** FAFSA. **Notification of Awards:** Applicants will be notified of awards on a rolling basis beginning 3/1. **Types of Aid:** *Need-based scholarships/grants:* Federal Pell, FSEOG, State

scholarships/grants, Private scholarships, College/university scholarship or grant aid from institutional funds. *Loans:* Direct Subsidized Stafford Loans, Direct Unsubsidized Stafford Loans, Direct PLUS loans, Federal Perkins Loans, State Loans. *Student Employment:* Federal Work-Study Program available. Institutional employment available. **Financial Aid Statistics:** 100% needy freshmen, 100% needy undergrads receive need-based scholarship or grant aid. 100% freshmen, 98% undergrads receive non-need-based scholarship or grant aid. 83% freshmen, 83% undergrads receive need-based self-help aid. 0% freshmen, 0% undergrads receive athletic scholarships. 99% freshmen receive any aid. 84% undergrads borrow to pay for school. Average cumulative indebtedness $36,818. **Criteria for awarding aid:** *Non-need-based:* Academics, Alumni affiliation, Leadership.

EMORY AND HENRY COLLEGE

PO Box 10, Emory, VA 24327
Phone: 276-944-6133 • **Financial Aid Phone:** 866-794-0010
E-mail: ehadmiss@ehc.edu • **CEEB Code:** 5185
Fax: 276-944-6935 • **Website:** http://www.ehc.edu • **ACT Code:** 4350

This private school, affiliated with the Methodist Church, was founded in 1836. It has a 331-acre campus.

RATINGS

Admissions Selectivity Rating: 81   **Fire Safety Rating:** 60*   **Green Rating:** 60*

STUDENTS AND FACULTY

Enrollment: 899. **Student Body:** 47% female, 53% male, 36% out-of-state, 1% international (5 countries represented). Asian 0%, African American 10%, Caucasian 80%, Hispanic 2%, Native American <1%, Pacific Islander 0%, Two or more races 2%, Race unknown 4%.
Retention and Graduation: 74% freshmen return for sophomore year. 35% freshmen graduate within 4 years. 48% freshmen graduate within 6 years. 37% grads go on to further study within 1 year. 24% grads pursue arts and sciences degrees. 31% grads pursue law degrees. 23% grads pursue business degrees. 12% grads pursue medical degrees. **Faculty:** Student/faculty ratio 10:1. 72 full-time faculty, 82% hold PhDs, 10% are are members of minority groups, 49% are women. 0% of classes are taught by teaching assistants.

ACADEMICS

Degrees: bachelor's, master's. **Classes:** Most classes have 10-19 students. **Most popular majors:** Education; Business Administration and Management; Pre-Medicine/Pre-Medical Studies. **Special Study Options:** cooperative education program, distance learning, double major, dual enrollment, honors program, independent study, internships, liberal arts/career combination, student-designed major, study abroad, teacher certification program. Combined degree programs: BA/MA. **Disability Services:** Special programs offered to physically disabled students, including reader services, tape recorders, tutors. **Career Services:** Career/job search classes, Career assessment, Internships.

FACILITIES

Housing: Coed dorms, special housing for disabled students, men's dorms, women's dorms, Theme Housing. **Special Academic Facilities/Equipment:** Language lab, capillary gas chromatograph, DNA vertical slab gel electrophoretic equipment, infrared spectrophotometer. Theatre Studio, Art gallery. **Computers:** 100% of classrooms, 100% of dorms, 100% of libraries, 100% of dining areas, 100% of student union, 100% of common outdoor areas have wireless network access.

CAMPUS LIFE

Environment: Rural. **Activities:** Choral groups, drama/theater, literary magazine, music ensembles, musical theater, opera, pep band, radio station, student government, student newspaper, television station, yearbook, Campus Ministries, Student Organization. 53 registered organizations, 7 honor societies, 4 religious organizations. 7 fraternities, 6 sororities. **Athletics (Intercollegiate):** *Men:* baseball, basketball, cross-country, football, golf, soccer, tennis. *Women:* basketball, cross-country, soccer, softball, swimming, tennis, volleyball. **On-Campus Highlights:** McGlothlin-Street Hall (new science buil, Memorial Chapel, Byars Hall (Arts, Music, and Theatre), King Athletic Center, Emory Mercantile (campus bookstore). **Environmental Initiatives:** Recycling is now in full swing, with a widespread distribution of recycling bins for paper, cardboard, aluminum, plastics and steel. There are thirty bins specially made for the college from sustainably-harvested local poplar. We have already reduced our trash volume significantly. We are a participant in the national Recyclemania competition, in the waste minimization category.

ADMISSIONS

Freshman Academic Profile: Average high school GPA 3.5. 20% in top 10% of high school class, 45% in top 25% of high school class, 80% in top 50% of high school class. 92% from public high schools. **Reported SAT (pre-2016 redesign) scores:** SAT Math middle 50% range 445-560. SAT Critical Reading middle 50% range 430-555. SAT Writing middle 50% range 425-540. **Concordant SAT scores:** SAT EBRW middle 50% 480–610. SAT Math middle 50% range 490–580. ACT middle 50% range 19-26. Minimum paper TOEFL 550. **Basis for Candidate Selection:** *Very important factors considered include:* rigor of secondary school record, academic GPA, recommendation(s), character/personal qualities, level of applicant's interest. *Important factors considered include:* standardized test scores, application essay, interview, extracurricular activities, talent/ability, geographical residence, state residency, volunteer work. *Other factors considered include:* class rank, first generation, alumni/ae relation, religious affiliation/commitment, racial/ethnic status, work experience. **Freshman Admission Requirements:** High school diploma is required and GED is accepted. *Academic units required:* 4 English, 3 math, 2 science, 2 science labs, 2 foreign language, 2 social studies. *Academic units recommended:* 1 visual/performing arts. **Freshman Admission Statistics:** 1,217 applied, 72.14% admitted, 28% enrolled. **Transfer Admission Requirements:** High school transcript, college transcript(s), statement of good standing from prior institution(s). Minimum college GPA of 2.5 required. Lowest grade transferable C. **General Admission Information:** Nonfall registration accepted. Admission may be deferred for a maximum of 1 year.

COSTS AND FINANCIAL AID

Annual tuition $23,860. Room and board $7,980. Average book expense $800. **Required Forms and Deadlines:** FAFSA, State aid form. **Notification of Awards:** Applicants will be notified of awards on a rolling basis beginning 3/1. **Types of Aid:** *Need-based scholarships/grants:* Federal Pell, FSEOG, State scholarships/grants, Private scholarships, College/university scholarship or grant aid from institutional funds. *Loans:* Federal Perkins Loans. *Student Employment:* Federal Work-Study Program available. Institutional employment available. **Financial Aid Statistics:** 80% needy freshmen, 87% needy undergrads receive need-based scholarship or grant aid. 20% freshmen, 13% undergrads receive non-need-based scholarship or grant aid. 70% freshmen, 0% undergrads receive need-based self-help aid. 0% freshmen, 0% undergrads receive athletic scholarships. **Criteria for awarding aid:** *Non-need-based:* Academics, Art, Music/drama, Religious affiliation, State/district residency.

EMORY UNIVERSITY

Emory University, Boiseuillet Jones Ctr, Atlanta, GA 30322
Phone: 404-727-6036 • **Financial Aid Phone:** 404-727-6039
E-mail: admiss@emory.edu • **CEEB Code:** 5186
Fax: 404-727-4303 • **Website:** www.emory.edu • **ACT Code:** 851

This private school, affiliated with the Methodist Church, was founded in 1836. It has a 56-acre campus.

RATINGS

Admissions Selectivity Rating: 97   **Fire Safety Rating:** 82   **Green Rating:** 97

STUDENTS AND FACULTY

Enrollment: 6,717. **Student Body:** 59% female, 41% male, 79% out-of-state, 16% international (106 countries represented). Asian 18%, African American 9%, Caucasian 42%, Hispanic 9%, Native American <1%, Pacific Islander <1%, Two or more races 4%, Race unknown 2%.
Retention and Graduation: 94% freshmen return for sophomore year. 85% freshmen graduate within 4 years. 91% freshmen graduate within 6 years. 43% grads go on to further study within 1 year. 22% grads pursue arts and sciences degrees. 16% grads pursue law degrees. 49% grads pursue medical degrees. **Faculty:** 1,028 full-time faculty, 96% hold PhDs, 21% are are members of minority groups, 40% are women. 10% of classes are taught by teaching assistants.

ACADEMICS

Degrees: bachelor's, doctoral/professional, doctoral/research, doctoral, master's, postbachelor's certificate, post-master's certificate. **Classes:** Most classes have 10-19 students. Most lab/discussion sessions have 10-19 students. **Most popular majors:** Biology/Biological Sciences; Business Administration and Management; Registered Nursing/Registered Nurse. **Special Study Options:** cooperative education program, cross-registration, double major,

dual enrollment, English as a Second Language (ESL), honors program, independent study, internships, liberal arts/career combination, study abroad, teacher certification program, Qualified undergraduates may take a semester of off-campus study in Washington D.C. Combined degree programs: BA/MA, 4 year BA/MA or BS/MS program. **Disability Services:** Special programs offered to physically disabled students, including note-taking services, reader services, tape recorders, tutors. **Career Services:** Alumni network, Alumni services, Career/job search classes, Career assessment, Internships, Regional alumni.

FACILITIES

Housing: Coed dorms, special housing for disabled students, special housing for international students, women's dorms, fraternity/sorority housing, apartments for married students, apartments for single students, Theme Housing. 90% of campus accessible to physically diasbled. **Computers:** Students can register for classes online. Administrative functions (other than registration) can be performed online.

CAMPUS LIFE

Environment: Town. **Activities:** Choral groups, concert band, dance, drama/theater, jazz band, literary magazine, marching band, music ensembles, musical theater, opera, pep band, radio station, student government, student newspaper, student-run film society, symphony orchestra, television station, Campus Ministries, Student Organization. 51 registered organizations, 30 honor societies, 27 religious organizations. 14 fraternities, 12 sororities. **Athletics (Intercollegiate):** *Men:* baseball, basketball, cross-country, diving, golf, soccer, swimming, tennis, track/field (outdoor). *Women:* basketball, cross-country, diving, soccer, softball, swimming, tennis, track/field (outdoor), volleyball. **On-Campus Highlights:** Michael C. Carlos Museum, Lullwater Park, Clifton Health Sciences Corridor, Top of Woodruff Library, Dooley's Den at the Depot, Candler Library Reading Room. **Environmental Initiatives:** Emory has among the highest number of square feet of LEED-certified space of any campus in America. Emory constructed the first LEED-certified building in the Southeast in the 1990, the first Good LEED-EB in the U.S., and since 2001 all new and future construction must be LEED (with Silver currently the minimum). We also are auditing and retrofitting exisiting buildings—roughly 1 million square feet are currently underway with additional 1 million in planning phase.

ADMISSIONS

Freshman Academic Profile: Average high school GPA 3.7. 83% in top 10% of high school class, 98% in top 25% of high school class, 100% in top 50% of high school class. 59% from public high schools. **Reported SAT (pre-2016 redesign) scores:** SAT Math middle 50% range 660-770. SAT Critical Reading middle 50% range 630-730. SAT Writing middle 50% range 650-740. **Concordant SAT scores:** SAT EBRW middle 50% 690–760. SAT Math middle 50% range 690–780. ACT middle 50% range 30-33. Minimum paper TOEFL 600. **Basis for Candidate Selection:** *Very important factors considered include:* academic GPA, recommendation(s), extracurricular activities, talent/ability, character/personal qualities. *Important factors considered include:* rigor of secondary school record, standardized test scores, application essay, volunteer work. *Other factors considered include:* class rank, interview, first generation, alumni/ae relation, geographical residence, state residency, racial/ethnic status, work experience. **Freshman Admission Requirements:** High school diploma is required and GED is not accepted. *Academic units recommended:* 4 English, 4 math, 4 science, 2 science labs, 4 foreign language, 2 social studies, 2 history, 1 visual/performing arts. **Freshman Admission Statistics:** 19,924 applied, 25.29% admitted, 27% enrolled. **Transfer Admission Requirements:** High school transcript, college transcript(s), essay or personal statement, standardized test scores, statement of good standing from prior institution(s). Minimum college GPA of 3.00 required. Lowest grade transferable C. **General Admission Information:** Application fee $75. Regular application deadline 1/1. Regular notification 4/1. Nonfall registration not accepted. Admission may be deferred for a maximum of 2 years.

COSTS AND FINANCIAL AID

Required Forms and Deadlines: FAFSA, CSS/Financial Aid PROFILE, Noncustodial PROFILE. **Notification of Awards:** Applicants will be notified of awards on or about 4/1. **Types of Aid:** *Need-based scholarships/grants:* Federal Pell, FSEOG, Private scholarships, College/university scholarship or grant aid from institutional funds. *Loans:* Direct Subsidized Stafford Loans, Direct Unsubsidized Stafford Loans, Direct PLUS loans, Federal Perkins Loans, Federal Nursing Loans, State Loans, College/university loans from institutional funds. *Student Employment:* Federal Work-Study Program available. Institutional employment available. **Financial Aid Statistics:** 90% needy freshmen, 94% needy undergrads receive need-based scholarship or grant aid. 36% freshmen, 25% undergrads receive non-need-based scholarship or grant aid. 87% freshmen, 91% undergrads receive need-based self-help aid. 0% freshmen, 0% undergrads receive athletic scholarships. 55% freshmen, 54% undergrads receive any aid. 39% undergrads borrow to pay for school. Average cumulative indebtedness $29,217. **Criteria for awarding aid:** *Need-based:* Religious affiliation. *Non-need-based:* Academics, Art, Leadership, Music/drama, Religious affiliation, State/district residency.

EMPORIA STATE UNIVERSITY

1 Kellogg Circle, Emporia, KS 66801-5087
Phone: 620-341-5465 • **Financial Aid Phone:** 620-341-5457
E-mail: go2esu@emporia.edu • **CEEB Code:** 6335
Fax: 620-341-5599 • **Website:** www.emporia.edu • **ACT Code:** 1430

This public school was founded in 1863. It has a 212-acre campus.

RATINGS

Admissions Selectivity Rating: 77   **Fire Safety Rating:** 77   **Green Rating:** 60*

STUDENTS AND FACULTY

Enrollment: 3,776. **Student Body:** 60% female, 40% male, 9% out-of-state, 8% international (40 countries represented). Asian 1%, African American 6%, Caucasian 71%, Hispanic 6%, Native American 1%, Pacific Islander <1%, Two or more races 6%, Race unknown 1%.
Retention and Graduation: 73% freshmen return for sophomore year. 20% grads go on to further study within 1 year. **Faculty:** Student/faculty ratio 17:1. 249 full-time faculty, 80% hold PhDs, 14% are are members of minority groups, 45% are women. 9% of classes are taught by teaching assistants.

ACADEMICS

Degrees: bachelor's, master's, postbachelor's certificate, post-master's certificate. **Classes:** Most classes have 20-29 students. Most lab/discussion sessions have 20-29 students. **Most popular majors:** Elementary Education and Teaching; Business/Commerce. **Special Study Options:** distance learning, double major, dual enrollment, honors program, independent study, internships, student-designed major, study abroad, teacher certification program, Continuing education courses, Evening courses, Interdisciplinary or interdepartmental course of study, Learning assistance program, Pass-Fail grading option, Student Exchange program, Summer sessions, Tutorial programs, Trio programs, Service members Opportunity College, Undergrads may take grad level classes, except 800 level. **Honors Programs:** Honors Programs Combined degree programs: MLS Legal studies with KU. **Disability Services:** Special programs offered to physically disabled students, including note-taking services, reader services, tape recorders, tutors. **Career Services:** Alumni network, Alumni services, Career assessment, Internships. Formal, for-credit internship program available to any student, any major.

FACILITIES

Housing: Coed dorms, special housing for disabled students, special housing for international students, fraternity/sorority housing, apartments for married students, apartments for single students, Wellness Housing, Theme Housing. 100% of campus accessible to physically diasbled. **Special Academic Facilities/Equipment:** Art gallery, geology and natural history museums, Great Plains study center, planetarium. **Computers:** 25% of classrooms, 100% of libraries, 50% of student union, have wireless network access. Students can register for classes online. Administrative functions (other than registration) can be performed online.

CAMPUS LIFE

Environment: Town. **Activities:** Choral groups, concert band, dance, drama/theater, jazz band, literary magazine, marching band, music ensembles, musical theater, opera, pep band, student government, student newspaper, student-run film society, symphony orchestra, yearbook, Campus Ministries, Student Organization. 141 registered organizations, 15 honor societies, 11 religious organizations. 6 fraternities, 4 sororities. **Athletics (Intercollegiate):** *Men:* baseball, basketball, cheerleading, cross-country, football, tennis, track/field (outdoor), track/field (indoor). *Women:* basketball, cheerleading, cross-country, soccer, softball, tennis, track/field (outdoor), track/field (indoor), volleyball. **On-Campus Highlights:** Student Recreation Center, The Memorial Student Union, Beach Music Hall, Wooser Lake, William Allen White Library.

ADMISSIONS

Freshman Academic Profile: Average high school GPA 3.3. 14% in top 10% of high school class, 35% in top 25% of high school class, 70% in top 50% of high school class. 96% from public high schools. **Reported SAT (pre-2016 redesign) scores:** SAT Math middle 50% range 430-585. SAT Critical Reading middle 50% range 400-495. SAT Writing middle 50% range 383-408. **Concordant SAT scores:** SAT EBRW middle 50% 440–500. SAT Math middle 50% range 470–610. ACT middle 50% range 19-24. Minimum paper TOEFL 450. **Basis for Candidate Selection:** *Very important factors considered include:* class rank, academic GPA, standardized test scores. *Important factors*

considered include: talent/ability. *Other factors considered include:* application essay, extracurricular activities. **Freshman Admission Requirements:** High school diploma is required and GED is accepted. *Academic units required:* 4 English, 3 math, 3 science, 3 social studies, 1 computer science. *Academic units recommended:* 4 English, 3 math, 3 science, 3 social studies, 1 computer science. **Freshman Admission Statistics:** 1,979 applied, 76.55% admitted, 50% enrolled. **Transfer Admission Requirements:** college transcript(s), Minimum college GPA of 2.0 required. Lowest grade transferable D. **General Admission Information:** Application fee $30. Nonfall registration accepted. Admission may be deferred for a maximum of 1 year.

COSTS AND FINANCIAL AID

Annual in-state tuition $4,500. Annual out-of-state tuition $16,650. Room and board $7,582. Required fees $1,246. Average book expense $800. **Required Forms and Deadlines:** FAFSA, State aid form. **Notification of Awards:** Applicants will be notified of awards on a rolling basis beginning 2/2. **Types of Aid:** *Need-based scholarships/grants:* Federal Pell, FSEOG, State scholarships/grants, Private scholarships, College/university scholarship or grant aid from institutional funds. *Loans:* Federal Perkins Loans. *Student Employment:* Federal Work-Study Program available. Institutional employment available. **Financial Aid Statistics:** 59% needy freshmen, 43% needy undergrads receive need-based scholarship or grant aid. 41% freshmen, 28% undergrads receive non-need-based scholarship or grant aid. 7% freshmen, 9% undergrads receive need-based self-help aid. 7% freshmen, 4% undergrads receive athletic scholarships. 61% freshmen, 57% undergrads receive any aid. **Criteria for awarding aid:** *Need-based:* Job skills, Minority status. *Non-need-based:* Academics, Alumni affiliation, Art, Athletics, Job skills, Leadership, Minority status, Music/drama, Religious affiliation, State/district residency.

ENDICOTT COLLEGE

376 Hale Street, Beverly, MA 1915
Phone: 978-921-1000 • **Financial Aid Phone:** 978-232-2060
E-mail: admissio@endicott.edu • **CEEB Code:** 3369
Fax: 978-232-2520 • **Website:** www.endicott.edu • **ACT Code:** 1824

This private school was founded in 1939. It has a 231-acre campus.

RATINGS

Admissions Selectivity Rating: 80   **Fire Safety Rating:** 97   **Green Rating:** 91

STUDENTS AND FACULTY

Enrollment: 3,081. **Student Body:** 61% female, 39% male, 52% out-of-state, 2% international (36 countries represented). Asian 1%, African American 3%, Caucasian 82%, Hispanic 5%, Native American <1%, Pacific Islander <1%, Two or more races 1%, Race unknown 6%.
Retention and Graduation: 86% freshmen return for sophomore year. 76% freshmen graduate within 4 years. 79% freshmen graduate within 6 years. 24% grads go on to further study within 1 year. **Faculty:** Student/faculty ratio 13:1. 102 full-time faculty, 59% hold PhDs, 10% are are members of minority groups, 61% are women. 0% of classes are taught by teaching assistants.

ACADEMICS

Degrees: associate, bachelor's, certificate, doctoral/research, doctoral, master's, postbachelor's certificate, terminal. **Classes:** Most classes have 10-19 students. Most lab/discussion sessions have 10-19 students. **Most popular majors:** Business Administration and Management; Sport and Fitness Administration/Management; Mass Communication/Media Studies. **Special Study Options:** Accelerated program, cross-registration, distance learning, dual enrollment, honors program, independent study, internships, liberal arts/career combination, student-designed major, study abroad, teacher certification program. **Honors Programs:** Alpha Phi Sigma, Eta Sigma Delta, Kappa Delta Pi, Lambda Pi Eta, Communications Mortar Board, Psi Chi, Sigma Beta Delta, National Honor Society for Criminal Justice Students, Endicott College Honors Program, Hospitality Management Society, National Honor Society for students in Senior Year Combined degree programs: BS/MBA, BS/MSN, BFA/MFA, BS/MA, BA/MED, BS/MS. **Disability Services:** Special programs offered to physically disabled students, including note-taking services, reader services, tape recorders, tutors. **Career Services:** Alumni network, Alumni services, Career/job search classes, Career assessment, Internships, Regional alumni, On-campus interviews. Three internships are required for all traditional undergraduate students.

FACILITIES

Housing: Coed dorms, special housing for disabled students, special housing for international students, women's dorms, apartments for single students, ThemeHousingSingle parent housing, suites, healthy living, academic. **Special Academic Facilities/Equipment:** Center for the Arts (galleries, theaters) http://www.endicott.edu/centerforthearts, Endicott Archives Museum http://

www.endicott.edu/archives, La Chanterelle, a student-run restaraunt http://www.endicott.edu/lachanterelle. **Computers:** 100% of classrooms, 96% of dorms, 100% of libraries, 100% of dining areas, 100% of student union, have wireless network access. Students can register for classes online. Administrative functions (other than registration) can be performed online.

CAMPUS LIFE

Environment: Town. **Activities:** Choral groups, concert band, dance, drama/theater, jazz band, literary magazine, music ensembles, musical theater, student government, student newspaper, student-run film society, television station, yearbook, Campus Ministries, Student Organization, Model UN. 47 registered organizations, 7 honor societies, 1 religious organization. **Athletics (Intercollegiate):** *Men:* baseball, basketball, cross-country, equestrian sports, football, golf, lacrosse, soccer, tennis, volleyball. *Women:* basketball, cross-country, equestrian sports, field hockey, lacrosse, soccer, softball, tennis, volleyball. **On-Campus Highlights:** Center for the Arts, The Lodge, Post Center—Sports Complex, Callahan Center, Endicott Beaches.

ADMISSIONS

Freshman Academic Profile: Average high school GPA 3.3. 16% in top 10% of high school class, 42% in top 25% of high school class, 79% in top 50% of high school class. 79% from public high schools. **Reported SAT (pre-2016 redesign) scores:** SAT Math middle 50% range 510-580. SAT Critical Reading middle 50% range 490-570. SAT Writing middle 50% range 480-570. **Concordant SAT scores:** SAT EBRW middle 50% 540–630. SAT Math middle 50% range 540–600. ACT middle 50% range 21-26. Minimum internet-based TOEFL 79. Minimum paper TOEFL 550. **Basis for Candidate Selection:** *Very important factors considered include:* rigor of secondary school record, academic GPA, character/personal qualities. *Important factors considered include:* class rank, standardized test scores, application essay, extracurricular activities, talent/ability, alumni/ae relation, geographical residence, volunteer work, work experience. *Other factors considered include:* recommendation(s), interview, first generation, state residency, racial/ethnic status, level of applicant's interest. **Freshman Admission Requirements:** High school diploma is required and GED is accepted. *Academic units recommended:* 4 English, 3 math, 2 science, 2 social studies, 1 history, 4 academic electives. **Freshman Admission Statistics:** 3,619 applied, 78.75% admitted, 26% enrolled. **Transfer Admission Requirements:** High school transcript, college transcript(s), essay or personal statement, standardized test scores, statement of good standing from prior institution(s). Minimum college GPA of 2.5 required. Lowest grade transferable C. **General Admission Information:** Application fee $50. Priority deadline 2/15. Regular application deadline 2/15. Nonfall registration accepted.

COSTS AND FINANCIAL AID

Annual tuition $30,612. Room and board $14,500. Required fees $700. Average book expense $1,252. **Required Forms and Deadlines:** FAFSA, Institution's own financial aid form. **Notification of Awards:** Applicants will be notified of awards on a rolling basis beginning 3/15. **Types of Aid:** *Need-based scholarships/grants:* Federal Pell, FSEOG, State scholarships/grants, Private scholarships, College/university scholarship or grant aid from institutional funds. *Loans:* Direct Subsidized Stafford Loans, Direct Unsubsidized Stafford Loans, Direct PLUS loans, Federal Perkins Loans. *Student Employment:* Federal Work-Study Program available. Institutional employment available. **Financial Aid Statistics:** 77% needy freshmen, 82% needy undergrads receive need-based scholarship or grant aid. 83% freshmen, 72% undergrads receive non-need-based scholarship or grant aid. 93% freshmen, 93% undergrads receive need-based self-help aid. 0% freshmen, 0% undergrads receive athletic scholarships. 91% freshmen, 88% undergrads receive any aid. 71% undergrads borrow to pay for school. Average cumulative indebtedness $41,901. **Criteria for awarding aid:** *Need-based:* Academics, Art, Leadership. *Non-need-based:* Academics, Alumni affiliation, Art, Job skills, Leadership, Music/drama, Religious affiliation, State/district residency.

ERSKINE COLLEGE

Erskine College, Due West, SC 29639
Phone: 864-379-8838 • **Financial Aid Phone:** 864-379-8832
E-mail: admissions@erskine.edu
Fax: 864-379-2172 • **Website:** www.erskine.edu

This private school, affiliated with the Presbyterian Church, was founded in 1839. It has a 85-acre campus.

RATINGS

Admissions Selectivity Rating: 84   **Fire Safety Rating:** 68   **Green Rating:** 60*

STUDENTS AND FACULTY

Enrollment: 548. **Student Body:** 53% female, 47% male, 24% out-of-state, 4% international (10 countries represented). Asian 1%, African American 8%, Caucasian 70%, Hispanic 1%, Native American 0%, Pacific Islander 0%, Two or more races 1%, Race unknown 16%.
Retention and Graduation: 77% freshmen return for sophomore year. 55% freshmen graduate within 4 years. 63% freshmen graduate within 6 years. **Faculty:** Student/faculty ratio 11:1. 41 full-time faculty, 85% hold PhDs, 7% are are members of minority groups, 39% are women. 0% of classes are taught by teaching assistants.

ACADEMICS

Degrees: bachelor's, certificate, doctoral/research, master's. **Classes:** Most classes have 10-19 students. Most lab/discussion sessions have 20-29 students. **Most popular majors:** Business/Commerce; Biology/Biological Sciences; Elementary Education and Teaching. **Special Study Options:** double major, independent study, internships, study abroad, teacher certification program. Combined degree programs: Medical Technology w/Medical Univ. of S. Carolina. **Disability Services:** Special programs offered to physically disabled students, including tutors. **Career Services:** Career/job search classes.

FACILITIES

Housing: men's dorms, women's dorms. 75% of campus accessible to physically diasbled. **Special Academic Facilities/Equipment:** Bowie Arts Center.

CAMPUS LIFE

Environment: Rural. **Activities:** Choral groups, concert band, dance, drama/theater, jazz band, literary magazine, music ensembles, musical theater, radio station, student government, student newspaper, yearbook, Campus Ministries. 51 registered organizations, 6 honor societies. **Athletics (Intercollegiate):** *Men:* baseball, basketball, cross-country, golf, soccer, tennis. *Women:* basketball, cross-country, golf, lacrosse, soccer, softball, tennis, volleyball. **On-Campus Highlights:** Java City, The Phoenix, Watkins Student Center, Bowie Arts Center.

ADMISSIONS

Freshman Academic Profile: 39% in top 10% of high school class, 65% in top 25% of high school class, 87% in top 50% of high school class. 85% from public high schools. **Reported SAT (pre-2016 redesign) scores:** SAT Math middle 50% range 480-605. SAT Critical Reading middle 50% range 460-590. **Concordant SAT scores:** SAT Math middle 50% range 510–630. ACT middle 50% range 21-26. Minimum paper TOEFL 550. **Basis for Candidate Selection:** *Very important factors considered include:* rigor of secondary school record, academic GPA, standardized test scores, application essay, recommendation(s), alumni/ae relation. *Important factors considered include:* extracurricular activities, talent/ability, character/personal qualities. *Other factors considered include:* class rank, interview, first generation, geographical residence, state residency, religious affiliation/commitment, racial/ethnic status, volunteer work, work experience, level of applicant's interest. **Freshman Admission Requirements:** High school diploma is required and GED is accepted. *Academic units required:* 4 English, 2 math, 2 science, 2 science labs. **Freshman Admission Statistics:** 500 applied, 74.60% admitted, 39% enrolled. **Transfer Admission Requirements:** college transcript(s), essay or personal statement, statement of good standing from prior institution(s). Minimum college GPA of 2.0 required. Lowest grade transferable C. **General Admission Information:** Application fee $25. Nonfall registration accepted. Admission may be deferred.

COSTS AND FINANCIAL AID

Required Forms and Deadlines: FAFSA, Institution's own financial aid form, State aid form. **Notification of Awards:** Applicants will be notified of awards on a rolling basis beginning 11/1. **Types of Aid:** *Need-based scholarships/grants:* Federal Pell, FSEOG, State scholarships/grants, Private scholarships, College/university scholarship or grant aid from institutional funds. *Loans:* Direct Subsidized Stafford Loans, Direct Unsubsidized Stafford Loans, Direct PLUS loans, Federal Perkins Loans, College/university loans from institutional funds. *Student Employment:* Federal Work-Study Program available. Institutional employment available. **Financial Aid Statistics:** 100% needy freshmen, 100% needy undergrads receive need-based scholarship or grant aid. 100% freshmen, 100% undergrads receive non-need-based scholarship or grant aid. 95% freshmen, 99% undergrads receive need-based self-help aid. 49% freshmen, 42% undergrads receive athletic scholarships. **Criteria for awarding aid:** *Need-based:* Academics, Alumni affiliation, Athletics, Leadership, Minority status, Religious affiliation. *Non-need-based:* Academics, Alumni affiliation, Athletics, Leadership, Minority status, Music/drama, Religious affiliation, State/district residency.

EUGENE LANG COLLEGE OF LIBERAL ARTS

72 5th Avenue, Floor 5, New York, NY 10003
Phone: 212-229-5150 • **Financial Aid Phone:** 212-229-8930
E-mail: admission@newschool.edu • **CEEB Code:** 2521
Website: www.newschool.edu/ • **ACT Code:** 2828

This private school was founded in 1978.

RATINGS

Admissions Selectivity Rating: 82   **Fire Safety Rating:** 89   **Green Rating:** 90

STUDENTS AND FACULTY

Enrollment: 1,535. **Student Body:** 73% female, 27% male, 70% out-of-state, 8% international (38 countries represented). Asian 5%, African American 8%, Caucasian 48%, Hispanic 17%, Native American 0%, Pacific Islander <1%, Two or more races 6%, Race unknown 8%.
Retention and Graduation: 74% freshmen return for sophomore year. 40% freshmen graduate within 4 years. 53% freshmen graduate within 6 years. 6% grads go on to further study within 1 year. **Faculty:** Student/faculty ratio 14:1. 71 full-time faculty, 82% hold PhDs, 23% are are members of minority groups, 49% are women. 0% of classes are taught by teaching assistants.

ACADEMICS

Degrees: bachelor's. **Classes:** Most classes have 10-19 students. Most lab/discussion sessions have 10-19 students. **Most popular majors:** Mass Communication/Media Studies; Liberal Arts and Sciences/Liberal Studies; Fine/Studio Arts. **Special Study Options:** Accelerated program, cross-registration, distance learning, double major, dual enrollment, English as a Second Language (ESL), exchange student program (domestic), independent study, internships, liberal arts/career combination, student-designed major, study abroad, Five year combined BA/BFA program. Combined degree programs: BA/BFA. **Disability Services:** Special programs offered to physically disabled students, including note-taking services, reader services, tape recorders. **Career Services:** Alumni network, Alumni services, Career/job search classes, Career assessment, Internships, Regional alumni. Both programs provide students with unique opportunities to explore future career paths, to learn new skills and to build strong communities.

FACILITIES

Housing: Coed dorms, special housing for disabled students, apartments for single students. 99% of campus accessible to physically diasbled. **Special Academic Facilities/Equipment:** Art gallery, photography gallery, extensive collections of contemporary art, concert hall, public lectures, conferences, cultural and intellectual events. **Computers:** 95% of classrooms, 100% of libraries, 100% of dining areas, na% of student union, 100% of common outdoor areas have wireless network access. Students can register for classes online. Administrative functions (other than registration) can be performed online.

CAMPUS LIFE

Environment: Metropolis. **Activities:** Choral groups, dance, drama/theater, jazz band, literary magazine, music ensembles, opera, radio station, student government, student newspaper, symphony orchestra, Student Organization. 34 registered organizations. **On-Campus Highlights:** Harry Scherman Library, Raymond Fogelman Library, Lang Courtyard, University Welcome Center, Sheila C. Johnson Design Center. **Environmental Initiatives:** Lighting Retrofits: 2W 13th St. and 66 5th Ave are in the midst of an ongoing replacement of all non-LED fixtures. The majority of the building's T8 fluorescent bulbs are being replaced with LED, stairwells are being replaced with dimming-occupancy based bi-level fixtures, and all rooms will be equiped with vacancy sensors. The main lobby and gallery spaces will also recieve significant upgrades as well. These same upgrades are being applied to 2 other large buildings, with a goal of completing the entire campus by early 2017.

ADMISSIONS

Freshman Academic Profile: Average high school GPA 3.5. 18% in top 10% of high school class, 32% in top 25% of high school class, 36% in top 50% of high school class. 52% from public high schools. **Reported SAT (pre-2016 redesign) scores:** SAT Math middle 50% range 500-630. SAT Critical Reading middle 50% range 500-620. SAT Writing middle 50% range 500-620. **Concordant SAT scores:** SAT EBRW middle 50% 560–670. SAT Math middle 50% range 530–650. ACT middle 50% range 22-27. Minimum internet-based TOEFL 92. **Basis for Candidate Selection:** *Very important factors considered include:* academic GPA, application essay, extracurricular activities. *Important factors considered include:* rigor of secondary school record, recommendation(s), character/personal qualities. *Other factors considered include:* class rank, standardized test scores, interview, talent/ability, volunteer work, work experience, level of applicant's interest. **Freshman Admission Requirements:** High school diploma is required and GED is accepted. *Academic units required:* 4 English. *Academic units recommended:* 4 math, 4

science, 4 foreign language, 4 social studies, 4 history. **Freshman Admission Statistics:** 3,449 applied, 70.63% admitted, 17% enrolled. **Transfer Admission Requirements:** High school transcript, college transcript(s), essay or personal statement, standardized test scores, Minimum college GPA of 3.0 required. Lowest grade transferable C. **General Admission Information:** Application fee $60. Priority deadline 1/15. Regular application deadline 8/1. Nonfall registration accepted. Admission may be deferred for a maximum of 1 year.

COSTS AND FINANCIAL AID

Annual tuition $42,080. Room and board $18,930. Required fees $926. Average book expense $920. **Required Forms and Deadlines:** FAFSA, State aid form. **Types of Aid:** *Need-based scholarships/grants:* Federal Pell, FSEOG, State scholarships/grants, Private scholarships, College/university scholarship or grant aid from institutional funds. *Loans:* Direct Subsidized Stafford Loans, Direct Unsubsidized Stafford Loans, Direct PLUS loans, Federal Perkins Loans. *Student Employment:* Federal Work-Study Program available. Institutional employment available. **Financial Aid Statistics:** 96% needy freshmen, 97% needy undergrads receive need-based scholarship or grant aid. 78% freshmen, 74% undergrads receive non-need-based scholarship or grant aid. 78% freshmen, 83% undergrads receive need-based self-help aid. 0% freshmen, 0% undergrads receive athletic scholarships. 58% freshmen, 57% undergrads receive any aid. 69% undergrads borrow to pay for school. Average cumulative indebtedness $26,583. **Criteria for awarding aid:** *Need-based:* Academics, Art, Leadership, Minority status, Music/drama. *Non-need-based:* Academics, Art, Leadership, Minority status, Music/drama, State/district residency.

THE EVERGREEN STATE COLLEGE

2700 Evergreen Pkwy NW, Olympia, WA 98505
Phone: 360-867-6170 • **Financial Aid Phone:** 360-867-6205
E-mail: admissions@evergreen.edu • **CEEB Code:** 4292
Fax: 360-867-5114 • **Website:** www.evergreen.edu • **ACT Code:** 4457

This public school was founded in 1967. It has a 1000-acre campus.

RATINGS

Admissions Selectivity Rating: 76   **Fire Safety Rating:** 90   **Green Rating:** 60*

STUDENTS AND FACULTY

Enrollment: 3,732. **Student Body:** 57% female, 43% male, 25% out-of-state, 1% international (22 countries represented). Asian 3%, African American 5%, Caucasian 66%, Hispanic 11%, Native American 2%, Pacific Islander <1%, Two or more races 8%, Race unknown 4%.
Retention and Graduation: 65% freshmen return for sophomore year. 43% freshmen graduate within 4 years. 56% freshmen graduate within 6 years. 20% grads go on to further study within 1 year. 12% grads pursue arts and sciences degrees. 2% grads pursue business degrees. **Faculty:** Student/faculty ratio 22:1. 157 full-time faculty, 96% hold PhDs, 43% are are members of minority groups, 55% are women. 0% of classes are taught by teaching assistants.

ACADEMICS

Degrees: bachelor's, master's. **Classes:** Most classes have 20-29 students. **Most popular majors:** Social Sciences; Liberal Arts and Sciences/Liberal Studies; Natural Sciences. **Special Study Options:** Accelerated program, double major, exchange student program (domestic), independent study, internships, student-designed major, study abroad, teacher certification program, weekend college, Learning disabilities services, summer session for credit, off-campus study. Combined degree programs: BA/BS in Liberal Arts. **Disability Services:** Special programs offered to physically disabled students, including note-taking services, tape recorders, tutors. **Career Services:** Alumni network, Alumni services, Career/job search classes, Career assessment, Internships, Regional alumni, On-campus interviews.

FACILITIES

Housing: Coed dorms, special housing for disabled students, special housing for international students, apartments for married students, apartments for single students, Wellness Housing, Theme Housing, First-Year/Freshman residence halls, Quiet housing, Substance-free housing, Gender Neutral Housing, Community Action House, Sustainability House. 85% of campus accessible to physically diasbled. **Special Academic Facilities/Equipment:** Longhouse Cultural Center, 4 computer music labs, 3 digital studio production studios, 4 analog audio recording studio/control room clusters, digital still imaging lab, multimedia lab, 3 nonlinear video editing suites, 4 linear analog video editing suites, color and BandW photography labs, animation stand, 2 digital animation suites, film mixing studio with 5 editing suites, 2 flatbed film edit rooms, 3 A/V classrooms, 5 A/V lecture halls, Media Loan equipment checkout facility, academic sailing fleet (two 40' wooden sailboats), organic farm, scanning electron microscope, gas chromatography mass spectrometer, FTNMR, FTIR, scientific computing laboratory, printmaking studio, ceramics studio, academic wood and metal shops, weaving studio, fine metal studio, two art galleries. **Computers:** 100% of classrooms, 95% of dorms, 100% of libraries, 100% of dining areas, 100% of student union, 80% of common outdoor areas have wireless network access. Students can register for classes online. Administrative functions (other than registration) can be performed online.

CAMPUS LIFE

Environment: City. **Activities:** Choral groups, dance, drama/theater, literary magazine, music ensembles, pep band, radio station, student government, student newspaper, student-run film society, television station, Campus Ministries, Model UN. 61 registered organizations, 3 religious organizations. **Athletics (Intercollegiate):** *Men:* basketball, cross-country, soccer, track/field (outdoor), track/field (indoor). *Women:* basketball, cross-country, soccer, track/field (outdoor), track/field (indoor), volleyball. **On-Campus Highlights:** Longhouse Cultural and Education Center, Organic Farm, College Library, College Activities Building, New Seminar II Building, The Flaming Eggplant, a student-run cafe featuring organic, local, and vegan food. **Environmental Initiatives:** We have completed the planning and begun implementation of our Climate Action Plan—Carbon Neutrality by 2020.

ADMISSIONS

Freshman Academic Profile: Average high school GPA 3.0. 5% in top 10% of high school class, 26% in top 25% of high school class, 54% in top 50% of high school class. **Reported SAT (pre-2016 redesign) scores:** SAT Math middle 50% range 440-560. SAT Critical Reading middle 50% range 480-620. SAT Writing middle 50% range 440-570. **Concordant SAT scores:** SAT EBRW middle 50% 510–650. SAT Math middle 50% range 480–580. ACT middle 50% range 20-26. Minimum internet-based TOEFL 79. Minimum paper TOEFL 550. **Basis for Candidate Selection:** *Very important factors considered include:* rigor of secondary school record, academic GPA, application essay. *Important factors considered include:* standardized test scores, first generation, level of applicant's interest. *Other factors considered include:* recommendation(s), interview, extracurricular activities, volunteer work, work experience. **Freshman Admission Requirements:** High school diploma is required and GED is accepted. *Academic units required:* 4 English, 3 math, 2 science, 2 science labs, 2 foreign language, 3 social studies, 1 academic elective, and 1 unit from above areas or other academic areas. **Freshman Admission Statistics:** 1,901 applied, 97.48% admitted, 31% enrolled. **Transfer Admission Requirements:** college transcript(s), Minimum college GPA of 2 required. Lowest grade transferable 2. **General Admission Information:** Application fee $50. Priority deadline 2/1. Nonfall registration accepted. Admission may be deferred for a maximum of 1 quarter.

COSTS AND FINANCIAL AID

Annual in-state tuition $6,534. Annual out-of-state tuition $23,007. Room and board $9,360. Required fees $705. Average book expense $750. **Required Forms and Deadlines:** FAFSA. **Notification of Awards:** Applicants will be notified of awards on a rolling basis beginning 4/1. **Types of Aid:** *Need-based scholarships/grants:* Federal Pell, FSEOG, State scholarships/grants, Private scholarships, College/university scholarship or grant aid from institutional funds. *Loans:* Direct Subsidized Stafford Loans, Direct Unsubsidized Stafford Loans, Direct PLUS loans, Federal Perkins Loans, College/university loans from institutional funds. *Student Employment:* Federal Work-Study Program available. Institutional employment available. **Financial Aid Statistics:** 85% needy freshmen, 84% needy undergrads receive need-based scholarship or grant aid. 3% freshmen, 1% undergrads receive non-need-based scholarship or grant aid. 71% freshmen, 79% undergrads receive need-based self-help aid. 1% freshmen, 1% undergrads receive athletic scholarships. 61% freshmen, 65% undergrads receive any aid. 56% undergrads borrow to pay for school. Average cumulative indebtedness $21,131. **Criteria for awarding aid:** *Non-need-based:* Academics, Art, Athletics, Leadership, State/district residency.

EXCELSIOR COLLEGE

7 Columbia Circle, Albany, NY 12203-5159
Phone: 518-464-8500 • **Financial Aid Phone:** 518-464-8500
E-mail: admissions@excelsior.edu • **CEEB Code:** 759
Fax: 518-464-8777 • **Website:** https://www.excelsior.edu/ • **ACT Code:** 20214

This private school was founded in 1970.

RATINGS
Admissions Selectivity Rating: 62   **Fire Safety Rating:** 60*   **Green Rating:** 60*

STUDENTS AND FACULTY

Enrollment: 32,133. **Student Body:** 58% female, 42% male, 90% out-of-state, <1% international (56 countries represented). Asian 4%, African American 17%, Caucasian 58%, Hispanic 5%, Native American 1%, Pacific Islander 0%, Two or more races 0%, Race unknown 14%.

ACADEMICS

Degrees: associate, bachelor's, master's, postbachelor's certificate, post-master's certificate. **Classes:** Most classes have 10-19 students. **Most popular majors:** Liberal Arts and Sciences/Liberal Studies Business Administration and Management. **Special Study Options:** Accelerated program, distance learning, external degree program, honors program, independent study. Combined degree programs: RN/MSN. **Career Services:** Alumni network, Alumni services, Career assessment, On-campus interviews.

FACILITIES

Housing: no housing available on campus. **Computers:** Students can register for classes online. Administrative functions (other than registration) can be performed online.

CAMPUS LIFE

Environment: City. **Activities:** 1 honor society. **Environmental Initiatives:** EC has a staff created and led committee that looks for opportunites to create a more 'green' environment.

ADMISSIONS

Freshman Admission Requirements: High school diploma is required and GED is accepted. **Freshman Admission Statistics:** Lowest grade transferable C. **General Admission Information:** Application fee $75. Nonfall registration accepted.

COSTS AND FINANCIAL AID

Required fees $0. Average book expense $0. **Required Forms and Deadlines:** FAFSA, Institution's own financial aid form. **Notification of Awards:** Applicants will be notified of awards on a rolling basis beginning 8/1. **Types of Aid:** *Need-based scholarships/grants:* Federal Pell, State scholarships/grants, Private scholarships, College/university scholarship or grant aid from institutional funds. *Loans:* Direct Subsidized Stafford Loans, Direct Unsubsidized Stafford Loans, Direct PLUS loans. **Financial Aid Statistics:** 3% undergrads receive any aid.

FAIRFIELD UNIVERSITY

1073 North Benson Road, Fairfield, CT 6824
Phone: 203-254-4100 • **Financial Aid Phone:** 203-254-4125
E-mail: admis@fairfield.edu • **CEEB Code:** 3390
Fax: 203-254-4199 • **Website:** www.fairfield.edu • **ACT Code:** 560

This private school, affiliated with the Roman Catholic-Jesuit Church, was founded in 1942. It has a 200-acre campus.

RATINGS
Admissions Selectivity Rating: 87   **Fire Safety Rating:** 93   **Green Rating:** 79

STUDENTS AND FACULTY

Enrollment: 3,955. **Student Body:** 61% female, 39% male, 71% out-of-state, 3% international (39 countries represented). Asian 2%, African American 2%, Caucasian 77%, Hispanic 8%, Native American <1%, Pacific Islander <1%, Two or more races 1%, Race unknown 6%.
Retention and Graduation: 89% freshmen return for sophomore year. 78% freshmen graduate within 4 years. 82% freshmen graduate within 6 years. 22% grads go on to further study within 1 year. 13% grads pursue arts and sciences degrees. 14% grads pursue law degrees. 34% grads pursue business degrees. 5% grads pursue medical degrees. **Faculty:** Student/faculty ratio 12:1. 271 full-time faculty, 93% hold PhDs, 9% are are members of minority groups, 54% are women. 0% of classes are taught by teaching assistants.

ACADEMICS

Degrees: bachelor's, doctoral/professional, master's, postbachelor's certificate, post-master's certificate. **Classes:** Most classes have 20-29 students. **Most popular majors:** Registered Nursing/Registered Nurse; Finance; Marketing/Marketing Management. **Special Study Options:** cross-registration, double major, exchange student program (domestic), honors program, independent study, internships, liberal arts/career combination, student-designed major, study abroad, teacher certification program, 3/2 Program with UConn,

Rensselaer Polytechnic Institute of Technology, Columbia and Stevens Institute of Technology. **Honors Programs:** Magis Scholars Four year Honors Program Corrigan Research Scholars Combined degree programs: BA/MA, BA/MEng, 5th year Graduate Programs in Education, Psychology, and Engineering. **Disability Services:** Special programs offered to physically disabled students, including note-taking services, reader services, tape recorders, tutors. **Career Services:** Alumni network, Alumni services, Career/job search classes, Career assessment, Internships. Fairfield's proximity to NYC,Stamford and Bridgeport maximizes student opportunities for internships in all majors from Finance to Psychology.

FACILITIES

Housing: Coed dorms, special housing for disabled students, apartments for single students, Wellness Floor; Sophomore College; Women in Math & Science; Freshmen Residence Halls; Diversity & Social Justice Floor (for Sophmores); Leadership House; Community Service House; The Green House; Empowering Women House; Extensive theme based living-learning options for sophomores. 95% of campus accessible to physically diasbled. **Special Academic Facilities/Equipment:** Quick Center for the arts, 2 art galleries, media center, TV studio, language labs, computer center for teacher education, Business Experiential, Simulation & Trading Floor (BEST) at the School of Business. School of Nursing Learning Resouce center is a simulated hospital environment with a Human Patient Simulator (SimMan) for simulation based learning. **Computers:** 50% of classrooms, 100% of dorms, 100% of libraries, 100% of dining areas, 100% of student union, 5% of common outdoor areas have wireless network access. Students can register for classes online. Administrative functions (other than registration) can be performed online.

CAMPUS LIFE

Environment: Town. **Activities:** Choral groups, concert band, dance, drama/theater, jazz band, literary magazine, music ensembles, pep band, radio station, student government, student newspaper, student-run film society, television station, yearbook, Campus Ministries, Student Organization, Model UN. 110 registered organizations, 21 honor societies, 3 religious organizations. **Athletics (Intercollegiate):** Men: baseball, basketball, crew/rowing, cross-country, diving, golf, lacrosse, soccer, swimming, tennis. Women: basketball, crew/rowing, cross-country, diving, field hockey, golf, lacrosse, soccer, softball, swimming, tennis, volleyball. **On-Campus Highlights:** Quick Center for the Arts(includes Walsh Art Gallery, Kelley Theatre and Wien Theatre, Egan/Loyola Chapel, DiMenna-Nyselius Library, Leslie C. Quick, Jr. Recreation Complex, Barone Campus Center (Student Center), Jazzman's Coffee Bar. **Environmental Initiatives:** Built a Co-generation facility providing 90% of campus electricity; 60% campus heating.

ADMISSIONS

Freshman Academic Profile: Average high school GPA 3.5. 35% in top 10% of high school class, 67% in top 25% of high school class, 93% in top 50% of high school class. 60% from public high schools. **Reported SAT (pre-2016 redesign) scores:** SAT Math middle 50% range 560-640. SAT Critical Reading middle 50% range 550-630. SAT Writing middle 50% range 550-640. **Concordant SAT scores:** SAT EBRW middle 50% 610–680. SAT Math middle 50% range 580–660. ACT middle 50% range 25-28. Minimum internet-based TOEFL 80. Minimum paper TOEFL 550. **Basis for Candidate Selection:** Very important factors considered include: rigor of secondary school record, academic GPA, application essay, recommendation(s). Important factors considered include: interview, extracurricular activities, talent/ability, character/personal qualities, first generation, volunteer work, work experience, level of applicant's interest. Other factors considered include: class rank, standardized test scores, alumni/ae relation, geographical residence, racial/ethnic status. **Freshman Admission Requirements:** High school diploma is required and GED is not accepted. Academic units required: 4 English, 3 math, 3 science, 2 science labs, 2 foreign language, 2 social studies, 2 history. Academic units recommended: 4 English, 4 math, 4 science, 4 foreign language, 2 social studies, 2 history. **Freshman Admission Statistics:** 11,055 applied, 61.47% admitted, 16% enrolled. **Transfer Admission Requirements:** High school transcript, college transcript(s), essay or personal statement, statement of good standing from prior institution(s). Lowest grade transferable C. **General Admission Information:** Application fee $60. Regular application deadline 1/15. Regular notification 4/1. Nonfall registration accepted. Admission may be deferred for a maximum of 1 Year.

COSTS AND FINANCIAL AID

Annual tuition $45,350. Room and board $13,860. Required fees $650. Average book expense $1,150. **Required Forms and Deadlines:** FAFSA, CSS/Financial Aid PROFILE, Noncustodial PROFILE, Business/Farm Supplement. **Notification of Awards:** Applicants will be notified of awards on or about 4/1. **Types of Aid:** Need-based scholarships/grants: Federal Pell, FSEOG, State scholarships/grants, Private scholarships, College/university scholarship or grant aid from institutional funds, Federal Nursing Scholarships. Loans: Direct Subsidized Stafford Loans, Direct Unsubsidized Stafford Loans, Direct PLUS loans, Federal Perkins Loans, Federal Nursing Loans. Student Employment: Federal Work-Study Program available. Institutional employment available. **Financial Aid Statistics:** 98% needy freshmen, 85% needy undergrads receive

need-based scholarship or grant aid. 92% freshmen, 88% undergrads receive non-need-based scholarship or grant aid. 83% freshmen, 82% undergrads receive need-based self-help aid. 6% freshmen, 7% undergrads receive athletic scholarships. 92% freshmen, 78% undergrads receive any aid. 66% undergrads borrow to pay for school. Average cumulative indebtedness $37,910. **Criteria for awarding aid:** Need-based: Academics. Non-need-based: Academics, Alumni affiliation, Art, Athletics, Leadership, Music/drama.

FAIRLEIGH DICKINSON UNIVERSITY, COLLEGE AT FLORHAM

285 Madison Ave, Madison, NJ 7940
Phone: 800-338-8803
E-mail: globaleducation@fdu.edu • **CEEB Code:** 226241
Fax: 973-443-8088 • **Website:** www.fdu.edu • **ACT Code:** 2554

This private school was founded in 1942. It has a 178-acre campus.

RATINGS

Admissions Selectivity Rating: 77   **Fire Safety Rating:** 91   **Green Rating:** 60*

STUDENTS AND FACULTY

Enrollment: 2,356. **Student Body:** 55% female, 45% male, 16% out-of-state, 1% international (25 countries represented). Asian 4%, African American 11%, Caucasian 62%, Hispanic 13%, Native American 1%, Pacific Islander 0%, Two or more races 1%, Race unknown 8%.
Retention and Graduation: 76% freshmen return for sophomore year. 43% freshmen graduate within 4 years. 58% freshmen graduate within 6 years.
Faculty: Student/faculty ratio 12:1. 141 full-time faculty, 0% hold PhDs, 0% are are members of minority groups, 45% are women.

ACADEMICS

Degrees: bachelor's, doctoral/professional, master's, postbachelor's certifiate, post-master's certificate. **Most popular majors:** Business Administration and Management; Psychology; Speech Communication and Rhetoric. **Special Study Options:** Accelerated program, cooperative education program, cross-registration, distance learning, double major, external degree program, honors program, independent study, internships, liberal arts/career combination, student-designed major, teacher certification program, weekend college. Combined degree programs: BA/MD, BA/MA, BA/DDS, BA or BS/MAT, BA or BS/MBA, BA/MPA. **Disability Services:** Special programs offered to physically disabled students, including note-taking services, reader services, tape recorders, tutors. **Career Services:** Alumni network, Alumni services, Career/job search classes, Career assessment, Internships. Experiential learning

FACILITIES

Housing: Coed dorms, special housing for disabled students. 34% of campus accessible to physically diasbled. **Computers:** 100% of classrooms, 100% of libraries, 100% of dining areas, 100% of student union, have wireless network access. Students can register for classes online. Administrative functions (other than registration) can be performed online.

CAMPUS LIFE

Environment: Village. **Activities:** Choral groups, dance, drama/theater, literary magazine, musical theater, radio station, student government, student newspaper, student-run film society, yearbook, Campus Ministries, Student Organization. 44 registered organizations, 9 honor societies, 3 religious organizations. 6 fraternities, 4 sororities. **Athletics (Intercollegiate):** Men: baseball, basketball, cross-country, football, golf, lacrosse, soccer, swimming, tennis. Women: basketball, cross-country, field hockey, lacrosse, soccer, softball, swimming, tennis, volleyball. **On-Campus Highlights:** Recreation Center, Bottle Hill Pub, Florham Perks, L'Orangerie of Library, Mansion gardens. **Environmental Initiatives:** Recyclemania, Recycling Bins

ADMISSIONS

Freshman Academic Profile: Average high school GPA 3.1. 14% in top 10% of high school class, 36% in top 25% of high school class, 75% in top 50% of high school class. **Reported SAT (pre-2016 redesign) scores:** SAT Math middle 50% range 460-570. SAT Critical Reading middle 50% range 450-560. SAT Writing middle 50% range 460-560. **Concordant SAT scores:** SAT EBRW middle 50% 510–620. SAT Math middle 50% range 500–590. Minimum internet-based TOEFL 79. Minimum paper TOEFL 550. **Basis for Candidate Selection:** Very important factors considered include: academic GPA, standardized test scores. Important factors considered include: rigor of secondary school record, recommendation(s). Other factors considered include: class rank, application essay, interview, extracurricular activities, talent/ability, character/personal qualities, alumni/ae relation, volunteer work, level of applicant's interest. **Freshman Admission Requirements:** High school diploma is required and GED is accepted. *Academic units required:* 4 English, 3 math, 2 science, 2 science labs, 2 history, 3 academic electives. *Academic units recommended:* 4 English, 3 math, 3 science, 2 science labs, 2 foreign language, 2 history, 4 academic electives. **Freshman Admission Statistics:** 3,647 applied, 77.74% admitted, 21% enrolled. **Transfer Admission Requirements:** college transcript(s), Minimum college GPA of 2.0 required. Lowest grade transferable C. **General Admission Information:** Application fee $40. Priority deadline 1/15. Nonfall registration accepted.

COSTS AND FINANCIAL AID

Annual tuition $36,386. Room and board $12,294. Required fees $958. *Student Employment:* Federal Work-Study Program available. Institutional employment available.

FAIRLEIGH DICKINSON UNIVERSITY, METROPOLITAN CAMPUS

1000 River Road, Teaneck, NJ 07666-1966
Phone: 201-692-2553
E-mail: globaleducation@fdu.edu • **CEEB Code:** 226341
Fax: 201-692-7319 • **Website:** www.fdu.edu • **ACT Code:** 2552

This private school was founded in 1942. It has a 68-acre campus.

RATINGS

Admissions Selectivity Rating: 78   **Fire Safety Rating:** 91   **Green Rating:** 60*

STUDENTS AND FACULTY

Enrollment: 4,101. **Student Body:** 57% female, 43% male, 14% out-of-state, 7% international (83 countries represented). Asian 5%, African American 14%, Caucasian 29%, Hispanic 34%, Native American <1%, Pacific Islander <1%, Two or more races 1%, Race unknown 11%.
Retention and Graduation: 70% freshmen return for sophomore year. 28% freshmen graduate within 4 years. 47% freshmen graduate within 6 years.
Faculty: Student/faculty ratio 15:1. 190 full-time faculty, 0% hold PhDs, 0% are are members of minority groups, 46% are women.

ACADEMICS

Degrees: associate, bachelor's, certificate, doctoral/professional, doctoral/research, master's, postbachelor's certificate, post-master's certificate. **Most popular majors:** Psychology; Registered Nursing/Registered Nurse; Criminal Justice/Law Enforcement Administration. **Special Study Options:** Accelerated program, cooperative education program, cross-registration, distance learning, English as a Second Language (ESL), external degree program, honors program, independent study, internships, liberal arts/career combination, student-designed major, study abroad, teacher certification program, weekend college. Combined degree programs: BA/MD, BA/MA, BA/DDS, BA/MPA, BA/BS-MAT,BA/MBA,BS/DMD,BS/DC,BSEE/MSEE,BSEE/MSCE, BA/MSW. **Disability Services:** Special programs offered to physically disabled students, including note-taking services, reader services, tape recorders, tutors. **Career Services:** Alumni network, Alumni services, Career/job search classes, Career assessment, Internships. Experiential Learning

FACILITIES

Housing: Coed dorms, special housing for disabled students, °LIFE House—Substance Free Living °Global Scholars Hall °Honor's House °Academic Year Round Housing. 41% of campus accessible to physically diasbled. **Computers:** 90% of classrooms, 100% of libraries, 100% of dining areas, 100% of student union, have wireless network access. Students can register for classes online. Administrative functions (other than registration) can be performed online.

CAMPUS LIFE

Environment: Town. **Activities:** Choral groups, dance, drama/theater, literary magazine, pep band, radio station, student government, student newspaper, student-run film society, yearbook, Campus Ministries, Student Organization, Model UN. 72 registered organizations, 10 honor societies, 4 religious organizations. 5 fraternities, 7 sororities. **Athletics (Intercollegiate):** *Men:* baseball, basketball, cross-country, golf, soccer, tennis, track/field (indoor). *Women:* basketball, bowling, cross-country, fencing, golf, soccer, softball, tennis, track/field (indoor), volleyball. **On-Campus Highlights:** Weiner Library, Fitness Center, Jeepers (Wireless Cafe), Knight Club, Hackensack River. **Environmental Initiatives:** Recyclemania, Recycling Bins.

ADMISSIONS

Freshman Academic Profile: Average high school GPA 3.2. 18% in top 10% of high school class, 45% in top 25% of high school class, 83% in top 50% of high school class. **Reported SAT (pre-2016 redesign) scores:** SAT Math middle 50% range 450-550. SAT Critical Reading middle 50% range

440-530. SAT Writing middle 50% range 430-540. **Concordant SAT scores:** SAT EBRW middle 50% 490–590. SAT Math middle 50% range 490–570. Minimum internet-based TOEFL 79. Minimum paper TOEFL 550. **Basis for Candidate Selection:** *Very important factors considered include:* academic GPA, standardized test scores. *Important factors considered include:* rigor of secondary school record, recommendation(s). *Other factors considered include:* class rank, application essay, interview, extracurricular activities, talent/ability, character/personal qualities, alumni/ae relation, volunteer work, level of applicant's interest. **Freshman Admission Requirements:** High school diploma is required and GED is accepted. *Academic units required:* 4 English, 3 math, 2 science, 2 science labs, 2 history, 3 academic electives. *Academic units recommended:* 4 English, 3 math, 3 science, 2 science labs, 2 foreign language, 2 history, 4 academic electives. **Freshman Admission Statistics:** 5,193 applied, 73.41% admitted, 20% enrolled. **Transfer Admission Requirements:** college transcript(s), Minimum college GPA of 2.0 required. Lowest grade transferable C. **General Admission Information:** Application fee $40. Priority deadline 1/15. Nonfall registration accepted.

COSTS AND FINANCIAL AID

Annual tuition $33,920. Room and board $12,742. Required fees $958. *Student Employment:* Federal Work-Study Program available. Institutional employment available.

FAIRMONT STATE UNIVERSITY, INCLUDING PIERPONT COMMUNITY & TECHNICAL COLLEGE

Office of Admissions, Fairmont State, Fairmont, WV 26554
Phone: 304-367-4892 • **Financial Aid Phone:** 304-367-4813
E-mail: admit@fairmontstate.edu • **CEEB Code:** 4520
Website: http://www.fairmontstate.edu • **ACT Code:** 4520

This public school was founded in 1865.

RATINGS

Admissions Selectivity Rating: 73   **Fire Safety Rating:** 60*   **Green Rating:** 60*

STUDENTS AND FACULTY

Enrollment: 6,227. **Student Body:** 57% female, 43% male, 4% out-of-state, 1% international. Asian 0%, African American 4%, Caucasian 91%, Hispanic 1%, Native American <1%, Pacific Islander 0%, Two or more races 0%, Race unknown 3%.
Retention and Graduation: 70% freshmen return for sophomore year. 11% freshmen graduate within 4 years. 35% freshmen graduate within 6 years.
Faculty: Student/faculty ratio 18:1. 232 full-time faculty, 48% hold PhDs, 6% are are members of minority groups, 45% are women. 0% of classes are taught by teaching assistants.

ACADEMICS

Degrees: associate, bachelor's, certificate, master's, terminal, transfer. **Classes:** Most classes have 10-19 students. Most lab/discussion sessions have fewer than 10 students. **Most popular majors:** Business Administration and Management; Teacher Education and Professional Development, Specific Levels and Methods; Criminal Justice/Safety Studies. **Special Study Options:** Accelerated program, cooperative education program, cross-registration, distance learning, double major, dual enrollment, English as a Second Language (ESL), honors program, independent study, internships, liberal arts/career combination, study abroad, teacher certification program, weekend college. **Disability Services:** Special programs offered to physically disabled students, including note-taking services, reader services, tutors. **Career Services:** Career/job search classes, Career assessment.

FACILITIES

Housing: Coed dorms, men's dorms, women's dorms, apartments for married students, apartments for single students. 100% of campus accessible to physically diasbled. **Special Academic Facilities/Equipment:** Folk Life Center **Computers:** Students can register for classes online. Administrative functions (other than registration) can be performed online.

CAMPUS LIFE

Environment: Town. **Activities:** Choral groups, concert band, dance, drama/theater, jazz band, literary magazine, marching band, music ensembles, musical theater, student government, student newspaper, symphony orchestra, yearbook, Campus Ministries, Student Organization. 90 registered organizations, 4 religious organizations. 4 fraternities, 3 sororities. **Athletics (Intercollegiate):** *Men:* baseball, basketball, cross-country, football, golf, swimming, tennis. *Women:* basketball, cheerleading, cross-country, golf, softball, tennis, volleyball.

ADMISSIONS

Freshman Academic Profile: Average high school GPA 3.0. 7% in top 10% of high school class, 24% in top 25% of high school class, 57% in top 50% of high school class. **Reported SAT (pre-2016 redesign) scores:** SAT Math middle 50% range 390-500. SAT Critical Reading middle 50% range 400-507.5. **Concordant SAT scores:** SAT Math middle 50% range 430-530. ACT middle 50% range 17-22. Minimum paper TOEFL 500. **Basis for Candidate Selection:** *Very important factors considered include:* academic GPA, standardized test scores. **Freshman Admission Requirements:** High school diploma is required and GED is accepted. *Academic units required:* 4 English, 3 math, 3 science, 2 science labs, 3 social studies, 1 history. *Academic units recommended:* 2 foreign language. **Freshman Admission Statistics:** 3,400 applied, 79.18% admitted, 45% enrolled. **Transfer Admission Requirements:** college transcript(s), Minimum college GPA of 2.00 required. Lowest grade transferable D. **General Admission Information:** Nonfall registration accepted.

COSTS AND FINANCIAL AID

Annual in-state tuition $4,656. Annual out-of-state tuition $9,956. Room and board $5,990. Average book expense $900. *Student Employment:* Federal Work-Study Program available. Institutional employment available. **Financial Aid Statistics:** 85% freshmen, 80% undergrads receive any aid.

FAITH BAPTIST BIBLE COLLEGE AND THEOLOGICAL SEMINARY

1900 NW 4th Street, Ankeny, IA 50023
Phone: 1.888.faith.4.u • **Financial Aid Phone:** 515-964-0601
E-mail: admissions@faith.edu • **CEEB Code:** 6214
Fax: 515-964-1638 • **Website:** http://www.faith.edu/ • **ACT Code:** 1315

This private school, affiliated with the Baptist Church, was founded in 1921. It has a 52-acre campus.

RATINGS

Admissions Selectivity Rating: 82   **Fire Safety Rating:** 97   **Green Rating:** 60*

STUDENTS AND FACULTY

Enrollment: 232. **Student Body:** 55% female, 45% male, 56% out-of-state, 0% international. Asian 0%, African American 2%, Caucasian 92%, Hispanic 1%, Native American 1%, Pacific Islander 1%, Two or more races 1%, Race unknown <1%.
Retention and Graduation: 65% freshmen return for sophomore year. 39% freshmen graduate within 4 years. 23% grads go on to further study within 1 year. **Faculty:** Student/faculty ratio 13:1. 17 full-time faculty, 65% hold PhDs, 0% are are members of minority groups, 12% are women. 0% of classes are taught by teaching assistants.

ACADEMICS

Degrees: associate, bachelor's, master's. **Classes:** Most classes have fewer than 10 students. **Most popular majors:** Elementary Education and Teaching; Bible/Biblical Studies; Religious Education. **Special Study Options:** independent study, internships, teacher certification program. **Career Services:** Alumni services, Internships, On-campus interviews.

FACILITIES

Housing: special housing for disabled students, men's dorms, women's dorms, apartments for married students, apartments for single students. **Computers:** 75% of classrooms, 100% of dorms, 100% of libraries, 100% of dining areas, 100% of student union, 60% of common outdoor areas have wireless network access.

CAMPUS LIFE

Environment: Town. **Activities:** Choral groups, concert band, dance, drama/theater, music ensembles, student government, symphony orchestra, yearbook, Campus Ministries, Student Organization. 1 registered organization, 1 religious organization. **Athletics (Intercollegiate):** *Men:* basketball, soccer. *Women:* basketball, soccer, volleyball. **On-Campus Highlights:** Convocation Building, Benson Hall, Library, Gray Hall, Residence Halls.

ADMISSIONS

Freshman Academic Profile: Average high school GPA 3.5. 9% in top 10% of high school class, 40% in top 25% of high school class, 60% in top 50% of high school class. 33% from public high schools. **Reported SAT (pre-2016 redesign) scores:** SAT Math middle 50% range 390-560. SAT Critical Reading middle 50% range 410-550. SAT Writing middle 50% range 400-470. **Concordant SAT scores:** SAT EBRW middle 50% 450-570. SAT Math middle 50% range 430-580. ACT middle 50% range 19-24. Minimum internet-

based TOEFL 173. Minimum paper TOEFL 500. **Basis for Candidate Selection:** *Very important factors considered include:* religious affiliation/commitment. *Important factors considered include:* application essay. *Other factors considered include:* class rank, academic GPA, standardized test scores, recommendation(s), interview, extracurricular activities, talent/ability, character/personal qualities, volunteer work, level of applicant's interest. **Freshman Admission Requirements:** High school diploma is required and GED is accepted. *Academic units recommended:* 4 English, 4 math, 2 science, 2 social studies, 2 history. **Freshman Admission Statistics:** 150 applied, 67.33% admitted, 87% enrolled. **Transfer Admission Requirements:** college transcript(s), essay or personal statement, statement of good standing from prior institution(s). Minimum college GPA of 2.0 required. Lowest grade transferable C. **General Admission Information:** Application fee $45. Nonfall registration accepted. Admission may be deferred for a maximum of 1 year.

COSTS AND FINANCIAL AID

Required Forms and Deadlines: FAFSA. **Types of Aid:** *Need-based scholarships/grants:* Federal Pell, State scholarships/grants, Private scholarships, College/university scholarship or grant aid from institutional funds. *Student Employment:* Institutional employment available. **Financial Aid Statistics:** 70% freshmen, 95% undergrads receive any aid. **Criteria for awarding aid:** *Need-based:* Academics, Leadership, Music/drama. *Non-need-based:* Academics, Leadership, Music/drama, State/district residency.

FARMINGDALE STATE COLLEGE

Admissions Office, Farmingdale, NY 11735
Phone: 631-420-2200 • **Financial Aid Phone:** 631-420-2578
E-mail: admissions@farmingdale.edu • **CEEB Code:** 2526
Fax: 631-420-2633 • **Website:** www.farmingdale.edu • **ACT Code:** 2918

This public school was founded in 1912. It has a 380-acre campus.

RATINGS

Admissions Selectivity Rating: 78   **Fire Safety Rating:** 60*   **Green Rating:** 75

STUDENTS AND FACULTY

Enrollment: 8,591. **Student Body:** 43% female, 57% male, 0% out-of-state, 2% international (73 countries represented). Asian 8%, African American 10%, Caucasian 59%, Hispanic 18%, Native American <1%, Pacific Islander <1%, Two or more races 2%, Race unknown <1%.
Retention and Graduation: 81% freshmen return for sophomore year. 31% freshmen graduate within 4 years. 53% freshmen graduate within 6 years. **Faculty:** Student/faculty ratio 20:1. 221 full-time faculty, 76% hold PhDs, 0% are are members of minority groups, 49% are women. 0% of classes are taught by teaching assistants.

ACADEMICS

Degrees: associate, bachelor's, certificate. **Classes:** Most classes have 20-29 students. **Most popular majors:** Computer and Information Sciences and Support Services; Registered Nursing/Registered Nurse; Business, Management, Marketing, and Related Support Services. **Special Study Options:** distance learning, double major, dual enrollment, internships, study abroad. **Disability Services:** Special programs offered to physically disabled students, including reader services, tutors. **Career Services:** Alumni services, Career/job search classes, Career assessment, Internships, On-campus interviews.

FACILITIES

Housing: 90% of campus accessible to physically diasbled. **Computers:** Students can register for classes online. Administrative functions (other than registration) can be performed online.

CAMPUS LIFE

Environment: Village. **Activities:** literary magazine. **Athletics (Intercollegiate):** *Men:* baseball, basketball, cross-country, golf, lacrosse, soccer, track/field (outdoor), track/field (indoor). *Women:* basketball, cross-country, soccer, softball, track/field (outdoor), track/field (indoor), volleyball. **Environmental Initiatives:** A 80 KW solar car port and the 7.2 KW wind farm.

ADMISSIONS

Freshman Academic Profile: Average high school GPA 3.2. 6% in top 10% of high school class, 24% in top 25% of high school class, 65% in top 50% of high school class. 93% from public high schools. **Reported SAT (pre-2016 redesign) scores:** SAT Math middle 50% range 450-540. SAT Critical Reading middle 50% range 430-520. **Concordant SAT scores:** SAT Math middle 50% range 490-570. ACT middle 50% range 19-23. **Basis for Candidate Selection:** *Very important factors considered include:* academic

GPA. *Important factors considered include:* rigor of secondary school record, standardized test scores, application essay, recommendation(s). *Other factors considered include:* interview, extracurricular activities, talent/ability, character/personal qualities, first generation, alumni/ae relation, volunteer work, work experience, level of applicant's interest. **Freshman Admission Requirements:** High school diploma is required and GED is accepted. *Academic units required:* 4 English, 3 math, 3 science, 4 social studies. *Academic units recommended:* 1 foreign language. **Freshman Admission Statistics:** 6,169 applied, 58.02% admitted, 36% enrolled. **Transfer Admission Requirements:** High school transcript, college transcript(s), statement of good standing from prior institution(s). Minimum college GPA of 2.0 required. Lowest grade transferable C. **General Admission Information:** Application fee $50. Priority deadline 1/1. Regular application deadline 6/1. Nonfall registration accepted. Admission may be deferred for a maximum of 1 year.

COSTS AND FINANCIAL AID

Annual in-state tuition $6,470. Annual out-of-state tuition $16,320. Room and board $12,500. Required fees $1,338. Average book expense $1,200. **Required Forms and Deadlines:** FAFSA. **Notification of Awards:** Applicants will be notified of awards on a rolling basis beginning 3/1. *Types of Aid: Need-based scholarships/grants:* Federal Pell, FSEOG, State scholarships/grants, Private scholarships, College/university scholarship or grant aid from institutional funds. *Loans:* Direct Subsidized Stafford Loans, Direct Unsubsidized Stafford Loans, Direct PLUS loans, Federal Perkins Loans. *Student Employment:* Federal Work-Study Program available. Institutional employment available. **Financial Aid Statistics:** 80% needy freshmen, 81% needy undergrads receive need-based scholarship or grant aid. 8% freshmen, 6% undergrads receive non-need-based scholarship or grant aid. 43% freshmen, 52% undergrads receive need-based self-help aid. 0% freshmen, 0% undergrads receive athletic scholarships.

FAULKNER UNIVERSITY

5345 Atlanta Highway, Montgomery, AL 36109-3398
Phone: 334-386-7200 • **Financial Aid Phone:** 334-386-7195
E-mail: admissions@faulkner.edu • **CEEB Code:** 1034
Fax: 334-386-7137 • **Website:** www.faulkner.edu • **ACT Code:** 3

This private school, affiliated with the Church of Christ Church, was founded in 1942. It has a 78-acre campus.

RATINGS

Admissions Selectivity Rating: 75   **Fire Safety Rating:** 79   **Green Rating:** 60*

STUDENTS AND FACULTY

Enrollment: 2,282. **Student Body:** 61% female, 39% male, 14% out-of-state, 2% international (15 countries represented). Asian 0%, African American 51%, Caucasian 40%, Hispanic 2%, Native American 1%, Pacific Islander <1%, Two or more races 2%, Race unknown 2%.
Retention and Graduation: 57% freshmen return for sophomore year. 9% freshmen graduate within 4 years. 21% freshmen graduate within 6 years. 80% grads go on to further study within 1 year. 35% grads pursue arts and sciences degrees. 12% grads pursue law degrees. 32% grads pursue business degrees. 19% grads pursue medical degrees. **Faculty:** Student/faculty ratio 15:1. 120 full-time faculty, 66% hold PhDs, 10% are are members of minority groups, 40% are women. 0% of classes are taught by teaching assistants.

ACADEMICS

Degrees: associate, bachelor's, doctoral/professional, doctoral/research, master's. **Classes:** Most classes have fewer than 10 students. Most lab/discussion sessions have fewer than 10 students. **Most popular majors:** Business/Commerce; Management Information Systems. **Special Study Options:** Accelerated program, cooperative education program, cross-registration, distance learning, double major, dual enrollment, honors program, independent study, internships, liberal arts/career combination, study abroad, teacher certification program, weekend college. **Honors Programs:** Great Books Honors College. **Disability Services:** Special programs offered to physically disabled students, including note-taking services, reader services, tape recorders, tutors. **Career Services:** Alumni services, Career/job search classes, Career assessment, Internships. All undergraduate programs have an internship. In Fall 2009 the University is starting a Spiritual Formation Program with a service-learning component.

FACILITIES

Housing: special housing for disabled students, men's dorms, women's dorms, apartments for single students. 75% of campus accessible to physically diasbled. **Computers:** 100% of classrooms, 100% of dorms, 100% of libraries, 100% of dining areas, 100% of student union, 100% of common outdoor areas have

wireless network access. Administrative functions (other than registration) can be performed online.

CAMPUS LIFE

Environment: City. **Activities:** Choral groups, drama/theater, music ensembles, musical theater, pep band, student government, student newspaper, yearbook, Campus Ministries. 12 registered organizations, 5 honor societies, 3 religious organizations. 5 fraternities, 5 sororities. **Athletics (Intercollegiate):** *Men:* baseball, basketball, cheerleading, fishing, football, golf, soccer. *Women:* cheerleading, fishing, soccer, softball, volleyball. **On-Campus Highlights:** Cafe Sienna, Student Multiplex, Dorm Lobbies, Perry Cafeteria, Dinner Theatre.

ADMISSIONS

Freshman Academic Profile: Average high school GPA 3.3. 75% from public high schools. **Reported SAT (pre-2016 redesign) scores:** SAT Math middle 50% range 440-510. SAT Critical Reading middle 50% range 430-520. SAT Writing middle 50% range 430-510. **Concordant SAT scores:** SAT EBRW middle 50% 480–570. SAT Math middle 50% 480–540. ACT middle 50% range 18-24. Minimum paper TOEFL 450. **Basis for Candidate Selection:** *Very important factors considered include:* academic GPA, standardized test scores. *Important factors considered include:* rigor of secondary school record, class rank, recommendation(s), interview, character/personal qualities, religious affiliation/commitment, level of applicant's interest. *Other factors considered include:* application essay, extracurricular activities, talent/ability, first generation, alumni/ae relation, volunteer work, work experience. **Freshman Admission Requirements:** High school diploma is required and GED is accepted. *Academic units required:* 3 English, 3 math, 3 science, 3 history. *Academic units recommended:* 4 English, 4 math, 4 science, 1 science lab, 1 foreign language, 2 social studies, 2 history. **Freshman Admission Statistics:** 1,712 applied, 57.30% admitted, 30% enrolled. **Transfer Admission Requirements:** High school transcript, college transcript(s), standardized test scores, statement of good standing from prior institution(s). Minimum college GPA of 2.0 required. Lowest grade transferable C. **General Admission Information:** Regular application deadline 8/1. Nonfall registration accepted. Admission may be deferred.

COSTS AND FINANCIAL AID

Annual tuition $17,500. Room and board $7,130. Required fees $1,780. Average book expense $1,800. **Required Forms and Deadlines:** FAFSA, Institution's own financial aid form, State aid form. **Notification of Awards:** Applicants will be notified of awards on or about 5/1. *Types of Aid: Need-based scholarships/grants:* Federal Pell, FSEOG, State scholarships/grants, Private scholarships, College/university scholarship or grant aid from institutional funds. *Loans:* Direct Subsidized Stafford Loans, Direct Unsubsidized Stafford Loans, Direct PLUS loans, Federal Perkins Loans. *Student Employment:* Federal Work-Study Program available. Institutional employment available. **Financial Aid Statistics:** 100% needy freshmen, 96% needy undergrads receive need-based scholarship or grant aid. 7% freshmen, 7% undergrads receive non-need-based scholarship or grant aid. 84% freshmen, 57% undergrads receive need-based self-help aid. 10% freshmen, 9% undergrads receive athletic scholarships. 95% freshmen, 93% undergrads receive any aid. **Criteria for awarding aid:** *Need-based:* Academics, Alumni affiliation, Art, Athletics, Leadership, Music/drama, Religious affiliation.

FERRIS STATE UNIVERSITY

1201 South State Street, Big Rapids, MI 49307
Phone: 231-591-2100 • **Financial Aid Phone:** 231-591-22115
E-mail: admissions@ferris.edu • **CEEB Code:** 1222
Fax: 231-591-3944 • **Website:** www.ferris.edu • **ACT Code:** 1994

This public school was founded in 1884. It has a 880-acre campus.

RATINGS

Admissions Selectivity Rating: 72   **Fire Safety Rating:** 96   **Green Rating:** 72

STUDENTS AND FACULTY

Enrollment: 12,006. **Student Body:** 51% female, 49% male, 7% out-of-state, 1% international (43 countries represented). Asian 2%, African American 7%, Caucasian 80%, Hispanic 5%, Native American 1%, Pacific Islander <1%, Two or more races 3%, Race unknown 1%.
Retention and Graduation: 75% freshmen return for sophomore year. 24% freshmen graduate within 4 years. 47% freshmen graduate within 6 years. **Faculty:** Student/faculty ratio 16:1. 592 full-time faculty, 0% hold PhDs, 0% are are members of minority groups, 45% are women. 0% of classes are taught by teaching assistants.

ACADEMICS

Degrees: associate, bachelor's, certificate, doctoral/professional, master's, postbachelor's certificate, terminal, transfer. **Classes:** Most classes have 20-29 students. Most lab/discussion sessions have 10-19 students. **Most popular majors:** Criminal Justice/Law Enforcement Administration; Pharmacy; Registered Nursing/Registered Nurse. **Special Study Options:** Accelerated program, cooperative education program, cross-registration, distance learning, double major, dual enrollment, exchange student program (domestic), external degree program, honors program, independent study, internships, liberal arts/career combination, study abroad, teacher certification program, weekend college. Combined degree programs: BA/MA. **Disability Services:** Special programs offered to physically disabled students, including note-taking services, reader services, tape recorders, tutors. **Career Services:** Career assessment.

FACILITIES

Housing: Coed dorms, special housing for disabled students, special housing for international students, apartments for married students, apartments for single students, Honors, smoke-free, alcohol-free, quiet residence halls, living/earning communities. 98% of campus accessible to physically diasbled. **Special Academic Facilities/Equipment:** Rankin Art Gallery, Student Recreation Center, Card Wildlife Museum, Jim Crowe Museum, Elastomer Center, FLITE **Computers:** Students can register for classes online. Administrative functions (other than registration) can be performed online.

CAMPUS LIFE

Environment: Village. **Activities:** Choral groups, concert band, dance, drama/theater, jazz band, literary magazine, music ensembles, pep band, radio station, student government, student newspaper, symphony orchestra, television station 180 registered organizations, 11 honor societies, 14 religious organizations. 8 fraternities, 6 sororities. **Athletics (Intercollegiate):** *Men:* basketball, cheerleading, cross-country, football, golf, ice hockey, tennis, track/field (outdoor). *Women:* basketball, cheerleading, cross-country, golf, soccer, softball, tennis, track/field (outdoor), volleyball. **On-Campus Highlights:** FLITE Library, Student Recreation Center, Card Wildlife Center, Center for Student Services, Ewigleben Ice Arena.

ADMISSIONS

Freshman Academic Profile: Average high school GPA 3.3. ACT middle 50% range 19-25. Minimum internet-based TOEFL 61. Minimum paper TOEFL 500. **Basis for Candidate Selection:** *Very important factors considered include:* rigor of secondary school record. *Important factors considered include:* academic GPA, standardized test scores, character/personal qualities. *Other factors considered include:* class rank, first generation, alumni/ae relation, geographical residence, volunteer work. **Freshman Admission Requirements:** High school diploma is required and GED is accepted. *Academic units recommended:* 4 English, 4 math, 3 science, 2 foreign language, 3 social studies, 1 visual/performing arts, and 1 unit from above areas or other academic areas. **Freshman Admission Statistics:** 10,883 applied, 77.69% admitted, 22% enrolled. **Transfer Admission Requirements:** college transcript(s), statement of good standing from prior institution(s). Minimum college GPA of 2.0 required. Lowest grade transferable C. **General Admission Information:** Application fee $30. Regular application deadline 8/1. Nonfall registration accepted.

COSTS AND FINANCIAL AID

Annual in-state tuition $11,760. Annual out-of-state tuition $17,640. Room and board $9,652. Average book expense $914. **Required Forms and Deadlines:** FAFSA. **Notification of Awards:** Applicants will be notified of awards on a rolling basis beginning 3/15. **Types of Aid:** *Need-based scholarships/grants:* Federal Pell, FSEOG, State scholarships/grants, Private scholarships, College/university scholarship or grant aid from institutional funds. *Loans:* Direct Subsidized Stafford Loans, Direct Unsubsidized Stafford Loans, Direct PLUS loans, Federal Perkins Loans, Federal Nursing Loans, College/university loans from institutional funds. *Student Employment:* Federal Work-Study Program available. Institutional employment available. **Financial Aid Statistics:** 84% needy freshmen, 76% needy undergrads receive need-based scholarship or grant aid. 79% freshmen, 60% undergrads receive non-need-based scholarship or grant aid. 78% freshmen, 80% undergrads receive need-based self-help aid. 4% freshmen, 3% undergrads receive athletic scholarships. 93% freshmen, 80% undergrads receive any aid. 72% undergrads borrow to pay for school. Average cumulative indebtedness $35,710. **Criteria for awarding aid:** *Need-based:* Academics, Athletics, Job skills, Leadership, Minority status. *Non-need-based:* Academics, Alumni affiliation, Art, Athletics, Job skills, Leadership, Minority status, Music/drama, State/district residency.

FISK UNIVERSITY

Phone: 1-800-443-3475 • **Website:**www.fisk.edu

RATINGS

Admissions Selectivity Rating: 82   **Fire Safety Rating:** 60*   **Green Rating:** 60*

ACADEMICS

Degrees: Special Study Options: cross-registration, double major, exchange student program (domestic), honors program, independent study, internships, student-designed major, study abroad, teacher certification program.

ADMISSIONS

Freshman Academic Profile: Average high school GPA 3.3. 10% in top 10% of high school class, 30% in top 25% of high school class, 75% in top 50% of high school class. 92% from public high schools. **Reported SAT (pre-2016 redesign) scores:** SAT Math middle 50% range 455-540. SAT Critical Reading middle 50% range 467-546. SAT Writing middle 50% range 447-547. **Concordant SAT scores:** SAT EBRW middle 50% 510–600. SAT Math middle 50% range 500–570. ACT middle 50% range 18-23. Minimum paper TOEFL 550. **Basis for Candidate Selection:** *Very important factors considered include:* rigor of secondary school record. *Important factors considered include:* class rank, academic GPA, standardized test scores, application essay, interview, extracurricular activities, character/personal qualities. *Other factors considered include:* recommendation(s), talent/ability, alumni/ae relation, geographical residence, volunteer work, level of applicant's interest. **Freshman Admission Requirements:** High school diploma is required and GED is accepted. *Academic units required:* 4 English, 3 math, 3 science, 2 science labs, 1 foreign language, 1 history. *Academic units recommended:* 4 English, 4 math, 3 science, 2 science labs, 2 foreign language, 1 history. **Freshman Admission Statistics:** 2,700 applied, 44.52% admitted, 51% enrolled. **Transfer Admission Requirements:** college transcript(s), essay or personal statement, statement of good standing from prior institution(s). Minimum college GPA of 2.5 required. Lowest grade transferable C. **General Admission Information:** Application fee $50. Priority deadline 3/1. Regular application deadline 3/1. Admission may be deferred for a maximum of 1 year.

COSTS AND FINANCIAL AID

Annual tuition $15,140. Room and board $7,730. Required fees $1,100. Average book expense $1,500. *Student Employment:* Federal Work-Study Program available. Institutional employment available.

FITCHBURG STATE COLLEGE

160 Pearl Street, Fitchburg, MA 01420-2697
Phone: 978-665-3144 • **Financial Aid Phone:** 978-665-3156
E-mail: admissions@fitchburgstate.edu • **CEEB Code:** 3518
Fax: 978-665-4540 • **Website:** www.fitchburgstate.edu • **ACT Code:** 1902

This public school was founded in 1894. It has a 78-acre campus.

RATINGS

Admissions Selectivity Rating: 74   **Fire Safety Rating:** 94   **Green Rating:** 60*

STUDENTS AND FACULTY

Enrollment: 3,958. **Student Body:** 54% female, 46% male, 8% out-of-state, <1% international (6 countries represented). Asian 2%, African American 4%, Caucasian 81%, Hispanic 6%, Native American <1%, Pacific Islander <1%, Two or more races 2%, Race unknown 5%.
Retention and Graduation: 73% freshmen return for sophomore year. 21% freshmen graduate within 4 years. 47% freshmen graduate within 6 years. 10% grads go on to further study within 1 year. **Faculty:** Student/faculty ratio 16:1. 184 full-time faculty, 91% hold PhDs, 11% are are members of minority groups, 46% are women. 0% of classes are taught by teaching assistants.

ACADEMICS

Degrees: bachelor's, certificate, master's, postbachelor's certificate, post-master's certificate. **Classes:** Most classes have 20-29 students. **Most popular majors:** Business Administration and Management; Speech Communication and Rhetoric; Education. **Special Study Options:** cross-registration, distance learning, double major, dual enrollment, honors program, independent study, internships, liberal arts/career combination, student-designed major, study abroad, teacher certification program. **Honors Programs:** Leadership Academy Honors Program. **Disability Services:** Special programs offered to physically disabled students, including note-taking services, reader services, tape recorders, tutors. **Career Services:** Alumni network, Alumni services, Career/job search classes, Career assessment, Internships.

FACILITIES

Housing: Coed dorms, special housing for disabled students, apartments for single students, Alcohol and Tobacco free housing. 90% of campus accessible to physically diasbled. **Special Academic Facilities/Equipment:** Art gallery, on-campus teacher education school, 120-acre conservation area. **Computers:** 100% of classrooms, 10% of dorms, 100% of libraries, 40% of dining areas, 100% of student union, 90% of common outdoor areas have wireless network access. Students can register for classes online. Administrative functions (other than registration) can be performed online. Undergraduates are required to own a computer.

CAMPUS LIFE

Environment: Town. **Activities:** Choral groups, concert band, dance, drama/ theater, jazz band, radio station, student government, student newspaper, student-run film society, Campus Ministries, Student Organization, Model UN. 60 registered organizations, 8 honor societies, 1 religious organization. 2 fraternities, 3 sororities. **Athletics (Intercollegiate):** *Men:* baseball, basketball, cross-country, football, ice hockey, soccer, track/field (outdoor), track/field (indoor). *Women:* basketball, cross-country, field hockey, lacrosse, soccer, softball, track/field (outdoor), track/field (indoor). **On-Campus Highlights:** Campus Recreation Center, Student Center Lounge, Campus Dining Hall, Commuter Cafe, Computer Labs. **Environmental Initiatives:** Single stream recycling program.

ADMISSIONS

Freshman Academic Profile: Average high school GPA 3.1. 90% from public high schools. **Reported SAT (pre-2016 redesign) scores:** SAT Math middle 50% range 460-560. SAT Critical Reading middle 50% range 450-560. SAT Writing middle 50% range 450-540. **Concordant SAT scores:** SAT EBRW middle 50% 500–610. SAT Math middle 50% range 500–580. ACT middle 50% range 19-23. Minimum paper TOEFL 550. **Basis for Candidate Selection:** *Very important factors considered include:* rigor of secondary school record. *Important factors considered include:* academic GPA, standardized test scores, application essay. *Other factors considered include:* recommendation(s), extracurricular activities, talent/ability, character/personal qualities, alumni/ ae relation, volunteer work, work experience, level of applicant's interest. **Freshman Admission Requirements:** High school diploma is required and GED is accepted. *Academic units required:* 4 English, 3 math, 3 science, 2 science labs, 2 foreign language, 1 social studies, 1 history, 2 academic electives. **Freshman Admission Statistics:** 3,104 applied, 69.68% admitted, 32% enrolled. **Transfer Admission Requirements:** college transcript(s), essay or personal statement, Minimum college GPA of 2.0 required. Lowest grade transferable C. **General Admission Information:** Application fee $25. Nonfall registration accepted. Admission may be deferred for a maximum of 1 year.

COSTS AND FINANCIAL AID

Annual in-state tuition $970. Annual out-of-state tuition $7,050. Room and board $8,256. Required fees $7,330. Average book expense $800. **Required Forms and Deadlines:** FAFSA. **Notification of Awards:** Applicants will be notified of awards on a rolling basis beginning 3/15. **Types of Aid:** *Need-based scholarships/grants:* Federal Pell, FSEOG, State scholarships/grants, Private scholarships, College/university scholarship or grant aid from institutional funds. *Loans:* Direct Subsidized Stafford Loans, Direct Unsubsidized Stafford Loans, Direct PLUS loans, Federal Perkins Loans, Federal Nursing Loans, State Loans. *Student Employment:* Federal Work-Study Program available. Institutional employment available. **Criteria for awarding aid:** *Need-based:* Academics, Alumni affiliation, Job skills. *Non-need-based:* Academics, Alumni affiliation, Job skills, Leadership.

FIVE TOWNS COLLEGE

Five Towns College, Dix Hills, NY 11746
Phone: 631-656-2110 • **Financial Aid Phone:** 631-656-2164
E-mail: admissions@ftc.edu • **CEEB Code:** 3142
Fax: 631-656-2172 • **Website:** http://www.ftc.edu/

This proprietary school was founded in 1972. It has a 35-acre campus.

RATINGS

Admissions Selectivity Rating: 73   **Fire Safety Rating:** 99   **Green Rating:** 60*

STUDENTS AND FACULTY

Enrollment: 630. **Student Body:** 32% female, 68% male, 8% out-of-state, 0% international (4 countries represented). Asian 4%, African American 20%, Caucasian 50%, Hispanic 15%, Native American 1%, Pacific Islander <1%, Two or more races 4%, Race unknown 5%.
Retention and Graduation: 74% freshmen return for sophomore year. 21% freshmen graduate within 4 years. 28% freshmen graduate within 6 years.

Faculty: Student/faculty ratio 15:1. 22 full-time faculty, 45% hold PhDs, 14% are are members of minority groups, 36% are women. 0% of classes are taught by teaching assistants.

ACADEMICS

Degrees: associate, bachelor's, doctoral, master's. **Classes:** Most classes have 20-29 students. **Most popular majors:** Recording Arts Technology/ Technician; Music; Film/Cinema/Video Studies. **Special Study Options:** distance learning, dual enrollment, internships, liberal arts/career combination, teacher certification program. **Disability Services:** Special programs offered to physically disabled students, including note-taking services, reader services, tape recorders, tutors. **Career Services:** Career/job search classes, Career assessment, Internships. Internships.

FACILITIES

Housing: Coed dorms, Wellness Housing. 100% of campus accessible to physically diasbled. **Computers:** 100% of classrooms, 100% of dorms, 100% of libraries, 100% of dining areas, 100% of common outdoor areas have wireless network access. Administrative functions (other than registration) can be performed online.

CAMPUS LIFE

Environment: Village. **Activities:** Choral groups, concert band, dance, drama/ theater, jazz band, music ensembles, musical theater, radio station, student government, student newspaper, student-run film society, symphony orchestra, television station, yearbook. **On-Campus Highlights:** Student Center, Audio Studios, Film Video Studios, Radio Station, Court Yard.

ADMISSIONS

Freshman Academic Profile: Average high school GPA 80.0. 91% from public high schools. **Reported SAT (pre-2016 redesign) scores:** SAT Math middle 50% range 380-490. SAT Critical Reading middle 50% range 390-490. SAT Writing middle 50% range 380-500. **Concordant SAT scores:** SAT EBRW middle 50% 430–550. SAT Math middle 50% range 420–520. ACT middle 50% range 16-24. **Basis for Candidate Selection:** *Very important factors considered include:* rigor of secondary school record, academic GPA, application essay, recommendation(s), talent/ability, character/ personal qualities. *Important factors considered include:* class rank, interview, extracurricular activities, level of applicant's interest. *Other factors considered include:* standardized test scores, volunteer work, work experience. **Freshman Admission Requirements:** High school diploma is required and GED is accepted. *Academic units required:* 4 English, 3 math, 3 science, 2 science labs, 2 foreign language, 4 social studies, 4 academic electives. *Academic units recommended:* 4 English, 3 math, 3 science, 2 science labs, 2 foreign language, 4 social studies, 4 academic electives. **Freshman Admission Statistics:** 379 applied, 62.80% admitted, 50% enrolled. **Transfer Admission Requirements:** High school transcript, college transcript(s), essay or personal statement, statement of good standing from prior institution(s). Minimum college GPA of 2.5 required. Lowest grade transferable C. **General Admission Information:** Application fee $35. Nonfall registration accepted. Admission may be deferred for a maximum of 1 year.

COSTS AND FINANCIAL AID

Annual tuition $21,000. Room and board $12,270. Required fees $700. Average book expense $1,400. **Required Forms and Deadlines:** FAFSA, State aid form. **Notification of Awards:** Applicants will be notified of awards on a rolling basis beginning 4/30. **Types of Aid:** *Need-based scholarships/ grants:* Federal Pell, FSEOG, State scholarships/grants, Private scholarships, College/university scholarship or grant aid from institutional funds. *Loans:* Direct Subsidized Stafford Loans, Direct Unsubsidized Stafford Loans, Direct PLUS loans, State Loans. *Student Employment:* Federal Work-Study Program available. Institutional employment available. **Financial Aid Statistics:** 73% needy freshmen, 73% needy undergrads receive need-based scholarship or grant aid. 91% freshmen, 81% undergrads receive non-need-based scholarship or grant aid. 78% freshmen, 80% undergrads receive need-based self-help aid. 0% freshmen, 0% undergrads receive athletic scholarships. 78% freshmen, 75% undergrads receive any aid. 88% undergrads borrow to pay for school. Average cumulative indebtedness $35,340. **Criteria for awarding aid:** *Need-based:* Academics, Art, Music/drama. *Non-need-based:* Academics, Art, Leadership, Music/drama.

FLAGLER COLLEGE

74 King Street, St. Augustine, FL 32085-1027
Phone: 904-819-6220 • **Financial Aid Phone:** 904-819-6225
E-mail: admissions@flagler.edu • **CEEB Code:** 5235
Fax: 904-819-6466 • **Website:** www.flagler.edu • **ACT Code:** 772

This private school was founded in 1968. It has a 42-acre campus.

RATINGS

Admissions Selectivity Rating: 86   **Fire Safety Rating:** 80   **Green Rating:** 68

STUDENTS AND FACULTY

Enrollment: 2,611. **Student Body:** 63% female, 37% male, 59% out-of-state, 3% international (45 countries represented). Asian 0%, African American <1%, Caucasian 1%, Hispanic 5%, Native American 4%, Pacific Islander 78%, Two or more races 2%, Race unknown 6%.
Retention and Graduation: 71% freshmen return for sophomore year. 54% freshmen graduate within 4 years. 60% freshmen graduate within 6 years. 15% grads go on to further study within 1 year. 4% grads pursue arts and sciences degrees. 3% grads pursue law degrees. 1% grads pursue business degrees. **Faculty:** Student/faculty ratio 15:1. 116 full-time faculty, 76% hold PhDs, 11% are are members of minority groups, 49% are women. 0% of classes are taught by teaching assistants.

ACADEMICS

Degrees: bachelor's. **Classes:** Most classes have 20-29 students. **Most popular majors:** Psychology; Business Administration and Management; Public Administration. **Special Study Options:** double major, external degree program, independent study, internships, liberal arts/career combination, study abroad, teacher certification program. Combined degree programs: **Disability Services:** Special programs offered to physically disabled students, including note-taking services, reader services, tape recorders, tutors. **Career Services:** Alumni network, Alumni services, Career/job search classes, Career assessment, Internships, Regional alumni. Most majors require students to gain internship experience.

FACILITIES

Housing: men's dorms, women's dorms. 95% of campus accessible to physically disabled. **Special Academic Facilities/Equipment:** Museum/theatre; learning disabilities clinic for student teachers; NorthEast Florida Archeological Association; Crisp-Ellert Art Gallery. **Computers:** 30% of classrooms, 100% of dorms, 100% of libraries, 100% of dining areas, 100% of student union, 80% of common outdoor areas have wireless network access. Students can register for classes online. Administrative functions (other than registration) can be performed online.

CAMPUS LIFE

Environment: Town. **Activities:** Choral groups, drama/theater, literary magazine, radio station, student government, student newspaper, Campus Ministries. 7 honor societies, 3 religious organizations. **Athletics (Intercollegiate):** *Men:* baseball, basketball, cross-country, golf, soccer, tennis. *Women:* basketball, cross-country, golf, soccer, softball, tennis, volleyball. **On-Campus Highlights:** The Student Center, Proctor Library, Campus Courtyard, Flagler College Tennis Complex, Flagler College Sports Complex. **Environmental Initiatives:** Chiller upgrades

ADMISSIONS

Freshman Academic Profile: Average high school GPA 3.4. 78% from public high schools. **Reported SAT (pre-2016 redesign) scores:** SAT Math middle 50% range 470-560. SAT Critical Reading middle 50% range 490-590. SAT Writing middle 50% range 480-570. **Concordant SAT scores:** SAT EBRW middle 50% 540–640. SAT Math middle 50% range 510–580. ACT middle 50% range 22-26. Minimum internet-based TOEFL 75. Minimum paper TOEFL 550. **Basis for Candidate Selection:** *Very important factors considered include:* rigor of secondary school record. *Important factors considered include:* academic GPA, standardized test scores, application essay, recommendation(s), extracurricular activities, talent/ability, character/personal qualities, alumni/ae relation, volunteer work. *Other factors considered include:* first generation, geographical residence, state residency, racial/ethnic status, work experience, level of applicant's interest. **Freshman Admission Requirements:** High school diploma is required and GED is accepted. *Academic units required:* 4 English, 3 math, 2 science, 1 science lab, 3 social studies, 1 history, 2 academic electives. *Academic units recommended:* 4 English, 4 math, 4 science, 2 science labs, 2 foreign language, 4 social studies, 4 history. **Freshman Admission Statistics:** 4,794 applied, 55.05% admitted, 23% enrolled. **Transfer Admission**

Requirements: college transcript(s), essay or personal statement, Minimum college GPA of 2.0 required. Lowest grade transferable C. **General Admission Information:** Application fee $50. Priority deadline 11/1. Regular application deadline 3/1. Regular notification 3/31. Nonfall registration accepted. Admission may be deferred for a maximum of 1 semester.

COSTS AND FINANCIAL AID

Annual tuition $18,200. Room and board $10,688. Average book expense $1,000. **Required Forms and Deadlines:** FAFSA, State aid form. **Notification of Awards:** Applicants will be notified of awards on a rolling basis beginning 3/1. **Types of Aid:** *Need-based scholarships/grants:* Federal Pell, FSEOG, State scholarships/grants, Private scholarships, College/university scholarship or grant aid from institutional funds. *Loans:* Direct Subsidized Stafford Loans, Direct Unsubsidized Stafford Loans, Direct PLUS loans, Federal Perkins Loans. *Student Employment:* Federal Work-Study Program available. Institutional employment available. **Financial Aid Statistics:** 100% needy freshmen receive need-based scholarship or grant aid. 12% freshmen, 7% undergrads receive non-need-based scholarship or grant aid. 92% undergrads receive need-based self-help aid. 3% freshmen, 4% undergrads receive athletic scholarships. 88% freshmen, 87% undergrads receive any aid. 69% undergrads borrow to pay for school. Average cumulative indebtedness $29,267. **Criteria for awarding aid:** *Need-based:* Academics, Art, Athletics, Job skills, Leadership, Minority status, Music/drama. *Non-need-based:* Academics, Art, Athletics, Job skills, Leadership, Minority status, Music/drama, Religious affiliation, State/district residency.

FLORIDA AGRICULTURE AND MECHANICAL UNIVERSITY

Room 204, Tallahassee, FL 32307-3200
Phone: 850-599-3796 • **Financial Aid Phone:** 850-599-3730
E-mail: ugrdadmissions@famu.edu • **CEEB Code:** 5215
Fax: 850-599-3069 • **Website:** www.famu.edu • **ACT Code:** 726

This public school was founded in 1887. It has a 419-acre campus.

RATINGS

Admissions Selectivity Rating: 86   **Fire Safety Rating:** 98   **Green Rating:** 60*

STUDENTS AND FACULTY

Enrollment: 7,365. **Student Body:** 65% female, 35% male, 13% out-of-state, 1% international (42 countries represented). Asian 1%, African American 90%, Caucasian 3%, Hispanic 2%, Native American <1%, Pacific Islander <1%, Two or more races 3%, Race unknown 0%.
Retention and Graduation: 83% freshmen return for sophomore year. 35% grads go on to further study within 1 year. 7% grads pursue arts and sciences degrees. 2% grads pursue law degrees. 6% grads pursue business degrees. 4% grads pursue medical degrees. **Faculty:** 544 full-time faculty, 74% hold PhDs, 81% are are members of minority groups, 46% are women. 0% of classes are taught by teaching assistants.

ACADEMICS

Degrees: associate, bachelor's, doctoral/professional, doctoral/research, master's, post-master's certificate. **Classes:** Most classes have fewer than 10 students. **Most popular majors:** Criminal Justice/Safety Studies; Business Administration and Management; Biology/Biological Sciences. **Special Study Options:** Accelerated program, cooperative education program, distance learning, double major, dual enrollment, honors program, independent study, internships, study abroad, teacher certification program, weekend college. **Honors Programs:** Florida Agricultural and Mechanical University Honors Program provides a series of challenging courses and academic enhancement experiences for undergraduate students who excel. Enhancement of academic performance in critical thinking skills, in essence, will lead to consummate intellectual engagement and strong research orientation as a launch to both graduate and professional schools, as well as career paths. The program stresses four major areas of concentration: academic achievement, development of leadership potential, community service and cultural enrichment. Combined degree programs: Occupational Therapy, MBA. **Disability Services:** Special programs offered to physically disabled students, including note-taking services, reader services, tape recorders, tutors. **Career Services:** Alumni network, Alumni services, Career/job search classes, Career assessment, Internships, Regional alumni. Internship and permanent placement opportunities.

FACILITIES

Housing: Coed dorms, men's dorms, women's dorms, apartments for married students, Outside housing (Apartment Complexes) agreement through the University. 90% of campus accessible to physically disabled. **Special Academic Facilities/Equipment:** Black Archives and Resource Ctr. Coleman Memorial

Library Foster Tanner Music/Art Bldg. **Computers:** 90% of classrooms, 100% of dorms, 100% of libraries, 100% of dining areas, 100% of student union, 60% of common outdoor areas have wireless network access. Students can register for classes online. Administrative functions (other than registration) can be performed online.

CAMPUS LIFE

Environment: City. **Activities:** Choral groups, concert band, dance, drama/theater, jazz band, marching band, music ensembles, pep band, radio station, student government, student newspaper, symphony orchestra, television station, yearbook. 145 registered organizations, 16 honor societies, 11 religious organizations. 4 fraternities, 4 sororities. **Athletics (Intercollegiate):** *Men:* baseball, basketball, cheerleading, cross-country, football, golf, swimming, tennis, track/field (outdoor), track/field (indoor). *Women:* basketball, bowling, cheerleading, cross-country, golf, softball, swimming, tennis, track/field (outdoor), track/field (indoor), volleyball. **On-Campus Highlights:** The Black Archives, FAMU/FSU College of Engineering, Athletic Department, Army/Navy ROTC, Alfred Lawson Jr. Multipurpose Center and Teaching Gymnasium. **Environmental Initiatives:** Establishment of an advisory body—the Environment & Sustainability Council to design and oversee the implementation of a sustainability strategic plan which informs and guides the various operatives on campus of the principles of sustainability as they apply specifically to the respective facets of the University—Administrative, Academic, Operations and Community.

ADMISSIONS

Freshman Academic Profile: Average high school GPA 3.5. 16% in top 10% of high school class, 48% in top 25% of high school class, 85% in top 50% of high school class. 87% from public high schools. **Reported SAT (pre-2016 redesign) scores:** SAT Math middle 50% range 440-530. SAT Critical Reading middle 50% range 460-550. SAT Writing middle 50% range 440-520. **Concordant SAT scores:** SAT EBRW middle 50% 500–590. SAT Math middle 50% range 480–560. ACT middle 50% range 19-24. Minimum internet-based TOEFL 61. Minimum paper TOEFL 500. **Basis for Candidate Selection:** *Very important factors considered include:* rigor of secondary school record, academic GPA, standardized test scores, application essay, recommendation(s), first generation. *Important factors considered include:* extracurricular activities, talent/ability, character/personal qualities, state residency. *Other factors considered include:* alumni/ae relation, volunteer work, work experience. **Freshman Admission Requirements:** High school diploma is required and GED is accepted. *Academic units required:* 4 English, 4 math, 3 science, 2 science labs, 2 foreign language, 3 social studies, 2 academic electives. **Freshman Admission Statistics:** 6,988 applied, 31.11% admitted, 50% enrolled. **Transfer Admission Requirements:** college transcript(s), Minimum college GPA of 2.0 required. Lowest grade transferable C. **General Admission Information:** Application fee $30. Regular application deadline 5/15. Nonfall registration accepted.

COSTS AND FINANCIAL AID

Annual in-state tuition $5,645. Annual out-of-state tuition $17,585. Room and board $10,058. Required fees $140. Average book expense $1,138. **Required Forms and Deadlines:** FAFSA. **Notification of Awards:** Applicants will be notified of awards on a rolling basis beginning 4/15. **Types of Aid:** *Need-based scholarships/grants:* Federal Pell, FSEOG, State scholarships/grants, Private scholarships, College/university scholarship or grant aid from institutional funds, United Negro College Fund. *Loans:* Direct Subsidized Stafford Loans, Direct Unsubsidized Stafford Loans, Direct PLUS loans, Federal Perkins Loans. *Student Employment:* Federal Work-Study Program available. Institutional employment available. **Financial Aid Statistics:** 90% needy freshmen, 86% needy undergrads receive need-based scholarship or grant aid. 50% freshmen, 39% undergrads receive non-need-based scholarship or grant aid. 75% freshmen, 75% undergrads receive need-based self-help aid. 3% freshmen, 3% undergrads receive athletic scholarships. 96% freshmen, 70% undergrads receive any aid. Average cumulative indebtedness $34. **Criteria for awarding aid:** *Need-based:* Academics, Art, Leadership. *Non-need-based:* Academics, Art, Athletics, Leadership, Music/drama.

FLORIDA ATLANTIC UNIVERSITY

777 Glades Road, Boca Raton, FL 33431-0991
Phone: 561-297-3040 • **Financial Aid Phone:** 561-297-3530
E-mail: admissions@fau.edu • **CEEB Code:** 5229
Fax: 561-297-2758 • **Website:** www.fau.edu • **ACT Code:** 729

This public school was founded in 1961. It has a 860-acre campus.

RATINGS

Admissions Selectivity Rating: 84   **Fire Safety Rating:** 98   **Green Rating:** 60*

STUDENTS AND FACULTY

Enrollment: 24,228. **Student Body:** 57% female, 43% male, 5% out-of-state, 2% international. Asian 4%, African American 20%, Caucasian 45%, Hispanic 25%, Native American <1%, Pacific Islander <1%, Two or more races 3%, Race unknown 1%.
Retention and Graduation: 16% freshmen graduate within 4 years. **Faculty:** Student/faculty ratio 20:1. 730 full-time faculty, 87% hold PhDs, 26% are are members of minority groups, 42% are women. 15% of classes are taught by teaching assistants.

ACADEMICS

Degrees: associate, bachelor's, certificate, doctoral/professional, doctoral/research, doctoral, master's, post-master's certificate, transfer. **Classes:** Most classes have 20-29 students. Most lab/discussion sessions have 20-29 students. **Most popular majors:** Education; Biology/Biological Sciences; Psychology. **Special Study Options:** Accelerated program, cooperative education program, cross-registration, distance learning, double major, dual enrollment, English as a Second Language (ESL), honors program, independent study, internships, liberal arts/career combination, study abroad, teacher certification program, weekend college. **Honors Programs:** The Harriet L. Wilkes Honors College of Florida Atlantic University, which opened in the Fall of 1999, is the first public honors institution to be built from the ground up in the United States. Its intellectual foundation is a belief in liberal arts education as the best preparation for a full and productive life. The University Scholars Program is the honors program located on the Boca Raton campus. It is for freshman and sophomore students. The historical mission of a liberal arts education has been to develop the qualities of a free and responsible citizen, one who can reason clearly, read analytically, argue persuasively in speech and in writing, and contribute in fundamental and innovative ways to a chosen field of study or work. Combined degree programs: BA/MEng. **Disability Services:** Special programs offered to physically disabled students, including note-taking services, reader services, tape recorders, tutors. **Career Services:** Alumni network, Alumni services, Career/job search classes, Career assessment, Internships, Regional alumni.

FACILITIES

Housing: Coed dorms, apartments for married students, apartments for single students. 100% of campus accessible to physically diasbled. **Special Academic Facilities/Equipment:** Art gallery, on-campus elementary school, robotics lab, marine research facilities. **Computers:** Students can register for classes online. Administrative functions (other than registration) can be performed online.

CAMPUS LIFE

Environment: City. **Activities:** Choral groups, dance, drama/theater, jazz band, literary magazine, marching band, music ensembles, musical theater, opera, radio station, student government, student newspaper, television station 150 registered organizations, 11 honor societies, 6 religious organizations. 9 fraternities, 4 sororities. **Athletics (Intercollegiate):** *Men:* baseball, basketball, cheerleading, cross-country, diving, football, golf, soccer, swimming, tennis. *Women:* basketball, cheerleading, cross-country, diving, golf, soccer, softball, swimming, tennis, track/field (outdoor), volleyball. **On-Campus Highlights:** Student Services Building, Student Union, Dining Hall, Breezeway, Residence Halls. **Environmental Initiatives:** All new construction is designed and built to a minimum LEED silver certification level. This has been surpassed on every project to date, FAU currently has 1 platinum, 5 gold, and 2 pending gold certified buildings.

ADMISSIONS

Freshman Academic Profile: Average high school GPA 3.5. 11% in top 10% of high school class, 35% in top 25% of high school class, 78% in top 50% of high school class. **Reported SAT (pre-2016 redesign) scores:** SAT Math middle 50% range 490-580. SAT Critical Reading middle 50% range 480-570. SAT Writing middle 50% range 480-560. **Concordant SAT scores:** SAT EBRW middle 50% 540–620. SAT Math middle 50% range 520–600. ACT middle 50% range 21-25. Minimum internet-based TOEFL 80. Minimum paper TOEFL 550. **Basis for Candidate Selection:** *Very important factors considered include:* academic GPA, standardized test scores. *Important factors considered include:* rigor of secondary school record, class rank. *Other factors considered include:* application essay, recommendation(s), extracurricular activities, talent/ability, character/personal qualities, first generation, alumni/ae relation, volunteer work, level of applicant's interest. **Freshman Admission Requirements:** High school diploma is required and GED is accepted. *Academic units required:* 4 English, 4 math, 3 science, 2 science labs, 2 foreign language, 3 social studies, 3 academic electives. *Academic units recommended:* 4 English, 4 math, 3 science, 2 science labs, 2 foreign language, 3 social studies, 3 academic electives. **Freshman Admission Statistics:** 27,888 applied, 39.00% admitted, 30% enrolled. **Transfer Admission Requirements:** college transcript(s), Minimum college GPA of 3.0 required. Lowest grade transferable D-. **General Admission Information:** Application fee $30. Priority deadline 2/15. Regular application deadline 5/1. Nonfall registration accepted. Admission may be deferred for a maximum of 3 semesters.

COSTS AND FINANCIAL AID

Annual in-state tuition $5,986. Annual out-of-state tuition $21,543. Room and board $11,353. Average book expense $1,203. **Required Forms and Deadlines:** FAFSA. **Notification of Awards:** Applicants will be notified of awards on a rolling basis beginning 5/1. **Types of Aid:** *Need-based scholarships/grants:* Federal Pell, FSEOG, State scholarships/grants, Private scholarships, College/university scholarship or grant aid from institutional funds, Federal Nursing Scholarships. *Loans:* Federal Perkins Loans, College/university loans from institutional funds. *Student Employment:* Federal Work-Study Program available. Institutional employment available. **Financial Aid Statistics:** 91% needy freshmen, 86% needy undergrads receive need-based scholarship or grant aid. 7% freshmen, 5% undergrads receive non-need-based scholarship or grant aid. 71% freshmen, 75% undergrads receive need-based self-help aid. 1% freshmen, 1% undergrads receive athletic scholarships. **Criteria for awarding aid:** *Need-based:* Academics. *Non-need-based:* Academics, Athletics, Music/drama, State/district residency.

FLORIDA COLLEGE

Admissions Office, Temple Terrace, FL 33617-5578
Phone: 813-988-5131 • **Financial Aid Phone:** 813-988-5131
E-mail: Admissions@FloridaCollege.edu • **CEEB Code:** 1562
Fax: 813-899-6722 • **Website:** www.floridacollege.edu • **ACT Code:** 1482

This private school was founded in 1946.

RATINGS

Admissions Selectivity Rating: 78   **Fire Safety Rating:** 97   **Green Rating:** 60*

STUDENTS AND FACULTY

Enrollment: 533. **Student Body:** 51% female, 49% male, 63% out-of-state, 4% international (6 countries represented). Asian 0%, African American 6%, Caucasian 77%, Hispanic 7%, Native American 1%, Pacific Islander 0%, Two or more races 5%, Race unknown 1%.
Faculty: Student/faculty ratio 13:1. 34 full-time faculty, 44% hold PhDs, 9% are are members of minority groups, 21% are women. 0% of classes are taught by teaching assistants.

ACADEMICS

Degrees: associate, bachelor's, transfer. **Classes:** Most classes have fewer than 10 students. Most lab/discussion sessions have 10-19 students. **Most popular majors:** Elementary Education and Teaching; Liberal Arts and Sciences/Liberal Studies; Business Administration and Management. **Special Study Options:** cross-registration, double major, independent study, teacher certification program. **Disability Services:** Special programs offered to physically disabled students, including tape recorders, tutors. **Career Services:** On-campus interviews.

FACILITIES

Housing: special housing for disabled students, men's dorms, women's dorms.

CAMPUS LIFE

Environment: Town. **Activities:** Choral groups, concert band, drama/theater, jazz band, literary magazine, music ensembles, musical theater, pep band, student government, yearbook. **Athletics (Intercollegiate):** *Men:* basketball, cross-country, soccer. *Women:* cheerleading, cross-country, soccer, volleyball. **On-Campus Highlights:** Riverwalk, Student Center.

ADMISSIONS

Reported SAT (pre-2016 redesign) scores: SAT Math middle 50% range 460-580. SAT Critical Reading middle 50% range 460-630. SAT Writing middle 50% range 515-640. **Concordant SAT scores:** SAT EBRW middle 50% 550–680. SAT Math middle 50% range 500–600. ACT middle 50% range 20-26. Minimum paper TOEFL 550. **Basis for Candidate Selection:** *Very important factors considered include:* rigor of secondary school record, academic GPA, standardized test scores, recommendation(s), character/personal qualities, religious affiliation/commitment. *Important factors considered include:* class rank, level of applicant's interest. *Other factors considered include:* talent/ability, alumni/ae relation. **Freshman Admission Requirements:** High school diploma is required and GED is accepted. *Academic units required:* 4 English, 3 math, 2 science, 2 science labs, 2 social studies. *Academic units recommended:* 2 foreign language, 3 social studies. **Freshman Admission Statistics:** 284 applied, 78.52% admitted, 71% enrolled. **Transfer Admission Requirements:** High school transcript, college transcript(s), standardized test scores, statement of good standing from prior institution(s). Minimum college GPA of 2.0 required. Lowest grade transferable C. **General Admission Information:** Application fee $40. Regular application deadline 8/1. Nonfall registration accepted.

COSTS AND FINANCIAL AID

Annual tuition $15,670. Room and board $8,230. Required fees $880. Average book expense $1,300. **Required Forms and Deadlines:** FAFSA, State aid form. **Notification of Awards:** Applicants will be notified of awards on a rolling basis beginning 9/30. **Types of Aid:** *Need-based scholarships/grants:* Federal Pell, FSEOG, State scholarships/grants, Private scholarships, College/university scholarship or grant aid from institutional funds. *Loans:* Federal Perkins Loans. **Financial Aid Statistics:** 83% needy freshmen, 86% needy undergrads receive need-based scholarship or grant aid. 94% freshmen, 92% undergrads receive non-need-based scholarship or grant aid. 76% freshmen, 77% undergrads receive need-based self-help aid. 3% freshmen, 13% undergrads receive athletic scholarships. **Criteria for awarding aid:** *Need-based:* Academics, Athletics, Music/drama. *Non-need-based:* Academics, Athletics, Music/drama, State/district residency.

FLORIDA GULF COAST UNIVERSITY

10501 FGCU Blvd. South, Fort Myers, FL 33965-6565
Phone: 239-590-7878 • **Financial Aid Phone:** 239-590-7920
E-mail: admissions@fgcu.edu • **CEEB Code:** 5221
Fax: 239-590-7894 • **ACT Code:** 733

This public school was founded in 1991. It has a 760-acre campus.

RATINGS

Admissions Selectivity Rating: 79   **Fire Safety Rating:** 95   **Green Rating:** 90

STUDENTS AND FACULTY

Enrollment: 12,773. **Student Body:** 55% female, 45% male, 7% out-of-state, 2% international (89 countries represented). Asian 2%, African American 7%, Caucasian 67%, Hispanic 19%, Native American <1%, Pacific Islander <1%, Two or more races 2%, Race unknown 1%.
Retention and Graduation: 76% freshmen return for sophomore year.
Faculty: Student/faculty ratio 23:1. 429 full-time faculty, 72% hold PhDs, 17% are are members of minority groups, 45% are women. 0% of classes are taught by teaching assistants.

ACADEMICS

Degrees: associate, bachelor's, certificate, doctoral/professional, master's, transfer. **Classes:** Most classes have 20-29 students. **Most popular majors:** Elementary Education and Teaching; Liberal Arts and Sciences/Liberal Studies; Business/Commerce. **Special Study Options:** Accelerated program, cross-registration, distance learning, double major, dual enrollment, honors program, independent study, internships, student-designed major, study abroad, teacher certification program. **Honors Programs:** The University Honors Program at Florida Gulf Coast University offers special opportunities for superior students to pursue academic work that challenges their interests and abilities. The program is university-wide, which gives students full access to the faculty and the entire range of programs at FGCU. Since the honors program at Florida Gulf Coast University is exclusive, we have the ability to design a unique program for each individual student. Scholarship opportunities and special programs that support the honors student's educational, intellectual, and personal goals will be designed individually with the student and his or her faculty mentor. Combined degree programs: Nursing, BS/MS. **Disability Services:** Special programs offered to physically disabled students, including note-taking services, reader services, tape recorders, tutors. **Career Services:** Alumni network, Alumni services, Career/job search classes, Career assessment, Internships, On-campus interviews.

FACILITIES

Housing: Coed dorms, special housing for disabled students, apartments for single students. 100% of campus accessible to physically diasbled. **Special Academic Facilities/Equipment:** Art Gallery, Observatory **Computers:** Students can register for classes online. Administrative functions (other than registration) can be performed online.

CAMPUS LIFE

Environment: City. **Activities:** Choral groups, dance, drama/theater, literary magazine, radio station, student government, student newspaper. 105 registered organizations, 7 honor societies, 8 religious organizations. 4 fraternities, 4 sororities. **Athletics (Intercollegiate):** *Men:* baseball, basketball, cross-country, golf, soccer, tennis. *Women:* basketball, cross-country, diving, golf, soccer, softball, swimming, tennis, volleyball. **On-Campus Highlights:** Alico Arena, Student Union, The Quad, The Library, Baseball/Softball fields.

ADMISSIONS

Freshman Academic Profile: Average high school GPA 3.3. 11% in top 10% of high school class, 36% in top 25% of high school class, 77% in top 50% of high school class. **Reported SAT (pre-2016 redesign) scores:** SAT Math middle 50% range 470-550. SAT Critical Reading middle 50% range 470-550. SAT Writing middle 50% range 450-540. **Concordant SAT scores:** SAT EBRW middle 50% 510–600. SAT Math middle 50% range 510–570. ACT middle 50% range 20-24. Minimum internet-based TOEFL 79. Minimum paper TOEFL 550. **Basis for Candidate Selection:** *Very important factors considered include:* academic GPA, standardized test scores. *Important factors considered include:* rigor of secondary school record. *Other factors considered include:* class rank, recommendation(s). **Freshman Admission Requirements:** High school diploma is required and GED is accepted. *Academic units required:* 4 English, 3 math, 3 science, 2 science labs, 2 foreign language, 3 social studies, and 3 units from above areas or other academic areas. **Freshman Admission Statistics:** 10,804 applied, 65.79% admitted, 39% enrolled. **Transfer Admission Requirements:** college transcript(s), Minimum college GPA of 2.0 required. Lowest grade transferable D. **General Admission Information:** Application fee $30. Priority deadline 2/15. Regular application deadline 5/1. Nonfall registration accepted. Admission may be deferred for a maximum of 2 Semesters.

COSTS AND FINANCIAL AID

Average book expense $1,200. **Required Forms and Deadlines:** FAFSA. **Types of Aid:** *Need-based scholarships/grants:* Federal Pell, FSEOG, State scholarships/grants, Private scholarships, College/university scholarship or grant aid from institutional funds. *Student Employment:* Federal Work-Study Program available. Institutional employment available. **Financial Aid Statistics:** 62% needy freshmen, 64% needy undergrads receive need-based scholarship or grant aid. 67% freshmen, 31% undergrads receive non-need-based scholarship or grant aid. 61% freshmen, 66% undergrads receive need-based self-help aid. 1% freshmen, 1% undergrads receive athletic scholarships. 88% freshmen, 35% undergrads receive any aid. **Criteria for awarding aid:** *Need-based:* Academics, Athletics, Leadership, Minority status, Religious affiliation. *Non-need-based:* Academics, Alumni affiliation, Athletics, Leadership, Minority status, Music/drama, Religious affiliation, State/district residency.

FLORIDA INSTITUTE OF TECHNOLOGY

150 West University Boulevard, Melbourne, FL 32901-6975
Phone: 321-674-8030 • **Financial Aid Phone:** 800-666-4348
E-mail: admission@fit.edu • **CEEB Code:** 5080
Fax: 321-674-8004 • **Website:** http://www.fit.edu • **ACT Code:** 716

This private school was founded in 1958. It has a 130-acre campus.

RATINGS

Admissions Selectivity Rating: 87   **Fire Safety Rating:** 86   **Green Rating:** 80

STUDENTS AND FACULTY

Enrollment: 3,419. **Student Body:** 30% female, 70% male, 49% out-of-state, 33% international (112 countries represented). Asian 2%, African American 6%, Caucasian 44%, Hispanic 7%, Native American <1%, Pacific Islander <1%, Two or more races 2%, Race unknown 4%.
Retention and Graduation: 83% freshmen return for sophomore year. 45% freshmen graduate within 4 years. 58% freshmen graduate within 6 years. 35% grads go on to further study within 1 year. 13% grads pursue arts and sciences degrees. 1% grads pursue law degrees. 5% grads pursue business degrees. **Faculty:** Student/faculty ratio 14:1. 311 full-time faculty, 86% hold PhDs, 22% are are members of minority groups, 25% are women. 0% of classes are taught by teaching assistants.

ACADEMICS

Degrees: bachelor's, doctoral/professional, doctoral/research, master's, post-master's certificate. **Classes:** Most classes have 10-19 students. Most lab/discussion sessions have 10-19 students. **Most popular majors:** Mechanical Engineering; Aerospace, Aeronautical and Astronautical/Space Engineering; Computer Science. **Special Study Options:** Accelerated program, cooperative education program, cross-registration, distance learning, double major, dual enrollment, English as a Second Language (ESL), independent study, internships, study abroad, teacher certification program, Dual degrees in computer engineering/electrical engineering, chemical engineering/chemistry, molecular/marine biology. **Disability Services:** Special programs offered to physically disabled students, including note-taking services, reader services, tutors. **Career Services:** Alumni services, Career/job search classes, Internships. Internships.

FACILITIES

Housing: Coed dorms, apartments for single students, Wellness Housing. 99% of campus accessible to physically disabled. **Special Academic Facilities/Equipment:** New facility openings have been the highlight of 2009, beginning

in February with the dedication of the Emil Buehler Center for Aviation Training and Research at Melbourne International Airport. The center, valued at $5.1 million, consists of a main building and 17,600-square-foot hanger, located on eight acres at the airport. The new building houses the operations of F.I.T. Aviation. In August, the university's Department of Humanities got a boost with the opening of the 3,000-square-foot Ruth Funk Center for Textile Arts. The only textiles center in the state of Florida, the facility is dedicated to furthering the understanding of cultural and creative achievements in the textile and fine arts. October gave another boost to the College of Psychology and Liberal Arts with the opening of the Scott Center for Autism Treatment. The 18,000-square-foot center provides services for individuals with autism spectrum disorder, training for parents, teachers and other professionals and research on effective treatments for autism. The College of Engineering and College of Science also gained a new building in October with the opening of the Harris Center for Science and Engineering. While computer science and marine biology laboratories fill two-thirds of the building, the rest is dedicated to the Harris Institute for Assured Information. The institute is already recognized for its work and numerous government and national foundation contracts. The College of Business received a tremendous boost in 2009 with a $5 million gift from Nathan M. Bisk, a leader in continuing education and online learning. The gift enhances business programs offerings and strengthens online education and marks the start of fund-raising for a new building, to be named the Nathan M. Bisk College of Business. **Computers:** 100% of classrooms, 30% of dorms, 100% of libraries, 100% of dining areas, 100% of student union, 5% of common outdoor areas have wireless network access. Students can register for classes online. Administrative functions (other than registration) can be performed online.

CAMPUS LIFE

Environment: Town. **Activities:** Choral groups, dance, drama/theater, literary magazine, pep band, radio station, student government, student newspaper, television station, Campus Ministries, Student Organization. 106 registered organizations, 8 honor societies, 3 religious organizations. 7 fraternities, 3 sororities. **Athletics (Intercollegiate):** *Men:* baseball, basketball, cross-country, golf, soccer, tennis. *Women:* basketball, crew/rowing, cross-country, golf, soccer, softball, tennis, volleyball. **On-Campus Highlights:** Student Union Building, Clemente Center for Sports & Recreation, Olin Engineering Complex, Harris Village, Botanical Gardens. **Environmental Initiatives:** The university recently created a Sustainability office with the university's first Sustainability Officer. The office is tasked to: -Develop, plan, coordinate and implement activities related to sustainability systems. -Utility analytics -Develop and lead campus-wide campaign to reduce energy consumption. -Integrate sustainable practices into Facilities' standard practices while encouraging and facilitating other sustainability programs across campus.

ADMISSIONS

Freshman Academic Profile: Average high school GPA 3.7. 33% in top 10% of high school class, 60% in top 25% of high school class, 89% in top 50% of high school class. 41% from public high schools. **Reported SAT (pre-2016 redesign) scores:** SAT Math middle 50% range 560-650. SAT Critical Reading middle 50% range 500-610. **Concordant SAT scores:** SAT Math middle 50% range 580–670. ACT middle 50% range 24-29. Minimum internet-based TOEFL 79. **Basis for Candidate Selection:** *Very important factors considered include:* rigor of secondary school record, academic GPA, standardized test scores. *Important factors considered include:* level of applicant's interest. *Other factors considered include:* class rank, application essay, recommendation(s), interview, extracurricular activities, character/personal qualities, alumni/ae relation, work experience. **Freshman Admission Requirements:** High school diploma is required and GED is accepted. *Academic units required:* 4 English, 3 math, 3 science, 3 science labs, 2 social studies, 2 history, 2 academic electives. *Academic units recommended:* 4 English, 4 math, 4 science, 3 science labs, 2 foreign language, 2 social studies, 2 history, 2 academic electives, 2 computer science. **Freshman Admission Statistics:** 9,503 applied, 61.33% admitted, 13% enrolled. **Transfer Admission Requirements:** college transcript(s), Minimum college GPA of 2.5 required. Lowest grade transferable C. **General Admission Information:** Priority deadline 2/1. Nonfall registration accepted. Admission may be deferred for a maximum of 12 month.

COSTS AND FINANCIAL AID

Required Forms and Deadlines: FAFSA, CSS/Financial Aid PROFILE. **Notification of Awards:** Applicants will be notified of awards on a rolling basis beginning 2/15. **Types of Aid:** *Need-based scholarships/grants:* Federal Pell, FSEOG, State scholarships/grants, Private scholarships, College/university scholarship or grant aid from institutional funds. *Loans:* Direct Subsidized Stafford Loans, Direct Unsubsidized Stafford Loans, Direct PLUS loans, Federal Perkins Loans. *Student Employment:* Federal Work-Study Program available. Institutional employment available. **Financial Aid Statistics:** 100% needy freshmen, 100% needy undergrads receive need-based scholarship or grant aid. 100% freshmen, 97% undergrads receive non-need-based scholarship or grant aid. 71% freshmen, 72% undergrads receive need-based self-help aid. 5% freshmen, 5% undergrads receive athletic scholarships. 97% freshmen, 85%

undergrads receive any aid. 52% undergrads borrow to pay for school. Average cumulative indebtedness $36,678. **Criteria for awarding aid:** *Need-based:* Academics, Minority status. *Non-need-based:* Academics, Alumni affiliation, Athletics, Music/drama, State/district residency.

FLORIDA INTERNATIONAL UNIVERSITY

Modesto Maidique Campus, Miami, FL 33199
Phone: 305-348-2363 • **Financial Aid Phone:** 305-348-7272
E-mail: admiss@fiu.edu • **CEEB Code:** 5206
Fax: 305-348-3648 • **Website:** www.fiu.edu • **ACT Code:** 776

This public school was founded in 1965. It has a 573-acre campus.

RATINGS
Admissions Selectivity Rating: 86   **Fire Safety Rating:** 97   **Green Rating:** 60*

STUDENTS AND FACULTY
Enrollment: 41,133. **Student Body:** 56% female, 44% male, 3% out-of-state, 6% international (151 countries represented). Asian 3%, African American 12%, Caucasian 9%, Hispanic 67%, Native American <1%, Pacific Islander <1%, Two or more races 3%, Race unknown 1%.
Retention and Graduation: 88% freshmen return for sophomore year. 25% freshmen graduate within 4 years. 56% freshmen graduate within 6 years.
Faculty: Student/faculty ratio 26:1. 1,275 full-time faculty, 86% hold PhDs, 39% are are members of minority groups, 42% are women.

ACADEMICS
Degrees: associate, bachelor's, certificate, doctoral/professional, doctoral/research, master's, postbachelor's certificate. **Classes:** Most classes have 20-29 students. Most lab/discussion sessions have 20-29 students. **Most popular majors:** Business Administration and Management; Biology/Biological Sciences; Psychology. **Special Study Options:** Accelerated program, cooperative education program, distance learning, double major, dual enrollment, exchange student program (domestic), honors program, independent study, internships, study abroad, teacher certification program, weekend college. Combined degree programs: BA/JD, BA/MA, BA/MEng, Computer,Economics, Asian Studies, Relations, Political Science, Spanish, Art History, Lideral Studies. **Disability Services:** Special programs offered to physically disabled students, including note-taking services, reader services, tape recorders, tutors. **Career Services:** Alumni services, Career/job search classes, Career assessment, Internships, Regional alumni. We are particularly proud of our Executive Protege Initiative that is designed for students who commit quality time to attend career readiness presentations and professional development activities. We are also proud of our yearly Federal Government Statewide Conference that brings together FIU students and federal agencies to help students freshman-graduate learn about internship and full-time opportunities in the federal government.

FACILITIES
Housing: Coed dorms, fraternity/sorority housing, apartments for married students, apartments for single students. 100% of campus accessible to physically diasbled. **Special Academic Facilities/Equipment:** The Frost Art Museum, The Wolfsonian Art Museum, Natural Preserve, Biscayne Bay Preserve **Computers:** 100% of classrooms, 100% of dorms, 1000% of libraries, 100% of dining areas, 100% of student union, 100% of common outdoor areas have wireless network access. Students can register for classes online. Administrative functions (other than registration) can be performed online.

CAMPUS LIFE
Environment: Metropolis. **Activities:** Choral groups, drama/theater, jazz band, music ensembles, opera, radio station, student government, student newspaper, symphony orchestra, yearbook, Campus Ministries, Student Organization, Model UN. 250 registered organizations, 40 honor societies, 5 religious organizations. 21 fraternities, 17 sororities. **Athletics (Intercollegiate):** *Men:* baseball, basketball, cross-country, football, soccer, track/field (outdoor), track/field (indoor). *Women:* basketball, cross-country, diving, golf, soccer, softball, swimming, tennis, track/field (outdoor), track/field (indoor), volleyball. **On-Campus Highlights:** The Frost Museum, The Wolfsonian Museum, Steven and Dorothea Green Library, Graham University Center, Biscayne Bay Campus Library, The Recreational Center. **Environmental Initiatives:** Spring 2011, FIU has officially become a smoking-free campus. Providing clean and smoke-free air to it's community.

ADMISSIONS
Freshman Academic Profile: Average high school GPA 3.9. 18% in top 10% of high school class, 47% in top 25% of high school class, 83% in top 50% of high school class. **Reported SAT (pre-2016 redesign) scores:** SAT Math middle 50% range 510-600. SAT Critical Reading middle 50% range 520-610.

SAT Writing middle 50% range 510-590. **Concordant SAT scores:** SAT EBRW middle 50% 570–650. SAT Math middle 50% range 540–620. ACT middle 50% range 23-27. Minimum paper TOEFL 500. **Basis for Candidate Selection:** *Very important factors considered include:* rigor of secondary school record, class rank, academic GPA, standardized test scores. *Other factors considered include:* application essay, recommendation(s), extracurricular activities, talent/ability, character/personal qualities, first generation, alumni/ae relation, geographical residence, state residency, volunteer work, work experience, level of applicant's interest. **Freshman Admission Requirements:** High school diploma is required and GED is accepted. *Academic units required:* 4 English, 4 math, 3 science, 2 science labs, 2 foreign language, 3 social studies, 2 academic electives. *Academic units recommended:* 4 English, 4 math, 3 science, 2 science labs, 2 foreign language, 3 social studies, 4 academic electives. **Freshman Admission Statistics:** 17,218 applied, 49.36% admitted, 37% enrolled. **Transfer Admission Requirements:** college transcript(s), statement of good standing from prior institution(s). Minimum college GPA of 2.0 required. Lowest grade transferable D. **General Admission Information:** Application fee $30. Regular application deadline 5/1. Regular notification 7/1. Nonfall registration accepted. Admission may be deferred for a maximum of 1 year.

COSTS AND FINANCIAL AID
Annual in-state tuition $6,168. Annual out-of-state tuition $18,566. Room and board $10,846. Required fees $390. Average book expense $1,540. **Required Forms and Deadlines:** FAFSA. **Types of Aid:** *Need-based scholarships/grants:* Federal Pell, FSEOG, State scholarships/grants, Private scholarships, College/university scholarship or grant aid from institutional funds. *Loans:* Direct Subsidized Stafford Loans, Direct Unsubsidized Stafford Loans, Direct PLUS loans, Federal Perkins Loans, College/university loans from institutional funds. *Student Employment:* Federal Work-Study Program available. Institutional employment available. **Financial Aid Statistics:** 66% needy freshmen, 79% needy undergrads receive need-based scholarship or grant aid. 45% freshmen, 32% undergrads receive non-need-based scholarship or grant aid. 41% freshmen, 53% undergrads receive need-based self-help aid. 1% freshmen, 1% undergrads receive athletic scholarships. 50% undergrads borrow to pay for school. Average cumulative indebtedness $19,915. **Criteria for awarding aid:** *Need-based:* Academics. *Non-need-based:* Academics, Art, Athletics, Minority status, Music/drama, State/district residency.

FLORIDA SOUTHERN COLLEGE

111 Lake Hollingworth Drive, Lakeland, FL 33801
Phone: 863-680-4131 • **Financial Aid Phone:** 863-680-4140
E-mail: fscadm@flsouthern.edu • **CEEB Code:** 5218
Fax: 863-680-4120 • **Website:** www.flsouthern.edu • **ACT Code:** 732

This private school, affiliated with the Methodist Church, was founded in 1883. It has a 100-acre campus.

RATINGS
Admissions Selectivity Rating: 89   **Fire Safety Rating:** 93   **Green Rating:** 69

STUDENTS AND FACULTY
Enrollment: 2,370. **Student Body:** 63% female, 37% male, 36% out-of-state, 4% international (40 countries represented). Asian 2%, African American 5%, Caucasian 74%, Hispanic 11%, Native American 1%, Pacific Islander <1%, Two or more races 2%, Race unknown 1%.
Retention and Graduation: 81% freshmen return for sophomore year. 53% freshmen graduate within 4 years. 60% freshmen graduate within 6 years. 24% grads go on to further study within 1 year. 6% grads pursue arts and sciences degrees. 1% grads pursue law degrees. 2% grads pursue business degrees. 2% grads pursue medical degrees. **Faculty:** Student/faculty ratio 14:1. 153 full-time faculty, 80% hold PhDs, 15% are are members of minority groups, 48% are women. 0% of classes are taught by teaching assistants.

ACADEMICS
Degrees: bachelor's, master's. **Classes:** Most classes have 10-19 students. Most lab/discussion sessions have 10-19 students. **Most popular majors:** Business Administration and Management; Biology/Biological Sciences; Registered Nursing/Registered Nurse. **Special Study Options:** double major, dual enrollment, honors program, independent study, internships, liberal arts/career combination, student-designed major, study abroad, teacher certification program, FSC Honors Program – USF College of Medicine Medical Education Program. **Honors Programs:** The mission of the Florida Southern College

Honors Program is to offer academically talented and highly motivated students opportunities to explore special topics through carefully constructed courses. Professors employ innovative teaching techniques that challenge students to explore subjects through multiple perspectives. The Honors Program fosters an interactive learning environment within a community of scholars. Combined degree programs: BA/MD, BA/MA, 3/2 Business Admin/MBA, 3/2 Enviromental Sci, 3/2 Accounting/Master of Accountancy, Pre-Med Honor's Program with USF College of Medicine Medical Education Program 3+/4+ Pharmacy 3+4/4+4 DO 4+4 Dental. **Career Services:** Alumni network, Alumni services, Career/job search classes, Career assessment, Internships, Regional alumni. Florida Southern College's Career Center guarantees each undergraduate student an internship, creating a bridge between a one's education and one's future. Faculty and Career Center staff members work with each student to procure an internship in his or her field, providing real-world, resume-building experience for each undergraduate. The center offers a four-year approach to success that guides each student into the best position to secure his or her future success by exploring career options, gaining hands-on experience, building their professional networks, investigating graduate school options, polishing their resumes, and honing interview skills. When it's time to graduate, students are prepared with job-relevant experience, a built-in professional network, and the confidence to launch successful careers.

FACILITIES

Housing: Coed dorms, special housing for disabled students, men's dorms, women's dorms, fraternity/sorority housing, apartments for married students, apartments for single students, Theme Housing. 85% of campus accessible to physically diasbled. **Special Academic Facilities/Equipment:** Campus designed by Frank Lloyd Wright; contains world's largest collection of Wright-designed structures at a single site. Also home to three buildings designed by world renowned architect Robert A.M. Stern: 2 residence halls and 1 classroom building, which includes an art gallery and film studies center. The science building features a planetarium; the communication building features a television studio. The latest two building additions are 1) a 24-hour, state-of-the-art Technology and Learning Center; and 2) a high-tech nursing building featuring virtual patient simulators. The college houses two newly renovated art galleries'—the Melvin and Burke Galleries. Also of note, FSC has a world-class performing arts venue seating 2200. Students enjoy a Wellness Center accompanied by an outdoor pool and a boathouse for water-skiing, sailing, and kayaking. At the center of campus is a spectacular, 50-foot high Water Dome, which is next to the library's Cyber Café, ewhich serves Starbuck's products. A spectacular Archives Center, also adjacent to the library, was completed within the past year. **Computers:** 20% of classrooms, 20% of dorms, 100% of libraries, 100% of dining areas, 50% of student union, 50% of common outdoor areas have wireless network access. Students can register for classes online. Administrative functions (other than registration) can be performed online.

CAMPUS LIFE

Environment: City. **Activities:** Choral groups, concert band, dance, drama/theater, jazz band, literary magazine, music ensembles, musical theater, opera, pep band, student government, student newspaper, symphony orchestra, television station, yearbook, Campus Ministries, Student Organization. 70 registered organizations, 22 honor societies, 9 religious organizations. 7 fraternities, 7 sororities. **Athletics (Intercollegiate):** *Men:* baseball, basketball, cross-country, golf, lacrosse, soccer, swimming, tennis, track/field (outdoor). *Women:* basketball, cross-country, golf, soccer, softball, swimming, tennis, track/field (outdoor), volleyball. **On-Campus Highlights:** Tutu's Cyber Cafe, Wellness Center and Pool, Badcock Garden's "outdoor living room", The Terrace Cafe, Field House, Our sunny campus offers something for everyone, including more than 70 clubs and organizations that cater to every interest. On beautiful Lake Hollingsworth, students enjoy free kayaking, sailing, and canoeing. Our state-of-the-art Wellness Center offers classes in everything from yoga to Pilates to water aerobics in our Olympic-sized pool. If the arts are more your speed, visit the Melvin Art Gallery, which exhibits the works of students and internationally recognized artists. Take in an opera, play, or concert through the renowned Festival of Fine Arts series, or catch a movie on the Badcock Garden lawn. Our championship Division II NCAA sports programs mean there's always something to cheer about, and intramural sports such as flag football, tennis, and soccer give you a chance to get in the game. And if you've worked up an appetite, grab lunch from the Grillmaster in the Badcock Garden or enjoy a cup of Starbuck's coffee and a bagel on the patio overlooking the Water Dome at the Cyber Café. **Environmental Initiatives:** Florida Southern College has installed filtered water bottle stations throughout campus that provide users with an opportunity to fill and refill reusable bottles rather than purchasing new filtered water bottles. Additionally, FSC Student Government Association distributes refillable water bottles to each new class at Orientation, encouraging new students to make use of the stations and to be environmentally minded from the start.

ADMISSIONS

Freshman Academic Profile: Average high school GPA 3.7. 29% in top 10% of high school class, 60% in top 25% of high school class, 89% in top 50% of high school class. 82% from public high schools. **Reported SAT**

(pre-2016 redesign) scores: SAT Math middle 50% range 520-620. SAT Critical Reading middle 50% range 520-610. SAT Writing middle 50% range 490-580. **Concordant SAT scores:** SAT EBRW middle 50% 560-650. SAT Math middle 50% range 550-640. ACT middle 50% range 24-29. Minimum paper TOEFL 550. **Basis for Candidate Selection:** *Very important factors considered include:* rigor of secondary school record, academic GPA. *Important factors considered include:* standardized test scores, application essay, recommendation(s), extracurricular activities, talent/ability, character/personal qualities, level of applicant's interest. *Other factors considered include:* class rank, interview, first generation, alumni/ae relation, religious affiliation/commitment, racial/ethnic status, volunteer work, work experience. **Freshman Admission Requirements:** High school diploma is required and GED is accepted. *Academic units required:* 4 English, 3 math, 2 science, 2 science labs, 3 social studies, 3 history, 1 academic elective. *Academic units recommended:* 2 foreign language. **Freshman Admission Statistics:** 6,192 applied, 45.54% admitted, 23% enrolled. **Transfer Admission Requirements:** college transcript(s), essay or personal statement, statement of good standing from prior institution(s). Minimum college GPA of 2.0 required. Lowest grade transferable C. **General Admission Information:** Application fee $30. Priority deadline 3/1. Nonfall registration accepted. Admission may be deferred for a maximum of 1 Year.

COSTS AND FINANCIAL AID

Required Forms and Deadlines: FAFSA, Institution's own financial aid form. **Notification of Awards:** Applicants will be notified of awards on a rolling basis beginning 3/1. **Types of Aid:** *Need-based scholarships/grants:* Federal Pell, FSEOG, State scholarships/grants, Private scholarships, College/university scholarship or grant aid from institutional funds, Federal Nursing Scholarships. *Loans:* Direct Subsidized Stafford Loans, Direct Unsubsidized Stafford Loans, Direct PLUS loans, Federal Perkins Loans. *Student Employment:* Federal Work-Study Program available. Institutional employment available. **Financial Aid Statistics:** 100% needy freshmen, 99% needy undergrads receive need-based scholarship or grant aid. 65% freshmen, 68% undergrads receive non-need-based scholarship or grant aid. 4% freshmen, 11% undergrads receive need-based self-help aid. 4% freshmen, 6% undergrads receive athletic scholarships. 99% freshmen, 98% undergrads receive any aid. 81% undergrads borrow to pay for school. Average cumulative indebtedness $26,637. **Criteria for awarding aid:** *Need-based:* Academics, Alumni affiliation, Art, Athletics, Job skills, Leadership, Minority status, Music/drama, Religious affiliation. *Non-need-based:* Academics, Alumni affiliation, Art, Athletics, Job skills, Leadership, Minority status, Music/drama, Religious affiliation, State/district residency.

FLORIDA STATE UNIVERSITY

PO Box 3062400, Tallahassee, FL 32306-2400
Phone: 850-644-6200 • **Financial Aid Phone:** 850-644-5716
E-mail: admissions@admin.fsu.edu • **CEEB Code:** 5219
Fax: 850-644-0197 • **Website:** www.fsu.edu • **ACT Code:** 734

This public school was founded in 1851. It has a 452-acre campus.

RATINGS

Admissions Selectivity Rating: 89   **Fire Safety Rating:** 86   **Green Rating:** 60*

STUDENTS AND FACULTY

Enrollment: 32,562. **Student Body:** 55% female, 45% male, 10% out-of-state, 1% international (106 countries represented). Asian 2%, African American 8%, Caucasian 63%, Hispanic 20%, Native American <1%, Pacific Islander <1%, Two or more races 3%, Race unknown 1%.
Retention and Graduation: 93% freshmen return for sophomore year. 61% freshmen graduate within 4 years. 80% freshmen graduate within 6 years. 42% grads go on to further study within 1 year. **Faculty:** Student/faculty ratio 26:1. 1,423 full-time faculty, 89% hold PhDs, 20% are are members of minority groups, 40% are women. 28% of classes are taught by teaching assistants.

ACADEMICS

Degrees: associate, bachelor's, certificate, doctoral/professional, doctoral/research, doctoral, master's, postbachelor's certifiate, post-master's certificate, transfer. **Classes:** Most classes have 20-29 students. Most lab/discussion sessions have 20-29 students. **Most popular majors:** Psychology; Criminal Justice/Safety Studies; Finance. **Special Study Options:** Accelerated program, cooperative education program, cross-registration, distance learning, double major, dual enrollment, English as a Second Language (ESL), honors program, independent study, internships, study abroad, teacher certification program. **Honors Programs:** The Florida State University Honors Program provides an enriched curriculum and special opportunities for exceptional, high-achieving students who are entering college for the first time. Each fall, freshmen who are admitted into this program attend the University Honors Colloquium, a weekly forum that features stimulating lectures by distinguished faculty as well as informative presentations from directors of academic programs. As they work to meet their liberal study requirements, University Honors students then have the chance to take small, honors-only courses and special topic seminars with some of the university's best researchers and teachers. With its emphasis on small classes taught by top faculty, this program provides the atmosphere of a small liberal arts college within a large research university. Combined degree programs: BA/MA. **Disability Services:** Special programs offered to physically disabled students, including note-taking services, reader services, tape recorders, tutors. **Career Services:** Alumni network, Alumni services, Career/job search classes, Career assessment, Internships, Regional alumni. Florida State University is committed to graduating engaged, career-ready students emphasizing skill building through experiential learning. Upon arrival at FSU, students are encouraged to request a Peer Involvement Mentor consultation to create a personalized #MyFSUExperience featuring on-campus experiential learning opportunities that align with career interests and post-graduation goals. During their time at FSU, The Career Center facilitates and recognizes student engagement in experiential learning, including:

1:1 Career Advising

Additionally, the Career Center refers students to offices across campus that specialize in high-impact specialized experiential learning opportunities in undergraduate research, global and intercultural experiences, fellowships, sustained service, and leadership. Prior to gradaution, the well-rounded undergraduate student who excels within and beyond the classroom can apply for induction into the prestigious Garnet & Gold Scholar Society (GGSS). All GGSS inductees synthesize how they developed their leadership, professional, citizenship and/or research skills while building collaborative relationships in the academic, local or global community.

FACILITIES

Housing: Coed dorms, special housing for disabled students, women's dorms, fraternity/sorority housing, apartments for married students, apartments for single students, On-campus: Honors Residences; Living Learning Communities Off-campus: Cooperative housing through Southern Scholarship Foundation; off-campus private residence halls. 99% of campus accessible to physically diasbled. **Special Academic Facilities/Equipment:** Art gallery, museum, developmental research school, marine lab, oceanographic institute, tandem Van de Graaff accelerator, national high magnetic field lab. **Computers:** 50% of classrooms, 25% of dorms, 90% of libraries, 100% of dining areas, 90% of student union, 70% of common outdoor areas have wireless network access. Students can register for classes online. Administrative functions (other than registration) can be performed online. Undergraduates are required to own a computer.

CAMPUS LIFE

Environment: City. **Activities:** Choral groups, concert band, dance, drama/theater, jazz band, literary magazine, marching band, music ensembles, musical theater, opera, pep band, radio station, student government, student newspaper, student-run film society, symphony orchestra, television station, yearbook, Campus Ministries, Student Organization, Model UN. 520 registered organizations, 23 honor societies, 30 religious organizations. 32 fraternities, 28 sororities. **Athletics (Intercollegiate):** *Men:* baseball, basketball, cheerleading, cross-country, diving, football, golf, swimming, tennis, track/field (outdoor), track/field (indoor). *Women:* basketball, cheerleading, cross-country, diving, golf, soccer, softball, swimming, tennis, track/field (outdoor), track/field (indoor), volleyball. **On-Campus Highlights:** Suwannee Dining Hall, Bobby E. Leach Student Recreation Center, Bobby Bowden Field at Doak Campbell Stadium, National High Magnetic Field Laboratory, FSU Reservation. **Environmental Initiatives:** Creation of the FSU Office of Sustainability and the hiring of a full-time Director of Campus Sustainability to help build a comprehensive sustainable campus program.

ADMISSIONS

Freshman Academic Profile: Average high school GPA 4.0. 41% in top 10% of high school class, 77% in top 25% of high school class, 98% in top 50% of high school class. 84% from public high schools. **Reported SAT (pre-2016 redesign) scores:** SAT Math middle 50% range 550-640. SAT Critical Reading middle 50% range 560-640. SAT Writing middle 50% range 550-630. **Concordant SAT scores:** SAT EBRW middle 50% 610–680. SAT Math middle 50% range 570–660. ACT middle 50% range 25-29. Minimum internet-based TOEFL 80. Minimum paper TOEFL 550. **Basis for Candidate Selection:** *Very important factors considered include:* rigor of secondary school record, academic GPA. *Important factors considered include:* standardized test scores, talent/ability, state residency. *Other factors considered include:* class rank, application essay, recommendation(s), extracurricular activities, character/personal qualities, first generation, alumni/ae relation, geographical residence, volunteer work, work experience. **Freshman Admission Requirements:** High

school diploma is required and GED is accepted. *Academic units required:* 4 English, 4 math, 3 science, 2 science labs, 2 foreign language, 1 social studies, 2 history, 3 academic electives. *Academic units recommended:* 4 English, 4 math, 4 science, 2 science labs, 4 foreign language, 2 social studies, 2 history, 3 academic electives. **Freshman Admission Statistics:** 29,027 applied, 58.01% admitted, 37% enrolled. **Transfer Admission Requirements:** college transcript(s), Minimum college GPA of 3.0 required. Lowest grade transferable D-. **General Admission Information:** Application fee $30. Regular application deadline 1/15. Nonfall registration accepted.

COSTS AND FINANCIAL AID

Annual in-state tuition $4,640. Annual out-of-state tuition $19,806. Room and board $10,304. Required fees $1,867. Average book expense $1,000. **Required Forms and Deadlines:** FAFSA, State aid form. **Notification of Awards:** Applicants will be notified of awards on a rolling basis beginning 4/5. **Types of Aid:** *Need-based scholarships/grants:* Federal Pell, FSEOG, State scholarships/grants, Private scholarships, College/university scholarship or grant aid from institutional funds. *Loans:* Direct Subsidized Stafford Loans, Direct Unsubsidized Stafford Loans, Direct PLUS loans, Federal Perkins Loans. *Student Employment:* Federal Work-Study Program available. Institutional employment available. **Financial Aid Statistics:** 94% needy freshmen, 89% needy undergrads receive need-based scholarship or grant aid. 74% freshmen, 77% undergrads receive non-need-based scholarship or grant aid. 54% freshmen, 82% undergrads receive need-based self-help aid. 1% freshmen, 1% undergrads receive athletic scholarships. 96% freshmen, 87% undergrads receive any aid. Average cumulative indebtedness $22,912. **Criteria for awarding aid:** *Non-need-based:* Academics, Art, Athletics, Leadership, Music/drama.

FONTBONNE UNIVERSITY

6800 Wydown Boulevard, St. Louis, MO 63105
Phone: 314-889-1400 • **Financial Aid Phone:** 314-889-1414
E-mail: fcadmis@fontbonne.edu • **CEEB Code:** 6216
Fax: 314-889-1451 • **Website:** www.fontbonne.edu • **ACT Code:** 2298

This private school, affiliated with the Roman Catholic Church, was founded in 1917. It has a 13-acre campus.

RATINGS
Admissions Selectivity Rating: 77   **Fire Safety Rating:** 90   **Green Rating:** 60*

STUDENTS AND FACULTY

Enrollment: 1,993. **Student Body:** 72% female, 28% male, 12% out-of-state, 1% international (23 countries represented). Asian 1%, African American 34%, Caucasian 62%, Hispanic 1%, Native American <1%, Pacific Islander 0%, Two or more races 0%, Race unknown 1%.
Retention and Graduation: 58% freshmen return for sophomore year. 33% freshmen graduate within 4 years. 49% freshmen graduate within 6 years. 25% grads go on to further study within 1 year. **Faculty:** Student/faculty ratio 16:1. 73 full-time faculty, 71% hold PhDs, 10% are are members of minority groups, 68% are women. 0% of classes are taught by teaching assistants.

ACADEMICS

Degrees: bachelor's, certificate, master's, postbachelor's certificate. **Classes:** Most classes have 10-19 students. Most lab/discussion sessions have 10-19 students. **Most popular majors:** Special Education and Teaching; Elementary Education and Teaching; Business Administration and Management. **Special Study Options:** Accelerated program, cooperative education program, cross-registration, distance learning, double major, English as a Second Language (ESL), exchange student program (domestic), honors program, independent study, internships, liberal arts/career combination, student-designed major, study abroad, teacher certification program, weekend college. Combined degree programs: BA/MEng, BS/MS with Washington University. **Disability Services:** Special programs offered to physically disabled students, including note-taking services, reader services, tape recorders, tutors. **Career Services:** Alumni services, Career/job search classes, Career assessment, Internships, On-campus interviews.

FACILITIES

Housing: Coed dorms, special housing for international students, apartments for single students, Off campus house which holds 13 females. 85% of campus accessible to physically diasbled. **Special Academic Facilities/Equipment:** Art gallery. **Computers:** 75% of classrooms, 100% of dorms, 100% of libraries, 100% of dining areas, 100% of student union, 100% of common outdoor areas have wireless network access. Students can register for classes online. Administrative functions (other than registration) can be performed online.

CAMPUS LIFE

Environment: Metropolis. **Activities:** Choral groups, dance, drama/theater, literary magazine, music ensembles, radio station, student government, student newspaper, Campus Ministries. 34 registered organizations, 7 honor societies, 4 religious organizations. **Athletics (Intercollegiate):** *Men:* baseball, basketball, cross-country, field hockey, golf, lacrosse, soccer, tennis. *Women:* basketball, bowling, cross-country, field hockey, golf, lacrosse, soccer, softball, tennis, volleyball. **On-Campus Highlights:** Ryan Hall, Dunham Student Activity Center, Library, Medaille Hall, Fine Arts Center, Message from the President. On behalf of the entire Fontbonne University family, I am pleased to welcome you to our web site. As you navigate these electronic pages, I trust that you will find whatever information you seek about our University. When you explore the Fontbonne University campus, either in person or on a virtual visit like this, you will learn that Fontbonne has certain advantages that are evidenced in the following ways: Location Our campus is located in the heart of Clayton, Missouri, which is one of the most beautiful suburbs in the United States. There is easy access from our campus to Forest Park, the St. Louis Zoo, the Art Museum and the History Museum. In addition, you are approximately fifteen minutes from downtown St. Louis, home of the St. Louis Cardinals, NFL Rams and NHL Blues. Academics The academic programs are excellent, and they are taught in a values-based, student-centered context. Because of our student-faculty ratio, the faculty know you as an individual and will help you incorporate experiential learning in your academic program. Focus The individual student is the primary focus at Fontbonne University. You are the central focus of the administration, faculty and staff. We are dedicated to your academic, moral, emotional, spiritual, social, cultural, career and co-curricular development. Ultimate Goal At Fontbonne, we strive to achieve strength of curriculum and strength of character. Therefore, we will teach you not only how to make a living but also how to live a life so that you are prepared to face the challenges of the 21st century and to prevail. Fontbonne is a Catholic University sponsored by the Sisters of St. Joseph of Carondelet. We are co-educational with 2,800 students, and a student body comprised of both traditional-aged undergraduate students as well as adult learners. All of our students are taught to think critically, to act ethically and to assume responsibility as citizens and leaders for a world in need. If you are seeking a university education where the individual student is at the epicenter of all activity, then Fontbonne is for you. I invite you to visit our campus in person and come to know and value, as we do, the advantage that is a Fontbonne University education. Dennis C. Golden President.

ADMISSIONS

Freshman Academic Profile: Average high school GPA 3.1. 7% in top 10% of high school class, 28% in top 25% of high school class, 61% in top 50% of high school class. 56% from public high schools. **Reported SAT (pre-2016 redesign) scores:** SAT Math middle 50% range 470-625. SAT Critical Reading middle 50% range 500-625. **Concordant SAT scores:** SAT Math middle 50% range 510–650. ACT middle 50% range 18-24. Minimum paper TOEFL 525. **Basis for Candidate Selection:** *Very important factors considered include:* rigor of secondary school record, class rank, academic GPA, standardized test scores, character/personal qualities. *Other factors considered include:* application essay, recommendation(s), interview, extracurricular activities, talent/ability, first generation, alumni/ae relation, volunteer work, work experience, level of applicant's interest. **Freshman Admission Requirements:** High school diploma is required and GED is accepted. *Academic units required:* 4 English, 3 math, 3 science, 1 science lab, 3 social studies, 3 academic electives. **Freshman Admission Statistics:** 588 applied, 75.51% admitted, 45% enrolled. **Transfer Admission Requirements:** college transcript(s), essay or personal statement, Minimum college GPA of 2.0 required. Lowest grade transferable D. **General Admission Information:** Application fee $25. Priority deadline 1/15. Regular application deadline 8/1. Nonfall registration accepted. Admission may be deferred for a maximum of 1 year.

COSTS AND FINANCIAL AID

Annual tuition $20,860. Room and board $8,319. Required fees $440. Average book expense $650. **Required Forms and Deadlines:** FAFSA, Institution's own financial aid form. **Types of Aid:** *Need-based scholarships/grants:* Federal Pell, FSEOG, State scholarships/grants, Private scholarships, College/university scholarship or grant aid from institutional funds. *Loans:* Federal Perkins Loans, State Loans, College/university loans from institutional funds. *Student Employment:* Federal Work-Study Program available. Institutional employment available. **Financial Aid Statistics:** 96% needy freshmen, 98% needy undergrads receive need-based scholarship or grant aid. 99% freshmen, 68% undergrads receive non-need-based scholarship or grant aid. 93% freshmen, 91% undergrads receive need-based self-help aid. 0% freshmen, 0% undergrads receive athletic scholarships. **Criteria for awarding aid:** *Need-based:* Job skills. *Non-need-based:* Academics, Alumni affiliation, Art, Job skills, Leadership, Minority status, Religious affiliation.

FORDHAM UNIVERSITY

441 East Fordham Road, Bronx, NY 10458
Phone: 718-817-4000 • **Financial Aid Phone:** 718-817-3800
E-mail: enroll@fordham.edu • **CEEB Code:** 2259
Fax: 718-817-0549 • **Website:** www.fordham.edu • **ACT Code:** 2748

This private school, affiliated with the Roman Catholic Church, was founded in 1841. It has a 93-acre campus.

RATINGS

Admissions Selectivity Rating: 91 **Fire Safety Rating:** 96 **Green Rating:** 60*

STUDENTS AND FACULTY

Enrollment: 9,096. **Student Body:** 57% female, 43% male, 57% out-of-state, 8% international (68 countries represented). Asian 10%, African American 4%, Caucasian 59%, Hispanic 14%, Native American <1%, Pacific Islander <1%, Two or more races 3%, Race unknown 2%.
Retention and Graduation: 91% freshmen return for sophomore year. 74% freshmen graduate within 4 years. 80% freshmen graduate within 6 years. 20% grads go on to further study within 1 year. **Faculty:** Student/faculty ratio 14:1. 736 full-time faculty, 95% hold PhDs, 14% are are members of minority groups, 43% are women.

ACADEMICS

Degrees: bachelor's, doctoral/professional, doctoral/research, doctoral, master's, postbachelor's certificate, post-master's certificate. **Classes:** Most classes have 10-19 students. Most lab/discussion sessions have 10-19 students. **Most popular majors:** Speech Communication and Rhetoric; Finance; Business Administration and Management. **Special Study Options:** double major, English as a Second Language (ESL), exchange student program (domestic), honors program, independent study, internships, student-designed major, study abroad, teacher certification program, Globe Program in International Business. 3:2 Engineering Cooperative with Columbia University or Case Western Reserve University. **Honors Programs:** Each undergraduate college has its own Honors Program. All four programs offer enriched academic opportunity for qualified and interested students. Additionally, there are major programs of study designated as selective. Students must be invited into those programs and meet minimum GPA requirements for consideration. Many more majors offer Honors designation at graduation usually based upon completion of a thesis or senior project. Combined degree programs: BA/JD, BA/MA, BS/MSW, BS/MBA, BS/MS Finance, 3:2 Engineering. **Disability Services:** Special programs offered to physically disabled students, including note-taking services, reader services, tape recorders, tutors. **Career Services:** Alumni network, Alumni services, Career/job search classes, Career assessment, Internships, Regional alumni. Our alumni are a tremendous asset to our student body. They assist with informational interviews, panel presentations, networking, and as members of our Fordham Alumni Networking Program.

FACILITIES

Housing: Coed dorms, special housing for disabled students, apartments for single students, Residential Colleges. 80% of campus accessible to physically diasbled. **Special Academic Facilities/Equipment:** television station, radio station, theaters, white and black box studio spaces, media and visual arts labs and design space, art gallery, University Church, seismic station, 113 biological field station The Louis Calder Center, in Armonk, NY **Computers:** 90% of classrooms, 98% of dorms, 95% of libraries, 100% of dining areas, 80% of common outdoor areas have wireless network access. Students can register for classes online. Administrative functions (other than registration) can be performed online.

CAMPUS LIFE

Environment: Metropolis. **Activities:** Choral groups, concert band, dance, drama/theater, jazz band, literary magazine, music ensembles, musical theater, pep band, radio station, student government, student newspaper, student-run film society, symphony orchestra, television station, yearbook. 133 registered organizations, 12 honor societies, 3 religious organizations. **Athletics (Intercollegiate):** *Men:* baseball, basketball, cross-country, diving, football, golf, soccer, squash, swimming, tennis, track/field (outdoor), track/field (indoor), water polo. *Women:* basketball, cheerleading, crew/rowing, cross-country, diving, soccer, softball, swimming, tennis, track/field (outdoor), track/field (indoor), volleyball. **On-Campus Highlights:** William D. Walsh Family Library (Rose Hill), O'Hare Hall (Residential College at Rose Hill), Edwards Parade/Keating Hall (Rose Hill), McMahon Hall (Lincoln Center), Pope Auditorium (Lincoln Center), With three distinct campuses, there are numerous noteworthy buildings including new and recently renovated academic and extracurricular space, residence halls and athletic centers/fields. Additional space to note includes student-run coffee houses, white and black box studio spaces and historic buildings designated as NYC landmarks.

ADMISSIONS

Freshman Academic Profile: Average high school GPA 3.6. 46% in top 10% of high school class, 81% in top 25% of high school class, 98% in top 50% of high school class. 61% from public high schools. **Reported SAT (pre-2016 redesign) scores:** SAT Math middle 50% range 590–690. SAT Critical Reading middle 50% range 580–680. SAT Writing middle 50% range 580–680. **Concordant SAT scores:** SAT EBRW middle 50% 640–720. SAT Math middle 50% range 610–720. ACT middle 50% range 27–31. Minimum internet-based TOEFL 90. Minimum paper TOEFL 575. **Basis for Candidate Selection:** *Very important factors considered include:* rigor of secondary school record, academic GPA, standardized test scores. *Important factors considered include:* application essay, recommendation(s), extracurricular activities, talent/ability, character/personal qualities, volunteer work. *Other factors considered include:* class rank, first generation, alumni/ae relation, geographical residence, racial/ethnic status, work experience, level of applicant's interest. **Freshman Admission Requirements:** High school diploma is required and GED is accepted. *Academic units required:* 4 English, 3 math, 3 science, 2 foreign language, 3 social studies. *Academic units recommended:* 4 English, 4 math, 4 science, 4 foreign language, 4 social studies. **Freshman Admission Statistics:** 44,816 applied, 45.22% admitted, 11% enrolled. **Transfer Admission Requirements:** High school transcript, college transcript(s), essay or personal statement, statement of good standing from prior institution(s). Minimum college GPA of 3.0 required. Lowest grade transferable C. **General Admission Information:** Application fee $70. Priority deadline 11/1. Regular application deadline 1/1. Regular notification 4/1. Nonfall registration accepted. Admission may be deferred for a maximum of 1 year.

COSTS AND FINANCIAL AID

Annual tuition $47,850. Room and board $16,845. Required fees $838. Average book expense $1,012. **Required Forms and Deadlines:** FAFSA, CSS/Financial Aid PROFILE, State aid form, Noncustodial PROFILE, Business/Farm Supplement. **Notification of Awards:** Applicants will be notified of awards on a rolling basis beginning 3/31. **Types of Aid:** *Need-based scholarships/grants:* Federal Pell, FSEOG, State scholarships/grants, Private scholarships, College/university scholarship or grant aid from institutional funds. *Loans:* Direct Subsidized Stafford Loans, Direct Unsubsidized Stafford Loans, Direct PLUS loans, Federal Perkins Loans. *Student Employment:* Federal Work-Study Program available. Institutional employment available. **Financial Aid Statistics:** 98% needy freshmen, 96% needy undergrads receive need-based scholarship or grant aid. 23% freshmen, 19% undergrads receive non-need-based scholarship or grant aid. 66% freshmen, 69% undergrads receive need-based self-help aid. 2% freshmen, 2% undergrads receive athletic scholarships. 90% freshmen, 80% undergrads receive any aid. 60% undergrads borrow to pay for school. Average cumulative indebtedness $25,069. **Criteria for awarding aid:** *Need-based:* Academics, Athletics. *Non-need-based:* Academics, Athletics.

FORT HAYS STATE UNIVERSITY

600 Park Street, Hays, KS 67601-4099
Phone: 785.628.3478 • **Financial Aid Phone:** 785-628-4408
E-mail: tigers@fhsu.edu • **CEEB Code:** 6218
Fax: 800.432.0248 • **Website:** www.fhsu.edu • **ACT Code:** 1408

This public school was founded in 1902. It has a 4160-acre campus.

RATINGS
Admissions Selectivity Rating: 75   **Fire Safety Rating:** 76   **Green Rating:** 60*

STUDENTS AND FACULTY
Enrollment: 11,503. **Student Body:** 61% female, 39% male, 31% out-of-state, 29% international. Asian 1%, African American 4%, Caucasian 57%, Hispanic 7%, Native American <1%, Pacific Islander <1%, Two or more races 2%, Race unknown 1%.
Retention and Graduation: 69% freshmen return for sophomore year. 19% freshmen graduate within 4 years. 42% freshmen graduate within 6 years. 20% grads go on to further study within 1 year. **Faculty:** Student/faculty ratio 16:1. 315 full-time faculty, 61% hold PhDs, 10% are are members of minority groups, 45% are women. 1% of classes are taught by teaching assistants.

ACADEMICS
Degrees: associate, bachelor's, certificate, master's, post-master's certificate. **Classes:** Most classes have 10-19 students. Most lab/discussion sessions have fewer than 10 students. **Most popular majors:** Elementary Education

and Teaching; Health and Physical Education/Fitness; Business/Commerce. **Special Study Options:** distance learning, double major, dual enrollment, English as a Second Language (ESL), exchange student program (domestic), external degree program, independent study, internships, liberal arts/career combination, student-designed major, study abroad, teacher certification program. Combined degree programs: BA/MEng, 3-1 progs in allied health, dentistry, and eng. **Disability Services:** Special programs offered to physically disabled students, including note-taking services, reader services, tutors. **Career Services:** Alumni network, Alumni services, Career/job search classes, Career assessment, Internships.

FACILITIES
Housing: Coed dorms, men's dorms, women's dorms, fraternity/sorority housing, apartments for married students, apartments for single students. 100% of campus accessible to physically diasbled. **Special Academic Facilities/Equipment:** Paleontology, natural history, visual arts and media center, farm, NMR gas analyzer, telescope (HG). **Computers:** 100% of classrooms, 100% of dorms, 100% of libraries, 100% of dining areas, 100% of student union, 100% of common outdoor areas have wireless network access.

CAMPUS LIFE
Environment: Village. **Activities:** Choral groups, concert band, dance, drama/theater, jazz band, marching band, music ensembles, musical theater, pep band, radio station, student government, student newspaper, symphony orchestra, television station, yearbook. 103 registered organizations, 20 honor societies, 2 religious organizations. 3 fraternities, 3 sororities. **Athletics (Intercollegiate):** *Men:* baseball, basketball, cheerleading, cross-country, football, golf, track/field (outdoor), track/field (indoor), wrestling. *Women:* basketball, cheerleading, cross-country, golf, softball, tennis, track/field (outdoor), track/field (indoor), volleyball. **On-Campus Highlights:** www.tigersportszone.com, www.fhsu.edu/sternberg/, www.fhsu.edu/int/kfhsradio/, www.fhsu.edu/int/kfhstv/, www.fhsu.edu/leader. **Environmental Initiatives:** Clean up of Big Creek

ADMISSIONS
Freshman Academic Profile: Average high school GPA 3.4. 13% in top 10% of high school class, 32% in top 25% of high school class, 64% in top 50% of high school class. 95% from public high schools. ACT middle 50% range 18-24. Minimum internet-based TOEFL 61. Minimum paper TOEFL 500. **Basis for Candidate Selection:** *Other factors considered include:* rigor of secondary school record, class rank, academic GPA, standardized test scores. **Freshman Admission Requirements:** High school diploma is required and GED is accepted. *Academic units recommended:* 4 English, 3 math, 3 science, 2 social studies, 1 history, 1 computer science. **Freshman Admission Statistics:** 2,337 applied, 85.88% admitted, 24% enrolled. **Transfer Admission Requirements:** college transcript(s), Minimum college GPA of 2.0 required. Lowest grade transferable D. **General Admission Information:** Application fee $30. Nonfall registration accepted. Admission may be deferred for a maximum of 1 year.

COSTS AND FINANCIAL AID
Required Forms and Deadlines: FAFSA, Institution's own financial aid form. **Notification of Awards:** Applicants will be notified of awards on a rolling basis beginning 3/15. **Types of Aid:** *Need-based scholarships/grants:* Federal Pell, FSEOG, State scholarships/grants, Private scholarships, College/university scholarship or grant aid from institutional funds. *Loans:* Direct Subsidized Stafford Loans, Direct Unsubsidized Stafford Loans, Direct PLUS loans, Federal Perkins Loans, College/university loans from institutional funds. *Student Employment:* Federal Work-Study Program available. Institutional employment available. **Financial Aid Statistics:** 82% needy freshmen, 80% needy undergrads receive need-based scholarship or grant aid. 3% freshmen, 3% undergrads receive non-need-based scholarship or grant aid. 85% freshmen, 10% undergrads receive need-based self-help aid. 4% freshmen, 3% undergrads receive athletic scholarships. Average cumulative indebtedness $27,462. **Criteria for awarding aid:** *Non-need-based:* Academics, Alumni affiliation, Art, Athletics, Job skills, Leadership, Minority status, Music/drama, State/district residency.

FORT LEWIS COLLEGE

1000 Rim Drive, Durango, CO 81301
Phone: 970-247-7184 • **Financial Aid Phone:** 970-247-7142
E-mail: admisson@fortlewis.edu • **CEEB Code:** 4310
Fax: 970-247-7179 • **Website:** www.fortlewis.edu • **ACT Code:** 510

This public school was founded in 1911. It has a 362-acre campus.

RATINGS
Admissions Selectivity Rating: 73   **Fire Safety Rating:** 90   **Green Rating:** 90

STUDENTS AND FACULTY

Enrollment: 3,458. **Student Body:** 49% female, 51% male, 51% out-of-state, 1% international (22 countries represented). Asian 1%, African American 1%, Caucasian 50%, Hispanic 11%, Native American 26%, Pacific Islander <1%, Two or more races 8%, Race unknown 3%.

Retention and Graduation: 66% freshmen return for sophomore year. 24% freshmen graduate within 4 years. 45% freshmen graduate within 6 years. 13% grads go on to further study within 1 year. **Faculty:** Student/faculty ratio 18:1. 163 full-time faculty, 93% hold PhDs, 9% are are members of minority groups, 56% are women. 0% of classes are taught by teaching assistants.

ACADEMICS

Degrees: bachelor's, master's, postbachelor's certificate. **Classes:** Most classes have 10-19 students. Most lab/discussion sessions have 10-19 students. **Most popular majors:** Business Administration and Management; Kinesiology and Exercise Science; Biology/Biological Sciences. **Special Study Options:** Accelerated program, cooperative education program, distance learning, double major, dual enrollment, English as a Second Language (ESL), exchange student program (domestic), honors program, independent study, internships, liberal arts/career combination, student-designed major, study abroad, teacher certification program. **Honors Programs:** The John F. Reed honors program selects outstanding first and second-year students who demonstrate ability and interest in pursuing additional academic achievements and challenges. The program requires honors courses called forums which ask students to study innovative thinkers, intellectual foundations, and multidisciplinary perspectives. All of the student's work culminates in an honors thesis presented in a public forum. Students in the honors program also benefit from the honors lounge (computers, tv, fridge, reference materials, etc.), free tickets to events and mentoring by professional associates. Upon graduation, the students receive a minor in Honors called "Rhetoric of Inquiry". **Disability Services:** Special programs offered to physically disabled students, including note-taking services, reader services, tape recorders, tutors. **Career Services:** Alumni services, Career/job search classes, Career assessment, Internships, Regional alumni. The Career Services career/job search classes were modified to include area, regional and national employers partnering in the presentations. This gave a new energy to the classes and permitted students to network with professionals in a wide variety of careers. The change was very well received by both populations. This has not only increased employer exposure on campus, but made the relationship between Career Services and these professionals stronger.

FACILITIES

Housing: Coed dorms, special housing for disabled students, apartments for married students, apartments for single students, Wellness Housing, Theme Housing. 90% of campus accessible to physically diasbled. **Special Academic Facilities/Equipment:** Center of Southwest Studies, Community Concert Hall **Computers:** 100% of classrooms, 100% of dorms, 100% of libraries, 100% of dining areas, 100% of student union, 10% of common outdoor areas have wireless network access. Students can register for classes online. Administrative functions (other than registration) can be performed online.

CAMPUS LIFE

Environment: Town. **Activities:** Choral groups, concert band, drama/theater, jazz band, literary magazine, musical theater, pep band, radio station, student government, student newspaper, Campus Ministries. 65 registered organizations, 5 honor societies, 3 religious organizations. **Athletics (Intercollegiate):** Men: basketball, cross-country, football, golf, soccer. Women: basketball, cross-country, lacrosse, soccer, softball, volleyball. **On-Campus Highlights:** Center of Southwest Studies, Student Life Center, College Union Building, Residence Halls, Academic buildings, Highly qualified, committed faculty who are available, helpful, and engaged. Emphasis on active, experiential learning through community service, undergraduate research, study abroad, and internships. Student-faculty ratio of 17:1. Collaborative campus culture where student voices are heard and respected. Graduates who are twice as likely as those other schools to say their education was "excellent." Cultural diversity is a core value and key feature of Fort Lewis College. Approximately 28% of our students are from ethnic minority backgrounds. **Environmental Initiatives:** All new construction or renovation follow at minimum LEED Silver standards.

ADMISSIONS

Freshman Academic Profile: Average high school GPA 3.3. 9% in top 10% of high school class, 27% in top 25% of high school class, 64% in top 50% of high school class. **Reported SAT (pre-2016 redesign) scores:** SAT Math middle 50% range 470-550. SAT Critical Reading middle 50% range 470-570. **Concordant SAT scores:** SAT Math middle 50% range 510–570. ACT middle 50% range 19-24. Minimum internet-based TOEFL 61. Minimum paper TOEFL 500. **Basis for Candidate Selection:** *Very important factors considered include:* rigor of secondary school record, class rank, academic GPA, standardized test scores. *Other factors considered include:* application essay, recommendation(s), interview, extracurricular activities, talent/ability, character/personal qualities, first generation, alumni/ae relation, level of applicant's interest. **Freshman Admission Requirements:** High school diploma is required and GED is accepted. *Academic units required:* 4 English, 4 math, 3

science, 2 science labs, 1 foreign language, 2 social studies, 1 history, 2 academic electives. **Freshman Admission Statistics:** 4,164 applied, 96.93% admitted, 19% enrolled. **Transfer Admission Requirements:** college transcript(s), Minimum college GPA of 2.40 required. Lowest grade transferable C-. **General Admission Information:** Application fee $40. Regular application deadline 8/1. Nonfall registration accepted. Admission may be deferred.

COSTS AND FINANCIAL AID

Annual in-state tuition $6,360. Annual out-of-state tuition $16,072. Room and board $9,328. Required fees $1,745. Average book expense $1,208. **Required Forms and Deadlines:** FAFSA. **Notification of Awards:** Applicants will be notified of awards on a rolling basis beginning 3/1. **Types of Aid:** *Need-based scholarships/grants:* Federal Pell, FSEOG, State scholarships/grants, Private scholarships, College/university scholarship or grant aid from institutional funds. *Loans:* Direct Subsidized Stafford Loans, Direct Unsubsidized Stafford Loans, Direct PLUS loans, Federal Perkins Loans. *Student Employment:* Federal Work-Study Program available. Institutional employment available. **Financial Aid Statistics:** 90% needy freshmen, 88% needy undergrads receive need-based scholarship or grant aid. 7% freshmen, 5% undergrads receive non-need-based scholarship or grant aid. 70% freshmen, 72% undergrads receive need-based self-help aid. 10% freshmen, 8% undergrads receive athletic scholarships. 92% freshmen, 82% undergrads receive any aid. 63% undergrads borrow to pay for school. Average cumulative indebtedness $22,265. **Criteria for awarding aid:** *Need-based:* Academics, Alumni affiliation, Art, Athletics, Leadership, Music/drama. *Non-need-based:* Academics, Alumni affiliation, Art, Athletics, Leadership, Music/drama, State/district residency.

FRAMINGHAM STATE UNIVERSITY

100 State Street, Framingham, MA 01701-9101
Phone: 508-626-4500 • **Financial Aid Phone:** 508-626-4534
E-mail: admissions@framingham.edu • **CEEB Code:** 3519
Fax: 508-626-4017 • **Website:** www.framingham.edu • **ACT Code:** 1904

This public school was founded in 1839. It has a 73-acre campus.

RATINGS

Admissions Selectivity Rating: 74   **Fire Safety Rating:** 99   **Green Rating:** 88

STUDENTS AND FACULTY

Enrollment: 4,100. **Student Body:** 61% female, 39% male, 6% out-of-state, <1% international (21 countries represented). Asian 3%, African American 11%, Caucasian 69%, Hispanic 12%, Native American <1%, Pacific Islander <1%, Two or more races 4%, Race unknown 2%.

Retention and Graduation: 74% freshmen return for sophomore year. 34% freshmen graduate within 4 years. 55% freshmen graduate within 6 years. 22% grads go on to further study within 1 year. **Faculty:** Student/faculty ratio 14:1. 198 full-time faculty, 0% hold PhDs, 19% are are members of minority groups, 57% are women. 0% of classes are taught by teaching assistants.

ACADEMICS

Degrees: bachelor's, master's, postbachelor's certificate. **Classes:** Most classes have 20-29 students. **Most popular majors:** Business/Commerce; Family and Consumer Sciences/Human Sciences; Sociology. **Special Study Options:** cross-registration, distance learning, double major, honors program, independent study, internships, liberal arts/career combination, study abroad, teacher certification program, Pre-engineering program in conjunction with University of Massachusetts Amherst, University of Massachusetts Dartmouth, and University of Massachusetts Lowell. **Honors Programs:** The Honors Program offers challenging courses and projects for qualified students,and sponsors events which contribute to the intellectual life of the College community. **Disability Services:** Special programs offered to physically disabled students, including note-taking services, reader services, tape recorders, tutors. **Career Services:** Alumni network, Alumni services, Career/job search classes, Career assessment, Internships. Current working relationships with key employers in the MetroWest area, Boston and Worcester.

FACILITIES

Housing: Coed dorms, women's dorms, Wellness Housing, Theme Housing. 95% of campus accessible to physically diasbled. **Special Academic Facilities/Equipment:** Mazmanian Art Gallery, McAuliffe Challenger Learning Center, Greenhouse, Early Childhood Development Lab, Education Curriculum Library,Planetarium **Computers:** 100% of classrooms, 100% of dorms, 100% of libraries, 100% of dining areas, 100% of student union, have wireless network access. Students can register for classes online. Administrative functions (other than registration) can be performed online. Undergraduates are required to own a computer.

CAMPUS LIFE

Environment: City. **Activities:** Choral groups, dance, drama/theater, literary magazine, musical theater, radio station, student government, student newspaper, Campus Ministries, Student Organization. 55 registered organizations, 11 honor societies, 4 religious organizations. **Athletics (Intercollegiate):** *Men:* baseball, basketball, cross-country, football, ice hockey, soccer. *Women:* basketball, cross-country, field hockey, lacrosse, soccer, softball, volleyball. **On-Campus Highlights:** Residence Halls, Athletic Facility, College Center, Academic Buildings, Library. **Environmental Initiatives:** Conversion of our power plant from #6 oil to natural gas, decreasing our carbon footprint from the plant by 30%.

ADMISSIONS

Reported SAT (pre-2016 redesign) scores: SAT Math middle 50% range 450-550. SAT Critical Reading middle 50% range 440-540. SAT Writing middle 50% range 430-530. **Concordant SAT scores:** SAT Math middle 50% range 510–570. ACT middle 50% range 20-55. Minimum internet-based TOEFL 61. Minimum paper TOEFL 500. **Basis for Candidate Selection:** *Very important factors considered include:* rigor of secondary school record, class rank, academic GPA, standardized test scores. *Other factors considered include:* application essay, recommendation(s), interview, extracurricular activities, talent/ability, character/personal qualities, first generation, alumni/ae relation, level of applicant's interest. **Freshman Admission Requirements:** High school diploma is required and GED is accepted. *Academic units required:* 4 English, 4 math, 3 science, 2 science labs, 1 foreign language, 2 social studies, 1 history, 2 academic electives. **Freshman Admission Statistics:** 6,204 applied, 64.81% admitted, 19% enrolled. **Transfer Admission Requirements:** college transcript(s), Minimum college GPA of 2.40 required. Lowest grade transferable C-. **General Admission Information:** Application fee $40. Regular application deadline 8/1. Nonfall registration accepted. Admission may be deferred.

COSTS AND FINANCIAL AID

Annual in-state tuition $6,360. Annual out-of-state tuition $16,072. Room and board $9,328. Required fees $1,745. Average book expense $1,208. **Required Forms and Deadlines:** FAFSA. **Notification of Awards:** Applicants will be notified of awards on a rolling basis beginning 3/1. **Types of Aid:** *Need-based scholarships/grants:* Federal Pell, FSEOG, State scholarships/grants, Private scholarships, College/university scholarship or grant aid from institutional funds. *Loans:* Direct Subsidized Stafford Loans, Direct Unsubsidized Stafford Loans, Direct PLUS loans, Federal Perkins Loans. *Student Employment:* Federal Work-Study Program available. Institutional employment available. **Financial Aid Statistics:** 90% needy freshmen, 88% needy undergrads receive need-based scholarship or grant aid. 7% freshmen, 5% undergrads receive non-need-based scholarship or grant aid. 70% freshmen, 72% undergrads receive need-based self-help aid. 10% freshmen, 8% undergrads receive athletic scholarships. 92% freshmen, 82% undergrads receive any aid. 63% undergrads borrow to pay for school. Average cumulative indebtedness $22,265. **Criteria for awarding aid:** *Need-based:* Academics, Alumni affiliation, Art, Athletics, Leadership, Music/drama. *Non-need-based:* Academics, Alumni affiliation, Art, Athletics, Leadership, Music/drama, State/district residency.

FRANCIS MARION UNIVERSITY

Office of Admissions, Florence, SC 29502-0547
Phone: 843-661-1231 • **Financial Aid Phone:** 843-661-1190
E-mail: admissions@fmarion.edu • **CEEB Code:** 5442
Fax: 843-661-4635 • **Website:** www.fmarion.edu • **ACT Code:** 3856

This public school was founded in 1970. It has a 300-acre campus.

RATINGS

Admissions Selectivity Rating: 78   **Fire Safety Rating:** 84   **Green Rating:** 65

STUDENTS AND FACULTY

Enrollment: 3,380. **Student Body:** 68% female, 32% male, 3% out-of-state, 1% international (19 countries represented). Asian 1%, African American 50%, Caucasian 45%, Hispanic 1%, Native American <1%, Pacific Islander <1%, Two or more races <1%, Race unknown 1%.
Retention and Graduation: 67% freshmen return for sophomore year. 16% freshmen graduate within 4 years. 41% freshmen graduate within 6 years.
Faculty: Student/faculty ratio 15:1. 204 full-time faculty, 79% hold PhDs, 11% are are members of minority groups, 49% are women. 0% of classes are taught by teaching assistants.

ACADEMICS

Degrees: bachelor's, master's, post-master's certificate. **Classes:** Most classes have 20-29 students. **Most popular majors:** Registered Nursing/Registered Nurse; Biology/Biological Sciences; Psychology. **Special Study Options:**

Accelerated program, cross-registration, distance learning, double major, dual enrollment, honors program, independent study, internships, study abroad, teacher certification program. Combined degree programs: 2-2 Forestry prog with Clemson U.; engineering,BSN. **Disability Services:** Special programs offered to physically disabled students, including note-taking services, reader services, tape recorders, tutors. **Career Services:** Alumni network, Career/job search classes, Career assessment, Internships, Regional alumni.

FACILITIES

Housing: special housing for disabled students, men's dorms, women's dorms, apartments for single students. 100% of campus accessible to physically diasbled. **Special Academic Facilities/Equipment:** Media center, planetarium, observatory. **Computers:** Students can register for classes online.

CAMPUS LIFE

Environment: Rural. **Activities:** Choral groups, drama/theater, jazz band, literary magazine, music ensembles, student government, student newspaper, television station 56 registered organizations, 13 honor societies, 5 religious organizations. 7 fraternities, 7 sororities. **Athletics (Intercollegiate):** *Men:* baseball, basketball, cross-country, golf, soccer, tennis, track/field (outdoor). *Women:* basketball, cross-country, soccer, softball, tennis, track/field (outdoor), volleyball. **On-Campus Highlights:** The Cottage, The Smith University Center, The Dooley Planetarium, The Hyman Fine Arts Center, The Hewn Timber Cabins.

ADMISSIONS

Freshman Academic Profile: Average high school GPA 3.6. 15% in top 10% of high school class, 15% in top 25% of high school class, 81% in top 50% of high school class. 91% from public high schools. **Reported SAT (pre-2016 redesign) scores:** SAT Math middle 50% range 420-530. SAT Critical Reading middle 50% range 410-530. SAT Writing middle 50% range 390-500. **Concordant SAT scores:** SAT EBRW middle 50% 450–570. SAT Math middle 50% range 460–560. ACT middle 50% range 17-22. Minimum internet-based TOEFL 61. Minimum paper TOEFL 500. **Basis for Candidate Selection:** *Very important factors considered include:* rigor of secondary school record, academic GPA, standardized test scores. *Important factors considered include:* class rank. *Other factors considered include:* recommendation(s). **Freshman Admission Requirements:** High school diploma is required and GED is accepted. *Academic units required:* 4 English, 4 math, 3 science, 3 science labs, 2 foreign language, 2 social studies, 1 history, 1 academic elective, 1 visual/performing arts, and 1 unit from above areas or other academic areas. **Freshman Admission Statistics:** 3,952 applied, 56.65% admitted, 33% enrolled. **Transfer Admission Requirements:** High school transcript, college transcript(s), statement of good standing from prior institution(s). Minimum college GPA of 2.0 required. Lowest grade transferable C. **General Admission Information:** Application fee $33. Priority deadline 7/1. Regular application deadline 8/15. Nonfall registration accepted. Admission may be deferred for a maximum of 1 year.

COSTS AND FINANCIAL AID

Annual in-state tuition $9,266. Annual out-of-state tuition $18,532. Room and board $7,256. Required fees $472. Average book expense $999. **Required Forms and Deadlines:** FAFSA. **Notification of Awards:** Applicants will be notified of awards on a rolling basis beginning 1/30. **Types of Aid:** *Need-based scholarships/grants:* Federal Pell, FSEOG, State scholarships/grants, Private scholarships, College/university scholarship or grant aid from institutional funds. *Loans:* Direct Subsidized Stafford Loans, Direct Unsubsidized Stafford Loans, Direct PLUS loans, Federal Perkins Loans, State Loans. *Student Employment:* Federal Work-Study Program available. Institutional employment available. **Financial Aid Statistics:** 99% needy freshmen, 76% needy undergrads receive need-based scholarship or grant aid. 7% freshmen, 4% undergrads receive non-need-based scholarship or grant aid. 75% freshmen, 97% undergrads receive need-based self-help aid. 0% freshmen, 0% undergrads receive athletic scholarships. 88% freshmen, 82% undergrads receive any aid. **Criteria for awarding aid:** *Non-need-based:* Academics, Alumni affiliation, Art, Athletics, Job skills, Leadership, Minority status, Music/drama, Religious affiliation, State/district residency.

FRANCISCAN UNIVERSITY OF STEUBENVILLE

1235 University Boulevard, Steubenville, OH 43952-1763
Phone: 740-283-6226 • **Financial Aid Phone:** 740-283-6226
E-mail: admissions@franciscan.edu • **CEEB Code:** 1133
Fax: 740-284-5456 • **Website:** www.franciscan.edu • **ACT Code:** 3258

This private school, affiliated with the Roman Catholic Church, was founded in 1946. It has a 124-acre campus.

RATINGS

Admissions Selectivity Rating: 85   **Fire Safety Rating:** 84   **Green Rating:** 60*

STUDENTS AND FACULTY

Enrollment: 2,038. **Student Body:** 61% female, 39% male, 80% out-of-state, 1% international (20 countries represented). Asian 2%, African American 1%, Caucasian 82%, Hispanic 11%, Native American <1%, Pacific Islander <1%, Two or more races 2%, Race unknown 2%.
Retention and Graduation: 84% freshmen return for sophomore year. 67% freshmen graduate within 4 years. 76% freshmen graduate within 6 years. 20% grads go on to further study within 1 year. 9% grads pursue arts and sciences degrees. 1% grads pursue business degrees. 1% grads pursue medical degrees.
Faculty: Student/faculty ratio 14:1. 127 full-time faculty, 82% hold PhDs, 2% are are members of minority groups, 24% are women. 0% of classes are taught by teaching assistants.

ACADEMICS

Degrees: associate, bachelor's, master's. **Classes:** Most classes have 10-19 students. Most lab/discussion sessions have 10-19 students. **Most popular majors:** Theology/Theological Studies; Business Administration, Management and Operations; Registered Nursing/Registered Nurse. **Special Study Options:** Accelerated program, distance learning, double major, dual enrollment, honors program, independent study, internships, liberal arts/career combination, study abroad, teacher certification program. **Honors Programs:** We have a Great Books program. Combined degree programs: BA/MA, 4+1 in Business, Clinical Counseling, Theology and Philosophy. **Disability Services:** Special programs offered to physically disabled students, including note-taking services, reader services, tape recorders, tutors. **Career Services:** Career/job search classes, Career assessment, Internships.

FACILITIES

Housing: men's dorms, women's dorms, apartments for single students. 75% of campus accessible to physically diasbled. **Special Academic Facilities/Equipment:** Art Gallery. **Computers:** Students can register for classes online. Administrative functions (other than registration) can be performed online.

CAMPUS LIFE

Environment: Village. **Activities:** Choral groups, drama/theater, literary magazine, music ensembles, radio station, student government, student newspaper, yearbook, Campus Ministries, Student Organization. 31 registered organizations, 3 honor societies, 6 religious organizations. 1 fraternity, 1 sorority. **On-Campus Highlights:** Heavenly Grounds Coffee Shop, Sts. Cosmas and Damian Hall-Science Building, Finnegan Fieldhouse, Christ The King Chapel, Portiuncula Chapel.

ADMISSIONS

Freshman Academic Profile: Average high school GPA 3.6. 25% in top 10% of high school class, 50% in top 25% of high school class, 81% in top 50% of high school class. 37% from public high schools. **Reported SAT (pre-2016 redesign) scores:** SAT Math middle 50% range 500-630. SAT Critical Reading middle 50% range 540-670. SAT Writing middle 50% range 510-620. **Concordant SAT scores:** SAT EBRW middle 50% 580–690. SAT Math middle 50% range 530–650. ACT middle 50% range 22-28. Minimum paper TOEFL 550. **Basis for Candidate Selection:** *Very important factors considered include:* rigor of secondary school record, academic GPA, standardized test scores, interview, character/personal qualities. *Important factors considered include:* extracurricular activities, talent/ability. *Other factors considered include:* recommendation(s). **Freshman Admission Requirements:** High school diploma is required and GED is accepted. *Academic units recommended:* 4 English, 3 math, 3 science, 3 science labs, 2 foreign language, 2 social studies, 1 history. **Freshman Admission Statistics:** 1,760 applied, 78.75% admitted, 33% enrolled. **Transfer Admission Requirements:** High school transcript, college transcript(s), essay or personal statement, Minimum college GPA of 2.2 required. Lowest grade transferable C. **General Admission Information:** Application fee $20. Priority deadline 1/31. Regular application deadline 5/1. Nonfall registration accepted. Admission may be deferred for a maximum of one year.

COSTS AND FINANCIAL AID

Required Forms and Deadlines: FAFSA. **Notification of Awards:** Applicants will be notified of awards on a rolling basis beginning 2/15.

Types of Aid: *Need-based scholarships/grants:* Federal Pell, FSEOG, State scholarships/grants, Private scholarships, College/university scholarship or grant aid from institutional funds. *Loans:* Direct Subsidized Stafford Loans, Direct Unsubsidized Stafford Loans, Direct PLUS loans, Federal Perkins Loans, Federal Nursing Loans. *Student Employment:* Federal Work-Study Program available. Institutional employment available. **Financial Aid Statistics:** 98% needy freshmen, 99% needy undergrads receive need-based scholarship or grant aid. 10% freshmen, 9% undergrads receive non-need-based scholarship or grant aid. 89% freshmen, 90% undergrads receive need-based self-help aid. 0% freshmen, 0% undergrads receive athletic scholarships. 63% freshmen, 62% undergrads receive any aid. **Criteria for awarding aid:** *Need-based:* Leadership, Religious affiliation. *Non-need-based:* Academics, Alumni affiliation, Leadership, Religious affiliation.

FRANKLIN AND MARSHALL COLLEGE

P.O. Box 3003, Lancaster, PA 17604-3003
Phone: 717-358-3953 • **Financial Aid Phone:** 717-291-3991
E-mail: admission@fandm.edu • **CEEB Code:** 2261
Fax: 717-358-4389 • **Website:** www.fandm.edu • **ACT Code:** 3574

This private school was founded in 1787. It has a 180-acre campus.

RATINGS

Admissions Selectivity Rating: 93   **Fire Safety Rating:** 97   **Green Rating:** 93

STUDENTS AND FACULTY

Enrollment: 2,222. **Student Body:** 53% female, 47% male, 73% out-of-state, 15% international (49 countries represented). Asian 5%, African American 6%, Caucasian 57%, Hispanic 9%, Native American <1%, Pacific Islander <1%, Two or more races 2%, Race unknown 6%.
Retention and Graduation: 91% freshmen return for sophomore year. 83% freshmen graduate within 4 years. 87% freshmen graduate within 6 years.
Faculty: Student/faculty ratio 9:1. 243 full-time faculty, 93% hold PhDs, 13% are are members of minority groups, 48% are women. 0% of classes are taught by teaching assistants.

ACADEMICS

Degrees: bachelor's. **Classes:** Most classes have 10-19 students. Most lab/discussion sessions have 10-19 students. **Most popular majors:** Political Science and Government; Psychology; Business Administration, Management and Operations. **Special Study Options:** Accelerated program, cross-registration, double major, dual enrollment, exchange student program (domestic), honors program, independent study, internships, student-designed major, study abroad, teacher certification program. **Disability Services:** Special programs offered to physically disabled students, including note-taking services, tutors. **Career Services:** Alumni network, Alumni services, Career/job search classes, Career assessment, Internships, Regional alumni.

FACILITIES

Housing: Coed dorms, special housing for disabled students, men's dorms, special housing for international students, women's dorms, fraternity/sorority housing, apartments for single students, Arts House, French House, Community Outreach House, Sustainability House. 80% of campus accessible to physically diasbled. **Special Academic Facilities/Equipment:** Art gallery, associated with natural history museums, bronze casting foundry, retail sales complex, psychology and language labs, TV and radio station, observatory/planetarium, Writers House **Computers:** 100% of classrooms, 100% of dorms, 100% of libraries, 100% of dining areas, 100% of student union, 100% of common outdoor areas have wireless network access. Students can register for classes online. Administrative functions (other than registration) can be performed online.

CAMPUS LIFE

Environment: Town. **Activities:** Choral groups, concert band, dance, drama/theater, jazz band, literary magazine, music ensembles, musical theater, radio station, student government, student newspaper, symphony orchestra, yearbook, Campus Ministries, Student Organization, Model UN. 90 registered organizations, 13 honor societies, 8 religious organizations. 7 fraternities, 3 sororities. **Athletics (Intercollegiate):** *Men:* baseball, basketball, crew/rowing, cross-country, football, golf, lacrosse, soccer, squash, swimming, tennis, track/field (outdoor), track/field (indoor), wrestling. *Women:* basketball, crew/rowing, cross-country, field hockey, golf, lacrosse, soccer, softball, squash, swimming, tennis, track/field (outdoor), track/field (indoor), volleyball. **On-Campus Highlights:** Alumni Sport and Fitness Center, Barshinger Center in Hensel Hall, Barnes and Noble Bookstore and Jazzman's Cafe, Roschel Performing Arts Center, Writers House. **Environmental Initiatives:** We have established the Wohlsen Center for the Sustainable Environment, including a Director, student staff member, and Artist-in-Residence, and partnership with the Millport Conservancy.

ADMISSIONS

Freshman Academic Profile: 67% in top 10% of high school class, 88% in top 25% of high school class, 96% in top 50% of high school class, 63% from public high schools. **Reported SAT (pre-2016 redesign) scores:** SAT Math middle 50% range 630-730. SAT Critical Reading middle 50% range 570-680. **Concordant SAT scores:** SAT Math middle 50% range 650–760. ACT middle 50% range 28-31. Minimum paper TOEFL 600. **Basis for Candidate Selection:** *Very important factors considered include:* rigor of secondary school record, class rank, academic GPA, character/personal qualities. *Important factors considered include:* standardized test scores, application essay, recommendation(s), interview, extracurricular activities, talent/ability, volunteer work. *Other factors considered include:* alumni/ae relation, geographical residence, racial/ethnic status, work experience, level of applicant's interest. **Freshman Admission Requirements:** High school diploma is required and GED is accepted. *Academic units required:* 4 English, 3 math, 2 science, 2 science labs, 2 foreign language, 1 social studies, 2 history, 1 visual/performing arts. *Academic units recommended:* 4 math, 3 science, 3 science labs, 4 foreign language, 3 social studies, 3 history. **Freshman Admission Statistics:** 6,956 applied, 36.36% admitted, 25% enrolled. **Transfer Admission Requirements:** High school transcript, college transcript(s) or personal statement, interview, standardized test scores, statement of good standing from prior institution(s). Lowest grade transferable C-. **General Admission Information:** Application fee $60. Regular application deadline 1/15. Regular notification 4/1. Nonfall registration accepted. Admission may be deferred for a maximum of one year.

COSTS AND FINANCIAL AID

Annual tuition $52,190. Room and board $13,120. Required fees $100. Average book expense $1,200. **Required Forms and Deadlines:** FAFSA, CSS/Financial Aid PROFILE, Noncustodial PROFILE. **Notification of Awards:** Applicants will be notified of awards on or about 4/1. **Types of Aid:** *Need-based scholarships/grants:* Federal Pell, FSEOG, State scholarships/grants, Private scholarships, College/university scholarship or grant aid from institutional funds. *Loans:* Direct Subsidized Stafford Loans, Direct Unsubsidized Stafford Loans, Direct PLUS loans, Federal Perkins Loans, College/university loans from institutional funds. *Student Employment:* Federal Work-Study Program available. **Financial Aid Statistics:** 100% needy freshmen, 100% needy undergrads receive need-based scholarship or grant aid. 26% freshmen, 29% undergrads receive non-need-based scholarship or grant aid. 90% freshmen, 98% undergrads receive need-based self-help aid. 0% freshmen, 0% undergrads receive athletic scholarships. 51% freshmen, 53% undergrads receive any aid. 60% undergrads borrow to pay for school. Average cumulative indebtedness $27,133. **Criteria for awarding aid:** *Need-based:* Academics, Religious affiliation. *Non-need-based:* Music/drama.

FRANKLIN COLLEGE

101 Branigin Blvd, Franklin, IN 46131-2623
Phone: 317-738-8075 • **Financial Aid Phone:** 317-738-8075
E-mail: admissions@franklincollege.edu • **CEEB Code:** 1228
Fax: 317-738-8274 • **Website:** www.franklincollege.edu • **ACT Code:** 1194

This private school, affiliated with the American Baptist Church, was founded in 1834. It has a 156-acre campus.

RATINGS

Admissions Selectivity Rating: 80   **Fire Safety Rating:** 85   **Green Rating:** 61

STUDENTS AND FACULTY

Enrollment: 977. **Student Body:** 51% female, 49% male, 8% out-of-state, 1% international (13 countries represented). Asian 1%, African American 5%, Caucasian 84%, Hispanic 3%, Native American <1%, Pacific Islander 0%, Two or more races 4%, Race unknown 2%.
Retention and Graduation: 74% freshmen return for sophomore year. 60% freshmen graduate within 4 years. 66% freshmen graduate within 6 years. 20% grads go on to further study within 1 year. 14% grads pursue arts and sciences degrees. 2% grads pursue law degrees. 1% grads pursue business degrees. 3% grads pursue medical degrees. **Faculty:** Student/faculty ratio 11:1. 78 full-time faculty, 88% hold PhDs, 13% are are members of minority groups, 42% are women. 0% of classes are taught by teaching assistants.

ACADEMICS

Degrees: bachelor's. **Classes:** Most classes have 10-19 students. **Most popular majors:** Elementary Education and Teaching; Biology/Biological Sciences; Business/Commerce. **Special Study Options:** double major, dual enrollment, exchange student program (domestic), independent study, internships, study abroad, teacher certification program. **Honors Programs:** The intercultural Honors Experience is a freshman-year program designed to attract and retain superior students and faculty to FC while internationalizing the FC community. The program is designed to help students build a solid intercultural foundation, introduce them to interdisciplinary learning, and provide them with opportunities and incentives to study abroad. Faculty development is an integral part of the project. Combined degree programs: BA/MA, Athletic Training. **Disability Services:** Special programs offered to physically disabled students, including note-taking services, reader services, tape recorders, tutors. **Career Services:** Alumni services, Career/job search classes, Career assessment.

FACILITIES

Housing: Coed dorms, special housing for disabled students, men's dorms, women's dorms, fraternity/sorority housing. 100% of campus accessible to physically diasbled. **Special Academic Facilities/Equipment:** Pulliam School of Journalism, Dietz Center for Professional Development, Leadership Center. **Computers:** 100% of classrooms, 100% of libraries, 100% of dining areas, 100% of student union, have wireless network access. Students can register for classes online. Administrative functions (other than registration) can be performed online.

CAMPUS LIFE

Environment: Village. **Activities:** Choral groups, dance, drama/theater, literary magazine, musical theater, pep band, radio station, student government, student newspaper, yearbook. 66 registered organizations, 13 honor societies, 3 religious organizations. 5 fraternities, 4 sororities. **Athletics (Intercollegiate):** *Men:* baseball, basketball, cross-country, diving, football, golf, soccer, swimming, tennis, track/field (outdoor). *Women:* basketball, cheerleading, cross-country, diving, golf, soccer, softball, swimming, tennis, track/field (outdoor), volleyball. **On-Campus Highlights:** Student Center, Sprulock Center (athletic facility), library, residence hall, fraternity houses. **Environmental Initiatives:** Completing green house car emissions inventory.

ADMISSIONS

Freshman Academic Profile: Average high school GPA 3.5. 26% in top 10% of high school class, 54% in top 25% of high school class, 85% in top 50% of high school class. 90% from public high schools. **Reported SAT (pre-2016 redesign) scores:** SAT Math middle 50% range 430-550. SAT Critical Reading middle 50% range 420-530. SAT Writing middle 50% range 410-520. **Concordant SAT scores:** SAT EBRW middle 50% 460–580. SAT Math middle 50% range 470–570. ACT middle 50% range 19-25. Minimum internet-based TOEFL 79. Minimum paper TOEFL 550. **Basis for Candidate Selection:** *Very important factors considered include:* rigor of secondary school record, class rank, academic GPA, standardized test scores. *Important factors considered include:* application essay, extracurricular activities, alumni/ae relation. *Other factors considered include:* recommendation(s), interview, talent/ability, first generation, geographical residence, state residency, religious affiliation/commitment, racial/ethnic status, volunteer work, work experience, level of applicant's interest. **Freshman Admission Requirements:** High school diploma is required and GED is accepted. *Academic units required:* 4 English, 4 math, 2 science, 3 social studies. *Academic units recommended:* 2 foreign language. **Freshman Admission Statistics:** 1,479 applied, 78.09% admitted, 21% enrolled. **Transfer Admission Requirements:** High school transcript, college transcript(s), essay or personal statement, statement of good standing from prior institution(s). Minimum college GPA of 2.0 required. Lowest grade transferable C-. **General Admission Information:** Application fee $40. Priority deadline 12/1. Nonfall registration accepted. Admission may be deferred for a maximum of 1 year.

COSTS AND FINANCIAL AID

Annual tuition $29,840. Room and board $9,040. Required fees $185. Average book expense $1,200. **Required Forms and Deadlines:** FAFSA, Institution's own financial aid form. **Notification of Awards:** Applicants will be notified of awards on or about 3/1. **Types of Aid:** *Need-based scholarships/grants:* Federal Pell, FSEOG, State scholarships/grants, Private scholarships, College/university scholarship or grant aid from institutional funds. *Loans:* Direct Subsidized Stafford Loans, Direct Unsubsidized Stafford Loans, Direct PLUS loans, Federal Perkins Loans, College/university loans from institutional funds. *Student Employment:* Federal Work-Study Program available. Institutional employment available. **Financial Aid Statistics:** 100% needy freshmen, 100% needy undergrads receive need-based scholarship or grant aid. 17% freshmen, 14% undergrads receive non-need-based scholarship or grant aid. 83% freshmen, 85% undergrads receive need-based self-help aid. 0% freshmen, 0% undergrads receive athletic scholarships. 100% freshmen, 96% undergrads receive any aid. 86% undergrads borrow to pay for school. Average cumulative indebtedness $34,884. **Criteria for awarding aid:** *Need-based:* Minority status, Religious affiliation. *Non-need-based:* Academics, Alumni affiliation, Art, Minority status, Music/drama, Religious affiliation, State/district residency.

FRANKLIN PIERCE UNIVERSITY

Admissions Office, Rindge, NH 3461
Phone: 603-899-4050 • **Financial Aid Phone:** 603-899-4180
E-mail: admissions@franklinpierce.edu • **CEEB Code:** 3395
Fax: 603-889-4394 • **Website:** www.franklinpierce.edu • **ACT Code:** 2509

This private school was founded in 1962. It has a 1200-acre campus.

RATINGS
Admissions Selectivity Rating: 63   **Fire Safety Rating:** 93   **Green Rating:** 60*

STUDENTS AND FACULTY
Student Body: 52% female, 48% male, % out-of-state.
Retention and Graduation: 26% grads go on to further study within 1 year. 5% grads pursue arts and sciences degrees. 3% grads pursue law degrees. 7% grads pursue business degrees. 1% grads pursue medical degrees. **Faculty:** Student/faculty ratio 18:1. 100 full-time faculty, 68% hold PhDs, 1% are are members of minority groups, 45% are women. 0% of classes are taught by teaching assistants.

ACADEMICS
Degrees: associate, bachelor's, certificate, doctoral, master's, post-master's certificate. **Classes:** Most classes have 10-19 students. Most lab/discussion sessions have fewer than 10 students. **Most popular majors:** Education; Criminal Justice/Safety Studies; Mass Communication/Media Studies. **Special Study Options:** distance learning, double major, dual enrollment, English as a Second Language (ESL), exchange student program (domestic), honors program, independent study, internships, liberal arts/career combination, student-designed major, study abroad, teacher certification program, Walk Across Europe Program, Washington Semester, Arcadia Study Abroad. **Honors Programs:** Honors Program. **Disability Services:** Special programs offered to physically disabled students, including note-taking services, reader services, tape recorders, tutors. **Career Services:** Alumni network, Alumni services, Career/job search classes, Career assessment, Internships, Regional alumni.

FACILITIES
Housing: Coed dorms, special housing for disabled students, apartments for single students, Wellness Housing, Condominiums (townhouses). 67% of campus accessible to physically diasbled. **Special Academic Facilities/ Equipment:** Thoreau Art Gallery; Flynt Center; Fitzwater Communications Center; Dance Studio; Pottery Kiln; Glass Blowing Studio; TV Station; Radio Station; Grimshaw-Gudewicz Activities Center: Lakeside Activity Center **Computers:** 20% of classrooms, 20% of dorms, 100% of libraries, 80% of dining areas, 100% of student union, 50% of common outdoor areas have wireless network access. Administrative functions (other than registration) can be performed online.

CAMPUS LIFE
Environment: Rural. **Activities:** Choral groups, dance, drama/theater, literary magazine, music ensembles, musical theater, radio station, student government, student newspaper, television station, yearbook, Campus Ministries. 35 registered organizations, 8 honor societies, 3 religious organizations. **Athletics (Intercollegiate):** *Men:* baseball, basketball, crew/rowing, golf, ice hockey, rugby, soccer, tennis. *Women:* basketball, crew/rowing, cross-country, field hockey, lacrosse, soccer, softball, volleyball. **On-Campus Highlights:** Peterson Hall, The Campus Center, The Northfields Activity Center, The Fitzwater Center for Communications, The Pub. **Environmental Initiatives:** Development of on enhanced on-campus recycling program.

ADMISSIONS
Freshman Academic Profile: Average high school GPA 2.8. 89% from public high schools. Minimum internet-based TOEFL 61. Minimum paper TOEFL 500. **Basis for Candidate Selection:** *Very important factors considered include:* academic GPA, recommendation(s), character/personal qualities. *Important factors considered include:* rigor of secondary school record, application essay. *Other factors considered include:* class rank, standardized test scores, interview, extracurricular activities, talent/ability, volunteer work, work experience. **Freshman Admission Requirements:** High school diploma is required and GED is accepted. *Academic units required:* 4 English, 3 math, 2 science, 2 science labs, 3 social studies, 4 academic electives, and 4 units from above areas or other academic areas. **Freshman Admission Statistics:** 3,740 applied, 79.71% admitted, 16% enrolled. **Transfer Admission Requirements:** college transcript(s), essay or personal statement, Minimum college GPA of 2.0 required. Lowest grade transferable C-. **General Admission Information:** Nonfall registration accepted. Admission may be deferred for a maximum of 1 year.

COSTS AND FINANCIAL AID
Annual tuition $30,870. Room and board $12,546. Required fees $2,450. Average book expense $1,000. **Required Forms and Deadlines:** FAFSA.

Notification of Awards: Applicants will be notified of awards on a rolling basis beginning 2/1. **Types of Aid:** *Need-based scholarships/grants:* Federal Pell, FSEOG, State scholarships/grants, Private scholarships, College/university scholarship or grant aid from institutional funds. *Loans:* Federal Perkins Loans. *Student Employment:* Federal Work-Study Program available. Institutional employment available. **Financial Aid Statistics:** 99% needy freshmen, 99% needy undergrads receive need-based scholarship or grant aid. 10% freshmen, 9% undergrads receive non-need-based scholarship or grant aid. 90% freshmen, 90% undergrads receive need-based self-help aid. 4% freshmen, 5% undergrads receive athletic scholarships. 99% freshmen, 87% undergrads receive any aid. **Criteria for awarding aid:** *Need-based:* Academics, Athletics. *Non-needbased:* Academics, Alumni affiliation, Athletics, Leadership, Minority status, Music/drama.

FRANKLIN UNIVERSITY

201 S Grant Ave, Columbus, OH 43215
Phone: 614-797-4700
E-mail: info@franklin.edu • **CEEB Code:** 1229
Fax: 614-224-8027 • **ACT Code:** 3275

This private school was founded in 1902. It has a 14-acre campus.

RATINGS
Admissions Selectivity Rating: 62   **Fire Safety Rating:** 60*   **Green Rating:** 60*

STUDENTS AND FACULTY
Enrollment: 5,147. **Student Body:** 55% female, 45% male, 26% out-of-state, 6% international. Asian 3%, African American 21%, Caucasian 73%, Hispanic 2%, Native American <1%, Pacific Islander 0%, Two or more races 0%, Race unknown 5%.
Retention and Graduation: 72% freshmen return for sophomore year. **Faculty:** Student/faculty ratio 19:1. 36 full-time faculty, 64% hold PhDs, 6% are are members of minority groups, 44% are women.

ACADEMICS
Degrees: associate, bachelor's, master's. **Classes:** Most classes have 10-19 students. **Special Study Options:** Accelerated program, cooperative education program, cross-registration, distance learning, double major, dual enrollment, English as a Second Language (ESL), independent study, internships, study abroad, weekend college. Combined degree programs: BS/MBA. **Disability Services:** Special programs offered to physically disabled students, including note-taking services, reader services, tape recorders, tutors. **Career Services:** Alumni network, Alumni services, Internships, On-campus interviews.

FACILITIES
Housing: 100% of campus accessible to physically diasbled. **Computers:** Students can register for classes online.

CAMPUS LIFE
Activities: 6 registered organizations.

ADMISSIONS
Minimum paper TOEFL 430. **Freshman Admission Requirements:** High school diploma is required and GED is accepted. *Academic units recommended:* 3 math. **Freshman Admission Statistics:** 262 applied, 100.00% admitted, 47% enrolled. **Transfer Admission Requirements:** college transcript(s), Lowest grade transferable C-. **General Admission Information:** Nonfall registration accepted. Admission may be deferred.

COSTS AND FINANCIAL AID
Annual tuition $6,990. Required fees $0. Average book expense $0. **Required Forms and Deadlines:** FAFSA. **Types of Aid:** *Need-based scholarships/ grants:* Federal Pell, FSEOG, State scholarships/grants, Private scholarships, College/university scholarship or grant aid from institutional funds. *Loans:* College/university loans from institutional funds. *Student Employment:* Federal Work-Study Program available. Institutional employment available. **Financial Aid Statistics:** 72% needy freshmen, 64% needy undergrads receive need-based scholarship or grant aid. 89% freshmen, 84% undergrads receive non-need-based scholarship or grant aid. 97% freshmen, 96% undergrads receive need-based self-help aid. 0% freshmen, 0% undergrads receive athletic scholarships. **Criteria for awarding aid:** *Need-based:* Academics. *Non-needbased:* Academics, Leadership, Minority status.

FRANKLIN W. OLIN COLLEGE OF ENGINEERING

Needham, MA 02492-1245
Phone: 781-292-2222 • **Financial Aid Phone:** 781-292-2343
E-mail: info@olin.edu • **CEEB Code:** 2824
Fax: 781-292-2210 • **Website:** www.olin.edu • **ACT Code:** 1883

This private school was founded in 1997.

RATINGS

Admissions Selectivity Rating: 99   **Fire Safety Rating:** 91   **Green Rating:** 70

STUDENTS AND FACULTY

Enrollment: 333. **Student Body:** 48% female, 52% male, 86% out-of-state, 8% international (13 countries represented). Asian 16%, African American <1%, Caucasian 53%, Hispanic 5%, Native American <1%, Pacific Islander 0%, Two or more races 7%, Race unknown 11%.
Retention and Graduation: 91% freshmen return for sophomore year. 76% freshmen graduate within 4 years. 93% freshmen graduate within 6 years. 18% grads go on to further study within 1 year. 14% grads pursue arts and sciences degrees. 1% grads pursue law degrees. 1% grads pursue business degrees. 1% grads pursue medical degrees. **Faculty:** Student/faculty ratio 8:1. 37 full-time faculty, 97% hold PhDs, 22% are are members of minority groups, 46% are women. 0% of classes are taught by teaching assistants.

ACADEMICS

Degrees: bachelor's. **Classes:** Most classes have 20-29 students. **Most popular majors:** Engineering; Electrical and Electronics Engineering; Mechanical Engineering. **Special Study Options:** cross-registration, exchange student program (domestic), independent study, internships, liberal arts/career combination, student-designed major, study abroad, Passionate Pursuits program. **Career Services:** Alumni network, Alumni services, Career/job search classes, Internships, Regional alumni. Because we are a fairly new school, our network of alumni remains small but powerful. Many are now at prestigious companies or graduate school programs, and they often return to campus to talk about their company, career, grad school experience, or they perform mock interviews and/or provide advice to our current students. Due to our young age, our students are especially interested in hearing of our alumni's tales of continued development and success.

FACILITIES

Housing: Coed dorms, special housing for disabled students. 100% of campus accessible to physically diasbled. **Computers:** 100% of classrooms, 100% of dorms, 100% of libraries, 100% of dining areas, 100% of student union, 100% of common outdoor areas have wireless network access. Students can register for classes online. Administrative functions (other than registration) can be performed online. Undergraduates are required to own a computer.

CAMPUS LIFE

Environment: Town. **Activities:** Choral groups, dance, drama/theater, jazz band, music ensembles, musical theater, student government, student-run film society, symphony orchestra, yearbook. 55 registered organizations.
Environmental Initiatives: Replacing site-wide external lighting with LED's

ADMISSIONS

Freshman Academic Profile: Average high school GPA 3.9. **Reported SAT (pre-2016 redesign) scores:** SAT Math middle 50% range 730-800. SAT Critical Reading middle 50% range 710-800. SAT Writing middle 50% range 680-770. **Concordant SAT scores:** SAT EBRW middle 50% 730–790. SAT Math middle 50% range 760–800. ACT middle 50% range 32-35. **Basis for Candidate Selection:** *Very important factors considered include:* rigor of secondary school record, academic GPA, application essay, recommendation(s), interview, extracurricular activities, talent/ability, character/personal qualities, level of applicant's interest. *Important factors considered include:* class rank, standardized test scores, racial/ethnic status, volunteer work. *Other factors considered include:* first generation, alumni/ae relation, geographical residence, state residency, work experience. **Freshman Admission Requirements:** High school diploma is required and GED is accepted. *Academic units recommended:* 4 English, 4 math, 4 science, 3 science labs, 2 foreign language, 2 social studies, 2 history. **Freshman Admission Statistics:** 1,075 applied, 10.98% admitted, 64% enrolled. **Transfer Admission Requirements:** college transcript(s), Minimum college GPA of 2.0 required. Lowest grade transferable C. **General Admission Information:** Application fee $80. Regular application deadline 1/1. Regular notification 3/21. Nonfall registration not accepted. Admission may be deferred for a maximum of 2 years.

COSTS AND FINANCIAL AID

Annual tuition $46,800. Required fees $530. Average book expense $300.
Required Forms and Deadlines: FAFSA. **Notification of Awards:** Applicants will be notified of awards on or about 3/21. **Types of Aid:** *Need-based scholarships/grants:* Federal Pell, FSEOG, College/university scholarship or grant aid from institutional funds. *Loans:* Direct Subsidized Stafford Loans, Direct Unsubsidized Stafford Loans, Direct PLUS loans. *Student Employment:* Institutional employment available. **Financial Aid Statistics:** 100% needy freshmen, 100% needy undergrads receive need-based scholarship or grant aid. 100% freshmen, 100% undergrads receive non-need-based scholarship or grant aid. 81% freshmen, 88% undergrads receive need-based self-help aid. 0% freshmen, 0% undergrads receive athletic scholarships. 100% freshmen, 100% undergrads receive any aid. 43% undergrads borrow to pay for school. Average cumulative indebtedness $19,196. **Criteria for awarding aid:** *Non-need-based:* Academics, Leadership.

FREED-HARDEMAN UNIVERSITY

158 East Main Street, Henderson, TN 38340
Phone: 731-989-6651 • **Financial Aid Phone:** 731-989-6662
E-mail: jathoms1@yahoo.com • **CEEB Code:** 1230
Fax: 731-989-6047 • **Website:** web.fhu.edu • **ACT Code:** 3962

This private school, affiliated with the Church of Christ Church, was founded in 1869. It has a 122-acre campus.

RATINGS

Admissions Selectivity Rating: 86   **Fire Safety Rating:** 66   **Green Rating:** 60*

STUDENTS AND FACULTY

Enrollment: 1,427. **Student Body:** 55% female, 45% male, 50% out-of-state, 3% international (26 countries represented). Asian 0%, African American 4%, Caucasian 91%, Hispanic 1%, Native American <1%, Pacific Islander 0%, Two or more races 0%, Race unknown <1%.
Retention and Graduation: 74% freshmen return for sophomore year. 41% freshmen graduate within 4 years. 58% freshmen graduate within 6 years. 40% grads go on to further study within 1 year. **Faculty:** Student/faculty ratio 14:1. 108 full-time faculty, 69% hold PhDs, 5% are are members of minority groups, 31% are women. 0% of classes are taught by teaching assistants.

ACADEMICS

Degrees: bachelor's, doctoral, master's, postbachelor's certifiate, post-master's certificate. **Classes:** Most classes have 10-19 students. Most lab/discussion sessions have 10-19 students. **Most popular majors:** Liberal Arts and Sciences Studies and Humanities; Biology/Biological Sciences; Bible/Biblical Studies. **Special Study Options:** Accelerated program, cooperative education program, cross-registration, distance learning, double major, dual enrollment, honors program, independent study, internships, liberal arts/career combination, student-designed major, study abroad, teacher certification program, 3-2 engineering, Honors College, study abroad in Belgium and Italy. **Honors Programs:** Exceptional students may be admitted to the Honors College, where he or she may graduate as an Honors College Scholar, or as an Honors College Scholar with University Honors. Combined degree programs: BBA/MBA. **Disability Services:** Special programs offered to physically disabled students, including note-taking services, reader services, tutors. **Career Services:** Alumni network, Career assessment, Internships.

FACILITIES

Housing: men's dorms, women's dorms, apartments for single students, Some student teacher housing is available. 70% of campus accessible to physically diasbled. **Special Academic Facilities/Equipment:** Child development lab, nursery school. **Computers:** Students can register for classes online. Administrative functions (other than registration) can be performed online.

CAMPUS LIFE

Environment: Rural. **Activities:** Choral groups, concert band, drama/theater, jazz band, music ensembles, musical theater, pep band, radio station, student government, student newspaper, television station, yearbook. 52 registered organizations, 4 honor societies, 5 religious organizations. 6 fraternities, 6 sororities. **Athletics (Intercollegiate):** *Men:* baseball, basketball, cheerleading, soccer. *Women:* basketball, cheerleading, soccer, softball, volleyball. **On-Campus Highlights:** The Commons, The Student Center, The Sports Center, Brown-Kopel Business Center, The Library.

ADMISSIONS

Freshman Academic Profile: Average high school GPA 3.4. 25% in top 10% of high school class, 51% in top 25% of high school class, 79% in top 50% of high school class. **Reported SAT (pre-2016 redesign) scores:** SAT Math middle 50% range 480-600. SAT Critical Reading middle 50% range 480-

640. **Concordant SAT scores:** SAT Math middle 50% range 510–620. ACT middle 50% range 20-26. **Basis for Candidate Selection:** *Very important factors considered include:* rigor of secondary school record, academic GPA, standardized test scores. *Other factors considered include:* recommendation(s), extracurricular activities, character/personal qualities, alumni/ae relation, religious affiliation/commitment, racial/ethnic status, volunteer work, work experience. **Freshman Admission Requirements:** High school diploma is required and GED is accepted. *Academic units recommended:* 4 English, 2 math, 2 science, 2 social studies, 10 academic electives. **Freshman Admission Statistics:** 1,326 applied, 54.83% admitted, 53% enrolled. **Transfer Admission Requirements:** college transcript(s), statement of good standing from prior institution(s). Lowest grade transferable D. **General Admission Information:** Nonfall registration accepted. Admission may be deferred for a maximum of 2 years.

COSTS AND FINANCIAL AID
Annual tuition $13,192. Room and board $6,560. Average book expense $1,710. **Required Forms and Deadlines:** FAFSA. **Notification of Awards:** Applicants will be notified of awards on a rolling basis beginning 3/1. **Types of Aid:** *Need-based scholarships/grants:* Federal Pell, FSEOG, State scholarships/grants, Private scholarships, College/university scholarship or grant aid from institutional funds. *Loans:* Federal Perkins Loans. *Student Employment:* Federal Work-Study Program available. Institutional employment available. **Financial Aid Statistics:** 97% needy freshmen, 91% needy undergrads receive need-based scholarship or grant aid. 19% freshmen, 17% undergrads receive non-need-based scholarship or grant aid. 74% freshmen, 78% undergrads receive need-based self-help aid. 4% freshmen, 4% undergrads receive athletic scholarships. 86% freshmen receive any aid. **Criteria for awarding aid:** *Non-need-based:* Academics, Art, Athletics, Leadership, Minority status, Music/drama, State/district residency.

FRESNO PACIFIC UNIVERSITY

1717 S. Chestnut Ave, Fresno, CA 93702
Phone: 559-453-2039 • **Financial Aid Phone:** 559-453-2041
E-mail: ugadmis@fresno.edu
Fax: 559-453-2007 • **Website:** http://www.fresno.edu/

This private school, affiliated with the Mennonite Church, was founded in 1944. It has a 42-acre campus.

RATINGS
Admissions Selectivity Rating: 60*   **Fire Safety Rating:** 60*   **Green Rating:** 60*

STUDENTS AND FACULTY
Enrollment: 1,459. **Student Body:** 68% female, 32% male, 2% international. Asian 4%, African American 4%, Caucasian 53%, Hispanic 26%, Native American 1%, Pacific Islander 0%, Two or more races 0%, Race unknown 10%. **Retention and Graduation:** 70% freshmen return for sophomore year. 48% freshmen graduate within 4 years. 62% freshmen graduate within 6 years.

ACADEMICS
Degrees: associate, bachelor's, certificate, master's, postbachelor's certificate. **Classes:** Most classes have fewer than 10 students. Most lab/discussion sessions have fewer than 10 students. **Most popular majors:** Education; Bible/Biblical Studies; Business/Commerce. **Special Study Options:** Accelerated program, cooperative education program, cross-registration, distance learning, double major, English as a Second Language (ESL), independent study, internships, liberal arts/career combination, student-designed major, study abroad, teacher certification program. **Disability Services:** Special programs offered to physically disabled students, including note-taking services, reader services, tutors. **Career Services:** Alumni services, Career/job search classes, Career assessment, Internships, On-campus interviews.

FACILITIES
Housing: special housing for disabled students, men's dorms, women's dorms, apartments for single students, Houses. 100% of campus accessible to physically diasbled. **Special Academic Facilities/Equipment:** English Language Training Institute

CAMPUS LIFE
Environment: Metropolis. **Activities:** Choral groups, concert band, dance, drama/theater, jazz band, music ensembles, pep band, student government, student newspaper, yearbook. 36 registered organizations, 1 honor society, 11 religious organizations. **Athletics (Intercollegiate):** *Men:* baseball, basketball, cross-country, soccer, tennis, track/field (outdoor). *Women:* basketball, cross-country, soccer, tennis, track/field (outdoor), volleyball. **On-Campus Highlights:** Special Events Center (Gym), Steinert Campus Center, The Green (students hang out there), Bookshop, New AIMS Building.

ADMISSIONS
Basis for Candidate Selection: *Very important factors considered include:* rigor of secondary school record, standardized test scores. *Important factors considered include:* class rank, academic GPA, application essay, recommendation(s), religious affiliation/commitment. *Other factors considered include:* character/personal qualities. **Freshman Admission Requirements:** High school diploma is required and GED is accepted. *Academic units required:* 4 English, 3 math, 1 science, 1 science lab, 2 foreign language, 2 social studies. *Academic units recommended:* 1 unit from above areas or other academic areas. **Transfer Admission Requirements:** High school transcript, college transcript(s), essay or personal statement, Minimum college GPA of 2.4 required. Lowest grade transferable C. **General Admission Information:** Application fee $40. Priority deadline 12/1. Regular application deadline 7/31. Nonfall registration accepted. Admission may be deferred.

COSTS AND FINANCIAL AID
Annual tuition $24,960. Required fees $276. Average book expense $1,665. **Required Forms and Deadlines:** FAFSA. **Notification of Awards:** Applicants will be notified of awards on a rolling basis beginning 2/21. **Types of Aid:** *Need-based scholarships/grants:* Federal Pell, FSEOG, State scholarships/grants, Private scholarships, College/university scholarship or grant aid from institutional funds. *Loans:* Direct Subsidized Stafford Loans, Direct Unsubsidized Stafford Loans, Direct PLUS loans, Federal Perkins Loans. *Student Employment:* Federal Work-Study Program available. Institutional employment available. **Financial Aid Statistics:** 81% needy freshmen, 81% needy undergrads receive need-based scholarship or grant aid. 98% freshmen, 52% undergrads receive non-need-based scholarship or grant aid. 74% freshmen, 80% undergrads receive need-based self-help aid. 14% freshmen, 9% undergrads receive athletic scholarships. **Criteria for awarding aid:** *Non-need-based:* Academics, Alumni affiliation, Art, Athletics, Leadership, Minority status, Music/drama, Religious affiliation.

FRIENDS UNIVERSITY

2100 University Avenue, Wichita, KS 67213
Phone: 316-295-5100 • **Financial Aid Phone:** 316-295-5200
E-mail: learn@friends.edu • **CEEB Code:** 6224
Fax: 316-295-5101 • **Website:** www.friends.edu • **ACT Code:** 1918

This private school, affiliated with the Quaker Church, was founded in 1898. It has a 45-acre campus.

RATINGS
Admissions Selectivity Rating: 81   **Fire Safety Rating:** 89   **Green Rating:** 60*

STUDENTS AND FACULTY
Enrollment: 1,737. **Student Body:** 56% female, 44% male, 19% out-of-state, 0% international (13 countries represented). Asian 3%, African American 11%, Caucasian 71%, Hispanic 4%, Native American 2%, Pacific Islander <1%, Two or more races 5%, Race unknown 4%. **Retention and Graduation:** 60% freshmen return for sophomore year. 10% freshmen graduate within 4 years. 33% freshmen graduate within 6 years. **Faculty:** Student/faculty ratio 11:1. 75 full-time faculty, 71% hold PhDs, 5% are are members of minority groups, 41% are women. 0% of classes are taught by teaching assistants.

ACADEMICS
Degrees: associate, bachelor's, master's, postbachelor's certificate. **Most popular majors:** Business Administration and Management; Wildlife Biology; Psychology. **Special Study Options:** cooperative education program, cross-registration, double major, dual enrollment, external degree program, honors program, independent study, internships, student-designed major, study abroad, teacher certification program, Degree completion program for working adults. **Career Services:** Alumni network, Alumni services, Career/job search classes, Career assessment, Internships, Regional alumni.

FACILITIES
Housing: men's dorms, women's dorms, apartments for married students, apartments for single students, University-owned houses. 95% of campus accessible to physically diasbled.

CAMPUS LIFE
Activities: Choral groups, concert band, dance, drama/theater, jazz band, literary magazine, music ensembles, musical theater, pep band, student government, symphony orchestra, yearbook. 32 registered organizations, 4 honor societies, 3 religious organizations. 2 fraternities, 1 sorority. **Athletics (Intercollegiate):** *Men:* baseball, basketball, cheerleading, cross-country, football, golf, soccer, tennis, track/field (outdoor). *Women:* basketball, cheerleading, cross-country, soccer, softball, tennis, track/field (outdoor), volleyball.

ADMISSIONS

Freshman Academic Profile: Average high school GPA 3.4. 20% in top 10% of high school class, 36% in top 25% of high school class, 68% in top 50% of high school class. 84% from public high schools. **Reported SAT (pre-2016 redesign) scores:** SAT Math middle 50% range 400-510. SAT Critical Reading middle 50% range 390-515. **Concordant SAT scores:** SAT Math middle 50% range 440–540. ACT middle 50% range 18-26. Minimum internet-based TOEFL 63. Minimum paper TOEFL 500. **Basis for Candidate Selection:** *Very important factors considered include:* academic GPA, standardized test scores. *Important factors considered include:* rigor of secondary school record, class rank, extracurricular activities, talent/ability, character/personal qualities, alumni/ae relation, work experience. *Other factors considered include:* interview. **Freshman Admission Requirements:** High school diploma is required and GED is accepted. *Academic units required:* 2 foreign language, 2 social studies, 2 history. *Academic units recommended:* 3 English, 3 math, 1 science, 1 science lab, 2 foreign language, 2 social studies, 2 history, 1 computer science. **Freshman Admission Statistics:** 786 applied, 58.02% admitted, 43% enrolled. **Transfer Admission Requirements:** college transcript(s), statement of good standing from prior institution(s). Minimum college GPA of 2.0 required. Lowest grade transferable C. **General Admission Information:** Application fee $35. Regular application deadline 8/28. Nonfall registration accepted.

COSTS AND FINANCIAL AID

Annual tuition $23,250. Room and board $6,800. Required fees $180. Average book expense $1,500. **Required Forms and Deadlines:** FAFSA. **Notification of Awards:** Applicants will be notified of awards on a rolling basis beginning 3/1. **Types of Aid:** *Need-based scholarships/grants:* Federal Pell, FSEOG, State scholarships/grants, Private scholarships, College/university scholarship or grant aid from institutional funds. *Loans:* Direct Subsidized Stafford Loans, Direct Unsubsidized Stafford Loans, Direct PLUS loans, Federal Perkins Loans. *Student Employment:* Federal Work-Study Program available. Institutional employment available. **Financial Aid Statistics:** 100% needy freshmen, 84% needy undergrads receive need-based scholarship or grant aid. 24% freshmen, 13% undergrads receive non-need-based scholarship or grant aid. 78% freshmen, 89% undergrads receive need-based self-help aid. 21% freshmen, 3% undergrads receive athletic scholarships. 87% freshmen, 77% undergrads receive any aid. **Criteria for awarding aid:** *Non-need-based:* Academics, Alumni affiliation, Art, Athletics, Leadership, Music/drama, Religious affiliation.

FROSTBURG STATE UNIVERSITY

FSU, 101 Braddock Road, Frostburg, MD 21532
Phone: 301-687-4201 • **Financial Aid Phone:** 301-687-4301
E-mail: fsuadmissions@frostburg.edu • **CEEB Code:** 5402
Fax: 301-687-7074 • **Website:** www.frostburg.edu • **ACT Code:** 1714

This public school was founded in 1898. It has a 260-acre campus.

RATINGS

Admissions Selectivity Rating: 79   **Fire Safety Rating:** 87   **Green Rating:** 87

STUDENTS AND FACULTY

Enrollment: 4,522. **Student Body:** 49% female, 51% male, 8% out-of-state, 1% international (25 countries represented). Asian 1%, African American 26%, Caucasian 64%, Hispanic 3%, Native American <1%, Pacific Islander <1%, Two or more races 4%, Race unknown 1%.
Retention and Graduation: 72% freshmen return for sophomore year. 20% freshmen graduate within 4 years. 45% freshmen graduate within 6 years.
Faculty: Student/faculty ratio 17:1. 245 full-time faculty, 0% hold PhDs, 13% are are members of minority groups, 41% are women.

ACADEMICS

Degrees: bachelor's, certificate, master's, postbachelor's certificate, post-master's certificate. **Classes:** Most classes have 20-29 students. Most lab/discussion sessions have 10-19 students. **Most popular majors:** Elementary Education and Teaching; Psychology; Business/Commerce. **Special Study Options:** Accelerated program, distance learning, double major, dual enrollment, honors program, independent study, internships, liberal arts/career combination, study abroad, teacher certification program, Learning Communities, Dual Degree Program. Combined degree programs: MBA/BS in Accounting. **Disability Services:** Special programs offered to physically disabled students, including note-taking services, reader services, tape recorders, tutors. **Career Services:** Alumni network, Alumni services, Career/job search classes, Career assessment, Internships, Regional alumni, Internships.

FACILITIES

Housing: Coed dorms, women's dorms, Special interest **Housing:** Leadership Hall Honors Housing Community Service. 100% of campus accessible to physically diasbled. **Special Academic Facilities/Equipment:** Art gallery, planetarium, electron microscope. **Computers:** Students can register for classes online. Administrative functions (other than registration) can be performed online.

CAMPUS LIFE

Environment: Rural. **Activities:** Choral groups, concert band, dance, drama/theater, jazz band, literary magazine, marching band, music ensembles, musical theater, pep band, radio station, student government, student newspaper, symphony orchestra, television station 95 registered organizations, 18 honor societies, 6 religious organizations. 9 fraternities, 6 sororities. **Athletics (Intercollegiate):** *Men:* baseball, basketball, cross-country, diving, football, golf, soccer, swimming, tennis, track/field (outdoor), track/field (indoor). *Women:* basketball, cross-country, diving, field hockey, lacrosse, soccer, softball, swimming, tennis, track/field (outdoor), track/field (indoor), volleyball. **On-Campus Highlights:** Lane University Center, Cordts PE Center, Performing Arts Center, Stephanie Roper Art Gallery, Compton Science Center. **Environmental Initiatives:** Adopted an energy-efficient appliance purchasing policy requiring purchase of ENERGY STAR-certified products in all areas for which such ratings exist.

ADMISSIONS

Freshman Academic Profile: Average high school GPA 3.2. 11% in top 10% of high school class, 31% in top 25% of high school class, 66% in top 50% of high school class. **Reported SAT (pre-2016 redesign) scores:** SAT Math middle 50% range 440-540. SAT Critical Reading middle 50% range 440-530. SAT Writing middle 50% range 420-520. **Concordant SAT scores:** SAT EBRW middle 50% 480–580. SAT Math middle 50% range 480–570. ACT middle 50% range 18-22. Minimum paper TOEFL 550. **Basis for Candidate Selection:** *Very important factors considered include:* rigor of secondary school record, academic GPA, standardized test scores. *Important factors considered include:* recommendation(s), interview. *Other factors considered include:* extracurricular activities, talent/ability, character/personal qualities, alumni/ae relation. **Freshman Admission Requirements:** High school diploma is required and GED is accepted. *Academic units required:* 4 English, 3 math, 3 science, 2 science labs, 2 foreign language, 3 history. **Freshman Admission Statistics:** 3,951 applied, 59.23% admitted, 35% enrolled. **Transfer Admission Requirements:** college transcript(s), Minimum college GPA of 2.0 required. Lowest grade transferable C. **General Admission Information:** Application fee $30. Priority deadline 6/1. Nonfall registration accepted.

COSTS AND FINANCIAL AID

Annual in-state tuition $5,464. Annual out-of-state tuition $15,652. Room and board $7,796. Required fees $1,972. Average book expense $1,200. **Required Forms and Deadlines:** FAFSA. **Notification of Awards:** Applicants will be notified of awards on a rolling basis beginning 3/15. **Types of Aid:** *Need-based scholarships/grants:* Federal Pell, FSEOG, State scholarships/grants, Private scholarships, College/university scholarship or grant aid from institutional funds. *Loans:* Direct Subsidized Stafford Loans, Direct Unsubsidized Stafford Loans, Direct PLUS loans, Federal Perkins Loans, College/university loans from institutional funds. *Student Employment:* Federal Work-Study Program available. Institutional employment available. **Financial Aid Statistics:** 75% needy freshmen, 73% needy undergrads receive need-based scholarship or grant aid. 30% freshmen, 28% undergrads receive non-need-based scholarship or grant aid. 78% freshmen, 80% undergrads receive need-based self-help aid. 0% freshmen, 0% undergrads receive athletic scholarships. 72% freshmen, 65% undergrads receive any aid. **Criteria for awarding aid:** *Need-based:* Academics. *Non-need-based:* Academics, Alumni affiliation, Art, Leadership, Music/drama, State/district residency.

FULL SAIL UNIVERSITY

3300 University Blvd, Winter Park, FL 32792
Phone: 800-226-7625
E-mail: admissions@fullsail.com
Website: http://www.fullsail.edu/

This proprietary school was founded in 1979. It has a 91-acre campus.

RATINGS

Admissions Selectivity Rating: 60*   **Fire Safety Rating:** 60*   **Green Rating:** 60*

ACADEMICS

Degrees: associate, bachelor's, master's, terminal. **Most popular majors:** Recording Arts Technology/Technician; Animation, Interactive Technology, Video Graphics and Special Effects; Cinematography and Film/Video Production. **Special Study Options:** Accelerated program.

FACILITIES

Housing: Full Sail does not feature on-campus living arrangements, but does employ a Housing Manager who is dedicated to providing information about affordable accommodations in one of the many apartment complexes near the school. The Housing Manager can also help with information regarding roommates (other incoming Full Sail students), power, phones, furniture, and helpful community programs in the Central Florida area.

CAMPUS LIFE

Environment: Metropolis.

ADMISSIONS

Freshman Admission Requirements: High school diploma is required and GED is accepted. **Transfer Admission Requirements:** college transcript(s), essay or personal statement, statement of good standing from prior institution(s). Minimum college GPA of 2.6 required. Lowest grade transferable c.

COSTS AND FINANCIAL AID

Student Employment: Federal Work-Study Program available. Institutional employment available.

FURMAN UNIVERSITY

3300 Poinsett Highway, Greenville, SC 29613
Phone: 864-294-2034 • **Financial Aid Phone:** 864-294-2204
E-mail: admissions@furman.edu • **CEEB Code:** 5222
Fax: 864-294-2018 • **Website:** www.furman.edu • **ACT Code:** 3858

This private school was founded in 1826. It has a 800-acre campus.

RATINGS

Admissions Selectivity Rating: 88   **Fire Safety Rating:** 90   **Green Rating:** 97

STUDENTS AND FACULTY

Enrollment: 2,780. **Student Body:** 58% female, 42% male, 72% out-of-state, 5% international (54 countries represented). Asian 2%, African American 5%, Caucasian 78%, Hispanic 5%, Native American <1%, Pacific Islander 0%, Two or more races 3%, Race unknown 3%.
Retention and Graduation: 90% freshmen return for sophomore year. 78% freshmen graduate within 4 years. 84% freshmen graduate within 6 years. 38% grads go on to further study within 1 year. 28% grads pursue arts and sciences degrees. 3% grads pursue law degrees. 2% grads pursue business degrees. 4% grads pursue medical degrees. **Faculty:** Student/faculty ratio 11:1. 233 full-time faculty, 98% hold PhDs, 12% are are members of minority groups, 36% are women. 0% of classes are taught by teaching assistants.

ACADEMICS

Degrees: bachelor's, master's. **Classes:** Most classes have 20-29 students. **Most popular majors:** Political Science and Government; Business/Commerce; Health Professions and Related Clinical Sciences. **Special Study Options:** double major, independent study, internships, student-designed major, study abroad, teacher certification program. Combined degree programs: BA/MD, BA/MA, BA/DDS, Environmental Studies, Pharmacy, Nursing. **Disability Services:** Special programs offered to physically disabled students, including note-taking services, reader services, tape recorders, tutors. **Career Services:** Alumni network, Alumni services, Career/job search classes, Career assessment, Internships. Furman's internships, both paid and unpaid, are available to virtually every student. They run the gamut from medical research to international business opportunities.

FACILITIES

Housing: Coed dorms, men's dorms, special housing for international students, women's dorms, apartments for single students, Wellness Housing, Theme Housing, lakeside cottages, language houses, eco-cottage. 98% of campus accessible to physically diasbled. **Special Academic Facilities/Equipment:** Visual arts gallery and teaching facility, language lab. Astronomical lab; Center for Engaged Learning; and Center for Collaborative Learning and Communication. **Computers:** 100% of classrooms, 100% of libraries, 100% of dining areas, 100% of student union, have wireless network access. Students can register for classes online. Administrative functions (other than registration) can be performed online.

CAMPUS LIFE

Environment: City. **Activities:** Choral groups, concert band, dance, drama/theater, jazz band, literary magazine, marching band, music ensembles, musical

theater, opera, pep band, radio station, student government, student newspaper, student-run film society, symphony orchestra, television station, yearbook, Campus Ministries, Student Organization. 143 registered organizations, 29 honor societies, 17 religious organizations. 7 fraternities, 7 sororities. **Athletics (Intercollegiate):** *Men:* baseball, basketball, cheerleading, cross-country, football, golf, soccer, tennis, track/field (outdoor), track/field (indoor). *Women:* basketball, cheerleading, cross-country, golf, soccer, softball, tennis, track/field (outdoor), track/field (indoor), volleyball. **On-Campus Highlights:** Charles Townes Science Center, Timmons Arena, Library, 18-hole Golf Course, Physical Activities Center, Place of Peace, David Shi Center for Sustainability. **Environmental Initiatives:** Sustainable Furman: The approval of Sustainable Furman, the university comprehensive sustainability master plan. The plan covers all aspects of the university; the 8 goals of Sustainable Furman address sustainability in the curriculum, co-curricular activities, campus culture, renewable energy, efficiency in operations and maintenance, transportation, sustainability service, and continuing national leadership in the sustainability arena. In addition, the plan sets out a path for the university to reach carbon neutrality by 2026.

ADMISSIONS

Freshman Academic Profile: 45% in top 10% of high school class, 77% in top 25% of high school class, 96% in top 50% of high school class. 59% from public high schools. **Reported SAT (pre-2016 redesign) scores:** SAT Math middle 50% range 560-650. SAT Critical Reading middle 50% range 560-670. SAT Writing middle 50% range 550-660. **Concordant SAT scores:** SAT EBRW middle 50% 610-710. SAT Math middle 50% range 580-670. ACT middle 50% range 25-31. **Basis for Candidate Selection:** *Very important factors considered include:* rigor of secondary school record. *Important factors considered include:* class rank, academic GPA, application essay, extracurricular activities, character/personal qualities. *Other factors considered include:* standardized test scores, recommendation(s), interview, talent/ability, first generation, alumni/ae relation, racial/ethnic status, volunteer work, work experience, level of applicant's interest. **Freshman Admission Requirements:** High school diploma is required and GED is accepted. *Academic units required:* 4 English, 3 math, 2 science, 2 science labs, 2 foreign language, 3 social studies. *Academic units recommended:* 4 English, 4 math, 3 science, 2 science labs, 3 foreign language, 4 social studies. **Freshman Admission Statistics:** 5,232 applied, 67.76% admitted, 21% enrolled. **Transfer Admission Requirements:** High school transcript, college transcript(s), essay or personal statement, standardized test scores, statement of good standing from prior institution(s). Minimum college GPA of 3.0 required. Lowest grade transferable C. **General Admission Information:** Application fee $50. Regular application deadline 1/15. Regular notification 3/1. Nonfall registration not accepted.

COSTS AND FINANCIAL AID

Annual tuition $46,784. Room and board $11,864. Required fees $380. Average book expense $1,270. **Required Forms and Deadlines:** FAFSA, Institution's own financial aid form, CSS/Financial Aid PROFILE, State aid form. **Notification of Awards:** Applicants will be notified of awards on or about 4/1. **Types of Aid:** *Need-based scholarships/grants:* Federal Pell, FSEOG, State scholarships/grants, Private scholarships, College/university scholarship or grant aid from institutional funds. *Loans:* Direct Subsidized Stafford Loans, Direct Unsubsidized Stafford Loans, Direct PLUS loans, Federal Perkins Loans, State Loans. *Student Employment:* Federal Work-Study Program available. Institutional employment available. **Financial Aid Statistics:** 100% needy freshmen, 100% needy undergrads receive need-based scholarship or grant aid. 100% freshmen, 100% undergrads receive non-need-based scholarship or grant aid. 71% freshmen, 69% undergrads receive need-based self-help aid. 11% freshmen, 12% undergrads receive athletic scholarships. 98% freshmen, 94% undergrads receive any aid. 35% undergrads borrow to pay for school. Average cumulative indebtedness $36,846. **Criteria for awarding aid:** *Need-based:* Academics, Alumni affiliation, Art, Athletics, Leadership, Music/drama, Religious affiliation. *Non-need-based:* Academics, Alumni affiliation, Art, Athletics, Leadership, Music/drama, Religious affiliation, State/district residency.

GALLAUDET UNIVERSITY

800 Florida Avenue, NE, Washington DC, DC 20002
Phone: 202-651-5750 • **Financial Aid Phone:** 202-651-5290
E-mail: admissions.office@gallaudet.edu • **CEEB Code:** 5240
Fax: 202-651-5744 • **Website:** http://www.gallaudet.edu/ • **ACT Code:** 662

This private school was founded in 1864. It has a 99-acre campus.

RATINGS

Admissions Selectivity Rating: 76   **Fire Safety Rating:** 91   **Green Rating:** 60*

STUDENTS AND FACULTY

Enrollment: 1,001. **Student Body:** 54% female, 46% male, 97% out-of-state, 8% international (31 countries represented). Asian 4%, African American 12%, Caucasian 56%, Hispanic 15%, Native American <1%, Pacific Islander <1%, Two or more races 3%, Race unknown 1%.
Retention and Graduation: 67% freshmen return for sophomore year. 16% freshmen graduate within 4 years. 46% freshmen graduate within 6 years.
Faculty: Student/faculty ratio 6:1. 181 full-time faculty, 88% hold PhDs, 24% are are members of minority groups, 62% are women.

ACADEMICS

Degrees: bachelor's, certificate, doctoral/research, doctoral, master's, postbachelor's certificate, post-master's certificate. **Classes:** Most classes have 10-19 students. Most lab/discussion sessions have fewer than 10 students. **Most popular majors:** Psychology; Business Administration and Management; Ethnic, Cultural Minority, Gender, and Group Studies. **Special Study Options:** Accelerated program, cross-registration, distance learning, double major, English as a Second Language (ESL), exchange student program (domestic), honors program, independent study, internships, student-designed major, study abroad, teacher certification program, Experiential programs off-campus including orientation program for employers of deaf students and paraprofessional jobs on campus, programs for interpreter-assisted mainstreaming of students into area colleges such as Georgetown University, George Mason University, Catholic University, and Howard University. **Honors Programs:** The Gallaudet Honors Program is a Learning Community for the most academically capable and motivated students. The overall goal is to foster skills, work habits, and attitudes conducive to future achievement and lifelong learning. To this end, the Program focuses on linking rigorous, challenging, and innovative curricular offerings with co-curricular activities. It also serves as a leader in and test laboratory of curricular, co-curricular, and extracurricular innovations; successes may then be replicated for all students. **Disability Services:** Special programs offered to physically disabled students, including tutors. **Career Services:** Alumni network, Alumni services, Career/job search classes, Career assessment, Internships.

FACILITIES

Housing: Coed dorms, special housing for disabled students, apartments for married students, Theme Housing. 100% of campus accessible to physically disabled. **Special Academic Facilities/Equipment:** Kendall Demonstration Elementary School and Model Secondary School for the Deaf **Computers:** 100% of classrooms, 100% of dorms, 100% of libraries, 100% of dining areas, 100% of student union, 20% of common outdoor areas have wireless network access. Students can register for classes online. Administrative functions (other than registration) can be performed online.

CAMPUS LIFE

Environment: Metropolis. **Activities:** dance, drama/theater, literary magazine, student government, student newspaper, student-run film society, yearbook, Campus Ministries, Student Organization. 25 registered organizations, 1 honor society, 1 religious organization. 5 fraternities, 4 sororities. **Athletics (Intercollegiate):** *Men:* baseball, basketball, cross-country, diving, football, soccer, swimming, tennis, track/field (outdoor), wrestling. *Women:* basketball, cross-country, diving, soccer, softball, swimming, tennis, track/field (outdoor), volleyball. **On-Campus Highlights:** Rathskellar, Cafeteria, Bison Shop, Starbucks, Student Academic Center.

ADMISSIONS

Freshman Academic Profile: Average high school GPA 3.2. **Reported SAT (pre-2016 redesign) scores:** SAT Math middle 50% range 405-485. SAT Critical Reading middle 50% range 385-475. **Concordant SAT scores:** SAT Math middle 50% range 450-520. ACT middle 50% range 15-20. **Basis for Candidate Selection:** *Very important factors considered include:* rigor of secondary school record, class rank, academic GPA, standardized test scores, application essay, recommendation(s). *Other factors considered include:* interview, extracurricular activities, talent/ability, character/personal qualities, first generation, alumni/ae relation, geographical residence, state residency, religious affiliation/commitment, racial/ethnic status, volunteer work, work experience, level of applicant's interest. **Freshman Admission Requirements:** High school diploma is required and GED is accepted. *Academic units recommended:* 4 English, 3 math, 2 science, 2 foreign language, 2 social studies, 1 visual/performing arts, and 1 unit from above areas or other academic areas. **Freshman Admission Statistics:** 496 applied, 65.32% admitted, 56% enrolled. **Transfer Admission Requirements:** college transcript(s), essay or personal statement, Lowest grade transferable C-. **General Admission Information:** Application fee $50. Nonfall registration accepted. Admission may be deferred for a maximum of 2 years.

COSTS AND FINANCIAL AID

Annual tuition $15,078. Room and board $12,630. Required fees $526. Average book expense $1,800. **Required Forms and Deadlines:** FAFSA. **Notification of Awards:** Applicants will be notified of awards on a rolling basis beginning 3/1. **Types of Aid:** *Need-based scholarships/grants:* Federal Pell, FSEOG, State scholarships/grants, Private scholarships, College/university scholarship or grant

aid from institutional funds. *Loans:* Direct Subsidized Stafford Loans, Direct Unsubsidized Stafford Loans, Direct PLUS loans, Federal Perkins Loans. *Student Employment:* Federal Work-Study Program available. Institutional employment available. **Financial Aid Statistics:** 99% needy freshmen, 91% needy undergrads receive need-based scholarship or grant aid. 18% freshmen, 18% undergrads receive non-need-based scholarship or grant aid. 45% freshmen, 46% undergrads receive need-based self-help aid. 0% freshmen, 0% undergrads receive athletic scholarships. 94% freshmen, 85% undergrads receive any aid. **Criteria for awarding aid:** *Need-based:* Academics. *Non-need-based:* Academics.

GANNON UNIVERSITY

109 University Square, Erie, PA 16541
Phone: 814-871-7240 • **Financial Aid Phone:** 814-871-7337
E-mail: admissions@gannon.edu • **CEEB Code:** 2270
Fax: 814-871-5803 • **Website:** www.gannon.edu • **ACT Code:** 3576

This private school, affiliated with the Roman Catholic Church, was founded in 1925. It has a 13-acre campus.

RATINGS

Admissions Selectivity Rating: 80 **Fire Safety Rating:** 97 **Green Rating:** 71

STUDENTS AND FACULTY

Enrollment: 2,597. **Student Body:** 56% female, 44% male, 29% out-of-state, 9% international (33 countries represented). Asian 2%, African American 5%, Caucasian 74%, Hispanic 3%, Native American <1%, Pacific Islander <1%, Two or more races 2%, Race unknown 5%.
Retention and Graduation: 78% freshmen return for sophomore year. 47% freshmen graduate within 4 years. 64% freshmen graduate within 6 years. 47% grads go on to further study within 1 year. 2% grads pursue law degrees. 4% grads pursue business degrees. 8% grads pursue medical degrees. **Faculty:** Student/faculty ratio 12:1. 238 full-time faculty, 78% hold PhDs, 14% are members of minority groups, 48% are women. 1% of classes are taught by teaching assistants.

ACADEMICS

Degrees: associate, bachelor's, certificate, doctoral/professional, doctoral/research, master's, postbachelor's certificate, post-master's certificate, terminal. **Classes:** Most classes have 10-19 students. Most lab/discussion sessions have 10-19 students. **Most popular majors:** Health Professions and Related Clinical Sciences; Registered Nursing/Registered Nurse; Kinesiology and Exercise Science. **Special Study Options:** Accelerated program, distance learning, double major, dual enrollment, honors program, independent study, internships, liberal arts/career combination, study abroad, teacher certification program. **Honors Programs:** Gannon offers an honors program for the academically talented and highly motivated students. Last year, 246 students participated in honors classes that were small in size and staffed by Gannon's best teachers. Combined degree programs: BA/MD, BA/JD, BA/MA, BS/MBA, BS/DMD, BS/DO, BS/Pharm.D, BS/OD, BS/MS, BS/DPM, BS/DVM, RN/BSN, RN/MSN. **Disability Services:** Special programs offered to physically disabled students, including note-taking services, reader services, tape recorders, tutors. **Career Services:** Alumni network, Alumni services, Career/job search classes, Career assessment, Internships, Regional alumni. The Career Road Show program we offer—it has the Career Development staff making over 78 in-class career and job search presentations each year. The program continues to grow and students benefit from learning valuable career information taught in classes within their major.

FACILITIES

Housing: Coed dorms, special housing for disabled students, apartments for single students. 70% of campus accessible to physically disabled. **Special Academic Facilities/Equipment:** Laser and spectrographic labs, Patient Simulation Center, metallurgy institute, computer-integrated manufacturing facilities, Schuster Art Gallery, Schuster Theatres, Erie Technology Incubator. **Computers:** 100% of classrooms, 100% of dorms, 100% of libraries, 100% of dining areas, 100% of student union, 100% of common outdoor areas have wireless network access. Students can register for classes online. Administrative functions (other than registration) can be performed online.

CAMPUS LIFE

Environment: City. **Activities:** Choral groups, concert band, dance, drama/theater, literary magazine, music ensembles, musical theater, pep band, radio station, student government, student newspaper, yearbook, Campus Ministries, Student Organization, Model UN. 71 registered organizations, 11 honor societies, 6 religious organizations. 5 fraternities, 5 sororities. **Athletics (Intercollegiate):** *Men:* baseball, basketball, cheerleading, cross-country, football, golf, soccer, swimming, water polo, wrestling. *Women:* basketball, cheerleading, cross-country, golf, lacrosse, soccer, softball, swimming, volleyball, water polo. **On-Campus Highlights:** Multi-purpose Athletic Field, Waldron Campus Center, A.J. Palumbo Academic Center, Carnaval Athletic Pavilion, Zurn Science Center, Schuster Art Gallery Morosky College of Health Professions and Science. **Environmental Initiatives:** Switching out all campus light bulbs to compact flourescent.

ADMISSIONS

Freshman Academic Profile: Average high school GPA 3.6. 22% in top 10% of high school class, 49% in top 25% of high school class, 83% in top 50% of high school class. 83% from public high schools. **Reported SAT (pre-2016 redesign) scores:** SAT Math middle 50% range 470-570. SAT Critical Reading middle 50% range 450-560. SAT Writing middle 50% range 433-550. **Concordant SAT scores:** SAT EBRW middle 50% 490–610. SAT Math middle 50% range 510–590. ACT middle 50% range 20-26. Minimum internet-based TOEFL 79. Minimum paper TOEFL 550. **Basis for Candidate Selection:** *Very important factors considered include:* rigor of secondary school record, class rank, academic GPA, standardized test scores. *Other factors considered include:* application essay, recommendation(s), interview, extracurricular activities, character/personal qualities, alumni/ae relation, work experience. **Freshman Admission Requirements:** High school diploma is required and GED is accepted. *Academic units required:* 4 English, 2 social studies, 1 history, 3 academic electives. *Academic units recommended:* 4 English, 4 math, 4 science, 3 science labs, 2 foreign language, 2 social studies, 1 history, 3 academic electives, 1 computer science, 1 visual/performing arts. **Freshman Admission Statistics:** 4,710 applied, 77.75% admitted, 17% enrolled. **Transfer Admission Requirements:** college transcript(s), statement of good standing from prior institution(s). Minimum college GPA of 2.0 required. Lowest grade transferable C. **General Admission Information:** Application fee $25. Nonfall registration accepted. Admission may be deferred for a maximum of 1 year.

COSTS AND FINANCIAL AID

Required Forms and Deadlines: FAFSA. **Notification of Awards:** Applicants will be notified of awards on a rolling basis beginning 11/1. **Types of Aid:** *Need-based scholarships/grants:* Federal Pell, FSEOG, State scholarships/grants, Private scholarships, College/university scholarship or grant aid from institutional funds, Federal Nursing Scholarships. *Loans:* Direct Subsidized Stafford Loans, Direct Unsubsidized Stafford Loans, Direct PLUS loans, Federal Perkins Loans, Federal Nursing Loans. *Student Employment:* Federal Work-Study Program available. Institutional employment available. **Financial Aid Statistics:** 99% needy freshmen, 98% needy undergrads receive need-based scholarship or grant aid. 15% freshmen, 15% undergrads receive non-need-based scholarship or grant aid. 82% freshmen, 77% undergrads receive need-based self-help aid. 4% freshmen, 35% undergrads receive athletic scholarships. 98% freshmen, 96% undergrads receive any aid. **Criteria for awarding aid:** *Non-need-based:* Academics, Athletics, Leadership, Music/drama, Religious affiliation.

GARDNER-WEBB UNIVERSITY

PO Box 817, Boiling Springs, NC 28017
Phone: 704-406-4498 • **Financial Aid Phone:** 704-406-4243
E-mail: admissions@gardner-webb.edu • **CEEB Code:** 5242
Fax: 704-406-4488 • **Website:** www.gardner-webb.edu • **ACT Code:** 3102

This private school, affiliated with the Baptist Church, was founded in 1905. It has a 250-acre campus.

RATINGS

Admissions Selectivity Rating: 83 **Fire Safety Rating:** 91 **Green Rating:** 60*

STUDENTS AND FACULTY

Enrollment: 2,680. **Student Body:** 65% female, 35% male, 21% out-of-state, <1% international (22 countries represented). Asian 0%, African American 19%, Caucasian 72%, Hispanic 2%, Native American 1%, Pacific Islander 0%, Two or more races 0%, Race unknown 6%. **Retention and Graduation:** 74% freshmen return for sophomore year. 36% freshmen graduate within 4 years. 49% freshmen graduate within 6 years. **Faculty:** Student/faculty ratio 13:1. 140 full-time faculty, 80% hold PhDs, 4% are are members of minority groups, 46% are women. 0% of classes are taught by teaching assistants.

ACADEMICS

Degrees: associate, bachelor's, doctoral, master's. **Classes:** Most classes have fewer than 10 students. **Most popular majors:** Social Sciences; Business/Commerce; Religion/Religious Studies. **Special Study Options:** Accelerated program, distance learning, double major, dual enrollment, English as a Second Language (ESL), honors program, independent study, internships, liberal arts/career combination, study abroad, teacher certification program. **Honors**

Programs: Alpha Chi Honors Program Beta Beta Beta Delta Mu Delta Sigma Delta Pi Sigma Tau Delta Theta Alpha Kappa Pi Delta Phi Psi Chi Sigma Zeta Sigma Theta Tau Who's Who Combined degree programs: Music-Business—BM/MBA. **Disability Services:** Special programs offered to physically disabled students, including note-taking services, reader services, tape recorders, tutors. **Career Services:** Alumni network, Career/job search classes, Career assessment, Internships, On-campus interviews. Our Career Services office organizes a mock formal dinner interview and sponsors the Metrolina Career Fair and a Nursing Career Fair.

FACILITIES

Housing: special housing for disabled students, men's dorms, women's dorms, apartments for single students, Wellness Housing, Housing for Honor Students. 100% of campus accessible to physically disabled. **Special Academic Facilities/Equipment:** Williams Observatory, Millennium Playhouse, Broyhill Adventure Course, Lake Hollifield Complex and Carillon **Computers:** 100% of classrooms, 100% of dorms, 100% of libraries, 100% of dining areas, 100% of student union, 100% of common outdoor areas have wireless network access. Students can register for classes online. Administrative functions (other than registration) can be performed online.

CAMPUS LIFE

Environment: Rural. **Activities:** Choral groups, concert band, dance, drama/theater, jazz band, literary magazine, marching band, music ensembles, musical theater, opera, pep band, radio station, student government, student newspaper, symphony orchestra, yearbook, Campus Ministries, Student Organization. 65 registered organizations, 12 honor societies, 11 religious organizations. **Athletics (Intercollegiate):** *Men:* baseball, basketball, cheerleading, cross-country, football, golf, soccer, swimming, tennis, track/field (outdoor), track/field (indoor), wrestling. *Women:* basketball, cheerleading, cross-country, golf, soccer, softball, swimming, tennis, track/field (outdoor), track/field (indoor), volleyball. **On-Campus Highlights:** Dover Campus Center, Suttle Wellness Center, Cafeteria, Lutz-Yelton Convocation Center, Kennel Snack Bar. **Environmental Initiatives:** recycling programs.

ADMISSIONS

Freshman Academic Profile: Average high school GPA 3.5. 32% in top 10% of high school class, 49% in top 25% of high school class, 72% in top 50% of high school class. 84% from public high schools. **Reported SAT (pre-2016 redesign) scores:** SAT Math middle 50% range 420-550. SAT Critical Reading middle 50% range 440-560. **Concordant SAT scores:** SAT Math middle 50% range 460–570. ACT middle 50% range 18-23. Minimum internet-based TOEFL 61. Minimum paper TOEFL 500. **Basis for Candidate Selection:** *Very important factors considered include:* rigor of secondary school record, academic GPA, standardized test scores, level of applicant's interest. *Important factors considered include:* class rank, recommendation(s), extracurricular activities, character/personal qualities. *Other factors considered include:* application essay, interview, talent/ability, volunteer work. **Freshman Admission Requirements:** High school diploma is required and GED is accepted. *Academic units recommended:* 4 English, 3 math, 3 science, 2 science labs, 2 foreign language, 1 social studies, 1 history. **Freshman Admission Statistics:** 3,277 applied, 61.52% admitted, 22% enrolled. **Transfer Admission Requirements:** college transcript(s), statement of good standing from prior institution(s). Minimum college GPA of 2.25 required. Lowest grade transferable C. **General Admission Information:** Application fee $40. Nonfall registration accepted. Admission may be deferred for a maximum of 2 Semesters.

COSTS AND FINANCIAL AID

Annual tuition $22,050. Room and board $7,195. Required fees $390. Average book expense $1,000. **Required Forms and Deadlines:** FAFSA, State aid form. **Notification of Awards:** Applicants will be notified of awards on a rolling basis beginning 3/1. **Types of Aid:** *Need-based scholarships/grants:* Federal Pell, FSEOG, State scholarships/grants, Private scholarships, College/university scholarship or grant aid from institutional funds. *Loans:* Federal Perkins Loans, Federal Nursing Loans, State Loans. *Student Employment:* Federal Work-Study Program available. Institutional employment available. **Financial Aid Statistics:** 96% needy freshmen, 34% needy undergrads receive need-based scholarship or grant aid. 77% freshmen, 70% undergrads receive non-need-based scholarship or grant aid. 66% freshmen, 75% undergrads receive need-based self-help aid. 100% freshmen receive any aid. **Criteria for awarding aid:** *Need-based:* Academics, Leadership, Minority status, Music/drama, Religious affiliation. *Non-need-based:* Academics, Athletics, Leadership, Music/drama, State/district residency.

GEORGE FOX UNIVERSITY

414 N. Meridian St., Newberg, OR 97132
Phone: 503-554-2240 • **Financial Aid Phone:** 503-554-2300
E-mail: admissions@georgefox.edu • **CEEB Code:** 4325
Fax: 503-554-3110 • **Website:** www.georgefox.edu • **ACT Code:** 3462

This private school was founded in 1891. It has a 85-acre campus.

RATINGS
Admissions Selectivity Rating: 83   **Fire Safety Rating:** 88   **Green Rating:** 60*

STUDENTS AND FACULTY
Enrollment: 2,358. **Student Body:** 57% female, 43% male, 35% out-of-state, 6% international (43 countries represented). Asian 4%, African American 2%, Caucasian 70%, Hispanic 7%, Native American <1%, Pacific Islander <1%, Two or more races 5%, Race unknown 4%.
Retention and Graduation: 82% freshmen return for sophomore year. 52% freshmen graduate within 4 years. 62% freshmen graduate within 6 years. 11% grads go on to further study within 1 year. 6% grads pursue arts and sciences degrees. 2% grads pursue business degrees. 2% grads pursue medical degrees.
Faculty: Student/faculty ratio 14:1. 168 full-time faculty, 76% hold PhDs, 14% are are members of minority groups, 40% are women. 0% of classes are taught by teaching assistants.

ACADEMICS
Degrees: bachelor's, doctoral/professional, master's, postbachelor's certificate, post-master's certificate. **Classes:** Most classes have 10-19 students. Most lab/discussion sessions have 10-19 students. **Most popular majors:** Business Administration and Management; Registered Nursing/Registered Nurse; Elementary Education and Teaching. **Special Study Options:** Accelerated program, cross-registration, double major, dual enrollment, English as a Second Language (ESL), exchange student program (domestic), honors program, independent study, internships, student-designed major, study abroad, teacher certification program. **Honors Programs:** University Scholars, Richter Scholars, Honors Scholarships, Advance Leadership Development Program. **Disability Services:** Special programs offered to physically disabled students, including note-taking services, reader services, tape recorders, tutors. **Career Services:** Alumni network, Alumni services, Career/job search classes, Career assessment, Internships, Regional alumni.

FACILITIES
Housing: special housing for disabled students, men's dorms, women's dorms, apartments for single students, Wellness Housing, Theme Housing. 98% of campus accessible to physically diasbled. **Special Academic Facilities/Equipment:** nuclear magnetic resonance spectrometer, Providence Nursing Learning Lab, language lab, electron microscope. **Computers:** 100% of classrooms, 90% of dorms, 100% of libraries, 100% of dining areas, 100% of student union, 50% of common outdoor areas have wireless network access. Students can register for classes online. Administrative functions (other than registration) can be performed online.

CAMPUS LIFE
Environment: Village. **Activities:** Choral groups, concert band, drama/theater, jazz band, literary magazine, music ensembles, musical theater, pep band, radio station, student government, student newspaper, symphony orchestra, yearbook, Campus Ministries, Student Organization. 20 registered organizations, 3 honor societies, 3 religious organizations. **Athletics (Intercollegiate):** *Men:* baseball, basketball, cross-country, golf, soccer, tennis, track/field (outdoor). *Women:* basketball, cross-country, golf, soccer, softball, tennis, track/field (outdoor), volleyball. **On-Campus Highlights:** Bruin Den-Cafe in the Student Union Bldg, The Foxhole-Student-run coffee house, Dorm Movie Rooms-most have movie areas, Wheeler Sports Center. **Environmental Initiatives:** LEED-certified residence hall.

ADMISSIONS
Freshman Academic Profile: Average high school GPA 3.6. 27% in top 10% of high school class, 57% in top 25% of high school class, 85% in top 50% of high school class. 73% from public high schools. **Reported SAT (pre-2016 redesign) scores:** SAT Math middle 50% range 470-600. SAT Critical Reading middle 50% range 470-600. SAT Writing middle 50% range 460-590. **Concordant SAT scores:** SAT EBRW middle 50% 520-650. SAT Math middle 50% range 510-620. ACT middle 50% range 20-26. Minimum internet-based TOEFL 80. Minimum paper TOEFL 550. **Basis for Candidate Selection:** *Very important factors considered include:* rigor of secondary school record, academic GPA, standardized test scores, application essay, recommendation(s). *Important factors considered include:* character/personal qualities. *Other factors considered include:* class rank, interview, extracurricular activities, talent/ability, religious affiliation/commitment, volunteer work, work experience. **Freshman Admission Requirements:** High school diploma is required and GED is accepted. *Academic units recommended:* 4 English, 2 math, 2 science, 2 science

labs, 2 foreign language, 3 social studies, 2 history, and 1 unit from above areas or other academic areas. **Freshman Admission Statistics:** 2,431 applied, 75.28% admitted, 35% enrolled. **Transfer Admission Requirements:** college transcript(s), essay or personal statement, statement of good standing from prior institution(s). Minimum college GPA of 2.6 required. Lowest grade transferable C-. **General Admission Information:** Application fee $40. Priority deadline 2/1. Nonfall registration accepted. Admission may be deferred for a maximum of 1 yr.

COSTS AND FINANCIAL AID
Annual tuition $33,370. Room and board $10,528. Required fees $360. Average book expense $950. **Required Forms and Deadlines:** FAFSA, State aid form. **Notification of Awards:** Applicants will be notified of awards on a rolling basis beginning 3/1. **Types of Aid:** *Need-based scholarships/grants:* Federal Pell, FSEOG, State scholarships/grants, Private scholarships, College/university scholarship or grant aid from institutional funds. *Loans:* Direct Subsidized Stafford Loans, Direct Unsubsidized Stafford Loans, Direct PLUS loans, Federal Perkins Loans. *Student Employment:* Federal Work-Study Program available. Institutional employment available. **Financial Aid Statistics:** 84% needy freshmen, 96% needy undergrads receive need-based scholarship or grant aid. 7% freshmen, 6% undergrads receive non-need-based scholarship or grant aid. 87% freshmen, 88% undergrads receive need-based self-help aid. 0% freshmen, 0% undergrads receive athletic scholarships. 100% freshmen, 96% undergrads receive any aid. 79% undergrads borrow to pay for school. Average cumulative indebtedness $22,996. **Criteria for awarding aid:** *Need-based:* Minority status, Religious affiliation. *Non-need-based:* Academics, Alumni affiliation, Art, Job skills, Leadership, Minority status, Music/drama, Religious affiliation.

GEORGE MASON UNIVERSITY

4400 University Drive, Fairfax, VA 22030-4444
Phone: 703-993-2400 • **Financial Aid Phone:** 703-993-2349
E-mail: admissions@gmu.edu • **CEEB Code:** 5827
Fax: 703-993-4622 • **Website:** https://www2.gmu.edu • **ACT Code:** 4357

This public school was founded in 1972. It has a 806-acre campus.

RATINGS
Admissions Selectivity Rating: 82   **Fire Safety Rating:** 94   **Green Rating:** 91

STUDENTS AND FACULTY
Enrollment: 23,174. **Student Body:** 51% female, 49% male, 10% out-of-state, 5% international (97 countries represented). Asian 19%, African American 11%, Caucasian 43%, Hispanic 14%, Native American <1%, Pacific Islander <1%, Two or more races 5%, Race unknown 3%.
Retention and Graduation: 88% freshmen return for sophomore year. 46% freshmen graduate within 4 years. 70% freshmen graduate within 6 years.
Faculty: Student/faculty ratio 16:1. 1,260 full-time faculty, 90% hold PhDs, 20% are are members of minority groups, 42% are women. 7% of classes are taught by teaching assistants.

ACADEMICS
Degrees: bachelor's, doctoral/professional, doctoral/research, doctoral, master's, postbachelor's certificate, post-master's certificate. **Classes:** Most classes have 20-29 students. Most lab/discussion sessions have 20-29 students. **Most popular majors:** Biology/Biological Sciences; Psychology; Information Technology. **Special Study Options:** Accelerated program, cooperative education program, cross-registration, distance learning, double major, dual enrollment, English as a Second Language (ESL), exchange student program (domestic), external degree program, honors program, independent study, internships, liberal arts/career combination, student-designed major, study abroad, teacher certification program. **Honors Programs:** Honors Program in General Education provides small courses with outstanding faculty. The University Scholars program provides an elite group of students with exceptional academic and research oppotunities in a dynamic community of learners. Combined degree programs: BA/MA, BS/MS, BS/MEd, BA/MEd, BA/MAIS, BS/MAIS. **Disability Services:** Special programs offered to physically disabled students, including note-taking services, reader services, tape recorders. **Career Services:** Alumni network, Alumni services, Career/job search classes, Career assessment, Internships, Regional alumni. Increasing student uptake of federal government internship opportunities (Federal Student Career Experience Program-SCEP) and post-grad internships. Students enroll for SCEP positions through Mason's Cooperative Education

program. Cooperative Education employs students in the DC metro area and adds value to student degree. Internships can be taken in concert with Co-op or stand alone.

FACILITIES

Housing: Coed dorms, special housing for disabled students, men's dorms, women's dorms, apartments for single students. 95% of campus accessible to physically diasbled. **Special Academic Facilities/Equipment:** Center for the Arts, science/technology building, television studio, art galleries in Mason Hall and Johnson Center, astronomy observatory, Smithsonian Conservation and Research Center. **Computers:** 30% of classrooms, 100% of dorms, 100% of libraries, 100% of dining areas, 100% of student union, 5% of common outdoor areas have wireless network access. Students can register for classes online. Administrative functions (other than registration) can be performed online.

CAMPUS LIFE

Environment: City. **Activities:** Choral groups, concert band, dance, drama/theater, jazz band, literary magazine, music ensembles, musical theater, opera, pep band, radio station, student government, student newspaper, student-run film society, symphony orchestra, television station, yearbook, Campus Ministries, Student Organization. 250 registered organizations, 7 honor societies, 29 religious organizations. 22 fraternities, 13 sororities. **Athletics (Intercollegiate):** *Men:* baseball, basketball, cheerleading, cross-country, diving, golf, soccer, swimming, tennis, track/field (outdoor), track/field (indoor), volleyball, wrestling. *Women:* basketball, cheerleading, crew/rowing, cross-country, diving, lacrosse, soccer, softball, swimming, tennis, track/field (outdoor), track/field (indoor), volleyball. **On-Campus Highlights:** Johnson Center, Aquatic and Fitness Center, Center for the Arts, Patriot Center, Freedom Aquatic Center at Prince William.

ADMISSIONS

Freshman Academic Profile: Average high school GPA 3.7. 21% in top 10% of high school class, 52% in top 25% of high school class, 88% in top 50% of high school class. 77% from public high schools. **Reported SAT (pre-2016 redesign) scores:** SAT Math middle 50% range 530-630. SAT Critical Reading middle 50% range 530-620. **Concordant SAT scores:** SAT Math middle 50% range 560–650. ACT middle 50% range 24-29. Minimum internet-based TOEFL 80. Minimum paper TOEFL 570. **Basis for Candidate Selection:** *Very important factors considered include:* rigor of secondary school record, academic GPA. *Important factors considered include:* class rank, standardized test scores, talent/ability, character/personal qualities. *Other factors considered include:* application essay, recommendation(s), extracurricular activities, first generation, alumni/ae relation, volunteer work, work experience, level of applicant's interest. **Freshman Admission Requirements:** High school diploma is required and GED is accepted. *Academic units required:* 4 English, 3 math, 2 science, 2 science labs, 2 foreign language, 3 social studies, 3 academic electives. *Academic units recommended:* 4 English, 4 math, 3 science, 3 science labs, 3 foreign language, 4 social studies, 5 academic electives. **Freshman Admission Statistics:** 15,548 applied, 80.99% admitted, 26% enrolled. **Transfer Admission Requirements:** college transcript(s), Minimum college GPA of 2.0 required. Lowest grade transferable C. **General Admission Information:** Application fee $60. Priority deadline 11/1. Regular application deadline 1/15. Nonfall registration accepted. Admission may be deferred for a maximum of 1 semester.

COSTS AND FINANCIAL AID

Annual in-state tuition $8,204. Annual out-of-state tuition $29,486. Room and board $10,730. Required fees $3,096. Average book expense $1,200. **Required Forms and Deadlines:** FAFSA. **Notification of Awards:** Applicants will be notified of awards on a rolling basis beginning 4/1. **Types of Aid:** *Need-based scholarships/grants:* Federal Pell, FSEOG, State scholarships/grants, Private scholarships, College/university scholarship or grant aid from institutional funds. *Loans:* Direct Subsidized Stafford Loans, Direct Unsubsidized Stafford Loans, Direct PLUS loans, Federal Perkins Loans, Federal Nursing Loans. *Student Employment:* Federal Work-Study Program available. Institutional employment available. **Financial Aid Statistics:** 77% needy freshmen, 78% needy undergrads receive need-based scholarship or grant aid. 38% freshmen, 19% undergrads receive non-need-based scholarship or grant aid. 79% freshmen, 79% undergrads receive need-based self-help aid. 1% freshmen, 1% undergrads receive athletic scholarships. 70% freshmen, 59% undergrads receive any aid. 56% undergrads borrow to pay for school. Average cumulative indebtedness $30,132. **Criteria for awarding aid:** *Non-need-based:* Academics, Athletics, Minority status, Music/drama.

THE GEORGE WASHINGTON UNIVERSITY

2121 Eye Street NW, Suite 201, Washington, DC 20052
Phone: 202-994-6040
E-mail: gwadm@gwu.edu • **CEEB Code:** 5246
Fax: 202-994-0325 • **Website:** www.gwu.edu • **ACT Code:** 664

This private school was founded in 1821. It has a 45-acre campus.

RATINGS

Admissions Selectivity Rating: 92   **Fire Safety Rating:** 60*   **Green Rating:** 96

STUDENTS AND FACULTY

Enrollment: 10,901. **Student Body:** 56% female, 44% male, 97% out-of-state, 10% international (122 countries represented). Asian 10%, African American 6%, Caucasian 56%, Hispanic 8%, Native American <1%, Pacific Islander <1%, Two or more races 4%, Race unknown 5%.
Retention and Graduation: 94% freshmen return for sophomore year. 76% freshmen graduate within 4 years. 83 22% grads go on to further study within 1 year. 48% grads pursue arts and sciences degrees. 31% grads pursue law degrees. 2% grads pursue business degrees. 18% grads pursue medical degrees. **Faculty:** Student/faculty ratio 13:1. 1,095 full-time faculty, 93% hold PhDs, 24% are are members of minority groups, 43% are women. 3% of classes are taught by teaching assistants.

ACADEMICS

Degrees: associate, bachelor's, certificate, doctoral/professional, doctoral/research, master's, postbachelor's certificate, post-master's certificate, terminal. **Classes:** Most classes have 10-19 students. Most lab/discussion sessions have 20-29 students. **Most popular majors:** International Relations and Affairs; Business Administration and Management; Psychology. **Special Study Options:** Accelerated program, cooperative education program, cross-registration, distance learning, double major, dual enrollment, honors program, independent study, internships, liberal arts/career combination, student-designed major, study abroad. Combined degree programs: BA/MD, BA/JD, BA/MA. **Disability Services:** Special programs offered to physically disabled students, including note-taking services, reader services, tape recorders, tutors. **Career Services:** Alumni network, Alumni services, Career/job search classes, Career assessment, Internships, Regional alumni. The F.David Fowler Career Center, of The George Washington University School of Business, prepares students to compete for internships by equipping them with the highest level of professional career-management training and services available. 76% of GWSB undergraduates hold internships in the private, public and nonprofit sectors. Student favorites include: Deloitte, The World Bank Group and The U.S. Department of the Treasury. Students who take full advantage of the many paid an unpaid internship opportunities develop the practical competencies necessary to compete and promptly contribute to an organization's success upon graduation from GW's School of Business.

FACILITIES

Housing: Coed dorms, fraternity/sorority housing, apartments for single students, Theme Housing. 95% of campus accessible to physically diasbled. **Special Academic Facilities/Equipment:** Art gallery, language lab, word processing center. **Computers:** Students can register for classes online. Administrative functions (other than registration) can be performed online.

CAMPUS LIFE

Environment: Metropolis. **Activities:** Choral groups, concert band, dance, drama/theater, jazz band, literary magazine, marching band, music ensembles, musical theater, pep band, radio station, student government, student newspaper, student-run film society, television station, yearbook, Student Organization, Model UN. 220 registered organizations, 3 honor societies, 5 religious organizations. 12 fraternities, 9 sororities. **Athletics (Intercollegiate):** *Men:* baseball, basketball, crew/rowing, cross-country, diving, fencing, golf, rugby, soccer, squash, swimming, tennis, water polo. *Women:* basketball, crew/rowing, cross-country, fencing, gymnastics, soccer, swimming, tennis, volleyball. **On-Campus Highlights:** The Smith Center, The Hippo, Media and Public Affairs Building, Kogan Plaza, Gelman Library. **Environmental Initiatives:** 1. GW mission is to be the premier university on policy and governance for sustainable systems through practice, teaching, research, and outreach. The University is deploying a pan-university approach that bridges traditional disciplines. In Fall 2012 GW will offer an interdisciplinary Minor in Sustainability to all undergraduate students. The minor is a pan-university offering that provides students with inter-disciplinary teaching (with a team-taught course taught by faculty representing several schools) and experiential learning (which challenges students to apply knowledge, theory and methods learned in the classroom to analyze a real-world sustainability issue and/or practice).

ADMISSIONS

Freshman Academic Profile: 56% in top 10% of high school class, 86% in top 25% of high school class, 99% in top 50% of high school class. 70% from public high schools. **Reported SAT (pre-2016 redesign) scores:** SAT Math middle 50% range 600-700. SAT Critical Reading middle 50% range 590-690. SAT Writing middle 50% range 600-690. **Concordant SAT scores:** SAT EBRW middle 50% 650–730. SAT Math middle 50% range 620–730. ACT middle 50% range 27-31. Minimum paper TOEFL 550. **Basis for Candidate Selection:** *Very important factors considered include:* rigor of secondary school record, academic GPA. *Important factors considered include:* standardized test scores, application essay, recommendation(s), interview, extracurricular activities, talent/ability, volunteer work. *Other factors considered include:* character/ personal qualities, first generation, alumni/ae relation, geographical residence, racial/ethnic status, work experience, level of applicant's interest. **Freshman Admission Requirements:** High school diploma is required and GED is not accepted. *Academic units required:* 4 English, 2 math, 2 science, 1 science lab, 2 foreign language, 2 social studies. *Academic units recommended:* 4 English, 4 math, 4 science, 4 foreign language, 4 social studies. **Freshman Admission Statistics:** 19,837 applied, 46.46% admitted, 28% enrolled. **Transfer Admission Requirements:** High school transcript, college transcript(s), essay or personal statement, standardized test scores, Lowest grade transferable C. **General Admission Information:** Application fee $75. Priority deadline 11/1. Regular application deadline 1/1. Regular notification 4/1. Nonfall registration accepted. Admission may be deferred.

COSTS AND FINANCIAL AID

Annual tuition $49,772. Room and board $15,205. Required fees $65. Average book expense $1,275. **Required Forms and Deadlines:** FAFSA, CSS/Financial Aid PROFILE. **Notification of Awards:** Applicants will be notified of awards on a rolling basis beginning 3/24. **Types of Aid:** *Need-based scholarships/grants:* Federal Pell, FSEOG, State scholarships/grants, College/university scholarship or grant aid from institutional funds. *Loans:* Direct Subsidized Stafford Loans, Direct Unsubsidized Stafford Loans, Direct PLUS loans, Federal Perkins Loans. *Student Employment:* Federal Work-Study Program available. Institutional employment available. **Financial Aid Statistics:** 96% needy freshmen, 94% needy undergrads receive need-based scholarship or grant aid. 63% freshmen, 34% undergrads receive non-need-based scholarship or grant aid. 76% freshmen, 81% undergrads receive need-based self-help aid. 2% freshmen, 2% undergrads receive athletic scholarships. Average cumulative indebtedness $33,081. **Criteria for awarding aid:** *Need-based:* Minority status. *Non-need-based:* Academics, Art, Athletics, Music/ drama.

See page 958.

GEORGETOWN COLLEGE

400 East College Street, Georgetown, KY 40324
Phone: 502-863-8009 • **Financial Aid Phone:** 502-863-8027
E-mail: admissions@georgetowncollege.edu • **CEEB Code:** 1249
Fax: 502-868-7733 • **Website:** www.georgetowncollege.edu • **ACT Code:** 1514

This private school was founded in 1787. It has a 104-acre campus.

RATINGS

Admissions Selectivity Rating: 74   **Fire Safety Rating:** 82   **Green Rating:** 67

STUDENTS AND FACULTY

Enrollment: 942. **Student Body:** 53% female, 47% male, 23% out-of-state, 1% international (12 countries represented). Asian 1%, African American 9%, Caucasian 79%, Hispanic 1%, Native American <1%, Pacific Islander 0%, Two or more races 4%, Race unknown 5%.
Retention and Graduation: 71% freshmen return for sophomore year. 52% freshmen graduate within 4 years. **Faculty:** Student/faculty ratio 11:1. 77 full-time faculty, 95% hold PhDs, 6% are are members of minority groups, 47% are women. 0% of classes are taught by teaching assistants.

ACADEMICS

Degrees: bachelor's, master's, post-master's certificate. **Classes:** Most classes have 20-29 students. Most lab/discussion sessions have 10-19 students. **Most popular majors:** Psychology; Biology/Biological Sciences; Athletic Training/ Trainer. **Special Study Options:** Accelerated program, cooperative education program, double major, dual enrollment, honors program, independent study, internships, liberal arts/career combination, student-designed major, study abroad, teacher certification program. **Honors Programs:** Georgetown College Academic Honors Program Combined degree programs: Nursing Arts, (UK); BA/BTh Religion (Oxford Univ). **Disability Services:** Special programs

offered to physically disabled students, including note-taking services, reader services, tape recorders, tutors. **Career Services:** Alumni network, Alumni services, Career/job search classes, Career assessment, Internships, Regional alumni. Georgetown College also hosts the Kentucky Governor's School for Entrepreneurs

FACILITIES

Housing: men's dorms, women's dorms, fraternity/sorority housing, Apartments for upper classmen. **Special Academic Facilities/Equipment:** To name only some: the Anna Ashcraft Ensor Learning Resource Center, an aboretum, three antebellum buildings, the Asher Science Center, the Anne Wright Wilson Fine Arts Building, and the Wilson Laboratory Theatre. **Computers:** 10% of classrooms, 60% of dorms, 90% of libraries, 100% of dining areas, 100% of student union, have wireless network access. Students can register for classes online. Administrative functions (other than registration) can be performed online.

CAMPUS LIFE

Environment: Town. **Activities:** Choral groups, concert band, dance, drama/ theater, literary magazine, music ensembles, musical theater, pep band, radio station, student government, student newspaper, yearbook, Campus Ministries. 110 registered organizations, 20 honor societies, 8 religious organizations. 5 fraternities, 4 sororities. **Athletics (Intercollegiate):** *Men:* baseball, basketball, cross-country, football, golf, soccer, tennis, track/field (outdoor), track/field (indoor). *Women:* basketball, cheerleading, cross-country, golf, soccer, softball, tennis, track/field (outdoor), track/field (indoor), volleyball. **On-Campus Highlights:** The Ensor Learning Resource Center, Starbucks—in the Learning Resource Center, The Grille **Environmental Initiatives:** Recycling with Pepsi Co.

ADMISSIONS

Freshman Academic Profile: 80% from public high schools. **Reported SAT (pre-2016 redesign) scores:** SAT Math middle 50% range 420-530. SAT Critical Reading middle 50% range 450-530. **Concordant SAT scores:** SAT Math middle 50% range 460–560. ACT middle 50% range 20-26. Minimum internet-based TOEFL 68. Minimum paper TOEFL 520. **Basis for Candidate Selection:** *Very important factors considered include:* academic GPA. *Important factors considered include:* rigor of secondary school record, standardized test scores. *Other factors considered include:* class rank, application essay, recommendation(s), interview, extracurricular activities, talent/ability, character/personal qualities, volunteer work, work experience. **Freshman Admission Requirements:** High school diploma is required and GED is accepted. *Academic units recommended:* 4 English, 3 math, 3 science, 2 foreign language, 2 social studies. **Freshman Admission Statistics:** 2,127 applied, 66.48% admitted, 21% enrolled. **Transfer Admission Requirements:** High school transcript, college transcript(s), statement of good standing from prior institution(s). Minimum college GPA of 2.5 required. Lowest grade transferable C. **General Admission Information:** Application fee $30. Priority deadline 5/1. Regular application deadline 8/15. Nonfall registration accepted. Admission may be deferred for a maximum of 1 year.

COSTS AND FINANCIAL AID

Annual tuition $35,650. Room and board $9,050. Required fees $0. Average book expense $1,250. **Required Forms and Deadlines:** FAFSA. **Notification of Awards:** Applicants will be notified of awards on a rolling basis beginning 3/1. **Types of Aid:** *Need-based scholarships/grants:* Federal Pell, FSEOG, State scholarships/grants, Private scholarships, College/university scholarship or grant aid from institutional funds. *Loans:* Direct Subsidized Stafford Loans, Direct Unsubsidized Stafford Loans, Direct PLUS loans, Federal Perkins Loans, College/university loans from institutional funds. *Student Employment:* Federal Work-Study Program available. Institutional employment available. **Financial Aid Statistics:** 100% needy freshmen, 100% needy undergrads receive need-based scholarship or grant aid. 89% freshmen, 86% undergrads receive non-need-based scholarship or grant aid. 78% freshmen, 80% undergrads receive need-based self-help aid. 3% freshmen, 3% undergrads receive athletic scholarships. 100% freshmen, 96% undergrads receive any aid. 76% undergrads borrow to pay for school. Average cumulative indebtedness $31,267. **Criteria for awarding aid:** *Need-based:* Academics, Alumni affiliation, Athletics, Leadership, Music/drama, Religious affiliation. *Non-need-based:* Academics, Alumni affiliation, Art, Athletics, Leadership, Music/drama, Religious affiliation, State/district residency.

GEORGETOWN UNIVERSITY

103 White Gravenor Hall, 37th and O, Washington, DC 20057
Phone: 202-687-3600 • **Financial Aid Phone:** 202-687-4547
E-mail: guadmiss@georgetown.edu • **CEEB Code:** 5244
Fax: 202-687-5084 • **Website:** www.georgetown.edu • **ACT Code:** 668

This private school, affiliated with the Roman Catholic Church, was founded in 1789. It has a 104-acre campus.

RATINGS
Admissions Selectivity Rating: 98 **Fire Safety Rating:** 88 **Green Rating:** 60*

STUDENTS AND FACULTY
Enrollment: 7,112. **Student Body:** 56% female, 44% male, 96% out-of-state, 12% international (138 countries represented). Asian 10%, African American 6%, Caucasian 56%, Hispanic 9%, Native American <1%, Pacific Islander <1%, Two or more races 5%, Race unknown 2%.
Retention and Graduation: 96% freshmen return for sophomore year. 94% freshmen graduate within 6 years. **Faculty:** Student/faculty ratio 11:1. 1,004 full-time faculty, 87% hold PhDs, 14% are are members of minority groups, 44% are women. 8% of classes are taught by teaching assistants.

ACADEMICS
Degrees: bachelor's, certificate, doctoral/professional, doctoral/research, doctoral, master's, postbachelor's certifiate, post-master's certificate. **Classes:** Most classes have 10-19 students. Most lab/discussion sessions have 10-19 students. **Most popular majors:** Political Science and Government; International Relations and Affairs; English Language and Literature. **Special Study Options:** cross-registration, double major, English as a Second Language (ESL), honors program, independent study, internships, student-designed major, study abroad. **Honors Programs:** The John Carroll Programs guide and support a highly selective group of academically talented and ambitious students from around the world. The Programs seek individuals who desire to make a lasting difference in the fields and communities they touch. For these young men and women, the Programs provide models and skills to·help them make the most effective use of their undergraduate years, and to assists them in moving from the undergraduate experience to their post-graduate academic and professional lives. The Programs invite students to take as their own the Carroll motto, mentis vita pro vita mundi: the life of the mind for the life of the world. Combined degree programs: BA/MA. **Disability Services:** Special programs offered to physically disabled students, including note-taking services, reader services, tape recorders, tutors. **Career Services:** Alumni network, Alumni services, Career/job search classes, Career assessment, Internships, Regional alumni.

FACILITIES
Housing: Coed dorms, special housing for disabled students, apartments for single students, Freshmen and sophomores are required to live on campus. 92% of campus accessible to physically diasbled. **Special Academic Facilities/ Equipment:** Language lab, seismological observatory. **Computers:** Students can register for classes online. Administrative functions (other than registration) can be performed online.

CAMPUS LIFE
Environment: Metropolis. **Activities:** Choral groups, concert band, dance, drama/theater, jazz band, literary magazine, music ensembles, musical theater, pep band, radio station, student government, student newspaper, student-run film society, symphony orchestra, television station, yearbook. 139 registered organizations, 14 honor societies, 20 religious organizations. **Athletics (Intercollegiate):** *Men:* baseball, basketball, crew/rowing, cross-country, diving, football, golf, lacrosse, sailing, soccer, swimming, tennis, track/field (outdoor), track/field (indoor). *Women:* basketball, crew/rowing, cross-country, diving, field hockey, golf, lacrosse, sailing, soccer, softball, swimming, tennis, track/field (outdoor), track/field (indoor), volleyball. **On-Campus Highlights:** Yates Field House, Uncommon Grounds, The Observatory, The Quadrangle, Healy Hall. **Environmental Initiatives:** Set LEED certification as the standard for new constructions & major renovations.

ADMISSIONS
Freshman Academic Profile: 91% in top 10% of high school class, 97% in top 25% of high school class, 99% in top 50% of high school class. 49% from public high schools. **Reported SAT (pre-2016 redesign) scores:** SAT Math middle 50% range 660-760. SAT Critical Reading middle 50% range 660-760. **Concordant SAT scores:** SAT Math middle 50% range 690–780. ACT middle 50% range 30-34. **Basis for Candidate Selection:** *Very important factors*

considered include: rigor of secondary school record, class rank, academic GPA, standardized test scores, application essay, recommendation(s), talent/ability, character/personal qualities, first generation. *Important factors considered include:* interview, extracurricular activities, volunteer work. *Other factors considered include:* alumni/ae relation, geographical residence, state residency, racial/ethnic status, work experience. **Freshman Admission Requirements:** High school diploma is required and GED is accepted. **Freshman Admission Statistics:** 19,997 applied, 16.85% admitted, 47% enrolled. **Transfer Admission Requirements:** High school transcript, college transcript(s), essay or personal statement, standardized test scores, statement of good standing from prior institution(s). Minimum college GPA of 3.0 required. Lowest grade transferable C. **General Admission Information:** Application fee $75. Regular application deadline 1/10. Regular notification 4/1. Nonfall registration not accepted. Admission may be deferred for a maximum of 1 year.

COSTS AND FINANCIAL AID
Annual tuition $49,968. Required fees $579. Average book expense $1,200. **Required Forms and Deadlines:** FAFSA, CSS/Financial Aid PROFILE, Business/Farm Supplement. **Notification of Awards:** Applicants will be notified of awards on or about 4/1. *Types of Aid: Need-based scholarships/ grants:* Federal Pell, FSEOG, State scholarships/grants, Private scholarships, College/university scholarship or grant aid from institutional funds. *Loans:* Direct Subsidized Stafford Loans, Direct Unsubsidized Stafford Loans, Direct PLUS loans, Federal Perkins Loans, Federal Nursing Loans. *Student Employment:* Federal Work-Study Program available. Institutional employment available. **Financial Aid Statistics:** 89% needy freshmen, 90% needy undergrads receive need-based scholarship or grant aid. 40% freshmen, 30% undergrads receive non-need-based scholarship or grant aid. 79% freshmen, 84% undergrads receive need-based self-help aid. 6% freshmen, 4% undergrads receive athletic scholarships. 38% undergrads borrow to pay for school. Average cumulative indebtedness $23,067. **Criteria for awarding aid:** *Non-need-based:* Athletics.

GEORGIA COLLEGE & STATE UNIVERSITY

Campus Box 23, Milledgeville, GA 31061
Phone: 478-445-1283 • **Financial Aid Phone:** 478-445-5149
E-mail: admissions@gcsu.edu • **CEEB Code:** 5252
Fax: 478-445-1914 • **Website:** www.gcsu.edu • **ACT Code:** 828

This public school was founded in 1889. It has a 590-acre campus.

RATINGS
Admissions Selectivity Rating: 74 **Fire Safety Rating:** 99 **Green Rating:** 78

STUDENTS AND FACULTY
Enrollment: 5,923. **Student Body:** 61% female, 39% male, 1% out-of-state, 1% international (31 countries represented). Asian 2%, African American 5%, Caucasian 84%, Hispanic 5%, Native American <1%, Pacific Islander <1%, Two or more races 3%, Race unknown <1%.
Retention and Graduation: 85% freshmen return for sophomore year. 42% freshmen graduate within 4 years. 59% freshmen graduate within 6 years. **Faculty:** Student/faculty ratio 17:1. 336 full-time faculty, 80% hold PhDs, 18% are are members of minority groups, 55% are women.

ACADEMICS
Degrees: bachelor's, doctoral/professional, master's, post-master's certificate. **Classes:** Most classes have 20-29 students. Most lab/discussion sessions have 20-29 students. **Most popular majors:** Registered Nursing/Registered Nurse; Business Administration and Management; Health Teacher Education. **Special Study Options:** Accelerated program, distance learning, double major, English as a Second Language (ESL), honors program, independent study, internships, study abroad, teacher certification program. **Honors Programs:** Honors and/or Scholars Program. **Disability Services:** Special programs offered to physically disabled students, including note-taking services, reader services, tape recorders, tutors. **Career Services:** Alumni network, Career/job search classes, Career assessment, Internships.

FACILITIES
Housing: Coed dorms, special housing for international students, apartments for single students, Theme Housing. 90% of campus accessible to physically diasbled. **Special Academic Facilities/Equipment:** Education archives museum, old governor's mansion, Museum of Fine Arts, Natural History Museum and Planetarium **Computers:** 98% of classrooms, 98% of dorms, 100% of libraries, 98% of dining areas, 100% of student union, 100% of common outdoor areas have wireless network access. Students can register for classes online. Administrative functions (other than registration) can be performed online.

CAMPUS LIFE

Environment: Town. **Activities:** Choral groups, concert band, dance, drama/theater, jazz band, literary magazine, music ensembles, musical theater, radio station, student government, student newspaper, television station, Campus Ministries, Student Organization. 238 registered organizations, 8 religious organizations. 8 fraternities, 6 sororities. **Athletics (Intercollegiate):** Men: baseball, basketball, cross-country, golf, tennis. Women: basketball, cross-country, softball, speed skating, tennis. **On-Campus Highlights:** The Depot (Wellness Center), The Centennial Center (Gymnasium), Cafeteria, Libary and Information Technology Center **Environmental Initiatives:** recycling program.

ADMISSIONS

Freshman Academic Profile: Average high school GPA 3.5. **Reported SAT (pre-2016 redesign) scores:** SAT Math middle 50% range 510-610. SAT Critical Reading middle 50% range 520-610. SAT Writing middle 50% range 500-590. **Concordant SAT scores:** SAT EBRW middle 50% 570–650. SAT Math middle 50% range 540–630. ACT middle 50% range 22-26. Minimum internet-based TOEFL 61. Minimum paper TOEFL 500. **Basis for Candidate Selection:** *Very important factors considered include:* rigor of secondary school record, academic GPA, standardized test scores, application essay, recommendation(s), first generation, level of applicant's interest. *Important factors considered include:* extracurricular activities, talent/ability, character/personal qualities, state residency. *Other factors considered include:* class rank, interview, alumni/ae relation, geographical residence, racial/ethnic status, volunteer work, work experience. **Freshman Admission Requirements:** High school diploma is required and GED is accepted. *Academic units required:* 4 English, 4 math, 4 science, 2 science labs, 2 foreign language, 3 social studies. **Freshman Admission Statistics:** 3,980 applied, 84.52% admitted, 41% enrolled. **Transfer Admission Requirements:** college transcript(s), statement of good standing from prior institution(s). Minimum college GPA of 2.0 required. **General Admission Information:** Application fee $40. Priority deadline 4/1. Nonfall registration accepted. Admission may be deferred for a maximum of 1 year.

COSTS AND FINANCIAL AID

Annual in-state tuition $7,180. Annual out-of-state tuition $25,528. Room and board $11,946. Required fees $2,022. Average book expense $1,500. **Required Forms and Deadlines:** FAFSA, State aid form. **Notification of Awards:** Applicants will be notified of awards on a rolling basis beginning 3/1. **Types of Aid:** *Need-based scholarships/grants:* Federal Pell, FSEOG, State scholarships/grants, Private scholarships, College/university scholarship or grant aid from institutional funds. *Loans:* Direct Subsidized Stafford Loans, Direct Unsubsidized Stafford Loans, Direct PLUS loans, Federal Perkins Loans, State Loans. *Student Employment:* Federal Work-Study Program available. Institutional employment available. **Financial Aid Statistics:** 34% needy freshmen, 37% needy undergrads receive need-based scholarship or grant aid. 94% freshmen, 78% undergrads receive non-need-based scholarship or grant aid. 53% freshmen, 61% undergrads receive need-based self-help aid. 2% freshmen, 2% undergrads receive athletic scholarships. 96% freshmen, 86% undergrads receive any aid. 56% undergrads borrow to pay for school. Average cumulative indebtedness $24,774. **Criteria for awarding aid:** *Non-need-based:* Academics, Alumni affiliation, Art, Athletics, Leadership, Music/drama, State/district residency.

GEORGIA INSTITUTE OF TECHNOLOGY

Office of Undergraduate Admissions, Atlanta, GA 30332-0320
Phone: 404-894-4154 • **Financial Aid Phone:** 404-894-4160
E-mail: admission@gatech.edu • **CEEB Code:** 5248
Fax: 404-894-9511 • **Website:** www.gatech.edu • **ACT Code:** 818

This public school was founded in 1885. It has a 450-acre campus.

RATINGS

Admissions Selectivity Rating: 97   **Fire Safety Rating:** 96   **Green Rating:** 96

STUDENTS AND FACULTY

Enrollment: 14,766. **Student Body:** 37% female, 63% male, 34% out-of-state, 10% international (95 countries represented). Asian 20%, African American 7%, Caucasian 50%, Hispanic 7%, Native American <1%, Pacific Islander <1%, Two or more races 4%, Race unknown 3%.

Retention and Graduation: 97% freshmen return for sophomore year. 41% freshmen graduate within 4 years. 86% freshmen graduate within 6 years. 19% grads go on to further study within 1 year. 2% grads pursue arts and sciences degrees. 1% grads pursue business degrees. 2% grads pursue medical degrees. **Faculty:** Student/faculty ratio 20:1. 1,075 full-time faculty, 81% hold PhDs, 29% are are members of minority groups, 27% are women. 3% of classes are taught by teaching assistants.

ACADEMICS

Degrees: bachelor's, doctoral/research, master's. **Classes:** Most classes have 10-19 students. Most lab/discussion sessions have 20-29 students. **Most popular majors:** Mechanical Engineering; Industrial Engineering; Computer and Information Sciences. **Special Study Options:** Accelerated program, cooperative education program, cross-registration, distance learning, double major, dual enrollment, English as a Second Language (ESL), honors program, independent study, internships, student-designed major, study abroad, Dual degree program (3-2); Regent's Engineering Transfer Program with 14 colleges in the University System of Georgia; Georgia Tech Regional Engineering Program (GTREP) offers undergraduate and graduate Engineering degrees in collaboration with Armstrong Atlantic state University, Georgia Southern University, and Savannah State University. **Honors Programs:** The Georgia Tech Honors Program combines the challenging academic standards of one of the finest technological universities in the world with the closer connections between students and faculty that one might expect to find in a smaller college. Our mission is to create a lively environment in which students and faculty members learn from each other through a common commitment to intellectual inquiry, careful analysis, and energetic exchange of ideas. To promote and sustain this close engagement between students and faculty, the Honors Program will offer unique opportunities to students in the first two years of their studies at Georgia Tech: 1) An Honors Program Residence where first-year students can find a supportive community of interesting people, continue their conversations beyond the classroom, and develop connections to Georgia Tech and the surrounding community; 2) Small sections of introductory core courses designed to emphasize not just mastery of the material, but innovative inquiry and exploration within the discipline and often beyond; 3) A selection of small special topics courses, each with an enrollment limit of twenty HP students, that encourage critical thinking and an interdisciplinary approach to some of the most significant issues facing the world today; 4) A program of well-coordinated advising that will help students build upon their first two years in the Honors Program as they move into their chosen undergraduate majors in the third and fourth years. Combined degree programs: BS/MS. **Disability Services:** Special programs offered to physically disabled students, including note-taking services, reader services, tape recorders, tutors. **Career Services:** Alumni network, Career/job search classes, Career assessment, Internships. We are proud that our experiential learning program affords opportunities for every level of student, from freshman through PhD, and reaches every department on our campus. We help thousands annually find full-time careers and internships, and our award-winning co-op program is over one hundred years old, and far outpaces others.

FACILITIES

Housing: Coed dorms, special housing for disabled students, men's dorms, special housing for international students, women's dorms, fraternity/sorority housing, apartments for married students, apartments for single students, ThemeHousingFirst Year housing is guaranteed to all new freshman and transfer students who submit an application by May 1. 75% of campus accessible to physically disabled. **Special Academic Facilities/Equipment:** Nuclear Magnetic Resonance Spectroscopy Center, Georgia Tech Research Institute, Ovarian Cancer Institute, Paper Museum, Mechanical Properties Research Laboratory with scanning electron microscope, Virtual Factory Laboratory, Ferris-Goldsmith Trading Floor, Advanced Technology Development Center, Klaus Advanced Computing Building, Electron Microscope, Marcus Nanotechnology Research Center, Solar Decathlon House at College of Architecture, Wind Tunnel, GT Smart House, Clough Undergraduates Learning Commons (under construction) **Computers:** 100% of classrooms, 100% of dorms, 100% of libraries, 100% of dining areas, 100% of student union, 65% of common outdoor areas have wireless network access. Students can register for classes online. Administrative functions (other than registration) can be performed online. Undergraduates are required to own a computer.

CAMPUS LIFE

Environment: Metropolis. **Activities:** Choral groups, concert band, dance, drama/theater, jazz band, literary magazine, marching band, music ensembles, musical theater, pep band, radio station, student government, student newspaper, student-run film society, symphony orchestra, television station, yearbook, Campus Ministries, Student Organization, Model UN. 429 registered organizations, 24 honor societies, 39 religious organizations. 38 fraternities, 14 sororities. **Athletics (Intercollegiate):** Men: baseball, basketball, cheerleading, cross-country, diving, football, golf, swimming, tennis, track/field (outdoor), track/field (indoor). Women: basketball, cheerleading, cross-country, diving, softball, swimming, tennis, track/field (outdoor), track/field (indoor), volleyball.

On-Campus Highlights: Tech Square—Bookstore/Hotel/College of, Olympic Aquatic Center/Campus Recreation, The Hill/Tech Tower, Student Center Commons and the Library W, Ferst Center for the Arts. **Environmental Initiatives:** Education: Over 200 courses across all colleges with a goal of having every student who graduates have at least one sustainability course o Many degree programs at the undergraduate and graduate levels, many continuing education and certificate programs also focus on sustainability and major areas of sustainability. Sustainability included in Mission Statement and Strategic Plan since 1994. Updated Strategic Plan in 2010. Have included addressing the Grand Challenges in the Strategic Plan to go along with Improving the Human Condition and a Sustainable Global Economy.

ADMISSIONS

Freshman Academic Profile: Average high school GPA 4.0. 87% in top 10% of high school class, 97% in top 25% of high school class, 99% in top 50% of high school class. **Reported SAT (pre-2016 redesign) scores:** SAT Math middle 50% range 680-770. SAT Critical Reading middle 50% range 640-730. SAT Writing middle 50% range 640-730. **Concordant SAT scores:** SAT EBRW middle 50% 690–750. SAT Math middle 50% range 710–780. ACT middle 50% range 30-34. **Basis for Candidate Selection:** *Very important factors considered include:* rigor of secondary school record, academic GPA, extracurricular activities. *Important factors considered include:* standardized test scores, application essay, talent/ability, character/personal qualities, geographical residence, state residency, volunteer work, work experience. *Other factors considered include:* recommendation(s), interview, first generation, alumni/ae relation, racial/ethnic status. **Freshman Admission Requirements:** High school diploma is required and GED is accepted. *Academic units required:* 4 English, 4 math, 4 science, 2 science labs, 2 foreign language, 3 social studies. **Freshman Admission Statistics:** 30,528 applied, 25.77% admitted, 37% enrolled. **Transfer Admission Requirements:** college transcript(s), statement of good standing from prior institution(s). Minimum college GPA of 2.7 required. Lowest grade transferable C. **General Admission Information:** Application fee $75. Priority deadline 10/15. Regular application deadline 1/10. Regular notification 3/14. Nonfall registration accepted. Admission may be deferred for a maximum of 1 Year.

COSTS AND FINANCIAL AID

Required Forms and Deadlines: FAFSA, Institution's own financial aid form, CSS/Financial Aid PROFILE. **Notification of Awards:** Applicants will be notified of awards on or about 4/15. **Types of Aid:** *Need-based scholarships/ grants:* Federal Pell, FSEOG, State scholarships/grants, Private scholarships, College/university scholarship or grant aid from institutional funds, United Negro College Fund. *Loans:* Direct Subsidized Stafford Loans, Direct Unsubsidized Stafford Loans, Direct PLUS loans, Federal Perkins Loans, State Loans, College/university loans from institutional funds. *Student Employment:* Federal Work-Study Program available. Institutional employment available. **Financial Aid Statistics:** 86% needy freshmen, 87% needy undergrads receive need-based scholarship or grant aid. 72% freshmen, 62% undergrads receive non-need-based scholarship or grant aid. 55% freshmen, 66% undergrads receive need-based self-help aid. 1% freshmen, 1% undergrads receive athletic scholarships. 63% freshmen, 72% undergrads receive any aid. 39% undergrads borrow to pay for school. Average cumulative indebtedness $32,169. **Criteria for awarding aid:** *Need-based:* Academics, Leadership, Minority status. *Non-need-based:* Academics, Athletics, Leadership, Music/drama, State/district residency.

GEORGIA SOUTHERN UNIVERSITY

P.O. Box 8024, Statesboro, GA 30460
Phone: 912-478-5391 • **Financial Aid Phone:** 912-478-5413
E-mail: admissions@georgiasouthern.edu • **CEEB Code:** 5253
Fax: 912-478-7240 • **Website:** http://www.georgiasouthern.edu/ • **ACT Code:** 830

This public school was founded in 1906. It has a 700-acre campus.

RATINGS

Admissions Selectivity Rating: 83   **Fire Safety Rating:** 97   **Green Rating:** 85

STUDENTS AND FACULTY

Enrollment: 17,349. **Student Body:** 51% female, 49% male, 4% out-of-state, 2% international (73 countries represented). Asian 2%, African American 26%, Caucasian 62%, Hispanic 5%, Native American <1%, Pacific Islander <1%, Two or more races 2%, Race unknown 1%.
Retention and Graduation: 81% freshmen return for sophomore year. 26% freshmen graduate within 4 years. 51% freshmen graduate within 6 years.
Faculty: Student/faculty ratio 21:1. 794 full-time faculty, 84% hold PhDs, 17% are are members of minority groups, 48% are women. 3% of classes are taught by teaching assistants.

ACADEMICS

Degrees: bachelor's, doctoral/research, master's, postbachelor's certificate, post-master's certificate. **Classes:** Most classes have 20-29 students. Most lab/discussion sessions have 20-29 students. **Most popular majors:** General Studies; Biology/Biological Sciences; Mechanical Engineering. **Special Study Options:** Accelerated program, cooperative education program, distance learning, double major, English as a Second Language (ESL), honors program, independent study, internships, student-designed major, study abroad, teacher certification program. **Honors Programs:** Georgia Southern University offers University Honors Program (UHP) and 1906 Scholars. The UHP is designed to offer exceptionally able and diligent students the opportunity to enroll in particularly stimulating classes and to integrate their classroom learning with the needs of the community in which they live. The 1906 Scholars, a selective group within the UHP, accepts 15-18 freshmen from the pool of approximately 400 UHP applicants. The program offers interdisciplinary course options. Weekly seminars and colloquia emphasize discussion and independent endeavor, and nurture curiosity and the sharing of ideas among students and faculty. Selected students receive a full tuition scholarship, including out-of-state fees. Combined degree programs: Bachelor's/Graduate in Nursing. **Disability Services:** Special programs offered to physically disabled students, including note-taking services, reader services, tape recorders, tutors. **Career Services:** Alumni network, Alumni services, Career/job search classes, Career assessment, Internships. Experiential learning encompasses internships and cooperative learning at Georgia Southern University. Students can also enroll in a specialized soft skills course which enhances a student's practical learning and sets them apart from other students while on their internship or co-op experience.

FACILITIES

Housing: Coed dorms, special housing for disabled students, special housing for international students, apartments for single students, Theme Housing. 97% of campus accessible to physically diasbled. **Special Academic Facilities/ Equipment:** Art galleries, teaching museum, performing arts center, wildlife education center, eagle cinema, broadcasting studios, planetarium, botanical garden, radio station, black box theatre, and Recreation Activity Center. **Computers:** 80% of classrooms, 45% of dorms, 100% of libraries, 100% of dining areas, 100% of student union, 20% of common outdoor areas have wireless network access. Students can register for classes online. Administrative functions (other than registration) can be performed online.

CAMPUS LIFE

Environment: Village. **Activities:** Choral groups, concert band, dance, drama/ theater, jazz band, literary magazine, marching band, music ensembles, musical theater, pep band, radio station, student government, student newspaper, student-run film society, symphony orchestra, television station, Campus Ministries, Student Organization. 235 registered organizations, 17 honor societies, 20 religious organizations. 20 fraternities, 9 sororities. **Athletics (Intercollegiate):** *Men:* baseball, basketball, cheerleading, football, golf, soccer, tennis. *Women:* basketball, cheerleading, cross-country, diving, soccer, softball, swimming, tennis, track/field (outdoor), volleyball. **On-Campus Highlights:** Russell Union, Recreation Activity Center, Center for Wildlife Education, Georgia Southern Museum, Paulson Stadium, Performing Arts Center, Lamar Q. Ball Raptor Center, Georgia Southern Planetarium, Gallery 303, the Georgia Southern Botanical Gardens, Eagle Cinema, College of Information Technology and Eagle Village. **Environmental Initiatives:** Georgia Southern Student Sustainability Fee Committee allocated $250,000 in funding for 14 sustainability projects at Georgia Southern University for FY2016. The 23 grant winners from FY15 displayed their funded projects in a Sustainability Showcase Exhibit in the university library, viewed by thousands in the campus community over the two weeks that they were displayed.

ADMISSIONS

Freshman Academic Profile: Average high school GPA 3.3. 18% in top 10% of high school class, 47% in top 25% of high school class, 78% in top 50% of high school class. **Reported SAT (pre-2016 redesign) scores:** SAT Math middle 50% range 510-600. SAT Critical Reading middle 50% range 520-590. SAT Writing middle 50% range 480-570. **Concordant SAT scores:** SAT EBRW middle 50% 560–640. SAT Math middle 50% range 560–620. ACT middle 50% range 22-26. Minimum internet-based TOEFL 69. Minimum paper TOEFL 523. **Basis for Candidate Selection:** *Very important factors considered include:* rigor of secondary school record, academic GPA, standardized test scores. *Other factors considered include:* class rank. **Freshman Admission Requirements:** High school diploma is required and GED is not accepted. *Academic units required:* 4 English, 4 math, 4 science, 2 science labs, 2 foreign language, 3 social studies. **Freshman Admission Statistics:** 9,834 applied, 64.55% admitted, 57% enrolled. **Transfer Admission Requirements:** college transcript(s), statement of good standing from prior institution(s). Minimum college GPA of 2.0 required. Lowest grade transferable D. **General Admission Information:** Application fee $30. Priority deadline 4/1. Regular application deadline 5/1. Nonfall registration accepted. Admission may be deferred.

COSTS AND FINANCIAL AID

Annual in-state tuition $4,704. Annual out-of-state tuition $16,600. Room and board $9,800. Required fees $2,092. Average book expense $1,200. **Required Forms and Deadlines:** FAFSA. **Notification of Awards:** Applicants will be notified of awards on a rolling basis beginning 4/20. **Types of Aid:** *Need-based scholarships/grants:* Federal Pell, FSEOG, State scholarships/grants, Private scholarships, College/university scholarship or grant aid from institutional funds. *Loans:* Direct Subsidized Stafford Loans, Direct Unsubsidized Stafford Loans, Direct PLUS loans, Federal Perkins Loans, State Loans. *Student Employment:* Federal Work-Study Program available. Institutional employment available. **Financial Aid Statistics:** 89% needy freshmen, 82% needy undergrads receive need-based scholarship or grant aid. 2% freshmen, 1% undergrads receive non-need-based scholarship or grant aid. 74% freshmen, 82% undergrads receive need-based self-help aid. 1% freshmen, 1% undergrads receive athletic scholarships. 92% freshmen, 89% undergrads receive any aid. 72% undergrads borrow to pay for school. Average cumulative indebtedness $28,098. **Criteria for awarding aid:** *Non-need-based:* Academics, Alumni affiliation, Art, Athletics, Leadership, Minority status, Music/drama, State/district residency.

GEORGIA SOUTHWESTERN STATE UNIVERSITY

800 Georgia Southwestern State University Dr., Americus, GA 31709-4693
Phone: 229-928-1273 • **Financial Aid Phone:** 229-928-1378
E-mail: admissions@gsw.edu • **CEEB Code:** 5250
Fax: 229-931-2983 • **Website:** www.gsw.edu • **ACT Code:** 824

This public school was founded in 1906. It has a 325-acre campus.

RATINGS
Admissions Selectivity Rating: 79   **Fire Safety Rating:** 88   **Green Rating:** 60*

STUDENTS AND FACULTY
Enrollment: 2,413. **Student Body:** 62% female, 38% male, 4% out-of-state, 2% international (37 countries represented). Asian 1%, African American 27%, Caucasian 63%, Hispanic 4%, Native American <1%, Pacific Islander <1%, Two or more races 2%, Race unknown <1%.
Retention and Graduation: 70% freshmen return for sophomore year. 14% freshmen graduate within 4 years. 32% freshmen graduate within 6 years.
Faculty: Student/faculty ratio 18:1. 112 full-time faculty, 73% hold PhDs, 14% are are members of minority groups, 51% are women. 0% of classes are taught by teaching assistants.

ACADEMICS
Degrees: bachelor's, master's, postbachelor's certificate, post-master's certificate. **Classes:** Most classes have 20-29 students. **Most popular majors:** Registered Nursing/Registered Nurse; Business Administration and Management; Accounting. **Special Study Options:** Accelerated program, cooperative education program, distance learning, double major, dual enrollment, English as a Second Language (ESL), honors program, internships, study abroad, teacher certification program. **Disability Services:** Special programs offered to physically disabled students, including note-taking services, reader services, tape recorders, tutors.

FACILITIES
Housing: Coed dorms, Apartment housing for upperclassmen. 99% of campus accessible to physically diasbled. **Special Academic Facilities/Equipment:** Observatory, Glass-blowing studio **Computers:** Students can register for classes online. Administrative functions (other than registration) can be performed online.

CAMPUS LIFE
Environment: Village. **Activities:** Choral groups, concert band, drama/ theater, jazz band, literary magazine, music ensembles, musical theater, student government, student newspaper, television station, Student Organization. 12 honor societies, 7 fraternities, 6 sororities. **Athletics (Intercollegiate):** *Men:* baseball, basketball, golf, soccer, tennis. *Women:* basketball, cross-country, soccer, softball, tennis.

ADMISSIONS
Freshman Academic Profile: Average high school GPA 3.3. 15% in top 10% of high school class, 42% in top 25% of high school class, 75% in top 50% of high school class. 82% from public high schools. **Reported SAT (pre-2016 redesign) scores:** SAT Math middle 50% range 430-520. SAT Critical Reading middle 50% range 440-540. **Concordant SAT scores:** SAT Math middle 50% range 470–550. ACT middle 50% range 19-23. Minimum internet-based TOEFL 70. Minimum paper TOEFL 523. **Basis for Candidate Selection:** *Very important factors considered include:* rigor of secondary school record, academic GPA, standardized test scores. *Important factors considered include:* class rank. *Other factors considered include:* application

essay, recommendation(s), interview, extracurricular activities, talent/ability.
Freshman Admission Requirements: High school diploma is required and GED is accepted. *Academic units required:* 4 English, 4 math, 4 science, 2 science labs, 2 foreign language, and 3 units from above areas or other academic areas. *Academic units recommended:* 2 academic electives. **Freshman Admission Statistics:** 1,389 applied, 68.18% admitted, 51% enrolled. **Transfer Admission Requirements:** college transcript(s), Minimum college GPA of 2.0 required. Lowest grade transferable D. **General Admission Information:** Application fee $25. Regular application deadline 7/21. Nonfall registration accepted. Admission may be deferred for a maximum of 12 months.

COSTS AND FINANCIAL AID
Annual in-state tuition $4,858. Annual out-of-state tuition $17,678. Room and board $8,952. Required fees $1,340. Average book expense $1,400. **Required Forms and Deadlines:** FAFSA, Institution's own financial aid form, State aid form. **Notification of Awards:** Applicants will be notified of awards on a rolling basis beginning 5/1. **Types of Aid:** *Need-based scholarships/grants:* Federal Pell, FSEOG, State scholarships/grants, Private scholarships, College/ university scholarship or grant aid from institutional funds. *Loans:* Direct Subsidized Stafford Loans, Direct Unsubsidized Stafford Loans, Direct PLUS loans, Federal Perkins Loans, State Loans. *Student Employment:* Federal Work-Study Program available. Institutional employment available. **Financial Aid Statistics:** 65% needy freshmen, 67% needy undergrads receive need-based scholarship or grant aid. 69% freshmen, 47% undergrads receive non-need-based scholarship or grant aid. 87% freshmen, 86% undergrads receive need-based self-help aid. 2% freshmen, 3% undergrads receive athletic scholarships. 76% undergrads borrow to pay for school. Average cumulative indebtedness $27,939. **Criteria for awarding aid:** *Non-need-based:* Academics, Alumni affiliation, Art, Athletics, Leadership, Music/drama, State/district residency.

GEORGIA STATE UNIVERSITY

PO Box 4009, Atlanta, GA 30302-4009
Phone: 404-413-2500 • **Financial Aid Phone:** 404-413-2600
E-mail: admissions@gsu.edu • **CEEB Code:** 5251
Fax: 404-413-2002 • **Website:** www.gsu.edu • **ACT Code:** 826

This public school was founded in 1913. It has a 33-acre campus.

RATINGS
Admissions Selectivity Rating: 84   **Fire Safety Rating:** 88   **Green Rating:** 79

STUDENTS AND FACULTY
Enrollment: 24,729. **Student Body:** 59% female, 41% male, 5% out-of-state, 2% international (159 countries represented). Asian 13%, African American 42%, Caucasian 25%, Hispanic 10%, Native American <1%, Pacific Islander <1%, Two or more races 6%, Race unknown 1%.
Retention and Graduation: 83% freshmen return for sophomore year. 23% freshmen graduate within 4 years. 53% freshmen graduate within 6 years.
Faculty: Student/faculty ratio 22:1. 1,219 full-time faculty, 90% hold PhDs, 26% are are members of minority groups, 46% are women.

ACADEMICS
Degrees: bachelor's, certificate, doctoral/professional, doctoral/research, master's, postbachelor's certificate, post-master's certificate. **Classes:** Most classes have 20-29 students. **Most popular majors:** Biology/Biological Sciences; Accounting; Psychology. **Special Study Options:** Accelerated program, cooperative education program, cross-registration, distance learning, double major, dual enrollment, English as a Second Language (ESL), honors program, independent study, internships, student-designed major, study abroad, teacher certification program, Freshman Learning Communities. **Honors Programs:** Students have the advantage of small classes and close contact with faculty members. Combined degree programs: BA/JD, BA/MA, BA/MIB; BBA/ MSISAC; BS/MAT. **Disability Services:** Special programs offered to physically disabled students, including note-taking services, reader services, tape recorders, tutors. **Career Services:** Alumni network, Alumni services, Career/ job search classes, Career assessment, Internships.

FACILITIES
Housing: Coed dorms, special housing for disabled students, special housing for international students, apartments for married students, apartments for single students, Some arrangments for visiting faculty/scholars. 100% of campus accessible to physically diasbled. **Special Academic Facilities/Equipment:** Cartography Production Laboratory,Commuter Student Services,Cooperative Learning Laboratory,Economic Forecasting Center,Ernest G. Welch School of Art and Design Gallery, Instructional Technology Center, James M. Cox, Jr. Multi-Media Instructional Lab and Satellite Downlink Facility,Kopleff Recital Hall,Lanette L. Suttles Child Development Center,Language Acquisition and Resource Center, Mathematics Assistance Complex, Mathematics Interactive

Learning Environment, Music Media Center, Rialto Center for the Performing Arts, Small Business Development Center, Visual Resource Center, Writing Studio. **Computers:** Students can register for classes online. Administrative functions (other than registration) can be performed online.

CAMPUS LIFE

Environment: Metropolis. **Activities:** Choral groups, concert band, dance, drama/theater, jazz band, literary magazine, music ensembles, pep band, radio station, student government, student newspaper, student-run film society, television station 201 registered organizations, 19 honor societies, 21 religious organizations. 9 fraternities, 15 sororities. **Athletics (Intercollegiate):** *Men:* baseball, basketball, cross-country, golf, soccer, tennis, track/field (outdoor), volleyball. *Women:* basketball, cross-country, golf, soccer, softball, tennis, track/field (outdoor), volleyball. **On-Campus Highlights:** Recreatoin Center, Student Housing, Aderhold Learning Center, The Rialto Center for the Performing Arts, The Student Center.

ADMISSIONS

Freshman Academic Profile: Average high school GPA 3.4. 17% in top 10% of high school class, 45% in top 25% of high school class, 82% in top 50% of high school class. **Reported SAT (pre-2016 redesign) scores:** SAT Math middle 50% range 470-590. SAT Critical Reading middle 50% range 480-590. SAT Writing middle 50% range 460-570. **Concordant SAT scores:** SAT EBRW middle 50% 530–640. SAT Math middle 50% range 510–610. ACT middle 50% range 20-26. Minimum internet-based TOEFL 79. Minimum paper TOEFL 550. **Basis for Candidate Selection:** *Very important factors considered include:* rigor of secondary school record, academic GPA, standardized test scores. *Other factors considered include:* application essay, recommendation(s), talent/ability. **Freshman Admission Requirements:** High school diploma is required and GED is not accepted. *Academic units required:* 4 English, 4 math, 4 science, 2 science labs, 2 foreign language, 3 social studies. *Academic units recommended:* 4 English, 4 math, 4 science, 2 science labs, 2 foreign language, 3 social studies. **Freshman Admission Statistics:** 17,467 applied, 52.74% admitted, 43% enrolled. **Transfer Admission Requirements:** college transcript(s), Minimum college GPA of 2.5 required. Lowest grade transferable D. **General Admission Information:** Application fee $60. Regular application deadline 3/1. Regular notification 5/1. Nonfall registration accepted. Admission may be deferred for a maximum of 2 terms.

COSTS AND FINANCIAL AID

Annual in-state tuition $8,112. Annual out-of-state tuition $26,322. Room and board $13,342. Required fees $2,128. Average book expense $1,200. **Required Forms and Deadlines:** FAFSA. **Notification of Awards:** Applicants will be notified of awards on a rolling basis beginning 3/1. **Types of Aid:** *Need-based scholarships/grants:* Federal Pell, FSEOG, State scholarships/grants, Private scholarships, College/university scholarship or grant aid from institutional funds, United Negro College Fund. *Loans:* Direct Subsidized Stafford Loans, Direct Unsubsidized Stafford Loans, Direct PLUS loans, Federal Perkins Loans, Federal Nursing Loans, State Loans. *Student Employment:* Federal Work-Study Program available. Institutional employment available. **Financial Aid Statistics:** 72% needy freshmen, 73% needy undergrads receive need-based scholarship or grant aid. 91% freshmen, 94% undergrads receive non-need-based scholarship or grant aid. 59% freshmen, 68% undergrads receive need-based self-help aid. 0% freshmen, 0% undergrads receive athletic scholarships. 70% undergrads borrow to pay for school. Average cumulative indebtedness $29,959. **Criteria for awarding aid:** *Non-need-based:* Academics, Alumni affiliation, Art, Athletics, Job skills, Leadership, Minority status, Music/drama, Religious affiliation, State/district residency.

GEORGIAN COURT UNIVERSITY

900 Lakewood Avenue, Lakewood, NJ 08701-2697
Phone: 732-987-2700 • **Financial Aid Phone:** 732-987-2258
E-mail: admissions@georgian.edu • **CEEB Code:** 2274
Fax: 732-987-2000 • **Website:** georgian.edu • **ACT Code:** 2562

This private school, affiliated with the Roman Catholic Church, was founded in 1908. It has a 156-acre campus.

RATINGS

Admissions Selectivity Rating: 75   Fire Safety Rating: 95   Green Rating: 60*

STUDENTS AND FACULTY

Enrollment: 1,409. **Student Body:** 75% female, 25% male, 6% out-of-state, 1% international (11 countries represented). Asian 3%, African American 12%, Caucasian 61%, Hispanic 11%, Native American <1%, Pacific Islander <1%, Two or more races 2%, Race unknown 9%.

Retention and Graduation: 85% freshmen return for sophomore year. 26% freshmen graduate within 4 years. 42% freshmen graduate within 6 years. **Faculty:** Student/faculty ratio 12:1. 85 full-time faculty, 91% hold PhDs, 22% are are members of minority groups, 61% are women. 0% of classes are taught by teaching assistants.

ACADEMICS

Degrees: bachelor's, certificate, master's, postbachelor's certificate, post-master's certificate. **Classes:** Most classes have 10-19 students. **Most popular majors:** Elementary Education and Teaching; Psychology; Registered Nursing/Registered Nurse. **Special Study Options:** Accelerated program, distance learning, double major, dual enrollment, English as a Second Language (ESL), honors program, independent study, internships, liberal arts/career combination, study abroad, teacher certification program, Undergrads may take grad level classes. Co-Op Programs: Arts, Business, Health Professions, Natural Science, Social/Behavioral Science. **Honors Programs:** Members of the University Honors Program receive an enriched academic curriculum featuring: ° Faculty chosen for their excellence as teaching-scholars ° Challenging interactive classroom format ° Emphasis on primary texts and sources ° Rigorous scholarly writing assignments and oral presentations ° Close faculty mentoring ° Preference in academic advisement and course registration ° A strong sense of belonging to a community of scholars ° Sponsorship in funding presentations at regional and national conferences ° Special advisement by faculty regarding graduate and professional school applications and prestigious fellowship opportunities ° Special recognition at commencement ceremonies Combined degree programs: BS/MBA. **Disability Services:** Special programs offered to physically disabled students, including note-taking services, reader services, tape recorders, tutors. **Career Services:** Alumni network, Alumni services, Career/job search classes, Career assessment, Internships, On-campus interviews. Every individual appointment, program and written resource integrates the tactical elements of the job search process with the emotional/spiritual side of identifying one's life purpose and true calling. Our approach is based on helping students identify their dreams and aspirations, explore their gifts and talents through classes, activities, internships and coaching, and create a tactical plan enabling them to achieve success as they have defined for themselves.

FACILITIES

Housing: women's dorms, Wellness Housing. 77% of campus accessible to physically diasbled. **Special Academic Facilities/Equipment:** Art gallery, arboretum, Wellness Center, NASA ERC. **Computers:** 98% of classrooms, 77% of dorms, 100% of libraries, 50% of dining areas, 100% of student union, have wireless network access. Students can register for classes online. Administrative functions (other than registration) can be performed online.

CAMPUS LIFE

Environment: Town. **Activities:** Choral groups, concert band, dance, jazz band, literary magazine, music ensembles, student government, student newspaper, yearbook, Campus Ministries, Student Organization, Model UN. 48 registered organizations, 18 honor societies, 1 religious organization. **Athletics (Intercollegiate):** *Women:* basketball, cross-country, lacrosse, soccer, softball, tennis, track/field (outdoor), volleyball. **On-Campus Highlights:** Arboretum, NASA Educational Resource Center, Art Gallery, Library, Wellness Center. **Environmental Initiatives:** We have included a sustainability commitment in our strategic plan.

ADMISSIONS

Freshman Academic Profile: Average high school GPA 3.3. 8% in top 10% of high school class, 24% in top 25% of high school class, 60% in top 50% of high school class. 71% from public high schools. **Reported SAT (pre-2016 redesign) scores:** SAT Math middle 50% range 430-530. SAT Critical Reading middle 50% range 420-510. SAT Writing middle 50% range 400-510. **Concordant SAT scores:** SAT EBRW middle 50% 460–570. SAT Math middle 50% range 440–560. ACT middle 50% range 17-23. Minimum internet-based TOEFL 79. Minimum paper TOEFL 550. **Basis for Candidate Selection:** *Very important factors considered include:* rigor of secondary school record, academic GPA. *Important factors considered include:* standardized test scores. *Other factors considered include:* class rank, application essay, recommendation(s), interview, extracurricular activities, talent/ability, character/personal qualities, first generation, alumni/ae relation, volunteer work, work experience, level of applicant's interest. **Freshman Admission Requirements:** High school diploma is required and GED is accepted. *Academic units required:* 4 English, 2 math, 1 science, 1 science lab, 2 foreign language, 1 history, 6 academic electives. **Freshman Admission Statistics:** 1,609 applied, 74.46% admitted, 18% enrolled. **Transfer Admission Requirements:** college transcript(s), Minimum college GPA of 2.0 required. Lowest grade transferable c. **General Admission Information:** Application fee $40. Regular application deadline 8/1. Nonfall registration accepted. Admission may be deferred.

COSTS AND FINANCIAL AID

Annual tuition $30,158. Room and board $10,808. Required fees $1,460. Average book expense $1,350. **Required Forms and Deadlines:** FAFSA. **Types of Aid:** *Need-based scholarships/grants:* Federal Pell, FSEOG, State scholarships/grants, Private scholarships, College/university scholarship or grant aid from institutional funds. *Loans:* Direct Subsidized Stafford Loans, Direct Unsubsidized Stafford Loans, Direct PLUS loans, State Loans. *Student Employment:* Federal Work-Study Program available. Institutional employment available. **Financial Aid Statistics:** 96% needy freshmen, 97% needy undergrads receive need-based scholarship or grant aid. 7% freshmen, 5% undergrads receive non-need-based scholarship or grant aid. 84% freshmen, 82% undergrads receive need-based self-help aid. 2% freshmen, 3% undergrads receive athletic scholarships. 99% freshmen, 95% undergrads receive any aid. Average cumulative indebtedness $40,267. **Criteria for awarding aid:** *Need-based:* Academics, Alumni affiliation, Art, Athletics, Leadership, Religious affiliation. *Non-need-based:* Academics, Alumni affiliation, Art, Athletics, Leadership, Religious affiliation, State/district residency.

See page 960.

GETTYSBURG COLLEGE

Admissions Office, Gettysburg, PA 17325-1484
Phone: 717-337-6100 • **Financial Aid Phone:** 717-337-6611
E-mail: admiss@gettysburg.edu • **CEEB Code:** 2275
Fax: 717-337-6145 • **Website:** www.gettysburg.edu • **ACT Code:** 3580

This private school, affiliated with the Lutheran Church, was founded in 1832. It has a 200-acre campus.

RATINGS
Admissions Selectivity Rating: 92   **Fire Safety Rating:** 91   **Green Rating:** 75

STUDENTS AND FACULTY
Enrollment: 2,379. **Student Body:** 53% female, 47% male, 75% out-of-state, 7% international (36 countries represented). Asian 2%, African American 3%, Caucasian 76%, Hispanic 6%, Native American <1%, Pacific Islander 0%, Two or more races 3%, Race unknown 2%.
Retention and Graduation: 90% freshmen return for sophomore year. 84% freshmen graduate within 4 years. 87 30% grads go on to further study within 1 year. **Faculty:** Student/faculty ratio 9:1. 223 full-time faculty, 96% hold PhDs, 17% are are members of minority groups, 42% are women. 0% of classes are taught by teaching assistants.

ACADEMICS
Degrees: bachelor's. **Classes:** Most classes have 10-19 students. **Most popular majors:** Psychology; Political Science and Government; Business/Commerce. **Special Study Options:** double major, independent study, internships, student-designed major, study abroad, teacher certification program. Combined degree programs: Optometry, Nursing, Forestry, Environmental Management. **Disability Services:** Special programs offered to physically disabled students, including tape recorders. **Career Services:** Alumni network, Alumni services, Career/job search classes, Career assessment, Internships, Regional alumni.

FACILITIES
Housing: Coed dorms, women's dorms, fraternity/sorority housing, apartments for single students, Theme Housing, Special interest and theme housing. **Special Academic Facilities/Equipment:** Art gallery, language lab, Child Study lab, Majestic Theatre, Sunderman Conservatory, planetarium, observatory, electron microscopes, NMR spectrometer, greenhouse,digital classrooms, wireless network, Plasma Physics labs, Science Center. **Computers:** 100% of classrooms, 100% of dorms, 100% of libraries, 100% of dining areas, 100% of student union, 90% of common outdoor areas have wireless network access. Students can register for classes online. Administrative functions (other than registration) can be performed online.

CAMPUS LIFE
Environment: Village. **Activities:** Choral groups, concert band, dance, drama/theater, jazz band, literary magazine, marching band, music ensembles, radio station, student government, student newspaper, student-run film society, symphony orchestra, television station, yearbook, Campus Ministries, Student Organization, Model UN. 120 registered organizations, 16 honor societies, 7 religious organizations. 10 fraternities, 6 sororities. **Athletics (Intercollegiate):** *Men:* baseball, basketball, cheerleading, cross-country, football, golf, lacrosse, soccer, swimming, tennis, track/field (outdoor), track/field (indoor), wrestling. *Women:* basketball, cheerleading, cross-country, field hockey, golf, lacrosse, soccer, softball, swimming, tennis, track/field (outdoor), track/field (indoor), volleyball. **On-Campus Highlights:** Beautiful 200-acre campus, Musselman

Library, Science Center, Center for Athletics, Recreation, and Fitness, College Union Building. **Environmental Initiatives:** The Center for Athletics, Recreation, and Fitness has received LEED Gold certification.

ADMISSIONS
Freshman Academic Profile: 64% in top 10% of high school class, 82% in top 25% of high school class, 99% in top 50% of high school class. 70% from public high schools. **Reported SAT (pre-2016 redesign) scores:** SAT Math middle 50% range 610-680. SAT Critical Reading middle 50% range 600-680. **Concordant SAT scores:** SAT Math middle 50% range 630–710. ACT middle 50% range 26-30. **Basis for Candidate Selection:** *Very important factors considered include:* rigor of secondary school record, class rank, academic GPA, recommendation(s). *Important factors considered include:* standardized test scores, application essay, interview, extracurricular activities, talent/ability, character/personal qualities, volunteer work. *Other factors considered include:* first generation, alumni/ae relation, geographical residence, racial/ethnic status, work experience, level of applicant's interest. **Freshman Admission Requirements:** High school diploma is required and GED is accepted. *Academic units required:* 4 English, 3 math, 3 science, 3 science labs, 3 foreign language, 3 social studies, 3 history. *Academic units recommended:* 4 English, 4 math, 4 science, 4 science labs, 4 foreign language, 4 social studies, 4 history. **Freshman Admission Statistics:** 6,816 applied, 42.63% admitted, 24% enrolled. **Transfer Admission Requirements:** High school transcript, college transcript(s), essay or personal statement, standardized test scores, statement of good standing from prior institution(s). Minimum college GPA of 2.5 required. Lowest grade transferable C. **General Admission Information:** Application fee $60. Priority deadline 1/15. Regular application deadline 1/15. Regular notification 4/1. Nonfall registration accepted. Admission may be deferred for a maximum of 1 year.

COSTS AND FINANCIAL AID
Annual tuition $50,860. Room and board $12,140. Average book expense $500. **Required Forms and Deadlines:** FAFSA, CSS/Financial Aid PROFILE. **Notification of Awards:** Applicants will be notified of awards on or about 4/1. **Types of Aid:** *Need-based scholarships/grants:* Federal Pell, FSEOG, State scholarships/grants, Private scholarships, College/university scholarship or grant aid from institutional funds. *Loans:* Direct Subsidized Stafford Loans, Direct Unsubsidized Stafford Loans, Direct PLUS loans, Federal Perkins Loans, College/university loans from institutional funds. *Student Employment:* Federal Work-Study Program available. Institutional employment available. **Financial Aid Statistics:** 96% needy freshmen, 95% needy undergrads receive need-based scholarship or grant aid. 45% freshmen, 38% undergrads receive non-need-based scholarship or grant aid. 92% freshmen, 91% undergrads receive need-based self-help aid. 0% freshmen, 0% undergrads receive athletic scholarships. 60% freshmen, 60% undergrads receive any aid. 63% undergrads borrow to pay for school. Average cumulative indebtedness $31,169. **Criteria for awarding aid:** *Need-based:* Academics, Leadership, Minority status, Music/drama. *Non-need-based:* Academics, Music/drama.

GODDARD COLLEGE

123 Pitkin Road, Plainfield, VT 5667
Phone: 802-454-8311
E-mail: admissions@goddard.edu
Fax: 802-454-1029 • **Website:** www.goddard.edu

RATINGS
Admissions Selectivity Rating: 64   **Fire Safety Rating:** 60*   **Green Rating:** 88

STUDENTS AND FACULTY
Enrollment: 186. **Student Body:** 70% female, 30% male, 0% out-of-state, 0% international. Asian 0%, African American 1%, Caucasian 68%, Hispanic 2%, Native American 3%, Pacific Islander 0%, Two or more races 5%, Race unknown 17%.
Faculty: 16 full-time faculty, 0% hold PhDs, 0% are are members of minority groups, 69% are women.

ACADEMICS
Degrees: bachelor's, master's. Combined degree programs: BA/MA, Psychology.

CAMPUS LIFE
Environmental Initiatives: Reducing emissions by 30% since 2007.

ADMISSIONS
Basis for Candidate Selection: *Very important factors considered include:* application essay, interview, character/personal qualities, level of applicant's interest. *Important factors considered include:* recommendation(s), talent/ability, volunteer work. *Other factors considered include:* rigor of secondary school record, academic GPA, extracurricular activities, first generation, alumni/ae relation, racial/ethnic status, work experience. **Freshman Admission**

Requirements: *Academic units recommended:* 4 English, 4 math, 4 science, 3 science labs, 2 foreign language, 4 social studies. **Freshman Admission Statistics:** 5 applied, 80.00% admitted, 100% enrolled. **General Admission Information:** Application fee $40. Priority deadline 6/15. Regular application deadline 7/15. Nonfall registration accepted. Admission may be deferred for a maximum of 2 semesters.

COSTS AND FINANCIAL AID

Annual tuition $15,786. Average book expense $600. **Required Forms and Deadlines:** FAFSA. **Types of Aid:** *Need-based scholarships/grants:* Federal Pell, FSEOG, State scholarships/grants, Private scholarships, College/university scholarship or grant aid from institutional funds. *Student Employment:* Federal Work-Study Program available. Institutional employment available. **Financial Aid Statistics:** 100% needy freshmen, 82% needy undergrads receive need-based scholarship or grant aid. 0% undergrads receive non-need-based scholarship or grant aid. 100% freshmen, 89% undergrads receive need-based self-help aid. 0% freshmen, 0% undergrads receive athletic scholarships.

GOLDEN GATE UNIVERSITY

536 Mission Street, San Francisco, CA 94105
Phone: 415-442-7800
E-mail: info@ggu.edu • **CEEB Code:** 4329
Fax: 415-442-7807 • **Website:** www.ggu.edu • **ACT Code:** 278

This private school was founded in 1901.

RATINGS

Admissions Selectivity Rating: 61   **Fire Safety Rating:** 60*   **Green Rating:** 60*

STUDENTS AND FACULTY

Student Body: 5% out-of-state, (61 countries represented). **Retention and Graduation:** 15% grads go on to further study within 1 year. 30% grads pursue business degrees. **Faculty:** Student/faculty ratio 13:1. 81 full-time faculty, 0% hold PhDs, 0% are are members of minority groups, 0% 0% of classes are taught by teaching assistants.

ACADEMICS

Degrees: bachelor's, certificate, doctoral/professional, doctoral/research, master's, postbachelor's certifiate, post-master's certificate. **Classes:** Most classes have 10-19 students. **Special Study Options:** Accelerated program, cooperative education program, distance learning, dual enrollment, English as a Second Language (ESL), independent study, internships, weekend college. **Disability Services:** Special programs offered to physically disabled students, including tape recorders. **Career Services:** Alumni network, Alumni services, Career/job search classes, Career assessment, Internships. Virtual career center—ggucareer.com. 24/7 access to career maanagement tools and resources including self assessment, company contact databases, industry reports and job board.

FACILITIES

Housing: 100% of campus accessible to physically diasbled. **Computers:** Students can register for classes online. Administrative functions (other than registration) can be performed online.

CAMPUS LIFE

Activities: student government, student newspaper. 16 registered organizations, 5 honor societies.

ADMISSIONS

Freshman Academic Profile: Average high school GPA 2.7. Minimum paper TOEFL 525. **Basis for Candidate Selection:** *Very important factors considered include:* rigor of secondary school record. *Other factors considered include:* class rank, standardized test scores, application essay, recommendation(s). **Freshman Admission Requirements:** High school diploma is required and GED is accepted. *Academic units recommended:* 4 English, 3 math, 2 science, 1 science lab, 2 foreign language, 1 social studies, 1 history. **Transfer Admission Requirements:** college transcript(s), Minimum college GPA of 2.0 required. Lowest grade transferable c-. **General Admission Information:** Application fee $55. Priority deadline 7/1. Nonfall registration accepted. Admission may be deferred for a maximum of 12 months.

COSTS AND FINANCIAL AID

Annual tuition $18,000. Average book expense $1,920. **Required Forms and Deadlines:** FAFSA, Institution's own financial aid form. **Notification of Awards:** Applicants will be notified of awards on a rolling basis beginning 7/15. **Types of Aid:** *Need-based scholarships/grants:* Federal Pell, FSEOG, State scholarships/grants, Private scholarships, College/university scholarship or grant aid from institutional funds. *Loans:* Direct Subsidized Stafford Loans, Direct Unsubsidized Stafford Loans, Federal Perkins Loans, State Loans. *Student*

Employment: Federal Work-Study Program available. Institutional employment available. **Financial Aid Statistics:** 20% needy undergrads receive need-based scholarship or grant aid. 24% undergrads receive non-need-based scholarship or grant aid. 100% undergrads receive need-based self-help aid. 0% undergrads receive athletic scholarships. **Criteria for awarding aid:** *Need-based:* Academics, Alumni affiliation, Leadership, Minority status. *Non-need-based:* Academics, Alumni affiliation, Leadership.

GONZAGA UNIVERSITY

502 E. Boone Avenue, Spokane, WA 99258
Phone: 509-313-6572 • **Financial Aid Phone:** 509-313-6582
E-mail: admissions@gonzaga.edu • **CEEB Code:** 4330
Fax: 509-313-5780 • **Website:** www.gonzaga.edu • **ACT Code:** 4458

This private school, affiliated with the Roman Catholic Church, affiliated with the Catholic-Jesuit Church, was founded in 1887. It has a 108-acre campus.

RATINGS

Admissions Selectivity Rating: 88   **Fire Safety Rating:** 82   **Green Rating:** 92

STUDENTS AND FACULTY

Enrollment: 5,084. **Student Body:** 52% female, 48% male, 51% out-of-state, 1% international (34 countries represented). Asian 5%, African American 1%, Caucasian 72%, Hispanic 10%, Native American 1%, Pacific Islander <1%, Two or more races 6%, Race unknown 3%. **Retention and Graduation:** 92% freshmen return for sophomore year. 74% freshmen graduate within 4 years. 84% freshmen graduate within 6 years. **Faculty:** Student/faculty ratio 12:1. 441 full-time faculty, 85% hold PhDs, 11% are are members of minority groups, 46% are women. 0% of classes are taught by teaching assistants.

ACADEMICS

Degrees: bachelor's, doctoral/professional, doctoral/research, master's. **Classes:** Most classes have 20-29 students. Most lab/discussion sessions have 10-19 students. **Most popular majors:** Business/Commerce; Psychology; Biology/Biological Sciences. **Special Study Options:** Accelerated program, double major, dual enrollment, English as a Second Language (ESL), exchange student program (domestic), honors program, independent study, internships, study abroad, teacher certification program. **Honors Programs:** Hogan Entrepreneurial Leadership Program- Immerses students in the fundamentals of creating and managing new ventures in the public and private sectors Combined degree programs: MAcc/JD, MBA/JD, RN/MSN. **Disability Services:** Special programs offered to physically disabled students, including note-taking services, reader services, tape recorders. **Career Services:** Alumni network, Alumni services, Career/job search classes, Career assessment, Internships, Regional alumni. Alumni Networking and Services.

FACILITIES

Housing: Coed dorms, special housing for disabled students, men's dorms, special housing for international students, women's dorms, apartments for married students, apartments for single students, Theme Housing. 95% of campus accessible to physically diasbled. **Special Academic Facilities/Equipment:** Art center, museum, language lab, TV production center, educational center, two electron microscopes. **Computers:** 75% of classrooms, 90% of dorms, 100% of libraries, 100% of student union, 75% of common outdoor areas have wireless network access. Students can register for classes online. Administrative functions (other than registration) can be performed online.

CAMPUS LIFE

Environment: City. **Activities:** Choral groups, concert band, dance, drama/theater, jazz band, literary magazine, music ensembles, pep band, radio station, student government, student newspaper, symphony orchestra, television station, yearbook, Campus Ministries. 86 registered organizations, 10 honor societies, 4 religious organizations. **Athletics (Intercollegiate):** *Men:* baseball, basketball, crew/rowing, cross-country, golf, soccer, tennis, track/field (outdoor). *Women:* basketball, crew/rowing, cross-country, golf, soccer, tennis, track/field (outdoor), volleyball. **On-Campus Highlights:** St Aloysius Cathedral, McCarthy Athletic Center, Jundt Art Museum, Bing Crosby Museum in the Crosby Student Center, The Gonzaga University Bookstore. **Environmental Initiatives:** Developing an emission inventory and a comprehensive Climate Action Plan.

ADMISSIONS

Freshman Academic Profile: Average high school GPA 3.8. 36% in top 10% of high school class, 69% in top 25% of high school class, 93% in top 50% of high school class. 61% from public high schools. **Reported SAT (pre-2016 redesign) scores:** SAT Math middle 50% range 560-650. SAT Critical Reading middle 50% range 550-650. **Concordant SAT scores:** SAT Math middle 50% range 580–670. ACT middle 50% range 25-30. Minimum paper TOEFL 550. **Basis for Candidate Selection:** *Very important factors considered include:* rigor of secondary school record, academic GPA, character/personal qualities, first generation. *Important factors considered include:* standardized test scores, application essay, recommendation(s), extracurricular activities, talent/ability. *Other factors considered include:* interview, alumni/ae relation, racial/ethnic status, volunteer work, work experience, level of applicant's interest. **Freshman Admission Requirements:** High school diploma is required and GED is not accepted. *Academic units required:* 4 English, 3 math, 3 science, 3 science labs, 2 foreign language, 2 social studies, 2 history, 2 academic electives. *Academic units recommended:* 4 English, 4 math, 4 science, 4 science labs, 3 foreign language, 3 social studies, 3 history, 3 academic electives. **Freshman Admission Statistics:** 7,324 applied, 67.29% admitted, 26% enrolled. **Transfer Admission Requirements:** college transcript(s), essay or personal statement, statement of good standing from prior institution(s). Minimum college GPA of 2.7 required. Lowest grade transferable C. **General Admission Information:** Application fee $50. Priority deadline 11/15. Regular application deadline 2/1. Regular notification 3/15. Nonfall registration accepted. Admission may be deferred for a maximum of 1 year.

COSTS AND FINANCIAL AID

Annual tuition $38,980. Room and board $11,158. Required fees $750. Average book expense $1,092. **Required Forms and Deadlines:** FAFSA. **Notification of Awards:** Applicants will be notified of awards on a rolling basis beginning 3/1. **Types of Aid:** *Need-based scholarships/grants:* Federal Pell, FSEOG, State scholarships/grants, Private scholarships, College/university scholarship or grant aid from institutional funds. *Loans:* Direct Subsidized Stafford Loans, Direct Unsubsidized Stafford Loans, Direct PLUS loans, Federal Perkins Loans, Federal Nursing Loans, College/university loans from institutional funds. *Student Employment:* Federal Work-Study Program available. Institutional employment available. **Financial Aid Statistics:** 100% needy freshmen, 100% needy undergrads receive need-based scholarship or grant aid. 24% freshmen, 21% undergrads receive non-need-based scholarship or grant aid. 65% freshmen, 68% undergrads receive need-based self-help aid. 3% freshmen, 4% undergrads receive athletic scholarships. 99% freshmen, 98% undergrads receive any aid. Average cumulative indebtedness $30,700. **Criteria for awarding aid:** *Need-based:* Academics, Leadership, Minority status. *Non-need-based:* Academics, Alumni affiliation, Athletics, Leadership, Minority status, Music/drama.

See page 962.

GORDON COLLEGE

255 Grapevine Road, Wenham, MA 01984-1899
Phone: 978-867-4218 • **Financial Aid Phone:** 978-867-4246
E-mail: admissions@gordon.edu • **CEEB Code:** 3417
Fax: 978-867-4682 • **Website:** www.gordon.edu • **ACT Code:** 1838

This private school, affiliated with the Protestant Church, was founded in 1889. It has a 500-acre campus.

RATINGS

Admissions Selectivity Rating: 82 **Fire Safety Rating:** 97 **Green Rating:** 84

STUDENTS AND FACULTY

Enrollment: 1,631. **Student Body:** 63% female, 37% male, 65% out-of-state, 9% international (55 countries represented). Asian 5%, African American 5%, Caucasian 69%, Hispanic 7%, Native American <1%, Pacific Islander <1%, Two or more races 4%, Race unknown 0%.
Retention and Graduation: 86% freshmen return for sophomore year. 61% freshmen graduate within 4 years. 71% freshmen graduate within 6 years. 23% grads go on to further study within 1 year. 9% grads pursue arts and sciences degrees. 5% grads pursue law degrees. 9% grads pursue business degrees. 9% grads pursue medical degrees. **Faculty:** Student/faculty ratio 12:1. 90 full-time faculty, 86% hold PhDs, 16% are are members of minority groups, 40% are women. 0% of classes are taught by teaching assistants.

ACADEMICS

Degrees: bachelor's, master's. **Classes:** Most classes have 10-19 students. Most lab/discussion sessions have 10-19 students. **Most popular majors:** Psychology; Biology/Biological Sciences; Business Administration, Management and Operations. **Special Study Options:** cooperative education program, cross-registration, double major, honors program, independent study, internships, liberal arts/career combination, student-designed major, study abroad, teacher certification program, Gordon-in-Boston Urban Semester; Gordon-in-France; Italian Semester in Orvieto, Italy; Oregon Extension; Outdoor Education Immersion Semester; LaVida Wilderness Expedition; Co-Op Programs: Arts, Business, Computer Science, Education, Engineering, Health Professions, Humanities, Natural Science, Social/Behavioral Science. **Honors Programs:** The Jerusalem and Athens Forum is a new interdisciplinary honors program at Gordon College, beginning in the academic year 2004-05. Through a variety of program components, but principally a great books course in the history of Christian thought and literature, the program strives to help students reflect on the relationship between faith and intellect, deepen their own sense of vocation, and awaken their capacities for intellectual and moral leadership. (Description taken from www.gordon.edu/jaf) The Kenneth L. Pike Honors Program provides exceptional students with an opportunity to meet unique academic goals not possible under existing Gordon programs by designing individualized, disciplined and chalenging interdisciplinary academic experiences. (Description taken from the Gordon College Academic Catalog). **Disability Services:** Special programs offered to physically disabled students, including tape recorders, tutors. **Career Services:** Alumni network, Alumni services, Career/job search classes, Career assessment, Internships, Regional alumni. Growth of internship opportunities and student participation (including the approval of a new internship program). Human resources programs (4) for resume review and mock interview preparation (meetings between an HR professional or recruiter and a Gordon student for skills development and feedback). Alternative convocation sessions (4 in 2013-2014) with guest speakers on career and professional development topics.

FACILITIES

Housing: Coed dorms, special housing for disabled students, men's dorms, apartments for married students, apartments for single students, Theme Housing International hall, mentoring hall, theme houses. Also Gordon's dorms are coed by floors and/or wings. Men and women do not live together or share facilities. 84% of campus accessible to physically diasbled. **Special Academic Facilities/Equipment:** Barrington Center for the Arts; Phillips Music Center; Center for Balance and Mobility; an electron microscope; a gene sequencer; papers of British Statesman/Reformer, William Wilberforce; East-West Institute; Center for Student Leadership; Center for Christian Studies; international office for Christians in the Visual Arts (CIVA). **Computers:** Administrative functions (other than registration) can be performed online.

CAMPUS LIFE

Environment: Village. **Activities:** Choral groups, concert band, drama/theater, jazz band, literary magazine, music ensembles, musical theater, student government, student newspaper, student-run film society, symphony orchestra, yearbook, Campus Ministries, Student Organization, Model UN. 35 registered organizations, 17 honor societies, 15 religious organizations. **Athletics (Intercollegiate):** *Men:* baseball, basketball, cross-country, lacrosse, soccer, swimming, tennis, track/field (outdoor), track/field (indoor). *Women:* basketball, cross-country, field hockey, lacrosse, soccer, softball, swimming, tennis, track/field (outdoor), track/field (indoor), volleyball. **On-Campus Highlights:** Gillies Lounge/Claymore Cafe, Hiking/biking/cross country ski trails, Bennett Athletic and Recreation Center, Barrington Center for the Arts, Canoeing/swimming ponds, Gordon's campus had many lakes and trails for use by the student body. On campus recreational activities are regularly planned and/or available. **Environmental Initiatives:** Winner of MA College/University Recycling Award 2008

ADMISSIONS

Freshman Academic Profile: Average high school GPA 3.6. 27% in top 10% of high school class, 58% in top 25% of high school class, 87% in top 50% of high school class. 63% from public high schools. **Reported SAT (pre-2016 redesign) scores:** SAT Math middle 50% range 440-610. SAT Critical Reading middle 50% range 450-600. SAT Writing middle 50% range 430-600. **Concordant SAT scores:** SAT EBRW middle 50% range 490–650. SAT Math middle 50% range 480–630. ACT middle 50% range 22-29. Minimum internet-based TOEFL 85. **Basis for Candidate Selection:** *Very important factors considered include:* rigor of secondary school record, academic GPA, standardized test scores, recommendation(s), interview, extracurricular activities, talent/ability, character/personal qualities, religious affiliation/commitment. *Important factors considered include:* class rank, application essay, first generation, alumni/ae relation, volunteer work, work experience, level of applicant's interest. *Other factors considered include:* geographical residence, racial/ethnic status. **Freshman Admission Requirements:** High school diploma is required and GED is accepted. *Academic units required:* 4 English, 2 math, 2 science, 1 science lab, 2 foreign language, 2 social studies, 5 academic electives. *Academic units recommended:* 4 English, 3 math, 3 science, 1 science lab, 4 foreign language, 2 social studies, 5 academic electives. **Freshman Admission Statistics:** 2,714 applied, 91.97% admitted, 17% enrolled. **Transfer Admission Requirements:** college transcript(s), essay or personal statement, interview, statement of good standing from prior institution(s). Minimum college GPA of 2.0 required. Lowest grade transferable C. **General Admission Information:** Application fee $50. Priority deadline 2/1. Regular application deadline 8/1. Nonfall registration accepted. Admission may be deferred for a maximum of 2 semesters.

COSTS AND FINANCIAL AID

Annual tuition $35,180. Room and board $11,000. Required fees $1,560. Average book expense $884. **Required Forms and Deadlines:** FAFSA. **Notification of Awards:** Applicants will be notified of awards on a rolling basis beginning 2/15. **Types of Aid:** *Need-based scholarships/grants:* Federal Pell, FSEOG, State scholarships/grants, Private scholarships, College/university scholarship or grant aid from institutional funds. *Loans:* Direct Subsidized Stafford Loans, Direct Unsubsidized Stafford Loans, Direct PLUS loans, Federal Perkins Loans, State Loans. *Student Employment:* Federal Work-Study Program available. Institutional employment available. **Financial Aid Statistics:** 100% needy freshmen, 100% needy undergrads receive need-based scholarship or grant aid. 11% freshmen, 12% undergrads receive non-need-based scholarship or grant aid. 88% freshmen, 87% undergrads receive need-based self-help aid. 0% freshmen, 0% undergrads receive athletic scholarships. 99% freshmen, 99% undergrads receive any aid. 86% undergrads borrow to pay for school. Average cumulative indebtedness $36,557. **Criteria for awarding aid:** *Need-based:* Academics, Alumni affiliation, Art, Leadership, Minority status, Music/drama, Religious affiliation. *Non-need-based:* Academics, Alumni affiliation, Art, Leadership, Minority status, Music/drama, State/district residency.

GOSHEN COLLEGE

1700 South Main Street, Goshen, IN 46526-4794
Phone: 574-535-7535 • **Financial Aid Phone:** 574-535-7525
E-mail: admission@goshen.edu • **CEEB Code:** 1251
Fax: 574-535-7609 • **Website:** www.goshen.edu • **ACT Code:** 1196

This private school, affiliated with the Mennonite Church, was founded in 1894. It has a 135-acre campus.

RATINGS

Admissions Selectivity Rating: 88   **Fire Safety Rating:** 97   **Green Rating:** 60*

STUDENTS AND FACULTY

Enrollment: 750. **Student Body:** 58% female, 42% male, 48% out-of-state, 9% international (25 countries represented). Asian 2%, African American 4%, Caucasian 68%, Hispanic 13%, Native American 0%, Pacific Islander 0%, Two or more races 3%, Race unknown 1%.
Retention and Graduation: 77% freshmen return for sophomore year. 56% freshmen graduate within 4 years. 72% freshmen graduate within 6 years. 15% grads go on to further study within 1 year. 13% grads pursue arts and sciences degrees. 3% grads pursue law degrees. 1% grads pursue business degrees. 3% grads pursue medical degrees. **Faculty:** Student/faculty ratio 10:1. 65 full-time faculty, 66% hold PhDs, 9% are are members of minority groups, 49% are women. 0% of classes are taught by teaching assistants.

ACADEMICS

Degrees: bachelor's, master's. **Classes:** Most classes have 10-19 students. Most lab/discussion sessions have 10-19 students. **Most popular majors:** Biology/Biological Sciences; Registered Nursing/Registered Nurse; Music. **Special Study Options:** cross-registration, double major, dual enrollment, independent study, internships, liberal arts/career combination, student-designed major, study abroad, teacher certification program, Adult degree completion program (one evening per week, concentrated study). Combined degree programs: BA/BS Eng. **Disability Services:** Special programs offered to physically disabled students, including note-taking services, reader services, tape recorders, tutors. **Career Services:** Alumni network, Career/job search classes, Internships, Regional alumni.

FACILITIES

Housing: Coed dorms, special housing for disabled students, men's dorms, women's dorms, apartments for married students, apartments for single students, Wellness Housing. 90% of campus accessible to physically diasbled. **Special Academic Facilities/Equipment:** X-ray precision lab, lab kindergarten, Mennonite Historical Library. **Computers:** 100% of classrooms, 25% of dorms, 80% of libraries, 75% of dining areas, 100% of student union, have wireless network access. Students can register for classes online. Administrative functions (other than registration) can be performed online.

CAMPUS LIFE

Environment: Town. **Activities:** Choral groups, concert band, drama/theater, jazz band, music ensembles, musical theater, opera, radio station, student government, student newspaper, student-run film society, symphony orchestra, yearbook, Campus Ministries, Student Organization. 21 registered organizations, 4 religious organizations. **Athletics (Intercollegiate):** *Men:* baseball, basketball, cross-country, golf, soccer, tennis, track/field (outdoor), track/field (indoor). *Women:* basketball, cross-country, soccer, softball, tennis, track/field (outdoor), track/field (indoor), volleyball. **On-Campus Highlights:** Music Center, Gingerich Rec-Fitness Center, Science Building, Residential Halls Connector, Good Library. **Environmental Initiatives:** Built the first Platinum LEED Certified facility in Indiana at our Merry Lea Environmental Center. www.goshen.edu/merrylea

ADMISSIONS

Freshman Academic Profile: Average high school GPA 3.5. 38% in top 10% of high school class, 63% in top 25% of high school class, 85% in top 50% of high school class. 90% from public high schools. **Reported SAT (pre-2016 redesign) scores:** SAT Math middle 50% range 500-635. SAT Critical Reading middle 50% range 475-620. SAT Writing middle 50% range 450-610. **Concordant SAT scores:** SAT EBRW middle 50% 520–670. SAT Math middle 50% range 530–660. ACT middle 50% range 21-28. Minimum internet-based TOEFL 79. Minimum paper TOEFL 550. **Basis for Candidate Selection:** *Very important factors considered include:* academic GPA, standardized test scores. *Important factors considered include:* rigor of secondary school record, class rank. *Other factors considered include:* application essay, recommendation(s), extracurricular activities, talent/ability, character/personal qualities, first generation, alumni/ae relation, volunteer work, work experience, level of applicant's interest. **Freshman Admission Requirements:** High school diploma is required and GED is accepted. *Academic units recommended:* 4 English. **Freshman Admission Statistics:** 900 applied, 54.00% admitted, 33% enrolled. **Transfer Admission Requirements:** college transcript(s), essay or personal statement, statement of good standing from prior institution(s). Lowest grade transferable C. **General Admission Information:** Application fee $25. Regular application deadline 8/15. Nonfall registration accepted. Admission may be deferred for a maximum of 1 year.

COSTS AND FINANCIAL AID

Annual tuition $29,700. Room and board $9,700. Required fees $0. Average book expense $900. **Required Forms and Deadlines:** FAFSA. **Notification of Awards:** Applicants will be notified of awards on a rolling basis beginning 2/1. **Types of Aid:** *Need-based scholarships/grants:* Federal Pell, FSEOG, State scholarships/grants, Private scholarships, College/university scholarship or grant aid from institutional funds. *Loans:* Direct Subsidized Stafford Loans, Direct Unsubsidized Stafford Loans, Direct PLUS loans, Federal Perkins Loans, Federal Nursing Loans. *Student Employment:* Federal Work-Study Program available. Institutional employment available. **Financial Aid Statistics:** 100% needy freshmen, 98% needy undergrads receive need-based scholarship or grant aid. 20% freshmen, 16% undergrads receive non-need-based scholarship or grant aid. 77% freshmen, 81% undergrads receive need-based self-help aid. 5% freshmen, 9% undergrads receive athletic scholarships. 100% freshmen, 99% undergrads receive any aid. **Criteria for awarding aid:** *Need-based:* Academics, Minority status, Religious affiliation. *Non-need-based:* Academics, Art, Athletics, Leadership, Minority status, Music/drama.

GOUCHER COLLEGE

1021 Dulaney Valley Road, Baltimore, MD 21204-2794
Phone: 410-337-6100 • **Financial Aid Phone:** 410-337-6141
E-mail: admissions@goucher.edu • **CEEB Code:** 5257
Fax: 410-337-6354 • **Website:** www.goucher.edu • **ACT Code:** 1696

This private school was founded in 1885. It has a 287-acre campus.

RATINGS

Admissions Selectivity Rating: 81   **Fire Safety Rating:** 95   **Green Rating:** 97

STUDENTS AND FACULTY

Enrollment: 1,461. **Student Body:** 68% female, 32% male, 72% out-of-state, 3% international (38 countries represented). Asian 4%, African American 13%, Caucasian 62%, Hispanic 6%, Native American 0%, Pacific Islander <1%, Two or more races 6%, Race unknown 5%.
Retention and Graduation: 79% freshmen return for sophomore year. 54% freshmen graduate within 4 years. 68% freshmen graduate within 6 years. 27% grads go on to further study within 1 year. 2% grads pursue law degrees. 2%

grads pursue business degrees. 1% grads pursue medical degrees. **Faculty:** Student/faculty ratio 10:1. 129 full-time faculty, 91% hold PhDs, 14% are are members of minority groups, 61% are women. 0% of classes are taught by teaching assistants.

ACADEMICS

Degrees: bachelor's, master's, postbachelor's certificate. **Classes:** Most classes have 10-19 students. **Most popular majors:** Psychology; English Language and Literature; Business Administration and Management. **Special Study Options:** cross-registration, distance learning, double major, dual enrollment, independent study, internships, student-designed major, study abroad, teacher certification program. Combined degree programs: 3-2 in Engineering with Johns Hopkins School of Engineering, BA/BS in Engineering with Columbia University FU Foundation School of Engineering and Applied Science. **Career Services:** Alumni network, Alumni services, Career assessment, Internships. Goucher has been linking liberal arts education with internships for more than 75 years. Through our internship program, we help students explore career paths, enhance skills, and experience the world of work.

FACILITIES

Housing: Coed dorms, special housing for disabled students, women's dorms, apartments for single students, Wellness Housing, Theme Housing. 100% of campus accessible to physically diasbled. **Special Academic Facilities/ Equipment:** The Athenaeum is a 103,000-square-foot building which is open 24 hours a day and features a new, technologically superior library; a spacious open forum for performances, public discussions, and other events; a Café, art gallery; a center for community service and multicultural affairs programming; and spaces for exercise, conversation, and quiet reflection and relaxation. Goucher, in collaboration with the architecture firm RMJM, approached every aspect of the Athenaeum project with an eye toward sustainable design strategies, and the project is in the process of applying for Silver certification from the Leadership in Energy and Environmental Design (LEED) Green-Building Rating System. The Silber Art Gallery in the Athenaeum provides a suitably secure gallery dedicated solely to the exhibition of art, both from the Goucher collection and from contemporary artists and collectors outside the campus. The 1,000-square-foot gallery is the new home to Goucher's permanent collection and its critically acclaimed program of contemporary art exhibitions. In addition to enabling us to display selections from the college's permanent collection, the gallery hosts a range of programming, from the traditional to the experimental, featuring the work of students, emerging artists, and established names alike. Additionally, Goucher has the Rosenberg Art Gallery and the Scientific Visualization Lab. **Computers:** 95% of classrooms, 40% of dorms, 100% of libraries, 100% of dining areas, 100% of student union, 80% of common outdoor areas have wireless network access. Students can register for classes online. Administrative functions (other than registration) can be performed online.

CAMPUS LIFE

Environment: City. **Activities:** Choral groups, dance, drama/theater, jazz band, literary magazine, music ensembles, musical theater, opera, radio station, student government, student newspaper, student-run film society, symphony orchestra, television station, yearbook, Campus Ministries, Student Organization, Model UN. 60 registered organizations, 1 honor society, 8 religious organizations. **Athletics (Intercollegiate):** *Men:* basketball, cross-country, lacrosse, soccer, swimming, tennis, track/field (outdoor), track/field (indoor). *Women:* basketball, cross-country, equestrian sports, field hockey, lacrosse, soccer, swimming, tennis, track/field (outdoor), track/field (indoor), volleyball. **On-Campus Highlights:** The Library at the Athenaeum, Alice's Cafe, Sports and Recreation Center, Pearlstone Cafe, Gopher Hole. **Environmental Initiatives:** Our newest building, the Athenaeum, was awarded Gold certification from the Leadership in Energy and Environmental Design (LEED) rating system, the national recognized standard for measuring a building's environmental sustainability, and committing that future buildings and renovations will also be LEED certified. Goucher, in collaboration with the architecture firm RMJM, approached every aspect of the Athenaeum project with an eye toward sustainable design strategies.

ADMISSIONS

Freshman Academic Profile: Average high school GPA 3.1. 13% in top 10% of high school class, 47% in top 25% of high school class, 76% in top 50% of high school class. 90% from public high schools. **Reported SAT (pre-2016 redesign) scores:** SAT Math middle 50% range 500-610. SAT Critical Reading middle 50% range 500-630. SAT Writing middle 50% range 480-610. **Concordant SAT scores:** SAT EBRW middle 50% 520–670. SAT Math middle 50% range 530–660. ACT middle 50% range 21-28. Minimum internet-based TOEFL 79. Minimum paper TOEFL 550. **Basis for Candidate Selection:** *Very important factors considered include:* academic GPA, standardized test scores. *Important factors considered include:* rigor of secondary school record, class rank. *Other factors considered include:* application essay, recommendation(s), extracurricular activities, talent/ability, character/ personal qualities, first generation, alumni/ae relation, volunteer work, work experience, level of applicant's interest. **Freshman Admission Requirements:** High school diploma is required and GED is accepted. *Academic units*

recommended: 4 English. **Freshman Admission Statistics:** 3,443 applied, 79.23% admitted, 16% enrolled. **Transfer Admission Requirements:** college transcript(s), essay or personal statement, statement of good standing from prior institution(s). Lowest grade transferable C. **General Admission Information:** Application fee $25. Regular application deadline 8/15. Nonfall registration accepted. Admission may be deferred for a maximum of 1 year.

COSTS AND FINANCIAL AID

Annual tuition $29,700. Room and board $9,700. Required fees $0. Average book expense $900. **Required Forms and Deadlines:** FAFSA. **Notification of Awards:** Applicants will be notified of awards on a rolling basis beginning 2/1. **Types of Aid:** *Need-based scholarships/grants:* Federal Pell, FSEOG, State scholarships/grants, Private scholarships, College/university scholarship or grant aid from institutional funds. *Loans:* Direct Subsidized Stafford Loans, Direct Unsubsidized Stafford Loans, Direct PLUS loans, Federal Perkins Loans, Federal Nursing Loans. *Student Employment:* Federal Work-Study Program available. Institutional employment available. **Financial Aid Statistics:** 100% needy freshmen, 98% needy undergrads receive need-based scholarship or grant aid. 20% freshmen, 16% undergrads receive non-need-based scholarship or grant aid. 77% freshmen, 81% undergrads receive need-based self-help aid. 5% freshmen, 9% undergrads receive athletic scholarships. 100% freshmen, 99% undergrads receive any aid. **Criteria for awarding aid:** *Need-based:* Academics, Minority status, Religious affiliation. *Non-need-based:* Academics, Art, Athletics, Leadership, Minority status, Music/drama.

GOVERNORS STATE UNIVERSITY

1 University Parkway, University Park, IL 60484
Phone: 708-534-4490 • **Financial Aid Phone:** 708-534-4480
E-mail: gsunow@govst.edu
Fax: 708-534-1640 • **Website:** www.govst.edu

This public school was founded in 1969. It has a 720-acre campus.

RATINGS

Admissions Selectivity Rating: 61 **Fire Safety Rating:** 60* **Green Rating:** 60*

STUDENTS AND FACULTY

Enrollment: 3,103. **Student Body:** 68% female, 32% male, 3% out-of-state, <1% international (17 countries represented). Asian 2%, African American 37%, Caucasian 44%, Hispanic 10%, Native American <1%, Pacific Islander <1%, Two or more races 1%, Race unknown 7%.
Retention and Graduation: 34% grads go on to further study within 1 year. 17% grads pursue arts and sciences degrees. 1% grads pursue law degrees. 16% grads pursue business degrees. **Faculty:** Student/faculty ratio 11:1. 211 full-time faculty, 59% hold PhDs, 37% are are members of minority groups, 59% are women. 0% of classes are taught by teaching assistants.

ACADEMICS

Degrees: bachelor's, doctoral/professional, master's, post-master's certificate. **Most popular majors:** Communication and Media Studies; Elementary Education and Teaching; Business/Commerce. **Special Study Options:** cross-registration, distance learning, dual enrollment, external degree program, honors program, independent study, internships, student-designed major, study abroad, teacher certification program. **Disability Services:** Special programs offered to physically disabled students, including note-taking services, reader services, tape recorders, tutors. **Career Services:** Alumni network, Alumni services, Career/job search classes, Career assessment, Internships.

FACILITIES

Housing: 99% of campus accessible to physically diasbled. **Special Academic Facilities/Equipment:** Manilow Sculpture Park **Computers:** Students can register for classes online. Administrative functions (other than registration) can be performed online.

CAMPUS LIFE

Environment: Village. **Activities:** drama/theater, literary magazine, student government, student newspaper, student-run film society. 7 honor societies.

ADMISSIONS

Freshman Academic Profile: 0% from public high schools. **Concordant SAT scores:** **Transfer Admission Requirements:** college transcript(s), statement of good standing from prior institution(s). Minimum college GPA of 2.0 required. Lowest grade transferable C. **General Admission Information:** Nonfall registration not accepted.

COSTS AND FINANCIAL AID

Types of Aid: *Need-based scholarships/grants:* Federal Pell, FSEOG, State scholarships/grants, Private scholarships, College/university scholarship or grant aid from institutional funds, Federal Nursing Scholarships. *Loans:* Direct Subsidized Stafford Loans, Federal Perkins Loans, Federal Nursing

Loans, State Loans, College/university loans from institutional funds. *Student Employment:* Federal Work-Study Program available. Institutional employment available. **Criteria for awarding aid:** *Need-based:* Academics. *Non-need-based:* Academics.

GRACE COLLEGE AND SEMINARY

200 Seminary Drive, Winona Lake, IN 46590
Phone: 800-544-7223 • **Financial Aid Phone:** 574-372-5100
E-mail: enroll@grace.edu • **CEEB Code:** 1252
Fax: 574-372-5120 • **Website:** www.grace.edu • **ACT Code:** 1198

This private school was founded in 1948. It has a 150-acre campus.

RATINGS

Admissions Selectivity Rating: 81   **Fire Safety Rating:** 83   **Green Rating:** 60*

STUDENTS AND FACULTY

Enrollment: 1,614. **Student Body:** 56% female, 44% male, 24% out-of-state, 1% international (9 countries represented). Asian 1%, African American 6%, Caucasian 80%, Hispanic 5%, Native American 0%, Pacific Islander 0%, Two or more races 3%, Race unknown 4%.
Retention and Graduation: 83% freshmen return for sophomore year. 57% freshmen graduate within 4 years. 61% freshmen graduate within 6 years.
Faculty: Student/faculty ratio 22:1. 49 full-time faculty, 71% hold PhDs, 4% are are members of minority groups, 35% are women. 0% of classes are taught by teaching assistants.

ACADEMICS

Degrees: associate, bachelor's, certificate, diploma, doctoral, master's, postbachelor's certificate. **Classes:** Most classes have 10-19 students. Most lab/discussion sessions have 10-19 students. **Most popular majors:** Elementary Education and Teaching; Business/Commerce; Psychology. **Special Study Options:** cooperative education program, cross-registration, distance learning, double major, dual enrollment, exchange student program (domestic), honors program, independent study, internships, liberal arts/career combination, study abroad, teacher certification program, Degree completion. **Disability Services:** Special programs offered to physically disabled students, including note-taking services, reader services, tape recorders, tutors. **Career Services:** Career assessment.

FACILITIES

Housing: men's dorms, women's dorms, apartments for single students. 85% of campus accessible to physically diasbled. **Special Academic Facilities/ Equipment:** Reneker Museum of Winona History **Computers:** 100% of classrooms, 100% of dorms, 100% of libraries, 100% of dining areas, 100% of student union, 33% of common outdoor areas have wireless network access. Students can register for classes online. Administrative functions (other than registration) can be performed online.

CAMPUS LIFE

Environment: Village. **Activities:** Choral groups, concert band, drama/theater, music ensembles, musical theater, opera, pep band, student government, student newspaper, symphony orchestra, yearbook, Campus Ministries. 9 registered organizations, 1 honor society, 8 religious organizations. **Athletics (Intercollegiate):** *Men:* baseball, basketball, cheerleading, cross-country, golf, soccer, tennis, track/field (outdoor). *Women:* basketball, cheerleading, cross-country, soccer, softball, tennis, track/field (outdoor), volleyball. **On-Campus Highlights:** Gordon Recreation Center, Tree of Life Coffee shop, Westminster Grille, Orthopedic Capital Center.

ADMISSIONS

Freshman Academic Profile: Average high school GPA 3.6. 24% in top 10% of high school class, 52% in top 25% of high school class, 80% in top 50% of high school class. 71% from public high schools. **Reported SAT (pre-2016 redesign) scores:** SAT Math middle 50% range 460-580. SAT Critical Reading middle 50% range 470-590. **Concordant SAT scores:** SAT Math middle 50% range 500–600. ACT middle 50% range 21-27. **Basis for Candidate Selection:** *Very important factors considered include:* rigor of secondary school record, standardized test scores, application essay, recommendation(s), religious affiliation/commitment. *Important factors considered include:* academic GPA, character/personal qualities. *Other factors considered include:* class rank, interview, extracurricular activities, talent/ability, alumni/ae relation. **Freshman Admission Requirements:** High school diploma is required and GED is accepted. *Academic units recommended:* 4 English, 2 math, 2 science, 1 science lab, 2 foreign language, 2 social studies, 1 history. **Freshman Admission Statistics:** 4,204 applied, 78.47% admitted, 29% enrolled. **Transfer Admission Requirements:** college transcript(s), essay or personal statement, standardized test scores, Minimum college GPA of 2.0 required. Lowest grade transferable

C-. General Admission Information: Application fee $30. Priority deadline 6/1. Regular application deadline 8/15. Nonfall registration accepted. Admission may be deferred for a maximum of 1 semester.

COSTS AND FINANCIAL AID

Annual tuition $23,120. Room and board $8,404. Average book expense $1,000. **Required Forms and Deadlines:** FAFSA. **Notification of Awards:** Applicants will be notified of awards on a rolling basis beginning 3/1. **Types of Aid:** *Need-based scholarships/grants:* Federal Pell, FSEOG, State scholarships/grants, Private scholarships, College/university scholarship or grant aid from institutional funds. *Loans:* Federal Perkins Loans. *Student Employment:* Federal Work-Study Program available. Institutional employment available. **Financial Aid Statistics:** 89% needy freshmen, 89% needy undergrads receive need-based scholarship or grant aid. 99% freshmen, 86% undergrads receive non-need-based scholarship or grant aid. 77% freshmen, 78% undergrads receive need-based self-help aid. 0% freshmen, 0% undergrads receive athletic scholarships. **Criteria for awarding aid:** *Need-based:* Minority status, Religious affiliation. *Non-need-based:* Academics, Art, Athletics, Leadership, Music/drama.

GRACELAND UNIVERSITY

1 University Place, Lamoni, IA 50140
Phone: 641-784-5196 • **Financial Aid Phone:** 641-784-5140
E-mail: admissions@graceland.edu • **CEEB Code:** 6249
Fax: 641-784-5480 • **Website:** www.graceland.edu • **ACT Code:** 1314

This private school was founded in 1895. It has a 170-acre campus.

RATINGS

Admissions Selectivity Rating: 81   **Fire Safety Rating:** 88   **Green Rating:** 76

STUDENTS AND FACULTY

Enrollment: 1,328. **Student Body:** 58% female, 42% male, 75% out-of-state, 2% international (23 countries represented). Asian 1%, African American 10%, Caucasian 62%, Hispanic 11%, Native American <1%, Pacific Islander 1%, Two or more races 4%, Race unknown 8%.
Retention and Graduation: 66% freshmen return for sophomore year. 24% freshmen graduate within 4 years. 43% freshmen graduate within 6 years.
Faculty: Student/faculty ratio 14:1. 78 full-time faculty, 74% hold PhDs, 12% are are members of minority groups, 51% are women. 0% of classes are taught by teaching assistants.

ACADEMICS

Degrees: bachelor's, certificate, master's, postbachelor's certificate, post-master's certificate. **Classes:** Most classes have 10-19 students. Most lab/discussion sessions have 20-29 students. **Most popular majors:** Elementary Education and Teaching; Business Administration and Management; Registered Nursing/Registered Nurse. **Special Study Options:** Accelerated program, distance learning, double major, dual enrollment, English as a Second Language (ESL), honors program, independent study, internships, liberal arts/career combination, student-designed major, study abroad, teacher certification program. **Honors Programs:** The Graceland University Honors Program includes courses in Honors English, Honors Humanities, Honors Advanced Composition, the combined Jr. and Sr. Honors Seminar, a Sr. Honors Thesis, and Honors Contracts to be created with instructors in any academic course the students choose. Completion of the Honors Program requires 21 hours of honors credit, completion of the Jr. and Sr. Honors Seminars, a Sr. Honors Thesis, and a minimum 3.5 gpa overall and in their honors work. Honors Students with a 3.75 gpa or higher are eligible for an Honors Scholarship. Incoming students with a 3.75 gap and an ACT of 27 or higher may apply for full tuition Prestigious Honors Scholarship, which are available on a competitive basis, and require an interview. Graceland University offers an Excellent Education in a caring community. So we believe the best reason to participate in the Honors Program is the people in it, and to participate in the Honors community. Combined degree programs: BSN/MSN. **Disability Services:** Special programs offered to physically disabled students, including note-taking services, reader services, tape recorders, tutors. **Career Services:** Alumni network, Alumni services, Career/job search classes, Career assessment, Internships. We offer a number of classes on campus for credit that address issues of personal exploration in regards to career. We also provide opportunities for students to take classes that allow students to gain credit while they learn to write resumes and engage in the job search. Every student participating in our upper division class does a mock interview, learns about personal finance, professional dress, professional networking, dining etiquette, and what to expect after graduation. We provide opportunities for students to participate in an internship in gaining experience in the work environment.

FACILITIES

Housing: men's dorms, women's dorms, apartments for married students. 95% of campus accessible to physically disabled. **Computers:** 100% of classrooms, 91% of dorms, 100% of libraries, 100% of dining areas, 100% of student union, 30% of common outdoor areas have wireless network access. Students can register for classes online. Administrative functions (other than registration) can be performed online.

CAMPUS LIFE

Environment: Rural. **Activities:** Choral groups, concert band, dance, drama/theater, jazz band, music ensembles, musical theater, pep band, radio station, student government, student newspaper, symphony orchestra, yearbook, Campus Ministries, Student Organization. 54 registered organizations, 1 religious organization. **Athletics (Intercollegiate):** *Men:* baseball, basketball, cross-country, football, golf, soccer, tennis, track/field (outdoor), track/field (indoor), volleyball. *Women:* basketball, cross-country, golf, soccer, softball, tennis, track/field (outdoor), track/field (indoor), volleyball. **On-Campus Highlights:** Resch Science & Technology Hall, The Helene Center for Visual Arts, The Closson Center, The Shaw Center for Performing Arts, The Higdon Administration Building. **Environmental Initiatives:** Installation of Hoop House garden to produce vegetables for campus dining services.

ADMISSIONS

Freshman Academic Profile: Average high school GPA 3.2. 10% in top 10% of high school class, 27% in top 25% of high school class, 67% in top 50% of high school class. 43% from public high schools. **Reported SAT (pre-2016 redesign) scores:** SAT Math middle 50% range 410-510. SAT Critical Reading middle 50% range 400-510. **Concordant SAT scores:** SAT Math middle 50% range 450–540. ACT middle 50% range 18-24. Minimum internet-based TOEFL 80. Minimum paper TOEFL 550. **Basis for Candidate Selection:** *Very important factors considered include:* academic GPA, standardized test scores. *Important factors considered include:* rigor of secondary school record, class rank. *Other factors considered include:* application essay, recommendation(s), interview, talent/ability. **Freshman Admission Requirements:** High school diploma is required and GED is accepted. *Academic units recommended:* 4 English, 3 math, 2 science, 1 foreign language, 3 social studies. **Freshman Admission Statistics:** 2,440 applied, 48.40% admitted, 22% enrolled. **Transfer Admission Requirements:** college transcript(s), Minimum college GPA of 2.0 required. Lowest grade transferable D. **General Admission Information:** Nonfall registration accepted.

COSTS AND FINANCIAL AID

Annual tuition $27,500. Room and board $8,480. Required fees $610. Average book expense $1,250. **Required Forms and Deadlines:** FAFSA. **Notification of Awards:** Applicants will be notified of awards on a rolling basis beginning 2/1. **Types of Aid:** *Need-based scholarships/grants:* Federal Pell, FSEOG, State scholarships/grants, Private scholarships, College/university scholarship or grant aid from institutional funds. *Loans:* Direct Subsidized Stafford Loans, Direct Unsubsidized Stafford Loans, Direct PLUS loans, Federal Perkins Loans, College/university loans from institutional funds. *Student Employment:* Federal Work-Study Program available. Institutional employment available. **Financial Aid Statistics:** 100% needy freshmen, 93% needy undergrads receive need-based scholarship or grant aid. 33% freshmen, 30% undergrads receive non-need-based scholarship or grant aid. 88% freshmen, 89% undergrads receive need-based self-help aid. 14% freshmen, 13% undergrads receive athletic scholarships. 99% freshmen, 93% undergrads receive any aid. 76% undergrads borrow to pay for school. Average cumulative indebtedness $32,720. **Criteria for awarding aid:** *Need-based:* Job skills, Minority status. *Non-need-based:* Academics, Alumni affiliation, Art, Athletics, Job skills, Leadership, Music/drama, Religious affiliation.

See page 964.

GRAND RAPIDS THEOLOGICAL SEMINARY

1001 E Beltline Ave. NE, Grand Rapids, MI 49525
Phone: 1-800-697-1133 • **Financial Aid Phone:** 616-949-5300
E-mail: grts@cornerstone.edu
Fax: 616-254-1623 • **Website:** http://grts.cornerstone.edu

This is a private school.

RATINGS

Admissions Selectivity Rating: 60*   **Fire Safety Rating:** 96   **Green Rating:** 60*

STUDENTS AND FACULTY

Retention and Graduation: 15% grads go on to further study within 1 year. 10% grads pursue arts and sciences degrees. 1% grads pursue law degrees. 3% grads pursue business degrees. 1% grads pursue medical degrees. **Faculty:**

Student/faculty ratio 17:1. 9 full-time faculty, 0% are are members of minority groups, 56% 0% of classes are taught by teaching assistants.

ACADEMICS

Degrees: certificate, master's. **Most popular majors:** Education; Psychology; Business/Commerce. **Special Study Options:** distance learning, double major, dual enrollment, honors program, independent study, internships, study abroad. **Honors Programs:** Honors Program based on a "great books" curriculum. **Disability Services:** Special programs offered to physically disabled students, including note-taking services, reader services, tape recorders, tutors. **Career Services:** Career/job search classes, Career assessment, Internships. The required internship of all students as part of the graduation requirements.

FACILITIES

Housing: special housing for disabled students, men's dorms, women's dorms, apartments for married students, apartments for single students. 100% of campus accessible to physically disabled. **Computers:** Students can register for classes online. Administrative functions (other than registration) can be performed online. Undergraduates are required to own a computer.

CAMPUS LIFE

Activities: student government, Campus Ministries, Student Organization. 11 registered organizations, 2 honor societies, 1 religious organization. **Athletics (Intercollegiate):** *Men:* basketball, cross-country, golf, soccer, track/field (outdoor), track/field (indoor). *Women:* basketball, cross-country, golf, soccer, softball, track/field (outdoor), track/field (indoor), volleyball. **On-Campus Highlights:** Corum Student Union, Bernice Hansen Athletic Center, Campus Bookstore Atrium, Faber Hall Seating Area, Gordon Music Hall. **Environmental Initiatives:** On campus dialogue and focus on sustainability issues.

ADMISSIONS

Freshman Academic Profile: 60% from public high schools. Minimum paper TOEFL 500. **Basis for Candidate Selection:** *Very important factors considered include:* academic GPA, application essay, recommendation(s), religious affiliation/commitment. *Important factors considered include:* standardized test scores, extracurricular activities, character/personal qualities, volunteer work, level of applicant's interest. *Other factors considered include:* rigor of secondary school record, talent/ability, work experience. **Freshman Admission Requirements:** High school diploma is required and GED is accepted. **Transfer Admission Requirements:** college transcript(s), essay or personal statement, Minimum college GPA of 2.5 required. Lowest grade transferable C.

COSTS AND FINANCIAL AID

Types of Aid: *Need-based scholarships/grants:* State scholarships/grants, Private scholarships, College/university scholarship or grant aid from institutional funds. *Loans:* Direct Subsidized Stafford Loans, Direct Unsubsidized Stafford Loans. *Student Employment:* Federal Work-Study Program available. Institutional employment available. **Financial Aid Statistics:** 100% freshmen, 98% undergrads receive any aid. **Criteria for awarding aid:** *Need-based:* Academics, Job skills, Leadership, Minority status, Religious affiliation. *Non-need-based:* Academics, Job skills, Leadership, Minority status, Religious affiliation.

GRAND VALLEY STATE UNIVERSITY

1 Campus Drive, Allendale, MI 49401
Phone: 616-331-2025 • **Financial Aid Phone:** 616-331-3234
E-mail: admissions@gvsu.edu • **CEEB Code:** 1258
Fax: 616-331-2000 • **Website:** www.gvsu.edu • **ACT Code:** 2005

This public school was founded in 1960. It has a 1275-acre campus.

RATINGS

Admissions Selectivity Rating: 78   **Fire Safety Rating:** 90   **Green Rating:** 96

STUDENTS AND FACULTY

Enrollment: 21,839. **Student Body:** 59% female, 41% male, 6% out-of-state, 1% international (82 countries represented). Asian 2%, African American 5%, Caucasian 83%, Hispanic 5%, Native American <1%, Pacific Islander <1%, Two or more races 3%, Race unknown <1%.
Retention and Graduation: 84% freshmen return for sophomore year. **Faculty:** Student/faculty ratio 17:1. 1,137 full-time faculty, 76% hold PhDs, 16% are are members of minority groups, 50% are women. 0% of classes are taught by teaching assistants.

ACADEMICS

Degrees: bachelor's, certificate, doctoral/professional, master's, postbachelor's certificate, post-master's certificate. **Classes:** Most classes have 20-29 students. Most lab/discussion sessions have 20-29 students. **Most popular majors:**

Health Services/Allied Health/Health Sciences; Business/Commerce. **Special Study Options:** distance learning, double major, dual enrollment, English as a Second Language (ESL), honors program, independent study, internships, student-designed major, study abroad, teacher certification program. **Honors Programs:** Honor's College Combined degree programs: BA/JD, BA/MEng, Physical therapy program; Occupational Therapy; Ph. **Disability Services:** Special programs offered to physically disabled students, including reader services, tape recorders, tutors. **Career Services:** Alumni network, Alumni services, Career/job search classes, Career assessment, Internships, Regional alumni. We have a very strong cooperative education program in engineering that is mature and provides one year of full-time work for students. We also have very strong internship programs in the following departments: computer science, hospitality, communications, education, health majors, and social work.

FACILITIES

Housing: Coed dorms, fraternity/sorority housing, apartments for married students, apartments for single students, Theme Housing. 99% of campus accessible to physically disabled. **Special Academic Facilities/Equipment:** two Great Lakes research vessels, audio-visual center, performance/recital hall, pipe organ, physical therapy/human performance lab. **Computers:** 100% of classrooms, 63% of dorms, 100% of libraries, 100% of dining areas, 100% of student union, have wireless network access. Students can register for classes online. Administrative functions (other than registration) can be performed online.

CAMPUS LIFE

Environment: City. **Activities:** Choral groups, concert band, dance, drama/theater, jazz band, literary magazine, marching band, music ensembles, musical theater, pep band, radio station, student government, student newspaper, symphony orchestra, television station, Campus Ministries, Student Organization. 301 registered organizations, 20 honor societies, 20 religious organizations. 11 fraternities, 11 sororities. **Athletics (Intercollegiate):** *Men:* baseball, basketball, cross-country, diving, football, golf, swimming, tennis, track/field (outdoor), track/field (indoor). *Women:* basketball, cross-country, diving, golf, soccer, softball, swimming, tennis, track/field (outdoor), track/field (indoor), volleyball. **On-Campus Highlights:** Living Centers, Cook DeVos Center for Health Sciences, Recreation Center and Fieldhouse, Laker Turf Building, Kirkhof Center. **Environmental Initiatives:** Climate Mitigation: GVSU is a signatory to American College and University Presidents Climate Commitment and has recently completed its Climate Action Plan and set a goal of climate neutrality by 2037. The climate action plan is available online. Currently there are over 650 colleges and universities that have signed on to this agreement. LEED construction projects and bus transportation are both important climate mitigation strategies. GVSU has completed and certified 10 LEED projects with 2 more LEED projects under construction. These 12 LEED projects represent over 925,000 square feet and ~19% of total square footage. Annual bus ridership is over ~ 2MM bus rides per year for faculty and students and saves millions of dollars in annual fuel purchases and vehicle maintenance costs while reducing our carbon footprint.

ADMISSIONS

Freshman Academic Profile: Average high school GPA 3.5. 17% in top 10% of high school class, 46% in top 25% of high school class, 85% in top 50% of high school class. ACT middle 50% range 21-26. Minimum paper TOEFL 550. **Basis for Candidate Selection:** *Very important factors considered include:* rigor of secondary school record, academic GPA. *Important factors considered include:* standardized test scores. *Other factors considered include:* class rank, application essay, recommendation(s), extracurricular activities, talent/ability, first generation, alumni/ae relation, volunteer work, work experience. **Freshman Admission Requirements:** High school diploma is required and GED is accepted. *Academic units required:* 4 English, 3 math, 3 science, 2 science labs, 2 foreign language, 3 social studies. **Freshman Admission Statistics:** 16,987 applied, 81.14% admitted, 30% enrolled. **Transfer Admission Requirements:** college transcript(s), statement of good standing from prior institution(s). Minimum college GPA of 2.5 required. Lowest grade transferable D. **General Admission Information:** Application fee $30. Priority deadline 5/1. Nonfall registration accepted.

COSTS AND FINANCIAL AID

Annual in-state tuition $11,832. Annual out-of-state tuition $16,704. Required fees $0. Average book expense $700. **Required Forms and Deadlines:** FAFSA. **Notification of Awards:** Applicants will be notified of awards on a rolling basis beginning 3/10. **Types of Aid:** *Need-based scholarships/grants:* Federal Pell, FSEOG, State scholarships/grants, Private scholarships, College/university scholarship or grant aid from institutional funds. *Loans:* Direct Subsidized Stafford Loans, Direct Unsubsidized Stafford Loans, Direct PLUS loans, Federal Perkins Loans, Federal Nursing Loans. *Student Employment:* Federal Work-Study Program available. Institutional employment available. **Financial Aid Statistics:** 86% needy freshmen, 84% needy undergrads receive need-based scholarship or grant aid. 6% freshmen, 4% undergrads receive non-need-based scholarship or grant aid. 86% freshmen, 88% undergrads receive need-based self-help aid. 1% freshmen, 1% undergrads receive athletic

scholarships. 86% freshmen, 83% undergrads receive any aid. 74% undergrads borrow to pay for school. Average cumulative indebtedness $29,656. **Criteria for awarding aid:** *Non-need-based:* Academics, Alumni affiliation, Art, Athletics, Music/drama, State/district residency.

GRAND VIEW UNIVERSITY

1200 Grandview Avenue, Des Moines, IA 50316-1599
Phone: 515-263-2810 • **Financial Aid Phone:** 515-263-2963
E-mail: admissions@GrandView.edu • **CEEB Code:** 6251
Fax: 515-263-2974 • **Website:** www.admissions.grandview.edu • **ACT Code:** 1316

This private school, affiliated with the Lutheran Church, was founded in 1896. It has a 35-acre campus.

RATINGS

Admissions Selectivity Rating: 73   **Fire Safety Rating:** 60*   **Green Rating:** 60*

STUDENTS AND FACULTY

Enrollment: 2,079. **Student Body:** 58% female, 42% male, 13% out-of-state, 2% international (16 countries represented). Asian 3%, African American 8%, Caucasian 74%, Hispanic 3%, Native American <1%, Pacific Islander <1%, Two or more races 3%, Race unknown 7%.
Retention and Graduation: 69% freshmen return for sophomore year. 28% freshmen graduate within 4 years. 48% freshmen graduate within 6 years. **Faculty:** Student/faculty ratio 13:1. 95 full-time faculty, 68% hold PhDs, 7% are are members of minority groups, 56% are women. 0% of classes are taught by teaching assistants.

ACADEMICS

Degrees: bachelor's, certificate, master's, postbachelor's certificate. **Classes:** Most classes have 10-19 students. Most lab/discussion sessions have 10-19 students. **Most popular majors:** Education Business/Commerce. **Special Study Options:** Accelerated program, cooperative education program, cross-registration, distance learning, double major, dual enrollment, honors program, independent study, internships, liberal arts/career combination, student-designed major, study abroad, teacher certification program, weekend college. **Honors Programs:** Logos Honors Program Combined degree programs: Dual Degrees.

FACILITIES

Housing: Coed dorms, apartments for single students. **Special Academic Facilities/Equipment:** Danish American Archives. **Computers:** Administrative functions (other than registration) can be performed online.

CAMPUS LIFE

Activities: Choral groups, concert band, dance, drama/theater, literary magazine, music ensembles, radio station, student government, student newspaper, television station, Campus Ministries, Student Organization. 28 registered organizations, 1 religious organization. **Athletics (Intercollegiate):** *Men:* baseball, basketball, cross-country, golf, soccer. *Women:* basketball, cross-country, golf, soccer, softball, volleyball.

ADMISSIONS

Freshman Academic Profile: Average high school GPA 3.2. 15% in top 10% of high school class, 33% in top 25% of high school class, 64% in top 50% of high school class. **Reported SAT (pre-2016 redesign) scores:** SAT Math middle 50% range 400-480. SAT Critical Reading middle 50% range 380-450. SAT Writing middle 50% range 360-440. **Concordant SAT scores:** SAT EBRW middle 50% 420–500. SAT Math middle 50% range 440–510. ACT middle 50% range 19-23. Minimum paper TOEFL 550. **Basis for Candidate Selection:** *Very important factors considered include:* rigor of secondary school record, class rank, academic GPA, character/personal qualities. *Important factors considered include:* standardized test scores. *Other factors considered include:* extracurricular activities, talent/ability, alumni/ae relation, volunteer work, work experience. **Freshman Admission Requirements:** High school diploma is required and GED is accepted. *Academic units recommended:* 4 English, 3 math, 3 science, 2 foreign language, 3 social studies. **Freshman Admission Statistics:** 805 applied, 95.65% admitted, 39% enrolled. **Transfer Admission Requirements:** college transcript(s), Minimum college GPA of 2.0 required. Lowest grade transferable D. **General Admission Information:** Regular application deadline 8/15. Nonfall registration accepted. Admission may be deferred for a maximum of 1 semester.

COSTS AND FINANCIAL AID

Annual tuition $22,986. Room and board $7,554. Required fees $530. Average book expense $880. **Required Forms and Deadlines:** FAFSA. **Notification of Awards:** Applicants will be notified of awards on a rolling basis beginning

3/1. **Types of Aid:** *Need-based scholarships/grants:* Federal Pell, FSEOG, State scholarships/grants, Private scholarships, College/university scholarship or grant aid from institutional funds. *Loans:* Federal Perkins Loans. *Student Employment:* Federal Work-Study Program available. Institutional employment available. **Financial Aid Statistics:** 88% needy freshmen, 92% needy undergrads receive need-based scholarship or grant aid. 20% freshmen, 11% undergrads receive non-need-based scholarship or grant aid. 80% freshmen, 88% undergrads receive need-based self-help aid. 63% freshmen, 10% undergrads receive athletic scholarships. 97% freshmen, 99% undergrads receive any aid. **Criteria for awarding aid:** *Need-based:* Academics, Leadership. *Non-need-based:* Academics, Alumni affiliation, Art, Athletics, Leadership, Music/drama.

GRANTHAM UNIVERSITY

7200 NW 86th Street, Kansas City, MO 64153
E-mail: admissions@grantham.edu
Fax: 816-595-5757 • **Website:** http://www.grantham.edu/

This is a proprietary school.

RATINGS

Admissions Selectivity Rating: 60*   **Fire Safety Rating:** 60*   **Green Rating:** 60*

ACADEMICS

Degrees: associate, bachelor's, master's. **Special Study Options:** Accelerated program, distance learning, external degree program, independent study.

ADMISSIONS

Freshman Admission Requirements: High school diploma is required and GED is accepted. **Transfer Admission Requirements:** High school transcript, college transcript(s), Minimum college GPA of 2.0 required. Lowest grade transferable C. **General Admission Information:** Nonfall registration accepted.

COSTS AND FINANCIAL AID

Annual tuition $7,500. *Student Employment:* Federal Work-Study Program available. Institutional employment available.

GREEN MOUNTAIN COLLEGE

One Brennan Circle, Poultney, VT 05764-1199
Phone: 802-287-8000 • **Financial Aid Phone:** 802-287-8209
E-mail: admiss@greenmtn.edu • **CEEB Code:** 3418
Fax: 802-287-8099 • **Website:** www.greenmtn.edu • **ACT Code:** 4302

This private school, affiliated with the Methodist Church, was founded in 1834. It has a 155-acre campus.

RATINGS

Admissions Selectivity Rating: 84   **Fire Safety Rating:** 97   **Green Rating:** 99

STUDENTS AND FACULTY

Enrollment: 582. **Student Body:** 51% female, 49% male, 85% out-of-state, 3% international (12 countries represented). Asian 1%, African American 4%, Caucasian 53%, Hispanic 3%, Native American 1%, Pacific Islander 0%, Two or more races 1%, Race unknown 33%.
Retention and Graduation: 66% freshmen return for sophomore year. 34% freshmen graduate within 4 years. 38% freshmen graduate within 6 years.
Faculty: Student/faculty ratio 14:1. 40 full-time faculty, 93% hold PhDs, 5% are are members of minority groups, 35% are women. 0% of classes are taught by teaching assistants.

ACADEMICS

Degrees: bachelor's, certificate, master's. **Classes:** Most classes have 10-19 students. Most lab/discussion sessions have 10-19 students. **Most popular majors:** Environmental Studies; Parks, Recreation and Leisure Studies; Agroecology and Sustainable Agriculture. **Special Study Options:** cooperative education program, distance learning, double major, exchange student program (domestic), honors program, independent study, internships, liberal arts/career combination, student-designed major, study abroad, teacher certification

program. **Honors Programs:** College Honors Program Combined degree programs: BA/JD, Masters of Environmental Law & Policy, Masters of Energy Regulation & Law. **Disability Services:** Special programs offered to physically disabled students, including note-taking services, tape recorders, tutors. **Career Services:** Alumni network, Alumni services, Career/job search classes, Career assessment, Internships, Regional alumni, On-campus interviews. Creation of 4-year academic plans for all programs with explicit ties to academic award preparation and career placement

FACILITIES

Housing: Coed dorms, special housing for disabled students, substance free theme floors—recreation, education, community, Honors. **Special Academic Facilities/Equipment:** Welsh Heritage Collection, Rare Books Room, Feick Arts Center **Computers:** Students can register for classes online. Administrative functions (other than registration) can be performed online.

CAMPUS LIFE

Environment: Rural. **Activities:** Choral groups, concert band, drama/theater, jazz band, literary magazine, music ensembles, radio station, student government, student newspaper, student-run film society, yearbook. 25 registered organizations, 2 honor societies, 2 religious organizations. **Athletics (Intercollegiate):** *Men:* basketball, cross-country, golf, lacrosse, skiing (downhill/alpine), soccer, tennis. *Women:* basketball, cross-country, lacrosse, skiing (downhill/alpine), soccer, softball, tennis, volleyball. **On-Campus Highlights:** Withey Student Center, Moses Coffeehouse, Surdam Art Building, Griswold Library, The Farm. **Environmental Initiatives:** 1) In 2011, Green Mountain College became the second college in the country to achieve climate neutrality under the ACUPCC agreement and the first to do it by reducing emissions by 50%. The reductions came from an integrated approach of replacing windows, upgrading to more efficient lights and appliances, and building a $5.8 million combined heat and power plant to shift the primary heat source from number six fuel oil to locally sourced woodchips, while also producing electricity with high pressure steam.

ADMISSIONS

Reported SAT (pre-2016 redesign) scores: SAT Math middle 50% range 460-530. SAT Critical Reading middle 50% range 480-590. SAT Writing middle 50% range 430-580. **Concordant SAT scores:** SAT EBRW middle 50% 510–640. SAT Math middle 50% range 500–560. ACT middle 50% range 18-24. Minimum internet-based TOEFL 61. Minimum paper TOEFL 500. **Basis for Candidate Selection:** *Very important factors considered include:* academic GPA, recommendation(s). *Important factors considered include:* rigor of secondary school record, class rank, standardized test scores, application essay, interview, extracurricular activities, volunteer work, level of applicant's interest. *Other factors considered include:* talent/ability, character/personal qualities, alumni/ae relation, religious affiliation/commitment, racial/ethnic status, work experience. **Freshman Admission Requirements:** High school diploma is required and GED is accepted. *Academic units required:* 4 English, 3 math, 3 science, 2 science labs, 1 foreign language, 3 social studies, 1 history, 5 academic electives. *Academic units recommended:* 4 math, 4 science, 2 foreign language, 2 history. **Freshman Admission Statistics:** 825 applied, 65.94% admitted, 24% enrolled. **Transfer Admission Requirements:** High school transcript, college transcript(s), essay or personal statement, statement of good standing from prior institution(s). Minimum college GPA of 2.0 required. Lowest grade transferable C-. **General Admission Information:** Application fee $30. Priority deadline 3/1. Nonfall registration accepted. Admission may be deferred for a maximum of 1 year.

COSTS AND FINANCIAL AID

Annual tuition $33,898. Room and board $11,492. Required fees $1,442. Average book expense $0. **Required Forms and Deadlines:** FAFSA. **Notification of Awards:** Applicants will be notified of awards on a rolling basis beginning 11/1. **Types of Aid:** *Need-based scholarships/grants:* Federal Pell, FSEOG, State scholarships/grants, Private scholarships, College/university scholarship or grant aid from institutional funds. *Loans:* Direct Subsidized Stafford Loans, Direct Unsubsidized Stafford Loans, Direct PLUS loans. *Student Employment:* Federal Work-Study Program available. Institutional employment available. **Financial Aid Statistics:** 100% needy freshmen, 100% needy undergrads receive need-based scholarship or grant aid. 14% freshmen, 11% undergrads receive non-need-based scholarship or grant aid. 82% freshmen, 84% undergrads receive need-based self-help aid. 0% freshmen, 0% undergrads receive athletic scholarships. 96% freshmen, 94% undergrads receive any aid. 74% undergrads borrow to pay for school. Average cumulative indebtedness $38,701. **Criteria for awarding aid:** *Need-based:* Academics, Alumni affiliation, Religious affiliation. *Non-need-based:* Academics, Alumni affiliation, Religious affiliation, State/district residency.

GREENVILLE COLLEGE

315 East College Avenue, Greenville, IL 62246
Phone: 618-664-7100 • **Financial Aid Phone:** 618-664-7110
E-mail: admissions@greenville.edu • **CEEB Code:** 1256
Fax: 618-664-9841 • **Website:** www.greenville.edu • **ACT Code:** 1032

This private school, affiliated with the Free Methodist Church, was founded in 1892. It has a 40-acre campus.

RATINGS

Admissions Selectivity Rating: 76   **Fire Safety Rating:** 97   **Green Rating:** 60*

STUDENTS AND FACULTY

Enrollment: 961. **Student Body:** 50% female, 50% male, 33% out-of-state, 3% international (7 countries represented). Asian 1%, African American 11%, Caucasian 68%, Hispanic 5%, Native American <1%, Pacific Islander <1%, Two or more races 1%, Race unknown 10%.
Retention and Graduation: 40% freshmen graduate within 4 years. 47% freshmen graduate within 6 years. **Faculty:** Student/faculty ratio 14:1. 57 full-time faculty, 74% hold PhDs, 11% are are members of minority groups, 39% are women. 0% of classes are taught by teaching assistants.

ACADEMICS

Degrees: bachelor's, master's. **Classes:** Most classes have 10-19 students. **Most popular majors:** Elementary Education and Teaching; Biology/Biological Sciences; Music Management. **Special Study Options:** Accelerated program, cooperative education program, cross-registration, double major, external degree program, honors program, independent study, internships, liberal arts/career combination, student-designed major, study abroad, teacher certification program. **Honors Programs:** Greenville College's Honors Program is an academic program that was established in 1995 to provide a "value-added" dimension to the excellent, Christ-centered education students regularly receive at Greenville College. The Honors Program consists of a blend of enriched sections of several general education classes, special honors seminars, and experiential learning opportunities offered in an enhanced educational environment that strives for small class sizes to encourage total student participation, facilitate spirited discussions and promote greater student-faculty interaction. Outside the classroom, the Honors Programs offers a co-curricular program consisting of diversified cultural, social and educationally-oriented activities and events developed especially for program members. The Honors Program encourages its members to be persons with multi-dimensional interests who participate in a wide range of College sponsored events, activities, and organizations. Students admitted to The Honors Program automatically become members of The Honors Society, the student organization within the program which elects officers who assist with the planning and implementation of the aforementioned activities and other community building opportunities. The Greenville College Honors Program strives to emulate the guidelines, "Basic Characteristics of a Fully-Developed Honors Program," developed by the National Collegiate Honors Council. It, also, cooperates with member institutions of the Council of Christian Colleges and Universities by encouraging GC students to participate in one of the nearly twenty semester-long academic programs coordinated and promoted by CCCU that are offered at off-campus sites, both domestic and abroad. Locally, The Honors Program is administered by a director who is assisted by an Honors Council composed of faculty and students. To graduate with Honors Program recognition, students must fulfill the requirements of their academic major, earn a minimum of 25 credit hours of honors work, maintain a cumulative grade point average of 3.50 and complete a Departmental Honors Thesis under the supervision of a three-person faculty thesis committee. Graduates of the Honors Program are awarded a special medallion and receive special recognition at commencement. For additional information about The Honors Program, contact the director at (618) 664-6610. **Disability Services:** Special programs offered to physically disabled students, including note-taking services, reader services, tutors.

FACILITIES

Housing: men's dorms, women's dorms, apartments for single students, All single students not living at home must live in college approved housing. 40% of campus accessible to physically disabled. **Special Academic Facilities/Equipment:** Sculpture museum, sports training annex. **Computers:** Administrative functions (other than registration) can be performed online.

CAMPUS LIFE

Environment: Village. **Activities:** Choral groups, concert band, drama/theater, jazz band, music ensembles, musical theater, pep band, radio station, student government, student newspaper, yearbook. 25 registered organizations, 6 honor societies, 2 religious organizations. **Athletics (Intercollegiate):** *Men:* baseball, basketball, cross-country, football, soccer, tennis, track/field (outdoor), track/field (indoor). *Women:* basketball, cross-country, soccer, softball, tennis, track/field (outdoor), track/field (indoor), volleyball. **On-Campus Highlights:** Hogue Hall, Family Christian Bookstore, Jo's Java, Maves Art Center, Fitness Center.

ADMISSIONS

Freshman Academic Profile: Average high school GPA 3.3. **Reported SAT (pre-2016 redesign) scores:** SAT Math middle 50% range 440-540. SAT Critical Reading middle 50% range 400-540. SAT Writing middle 50% range 360-500. **Concordant SAT scores:** SAT EBRW middle 50% 430-580. SAT Math middle 50% range 480-570. ACT middle 50% range 18-25. Minimum internet-based TOEFL 79. **Basis for Candidate Selection:** *Very important factors considered include:* academic GPA, standardized test scores, application essay. *Important factors considered include:* character/personal qualities, religious affiliation/commitment. **Freshman Admission Requirements:** High school diploma is required and GED is accepted. *Academic units recommended:* 4 English, 2 math, 1 science, 1 science lab, 2 foreign language, 1 history. **Freshman Admission Statistics:** 1,093 applied, 57.82% admitted, 32% enrolled. **Transfer Admission Requirements:** High school transcript, college transcript(s), essay or personal statement, Minimum college GPA of 2.0 required. Lowest grade transferable C. **General Admission Information:** Priority deadline 5/1. Regular application deadline 8/15. Nonfall registration accepted. Admission may be deferred for a maximum of 1 year.

COSTS AND FINANCIAL AID

Annual tuition $26,124. Room and board $9,322. Required fees $232. Average book expense $900. **Required Forms and Deadlines:** FAFSA. **Notification of Awards:** Applicants will be notified of awards on a rolling basis beginning 3/1. **Types of Aid:** *Need-based scholarships/grants:* Federal Pell, FSEOG, State scholarships/grants, Private scholarships, College/university scholarship or grant aid from institutional funds. *Loans:* Direct Subsidized Stafford Loans, Direct Unsubsidized Stafford Loans, Direct PLUS loans, Federal Perkins Loans, College/university loans from institutional funds. *Student Employment:* Federal Work-Study Program available. Institutional employment available. **Financial Aid Statistics:** 100% needy freshmen, 100% needy undergrads receive need-based scholarship or grant aid. 13% freshmen, 10% undergrads receive non-need-based scholarship or grant aid. 83% freshmen, 84% undergrads receive need-based self-help aid. 0% freshmen, 0% undergrads receive athletic scholarships. 94% freshmen, 92% undergrads receive any aid. 82% undergrads borrow to pay for school. Average cumulative indebtedness $33,083. **Criteria for awarding aid:** *Need-based:* Academics, Alumni affiliation, Leadership, Music/drama, Religious affiliation. *Non-need-based:* Academics, Alumni affiliation, Leadership, Music/drama, Religious affiliation.

GRINNELL COLLEGE

1103 Park Street, Grinnell, IA 50112-1690
Phone: 641-269-3600 • **Financial Aid Phone:** 641-269-3250
E-mail: admission@grinnell.edu • **CEEB Code:** 6252
Fax: 641-269-4800 • **Website:** www.grinnell.edu • **ACT Code:** 1318

This private school was founded in 1846. It has a 120-acre campus.

RATINGS

Admissions Selectivity Rating: 96   **Fire Safety Rating:** 91   **Green Rating:** 76

STUDENTS AND FACULTY

Enrollment: 1,657. **Student Body:** 55% female, 45% male, 90% out-of-state, 18% international (47 countries represented). Asian 8%, African American 6%, Caucasian 52%, Hispanic 8%, Native American <1%, Pacific Islander 0%, Two or more races 5%, Race unknown 4%.
Retention and Graduation: 93% freshmen return for sophomore year. 81% freshmen graduate within 4 years. 86% freshmen graduate within 6 years. 19% grads go on to further study within 1 year. 29% grads pursue arts and sciences degrees. 3% grads pursue law degrees. 1% grads pursue business degrees. 3% grads pursue medical degrees. **Faculty:** Student/faculty ratio 8:1. 172 full-time faculty, 99% hold PhDs, 20% are are members of minority groups, 45% are women. 0% of classes are taught by teaching assistants.

ACADEMICS

Degrees: bachelor's. **Classes:** Most classes have 10-19 students. Most lab/discussion sessions have 10-19 students. **Most popular majors:** Political Science and Government; Economics; Biology/Biological Sciences. **Special Study Options:** Accelerated program, double major, independent study, internships, liberal arts/career combination, student-designed major, study abroad, teacher certification program, Study abroad available in 32 countries, including Grinnell-in-London, Grinnell-in-Washington program, 3-2 programs available in engineering, architecture, and law. Combined degree programs:

Architecture With Washington Univ,St.Louis Law Col. **Disability Services:** Special programs offered to physically disabled students, including note-taking services, reader services, tape recorders, tutors. **Career Services:** Alumni network, Alumni services, Career assessment, Internships, Regional alumni. Support 12+ funded internships each summer.

FACILITIES

Housing: Coed dorms, special housing for disabled students, cooperative housing, Wellness Housing, Theme Housing. 85% of campus accessible to physically diasbled. **Special Academic Facilities/Equipment:** Art galleries, language lab, nuclear magnetic resonance spectrometer, electron microscope, 24-inch reflecting telescope, 365-acre environmental research area. **Computers:** 100% of classrooms, 100% of dorms, 100% of libraries, 100% of dining areas, 100% of student union, 100% of common outdoor areas have wireless network access. Administrative functions (other than registration) can be performed online.

CAMPUS LIFE

Environment: Village. **Activities:** Choral groups, concert band, dance, drama/theater, jazz band, literary magazine, music ensembles, musical theater, pep band, radio station, student government, student newspaper, student-run film society, symphony orchestra, yearbook, Campus Ministries, Student Organization, Model UN. 240 registered organizations, 2 honor societies, 12 religious organizations. **Athletics (Intercollegiate):** *Men:* baseball, basketball, cross-country, diving, football, golf, soccer, swimming, tennis, track/field (outdoor), track/field (indoor). *Women:* basketball, cross-country, diving, golf, soccer, softball, swimming, tennis, track/field (outdoor), track/field (indoor), volleyball. **On-Campus Highlights:** Two building on campus are listed on the National Register of Historic Places: Mears Cottage and Goodnow Hall, Faulconer Gallery, Burling Library, Joe Rosenfield '25 Center, Bucksbaum Center for the Arts, Robert N. Noyce '49 Science Center; Athletic Center. **Environmental Initiatives:** All new buildings are LEED certified.

ADMISSIONS

Freshman Academic Profile: 66% in top 10% of high school class, 91% in top 25% of high school class, 99% in top 50% of high school class. 59% from public high schools. **Reported SAT (pre-2016 redesign) scores:** SAT Math middle 50% range 680-780. SAT Critical Reading middle 50% range 640-750. **Concordant SAT scores:** SAT Math middle 50% range 710–790. ACT middle 50% range 30-33. **Basis for Candidate Selection:** *Very important factors considered include:* rigor of secondary school record, class rank, academic GPA, recommendation(s). *Important factors considered include:* standardized test scores, application essay, extracurricular activities, talent/ability. *Other factors considered include:* interview, character/personal qualities, first generation, alumni/ae relation, geographical residence, state residency, racial/ethnic status, volunteer work, work experience, level of applicant's interest. **Freshman Admission Requirements:** High school diploma is required and GED is accepted. *Academic units recommended:* 4 English, 4 math, 3 science, 3 science labs, 3 foreign language, 3 social studies, 3 history. **Freshman Admission Statistics:** 7,370 applied, 20.19% admitted, 28% enrolled. **Transfer Admission Requirements:** High school transcript, college transcript(s), essay or personal statement, standardized test scores, statement of good standing from prior institution(s). Lowest grade transferable C. **General Admission Information:** Regular application deadline 1/15. Nonfall registration not accepted. Admission may be deferred for a maximum of 1 year.

COSTS AND FINANCIAL AID

Annual tuition $50,014. Room and board $12,400. Required fees $450. Average book expense $900. **Required Forms and Deadlines:** FAFSA, CSS/Financial Aid PROFILE, Noncustodial PROFILE. **Notification of Awards:** Applicants will be notified of awards on or about 4/1. **Types of Aid:** *Need-based scholarships/grants:* Federal Pell, FSEOG, State scholarships/grants, Private scholarships, College/university scholarship or grant aid from institutional funds. *Loans:* Direct Subsidized Stafford Loans, Direct Unsubsidized Stafford Loans, Direct PLUS loans, Federal Perkins Loans, College/university loans from institutional funds. *Student Employment:* Federal Work-Study Program available. Institutional employment available. **Financial Aid Statistics:** 99% needy freshmen, 100% needy undergrads receive need-based scholarship or grant aid. 14% freshmen, 11% undergrads receive non-need-based scholarship or grant aid. 100% freshmen, 100% undergrads receive need-based self-help aid. 0% freshmen, 0% undergrads receive athletic scholarships. 88% freshmen, 87% undergrads receive any aid. 50% undergrads borrow to pay for school. Average cumulative indebtedness $18,780. **Criteria for awarding aid:** *Non-need-based:* Academics, State/district residency.

100 Campus Drive, Grove City, PA 16127-2104
Phone: 724-458-2100 • **Financial Aid Phone:** 724-458-3300
E-mail: admissions@gcc.edu • **CEEB Code:** 2277
Fax: 724-458-3395 • **Website:** www.gcc.edu • **ACT Code:** 3582

This private school, affiliated with the Presbyterian Church, was founded in 1876. It has a 150-acre campus.

RATINGS

Admissions Selectivity Rating: 86   **Fire Safety Rating:** 94   **Green Rating:** 67

STUDENTS AND FACULTY

Enrollment: 2,346. **Student Body:** 50% female, 50% male, 54% out-of-state, 1% international (14 countries represented). Asian 2%, African American <1%, Caucasian 92%, Hispanic 1%, Native American <1%, Pacific Islander 0%, Two or more races 3%, Race unknown 0%.
Retention and Graduation: 94% freshmen return for sophomore year. 78% freshmen graduate within 4 years. 81% freshmen graduate within 6 years. 16% grads go on to further study within 1 year. 13% grads pursue arts and sciences degrees. 2% grads pursue law degrees. 2% grads pursue medical degrees. **Faculty:** Student/faculty ratio 13:1. 153 full-time faculty, 84% hold PhDs, 5% are are members of minority groups, 33% are women. 0% of classes are taught by teaching assistants.

ACADEMICS

Degrees: bachelor's. **Classes:** Most classes have 10-19 students. Most lab/discussion sessions have 20-29 students. **Most popular majors:** Mechanical Engineering; Biology/Biological Sciences; Speech Communication and Rhetoric. **Special Study Options:** Accelerated program, double major, independent study, internships, study abroad, teacher certification program. Combined degree programs: BS/BA; BEE/BA; BEE/BS; BM/BA; BM/BS; BME/BA; BME/BS. **Disability Services:** Special programs offered to physically disabled students, including tutors. **Career Services:** Alumni network, Alumni services, Career/job search classes, Career assessment, Internships, Regional alumni. Our program has a heavy emphasis on experiential learning. Students participate in campus-wide elevator pitch and business plan competitions as well as a variety of challenging curriculum exercises such as our $10 Startup Competition. In this exercise, all first-year entrepreneurship students are placed in teams and given only $10 to start and operate an exclusively on-campus business over a condensed 72-hour period. All proceeds are donated to a charity chosen by the class.

FACILITIES

Housing: men's dorms, women's dorms, fraternity/sorority housing, apartments for single students, Theme Housing. 10% of campus accessible to physically diasbled. **Special Academic Facilities/Equipment:** Fine arts center, language lab, on-campus preschool, technological learning center. **Computers:** 100% of classrooms, 15% of dorms, 100% of libraries, 33% of dining areas, 100% of student union, 10% of common outdoor areas have wireless network access. Students can register for classes online. Administrative functions (other than registration) can be performed online. Undergraduates are required to own a computer.

CAMPUS LIFE

Environment: Rural. **Activities:** Choral groups, concert band, dance, drama/theater, jazz band, literary magazine, marching band, music ensembles, musical theater, opera, pep band, radio station, student government, student newspaper, symphony orchestra, television station, yearbook, Campus Ministries, Student Organization. 130 registered organizations, 19 honor societies, 22 religious organizations. 8 fraternities, 8 sororities. **Athletics (Intercollegiate):** *Men:* baseball, basketball, cross-country, diving, football, golf, soccer, swimming, tennis, track/field (outdoor). *Women:* basketball, cheerleading, cross-country, diving, golf, soccer, softball, swimming, tennis, track/field (outdoor), volleyball, water polo. **On-Campus Highlights:** Student Union, Chapel, Hall of Arts and Letters, Fitness Center, Ketler Recreation Room. **Environmental Initiatives:** Use of high-efficiency condensing boilers in newer construction or existing retrofits.

ADMISSIONS

Freshman Academic Profile: Average high school GPA 3.7. 39% in top 10% of high school class, 67% in top 25% of high school class, 89% in top 50% of high school class. 61% from public high schools. **Reported SAT (pre-2016 redesign) scores:** SAT Math middle 50% range 529-657. SAT Critical Reading middle 50% range 531-668. **Concordant SAT scores:** SAT Math middle

50% range 560–690. ACT middle 50% range 23-29. Minimum internet-based TOEFL 79. Minimum paper TOEFL 550. **Basis for Candidate Selection:** *Very important factors considered include:* rigor of secondary school record, academic GPA, standardized test scores, application essay, interview, character/personal qualities, level of applicant's interest. *Important factors considered include:* recommendation(s), extracurricular activities. *Other factors considered include:* class rank, talent/ability, first generation, alumni/ae relation, geographical residence, state residency, religious affiliation/commitment, racial/ethnic status, volunteer work, work experience. **Freshman Admission Requirements:** High school diploma is required and GED is accepted. *Academic units recommended:* 4 English, 3 math, 3 science, 2 science labs, 3 foreign language, 3 social studies, 2 history. **Freshman Admission Statistics:** 1,517 applied, 82.47% admitted, 47% enrolled. **Transfer Admission Requirements:** High school transcript, college transcript(s), essay or personal statement, standardized test scores, statement of good standing from prior institution(s). Minimum college GPA of 2.0 required. Lowest grade transferable C. **General Admission Information:** Application fee $50. Regular application deadline 2/1. Regular notification 3/15. Nonfall registration accepted. Admission may be deferred for a maximum of 1 year.

COSTS AND FINANCIAL AID
Average book expense $1,000. **Required Forms and Deadlines:** Institution's own financial aid form. **Notification of Awards:** Applicants will be notified of awards on a rolling basis beginning 3/15. **Types of Aid:** *Need-based scholarships/grants:* State scholarships/grants, Private scholarships, College/university scholarship or grant aid from institutional funds. *Loans:* State Loans. *Student Employment:* Institutional employment available. **Financial Aid Statistics:** 100% needy freshmen, 98% needy undergrads receive need-based scholarship or grant aid. 12% freshmen, 9% undergrads receive non-need-based scholarship or grant aid. 58% freshmen, 66% undergrads receive need-based self-help aid. 0% freshmen, 0% undergrads receive athletic scholarships. 77% freshmen, 79% undergrads receive any aid. 54% undergrads borrow to pay for school. Average cumulative indebtedness $37,655. **Criteria for awarding aid:** *Need-based:* Academics, Art, Leadership, Minority status, Music/drama, Religious affiliation. *Non-need-based:* Academics, Leadership, Music/drama.

See page 966.

GUILFORD COLLEGE

Best Colleges

5800 West Friendly Avenue, Greensboro, NC 27410
Phone: 336-316-2100 • **Financial Aid Phone:** 336-316-2410
E-mail: admission@guilford.edu • **CEEB Code:** 5261
Fax: 336-316-2954 • **Website:** http://www.guilford.edu/ • **ACT Code:** 3106

This private school, affiliated with the Quaker Church, was founded in 1837. It has a 340-acre campus.

RATINGS
Admissions Selectivity Rating: 84   **Fire Safety Rating:** 88   **Green Rating:** 88

STUDENTS AND FACULTY
Enrollment: 1,768. **Student Body:** 53% female, 47% male, 29% out-of-state, 2% international (23 countries represented). Asian 3%, African American 22%, Caucasian 63%, Hispanic 7%, Native American <1%, Pacific Islander <1%, Two or more races 3%, Race unknown 1%.
Retention and Graduation: 67% freshmen return for sophomore year. 43% freshmen graduate within 4 years. 58 20% grads go on to further study within 1 year. 55% grads pursue arts and sciences degrees. 1% grads pursue law degrees. 18% grads pursue business degrees. 1% grads pursue medical degrees. **Faculty:** Student/faculty ratio 14:1. 104 full-time faculty, 92% hold PhDs, 9% are are members of minority groups, 50% are women. 0% of classes are taught by teaching assistants.

ACADEMICS
Degrees: bachelor's, certificate. **Classes:** Most classes have 10-19 students. Most lab/discussion sessions have 10-19 students. **Most popular majors:** Psychology; Criminal Justice/Safety Studies; Business Administration and Management. **Special Study Options:** Accelerated program, cooperative education program, cross-registration, double major, honors program, independent study, internships, liberal arts/career combination, student-designed major, study abroad, teacher certification program, weekend college. There are 3-2 degree programs available in forestry and environmental studies with Duke University, and in physician assistant training with Bowman Gray

School of Medicine at Wake Forest University. Guilford also offers many internships, a Washington semester, work-study programs, accelerated degree programs in business management, computer information systems, psychology, and biology, dual majors, student-designed majors, study abroad in 9 countries, and cross-registration with members of the Greater Greensboro Consortium (8 colleges/universities). **Honors Programs:** Guilford College is a participating member of the National Collegiate Honors Council. Membership in the NCHC means that students in the Guilford College Honors Program can participate in the NCHC Honors Semesters. These semester programs are regularly offered in different sites around the world and enable Honors students from across the country to meet and learn in unique settings. In recent years, Guilford College students have participated in the Study Abroad programs sponsored by Honors Programs at other colleges and universities. The University of North Carolina at Wilmington offers an Honors Semester Program at the University of Wales Swansea. For more information visit the following site: www.swan.ac.uk. Eastern Illinois University offers a n Honors Summer Program at the Universite Catholique de Louvain in Belgium that features archaeological study of historic sites. For more information, one can visit: www.eiu.edu/~honprog/abroad.htm. Both these programs offer college credit courses that are transferable. Combined degree programs: 3-1 Physician's asst program, 3-2 Forestry/environ. **Disability Services:** Special programs offered to physically disabled students, including note-taking services, reader services, tape recorders, tutors. **Career Services:** Alumni network, Alumni services, Career/job search classes, Career assessment, Internships. Internships offer students up top 12 credit hours. Local, national, and international opportunities are available. Program is centralized and provides a coordinator to assist students with the process and reflection.

FACILITIES
Housing: Coed dorms, special housing for disabled students, men's dorms, special housing for international students, women's dorms, cooperative housing, apartments for single students, Theme Housing, Special interest housing available. Alternative houses with themes and community service project requirements. 97% of campus accessible to physically diasbled. Friends Historical Collection, Frank Family Science Center, art gallery, language lab, research-grade observatory + planetarium, **Computers:** 15% of classrooms, 10% of dorms, 100% of libraries, 100% of dining areas, 50% of student union, 10% of common outdoor areas have wireless network access. Students can register for classes online. Administrative functions (other than registration) can be performed online.

CAMPUS LIFE
Environment: City. **Activities:** Choral groups, concert band, dance, drama/theater, jazz band, literary magazine, music ensembles, musical theater, pep band, radio station, student government, student newspaper, student-run film society, yearbook, Campus Ministries. 47 registered organizations, 1 honor society, 8 religious organizations. **Athletics (Intercollegiate):** *Men:* baseball, basketball, cross-country, football, golf, lacrosse, rugby, soccer, tennis. *Women:* basketball, cross-country, lacrosse, rugby, soccer, softball, swimming, tennis, volleyball. **On-Campus Highlights:** Hege Library and Art Gallery, Community Center, Frank Family Science Center, Founders Student Center and the new Grill 155, The Greenleaf Cafe—coffee co-op, The Guilford College campus is a beautiful 340 acre campus situated in the western residential area of Greensboro, North Carolina. The college is bordered by woods on one end and easy access to stores on the other. **Environmental Initiatives:** Purchasing policy that only allows Energy Star rated appliances.

ADMISSIONS
Freshman Academic Profile: Average high school GPA 3.2. 14% in top 10% of high school class, 39% in top 25% of high school class, 76% in top 50% of high school class. 75% from public high schools. **Reported SAT (pre-2016 redesign) scores:** SAT Math middle 50% range 460-570. SAT Critical Reading middle 50% range 450-600. SAT Writing middle 50% range 430-570. **Concordant SAT scores:** SAT EBRW middle 50% 490–640. SAT Math middle 50% range 500–590. ACT middle 50% range 18-22. Minimum paper TOEFL 550. **Basis for Candidate Selection:** *Very important factors considered include:* rigor of secondary school record, academic GPA, application essay. *Important factors considered include:* class rank, standardized test scores, recommendation(s), extracurricular activities, character/personal qualities, volunteer work. *Other factors considered include:* interview, talent/ability, first generation, alumni/ae relation, geographical residence, state residency, religious affiliation/commitment, racial/ethnic status, work experience, level of applicant's interest. **Freshman Admission Requirements:** High school diploma is required and GED is accepted. *Academic units recommended:* 4 English, 3 math, 3 science, 2 foreign language, 3 social studies, 3 history. **Freshman Admission Statistics:** 2,775 applied, 62.81% admitted, 19% enrolled. **Transfer Admission Requirements:** High school transcript, college transcript(s), essay or personal statement, standardized test scores, statement of good standing from prior institution(s). Minimum college GPA of 2.5 required. Lowest grade transferable C. **General Admission Information:** Priority deadline 11/15. Regular application deadline 2/15. Nonfall registration accepted. Admission may be deferred for a maximum of 1 year.

COSTS AND FINANCIAL AID

Annual tuition $33,710. Room and board $9,560. Required fees $380. Average book expense $1,650. **Required Forms and Deadlines:** FAFSA. **Notification of Awards:** Applicants will be notified of awards on a rolling basis beginning 2/15. **Types of Aid:** *Need-based scholarships/grants:* Federal Pell, FSEOG, State scholarships/grants, Private scholarships, College/university scholarship or grant aid from institutional funds. *Loans:* Direct Subsidized Stafford Loans, Direct Unsubsidized Stafford Loans, Direct PLUS loans, Federal Perkins Loans. *Student Employment:* Federal Work-Study Program available. Institutional employment available. **Financial Aid Statistics:** 91% needy freshmen, 70% needy undergrads receive need-based scholarship or grant aid. 100% freshmen, 71% undergrads receive non-need-based scholarship or grant aid. 80% freshmen, 83% undergrads receive need-based self-help aid. 0% freshmen, 0% undergrads receive athletic scholarships. 98% freshmen, 86% undergrads receive any aid. 88% undergrads borrow to pay for school. Average cumulative indebtedness $26,058. **Criteria for awarding aid:** *Need-based:* Academics. *Non-need-based:* Academics.

GUSTAVUS ADOLPHUS COLLEGE

800 College Avenue, Saint Peter, MN 56082
Phone: 507-933-7676 • **Financial Aid Phone:** 507-933-7527
E-mail: admission@gustavus.edu • **CEEB Code:** 6253
Fax: 507-933-7474 • **Website:** www.gustavus.edu • **ACT Code:** 2112

This private school, affiliated with the Lutheran Church, was founded in 1862. It has a 340-acre campus.

RATINGS
Admissions Selectivity Rating: 86   **Fire Safety Rating:** 96   **Green Rating:** 60*

STUDENTS AND FACULTY
Enrollment: 2,342. **Student Body:** 53% female, 47% male, 18% out-of-state, 4% international (22 countries represented). Asian 4%, African American 2%, Caucasian 82%, Hispanic 4%, Native American <1%, Pacific Islander <1%, Two or more races 3%, Race unknown <1%.
Retention and Graduation: 89% freshmen return for sophomore year. 82% freshmen graduate within 4 years. 83% freshmen graduate within 6 years. 32% grads go on to further study within 1 year. 11% grads pursue arts and sciences degrees. 3% grads pursue law degrees. 4% grads pursue business degrees. 4% grads pursue medical degrees. **Faculty:** Student/faculty ratio 11:1. 189 full-time faculty, 95% hold PhDs, 19% are are members of minority groups, 54% are women. 0% of classes are taught by teaching assistants.

ACADEMICS
Degrees: bachelor's. **Classes:** Most classes have 10-19 students. Most lab/discussion sessions have 10-19 students. **Most popular majors:** Psychology; Business/Commerce; Biology/Biological Sciences. **Special Study Options:** cooperative education program, cross-registration, double major, dual enrollment, exchange student program (domestic), honors program, independent study, internships, liberal arts/career combination, student-designed major, study abroad, teacher certification program. **Honors Programs:** Curriculum II. **Disability Services:** Special programs offered to physically disabled students, including note-taking services, reader services, tape recorders, tutors. **Career Services:** Alumni network, Alumni services, Career assessment, Internships. We have a well developed internship program offering month-long career explorations as well as full-semester and summer full-time and part-time internships for academic credit. Forty-eight percent of our graduates participate in an internship for academic credit and 93.4% participated in some type of experiential learning during their college experience.

FACILITIES
Housing: Coed dorms, special housing for disabled students, special housing for international students, apartments for single students, Wellness Housing, Theme Housing. 100% of campus accessible to physically diasbled. **Special Academic Facilities/Equipment:** Art gallery, mineral museum, electron microscopes, arboretum, 14-inch computer-guided Celestron telescope, artificial intelligence laboratory, materials science laboratory, 300-MHz NMR spectrometer, five-section greenhouse. **Computers:** 100% of dorms, 100% of libraries, 100% of dining areas, 100% of student union, 50% of common outdoor areas have wireless network access. Students can register for classes online. Administrative functions (other than registration) can be performed online.

CAMPUS LIFE
Environment: Village. **Activities:** Choral groups, concert band, dance, drama/theater, jazz band, literary magazine, music ensembles, musical theater, pep band, radio station, student government, student newspaper, symphony orchestra, television station, yearbook. 120 registered organizations, 11 honor societies, 8 religious organizations. 5 fraternities, 5 sororities. **Athletics (Intercollegiate):** *Men:* baseball, basketball, cross-country, diving, football, golf, ice hockey, skiing (nordic/cross-country), soccer, swimming, tennis, track/field (outdoor), track/field (indoor). *Women:* basketball, cross-country, diving, golf, gymnastics, ice hockey, skiing (nordic/cross-country), soccer, softball, swimming, tennis, track/field (outdoor), track/field (indoor), volleyball. **On-Campus Highlights:** Campus Center, Courtyard Cafe, Lund Athletic Center, Christ Chapel, Linnaeus Arboretum, With over 75% of students remaining on campus during a typical weekend (according to our Dining Service), our students actively use the entire campus. As there are no city streets intersecting our campus, Gusties enjoy their home on the hill. **Environmental Initiatives:** Seeking to acquire 5 MW of wind generator capacity.

ADMISSIONS
Freshman Academic Profile: Average high school GPA 3.6. 30% in top 10% of high school class, 65% in top 25% of high school class, 94% in top 50% of high school class. 94% from public high schools. **Reported SAT (pre-2016 redesign) scores:** SAT Math middle 50% range 530-675. SAT Critical Reading middle 50% range 550-620. **Concordant SAT scores:** SAT Math middle 50% range 560–710. ACT middle 50% range 24-30. Minimum internet-based TOEFL 80. Minimum paper TOEFL 550. **Basis for Candidate Selection:** *Very important factors considered include:* rigor of secondary school record, academic GPA. *Important factors considered include:* class rank, application essay, recommendation(s), interview. *Other factors considered include:* standardized test scores, extracurricular activities, talent/ability, character/personal qualities, first generation, alumni/ae relation, geographical residence, state residency, religious affiliation/commitment, racial/ethnic status, volunteer work, work experience, level of applicant's interest. **Freshman Admission Requirements:** High school diploma is required and GED is accepted. *Academic units required:* 4 English, 3 math, 2 science, 2 science labs, 2 foreign language, 2 social studies, 2 history. *Academic units recommended:* 4 math, 3 science, 3 science labs, 3 foreign language, 2 academic electives. **Freshman Admission Statistics:** 4,657 applied, 67.06% admitted, 20% enrolled. **Transfer Admission Requirements:** High school transcript, college transcript(s), essay or personal statement, standardized test scores, statement of good standing from prior institution(s). Minimum college GPA of 2.4 required. Lowest grade transferable 2. **General Admission Information:** Regular application deadline 4/1. Nonfall registration accepted. Admission may be deferred for a maximum of 1 year.

COSTS AND FINANCIAL AID
Required Forms and Deadlines: FAFSA. **Notification of Awards:** Applicants will be notified of awards on a rolling basis beginning 3/15. **Types of Aid:** *Need-based scholarships/grants:* Federal Pell, FSEOG, State scholarships/grants, Private scholarships, College/university scholarship or grant aid from institutional funds. *Loans:* Direct Subsidized Stafford Loans, Direct Unsubsidized Stafford Loans, Direct PLUS loans, State Loans. *Student Employment:* Federal Work-Study Program available. Institutional employment available. **Financial Aid Statistics:** 100% needy freshmen, 100% needy undergrads receive need-based scholarship or grant aid. 14% freshmen, 9% undergrads receive non-need-based scholarship or grant aid. 100% freshmen, 100% undergrads receive need-based self-help aid. 0% freshmen, 0% undergrads receive athletic scholarships. 96% freshmen, 95% undergrads receive any aid. Average cumulative indebtedness $35,247. **Criteria for awarding aid:** *Need-based:* Minority status, Religious affiliation. *Non-need-based:* Academics, Alumni affiliation, Art, Minority status, Music/drama, Religious affiliation.

GWYNEDD MERCY UNIVERSITY

1325 Sumneytown Pike, Gwynedd Valley, PA 19437-0901
Phone: 215-641-5510 • **Financial Aid Phone:** 215-646-7300
E-mail: admissions@gmercyu.edu • **CEEB Code:** 2278
Fax: 215-641-5556 • **Website:** www.gmercyu.edu

This private school, affiliated with the Roman Catholic Church, was founded in 1948. It has a 160-acre campus.

RATINGS
Admissions Selectivity Rating: 74   **Fire Safety Rating:** 82   **Green Rating:** 60*

STUDENTS AND FACULTY
Enrollment: 2,130. **Student Body:** 74% female, 26% male, 8% out-of-state, <1% international (28 countries represented). Asian 2%, African American 21%, Caucasian 69%, Hispanic 1%, Native American <1%, Pacific Islander 0%, Two or more races 0%, Race unknown 6%.
Retention and Graduation: 76% freshmen return for sophomore year. 50% freshmen graduate within 4 years. 69% freshmen graduate within 6 years. 60%

grads go on to further study within 1 year. **Faculty:** Student/faculty ratio 13:1. 75 full-time faculty, 63% hold PhDs, 0% are are members of minority groups, 71% are women. 0% of classes are taught by teaching assistants.

ACADEMICS

Degrees: associate, bachelor's, certificate, doctoral/professional, doctoral, master's, postbachelor's certificate, post-master's certificate. **Classes:** Most classes have 10-19 students. Most lab/discussion sessions have 10-19 students. **Most popular majors:** Education; Business Administration and Management; Registered Nursing, Nursing Administration, Nursing Research and Clinical Nursing. **Special Study Options:** Accelerated program, cross-registration, double major, English as a Second Language (ESL), honors program, independent study, internships, liberal arts/career combination, study abroad, teacher certification program, weekend college. **Honors Programs:** The Honors Program in Liberal Studies consists of six interdisciplinary, team-taught courses developing the theme of "The Quest for Community and Freedom: The Individual and Society." Combined degree programs: BSN/MSN. **Disability Services:** Special programs offered to physically disabled students, including reader services, tutors. **Career Services:** Alumni services, Career assessment, Internships.

FACILITIES

Housing: Coed dorms, special housing for international students 95% of campus accessible to physically diasbled. **Special Academic Facilities/Equipment:** Keiss Hall (Health and Science Center), television production room and small theater, computer labs. **Computers:** Students can register for classes online.

CAMPUS LIFE

Environment: City. **Activities:** Choral groups, literary magazine, student government, student newspaper, yearbook, Campus Ministries. 22 registered organizations, 10 honor societies, 1 religious organization. **Athletics (Intercollegiate):** *Men:* baseball, basketball, cross-country, golf, soccer, tennis, track/field (outdoor), track/field (indoor). *Women:* basketball, cross-country, field hockey, lacrosse, soccer, softball, tennis, track/field (outdoor), track/field (indoor), volleyball. **On-Campus Highlights:** Assumption Hall, The Sister Isabelle Keiss Center for Health and Sciences, The Griffin Complex Student Union and Athletic Facility, Saint Bernard Lobby and Snack Bar, Loyola Hall and Saint Brigid's Hall—Residence Halls.

ADMISSIONS

Freshman Academic Profile: 4% in top 10% of high school class, 14% in top 25% of high school class, 40% in top 50% of high school class. 57% from public high schools. **Reported SAT (pre-2016 redesign) scores:** SAT Math middle 50% range 430-530. SAT Critical Reading middle 50% range 440-530. **Concordant SAT scores:** SAT Math middle 50% range 470–560. ACT middle 50% range 0-0. Minimum paper TOEFL 525. **Basis for Candidate Selection:** *Very important factors considered include:* rigor of secondary school record. *Important factors considered include:* class rank, academic GPA, standardized test scores, recommendation(s), extracurricular activities. *Other factors considered include:* application essay, interview, character/personal qualities, alumni/ae relation, volunteer work, work experience. **Freshman Admission Requirements:** High school diploma is required and GED is accepted. *Academic units required:* 4 English, 3 math, 3 science, 1 history, 3 academic electives. **Freshman Admission Statistics:** 1,844 applied, 67.08% admitted, 25% enrolled. **Transfer Admission Requirements:** High school transcript, college transcript(s), Minimum college GPA of 2.0 required. Lowest grade transferable c. **General Admission Information:** Application fee $25. Regular application deadline 8/20. Nonfall registration accepted. Admission may be deferred for a maximum of 12 months.

COSTS AND FINANCIAL AID

Annual tuition $25,160. Room and board $9,760. Required fees $450. Average book expense $600. **Required Forms and Deadlines:** FAFSA, Institution's own financial aid form. **Notification of Awards:** Applicants will be notified of awards on a rolling basis beginning 3/1. **Types of Aid:** *Need-based scholarships/grants:* Federal Pell, FSEOG, State scholarships/grants, Private scholarships, College/university scholarship or grant aid from institutional funds. *Loans:* Direct Subsidized Stafford Loans, Direct Unsubsidized Stafford Loans, Direct PLUS loans, Federal Perkins Loans, Federal Nursing Loans. *Student Employment:* Federal Work-Study Program available. Institutional employment available. **Financial Aid Statistics:** 97% needy freshmen, 98% needy undergrads receive need-based scholarship or grant aid. 77% freshmen, 77% undergrads receive non-need-based scholarship or grant aid. 91% freshmen, 83% undergrads receive need-based self-help aid. 0% freshmen, 0% undergrads receive athletic scholarships. 97% freshmen, 92% undergrads receive any aid. **Criteria for awarding aid:** *Need-based:* Alumni affiliation. *Non-need-based:* Academics, Leadership.

HAMILTON COLLEGE

Office of Admission, Clinton, NY 13323
Phone: 315-859-4421 • **Financial Aid Phone:** 800-859-4413
E-mail: admission@hamilton.edu • **CEEB Code:** 2286
Fax: 315-859-4457 • **Website:** www.hamilton.edu • **ACT Code:** 2754

This private school was founded in 1812. It has a 1300-acre campus.

RATINGS

Admissions Selectivity Rating: 95   **Fire Safety Rating:** 92   **Green Rating:** 60*

STUDENTS AND FACULTY

Enrollment: 1,867. **Student Body:** 51% female, 49% male, 71% out-of-state, 7% international (45 countries represented). Asian 7%, African American 4%, Caucasian 64%, Hispanic 8%, Native American <1%, Pacific Islander 0%, Two or more races 3%, Race unknown 7%.
Retention and Graduation: 94% freshmen return for sophomore year. 89% freshmen graduate within 4 years. 92% freshmen graduate within 6 years. 10% grads go on to further study within 1 year. 7% grads pursue arts and sciences degrees. 1% grads pursue law degrees. 1% grads pursue business degrees. 1% grads pursue medical degrees. **Faculty:** Student/faculty ratio 9:1. 186 full-time faculty, 96% hold PhDs, 18% are are members of minority groups, 47% are women. 0% of classes are taught by teaching assistants.

ACADEMICS

Degrees: bachelor's. **Classes:** Most classes have 10-19 students. Most lab/discussion sessions have 10-19 students. **Most popular majors:** Economics; Mathematics; Political Science and Government. **Special Study Options:** Accelerated program, cross-registration, double major, English as a Second Language (ESL), independent study, internships, student-designed major, study abroad, 3-2 program in Engineering with Columbia University, Rensselaer Polytechnic Institute, and Washington University(St. Louis); 3-3 program in Law with Columbia University. Combined degree programs: BA/JD, Columbia University School of Law. **Disability Services:** Special programs offered to physically disabled students, including note-taking services, reader services, tape recorders, tutors. **Career Services:** Alumni network, Alumni services, Career/job search classes, Career assessment, Internships, Regional alumni. The Summer Internship Fund, launched with a $1.6 million endowment in 2006, provides cost-of-living stipends each summer to a number of undergraduates who accept unpaid internships in any career field.

FACILITIES

Housing: Coed dorms, special housing for disabled students, apartments for married students, cooperative housing, apartments for single students, Wellness Housing. **Special Academic Facilities/Equipment:** Art gallery, language lab, fitness center, observatory, two electron microscopes. Arthur Levitt Public Affairs Center. **Computers:** 100% of classrooms, 100% of dorms, 100% of libraries, 100% of dining areas, 100% of student union, 100% of common outdoor areas have wireless network access. Students can register for classes online. Administrative functions (other than registration) can be performed online.

CAMPUS LIFE

Environment: Rural. **Activities:** Choral groups, concert band, dance, drama/theater, jazz band, literary magazine, music ensembles, musical theater, radio station, student government, student newspaper, student-run film society, symphony orchestra, yearbook, Campus Ministries, Student Organization, Model UN. 117 registered organizations, 8 honor societies, 4 religious organizations. 11 fraternities, 7 sororities. **Athletics (Intercollegiate):** *Men:* baseball, basketball, crew/rowing, cross-country, diving, football, golf, ice hockey, lacrosse, soccer, squash, swimming, tennis, track/field (outdoor), track/field (indoor). *Women:* basketball, crew/rowing, cross-country, diving, field hockey, ice hockey, lacrosse, soccer, softball, squash, swimming, tennis, track/field (outdoor), track/field (indoor), volleyball. **On-Campus Highlights:** Blood Fitness and Dance Center, Kirner-Johnson Commons, Outdoor Leadership Center/Root Glen, Science Center, Cafe Opus.

ADMISSIONS

Freshman Academic Profile: 65% in top 10% of high school class, 91% in top 25% of high school class, 98% in top 50% of high school class. 61% from public high schools. **Reported SAT (pre-2016 redesign) scores:** SAT Math middle 50% range 650-740. SAT Critical Reading middle 50% range 650-740. SAT Writing middle 50% range 650-740. **Concordant SAT scores:** SAT EBRW middle 50% 700–760. SAT Math middle 50% range 670–760. ACT middle 50% range 31-33. **Basis for Candidate Selection:** *Very important* factors considered include: rigor of secondary school record, class rank, academic GPA. *Important factors considered include:* standardized test scores, application essay, recommendation(s), interview, extracurricular activities, character/personal qualities. *Other factors considered include:* talent/ability, first generation, alumni/ae relation, geographical residence, racial/ethnic status, volunteer work, work experience, level of applicant's interest. **Freshman Admission Requirements:** High school diploma is required and GED is accepted. *Academic units recommended:* 4 English, 3 math, 3 science, 3 foreign language, 3 social studies. **Freshman Admission Statistics:** 5,230 applied, 26.08% admitted, 35% enrolled. **Transfer Admission Requirements:** High school transcript, college transcript(s), essay or personal statement, standardized test scores, statement of good standing from prior institution(s). Lowest grade transferable C. **General Admission Information:** Application fee $50. Regular application deadline 1/1. Regular notification 4/1. Nonfall registration accepted. Admission may be deferred.

COSTS AND FINANCIAL AID

Required Forms and Deadlines: FAFSA, Institution's own financial aid form, CSS/Financial Aid PROFILE, State aid form, Noncustodial PROFILE, Business/Farm Supplement. **Notification of Awards:** Applicants will be notified of awards on or about 4/1. **Types of Aid:** *Need-based scholarships/grants:* Federal Pell, FSEOG, State scholarships/grants, Private scholarships, College/university scholarship or grant aid from institutional funds. *Loans:* Direct Subsidized Stafford Loans, Direct Unsubsidized Stafford Loans, Direct PLUS loans, Federal Perkins Loans, College/university loans from institutional funds. *Student Employment:* Federal Work-Study Program available. Institutional employment available. **Financial Aid Statistics:** 100% needy freshmen, 100% needy undergrads receive need-based scholarship or grant aid. 0% undergrads receive non-need-based scholarship or grant aid. 83% freshmen, 81% undergrads receive need-based self-help aid. 0% freshmen, 0% undergrads receive athletic scholarships. 53% freshmen, 48% undergrads receive any aid. 45% undergrads borrow to pay for school. Average cumulative indebtedness $21,491.

HAMLINE UNIVERSITY

Saint Paul, MN 55104
Phone: 651-523-2207 • **Financial Aid Phone:** 651-523-3000
E-mail: CLA-admis@hamline.edu • **CEEB Code:** 6265
Fax: 651-523-2458 • **Website:** www.hamline.edu • **ACT Code:** 2114

This private school, affiliated with the Methodist Church, was founded in 1854. It has a 77-acre campus.

RATINGS

Admissions Selectivity Rating: 81   **Fire Safety Rating:** 89   **Green Rating:** 60*

STUDENTS AND FACULTY

Enrollment: 1,986. **Student Body:** 58% female, 42% male, 15% out-of-state, 3% international (53 countries represented). Asian 6%, African American 5%, Caucasian 75%, Hispanic 2%, Native American 1%, Pacific Islander 0%, Two or more races 0%, Race unknown 9%.
Retention and Graduation: 82% freshmen return for sophomore year. 61% freshmen graduate within 4 years. 68% freshmen graduate within 6 years. 27% grads go on to further study within 1 year. 17% grads pursue arts and sciences degrees. 4% grads pursue law degrees. 2% grads pursue business degrees. 1% grads pursue medical degrees. **Faculty:** Student/faculty ratio 14:1. 173 full-time faculty, 87% hold PhDs, 11% are are members of minority groups, 49% are women. 0% of classes are taught by teaching assistants.

ACADEMICS

Degrees: bachelor's, master's, postbachelor's certificate. **Classes:** Most classes have 10-19 students. Most lab/discussion sessions have 10-19 students. **Most popular majors:** Psychology; Criminal Justice/Police Science; Business/Commerce. **Special Study Options:** cross-registration, double major, dual enrollment, English as a Second Language (ESL), exchange student program (domestic), honors program, independent study, internships, student-designed major, study abroad, teacher certification program. Combined degree programs: BA/JD, BA/MEng, 3-3 prog with Hamline School of Law. **Disability Services:** Special programs offered to physically disabled students, including note-taking services, reader services, tape recorders, tutors. **Career Services:** Alumni network, Alumni services, Career/job search classes, Career assessment, Internships, Regional alumni. All students must fulfill the Leadership, Education, and Development (LEAD) requirement which integrates the liberal arts with the world of work. Most students choose an internship to fulfill this requirement.

FACILITIES

Housing: Coed dorms, fraternity/sorority housing, apartments for married students, cooperative housing, apartments for single students, PRIDE (African-American), Spectrum (GLBT), Hmong, foreign language interest, theme housing (floors organized around areas like Arts, Weekends on Campus, GLBT, and Social Justice). 80% of campus accessible to physically diasbled. **Special Academic Facilities/Equipment:** theatre, music hall, art gallery, science center. **Computers:** 100% of classrooms, 100% of dorms, 100% of libraries, 100% of dining areas, 100% of student union, 100% of common outdoor areas have wireless network access. Students can register for classes online. Administrative functions (other than registration) can be performed online.

CAMPUS LIFE

Environment: Metropolis. **Activities:** Choral groups, concert band, dance, drama/theater, jazz band, literary magazine, music ensembles, musical theater, pep band, radio station, student government, student newspaper, symphony orchestra, television station, yearbook, Campus Ministries, Student Organization, Model UN. 77 registered organizations, 11 honor societies, 9 religious organizations. 1 fraternity, 2 sororities. **Athletics (Intercollegiate):** *Men:* baseball, basketball, cross-country, diving, football, ice hockey, soccer, swimming, tennis, track/field (outdoor), track/field (indoor). *Women:* basketball, cross-country, diving, gymnastics, ice hockey, soccer, softball, swimming, tennis, track/field (outdoor), track/field (indoor), volleyball. **On-Campus Highlights:** Klas Center (stadium and food service), Walker Field House, Sorin Dining Hall, Sundin Music Hall, Bush Student Center. **Environmental Initiatives:** Recycling program.

ADMISSIONS

Freshman Academic Profile: Average high school GPA 3.4. 20% in top 10% of high school class, 49% in top 25% of high school class, 79% in top 50% of high school class. 90% from public high schools. **Reported SAT (pre-2016 redesign) scores:** SAT Math middle 50% range 540-640. SAT Critical Reading middle 50% range 512.5-645. SAT Writing middle 50% range 510-615. **Concordant SAT scores:** SAT EBRW middle 50% 570–680. SAT Math middle 50% range 570–660. ACT middle 50% range 21-27. Minimum paper TOEFL 550. **Basis for Candidate Selection:** *Very important factors considered include:* rigor of secondary school record, class rank. *Important factors considered include:* academic GPA, standardized test scores, application essay, recommendation(s), interview, extracurricular activities, talent/ability. *Other factors considered include:* character/personal qualities, first generation, alumni/ae relation, racial/ethnic status, volunteer work, work experience. **Freshman Admission Requirements:** High school diploma is required and GED is accepted. *Academic units recommended:* 4 English, 3 math, 3 science, 3 science labs, 2 foreign language, 4 social studies, 4 academic electives. **Freshman Admission Statistics:** 2,018 applied, 77.80% admitted, 29% enrolled. **Transfer Admission Requirements:** college transcript(s), essay or personal statement, Minimum college GPA of 2.0 required. Lowest grade transferable C-. **General Admission Information:** Priority deadline 5/1. Nonfall registration accepted. Admission may be deferred for a maximum of 2 years.

COSTS AND FINANCIAL AID

Annual tuition $36,888. Room and board $9,736. Required fees $998. **Required Forms and Deadlines:** FAFSA. **Notification of Awards:** Applicants will be notified of awards on a rolling basis beginning 3/15. **Types of Aid:** *Need-based scholarships/grants:* Federal Pell, FSEOG, State scholarships/grants, Private scholarships, College/university scholarship or grant aid from institutional funds. *Loans:* Direct Subsidized Stafford Loans, Direct Unsubsidized Stafford Loans, Direct PLUS loans, Federal Perkins Loans, State Loans. *Student Employment:* Federal Work-Study Program available. Institutional employment available. **Financial Aid Statistics:** 100% needy freshmen, 99% needy undergrads receive need-based scholarship or grant aid. 15% freshmen, 10% undergrads receive non-need-based scholarship or grant aid. 87% freshmen, 91% undergrads receive need-based self-help aid. 0% freshmen, 0% undergrads receive athletic scholarships. 98% freshmen, 95% undergrads receive any aid. **Criteria for awarding aid:** *Need-based:* Academics, Alumni affiliation, Art, Minority status, Music/drama, Religious affiliation. *Non-need-based:* Academics, Alumni affiliation, Art, Leadership, Minority status, Music/drama, Religious affiliation.

HAMPDEN-SYDNEY COLLEGE

PO Box 667, Hampden-Sydney, VA 23943-0667
Phone: 434-223-6120 • **Financial Aid Phone:** 434-223-6119
E-mail: hsapp@hsc.edu • **CEEB Code:** 5291
Fax: 434-223-6346 • **Website:** www.hsc.edu • **ACT Code:** 4356

This private school, affiliated with the Presbyterian Church, was founded in 1775. It has a 1200-acre campus.

RATINGS

Admissions Selectivity Rating: 87   **Fire Safety Rating:** 88   **Green Rating:** 69

STUDENTS AND FACULTY

Enrollment: 1,027. **Student Body:** 0% female, 100% male, 30% out-of-state, 1% international (11 countries represented). Asian 1%, African American 5%, Caucasian 84%, Hispanic 4%, Native American <1%, Pacific Islander <1%, Two or more races 4%, Race unknown 2%.
Retention and Graduation: 83% freshmen return for sophomore year. 66% freshmen graduate within 6 years. 22% grads go on to further study within 1 year. 8% grads pursue arts and sciences degrees. 1% grads pursue law degrees. 2% grads pursue business degrees. **Faculty:** Student/faculty ratio 10:1. 87 full-time faculty, 93% hold PhDs, 5% are are members of minority groups, 29% are women. 0% of classes are taught by teaching assistants.

ACADEMICS

Degrees: bachelor's. **Classes:** Most classes have 10-19 students. **Most popular majors:** Economics; History; Business/Managerial Economics. **Special Study Options:** cooperative education program, cross-registration, double major, dual enrollment, exchange student program (domestic), honors program, independent study, internships, study abroad, Appalachian semester, junior year exchange with members of Virginia consortium. Semester at sea and Washington semester also available. **Honors Programs:** Student Summer Research programs, Departmental Honors. **Disability Services:** Special programs offered to physically disabled students, including note-taking services, reader services, tape recorders, tutors. **Career Services:** Alumni network, Alumni services, Career assessment, Internships, Regional alumni. While we don't offer career classes, we are most proud of the Professional Development which is a conference-style workshop that takes place prior to the Spring semester. Students come back early from break to engage in career development and networking activities with alumni and employers. We also host the Career Fair where approximately 25 employers and graduate schools participate with over 200 students in attendance. Additionally, we have a Minority Alumni Mentorship weekend where a networking fair occurs.

FACILITIES

Housing: men's dorms, special housing for international students, fraternity/sorority housing, apartments for married students, apartments for single students, Theme Housing, Language Houses. 50% of campus accessible to physically diasbled. **Special Academic Facilities/Equipment:** History museum, language lab, communications center, observatory. **Computers:** 15% of classrooms, 100% of libraries, 100% of dining areas, 100% of student union, 20% of common outdoor areas have wireless network access. Students can register for classes online. Administrative functions (other than registration) can be performed online.

CAMPUS LIFE

Environment: Rural. **Activities:** Choral groups, drama/theater, literary magazine, music ensembles, pep band, radio station, student government, student newspaper, yearbook, Campus Ministries, Student Organization. 45 registered organizations, 14 honor societies, 6 religious organizations. 11 fraternities. **Athletics (Intercollegiate):** *Men:* baseball, basketball, cross-country, football, golf, lacrosse, soccer, tennis. **On-Campus Highlights:** Bortz Library, Kirby Fieldhouse (athletic facility), Gammon gym/Hall of Fame, Tiger Inn, Campus Museum. **Environmental Initiatives:** Electrical energy conservation.

ADMISSIONS

Freshman Academic Profile: Average high school GPA 3.6. 10% in top 10% of high school class, 40% in top 25% of high school class, 77% in top 50% of high school class. 68% from public high schools. **Reported SAT (pre-2016 redesign) scores:** SAT Math middle 50% range 510-615. SAT Critical Reading middle 50% range 500-615. SAT Writing middle 50% range 460-570. **Concordant SAT scores:** SAT EBRW middle 50% 540–650. SAT Math middle 50% range 540–640. ACT middle 50% range 21-28. Minimum internet-based TOEFL 100. Minimum paper TOEFL 600. **Basis for Candidate Selection:**

Very important factors considered include: rigor of secondary school record, academic GPA, standardized test scores, application essay, recommendation(s), character/personal qualities. *Important factors considered include:* class rank, extracurricular activities. *Other factors considered include:* interview, talent/ability, first generation, alumni/ae relation, volunteer work, work experience, level of applicant's interest. **Freshman Admission Requirements:** High school diploma is required and GED is accepted. *Academic units required:* 4 English, 3 math, 2 science, 1 science lab, 2 foreign language, 1 social studies, 1 history, 3 academic electives. *Academic units recommended:* 4 math, 3 science, 3 foreign language. **Freshman Admission Statistics:** 3,403 applied, 55.60% admitted, 16% enrolled. **Transfer Admission Requirements:** High school transcript, college transcript(s), essay or personal statement, standardized test scores, statement of good standing from prior institution(s). Minimum college GPA of 2.5 required. Lowest grade transferable C. **General Admission Information:** Application fee $30. Regular application deadline 3/1. Regular notification 4/15. Nonfall registration accepted.

COSTS AND FINANCIAL AID

Annual tuition $41,516. Room and board $13,286. Required fees $1,446. Average book expense $1,000. **Required Forms and Deadlines:** FAFSA, State aid form. **Notification of Awards:** Applicants will be notified of awards on or about 3/15. **Types of Aid:** *Need-based scholarships/grants:* Federal Pell, FSEOG, State scholarships/grants, Private scholarships, College/university scholarship or grant aid from institutional funds. *Loans:* Direct Subsidized Stafford Loans, Direct Unsubsidized Stafford Loans, Direct PLUS loans, Federal Perkins Loans, College/university loans from institutional funds. *Student Employment:* Federal Work-Study Program available. Institutional employment available. **Financial Aid Statistics:** 100% needy freshmen, 100% needy undergrads receive need-based scholarship or grant aid. 26% freshmen, 18% undergrads receive non-need-based scholarship or grant aid. 73% freshmen, 75% undergrads receive need-based self-help aid. 0% freshmen, 0% undergrads receive athletic scholarships. 100% freshmen, 99% undergrads receive any aid. 68% undergrads borrow to pay for school. Average cumulative indebtedness $34,334. **Criteria for awarding aid:** *Need-based:* Academics, Leadership, Minority status, Music/drama. *Non-need-based:* Academics, Leadership, Minority status, Music/drama, State/district residency.

HAMPSHIRE COLLEGE

Admissions Office, Amherst, MA 1002
Phone: 413-559-5471 • **Financial Aid Phone:** 413-559-5484
E-mail: admissions@hampshire.edu • **CEEB Code:** 3447
Fax: 413-559-5631 • **Website:** https://www.hampshire.edu/ • **ACT Code:** 1842

This private school was founded in 1965. It has a 850-acre campus.

RATINGS

Admissions Selectivity Rating: 77   **Fire Safety Rating:** 79   **Green Rating:** 94

STUDENTS AND FACULTY

Enrollment: 1,357. **Student Body:** 59% female, 41% male, 5% international (31 countries represented). Asian 2%, African American 4%, Caucasian 68%, Hispanic 10%, Native American <1%, Pacific Islander <1%, Two or more races 6%, Race unknown 5%.
Retention and Graduation: 78% freshmen return for sophomore year. 63% freshmen graduate within 4 years. 74% freshmen graduate within 6 years. 10% grads go on to further study within 1 year. 8% grads pursue arts and sciences degrees. 1% grads pursue law degrees. 1% grads pursue medical degrees. **Faculty:** Student/faculty ratio 11:1. 112 full-time faculty, 0% hold PhDs, 0% are are members of minority groups, 0% are women. 0% of classes are taught by teaching assistants.

ACADEMICS

Degrees: bachelor's. **Classes:** Most classes have 10-19 students. Most lab/discussion sessions have 10-19 students. **Most popular majors:** Film/Video and Photographic Arts; Creative Writing; Cultural Studies/Critical Theory and Analysis. **Special Study Options:** exchange student program (domestic), independent study, internships, student-designed major, study abroad, teacher certification program. **Disability Services:** Special programs offered to physically disabled students, including note-taking services, reader services, tape recorders. **Career Services:** Alumni network, Alumni services, Career/job search classes, Career assessment, Internships, Regional alumni.

FACILITIES

Housing: Coed dorms, special housing for disabled students, special housing for international students, women's dorms, apartments for single students, Theme Housing. 50% of campus accessible to physically disabled. **Special Academic Facilities/Equipment:** Performing and visual arts center, bioshelter (integrated greenhouse/aquaculture facility), farm center, electronic music and TV production studios, extensive film and photography facilities, multimedia center. **Computers:** 100% of classrooms, 10% of dorms, 100% of libraries, 100% of dining areas, n/a% of student union, 50% of common outdoor areas have wireless network access. Students can register for classes online. Administrative functions (other than registration) can be performed online.

CAMPUS LIFE

Environment: Town. **Activities:** Choral groups, dance, drama/theater, jazz band, student newspaper, student-run film society, Student Organization. 94 registered organizations, 3 religious organizations. **On-Campus Highlights:** Bridge Cafe, Bookstore, Library, Eric Carle Museum of Picture Book Art, Liebling Center—Film/Photo. **Environmental Initiatives:** Constructing a new facility addition to LEED standards (minimum silver; hopefully gold); constructing a condominium community to be LEED certified.

ADMISSIONS

Freshman Academic Profile: Average high school GPA 3.5. 74% from public high schools. **Reported SAT (pre-2016 redesign) scores:** SAT Math middle 50% range 530-660. SAT Critical Reading middle 50% range 580-700. SAT Writing middle 50% range 560-670. **Concordant SAT scores:** SAT EBRW middle 50% 630–720. SAT Math middle 50% range 560–690. ACT middle 50% range 25-30. Minimum internet-based TOEFL 91. Minimum paper TOEFL 577. **Basis for Candidate Selection:** *Very important factors considered include:* application essay, recommendation(s), character/personal qualities. *Important factors considered include:* rigor of secondary school record, academic GPA, interview, extracurricular activities, talent/ability, volunteer work, work experience, level of applicant's interest. *Other factors considered include:* class rank, first generation, alumni/ae relation, racial/ethnic status. **Freshman Admission Requirements:** High school diploma is required and GED is accepted. *Academic units required:* 4 English, 3 math, 3 science, 2 science labs, 3 foreign language, 3 history. *Academic units recommended:* 4 English, 4 math, 4 science, 2 science labs, 4 foreign language, 4 history. **Freshman Admission Statistics:** 2,671 applied, 66.64% admitted, 19% enrolled. **Transfer Admission Requirements:** High school transcript, college transcript(s), essay or personal statement, Lowest grade transferable C. **General Admission Information:** Regular application deadline 1/15. Regular notification 4/1. Nonfall registration accepted. Admission may be deferred for a maximum of 1 year.

COSTS AND FINANCIAL AID

Annual tuition $47,620. Room and board $12,950. Required fees $1,380. Average book expense $850. **Required Forms and Deadlines:** FAFSA, CSS/Financial Aid PROFILE, Noncustodial PROFILE. **Notification of Awards:** Applicants will be notified of awards on or about 4/1. **Types of Aid:** *Need-based scholarships/grants:* Federal Pell, FSEOG, State scholarships/grants, Private scholarships, College/university scholarship or grant aid from institutional funds. *Loans:* Direct Subsidized Stafford Loans, Direct Unsubsidized Stafford Loans, Direct PLUS loans, Federal Perkins Loans. *Student Employment:* Federal Work-Study Program available. Institutional employment available. **Financial Aid Statistics:** 97% needy freshmen, 98% needy undergrads receive need-based scholarship or grant aid. 14% freshmen, 14% undergrads receive non-need-based scholarship or grant aid. 96% freshmen, 96% undergrads receive need-based self-help aid. 0% freshmen, 0% undergrads receive athletic scholarships. 70% freshmen, 76% undergrads receive any aid. **Criteria for awarding aid:** *Non-need-based:* Academics, Art, Leadership, Music/drama.

HAMPTON UNIVERSITY

Office of Admissions, Hampton, VA 23668
Phone: 757-727-5328 • **Financial Aid Phone:** 757-727-5332
E-mail: admit@hamptonu.edu • **CEEB Code:** 5292
Fax: 757-727-5095 • **Website:** www.hamptonu.edu • **ACT Code:** 4358

This private school was founded in 1868. It has a 255-acre campus.

RATINGS

Admissions Selectivity Rating: 82   **Fire Safety Rating:** 72   **Green Rating:** 60*

STUDENTS AND FACULTY

Enrollment: 3,836. **Student Body:** 67% female, 33% male, 71% out-of-state, 1% international (33 countries represented). Asian 0%, African American 96%, Caucasian 2%, Hispanic 1%, Native American <1%, Pacific Islander <1%, Two or more races 0%, Race unknown <1%.

Retention and Graduation: 80% freshmen return for sophomore year. 63% freshmen graduate within 6 years. **Faculty:** Student/faculty ratio 13:1. 303 full-time faculty, 75% hold PhDs, 75% are are members of minority groups, 45% are women. 0% of classes are taught by teaching assistants.

ACADEMICS

Degrees: associate, bachelor's, certificate, doctoral/professional, doctoral/research, doctoral, master's, post-master's certificate. **Classes:** Most classes have fewer than 10 students. **Most popular majors:** Psychology; Business Administration, Management and Operations; Biology. **Special Study Options:** Accelerated program, cooperative education program, cross-registration, distance learning, double major, dual enrollment, honors program, independent study, internships, study abroad, teacher certification program, Undergrads may take grad level programs. Co-Op Programs: Arts, Business, Education, Engineering,Social/Behavioral Science, Pre-college, Army ROTC, Navy ROTC. Member Tidewater Consortium. **Honors Programs:** Honors College-Designed to augment, enhance and extend the undergraduate academic experience through community, exposure and expectations. Leadership Institute—Offers the undergraduate student a curricular option that enhances the university experience. Combined degree programs: Bachelor of Arts/Master in Teaching. **Disability Services:** Special programs offered to physically disabled students, including note-taking services, reader services, tape recorders, tutors. **Career Services:** Alumni network, Alumni services, Career/job search classes, Career assessment, Internships. Students who experience jobs through Cooperative Education have a chance to determine their life's work while earning academic credit.

FACILITIES

Housing: Coed dorms, men's dorms, special housing for international students, women's dorms. 90% of campus accessible to physically disabled. **Special Academic Facilities/Equipment:** African, Native American, and Oceanic museums, and gallery. New Student Center **Computers:** 100% of classrooms, 100% of dorms, 100% of libraries, 100% of dining areas, 100% of student union, 100% of common outdoor areas have wireless network access. Students can register for classes online. Administrative functions (other than registration) can be performed online.

CAMPUS LIFE

Environment: City. **Activities:** Choral groups, concert band, dance, drama/theater, jazz band, marching band, music ensembles, musical theater, opera, pep band, radio station, student government, student newspaper, symphony orchestra, television station, yearbook. 85 registered organizations, 16 honor societies, 3 religious organizations. 6 fraternities, 3 sororities. **Athletics (Intercollegiate):** *Men:* basketball, cross-country, football, golf, sailing, tennis, track/field (outdoor), track/field (indoor). *Women:* basketball, bowling, cross-country, golf, sailing, softball, tennis, track/field (outdoor), track/field (indoor), volleyball. **On-Campus Highlights:** Emancipation Oak, Memorial Chapel, Huntington Memorial Museum, Booker T. Washington Monument, Student Center: bowling, fitness and movie.

ADMISSIONS

Freshman Academic Profile: Average high school GPA 3.3. 10% in top 10% of high school class, 14% in top 25% of high school class, 52% in top 50% of high school class. 90% from public high schools. **Reported SAT (pre-2016 redesign) scores:** SAT Math middle 50% range 430-530. SAT Critical Reading middle 50% range 430-510. **Concordant SAT scores:** SAT Math middle 50% range 470–560. ACT middle 50% range 19-24. Minimum paper TOEFL 525. **Basis for Candidate Selection:** *Very important factors considered include:* rigor of secondary school record, academic GPA, application essay, character/personal qualities. *Important factors considered include:* class rank, recommendation(s). *Other factors considered include:* extracurricular activities, talent/ability, alumni/ae relation, volunteer work, work experience, level of applicant's interest. **Freshman Admission Requirements:** High school diploma is required and GED is accepted. *Academic units required:* 4 English, 3 math, 2 science, 2 science labs, 2 social studies, 6 academic electives. *Academic units recommended:* 2 foreign language. **Freshman Admission Statistics:** 11,165 applied, 64.82% admitted, 18% enrolled. **Transfer Admission Requirements:** college transcript(s), essay or personal statement, statement of good standing from prior institution(s). Minimum college GPA of 2.3 required. Lowest grade transferable C. **General Admission Information:** Application fee $35. Priority deadline 3/1. Nonfall registration accepted. Admission may be deferred for a maximum of one year.

COSTS AND FINANCIAL AID

Annual tuition $21,552. Room and board $10,684. Required fees $2,690. Average book expense $1,300. **Required Forms and Deadlines:** FAFSA. **Notification of Awards:** Applicants will be notified of awards on a rolling basis beginning 4/15. **Types of Aid:** *Need-based scholarships/grants:* Federal Pell, FSEOG, State scholarships/grants, Private scholarships, College/university scholarship or grant aid from institutional funds, United Negro College Fund. *Loans:* Direct Subsidized Stafford Loans, Direct Unsubsidized Stafford Loans, Direct PLUS loans, Federal Perkins Loans, Federal Nursing Loans. *Student*

Employment: Federal Work-Study Program available. **Financial Aid Statistics:** 95% needy freshmen, 98% needy undergrads receive need-based scholarship or grant aid. 91% freshmen, 69% undergrads receive non-need-based scholarship or grant aid. 88% freshmen, 88% undergrads receive need-based self-help aid. 8% freshmen, 2% undergrads receive athletic scholarships. 39% freshmen, 43% undergrads receive any aid. 73% undergrads borrow to pay for school. Average cumulative indebtedness $1,902. **Criteria for awarding aid:** *Non-need-based:* Academics, Athletics, Job skills, Leadership, Music/drama.

HANNIBAL-LAGRANGE UNIVERSITY

2800 Palmyra Road, Hannibal, MO 63401
Phone: 573-221-3113 • **Financial Aid Phone:** 573-629-3280
E-mail: admissio@hlg.edu
Fax: 573-221-6594 • **Website:** http://www.hlg.edu/ • **ACT Code:** 2320

This private school, affiliated with the Southern Baptist Church, was founded in 1858. It has a 110-acre campus.

RATINGS
Admissions Selectivity Rating: 72   **Fire Safety Rating:** 78   **Green Rating:** 60*

STUDENTS AND FACULTY
Student Body: 26% out-of-state, (11 countries represented).
Retention and Graduation: 58% freshmen return for sophomore year.
Faculty: Student/faculty ratio 11:1. 60 full-time faculty, 28% hold PhDs, 2% are are members of minority groups, 0% of classes are taught by teaching assistants.

ACADEMICS
Degrees: associate, bachelor's, certificate, master's. **Most popular majors:** Secondary Education and Teaching; Elementary Education and Teaching; Non. **Special Study Options:** Accelerated program, distance learning, dual enrollment, English as a Second Language (ESL), honors program, independent study, internships, liberal arts/career combination, student-designed major, study abroad, teacher certification program, weekend college, Adult Program. **Honors Programs:** Honors Program qualifies a student for a semester of study at Harlaxton College, Grantham, England. **Disability Services:** Special programs offered to physically disabled students, including tape recorders, tutors. **Career Services:** Career assessment, Internships, Career Beam online employment exploration and tools.

FACILITIES
Housing: special housing for disabled students, men's dorms, women's dorms, apartments for single students. 98% of campus accessible to physically diasbled. **Special Academic Facilities/Equipment:** L.A. Foster Library, T.M. Matthews Science Building, Mary Wiehe Science Building, Partee Tech. Center, Roland Fine Arts Center. **Computers:** Students can register for classes online.

CAMPUS LIFE
Environment: Village. **Activities:** Choral groups, concert band, drama/theater, jazz band, music ensembles, musical theater, student government, student newspaper, yearbook, Campus Ministries, Student Organization. 22 registered organizations, 1 honor society, 3 religious organizations. **Athletics (Intercollegiate):** *Men:* baseball, basketball, cross-country, golf, soccer, swimming, track/field (outdoor), volleyball, wrestling. *Women:* basketball, cheerleading, cross-country, golf, soccer, softball, swimming, track/field (outdoor), volleyball. **On-Campus Highlights:** Roland Fine Arts Center, Mabee Sports Complex, Common Grounds, Snack Shack, Carroll Mission Center.

ADMISSIONS
Freshman Academic Profile: 21% in top 10% of high school class, 37% in top 25% of high school class, 52% in top 50% of high school class. **Reported SAT (pre-2016 redesign) scores:** SAT Math middle 50% range 440–480. SAT Critical Reading middle 50% range 260–490. SAT Writing middle 50% range 420–480. **Concordant SAT scores:** SAT EBRW middle 50% 390–540. SAT Math middle 50% range 480–510. ACT middle 50% range 19-24. Minimum paper TOEFL 520. **Basis for Candidate Selection:** *Very important factors considered include:* academic GPA, standardized test scores. *Important factors considered include:* rigor of secondary school record. *Other factors considered include:* class rank, recommendation(s), talent/ability, character/personal qualities, religious affiliation/commitment, level of applicant's interest. **Freshman Admission Requirements:** High school diploma is required and GED is accepted. *Academic units recommended:* 4 English, 3 math, 2 science, 1 science lab, 3 history. **Transfer Admission Requirements:** college transcript(s), Minimum college GPA of 2.0 required. Lowest grade transferable 1. **General Admission Information:** Application fee $25. Nonfall registration accepted. Admission may be deferred for a maximum of 1 semester.

COSTS AND FINANCIAL AID
Annual tuition $20,010. Room and board $5,608. Required fees $550. Average book expense $800. **Required Forms and Deadlines:** FAFSA, Institution's own financial aid form. **Types of Aid:** *Need-based scholarships/grants:* Federal Pell, FSEOG, State scholarships/grants, Private scholarships, College/university scholarship or grant aid from institutional funds. *Loans:* Federal Perkins Loans. *Student Employment:* Federal Work-Study Program available. Institutional employment available. **Criteria for awarding aid:** *Non-need-based:* Academics, Art, Athletics, Music/drama, Religious affiliation.

HANOVER COLLEGE

P.O. Box 108, Hanover, IN 47243-0108
Phone: 800-213-2178 • **Financial Aid Phone:** 812-866-7029
E-mail: admission@hanover.edu • **CEEB Code:** 1290
Fax: 812-866-7098 • **Website:** www.hanover.edu • **ACT Code:** 1200

This private school, affiliated with the Presbyterian Church, was founded in 1827. It has a 650-acre campus.

RATINGS
Admissions Selectivity Rating: 85   **Fire Safety Rating:** 94   **Green Rating:** 79

STUDENTS AND FACULTY
Enrollment: 1,083. **Student Body:** 57% female, 43% male, 32% out-of-state, 4% international (25 countries represented). Asian 1%, African American 5%, Caucasian 81%, Hispanic 3%, Native American 1%, Pacific Islander <1%, Two or more races 1%, Race unknown 4%.
Retention and Graduation: 82% freshmen return for sophomore year. 67% freshmen graduate within 4 years. 71% freshmen graduate within 6 years. 22% grads go on to further study within 1 year. 16% grads pursue arts and sciences degrees. 3% grads pursue law degrees. 2% grads pursue business degrees. 2% grads pursue medical degrees. **Faculty:** Student/faculty ratio 12:1. 87 full-time faculty, 99% hold PhDs, 7% are are members of minority groups, 43% are women. 0% of classes are taught by teaching assistants.

ACADEMICS
Degrees: bachelor's. **Classes:** Most classes have 10-19 students. **Most popular majors:** Speech Communication and Rhetoric; Economics; Psychology. **Special Study Options:** double major, dual enrollment, independent study, internships, student-designed major, study abroad, teacher certification program, CBP (Center for Business Preparation) Business Scholar Program, Philadelphia Center and Washington Center Internship Programs. **Disability Services:** Special programs offered to physically disabled students, including note-taking services, tutors. **Career Services:** Alumni network, Alumni services, Career/job search classes, Career assessment, Internships, Regional alumni. Hanover College curriculum teaches students to communicate effectively, think critically, and solve problems creatively. Through a variety of experiential learning opportunities and networking events, the Business Scholars Program builds upon the liberal arts foundation by emphasizing personal leadership development and team working skills.

FACILITIES
Housing: Coed dorms, men's dorms, women's dorms, fraternity/sorority housing, apartments for single students, Wellness Housing, Theme Housing. 50% of campus accessible to physically diasbled. **Special Academic Facilities/Equipment:** cadaver lab, geological museum, electronic language lab, observatory **Computers:** 80% of classrooms, 100% of dorms, 50% of libraries, 100% of dining areas, 100% of student union, 20% of common outdoor areas have wireless network access. Students can register for classes online. Administrative functions (other than registration) can be performed online.

CAMPUS LIFE
Environment: Rural. **Activities:** Choral groups, concert band, dance, drama/theater, jazz band, literary magazine, music ensembles, musical theater, pep band, radio station, student government, student newspaper, student-run film society, symphony orchestra, television station, yearbook, Campus Ministries, Student Organization. 60 registered organizations, 8 honor societies, 4 religious organizations. 4 fraternities, 4 sororities. **Athletics (Intercollegiate):** *Men:* baseball, basketball, cross-country, football, golf, lacrosse, soccer, tennis, track/field (outdoor). *Women:* basketball, cross-country, golf, soccer, softball, tennis, track/field (outdoor), volleyball. **On-Campus Highlights:** Science Center, Horner Health and Recreation Center (Collier Arena), Campus Center, The

Shoebox, The Point-River View, The Shoebox serves food and drinks, as does the new coffee house in Crowe Hall. **Environmental Initiatives:** The College is currently developing a new strategic plan and re-evaluating our green initiatives and sustainability program as an integral component of the plan.

ADMISSIONS

Freshman Academic Profile: Average high school GPA 3.7. 25% in top 10% of high school class, 55% in top 25% of high school class, 91% in top 50% of high school class. 85% from public high schools. **Reported SAT (pre-2016 redesign) scores:** SAT Math middle 50% range 470-570. SAT Critical Reading middle 50% range 470-580. SAT Writing middle 50% range 440-560. **Concordant SAT scores:** SAT EBRW middle 50% 510-630. SAT Math middle 50% range 510-590. ACT middle 50% range 22-27. Minimum internet-based TOEFL 80. Minimum paper TOEFL 550. **Basis for Candidate Selection:** *Very important factors considered include:* rigor of secondary school record, class rank, academic GPA. *Important factors considered include:* standardized test scores, recommendation(s), talent/ability. *Other factors considered include:* application essay, interview, extracurricular activities, character/personal qualities, first generation, alumni/ae relation, geographical residence, state residency, racial/ethnic status, volunteer work, work experience, level of applicant's interest. **Freshman Admission Requirements:** High school diploma is required and GED is not accepted. *Academic units required:* 4 English, 3 math, 3 science, 2 science labs, 2 foreign language, 2 social studies, 2 history, 2 academic electives. *Academic units recommended:* 4 English, 4 math, 4 science, 4 science labs, 4 foreign language, 3 social studies, 3 history, 3 academic electives, 1 visual/performing arts. **Freshman Admission Statistics:** 3,696 applied, 57.33% admitted, 15% enrolled. **Transfer Admission Requirements:** High school transcript, college transcript(s), essay or personal statement, standardized test scores, statement of good standing from prior institution(s). Minimum college GPA of 2.0 required. Lowest grade transferable C-. **General Admission Information:** Nonfall registration accepted. Admission may be deferred for a maximum of 1 year.

COSTS AND FINANCIAL AID

Annual tuition $34,744. Room and board $10,850. Required fees $770. Average book expense $1,200. **Required Forms and Deadlines:** FAFSA. **Notification of Awards:** Applicants will be notified of awards on or about 3/1. **Types of Aid:** *Need-based scholarships/grants:* Federal Pell, FSEOG, State scholarships/grants, Private scholarships, College/university scholarship or grant aid from institutional funds. *Loans:* Direct Subsidized Stafford Loans, Direct Unsubsidized Stafford Loans, Direct PLUS loans, College/university loans from institutional funds. *Student Employment:* Federal Work-Study Program available. Institutional employment available. **Financial Aid Statistics:** 100% needy freshmen, 100% needy undergrads receive need-based scholarship or grant aid. 21% freshmen, 16% undergrads receive non-need-based scholarship or grant aid. 67% freshmen, 76% undergrads receive need-based self-help aid. 0% freshmen, 0% undergrads receive athletic scholarships. 100% freshmen, 100% undergrads receive any aid. 76% undergrads borrow to pay for school. Average cumulative indebtedness $29,745. **Criteria for awarding aid:** *Need-based:* Academics, Alumni affiliation, Art, Leadership, Minority status, Music/drama, Religious affiliation. *Non-need-based:* Academics, Alumni affiliation, Art, Leadership, Minority status, Music/drama, Religious affiliation, State/district residency.

HARDIN-SIMMONS UNIVERSITY

Box 16050, Abilene, TX 79698
Phone: 325-670-1206 • **Financial Aid Phone:** 325-670-1206
E-mail: enroll@hsutx.edu • **CEEB Code:** 6268
Fax: 325-671-2115 • **Website:** www.hsutx.edu • **ACT Code:** 4096

This private school was founded in 1891. It has a 209-acre campus.

RATINGS

Admissions Selectivity Rating: 78   **Fire Safety Rating:** 76   **Green Rating:** 71

STUDENTS AND FACULTY

Enrollment: 1,621. **Student Body:** 55% female, 45% male, 4% out-of-state, 1% international (26 countries represented). Asian 1%, African American 7%, Caucasian 69%, Hispanic 17%, Native American <1%, Pacific Islander <1%, Two or more races 4%, Race unknown 1%.
Retention and Graduation: 71% freshmen return for sophomore year. 37% freshmen graduate within 4 years. 52% freshmen graduate within 6 years. 45% grads go on to further study within 1 year. 17% grads pursue arts and sciences degrees. 3% grads pursue law degrees. 2% grads pursue business degrees. 7% grads pursue medical degrees. **Faculty:** Student/faculty ratio 12:1. 136 full-time faculty, 90% hold PhDs, 4% are are members of minority groups, 38% are women. 0% of classes are taught by teaching assistants.

ACADEMICS

Degrees: bachelor's, doctoral/professional, doctoral/research, doctoral, master's, post-master's certificate. **Classes:** Most classes have 10-19 students. Most lab/discussion sessions have 20-29 students. **Most popular majors:** Business, Management, Marketing, and Related Support Services; Registered Nursing/Registered Nurse; Education. **Special Study Options:** Accelerated program, cross-registration, distance learning, double major, dual enrollment, honors program, independent study, internships, study abroad, teacher certification program. **Honors Programs:** The Hardin-Simmons University Honors Program provides an enriched educational environment for undergraduate students of exceptional promise who have a wide variety of interests and seek an enhanced learning opportunity. The Honors Program promotes creative and critical thinking skills to equip individuals for success in today's world. The Program, which serves as an integral part of the academic community, includes courses taught by selected faculty members interested in working with highly motivated students. The Honors Program expects participants to strive for excellence and assume personal accountability for their intellectual growth. **Disability Services:** Special programs offered to physically disabled students, including note-taking services, reader services, tape recorders, tutors. **Career Services:** Alumni network, Alumni services, Career/job search classes, Career assessment, Internships, Regional alumni. Internship program—the Office of Career Services at HSU hosts internship listings through our online service, College Central Network. In addition, many academic departments have a specific faculty person designated to help students find internship opportunities within their field of study.

FACILITIES

Housing: special housing for disabled students, men's dorms, women's dorms, apartments for married students, apartments for single students, Single and Duplex housing with priority given to families. 100% of campus accessible to physically diasbled. **Special Academic Facilities/Equipment:** Art center, observatory with 14-inch telescope, rare and fine book room, Six White Horse facility, Holland Health Science Medical High School **Computers:** 90% of classrooms, 100% of dorms, 80% of libraries, 100% of dining areas, 100% of student union, 50% of common outdoor areas have wireless network access.

CAMPUS LIFE

Environment: City. **Activities:** Choral groups, concert band, drama/theater, jazz band, literary magazine, marching band, music ensembles, musical theater, opera, student government, student newspaper, symphony orchestra, yearbook, Campus Ministries, Student Organization, Model UN. 15 honor societies, 1 religious organization. 4 fraternities, 4 sororities. **Athletics (Intercollegiate):** *Men:* baseball, basketball, cheerleading, cross-country, football, golf, soccer, tennis, track/field (outdoor). *Women:* basketball, cheerleading, cross-country, golf, soccer, softball, tennis, track/field (outdoor), volleyball. **On-Campus Highlights:** Moody Center (Student Center), Java City Coffee House, The Pond/Gazebo, Dorm Lobbies, The Pool, Gym/Fitness Center; Connally Mission Center; Skiles Social Science Building. **Environmental Initiatives:** Estabishing a recycling program.

ADMISSIONS

Freshman Academic Profile: Average high school GPA 3.7. 19% in top 10% of high school class, 53% in top 25% of high school class, 84% in top 50% of high school class. 91% from public high schools. **Reported SAT (pre-2016 redesign) scores:** SAT Math middle 50% range 470-580. SAT Critical Reading middle 50% range 450-560. SAT Writing middle 50% range 440-538. **Concordant SAT scores:** SAT EBRW middle 50% 500-610. SAT Math middle 50% range 510-600. ACT middle 50% range 19-24. Minimum internet-based TOEFL 75. Minimum paper TOEFL 550. **Basis for Candidate Selection:** *Very important factors considered include:* class rank, academic GPA, standardized test scores. *Important factors considered include:* rigor of secondary school record, recommendation(s), talent/ability, character/personal qualities. *Other factors considered include:* extracurricular activities, alumni/ae relation, religious affiliation/commitment, level of applicant's interest. **Freshman Admission Requirements:** High school diploma is required and GED is accepted. *Academic units required:* 4 English, 4 math, 4 science, 2 foreign language, 4 social studies, 1 visual/performing arts. **Freshman Admission Statistics:** 1,149 applied, 87.99% admitted, 39% enrolled. **Transfer Admission Requirements:** college transcript(s), Minimum college GPA of 2.0 required. Lowest grade transferable C. **General Admission Information:** Nonfall registration accepted. Admission may be deferred for a maximum of 12 months.

COSTS AND FINANCIAL AID

Annual tuition $26,240. Room and board $8,420. Required fees $1,200. Average book expense $800. **Required Forms and Deadlines:** FAFSA. **Notification of Awards:** Applicants will be notified of awards on a rolling basis beginning 3/1. **Types of Aid:** *Need-based scholarships/grants:* Federal Pell, FSEOG, State scholarships/grants, Private scholarships, College/university scholarship or grant aid from institutional funds. *Loans:* Direct Subsidized Stafford Loans, Direct Unsubsidized Stafford Loans, Direct PLUS loans, Federal Perkins Loans, Federal Nursing Loans, State Loans, College/university loans from institutional funds. *Student Employment:* Federal Work-Study Program available. Institutional employment available. **Financial Aid Statistics:** 72% needy freshmen, 76% needy undergrads receive need-based scholarship or grant aid. 100% freshmen, 96% undergrads receive non-need-based scholarship or grant aid. 88% freshmen, 90% undergrads receive need-based self-help aid. 0% freshmen, 0% undergrads receive athletic scholarships. 99% freshmen, 98% undergrads receive any aid. 66% undergrads borrow to pay for school. Average cumulative indebtedness $39,597. **Criteria for awarding aid:** *Non-need-based:* Academics, Alumni affiliation, Art, Leadership, Minority status, Music/drama, Religious affiliation.

HARDING UNIVERSITY

Box 12255, Searcy, AR 72149
Phone: 501-279-4407 • **Financial Aid Phone:** 501-279-4257
E-mail: admissions@harding.edu • **CEEB Code:** 10311
Fax: 501-279-4129 • **Website:** www.harding.edu • **ACT Code:** 124

This private school, affiliated with the Church of Christ Church, was founded in 1924. It has a 275-acre campus.

RATINGS
Admissions Selectivity Rating: 84   **Fire Safety Rating:** 91   **Green Rating:** 60*

STUDENTS AND FACULTY
Enrollment: 3,399. **Student Body:** 56% female, 44% male, 68% out-of-state, 8% international (44 countries represented). Asian 1%, African American 5%, Caucasian 81%, Hispanic 3%, Native American 1%, Pacific Islander 0%, Two or more races 2%, Race unknown <1%.
Retention and Graduation: 82% freshmen return for sophomore year. 43% freshmen graduate within 4 years. 64% freshmen graduate within 6 years. **Faculty:** Student/faculty ratio 15:1. 332 full-time faculty, 67% hold PhDs, 5% are are members of minority groups, 32% are women. 0% of classes are taught by teaching assistants.

ACADEMICS
Degrees: bachelor's, doctoral/professional, doctoral/research, master's, post-master's certificate. **Classes:** Most classes have 10-19 students. Most lab/discussion sessions have 10-19 students. **Most popular majors:** Early Childhood Education and Teaching; Business Administration and Management; Accounting. **Special Study Options:** Accelerated program, cooperative education program, distance learning, double major, dual enrollment, English as a Second Language (ESL), honors program, independent study, internships, liberal arts/career combination, study abroad, teacher certification program. Combined degree programs: BA/PharmD. **Disability Services:** Special programs offered to physically disabled students, including note-taking services, reader services, tape recorders, tutors. **Career Services:** Alumni network, Alumni services, Career/job search classes, Career assessment, Internships.

FACILITIES
Housing: special housing for disabled students, men's dorms, women's dorms, apartments for married students, apartments for single students, Approved Off-Campus Housing. 95% of campus accessible to physically diasbled. **Special Academic Facilities/Equipment:** On-campus academy (prep school grades K-12). **Computers:** 95% of classrooms, 100% of libraries, 100% of dining areas, 100% of student union, 80% of common outdoor areas have wireless network access. Students can register for classes online. Administrative functions (other than registration) can be performed online.

CAMPUS LIFE
Environment: Village. **Activities:** Choral groups, concert band, drama/theater, jazz band, marching band, music ensembles, pep band, radio station, student government, student newspaper, symphony orchestra, television station, yearbook, Campus Ministries, Student Organization. 100 registered organizations, 12 honor societies, 10 religious organizations. 14 fraternities, 15 sororities. **Athletics (Intercollegiate):** *Men:* baseball, basketball, cross-country, football, golf, soccer, tennis, track/field (outdoor). *Women:* basketball, cheerleading, cross-country, golf, soccer, tennis, track/field (outdoor), volleyball. **On-Campus Highlights:** Cyber Cafe in Student Center, Front Lawn with Swings, Campus Dining until 9:00pm, Rhodes Memorial Field House, First Security Stadium. **Environmental Initiatives:** Recycling.

ADMISSIONS
Freshman Academic Profile: Average high school GPA 3.6. 24% in top 10% of high school class, 42% in top 25% of high school class, 61% in top 50% of high school class. 66% from public high schools. **Reported SAT (pre-2016 redesign) scores:** SAT Math middle 50% range 480-610. SAT Critical Reading middle 50% range 500-610. **Concordant SAT scores:** SAT Math middle 50% range 510–630. ACT middle 50% range 22-28. Minimum internet-based

---

TOEFL 79. Minimum paper TOEFL 550. **Basis for Candidate Selection:** *Very important factors considered include:* rigor of secondary school record, standardized test scores, recommendation(s), interview, character/personal qualities. *Important factors considered include:* class rank, academic GPA, talent/ability. *Other factors considered include:* application essay, extracurricular activities, first generation, alumni/ae relation, geographical residence, state residency, volunteer work, work experience, level of applicant's interest. **Freshman Admission Requirements:** High school diploma is required and GED is accepted. *Academic units required:* 4 English, 3 math, 2 science, 3 social studies, 3 academic electives. *Academic units recommended:* 4 English, 4 math, 4 science, 2 foreign language, 4 social studies, 2 academic electives. **Freshman Admission Statistics:** 2,184 applied, 76.14% admitted, 61% enrolled. **Transfer Admission Requirements:** college transcript(s), essay or personal statement, statement of good standing from prior institution(s). Minimum college GPA of 2 required. Lowest grade transferable C. **General Admission Information:** Application fee $50. Nonfall registration accepted. Admission may be deferred for a maximum of One Year.

COSTS AND FINANCIAL AID
Annual tuition $17,940. Room and board $6,756. Required fees $500. Average book expense $1,200. **Required Forms and Deadlines:** FAFSA. **Notification of Awards:** Applicants will be notified of awards on a rolling basis beginning 2/15. **Types of Aid:** *Need-based scholarships/grants:* Federal Pell, FSEOG, State scholarships/grants, Private scholarships, College/university scholarship or grant aid from institutional funds. *Loans:* Direct Subsidized Stafford Loans, Direct Unsubsidized Stafford Loans, Direct PLUS loans, Federal Perkins Loans, Federal Nursing Loans, College/university loans from institutional funds. *Student Employment:* Federal Work-Study Program available. Institutional employment available. **Financial Aid Statistics:** 98% needy freshmen, 92% needy undergrads receive need-based scholarship or grant aid. 21% freshmen, 17% undergrads receive non-need-based scholarship or grant aid. 69% freshmen, 77% undergrads receive need-based self-help aid. 4% freshmen, 4% undergrads receive athletic scholarships. 99% freshmen, 94% undergrads receive any aid. 66% undergrads borrow to pay for school. Average cumulative indebtedness $30,570. **Criteria for awarding aid:** *Need-based:* Academics, Alumni affiliation, Job skills, Minority status. *Non-need-based:* Academics, Alumni affiliation, Art, Athletics, Leadership, Music/drama, Religious affiliation, State/district residency.

HARRISBURG UNIVERSITY OF SCIENCE AND TECHNOLOGY

326 Market Street, Harrisburg, PA 17101
Phone: 717-901-5101 • **Financial Aid Phone:** 717-901-5115
E-mail: admissions@HarrisburgU.edu • **CEEB Code:** 4511
Fax: 717-901-3101 • **Website:** www.HarrisburgU.edu • **ACT Code:** 3637

This private school was founded in 2001. It has a 2-acre campus.

RATINGS
Admissions Selectivity Rating: 76   **Fire Safety Rating:** 60*   **Green Rating:** 60*

STUDENTS AND FACULTY
Enrollment: 272. **Student Body:** 46% female, 54% male, 17% out-of-state, 1% international (3 countries represented). Asian 4%, African American 32%, Caucasian 49%, Hispanic 8%, Native American <1%, Pacific Islander 0%, Two or more races 3%, Race unknown 2%.
Retention and Graduation: 54% freshmen return for sophomore year. 12% freshmen graduate within 4 years. 20% freshmen graduate within 6 years. 10% grads go on to further study within 1 year. 10% grads pursue arts and sciences degrees. **Faculty:** Student/faculty ratio 11:1. 10 full-time faculty, 100% hold PhDs, 40% are are members of minority groups, 50% are women. 0% of classes are taught by teaching assistants.

ACADEMICS
Degrees: bachelor's, master's. **Most popular majors:** Computer and Information Sciences; Biotechnology; Physical Sciences. **Special Study Options:** dual enrollment, internships, student-designed major. **Career Services:** Internships, On-campus interviews.

FACILITIES
Housing: 100% of campus accessible to physically diasbled. **Computers:** 100% of classrooms, 100% of libraries, 100% of dining areas, 100% of student union, 100% of common outdoor areas have wireless network access. Students can register for classes online. Administrative functions (other than registration) can be performed online. Undergraduates are required to own a computer.

CAMPUS LIFE
Environment: City. **Activities: On-Campus Highlights:** Conference Center.

ADMISSIONS
Freshman Academic Profile: 90% from public high schools. **Reported SAT (pre-2016 redesign) scores:** SAT Math middle 50% range 420-550. SAT Critical Reading middle 50% range 440-530. SAT Writing middle 50% range 390-510. **Concordant SAT scores:** SAT EBRW middle 50% 460–580. SAT Math middle 50% range 460–570. ACT middle 50% range 20-24. Minimum paper TOEFL 80. **Basis for Candidate Selection:** *Very important factors considered include:* academic GPA, application essay. *Important factors considered include:* interview. *Other factors considered include:* standardized test scores, recommendation(s). **Freshman Admission Statistics:** 1,827 applied, 47.40% admitted, 15% enrolled. **General Admission Information:** Nonfall registration accepted.

COSTS AND FINANCIAL AID
Annual tuition $23,800. Required fees $0. Average book expense $1,500. **Required Forms and Deadlines:** FAFSA. **Types of Aid:** *Need-based scholarships/grants:* Federal Pell, FSEOG, State scholarships/grants, Private scholarships, College/university scholarship or grant aid from institutional funds. *Loans:* Direct Subsidized Stafford Loans, Direct Unsubsidized Stafford Loans, Direct PLUS loans. *Student Employment:* Federal Work-Study Program available. Institutional employment available. **Financial Aid Statistics:** 99% needy freshmen, 100% needy undergrads receive need-based scholarship or grant aid. 9% freshmen, 6% undergrads receive non-need-based scholarship or grant aid. 87% freshmen, 82% undergrads receive need-based self-help aid. 0% freshmen, 0% undergrads receive athletic scholarships. 98% freshmen, 94% undergrads receive any aid. **Criteria for awarding aid:** *Non-need-based:* Academics.

HARTWICK COLLEGE

PO Box 4022, Oneonta, NY 13820-4020
Phone: 607-431-4154 • **Financial Aid Phone:** 607-431-4130
E-mail: admissions@hartwick.edu • **CEEB Code:** 2288
Fax: 607-431-4102 • **Website:** www.hartwick.edu/ • **ACT Code:** 2756

This private school was founded in 1797. It has a 425-acre campus.

RATINGS
Admissions Selectivity Rating: 73   **Fire Safety Rating:** 93   **Green Rating:** 68

STUDENTS AND FACULTY
Enrollment: 1,382. **Student Body:** 60% female, 40% male, 23% out-of-state, 3% international (35 countries represented). Asian 2%, African American 9%, Caucasian 65%, Hispanic 8%, Native American <1%, Pacific Islander <1%, Two or more races 2%, Race unknown 11%.
Retention and Graduation: 75% freshmen return for sophomore year. 54% freshmen graduate within 4 years. 61% freshmen graduate within 6 years. 29% grads go on to further study within 1 year. 21% grads pursue arts and sciences degrees. **Faculty:** Student/faculty ratio 10:1. 110 full-time faculty, 88% hold PhDs, 12% are are members of minority groups, 45% are women. 0% of classes are taught by teaching assistants.

ACADEMICS
Degrees: bachelor's. **Classes:** Most classes have 10-19 students. Most lab/discussion sessions have 30-39 students. **Most popular majors:** Psychology; Business Administration and Management; Registered Nursing, Nursing Administration, Nursing Research and Clinical Nursing. **Special Study Options:** Accelerated program, cross-registration, double major, exchange student program (domestic), honors program, independent study, internships, student-designed major, study abroad, teacher certification program, January thematic term, study abroad/international internships. **Honors Programs:** Requirements for the Honors Program are: Challenges—4 must be completed by graduation; Divisions—3 must be represented in Challenges; Honors Forum—a presentation of a project; Academic Excellence—a 3.50 Grade Point Average. Also, students in the Honors program can choose to live on the Honors floor in a campus residence hall. Combined degree programs: BA/JD, BA/MEng, JD with Albany Law School. **Disability Services:** Special programs offered to physically disabled students, including reader services, tape recorders, tutors. **Career Services:** Alumni network, Career/job search classes, Internships, On-campus interviews. Learning outside the classroom is an integral part of preparing our students for careers after graduation and why we've designed our curriculum and teaching approaches to break down the barriers that separate the classroom from the world. As a Hartwick student, you'll get to learn "out there" and bring that experience back, making your time in the classroom more engaging and effective.

FACILITIES
Housing: Coed dorms, women's dorms, fraternity/sorority housing, apartments for single students, Housing at Pine Lake environmental campus (lodge and cabins) also available. 50% of campus accessible to physically diasbled. **Special Academic Facilities/Equipment:** Art and history museums, Indian artifact collection, environmental center, observatory, electron microscope, tissue culture lab, spectrophotometers. **Computers:** 100% of classrooms, 100% of dorms, 100% of libraries, 50% of dining areas, 50% of student union, have wireless network access. Students can register for classes online. Administrative functions (other than registration) can be performed online.

CAMPUS LIFE
Environment: Village. **Activities:** Choral groups, dance, drama/theater, literary magazine, music ensembles, pep band, radio station, student government, student newspaper, yearbook, Campus Ministries. 70 registered organizations, 30 honor societies, 3 religious organizations. 3 fraternities, 3 sororities. **Athletics (Intercollegiate):** *Men:* basketball, cross-country, diving, football, lacrosse, soccer, swimming, tennis. *Women:* basketball, cheerleading, cross-country, diving, equestrian sports, field hockey, lacrosse, soccer, swimming, tennis, volleyball, water polo. **On-Campus Highlights:** Yager Museum, Stevens-German Library, Johnstone Science Center, Binder Athletic Facility, Dewar Student Union. **Environmental Initiatives:** Hartwick is a signatory of the Talloires Declaration and is a member of the Association for the Advancement of Sustainability in Higher Education. In 2005, the College received a Kresge Green Building Iniative planning grant to partially fund green design of its first LEED-certified building, Golisano Hall. In keeping with Hartwick's emphasis on hands-on learning, the project provided the basis for a course entitled "Sustainable Design", taught by Richard Rittelman, FAIA principal architect and Karl Seeley, PhD. of Hartwick's economics department. The LEED-certification process for Golisano Hall is currently underway. The process involves commissioning the building's systems, which are estimated to use 75% less energy than the average building on Hartwick's campus.

ADMISSIONS
Freshman Academic Profile: Average high school GPA 86.5. 9% in top 10% of high school class, 36% in top 25% of high school class, 71% in top 50% of high school class. 86% from public high schools. **Reported SAT (pre-2016 redesign) scores:** SAT Math middle 50% range 450-550. SAT Critical Reading middle 50% range 450-540. **Concordant SAT scores:** SAT Math middle 50% range 490–570. ACT middle 50% range 19-25. Minimum internet-based TOEFL 79. Minimum paper TOEFL 550. **Basis for Candidate Selection:** *Very important factors considered include:* rigor of secondary school record, academic GPA. *Important factors considered include:* extracurricular activities, character/personal qualities, alumni/ae relation, volunteer work, work experience. *Other factors considered include:* class rank, standardized test scores, application essay, recommendation(s), interview, talent/ability, level of applicant's interest. **Freshman Admission Requirements:** High school diploma is required and GED is accepted. *Academic units recommended:* 4 English, 3 math, 3 science, 2 science labs, 3 foreign language, 2 social studies, 2 history. **Freshman Admission Statistics:** 3,085 applied, 93.65% admitted, 14% enrolled. **Transfer Admission Requirements:** college transcript(s), essay or personal statement, statement of good standing from prior institution(s). Minimum college GPA of 2.0 required. Lowest grade transferable C-. **General Admission Information:** Nonfall registration accepted. Admission may be deferred for a maximum of 12 months.

COSTS AND FINANCIAL AID
Required Forms and Deadlines: FAFSA. **Notification of Awards:** Applicants will be notified of awards on a rolling basis beginning 1/15. **Types of Aid:** *Need-based scholarships/grants:* Federal Pell, FSEOG, State scholarships/grants, Private scholarships, College/university scholarship or grant aid from institutional funds. *Loans:* Direct Subsidized Stafford Loans, Direct Unsubsidized Stafford Loans, Direct PLUS loans, Federal Perkins Loans, Federal Nursing Loans, College/university loans from institutional funds. *Student Employment:* Federal Work-Study Program available. Institutional employment available. **Financial Aid Statistics:** 99% needy freshmen, 99% needy undergrads receive need-based scholarship or grant aid. 14% freshmen, 12% undergrads receive non-need-based scholarship or grant aid. 86% freshmen, 86% undergrads receive need-based self-help aid. 2% freshmen, 2% undergrads receive athletic scholarships. 87% freshmen, 83% undergrads receive any aid. 71% undergrads borrow to pay for school. Average cumulative indebtedness $27,653. **Criteria for awarding aid:** *Need-based:* Music/drama. *Non-need-based:* Academics, Alumni affiliation, Art, Athletics, Music/drama.

HARVARD COLLEGE

86 Brattle Street, Cambridge, MA 2138
Phone: 617-495-1551 • **Financial Aid Phone:** 617-495-1581
E-mail: college@fas.harvard.edu • **CEEB Code:** 3434
Fax: 617-495-8821 • **Website:** www.college.harvard.edu • **ACT Code:** 1840

This private school was founded in 1636. It has a 380-acre campus.

RATINGS
Admissions Selectivity Rating: 99   **Fire Safety Rating:** 60*   **Green Rating:** 97

STUDENTS AND FACULTY
Enrollment: 6,648. **Student Body:** 47% female, 53% male, 84% out-of-state, 12% international (100 countries represented). Asian 20%, African American 7%, Caucasian 41%, Hispanic 11%, Native American <1%, Pacific Islander <1%, Two or more races 7%, Race unknown 2%.
Retention and Graduation: 97% freshmen return for sophomore year. 86% freshmen graduate within 4 years. 96% freshmen graduate within 6 years.
Faculty: Student/faculty ratio 7:1. 973 full-time faculty, 86% hold PhDs, 21% are are members of minority groups, 33% are women. 0% of classes are taught by teaching assistants.

ACADEMICS
Degrees: bachelor's, doctoral/research, master's. **Classes:** Most classes have fewer than 10 students. Most lab/discussion sessions have 20-29 students. **Most popular majors:** Political Science and Government; Economics; Social Sciences. **Special Study Options:** Accelerated program, cross-registration, double major, exchange student program (domestic), honors program, independent study, internships, student-designed major, study abroad, teacher certification program. Combined degree programs: BA/MA, BA/MEng. **Disability Services:** Special programs offered to physically disabled students, including note-taking services, reader services, tape recorders, tutors. **Career Services:** Alumni network, Alumni services.

FACILITIES
Housing: Coed dorms, special housing for disabled students, apartments for married students, cooperative housing **Special Academic Facilities/ Equipment:** Museums (University Arts Museums, Museums of Cultural History, many others), language labs, observatory, many science and research laboratories and facilities, new state-of-the-art computer science facility. **Computers:** 98% of classrooms, 100% of dorms, 100% of libraries, have wireless network access. Students can register for classes online. Administrative functions (other than registration) can be performed online.

CAMPUS LIFE
Environment: City. **Activities:** Choral groups, concert band, dance, drama/theater, jazz band, literary magazine, marching band, music ensembles, musical theater, opera, pep band, radio station, student government, student newspaper, student-run film society, symphony orchestra, television station, yearbook, Campus Ministries, Student Organization, Model UN. 393 registered organizations, 1 honor society, 28 religious organizations. **Athletics (Intercollegiate):** *Men:* baseball, basketball, crew/rowing, cross-country, diving, fencing, football, golf, ice hockey, lacrosse, sailing, skiing (downhill/alpine), skiing (nordic/cross-country), soccer, squash, swimming, tennis, track/field (outdoor), track/field (indoor), volleyball, water polo, wrestling. *Women:* basketball, crew/rowing, cross-country, diving, fencing, field hockey, golf, ice hockey, lacrosse, sailing, skiing (downhill/alpine), skiing (nordic/cross-country), soccer, softball, squash, swimming, tennis, track/field (outdoor), track/field (indoor), volleyball, water polo. **On-Campus Highlights:** Widener Library, Harvard Yard, Fogg Museum, Annenburg/Memorial Hall, Science Center. **Environmental Initiatives:** Campus-wide Sustainability Principles that provide a broad vision to guide University operations and planning (adopted in 2004) and an established University-wide Office for Sustainability (green.harvard.edu) that oversees implementation of Harvard GHG reduction goal and sustainability commitments. The University has had a formal sustainability office for a decade initially created by a faculty and staff initiative with strong student involvement.

ADMISSIONS
Freshman Academic Profile: Average high school GPA 4.2. 95% in top 10% of high school class, 99% in top 25% of high school class, 100% in top 50% of high school class. 58% from public high schools. **Reported SAT (pre-2016 redesign) scores:** SAT Math middle 50% range 720-800. SAT Critical Reading middle 50% range 710-800. SAT Writing middle 50% range 710-800. **Concordant SAT scores:** SAT EBRW middle 50% 740–800. SAT Math middle 50% range 750–800. ACT middle 50% range 32-35. **Basis for Candidate Selection:** *Other factors considered include:* rigor of secondary school record, academic GPA, standardized test scores, application essay, recommendation(s), interview, extracurricular activities, talent/ability, character/personal qualities, first generation, alumni/ae relation, geographical residence, racial/ethnic status, volunteer work, work experience. **Freshman Admission Requirements:** High school diploma or equivalent is not required. *Academic units recommended:* 4 English, 4 math, 4 science, 4 foreign language, 3 social studies, 2 history. **Freshman Admission Statistics:** 39,041 applied, 5.40% admitted, 79% enrolled. **General Admission Information:** Application fee $75. Regular application deadline 1/1. Regular notification 4/1. Nonfall registration not accepted. Admission may be deferred for a maximum of 1 Year.

COSTS AND FINANCIAL AID
Annual tuition $43,280. Room and board $15,951. Required fees $3,794. Average book expense $1,000. **Required Forms and Deadlines:** FAFSA, CSS/Financial Aid PROFILE, Noncustodial PROFILE, Business/Farm Supplement. **Notification of Awards:** Applicants will be notified of awards on or about 4/1. **Types of Aid:** *Need-based scholarships/grants:* Federal Pell, FSEOG, State scholarships/grants, Private scholarships, College/university scholarship or grant aid from institutional funds. *Loans:* Direct Subsidized Stafford Loans, Direct Unsubsidized Stafford Loans, Direct PLUS loans, Federal Perkins Loans, State Loans, College/university loans from institutional funds. *Student Employment:* Federal Work-Study Program available. Institutional employment available. **Financial Aid Statistics:** 100% needy freshmen, 100% needy undergrads receive need-based scholarship or grant aid. 0% undergrads receive non-need-based scholarship or grant aid. 70% freshmen, 85% undergrads receive need-based self-help aid. 0% freshmen, 0% undergrads receive athletic scholarships. 54% freshmen, 56% undergrads receive any aid. 23% undergrads borrow to pay for school. Average cumulative indebtedness $16,702.

HARVEY MUDD COLLEGE

301 Platt Boulevard, Claremont, CA 91711
Phone: 909-621-8011 • **Financial Aid Phone:** 909-621-8055
E-mail: admission@hmc.edu • **CEEB Code:** 4341
Fax: 909-607-7046 • **Website:** www.hmc.edu

This private school was founded in 1955. It has a 33-acre campus.

RATINGS
Admissions Selectivity Rating: 98   **Fire Safety Rating:** 84   **Green Rating:** 60*

STUDENTS AND FACULTY
Enrollment: 829. **Student Body:** 46% female, 54% male, 56% out-of-state, 11% international (26 countries represented). Asian 19%, African American 3%, Caucasian 36%, Hispanic 16%, Native American <1%, Pacific Islander <1%, Two or more races 10%, Race unknown 5%.
Retention and Graduation: 98% freshmen return for sophomore year. 85% freshmen graduate within 4 years. 93% freshmen graduate within 6 years.
Faculty: Student/faculty ratio 8:1. 99 full-time faculty, 100% hold PhDs, 22% are are members of minority groups, 38% are women. 0% of classes are taught by teaching assistants.

ACADEMICS
Degrees: bachelor's. **Classes:** Most classes have 10-19 students. Most lab/discussion sessions have 10-19 students. **Most popular majors:** Engineering; Computer and Information Sciences; Mathematics. **Special Study Options:** cross-registration, double major, dual enrollment, exchange student program (domestic), independent study, internships, liberal arts/career combination, student-designed major, study abroad, Innovative client-sponsored design projects. Combined degree programs: BS/MS math, BS/MBA, BS/MIS, BA/BS. **Career Services:** Alumni network, Alumni services, Career assessment, Internships.

FACILITIES
Housing: Coed dorms, apartments for married students, apartments for single students, Housing exchange program w/ Pomona College, Pitzer College, Scripps College, and Claremont McKenna College. 90% of campus accessible to physically disabled. **Computers:** 100% of classrooms, 100% of dorms, 100% of libraries, 100% of dining areas, 100% of student union, 75% of common outdoor areas have wireless network access. Students can register for classes online. Administrative functions (other than registration) can be performed online.

CAMPUS LIFE

Environment: Town. **Activities:** Choral groups, concert band, dance, drama/theater, jazz band, literary magazine, music ensembles, musical theater, pep band, radio station, student government, student newspaper, student-run film society, symphony orchestra, yearbook, Campus Ministries, Student Organization, Model UN. 109 registered organizations, 4 honor societies, 6 religious organizations. **Athletics (Intercollegiate):** *Men:* baseball, basketball, cross-country, diving, football, golf, soccer, swimming, tennis, track/field (outdoor), water polo. *Women:* basketball, cross-country, diving, golf, lacrosse, soccer, softball, swimming, tennis, track/field (outdoor), volleyball, water polo. **On-Campus Highlights:** Dorm Lounges, Platt Campus Center Living Room, Liquidamber mall, Jay's Pizza Place, Linde Student Activities Center. **Environmental Initiatives:** In February 2008 Harvey Mudd College President Maria Klawe signed the American College & University Presidents Climate Commitment and Harvey Mudd College Board of Trustees adopted HMC Sustainability Policy Statement. Additionally, the Board of Trustees passed a resolution where the standard for new buildings will be at least U.S. Green Building Council LEED Silver standard or equivalent and premium rated or ENERGY STAR certified products are purchased for use on campus where possible.

ADMISSIONS

Freshman Academic Profile: 88% in top 10% of high school class, 95% in top 25% of high school class, 98% in top 50% of high school class. 65% from public high schools. **Reported SAT (pre-2016 redesign) scores:** SAT Math middle 50% range 740-800. SAT Critical Reading middle 50% range 680-780. SAT Writing middle 50% range 670-760. **Concordant SAT scores:** SAT EBRW middle 50% 710–780. SAT Math middle 50% range 760–800. ACT middle 50% range 32-35. Minimum internet-based TOEFL 100. Minimum paper TOEFL 600. **Basis for Candidate Selection:** *Very important factors considered include:* rigor of secondary school record, academic GPA, application essay, recommendation(s), talent/ability, character/personal qualities. *Important factors considered include:* class rank, standardized test scores, extracurricular activities, first generation. *Other factors considered include:* interview, alumni/ae relation, geographical residence, state residency, racial/ethnic status, volunteer work, work experience, level of applicant's interest. **Freshman Admission Requirements:** High school diploma is required and GED is accepted.High school diploma or equivalent is not required. *Academic units required:* 4 English, 4 math, 3 science, 1 history. *Academic units recommended:* 4 English, 4 math, 4 science, 2 science labs, 2 foreign language, 2 social studies, 2 history, 2 academic electives. **Freshman Admission Statistics:** 4,180 applied, 12.87% admitted, 40% enrolled. **Transfer Admission Requirements:** High school transcript, college transcript(s), essay or personal statement, statement of good standing from prior institution(s). Minimum college GPA of 3.0 required. Lowest grade transferable C. **General Admission Information:** Application fee $70. Regular application deadline 1/1. Regular notification 4/1. Nonfall registration not accepted. Admission may be deferred.

COSTS AND FINANCIAL AID

Annual tuition $52,383. Room and board $17,051. Required fees $283. Average book expense $800. **Required Forms and Deadlines:** FAFSA, CSS/Financial Aid PROFILE, State aid form, Noncustodial PROFILE, Business/Farm Supplement. **Notification of Awards:** Applicants will be notified of awards on or about 4/1. **Types of Aid:** *Need-based scholarships/grants:* Federal Pell, FSEOG, State scholarships/grants, Private scholarships, College/university scholarship or grant aid from institutional funds. *Loans:* Direct Subsidized Stafford Loans, Direct Unsubsidized Stafford Loans, Direct PLUS loans, Federal Perkins Loans, College/university loans from institutional funds. *Student Employment:* Federal Work-Study Program available. Institutional employment available. **Financial Aid Statistics:** 98% needy freshmen, 95% needy undergrads receive need-based scholarship or grant aid. 26% freshmen, 16% undergrads receive non-need-based scholarship or grant aid. 62% freshmen, 73% undergrads receive need-based self-help aid. 0% freshmen, 0% undergrads receive athletic scholarships. 84% freshmen, 76% undergrads receive any aid. 42% undergrads borrow to pay for school. Average cumulative indebtedness $25,412. **Criteria for awarding aid:** *Non-need-based:* Academics.

HASTINGS COLLEGE

Hastings College, Hastings, NE 68901
Phone: 402-461-7403 • **Financial Aid Phone:** 402-461-7431
E-mail: mmolliconi@hastings.edu • **CEEB Code:** 6270
Fax: 402-461-7490 • **Website:** www.hastings.edu • **ACT Code:** 2456

This private school, affiliated with the Presbyterian Church, was founded in 1882. It has a 109-acre campus.

RATINGS

Admissions Selectivity Rating: 79   **Fire Safety Rating:** 79   **Green Rating:** 60*

STUDENTS AND FACULTY

Enrollment: 1,059. **Student Body:** 46% female, 54% male, 28% out-of-state, 1% international (7 countries represented). Asian 1%, African American 2%, Caucasian 92%, Hispanic 3%, Native American <1%, Pacific Islander 0%, Two or more races 0%, Race unknown 1%.
Retention and Graduation: 76% freshmen return for sophomore year. 52% freshmen graduate within 4 years. 61% freshmen graduate within 6 years. 24% grads go on to further study within 1 year. 16% grads pursue arts and sciences degrees. 2% grads pursue law degrees. 1% grads pursue business degrees. 1% grads pursue medical degrees. **Faculty:** Student/faculty ratio 11:1. 87 full-time faculty, 71% hold PhDs, 1% are are members of minority groups, 34% are women. 0% of classes are taught by teaching assistants.

ACADEMICS

Degrees: bachelor's, master's. **Classes:** Most classes have 10-19 students. Most lab/discussion sessions have fewer than 10 students. **Most popular majors:** Education; Psychology; Business/Commerce. **Special Study Options:** double major, exchange student program (domestic), independent study, internships, student-designed major, study abroad, teacher certification program. Combined degree programs: BA/BM. **Disability Services:** Special programs offered to physically disabled students, including note-taking services, reader services, tape recorders, tutors. **Career Services:** Alumni network, Alumni services, Career/job search classes, Career assessment, Internships, Regional alumni, Service Learning program.

FACILITIES

Housing: Coed dorms, men's dorms, women's dorms, apartments for single students, Honors housing, one apartment complex is for quiet and alcohol-free living. 90% of campus accessible to physically diasbled. **Special Academic Facilities/Equipment:** center for communication arts, glass-blowing studio, observatory, art gallery. **Computers:** 95% of classrooms, 100% of libraries, 100% of dining areas, 100% of student union, have wireless network access. Administrative functions (other than registration) can be performed online.

CAMPUS LIFE

Environment: Village. **Activities:** Choral groups, concert band, dance, drama/theater, jazz band, literary magazine, marching band, music ensembles, musical theater, pep band, radio station, student government, student newspaper, symphony orchestra, television station, yearbook, Campus Ministries. 85 registered organizations, 13 honor societies, 10 religious organizations. 4 fraternities, 4 sororities. **Athletics (Intercollegiate):** *Men:* baseball, basketball, cross-country, football, golf, soccer, tennis, track/field (outdoor), track/field (indoor), wrestling. *Women:* basketball, cheerleading, cross-country, golf, soccer, softball, tennis, track/field (outdoor), track/field (indoor), volleyball. **On-Campus Highlights:** Fleharty Educational Center and weight room, Hazelrigg Student Union, Perkins Library, Gray Center of Communication Arts, Dorm lounges.

ADMISSIONS

Freshman Academic Profile: Average high school GPA 3.2. 16% in top 10% of high school class, 40% in top 25% of high school class, 65% in top 50% of high school class. 88% from public high schools. **Reported SAT (pre-2016 redesign) scores:** SAT Math middle 50% range 490-605. SAT Critical Reading middle 50% range 500-600. **Concordant SAT scores:** SAT Math middle 50% range 520–630. ACT middle 50% range 20-26. Minimum paper TOEFL 600. **Basis for Candidate Selection:** *Very important factors considered include:* rigor of secondary school record, class rank, academic GPA, standardized test scores, recommendation(s). *Important factors considered include:* extracurricular activities, talent/ability, character/personal qualities. *Other factors considered include:* application essay, interview, alumni/ae relation, racial/ethnic status, level of applicant's interest. **Freshman Admission Requirements:** High school diploma is required and GED is accepted. *Academic units required:* 3 English, 3 math, 3 science, 3 science labs, 4 social studies, 3 history. *Academic units recommended:* 4 English, 4 math, 4 science, 4 science labs, 2 foreign language, 4 social studies, 4 history. **Freshman Admission Statistics:** 1,210 applied, 81.40% admitted, 32% enrolled. **Transfer Admission Requirements:** High school transcript, college transcript(s), statement of good standing from prior institution(s). Minimum college GPA of

2.0 required. Lowest grade transferable C. **General Admission Information:** Application fee $20. Nonfall registration accepted.

COSTS AND FINANCIAL AID

Annual tuition $27,300. Room and board $8,080. Average book expense $730. **Required Forms and Deadlines:** FAFSA, Institution's own financial aid form. **Notification of Awards:** Applicants will be notified of awards on a rolling basis beginning 3/1. **Types of Aid:** *Need-based scholarships/grants:* Federal Pell, FSEOG, State scholarships/grants, Private scholarships, College/university scholarship or grant aid from institutional funds. *Loans:* Federal Perkins Loans. *Student Employment:* Federal Work-Study Program available. Institutional employment available. **Financial Aid Statistics:** 100% needy freshmen, 98% needy undergrads receive need-based scholarship or grant aid. 20% freshmen, 16% undergrads receive non-need-based scholarship or grant aid. 73% freshmen, 79% undergrads receive need-based self-help aid. 23% freshmen, 16% undergrads receive athletic scholarships. 97% freshmen, 98% undergrads receive any aid. **Criteria for awarding aid:** *Need-based:* Academics, Art, Athletics, Leadership, Music/drama. *Non-need-based:* Academics, Art, Athletics, Leadership, Music/drama.

HAVERFORD COLLEGE

Best Colleges

370 Lancaster Avenue, Haverford, PA 19041
Phone: 610-896-1350 • **Financial Aid Phone:** 610-896-1350
E-mail: http://www.haverford.edu/admission/ • **CEEB Code:** 2289
Fax: 610-896-1338 • **Website:** www.haverford.edu • **ACT Code:** 3409

This private school was founded in 1833. It has a 200-acre campus.

RATINGS

Admissions Selectivity Rating: 98   **Fire Safety Rating:** 88   **Green Rating:** 89

STUDENTS AND FACULTY

Enrollment: 1,261. **Student Body:** 52% female, 48% male, 88% out-of-state, 9% international (36 countries represented). Asian 10%, African American 7%, Caucasian 59%, Hispanic 8%, Native American <1%, Pacific Islander 0%, Two or more races 4%, Race unknown 2%.
Retention and Graduation: 97% freshmen return for sophomore year. 86% freshmen graduate within 4 years. 90% freshmen graduate within 6 years. 16% grads go on to further study within 1 year. 9% grads pursue arts and sciences degrees. 1% grads pursue law degrees. 1% grads pursue business degrees. 3% grads pursue medical degrees. **Faculty:** Student/faculty ratio 9:1. 132 full-time faculty, 98% hold PhDs, 23% are are members of minority groups, 47% are women. 0% of classes are taught by teaching assistants.

ACADEMICS

Degrees: bachelor's. **Classes:** Most classes have 10-19 students. Most lab/discussion sessions have fewer than 10 students. **Most popular majors:** Biology/Biological Sciences; English Language and Literature; Psychology. **Special Study Options:** cross-registration, double major, exchange student program (domestic), independent study, internships, liberal arts/career combination, student-designed major, study abroad, teacher certification program. Combined degree programs: BA/MEng, 4+1 M.S. in Bioethics (UPenn); 4+1 M.S. in Engineering (UPenn); 3-2 program in City Planning with UPENN; 1-yr Masters in Finance (Claremont McKenna); 5-year Latin American Studies (Georgetown). **Disability Services:** Special programs offered to physically disabled students, including note-taking services, tape recorders. **Career Services:** Alumni network, Alumni services, Career assessment, Internships, Regional alumni. We have a strong alumni network and numerous ongoing programs providing student/alumni interaction.

FACILITIES

Housing: Coed dorms, men's dorms, women's dorms, apartments for single students, Theme Housing. 66% of campus accessible to physically disabled. **Special Academic Facilities/Equipment:** Art gallery, center for cross-cultural study of religion, arboretum, observatory, foundry. **Computers:** 75% of classrooms, 75% of libraries, 100% of dining areas, 100% of student union, 80% of common outdoor areas have wireless network access. Students can register for classes online. Administrative functions (other than registration) can be performed online.

CAMPUS LIFE

Environment: Town. **Activities:** Choral groups, dance, drama/theater, literary magazine, music ensembles, musical theater, student government,

student newspaper, yearbook, Campus Ministries, Student Organization. 144 registered organizations, 1 honor society, 6 religious organizations. **Athletics (Intercollegiate):** *Men:* baseball, basketball, cross-country, fencing, lacrosse, soccer, squash, tennis, track/field (outdoor), track/field (indoor). *Women:* basketball, cross-country, fencing, field hockey, lacrosse, soccer, softball, squash, tennis, track/field (outdoor), track/field (indoor), volleyball. **On-Campus Highlights:** Integrated Natural Sciences Center, John Whitehead Campus Center, Cantor Fitzgerald Gallery, Arboretum, Douglas B. Gardner Athletic Center. **Environmental Initiatives:** The athletic center is the 1st gold LEED certified recreation center in the US (opened in 2005).

ADMISSIONS

Freshman Academic Profile: 94% in top 10% of high school class, 99% in top 25% of high school class, 100% in top 50% of high school class. 54% from public high schools. **Reported SAT (pre-2016 redesign) scores:** SAT Math middle 50% range 660-760. SAT Critical Reading middle 50% range 660-760. SAT Writing middle 50% range 660-760. **Concordant SAT scores:** SAT EBRW middle 50% 700–770. SAT Math middle 50% range 690–780. ACT middle 50% range 31-34. Minimum internet-based TOEFL 100. **Basis for Candidate Selection:** *Very important factors considered include:* rigor of secondary school record, academic GPA, application essay, recommendation(s), extracurricular activities, character/personal qualities. *Important factors considered include:* class rank, standardized test scores, talent/ability, volunteer work, work experience. *Other factors considered include:* interview, first generation, alumni/ae relation, geographical residence, racial/ethnic status, level of applicant's interest. **Freshman Admission Requirements:** High school diploma or equivalent is not required. *Academic units recommended:* 4 English, 3 math, 3 science, 3 science labs, 3 foreign language, 3 social studies. **Freshman Admission Statistics:** 4,066 applied, 21.40% admitted, 40% enrolled. **Transfer Admission Requirements:** college transcript(s), essay or personal statement, standardized test scores, statement of good standing from prior institution(s). Minimum college GPA of 3.0 required. Lowest grade transferable C. **General Admission Information:** Application fee $65. Regular application deadline 1/15. Regular notification 4/1. Nonfall registration not accepted. Admission may be deferred for a maximum of 1 year.

COSTS AND FINANCIAL AID

Required Forms and Deadlines: FAFSA, CSS/Financial Aid PROFILE, Noncustodial PROFILE, Business/Farm Supplement. **Notification of Awards:** Applicants will be notified of awards on or about 4/1. **Types of Aid:** *Need-based scholarships/grants:* Federal Pell, FSEOG, State scholarships/grants, College/university scholarship or grant aid from institutional funds. *Loans:* Direct Subsidized Stafford Loans, Direct Unsubsidized Stafford Loans, Direct PLUS loans. *Student Employment:* Federal Work-Study Program available. Institutional employment available. **Financial Aid Statistics:** 98% needy freshmen, 100% needy undergrads receive need-based scholarship or grant aid. 0% undergrads receive non-need-based scholarship or grant aid. 94% freshmen, 93% undergrads receive need-based self-help aid. 0% freshmen, 0% undergrads receive athletic scholarships. 51% freshmen, 51% undergrads receive any aid. 29% undergrads borrow to pay for school. Average cumulative indebtedness $18,932.

HAWAI'I PACIFIC UNIVERSITY

1 Aloha Tower Drive, Honolulu, HI 96813
Phone: 808-544-0238 • **Financial Aid Phone:** 808-544-0253
E-mail: admissions@hpu.edu • **CEEB Code:** 4352
Fax: 808-544-1136 • **Website:** www.hpu.edu • **ACT Code:** 4352

This private school was founded in 1965. It has a 135-acre campus.

RATINGS

Admissions Selectivity Rating: 73   **Fire Safety Rating:** 92   **Green Rating:** 60*

STUDENTS AND FACULTY

Enrollment: 3,384. **Student Body:** 58% female, 42% male, 44% out-of-state, 11% international (80 countries represented). Asian 14%, African American 5%, Caucasian 20%, Hispanic 15%, Native American 1%, Pacific Islander 2%, Two or more races 12%, Race unknown 21%.
Retention and Graduation: 65% freshmen return for sophomore year. 22% freshmen graduate within 4 years. 42% freshmen graduate within 6 years. **Faculty:** Student/faculty ratio 12:1. 225 full-time faculty, 0% hold PhDs, 0% are are members of minority groups, 44% are women. 0% of classes are taught by teaching assistants.

ACADEMICS

Degrees: associate, bachelor's, certificate, master's, postbachelor's certificate, post-master's certificate. **Classes:** Most classes have 10-19 students. Most lab/discussion sessions have fewer than 10 students. **Special Study Options:**

Accelerated program, cooperative education program, distance learning, double major, dual enrollment, English as a Second Language (ESL), honors program, independent study, internships, liberal arts/career combination, student-designed major, study abroad, weekend college. **Honors Programs:** University Scholars Honors Program: During the freshman and sophomore years University Scholars enroll in honors sections of many courses required in the general education curriculum. Normally, University Scholars are required to complete at least six of these courses, but exceptions can be made for students who have completed certain requirements through AP courses in high school or for majors with different general education requirements. At the upper-division level, University Scholars enroll in three honors seminars. The Certificate of Merit is awarded at the time of graduation to students who fulfill the University Scholars requirements. Combined degree programs: BA/MA.

FACILITIES

Housing: Coed dorms, women's dorms, apartments for married students, apartments for single students, Apartment search and referral service. **Special Academic Facilities/Equipment:** Hawaii Pacific University Art Gallery, Hawaii Pacific University Theatre. **Computers:** Students can register for classes online. Administrative functions (other than registration) can be performed online.

CAMPUS LIFE

Environment: Metropolis. **Activities:** Choral groups, dance, drama/theater, literary magazine, music ensembles, musical theater, pep band, student government, student newspaper, student-run film society 80 registered organizations, 18 honor societies, 3 religious organizations. **Athletics (Intercollegiate):** *Men:* baseball, basketball, cheerleading, cross-country, golf, tennis. *Women:* cheerleading, cross-country, golf, softball, tennis, volleyball. **On-Campus Highlights:** Frear Center, Sea Warrior Center, Windward Campus, Art Gallery, Fort Street Mall.

ADMISSIONS

Freshman Academic Profile: Average high school GPA 3.4. **Reported SAT (pre-2016 redesign) scores:** SAT Math middle 50% range 450-550. SAT Critical Reading middle 50% range 450-540. SAT Writing middle 50% range 440-540. **Concordant SAT scores:** SAT EBRW middle 50% 500–600. SAT Math middle 50% range 490–570. ACT middle 50% range 19-24. Minimum paper TOEFL 550. **Basis for Candidate Selection:** *Very important factors considered include:* rigor of secondary school record, academic GPA. *Important factors considered include:* standardized test scores, application essay, extracurricular activities. *Other factors considered include:* recommendation(s), interview, talent/ability, character/personal qualities, first generation, volunteer work, work experience. **Freshman Admission Requirements:** High school diploma is required and GED is accepted. *Academic units recommended:* 4 English, 3 math, 3 science, 1 science lab, 2 foreign language, 2 social studies, 2 history. **Freshman Admission Statistics:** 5,452 applied, 75.37% admitted, 12% enrolled. **Transfer Admission Requirements:** college transcript(s), Minimum college GPA of 2.0 required. Lowest grade transferable C. **General Admission Information:** Application fee $50. Nonfall registration accepted. Admission may be deferred for a maximum of 2 years.

COSTS AND FINANCIAL AID

Annual tuition $23,160. Room and board $13,898. Required fees $280. Average book expense $1,200. **Required Forms and Deadlines:** FAFSA. **Types of Aid:** *Need-based scholarships/grants:* Federal Pell, FSEOG, State scholarships/grants, Private scholarships, College/university scholarship or grant aid from institutional funds, Federal Nursing Scholarships. *Loans:* Direct Subsidized Stafford Loans, Direct Unsubsidized Stafford Loans, Direct PLUS loans, Federal Perkins Loans, Federal Nursing Loans. *Student Employment:* Federal Work-Study Program available. Institutional employment available. **Financial Aid Statistics:** 68% needy undergrads receive need-based scholarship or grant aid. 100% freshmen, 83% undergrads receive non-need-based scholarship or grant aid. 96% freshmen, 98% undergrads receive need-based self-help aid. 8% freshmen, 7% undergrads receive athletic scholarships. 59% undergrads borrow to pay for school. Average cumulative indebtedness $26,216. **Criteria for awarding aid:** *Non-need-based:* Academics, Alumni affiliation, Athletics, Job skills, Leadership, Music/drama, Religious affiliation.

HEIDELBERG UNIVERSITY

310 East Market Street, Tiffin, OH 44883
Phone: 419-448-2330 • **Financial Aid Phone:** 419-448-2293
E-mail: adminfo@heidelberg.edu • **CEEB Code:** 1292
Fax: 419-448-2334 • **Website:** www.heidelberg.edu • **ACT Code:** 3278

This private school, affiliated with the United Church of Christ Church, was founded in 1850. It has a 120-acre campus.

RATINGS
Admissions Selectivity Rating: 78 **Fire Safety Rating:** 63 **Green Rating:** 60*

STUDENTS AND FACULTY

Enrollment: 1,089. **Student Body:** 48% female, 52% male, 15% out-of-state, 1% international. Asian 1%, African American 7%, Caucasian 78%, Hispanic 2%, Native American <1%, Pacific Islander 0%, Two or more races 2%, Race unknown 9%.
Retention and Graduation: 61% freshmen return for sophomore year. 39% freshmen graduate within 4 years. 51% freshmen graduate within 6 years. 25% grads go on to further study within 1 year. 15% grads pursue arts and sciences degrees. 2% grads pursue law degrees. 5% grads pursue business degrees. 3% grads pursue medical degrees. **Faculty:** Student/faculty ratio 12:1. 50 full-time faculty, 86% hold PhDs, 6% are are members of minority groups, 46% are women. 0% of classes are taught by teaching assistants.

ACADEMICS

Degrees: bachelor's, master's. **Classes:** Most classes have fewer than 10 students. Most lab/discussion sessions have 10-19 students. **Most popular majors:** Education; Biological and Physical Sciences; Business/Commerce. **Special Study Options:** cross-registration, double major, dual enrollment, English as a Second Language (ESL), exchange student program (domestic), honors program, independent study, internships, liberal arts/career combination, study abroad, teacher certification program. **Honors Programs:** The Honors Program, entitled "The Life of the Mind," integrates learning and life experiences, stems from the mission of the University. It features extensive contact with the fundamental values that underpin self-worth and integrity, free inquiry, and intellectual rigor, an understanding of other cultures and traditions, and a lifelong habit of commitment to the community and concern for social responsibility. **Disability Services:** Special programs offered to physically disabled students, including tutors. **Career Services:** Alumni network, Career assessment, Internships.

FACILITIES

Housing: Coed dorms, special housing for disabled students, women's dorms, cooperative housing, apartments for single students, Theme Housing. 65% of campus accessible to physically diasbled. **Special Academic Facilities/Equipment:** Forest research lots, water quality lab, Center for Historic and Military Archaeology. **Computers:** 80% of classrooms, 70% of dorms, 100% of libraries, 100% of dining areas, 100% of student union, have wireless network access. Students can register for classes online. Administrative functions (other than registration) can be performed online.

CAMPUS LIFE

Environment: Village. **Activities:** Choral groups, concert band, dance, drama/theater, jazz band, literary magazine, music ensembles, musical theater, opera, pep band, radio station, student government, student newspaper, student-run film society, symphony orchestra, television station, yearbook, Campus Ministries, Student Organization, Model UN. 75 registered organizations, 6 honor societies, 3 religious organizations. 5 fraternities, 4 sororities. **Athletics (Intercollegiate):** *Men:* baseball, basketball, cheerleading, cross-country, football, golf, soccer, tennis, track/field (outdoor), track/field (indoor), wrestling. *Women:* basketball, cheerleading, cross-country, golf, soccer, softball, tennis, track/field (outdoor), track/field (indoor), volleyball. **On-Campus Highlights:** Gillmor Science Center, Campus Center, Seiberling Gymnasium, Education Center.

ADMISSIONS

Freshman Academic Profile: Average high school GPA 3.2. 14% in top 10% of high school class, 33% in top 25% of high school class, 62% in top 50% of high school class. 61% from public high schools. **Reported SAT (pre-2016 redesign) scores:** SAT Math middle 50% range 420-570. SAT Critical Reading middle 50% range 420-590. SAT Writing middle 50% range 400-550. **Concordant SAT scores:** SAT EBRW middle 50% 460–630. SAT Math middle 50% range 460–590. ACT middle 50% range 19-25. Minimum paper TOEFL 550. **Basis for Candidate Selection:** *Very important factors considered include:* rigor of secondary school record, academic GPA, standardized test scores, interview, talent/ability, character/personal qualities. *Important factors considered include:* class rank, application essay, extracurricular activities, level of applicant's interest. *Other factors considered include:* recommendation(s), first generation, alumni/ae relation, geographical residence, volunteer work,

work experience. **Freshman Admission Requirements:** High school diploma is required and GED is accepted. *Academic units recommended:* 4 English, 3 math, 3 science, 1 science lab, 2 foreign language, 3 social studies, 2 history, 3 academic electives. **Freshman Admission Statistics:** 1,726 applied, 70.97% admitted, 29% enrolled. **Transfer Admission Requirements:** High school transcript, college transcript(s), standardized test scores, statement of good standing from prior institution(s). Minimum college GPA of 2.0 required. Lowest grade transferable C-. **General Admission Information:** Application fee $25. Priority deadline 1/1. Regular application deadline 8/1. Nonfall registration accepted. Admission may be deferred for a maximum of 3 yrs.

COSTS AND FINANCIAL AID

Average book expense $1,500. **Required Forms and Deadlines:** FAFSA. **Notification of Awards:** Applicants will be notified of awards on a rolling basis beginning 3/1. **Types of Aid:** *Need-based scholarships/grants:* Federal Pell, FSEOG, State scholarships/grants, Private scholarships, College/university scholarship or grant aid from institutional funds. *Loans:* Direct Subsidized Stafford Loans, Direct Unsubsidized Stafford Loans, Direct PLUS loans, Federal Perkins Loans. *Student Employment:* Federal Work-Study Program available. Institutional employment available. **Financial Aid Statistics:** 100% needy freshmen, 100% needy undergrads receive need-based scholarship or grant aid. 89% freshmen, 70% undergrads receive non-need-based scholarship or grant aid. 89% freshmen, 89% undergrads receive need-based self-help aid. 0% freshmen, 0% undergrads receive athletic scholarships. 99% freshmen, 97% undergrads receive any aid. **Criteria for awarding aid:** *Non-need-based:* Academics, Music/drama, Religious affiliation, State/district residency.

HELLENIC COLLEGE

50 Goddard Avenue, Brookline, MA 2445
Phone: 617-850-1260 • **Financial Aid Phone:** 617-850-1317
E-mail: admissions@hchc.edu
Fax: 617-850-1460 • **Website:** www.hchc.edu • **ACT Code:** 1843

This private school, affiliated with the Greek Orthodox Church, was founded in 1937. It has a 59-acre campus.

RATINGS

Admissions Selectivity Rating: 71 **Fire Safety Rating:** 99 **Green Rating:** 60*

STUDENTS AND FACULTY

Enrollment: 100. **Student Body:** 40% female, 60% male, 86% out-of-state, 5% international (9 countries represented). Asian 0%, African American 1%, Caucasian 75%, Hispanic 6%, Native American 1%, Pacific Islander 0%, Two or more races 1%, Race unknown 11%.
Retention and Graduation: 80% freshmen return for sophomore year. 24% grads go on to further study within 1 year. **Faculty:** Student/faculty ratio 8:1. 21 full-time faculty, 95% hold PhDs, 0% are are members of minority groups, 29% are women.

ACADEMICS

Degrees: bachelor's, master's. **Classes:** Most classes have 20-29 students. **Most popular majors:** Religion/Religious Studies; Business/Commerce; Psychology. **Special Study Options:** honors program, liberal arts/career combination. Combined degree programs: BA/MDiv. **Disability Services:** Special programs offered to physically disabled students, including tutors. **Career Services:** Alumni network, Alumni services, Career/job search classes, Career assessment, Internships, Regional alumni, On-campus interviews. Experiential learning: study abroad experiences, Personalized counseling & professional development.

FACILITIES

Housing: Coed dorms, apartments for married students. 20% of campus accessible to physically diasbled. **Computers:** 100% of dorms, have wireless network access.

CAMPUS LIFE

Environment: Village. **Activities:** Choral groups, student government, yearbook, Campus Ministries. **Athletics (Intercollegiate):** *Men:* basketball. *Women:* tennis.

ADMISSIONS

Freshman Academic Profile: Average high school GPA 3.1. 97% from public high schools. Minimum internet-based TOEFL 61. Minimum paper TOEFL 500. **Basis for Candidate Selection:** *Very important factors considered include:* rigor of secondary school record, academic GPA, standardized test scores, application essay, recommendation(s), interview. *Important factors considered include:* class rank. *Other factors considered include:* extracurricular activities, character/personal qualities, alumni/ae relation. **Freshman Admission Requirements:** High school diploma is required and GED is accepted. *Academic units required:* 4 English, 2 math, 2 science, 2 foreign

language, 2 social studies, 2 history. **Freshman Admission Statistics:** 51 applied, 68.63% admitted, 46% enrolled. **Transfer Admission Requirements:** college transcript(s), essay or personal statement, interview, Minimum college GPA of 2.0 required. Lowest grade transferable C+. **General Admission Information:** Application fee $50. Regular application deadline 8/15. Nonfall registration accepted. Admission may be deferred.

COSTS AND FINANCIAL AID

Annual tuition $21,940. Room and board $12,142. Required fees $550. Average book expense $600. **Required Forms and Deadlines:** FAFSA, Institution's own financial aid form. **Notification of Awards:** Applicants will be notified of awards on a rolling basis beginning 4/1. **Types of Aid:** *Need-based scholarships/grants:* Federal Pell, FSEOG, State scholarships/grants, Private scholarships, College/university scholarship or grant aid from institutional funds. *Student Employment:* Federal Work-Study Program available. Institutional employment available. **Financial Aid Statistics:** 100% needy freshmen, 100% needy undergrads receive need-based scholarship or grant aid. 0% undergrads receive non-need-based scholarship or grant aid. 100% freshmen, 100% undergrads receive need-based self-help aid. 0% freshmen, 0% undergrads receive athletic scholarships. 98% freshmen, 96% undergrads receive any aid. 100% undergrads borrow to pay for school. Average cumulative indebtedness $15,500. **Criteria for awarding aid:** *Need-based:* Academics, Leadership, Religious affiliation. *Non-need-based:* Academics, Alumni affiliation, Religious affiliation.

HENDERSON STATE UNIVERSITY

1100 Henderson Street, Arkadelphia, AR 71999-0001
Phone: 870-230-5028 • **Financial Aid Phone:** 870-230-5148
E-mail: admissions@hsu.edu • **CEEB Code:** 6272
Fax: 870-230-5066 • **ACT Code:** 126

This public school was founded in 1890. It has a 151-acre campus.

RATINGS

Admissions Selectivity Rating: 79 **Fire Safety Rating:** 88 **Green Rating:** 60*

STUDENTS AND FACULTY

Enrollment: 3,190. **Student Body:** 56% female, 44% male, 13% out-of-state, 1% international (35 countries represented). Asian 1%, African American 24%, Caucasian 66%, Hispanic 3%, Native American <1%, Pacific Islander 0%, Two or more races 5%, Race unknown <1%.
Retention and Graduation: 58% freshmen return for sophomore year. 15% freshmen graduate within 4 years. 29% freshmen graduate within 6 years. **Faculty:** Student/faculty ratio 15:1. 164 full-time faculty, 69% hold PhDs, 17% are are members of minority groups, 44% are women. 0% of classes are taught by teaching assistants.

ACADEMICS

Degrees: bachelor's, master's, postbachelor's certificate, post-master's certificate. **Most popular majors:** Business/Commerce; Biology/Biological Sciences; General Studies. **Special Study Options:** cross-registration, distance learning, English as a Second Language (ESL), honors program, internships, liberal arts/career combination, teacher certification program. **Honors Programs:** The overarching purpose of the Honors College is summed up in the single ancient Greek word, aretÃ© (highest excellence), which the students and faculty of the College have taken as their motto. In working to achieve this purpose, the Honors College shares the university's goal "to excel in undergraduate education, always striving to enrich the quality of learning and teaching." The program is directly involved in "actively recruiting, challenging, and supporting those students" who are among the most "highly motivated toward achieving academic success." **Disability Services:** Special programs offered to physically disabled students, including note-taking services, tutors. **Career Services:** Alumni services, Career assessment, Internships.

FACILITIES

Housing: Coed dorms, men's dorms, special housing for international students, women's dorms, cooperative housing, honors dorm. 95% of campus accessible to physically diasbled. **Special Academic Facilities/Equipment:** closed-circuit TV studio, Planetarium. **Computers:** Students can register for classes online. Administrative functions (other than registration) can be performed online.

CAMPUS LIFE

Environment: Rural. **Activities:** Choral groups, concert band, dance, drama/theater, jazz band, literary magazine, marching band, music ensembles, radio station, student government, student newspaper, symphony orchestra, television station, yearbook, Student Organization. 80 registered organizations, 11 honor societies, 7 religious organizations. 9 fraternities, 6 sororities. **Athletics (Intercollegiate):** *Men:* baseball, basketball, cross-country, football, golf, swimming. *Women:* basketball, cross-country, golf, softball, swimming, tennis, volleyball. **On-Campus Highlights:** HSU Planetarium, New Reddie Athletic Center, Newly Renovated Arkansas Hall, Henderson House Bed and Breakfast, Java Spot Coffee House. **Environmental Initiatives:** Recycling paper, cans and bottles on campus.

ADMISSIONS

Freshman Academic Profile: Average high school GPA 3.2. 12% in top 10% of high school class, 26% in top 25% of high school class, 52% in top 50% of high school class. 92% from public high schools. **Reported SAT (pre-2016 redesign) scores:** SAT Math middle 50% range 485-573. SAT Critical Reading middle 50% range 465-538. **Concordant SAT scores:** SAT Math middle 50% range 520–590. ACT middle 50% range 19-24. Minimum internet-based TOEFL 61. Minimum paper TOEFL 500. **Basis for Candidate Selection:** *Very important factors considered include:* rigor of secondary school record, academic GPA, standardized test scores. *Important factors considered include:* class rank. **Freshman Admission Requirements:** High school diploma is required and GED is accepted. *Academic units required:* 4 English, 4 math, 3 science, 2 social studies, 1 history, and 8 units from above areas or other academic areas. *Academic units recommended:* 4 English, 4 math, 4 science, 2 foreign language, 2 social studies, 2 history, and 8 units from above areas or other academic areas. **Freshman Admission Statistics:** 3,388 applied, 62.16% admitted, 33% enrolled. **Transfer Admission Requirements:** college transcript(s), Lowest grade transferable C. **General Admission Information:** Regular application deadline 7/15. Nonfall registration accepted. Admission may be deferred for a maximum of 1+.

COSTS AND FINANCIAL AID

Annual in-state tuition $5,730. Annual out-of-state tuition $11,850. Room and board $6,350. Required fees $1,554. Average book expense $1,200. **Required Forms and Deadlines:** FAFSA. **Notification of Awards:** Applicants will be notified of awards on a rolling basis beginning 3/1. **Types of Aid:** *Need-based scholarships/grants:* Federal Pell, FSEOG, State scholarships/grants, Private scholarships, College/university scholarship or grant aid from institutional funds. *Loans:* Direct Subsidized Stafford Loans, Direct Unsubsidized Stafford Loans, Direct PLUS loans, Federal Perkins Loans. *Student Employment:* Federal Work-Study Program available. **Financial Aid Statistics:** 69% needy freshmen, 69% needy undergrads receive need-based scholarship or grant aid. 87% freshmen, 72% undergrads receive non-need-based scholarship or grant aid. 63% freshmen, 71% undergrads receive need-based self-help aid. 8% freshmen, 8% undergrads receive athletic scholarships. **Criteria for awarding aid:** *Non-need-based:* Academics, Alumni affiliation, Art, Athletics, Leadership, Minority status, Music/drama.

HENDRIX COLLEGE

1600 Washington Avenue, Conway, AR 72032
Phone: 501-450-1362 • **Financial Aid Phone:** 501-450-1368
E-mail: adm@hendrix.edu • **CEEB Code:** 6273
Fax: 501-450-3843 • **Website:** www.hendrix.edu • **ACT Code:** 128

This private school, affiliated with the Methodist Church, was founded in 1876. It has a 160-acre campus.

RATINGS

Admissions Selectivity Rating: 83   **Fire Safety Rating:** 81   **Green Rating:** 60*

STUDENTS AND FACULTY

Enrollment: 1,303. **Student Body:** 53% female, 47% male, 52% out-of-state, 3% international (13 countries represented). Asian 5%, African American 5%, Caucasian 78%, Hispanic 5%, Native American 1%, Pacific Islander <1%, Two or more races 3%, Race unknown 1%.
Retention and Graduation: 79% freshmen return for sophomore year. 64% freshmen graduate within 4 years. 68% freshmen graduate within 6 years. 63% grads go on to further study within 1 year. 43% grads pursue arts and sciences degrees. 10% grads pursue law degrees. 3% grads pursue business degrees. 6% grads pursue medical degrees. **Faculty:** Student/faculty ratio 11:1. 107 full-time faculty, 93% hold PhDs, 13% are are members of minority groups, 44% are women. 0% of classes are taught by teaching assistants.

ACADEMICS

Degrees: bachelor's, master's. **Classes:** Most classes have 10-19 students. Most lab/discussion sessions have 20-29 students. **Most popular majors:** Psychology; Biology/Biological Sciences. **Special Study Options:** cooperative education program, double major, English as a Second Language (ESL), independent study, internships, student-designed major, study abroad, teacher certification program, Hendrix-in-Brussels (Belgium), Hendrix-in-Costa Rica, Hendrix-in-Heilongjiang (China), Hendrix-in-Graz (Austria), Hendrix-in-London (UK), Hendrix-in-Madrid (Spain), Hendrix-in-Oxford (UK), Accademia dell'Arte,

other programs with 140 colleges and universities on 6 continents including countries such as Australia, Finland, France, Ghana, Japan etc. Combined degree programs: BA/MEng, 4-1 BA/MPH Program in Public Health with UAMS. **Disability Services:** Special programs offered to physically disabled students, including note-taking services, reader services, tape recorders, tutors. **Career Services:** Alumni network, Alumni services, Career/job search classes, Career assessment, Internships, Career discovery and counseling, Graduate and Career Fairs, FACT Program: Friday Alumni Connection Time.

FACILITIES

Housing: Coed dorms, special housing for disabled students, men's dorms, women's dorms, cooperative housing, apartments for single students, Wellness Housing, Theme Housing, co-educational foreign language house (Spanish, German, French alternating years) available; suite-style small houses; Ecology house; Christian House. 49% of campus accessible to physically diasbled. **Special Academic Facilities/Equipment:** Herbarium, Wilbur A. Mills Library. **Computers:** 100% of classrooms, 100% of dorms, 100% of libraries, 100% of dining areas, 100% of student union, 100% of common outdoor areas have wireless network access. Students can register for classes online. Administrative functions (other than registration) can be performed online.

CAMPUS LIFE

Environment: Town. **Activities:** Choral groups, concert band, dance, drama/theater, jazz band, literary magazine, music ensembles, musical theater, pep band, radio station, student government, student newspaper, student-run film society, symphony orchestra, yearbook, Campus Ministries, Student Organization, Model UN. 80 registered organizations, 6 honor societies, 5 religious organizations. **Athletics (Intercollegiate):** *Men:* baseball, basketball, cross-country, diving, golf, lacrosse, soccer, swimming, tennis, track/field (outdoor). *Women:* basketball, cross-country, diving, field hockey, golf, soccer, softball, swimming, tennis, track/field (outdoor), volleyball. **On-Campus Highlights:** Student Life & Technology Center, Village at Hendrix Apartments, Wellness & Athletic Center, Charles D. Morgan Center for Physical Sc, D.W. Reynolds building for the life scie, Art Complex, Butler Plaza Fountain, the Burrow (campus center). **Environmental Initiatives:** Reduction in paper utilization

ADMISSIONS

Freshman Academic Profile: Average high school GPA 3.9. 48% in top 10% of high school class, 96% in top 50% of high school class. 77% from public high schools. **Reported SAT (pre-2016 redesign) scores:** SAT Math middle 50% range 580-660. SAT Critical Reading middle 50% range 640-680. **Concordant SAT scores:** SAT Math middle 50% range 600–690. ACT middle 50% range 25-32. Minimum internet-based TOEFL 79. Minimum paper TOEFL 550. **Basis for Candidate Selection:** *Very important factors considered include:* rigor of secondary school record, academic GPA, standardized test scores, application essay. *Important factors considered include:* class rank, recommendation(s), interview, extracurricular activities. *Other factors considered include:* talent/ability, racial/ethnic status, volunteer work. **Freshman Admission Requirements:** High school diploma is required and GED is accepted. *Academic units recommended:* 4 English, 3 math, 2 science, 2 foreign language, 3 social studies. **Freshman Admission Statistics:** 1,656 applied, 82.97% admitted, 29% enrolled. **Transfer Admission Requirements:** college transcript(s), essay or personal statement, statement of good standing from prior institution(s). Minimum college GPA of 2.5 required. Lowest grade transferable C. **General Admission Information:** Application fee $40. Priority deadline 2/1. Regular application deadline 6/1. Nonfall registration accepted.

COSTS AND FINANCIAL AID

Required Forms and Deadlines: FAFSA. **Notification of Awards:** Applicants will be notified of awards on a rolling basis beginning 3/1. **Types of Aid:** *Need-based scholarships/grants:* Federal Pell, FSEOG, State scholarships/grants, Private scholarships, College/university scholarship or grant aid from institutional funds. *Loans:* Direct Subsidized Stafford Loans, Direct Unsubsidized Stafford Loans, Direct PLUS loans, Federal Perkins Loans. *Student Employment:* Federal Work-Study Program available. Institutional employment available. **Financial Aid Statistics:** 100% needy freshmen, 100% needy undergrads receive need-based scholarship or grant aid. 31% freshmen, 34% undergrads receive non-need-based scholarship or grant aid. 69% freshmen, 65% undergrads receive need-based self-help aid. 0% freshmen, 0% undergrads receive athletic scholarships. 100% freshmen, 100% undergrads receive any aid. Average cumulative indebtedness $30,213. **Criteria for awarding aid:** *Non-need-based:* Academics, Art, Leadership, Music/drama, State/district residency.

HIGH POINT UNIVERSITY

University Station 3598, High Point, NC 27268
Phone: 336-841-9216 • **Financial Aid Phone:** 336-841-9128
E-mail: admiss@highpoint.edu • **CEEB Code:** 5293
Fax: 336-888-6382 • **Website:** www.highpoint.edu • **ACT Code:** 3108

This private school, affiliated with the Methodist Church, was founded in 1924. It has a 135-acre campus.

RATINGS
Admissions Selectivity Rating: 81 **Fire Safety Rating:** 87 **Green Rating:** 60*

STUDENTS AND FACULTY
Enrollment: 4,510. **Student Body:** 59% female, 41% male, 79% out-of-state, 2% international (42 countries represented). Asian 2%, African American 5%, Caucasian 78%, Hispanic 5%, Native American <1%, Pacific Islander <1%, Two or more races 6%, Race unknown 1%.
Retention and Graduation: 82% freshmen return for sophomore year. 60% freshmen graduate within 4 years. 64% freshmen graduate within 6 years. 15% grads go on to further study within 1 year. 17% grads pursue arts and sciences degrees. 1% grads pursue law degrees. 2% grads pursue business degrees. 5% grads pursue medical degrees. **Faculty:** Student/faculty ratio 15:1. 301 full-time faculty, 78% hold PhDs, 11% are are members of minority groups, 49% are women. 0% of classes are taught by teaching assistants.

ACADEMICS
Degrees: bachelor's, doctoral, master's, postbachelor's certificate. **Classes:** Most classes have 10-19 students. **Most popular majors:** Business Administration and Management; Communication; Biology/Biological Sciences. **Special Study Options:** Accelerated program, cooperative education program, cross-registration, double major, dual enrollment, English as a Second Language (ESL), honors program, independent study, internships, liberal arts/career combination, student-designed major, study abroad, teacher certification program, Joint degree programs in environmental science, forestry and medical technology. **Honors Programs:** More than 200 students are enrolled in the university's Honors Program. In addition to enrollment in honors courses, members of the Honors Program often present the results of their research at the Honors Symposium sponsored annually by the university's Odyssey Club, an organization of students enrolled in the Honors Program. In addition to activities for members of the Honors Program, the Odyssey Club sponsors a number of activities annually for the campus at large, including academic bowls and visiting lecturers. Combined degree programs: BA/MA, BA/MEng, BA/MA Communication; BA.M.Ed. Education. **Disability Services:** Special programs offered to physically disabled students, including tape recorders, tutors. **Career Services:** Alumni network, Alumni services, Career/job search classes, Career assessment, Internships, Regional alumni, On-campus interviews. The mission of the Service Learning Program at High Point University is to engage students in an experiential and interdisciplinary learning environment that promotes their understanding of and commitment to responsible civic leadership. In our turbulent global times, HPU employs its liberal arts mission to prepare students to be active, knowledgeable, and responsible citizens. The Service Learning Program engages students in connecting the theory of the classroom with the practices of good citizens, encouraging community-based research, active problem-solving, and a growth mindset that fosters creativity and social innovation. Service Learning courses can be found in the Liberal Arts Core Curriculum of the University, in Liberal Arts majors courses, and throughout the University's professional schools. But wherever these courses are found, students will be active participants in their education and community.

FACILITIES
Housing: Coed dorms, special housing for disabled students, men's dorms, women's dorms, fraternity/sorority housing, apartments for married students, cooperative housing, apartments for single studentsThe number of apartments/houses are available for married students is limited. 98% of campus accessible to physically disabled. **Special Academic Facilities/Equipment:** Hayworth Chapel; Hayworth Fine Arts Center; Sechrest Gallery; Smith Library; Campus Television Studio; Radio Studio/Station (WHPU) Beginning a $100 million new-construction and renovation program, the campus of High Point University is currently experiencing the greatest period of growth in our 81-year history. Currently under construction are: Blessing Residence Hall is a $10-million facility which is made possible by the generous lead gift of one anonymous donor who requested we call it the "Blessing" residence hall. It will be loaded with amenities that make it a prototype for 21st Century college residence halls. It will offer 240 fully furnished, private bedrooms arranged in suites with living rooms,kitchens and dining areas. Residents will enjoy spacious common areas, computer lounges, conference areas, laundry rooms and elevators. Slane Student Life & Wellness Center will be a centerpiece of campus. This $6.5 million, 45,000-square-foot building will connect to the current Slane Student Center via a two-story atrium, and will feature a high-performance aerobics room, rock-climbing wall, indoor track, fully equipped weight room, food court, dramatic inside & outside basketball courts, outdoor swimming pool, sand volleyball courts, and a grand student atrium with billiard tables and sitting areas. The Earl N. Phillips School of Business will be a new 27,000-square-foot building which will become the home for the more than 1,000 undergraduate students pursuing a degree in one of High Point University's 12 undergraduate majors and Master of Business Administration graduate degree. The facility will feature a 200-seat, tiered lecture hall, four smaller lecture rooms, as well as traditional classrooms, a spacious auditorium, private study rooms, computer labs and faculty offices. The Jerry & Kitty Steele Sports Center will be a $5 million, 2-story, 27,000-square-foot facility featuring training & weight rooms, a hospitality/conference room, locker rooms, and an academic services room. In addition, another $5 million is being invested to build a new soccer stadium, baseball stadium, and eight-lane track. University Park will be an extraordinary outdoor experience. Featuring a network of trails and bridges, spectacular waterfalls, a 15-foot overhead trellis, multi-level reflecting pools, 65' covered walkway, and an amphitheatre, this will be the perfect place for an outdoor class, receptions, plays and programs. **Computers:** 100% of classrooms, 100% of dorms, 100% of libraries, 100% of dining areas, 100% of student union, 100% of common outdoor areas have wireless network access. Students can register for classes online. Administrative functions (other than registration) can be performed online.

CAMPUS LIFE
Environment: City. **Activities:** Choral groups, concert band, dance, drama/theater, literary magazine, music ensembles, musical theater, pep band, radio station, student government, student newspaper, symphony orchestra, television station, yearbook, Campus Ministries, Model UN. 109 registered organizations, 14 honor societies, 8 religious organizations. 4 fraternities, 5 sororities. **Athletics (Intercollegiate):** *Men:* baseball, basketball, cheerleading, cross-country, golf, soccer, tennis, track/field (outdoor), track/field (indoor). *Women:* basketball, cheerleading, cross-country, golf, soccer, tennis, track/field (outdoor), track/field (indoor), volleyball. **On-Campus Highlights:** Slane University Center, Hayworth Fine Arts Center, Millis Athletic/Convocation Center, Hayworth Chapel, The International Promenade, High Point University is in the midst of a 5-year, $250 million campus development plan that will result in the construction of a new building for the School of Business, a new Student Activity Center, a new soccer stadium and track, a new residence hall, a new Sports Center, a new University Park, and dozens of renovations across campus. **Environmental Initiatives:** Arboreatum and Tree Campus USA.

ADMISSIONS
Freshman Academic Profile: Average high school GPA 3.3. 17% in top 10% of high school class, 46% in top 25% of high school class, 81% in top 50% of high school class. 67% from public high schools. **Reported SAT (pre-2016 redesign) scores:** SAT Math middle 50% range 503-605. SAT Critical Reading middle 50% range 492-595. SAT Writing middle 50% range 482-585. **Concordant SAT scores:** SAT EBRW middle 50% 540–650. SAT Math middle 50% range 530–630. ACT middle 50% range 21-26. Minimum internet-based TOEFL 79. Minimum paper TOEFL 550. **Basis for Candidate Selection:** *Very important factors considered include:* academic GPA, standardized test scores. *Important factors considered include:* rigor of secondary school record, application essay, recommendation(s), interview, extracurricular activities, talent/ability, character/personal qualities, volunteer work, work experience, level of applicant's interest. *Other factors considered include:* first generation, alumni/ae relation. **Freshman Admission Requirements:** High school diploma is required and GED is accepted. *Academic units required:* 4 English, 3 math, 3 science, 1 science lab, 2 foreign language, 3 social studies. *Academic units recommended:* 4 English, 4 math, 3 science, 1 science lab, 3 foreign language, 3 social studies. **Freshman Admission Statistics:** 9,683 applied, 79.08% admitted, 18% enrolled. **Transfer Admission Requirements:** High school transcript, college transcript(s), standardized test scores, statement of good standing from prior institution(s). Minimum college GPA of 2.0 required. Lowest grade transferable C. **General Admission Information:** Application fee $50. Priority deadline 3/1. Regular application deadline 3/1. Nonfall registration accepted. Admission may be deferred for a maximum of 1 year.

COSTS AND FINANCIAL AID
Annual tuition $29,450. Room and board $12,572. Required fees $3,955. Average book expense $1,500. **Required Forms and Deadlines:** FAFSA, State aid form. **Notification of Awards:** Applicants will be notified of awards on a rolling basis beginning 4/1. **Types of Aid:** *Need-based scholarships/grants:* Federal Pell, FSEOG, State scholarships/grants, Private scholarships, College/university scholarship or grant aid from institutional funds. *Loans:* Direct Subsidized Stafford Loans, Direct Unsubsidized Stafford Loans, Direct PLUS loans, Federal Perkins Loans. *Student Employment:* Federal Work-Study Program available. Institutional employment available. **Financial Aid

Statistics: 96% needy freshmen, 69% needy undergrads receive need-based scholarship or grant aid. 83% freshmen, 79% undergrads receive non-need-based scholarship or grant aid. 70% freshmen, 78% undergrads receive need-based self-help aid. 5% freshmen, 6% undergrads receive athletic scholarships. 85% freshmen, 77% undergrads receive any aid. 58% undergrads borrow to pay for school. Average cumulative indebtedness $35,897. **Criteria for awarding aid:** *Non-need-based:* Academics, Alumni affiliation, Art, Athletics, Leadership, Music/drama, Religious affiliation, State/district residency.

HILBERT COLLEGE

5200 South Park Avenue, Hamburg, NY 14075-1597
Phone: 716-649-7900 • **Financial Aid Phone:** 716-649-7900
E-mail: admissions@hilbert.edu • **CEEB Code:** 2334
Fax: 716-649-0702 • **Website:** www.hilbert.edu • **ACT Code:** 2759

This private school, affiliated with the Roman Catholic Church, was founded in 1957. It has a 40-acre campus.

RATINGS
Admissions Selectivity Rating: 72 **Fire Safety Rating:** 93 **Green Rating:** 60*

STUDENTS AND FACULTY
Enrollment: 999. **Student Body:** 60% female, 40% male, 10% out-of-state, <1% international (4 countries represented). Asian 0%, African American 6%, Caucasian 82%, Hispanic 2%, Native American 2%, Pacific Islander 0%, Two or more races 0%, Race unknown 7%.
Retention and Graduation: 70% freshmen return for sophomore year. 49% freshmen graduate within 4 years. 50% freshmen graduate within 6 years. 15% grads go on to further study within 1 year. 4% grads pursue arts and sciences degrees. 4% grads pursue law degrees. 4% grads pursue business degrees.
Faculty: Student/faculty ratio 13:1. 48 full-time faculty, 50% hold PhDs, 2% are are members of minority groups, 48% are women. 0% of classes are taught by teaching assistants.

ACADEMICS
Degrees: associate, bachelor's, certificate, terminal. **Classes:** Most classes have 10-19 students. Most lab/discussion sessions have fewer than 10 students. **Most popular majors:** Criminal Justice/Law Enforcement Administration; Forensic Science and Technology; Business/Commerce. **Special Study Options:** cross-registration, distance learning, dual enrollment, honors program, independent study, internships, study abroad, Member of Western New York consortium of colleges. **Honors Programs:** The Hilbert Honors Program will give you more from your college experience. You will enroll in regular classes and fulfill honors credit requirements by doing advanced work, or in lieu of projects. These special projects allow you to work one-on-one with Hilbert's outstanding honors faculty in your major and in other academic areas. As an honors student, you will also have a student mentor for your first semester and personal faculty advisement. **Disability Services:** Special programs offered to physically disabled students, including note-taking services, reader services, tape recorders, tutors. **Career Services:** Alumni network, Alumni services, Career assessment, Internships. Internships are available with agencies in most majors.

FACILITIES
Housing: Coed dorms, apartments for single studentsCampus Apartments. 95% of campus accessible to physically diasbled. Honors Lounge, Institute for Law and Justice, Center for Creative Media, **Computers:** 100% of classrooms, 100% of dorms, 100% of libraries, 100% of dining areas, 100% of student union, 100% of common outdoor areas have wireless network access. Students can register for classes online. Administrative functions (other than registration) can be performed online.

CAMPUS LIFE
Environment: Village. **Activities:** Choral groups, drama/theater, literary magazine, student government, student newspaper, Campus Ministries. 20 registered organizations, 5 honor societies, 1 religious organization. **Athletics (Intercollegiate):** *Men:* baseball, basketball, cross-country, golf, soccer, volleyball. *Women:* basketball, cross-country, golf, soccer, softball, volleyball. **On-Campus Highlights:** Hafner Recreation Center, Franciscan Hall Atrium, Campus Apartments, Swan Auditorium, Paczesny Hall.

ADMISSIONS
Freshman Academic Profile: Average high school GPA 2.8. 2% in top 10% of high school class, 13% in top 25% of high school class, 40% in top 50% of high school class. 85% from public high schools. **Reported SAT (pre-2016 redesign) scores:** SAT Math middle 50% range 400-510. SAT Critical Reading middle 50% range 400-510. **Concordant SAT scores:** SAT Math middle 50% range 440–540. ACT middle 50% range 17-22. Minimum paper TOEFL 500. **Basis for Candidate Selection:** *Very important factors considered include:*

rigor of secondary school record, academic GPA. *Important factors considered include:* recommendation(s). *Other factors considered include:* application essay, interview, extracurricular activities, talent/ability, character/personal qualities, volunteer work, work experience. **Freshman Admission Requirements:** High school diploma is required and GED is accepted. *Academic units required:* 4 English, 2 math, 2 science, 1 science lab, 2 social studies, 2 history, 4 academic electives. *Academic units recommended:* 4 English, 3 math, 3 science, 1 foreign language, 3 social studies, 3 history, 3 academic electives. **Freshman Admission Statistics:** 726 applied, 84.71% admitted, 35% enrolled. **Transfer Admission Requirements:** High school transcript, college transcript(s), Minimum college GPA of 2.0 required. Lowest grade transferable C. **General Admission Information:** Application fee $20. Priority deadline 6/30. Regular application deadline 9/1. Nonfall registration accepted. Admission may be deferred for a maximum of 1 year.

COSTS AND FINANCIAL AID
Annual tuition $16,000. Room and board $6,600. Required fees $600. Average book expense $700. **Required Forms and Deadlines:** FAFSA, State aid form. **Notification of Awards:** Applicants will be notified of awards on a rolling basis beginning 3/1. **Types of Aid:** *Need-based scholarships/grants:* Federal Pell, FSEOG, State scholarships/grants, Private scholarships, College/university scholarship or grant aid from institutional funds. *Loans:* Federal Perkins Loans. *Student Employment:* Federal Work-Study Program available. Institutional employment available. **Financial Aid Statistics:** 99% needy freshmen, 98% needy undergrads receive need-based scholarship or grant aid. 4% freshmen, 5% undergrads receive non-need-based scholarship or grant aid. 90% freshmen, 88% undergrads receive need-based self-help aid. 0% freshmen, 0% undergrads receive athletic scholarships. 92% freshmen, 87% undergrads receive any aid. **Criteria for awarding aid:** *Non-need-based:* Academics, Leadership, Minority status.

HILLSDALE COLLEGE

33 East College Street, Hillsdale, MI 49242
Phone: 517-607-2327 • **Financial Aid Phone:** 517-607-2350
E-mail: admissions@hillsdale.edu • **CEEB Code:** 1295
Fax: 517-607-2223 • **Website:** www.hillsdale.edu • **ACT Code:** 2010

This private school was founded in 1844. It has a 200-acre campus.

RATINGS
Admissions Selectivity Rating: 93 **Fire Safety Rating:** 89 **Green Rating:** 65

STUDENTS AND FACULTY
Enrollment: 1,482. **Student Body:** 50% female, 50% male, 65% out-of-state, 0% international (9 countries represented). Asian 0%, African American 0%, Caucasian 0%, Hispanic 0%, Native American 0%, Pacific Islander 0%, Two or more races 0%, Race unknown 100%.
Retention and Graduation: 94% freshmen return for sophomore year. 73% freshmen graduate within 4 years. 83% freshmen graduate within 6 years. 8% grads pursue arts and sciences degrees. 3% grads pursue law degrees. 1% grads pursue business degrees. 6% grads pursue medical degrees. **Faculty:** Student/faculty ratio 10:1. 127 full-time faculty, 95% hold PhDs, 0% are are members of minority groups, 21% are women. 0% of classes are taught by teaching assistants.

ACADEMICS
Degrees: bachelor's, doctoral, master's. **Classes:** Most classes have 10-19 students. Most lab/discussion sessions have 10-19 students. **Most popular majors:** History; English Language and Literature; Economics. **Special Study Options:** double major, dual enrollment, honors program, independent study, internships, student-designed major, study abroad, teacher certification program. **Honors Programs:** Honors Program available. **Career Services:** Alumni network, Alumni services, Career assessment, Internships, Regional alumni. Our office executes signature programs titled 'Living and Working' where we offer students the opportunity to travel, live, and experience what it is like to work in major cities across the country. On average, the trips last two full days and include: an exciting city-specific activity (e.g. tour of the Pentagon, a Chicago River architectural tour, etc.); an intensive career workshop, where we teach networking skills and effective elevator pitches; a local alumni networking event, hosted in partnership with our Alumni Association, where the students put their new skills to the test; and job shadows and/or employer visits at partner companies in the area. In the past we have visited Chicago, IL, Detroit,

MI, Grand Rapids, MI, Lansing, MI, New York, NY, and Washington, D.C., and we intend to expand the program to include Seattle, WA, Cincinnati, OH, Denver, CO, and Omaha, NE. Each academic year we offer multiple city trips on a rotating basis. In 2016, we took students to four locations and had over 60 students and 250 alumni participate. We are proud of this program for the meaningful impact it has on our students and our alumni, and the wide-range of objectives it accomplishes for our office.

FACILITIES

Housing: men's dorms, women's dorms, fraternity/sorority housing, apartments for single students. 85% of campus accessible to physically diasbled. **Special Academic Facilities/Equipment:** Early childhood education lab, media center, K-8 private academy, Slayton Arboretum, rare books library **Computers:** 100% of classrooms, 85% of dorms, 100% of libraries, 100% of dining areas, 100% of student union, 100% of common outdoor areas have wireless network access.

CAMPUS LIFE

Environment: Village. **Activities:** Choral groups, concert band, dance, drama/theater, jazz band, literary magazine, music ensembles, musical theater, pep band, student government, student newspaper, symphony orchestra, yearbook, Campus Ministries, Student Organization. 50 registered organizations, 26 honor societies, 4 religious organizations. 3 fraternities, 3 sororities. **Athletics (Intercollegiate):** *Men:* baseball, basketball, cheerleading, cross-country, football, track/field (outdoor), track/field (indoor). *Women:* basketball, cheerleading, cross-country, diving, equestrian sports, softball, swimming, track/field (outdoor), track/field (indoor), volleyball. **On-Campus Highlights:** Student Union, Quad (outdoor quadrangle), Sage Center for the Arts, Howard Music Hall, Sports Complex.

ADMISSIONS

Freshman Academic Profile: Average high school GPA 3.8. 56% from public high schools. **Reported SAT (pre-2016 redesign) scores:** SAT Math middle 50% range 670-690. SAT Critical Reading middle 50% range 620-750. SAT Writing middle 50% range 610-730. **Concordant SAT scores:** SAT EBRW middle 50% 670–760. SAT Math middle 50% range 700–720. ACT middle 50% range 28-32. Minimum internet-based TOEFL 83. Minimum paper TOEFL 560. **Basis for Candidate Selection:** *Very important factors considered include:* rigor of secondary school record, academic GPA, standardized test scores, application essay, interview, extracurricular activities, character/personal qualities, level of applicant's interest. *Important factors considered include:* recommendation(s), volunteer work, work experience. *Other factors considered include:* talent/ability, alumni/ae relation. **Freshman Admission Requirements:** High school diploma is required and GED is accepted. *Academic units required:* 4 English, 3 math, 3 science, 2 social studies, 3 history. *Academic units recommended:* 4 English, 4 math, 4 science, 2 science labs, 3 foreign language, 4 social studies, 4 history. **Freshman Admission Statistics:** 1,934 applied, 45.19% admitted, 43% enrolled. **Transfer Admission Requirements:** High school transcript, college transcript(s), essay or personal statement, standardized test scores, statement of good standing from prior institution(s). Minimum college GPA of 3.25 required. Lowest grade transferable C. **General Admission Information:** Application fee $35. Priority deadline 1/1. Regular application deadline 4/1. Nonfall registration accepted.

COSTS AND FINANCIAL AID

Annual tuition $24,670. Room and board $10,200. Required fees $852. Average book expense $1,200. **Required Forms and Deadlines:** Institution's own financial aid form. **Notification of Awards:** Applicants will be notified of awards on a rolling basis beginning 12/1. **Types of Aid:** *Need-based scholarships/grants:* Private scholarships, College/university scholarship or grant aid from institutional funds. *Loans:* College/university loans from institutional funds. *Student Employment:* Institutional employment available. **Financial Aid Statistics:** 65% needy freshmen, 64% needy undergrads receive need-based scholarship or grant aid. 91% freshmen, 93% undergrads receive non-need-based scholarship or grant aid. 63% freshmen, 72% undergrads receive need-based self-help aid. 21% freshmen, 16% undergrads receive athletic scholarships. 97% freshmen, 98% undergrads receive any aid. **Criteria for awarding aid:** *Non-need-based:* Academics, Alumni affiliation, Art, Athletics, Leadership, Music/drama.

See page 968.

HIRAM COLLEGE

PO Box 96, Hiram, OH 44234
Phone: 330-569-5169
E-mail: admission@hiram.edu • **CEEB Code:** 1297
Fax: 330-569-5944 • **Website:** www.hiram.edu • **ACT Code:** 3280

This private school, affiliated with the Disciples of Christ Church, was founded in 1850. It has a 110-acre campus.

RATINGS

Admissions Selectivity Rating: 80   **Fire Safety Rating:** 60*   **Green Rating:** 60*

STUDENTS AND FACULTY

Enrollment: 974. **Student Body:** 49% female, 51% male, 19% out-of-state, 2% international (18 countries represented). Asian 1%, African American 17%, Caucasian 65%, Hispanic 4%, Native American <1%, Pacific Islander <1%, Two or more races 3%, Race unknown 7%.
Retention and Graduation: 70% freshmen return for sophomore year. 54% freshmen graduate within 4 years. 61% freshmen graduate within 6 years.
Faculty: Student/faculty ratio 10:1. 81 full-time faculty, 95% hold PhDs, 10% are are members of minority groups, 57% are women. 0% of classes are taught by teaching assistants.

ACADEMICS

Degrees: bachelor's, master's. **Classes:** Most classes have 10-19 students. Most lab/discussion sessions have 10-19 students. **Most popular majors:** Registered Nursing/Registered Nurse; Business Administration and Management; Accounting and Finance. **Special Study Options:** Accelerated program, cross-registration, double major, English as a Second Language (ESL), exchange student program (domestic), independent study, internships, student-designed major, study abroad, teacher certification program, weekend college. Combined degree programs: BA(Hiram)/BS(Engineering) 5 years. **Disability Services:** Special programs offered to physically disabled students, including note-taking services, reader services, tape recorders, tutors. **Career Services:** Alumni network, Alumni services, Career/job search classes, Career assessment, Internships. Hiram Connect is a new program guaranteeing that each student completes an internship, study away trip, or guided research project before graduation. It helps students reflect on who they want to be and the type of career that will help them achieve it.

FACILITIES

Housing: Coed dorms, special housing for disabled students, women's dorms, Theme Housing, suite style housing. 55% of campus accessible to physically diasbled. **Special Academic Facilities/Equipment:** Psychology lab, language lab, center, center for literature and medicine, fitness center, health center, observatory, electron microscope, two field stations for study and research.

CAMPUS LIFE

Environment: Rural. **Activities:** Choral groups, concert band, dance, drama/theater, jazz band, literary magazine, marching band, music ensembles, opera, pep band, radio station, student government, student newspaper, symphony orchestra, yearbook, Campus Ministries, Student Organization, Model UN. 55 registered organizations, 7 honor societies, 6 religious organizations. 3 fraternities, 3 sororities. **Athletics (Intercollegiate):** *Men:* baseball, basketball, cheerleading, cross-country, diving, football, golf, soccer, swimming, tennis, track/field (outdoor), track/field (indoor). *Women:* basketball, cheerleading, cross-country, diving, golf, soccer, softball, swimming, tennis, track/field (outdoor), track/field (indoor), volleyball. **On-Campus Highlights:** James H. Barrow Field Station, The Hiram College Library, Kennedy Center(Food Court, Bookstore, ballroom, and other facilities), Hiram Church, Stevens Memorial Observatory.

ADMISSIONS

Freshman Academic Profile: Average high school GPA 3.3. 16% in top 10% of high school class, 33% in top 25% of high school class, 61% in top 50% of high school class. **Reported SAT (pre-2016 redesign) scores:** SAT Math middle 50% range 433-525. SAT Critical Reading middle 50% range 430-520. SAT Writing middle 50% range 415-520. **Concordant SAT scores:** SAT EBRW middle 50% 480–580. SAT Math middle 50% range 470–560. ACT middle 50% range 19-25. Minimum internet-based TOEFL 61. Minimum paper TOEFL 500. **Basis for Candidate Selection:** *Very important factors considered include:* rigor of secondary school record, academic GPA, character/personal qualities, level of applicant's interest. *Important factors considered include:* standardized test scores, application essay, recommendation(s), interview, extracurricular activities, talent/ability. *Other factors considered include:* class rank, alumni/ae relation, volunteer work, work experience. **Freshman Admission Requirements:** *Academic units required:* 4 English, 4 math, 3 science, 1 science lab, 1 foreign language, 1 social studies, 1 history, 1 academic elective. *Academic units recommended:* 4 English, 4 math, 3 science, 1 science lab, 2 foreign language, 1 social studies, 1 history, 2 academic electives. **Freshman Admission Statistics:** 2,521 applied, 54.18% admitted, 15% enrolled. **General Admission Information:** Application fee $25. Priority deadline 12/15. Nonfall registration accepted. Admission may be deferred.

COSTS AND FINANCIAL AID
Required Forms and Deadlines: FAFSA. **Types of Aid:** *Need-based scholarships/grants:* Federal Pell, FSEOG, State scholarships/grants, Private scholarships, College/university scholarship or grant aid from institutional funds. *Loans:* Direct Subsidized Stafford Loans, Direct Unsubsidized Stafford Loans, Direct PLUS loans, Federal Perkins Loans, College/university loans from institutional funds. *Student Employment:* Federal Work-Study Program available. Institutional employment available. **Criteria for awarding aid:** *Non-need-based:* Academics, Alumni affiliation, Art, Music/drama, Religious affiliation.

HOBART AND WILLIAM SMITH COLLEGES

629 South Main Street, Geneva, NY 14456
Phone: 315-781-3622 • **Financial Aid Phone:** 315-781-3315
E-mail: admissions@hws.edu • **CEEB Code:** 2294
Fax: 315-781-3914 • **Website:** www.hws.edu • **ACT Code:** 2758

This private school was founded in 1822. It has a 170-acre campus.

RATINGS
Admissions Selectivity Rating: 89 **Fire Safety Rating:** 95 **Green Rating:** 94

STUDENTS AND FACULTY
Enrollment: 2,241. **Student Body:** 50% female, 50% male, 60% out-of-state, 6% international (30 countries represented). Asian 4%, African American 6%, Caucasian 73%, Hispanic 5%, Native American <1%, Pacific Islander <1%, Two or more races 0%, Race unknown 6%.
Retention and Graduation: 85% freshmen return for sophomore year. 72% freshmen graduate within 4 years. 77 **Faculty:** Student/faculty ratio 10:1. 221 full-time faculty, 100% hold PhDs, 17% are are members of minority groups, 49% are women. 0% of classes are taught by teaching assistants.

ACADEMICS
Degrees: bachelor's, master's. **Classes:** Most classes have 10-19 students. Most lab/discussion sessions have 10-19 students. **Most popular majors:** Environmental Studies; Economics; Mass Communication/Media Studies. **Special Study Options:** cross-registration, double major, dual enrollment, English as a Second Language (ESL), exchange student program (domestic), honors program, independent study, internships, student-designed major, study abroad, teacher certification program. Combined degree programs: BA/MA, 3-2 Engineer; 4-1 MBA; Nursing 4+3; 4-1 MAT. **Disability Services:** Special programs offered to physically disabled students, including note-taking services, reader services, tape recorders, tutors. **Career Services:** Alumni network, Alumni services, Career/job search classes, Career assessment, Internships, Regional alumni. The Salisbury: Created by gifts from Charles Salisbury Jr. '63, P'94, L.H.D.'08, the Salisbury Summer International Internship Stipend Award provides financial support of up to $20,000 for three students interested in pursuing an international internship experience in a location of the student's choice. Guaranteed Internship Program: the Colleges guarantee that students of good academic and social standing who have successfully completed the Pathways Program, will be able to participate in one internship or research opportunity. In most cases, the internship will happen in the summer after the junior year. For summer internships that are unpaid, the Colleges will provide a stipend. Pathways: Our approach to career preparation is wrapped up in our Pathways program. It's a comprehensive, action-packed approach that gets you thinking about and acting on your future. You'll research careers, spend time with professionals in the career you're pursuing, take backstage tours of certain fields and find internships and jobs. Students who complete the program make connections that lead to promising careers or graduate school.

FACILITIES
Housing: Coed dorms, men's dorms, special housing for international students, women's dorms, fraternity/sorority housing, cooperative housing, apartments for single students, Upperclass townhouses; Theme Houses; Honors Houses. 69% of campus accessible to physically disabled. **Special Academic Facilities/ Equipment:** Houghton Gallery, HWS Explorer (research vessel), 100 Acre Nature Preserve, Melly Academic Center, Rosenberg science center. **Computers:** Students can register for classes online. Administrative functions (other than registration) can be performed online.

CAMPUS LIFE
Environment: Village. **Activities:** Choral groups, dance, drama/theater, jazz band, literary magazine, music ensembles, radio station, student government, student newspaper, student-run film society, symphony orchestra, yearbook. 77 registered organizations, 12 honor societies, 4 religious organizations. 5 fraternities. **Athletics (Intercollegiate):** *Men:* basketball, crew/rowing, cross-country, football, golf, ice hockey, lacrosse, sailing, soccer, squash, tennis. *Women:* basketball, crew/rowing, cross-country, diving, field hockey, golf, lacrosse, sailing, soccer, squash, swimming, tennis. **On-Campus Highlights:** Scandling Center, South Hall, Stern Hall, North Hall, Bristol Field House, Trinity Hall, with the newly remodeled Salisbury Center, houses the Offices of Career Development, Public Service and Global Education. The building re-opened in January 2004. **Environmental Initiatives:** Integrating the Colleges' Sustainability living laboratory approach in the Climate Action Plan. The living laboratory approach is exemplified through student projects—class, independent study or volunteer that directly effect the colleges' impact on the environment and culture of environmental sustainability. For example, The Finger Lakes Institute renovation was directed by a first year Energy class project that identified specific environmental parameters to be incorporated into the building. These students' vision and project qualified the Finger Lakes Institute for the Energy Star Small Business Award. This living laboratory, student oriented learning approach is at the core of the Colleges Sustainability Program and enhanced by the Colleges Climate Action Plan.

ADMISSIONS
Freshman Academic Profile: Average high school GPA 3.5. 32% in top 10% of high school class, 64% in top 25% of high school class, 88% in top 50% of high school class. 60% from public high schools. **Reported SAT (pre-2016 redesign) scores:** SAT Math middle 50% range 580-670. SAT Critical Reading middle 50% range 580-680. SAT Writing middle 50% range 570-670. **Concordant SAT scores:** SAT EBRW middle 50% 630–710. SAT Math middle 50% range 600–700. ACT middle 50% range 26-30. Minimum internet-based TOEFL 80. Minimum paper TOEFL 550. **Basis for Candidate Selection:** *Very important factors considered include:* rigor of secondary school record, academic GPA. *Important factors considered include:* application essay, recommendation(s), interview, extracurricular activities, character/personal qualities, volunteer work, work experience. *Other factors considered include:* class rank, standardized test scores, talent/ability, first generation, alumni/ ae relation, geographical residence, state residency, racial/ethnic status, level of applicant's interest. **Freshman Admission Requirements:** High school diploma is required and GED is accepted. *Academic units required:* 4 English, 3 math, 3 science, 2 science labs, 2 foreign language, 2 social studies, 2 academic electives. *Academic units recommended:* 3 foreign language, 3 social studies, 4 academic electives. **Freshman Admission Statistics:** 4,614 applied, 54.51% admitted, 23% enrolled. **Transfer Admission Requirements:** High school transcript, college transcript(s), essay or personal statement, standardized test scores, Minimum college GPA of 2.5 required. Lowest grade transferable C. **General Admission Information:** Application fee $45. Regular application deadline 2/1. Regular notification 4/1. Nonfall registration accepted. Admission may be deferred for a maximum of 1 Year.

COSTS AND FINANCIAL AID
Annual tuition $50,432. Room and board $13,050. Required fees $1,091. Average book expense $1,300. **Required Forms and Deadlines:** FAFSA, CSS/Financial Aid PROFILE, State aid form, Noncustodial PROFILE. **Types of Aid:** *Need-based scholarships/grants:* Federal Pell, FSEOG, State scholarships/grants, Private scholarships, College/university scholarship or grant aid from institutional funds. *Loans:* Direct Subsidized Stafford Loans, Direct Unsubsidized Stafford Loans, Direct PLUS loans, Federal Perkins Loans. *Student Employment:* Federal Work-Study Program available. Institutional employment available. **Financial Aid Statistics:** 99% needy freshmen, 99% needy undergrads receive need-based scholarship or grant aid. 20% freshmen, 18% undergrads receive non-need-based scholarship or grant aid. 81% freshmen, 81% undergrads receive need-based self-help aid. 0% freshmen, 0% undergrads receive athletic scholarships. 90% freshmen, 88% undergrads receive any aid. Average cumulative indebtedness $34,935. **Criteria for awarding aid:** *Need-based:* Academics, Alumni affiliation, Art, Leadership, Music/drama, Religious affiliation. *Non-need-based:* Academics, Alumni affiliation, Art, Leadership, Music/drama, Religious affiliation.

HODGES UNIVERSITY

2655 Northbrooke Drive, Naples, FL 34119
Phone: 239-513-1122 • **Financial Aid Phone:** 239-513-1122
E-mail: admit@internationalcollege.edu • **CEEB Code:** 7113
Fax: 239-598-6254 • **Website:** www.hodges.edu • **ACT Code:** 4775

This private school was founded in 1990.

RATINGS
Admissions Selectivity Rating: 65 **Fire Safety Rating:** 60* **Green Rating:** 60*

STUDENTS AND FACULTY
Enrollment: 1,475. **Student Body:** 68% female, 32% male, 0% out-of-state, <1% international (40 countries represented). Asian 2%, African American 16%, Caucasian 55%, Hispanic 24%, Native American <1%, Pacific Islander 0%, Two or more races 0%, Race unknown 2%.
Faculty: Student/faculty ratio 17:1. 61 full-time faculty, 66% hold PhDs, 8% are are members of minority groups, 33% are women. 0% of classes are taught by teaching assistants.

ACADEMICS
Degrees: associate, bachelor's, certificate, master's. **Classes:** Most classes have 10-19 students. **Most popular majors:** Business, Management, Marketing, and Related Support Services; Multi-/Interdisciplinary Studies; Health Professions and Related Clinical Sciences. **Special Study Options:** Accelerated program, cooperative education program, distance learning, double major, English as a Second Language (ESL), independent study, internships, weekend college. **Career Services:** Alumni services, Career/job search classes, Career assessment, On-campus interviews.

FACILITIES
Housing: 100% of campus accessible to physically disabled. **Computers:** 100% of classrooms, 100% of libraries, have wireless network access. Students can register for classes online. Administrative functions (other than registration) can be performed online.

CAMPUS LIFE
Environment: City. **Activities:** literary magazine 1 honor society.
Environmental Initiatives: Reduction in energy usage.

ADMISSIONS
Minimum paper TOEFL 500. **Basis for Candidate Selection:** *Important factors considered include:* interview, level of applicant's interest. **Freshman Admission Requirements:** High school diploma is required and GED is accepted. **Freshman Admission Statistics:** 210 applied, 79.05% admitted, 94% enrolled. **Transfer Admission Requirements:** High school transcript, essay or personal statement, Lowest grade transferable C. **General Admission Information:** Application fee $20. Nonfall registration accepted. Admission may be deferred for a maximum of 1 year.

COSTS AND FINANCIAL AID
Required Forms and Deadlines: FAFSA. **Types of Aid:** *Need-based scholarships/grants:* Federal Pell, FSEOG, State scholarships/grants, Private scholarships, College/university scholarship or grant aid from institutional funds. *Student Employment:* Federal Work-Study Program available. Institutional employment available. **Financial Aid Statistics:** 90% needy freshmen, 94% needy undergrads receive need-based scholarship or grant aid. 41% freshmen, 66% undergrads receive non-need-based scholarship or grant aid. 87% freshmen, 91% undergrads receive need-based self-help aid. 0% freshmen, 0% undergrads receive athletic scholarships. **Criteria for awarding aid:** *Non-need-based:* Academics, Leadership.

HOFSTRA UNIVERSITY

100 Hofstra University, Hempstead, NY 11549
Phone: 516-463-6700 • **Financial Aid Phone:** 516-463-8000
E-mail: admission@hofstra.edu • **CEEB Code:** 2295
Fax: 516-463-5100 • **Website:** http://www.hofstra.edu • **ACT Code:** 2760

This private school was founded in 1935. It has a 240-acre campus.

RATINGS
Admissions Selectivity Rating: 86 **Fire Safety Rating:** 98 **Green Rating:** 78

STUDENTS AND FACULTY
Enrollment: 6,810. **Student Body:** 54% female, 46% male, 37% out-of-state, 5% international (53 countries represented). Asian 10%, African American 8%, Caucasian 56%, Hispanic 14%, Native American <1%, Pacific Islander 1%, Two or more races 2%, Race unknown 2%.
Retention and Graduation: 82% freshmen return for sophomore year. 53% freshmen graduate within 4 years. 64% freshmen graduate within 6 years. 30% grads go on to further study within 1 year. 5% grads pursue arts and sciences degrees. 3% grads pursue law degrees. 3% grads pursue business degrees. 2% grads pursue medical degrees. **Faculty:** Student/faculty ratio 14:1. 489 full-time faculty, 93% hold PhDs, 20% are are members of minority groups, 44% are women. 0% of classes are taught by teaching assistants.

ACADEMICS
Degrees: bachelor's, certificate, doctoral/professional, doctoral/research, doctoral, master's, postbachelor's certificate, post-master's certificate. **Classes:** Most classes have 10-19 students. Most lab/discussion sessions have 20-29 students. **Most popular majors:** Psychology; Biology/Biological Sciences; Radio, Television, and Digital Communication. **Special Study Options:** Accelerated program, cross-registration, distance learning, double major, dual enrollment, English as a Second Language (ESL), external degree program, honors program, independent study, internships, liberal arts/career combination, student-designed major, study abroad, teacher certification program. **Honors Programs:** Hofstra University's Honors College (HUHC) is the leading edge of Hofstra University's pursuit of academic excellence. Serving the highly motivated, high achieving student, every aspect of its curriculum is designed to provide them with the resources they need to meet their academic objectives. Combining the support of a strong community with the freedom to pursue individual goals HUHC emphasizes student ownership and direction of their own education. At the same time, HUHC recognizes its responsibility to support students so that they can explore, reflect upon and achieve their educational objectives. HUHC is an intimate community of students, faculty and administrators committed to challenging and supporting one another in the pursuit of excellence at all levels. Its students are connected to every college, department, major and program on campus and engaged in every aspect of campus life. All entering HUHC students begin their Hofstra careers with Culture and Expression (C&E) a four-course, year-long sequence designed specifically for the honors college community. C&E is our primary tool for establishing a community among the students of each entering class. Together, they follow a common reading list, attend common lectures and take ownership of the materials via small group discussions with some of Hofstra's best faculty. C&E addresses life's biggest questions with rigor. Most importantly, it provides a broad foundation for a lifetime of learning in college and beyond. After the first year, Honors College students pursue honors work in those Hofstra courses that they find most exciting. Each semester HUHC offers an array of small, discussion based seminars, taught by professors from around the university, who are invited to offer their dream course. In addition, HUHC's Honors Option program allows students to enrich regular courses that align with their personal and intellectual passions. These honors experiences are all recognized on the transcript and count toward completion of an HUHC designation which is applied to both the student's transcript and diploma. Thus, HUHC students may choose from among any of Hofstra's more than 145 undergraduate majors and upon graduation receive a bachelor"s degree with a special designation marking it as having been achieved with an extraordinary level of distinction. HUHC sponsors a rich array of cultural and social experiences, including trips to New York City to visit museums, Broadway shows, concerts, and major league sporting events. Given our location, HUHC faculty mentors regularly organize outdoor adventures, such as sea kayaking, hiking and visits to ocean beaches. A significant percentage of HUHC students participate in a variety of HUHC-based social service programs, including those focused on serving the homeless, promoting early literacy and working toward environmental responsibility. HUHC students can be found in leadership roles in virtually every club and activity on the Hofstra campus. They are student government

leaders, newspaper editors, and champions of social and political causes. They are committed to the arts and to sports (including Division I) and can be found in just about every form of meaningful activity imaginable. They come from across the United States, and increasingly from abroad. Most of all, they are curious about one another and the wider world. Many HUHC students opt to live in honors housing, where they enjoy an even greater sense of community and an exceptional level of support from a professional staff and specially selected student leaders. HUHC graduates have won prestigious grants and fellowships such as the Fulbright, the National Science Fellowship, and the Jack Kent Cooke fellowship. They've also been admitted to the most prestigious graduate and professional schools. Hofstra University also recognizes high-achieving students in many other ways, including Dean's List, Provost's Scholars, Phi Beta Kappa, Phi Eta Sigma, Golden Key, and the chance to earn baccalaureate degrees with distinction and departmental honors. Combined degree programs: BA/MD, BA/JD, BA/MA, BA/MBA, BA/MS, BA/MSED, BS/MBA, BS/MS, BS/MD, BBA/MBA, BBA/MS, BBA/MSED, JD/MBA, JD/MPH, MD/PHD. **Disability Services:** Special programs offered to physically disabled students, including note-taking services, reader services, tape recorders, tutors. **Career Services:** Alumni network, Alumni services, Career/job search classes, Career assessment, Internships, Regional alumni. Service Networking: A finalist for a 2016 National Association of Colleges and Employers Member's Choice Award and winner of a 2016 Long Island Council of Student Personnel Administrators, Service Networking brings together students in a particular major with employer related to that field to provide service in the Hempstead/Nassau Community. Through the hours of service, students and employers get to know one another outside the traditional confines of recruiting. We run this program in the fall and spring and target students in majors with traditionally low participation in career center programming.

FACILITIES

Housing: Coed dorms, special housing for disabled students, apartments for single students, Theme Housing, Living-Learning Center, Honors Housing, Quiet Floors, and Women's Floors. 100% of campus accessible to physically diasbled. **Special Academic Facilities/Equipment:** New state-of-the-art medical school, financial trading room, multi-media converged news room, comprehensive media production facility including a 24 hour radio station, linux beowolf cluster, digital language lab, technology, science and engineering labs, a rooftop observatory, 6 theaters including a black box teaching theater, assessment centers for client observation and counseling, child care institute, cultural center, museum, arboretum, and bird sanctuary. **Computers:** 57% of classrooms, 100% of dorms, 100% of libraries, 100% of dining areas, 100% of student union, 60% of common outdoor areas have wireless network access. Students can register for classes online. Administrative functions (other than registration) can be performed online.

CAMPUS LIFE

Environment: City. **Activities:** Choral groups, concert band, dance, drama/theater, jazz band, literary magazine, music ensembles, musical theater, opera, pep band, radio station, student government, student newspaper, student-run film society, symphony orchestra, television station, yearbook, Campus Ministries, Student Organization. 135 registered organizations, 32 honor societies, 9 religious organizations. 13 fraternities, 12 sororities. **Athletics (Intercollegiate):** *Men:* baseball, basketball, cross-country, golf, lacrosse, soccer, tennis, wrestling. *Women:* basketball, cross-country, field hockey, golf, lacrosse, soccer, softball, tennis, volleyball. **Environmental Initiatives:** New construction complies with LEED standards where feasible. The new School of Business Building will be built to obtain LEED Silver Certification. The approximate 50,000 sq. ft building is expected to open in 2018.

ADMISSIONS

Freshman Academic Profile: Average high school GPA 3.6. 27% in top 10% of high school class, 60% in top 25% of high school class, 90% in top 50% of high school class. **Reported SAT (pre-2016 redesign) scores:** SAT Math middle 50% range 540-630. SAT Critical Reading middle 50% range 530-630. **Concordant SAT scores:** SAT Math middle 50% range 570–650. ACT middle 50% range 24-29. Minimum internet-based TOEFL 80. Minimum paper TOEFL 550. **Basis for Candidate Selection:** *Very important factors considered include:* rigor of secondary school record, class rank, academic GPA, application essay, recommendation(s). *Important factors considered include:* interview, extracurricular activities, talent/ability, character/personal qualities. *Other factors considered include:* standardized test scores, first generation, alumni/ae relation, geographical residence, racial/ethnic status, volunteer work, work experience, level of applicant's interest. **Freshman Admission Requirements:** High school diploma is required and GED is accepted. *Academic units required:* 4 English, 3 math, 3 science, 1 science lab, 2 foreign language, 3 social studies. *Academic units recommended:* 4 math, 4 science, 2 science labs, 3 foreign language, 4 social studies. **Freshman Admission Statistics:** 28,617 applied, 62.22% admitted, 9% enrolled. **Transfer Admission Requirements:** college transcript(s), statement of good standing from prior institution(s). Lowest grade transferable C-. **General Admission Information:** Application fee $70. Nonfall registration accepted. Admission may be deferred for a maximum of 1 year.

COSTS AND FINANCIAL AID

Annual tuition $41,100. Room and board $14,460. Required fees $1,060. Average book expense $1,000. **Required Forms and Deadlines:** FAFSA, State aid form. **Notification of Awards:** Applicants will be notified of awards on a rolling basis beginning 3/1. **Types of Aid:** *Need-based scholarships/grants:* Federal Pell, FSEOG, State scholarships/grants, Private scholarships, College/university scholarship or grant aid from institutional funds, United Negro College Fund. *Loans:* Direct Subsidized Stafford Loans, Direct Unsubsidized Stafford Loans, Direct PLUS loans, Federal Perkins Loans, State Loans, College/university loans from institutional funds. *Student Employment:* Federal Work-Study Program available. Institutional employment available. **Financial Aid Statistics:** 96% needy freshmen, 94% needy undergrads receive need-based scholarship or grant aid. 22% freshmen, 16% undergrads receive non-need-based scholarship or grant aid. 81% freshmen, 76% undergrads receive need-based self-help aid. 1% freshmen, 1% undergrads receive athletic scholarships. 96% freshmen, 91% undergrads receive any aid. 69% undergrads borrow to pay for school. **Criteria for awarding aid:** *Need-based:* Academics, Alumni affiliation, Art, Leadership, Music/drama. *Non-need-based:* Academics, Alumni affiliation, Art, Athletics, Leadership, Minority status, Music/drama, State/district residency.

See page 970.

HOLLINS UNIVERSITY

7916 Williamson Road, Box 9707, Roanoke, VA 24020-1707
Phone: 540-362-6401 • **Financial Aid Phone:** 540-362-6332
E-mail: huadm@hollins.edu • **CEEB Code:** 5294
Fax: 540-362-6218 • **Website:** www.hollins.edu • **ACT Code:** 4360

This private school was founded in 1842. It has a 475-acre campus.

RATINGS

Admissions Selectivity Rating: 85   **Fire Safety Rating:** 85   **Green Rating:** 80

STUDENTS AND FACULTY

Enrollment: 647. **Student Body:** 100% female, 0% male, 47% out-of-state, 5% international (17 countries represented). Asian 2%, African American 12%, Caucasian 65%, Hispanic 6%, Native American 1%, Pacific Islander <1%, Two or more races 5%, Race unknown 4%.
Retention and Graduation: 69% freshmen return for sophomore year. 50% freshmen graduate within 4 years. 53 10% grads go on to further study within 1 year. 16% grads pursue arts and sciences degrees. 1% grads pursue law degrees. 1% grads pursue business degrees. 3% grads pursue medical degrees. **Faculty:** Student/faculty ratio 9:1. 70 full-time faculty, 97% hold PhDs, 14% are members of minority groups, 59% are women. 1% of classes are taught by teaching assistants.

ACADEMICS

Degrees: bachelor's, master's, postbachelor's certificate, post-master's certificate. **Classes:** Most classes have 10-19 students. Most lab/discussion sessions have fewer than 10 students. **Most popular majors:** English Language and Literature; Psychology; Business/Commerce. **Special Study Options:** Accelerated program, cross-registration, double major, dual enrollment, exchange student program (domestic), independent study, internships, student-designed major, study abroad, teacher certification program. **Honors Programs:** A number of university departments offer honors programs. The specific nature of departmental honors varies from department to department. The programs, which are undertaken for at least the full senior year, may involve research, theses, oral or written examinations, seminars, reading programs, or any combination thereof. **Disability Services:** Special programs offered to physically disabled students, including tape recorders. **Career Services:** Alumni network, Alumni services, Career/job search classes, Career assessment, Internships, Regional alumni, On-campus interviews. Signature Internship Program: Sophomores, juniors, and seniors may apply for an exceptional number of internships offered by alumnae in various fields. These internships carry academic credit and offer a stipend of $300. Housing is often provided.

FACILITIES

Housing: special housing for disabled students, women's dorms, apartments for single students, Wellness Housing, Theme Housing. 44% of campus accessible to physically diasbled. **Special Academic Facilities/Equipment:** Athletic complex, a writing center, language labs, campus-wide computer network, scientific equipment and instrumentation, art museum, and a state-of-the-art library. **Computers:** 90% of classrooms, 100% of dorms, 100% of libraries, 100% of dining areas, 100% of student union, 100% of common outdoor areas have wireless network access. Students can register for classes online. Administrative functions (other than registration) can be performed online.

CAMPUS LIFE

Environment: City. **Activities:** Choral groups, dance, drama/theater, literary magazine, music ensembles, musical theater, student government, student newspaper, student-run film society, television station, yearbook, Campus Ministries, Student Organization, Model UN. 28 registered organizations, 15 honor societies, 5 religious organizations. **Athletics (Intercollegiate):** *Women:* basketball, equestrian sports, golf, lacrosse, soccer, swimming, tennis. **On-Campus Highlights:** Front Quadrangle, Wetherill Visual Arts Center and Wilson Museum, Wyndham Robertson Library, Moody Center, Gymnasium, Northen Swim Cntrr, Tayloe Fitness Cntr. **Environmental Initiatives:** Signing the President's Climate Agreement.

ADMISSIONS

Freshman Academic Profile: Average high school GPA 3.7. 23% in top 10% of high school class, 40% in top 25% of high school class, 91% in top 50% of high school class. 81% from public high schools. **Reported SAT (pre-2016 redesign) scores:** SAT Math middle 50% range 490-590. SAT Critical Reading middle 50% range 530-643. SAT Writing middle 50% range 490-600. **Concordant SAT scores:** SAT EBRW middle 50% 570–670. SAT Math middle 50% range 520–610. ACT middle 50% range 23-29. Minimum internet-based TOEFL 80. Minimum paper TOEFL 550. **Basis for Candidate Selection:** *Very important factors considered include:* academic GPA, standardized test scores. *Important factors considered include:* application essay, recommendation(s). *Other factors considered include:* rigor of secondary school record, class rank, interview, extracurricular activities, talent/ability, character/ personal qualities, first generation, alumni/ae relation, volunteer work, work experience, level of applicant's interest. **Freshman Admission Requirements:** High school diploma is required and GED is accepted. *Academic units required:* 4 English, 3 math, 3 science, 2 foreign language, 3 social studies. **Freshman Admission Statistics:** 2,901 applied, 59.88% admitted, 13% enrolled. **Transfer Admission Requirements:** High school transcript, college transcript(s), essay or personal statement, Minimum college GPA of 2.5 required. Lowest grade transferable C. **General Admission Information:** Priority deadline 2/1. Nonfall registration accepted. Admission may be deferred for a maximum of 1 year.

COSTS AND FINANCIAL AID

Annual tuition $36,200. Room and board $12,800. Required fees $635. Average book expense $600. **Required Forms and Deadlines:** FAFSA, State aid form. **Notification of Awards:** Applicants will be notified of awards on a rolling basis beginning 3/1. **Types of Aid:** *Need-based scholarships/grants:* Federal Pell, FSEOG, State scholarships/grants, Private scholarships, College/ university scholarship or grant aid from institutional funds. *Loans:* Direct Subsidized Stafford Loans, Direct Unsubsidized Stafford Loans, Direct PLUS loans, Federal Perkins Loans, College/university loans from institutional funds. *Student Employment:* Federal Work-Study Program available. Institutional employment available. **Financial Aid Statistics:** 100% needy freshmen, 100% needy undergrads receive need-based scholarship or grant aid. 100% freshmen, 100% undergrads receive non-need-based scholarship or grant aid. 70% freshmen, 73% undergrads receive need-based self-help aid. 0% freshmen, 0% undergrads receive athletic scholarships. 99% freshmen, 96% undergrads receive any aid. 76% undergrads borrow to pay for school. Average cumulative indebtedness $34,414. **Criteria for awarding aid:** *Need-based:* Academics, Alumni affiliation, Art, Leadership, Minority status, Music/drama. *Non-need-based:* Academics, Alumni affiliation, Art, Leadership, Music/drama, State/ district residency.

HOLY FAMILY UNIVERSITY

9801 Frankford Avenue, Philadephia, PA 19114-2009
Phone: 215-637-7700 • **Financial Aid Phone:** 267-341-3234
E-mail: admissions@holyfamily.edu gradstudy@holyfamily.edu • **CEEB Code:** 2297
Fax: 215-281-1022 • **Website:** www.holyfamily.edu • **ACT Code:** 3592

This private school, affiliated with the Roman Catholic Church, was founded in 1954. It has a 46-acre campus.

RATINGS

Admissions Selectivity Rating: 76   **Fire Safety Rating:** 99   **Green Rating:** 65

STUDENTS AND FACULTY

Enrollment: 1,766. **Student Body:** 74% female, 26% male, 14% out-of-state, <1% international (5 countries represented). Asian 5%, African American 12%,

Caucasian 62%, Hispanic 6%, Native American <1%, Pacific Islander <1%, Two or more races 0%, Race unknown 15%.
Retention and Graduation: 76% freshmen return for sophomore year. 44% freshmen graduate within 4 years. **Faculty:** Student/faculty ratio 13:1. 76 full-time faculty, 82% hold PhDs, 13% are are members of minority groups, 71% are women. 0% of classes are taught by teaching assistants.

ACADEMICS

Degrees: associate, bachelor's, certificate, doctoral, master's, postbachelor's certificate, post-master's certificate. **Classes:** Most classes have 10-19 students. **Most popular majors:** Registered Nursing/Registered Nurse; Business Administration and Management; Education. **Special Study Options:** Accelerated program, cooperative education program, double major, dual enrollment, English as a Second Language (ESL), independent study, internships, study abroad, teacher certification program. Combined degree programs: BA/MA, BABA/MS. **Disability Services:** Special programs offered to physically disabled students, including note-taking services, reader services, tape recorders, tutors. **Career Services:** Alumni services, Career/job search classes, Career assessment, Internships, Co-op Program.

FACILITIES

Housing: Coed dorms, of campus accessible to physically diasbled. **Special Academic Facilities/Equipment:** On-campus nursery school, art gallery. **Computers:** 100% of classrooms, 100% of dorms, 100% of libraries, 100% of dining areas, 100% of student union, 100% of common outdoor areas have wireless network access. Students can register for classes online. Administrative functions (other than registration) can be performed online.

CAMPUS LIFE

Environment: Metropolis. **Activities:** Choral groups, drama/theater, literary magazine, radio station, student government, student newspaper, television station, yearbook, Campus Ministries, Student Organization. 15 registered organizations, 14 honor societies, 1 religious organization. **Athletics (Intercollegiate):** *Men:* basketball, cross-country, golf, soccer, track/field (outdoor), track/field (indoor). *Women:* basketball, cross-country, lacrosse, soccer, softball, tennis, track/field (outdoor), track/field (indoor), volleyball. **On-Campus Highlights:** Campus Center, Education / Technology Center, Library, Student Residence Halls, Nurse Education Building.

ADMISSIONS

Freshman Academic Profile: Average high school GPA 3.1. 10% in top 10% of high school class, 25% in top 25% of high school class, 62% in top 50% of high school class. 60% from public high schools. **Reported SAT (pre-2016 redesign) scores:** SAT Math middle 50% range 410-520. SAT Critical Reading middle 50% range 420-510. SAT Writing middle 50% range 410-500. **Concordant SAT scores:** SAT EBRW middle 50% 460–560. SAT Math middle 50% range 450–550. Minimum paper TOEFL 550. **Basis for Candidate Selection:** *Very important factors considered include:* academic GPA. *Important factors considered include:* standardized test scores. *Other factors considered include:* rigor of secondary school record, class rank, application essay, recommendation(s), interview, extracurricular activities, character/ personal qualities, alumni/ae relation, volunteer work. **Freshman Admission Requirements:** High school diploma is required and GED is accepted. *Academic units required:* 4 English, 3 math, 2 science, 2 foreign language, 2 history, 3 academic electives. **Freshman Admission Statistics:** 1,441 applied, 68.49% admitted, 35% enrolled. **Transfer Admission Requirements:** High school transcript, college transcript(s), essay or personal statement, statement of good standing from prior institution(s). Minimum college GPA of 2.5 required. Lowest grade transferable C. **General Admission Information:** Application fee $25. Nonfall registration accepted. Admission may be deferred for a maximum of 1 year.

COSTS AND FINANCIAL AID

Annual tuition $29,338. Room and board $13,576. Required fees $1,008. Average book expense $1,090. **Required Forms and Deadlines:** FAFSA. **Notification of Awards:** Applicants will be notified of awards on a rolling basis beginning 3/15. **Types of Aid:** *Need-based scholarships/grants:* Federal Pell, FSEOG, State scholarships/grants, Private scholarships, College/ university scholarship or grant aid from institutional funds. *Loans:* Direct Subsidized Stafford Loans, Direct Unsubsidized Stafford Loans, Direct PLUS loans, Federal Perkins Loans, Federal Nursing Loans. *Student Employment:* Federal Work-Study Program available. **Financial Aid Statistics:** 100% needy freshmen, 94% needy undergrads receive need-based scholarship or grant aid. 99% freshmen, 92% undergrads receive non-need-based scholarship or grant aid. 96% freshmen, 93% undergrads receive need-based self-help aid. 14% freshmen, 9% undergrads receive athletic scholarships. 83% freshmen, 97% undergrads receive any aid. 86% undergrads borrow to pay for school. Average cumulative indebtedness $39,664. **Criteria for awarding aid:** *Need-based:* Academics. *Non-need-based:* Academics, Athletics, Leadership.

HOOD COLLEGE

401 Rosemont Avenue, Frederick, MD 21701
Phone: 301-696-3400 • **Financial Aid Phone:** 301-696-3411
E-mail: admission@hood.edu • **CEEB Code:** 5296
Fax: 301-696-3819 • **Website:** www.hood.edu • **ACT Code:** 1702

This private school, affiliated with the United Church of Christ Church, was founded in 1893. It has a 50-acre campus.

RATINGS

Admissions Selectivity Rating: 80   **Fire Safety Rating:** 96   **Green Rating:** 65

STUDENTS AND FACULTY

Enrollment: 1,151. **Student Body:** 61% female, 39% male, 24% out-of-state, 2% international (21 countries represented). Asian 3%, African American 14%, Caucasian 61%, Hispanic 10%, Native American 0%, Pacific Islander <1%, Two or more races 5%, Race unknown 5%.
Retention and Graduation: 81% freshmen return for sophomore year. 50% freshmen graduate within 4 years. 65% freshmen graduate within 6 years. 38% grads go on to further study within 1 year. 57% grads pursue arts and sciences degrees. 9% grads pursue law degrees. 15% grads pursue business degrees. **Faculty:** Student/faculty ratio 10:1. 103 full-time faculty, 94% hold PhDs, 18% are are members of minority groups, 59% are women. 0% of classes are taught by teaching assistants.

ACADEMICS

Degrees: bachelor's, certificate, master's, postbachelor's certificate. **Classes:** Most classes have 10-19 students. Most lab/discussion sessions have 10-19 students. **Most popular majors:** Psychology; Business Administration, Management and Operations; Biology/Biological Sciences. **Special Study Options:** double major, dual enrollment, honors program, independent study, internships, liberal arts/career combination, student-designed major, study abroad, teacher certification program. **Honors Programs:** Our award-winning program offers exceptional undergraduate students four years of exciting coursework and co-curriuclar activities. Classes are small, discussion oriented, and enhanced by guest speakers and field trips. Interdisciplinary in approach, students are encouraged to engage in personal and intellectual development in the context of community memebership and service. Combined degree programs: BA/MA, BA Biology/MS Environmental Biology; BA Bus Admin/MBA. **Disability Services:** Special programs offered to physically disabled students, including note-taking services, reader services, tape recorders, tutors. **Career Services:** Alumni network, Alumni services, Career assessment, Internships, Regional alumni. Hood College has a very active internship program. In 2016-17,more than 200 students completed internships at a variety of sites throughout the Baltimore/Washington/Frederick area.

FACILITIES

Housing: Coed dorms, women's dorms, Theme Housing. 50% of campus accessible to physically diasbled. **Special Academic Facilities/Equipment:** Art gallery, child development lab, language lab, observatory, science labs. **Computers:** 100% of classrooms, 100% of dorms, 100% of libraries, 100% of dining areas, 100% of student union, 100% of common outdoor areas have wireless network access. Students can register for classes online. Administrative functions (other than registration) can be performed online.

CAMPUS LIFE

Environment: Town. **Activities:** Choral groups, dance, drama/theater, jazz band, literary magazine, music ensembles, musical theater, radio station, student government, student newspaper, student-run film society, Campus Ministries, Student Organization, Model UN. 92 registered organizations, 14 honor societies, 6 religious organizations. **Athletics (Intercollegiate):** *Men:* basketball, cross-country, golf, lacrosse, soccer, swimming, tennis, track/field (outdoor). *Women:* basketball, cross-country, field hockey, golf, lacrosse, soccer, softball, swimming, tennis, track/field (outdoor), volleyball. **On-Campus Highlights:** Whitaker Campus Center, Hodson Science and Technology Building, Coblentz Dining Hall, Beneficial-Hodson Library, The Residence Halls. **Environmental Initiatives:** Reduction of natural gas consumption through the use of new decentralized building heating boilers and software controls programming.

ADMISSIONS

Freshman Academic Profile: Average high school GPA 3.5. 17% in top 10% of high school class, 46% in top 25% of high school class, 82% in top 50% of high school class. 81% from public high schools. **Reported SAT (pre-2016 redesign) scores:** SAT Math middle 50% range 450-540. SAT Critical Reading middle 50% range 450-560. SAT Writing middle 50% range 430-530. **Concordant SAT scores:** SAT EBRW middle 50% 490–600. SAT Math middle 50% range 490–570. ACT middle 50% range 20-24. Minimum internet-based TOEFL 79. Minimum paper TOEFL 550. **Basis for Candidate Selection:** *Very important factors considered include:* rigor of secondary school record,

academic GPA. *Important factors considered include:* standardized test scores, application essay, recommendation(s), interview, extracurricular activities. *Other factors considered include:* class rank, talent/ability, character/personal qualities, volunteer work, work experience, level of applicant's interest. **Freshman Admission Requirements:** High school diploma is required and GED is accepted. *Academic units required:* 4 English, 3 math, 3 science, 2 science labs, 2 foreign language, 3 social studies, 3 history, 1 academic elective. *Academic units recommended:* 4 English, 4 math, 4 science, 2 science labs, 3 foreign language, 1 social studies, 3 history, 1 academic elective, 1 computer science, 1 visual/performing arts. **Freshman Admission Statistics:** 1,727 applied, 70.53% admitted, 18% enrolled. **Transfer Admission Requirements:** college transcript(s), Minimum college GPA of 2.5 required. Lowest grade transferable C-. **General Admission Information:** Application fee $35. Priority deadline 2/1. Nonfall registration accepted. Admission may be deferred for a maximum of 1 yr.

COSTS AND FINANCIAL AID

Annual tuition $37,400. Room and board $12,580. Required fees $560. Average book expense $1,200. **Required Forms and Deadlines:** FAFSA. **Notification of Awards:** Applicants will be notified of awards on a rolling basis beginning 3/1. **Types of Aid:** *Need-based scholarships/grants:* Federal Pell, FSEOG, State scholarships/grants, Private scholarships, College/university scholarship or grant aid from institutional funds. *Loans:* Direct Subsidized Stafford Loans, Direct Unsubsidized Stafford Loans, Direct PLUS loans, Federal Perkins Loans. *Student Employment:* Federal Work-Study Program available. Institutional employment available. **Financial Aid Statistics:** 100% needy freshmen, 100% needy undergrads receive need-based scholarship or grant aid. 15% freshmen, 17% undergrads receive non-need-based scholarship or grant aid. 81% freshmen, 79% undergrads receive need-based self-help aid. 0% freshmen, 0% undergrads receive athletic scholarships. 98% freshmen, 97% undergrads receive any aid. 71% undergrads borrow to pay for school. Average cumulative indebtedness $30,554. **Criteria for awarding aid:** *Need-based:* Leadership, Minority status, Music/drama, Religious affiliation. *Non-need-based:* Academics, Alumni affiliation, Leadership, Minority status, Music/drama, Religious affiliation, State/district residency.

HOPE COLLEGE

69 East 10th, Holland, MI 49422-9000
Phone: 616-395-7850 • **Financial Aid Phone:** 616-395-7765
E-mail: admissions@hope.edu • **CEEB Code:** 1301
Fax: 616-395-7130 • **Website:** www.hope.edu • **ACT Code:** 2012

This private school, affiliated with the Reformed Church Church, was founded in 1862. It has a 120-acre campus.

RATINGS

Admissions Selectivity Rating: 87   **Fire Safety Rating:** 89   **Green Rating:** 84

STUDENTS AND FACULTY

Enrollment: 3,238. **Student Body:** 60% female, 40% male, 32% out-of-state, 1% international (35 countries represented). Asian 2%, African American 3%, Caucasian 84%, Hispanic 8%, Native American <1%, Pacific Islander 0%, Two or more races 2%, Race unknown 0%.
Retention and Graduation: 86% freshmen return for sophomore year. 65% freshmen graduate within 4 years. 76% freshmen graduate within 6 years. 24% grads go on to further study within 1 year. 17% grads pursue arts and sciences degrees. 2% grads pursue law degrees. 6% grads pursue business degrees. 5% grads pursue medical degrees. **Faculty:** Student/faculty ratio 11:1. 244 full-time faculty, 0% hold PhDs, 16% are are members of minority groups, 47% are women. 0% of classes are taught by teaching assistants.

ACADEMICS

Degrees: bachelor's. **Classes:** Most classes have 10-19 students. Most lab/discussion sessions have 20-29 students. **Most popular majors:** Business/Commerce; Speech Communication and Rhetoric; Psychology. **Special Study Options:** distance learning, double major, English as a Second Language (ESL), independent study, internships, student-designed major, study abroad, teacher certification program. **Disability Services:** Special programs offered to physically disabled students, including note-taking services, reader services, tape recorders, tutors. **Career Services:** Alumni network, Alumni services, Career/job search classes, Career assessment, Internships, Regional alumni. Hope has an extensive undergraduate research program engaging more than 200 students each summer.

FACILITIES

Housing: Coed dorms, special housing for disabled students, men's dorms, special housing for international students, women's dorms, fraternity/sorority housing, apartments for single students, Wellness Housing, Theme Housing.

95% of campus accessible to physically disabled. **Special Academic Facilities/Equipment:** Art gallery, particle accelerator, computational chemistry lab, electron microscopes, spectrometers, ultracentrifuge, observatory, new $38M science building. **Computers:** 70% of classrooms, 100% of libraries, 34% of dining areas, 100% of student union, 40% of common outdoor areas have wireless network access. Students can register for classes online. Administrative functions (other than registration) can be performed online.

CAMPUS LIFE

Environment: Town. **Activities:** Choral groups, concert band, dance, drama/theater, jazz band, literary magazine, music ensembles, radio station, student government, student newspaper, symphony orchestra, television station, yearbook, Campus Ministries, Student Organization, Model UN. 67 registered organizations, 22 honor societies, 6 religious organizations. 6 fraternities, 7 sororities. **Athletics (Intercollegiate):** *Men:* baseball, basketball, cheerleading, cross-country, diving, football, golf, soccer, swimming, tennis, track/field (outdoor), track/field (indoor). *Women:* basketball, cheerleading, cross-country, diving, golf, soccer, softball, swimming, tennis, track/field (outdoor), track/field (indoor), volleyball. **On-Campus Highlights:** DeWitt Student Center, Martha Miller Center for Global Communic, Library, Paul A Schaap Science Center, DeVos Fieldhouse, Kletz—student grill. **Environmental Initiatives:** electrical use reduction.

ADMISSIONS

Freshman Academic Profile: Average high school GPA 3.7. 34% in top 10% of high school class, 65% in top 25% of high school class, 92% in top 50% of high school class. 88% from public high schools. **Reported SAT (pre-2016 redesign) scores:** SAT Math middle 50% range 550-670. SAT Critical Reading middle 50% range 540-650. **Concordant SAT scores:** SAT Math middle 50% range 570–700. ACT middle 50% range 24-29. Minimum internet-based TOEFL 80. **Basis for Candidate Selection:** *Very important factors considered include:* academic GPA, standardized test scores. *Important factors considered include:* rigor of secondary school record. *Other factors considered include:* class rank, application essay, recommendation(s), interview, extracurricular activities, talent/ability, character/personal qualities, first generation, alumni/ae relation, geographical residence, state residency, religious affiliation/commitment, racial/ethnic status, volunteer work, work experience, level of applicant's interest. **Freshman Admission Requirements:** High school diploma is required and GED is accepted. *Academic units recommended:* 4 English. **Freshman Admission Statistics:** 4,420 applied, 72.04% admitted, 25% enrolled. **Transfer Admission Requirements:** High school transcript, college transcript(s), essay or personal statement, standardized test scores, statement of good standing from prior institution(s). Minimum college GPA of 2.5 required. Lowest grade transferable C. **General Admission Information:** Application fee $35. Priority deadline 3/1. Nonfall registration accepted. Admission may be deferred for a maximum of 1 year.

COSTS AND FINANCIAL AID

Annual tuition $31,380. Room and board $9,690. Required fees $180. Average book expense $920. **Required Forms and Deadlines:** FAFSA, Institution's own financial aid form. **Notification of Awards:** Applicants will be notified of awards on a rolling basis beginning 3/15. **Types of Aid:** *Need-based scholarships/grants:* Federal Pell, FSEOG, State scholarships/grants, Private scholarships, College/university scholarship or grant aid from institutional funds. *Loans:* Direct Subsidized Stafford Loans, Direct Unsubsidized Stafford Loans, Direct PLUS loans, Federal Perkins Loans. *Student Employment:* Federal Work-Study Program available. Institutional employment available. **Financial Aid Statistics:** 87% needy freshmen, 88% needy undergrads receive need-based scholarship or grant aid. 81% freshmen, 73% undergrads receive non-need-based scholarship or grant aid. 77% freshmen, 82% undergrads receive need-based self-help aid. 0% freshmen, 0% undergrads receive athletic scholarships. 95% freshmen, 95% undergrads receive any aid. Average cumulative indebtedness $32,188. **Criteria for awarding aid:** *Need-based:* Academics, Minority status. *Non-need-based:* Academics, Art, Minority status, Music/drama, Religious affiliation.

HOPE INTERNATIONAL UNIVERSITY

Undergraduate Admissions, Fullerton, CA 92831
Phone: 866-722-4673 • **Financial Aid Phone:** 714-879-3901
E-mail: pccadmissions@hiu.edu
Fax: 714-681-7423 • **Website:** www.hiu.edu • **ACT Code:** 356

This private school, affiliated with the Church of Christ Church, was founded in 1928. It has a 18-acre campus.

RATINGS

Admissions Selectivity Rating: 85   **Fire Safety Rating:** 70   **Green Rating:** 60*

STUDENTS AND FACULTY

Enrollment: 500. **Student Body:** 60% female, 40% male, 24% out-of-state, 2% international. Asian 5%, African American 5%, Caucasian 63%, Hispanic 16%, Native American 1%, Pacific Islander 0%, Two or more races 0%, Race unknown 7%.
Retention and Graduation: 71% freshmen return for sophomore year. 1% freshmen graduate within 4 years. 50% freshmen graduate within 6 years.
Faculty: Student/faculty ratio 15:1. 32 full-time faculty, 59% hold PhDs, 6% are are members of minority groups, 25% are women. 0% of classes are taught by teaching assistants.

ACADEMICS

Degrees: associate, bachelor's, certificate, master's, postbachelor's certificate.
Classes: Most classes have fewer than 10 students. Most lab/discussion sessions have fewer than 10 students. **Most popular majors:** Teacher Education, Multiple Levels; Youth Ministry; Psychology. **Special Study Options:** Accelerated program, cross-registration, distance learning, double major, dual enrollment, English as a Second Language (ESL), independent study, internships, liberal arts/career combination, student-designed major, study abroad, teacher certification program. **Disability Services:** Special programs offered to physically disabled students, including note-taking services, tape recorders, tutors.

FACILITIES

Housing: men's dorms, women's dorms. 95% of campus accessible to physically disabled.

CAMPUS LIFE

Environment: City. **Activities:** Choral groups, drama/theater, jazz band, music ensembles, musical theater, student government, student newspaper, yearbook. **Athletics (Intercollegiate):** *Men:* basketball, soccer, tennis, volleyball. *Women:* basketball, soccer, softball, tennis, volleyball. **On-Campus Highlights:** Lawson-Fulton Student Center, Darling Library, Lambda Lounge, Auditorium, The Commons.

ADMISSIONS

Freshman Academic Profile: Average high school GPA 3.3. 20% in top 10% of high school class, 37% in top 25% of high school class, 77% in top 50% of high school class. 95% from public high schools. **Reported SAT (pre-2016 redesign) scores:** SAT Math middle 50% range 420-530. SAT Critical Reading middle 50% range 440-540. SAT Writing middle 50% range 420-520. **Concordant SAT scores:** SAT EBRW middle 50% 480–590. SAT Math middle 50% range 460–560. ACT middle 50% range 18-21. Minimum paper TOEFL 500. **Basis for Candidate Selection:** *Very important factors considered include:* rigor of secondary school record, class rank, academic GPA, standardized test scores, application essay, recommendation(s). *Important factors considered include:* level of applicant's interest. *Other factors considered include:* interview, extracurricular activities, talent/ability, character/personal qualities, religious affiliation/commitment, volunteer work. **Freshman Admission Requirements:** High school diploma is required and GED is accepted. *Academic units recommended:* 4 English, 2 math, 1 science, 1 science lab, 1 foreign language, 1 social studies, 1 history, 3 academic electives. **Freshman Admission Statistics:** 413 applied, 32.45% admitted. **Transfer Admission Requirements:** college transcript(s), essay or personal statement, statement of good standing from prior institution(s). Minimum college GPA of 2.5 required. Lowest grade transferable C. **General Admission Information:** Application fee $40. Nonfall registration accepted. Admission may be deferred.

COSTS AND FINANCIAL AID

Annual tuition $21,560. Room and board $6,940. Required fees $325. Average book expense $1,386. **Required Forms and Deadlines:** FAFSA, Institution's own financial aid form. **Notification of Awards:** Applicants will be notified of awards on a rolling basis beginning 3/15. **Types of Aid:** *Need-based scholarships/grants:* Federal Pell, FSEOG, State scholarships/grants, Private scholarships, College/university scholarship or grant aid from institutional funds. *Loans:* Direct Subsidized Stafford Loans, Direct Unsubsidized Stafford Loans, Direct PLUS loans, Federal Perkins Loans, State Loans, College/university loans from institutional funds. *Student Employment:* Federal Work-Study Program available. Institutional employment available. **Financial Aid Statistics:** 98% needy freshmen, 96% needy undergrads receive need-based scholarship or grant aid. 19% freshmen, 15% undergrads receive non-need-based scholarship or grant aid. 74% freshmen, 79% undergrads receive need-based self-help aid. 0% freshmen, 0% undergrads receive athletic scholarships. 67% freshmen, 73% undergrads receive any aid. **Criteria for awarding aid:** *Need-based:* Academics, Alumni affiliation, Athletics, Job skills, Leadership, Music/drama, Religious affiliation. *Non-need-based:* Academics, Alumni affiliation, Athletics, Leadership, Music/drama, Religious affiliation.

HOUGHTON COLLEGE

PO Box 128, Houghton, NY 14744
Phone: 585-567-9353 • **Financial Aid Phone:** 585-567-9328
E-mail: admission@houghton.edu • **CEEB Code:** 2299
Fax: 716-567-9522 • **Website:** www.houghton.edu • **ACT Code:** 2766

*This private school, affiliated with the Wesleyan Church, was founded in
1883. It has a 1300-acre campus.*

RATINGS

Admissions Selectivity Rating: 82   **Fire Safety Rating:** 82   **Green Rating:** 75

STUDENTS AND FACULTY

Enrollment: 1,047. **Student Body:** 65% female, 35% male, 38% out-of-state,
6% international (31 countries represented). Asian 1%, African American 3%,
Caucasian 85%, Hispanic 2%, Native American <1%, Pacific Islander 0%, Two
or more races 3%, Race unknown <1%.
Retention and Graduation: 88% freshmen return for sophomore year. 65%
freshmen graduate within 4 years. 73% freshmen graduate within 6 years. 18%
grads go on to further study within 1 year. 11% grads pursue arts and sciences
degrees. 1% grads pursue business degrees. 1% grads pursue medical degrees.
Faculty: Student/faculty ratio 12:1. 73 full-time faculty, 88% hold PhDs, 4% are
are members of minority groups, 36% are women. 0% of classes are taught by
teaching assistants.

ACADEMICS

Degrees: associate, bachelor's, master's. **Classes:** Most classes have 10-19
students. Most lab/discussion sessions have 10-19 students. **Most popular
majors:** Business Administration and Management; Biology/Biological
Sciences; Digital Communication and Media/Multimedia. **Special Study
Options:** cross-registration, double major, exchange student program
(domestic), honors program, independent study, internships, liberal arts/
career combination, study abroad, teacher certification program. **Honors
Programs:** First-year honors program in London, England; first-year honors
program in Eastern Europe; first-year honors program in math and science
Combined degree programs: BA/PharmD, 4+1 MBA. **Disability Services:**
Special programs offered to physically disabled students, including note-taking
services, tape recorders, tutors. **Career Services:** Alumni network, Alumni
services, Career/job search classes, Career assessment, Internships, Regional
alumni. Our Off-Campus Programs truly combine the best in off-campus and
experiential learning. Most trips fit right within a student's degree plan and
provide exceptional preparation for their careers on top of a once-in-a-lifetime
opportunity.

FACILITIES

Housing: men's dorms, special housing for international students, women's
dorms, apartments for married students, apartments for single students. 80%
of campus accessible to physically disabled. **Special Academic Facilities/
Equipment:** Electron microscope, Art Gallery, Greenhouse. **Computers:**
100% of classrooms, 100% of dorms, 100% of libraries, 100% of dining areas,
100% of student union, 50% of common outdoor areas have wireless network
access. Students can register for classes online. Administrative functions (other
than registration) can be performed online.

CAMPUS LIFE

Environment: Rural. **Activities:** Choral groups, concert band, dance, drama/
theater, jazz band, literary magazine, music ensembles, musical theater, opera,
student government, student newspaper, symphony orchestra, yearbook,
Campus Ministries, Student Organization. 34 registered organizations, 2
honor societies, 9 religious organizations. **Athletics (Intercollegiate):** *Men:*
basketball, cross-country, soccer, track/field (outdoor), track/field (indoor).
Women: basketball, cross-country, field hockey, soccer, track/field (outdoor),
track/field (indoor), volleyball. **On-Campus Highlights:** Center for the Arts,
Nielsen Physical Education Center, Wesley Chapel, Campus Center, Library.
Environmental Initiatives: Achieving carbon neutrality by 2050.

ADMISSIONS

Freshman Academic Profile: Average high school GPA 3.5. 35% in top 10%
of high school class, 61% in top 25% of high school class, 88% in top 50%
of high school class. 66% from public high schools. **Reported SAT (pre-
2016 redesign) scores:** SAT Math middle 50% range 490-605. SAT Critical
Reading middle 50% range 490-630. SAT Writing middle 50% range 470-600.
Concordant SAT scores: SAT EBRW middle 50% 540-670. SAT Math middle
50% range 520-630. ACT middle 50% range 21-28. Minimum internet-
based TOEFL 80. Minimum paper TOEFL 550. **Basis for Candidate
Selection:** *Very important factors considered include:* class rank, academic
GPA, religious affiliation/commitment. *Important factors considered include:*
rigor of secondary school record, standardized test scores, application essay,
recommendation(s), character/personal qualities. *Other factors considered
include:* interview, extracurricular activities, talent/ability, first generation,

alumni/ae relation, racial/ethnic status, volunteer work, work experience, level
of applicant's interest. **Freshman Admission Requirements:** High school
diploma is required and GED is accepted. *Academic units recommended:* 4
English, 3 math, 2 science, 2 science labs, 2 foreign language, 1 social studies,
3 history. **Freshman Admission Statistics:** 807 applied, 91.08% admitted,
30% enrolled. **Transfer Admission Requirements:** college transcript(s), essay
or personal statement, Lowest grade transferable C-. **General Admission
Information:** Application fee $40. Priority deadline 3/1. Nonfall registration
accepted. Admission may be deferred for a maximum of 2 years.

COSTS AND FINANCIAL AID

Annual tuition $27,578. Room and board $8,012. Required fees $150. Average
book expense $1,000. **Required Forms and Deadlines:** FAFSA, State aid
form. **Notification of Awards:** Applicants will be notified of awards on a rolling
basis beginning 3/1. **Types of Aid:** *Need-based scholarships/grants:* Federal
Pell, FSEOG, State scholarships/grants, Private scholarships, College/university
scholarship or grant aid from institutional funds. *Loans:* Direct Subsidized
Stafford Loans, Direct Unsubsidized Stafford Loans, Direct PLUS loans,
Federal Perkins Loans. *Student Employment:* Federal Work-Study Program
available. Institutional employment available. **Financial Aid Statistics:** 90%
needy freshmen, 88% needy undergrads receive need-based scholarship or
grant aid. 76% freshmen, 76% undergrads receive non-need-based scholarship
or grant aid. 90% freshmen, 89% undergrads receive need-based self-help aid.
0% freshmen, 5% undergrads receive athletic scholarships. 100% freshmen,
98% undergrads receive any aid. **Criteria for awarding aid:** *Need-based:*
Academics, Leadership, Minority status, Religious affiliation. *Non-need-based:*
Academics, Alumni affiliation, Art, Music/drama, Religious affiliation, State/
district residency.

HOUSTON BAPTIST UNIVERSITY

7502 Fondren Road, Houston, TX 77074
Phone: 281-649-3211 • **Financial Aid Phone:** 281-649-3749
E-mail: admissions@hbu.edu • **CEEB Code:** 6282
Fax: 281-649-3217 • **Website:** www.hbu.edu • **ACT Code:** 4101

*This private school, affiliated with the Southern Baptist Church, was
founded in 1960. It has a 100-acre campus.*

RATINGS

Admissions Selectivity Rating: 79   **Fire Safety Rating:** 65   **Green Rating:** 60*

STUDENTS AND FACULTY

Enrollment: 2,313. **Student Body:** 63% female, 37% male, 4% out-of-state,
3% international (28 countries represented). Asian 10%, African American 18%,
Caucasian 26%, Hispanic 33%, Native American <1%, Pacific Islander <1%,
Two or more races 4%, Race unknown 5%.
Retention and Graduation: 68% freshmen return for sophomore year. 25%
freshmen graduate within 4 years. 44% freshmen graduate within 6 years.
Faculty: Student/faculty ratio 16:1. 136 full-time faculty, 85% hold PhDs, 21%
are are members of minority groups, 46% are women. 0% of classes are taught
by teaching assistants.

ACADEMICS

Degrees: bachelor's, master's. **Classes:** Most classes have 10-19 students.
Most lab/discussion sessions have fewer than 10 students. **Most popular
majors:** Registered Nursing/Registered Nurse; Kinesiology and Exercise
Science; Biology/Biological Sciences. **Special Study Options:** Accelerated
program, double major, dual enrollment, English as a Second Language
(ESL), independent study, internships, liberal arts/career combination, teacher
certification program. Combined degree programs: Masters of Accountancy
(with BBA). **Career Services:** Career/job search classes, Career assessment,
Internships.

FACILITIES

Housing: men's dorms, women's dorms, apartments for single students. 90%
of campus accessible to physically disabled. **Special Academic Facilities/
Equipment:** Museum of architecture/decorative arts, language lab, research
center. **Computers:** Students can register for classes online.

CAMPUS LIFE

Environment: Metropolis. **Activities:** Choral groups, concert band,
drama/theater, music ensembles, pep band, student government, student
newspaper, yearbook. 36 registered organizations, 9 honor societies, 3 religious
organizations. 2 fraternities, 2 sororities. **Athletics (Intercollegiate):** *Men:*
baseball, basketball, cheerleading. *Women:* basketball, cheerleading, softball,
volleyball. **On-Campus Highlights:** Hinton Center, Baugh Center and the
Bone Appetit Cafe, Bible Museum, Wellness Center, Admissions Office.

ADMISSIONS

Freshman Academic Profile: Average high school GPA 3.4. **Reported SAT (pre-2016 redesign) scores:** SAT Math middle 50% range 470-570. SAT Critical Reading middle 50% range 470-570. **Concordant SAT scores:** SAT Math middle 50% range 510–590. ACT middle 50% range 21-26. Minimum internet-based TOEFL 80. Minimum paper TOEFL 80. **Basis for Candidate Selection:** *Important factors considered include:* class rank, academic GPA, standardized test scores. *Other factors considered include:* rigor of secondary school record, recommendation(s), extracurricular activities, religious affiliation/commitment. **Freshman Admission Requirements:** High school diploma is required and GED is accepted. *Academic units recommended:* 4 English, 4 math, 4 science, 2 foreign language, 2 social studies, 2 history, and 5 units from above areas or other academic areas. **Freshman Admission Statistics:** 15,256 applied, 34.56% admitted, 11% enrolled. **Transfer Admission Requirements:** college transcript(s), essay or personal statement, statement of good standing from prior institution(s). Minimum college GPA of 2.0 required. Lowest grade transferable C. **General Admission Information:** Application fee $25. Nonfall registration accepted. Admission may be deferred.

COSTS AND FINANCIAL AID

Average book expense $1,000. **Required Forms and Deadlines:** FAFSA. **Notification of Awards:** Applicants will be notified of awards on a rolling basis beginning 3/15. **Types of Aid:** *Need-based scholarships/grants:* Federal Pell, FSEOG, College/university scholarship or grant aid from institutional funds. *Loans:* Direct Subsidized Stafford Loans, Direct Unsubsidized Stafford Loans, Direct PLUS loans, State Loans. *Student Employment:* Federal Work-Study Program available. **Financial Aid Statistics:** 99% needy freshmen, 99% needy undergrads receive need-based scholarship or grant aid. 100% freshmen, 93% undergrads receive non-need-based scholarship or grant aid. 84% freshmen, 82% undergrads receive need-based self-help aid. 10% freshmen, 14% undergrads receive athletic scholarships. 66% undergrads borrow to pay for school. Average cumulative indebtedness $32,027. **Criteria for awarding aid:** *Need-based:* Religious affiliation. *Non-need-based:* Academics, Alumni affiliation, Art, Athletics, Leadership, Music/drama.

HOWARD UNIVERSITY

2400 Sixth Street, NW, Suite 111, Washington, DC 20059
Phone: 202-806-2755 • **Financial Aid Phone:** 202-806-2840
E-mail: admission@howard.edu • **CEEB Code:** 5297
Fax: 202-806-4465 • **Website:** www.howard.edu • **ACT Code:** 674

This private school was founded in 1867. It has a 258-acre campus.

RATINGS

Admissions Selectivity Rating: 88   **Fire Safety Rating:** 98   **Green Rating:** 60*

STUDENTS AND FACULTY

Enrollment: 6,965. **Student Body:** 67% female, 33% male, 95% out-of-state, 4% international (86 countries represented). Asian 2%, African American 91%, Caucasian 1%, Hispanic <1%, Native American 1%, Pacific Islander <1%, Two or more races 0%, Race unknown 0%.
Retention and Graduation: 85% freshmen return for sophomore year. 42% freshmen graduate within 4 years. 60% grads go on to further study within 1 year. 42% grads pursue arts and sciences degrees. 12% grads pursue law degrees. 15% grads pursue business degrees. 11% grads pursue medical degrees. **Faculty:** Student/faculty ratio 10:1. 1,094 full-time faculty, 0% hold PhDs, 87% are are members of minority groups, 42% are women.

ACADEMICS

Degrees: bachelor's, certificate, doctoral/professional, doctoral/research, doctoral, master's, post-master's certificate. **Classes:** Most classes have fewer than 10 students. Most lab/discussion sessions have 10-19 students. **Most popular majors:** Journalism; Radio and Television; Biology/Biological Sciences. **Special Study Options:** Accelerated program, cooperative education program, distance learning, double major, English as a Second Language (ESL), exchange student program (domestic), honors program, independent study, internships, study abroad, teacher certification program, Tutorial program, advanced placement, continuing education. Combined degree programs: BA/MD, BA/DDS, MBA / JD, MD / PHD. **Disability Services:** Special programs offered to physically disabled students, including note-taking services, reader services. **Career Services:** Career/job search classes, Career assessment, Internships. Rangel Scholars Program Internships offer exposure to Capital Hii and countries abroad. Students get personal experiences regarding the working

of our political system and those of other countries from experienced state department professionals and elected government officials.

FACILITIES

Housing: Coed dorms, men's dorms, women's dorms, apartments for married students, apartments for single students. 100% of campus accessible to physically diasbled. **Special Academic Facilities/Equipment:** Three art galleries, language labs, hospital. Research center with comprehensive collection on Africa and persons of African descent. **Computers:** 10% of classrooms, 100% of dorms, 100% of libraries, 10% of dining areas, 50% of student union, 10% of common outdoor areas have wireless network access. Students can register for classes online. Administrative functions (other than registration) can be performed online.

CAMPUS LIFE

Environment: Metropolis. **Activities:** Choral groups, concert band, dance, drama/theater, jazz band, literary magazine, marching band, music ensembles, musical theater, opera, pep band, radio station, student government, student newspaper, student-run film society, symphony orchestra, television station, yearbook, Campus Ministries, Student Organization. 150 registered organizations, 15 honor societies, 3 religious organizations. 10 fraternities, 8 sororities. **Athletics (Intercollegiate):** *Men:* basketball, cheerleading, cross-country, diving, football, soccer, swimming, tennis, track/field (outdoor). *Women:* basketball, bowling, boxing, cheerleading, cross-country, diving, lacrosse, soccer, softball, swimming, tennis, track/field (outdoor), volleyball. **On-Campus Highlights:** Founders Library, Rankin Chapel, Punchout, Ira Aldridge Theatre, Burr Gymnasium.

ADMISSIONS

Freshman Academic Profile: Average high school GPA 3.3. 26% in top 10% of high school class, 55% in top 25% of high school class, 86% in top 50% of high school class. 80% from public high schools. **Reported SAT (pre-2016 redesign) scores:** SAT Math middle 50% range 490-610. SAT Critical Reading middle 50% range 500-610. SAT Writing middle 50% range 490-600. **Concordant SAT scores:** SAT EBRW middle 50% 550–660. SAT Math middle 50% range 520–630. ACT middle 50% range 21-27. Minimum paper TOEFL 550. **Basis for Candidate Selection:** *Very important factors considered include:* rigor of secondary school record, class rank, academic GPA, standardized test scores. *Other factors considered include:* application essay, recommendation(s), extracurricular activities, talent/ability, first generation, alumni/ae relation, volunteer work, work experience, level of applicant's interest. **Freshman Admission Requirements:** High school diploma is required and GED is accepted. *Academic units required:* 4 English, 3 math, 2 science, 2 science labs, 2 foreign language, 2 social studies, 4 academic electives. **Freshman Admission Statistics:** 13,760 applied, 48.41% admitted, 22% enrolled. **Transfer Admission Requirements:** college transcript(s), statement of good standing from prior institution(s). Minimum college GPA of 2.5 required. Lowest grade transferable C. **General Admission Information:** Application fee $45. Priority deadline 2/15. Regular application deadline 2/15. Nonfall registration accepted. Admission may be deferred for a maximum of 1 Semester.

COSTS AND FINANCIAL AID

Annual tuition $22,737. Room and board $13,814. Required fees $1,233. Average book expense $3,000. **Required Forms and Deadlines:** FAFSA. **Notification of Awards:** Applicants will be notified of awards on a rolling basis beginning 2/16. **Types of Aid:** *Need-based scholarships/grants:* Federal Pell, FSEOG, State scholarships/grants, Private scholarships, College/university scholarship or grant aid from institutional funds, Federal Nursing Scholarships. *Loans:* Direct Subsidized Stafford Loans, Direct Unsubsidized Stafford Loans, Direct PLUS loans, Federal Perkins Loans, Federal Nursing Loans, State Loans, College/university loans from institutional funds. *Student Employment:* Federal Work-Study Program available. Institutional employment available. **Financial Aid Statistics:** 62% needy freshmen, 63% needy undergrads receive need-based scholarship or grant aid. 57% freshmen, 47% undergrads receive non-need-based scholarship or grant aid. 72% freshmen, 77% undergrads receive need-based self-help aid. 3% freshmen, 4% undergrads receive athletic scholarships. 96% freshmen, 96% undergrads receive any aid. **Criteria for awarding aid:** *Need-based:* Academics, Leadership, Music/drama. *Non-need-based:* Academics, Art, Athletics, Leadership, Music/drama.

HULT INTERNATIONAL BUSINESS SCHOOL

Financial Aid Phone: 617-619-1097
CEEB Code: San Francisco: 7754 London: 6385 • **ACT Code:** 1835

RATINGS

Admissions Selectivity Rating: 60*   **Fire Safety Rating:** 60*   **Green Rating:** 60*

STUDENTS AND FACULTY

Faculty: 0% of classes are taught by teaching assistants.

ACADEMICS

Degrees: bachelor's, master's.

ADMISSIONS

Basis for Candidate Selection: *Important factors considered include:* rigor of secondary school record, academic GPA, application essay, interview, talent/ ability, character/personal qualities, level of applicant's interest. *Other factors considered include:* class rank, standardized test scores, recommendation(s), extracurricular activities, volunteer work, work experience. **General Admission Information:** Application fee $75. Nonfall registration accepted. Admission may be deferred for a maximum of 1 year.

COSTS AND FINANCIAL AID

Required Forms and Deadlines: Institution's own financial aid form. **Types of Aid:** *Need-based scholarships/grants:* College/university scholarship or grant aid from institutional funds. *Student Employment:* Institutional employment available. **Financial Aid Statistics:** 100% needy freshmen receive need-based scholarship or grant aid. 74% freshmen, 77% undergrads receive any aid. **Criteria for awarding aid:** *Need-based:* Academics, Leadership. *Non-need-based:* Academics, Leadership, State/district residency.

HUMBOLDT STATE UNIVERSITY

1 Harpst Street, Arcata, CA 95521-8299
Phone: 707-826-4402 • **Financial Aid Phone:** 707-826-4321
E-mail: hsuinfo@humboldt.edu • **CEEB Code:** 4345
Fax: 707-826-6190 • **Website:** www.humboldt.edu • **ACT Code:** 286

This public school was founded in 1913. It has a 161-acre campus.

RATINGS

Admissions Selectivity Rating: 77   **Fire Safety Rating:** 92   **Green Rating:** 92

STUDENTS AND FACULTY

Enrollment: 6,647. **Student Body:** 56% female, 44% male, 6% out-of-state, 1% international (50 countries represented). Asian 3%, African American 3%, Caucasian 44%, Hispanic 34%, Native American 1%, Pacific Islander <1%, Two or more races 7%, Race unknown 6%.
Retention and Graduation: 71% freshmen return for sophomore year. 15% freshmen graduate within 4 years. 46% freshmen graduate within 6 years. **Faculty:** Student/faculty ratio 23:1. 241 full-time faculty, 99% hold PhDs, 16% are are members of minority groups, 44% are women.

ACADEMICS

Degrees: bachelor's, master's, postbachelor's certificate. **Classes:** Most classes have 20-29 students. Most lab/discussion sessions have 20-29 students. **Most popular majors:** Biology/Biological Sciences; Business Administration and Management; Psychology. **Special Study Options:** double major, English as a Second Language (ESL), exchange student program (domestic), student-designed major, study abroad, teacher certification program. **Disability Services:** Special programs offered to physically disabled students, including note-taking services, reader services, tape recorders, tutors. **Career Services:** Alumni services, Career/job search classes, Career assessment, Internships, Regional alumni. Internship Peer Advising offers one-on-one appointments with students who are interested in seeking an internship. They do an assessment of each student's 'internship search readiness', an initial resume critique, and an introduction to the search process and resources. Internship Peer Advisors also offer 'How to Find an Internship' workshops and short presentations in academic classes requested by faculty.

FACILITIES

Housing: Coed dorms. 85% of campus accessible to physically disabled. **Special Academic Facilities/Equipment:** Art and geology museums, marine research lab, fish hatchery, wildlife game pen, observatory, First Street Gallery **Computers:** 85% of classrooms, 100% of dorms, 100% of libraries, 100% of dining areas, 100% of student union, 80% of common outdoor areas have wireless network access. Students can register for classes online. Administrative functions (other than registration) can be performed online.

CAMPUS LIFE

Environment: Village. **Activities:** Choral groups, concert band, dance, drama/theater, jazz band, literary magazine, music ensembles, pep band, radio station, student government, student newspaper, symphony orchestra, Student Organization, Model UN. 160 registered organizations, 6 honor societies, 8 religious organizations. 2 fraternities, 4 sororities. **Athletics (Intercollegiate):** *Men:* basketball, cross-country, football, soccer, track/field (outdoor). *Women:* basketball, crew/rowing, cross-country, soccer, softball, track/field (outdoor),

volleyball. **On-Campus Highlights:** Founders Hall, Campus Center for Appropriate Technology, University Center, Redwood Bowl, University Library. **Environmental Initiatives:** Campus Center for Appropriate Technology (CCAT): For 35 years, the Campus Center for Appropriate Technology live-in demonstration home for sustainability annually exposes over 2,000 students, faculty, staff, and visitors through tours, student-taught courses, workshops, presentations and hands-on projects. The first of its kind, CCAT has been the inspiration for similar projects on college campuses across the nation. http:// www.humboldt.edu/~ccat/

ADMISSIONS

Freshman Academic Profile: Average high school GPA 3.2. 13% in top 10% of high school class, 46% in top 25% of high school class, 80% in top 50% of high school class. 90% from public high schools. **Reported SAT (pre-2016 redesign) scores:** SAT Math middle 50% range 430-540. SAT Critical Reading middle 50% range 440-550. SAT Writing middle 50% range 420-540. **Concordant SAT scores:** SAT EBRW middle 50% 480–600. SAT Math middle 50% range 470–570. ACT middle 50% range 18-24. Minimum internet-based TOEFL 71. Minimum paper TOEFL 525. **Basis for Candidate Selection:** *Very important factors considered include:* rigor of secondary school record, academic GPA. *Important factors considered include:* geographical residence, state residency. *Other factors considered include:* standardized test scores. **Freshman Admission Requirements:** High school diploma is required and GED is accepted. *Academic units required:* 4 English, 3 math, 2 science, 2 science labs, 2 foreign language, 1 social studies, 1 history, 1 academic elective, 1 visual/performing arts. **Freshman Admission Statistics:** 12,967 applied, 76.31% admitted, 13% enrolled. **Transfer Admission Requirements:** college transcript(s), statement of good standing from prior institution(s). Minimum college GPA of 2.00 required. Lowest grade transferable D-. **General Admission Information:** Application fee $55. Priority deadline 10/31. Regular application deadline 12/6. Nonfall registration accepted.

COSTS AND FINANCIAL AID

Annual in-state tuition $5,472. Annual out-of-state tuition $16,632. Room and board $12,712. Required fees $1,740. Average book expense $1,660. **Required Forms and Deadlines:** FAFSA. **Notification of Awards:** Applicants will be notified of awards on a rolling basis beginning 4/1. **Types of Aid:** *Need-based scholarships/grants:* Federal Pell, State scholarships/grants, Private scholarships, College/university scholarship or grant aid from institutional funds. *Loans:* Direct Subsidized Stafford Loans, Direct Unsubsidized Stafford Loans, Direct PLUS loans, Federal Perkins Loans. *Student Employment:* Federal Work-Study Program available. Institutional employment available. **Financial Aid Statistics:** 93% needy freshmen, 93% needy undergrads receive need-based scholarship or grant aid. 2% freshmen, 2% undergrads receive non-need-based scholarship or grant aid. 77% freshmen, 73% undergrads receive need-based self-help aid. 1% freshmen, 1% undergrads receive athletic scholarships. 72% freshmen, 74% undergrads receive any aid. 73% undergrads borrow to pay for school. Average cumulative indebtedness $23,834. **Criteria for awarding aid:** *Non-need-based:* Academics, Alumni affiliation, Athletics, Leadership, Minority status, State/district residency.

HUMPHREYS COLLEGE

6650 Inglewood Avenue, Stockton, CA 95207
Phone: 209-478-0800 • **Financial Aid Phone:** 209-478-0800
E-mail: slopez@humphreys.edu
Fax: 209-478-0800 • **Website:** http://www.humphreys.edu/

This private school was founded in 1896. It has a 10-acre campus.

RATINGS

Admissions Selectivity Rating: 65   **Fire Safety Rating:** 60*   **Green Rating:** 60*

STUDENTS AND FACULTY

Enrollment: 610. **Student Body:** 85% female, 15% male, 0% out-of-state, <1% international. Asian 13%, African American 17%, Caucasian 29%, Hispanic 37%, Native American 1%, Pacific Islander 0%, Two or more races 0%, Race unknown 2%.
Retention and Graduation: 64% freshmen return for sophomore year. 100% freshmen graduate within 6 years. 54% grads go on to further study within 1 year. 20% grads pursue arts and sciences degrees. 30% grads pursue law degrees. 40% grads pursue business degrees. 1% grads pursue medical degrees. **Faculty:** Student/faculty ratio 18:1. 18 full-time faculty, 17% hold PhDs, 6% are are members of minority groups, 67% are women. 0% of classes are taught by teaching assistants.

ACADEMICS

Degrees: associate, bachelor's, certificate. **Classes:** Most classes have greater than 100 students. **Special Study Options:** distance learning, double major, dual enrollment, independent study, internships. **Career Services:** Alumni services, Internships, On-campus interviews.

FACILITIES
Housing: apartments for single students. 100% of campus accessible to physically diasbled.

CAMPUS LIFE
Environment: Village. **Activities:** literary magazine, student newspaper. 3 registered organizations.

ADMISSIONS
Freshman Academic Profile: Average high school GPA 3.0. 0% in top 10% of high school class, 0% in top 25% of high school class, 15% in top 50% of high school class. 95% from public high schools. ACT middle 50% range 0-0. Minimum paper TOEFL 450. **Basis for Candidate Selection:** *Very important factors considered include:* interview. *Important factors considered include:* character/personal qualities. *Other factors considered include:* level of applicant's interest. **Freshman Admission Requirements:** High school diploma is required and GED is accepted. **Freshman Admission Statistics:** 143 applied, 81.12% admitted, 100% enrolled. **Transfer Admission Requirements:** High school transcript, college transcript(s), interview, Minimum college GPA of 2.0 required. Lowest grade transferable C-. **General Admission Information:** Application fee $35. Nonfall registration accepted. Admission may be deferred.

COSTS AND FINANCIAL AID
Required Forms and Deadlines: FAFSA. **Types of Aid:** *Need-based scholarships/grants:* Federal Pell, FSEOG, State scholarships/grants, Private scholarships. *Student Employment:* Federal Work-Study Program available. Institutional employment available. **Financial Aid Statistics:** 100% needy freshmen, 100% needy undergrads receive need-based scholarship or grant aid. 0% undergrads receive non-need-based scholarship or grant aid. 23% freshmen, 7% undergrads receive need-based self-help aid. 0% freshmen, 0% undergrads receive athletic scholarships. 98% freshmen, 98% undergrads receive any aid. **Criteria for awarding aid:** *Need-based:* Academics.

HUNTINGDON COLLEGE

1500 East Fairview Avenue, Montgomery, AL 36106-2148
Phone: 334-833-4497 • **Financial Aid Phone:** 334-833-4428
E-mail: admiss@huntingdon.edu • **CEEB Code:** 1303
Fax: 334-833-4347 • **Website:** www.huntingdon.edu • **ACT Code:** 18

This private school, affiliated with the Methodist Church, was founded in 1854. It has a 71-acre campus.

RATINGS
Admissions Selectivity Rating: 79   **Fire Safety Rating:** 95   **Green Rating:** 60*

STUDENTS AND FACULTY
Enrollment: 1,140. **Student Body:** 49% female, 51% male, 19% out-of-state, <1% international (5 countries represented). Asian 0%, African American 21%, Caucasian 64%, Hispanic 4%, Native American 1%, Pacific Islander <1%, Two or more races 4%, Race unknown 5%.
Retention and Graduation: 62% freshmen return for sophomore year. 26% freshmen graduate within 4 years. 39% freshmen graduate within 6 years.
Faculty: Student/faculty ratio 14:1. 46 full-time faculty, 80% hold PhDs, 4% are are members of minority groups, 48% are women. 0% of classes are taught by teaching assistants.

ACADEMICS
Degrees: bachelor's. **Classes:** Most classes have fewer than 10 students. Most lab/discussion sessions have 10-19 students. **Most popular majors:** Kinesiology and Exercise Science; Biology/Biological Sciences; Business/Commerce. **Special Study Options:** cross-registration, double major, honors program, independent study, internships, liberal arts/career combination, student-designed major, study abroad, teacher certification program, Adult Degree Completion Program in which students take classes only in the evening, all year long, dual engineering degree with Auburn University and exchange student program with universities Ireland; travel opportunities to all full-time junior and seniors within regular educational costs or for nominal additional fees. **Honors Programs:** Program Honors—An outstanding student in a particular major has the opportunity to create an individualized honors project within the major to meet a particular need and interest. **Disability Services:** Special programs offered to physically disabled students, including note-taking services, reader services, tape recorders, tutors. **Career Services:** Alumni network, Alumni services, Career/job search classes, Career assessment, Internships. The Internship program is exceptional. The Center for Career and Vocation currently has more internships and jobs than there are students and

alumni needing such opportunities. Huntingdon College's partnership with the community and local business and industry is paying huge dividends for Huntingdon students, alumni and the College.

FACILITIES
Housing: Coed dorms, men's dorms, women's dorms. 85% of campus accessible to physically diasbled. **Special Academic Facilities/Equipment:** 1. The Bowman Ecological Center is a protected area in Prattville, AL that provides space for students to collect and study samples of plants, trees, and aquatic life. 2. Sybil Smith Hall is a fully equipped music facility housing the Lucile Crowell Delchamps Recital Hall, the Julia Lightfoot Sellers Reception Hall, faculty offices and studios, rehersal rooms, classrooms, a modern electronic music laboratory, and one of the most extensive music collections in the South, with more than 10,000 records, CDs and tapes. 3. The Staton Center for Learning Enrichment Center oversees the Academic Success Centers, advises students who have not declared majors, provides academic counseling for students with provisional enrollment, serves as a resource for study halls as related to study skills and time management skills, and advises staff and faculty serving the First Year Experience (FYEx) program. 4. Leon and Myra Allman Ligon Chapel contains the newly expanded and installed Bellingrath Memorial Organ, which Dr. Harold Rohlig, professor of music, designed. The Bellingrath Memorial Organ is one of the largest of its kind among private colleges in the Southeast, with 141 ranks and a four-manual keyboard. The Chapel's Green Window, revered by alumni as a symbol of the Huntingdon experience, is framed by the new organ pipes, some of which are 32 feet in length. Ligon Chapel is the site of pageants, performances, lectures, convocations, concerts, and countless traditions at Huntingdon College. **Computers:** 40% of classrooms, 33% of dorms, 100% of libraries, 100% of dining areas, 100% of student union, have wireless network access. Administrative functions (other than registration) can be performed online. Undergraduates are required to own a computer.

CAMPUS LIFE
Environment: City. **Activities:** Choral groups, concert band, dance, drama/theater, literary magazine, marching band, music ensembles, pep band, student government, student newspaper, yearbook, Campus Ministries, Student Organization, Model UN. 50 registered organizations, 15 honor societies, 3 religious organizations. 4 fraternities, 4 sororities. **Athletics (Intercollegiate):** *Men:* baseball, basketball, cross-country, football, golf, soccer, tennis. *Women:* basketball, cross-country, golf, soccer, softball, tennis, volleyball. **On-Campus Highlights:** Flowers Hall, Houghton Memorial Library, Wilson Center, Carolyn & Wynton Blount (Residence) Hall, Julia Walker Russell Dining Hall.

ADMISSIONS
Freshman Academic Profile: Average high school GPA 3.4. 8% in top 10% of high school class, 29% in top 25% of high school class, 63% in top 50% of high school class. 86% from public high schools. **Reported SAT (pre-2016 redesign) scores:** SAT Math middle 50% range 425-525. SAT Critical Reading middle 50% range 420-525. **Concordant SAT scores:** SAT Math middle 50% range 470–560. ACT middle 50% range 19-24. Minimum internet-based TOEFL 45. Minimum paper TOEFL 500. **Basis for Candidate Selection:** *Very important factors considered:* rigor of secondary school record, academic GPA, standardized test scores. *Other factors considered include:* class rank, application essay, recommendation(s), interview. **Freshman Admission Requirements:** High school diploma is required and GED is accepted. *Academic units recommended:* 4 English, 3 math, 2 science, 2 foreign language, 3 social studies, 3 history. **Freshman Admission Statistics:** 1,716 applied, 56.76% admitted, 28% enrolled. **Transfer Admission Requirements:** High school transcript, college transcript(s), statement of good standing from prior institution(s). Minimum college GPA of 2.25 required. Lowest grade transferable C. **General Admission Information:** Nonfall registration accepted. Admission may be deferred for a maximum of 1 semester.

COSTS AND FINANCIAL AID
Required Forms and Deadlines: FAFSA. **Notification of Awards:** Applicants will be notified of awards on a rolling basis beginning 3/1. **Types of Aid:** *Need-based scholarships/grants:* Federal Pell, FSEOG, State scholarships/grants, Private scholarships, College/university scholarship or grant aid from institutional funds. *Loans:* Direct Subsidized Stafford Loans, Direct Unsubsidized Stafford Loans, Direct PLUS loans, Federal Perkins Loans. *Student Employment:* Federal Work-Study Program available. Institutional employment available. **Financial Aid Statistics:** 100% needy freshmen, 100% needy undergrads receive need-based scholarship or grant aid. 11% freshmen, 11% undergrads receive non-need-based scholarship or grant aid. 82% freshmen, 81% undergrads receive need-based self-help aid. 0% freshmen, 0% undergrads receive athletic scholarships. 100% freshmen, 100% undergrads receive any aid. 81% undergrads borrow to pay for school. Average cumulative indebtedness $33,503. **Criteria for awarding aid:** *Need-based:* Art, Music/drama, Religious affiliation. *Non-need-based:* Academics, Alumni affiliation, Leadership, Music/drama, Religious affiliation, State/district residency.

HUNTINGTON UNIVERSITY

2303 College Avenue, Huntington, IN 46750
Phone: (260) 359-4000 • **Financial Aid Phone:** 800-642-6493
E-mail: admissions@huntington.edu • **CEEB Code:** 1304
Fax: (260) 358-3699 • **Website:** www.huntington.edu • **ACT Code:** 1202

This private school, affiliated with the Protestant Church, was founded in 1897. It has a 170-acre campus.

RATINGS
Admissions Selectivity Rating: 79   **Fire Safety Rating:** 96   **Green Rating:** 60*

STUDENTS AND FACULTY
Enrollment: 1,030. **Student Body:** 57% female, 43% male, 35% out-of-state, 4% international (20 countries represented). Asian 0%, African American 2%, Caucasian 88%, Hispanic 3%, Native American <1%, Pacific Islander <1%, Two or more races 1%, Race unknown 0%.
Retention and Graduation: 79% freshmen return for sophomore year. 57% freshmen graduate within 4 years. 62% freshmen graduate within 6 years. 14% grads go on to further study within 1 year. 13% grads pursue arts and sciences degrees. 1% grads pursue medical degrees. **Faculty:** Student/faculty ratio 13:1. 55 full-time faculty, 87% hold PhDs, 2% are are members of minority groups, 38% are women. 0% of classes are taught by teaching assistants.

ACADEMICS
Degrees: associate, bachelor's, doctoral, master's. **Classes:** Most classes have 10-19 students. Most lab/discussion sessions have 10-19 students. **Most popular majors:** Animation, Interactive Technology, Video Graphics and Special Effects; Practical Nursing, Vocational Nursing and Nursing Assistants; Cinematography and Film/Video Production. **Special Study Options:** Accelerated program, double major, independent study, internships, study abroad, teacher certification program, Bible and religion. Combined degree programs: BS/MAT. **Disability Services:** Special programs offered to physically disabled students, including note-taking services, reader services, tutors. **Career Services:** Alumni network, Alumni services, Career/job search classes, Career assessment, Internships, Regional alumni. We have an Enterprise Resource Center that prepares students with job training, resume building and interview training and it also finds and prepares student for internships.

FACILITIES
Housing: special housing for disabled students, men's dorms, women's dorms, apartments for single students, college-owned houses. 61% of campus accessible to physically diasbled. **Special Academic Facilities/Equipment:** Thornhill Nature Preserve **Computers:** 100% of classrooms, 100% of dorms, 100% of libraries, 100% of dining areas, 100% of student union, have wireless network access. Students can register for classes online. Administrative functions (other than registration) can be performed online.

CAMPUS LIFE
Environment: Town. **Activities:** Choral groups, concert band, dance, drama/theater, jazz band, literary magazine, music ensembles, musical theater, pep band, radio station, student government, student newspaper, student-run film society, television station, yearbook, Campus Ministries, Student Organization. 6 honor societies, 4 religious organizations. **Athletics (Intercollegiate):** *Men:* baseball, basketball, cheerleading, cross-country, golf, soccer, tennis, track/field (outdoor), track/field (indoor). *Women:* basketball, cheerleading, cross-country, golf, soccer, softball, tennis, track/field (outdoor), track/field (indoor), volleyball. **On-Campus Highlights:** Residence Halls-lounges, Habecker Dining Commons, Norm's Place-snack lounge, Merillat Complex for Physical EducationandRecreation, Merillat Centre for the Arts. **Environmental Initiatives:** Campus recycling program.

ADMISSIONS
Freshman Academic Profile: Average high school GPA 3.5. 26% in top 10% of high school class, 53% in top 25% of high school class, 80% in top 50% of high school class. 81% from public high schools. **Reported SAT (pre-2016 redesign) scores:** SAT Math middle 50% range 440-560. SAT Critical Reading middle 50% range 440-570. SAT Writing middle 50% range 423-550. **Concordant SAT scores:** SAT EBRW middle 50% 480–620. SAT Math middle 50% range 480–580. ACT middle 50% range 21-27. Minimum internet-based TOEFL 65. Minimum paper TOEFL 525. **Basis for Candidate Selection:** *Very important factors considered include:* academic GPA, standardized test scores. *Important factors considered include:* rigor of secondary school record, class rank, application essay. *Other factors considered include:* recommendation(s), interview, extracurricular activities, talent/ability, character/personal qualities, first generation, alumni/ae relation, geographical residence, state residency, religious affiliation/commitment, racial/ethnic status, volunteer work, work experience, level of applicant's interest. **Freshman Admission Requirements:** High school diploma is required and GED is accepted. *Academic units recommended:* 4 English, 2 math, 3 social studies. **Freshman**

Admission Statistics: 780 applied, 97.31% admitted, 30% enrolled. **Transfer Admission Requirements:** college transcript(s), essay or personal statement, Minimum college GPA of 2.0 required. Lowest grade transferable C. **General Admission Information:** Application fee $20. Priority deadline 3/1. Regular application deadline 8/1. Nonfall registration accepted. Admission may be deferred for a maximum of 1 year.

COSTS AND FINANCIAL AID
Annual tuition $23,976. Room and board $8,306. Required fees $795. Average book expense $1,000. **Required Forms and Deadlines:** FAFSA. **Notification of Awards:** Applicants will be notified of awards on a rolling basis beginning 2/15. **Types of Aid:** *Need-based scholarships/grants:* Federal Pell, FSEOG, State scholarships/grants, Private scholarships, College/university scholarship or grant aid from institutional funds. *Loans:* Direct Subsidized Stafford Loans, Direct Unsubsidized Stafford Loans, Direct PLUS loans, Federal Perkins Loans. *Student Employment:* Federal Work-Study Program available. Institutional employment available. **Financial Aid Statistics:** 94% needy freshmen, 94% needy undergrads receive need-based scholarship or grant aid. 22% freshmen, 17% undergrads receive non-need-based scholarship or grant aid. 88% freshmen, 90% undergrads receive need-based self-help aid. 6% freshmen, 5% undergrads receive athletic scholarships. 98% freshmen, 94% undergrads receive any aid. **Criteria for awarding aid:** *Need-based:* Minority status, Religious affiliation. *Non-need-based:* Academics, Alumni affiliation, Art, Athletics, Leadership, Minority status, Music/drama, Religious affiliation.

HUSSON UNIVERSITY

1 College Circle, Bangor, ME 4401
Phone: 207-941-7100 • **Financial Aid Phone:** 207-973-1090
E-mail: admit@husson.edu • **CEEB Code:** 3440
Fax: 207-941-7935 • **Website:** www.husson.edu • **ACT Code:** 1646

This private school was founded in 1898. It has a 170-acre campus.

RATINGS
Admissions Selectivity Rating: 76   **Fire Safety Rating:** 99   **Green Rating:** 86

STUDENTS AND FACULTY
Enrollment: 2,724. **Student Body:** 54% female, 46% male, 22% out-of-state, 3% international (19 countries represented). Asian 1%, African American 4%, Caucasian 86%, Hispanic 2%, Native American 1%, Pacific Islander <1%, Two or more races 2%, Race unknown 2%.
Retention and Graduation: 76% freshmen return for sophomore year. 29% freshmen graduate within 4 years. 53% freshmen graduate within 6 years. 20% grads go on to further study within 1 year. 1% grads pursue arts and sciences degrees. 1% grads pursue law degrees. 10% grads pursue business degrees. 1% grads pursue medical degrees. **Faculty:** Student/faculty ratio 14:1. 147 full-time faculty, 64% hold PhDs, 6% are are members of minority groups, 48% are women. 0% of classes are taught by teaching assistants.

ACADEMICS
Degrees: associate, bachelor's, certificate, doctoral/professional, master's, postbachelor's certificate, post-master's certificate, transfer. **Classes:** Most classes have 20-29 students. Most lab/discussion sessions have fewer than 10 students. **Most popular majors:** Business/Commerce; Registered Nursing/Registered Nurse; Criminal Justice/Law Enforcement Administration. **Special Study Options:** Accelerated program, cooperative education program, distance learning, double major, dual enrollment, independent study, internships, liberal arts/career combination, student-designed major, teacher certification program, weekend college. Combined degree programs: BS/BS, BS/MBA, BS/MS, BS/MSOT, BS/DPT. **Disability Services:** Special programs offered to physically disabled students, including note-taking services, tape recorders, tutors. **Career Services:** Alumni network, Alumni services, Career/job search classes, Career assessment, Internships, Regional alumni. Every student is required to complete at last one experiential learning experience. Many of these experiences lead to a future job.

FACILITIES
Housing: Coed dorms, special housing for disabled students. 100% of campus accessible to physically diasbled. **Special Academic Facilities/Equipment:** White Art Gallery Dahl Anatomy Lab Kenduskeag Research Institute Gracie Theater **Computers:** 100% of classrooms, 100% of dorms, 100% of libraries, 100% of student union, have wireless network access. Students can register for classes online. Administrative functions (other than registration) can be performed online.

CAMPUS LIFE
Environment: City. **Activities:** drama/theater, literary magazine, pep band, radio station, student government, student newspaper, television

station, yearbook, Campus Ministries, Student Organization. 30 registered organizations, 1 honor society, 2 religious organizations. 2 fraternities, 3 sororities. **Athletics (Intercollegiate):** *Men:* baseball, basketball, football, golf, lacrosse, soccer. *Women:* basketball, field hockey, lacrosse, soccer, softball, swimming, tennis, volleyball. **On-Campus Highlights:** Swan Fitness Center, Campus Center, Student Lounge, Newman Gym, Library, The Meeting House, a new academic building, opened in the fall of 2008. The attached 500-seat balconied, performing arts center opened in the fall of 2009. **Environmental Initiatives:** Green Cleaning Supplies.

ADMISSIONS

Freshman Academic Profile: Average high school GPA 3.3. 10% in top 10% of high school class, 39% in top 25% of high school class, 77% in top 50% of high school class. 90% from public high schools. **Reported SAT (pre-2016 redesign) scores:** SAT Math middle 50% range 430-540. SAT Critical Reading middle 50% range 430-530. SAT Writing middle 50% range 420-530. **Concordant SAT scores:** SAT EBRW middle 50% 480-590. SAT Math middle 50% range 470-570. ACT middle 50% range 17-23. Minimum internet-based TOEFL 75. Minimum paper TOEFL 500. **Basis for Candidate Selection:** *Very important factors considered include:* rigor of secondary school record, academic GPA. *Important factors considered include:* class rank, standardized test scores, application essay, recommendation(s), interview, extracurricular activities, character/personal qualities. *Other factors considered include:* alumni/ae relation, volunteer work, work experience, level of applicant's interest. **Freshman Admission Requirements:** High school diploma is required and GED is accepted. *Academic units recommended:* 4 English, 3 math, 3 science, 2 science labs, 1 social studies, 1 history. **Freshman Admission Statistics:** 2,460 applied, 80.24% admitted, 32% enrolled. **Transfer Admission Requirements:** High school transcript, college transcript(s), essay or personal statement, Minimum college GPA of 2.0 required. Lowest grade transferable C. **General Admission Information:** Application fee $40. Priority deadline 3/1. Regular application deadline 8/15. Nonfall registration accepted. Admission may be deferred for a maximum of 1 year.

COSTS AND FINANCIAL AID

Annual tuition $16,530. Room and board $9,498. Required fees $480. Average book expense $1,150. **Required Forms and Deadlines:** FAFSA. **Notification of Awards:** Applicants will be notified of awards on a rolling basis beginning 4/1. **Types of Aid:** *Need-based scholarships/grants:* Federal Pell, FSEOG, State scholarships/grants, Private scholarships, College/university scholarship or grant aid from institutional funds. *Loans:* Direct Subsidized Stafford Loans, Direct Unsubsidized Stafford Loans, Direct PLUS loans, Federal Perkins Loans, State Loans. *Student Employment:* Federal Work-Study Program available. **Financial Aid Statistics:** 94% needy freshmen, 84% needy undergrads receive need-based scholarship or grant aid. 98% freshmen, 79% undergrads receive non-need-based scholarship or grant aid. 93% freshmen, 93% undergrads receive need-based self-help aid. 0% freshmen, 0% undergrads receive athletic scholarships. 85% freshmen, 86% undergrads receive any aid. 88% undergrads borrow to pay for school. Average cumulative indebtedness $9,088,119. **Criteria for awarding aid:** *Need-based:* Academics, Leadership. *Non-need-based:* Academics, Leadership.

HUSTON-TILLOTSON UNIVERSITY

900 Chicon Street, Austin, TX 78702
Phone: 512-505-3028 • **Financial Aid Phone:** 512-505-3028
E-mail: admission@htu.edu • **CEEB Code:** 6280
Fax: 512-505-3192 • **Website:** www.htu.edu./ • **ACT Code:** 4104

This private school was founded in 1875. It has a 35-acre campus.

RATINGS

Admissions Selectivity Rating: 71   Fire Safety Rating: 60*   Green Rating: 60*

STUDENTS AND FACULTY

Enrollment: 889. **Student Body:** 51% female, 49% male, 3% out-of-state, 3% international (11 countries represented). Asian 0%, African American 72%, Caucasian 5%, Hispanic 19%, Native American 0%, Pacific Islander 0%, Two or more races <1%, Race unknown 0%.
Retention and Graduation: 50% freshmen return for sophomore year. 12% freshmen graduate within 4 years. 24% freshmen graduate within 6 years.
Faculty: Student/faculty ratio 15:1. 47 full-time faculty, 70% hold PhDs, 57% are members of minority groups, 53% are women. 0% of classes are taught by teaching assistants.

ACADEMICS

Degrees: bachelor's, postbachelor's certificate. **Classes:** Most classes have fewer than 10 students. Most lab/discussion sessions have fewer than 10 students. **Special Study Options:** cross-registration, distance learning, double major,

dual enrollment, external degree program, honors program, independent study, internships, liberal arts/career combination, study abroad, teacher certification program, 3-2 Engineering Program with Prairie View A&M University.

FACILITIES

Housing: men's dorms, women's dorms.

CAMPUS LIFE

Activities: Choral groups, dance, jazz band, literary magazine, music ensembles, student government, student-run film society, Campus Ministries, Student Organization. 17 registered organizations, 5 honor societies, 5 religious organizations. **Athletics (Intercollegiate):** *Men:* baseball, basketball, soccer, track/field (outdoor). *Women:* basketball, track/field (outdoor), volleyball.

ADMISSIONS

Freshman Academic Profile: Average high school GPA 2.8. 6% in top 10% of high school class, 12% in top 25% of high school class, 53% in top 50% of high school class. **Reported SAT (pre-2016 redesign) scores:** SAT Math middle 50% range 360-460. SAT Critical Reading middle 50% range 350-460. **Concordant SAT scores:** SAT Math middle 50% range 400-500. ACT middle 50% range 14-19. Minimum internet-based TOEFL 61. Minimum paper TOEFL 500. **Basis for Candidate Selection:** *Very important factors considered include:* rigor of secondary school record, academic GPA. *Important factors considered include:* class rank, standardized test scores, interview. *Other factors considered include:* application essay, recommendation(s), extracurricular activities, talent/ability, first generation, alumni/ae relation, work experience. **Freshman Admission Requirements:** High school diploma is required and GED is accepted. *Academic units required:* 4 English, 3 math, 2 science, 3 social studies, 1 computer science, and 2 units from above areas or other academic areas. *Academic units recommended:* 2 foreign language. **Freshman Admission Statistics:** 652 applied, 96.32% admitted, 43% enrolled. **Transfer Admission Requirements:** college transcript(s), essay or personal statement, Minimum college GPA of 2.0 required. Lowest grade transferable C. **General Admission Information:** Application fee $25. Priority deadline 3/15. Regular application deadline 7/1. Nonfall registration accepted. Admission may be deferred for a maximum of 1 semester.

COSTS AND FINANCIAL AID

Annual tuition $10,396. Room and board $6,946. Required fees $2,034. Average book expense $600. **Required Forms and Deadlines:** FAFSA. **Notification of Awards:** Applicants will be notified of awards on a rolling basis beginning 3/1. **Types of Aid:** *Need-based scholarships/grants:* Federal Pell, FSEOG, State scholarships/grants, Private scholarships, College/university scholarship or grant aid from institutional funds, United Negro College Fund. *Loans:* Direct Subsidized Stafford Loans, Direct Unsubsidized Stafford Loans, Direct PLUS loans, State Loans. *Student Employment:* Federal Work-Study Program available. **Financial Aid Statistics:** 25% needy freshmen, 33% needy undergrads receive need-based scholarship or grant aid. 33% freshmen, 35% undergrads receive non-need-based scholarship or grant aid. 100% freshmen, 100% undergrads receive need-based self-help aid. 15% freshmen, 14% undergrads receive athletic scholarships. 97% undergrads receive any aid. **Criteria for awarding aid:** *Non-need-based:* Academics, Alumni affiliation, Art, Athletics, Job skills, Leadership, Minority status, Music/drama, Religious affiliation, State/district residency.

IDAHO STATE UNIVERSITY

Museum of Natural History 319, Pocatello, ID 83209-8270
Phone: 208-282-2475 • **Financial Aid Phone:** 208-282-2981
E-mail: admiss@isu.edu • **CEEB Code:** 4355
Fax: 208-282-4511 • **Website:** www.isu.edu • **ACT Code:** 918

This public school was founded in 1901. It has a 1100-acre campus.

RATINGS

Admissions Selectivity Rating: 82   Fire Safety Rating: 73   Green Rating: 60*

STUDENTS AND FACULTY

Enrollment: 8,977. **Student Body:** 50% female, 50% male, 8% out-of-state, 14% international (63 countries represented). Asian 1%, African American 1%, Caucasian 67%, Hispanic 10%, Native American 1%, Pacific Islander <1%, Two or more races 3%, Race unknown 2%.
Retention and Graduation: 71% freshmen return for sophomore year. 22% freshmen graduate within 4 years. 31% freshmen graduate within 6 years.
Faculty: Student/faculty ratio 15:1. 585 full-time faculty, 51% hold PhDs, 9% are members of minority groups, 45% are women.

ACADEMICS

Degrees: associate, bachelor's, certificate, doctoral/professional, doctoral/research, doctoral, master's, postbachelor's certificate, post-master's certificate.

Classes: Most classes have 10-19 students. Most lab/discussion sessions have 20-29 students. **Most popular majors:** Secondary Education and Teaching; Elementary Education and Teaching; Biology/Biological Sciences. **Special Study Options:** Accelerated program, cooperative education program, cross-registration, distance learning, double major, dual enrollment, English as a Second Language (ESL), exchange student program (domestic), honors program, independent study, internships, liberal arts/career combination, student-designed major, study abroad, teacher certification program, weekend college. **Honors Programs:** Honors courses are offered in small classes and deal with interdisciplinary issues and confront some aspect of the human condition. Innovative teaching and assignments are encourages and interaction with faculty and class members is lively. Combined degree programs: BS/MS in chemistry. **Disability Services:** Special programs offered to physically disabled students, including note-taking services, reader services, tape recorders, tutors. **Career Services:** Career/job search classes, Career assessment.

FACILITIES
Housing: Coed dorms, special housing for disabled students, men's dorms, women's dorms, fraternity/sorority housing, apartments for married students, apartments for single students, Graduate Student Housing. 100% of campus accessible to physically diasbled. **Special Academic Facilities/Equipment:** Museum of Natural History, Idaho Accelerator Center, Rendezvous Center **Computers:** Students can register for classes online. Administrative functions (other than registration) can be performed online.

CAMPUS LIFE
Environment: Town. **Activities:** Choral groups, concert band, dance, drama/theater, jazz band, marching band, music ensembles, musical theater, opera, pep band, radio station, student government, student newspaper, symphony orchestra, television station, yearbook, Campus Ministries, Student Organization. 134 registered organizations, 8 honor societies, 7 religious organizations. 2 fraternities, 3 sororities. **Athletics (Intercollegiate):** *Men:* basketball, cheerleading, cross-country, football, golf, tennis, track/field (outdoor). *Women:* basketball, cheerleading, cross-country, golf, soccer, softball, tennis, track/field (outdoor), volleyball. **On-Campus Highlights:** Idaho Museum of Natural History, Rock Climbing Wall at Reed Gym, L.E. and Thelma E Stephens performing Ar, Rendezvous Center, Particle Accelerator.

ADMISSIONS
Freshman Academic Profile: Average high school GPA 3.2. 11% in top 10% of high school class, 30% in top 25% of high school class, 59% in top 50% of high school class. **Reported SAT (pre-2016 redesign) scores:** SAT Math middle 50% range 420-530. SAT Critical Reading middle 50% range 420-540. SAT Writing middle 50% range 400-510. **Concordant SAT scores:** SAT EBRW middle 50% 460–580. SAT Math middle 50% range 460–560. ACT middle 50% range 19-25. Minimum internet-based TOEFL 61. Minimum paper TOEFL 500. **Basis for Candidate Selection:** *Other factors considered include:* academic GPA, standardized test scores. **Freshman Admission Requirements:** High school diploma is required and GED is accepted. *Academic units required:* 4 English, 3 math, 3 science, 1 science lab, 1 foreign language. *Academic units recommended:* 4 math. **Freshman Admission Statistics:** 3,057 applied, 53.25% admitted, 90% enrolled. **Transfer Admission Requirements:** High school transcript, college transcript(s), standardized test scores, Minimum college GPA of 2.0 required. Lowest grade transferable D. **General Admission Information:** Application fee $50. Nonfall registration accepted. Admission may be deferred for a maximum of 3 years.

COSTS AND FINANCIAL AID
Annual in-state tuition $5,106. Annual out-of-state tuition $18,504. Room and board $6,338. Required fees $1,678. Average book expense $1,000. **Required Forms and Deadlines:** FAFSA. **Notification of Awards:** Applicants will be notified of awards on a rolling basis beginning 4/1. **Types of Aid:** *Need-based scholarships/grants:* Federal Pell, FSEOG, State scholarships/grants, Private scholarships, College/university scholarship or grant aid from institutional funds, Federal Nursing Scholarships. *Loans:* Direct Subsidized Stafford Loans, Direct Unsubsidized Stafford Loans, Direct PLUS loans, Federal Perkins Loans, Federal Nursing Loans. *Student Employment:* Federal Work-Study Program available. Institutional employment available. **Financial Aid Statistics:** 77% needy freshmen, 77% needy undergrads receive need-based scholarship or grant aid. 56% freshmen, 31% undergrads receive non-need-based scholarship or grant aid. 72% freshmen, 79% undergrads receive need-based self-help aid. 3% freshmen, 3% undergrads receive athletic scholarships. 73% freshmen, 74% undergrads receive any aid. 69% undergrads borrow to pay for school. Average cumulative indebtedness $29,983. **Criteria for awarding aid:** *Non-need-based:* Academics, Alumni affiliation, Art, Athletics, Leadership, Minority status, Music/drama, State/district residency.

ILLINOIS COLLEGE

1101 West College Avenue, Jacksonville, IL 62650
Phone: 217-245-3030
E-mail: admissions@mail.ic.edu • **CEEB Code:** 1315
Fax: 217-245-3034 • **Website:** www.ic.edu • **ACT Code:** 1034

This private school, affiliated with the Presbyterian Church, was founded in 1829. It has a 62-acre campus.

RATINGS
Admissions Selectivity Rating: 82   **Fire Safety Rating:** 60*   **Green Rating:** 60*

STUDENTS AND FACULTY
Enrollment: 942. **Student Body:** 52% female, 48% male, 16% out-of-state, 4% international. Asian 1%, African American 12%, Caucasian 68%, Hispanic 10%, Native American <1%, Pacific Islander <1%, Two or more races 4%, Race unknown 1%.
Retention and Graduation: 79% freshmen return for sophomore year. 62% freshmen graduate within 4 years. 71% freshmen graduate within 6 years. 22% grads go on to further study within 1 year. 13% grads pursue arts and sciences degrees. 5% grads pursue law degrees. 2% grads pursue business degrees. 4% grads pursue medical degrees. **Faculty:** Student/faculty ratio 10:1. 84 full-time faculty, 83% hold PhDs, 10% are are members of minority groups, 43% are women.

ACADEMICS
Degrees: bachelor's, master's. **Classes:** Most classes have 10-19 students. Most lab/discussion sessions have 10-19 students. **Special Study Options:** cross-registration, double major, dual enrollment, independent study, internships, liberal arts/career combination, student-designed major, study abroad, teacher certification program. Combined degree programs: 3-2 nursing, 3-2 occupational ther and 3-1 med-tech. **Career Services:** Career/job search classes, Career assessment, Internships.

FACILITIES
Housing: Coed dorms, men's dorms, women's dorms, apartments for single students. **Special Academic Facilities/Equipment:** Art gallery, language lab.

CAMPUS LIFE
Environment: Rural. **Activities:** Choral groups, concert band, drama/theater, literary magazine, music ensembles, student government, student newspaper, yearbook, Campus Ministries, Student Organization, Model UN. 72 registered organizations, 12 honor societies, 3 religious organizations. 4 fraternities, 3 sororities. **Athletics (Intercollegiate):** *Men:* baseball, basketball, cross-country, football, golf, soccer, tennis, track/field (outdoor), track/field (indoor), wrestling. *Women:* basketball, cheerleading, cross-country, golf, soccer, softball, tennis, track/field (outdoor), track/field (indoor), volleyball.

ADMISSIONS
Freshman Academic Profile: Average high school GPA 3.5. 23% in top 10% of high school class, 51% in top 25% of high school class, 89% in top 50% of high school class. 80% from public high schools. **Reported SAT (pre-2016 redesign) scores:** SAT Math middle 50% range 430-630. SAT Critical Reading middle 50% range 430-530. SAT Writing middle 50% range 400-550. **Concordant SAT scores:** SAT EBRW middle 50% 460–600. SAT Math middle 50% range 470–650. ACT middle 50% range 18-25. Minimum paper TOEFL 550. **Basis for Candidate Selection:** *Very important factors considered include:* rigor of secondary school record, academic GPA, character/personal qualities. *Important factors considered include:* class rank, application essay, recommendation(s), interview, extracurricular activities, talent/ability. *Other factors considered include:* standardized test scores, first generation, alumni/ae relation, geographical residence, racial/ethnic status, volunteer work, work experience, level of applicant's interest. **Freshman Admission Requirements:** High school diploma is required and GED is accepted. *Academic units required:* 4 English, 3 math, 2 science, 2 science labs, 1 history, 3 academic electives. *Academic units recommended:* 4 English, 3 math, 3 science, 3 science labs, 2 foreign language, 1 social studies, 1 history, 3 academic electives. **Freshman Admission Statistics:** 2,431 applied, 60.51% admitted, 16% enrolled. **Transfer Admission Requirements:** High school transcript, college transcript(s), Minimum college GPA of 2.50 required. Lowest grade transferable C. **General Admission Information:** Priority deadline 12/1. Nonfall registration accepted. Admission may be deferred for a maximum of 1 year.

COSTS AND FINANCIAL AID
Annual tuition $31,590. Room and board $9,190. Required fees $550. **Required Forms and Deadlines:** FAFSA. **Notification of Awards:** Applicants will be notified of awards on a rolling basis beginning 2/15. **Types of Aid:** *Need-based scholarships/grants:* Federal Pell, FSEOG, State scholarships/grants, Private scholarships, College/university scholarship or grant

aid from institutional funds. *Loans:* Direct Subsidized Stafford Loans, Direct Unsubsidized Stafford Loans, Direct PLUS loans, Federal Perkins Loans. *Student Employment:* Federal Work-Study Program available. Institutional employment available. **Financial Aid Statistics:** 100% needy freshmen, 100% needy undergrads receive need-based scholarship or grant aid. 11% freshmen, 12% undergrads receive non-need-based scholarship or grant aid. 89% freshmen, 87% undergrads receive need-based self-help aid. 0% freshmen, 0% undergrads receive athletic scholarships. 78% undergrads borrow to pay for school. Average cumulative indebtedness $32,000. **Criteria for awarding aid:** *Non-need-based:* Academics, Art, Music/drama.

ILLINOIS INSTITUTE OF TECHNOLOGY

10 West 33rd Street, Chicago, IL 60616
Phone: 312-567-3025 • **Financial Aid Phone:** 312-567-7219
E-mail: admission@iit.edu • **CEEB Code:** 1318
Fax: 312-567-6939 • **Website:** http://www.iit.edu/ • **ACT Code:** 1040

This private school was founded in 1892. It has a 120-acre campus.

RATINGS

Admissions Selectivity Rating: 88   **Fire Safety Rating:** 83   **Green Rating:** 60*

STUDENTS AND FACULTY

Enrollment: 2,800. **Student Body:** 30% female, 70% male, 22% out-of-state, 22% international (74 countries represented). Asian 14%, African American 6%, Caucasian 35%, Hispanic 17%, Native American <1%, Pacific Islander <1%, Two or more races 3%, Race unknown 4%.
Retention and Graduation: 92% freshmen return for sophomore year. 36% freshmen graduate within 4 years. 71% freshmen graduate within 6 years.
Faculty: Student/faculty ratio 13:1. 412 full-time faculty, 94% hold PhDs, 21% are are members of minority groups, 27% are women. 0% of classes are taught by teaching assistants.

ACADEMICS

Degrees: bachelor's, doctoral/professional, doctoral/research, master's, postbachelor's certificate, post-master's certificate. **Classes:** Most classes have 10-19 students. Most lab/discussion sessions have 20-29 students. **Most popular majors:** Architecture; Mechanical Engineering; Computer and Information Sciences. **Special Study Options:** cooperative education program, cross-registration, distance learning, double major, English as a Second Language (ESL), independent study, liberal arts/career combination, study abroad, teacher certification program, Joint **Enrollment:** Enrollment at 2 institutions for 2 degrees. **Honors Programs:** Honors Pharmacy Program, and Honors Medical Program, Honors Law Program, Business Honors Law Program Combined degree programs: BA/JD, BA/MA, BS/MBA; BS/JD; BS/DO; PharmD; BArch/MBA; BArch/MCE; BS/MS; BS/MPA. **Disability Services:** Special programs offered to physically disabled students, including note-taking services, reader services, tape recorders, tutors. **Career Services:** Alumni network, Alumni services, Career/job search classes, Career assessment, Internships, Regional alumni. Illinois Tech provides students a wide variety of hands-on, experiential learning opportunities as a part of the curriculum'each designed to prepare students for success in multidisciplinary work environments. Our Introduction to the Profession coursework prepares students for research and professional projects in specific disciplines during their first semester. In the third and fourth years IIT's flagship Interprofessional Projects (IPRO) Program brings together interdisciplinary teams of students to work on real-world projects sponsored by companies, municipalities, and nonprofit organizations.

FACILITIES

Housing: Coed dorms, fraternity/sorority housing, Men's/women's floors in residence halls, university apartments, arrangements for disabled students. 90% of campus accessible to physically diasbled. **Special Academic Facilities/Equipment:** The Center for Accelerator and Particle Physics (CAPP), The Center for Complex Systems and Dynamics (CCSD), The Center for Digital Design and Manufacturing (CDDM), The Center for Electrochemical Science and Engineering, The Center for Excellence in Polymer Science and Engineering, The Center for Integrative Neuroscience and Neuroengineering Research, The Center for the Management of Medical Technology (CMMT), The Center for Molecular Study of Soft Condensed Matter (CMS2), The Center for Strategic Competitiveness (CSC), The Center for the Study of Ethics in the Professions (CSEP), The Center for Synchrotron Radiation

Research and Instrumentation, The Center for Work Zone Safety and Mobility (CWZSM), Electric Power and Power Electronics Center (EPPEC), Energy + Power Center, Energy and Sustainability Institute, The Engineering Center For Diabetes Research and Education (ECDRE), The Fluid Dynamics Research Center, The High Performance Computing Center (HPCC), IIT Research Institute (IITRI), The International Center for Sensor Science and Engineering (ICSSE), The International Center for Sustainable New Cities (ICSNC), The Medical Imaging Research Center (MIRC), The National Center for Food Safety and Technology (NCFST), The Particle Technology and Crystallization Center (PTCC), The Pritzker Institute of Biomedical Science and Engineering, The Thermal Processing Technology Center (TPTC), The Wireless Network and Communications Research Center (WiNCom), Main Campus design by Ludwig Mies van der Rohe, McCormick Tribune Campus Center (MTCC) design by Rem Koolhaas, residence hall designed by Helmut Jahn, IIT Research Institute (IITRI), University Technology Park At IIT (UTP), Kemper Room Art Gallery, Illinois Tech Model Railroad (ITMR) **Computers:** 100% of classrooms, 100% of dorms, 100% of libraries, 100% of dining areas, 100% of student union, have wireless network access. Students can register for classes online. Administrative functions (other than registration) can be performed online.

CAMPUS LIFE

Environment: Metropolis. **Activities:** Choral groups, concert band, dance, drama/theater, literary magazine, music ensembles, musical theater, radio station, student government, student newspaper, student-run film society, television station, yearbook, Campus Ministries, Student Organization. 100 registered organizations, 4 honor societies, 10 religious organizations. 7 fraternities, 3 sororities. **Athletics (Intercollegiate):** *Men:* baseball, cross-country, diving, soccer, swimming. *Women:* cross-country, diving, soccer, swimming, volleyball. **On-Campus Highlights:** S.R. Crown Hall (Architecture Building), McCormick Tribune Center, Keating Athletic Center, Hermann Hall, State Street Village. **Environmental Initiatives:** Creation of an Office of Campus Energy and Sustainability and the Wanger Institute of Sustainable Energy Research bringing students, faculty, staff, and alumni together to address complex sustainability issues.

ADMISSIONS

Freshman Academic Profile: 56% in top 10% of high school class, 67% in top 25% of high school class, 99% in top 50% of high school class. 90% from public high schools. **Reported SAT (pre-2016 redesign) scores:** SAT Math middle 50% range 620-720. SAT Critical Reading middle 50% range 510-640. SAT Writing middle 50% range 530-640. **Concordant SAT scores:** SAT EBRW middle 50% 580–690. SAT Math middle 50% range 640–750. ACT middle 50% range 26-31. Minimum internet-based TOEFL 80. Minimum paper TOEFL 550. **Basis for Candidate Selection:** *Very important factors considered include:* rigor of secondary school record, academic GPA, standardized test scores. *Important factors considered include:* class rank, recommendation(s). *Other factors considered include:* application essay, interview, extracurricular activities, talent/ability, character/personal qualities, first generation, alumni/ae relation, volunteer work, work experience, level of applicant's interest. **Freshman Admission Requirements:** High school diploma is required and GED is accepted. *Academic units required:* 4 English, 4 math, 3 science, 2 science labs, 2 foreign language, 2 social studies. *Academic units recommended:* 4 English, 4 math, 3 science, 2 science labs, 2 foreign language, 2 social studies, 2 history, 1 computer science, 1 visual/performing arts. **Freshman Admission Statistics:** 4,288 applied, 57.11% admitted, 21% enrolled. **Transfer Admission Requirements:** college transcript(s), essay or personal statement, statement of good standing from prior institution(s). Minimum college GPA of 3.0 required. Lowest grade transferable C. **General Admission Information:** Priority deadline 12/1. Regular application deadline 8/1. Nonfall registration accepted. Admission may be deferred.

COSTS AND FINANCIAL AID

Required Forms and Deadlines: FAFSA. **Notification of Awards:** Applicants will be notified of awards on a rolling basis beginning 3/15. **Types of Aid:** *Need-based scholarships/grants:* Federal Pell, FSEOG, State scholarships/grants, Private scholarships, College/university scholarship or grant aid from institutional funds. *Loans:* Direct Subsidized Stafford Loans, Direct Unsubsidized Stafford Loans, Direct PLUS loans, Federal Perkins Loans. *Student Employment:* Federal Work-Study Program available. Institutional employment available. **Financial Aid Statistics:** 100% needy freshmen receive need-based scholarship or grant aid. 100% freshmen, 99% undergrads receive any aid. **Criteria for awarding aid:** *Non-need-based:* Academics, Alumni affiliation, Leadership.

ILLINOIS STATE UNIVERSITY

Office of Admissions, Normal, IL 61790-2200
Phone: 309-438-2181 • **Financial Aid Phone:** 309-438-2231
E-mail: admissions@illinoisstate.edu • **CEEB Code:** 1319
Fax: 309-438-3932 • **Website:** www.ilstu.edu • **ACT Code:** 1042

This public school was founded in 1857. It has a 850-acre campus.

RATINGS
Admissions Selectivity Rating: 72   **Fire Safety Rating:** 91   **Green Rating:** 88

STUDENTS AND FACULTY
Enrollment: 18,571. **Student Body:** 55% female, 45% male, 2% out-of-state, <1% international (59 countries represented). Asian 2%, African American 8%, Caucasian 76%, Hispanic 10%, Native American <1%, Pacific Islander <1%, Two or more races 3%, Race unknown <1%.
Retention and Graduation: 81% freshmen return for sophomore year. 48% freshmen graduate within 4 years. 72% freshmen graduate within 6 years. **Faculty:** Student/faculty ratio 18:1. 882 full-time faculty, 82% hold PhDs, 16% are are members of minority groups, 52% are women. 8% of classes are taught by teaching assistants.

ACADEMICS
Degrees: bachelor's, doctoral/professional, doctoral/research, master's, postbachelor's certificate, post-master's certificate. **Classes:** Most classes have 20-29 students. Most lab/discussion sessions have 20-29 students. **Most popular majors:** Elementary Education and Teaching; Special Education and Teaching; Business Administration and Management. **Special Study Options:** Accelerated program, cooperative education program, distance learning, double major, dual enrollment, English as a Second Language (ESL), exchange student program (domestic), honors program, independent study, internships, student-designed major, study abroad, teacher certification program. Combined degree programs: BA/MA, Integrated BS/MPA—Accountancy. **Disability Services:** Special programs offered to physically disabled students, including note-taking services, reader services, tape recorders, tutors. **Career Services:** Alumni services, Career assessment, Internships.

FACILITIES
Housing: Coed dorms, special housing for disabled students, special housing for international students, women's dorms, fraternity/sorority housing, apartments for married students, apartments for single students. 100% of campus accessible to physically disabled. **Special Academic Facilities/ Equipment:** Art gallery, cultural museums, on-campus elementary and secondary schools, greenhouse, farm, planetarium. **Computers:** 100% of classrooms, 100% of dorms, 100% of libraries, 100% of dining areas, 100% of student union, have wireless network access. Students can register for classes online. Administrative functions (other than registration) can be performed online. Undergraduates are required to own a computer.

CAMPUS LIFE
Environment: City. **Activities:** Choral groups, concert band, dance, drama/ theater, jazz band, literary magazine, marching band, music ensembles, musical theater, pep band, radio station, student government, student newspaper, student-run film society, symphony orchestra, television station 270 registered organizations, 23 honor societies, 22 religious organizations. 21 fraternities, 17 sororities. **Athletics (Intercollegiate):** *Men:* baseball, basketball, cheerleading, cross-country, football, golf, tennis, track/field (outdoor), track/field (indoor). *Women:* basketball, cheerleading, cross-country, diving, golf, gymnastics, soccer, softball, swimming, tennis, track/field (outdoor), track/field (indoor), volleyball. **On-Campus Highlights:** College of Business Building, Science Laboratory Building, Redbird Arena **Environmental Initiatives:** Establishing a formal Office of Sustainability with 2 full time staff, 1 graduate assistant and multiple interns.

ADMISSIONS
Freshman Academic Profile: Average high school GPA 3.4. 86% from public high schools. ACT middle 50% range 21-26. Minimum internet-based TOEFL 79. Minimum paper TOEFL 550. **Basis for Candidate Selection:** *Very important factors considered include:* rigor of secondary school record, academic GPA, standardized test scores. *Important factors considered include:* application essay. *Other factors considered include:* talent/ability, character/ personal qualities, level of applicant's interest. **Freshman Admission Requirements:** High school diploma is required and GED is accepted. *Academic units required:* 4 English, 3 math, 2 science, 2 science labs, 2 foreign language, 2 social studies, 2 academic electives. **Freshman Admission Statistics:** 12,078 applied, 88.88% admitted, 34% enrolled. **Transfer Admission Requirements:** college transcript(s), essay or personal statement, Minimum college GPA of 3.0 required. Lowest grade transferable D. **General Admission Information:** Application fee $50. Priority deadline 11/15. Regular application deadline 4/1. Nonfall registration accepted. Admission may be deferred for a maximum of 2 semesters.

COSTS AND FINANCIAL AID
Annual in-state tuition $11,108. Annual out-of-state tuition $22,215. Room and board $9,948. Required fees $2,953. Average book expense $942. **Required Forms and Deadlines:** FAFSA. **Notification of Awards:** Applicants will be notified of awards on a rolling basis beginning 4/1. **Types of Aid:** *Need-based scholarships/grants:* Federal Pell, FSEOG, State scholarships/grants, Private scholarships, College/university scholarship or grant aid from institutional funds, Federal Nursing Scholarships. *Loans:* Direct Subsidized Stafford Loans, Direct Unsubsidized Stafford Loans, Direct PLUS loans, Federal Perkins Loans, Federal Nursing Loans. *Student Employment:* Federal Work-Study Program available. Institutional employment available. **Criteria for awarding aid:** *Need-based:* Academics, Art, Music/drama. *Non-need-based:* Academics, Art, Athletics, Music/drama.

ILLINOIS WESLEYAN UNIVERSITY

P.O. Box 2900, Bloomington, IL 61702-2900
Phone: 309-556-3031 • **Financial Aid Phone:** 309-556-3096
E-mail: iwuadmit@iwu.edu • **CEEB Code:** 1320
Fax: 309-556-3820 • **Website:** www.iwu.edu • **ACT Code:** 1044

This private school was founded in 1850. It has a 80-acre campus.

RATINGS
Admissions Selectivity Rating: 87   **Fire Safety Rating:** 94   **Green Rating:** 68

STUDENTS AND FACULTY
Enrollment: 1,763. **Student Body:** 54% female, 46% male, 14% out-of-state, 9% international (24 countries represented). Asian 4%, African American 4%, Caucasian 71%, Hispanic 7%, Native American 0%, Pacific Islander <1%, Two or more races 3%, Race unknown 2%.
Retention and Graduation: 93% freshmen return for sophomore year. 74% freshmen graduate within 4 years. 81% freshmen graduate within 6 years. 25% grads go on to further study within 1 year. **Faculty:** Student/faculty ratio 10:1. 148 full-time faculty, 97% hold PhDs, 9% are are members of minority groups, 42% are women. 0% of classes are taught by teaching assistants.

ACADEMICS
Degrees: bachelor's. **Classes:** Most classes have 10-19 students. Most lab/ discussion sessions have fewer than 10 students. **Most popular majors:** Business/Commerce; Biology/Biological Sciences; Accounting. **Special Study Options:** double major, exchange student program (domestic), honors program, independent study, internships, student-designed major, study abroad, teacher certification program. **Honors Programs:** IWU offers a research honors designation to eligible senior students who successfully complete and defend an intensive, advanced research or creative project under the direction of an interdisciplinary faculty committee. Performance Honors designations are also available in the Art, Music, and Theatre Arts. Combined degree programs: 3-2 prgrms—Engrng, Forestry, or Environ. **Disability Services:** Special programs offered to physically disabled students, including note-taking services, reader services, tape recorders, tutors. **Career Services:** Alumni network, Alumni services, Career/job search classes, Career assessment, Internships, Regional alumni. The Action Research Center links students in seminar and internships classes with community partners, such as social service and non-profit agencies. Students in these classes work with the partners on major projects intended to have a lasting, positive impact on the community. Projects have been as varied as those on environmental issues, historic preservation, pre-school education, crisis intervention, mentoring troubled youth, drug courts, living wage legislation, and ESL tutoring.

FACILITIES
Housing: Coed dorms, special housing for disabled students, special housing for international students, fraternity/sorority housing, apartments for single students, Groups of students with common curricular or cocurricular interests can propose and implement theme housing consistent with their educational goals in a limited number of residential buildings. Examples of past and current interest areas include the arts, languages, environmentalism, multi-faith issues, wellness, culinary arts, and internationalism. 80% of campus accessible to physically disabled. **Special Academic Facilities/Equipment:** observatory, computerized music lab, graphic design studio, Ames Library archives and special collections, visual anthropology lab, social science lab **Computers:** 60% of classrooms, 100% of libraries, 100% of dining areas, 100% of student union, have wireless network access. Students can register for classes online. Administrative functions (other than registration) can be performed online.

CAMPUS LIFE

Environment: City. **Activities:** Choral groups, concert band, dance, drama/theater, jazz band, literary magazine, music ensembles, musical theater, opera, pep band, radio station, student government, student newspaper, student-run film society, symphony orchestra, television station, yearbook, Campus Ministries, Student Organization, Model UN. 165 registered organizations, 29 honor societies, 15 religious organizations. 6 fraternities, 5 sororities. **Athletics (Intercollegiate):** *Men:* baseball, basketball, cross-country, diving, football, golf, soccer, swimming, tennis, track/field (outdoor), track/field (indoor). *Women:* basketball, cross-country, diving, golf, soccer, softball, swimming, tennis, track/field (outdoor), track/field (indoor), volleyball. **On-Campus Highlights:** Ames Library, Hansen Student Center, Shirk Center for Athletics and Wellness, Center for Natural Science, The Dugout (snack bar and coffee shop). **Environmental Initiatives:** IWU has a commitment to environmental sustainability in its mission statement.

ADMISSIONS

Freshman Academic Profile: Average high school GPA 3.8. 34% in top 10% of high school class, 71% in top 25% of high school class, 96% in top 50% of high school class. 73% from public high schools. ACT middle 50% range 25-29. Minimum internet-based TOEFL 80. Minimum paper TOEFL 550. **Basis for Candidate Selection:** *Very important factors considered include:* rigor of secondary school record, academic GPA, interview. *Important factors considered include:* class rank, standardized test scores, application essay, extracurricular activities, talent/ability, character/personal qualities. *Other factors considered include:* recommendation(s), first generation, alumni/ae relation, geographical residence, state residency, racial/ethnic status, volunteer work, work experience, level of applicant's interest. **Freshman Admission Requirements:** High school diploma is required and GED is accepted. *Academic units recommended:* 4 English, 3 math, 3 science, 2 science labs, 3 foreign language, 2 social studies. **Freshman Admission Statistics:** 3,841 applied, 58.21% admitted, 19% enrolled. **Transfer Admission Requirements:** High school transcript, college transcript(s), essay or personal statement, standardized test scores, Minimum college GPA of 2.0 required. Lowest grade transferable C-. **General Admission Information:** Nonfall registration accepted. Admission may be deferred for a maximum of 1 year.

COSTS AND FINANCIAL AID

Annual tuition $45,654. Room and board $10,574. Average book expense $800. **Required Forms and Deadlines:** FAFSA, Institution's own financial aid form. **Notification of Awards:** Applicants will be notified of awards on a rolling basis beginning 3/1. **Types of Aid:** *Need-based scholarships/grants:* Federal Pell, FSEOG, State scholarships/grants, Private scholarships, College/university scholarship or grant aid from institutional funds. *Loans:* Direct Subsidized Stafford Loans, Direct Unsubsidized Stafford Loans, Direct PLUS loans, Federal Perkins Loans, Federal Nursing Loans, College/university loans from institutional funds. *Student Employment:* Federal Work-Study Program available. Institutional employment available. **Financial Aid Statistics:** 100% needy freshmen, 100% needy undergrads receive need-based scholarship or grant aid. 19% freshmen, 12% undergrads receive non-need-based scholarship or grant aid. 72% freshmen, 81% undergrads receive need-based self-help aid. 0% freshmen, 0% undergrads receive athletic scholarships. 100% freshmen, 100% undergrads receive any aid. 73% undergrads borrow to pay for school. Average cumulative indebtedness $34,999. **Criteria for awarding aid:** *Need-based:* Academics, Art, Music/drama. *Non-need-based:* Academics, Art, Music/drama.

IMMACULATA UNIVERSITY

1145 King Road, Immaculata, PA 19345-0642
Phone: 610-647-4400 x3060 • **Financial Aid Phone:** 877-428-6329
E-mail: admiss@immaculata.edu • **CEEB Code:** 2320
Fax: 610-640-0836 • **Website:** www.immaculata.edu • **ACT Code:** 3596

This private school, affiliated with the Roman Catholic Church, was founded in 2000. It has a 400-acre campus.

RATINGS

Admissions Selectivity Rating: 72   **Fire Safety Rating:** 86   **Green Rating:** 60*

STUDENTS AND FACULTY

Enrollment: 1,693. **Student Body:** 73% female, 27% male, 229% out-of-state, 1% international. Asian 2%, African American 14%, Caucasian 74%, Hispanic 5%, Native American <1%, Pacific Islander <1%, Two or more races 2%, Race unknown 2%.
Retention and Graduation: 83% freshmen return for sophomore year. 58% freshmen graduate within 4 years. 20% grads go on to further study within 1 year. **Faculty:** Student/faculty ratio 9:1. 71 full-time faculty, 77% hold PhDs,

3% are are members of minority groups, 79% are women. 0% of classes are taught by teaching assistants.

ACADEMICS

Degrees: associate, bachelor's, certificate, doctoral/research, master's. **Most popular majors:** Business Administration and Management; Kinesiology and Exercise Science; Registered Nursing/Registered Nurse. **Special Study Options:** Accelerated program, cooperative education program, cross-registration, distance learning, double major, dual enrollment, external degree program, honors program, independent study, internships, liberal arts/career combination, study abroad, teacher certification program. **Disability Services:** Special programs offered to physically disabled students, including note-taking services, reader services, tape recorders, tutors. **Career Services:** Alumni network, Alumni services, Career/job search classes, Career assessment, Internships.

FACILITIES

Housing: No housing is available for CLL students. 100% of campus accessible to physically disabled. **Special Academic Facilities/Equipment:** Annual art show on-campus. **Computers:** Administrative functions (other than registration) can be performed online.

CAMPUS LIFE

Environment: Town. **Activities:** Choral groups, dance, drama/theater, literary magazine, music ensembles, musical theater, student government, student newspaper, symphony orchestra, yearbook. 28 registered organizations, 14 honor societies, 1 religious organization. **Athletics (Intercollegiate):** *Men:* basketball, golf, soccer, tennis. *Women:* basketball, cross-country, field hockey, golf, lacrosse, soccer, softball, tennis, volleyball. **On-Campus Highlights:** Java Hut, Pool, Weight Room.

ADMISSIONS

Freshman Academic Profile: Average high school GPA 3.3. **Reported SAT (pre-2016 redesign) scores:** SAT Math middle 50% range 420-550. SAT Critical Reading middle 50% range 440-530. SAT Writing middle 50% range 430-550. **Concordant SAT scores:** SAT EBRW middle 50% 490–600. SAT Math middle 50% range 460–570. ACT middle 50% range 20-23. Minimum paper TOEFL 500. **Basis for Candidate Selection:** *Very important factors considered include:* rigor of secondary school record, academic GPA. *Important factors considered include:* class rank, standardized test scores, application essay, recommendation(s), first generation. *Other factors considered include:* interview, extracurricular activities, talent/ability, character/personal qualities, alumni/ae relation, geographical residence, religious affiliation/commitment, volunteer work, work experience, level of applicant's interest. **Freshman Admission Requirements:** High school diploma is required and GED is accepted. *Academic units required:* 4 English, 2 math, 2 science, 1 science lab, 2 foreign language, 2 social studies, and 4 units from above areas or other academic areas. **Freshman Admission Statistics:** 1,586 applied, 78.81% admitted, 15% enrolled. **Transfer Admission Requirements:** High school transcript, college transcript(s), Minimum college GPA of 2.0 required. Lowest grade transferable C. **General Admission Information:** Nonfall registration accepted. Admission may be deferred.

COSTS AND FINANCIAL AID

Annual tuition $33,280. Room and board $13,210. Required fees $0. Average book expense $1,974. **Required Forms and Deadlines:** FAFSA. **Notification of Awards:** Applicants will be notified of awards on a rolling basis beginning 2/1. **Types of Aid:** *Need-based scholarships/grants:* Federal Pell, State scholarships/grants, Private scholarships, United Negro College Fund. *Loans:* Federal Perkins Loans. *Student Employment:* Federal Work-Study Program available. Institutional employment available. **Financial Aid Statistics:** 34% undergrads receive any aid.

INDIANA STATE UNIVERSITY

Office of Admissions, 318 N 6th Street, Terre Haute, IN 47809
Phone: 812-237-2121 • **Financial Aid Phone:** 812-237-2215
E-mail: http://www.indstate.edu/admissions • **CEEB Code:** 1322
Fax: 812-237-8023 • **Website:** www.indstate.edu • **ACT Code:** 1206

This public school was founded in 1865. It has a 92-acre campus.

RATINGS

Admissions Selectivity Rating: 72   **Fire Safety Rating:** 92   **Green Rating:** 88

STUDENTS AND FACULTY

Enrollment: 10,601. **Student Body:** 54% female, 46% male, 17% out-of-state, 6% international (63 countries represented). Asian 1%, African American 19%, Caucasian 65%, Hispanic 4%, Native American <1%, Pacific Islander <1%, Two or more races 4%, Race unknown 1%.

Retention and Graduation: 64% freshmen return for sophomore year. 17% freshmen graduate within 4 years. 35% freshmen graduate within 6 years. **Faculty:** Student/faculty ratio 21:1. 495 full-time faculty, 77% hold PhDs, 15% are are members of minority groups, 46% are women. 4% of classes are taught by teaching assistants.

ACADEMICS

Degrees: bachelor's, certificate, doctoral/professional, doctoral/research, master's, postbachelor's certificate, post-master's certificate. **Classes:** Most classes have 20-29 students. **Most popular majors:** Business Administration and Management; Criminology; Registered Nursing/Registered Nurse. **Special Study Options:** Accelerated program, cooperative education program, distance learning, double major, dual enrollment, English as a Second Language (ESL), honors program, independent study, internships, study abroad, teacher certification program. **Honors Programs:** University Honors Program. **Disability Services:** Special programs offered to physically disabled students, including note-taking services, tape recorders, tutors. **Career Services:** Alumni network, Alumni services, Career assessment, Internships, Regional alumni. At Indiana State, students from every discipline are able to apply what they are learning through hands-on inquiry and research, and life-changing field experiences. Our students program robots, conduct research alongside expert faculty, assist K-12 teachers in the classroom, analyze artifacts from a major archaeological dig, compose, dance, write and perform. They assist non-profit organizations, sample deep-ocean sediments off the California coast, and care for patients at our community health education center.

Experiential learning brings knowledge to life and gives student the kind of real-world understanding that sets you apart from students at other institutions.

FACILITIES

Housing: Coed dorms, special housing for disabled students, men's dorms, women's dorms, fraternity/sorority housing, apartments for married students, apartments for single students, Theme Housing, Special housing for freshmen, and apartments for students with dependent children. 98% of campus accessible to physically diasbled. **Special Academic Facilities/Equipment:** Music hall, art gallery, civic center, museum,flight simulator, audio-visual center, observatory, theaters. **Computers:** 100% of classrooms, 100% of dorms, 100% of libraries, 100% of dining areas, 100% of student union, have wireless network access. Students can register for classes online. Administrative functions (other than registration) can be performed online. Undergraduates are required to own a computer.

CAMPUS LIFE

Environment: Town. **Activities:** Choral groups, concert band, dance, drama/theater, jazz band, literary magazine, marching band, music ensembles, musical theater, pep band, radio station, student government, student newspaper, student-run film society, symphony orchestra, yearbook, Campus Ministries, Student Organization. 130 registered organizations, 19 honor societies, 13 religious organizations. 11 fraternities, 10 sororities. **Athletics (Intercollegiate):** *Men:* baseball, basketball, cross-country, football, track/field (outdoor), track/field (indoor). *Women:* basketball, cross-country, golf, soccer, softball, track/field (outdoor), track/field (indoor), volleyball. **On-Campus Highlights:** Hulman Memorial Student Union, Student Recreation Center, John C. Hook's Memorial Observatory, Cunningham Memorial Library, Three Art Galleries, The Hulman Memorial Student Union Building contains the University Bookstore, The Commons(food court), Le Club (exercise club), etc. Various Libraries—Cunningham Memorial (main), Women Study, Arts and Science, etc. **Environmental Initiatives:** The signing of the American Colleges & Universities President's Climate Commitment that resulted in the development of a Climate Action Plan and three rounds of carbon footprint analyses.

ADMISSIONS

Freshman Academic Profile: Average high school GPA 3.1. 9% in top 10% of high school class, 25% in top 25% of high school class, 62% in top 50% of high school class. **Reported SAT (pre-2016 redesign) scores:** SAT Math middle 50% range 390-510. SAT Critical Reading middle 50% range 400-510. SAT Writing middle 50% range 380-490. **Concordant SAT scores:** SAT EBRW middle 50% 440–560. SAT Math middle 50% range 430–540. ACT middle 50% range 16-22. Minimum internet-based TOEFL 61. Minimum paper TOEFL 500. **Basis for Candidate Selection:** *Very important factors considered include:* rigor of secondary school record, class rank, academic GPA. *Important factors considered include:* standardized test scores, application essay, recommendation(s). *Other factors considered include:* interview, extracurricular activities, talent/ability, character/personal qualities. **Freshman Admission Requirements:** High school diploma is required and GED is accepted. *Academic units recommended:* 4 English, 3 science, 3 science labs, 1 foreign language, 2 social studies, 1 history. **Freshman Admission Statistics:** 11,101 applied, 85.88% admitted, 26% enrolled. **Transfer Admission Requirements:** college transcript(s), Minimum college GPA of 2.0 required. Lowest grade transferable C. **General Admission Information:** Application fee $25. Priority deadline 7/1. Regular application deadline 8/15. Nonfall registration accepted. Admission may be deferred for a maximum of 12 months.

COSTS AND FINANCIAL AID

Annual in-state tuition $8,546. Annual out-of-state tuition $18,876. Room and board $9,785. Required fees $200. Average book expense $1,170. **Required Forms and Deadlines:** FAFSA. **Notification of Awards:** Applicants will be notified of awards on a rolling basis beginning 3/15. **Types of Aid:** *Need-based scholarships/grants:* Federal Pell, FSEOG, State scholarships/grants, Private scholarships, College/university scholarship or grant aid from institutional funds. *Loans:* Direct Subsidized Stafford Loans, Direct Unsubsidized Stafford Loans, Direct PLUS loans, Federal Perkins Loans. *Student Employment:* Federal Work-Study Program available. Institutional employment available. **Financial Aid Statistics:** 68% needy freshmen, 64% needy undergrads receive need-based scholarship or grant aid. 70% freshmen, 56% undergrads receive non-need-based scholarship or grant aid. 75% freshmen, 78% undergrads receive need-based self-help aid. 3% freshmen, 3% undergrads receive athletic scholarships. 76% freshmen, 69% undergrads receive any aid. Average cumulative indebtedness $27,457. **Criteria for awarding aid:** *Need-based:* Academics. *Non-need-based:* Academics, Alumni affiliation, Art, Athletics, Minority status, Music/drama, State/district residency.

INDIANA UNIVERSITY BLOOMINGTON

300 North Jordan Avenue, Bloomington, IN 47405-1106
Phone: 812-855-0661 • **Financial Aid Phone:** 812-855-6500
E-mail: iuadmit@indiana.edu • **CEEB Code:** 1324
Fax: 812-855-5102 • **Website:** www.iub.edu • **ACT Code:** 1210

This public school was founded in 1820. It has a 1937-acre campus.

RATINGS

Admissions Selectivity Rating: 86   **Fire Safety Rating:** 88   **Green Rating:** 95

STUDENTS AND FACULTY

Enrollment: 32,924. **Student Body:** 49% female, 51% male, 33% out-of-state, 11% international (126 countries represented). Asian 5%, African American 4%, Caucasian 70%, Hispanic 6%, Native American <1%, Pacific Islander <1%, Two or more races 4%, Race unknown <1%.
Retention and Graduation: 91% freshmen return for sophomore year. 60% freshmen graduate within 4 years. 76% freshmen graduate within 6 years.
Faculty: Student/faculty ratio 17:1. 2,144 full-time faculty, 82% hold PhDs, 20% are are members of minority groups, 40% are women.

ACADEMICS

Degrees: bachelor's, certificate, doctoral/professional, doctoral/research, doctoral, master's, postbachelor's certificate, terminal. **Classes:** Most classes have 20-29 students. Most lab/discussion sessions have 20-29 students. **Most popular majors:** Public Administration; Business/Commerce; Informatics. **Special Study Options:** Accelerated program, cooperative education program, distance learning, double major, dual enrollment, English as a Second Language (ESL), external degree program, honors program, independent study, internships, liberal arts/career combination, student-designed major, study abroad, teacher certification program. **Honors Programs:** Hutton Honors College and the Hudson/Holland Scholar Programs Combined degree programs: JD/MD, MIS/MLS, MA/MPH, JD/MBA, MPA/MSES, MD/MPH. **Disability Services:** Special programs offered to physically disabled students, including note-taking services, reader services, tape recorders, tutors. **Career Services:** Alumni network, Alumni services, Career/job search classes, Career assessment, Internships. The IU Alumni Connections Program that we host each year brings back successful alumni to work with current students.

FACILITIES

Housing: Coed dorms, special housing for disabled students, men's dorms, special housing for international students, women's dorms, fraternity/sorority housing, apartments for married students, cooperative housing, apartments for single students, Apartments for students with dependent children. Residential language houses, and living/learning centers available, wellness center, African-American living/learning. Honor College floors, First-Year Academic Interest Group Housing; Suites for 2, 3 students. 95% of campus accessible to physically diasbled. **Special Academic Facilities/Equipment:** Art Gallery, folklore, radio station, natural history museum, TV station, art museum, Mathers Museum of World Cultures, Kirkwood Observatory, Hilltop Garden and Nature Center, Arboretum, Student Recreational Sports and Aquatic Center, Auditorium, Beck Chapel, Golf Driving Range, Musical Arts Center, Health Physical Education and Recreation facilities (HPER), indoor swimming, outdoor swimming, Wildermuth Intramural Center (in HPER complex), cyclotron, Lilly Library, and more than 70 research centers. **Computers:** Students can register for classes online. Administrative functions (other than registration) can be performed online.

CAMPUS LIFE

Environment: City. **Activities:** Choral groups, concert band, dance, drama/theater, jazz band, literary magazine, marching band, music ensembles, musical theater, opera, radio station, student government, student newspaper, symphony orchestra, television station, yearbook, Campus Ministries, Student Organization. 9 religious organizations. **Athletics (Intercollegiate):** *Men:* baseball, basketball, cheerleading, cross-country, diving, football, golf, soccer, swimming, tennis, track/field (outdoor), wrestling. *Women:* basketball, cheerleading, cross-country, diving, field hockey, golf, soccer, softball, swimming, tennis, track/field (outdoor), volleyball, water polo. **On-Campus Highlights:** Indiana Memorial Union, Art Museum, Lilly Library, Assembly Hall, Student Recreational Sports Center. **Environmental Initiatives:** The Bicentennial Strategic Plan (IU turns 200 in 2020) was adopted by the Board of Trustees in December establishing Core Value 7: Sustainability, stewardship and accountability for the natural, human, and economic resources and relationships entrusted to IU. Bicentennial Priority 3: Support innovative campus living laboratory initiatives that provide opportunities to integrate campus operations, faculty and student research, education, student life, and community engagement to applied, solutions-oriented sustainability research. Bicentennial Priority 8: Building for Excellence—IU has also become a leader in high‐quality environmentally conscious design, and leads the Big Ten in LEED certified green buildings with twelve certified to date, including four at the gold level (platinum is the highest certification). This strategy pays dividends for the life of each building in terms of occupant health and productivity, resource efficiency, life cycle cost savings and retention of human capital. Bicentennial Action Item 3: IU will implement plans to solidify IU Focus on efficient and environmentally conscious campus design and operation by: a. Completing and implementing pedestrian, transportation, and bicycle sub-master plans on each campus. b. Certifying all major new buildings with the LEED Green Building Certification System and elevate the minimum certification level to Gold. c. Continuing to explore and research a variety of energy and utility supply and delivery options that reflect changes in economies, demand, and climate variables. d. Achieving the goals for energy efficiency and emissions reductions called for in the Campus Master Plan and the Integrated Energy Master Plan for the IU Bloomington campus; expand that analysis to all campuses. e. Increasing energy and utility system efficiency while reducing demand and consumption. Continuing Priorities Give special emphasis on all campuses to improving traffic flow, making them more pedestrian and bicycle friendly, and to improving parking and alternative modes of transportation for students, faculty, and staff. Expand efforts to make all IU campuses more energy efficient and sustainable.

ADMISSIONS

Freshman Academic Profile: Average high school GPA 3.7. 35% in top 10% of high school class, 72% in top 25% of high school class, 96% in top 50% of high school class. **Reported SAT (pre-2016 redesign) scores:** SAT Math middle 50% range 540-660. SAT Critical Reading middle 50% range 520-630. SAT Writing middle 50% range 510-620. **Concordant SAT scores:** SAT EBRW middle 50% 570–680. SAT Math middle 50% range 570–690. ACT middle 50% range 24-30. Minimum internet-based TOEFL 79. Minimum paper TOEFL 550. **Basis for Candidate Selection:** *Very important factors considered include:* rigor of secondary school record, class rank, academic GPA, standardized test scores. *Important factors considered include:* application essay. *Other factors considered include:* recommendation(s), interview, extracurricular activities, talent/ability, character/personal qualities, first generation, alumni/ae relation, geographical residence, state residency, racial/ethnic status, volunteer work, work experience. **Freshman Admission Requirements:** High school diploma is required and GED is accepted. *Academic units required:* 4 English, 3 science, 2 science labs, 2 foreign language, 3 social studies. **Freshman Admission Statistics:** 34,646 applied, 78.72% admitted, 28% enrolled. **Transfer Admission Requirements:** college transcript(s), Minimum college GPA of 2.0 required. Lowest grade transferable C. **General Admission Information:** Application fee $60. Priority deadline 2/1. Nonfall registration accepted. Admission may be deferred for a maximum of 1 year.

COSTS AND FINANCIAL AID

Annual in-state tuition $9,087. Annual out-of-state tuition $32,945. Room and board $10,041. Required fees $1,301. Average book expense $1,290. **Required Forms and Deadlines:** FAFSA. **Notification of Awards:** Applicants will be notified of awards on a rolling basis beginning 4/1. **Types of Aid:** *Need-based scholarships/grants:* Federal Pell, FSEOG, State scholarships/grants, Private scholarships, College/university scholarship or grant aid from institutional funds. *Loans:* Direct Subsidized Stafford Loans, Direct Unsubsidized Stafford Loans, Direct PLUS loans, Federal Perkins Loans, Federal Nursing Loans, College/university loans from institutional funds. *Student Employment:* Federal Work-Study Program available. Institutional employment available. **Financial Aid Statistics:** 77% needy freshmen, 80% needy undergrads receive

need-based scholarship or grant aid. 19% freshmen, 16% undergrads receive non-need-based scholarship or grant aid. 62% freshmen, 65% undergrads receive need-based self-help aid. 1% freshmen, 1% undergrads receive athletic scholarships. 72% freshmen, 75% undergrads receive any aid. 44% undergrads borrow to pay for school. Average cumulative indebtedness $28,039. **Criteria for awarding aid:** *Need-based:* Academics, Alumni affiliation, Art, Athletics, Leadership, Minority status, Music/drama. *Non-need-based:* Academics, Art, Athletics, Leadership, Minority status, Music/drama, Religious affiliation.

INDIANA UNIVERSITY EAST

2325 Chester Boulevard, Richmond, IN 47374-1289
Phone: 765-973-8208 • **Financial Aid Phone:** 765-973-8206
E-mail: applynow@iue.edu • **CEEB Code:** 1194
Fax: 765-973-8209 • **Website:** www.iue.edu • **ACT Code:** 1216

This public school was founded in 1971. It has a 182-acre campus.

RATINGS
Admissions Selectivity Rating: 78   **Fire Safety Rating:** 60*   **Green Rating:** 60*

STUDENTS AND FACULTY

Enrollment: 3,082. **Student Body:** 65% female, 35% male, 24% out-of-state, 1% international (34 countries represented). Asian 1%, African American 4%, Caucasian 86%, Hispanic 3%, Native American <1%, Pacific Islander <1%, Two or more races 3%, Race unknown 1%.
Retention and Graduation: 67% freshmen return for sophomore year. 14% freshmen graduate within 4 years. 32% freshmen graduate within 6 years.
Faculty: Student/faculty ratio 14:1. 108 full-time faculty, 75% hold PhDs, 15% are are members of minority groups, 61% are women.

ACADEMICS

Degrees: bachelor's, certificate, master's, postbachelor's certifiate. **Classes:** Most classes have 10-19 students. **Most popular majors:** Registered Nursing/Registered Nurse; Business/Commerce; Psychology. **Special Study Options:** cooperative education program, cross-registration, distance learning, double major, dual enrollment, external degree program, honors program, independent study, internships, teacher certification program, weekend college, State-wide technology program with Purdue University. **Disability Services:** Special programs offered to physically disabled students, including note-taking services, reader services, tape recorders, tutors. **Career Services:** Alumni network, Alumni services, Career/job search classes, Career assessment, Internships, Regional alumni.

FACILITIES

Computers: Students can register for classes online. Administrative functions (other than registration) can be performed online.

CAMPUS LIFE

Environment: Town. **Activities:** drama/theater, literary magazine, student government, student newspaper, television station. **Athletics (Intercollegiate):** *Men:* basketball, golf. *Women:* volleyball.

ADMISSIONS

Freshman Academic Profile: Average high school GPA 3.1. 8% in top 10% of high school class, 27% in top 25% of high school class, 67% in top 50% of high school class. **Reported SAT (pre-2016 redesign) scores:** SAT Math middle 50% range 410-520. SAT Critical Reading middle 50% range 420-520. SAT Writing middle 50% range 410-500. **Concordant SAT scores:** SAT EBRW middle 50% 460–570. SAT Math middle 50% range 450–550. ACT middle 50% range 18-23. Minimum internet-based TOEFL 79. Minimum paper TOEFL 550. **Basis for Candidate Selection:** *Very important factors considered include:* rigor of secondary school record, class rank, standardized test scores. *Important factors considered include:* academic GPA. *Other factors considered include:* recommendation(s), geographical residence, state residency. **Freshman Admission Requirements:** High school diploma is required and GED is accepted. *Academic units required:* 4 English, 3 math, 3 science, 3 science labs, 3 social studies, 4 academic electives. **Freshman Admission Statistics:** 1,226 applied, 60.28% admitted, 49% enrolled. **Transfer Admission Requirements:** college transcript(s), Minimum college GPA of 2.0 required. Lowest grade transferable C. **General Admission Information:** Application fee $35. Nonfall registration accepted. Admission may be deferred.

COSTS AND FINANCIAL AID

Annual in-state tuition $6,478. Annual out-of-state tuition $18,088. Required fees $595. **Required Forms and Deadlines:** FAFSA, Institution's own financial aid form. **Notification of Awards:** Applicants will be notified of awards on a rolling basis beginning 5/1. **Types of Aid:** *Need-based scholarships/grants:* Federal Pell, FSEOG, State scholarships/grants, Private scholarships, College/university scholarship or grant aid from institutional funds. *Loans:*

Direct Subsidized Stafford Loans, Direct Unsubsidized Stafford Loans, Direct PLUS loans, Federal Perkins Loans, College/university loans from institutional funds. *Student Employment:* Federal Work-Study Program available. Institutional employment available. **Financial Aid Statistics:** 91% needy freshmen, 84% needy undergrads receive need-based scholarship or grant aid. 18% freshmen, 9% undergrads receive non-need-based scholarship or grant aid. 41% freshmen, 66% undergrads receive need-based self-help aid. 5% freshmen, 3% undergrads receive athletic scholarships. 96% freshmen, 82% undergrads receive any aid. 78% undergrads borrow to pay for school. Average cumulative indebtedness $27,379. **Criteria for awarding aid:** *Need-based:* Academics, Alumni affiliation, Leadership. *Non-need-based:* Academics, Alumni affiliation, Leadership.

INDIANA UNIVERSITY—KOKOMO

2300 South Washington Street, Kokomo, IN 46902-9003
Phone: 765-455-9217 • **Financial Aid Phone:** 765-455-9216
E-mail: iuadmis@iuk.edu • **CEEB Code:** 1337
Fax: 765-455-9537 • **Website:** www.iuk.edu • **ACT Code:** 1219

This public school was founded in 1945. It has a 51-acre campus.

RATINGS

Admissions Selectivity Rating: 75   **Fire Safety Rating:** 60*   **Green Rating:** 60*

STUDENTS AND FACULTY

Enrollment: 2,771. **Student Body:** 67% female, 33% male, 1% out-of-state, 1% international (29 countries represented). Asian 1%, African American 4%, Caucasian 84%, Hispanic 5%, Native American <1%, Pacific Islander <1%, Two or more races 3%, Race unknown 2%.
Retention and Graduation: 63% freshmen return for sophomore year. 17% freshmen graduate within 4 years. 39% freshmen graduate within 6 years.
Faculty: Student/faculty ratio 15:1. 123 full-time faculty, 63% hold PhDs, 14% are are members of minority groups, 65% are women.

ACADEMICS

Degrees: associate, bachelor's, certificate, master's, postbachelor's certificate.
Classes: Most classes have 20-29 students. Most lab/discussion sessions have 20-29 students. **Most popular majors:** Business/Commerce; Registered Nursing/Registered Nurse; Liberal Arts and Sciences Studies and Humanities.
Special Study Options: Accelerated program, cross-registration, distance learning, double major, dual enrollment, external degree program, honors program, independent study, internships, liberal arts/career combination, study abroad, teacher certification program. **Disability Services:** Special programs offered to physically disabled students, including note-taking services, reader services, tutors. **Career Services:** Alumni network, Alumni services, Career/job search classes, Career assessment, Internships.

FACILITIES

Special Academic Facilities/Equipment: Observatory, Art Gallery
Computers: Students can register for classes online. Administrative functions (other than registration) can be performed online.

CAMPUS LIFE

Environment: Village. **Activities:** Choral groups, drama/theater, music ensembles, student government, student newspaper.

ADMISSIONS

Freshman Academic Profile: Average high school GPA 3.1. 7% in top 10% of high school class, 25% in top 25% of high school class, 63% in top 50% of high school class. **Reported SAT (pre-2016 redesign) scores:** SAT Math middle 50% range 420-510. SAT Critical Reading middle 50% range 410-520. SAT Writing middle 50% range 390-490. **Concordant SAT scores:** SAT EBRW middle 50% 450–560. SAT Math middle 50% range 460–540. ACT middle 50% range 18-23. Minimum internet-based TOEFL 61. Minimum paper TOEFL 530. **Basis for Candidate Selection:** *Very important factors considered include:* rigor of secondary school record, class rank, standardized test scores. *Important factors considered include:* academic GPA. *Other factors considered include:* recommendation(s). **Freshman Admission Requirements:** High school diploma is required and GED is accepted. *Academic units required:* 4 English, 3 math, 3 science, 3 science labs, 3 social studies, 7 academic electives. *Academic units recommended:* 2 foreign language. **Freshman Admission Statistics:** 1,513 applied, 69.13% admitted, 48% enrolled. **Transfer Admission Requirements:** college transcript(s), Minimum college GPA of 2.0 required. Lowest grade transferable C. **General Admission Information:** Application fee $35. Priority deadline 3/1. Nonfall registration accepted. Admission may be deferred for a maximum of 1 year.

COSTS AND FINANCIAL AID

Annual in-state tuition $6,478. Annual out-of-state tuition $18,088. Required fees $595. **Required Forms and Deadlines:** FAFSA. **Notification of Awards:** Applicants will be notified of awards on a rolling basis beginning 3/30. **Types of Aid:** *Need-based scholarships/grants:* Federal Pell, FSEOG, State scholarships/grants, Private scholarships, College/university scholarship or grant aid from institutional funds. *Loans:* Direct Subsidized Stafford Loans, Direct Unsubsidized Stafford Loans, Direct PLUS loans, Federal Perkins Loans, Federal Nursing Loans, College/university loans from institutional funds. *Student Employment:* Federal Work-Study Program available. Institutional employment available. **Financial Aid Statistics:** 84% needy freshmen, 82% needy undergrads receive need-based scholarship or grant aid. 9% freshmen, 5% undergrads receive non-need-based scholarship or grant aid. 50% freshmen, 64% undergrads receive need-based self-help aid. 1% freshmen, 1% undergrads receive athletic scholarships. 89% freshmen, 85% undergrads receive any aid. 74% undergrads borrow to pay for school. Average cumulative indebtedness $25,675. **Criteria for awarding aid:** *Need-based:* Academics, Athletics, Leadership. *Non-need-based:* Academics, Athletics, Leadership.

INDIANA UNIVERSITY—NORTHWEST

3400 Broadway, Gary, IN 46408-1197
Phone: 219-980-6991 • **Financial Aid Phone:** 219-980-6778
E-mail: admit@iun.edu • **CEEB Code:** 1338
Fax: 219-981-4219 • **Website:** www.iun.edu • **ACT Code:** 1218

This public school was founded in 1948. It has a 38-acre campus.

RATINGS

Admissions Selectivity Rating: 75   **Fire Safety Rating:** 60*   **Green Rating:** 60*

STUDENTS AND FACULTY

Enrollment: 3,727. **Student Body:** 69% female, 31% male, 3% out-of-state, <1% international (34 countries represented). Asian 2%, African American 16%, Caucasian 55%, Hispanic 22%, Native American <1%, Pacific Islander <1%, Two or more races 3%, Race unknown 1%.
Retention and Graduation: 65% freshmen return for sophomore year. 7% freshmen graduate within 4 years. 23% freshmen graduate within 6 years.
Faculty: Student/faculty ratio 14:1. 167 full-time faculty, 74% hold PhDs, 28% are are members of minority groups, 54% are women.

ACADEMICS

Degrees: associate, bachelor's, certificate, master's, postbachelor's certificate.
Classes: Most classes have 20-29 students. Most lab/discussion sessions have 20-29 students. **Most popular majors:** Business/Commerce; Registered Nursing/Registered Nurse; Liberal Arts and Sciences Studies and Humanities.
Special Study Options: Accelerated program, cooperative education program, distance learning, double major, dual enrollment, external degree program, independent study, internships, liberal arts/career combination, student-designed major, study abroad, teacher certification program, weekend college.
Disability Services: Special programs offered to physically disabled students, including reader services, tape recorders, tutors. **Career Services:** Alumni network, Alumni services, Career/job search classes, Career assessment, Internships.

FACILITIES

Computers: Students can register for classes online. Administrative functions (other than registration) can be performed online.

CAMPUS LIFE

Activities: Choral groups, dance, drama/theater, literary magazine, musical theater, radio station, student government, student newspaper, Student Organization. 60 registered organizations, 4 honor societies, 2 religious organizations. 2 fraternities, 3 sororities. **Athletics (Intercollegiate):** *Men:* baseball, basketball, cheerleading, golf. *Women:* basketball, cheerleading, volleyball.

ADMISSIONS

Freshman Academic Profile: Average high school GPA 3.0. 13% in top 10% of high school class, 32% in top 25% of high school class, 72% in top 50% of high school class. **Reported SAT (pre-2016 redesign) scores:** SAT Math middle 50% range 400-510. SAT Critical Reading middle 50% range 420-500. SAT Writing middle 50% range 400-500. **Concordant SAT scores:** SAT EBRW middle 50% 460–560. SAT Math middle 50% range 440–540. ACT middle 50% range 18-23. Minimum internet-based TOEFL 71. Minimum paper TOEFL 530. **Basis for Candidate Selection:** *Very important factors considered include:* rigor of secondary school record, academic GPA, standardized test scores. *Important factors considered include:* class rank. *Other factors considered include:* recommendation(s). **Freshman Admission**

Requirements: High school diploma is required and GED is accepted. *Academic units required:* 4 English, 3 math, 3 science, 3 science labs, 2 social studies, 1 history, 7 academic electives. *Academic units recommended:* 2 foreign language. **Freshman Admission Statistics:** 1,723 applied, 75.80% admitted, 46% enrolled. **Transfer Admission Requirements:** High school transcript, college transcript(s), Minimum college GPA of 2.0 required. Lowest grade transferable C. **General Admission Information:** Application fee $35. Priority deadline 7/1. Nonfall registration accepted. Admission may be deferred for a maximum of 1 years.

COSTS AND FINANCIAL AID

Annual in-state tuition $6,478. Annual out-of-state tuition $18,088. Required fees $595. **Required Forms and Deadlines:** FAFSA. **Notification of Awards:** Applicants will be notified of awards on a rolling basis beginning 4/15. **Types of Aid:** *Need-based scholarships/grants:* Federal Pell, FSEOG, State scholarships/grants, Private scholarships, College/university scholarship or grant aid from institutional funds, United Negro College Fund, Federal Nursing Scholarships. *Loans:* Direct Subsidized Stafford Loans, Direct Unsubsidized Stafford Loans, Direct PLUS loans, Federal Perkins Loans, College/university loans from institutional funds. *Student Employment:* Federal Work-Study Program available. Institutional employment available. **Financial Aid Statistics:** 78% needy freshmen, 78% needy undergrads receive need-based scholarship or grant aid. 7% freshmen, 4% undergrads receive non-need-based scholarship or grant aid. 48% freshmen, 63% undergrads receive need-based self-help aid. 1% freshmen, 0% undergrads receive athletic scholarships. 82% freshmen, 79% undergrads receive any aid. 68% undergrads borrow to pay for school. Average cumulative indebtedness $29,701. **Criteria for awarding aid:** *Need-based:* Academics, Minority status. *Non-need-based:* Academics, Athletics.

INDIANA UNIVERSITY OF PENNSYLVANIA

1011 South Drive, Indiana, PA 15705
Phone: 724-357-2230 • **Financial Aid Phone:** 724-357-2218
E-mail: admissions-inquiry@iup.edu • **CEEB Code:** 2652
Fax: 724-357-6281 • **Website:** www.iup.edu • **ACT Code:** 3704

This public school was founded in 1875. It has a 342-acre campus.

RATINGS

Admissions Selectivity Rating: 75   **Fire Safety Rating:** 96   **Green Rating:** 60*

STUDENTS AND FACULTY

Enrollment: 10,357. **Student Body:** 56% female, 44% male, 5% out-of-state, 4% international (34 countries represented). Asian 1%, African American 12%, Caucasian 74%, Hispanic 4%, Native American <1%, Pacific Islander <1%, Two or more races 4%, Race unknown 1%.
Retention and Graduation: 75% freshmen return for sophomore year. 55 **Faculty:** Student/faculty ratio 16:1. 576 full-time faculty, 0% hold PhDs, 15% are are members of minority groups, 46% are women. 0% of classes are taught by teaching assistants.

ACADEMICS

Degrees: associate, bachelor's, certificate, doctoral/professional, doctoral/research, master's, postbachelor's certificate, post-master's certificate. **Classes:** Most classes have 20-29 students. Most lab/discussion sessions have 10-19 students. **Most popular majors:** Criminology; Business Administration and Management; Speech Communication and Rhetoric. **Special Study Options:** Accelerated program, cooperative education program, cross-registration, distance learning, double major, dual enrollment, English as a Second Language (ESL), exchange student program (domestic), external degree program, honors program, independent study, internships, liberal arts/career combination, student-designed major, study abroad, teacher certification program, weekend college. **Honors Programs:** Robert E. Cook Honors College. **Disability Services:** Special programs offered to physically disabled students, including note-taking services, reader services, tape recorders. **Career Services:** Alumni services, Career/job search classes, Career assessment, Internships. IUP partners with The Washington Center (TWC) to provide students with internship and educational opportunities for academic semesters, summer terms, and seminars in Washington, DC. TWC gives students an invaluable chance to test drive a career by mentoring those who may one day lead an organization or industry. IUP has garnered more than $1.2 million dollars in TWC scholarships for our students, making this an affordable life-changing experience.

FACILITIES

Housing: Coed dorms, special housing for disabled students, special housing for international students, apartments for married students, apartments for single students, Wellness Housing, Theme Housing, Living Learning Communities. 98% of campus accessible to physically diasbled. **Special Academic Facilities/Equipment:** Art museum, natural history museum, on-campus elementary school, lodge, farm, co-generation plant, ski slope, sailing base. **Computers:** 90% of classrooms, 60% of dorms, 100% of libraries, 100% of dining areas, 80% of student union, 100% of common outdoor areas have wireless network access. Students can register for classes online. Administrative functions (other than registration) can be performed online.

CAMPUS LIFE

Environment: Village. **Activities:** Choral groups, concert band, dance, drama/theater, jazz band, marching band, music ensembles, musical theater, radio station, student government, student newspaper, symphony orchestra, television station, Campus Ministries, Student Organization. 210 registered organizations, 23 honor societies, 18 religious organizations. 18 fraternities, 14 sororities. **Athletics (Intercollegiate):** *Men:* baseball, basketball, cross-country, diving, football, golf, swimming, track/field (outdoor), track/field (indoor). *Women:* basketball, cross-country, diving, field hockey, lacrosse, soccer, softball, swimming, tennis, track/field (outdoor), track/field (indoor), volleyball. **On-Campus Highlights:** Suites on Grant, Oak Grove, Hadley Union Building Fitness Center/Foo, Stapleton Library, Miller Stadium.

ADMISSIONS

Freshman Academic Profile: 8% in top 10% of high school class, 27% in top 25% of high school class, 60% in top 50% of high school class. **Reported SAT (pre-2016 redesign) scores:** SAT Math middle 50% range 420-520. SAT Critical Reading middle 50% range 420-530. SAT Writing middle 50% range 400-510. **Concordant SAT scores:** SAT EBRW middle 50% 460-580. SAT Math middle 50% range 460-550. Minimum internet-based TOEFL 61. Minimum paper TOEFL 500. **Basis for Candidate Selection:** *Very important factors considered include:* academic GPA. *Important factors considered include:* rigor of secondary school record, standardized test scores. *Other factors considered include:* class rank, application essay, recommendation(s), interview, extracurricular activities, talent/ability, character/personal qualities, first generation, volunteer work, work experience, level of applicant's interest. **Freshman Admission Requirements:** High school diploma is required and GED is accepted. *Academic units required:* 4 English, 3 math, 3 science, 2 science labs. *Academic units recommended:* 2 foreign language, 3 social studies, 2 history. **Freshman Admission Statistics:** 8,943 applied, 91.54% admitted, 27% enrolled. **Transfer Admission Requirements:** High school transcript, college transcript(s), statement of good standing from prior institution(s). Minimum college GPA of 2.0 required. Lowest grade transferable C-. **General Admission Information:** Application fee $50. Nonfall registration accepted. Admission may be deferred for a maximum of 1 year.

COSTS AND FINANCIAL AID

Annual in-state tuition $8,430. Annual out-of-state tuition $18,096. Room and board $12,402. Required fees $2,938. Average book expense $1,100. **Required Forms and Deadlines:** FAFSA. **Notification of Awards:** Applicants will be notified of awards on a rolling basis beginning 3/14. **Types of Aid:** *Need-based scholarships/grants:* Federal Pell, FSEOG, State scholarships/grants, Private scholarships, College/university scholarship or grant aid from institutional funds, United Negro College Fund. *Loans:* Direct Subsidized Stafford Loans, Direct Unsubsidized Stafford Loans, Direct PLUS loans, Federal Perkins Loans. *Student Employment:* Federal Work-Study Program available. Institutional employment available. **Financial Aid Statistics:** 67% needy freshmen, 67% needy undergrads receive need-based scholarship or grant aid. 51% freshmen, 27% undergrads receive non-need-based scholarship or grant aid. 92% freshmen, 92% undergrads receive need-based self-help aid. 3% freshmen, 3% undergrads receive athletic scholarships. 80% freshmen, 81% undergrads receive any aid. 83% undergrads borrow to pay for school. Average cumulative indebtedness $36,514. **Criteria for awarding aid:** *Need-based:* Academics, Alumni affiliation, Art, Job skills, Leadership, Music/drama. *Non-need-based:* Academics, Alumni affiliation, Art, Athletics, Job skills, Leadership, Music/drama, State/district residency.

INDIANA UNIVERSITY—PURDUE UNIVERSITY INDIANAPOLIS

420 N University Boulevard, Indianapolis, IN 46202
Phone: 317-274-4591 • **Financial Aid Phone:** 317-274-4162
E-mail: apply@iupui.edu • **CEEB Code:** 1325
Fax: 317-278-1862 • **Website:** www.iupui.edu • **ACT Code:** 1214

This public school was founded in 1969. It has a 509-acre campus.

RATINGS

Admissions Selectivity Rating: 79   **Fire Safety Rating:** 93   **Green Rating:** 95

STUDENTS AND FACULTY

Enrollment: 21,001. **Student Body:** 56% female, 44% male, 3% out-of-state, 4% international (134 countries represented). Asian 4%, African American 10%, Caucasian 71%, Hispanic 7%, Native American <1%, Pacific Islander <1%, Two or more races 4%, Race unknown 1%.
Retention and Graduation: 74% freshmen return for sophomore year. 19% freshmen graduate within 4 years. 47% freshmen graduate within 6 years.
Faculty: Student/faculty ratio 17:1. 2,329 full-time faculty, 85% hold PhDs, 24% are are members of minority groups, 42% are women.

ACADEMICS

Degrees: associate, bachelor's, certificate, doctoral/professional, doctoral/research, doctoral, master's, postbachelor's certificate, post-master's certificate.
Classes: Most classes have 20-29 students. Most lab/discussion sessions have 10-19 students. **Most popular majors:** Registered Nursing/Registered Nurse; Business/Commerce; Liberal Arts and Sciences Studies and Humanities.
Special Study Options: Accelerated program, cooperative education program, cross-registration, distance learning, double major, dual enrollment, English as a Second Language (ESL), exchange student program (domestic), external degree program, honors program, independent study, internships, student-designed major, study abroad, teacher certification program, weekend college.
Honors Programs: The Honors Program provides a challenging campus-wide program for high achieving students from all academic disciplines. Honors Program students have the opportunity to enroll in smaller dynamic classes and to collaborate with faculty in independent study and research projects. Participants in the IUPUI Honors Program will be required to complete at least three credit hours of honors course work each semester. Combined degree programs: BA/MEng; BS/MS; MD/PhD; MA/MPA; MBA/JD; MA/MPH; MA/MA; JD/MD; MBA/MSE; MLS/MA. **Disability Services:** Special programs offered to physically disabled students, including note-taking services, reader services, tape recorders, tutors. **Career Services:** Alumni network, Alumni services, Career/job search classes, Career assessment, Internships, Regional alumni.

FACILITIES

Housing: Coed dorms, special housing for international students, apartments for married students, apartments for single students. 90% of campus accessible to physically diasbled. **Special Academic Facilities/Equipment:** Inlow Hall-Law School, Eskenazi Hall-Herron School of Art and Design, Cavanagh Hall-School of Liberal Arts, and IUPUI Enrollment Center University Library-Most high tech library in North America, IUPUI Sport Complex-host of 11 Olympic Team Trails, White River State Park-Indianapolis' version of the mall in Washington, D.C. **Computers:** 100% of classrooms, 100% of dorms, 100% of libraries, 100% of dining areas, 100% of student union, 100% of common outdoor areas have wireless network access. Students can register for classes online. Administrative functions (other than registration) can be performed online.

CAMPUS LIFE

Environment: Metropolis. **Activities:** Choral groups, concert band, dance, drama/theater, jazz band, literary magazine, music ensembles, pep band, student government, student newspaper, Campus Ministries, Student Organization. 154 registered organizations, 9 honor societies, 10 religious organizations. 2 fraternities, 1 sorority. **Athletics (Intercollegiate):** *Men:* basketball, cross-country, diving, golf, soccer, swimming, tennis. *Women:* basketball, cross-country, diving, golf, soccer, softball, swimming, tennis, volleyball. **On-Campus Highlights:** IUPUI Sport Complex, University College, Cavanaugh Hall, University Library, Eskenazi Hall, IU Medical Center.

ADMISSIONS

Freshman Academic Profile: Average high school GPA 3.5. 16% in top 10% of high school class, 44% in top 25% of high school class, 87% in top 50% of high school class. **Reported SAT (pre-2016 redesign) scores:** SAT Math middle 50% range 450-570. SAT Critical Reading middle 50% range 440-560. SAT Writing middle 50% range 430-530. **Concordant SAT scores:** SAT EBRW middle 50% 490–600. SAT Math middle 50% 490–590. ACT middle 50% range 19-26. Minimum internet-based TOEFL 80. **Basis**

for Candidate Selection: *Very important factors considered include:* rigor of secondary school record, academic GPA, standardized test scores. *Important factors considered include:* class rank. *Other factors considered include:* character/personal qualities, first generation, volunteer work, work experience. **Freshman Admission Requirements:** High school diploma is required and GED is accepted. *Academic units required:* 4 English, 3 math, 3 science, 3 science labs, 3 social studies, 7 academic electives. **Freshman Admission Statistics:** 13,301 applied, 73.97% admitted, 41% enrolled. **Transfer Admission Requirements:** college transcript(s), Minimum college GPA of 2.0 required. Lowest grade transferable C. **General Admission Information:** Application fee $55. Regular application deadline 5/1. Nonfall registration accepted.

COSTS AND FINANCIAL AID

Annual in-state tuition $8,141. Annual out-of-state tuition $28,727. Room and board $8,462. Required fees $1,064. Average book expense $1,204. **Required Forms and Deadlines:** FAFSA. **Notification of Awards:** Applicants will be notified of awards on a rolling basis beginning 4/1. **Types of Aid:** *Need-based scholarships/grants:* Federal Pell, FSEOG, State scholarships/grants, Private scholarships, College/university scholarship or grant aid from institutional funds. *Loans:* Direct Subsidized Stafford Loans, Direct Unsubsidized Stafford Loans, Direct PLUS loans, Federal Perkins Loans, Federal Nursing Loans, College/university loans from institutional funds. *Student Employment:* Federal Work-Study Program available. Institutional employment available. **Financial Aid Statistics:** 83% needy freshmen, 80% needy undergrads receive need-based scholarship or grant aid. 14% freshmen, 10% undergrads receive non-need-based scholarship or grant aid. 56% freshmen, 67% undergrads receive need-based self-help aid. 0% freshmen, 1% undergrads receive athletic scholarships. 89% freshmen, 83% undergrads receive any aid. 70% undergrads borrow to pay for school. Average cumulative indebtedness $28,951. **Criteria for awarding aid:** *Need-based:* Academics. *Non-need-based:* Academics, Alumni affiliation, Art, Athletics, Leadership, State/district residency.

INDIANA UNIVERSITY—PURDUE UNIVERSITY FORT WAYNE

2101 East Coliseum Boulevard, Fort Wayne, IN 46805-1499
Phone: 260-481-6812
E-mail: ipfwadms@ipfw.edu • **CEEB Code:** 1336
Fax: 260-481-6880 • **Website:** www.ipfw.edu • **ACT Code:** 1217

This public school was founded in 1917. It has a 565-acre campus.

RATINGS

Admissions Selectivity Rating: 72   **Fire Safety Rating:** 60*   **Green Rating:** 60*

STUDENTS AND FACULTY

Enrollment: 10,587. **Student Body:** 58% female, 42% male, 5% out-of-state, 2% international (71 countries represented). Asian 2%, African American 5%, Caucasian 87%, Hispanic 2%, Native American <1%, Pacific Islander 0%, Two or more races 0%, Race unknown 2%.
Retention and Graduation: 60% freshmen return for sophomore year.
Faculty: Student/faculty ratio 19:1. 329 full-time faculty, 83% hold PhDs, 13% are are members of minority groups, 37% are women. 1% of classes are taught by teaching assistants.

ACADEMICS

Degrees: associate, bachelor's, certificate, master's, postbachelor's certifiate, post-master's certificate, terminal, transfer. **Classes:** Most classes have 20-29 students. Most lab/discussion sessions have 20-29 students. **Most popular majors:** Elementary Education and Teaching Business/Commerce. **Special Study Options:** cooperative education program, distance learning, double major, English as a Second Language (ESL), exchange student program (domestic), honors program, independent study, internships, liberal arts/career combination, student-designed major, study abroad, teacher certification program, weekend college. **Disability Services:** Special programs offered to physically disabled students, including note-taking services, reader services, tape recorders, tutors. **Career Services:** Alumni network, Alumni services, Career/job search classes, Career assessment, Internships, Regional alumni.

FACILITIES

Housing: Coed dorms. 100% of campus accessible to physically diasbled. **Special Academic Facilities/Equipment:** Williams theatre, recital hall, anthropology and geology exhibits, art gallery. **Computers:** Students can register for classes online. Administrative functions (other than registration) can be performed online.

CAMPUS LIFE

Environment: Village. **Activities:** Choral groups, concert band, dance, drama/theater, jazz band, literary magazine, music ensembles, musical theater, opera, pep band, student government, student newspaper, symphony orchestra, television station 65 registered organizations, 7 honor societies, 3 religious organizations. 2 fraternities, 3 sororities. **Athletics (Intercollegiate):** *Men:* baseball, basketball, cross-country, soccer, tennis, track/field (outdoor), volleyball. *Women:* basketball, cross-country, soccer, softball, tennis, track/field (outdoor), volleyball.

ADMISSIONS

Freshman Academic Profile: Average high school GPA 2.6. 7% in top 10% of high school class, 24% in top 25% of high school class, 57% in top 50% of high school class. **Reported SAT (pre-2016 redesign) scores:** SAT Math middle 50% range 430-550. SAT Critical Reading middle 50% range 420-540. **Concordant SAT scores:** SAT Math middle 50% range 470–570. ACT middle 50% range 17-23. Minimum paper TOEFL 550. **Basis for Candidate Selection:** *Very important factors considered include:* rigor of secondary school record, class rank, standardized test scores. *Other factors considered include:* recommendation(s), state residency. **Freshman Admission Requirements:** High school diploma is required and GED is accepted. *Academic units required:* 4 English, 3 math, 1 science, 1 foreign language, 1 social studies. *Academic units recommended:* 3 science, 1 science lab, 3 foreign language, 3 social studies. **Freshman Admission Statistics:** 2,471 applied, 96.92% admitted, 71% enrolled. **Transfer Admission Requirements:** High school transcript, college transcript(s), Minimum college GPA of 2.0 required. Lowest grade transferable C-. **General Admission Information:** Application fee $30. Priority deadline 3/1. Regular application deadline 8/1. Nonfall registration accepted.

COSTS AND FINANCIAL AID

Annual in-state tuition $3,100. Annual out-of-state tuition $7,728. Required fees $384. Average book expense $800. **Required Forms and Deadlines:** FAFSA. **Notification of Awards:** Applicants will be notified of awards on or about 4/30. **Types of Aid:** *Need-based scholarships/grants:* Federal Pell, FSEOG, State scholarships/grants, Private scholarships, Federal Nursing Scholarships. *Loans:* Federal Perkins Loans, Federal Nursing Loans. *Student Employment:* Federal Work-Study Program available. Institutional employment available. **Financial Aid Statistics:** 56% needy freshmen, 69% needy undergrads receive need-based scholarship or grant aid. 28% freshmen, 23% undergrads receive non-need-based scholarship or grant aid. 46% freshmen, 50% undergrads receive need-based self-help aid. 3% freshmen, 3% undergrads receive athletic scholarships. **Criteria for awarding aid:** *Need-based:* Athletics, Job skills. *Non-need-based:* Academics, Alumni affiliation, Art, Athletics.

INDIANA UNIVERSITY SOUTH BEND

1700 Mishawaka Avenue, South Bend, IN 46634-7111
Phone: 574-520-4839 • **Financial Aid Phone:** 574-520-4357
E-mail: admissions@iusb.edu • **CEEB Code:** 1339
Fax: 574-520-4834 • **Website:** www.iusb.edu • **ACT Code:** 1225

This public school was founded in 1922. It has a 80-acre campus.

RATINGS

Admissions Selectivity Rating: 75   **Fire Safety Rating:** 91   **Green Rating:** 68

STUDENTS AND FACULTY

Enrollment: 4,981. **Student Body:** 61% female, 39% male, 4% out-of-state, 3% international (68 countries represented). Asian 1%, African American 8%, Caucasian 73%, Hispanic 10%, Native American <1%, Pacific Islander <1%, Two or more races 4%, Race unknown 1%.
Retention and Graduation: 64% freshmen return for sophomore year. 7% freshmen graduate within 4 years. 28% freshmen graduate within 6 years.
Faculty: Student/faculty ratio 14:1. 263 full-time faculty, 76% hold PhDs, 22% are are members of minority groups, 50% are women.

ACADEMICS

Degrees: associate, bachelor's, certificate, diploma, master's, postbachelor's certificate. **Classes:** Most classes have 20-29 students. Most lab/discussion sessions have 20-29 students. **Most popular majors:** Registered Nursing/Registered Nurse; Business/Commerce; Liberal Arts and Sciences Studies and Humanities. **Special Study Options:** Accelerated program, cross-registration, distance learning, double major, English as a Second Language (ESL), external degree program, honors program, internships, liberal arts/career combination, study abroad, teacher certification program, weekend college, Electrical, Mechanical Engineering, Computer Technology with Purdue University on Indiana University South Bend Campus. Northern Indiana Consortium for Education (NICE)—IUSB is one of six member institutions sharing library

resources, faculty expertise, and academic strengths resulting in broadened course opportunities to students. **Disability Services:** Special programs offered to physically disabled students, including note-taking services, reader services, tape recorders, tutors. **Career Services:** Alumni network, Alumni services, Career/job search classes, Career assessment, Internships.

FACILITIES

Housing: Coed dorms, special housing for international students, apartments for single students. **Computers:** Students can register for classes online. Administrative functions (other than registration) can be performed online.

CAMPUS LIFE

Activities: Choral groups, drama/theater, jazz band, literary magazine, music ensembles, musical theater, opera, student government, student newspaper, student-run film society, symphony orchestra 30 registered organizations, 1 religious organization. 2 fraternities, 1 sorority. **Athletics (Intercollegiate):** *Men:* basketball. *Women:* basketball.

ADMISSIONS

Freshman Academic Profile: Average high school GPA 3.1. 10% in top 10% of high school class, 29% in top 25% of high school class, 65% in top 50% of high school class. **Reported SAT (pre-2016 redesign) scores:** SAT Math middle 50% range 420-530. SAT Critical Reading middle 50% range 420-520. SAT Writing middle 50% range 400-500. **Concordant SAT scores:** SAT EBRW middle 50% 460–570. SAT Math middle 50% range 460–560. ACT middle 50% range 18-23. Minimum internet-based TOEFL 71. Minimum paper TOEFL 530. **Basis for Candidate Selection:** *Very important factors considered include:* rigor of secondary school record. *Important factors considered include:* class rank, academic GPA, standardized test scores. *Other factors considered include:* recommendation(s), interview, extracurricular activities, geographical residence, state residency. **Freshman Admission Requirements:** High school diploma is required and GED is accepted. *Academic units required:* 4 English, 3 math, 3 science, 3 science labs, 3 social studies, 7 academic electives. *Academic units recommended:* 2 foreign language. **Freshman Admission Statistics:** 2,451 applied, 77.03% admitted, 48% enrolled. **Transfer Admission Requirements:** college transcript(s), Minimum college GPA of 2.0 required. Lowest grade transferable C. **General Admission Information:** Application fee $35. Priority deadline 7/31. Nonfall registration accepted. Admission may be deferred.

COSTS AND FINANCIAL AID

Annual in-state tuition $6,478. Annual out-of-state tuition $18,088. Required fees $595. Average book expense $1,204. **Required Forms and Deadlines:** FAFSA, Institution's own financial aid form. **Notification of Awards:** Applicants will be notified of awards on a rolling basis beginning 5/1. **Types of Aid:** *Need-based scholarships/grants:* Federal Pell, FSEOG, State scholarships/grants, Private scholarships, College/university scholarship or grant aid from institutional funds. *Loans:* Direct Subsidized Stafford Loans, Direct Unsubsidized Stafford Loans, Direct PLUS loans, Federal Perkins Loans, State Loans. *Student Employment:* Federal Work-Study Program available. Institutional employment available. **Financial Aid Statistics:** 86% needy freshmen, 82% needy undergrads receive need-based scholarship or grant aid. 6% freshmen, 6% undergrads receive non-need-based scholarship or grant aid. 49% freshmen, 63% undergrads receive need-based self-help aid. 6% freshmen, 2% undergrads receive athletic scholarships. 90% freshmen, 82% undergrads receive any aid. 76% undergrads borrow to pay for school. Average cumulative indebtedness $27,306. **Criteria for awarding aid:** *Need-based:* Academics, Alumni affiliation, Art, Athletics, Job skills, Leadership, Minority status. *Non-need-based:* Academics, Athletics.

INDIANA UNIVERSITY SOUTHEAST

4201 Grant Line Road, New Albany, IN 47150
Phone: 812-941-2212 • **Financial Aid Phone:** 812-941-2246
E-mail: admissions@ius.edu • **CEEB Code:** 1314
Fax: 812-941-2595 • **Website:** www.ius.edu • **ACT Code:** 1229

This public school was founded in 1941. It has a 177-acre campus.

RATINGS

Admissions Selectivity Rating: 75   **Fire Safety Rating:** 91   **Green Rating:** 67

STUDENTS AND FACULTY

Enrollment: 4,964. **Student Body:** 60% female, 40% male, 30% out-of-state, <1% international (34 countries represented). Asian 1%, African American 7%, Caucasian 84%, Hispanic 3%, Native American <1%, Pacific Islander <1%, Two or more races 3%, Race unknown <1%.
Retention and Graduation: 62% freshmen return for sophomore year. 12% freshmen graduate within 4 years. 31% freshmen graduate within 6 years.

Faculty: Student/faculty ratio 13:1. 218 full-time faculty, 78% hold PhDs, 17% are are members of minority groups, 52% are women.

ACADEMICS
Degrees: associate, bachelor's, certificate, master's, postbachelor's certificate. **Classes:** Most classes have 20-29 students. Most lab/discussion sessions have 10-19 students. **Most popular majors:** Registered Nursing/Registered Nurse; Business/Commerce; Psychology. **Special Study Options:** Accelerated program, cross-registration, distance learning, double major, dual enrollment, external degree program, honors program, independent study, internships, student-designed major, study abroad, teacher certification program, weekend college. **Disability Services:** Special programs offered to physically disabled students, including note-taking services, reader services, tutors. **Career Services:** Alumni network, Alumni services, Career/job search classes, Career assessment, Internships.

FACILITIES
Housing: Coed dorms. 95% of campus accessible to physically diasbled. **Special Academic Facilities/Equipment:** Paul W. Ogle Center, Concert Hall, Theatre, Recital Hall, Japanese Cultural Center, Ronald L. Barr Art Gallery **Computers:** Students can register for classes online. Administrative functions (other than registration) can be performed online.

CAMPUS LIFE
Environment: Village. **Activities:** Choral groups, concert band, drama/theater, literary magazine, music ensembles, student government, student newspaper, symphony orchestra 76 registered organizations, 1 religious organization. 2 fraternities, 4 sororities. **Athletics (Intercollegiate):** *Men:* baseball, basketball, cross-country, tennis. *Women:* basketball, cross-country, softball, tennis, volleyball. **Environmental Initiatives:** Single stream waste Recycling.

ADMISSIONS
Freshman Academic Profile: Average high school GPA 3.2. 10% in top 10% of high school class, 31% in top 25% of high school class, 67% in top 50% of high school class. **Reported SAT (pre-2016 redesign) scores:** SAT Math middle 50% range 410-510. SAT Critical Reading middle 50% range 420-530. SAT Writing middle 50% range 410-500. **Concordant SAT scores:** SAT EBRW middle 50% 460–570. SAT Math middle 50% range 450–540. ACT middle 50% range 17-23. Minimum internet-based TOEFL 75. Minimum paper TOEFL 530. **Basis for Candidate Selection:** *Very important factors considered include:* rigor of secondary school record, class rank. *Important factors considered include:* academic GPA, standardized test scores. *Other factors considered include:* recommendation(s), interview. **Freshman Admission Requirements:** High school diploma is required and GED is accepted. *Academic units required:* 4 English, 3 math, 3 science, 3 science labs, 3 social studies, 7 academic electives. *Academic units recommended:* 2 foreign language. **Freshman Admission Statistics:** 2,177 applied, 84.01% admitted, 51% enrolled. **Transfer Admission Requirements:** college transcript(s), Lowest grade transferable C. **General Admission Information:** Application fee $35. Priority deadline 8/17. Nonfall registration accepted. Admission may be deferred.

COSTS AND FINANCIAL AID
Annual in-state tuition $6,478. Annual out-of-state tuition $18,088. Required fees $595. Average book expense $1,204. **Required Forms and Deadlines:** FAFSA. **Notification of Awards:** Applicants will be notified of awards on a rolling basis beginning 5/1. **Types of Aid:** *Need-based scholarships/grants:* Federal Pell, FSEOG, State scholarships/grants, Private scholarships, College/university scholarship or grant aid from institutional funds. *Loans:* Direct Subsidized Stafford Loans, Direct Unsubsidized Stafford Loans, Direct PLUS loans, Federal Perkins Loans, College/university loans from institutional funds. *Student Employment:* Federal Work-Study Program available. Institutional employment available. **Financial Aid Statistics:** 83% needy freshmen, 81% needy undergrads receive need-based scholarship or grant aid. 6% freshmen, 5% undergrads receive non-need-based scholarship or grant aid. 50% freshmen, 63% undergrads receive need-based self-help aid. 1% freshmen, 1% undergrads receive athletic scholarships. 90% freshmen, 78% undergrads receive any aid. 71% undergrads borrow to pay for school. Average cumulative indebtedness $22,612. **Criteria for awarding aid:** *Need-based:* Academics, Alumni affiliation, Art, Athletics, Leadership, Minority status. *Non-need-based:* Academics, Art, Athletics, Leadership, Minority status, Music/drama.

INDIANA WESLEYAN UNIVERSITY

4201 South Washington Street, Marion, IN 46953
Phone: 765-677-2138 • **Financial Aid Phone:** 765-677-2116
E-mail: admissions@indwes.edu • **CEEB Code:** 1446
Fax: 765-677-2333 • **Website:** www.indwes.edu • **ACT Code:** 1226

This private school, affiliated with the Wesleyan Church, was founded in 1920. It has a 220-acre campus.

RATINGS
Admissions Selectivity Rating: 84   **Fire Safety Rating:** 96   **Green Rating:** 60*

STUDENTS AND FACULTY
Enrollment: 2,679. **Student Body:** 66% female, 34% male, 46% out-of-state, 1% international (21 countries represented). Asian 1%, African American 3%, Caucasian 82%, Hispanic 4%, Native American <1%, Pacific Islander <1%, Two or more races 3%, Race unknown 5%.
Retention and Graduation: 82% freshmen return for sophomore year. 51% freshmen graduate within 4 years. **Faculty:** Student/faculty ratio 14:1. 163 full-time faculty, 75% hold PhDs, 9% are are members of minority groups, 44% are women. 0% of classes are taught by teaching assistants.

ACADEMICS
Degrees: associate, bachelor's, doctoral/research, doctoral, master's, postbachelor's certificate, post-master's certificate. **Classes:** Most classes have 10-19 students. Most lab/discussion sessions have 10-19 students. **Most popular majors:** Registered Nursing/Registered Nurse; Business Administration and Management; Psychology. **Special Study Options:** double major, dual enrollment, honors program, independent study, internships, study abroad, teacher certification program. **Honors Programs:** John Wesley Honors College. **Disability Services:** Special programs offered to physically disabled students, including note-taking services, reader services, tape recorders, tutors. **Career Services:** Alumni network, Alumni services, Career/job search classes, Career assessment, Internships, Regional alumni, On-campus interviews. The Center for Life Calling and Leadership enables individuals to find an overriding purpose for their lives, equips them to make life decisions based on this purpose, and empowers them to develop this purpose into world changing leadership.

FACILITIES
Housing: men's dorms, women's dorms, apartments for married students, apartments for single students. 99% of campus accessible to physically diasbled. **Special Academic Facilities/Equipment:** Lee Howard art collection (European artists) Lewis Jackson Library (2003) Tom and Joanne Phillippe Performing Arts Center (1998) Bronze statues from Israel (1998-2002) Williams chapel–medieval replica (2001) Burns Hall of Science and Nursing (2000) Luckey Recreation and Wellness Center (2001) John Maxwell Business Center (1999) **Computers:** 100% of classrooms, 100% of dorms, 100% of libraries, 100% of dining areas, 100% of student union, 100% of common outdoor areas have wireless network access. Students can register for classes online. Administrative functions (other than registration) can be performed online.

CAMPUS LIFE
Environment: Town. **Activities:** Choral groups, concert band, drama/theater, jazz band, literary magazine, music ensembles, musical theater, pep band, radio station, student government, student newspaper, symphony orchestra, television station, yearbook, Campus Ministries, Student Organization. 35 registered organizations, 1 honor society, 5 religious organizations. **Athletics (Intercollegiate):** *Men:* baseball, basketball, cheerleading, cross-country, golf, soccer, tennis, track/field (outdoor), track/field (indoor). *Women:* basketball, cheerleading, cross-country, soccer, softball, tennis, track/field (outdoor), track/field (indoor), volleyball. **On-Campus Highlights:** McConn Coffee Shop, Recreation and Wellness Center, Globe Theater, The 1920 Art Gallery, Williams Chapel, The McCoon Coffee Shop is one of the more striking facilities on any college campus–situated in a long indoor mall area of the student center–and includes a fireplace and numerous seating configurations. **Environmental Initiatives:** Creation of a multi-disciplinary Task Force for Campus Sustainabilty.

ADMISSIONS
Freshman Academic Profile: Average high school GPA 3.6. 27% in top 10% of high school class, 53% in top 25% of high school class, 85% in top 50% of high school class. **Reported SAT (pre-2016 redesign) scores:** SAT Math middle 50% range 460-580. SAT Critical Reading middle 50% range 460-590. SAT Writing middle 50% range 450-570. **Concordant SAT scores:** SAT EBRW middle 50% 510–640. SAT Math middle 50% range 500–600. ACT middle 50% range 21-27. Minimum internet-based TOEFL 79. Minimum paper TOEFL 550. **Basis for Candidate Selection:** *Important factors considered include:* rigor of secondary school record, class rank, academic GPA, standardized test scores, recommendation(s), character/

personal qualities, religious affiliation/commitment. *Other factors considered include:* extracurricular activities, talent/ability, first generation, alumni/ae relation, geographical residence, state residency, racial/ethnic status, volunteer work, work experience, level of applicant's interest. **Freshman Admission Requirements:** High school diploma is required and GED is accepted. *Academic units recommended:* 4 English, 3 math, 3 science, 2 foreign language, 3 social studies, 5 academic electives, and 1 unit from above areas or other academic areas. **Freshman Admission Statistics:** 3,323 applied, 73.88% admitted, 28% enrolled. **Transfer Admission Requirements:** college transcript(s), statement of good standing from prior institution(s). Minimum college GPA of 2.0 required. Lowest grade transferable C. **General Admission Information:** Nonfall registration accepted.

COSTS AND FINANCIAL AID

Annual tuition $25,346. Average book expense $1,380. **Required Forms and Deadlines:** FAFSA, Institution's own financial aid form. **Types of Aid:** *Need-based scholarships/grants:* Federal Pell, FSEOG, State scholarships/grants, Private scholarships, College/university scholarship or grant aid from institutional funds, Federal Nursing Scholarships. *Loans:* Direct Subsidized Stafford Loans, Direct Unsubsidized Stafford Loans, Direct PLUS loans, Federal Perkins Loans, Federal Nursing Loans, State Loans, College/university loans from institutional funds. *Student Employment:* Federal Work-Study Program available. Institutional employment available. **Financial Aid Statistics:** 100% needy freshmen, 83% needy undergrads receive need-based scholarship or grant aid. 92% freshmen, 88% undergrads receive non-need-based scholarship or grant aid. 86% freshmen, 88% undergrads receive need-based self-help aid. 10% freshmen, 8% undergrads receive athletic scholarships. 94% freshmen, 95% undergrads receive any aid. Average cumulative indebtedness $28,907. **Criteria for awarding aid:** *Need-based:* Alumni affiliation, Minority status, Religious affiliation. *Non-need-based:* Academics, Alumni affiliation, Art, Athletics, Music/drama, State/district residency.

IONA COLLEGE

715 North Avenue, New Rochelle, NY 10801
Phone: 914-633-2502 • **Financial Aid Phone:** 914-633-2497
E-mail: admissions@iona.edu • **CEEB Code:** 2324
Fax: 914-633-2182 • **Website:** www.iona.edu • **ACT Code:** 2770

This private school, affiliated with the Roman Catholic Church, was founded in 1940. It has a 35-acre campus.

RATINGS

Admissions Selectivity Rating: 73   **Fire Safety Rating:** 92   **Green Rating:** 71

STUDENTS AND FACULTY

Enrollment: 3,120. **Student Body:** 52% female, 48% male, 24% out-of-state, 3% international (37 countries represented). Asian 2%, African American 10%, Caucasian 56%, Hispanic 23%, Native American <1%, Pacific Islander <1%, Two or more races 2%, Race unknown 4%.
Retention and Graduation: 77% freshmen return for sophomore year. 60% freshmen graduate within 4 years. 68% freshmen graduate within 6 years. 40% grads go on to further study within 1 year. **Faculty:** Student/faculty ratio 15:1. 174 full-time faculty, 90% hold PhDs, 18% are are members of minority groups, 44% are women. 0% of classes are taught by teaching assistants.

ACADEMICS

Degrees: bachelor's, certificate, master's, postbachelor's certificate, post-master's certificate. **Classes:** Most classes have 20-29 students. Most lab/discussion sessions have 10-19 students. **Most popular majors:** Mass Communication/Media Studies; Psychology; Business Administration and Management.
Special Study Options: Accelerated program, distance learning, double major, honors program, independent study, internships, liberal arts/career combination, study abroad, teacher certification program, weekend college.
Honors Programs: The Iona College Honors Degree Program is designed to meet the educational needs of the ablest and most highly motivated students at Iona. Grounded in a challenging curriculum, the program offers gifted students the resources and opportunities to develop their talents and to perform at the peak of their capabilities. The course of study is designed to develop intellectual curiosity, analytic abilities, and awareness of ethical and civic responsibilities. The program encourages the development of a nucleus of independent learners able to inspire each other academically and fosters a sense of self-respect in students, encouraging them to stretch their abilities in pursuit of lifelong learning, independent thinking, and personal fulfillment. The Honors Degree Program seeks to establish a core academic community that enriches and serves the wider college community. The program endeavors to create an intellectual atmosphere to attract and challenge superior students and faculty and to enhance the public image of the College by promoting the

concept of excellence in education. The curriculum promotes an appreciation and understanding of the interrelatedness of knowledge and culture by providing a wide range of interdisciplinary courses and opportunities to study abroad. Students in the program take specially designed honors courses and advanced courses in other areas, and engage in independent research under the guidance of faculty mentors. Small class sizes encourage student participation and promote a close student-faculty relationship. Students are offered close individual guidance, both academically and in terms of career preparation. There is a faculty committee that works with students interested in applying for competitive grants and fellowships and advises them regarding graduate and professional studies. A career mentoring program affords students a unique chance to explore career opportunities by matching them with an appropriate alumnus/alumna or corporate liaison. Combined degree programs: BA/MA, BA/MS,BS/MS,BS/MST, BA/MBA, BS/MBA. **Disability Services:** Special programs offered to physically disabled students, including note-taking services, reader services, tape recorders, tutors. **Career Services:** Alumni network, Alumni services, Career/job search classes, Career assessment, Internships, Regional alumni. Career/job search **Classes:** presentations/workshops covering a range of topics including exploring majors; resume writing, interview preparation, and job/internship search strategies.

FACILITIES

Housing: Coed dorms, special housing for disabled students, apartments for single students, Living learning communities in Science, Education, wellness housing to Honors Program Students. 70% of campus accessible to physically diasbled. **Special Academic Facilities/Equipment:** Iona College Art Center, Br. Kenneth Chapman Public Art Gallary, Murphy Science Technology Center, Hynes Natural Science Center, Advanced Computer Laboratory, TV Production Studio, LaPenta Student Union,Hynes Athletic Center, Rowing tank, Arrigoni center **Computers:** 100% of classrooms, 100% of dorms, 100% of libraries, 100% of dining areas, 100% of student union, 100% of common outdoor areas have wireless network access. Students can register for classes online. Administrative functions (other than registration) can be performed online.

CAMPUS LIFE

Environment: City. **Activities:** Choral groups, dance, drama/theater, literary magazine, musical theater, pep band, radio station, student government, student newspaper, student-run film society, television station, yearbook, Campus Ministries, Student Organization, Model UN. 65 registered organizations, 9 honor societies, 4 religious organizations. 4 fraternities, 6 sororities. **Athletics (Intercollegiate):** *Men:* baseball, basketball, crew/rowing, cross-country, diving, golf, soccer, swimming, track/field (outdoor), track/field (indoor), water polo. *Women:* basketball, crew/rowing, cross-country, diving, lacrosse, soccer, softball, swimming, track/field (outdoor), track/field (indoor), volleyball, water polo. **On-Campus Highlights:** Lapenta Student Union, Hynes Athletics Center, Ryan Library, North Residence Hall, Loftus Courtyard.

ADMISSIONS

Freshman Academic Profile: Average high school GPA 3.0. 10% in top 10% of high school class, 28% in top 25% of high school class, 58% in top 50% of high school class. 64% from public high schools. **Reported SAT (pre-2016 redesign) scores:** SAT Math middle 50% range 440-550. SAT Critical Reading middle 50% range 450-550. **Concordant SAT scores:** SAT Math middle 50% range 480–570. ACT middle 50% range 20-25. Minimum internet-based TOEFL 80. Minimum paper TOEFL 550. **Basis for Candidate Selection:** *Very important factors considered include:* rigor of secondary school record, academic GPA. *Important factors considered include:* standardized test scores, application essay, character/personal qualities, level of applicant's interest. *Other factors considered include:* class rank, recommendation(s), interview, extracurricular activities, talent/ability, first generation, alumni/ae relation, geographical residence, volunteer work, work experience. **Freshman Admission Requirements:** High school diploma is required and GED is accepted. *Academic units required:* 4 English, 3 math, 3 science, 2 science labs, 2 foreign language, 2 social studies, 1 history, 1 academic elective. *Academic units recommended:* 4 math, 2 history, 3 academic electives. **Freshman Admission Statistics:** 10,896 applied, 91.46% admitted, 9% enrolled. **Transfer Admission Requirements:** High school transcript, college transcript(s), essay or personal statement, Minimum college GPA of 2.5 required. Lowest grade transferable C. **General Admission Information:** Application fee $50. Priority deadline 2/15. Regular application deadline 2/15. Nonfall registration accepted. Admission may be deferred for a maximum of 12 months.

COSTS AND FINANCIAL AID

Annual tuition $34,384. Room and board $14,400. Required fees $2,200. Average book expense $1,500. **Required Forms and Deadlines:** FAFSA, State aid form. **Notification of Awards:** Applicants will be notified of awards on a rolling basis beginning 3/1. **Types of Aid:** *Need-based scholarships/grants:* Federal Pell, FSEOG, State scholarships/grants, Private scholarships, College/university scholarship or grant aid from institutional funds. *Loans:* Direct Subsidized Stafford Loans, Direct Unsubsidized Stafford Loans, Direct PLUS loans, Federal Perkins Loans. *Student Employment:* Federal Work-Study Program available. Institutional employment available. **Financial Aid**

Statistics: 42% needy freshmen, 41% needy undergrads receive need-based scholarship or grant aid. 100% freshmen, 99% undergrads receive non-need-based scholarship or grant aid. 73% freshmen, 74% undergrads receive need-based self-help aid. 6% freshmen, 7% undergrads receive athletic scholarships. 99% freshmen, 96% undergrads receive any aid. 76% undergrads borrow to pay for school. Average cumulative indebtedness $34,199. **Criteria for awarding aid:** *Non-need-based:* Academics, Alumni affiliation, Athletics.

IOWA STATE UNIVERSITY

100 Enrollment Services Center, Ames, IA 50011-2011
Phone: 515-294-5836 • **Financial Aid Phone:** 515-294-2223
E-mail: admissions@iastate.edu • **CEEB Code:** 6306
Fax: 515-294-2592 • **Website:** www.iastate.edu • **ACT Code:** 1320

This public school was founded in 1858. It has a 1794-acre campus.

RATINGS

Admissions Selectivity Rating: 81   Fire Safety Rating: 91   Green Rating: 97

STUDENTS AND FACULTY

Enrollment: 30,224. **Student Body:** 43% female, 57% male, 31% out-of-state, 7% international (116 countries represented). Asian 3%, African American 3%, Caucasian 75%, Hispanic 5%, Native American <1%, Pacific Islander <1%, Two or more races 2%, Race unknown 5%.
Retention and Graduation: 88% freshmen return for sophomore year. 44% freshmen graduate within 4 years. 74% freshmen graduate within 6 years. 17% grads go on to further study within 1 year. 6% grads pursue arts and sciences degrees. 1% grads pursue law degrees. 2% grads pursue business degrees. 2% grads pursue medical degrees. **Faculty:** Student/faculty ratio 19:1. 1,545 full-time faculty, 93% hold PhDs, 22% are are members of minority groups, 36% are women. 11% of classes are taught by teaching assistants.

ACADEMICS

Degrees: bachelor's, doctoral/professional, doctoral/research, master's, postbachelor's certificate, post-master's certificate. **Classes:** Most classes have 20-29 students. Most lab/discussion sessions have 20-29 students. **Special Study Options:** Accelerated program, cooperative education program, cross-registration, distance learning, double major, dual enrollment, English as a Second Language (ESL), exchange student program (domestic), external degree program, honors program, independent study, internships, liberal arts/career combination, student-designed major, study abroad, teacher certification program, weekend college. **Honors Programs:** ISU offers both a University Honors Program and a Freshman Honors Program. Each program promotes an enhanced academic environment for students of high ability and emphasizes the development of an enriched, individualized program study that meets each student's particular needs, interests and abilities. Honors gives students a supportive community in which to pursue their goals and stretch their horizons. Benefits include uniques courses, small class sizes, research opportunities and funding, access to graduate-level courses, and priority registration. Combined degree programs: BA/MEng. **Disability Services:** Special programs offered to physically disabled students, including note-taking services, reader services, tape recorders, tutors. **Career Services:** Alumni network, Alumni services, Career/job search classes, Career assessment, Internships. Our Learning Communities, in which students who have similar career goals live together and share academic courses, are ranked high nationally.

FACILITIES

Housing: Coed dorms, special housing for disabled students, men's dorms, special housing for international students, women's dorms, fraternity/sorority housing, apartments for married students, apartments for single students, Theme Housing, Learning Communities; family housing; quiet, non-smoking, or alcohol-free floors; graduate/adult undergraduate housing. 96% of campus accessible to physically diasbled. **Special Academic Facilities/Equipment:** Brunnier art museum, Farm House museum, observatory, numerous institutes, research centers, College of Design Gallery, Virtual Reality Application Center, Pappajohn Center for Entrepreneurship **Computers:** 100% of classrooms, 75% of dorms, 100% of libraries, 100% of dining areas, 100% of student union, 40% of common outdoor areas have wireless network access. Students can register for classes online. Administrative functions (other than registration) can be performed online.

CAMPUS LIFE

Environment: Town. **Activities:** Choral groups, concert band, dance, drama/theater, jazz band, literary magazine, marching band, music ensembles, musical theater, opera, pep band, radio station, student government, student newspaper, student-run film society, symphony orchestra, television station 799 registered organizations, 43 honor societies, 34 religious organizations. 34 fraternities, 19 sororities. **Athletics (Intercollegiate):** *Men:* basketball, cross-country, football, golf, track/field (outdoor), track/field (indoor), wrestling. *Women:* basketball, cross-country, diving, golf, gymnastics, soccer, softball, swimming, tennis, track/field (outdoor), track/field (indoor), volleyball. **On-Campus Highlights:** Union Drive Community Center (dining center), Reiman Gardens, Lied Recreation Center, Memorial Union, Virtual Reality Lab (available to visitors also), 6. Campanile. **Environmental Initiatives:** Establishment of the Live Green Initiative (http://www.livegreen.iastate.edu/about/)that has included: 1. Hiring of a Director of Sustainability (http://www.iastate.edu/Inside/2008/1212/rankin.shtml) 2. Creation of a 13 member (students, staff, and faculty) President's Advisory Committee on Energy Conservation and Global Climate Change (http://www.committees.iastate.edu/comm-info.php?id=136) 3. Creation of a Live Green Loan Fund for energy conservation and sustainability projects (http://www.livegreen.iastate.edu/loan/) 4. Completion of an annual Symposium on Sustainability (http://www.livegreen.iastate.edu/symposium/archive/).

ADMISSIONS

Freshman Academic Profile: Average high school GPA 3.6. 22% in top 10% of high school class, 55% in top 25% of high school class, 92% in top 50% of high school class. **Reported SAT (pre-2016 redesign) scores:** SAT Math middle 50% range 520-660. SAT Critical Reading middle 50% range 460-610. **Concordant SAT scores:** SAT Math middle 50% range 550–690. ACT middle 50% range 22-28. Minimum internet-based TOEFL 71. Minimum paper TOEFL 530. **Basis for Candidate Selection:** *Very important factors considered include:* rigor of secondary school record, class rank, academic GPA, standardized test scores. *Other factors considered include:* application essay, recommendation(s), interview, extracurricular activities, talent/ability, character/personal qualities, geographical residence, state residency, volunteer work, work experience. **Freshman Admission Requirements:** High school diploma is required and GED is accepted. *Academic units required:* 4 English, 3 math, 3 science, 2 science labs, 2 foreign language, 2 social studies. *Academic units recommended:* 4 English, 4 math, 4 science, 3 science labs, 3 foreign language, 4 social studies. **Freshman Admission Statistics:** 19,433 applied, 87.49% admitted, 37% enrolled. **Transfer Admission Requirements:** college transcript(s), statement of good standing from prior institution(s). Minimum college GPA of 2.0 required. Lowest grade transferable D. **General Admission Information:** Application fee $40. Nonfall registration accepted. Admission may be deferred for a maximum of 1 year.

COSTS AND FINANCIAL AID

Annual in-state tuition $7,240. Annual out-of-state tuition $21,076. Room and board $8,356. Required fees $1,180. Average book expense $994. **Required Forms and Deadlines:** FAFSA. **Notification of Awards:** Applicants will be notified of awards on a rolling basis beginning 4/1. **Types of Aid:** *Need-based scholarships/grants:* Federal Pell, FSEOG, State scholarships/grants, College/university scholarship or grant aid from institutional funds. *Loans:* Direct Subsidized Stafford Loans, Direct Unsubsidized Stafford Loans, Direct PLUS loans, Federal Perkins Loans, College/university loans from institutional funds. *Student Employment:* Federal Work-Study Program available. Institutional employment available. **Financial Aid Statistics:** 98% needy freshmen, 97% needy undergrads receive need-based scholarship or grant aid. 48% freshmen, 46% undergrads receive non-need-based scholarship or grant aid. 62% freshmen, 74% undergrads receive need-based self-help aid. 1% freshmen, 1% undergrads receive athletic scholarships. 88% freshmen, 79% undergrads receive any aid. Average cumulative indebtedness $28,617. **Criteria for awarding aid:** *Need-based:* Academics, Minority status. *Non-need-based:* Academics, Alumni affiliation, Art, Athletics, Leadership, Minority status, Music/drama, State/district residency.

ITHACA COLLEGE

Ithaca College, Office of Admission, Ithaca, NY 14850-7002
Phone: 607-274-3124 • **Financial Aid Phone:** 607-274-3131
E-mail: admission@ithaca.edu • **CEEB Code:** 2325
Fax: 607-274-1900 • **Website:** www.ithaca.edu • **ACT Code:** 2772

This private school was founded in 1892. It has a 650-acre campus.

RATINGS
Admissions Selectivity Rating: 85   **Fire Safety Rating:** 93   **Green Rating:** 89

STUDENTS AND FACULTY
Enrollment: 6,181. **Student Body:** 58% female, 42% male, 54% out-of-state, 2% international (52 countries represented). Asian 4%, African American 6%, Caucasian 72%, Hispanic 8%, Native American <1%, Pacific Islander 0%, Two or more races 3%, Race unknown 5%.
Retention and Graduation: 85% freshmen return for sophomore year. 66% freshmen graduate within 4 years. 75% freshmen graduate within 6 years. 23% grads go on to further study within 1 year. 15% grads pursue arts and sciences degrees. 1% grads pursue business degrees. **Faculty:** Student/faculty ratio 11:1. 515 full-time faculty, 88% hold PhDs, 13% are members of minority groups, 47% are women. 2% of classes are taught by teaching assistants.

ACADEMICS
Degrees: bachelor's, certificate, doctoral/professional, master's. **Classes:** Most classes have 10-19 students. **Most popular majors:** Radio and Television; Music; Business Administration, Management and Operations. **Special Study Options:** Accelerated program, cross-registration, distance learning, double major, dual enrollment, honors program, independent study, internships, liberal arts/career combination, student-designed major, study abroad, teacher certification program, London Center (London, England), Los Angeles Program, Washington D.C. semester program, Walkabout Down Under Program(Australia),opportunities to study in over 50 countries around the world. **Honors Programs:** Students in the Humanities and Sciences Honors Program participate in a series of special intensive seminars complemented by an array of out-of-class activities. Starting in the fall of the first year, honors students begin a sequence of eight honors seminar courses that help them meet general requirements of the school. The sequence includes: a first-year seminar taken in the first semester, four intermediate seminars normally taken in the second, third and fourth semesters, a seminar on cultural themes taken in the junior year, and a capstone seminar on contemporary issues, taken in the senior year. Combined degree programs: BS/MS-Occup. Therapy and BS/DPT in Physical Therapy. **Disability Services:** Special programs offered to physically disabled students, including note-taking services, reader services, tape recorders. **Career Services:** Alumni network, Alumni services, Career/job search classes, Career assessment, Internships, Regional alumni. From your first day on campus at Ithaca, you'll have a full-immersion learning experience. Students have the opportunity to intern, do fieldwork related to classes, and conduct hands-on research side-by-side with professors. Most Ithaca College students participate in at least one fieldwork or internship experience before they graduate, and Ithaca has internship connections around the globe. Each school can assist students with internship placements during the academic year and in the summer. The school has centers in Los Angeles, New York, and London where students study for a semester while completing internships. Recent placements include: American Red Cross, CBS News, Ernst & Young, JPMorgan Chase, Late Show with David Letterman, Madison Square Garden, NBC News, New York Rangers, Pricewater-houseCoopers, U.S. Department of Defense, and many more.

FACILITIES
Housing: Coed dorms, special housing for disabled students, women's dorms, fraternity/sorority housing, apartments for single students, Theme Housing. **Special Academic Facilities/Equipment:** Two newly-constructed Platinum LEED certified buildings(the Business School and the Peggy Williams Center, Art Gallery, Radio and TV stations, digital technology throughout Communications building, Observatory, Wellness Clinic, Fitness Center, Trading Room, Speech and Hearing Handicapped Clinic, Physical Therapy Clinic, Performing Arts Centers (Music And Theater), Music Recording Facility. **Computers:** 50% of classrooms, 100% of dorms, 100% of libraries, 100% of dining areas, 100% of student union, have wireless network access. Students can register for classes online. Administrative functions (other than registration) can be performed online.

CAMPUS LIFE
Environment: Town. **Activities:** Choral groups, concert band, dance, drama/theater, jazz band, literary magazine, music ensembles, musical theater, opera, pep band, radio station, student government, student newspaper, student-run film society, symphony orchestra, television station, yearbook, Campus Ministries, Student Organization. 180 registered organizations, 28 honor societies, 8 religious organizations. 3 fraternities, 1 sorority. **Athletics (Intercollegiate):** *Men:* baseball, basketball, crew/rowing, cross-country, diving, football, lacrosse, soccer, swimming, tennis, track/field (outdoor), wrestling. *Women:* basketball, crew/rowing, cross-country, diving, field hockey, golf, gymnastics, lacrosse, soccer, softball, swimming, tennis, track/field (outdoor), volleyball. **On-Campus Highlights:** IC Square and Food Court, Handwerker Gallery, Fitness Center, Business School Atrium, Library. **Environmental Initiatives:** Sustainability Initiative that spurs and chronicles progress in three separate but highly inter-related areas: development of curriculum to infuse considerations of sustainability and applied research opportunities to study and solve sustainability challenges; modification of campus operations to incorporate more sustainable decision-making; and campus in-reach and community outreach to share our experiences as a learning organization seeking to become more sustainable.

ADMISSIONS
Freshman Academic Profile: 27% in top 10% of high school class, 57% in top 25% of high school class, 89% in top 50% of high school class. 83% from public high schools. **Reported SAT (pre-2016 redesign) scores:** SAT Math middle 50% range 540-640. SAT Critical Reading middle 50% range 550-640. SAT Writing middle 50% range 540-630. **Concordant SAT scores:** SAT EBRW middle 50% 600–680. SAT Math middle 50% range 570–660. ACT middle 50% range 25-29. Minimum internet-based TOEFL 80. Minimum paper TOEFL 550. **Basis for Candidate Selection:** *Very important factors considered include:* rigor of secondary school record, academic GPA, level of applicant's interest. *Important factors considered include:* application essay, recommendation(s), extracurricular activities, talent/ability, character/personal qualities. *Other factors considered include:* class rank, standardized test scores, interview, first generation, alumni/ae relation, volunteer work, work experience. **Freshman Admission Requirements:** High school diploma is required and GED is accepted. *Academic units required:* 4 English, 3 math, 3 science, 2 foreign language, 3 social studies, 1 academic elective. *Academic units recommended:* 4 English, 4 math, 4 science, 3 foreign language, 4 social studies, 1 academic elective. **Freshman Admission Statistics:** 14,380 applied, 69.92% admitted, 16% enrolled. **Transfer Admission Requirements:** High school transcript, college transcript(s), essay or personal statement, statement of good standing from prior institution(s). Minimum college GPA of 2.75 required. Lowest grade transferable C-. **General Admission Information:** Application fee $60. Regular application deadline 2/1. Regular notification 4/15. Nonfall registration accepted. Admission may be deferred for a maximum of 1 year.

COSTS AND FINANCIAL AID
Annual tuition $42,884. Room and board $15,274. Required fees $0. Average book expense $1,200. **Required Forms and Deadlines:** FAFSA, CSS/Financial Aid PROFILE. **Notification of Awards:** Applicants will be notified of awards on a rolling basis beginning 2/15. **Types of Aid:** *Need-based scholarships/grants:* Federal Pell, FSEOG, State scholarships/grants, Private scholarships, College/university scholarship or grant aid from institutional funds. *Loans:* Direct Subsidized Stafford Loans, Direct Unsubsidized Stafford Loans, Direct PLUS loans, Federal Perkins Loans. *Student Employment:* Federal Work-Study Program available. Institutional employment available. **Financial Aid Statistics:** 97% needy freshmen, 98% needy undergrads receive need-based scholarship or grant aid. 33% freshmen, 16% undergrads receive non-need-based scholarship or grant aid. 88% freshmen, 89% undergrads receive need-based self-help aid. 0% freshmen, 0% undergrads receive athletic scholarships. 96% freshmen, 93% undergrads receive any aid. 70% undergrads borrow to pay for school. Average cumulative indebtedness $40,595. **Criteria for awarding aid:** *Need-based:* Academics, Minority status, Music/drama. *Non-need-based:* Academics, Alumni affiliation, Leadership, Minority status, Music/drama.

JACKSON STATE UNIVERSITY

1400 J. R. Lynch Street, Jackson, MS 39217
Phone: 601-979-2100 • **Financial Aid Phone:** 601-979-2227
E-mail: admappl@jsums.edu • **CEEB Code:** 1341
Fax: 601-979-3445 • **Website:** www.jsums.edu • **ACT Code:** 2204

This public school was founded in 1877. It has a 150-acre campus.

RATINGS
Admissions Selectivity Rating: 72   **Fire Safety Rating:** 89   **Green Rating:** 60*

STUDENTS AND FACULTY

Enrollment: 6,844. **Student Body:** 62% female, 38% male, 17% out-of-state, 2% international (35 countries represented). Asian 0%, African American 93%, Caucasian 3%, Hispanic <1%, Native American <1%, Pacific Islander 0%, Two or more races 1%, Race unknown 0%.
Retention and Graduation: 78% freshmen return for sophomore year. 22% freshmen graduate within 4 years. 42% freshmen graduate within 6 years.
Faculty: Student/faculty ratio 17:1. 378 full-time faculty, 81% hold PhDs, 81% are are members of minority groups, 46% are women.

ACADEMICS

Degrees: bachelor's, doctoral, master's, post-master's certificate. **Most popular majors:** Elementary Education and Teaching; Biology/Biological Sciences; Criminal Justice/Safety Studies. **Special Study Options:** cooperative education program, distance learning, double major, dual enrollment, English as a Second Language (ESL), honors program, independent study, internships, study abroad, teacher certification program, weekend college, Undergrads may take grad level classes. Off-Campus Programs: Research semester at Lawrence Berkeley Lab. Co-Op Programs: Business, Computer Science, Natural Science. **Honors Programs:** Honors College. **Disability Services:** Special programs offered to physically disabled students, including note-taking services, tape recorders, tutors. **Career Services:** Career/job search classes, Career assessment, Internships. All are important in assisting students for job placement after graduation.

FACILITIES

Housing: men's dorms, women's dorms. 100% of campus accessible to physically diasbled. **Special Academic Facilities/Equipment:** Research center. **Computers:** Students can register for classes online. Administrative functions (other than registration) can be performed online.

CAMPUS LIFE

Environment: Metropolis. **Activities:** Choral groups, concert band, dance, drama/theater, jazz band, literary magazine, marching band, music ensembles, opera, pep band, radio station, student government, student newspaper, student-run film society, symphony orchestra, television station, yearbook. 150 registered organizations, 20 honor societies, 11 religious organizations. 4 fraternities, 4 sororities. **Athletics (Intercollegiate):** *Men:* baseball, basketball, cross-country, football, golf, soccer, tennis, track/field (outdoor), track/field (indoor), volleyball. *Women:* basketball, cross-country, golf, soccer, softball, tennis, track/field (outdoor), track/field (indoor), volleyball.

ADMISSIONS

Freshman Academic Profile: Average high school GPA 2.9. 85% from public high schools. ACT middle 50% range 17-20. Minimum paper TOEFL 525.
Basis for Candidate Selection: *Very important factors considered include:* rigor of secondary school record, academic GPA, standardized test scores. *Important factors considered include:* level of applicant's interest. **Freshman Admission Requirements:** High school diploma is required and GED is accepted. *Academic units required:* 4 English, 3 math, 3 science, 3 social studies, 2 academic electives. **Freshman Admission Statistics:** 7,265 applied, 74.45% admitted, 19% enrolled. **Transfer Admission Requirements:** High school transcript, college transcript(s), Minimum college GPA of 2.0 required. Lowest grade transferable C. **General Admission Information:** Priority deadline 8/1. Regular application deadline 8/1. Nonfall registration accepted.

COSTS AND FINANCIAL AID

Annual in-state tuition $5,504. Annual out-of-state tuition $13,494. Room and board $6,494. Average book expense $800. **Required Forms and Deadlines:** FAFSA, Institution's own financial aid form, State aid form. **Notification of Awards:** Applicants will be notified of awards on a rolling basis beginning 2/15. **Types of Aid:** *Need-based scholarships/grants:* Federal Pell, FSEOG, State scholarships/grants, Private scholarships, College/university scholarship or grant aid from institutional funds. *Loans:* Federal Perkins Loans, College/university loans from institutional funds. *Student Employment:* Federal Work-Study Program available. Institutional employment available. **Criteria for awarding aid:** *Need-based:* Academics.

JACKSONVILLE UNIVERSITY

Office of Admissions, Jacksonville, FL 32211
Phone: 904-256-7000 • **Financial Aid Phone:** 800-558-3467
E-mail: admissions@ju.edu • **CEEB Code:** 5331
Website: http://www.ju.edu/ • **ACT Code:** 740

This private school was founded in 1934. It has a 198-acre campus.

RATINGS

Admissions Selectivity Rating: 80   **Fire Safety Rating:** 82   **Green Rating:** 60*

STUDENTS AND FACULTY

Enrollment: 3,122. **Student Body:** 59% female, 41% male, 29% out-of-state, 1% international (50 countries represented). Asian 4%, African American 19%, Caucasian 60%, Hispanic 7%, Native American 1%, Pacific Islander <1%, Two or more races 8%, Race unknown 0%.
Retention and Graduation: 60% freshmen return for sophomore year. 23% freshmen graduate within 4 years. 40% freshmen graduate within 6 years. 22% grads go on to further study within 1 year. **Faculty:** Student/faculty ratio 13:1. 180 full-time faculty, 79% hold PhDs, 9% are members of minority groups, 43% are women. 0% of classes are taught by teaching assistants.

ACADEMICS

Degrees: bachelor's, master's, post-master's certificate. **Classes:** Most classes have 10-19 students. **Most popular majors:** Aviation/Airway Management and Operations Business/Commerce. **Special Study Options:** Accelerated program, cooperative education program, distance learning, double major, dual enrollment, honors program, independent study, internships, liberal arts/career combination, student-designed major, study abroad, teacher certification program. **Honors Programs:** University Honors Program. **Disability Services:** Special programs offered to physically disabled students, including note-taking services, reader services, tutors.

FACILITIES

Housing: Coed dorms, special housing for disabled students, men's dorms, women's dorms, fraternity/sorority housing, apartments for single students. **Special Academic Facilities/Equipment:** Art museum, dance pavilion, concert hall, on-campus pre-school. **Computers:** Students can register for classes online. Administrative functions (other than registration) can be performed online.

CAMPUS LIFE

Environment: Metropolis. **Activities:** Choral groups, concert band, dance, drama/theater, jazz band, literary magazine, music ensembles, musical theater, pep band, radio station, student government, student newspaper, symphony orchestra, television station, yearbook, Campus Ministries, Student Organization. 60 registered organizations, 16 honor societies, 9 fraternities, 6 sororities. **Athletics (Intercollegiate):** *Men:* baseball, basketball, crew/rowing, cross-country, football, golf, soccer, tennis. *Women:* basketball, crew/rowing, cross-country, golf, soccer, softball, tennis, track/field (outdoor), track/field (indoor), volleyball. **On-Campus Highlights:** Alexander Brest Fine Arts Museum, Davis College of Business/ Jazzman's Cafe (New), JU Baseball Complex, Lazzara Health Sciences Center (New), Residential Apartment Village (New).

ADMISSIONS

Freshman Academic Profile: Average high school GPA 3.5. **Reported SAT (pre-2016 redesign) scores:** SAT Math middle 50% range 480-570. SAT Critical Reading middle 50% range 470-560. **Concordant SAT scores:** SAT Math middle 50% range 510–590. ACT middle 50% range 20-26. Minimum paper TOEFL 540. **Basis for Candidate Selection:** *Very important factors considered include:* academic GPA, standardized test scores. *Important factors considered include:* rigor of secondary school record, talent/ability. *Other factors considered include:* application essay, recommendation(s), interview, extracurricular activities, character/personal qualities, volunteer work, work experience. **Freshman Admission Requirements:** High school diploma is required and GED is accepted. *Academic units required:* 4 English, 3 math, 3 science, 2 science labs, 3 social studies. *Academic units recommended:* 4 English, 4 math, 3 science, 2 science labs, 2 foreign language, 3 social studies. **Freshman Admission Statistics:** 8,096 applied, 41.61% admitted, 16% enrolled. **Transfer Admission Requirements:** college transcript(s), essay or personal statement, statement of good standing from prior institution(s). Minimum college GPA of 2.0 required. Lowest grade transferable C. **General Admission Information:** Application fee $30. Priority deadline 3/1. Nonfall registration accepted. Admission may be deferred.

COSTS AND FINANCIAL AID

Required Forms and Deadlines: FAFSA, Institution's own financial aid form, State aid form. **Notification of Awards:** Applicants will be notified of awards on a rolling basis beginning 2/15. **Types of Aid:** *Need-based scholarships/grants:* Federal Pell, FSEOG, State scholarships/grants, Private scholarships, College/university scholarship or grant aid from institutional funds. *Loans:* Federal Perkins Loans, State Loans, College/university loans from institutional funds. *Student Employment:* Federal Work-Study Program available. Institutional employment available. **Financial Aid Statistics:** 98% needy freshmen, 99% needy undergrads receive need-based scholarship or grant aid. 1% freshmen, 1% undergrads receive non-need-based scholarship or grant aid. 62% freshmen, 69% undergrads receive need-based self-help aid. 2% freshmen, 4% undergrads receive athletic scholarships. 97% freshmen, 87% undergrads receive any aid. **Criteria for awarding aid:** *Need-based:* Job skills, Leadership. *Non-need-based:* Academics, Art, Athletics, Job skills, Leadership, Music/drama, State/district residency.

JAMES MADISON UNIVERSITY

Best Colleges

Sonner Hall, Harrisonburg, VA 22807
Phone: 540-568-5681 • **Financial Aid Phone:** 540-568-7820
E-mail: admissions@jmu.edu • **CEEB Code:** 5392
Fax: 540-568-3332 • **Website:** www.jmu.edu • **ACT Code:** 4370

This public school was founded in 1908. It has a 712-acre campus.

RATINGS
Admissions Selectivity Rating: 85 **Fire Safety Rating:** 85 **Green Rating:** 89

STUDENTS AND FACULTY
Enrollment: 19,262. **Student Body:** 59% female, 41% male, 23% out-of-state, 2% international (68 countries represented). Asian 5%, African American 5%, Caucasian 75%, Hispanic 6%, Native American <1%, Pacific Islander <1%, Two or more races 4%, Race unknown 3%.
Retention and Graduation: 91% freshmen return for sophomore year. 82% freshmen graduate within 6 years. 29% grads go on to further study within 1 year. 14% grads pursue arts and sciences degrees. 1% grads pursue law degrees. 2% grads pursue business degrees. 1% grads pursue medical degrees. **Faculty:** Student/faculty ratio 16:1. 1,028 full-time faculty, 76% hold PhDs, 12% are are members of minority groups, 48% are women. 1% of classes are taught by teaching assistants.

ACADEMICS
Degrees: bachelor's, doctoral/professional, doctoral/research, doctoral, master's. **Classes:** Most classes have 20-29 students. Most lab/discussion sessions have 20-29 students. **Most popular majors:** Community Health Services/Liaison/Counseling; Speech Communication and Rhetoric; Psychology. **Special Study Options:** Accelerated program, distance learning, double major, English as a Second Language (ESL), honors program, independent study, internships, study abroad, teacher certification program, Continuing education programs offered on campus. **Honors Programs:** Academic honors program, honors scholars (3.25 or above),honors courses, and senior honors project (3.25) Combined degree programs: BS in Bio. JMU/Master of Forestry VA Tech 3-2. **Disability Services:** Special programs offered to physically disabled students, including note-taking services, reader services, tape recorders. **Career Services:** Alumni network, Alumni services, Career/job search classes, Career assessment, Internships, Regional alumni. We offer innovative outreach programs to help students connect with employers, and with our services. Practice Interviews and Resume PREP programs allow students to gain employer feedback on their resume or interview skills. Panel presentations on various topics feature employers sharing their perspective, expertise and industry knowledge. Career Fair events held each semester allow students to make personal connections and learn about full-time jobs and internships. Ask A Career Coach tables are scheduled weekly in locations with high student traffic, making our services more accessible to students.

FACILITIES
Housing: Coed dorms, special housing for disabled students, fraternity/sorority housing, apartments for single students, Wellness Housing, Theme Housing. 90% of campus accessible to physically diasbled. **Special Academic Facilities/Equipment:** language lab, music and fine arts buildings, herbarium, university farm, planetarium, arboretum,mineral museum, Science on a Sphere. **Computers:** 25% of classrooms, 100% of dorms, 100% of libraries, 50% of dining areas, 100% of student union, 25% of common outdoor areas have wireless network access. Students can register for classes online. Administrative functions (other than registration) can be performed online.

CAMPUS LIFE
Environment: Town. **Activities:** Choral groups, concert band, dance, drama/theater, jazz band, literary magazine, marching band, music ensembles, musical theater, opera, pep band, radio station, student government, student newspaper, student-run film society, symphony orchestra, yearbook, Campus Ministries, Student Organization. 298 registered organizations, 28 honor societies, 28 religious organizations. 15 fraternities, 9 sororities. **Athletics (Intercollegiate):** *Men:* baseball, basketball, cheerleading, football, golf, soccer, tennis. *Women:* basketball, cheerleading, cross-country, diving, field hockey, golf, lacrosse, soccer, softball, swimming, tennis, track/field (outdoor), volleyball. **On-Campus Highlights:** Quad, Taylor Down Under, UREC, East Campus Library, Festival Student Center. **Environmental Initiatives:** Development of student learning outcomes for environmental literacy and an assessment.

ADMISSIONS
Freshman Academic Profile: 19% in top 10% of high school class, 38% in top 25% of high school class, 94% in top 50% of high school class. 60% from public high schools. **Reported SAT (pre-2016 redesign) scores:** SAT Math middle 50% range 520-610. SAT Critical Reading middle 50% range 510-610. **Concordant SAT scores:** SAT Math middle 50% range 550–630. Minimum paper TOEFL 550. **Basis for Candidate Selection:** *Very important factors considered include:* rigor of secondary school record, academic GPA. *Important factors considered include:* standardized test scores. *Other factors considered include:* application essay, recommendation(s). **Freshman Admission Requirements:** High school diploma is required and GED is accepted. *Academic units required:* 4 English, 4 math, 2 social studies, 2 history. **Freshman Admission Statistics:** 21,304 applied, 72.13% admitted, 29% enrolled. **Transfer Admission Requirements:** High school transcript, college transcript(s), Minimum college GPA of 2.0 required. Lowest grade transferable C. **General Admission Information:** Application fee $70. Regular application deadline 1/15. Regular notification 4/1. Nonfall registration not accepted. Admission may be deferred for a maximum of 1 year.

COSTS AND FINANCIAL AID
Annual in-state tuition $5,896. Annual out-of-state tuition $21,670. Room and board $9,334. Required fees $4,446. Average book expense $976. **Required Forms and Deadlines:** FAFSA. **Notification of Awards:** Applicants will be notified of awards on a rolling basis beginning 4/1. **Types of Aid:** *Need-based scholarships/grants:* Federal Pell, FSEOG, State scholarships/grants, Private scholarships, College/university scholarship or grant aid from institutional funds. *Loans:* Direct Subsidized Stafford Loans, Direct Unsubsidized Stafford Loans, Direct PLUS loans, Federal Perkins Loans. *Student Employment:* Federal Work-Study Program available. Institutional employment available. **Financial Aid Statistics:** 53% needy freshmen, 51% needy undergrads receive need-based scholarship or grant aid. 8% freshmen, 9% undergrads receive non-need-based scholarship or grant aid. 88% freshmen, 86% undergrads receive need-based self-help aid. 2% freshmen, 2% undergrads receive athletic scholarships. 59% freshmen, 56% undergrads receive any aid. 52% undergrads borrow to pay for school. Average cumulative indebtedness $28,407. **Criteria for awarding aid:** *Need-based:* Academics, Leadership, Minority status, Religious affiliation. *Non-need-based:* Academics, Alumni affiliation, Art, Athletics, Leadership, Minority status, Music/drama, State/district residency.

JARVIS CHRISTIAN COLLEGE

P.O.BOX 1470, Hawkins, TX 75765-1470
Phone: 903-769-5730 • **Financial Aid Phone:** 903-769-5740
E-mail: felecia_tyiska@jarvis.edu
Fax: 903-769-1282 • **Website:** http://www.jarvis.edu/ • **ACT Code:** 4110

This private school, affiliated with the Disciples of Christ Church, was founded in 1912. It has a 243-acre campus.

RATINGS
Admissions Selectivity Rating: 62 **Fire Safety Rating:** 92 **Green Rating:** 60*

STUDENTS AND FACULTY
Enrollment: 617. **Student Body:** 60% female, 40% male, 15% out-of-state, <1% international (2 countries represented). Asian 0%, African American 95%, Caucasian 1%, Hispanic 3%, Native American <1%, Pacific Islander 0%, Two or more races 0%, Race unknown 0%.
Retention and Graduation: 41% freshmen return for sophomore year. 17% freshmen graduate within 4 years. 19% freshmen graduate within 6 years. 2% grads go on to further study within 1 year. 1% grads pursue business degrees. **Faculty:** Student/faculty ratio 13:1. 35 full-time faculty, 46% hold PhDs, 63% are are members of minority groups, 49% are women. 0% of classes are taught by teaching assistants.

ACADEMICS
Degrees: bachelor's. **Classes:** Most classes have fewer than 10 students. Most lab/discussion sessions have 10-19 students. **Most popular majors:** Biology/Biological Sciences; Criminal Justice/Law Enforcement Administration; Health and Physical Education/Fitness. **Special Study Options:** cross-registration, distance learning, double major, dual enrollment, English as a Second Language (ESL), honors program, independent study, internships, liberal arts/career combination, student-designed major, teacher certification program. **Honors Programs:** JETS Honors Program. **Disability Services:** Special programs offered to physically disabled students, including reader services, tutors. **Career Services:** Alumni network, Alumni services

FACILITIES
Housing: special housing for disabled students, men's dorms, women's dorms, apartments for married students, apartments for single students. 95% of campus

accessible to physically diasbled. **Special Academic Facilities/Equipment:** Archives **Computers:** 100% of classrooms, 100% of dorms, 100% of libraries, 100% of dining areas, 100% of student union, 20% of common outdoor areas have wireless network access. Students can register for classes online.

CAMPUS LIFE

Environment: Rural. **Activities:** Choral groups, drama/theater, music ensembles, pep band, student government, Student Organization. 33 registered organizations, 6 honor societies, 5 religious organizations. 4 fraternities, 4 sororities. **Athletics (Intercollegiate):** *Men:* baseball, basketball. *Women:* basketball, volleyball. **On-Campus Highlights:** E. W. Rand Health, Physical Education, and Recreat, J. N. Ervin Religion Center, Walk of Fame, Community and Technology Center, Meyer Science and Mathematics Center, Archives of the Texas Christian Missionary Fellowship of the Christian Church (Disciples of Christ).

ADMISSIONS

Freshman Academic Profile: Average high school GPA 2.6. 0% in top 10% of high school class, 6% in top 25% of high school class, 23% in top 50% of high school class. 99% from public high schools. Minimum paper TOEFL 500. **Basis for Candidate Selection:** *Other factors considered include:* rigor of secondary school record, class rank, academic GPA, standardized test scores, extracurricular activities, talent/ability, character/personal qualities. **Freshman Admission Requirements:** High school diploma is required and GED is accepted. *Academic units required:* 3 English, 2 math, 1 science, 3 social studies, 7 academic electives. *Academic units recommended:* 3 English, 2 math, 1 science, 3 social studies, 7 academic electives. **Freshman Admission Statistics:** 525 applied, 92.38% admitted, 25% enrolled. **Transfer Admission Requirements:** High school transcript, college transcript(s), standardized test scores, Lowest grade transferable F. **General Admission Information:** Application fee $50. Priority deadline 5/1. Nonfall registration accepted. Admission may be deferred for a maximum of one year.

COSTS AND FINANCIAL AID

Annual tuition $8,528. Room and board $6,715. Required fees $1,080. Average book expense $1,000. **Required Forms and Deadlines:** FAFSA, Institution's own financial aid form, State aid form. **Notification of Awards:** Applicants will be notified of awards on a rolling basis beginning 5/1. **Types of Aid:** *Need-based scholarships/grants:* Federal Pell, FSEOG, State scholarships/grants, Private scholarships, College/university scholarship or grant aid from institutional funds, United Negro College Fund. *Loans:* Direct Subsidized Stafford Loans, Direct Unsubsidized Stafford Loans, Direct PLUS loans, Federal Perkins Loans. *Student Employment:* Federal Work-Study Program available. **Financial Aid Statistics:** 94% needy freshmen, 100% needy undergrads receive need-based scholarship or grant aid. 41% freshmen, 23% undergrads receive non-need-based scholarship or grant aid. 79% freshmen, 89% undergrads receive need-based self-help aid. 3% freshmen, 6% undergrads receive athletic scholarships. 98% freshmen, 98% undergrads receive any aid. **Criteria for awarding aid:** *Non-need-based:* Academics, Athletics, Religious affiliation, State/district residency.

JEWISH THEOLOGICAL SEMINARY, ALBERT A. LIST COLLEGE

3080 Broadway, New York, NY 10027
Phone: 212-678-8832 • **Financial Aid Phone:** 212-678-8007
E-mail: lcadmissions@jtsa.edu • **CEEB Code:** 2339
Fax: 212-280-6022 • **Website:** www.jtsa.edu • **ACT Code:** 2776

This private school, affiliated with the Jewish Church, was founded in 1886. It has a 1-acre campus.

RATINGS

Admissions Selectivity Rating: 85   **Fire Safety Rating:** 60*   **Green Rating:** 60*

STUDENTS AND FACULTY

Enrollment: 177. **Student Body:** 54% female, 46% male, 84% out-of-state, 3% international (10 countries represented). Asian 0%, African American 0%, Caucasian 94%, Hispanic 1%, Native American 0%, Pacific Islander 0%, Two or more races 0%, Race unknown 2%.
Retention and Graduation: 89% freshmen return for sophomore year. 15% grads go on to further study within 1 year. 6% grads pursue arts and sciences degrees. 6% grads pursue law degrees. 3% grads pursue medical degrees.
Faculty: Student/faculty ratio 6:1. 52 full-time faculty, 0% are are members of minority groups, 29% are women. 0% of classes are taught by teaching assistants.

ACADEMICS

Degrees: bachelor's, doctoral/professional, doctoral/research, master's. **Classes:** Most classes have fewer than 10 students. **Most popular majors:** Jewish/Judaic Studies; Bible/Biblical Studies; Talmudic Studies. **Special Study Options:** cross-registration, distance learning, double major, exchange student program (domestic), honors program, independent study, internships, liberal arts/career combination, student-designed major, study abroad, BA/MA program with JTS Graduate School or William Davidson School of Jewish Education. Combined degree programs: BA/MA, BA/BA and BA/BS programs with Columbia University and Barnard College. **Disability Services:** Special programs offered to physically disabled students, including tape recorders, tutors. **Career Services:** Alumni network, Alumni services, Career/job search classes, Internships. Career/Job search classes and alumni network

FACILITIES

Housing: Coed dorms, apartments for married students, apartments for single students. **Special Academic Facilities/Equipment:** The Jewish Museum and the Rare Book Room of the Library **Computers:** 100% of classrooms, 100% of dorms, 80% of libraries, 100% of dining areas, 50% of common outdoor areas have wireless network access. Students can register for classes online. Administrative functions (other than registration) can be performed online.

CAMPUS LIFE

Environment: Metropolis. **Activities:** Choral groups, concert band, dance, drama/theater, jazz band, literary magazine, music ensembles, musical theater, radio station, student government, student newspaper, yearbook. 1 religious organization. **Athletics (Intercollegiate):** *Men:* baseball, basketball, crew/rowing, soccer, tennis, track/field (outdoor), volleyball. *Women:* baseball, basketball, crew/rowing, soccer, tennis, track/field (outdoor), volleyball. **On-Campus Highlights:** The Library of the Jewish Theological Seminary **Environmental Initiatives:** 4-Day work week to save on electricity.

ADMISSIONS

Freshman Academic Profile: Average high school GPA 3.7. **Reported SAT (pre-2016 redesign) scores:** SAT Math middle 50% range 620-660. SAT Critical Reading middle 50% range 640-700. SAT Writing middle 50% range 620-720. **Concordant SAT scores:** SAT EBRW middle 50% 680–740. SAT Math middle 50% range 640–690. ACT middle 50% range 30-32. Minimum paper TOEFL 600. **Basis for Candidate Selection:** *Very important factors considered include:* rigor of secondary school record, academic GPA, standardized test scores. *Important factors considered include:* class rank, application essay, recommendation(s), interview. *Other factors considered include:* extracurricular activities, talent/ability, character/personal qualities, first generation, alumni/ae relation, religious affiliation/commitment, volunteer work, level of applicant's interest. **Freshman Admission Requirements:** High school diploma is required and GED is not accepted. *Academic units recommended:* 4 English, 4 math, 4 science, 4 foreign language, 1 social studies, 3 history, 4 academic electives. **Freshman Admission Statistics:** 102 applied, 61.76% admitted, 65% enrolled. **Transfer Admission Requirements:** High school transcript, college transcript(s), essay or personal statement, standardized test scores, statement of good standing from prior institution(s). **General Admission Information:** Application fee $65. Priority deadline 1/15. Regular application deadline 2/15. Regular notification 4/1. Nonfall registration accepted. Admission may be deferred.

COSTS AND FINANCIAL AID

Annual tuition $14,200. Required fees $800. Average book expense $500. **Required Forms and Deadlines:** FAFSA, Institution's own financial aid form, CSS/Financial Aid PROFILE, State aid form, Noncustodial PROFILE, Business/Farm Supplement. **Notification of Awards:** Applicants will be notified of awards on a rolling basis beginning 4/1. **Types of Aid:** *Need-based scholarships/grants:* Private scholarships, College/university scholarship or grant aid from institutional funds. *Loans:* Direct Subsidized Stafford Loans, Direct Unsubsidized Stafford Loans, College/university loans from institutional funds. *Student Employment:* Federal Work-Study Program available. Institutional employment available. **Financial Aid Statistics:** 100% needy freshmen, 100% needy undergrads receive need-based scholarship or grant aid. 50% freshmen, 41% undergrads receive non-need-based scholarship or grant aid. 86% freshmen, 97% undergrads receive need-based self-help aid. 0% freshmen, 0% undergrads receive athletic scholarships. **Criteria for awarding aid:** *Non-need-based:* Academics, Alumni affiliation, Leadership.

JOHN BROWN UNIVERSITY

2000 West University Street, Siloam Springs, AR 72761
Phone: 479-524-7454 • **Financial Aid Phone:** 479-524-7424
E-mail: jbuinfo@jbu.edu • **CEEB Code:** 6321
Fax: 479-524-4196 • **Website:** www.jbu.edu • **ACT Code:** 130

This private school was founded in 1919. It has a 200-acre campus.

RATINGS

Admissions Selectivity Rating: 85   **Fire Safety Rating:** 88   **Green Rating:** 72

STUDENTS AND FACULTY

Enrollment: 1,662. **Student Body:** 58% female, 42% male, 47% out-of-state, 6% international (40 countries represented). Asian 2%, African American 3%, Caucasian 75%, Hispanic 6%, Native American 2%, Pacific Islander <1%, Two or more races 3%, Race unknown 4%.
Retention and Graduation: 85% freshmen return for sophomore year. 55% freshmen graduate within 4 years. 65% freshmen graduate within 6 years. 18% grads go on to further study within 1 year. **Faculty:** Student/faculty ratio 13:1. 80 full-time faculty, 74% hold PhDs, 4% are are members of minority groups, 25% are women. 0% of classes are taught by teaching assistants.

ACADEMICS

Degrees: associate, bachelor's, master's. **Classes:** Most classes have 10-19 students. Most lab/discussion sessions have 10-19 students. **Most popular majors:** Graphic Design; Engineering; Registered Nursing/Registered Nurse. **Special Study Options:** Accelerated program, distance learning, double major, dual enrollment, English as a Second Language (ESL), honors program, independent study, internships, liberal arts/career combination, student-designed major, study abroad, teacher certification program.
Honors Programs: The Honors Scholars Program consists of enriched Core Curriculum courses developed especially for gifted and highly motivated students. Emphasizing the use of primary texts, instructors challenge students through individual research, critical reflection, incisive discussion, interactive projects, and professional presentations. **Disability Services:** Special programs offered to physically disabled students, including note-taking services, reader services, tutors. **Career Services:** Alumni network, Career/job search classes, Career assessment.

FACILITIES

Housing: Coed dorms, men's dorms, women's dorms, apartments for married students, apartments for single students. 90% of campus accessible to physically diasbled. **Special Academic Facilities/Equipment:** Art Gallery, Human Anatomy Lab, TV Studio, Radio Station, Outdoor Learning Center, Center for Relationship Enrichment, Soderquist Center for Business and Ethics **Computers:** 100% of classrooms, 100% of dorms, 100% of libraries, 100% of dining areas, 100% of student union, 30% of common outdoor areas have wireless network access. Students can register for classes online. Administrative functions (other than registration) can be performed online.

CAMPUS LIFE

Environment: Village. **Activities:** Choral groups, dance, drama/theater, jazz band, literary magazine, music ensembles, musical theater, pep band, radio station, student government, student newspaper, student-run film society, yearbook, Campus Ministries, Student Organization, 20 registered organizations, 3 honor societies. **Athletics (Intercollegiate):** *Men:* basketball, golf, soccer, tennis. *Women:* basketball, soccer, swimming, tennis, volleyball. **On-Campus Highlights:** Walker Student Center, California Cafe, Chapel, Walton Lifetime Health Complex, Intrumural Sports.

ADMISSIONS

Freshman Academic Profile: Average high school GPA 3.7. 30% in top 10% of high school class, 62% in top 25% of high school class, 84% in top 50% of high school class. **Reported SAT (pre-2016 redesign) scores:** SAT Math middle 50% range 480-300. SAT Writing middle 50% range 490-605. **Concordant SAT scores:** SAT EBRW middle 50% 570–750. SAT Math middle 50% range 510–350. ACT middle 50% range 23-29. Minimum internet-based TOEFL 85. Minimum paper TOEFL 560. **Basis for Candidate Selection:** *Very important factors considered include:* academic GPA, standardized test scores, recommendation(s). *Important factors considered include:* class rank, application essay, interview, character/personal qualities, religious affiliation/commitment. *Other factors considered include:* rigor of secondary school record, extracurricular activities, talent/ability, first generation, alumni/ae relation, level of applicant's interest. **Freshman Admission Requirements:** High school diploma is required and GED is accepted. *Academic units recommended:* 4 English, 3 math, 2 science, 1 science lab, 2 foreign language, 2 social studies, 1 history. **Freshman Admission Statistics:** 1,206 applied, 77.11% admitted, 35% enrolled. **Transfer Admission Requirements:** High school transcript, college transcript(s), essay or personal statement, Minimum college GPA of 2.5 required. Lowest grade transferable C. **General Admission**

Information: Application fee $25. Priority deadline 5/1. Nonfall registration accepted. Admission may be deferred for a maximum of 1 year.

COSTS AND FINANCIAL AID

Annual tuition $24,218. Room and board $8,840. Required fees $1,106. Average book expense $800. **Required Forms and Deadlines:** FAFSA, State aid form. **Notification of Awards:** Applicants will be notified of awards on or about 3/1. **Types of Aid:** *Need-based scholarships/grants:* Federal Pell, FSEOG, State scholarships/grants, Private scholarships, College/university scholarship or grant aid from institutional funds. *Loans:* Direct Subsidized Stafford Loans, Direct Unsubsidized Stafford Loans, Direct PLUS loans, Federal Perkins Loans, College/university loans from institutional funds. *Student Employment:* Federal Work-Study Program available. Institutional employment available. **Financial Aid Statistics:** 90% needy freshmen, 91% needy undergrads receive need-based scholarship or grant aid. 89% freshmen, 69% undergrads receive non-need-based scholarship or grant aid. 81% freshmen, 59% undergrads receive need-based self-help aid. 7% freshmen, 5% undergrads receive athletic scholarships. 90% freshmen, 91% undergrads receive any aid. 59% undergrads borrow to pay for school. Average cumulative indebtedness $26,651. **Criteria for awarding aid:** *Non-need-based:* Academics, Alumni affiliation, Art, Athletics, Leadership, Music/drama.

JOHN CARROLL UNIVERSITY

1 John Carroll Boulevard, University Heights, OH 44118-4581
Phone: 216-397-4294 • **Financial Aid Phone:** 216-397-4270 • **CEEB Code:** 1342
Fax: 216-397-4981 • **Website:** http://sites.jcu.edu/ • **ACT Code:** 3282

This private school, affiliated with the Roman Catholic Church, was founded in 1886. It has a 60-acre campus.

RATINGS

Admissions Selectivity Rating: 80   **Fire Safety Rating:** 85   **Green Rating:** 76

STUDENTS AND FACULTY

Enrollment: 3,080. **Student Body:** 47% female, 53% male, 31% out-of-state, 2% international (23 countries represented). Asian 2%, African American 4%, Caucasian 85%, Hispanic 3%, Native American <1%, Pacific Islander 0%, Two or more races 2%, Race unknown 1%.
Retention and Graduation: 85% freshmen return for sophomore year. 60% freshmen graduate within 4 years. 28% grads go on to further study within 1 year. 48% grads pursue arts and sciences degrees. 7% grads pursue law degrees. 28% grads pursue business degrees. 9% grads pursue medical degrees. **Faculty:** Student/faculty ratio 13:1. 190 full-time faculty, 98% hold PhDs, 17% are are members of minority groups, 43% are women. 1% of classes are taught by teaching assistants.

ACADEMICS

Degrees: bachelor's, certificate, master's, postbachelor's certifiate, post-master's certificate. **Classes:** Most classes have 20-29 students. Most lab/discussion sessions have 10-19 students. **Most popular majors:** Speech Communication and Rhetoric; Psychology; Marketing/Marketing Management. **Special Study Options:** Accelerated program, cooperative education program, cross-registration, double major, dual enrollment, exchange student program (domestic), honors program, independent study, internships, liberal arts/career combination, student-designed major, study abroad, teacher certification program, Undergrads may take grad level classes. Co-Op Programs: All majors. Combined degree programs: BA/MA, 3-4 Doctor of Nursing prog with Case Western Reserve U. **Disability Services:** Special programs offered to physically disabled students, including note-taking services, reader services, tape recorders. **Career Services:** Alumni network, Alumni services, Career/job search classes, Career assessment, Internships, Regional alumni. Internships are available to our students for 0-3 credits and they can be paid or unpaid. We have a large number of students working at non-profits and are eligible for scholarships.

FACILITIES

Housing: Coed dorms, special housing for disabled students, women's dorms, fraternity/sorority housing, apartments for single students, Theme Housing. 94% of campus accessible to physically diasbled. **Computers:** 100% of classrooms, 100% of dorms, 100% of libraries, 100% of dining areas, 100% of student union, 100% of common outdoor areas have wireless network access. Students can register for classes online. Administrative functions (other than registration) can be performed online.

CAMPUS LIFE

Environment: Metropolis. **Activities:** Choral groups, dance, drama/theater, literary magazine, music ensembles, pep band, radio station, student government, student newspaper, television station, yearbook, Campus Ministries. 95 registered organizations, 12 honor societies, 2 religious organizations. 4 fraternities, 5 sororities. **Athletics (Intercollegiate):** *Men:* baseball, basketball, cross-country, diving, football, golf, soccer, swimming, tennis, track/field (outdoor), track/field (indoor), wrestling. *Women:* basketball, cheerleading, cross-country, diving, golf, soccer, softball, swimming, tennis, track/field (outdoor), track/field (indoor), volleyball. **On-Campus Highlights:** Einstein Bagel Bros, Dolan Center for Science and Technology, Inn-Between Cafe, Grasselli Library, Student Center Atrium. **Environmental Initiatives:** Reuse building materials on campus or divert from landfills

ADMISSIONS

Freshman Academic Profile: Average high school GPA 3.5. 20% in top 10% of high school class, 44% in top 25% of high school class, 79% in top 50% of high school class. 57% from public high schools. **Reported SAT (pre-2016 redesign) scores:** SAT Math middle 50% range 500-610. SAT Critical Reading middle 50% range 500-590. SAT Writing middle 50% range 480-590. **Concordant SAT scores:** SAT EBRW middle 50% 550–650. SAT Math middle 50% range 530–630. ACT middle 50% range 22-27. Minimum internet-based TOEFL 79. Minimum paper TOEFL 550. **Basis for Candidate Selection:** *Very important factors considered include:* rigor of secondary school record, academic GPA. *Important factors considered include:* standardized test scores, application essay, extracurricular activities, talent/ability, character/ personal qualities, volunteer work. *Other factors considered include:* class rank, recommendation(s), interview, first generation, alumni/ae relation, geographical residence, work experience, level of applicant's interest. **Freshman Admission Requirements:** High school diploma is required and GED is accepted. *Academic units required:* 4 English, 3 math, 2 science, 2 science labs, 2 foreign language, 2 history, 3 academic electives, and 2 units from above areas or other academic areas. *Academic units recommended:* 4 English, 4 math, 3 science, 3 science labs, 3 foreign language, 4 history, and 4 units from above areas or other academic areas. **Freshman Admission Statistics:** 3,873 applied, 82.91% admitted, 25% enrolled. **Transfer Admission Requirements:** High school transcript, college transcript(s), essay or personal statement, standardized test scores, statement of good standing from prior institution(s). Lowest grade transferable 2. **General Admission Information:** Priority deadline 12/1. Regular application deadline 2/1. Nonfall registration accepted. Admission may be deferred for a maximum of 1 year.

COSTS AND FINANCIAL AID

Annual tuition $35,930. Room and board $10,920. Required fees $1,250. Average book expense $1,000. **Required Forms and Deadlines:** FAFSA. **Notification of Awards:** Applicants will be notified of awards on a rolling basis beginning 2/15. **Types of Aid:** *Need-based scholarships/grants:* Federal Pell, FSEOG, State scholarships/grants, Private scholarships, College/university scholarship or grant aid from institutional funds. *Loans:* Direct Subsidized Stafford Loans, Direct Unsubsidized Stafford Loans, Direct PLUS loans, Federal Perkins Loans. *Student Employment:* Federal Work-Study Program available. Institutional employment available. **Financial Aid Statistics:** 92% needy freshmen, 98% needy undergrads receive need-based scholarship or grant aid. 99% freshmen, 99% undergrads receive non-need-based scholarship or grant aid. 82% freshmen, 85% undergrads receive need-based self-help aid. 0% freshmen, 0% undergrads receive athletic scholarships. 100% freshmen, 95% undergrads receive any aid. **Criteria for awarding aid:** *Non-need-based:* Academics, Leadership.

JOHNS HOPKINS UNIVERSITY

3400 North Charles Street, Baltimore, MD 21218
Phone: 410-516-8171 • **Financial Aid Phone:** 410-516-8028
E-mail: gotojhu@jhu.edu • **CEEB Code:** 5332
Fax: 410-516-6025 • **Website:** www.jhu.edu

This private school was founded in 1876. It has a 140-acre campus.

RATINGS

Admissions Selectivity Rating: 99   **Fire Safety Rating:** 98   **Green Rating:** 91

STUDENTS AND FACULTY

Enrollment: 5,334. **Student Body:** 49% female, 51% male, 88% out-of-state, 10% international (65 countries represented). Asian 23%, African American 6%, Caucasian 40%, Hispanic 13%, Native American <1%, Pacific Islander <1%, Two or more races 5%, Race unknown 3%.
Retention and Graduation: 97% freshmen return for sophomore year. 88% freshmen graduate within 4 years. 94% freshmen graduate within 6 years. 37% grads go on to further study within 1 year. 28% grads pursue arts and sciences

degrees. 3% grads pursue law degrees. 1% grads pursue business degrees. 18% grads pursue medical degrees. **Faculty:** Student/faculty ratio 10 707 full-time faculty, 94% hold PhDs, 14% are are members of minority groups, 32% are women.

ACADEMICS

Degrees: bachelor's, certificate, diploma, doctoral/professional, doctoral/ research, doctoral, master's, postbachelor's certificate, post-master's certificate. **Classes:** Most classes have 10-19 students. Most lab/discussion sessions have 20-29 students. **Most popular majors:** Bioengineering and Biomedical Engineering; Neuroscience; Public Health. **Special Study Options:** cross-registration, double major, dual enrollment, independent study, internships, student-designed major, study abroad, Combined Bachelor's/Master's programs. Combined degree programs: BA/MA, BA/MEng, Accelerated Bachelor's/ Masters Programs. **Disability Services:** Special programs offered to physically disabled students, including note-taking services, reader services, tape recorders, tutors. **Career Services:** Alumni network, Alumni services, Career/ job search classes, Career assessment, Internships, Regional alumni. Second Decade Society summer internship grants;
Medical tutorial program, wherein students shadow physicians; Intersession classes and employer visits in Finance, Public Health, Globalization and Media.

FACILITIES

Housing: Coed dorms, men's dorms, women's dorms, fraternity/sorority housing, apartments for single students. **Special Academic Facilities/ Equipment:** Baltimore Museum of Art, on-campus Digital Media Center, art gallery, electron microscope, Space Telescope Science Institute, four major research centers **Computers:** 95% of classrooms, 100% of dorms, 100% of libraries, 90% of dining areas, 100% of student union, 50% of common outdoor areas have wireless network access. Students can register for classes online. Administrative functions (other than registration) can be performed online.

CAMPUS LIFE

Environment: Metropolis. **Activities:** Choral groups, concert band, dance, drama/theater, jazz band, literary magazine, music ensembles, musical theater, pep band, radio station, student government, student newspaper, student-run film society, symphony orchestra, yearbook, Campus Ministries, Model UN. 250 registered organizations, 17 honor societies, 20 religious organizations. 12 fraternities, 7 sororities. **Athletics (Intercollegiate):** *Men:* baseball, basketball, cross-country, diving, fencing, football, lacrosse, soccer, swimming, tennis, track/ field (outdoor), track/field (indoor), water polo, wrestling. *Women:* basketball, cross-country, diving, fencing, field hockey, lacrosse, soccer, swimming, tennis, track/field (outdoor), track/field (indoor), volleyball. **On-Campus Highlights:** Mason Hall—new Visitor's Center, Mattin Student Arts Center, Homewood House Museum, Lacrosse Hall of Fame and Museum, Ralph S. O'Connor Recreation Center, Also, Charles Commons, a new building that houses 618 upperclassmen, as well as a new dining facility and retail spaces, opened in the Fall of 2007. **Environmental Initiatives:** Comprehensive climate commitment includes reaching a 51% reduction in GHG by 2025, investing over $73 million in GHG reduction projects, and seed grants for climate researchers.

ADMISSIONS

Freshman Academic Profile: Average high school GPA 3.9. 92% in top 10% of high school class, 99% in top 25% of high school class, 100% in top 50% of high school class. 57% from public high schools. **Reported SAT (pre-2016 redesign) scores:** SAT Math middle 50% range 710-790. SAT Critical Reading middle 50% range 690-760. SAT Writing middle 50% range 690-770. **Concordant SAT scores:** SAT EBRW middle 50% 730–780. SAT Math middle 50% range 740–800. ACT middle 50% range 32-34. Minimum paper TOEFL 600. **Basis for Candidate Selection:** *Very important factors considered include:* rigor of secondary school record, academic GPA, application essay, recommendation(s), character/personal qualities. *Important factors considered include:* class rank, standardized test scores, extracurricular activities, talent/ ability. *Other factors considered include:* interview, first generation, alumni/ ae relation, geographical residence, state residency, racial/ethnic status, volunteer work, work experience. **Freshman Admission Requirements:** High school diploma or equivalent is not required. *Academic units recommended:* 4 English, 4 math, 4 science, 4 foreign language, 2 social studies, 2 history. **Freshman Admission Statistics:** 24,716 applied, 13.15% admitted, 40% enrolled. **Transfer Admission Requirements:** High school transcript, college transcript(s), essay or personal statement, statement of good standing from prior institution(s). Minimum college GPA of 3.0 required. Lowest grade transferable C. **General Admission Information:** Application fee $70. Regular application deadline 1/1. Regular notification 4/1. Nonfall registration not accepted. Admission may be deferred for a maximum of 2 Years.

COSTS AND FINANCIAL AID

Annual tuition $50,410. Room and board $14,976. Average book expense $1,220. **Required Forms and Deadlines:** FAFSA, CSS/Financial Aid PROFILE, Noncustodial PROFILE. **Notification of Awards:** Applicants will be notified of awards on or about 4/1. **Types of Aid:** *Need-based scholarships/ grants:* Federal Pell, FSEOG, State scholarships/grants, Private scholarships, College/university scholarship or grant aid from institutional funds. *Loans:*

Direct Subsidized Stafford Loans, Direct Unsubsidized Stafford Loans, Direct PLUS loans, Federal Perkins Loans, College/university loans from institutional funds. *Student Employment:* Federal Work-Study Program available. Institutional employment available. **Financial Aid Statistics:** 93% needy freshmen, 92% needy undergrads receive need-based scholarship or grant aid. 33% freshmen, 20% undergrads receive non-need-based scholarship or grant aid. 80% freshmen, 84% undergrads receive need-based self-help aid. 1% freshmen, 1% undergrads receive athletic scholarships. 42% undergrads borrow to pay for school. Average cumulative indebtedness $24,702. **Criteria for awarding aid:** *Need-based:* Academics, Leadership. *Non-need-based:* Academics, Athletics, Leadership, State/district residency.

See page 972.

JOHNSON & WALES UNIVERSITY— CHARLOTTE CAMPUS

Phone: 980-598-1100
E-mail: clt@admissions.jwu.edu
Fax: 980-598-1111 • **Website:** https://www1.jwu.edu/charlotte/

RATINGS
Admissions Selectivity Rating: 70   **Fire Safety Rating:** 60*   **Green Rating:** 60*

STUDENTS AND FACULTY
Enrollment: 2,218. **Student Body:** 66% female, 34% male, 62% out-of-state, 1% international. Asian 1%, African American 37%, Caucasian 43%, Hispanic 6%, Native American <1%, Pacific Islander 0%, Two or more races 7%, Race unknown 5%.
Retention and Graduation: 76% freshmen return for sophomore year. 39% freshmen graduate within 4 years. **Faculty:** Student/faculty ratio 23:1. 83 full-time faculty, 0% hold PhDs, 0% are are members of minority groups, 0% are women.

ACADEMICS
Degrees: associate, bachelor's.

ADMISSIONS
Freshman Academic Profile: Average high school GPA 3.5. **Basis for Candidate Selection:** *Very important factors considered include:* rigor of secondary school record, class rank, academic GPA. *Important factors considered include:* interview, extracurricular activities. *Other factors considered include:* standardized test scores, recommendation(s), alumni/ae relation, volunteer work, work experience, level of applicant's interest. **Freshman Admission Requirements:** *Academic units required:* 4 English, 3 math, 3 science, 2 social studies. **Freshman Admission Statistics:** 4,537 applied, 72.45% admitted, 20% enrolled. **General Admission Information:** Nonfall registration accepted. Admission may be deferred.

COSTS AND FINANCIAL AID
Annual tuition $30,396. Average book expense $1,500. *Student Employment:* Federal Work-Study Program available. Institutional employment available.

JOHNSON AND WALES UNIVERSITY AT NORTH MIAMI

1701 NE 127th Street, North Miami, FL 33181
Phone: 1-866-598-3567
E-mail: mia@admissions.jwu.edu
Fax: 305-892-7020 • **Website:** http://admissions.jwu.edu

This is a private school.

RATINGS
Admissions Selectivity Rating: 65   **Fire Safety Rating:** 60*   **Green Rating:** 60*

STUDENTS AND FACULTY
Enrollment: 1,743. **Student Body:** 63% female, 37% male, 53% out-of-state, 10% international. Asian 0%, African American 31%, Caucasian 24%, Hispanic 23%, Native American <1%, Pacific Islander <1%, Two or more races 8%, Race unknown 5%.
Retention and Graduation: 69% freshmen return for sophomore year. 32% freshmen graduate within 4 years. 41% freshmen graduate within 6 years. **Faculty:** Student/faculty ratio 25:1. 57 full-time faculty, 0% hold PhDs, 0% are are members of minority groups, 0% are women.

ACADEMICS
Degrees: associate, bachelor's. **Classes:** Most classes have 10-19 students. Most lab/discussion sessions have 20-29 students. **Special Study Options:** Accelerated program, cooperative education program, honors program, independent study, internships, study abroad, weekend college.

FACILITIES
Housing: Coed dorms, special housing for disabled students.

CAMPUS LIFE
Activities: dance, drama/theater, student government, student newspaper, yearbook.

ADMISSIONS
Freshman Academic Profile: Average high school GPA 3.2. **Basis for Candidate Selection:** *Very important factors considered include:* rigor of secondary school record, class rank, academic GPA. *Important factors considered include:* application essay, interview, extracurricular activities, work experience. *Other factors considered include:* standardized test scores, recommendation(s), alumni/ae relation, volunteer work, level of applicant's interest. **Freshman Admission Requirements:** High school diploma is required and GED is accepted. *Academic units required:* 4 English, 3 math, 3 science, 2 social studies. **Freshman Admission Statistics:** 4,049 applied, 75.85% admitted, 14% enrolled. **Transfer Admission Requirements:** High school transcript, college transcript(s), Minimum college GPA of 2.0 required. Lowest grade transferable C. **General Admission Information:** Nonfall registration accepted. Admission may be deferred.

COSTS AND FINANCIAL AID
Annual tuition $30,396. Room and board $8,268. Average book expense $1,500. **Required Forms and Deadlines:** FAFSA. **Notification of Awards:** Applicants will be notified of awards on a rolling basis beginning 3/1. **Types of Aid:** *Need-based scholarships/grants:* Federal Pell, FSEOG, State scholarships/grants, Private scholarships, College/university scholarship or grant aid from institutional funds. *Loans:* Federal Perkins Loans, State Loans, College/university loans from institutional funds. *Student Employment:* Federal Work-Study Program available. Institutional employment available. **Financial Aid Statistics:** 94% needy undergrads receive need-based scholarship or grant aid. 72% freshmen, 63% undergrads receive non-need-based scholarship or grant aid. 98% freshmen, 97% undergrads receive need-based self-help aid. 0% freshmen, 0% undergrads receive athletic scholarships. **Criteria for awarding aid:** *Need-based:* Academics. *Non-need-based:* Academics, Alumni affiliation, Job skills, Leadership, State/district residency.

JOHNSON AND WALES UNIVERSITY—DENVER

7150 Montview Boulevard, Denver, CO 80220
Phone: 303-256-9300
E-mail: den@admissions.jwu.edu
Fax: 303-256-9333 • **Website:** http://www.jwu.edu/denver

This private school was founded in 1914.

RATINGS
Admissions Selectivity Rating: 65   **Fire Safety Rating:** 60*   **Green Rating:** 60*

STUDENTS AND FACULTY
Enrollment: 1,356. **Student Body:** 59% female, 41% male, 63% out-of-state, 1% international. Asian 2%, African American 9%, Caucasian 54%, Hispanic 19%, Native American <1%, Pacific Islander <1%, Two or more races 8%, Race unknown 6%.
Retention and Graduation: 75% freshmen return for sophomore year. 37% freshmen graduate within 4 years. 43 **Faculty:** Student/faculty ratio 16:1. 52 full-time faculty, 0% hold PhDs, 0% are are members of minority groups, 0% are women.

ACADEMICS
Degrees: associate, bachelor's, certificate, master's. **Classes:** Most classes have 10-19 students. Most lab/discussion sessions have 20-29 students. **Most popular majors:** Business/Commerce; Hotel/Motel Administration/Management; Restaurant/Food Services Management. **Special Study Options:** cooperative education program, double major, honors program, independent study, internships, study abroad.

FACILITIES
Housing: Coed dorms, Living-Learning Communities (LLCs) and Theme Floors, are an exciting approach to combining residential and academic life at Johnson & Wales University, Denver. LLCs and theme floors provide students with an opportunity to interact with faculty, staff, and other students around a theme or academic discipline in an active and collaborative program that

enhances the teaching and learning process by incorporating all aspects of a Student's collegiate experience.

CAMPUS LIFE

Activities: Choral groups, dance, literary magazine, student government, yearbook.

ADMISSIONS

Freshman Academic Profile: Average high school GPA 3.2. **Basis for Candidate Selection:** *Very important factors considered include:* rigor of secondary school record, class rank, academic GPA. *Important factors considered include:* application essay, interview, extracurricular activities. *Other factors considered include:* standardized test scores, recommendation(s), alumni/ae relation, volunteer work, work experience, level of applicant's interest. **Freshman Admission Requirements:** High school diploma is required and GED is accepted. *Academic units required:* 4 English, 3 math, 3 science, 2 social studies. **Freshman Admission Statistics:** 2,319 applied, 81.20% admitted, 18% enrolled. **Transfer Admission Requirements:** High school transcript, college transcript(s), Minimum college GPA of 2.0 required. Lowest grade transferable C. **General Admission Information:** Nonfall registration accepted. Admission may be deferred.

COSTS AND FINANCIAL AID

Annual tuition $30,396. Average book expense $1,500. **Required Forms and Deadlines:** FAFSA. **Notification of Awards:** Applicants will be notified of awards on a rolling basis beginning 3/1. **Types of Aid:** *Need-based scholarships/ grants:* Federal Pell, FSEOG, State scholarships/grants, Private scholarships, College/university scholarship or grant aid from institutional funds. *Loans:* Federal Perkins Loans, State Loans, College/university loans from institutional funds. *Student Employment:* Federal Work-Study Program available. Institutional employment available. **Financial Aid Statistics:** 91% needy freshmen, 84% needy undergrads receive need-based scholarship or grant aid. 85% freshmen, 75% undergrads receive non-need-based scholarship or grant aid. 90% freshmen, 94% undergrads receive need-based self-help aid. 0% freshmen, 0% undergrads receive athletic scholarships. **Criteria for awarding aid:** *Need-based:* Academics. *Non-need-based:* Academics, Alumni affiliation, Job skills, Leadership, State/district residency.

JOHNSON AND WALES UNIVERSITY— PROVIDENCE CAMPUS

Phone: 1-401-598-1000
E-mail: pvd@admissions.jwu.edu
Website: http://admissions.jwu.edu/ • **ACT Code:** 3804

This private school was founded in 1914. It has a 50-acre campus.

RATINGS

Admissions Selectivity Rating: 70   **Fire Safety Rating:** 60*   **Green Rating:** 60*

STUDENTS AND FACULTY

Enrollment: 8,718. **Student Body:** 60% female, 40% male, 81% out-of-state, 9% international. Asian 1%, African American 11%, Caucasian 56%, Hispanic 11%, Native American <1%, Pacific Islander <1%, Two or more races 8%, Race unknown 4%.
Retention and Graduation: 78% freshmen return for sophomore year. 46% freshmen graduate within 4 years. **Faculty:** Student/faculty ratio 20:1. 294 full-time faculty, 0% hold PhDs, 0% are are members of minority groups, 0% are women.

ACADEMICS

Degrees: associate, bachelor's, certificate, doctoral, master's, post-master's certificate. **Classes:** Most classes have 10-19 students. Most lab/discussion sessions have 10-19 students. **Special Study Options:** Accelerated program, cooperative education program, English as a Second Language (ESL), exchange student program (domestic), external degree program, honors program, independent study, study abroad, weekend college.

FACILITIES

Housing: Coed dorms, special housing for disabled students, special housing for international students, Technology Living/Learning Community at Snowden Hall—A wing for first-year technology majors (among other upperclassman technology majors) interested in living with other students in the same academic program. The floor Resident Assistant is an upperclassman Technology Major. Faculty from the School of Technology will be involved in programming and mentorship in this community, providing out of classroom contact with instructors and academic program content. **Special Academic Facilities/Equipment:** Culinary Archives and Museum. **Computers:** Students

can register for classes online. Administrative functions (other than registration) can be performed online.

CAMPUS LIFE

Environment: City. **Activities:** Choral groups, dance, drama/theater, pep band, student government, student newspaper, yearbook. **Athletics (Intercollegiate):** *Men:* baseball, basketball, cheerleading, cross-country, equestrian sports, golf, ice hockey, soccer, tennis, volleyball, wrestling. *Women:* basketball, cheerleading, cross-country, equestrian sports, golf, ice hockey, soccer, softball, tennis, volleyball.

ADMISSIONS

Freshman Academic Profile: Average high school GPA 3.1. **Basis for Candidate Selection:** *Very important factors considered include:* rigor of secondary school record, class rank, academic GPA. *Important factors considered include:* application essay, interview, extracurricular activities. *Other factors considered include:* standardized test scores, recommendation(s), talent/ ability, character/personal qualities, alumni/ae relation, volunteer work, work experience, level of applicant's interest. **Freshman Admission Requirements:** High school diploma is required and GED is accepted. *Academic units required:* 4 English, 3 math, 3 science, 2 social studies. **Freshman Admission Statistics:** 11,971 applied, 81.92% admitted, 20% enrolled. **Transfer Admission Requirements:** High school transcript, college transcript(s), Minimum college GPA of 2.0 required. Lowest grade transferable C. **General Admission Information:** Nonfall registration accepted. Admission may be deferred.

COSTS AND FINANCIAL AID

Annual tuition $30,396. Average book expense $1,500. **Required Forms and Deadlines:** FAFSA. **Notification of Awards:** Applicants will be notified of awards on a rolling basis beginning 3/1. **Types of Aid:** *Need-based scholarships/ grants:* Federal Pell, FSEOG, State scholarships/grants, Private scholarships, College/university scholarship or grant aid from institutional funds. *Loans:* Federal Perkins Loans, State Loans, College/university loans from institutional funds. *Student Employment:* Federal Work-Study Program available. Institutional employment available. **Financial Aid Statistics:** 90% needy freshmen, 84% needy undergrads receive need-based scholarship or grant aid. 71% freshmen, 59% undergrads receive non-need-based scholarship or grant aid. 94% freshmen, 95% undergrads receive need-based self-help aid. 0% freshmen, 0% undergrads receive athletic scholarships. **Criteria for awarding aid:** *Need-based:* Academics. *Non-need-based:* Academics, Alumni affiliation, Job skills, Leadership, State/district residency.

JOHNSON STATE COLLEGE

337 College Hill, Johnson, VT 05656-9408
Phone: 802-635-1219 • **Financial Aid Phone:** 802-635-1380
E-mail: jscadmissions@jsc.edu • **CEEB Code:** 3766
Fax: 802-635-1230 • **Website:** www.jsc.edu • **ACT Code:** 4316

This public school was founded in 1828. It has a 350-acre campus.

RATINGS

Admissions Selectivity Rating: 80   **Fire Safety Rating:** 80   **Green Rating:** 60*

STUDENTS AND FACULTY

Enrollment: 1,640. **Student Body:** 62% female, 38% male, 28% out-of-state, <1% international (2 countries represented). Asian 1%, African American 3%, Caucasian 85%, Hispanic 1%, Native American 1%, Pacific Islander 0%, Two or more races 0%, Race unknown 8%.
Retention and Graduation: 64% freshmen return for sophomore year. 15% freshmen graduate within 4 years. 35% freshmen graduate within 6 years. **Faculty:** Student/faculty ratio 16:1. 50 full-time faculty, 98% hold PhDs, 4% are are members of minority groups, 36% are women. 0% of classes are taught by teaching assistants.

ACADEMICS

Degrees: associate, bachelor's, master's, postbachelor's certificate, terminal. **Classes:** Most classes have 10-19 students. **Most popular majors:** Elementary Education and Teaching; Visual and Performing Arts; Tourism and Travel Services Management. **Special Study Options:** cross-registration, double major, dual enrollment, English as a Second Language (ESL), exchange student program (domestic), external degree program, honors program, independent study, internships, study abroad, teacher certification program. **Disability Services:** Special programs offered to physically disabled students, including note-taking services, reader services, tape recorders, tutors. **Career Services:** Alumni network, Alumni services, Career/job search classes, Career assessment, Internships, Regional alumni, On-campus interviews. Internships.

FACILITIES

Housing: Coed dorms, apartments for married students, apartments for single students, Apartments for students who have 60 credits and a 3.0 average GPA. 80% of campus accessible to physically disabled. **Special Academic Facilities/Equipment:** Art gallery, visual arts center, child development center, human performance lab, 1,000-acre nature preserve, snowboard terrain park, dance studio **Computers:** Students can register for classes online. Administrative functions (other than registration) can be performed online.

CAMPUS LIFE

Environment: Rural. **Activities:** Choral groups, concert band, dance, drama/theater, jazz band, literary magazine, music ensembles, musical theater, pep band, radio station, student government, student newspaper, yearbook, Student Organization. 30 registered organizations, 1 honor society, 4 religious organizations. **Athletics (Intercollegiate):** *Men:* basketball, cross-country, golf, lacrosse, soccer, tennis. *Women:* basketball, cross-country, soccer, softball, tennis, volleyball. **On-Campus Highlights:** Dibden Center For the Arts, Snowboarding Hill, Baselodge, Disc Golf Course, SHAPE Athletic Facility, Located in the heart of the Green Mountains, 1 hour from Vermont largest city, Burlington. JSC has 14 buildings on 1,350 acres (including our nature preserve). **Environmental Initiatives:** We compost.

ADMISSIONS

Freshman Academic Profile: 34% in top 10% of high school class, 66% in top 25% of high school class, 68% in top 50% of high school class. **Reported SAT (pre-2016 redesign) scores:** SAT Math middle 50% range 430-550. SAT Critical Reading middle 50% range 430-550. **Concordant SAT scores:** SAT Math middle 50% range 470–570. ACT middle 50% range 20-28. Minimum internet-based TOEFL 61. Minimum paper TOEFL 500. **Basis for Candidate Selection:** *Very important factors considered include:* rigor of secondary school record, standardized test scores. *Important factors considered include:* class rank, academic GPA, application essay, recommendation(s), talent/ability, character/personal qualities. *Other factors considered include:* interview, extracurricular activities, volunteer work, work experience. **Freshman Admission Requirements:** High school diploma is required and GED is accepted. *Academic units required:* 4 English, 2 math, 2 science, 1 science lab, 3 social studies, 2 history. *Academic units recommended:* 4 English, 3 math, 3 science, 2 science labs, 1 foreign language, 3 social studies, 3 history. **Freshman Admission Statistics:** 973 applied, 86.64% admitted, 34% enrolled. **Transfer Admission Requirements:** High school transcript, college transcript(s), essay or personal statement, statement of good standing from prior institution(s). Minimum college GPA of 2.0 required. Lowest grade transferable C-. **General Admission Information:** Application fee $40. Priority deadline 3/1. Nonfall registration accepted. Admission may be deferred for a maximum of 1 year.

COSTS AND FINANCIAL AID

Annual in-state tuition $8,568. Annual out-of-state tuition $19,008. Room and board $8,446. Required fees $1,113. Average book expense $1,000. **Required Forms and Deadlines:** FAFSA, State aid form. **Notification of Awards:** Applicants will be notified of awards on a rolling basis beginning 4/1. **Types of Aid:** *Need-based scholarships/grants:* Federal Pell, FSEOG, State scholarships/grants, Private scholarships, College/university scholarship or grant aid from institutional funds. *Loans:* Direct Subsidized Stafford Loans, Direct Unsubsidized Stafford Loans, Direct PLUS loans, Federal Perkins Loans. *Student Employment:* Federal Work-Study Program available. Institutional employment available. **Financial Aid Statistics:** 93% needy freshmen, 89% needy undergrads receive need-based scholarship or grant aid. 4% freshmen, 3% undergrads receive non-need-based scholarship or grant aid. 95% freshmen, 95% undergrads receive need-based self-help aid. 0% freshmen, 0% undergrads receive athletic scholarships. 87% freshmen, 82% undergrads receive any aid. **Criteria for awarding aid:** *Need-based:* Academics, Alumni affiliation, Art, Leadership, Music/drama. *Non-need-based:* Academics, Art, Leadership, Music/drama, State/district residency.

JOHNSON UNIVERSITY

7900 Johnson Drive, Knoxville, TN 37998
Phone: 800-827-2122 • **Financial Aid Phone:** 865-251-2303
E-mail: http://www.johnsonu.edu/ • **CEEB Code:** 1345
Fax: 865-251-2336 • **Website:** http://www.johnsonu.edu/ • **ACT Code:** 3968

This private school, affiliated with the Christian (Nondenominational) Church, was founded in 1893. It has a 350-acre campus.

RATINGS

Admissions Selectivity Rating: 80   **Fire Safety Rating:** 81   **Green Rating:** 60*

STUDENTS AND FACULTY

Enrollment: 100. **Student Body:** 78% out-of-state, 2% international (12 countries represented). Asian 1%, African American 2%, Caucasian 90%, Hispanic 2%, Native American 1%, Pacific Islander 0%, Two or more races 2%, Race unknown 0%.
Retention and Graduation: 73% freshmen return for sophomore year. 57% freshmen graduate within 6 years. **Faculty:** Student/faculty ratio 21:1. 30 full-time faculty, 63% hold PhDs, 0% are are members of minority groups, 17% 0% of classes are taught by teaching assistants.

ACADEMICS

Degrees: associate, bachelor's, certificate, master's. **Special Study Options:** Accelerated program, cooperative education program, distance learning, double major, English as a Second Language (ESL), honors program, independent study, internships, teacher certification program. **Disability Services:** Special programs offered to physically disabled students, including reader services, tape recorders.

FACILITIES

Housing: men's dorms, women's dorms, apartments for married students. **Computers:** Students can register for classes online. Administrative functions (other than registration) can be performed online.

CAMPUS LIFE

Environment: Rural. **Activities:** Choral groups, music ensembles, musical theater, radio station, student government, yearbook. 3 honor societies, 3 religious organizations. **Athletics (Intercollegiate):** *Men:* baseball, basketball, cheerleading, soccer. *Women:* basketball, cheerleading, volleyball. **On-Campus Highlights:** women's residence hall, men's residence hall, global-education-tech building

ADMISSIONS

Freshman Academic Profile: Average high school GPA 3.0. 21% in top 10% of high school class, 48% in top 25% of high school class, 78% in top 50% of high school class. **Reported SAT (pre-2016 redesign) scores:** SAT Math middle 50% range 470-560. SAT Critical Reading middle 50% range 480-612. SAT Writing middle 50% range 487-562. **Concordant SAT scores:** SAT EBRW middle 50% 540–640. SAT Math middle 50% range 510–580. ACT middle 50% range 20-26. Minimum paper TOEFL 500. **Basis for Candidate Selection:** *Very important factors considered include:* rigor of secondary school record, class rank, standardized test scores, recommendation(s), character/personal qualities, religious affiliation/commitment. *Important factors considered include:* application essay, interview. *Other factors considered include:* extracurricular activities, talent/ability, alumni/ae relation, volunteer work. **Freshman Admission Requirements:** High school diploma is required and GED is accepted. **Freshman Admission Statistics:** 296 applied, 94.59% admitted, 57% enrolled. **Transfer Admission Requirements:** High school transcript, college transcript(s), essay or personal statement, statement of good standing from prior institution(s). Lowest grade transferable C. **General Admission Information:** Application fee $35. Regular application deadline 7/1. Regular notification 9/1. Nonfall registration accepted. Admission may be deferred for a maximum of one year.

COSTS AND FINANCIAL AID

Annual tuition $7,000. Room and board $4,890. Required fees $770. Average book expense $1,300. **Required Forms and Deadlines:** FAFSA, Institution's own financial aid form. **Notification of Awards:** Applicants will be notified of awards on or about 3/30. **Types of Aid:** *Need-based scholarships/grants:* Federal Pell, FSEOG, State scholarships/grants, Private scholarships, College/university scholarship or grant aid from institutional funds. *Student Employment:* Federal Work-Study Program available. Institutional employment available. **Financial Aid Statistics:** 97% needy freshmen, 98% needy undergrads receive need-based scholarship or grant aid. 24% freshmen, 26% undergrads receive non-need-based scholarship or grant aid. 59% freshmen, 58% undergrads receive need-based self-help aid. 0% freshmen, 0% undergrads receive athletic scholarships. 97% undergrads receive any aid. **Criteria for awarding aid:** *Non-need-based:* Academics, Minority status, Music/drama, Religious affiliation, State/district residency.

JONES INTERNATIONAL UNIVERSITY

9697 E. Mineral Avenue, Centennial, CO 80112
Phone: 800-811-5663
E-mail: admissions@international.edu
Fax: 303-799-0966 • **Website:** www.jonesinternational.edu

This is a private school.

RATINGS

Admissions Selectivity Rating: 62   Fire Safety Rating: 60*   Green Rating: 60*

STUDENTS AND FACULTY

Student Body: 50% female, 50% male, % out-of-state.
Retention and Graduation: 97% freshmen return for sophomore year.

ACADEMICS

Degrees: bachelor's, certificate, master's. **Special Study Options:** Accelerated program, distance learning, external degree program.

ADMISSIONS

Freshman Admission Requirements: High school diploma is required and GED is accepted. **Freshman Admission Statistics:** 22 applied, 100.00% admitted, 86% enrolled. **Transfer Admission Requirements:** High school transcript, college transcript(s), Lowest grade transferable C. **General Admission Information:** Application fee $75. Nonfall registration accepted. Admission may be deferred for a maximum of 1 Year.

COSTS AND FINANCIAL AID

Annual tuition $835. Required fees $75. Average book expense $100. *Student Employment:* Federal Work-Study Program available. Institutional employment available.

JUDSON COLLEGE (AL)

302 Bibb Street, Marion, AL 36756
Phone: 334-683-5110 • **Financial Aid Phone:** 334-683-5157
E-mail: admissions@judson.edu • **CEEB Code:** 1349
Fax: 334-683-5282 • **Website:** www.judson.edu • **ACT Code:** 22

This private school, affiliated with the Baptist Church, was founded in 1838. It has a 80-acre campus.

RATINGS

Admissions Selectivity Rating: 79   Fire Safety Rating: 75   Green Rating: 60*

STUDENTS AND FACULTY

Enrollment: 315. **Student Body:** 97% female, 3% male, 29% out-of-state, 1% international (3 countries represented). Asian 0%, African American 12%, Caucasian 83%, Hispanic 1%, Native American 1%, Pacific Islander 0%, Two or more races 0%, Race unknown 1%.
Retention and Graduation: 61% freshmen return for sophomore year. 49% freshmen graduate within 4 years. 49% freshmen graduate within 6 years. 15% grads go on to further study within 1 year. 83% grads pursue arts and sciences degrees. 17% grads pursue medical degrees. **Faculty:** Student/faculty ratio 11:1. 18 full-time faculty, 83% hold PhDs, 0% are are members of minority groups, 39% are women. 0% of classes are taught by teaching assistants.

ACADEMICS

Degrees: bachelor's. **Classes:** Most classes have fewer than 10 students. Most lab/discussion sessions have fewer than 10 students. **Most popular majors:** Elementary Education and Teaching; Biology/Biological Sciences; Psychology. **Special Study Options:** Accelerated program, cross-registration, distance learning, double major, dual enrollment, independent study, internships, student-designed major, study abroad, teacher certification program. **Disability Services:** Special programs offered to physically disabled students, including tutors. **Career Services:** Alumni services, Career assessment, Internships, On-campus interviews.

FACILITIES

Housing: women's dorms. 50% of campus accessible to physically diasbled. **Special Academic Facilities/Equipment:** Alabama Women's Hall of Fame. **Computers:** 50% of classrooms, 100% of dorms, 100% of libraries, 100% of student union, have wireless network access.

CAMPUS LIFE

Environment: Rural. **Activities:** Choral groups, drama/theater, literary magazine, marching band, music ensembles, student government, student newspaper, yearbook, Campus Ministries. 23 registered organizations, 8 honor societies, 1 religious organization. **Athletics (Intercollegiate):** *Women:* basketball, equestrian sports, soccer, softball, volleyball. **On-Campus Highlights:** Residence Hall Lobbies, Gym, Computer Labs, Club House, Student Center.

ADMISSIONS

Freshman Academic Profile: Average high school GPA 3.4. 32% in top 10% of high school class, 22% in top 25% of high school class, 84% in top 50% of high school class. 78% from public high schools. **Reported SAT (pre-2016 redesign) scores:** SAT Math middle 50% range 470-590. SAT Critical Reading middle 50% range 540-590. SAT Writing middle 50% range 520-630. **Concordant SAT scores:** SAT EBRW middle 50% 590–660. SAT Math middle 50% range 510–610. ACT middle 50% range 19-26. Minimum paper TOEFL 500. **Basis for Candidate Selection:** *Very important factors considered include:* class rank, academic GPA, standardized test scores. *Other factors considered include:* rigor of secondary school record, recommendation(s), extracurricular activities, talent/ability, character/personal qualities, alumni/ae relation, level of applicant's interest. **Freshman Admission Requirements:** High school diploma is required and GED is accepted. *Academic units required:* 4 English, 2 math, 2 science, 3 social studies, 5 academic electives. *Academic units recommended:* 4 English, 4 math, 4 science, 2 foreign language, 4 social studies, 2 history. **Freshman Admission Statistics:** 306 applied, 83.66% admitted, 38% enrolled. **Transfer Admission Requirements:** college transcript(s), Minimum college GPA of 2.0 required. Lowest grade transferable C-. **General Admission Information:** Application fee $35. Nonfall registration accepted. Admission may be deferred for a maximum of 1 Year.

COSTS AND FINANCIAL AID

Annual tuition $12,327. Room and board $7,969. Required fees $220. Average book expense $1,200. **Required Forms and Deadlines:** FAFSA, Institution's own financial aid form, State aid form. **Notification of Awards:** Applicants will be notified of awards on a rolling basis beginning 11/15. **Types of Aid:** *Need-based scholarships/grants:* Federal Pell, FSEOG, State scholarships/grants, Private scholarships, College/university scholarship or grant aid from institutional funds. *Loans:* Federal Perkins Loans, College/university loans from institutional funds. *Student Employment:* Federal Work-Study Program available. Institutional employment available. **Financial Aid Statistics:** 97% needy freshmen, 97% needy undergrads receive need-based scholarship or grant aid. 11% freshmen, 12% undergrads receive non-need-based scholarship or grant aid. 75% freshmen, 86% undergrads receive need-based self-help aid. 12% freshmen, 12% undergrads receive athletic scholarships. 99% freshmen, 96% undergrads receive any aid. **Criteria for awarding aid:** *Need-based:* Academics, Alumni affiliation, Art, Athletics, Leadership, Music/drama. *Non-need-based:* Academics, Alumni affiliation, Art, Athletics, Music/drama, Religious affiliation, State/district residency.

THE JUILLIARD SCHOOL

60 Lincoln Center Plaza, New York, NY 10023-6588
Phone: 212-799-2000 ext.223 • **Financial Aid Phone:** 212-799-5000
E-mail: admissions@juilliard.edu • **CEEB Code:** 2340
Fax: 212-769-6420 • **Website:** www.juilliard.edu

This private school was founded in 1905.

RATINGS

Admissions Selectivity Rating: 74   Fire Safety Rating: 69   Green Rating: 60*

STUDENTS AND FACULTY

Enrollment: 499. **Student Body:** 49% female, 51% male, 89% out-of-state, 26% international (40 countries represented). Asian 14%, African American 5%, Caucasian 40%, Hispanic 7%, Native American 0%, Pacific Islander 0%, Two or more races 6%, Race unknown 1%.
Retention and Graduation: 83% freshmen graduate within 4 years. **Faculty:** Student/faculty ratio 4:1. 136 full-time faculty, 0% hold PhDs, 15% are members of minority groups, 39% are women.

ACADEMICS

Degrees: bachelor's, diploma, doctoral/research, doctoral, master's, postbachelor's certificate, post-master's certificate. **Classes:** Most classes have fewer than 10 students. **Most popular majors:** Keyboard Instruments; Voice and Opera; Stringed Instruments.

FACILITIES

Housing: Coed dorms. **Special Academic Facilities/Equipment:** 2 recital halls, 1 theater (1000 ppl), 1 drama theater (200 ppl), 15 two-story studios, 35 private teaching studios, 106 practice rooms, organ studios, 200+ pianos, recording studio, The Peter Jay Sharp Special Collections Room. **Computers:**

Students can register for classes online. Administrative functions (other than registration) can be performed online.

CAMPUS LIFE
Environment: Metropolis. **Activities:** student government 5 registered organizations, 2 religious organizations. **On-Campus Highlights:** Lila Acheson Wallace Library, Lincoln Center, Rose Building—cafeteria, Juilliard Bookstore.

ADMISSIONS
Minimum paper TOEFL 533. **Basis for Candidate Selection:** *Very important factors considered include:* interview, talent/ability. *Other factors considered include:* academic GPA, application essay, recommendation(s), extracurricular activities. **Freshman Admission Requirements:** High school diploma is required and GED is accepted. *Academic units recommended:* 4 visual/performing arts. **Freshman Admission Statistics:** 2,533 applied, 6.55% admitted, 69% enrolled. **Transfer Admission Requirements:** college transcript(s), essay or personal statement, interview, Lowest grade transferable C. **General Admission Information:** Application fee $110. Priority deadline 12/1. Regular application deadline 12/1. Regular notification 4/1. Nonfall registration not accepted.

COSTS AND FINANCIAL AID
Annual tuition $41,310. Required fees $100. Average book expense $580. **Required Forms and Deadlines:** FAFSA, CSS/Financial Aid PROFILE. **Notification of Awards:** Applicants will be notified of awards on or about 4/1. **Types of Aid:** *Need-based scholarships/grants:* Federal Pell, FSEOG, State scholarships/grants, Private scholarships, College/university scholarship or grant aid from institutional funds. *Loans:* Direct Subsidized Stafford Loans, Direct Unsubsidized Stafford Loans, Direct PLUS loans, Federal Perkins Loans. *Student Employment:* Federal Work-Study Program available. Institutional employment available. **Financial Aid Statistics:** 94% needy freshmen, 97% needy undergrads receive need-based scholarship or grant aid. 7% freshmen, 2% undergrads receive non-need-based scholarship or grant aid. 100% freshmen, 100% undergrads receive need-based self-help aid. 0% freshmen, 0% undergrads receive athletic scholarships. Average cumulative indebtedness $32,493. **Criteria for awarding aid:** *Need-based:* Music/drama. *Non-need-based:* Music/drama.

JUNIATA COLLEGE

1700 Moore Street, Huntingdon, PA 16652
Phone: 814-641-3420 • **Financial Aid Phone:** 814-641-3142
E-mail: admissions@juniata.edu • **CEEB Code:** 2341
Fax: 814-641-3100 • **Website:** www.juniata.edu • **ACT Code:** 3600

This private school was founded in 1876. It has a 800-acre campus.

RATINGS
Admissions Selectivity Rating: 84 **Fire Safety Rating:** 88 **Green Rating:** 61

STUDENTS AND FACULTY
Enrollment: 1,454. **Student Body:** 56% female, 44% male, 34% out-of-state, 7% international (29 countries represented). Asian 4%, African American 3%, Caucasian 73%, Hispanic 4%, Native American <1%, Pacific Islander 0%, Two or more races 3%, Race unknown 5%.
Retention and Graduation: 85% freshmen return for sophomore year. 72% freshmen graduate within 4 years. 75% freshmen graduate within 6 years. 27% grads go on to further study within 1 year. 37% grads pursue arts and sciences degrees. 7% grads pursue law degrees. 33% grads pursue business degrees. 15% grads pursue medical degrees. **Faculty:** Student/faculty ratio 12:1. 117 full-time faculty, 89% hold PhDs, 9% are are members of minority groups, 48% are women. 0% of classes are taught by teaching assistants.

ACADEMICS
Degrees: bachelor's, master's. **Classes:** Most classes have 10-19 students. Most lab/discussion sessions have 10-19 students. **Most popular majors:** Biology/Biological Sciences; Physical Sciences; Business/Commerce. **Special Study Options:** double major, dual enrollment, English as a Second Language (ESL), exchange student program (domestic), honors program, independent study, internships, student-designed major, study abroad, teacher certification program, Philadelphia Urban Semester, Marine Science Semester, Washington Semester, Cooperative Degree Programs (3-1, 3-2, etc.). **Honors Programs:** Entire college is considered to be an honors program. Combined degree programs: BA/MD, BA/JD, BA/MA, BA/DDS, BA/MEng, Dentistry,Optometry,Podiatry,Alli

ed Health,Nursing. **Disability Services:** Special programs offered to physically disabled students, including reader services, tape recorders, tutors. **Career Services:** Alumni network, Alumni services, Career/job search classes, Career assessment, Internships. At Juniata, countless opportunities abound to learn by doing. Whether students are participating in internships, studying abroad, volunteering for local charities, leading student organizations, starting their own business, designing a play, or working on individual research, Juniata students learn early in their education how to make things happen.

FACILITIES
Housing: Coed dorms, special housing for international students, women's dorms, apartments for single students, Substance-Free Housing. 75% of campus accessible to physically diasbled. **Special Academic Facilities/Equipment:** Environmental Studies Field Station,Juniata Museum of Art, Early Childhood Education Center, Ceramics studio and Anagama Kiln, Nature preserve and Peace Chapel, Observatory, Electron microscopes, Nuclear magnetic resonance spectrometers, Human Interaction Lab. three story, free form theater. **Computers:** 100% of classrooms, 100% of dorms, 100% of libraries, 100% of dining areas, 100% of student union, 100% of common outdoor areas have wireless network access. Students can register for classes online. Administrative functions (other than registration) can be performed online. Undergraduates are required to own a computer.

CAMPUS LIFE
Environment: Village. **Activities:** Choral groups, concert band, dance, drama/theater, jazz band, literary magazine, music ensembles, musical theater, radio station, student government, student newspaper, symphony orchestra, television station, Campus Ministries, Student Organization, Model UN. 94 registered organizations, 12 honor societies, 7 religious organizations. **Athletics (Intercollegiate): Men:** baseball, basketball, cross-country, football, soccer, tennis, track/field (outdoor), track/field (indoor), volleyball. *Women:* basketball, cross-country, field hockey, soccer, softball, swimming, tennis, track/field (outdoor), track/field (indoor), volleyball. **On-Campus Highlights:** von Liebig Science Center, Juniata College Museum of Art, Ceramics Studio w/Anagama Kiln, Sill Business Incubator and Juniata College Center, Suzanne von Liebig Theatre. **Environmental Initiatives:** 60% today and 75% by 2012 Electric in Wind RECS.

ADMISSIONS
Freshman Academic Profile: Average high school GPA 3.7. 28% in top 10% of high school class, 56% in top 25% of high school class, 91% in top 50% of high school class. 81% from public high schools. **Reported SAT (pre-2016 redesign) scores:** SAT Math middle 50% range 520-620. SAT Critical Reading middle 50% range 520-620. SAT Writing middle 50% range 480-603. **Concordant SAT scores:** SAT EBRW middle 50% 560–660. SAT Math middle 50% range 550–640. ACT middle 50% range 23-29. Minimum internet-based TOEFL 79. Minimum paper TOEFL 550. **Basis for Candidate Selection:** *Very important factors considered include:* rigor of secondary school record, academic GPA, standardized test scores, application essay, recommendation(s), character/personal qualities. *Important factors considered include:* interview, extracurricular activities, talent/ability, first generation, volunteer work. *Other factors considered include:* alumni/ae relation, geographical residence, state residency, racial/ethnic status, level of applicant's interest. **Freshman Admission Requirements:** High school diploma is required and GED is accepted. *Academic units required:* 4 English, 3 math, 3 science, 2 science labs, 1 social studies, 3 history. **Freshman Admission Statistics:** 2,386 applied, admitted, 14% enrolled. **Transfer Admission Requirements:** High school transcript, college transcript(s), essay or personal statement, Minimum college GPA of 2.5 required. Lowest grade transferable C-. **General Admission Information:** Priority deadline 11/15. Regular application deadline 2/15. Regular notification 2/1. Nonfall registration accepted. Admission may be deferred for a maximum of 1 year.

COSTS AND FINANCIAL AID
Annual tuition $43,050. Room and board $12,040. Required fees $825. Average book expense $1,000. **Required Forms and Deadlines:** FAFSA. **Notification of Awards:** Applicants will be notified of awards on a rolling basis beginning 3/1. **Types of Aid:** *Need-based scholarships/grants:* Federal Pell, FSEOG, State scholarships/grants, Private scholarships, College/university scholarship or grant aid from institutional funds. *Loans:* Direct Subsidized Stafford Loans, Direct Unsubsidized Stafford Loans, Direct PLUS loans, Federal Perkins Loans, College/university loans from institutional funds. *Student Employment:* Federal Work-Study Program available. Institutional employment available. **Financial Aid Statistics:** 99% needy freshmen, 98% needy undergrads receive need-based scholarship or grant aid. 97% freshmen, 100% undergrads receive non-need-based scholarship or grant aid. 86% freshmen, 89% undergrads receive need-based self-help aid. 0% freshmen receive athletic scholarships. 100% freshmen, 100% undergrads receive any aid. 73% undergrads borrow to pay for school. Average cumulative indebtedness $36,338. **Criteria for awarding aid:** *Need-based:* Academics, Minority status, Music/drama. *Non-need-based:* Academics, Alumni affiliation, Art, Minority status, Music/drama.

KALAMAZOO COLLEGE

1200 Academy Street, Kalamazoo, MI 49006
Phone: 269-337-7166 • **Financial Aid Phone:** 269-337-7192
E-mail: admission@kzoo.edu • **CEEB Code:** 1365
Fax: 269-337-7390 • **Website:** www.kzoo.edu • **ACT Code:** 2018

This private school was founded in 1833. It has a 60-acre campus.

RATINGS

Admissions Selectivity Rating: 89 **Fire Safety Rating:** 79 **Green Rating:** 60*

STUDENTS AND FACULTY

Enrollment: 1,417. **Student Body:** 55% female, 45% male, 33% out-of-state, 8% international (32 countries represented). Asian 7%, African American 6%, Caucasian 59%, Hispanic 10%, Native American <1%, Pacific Islander <1%, Two or more races 5%, Race unknown 5%.
Retention and Graduation: 88% freshmen return for sophomore year. 73% freshmen graduate within 4 years. 81 **Faculty:** Student/faculty ratio 13:1. 105 full-time faculty, 90% hold PhDs, 28% are are members of minority groups, 52% are women. 0% of classes are taught by teaching assistants.

ACADEMICS

Degrees: bachelor's. **Classes:** Most classes have 10-19 students. Most lab/discussion sessions have 10-19 students. **Most popular majors:** English Language and Literature; Psychology; Economics. **Special Study Options:** cross-registration, double major, dual enrollment, English as a Second Language (ESL), exchange student program (domestic), independent study, internships, student-designed major, study abroad. **Disability Services:** Special programs offered to physically disabled students, including note-taking services, tape recorders, tutors. **Career Services:** Alumni network, Alumni services, Career/job search classes, Career assessment, Internships, Regional alumni.

FACILITIES

Housing: Coed dorms, Wellness Housing, Theme Housing. 25% of campus accessible to physically diasbled. **Special Academic Facilities/Equipment:** Science center, Rare book room **Computers:** 100% of classrooms, 70% of dorms, 100% of libraries, 100% of dining areas, 100% of student union, have wireless network access. Students can register for classes online. Administrative functions (other than registration) can be performed online.

CAMPUS LIFE

Environment: City. **Activities:** Choral groups, concert band, dance, drama/theater, jazz band, literary magazine, music ensembles, musical theater, pep band, radio station, student government, student newspaper, symphony orchestra, yearbook, Campus Ministries, Student Organization, Model UN. 50 registered organizations, 3 honor societies, 5 religious organizations. **Athletics (Intercollegiate):** *Men:* baseball, basketball, cross-country, diving, football, golf, soccer, swimming, tennis. *Women:* basketball, cross-country, diving, golf, soccer, softball, swimming, tennis, volleyball. **On-Campus Highlights:** Upjohn Library Commons, The Quad, Biggby Coffee Shop, Hicks Student Center, Anderson Athletic Center. **Environmental Initiatives:** The College is currently involved in a LEED registered expansion and renovation of Hicks Student Center. The project is expected to receive Silver certification when completed in summer 2008.

ADMISSIONS

Freshman Academic Profile: Average high school GPA 3.7. 52% in top 10% of high school class, 81% in top 25% of high school class, 95% in top 50% of high school class. 80% from public high schools. **Reported SAT (pre-2016 redesign) scores:** SAT Math middle 50% range 560-680. SAT Critical Reading middle 50% range 540-670. SAT Writing middle 50% range 550-660. **Concordant SAT scores:** SAT EBRW middle 50% 600–710. SAT Math middle 50% range 580–710. ACT middle 50% range 26-30. Minimum internet-based TOEFL 84. Minimum paper TOEFL 550. **Basis for Candidate Selection:** *Very important factors considered include:* rigor of secondary school record, academic GPA, extracurricular activities. *Important factors considered include:* application essay, recommendation(s). *Other factors considered include:* standardized test scores, interview, talent/ability, character/personal qualities, first generation, alumni/ae relation, geographical residence, state residency, racial/ethnic status, volunteer work, work experience, level of applicant's interest. **Freshman Admission Requirements:** High school diploma is required and GED is accepted. *Academic units required:* 4 English, 3 math, 3 science, 3 foreign language, 2 social studies, 2 history. *Academic units recommended:* 4 English, 4 math, 4 science, 4 foreign language, 2 social studies, 2 history. **Freshman Admission Statistics:** 3,626 applied, 65.66% admitted,

15% enrolled. **Transfer Admission Requirements:** High school transcript, college transcript(s), essay or personal statement, standardized test scores, statement of good standing from prior institution(s). Lowest grade transferable C. **General Admission Information:** Priority deadline 11/15. Regular application deadline 2/15. Regular notification 4/1. Nonfall registration not accepted. Admission may be deferred for a maximum of 1 year.

COSTS AND FINANCIAL AID

Annual tuition $42,510. Room and board $8,886. Required fees $336. Average book expense $720. **Required Forms and Deadlines:** FAFSA. **Notification of Awards:** Applicants will be notified of awards on a rolling basis beginning 3/23. **Types of Aid:** *Need-based scholarships/grants:* Federal Pell, FSEOG, State scholarships/grants, Private scholarships, College/university scholarship or grant aid from institutional funds. *Loans:* Direct Subsidized Stafford Loans, Direct Unsubsidized Stafford Loans, Direct PLUS loans, Federal Perkins Loans. *Student Employment:* Federal Work-Study Program available. Institutional employment available. **Financial Aid Statistics:** 97% needy freshmen, 99% needy undergrads receive need-based scholarship or grant aid. 23% freshmen, 17% undergrads receive non-need-based scholarship or grant aid. 79% freshmen, 82% undergrads receive need-based self-help aid. 0% freshmen, 0% undergrads receive athletic scholarships. 98% freshmen, 97% undergrads receive any aid. 61% undergrads borrow to pay for school. Average cumulative indebtedness $27,653. **Criteria for awarding aid:** *Need-based:* Academics. *Non-need-based:* Academics, Alumni affiliation, Art, Leadership, Music/drama.

KANSAS CITY ART INSTITUTE

4415 Warwick Boulevard, Kansas City, MO 64111
Phone: 800-522-5224 • **Financial Aid Phone:** 816-802-3337
E-mail: admiss@kcai.edu • **CEEB Code:** 6330
Fax: 816-802-3309 • **Website:** www.kcai.edu • **ACT Code:** 2277

This private school was founded in 1885. It has a 15-acre campus.

RATINGS

Admissions Selectivity Rating: 80 **Fire Safety Rating:** 71 **Green Rating:** 60*

STUDENTS AND FACULTY

Enrollment: 671. **Student Body:** 55% female, 45% male, 62% out-of-state, 1% international (6 countries represented). Asian 4%, African American 3%, Caucasian 80%, Hispanic 6%, Native American 1%, Pacific Islander 0%, Two or more races 0%, Race unknown 6%.
Retention and Graduation: 78% freshmen return for sophomore year. 43% freshmen graduate within 4 years. 53% freshmen graduate within 6 years. 40% grads go on to further study within 1 year. **Faculty:** Student/faculty ratio 12:1. 51 full-time faculty, 84% hold PhDs, 2% are are members of minority groups, 37% are women. 0% of classes are taught by teaching assistants.

ACADEMICS

Degrees: bachelor's. **Classes:** Most classes have 20-29 students. **Most popular majors:** Design and Visual Communications; Film/Video and Photographic Arts; Painting. **Special Study Options:** cross-registration, double major, exchange student program (domestic), independent study, internships, student-designed major, study abroad. **Disability Services:** Special programs offered to physically disabled students, including tape recorders, tutors. **Career Services:** Alumni network, Alumni services, Career/job search classes, Career assessment, Internships, Regional alumni, On-campus interviews, Community Arts and Service Learning program (CASL).

FACILITIES

Housing: Coed dorms, apartments for single students. **Special Academic Facilities/Equipment:** H and R Block Art Space **Computers:** Students can register for classes online. Administrative functions (other than registration) can be performed online.

CAMPUS LIFE

Environment: Metropolis. **Activities:** student government. **On-Campus Highlights:** Dodge Painting Building, Cafe Nerman, Jannes Library-Learning Center, H&R Block Artspace, Green space in center of campus.

ADMISSIONS

Freshman Academic Profile: Average high school GPA 3.2. 11% in top 10% of high school class, 39% in top 25% of high school class, 73% in top 50% of high school class. 80% from public high schools. **Reported SAT (pre-2016 redesign) scores:** SAT Math middle 50% range 430-590. SAT Critical Reading middle 50% range 430-580. SAT Writing middle 50% range 420-570. **Concordant SAT scores:** SAT EBRW middle 50% 480–630. SAT Math middle 50% range 470–610. ACT middle 50% range 20-25. Minimum internet-based TOEFL 79. Minimum paper TOEFL 550. **Basis for Candidate Selection:**

Very important factors considered include: recommendation(s). *Important factors considered include:* rigor of secondary school record, academic GPA, standardized test scores, application essay. *Other factors considered include:* interview, extracurricular activities, talent/ability, character/personal qualities, first generation, volunteer work, work experience, level of applicant's interest. **Freshman Admission Requirements:** High school diploma is required and GED is accepted. *Academic units recommended:* 4 English, 3 math, 3 science, 3 social studies, 3 academic electives, and 4 units from above areas or other academic areas. **Freshman Admission Statistics:** 603 applied, 72.31% admitted, 44% enrolled. **Transfer Admission Requirements:** High school transcript, college transcript(s), essay or personal statement, statement of good standing from prior institution(s). Minimum college GPA of 2.5 required. Lowest grade transferable C. **General Admission Information:** Application fee $35. Priority deadline 1/15. Nonfall registration accepted. Admission may be deferred.

COSTS AND FINANCIAL AID
Annual tuition $27,220. Room and board $8,294. Average book expense $1,500. **Required Forms and Deadlines:** FAFSA. **Notification of Awards:** Applicants will be notified of awards on a rolling basis beginning 4/1. **Types of Aid:** *Need-based scholarships/grants:* Federal Pell, FSEOG, State scholarships/grants, College/university scholarship or grant aid from institutional funds. *Loans:* Federal Perkins Loans. *Student Employment:* Federal Work-Study Program available. Institutional employment available. **Financial Aid Statistics:** 100% needy freshmen, 100% needy undergrads receive need-based scholarship or grant aid. 15% freshmen, 9% undergrads receive non-need-based scholarship or grant aid. 78% freshmen, 87% undergrads receive need-based self-help aid. 0% freshmen, 0% undergrads receive athletic scholarships. 99% freshmen, 95% undergrads receive any aid. **Criteria for awarding aid:** *Need-based:* Academics, Art. *Non-need-based:* Academics, Art.

KANSAS STATE UNIVERSITY

119 Anderson Hall, Manhattan, KS 66506
Phone: 785-532-6250 • **Financial Aid Phone:** 785-532-6420
E-mail: k-state@k-state.edu • **CEEB Code:** 6334
Fax: 785-532-6393 • **Website:** www.k-state.edu • **ACT Code:** 1428

This public school was founded in 1863. It has a 668-acre campus.

RATINGS
Admissions Selectivity Rating: 79   **Fire Safety Rating:** 60*   **Green Rating:** 60*

STUDENTS AND FACULTY
Enrollment: 19,151. **Student Body:** 48% female, 52% male, 18% out-of-state, 5% international (107 countries represented). Asian 1%, African American 4%, Caucasian 78%, Hispanic 7%, Native American <1%, Pacific Islander <1%, Two or more races 3%, Race unknown 1%.
Retention and Graduation: 85% freshmen return for sophomore year. 31% freshmen graduate within 4 years. 63% freshmen graduate within 6 years. 22% grads go on to further study within 1 year. **Faculty:** Student/faculty ratio 18:1. 1,104 full-time faculty, 83% hold PhDs, 17% are are members of minority groups, 42% are women. 17% of classes are taught by teaching assistants.

ACADEMICS
Degrees: associate, bachelor's, doctoral/professional, doctoral/research, master's, postbachelor's certificate. **Classes:** Most classes have 20-29 students. **Most popular majors:** Business Administration and Management; Animal Sciences; Mechanical Engineering. **Special Study Options:** Accelerated program, cooperative education program, distance learning, double major, English as a Second Language (ESL), exchange student program (domestic), honors program, independent study, internships, study abroad, teacher certification program, Minors. **Honors Programs:** The University Honors Program is an opportunity for undergraduate students from all colleges to enhance their education with special classes and opportunities for personal growth. Combined degree programs: BS/MS Arch. Eng., Indstrl Eng., Biol, Kineslgy, Horticltr, Pub. Health. **Disability Services:** Special programs offered to physically disabled students, including note-taking services, reader services, tape recorders, tutors. **Career Services:** Career/job search classes, Career assessment. Alumni career services partnership with the K-State Alumni association provides lifelong career services.

FACILITIES
Housing: Coed dorms, men's dorms, women's dorms, fraternity/sorority housing, apartments for married students, cooperative housing, apartments for single students. **Special Academic Facilities/Equipment:** South Asian area study center, education communications center, center for cancer research, planetarium, nuclear reactor/accelerator, Beach Art museum. **Computers:** 85% of classrooms, 100% of dorms, 100% of libraries, 100% of dining areas, 100% of student union, 10% of common outdoor areas have wireless network access. Students can register for classes online. Administrative functions (other than registration) can be performed online.

CAMPUS LIFE
Environment: Town. **Activities:** Choral groups, concert band, dance, drama/theater, jazz band, marching band, music ensembles, musical theater, pep band, radio station, student government, student newspaper, symphony orchestra, television station, yearbook, Campus Ministries, Student Organization, Model UN. 594 registered organizations, 36 honor societies, 37 religious organizations. 28 fraternities, 16 sororities. **Athletics (Intercollegiate):** *Men:* baseball, basketball, cheerleading, cross-country, football, golf, track/field (outdoor), track/field (indoor). *Women:* basketball, cheerleading, crew/rowing, cross-country, equestrian sports, golf, tennis, track/field (outdoor), track/field (indoor), volleyball. **On-Campus Highlights:** Peters Recreation Complex, Sports Complexes: Wagner Field, Bramlage Coliseum, K-State Student Union, Ahearn Fieldhouse, Beach Museum of Art. **Environmental Initiatives:** A university-wide task force for long-term visioning and planning in all areas of the university, including campus operations, curriculum, research, and external relations/outreach.

ADMISSIONS
Freshman Academic Profile: Average high school GPA 3.5. 24% in top 10% of high school class, 47% in top 25% of high school class, 77% in top 50% of high school class. 80% from public high schools. ACT middle 50% range 22-28. **Basis for Candidate Selection:** *Very important factors considered include:* rigor of secondary school record, class rank, academic GPA, standardized test scores. *Other factors considered include:* recommendation(s). **Freshman Admission Requirements:** High school diploma is required and GED is accepted. *Academic units required:* 4 English, 3 math, 3 science, 3 social studies, 3 academic electives. **Freshman Admission Statistics:** 9,018 applied, 94.38% admitted, 42% enrolled. **Transfer Admission Requirements:** college transcript(s), Minimum college GPA of 2.0 required. Lowest grade transferable C. **General Admission Information:** Application fee $30. Nonfall registration accepted.

COSTS AND FINANCIAL AID
Annual in-state tuition $9,012. Annual out-of-state tuition $23,913. Room and board $9,150. Required fees $862. Average book expense $856. **Required Forms and Deadlines:** FAFSA. **Notification of Awards:** Applicants will be notified of awards on a rolling basis beginning 4/1. **Types of Aid:** *Need-based scholarships/grants:* Federal Pell, FSEOG, State scholarships/grants, Private scholarships, College/university scholarship or grant aid from institutional funds. *Loans:* Direct Subsidized Stafford Loans, Direct Unsubsidized Stafford Loans, Direct PLUS loans, Federal Perkins Loans, College/university loans from institutional funds. *Student Employment:* Federal Work-Study Program available. Institutional employment available. **Financial Aid Statistics:** 54% needy freshmen, 56% needy undergrads receive need-based scholarship or grant aid. 77% freshmen, 52% undergrads receive non-need-based scholarship or grant aid. 66% freshmen, 75% undergrads receive need-based self-help aid. 2% freshmen, 2% undergrads receive athletic scholarships. 57% undergrads borrow to pay for school. Average cumulative indebtedness $27,198. **Criteria for awarding aid:** *Non-need-based:* Academics, Alumni affiliation, Art, Athletics, Leadership, Music/drama, State/district residency.

KANSAS WESLEYAN UNIVERSITY

100 E. Claflin, Salina, KS 67401
Financial Aid Phone: 785-827-5541
Fax: 785-827-0927 • **Website:** www.kwu.edu • **ACT Code:** 1434

This private school, affiliated with the Methodist Church, was founded in 1886. It has a 28-acre campus.

RATINGS
Admissions Selectivity Rating: 79   **Fire Safety Rating:** 80   **Green Rating:** 60*

STUDENTS AND FACULTY
Enrollment: 556. **Student Body:** 57% female, 43% male, 29% out-of-state, 2% international (8 countries represented). Asian 1%, African American 9%,

Caucasian 77%, Hispanic 9%, Native American 1%, Pacific Islander 0%, Two or more races 0%, Race unknown 0%.
Retention and Graduation: 53% freshmen return for sophomore year. 30% grads go on to further study within 1 year. 24% grads pursue arts and sciences degrees. **Faculty:** Student/faculty ratio 15:1. 42 full-time faculty, 67% hold PhDs, 0% are are members of minority groups, 38% are women. 0% of classes are taught by teaching assistants.

ACADEMICS
Degrees: associate, bachelor's, master's. **Classes:** Most classes have 10-19 students. **Special Study Options:** cross-registration, double major, honors program, independent study, internships, student-designed major, study abroad, teacher certification program. **Honors Programs:** Alpha Chi Beta Beta Beta Sigma Pi Sigma Alpha Psi Omega Phi Alpha Theta. **Career Services:** Alumni services, Career assessment, Internships, Regional alumni.

FACILITIES
Housing: Coed dorms, special housing for disabled students, men's dorms, women's dorms, apartments for married students, apartments for single students. 95% of campus accessible to physically diasbled.

CAMPUS LIFE
Environment: Town. **Activities:** Choral groups, concert band, dance, drama/theater, jazz band, literary magazine, music ensembles, musical theater, pep band, student government, student newspaper, symphony orchestra, yearbook, Campus Ministries, Student Organization, Model UN. 20 registered organizations, 5 honor societies, 3 religious organizations. **Athletics (Intercollegiate):** *Men:* baseball, basketball, cheerleading, cross-country, football, golf, racquetball, soccer, tennis, track/field (outdoor). *Women:* basketball, cheerleading, cross-country, golf, racquetball, soccer, softball, tennis, track/field (outdoor), volleyball. **On-Campus Highlights:** NEW Student Center & Gym, Sam's Chapel, dorms, library, Science Hall.

ADMISSIONS
Freshman Academic Profile: Average high school GPA 3.2. 9% in top 10% of high school class, 32% in top 25% of high school class, 62% in top 50% of high school class. **Reported SAT (pre-2016 redesign) scores:** SAT Math middle 50% range 500-590. SAT Critical Reading middle 50% range 420-520. **Concordant SAT scores:** SAT Math middle 50% range 530–610. ACT middle 50% range 22-. **Basis for Candidate Selection:** *Very important factors considered include:* academic GPA, standardized test scores. **Freshman Admission Requirements:** High school diploma is required and GED is accepted. **Freshman Admission Statistics:** 442 applied, 60.63% admitted, 43% enrolled. **Transfer Admission Requirements:** college transcript(s), Minimum college GPA of 2.0 required. Lowest grade transferable D. **General Admission Information:** Application fee $20. Nonfall registration accepted. Admission may be deferred.

COSTS AND FINANCIAL AID
Annual tuition $18,200. Room and board $6,400. Average book expense $800. **Required Forms and Deadlines:** FAFSA. **Types of Aid:** *Need-based scholarships/grants:* Federal Pell, FSEOG, State scholarships/grants, Private scholarships, College/university scholarship or grant aid from institutional funds. *Loans:* Direct Subsidized Stafford Loans, Direct Unsubsidized Stafford Loans, Direct PLUS loans, Federal Perkins Loans. *Student Employment:* Federal Work-Study Program available. Institutional employment available. **Financial Aid Statistics:** freshmen, 0% undergrads receive non-need-based scholarship or grant aid. 0% freshmen, 0% undergrads receive need-based self-help aid. 0% freshmen, 0% undergrads receive athletic scholarships. 75% undergrads receive any aid. **Criteria for awarding aid:** *Need-based:* Academics, Alumni affiliation, Art, Athletics, Music/drama. *Non-need-based:* Academics, Alumni affiliation, Art, Athletics, Music/drama.

KEAN UNIVERSITY

Office of Admissions -Kean Hall, Union, NJ 07083-0411
Phone: 908-737-7100 • **Financial Aid Phone:** 908-737-3190
E-mail: admitme@kean.edu • **CEEB Code:** 2517
Fax: 908-737-7105 • **Website:** www.kean.edu • **ACT Code:** 2582

This public school was founded in 1855. It has a 186-acre campus.

RATINGS
Admissions Selectivity Rating: 72   **Fire Safety Rating:** 98   **Green Rating:** 73

STUDENTS AND FACULTY
Enrollment: 11,656. **Student Body:** 61% female, 39% male, 2% out-of-state, 2% international (50 countries represented). Asian 5%, African American 19%, Caucasian 35%, Hispanic 27%, Native American <1%, Pacific Islander <1%, Two or more races 2%, Race unknown 8%.

Retention and Graduation: 73% freshmen return for sophomore year. 21% freshmen graduate within 4 years. 50% freshmen graduate within 6 years. **Faculty:** Student/faculty ratio 16:1. 331 full-time faculty, 82% hold PhDs, 30% are are members of minority groups, 54% are women. 0% of classes are taught by teaching assistants.

ACADEMICS
Degrees: bachelor's, doctoral/research, master's, post-master's certificate. **Classes:** Most classes have 20-29 students. **Most popular majors:** Business Administration and Management; Psychology; Biology/Biological Sciences. **Special Study Options:** Accelerated program, cooperative education program, distance learning, double major, dual enrollment, English as a Second Language (ESL), honors program, independent study, internships, liberal arts/career combination, study abroad, teacher certification program, weekend college, 2-year bachelor's degree program for RNs, Foreign Transfer Programs, Travelearn. **Honors Programs:** NJCSTME -THE NEW JERSEY CENTER FOR SCIENCE, TECHNOLOGY and MATHEMATICS EDUCATION: 5 year B.S. / M.S. –B.S. / M.A. Scholars programs- There is a critical and immediate need for highly qualified Science and Mathematics teachers in New Jersey, especially in urban school districts. There is also a need for highly trained research technicians to work in the pharmaceutical and biotechnology industries in New Jersey. Kean University created The New Jersey Center for Science, Technology and Mathematics Education (NJCSTME) to respond to both these needs. Through NJCSTME, Kean University offers an innovative and rigorous five year combined bachelor/master degree program to qualified students who are interested either in teaching science or mathematics (teacher track) or in a career in biotechnology or computational mathematics (research track). This program prepares graduates for immediate, well paid employment, and helps future generations of New Jersey students by putting highly qualified science and math teachers in the classroom and researchers in industry laboratories. These are some of the programs important features: It is the only program in New Jersey that offers a core curriculum that links science and math laboratory courses with a team teaching approach. This program is a great opportunity for any student interested in both mathematics and science. -Each student has both an academic advisor and a career mentor. The progress of every student in the program is closely tracked by dedicated faculty who offer personal attention and support. It is a rigorous but highly structured and very supportive program that is designed for ensuring student success. Students participate in research seminars and presentations, team research projects under faculty leadership, and educational outreach enrichment programs at area schools to help them appreciate the career choice between teaching and research. 4 + 4 B.S. / M.D. Scholars Program-Kean University's NJ Center for Science, Technology and Mathematics Education (NJCSTME), Drexel University College of Medicine and St. Peter's University Hospital have partnered to offer a four-plus -four Bachelor of Science / Medical Degree (4 + 4 B.S./M.D.) Scholars Program to highly qualified incoming freshmen. Students who meet all the requirements of this joint program while in college are awarded the B.S. in science and technology degree from NJCSTME at the end of their fourth year, then proceed to enter the first year medical school class at DCOM. Combined degree programs: BA/MA, BA/MPA,BA/MS,BS/MS,BS/MA. **Disability Services:** Special programs offered to physically disabled students, including note-taking services, reader services, tape recorders, tutors. **Career Services:** Alumni network, Alumni services, Career/job search classes, Career assessment, Internships. Interviewing Workshops & Mock Interviews. Each Student writes and prepares their own answer for each interviewing questions, then sets up a meeting for Mock Interview.

FACILITIES
Housing: Coed dorms, special housing for disabled students, apartments for single students, Freshmen Housing, Floor for women-only housing. 100% of campus accessible to physically diasbled. **Special Academic Facilities/Equipment:** Liberty Hall Museum, Holocaust Resource Center, Center for Academic Success, Harwood Arena,Human Rights Institute Wynona Moore Lipman Ethnic Studies Center **Computers:** 100% of classrooms, 100% of dorms, 100% of libraries, 100% of dining areas, 100% of student union, 100% of common outdoor areas have wireless network access. Students can register for classes online. Administrative functions (other than registration) can be performed online.

CAMPUS LIFE
Environment: City. **Activities:** Choral groups, concert band, dance, drama/theater, jazz band, literary magazine, music ensembles, musical theater, pep band, radio station, student government, student newspaper, student-run film society, symphony orchestra, television station, yearbook, Campus Ministries, Student Organization. 143 registered organizations, 23 honor societies, 6 religious organizations. 16 fraternities, 17 sororities. **Athletics (Intercollegiate):** *Men:* baseball, basketball, football, lacrosse, soccer, track/field (outdoor). *Women:* basketball, field hockey, lacrosse, soccer, softball, tennis, track/field (outdoor), volleyball. **On-Campus Highlights:** University Center, Harwood Arena and Football Field, Center for Academic Success (CAS), Kean Hall, One Stop Service Center, Liberty Hall Museum Weather Station Holocaust Resource Center Wynona Moore Lipman Ethnic Studies

Center Planetarium CAS and Vaughn Eames—Art Gallaries. **Environmental Initiatives:** Creation of a bachelor of science degree in sustainability.

ADMISSIONS

Freshman Academic Profile: Average high school GPA 3.1. **Reported SAT (pre-2016 redesign) scores:** SAT Math middle 50% range 420-510. SAT Critical Reading middle 50% range 410-500. **Concordant SAT scores:** SAT Math middle 50% range 460–540. ACT middle 50% range 17-22. Minimum internet-based TOEFL 79. Minimum paper TOEFL 550. **Basis for Candidate Selection:** *Very important factors considered include:* rigor of secondary school record, academic GPA. *Important factors considered include:* standardized test scores. *Other factors considered include:* application essay, recommendation(s), interview, extracurricular activities, talent/ability, character/personal qualities, alumni/ae relation, volunteer work, work experience. **Freshman Admission Requirements:** High school diploma is required and GED is accepted. *Academic units required:* 4 English, 3 math, 2 science, 2 science labs, 2 history, 5 academic electives. *Academic units recommended:* 4 English, 3 math, 2 science, 2 science labs, 2 foreign language, 2 social studies, 2 history, 5 academic electives. **Freshman Admission Statistics:** 8,785 applied, 74.40% admitted, 23% enrolled. **Transfer Admission Requirements:** college transcript(s), statement of good standing from prior institution(s). Minimum college GPA of 2.0 required. Lowest grade transferable C. **General Admission Information:** Application fee $75. Priority deadline 4/30. Regular application deadline 8/15. Nonfall registration accepted. Admission may be deferred for a maximum of 1 semester.

COSTS AND FINANCIAL AID

Required Forms and Deadlines: FAFSA. **Notification of Awards:** Applicants will be notified of awards on a rolling basis beginning 3/1. **Types of Aid:** *Need-based scholarships/grants:* Federal Pell, FSEOG, State scholarships/grants, Private scholarships, College/university scholarship or grant aid from institutional funds. *Loans:* Direct Subsidized Stafford Loans, Direct Unsubsidized Stafford Loans, Direct PLUS loans, Federal Perkins Loans. *Student Employment:* Federal Work-Study Program available. Institutional employment available. **Financial Aid Statistics:** 67% needy freshmen, 70% needy undergrads receive need-based scholarship or grant aid. 17% freshmen, 11% undergrads receive non-need-based scholarship or grant aid. 98% freshmen, 97% undergrads receive need-based self-help aid. 0% freshmen, 0% undergrads receive athletic scholarships. 82% freshmen, 74% undergrads receive any aid. 75% undergrads borrow to pay for school. Average cumulative indebtedness $33,693. **Criteria for awarding aid:** *Non-need-based:* Academics, Art, Leadership, Music/drama.

KEENE STATE COLLEGE

229 Main Street, Keene, NH 03435-2604
Phone: 603-358-2276 • **Financial Aid Phone:** 603-358-2280
E-mail: admissions@keene.edu • **CEEB Code:** 3472
Fax: 603-358-2767 • **Website:** www.keene.edu • **ACT Code:** 2510

This public school was founded in 1909. It has a 150-acre campus.

RATINGS

Admissions Selectivity Rating: 74   **Fire Safety Rating:** 93   **Green Rating:** 94

STUDENTS AND FACULTY

Enrollment: 4,068. **Student Body:** 55% female, 45% male, 57% out-of-state, <1% international (4 countries represented). Asian 1%, African American 1%, Caucasian 87%, Hispanic 4%, Native American <1%, Pacific Islander <1%, Two or more races 2%, Race unknown 5%.
Retention and Graduation: 73% freshmen return for sophomore year. 53% freshmen graduate within 4 years. 63% freshmen graduate within 6 years.
Faculty: 0% of classes are taught by teaching assistants.

ACADEMICS

Degrees: bachelor's, certificate, master's, postbachelor's certificate, post-master's certificate. **Classes:** Most classes have 10-19 students. **Most popular majors:** Elementary Education and Teaching; Occupational Safety and Health Technology/Technician; Psychology. **Special Study Options:** cooperative education program, double major, English as a Second Language (ESL), exchange student program (domestic), honors program, independent study, internships, liberal arts/career combination, student-designed major, study abroad, teacher certification program. **Honors Programs:** The Keene State College Honors Program; National Society of Collegiate Scholars in addition to Honors Programs in: Psychology, Safety Studies. **Disability Services:** Special programs offered to physically disabled students, including note-taking services, reader services, tape recorders, tutors. **Career Services:** Alumni network, Alumni services, Career/job search classes, Career assessment, Internships.

Experiential learning/service learning and commitment to the community. Students apply what they learn from their course work by working in the local community. These real-life working situations enhance student learning and help students meet their course goals.

FACILITIES

Housing: Coed dorms, women's dorms, fraternity/sorority housing, apartments for married students, apartments for single students, Wellness Housing, Theme Housing, Honors, Language/Culture, Leadership, Quiet Study, Substance Free. 98% of campus accessible to physically diasbled. **Special Academic Facilities/Equipment:** Thorne-Sagendorph Art gallery, Redfern Arts Center, Recreational Center,Science Center, Mason Library, Media Arts Center, Cohen Center for Holocaust Studies, Center for Writing, Child Development Center **Computers:** 10% of classrooms, 100% of libraries, 50% of dining areas, 80% of student union, have wireless network access. Students can register for classes online. Administrative functions (other than registration) can be performed online.

CAMPUS LIFE

Environment: Village. **Activities:** Choral groups, concert band, dance, drama/theater, jazz band, literary magazine, music ensembles, musical theater, radio station, student government, student newspaper, student-run film society, television station, yearbook, Campus Ministries, Student Organization. 100 registered organizations, 21 honor societies, 4 religious organizations. 4 fraternities, 5 sororities. **Athletics (Intercollegiate):** *Men:* baseball, basketball, cheerleading, cross-country, diving, lacrosse, soccer, swimming, track/field (outdoor), track/field (indoor). *Women:* basketball, cheerleading, cross-country, diving, field hockey, lacrosse, soccer, softball, swimming, track/field (outdoor), track/field (indoor), volleyball. **On-Campus Highlights:** Science Building, Mason Library, Young Student Center, Night Owl Cafe, Arts Center on Brickyard Pond, Spaulding Gymnasium, Zorn Dining Commons new facility, New Pondside residence hall,Bodyworks Fitness Center, New Alumni Center in progress. **Environmental Initiatives:** LEED Silver residence hall (awarded 2008).

ADMISSIONS

Freshman Academic Profile: Average high school GPA 3.0. 5% in top 10% of high school class, 28% in top 25% of high school class, 58% in top 50% of high school class. **Reported SAT (pre-2016 redesign) scores:** SAT Math middle 50% range 440-530. SAT Critical Reading middle 50% range 440-540. SAT Writing middle 50% range 430-530. **Concordant SAT scores:** SAT EBRW middle 50% 490–590. SAT Math middle 50% range 480–560. ACT middle 50% range 18-24. Minimum internet-based TOEFL 61. Minimum paper TOEFL 550. **Basis for Candidate Selection:** *Important factors considered include:* rigor of secondary school record, academic GPA, application essay, recommendation(s). *Other factors considered include:* class rank, standardized test scores, extracurricular activities, talent/ability, character/personal qualities, first generation, alumni/ae relation, racial/ethnic status, volunteer work, work experience, level of applicant's interest. **Freshman Admission Requirements:** High school diploma is required and GED is accepted. *Academic units required:* 4 English, 3 math, 3 science, 2 social studies, 2 academic electives. **Freshman Admission Statistics:** 5,466 applied, 82.53% admitted, 23% enrolled. **Transfer Admission Requirements:** High school transcript, college transcript(s), essay or personal statement, statement of good standing from prior institution(s). Minimum college GPA of 2.0 required. Lowest grade transferable C. **General Admission Information:** Application fee $50. Regular application deadline 4/1. Nonfall registration accepted. Admission may be deferred for a maximum of 1 year.

COSTS AND FINANCIAL AID

Average book expense $900. **Required Forms and Deadlines:** FAFSA. **Types of Aid:** *Need-based scholarships/grants:* Federal Pell, FSEOG, State scholarships/grants, Private scholarships, College/university scholarship or grant aid from institutional funds. *Loans:* Direct Subsidized Stafford Loans, Direct Unsubsidized Stafford Loans, Direct PLUS loans, Federal Perkins Loans, College/university loans from institutional funds. *Student Employment:* Federal Work-Study Program available. Institutional employment available. **Financial Aid Statistics:** 70% needy freshmen, 70% needy undergrads receive need-based scholarship or grant aid. 65% freshmen, 50% undergrads receive non-need-based scholarship or grant aid. 89% freshmen, 91% undergrads receive need-based self-help aid. 0% freshmen, 0% undergrads receive athletic scholarships. 94% freshmen, 89% undergrads receive any aid. 84% undergrads borrow to pay for school. Average cumulative indebtedness $41,016. **Criteria for awarding aid:** *Need-based:* Alumni affiliation. *Non-need-based:* Academics, Alumni affiliation, Art, Music/drama.

KENDALL COLLEGE OF ART AND DESIGN OF FERRIS STATE UNIVERSITY

17 Fountain Street NW, Grand Rapids, MI 49503-3002
Phone: 616-451-2787 • **Financial Aid Phone:** 616-451-2787
E-mail: brittons@ferris.edu • **CEEB Code:** 1983
Fax: 616-831-9689 • **Website:** www.kcad.edu • **ACT Code:** 1983

This public school was founded in 1928. It has a 2-acre campus.

RATINGS
Admissions Selectivity Rating: 70   **Fire Safety Rating:** 60*   **Green Rating:** 60*

STUDENTS AND FACULTY
Enrollment: 1,141. **Student Body:** 13% out-of-state, 0% international (15 countries represented). Asian 0%, African American 0%, Caucasian 0%, Hispanic 0%, Native American 0%, Pacific Islander 0%, Two or more races 0%, Race unknown 0%.
Retention and Graduation: 12% grads go on to further study within 1 year. 12% grads pursue arts and sciences degrees. **Faculty:** Student/faculty ratio 15:1. 50 full-time faculty, 6% hold PhDs, 4% are are members of minority groups, 0% 0% of classes are taught by teaching assistants.

ACADEMICS
Degrees: bachelor's, master's. **Most popular majors:** Interior Design; Graphic Design; Illustration. **Special Study Options:** cooperative education program, double major, dual enrollment, independent study, internships, liberal arts/career combination, study abroad, teacher certification program. **Disability Services:** Special programs offered to physically disabled students, including note-taking services, reader services, tape recorders, tutors. **Career Services:** Alumni network, Alumni services, Career/job search classes, Internships, Regional alumni.

FACILITIES
Housing: apartments for married students, apartments for single students, Fabulous historic district with rental apartments nearby. 100% of campus accessible to physically diasbled. **Computers:** 100% of classrooms, 100% of libraries, 100% of student union, have wireless network access. Students can register for classes online. Administrative functions (other than registration) can be performed online. Undergraduates are required to own a computer.

CAMPUS LIFE
Environment: Metropolis. **Activities:** 12 registered organizations, 1 religious organization. **On-Campus Highlights:** Studio Spaces, Studio Class Rooms, Library, Student Commons, Labs.

ADMISSIONS
Freshman Academic Profile: Average high school GPA 3.1. 10% in top 10% of high school class, 20% in top 25% of high school class, 75% in top 50% of high school class. Minimum internet-based TOEFL 61. Minimum paper TOEFL 500. **Basis for Candidate Selection:** *Very important factors considered include:* rigor of secondary school record, academic GPA, standardized test scores, application essay, talent/ability. *Important factors considered include:* interview, character/personal qualities. *Other factors considered include:* class rank, recommendation(s), extracurricular activities. **Freshman Admission Requirements:** High school diploma is required and GED is accepted. **Freshman Admission Statistics:** 338 applied, 78.11% admitted, 91% enrolled. **Transfer Admission Requirements:** High school transcript, college transcript(s), essay or personal statement, Lowest grade transferable C. **General Admission Information:** Application fee $30. Nonfall registration accepted. Admission may be deferred for a maximum of one semester.

COSTS AND FINANCIAL AID
Annual in-state tuition $12,674. Annual out-of-state tuition $19,220. Required fees $420. Average book expense $3,604. **Required Forms and Deadlines:** FAFSA. **Notification of Awards:** Applicants will be notified of awards on a rolling basis beginning 4/1. **Types of Aid:** *Need-based scholarships/grants:* Federal Pell, FSEOG, State scholarships/grants, Private scholarships, College/university scholarship or grant aid from institutional funds. *Loans:* Direct Subsidized Stafford Loans, Direct Unsubsidized Stafford Loans, Direct PLUS loans, Federal Perkins Loans. *Student Employment:* Federal Work-Study Program available. Institutional employment available. **Criteria for awarding aid:** *Non-need-based:* Academics, Alumni affiliation, Art.

KENNESAW STATE UNIVERSITY

3391 Town Point Drive, Suite 1000, Kennesaw, GA 30144-5591
Phone: 770-423-6300 • **Financial Aid Phone:** 770-423-6074
E-mail: ksuadmit@kennesaw.edu • **CEEB Code:** 5359
Fax: 470-578-9169 • **Website:** http://www.kennesaw.edu • **ACT Code:** 833

This public school was founded in 1963. It has a 384-acre campus.

RATINGS
Admissions Selectivity Rating: 85   **Fire Safety Rating:** 92   **Green Rating:** 98

STUDENTS AND FACULTY
Enrollment: 31,613. **Student Body:** 48% female, 52% male, 8% out-of-state, 2% international (143 countries represented). Asian 5%, African American 21%, Caucasian 57%, Hispanic 9%, Native American <1%, Pacific Islander <1%, Two or more races 4%, Race unknown 2%.
Retention and Graduation: 80% freshmen return for sophomore year. 13% freshmen graduate within 4 years. 42% freshmen graduate within 6 years. **Faculty:** Student/faculty ratio 20:1. 1,119 full-time faculty, 78% hold PhDs, 24% are are members of minority groups, 50% are women. 0% of classes are taught by teaching assistants.

ACADEMICS
Degrees: bachelor's, certificate, doctoral/research, master's, postbachelor's certifiate, post-master's certificate. **Classes:** Most classes have 20-29 students. Most lab/discussion sessions have 20-29 students. **Most popular majors:** Registered Nursing/Registered Nurse; Biology/Biological Sciences; Psychology. **Special Study Options:** cooperative education program, cross-registration, distance learning, double major, English as a Second Language (ESL), honors program, internships, study abroad, teacher certification program, weekend college. **Honors Programs:** The Honors Program at KSU provides a unique opportunity for exceptional students to customize their college experience. Through colloquia, seminars and directed studies, honor students can tailor their experience to meet their needs and interest. Instead of being restricted to the guidelines of a course catalog, students are encouraged to think outside the box and stretch themselves in academic directions that appeal to them. To guide them in their journey, a faculty mentor is assigned to each student. Most students only know faculty in a classroom setting, but honor students develop a one-on-one relationship designed to enhance their collegiate experience. **Disability Services:** Special programs offered to physically disabled students, including note-taking services, reader services, tape recorders, tutors. **Career Services:** Alumni network, Alumni services, Internships. The Department of Career Planning & Development at Kennesaw State shares in the mission of the University by educating and facilitating the career development of students and alumni, in preparation for the ever-changing work environment. Through strategic engagement with internal and external partners, we provide access to services, programs, and experiences that develop competent and competitive professionals who will contribute to local and global communities.

FACILITIES
Housing: apartments for single students. 100% of campus accessible to physically diasbled. **Computers:** 100% of classrooms, 100% of libraries, 100% of dining areas, 100% of student union, 5% of common outdoor areas have wireless network access. Students can register for classes online. Administrative functions (other than registration) can be performed online.

CAMPUS LIFE
Environment: Town. **Activities:** Choral groups, concert band, dance, drama/theater, jazz band, music ensembles, musical theater, radio station, student government, student newspaper, symphony orchestra, Campus Ministries, Student Organization, Model UN. 151 registered organizations, 20 honor societies, 18 religious organizations. 10 fraternities, 8 sororities. **Athletics (Intercollegiate):** *Men:* baseball, basketball, cross-country, golf, tennis, track/field (outdoor), track/field (indoor). *Women:* basketball, cheerleading, cross-country, golf, soccer, softball, tennis, track/field (outdoor), track/field (indoor), volleyball. **On-Campus Highlights:** Student Dining Hall, Lounge in Student Center, Game Room in Student Center, Student Recreation Center, Campus Green. **Environmental Initiatives:** Commitment by KSU President Daniel S. Papp to reduce the university's carbon footprint, in line with a national coalition of college and university presidents.

ADMISSIONS
Freshman Academic Profile: Average high school GPA 3.3. 21% in top 10% of high school class, 53% in top 25% of high school class, 81% in top 50% of high school class. **Reported SAT (pre-2016 redesign) scores:** SAT Math middle 50% range 500-590. SAT Critical Reading middle 50% range 500-590. SAT Writing middle 50% range 470-570. **Concordant SAT scores:** SAT EBRW middle 50% 540–640. SAT Math middle 50% range 530–610. ACT middle 50% range 21-26. Minimum internet-based TOEFL 79. **Basis for Candidate Selection:** *Very important factors considered include:* academic

GPA, standardized test scores. **Freshman Admission Requirements:** High school diploma is required and GED is not accepted. *Academic units required:* 4 English, 4 math, 4 science, 2 science labs, 2 foreign language, 3 social studies. **Freshman Admission Statistics:** 15,122 applied, 58.50% admitted, 60% enrolled. **Transfer Admission Requirements:** college transcript(s), Minimum college GPA of 2.0 required. Lowest grade transferable D. **General Admission Information:** Application fee $40. Priority deadline 10/30. Regular application deadline 5/6. Nonfall registration accepted. Admission may be deferred for a maximum of 12 months.

COSTS AND FINANCIAL AID
Required Forms and Deadlines: FAFSA. **Notification of Awards:** Applicants will be notified of awards on a rolling basis beginning 4/1. **Types of Aid:** *Need-based scholarships/grants:* Federal Pell, FSEOG, State scholarships/grants, Private scholarships, College/university scholarship or grant aid from institutional funds. *Loans:* Direct Subsidized Stafford Loans, Direct Unsubsidized Stafford Loans, Direct PLUS loans, Federal Perkins Loans. *Student Employment:* Federal Work-Study Program available. Institutional employment available. **Financial Aid Statistics:** 58% needy undergrads receive need-based scholarship or grant aid. 77% freshmen, 50% undergrads receive non-need-based scholarship or grant aid. 73% freshmen, 77% undergrads receive need-based self-help aid. 0% freshmen, 0% undergrads receive athletic scholarships. 63% undergrads borrow to pay for school. Average cumulative indebtedness $25,123. **Criteria for awarding aid:** *Need-based:* Academics, Art, Athletics, Job skills, Leadership, Minority status. *Non-need-based:* Academics, Alumni affiliation, Art, Athletics, Job skills, Leadership, Minority status, Music/drama, State/district residency.

KENT STATE UNIVERSITY-KENT CAMPUS

161 Schwartz Center, Kent, OH 44242-0001
Phone: 330-672-2444 • **Financial Aid Phone:** 330-672-2972
E-mail: kentadm@kent.edu • **CEEB Code:** 1367
Fax: 330-672-2499 • **Website:** http://www.kent.edu • **ACT Code:** 3284

This public school was founded in 1910. It has a 1200-acre campus.

RATINGS
Admissions Selectivity Rating: 77   **Fire Safety Rating:** 92   **Green Rating:** 81

STUDENTS AND FACULTY
Enrollment: 22,907. **Student Body:** 61% female, 39% male, 14% out-of-state, 5% international (75 countries represented). Asian 2%, African American 9%, Caucasian 75%, Hispanic 3%, Native American <1%, Pacific Islander <1%, Two or more races 4%, Race unknown 3%.
Retention and Graduation: 82% freshmen return for sophomore year. 46% freshmen graduate within 4 years. 80% freshmen graduate within 6 years. 23% grads go on to further study within 1 year. **Faculty:** Student/faculty ratio 21:1. 973 full-time faculty, 0% hold PhDs, 13% are are members of minority groups, 53% are women. 9% of classes are taught by teaching assistants.

ACADEMICS
Degrees: bachelor's, certificate, doctoral/professional, doctoral/research, doctoral, master's, postbachelor's certifiate, post-master's certificate. **Classes:** Most classes have 20-29 students. **Most popular majors:** Psychology; Registered Nursing/Registered Nurse; Fashion Merchandising. **Special Study Options:** Accelerated program, cooperative education program, cross-registration, distance learning, double major, dual enrollment, English as a Second Language (ESL), exchange student program (domestic), external degree program, honors program, independent study, internships, liberal arts/career combination, student-designed major, study abroad, teacher certification program, weekend college. **Honors Programs:** Honors College membership at Kent State University is open to all majors and hosts approximately 1,350 students at the Kent Campus and five Regional Campuses. Honors College classes emphasize the intellectual value in the pursuit of knowledge. Every effort is made to show students the connections between disciplines. Honors College classes are small, taught by carefully chosen faculty, and emphasize students" active involvement in their learning. Plentiful opportunities for individual study, including the Senior Honors Thesis/Project give students exciting experiences in following their intellectual curiosity. An Honors College residence complex, state-of-the-art facilities, experiences including study abroad/away opportunities and cultural programming all support bright and motivated students seeking an intellectual home within the larger university. Combined degree programs: BA/MD, BA/MA, BBA/MBA; BS/MBA Fashion Merch; BSN/MSN; BS/MPH. **Disability Services:** Special programs offered to physically disabled students, including note-taking services, reader services, tape recorders, tutors. **Career Services:** Alumni network, Alumni services, Career/job search classes, Career assessment, Internships,

Regional alumni. The entrepreneurship initiative at Kent State University is designed to give students the opportunities, educational training, and real life experiences they need to develop their entrepreneurial spirit. Through a range of hands-on activities afforded by class projects, working in the John S. Brinzo Entrepreneurship Lab with entrepreneurs-in-residence, pitching concepts in business idea competitions, talking with entrepreneurs at the E (Entrepreneurship) Extravaganza and Solomon speaker series events, participating in entrepreneurship immersion week during the summer, working in a student-run business or initiating one of their own, KSU students can experience the world of entrepreneurship directly and meaningfully. These rich experiences help us develop individuals who will have the disposition, skills, abilities, and knowledge needed to be competitive in the world of business upon graduation.

FACILITIES
Housing: Coed dorms, special housing for disabled students, men's dorms, special housing for international students, women's dorms, fraternity/sorority housing, apartments for married students, apartments for single students. 95% of campus accessible to physically diasbled. **Special Academic Facilities/Equipment:** Fashion museum, herbarium, liquid crystal institute, planetarium, airport. **Computers:** 90% of classrooms, 20% of dorms, 40% of libraries, 70% of dining areas, 100% of student union, 10% of common outdoor areas have wireless network access. Students can register for classes online. Administrative functions (other than registration) can be performed online.

CAMPUS LIFE
Environment: Town. **Activities:** Choral groups, concert band, dance, drama/theater, jazz band, literary magazine, marching band, music ensembles, pep band, radio station, student government, student newspaper, television station, Campus Ministries, Student Organization. 214 registered organizations, 10 honor societies, 15 religious organizations. 17 fraternities, 6 sororities. **Athletics (Intercollegiate):** *Men:* baseball, basketball, cheerleading, cross-country, football, golf, track/field (outdoor), track/field (indoor), wrestling. *Women:* basketball, cheerleading, cross-country, field hockey, football, golf, gymnastics, soccer, softball, track/field (outdoor), track/field (indoor), volleyball. **On-Campus Highlights:** Student Recreation and Wellness Center, Kent State University Museum, Kent Student Center Plaza, Pan African Center Gallery, May 4 Memorial. **Environmental Initiatives:** Energy production on campus including a combined heat and power plant and a solar array installed in spring 2012 as part of our renewable energy master plan.

ADMISSIONS
Freshman Academic Profile: Average high school GPA 3.4. 15% in top 10% of high school class, 41% in top 25% of high school class, 77% in top 50% of high school class. **Reported SAT (pre-2016 redesign) scores:** SAT Math middle 50% range 480-580. SAT Critical Reading middle 50% range 470-580. SAT Writing middle 50% range 440-560. **Concordant SAT scores:** SAT EBRW middle 50% 510–630. SAT Math middle 50% range 510–600. ACT middle 50% range 21-25. Minimum internet-based TOEFL 71. Minimum paper TOEFL 525. **Basis for Candidate Selection:** *Very important factors considered include:* academic GPA, standardized test scores. *Important factors considered include:* rigor of secondary school record. *Other factors considered include:* application essay, recommendation(s), interview, talent/ability, level of applicant's interest. **Freshman Admission Requirements:** High school diploma is required and GED is accepted. *Academic units recommended:* 4 English, 4 math, 3 science, 2 science labs, 2 foreign language, 3 social studies, 1 visual/performing arts. **Freshman Admission Statistics:** 16,145 applied, 85.36% admitted, 32% enrolled. **Transfer Admission Requirements:** college transcript(s), Minimum college GPA of 2.0 required. Lowest grade transferable C. **General Admission Information:** Application fee $45. Priority deadline 3/1. Regular application deadline 5/1. Nonfall registration accepted. Admission may be deferred for a maximum of 1 year.

COSTS AND FINANCIAL AID
Required Forms and Deadlines: FAFSA. **Notification of Awards:** Applicants will be notified of awards on or about 3/15. **Types of Aid:** *Need-based scholarships/grants:* Federal Pell, FSEOG, State scholarships/grants, Private scholarships, College/university scholarship or grant aid from institutional funds. *Loans:* Direct Subsidized Stafford Loans, Direct Unsubsidized Stafford Loans, Direct PLUS loans, Federal Perkins Loans, Federal Nursing Loans, State Loans, College/university loans from institutional funds. *Student Employment:* Federal Work-Study Program available. Institutional employment available. **Financial Aid Statistics:** 52% needy freshmen, 54% needy undergrads receive need-based scholarship or grant aid. 74% freshmen, 55% undergrads receive non-need-based scholarship or grant aid. 80% freshmen, 83% undergrads receive need-based self-help aid. 1% freshmen, 1% undergrads receive athletic scholarships. 76% undergrads borrow to pay for school. Average cumulative indebtedness $33,234. **Criteria for awarding aid:** *Need-based:* Academics, Alumni affiliation, Athletics, Leadership, Minority status. *Non-need-based:* Academics, Alumni affiliation, Art, Athletics, Leadership, Minority status, Music/drama, State/district residency.

KENTUCKY STATE UNIVERSITY

400 East Main Street, Frankfort, KY 40601
Phone: 502-597-6813 • **Financial Aid Phone:** 502-597-5960
E-mail: admissions@kysu.edu • **CEEB Code:** 1368
Fax: 502-597-5814 • **Website:** www.kysu.edu • **ACT Code:** 1516

This public school was founded in 1886. It has a 915-acre campus.

RATINGS

Admissions Selectivity Rating: 80   **Fire Safety Rating:** 97   **Green Rating:** 75

STUDENTS AND FACULTY

Enrollment: 1,286. **Student Body:** 59% female, 41% male, 32% out-of-state, <1% international (9 countries represented). Asian 1%, African American 57%, Caucasian 27%, Hispanic 3%, Native American <1%, Pacific Islander <1%, Two or more races 2%, Race unknown 9%.
Retention and Graduation: 60% freshmen return for sophomore year. 6% freshmen graduate within 4 years. 22% freshmen graduate within 6 years.
Faculty: Student/faculty ratio 11:1. 121 full-time faculty, 79% hold PhDs, 42% are are members of minority groups, 35% are women. 0% of classes are taught by teaching assistants.

ACADEMICS

Degrees: associate, bachelor's, doctoral/professional, master's, terminal, transfer. **Classes:** Most classes have 20-29 students. Most lab/discussion sessions have fewer than 10 students. **Most popular majors:** Registered Nursing/Registered Nurse; Business/Commerce; Criminal Justice/Safety Studies. **Special Study Options:** cooperative education program, distance learning, double major, dual enrollment, English as a Second Language (ESL), honors program, independent study, internships, liberal arts/career combination, student-designed major, study abroad, teacher certification program. **Honors Programs:** The Whitney Young School of Honors and Liberal Studies. The Honors Program is an integrated liberal arts program that emphasizes student discussion of excellent books. Combined degree programs: Applied Math/Pre-engineering joint program. **Disability Services:** Special programs offered to physically disabled students, including note-taking services, reader services, tape recorders, tutors. **Career Services:** Alumni network, Alumni services, Career/job search classes, Career assessment, Internships, Regional alumni. The Cooperative Education and Internship program gives our undergraduates hands on experience in their major field.

FACILITIES

Housing: Coed dorms, men's dorms, women's dorms. 100% of campus accessible to physically diasbled. **Special Academic Facilities/Equipment:** Art gallery, nutrition lab, agriculture research building, research farm, fish hatchery, electron microscope. **Computers:** 100% of classrooms, 100% of dorms, 100% of libraries, 100% of dining areas, 100% of student union, 60% of common outdoor areas have wireless network access. Students can register for classes online. Administrative functions (other than registration) can be performed online.

CAMPUS LIFE

Environment: Town. **Activities:** Choral groups, concert band, dance, drama/theater, jazz band, marching band, music ensembles, musical theater, opera, pep band, student government, student newspaper, Campus Ministries, Student Organization. 30 registered organizations, 5 honor societies, 4 religious organizations. 6 fraternities, 5 sororities. **Athletics (Intercollegiate):** *Men:* baseball, basketball, cross-country, football, golf, track/field (outdoor), track/field (indoor). *Women:* basketball, cross-country, softball, track/field (outdoor), track/field (indoor), volleyball. **On-Campus Highlights:** Jackson Hall, Carl Hill Student Center, William Exum Building, Whitney Young Residence Hall, Hume Hall. **Environmental Initiatives:** Energy efficient fixtures for power & water.

ADMISSIONS

Freshman Academic Profile: 4% in top 10% of high school class, 26% in top 25% of high school class, 58% in top 50% of high school class. **Reported SAT (pre-2016 redesign) scores:** SAT Math middle 50% range 450-570. SAT Critical Reading middle 50% range 380-480. SAT Writing middle 50% range 380-480. **Concordant SAT scores:** SAT EBRW middle 50% 430-540. SAT Math middle 50% range 490-590. ACT middle 50% range 17-22. Minimum internet-based TOEFL 70. Minimum paper TOEFL 525. **Basis for Candidate Selection:** *Very important factors considered include:* academic GPA, standardized test scores. *Important factors considered include:* rigor of secondary school record, class rank, extracurricular activities, first generation, alumni/ae relation, level of applicant's interest. *Other factors considered include:* recommendation(s), character/personal qualities, geographical residence, state residency, volunteer work, work experience. **Freshman Admission Requirements:** High school diploma is required and GED is accepted.

Academic units required: 4 English, 3 math, 3 science, 2 foreign language, 3 social studies, 3 history. **Freshman Admission Statistics:** 4,666 applied, 38.30% admitted, 12% enrolled. **Transfer Admission Requirements:** college transcript(s), Minimum college GPA of 2.0 required. Lowest grade transferable C. **General Admission Information:** Application fee $30. Priority deadline 11/1. Regular application deadline 7/1. Nonfall registration accepted. Admission may be deferred.

COSTS AND FINANCIAL AID

Annual in-state tuition $7,364. Annual out-of-state tuition $17,666. Room and board $6,690. Required fees $390. Average book expense $1,300. **Required Forms and Deadlines:** FAFSA. **Notification of Awards:** Applicants will be notified of awards on a rolling basis beginning 3/15. **Types of Aid:** *Need-based scholarships/grants:* Federal Pell, FSEOG, State scholarships/grants, College/university scholarship or grant aid from institutional funds. *Loans:* Direct Subsidized Stafford Loans, Direct Unsubsidized Stafford Loans, Direct PLUS loans, Federal Perkins Loans. *Student Employment:* Federal Work-Study Program available. Institutional employment available. **Financial Aid Statistics:** 95% needy freshmen, 89% needy undergrads receive need-based scholarship or grant aid. 4% freshmen, 3% undergrads receive non-need-based scholarship or grant aid. 69% freshmen, 76% undergrads receive need-based self-help aid. 3% freshmen, 2% undergrads receive athletic scholarships. 94% freshmen, 83% undergrads receive any aid. 66% undergrads borrow to pay for school. Average cumulative indebtedness $32,813. **Criteria for awarding aid:** *Non-need-based:* Academics, Alumni affiliation, Art, Athletics, Leadership, Music/drama.

KENTUCKY WESLEYAN COLLEGE

3000 Frederica Street, Owensboro, KY 42301
Phone: 270-852-3120 • **Financial Aid Phone:** 270-852-3130
E-mail: http://www.kwc.edu • **CEEB Code:** 1369
Fax: 270-852-3133 • **Website:** www.kwc.edu • **ACT Code:** 1518

This private school, affiliated with the Methodist Church, was founded in 1858. It has a 52-acre campus.

RATINGS

Admissions Selectivity Rating: 81   **Fire Safety Rating:** 85   **Green Rating:** 60*

STUDENTS AND FACULTY

Enrollment: 650. **Student Body:** 48% female, 52% male, 28% out-of-state, 2% international (8 countries represented). Asian 0%, African American 12%, Caucasian 74%, Hispanic 2%, Native American <1%, Pacific Islander 0%, Two or more races 0%, Race unknown 10%.
Retention and Graduation: 54% freshmen return for sophomore year. 29% freshmen graduate within 4 years. 25% grads go on to further study within 1 year. **Faculty:** Student/faculty ratio 12:1. 48 full-time faculty, 71% hold PhDs, 6% are are members of minority groups, 48% are women. 0% of classes are taught by teaching assistants.

ACADEMICS

Degrees: bachelor's. **Classes:** Most classes have 10-19 students. Most lab/discussion sessions have 10-19 students. **Most popular majors:** Business/Commerce; Biology/Biological Sciences; Criminal Justice/Safety Studies. **Special Study Options:** double major, independent study, internships, liberal arts/career combination, student-designed major, study abroad, teacher certification program, Online Program. Combined degree programs: University of Louisville and Auburn University. **Disability Services:** Special programs offered to physically disabled students, including note-taking services, tutors. **Career Services:** Alumni network, Alumni services, Career/job search classes, Career assessment, Internships, Regional alumni.

FACILITIES

Housing: Coed dorms, special housing for disabled students, men's dorms, women's dorms, fraternity/sorority housing, apartments for married students, apartments for single students. 100% of campus accessible to physically diasbled. **Special Academic Facilities/Equipment:** President's Hall/Library Learning Center Ralph Center for Fine Arts. Woodward Health and Recreation Center. Yu Hak Hahn Center for the Sciences. **Computers:** 100% of classrooms, 100% of dorms, 100% of libraries, 100% of dining areas, 100% of student union, have wireless network access. Students can register for classes online. Administrative functions (other than registration) can be performed online.

CAMPUS LIFE

Environment: Town. **Activities:** Choral groups, dance, drama/theater, literary magazine, music ensembles, pep band, radio station, student government, student newspaper, yearbook, Campus Ministries. 42 registered organizations,

6 honor societies, 6 religious organizations. 3 fraternities, 2 sororities. **Athletics (Intercollegiate): Men:** baseball, basketball, cheerleading, cross-country, football, golf, soccer. **Women:** basketball, cheerleading, cross-country, golf, soccer, softball, tennis, volleyball. **On-Campus Highlights:** Winchester Center-New Campus Center, Ralph Fine Arts Center, Yu Hak Hahn Center for the Sciences, Woodward Health and Recreation Center, The Quad, For virtual tours, visit www.kwc.edu.

ADMISSIONS

Freshman Academic Profile: Average high school GPA 3.2. 20% in top 10% of high school class, 44% in top 25% of high school class, 68% in top 50% of high school class. 90% from public high schools. **Reported SAT (pre-2016 redesign) scores:** SAT Math middle 50% range 410-555. SAT Critical Reading middle 50% range 410-540. SAT Writing middle 50% range 450-660. **Concordant SAT scores:** SAT EBRW middle 50% 480–650. SAT Math middle 50% range 450–580. ACT middle 50% range 19-25. Minimum paper TOEFL 500. **Basis for Candidate Selection:** *Very important factors considered include:* academic GPA, standardized test scores. *Important factors considered include:* rigor of secondary school record, interview, extracurricular activities. *Other factors considered include:* class rank, recommendation(s), talent/ability, character/personal qualities, alumni/ae relation, volunteer work, work experience, level of applicant's interest. **Freshman Admission Requirements:** High school diploma is required and GED is accepted. *Academic units required:* 4 English, 3 math, 3 science, 3 social studies. *Academic units recommended:* 2 foreign language. **Freshman Admission Statistics:** 1,006 applied, 67.10% admitted, 24% enrolled. **Transfer Admission Requirements:** college transcript(s), Minimum college GPA of 2.0 required. Lowest grade transferable C. **General Admission Information:** Nonfall registration accepted. Admission may be deferred for a maximum of 12 mo.

COSTS AND FINANCIAL AID

Annual tuition $21,400. Room and board $7,800. Required fees $600. Average book expense $1,400. **Required Forms and Deadlines:** FAFSA. **Notification of Awards:** Applicants will be notified of awards on a rolling basis beginning 2/15. **Types of Aid:** *Need-based scholarships/grants:* Federal Pell, FSEOG, State scholarships/grants, Private scholarships, College/university scholarship or grant aid from institutional funds. *Loans:* Direct Subsidized Stafford Loans, Direct Unsubsidized Stafford Loans, Direct PLUS loans, Federal Perkins Loans, College/university loans from institutional funds. *Student Employment:* Federal Work-Study Program available. Institutional employment available. **Financial Aid Statistics:** 99% needy freshmen, 98% needy undergrads receive need-based scholarship or grant aid. 8% freshmen, 11% undergrads receive non-need-based scholarship or grant aid. 81% freshmen, 77% undergrads receive need-based self-help aid. 0% freshmen, 0% undergrads receive athletic scholarships. 99% freshmen, 85% undergrads receive any aid. **Criteria for awarding aid:** *Need-based:* Academics, Alumni affiliation, Art, Athletics, Leadership, Music/drama, Religious affiliation. *Non-need-based:* Academics, Alumni affiliation, Art, Athletics, Leadership, Music/drama, Religious affiliation, State/district residency.

KENYON COLLEGE

Kenyon College Admissions Office, Gambier, OH 43022-9623
Phone: 740-427-5776 • **Financial Aid Phone:** 740-427-5240
E-mail: admissions@kenyon.edu • **CEEB Code:** 1370
Fax: 740-427-5770 • **Website:** www.kenyon.edu • **ACT Code:** 3286

This private school was founded in 1824. It has a 1200-acre campus.

RATINGS

Admissions Selectivity Rating: 96   **Fire Safety Rating:** 88   **Green Rating:** 80

STUDENTS AND FACULTY

Enrollment: 1,688. **Student Body:** 55% female, 45% male, 85% out-of-state, 5% international (41 countries represented). Asian 4%, African American 3%, Caucasian 73%, Hispanic 5%, Native American 0%, Pacific Islander 0%, Two or more races 8%, Race unknown 3%.
Retention and Graduation: 92% freshmen return for sophomore year. 89% freshmen graduate within 4 years. 90% freshmen graduate within 6 years. 19% grads go on to further study within 1 year. **Faculty:** Student/faculty ratio 9:1. 166 full-time faculty, 99% hold PhDs, 21% are are members of minority groups, 43% are women. 0% of classes are taught by teaching assistants.

ACADEMICS

Degrees: bachelor's. **Classes:** Most classes have 10-19 students. **Most popular majors:** Economics; Psychology; English Language and Literature. **Special Study Options:** Accelerated program, double major, exchange student program (domestic), honors program, independent study, internships, liberal arts/career combination, student-designed major, study abroad. **Honors Programs:** Honors programs are offered by all departmental and interdepartmental majors. Combined degree programs: 3-2 Engineering, Education, Environmental Studies. **Disability Services:** Special programs offered to physically disabled students, including note-taking services, reader services, tape recorders, tutors. **Career Services:** Alumni network, Alumni services, Career/job search classes, Career assessment, Internships, Regional alumni. Our Extern program enables students to explore career options through an experiential week of job-showing during winter or spring breaks. This often helps students decide what internships and/or career paths they'd like to pursue while building a network of contacts.

FACILITIES

Housing: Coed dorms, special housing for disabled students, women's dorms, fraternity/sorority housing, apartments for single students, Wellness Housing, Theme Housing, Housing options for community service, substance-free, wellness, wing, Kosher, twp. fire dept. groups. 70% of campus accessible to physically disabled. **Special Academic Facilities/Equipment:** Horn and Olin art galleries; Bolton and Hill theaters; Black Box Theater; Rosse and Storer halls for music; new sciences quadrangle; greenhouse and observatory; environmental center; $70-million fitness, recreation, and athletics facility. New art history building under construction. **Computers:** 100% of classrooms, 100% of dorms, 100% of libraries, 100% of dining areas, NA% of student union, 33% of common outdoor areas have wireless network access. Administrative functions (other than registration) can be performed online.

CAMPUS LIFE

Environment: Rural. **Activities:** Choral groups, concert band, dance, drama/theater, jazz band, literary magazine, music ensembles, musical theater, opera, pep band, radio station, student government, student newspaper, student-run film society, symphony orchestra, yearbook, Campus Ministries, Student Organization, Model UN. 140 registered organizations, 5 honor societies, 6 religious organizations. 8 fraternities, 4 sororities. **Athletics (Intercollegiate): Men:** baseball, basketball, cross-country, diving, football, golf, lacrosse, soccer, swimming, tennis, track/field (outdoor), track/field (indoor). **Women:** basketball, cross-country, diving, field hockey, lacrosse, soccer, softball, swimming, tennis, track/field (outdoor), track/field (indoor), volleyball. **On-Campus Highlights:** Kenyon College Bookstore, Fitness/Recreation, Athletic Facility, Middle Ground Coffee Shop, Brown Family Environmental Center, Horn Gallery. **Environmental Initiatives:** 1 Food for Thought (purchase of local foods for dining hall and building a county-wide sustainable food system) http://rurallife.kenyon.edu.

ADMISSIONS

Freshman Academic Profile: Average high school GPA 3.9. 63% in top 10% of high school class, 90% in top 25% of high school class, 99% in top 50% of high school class. 50% from public high schools. **Reported SAT (pre-2016 redesign) scores:** SAT Math middle 50% range 610-710. SAT Critical Reading middle 50% range 620-730. SAT Writing middle 50% range 630-730. **Concordant SAT scores:** SAT EBRW middle 50% 680–750. SAT Math middle 50% range 630–740. ACT middle 50% range 29-33. Minimum internet-based TOEFL 100. **Basis for Candidate Selection:** *Very important factors considered include:* rigor of secondary school record, academic GPA, application essay, recommendation(s), character/personal qualities. *Important factors considered include:* class rank, standardized test scores, interview, extracurricular activities, talent/ability, level of applicant's interest. *Other factors considered include:* first generation, alumni/ae relation, geographical residence, state residency, racial/ethnic status, volunteer work, work experience. **Freshman Admission Requirements:** High school diploma is required and GED is accepted. *Academic units required:* 4 English, 4 math, 3 science, 3 science labs, 3 foreign language, 3 social studies, 3 academic electives. *Academic units recommended:* 4 English, 4 math, 4 science, 3 science labs, 4 foreign language, 3 social studies, 3 academic electives, and 1 unit from above areas or other academic areas. **Freshman Admission Statistics:** 5,927 applied, 28.72% admitted, 29% enrolled. **Transfer Admission Requirements:** High school transcript, college transcript(s), essay or personal statement, standardized test scores, statement of good standing from prior institution(s). Minimum college GPA of 3.0 required. Lowest grade transferable C. **General Admission Information:** Priority deadline 1/15. Regular application deadline 1/15. Regular notification 4/1. Nonfall registration not accepted. Admission may be deferred for a maximum of 1 year.

COSTS AND FINANCIAL AID

Annual tuition $49,220. Room and board $12,130. Required fees $1,980. Average book expense $1,900. **Required Forms and Deadlines:** FAFSA, CSS/Financial Aid PROFILE, Noncustodial PROFILE. **Types of Aid:** *Need-based scholarships/grants:* Federal Pell, FSEOG, State scholarships/

grants, Private scholarships, College/university scholarship or grant aid from institutional funds. *Loans:* Direct Subsidized Stafford Loans, Direct Unsubsidized Stafford Loans, Direct PLUS loans, Federal Perkins Loans, College/university loans from institutional funds. *Student Employment:* Federal Work-Study Program available. Institutional employment available. **Financial Aid Statistics:** 97% needy freshmen, 98% needy undergrads receive need-based scholarship or grant aid. 30% freshmen, 21% undergrads receive non-need-based scholarship or grant aid. 90% freshmen, 87% undergrads receive need-based self-help aid. 0% freshmen, 0% undergrads receive athletic scholarships. 53% freshmen, 42% undergrads receive any aid. 36% undergrads borrow to pay for school. Average cumulative indebtedness $26,746. **Criteria for awarding aid:** *Non-need-based:* Academics, Art, Minority status, Music/drama.

KETTERING UNIVERSITY

1700 University Ave., Flint, MI 48504-6214
Phone: 810-762-9500 • **Financial Aid Phone:** 810-762-7859
E-mail: admissions@kettering.edu • **CEEB Code:** 1246
Fax: 810-762-9837 • **Website:** www.kettering.edu • **ACT Code:** 1998

This private school was founded in 1919. It has a 85-acre campus.

RATINGS

Admissions Selectivity Rating: 86   **Fire Safety Rating:** 78   **Green Rating:** 61

STUDENTS AND FACULTY

Enrollment: 1,866. **Student Body:** 18% female, 82% male, 16% out-of-state, 4% international (29 countries represented). Asian 4%, African American 3%, Caucasian 76%, Hispanic 5%, Native American <1%, Pacific Islander <1%, Two or more races 3%, Race unknown 6%.
Retention and Graduation: 95% freshmen return for sophomore year. 9% freshmen graduate within 4 years. 53% freshmen graduate within 6 years. **Faculty:** Student/faculty ratio 14:1. 116 full-time faculty, 84% hold PhDs, 26% are are members of minority groups, 27% are women. 0% of classes are taught by teaching assistants.

ACADEMICS

Degrees: bachelor's, master's, postbachelor's certificate. **Classes:** Most classes have 20-29 students. Most lab/discussion sessions have 10-19 students. **Most popular majors:** Mechanical Engineering; Electrical and Electronics Engineering; Chemical Engineering. **Special Study Options:** Accelerated program, cooperative education program, distance learning, double major, dual enrollment, independent study, study abroad, Co-op is required of all undergraduate students and typically begins in the first year. Each 24 week semester is divided into 11-weeks of classes and 12-13 weeks of paid professional co-op experience in industry. Students co-op with employers in 43 states and several countries. Income from co-op is a major resource for Kettering students whose total co-op income over their 4 and 1/2-year program typically ranges between $40,000 and $65,000. In addition to study abroad some Kettering students also gain experience in foreign locations for their co-op employer. Accelerated Program, Cooperative (work-study)program, distance learning, double major, independent study. Distance learing is for graduate students only. Combined degree programs: BS/MS Engineering. **Disability Services:** Special programs offered to physically disabled students, including note-taking services, reader services, tape recorders, tutors. **Career Services:** Kettering University is a premier cooperative education program. All students are required to complete a specified number of co-op terms to graduate.

FACILITIES

Housing: Coed dorms, fraternity/sorority housing, apartments for single students. 100% of campus accessible to physically diasbled. **Special Academic Facilities/Equipment:** Art museum, Scharschburg Archieves and Industrial History Museum (principal repository for SAE Patents and Technical Papers). Kettering is renown for the variety and quality of its laboratories for student use and teaching. Labs are required in nearly all science and engineering courses. Of special note are the Bosch Automotive Electronics Systems Lab, Ford Design Simulation Studio, the GM/PACE e-Design and e-Manufacturing Studio, Center for Fuel Cell Systems and Powertrain Integration, the Crash Test Safety, Computer Intergrated Manufacturing (CIM), Polymer Processing, and Mechatronics Labs, the Lubrizol Engine Test Center, SAE Project Vehicle facilities, Biomedical, and the Environmental Scanning Electron Microscopy Lab. The Connie and Jim John Recreation Center and Kettering Park (outdoor recreation). **Computers:** 100% of classrooms, 100% of libraries, 100% of dining areas, have wireless network access. Students can register for classes online. Administrative functions (other than registration) can be performed online.

CAMPUS LIFE

Environment: City. **Activities:** drama/theater, music ensembles, radio station, student government, student newspaper, yearbook. 43 registered organizations, 13 honor societies, 1 religious organization. 13 fraternities, 6 sororities. **On-Campus Highlights:** CS Mott Engineering and Science Center, Connie and Jim John Recreation Center, Frances Willson Thompson Residence Hall, Cemistry and Physics Laboratories, Engineering Laboratories, Kettering University takes great pride in our TOP ranked programs and one-of-a-kind co-op program. Kettering students earn on average $40,000-$65,000 and up to 2 1/2 years of relevant work experience while working for one of our 600+ co-op employers. Prospective students are encouraged to visit campus to learn more about our academic programs, one-of-a-kind co-op program and to meet our faculty, students and staff.

ADMISSIONS

Freshman Academic Profile: Average high school GPA 3.7. 31% in top 10% of high school class, 68% in top 25% of high school class, 93% in top 50% of high school class. 84% from public high schools. **Reported SAT (pre-2016 redesign) scores:** SAT Math middle 50% range 580-700. SAT Critical Reading middle 50% range 540-640. **Concordant SAT scores:** SAT Math middle 50% range 600–730. ACT middle 50% range 25-29. Minimum internet-based TOEFL 79. Minimum paper TOEFL 550. **Basis for Candidate Selection:** *Very important factors considered include:* rigor of secondary school record, academic GPA, standardized test scores. *Important factors considered include:* extracurricular activities. *Other factors considered include:* class rank, application essay, recommendation(s), talent/ability, racial/ethnic status, volunteer work, work experience. **Freshman Admission Requirements:** High school diploma is required and GED is not accepted. *Academic units required:* 3 English, 2 science, 2 science labs. *Academic units recommended:* 4 English, 4 math, 3 science, 3 science labs, 2 foreign language, 2 social studies, 2 history, 1 academic elective. **Freshman Admission Statistics:** 2,251 applied, 71.83% admitted, 26% enrolled. **Transfer Admission Requirements:** college transcript(s), Minimum college GPA of 3.0 required. Lowest grade transferable C. **General Admission Information:** Nonfall registration accepted. Admission may be deferred for a maximum of 1 year.

COSTS AND FINANCIAL AID

Annual tuition $39,790. Room and board $7,780. **Required Forms and Deadlines:** FAFSA. **Notification of Awards:** Applicants will be notified of awards on a rolling basis beginning 3/1. **Types of Aid:** *Need-based scholarships/grants:* Federal Pell, FSEOG, State scholarships/grants, Private scholarships, College/university scholarship or grant aid from institutional funds. *Loans:* Direct Subsidized Stafford Loans, Direct Unsubsidized Stafford Loans, Direct PLUS loans. *Student Employment:* Federal Work-Study Program available. Institutional employment available. **Financial Aid Statistics:** 100% needy freshmen, 100% needy undergrads receive need-based scholarship or grant aid. 12% freshmen, 9% undergrads receive non-need-based scholarship or grant aid. 73% freshmen, 68% undergrads receive need-based self-help aid. 99% freshmen, 88% undergrads receive any aid. **Criteria for awarding aid:** *Non-need-based:* Academics, Leadership.

See page 974.

KEUKA COLLEGE

Office of Admissions, Keuka Park, NY 14478-0098
Phone: 315-279-5254 • **Financial Aid Phone:** 315-279-5646
E-mail: admissions@mail.keuka.edu • **CEEB Code:** 2744
Fax: 315-536-5386 • **Website:** www.keuka.edu • **ACT Code:** 2782

This private school, affiliated with the American Baptist Church, was founded in 1890. It has a 203-acre campus.

RATINGS

Admissions Selectivity Rating: 73   **Fire Safety Rating:** 87   **Green Rating:** 60*

STUDENTS AND FACULTY

Enrollment: 720. **Student Body:** 76% female, 24% male, 6% out-of-state, 0% international (3 countries represented). Asian 1%, African American 8%, Caucasian 84%, Hispanic <1%, Native American 1%, Pacific Islander <1%, Two or more races 1%, Race unknown 6%.
Retention and Graduation: 72% freshmen return for sophomore year. 36% freshmen graduate within 4 years. 48% freshmen graduate within 6 years. 28% grads go on to further study within 1 year. **Faculty:** Student/faculty ratio 15:1. 90 full-time faculty, 70% hold PhDs, 18% are are members of minority groups, 61% are women. 0% of classes are taught by teaching assistants.

ACADEMICS

Degrees: bachelor's, master's. **Classes:** Most classes have 20-29 students. Most lab/discussion sessions have 10-19 students. **Most popular majors:**

Special Education and Teaching; Occupational Therapy/Therapist; Business Administration and Management. **Special Study Options:** Accelerated program, cooperative education program, cross-registration, double major, dual enrollment, independent study, internships, student-designed major, study abroad, teacher certification program. Combined degree programs: Clinical Science to Chiropractic with NY Chiroprac. **Disability Services:** Special programs offered to physically disabled students, including note-taking services, reader services, tape recorders, tutors. **Career Services:** Alumni network, Alumni services, Career/job search classes, Career assessment, Internships, Regional alumni. Experiential learning—National Leader in Experiential, Hands-on Learning.

FACILITIES

Housing: Coed dorms, special housing for disabled students, men's dorms, women's dorms, cooperative housing, Theme housing. 61% of campus accessible to physically diasbled. **Special Academic Facilities/Equipment:** Bird Museum, Lightner Gallery.

CAMPUS LIFE

Environment: Rural. **Activities:** Choral groups, concert band, dance, drama/theater, literary magazine, musical theater, radio station, student government, student newspaper, student-run film society, yearbook. 32 registered organizations, 7 honor societies, 2 religious organizations. **Athletics (Intercollegiate):** *Men:* baseball, basketball, cross-country, golf, lacrosse, soccer, tennis. *Women:* basketball, cross-country, golf, lacrosse, soccer, softball, synchronized swimming, tennis, volleyball. **On-Campus Highlights:** The Weed Physical Arts Center (Gym, pool, fitness rooms, coaches offices), Dahstrom Student Center (bookstore, club offices, student affairs), Ostrander Field (soccer, lacrosse games), Hegeman Hall (classes, faculty offices), Jephson Hall (sciences, greenhouse, labs, electronic classroom).

ADMISSIONS

Freshman Academic Profile: Average high school GPA 3.1. 7% in top 10% of high school class, 27% in top 25% of high school class, 75% in top 50% of high school class. 96% from public high schools. **Reported SAT (pre-2016 redesign) scores:** SAT Math middle 50% range 430-530. SAT Critical Reading middle 50% range 430-520. SAT Writing middle 50% range 400-500. **Concordant SAT scores:** SAT EBRW middle 50% 460–570. SAT Math middle 50% range 470–560. ACT middle 50% range 18-23. Minimum paper TOEFL 500. **Basis for Candidate Selection:** *Very important factors considered include:* rigor of secondary school record, standardized test scores. *Important factors considered include:* class rank, academic GPA, application essay, recommendation(s), interview, extracurricular activities. *Other factors considered include:* talent/ability, alumni/ae relation, volunteer work, work experience, level of applicant's interest. **Freshman Admission Requirements:** High school diploma is required and GED is accepted. *Academic units recommended:* 4 English, 3 math, 3 science, 2 science labs, 3 foreign language, 3 social studies, 2 history. **Freshman Admission Statistics:** 1,371 applied, 82.86% admitted, 19% enrolled. **Transfer Admission Requirements:** college transcript(s), essay or personal statement, Minimum college GPA of 2.0 required. Lowest grade transferable C. **General Admission Information:** Application fee $50. Nonfall registration accepted. Admission may be deferred.

COSTS AND FINANCIAL AID

Annual tuition $26,490. Room and board $10,590. Required fees $790. Average book expense $1,500. **Required Forms and Deadlines:** FAFSA. **Notification of Awards:** Applicants will be notified of awards on a rolling basis beginning 3/1. **Types of Aid:** *Need-based scholarships/grants:* Federal Pell, FSEOG, State scholarships/grants, College/university scholarship or grant aid from institutional funds. *Loans:* Direct Subsidized Stafford Loans, Direct Unsubsidized Stafford Loans, Direct PLUS loans, Federal Perkins Loans, State Loans. *Student Employment:* Federal Work-Study Program available. Institutional employment available. **Financial Aid Statistics:** 91% needy freshmen, 80% needy undergrads receive need-based scholarship or grant aid. 83% freshmen, 58% undergrads receive non-need-based scholarship or grant aid. 97% freshmen, 93% undergrads receive need-based self-help aid. 0% freshmen, 0% undergrads receive athletic scholarships. 92% freshmen, 93% undergrads receive any aid. **Criteria for awarding aid:** *Need-based:* Academics, Alumni affiliation, Leadership, Minority status, Religious affiliation. *Non-need-based:* Academics, Alumni affiliation, Leadership, Minority status, Religious affiliation.

KEYSTONE COLLEGE

One College Green, La Plume, PA 18440
Phone: 570-945-8111 • **Financial Aid Phone:** 570-945-8132
E-mail: admissions@keystone.edu • **CEEB Code:** 2351
Fax: 570-945-7916 • **Website:** www.keystone.edu • **ACT Code:** 2602

This private school was founded in 1868. It has a 270-acre campus.

RATINGS

Admissions Selectivity Rating: 72   **Fire Safety Rating:** 97   **Green Rating:** 60*

STUDENTS AND FACULTY

Enrollment: 1,647. **Student Body:** 60% female, 40% male, 13% out-of-state, 1% international (9 countries represented). Asian 1%, African American 5%, Caucasian 72%, Hispanic 3%, Native American <1%, Pacific Islander <1%, Two or more races 2%, Race unknown 16%.
Retention and Graduation: 61% freshmen return for sophomore year. 29% freshmen graduate within 4 years. 42% freshmen graduate within 6 years. 25% grads go on to further study within 1 year. 1% grads pursue arts and sciences degrees. 1% grads pursue law degrees. 1% grads pursue business degrees. 1% grads pursue medical degrees. **Faculty:** Student/faculty ratio 11:1. 68 full-time faculty, 49% hold PhDs, 1% are are members of minority groups, 63% are women. 0% of classes are taught by teaching assistants.

ACADEMICS

Degrees: associate, bachelor's, certificate, postbachelor's certificate. **Classes:** Most classes have 10-19 students. Most lab/discussion sessions have fewer than 10 students. **Most popular majors:** Business Administration and Management; Homeland Security, Law Enforcement, Firefighting and Related Protective Services; Education. **Special Study Options:** cooperative education program, cross-registration, distance learning, double major, dual enrollment, English as a Second Language (ESL), honors program, independent study, internships, study abroad, teacher certification program, weekend college. **Honors Programs:** Freshmen Honor's Program. **Disability Services:** Special programs offered to physically disabled students, including note-taking services, reader services, tutors. **Career Services:** Alumni network, Alumni services, Career/job search classes, Career assessment, Internships, Regional alumni. Student intership placements have included NBC Dateline, Late Night with Conan O'Brien, US Olympic Training Committee, US Secret Service, ESPN Radio, Glacier National Park, Atlantic Records, and placements abroad in several countries.

FACILITIES

Housing: Coed dorms, special housing for disabled students, women's dorms. 80% of campus accessible to physically diasbled. **Special Academic Facilities/Equipment:** Linder Art Gallery; Cupillari Astronomical Observatory; Willary Water Resource Center **Computers:** 100% of classrooms, 50% of dorms, 100% of libraries, 100% of dining areas, 100% of student union, 50% of common outdoor areas have wireless network access. Students can register for classes online. Administrative functions (other than registration) can be performed online.

CAMPUS LIFE

Environment: Rural. **Activities:** Choral groups, drama/theater, literary magazine, musical theater, radio station, student government, student newspaper, yearbook, Campus Ministries, Student Organization. 22 registered organizations, 1 religious organization. **Athletics (Intercollegiate):** *Men:* baseball, basketball, cross-country, golf, soccer, tennis, track/field (outdoor), track/field (indoor). *Women:* basketball, cross-country, field hockey, soccer, softball, tennis, track/field (outdoor), track/field (indoor), volleyball. **On-Campus Highlights:** Linder Art Gallery, 270 acre woodlands campus (trail system), Astronomical Observatory, Giants' Den, Keystone Commons. **Environmental Initiatives:** A recycling program.

ADMISSIONS

Reported SAT (pre-2016 redesign) scores: SAT Math middle 50% range 400-500. SAT Critical Reading middle 50% range 400-500. SAT Writing middle 50% range 380-480. **Concordant SAT scores:** SAT EBRW middle 50% 440–550. SAT Math middle 50% range 440–530. ACT middle 50% range 17-22. Minimum internet-based TOEFL 80. Minimum paper TOEFL 550. **Basis for Candidate Selection:** *Very important factors considered include:* rigor of secondary school record, academic GPA, interview, talent/ability. *Important factors considered include:* standardized test scores, application essay, extracurricular activities, character/personal qualities, volunteer work, work experience. *Other factors considered include:* class rank, recommendation(s), first generation, alumni/ae relation, level of applicant's interest. **Freshman Admission Requirements:** High school diploma is required and GED is accepted. *Academic units required:* 4 English, 3 math, 2 science, 1 science lab, 2 social studies, 4 academic electives. *Academic units recommended:* 4 English,

3 math, 3 science, 1 science lab, 2 foreign language, 2 social studies, 2 history, 4 academic electives, 1 computer science, 1 visual/performing arts. **Freshman Admission Statistics:** 1,192 applied, 70.22% admitted, 43% enrolled. **Transfer Admission Requirements:** college transcript(s), essay or personal statement, standardized test scores, statement of good standing from prior institution(s). Minimum college GPA of 2 required. Lowest grade transferable 2. **General Admission Information:** Application fee $30. Priority deadline 4/1. Regular application deadline 6/1. Nonfall registration accepted. Admission may be deferred for a maximum of 1 year.

COSTS AND FINANCIAL AID

Annual tuition $20,300. Room and board $9,800. Required fees $900. Average book expense $1,900. **Required Forms and Deadlines:** FAFSA, State aid form. **Notification of Awards:** Applicants will be notified of awards on or about 3/1. **Types of Aid:** *Need-based scholarships/grants:* Federal Pell, FSEOG, State scholarships/grants, Private scholarships, College/university scholarship or grant aid from institutional funds. *Loans:* Direct Subsidized Stafford Loans, Direct Unsubsidized Stafford Loans, Direct PLUS loans, Federal Perkins Loans. *Student Employment:* Federal Work-Study Program available. Institutional employment available. **Financial Aid Statistics:** 100% needy freshmen, 99% needy undergrads receive need-based scholarship or grant aid. 76% freshmen, 72% undergrads receive non-need-based scholarship or grant aid. 90% freshmen, 91% undergrads receive need-based self-help aid. 0% freshmen, 0% undergrads receive athletic scholarships. 88% freshmen, 91% undergrads receive any aid. **Criteria for awarding aid:** *Non-need-based:* Academics, Alumni affiliation, Art.

See page 976.

KING'S COLLEGE (PA)

133 North River Street, Wilkes-Barre, PA 18711
Phone: 570-208-5858 • **Financial Aid Phone:** 570-208-5868
E-mail: admissions@kings.edu • **CEEB Code:** 2353
Fax: 570-208-5971 • **Website:** www.kings.edu • **ACT Code:** 3604

This private school, affiliated with the Roman Catholic Church, was founded in 1946. It has a 48-acre campus.

RATINGS
Admissions Selectivity Rating: 80   **Fire Safety Rating:** 96   **Green Rating:** 65

STUDENTS AND FACULTY
Enrollment: 1,903. **Student Body:** 46% female, 54% male, 30% out-of-state, 6% international (5 countries represented). Asian 2%, African American 3%, Caucasian 74%, Hispanic 7%, Native American <1%, Pacific Islander 0%, Two or more races 2%, Race unknown 5%.
Retention and Graduation: 77% freshmen return for sophomore year. 59% freshmen graduate within 4 years. 65% freshmen graduate within 6 years. 29% grads go on to further study within 1 year. 17% grads pursue arts and sciences degrees. 1% grads pursue law degrees. 1% grads pursue business degrees. 3% grads pursue medical degrees. **Faculty:** Student/faculty ratio 13:1. 131 full-time faculty, 88% hold PhDs, 3% are are members of minority groups, 49% are women. 0% of classes are taught by teaching assistants.

ACADEMICS
Degrees: bachelor's, master's, postbachelor's certificate. **Classes:** Most classes have 10-19 students. Most lab/discussion sessions have 10-19 students. **Most popular majors:** Physician Assistant; Accounting; Criminal Justice/Safety Studies. **Special Study Options:** Accelerated program, cross-registration, distance learning, double major, dual enrollment, English as a Second Language (ESL), honors program, independent study, internships, student-designed major, study abroad, teacher certification program, weekend college. Combined degree programs: BS Med Studies/MS Phys Asst. **Disability Services:** Special programs offered to physically disabled students, including note-taking services, reader services, tape recorders, tutors. **Career Services:** Alumni network, Alumni services, Career/job search classes, Career assessment, Internships, Regional alumni.

FACILITIES
Housing: Coed dorms, special housing for disabled students, men's dorms, women's dorms, apartments for single students, Wellness Housing, Theme Housing. 99% of campus accessible to physically disabled. **Special Academic Facilities/Equipment:** Electron microscope, rooftop greenhouse, molecular biology lab, computer graphics lab **Computers:** 50% of classrooms, 25% of dorms, 100% of libraries, 100% of dining areas, 100% of student union, 100% of common outdoor areas have wireless network access. Students can register for classes online. Administrative functions (other than registration) can be performed online.

CAMPUS LIFE
Environment: City. **Activities:** Choral groups, dance, drama/theater, literary magazine, music ensembles, pep band, radio station, student government, student newspaper, yearbook, Campus Ministries. 50 registered organizations, 15 honor societies, 2 religious organizations. **Athletics (Intercollegiate):** *Men:* baseball, basketball, cheerleading, cross-country, football, golf, lacrosse, soccer, swimming, tennis, wrestling. *Women:* basketball, cheerleading, cross-country, field hockey, lacrosse, soccer, softball, swimming, tennis, volleyball. **On-Campus Highlights:** Sheehy-Farmer Campus Center, McGowan School of Business, Scandlon Physical Education Center, Betzler Fields (Athletic Complex), Gateway Corners.

ADMISSIONS
Freshman Academic Profile: Average high school GPA 3.4. 18% in top 10% of high school class, 43% in top 25% of high school class, 72% in top 50% of high school class. 75% from public high schools. **Reported SAT (pre-2016 redesign) scores:** SAT Math middle 50% range 480-590. SAT Critical Reading middle 50% range 460-570. SAT Writing middle 50% range 440-550. **Concordant SAT scores:** SAT EBRW middle 50% 500–620. SAT Math middle 50% range 510–610. ACT middle 50% range 21-25. Minimum internet-based TOEFL 71. Minimum paper TOEFL 530. **Basis for Candidate Selection:** *Very important factors considered include:* rigor of secondary school record, class rank, academic GPA. *Important factors considered include:* standardized test scores, application essay, character/personal qualities. *Other factors considered include:* recommendation(s), interview, extracurricular activities, alumni/ae relation, volunteer work, work experience. **Freshman Admission Requirements:** High school diploma is required and GED is accepted. *Academic units required:* 4 English, 3 math, 3 science, 2 science labs, 2 foreign language, 3 social studies, 1 history. *Academic units recommended:* 4 English, 4 math, 4 science, 2 science labs, 4 foreign language, 3 social studies, 1 history, 2 academic electives, 2 computer science. **Freshman Admission Statistics:** 3,852 applied, 70.90% admitted, 21% enrolled. **Transfer Admission Requirements:** High school transcript, college transcript(s), essay or personal statement, Minimum college GPA of 2.0 required. Lowest grade transferable C. **General Admission Information:** Application fee $30. Nonfall registration accepted. Admission may be deferred for a maximum of 1 year.

COSTS AND FINANCIAL AID
Required Forms and Deadlines: FAFSA. **Notification of Awards:** Applicants will be notified of awards on a rolling basis beginning 3/1. **Types of Aid:** *Need-based scholarships/grants:* Federal Pell, FSEOG, State scholarships/grants, Private scholarships, College/university scholarship or grant aid from institutional funds. *Loans:* Direct Subsidized Stafford Loans, Direct Unsubsidized Stafford Loans, Direct PLUS loans, Federal Perkins Loans. *Student Employment:* Federal Work-Study Program available. Institutional employment available. **Financial Aid Statistics:** 97% needy freshmen, 100% needy undergrads receive need-based scholarship or grant aid. 15% freshmen, 14% undergrads receive non-need-based scholarship or grant aid. 82% freshmen, 83% undergrads receive need-based self-help aid. 0% freshmen, 0% undergrads receive athletic scholarships. 98% freshmen, 96% undergrads receive any aid. 86% undergrads borrow to pay for school. Average cumulative indebtedness $37,874. **Criteria for awarding aid:** *Non-need-based:* Academics, Leadership.

See page 978.

KING UNIVERSITY

1350 King College Road, Bristol, TN 37620-2699
Phone: 423-652-4861 • **Financial Aid Phone:** 423-652-4728
E-mail: admissions@king.edu • **CEEB Code:** 1371
Fax: 423-652-4727 • **Website:** www.king.edu • **ACT Code:** 3970

This private school, affiliated with the Presbyterian Church, was founded in 1867. It has a 135-acre campus.

RATINGS
Admissions Selectivity Rating: 83   **Fire Safety Rating:** 68   **Green Rating:** 60*

STUDENTS AND FACULTY
Enrollment: 2,357. **Student Body:** 65% female, 35% male, 35% out-of-state, 3% international (29 countries represented). Asian 0%, African American 6%, Caucasian 81%, Hispanic 3%, Native American <1%, Pacific Islander <1%, Two or more races 2%, Race unknown 4%.
Retention and Graduation: 73% freshmen return for sophomore year. 29% freshmen graduate within 4 years. 45% freshmen graduate within 6 years. 21% grads go on to further study within 1 year. 39% grads pursue arts and sciences degrees. 3% grads pursue law degrees. 42% grads pursue business degrees. 5%

grads pursue medical degrees. **Faculty:** Student/faculty ratio 14:1. 135 full-time faculty, 55% hold PhDs, 10% are are members of minority groups, 56% are women. 0% of classes are taught by teaching assistants.

ACADEMICS

Degrees: associate, bachelor's, master's. **Classes:** Most classes have 10-19 students. Most lab/discussion sessions have fewer than 10 students. **Special Study Options:** Accelerated program, cross-registration, double major, dual enrollment, exchange student program (domestic), honors program, independent study, internships, student-designed major, study abroad, teacher certification program. **Honors Programs:** The Jack E. Snider Honors Center allows students to interact with other students and faculty of diverse interests. Participants take selected courses that stimulate thinking and allow for creative response while engaging in special opportunities such as meeting with faculty members and outside guests. Other courses may allow honors students, for extra credit, to develop more extensive research projects. The honors seminars also examine ideas from a variety of academic disciplines. Participants serve both the campus and the larger community by tutoring and mentoring and are encouraged to explore other perspectives through study abroad experiences. Combined degree programs: MBA/MSN. **Disability Services:** Special programs offered to physically disabled students, including tutors. **Career Services:** Alumni network, Alumni services, Career/job search classes, Career assessment, Internships, Regional alumni.

FACILITIES

Housing: special housing for disabled students, men's dorms, women's dorms. 53% of campus accessible to physically diasbled. **Special Academic Facilities/ Equipment:** Electron microscope, observatory with two reflecting telescopes, solar telescope.

CAMPUS LIFE

Environment: Town. **Activities:** Choral groups, concert band, dance, drama/ theater, literary magazine, music ensembles, musical theater, pep band, student government, student newspaper, yearbook, Campus Ministries, Student Organization. 35 registered organizations, 5 honor societies, 9 religious organizations. **Athletics (Intercollegiate):** *Men:* baseball, basketball, bowling, cheerleading, cross-country, cycling, diving, golf, soccer, swimming, tennis, track/field (outdoor), track/field (indoor), wrestling. *Women:* basketball, bowling, cheerleading, cross-country, cycling, diving, golf, soccer, softball, swimming, tennis, track/field (outdoor), track/field (indoor), volleyball, wrestling. **On-Campus Highlights:** New Student Center/Athletic Complex, Campus oval, Library, Residence hall lobbies, Entrance way and sporting fields.

ADMISSIONS

Freshman Academic Profile: Average high school GPA 3.6. 14% in top 10% of high school class, 43% in top 25% of high school class, 85% in top 50% of high school class. 89% from public high schools. **Reported SAT (pre-2016 redesign) scores:** SAT Math middle 50% range 438-565. SAT Critical Reading middle 50% range 440-540. SAT Writing middle 50% range 420-515. **Concordant SAT scores:** SAT EBRW middle 50% 480–590. SAT Math middle 50% range 480–590. ACT middle 50% range 19.25-24. Minimum internet-based TOEFL 84. Minimum paper TOEFL 563. **Basis for Candidate Selection:** *Very important factors considered include:* rigor of secondary school record, academic GPA, standardized test scores. *Other factors considered include:* application essay, first generation. **Freshman Admission Requirements:** High school diploma is required and GED is accepted. *Academic units required:* 4 English, 2 math, 1 science, 1 science lab, 2 foreign language, 1 social studies, 1 history, 4 academic electives. *Academic units recommended:* 4 English, 4 math, 4 science, 4 science labs, 2 foreign language, 2 social studies, 2 history. **Freshman Admission Statistics:** 1,601 applied, 51.41% admitted, 19% enrolled. **Transfer Admission Requirements:** college transcript(s), Minimum college GPA of 2.0 required. Lowest grade transferable C-. **General Admission Information:** Application fee $20. Nonfall registration accepted. Admission may be deferred for a maximum of 1 year.

COSTS AND FINANCIAL AID

Annual tuition $25,798. Room and board $8,180. Required fees $1,478. Average book expense $1,420. **Required Forms and Deadlines:** FAFSA. **Notification of Awards:** Applicants will be notified of awards on a rolling basis beginning 3/1. **Types of Aid:** *Need-based scholarships/grants:* Federal Pell, FSEOG, State scholarships/grants, College/university scholarship or grant aid from institutional funds. *Loans:* Direct Subsidized Stafford Loans, Direct Unsubsidized Stafford Loans, Direct PLUS loans, Federal Perkins Loans, State Loans. *Student Employment:* Federal Work-Study Program available. Institutional employment available. **Financial Aid Statistics:** 95% needy freshmen, 80% needy undergrads receive need-based scholarship or grant aid. 13% freshmen, 7% undergrads receive non-need-based scholarship or grant aid. 87% freshmen, 93% undergrads receive need-based self-help aid. 20% freshmen, 6% undergrads receive athletic scholarships. 98% freshmen, 94% undergrads receive any aid. Average cumulative indebtedness $23,950. **Criteria for awarding aid:** *Need-based:* Alumni affiliation. *Non-need-based:* Academics, Art, Athletics, Job skills, Music/drama, State/district residency.

KNOX COLLEGE

2 East South Street, Campus Box 148, Galesburg, IL 61401
Phone: 309-341-7100 • **Financial Aid Phone:** 309-341-7149
E-mail: admission@knox.edu • **CEEB Code:** 1372
Fax: 309-341-7070 • **Website:** www.knox.edu • **ACT Code:** 1052

This private school was founded in 1837. It has a 82-acre campus.

RATINGS

Admissions Selectivity Rating: 87   **Fire Safety Rating:** 96   **Green Rating:** 90

STUDENTS AND FACULTY

Enrollment: 1,334. **Student Body:** 59% female, 41% male, 44% out-of-state, 14% international (44 countries represented). Asian 6%, African American 8%, Caucasian 49%, Hispanic 15%, Native American 0%, Pacific Islander 0%, Two or more races 5%, Race unknown 3%.
Retention and Graduation: 87% freshmen return for sophomore year. 69% freshmen graduate within 4 years. 77% freshmen graduate within 6 years. 17% grads go on to further study within 1 year. 13% grads pursue arts and sciences degrees. 1% grads pursue law degrees. 2% grads pursue business degrees. 3% grads pursue medical degrees. **Faculty:** Student/faculty ratio 11:1. 112 full-time faculty, 96% hold PhDs, 15% are are members of minority groups, 42% are women. 0% of classes are taught by teaching assistants.

ACADEMICS

Degrees: bachelor's. **Classes:** Most classes have 10-19 students. Most lab/ discussion sessions have 10-19 students. **Most popular majors:** Creative Writing; Economics; Psychology. **Special Study Options:** double major, dual enrollment, honors program, independent study, internships, student-designed major, study abroad, teacher certification program. **Honors Programs:** Knox College is an "honors college". If you compare Knox's academic requirements, student profile, educational opportunities, and student experiences with those of an honors program at a university, Knox provides comparable and often much richer opportunities for its students. Combined degree programs: BA/JD 3-3 prog-Law Columbia Univ & Univ of Chicago; BA/MS prog-Occup Therapy Washington Univ; BA/OD prog-Optometry Illinois Coll of Optometry;BA/ Master-Forestry & BA/Master of Environ Mgmt Duke Univ. **Disability Services:** Special programs offered to physically disabled students, including note-taking services, tape recorders, tutors. **Career Services:** Alumni network, Alumni services, Career/job search classes, Career assessment, Internships, Regional alumni. Our annual alumni/student mock interview and networking events held during homecoming. In one evening we hold 50 interviews conducted by alumni with students, followed by approximately 100 students attending a networking event with alumni.

FACILITIES

Housing: Coed dorms, special housing for disabled students, men's dorms, special housing for international students, women's dorms, fraternity/sorority housing, apartments for single students, Wellness Housing, Theme Housing. 55% of campus accessible to physically diasbled. **Special Academic Facilities/ Equipment:** Anthropology, art, and field museums, theatre with revolving stage and computerized lighting, ceramics, sculpture, painting, and printmaking studios, 760-acre biological field station, environmental climate chambers, electron microscope. **Computers:** 100% of classrooms, 100% of dorms, 100% of libraries, 100% of dining areas, 100% of student union, 90% of common outdoor areas have wireless network access. Students can register for classes online. Administrative functions (other than registration) can be performed online.

CAMPUS LIFE

Environment: Town. **Activities:** Choral groups, dance, drama/theater, jazz band, literary magazine, music ensembles, radio station, student government, student newspaper, symphony orchestra, Campus Ministries, Student Organization, Model UN. 102 registered organizations, 8 honor societies, 6 religious organizations. 5 fraternities, 3 sororities. **Athletics (Intercollegiate):** *Men:* baseball, basketball, cross-country, football, golf, soccer, swimming, tennis, track/field (outdoor), track/field (indoor), wrestling. *Women:* basketball, cross-country, golf, soccer, softball, swimming, tennis, track/field (outdoor), track/field (indoor), volleyball. **On-Campus Highlights:** Gizmo Snack Bar, Andrew Fitness Center, Hard Knox Cafe, Gizmo Patio, Seymour Library. **Environmental Initiatives:** GOVERNANCE: The President's Sustainability Task Force, established in 2008, has now been re-formed as a permanent President Council on Sustainability. This group addresses campus sustainability on a large scale by reviewing, recommending, and promoting sustainable initiatives. In addition to introducing the new initiatives outlined in the next numbered point, the Council is currently finalizing a three-year sustainability plan that outlines their goals, in line with the College Strategic Plan for 2018. Also, in 2008, Knox students established a fund for sustainability projects to help them embrace sustainability by implementing their own initiatives. Drawn from student activity fees, the Fund can be petitioned by any student to purchase services or products that directly increase the sustainability of the Knox College campus. The Student Senate Sustainability Committee administers this fund and has recently supported initiatives including a campus community garden, water bottle filling stations throughout campus, improved sports-field recycling options, compost tumblers in the residential quad, and light switch timers for restrooms.

ADMISSIONS

Freshman Academic Profile: 46% in top 10% of high school class, 71% in top 25% of high school class, 95% in top 50% of high school class. 74% from public high schools. **Reported SAT (pre-2016 redesign) scores:** SAT Math middle 50% range 670-530. SAT Critical Reading middle 50% range 650-500. SAT Writing middle 50% range 620-527. **Concordant SAT scores:** SAT EBRW middle 50% 680–570. SAT Math middle 50% range 700–560. ACT middle 50% range 30-24. Minimum internet-based TOEFL 80. Minimum paper TOEFL 550. **Basis for Candidate Selection:** *Very important factors considered include:* rigor of secondary school record, academic GPA, application essay. *Important factors considered include:* class rank, recommendation(s), interview, character/personal qualities. *Other factors considered include:* standardized test scores, extracurricular activities, talent/ability, first generation, alumni/ae relation, geographical residence, racial/ethnic status, volunteer work, level of applicant's interest. **Freshman Admission Requirements:** High school diploma is required and GED is accepted. *Academic units recommended:* 4 English, 4 math, 4 science, 2 science labs, 3 foreign language, 2 social studies, 2 history, 1 academic elective. **Freshman Admission Statistics:** 3,514 applied, 65.22% admitted, 15% enrolled. **Transfer Admission Requirements:** High school transcript, college transcript(s), essay or personal statement, statement of good standing from prior institution(s). Minimum college GPA of 3.0 required. Lowest grade transferable C. **General Admission Information:** Application fee $50. Regular application deadline 1/15. Regular notification 3/30. Nonfall registration not accepted. Admission may be deferred for a maximum of 1 year.

COSTS AND FINANCIAL AID

Annual tuition $44,191. Room and board $9,666. Required fees $767. Average book expense $900. **Required Forms and Deadlines:** FAFSA, Institution's own financial aid form. **Notification of Awards:** Applicants will be notified of awards on a rolling basis beginning 2/15. **Types of Aid:** *Need-based scholarships/grants:* Federal Pell, FSEOG, State scholarships/grants, Private scholarships, College/university scholarship or grant aid from institutional funds. *Loans:* Direct Subsidized Stafford Loans, Direct Unsubsidized Stafford Loans, Direct PLUS loans, Federal Perkins Loans, College/university loans from institutional funds. *Student Employment:* Federal Work-Study Program available. Institutional employment available. **Financial Aid Statistics:** 99% needy freshmen, 98% needy undergrads receive need-based scholarship or grant aid. 11% freshmen, 9% undergrads receive non-need-based scholarship or grant aid. 85% freshmen, 87% undergrads receive need-based self-help aid. 0% freshmen, 0% undergrads receive athletic scholarships. 99% freshmen, 98% undergrads receive any aid. 64% undergrads borrow to pay for school. Average cumulative indebtedness $30,638. **Criteria for awarding aid:** *Non-need-based:* Academics, Art, Leadership, Music/drama.

See page 980.

KUTZTOWN UNIVERSITY OF PENNSYLVANIA

Admissions Office, Kutztown, PA 19530-0730
Phone: 610-683-4060 • **Financial Aid Phone:** 610-683-4032
E-mail: admissions@kutztown.edu • **CEEB Code:** 2653
Fax: 610-683-1375 • **Website:** www.kutztown.edu • **ACT Code:** 3706

This public school was founded in 1866. It has a 325-acre campus.

RATINGS

Admissions Selectivity Rating: 74   **Fire Safety Rating:** 98   **Green Rating:** 60*

STUDENTS AND FACULTY

Enrollment: 7,683. **Student Body:** 54% female, 46% male, 12% out-of-state, 1% international (32 countries represented). Asian 1%, African American 8%, Caucasian 78%, Hispanic 8%, Native American <1%, Pacific Islander <1%, Two or more races 3%, Race unknown 1%.
Retention and Graduation: 73% freshmen return for sophomore year. 34% freshmen graduate within 4 years. 55% freshmen graduate within 6 years. 25%

grads go on to further study within 1 year. 26% grads pursue arts and sciences degrees. 4% grads pursue law degrees. 4% grads pursue business degrees. 16% grads pursue medical degrees. **Faculty:** Student/faculty ratio 18:1. 410 full-time faculty, 87% hold PhDs, 19% are are members of minority groups, 50% are women. 0% of classes are taught by teaching assistants.

ACADEMICS

Degrees: bachelor's, doctoral, master's, postbachelor's certificate. **Classes:** Most classes have 20-29 students. Most lab/discussion sessions have 20-29 students. **Most popular majors:** Business Administration and Management; Psychology; English Language and Literature. **Special Study Options:** cross-registration, distance learning, double major, dual enrollment, honors program, independent study, internships, liberal arts/career combination, student-designed major, study abroad, teacher certification program. **Honors Programs:** 1)University Honors Program 2)Various Honor Societies Combined degree programs: BS/MS Computer Information Science; BSW/MSW Social Work. **Disability Services:** Special programs offered of physically disabled students, including note-taking services, reader services, tape recorders, tutors. **Career Services:** Alumni network, Alumni services, Career/job search classes, Career assessment, Internships, Regional alumni. Proudest of the wide array of services and events for Kutztown University students.

FACILITIES

Housing: Coed dorms, women's dorms, cooperative housing, apartments for single students, Apartment Units. 90% of campus accessible to physically diasbled. **Special Academic Facilities/Equipment:** Art Gallery, German Cultural Heritage Center, Early Childhood Learning Center, Cartography Lab, Observatory, Planetarium, Daycare Center **Computers:** 25% of classrooms, 95% of dorms, 100% of libraries, 75% of dining areas, 100% of student union, 65% of common outdoor areas have wireless network access. Students can register for classes online. Administrative functions (other than registration) can be performed online.

CAMPUS LIFE

Environment: Rural. **Activities:** Choral groups, concert band, dance, drama/theater, jazz band, literary magazine, marching band, music ensembles, musical theater, radio station, student government, student newspaper, student-run film society, symphony orchestra, television station, yearbook, Campus Ministries, Student Organization, Model UN. 218 registered organizations, 15 honor societies, 11 religious organizations. 9 fraternities, 8 sororities. **Athletics (Intercollegiate):** *Men:* baseball, basketball, cross-country, football, tennis, track/field (outdoor), track/field (indoor), wrestling. *Women:* basketball, bowling, cross-country, field hockey, golf, lacrosse, soccer, softball, swimming, tennis, track/field (outdoor), track/field (indoor), volleyball. **On-Campus Highlights:** Taylor and Burnes Gourmet Coffee, Student Rec Center, Alumni Plaza-new walkway with outdoor amphitheater, Pennsylvania German Cultural Heritage Center, Academic Forum. **Environmental Initiatives:** Recycling program.

ADMISSIONS

Freshman Academic Profile: Average high school GPA 3.2. 6% in top 10% of high school class, 22% in top 25% of high school class, 57% in top 50% of high school class. 92% from public high schools. **Reported SAT (pre-2016 redesign) scores:** SAT Math middle 50% range 440-530. SAT Critical Reading middle 50% range 440-540. SAT Writing middle 50% range 420-510. **Concordant SAT scores:** SAT EBRW middle 50% 480–580. SAT Math middle 50% range 480–560. ACT middle 50% range 18-22. Minimum internet-based TOEFL 79. Minimum paper TOEFL 550. **Basis for Candidate Selection:** *Very important factors considered include:* rigor of secondary school record, class rank, standardized test scores. *Other factors considered include:* academic GPA, recommendation(s), interview, extracurricular activities, talent/ability, character/personal qualities, geographical residence, state residency, racial/ethnic status, volunteer work, work experience. **Freshman Admission Requirements:** High school diploma is required and GED is accepted. *Academic units required:* 4 English, 3 math, 3 science, 2 science labs, 3 social studies. **Freshman Admission Statistics:** 7,668 applied, 79.77% admitted, 28% enrolled. **Transfer Admission Requirements:** college transcript(s), statement of good standing from prior institution(s). Minimum college GPA of 2.0 required. Lowest grade transferable C-. **General Admission Information:** Application fee $35. Priority deadline 12/1. Nonfall registration accepted. Admission may be deferred for a maximum of 1 year.

COSTS AND FINANCIAL AID

Annual in-state tuition $7,238. Annual out-of-state tuition $18,096. Room and board $9,438. Required fees $2,380. Average book expense $1,628. **Required Forms and Deadlines:** FAFSA. **Notification of Awards:** Applicants will be notified of awards on a rolling basis beginning 3/30. **Types of Aid:** *Need-based scholarships/grants:* Federal Pell, FSEOG, State scholarships/grants, Private scholarships, College/university scholarship or grant aid from institutional funds. *Loans:* Direct Subsidized Stafford Loans, Direct Unsubsidized Stafford Loans, Direct PLUS loans, Federal Perkins Loans. *Student Employment:* Federal Work-Study Program available. Institutional employment available. **Financial Aid Statistics:** 62% needy freshmen, 62% needy undergrads receive need-based scholarship or grant aid. 67% freshmen, 27% undergrads receive non-need-based scholarship or grant aid. 89% freshmen, 90% undergrads receive need-based self-help aid. 5% freshmen, 4% undergrads receive athletic scholarships. 88% freshmen, 82% undergrads receive any aid. 80% undergrads borrow to pay for school. Average cumulative indebtedness $39,230. **Criteria for awarding aid:** *Need-based:* Academics. *Non-need-based:* Academics, Art, Athletics, Leadership, Minority status, Music/drama.

LA ROCHE COLLEGE

9000 Babcock Boulevard, Pittsburgh, PA 15237
Phone: 412-536-1271 • **Financial Aid Phone:** 412-536-1120
E-mail: admissions@laroche.edu • **CEEB Code:** 2379
Fax: 412-847-1820 • **Website:** www.laroche.edu • **ACT Code:** 3607

This private school, affiliated with the Roman Catholic Church, was founded in 1963. It has a 43-acre campus.

RATINGS
Admissions Selectivity Rating: 73   Fire Safety Rating: 93   Green Rating: 60*

STUDENTS AND FACULTY
Enrollment: 1,406. **Student Body:** 55% female, 45% male, 9% out-of-state, 16% international (35 countries represented). Asian 1%, African American 10%, Caucasian 60%, Hispanic 3%, Native American <1%, Pacific Islander <1%, Two or more races 2%, Race unknown 8%.
Retention and Graduation: 68% freshmen return for sophomore year. 40% freshmen graduate within 4 years. 55% freshmen graduate within 6 years.
Faculty: Student/faculty ratio 13:1. 61 full-time faculty, 84% hold PhDs, 11% are are members of minority groups, 59% are women. 0% of classes are taught by teaching assistants.

ACADEMICS
Degrees: associate, bachelor's, certificate, master's, postbachelor's certificate, post-master's certificate, terminal. **Classes:** Most classes have 10-19 students. Most lab/discussion sessions have 10-19 students. **Most popular majors:** Psychology; Criminal Justice/Safety Studies; Accounting. **Special Study Options:** Accelerated program, cross-registration, distance learning, double major, English as a Second Language (ESL), honors program, independent study, internships, student-designed major, study abroad, teacher certification program. Combined degree programs: BA/MA. **Disability Services:** Special programs offered to physically disabled students, including note-taking services, reader services, tutors. **Career Services:** Career/job search classes, Career assessment, Internships, Regional alumni.

FACILITIES
Housing: Coed dorms. 100% of campus accessible to physically disabled. **Special Academic Facilities/Equipment:** Cantellopes Art Gallery; College Center extension has state of the art smart classrooms **Computers:** 100% of classrooms, 10% of dorms, 100% of libraries, 100% of dining areas, 100% of student union, 25% of common outdoor areas have wireless network access. Students can register for classes online. Administrative functions (other than registration) can be performed online.

CAMPUS LIFE
Environment: City. **Activities:** Choral groups, dance, drama/theater, literary magazine, musical theater, radio station, student government, student newspaper, Campus Ministries, Student Organization. 40 registered organizations, 4 honor societies, 2 religious organizations. **Athletics (Intercollegiate):** *Men:* baseball, basketball, cross-country, golf, lacrosse, soccer. *Women:* basketball, cheerleading, cross-country, soccer, softball, tennis, volleyball. **On-Campus Highlights:** Sports and Fitness Center, College bookstore, Magdalen Chapel, College Center Annex.

ADMISSIONS
Freshman Academic Profile: Average high school GPA 3.2. 15% in top 10% of high school class, 30% in top 25% of high school class, 68% in top 50% of high school class. 77% from public high schools. **Reported SAT (pre-2016 redesign) scores:** SAT Math middle 50% range 410-510. SAT Critical Reading middle 50% range 400-510. SAT Writing middle 50% range 400-500. **Concordant SAT scores:** SAT EBRW middle 50% 450–560. SAT Math middle 50% range 450–540. ACT middle 50% range 17-23. **Basis for Candidate Selection:** *Very important factors considered include:* rigor of secondary school record, academic GPA. *Important factors considered include:* standardized test scores. *Other factors considered include:* class rank, application essay, recommendation(s), interview, extracurricular activities, talent/ability, character/personal qualities, first generation, alumni/ae relation, volunteer work, work experience, level of applicant's interest. **Freshman Admission Requirements:** High school diploma is required and GED is accepted. *Academic units*

required: 4 English, 2 math, 3 science, 2 science labs, 2 social studies, 2 history, 2 academic electives. *Academic units recommended:* 4 English, 3 math, 4 science, 3 science labs, 2 foreign language, 2 social studies, 2 history, 3 academic electives, 1 computer science. **Freshman Admission Statistics:** 1,320 applied, 92.27% admitted, 24% enrolled. **Transfer Admission Requirements:** college transcript(s), essay or personal statement, Minimum college GPA of 2.0 required. Lowest grade transferable C. **General Admission Information:** Application fee $50. Nonfall registration accepted. Admission may be deferred for a maximum of 1 year.

COSTS AND FINANCIAL AID
Annual tuition $26,200. Room and board $10,924. Required fees $800. Average book expense $1,200. **Required Forms and Deadlines:** FAFSA. **Notification of Awards:** Applicants will be notified of awards on a rolling basis beginning 2/15. **Types of Aid:** *Need-based scholarships/grants:* Federal Pell, FSEOG, State scholarships/grants, Private scholarships, College/university scholarship or grant aid from institutional funds. *Loans:* Direct Subsidized Stafford Loans, Direct Unsubsidized Stafford Loans, Direct PLUS loans, Federal Perkins Loans. *Student Employment:* Federal Work-Study Program available. **Financial Aid Statistics:** 98% needy freshmen, 80% needy undergrads receive need-based scholarship or grant aid. 100% freshmen, 92% undergrads receive non-need-based scholarship or grant aid. 82% freshmen, 74% undergrads receive need-based self-help aid. 0% freshmen, 0% undergrads receive athletic scholarships. 91% freshmen, 91% undergrads receive any aid. 79% undergrads borrow to pay for school. Average cumulative indebtedness $34,992. **Criteria for awarding aid:** *Non-need-based:* Academics, Religious affiliation.

LA SALLE UNIVERSITY

1900 West Olney Avenue, Philadelphia, PA 19141-1199
Phone: 215-951-1500 • **Financial Aid Phone:** 215-951-1070
E-mail: admiss@lasalle.edu • **CEEB Code:** 2363
Fax: 215-951-1656 • **Website:** http://www.lasalle.edu • **ACT Code:** 3608

This private school, affiliated with the Roman Catholic Church, was founded in 1863. It has a 120-acre campus.

RATINGS
Admissions Selectivity Rating: 78   Fire Safety Rating: 86   Green Rating: 67

STUDENTS AND FACULTY
Enrollment: 3,543. **Student Body:** 61% female, 39% male, 34% out-of-state, 2% international (47 countries represented). Asian 5%, African American 19%, Caucasian 51%, Hispanic 14%, Native American <1%, Pacific Islander <1%, Two or more races 3%, Race unknown 6%.
Retention and Graduation: 75% freshmen return for sophomore year. 57% freshmen graduate within 4 years. 65% freshmen graduate within 6 years.
Faculty: Student/faculty ratio 11:1. 226 full-time faculty, 81% hold PhDs, 12% are are members of minority groups, 58% are women. 0% of classes are taught by teaching assistants.

ACADEMICS
Degrees: associate, bachelor's, doctoral/professional, master's, postbachelor's certificate, post-master's certificate. **Classes:** Most classes have 20-29 students. Most lab/discussion sessions have fewer than 10 students. **Most popular majors:** Communication; Registered Nursing/Registered Nurse; Marketing/Marketing Management. **Special Study Options:** Accelerated program, cooperative education program, cross-registration, double major, dual enrollment, English as a Second Language (ESL), exchange student program (domestic), honors program, independent study, internships, student-designed major, study abroad, teacher certification program, 2+2 with Thomas Jefferson University. Combined degree programs: BA/MA, La Salle offers several combined degree programs. **Disability Services:** Special programs offered to physically disabled students, including note-taking services, reader services, tape recorders, tutors. **Career Services:** Alumni network, Alumni services, Career/job search classes, Career assessment, Internships, Regional alumni.

FACILITIES
Housing: Coed dorms, special housing for disabled students, fraternity/sorority housing, apartments for single students. 95% of campus accessible to physically disabled. **Special Academic Facilities/Equipment:** Art museum, Japanese tea house, language lab, child development center. **Computers:** Students can register for classes online. Administrative functions (other than registration) can be performed online.

CAMPUS LIFE
Environment: Metropolis. **Activities:** Choral groups, concert band, drama/theater, jazz band, literary magazine, music ensembles, musical theater, pep band, radio station, student government, student newspaper, student-run

film society, television station, yearbook. 100 registered organizations, 10 honor societies, 4 religious organizations. 7 fraternities, 5 sororities. **Athletics (Intercollegiate):** *Men:* baseball, basketball, cheerleading, crew/rowing, cross-country, diving, football, golf, soccer, swimming, tennis, track/field (outdoor), wrestling. *Women:* basketball, cheerleading, crew/rowing, cross-country, diving, field hockey, golf, lacrosse, soccer, softball, swimming, tennis, track/field (outdoor), volleyball. **On-Campus Highlights:** Hayman Center (sports facility), Connelly Library, Student Union Building-food court, coffee house, restaurant, La Salle University Art Museum, Japanese Tea Ceremony House.

ADMISSIONS

Freshman Academic Profile: Average high school GPA 3.3. 15% in top 10% of high school class, 35% in top 25% of high school class, 68% in top 50% of high school class. 42% from public high schools. **Reported SAT (pre-2016 redesign) scores:** SAT Math middle 50% range 430-540. SAT Critical Reading middle 50% range 440-540. **Concordant SAT scores:** SAT Math middle 50% range 470–570. ACT middle 50% range 19-25. Minimum internet-based TOEFL 76. Minimum paper TOEFL 540. **Basis for Candidate Selection:** *Very important factors considered include:* rigor of secondary school record, academic GPA, standardized test scores. *Important factors considered include:* extracurricular activities. *Other factors considered include:* application essay, recommendation(s), interview, talent/ability, character/personal qualities, alumni/ae relation, volunteer work, work experience. **Freshman Admission Requirements:** High school diploma is required and GED is accepted. *Academic units required:* 4 English, 3 math, 1 science, 1 science lab, 2 foreign language, 1 history, 5 academic electives. **Freshman Admission Statistics:** 5,673 applied, 76.84% admitted, 20% enrolled. **Transfer Admission Requirements:** High school transcript, college transcript(s), essay or personal statement, standardized test scores, statement of good standing from prior institution(s). Minimum college GPA of 2.5 required. Lowest grade transferable C. **General Admission Information:** Application fee $35. Nonfall registration accepted. Admission may be deferred for a maximum of 1 Year.

COSTS AND FINANCIAL AID

Annual tuition $28,800. Room and board $7,160. Required fees $700. Average book expense $500. **Required Forms and Deadlines:** FAFSA. **Notification of Awards:** Applicants will be notified of awards on a rolling basis beginning 3/15. **Types of Aid:** *Need-based scholarships/grants:* Federal Pell, FSEOG, State scholarships/grants, Private scholarships, College/university scholarship or grant aid from institutional funds, Federal Nursing Scholarships. *Loans:* Direct Subsidized Stafford Loans, Direct Unsubsidized Stafford Loans, Direct PLUS loans, Federal Perkins Loans, Federal Nursing Loans. *Student Employment:* Federal Work-Study Program available. Institutional employment available. **Financial Aid Statistics:** 99% needy freshmen, 97% needy undergrads receive need-based scholarship or grant aid. 7% freshmen, 7% undergrads receive non-need-based scholarship or grant aid. 77% freshmen, 81% undergrads receive need-based self-help aid. 4% freshmen, 5% undergrads receive athletic scholarships. 97% freshmen, 93% undergrads receive any aid. 77% undergrads borrow to pay for school. Average cumulative indebtedness $36,907. **Criteria for awarding aid:** *Need-based:* Academics. *Non-need-based:* Academics, Athletics.

LA SIERRA UNIVERSITY

4500 Riverwalk Parkway, Riverside, CA 92515
Phone: 951-785-2176
E-mail: admissions@lasierra.edu
Fax: 951-785-2477 • **Website:** www.lasierra.edu • **ACT Code:** 294

RATINGS

Admissions Selectivity Rating: 81 **Fire Safety Rating:** 60* **Green Rating:** 60*

STUDENTS AND FACULTY

Enrollment: 2,060. **Student Body:** 58% female, 42% male, 6% out-of-state, 12% international. Asian 16%, African American 7%, Caucasian 16%, Hispanic 42%, Native American <1%, Pacific Islander 2%, Two or more races 4%, Race unknown <1%.
Retention and Graduation: 76% freshmen return for sophomore year. 30% freshmen graduate within 4 years. 59% freshmen graduate within 6 years.
Faculty: Student/faculty ratio 14:1. 103 full-time faculty, 95% hold PhDs, 32% are are members of minority groups, 44% are women.

ACADEMICS

Degrees: bachelor's, certificate, doctoral/research, master's, postbachelor's certificate, post-master's certificate.

ADMISSIONS

Freshman Academic Profile: Average high school GPA 3.3. 10% in top 10% of high school class, 41% in top 25% of high school class, 63% in top 50% of high school class. **Reported SAT (pre-2016 redesign) scores:** SAT Math middle 50% range 410-530. SAT Critical Reading middle 50% range 400-510. SAT Writing middle 50% range 410-520. **Concordant SAT scores:** SAT EBRW middle 50% 450–570. SAT Math middle 50% range 450–560. ACT middle 50% range 17-22. Minimum paper TOEFL 525. **Basis for Candidate Selection:** *Very important factors considered include:* rigor of secondary school record, academic GPA, standardized test scores, character/personal qualities. *Important factors considered include:* application essay, recommendation(s), religious affiliation/commitment, level of applicant's interest. **Freshman Admission Requirements:** *Academic units required:* 4 English, 3 math, 2 science, 2 science labs, 2 foreign language, 2 social studies, 1 visual/performing arts, and 1 unit from above areas or other academic areas. *Academic units recommended:* 4 math, 3 science, 3 science labs, 3 foreign language. **Freshman Admission Statistics:** 3,479 applied, 46.77% admitted, 29% enrolled. **General Admission Information:** Application fee $30. Regular application deadline 8/15. Nonfall registration accepted. Admission may be deferred.

COSTS AND FINANCIAL AID

Annual tuition $27,972. Room and board $7,500. Required fees $1,131. Average book expense $1,710. *Student Employment:* Federal Work-Study Program available. Institutional employment available.

LAFAYETTE COLLEGE

730 High Street, Easton, PA 18042
Phone: 610-330-5100 • **Financial Aid Phone:** 610-330-5055
E-mail: admissions@lafayette.edu • **CEEB Code:** 2361
Fax: 610-330-5355 • **Website:** http://www.lafayette.edu/

This private school, affiliated with the Presbyterian Church, was founded in 1826. It has a 340-acre campus.

RATINGS

Admissions Selectivity Rating: 95 **Fire Safety Rating:** 97 **Green Rating:** 89

STUDENTS AND FACULTY

Enrollment: 2,518. **Student Body:** 51% female, 49% male, 82% out-of-state, 10% international (46 countries represented). Asian 4%, African American 5%, Caucasian 66%, Hispanic 7%, Native American 0%, Pacific Islander <1%, Two or more races 2%, Race unknown 6%.
Retention and Graduation: 94% freshmen return for sophomore year. 85% freshmen graduate within 4 years. 89 16% grads go on to further study within 1 year. 2% grads pursue law degrees. 2% grads pursue medical degrees. **Faculty:** Student/faculty ratio 10:1. 229 full-time faculty, 98% hold PhDs, 16% are members of minority groups, 36% are women. 0% of classes are taught by teaching assistants.

ACADEMICS

Degrees: bachelor's. **Classes:** Most classes have 10-19 students. Most lab/discussion sessions have 10-19 students. **Most popular majors:** Economics; Mechanical Engineering; Biology/Biological Sciences. **Special Study Options:** cross-registration, double major, dual enrollment, exchange student program (domestic), honors program, independent study, internships, student-designed major, study abroad, interim sessions here and abroad. Combined degree programs: BA/BS. **Disability Services:** Special programs offered to physically disabled students, including tutors. **Career Services:** Alumni network, Alumni services, Career/job search classes, Career assessment, Internships, Regional alumni. Our Gateway Program which engages the majority of our students in their first year at Lafayette. Students work with the same career advisor over their four years, and have many opportunities to interact with alumni to enhance their career exploration and experiences outside the classroom. As part of this, students of all class years can participate in our January Externship program, now in its 31st year. Ninety-nine percent of students who participated felt that the Externship helped them clarify their career goals.

FACILITIES

Housing: Coed dorms, special housing for disabled students, men's dorms, women's dorms, fraternity/sorority housing, apartments for single students, Wellness Housing, Theme Housing, scholars houses, Hillel House, arts houses.
Special Academic Facilities/Equipment: Art and geological museums,

center for the arts, engineering labs, INSTRON materials testing machine, electron microscopes, transform nuclear magnetic resonance spectrometer, computerized gas chromatograph/mass spectrometer. **Computers:** Students can register for classes online. Administrative functions (other than registration) can be performed online.

CAMPUS LIFE

Environment: Village. **Activities:** Choral groups, concert band, dance, drama/theater, jazz band, literary magazine, music ensembles, musical theater, pep band, radio station, student government, student newspaper, student-run film society, symphony orchestra, yearbook, Campus Ministries, Student Organization. 250 registered organizations, 14 honor societies, 7 religious organizations. 7 fraternities, 6 sororities. **Athletics (Intercollegiate):** *Men:* baseball, basketball, cheerleading, crew/rowing, cross-country, diving, equestrian sports, fencing, football, golf, gymnastics, ice hockey, lacrosse, soccer, softball, swimming, tennis, track/field (outdoor), track/field (indoor), volleyball, wrestling. *Women:* basketball, cheerleading, crew/rowing, cross-country, diving, equestrian sports, fencing, field hockey, golf, gymnastics, softball, swimming, tennis, track/field (outdoor), track/field (indoor), volleyball. **On-Campus Highlights:** Skillman and Kirby Libraries, Farinon College Center, Williams Center for the Arts. **Environmental Initiatives:** In addition to signing American College and University Presidents Climate Commitment, three undertakings summarize the College efforts towards responsible stewardship of the **Environment:** 1. Waste Reduction—Recycling, including composting.—Purchases of materials/goods made from recycled materials and/or virgin material that is recyclable and produced from renewable sources.

ADMISSIONS

Freshman Academic Profile: Average high school GPA 3.5. 60% in top 10% of high school class, 91% in top 25% of high school class, 99% in top 50% of high school class. 60% from public high schools. **Reported SAT (pre-2016 redesign) scores:** SAT Math middle 50% range 620-710. SAT Critical Reading middle 50% range 580-680. SAT Writing middle 50% range 590-690. **Concordant SAT scores:** SAT EBRW middle 50% 640–720. SAT Math middle 50% range 640–740. ACT middle 50% range 27-31. Minimum internet-based TOEFL 80. Minimum paper TOEFL 550. **Basis for Candidate Selection:** *Very important factors considered include:* rigor of secondary school record, academic GPA. *Important factors considered include:* class rank, standardized test scores, application essay, recommendation(s), interview, extracurricular activities, talent/ability, character/personal qualities. *Other factors considered include:* first generation, alumni/ae relation, geographical residence, racial/ethnic status, volunteer work, work experience, level of applicant's interest. **Freshman Admission Requirements:** High school diploma or equivalent is not required. *Academic units recommended:* 4 English, 3 math, 2 science, 2 science labs, 2 foreign language, 5 academic electives. **Freshman Admission Statistics:** 8,123 applied, 28.29% admitted, 28% enrolled. **Transfer Admission Requirements:** High school transcript, college transcript(s), essay or personal statement, statement of good standing from prior institution(s). Lowest grade transferable C. **General Admission Information:** Application fee $65. Regular application deadline 1/15. Regular notification 4/1. Nonfall registration accepted. Admission may be deferred for a maximum of 1 year.

COSTS AND FINANCIAL AID

Annual tuition $48,450. Room and board $14,470. Required fees $435. Average book expense $1,000. **Required Forms and Deadlines:** FAFSA, CSS/Financial Aid PROFILE, Noncustodial PROFILE. **Notification of Awards:** Applicants will be notified of awards on or about 4/1. **Types of Aid:** *Need-based scholarships/grants:* Federal Pell, FSEOG, State scholarships/grants, Private scholarships, College/university scholarship or grant aid from institutional funds. *Loans:* Direct Subsidized Stafford Loans, Direct Unsubsidized Stafford Loans, Direct PLUS loans, Federal Perkins Loans, College/university loans from institutional funds. *Student Employment:* Federal Work-Study Program available. Institutional employment available. **Financial Aid Statistics:** 95% needy freshmen, 94% needy undergrads receive need-based scholarship or grant aid. 26% freshmen, 21% undergrads receive non-need-based scholarship or grant aid. 88% freshmen, 92% undergrads receive need-based self-help aid. 10% freshmen, 9% undergrads receive athletic scholarships. 61% freshmen, 58% undergrads receive any aid. 48% undergrads borrow to pay for school. Average cumulative indebtedness $29,324. **Criteria for awarding aid:** *Need-based:* Academics, Athletics, Leadership. *Non-need-based:* Academics, Athletics, Leadership.

LAGRANGE COLLEGE

Office of Admission, LaGrange, GA 30240
Phone: 706-880-8005 • **Financial Aid Phone:** 888-253-9918
E-mail: lgcadmis@lagrange.edu • **CEEB Code:** 5362
Fax: 706-880-8010 • **Website:** www.lagrange.edu • **ACT Code:** 834

This private school, affiliated with the Methodist Church, was founded in 1831. It has a 120-acre campus.

RATINGS

Admissions Selectivity Rating: 83   **Fire Safety Rating:** 60*   **Green Rating:** 60*

STUDENTS AND FACULTY

Enrollment: 860. **Student Body:** 55% female, 45% male, 11% out-of-state, 2% international (10 countries represented). Asian 1%, African American 22%, Caucasian 72%, Hispanic 2%, Native American <1%, Pacific Islander 0%, Two or more races 0%, Race unknown 1%.
Retention and Graduation: 71% freshmen return for sophomore year. 39% freshmen graduate within 4 years. 55% freshmen graduate within 6 years. **Faculty:** Student/faculty ratio 10:1. 65 full-time faculty, 83% hold PhDs, 0% are are members of minority groups, 48% are women. 0% of classes are taught by teaching assistants.

ACADEMICS

Degrees: associate, bachelor's, master's. **Classes:** Most classes have 10-19 students. Most lab/discussion sessions have 10-19 students. **Most popular majors:** Organizational Behavior Studies; Business Administration and Management; Teacher Education, Multiple Levels. **Special Study Options:** double major, dual enrollment, independent study, internships, liberal arts/career combination, study abroad, teacher certification program. **Career Services:** Alumni network, Alumni services, Career/job search classes, Career assessment, Internships.

FACILITIES

Housing: Coed dorms, men's dorms, women's dorms, fraternity/sorority housing, apartments for single students, Theme Housing. 75% of campus accessible to physically diasbled. **Special Academic Facilities/Equipment:** Lamar Dodd Art Center, Price Theater, Callaway Auditorium. **Computers:** Students can register for classes online. Administrative functions (other than registration) can be performed online.

CAMPUS LIFE

Environment: Village. **Activities:** Choral groups, drama/theater, literary magazine, music ensembles, musical theater, pep band, student government, student newspaper, symphony orchestra, yearbook, Campus Ministries, Student Organization. 49 registered organizations, 11 honor societies, 8 religious organizations. 3 fraternities, 6 sororities. **Athletics (Intercollegiate):** *Men:* baseball, basketball, cross-country, football, golf, soccer, swimming, tennis. *Women:* basketball, cheerleading, cross-country, soccer, softball, swimming, tennis, volleyball. **On-Campus Highlights:** Turner Student Center, Smith Hall, Academic Quadrangle, Smith Patio, Callaway Sports Facilities. **Environmental Initiatives:** Building a LEED library

ADMISSIONS

Freshman Academic Profile: Average high school GPA 3.5. 25% in top 10% of high school class, 54% in top 25% of high school class, 92% in top 50% of high school class. **Reported SAT (pre-2016 redesign) scores:** SAT Math middle 50% range 460-570. SAT Critical Reading middle 50% range 460-570. **Concordant SAT scores:** SAT Math middle 50% range 500–590. ACT middle 50% range 20-25. Minimum paper TOEFL 500. **Basis for Candidate Selection:** *Very important factors considered include:* academic GPA, standardized test scores, character/personal qualities. *Important factors considered include:* class rank, recommendation(s), extracurricular activities, level of applicant's interest. *Other factors considered include:* rigor of secondary school record, application essay, interview, talent/ability, alumni/ae relation, geographical residence, volunteer work. **Freshman Admission Requirements:** High school diploma is required and GED is accepted. *Academic units required:* 4 English, 4 math, 3 science, 3 social studies. *Academic units recommended:* 4 English, 4 math, 3 science, 2 foreign language, 3 social studies. **Freshman Admission Statistics:** 1,342 applied, 64.75% admitted, 27% enrolled. **Transfer Admission Requirements:** college transcript(s), statement of good standing from prior institution(s). Minimum college GPA of 2.0 required. Lowest grade transferable I. **General Admission Information:** Application fee $30. Priority deadline 3/1. Nonfall registration accepted. Admission may be deferred for a maximum of one term.

COSTS AND FINANCIAL AID

Annual tuition $19,900. Room and board $8,168. Required fees $0. **Required Forms and Deadlines:** FAFSA, State aid form. **Notification of Awards:** Applicants will be notified of awards on a rolling basis beginning 3/15. **Types of**

Aid: *Need-based scholarships/grants:* Federal Pell, FSEOG, State scholarships/grants, Private scholarships, College/university scholarship or grant aid from institutional funds. *Loans:* Federal Perkins Loans, State Loans. *Student Employment:* Federal Work-Study Program available. Institutional employment available. **Financial Aid Statistics:** 100% needy freshmen, 100% needy undergrads receive need-based scholarship or grant aid. 24% freshmen, 17% undergrads receive non-need-based scholarship or grant aid. 69% freshmen, 77% undergrads receive need-based self-help aid. 0% freshmen, 0% undergrads receive athletic scholarships. **Criteria for awarding aid:** *Need-based:* Minority status, Religious affiliation. *Non-need-based:* Academics, Art, Leadership, Music/drama, Religious affiliation, State/district residency.

LAKE ERIE COLLEGE

391 West Washington Street, Painesville, OH 44077-3389
Phone: 440-375-7050 • **Financial Aid Phone:** 440-375-7100
E-mail: admissions@lec.edu • **CEEB Code:** 1391
Fax: 440-375-7005 • **Website:** www.lec.edu • **ACT Code:** 3288

This is a private school.

RATINGS
Admissions Selectivity Rating: 76   **Fire Safety Rating:** 93   **Green Rating:** 60*

STUDENTS AND FACULTY
Enrollment: 783. **Student Body:** 47% female, 53% male, 25% out-of-state, 4% international. Asian 0%, African American 10%, Caucasian 77%, Hispanic 2%, Native American <1%, Pacific Islander 0%, Two or more races 3%, Race unknown 3%.
Retention and Graduation: 68% freshmen return for sophomore year. 36% freshmen graduate within 4 years. 52% freshmen graduate within 6 years. 23% grads go on to further study within 1 year. **Faculty:** Student/faculty ratio 15:1. 45 full-time faculty, 87% hold PhDs, 0% are are members of minority groups, 60% are women. 0% of classes are taught by teaching assistants.

ACADEMICS
Degrees: bachelor's, master's, postbachelor's certificate. **Classes:** Most classes have fewer than 10 students. **Most popular majors:** Business Administration and Management; Criminal Justice/Law Enforcement Administration; Biology/Biological Sciences. **Special Study Options:** Accelerated program, cross-registration, double major, dual enrollment, honors program, independent study, internships, liberal arts/career combination, student-designed major, study abroad, teacher certification program, weekend college. **Honors Programs:** LEC Scholars Program. **Disability Services:** Special programs offered to physically disabled students, including note-taking services, reader services, tape recorders, tutors. **Career Services:** Alumni network, Alumni services, Career/job search classes, Career assessment, Internships.

FACILITIES
Housing: Coed dorms, women's dorms, apartments for single students, Theme Housing. 90% of campus accessible to physically disabled. **Computers:** Students can register for classes online. Administrative functions (other than registration) can be performed online.

CAMPUS LIFE
Activities: Choral groups, dance, drama/theater, pep band, student government, student newspaper, yearbook, Student Organization. 15 registered organizations, 3 honor societies, 1 sorority. **Athletics (Intercollegiate):** *Men:* baseball, basketball, cross-country, equestrian sports, football, golf, soccer. *Women:* basketball, cross-country, equestrian sports, soccer, softball, volleyball.

ADMISSIONS
Freshman Academic Profile: Average high school GPA 3.1, 89% from public high schools. **Reported SAT (pre-2016 redesign) scores:** SAT Math middle 50% range 450-540. SAT Critical Reading middle 50% range 440-540. SAT Writing middle 50% range 425-520. **Concordant SAT scores:** SAT EBRW middle 50% range 490-590. SAT Math middle 50% range 490-570. ACT middle 50% range 19-23. Minimum internet-based TOEFL 79. Minimum paper TOEFL 550. **Basis for Candidate Selection:** *Very important factors considered include:* rigor of secondary school record, academic GPA, recommendation(s), interview, character/personal qualities. *Important factors considered include:* class rank, standardized test scores, application essay, extracurricular activities, talent/ability. *Other factors considered include:* alumni/ae relation, volunteer work, work experience, level of applicant's interest. **Freshman Admission Requirements:** High school diploma is required and GED is accepted. *Academic units required:* 4 English, 3 math, 3 science, 2 science labs, 2 foreign language, 3 social studies. *Academic units recommended:* 4 English, 3 math, 3 science, 2 science labs, 2 foreign language, 3 social studies. **Freshman Admission Statistics:** 1,712 applied, 56.31% admitted, 22% enrolled. **Transfer**

Admission Requirements: High school transcript, college transcript(s), statement of good standing from prior institution(s). Minimum college GPA of 2.0 required. Lowest grade transferable C. **General Admission Information:** Application fee $30. Priority deadline 5/1. Regular application deadline 8/1. Nonfall registration accepted. Admission may be deferred for a maximum of 1 year.

COSTS AND FINANCIAL AID
Annual tuition $28,568. Room and board $9,178. Required fees $1,392. Average book expense $1,100. **Required Forms and Deadlines:** FAFSA. **Notification of Awards:** Applicants will be notified of awards on a rolling basis beginning 2/15. **Types of Aid:** *Need-based scholarships/grants:* Federal Pell, FSEOG, State scholarships/grants, Private scholarships, College/university scholarship or grant aid from institutional funds. *Loans:* Direct Subsidized Stafford Loans, Direct Unsubsidized Stafford Loans, Direct PLUS loans, Federal Perkins Loans. *Student Employment:* Federal Work-Study Program available. Institutional employment available. **Financial Aid Statistics:** 100% needy freshmen, 100% needy undergrads receive need-based scholarship or grant aid. 7% freshmen, 12% undergrads receive non-need-based scholarship or grant aid. 92% freshmen, 87% undergrads receive need-based self-help aid. 8% freshmen, 11% undergrads receive athletic scholarships. 100% freshmen, 99% undergrads receive any aid. **Criteria for awarding aid:** *Need-based:* Academics, Athletics, Leadership. *Non-need-based:* Academics, Art, Athletics, Leadership, Music/drama, State/district residency.

LAKE FOREST COLLEGE

Best Colleges

555 North Sheridan Road, Lake Forest, IL 60045
Phone: 847-735-5000 • **Financial Aid Phone:** 847-725-5103
E-mail: admissions@lakeforest.edu • **CEEB Code:** 1392
Fax: 847-735-6291 • **Website:** www.lakeforest.edu • **ACT Code:** 1054

This private school was founded in 1857. It has a 107-acre campus.

RATINGS
Admissions Selectivity Rating: 87   **Fire Safety Rating:** 82   **Green Rating:** 60*

STUDENTS AND FACULTY
Enrollment: 1,514. **Student Body:** 57% female, 43% male, 39% out-of-state, 8% international (76 countries represented). Asian 6%, African American 6%, Caucasian 58%, Hispanic 16%, Native American <1%, Pacific Islander 0%, Two or more races 3%, Race unknown 3%.
Retention and Graduation: 83% freshmen return for sophomore year. 64% freshmen graduate within 4 years. 70% freshmen graduate within 6 years. 16% grads go on to further study within 1 year. 65% grads pursue arts and sciences degrees. 15% grads pursue law degrees. 6% grads pursue business degrees. 6% grads pursue medical degrees. **Faculty:** Student/faculty ratio 12:1. 98 full-time faculty, 98% hold PhDs, 14% are are members of minority groups, 42% are women. 0% of classes are taught by teaching assistants.

ACADEMICS
Degrees: bachelor's, master's, postbachelor's certificate. **Classes:** Most classes have 10-19 students. Most lab/discussion sessions have 10-19 students. **Most popular majors:** Business/Commerce; Finance; Psychology. **Special Study Options:** Accelerated program, double major, honors program, independent study, internships, liberal arts/career combination, student-designed major, study abroad, teacher certification program. **Honors Programs:** The Honors Fellows program recognizes those students admitted to Lake Forest College with exemplary high school careers and high promise for independent study and research at the College. Fellows are expected to think deeply and broadly, and to join their teachers and fellow students in serious intellectual inquiry and debate. They will produce independent work, research, Student Symposium presentations, Independent Scholar majors, distinguished senior theses, and provide intellectual leadership. The Richter Apprentice Scholars Program provides students, early in their academic careers, with the opportunity to conduct independent, individual research with Lake Forest College faculty. In the summer between their first and second year, each student in the Richter Program is employed for a ten week period and works one-on-one with a faculty member, doing independent research in a particular field. As the Richter Apprentice Scholars live and work together and participate in a weekly colloquium, they become a community of peers providing encouragement and support for each other's present and future intellectual and research endeavors. Combined degree programs: BA/JD, BA/MA, Accelerated BA/JD with select

law schools; BA/MA with Monterey Inst.; BA/MAcc w/ William and Mary; BA/PharmD with RFUMS. **Disability Services:** Special programs offered to physically disabled students, including note-taking services, reader services, tape recorders, tutors. **Career Services:** Alumni network, Alumni services, Career/job search classes, Career assessment, Internships, Regional alumni. Internships: Due to our location near Chicago and the many partnerships Lake Forest College has developed with Chicago institutions over the years, there are a myriad of internship opportunities available to our students. Experiential learning: Again, due to our location near Chicago and the relationships with area institutions we offer dozens of courses that have been developed to utilize the rich resources of Chicago to enhance the curriculum. Beginning with our innovative First-Year Studies program students travel downtown to Chicago with professors and take advantage of the many resources.

FACILITIES

Housing: Coed dorms, special housing for disabled students, women's dorms, apartments for single students, Wellness Housing. 75% of campus accessible to physically diasbled. **Special Academic Facilities/Equipment:** Center for Chicago Programs, art galleries, language labs, technology resource center, speech and video production room, "smart" classrooms, music/recording studio with synthesizers, public access computer labs, electron microscope, computer molecular modeling equipment, high-resolution FT-IR, NMR spectrometer, neutron howitzer, digital storage oscilloscopes, flourescence microscope **Computers:** 90% of classrooms, 100% of dorms, 100% of libraries, 75% of dining areas, 100% of student union, 10% of common outdoor areas have wireless network access. Administrative functions (other than registration) can be performed online.

CAMPUS LIFE

Environment: Village. **Activities:** Choral groups, concert band, dance, drama/theater, jazz band, literary magazine, music ensembles, musical theater, radio station, student government, student newspaper, symphony orchestra, Campus Ministries, Student Organization, Model UN. 80 registered organizations, 12 honor societies, 6 religious organizations. 2 fraternities, 4 sororities. **Athletics (Intercollegiate):** *Men:* basketball, cross-country, diving, football, handball, ice hockey, soccer, swimming, tennis. *Women:* basketball, cross-country, diving, handball, ice hockey, soccer, softball, swimming, tennis, volleyball. **On-Campus Highlights:** Donnelley and Lee Library, Mohr Student Center, Sports Center, Center for Chicago Programs, Career Advancement Center. **Environmental Initiatives:** The organic campus garden provides internship opportunities for students and it supplies the campus cafeteria with food during the summer and fall.

ADMISSIONS

Freshman Academic Profile: Average high school GPA 3.6. 33% in top 10% of high school class, 57% in top 25% of high school class, 86% in top 50% of high school class. 73% from public high schools. **Reported SAT (pre-2016 redesign) scores:** SAT Math middle 50% range 520-600. SAT Critical Reading middle 50% range 520-620. SAT Writing middle 50% range 500-600. **Concordant SAT scores:** SAT EBRW middle 50% 570–660. SAT Math middle 50% range 550–620. ACT middle 50% range 24-29. Minimum internet-based TOEFL 83. Minimum paper TOEFL 550. **Basis for Candidate Selection:** *Very important factors considered include:* rigor of secondary school record, application essay, interview, extracurricular activities, talent/ability, character/personal qualities. *Important factors considered include:* academic GPA. *Other factors considered include:* class rank, standardized test scores, recommendation(s), first generation, alumni/ae relation, geographical residence, volunteer work, work experience, level of applicant's interest. **Freshman Admission Requirements:** High school diploma is required and GED is accepted. *Academic units required:* 4 English, 3 math, 3 science, 3 science labs, 2 foreign language, 2 social studies, 2 history, 3 academic electives. *Academic units recommended:* 4 English, 4 math, 4 science, 4 science labs, 4 foreign language, 2 social studies, 2 history, 3 academic electives, and 1 unit from above areas or other academic areas. **Freshman Admission Statistics:** 4,227 applied, 56.94% admitted, 15% enrolled. **Transfer Admission Requirements:** High school transcript, college transcript(s), essay or personal statement, Minimum college GPA of 2.5 required. Lowest grade transferable C-. **General Admission Information:** Priority deadline 2/15. Nonfall registration accepted. Admission may be deferred for a maximum of 12 months.

COSTS AND FINANCIAL AID

Annual tuition $43,392. Room and board $9,810. Required fees $724. Average book expense $1,000. **Required Forms and Deadlines:** FAFSA. **Notification of Awards:** Applicants will be notified of awards on a rolling basis beginning 3/1. **Types of Aid:** *Need-based scholarships/grants:* Federal Pell, FSEOG, State scholarships/grants, Private scholarships, College/university scholarship or grant aid from institutional funds. *Loans:* Direct Subsidized Stafford Loans, Direct Unsubsidized Stafford Loans, Direct PLUS loans, Federal Perkins Loans, College/university loans from institutional funds. *Student Employment:* Federal Work-Study Program available. Institutional employment available. **Financial Aid Statistics:** 100% needy freshmen, 100% needy undergrads receive need-based scholarship or grant aid. 0% undergrads receive non-need-based

scholarship or grant aid. 90% freshmen, 88% undergrads receive need-based self-help aid. 0% freshmen, 0% undergrads receive athletic scholarships. 94% freshmen, 95% undergrads receive any aid. **Criteria for awarding aid:** *Non-need-based:* Academics, Alumni affiliation, Art, Leadership, Music/drama.

See page 982.

LAKE REGION STATE COLLEGE

1801 College Drive N, Devils Lake, ND 58301-1598
Phone: 701-662-1514 • **Financial Aid Phone:** 701-662-1516
E-mail: lrsc.admissions@lrsc.edu
Fax: 701-662-1581 • **Website:** www.lrsc.edu • **ACT Code:** 3198

This public school was founded in 1941. It has a 120-acre campus.

RATINGS
Admissions Selectivity Rating: 71   **Fire Safety Rating:** 96   **Green Rating:** 60*

STUDENTS AND FACULTY
Enrollment: 696. **Student Body:** 53% female, 47% male, 12% out-of-state, 3% international (14 countries represented). Asian 2%, African American 4%, Caucasian 82%, Hispanic 2%, Native American 5%, Pacific Islander 0%, Two or more races 0%, Race unknown 3%.
Faculty: Student/faculty ratio 13:1. 35 full-time faculty, 14% hold PhDs, 3% are are members of minority groups, 51% are women. 0% of classes are taught by teaching assistants.

ACADEMICS
Degrees: associate, certificate, diploma, terminal, transfer. **Classes:** Most classes have fewer than 10 students. **Most popular majors:** Liberal Arts and Sciences/Liberal Studies; Criminal Justice/Police Science; Business Administration and Management. **Special Study Options:** cooperative education program, cross-registration, distance learning, dual enrollment, English as a Second Language (ESL), internships, liberal arts/career combination. **Disability Services:** Special programs offered to physically disabled students, including note-taking services, reader services, tape recorders, tutors. **Career Services:** Career/job search classes, Internships.

FACILITIES
Housing: special housing for disabled students, men's dorms, women's dorms, apartments for married students, apartments for single students, Coed dorms. for adult students. 100% of campus accessible to physically diasbled. **Special Academic Facilities/Equipment:** Paul Hoghaug Library and Law Library. **Computers:** 100% of classrooms, 100% of dorms, 100% of libraries, 100% of dining areas, 100% of student union, have wireless network access. Students can register for classes online. Administrative functions (other than registration) can be performed online.

CAMPUS LIFE
Environment: Village. **Activities:** drama/theater, literary magazine, musical theater, student government, symphony orchestra 12 registered organizations, 1 religious organization. **Athletics (Intercollegiate):** *Men:* basketball. *Women:* basketball. **On-Campus Highlights:** Student Union, Computer Lab, Recreational Area, Library, Gymnasium.

ADMISSIONS
Freshman Academic Profile: 98% from public high schools. ACT middle 50% range 18-25. Minimum internet-based TOEFL 65. Minimum paper TOEFL 510. **Freshman Admission Requirements:** High school diploma is required and GED is accepted. *Academic units recommended:* 4 English, 3 math, 3 science, 2 science labs, 2 foreign language, 3 social studies. **Freshman Admission Statistics:** 233 applied, 98.71% admitted, 95% enrolled. **Transfer Admission Requirements:** High school transcript, college transcript(s), statement of good standing from prior institution(s). Minimum college GPA of 2.0 required. Lowest grade transferable D. **General Admission Information:** Application fee $35. Nonfall registration accepted. Admission may be deferred for a maximum of one semester.

COSTS AND FINANCIAL AID
Annual in-state tuition $3,065. Annual out-of-state tuition $3,065. Room and board $5,230. Required fees $843. Average book expense $900. **Required Forms and Deadlines:** FAFSA. **Notification of Awards:** Applicants will be notified of awards on a rolling basis beginning 5/15. **Types of Aid:** *Need-based scholarships/grants:* Federal Pell, FSEOG, State scholarships/grants, Private scholarships, College/university scholarship or grant aid from institutional funds. *Loans:* Federal Perkins Loans, State Loans. *Student Employment:* Federal Work-Study Program available. Institutional employment available. **Financial Aid Statistics:** 93% needy freshmen, 87% needy undergrads receive need-based scholarship or grant aid. 1% freshmen, 0% undergrads receive

non-need-based scholarship or grant aid. 86% freshmen, 90% undergrads receive need-based self-help aid. 6% freshmen, 6% undergrads receive athletic scholarships. 80% undergrads receive any aid. **Criteria for awarding aid:** *Need-based:* Academics, Athletics, Minority status. *Non-need-based:* Academics, Athletics, Leadership, Minority status, Music/drama.

LAKE SUPERIOR STATE UNIVERSITY

650 W. Easterday Avenue, Sault Ste. Marie, MI 49783-1699
Phone: 906-635-2231 • **Financial Aid Phone:** 906-635-2678
E-mail: admissions@lssu.edu • **CEEB Code:** 1421
Fax: 906-635-6669 • **ACT Code:** 2031

This public school was founded in 1946. It has a 115-acre campus.

RATINGS
Admissions Selectivity Rating: 74   **Fire Safety Rating:** 60*   **Green Rating:** 60*

STUDENTS AND FACULTY
Enrollment: 2,446. **Student Body:** 50% female, 50% male, 5% out-of-state, 7% international. Asian 1%, African American 1%, Caucasian 79%, Hispanic 2%, Native American 8%, Pacific Islander 0%, Two or more races <1%, Race unknown 2%.
Retention and Graduation: 70% freshmen return for sophomore year. 13% freshmen graduate within 4 years. 33% freshmen graduate within 6 years.
Faculty: Student/faculty ratio 17:1. 114 full-time faculty, 53% hold PhDs, 5% are members of minority groups, 46% are women. 0% of classes are taught by teaching assistants.

ACADEMICS
Degrees: associate, bachelor's, certificate, master's. **Classes:** Most classes have 20-29 students. Most lab/discussion sessions have 10-19 students. **Special Study Options:** cooperative education program, cross-registration, distance learning, double major, dual enrollment, honors program, independent study, internships, student-designed major, teacher certification program, weekend college. **Disability Services:** Special programs offered to physically disabled students, including note-taking services, reader services, tape recorders, tutors.

FACILITIES
Housing: Coed dorms, men's dorms, women's dorms, fraternity/sorority housing, apartments for married students, apartments for single students. 90% of campus accessible to physically disabled. **Special Academic Facilities/Equipment:** Natural science, Michigan history, and Great Lakes shipping museums, planetarium, industrial robots, atomic absorption/flame emission spectrophotometer. **Computers:** Students can register for classes online.

CAMPUS LIFE
Environment: City. **Activities:** Choral groups, concert band, dance, drama/theater, jazz band, literary magazine, music ensembles, pep band, radio station, student government, student newspaper, symphony orchestra 60 registered organizations, 4 fraternities, 4 sororities. **Athletics (Intercollegiate):** *Men:* basketball, cross-country, ice hockey, tennis, track/field (outdoor), track/field (indoor). *Women:* basketball, cross-country, softball, tennis, track/field (outdoor), track/field (indoor), volleyball.

ADMISSIONS
Freshman Academic Profile: Average high school GPA 3.3. 14% in top 10% of high school class, 40% in top 25% of high school class, 75% in top 50% of high school class. ACT middle 50% range 20-25. Minimum paper TOEFL 550. **Basis for Candidate Selection:** *Very important factors considered include:* rigor of secondary school record, academic GPA, standardized test scores. *Other factors considered include:* class rank, recommendation(s), interview, geographical residence. **Freshman Admission Requirements:** High school diploma is required and GED is accepted. *Academic units recommended:* 4 English, 3 math, 3 science, 3 science labs, 2 foreign language, 2 social studies, 1 history. **Freshman Admission Statistics:** 1,425 applied, 89.68% admitted, 34% enrolled. **Transfer Admission Requirements:** college transcript(s), Minimum college GPA of 2.0 required. Lowest grade transferable C-. **General Admission Information:** Application fee $35. Priority deadline 3/1. Nonfall registration accepted. Admission may be deferred for a maximum of 1 Year.

COSTS AND FINANCIAL AID
Annual in-state tuition $9,540. Annual out-of-state tuition $14,410. Room and board $8,481. Required fees $100. Average book expense $1,200. **Required Forms and Deadlines:** FAFSA. **Notification of Awards:** Applicants will be notified of awards on a rolling basis beginning 10/11. **Types of Aid:** *Need-based scholarships/grants:* Federal Pell, FSEOG, State scholarships/grants, Private scholarships, College/university scholarship or grant aid from institutional funds, Federal Nursing Scholarships. *Loans:* Direct Subsidized Stafford Loans, Direct

Unsubsidized Stafford Loans, Direct PLUS loans, Federal Perkins Loans, Federal Nursing Loans. *Student Employment:* Federal Work-Study Program available. Institutional employment available. **Financial Aid Statistics:** 75% needy freshmen, 75% needy undergrads receive need-based scholarship or grant aid. 61% freshmen, 40% undergrads receive non-need-based scholarship or grant aid. 82% freshmen, 90% undergrads receive need-based self-help aid. 10% freshmen, 9% undergrads receive athletic scholarships. 83% undergrads receive any aid. **Criteria for awarding aid:** *Need-based:* Academics, Alumni affiliation, Athletics, Job skills, Leadership, Minority status. *Non-need-based:* Academics, Athletics, State/district residency.

LAKEHEAD UNIVERSITY

955 Oliver Road, Thunder Bay, ON P7B 5E1
Phone: 807-343-8500 • **Financial Aid Phone:** 807-343-8206
E-mail: admissions@lakeheadu.ca
Fax: 807-766-7209 • **Website:** www.lakeheadu.ca

This public school was founded in 1965. It has a 288-acre campus.

RATINGS
Admissions Selectivity Rating: 60*   **Fire Safety Rating:** 60*   **Green Rating:** 60*

STUDENTS AND FACULTY
Retention and Graduation: 85% freshmen return for sophomore year.
Faculty: Student/faculty ratio 24:1.

ACADEMICS
Degrees: bachelor's, certificate, diploma, master's. **Classes:** Most classes have 30-39 students. **Most popular majors:** Engineering; Forestry; Business Administration and Management.

FACILITIES
Housing: Coed dorms, special housing for disabled students, apartments for single students, Wellness Housing. **Computers:** Students can register for classes online.

CAMPUS LIFE
Environment: City. **Activities:** Choral groups, concert band, dance, drama/theater, jazz band, literary magazine, music ensembles, musical theater, radio station, student government, student newspaper, Campus Ministries, Student Organization, Model UN. **Athletics (Intercollegiate):** *Men:* basketball, cross-country, ice hockey, skiing (nordic/cross-country), track/field (outdoor), track/field (indoor), wrestling. *Women:* basketball, cross-country, skiing (nordic/cross-country), track/field (outdoor), track/field (indoor), volleyball, wrestling.

ADMISSIONS
Freshman Admission Requirements: High school diploma is required and GED is accepted. **General Admission Information:** Application fee $105. Priority deadline 6/1. Regular application deadline 9/24. Nonfall registration accepted. Admission may be deferred for a maximum of one year.

COSTS AND FINANCIAL AID
Annual in-state tuition $4,670. Annual out-of-state tuition $4,670. Required fees $825. *Student Employment:* Federal Work-Study Program available. Institutional employment available.

LAMAR UNIVERSITY

P.O. Box 10009, Beaumont, TX 77710
Phone: 409-880-8888
E-mail: admissions@hal.lamar.edu • **CEEB Code:** 6360
Fax: 409-880-8463 • **Website:** www.lamar.edu • **ACT Code:** 4114

This public school was founded in 1923. It has a 200-acre campus.

RATINGS
Admissions Selectivity Rating: 62   **Fire Safety Rating:** 60*   **Green Rating:** 60*

STUDENTS AND FACULTY
Enrollment: 9,551. **Student Body:** 55% female, 45% male, 1% out-of-state, 1% international. Asian 3%, African American 21%, Caucasian 70%, Hispanic 4%, Native American 1%, Pacific Islander 0%, Two or more races 0%, Race unknown 0%.

ACADEMICS

Degrees: bachelor's, master's. **Special Study Options:** cooperative education program, distance learning, double major, dual enrollment, English as a Second Language (ESL), honors program, internships, study abroad, teacher certification program, Texas Academy for Leadership in the Humanities, a two-year residential, early admission program for gifted high school students. Students are selected during the sophomore year of high school and enter the University at the end of their junior year. Combined degree programs: 3-1 program Medicine/Dentistry 3-2 Pharmacy prog. **Disability Services:** Special programs offered to physically disabled students, including note-taking services, reader services, tape recorders, tutors. **Career Services:** Alumni services, Career/job search classes, Career assessment.

FACILITIES

Housing: Coed dorms, men's dorms, women's dorms, fraternity/sorority housing, apartments for single students. **Special Academic Facilities/Equipment:** Museum.

CAMPUS LIFE

Environment: Village. **Activities:** student government, student newspaper. 145 registered organizations, 11 fraternities, 8 sororities. **Athletics (Intercollegiate):** *Men:* baseball, basketball, cross-country, golf, tennis, track/field (outdoor). *Women:* basketball, cross-country, golf, tennis, track/field (outdoor), volleyball.

ADMISSIONS

Freshman Academic Profile: 10% in top 10% of high school class, 27% in top 25% of high school class, 90% in top 50% of high school class. 96% from public high schools. Minimum paper TOEFL 500. **Freshman Admission Requirements:** High school diploma is required and GED is accepted. High school diploma is required and GED is not accepted. *Academic units recommended:* 4 English, 3 math, 2 science, 2 social studies, 2 academic electives. **Freshman Admission Statistics:** Minimum college GPA of 2.0 required. Lowest grade transferable D. **General Admission Information:** Regular application deadline 8/1. Nonfall registration accepted.

COSTS AND FINANCIAL AID

Annual in-state tuition $864. Annual out-of-state tuition $5,976. Room and board $3,040. Required fees $840. **Required Forms and Deadlines:** FAFSA, Institution's own financial aid form, State aid form. *Student Employment:* Federal Work-Study Program available. Institutional employment available.

LAMBUTH UNIVERSITY

705 Lambuth Boulevard, Jackson, TN 38301-5296
Phone: 731-425-3223 • **Financial Aid Phone:** 731-425-3332
E-mail: admit@lambuth.edu • **CEEB Code:** 1394
Fax: 731-425-3496 • **Website:** www.lambuth.edu • **ACT Code:** 3974

This private school, affiliated with the Methodist Church, was founded in 1843. It has a 50-acre campus.

RATINGS

Admissions Selectivity Rating: 84   **Fire Safety Rating:** 87   **Green Rating:** 60*

STUDENTS AND FACULTY

Student Body: 47% female, 53% male, 21% out-of-state, (9 countries represented).
Retention and Graduation: 60% freshmen return for sophomore year. 29% freshmen graduate within 4 years. 39% freshmen graduate within 6 years. 20% grads go on to further study within 1 year. 5% grads pursue arts and sciences degrees. 5% grads pursue law degrees. 5% grads pursue business degrees. 5% grads pursue medical degrees. **Faculty:** Student/faculty ratio 12:1. 51 full-time faculty, 78% hold PhDs, 2% are members of minority groups, 41% are women. 0% of classes are taught by teaching assistants.

ACADEMICS

Degrees: bachelor's. **Classes:** Most classes have fewer than 10 students. Most lab/discussion sessions have 20-29 students. **Most popular majors:** Business/Commerce; Psychology; Health and Physical Education/Fitness. **Special Study Options:** cross-registration, double major, honors program, independent study, internships, student-designed major, study abroad, teacher certification program, Washington Semester. Tennessee Legislative Internship. Interdisciplinary courses. Lambuth in London. **Honors Programs:** University Honors is a 3 semester sequence of courses designed to offer more in-depth study of classic literature and themes. Various topics are considered including art, psychology, ecology, history, ethics, politics, science, sociology, business, religion, and literature. Honors study is available in most disciplines and consists of an 8 hour sequence of research over the last 3 semesters of study in a particular discipline. **Disability Services:** Special programs offered to physically disabled students, including tape recorders, tutors. **Career Services:** Alumni network, Alumni services, Career/job search classes, Career assessment, Internships, Regional alumni. Excellent internships for business, communications, psychology, education and social science majors.

FACILITIES

Housing: Coed dorms, special housing for disabled students, men's dorms, women's dorms, fraternity/sorority housing, apartments for single students. 80% of campus accessible to physically disabled. **Special Academic Facilities/Equipment:** Academic Support Center, Interior Design lab, M.D. Anderson Planetarium, Oxley Biological Field Station **Computers:** 40% of classrooms, 10% of dorms, 100% of libraries, 100% of dining areas, 100% of student union, 50% of common outdoor areas have wireless network access.

CAMPUS LIFE

Environment: City. **Activities:** Choral groups, concert band, dance, drama/theater, jazz band, literary magazine, music ensembles, musical theater, student government, student newspaper, yearbook, Campus Ministries, Student Organization, Model UN. 41 registered organizations, 6 honor societies, 3 religious organizations. 3 fraternities, 3 sororities. **Athletics (Intercollegiate):** *Men:* baseball, basketball, football, golf, soccer, tennis. *Women:* basketball, golf, soccer, softball, tennis. **On-Campus Highlights:** Eagle's Nest Bistro, E/MI Studio, The Quadrangle, Eickoff Plaza, M.D. Anderson Planetarium, Oxley Square (apartment-style dorms) Computer Center Hamilton Performing Arts Center R. E. Womack Memorial Chapel Greek houses Wellness Center Athletic Center/Olympic Pool.

ADMISSIONS

Freshman Academic Profile: Average high school GPA 3.3. 21% in top 10% of high school class, 42% in top 25% of high school class, 71% in top 50% of high school class. 85% from public high schools. **Reported SAT (pre-2016 redesign) scores:** SAT Math middle 50% range 460-570. SAT Critical Reading middle 50% range 440-570. **Concordant SAT scores:** SAT Math middle 50% range 500–590. ACT middle 50% range 20-25. Minimum paper TOEFL 425. **Basis for Candidate Selection:** *Very important factors considered include:* rigor of secondary school record, academic GPA, standardized test scores. *Important factors considered include:* application essay, recommendation(s), interview, extracurricular activities, level of applicant's interest. *Other factors considered include:* class rank, talent/ability, first generation, alumni/ae relation, geographical residence, state residency, religious affiliation/commitment, volunteer work, work experience. **Freshman Admission Requirements:** High school diploma is required and GED is accepted. *Academic units recommended:* 4 English, 3 math, 3 science, 1 foreign language, 2 social studies, 1 history. **Freshman Admission Statistics:** 1,042 applied, 52.69% admitted, 37% enrolled. **Transfer Admission Requirements:** college transcript(s), essay or personal statement, statement of good standing from prior institution(s). Minimum college GPA of 2.0 required. Lowest grade transferable D. **General Admission Information:** Application fee $25. Nonfall registration accepted. Admission may be deferred for a maximum of one year.

COSTS AND FINANCIAL AID

Annual tuition $17,000. Room and board $7,160. Required fees $400. Average book expense $1,200. **Required Forms and Deadlines:** FAFSA, Institution's own financial aid form. **Notification of Awards:** Applicants will be notified of awards on a rolling basis beginning 2/15. **Types of Aid:** *Need-based scholarships/grants:* Federal Pell, FSEOG, State scholarships/grants, Private scholarships, College/university scholarship or grant aid from institutional funds. *Loans:* Federal Perkins Loans. *Student Employment:* Federal Work-Study Program available. Institutional employment available. **Financial Aid Statistics:** 98% needy freshmen, 97% needy undergrads receive need-based scholarship or grant aid. 24% freshmen, 22% undergrads receive non-need-based scholarship or grant aid. 66% freshmen, 69% undergrads receive need-based self-help aid. 9% freshmen, 9% undergrads receive athletic scholarships. 99% freshmen, 99% undergrads receive any aid. **Criteria for awarding aid:** *Need-based:* Academics, Alumni affiliation, Art, Athletics, Job skills, Leadership, Music/drama, Religious affiliation. *Non-need-based:* Academics, Alumni affiliation, Art, Athletics, Job skills, Leadership, Music/drama, Religious affiliation.

LANCASTER BIBLE COLLEGE

901 Eden Rd, Lancaster, PA 17601-5036
Phone: 717-560-8271 • **Financial Aid Phone:** 717-560-8254
E-mail: admissions@lbc.edu • **CEEB Code:** 2388
Fax: 717-560-8213 • **Website:** www.lbc.edu • **ACT Code:** 3707

This private school was founded in 1933. It has a 100-acre campus.

RATINGS

Admissions Selectivity Rating: 62   **Fire Safety Rating:** 77   **Green Rating:** 60*

STUDENTS AND FACULTY

Enrollment: 680. **Student Body:** 47% female, 53% male, 26% out-of-state, 1% international. Asian 1%, African American 3%, Caucasian 73%, Hispanic 1%, Native American <1%, Pacific Islander 0%, Two or more races 0%, Race unknown 20%.
Retention and Graduation: 77% freshmen return for sophomore year.
Faculty: Student/faculty ratio 10:1. 48 full-time faculty, 52% hold PhDs, 2% are are members of minority groups, 25% are women. 0% of classes are taught by teaching assistants.

ACADEMICS

Degrees: associate, bachelor's, certificate, master's, postbachelor's certificate.
Classes: Most classes have fewer than 10 students. Most lab/discussion sessions have 10-19 students. **Most popular majors:** Elementary Education and Teaching; Bible/Biblical Studies; Theology and Religious Vocations. **Special Study Options:** Accelerated program, double major, independent study, internships, study abroad, teacher certification program. **Disability Services:** Special programs offered to physically disabled students, including note-taking services, reader services, tape recorders, tutors. **Career Services:** Alumni network, Internships, On-campus interviews.

FACILITIES

Housing: men's dorms, women's dorms. 80% of campus accessible to physically diasbled.

CAMPUS LIFE

Environment: Village. **Activities:** Choral groups, concert band, drama/theater, music ensembles, musical theater, student government, student newspaper, yearbook. 20 registered organizations. **Athletics (Intercollegiate):** *Men:* baseball, basketball, cheerleading, soccer, volleyball. *Women:* basketball, cheerleading, lacrosse, soccer, volleyball.

ADMISSIONS

Freshman Academic Profile: 60% from public high schools. Minimum paper TOEFL 550. **Basis for Candidate Selection:** *Very important factors considered include:* rigor of secondary school record, standardized test scores, application essay, recommendation(s), character/personal qualities, religious affiliation/commitment. *Important factors considered include:* extracurricular activities. *Other factors considered include:* interview, talent/ability, volunteer work. **Freshman Admission Requirements:** High school diploma is required and GED is accepted. **Freshman Admission Statistics:** 314 applied, 96.82% admitted, 44% enrolled. **Transfer Admission Requirements:** High school transcript, college transcript(s), essay or personal statement, standardized test scores, statement of good standing from prior institution(s). Minimum college GPA of 2.0 required. Lowest grade transferable C. **General Admission Information:** Application fee $25. Priority deadline 8/1. Nonfall registration accepted. Admission may be deferred for a maximum of 1 year.

COSTS AND FINANCIAL AID

Annual tuition $15,930. Room and board $7,110. Required fees $630. Average book expense $1,000. **Required Forms and Deadlines:** FAFSA, State aid form. **Notification of Awards:** Applicants will be notified of awards on a rolling basis beginning 3/1. **Types of Aid:** *Need-based scholarships/grants:* Federal Pell, FSEOG, State scholarships/grants, Private scholarships, College/university scholarship or grant aid from institutional funds. *Loans:* Federal Perkins Loans. *Student Employment:* Federal Work-Study Program available. Institutional employment available. **Financial Aid Statistics:** 98% needy freshmen, 94% needy undergrads receive need-based scholarship or grant aid. 97% freshmen, 79% undergrads receive non-need-based scholarship or grant aid. 83% freshmen, 88% undergrads receive need-based self-help aid. 0% freshmen, 0% undergrads receive athletic scholarships. **Criteria for awarding aid:** *Non-need-based:* Academics, Alumni affiliation, Leadership, Music/drama.

LANDMARK COLLEGE

P.O. Box 820, Putney, VT 05346-0820
Phone: 802-387-6718 • **Financial Aid Phone:** 802-387-6736
E-mail: admissions@landmark.edu
Fax: 802-387-6868 • **Website:** http://www.landmark.edu/ • **ACT Code:** 4317

This private school was founded in 1984. It has a 128-acre campus.

RATINGS

Admissions Selectivity Rating: 71   **Fire Safety Rating:** 83   **Green Rating:** 60*

STUDENTS AND FACULTY

Enrollment: 487. **Student Body:** 32% female, 68% male, 95% out-of-state, 3% international (14 countries represented). Asian 1%, African American 5%, Caucasian 70%, Hispanic 3%, Native American 0%, Pacific Islander 1%, Two or more races 3%, Race unknown 14%.

Retention and Graduation: 95% grads go on to further study within 1 year.
Faculty: Student/faculty ratio 6:1. 86 full-time faculty, 0% hold PhDs, 1% are are members of minority groups, 64% are women. 0% of classes are taught by teaching assistants.

ACADEMICS

Degrees: associate, terminal, transfer. **Classes:** Most classes have 10-19 students. **Special Study Options:** internships, study abroad.

FACILITIES

Housing: Coed dorms, special housing for disabled students, Wellness Housing. 65% of campus accessible to physically diasbled.

CAMPUS LIFE

Environment: Rural. **Activities:** Choral groups, dance, drama/theater, jazz band, literary magazine, music ensembles, radio station, student government.

ADMISSIONS

Freshman Academic Profile: 70% from public high schools. Minimum paper TOEFL 200. **Basis for Candidate Selection:** *Very important factors considered include:* recommendation(s), interview. *Important factors considered include:* character/personal qualities, level of applicant's interest. *Other factors considered include:* rigor of secondary school record, class rank, academic GPA, standardized test scores, application essay, extracurricular activities, talent/ability. **Freshman Admission Requirements:** High school diploma is required and GED is accepted. *Academic units recommended:* 4 English, 3 math, 3 science, 1 foreign language, 3 social studies, 3 history, 1 academic elective, 1 visual/performing arts. **Freshman Admission Statistics:** 395 applied, 53.67% admitted, 54% enrolled. **Transfer Admission Requirements:** High school transcript, college transcript(s), essay or personal statement, interview, Lowest grade transferable C-. **General Admission Information:** Application fee $75. Priority deadline 5/15. Nonfall registration accepted. Admission may be deferred for a maximum of 1 calendar year.

COSTS AND FINANCIAL AID

Annual tuition $48,210. Room and board $8,620. Required fees $500. Average book expense $1,200. **Required Forms and Deadlines:** FAFSA. **Notification of Awards:** Applicants will be notified of awards on a rolling basis beginning 3/15. **Types of Aid:** *Need-based scholarships/grants:* Federal Pell, FSEOG, State scholarships/grants, Private scholarships, College/university scholarship or grant aid from institutional funds. *Loans:* Direct Subsidized Stafford Loans, Direct Unsubsidized Stafford Loans, Direct PLUS loans. *Student Employment:* Federal Work-Study Program available. Institutional employment available. **Financial Aid Statistics:** 100% needy undergrads receive need-based scholarship or grant aid. 4% undergrads receive non-need-based scholarship or grant aid. 100% undergrads receive need-based self-help aid. 0% undergrads receive athletic scholarships. 35% freshmen, 42% undergrads receive any aid. **Criteria for awarding aid:** *Non-need-based:* Academics, Art, Athletics, Leadership, Minority status, Music/drama.

LANE COLLEGE

545 Lane Avenue, Jackson, TN 38301
Phone: 731-426-7533 • **Financial Aid Phone:** 731-426-7536
E-mail: admissions@lanecollege.edu
Fax: 731-426-7559 • **Website:** www.lanecollege.edu • **ACT Code:** 3976

This private school, affiliated with the Methodist Church, was founded in 1882. It has a 25-acre campus.

RATINGS

Admissions Selectivity Rating: 74   **Fire Safety Rating:** 95   **Green Rating:** 60*

STUDENTS AND FACULTY

Enrollment: 972. **Student Body:** 47% female, 53% male, 40% out-of-state, <1% international (1 countries represented). Asian 0%, African American 90%, Caucasian <1%, Hispanic <1%, Native American <1%, Pacific Islander 0%, Two or more races 1%, Race unknown 8%.
Retention and Graduation: 62% freshmen return for sophomore year. 35% grads go on to further study within 1 year. 37% grads pursue arts and sciences degrees. 6% grads pursue law degrees. 10% grads pursue business degrees. 7% grads pursue medical degrees. **Faculty:** Student/faculty ratio 19:1. 65 full-time faculty, 65% hold PhDs, 57% are are members of minority groups, 38% are women. 0% of classes are taught by teaching assistants.

ACADEMICS

Degrees: bachelor's. **Classes:** Most classes have 20-29 students. **Most popular majors:** Criminal Justice/Law Enforcement Administration; Business/Commerce; Biology/Biological Sciences. **Special Study Options:** Accelerated program, independent study, internships, study abroad, teacher certification program. **Disability Services:** Special programs offered to physically disabled students, including tutors. **Career Services:** Alumni services, Career/job search classes, Career assessment, Internships.

FACILITIES

Housing: men's dorms, women's dorms. 98% of campus accessible to physically diasbled. **Special Academic Facilities/Equipment:** The Grand Student Center, The Cyber Cafe. **Computers:** 50% of classrooms, 100% of libraries, 100% of student union, 25% of common outdoor areas have wireless network access.

CAMPUS LIFE

Environment: Town. **Activities:** Choral groups, concert band, dance, drama/theater, marching band, music ensembles, student government, student newspaper, yearbook, Campus Ministries. 21 registered organizations, 6 honor societies, 4 religious organizations. 4 fraternities, 4 sororities. **Athletics (Intercollegiate):** *Men:* baseball, basketball, cross-country, football, tennis, track/field (outdoor). *Women:* basketball, cheerleading, cross-country, softball, tennis, track/field (outdoor), volleyball. **On-Campus Highlights:** Pond at the Plain, Williams/Boyd Campus Center, The Cyber Cafe, Phillips Dining Hall, The Grand.

ADMISSIONS

Freshman Academic Profile: Average high school GPA 2.6. 5% in top 10% of high school class, 17% in top 25% of high school class, 52% in top 50% of high school class. 96% from public high schools. ACT middle 50% range 14-16. Minimum paper TOEFL 339. **Basis for Candidate Selection:** *Very important factors considered include:* rigor of secondary school record, recommendation(s), first generation. *Important factors considered include:* academic GPA, standardized test scores. *Other factors considered include:* class rank, character/personal qualities, level of applicant's interest. **Freshman Admission Requirements:** High school diploma is required and GED is accepted. *Academic units recommended:* 4 English, 2 math, 2 science, 2 foreign language, 2 social studies. **Freshman Admission Statistics:** 5,311 applied, 50.27% admitted, 15% enrolled. **Transfer Admission Requirements:** college transcript(s), standardized test scores, statement of good standing from prior institution(s). Lowest grade transferable C. **General Admission Information:** Regular application deadline 7/1. Nonfall registration accepted. Admission may be deferred for a maximum of 2 semesters.

COSTS AND FINANCIAL AID

Annual tuition $9,000. Required fees $1,690. Average book expense $1,300. **Required Forms and Deadlines:** FAFSA. **Notification of Awards:** Applicants will be notified of awards on a rolling basis beginning 3/1. **Types of Aid:** *Need-based scholarships/grants:* Federal Pell, FSEOG, State scholarships/grants, Private scholarships, College/university scholarship or grant aid from institutional funds, United Negro College Fund. *Loans:* Direct Subsidized Stafford Loans, Direct Unsubsidized Stafford Loans, Direct PLUS loans. *Student Employment:* Federal Work-Study Program available. Institutional employment available. **Financial Aid Statistics:** 98% needy freshmen, 94% needy undergrads receive need-based scholarship or grant aid. 87% freshmen, 85% undergrads receive non-need-based scholarship or grant aid. 96% freshmen, 92% undergrads receive need-based self-help aid. 12% freshmen, 10% undergrads receive athletic scholarships. 96% freshmen, 98% undergrads receive any aid. **Criteria for awarding aid:** *Need-based:* Academics, Athletics, Religious affiliation. *Non-need-based:* Academics, Athletics, Religious affiliation.

LASELL COLLEGE

Office of Undergraduate Admissions, Newton, MA 2466
Phone: 617-243-2225 • **Financial Aid Phone:** 617-243-2227
E-mail: info@lasell.edu • **CEEB Code:** 3481
Fax: 617-243-2380 • **Website:** www.lasell.edu • **ACT Code:** 1848

This private school was founded in 1851. It has a 55-acre campus.

RATINGS

Admissions Selectivity Rating: 73   Fire Safety Rating: 78   Green Rating: 67

STUDENTS AND FACULTY

Enrollment: 1,778. **Student Body:** 65% female, 35% male, 42% out-of-state, 6% international (15 countries represented). Asian 2%, African American 5%, Caucasian 71%, Hispanic 9%, Native American <1%, Pacific Islander <1%, Two or more races 2%, Race unknown 4%.
Retention and Graduation: 80% freshmen return for sophomore year. 46% freshmen graduate within 4 years. 51% freshmen graduate within 6 years. 12% grads go on to further study within 1 year. 13% grads pursue arts and sciences degrees. 5% grads pursue business degrees. **Faculty:** Student/faculty ratio 13:1. 93 full-time faculty, 78% hold PhDs, 18% are are members of minority groups, 66% are women. 0% of classes are taught by teaching assistants.

ACADEMICS

Degrees: bachelor's, master's. **Classes:** Most classes have 10-19 students. Most lab/discussion sessions have 10-19 students. **Most popular majors:** Fashion/Apparel Design; Sport and Fitness Administration/Management; Psychology. **Special Study Options:** double major, honors program, internships, liberal arts/career combination, study abroad. **Honors Programs:** Lasell College Honor's Program. **Career Services:** Alumni services, Career/job search classes, Career assessment, Internships.

FACILITIES

Housing: Coed dorms, women's dorms, Special interst (human services). Some houses Alcohol free. All houses Smoke free. 30% of campus accessible to physically diasbled. **Special Academic Facilities/Equipment:** Center for Public Service—Yamawaki Art/Cultural Center.

CAMPUS LIFE

Environment: City. **Activities:** Choral groups, dance, drama/theater, literary magazine, music ensembles, musical theater, radio station, student government, student newspaper, television station, yearbook. 30 registered organizations, 1 honor society. **Athletics (Intercollegiate):** *Men:* basketball, cross-country, lacrosse, soccer, volleyball. *Women:* basketball, cross-country, field hockey, lacrosse, soccer, softball, volleyball. **On-Campus Highlights:** Yamawaki Art and Cultural Center, Campus Center, Athletic Center, Winslow Academic Center, Edwards Student Center.

ADMISSIONS

Freshman Academic Profile: Average high school GPA 3.0. 80% from public high schools. **Reported SAT (pre-2016 redesign) scores:** SAT Math middle 50% range 430-530. SAT Critical Reading middle 50% range 440-530. SAT Writing middle 50% range 430-520. **Concordant SAT scores:** SAT EBRW middle 50% 490–580. SAT Math middle 50% range 470–560. ACT middle 50% range 19-22. Minimum paper TOEFL 500. **Basis for Candidate Selection:** *Very important factors considered include:* rigor of secondary school record, academic GPA, interview. *Important factors considered include:* standardized test scores, application essay, recommendation(s), extracurricular activities, volunteer work, work experience. *Other factors considered include:* talent/ability, character/personal qualities, alumni/ae relation. **Freshman Admission Requirements:** High school diploma is required and GED is accepted. *Academic units required:* 4 English, 3 math, 2 science, 2 science labs, 1 social studies, 1 history. *Academic units recommended:* 4 English, 4 math, 3 science, 3 science labs, 2 foreign language, 2 social studies, 2 history. **Freshman Admission Statistics:** 3,221 applied, 76.06% admitted, 18% enrolled. **Transfer Admission Requirements:** college transcript(s), standardized test scores, statement of good standing from prior institution(s). Minimum college GPA of 2.3 required. Lowest grade transferable C. **General Admission Information:** Application fee $40. Priority deadline 11/15. Nonfall registration accepted. Admission may be deferred for a maximum of 1 year.

COSTS AND FINANCIAL AID

Required Forms and Deadlines: FAFSA. **Notification of Awards:** Applicants will be notified of awards on a rolling basis beginning 2/15. **Types of Aid:** *Need-based scholarships/grants:* Federal Pell, FSEOG, State scholarships/grants, Private scholarships, College/university scholarship or grant aid from institutional funds. *Loans:* Direct Subsidized Stafford Loans, Direct Unsubsidized Stafford Loans, Direct PLUS loans, Federal Perkins Loans. *Student Employment:* Federal Work-Study Program available. Institutional employment available. **Financial Aid Statistics:** 100% needy freshmen receive need-based scholarship or grant aid. 87% freshmen, 85% undergrads receive any aid. **Criteria for awarding aid:** *Need-based:* Academics, Alumni affiliation, Leadership. *Non-need-based:* Academics, Alumni affiliation, Leadership.

LAWRENCE TECHNOLOGICAL UNIVERSITY

21000 West Ten Mile Rd., Southfield, MI 48075-1058
Phone: 248-204-3160 • **Financial Aid Phone:** 248-204-2280
E-mail: admissions@ltu.edu • **CEEB Code:** 1399
Fax: 248-204-3188 • **Website:** www.ltu.edu • **ACT Code:** 2020

This private school was founded in 1932. It has a 102-acre campus.

RATINGS

Admissions Selectivity Rating: 84   Fire Safety Rating: 93   Green Rating: 77

STUDENTS AND FACULTY

Enrollment: 2,004. **Student Body:** 27% female, 73% male, 6% out-of-state, 16% international (37 countries represented). Asian 2%, African American 6%, Caucasian 64%, Hispanic 4%, Native American <1%, Pacific Islander 0%, Two or more races 2%, Race unknown 4%.

Retention and Graduation: 80% freshmen return for sophomore year. 10% grads go on to further study within 1 year. **Faculty:** Student/faculty ratio 11:1. 122 full-time faculty, 67% hold PhDs, 26% are are members of minority groups, 28% are women. 0% of classes are taught by teaching assistants.

ACADEMICS

Degrees: associate, bachelor's, certificate, doctoral/research, doctoral, master's, postbachelor's certifiate. **Classes:** Most classes have 10-19 students. Most lab/discussion sessions have fewer than 10 students. **Most popular majors:** Mechanical Engineering; Architecture; Business Administration and Management. **Special Study Options:** cooperative education program, cross-registration, distance learning, double major, dual enrollment, English as a Second Language (ESL), honors program, independent study, internships, liberal arts/career combination, study abroad, weekend college. **Honors Programs:** The LTU Honors Program is designed for highly qualified students who want an educational experience that will take full advantage of the challenging curricula offered at Lawrence Tech. Combined degree programs: BA/MEng, Many dual degree combinations. **Disability Services:** Special programs offered to physically disabled students, including note-taking services, reader services, tape recorders, tutors. **Career Services:** Alumni network, Alumni services, Career/job search classes, Career assessment, Internships, Regional alumni. Career Services maintains an agile job search database that is available and used by current students as well as alumni. Employers are engaged and actively recruiting students and alumni in a very dynamic job market and career staff members work closely with student and alumni candidates to connect them to a myriad of job opportunities utilizing career planning, job search assistance and resume and interview coaching.

FACILITIES

Housing: special housing for disabled students, fraternity/sorority housing, apartments for married students, apartments for single students. 97% of campus accessible to physically diasbled. **Special Academic Facilities/Equipment:** Albert Kahn Library Center for Innovative Materials Research **Computers:** 100% of classrooms, 100% of dorms, 100% of libraries, 100% of dining areas, 100% of student union, 75% of common outdoor areas have wireless network access. Students can register for classes online. Administrative functions (other than registration) can be performed online. Undergraduates are required to own a computer.

CAMPUS LIFE

Environment: City. **Activities:** drama/theater, literary magazine, music ensembles, student government, student newspaper. 54 registered organizations, 7 honor societies, 1 religious organization. 6 fraternities, 3 sororities. **On-Campus Highlights:** Atrium, Field House, Engineering Lounge, Larry Joe Coffee Bar, Housing. **Environmental Initiatives:** A. Alfred Taubman Student Services Center is a green building including geothermal wells and a vegetated roof. It serves as a living laboratory for sustainability education of architects and engineers.

ADMISSIONS

Freshman Academic Profile: Average high school GPA 3.5. 26% in top 10% of high school class, 53% in top 25% of high school class, 83% in top 50% of high school class. **Reported SAT (pre-2016 redesign) scores:** SAT Math middle 50% range 560-660. SAT Critical Reading middle 50% range 480-600. SAT Writing middle 50% range 480-570. **Concordant SAT scores:** SAT EBRW middle 50% 540–640. SAT Math middle 50% range 580–690. ACT middle 50% range 22-29. Minimum internet-based TOEFL 79. Minimum paper TOEFL 550. **Basis for Candidate Selection:** *Very important factors considered include:* rigor of secondary school record, academic GPA, standardized test scores. *Other factors considered include:* application essay, recommendation(s), interview. **Freshman Admission Requirements:** High school diploma is required and GED is accepted. *Academic units required:* 4 English, 3 math, 2 science, 3 social studies. *Academic units recommended:* 4 English, 4 math, 4 science, 2 science labs, 2 history. **Freshman Admission Statistics:** 2,318 applied, 69.33% admitted, 23% enrolled. **Transfer Admission Requirements:** High school transcript, college transcript(s), Minimum college GPA of 2.2 required. Lowest grade transferable C. **General Admission Information:** Application fee $30. Nonfall registration accepted. Admission may be deferred for a maximum of 3 years.

COSTS AND FINANCIAL AID

Required Forms and Deadlines: FAFSA. **Notification of Awards:** Applicants will be notified of awards on a rolling basis beginning 3/1. **Types of Aid:** *Need-based scholarships/grants:* Federal Pell, FSEOG, State scholarships/grants, Private scholarships, College/university scholarship or grant aid from institutional funds. *Loans:* Direct Subsidized Stafford Loans, Direct Unsubsidized Stafford Loans, Direct PLUS loans, Federal Perkins Loans, State Loans. *Student Employment:* Federal Work-Study Program available. Institutional employment available. **Financial Aid Statistics:** 99% needy freshmen, 97% needy undergrads receive need-based scholarship or grant aid. 91% freshmen, 83% undergrads receive non-need-based scholarship or grant aid. 81% freshmen, 85% undergrads receive need-based self-help aid. 15% freshmen, 13% undergrads receive athletic scholarships. 94% freshmen, 54%

undergrads receive any aid. 66% undergrads borrow to pay for school. Average cumulative indebtedness $35,810. **Criteria for awarding aid:** *Non-need-based:* Academics, Alumni affiliation, Athletics, Leadership, Minority status, State/district residency.

See page 984.

LAWRENCE UNIVERSITY

711 East Boldt Way, Appleton, WI 54911-5699
Phone: 920-832-6500 • **Financial Aid Phone:** 920-832-6583
E-mail: admissions@lawrence.edu • **CEEB Code:** 1398
Fax: 920-832-6782 • **Website:** www.lawrence.edu • **ACT Code:** 4596

This private school was founded in 1847. It has a 84-acre campus.

RATINGS

Admissions Selectivity Rating: 89   **Fire Safety Rating:** 83   **Green Rating:** 73

STUDENTS AND FACULTY

Enrollment: 1,527. **Student Body:** 55% female, 45% male, 71% out-of-state, 10% international (32 countries represented). Asian 5%, African American 3%, Caucasian 70%, Hispanic 7%, Native American <1%, Pacific Islander <1%, Two or more races 4%, Race unknown 1%.
Retention and Graduation: 89% freshmen return for sophomore year. 63% freshmen graduate within 4 years. 76% freshmen graduate within 6 years. 22% grads go on to further study within 1 year. 11% grads pursue arts and sciences degrees. 3% grads pursue law degrees. 2% grads pursue medical degrees. **Faculty:** Student/faculty ratio 9:1. 166 full-time faculty, 91% hold PhDs, 11% are are members of minority groups, 40% are women. 0% of classes are taught by teaching assistants.

ACADEMICS

Degrees: bachelor's. **Classes:** Most classes have fewer than 10 students. **Most popular majors:** Music Performance; Biology/Biological Sciences; Psychology. **Special Study Options:** double major, independent study, internships, student-designed major, study abroad, teacher certification program. Combined degree programs: BA/BMus. **Disability Services:** Special programs offered to physically disabled students, including note-taking services, reader services, tape recorders, tutors. **Career Services:** Alumni network, Alumni services, Career/job search classes, Career assessment, Internships, Regional alumni. Launched in 2008, Lawrence Scholars in Business (LSB) is designed for students who are interested in distinguishing themselves as strong candidates for careers in the competitive world of business, including: banking, consulting, marketing, arts management, insurance, finance, entrepreneurship, and investment management.

FACILITIES

Housing: Coed dorms, special housing for disabled students, men's dorms, women's dorms, apartments for married students, Theme Housing, theme/group houses available. 95% of campus accessible to physically diasbled. **Special Academic Facilities/Equipment:** Art galleries, anthropology collection, 425-acre estate on Lake Michigan hosting retreats and seminars for students, new student center (Warch Center) electron microscope, laser physics lab, physics/computational graphics lab, nuclear magnetic resonance spectrometer. **Computers:** 100% of classrooms, 20% of dorms, 100% of libraries, 100% of dining areas, 100% of student union, have wireless network access. Students can register for classes online. Administrative functions (other than registration) can be performed online.

CAMPUS LIFE

Environment: City. **Activities:** Choral groups, concert band, dance, drama/theater, jazz band, literary magazine, music ensembles, musical theater, opera, pep band, radio station, student government, student newspaper, student-run film society, symphony orchestra, yearbook, Campus Ministries, Student Organization, Model UN. 90 registered organizations, 5 honor societies, 3 religious organizations. 5 fraternities, 3 sororities. **Athletics (Intercollegiate):** *Men:* baseball, basketball, cross-country, diving, fencing, football, golf, ice hockey, soccer, swimming, tennis, track/field (outdoor), track/field (indoor), wrestling. *Women:* basketball, cross-country, diving, fencing, soccer, softball, swimming, tennis, track/field (outdoor), track/field (indoor), volleyball. **On-Campus Highlights:** Wriston Art Gallery, Music Conservatory, New Warch Campus Center -opening '09, New $18 million Science Building, Hiett Hall (new $8 million residence hall). **Environmental Initiatives:** Construction of LEED certified Student Center—Gold!

ADMISSIONS

Freshman Academic Profile: Average high school GPA 3.6. 42% in top 10% of high school class, 77% in top 25% of high school class, 97% in top 50% of high school class. **Reported SAT (pre-2016 redesign) scores:** SAT Math middle 50% range 610-730. SAT Critical Reading middle 50% range 560-690. SAT Writing middle 50% range 580-690. **Concordant SAT scores:** SAT EBRW middle 50% 630–730. SAT Math middle 50% range 630–760. ACT middle 50% range 26-32. Minimum internet-based TOEFL 90. Minimum paper TOEFL 577. **Basis for Candidate Selection:** *Very important factors considered include:* rigor of secondary school record, class rank, academic GPA, talent/ability, character/personal qualities. *Important factors considered include:* application essay, recommendation(s), interview, extracurricular activities. *Other factors considered include:* standardized test scores, first generation, alumni/ae relation, geographical residence, racial/ethnic status, volunteer work, work experience, level of applicant's interest. **Freshman Admission Requirements:** High school diploma is required and GED is not accepted. *Academic units recommended:* 4 English, 3 math, 3 science, 2 foreign language, 2 social studies, 2 history. **Freshman Admission Statistics:** 3,014 applied, 68.25% admitted, 19% enrolled. **Transfer Admission Requirements:** High school transcript, college transcript(s), essay or personal statement, Minimum college GPA of 2.75 required. Lowest grade transferable C-. **General Admission Information:** Regular application deadline 1/15. Regular notification 4/1. Nonfall registration accepted. Admission may be deferred for a maximum of 1 year.

COSTS AND FINANCIAL AID

Annual tuition $44,544. Room and board $9,654. Required fees $300. Average book expense $900. **Required Forms and Deadlines:** FAFSA, CSS/Financial Aid PROFILE, Noncustodial PROFILE. **Notification of Awards:** Applicants will be notified of awards on a rolling basis beginning 3/1. **Types of Aid:** *Need-based scholarships/grants:* Federal Pell, FSEOG, State scholarships/grants, Private scholarships, College/university scholarship or grant aid from institutional funds. *Loans:* Direct Subsidized Stafford Loans, Direct Unsubsidized Stafford Loans, Direct PLUS loans, Federal Perkins Loans. *Student Employment:* Federal Work-Study Program available. Institutional employment available. **Financial Aid Statistics:** 96% needy freshmen, 99% needy undergrads receive need-based scholarship or grant aid. 0% undergrads receive non-need-based scholarship or grant aid. 80% freshmen, 80% undergrads receive need-based self-help aid. 0% freshmen, 0% undergrads receive athletic scholarships. 97% freshmen, 97% undergrads receive any aid. 62% undergrads borrow to pay for school. Average cumulative indebtedness $33,343. **Criteria for awarding aid:** *Need-based:* Academics, Music/drama. *Non-need-based:* Academics, Alumni affiliation, Leadership, Minority status, Music/drama.

LE MOYNE COLLEGE

1419 Salt Springs Rd., Syracuse, NY 13214-1301
Phone: 315-445-4300 • **Financial Aid Phone:** 315-445-4400
E-mail: admission@lemoyne.edu • **CEEB Code:** 2366
Fax: 315-445-4711 • **Website:** www.lemoyne.edu • **ACT Code:** 2790

This private school, affiliated with the Roman Catholic Church, was founded in 1946. It has a 161-acre campus.

RATINGS

Admissions Selectivity Rating: 84   Fire Safety Rating: 90   Green Rating: 74

STUDENTS AND FACULTY

Enrollment: 2,793. **Student Body:** 60% female, 40% male, 5% out-of-state, 1% international (36 countries represented). Asian 2%, African American 6%, Caucasian 79%, Hispanic 5%, Native American <1%, Pacific Islander <1%, Two or more races 2%, Race unknown 4%.
Retention and Graduation: 86% freshmen return for sophomore year. 58% freshmen graduate within 4 years. 67% freshmen graduate within 6 years. 41% grads go on to further study within 1 year. 9% grads pursue arts and sciences degrees. 3% grads pursue law degrees. 3% grads pursue business degrees. 4% grads pursue medical degrees. **Faculty:** Student/faculty ratio 13:1. 170 full-time faculty, 91% hold PhDs, 15% are are members of minority groups, 43% are women. 0% of classes are taught by teaching assistants.

ACADEMICS

Degrees: bachelor's, master's, postbachelor's certificate, post-master's certificate.
Classes: Most classes have 10-19 students. Most lab/discussion sessions

have 10-19 students. **Most popular majors:** Biology/Biological Sciences; Psychology; Accounting. **Special Study Options:** Accelerated program, double major, dual enrollment, honors program, independent study, internships, study abroad, teacher certification program, Certificate of Advanced Studies in Educational Leadership and Certificate of Advanced Studies in Nursing. **Honors Programs:** Students in the program complete a 21-hour sequence of interdisciplinary humanities courses that replaces the standard core requirements in English, history, philosophy, and religious studies. Seniors complete an honors project working in close collaboration with a faculty advisor. Combined degree programs: BA/MD, BA/JD, BA/MA, BA/DDS, BA/MEng, Pre-Dental, Pre-Optometry, Pre-Podiatry; Dr. of Physical Therapy. **Disability Services:** Special programs offered to physically disabled students, including note-taking services, reader services, tape recorders, tutors. **Career Services:** Alumni network, Alumni services, Career/job search classes, Career assessment, Internships, Regional alumni. Business Internship Programs, Health Profession Fair, Teacher Recruitment Days and Annual Internship and Career Fairs.

FACILITIES

Housing: Coed dorms, special housing for disabled students, men's dorms, women's dorms, apartments for single students, Living/Learning Communities. 98% of campus accessible to physically diasbled. **Special Academic Facilities/Equipment:** Art gallery, audiovisual center, electron microscopes and Academic Support Center. **Computers:** 100% of classrooms, 75% of dorms, 100% of libraries, 100% of dining areas, 100% of student union, 100% of common outdoor areas have wireless network access. Students can register for classes online. Administrative functions (other than registration) can be performed online.

CAMPUS LIFE

Environment: City. **Activities:** Choral groups, concert band, dance, drama/theater, jazz band, literary magazine, music ensembles, musical theater, pep band, radio station, student government, student newspaper, student-run film society, television station, yearbook, Campus Ministries, Student Organization, Model UN. 70 registered organizations, 14 honor societies, 11 religious organizations. **Athletics (Intercollegiate):** *Men:* baseball, basketball, cross-country, diving, golf, lacrosse, soccer, swimming, tennis. *Women:* basketball, cross-country, diving, golf, lacrosse, soccer, softball, swimming, tennis, volleyball. **On-Campus Highlights:** The Thomas J. Niland Athletic Complex, Campus Center, The W.Carroll Coyne Center for the Performing Arts, Panasci Family Chapel, Noreen Reale Falcone Library. **Environmental Initiatives:** LEED GOLD certification on new science building.

ADMISSIONS

Freshman Academic Profile: Average high school GPA 3.5. 25% in top 10% of high school class, 54% in top 25% of high school class, 86% in top 50% of high school class. 87% from public high schools. **Reported SAT (pre-2016 redesign) scores:** SAT Math middle 50% range 510-610. SAT Critical Reading middle 50% range 490-600. **Concordant SAT scores:** SAT Math middle 50% range 540–630. ACT middle 50% range 22-28. Minimum internet-based TOEFL 79. Minimum paper TOEFL 550. **Basis for Candidate Selection:** *Very important factors considered include:* rigor of secondary school record, academic GPA. *Important factors considered include:* class rank, application essay, recommendation(s), interview, extracurricular activities, talent/ability, work experience. *Other factors considered include:* standardized test scores, character/personal qualities, alumni/ae relation, geographical residence, state residency, volunteer work, level of applicant's interest. **Freshman Admission Requirements:** High school diploma is required and GED is accepted. *Academic units required:* 4 English, 3 math, 3 science, 3 foreign language, 4 social studies. *Academic units recommended:* 4 math, 4 science, 3 science labs. **Freshman Admission Statistics:** 6,832 applied, 65.31% admitted, 14% enrolled. **Transfer Admission Requirements:** college transcript(s), essay or personal statement, Minimum college GPA of 2.6 required. Lowest grade transferable C-. **General Admission Information:** Application fee $35. Priority deadline 2/1. Nonfall registration accepted. Admission may be deferred for a maximum of 12 months.

COSTS AND FINANCIAL AID

Annual tuition $32,040. Room and board $12,970. Required fees $990. Average book expense $1,300. **Required Forms and Deadlines:** FAFSA, State aid form. **Notification of Awards:** Applicants will be notified of awards on or about 3/15. **Types of Aid:** *Need-based scholarships/grants:* Federal Pell, FSEOG, State scholarships/grants, Private scholarships, College/university scholarship or grant aid from institutional funds. *Loans:* Direct Subsidized Stafford Loans, Direct Unsubsidized Stafford Loans, Direct PLUS loans, Federal Perkins Loans. *Student Employment:* Federal Work-Study Program available. Institutional employment available. **Financial Aid Statistics:** 100% needy freshmen, 100% needy undergrads receive need-based scholarship or grant aid. 16% freshmen, 14% undergrads receive non-need-based scholarship or grant aid. 78% freshmen, 80% undergrads receive need-based self-help aid. 3% freshmen, 3% undergrads receive athletic scholarships. 88% freshmen, 91% undergrads receive any aid. 84% undergrads borrow to pay for school. Average cumulative indebtedness $37,337. **Criteria for awarding aid:** *Non-need-based:* Academics, Alumni affiliation, Athletics, Leadership, Minority status.

See page 986.

LEBANON VALLEY COLLEGE

101 North College Avenue, Annville, PA 17003-1400
Phone: 717-867-6181 • **Financial Aid Phone:** 717-867-6126
E-mail: admission@lvc.edu • **CEEB Code:** 2364
Fax: 717-867-6026 • **Website:** www.lvc.edu • **ACT Code:** 3610

This private school, affiliated with the Methodist Church, was founded in 1866. It has a 340-acre campus.

RATINGS
Admissions Selectivity Rating: 84   **Fire Safety Rating:** 94   **Green Rating:** 85

STUDENTS AND FACULTY
Enrollment: 1,649. **Student Body:** 54% female, 46% male, 20% out-of-state, <1% international (5 countries represented). Asian 2%, African American 3%, Caucasian 83%, Hispanic 5%, Native American <1%, Pacific Islander <1%, Two or more races 3%, Race unknown 3%.
Retention and Graduation: 82% freshmen return for sophomore year. 72% freshmen graduate within 4 years. 76 33% grads go on to further study within 1 year. 21% grads pursue arts and sciences degrees. 3% grads pursue law degrees. 1% grads pursue business degrees. 3% grads pursue medical degrees. **Faculty:** Student/faculty ratio 11:1. 113 full-time faculty, 88% hold PhDs, 12% are are members of minority groups, 42% are women. 0% of classes are taught by teaching assistants.

ACADEMICS
Degrees: bachelor's, doctoral/professional, master's, postbachelor's certificate. **Classes:** Most classes have 10-19 students. Most lab/discussion sessions have 10-19 students. **Most popular majors:** Health Services/Allied Health/Health Sciences; Early Childhood Education and Teaching; Business Administration and Management. **Special Study Options:** double major, dual enrollment, independent study, internships, liberal arts/career combination, student-designed major, study abroad, teacher certification program. Combined degree programs: 3+1 Account/MBA at LVC. **Disability Services:** Special programs offered to physically disabled students, including note-taking services, reader services, tape recorders, tutors. **Career Services:** Alumni network, Career assessment, Internships. Handshake, our online Career Management Platform, that provides students with the opportunity to perform a national search for jobs/internships, apply for and schedule on-campus interviews with recruiters, track and attend events and fairs hosted by the center for career development, and connect with alumni through the mentoring database.

FACILITIES
Housing: Coed dorms, special housing for disabled students, women's dorms, apartments for single students, Theme Housing, suites. 78% of campus accessible to physically diasbled. **Special Academic Facilities/Equipment:** Electric pianos, sound recording studio, transmission electron microscope, scanning electron microscope, Fourier transform infrared spectrometer, atomic absorption spectrometer, nuclear magnetic resonance spectrometer, molecular modeling lab, campus Arboretum, art gallery, therapy pool **Computers:** 100% of classrooms, 100% of dorms, 100% of libraries, 100% of dining areas, 100% of student union, 90% of common outdoor areas have wireless network access. Students can register for classes online. Administrative functions (other than registration) can be performed online.

CAMPUS LIFE
Environment: Rural. **Activities:** Choral groups, drama/theater, jazz band, literary magazine, marching band, music ensembles, musical theater, radio station, student government, student newspaper, symphony orchestra, yearbook, Campus Ministries. 79 registered organizations, 6 honor societies, 14 religious organizations. 4 fraternities, 4 sororities. **Athletics (Intercollegiate):** *Men:* baseball, basketball, cross-country, football, golf, ice hockey, lacrosse, soccer, swimming, tennis, track/field (outdoor), track/field (indoor). *Women:* basketball, cross-country, field hockey, lacrosse, soccer, softball, swimming, tennis, track/field (outdoor), track/field (indoor), volleyball. **On-Campus Highlights:** Neidig Garber Science Center, Lynch Memorial—Synodinos Commons, The Peace Garden, Bishop Library, Suzanne Arnold Art Gallery and Zimmerman Recital Hall, Athletic fields are outstanding. Stanson Residence Hall, with 148 beds, was opened in Fall 2009. **Environmental Initiatives:** energy conservation.

ADMISSIONS
Freshman Academic Profile: Average high school GPA 3.7. 30% in top 10% of high school class, 59% in top 25% of high school class, 86% in top 50% of high school class. **Reported SAT (pre-2016 redesign) scores:** SAT Math

middle 50% range 490-620. SAT Critical Reading middle 50% range 480-600. SAT Writing middle 50% range 455-580. **Concordant SAT scores:** SAT EBRW middle 50% 530–650. SAT Math middle 50% range 520–640. Minimum internet-based TOEFL 80. Minimum paper TOEFL 550. **Basis for Candidate Selection:** *Very important factors considered include:* rigor of secondary school record, class rank, academic GPA. *Important factors considered include:* interview, extracurricular activities, talent/ability, character/personal qualities, level of applicant's interest. *Other factors considered include:* standardized test scores, application essay, recommendation(s), first generation, alumni/ae relation, geographical residence, state residency, racial/ethnic status, volunteer work, work experience. **Freshman Admission Requirements:** High school diploma is required and GED is accepted. *Academic units required:* 4 English, 3 math, 3 science, 2 foreign language, 3 social studies, and 1 unit from above areas or other academic areas. *Academic units recommended:* 2 science labs, 3 foreign language, 2 history. **Freshman Admission Statistics:** 2,561 applied, 76.06% admitted, 22% enrolled. **Transfer Admission Requirements:** High school transcript, college transcript(s), essay or personal statement, statement of good standing from prior institution(s). Minimum college GPA of 2.0 required. Lowest grade transferable C-. **General Admission Information:** Priority deadline 3/1. Nonfall registration accepted.

COSTS AND FINANCIAL AID
Annual tuition $40,990. Room and board $11,410. Required fees $1,190. Average book expense $1,150. **Required Forms and Deadlines:** FAFSA. **Notification of Awards:** Applicants will be notified of awards on a rolling basis beginning 3/1. **Types of Aid:** *Need-based scholarships/grants:* Federal Pell, FSEOG, State scholarships/grants, Private scholarships, College/university scholarship or grant aid from institutional funds. *Loans:* Direct Subsidized Stafford Loans, Direct Unsubsidized Stafford Loans, Direct PLUS loans, Federal Perkins Loans, College/university loans from institutional funds. *Student Employment:* Federal Work-Study Program available. Institutional employment available. **Financial Aid Statistics:** 100% needy freshmen, 99% needy undergrads receive need-based scholarship or grant aid. 12% freshmen, 11% undergrads receive non-need-based scholarship or grant aid. 86% freshmen, 84% undergrads receive need-based self-help aid. 0% freshmen, 0% undergrads receive athletic scholarships. 99% freshmen, 99% undergrads receive any aid. Average cumulative indebtedness $46,346. **Criteria for awarding aid:** *Need-based:* Academics, Minority status. *Non-need-based:* Academics, Alumni affiliation, Music/drama.

LEE UNIVERSITY

P.O. Box 3450, Cleveland, TN 37320-3450
Phone: 423-614-8500 • **Financial Aid Phone:** 423-614-8300
E-mail: admissions@leeuniversity.edu • **CEEB Code:** 1401
Fax: 423-614-8533 • **Website:** www.leeuniversity.edu • **ACT Code:** 3978

This private school, affiliated with the Church of God Church, was founded in 1918. It has a 115-acre campus.

RATINGS
Admissions Selectivity Rating: 82   **Fire Safety Rating:** 93   **Green Rating:** 60*

STUDENTS AND FACULTY
Enrollment: 4,261. **Student Body:** 61% female, 39% male, 56% out-of-state, 4% international (50 countries represented). Asian 1%, African American 6%, Caucasian 80%, Hispanic 3%, Native American <1%, Pacific Islander <1%, Two or more races 2%, Race unknown 4%.
Retention and Graduation: 76% freshmen return for sophomore year. 34% freshmen graduate within 4 years. 50% freshmen graduate within 6 years. 17% grads pursue arts and sciences degrees. 1% grads pursue law degrees. 3% grads pursue business degrees. 2% grads pursue medical degrees. **Faculty:** Student/faculty ratio 17:1. 175 full-time faculty, 74% hold PhDs, 10% are are members of minority groups, 36% are women. 0% of classes are taught by teaching assistants.

ACADEMICS
Degrees: bachelor's, master's, post-master's certificate. **Classes:** Most classes have 20-29 students. Most lab/discussion sessions have fewer than 10 students. **Most popular majors:** Psychology; Business Administration and Management; Pastoral Studies/Counseling. **Special Study Options:** distance learning, double major, dual enrollment, English as a Second Language (ESL), exchange student program (domestic), external degree program, honors program, independent study, internships, liberal arts/career combination, study abroad, teacher certification program. **Honors Programs:** The Kairos Scholars Honors Program. Also, several academic subject honors societies like Psychology, Business, Music and Pre-Med. **Disability Services:** Special programs offered to physically disabled students, including reader services, tape recorders,

tutors. **Career Services:** Alumni network, Alumni services, Career assessment, Internships, On-campus interviews.

FACILITIES

Housing: men's dorms, women's dorms, apartments for married students, apartments for single students, Wellness HousingLee University leases apartments and houses for students. 76.92% of campus accessible to physically diasbled. **Special Academic Facilities/Equipment:** Curriculum Library in the College of Education. **Computers:** 80% of classrooms, 50% of dorms, 100% of libraries, 100% of dining areas, 100% of student union, 50% of common outdoor areas have wireless network access. Students can register for classes online. Administrative functions (other than registration) can be performed online.

CAMPUS LIFE

Environment: Town. **Activities:** Choral groups, concert band, drama/theater, jazz band, literary magazine, music ensembles, musical theater, opera, pep band, student government, student newspaper, symphony orchestra, yearbook, Campus Ministries, Student Organization, Model UN. 72 registered organizations, 16 honor societies, 10 religious organizations. 5 fraternities, 4 sororities. **Athletics (Intercollegiate):** *Men:* baseball, basketball, cheerleading, cross-country, golf, soccer, tennis. *Women:* basketball, cheerleading, cross-country, soccer, softball, tennis, volleyball. **On-Campus Highlights:** Paul Conn Student Union-Bookstore, Pizza Hut, Chickfil, Conn Center-Home of Chapels, Concerts, etc., Dixon Center plays, recitals, community eents, De Vos Recreaction Center, The House-Coffee House, and Jazzman's Cafe.

ADMISSIONS

Freshman Academic Profile: Average high school GPA 3.6. 25% in top 10% of high school class, 52% in top 25% of high school class, 76% in top 50% of high school class. **Reported SAT (pre-2016 redesign) scores:** SAT Math middle 50% range 450-580. SAT Critical Reading middle 50% range 470-600. **Concordant SAT scores:** SAT Math middle 50% range 490–600. ACT middle 50% range 21-28. Minimum paper TOEFL 450. **Basis for Candidate Selection:** *Very important factors considered include:* rigor of secondary school record, academic GPA, standardized test scores. *Important factors considered include:* class rank, character/personal qualities, level of applicant's interest. *Other factors considered include:* application essay, recommendation(s), interview, extracurricular activities, talent/ability, first generation, alumni/ae relation. **Freshman Admission Requirements:** High school diploma is required and GED is accepted. *Academic units required:* 4 English, 3 math, 2 science, 1 foreign language, 2 social studies, 1 history. *Academic units recommended:* 4 English, 3 math, 2 science, 1 foreign language, 2 social studies, 1 history, 1 computer science. **Freshman Admission Statistics:** 2,277 applied, 87.22% admitted, 45% enrolled. **Transfer Admission Requirements:** college transcript(s), Minimum college GPA of 2.0 required. Lowest grade transferable D. **General Admission Information:** Application fee $25. Priority deadline 4/15. Nonfall registration accepted. Admission may be deferred for a maximum of 1 semester.

COSTS AND FINANCIAL AID

Annual tuition $15,170. Room and board $7,880. Required fees $600. Average book expense $1,200. **Required Forms and Deadlines:** FAFSA. **Notification of Awards:** Applicants will be notified of awards on a rolling basis beginning 2/1. **Types of Aid:** *Need-based scholarships/grants:* Federal Pell, FSEOG, State scholarships/grants, Private scholarships, College/university scholarship or grant aid from institutional funds. *Loans:* Direct Subsidized Stafford Loans, Direct Unsubsidized Stafford Loans, Direct PLUS loans, Federal Perkins Loans, College/university loans from institutional funds. *Student Employment:* Federal Work-Study Program available. Institutional employment available. **Financial Aid Statistics:** 95% needy freshmen, 89% needy undergrads receive need-based scholarship or grant aid. 40% freshmen, 14% undergrads receive non-need-based scholarship or grant aid. 59% freshmen, 80% undergrads receive need-based self-help aid. 5% freshmen, 4% undergrads receive athletic scholarships. 95% freshmen, 85% undergrads receive any aid. 60% undergrads borrow to pay for school. Average cumulative indebtedness $31,630. **Criteria for awarding aid:** *Non-need-based:* Academics, Alumni affiliation, Athletics, Leadership, Minority status, Music/drama, Religious affiliation, State/district residency.

LEHIGH UNIVERSITY

27 Memorial Drive West, Bethlehem, PA 18015
Phone: 610-758-3100 • **Financial Aid Phone:** 610-758-3181
E-mail: admissions@lehigh.edu • **CEEB Code:** 2365
Fax: 610-758-4361 • **Website:** www.lehigh.edu • **ACT Code:** 3612

This private school was founded in 1865. It has a 1600-acre campus.

RATINGS

Admissions Selectivity Rating: 94   **Fire Safety Rating:** 90   **Green Rating:** 92

STUDENTS AND FACULTY

Enrollment: 5,061. **Student Body:** 44% female, 56% male, 74% out-of-state, 8% international (60 countries represented). Asian 8%, African American 4%, Caucasian 65%, Hispanic 9%, Native American <1%, Pacific Islander <1%, Two or more races 3%, Race unknown 3%.
Retention and Graduation: 95% freshmen return for sophomore year. 77% freshmen graduate within 4 years. 89% freshmen graduate within 6 years. 24% grads go on to further study within 1 year. 26% grads pursue arts and sciences degrees. 5% grads pursue law degrees. 10% grads pursue business degrees. 11% grads pursue medical degrees. **Faculty:** Student/faculty ratio 9:1. 540 full-time faculty, 96% hold PhDs, 22% are are members of minority groups, 33% are women.

ACADEMICS

Degrees: bachelor's, doctoral/research, doctoral, master's, postbachelor's certificate, post-master's certificate. **Classes:** Most classes have 10-19 students. Most lab/discussion sessions have 10-19 students. **Most popular majors:** Mechanical Engineering; Finance; Accounting. **Special Study Options:** Accelerated program, cooperative education program, cross-registration, distance learning, double major, English as a Second Language (ESL), exchange student program (domestic), external degree program, honors program, independent study, internships, liberal arts/career combination, study abroad. **Honors Programs:** Integrated Business and Engineering (IBE) Honors Program, program description available http://www.lehigh.edu/~inibep/ Combined degree programs: BA/MD, BA/DDS, Pre-Optometry/SUNY(BA/OD), Pre-Dental/UPenn(BA/DMD), Pre-Med/Drexel(BA/MD). **Disability Services:** Special programs offered to physically disabled students, including note-taking services, reader services, tape recorders, tutors. **Career Services:** Alumni network, Alumni services, Career/job search classes, Career assessment, Internships, Regional alumni. LUCID Mentoring Program (Lehigh University Career Insight on Demand) connects current students with alumni for flash mentoring opportunities and semester-long mentor relationships. Flash mentoring includes alumni who provide an externship, resume review, mock interview or quick career insight.

FACILITIES

Housing: Coed dorms, special housing for disabled students, special housing for international students, fraternity/sorority housing, apartments for married students, apartments for single students, Wellness Housing, Theme Housing. **Special Academic Facilities/Equipment:** Art Museum, Zoellner Arts Center Electron optical labs civil engineering lab particle accelerator electron optical labs **Computers:** 70% of classrooms, 100% of dorms, 100% of libraries, 100% of dining areas, 75% of student union, 80% of common outdoor areas have wireless network access. Students can register for classes online. Administrative functions (other than registration) can be performed online.

CAMPUS LIFE

Environment: City. **Activities:** Choral groups, concert band, dance, drama/theater, jazz band, literary magazine, marching band, music ensembles, musical theater, pep band, radio station, student government, student newspaper, student-run film society, symphony orchestra, yearbook, Campus Ministries, Student Organization, Model UN. 18 honor societies, 10 religious organizations. 21 fraternities, 9 sororities. **Athletics (Intercollegiate):** *Men:* baseball, basketball, cross-country, diving, football, golf, lacrosse, soccer, swimming, tennis, track/field (outdoor), track/field (indoor), wrestling. *Women:* basketball, crew/rowing, cross-country, diving, field hockey, golf, lacrosse, soccer, softball, swimming, tennis, track/field (outdoor), track/field (indoor), volleyball. **On-Campus Highlights:** Zoellner Arts Center LU Art Galleries, Campus Square, Taylor Gymnasium, Ulrich Student Center, Goodman Campus.

ADMISSIONS

Freshman Academic Profile: 64% in top 10% of high school class, 89% in top 25% of high school class, 98% in top 50% of high school class. **Reported**

SAT (pre-2016 redesign) scores: SAT Math middle 50% range 640-740. SAT Critical Reading middle 50% range 590-680. **Concordant SAT scores:** SAT Math middle 50% range 660–760. ACT middle 50% range 29-32. Minimum internet-based TOEFL 90. Minimum paper TOEFL 570. **Basis for Candidate Selection:** *Very important factors considered include:* rigor of secondary school record, recommendation(s). *Important factors considered include:* standardized test scores, application essay, extracurricular activities, talent/ability, character/personal qualities, volunteer work, level of applicant's interest. *Other factors considered include:* class rank, academic GPA, interview, first generation, alumni/ae relation, geographical residence, racial/ethnic status, work experience. **Freshman Admission Requirements:** High school diploma or equivalent is not required. *Academic units required:* 4 English, 3 math, 2 science, 2 science labs, 2 foreign language, 2 social studies, 3 academic electives. **Freshman Admission Statistics:** 13,403 applied, 26.11% admitted, 36% enrolled. **Transfer Admission Requirements:** High school transcript, college transcript(s), essay or personal statement, statement of good standing from prior institution(s). Minimum college GPA of 3.25 required. **General Admission Information:** Application fee $70. Regular application deadline 1/1. Regular notification 4/1. Nonfall registration accepted. Admission may be deferred for a maximum of 1 year.

COSTS AND FINANCIAL AID

Annual tuition $47,920. Room and board $12,690. Required fees $400. Average book expense $1,000. **Required Forms and Deadlines:** FAFSA, CSS/Financial Aid PROFILE, Noncustodial PROFILE, Business/Farm Supplement. **Notification of Awards:** Applicants will be notified of awards on or about 3/30. **Types of Aid:** *Need-based scholarships/grants:* Federal Pell, FSEOG, State scholarships/grants, Private scholarships, College/university scholarship or grant aid from institutional funds, United Negro College Fund. *Loans:* Direct Subsidized Stafford Loans, Direct Unsubsidized Stafford Loans, Direct PLUS loans, Federal Perkins Loans, College/university loans from institutional funds. *Student Employment:* Federal Work-Study Program available. Institutional employment available. **Financial Aid Statistics:** 96% needy freshmen, 98% needy undergrads receive need-based scholarship or grant aid. 20% freshmen, 17% undergrads receive non-need-based scholarship or grant aid. 93% freshmen, 94% undergrads receive need-based self-help aid. 6% freshmen, 5% undergrads receive athletic scholarships. 57% freshmen, 62% undergrads receive any aid. 53% undergrads borrow to pay for school. Average cumulative indebtedness $34,215. **Criteria for awarding aid:** *Need-based:* Academics, Athletics, Minority status, Religious affiliation. *Non-need-based:* Academics, Art, Athletics, Leadership, Music/drama.

LENOIR RHYNE UNIVERSITY

524 7th Ave NE, Hickory, NC 28603
Phone: 828-328-7300 • **Financial Aid Phone:** 828-328-7300
E-mail: admission@lr.edu • **CEEB Code:** 5365
Website: www.lr.edu • **ACT Code:** 2941

This private school, affiliated with the Lutheran Church, was founded in 1891. It has a 100-acre campus.

RATINGS

Admissions Selectivity Rating: 73   **Fire Safety Rating:** 60*   **Green Rating:** 70

STUDENTS AND FACULTY

Enrollment: 1,590. **Student Body:** 60% female, 40% male, 17% out-of-state, 2% international (18 countries represented). Asian 2%, African American 13%, Caucasian 68%, Hispanic 7%, Native American 1%, Pacific Islander <1%, Two or more races 4%, Race unknown 4%.
Retention and Graduation: 72% freshmen return for sophomore year. 35% freshmen graduate within 4 years. 22% grads go on to further study within 1 year. **Faculty:** Student/faculty ratio 13:1. 128 full-time faculty, 87% hold PhDs, 9% are are members of minority groups, 49% are women. 0% of classes are taught by teaching assistants.

ACADEMICS

Degrees: bachelor's, master's, postbachelor's certificate. **Most popular majors:** Registered Nursing/Registered Nurse; Health and Wellness; Health and Physical Education/Fitness. **Special Study Options:** Accelerated program, double major, dual enrollment, English as a Second Language (ESL), honors program, independent study, internships, student-designed major, study abroad, teacher certification program. Combined degree programs: BA/MEng. **Disability Services:** Special programs offered to physically disabled students, including note-taking services, tutors. **Career Services:** Alumni network, Alumni services, Career/job search classes, Career assessment, Internships.

FACILITIES

Housing: Coed dorms, special housing for disabled students, men's dorms, women's dorms, fraternity/sorority housing, Honors, Hearing Impaired. 75% of campus accessible to physically disabled. **Special Academic Facilities/Equipment:** Language lab.

CAMPUS LIFE

Environment: Village. **Activities:** Choral groups, concert band, dance, drama/theater, jazz band, music ensembles, musical theater, pep band, radio station, student government, student newspaper, television station, yearbook. 54 registered organizations, 10 honor societies, 6 religious organizations. 4 fraternities, 4 sororities. **Athletics (Intercollegiate):** *Men:* baseball, basketball, cheerleading, cross-country, football, golf, soccer. *Women:* basketball, cheerleading, cross-country, golf, soccer, softball, volleyball. **On-Campus Highlights:** McCrorie Center, Cromer College Center, Shuford Fitness Center, Living and Learning Center, Quad.

ADMISSIONS

Freshman Academic Profile: Average high school GPA 3.3. 87% from public high schools. **Reported SAT (pre-2016 redesign) scores:** SAT Math middle 50% range 440-550. SAT Critical Reading middle 50% range 430-540. **Concordant SAT scores:** SAT Math middle 50% range 480–570. Minimum internet-based TOEFL 79. Minimum paper TOEFL 500. **Basis for Candidate Selection:** *Very important factors considered include:* academic GPA, standardized test scores. *Important factors considered include:* rigor of secondary school record. *Other factors considered include:* extracurricular activities, character/personal qualities, volunteer work. **Freshman Admission Requirements:** High school diploma is required and GED is accepted. *Academic units required:* 4 English, 3 math, 1 science, 1 science lab, 2 foreign language, 1 history. *Academic units recommended:* 4 English, 4 math, 2 science, 1 science lab, 3 foreign language, 2 history. **Freshman Admission Statistics:** 6,300 applied, 70.11% admitted, 11% enrolled. **Transfer Admission Requirements:** college transcript(s), statement of good standing from prior institution(s). Minimum college GPA of 2.5 required. Lowest grade transferable C. **General Admission Information:** Application fee $35. Nonfall registration accepted. Admission may be deferred for a maximum of 1 year.

COSTS AND FINANCIAL AID

Annual tuition $35,350. Room and board $12,150. Average book expense $1,160. **Required Forms and Deadlines:** FAFSA. **Types of Aid:** *Need-based scholarships/grants:* Federal Pell, FSEOG, State scholarships/grants, Private scholarships, College/university scholarship or grant aid from institutional funds. *Loans:* Direct Subsidized Stafford Loans, Direct Unsubsidized Stafford Loans, Direct PLUS loans, Federal Perkins Loans, State Loans. *Student Employment:* Federal Work-Study Program available. Institutional employment available. **Financial Aid Statistics:** 100% needy freshmen, 99% needy undergrads receive need-based scholarship or grant aid. 16% freshmen, 12% undergrads receive non-need-based scholarship or grant aid. 81% freshmen, 85% undergrads receive need-based self-help aid. 15% freshmen, 12% undergrads receive athletic scholarships. 99% freshmen, 88% undergrads receive any aid. Average cumulative indebtedness $28,104. **Criteria for awarding aid:** *Need-based:* Academics, Alumni affiliation, Athletics, Leadership, Minority status, Music/drama, Religious affiliation. *Non-need-based:* Academics, Alumni affiliation, Athletics, Leadership, Religious affiliation.

LESLEY UNIVERSITY

Lesley University Undergraduate Admissio, Cambridge, MA 2140
Phone: 617-349-8800 • **Financial Aid Phone:** 617-349-8710
E-mail: admissions@lesley.edu • **CEEB Code:** 3483
Fax: 617-349-8810 • **Website:** www.lesley.edu • **ACT Code:** 1850

This private school was founded in 1909. It has a 1-acre campus.

RATINGS

Admissions Selectivity Rating: 81   **Fire Safety Rating:** 91   **Green Rating:** 60*

STUDENTS AND FACULTY

Enrollment: 1,418. **Student Body:** 75% female, 25% male, 57% out-of-state, 2% international (30 countries represented). Asian 4%, African American 4%, Caucasian 71%, Hispanic 10%, Native American <1%, Pacific Islander <1%, Two or more races 4%, Race unknown 5%.
Retention and Graduation: 78% freshmen return for sophomore year. 41% freshmen graduate within 4 years. 54% freshmen graduate within 6 years. **Faculty:** Student/faculty ratio 9:1. 80 full-time faculty, 80% hold PhDs, 16% are are members of minority groups, 50% are women. 0% of classes are taught by teaching assistants.

ACADEMICS

Degrees: associate, bachelor's, certificate, doctoral/research, master's, postbachelor's certificate, post-master's certificate. **Classes:** Most classes have 10-19 students. **Most popular majors:** Elementary Education and Teaching Marketing/Marketing Management. **Special Study Options:** Accelerated program, cross-registration, distance learning, double major, dual enrollment, exchange student program (domestic), honors program, independent study, internships, liberal arts/career combination, student-designed major, study abroad, teacher certification program, Studio courses. Combined degree programs: BA/MA, BS/M.Ed. **Disability Services:** Special programs offered to physically disabled students, including note-taking services, reader services, tape recorders, tutors. **Career Services:** Alumni network, Alumni services, Career/job search classes, Career assessment, Internships, Regional alumni. Wellesley College funded at least one internship for more than half the class of 2016. This included grants of up $3,500 for what otherwise would have been unpaid internships over the summer.

FACILITIES

Housing: Coed dorms, women's dorms, Special Interest and themed housing. 85% of campus accessible to physically diasbled. **Special Academic Facilities/Equipment:** Kresge Center for Teaching Resources and Educational Software Collection, Marran Art Gallery, Porter Exchange Gallery, AIB Main Gallery **Computers:** 100% of classrooms, 100% of libraries, 100% of dining areas, 100% of student union, 20% of common outdoor areas have wireless network access. Students can register for classes online. Administrative functions (other than registration) can be performed online.

CAMPUS LIFE

Environment: Metropolis. **Activities:** Choral groups, dance, drama/theater, literary magazine, musical theater, student government, student newspaper, Campus Ministries, Student Organization. 25 registered organizations, 2 honor societies, 2 religious organizations. **Athletics (Intercollegiate):** *Men:* basketball, cross-country, soccer, tennis, volleyball. *Women:* basketball, crew/rowing, cross-country, soccer, softball, tennis, volleyball. **On-Campus Highlights:** Student Center, Ludke Library, Porter Exchange Building, Stebbins Fitness Room, Kresge Center for Teaching Resources. **Environmental Initiatives:** The continual enhancement of recycling, waste management and composting programs on campus.

ADMISSIONS

Freshman Academic Profile: Average high school GPA 3.3. 15% in top 10% of high school class, 44% in top 25% of high school class, 80% in top 50% of high school class. 83% from public high schools. **Reported SAT (pre-2016 redesign) scores:** SAT Math middle 50% range 460-570. SAT Critical Reading middle 50% range 490-600. SAT Writing middle 50% range 490-590. **Concordant SAT scores:** SAT EBRW middle 50% 550-650. SAT Math middle 50% range 500–590. ACT middle 50% range 21-25. Minimum internet-based TOEFL 61. Minimum paper TOEFL 500. **Basis for Candidate Selection:** *Very important factors considered include:* rigor of secondary school record, academic GPA, interview. *Important factors considered include:* class rank, standardized test scores, application essay, recommendation(s), extracurricular activities, talent/ability, character/personal qualities, volunteer work, level of applicant's interest. *Other factors considered include:* first generation, alumni/ae relation, racial/ethnic status, work experience. **Freshman Admission Requirements:** High school diploma is required and GED is accepted. *Academic units required:* 4 English, 3 math, 3 science, 2 science labs, 1 social studies, 1 history, 4 academic electives. *Academic units recommended:* 4 English, 4 math, 4 science, 2 science labs, 2 foreign language, 2 social studies, 2 history, and 2 units from above areas or other academic areas. **Freshman Admission Statistics:** 3,115 applied, 68.54% admitted, 18% enrolled. **Transfer Admission Requirements:** High school transcript, college transcript(s), essay or personal statement, statement of good standing from prior institution(s). Minimum college GPA of 2.5 required. Lowest grade transferable C. **General Admission Information:** Priority deadline 2/15. Regular notification 12/23. Nonfall registration accepted. Admission may be deferred for a maximum of 1 year.

COSTS AND FINANCIAL AID

Annual tuition $25,500. Room and board $15,300. **Required Forms and Deadlines:** FAFSA. **Notification of Awards:** Applicants will be notified of awards on a rolling basis beginning 2/1. **Types of Aid:** *Need-based scholarships/grants:* Federal Pell, FSEOG, State scholarships/grants, Private scholarships, College/university scholarship or grant aid from institutional funds. *Loans:* Direct Subsidized Stafford Loans, Direct Unsubsidized Stafford Loans, Direct PLUS loans, Federal Perkins Loans. *Student Employment:* Federal Work-Study Program available. Institutional employment available. **Financial Aid Statistics:** 96% needy freshmen, 97% needy undergrads receive need-based scholarship or grant aid. 8% freshmen, 5% undergrads receive non-need-based scholarship or grant aid. 86% freshmen, 91% undergrads receive need-based self-help aid. 0% freshmen, 0% undergrads receive athletic scholarships. 70% freshmen, 70% undergrads receive any aid. 75% undergrads borrow to pay for school. Average cumulative indebtedness $2,300.

LETOURNEAU UNIVERSITY

PO Box 7001, Longview, TX 75607-7001
Phone: 903-233-4300
E-mail: admissions@letu.edu • **CEEB Code:** 6365
Fax: 903-233-4301 • **Website:** www.letu.edu • **ACT Code:** 4120

This private school was founded in 1946. It has a 162-acre campus.

RATINGS

Admissions Selectivity Rating: 88 **Fire Safety Rating:** 60* **Green Rating:** 60*

STUDENTS AND FACULTY

Enrollment: 1,823. **Student Body:** 45% female, 55% male, 31% out-of-state, 3% international (32 countries represented). Asian 1%, African American 9%, Caucasian 62%, Hispanic 10%, Native American <1%, Pacific Islander 0%, Two or more races 4%, Race unknown 10%.
Retention and Graduation: 78% freshmen return for sophomore year. **Faculty:** Student/faculty ratio 14:1. 83 full-time faculty, 84% hold PhDs, 12% are are members of minority groups, 20% are women.

ACADEMICS

Degrees: associate, bachelor's, master's. **Classes:** Most classes have fewer than 10 students. Most lab/discussion sessions have 10-19 students. **Special Study Options:** Accelerated program, cooperative education program, distance learning, double major, dual enrollment, honors program, independent study, internships, study abroad, teacher certification program, weekend college. **Career Services:** Alumni network, Alumni services, Career/job search classes, Career assessment, Internships.

FACILITIES

Housing: special housing for disabled students, men's dorms, special housing for international students, women's dorms, apartments for married students, apartments for single students, Theme Housing, Residential societies available. **Special Academic Facilities/Equipment:** Longview Citizens Resource Center; R.G. LeTourneau Memorial Museum **Computers:** Students can register for classes online. Administrative functions (other than registration) can be performed online.

CAMPUS LIFE

Environment: Town. **Activities:** Choral groups, drama/theater, jazz band, literary magazine, music ensembles, musical theater, student government, student newspaper, student-run film society, yearbook, Campus Ministries, Student Organization. 44 registered organizations, 4 honor societies, 10 religious organizations. **Athletics (Intercollegiate):** *Men:* baseball, basketball, cross-country, golf, soccer, tennis. *Women:* basketball, cross-country, golf, soccer, softball, tennis, volleyball.

ADMISSIONS

Freshman Academic Profile: Average high school GPA 3.6. 27% in top 10% of high school class, 55% in top 25% of high school class, 86% in top 50% of high school class. **Reported SAT (pre-2016 redesign) scores:** SAT Math middle 50% range 520-640. SAT Critical Reading middle 50% range 510-640. SAT Writing middle 50% range 470-600. **Concordant SAT scores:** SAT EBRW middle 50% 550-670. SAT Math middle 50% range 550–660. ACT middle 50% range 22-28. **Basis for Candidate Selection:** *Very important factors considered include:* rigor of secondary school record, academic GPA, standardized test scores, character/personal qualities. *Important factors considered include:* religious affiliation/commitment. *Other factors considered include:* class rank, interview, extracurricular activities, talent/ability, first generation, alumni/ae relation, volunteer work, work experience, level of applicant's interest. **Freshman Admission Requirements:** High school diploma is required and GED is accepted. **Freshman Admission Statistics:** 1,842 applied, 44.19% admitted, 34% enrolled. **Transfer Admission Requirements:** college transcript(s), essay or personal statement, Minimum college GPA of 2.0 required. Lowest grade transferable C. **General Admission Information:** Nonfall registration accepted. Admission may be deferred.

COSTS AND FINANCIAL AID

Annual tuition $28,770. Room and board $9,870. Required fees $550. Average book expense $1,564. **Required Forms and Deadlines:** FAFSA. **Notification of Awards:** Applicants will be notified of awards on a rolling basis beginning 3/1. **Types of Aid:** *Need-based scholarships/grants:* Federal Pell, FSEOG, State scholarships/grants, Private scholarships, College/university scholarship or grant aid from institutional funds, United Negro College Fund. *Loans:* Direct Subsidized Stafford Loans, Direct Unsubsidized Stafford Loans, Direct PLUS loans, Federal Perkins Loans, State Loans. *Student Employment:* Federal Work-Study Program available. Institutional employment available. **Financial Aid Statistics:** 100% needy freshmen, 96% needy undergrads receive need-based scholarship or grant aid. 18% freshmen, 9% undergrads receive non-need-based scholarship or grant aid. 75% freshmen, 84% undergrads receive need-based

---

self-help aid. 0% freshmen, 0% undergrads receive athletic scholarships. 69% undergrads borrow to pay for school. Average cumulative indebtedness $38,988. **Criteria for awarding aid:** *Need-based:* Academics, Alumni affiliation, Leadership, Minority status, Religious affiliation. *Non-need-based:* Academics, Alumni affiliation, Leadership, Minority status, Religious affiliation, State/district residency.

LEWIS & CLARK COLLEGE

0615 SW Palatine Hill Road, Portland, OR 97219-7899
Phone: 503-768-7040 • **Financial Aid Phone:** 503-768-7090
E-mail: admissions@lclark.edu • **CEEB Code:** 4384
Fax: 503-768-7055 • **Website:** www.lclark.edu • **ACT Code:** 3464

This private school was founded in 1867. It has a 137-acre campus.

RATINGS

Admissions Selectivity Rating: 88   Fire Safety Rating: 87   Green Rating: 99

STUDENTS AND FACULTY

Enrollment: 2,033. **Student Body:** 62% female, 38% male, 89% out-of-state, 5% international (80 countries represented). Asian 6%, African American 2%, Caucasian 66%, Hispanic 11%, Native American 1%, Pacific Islander <1%, Two or more races 3%, Race unknown 5%.
Retention and Graduation: 85% freshmen return for sophomore year. 74% freshmen graduate within 4 years. 79% freshmen graduate within 6 years. **Faculty:** Student/faculty ratio 11:1. 211 full-time faculty, 92% hold PhDs, 18% are are members of minority groups, 53% are women. 0% of classes are taught by teaching assistants.

ACADEMICS

Degrees: bachelor's, doctoral/professional, master's, post-master's certificate. **Classes:** Most classes have 10-19 students. Most lab/discussion sessions have 20-29 students. **Most popular majors:** Psychology; Biology/Biological Sciences; Sociology and Anthropology. **Special Study Options:** Accelerated program, cross-registration, double major, dual enrollment, English as a Second Language (ESL), honors program, independent study, internships, student-designed major, study abroad, teacher certification program, Teacher certification is graduate level only. **Honors Programs:** Honors are designated by each department. **Disability Services:** Special programs offered to physically disabled students, including note-taking services, reader services, tape recorders, tutors. **Career Services:** Alumni network, Alumni services, Career/job search classes, Career assessment, Internships, Regional alumni, On-campus interviews.

FACILITIES

Housing: Coed dorms, women's dorms, Theme Floors, Apartment-style residence halls for upper-class students. 85% of campus accessible to physically disabled. **Special Academic Facilities/Equipment:** Art gallery, observatory, world music room, 85 Rank Casavant organ, renovated greenhouse. **Computers:** 50% of classrooms, 20% of dorms, 100% of libraries, 25% of common outdoor areas have wireless network access. Students can register for classes online. Administrative functions (other than registration) can be performed online.

CAMPUS LIFE

Environment: City. **Activities:** Choral groups, concert band, dance, drama/theater, jazz band, literary magazine, music ensembles, musical theater, radio station, student government, student newspaper, symphony orchestra, television station, yearbook, Campus Ministries, Student Organization, Model UN. 70 registered organizations, 5 honor societies, 9 religious organizations. **Athletics (Intercollegiate): Men:** baseball, basketball, crew/rowing, cross-country, football, golf, swimming, tennis, track/field (outdoor). *Women:* basketball, crew/rowing, cross-country, golf, soccer, softball, swimming, tennis, track/field (outdoor), volleyball. **On-Campus Highlights:** Gallery of Contemporary Art, New residence halls/Maggie's Cafe, Library, Templeton Student Center, Pamplin Sports Center, Howard Hall, newest academic building. **Environmental Initiatives:** Lewis & Clark provides students, faculty, and staff with a fare-free shuttle bus system that allows access to downtown Portland, local neighborhoods, and retail stores. We installed a 100KW photovoltaic system. Students funds are used to purchase green power.

ADMISSIONS

Freshman Academic Profile: Average high school GPA 3.9. 75% from public high schools. **Reported SAT (pre-2016 redesign) scores:** SAT Math middle 50% range 590-680. SAT Critical Reading middle 50% range 600-690. SAT Writing middle 50% range 580-670. **Concordant SAT scores:** SAT EBRW middle 50% 650–720. SAT Math middle 50% range 610–710. ACT middle 50% range 27-31. Minimum internet-based TOEFL 91. Minimum paper TOEFL 575. **Basis for Candidate Selection:** *Very important factors considered include:* rigor of secondary school record, academic GPA. *Important factors considered include:* class rank, standardized test scores, application essay, recommendation(s), extracurricular activities, talent/ability, character/personal qualities, volunteer work, work experience. *Other factors considered include:* interview, first generation, alumni/ae relation, geographical residence, racial/ethnic status, level of applicant's interest. **Freshman Admission Requirements:** High school diploma is required and GED is accepted. *Academic units recommended:* 4 English, 4 math, 3 science, 2 science labs, 2 foreign language, 3 social studies, 1 visual/performing arts. **Freshman Admission Statistics:** 7,796 applied, 54.95% admitted, 12% enrolled. **Transfer Admission Requirements:** High school transcript, college transcript(s), essay or personal statement, statement of good standing from prior institution(s). Minimum college GPA of 2.0 required. Lowest grade transferable C. **General Admission Information:** Priority deadline 1/15. Regular application deadline 3/1. Regular notification 4/1. Nonfall registration accepted. Admission may be deferred for a maximum of One year.

COSTS AND FINANCIAL AID

Annual tuition $46,534. Room and board $11,540. Required fees $360. Average book expense $1,050. **Required Forms and Deadlines:** FAFSA, CSS/Financial Aid PROFILE. **Notification of Awards:** Applicants will be notified of awards on a rolling basis beginning 3/15. **Types of Aid:** *Need-based scholarships/grants:* Federal Pell, FSEOG, State scholarships/grants, Private scholarships, College/university scholarship or grant aid from institutional funds. *Loans:* Direct Subsidized Stafford Loans, Direct Unsubsidized Stafford Loans, Direct PLUS loans, Federal Perkins Loans. *Student Employment:* Federal Work-Study Program available. Institutional employment available. **Financial Aid Statistics:** 98% needy freshmen, 99% needy undergrads receive need-based scholarship or grant aid. 16% freshmen, 8% undergrads receive non-need-based scholarship or grant aid. 91% freshmen, 92% undergrads receive need-based self-help aid. 0% freshmen, 0% undergrads receive athletic scholarships. 94% freshmen, 91% undergrads receive any aid. 55% undergrads borrow to pay for school. Average cumulative indebtedness $29,913. **Criteria for awarding aid:** *Need-based:* Academics. *Non-need-based:* Academics, Leadership, Music/drama.

See page 988.

LEWIS-CLARK STATE COLLEGE

500 Eighth Avenue, Lewiston, ID 83501
Phone: 208-792-2210 • **Financial Aid Phone:** 208-792-2224
E-mail: admissions@lcsc.edu • **CEEB Code:** 4385
Fax: 208-792-2876 • **Website:** www.lcsc.edu • **ACT Code:** 920

This public school was founded in 1893. It has a 44-acre campus.

RATINGS

Admissions Selectivity Rating: 72   Fire Safety Rating: 78   Green Rating: 60*

STUDENTS AND FACULTY

Enrollment: 3,083. **Student Body:** 61% female, 39% male, 20% out-of-state, 4% international (32 countries represented). Asian 1%, African American 1%, Caucasian 82%, Hispanic 6%, Native American 2%, Pacific Islander <1%, Two or more races 3%, Race unknown 2%.
Retention and Graduation: 61% freshmen return for sophomore year. 18% freshmen graduate within 4 years. 31% freshmen graduate within 6 years. 7% grads go on to further study within 1 year. **Faculty:** Student/faculty ratio 18:1. 159 full-time faculty, 47% hold PhDs, 4% are are members of minority groups, 53% are women. 0% of classes are taught by teaching assistants.

ACADEMICS

Degrees: associate, bachelor's, certificate, terminal, transfer. **Classes:** Most classes have fewer than 10 students. **Most popular majors:** Elementary Education and Teaching Business/Commerce. **Special Study Options:** Accelerated program, cooperative education program, distance learning, double major, dual enrollment, English as a Second Language (ESL), independent study, internships, study abroad, teacher certification program. **Disability Services:** Special programs offered to physically disabled students, including note-taking services, reader services, tape recorders, tutors.

FACILITIES

Housing: Coed dorms, apartments for married students, apartments for single students. 95% of campus accessible to physically diasbled. **Special Academic Facilities/Equipment:** Museum/art gallery, Media Services. **Computers:** Students can register for classes online. Administrative functions (other than registration) can be performed online.

CAMPUS LIFE

Environment: Town. **Activities:** drama/theater, jazz band, literary magazine, radio station, student government, student newspaper, Campus Ministries, Student Organization. 52 registered organizations, 1 honor society, 3 religious organizations. **Athletics (Intercollegiate):** *Men:* baseball, basketball, cross-country, golf, tennis. *Women:* basketball, cross-country, golf, tennis, volleyball. **On-Campus Highlights:** Information Commons in the Library, Student Union Building, Athletic Center which is under construction, Centennial Mall, Yo Espresso or Jitterz.

ADMISSIONS

Freshman Academic Profile: Average high school GPA 3.1. 5% in top 10% of high school class, 18% in top 25% of high school class, 46% in top 50% of high school class. 99% from public high schools. **Reported SAT (pre-2016 redesign) scores:** SAT Math middle 50% range 400-520. SAT Critical Reading middle 50% range 410-510. **Concordant SAT scores:** SAT Math middle 50% range 440–550. ACT middle 50% range 17-22. Minimnm paper TOEFL 500. **Basis for Candidate Selection:** *Other factors considered include:* academic GPA, standardized test scores. **Freshman Admission Requirements:** High school diploma is required and GED is accepted. *Academic units required:* 4 English, 3 math, 3 science, 1 science lab, and 1 unit from above areas or other academic areas. **Freshman Admission Statistics:** 852 applied, 99.06% admitted, 61% enrolled. **Transfer Admission Requirements:** college transcript(s), Minimum college GPA of 2.0 required. Lowest grade transferable D. **General Admission Information:** Regular application deadline 8/8. Nonfall registration accepted. Admission may be deferred for a maximum of 1 year.

COSTS AND FINANCIAL AID

Annual in-state tuition $5,900. Room and board $6,194. Required fees $2,724. **Required Forms and Deadlines:** FAFSA. **Notification of Awards:** Applicants will be notified of awards on a rolling basis beginning 4/15. **Types of Aid:** *Need-based scholarships/grants:* Federal Pell, FSEOG, State scholarships/grants, Private scholarships, College/university scholarship or grant aid from institutional funds. *Loans:* Federal Perkins Loans, Federal Nursing Loans. *Student Employment:* Federal Work-Study Program available. Institutional employment available. **Financial Aid Statistics:** 58% needy freshmen, 66% needy undergrads receive need-based scholarship or grant aid. 55% freshmen, 24% undergrads receive non-need-based scholarship or grant aid. 77% freshmen, 82% undergrads receive need-based self-help aid. 5% freshmen, 8% undergrads receive athletic scholarships. 85% freshmen, 76% undergrads receive any aid. **Criteria for awarding aid:** *Need-based:* Academics, Alumni affiliation, Minority status. *Non-need-based:* Academics, Alumni affiliation, Art, Athletics, Leadership, Minority status, Music/drama.

LEWIS UNIVERSITY

One University Parkway, Romeoville, IL 60446
Phone: 815-836-5250 • **Financial Aid Phone:** 815-836-5263
E-mail: admissions@lewisu.edu • **CEEB Code:** 1404
Fax: 815-836-5002 • **Website:** www.lewisu.edu • **ACT Code:** 1058

This private school, affiliated with the Roman Catholic Church, was founded in 1932. It has a 375-acre campus.

RATINGS

Admissions Selectivity Rating: 83   **Fire Safety Rating:** 97   **Green Rating:** 83

STUDENTS AND FACULTY

Enrollment: 4,433. **Student Body:** 54% female, 46% male, 8% out-of-state, 1% international (26 countries represented). Asian 4%, African American 6%, Caucasian 62%, Hispanic 19%, Native American <1%, Pacific Islander <1%, Two or more races 3%, Race unknown 4%.
Retention and Graduation: 79% freshmen return for sophomore year. 41% freshmen graduate within 4 years. 61% freshmen graduate within 6 years.
Faculty: Student/faculty ratio 13:1. 228 full-time faculty, 82% hold PhDs, 15% are are members of minority groups, 49% are women. 0% of classes are taught by teaching assistants.

ACADEMICS

Degrees: associate, bachelor's, certificate, doctoral/research, master's, postbachelor's certifiate, post-master's certificate. **Classes:** Most classes

have 10-19 students. Most lab/discussion sessions have 10-19 students.
Most popular majors: Registered Nursing/Registered Nurse; Criminal Justice/Safety Studies; Business Administration and Management. **Special Study Options:** Accelerated program, distance learning, double major, dual enrollment, English as a Second Language (ESL), exchange student program (domestic), honors program, independent study, internships, liberal arts/career combination, student-designed major, study abroad, teacher certification program. **Honors Programs:** Honors Program offers academically motivated students opportunities for active and collaborative learning. Students have the opporuntiy to fulfill many of their general education requirements in a "paired course" arrangement that allows for greater integration of material and content. Combined degree programs: BA/MA, BS/MS Chemistry; BS/MS Physics; BS/MS Chemical Physics; BA/MBA; BS/MBA; BS/MS Finance; BSIS/MSIS; BS/MS Aviation; BA/MS CSJ; BSCS/MSDataScience; BSCS/MSIS; ITM/MSIS; BAOL/MAOL. **Disability Services:** Special programs offered to physically disabled students, including note-taking services, tape recorders, tutors. **Career Services:** Alumni network, Alumni services, Career/job search classes, Career assessment, Internships, Regional alumni. Career assessments, career preparation workshops, internships, job placement, employer recruitment, online JOBNET, member of Illinois Small College Placement Association.

FACILITIES

Housing: Coed dorms, special housing for disabled students, Theme Housing. 90% of campus accessible to physically diasbled. **Special Academic Facilities/Equipment:** Lewis University is located immediately adjacent to the Lewis University airport, and contains an aviation complex, which includes a Boeing 737 located on campus for use by students studying aviation maintenance. Special collections on campus include: Curriculum Collection, Eva White Memorial Aviation Collection, Library of American Civilization (ultrafiche), Library of English Literature (ultrafiche), ERIC fiche, Government Documents (Lewis University has housed a selective Federal Depository since 1952, and possesses a strong collection of the public documents generated during each decennial census), and Canal and Regional History Collection/I and M Canal Archives (one of the largest collections of documents, photographs, and artifacts pertaining to the canal era in the U.S.). **Computers:** 100% of classrooms, 100% of dorms, 100% of libraries, 100% of dining areas, 100% of student union, 100% of common outdoor areas have wireless network access. Students can register for classes online. Administrative functions (other than registration) can be performed online.

CAMPUS LIFE

Environment: Metropolis. **Activities:** Choral groups, dance, drama/theater, jazz band, literary magazine, music ensembles, musical theater, radio station, student government, student newspaper, television station, Campus Ministries, Student Organization. 45 registered organizations, 10 honor societies, 7 religious organizations. 7 fraternities, 6 sororities. **Athletics (Intercollegiate):** *Men:* baseball, basketball, cheerleading, cross-country, golf, soccer, swimming, tennis, track/field (outdoor), track/field (indoor), volleyball. *Women:* basketball, cheerleading, cross-country, golf, soccer, softball, swimming, tennis, track/field (outdoor), track/field (indoor), volleyball. **On-Campus Highlights:** Harold E. White Aviation Center, Student Recreation and Fitness Center, Philip Lynch Theatre, Student Union/Bookstore, Flyer's Den. **Environmental Initiatives:** The Lewis University Environment and Energy Conservation Council sponsors annual events such as an Earth Day event in spring where we clear out Buckthorn (an invasive plant species) from the nature trail here on campus and the Arbor Day Initiative in which we plant an assortment of native trees back into the University nature trail.

ADMISSIONS

Freshman Academic Profile: Average high school GPA 3.4. 20% in top 10% of high school class, 46% in top 25% of high school class, 83% in top 50% of high school class. **Reported SAT (pre-2016 redesign) scores:** SAT Math middle 50% range 520-610. SAT Critical Reading middle 50% range 460-600. **Concordant SAT scores:** SAT Math middle 50% range 550–630. ACT middle 50% range 21-26. Minimum internet-based TOEFL 79. Minimum paper TOEFL 550. **Basis for Candidate Selection:** *Very important factors considered include:* rigor of secondary school record, academic GPA, standardized test scores. *Important factors considered include:* application essay. *Other factors considered include:* class rank, recommendation(s), interview, extracurricular activities, talent/ability, character/personal qualities, first generation, alumni/ae relation, geographical residence, racial/ethnic status, volunteer work, work experience, level of applicant's interest. **Freshman Admission Requirements:** High school diploma is required and GED is accepted. *Academic units required:* 3 English, 2 math, 2 science, 1 science lab, 2 social studies, 1 history, 8 academic electives. *Academic units recommended:* 4 English, 3 math, 2 science, 1 science lab, 2 foreign language, 2 social studies, 1 history, 8 academic electives. **Freshman Admission Statistics:** 6,199 applied, 59.19% admitted, 17% enrolled. **Transfer Admission Requirements:** college transcript(s), Minimum college GPA of 2.0 required. Lowest grade transferable D. **General Admission Information:** Application fee $40. Priority deadline 4/15. Nonfall registration accepted. Admission may be deferred for a maximum of 1 year.

COSTS AND FINANCIAL AID

Annual tuition $31,100. Room and board $10,460. Required fees $150. Average book expense $1,500. **Required Forms and Deadlines:** FAFSA. **Notification of Awards:** Applicants will be notified of awards on a rolling basis beginning 2/1. **Types of Aid:** *Need-based scholarships/grants:* Federal Pell, FSEOG, State scholarships/grants, Private scholarships, College/university scholarship or grant aid from institutional funds, Federal Nursing Scholarships. *Loans:* Direct Subsidized Stafford Loans, Direct Unsubsidized Stafford Loans, Direct PLUS loans, Federal Perkins Loans. *Student Employment:* Federal Work-Study Program available. Institutional employment available. **Financial Aid Statistics:** 100% needy freshmen, 95% needy undergrads receive need-based scholarship or grant aid. 15% freshmen, 11% undergrads receive non-need-based scholarship or grant aid. 86% freshmen, 90% undergrads receive need-based self-help aid. 4% freshmen, 2% undergrads receive athletic scholarships. 99% freshmen, 88% undergrads receive any aid. 81% undergrads borrow to pay for school. Average cumulative indebtedness $36,073. **Criteria for awarding aid:** *Non-need-based:* Academics, Alumni affiliation, Art, Athletics, Music/drama, Religious affiliation.

LIBERTY UNIVERSITY

1971 University Blvd, Lynchburg, VA 24515
Phone: 434-582-2000 • **Financial Aid Phone:** 434-582-2270
E-mail: admissions@liberty.edu • **CEEB Code:** 5385
Fax: 800-628-7977 • **Website:** https://www.liberty.edu/ • **ACT Code:** 4364

This private school, affiliated with the Baptist Church, was founded in 1971. It has a 4400-acre campus.

RATINGS

Admissions Selectivity Rating: 89   **Fire Safety Rating:** 84   **Green Rating:** 60*

STUDENTS AND FACULTY

Enrollment: 13,596. **Student Body:** 53% female, 47% male, 60% out-of-state, 5% international (125 countries represented). Asian 2%, African American 5%, Caucasian 66%, Hispanic 5%, Native American 1%, Pacific Islander <1%, Two or more races 2%, Race unknown 15%.
Retention and Graduation: 88% freshmen return for sophomore year. 36% freshmen graduate within 4 years. 59% freshmen graduate within 6 years.
Faculty: 0% of classes are taught by teaching assistants.

ACADEMICS

Degrees: associate, bachelor's, certificate, doctoral/professional, doctoral/research, doctoral, master's, postbachelor's certificate, post-master's certificate, terminal. **Classes:** Most classes have 20-29 students. **Most popular majors:** Religion/Religious Studies; Psychology; Business/Commerce. **Special Study Options:** Accelerated program, cooperative education program, distance learning, double major, dual enrollment, English as a Second Language (ESL), external degree program, honors program, independent study, internships, student-designed major, teacher certification program, weekend college. **Honors Programs:** An early class registration period, smaller class size (15:1) for general education Honors seminars, and a generous scholarship based on grade point average are just a few of the benefits enjoyed by our Honors students. Once Honors students reach junior status, they petition one Honors course per semester in their desired major field of study. **Disability Services:** Special programs offered to physically disabled students, including tutors. **Career Services:** Career assessment, Internships, On-campus interviews.

FACILITIES

Housing: special housing for disabled students, men's dorms, women's dorms, apartments for single students. 98% of campus accessible to physically disabled. **Special Academic Facilities/Equipment:** Displays from the Museum of Life and Earth History are located in the Library. The Jerry Falwell Museum located in the main lobby of DeMoss Hall. **Computers:** 90% of classrooms, have wireless network access. Students can register for classes online. Administrative functions (other than registration) can be performed online.

CAMPUS LIFE

Environment: Town. **Activities:** Choral groups, concert band, drama/theater, literary magazine, marching band, music ensembles, musical theater, pep band, radio station, student government, student newspaper, symphony orchestra, television station, yearbook, Campus Ministries. 25 registered organizations, 8 honor societies, 10 religious organizations. **Athletics (Intercollegiate):** *Men:* baseball, basketball, cheerleading, cross-country, football, golf, soccer, tennis, track/field (outdoor), track/field (indoor), wrestling. *Women:* basketball, cheerleading, cross-country, soccer, softball, tennis, track/field (outdoor), track/field (indoor), volleyball. **On-Campus Highlights:** LaHaye Student Center, Bookstore, Hangar (Food Court), ILRC Computer Lab, LaHaye Ice Center (Ice Arena).

ADMISSIONS

Freshman Academic Profile: Average high school GPA 3.5. 26% in top 10% of high school class, 50% in top 25% of high school class, 78% in top 50% of high school class. **Reported SAT (pre-2016 redesign) scores:** SAT Math middle 50% range 470-590. SAT Critical Reading middle 50% range 480-600. SAT Writing middle 50% range 460-580. **Concordant SAT scores:** SAT EBRW middle 50% 530-650. SAT Math middle 50% range 510-610. ACT middle 50% range 21-28. Minimum internet-based TOEFL 60. Minimum paper TOEFL 500. **Basis for Candidate Selection:** *Very important factors considered include:* rigor of secondary school record, academic GPA. *Important factors considered include:* standardized test scores, character/personal qualities. *Other factors considered include:* class rank, application essay, recommendation(s), extracurricular activities, talent/ability, level of applicant's interest. **Freshman Admission Requirements:** High school diploma is required and GED is accepted. *Academic units recommended:* 4 English, 3 math, 2 science, 2 science labs, 2 foreign language, 2 social studies, 4 academic electives. **Freshman Admission Statistics:** 22,984 applied, 27.71% admitted, 46% enrolled. **Transfer Admission Requirements:** High school transcript, college transcript(s), essay or personal statement, statement of good standing from prior institution(s). Minimum college GPA of 2.0 required. Lowest grade transferable C. **General Admission Information:** Application fee $40. Priority deadline 1/31. Nonfall registration accepted. Admission may be deferred for a maximum of 12 months.

COSTS AND FINANCIAL AID

Annual tuition $22,000. Room and board $9,306. Required fees $1,020. Average book expense $1,700. **Required Forms and Deadlines:** FAFSA, State aid form. **Notification of Awards:** Applicants will be notified of awards on a rolling basis beginning 3/15. **Types of Aid:** *Need-based scholarships/grants:* Federal Pell, FSEOG, State scholarships/grants, Private scholarships, College/university scholarship or grant aid from institutional funds. *Loans:* Direct Subsidized Stafford Loans, Direct Unsubsidized Stafford Loans, Direct PLUS loans, State Loans, College/university loans from institutional funds. *Student Employment:* Federal Work-Study Program available. Institutional employment available. **Financial Aid Statistics:** 99% needy freshmen receive need-based scholarship or grant aid. 95% freshmen, 87% undergrads receive any aid. **Criteria for awarding aid:** *Non-need-based:* Academics, Alumni affiliation, Athletics, Leadership, Music/drama, Religious affiliation, State/district residency.

LIFE UNIVERSITY

1269 Barclay Circle, Marietta, GA 30060
Phone: 770-426-2884 • **Financial Aid Phone:** 770-426-2667
E-mail: admissions@life.edu
Website: http://www.life.edu/

RATINGS

Admissions Selectivity Rating: 65   **Fire Safety Rating:** 60*   **Green Rating:** 60*

STUDENTS AND FACULTY

Enrollment: 811. **Student Body:** 48% female, 52% male, 0% international (31 countries represented). Asian 3%, African American 25%, Caucasian 34%, Hispanic 8%, Native American 1%, Pacific Islander 0%, Two or more races 0%, Race unknown 29%.
Retention and Graduation: 12% freshmen graduate within 4 years. **Faculty:** Student/faculty ratio 17:1. 124 full-time faculty, 86% hold PhDs, 0% are are members of minority groups, 44% are women.

ACADEMICS

Degrees: associate, bachelor's, certificate, doctoral, master's. **Career Services:** Alumni network, Internships, Regional alumni. PEAK Clinic Program: The PEAK (Practice, Excellence, Art and Knowledge) program is a program designed to allow senior interns to complete their clinic requirements under the direction of an off-campus doctor. The doctor has qualified to become a Life University Extension Faculty member and serves as a mentor to help the intern not only develop clinically, but also prepare to make the transition from school to practice. The PEAK Program is for student interns in their 13th or 14th quarters of study, in good academic standing and having passed the 12th quarter OSCE exam. Doctors of Chiropractic are credentialed through an application process to become a PEAK Doctor. The student intern works with the PEAK Doctor to provide patient care and fulfill other assignments given by the PEAK Doctor. Students are a participating team member of the clinic, and a valuable part of the practice team. Interns perform history, examinations, diagnosis, X-ray, provide chiropractic adjustments and complete a Learning Objective Worksheet each week. In many other programs, student interns mostly just observe a practice. This is clearly not the case in the LIFE PEAK Program. This experience allows the intern to gain valuable insights into the nuances of running a profitable practice and the rewards of providing quality chiropractic care. The PEAK Doctor acts as a mentor to the intern, helping to bridge the gap between the classroom, the college clinic and private practice. In many cases, the PEAK Doctor is not only a facilitator in the student intern's development, but also becomes a lifelong mentor. Our options in the PEAK Program include: International Clinic Program: Read more about our amazing options to work in clinics in Ghana, Peru, Sweden, Argentina and New Zealand. Outreach Clinics: LIFE operates a clinic which provides free care to populations who cannot afford to seek out care in private practices. This clinic allows our students to give back while learning the clinical art of chiropractic practice. Private Chiropractic Offices: We have PEAK Clinics not only in Georgia, but also in 27 other states. One of the things that sets our private practice experience apart from many other schools is that our students are able to not just observe, but actually adjust in all of our PEAK offices. In a private practice, our students hone their patient care skills by caring for and adjusting real-world patients, and they also learn many details of real-life practice, like front and back office procedures that work and how to manage a private practice.

ADMISSIONS

Basis for Candidate Selection: *Important factors considered include:* academic GPA, extracurricular activities, talent/ability, alumni/ae relation. *Other factors considered include:* rigor of secondary school record, class rank, character/personal qualities, work experience. **Freshman Admission Statistics:** 259 applied, 67.57% admitted, 43% enrolled. **General Admission Information:** Application fee $50. Nonfall registration accepted. Admission may be deferred.

COSTS AND FINANCIAL AID

Annual tuition $9,874. Room and board $12,480. Required fees $747. **Required Forms and Deadlines:** FAFSA. *Types of Aid: Need-based scholarships/grants:* Federal Pell, FSEOG. *Loans:* Direct Subsidized Stafford Loans, Direct Unsubsidized Stafford Loans, Direct PLUS loans, Federal Perkins Loans, State Loans, College/university loans from institutional funds. *Student Employment:* Federal Work-Study Program available. Institutional employment available. **Financial Aid Statistics:** 74% needy freshmen, 66% needy undergrads receive need-based scholarship or grant aid. 85% freshmen, 70% undergrads receive non-need-based scholarship or grant aid. 91% freshmen, 90% undergrads receive need-based self-help aid. 32% freshmen, 16% undergrads receive athletic scholarships. **Criteria for awarding aid:** *Non-need-based:* Academics, Alumni affiliation, Athletics, Leadership, State/district residency.

LIM COLLEGE

12 East 53rd Street, New York, NY 10022
Phone: 212-310-0639 • **Financial Aid Phone:** 212-752-1530
E-mail: admissions@limcollege.edu • **CEEB Code:** 2380
Website: www.limcollege.edu • **ACT Code:** 4807

This proprietary school was founded in 1939.

RATINGS

Admissions Selectivity Rating: 73   **Fire Safety Rating:** 81   **Green Rating:** 60*

STUDENTS AND FACULTY

Enrollment: 1,515. **Student Body:** 93% female, 7% male, 61% out-of-state, 4% international (13 countries represented). Asian 6%, African American 15%, Caucasian 55%, Hispanic 12%, Native American 1%, Pacific Islander 1%, Two or more races 1%, Race unknown 5%.
Retention and Graduation: 73% freshmen return for sophomore year. 45% freshmen graduate within 4 years. 50% freshmen graduate within 6 years.
Faculty: Student/faculty ratio 8:1. 32 full-time faculty, 0% hold PhDs, 0% are are members of minority groups, 0% are women. 0% of classes are taught by teaching assistants.

ACADEMICS

Degrees: associate, bachelor's, certificate, master's, postbachelor's certificate. **Classes:** Most classes have 10-19 students. **Most popular majors:** Marketing/Marketing Management; Fashion Merchandising. **Special Study Options:** cooperative education program, internships, study abroad, 3 credit trip in winter/summer to Europe. **Disability Services:** Special programs offered to physically disabled students, including tape recorders, tutors. **Career Services:** Alumni network, Alumni services, Career/job search classes, Career assessment, Internships. All first and second year students must participate in a 5 week internship between Thanksgiving and Christmas. All seniors must participate in a full-semester co-op.

FACILITIES

Housing: Coed dorms. 100% of campus accessible to physically diasbled. **Computers:** 100% of classrooms, 100% of dorms, 100% of libraries, 100% of dining areas, 100% of student union, have wireless network access. Students can register for classes online. Administrative functions (other than registration) can be performed online.

CAMPUS LIFE

Environment: Metropolis. **Activities:** student government, yearbook. 12 registered organizations, 1 honor society. **On-Campus Highlights:** Library, Cafe 45, Cyber Lounge, 1760 Third Ave.

ADMISSIONS

Freshman Academic Profile: Average high school GPA 3.0. 73% from public high schools. **Reported SAT (pre-2016 redesign) scores:** SAT Math middle 50% range 410-510. SAT Critical Reading middle 50% range 430-520. SAT Writing middle 50% range 410-510. **Concordant SAT scores:** SAT EBRW middle 50% 470–570. SAT Math middle 50% range 450–540. Minimum paper TOEFL 550. **Basis for Candidate Selection:** *Very important factors considered include:* academic GPA, standardized test scores. *Important factors considered include:* rigor of secondary school record, application essay, recommendation(s), level of applicant's interest. *Other factors considered include:* class rank, interview, extracurricular activities, talent/ability, character/personal qualities, alumni/ae relation, volunteer work, work experience. **Freshman Admission Requirements:** High school diploma is required and GED is accepted. **Freshman Admission Statistics:** 1,389 applied, 74.15% admitted, 26% enrolled. **Transfer Admission Requirements:** High school transcript, college transcript(s), essay or personal statement, Minimum college GPA of 2.0 required. Lowest grade transferable D-. **General Admission Information:** Nonfall registration accepted. Admission may be deferred for a maximum of 1 year.

COSTS AND FINANCIAL AID

Annual tuition $24,950. Room and board $20,350. Required fees $775. Average book expense $900. **Required Forms and Deadlines:** FAFSA, State aid form. **Notification of Awards:** Applicants will be notified of awards on a rolling basis beginning 2/25. **Types of Aid:** *Need-based scholarships/grants:* Federal Pell, FSEOG, State scholarships/grants, Private scholarships, College/university scholarship or grant aid from institutional funds. *Loans:* Direct Subsidized Stafford Loans, Direct Unsubsidized Stafford Loans, Direct PLUS loans. *Student Employment:* Federal Work-Study Program available. Institutional employment available. **Financial Aid Statistics:** 76% needy freshmen, 74% needy undergrads receive need-based scholarship or grant aid. 60% freshmen, 50% undergrads receive non-need-based scholarship or grant aid. 77% freshmen, 90% undergrads receive need-based self-help aid. 0% freshmen, 0% undergrads receive athletic scholarships. 85% freshmen, 85% undergrads receive any aid. 75% undergrads borrow to pay for school. Average cumulative indebtedness $37,238. **Criteria for awarding aid:** *Need-based:* Academics, Alumni affiliation, Minority status. *Non-need-based:* Academics, Leadership, State/district residency.

See page 990.

LIMESTONE COLLEGE

1115 College Drive, Gaffney, SC 29340-3799
Phone: 864-488-4549 • **Financial Aid Phone:** 864-488-8800
E-mail: admiss@limestone.edu • **CEEB Code:** 5366
Fax: 864-487-8706 • **Website:** www.limestone.edu • **ACT Code:** 3862

This private school was founded in 1845. It has a 115-acre campus.

RATINGS

Admissions Selectivity Rating: 80   **Fire Safety Rating:** 81   **Green Rating:** 60*

STUDENTS AND FACULTY

Enrollment: 1,052. **Student Body:** 38% female, 62% male, 42% out-of-state, 9% international. Asian 0%, African American 29%, Caucasian 54%, Hispanic 4%, Native American <1%, Pacific Islander 0%, Two or more races 2%, Race unknown 1%.
Retention and Graduation: 57% freshmen return for sophomore year. 21% freshmen graduate within 4 years. 37% freshmen graduate within 6 years.
Faculty: Student/faculty ratio 13:1. 75 full-time faculty, 80% hold PhDs, 5% are are members of minority groups, 51% are women. 0% of classes are taught by teaching assistants.

ACADEMICS

Degrees: bachelor's, master's, transfer. **Classes:** Most classes have 20-29 students. Most lab/discussion sessions have fewer than 10 students. **Most**

popular majors: Business/Managerial Economics; Elementary Education and Teaching; Health and Physical Education/Fitness. **Special Study Options:** Accelerated program, distance learning, double major, honors program, independent study, internships, liberal arts/career combination, student-designed major, teacher certification program. **Honors Programs:** The Honors Program was established at Limestone College in 1983 to create a challenging academic environment for gifted and special ability students. **Disability Services:** Special programs offered to physically disabled students, including tape recorders, tutors. **Career Services:** Alumni services, Career assessment, On-campus interviews. The student is placed in a local private or public enterprise to gain work-related experience consistent with their field of study.

FACILITIES

Housing: men's dorms, women's dorms, apartments for single students. 90% of campus accessible to physically disabled. **Special Academic Facilities/Equipment:** Computer graphic arts lab; museum of Southern history in Winnie Davis Hall **Computers:** 20% of classrooms, 20% of dorms, 100% of libraries, 100% of student union, 5% of common outdoor areas have wireless network access. Students can register for classes online. Administrative functions (other than registration) can be performed online.

CAMPUS LIFE

Environment: Town. **Activities:** Choral groups, concert band, drama/theater, jazz band, literary magazine, music ensembles, musical theater, pep band, student government, yearbook, Campus Ministries. 2 religious organizations. **Athletics (Intercollegiate):** *Men:* baseball, basketball, cross-country, golf, lacrosse, soccer, swimming, tennis, track/field (outdoor), volleyball, wrestling. *Women:* basketball, cross-country, field hockey, golf, lacrosse, soccer, softball, swimming, tennis, track/field (outdoor), volleyball. **On-Campus Highlights:** Dixie Lodge, Stephenson Dining Hall, Timken Gym and Pool, Eastwood Library, Curtis Administration Building, The Walt Griffin Physical Education Center, Limestone Learning Center, Winnie Davis Hall of History. **Environmental Initiatives:** Community Garden

ADMISSIONS

Freshman Academic Profile: Average high school GPA 3.2. 3% in top 10% of high school class, 19% in top 25% of high school class, 51% in top 50% of high school class. 90% from public high schools. **Reported SAT (pre-2016 redesign) scores:** SAT Math middle 50% range 480-560. SAT Critical Reading middle 50% range 450-530. **Concordant SAT scores:** SAT Math middle 50% range 510–580. ACT middle 50% range 2-2.3. Minimum internet-based TOEFL 75. Minimum paper TOEFL 500. **Basis for Candidate Selection:** *Very important factors considered include:* rigor of secondary school record, academic GPA, standardized test scores. *Important factors considered include:* class rank. *Other factors considered include:* recommendation(s), interview. **Freshman Admission Requirements:** High school diploma is required and GED is accepted. *Academic units required:* 4 English, 3 math, 2 science, 2 science labs, 3 social studies. **Freshman Admission Statistics:** 2,318 applied, 53.67% admitted, 33% enrolled. **Transfer Admission Requirements:** college transcript(s), statement of good standing from prior institution(s). Minimum college GPA of 2.0 required. Lowest grade transferable C. **General Admission Information:** Application fee $25. Priority deadline 6/1. Regular application deadline 8/25. Nonfall registration accepted. Admission may be deferred for a maximum of 18 months.

COSTS AND FINANCIAL AID

Annual tuition $23,000. Room and board $7,800. Average book expense $2,304. **Required Forms and Deadlines:** FAFSA. **Notification of Awards:** Applicants will be notified of awards on a rolling basis beginning 1/15. **Types of Aid:** *Need-based scholarships/grants:* Federal Pell, FSEOG, State scholarships/grants, Private scholarships, College/university scholarship or grant aid from institutional funds. *Loans:* Direct Subsidized Stafford Loans, Direct Unsubsidized Stafford Loans, Direct PLUS loans, Federal Perkins Loans. *Student Employment:* Federal Work-Study Program available. Institutional employment available. **Financial Aid Statistics:** 100% needy freshmen, 100% needy undergrads receive need-based scholarship or grant aid. 8% freshmen, 10% undergrads receive non-need-based scholarship or grant aid. 86% freshmen, 85% undergrads receive need-based self-help aid. 12% freshmen, 16% undergrads receive athletic scholarships. 98% freshmen, 98% undergrads receive any aid. **Criteria for awarding aid:** *Need-based:* Academics, Art, Athletics, Leadership, Music/drama. *Non-need-based:* Academics, Art, Athletics, Leadership, Music/drama, State/district residency.

LINCOLN CHRISTIAN COLLEGE AND SEMINARY

100 Campus View Dr, Lincoln, IL 62656-2167
Phone: 217-732-3168 x:2251 • **Financial Aid Phone:** 217-732-3168
E-mail: coladmis@lccs.edu
Fax: 217-732-4199 • **Website:** www.lccs.edu • **ACT Code:** 1060

This private school, affiliated with the Church of Christ Church, was founded in 1944. It has a 100-acre campus.

RATINGS

Admissions Selectivity Rating: 79 **Fire Safety Rating:** 84 **Green Rating:** 60*

STUDENTS AND FACULTY

Enrollment: 601. **Student Body:** 51% female, 49% male, 40% out-of-state, 0% international (19 countries represented). Asian 0%, African American 5%, Caucasian 91%, Hispanic 2%, Native American <1%, Pacific Islander 0%, Two or more races 0%, Race unknown 1%.
Retention and Graduation: 66% freshmen return for sophomore year. 17% grads go on to further study within 1 year. **Faculty:** Student/faculty ratio 15:1. 44 full-time faculty, 45% hold PhDs, 5% are are members of minority groups, 18% are women. 0% of classes are taught by teaching assistants.

ACADEMICS

Degrees: associate, bachelor's, certificate, master's. **Special Study Options:** distance learning, double major, honors program, independent study, internships, study abroad, teacher certification program, weekend college, Teacher preparatory program through University of Illinois at Springfield, Illinois State University, and Greenville College. **Honors Programs:** Students with at least sophomore standing and a cumulative grade average of 3.5 or higher may apply for acceptance into an honors degree program. The honors degree requires 5 additional semester hours of study under a mentoring professor and the completion of a capstone project. The additional work may be completed in the area of the student's ministry specialization or in an area of interest outside the specialization. Since the program is funded by memorial gifts, honors degree students do not pay tuition for the additional 5 hours. For students who complet the honors degree requirements, special recognition will be given at the Commencement service, and an honors designation will be included on the academic transcript. **Disability Services:** Special programs offered to physically disabled students, including reader services, tape recorders, tutors.

FACILITIES

Housing: men's dorms, women's dorms, apartments for married students. 80% of campus accessible to physically disabled. **Computers:** 90% of classrooms, 100% of dorms, 80% of libraries, have wireless network access. Students can register for classes online. Administrative functions (other than registration) can be performed online.

CAMPUS LIFE

Environment: Village. **Activities:** Choral groups, drama/theater, music ensembles, musical theater, student government, student newspaper, Campus Ministries, Student Organization. 7 registered organizations. **Athletics (Intercollegiate):** *Men:* baseball, basketball, soccer. *Women:* basketball, softball, volleyball. **On-Campus Highlights:** The Warehouse, The CoffeeShop

ADMISSIONS

Freshman Academic Profile: 19% in top 10% of high school class, 45% in top 25% of high school class, 76% in top 50% of high school class. ACT middle 50% range 19-25. Minimum internet-based TOEFL 75. Minimum paper TOEFL 550. **Basis for Candidate Selection:** *Very important factors considered include:* rigor of secondary school record, standardized test scores, application essay, state residency, religious affiliation/commitment, level of applicant's interest. *Important factors considered include:* class rank, academic GPA, extracurricular activities, character/personal qualities, alumni/ae relation, geographical residence, racial/ethnic status, volunteer work. *Other factors considered include:* recommendation(s), interview, talent/ability, work experience. **Freshman Admission Requirements:** High school diploma is required and GED is accepted. *Academic units recommended:* 4 English, 3 math, 2 science, 2 foreign language, 3 social studies, 3 history. **Freshman Admission Statistics:** 195 applied, 84.10% admitted, 65% enrolled. **Transfer Admission Requirements:** High school transcript, college transcript(s), essay or personal statement, Minimum college GPA of 2.0 required. Lowest grade transferable 2. **General Admission Information:** Application fee $25. Nonfall registration accepted. Admission may be deferred for a maximum of 1 semester.

COSTS AND FINANCIAL AID

Annual tuition $11,790. Room and board $5,355. **Required Forms and Deadlines:** FAFSA. **Notification of Awards:** Applicants will be notified of awards on a rolling basis beginning 3/1. **Types of Aid:** *Need-based scholarships/*

grants: Federal Pell, FSEOG, State scholarships/grants. *Loans:* Federal Perkins Loans, College/university loans from institutional funds. *Student Employment:* Federal Work-Study Program available. Institutional employment available. **Financial Aid Statistics:** 55% needy freshmen, 64% needy undergrads receive need-based scholarship or grant aid. 84% freshmen, 79% undergrads receive non-need-based scholarship or grant aid. 67% freshmen, 72% undergrads receive need-based self-help aid. 0% freshmen, 0% undergrads receive athletic scholarships. 80% freshmen, 80% undergrads receive any aid. **Criteria for awarding aid:** *Non-need-based:* Academics.

LINCOLN MEMORIAL UNIVERSITY

6965 Cumberland Gap Parkway, Harrogate, TN 37752
Phone: 423-869-6280 • **Financial Aid Phone:** 423-869-6465
E-mail: admissions@lmunet.edu • **CEEB Code:** 1408
Fax: 423-869-6444 • **Website:** www.lmunet.edu • **ACT Code:** 3982

This private school was founded in 1897. It has a 1000-acre campus.

RATINGS
Admissions Selectivity Rating: 76   **Fire Safety Rating:** 60*   **Green Rating:** 60*

STUDENTS AND FACULTY
Enrollment: 1,749. **Student Body:** 73% female, 27% male, 36% out-of-state, 2% international (27 countries represented). Asian 1%, African American 4%, Caucasian 80%, Hispanic 2%, Native American <1%, Pacific Islander 0%, Two or more races <1%, Race unknown 10%.
Retention and Graduation: 66% freshmen return for sophomore year. 50% freshmen graduate within 4 years. **Faculty:** Student/faculty ratio 13:1. 256 full-time faculty, 97% hold PhDs, 8% are are members of minority groups, 53% are women. 0% of classes are taught by teaching assistants.

ACADEMICS
Degrees: associate, bachelor's, doctoral/professional, doctoral/research, master's, postbachelor's certificate, post-master's certificate. **Classes:** Most classes have fewer than 10 students. Most lab/discussion sessions have 10-19 students. **Most popular majors:** Athletic Training/Trainer; Osteopathic Medicine/Osteopathy; Veterinary/Animal Health Technology/Technician and Veterinary Assistant. **Special Study Options:** Accelerated program, distance learning, double major, dual enrollment, English as a Second Language (ESL), internships, teacher certification program. **Career Services:** Alumni services, Career/job search classes, Career assessment, Internships, On-campus interviews.

FACILITIES
Housing: Coed dorms, special housing for disabled students, men's dorms, women's dorms, apartments for married students, apartments for single students. 80% of campus accessible to physically disabled. **Special Academic Facilities/Equipment:** Civil War museum, including Abraham Lincoln memorabilia collection of over 6,000 books, paintings, and manuscripts.

CAMPUS LIFE
Environment: Rural. **Activities:** Choral groups, dance, drama/theater, literary magazine, music ensembles, pep band, radio station, student government, television station, yearbook, Campus Ministries, Student Organization. 26 registered organizations, 5 honor societies, 3 religious organizations, 3 fraternities, 3 sororities. **Athletics (Intercollegiate):** *Men:* baseball, basketball, cross-country, golf, soccer, tennis. *Women:* basketball, cross-country, golf, soccer, softball, tennis, volleyball.

ADMISSIONS
Freshman Academic Profile: Average high school GPA 3.4. 90% from public high schools. **Reported SAT (pre-2016 redesign) scores:** SAT Math middle 50% range 430-560. SAT Critical Reading middle 50% range 420-550. **Concordant SAT scores:** SAT Math middle 50% range 470–580. ACT middle 50% range 20-25. Minimum paper TOEFL 500. **Basis for Candidate Selection:** *Very important factors considered include:* rigor of secondary school record, academic GPA, standardized test scores. *Important factors considered include:* class rank, character/personal qualities, alumni/ae relation. *Other factors considered include:* extracurricular activities, first generation, religious affiliation/commitment, racial/ethnic status, volunteer work. **Freshman Admission Requirements:** High school diploma is required and GED is accepted. *Academic units required:* 4 English, 3 math, 2 science, 2 foreign language, 1 social studies, 1 history, 1 visual/performing arts. *Academic units recommended:* 4 English, 4 math, 2 science labs, 2 social studies, 7 academic electives. **Freshman Admission Statistics:** 984 applied, 65.24% admitted, 39% enrolled. **Transfer Admission Requirements:** High school transcript, college transcript(s), standardized test scores, Minimum college GPA of 2.0 required. Lowest grade transferable C. **General Admission Information:** Application fee $25. Priority deadline 6/1. Nonfall registration accepted.

COSTS AND FINANCIAL AID
Room and board $7,770. Required fees $530. Average book expense $1,250. **Required Forms and Deadlines:** FAFSA. **Types of Aid:** *Need-based scholarships/grants:* Federal Pell, FSEOG, State scholarships/grants, Private scholarships, College/university scholarship or grant aid from institutional funds. *Loans:* Federal Perkins Loans. *Student Employment:* Federal Work-Study Program available. **Financial Aid Statistics:** 100% needy freshmen, 97% needy undergrads receive need-based scholarship or grant aid. 17% freshmen, 9% undergrads receive non-need-based scholarship or grant aid. 42% freshmen, 59% undergrads receive need-based self-help aid. 2% freshmen, 1% undergrads receive athletic scholarships. **Criteria for awarding aid:** *Non-need-based:* Academics, Alumni affiliation, Athletics, Leadership, Music/drama.

LINCOLN UNIVERSITY (CA)

401 15th Street, Oakland, CA 94612
Phone: 510-628-8010 • **Financial Aid Phone:** 510-628-8023
E-mail: admissions@lincolnuca.edu
Fax: 510-628-8012 • **Website:** www.lincolnuca.edu

This private school was founded in 1919.

RATINGS
Admissions Selectivity Rating: 63   **Fire Safety Rating:** 60*   **Green Rating:** 60*

STUDENTS AND FACULTY
Student Body: 57% female, 43% male, % out-of-state.
Faculty: 11 full-time faculty, 82% hold PhDs, 0% are are members of minority groups, 9% are women.

ACADEMICS
Degrees: bachelor's, certificate, doctoral, master's. **Most popular majors:** Education; Bible/Biblical Studies; Youth Ministry. **Special Study Options:** cross-registration, double major, English as a Second Language (ESL), internships, student-designed major. **Career Services:** Alumni network, Internships, On-campus interviews.

FACILITIES
Housing: Universal Student Housing Placement.

CAMPUS LIFE
Environment: Metropolis. **Activities:** student government.

ADMISSIONS
Minimum paper TOEFL 500. **Basis for Candidate Selection:** *Very important factors considered include:* rigor of secondary school record. *Important factors considered include:* academic GPA. *Other factors considered include:* class rank, standardized test scores. **Freshman Admission Requirements:** High school diploma is required and GED is accepted. **Freshman Admission Statistics:** 130 applied, 81.54% admitted, 40% enrolled. **Transfer Admission Requirements:** college transcript(s), Minimum college GPA of 2.0 required. Lowest grade transferable C. **General Admission Information:** Application fee $75. Nonfall registration accepted. Admission may be deferred.

COSTS AND FINANCIAL AID
Annual tuition $9,600. Required fees $400. Average book expense $400. **Types of Aid:** *Need-based scholarships/grants:* Federal Pell. *Student Employment:* Federal Work-Study Program available. Institutional employment available.

LINCOLN UNIVERSITY (MO)

820 Chestnut Street, Jefferson City, MO 65101
Phone: 573-681-5599 • **Financial Aid Phone:** 573-681-6156
E-mail: enroll@lincolnu.edu
Fax: 573-681-5889 • **Website:** www.lincolnu.edu • **ACT Code:** 2322

This public school was founded in 1866. It has a 165-acre campus.

RATINGS
Admissions Selectivity Rating: 76   **Fire Safety Rating:** 91   **Green Rating:** 75

STUDENTS AND FACULTY
Enrollment: 2,113. **Student Body:** 58% female, 42% male, 24% out-of-state, 2% international (12 countries represented). Asian 1%, African American 53%, Caucasian 34%, Hispanic 2%, Native American 1%, Pacific Islander <1%, Two or more races 4%, Race unknown 4%.

Retention and Graduation: 47% freshmen return for sophomore year. 9% freshmen graduate within 4 years. 22% freshmen graduate within 6 years. **Faculty:** Student/faculty ratio 15:1. 127 full-time faculty, 66% hold PhDs, 27% are are members of minority groups, 44% are women.

ACADEMICS

Degrees: associate, bachelor's, master's, postbachelor's certificate, post-master's certificate. **Classes:** Most classes have 20-29 students. **Most popular majors:** Criminal Justice/Law Enforcement Administration; Registered Nursing/Registered Nurse. **Special Study Options:** Accelerated program, distance learning, double major, dual enrollment, exchange student program (domestic), honors program, independent study, internships, study abroad, teacher certification program, Senior Citizen Program; Learning in Retirement, Inc.; Intersession courses. **Honors Programs:** Lincoln University offers a 24-credit-hour Honors Program which features small classes, unique academic challenges, individual attention from Honors faculty, and association with other like-minded students. An Honors student has opportunities to compete for summer mentorships, work closely with a faculty member on a research or creative project; to do sustained research or creative work leading to a thesis in the student's major; and to present his/her work at regional, national, and international conferences. These students also qualify for Honors housing, certain restricted courses, and other activities. **Disability Services:** Special programs offered to physically disabled students, including note-taking services, reader services, tape recorders, tutors. **Career Services:** Alumni network, Alumni services, Career/job search classes, Career assessment, Internships.

FACILITIES

Housing: Coed dorms, men's dorms, women's dorms, Wellness HousingHonors Student Housing. 100% of campus accessible to physically diasbled. **Special Academic Facilities/Equipment:** University Archives/Ethnic Studies Center Media Center Student Support Services Center for Academic Enrichment Agriculture and Extension Information Center Education Curriculum Library **Computers:** 100% of classrooms, 100% of dorms, 100% of libraries, 100% of dining areas, 100% of student union, have wireless network access. Students can register for classes online. Administrative functions (other than registration) can be performed online.

CAMPUS LIFE

Environment: Town. **Activities:** Choral groups, concert band, dance, drama/theater, jazz band, literary magazine, marching band, music ensembles, pep band, radio station, student government, student newspaper, television station, yearbook, Campus Ministries, Student Organization. 24 registered organizations, 6 honor societies, 2 religious organizations. 4 fraternities, 2 sororities. **Athletics (Intercollegiate):** *Men:* baseball, basketball, football, golf, track/field (outdoor). *Women:* basketball, cheerleading, cross-country, golf, softball, tennis, track/field (outdoor). **On-Campus Highlights:** Clifford G. Scruggs University Center (SUC), Inman E. Page Library, Stamper Hall (Business and Economics), Richardson Fine Arts Center, Dwight T. Reed Stadium, University Farms used for agricultural research include: Busby Research Farm (273 acres); Carver Research Farm (173 acres); and Freeman Research Farm (199 acres). **Environmental Initiatives:** Lincoln University Composting Facility built to divert cafeteria food waste from landfills and convert it to soil amendment.

ADMISSIONS

Freshman Academic Profile: Average high school GPA 2.8. 5% in top 10% of high school class, 24% in top 25% of high school class, 56% in top 50% of high school class. ACT middle 50% range 15-20. Minimum internet-based TOEFL 61. Minimum paper TOEFL 500. **Basis for Candidate Selection:** *Other factors considered include:* rigor of secondary school record, academic GPA, standardized test scores, state residency. **Freshman Admission Requirements:** High school diploma is required and GED is accepted. *Academic units required:* 4 English, 3 math, 3 science, 1 science lab, 3 social studies, 3 academic electives, 1 visual/performing arts. *Academic units recommended:* 4 English, 3 math, 3 science, 1 science lab, 2 foreign language, 3 social studies, 3 academic electives, 1 visual/performing arts. **Freshman Admission Statistics:** 5,077 applied, 51.82% admitted, 17% enrolled. **Transfer Admission Requirements:** college transcript(s), Minimum college GPA of 2.0 required. Lowest grade transferable C. **General Admission Information:** Nonfall registration accepted. Admission may be deferred for a maximum of 1 semester.

COSTS AND FINANCIAL AID

Required Forms and Deadlines: FAFSA, Institution's own financial aid form. **Notification of Awards:** Applicants will be notified of awards on a rolling basis beginning 3/15. **Types of Aid:** *Need-based scholarships/grants:* Federal Pell, FSEOG, State scholarships/grants, Private scholarships, College/university scholarship or grant aid from institutional funds. *Loans:* Direct Subsidized Stafford Loans, Direct Unsubsidized Stafford Loans, Direct PLUS loans. *Student Employment:* Federal Work-Study Program available. Institutional employment available. **Financial Aid Statistics:** 91% needy freshmen, 88% needy undergrads receive need-based scholarship or grant aid. 48% freshmen, 40% undergrads receive non-need-based scholarship or grant

aid. 100% freshmen, 95% undergrads receive need-based self-help aid. 1% freshmen, 1% undergrads receive athletic scholarships. 95% freshmen, 82% undergrads receive any aid. Average cumulative indebtedness $32,691. **Criteria for awarding aid:** *Need-based:* Alumni affiliation. *Non-need-based:* Academics, Art, Athletics, Job skills, Leadership, Minority status, Music/drama, State/district residency.

THE LINCOLN UNIVERSITY (PA)

1570 Balitmore Pike, Lincoln University, PA 19352
Phone: 484-365-7206 • **Financial Aid Phone:** 800-561-2606
E-mail: admiss@lincoln.edu • **CEEB Code:** 2367
Fax: 484-365-8109 • **Website:** www.lincoln.edu • **ACT Code:** 3614

This public school was founded in 1854. It has a 422-acre campus.

RATINGS

Admissions Selectivity Rating: 75   **Fire Safety Rating:** 76   **Green Rating:** 71

STUDENTS AND FACULTY

Enrollment: 1,584. **Student Body:** 61% female, 39% male, 57% out-of-state, 4% international (28 countries represented). Asian 0%, African American 81%, Caucasian 2%, Hispanic 2%, Native American <1%, Pacific Islander 0%, Two or more races 1%, Race unknown 10%.

Retention and Graduation: 75% freshmen return for sophomore year. 23% freshmen graduate within 4 years. 20% grads go on to further study within 1 year. **Faculty:** Student/faculty ratio 17:1. 91 full-time faculty, 86% hold PhDs, 59% are are members of minority groups, 38% are women. 0% of classes are taught by teaching assistants.

ACADEMICS

Degrees: bachelor's, master's. **Classes:** Most classes have 20-29 students. Most lab/discussion sessions have 10-19 students. **Most popular majors:** Criminal Justice/Safety Studies; Human Services; Biology/Biological Sciences. **Special Study Options:** double major, exchange student program (domestic), honors program, independent study, internships, study abroad, teacher certification program, 3-2 in advanced science/egineering with Drexel University, Pennsylvania State University, Howard University, University of Delaware, Temple University, Widener University, and New Jersey Institute of Technology. **Disability Services:** Special programs offered to physically disabled students, including reader services, tutors. **Career Services:** Alumni services, Career/job search classes, Internships.

FACILITIES

Housing: Coed dorms, men's dorms, women's dorms, apartments for single students. 90% of campus accessible to physically diasbled. **Special Academic Facilities/Equipment:** African museum, fine arts center, hall for life sciences, learning resource center.

CAMPUS LIFE

Environment: Rural. **Activities:** Choral groups, dance, drama/theater, jazz band, music ensembles, radio station, student government, student newspaper, television station, yearbook. 30 registered organizations, 9 honor societies, 4 fraternities, 3 sororities. **Athletics (Intercollegiate):** *Men:* baseball, basketball, cross-country, soccer, tennis, track/field (outdoor), track/field (indoor). *Women:* basketball, cross-country, soccer, tennis, track/field (outdoor), track/field (indoor), volleyball. **On-Campus Highlights:** Langston Hughes Memorial Library, Thurgood Marshall Living and Learning Ce, John Miller Dickey Hall, Student Union Building, Fredrick Douglass Memorial statue area.

ADMISSIONS

Freshman Academic Profile: Average high school GPA 2.9. **Reported SAT (pre-2016 redesign) scores:** SAT Math middle 50% range 390-470. SAT Critical Reading middle 50% range 382-470. SAT Writing middle 50% range 360-450. **Concordant SAT scores:** SAT EBRW middle 50% 420–510. SAT Math middle 50% range 430–510. ACT middle 50% range 16-21. Minimum paper TOEFL 500. **Basis for Candidate Selection:** *Very important factors considered include:* application essay, recommendation(s). *Important factors considered include:* class rank, academic GPA, standardized test scores, talent/ability. *Other factors considered include:* rigor of secondary school record, interview, extracurricular activities, character/personal qualities, first generation, alumni/ae relation, geographical residence, state residency, religious affiliation/commitment, volunteer work, work experience, level of applicant's interest. **Freshman Admission Requirements:** High school diploma is required and GED is accepted. *Academic units required:* 4 English, 3 math, 3 science, 3 social studies, 5 academic electives, and 3 units from above areas or other academic areas. **Freshman Admission Statistics:** 2,790 applied, 50.39% admitted, 23% enrolled. **Transfer Admission Requirements:** college transcript(s), essay or personal statement, statement of good standing from prior institution(s). Minimum college GPA of 2.0 required. Lowest grade transferable C. **General Admission Information:** Application fee $20. Priority deadline 4/1. Nonfall registration accepted. Admission may be deferred for a maximum of 1 year.

COSTS AND FINANCIAL AID

Annual in-state tuition $7,160. Annual out-of-state tuition $11,836. Room and board $8,686. Required fees $3,378. Average book expense $1,520. **Required Forms and Deadlines:** FAFSA. **Notification of Awards:** Applicants will be notified of awards on a rolling basis beginning 4/1. **Types of Aid:** *Need-based scholarships/grants:* Federal Pell, FSEOG, State scholarships/grants, Private scholarships, College/university scholarship or grant aid from institutional funds, United Negro College Fund. *Loans:* Direct Subsidized Stafford Loans, Direct Unsubsidized Stafford Loans, Direct PLUS loans, Federal Perkins Loans, State Loans. *Student Employment:* Federal Work-Study Program available. Institutional employment available. **Financial Aid Statistics:** freshmen, 0% undergrads receive non-need-based scholarship or grant aid. 89% freshmen, 88% undergrads receive need-based self-help aid. 0% freshmen, 0% undergrads receive athletic scholarships. 99% freshmen, 93% undergrads receive any aid. **Criteria for awarding aid:** *Need-based:* Academics, Leadership. *Non-need-based:* Academics, Alumni affiliation, Leadership, Music/drama.

LINDENWOOD UNIVERSITY

209 South Kingshighway, Saint Charles, MO 63301-1695
Phone: 314-949-4949 • **Financial Aid Phone:** 636-949-4923
E-mail: admissions@lindenwood.edu • **CEEB Code:** 6367
Fax: 314-949-4989 • **Website:** www.lindenwood.edu • **ACT Code:** 2324

This private school, affiliated with the Presbyterian Church, was founded in 1827. It has a 172-acre campus.

RATINGS
Admissions Selectivity Rating: 82   **Fire Safety Rating:** 73   **Green Rating:** 60*

STUDENTS AND FACULTY
Enrollment: 7,787. **Student Body:** 55% female, 45% male, 36% out-of-state, 12% international. Asian 1%, African American 13%, Caucasian 56%, Hispanic 4%, Native American <1%, Pacific Islander <1%, Two or more races 3%, Race unknown 10%.
Retention and Graduation: 66% freshmen return for sophomore year. 28% freshmen graduate within 4 years. 49% freshmen graduate within 6 years. **Faculty:** Student/faculty ratio 17:1. 301 full-time faculty, 72% hold PhDs, 9% are are members of minority groups, 49% are women. 0% of classes are taught by teaching assistants.

ACADEMICS
Degrees: bachelor's, certificate, doctoral/research, master's, postbachelor's certificate, post-master's certificate. **Classes:** Most classes have 10-19 students. Most lab/discussion sessions have 20-29 students. **Most popular majors:** Business Administration and Management; Criminology; Education. **Special Study Options:** Accelerated program, cross-registration, double major, dual enrollment, English as a Second Language (ESL), honors program, independent study, internships, student-designed major, study abroad, teacher certification program. **Disability Services:** Special programs offered to physically disabled students, including reader services, tutors. **Career Services:** Alumni services, Career/job search classes, Career assessment, Internships. We are able to offer comprehensive career services to all alumni without cost.

FACILITIES
Housing: men's dorms, women's dorms, apartments for married students, apartments for single students. **Special Academic Facilities/Equipment:** University archives. Daniel Boone Campus

CAMPUS LIFE
Activities: Choral groups, concert band, dance, drama/theater, jazz band, literary magazine, marching band, music ensembles, musical theater, pep band, radio station, student government, student newspaper, symphony orchestra, television station, Campus Ministries, Student Organization. 72 registered organizations, 8 honor societies, 13 religious organizations. 1 fraternity, 1 sorority. **Athletics (Intercollegiate):** *Men:* baseball, basketball, cheerleading, cross-country, diving, football, golf, ice hockey, lacrosse, riflery, soccer, swimming, tennis, track/field (outdoor), track/field (indoor), volleyball, water polo, wrestling. *Women:* basketball, cheerleading, cross-country, diving, field hockey, golf, ice hockey, lacrosse, riflery, soccer, softball, swimming, tennis, track/field (outdoor), track/field (indoor), volleyball, water polo.
Environmental Initiatives: Paper Recycling.

ADMISSIONS
Freshman Academic Profile: Average high school GPA 3.2. 13% in top 10% of high school class, 33% in top 25% of high school class, 70% in top 50% of high school class. **Reported SAT (pre-2016 redesign) scores:** SAT Math middle 50% range 460-560. SAT Critical Reading middle 50% range 430-540. SAT Writing middle 50% range 400-500. **Concordant SAT scores:** SAT EBRW middle 50% 460–580. SAT Math middle 50% range 500–580. ACT middle 50% range 20-25. Minimum internet-based TOEFL 61. Minimum paper TOEFL 500. **Basis for Candidate Selection:** *Very important factors considered include:* academic GPA, standardized test scores. *Important factors considered include:* rigor of secondary school record, application essay, recommendation(s). *Other factors considered include:* class rank, interview, extracurricular activities, talent/ability, character/personal qualities, first generation, alumni/ae relation, volunteer work, work experience. **Freshman Admission Requirements:** High school diploma is required and GED is accepted. *Academic units recommended:* 4 English, 1 science lab, 2 foreign language, 1 history, 1 visual/performing arts. **Freshman Admission Statistics:** 4,156 applied, 55.39% admitted, 53% enrolled. **Transfer Admission Requirements:** college transcript(s), Minimum college GPA of 2.0 required. Lowest grade transferable D. **General Admission Information:** Application fee $30. Nonfall registration accepted. Admission may be deferred.

COSTS AND FINANCIAL AID
Annual tuition $15,672. Room and board $7,934. Required fees $350. Average book expense $1,800. **Required Forms and Deadlines:** FAFSA. **Types of Aid:** *Need-based scholarships/grants:* Federal Pell, FSEOG, State scholarships/grants, Private scholarships, College/university scholarship or grant aid from institutional funds. *Loans:* Direct Subsidized Stafford Loans, Direct Unsubsidized Stafford Loans, Direct PLUS loans, Federal Perkins Loans. *Student Employment:* Federal Work-Study Program available. Institutional employment available. **Financial Aid Statistics:** 94% needy freshmen, 83% needy undergrads receive need-based scholarship or grant aid. 66% freshmen, 51% undergrads receive non-need-based scholarship or grant aid. 89% freshmen, 91% undergrads receive need-based self-help aid. 6% freshmen, 4% undergrads receive athletic scholarships. 98% freshmen, 86% undergrads receive any aid. 70% undergrads borrow to pay for school. Average cumulative indebtedness $33,182. **Criteria for awarding aid:** *Non-need-based:* Academics, Art, Athletics, Leadership, Minority status, Music/drama, Religious affiliation, State/district residency.

LINFIELD COLLEGE

900 South East Baker Street, McMinnville, OR 97128-6894
Phone: 503-883-2213 • **Financial Aid Phone:** 503-883-2269
E-mail: admission@linfield.edu • **CEEB Code:** 4387
Fax: 503-883-2472 • **Website:** www.linfield.edu • **ACT Code:** 3466

This private school, affiliated with the American Baptist Church, was founded in 1858. It has a 193-acre campus.

RATINGS
Admissions Selectivity Rating: 82   **Fire Safety Rating:** 98   **Green Rating:** 94

STUDENTS AND FACULTY
Enrollment: 1,603. **Student Body:** 62% female, 38% male, 45% out-of-state, 3% international (25 countries represented). Asian 5%, African American 2%, Caucasian 60%, Hispanic 14%, Native American 1%, Pacific Islander 1%, Two or more races 12%, Race unknown 3%.
Retention and Graduation: 82% freshmen return for sophomore year. 57% freshmen graduate within 4 years. 70% freshmen graduate within 6 years. 13% grads go on to further study within 1 year. 3% grads pursue arts and sciences degrees. 1% grads pursue law degrees. 7% grads pursue business degrees. 1% grads pursue medical degrees. **Faculty:** Student/faculty ratio 11:1. 118 full-time faculty, 94% hold PhDs, 13% are members of minority groups, 51% are women. 0% of classes are taught by teaching assistants.

ACADEMICS
Degrees: bachelor's. **Classes:** Most classes have 10-19 students. **Most popular majors:** Kinesiology and Exercise Science; Psychology; Registered Nursing/Registered Nurse. **Special Study Options:** cross-registration, distance learning, double major, English as a Second Language (ESL), external degree program, independent study, internships, liberal arts/career combination, student-designed major, study abroad, teacher certification program, Unique January Term courses, widespread participation in off-campus international study. **Disability Services:** Special programs offered to physically disabled students, including note-taking services, reader services, tape recorders, tutors. **Career Services:** Alumni network, Alumni services, Career/job search classes, Career assessment, Internships, Regional alumni, On-campus interviews.

FACILITIES

Housing: Coed dorms, special housing for disabled students, men's dorms, women's dorms, fraternity/sorority housing, apartments for single students, Wellness Housing. 80% of campus accessible to physically diasbled. **Special Academic Facilities/Equipment:** New library, art gallery, anthropology museum, language classroom with murals, environmental field station, undergraduate research institute, electron microscope. **Computers:** 90% of classrooms, 90% of dorms, 100% of libraries, have wireless network access. Students can register for classes online. Administrative functions (other than registration) can be performed online.

CAMPUS LIFE

Environment: Town. **Activities:** Choral groups, concert band, dance, drama/theater, jazz band, literary magazine, music ensembles, musical theater, opera, pep band, radio station, student government, student newspaper, symphony orchestra, Campus Ministries, Student Organization, Model UN. 41 registered organizations, 18 honor societies, 5 religious organizations. 4 fraternities, 4 sororities. **Athletics (Intercollegiate):** *Men:* baseball, basketball, cross-country, football, golf, soccer, swimming, tennis, track/field (outdoor). *Women:* basketball, cross-country, golf, lacrosse, soccer, softball, swimming, tennis, track/field (outdoor), volleyball. **On-Campus Highlights:** Nicholson Library, Modern language rooms (Walker Hall, 3rd floor), Elkington and Terrell Halls, Food services and coffee shop, Athletic complex. **Environmental Initiatives:** Signatory on ACUPCC.

ADMISSIONS

Freshman Academic Profile: Average high school GPA 3.7. 27% in top 10% of high school class, 64% in top 25% of high school class, 94% in top 50% of high school class. 90% from public high schools. **Reported SAT (pre-2016 redesign) scores:** SAT Math middle 50% range 460-560. SAT Critical Reading middle 50% range 460-590. SAT Writing middle 50% range 450-570. **Concordant SAT scores:** SAT EBRW middle 50% 510–640. SAT Math middle 50% range 500–580. ACT middle 50% range 20-24. Minimum internet-based TOEFL 80. Minimum paper TOEFL 550. **Basis for Candidate Selection:** *Very important factors considered include:* rigor of secondary school record, academic GPA, standardized test scores. *Important factors considered include:* class rank, application essay, recommendation(s). *Other factors considered include:* extracurricular activities, talent/ability, character/personal qualities, first generation, alumni/ae relation, geographical residence, racial/ethnic status, volunteer work, work experience, level of applicant's interest. **Freshman Admission Requirements:** High school diploma is required and GED is accepted. *Academic units recommended:* 4 English, 4 math. **Freshman Admission Statistics:** 2,296 applied, 80.75% admitted, 26% enrolled. **Transfer Admission Requirements:** college transcript(s), essay or personal statement, Lowest grade transferable C. **General Admission Information:** Priority deadline 2/1. Regular notification 4/1. Nonfall registration accepted. Admission may be deferred for a maximum of 1 YEAR.

COSTS AND FINANCIAL AID

Annual tuition $39,700. Room and board $11,320. Required fees $370. Average book expense $900. **Required Forms and Deadlines:** FAFSA. **Notification of Awards:** Applicants will be notified of awards on or about 4/1. **Types of Aid:** *Need-based scholarships/grants:* Federal Pell, FSEOG, State scholarships/grants, Private scholarships, College/university scholarship or grant aid from institutional funds. *Loans:* Direct Subsidized Stafford Loans, Direct Unsubsidized Stafford Loans, Direct PLUS loans, Federal Perkins Loans. *Student Employment:* Federal Work-Study Program available. Institutional employment available. **Financial Aid Statistics:** 84% needy freshmen, 80% needy undergrads receive need-based scholarship or grant aid. 96% freshmen, 94% undergrads receive non-need-based scholarship or grant aid. 100% freshmen, 100% undergrads receive need-based self-help aid. 0% freshmen, 0% undergrads receive athletic scholarships. 99% freshmen, 95% undergrads receive any aid. 70% undergrads borrow to pay for school. Average cumulative indebtedness $34,320. **Criteria for awarding aid:** *Need-based:* Academics, Minority status, Music/drama. *Non-need-based:* Academics, Leadership, Minority status, Music/drama.

LIPSCOMB UNIVERSITY

One University Park Dr., Nashville, TN 37204-3951
Phone: 615-966-1776 • **Financial Aid Phone:** 615-966-1791
E-mail: admissions@lipscomb.edu • **CEEB Code:** 1161
Fax: 615-966-1804 • **Website:** http://www.lipscomb.edu • **ACT Code:** 3956

This private school, affiliated with the Church of Christ Church, was founded in 1891. It has a 65-acre campus.

RATINGS

Admissions Selectivity Rating: 86   **Fire Safety Rating:** 97   **Green Rating:** 77

STUDENTS AND FACULTY

Enrollment: 2,969. **Student Body:** 62% female, 38% male, 35% out-of-state, 3% international (44 countries represented). Asian 3%, African American 7%, Caucasian 76%, Hispanic 6%, Native American <1%, Pacific Islander <1%, Two or more races 3%, Race unknown 2%. **Retention and Graduation:** 85% freshmen return for sophomore year. 48% freshmen graduate within 4 years. 58% freshmen graduate within 6 years. 30% grads go on to further study within 1 year. **Faculty:** Student/faculty ratio 12:1. 220 full-time faculty, 83% hold PhDs, 8% are are members of minority groups, 41% are women. 0% of classes are taught by teaching assistants.

ACADEMICS

Degrees: associate, bachelor's, doctoral/professional, doctoral/research, master's, postbachelor's certificate. **Classes:** Most classes have 10-19 students. Most lab/discussion sessions have 20-29 students. **Most popular majors:** Biology/Biological Sciences; Business Administration and Management; Registered Nursing/Registered Nurse. **Special Study Options:** cross-registration, distance learning, double major, dual enrollment, honors program, independent study, internships, study abroad, teacher certification program, weekend college. Combined degree programs: BBA/MAcc; BS/MS in Molecular Biology/Biomolecular Science; BS/MS in Computing & Technology programs; BA/MA in Law Justice & Society/Conflict Management. **Disability Services:** Special programs offered to physically disabled students, including note-taking services, reader services, tape recorders, tutors. **Career Services:** Alumni network, Alumni services, Career/job search classes, Career assessment, Internships.

FACILITIES

Housing: men's dorms, women's dormsOut-of-town undergraduates required to live on campus except for seniors, students over 21, and married students. 100% of campus accessible to physically diasbled. **Special Academic Facilities/Equipment:** On-campus elementary, middle, and secondary schools. **Computers:** 100% of classrooms, 100% of dorms, 100% of libraries, 100% of dining areas, 100% of student union, 100% of common outdoor areas have wireless network access. Students can register for classes online. Administrative functions (other than registration) can be performed online.

CAMPUS LIFE

Environment: Metropolis. **Activities:** Choral groups, concert band, drama/theater, jazz band, literary magazine, marching band, music ensembles, musical theater, pep band, radio station, student government, student newspaper, yearbook, Campus Ministries, Student Organization. 65 registered organizations. **Athletics (Intercollegiate):** *Men:* baseball, basketball, cross-country, golf, soccer, tennis, track/field (outdoor). *Women:* basketball, cheerleading, cross-country, soccer, softball, tennis, track/field (outdoor), track/field (indoor), volleyball. **On-Campus Highlights:** Student Center, SAC—Student Activity Center, Allen Arena, Willard Collins Alumni Auditorium, Bison Square. **Environmental Initiatives:** Academic: First and only comprehensive sustainability academic program in the SE US.

ADMISSIONS

Freshman Academic Profile: Average high school GPA 3.6. 30% in top 10% of high school class, 57% in top 25% of high school class, 83% in top 50% of high school class. 70% from public high schools. **Reported SAT (pre-2016 redesign) scores:** SAT Math middle 50% range 490-630. SAT Critical Reading middle 50% range 500-638. **Concordant SAT scores:** SAT Math middle 50% range 520–650. ACT middle 50% range 22-28. Minimum internet-based TOEFL 80. Minimum paper TOEFL 550. **Basis for Candidate Selection:** *Very important factors considered include:* class rank, standardized test scores. *Important factors considered include:* rigor of secondary school record, academic GPA, recommendation(s). *Other factors considered include:* application essay, extracurricular activities, talent/ability, character/personal qualities, first generation, volunteer work, work experience. **Freshman Admission Requirements:** High school diploma is required and GED is accepted. **Freshman Admission Statistics:** 3,464 applied, 60.85% admitted, 30% enrolled. **Transfer Admission Requirements:** college transcript(s), interview, statement of good standing from prior institution(s). Minimum college GPA of 2.0 required. Lowest grade transferable C. **General Admission**

Information: Application fee $50. Nonfall registration accepted. Admission may be deferred for a maximum of 1 year.

COSTS AND FINANCIAL AID
Required Forms and Deadlines: FAFSA. **Notification of Awards:** Applicants will be notified of awards on a rolling basis beginning 3/1. **Types of Aid:** *Need-based scholarships/grants:* Federal Pell, FSEOG, State scholarships/grants, Private scholarships, College/university scholarship or grant aid from institutional funds. *Loans:* Direct Subsidized Stafford Loans, Direct Unsubsidized Stafford Loans, Direct PLUS loans, Federal Perkins Loans. *Student Employment:* Federal Work-Study Program available. Institutional employment available. **Financial Aid Statistics:** 43% needy freshmen, 98% needy undergrads receive need-based scholarship or grant aid. 100% freshmen, 87% undergrads receive non-need-based scholarship or grant aid. 76% freshmen, 78% undergrads receive need-based self-help aid. 3% freshmen, 3% undergrads receive athletic scholarships. 99% freshmen, 73% undergrads receive any aid. 55% undergrads borrow to pay for school. Average cumulative indebtedness $31,082. **Criteria for awarding aid:** *Need-based:* Leadership. *Non-need-based:* Academics, Art, Athletics, Job skills, Leadership, Minority status, Music/drama, Religious affiliation, State/district residency.

LOCK HAVEN UNIVERSITY OF PENNSYLVANIA

LHU Office of Admissions, Lock Haven, PA 17745
Phone: 570-484-2027
E-mail: admissions@lhup.edu • **CEEB Code:** 2654
Fax: 570-484-2201 • **Website:** www.lhup.edu • **ACT Code:** 3708

This public school was founded in 1870. It has a 175-acre campus.

RATINGS
Admissions Selectivity Rating: 73   **Fire Safety Rating:** 62   **Green Rating:** 60*

STUDENTS AND FACULTY
Enrollment: 4,158. **Student Body:** 57% female, 43% male, 5% out-of-state, 1% international (39 countries represented). Asian 1%, African American 9%, Caucasian 84%, Hispanic 2%, Native American <1%, Pacific Islander 0%, Two or more races 1%, Race unknown 2%.
Retention and Graduation: 30% freshmen graduate within 4 years. **Faculty:** Student/faculty ratio 19:1. 214 full-time faculty, 83% hold PhDs, 14% are are members of minority groups, 50% are women. 0% of classes are taught by teaching assistants.

ACADEMICS
Degrees: associate, bachelor's, master's. **Classes:** Most classes have 20-29 students. Most lab/discussion sessions have 20-29 students. **Most popular majors:** Elementary Education and Teaching; Health and Physical Education/Fitness; Health Professions and Related Clinical Sciences. **Special Study Options:** cross-registration, distance learning, double major, dual enrollment, honors program, independent study, internships, student-designed major, study abroad, teacher certification program. **Honors Programs:** The University Honors Program provides students and faculty opportunities for creative intellectual engagement through a mix of special curricular and co-curricular opportunities. Students may apply for entry as a first-year freshman or after completing 1-4 semesters of college-level work. Entry as a first-year freshman may be either directly into the University Honors or through the First Year Excellence Program. Students successfully completing the First Year Excellence Program receive certificate recognition. Students completing the University Honors Program receive recognition on their transcript, on their diploma and at commencement. Students in both the First Year Excellence and University Honors programs must participate in co-curricular activities and community service in addition to their curriculum. Engaging activity groups and Speaker Series allow students in the Honors Program to bond together and learn from each other, creating a community of both friends and scholars. **Disability Services:** Special programs offered to physically disabled students, including note-taking services, reader services, tape recorders, tutors. **Career Services:** Alumni network, Alumni services, Career/job search classes, Career assessment, Internships, Regional alumni.

FACILITIES
Housing: Coed dorms, apartments for single students. 98% of campus accessible to physically diasbled. **Special Academic Facilities/Equipment:** Planetarium, Sloan Art Gallery, Library Archives **Computers:** Students can register for classes online. Administrative functions (other than registration) can be performed online. Undergraduates are required to own a computer.

CAMPUS LIFE
Environment: Village. **Activities:** Choral groups, concert band, dance, drama/theater, jazz band, literary magazine, marching band, music ensembles, musical theater, pep band, radio station, student government, student newspaper, symphony orchestra, television station, yearbook, Campus Ministries, Student Organization. 96 registered organizations, 10 honor societies, 7 religious organizations. 6 fraternities, 4 sororities. **Athletics (Intercollegiate):** *Men:* baseball, basketball, football, soccer, track/field (outdoor), track/field (indoor), wrestling. *Women:* basketball, field hockey, lacrosse, soccer, softball, swimming, track/field (outdoor), track/field (indoor), volleyball. **On-Campus Highlights:** Student Recreation Center, Parsons Union Building, Library, Residence Halls, Bentley Dining Hall.

ADMISSIONS
Freshman Academic Profile: Average high school GPA 3.3. 9% in top 10% of high school class, 29% in top 25% of high school class, 64% in top 50% of high school class. **Reported SAT (pre-2016 redesign) scores:** SAT Math middle 50% range 430-530. SAT Critical Reading middle 50% range 420-520. SAT Writing middle 50% range 400-510. **Concordant SAT scores:** SAT EBRW middle 50% 460-570. SAT Math middle 50% range 470-560. ACT middle 50% range 17-22. Minimum paper TOEFL 550. **Basis for Candidate Selection:** *Very important factors considered include:* rigor of secondary school record, class rank, academic GPA, talent/ability, character/personal qualities. *Important factors considered include:* standardized test scores, racial/ethnic status. *Other factors considered include:* application essay, recommendation(s), interview, extracurricular activities, first generation, volunteer work, work experience, level of applicant's interest. **Freshman Admission Requirements:** High school diploma is required and GED is accepted. *Academic units required:* 4 English, 3 math, 3 science, 2 science labs, 2 social studies, 2 history. *Academic units recommended:* 4 English, 4 math, 4 science, 3 science labs, 2 foreign language, 2 social studies, 2 history. **Freshman Admission Statistics:** 3,415 applied, 91.74% admitted, 27% enrolled. **Transfer Admission Requirements:** college transcript(s), statement of good standing from prior institution(s). Minimum college GPA of 2.0 required. Lowest grade transferable C. **General Admission Information:** Application fee $25. Nonfall registration accepted. Admission may be deferred for a maximum of 1 year.

COSTS AND FINANCIAL AID
Annual in-state tuition $7,060. Annual out-of-state tuition $15,650. Room and board $9,344. Required fees $2,605. Average book expense $1,600. **Required Forms and Deadlines:** FAFSA, State aid form. **Notification of Awards:** Applicants will be notified of awards on a rolling basis beginning 4/10. **Types of Aid:** *Need-based scholarships/grants:* Federal Pell, FSEOG, State scholarships/grants, Private scholarships, College/university scholarship or grant aid from institutional funds. *Loans:* Direct Subsidized Stafford Loans, Direct Unsubsidized Stafford Loans, Direct PLUS loans, Federal Perkins Loans, College/university loans from institutional funds. *Student Employment:* Federal Work-Study Program available. Institutional employment available. **Financial Aid Statistics:** 70% needy freshmen, 87% needy undergrads receive need-based scholarship or grant aid. 31% freshmen, 19% undergrads receive non-need-based scholarship or grant aid. 87% freshmen, 88% undergrads receive need-based self-help aid. 6% freshmen, 4% undergrads receive athletic scholarships. 87% undergrads borrow to pay for school. Average cumulative indebtedness $31,806. **Criteria for awarding aid:** *Need-based:* Academics, Athletics, Leadership. *Non-need-based:* Academics, Art, Athletics, Leadership, Minority status, Music/drama, State/district residency.

LIU POST

720 Northern Blvd., Brookville, NY 11548
Phone: 318-487-7259 • **E-mail:** post-enroll@liu.edu
Fax: 516-299-2137 • **Website:** www.liu.edu/post

RATINGS
Admissions Selectivity Rating: 72   **Fire Safety Rating:** 98   **Green Rating:** 84

STUDENTS AND FACULTY
Enrollment: 6,815. **Student Body:** 51% female, 49% male, 7% international. Asian 21%, African American 5%, Caucasian 11%, Hispanic 51%, Native American <1%, Pacific Islander 1%, Two or more races 3%, Race unknown 1%.
Retention and Graduation: 78% freshmen return for sophomore year. 37% freshmen graduate within 4 years. 24% grads go on to further study within 1 year. **Faculty:** Student/faculty ratio 20 321 full-time faculty, 90% hold PhDs, 31% are are members of minority groups, 54% are women.

ACADEMICS
Degrees: **Most popular majors:** Business/Commerce; Education; Health Services/Allied Health/Health Sciences. Combined degree programs: BA/MA, 2-2 pre-pharm prog with Long Island U at Brooklyn. **Career Services:** Alumni network, Alumni services, Career/job search classes, Career assessment, Internships, Regional alumni. Career outcomes at LIU Post significantly outperform national norms for graduating students. At LIU Post, 91% of

graduates are employed or in graduate school, while LIU Post's top ranked business school is even higher at 94%. LIU Post is in its 14th year as one of the Princeton Review's 'Best Business Schools,' with programs accredited by AACSB, a distinction awarded to only five percent of the world's business schools. LIU's career outcomes are significantly higher than the national average of 82% of bachelor's degree graduates employed or in graduate school according to the National Association of Colleges and Employers (NACE). LIU's strong career outcomes are a result of an innovative experiential approach that encourages students to engage in real world experiences that extend outside the classroom, including internships, co-ops, student-run businesses, research and consulting opportunities with faculty. The University's experiential approach capitalizes not only on its robust student experiential learning platforms, but also on its proximity to premiere internship opportunities in New York City, and strong alumni connections across industries.

FACILITIES
Housing: 80% of campus accessible to physically diasbled.

ADMISSIONS
Freshman Academic Profile: Average high school GPA 3.2. **Reported SAT (pre-2016 redesign) scores:** SAT Math middle 50% range 440-500. SAT Critical Reading middle 50% range 420-520. SAT Writing middle 50% range 440-550. **Concordant SAT scores:** SAT EBRW middle 50% 500–610. SAT Math middle 50% range 510–590. ACT middle 50% range 21-26. **Freshman Admission Statistics:** 755 applied, 72% admitted, 13% enrolled.

COSTS AND FINANCIAL AID
Annual tuition $8,850. Room and board $13,426. Required fees $1,249. **Financial Aid Statistics:** 64% needy undergrads receive need-based scholarship or grant aid. 24% freshmen, 73% undergrads receive non-need-based scholarship or grant aid. 66% freshmen, 62% undergrads receive need-based self-help aid. 15% freshmen, 10% undergrads receive athletic scholarships.

LONGWOOD UNIVERSITY

Admissions Office, Farmville, VA 23909
Phone: 434-395-2060 • **Financial Aid Phone:** 800-281-4677
E-mail: admissions@longwood.edu • **CEEB Code:** 5368
Fax: 434-395-2332 • **Website:** www.whylongwood.com • **ACT Code:** 4366

This public school was founded in 1839. It has a 160-acre campus.

RATINGS
Admissions Selectivity Rating: 78   **Fire Safety Rating:** 89   **Green Rating:** 60*

STUDENTS AND FACULTY
Enrollment: 4,185. **Student Body:** 66% female, 34% male, 3% out-of-state, 1% international (46 countries represented). Asian 1%, African American 7%, Caucasian 81%, Hispanic 4%, Native American <1%, Pacific Islander <1%, Two or more races 3%, Race unknown 3%.
Retention and Graduation: 79% freshmen return for sophomore year. 40% freshmen graduate within 4 years. **Faculty:** Student/faculty ratio 18:1. 222 full-time faculty, 85% hold PhDs, 8% are are members of minority groups, 48% are women. 0% of classes are taught by teaching assistants.

ACADEMICS
Degrees: bachelor's, master's, postbachelor's certificate, post-master's certificate. **Classes:** Most classes have 20-29 students. Most lab/discussion sessions have 20-29 students. **Most popular majors:** Elementary Education and Teaching; Psychology; Business/Commerce. **Special Study Options:** Accelerated program, cross-registration, distance learning, double major, dual enrollment, English as a Second Language (ESL), honors program, independent study, internships, study abroad, teacher certification program. **Honors Programs:** The Longwood University Honors Program is designed to meet the needs of academically gifted and talented undergraduate students. Challenging courses with high academic standards enable students to expand their intellectual and creative horizons. The Honors Program focuses on the exchange of ideas and the enrichment of students' educational and cultural experiences. Learning takes place not only in the classroom, but also through cultural events, conferences, field trips, and study abroad. In keeping with the University's mission, the Longwood Honors Program strives to develop citizens who are committed to using their learning to provide service to their local communities as well as to the larger national and global communities. The concept of linking learning with the practice of citizenship is the distinctive feature of our Program. Combined degree programs: BA/MA, Special Education BA/MS and BS/MS. **Disability Services:** Special programs offered to physically disabled students, including note-taking services, reader services, tape recorders, tutors. **Career Services:** Alumni network, Career/job search classes, Career assessment, Internships. Students must complete either am internship, study abroad program or work on a research project to graduate.

FACILITIES
Housing: Coed dorms, special housing for disabled students, women's dorms, fraternity/sorority housing, apartments for single students, Honor Student Housing. 100% of campus accessible to physically diasbled. **Special Academic Facilities/Equipment:** Longwood Center for the Visual Arts **Computers:** 100% of classrooms, 100% of libraries, 100% of dining areas, 100% of student union, have wireless network access. Students can register for classes online. Administrative functions (other than registration) can be performed online. Undergraduates are required to own a computer.

CAMPUS LIFE
Environment: Village. **Activities:** Choral groups, concert band, dance, drama/theater, jazz band, literary magazine, music ensembles, pep band, radio station, student government, student newspaper, yearbook, Campus Ministries, Student Organization. 129 registered organizations, 17 honor societies, 11 religious organizations. 9 fraternities, 12 sororities **Athletics (Intercollegiate):** *Men:* baseball, basketball, cheerleading, cross-country, golf, soccer, tennis. *Women:* basketball, cheerleading, cross-country, field hockey, golf, lacrosse, soccer, softball, tennis. **On-Campus Highlights:** Brock Commons, Lankford Student Union, Health and Fitness Center, Greenwood Library, Dorrill Dining Hall, Science Building.

ADMISSIONS
Freshman Academic Profile: Average high school GPA 3.4. 12% in top 10% of high school class, 39% in top 25% of high school class, 79% in top 50% of high school class. 92% from public high schools. **Reported SAT (pre-2016 redesign) scores:** SAT Math middle 50% range 470-560. SAT Critical Reading middle 50% range 480-570. **Concordant SAT scores:** SAT Math middle 50% range 510–580. ACT middle 50% range 20-24. Minimum internet-based TOEFL 79. Minimum paper TOEFL 550. **Basis for Candidate Selection:** *Very important factors considered include:* rigor of secondary school record, academic GPA, standardized test scores, application essay. *Important factors considered include:* class rank, extracurricular activities, talent/ability, character/personal qualities, first generation, alumni/ae relation, geographical residence, racial/ethnic status, volunteer work. *Other factors considered include:* recommendation(s), state residency. **Freshman Admission Requirements:** High school diploma is required and GED is accepted. *Academic units required:* 4 English, 3 math, 3 science, 2 science labs, 2 foreign language, 2 social studies, 2 history, 1 visual/performing arts, and 2 units from above areas or other academic areas. *Academic units recommended:* 4 English, 4 math, 4 science, 3 science labs, 4 foreign language, 2 social studies, 2 history, 1 visual/performing arts, and 2 units from above areas or other academic areas. **Freshman Admission Statistics:** 4,166 applied, 77.63% admitted, 32% enrolled. **Transfer Admission Requirements:** High school transcript, college transcript(s), essay or personal statement, Minimum college GPA of 2.50 required. Lowest grade transferable C-. **General Admission Information:** Application fee $50. Priority deadline 3/1. Nonfall registration accepted. Admission may be deferred for a maximum of 1 year.

COSTS AND FINANCIAL AID
Annual in-state tuition $11,340. Annual out-of-state tuition $24,210. Room and board $9,584. Required fees $4,890. Average book expense $1,000. **Required Forms and Deadlines:** FAFSA. **Notification of Awards:** Applicants will be notified of awards on or about 4/1. *Types of Aid: Need-based scholarships/grants:* Federal Pell, FSEOG, State scholarships/grants, Private scholarships, College/university scholarship or grant aid from institutional funds. *Loans:* Direct Subsidized Stafford Loans, Direct Unsubsidized Stafford Loans, Direct PLUS loans, Federal Perkins Loans. *Student Employment:* Federal Work-Study Program available. Institutional employment available. **Financial Aid Statistics:** 85% needy freshmen, 79% needy undergrads receive need-based scholarship or grant aid. 2% freshmen, 2% undergrads receive non-need-based scholarship or grant aid. 87% freshmen, 86% undergrads receive need-based self-help aid. 3% freshmen, 3% undergrads receive athletic scholarships. 60% freshmen receive any aid. **Criteria for awarding aid:** *Non-need-based:* Academics, Alumni affiliation, Art, Athletics, Leadership, Music/drama, State/district residency.

LORAS COLLEGE

1450 Alta Vista, Dubuque, IA 52001
Phone: 563-588-7236 • **Financial Aid Phone:** 563-588-7136
E-mail: admissions@loras.edu • **CEEB Code:** 6370
Fax: 563-588-7119 • **Website:** www.loras.edu • **ACT Code:** 1328

This private school, affiliated with the Roman Catholic Church, was founded in 1839. It has a 60-acre campus.

RATINGS
Admissions Selectivity Rating: 79   **Fire Safety Rating:** 96   **Green Rating:** 70

STUDENTS AND FACULTY

Enrollment: 1,444. **Student Body:** 48% female, 52% male, 62% out-of-state, 1% international (9 countries represented). Asian 1%, African American 2%, Caucasian 84%, Hispanic 6%, Native American 0%, Pacific Islander <1%, Two or more races 2%, Race unknown 3%.

Retention and Graduation: 81% freshmen return for sophomore year. 57% freshmen graduate within 4 years. 70% freshmen graduate within 6 years. 20% grads go on to further study within 1 year. 4% grads pursue arts and sciences degrees. 1% grads pursue law degrees. 1% grads pursue business degrees. **Faculty:** Student/faculty ratio 12:1. 103 full-time faculty, 97% hold PhDs, 3% are are members of minority groups, 37% are women. 0% of classes are taught by teaching assistants.

ACADEMICS

Degrees: associate, bachelor's, master's. **Classes:** Most classes have 20-29 students. Most lab/discussion sessions have fewer than 10 students. **Most popular majors:** Marketing/Marketing Management; Psychology; Biology/Biological Sciences. **Special Study Options:** cooperative education program, cross-registration, double major, dual enrollment, English as a Second Language (ESL), honors program, independent study, internships, liberal arts/career combination, student-designed major, study abroad, teacher certification program, Undergrads may take graduate level classes if certain qualifications are met. Combined degree programs: Athletic Training (3+2) program at Loras College; Nursing (BSN) program with Allen College of Nursing; Pharmacy (PharmD) program with Creighton University. **Disability Services:** Special programs offered to physically disabled students, including note-taking services, reader services, tape recorders. **Career Services:** Alumni network, Alumni services, Career/job search classes, Career assessment, Internships. 95.9% of our 2014 graduates were employed or attending school within one year of graduating.

FACILITIES

Housing: Coed dorms, men's dorms, women's dorms, apartments for single students. 63% of campus accessible to physically diasbled. **Special Academic Facilities/Equipment:** Language lab, television studio, observatory and planetarium. **Computers:** Students can register for classes online. Administrative functions (other than registration) can be performed online. Undergraduates are required to own a computer.

CAMPUS LIFE

Environment: Town. **Activities:** Choral groups, concert band, dance, drama/theater, jazz band, music ensembles, musical theater, radio station, student government, student newspaper, television station, yearbook. 71 registered organizations, 710 honor societies, 5 religious organizations. 2 fraternities, 2 sororities. **Athletics (Intercollegiate):** *Men:* baseball, basketball, cross-country, diving, football, golf, soccer, swimming, tennis, track/field (outdoor), track/field (indoor), wrestling. *Women:* basketball, cross-country, diving, golf, soccer, softball, swimming, tennis, track/field (outdoor), track/field (indoor), volleyball. **On-Campus Highlights:** Academic Resource Center, Alumni Campus Center, The Pub and Cafeteria, The Grotto. **Environmental Initiatives:** Petal Certification through the Petal Project, a Dubuque-area green business initiative.

ADMISSIONS

Freshman Academic Profile: Average high school GPA 3.5. 22% in top 10% of high school class, 46% in top 25% of high school class, 77% in top 50% of high school class. 65% from public high schools. **Reported SAT (pre-2016 redesign) scores:** SAT Math middle 50% range 460-570. SAT Critical Reading middle 50% range 460-540. **Concordant SAT scores:** SAT Math middle 50% range 500–590. ACT middle 50% range 21-26. Minimum internet-based TOEFL 79. Minimum paper TOEFL 550. **Basis for Candidate Selection:** *Very important factors considered include:* rigor of secondary school record, academic GPA, standardized test scores. *Other factors considered include:* class rank, application essay, recommendation(s), interview, extracurricular activities, character/personal qualities, racial/ethnic status, volunteer work, work experience, level of applicant's interest. **Freshman Admission Requirements:** High school diploma is required and GED is accepted. *Academic units recommended:* 4 English, 4 math, 3 science, 2 science labs, 3 social studies, 2 academic electives. **Freshman Admission Statistics:** 1,250 applied, 94.96% admitted, 33% enrolled. **Transfer Admission Requirements:** High school transcript, college transcript(s), standardized test scores, Minimum college GPA of 2.0 required. Lowest grade transferable C. **General Admission Information:** Application fee $25. Nonfall registration accepted. Admission may be deferred for a maximum of 1 year.

COSTS AND FINANCIAL AID

Annual tuition $30,065. Room and board $7,697. Required fees $1,460. Average book expense $1,100. **Required Forms and Deadlines:** FAFSA. **Notification of Awards:** Applicants will be notified of awards on a rolling basis beginning 3/1. **Types of Aid:** *Need-based scholarships/grants:* Federal Pell, FSEOG, State scholarships/grants, Private scholarships, College/university scholarship or grant aid from institutional funds. *Loans:* Direct Subsidized Stafford Loans, Direct Unsubsidized Stafford Loans, Direct PLUS loans, Federal Perkins Loans, College/university loans from institutional funds. *Student Employment:* Federal

Work-Study Program available. Institutional employment available. **Financial Aid Statistics:** 100% needy freshmen, 100% needy undergrads receive need-based scholarship or grant aid. 47% freshmen, 58% undergrads receive non-need-based scholarship or grant aid. 66% freshmen, 70% undergrads receive need-based self-help aid. 0% freshmen, 0% undergrads receive athletic scholarships. 100% freshmen, 100% undergrads receive any aid. 71% undergrads borrow to pay for school. Average cumulative indebtedness $31,418. **Criteria for awarding aid:** *Non-need-based:* Academics, Art.

LOUISIANA COLLEGE

1140 College Drive, Pineville, LA 71359
Phone: 318-487-7259
E-mail: admissions@lacollege.edu
Fax: 419-434-4898 • **Website:** www.lacollege.edu

RATINGS

Admissions Selectivity Rating: 73   **Fire Safety Rating:** 81   **Green Rating:** 60*

STUDENTS AND FACULTY

Enrollment: 2,377. **Student Body:** 33% female, 67% male, 10% out-of-state, 3% international. Asian 1%, African American 29%, Caucasian 62%, Hispanic 2%, Native American 1%, Pacific Islander <1%, Two or more races 1%, Race unknown <1%.

Retention and Graduation: 50% freshmen return for sophomore year. 0.223367698 freshmen graduate within 4 years. 35 38% grads go on to further study within 1 year. **Faculty:** Student/faculty ratio 15 267 full-time faculty, 74% hold PhDs, 17% are are members of minority groups, 59% are women.

ACADEMICS

Degrees: Most popular majors: Health and Physical Education/Fitness; Registered Nursing, Nursing Administration, Nursing Research and Clinical Nursing; Education. **Career Services:** Career/job search classes, Career assessment, Internships, On-campus interviews. Several majors require internships to fulfill graduation requirements.

FACILITIES

Housing: 95% of campus accessible to physically diasbled.

ADMISSIONS

Reported SAT (pre-2016 redesign) scores: SAT Math middle 50% range 470-580. SAT Critical Reading middle 50% range 430-560. **Concordant SAT scores:** SAT Math middle 50% range 480–530. ACT middle 50% range 18-23. **Freshman Admission Statistics:** 6,724 applied, 81% admitted.

LOUISIANA STATE UNIVERSITY

1146 Pleasant Hall, Baton Rouge, LA 70803
Phone: 225-578-1175 • **Financial Aid Phone:** 225-578-3103
E-mail: admissions@lsu.edu • **CEEB Code:** 6373
Fax: 225-578-4433 • **Website:** www.lsu.edu • **ACT Code:** 1590

This public school was founded in 1860. It has a 2000-acre campus.

RATINGS

Admissions Selectivity Rating: 85   **Fire Safety Rating:** 98   **Green Rating:** 86

STUDENTS AND FACULTY

Enrollment: 23,904. **Student Body:** 52% female, 48% male, 17% out-of-state, 2% international (69 countries represented). Asian 4%, African American 8%, Caucasian 76%, Hispanic 6%, Native American <1%, Pacific Islander <1%, Two or more races 2%, Race unknown <1%.

Retention and Graduation: 85% freshmen return for sophomore year. 41% freshmen graduate within 4 years. 67 **Faculty:** Student/faculty ratio 23:1. 1,278 full-time faculty, 88% hold PhDs, 18% are are members of minority groups, 35% are women. 6% of classes are taught by teaching assistants.

ACADEMICS

Degrees: bachelor's, doctoral/professional, doctoral/research, master's, postbachelor's certificate, post-master's certificate. **Classes:** Most classes have

10-19 students. Most lab/discussion sessions have 10-19 students. **Most popular majors:** Physical Education Teaching and Coaching; Biology/Biological Sciences; Mass Communication/Media Studies. **Special Study Options:** Accelerated program, cooperative education program, cross-registration, distance learning, double major, dual enrollment, English as a Second Language (ESL), exchange student program (domestic), honors program, independent study, internships, liberal arts/career combination, student-designed major, study abroad, teacher certification program. **Honors Programs:** Admissions to the Honors College Combined degree programs: BS/MAT Elementary Education/Holmes. **Disability Services:** Special programs offered to physically disabled students, including note-taking services, reader services, tape recorders. **Career Services:** Alumni services, Career/job search classes, Career assessment, Internships, Regional alumni. Through Experiential Education our team has been able to assist students with gaining valuable work experience during their time as an LSU student. Given the job market today, it is ever more important that students have this opportunity. We are committed to expanding upon the opportunities available to students, and as a result we have several new programs and initiatives in place. Among these initiatives are the reinvigoration of the Cooperative Education Program (Co-op), the formation of the Internship Council, and the collaboration with the College of Engineering Global Internship Initiative.

FACILITIES

Housing: Coed dorms, special housing for disabled students, men's dorms, women's dorms, fraternity/sorority housing, apartments for married students, apartments for single students, Theme Housing. 75% of campus accessible to physically diasbled. **Special Academic Facilities/Equipment:** Art Museum, NAtural Science Museum, Rural Life Museum, Lichen/Bryophyte Mycological and Vascular Plant herbariums, on campus K-12 schools, geoscience and mycological museums, electron microscope, nuclear science center and civil war center. **Computers:** 100% of classrooms, 100% of dorms, 100% of libraries, 90% of dining areas, 100% of student union, 90% of common outdoor areas have wireless network access. Students can register for classes online. Administrative functions (other than registration) can be performed online.

CAMPUS LIFE

Environment: Metropolis. **Activities:** Choral groups, concert band, dance, drama/theater, jazz band, literary magazine, marching band, music ensembles, musical theater, opera, pep band, radio station, student government, student newspaper, student-run film society, symphony orchestra, television station, yearbook, Campus Ministries, Student Organization. 300 registered organizations, 32 honor societies, 25 religious organizations. 23 fraternities, 15 sororities. **Athletics (Intercollegiate):** *Men:* baseball, basketball, cheerleading, cross-country, diving, football, golf, swimming, tennis, track/field (outdoor), track/field (indoor). *Women:* basketball, cheerleading, cross-country, diving, golf, gymnastics, soccer, softball, swimming, tennis, track/field (outdoor), track/field (indoor), volleyball. **On-Campus Highlights:** LSU Student Union, Mike VI Tiger Habitat, Indian Mounds, Tiger Stadium, Alex Box Stadium, FACES Laboratory. **Environmental Initiatives:** Goal to increase recycling rate to 50%.

ADMISSIONS

Freshman Academic Profile: Average high school GPA 3.4. 26% in top 10% of high school class, 52% in top 25% of high school class, 82% in top 50% of high school class. 60% from public high schools. **Reported SAT (pre-2016 redesign) scores:** SAT Math middle 50% range 510-640. SAT Critical Reading middle 50% range 510-620. **Concordant SAT scores:** SAT Math middle 50% range 540–660. ACT middle 50% range 23-28. Minimum internet-based TOEFL 79. Minimum paper TOEFL 550. **Basis for Candidate Selection:** *Very important factors considered include:* rigor of secondary school record, academic GPA, standardized test scores. *Important factors considered include:* talent/ability. *Other factors considered include:* class rank, application essay, recommendation(s), extracurricular activities, first generation, alumni/ae relation. **Freshman Admission Requirements:** High school diploma is required and GED is accepted. *Academic units required:* 4 English, 4 math, 4 science, 2 foreign language, 3 social studies, 1 history, 1 visual/performing arts. **Freshman Admission Statistics:** 17,429 applied, 77.34% admitted, 42% enrolled. **Transfer Admission Requirements:** college transcript(s), Minimum college GPA of 2.5 required. Lowest grade transferable D. **General Admission Information:** Application fee $40. Priority deadline 11/15. Regular application deadline 4/15. Nonfall registration accepted. Admission may be deferred for a maximum of 1 acad. year.

COSTS AND FINANCIAL AID

Annual in-state tuition $8,038. Annual out-of-state tuition $24,715. Room and board $11,540. Required fees $2,776. Average book expense $1,160. **Required Forms and Deadlines:** FAFSA, Institution's own financial aid form. **Notification of Awards:** Applicants will be notified of awards on a rolling basis beginning 12/15. **Types of Aid:** *Need-based scholarships/grants:* Federal Pell, FSEOG, State scholarships/grants, Private scholarships, College/university scholarship or grant aid from institutional funds. *Loans:* Direct Subsidized Stafford Loans, Direct Unsubsidized Stafford Loans, Direct PLUS loans, Federal Perkins Loans, College/university loans from institutional funds.

Student Employment: Federal Work-Study Program available. Institutional employment available. **Financial Aid Statistics:** 95% needy freshmen, 84% needy undergrads receive need-based scholarship or grant aid. 4% freshmen, 3% undergrads receive non-need-based scholarship or grant aid. 66% freshmen, 73% undergrads receive need-based self-help aid. 2% freshmen, 2% undergrads receive athletic scholarships. 95% freshmen, 81% undergrads receive any aid. Average cumulative indebtedness $24,509. **Criteria for awarding aid:** *Need-based:* Academics. *Non-need-based:* Academics, Athletics, Music/drama.

LOUISIANA TECH UNIVERSITY

P. O. Box 3178, Ruston, LA 71272
Phone: 318-257-3036
E-mail: bulldog@latech.edu
Fax: 318-257-2499 • **Website:** www.latech.edu

This is a public school.

RATINGS

Admissions Selectivity Rating: 83   **Fire Safety Rating:** 60*   **Green Rating:** 60*

STUDENTS AND FACULTY

Enrollment: 7,047. **Student Body:** 43% female, 57% male, 10% out-of-state, 4% international. Asian 1%, African American 15%, Caucasian 68%, Hispanic 1%, Native American <1%, Pacific Islander <1%, Two or more races 1%, Race unknown 8%.
Retention and Graduation: 29% freshmen graduate within 4 years. **Faculty:** Student/faculty ratio 23:1. 352 full-time faculty, 79% hold PhDs, 0% are are members of minority groups, 39% are women.

ACADEMICS

Degrees: associate, bachelor's, doctoral/professional, doctoral/research, master's, postbachelor's certifiate, post-master's certificate. **Career Services:** Alumni network, Alumni services, Career/job search classes, Career assessment, Internships, Regional alumni. The mission of the Career Center is to educate and to serve the students and graduates of Louisiana Tech University in the career education, planning, and development processes. In support of the mission of the University, the Career Center functions as a vital component in the total educational experience of students, primarily in the development, evaluation, initiation, and implementation of career plans and opportunities. Career Center services and resources provide assistance to students in the cultivation and enhancement of skills to explore career options, master job search techniques and strategies, and research employment opportunities. The Career Center provides effective and efficient service to employers in recruitment programs and activities.

ADMISSIONS

Freshman Academic Profile: Average high school GPA 3.4. 24% in top 10% of high school class, 51% in top 25% of high school class, 80% in top 50% of high school class. 77% from public high schools. **Reported SAT (pre-2016 redesign) scores:** SAT Math middle 50% range 490-600. SAT Critical Reading middle 50% range 450-590. **Concordant SAT scores:** SAT Math middle 50% range 520–620. ACT middle 50% range 21-26. Minimum internet-based TOEFL 88. Minimum paper TOEFL 570. **Basis for Candidate Selection:** *Very important factors considered include:* rigor of secondary school record, class rank, academic GPA, standardized test scores. *Important factors considered include:* talent/ability, level of applicant's interest. *Other factors considered include:* recommendation(s), extracurricular activities, first generation, alumni/ae relation. **Freshman Admission Requirements:** *Academic units required:* 4 English, 4 math, 4 science, 2 foreign language, 4 social studies, 1 visual/performing arts. **Freshman Admission Statistics:** 5,077 applied, 67.44% admitted, 45% enrolled. **General Admission Information:** Application fee $20. Nonfall registration accepted.

COSTS AND FINANCIAL AID

Required Forms and Deadlines: FAFSA, Institution's own financial aid form. **Notification of Awards:** Applicants will be notified of awards on a rolling basis beginning 4/1. **Types of Aid:** *Need-based scholarships/grants:* Federal Pell, FSEOG, State scholarships/grants, Private scholarships, College/university scholarship or grant aid from institutional funds. *Loans:* Direct Subsidized Stafford Loans, Direct Unsubsidized Stafford Loans, Direct PLUS loans, Federal Perkins Loans. *Student Employment:* Federal Work-Study Program available. Institutional employment available. **Financial Aid Statistics:** 94% needy freshmen, 89% needy undergrads receive need-based scholarship or grant aid. 18% freshmen, 15% undergrads receive non-need-based scholarship or grant aid. 51% freshmen, 61% undergrads receive need-based self-help aid. 1% freshmen, 2% undergrads receive athletic scholarships. **Criteria for awarding aid:** *Non-need-based:* Academics, Alumni affiliation, Art, Athletics, Job skills, Leadership, Music/drama, State/district residency.

LOURDES UNIVERSITY

6832 Convent Road, Sylvania, OH 43560-2898
Phone: 419-885-5291 • **Financial Aid Phone:** 419-824-3732
E-mail: AdmissionsLCAdmits@lourdes.edu • **CEEB Code:** 1427
Fax: 419-824-3916 • **Website:** www.lourdes.edu • **ACT Code:** 3598

This private school, affiliated with the Roman Catholic Church, was founded in 1958. It has a 94-acre campus.

RATINGS
Admissions Selectivity Rating: 75   **Fire Safety Rating:** 85   **Green Rating:** 60*

STUDENTS AND FACULTY
Enrollment: 1,964. **Student Body:** 71% female, 29% male, 14% out-of-state, <1% international. Asian 1%, African American 18%, Caucasian 72%, Hispanic 6%, Native American <1%, Pacific Islander 0%, Two or more races 2%, Race unknown 2%.
Retention and Graduation: 63% freshmen return for sophomore year. **Faculty:** Student/faculty ratio 10:1. 100 full-time faculty, 59% hold PhDs, 10% are are members of minority groups, 67% are women. 2% of classes are taught by teaching assistants.

ACADEMICS
Degrees: associate, bachelor's, certificate, master's, postbachelor's certificate. **Classes:** Most classes have 10-19 students. Most lab/discussion sessions have fewer than 10 students. **Most popular majors:** Registered Nursing/Registered Nurse; Social Work; Business Administration and Management. **Special Study Options:** distance learning, double major, dual enrollment, independent study, internships, liberal arts/career combination, student-designed major, study abroad, teacher certification program. **Disability Services:** Special programs offered to physically disabled students, including note-taking services, reader services, tape recorders, tutors. **Career Services:** Career/job search classes, Career assessment, On-campus interviews.

FACILITIES
Special Academic Facilities/Equipment: Planetarium, Life Lab **Computers:** 100% of classrooms, 100% of libraries, 100% of dining areas, 100% of student union, have wireless network access. Students can register for classes online. Administrative functions (other than registration) can be performed online.

CAMPUS LIFE
Environment: Village. **Activities:** Choral groups, drama/theater, literary magazine, student government, Campus Ministries. 25 registered organizations, 2 honor societies. **Athletics (Intercollegiate):** *Men:* basketball, golf. *Women:* golf, volleyball. **On-Campus Highlights:** McAlear Hall, Ebied Center.

ADMISSIONS
Freshman Academic Profile: Average high school GPA 3.0. 8% in top 10% of high school class, 27% in top 25% of high school class, 59% in top 50% of high school class. **Reported SAT (pre-2016 redesign) scores:** SAT Math middle 50% range 350-500. SAT Critical Reading middle 50% range 410-540. **Concordant SAT scores:** SAT Math middle 50% range 390–530. ACT middle 50% range 17-22. Minimum internet-based TOEFL 173. Minimum paper TOEFL 500. **Basis for Candidate Selection:** *Very important factors considered include:* academic GPA, standardized test scores. *Other factors considered include:* interview. **Freshman Admission Requirements:** High school diploma is required and GED is accepted. *Academic units recommended:* 4 English, 3 math, 3 science, 2 foreign language, 3 social studies, 1 visual/performing arts, and 1 unit from above areas or other academic areas. **Freshman Admission Statistics:** 1,296 applied, 67.98% admitted, 29% enrolled. **Transfer Admission Requirements:** college transcript(s), Minimum college GPA of 2.0 required. Lowest grade transferable C. **General Admission Information:** Application fee $25. Nonfall registration accepted. Admission may be deferred for a maximum of 4 years.

COSTS AND FINANCIAL AID
Annual tuition $17,455. Room and board $8,400. Required fees $200. Average book expense $1,275. **Required Forms and Deadlines:** FAFSA. **Notification of Awards:** Applicants will be notified of awards on a rolling basis beginning 3/1. **Types of Aid:** *Need-based scholarships/grants:* Federal Pell, FSEOG, State scholarships/grants, Private scholarships, College/university scholarship or grant aid from institutional funds. *Loans:* Direct Subsidized Stafford Loans, Direct Unsubsidized Stafford Loans, Direct PLUS loans, Federal Perkins Loans, Federal Nursing Loans, State Loans, College/university loans from institutional funds. *Student Employment:* Federal Work-Study Program available. Institutional employment available. **Financial Aid Statistics:** 88% needy freshmen, 82% needy undergrads receive need-based scholarship or grant aid. 89% freshmen, 63% undergrads receive non-need-based scholarship or grant aid. 92% freshmen, 91% undergrads receive need-based self-help aid.

28% freshmen, 18% undergrads receive athletic scholarships. 96% freshmen, 84% undergrads receive any aid. **Criteria for awarding aid:** *Need-based:* Academics, Alumni affiliation, Art, Leadership, Minority status, Religious affiliation. *Non-need-based:* Academics, Art, Athletics, Minority status, Music/drama, Religious affiliation, State/district residency.

LOYOLA MARYMOUNT UNIVERSITY

1 LMU Drive, Los Angeles, CA 90045-8350
Phone: 310-338-2750 • **Financial Aid Phone:** 310-338-1949
E-mail: admissions@lmu.edu • **CEEB Code:** 4403
Fax: 310-338-2797 • **Website:** www.lmu.edu • **ACT Code:** 326

This private school, affiliated with the Roman Catholic Church, was founded in 1911. It has a 128-acre campus.

RATINGS
Admissions Selectivity Rating: 89   **Fire Safety Rating:** 89   **Green Rating:** 99

STUDENTS AND FACULTY
Enrollment: 6,126. **Student Body:** 56% female, 44% male, 26% out-of-state, 10% international (74 countries represented). Asian 11%, African American 6%, Caucasian 44%, Hispanic 21%, Native American <1%, Pacific Islander <1%, Two or more races 8%, Race unknown <1%.
Retention and Graduation: 88% freshmen return for sophomore year. 74% freshmen graduate within 4 years. 83% freshmen graduate within 6 years. 26% grads go on to further study within 1 year. 14% grads pursue arts and sciences degrees. 5% grads pursue law degrees. 1% grads pursue business degrees. 4% grads pursue medical degrees. **Faculty:** Student/faculty ratio 11:1. 561 full-time faculty, 96% hold PhDs, 29% are are members of minority groups, 45% are women. 1% of classes are taught by teaching assistants.

ACADEMICS
Degrees: bachelor's, certificate, doctoral/professional, doctoral/research, master's, postbachelor's certificate, post-master's certificate. **Classes:** Most classes have 10-19 students. Most lab/discussion sessions have 10-19 students. **Most popular majors:** Psychology; Marketing/Marketing Management; Speech Communication and Rhetoric. **Special Study Options:** cross-registration, double major, dual enrollment, honors program, independent study, internships, liberal arts/career combination, student-designed major, study abroad, teacher certification program, Encore program for adult students. Combined degree programs: BA/MEng, 5-year BS/MS Healthcare Systems Engineering. **Disability Services:** Special programs offered to physically disabled students, including note-taking services, reader services, tape recorders, tutors. **Career Services:** Alumni network, Alumni services, Career/job search classes, Career assessment, Internships, Regional alumni. The VOCAR' retreat is a unique opportunity for LMU sophomores and transfer students to step away from campus to reflect on where they have been, who they are, and where they are going within a supportive community of fellow students, staff, faculty and alumni.

FACILITIES
Housing: Coed dorms, special housing for disabled students, men's dorms, women's dorms, apartments for single students. 95% of campus accessible to physically diasbled. **Special Academic Facilities/Equipment:** Art gallery, theater, TV production labs, computer graphics lab. **Computers:** Students can register for classes online. Administrative functions (other than registration) can be performed online.

CAMPUS LIFE
Environment: Metropolis. **Activities:** Choral groups, dance, drama/theater, literary magazine, music ensembles, musical theater, pep band, radio station, student government, student newspaper, student-run film society, television station, yearbook. 120 registered organizations, 12 honor societies, 2 religious organizations. 6 fraternities, 8 sororities. **Athletics (Intercollegiate):** *Men:* baseball, basketball, crew/rowing, cross-country, golf, soccer, tennis, water polo. *Women:* basketball, crew/rowing, cross-country, soccer, softball, swimming, tennis, volleyball, water polo. **Environmental Initiatives:** LEED Building Program: LMU's new LEED Gold Life Science Building is a 120,000 GSF building is designed with state-of-the-art laboratory technologies, collaborative research space, and energy efficiency features, complementing our 5 other LEED-certified campus buildings and signifying LMU's commitment to continued leadership in environmental stewardship. The building will also

act as a 'living lab' for students studying with a 200,000 kwh Solar Array and a green roof with research functionality. the building also houses 9,000 SF of faculty research lab space, 24 teaching labs, lab support spaces, vivarium, faculty offices, classrooms, shared public spaces, conference rooms, and a 292-fixed seat auditorium.

ADMISSIONS

Freshman Academic Profile: Average high school GPA 3.7. 39% in top 10% of high school class, 73% in top 25% of high school class, 98% in top 50% of high school class. 49% from public high schools. **Reported SAT (pre-2016 redesign) scores:** SAT Math middle 50% range 570-670. SAT Critical Reading middle 50% range 550-660. SAT Writing middle 50% range 560-660. **Concordant SAT scores:** SAT EBRW middle 50% 610–700. SAT Math middle 50% range 590–700. ACT middle 50% range 26-30. Minimum internet-based TOEFL 80. Minimum paper TOEFL 550. **Basis for Candidate Selection:** *Very important factors considered include:* academic GPA. *Important factors considered include:* rigor of secondary school record, standardized test scores, application essay, talent/ability, character/personal qualities. *Other factors considered include:* class rank, recommendation(s), extracurricular activities, first generation, alumni/ae relation. **Freshman Admission Requirements:** High school diploma is required and GED is accepted. *Academic units recommended:* 4 English, 3 math, 2 science, 2 science labs, 3 foreign language, 3 social studies, 1 academic elective. **Freshman Admission Statistics:** 13,506 applied, 53.87% admitted, 18% enrolled. **Transfer Admission Requirements:** college transcript(s), essay or personal statement, statement of good standing from prior institution(s). Minimum college GPA of 2.8 required. Lowest grade transferable C. **General Admission Information:** Application fee $60. Regular application deadline 1/15. Nonfall registration accepted. Admission may be deferred for a maximum of 1 year.

COSTS AND FINANCIAL AID

Annual tuition $43,526. Room and board $14,485. Required fees $704. Average book expense $1,791. **Required Forms and Deadlines:** FAFSA. **Notification of Awards:** Applicants will be notified of awards on a rolling basis beginning 1/31. **Types of Aid:** *Need-based scholarships/grants:* Federal Pell, FSEOG, State scholarships/grants, Private scholarships, College/university scholarship or grant aid from institutional funds. *Loans:* Direct Subsidized Stafford Loans, Direct Unsubsidized Stafford Loans, Direct PLUS loans, Federal Perkins Loans, College/university loans from institutional funds. *Student Employment:* Federal Work-Study Program available. Institutional employment available. **Financial Aid Statistics:** 97% needy freshmen, 95% needy undergrads receive need-based scholarship or grant aid. 14% freshmen, 11% undergrads receive non-need-based scholarship or grant aid. 76% freshmen, 78% undergrads receive need-based self-help aid. 3% freshmen, 3% undergrads receive athletic scholarships. 92% freshmen, 87% undergrads receive any aid. 54% undergrads borrow to pay for school. Average cumulative indebtedness $30,698. **Criteria for awarding aid:** *Need-based:* Academics, Leadership, Minority status, Religious affiliation. *Non-need-based:* Academics, Alumni affiliation, Art, Athletics, Music/drama, Religious affiliation.

LOYOLA UNIVERSITY MARYLAND

Best Colleges

4501 North Charles Street, Baltimore, MD 21210
Phone: 410-617-5012 • **Financial Aid Phone:** 410-617-2576
E-mail: admissions@loyola.edu • **CEEB Code:** 5370
Fax: 410-617-2176 • **Website:** www.loyola.edu

This private school, affiliated with the Roman Catholic Church, was founded in 1852. It has a 89-acre campus.

RATINGS

Admissions Selectivity Rating: 87   **Fire Safety Rating:** 94   **Green Rating:** 73

STUDENTS AND FACULTY

Enrollment: 4,031. **Student Body:** 58% female, 42% male, 82% out-of-state, <1% international (37 countries represented). Asian 4%, African American 6%, Caucasian 78%, Hispanic 9%, Native American <1%, Pacific Islander <1%, Two or more races 2%, Race unknown <1%.
Retention and Graduation: 87% freshmen return for sophomore year. 76% freshmen graduate within 4 years. 81% freshmen graduate within 6 years. 21% grads go on to further study within 1 year. 35% grads pursue arts and sciences degrees. 13% grads pursue law degrees. 11% grads pursue business degrees. 2% grads pursue medical degrees. **Faculty:** Student/faculty ratio 11:1. 375 full-time faculty, 86% hold PhDs, 19% are are members of minority groups, 51% are women. 0% of classes are taught by teaching assistants.

ACADEMICS

Degrees: bachelor's, doctoral/professional, doctoral/research, master's, postbachelor's certifiate, post-master's certificate. **Classes:** Most classes have 20-29 students. Most lab/discussion sessions have 10-19 students. **Most popular majors:** Business Administration and Management; Communication; Social Sciences. **Special Study Options:** cross-registration, double major, dual enrollment, exchange student program (domestic), honors program, independent study, internships, liberal arts/career combination, study abroad, teacher certification program. **Honors Programs:** http://www.loyola.edu/undergraduate/academics/honors.aspx. **Disability Services:** Special programs offered to physically disabled students, including note-taking services, reader services, tape recorders, tutors. **Career Services:** Alumni network, Alumni services, Career/job search classes, Career assessment, Internships, Regional alumni.

FACILITIES

Housing: Coed dorms, cooperative housing, apartments for single students, Wellness Housing, Theme Housing. 100% of campus accessible to physically diasbled. **Special Academic Facilities/Equipment:** Art gallery, advanced biology lab, humanities building, speech pathology lab and audiology center, black box theater **Computers:** 75% of classrooms, 80% of dorms, 100% of libraries, 100% of dining areas, 50% of student union, 50% of common outdoor areas have wireless network access. Students can register for classes online. Administrative functions (other than registration) can be performed online.

CAMPUS LIFE

Environment: Village. **Activities:** Choral groups, dance, drama/theater, literary magazine, music ensembles, musical theater, radio station, student government, student newspaper, television station, yearbook, Campus Ministries, Student Organization. 185 registered organizations, 25 honor societies, 4 religious organizations. **Athletics (Intercollegiate):** *Men:* basketball, crew/rowing, cross-country, diving, golf, lacrosse, soccer, swimming, tennis. *Women:* basketball, crew/rowing, cross-country, diving, lacrosse, soccer, swimming, tennis, track/field (outdoor), track/field (indoor), volleyball. **On-Campus Highlights:** Loyola/Notre Dame Library, The Loyola University Art Gallery, Fitness and Aquatic Center, Boulder Garden Cafe, Primo's: The New Marketplace. **Environmental Initiatives:** Our commitment responsible building can be seen in our 100,000 sq. ft. green residential hall that was built in 2007. In 2010 we completed construction of an athletic facility that was built on a landfill and is considered an example of smart growth.

ADMISSIONS

Freshman Academic Profile: Average high school GPA 3.5. 26% in top 10% of high school class, 62% in top 25% of high school class, 91% in top 50% of high school class. **Reported SAT (pre-2016 redesign) scores:** SAT Math middle 50% range 560-640. SAT Critical Reading middle 50% range 550-640. **Concordant SAT scores:** SAT Math middle 50% range 580–660. ACT middle 50% range 25-29. Minimum internet-based TOEFL 79. Minimum paper TOEFL 550. **Basis for Candidate Selection:** *Very important factors considered include:* rigor of secondary school record, academic GPA, application essay, recommendation(s), character/personal qualities. *Important factors considered include:* extracurricular activities, talent/ability, volunteer work. *Other factors considered include:* class rank, standardized test scores, first generation, alumni/ae relation, geographical residence, racial/ethnic status, work experience, level of applicant's interest. **Freshman Admission Requirements:** High school diploma is required and GED is accepted. *Academic units required:* 4 English, 3 math, 3 science, 3 foreign language, 2 social studies, 2 history. *Academic units recommended:* 4 English, 4 math, 4 science, 4 foreign language, 3 social studies, 3 history, 1 computer science, 1 visual/performing arts. **Freshman Admission Statistics:** 13,867 applied, 60.93% admitted, 12% enrolled. **Transfer Admission Requirements:** High school transcript, college transcript(s), essay or personal statement, statement of good standing from prior institution(s). Minimum college GPA of 2.7 required. Lowest grade transferable C. **General Admission Information:** Application fee $50. Priority deadline 11/1. Regular application deadline 1/15. Regular notification 3/15. Nonfall registration accepted. Admission may be deferred.

COSTS AND FINANCIAL AID

Annual tuition $43,800. Room and board $14,200. Required fees $1,400. Average book expense $1,250. **Required Forms and Deadlines:** FAFSA, CSS/Financial Aid PROFILE, Noncustodial PROFILE. **Notification of Awards:** Applicants will be notified of awards on or about 3/15. **Types of Aid:** *Need-based scholarships/grants:* Federal Pell, FSEOG, State scholarships/grants, Private scholarships, College/university scholarship or grant aid from institutional funds. *Loans:* Direct Subsidized Stafford Loans, Direct Unsubsidized Stafford Loans, Direct PLUS loans, Federal Perkins Loans, College/university loans from institutional funds. *Student Employment:* Federal Work-Study Program available. Institutional employment available. **Financial Aid Statistics:** 89% needy freshmen, 89% needy undergrads receive need-based scholarship or grant aid. 33% freshmen, 29% undergrads receive non-need-based scholarship or grant aid. 96% freshmen, 95% undergrads receive need-based self-help aid. 3% freshmen, 3% undergrads receive athletic scholarships. 75% freshmen, 70% undergrads receive any aid. 61% undergrads borrow to pay for school. Average cumulative indebtedness $34,375. **Criteria for awarding aid:** *Non-need-based:* Academics, Athletics.

LOYOLA UNIVERSITY NEW ORLEANS

6363 St. Charles Avenue, New Orleans, LA 70118-6195
Phone: 504-865-3240 • **Financial Aid Phone:** 504-865-3231
E-mail: admit@loyno.edu • **CEEB Code:** 6374
Fax: 504-865-3383 • **Website:** www.loyno.edu • **ACT Code:** 1592

This private school, affiliated with the Roman Catholic Church, affiliated with the Jesuit Church, was founded in 1912. It has a 26-acre campus.

RATINGS

Admissions Selectivity Rating: 85   **Fire Safety Rating:** 98   **Green Rating:** 83

STUDENTS AND FACULTY

Enrollment: 2,399. **Student Body:** 61% female, 39% male, 57% out-of-state, 2% international (42 countries represented). Asian 3%, African American 16%, Caucasian 52%, Hispanic 17%, Native American <1%, Pacific Islander <1%, Two or more races 5%, Race unknown 4%.
Retention and Graduation: 79% freshmen return for sophomore year. 44% freshmen graduate within 4 years. 55% freshmen graduate within 6 years. 70% grads go on to further study within 1 year. **Faculty:** Student/faculty ratio 10:1. 243 full-time faculty, 91% hold PhDs, 15% are are members of minority groups, 45% are women. 0% of classes are taught by teaching assistants.

ACADEMICS

Degrees: bachelor's, doctoral/professional, master's, postbachelor's certificate, post-master's certificate. **Classes:** Most classes have 10-19 students. Most lab/discussion sessions have 10-19 students. **Most popular majors:** Music Management; Research and Experimental Psychology; Public Relations, Advertising, and Applied Communication. **Special Study Options:** Accelerated program, cross-registration, distance learning, double major, dual enrollment, English as a Second Language (ESL), exchange student program (domestic), honors program, independent study, internships, liberal arts/career combination, student-designed major, study abroad, teacher certification program, Advance placement credit. Limited weekend courses available. Evening Courses available. Also teacher certification program is available in music only. **Honors Programs:** The Loyola University Honors Program offers the opportunity for academically superior, highly motivated students to take challenging Honors courses and to participate in special cultural and intellectual enrichment activities. The University Honors Program is open to qualified students of all undergraduate colleges and majors. The Honors courses replace other required courses, and therefore do not add to the number of requirements for graduation. Combined degree programs: RN/MSN/DNP, JD/MBA, MPS/MS, Early Law Admission. **Disability Services:** Special programs offered to physically disabled students, including note-taking services, reader services, tape recorders, tutors. **Career Services:** Alumni network, Alumni services, Career/job search classes, Career assessment, Internships, Regional alumni. Discerning Minds: Experience. Reflect. Transform. The Quality Enhancement Plan (QEP), Discerning Minds: Experience. Reflect. Transform., is designed to improve student learning experiences within four high impact experiential learning activities to which large numbers of Loyola students have access: Collaborative Research, Scholarship, and Creative Activities (CRSCA); Internships; Service Learning; and Study Abroad. Discerning Minds, will address Student Learning Outcomes designed to enhance students' abilities to connect course material to related experiences via structured, critical reflection. In other words: students will engage in experiential learning, reflect on what they've done, and integrate those reflections into their plans for the future. The topic of the QEP is connected to the Jesuit tradition of discernment, which is central to the pedagogical mission of Loyola. In the Jesuit tradition, to 'discern' means to apply wisdom of our intuition to discover what is essential and true. Implementation initiatives focus on faculty development related to experiential learning and reflection, best practices specific to each of the four pedagogies, curriculum revisions, evaluation of assessment data, identifying and implementing modifications needed, providing incentives for all stakeholders, as well as developing infrastructure and resources to ensure sustainability.

FACILITIES

Housing: Coed dorms, special housing for disabled students, apartments for single students, Wellness Housing, Theme Housing, Honors floor available. 95% of campus accessible to physically diasbled. **Special Academic Facilities/Equipment:** Collins C. Diboll Art Gallery, Humanities Lab with Perseus Project and TLG TV, Multimedia Classrooms, 24-hour Microcomputer Labs, Computer Science Lab, Graphics Lab, Visual Arts Lab, Ad Club/Communications Lab, RATHE Business Computer Lab, Multi-Media Training Center, Donnelley Center for Non-Profit Communications, Chemistry Wing, Television Broadcast Studio, Multimedia Studio, Audio Recording Studio, Editing Studio, Library Learning Commons, Multimedia Exhibit Room, Satchmo's Deli and Performance Area, Center for International Education, University Sports Complex with Suspended Pool, Career Development Center, Jesuit Social Research Institute, Learning Communities. **Computers:** 50% of classrooms, 100% of dorms, 100% of libraries, 100% of dining areas, 100% of student union, 100% of common outdoor areas have wireless network access. Students can register for classes online. Administrative functions (other than registration) can be performed online.

CAMPUS LIFE

Environment: City. **Activities:** Choral groups, concert band, dance, drama/theater, jazz band, literary magazine, music ensembles, musical theater, opera, pep band, radio station, student government, student newspaper, student-run film society, symphony orchestra, yearbook, Campus Ministries, Student Organization. 90 registered organizations, 13 honor societies, 4 religious organizations. 7 fraternities, 7 sororities. **Athletics (Intercollegiate):** *Men:* baseball, basketball, cross-country, track/field (outdoor), track/field (indoor). *Women:* basketball, cross-country, track/field (outdoor), track/field (indoor), volleyball. **On-Campus Highlights:** J. Edgar and Louise S. Monroe Library, Danna Student Center, Recreational Sports Complex, Peace Quad, Residential Quad, Collins C. Diboll Art Gallery, Humanities Lab with Perseus Project and TLG TV, Multimedia Classrooms, 24-hour Microcomputer Labs, Computer Science Lab, Graphics Lab, Visual Arts Lab, Ad Club/Communications Lab, RATHE Business Computer Lab, Multi-Media Training Center, Donnelley Center for Non-Profit Communications, Chemistry Wing, Television Broadcast Studio, Multimedia Studio, Audio Recording Studio, Editing Studio, Library Learning Commons, Multimedia Exhibit Room, Satchmo's Deli and Performance Area, Center for International Education, University Sports Complex with Suspended Pool, Career Development Center, Jesuit Social Research Institute, Learning Communities. **Environmental Initiatives:** Formation of a committee that has representatives from important units on campus, including SGA and other student organizations. Full support of the Administration, starting with the President and Provost.

ADMISSIONS

Freshman Academic Profile: Average high school GPA 3.6. 27% in top 10% of high school class, 55% in top 25% of high school class, 85% in top 50% of high school class. 56% from public high schools. **Reported SAT (pre-2016 redesign) scores:** SAT Math middle 50% range 500-610. SAT Critical Reading middle 50% range 520-630. **Concordant SAT scores:** SAT Math middle 50% range 530–630. ACT middle 50% range 23-29. Minimum internet-based TOEFL 79. Minimum paper TOEFL 550. **Basis for Candidate Selection:** *Very important factors considered include:* rigor of secondary school record, academic GPA, standardized test scores. *Important factors considered include:* application essay, recommendation(s), extracurricular activities, talent/ability. *Other factors considered include:* class rank, interview, character/personal qualities, alumni/ae relation, geographical residence, racial/ethnic status, volunteer work, work experience, level of applicant's interest. **Freshman Admission Requirements:** High school diploma is required and GED is accepted. *Academic units required:* 4 English, 2 math, 2 science, 2 social studies. *Academic units recommended:* 4 English, 3 math, 3 science, 1 science lab, 2 foreign language, 2 social studies. **Freshman Admission Statistics:** 5,160 applied, 67.75% admitted, 18% enrolled. **Transfer Admission Requirements:** college transcript(s), essay or personal statement, statement of good standing from prior institution(s). Minimum college GPA of 2.25 required. Lowest grade transferable C. **General Admission Information:** Priority deadline 12/1. Nonfall registration accepted. Admission may be deferred for a maximum of 1 year.

COSTS AND FINANCIAL AID

Annual tuition $37,676. Room and board $13,214. Required fees $1,566. Average book expense $1,248. **Required Forms and Deadlines:** FAFSA. **Notification of Awards:** Applicants will be notified of awards on a rolling basis beginning 3/1. **Types of Aid:** *Need-based scholarships/grants:* Federal Pell, FSEOG, State scholarships/grants, Private scholarships, College/university scholarship or grant aid from institutional funds, United Negro College Fund. *Loans:* Direct Subsidized Stafford Loans, Direct Unsubsidized Stafford Loans, Direct PLUS loans, Federal Perkins Loans. *Student Employment:* Federal Work-Study Program available. Institutional employment available. **Financial Aid Statistics:** 100% needy freshmen, 99% needy undergrads receive need-based scholarship or grant aid. 13% freshmen, 11% undergrads receive non-need-based scholarship or grant aid. 85% freshmen, 84% undergrads receive need-based self-help aid. 3% freshmen, 3% undergrads receive athletic scholarships. 92% freshmen, 92% undergrads receive any aid. **Criteria for awarding aid:** *Need-based:* Academics, Alumni affiliation. *Non-need-based:* Academics, Alumni affiliation, Art, Athletics, Music/drama.

LOYOLA UNIVERSITY OF CHICAGO

820 North Michigan Avenue, Chicago, IL 60611
Phone: 312-915-6500 • **Financial Aid Phone:** 773-508-7704
E-mail: admission@luc.edu • **CEEB Code:** 1412
Fax: 312-915-7216 • **Website:** www.luc.edu/

This private school, affiliated with the Roman Catholic-Jesuit Church, was founded in 1870. It has a 105-acre campus.

RATINGS
Admissions Selectivity Rating: 86   **Fire Safety Rating:** 97   **Green Rating:** 97

STUDENTS AND FACULTY
Enrollment: 10,906. **Student Body:** 66% female, 34% male, 35% out-of-state, 5% international (97 countries represented). Asian 12%, African American 5%, Caucasian 56%, Hispanic 15%, Native American <1%, Pacific Islander <1%, Two or more races 4%, Race unknown 1%.
Retention and Graduation: 82% freshmen return for sophomore year. 65% freshmen graduate within 4 years. 75% freshmen graduate within 6 years.
Faculty: Student/faculty ratio 14:1. 799 full-time faculty, 93% hold PhDs, 16% are are members of minority groups, 48% are women. 0% of classes are taught by teaching assistants.

ACADEMICS
Degrees: associate, bachelor's, certificate, doctoral/professional, doctoral/research, master's, postbachelor's certificate, post-master's certificate. **Classes:** Most classes have 10-19 students. Most lab/discussion sessions have 20-29 students. **Most popular majors:** Registered Nursing/Registered Nurse; Biology/Biological Sciences; Psychology. **Special Study Options:** Accelerated program, distance learning, double major, dual enrollment, English as a Second Language (ESL), exchange student program (domestic), honors program, independent study, internships, study abroad, teacher certification program. **Honors Programs:** Loyola University Chicago offers an Interdisciplinary Honors Program that integrates a challenging academic program with service-learning opportunities. Taking a series of team-taught, interdisciplinary courses, students learn to perceive unexpected convergences among discrete facts, to synthesize information from many sources, and to use their knowledge to benefit society. Combined degree programs: BA/JD, BA/MA, BA/MEng, B.B.A./M.B.A. Business Administration; B.S. Biology/M.B.A.; B.B.A./M.S.A. Ac. **Disability Services:** Special programs offered to physically disabled students, including note-taking services, reader services, tape recorders, tutors. **Career Services:** Alumni network, Alumni services, Career/job search classes, Career assessment, Internships, Regional alumni. In 2015 we launched an online platform, free to students and alumni seeking career related mentoring and networking connections. LUConnect is a fully branded, self-contained program that is up and running 24/7 from anywhere in the world.

FACILITIES
Housing: Coed dorms, special housing for disabled students, apartments for single students, Honors floors; Living Learning Community floors. 90% of campus accessible to physically disabled. **Special Academic Facilities/ Equipment:** Renaissance art gallery, Loyola University Museum of Art (LUMA), Madonna Della Strada Chapel, The Quinlin Life Sciences Building Bio Deisel Labs, Mock Trial Room, Mundelein Auditorium **Computers:** 75% of classrooms, 60% of dorms, 95% of libraries, 50% of dining areas, 100% of student union, 40% of common outdoor areas have wireless network access. Students can register for classes online. Administrative functions (other than registration) can be performed online.

CAMPUS LIFE
Environment: Metropolis. **Activities:** concert band, dance, drama/theater, jazz band, literary magazine, music ensembles, musical theater, pep band, radio station, student government, student newspaper, student-run film society, television station, Campus Ministries, Student Organization, Model UN. 185 registered organizations, 11 honor societies, 9 religious organizations. 6 fraternities, 9 sororities. **Athletics (Intercollegiate):** *Men:* basketball, cheerleading, cross-country, golf, soccer, track/field (outdoor), track/field (indoor), volleyball. *Women:* basketball, cheerleading, cross-country, golf, soccer, softball, track/field (outdoor), track/field (indoor), volleyball. **On-Campus Highlights:** Information Commons, Lake front Residence Halls, Joseph J. Gentile Center, Halas Athletic Center/Alumni Gym, Quinlan Life Sciences Center, LAKE SHORE CAMPUS Loyola's main residential campus is located on Chicago's North Side, minutes from downtown Chicago and the Water Tower Campus, and is set along the shore of Lake Michigan. It's home to the College of Arts and Sciences, Graduate School and Marcella Niehoff School of Nursing. The School of Education offers academic courses, programs and student advising. More than 3,000 students live in residence halls. The Lake Shore Campus includes Cudahy Library, Madonna della Strada Chapel, Joseph J. Gentile Center and the Halas Sports Center. WATER TOWER CAMPUS Loyola's downtown campus is located along Pearson Street, just off North Michigan Avenue, Chicago's "Magnificent Mile." Here, both residential and commuter students can complete one of many undergraduate degree programs, as well as take advantage of internships at many of Chicago's business and cultural institutions. The Water Tower Campus is home to the Schools of Business Administration, Education, Law and Social Work, and to selected programs in the College of Arts and Sciences. **Environmental Initiatives:** Energy reduction and conservation, transportation: Adopt green building design standards for all new construction. Lighting, heating/cooling retrofits. Biodiesel production from dining hall's waste vegetable oil used in campus shuttles. (www. luc.edu/biodiesel) Transportation: walk-to-work program, bicycle program, electric vehicles, public transit passes for students, car sharing program.

ADMISSIONS
Freshman Academic Profile: Average high school GPA 3.7. 34% in top 10% of high school class, 70% in top 25% of high school class, 92% in top 50% of high school class. 64% from public high schools. **Reported SAT (pre-2016 redesign) scores:** SAT Math middle 50% range 510-630. SAT Critical Reading middle 50% range 520-630. SAT Writing middle 50% range 510-620. **Concordant SAT scores:** SAT EBRW middle 50% 570–680. SAT Math middle 50% range 540–650. ACT middle 50% range 24-29. Minimum internet-based TOEFL 79. Minimum paper TOEFL 550. **Basis for Candidate Selection:** *Very important factors considered include:* rigor of secondary school record, academic GPA, standardized test scores. *Important factors considered include:* application essay, recommendation(s), extracurricular activities, character/ personal qualities, volunteer work, level of applicant's interest. *Other factors considered include:* class rank, interview, talent/ability, first generation, alumni/ae relation, geographical residence, state residency, work experience. **Freshman Admission Requirements:** High school diploma is required and GED is accepted. *Academic units required:* 4 English, 3 math, 3 science, 2 foreign language, 2 social studies, 1 history. *Academic units recommended:* 4 English, 4 math, 3 science, 2 foreign language, 2 social studies, 3 history, 3 academic electives. **Freshman Admission Statistics:** 22,712 applied, 72.57% admitted, 16% enrolled. **Transfer Admission Requirements:** college transcript(s), Minimum college GPA of 2.0 required. Lowest grade transferable C. **General Admission Information:** Priority deadline 12/1. Nonfall registration accepted.

COSTS AND FINANCIAL AID
Annual tuition $41,470. Room and board $14,080. Required fees $1,358. Average book expense $1,200. **Required Forms and Deadlines:** FAFSA. **Notification of Awards:** Applicants will be notified of awards on a rolling basis beginning 2/15. **Types of Aid:** *Need-based scholarships/grants:* Federal Pell, FSEOG, State scholarships/grants, Private scholarships, College/ university scholarship or grant aid from institutional funds. *Loans:* Direct Subsidized Stafford Loans, Direct Unsubsidized Stafford Loans, Direct PLUS loans, Federal Perkins Loans, Federal Nursing Loans. *Student Employment:* Federal Work-Study Program available. Institutional employment available. **Financial Aid Statistics:** 98% needy freshmen, 95% needy undergrads receive need-based scholarship or grant aid. 11% freshmen, 9% undergrads receive non-need-based scholarship or grant aid. 83% freshmen, 83% undergrads receive need-based self-help aid. 1% freshmen, 1% undergrads receive athletic scholarships. 97% freshmen, 88% undergrads receive any aid. 71% undergrads borrow to pay for school. Average cumulative indebtedness $31,750. **Criteria for awarding aid:** *Non-need-based:* Academics, Art, Athletics, Leadership, Music/drama, Religious affiliation.

See page 992.

LUBBOCK CHRISTIAN UNIVERSITY

5601 19th Street, Lubbock, TX 79407
Phone: 800-720-7151 • **Financial Aid Phone:** 806-720-7176
E-mail: admissions@lcu.edu • **CEEB Code:** 6378
Fax: 806-720-7162 • **Website:** www.lcu.edu • **ACT Code:** 4123

This private school, affiliated with the Church of Christ Church, was founded in 1957. It has a 120-acre campus.

RATINGS
Admissions Selectivity Rating: 75   **Fire Safety Rating:** 72   **Green Rating:** 60*

STUDENTS AND FACULTY
Enrollment: 1,496. **Student Body:** 59% female, 41% male, 9% out-of-state, 2% international (21 countries represented). Asian 1%, African American 5%, Caucasian 66%, Hispanic 25%, Native American 1%, Pacific Islander <1%, Two or more races 0%, Race unknown 0%.
Retention and Graduation: 73% freshmen return for sophomore year. 26% freshmen graduate within 4 years. 42% freshmen graduate within 6 years. 16% grads go on to further study within 1 year. 14% grads pursue law degrees. 7% grads pursue business degrees. **Faculty:** Student/faculty ratio 13:1. 99 full-time faculty, 73% hold PhDs, 4% are are members of minority groups, 43% are women. 0% of classes are taught by teaching assistants.

ACADEMICS
Degrees: associate, bachelor's, master's. **Classes:** Most classes have 10-19 students. Most lab/discussion sessions have fewer than 10 students. **Special Study Options:** distance learning, double major, dual enrollment, honors program, internships, liberal arts/career combination, student-designed major, study abroad, teacher certification program, weekend college. **Honors Programs:** Honors program available to all majors. **Disability Services:** Special programs offered to physically disabled students, including tape recorders, tutors. **Career Services:** Alumni services, Career/job search classes, Career assessment, Internships. Education—experiential learning opportunities in local schools are required with each education course.

FACILITIES
Housing: special housing for disabled students, men's dorms, women's dorms, apartments for married students, apartments for single students. 78% of campus accessible to physically diasbled. **Computers:** Students can register for classes online.

CAMPUS LIFE
Environment: City. **Activities:** Choral groups, drama/theater, music ensembles, student government, student newspaper, yearbook. 24 registered organizations, 3 honor societies, 4 fraternities, 4 sororities. **Athletics (Intercollegiate):** *Men:* baseball, basketball, cheerleading, golf. *Women:* basketball, cheerleading, golf, volleyball. **On-Campus Highlights:** Student Union Building, Ramona Perrin Fitness Center, Rip Griffin Athletic Center, Library, Snackbar.

ADMISSIONS
Freshman Academic Profile: Average high school GPA 3.5. 19% in top 10% of high school class, 43% in top 25% of high school class, 74% in top 50% of high school class. 83% from public high schools. **Reported SAT (pre-2016 redesign) scores:** SAT Math middle 50% range 430-555. SAT Critical Reading middle 50% range 440-550. SAT Writing middle 50% range 420-548. **Concordant SAT scores:** SAT EBRW middle 50% 480–610. SAT Math middle 50% range 470–580. ACT middle 50% range 19-25. Minimum internet-based TOEFL 71. Minimum paper TOEFL 525. **Basis for Candidate Selection:** *Very important factors considered include:* standardized test scores. *Other factors considered include:* rigor of secondary school record, class rank, academic GPA, recommendation(s), extracurricular activities, talent/ability, character/personal qualities, first generation, alumni/ae relation, volunteer work, work experience, level of applicant's interest. **Freshman Admission Requirements:** High school diploma is required and GED is accepted. *Academic units recommended:* 4 English, 3 math, 3 science, 2 science labs, 2 foreign language, 1 social studies, 2 history, 2 academic electives, 1 computer science, 1 visual/performing arts. **Freshman Admission Statistics:** 867 applied, 96.08% admitted, 33% enrolled. **Transfer Admission Requirements:** college transcript(s), statement of good standing from prior institution(s). Lowest grade transferable C. **General Admission Information:** Application fee $25. Regular application deadline 6/1. Nonfall registration accepted.

COSTS AND FINANCIAL AID
Annual tuition $20,360. Room and board $6,070. Average book expense $1,100. **Required Forms and Deadlines:** FAFSA, Institution's own financial aid form. **Notification of Awards:** Applicants will be notified of awards on a rolling basis beginning 3/1. **Types of Aid:** *Need-based scholarships/grants:* Federal Pell, FSEOG, State scholarships/grants. *Loans:* Direct Subsidized

---

Stafford Loans, Direct Unsubsidized Stafford Loans, Direct PLUS loans, Federal Perkins Loans, State Loans. *Student Employment:* Federal Work-Study Program available. **Financial Aid Statistics:** 99% needy freshmen, 97% needy undergrads receive need-based scholarship or grant aid. 9% freshmen, 10% undergrads receive non-need-based scholarship or grant aid. 90% freshmen, 89% undergrads receive need-based self-help aid. 8% freshmen, 6% undergrads receive athletic scholarships. 98% freshmen, 83% undergrads receive any aid. **Criteria for awarding aid:** *Non-need-based:* Academics, Athletics, Leadership, Music/drama, Religious affiliation.

LUTHER COLLEGE

700 College Drive, Decorah, IA 52101-1042
Phone: 563-387-1287 • **Financial Aid Phone:** 563-387-1018
E-mail: admissions@luther.edu • **CEEB Code:** 6375
Fax: 563-387-2159 • **Website:** www.luther.edu • **ACT Code:** 1330

This private school, affiliated with the Lutheran Church, was founded in 1861. It has a 175-acre campus.

RATINGS
Admissions Selectivity Rating: 85   **Fire Safety Rating:** 87   **Green Rating:** 94

STUDENTS AND FACULTY
Enrollment: 2,121. **Student Body:** 55% female, 45% male, 65% out-of-state, 7% international (64 countries represented). Asian 2%, African American 2%, Caucasian 82%, Hispanic 5%, Native American <1%, Pacific Islander <1%, Two or more races 2%, Race unknown 0%.
Retention and Graduation: 84% freshmen return for sophomore year. 72% freshmen graduate within 4 years. 79% freshmen graduate within 6 years. 15% grads go on to further study within 1 year. 10% grads pursue arts and sciences degrees. 1% grads pursue law degrees. 2% grads pursue business degrees. 3% grads pursue medical degrees. **Faculty:** Student/faculty ratio 11:1. 175 full-time faculty, 95% hold PhDs, 11% are are members of minority groups, 49% are women. 0% of classes are taught by teaching assistants.

ACADEMICS
Degrees: bachelor's. **Classes:** Most classes have 10-19 students. Most lab/discussion sessions have 10-19 students. **Most popular majors:** Biology/Biological Sciences; Music; Psychology. **Special Study Options:** double major, dual enrollment, honors program, independent study, internships, student-designed major, study abroad, teacher certification program. **Disability Services:** Special programs offered to physically disabled students, including note-taking services, reader services, tutors. **Career Services:** Alumni network, Career/job search classes, Internships.

FACILITIES
Housing: Coed dorms, special housing for disabled students, apartments for married students, apartments for single students, Wellness Housing. 95% of campus accessible to physically diasbled. **Special Academic Facilities/Equipment:** Natural history museum, Norwegian-American museum, five art galleries, planetarium, live animal center, archaeological research center, computer music lab, two electron microscopes. **Computers:** 90% of classrooms, 75% of dorms, 90% of libraries, 90% of dining areas, 90% of student union, 25% of common outdoor areas have wireless network access. Students can register for classes online. Administrative functions (other than registration) can be performed online.

CAMPUS LIFE
Environment: Village. **Activities:** Choral groups, concert band, dance, drama/theater, jazz band, literary magazine, music ensembles, musical theater, pep band, radio station, student government, student newspaper, symphony orchestra, yearbook, Campus Ministries, Student Organization, Model UN. 83 registered organizations, 13 honor societies, 8 religious organizations. 1 fraternity, 3 sororities. **Athletics (Intercollegiate):** *Men:* baseball, basketball, cross-country, diving, football, golf, soccer, swimming, tennis, track/field (outdoor), track/field (indoor), wrestling. *Women:* basketball, cross-country, diving, golf, soccer, softball, swimming, tennis, track/field (outdoor), track/field (indoor), volleyball. **On-Campus Highlights:** Marty's Cyber Cafe, Legends Fitness Center, The Cafeteria, Residence Hall Lounges, Sunnyside Cafe in the Center for the Arts. **Environmental Initiatives:** Energy audit and efficiency upgrades totaling $1.5 million and has reduced campus carbon footprint by 15%.

ADMISSIONS
Freshman Academic Profile: Average high school GPA 3.7. 23% in top 10% of high school class, 52% in top 25% of high school class, 84% in top 50% of high school class. 90% from public high schools. **Reported SAT (pre-2016 redesign) scores:** SAT Math middle 50% range 480-625. SAT Critical

Reading middle 50% range 448-573. SAT Writing middle 50% range 450-578. **Concordant SAT scores:** SAT EBRW middle 50% 500–630. SAT Math middle 50% range 510–650. ACT middle 50% range 23-28. Minimum internet-based TOEFL 80. Minimum paper TOEFL 550. **Basis for Candidate Selection:** *Very important factors considered include:* rigor of secondary school record, class rank, academic GPA, standardized test scores, recommendation(s). *Important factors considered include:* extracurricular activities, talent/ability, character/personal qualities. *Other factors considered include:* application essay, interview, first generation, alumni/ae relation, racial/ethnic status, volunteer work, level of applicant's interest. **Freshman Admission Requirements:** High school diploma is required and GED is accepted. *Academic units recommended:* 4 English, 3 math, 2 science, 1 science lab, 2 foreign language, 3 social studies. **Freshman Admission Statistics:** 3,856 applied, 67.63% admitted, 20% enrolled. **Transfer Admission Requirements:** High school transcript, college transcript(s), essay or personal statement, standardized test scores, Minimum college GPA of 2.50 required. Lowest grade transferable C. **General Admission Information:** Nonfall registration accepted. Admission may be deferred for a maximum of 1 year.

COSTS AND FINANCIAL AID
Annual tuition $40,710. Required fees $310. Average book expense $1,040. **Required Forms and Deadlines:** FAFSA, Institution's own financial aid form. **Notification of Awards:** Applicants will be notified of awards on a rolling basis beginning 3/15. **Types of Aid:** *Need-based scholarships/grants:* Federal Pell, FSEOG, State scholarships/grants, Private scholarships, College/university scholarship or grant aid from institutional funds. *Loans:* Direct Subsidized Stafford Loans, Direct Unsubsidized Stafford Loans, Direct PLUS loans, Federal Perkins Loans, College/university loans from institutional funds. *Student Employment:* Federal Work-Study Program available. Institutional employment available. **Financial Aid Statistics:** 100% needy freshmen, 100% needy undergrads receive need-based scholarship or grant aid. 26% freshmen, 18% undergrads receive non-need-based scholarship or grant aid. 73% freshmen, 81% undergrads receive need-based self-help aid. 0% freshmen, 0% undergrads receive athletic scholarships. 98% freshmen, 97% undergrads receive any aid. 69% undergrads borrow to pay for school. Average cumulative indebtedness $35,642. **Criteria for awarding aid:** *Non-need-based:* Academics, Alumni affiliation, Art, Minority status, Music/drama.

LYCOMING COLLEGE

700 College Place, Williamsport, PA 17701
Phone: 570-321-4026 • **Financial Aid Phone:** 570-321-4040
E-mail: admissions@lycoming.edu • **CEEB Code:** 2372
Fax: 570-321-4317 • **Website:** www.lycoming.edu • **ACT Code:** 3622

This private school, affiliated with the Methodist Church, was founded in 1812. It has a 39-acre campus.

RATINGS
Admissions Selectivity Rating: 81   **Fire Safety Rating:** 88   **Green Rating:** 77

STUDENTS AND FACULTY
Enrollment: 1,246. **Student Body:** 52% female, 48% male, 39% out-of-state, 5% international (16 countries represented). Asian 1%, African American 10%, Caucasian 67%, Hispanic 9%, Native American <1%, Pacific Islander 0%, Two or more races 3%, Race unknown 5%.
Retention and Graduation: 79% freshmen return for sophomore year. 59% freshmen graduate within 4 years. 72% freshmen graduate within 6 years. 13% grads go on to further study within 1 year. **Faculty:** Student/faculty ratio 12:1. 90 full-time faculty, 94% hold PhDs, 4% are are members of minority groups, 44% are women. 0% of classes are taught by teaching assistants.

ACADEMICS
Degrees: bachelor's. **Classes:** Most classes have 10-19 students. Most lab/discussion sessions have 10-19 students. **Most popular majors:** Biology/Biological Sciences; Business Administration and Management; Psychology. **Special Study Options:** Accelerated program, cross-registration, double major, honors program, independent study, internships, student-designed major, study abroad, teacher certification program. **Honors Programs:** Scholars Program offered to students through admissions process; each major also provides an Honors major option for students who wish to graduate with honors within their field of study. Combined degree programs: 3-2 engineering partnership with the Watson School of Engineering at SUNY Binghamton. **Disability**

Services: Special programs offered to physically disabled students, including note-taking services, reader services, tape recorders, tutors. **Career Services:** Alumni network, Alumni services, Career/job search classes, Career assessment, Internships, Regional alumni. Lycoming College has a successful internship program with local businesses (WISE program). Williamsport, PA serves as the County Seat and offers a rich array of business and government opportunities for students. Lycoming also provides and supports unique opportunities for student research with faculty. In addition, Lycoming has successfully placed students in nationally competitive internship programs with the FBI, top 5 accounting firms, Datatel, and the National Science Foundation.

FACILITIES
Housing: Coed dorms, special housing for disabled students, women's dorms, fraternity/sorority housing, apartments for single students, ThemeHousingSubstance-free housing, Study-intensive housing, Creative Arts Society housing. **Special Academic Facilities/Equipment:** Language lab, tissue culture lab, TV studio, planetarium, video conferencing. **Computers:** 100% of classrooms, 100% of dorms, 100% of libraries, 100% of dining areas, 100% of student union, 100% of common outdoor areas have wireless network access. Students can register for classes online. Administrative functions (other than registration) can be performed online.

CAMPUS LIFE
Environment: Town. **Activities:** Choral groups, concert band, dance, drama/theater, jazz band, literary magazine, music ensembles, musical theater, pep band, radio station, student government, student newspaper, student-run film society, symphony orchestra, television station, yearbook, Campus Ministries, Student Organization. 78 registered organizations, 20 honor societies, 3 religious organizations. 5 fraternities, 5 sororities. **Athletics (Intercollegiate):** *Men:* basketball, cross-country, football, golf, lacrosse, soccer, swimming, tennis, wrestling. *Women:* basketball, cross-country, golf, lacrosse, soccer, softball, swimming, tennis, volleyball. **On-Campus Highlights:** Quad, Dining Hall, Jack's Place, Lamade Gymnasium, Recreation Center. **Environmental Initiatives:** The College has a Sustainability Committee that is comprised of faculty, administrators and students. Several initiatives have emerged from this group including using the grease waste from campus dining and converting it into biodiesel.

ADMISSIONS
Freshman Academic Profile: Average high school GPA 3.4. 18% in top 10% of high school class, 42% in top 25% of high school class, 73% in top 50% of high school class. 90% from public high schools. **Reported SAT (pre-2016 redesign) scores:** SAT Math middle 50% range 470-570. SAT Critical Reading middle 50% range 470-550. SAT Writing middle 50% range 430-530. **Concordant SAT scores:** SAT EBRW middle 50% 500–600. SAT Math middle 50% range 510–590. ACT middle 50% range 20-25. Minimum internet-based TOEFL 70. Minimum paper TOEFL 525. **Basis for Candidate Selection:** *Very important factors considered include:* rigor of secondary school record, recommendation(s). *Important factors considered include:* class rank, academic GPA, standardized test scores, application essay, interview, racial/ethnic status. *Other factors considered include:* extracurricular activities, talent/ability, character/personal qualities, first generation, alumni/ae relation, geographical residence, volunteer work, work experience, level of applicant's interest. **Freshman Admission Requirements:** High school diploma is required and GED is accepted. *Academic units required:* 4 English, 3 math, 3 science, 2 foreign language, 3 social studies, 2 academic electives. *Academic units recommended:* 4 English, 4 math, 3 science, 3 foreign language, 4 social studies, 3 academic electives. **Freshman Admission Statistics:** 1,876 applied, 69.56% admitted, 26% enrolled. **Transfer Admission Requirements:** college transcript(s), statement of good standing from prior institution(s). Minimum college GPA of 2.0 required. Lowest grade transferable C-. **General Admission Information:** Application fee $35. Priority deadline 12/1. Regular application deadline 3/1. Nonfall registration accepted. Admission may be deferred for a maximum of 1 year.

COSTS AND FINANCIAL AID
Annual tuition $36,432. Room and board $11,418. Average book expense $1,000. **Required Forms and Deadlines:** FAFSA. **Notification of Awards:** Applicants will be notified of awards on a rolling basis beginning 3/1. **Types of Aid:** *Need-based scholarships/grants:* Federal Pell, FSEOG, State scholarships/grants, Private scholarships, College/university scholarship or grant aid from institutional funds. *Loans:* Direct Subsidized Stafford Loans, Direct Unsubsidized Stafford Loans, Direct PLUS loans, Federal Perkins Loans, College/university loans from institutional funds. *Student Employment:* Federal Work-Study Program available. Institutional employment available. **Financial Aid Statistics:** 100% needy freshmen, 100% needy undergrads receive need-based scholarship or grant aid. 11% freshmen, 13% undergrads receive non-need-based scholarship or grant aid. 80% freshmen, 85% undergrads receive need-based self-help aid. 0% freshmen, 0% undergrads receive athletic scholarships. 100% freshmen, 100% undergrads receive any aid. **Criteria for awarding aid:** *Need-based:* Academics, Minority status. *Non-need-based:* Academics, Art, Minority status, Music/drama.

LYME ACADEMY COLLEGE OF FINE ARTS

84 Lyme St, Old Lyme, CT 6371
Phone: 860-434-3571 x118 • **Financial Aid Phone:** 860-434-5232
E-mail: admissions@lymeacademy.edu • **CEEB Code:** 1971
Fax: 860-434-8725 • **Website:** http://www.lymeacademy.edu/

This private school was founded in 1976. It has a 47-acre campus.

RATINGS

Admissions Selectivity Rating: 76   **Fire Safety Rating:** 60*   **Green Rating:** 60*

STUDENTS AND FACULTY

Enrollment: 77. **Student Body:** 63% female, 37% male, 47% out-of-state, 0% international (0 countries represented). Asian 1%, African American 4%, Caucasian 88%, Hispanic 1%, Native American 3%, Pacific Islander 1%, Two or more races 3%, Race unknown 0%.
Retention and Graduation: 89% freshmen return for sophomore year. 53% freshmen graduate within 4 years. 10% grads go on to further study within 1 year. **Faculty:** Student/faculty ratio 14:1. 8 full-time faculty, 75% hold PhDs, 0% are are members of minority groups, 38% are women. 0% of classes are taught by teaching assistants.

ACADEMICS

Degrees: bachelor's, certificate, postbachelor's certificate. **Classes:** Most classes have 10-19 students. **Most popular majors:** Sculpture; Painting; Illustration. **Special Study Options:** independent study.

FACILITIES

Housing: Currently, all housing is Off-campus. Students live in local homes as well as apartments. Contact Patti Broedlin in Student Services for assistance, lists and referrals. 95% of campus accessible to physically diasbled. **Special Academic Facilities/Equipment:** Sill House Gallery, Chauncey Stillman Gallery, Academy Wood Shop, Sculpture Casting rooms. **Computers:** 20% of classrooms, 100% of libraries, 100% of dining areas, 100% of student union, 40% of common outdoor areas have wireless network access.

CAMPUS LIFE

Environment: Village. **Activities:** literary magazine, student government, student-run film society. **On-Campus Highlights:** Chauncey Stillman Art Gallery, Cafe, Student Commons, Library, Sill House Art Gallery.

ADMISSIONS

Freshman Academic Profile: Average high school GPA 3.2. 85% from public high schools. **Reported SAT (pre-2016 redesign) scores:** SAT Math middle 50% range 395-555. SAT Critical Reading middle 50% range 440-650. SAT Writing middle 50% range 450-595. **Concordant SAT scores:** SAT EBRW middle 50% 500–680. SAT Math middle 50% range 440–580. Minimum paper TOEFL 550. **Basis for Candidate Selection:** *Very important factors considered include:* academic GPA, interview, talent/ability, character/personal qualities, level of applicant's interest. *Important factors considered include:* rigor of secondary school record, application essay, recommendation(s). *Other factors considered include:* standardized test scores, racial/ethnic status. **Freshman Admission Requirements:** High school diploma is required and GED is accepted. **Freshman Admission Statistics:** 82 applied, 68.29% admitted, 43% enrolled. **Transfer Admission Requirements:** college transcript(s), essay or personal statement, interview, Minimum college GPA of 2.0 required. Lowest grade transferable C. **General Admission Information:** Application fee $55. Nonfall registration accepted. Admission may be deferred for a maximum of 1 year.

COSTS AND FINANCIAL AID

Annual tuition $25,248. Required fees $1,536. Average book expense $1,500. **Required Forms and Deadlines:** FAFSA. **Notification of Awards:** Applicants will be notified of awards on a rolling basis beginning 3/1. **Types of Aid:** *Need-based scholarships/grants:* Federal Pell, FSEOG, State scholarships/grants, Private scholarships, College/university scholarship or grant aid from institutional funds. *Loans:* Direct Subsidized Stafford Loans, Direct Unsubsidized Stafford Loans, Direct PLUS loans. *Student Employment:* Federal Work-Study Program available. Institutional employment available. **Financial Aid Statistics:** 0% freshmen, 0% undergrads receive athletic scholarships. 88% freshmen, 84% undergrads receive any aid. **Criteria for awarding aid:** *Need-based:* Alumni affiliation, Art, Job skills, Minority status. *Non-need-based:* Academics, Art, Leadership.

LYNCHBURG COLLEGE

1501 Lakeside Drive, Lynchburg, VA 24501
Phone: 434-544-8300 • **Financial Aid Phone:** 434-544-8229
E-mail: admissions@lynchburg.edu • **CEEB Code:** 5372
Fax: 434-544-8653 • **Website:** www.lynchburg.edu • **ACT Code:** 4368

This private school, affiliated with the Disciples of Christ Church, was founded in 1903. It has a 214-acre campus.

RATINGS

Admissions Selectivity Rating: 84   **Fire Safety Rating:** 80   **Green Rating:** 60*

STUDENTS AND FACULTY

Enrollment: 1,999. **Student Body:** 60% female, 40% male, 31% out-of-state, 3% international (12 countries represented). Asian 1%, African American 12%, Caucasian 73%, Hispanic 5%, Native American <1%, Pacific Islander 0%, Two or more races 5%, Race unknown 2%.
Retention and Graduation: 81% freshmen return for sophomore year. 48% freshmen graduate within 4 years. 56 18% grads go on to further study within 1 year. 18% grads pursue arts and sciences degrees. 22% grads pursue business degrees. **Faculty:** Student/faculty ratio 10:1. 180 full-time faculty, 83% hold PhDs, 7% are are members of minority groups, 54% are women. 0% of classes are taught by teaching assistants.

ACADEMICS

Degrees: bachelor's, doctoral/professional, doctoral, master's, postbachelor's certificate, post-master's certificate. **Classes:** Most classes have 10-19 students. Most lab/discussion sessions have 10-19 students. **Most popular majors:** Teacher Education and Professional Development, Specific Levels and Methods; Speech Communication and Rhetoric; Registered Nursing, Nursing Administration, Nursing Research and Clinical Nursing. **Special Study Options:** Accelerated program, cross-registration, double major, dual enrollment, honors program, independent study, internships, study abroad, teacher certification program. **Honors Programs:** Westover Honors Program. **Disability Services:** Special programs offered to physically disabled students, including note-taking services, reader services, tape recorders, tutors. **Career Services:** Alumni network, Alumni services, Career/job search classes, Career assessment, Internships, Regional alumni. Experiential learning and internship programs are so numerous and diverse that it is impossible to select one that is most outstanding.

FACILITIES

Housing: Coed dorms, special housing for disabled students, men's dorms, special housing for international students, women's dorms, fraternity/sorority housing, apartments for single students, Wellness Housing, Theme Housing. 90% of campus accessible to physically diasbled. **Special Academic Facilities/Equipment:** Daura Art Gallery, Claytor Nature Study Center, Ramsey-Freer Herbarium, Forensics cadaver lab; Centennial Hall audio-visual and television studios, Dillard Fine Arts Center **Computers:** 20% of dorms, 100% of libraries, 100% of dining areas, 100% of student union, have wireless network access. Students can register for classes online. Administrative functions (other than registration) can be performed online.

CAMPUS LIFE

Environment: City. **Activities:** Choral groups, concert band, dance, drama/theater, jazz band, literary magazine, music ensembles, musical theater, pep band, student government, student newspaper, student-run film society, symphony orchestra, yearbook, Campus Ministries, Student Organization, Model UN. 90 registered organizations, 14 honor societies, 10 religious organizations. 4 fraternities, 6 sororities. **Athletics (Intercollegiate):** *Men:* baseball, basketball, cheerleading, cross-country, golf, lacrosse, soccer, tennis, track/field (outdoor), track/field (indoor). *Women:* basketball, cheerleading, cross-country, equestrian sports, field hockey, lacrosse, soccer, softball, tennis, track/field (outdoor), track/field (indoor), volleyball. **On-Campus Highlights:** Shellenberger Field, Burton Student Center, Claytor Nature Study Center, Stingers Coffee House, Schewel Hall. **Environmental Initiatives:** Recovery of College Lake. Working with the Army Corp of Engineers, and the state of Virginia, Lynchburg College is attempting to restore College Lake.

ADMISSIONS

Freshman Academic Profile: Average high school GPA 3.5. 80% from public high schools. **Reported SAT (pre-2016 redesign) scores:** SAT Math middle 50% range 460-560. SAT Critical Reading middle 50% range 460-560. **Concordant SAT scores:** SAT Math middle 50% range 500–580. ACT middle 50% range 19-25. Minimum internet-based TOEFL 78. Minimum paper TOEFL 550. **Basis for Candidate Selection:** *Very important factors considered include:* rigor of secondary school record, academic GPA, standardized test scores. *Important factors considered include:* interview. *Other factors considered include:* class rank, application essay, recommendation(s), extracurricular activities, talent/ability, character/personal qualities, volunteer work, work experience, level of applicant's interest. **Freshman Admission Requirements:** High school diploma is required and GED is accepted. *Academic units required:* 4 English, 3 math, 3 science, 2 science labs, 2 foreign language, 2 social studies, 2 history. *Academic units recommended:* 4 English, 4 math, 4 science, 2 science labs, 3 foreign language, 2 social studies, 2 history, 1 academic elective. **Freshman Admission Statistics:** 5,223 applied, 63.78% admitted, 16% enrolled. **Transfer Admission Requirements:** college transcript(s), Minimum college GPA of 2.0 required. Lowest grade transferable C. **General Admission Information:** Application fee $30. Nonfall registration accepted. Admission may be deferred for a maximum of 1 year.

COSTS AND FINANCIAL AID

Annual tuition $35,650. Room and board $10,120. Required fees $970. Average book expense $1,000. **Required Forms and Deadlines:** FAFSA, State aid form. **Notification of Awards:** Applicants will be notified of awards on a rolling basis beginning 3/5. **Types of Aid:** *Need-based scholarships/grants:* Federal Pell, FSEOG, State scholarships/grants, Private scholarships, College/university scholarship or grant aid from institutional funds. *Loans:* Direct Subsidized Stafford Loans, Direct Unsubsidized Stafford Loans, Direct PLUS loans, Federal Perkins Loans. *Student Employment:* Federal Work-Study Program available. Institutional employment available. **Financial Aid Statistics:** 100% needy freshmen, 99% needy undergrads receive need-based scholarship or grant aid. 19% freshmen, 14% undergrads receive non-need-based scholarship or grant aid. 80% freshmen, 85% undergrads receive need-based self-help aid. 0% freshmen, 0% undergrads receive athletic scholarships. 80% freshmen, 74% undergrads receive any aid. 77% undergrads borrow to pay for school. Average cumulative indebtedness $35,614. **Criteria for awarding aid:** *Need-based:* Minority status, Religious affiliation. *Non-need-based:* Academics, Art, Leadership, Music/drama, Religious affiliation, State/district residency.

LYNN UNIVERSITY

3601 North Military Trail, Boca Raton, FL 33431-5598
Phone: 561-237-7900 • **Financial Aid Phone:** 561-237-7973
E-mail: admission@lynn.edu • **CEEB Code:** 5437
Fax: 561-237-7100 • **Website:** www.lynn.edu • **ACT Code:** 706

This private school was founded in 1962. It has a 123-acre campus.

RATINGS

Admissions Selectivity Rating: 73   **Fire Safety Rating:** 98   **Green Rating:** 89

STUDENTS AND FACULTY

Enrollment: 2,053. **Student Body:** 49% female, 51% male, 53% out-of-state, 21% international (89 countries represented). Asian 1%, African American 9%, Caucasian 45%, Hispanic 16%, Native American <1%, Pacific Islander <1%, Two or more races 1%, Race unknown 5%.
Retention and Graduation: 68% freshmen return for sophomore year. 35% freshmen graduate within 4 years. 45% freshmen graduate within 6 years.
Faculty: Student/faculty ratio 21:1. 106 full-time faculty, 58% hold PhDs, 5% are members of minority groups, 42% are women. 0% of classes are taught by teaching assistants.

ACADEMICS

Degrees: bachelor's, doctoral, master's, postbachelor's certificate, post-master's certificate. **Classes:** Most classes have 10-19 students. **Most popular majors:** International Business/Trade/Commerce; Entrepreneurship/Entrepreneurial Studies; Sport and Fitness Administration/Management. **Special Study Options:** Accelerated program, cooperative education program, distance learning, double major, dual enrollment, English as a Second Language (ESL), honors program, independent study, internships, liberal arts/career combination, study abroad, teacher certification program. **Honors Programs:** Honors Program. **Disability Services:** Special programs offered to physically disabled students, including note-taking services, reader services, tape recorders. **Career Services:** Alumni network, Alumni services, Career/job search classes, Career assessment, Internships, Regional alumni. At the Hannifan Center for Career Connections, we do career preparation differently. We work with students one-on-one and early on to find the best opportunities, experiences, internships, jobs and careers. And we do it one connection at a time.

FACILITIES

Housing: Coed dorms, special housing for disabled students, special housing for international students, women's dorms. 99% of campus accessible to physically diasbled. **Computers:** Students can register for classes online. Administrative functions (other than registration) can be performed online.

CAMPUS LIFE

Environment: City. **Activities:** Choral groups, dance, drama/theater, literary magazine, music ensembles, radio station, student government, student newspaper, student-run film society, symphony orchestra, television station, yearbook, Campus Ministries, Student Organization. 25 registered organizations, 4 honor societies, 4 religious organizations. 2 fraternities, 1 sorority. **Athletics (Intercollegiate):** *Men:* baseball, basketball, golf, soccer, tennis. *Women:* basketball, golf, soccer, softball, tennis, volleyball. **On-Campus Highlights:** The de Hoernle Sports Complex, The de Hoernle Sports and Cultural Center, The Coleman Electronic Lab, The Lynn Student Center, The Eugene M. and Christine E. Lynn Library. **Environmental Initiatives:** Lynn Going Green initiatives include a complete campus retrofit of water fixtures and lighting equipment (over 7,500 light bulbs changed out in 2012). These projects also include building a new Central Energy Plant, complete retrofit of campus A/C equipment, boilers and hot water heaters, as well as other measures to save energy. This project was completed in January of 2015.

ADMISSIONS

Freshman Academic Profile: Average high school GPA 3.0. 2% in top 10% of high school class, 14% in top 25% of high school class, 44% in top 50% of high school class. **Reported SAT (pre-2016 redesign) scores:** SAT Math middle 50% range 430-530. SAT Critical Reading middle 50% range 440-530. SAT Writing middle 50% range 420-520. **Concordant SAT scores:** SAT EBRW middle 50% 480–580. SAT Math middle 50% range 470–560. ACT middle 50% range 19-24. Minimum internet-based TOEFL 71. Minimum paper TOEFL 525. **Basis for Candidate Selection:** *Very important factors considered include:* rigor of secondary school record, academic GPA, application essay. *Important factors considered include:* class rank, standardized test scores, recommendation(s), interview, extracurricular activities, character/personal qualities, volunteer work, work experience. *Other factors considered include:* level of applicant's interest. **Freshman Admission Requirements:** High school diploma is required and GED is accepted. *Academic units recommended:* 4 English, 4 math, 4 science, 2 social studies, 2 history. **Freshman Admission Statistics:** 3,514 applied, 81.73% admitted, 20% enrolled. **Transfer Admission Requirements:** college transcript(s), essay or personal statement, statement of good standing from prior institution(s). Minimum college GPA of 2.0 required. Lowest grade transferable C. **General Admission Information:** Application fee $45. Priority deadline 12/1. Regular application deadline 8/1. Nonfall registration accepted. Admission may be deferred.

COSTS AND FINANCIAL AID

Annual tuition $35,260. Room and board $11,970. Required fees $2,250. Average book expense $800. **Required Forms and Deadlines:** FAFSA. **Notification of Awards:** Applicants will be notified of awards on a rolling basis beginning 2/1. **Types of Aid:** *Need-based scholarships/grants:* Federal Pell, FSEOG, State scholarships/grants, Private scholarships, College/university scholarship or grant aid from institutional funds. *Loans:* Direct Subsidized Stafford Loans, Direct Unsubsidized Stafford Loans, Direct PLUS loans, Federal Perkins Loans, State Loans, College/university loans from institutional funds. *Student Employment:* Federal Work-Study Program available. Institutional employment available. **Financial Aid Statistics:** 84% needy freshmen, 84% needy undergrads receive need-based scholarship or grant aid. 96% freshmen, 88% undergrads receive non-need-based scholarship or grant aid. 80% freshmen, 76% undergrads receive need-based self-help aid. 12% freshmen, 7% undergrads receive athletic scholarships. 95% freshmen, 80% undergrads receive any aid. 30% undergrads borrow to pay for school. Average cumulative indebtedness $33,689. **Criteria for awarding aid:** *Need-based:* Leadership. *Non-need-based:* Academics, Alumni affiliation, Athletics, Leadership, Music/drama.

LYON COLLEGE

P.O. Box 2317, Batesville, AR 72503-2317
Phone: 870-307-7250 • **Financial Aid Phone:** 870-307-7257
E-mail: admissions@lyon.edu • **CEEB Code:** 1088
Website: www.lyon.edu • **ACT Code:** 112

This private school, affiliated with the Presbyterian Church, was founded in 1872. It has a 136-acre campus.

RATINGS

Admissions Selectivity Rating: 78   **Fire Safety Rating:** 83   **Green Rating:** 60*

STUDENTS AND FACULTY

Enrollment: 678. **Student Body:** 47% female, 53% male, 31% out-of-state, 3% international (12 countries represented). Asian 2%, African American 6%, Caucasian 73%, Hispanic 8%, Native American 2%, Pacific Islander 0%, Two or more races 0%, Race unknown 6%.

Retention and Graduation: 66% freshmen return for sophomore year. 31% freshmen graduate within 4 years. 39% freshmen graduate within 6 years. 26% grads go on to further study within 1 year. **Faculty:** Student/faculty ratio 12:1. 46 full-time faculty, 98% hold PhDs, 15% are are members of minority groups, 30% are women. 0% of classes are taught by teaching assistants.

ACADEMICS

Degrees: bachelor's. **Classes:** Most classes have 10-19 students. Most lab/discussion sessions have fewer than 10 students. **Most popular majors:** Biology/Biological Sciences; Psychology; English Language and Literature. **Special Study Options:** Accelerated program, cross-registration, double major, dual enrollment, independent study, internships, liberal arts/career combination, student-designed major, study abroad, teacher certification program. **Combined degree programs:** BA/MEng, BS/BEng (with U. MO. Rolla, University of Arkansas,University of Minnesota). **Disability Services:** Special programs offered to physically disabled students, including tape recorders. **Career Services:** Alumni network, Alumni services, Career/job search classes, Career assessment, Internships, Regional alumni.

FACILITIES

Housing: Coed dorms, special housing for disabled students, men's dorms, women's dorms, apartments for single students, Limited College-owned off campus housing. 80% of campus accessible to physically diasbled. **Special Academic Facilities/Equipment:** Ozark Regional Studies Center **Computers:** 100% of classrooms, 100% of dorms, 100% of libraries, 100% of dining areas, 100% of student union, 100% of common outdoor areas have wireless network access. Students can register for classes online. Administrative functions (other than registration) can be performed online.

CAMPUS LIFE

Environment: Village. **Activities:** Choral groups, concert band, drama/theater, literary magazine, music ensembles, student government, student newspaper, yearbook, Campus Ministries, Model UN. 44 registered organizations, 9 honor societies, 7 religious organizations. 3 fraternities, 2 sororities. **Athletics (Intercollegiate):** *Men:* baseball, basketball, cheerleading, cross-country, golf, soccer. *Women:* basketball, cheerleading, cross-country, golf, soccer, softball, volleyball. **On-Campus Highlights:** Derby Center for Science and Mathematics, Becknell Gymnasium, Holloway Theater, Edwards Commons / Bookstore, Mabee Simpson Library.

ADMISSIONS

Freshman Academic Profile: Average high school GPA 3.6. **Reported SAT (pre-2016 redesign) scores:** SAT Math middle 50% range 490-580. SAT Critical Reading middle 50% range 455-540. SAT Writing middle 50% range 445-530. **Concordant SAT scores:** SAT EBRW middle 50% 500–590. SAT Math middle 50% range 520–600. ACT middle 50% range 22-26. Minimum internet-based TOEFL 79. Minimum paper TOEFL 550. **Basis for Candidate Selection:** *Very important factors considered include:* academic GPA, standardized test scores. *Other factors considered include:* class rank. **Freshman Admission Requirements:** High school diploma is required and GED is accepted. *Academic units required:* 4 English, 3 math, 3 science, 2 science labs, 2 foreign language, 1 social studies, 2 history, 1 academic elective. *Academic units recommended:* 4 English, 4 math, 4 science, 2 science labs, 2 foreign language, 1 social studies, 2 history, 1 academic elective. **Freshman Admission Statistics:** 1,776 applied, 59.35% admitted, 19% enrolled. **Transfer Admission Requirements:** college transcript(s), statement of good standing from prior institution(s). Minimum college GPA of 2.75 required. Lowest grade transferable C. **General Admission Information:** Application fee $25. Nonfall registration accepted. Admission may be deferred for a maximum of 1 Fall term.

COSTS AND FINANCIAL AID

Annual tuition $26,050. Room and board $8,440. Required fees $240. Average book expense $1,000. **Required Forms and Deadlines:** FAFSA, State aid form. **Notification of Awards:** Applicants will be notified of awards on a rolling basis beginning 3/1. **Types of Aid:** *Need-based scholarships/grants:* Federal Pell, FSEOG, State scholarships/grants, Private scholarships, College/university scholarship or grant aid from institutional funds. *Loans:* Direct Subsidized Stafford Loans, Direct Unsubsidized Stafford Loans, Direct PLUS loans, Federal Perkins Loans. *Student Employment:* Federal Work-Study Program available. Institutional employment available. **Financial Aid Statistics:** 100% needy freshmen, 100% needy undergrads receive need-based scholarship or grant aid. 22% freshmen, 20% undergrads receive non-need-based scholarship or grant aid. 70% freshmen, 73% undergrads receive need-based self-help aid. 11% freshmen, 15% undergrads receive athletic scholarships. 100% freshmen, 99% undergrads receive any aid. 72% undergrads borrow to pay for school. Average cumulative indebtedness $1,764,757. **Criteria for awarding aid:**

Non-need-based: Academics, Alumni affiliation, Art, Athletics, Music/drama, Religious affiliation, State/district residency.

MACALESTER COLLEGE

1600 Grand Avenue, St. Paul, MN 55105
Phone: 651-696-6357 • **Financial Aid Phone:** 651-696-6214
E-mail: admissions@macalester.edu • **CEEB Code:** 6390
Fax: 651-696-6724 • **Website:** www.macalester.edu • **ACT Code:** 2122

This private school, affiliated with the Presbyterian Church, was founded in 1874. It has a 53-acre campus.

RATINGS

Admissions Selectivity Rating: 94   **Fire Safety Rating:** 98   **Green Rating:** 93

STUDENTS AND FACULTY

Enrollment: 2,122. **Student Body:** 60% female, 40% male, 83% out-of-state, 14% international (91 countries represented). Asian 7%, African American 3%, Caucasian 64%, Hispanic 6%, Native American <1%, Pacific Islander <1%, Two or more races 5%, Race unknown <1%.

Retention and Graduation: 93% freshmen return for sophomore year. 84% freshmen graduate within 4 years. 88% freshmen graduate within 6 years. 12% grads go on to further study within 1 year. 9% grads pursue arts and sciences degrees. 1% grads pursue law degrees. 1% grads pursue medical degrees. **Faculty:** Student/faculty ratio 10:1. 182 full-time faculty, 93% hold PhDs, 23% are are members of minority groups, 54% are women. 0% of classes are taught by teaching assistants.

ACADEMICS

Degrees: bachelor's. **Classes:** Most classes have 10-19 students. Most lab/discussion sessions have 10-19 students. **Most popular majors:** Mathematics; Biology/Biological Sciences; Political Science and Government. **Special Study Options:** cross-registration, double major, honors program, independent study, internships, student-designed major, study abroad, Combined bachelors/graduate programs: -BA/Master's in Architecture with Washington University, St. Louis, Missouri -BA/BS in Engineering with Washington University, St. Louis or the University of Minnesota. Combined degree programs: 3/3 BA/MA w/ Architecture Washington U. **Disability Services:** Special programs offered to physically disabled students, including note-taking services, reader services, tape recorders, tutors. **Career Services:** Alumni network, Alumni services, Career assessment, Internships, Regional alumni. Macalester's location in a thriving metropolitan area provides valuable opportunities for learning through first-hand experience. A broad range of programs help students learn through internships, summer fellowships, classes that include student-led data-driven studies to assist a wide variety of organizations as they plan for the future, off-campus work in non-profit settings or corporations, and countless volunteer service projects. Students gain important skills and experience, and they benefit from learning in an environment where civic engagement is a vital component of a high quality liberal arts education.

FACILITIES

Housing: Coed dorms, cooperative housing, apartments for single students, Theme Housing, Language Houses, Kosher Residence, EcoHouse. 90% of campus accessible to physically diasbled. **Special Academic Facilities/Equipment:** Humanities learning center, econometrics lab, cartography lab, 250-acre nature preserve, observatory and planetarium, two electron microscopes, nuclear magnetic resonance spectrometer, laser spectroscopy lab, X-ray diffractometer, Center, Center for Scholarship and Teaching, Ethnographic lab, GIS lab, State-of-the-Art science labs. **Computers:** 100% of classrooms, 98% of dorms, 100% of libraries, 100% of dining areas, 100% of student union, 90% of common outdoor areas have wireless network access. Students can register for classes online. Administrative functions (other than registration) can be performed online.

CAMPUS LIFE

Environment: Metropolis. **Activities:** Choral groups, concert band, dance, drama/theater, jazz band, literary magazine, music ensembles, radio station, student government, student newspaper, symphony orchestra, Campus Ministries, Student Organization, Model UN. 80 registered organizations, 15 honor societies, 10 religious organizations. **Athletics (Intercollegiate):** *Men:* baseball, basketball, cross-country, diving, football, golf, soccer, swimming, tennis, track/field (outdoor), track/field (indoor). *Women:* basketball, cross-country, diving, golf, soccer, softball, swimming, tennis, track/field (outdoor), track/field (indoor), volleyball, water polo. **On-Campus Highlights:** Second Floor Campus Center, Bateman Plaza (our front patio), The Quad (our front yard), Shaw Field, Smail Gallery in the Science Center. **Environmental Initiatives:** Developed a comprehensive sustainability plan.

ADMISSIONS
Freshman Academic Profile: 69% in top 10% of high school class, 94% in top 25% of high school class, 99% in top 50% of high school class. 59% from public high schools. **Reported SAT (pre-2016 redesign) scores:** SAT Math middle 50% range 630-750. SAT Critical Reading middle 50% range 630-740. SAT Writing middle 50% range 650-740. **Concordant SAT scores:** SAT EBRW middle 50% 690-760. SAT Math middle 50% range 650-770. ACT middle 50% range 29-33. Minimum internet-based TOEFL 100. Minimum paper TOEFL 600. **Basis for Candidate Selection:** *Very important factors considered include:* rigor of secondary school record, academic GPA. *Important factors considered include:* standardized test scores, application essay, recommendation(s), extracurricular activities, character/personal qualities. *Other factors considered include:* class rank, interview, talent/ability, first generation, alumni/ae relation, racial/ethnic status, volunteer work, work experience. **Freshman Admission Requirements:** High school diploma or equivalent is not required. *Academic units recommended:* 4 English, 3 math, 3 science, 3 science labs, 3 foreign language, 3 social studies. **Freshman Admission Statistics:** 5,946 applied, 37.10% admitted, 23% enrolled. **Transfer Admission Requirements:** High school transcript, college transcript(s), essay or personal statement, standardized test scores, statement of good standing from prior institution(s). Lowest grade transferable C-. **General Admission Information:** Application fee $40. Regular application deadline 1/15. Regular notification 3/30. Nonfall registration not accepted. Admission may be deferred for a maximum of 1 year.

COSTS AND FINANCIAL AID
Annual tuition $52,234. Room and board $11,672. Required fees $230. Average book expense $1,145. **Required Forms and Deadlines:** FAFSA, CSS/Financial Aid PROFILE, Noncustodial PROFILE. **Notification of Awards:** Applicants will be notified of awards on or about 4/1. **Types of Aid:** *Need-based scholarships/grants:* Federal Pell, FSEOG, State scholarships/grants, Private scholarships, College/university scholarship or grant aid from institutional funds. *Loans:* Direct Subsidized Stafford Loans, Direct Unsubsidized Stafford Loans, Direct PLUS loans, State Loans, College/university loans from institutional funds. *Student Employment:* Federal Work-Study Program available. Institutional employment available. **Financial Aid Statistics:** 99% needy freshmen, 99% needy undergrads receive need-based scholarship or grant aid. 6% freshmen, 4% undergrads receive non-need-based scholarship or grant aid. 91% freshmen, 93% undergrads receive need-based self-help aid. 0% freshmen, 0% undergrads receive athletic scholarships. 79% freshmen, 79% undergrads receive any aid. 63% undergrads borrow to pay for school. Average cumulative indebtedness $23,875. **Criteria for awarding aid:** *Non-need-based:* Academics, Minority status.

MACMURRAY COLLEGE

447 East College, Jacksonville, IL 62650
Phone: 217-479-7056 • **Financial Aid Phone:** 217-479-7041
E-mail: admissions@mac.edu • **CEEB Code:** 1435
Fax: 217-291-0702 • **Website:** www.mac.edu • **ACT Code:** 1068

This private school, affiliated with the Methodist Church, was founded in 1846. It has a 60-acre campus.

RATINGS
Admissions Selectivity Rating: 77 **Fire Safety Rating:** 72 **Green Rating:** 60* •

STUDENTS AND FACULTY
Enrollment: 581. **Student Body:** 66% female, 34% male, 11% out-of-state, <1% international (2 countries represented). Asian 1%, African American 13%, Caucasian 73%, Hispanic 3%, Native American 0%, Pacific Islander 0%, Two or more races 0%, Race unknown 10%.
Retention and Graduation: 72% freshmen return for sophomore year. 26% freshmen graduate within 4 years. 37% freshmen graduate within 6 years. 25% grads go on to further study within 1 year. 9% grads pursue arts and sciences degrees. 1% grads pursue law degrees. 12% grads pursue business degrees. 1% grads pursue medical degrees. **Faculty:** Student/faculty ratio 14:1. 35 full-time faculty, 63% hold PhDs, 3% are are members of minority groups, 74% are women. 0% of classes are taught by teaching assistants.

ACADEMICS
Degrees: associate, bachelor's. **Classes:** Most classes have 10-19 students. Most lab/discussion sessions have 10-19 students. **Most popular majors:**

Special Education and Teaching. **Special Study Options:** cooperative education program, double major, dual enrollment, independent study, internships, liberal arts/career combination, student-designed major, study abroad, teacher certification program. Combined degree programs: BA/MEng, 3-2 Occupational Therapy prog. w/Washington U. **Disability Services:** Special programs offered to physically disabled students, including note-taking services, reader services, tape recorders, tutors. **Career Services:** Alumni network, Alumni services, Career/job search classes, Career assessment, Internships, Regional alumni.

FACILITIES
Housing: Coed dorms, special housing for disabled students, women's dorms. 50% of campus accessible to physically diasbled. Art gallery, language lab, music hall, nursing labs.

CAMPUS LIFE
Environment: Village. **Activities:** Choral groups, dance, drama/theater, literary magazine, student government, yearbook, Campus Ministries. 37 registered organizations, 2 honor societies, 2 religious organizations. 2 fraternities, 1 sorority. **Athletics (Intercollegiate):** *Men:* baseball, basketball, football, golf, soccer, wrestling. *Women:* basketball, golf, soccer, softball, volleyball. **On-Campus Highlights:** Gamble Campus, Education Complex, Jane Hall, Putnam Center for the Arts, McClelland Dining Hall.

ADMISSIONS
Freshman Academic Profile: Average high school GPA 2.8. 4% in top 10% of high school class, 28% in top 25% of high school class, 55% in top 50% of high school class. 75% from public high schools. **Reported SAT (pre-2016 redesign) scores:** SAT Math middle 50% range 430-500. SAT Critical Reading middle 50% range 370-470. SAT Writing middle 50% range 340-430. **Concordant SAT scores:** SAT EBRW middle 50% 400-500. SAT Math middle 50% range 470-530. ACT middle 50% range 17-23. Minimum paper TOEFL 550. **Basis for Candidate Selection:** *Very important factors considered include:* rigor of secondary school record, academic GPA, standardized test scores. *Important factors considered include:* class rank, extracurricular activities, character/personal qualities. *Other factors considered include:* application essay, recommendation(s), interview, volunteer work, work experience. **Freshman Admission Requirements:** High school diploma is required and GED is accepted. *Academic units recommended:* 4 English, 3 math, 3 science, 2 science labs, 2 foreign language, 2 social studies, 3 history. **Freshman Admission Statistics:** 1,004 applied, 56.08% admitted, 31% enrolled. **Transfer Admission Requirements:** college transcript(s), Minimum college GPA of 2.0 required. Lowest grade transferable C. **General Admission Information:** Application fee $25. Priority deadline 5/1. Nonfall registration accepted. Admission may be deferred.

COSTS AND FINANCIAL AID
Annual tuition $15,500. Room and board $5,998. Required fees $250. Average book expense $775. **Required Forms and Deadlines:** FAFSA. **Notification of Awards:** Applicants will be notified of awards on a rolling basis beginning 2/1. **Types of Aid:** *Need-based scholarships/grants:* Federal Pell, FSEOG, State scholarships/grants, Private scholarships, College/university scholarship or grant aid from institutional funds, Federal Nursing Scholarships. *Loans:* Federal Perkins Loans. *Student Employment:* Federal Work-Study Program available. Institutional employment available. **Financial Aid Statistics:** 100% needy freshmen, 100% needy undergrads receive need-based scholarship or grant aid. 9% freshmen, 7% undergrads receive non-need-based scholarship or grant aid. 79% freshmen, 86% undergrads receive need-based self-help aid. 0% freshmen, 0% undergrads receive athletic scholarships. 95% freshmen, 97% undergrads receive any aid. **Criteria for awarding aid:** *Need-based:* Academics, Alumni affiliation, Art, Music/drama. *Non-need-based:* Academics, Alumni affiliation, Art, Leadership, Music/drama, Religious affiliation.

MAHARISHI UNIVERSITY OF MANAGEMENT

1000 North Fourth Street, Fairfield, IA 52557
Phone: 641-472-1110 • **Financial Aid Phone:** 641-472-1156
E-mail: admissions@mum.edu
Fax: 641-472-1179 • **Website:** www.mum.edu • **ACT Code:** 1317

This private school was founded in 1971. It has a 242-acre campus.

RATINGS
Admissions Selectivity Rating: 70 **Fire Safety Rating:** 60* **Green Rating:** 92

STUDENTS AND FACULTY
Enrollment: 199. **Student Body:** 43% female, 57% male, 65% out-of-state, 17% international. Asian 4%, African American 2%, Caucasian 71%, Hispanic 7%, Native American 0%, Pacific Islander 0%, Two or more races 0%, Race unknown 0%.

Retention and Graduation: 84% grads go on to further study within 1 year. **Faculty:** Student/faculty ratio 16:1. 52 full-time faculty, 98% hold PhDs, 13% are are members of minority groups, 21% are women. 0% of classes are taught by teaching assistants.

ACADEMICS

Degrees: associate, bachelor's, certificate, doctoral, master's. **Most popular majors:** Fine/Studio Arts; Business/Commerce; Environmental Studies. **Special Study Options:** double major, independent study, internships, study abroad, teacher certification program, Rotating University: several one-month blocks out of each academic year, a course is offered abroad-e.g. students spend a month with professor studying Art in Italy, Literature in Switzerland, or Business in Japan.

FACILITIES

Housing: special housing for disabled students, men's dorms, women's dorms, apartments for married students, apartments for single students, Apartments for students with dependent children; "quiet" dorms. 80% of campus accessible to physically diasbled. **Special Academic Facilities/Equipment:** art gallery; scanning electron microscope; real-time cell-imaging computer system; DNA synthesizer; rock-climbing wall

CAMPUS LIFE

Environment: Village. **Activities:** Choral groups, dance, drama/theater, music ensembles, musical theater, radio station, student government, student newspaper, yearbook. 25 registered organizations, 3 honor societies, 1 religious organization. **Athletics (Intercollegiate):** *Men:* golf. *Women:* golf. **On-Campus Highlights:** Golden Domes, Vedic Architecture, 60,000 sq. ft. Recreation Center, Student Cafe, Vedic Organic Greenhouses. **Environmental Initiatives:** Four-year bachelors of Science degree offered in Sustainable Living.

ADMISSIONS

Freshman Academic Profile: Average high school GPA 3.6. 0% in top 10% of high school class, 0% in top 25% of high school class, 80% in top 50% of high school class. Minimum paper TOEFL 550. **Basis for Candidate Selection:** *Very important factors considered include:* interview, character/personal qualities. *Important factors considered include:* rigor of secondary school record, academic GPA, application essay, recommendation(s), extracurricular activities, talent/ability, level of applicant's interest. *Other factors considered include:* standardized test scores, alumni/ae relation, volunteer work, work experience. **Freshman Admission Requirements:** High school diploma is required and GED is accepted. *Academic units recommended:* 4 English, 3 math, 3 science, 2 foreign language, 3 social studies. **Freshman Admission Statistics:** 51 applied, 66.67% admitted. **Transfer Admission Requirements:** High school transcript, college transcript(s), essay or personal statement, interview, Minimum college GPA of 2.5 required. Lowest grade transferable 2. **General Admission Information:** Application fee $30. Nonfall registration accepted. Admission may be deferred for a maximum of one semester.

COSTS AND FINANCIAL AID

Annual tuition $24,000. Room and board $6,000. Required fees $430. Average book expense $800. **Required Forms and Deadlines:** FAFSA. **Notification of Awards:** Applicants will be notified of awards on a rolling basis beginning 3/1. **Types of Aid:** *Need-based scholarships/grants:* Federal Pell, FSEOG, State scholarships/grants, Private scholarships, College/university scholarship or grant aid from institutional funds. *Loans:* Federal Perkins Loans, College/university loans from institutional funds. *Student Employment:* Federal Work-Study Program available. **Financial Aid Statistics:** 100% needy freshmen, 100% needy undergrads receive need-based scholarship or grant aid. 7% undergrads receive non-need-based scholarship or grant aid. 100% freshmen, 100% undergrads receive need-based self-help aid. 0% freshmen, 0% undergrads receive athletic scholarships. 93% freshmen, 98% undergrads receive any aid. **Criteria for awarding aid:** *Need-based:* Academics, Minority status, Music/drama. *Non-need-based:* Academics, Alumni affiliation, Music/drama, State/district residency.

MALONE UNIVERSITY

2600 Cleveland Avenue NW, Canton, OH 44709
Phone: 330-471-8145 • **Financial Aid Phone:** 330-471-8161
E-mail: admissions@malone.edu • **CEEB Code:** 1439
Fax: 330-471-8149 • **Website:** www.malone.edu • **ACT Code:** 3289

This private school was founded in 1892. It has a 87-acre campus.

RATINGS

Admissions Selectivity Rating: 80   **Fire Safety Rating:** 86   **Green Rating:** 61

STUDENTS AND FACULTY

Enrollment: 1,496. **Student Body:** 58% female, 42% male, 14% out-of-state, 1% international (17 countries represented). Asian 1%, African American 8%, Caucasian 84%, Hispanic 2%, Native American <1%, Pacific Islander <1%, Two or more races 2%, Race unknown <1%.
Retention and Graduation: 70% freshmen return for sophomore year. 38% freshmen graduate within 4 years. 51% freshmen graduate within 6 years.
Faculty: Student/faculty ratio 12:1. 95 full-time faculty, 78% hold PhDs, 4% are are members of minority groups, 52% are women. 0% of classes are taught by teaching assistants.

ACADEMICS

Degrees: bachelor's, master's, post-master's certificate. **Classes:** Most classes have 10-19 students. Most lab/discussion sessions have 10-19 students. **Most popular majors:** Early Childhood Education and Teaching; Business/Commerce; Registered Nursing, Nursing Administration, Nursing Research and Clinical Nursing. **Special Study Options:** Accelerated program, cross-registration, distance learning, double major, dual enrollment, exchange student program (domestic), honors program, independent study, internships, student-designed major, study abroad, teacher certification program, weekend college, 2 degree-completion programs for adults; management, nursing. NOTE: Weekend college is only for degree-completion programs and graduate programs. NOTE: Cooperative education credits are available; but, not entire program. **Honors Programs:** The purpose of the Malone University Honors Program is to support the university's intellectually gifted and highly motivated students, to create a community of students and faculty engaged in serious, substantive, and sustained critical inquiry, and to underscore the university's commitment to academic excellence. The Honors Program fulfills this purpose through pursuit of the following goals: 1. Challenging students to fulfill their intellectual and personal potential through enriching and stimulating experiences in and out of the classroom. 2. Cultivating an esprit de corps, committed to an earnest, cooperative, free, and open pursuit of truth. 3. Developing students' understanding of the unity of knowledge and the interrelationship of the academic disciplines. 4. Providing students the occasion for mentoring relationships with faculty. 5. Preparing students for the pursuit of original and advanced research, scholarship, and performance. 6. Equipping students for outstanding leadership in service to God, their communities, and the world. Combined degree programs: 3-1 Medical Technology program. **Disability Services:** Special programs offered to physically disabled students, including note-taking services, reader services, tape recorders, tutors. **Career Services:** Alumni network, Alumni services, Career/job search classes, Career assessment, Internships, On-campus interviews. The highest number of graduates who are hired by the employer providing experiential learning is in Nursing.

FACILITIES

Housing: special housing for disabled students, men's dorms, women's dorms, Theme Housing. **Special Academic Facilities/Equipment:** Child development center. **Computers:** 100% of classrooms, 85% of dorms, 100% of libraries, 100% of dining areas, 100% of student union, 40% of common outdoor areas have wireless network access. Students can register for classes online. Administrative functions (other than registration) can be performed online.

CAMPUS LIFE

Environment: City. **Activities:** Choral groups, concert band, dance, drama/theater, jazz band, literary magazine, marching band, music ensembles, musical theater, radio station, student government, student newspaper, student-run film society, television station, yearbook, Campus Ministries, Student Organization. 53 registered organizations, 11 honor societies, 9 religious organizations. **Athletics (Intercollegiate):** *Men:* baseball, basketball, cheerleading, cross-country, diving, football, golf, soccer, swimming, tennis, track/field (outdoor), track/field (indoor). *Women:* basketball, cheerleading, cross-country, diving, golf, soccer, softball, swimming, tennis, track/field (outdoor), track/field (indoor), volleyball. **On-Campus Highlights:** Hoover Dining Commons—Brehme Centennial Center, Randall Campus Center, Wellness Center, Froggy's & Regula Cafe, Classsrooms, Randall Campus Center houses the Office of Student Development; a game room, among other features. The Wellness Center houses equipment and laboratories to support the programs of the majors in the Health and Human Performance Department. Also, its aerobic exercise and weight room are available for all Malone University, students, faculty, and staff. It was just opened in Fall 2004. **Environmental Initiatives:** Recycling.

ADMISSIONS

Freshman Academic Profile: Average high school GPA 3.3. 18% in top 10% of high school class, 44% in top 25% of high school class, 76% in top 50% of high school class. 80% from public high schools. **Reported SAT (pre-2016 redesign) scores:** SAT Math middle 50% range 472.5-570. SAT Critical Reading middle 50% range 430-570. **Concordant SAT scores:** SAT Math middle 50% range 510–590. ACT middle 50% range 20-25. Minimum internet-based TOEFL 79. Minimum paper TOEFL 550. **Basis for Candidate Selection:** *Very important factors considered include:* rigor of secondary school record, academic GPA, standardized test scores, character/personal qualities.

Important factors considered include: class rank, talent/ability, religious affiliation/commitment. *Other factors considered include:* application essay, recommendation(s), interview, extracurricular activities, alumni/ae relation, racial/ethnic status, volunteer work, level of applicant's interest. **Freshman Admission Requirements:** High school diploma is required and GED is accepted. *Academic units required:* 4 English, 3 math, 3 science, 1 science lab, 2 foreign language, 2 social studies, 1 history, 2 academic electives, 1 visual/performing arts. **Freshman Admission Statistics:** 1,327 applied, 71.74% admitted, 33% enrolled. **Transfer Admission Requirements:** High school transcript, college transcript(s), statement of good standing from prior institution(s). Minimum college GPA of 2.0 required. **General Admission Information:** Application fee $20. Nonfall registration accepted. Admission may be deferred for a maximum of 2 years.

COSTS AND FINANCIAL AID
Annual tuition $26,456. Room and board $9,266. Required fees $984. Average book expense $1,200. **Required Forms and Deadlines:** FAFSA. **Notification of Awards:** Applicants will be notified of awards on a rolling basis beginning 3/1. **Types of Aid:** *Need-based scholarships/grants:* Federal Pell, FSEOG, State scholarships/grants, Private scholarships, College/university scholarship or grant aid from institutional funds. *Loans:* Direct Subsidized Stafford Loans, Direct Unsubsidized Stafford Loans, Direct PLUS loans, Federal Perkins Loans, State Loans, College/university loans from institutional funds. *Student Employment:* Federal Work-Study Program available. Institutional employment available. **Financial Aid Statistics:** 100% needy freshmen, 98% needy undergrads receive need-based scholarship or grant aid. 13% freshmen, 13% undergrads receive non-need-based scholarship or grant aid. 82% freshmen, 81% undergrads receive need-based self-help aid. 12% freshmen, 10% undergrads receive athletic scholarships. 100% freshmen, 95% undergrads receive any aid. **Criteria for awarding aid:** *Need-based:* Academics, Athletics, Leadership, Music/drama, Religious affiliation. *Non-need-based:* Academics, Athletics, Leadership, Music/drama, Religious affiliation.

MANCHESTER UNIVERSITY

604 E. College Avenue, N. Manchester, IN 46962
Phone: 260-982-5055 • **Financial Aid Phone:** 260-982-5066
E-mail: admitinfo@manchester.edu • **CEEB Code:** 1440
Fax: 260-982-5239 • **Website:** www.manchester.edu • **ACT Code:** 1222

This private school was founded in 1889. It has a 124-acre campus.

RATINGS
Admissions Selectivity Rating: 78   **Fire Safety Rating:** 84   **Green Rating:** 60*

STUDENTS AND FACULTY
Enrollment: 1,254. **Student Body:** 52% female, 48% male, 12% out-of-state, 4% international (19 countries represented). Asian 2%, African American 7%, Caucasian 77%, Hispanic 6%, Native American <1%, Pacific Islander 0%, Two or more races 4%, Race unknown 1%.
Retention and Graduation: 69% freshmen return for sophomore year. 14% grads go on to further study within 1 year. 16% grads pursue arts and sciences degrees. 7% grads pursue law degrees. 11% grads pursue business degrees. 11% grads pursue medical degrees. **Faculty:** Student/faculty ratio 14:1. 82 full-time faculty, 87% hold PhDs, 10% are are members of minority groups, 0% are women. 0% of classes are taught by teaching assistants.

ACADEMICS
Degrees: associate, bachelor's, doctoral/professional, master's. **Classes:** Most classes have 20-29 students. **Most popular majors:** Accounting and Business/Management; Education; Health Services/Allied Health/Health Sciences. **Special Study Options:** Accelerated program, cross-registration, double major, dual enrollment, exchange student program (domestic), honors program, independent study, internships, liberal arts/career combination, student-designed major, study abroad, teacher certification program. **Honors Programs:** An Honors Program for top students. **Disability Services:** Special programs offered to physically disabled students, including reader services, tape recorders, tutors. **Career Services:** Alumni network, Alumni services, Career/job search classes, Career assessment, Internships, Regional alumni. College-paid internships in regional businesses.

FACILITIES
Housing: Coed dorms, special housing for disabled students, apartments for married students, apartments for single students. **Special Academic Facilities/Equipment:** Language lab, observatory, environmental center and labs. **Computers:** 50% of classrooms, 100% of libraries, 100% of dining areas, 100% of student union, 5% of common outdoor areas have wireless network access. Students can register for classes online. Administrative functions (other than registration) can be performed online.

CAMPUS LIFE
Environment: Rural. **Activities:** Choral groups, concert band, dance, drama/theater, jazz band, literary magazine, music ensembles, musical theater, opera, pep band, radio station, student government, student newspaper, symphony orchestra, yearbook, Campus Ministries, Student Organization, Model UN. 47 registered organizations, 3 honor societies, 5 religious organizations. **Athletics (Intercollegiate):** *Men:* baseball, basketball, cheerleading, cross-country, football, golf, soccer, tennis, track/field (outdoor), wrestling. *Women:* basketball, cheerleading, cross-country, golf, soccer, softball, tennis, track/field (outdoor), volleyball. **On-Campus Highlights:** Athletic Facilities, Residence Halls, College Union, Petersime Chapel, Science Center, The campus is located on a well maintained wooded 125 acres. **Environmental Initiatives:** Over 25 years of active recyling on campus

ADMISSIONS
Freshman Academic Profile: Average high school GPA 3.3. 13% in top 10% of high school class, 34% in top 25% of high school class, 75% in top 50% of high school class. **Reported SAT (pre-2016 redesign) scores:** SAT Math middle 50% range 435-550. SAT Critical Reading middle 50% range 430-540. SAT Writing middle 50% range 420-510. **Concordant SAT scores:** SAT EBRW middle 50% 480-580. SAT Math middle 50% range 480-570. ACT middle 50% range 18-30. Minimum internet-based TOEFL 79. Minimum paper TOEFL 550. **Basis for Candidate Selection:** *Very important factors considered include:* rigor of secondary school record, class rank, academic GPA, standardized test scores, application essay, recommendation(s). *Important factors considered include:* extracurricular activities, talent/ability, character/personal qualities. *Other factors considered include:* interview, alumni/ae relation, volunteer work, work experience. **Freshman Admission Requirements:** High school diploma is required and GED is accepted. *Academic units required:* 4 English, 2 math, 2 science, 2 science labs, 1 social studies, 1 history, 2 academic electives. *Academic units recommended:* 4 English, 3 math, 3 science, 2 science labs, 2 foreign language, 2 social studies, 2 history, 2 academic electives, 1 computer science, 1 visual/performing arts. **Freshman Admission Statistics:** 2,431 applied, 70.55% admitted, 23% enrolled. **Transfer Admission Requirements:** High school transcript, college transcript(s), statement of good standing from prior institution(s). Minimum college GPA of 2.0 required. **General Admission Information:** Application fee $25. Priority deadline 12/31. Nonfall registration accepted. Admission may be deferred for a maximum of 1 year.

COSTS AND FINANCIAL AID
Annual tuition $30,450. Room and board $9,880. Required fees $1,210. Average book expense $1,000. **Required Forms and Deadlines:** FAFSA. **Notification of Awards:** Applicants will be notified of awards on a rolling basis beginning 3/20. **Types of Aid:** *Need-based scholarships/grants:* Federal Pell, FSEOG, State scholarships/grants, Private scholarships, College/university scholarship or grant aid from institutional funds. *Loans:* Direct Subsidized Stafford Loans, Direct Unsubsidized Stafford Loans, Direct PLUS loans, Federal Perkins Loans. *Student Employment:* Federal Work-Study Program available. Institutional employment available. **Financial Aid Statistics:** 100% needy freshmen, 99% needy undergrads receive need-based scholarship or grant aid. 11% freshmen, 12% undergrads receive non-need-based scholarship or grant aid. 89% freshmen, 88% undergrads receive need-based self-help aid. 0% freshmen, 0% undergrads receive athletic scholarships. 100% freshmen, 99% undergrads receive any aid. 87% undergrads borrow to pay for school. Average cumulative indebtedness $33,011. **Criteria for awarding aid:** *Non-need-based:* Academics, Alumni affiliation, Leadership, Minority status, Music/drama, Religious affiliation.

MANHATTAN COLLEGE

Manhattan College Parkway, Riverdale, NY 10471
Phone: 718-862-7200 • **Financial Aid Phone:** 718-862-7100
E-mail: admit@manhattan.edu • **CEEB Code:** 2395
Fax: 718-862-8019 • **Website:** www.manhattan.edu

This private school, affiliated with the Roman Catholic Church, was founded in 1853. It has a 22-acre campus.

RATINGS
Admissions Selectivity Rating: 84   **Fire Safety Rating:** 83   **Green Rating:** 69

STUDENTS AND FACULTY

Enrollment: 3,637. **Student Body:** 45% female, 55% male, 31% out-of-state, 3% international (46 countries represented). Asian 5%, African American 5%, Caucasian 57%, Hispanic 21%, Native American <1%, Pacific Islander <1%, Two or more races 2%, Race unknown 7%.

Retention and Graduation: 89% freshmen return for sophomore year. 57% freshmen graduate within 4 years. 71% freshmen graduate within 6 years. 28% grads go on to further study within 1 year. 1% grads pursue law degrees. 2% grads pursue business degrees. 1% grads pursue medical degrees. **Faculty:** Student/faculty ratio 13:1. 240 full-time faculty, 97% hold PhDs, 16% are are members of minority groups, 45% are women. 0% of classes are taught by teaching assistants.

ACADEMICS

Degrees: bachelor's, master's. **Classes:** Most classes have 20-29 students. Most lab/discussion sessions have 10-19 students. **Most popular majors:** Special Education and Teaching; Civil Engineering; Marketing/Marketing Management. **Special Study Options:** Accelerated program, cooperative education program, cross-registration, distance learning, double major, English as a Second Language (ESL), exchange student program (domestic), honors program, independent study, internships, liberal arts/career combination, student-designed major, study abroad, teacher certification program. **Honors Programs:** Honors Enrichment Program Combined degree programs: BA/MA, BA/MEng, Education. **Disability Services:** Special programs offered to physically disabled students, including note-taking services, reader services, tape recorders, tutors. **Career Services:** Alumni network, Alumni services, Career/job search classes, Career assessment, Internships. Manhattan College's Mentor program assists students in making career-related decisions by pairing them with professionals, generally alumni, who work in the students' intended careers. Having a Mentor provides them exposure to their intended industry/career at an early stage in their education. Approximately 200 college-wide students'and Mentors are matched up annually.

FACILITIES

Housing: Coed dorms. 100% of campus accessible to physically diasbled. **Special Academic Facilities/Equipment:** Research and learning center, 24-hour Internet cafe. **Computers:** 100% of classrooms, 50% of dorms, 100% of libraries, 100% of dining areas, 100% of student union, 100% of common outdoor areas have wireless network access. Students can register for classes online. Administrative functions (other than registration) can be performed online.

CAMPUS LIFE

Environment: Metropolis. **Activities:** Choral groups, concert band, dance, drama/theater, jazz band, literary magazine, music ensembles, musical theater, radio station, student government, student newspaper, symphony orchestra, television station, yearbook, Campus Ministries, Student Organization, Model UN. 64 registered organizations, 30 honor societies, 2 religious organizations. 2 fraternities, 2 sororities. **Athletics (Intercollegiate):** *Men:* baseball, basketball, cross-country, golf, lacrosse, soccer, tennis, track/field (outdoor), track/field (indoor). *Women:* basketball, cross-country, lacrosse, soccer, softball, swimming, tennis, track/field (outdoor), track/field (indoor), volleyball. **On-Campus Highlights:** Quadrangle, O'Malley Library, Internet Cafe, Galligan Exercise Center, Thomas Hall.

ADMISSIONS

Freshman Academic Profile: Average high school GPA 89.6. 25% in top 10% of high school class, 60% in top 25% of high school class, 86% in top 50% of high school class. 57% from public high schools. **Reported SAT (pre-2016 redesign) scores:** SAT Math middle 50% range 510-620. SAT Critical Reading middle 50% range 490-590. SAT Writing middle 50% range 490-590. **Concordant SAT scores:** SAT EBRW middle 50% 550–650. SAT Math middle 50% range 540–640. ACT middle 50% range 23-28. Minimum internet-based TOEFL 80. Minimum paper TOEFL 550. **Basis for Candidate Selection:** *Very important factors considered include:* rigor of secondary school record, class rank, academic GPA, standardized test scores. *Important factors considered include:* application essay, recommendation(s). *Other factors considered include:* interview, extracurricular activities, talent/ability, character/personal qualities, first generation, alumni/ae relation, geographical residence, volunteer work, work experience, level of applicant's interest. **Freshman Admission Requirements:** High school diploma is required and GED is accepted. *Academic units required:* 4 English, 3 math, 2 science, 2 science labs, 2 foreign language, 3 social studies, 2 academic electives. *Academic units recommended:* 4 English, 4 math, 4 science, 4 science labs, 3 foreign language, 4 social studies. **Freshman Admission Statistics:** 8,145 applied, 71.37% admitted, 14% enrolled. **Transfer Admission Requirements:** High school transcript, college transcript(s), standardized test scores, statement of good standing from prior institution(s). Minimum college GPA of 2.5 required. Lowest grade transferable C. **General Admission Information:** Application fee $60. Priority deadline 3/1. Nonfall registration accepted. Admission may be deferred for a maximum of 1 year.

COSTS AND FINANCIAL AID

Required Forms and Deadlines: FAFSA. **Notification of Awards:** Applicants will be notified of awards on a rolling basis beginning 2/15. **Types of Aid:** *Need-based scholarships/grants:* Federal Pell, FSEOG, State scholarships/grants, Private scholarships, College/university scholarship or grant aid from institutional funds. *Loans:* Direct Subsidized Stafford Loans, Direct Unsubsidized Stafford Loans, Direct PLUS loans, Federal Perkins Loans. *Student Employment:* Federal Work-Study Program available. Institutional employment available. **Financial Aid Statistics:** 80% needy undergrads receive need-based scholarship or grant aid. 14% freshmen, 11% undergrads receive non-need-based scholarship or grant aid. 56% freshmen, 58% undergrads receive need-based self-help aid. 3% freshmen, 3% undergrads receive athletic scholarships. 88% freshmen, 86% undergrads receive any aid. 97% undergrads borrow to pay for school. Average cumulative indebtedness $46,498. **Criteria for awarding aid:** *Need-based:* Academics, Music/drama. *Non-need-based:* Academics, Athletics, State/district residency.

See page 994.

MANHATTANVILLE COLLEGE

2900 Purchase Street, Purchase, NY 10577
Phone: 914-323-5464 • **Financial Aid Phone:** 914-323-5357
E-mail: admissions@mville.edu • **CEEB Code:** 2397
Fax: 914-694-1732 • **Website:** www.mville.edu • **ACT Code:** 2800

This private school was founded in 1841. It has a 100-acre campus.

RATINGS

Admissions Selectivity Rating: 77   **Fire Safety Rating:** 98   **Green Rating:** 60*

STUDENTS AND FACULTY

Enrollment: 1,735. **Student Body:** 64% female, 36% male, 29% out-of-state, 8% international (47 countries represented). Asian 1%, African American 8%, Caucasian 44%, Hispanic 18%, Native American <1%, Pacific Islander <1%, Two or more races 2%, Race unknown 17%.

Retention and Graduation: 76% freshmen return for sophomore year. 42% freshmen graduate within 4 years. 48 24% grads go on to further study within 1 year. 6% grads pursue arts and sciences degrees. 1% grads pursue law degrees. 1% grads pursue business degrees. 2% grads pursue medical degrees. **Faculty:** Student/faculty ratio 13:1. 113 full-time faculty, 82% hold PhDs, 15% are are members of minority groups, 52% are women. 0% of classes are taught by teaching assistants.

ACADEMICS

Degrees: bachelor's, doctoral, master's, post-master's certificate. **Classes:** Most classes have 10-19 students. **Most popular majors:** Business/Commerce; Psychology; Communication. **Special Study Options:** Accelerated program, cross-registration, double major, dual enrollment, English as a Second Language (ESL), exchange student program (domestic), honors program, independent study, internships, student-designed major, study abroad, teacher certification program, weekend college. **Honors Programs:** The Castle Scholars Program offers students of exceptional ability a broader and more intensive program of study than the usual college curriculum. It provides motivated students in any major field with challenging, cross-disciplinary courses that encourage their academic and personal growth. Participation in the Castle Scholars Program encourages intellectual exchange among students and faculty and fosters independent initiative in academic and creative realms. Advised and mentored by the Program Director, Castle Scholars are well prepared for success in graduate and professional schools, as well as in the professional world. Castle Scholars build relationships with each other and with the college's faculty in specially-designed Honors Seminars and other unique academic opportunities, as well as in a host of social events throughout the year. Through their studies, research, and service, the Scholars contribute to the intellectual and social life of the college. Studies are augmented by participation in the wider New York City community. The Castle Scholars Program complements a student's chosen major and minor and is distinct from honors options within the major. Castle Scholars are recognized annually at college-wide awards receptions, and honors courses are noted on student academic transcripts. Successful completion of the program will be noted on the final transcript as well as on printed graduation materials. Combined degree programs: BA/MA, Dual BS/MS Business Degrees, BA/MFA in Creative Writing, Dual BA/MAT education degrees. **Disability Services:** Special programs offered to physically disabled students, including note-taking services, reader services, tape recorders, tutors. **Career Services:** Alumni network, Alumni services, Career/job search classes, Career assessment, Internships, Regional alumni. The Center for Career Development engages students at the beginning of their first year to prepare them for the competitive work environment. One hundred percent of first year students attend a Career Development workshop. Further, Manhattanville's proximity to New York City and to the Purchase, NY headquarters of prestigious global companies such as MasterCard and Morgan Stanley allows students to choose from a variety of exceptional internship opportunities. Students are encouraged to complete at least one internship to gain experiential learning in their area of interest, create networking contacts for future job leads, and develop skills, confidence and professionalism in the workplace. Examples of past internship placements for Manhattanville include Morgan Stanley Wealth Management, MTV, NBC Universal, Central Park Zoo, New York Presbyterian Hospital, Clinton Foundation, PepsiCo, EMI Music, Pfizer, PGA Tour, Greenwich Historical Society, Rachel Maddow Show, Legal Services of the Hudson Valley, SONY, Make A Wish Foundation, Standard & Poor's, MasterCard Worldwide, Marvel Entertainment, Westchester County Human Rights Commission, Merrill Lynch, Westchester Magazine, Metropolitan Museum of Art.

FACILITIES

Housing: Coed dorms. 90% of campus accessible to physically diasbled. **Special Academic Facilities/Equipment:** Art gallery, art and music studios, Environmental Park, English language institute, two electron microscopes, library. **Computers:** Students can register for classes online. Administrative functions (other than registration) can be performed online.

CAMPUS LIFE

Environment: Town. **Activities:** Choral groups, concert band, dance, drama/theater, jazz band, literary magazine, music ensembles, musical theater, opera, radio station, student government, student newspaper, student-run film society, symphony orchestra, television station, yearbook, Campus Ministries, Student Organization. 46 registered organizations, 2 honor societies, 5 religious organizations. **Athletics (Intercollegiate): Men:** baseball, basketball, golf, ice hockey, lacrosse, soccer, tennis. **Women:** basketball, cheerleading, field hockey, ice hockey, lacrosse, soccer, softball, tennis, volleyball. **On-Campus Highlights:** The Castle, Library Cafe, Richard Berman Student Center, Kennedy Gymnasium, Quad, New Student Center. **Environmental Initiatives:** Environmental Classroom Building's Platinum Rating (LEED)

ADMISSIONS

Freshman Academic Profile: Average high school GPA 3.2. 12% in top 10% of high school class, 32% in top 25% of high school class, 68% in top 50% of high school class. **Reported SAT (pre-2016 redesign) scores:** SAT Math middle 50% range 480-570. SAT Critical Reading middle 50% range 470-580. SAT Writing middle 50% range 470-580. **Concordant SAT scores:** SAT EBRW middle 50% 530–640. SAT Math middle 50% range 510–590. ACT middle 50% range 21-27. Minimum internet-based TOEFL 80. Minimum paper TOEFL 550. **Basis for Candidate Selection:** *Very important factors considered include:* academic GPA, application essay, extracurricular activities, talent/ability, character/personal qualities, alumni/ae relation. *Important factors considered include:* rigor of secondary school record, standardized test scores, recommendation(s), interview, first generation, geographical residence, volunteer work, level of applicant's interest. *Other factors considered include:* class rank, state residency, work experience. **Freshman Admission Requirements:** High school diploma is required and GED is accepted. *Academic units required:* 4 English, 3 math, 2 science, 2 social studies, 5 academic electives. **Freshman Admission Statistics:** 4,132 applied, 77.40% admitted, 15% enrolled. **Transfer Admission Requirements:** college transcript(s), statement of good standing from prior institution(s). Minimum college GPA of 2.5 required. Lowest grade transferable C. **General Admission Information:** Application fee $50. Regular application deadline 3/1. Nonfall registration accepted. Admission may be deferred for a maximum of 1 year.

COSTS AND FINANCIAL AID

Annual tuition $36,460. Room and board $14,520. Required fees $1,450. Average book expense $800. **Required Forms and Deadlines:** FAFSA, State aid form. **Notification of Awards:** Applicants will be notified of awards on a rolling basis beginning 3/1. **Types of Aid:** *Need-based scholarships/grants:* Federal Pell, FSEOG, State scholarships/grants, College/university scholarship or grant aid from institutional funds. *Loans:* Direct Subsidized Stafford Loans, Direct Unsubsidized Stafford Loans, Direct PLUS loans, Federal Perkins Loans. *Student Employment:* Federal Work-Study Program available. Institutional employment available. **Financial Aid Statistics:** 69% needy freshmen, 85% needy undergrads receive need-based scholarship or grant aid. 99% freshmen, undergrads receive non-need-based scholarship or grant aid. 72% freshmen, 79% undergrads receive need-based self-help aid. 0% freshmen, 0% undergrads receive athletic scholarships. 97% freshmen, 94% undergrads receive any aid. 69% undergrads borrow to pay for school. Average cumulative indebtedness $32,212. **Criteria for awarding aid:** *Non-need-based:* Academics, Alumni affiliation, Art, Leadership, Music/drama.

MANSFIELD UNIVERSITY

71 Academy Street, Mansfield, PA 16933
Phone: 570-662-4243 • **Financial Aid Phone:** 570-664-4129
E-mail: admissions@mansfield.edu • **CEEB Code:** 2655
Fax: 570-662-4121 • **Website:** mansfield.edu • **ACT Code:** 3710

This public school was founded in 1857. It has a 174-acre campus.

RATINGS
Admissions Selectivity Rating: 77 **Fire Safety Rating:** 79 **Green Rating:** 60*

STUDENTS AND FACULTY
Enrollment: 2,052. **Student Body:** 60% female, 40% male, 18% out-of-state, 1% international (15 countries represented). Asian 1%, African American 10%, Caucasian 81%, Hispanic 3%, Native American <1%, Pacific Islander <1%, Two or more races 2%, Race unknown 2%.
Retention and Graduation: 72% freshmen return for sophomore year. 33% freshmen graduate within 4 years. 55% freshmen graduate within 6 years. 23% grads go on to further study within 1 year. **Faculty:** Student/faculty ratio 16:1. 109 full-time faculty, 86% hold PhDs, 9% are are members of minority groups, 50% are women. 0% of classes are taught by teaching assistants.

ACADEMICS
Degrees: associate, bachelor's, master's. **Classes:** Most classes have 20-29 students. Most lab/discussion sessions have 20-29 students. **Most popular majors:** Music Teacher Education; Criminal Justice/Law Enforcement Administration; Psychology. **Special Study Options:** cross-registration, distance learning, double major, dual enrollment, exchange student program (domestic), honors program, independent study, internships, liberal arts/career combination, student-designed major, study abroad, teacher certification program. **Disability Services:** Special programs offered to physically disabled students, including note-taking services, reader services, tape recorders, tutors. **Career Services:** Career/job search classes, Career assessment, Internships.

FACILITIES
Housing: Coed dorms, fraternity/sorority housing. 90% of campus accessible to physically diasbled. **Special Academic Facilities/Equipment:** Science museum, two art galleries, animal collection, planetarium, solar collector. **Computers:** Students can register for classes online.

CAMPUS LIFE
Environment: Rural. **Activities:** Choral groups, concert band, dance, drama/theater, jazz band, literary magazine, marching band, music ensembles, musical theater, pep band, radio station, student government, student newspaper, symphony orchestra, television station 108 registered organizations, 10 honor societies, 4 religious organizations. 6 fraternities, 4 sororities. **Athletics (Intercollegiate): Men:** baseball, basketball, cross-country, football, track/field (outdoor), track/field (indoor). **Women:** basketball, cheerleading, cross-country, diving, field hockey, soccer, softball, swimming, track/field (outdoor), track/field (indoor). **On-Campus Highlights:** North Hall Library, Fitness Center, Student Union

ADMISSIONS
Freshman Academic Profile: Average high school GPA 3.4. 31% in top 25% of high school class, 67% in top 50% of high school class. **Reported SAT (pre-2016 redesign) scores:** SAT Math middle 50% range 430-530. SAT Critical Reading middle 50% range 430-530. SAT Writing middle 50% range 390-510. **Concordant SAT scores:** SAT EBRW middle 50% 460–580. SAT Math middle 50% range 470–560. Minimum internet-based TOEFL 61. Minimum paper TOEFL 500. **Basis for Candidate Selection:** *Very important factors considered include:* rigor of secondary school record, class rank, academic GPA, standardized test scores. *Other factors considered include:* application essay, recommendation(s), interview, extracurricular activities, talent/ability, character/personal qualities, first generation, alumni/ae relation, geographical residence, volunteer work, work experience, level of applicant's interest. **Freshman Admission Requirements:** High school diploma is required and GED is accepted. *Academic units required:* 4 English, 3 math, 2 science, 2 science labs, 2 foreign language, 4 history, 6 academic electives. *Academic units recommended:* 4 English, 4 math, 3 science, 3 science labs, 4 foreign language. **Freshman Admission Statistics:** 2,997 applied, 65.70% admitted, 23% enrolled. **Transfer Admission Requirements:** college transcript(s). Minimum college GPA of 2.0 required. Lowest grade transferable D. **General Admission Information:** Application fee $25. Priority deadline 11/30. Nonfall registration accepted. Admission may be deferred for a maximum of 1 year.

COSTS AND FINANCIAL AID
Annual in-state tuition $9,150. Annual out-of-state tuition $15,090. Room and board $11,468. Required fees $2,758. Average book expense $1,800. **Required Forms and Deadlines:** FAFSA, State aid form. **Types of Aid:** *Need-based scholarships/grants:* Federal Pell, FSEOG, State scholarships/grants, Private

scholarships, College/university scholarship or grant aid from institutional funds. *Loans:* Direct Subsidized Stafford Loans, Direct Unsubsidized Stafford Loans, Direct PLUS loans, Federal Perkins Loans. *Student Employment:* Federal Work-Study Program available. Institutional employment available. **Financial Aid Statistics:** 69% needy freshmen, 69% needy undergrads receive need-based scholarship or grant aid. 46% freshmen, 36% undergrads receive non-need-based scholarship or grant aid. 91% freshmen, 90% undergrads receive need-based self-help aid. 0% freshmen, 1% undergrads receive athletic scholarships. 90% freshmen, 90% undergrads receive any aid. 80% undergrads borrow to pay for school. Average cumulative indebtedness $41,816. **Criteria for awarding aid:** *Need-based:* Academics. *Non-need-based:* Academics, Alumni affiliation, Art, Athletics, Job skills, Leadership, Minority status, Music/drama, Religious affiliation, State/district residency.

MARIAN UNIVERSITY

45 South National Avenue, Fond du Lac, WI 54935
Phone: 920-923-7650 • **Financial Aid Phone:** 920-923-7614
E-mail: admissions@marianuniversity.edu • **CEEB Code:** 1443
Fax: 920-923-8755 • **Website:** www.marianuniversity.edu • **ACT Code:** 4606

This private school, affiliated with the Roman Catholic Church, was founded in 1936. It has a 100-acre campus.

RATINGS

Admissions Selectivity Rating: 82   **Fire Safety Rating:** 82   **Green Rating:** 60*

STUDENTS AND FACULTY

Enrollment: 1,903. **Student Body:** 75% female, 25% male, 7% out-of-state, 1% international (13 countries represented). Asian 1%, African American 5%, Caucasian 88%, Hispanic 2%, Native American 1%, Pacific Islander 0%, Two or more races 0%, Race unknown 1%.
Retention and Graduation: 71% freshmen return for sophomore year. 21% freshmen graduate within 4 years. 41% freshmen graduate within 6 years. 16% grads go on to further study within 1 year. **Faculty:** Student/faculty ratio 12:1. 83 full-time faculty, 60% hold PhDs, 6% are are members of minority groups, 55% are women. 0% of classes are taught by teaching assistants.

ACADEMICS

Degrees: bachelor's, master's. **Classes:** Most classes have 10-19 students. Most lab/discussion sessions have 10-19 students. **Most popular majors:** Teacher Education and Professional Development, Specific Levels and Methods Business/Commerce. **Special Study Options:** Accelerated program, cooperative education program, distance learning, double major, dual enrollment, honors program, independent study, internships, liberal arts/career combination, student-designed major, study abroad, teacher certification program, Accelerated programs for adults in business, criminal justice, nursing, operations management, and radiologic technology. **Honors Programs:** Honors. **Disability Services:** Special programs offered to physically disabled students, including note-taking services, reader services, tape recorders, tutors. **Career Services:** Career/job search classes, Career assessment, Internships. 97% of students receive field experience.

FACILITIES

Housing: Coed dorms, special housing for disabled students, fraternity/sorority housing, apartments for single students, Townhouses, Penthouses and Suites. 95% of campus accessible to physically disabled. **Special Academic Facilities/Equipment:** On-campus child-care center, electron microscope. **Computers:** Students can register for classes online. Administrative functions (other than registration) can be performed online.

CAMPUS LIFE

Environment: Town. **Activities:** Choral groups, concert band, dance, drama/theater, jazz band, literary magazine, music ensembles, pep band, student government, student newspaper, symphony orchestra, Campus Ministries, Model UN. 40 registered organizations, 6 honor societies, 1 religious organization. 1 fraternity, 2 sororities. **Athletics (Intercollegiate):** *Men:* baseball, basketball, cross-country, golf, ice hockey, soccer, tennis. *Women:* basketball, cross-country, golf, ice hockey, soccer, softball, tennis, volleyball. **On-Campus Highlights:** Housing, Coffee House, Student Center, Stayer Center, Library and Academic buildings.

ADMISSIONS

Freshman Academic Profile: Average high school GPA 3.0. 9% in top 10% of high school class, 30% in top 25% of high school class, 66% in top 50% of high school class. 87% from public high schools. ACT middle 50% range 18-22. Minimum paper TOEFL 525. **Basis for Candidate Selection:** *Very important factors considered include:* rigor of secondary school record, class rank, academic GPA, standardized test scores. *Important factors considered include:*

interview, character/personal qualities, level of applicant's interest. *Other factors considered include:* application essay, recommendation(s), extracurricular activities, talent/ability, alumni/ae relation, volunteer work, work experience. **Freshman Admission Requirements:** High school diploma is required and GED is accepted. *Academic units required:* 4 English, 2 math, 1 science, 1 science lab, 1 history. *Academic units recommended:* 3 math, 2 science, 2 foreign language. **Freshman Admission Statistics:** 754 applied, 84.62% admitted, 45% enrolled. **Transfer Admission Requirements:** High school transcript, college transcript(s), Minimum college GPA of 2.0 required. Lowest grade transferable C. **General Admission Information:** Application fee $20. Priority deadline 4/1. Nonfall registration accepted. Admission may be deferred.

COSTS AND FINANCIAL AID

Annual tuition $19,590. Room and board $5,380. Required fees $350. Average book expense $700. **Required Forms and Deadlines:** FAFSA, Institution's own financial aid form. **Notification of Awards:** Applicants will be notified of awards on a rolling basis beginning 3/1. **Types of Aid:** *Need-based scholarships/grants:* Federal Pell, FSEOG, State scholarships/grants, Private scholarships, College/university scholarship or grant aid from institutional funds. *Loans:* Federal Perkins Loans, Federal Nursing Loans. *Student Employment:* Federal Work-Study Program available. Institutional employment available. **Financial Aid Statistics:** 100% needy freshmen, 97% needy undergrads receive need-based scholarship or grant aid. 91% freshmen, 85% undergrads receive non-need-based scholarship or grant aid. 89% freshmen, 91% undergrads receive need-based self-help aid. 0% freshmen, 0% undergrads receive athletic scholarships. 99% freshmen, 94% undergrads receive any aid. **Criteria for awarding aid:** *Need-based:* Academics, Alumni affiliation, Art, Leadership, Music/drama, Religious affiliation. *Non-need-based:* Academics, State/district residency.

MARIAN UNIVERSITY

3200 Cold Spring Rd., Indianapolis, IN 46222-1997
Phone: 317-955-6300 • **Financial Aid Phone:** 317-955-6040
E-mail: admissions@marian.edu • **CEEB Code:** 1442
Fax: 317-955-6401 • **Website:** www.marian.edu • **ACT Code:** 1224

This private school is, affiliated with the Roman Catholic Church.

RATINGS

Admissions Selectivity Rating: 73   **Fire Safety Rating:** 66   **Green Rating:** 60*

STUDENTS AND FACULTY

Enrollment: 2,019. **Student Body:** 61% female, 39% male, 21% out-of-state, 1% international (25 countries represented). Asian 2%, African American 12%, Caucasian 73%, Hispanic 5%, Native American <1%, Pacific Islander <1%, Two or more races 3%, Race unknown 4%.
Retention and Graduation: 77% freshmen return for sophomore year. 39% freshmen graduate within 4 years. 56% freshmen graduate within 6 years. 18% grads go on to further study within 1 year. 6% grads pursue arts and sciences degrees. 1% grads pursue law degrees. 1% grads pursue business degrees. 2% grads pursue medical degrees. **Faculty:** Student/faculty ratio 13:1. 148 full-time faculty, 66% hold PhDs, 11% are members of minority groups, 55% are women. 0% of classes are taught by teaching assistants.

ACADEMICS

Degrees: associate, bachelor's, doctoral/professional, master's. **Classes:** Most classes have fewer than 10 students. Most lab/discussion sessions have 10-19 students. **Most popular majors:** Management Science; Registered Nursing/Registered Nurse; Biology/Biological Sciences. **Special Study Options:** Accelerated program, cooperative education program, cross-registration, double major, dual enrollment, honors program, independent study, internships, liberal arts/career combination, study abroad, teacher certification program. **Disability Services:** Special programs offered to physically disabled students, including note-taking services, reader services, tape recorders, tutors. **Career Services:** Alumni network, Alumni services, Career/job search classes, Career assessment, Internships, Regional alumni. The Exchange–Its work centers on promoting Experience that Matters: connecting students to experiential learning opportunities of all types (internships, applied research, special projects) to help them hone their communication, problem-solving, team building, and leadership skills. We also teach students how to effectively translate their activities, achievements, and demonstrated abilities to advance their professional goals.
Specifically, we assist with:
Discussions of purpose and calling
Career exploration
Networking opportunities
Employer relations

Career fairs and on-campus recruiting
Mock interviews
Job/internship search assistance
Resume, cover letter, personal statement review
LinkedIn and professional online presence
Professional dress and etiquette; workplace expectations
Nationally competitive scholarships/fellowships for graduate study

FACILITIES

Housing: Coed dorms, cooperative housing, On-campus seminary, housing for Peace and Justice. 95% of campus accessible to physically diasbled. **Computers:** 15% of classrooms, 100% of dorms, 100% of libraries, 100% of dining areas, 100% of student union, 50% of common outdoor areas have wireless network access. Administrative functions (other than registration) can be performed online.

CAMPUS LIFE

Environment: Metropolis. **Activities:** Choral groups, concert band, dance, drama/theater, marching band, music ensembles, musical theater, pep band, student government, student newspaper, yearbook, Campus Ministries, Student Organization. **Athletics (Intercollegiate):** *Men:* baseball, basketball, cheerleading, cross-country, cycling, football, golf, tennis, track/field (outdoor), track/field (indoor). *Women:* basketball, cheerleading, cross-country, cycling, golf, softball, tennis, track/field (outdoor), track/field (indoor), volleyball.

ADMISSIONS

Freshman Academic Profile: Average high school GPA 3.4. 14% in top 10% of high school class, 38% in top 25% of high school class, 74% in top 50% of high school class. 71% from public high schools. **Reported SAT (pre-2016 redesign) scores:** SAT Math middle 50% range 470-600. SAT Critical Reading middle 50% range 470-570. SAT Writing middle 50% range 440-570. **Concordant SAT scores:** SAT EBRW middle 50% 510–630. SAT Math middle 50% range 510–620. ACT middle 50% range 19-25. Minimum internet-based TOEFL 80. Minimum paper TOEFL 550. **Basis for Candidate Selection:** *Very important factors considered include:* academic GPA, standardized test scores. *Important factors considered include:* rigor of secondary school record, class rank, recommendation(s). *Other factors considered include:* application essay, interview, extracurricular activities, talent/ability, character/personal qualities, alumni/ae relation, volunteer work, level of applicant's interest. **Freshman Admission Requirements:** High school diploma is required and GED is accepted. *Academic units required:* 4 English, 2 math, 2 science, 2 science labs, 1 social studies, 1 history, 9 academic electives. *Academic units recommended:* 4 English, 3 math, 3 science, 2 science labs, 1 foreign language, 1 social studies, 1 history, 8 academic electives. **Freshman Admission Statistics:** 2,181 applied, 59.74% admitted, 30% enrolled. **Transfer Admission Requirements:** college transcript(s), Minimum college GPA of 2 required. Lowest grade transferable C-. **General Admission Information:** Application fee $35. Priority deadline 3/1. Regular application deadline 8/1. Nonfall registration accepted. Admission may be deferred for a maximum of 1 yr.

COSTS AND FINANCIAL AID

Annual tuition $33,000. Room and board $10,206. Average book expense $1,200. **Required Forms and Deadlines:** FAFSA. **Notification of Awards:** Applicants will be notified of awards on a rolling basis beginning 3/20. **Types of Aid:** *Need-based scholarships/grants:* Federal Pell, FSEOG, State scholarships/grants, Private scholarships, College/university scholarship or grant aid from institutional funds. *Loans:* Direct Subsidized Stafford Loans, Direct Unsubsidized Stafford Loans, Direct PLUS loans, Federal Perkins Loans, College/university loans from institutional funds. *Student Employment:* Federal Work-Study Program available. Institutional employment available. **Criteria for awarding aid:** *Need-based:* Minority status. *Non-need-based:* Academics, Alumni affiliation, Art, Athletics, Leadership, Music/drama, Religious affiliation.

MARIETTA COLLEGE

215 Fifth Street, Marietta, OH 45750
Phone: 740-376-4600 • **Financial Aid Phone:** 740-376-4712
E-mail: admit@marietta.edu • **CEEB Code:** 1444
Fax: 740-376-8888 • **Website:** www.marietta.edu • **ACT Code:** 3290

This private school was founded in 1835. It has a 90-acre campus.

RATINGS

Admissions Selectivity Rating: 84   **Fire Safety Rating:** 88   **Green Rating:** 67

STUDENTS AND FACULTY

Enrollment: 1,470. **Student Body:** 43% female, 57% male, 36% out-of-state, 12% international (15 countries represented). Asian 1%, African American 6%, Caucasian 71%, Hispanic 2%, Native American <1%, Pacific Islander 0%, Two or more races 1%, Race unknown 6%.

Retention and Graduation: 75% freshmen return for sophomore year. 54% freshmen graduate within 4 years. 63% freshmen graduate within 6 years. 20% grads go on to further study within 1 year. 9% grads pursue arts and sciences degrees. 3% grads pursue law degrees. 2% grads pursue business degrees. 2% grads pursue medical degrees. **Faculty:** Student/faculty ratio 12:1. 110 full-time faculty, 89% hold PhDs, 7% are are members of minority groups, 45% are women. 0% of classes are taught by teaching assistants.

ACADEMICS

Degrees: associate, bachelor's, certificate, master's. **Classes:** Most classes have 10-19 students. **Most popular majors:** Education; Petroleum Engineering; Athletic Training/Trainer. **Special Study Options:** double major, dual enrollment, English as a Second Language (ESL), exchange student program (domestic), honors program, independent study, internships, liberal arts/career combination, student-designed major, study abroad, teacher certification program. **Honors Programs:** Four Year Program for Top Scholarship Winners Combined degree programs: BA/MA. **Disability Services:** Special programs offered to physically disabled students, including note-taking services, reader services, tape recorders, tutors. **Career Services:** Alumni network, Alumni services, Career/job search classes, Career assessment, Internships, Regional alumni. The Petroleum Engineering Department at Marietta College is unique in the nation—it is the only program of its kind located in a liberal arts college. This program is also significant because of its strong connection to the petroleum workforce, and thus its ability to link students with important experiential and lucrative internships throughout their college careers. These internships positively impact students' employment; nearly 100% of the department's graduates have jobs in the petroleum industry at graduation.

FACILITIES

Housing: Coed dorms, special housing for disabled students, men's dorms, women's dorms, fraternity/sorority housing, apartments for single students, Wellness Housing, Theme Housing is available. 90% of campus accessible to physically diasbled. **Special Academic Facilities/Equipment:** Mass media building, fine arts center, natural science field camp, observatory, special collections in library **Computers:** 100% of classrooms, 100% of dorms, 100% of libraries, 100% of dining areas, 100% of student union, have wireless network access. Students can register for classes online. Administrative functions (other than registration) can be performed online.

CAMPUS LIFE

Environment: Town. **Activities:** Choral groups, concert band, dance, drama/theater, jazz band, literary magazine, music ensembles, musical theater, radio station, student government, student newspaper, television station, yearbook, Campus Ministries, Student Organization, Model UN. 80 registered organizations, 23 honor societies, 2 religious organizations. 3 fraternities, 3 sororities. **Athletics (Intercollegiate):** *Men:* baseball, basketball, crew/rowing, cross-country, football, soccer, tennis, track/field (outdoor), track/field (indoor). *Women:* basketball, crew/rowing, cross-country, soccer, softball, tennis, track/field (outdoor), track/field (indoor), volleyball. **On-Campus Highlights:** Gathering Place, new Upper Class Residence Hall, Legacy Library, Hermann Fine Arts Center, Dyson Baudo Recreation Center, 6. New Rickey Science Center 7. New Soccer and Softball Fields 8. Andrews Hall—Izzy's Snack Place. **Environmental Initiatives:** Added Sustainable Energy Minor under the Petroleum Engineering Program.

ADMISSIONS

Freshman Academic Profile: Average high school GPA 3.5. 30% in top 10% of high school class, 56% in top 25% of high school class, 84% in top 50% of high school class. 89% from public high schools. **Reported SAT (pre-2016 redesign) scores:** SAT Math middle 50% range 490-610. SAT Critical Reading middle 50% range 480-610. SAT Writing middle 50% range 450-580. **Concordant SAT scores:** SAT EBRW middle 50% 520–650. SAT Math middle 50% range 520–630. ACT middle 50% range 21-26. Minimum internet-based TOEFL 79. Minimum paper TOEFL 550. **Basis for Candidate Selection:** *Very important factors considered include:* rigor of secondary school record, class rank, academic GPA, standardized test scores. *Important factors considered include:* application essay, recommendation(s), interview, character/personal qualities. *Other factors considered include:* extracurricular activities, talent/ability, first generation, alumni/ae relation, geographical residence, state residency, racial/ethnic status, volunteer work, work experience, level of applicant's interest. **Freshman Admission Requirements:** High school diploma is required and GED is accepted. *Academic units required:* 4 English, 3 math, 3 science, 2 science labs, 2 foreign language, 2 social studies, 2 history. **Freshman Admission Statistics:** 4,157 applied, 67.62% admitted, 14% enrolled. **Transfer Admission Requirements:** college transcript(s), essay or personal statement, statement of good standing from prior institution(s). Minimum college GPA of 2.3 required. Lowest grade transferable C. **General Admission Information:** Application fee $25. Priority deadline 3/1. Nonfall registration accepted. Admission may be deferred for a maximum of 12 months.

COSTS AND FINANCIAL AID

Annual tuition $30,090. Room and board $9,560. Required fees $850. Average book expense $1,136. **Required Forms and Deadlines:** FAFSA. **Notification**

of Awards: Applicants will be notified of awards on a rolling basis beginning 3/15. **Types of Aid:** *Need-based scholarships/grants:* Federal Pell, FSEOG, State scholarships/grants, Private scholarships, College/university scholarship or grant aid from institutional funds. *Loans:* Direct Subsidized Stafford Loans, Direct Unsubsidized Stafford Loans, Direct PLUS loans, Federal Perkins Loans, College/university loans from institutional funds. *Student Employment:* Federal Work-Study Program available. Institutional employment available. **Financial Aid Statistics:** 98% needy freshmen, 97% needy undergrads receive need-based scholarship or grant aid. 71% freshmen, 87% undergrads receive non-need-based scholarship or grant aid. 86% freshmen, 88% undergrads receive need-based self-help aid. 0% freshmen, 0% undergrads receive athletic scholarships. 98% freshmen, 94% undergrads receive any aid. **Criteria for awarding aid:** *Need-based:* Academics, Leadership. *Non-need-based:* Academics, Alumni affiliation, Art, Leadership, Minority status, Music/drama, State/district residency.

MARIST COLLEGE

3399 North Road, Poughkeepsie, NY 12601-1387
Phone: 845-575-3226 • **Financial Aid Phone:** 845-575-3230
E-mail: admission@marist.edu • **CEEB Code:** 2400
Fax: 845-575-3215 • **Website:** http://www.marist.edu/ • **ACT Code:** 2804

This private school was founded in 1929. It has a 180-acre campus.

RATINGS
Admissions Selectivity Rating: 90   **Fire Safety Rating:** 96   **Green Rating:** 74

STUDENTS AND FACULTY
Enrollment: 5,308. **Student Body:** 58% female, 42% male, 48% out-of-state, 2% international (46 countries represented). Asian 3%, African American 4%, Caucasian 77%, Hispanic 10%, Native American <1%, Pacific Islander <1%, Two or more races 2%, Race unknown 1%.
Retention and Graduation: 90% freshmen return for sophomore year. 75% freshmen graduate within 4 years. 83 23% grads go on to further study within 1 year. 7% grads pursue arts and sciences degrees. 1% grads pursue law degrees. 2% grads pursue business degrees. 1% grads pursue medical degrees. **Faculty:** Student/faculty ratio 16:1. 232 full-time faculty, 75% hold PhDs, 17% are are members of minority groups, 51% are women. 0% of classes are taught by teaching assistants.

ACADEMICS
Degrees: bachelor's, certificate, master's, postbachelor's certificate. **Classes:** Most classes have 20-29 students. Most lab/discussion sessions have 10-19 students. **Most popular majors:** Business Administration and Management; Communication; Psychology. **Special Study Options:** Accelerated program, cooperative education program, cross-registration, distance learning, double major, dual enrollment, English as a Second Language (ESL), honors program, independent study, internships, liberal arts/career combination, study abroad, teacher certification program, weekend college, Undergrads may take grad level classes. Cooperative ed- Arts, Business, Computer Science,Education, Humanities, Natural Science, Social/Behavioral Science, Technologies. **Honors Programs:** The Marist College Honors Program brings together talented students in honors-enriched classes that often coordinate with co-curricular activities such as field trips and lectures. The cultural enrichment exchange is a highlight of the Program. It encourages students to move beyond standard curricula and engage in a broader range of experience consonant with their interests. Combined degree programs: BA/MA, BS/MS. **Disability Services:** Special programs offered to physically disabled students, including note-taking services, reader services, tape recorders, tutors. **Career Services:** Alumni network, Alumni services, Career/job search classes, Career assessment, Internships, Regional alumni. We have a very extensive internship program that provides students with practical work experience and reinforces the lessons from the classroom.

FACILITIES
Housing: Coed dorms, special housing for disabled students, apartments for single students, Wellness Housing, garden apartments, townhouses, suites. 95% of campus accessible to physically diasbled. **Special Academic Facilities/Equipment:** Art gallery, language lab, estuarine and environmental studies lab, public opinion institute, audiovisual/TV center, communications center, high tech classroom,digital state of the art library. **Computers:** 100% of classrooms, 100% of dorms, 100% of libraries, 100% of dining areas, 100% of student union,

57% of common outdoor areas have wireless network access. Students can register for classes online. Administrative functions (other than registration) can be performed online.

CAMPUS LIFE
Environment: Town. **Activities:** Choral groups, concert band, dance, drama/theater, jazz band, literary magazine, marching band, music ensembles, musical theater, pep band, radio station, student government, student newspaper, student-run film society, television station, yearbook, Campus Ministries. 86 registered organizations, 16 honor societies, 6 religious organizations. 3 fraternities, 4 sororities. **Athletics (Intercollegiate):** *Men:* baseball, basketball, crew/rowing, cross-country, diving, football, lacrosse, soccer, swimming, tennis, track/field (outdoor). *Women:* basketball, crew/rowing, cross-country, diving, lacrosse, soccer, softball, swimming, tennis, track/field (outdoor), volleyball, water polo. **On-Campus Highlights:** James A Cannavino Library, James J McCann Recreation Center, Student Center, Newly Renovated Freshman Residence Halls, Tenney Stadium at Leonidoff Field. **Environmental Initiatives:** Sustainable food purchases.

ADMISSIONS
Freshman Academic Profile: Average high school GPA 3.3. 24% in top 10% of high school class, 58% in top 25% of high school class, 89% in top 50% of high school class. 68% from public high schools. **Reported SAT (pre-2016 redesign) scores:** SAT Math middle 50% range 540-640. SAT Critical Reading middle 50% range 530-630. SAT Writing middle 50% range 530-630. **Concordant SAT scores:** SAT EBRW middle 50% 590–680. SAT Math middle 50% range 570–660. ACT middle 50% range 24-29. Minimum internet-based TOEFL 80. Minimum paper TOEFL 550. **Basis for Candidate Selection:** *Very important factors considered include:* rigor of secondary school record, academic GPA. *Important factors considered include:* class rank, application essay, recommendation(s), extracurricular activities, talent/ability, character/personal qualities, geographical residence, state residency, volunteer work, work experience. *Other factors considered include:* standardized test scores, first generation, alumni/ae relation, racial/ethnic status, level of applicant's interest. **Freshman Admission Requirements:** High school diploma is required and GED is accepted. *Academic units required:* 4 English, 3 math, 3 science, 2 science labs, 2 foreign language, 2 social studies, 1 history, 2 academic electives. *Academic units recommended:* 4 math, 4 science, 3 science labs, 3 foreign language. **Freshman Admission Statistics:** 11,087 applied, 40.99% admitted, 27% enrolled. **Transfer Admission Requirements:** High school transcript, college transcript(s), essay or personal statement, Minimum college GPA of 2.8 required. Lowest grade transferable 2. **General Admission Information:** Application fee $50. Regular application deadline 2/1. Regular notification 4/1. Nonfall registration accepted. Admission may be deferred for a maximum of 1 year.

COSTS AND FINANCIAL AID
Annual tuition $34,550. Room and board $16,160. Required fees $560. Average book expense $1,000. **Required Forms and Deadlines:** FAFSA. **Notification of Awards:** Applicants will be notified of awards on a rolling basis beginning 4/1. **Types of Aid:** *Need-based scholarships/grants:* Federal Pell, FSEOG, State scholarships/grants, Private scholarships, College/university scholarship or grant aid from institutional funds. *Loans:* Direct Subsidized Stafford Loans, Direct Unsubsidized Stafford Loans, Direct PLUS loans. *Student Employment:* Federal Work-Study Program available. Institutional employment available. **Financial Aid Statistics:** 72% needy freshmen, 71% needy undergrads receive need-based scholarship or grant aid. 87% undergrads receive non-need-based scholarship or grant aid. 80% freshmen, 83% undergrads receive need-based self-help aid. 6% freshmen, 6% undergrads receive athletic scholarships. 66% freshmen, 64% undergrads receive any aid. 66% undergrads borrow to pay for school. Average cumulative indebtedness $39,584. **Criteria for awarding aid:** *Need-based:* Academics, Alumni affiliation, Art, Leadership, Minority status, Music/drama. *Non-need-based:* Academics, Athletics, Music/drama, State/district residency.

MARLBORO COLLEGE

PO Box A, Marlboro, VT 05344-0300
Phone: 802-258-9236 • **Financial Aid Phone:** 802-258-9312
E-mail: admissions@marlboro.edu • **CEEB Code:** 3509
Fax: 802-451-7555 • **Website:** www.marlboro.edu • **ACT Code:** 4304

This private school was founded in 1946. It has a 350-acre campus.

RATINGS
Admissions Selectivity Rating: 80   **Fire Safety Rating:** 82   **Green Rating:** 60*

STUDENTS AND FACULTY

Enrollment: 190. **Student Body:** 48% female, 52% male, 88% out-of-state, 2% international (5 countries represented). Asian 2%, African American 3%, Caucasian 77%, Hispanic 3%, Native American 1%, Pacific Islander 0%, Two or more races 5%, Race unknown 7%.
Retention and Graduation: 71% freshmen return for sophomore year. 58% freshmen graduate within 4 years. 24% grads go on to further study within 1 year. **Faculty:** Student/faculty ratio 5:1. 34 full-time faculty, 91% hold PhDs, 18% are are members of minority groups, 47% are women. 0% of classes are taught by teaching assistants.

ACADEMICS

Degrees: bachelor's, certificate, master's, postbachelor's certifiate. **Classes:** Most classes have fewer than 10 students. Most lab/discussion sessions have fewer than 10 students. **Most popular majors:** English Language and Literature; Social Sciences; Visual and Performing Arts. **Special Study Options:** double major, dual enrollment, independent study, internships, student-designed major, study abroad, World Studies Program for students interested in international relations while also integrating an internship with study abroad opportunities. Combined degree programs: BA/MA, BA/MS BA/ MBA. **Disability Services:** Special programs offered to physically disabled students, including note-taking services, reader services, tape recorders, tutors. **Career Services:** Alumni network, Alumni services, Career/job search classes, Career assessment, Internships, Regional alumni, On-campus interviews.

FACILITIES

Housing: Coed dorms, special housing for disabled students, women's dorms, apartments for married students, cooperative housing, apartments for single students, Housing is to a human scale; the largest residence hall accommodates about 30 students. 80% of campus accessible to physically diasbled. **Special Academic Facilities/Equipment:** Serkin Center for the Performing Arts, Drury art gallery, theater, dance studio, observatory, darkroom, art studios, music practice and performance spaces. **Computers:** 80% of classrooms, 85% of dorms, 100% of libraries, 100% of dining areas, 100% of student union, 80% of common outdoor areas have wireless network access. Students can register for classes online. Administrative functions (other than registration) can be performed online.

CAMPUS LIFE

Environment: Rural. **Activities:** Choral groups, dance, drama/theater, literary magazine, music ensembles, musical theater, radio station, student government, student newspaper, student-run film society 22 registered organizations. **On-Campus Highlights:** The Rice-Aron Library, Whittemore Theatre, Rod Gander World Studies Center, Serkin Center for the Performing Arts, Persons Auditorium. **Environmental Initiatives:** Energy audits of all campus buildings in preparation for efficiency upgrades.

ADMISSIONS

Freshman Academic Profile: Average high school GPA 3.1. 0% in top 10% of high school class, 0% in top 25% of high school class, 0% in top 50% of high school class. 66% from public high schools. **Reported SAT (pre-2016 redesign) scores:** SAT Math middle 50% range 510-600. SAT Critical Reading middle 50% range 580-760. SAT Writing middle 50% range 580-660. **Concordant SAT scores:** SAT EBRW middle 50% 640–740. SAT Math middle 50% range 540–620. Minimum internet-based TOEFL 90. Minimum paper TOEFL 577. **Basis for Candidate Selection:** *Very important factors considered include:* application essay, interview. *Important factors considered include:* rigor of secondary school record, academic GPA, recommendation(s), extracurricular activities, talent/ability, character/personal qualities, level of applicant's interest. *Other factors considered include:* class rank, standardized test scores, first generation, volunteer work, work experience. **Freshman Admission Requirements:** High school diploma is required and GED is accepted. *Academic units recommended:* 4 English, 3 math, 3 science, 2 foreign language, 2 social studies, 2 history, 2 academic electives. **Freshman Admission Statistics:** 161 applied, 95.65% admitted, 36% enrolled. **Transfer Admission Requirements:** High school transcript, college transcript(s), essay or personal statement, interview, Minimum college GPA of 2.0 required. Lowest grade transferable C-. **General Admission Information:** Application fee $50. Priority deadline 3/1. Nonfall registration accepted. Admission may be deferred for a maximum of 2 semesters.

COSTS AND FINANCIAL AID

Annual tuition $39,481. Room and board $11,930. Required fees $944. Average book expense $1,200. **Required Forms and Deadlines:** FAFSA. **Notification of Awards:** Applicants will be notified of awards on a rolling basis beginning 3/1. **Types of Aid:** *Need-based scholarships/grants:* Federal Pell, FSEOG, State scholarships/grants, Private scholarships, College/university scholarship or grant aid from institutional funds. *Loans:* Direct Subsidized Stafford Loans, Direct Unsubsidized Stafford Loans, Direct PLUS loans. *Student Employment:* Federal Work-Study Program available. Institutional employment available. **Financial Aid Statistics:** 100% needy freshmen, 98% needy undergrads receive need-based scholarship or grant aid. 72% freshmen, 77% undergrads receive non-need-based scholarship or grant aid. 100% freshmen, 99%

undergrads receive need-based self-help aid. 0% freshmen, 0% undergrads receive athletic scholarships. 98% freshmen, 94% undergrads receive any aid. 77% undergrads borrow to pay for school. Average cumulative indebtedness $31,747. **Criteria for awarding aid:** *Non-need-based:* Academics, Art, Leadership, Music/drama.

See page 996.

MARQUETTE UNIVERSITY

PO Box 1881, Milwaukee, WI 53201-1881
Phone: 414-288-7302 • **Financial Aid Phone:** 414-288-7390
E-mail: admissions@Marquette.edu • **CEEB Code:** 1448
Fax: 414-288-3764 • **Website:** www.marquette.edu • **ACT Code:** 4610

This private school, affiliated with the Roman Catholic-Jesuit Church, affiliated with the Jesuit Church, was founded in 1881. It has a 93-acre campus.

RATINGS

Admissions Selectivity Rating: 83   **Fire Safety Rating:** 98   **Green Rating:** 80

STUDENTS AND FACULTY

Enrollment: 8,053. **Student Body:** 54% female, 46% male, 68% out-of-state, 3% international (39 countries represented). Asian 6%, African American 4%, Caucasian 72%, Hispanic 11%, Native American <1%, Pacific Islander <1%, Two or more races 4%, Race unknown <1%.
Retention and Graduation: 89% freshmen return for sophomore year. 60% freshmen graduate within 4 years. 80% freshmen graduate within 6 years. **Faculty:** Student/faculty ratio 14:1. 648 full-time faculty, 91% hold PhDs, 16% are are members of minority groups, 42% are women.

ACADEMICS

Degrees: bachelor's, doctoral/professional, doctoral/research, doctoral, master's, postbachelor's certifiate, post-master's certificate. **Classes:** Most classes have 10-19 students. Most lab/discussion sessions have 10-19 students. **Most popular majors:** Biomedical Sciences; Registered Nursing/Registered Nurse; Mechanical Engineering. **Special Study Options:** Accelerated program, cooperative education program, cross-registration, double major, dual enrollment, honors program, independent study, internships, student-designed major, study abroad, teacher certification program, weekend college. **Honors Programs:** Pre-Law Scholars Program Pre-Dental Scholars Program Combined degree programs: BA/JD, BA/MA, BA/DDS, Physical Therapy, Physician Assistant Studies. **Disability Services:** Special programs offered to physically disabled students, including note-taking services, reader services, tape recorders, tutors. **Career Services:** Alumni network, Alumni services, Career/job search classes, Career assessment, Internships, Regional alumni. Career/job search classes.

FACILITIES

Housing: Coed dorms, special housing for disabled students, men's dorms, special housing for international students, women's dorms, fraternity/sorority housing, apartments for married students, apartments for single students, Specialty housing for honor students, engineering students, nursing students. 90% of campus accessible to physically diasbled. **Special Academic Facilities/Equipment:** Haggerty Museum of Art, Helfaer Theatre, Al McGuire Center Broadcast Facilities, Dental School/Clinic **Computers:** 30% of classrooms, 100% of dorms, 100% of libraries, 100% of dining areas, 100% of student union, 10% of common outdoor areas have wireless network access. Students can register for classes online. Administrative functions (other than registration) can be performed online.

CAMPUS LIFE

Environment: Metropolis. **Activities:** Choral groups, concert band, dance, drama/theater, jazz band, literary magazine, music ensembles, musical theater, pep band, radio station, student government, student newspaper, symphony orchestra, television station, yearbook, Campus Ministries, Student Organization, Model UN. 230 registered organizations, 21 honor societies, 11 religious organizations. 11 fraternities, 11 sororities. **Athletics (Intercollegiate):** *Men:* basketball, cheerleading, cross-country, golf, soccer, tennis, track/field (outdoor), track/field (indoor). *Women:* basketball, cheerleading, cross-country, soccer, tennis, track/field (outdoor), track/field (indoor), volleyball. **On-Campus Highlights:** The Raynor Memorial Library and the Law, Gesu Church, Haggerty Museum of Art, Al McGuire Center,

Helfaer Recreation Center, Other places of interest Alumni Memorial Union and the Golden Eagle giftshop. (Located in the AMU). **Environmental Initiatives:** All Full-Time undergraduate Students receive a UPASS (Allows unlimited use of Milwaukee County Transit System Buses).

ADMISSIONS

Freshman Academic Profile: 31% in top 10% of high school class, 65% in top 25% of high school class, 94% in top 50% of high school class. 58% from public high schools. **Reported SAT (pre-2016 redesign) scores:** SAT Math middle 50% range 520-640. SAT Critical Reading middle 50% range 520-630. SAT Writing middle 50% range 520-620. **Concordant SAT scores:** SAT EBRW middle 50% 580–680. SAT Math middle 50% range 550–660. ACT middle 50% range 24-29. Minimum internet-based TOEFL 78. Minimum paper TOEFL 530. **Basis for Candidate Selection:** *Very important factors considered include:* rigor of secondary school record, academic GPA. *Important factors considered include:* standardized test scores, application essay, extracurricular activities, volunteer work. *Other factors considered include:* class rank, recommendation(s), talent/ability, character/personal qualities, first generation, alumni/ae relation, racial/ethnic status, work experience. **Freshman Admission Requirements:** High school diploma is required and GED is accepted. *Academic units required:* 4 English, 2 science labs. *Academic units recommended:* 4 English, 3 science labs, 2 foreign language, 3 social studies, 2 history. **Freshman Admission Statistics:** 13,136 applied, 84.34% admitted, 18% enrolled. **Transfer Admission Requirements:** High school transcript, college transcript(s), essay or personal statement, Lowest grade transferable C. **General Admission Information:** Priority deadline 12/1. Regular application deadline 12/1. Nonfall registration accepted. Admission may be deferred for a maximum of 1 semester.

COSTS AND FINANCIAL AID

Annual tuition $38,000. Room and board $11,440. Required fees $470. Average book expense $1,008. **Required Forms and Deadlines:** FAFSA. **Notification of Awards:** Applicants will be notified of awards on a rolling basis beginning 3/5. **Types of Aid:** *Need-based scholarships/grants:* Federal Pell, FSEOG, State scholarships/grants, Private scholarships, College/university scholarship or grant aid from institutional funds. *Loans:* Direct Subsidized Stafford Loans, Direct Unsubsidized Stafford Loans, Direct PLUS loans, Federal Perkins Loans, Federal Nursing Loans, State Loans, College/university loans from institutional funds. *Student Employment:* Federal Work-Study Program available. Institutional employment available. **Financial Aid Statistics:** 98% needy freshmen, 98% needy undergrads receive need-based scholarship or grant aid. 14% freshmen, 12% undergrads receive non-need-based scholarship or grant aid. 79% freshmen, 81% undergrads receive need-based self-help aid. 2% freshmen, 2% undergrads receive athletic scholarships. 100% freshmen, 99% undergrads receive any aid. 56% undergrads borrow to pay for school. Average cumulative indebtedness $35,421. **Criteria for awarding aid:** *Need-based:* Minority status. *Non-need-based:* Academics, Athletics, Leadership, Music/drama.

MARSHALL UNIVERSITY

One John Marshall Drive, Huntington, WV 25755
Phone: 304-696-3160 • **Financial Aid Phone:** 304-696-3162
E-mail: admissions@marshall.edu • **CEEB Code:** 5396
Fax: 304-696-3135 • **Website:** www.marshall.edu • **ACT Code:** 4526

This public school was founded in 1837. It has a 70-acre campus.

RATINGS

Admissions Selectivity Rating: 72   Fire Safety Rating: 67   Green Rating: 60*

STUDENTS AND FACULTY

Enrollment: 8,699. **Student Body:** 57% female, 43% male, 20% out-of-state, 1% international. Asian 1%, African American 7%, Caucasian 84%, Hispanic 2%, Native American <1%, Pacific Islander <1%, Two or more races 3%, Race unknown 1%.
Retention and Graduation: 75% freshmen return for sophomore year. 27% grads go on to further study within 1 year. **Faculty:** Student/faculty ratio 18:1. 505 full-time faculty, 76% hold PhDs, 19% are are members of minority groups, 48% are women.

ACADEMICS

Degrees: associate, bachelor's, doctoral/professional, doctoral/research, master's, postbachelor's certificate, post-master's certificate. **Classes:** Most classes have 20-29 students. **Most popular majors:** Elementary Education and Teaching; Psychology; Business/Commerce. **Special Study Options:** Accelerated program, cooperative education program, cross-registration, distance learning, double major, dual enrollment, English as a Second Language (ESL), exchange student program (domestic), honors program, independent

study, internships, study abroad, teacher certification program. **Honors Programs:** John Marshall Scholars, Society of Yeager Scholars Combined degree programs: BS/MF Forestry (w/ Duke),BS/MEM Env Mgmt (w/ Duke). **Disability Services:** Special programs offered to physically disabled students, including note-taking services, reader services, tutors. **Career Services:** Alumni network, Alumni services, Career/job search classes, Career assessment, Internships, Regional alumni.

FACILITIES

Housing: Coed dorms, special housing for disabled students, women's dorms. 100% of campus accessible to physically diasbled. **Special Academic Facilities/Equipment:** Art gallery, audiovisual center, language lab, superconducting nuclear magnetic resonance spectrometer. **Computers:** Students can register for classes online. Administrative functions (other than registration) can be performed online.

CAMPUS LIFE

Environment: Town. **Activities:** Choral groups, concert band, dance, drama/theater, jazz band, literary magazine, marching band, music ensembles, musical theater, opera, pep band, radio station, student government, student newspaper, symphony orchestra, television station, Campus Ministries, Student Organization, Model UN. 100 registered organizations, 11 honor societies, 10 religious organizations. 12 fraternities, 7 sororities. **Athletics (Intercollegiate):** *Men:* baseball, basketball, cross-country, football, golf, soccer, track/field (outdoor). *Women:* basketball, cross-country, golf, soccer, softball, swimming, tennis, track/field (outdoor), volleyball. **On-Campus Highlights:** Memorial Student Center Plaza, Drinko Library, Marshall Stadium, Henderson Center, Buskirk Field.

ADMISSIONS

Freshman Academic Profile: Average high school GPA 3.4. **Reported SAT (pre-2016 redesign) scores:** SAT Math middle 50% range 430-480. SAT Critical Reading middle 50% range 440-490. **Concordant SAT scores:** SAT Math middle 50% range 470–510. ACT middle 50% range 20-25. Minimum paper TOEFL 500. **Basis for Candidate Selection:** *Very important factors considered include:* academic GPA, standardized test scores. *Other factors considered include:* rigor of secondary school record. **Freshman Admission Requirements:** High school diploma is required and GED is accepted. *Academic units required:* 4 English, 4 math, 3 science, 3 science labs, 2 foreign language, 3 social studies, 1 visual/performing arts. **Freshman Admission Statistics:** 4,891 applied, 89.43% admitted, 43% enrolled. **Transfer Admission Requirements:** college transcript(s). **General Admission Information:** Application fee $30. Nonfall registration accepted. Admission may be deferred for a maximum of 1 year.

COSTS AND FINANCIAL AID

Annual in-state tuition $6,032. Annual out-of-state tuition $15,260. Room and board $9,254. Required fees $1,122. Average book expense $1,100. **Required Forms and Deadlines:** FAFSA, State aid form. **Notification of Awards:** Applicants will be notified of awards on a rolling basis beginning 4/1. **Types of Aid:** *Need-based scholarships/grants:* Federal Pell, FSEOG, State scholarships/grants, Private scholarships, College/university scholarship or grant aid from institutional funds, Federal Nursing Scholarships. *Loans:* Direct Subsidized Stafford Loans, Direct Unsubsidized Stafford Loans, Direct PLUS loans, Federal Perkins Loans, Federal Nursing Loans. *Student Employment:* Federal Work-Study Program available. Institutional employment available. **Financial Aid Statistics:** 77% needy freshmen, 76% needy undergrads receive need-based scholarship or grant aid. 61% freshmen, 47% undergrads receive non-need-based scholarship or grant aid. 68% freshmen, 73% undergrads receive need-based self-help aid. 5% freshmen, 5% undergrads receive athletic scholarships. 69% undergrads borrow to pay for school. Average cumulative indebtedness $27,121. **Criteria for awarding aid:** *Non-need-based:* Academics, Alumni affiliation, Art, Athletics, Minority status, Music/drama, State/district residency.

MARY BALDWIN COLLEGE

PO Box 1500, Staunton, VA 24402
Phone: 540-887-7019 • **Financial Aid Phone:** 540-887-7022
E-mail: admit@mbc.edu • **CEEB Code:** 5397
Fax: 540-887-7292 • **Website:** www.mbc.edu • **ACT Code:** 4374

This private school, affiliated with the Presbyterian Church, was founded in 1842. It has a 54-acre campus.

RATINGS

Admissions Selectivity Rating: 82   Fire Safety Rating: 87   Green Rating: 60*

STUDENTS AND FACULTY

Enrollment: 1,298. **Student Body:** 94% female, 6% male, 31% out-of-state, <1% international (4 countries represented). Asian 3%, African American 25%, Caucasian 57%, Hispanic 7%, Native American <1%, Pacific Islander <1%, Two or more races 4%, Race unknown 4%.
Retention and Graduation: 68% freshmen return for sophomore year. 43% freshmen graduate within 4 years. 20% grads go on to further study within 1 year. 5% grads pursue law degrees. 5% grads pursue business degrees. 2% grads pursue medical degrees. **Faculty:** Student/faculty ratio 11:1. 86 full-time faculty, 84% hold PhDs, 19% are are members of minority groups, 63% are women. 0% of classes are taught by teaching assistants.

ACADEMICS

Degrees: bachelor's, certificate, doctoral, master's. **Classes:** Most classes have 10-19 students. Most lab/discussion sessions have 10-19 students. **Most popular majors:** Social Sciences; Psychology; Multi-/Interdisciplinary Studies. **Special Study Options:** Accelerated program, cooperative education program, cross-registration, distance learning, double major, dual enrollment, English as a Second Language (ESL), exchange student program (domestic), external degree program, honors program, independent study, internships, liberal arts/career combination, student-designed major, study abroad, teacher certification program, Summer exchange program with Doshisha Women's College in Kyoto, Japan. **Disability Services:** Special programs offered to physically disabled students, including tape recorders, tutors. **Career Services:** Alumni services, Career/job search classes, Career assessment, Internships, On-campus interviews.

FACILITIES

Housing: special housing for international students, women's dorms, apartments for single students, Special interest (club) housing focuses on students, honors, leadership and community services available. 75% of campus accessible to physically diasbled. **Special Academic Facilities/Equipment:** Audiovisual center, TV studio, communications lab, electron microscope, gas chromatoscope, greenhouse. **Computers:** 100% of classrooms, 100% of dorms, 100% of libraries, 100% of common outdoor areas have wireless network access. Students can register for classes online. Administrative functions (other than registration) can be performed online.

CAMPUS LIFE

Environment: Village. **Activities:** Choral groups, dance, drama/theater, literary magazine, marching band, music ensembles, musical theater, radio station, student government, student newspaper, student-run film society, television station, yearbook. 34 registered organizations, 9 honor societies, 4 religious organizations. **Athletics (Intercollegiate):** *Women:* basketball, field hockey, soccer, softball, swimming, tennis, volleyball. **On-Campus Highlights:** Coffee House (The Nut House), SMA (VWIL) Museum, The Library, Spencer Center for Civic & Global Engage, Computer Center Labs.

ADMISSIONS

Freshman Academic Profile: Average high school GPA 3.4. 14% in top 10% of high school class, 42% in top 25% of high school class, 82% in top 50% of high school class. 75% from public high schools. **Reported SAT (pre-2016 redesign) scores:** SAT Math middle 50% range 410-530. SAT Critical Reading middle 50% range 440-560. SAT Writing middle 50% range 420-540. **Concordant SAT scores:** SAT EBRW middle 50% 480-610. SAT Math middle 50% range 450–560. ACT middle 50% range 19-24. Minimum paper TOEFL 500. **Basis for Candidate Selection:** *Very important factors considered include:* rigor of secondary school record, standardized test scores. *Important factors considered include:* interview, extracurricular activities, character/personal qualities. *Other factors considered include:* class rank, application essay, recommendation(s), talent/ability, alumni/ae relation, volunteer work, work experience. **Freshman Admission Requirements:** High school diploma is required and GED is accepted. *Academic units required:* 4 English, 3 math, 2 science, 1 science lab, 2 foreign language, 3 social studies. *Academic units recommended:* 3 foreign language, 2 academic electives. **Freshman Admission Statistics:** 5,860 applied, 51.01% admitted, 9% enrolled. **Transfer Admission Requirements:** High school transcript, college transcript(s), statement of good standing from prior institution(s). Minimum college GPA of 2.0 required. Lowest grade transferable c-. **General Admission Information:** Nonfall registration accepted. Admission may be deferred for a maximum of 1 semester.

COSTS AND FINANCIAL AID

Annual tuition $29,210. Room and board $8,650. Required fees $385. Average book expense $1,000. **Required Forms and Deadlines:** FAFSA, State aid form. **Notification of Awards:** Applicants will be notified of awards on a rolling basis beginning 3/15. **Types of Aid:** *Need-based scholarships/grants:* Federal Pell, FSEOG, State scholarships/grants, Private scholarships, College/university scholarship or grant aid from institutional funds. *Loans:* Direct Subsidized Stafford Loans, Direct Unsubsidized Stafford Loans, Direct PLUS loans, Federal Perkins Loans, State Loans. *Student Employment:* Federal Work-Study Program available. Institutional employment available. **Financial Aid Statistics:** 98% needy freshmen, 99% needy undergrads receive need-based scholarship or grant aid. 7% freshmen, 7% undergrads receive non-need-based scholarship or grant aid. 87% freshmen, 88% undergrads receive need-based self-help aid. 0% freshmen, 0% undergrads receive athletic scholarships. 90% freshmen, 95% undergrads receive any aid. **Criteria for awarding aid:** *Need-based:* Academics, Leadership. *Non-need-based:* Academics, Leadership, State/district residency.

MARYLAND INSTITUTE COLLEGE OF ART

1300 West Mount Royal Avenue, Baltimore, MD 21217
Phone: 410-225-2222 • **Financial Aid Phone:** 410-225-2285
E-mail: admissions@mica.edu • **CEEB Code:** 5399
Fax: 410-225-2337 • **Website:** www.mica.edu • **ACT Code:** 1710

This private school was founded in 1826. It has a 12-acre campus.

RATINGS

Admissions Selectivity Rating: 78   **Fire Safety Rating:** 93   **Green Rating:** 69

STUDENTS AND FACULTY

Enrollment: 1,673. **Student Body:** 74% female, 26% male, 77% out-of-state, 18% international (62 countries represented). Asian 13%, African American 6%, Caucasian 45%, Hispanic 4%, Native American <1%, Pacific Islander <1%, Two or more races 11%, Race unknown 4%.
Retention and Graduation: 87% freshmen return for sophomore year. 68% freshmen graduate within 4 years. 73% freshmen graduate within 6 years. **Faculty:** Student/faculty ratio 9:1. 159 full-time faculty, 76% hold PhDs, 13% are are members of minority groups, 52% are women. 0% of classes are taught by teaching assistants.

ACADEMICS

Degrees: bachelor's, master's, postbachelor's certificate. **Classes:** Most classes have 10-19 students. **Most popular majors:** Illustration; Graphic Design; Painting. **Special Study Options:** Accelerated program, cross-registration, distance learning, double major, dual enrollment, exchange student program (domestic), independent study, internships, student-designed major, study abroad, teacher certification program, Cooperative exchange programs with Johns Hopkins University, Goucher College, The Peabody Conservatory of Music, University of Baltimore, Loyola College, Notre Dame College, University of Maryland Baltimore County, Morgan State University, and Towson University; 5-year BFA/MAT program is available. Combined degree programs: BA/MA, BFA/MAT; MA/MBA. **Disability Services:** Special programs offered to physically disabled students, including note-taking services, tape recorders, tutors. **Career Services:** Alumni network, Alumni services, Career/job search classes, Career assessment, Internships, Regional alumni, On-campus interviews. MICAnetwork is our free online database listing opportunities from employers across the United States who are actively seeking to hire MICA students and alumni.

FACILITIES

Housing: Coed dorms, special housing for disabled students, special housing for international students, apartments for single students. 85% of campus accessible to physically diasbled. **Special Academic Facilities/Equipment:** There are seven art galleries open to the public year-round featuring work by MICA faculty, students, and nationally/internationally known artists; a nature library; and an extensive slide library containing over 220,000 slides. **Computers:** 100% of libraries, 100% of dining areas, 80% of common outdoor areas have wireless network access. Students can register for classes online. Administrative functions (other than registration) can be performed online.

CAMPUS LIFE

Environment: Metropolis. **Activities:** Choral groups, dance, drama/theater, literary magazine, radio station, student government, student-run film society, Student Organization. 50 registered organizations, 3 religious organizations. **On-Campus Highlights:** The Gateway, our new dormitory, The Brown Center, our Digital Arts cente, The Meyerhoff House dormitory & dining, Various on-campus galleries/exhibitiions, Cafe Doris and Java Corner, two eateries. **Environmental Initiatives:** Single-Stream recycling of recyclable waste.

ADMISSIONS

Freshman Academic Profile: Average high school GPA 3.3. 70% from public high schools. **Reported SAT (pre-2016 redesign) scores:** SAT Math middle 50% range 500-630. SAT Critical Reading middle 50% range 520-660. SAT Writing middle 50% range 510-640. **Concordant SAT scores:** SAT EBRW middle 50% 570–700. SAT Math middle 50% range 530–650. Minimum internet-based TOEFL 80. Minimum paper TOEFL 550. **Basis for Candidate Selection:** *Very important factors considered include:* rigor of secondary school record, academic GPA, talent/ability, level of applicant's interest. *Important factors considered include:* class rank, standardized test scores, application essay, interview, extracurricular activities. *Other factors considered include:*

recommendation(s), character/personal qualities, alumni/ae relation, racial/ethnic status, volunteer work. **Freshman Admission Requirements:** High school diploma is required and GED is accepted. *Academic units required:* 4 English, 2 math, 2 science, 1 science lab, 4 social studies, 3 history, 6 academic electives, and 2 units from above areas or other academic areas. *Academic units recommended:* 4 English, 3 math, 3 science, 4 social studies, 4 history, and 5 units from above areas or other academic areas. **Freshman Admission Statistics:** 3,475 applied, 57.09% admitted, 18% enrolled. **Transfer Admission Requirements:** High school transcript, college transcript(s), essay or personal statement, Minimum college GPA of 2.8 required. Lowest grade transferable C. **General Admission Information:** Application fee $70. Regular application deadline 2/1. Regular notification 3/4. Nonfall registration accepted. Admission may be deferred for a maximum of 1 year.

COSTS AND FINANCIAL AID

Annual tuition $43,760. Room and board $12,450. Required fees $1,640. Average book expense $1,450. **Required Forms and Deadlines:** FAFSA, Institution's own financial aid form. **Notification of Awards:** Applicants will be notified of awards on or about 4/6. **Types of Aid:** *Need-based scholarships/grants:* Federal Pell, FSEOG, State scholarships/grants, Private scholarships, College/university scholarship or grant aid from institutional funds. *Loans:* Direct Subsidized Stafford Loans, Direct Unsubsidized Stafford Loans, Direct PLUS loans, Federal Perkins Loans. *Student Employment:* Federal Work-Study Program available. Institutional employment available. **Criteria for awarding aid:** *Need-based:* Academics, Art. *Non-need-based:* Academics, Art.

MARYLHURST UNIVERSITY

PO Box 261, Marylhurst, OR 97036
Phone: 503-699-6268 • **Financial Aid Phone:** 503-699-6253
E-mail: admissions@marylhurst.edu • **CEEB Code:** 440
Fax: 503-636-9526 • **Website:** www.marylhurst.edu • **ACT Code:** 3470

This private school, affiliated with the Roman Catholic Church, was founded in 1893. It has a 68-acre campus.

RATINGS

Admissions Selectivity Rating: 63   **Fire Safety Rating:** 60*   **Green Rating:** 67

STUDENTS AND FACULTY

Enrollment: 503. **Student Body:** 73% female, 27% male, 25% out-of-state, 3% international (10 countries represented). Asian 3%, African American 3%, Caucasian 70%, Hispanic 7%, Native American 1%, Pacific Islander <1%, Two or more races 3%, Race unknown 11%.
Retention and Graduation: 67% freshmen return for sophomore year. 20% freshmen graduate within 4 years. 40% freshmen graduate within 6 years.
Faculty: 0% of classes are taught by teaching assistants.

ACADEMICS

Degrees: bachelor's, certificate, master's, postbachelor's certifiate, post-master's certificate. **Classes:** Most classes have fewer than 10 students. **Most popular majors:** Multi-/Interdisciplinary Studies; Business Administration and Management; Psychology. **Special Study Options:** Accelerated program, cooperative education program, cross-registration, distance learning, double major, English as a Second Language (ESL), independent study, internships, student-designed major, study abroad, teacher certification program, weekend college. **Disability Services:** Special programs offered to physically disabled students, including note-taking services, reader services, tape recorders, tutors. **Career Services:** Career/job search classes, Internships.

FACILITIES

Housing: 90% of campus accessible to physically diasbled. **Special Academic Facilities/Equipment:** Art Gym, Art Gallery, Streff Gallery. **Computers:** Students can register for classes online. Administrative functions (other than registration) can be performed online.

CAMPUS LIFE

Environment: City. **Activities:** Choral groups, jazz band, literary magazine, music ensembles, symphony orchestra 6 registered organizations, 1 honor society.

ADMISSIONS

Freshman Admission Requirements: High school diploma is required and GED is accepted. **Freshman Admission Statistics:** 5 applied, 100.00% admitted, 100% enrolled. **Transfer Admission Requirements:** High school transcript, college transcript(s), Minimum college GPA of 2.0 required. Lowest grade transferable C-. **General Admission Information:** Application fee $50. Nonfall registration accepted. Admission may be deferred for a maximum of 1 yr.

COSTS AND FINANCIAL AID

Annual tuition $20,835. Required fees $0. **Required Forms and Deadlines:** FAFSA, Institution's own financial aid form. **Notification of Awards:** Applicants will be notified of awards on a rolling basis beginning 4/1. **Types of Aid:** *Need-based scholarships/grants:* Federal Pell, FSEOG, State scholarships/grants, Private scholarships, College/university scholarship or grant aid from institutional funds. *Loans:* Direct Subsidized Stafford Loans, Direct Unsubsidized Stafford Loans, Direct PLUS loans, Federal Perkins Loans. *Student Employment:* Federal Work-Study Program available. Institutional employment available. **Financial Aid Statistics:** 100% needy freshmen, 96% needy undergrads receive need-based scholarship or grant aid. 0% undergrads receive non-need-based scholarship or grant aid. 100% freshmen, 91% undergrads receive need-based self-help aid. 0% freshmen, 0% undergrads receive athletic scholarships. Average cumulative indebtedness $0. **Criteria for awarding aid:** *Need-based:* Academics, Art, Minority status, Music/drama. *Non-need-based:* Academics, Art, Music/drama.

MARYMOUNT CALIFORNIA UNIVERSITY

30800 Palos Verdes Drive East, Rancho Palos Verdes, CA 90275
Phone: 310-377-5501 • **Financial Aid Phone:** 310-303-7311
E-mail: admissions@marymountcalifornia.edu • **CEEB Code:** 4515
Fax: 310-265-0962 • **Website:** http://www.marymountcalifornia.edu/
ACT Code: 316

This private school, affiliated with the Roman Catholic Church, was founded in 1932. It has a 22-acre campus.

RATINGS

Admissions Selectivity Rating: 74   **Fire Safety Rating:** 93   **Green Rating:** 60*

STUDENTS AND FACULTY

Enrollment: 1,034. **Student Body:** 55% female, 45% male, 5% out-of-state, 14% international (42 countries represented). Asian 5%, African American 8%, Caucasian 25%, Hispanic 36%, Native American <1%, Pacific Islander 1%, Two or more races 4%, Race unknown 6%.
Retention and Graduation: 68% freshmen return for sophomore year.
Faculty: Student/faculty ratio 17:1. 28 full-time faculty, 68% hold PhDs, 18% are are members of minority groups, 43% are women. 0% of classes are taught by teaching assistants.

ACADEMICS

Degrees: associate, bachelor's, master's. **Classes:** Most classes have 10-19 students. **Most popular majors:** Business, Management, Marketing, and Related Support Services; Liberal Arts and Sciences Studies and Humanities; Psychology. **Special Study Options:** dual enrollment, English as a Second Language (ESL), honors program, internships, study abroad, weekend college. **Honors Programs:** Marymount Honors Program Phi Theta Kappa Combined degree programs: BA/MA. **Disability Services:** Special programs offered to physically disabled students, including note-taking services, reader services, tape recorders, tutors. **Career Services:** Alumni network, Alumni services, Career assessment, Internships, Regional alumni, On-campus interviews. Experiential Learning

FACILITIES

Housing: Coed dorms, special housing for disabled students. 100% of campus accessible to physically diasbled. **Computers:** 100% of classrooms, 100% of dorms, 100% of libraries, 100% of dining areas, 100% of student union, 75% of common outdoor areas have wireless network access. Administrative functions (other than registration) can be performed online.

CAMPUS LIFE

Environment: Town. **Activities:** Choral groups, dance, drama/theater, jazz band, literary magazine, musical theater, radio station, student government, student newspaper, student-run film society, Campus Ministries, Student Organization. 2 honor societies, 2 religious organizations. **Athletics (Intercollegiate):** *Men:* soccer. *Women:* soccer.

ADMISSIONS

Freshman Academic Profile: Average high school GPA 3.0. 30% from public high schools. **Reported SAT (pre-2016 redesign) scores:** SAT Math middle 50% range 390-520. SAT Critical Reading middle 50% range 410-520. SAT Writing middle 50% range 400-520. **Concordant SAT scores:** SAT EBRW middle 50% 450–580. SAT Math middle 50% range 430–550. ACT middle 50% range 16-22. Minimum internet-based TOEFL 61. **Basis for Candidate Selection:** *Very important factors considered include:* rigor of secondary school record, academic GPA. *Other factors considered include:* class rank, standardized test scores, application essay, recommendation(s), interview, extracurricular activities, talent/ability, character/personal qualities, alumni/ae relation, volunteer work, level of applicant's interest. **Freshman Admission Requirements:** High school diploma is required and GED is accepted. *Academic units recommended:* 4 English, 3 math, 2 science, 2 foreign language, 2 social studies, 2 history, 1 academic elective. **Freshman Admission Statistics:** 1,612 applied, 59.43% admitted, 30% enrolled. **Transfer Admission Requirements:** High school transcript, college transcript(s), Lowest grade transferable C-. **General Admission Information:** Application fee $50. Priority deadline 3/1. Nonfall registration accepted. Admission may be deferred for a maximum of 1 year.

COSTS AND FINANCIAL AID
Required Forms and Deadlines: FAFSA. **Notification of Awards:** Applicants will be notified of awards on or about 3/1. **Types of Aid:** *Need-based scholarships/grants:* Federal Pell, FSEOG, State scholarships/grants, Private scholarships, College/university scholarship or grant aid from institutional funds. *Loans:* Direct Subsidized Stafford Loans, Direct Unsubsidized Stafford Loans, Direct PLUS loans. *Student Employment:* Federal Work-Study Program available. Institutional employment available. **Financial Aid Statistics:** 100% needy freshmen, 100% needy undergrads receive need-based scholarship or grant aid. 86% freshmen, 88% undergrads receive non-need-based scholarship or grant aid. 1% freshmen, 6% undergrads receive need-based self-help aid. 5% freshmen, 5% undergrads receive athletic scholarships. 84% freshmen, 74% undergrads receive any aid. **Criteria for awarding aid:** *Need-based:* Academics. *Non-need-based:* Academics, Art, Athletics.

MARYMOUNT MANHATTAN COLLEGE

221 East 71 Street, New York, NY 10021
Phone: 212-517-0430 • **Financial Aid Phone:** 212-517-0500
E-mail: admissions@mmm.edu • **CEEB Code:** 2405
Fax: 212-517-0448 • **Website:** www.mmm.edu • **ACT Code:** 2810

This private school was founded in 1936. It has a 1-acre campus.

RATINGS
Admissions Selectivity Rating: 73   **Fire Safety Rating:** 60*   **Green Rating:** 60*

STUDENTS AND FACULTY
Enrollment: 1,875. **Student Body:** 77% female, 23% male, 59% out-of-state, 5% international (66 countries represented). Asian 4%, African American 10%, Caucasian 57%, Hispanic 18%, Native American 1%, Pacific Islander <1%, Two or more races 1%, Race unknown 5%.
Retention and Graduation: 74% freshmen return for sophomore year. 34% freshmen graduate within 4 years. 42% freshmen graduate within 6 years.
Faculty: Student/faculty ratio 11:1. 94 full-time faculty, 95% hold PhDs, 10% are are members of minority groups, 62% are women. 0% of classes are taught by teaching assistants.

ACADEMICS
Degrees: associate, bachelor's. **Classes:** Most classes have 10-19 students. **Most popular majors:** Visual and Performing Arts; Communication and Media Studies; Psychology. **Special Study Options:** Accelerated program, distance learning, double major, dual enrollment, exchange student program (domestic), independent study, internships, liberal arts/career combination, study abroad, teacher certification program. **Disability Services:** Special programs offered to physically disabled students, including note-taking services, reader services, tape recorders, tutors. **Career Services:** Alumni network, Alumni services, Career/job search classes, Career assessment, Internships, Regional alumni.

FACILITIES
Housing: Coed dorms. **Special Academic Facilities/Equipment:** Gallery, communications and learning center, theatre, media center, college skills center, mathematics lab, Samuel Freeman science center,Comm Arts multimedia suite. **Computers:** 40% of classrooms, 100% of libraries, have wireless network access. Students can register for classes online. Administrative functions (other than registration) can be performed online.

CAMPUS LIFE
Environment: Metropolis. **Activities:** Choral groups, dance, drama/theater, literary magazine, musical theater, radio station, student government, student newspaper, yearbook, Student Organization. 30 registered organizations, 7 honor societies, 2 religious organizations. **On-Campus Highlights:** Theresa Lang Theatre, Hewitt Gallery of Art, Science Laboratories, 55th Street Residence Hall, Shanahan Library, Student cafeterias. **Environmental Initiatives:** purchase of renewable energy.

ADMISSIONS
Freshman Academic Profile: Average high school GPA 3.3. **Reported SAT (pre-2016 redesign) scores:** SAT Math middle 50% range 440-550. SAT Critical Reading middle 50% range 470-590. SAT Writing middle 50% range

480-580. **Concordant SAT scores:** SAT EBRW middle 50% 530–640. SAT Math middle 50% range 480–570. ACT middle 50% range 20-26. Minimum internet-based TOEFL 80. **Basis for Candidate Selection:** *Very important factors considered include:* rigor of secondary school record, academic GPA, standardized test scores. *Important factors considered include:* application essay, recommendation(s), talent/ability, character/personal qualities, level of applicant's interest. *Other factors considered include:* interview, extracurricular activities, first generation, alumni/ae relation, geographical residence, state residency, volunteer work, work experience. **Freshman Admission Requirements:** High school diploma is required and GED is accepted. *Academic units required:* 4 English, 3 math, 3 science, 3 social studies, 4 academic electives. *Academic units recommended:* 2 science labs, 2 foreign language. **Freshman Admission Statistics:** 4,459 applied, 83.81% admitted, 14% enrolled. **Transfer Admission Requirements:** High school transcript, college transcript(s), essay or personal statement, statement of good standing from prior institution(s). Minimum college GPA of 2.5 required. Lowest grade transferable C-. **General Admission Information:** Application fee $60. Priority deadline 8/1. Nonfall registration accepted. Admission may be deferred.

COSTS AND FINANCIAL AID
Annual tuition $28,870. Room and board $15,990. Required fees $1,420. Average book expense $1,000. **Required Forms and Deadlines:** FAFSA, State aid form. **Notification of Awards:** Applicants will be notified of awards on a rolling basis beginning 3/15. **Types of Aid:** *Need-based scholarships/grants:* Federal Pell, FSEOG, State scholarships/grants, Private scholarships, College/university scholarship or grant aid from institutional funds. *Loans:* Direct Subsidized Stafford Loans, Direct Unsubsidized Stafford Loans, Direct PLUS loans. *Student Employment:* Federal Work-Study Program available. Institutional employment available. **Financial Aid Statistics:** 99% needy undergrads receive need-based scholarship or grant aid. 0% undergrads receive non-need-based scholarship or grant aid. 73% freshmen, 79% undergrads receive need-based self-help aid. 0% freshmen, 0% undergrads receive athletic scholarships. Average cumulative indebtedness $30,159. **Criteria for awarding aid:** *Need-based:* Academics. *Non-need-based:* Academics, Art, Leadership, Music/drama, State/district residency.

MARYMOUNT UNIVERSITY

2807 North Glebe Road, Arlington, VA 22207
Phone: 703-284-1500 • **Financial Aid Phone:** 703-284-1530
E-mail: admissions@marymount.edu • **CEEB Code:** 5405
Fax: 703-522-0349 • **Website:** http://www.marymount.edu • **ACT Code:** 4378

This private school, affiliated with the Roman Catholic Church, was founded in 1950. It has a 21-acre campus.

RATINGS
Admissions Selectivity Rating: 78   **Fire Safety Rating:** 86   **Green Rating:** 60*

STUDENTS AND FACULTY
Enrollment: 2,199. **Student Body:** 75% female, 25% male, 42% out-of-state, 6% international (70 countries represented). Asian 8%, African American 15%, Caucasian 46%, Hispanic 12%, Native American 1%, Pacific Islander 0%, Two or more races 0%, Race unknown 13%.
Retention and Graduation: 71% freshmen return for sophomore year.
Faculty: Student/faculty ratio 14:1. 138 full-time faculty, 89% hold PhDs, 5% are are members of minority groups, 74% are women. 0% of classes are taught by teaching assistants.

ACADEMICS
Degrees: bachelor's, certificate, doctoral, master's, postbachelor's certifiate, post-master's certificate. **Classes:** Most classes have 10-19 students. **Most popular majors:** Business Administration and Management; Fashion/Apparel Design; Biology/Biological Sciences. **Special Study Options:** Accelerated program, cross-registration, distance learning, double major, English as a Second Language (ESL), honors program, independent study, internships, student-designed major, study abroad, teacher certification program. **Honors Programs:** The Honors Program at Marymount University Combined degree programs: BBA/MBA, Health Promotion Mgt. BS/MS. **Disability Services:** Special programs offered to physically disabled students, including note-taking services, reader services, tape recorders, tutors. **Career Services:** Alumni network, Career/job search classes, Internships.

FACILITIES
Housing: Coed dorms, men's dorms, women's dorms. 75% of campus accessible to physically diasbled. **Special Academic Facilities/Equipment:** Art gallery, learning resource center, audiovisual center, studio, and computer labs **Computers:** Students can register for classes online. Administrative functions (other than registration) can be performed online.

CAMPUS LIFE

Environment: City. **Activities:** Choral groups, dance, drama/theater, literary magazine, student government, student newspaper, yearbook, Campus Ministries, Student Organization. 33 registered organizations, 11 honor societies, 2 religious organizations. **Athletics (Intercollegiate):** *Men:* basketball, cross-country, golf, lacrosse, soccer, swimming. *Women:* basketball, cross-country, lacrosse, soccer, swimming, volleyball. **On-Campus Highlights:** Student Center, Gym, Bernie's Cafe, Turf field, Ballston campus. **Environmental Initiatives:** Recycling program.

ADMISSIONS

Freshman Academic Profile: Average high school GPA 3.1. 15% in top 10% of high school class, 41% in top 25% of high school class, 81% in top 50% of high school class. 68% from public high schools. **Reported SAT (pre-2016 redesign) scores:** SAT Math middle 50% range 450-550. SAT Critical Reading middle 50% range 450-560. SAT Writing middle 50% range 450-550. **Concordant SAT scores:** SAT EBRW middle 50% 500–610. SAT Math middle 50% range 490–570. ACT middle 50% range 18-24. Minimum internet-based TOEFL 79. Minimum paper TOEFL 550. **Basis for Candidate Selection:** *Very important factors considered include:* rigor of secondary school record, academic GPA, standardized test scores. *Important factors considered include:* class rank, recommendation(s), interview, talent/ability. *Other factors considered include:* application essay, extracurricular activities, character/personal qualities, first generation, alumni/ae relation, volunteer work, work experience, level of applicant's interest. **Freshman Admission Requirements:** High school diploma is required and GED is accepted. *Academic units recommended:* 4 English, 3 math, 2 science, 3 foreign language, 3 social studies. **Freshman Admission Statistics:** 1,904 applied, 80.93% admitted, 26% enrolled. **Transfer Admission Requirements:** college transcript(s), statement of good standing from prior institution(s). Minimum college GPA of 2.0 required. Lowest grade transferable C. **General Admission Information:** Application fee $40. Priority deadline 5/1. Nonfall registration accepted. Admission may be deferred for a maximum of 1 year.

COSTS AND FINANCIAL AID

Annual tuition $23,700. Room and board $8,705. Required fees $220. Average book expense $800. **Required Forms and Deadlines:** FAFSA. **Notification of Awards:** Applicants will be notified of awards on a rolling basis beginning 3/15. **Types of Aid:** *Need-based scholarships/grants:* Federal Pell, FSEOG, State scholarships/grants, Private scholarships, College/university scholarship or grant aid from institutional funds. *Loans:* Direct Subsidized Stafford Loans, Direct Unsubsidized Stafford Loans, Federal Perkins Loans. *Student Employment:* Federal Work-Study Program available. Institutional employment available. **Financial Aid Statistics:** 83% needy freshmen, 74% needy undergrads receive need-based scholarship or grant aid. 80% freshmen, 73% undergrads receive non-need-based scholarship or grant aid. 78% freshmen, 83% undergrads receive need-based self-help aid. 0% freshmen, 0% undergrads receive athletic scholarships. 92% freshmen, 84% undergrads receive any aid. **Criteria for awarding aid:** *Need-based:* Academics, Religious affiliation. *Non-need-based:* Academics, Alumni affiliation, Leadership, State/district residency.

MARYVILLE COLLEGE

502 East Lamar Alexander Parkway, Maryville, TN 37804-5907
Phone: 865-981-8092 • **Financial Aid Phone:** 865-981-8100
E-mail: admissions@maryvillecollege.edu • **CEEB Code:** 1454
Fax: 865-981-8005 • **Website:** www.maryvillecollege.edu • **ACT Code:** 3988

This private school, affiliated with the Presbyterian Church, was founded in 1819. It has a 370-acre campus.

RATINGS

Admissions Selectivity Rating: 84   **Fire Safety Rating:** 92   **Green Rating:** 60*

STUDENTS AND FACULTY

Enrollment: 1,114. **Student Body:** 55% female, 45% male, 24% out-of-state, 4% international (20 countries represented). Asian 1%, African American 5%, Caucasian 86%, Hispanic 2%, Native American <1%, Pacific Islander 0%, Two or more races 0%, Race unknown 2%.
Retention and Graduation: 67% freshmen return for sophomore year. 43% freshmen graduate within 4 years. 51% freshmen graduate within 6 years. 28% grads go on to further study within 1 year. **Faculty:** Student/faculty ratio 12:1. 79 full-time faculty, 76% hold PhDs, 4% are are members of minority groups, 54% are women. 0% of classes are taught by teaching assistants.

ACADEMICS

Degrees: bachelor's. **Classes:** Most classes have 10-19 students. Most lab/discussion sessions have 10-19 students. **Most popular majors:** Education;

Biology/Biological Sciences; Business/Commerce. **Special Study Options:** double major, English as a Second Language (ESL), honors program, independent study, internships, liberal arts/career combination, student-designed major, study abroad, teacher certification program. **Honors Programs:** Presidential and Deans scholars participate in honors courses and honors tutorial practicum. Most courses may be taken with "honors" status. Combined degree programs: BA/MSN. **Disability Services:** Special programs offered to physically disabled students, including note-taking services, reader services, tape recorders, tutors. **Career Services:** Alumni network, Alumni services, Career/job search classes, Career assessment, Internships, Regional alumni. Internships and practica are available in almost all major fields.

FACILITIES

Housing: Coed dorms, special housing for disabled students, men's dorms, women's dorms, apartments for single students, Special Interest groups. 90% of campus accessible to physically diasbled. **Special Academic Facilities/Equipment:** Art gallery, theatre, greenhouse, College Woods **Computers:** 100% of classrooms, 100% of dorms, 100% of libraries, 100% of dining areas, 100% of student union, 50% of common outdoor areas have wireless network access. Students can register for classes online. Administrative functions (other than registration) can be performed online.

CAMPUS LIFE

Environment: Town. **Activities:** Choral groups, concert band, dance, drama/theater, jazz band, literary magazine, music ensembles, musical theater, student government, student newspaper, symphony orchestra, yearbook, Campus Ministries. 63 registered organizations, 15 honor societies, 5 religious organizations. **Athletics (Intercollegiate):** *Men:* baseball, basketball, cross-country, equestrian sports, football, soccer, tennis. *Women:* basketball, cross-country, equestrian sports, soccer, softball, tennis, volleyball. **On-Campus Highlights:** Isaacs Student Center, Mountain Challenge, Lloyd Beach, New Lloyd Residence Hall, Center for Calling and Career, Mountain Challenge includes a 60' Alpine Tower, rock climbing wall, ropes course, and kayak roll sessions on campus. In addition there are trips offered every Saturday to nearby attractions, i.e. rock climbing, white water rafting, camping, and caving. **Environmental Initiatives:** Steam plant boiler is fueled by recycled wood products.

ADMISSIONS

Freshman Academic Profile: Average high school GPA 3.6. 34% in top 10% of high school class, 65% in top 25% of high school class, 89% in top 50% of high school class. 91% from public high schools. **Reported SAT (pre-2016 redesign) scores:** SAT Math middle 50% range 480-610. SAT Critical Reading middle 50% range 470-630. SAT Writing middle 50% range 450-610. **Concordant SAT scores:** SAT EBRW middle 50% 510–670. SAT Math middle 50% range 510–630. ACT middle 50% range 21-28. Minimum paper TOEFL 525. **Basis for Candidate Selection:** *Very important factors considered include:* rigor of secondary school record, class rank, standardized test scores. *Important factors considered include:* academic GPA, recommendation(s), interview, extracurricular activities. *Other factors considered include:* application essay, talent/ability, character/personal qualities, first generation, alumni/ae relation, volunteer work, level of applicant's interest. **Freshman Admission Requirements:** High school diploma is required and GED is accepted. *Academic units required:* 4 English, 3 math, 2 science, 1 science lab, 2 foreign language, 2 social studies, 1 academic elective. *Academic units recommended:* 1 history. **Freshman Admission Statistics:** 1,291 applied, 77.69% admitted, 30% enrolled. **Transfer Admission Requirements:** college transcript(s), statement of good standing from prior institution(s). Minimum college GPA of 2.0 required. Lowest grade transferable C. **General Admission Information:** Priority deadline 1/15. Nonfall registration accepted. Admission may be deferred for a maximum of 1 year.

COSTS AND FINANCIAL AID

Annual tuition $26,272. Room and board $8,240. Required fees $675. Average book expense $880. **Required Forms and Deadlines:** FAFSA. **Types of Aid:** *Need-based scholarships/grants:* Federal Pell, FSEOG, State scholarships/grants, Private scholarships, College/university scholarship or grant aid from institutional funds. *Loans:* Direct Subsidized Stafford Loans, Direct Unsubsidized Stafford Loans, Direct PLUS loans, Federal Perkins Loans, State Loans, College/university loans from institutional funds. *Student Employment:* Federal Work-Study Program available. **Financial Aid Statistics:** 75% needy freshmen, 98% needy undergrads receive need-based scholarship or grant aid. 31% freshmen, 25% undergrads receive non-need-based scholarship or grant aid. 78% freshmen, 61% undergrads receive need-based self-help aid. 0% freshmen, 0% undergrads receive athletic scholarships. 100% freshmen, 98% undergrads receive any aid. **Criteria for awarding aid:** *Need-based:* Academics, Art, Leadership, Minority status, Music/drama, Religious affiliation. *Non-need-based:* Academics, Art, Leadership, Minority status, Music/drama, Religious affiliation, State/district residency.

MARYVILLE UNIVERSITY OF SAINT LOUIS

650 Maryville University Drive, St. Louis, MO 63141-7299
Phone: 314-529-9350 • **Financial Aid Phone:** 314-529-9360
E-mail: admissions@maryville.edu • **CEEB Code:** 6399
Fax: 314-529-9927 • **ACT Code:** 2326

This private school was founded in 1872. It has a 130-acre campus.

RATINGS
Admissions Selectivity Rating: 80   **Fire Safety Rating:** 93   **Green Rating:** 60*

STUDENTS AND FACULTY
Enrollment: 2,892. **Student Body:** 67% female, 33% male, 24% out-of-state, 5% international (14 countries represented). Asian 3%, African American 8%, Caucasian 73%, Hispanic 4%, Native American <1%, Pacific Islander <1%, Two or more races 2%, Race unknown 5%.
Retention and Graduation: 86% freshmen return for sophomore year. 57% freshmen graduate within 4 years. 75% freshmen graduate within 6 years. **Faculty:** Student/faculty ratio 13:1. 144 full-time faculty, 74% hold PhDs, 10% are members of minority groups, 64% are women. 0% of classes are taught by teaching assistants.

ACADEMICS
Degrees: bachelor's, doctoral/professional, doctoral/research, doctoral, master's, postbachelor's certificate, post-master's certificate. **Classes:** Most classes have 10-19 students. Most lab/discussion sessions have fewer than 10 students. **Most popular majors:** Physical Therapy/Therapist; Business/Commerce; Registered Nursing/Registered Nurse. **Special Study Options:** Accelerated program, cooperative education program, cross-registration, distance learning, double major, dual enrollment, honors program, independent study, internships, liberal arts/career combination, student-designed major, study abroad, teacher certification program, weekend college, Washington Center, Semester at Sea. **Honors Programs:** Bascom Honors Program Combined degree programs: MU-St. Louis Univ. M.S.W. Joint Degree Program. **Disability Services:** Special programs offered to physically disabled students, including note-taking services, reader services, tape recorders, tutors. **Career Services:** Alumni services, Career/job search classes, Career assessment, Internships, Cooperative Education.

FACILITIES
Housing: Coed dorms, apartments for single students, Wellness Housing, Theme Housing. 100% of campus accessible to physically disabled. **Special Academic Facilities/Equipment:** University Center, art galleries, auditorium, chapel, observatory, teaching lab, clinical labs, art and design labs, videoconferencing facility with downlinking and electronic multi-media capability for presentations. **Computers:** 100% of classrooms, 100% of dorms, 100% of libraries, 100% of dining areas, 100% of student union, 100% of common outdoor areas have wireless network access. Students can register for classes online. Administrative functions (other than registration) can be performed online.

CAMPUS LIFE
Environment: Metropolis. **Activities:** Choral groups, dance, drama/theater, jazz band, literary magazine, music ensembles, pep band, student government, student newspaper, symphony orchestra, Campus Ministries. 40 registered organizations, 3 honor societies, 4 religious organizations. **Athletics (Intercollegiate):** *Men:* baseball, basketball, cheerleading, cross-country, golf, soccer, tennis. *Women:* basketball, cheerleading, cross-country, golf, soccer, softball, tennis, volleyball.

ADMISSIONS
Freshman Academic Profile: Average high school GPA 3.6. 28% in top 10% of high school class, 59% in top 25% of high school class, 85% in top 50% of high school class. 77% from public high schools. ACT middle 50% range 22-27. Minimum paper TOEFL 500. **Basis for Candidate Selection:** *Very important factors considered include:* academic GPA, standardized test scores. *Important factors considered include:* rigor of secondary school record, extracurricular activities. *Other factors considered include:* class rank, application essay, recommendation(s), interview, talent/ability, character/personal qualities. **Freshman Admission Requirements:** High school diploma is required and GED is accepted. *Academic units required:* 4 English, 3 math, 2 science, 2 social studies, and 3 units from above areas or other academic areas. **Freshman Admission Statistics:** 1,846 applied, 92.80% admitted, 32% enrolled. **Transfer Admission Requirements:** college transcript(s), Minimum college GPA of 2.0 required. Lowest grade transferable C-. **General Admission Information:** Priority deadline 12/15. Regular application deadline 8/15. Nonfall registration accepted. Admission may be deferred for a maximum of 1 year.

COSTS AND FINANCIAL AID
Annual tuition $25,558. Room and board $10,088. Required fees $2,400. **Required Forms and Deadlines:** FAFSA. **Notification of Awards:**

Applicants will be notified of awards on a rolling basis beginning 3/1. **Types of Aid:** *Need-based scholarships/grants:* Federal Pell, FSEOG, State scholarships/grants, Private scholarships, College/university scholarship or grant aid from institutional funds. *Loans:* Direct Subsidized Stafford Loans, Direct Unsubsidized Stafford Loans, Direct PLUS loans, Federal Perkins Loans. *Student Employment:* Federal Work-Study Program available. Institutional employment available. **Financial Aid Statistics:** 98% needy freshmen, 97% needy undergrads receive need-based scholarship or grant aid. 15% freshmen, 9% undergrads receive non-need-based scholarship or grant aid. 59% freshmen, 71% undergrads receive need-based self-help aid. 10% freshmen, 7% undergrads receive athletic scholarships. 72% freshmen, 65% undergrads receive any aid. 84% undergrads borrow to pay for school. Average cumulative indebtedness $19,266. **Criteria for awarding aid:** *Need-based:* Academics, Art, Minority status, Music/drama. *Non-need-based:* Academics, Art, Athletics, Job skills, Leadership, Minority status, Music/drama, State/district residency.

MARYWOOD UNIVERSITY

Office of University Admissions, Scranton, PA 18509
Phone: 570-348-6234 • **Financial Aid Phone:** 866-279-9663
E-mail: yourfuture@marywood.edu • **CEEB Code:** 2407
Fax: 570-961-4763 • **Website:** www.marywood.edu • **ACT Code:** 3626

This private school, affiliated with the Roman Catholic Church, was founded in 1915. It has a 115-acre campus.

RATINGS
Admissions Selectivity Rating: 80   **Fire Safety Rating:** 95   **Green Rating:** 60*

STUDENTS AND FACULTY
Enrollment: 1,817. **Student Body:** 68% female, 32% male, 30% out-of-state, 1% international (8 countries represented). Asian 2%, African American 2%, Caucasian 79%, Hispanic 6%, Native American <1%, Pacific Islander <1%, Two or more races 2%, Race unknown 8%.
Retention and Graduation: 83% freshmen return for sophomore year. 56% freshmen graduate within 4 years. 70% freshmen graduate within 6 years. 40% grads go on to further study within 1 year. 6% grads pursue arts and sciences degrees, 1% grads pursue business degrees. 1% grads pursue medical degrees. **Faculty:** Student/faculty ratio 11:1. 160 full-time faculty, 91% hold PhDs, 14% are members of minority groups, 56% are women. 0% of classes are taught by teaching assistants.

ACADEMICS
Degrees: bachelor's, certificate, doctoral/professional, doctoral/research, master's, postbachelor's certificate, post-master's certificate. **Classes:** Most classes have 10-19 students. **Most popular majors:** Registered Nursing/Registered Nurse; Audiology/Audiologist and Speech; Psychology. **Special Study Options:** cross-registration, double major, dual enrollment, English as a Second Language (ESL), honors program, independent study, internships, student-designed major, study abroad, teacher certification program. **Honors Programs:** Open Door Honors program Combined degree programs: BA/MA, BS/MS. **Disability Services:** Special programs offered to physically disabled students, including note-taking services, reader services, tape recorders, tutors. **Career Services:** Alumni network, Alumni services, Career/job search classes, Career assessment, Internships, Regional alumni. We are most proud of our individual counseling on job search, internship search, resume and interview assistance.

FACILITIES
Housing: Coed dorms, special housing for disabled students, men's dorms, women's dorms, apartments for single students, 98% of campus accessible to physically disabled. **Special Academic Facilities/Equipment:** Mellow Athletic and Fitness Center, Mahady Gallery, Suraci Gallery, The Maslow Study Gallery for Contemporary Art, Performing Arts Center, O'Neill Center for Healthy Families, Insalaco Studio Arts Center, Center for Architectural Studies, Marywood University Arboretum, Curriculum Lab, electronic learning labs, Broadcast Studios, instructional media lab, interactive video lab, computerized editing facility, center for natural and health sciences, psycho-physiology experimental lab, psychology/education research lab, science multi-media lab, language lab, center for justice and peace, on-campus preschool and day care, video tele-conferencing lab. **Computers:** 75% of classrooms, 75% of dorms, 100% of libraries, 100% of dining areas, 100% of student union, 75% of common outdoor areas have wireless network access. Students can register for classes online. Administrative functions (other than registration) can be performed online.

CAMPUS LIFE
Environment: City. **Activities:** Choral groups, concert band, dance, drama/theater, jazz band, literary magazine, music ensembles, musical theater, radio

station, student government, student newspaper, television station, Campus Ministries, Student Organization. 43 registered organizations, 31 honor societies, 1 religious organization. 1 sororities. **Athletics (Intercollegiate):** *Men:* baseball, basketball, cross-country, diving, lacrosse, soccer, swimming, tennis. *Women:* basketball, cross-country, diving, field hockey, lacrosse, soccer, softball, swimming, tennis, volleyball. **On-Campus Highlights:** Mellow Center for Athletics and Wellness, Insalaco Center for Studio Arts, Liberal Arts Center Rotunda, Cafe Ritazza/Main Dining Room, Nazareth Student Center. **Environmental Initiatives:** Purchase of renewable fuel sources; wind and solar power $28,800 annually.

ADMISSIONS

Freshman Academic Profile: Average high school GPA 3.5. 13% in top 10% of high school class, 48% in top 25% of high school class, 80% in top 50% of high school class. 89% from public high schools. **Reported SAT (pre-2016 redesign) scores:** SAT Math middle 50% range 470-560. SAT Critical Reading middle 50% range 460-560. SAT Writing middle 50% range 450-550. **Concordant SAT scores:** SAT EBRW middle 50% 510–610. SAT Math middle 50% range 510–580. Minimum internet-based TOEFL 71. Minimum paper TOEFL 530. **Basis for Candidate Selection:** *Very important factors considered include:* rigor of secondary school record, class rank, academic GPA, standardized test scores, interview, character/personal qualities. *Important factors considered include:* application essay, recommendation(s), extracurricular activities, talent/ability. *Other factors considered include:* volunteer work, work experience, level of applicant's interest. **Freshman Admission Requirements:** High school diploma is required and GED is accepted. *Academic units required:* 4 English, 2 math, 1 science, 1 science lab, 3 social studies, 6 academic electives. **Freshman Admission Statistics:** 2,273 applied, 70.52% admitted, 23% enrolled. **Transfer Admission Requirements:** High school transcript, college transcript(s), Minimum college GPA of 2.25 required. Lowest grade transferable C. **General Admission Information:** Application fee $35. Nonfall registration accepted. Admission may be deferred for a maximum of 1 year.

COSTS AND FINANCIAL AID

Annual tuition $30,942. Room and board $13,900. Required fees $1,750. Average book expense $1,000. **Required Forms and Deadlines:** FAFSA, State aid form. **Notification of Awards:** Applicants will be notified of awards on a rolling basis beginning 3/15. **Types of Aid:** *Need-based scholarships/grants:* Federal Pell, FSEOG, State scholarships/grants, Private scholarships, College/university scholarship or grant aid from institutional funds. *Loans:* Direct Subsidized Stafford Loans, Direct Unsubsidized Stafford Loans, Direct PLUS loans, Federal Perkins Loans. *Student Employment:* Federal Work-Study Program available. **Financial Aid Statistics:** 100% needy freshmen, 99% needy undergrads receive need-based scholarship or grant aid. 16% freshmen, 12% undergrads receive non-need-based scholarship or grant aid. 79% freshmen, 84% undergrads receive need-based self-help aid. 0% freshmen, 0% undergrads receive athletic scholarships. 99% freshmen, 99% undergrads receive any aid. 83% undergrads borrow to pay for school. Average cumulative indebtedness $29,064. **Criteria for awarding aid:** *Need-based:* Academics, Art, Leadership, Music/drama. *Non-need-based:* Academics, Alumni affiliation, Art, Leadership, Music/drama.

MASSACHUSETTS COLLEGE OF ART AND DESIGN

621 Huntington Avenue, Boston, MA 2115
Phone: 617-879-7222 • **Financial Aid Phone:** 617-879-7850
E-mail: admissions@massart.edu • **CEEB Code:** 3516
Fax: 617-879-7250 • **ACT Code:** 1846

This public school was founded in 1873. It has a 5-acre campus.

RATINGS

Admissions Selectivity Rating: 76   **Fire Safety Rating:** 82   **Green Rating:** 60*

STUDENTS AND FACULTY

Enrollment: 1,736. **Student Body:** 71% female, 29% male, 33% out-of-state, 4% international. Asian 8%, African American 3%, Caucasian 63%, Hispanic 10%, Native American <1%, Pacific Islander <1%, Two or more races 1%, Race unknown 11%.
Retention and Graduation: 92% freshmen return for sophomore year. 53% freshmen graduate within 4 years. 72% freshmen graduate within 6 years.
Faculty: Student/faculty ratio 10:1. 115 full-time faculty, 0% hold PhDs, 0% are are members of minority groups, 0% are women. 0% of classes are taught by teaching assistants.

ACADEMICS

Degrees: bachelor's, certificate, master's, postbachelor's certificate. **Classes:** Most classes have 10-19 students. **Most popular majors:** Illustration; Graphic Design; Painting. **Special Study Options:** cross-registration, double major, exchange student program (domestic), independent study, internships, liberal arts/career combination, student-designed major, study abroad, teacher certification program. **Disability Services:** Special programs offered to physically disabled students, including note-taking services, reader services, tutors. **Career Services:** Alumni network, Alumni services, Career/job search classes, Career assessment, Internships.

FACILITIES

Housing: Coed dorms, apartments for single students, Off campus housing assistance from school. Additional housing available in Simmons College dorms. 95% of campus accessible to physically disabled. **Special Academic Facilities/Equipment:** Ten art galleries, foundry, glass furnaces, ceramic kilns, video and film studios, performance spaces, Polaroid 20x24 camera, individual studio spaces, design research unit, printmaking facilities, video and photography equipment and facilities, specialized computer labs, specialized equipment and facilities for all art and design programs and levels. **Computers:** 100% of classrooms, 100% of dorms, 100% of libraries, 100% of dining areas, 100% of student union, 100% of common outdoor areas have wireless network access. Students can register for classes online. Administrative functions (other than registration) can be performed online.

CAMPUS LIFE

Environment: Metropolis. **Activities:** dance, drama/theater, music ensembles, radio station, student government, student newspaper, student-run film society, television station, yearbook. 30 registered organizations, 1 honor society, 3 religious organizations. **Athletics (Intercollegiate):** *Men:* baseball, basketball, cross-country, golf, lacrosse, soccer, softball, tennis, volleyball. *Women:* basketball, cross-country, golf, lacrosse, soccer, softball, tennis, volleyball. **On-Campus Highlights:** 10 art galleries, student studios, courtyard, cafes, student center, see http://inside.massart.edu/x942.xml for a description of student activites. **Environmental Initiatives:** http://inside.massart.edu/Administration/Administration_and_Finance/Facilities/Sustainability.html

ADMISSIONS

Freshman Academic Profile: Average high school GPA 3.4. **Reported SAT (pre-2016 redesign) scores:** SAT Math middle 50% range 470-580. SAT Critical Reading middle 50% range 500-620. SAT Writing middle 50% range 480-600. **Concordant SAT scores:** SAT EBRW middle 50% range 550–660. SAT Math middle 50% range 510–600. ACT middle 50% range 21-26. Minimum internet-based TOEFL 85. Minimum paper TOEFL 530. **Basis for Candidate Selection:** *Very important factors considered include:* rigor of secondary school record, academic GPA, application essay, talent/ability. *Important factors considered include:* standardized test scores, state residency. *Other factors considered include:* recommendation(s), extracurricular activities, character/personal qualities, geographical residence, volunteer work, work experience. **Freshman Admission Requirements:** High school diploma is required and GED is accepted. *Academic units required:* 4 English, 2 math, 2 science, 2 science labs, 2 foreign language, 2 social studies, 2 academic electives, and 2 units from above areas or other academic areas. *Academic units recommended:* 1 history. **Freshman Admission Statistics:** 1,273 applied, 71.33% admitted, 32% enrolled. **Transfer Admission Requirements:** college transcript(s), essay or personal statement, statement of good standing from prior institution(s). Minimum college GPA of 2.5 required. Lowest grade transferable C. **General Admission Information:** Application fee $50. Regular application deadline 2/1. Nonfall registration not accepted. Admission may be deferred for a maximum of 12 months.

COSTS AND FINANCIAL AID

Annual in-state tuition $11,225. Annual out-of-state tuition $29,925. Room and board $13,000. Required fees $0. Average book expense $2,100. **Required Forms and Deadlines:** FAFSA. **Types of Aid:** *Need-based scholarships/grants:* Federal Pell, FSEOG, State scholarships/grants, Private scholarships, College/university scholarship or grant aid from institutional funds. *Loans:* Direct Subsidized Stafford Loans, Direct Unsubsidized Stafford Loans, Direct PLUS loans, Federal Perkins Loans, State Loans, College/university loans from institutional funds. *Student Employment:* Federal Work-Study Program available. Institutional employment available. **Financial Aid Statistics:** 85% needy freshmen, 74% needy undergrads receive need-based scholarship or grant aid. 27% freshmen, 21% undergrads receive non-need-based scholarship or grant aid. 89% freshmen, 91% undergrads receive need-based self-help aid. 0% freshmen, 0% undergrads receive athletic scholarships. **Criteria for awarding aid:** *Need-based:* Academics, Leadership. *Non-need-based:* Academics, Art, Leadership, State/district residency.

MASSACHUSETTS INSTITUTE OF TECHNOLOGY

77 Massachusetts Avenue, Cambridge, MA 2139
Phone: 617-253-3400 • **Financial Aid Phone:** 617-258-8600
E-mail: admissions@mit.edu • **CEEB Code:** 3514
Fax: 617-258-8304 • **Website:** web.mit.edu • **ACT Code:** 1858

This private school was founded in 1861. It has a 168-acre campus.

RATINGS

Admissions Selectivity Rating: 99   **Fire Safety Rating:** 90   **Green Rating:** 60*

STUDENTS AND FACULTY

Enrollment: 4,489. **Student Body:** 46% female, 54% male, 90% out-of-state, 10% international (91 countries represented). Asian 26%, African American 6%, Caucasian 35%, Hispanic 15%, Native American <1%, Pacific Islander <1%, Two or more races 7%, Race unknown 2%.
Retention and Graduation: 98% freshmen return for sophomore year. 84% freshmen graduate within 4 years. 93% freshmen graduate within 6 years. 39% grads go on to further study within 1 year. 25% grads pursue arts and sciences degrees. 14% grads pursue medical degrees. **Faculty:** Student/faculty ratio 3:1. 1,264 full-time faculty, 91% hold PhDs, 18% are are members of minority groups, 25% are women.

ACADEMICS

Degrees: bachelor's, doctoral/research, master's. **Classes:** Most classes have fewer than 10 students. Most lab/discussion sessions have 10-19 students. **Most popular majors:** Computer Science; Mechanical Engineering; Mathematics. **Special Study Options:** cooperative education program, cross-registration, double major, internships, study abroad, teacher certification program, Undergraduate Research Opportunitites Program (UROP); Independent Activities Period (IAP); freshman learning communities. Combined degree programs: SB/SM, SB/MEng, SB/MCP. **Disability Services:** Special programs offered to physically disabled students, including note-taking services, reader services, tape recorders. **Career Services:** Alumni network, Alumni services, Career/job search classes, Career assessment, Internships, Regional alumni. We have a very strong on-campus recruiting system. During 2015-2016, 260 employers recruited in MIT Global Education and Career Development. In addition, students have access to a strong database of over 5500+ companies if their interests are outside of the companies who recruit on campus.

FACILITIES

Housing: Coed dorms, special housing for disabled students, women's dorms, fraternity/sorority housing, apartments for married students, cooperative housing, apartments for single students, ThemeHousingindependent living group housing, apartments for students with dependent children, and living learning communities available. **Special Academic Facilities/Equipment:** List Visual Arts Center; MIT Museum; Ray and Maria Stata Center for Computer, Information and Intelligence Sciences; numerous labs and centers **Computers:** 100% of classrooms, 100% of dorms, 100% of libraries, 100% of dining areas, 100% of student union, 80-98% of common outdoor areas have wireless network access. Administrative functions (other than registration) can be performed online.

CAMPUS LIFE

Environment: City. **Activities:** Choral groups, concert band, dance, drama/theater, jazz band, literary magazine, marching band, music ensembles, musical theater, radio station, student government, student newspaper, student-run film society, symphony orchestra, television station, yearbook, Campus Ministries, Student Organization, Model UN. 400 registered organizations, 10 honor societies, 29 religious organizations. 27 fraternities, 6 sororities. **Athletics (Intercollegiate):** *Men:* baseball, basketball, crew/rowing, cross-country, diving, fencing, football, golf, gymnastics, lacrosse, pistol, riflery, sailing, skiing (downhill/alpine), skiing (nordic/cross-country), soccer, squash, swimming, tennis, track/field (outdoor), track/field (indoor), volleyball, water polo, wrestling. *Women:* basketball, crew/rowing, cross-country, diving, fencing, field hockey, gymnastics, ice hockey, lacrosse, pistol, riflery, sailing, skiing (downhill/alpine), skiing (nordic/cross-country), soccer, softball, swimming, tennis, track/field (outdoor), track/field (indoor), volleyball. **On-Campus Highlights:** Ray and Maria Stata Center, Zesiger Sports and Fitness Center, Killian Court, The Infinite Corridor, The Student Center (W20), Stata Center is a 720,000 square foot building designed by Frank Gehry. Zesiger Sports and Fitness Center is our state-of-the-art athletics facility. At 778.8 feet, the Infinite Corridor is reputed to be the longest straight hallway in the world–it connects many of the buildings on central campus and runs though two popular gathering spots:

Lobbies 7 and 10. **Environmental Initiatives:** In 2013, MIT created a new Office of Sustainability reporting directly to our Executive Vice President, which is the highest administrative for operations office. This creates an office at the highest level with a new director to scale up MIT's already robust sustainability programs. MIT has also launched a new Sustainability Executive Committee (comprised of the Provost, Directors of MIT's top sustainability research programs, Chancellor, and Vice President for Research) and a Campus Sustainability Task Force (comprised of respresentatives of all 5 schools, and key operational areas and students) to coordinate implementation of MIT's sustainability plans.

ADMISSIONS

Freshman Academic Profile: 97% in top 10% of high school class, 100% in top 25% of high school class, 100% in top 50% of high school class. 67% from public high schools. **Reported SAT (pre-2016 redesign) scores:** SAT Math middle 50% range 760-800. SAT Critical Reading middle 50% range 700-790. SAT Writing middle 50% range 690-790. **Concordant SAT scores:** SAT EBRW middle 50% 730–800. SAT Math middle 50% range 780–800. ACT middle 50% range 33-35. Minimum internet-based TOEFL 90. **Basis for Candidate Selection:** *Very important factors considered include:* character/personal qualities. *Important factors considered include:* rigor of secondary school record, academic GPA, standardized test scores, application essay, recommendation(s), interview, extracurricular activities, talent/ability. *Other factors considered include:* class rank, first generation, geographical residence, racial/ethnic status, volunteer work, work experience. **Freshman Admission Requirements:** High school diploma or equivalent is not required. *Academic units recommended:* 4 English, 4 math, 4 science, 2 foreign language, 2 social studies. **Freshman Admission Statistics:** 19,020 applied, 7.94% admitted, 73% enrolled. **Transfer Admission Requirements:** High school transcript, college transcript(s), essay or personal statement, standardized test scores, statement of good standing from prior institution(s). Lowest grade transferable B. **General Admission Information:** Application fee $75. Regular application deadline 1/1. Regular notification 3/20. Nonfall registration not accepted. Admission may be deferred for a maximum of 2 years.

COSTS AND FINANCIAL AID

Annual tuition $49,580. Room and board $14,720. Required fees $312. Average book expense $1,000. **Required Forms and Deadlines:** FAFSA, CSS/Financial Aid PROFILE, Noncustodial PROFILE, Business/Farm Supplement. **Notification of Awards:** Applicants will be notified of awards on or about 3/15. **Types of Aid:** *Need-based scholarships/grants:* Federal Pell, FSEOG, State scholarships/grants, Private scholarships, College/university scholarship or grant aid from institutional funds. *Loans:* Direct Subsidized Stafford Loans, Direct Unsubsidized Stafford Loans, Direct PLUS loans, Federal Perkins Loans, College/university loans from institutional funds. *Student Employment:* Federal Work-Study Program available. Institutional employment available. **Financial Aid Statistics:** 96% needy freshmen, 96% needy undergrads receive need-based scholarship or grant aid. 5% freshmen, 2% undergrads receive non-need-based scholarship or grant aid. 71% freshmen, 77% undergrads receive need-based self-help aid. 0% freshmen, 0% undergrads receive athletic scholarships. 86% freshmen, 76% undergrads receive any aid. 27% undergrads borrow to pay for school. Average cumulative indebtedness $24,954.

THE MASTER'S COLLEGE AND SEMINARY

21726 Placerita Canyon Road, Santa Clarita, CA 91321
Phone: 661-259-3540 • **Financial Aid Phone:** 661-362-2290
E-mail: admissions@masters.edu • **CEEB Code:** 4411
Fax: 661-288-1037 • **Website:** www.masters.edu • **ACT Code:** 303

This private school was founded in 1927. It has a 95-acre campus.

RATINGS

Admissions Selectivity Rating: 81   **Fire Safety Rating:** 85   **Green Rating:** 60*

STUDENTS AND FACULTY

Enrollment: 1,133. **Student Body:** 46% female, 54% male, 35% out-of-state, 6% international (19 countries represented). Asian 6%, African American 4%, Caucasian 64%, Hispanic 10%, Native American <1%, Pacific Islander 1%, Two or more races 7%, Race unknown 3%.
Retention and Graduation: 85% freshmen return for sophomore year. 55% freshmen graduate within 4 years. 68% freshmen graduate within 6 years. **Faculty:** Student/faculty ratio 10:1. 67 full-time faculty, 75% hold PhDs, 7% are are members of minority groups, 15% are women. 0% of classes are taught by teaching assistants.

ACADEMICS

Degrees: bachelor's, doctoral/professional, doctoral/research, doctoral, master's. **Classes:** Most classes have fewer than 10 students. **Most popular**

majors: Bible/Biblical Studies; Business/Commerce; Communication. **Special Study Options:** Accelerated program, cooperative education program, distance learning, double major, independent study, internships, liberal arts/career combination, study abroad, teacher certification program, Israel semester. **Disability Services:** Special programs offered to physically disabled students, including note-taking services, reader services, tape recorders, tutors. **Career Services:** Alumni network, Alumni services, Career/job search classes, Career assessment, Internships, Regional alumni. Alumni counseling and resume workshops for undergraduate students.

FACILITIES

Housing: men's dorms, special housing for international students, women's dorms, Wellness Housing. 95% of campus accessible to physically diasbled. **Computers:** 100% of classrooms, 100% of dorms, 100% of libraries, 100% of dining areas, 100% of student union, 95% of common outdoor areas have wireless network access. Students can register for classes online. Administrative functions (other than registration) can be performed online. Undergraduates are required to own a computer.

CAMPUS LIFE

Environment: City. **Activities:** Choral groups, concert band, drama/theater, jazz band, music ensembles, opera, pep band, student government, symphony orchestra. 15 registered organizations, 1 honor society, 11 religious organizations. **Athletics (Intercollegiate):** *Men:* baseball, basketball, cross-country, golf, soccer, track/field (outdoor). *Women:* basketball, cross-country, soccer, tennis, track/field (outdoor), volleyball. **On-Campus Highlights:** New All-Weather Field (2005), Dining Center Remodeled (2005), Music Center, Smith Hall Dormitory, Canyon Cafe.

ADMISSIONS

Freshman Academic Profile: Average high school GPA 3.7. 29% in top 10% of high school class, 52% in top 25% of high school class, 81% in top 50% of high school class. 40% from public high schools. **Reported SAT (pre-2016 redesign) scores:** SAT Math middle 50% range 480-590. SAT Critical Reading middle 50% range 480-620. SAT Writing middle 50% range 480-600. **Concordant SAT scores:** SAT EBRW middle 50% 540–660. SAT Math middle 50% range 510–610. ACT middle 50% range 21-27. Minimum internet-based TOEFL 80. **Basis for Candidate Selection:** *Very important factors considered include:* academic GPA, standardized test scores, application essay, recommendation(s), character/personal qualities, religious affiliation/commitment. *Important factors considered include:* rigor of secondary school record. *Other factors considered include:* extracurricular activities, talent/ability, alumni/ae relation, level of applicant's interest. **Freshman Admission Requirements:** High school diploma is required and GED is accepted. *Academic units required:* 4 English, 3 math, 2 science, 2 history. *Academic units recommended:* 3 academic electives. **Freshman Admission Statistics:** 490 applied, 94.69% admitted, 43% enrolled. **Transfer Admission Requirements:** High school transcript, college transcript(s), essay or personal statement, interview, statement of good standing from prior institution(s). Minimum college GPA of 2.5 required. Lowest grade transferable C. **General Admission Information:** Application fee $40. Priority deadline 3/2. Nonfall registration accepted. Admission may be deferred for a maximum of 2 semesters.

COSTS AND FINANCIAL AID

Annual tuition $31,550. Room and board $10,300. Required fees $420. Average book expense $1,791. **Required Forms and Deadlines:** FAFSA, Institution's own financial aid form, State aid form. **Notification of Awards:** Applicants will be notified of awards on a rolling basis beginning 2/18. **Types of Aid:** *Need-based scholarships/grants:* Federal Pell, FSEOG, State scholarships/grants, Private scholarships, College/university scholarship or grant aid from institutional funds. *Loans:* Direct Subsidized Stafford Loans, Direct Unsubsidized Stafford Loans, Direct PLUS loans. *Student Employment:* Federal Work-Study Program available. Institutional employment available. **Financial Aid Statistics:** 88% needy freshmen, 97% needy undergrads receive need-based scholarship or grant aid. 13% freshmen, 10% undergrads receive non-need-based scholarship or grant aid. 78% freshmen, 82% undergrads receive need-based self-help aid. 5% freshmen, 4% undergrads receive athletic scholarships. 95% freshmen, 90% undergrads receive any aid. **Criteria for awarding aid:** *Need-based:* Job skills. *Non-need-based:* Academics, Alumni affiliation, Art, Athletics, Music/drama.

MAYNOOTH UNIVERSITY

International Office Maynooth University, Maynooth, IR Co Kildare
Phone: +353 1 708 3868
E-mail: international.office@nuim.ie
Fax: 353 1 628 9063 • **Website:** www.maynoothuniversity.ie • **ACT Code:** 5483

This is a public school.

RATINGS
Admissions Selectivity Rating: 86   **Fire Safety Rating:** 89   **Green Rating:** 73

STUDENTS AND FACULTY
Student Body: 55% female, 45% male, (90 countries represented). **Retention and Graduation:** 88% freshmen return for sophomore year. 81% freshmen graduate within 6 years. **Faculty:** Student/faculty ratio 28:1. 363 full-time faculty, 0% hold PhDs, 0% are are members of minority groups, 0% are women. 0% of classes are taught by teaching assistants.

ACADEMICS
Degrees: bachelor's, doctoral/professional, doctoral/research, doctoral, master's, postbachelor's certificate, post-master's certificate. **Classes:** Most classes have 20-29 students. **Most popular majors:** Liberal Arts and Sciences Studies and Humanities; Business/Commerce; Multi-/Interdisciplinary Studies. **Career Services:** Alumni network, Career/job search classes, Internships, Regional alumni. Undergraduate and postgraduate students can avail of the great opportunity to work in Ireland or abroad on placement or internship as part of their degree. Maynooth University students have worked in major companies around the world such as Microsoft, Pfizer, IBM, Ericsson, Intel and Accenture. Maynooth University Placement students may undertake their placement in any country worldwide. NUIM students have enjoyed placement experiences in USA, New Zealand, Italy, France, Austria, China, Australia, Hungary etc. in the past three ' four years.

FACILITIES
Housing: 70% of campus accessible to physically diasbled.

CAMPUS LIFE
Environmental Initiatives: To provide and co-ordinate the travel strategy at Maynooth University to enable a lasting and maintained shift to sustainable travel in line with the University's vision of becoming a sustainable campus by providing the best range of travel options to staff, students and visitors.

ADMISSIONS
Freshman Academic Profile: Average high school GPA 3.2. Minimum internet-based TOEFL 80. Minimum paper TOEFL 550. **Basis for Candidate Selection:** *Very important factors considered include:* rigor of secondary school record, academic GPA, standardized test scores. *Other factors considered include:* class rank, application essay, recommendation(s), talent/ability, character/personal qualities, volunteer work, work experience, level of applicant's interest. **Freshman Admission Requirements:** *Academic units required:* 4 English, 4 math, and 16 units from above areas or other academic areas. *Academic units recommended:* 4 English, 4 math, 4 science, 4 foreign language, 4 social studies, 4 history, 4 computer science, and 4 units from above areas or other academic areas. **Freshman Admission Statistics:** 20,103 applied, 14.95% admitted, 91% enrolled. **General Admission Information:** Regular application deadline 7/1. Nonfall registration not accepted. Admission may be deferred for a maximum of 1 year.

COSTS AND FINANCIAL AID
Required Forms and Deadlines: FAFSA. **Notification of Awards:** Applicants will be notified of awards on a rolling basis beginning 3/1. **Types of Aid:** *Loans:* Direct Subsidized Stafford Loans, Direct Unsubsidized Stafford Loans, Direct PLUS loans. *Student Employment:* Federal Work-Study Program available. Institutional employment available. **Criteria for awarding aid:** *Need-based:* Academics. *Non-need-based:* Academics.

MAYVILLE STATE UNIVERSITY

330 Third Street Northeast, Mayville, ND 58257-1299
Phone: 701-788-4842 • **Financial Aid Phone:** 701-788-4767
E-mail: MaSU.admissions@mayvillestate.edu • **CEEB Code:** 6478
Fax: 701-788-4656 • **Website:** www.mayvillestate.edu • **ACT Code:** 3212

This public school was founded in 1889. It has a 55-acre campus.

RATINGS
Admissions Selectivity Rating: 77   **Fire Safety Rating:** 81   **Green Rating:** 60*

STUDENTS AND FACULTY

Enrollment: 1,091. **Student Body:** 56% female, 44% male, 43% out-of-state, 3% international (7 countries represented). Asian 0%, African American 8%, Caucasian 78%, Hispanic 5%, Native American 1%, Pacific Islander 1%, Two or more races 3%, Race unknown 1%.

Retention and Graduation: 49% freshmen return for sophomore year. 5% freshmen graduate within 4 years. 25% freshmen graduate within 6 years. 12% grads go on to further study within 1 year. 1% grads pursue arts and sciences degrees. 4% grads pursue business degrees. **Faculty:** Student/faculty ratio 13:1. 49 full-time faculty, 41% hold PhDs, 2% are are members of minority groups, 49% are women. 0% of classes are taught by teaching assistants.

ACADEMICS

Degrees: bachelor's, transfer. Classes: Most classes have 10-19 students. **Most popular majors:** Elementary Education and Teaching; Physical Education Teaching and Coaching; Business/Commerce. **Special Study Options:** Accelerated program, cooperative education program, distance learning, double major, dual enrollment, independent study, internships, student-designed major, teacher certification program. **Disability Services:** Special programs offered to physically disabled students, including note-taking services, tape recorders, tutors. **Career Services:** Alumni network, Alumni services, Career/job search classes, Career assessment, Internships, Regional alumni. The internship program provides opportunities for students to have related work experience with a variety of local, regional and national employers.

FACILITIES

Housing: men's dorms, women's dorms, apartments for married students, apartments for single students. 80% of campus accessible to physically diasbled. **Special Academic Facilities/Equipment:** Art gallery available in the Campus Center. **Computers:** 100% of classrooms, 25% of dorms, 100% of libraries, 100% of dining areas, 100% of student union, 25% of common outdoor areas have wireless network access. Students can register for classes online. Administrative functions (other than registration) can be performed online. Undergraduates are required to own a computer.

CAMPUS LIFE

Environment: Rural. **Activities:** Choral groups, concert band, drama/theater, jazz band, music ensembles, musical theater, radio station, student government, student newspaper. 118 registered organizations, 1 honor society, 2 religious organizations. **Athletics (Intercollegiate):** Men: baseball, basketball, football. Women: basketball, softball, volleyball. **On-Campus Highlights:** Lewy Lee Fieldhouse, Campus Center, Residence Halls, Library, West Hall.

ADMISSIONS

Freshman Academic Profile: Average high school GPA 3.0. 95% from public high schools. ACT middle 50% range 17-22. Minimum internet-based TOEFL 68. Minimum paper TOEFL 520. **Basis for Candidate Selection:** *Very important factors considered include:* rigor of secondary school record, academic GPA. *Important factors considered include:* standardized test scores. *Other factors considered include:* interview, character/personal qualities. **Freshman Admission Requirements:** High school diploma is required and GED is accepted. *Academic units required:* 4 English, 3 math, 3 science, 3 science labs, 3 social studies. *Academic units recommended:* 2 foreign language. **Freshman Admission Statistics:** 336 applied, 53.57% admitted, 76% enrolled. **Transfer Admission Requirements:** college transcript(s), statement of good standing from prior institution(s). Minimum college GPA of 2.0 required. Lowest grade transferable d. **General Admission Information:** Application fee $35. Nonfall registration accepted. Admission may be deferred.

COSTS AND FINANCIAL AID

Annual in-state tuition $4,930. Annual out-of-state tuition $7,395. Room and board $5,904. Required fees $1,450. Average book expense $1,000. **Required Forms and Deadlines:** FAFSA. **Notification of Awards:** Applicants will be notified of awards on a rolling basis beginning 5/1. **Types of Aid:** *Need-based scholarships/grants:* Federal Pell, FSEOG, State scholarships/grants, Private scholarships, College/university scholarship or grant aid from institutional funds. *Loans:* Direct Subsidized Stafford Loans, Direct Unsubsidized Stafford Loans, Direct PLUS loans, Federal Perkins Loans. *Student Employment:* Federal Work-Study Program available. Institutional employment available. **Financial Aid Statistics:** 94% needy freshmen, 88% needy undergrads receive need-based scholarship or grant aid. 9% freshmen, 6% undergrads receive non-need-based scholarship or grant aid. 79% freshmen, 83% undergrads receive need-based self-help aid. 8% freshmen, 8% undergrads receive athletic scholarships. 83% freshmen, 78% undergrads receive any aid. 71% undergrads borrow to pay for school. Average cumulative indebtedness $32,424. **Criteria for awarding aid:** *Need-based:* Academics, Athletics, Leadership, Minority status, Music/drama. *Non-need-based:* Academics, Athletics, Leadership, Minority status, Music/drama, State/district residency.

MCDANIEL COLLEGE

2 College Hill, Westminster, MD 21157
Phone: 410-857-2230 • **Financial Aid Phone:** 410-857-2233
E-mail: admissions@mcdaniel.edu • **CEEB Code:** 5898
Website: www.mcdaniel.edu • **ACT Code:** 1756

This is a private school.

RATINGS

Admissions Selectivity Rating: 80   **Fire Safety Rating:** 88   **Green Rating:** 60*

STUDENTS AND FACULTY

Enrollment: 1,528. **Student Body:** 51% female, 49% male, 35% out-of-state, 0% international (11 countries represented). Asian 4%, African American 15%, Caucasian 65%, Hispanic 7%, Native American <1%, Pacific Islander <1%, Two or more races 3%, Race unknown 6%.

Retention and Graduation: 79% freshmen return for sophomore year. 61% freshmen graduate within 4 years. 68% freshmen graduate within 6 years. **Faculty:** Student/faculty ratio 10:1. 133 full-time faculty, 89% hold PhDs, 8% are are members of minority groups, 55% are women. 0% of classes are taught by teaching assistants.

ACADEMICS

Degrees: bachelor's, master's, postbachelor's certificate. **Most popular majors:** Health and Physical Education/Fitness; Psychology; Biology/Biological Sciences. Combined degree programs: Five-Year BA/MS Programs. **Disability Services:** Special programs offered to physically disabled students, including note-taking services, reader services, tape recorders, tutors. **Career Services:** Alumni network, Alumni services, Career/job search classes, Career assessment, Internships, Regional alumni. The Center for Experience & Opportunity is a one-stop shop connecting McDaniel students with experiences and opportunities to ensure that every student has a significant out-of-class learning experience. The CEO provides students with information about a variety of experiential learning opportunities, including community outreach, service learning, internships, work/study, undergraduate research, post-graduate fellowships, pre-professional studies, and more, as well as a full range of career services for all McDaniel undergraduate and graduate students, and alumni.

FACILITIES

Housing: Coed dorms, special housing for disabled students, men's dorms, women's dorms, fraternity/sorority housing, apartments for married students, apartments for single studentsSingle family homes shared by 3-10 students. 85% of campus accessible to physically diasbled. **Special Academic Facilities/Equipment:** Art gallery, computer graphics and physiology labs, electron microscope, math spectrometer. **Computers:** Students can register for classes online. Administrative functions (other than registration) can be performed online.

CAMPUS LIFE

Activities: Choral groups, concert band, dance, drama/theater, jazz band, literary magazine, music ensembles, musical theater, pep band, radio station, student government, student newspaper, symphony orchestra, television station, yearbook. 136 registered organizations, 22 honor societies, 5 religious organizations. 6 fraternities, 4 sororities. **Athletics (Intercollegiate):** Men: baseball, basketball, cross-country, football, golf, lacrosse, soccer, swimming, tennis, track/field (outdoor), track/field (indoor), volleyball, wrestling. Women: basketball, cross-country, field hockey, golf, lacrosse, soccer, softball, swimming, tennis, track/field (outdoor), track/field (indoor), volleyball. **On-Campus Highlights:** The Hoover Library, Peterson Hall, Golf course, Bair stadium, Academic Hall.

ADMISSIONS

Freshman Academic Profile: Average high school GPA 3.5. 22% in top 10% of high school class, 44% in top 25% of high school class, 78% in top 50% of high school class. **Reported SAT (pre-2016 redesign) scores:** SAT Math middle 50% range 490-610. SAT Critical Reading middle 50% range 490-600. **Concordant SAT scores:** SAT Math middle 50% range 520–630. ACT middle 50% range 21-28. Minimum internet-based TOEFL 80. Minimum paper TOEFL 550. **Basis for Candidate Selection:** *Very important factors considered include:* rigor of secondary school record, academic GPA. *Important factors considered include:* standardized test scores, application essay, recommendation(s). *Other factors considered include:* class rank, interview, extracurricular activities, talent/ability, character/personal qualities, first generation, alumni/ae relation, volunteer work, work experience, level of applicant's interest. **Freshman Admission Requirements:** *Academic units required:* 4 English, 3 math, 3 science, 3 science labs, 3 foreign language, 3 social studies. *Academic units recommended:* 4 English, 4 math, 4 science, 4 foreign language, 3 social studies. **Freshman Admission Statistics:** 2,864 applied, 79.82% admitted, 19% enrolled. **General Admission Information:** Application fee $50. Priority deadline 2/15. Nonfall registration accepted. Admission may be deferred for a maximum of 1 year.

COSTS AND FINANCIAL AID

Annual tuition $41,800. Room and board $11,110. Average book expense $1,200. **Required Forms and Deadlines:** FAFSA. **Notification of Awards:** Applicants will be notified of awards on a rolling basis beginning 3/15. **Types of Aid:** *Need-based scholarships/grants:* Federal Pell, FSEOG, State scholarships/grants, Private scholarships, College/university scholarship or grant aid from institutional funds. *Loans:* Direct Subsidized Stafford Loans, Direct Unsubsidized Stafford Loans, Direct PLUS loans, Federal Perkins Loans. *Student Employment:* Federal Work-Study Program available. Institutional employment available. **Financial Aid Statistics:** 100% needy freshmen, 100% needy undergrads receive need-based scholarship or grant aid. 22% freshmen, 16% undergrads receive non-need-based scholarship or grant aid. 82% freshmen, 85% undergrads receive need-based self-help aid. 0% freshmen, 0% undergrads receive athletic scholarships. 100% freshmen, 98% undergrads receive any aid. 71% undergrads borrow to pay for school. Average cumulative indebtedness $35,397. **Criteria for awarding aid:** *Non-need-based:* Academics, State/district residency.

MCGILL UNIVERSITY

3415 McTavish St., Montreal, QC H3A 0C8
Phone: 514-398-7878 • **Financial Aid Phone:** 514-398-6013 • **CEEB Code:** 935
Fax: 514-398-5544 • **Website:** http://www.mcgill.ca/admissions/
ACT Code: 5231

This public school was founded in 1821. It has a 80-acre campus.

RATINGS
Admissions Selectivity Rating: 88   **Fire Safety Rating:** 79   **Green Rating:** 60*

STUDENTS AND FACULTY
Student Body: 37% out-of-state, (136 countries represented).
Retention and Graduation: 81 **Faculty:** Student/faculty ratio 16:1.

ACADEMICS
Degrees: bachelor's, certificate, diploma, doctoral, master's, postbachelor's certificate. **Classes:** Most classes have 10-19 students. Most lab/discussion sessions have 20-29 students. **Most popular majors:** Political Science and Government; Psychology; Business/Commerce. **Special Study Options:** Accelerated program, cooperative education program, cross-registration, distance learning, double major, English as a Second Language (ESL), exchange student program (domestic), honors program, independent study, internships, study abroad, teacher certification program. **Honors Programs:** McGill's Faculties of Arts, Science, and Engineering, the Desautels Faculty of Management, and the McGill School of Environment offer many outstanding honours and joint honours programs. Honours programs offer specialization and research in one academic discipline while joint honours programs offer specialization and research in a combination of disciplines. Combined degree programs: BSc/BEd; BMus/BEd; BCL/LLB; MSW/Law; MDCM/MBA; MDCM/PhD. **Disability Services:** Special programs offered to physically disabled students, including note-taking services, reader services, tape recorders, tutors. **Career Services:** Career/job search classes, Career assessment. Bilingual Mining and Materials Co-op Program.

FACILITIES
Housing: Coed dorms, special housing for disabled students, women's dorms, apartments for single students, Shared Facilities **Housing:** Similar to Cooperative Housing but chores and costs are not shared amongst the students. 90% of campus accessible to physically disabled. **Special Academic Facilities/Equipment:** McCord Museum of Canadian History, Redpath Museum of Natural History, Lyman Entomological Museum and Research Laboratory, Ecomuseum, Rutherford Museum, Lawrence Lande Collection of Canadiana, Canadian Architecture Collection, Morgan Arboretum, Gault Nature Reserve, Herbarium, McGill Archives (Canadian History), Islamic Studies Library, Bellairs Research Institute, McConnell Brain Imaging Centre, McConnell Winter Arena, McGill Sports Centre Gymnasiums, Percival Molson Stadium, Memorial Pool, Richard Tomlinson Fieldhouse, Outdoor Tennis Courts, McGill Arctic Research Station, McGill Subarctic Research Station, Phytotron, Schulich School of Music (world-class sound stage, recording studio), McGill

Centre for Interdisciplinary Research in Music, Media and Technology, Research Greenhouse, J. S. Marshall Weather Radar Observatory, Mountain and Glen Campuses (McGill University Health Centre Teaching Hospitals), McGill Medical Simulation Centre, McGill Reproductive Centre, McGill University and Genome Quebec Innovation Centre. **Computers:** 100% of classrooms, 100% of dorms, 100% of libraries, 100% of dining areas, 100% of student union, 100% of common outdoor areas have wireless network access. Students can register for classes online. Administrative functions (other than registration) can be performed online.

CAMPUS LIFE
Environment: Metropolis. **Activities:** Choral groups, concert band, dance, drama/theater, jazz band, literary magazine, marching band, music ensembles, musical theater, opera, pep band, radio station, student government, student newspaper, student-run film society, symphony orchestra, television station, yearbook, Student Organization. 250 registered organizations, 2 honor societies, 10 religious organizations. 8 fraternities, 4 sororities. **Athletics (Intercollegiate):** *Men:* badminton, baseball, basketball, cheerleading, crew/rowing, cross-country, curling, cycling, fencing, football, golf, ice hockey, lacrosse, rugby, sailing, skiing (downhill/alpine), skiing (nordic/cross-country), soccer, squash, swimming, tennis, track/field (indoor), ultimate frisbee, volleyball, wrestling. *Women:* badminton, basketball, cheerleading, crew/rowing, cross-country, curling, cycling, fencing, field hockey, golf, ice hockey, lacrosse, rugby, sailing, skiing (downhill/alpine), skiing (nordic/cross-country), soccer, squash, swimming, synchronized swimming, tennis, track/field (indoor), ultimate frisbee, volleyball, wrestling. **On-Campus Highlights:** Arts Building, Schulich School of Music, McGill Bookstore, MacDonald Campus, Redpath Museum, To get a big-picture view of the entire campus, take a walk up Mont-Royal. From the Chateau look-out it is possible to see the entire downtown campus. **Environmental Initiatives:** Excellence in environmental research and teaching (e.g. School of Environment, GEC3, Brace, VERT, etc.).

ADMISSIONS
Reported SAT (pre-2016 redesign) scores: SAT Math middle 50% range 650-720. SAT Critical Reading middle 50% range 640-740. SAT Writing middle 50% range 650-730. **Concordant SAT scores:** SAT EBRW middle 50% 690–760. SAT Math middle 50% range 670–750. ACT middle 50% range 29-32. Minimum internet-based TOEFL 90. Minimum paper TOEFL 577. **Basis for Candidate Selection:** *Very important factors considered include:* rigor of secondary school record, academic GPA, standardized test scores. *Important factors considered include:* class rank. *Other factors considered include:* recommendation(s). **Freshman Admission Requirements:** High school diploma is required and GED is not accepted. *Academic units recommended:* 4 English, 4 math, 3 science, 3 science labs, 3 foreign language, 2 social studies, 2 history. **Freshman Admission Statistics:** 24,901 applied, 56.13% admitted. **Transfer Admission Requirements:** High school transcript, college transcript(s), Minimum college GPA of 3.00 required. Lowest grade transferable C. **General Admission Information:** Application fee $102.2. Regular application deadline 1/15. Nonfall registration accepted. Admission may be deferred for a maximum of 1 year.

COSTS AND FINANCIAL AID
Required Forms and Deadlines: Institution's own financial aid form. **Notification of Awards:** Applicants will be notified of awards on a rolling basis beginning 3/1. **Types of Aid:** *Need-based scholarships/grants:* Private scholarships, College/university scholarship or grant aid from institutional funds. *Loans:* College/university loans from institutional funds. *Student Employment:* Institutional employment available. **Financial Aid Statistics:** 63% needy undergrads receive need-based scholarship or grant aid. 31% undergrads receive non-need-based scholarship or grant aid. 89% undergrads receive need-based self-help aid. 0% undergrads receive athletic scholarships. 28% undergrads receive any aid. **Criteria for awarding aid:** *Need-based:* Academics, Alumni affiliation, Leadership, Minority status. *Non-need-based:* Academics, Art, Athletics, Leadership, Music/drama, State/district residency.

MCMURRY UNIVERSITY

1 McMurry University, #278, Abilene, TX 79697
Phone: 325-793-4700 • **Financial Aid Phone:** 325-793-4713
E-mail: admissions@mcm.edu • **CEEB Code:** 3591
Fax: 325-793-4701 • **Website:** www.mcm.edu • **ACT Code:** 4130

RATINGS
Admissions Selectivity Rating: 82   **Fire Safety Rating:** 87   **Green Rating:** 62

STUDENTS AND FACULTY

Enrollment: 1,016. **Student Body:** 44% female, 56% male, 5% out-of-state, 7% international (7 countries represented). Asian 1%, African American 17%, Caucasian 47%, Hispanic 25%, Native American 1%, Pacific Islander <1%, Two or more races 2%, Race unknown <1%.
Retention and Graduation: 52% freshmen return for sophomore year. 28% freshmen graduate within 4 years. 36% freshmen graduate within 6 years. 19% grads go on to further study within 1 year. 12% grads pursue arts and sciences degrees. 1% grads pursue law degrees. 1% grads pursue business degrees. 1% grads pursue medical degrees. **Faculty:** Student/faculty ratio 12:1. 74 full-time faculty, 78% hold PhDs, 0% are are members of minority groups, 42% are women. 0% of classes are taught by teaching assistants.

ACADEMICS

Degrees: bachelor's, master's. Combined degree programs: BA/DDS. **Career Services:** Alumni network, Internships.

FACILITIES

Housing: 85% of campus accessible to physically diasbled.

CAMPUS LIFE

Environmental Initiatives: Effluent water—The University uses effluent water for all landscape irrigation.

ADMISSIONS

Freshman Academic Profile: Average high school GPA 3.5. 12% in top 10% of high school class, 39% in top 25% of high school class, 73% in top 50% of high school class. 95% from public high schools. **Reported SAT (pre-2016 redesign) scores:** SAT Math middle 50% range 430-530. SAT Critical Reading middle 50% range 390-500. SAT Writing middle 50% range 370-470. **Concordant SAT scores:** SAT EBRW middle 50% 430–540. SAT Math middle 50% range 470–560. ACT middle 50% range 18-22. Minimum internet-based TOEFL 79. Minimum paper TOEFL 550. **Basis for Candidate Selection:** *Very important factors considered include:* rigor of secondary school record, class rank, academic GPA, standardized test scores. *Important factors considered include:* application essay, interview, extracurricular activities, talent/ability, character/personal qualities, volunteer work. *Other factors considered include:* recommendation(s), first generation, alumni/ae relation, geographical residence, state residency, religious affiliation/commitment, work experience, level of applicant's interest. **Freshman Admission Requirements:** *Academic units required:* 4 English, 4 math, 4 science, 2 foreign language, 4 social studies. *Academic units recommended:* 4 English, 4 math, 4 science, 2 foreign language, 4 social studies. **Freshman Admission Statistics:** 1,884 applied, 48.04% admitted, 31% enrolled. **General Admission Information:** Application fee $25. Priority deadline 3/15. Regular application deadline 8/15. Nonfall registration accepted. Admission may be deferred for a maximum of 1 year.

COSTS AND FINANCIAL AID

Annual tuition $26,100. Room and board $8,244. Required fees $175. Average book expense $1,200. **Required Forms and Deadlines:** FAFSA, Institution's own financial aid form, State aid form. **Notification of Awards:** Applicants will be notified of awards on a rolling basis beginning 2/15. **Types of Aid:** *Need-based scholarships/grants:* Federal Pell, FSEOG, State scholarships/grants, Private scholarships, College/university scholarship or grant aid from institutional funds. *Loans:* Direct Subsidized Stafford Loans, Direct Unsubsidized Stafford Loans, Direct PLUS loans, Federal Perkins Loans, State Loans. *Student Employment:* Federal Work-Study Program available. Institutional employment available. **Financial Aid Statistics:** 100% needy freshmen, 99% needy undergrads receive need-based scholarship or grant aid. 6% freshmen, 9% undergrads receive non-need-based scholarship or grant aid. 93% freshmen, 91% undergrads receive need-based self-help aid. 0% freshmen, 2% undergrads receive athletic scholarships. 100% freshmen, 90% undergrads receive any aid. 69% undergrads borrow to pay for school. Average cumulative indebtedness $39,362. **Criteria for awarding aid:** *Need-based:* Minority status, Religious affiliation. *Non-need-based:* Academics, Art, Athletics, Job skills, Leadership, Music/drama, Religious affiliation.

MCNEESE STATE UNIVERSITY

Box 91740, Lake Charles, LA 70609
Phone: 337-475-5504 • **Financial Aid Phone:** 337-475-5065
E-mail: admissions@mcneese.edu
Fax: 337-475-5151 • **Website:** www.mcneese.edu • **ACT Code:** 1594

This is a public school.

RATINGS

Admissions Selectivity Rating: 77   **Fire Safety Rating:** 60*   **Green Rating:** 60*

STUDENTS AND FACULTY

Enrollment: 6,598. **Student Body:** 60% female, 40% male, 8% out-of-state, 7% international (53 countries represented). Asian 2%, African American 18%, Caucasian 68%, Hispanic 3%, Native American 1%, Pacific Islander <1%, Two or more races 2%, Race unknown <1%.
Retention and Graduation: 67% freshmen return for sophomore year. **Faculty:** Student/faculty ratio 20:1. 256 full-time faculty, 65% hold PhDs, 0% are are members of minority groups, 47% are women.

ACADEMICS

Degrees: associate, bachelor's, master's, postbachelor's certificate, post-master's certificate. **Classes:** Most classes have 20-29 students. Most lab/discussion sessions have 10-19 students. **Special Study Options:** Accelerated program, cooperative education program, distance learning, double major, dual enrollment, English as a Second Language (ESL), honors program, independent study, internships, study abroad, teacher certification program.

FACILITIES

Housing: Coed dorms, apartments for married students, apartments for single students.

CAMPUS LIFE

Activities: drama/theater, marching band, student government, student newspaper, yearbook.

ADMISSIONS

Freshman Academic Profile: 18% in top 10% of high school class, 41% in top 25% of high school class, 73% in top 50% of high school class. **Reported SAT (pre-2016 redesign) scores:** SAT Math middle 50% range 470-580. SAT Critical Reading middle 50% range 440-530. **Concordant SAT scores:** SAT Math middle 50% range 510–600. ACT middle 50% range 20-24. Minimum internet-based TOEFL 61. Minimum paper TOEFL 500. **Freshman Admission Requirements:** High school diploma is required and GED is accepted. **Freshman Admission Statistics:** 3,002 applied, 82.05% admitted, 58% enrolled. **Transfer Admission Requirements:** college transcript(s), statement of good standing from prior institution(s). Minimum college GPA of 2.00 required. Lowest grade transferable C.

COSTS AND FINANCIAL AID

Student Employment: Federal Work-Study Program available. Institutional employment available.

MCPHERSON COLLEGE

P.O. Box 1402, McPherson, KS 67460
Phone: 620-241-0731 • **Financial Aid Phone:** 800-365-7402
E-mail: admiss@mcpherson.edu • **CEEB Code:** 6404
Fax: 620-241-8443 • **ACT Code:** 1440

This private school, affiliated with the Church of Brethren Church, was founded in 1887. It has a 23-acre campus.

RATINGS

Admissions Selectivity Rating: 74   **Fire Safety Rating:** 60*   **Green Rating:** 60*

STUDENTS AND FACULTY

Enrollment: 566. **Student Body:** 43% female, 57% male, 5% out-of-state, 1% international. Asian 2%, African American 10%, Caucasian 77%, Hispanic 7%, Native American 3%, Pacific Islander 0%, Two or more races 0%, Race unknown 0%.
Retention and Graduation: 67% freshmen return for sophomore year. 36% freshmen graduate within 4 years. 48% freshmen graduate within 6 years. 9% grads go on to further study within 1 year. 9% grads pursue medical degrees. **Faculty:** Student/faculty ratio 15:1. 34 full-time faculty, 82% hold PhDs, 12% are are members of minority groups, 32% are women. 0% of classes are taught by teaching assistants.

ACADEMICS

Degrees: bachelor's. **Classes:** Most classes have 10-19 students. Most lab/discussion sessions have 10-19 students. **Special Study Options:** cross-registration, double major, dual enrollment, English as a Second Language (ESL), independent study, internships, student-designed major, study abroad, teacher certification program. Combined degree programs: 2-2 program with Hutchinson Com Col.

FACILITIES

Housing: Coed dorms, special housing for disabled students, men's dorms, women's dorms. **Special Academic Facilities/Equipment:** Natural history museum.

CAMPUS LIFE

Environment: Village. **Activities:** Choral groups, concert band, dance, drama/theater, jazz band, music ensembles, musical theater, pep band, student government, student newspaper, yearbook, Campus Ministries. **Athletics (Intercollegiate):** *Women:* basketball, cross-country, golf, tennis, track/field (outdoor), volleyball.

ADMISSIONS

Freshman Academic Profile: Average high school GPA 3.2. 9% in top 10% of high school class, 25% in top 25% of high school class, 60% in top 50% of high school class. 99% from public high schools. **Reported SAT (pre-2016 redesign) scores:** SAT Math middle 50% range 450-563. SAT Critical Reading middle 50% range 448-560. **Concordant SAT scores:** SAT Math middle 50% range 490–580. ACT middle 50% range 19-24. Minimum paper TOEFL 550. **Basis for Candidate Selection:** *Very important factors considered include:* rigor of secondary school record, academic GPA, standardized test scores. *Other factors considered include:* class rank, recommendation(s), interview, extracurricular activities, talent/ability, character/personal qualities, first generation, volunteer work, work experience, level of applicant's interest. **Freshman Admission Requirements:** High school diploma is required and GED is accepted. **Freshman Admission Statistics:** 474 applied, 86.71% admitted, 54% enrolled. **Transfer Admission Requirements:** High school transcript, college transcript(s), statement of good standing from prior institution(s). Minimum college GPA of 2.0 required. Lowest grade transferable C. **General Admission Information:** Application fee $25. Priority deadline 3/1. Nonfall registration accepted. Admission may be deferred.

COSTS AND FINANCIAL AID

Annual tuition $17,900. Room and board $6,910. Required fees $500. Average book expense $1,170. **Required Forms and Deadlines:** FAFSA, State aid form. **Notification of Awards:** Applicants will be notified of awards on a rolling basis beginning 3/1. **Types of Aid:** *Need-based scholarships/grants:* Federal Pell, FSEOG, State scholarships/grants, Private scholarships, College/university scholarship or grant aid from institutional funds, United Negro College Fund. *Loans:* Federal Perkins Loans. *Student Employment:* Federal Work-Study Program available. Institutional employment available. **Financial Aid Statistics:** 85% needy freshmen, 85% needy undergrads receive need-based scholarship or grant aid. 95% freshmen, 98% undergrads receive non-need-based scholarship or grant aid. 86% freshmen, 88% undergrads receive need-based self-help aid. 66% freshmen, 38% undergrads receive athletic scholarships. **Criteria for awarding aid:** *Non-need-based:* Academics, Alumni affiliation, Art, Athletics, Music/drama, Religious affiliation, State/district residency.

MCPHS UNIVERSITY

Office of Admissions, Boston, MA 2115
Phone: 617-732-2850 • **Financial Aid Phone:** 617-732-2864
E-mail: admissions@mcphs.edu • **CEEB Code:** 3512
Fax: 617-732-2118 • **Website:** www.mcphs.edu • **ACT Code:** 1860

This private school was founded in 1823. It has a 3-acre campus.

RATINGS

Admissions Selectivity Rating: 73   **Fire Safety Rating:** 97   **Green Rating:** 60*

STUDENTS AND FACULTY

Enrollment: 3,791. **Student Body:** 71% female, 29% male, 42% out-of-state, 13% international (32 countries represented). Asian 23%, African American 7%, Caucasian 41%, Hispanic 6%, Native American <1%, Pacific Islander <1%, Two or more races 2%, Race unknown 7%.
Retention and Graduation: 85% freshmen return for sophomore year. 68% freshmen graduate within 4 years. 78% freshmen graduate within 6 years.
Faculty: 309 full-time faculty, 91% hold PhDs, 0% are are members of minority groups, 0% are women. 0% of classes are taught by teaching assistants.

ACADEMICS

Degrees: bachelor's, certificate, doctoral/professional, doctoral/research, master's, postbachelor's certifiate, post-master's certificate. **Classes:** Most classes have 20-29 students. Most lab/discussion sessions have 10-19 students. **Special Study Options:** Accelerated program, cross-registration, distance learning, double major, independent study, internships, study abroad. Combined degree programs: BS/MS Pharmaceutical Chemistry. **Disability Services:** Special programs offered to physically disabled students, including note-taking services, reader services, tape recorders, tutors. **Career Services:** Alumni network, Alumni services, Regional alumni. Students in most majors have "rotations" in hospitals, pharmacies, clinics.

FACILITIES

Housing: Coed dorms, Wellness HousingSeparate all-women floors. 100% of campus accessible to physically diasbled. **Special Academic Facilities/Equipment:** Museum of Fine Arts and Isabella Stewart Gardner museum next door. **Computers:** 100% of classrooms, 100% of dorms, 100% of libraries, 100% of dining areas, 100% of student union, 100% of common outdoor areas have wireless network access. Students can register for classes online. Administrative functions (other than registration) can be performed online.

CAMPUS LIFE

Environment: Metropolis. **Activities:** Choral groups, concert band, dance, drama/theater, literary magazine, music ensembles, musical theater, student government, student newspaper, yearbook, Student Organization. 66 registered organizations, 5 honor societies, 2 religious organizations. **On-Campus Highlights:** New Building, residence hall, labs, Pharmacy Laboratory, Dental Hygiene Clinic, Cafeteria (located in Mass. College of Art), Student Lounge, In addition to the Boston campus, there are campuses in Worcester and Manchester NH with expanding program offerings.

ADMISSIONS

Freshman Academic Profile: Average high school GPA 3.5. **Reported SAT (pre-2016 redesign) scores:** SAT Math middle 50% range 490-620. SAT Critical Reading middle 50% range 460-560. SAT Writing middle 50% range 470-580. **Concordant SAT scores:** SAT EBRW middle 50% 520–630. SAT Math middle 50% range 520–640. ACT middle 50% range 21-27. Minimum internet-based TOEFL 79. Minimum paper TOEFL 550. **Basis for Candidate Selection:** *Very important factors considered include:* rigor of secondary school record, academic GPA, standardized test scores. *Other factors considered include:* class rank, application essay, recommendation(s), interview, extracurricular activities, talent/ability, character/personal qualities, first generation, alumni/ae relation, volunteer work, work experience, level of applicant's interest. **Freshman Admission Requirements:** High school diploma is required and GED is accepted. *Academic units required:* 4 English, 3 math, 2 science, 2 science labs, 1 social studies, 1 history, 5 academic electives. **Freshman Admission Statistics:** 5,530 applied, 84.45% admitted, 17% enrolled. **Transfer Admission Requirements:** college transcript(s), essay or personal statement, Minimum college GPA of 2.5 required. Lowest grade transferable C. **General Admission Information:** Nonfall registration accepted. Admission may be deferred.

COSTS AND FINANCIAL AID

Annual tuition $30,600. Room and board $15,834. Required fees $1,070. Average book expense $1,028. **Required Forms and Deadlines:** FAFSA. **Notification of Awards:** Applicants will be notified of awards on a rolling basis beginning 3/15. **Types of Aid:** *Need-based scholarships/grants:* Federal Pell, FSEOG, State scholarships/grants, Private scholarships, College/university scholarship or grant aid from institutional funds. *Loans:* Direct Subsidized Stafford Loans, Direct Unsubsidized Stafford Loans, Direct PLUS loans, Federal Perkins Loans. *Student Employment:* Federal Work-Study Program available. Institutional employment available. **Financial Aid Statistics:** 99% needy freshmen, 93% needy undergrads receive need-based scholarship or grant aid. 0% undergrads receive non-need-based scholarship or grant aid. 89% freshmen, 90% undergrads receive need-based self-help aid. 0% freshmen, 0% undergrads receive athletic scholarships. 90% freshmen, 90% undergrads receive any aid. **Criteria for awarding aid:** *Non-need-based:* Academics.

MEDCENTER ONE COLLEGE OF NURSING

512 North 7th Street, Bismarck, ND 58501
Phone: 701-323-6271 • **Financial Aid Phone:** 701-323-6270
E-mail: msmith@mohs.org
Fax: 701-323-6289 • **Website:** www.medcenterone.com/collegeofnursing
ACT Code: 3197

This private school was founded in 1988.

RATINGS

Admissions Selectivity Rating: 61   **Fire Safety Rating:** 60*   **Green Rating:** 60*

STUDENTS AND FACULTY

Enrollment: 91. **Student Body:** 91% female, 9% male, 6% out-of-state, 0% international (0 countries represented). Asian 1%, African American 4%, Caucasian 90%, Hispanic 1%, Native American 0%, Pacific Islander 0%, Two or more races 3%, Race unknown 0%.
Faculty: Student/faculty ratio 8:1. 10 full-time faculty, 10% hold PhDs, 0% are are members of minority groups, 100% are women. 0% of classes are taught by teaching assistants.

ACADEMICS

Degrees: bachelor's. **Classes:** Most classes have 40-49 students. Most lab/discussion sessions have fewer than 10 students. **Special Study Options:** independent study, internships. **Career Services:** On-campus interviews.

FACILITIES

Special Academic Facilities/Equipment: Alumni Corner **Computers:** 100% of classrooms, 100% of libraries, 100% of common outdoor areas have wireless network access.

CAMPUS LIFE

Environment: Rural. **Activities:** student government 2 registered organizations, 1 honor society. **On-Campus Highlights:** Simulation Lab

ADMISSIONS

Freshman Admission Requirements: High school diploma is required and GED is accepted. **Transfer Admission Requirements:** High school transcript, college transcript(s), essay or personal statement, interview, Minimum college GPA of 2.5 required. Lowest grade transferable C. **General Admission Information:** Application fee $40. Priority deadline 11/1.

COSTS AND FINANCIAL AID

Annual tuition $9,720. Required fees $889. Average book expense $1,169. **Notification of Awards:** Applicants will be notified of awards on a rolling basis beginning 6/1. **Types of Aid:** *Need-based scholarships/grants:* Federal Pell, FSEOG, State scholarships/grants, Private scholarships, College/university scholarship or grant aid from institutional funds. *Loans:* Federal Perkins Loans, Federal Nursing Loans, College/university loans from institutional funds. *Student Employment:* Federal Work-Study Program available. **Financial Aid Statistics:** 78% needy undergrads receive need-based scholarship or grant aid. 29% undergrads receive non-need-based scholarship or grant aid. 77% undergrads receive need-based self-help aid. 0% undergrads receive athletic scholarships. 0% freshmen receive any aid. **Criteria for awarding aid:** *Need-based:* Academics, Alumni affiliation, Leadership. *Non-need-based:* Academics, Alumni affiliation, Leadership.

MEDICAL UNIVERSITY OF SOUTH CAROLINA

41 Bee Street, Charleston, SC 29425-0203
Phone: 843-792-3281 • **Financial Aid Phone:** 843-792-2536
E-mail: oesadmis@musc.edu
Fax: 843-792-6615 • **Website:** www.musc.edu • **ACT Code:** 6440

This public school was founded in 1824. It has a 80-acre campus.

RATINGS

Admissions Selectivity Rating: 61   **Fire Safety Rating:** 60*   **Green Rating:** 60*

STUDENTS AND FACULTY

Enrollment: 198. **Student Body:** 79% female, 21% male, 12% out-of-state, 0% international (26 countries represented). Asian 3%, African American 11%, Caucasian 73%, Hispanic 6%, Native American 1%, Pacific Islander 0%, Two or more races 1%, Race unknown 5%.
Faculty: Student/faculty ratio 2:1. 153 full-time faculty, 92% hold PhDs, 10% are are members of minority groups, 56% are women. 0% of classes are taught by teaching assistants.

ACADEMICS

Degrees: bachelor's, doctoral/professional, doctoral/research, doctoral, master's, postbachelor's certificate, post-master's certificate. **Classes:** Most classes have 50-59 students. **Most popular majors:** Registered Nursing/Registered Nurse. **Special Study Options:** Accelerated program, distance learning, Varies with the academic program selected. **Disability Services:** Special programs offered to physically disabled students, including note-taking services, reader services, tape recorders, tutors. **Career Services:** Internships, On-campus interviews. We are an academic health science center and each specialty has various programs for placement of these highly specialized graduates. Internship refers to post-graduate programs and are not part of the degree curriculum.

FACILITIES

Housing: No on-campus housing available. Housing available in community and promoted to students via the Off-Campus Housing Service's website. 97% of campus accessible to physically diasbled. **Special Academic Facilities/Equipment:** Dental Museum, and Medical Museum, and Pharmacy Museum. **Computers:** 100% of classrooms, 100% of libraries, 100% of dining areas, 100% of common outdoor areas have wireless network access. Students can register for classes online. Administrative functions (other than registration) can be performed online.

CAMPUS LIFE

Environment: City. **Activities:** Choral groups, dance, literary magazine, music ensembles, student government, Campus Ministries, Student Organization. 77 registered organizations, 4 honor societies. **On-Campus Highlights:** Student Activity and Fitness Center, Library, Various Student Lounges, Classroom and Laboratories **Environmental Initiatives:** Installed ground source heat pump as first renewable energy project

ADMISSIONS

Minimum internet-based TOEFL 80. Minimum paper TOEFL 550. **General Admission Information:** Application fee $95. Regular application deadline 6/30. Admission may be deferred.

COSTS AND FINANCIAL AID

Annual in-state tuition $14,018. Annual out-of-state tuition $23,824. Required fees $1,140. **Required Forms and Deadlines:** FAFSA, Institution's own financial aid form. **Types of Aid:** *Need-based scholarships/grants:* Federal Pell, FSEOG, State scholarships/grants, Private scholarships, College/university scholarship or grant aid from institutional funds, Federal Nursing Scholarships. *Loans:* Federal Perkins Loans, Federal Nursing Loans, College/university loans from institutional funds. *Student Employment:* Federal Work-Study Program available. **Financial Aid Statistics:** 49% needy undergrads receive need-based scholarship or grant aid. 23% undergrads receive non-need-based scholarship or grant aid. 99% undergrads receive need-based self-help aid. 0% undergrads receive athletic scholarships. 0% freshmen, 75% undergrads receive any aid. **Criteria for awarding aid:** *Need-based:* Academics, Alumni affiliation, Minority status. *Non-need-based:* Academics, Alumni affiliation, Minority status, State/district residency.

MEMPHIS COLLEGE OF ART

Overton Park, 1930 Poplar Avenue, Memphis, TN 38104-2764
Phone: 901-272-5151 • **Financial Aid Phone:** 901-272-5136
E-mail: info@mca.edu • **CEEB Code:** 1511
Fax: 901-272-5158 • **Website:** www.mca.edu • **ACT Code:** 3991

This private school was founded in 1936. It has a 340-acre campus.

RATINGS

Admissions Selectivity Rating: 71   **Fire Safety Rating:** 82   **Green Rating:** 60*

STUDENTS AND FACULTY

Enrollment: 357. **Student Body:** 65% female, 35% male, 55% out-of-state, <1% international (13 countries represented). Asian 1%, African American 29%, Caucasian 57%, Hispanic 6%, Native American <1%, Pacific Islander 0%, Two or more races 4%, Race unknown 2%.
Retention and Graduation: 72% freshmen return for sophomore year. 47% freshmen graduate within 4 years. 49% freshmen graduate within 6 years. 10% grads go on to further study within 1 year. **Faculty:** Student/faculty ratio 10:1. 21 full-time faculty, 90% hold PhDs, 14% are are members of minority groups, 62% are women. 0% of classes are taught by teaching assistants.

ACADEMICS

Degrees: bachelor's, master's. **Classes:** Most classes have 10-19 students. **Special Study Options:** cross-registration, double major, exchange student program (domestic), independent study, internships, study abroad, teacher certification program, New York Studies Program. Arts Exchange possible with othe AICAD schools. **Disability Services:** Special programs offered to physically disabled students, including note-taking services, reader services, tape recorders, tutors. **Career Services:** Alumni network, Alumni services, Career/job search classes, Internships, Regional alumni. Give Back Community Service Program.

FACILITIES

Housing: Coed dorms, apartments for single students. 100% of campus accessible to physically diasbled. **Special Academic Facilities/Equipment:** Art museum, numerous galleries for student exhibition, Computer writing lab. **Computers:** 100% of classrooms, 100% of dorms, 100% of libraries, 100% of dining areas, have wireless network access.

CAMPUS LIFE

Environment: Metropolis. **Activities:** student government, student newspaper.

ADMISSIONS

Freshman Academic Profile: Average high school GPA 3.2. 80% from public high schools. Minimum paper TOEFL 500. **Basis for Candidate Selection:** *Very important factors considered include:* academic GPA, talent/ability. *Important factors considered include:* rigor of secondary school record, standardized test scores, interview. *Other factors considered include:* class rank, application essay, recommendation(s), extracurricular activities, character/personal qualities, volunteer work, work experience, level of applicant's interest. **Freshman Admission Requirements:** High school diploma is required and GED is accepted. *Academic units recommended:* 4 visual/performing arts. **Freshman Admission Statistics:** 843 applied, 30.72% admitted, 34% enrolled. **Transfer Admission Requirements:** college transcript(s), Minimum college GPA of 2.0 required. Lowest grade transferable C. **General Admission Information:** Priority deadline 3/31. Nonfall registration accepted. Admission may be deferred for a maximum of 1 year.

COSTS AND FINANCIAL AID

Annual tuition $28,170. Room and board $8,500. Required fees $650. Average book expense $1,650. **Required Forms and Deadlines:** FAFSA. **Notification of Awards:** Applicants will be notified of awards on a rolling basis beginning 1/15. **Types of Aid:** *Need-based scholarships/grants:* Federal Pell, FSEOG, State scholarships/grants, Private scholarships, College/university scholarship or grant aid from institutional funds. *Loans:* Direct Subsidized Stafford Loans, Direct Unsubsidized Stafford Loans, Direct PLUS loans, College/university loans from institutional funds. *Student Employment:* Federal Work-Study Program available. **Financial Aid Statistics:** 58% needy freshmen, 64% needy undergrads receive need-based scholarship or grant aid. 97% freshmen, 97% undergrads receive non-need-based scholarship or grant aid. 71% freshmen, 71% undergrads receive need-based self-help aid. 0% freshmen, 0% undergrads receive athletic scholarships. 95% freshmen, 95% undergrads receive any aid. **Criteria for awarding aid:** *Non-need-based:* Academics, Art.

MENLO COLLEGE

1000 El Camino Real, Atherton, CA 94027
Phone: 650-543-3753 • **Financial Aid Phone:** 650-543-3880
E-mail: admissions@menlo.edu • **CEEB Code:** 1236
Fax: 650-543-4103 • **Website:** www.menlo.edu • **ACT Code:** 330

This private school was founded in 1927. It has a 45-acre campus.

RATINGS

Admissions Selectivity Rating: 71   **Fire Safety Rating:** 74   **Green Rating:** 60*

STUDENTS AND FACULTY

Enrollment: 774. **Student Body:** 45% female, 55% male, 19% out-of-state, 14% international (34 countries represented). Asian 10%, African American 6%, Caucasian 26%, Hispanic 23%, Native American 1%, Pacific Islander 2%, Two or more races 9%, Race unknown 10%.
Retention and Graduation: 77% freshmen return for sophomore year. 43% freshmen graduate within 4 years. 53% freshmen graduate within 6 years. **Faculty:** Student/faculty ratio 14:1. 30 full-time faculty, 87% hold PhDs, 33% are are members of minority groups, 53% are women. 0% of classes are taught by teaching assistants.

ACADEMICS

Degrees: bachelor's. **Classes:** Most classes have 20-29 students. Most lab/discussion sessions have 10-19 students. **Most popular majors:** Sport and Fitness Administration/Management; Accounting; Marketing/Marketing Management. **Special Study Options:** Accelerated program, double major, independent study, internships, student-designed major, study abroad, Advanced Placement credit Learning disability services. **Disability Services:** Special programs offered to physically disabled students, including note-taking services, reader services, tape recorders, tutors. **Career Services:** Alumni network, Alumni services, Career/job search classes, Career assessment, Internships, Regional alumni.

FACILITIES

Housing: Coed dorms, special housing for disabled students, men's dorms, women's dorms. 95% of campus accessible to physically diasbled. **Computers:** 33% of classrooms, 100% of libraries, 100% of dining areas, 100% of student union, have wireless network access. Students can register for classes online. Administrative functions (other than registration) can be performed online.

CAMPUS LIFE

Environment: Town. **Activities:** radio station, student government, student newspaper, student-run film society, television station, yearbook, Student Organization. 30 registered organizations, 2 honor societies. **Athletics (Intercollegiate):** *Men:* baseball, basketball, cross-country, football, golf, soccer, wrestling. *Women:* basketball, cross-country, soccer, softball, volleyball, wrestling. **On-Campus Highlights:** Library, Student Union, Dining commons **Environmental Initiatives:** Plastic bottle and styrofoam cups free campus.

ADMISSIONS

Freshman Academic Profile: Average high school GPA 3.2. 80% from public high schools. Minimum internet-based TOEFL 61. Minimum paper TOEFL 500. **Basis for Candidate Selection:** *Very important factors considered include:* rigor of secondary school record, academic GPA, standardized test scores. *Important factors considered include:* class rank, application essay, recommendation(s), character/personal qualities, volunteer work. *Other factors considered include:* interview, alumni/ae relation, work experience, level of applicant's interest. **Freshman Admission Requirements:** High school diploma is required and GED is accepted. *Academic units recommended:* 4 English, 3 math, 3 science, 2 foreign language, 3 social studies. **Freshman Admission Statistics:** 2,195 applied, 40.87% admitted, 18% enrolled. **Transfer Admission Requirements:** college transcript(s), essay or personal statement, statement of good standing from prior institution(s). Minimum college GPA of 2.0 required. Lowest grade transferable C-. **General Admission Information:** Application fee $40. Priority deadline 2/1. Regular application deadline 4/1. Nonfall registration accepted. Admission may be deferred for a maximum of 2 semesters.

COSTS AND FINANCIAL AID

Annual tuition $40,625. Room and board $13,680. Required fees $725. Average book expense $550. **Required Forms and Deadlines:** FAFSA, State aid form. **Notification of Awards:** Applicants will be notified of awards on a rolling basis beginning 12/15. **Types of Aid:** *Need-based scholarships/grants:* Federal Pell, FSEOG, State scholarships/grants, College/university scholarship or grant aid from institutional funds. *Loans:* Direct Subsidized Stafford Loans, Direct Unsubsidized Stafford Loans, Direct PLUS loans. *Student Employment:* Federal Work-Study Program available. Institutional employment available. **Financial Aid Statistics:** 100% needy freshmen, 100% needy undergrads receive need-based scholarship or grant aid. 14% freshmen, 9% undergrads receive non-need-based scholarship or grant aid. 83% freshmen, 88% undergrads receive need-based self-help aid. 12% freshmen, 16% undergrads receive athletic scholarships. 97% freshmen, 96% undergrads receive any aid. 65% undergrads borrow to pay for school. Average cumulative indebtedness $30,145. **Criteria for awarding aid:** *Need-based:* Academics, Athletics. *Non-need-based:* Academics, Athletics.

MERCER UNIVERSITY—MACON

1501 Mercer University Drive, Macon, GA 31207-0001
Phone: 478-301-2650 • **Financial Aid Phone:** 478-301-2670
E-mail: admissions@mercer.edu • **CEEB Code:** 5409
Fax: 478-301-2828 • **Website:** www.mercer.edu • **ACT Code:** 838

This private school, affiliated with the Baptist Church, was founded in 1833. It has a 150-acre campus.

RATINGS

Admissions Selectivity Rating: 87   **Fire Safety Rating:** 89   **Green Rating:** 60*

STUDENTS AND FACULTY

Enrollment: 3,032. **Student Body:** 51% female, 49% male, 19% out-of-state, 3% international (37 countries represented). Asian 8%, African American 19%, Caucasian 58%, Hispanic 5%, Native American <1%, Pacific Islander <1%, Two or more races 4%, Race unknown 3%.
Retention and Graduation: 88% freshmen return for sophomore year. 49% freshmen graduate within 4 years. 67% freshmen graduate within 6 years. 37% grads go on to further study within 1 year. **Faculty:** Student/faculty ratio 13:1. 391 full-time faculty, 92% hold PhDs, 23% are are members of minority groups, 50% are women. 0% of classes are taught by teaching assistants.

ACADEMICS

Degrees: bachelor's, doctoral/professional, doctoral/research, master's, post-master's certificate. **Classes:** Most classes have 10-19 students. Most lab/discussion sessions have 20-29 students. **Most popular majors:** Engineering; Business/Commerce; Biology/Biological Sciences. **Special Study Options:** Accelerated program, cooperative education program, cross-registration, double major, dual enrollment, honors program, independent study, internships, liberal arts/career combination, student-designed major, study abroad, teacher certification program, Great Books program. **Honors Programs:** Qualified students may be admitted to the Honors Program in the College of Liberal Arts, the Stetson School of Business and Economics, the School of Engineering, and the Tift College of Education. The Honors Program includes honors courses, out of classroom activities, independent study, and other opportunities. Combined degree programs: BA/MEng. **Disability Services:** Special programs offered to physically disabled students, including note-taking services, reader services, tape recorders, tutors. **Career Services:** Alumni network, Alumni services, Career/job search classes, Career assessment, Internships, Regional alumni. Aproximately 65% of undergraduate students participate in some form of structured experiential education prior to graduation. These experiences serve to enhance the students' academic and leadership skills and also prepares them well for their chosen career paths.

FACILITIES

Housing: Coed dorms, special housing for disabled students, men's dorms, special housing for international students, women's dorms, fraternity/sorority housing, apartments for married students, apartments for single students. 85% of campus accessible to physically diasbled. **Special Academic Facilities/Equipment:** McCorkle Music Building **Computers:** 100% of classrooms, 100% of dorms, 100% of libraries, 100% of dining areas, 100% of student union, 100% of common outdoor areas have wireless network access. Students can register for classes online. Administrative functions (other than registration) can be performed online.

CAMPUS LIFE

Environment: City. **Activities:** Choral groups, concert band, dance, drama/theater, jazz band, literary magazine, music ensembles, musical theater, opera, pep band, student government, student newspaper, television station, Campus Ministries, Student Organization. 115 registered organizations, 18 honor societies, 7 religious organizations. 9 fraternities, 7 sororities. **Athletics (Intercollegiate):** *Men:* baseball, basketball, cross-country, golf, riflery, soccer, tennis. *Women:* basketball, cross-country, golf, soccer, softball, tennis, volleyball. **On-Campus Highlights:** University Center, Connell Student Center, Greek Village, Porter Patch, Jesse Mercer Plaza. **Environmental Initiatives:** We have long-standing community partnerships to improve and rehabilitate housing and commerical stock in Macon proper, which has significant positive impact on the sustability of the community.

ADMISSIONS

Freshman Academic Profile: Average high school GPA 3.8. 39% in top 10% of high school class, 70% in top 25% of high school class, 92% in top 50% of high school class. **Reported SAT (pre-2016 redesign) scores:** SAT Math middle 50% range 550-650. SAT Critical Reading middle 50% range 550-640. SAT Writing middle 50% range 520-630. **Concordant SAT scores:** SAT EBRW middle 50% 590–680. SAT Math middle 50% range 570–670. ACT middle 50% range 25-29. Minimum internet-based TOEFL 80. Minimum paper TOEFL 550. **Basis for Candidate Selection:** *Very important factors considered include:* rigor of secondary school record, academic GPA, standardized test scores, level of applicant's interest. *Important factors considered include:* application essay, extracurricular activities, talent/ability, character/personal qualities, volunteer work. *Other factors considered include:* class rank, recommendation(s), interview, alumni/ae relation, work experience. **Freshman Admission Requirements:** High school diploma is required and GED is accepted. *Academic units required:* 4 English, 4 math, 3 science, 2 science labs, 2 foreign language, 1 social studies, 2 history. **Freshman Admission Statistics:** 4,836 applied, 69.35% admitted, 25% enrolled. **Transfer Admission Requirements:** college transcript(s), statement of good standing from prior institution(s). Minimum college GPA of 2.5 required. Lowest grade transferable C. **General Admission Information:** Application fee $50. Priority deadline 3/1. Regular application deadline 4/1. Nonfall registration accepted. Admission may be deferred for a maximum of 1 year.

COSTS AND FINANCIAL AID

Annual tuition $34,830. Room and board $11,916. Required fees $300. Average book expense $1,200. **Required Forms and Deadlines:** FAFSA, Institution's own financial aid form, State aid form. **Notification of Awards:** Applicants will be notified of awards on a rolling basis beginning 3/15. **Types of Aid:** *Need-based scholarships/grants:* Federal Pell, FSEOG, State scholarships/grants, College/university scholarship or grant aid from institutional funds, Federal Nursing Scholarships. *Loans:* Direct Subsidized Stafford Loans, Direct Unsubsidized Stafford Loans, Direct PLUS loans, Federal Perkins Loans, Federal Nursing Loans, College/university loans from institutional funds. *Student Employment:* Federal Work-Study Program available. Institutional employment available. **Financial Aid Statistics:** 100% needy freshmen, 99% needy undergrads receive need-based scholarship or grant aid. 31% freshmen, 28% undergrads receive non-need-based scholarship or grant aid. 58% freshmen, 55% undergrads receive need-based self-help aid. 4% freshmen, 6% undergrads receive athletic scholarships. 99% freshmen, 97% undergrads receive any aid. 64% undergrads borrow to pay for school. Average cumulative indebtedness $28,194. **Criteria for awarding aid:** *Need-based:* Job skills. *Non-need-based:* Academics, Art, Athletics, Job skills, Leadership, Music/drama, State/district residency.

MERCY COLLEGE

555 Broadway, Dobbs Ferry, NY 10522
Phone: 877-637-2946 • **Financial Aid Phone:** 1-888-464-6737
E-mail: admissions@mercy.edu • **CEEB Code:** 2409
Fax: 914-674-7382 • **Website:** www.mercy.edu • **ACT Code:** 2814

This private school was founded in 1950. It has a 90-acre campus.

RATINGS

Admissions Selectivity Rating: 65   **Fire Safety Rating:** 97   **Green Rating:** 68

STUDENTS AND FACULTY

Enrollment: 6,410. **Student Body:** 69% female, 31% male, 7% out-of-state, 1% international (37 countries represented). Asian 4%, African American 23%, Caucasian 27%, Hispanic 35%, Native American <1%, Pacific Islander <1%, Two or more races 1%, Race unknown 7%.
Retention and Graduation: 76% freshmen return for sophomore year. 19% freshmen graduate within 4 years. 38 **Faculty:** Student/faculty ratio 17:1. 198 full-time faculty, 86% hold PhDs, 23% are are members of minority groups, 62% are women. 0% of classes are taught by teaching assistants.

ACADEMICS

Degrees: associate, bachelor's, certificate, doctoral/professional, master's, postbachelor's certificate. **Classes:** Most classes have 10-19 students. **Most popular majors:** Psychology; Social Sciences; Business Administration and Management. **Special Study Options:** Accelerated program, cooperative education program, distance learning, double major, dual enrollment, honors program, internships, teacher certification program, weekend college, Program for college students with learning disabilities. **Honors Programs:** Admission criteria to the Honors Program is a 87 or above high school average. One hundred and thirty new and transfer students were admitted in 2009-10. Students in the Honors Program take Honors versions of General Education courses (e.g., English, speech, and math) at the lower level and complete individualized Honors project in connection with their major for a total of 24 Honors credits. Combined degree programs: BA/MA, Accounting, Education, Nursing. **Disability Services:** Special programs offered to physically disabled students, including note-taking services, reader services, tape recorders, tutors. **Career Services:** Alumni network, Alumni services, Career/job search classes, Career assessment, Internships, Regional alumni, On-campus interviews.

FACILITIES

Housing: Coed dorms. 75% of campus accessible to physically diasbled. **Special Academic Facilities/Equipment:** Childcare center located at the Bronx campus. **Computers:** 40% of classrooms, 100% of dorms, 60% of libraries, 60% of dining areas, 60% of student union, have wireless network access. Students can register for classes online. Administrative functions (other than registration) can be performed online.

CAMPUS LIFE

Environment: Village. **Activities:** dance, student government, student newspaper, Campus Ministries, Model UN. 20 registered organizations, 1 religious organization. **Athletics (Intercollegiate):** *Men:* baseball, basketball, cross-country, lacrosse, soccer, tennis, track/field (outdoor). *Women:* basketball, cross-country, lacrosse, soccer, softball, track/field (outdoor), volleyball. **On-Campus Highlights:** Waterfront campus on the Hudson River, New State-of-the-Art Library, Student Cafe, Music and Recording Studio, Roy Disney Center for Computer Animation.

ADMISSIONS

Freshman Academic Profile: Average high school GPA 84.8. Minimum internet-based TOEFL 79. Minimum paper TOEFL 550. **Basis for Candidate Selection:** *Very important factors considered include:* academic GPA, extracurricular activities, talent/ability, character/personal qualities, volunteer work. *Important factors considered include:* rigor of secondary school record, application essay, recommendation(s), interview, level of applicant's interest. *Other factors considered include:* class rank, alumni/ae relation, work experience. **Freshman Admission Requirements:** High school diploma is required and GED is accepted. *Academic units required:* 4 English, 4 math, 3 science, 1 science lab, 3 foreign language, 2 social studies, 2 history, 3 academic electives. *Academic units recommended:* 4 English, 4 math, 3 science, 1 science lab, 3 foreign language, 2 social studies, 2 history, 3 academic electives. **Freshman Admission Statistics:** 5,573 applied, 65.69% admitted, 26% enrolled. **Transfer Admission Requirements:** college transcript(s), Minimum college GPA of 2.0 required. Lowest grade transferable C. **General Admission Information:** Application fee $40. Nonfall registration accepted. Admission may be deferred for a maximum of 1 year.

COSTS AND FINANCIAL AID

Annual tuition $17,466. Room and board $13,700. Required fees $610. Average book expense $1,492. **Required Forms and Deadlines:** FAFSA,

State aid form. **Notification of Awards:** Applicants will be notified of awards on a rolling basis beginning 2/20. **Types of Aid:** *Need-based scholarships/ grants:* Federal Pell, FSEOG, State scholarships/grants, Private scholarships, College/university scholarship or grant aid. *Loans:* Direct Subsidized Stafford Loans, Direct Unsubsidized Stafford Loans, Direct PLUS loans, Federal Nursing Loans, State Loans. *Student Employment:* Federal Work-Study Program available. Institutional employment available. **Financial Aid Statistics:** 90% needy freshmen, 89% needy undergrads receive need-based scholarship or grant aid. 52% freshmen, 29% undergrads receive non-need-based scholarship or grant aid. 72% freshmen, 82% undergrads receive need-based self-help aid. 8% freshmen, 4% undergrads receive athletic scholarships. 82% freshmen, 82% undergrads receive any aid. Average cumulative indebtedness $26,100. **Criteria for awarding aid:** *Non-need-based:* Academics, Athletics.

MERCYHURST UNIVERSITY

Admissions, Erie, PA 16546
Phone: 814-824-2202 • **Financial Aid Phone:** 814-824-2288
E-mail: admissions@mercyhurst.edu • **CEEB Code:** 2410
Fax: 814-824-2071 • **Website:** www.mercyhurst.edu • **ACT Code:** 3629

This private school, affiliated with the Roman Catholic Church, was founded in 1926. It has a 88-acre campus.

RATINGS
Admissions Selectivity Rating: 80   **Fire Safety Rating:** 91   **Green Rating:** 92

STUDENTS AND FACULTY
Enrollment: 2,680. **Student Body:** 56% female, 44% male, 48% out-of-state, 8% international. Asian 1%, African American 4%, Caucasian 77%, Hispanic 2%, Native American <1%, Pacific Islander 0%, Two or more races 0%, Race unknown 7%.
Retention and Graduation: 79% freshmen return for sophomore year. 55% freshmen graduate within 4 years. 61% freshmen graduate within 6 years.
Faculty: Student/faculty ratio 14:1. 164 full-time faculty, 68% hold PhDs, 9% are are members of minority groups, 44% are women. 0% of classes are taught by teaching assistants.

ACADEMICS
Degrees: bachelor's, doctoral, master's, postbachelor's certificate. **Classes:** Most classes have fewer than 10 students. Most lab/discussion sessions have 10-19 students. **Most popular majors:** Elementary Education and Teaching; International/Global Studies; Business Administration and Management. **Special Study Options:** Accelerated program, cooperative education program, cross-registration, double major, exchange student program (domestic), honors program, independent study, internships, liberal arts/career combination, student-designed major, study abroad, teacher certification program, weekend college, Arts, Business, Computer Science, Education, Health Professions, History, English Home Economics, Humanities, Natural Science, Social/ Behavioral Science. Off Campus Study: Washington D.C. Undergrads may take grad level classes. Combined degree programs: 3+4 Medical school program; 3+3 Pharmacy school program. **Disability Services:** Special programs offered to physically disabled students, including note-taking services, reader services, tape recorders, tutors. **Career Services:** Alumni network, Alumni services, Career/job search classes, Career assessment, Internships.

FACILITIES
Housing: special housing for disabled students, men's dorms, women's dorms, apartments for single students. **Special Academic Facilities/Equipment:** Art gallery, college-owned restaurant for hotel/restaurant management department, observatory, archaeology lab. **Computers:** Students can register for classes online. Administrative functions (other than registration) can be performed online.

CAMPUS LIFE
Environment: Village. **Activities:** Choral groups, concert band, dance, drama/ theater, literary magazine, music ensembles, musical theater, pep band, radio station, student government, student newspaper, television station, yearbook. 9 honor societies, 2 religious organizations. **Athletics (Intercollegiate):** *Men:* baseball, basketball, cheerleading, crew/rowing, cross-country, football, golf, ice hockey, lacrosse, soccer, tennis, volleyball, water polo, wrestling. *Women:* basketball, cheerleading, crew/rowing, cross-country, field hockey, golf, ice hockey, lacrosse, soccer, softball, tennis, volleyball, water polo. **On-Campus Highlights:** Performing Arts Center, Mercyhurst Athletic Center, Library, Student Union, Ice Rink. **Environmental Initiatives:** Sustainability Studies academic program.

ADMISSIONS
Freshman Academic Profile: Average high school GPA 3.4. 21% in top 10% of high school class, 29% in top 25% of high school class, 87% in top 50% of high school class. 55% from public high schools. **Reported SAT (pre-2016 redesign) scores:** SAT Math middle 50% range 470-570. SAT Critical Reading middle 50% range 470-580. SAT Writing middle 50% range 460-560. **Concordant SAT scores:** SAT EBRW middle 50% 520–630. SAT Math middle 50% range 510–590. ACT middle 50% range 21-26. Minimum internet-based TOEFL 79. Minimum paper TOEFL 550. **Basis for Candidate Selection:** *Very important factors considered include:* rigor of secondary school record, class rank, academic GPA, standardized test scores. *Important factors considered include:* application essay, recommendation(s), interview, extracurricular activities, talent/ability, character/personal qualities. *Other factors considered include:* alumni/ae relation, geographical residence, state residency, religious affiliation/commitment, racial/ethnic status, volunteer work, work experience, level of applicant's interest. **Freshman Admission Requirements:** High school diploma is required and GED is accepted. *Academic units required:* 4 English, 3 math, 2 science, 1 science lab, 2 foreign language, 5 social studies. *Academic units recommended:* 4 English, 3 math, 3 science, 2 science labs, 2 foreign language, 5 social studies. **Freshman Admission Statistics:** 2,938 applied, 75.36% admitted, 27% enrolled. **Transfer Admission Requirements:** High school transcript, college transcript(s), standardized test scores, Minimum college GPA of 2.0 required. Lowest grade transferable C. **General Admission Information:** Application fee $30. Priority deadline 5/1. Nonfall registration accepted. Admission may be deferred for a maximum of 1 year.

COSTS AND FINANCIAL AID
Annual tuition $29,600. Room and board $10,800. Required fees $1,885. Average book expense $1,000. **Notification of Awards:** Applicants will be notified of awards on a rolling basis beginning 2/15. **Types of Aid:** *Need-based scholarships/grants:* Federal Pell, FSEOG, State scholarships/grants, Private scholarships, College/university scholarship or grant aid from institutional funds. *Loans:* Direct Subsidized Stafford Loans, Direct Unsubsidized Stafford Loans, Direct PLUS loans, Federal Perkins Loans. *Student Employment:* Federal Work-Study Program available. Institutional employment available. **Financial Aid Statistics:** 95% needy freshmen, 94% needy undergrads receive need-based scholarship or grant aid. 75% freshmen, 66% undergrads receive non-need-based scholarship or grant aid. 82% freshmen, 87% undergrads receive need-based self-help aid. 5% freshmen, 5% undergrads receive athletic scholarships. 93% freshmen receive any aid. **Criteria for awarding aid:** *Need-based:* Academics, Alumni affiliation, Art, Athletics, Leadership, Music/ drama, Religious affiliation. *Non-need-based:* Academics, Alumni affiliation, Art, Athletics, Leadership, Music/drama, Religious affiliation.

MEREDITH COLLEGE

3800 Hillsborough Street, Raleigh, NC 27607
Phone: 919-760-8581 • **Financial Aid Phone:** 919-760-8565
E-mail: admissions@meredith.edu • **CEEB Code:** 5410
Fax: 919-760-2348 • **Website:** www.meredith.edu • **ACT Code:** 3126

This private school was founded in 1891. It has a 225-acre campus.

RATINGS
Admissions Selectivity Rating: 82   **Fire Safety Rating:** 88   **Green Rating:** 68

STUDENTS AND FACULTY
Enrollment: 1,649. **Student Body:** 100% female, 0% male, 9% out-of-state, 5% international (24 countries represented). Asian 3%, African American 10%, Caucasian 71%, Hispanic 3%, Native American 1%, Pacific Islander <1%, Two or more races 4%, Race unknown 2%.
Retention and Graduation: 79% freshmen return for sophomore year. 55% freshmen graduate within 4 years. 62% freshmen graduate within 6 years.
Faculty: Student/faculty ratio 12:1. 126 full-time faculty, 88% hold PhDs, 10% are are members of minority groups, 73% are women. 0% of classes are taught by teaching assistants.

ACADEMICS
Degrees: bachelor's, master's, postbachelor's certificate. **Classes:** Most classes have 10-19 students. Most lab/discussion sessions have fewer than 10 students. **Most popular majors:** Psychology; Biology/Biological Sciences; Interior Design. **Special Study Options:** Accelerated program, cooperative education program, cross-registration, double major, dual enrollment, honors program, independent study, internships, liberal arts/career combination, student-designed major, study abroad, teacher certification program, Semester Programs at American U., Drew U., Marymount Manhattan. **Honors Programs:**

Meredith offers an enriched academic and co-curricular Honors Program that spans the four years and involves honors courses in general education, in the major field, and a thesis or equivalent project. Interdisciplinary honors courses and weekend trips/programs enrich the experience, and a Focus on Excellence series offers a variety of outings to cultural/intellectual/entertainment venues. Scholarships are provided for Honors Program participants. Combined degree programs: BA/MEng. **Disability Services:** Special programs offered to physically disabled students, including note-taking services, reader services, tape recorders, tutors. **Career Services:** Alumni network, Alumni services, Career/job search classes, Career assessment, Internships.

FACILITIES

Housing: women's dorms, apartments for married students, apartments for single students. 80% of campus accessible to physically diasbled. **Special Academic Facilities/Equipment:** Art gallery, amphitheatre, child-care lab, learning center and fitness center. Experimental and clinical psychology labs including an autism lab. A new Science and Mathematics Building provides a roof top telescope platform for astronomy observations, an electron microscope suite, greenhouse, and 15 student/faculty research labs. **Computers:** Students can register for classes online. Administrative functions (other than registration) can be performed online.

CAMPUS LIFE

Environment: Metropolis. **Activities:** Choral groups, concert band, dance, drama/theater, literary magazine, music ensembles, musical theater, student government, student newspaper, symphony orchestra, yearbook, Model UN. 91 registered organizations, 22 honor societies, 7 religious organizations. **Athletics (Intercollegiate):** *Women:* basketball, cross-country, soccer, softball, tennis, volleyball. **On-Campus Highlights:** Science and Math Building, McIver Ampitheatre and Meredith Lake, Weatherspoon Physical Education -Dance Building, Belk Dining Hall, Cate Student Center/Bee Hive (snack bar).

ADMISSIONS

Freshman Academic Profile: Average high school GPA 3.4. 20% in top 10% of high school class, 468% in top 25% of high school class, 84% in top 50% of high school class. **Reported SAT (pre-2016 redesign) scores:** SAT Math middle 50% range 450-560. SAT Critical Reading middle 50% range 470-570. **Concordant SAT scores:** SAT Math middle 50% range 490–580. ACT middle 50% range 20-25. Minimum paper TOEFL 500. **Basis for Candidate Selection:** *Very important factors considered include:* class rank, academic GPA, application essay, recommendation(s), character/personal qualities. *Important factors considered include:* rigor of secondary school record, standardized test scores, interview, extracurricular activities, talent/ability, volunteer work, level of applicant's interest. *Other factors considered include:* first generation, alumni/ae relation, work experience. **Freshman Admission Requirements:** High school diploma is required and GED is not accepted. *Academic units required:* 4 English, 3 math, 3 science, 2 foreign language, 1 academic elective. **Freshman Admission Statistics:** 1,721 applied, 60.02% admitted, 42% enrolled. **Transfer Admission Requirements:** High school transcript, college transcript(s), statement of good standing from prior institution(s). Minimum college GPA of 2.0 required. Lowest grade transferable C. **General Admission Information:** Application fee $40. Priority deadline 2/15. Nonfall registration accepted. Admission may be deferred for a maximum of One year.

COSTS AND FINANCIAL AID

Annual tuition $34,807. Room and board $10,390. Required fees $100. Average book expense $850. **Required Forms and Deadlines:** FAFSA. **Notification of Awards:** Applicants will be notified of awards on a rolling basis beginning 3/15. **Types of Aid:** *Need-based scholarships/grants:* Federal Pell, FSEOG, State scholarships/grants, Private scholarships, College/university scholarship or grant aid from institutional funds. *Loans:* Federal Perkins Loans, College/university loans from institutional funds. *Student Employment:* Federal Work-Study Program available. Institutional employment available. **Financial Aid Statistics:** 100% needy freshmen, 100% needy undergrads receive need-based scholarship or grant aid. 0% undergrads receive non-need-based scholarship or grant aid. 83% freshmen, 83% undergrads receive need-based self-help aid. 0% freshmen, 0% undergrads receive athletic scholarships. 69% undergrads borrow to pay for school. Average cumulative indebtedness $33,993. **Criteria for awarding aid:** *Need-based:* Academics, Art, Leadership, Minority status, Music/drama, Religious affiliation. *Non-need-based:* Academics, Art, Leadership, Minority status, Music/drama, Religious affiliation, State/district residency.

MERRIMACK COLLEGE

Office of Admission, North Andover, MA 1845
Phone: 978-837-5100 • **Financial Aid Phone:** 978-837-5186
E-mail: admission@merrimack.edu • **CEEB Code:** 3525
Fax: 978-837-5133 • **Website:** www.merrimack.edu

This private school, affiliated with the Roman Catholic Church, was founded in 1947. It has a 220-acre campus.

RATINGS

Admissions Selectivity Rating: 64   **Fire Safety Rating:** 98   **Green Rating:** 67

STUDENTS AND FACULTY

Enrollment: 3,416. **Student Body:** 52% female, 48% male, 30% out-of-state, 3% international (30 countries represented). Asian 1%, African American 3%, Caucasian 76%, Hispanic 6%, Native American <1%, Pacific Islander <1%, Two or more races 2%, Race unknown 8%.
Retention and Graduation: 82% freshmen return for sophomore year. 68% freshmen graduate within 4 years. 73% freshmen graduate within 6 years. 29% grads go on to further study within 1 year. **Faculty:** Student/faculty ratio 14:1. 175 full-time faculty, 87% hold PhDs, 13% are are members of minority groups, 47% are women. 0% of classes are taught by teaching assistants.

ACADEMICS

Degrees: bachelor's, master's, post-master's certificate. **Classes:** Most classes have 10-19 students. **Most popular majors:** Human Development and Family Studies; Marketing; Accounting. **Special Study Options:** Accelerated program, cooperative education program, cross-registration, double major, dual enrollment, English as a Second Language (ESL), independent study, internships, liberal arts/career combination, student-designed major, study abroad, teacher certification program, Five-year combined BA/BS program, continuing education program, center for corporate education. ESL available through Kaplan with offices on the college campus. Cross-registration available through college's membership in 10-college consortium. **Honors Programs:** The Honors Program offers students with strong academic credentials, class standing, and leadership qualities the opportunity to study with other exceptional students in smaller classes. It is an innovative and exciting approach to fulfilling the college"s general education requirements and includes a variety of social and co-curricular activities. Combined degree programs: BS/MS. **Disability Services:** Special programs offered to physically disabled students, including note-taking services, reader services, tape recorders, tutors. **Career Services:** Alumni network, Alumni services, Career/job search classes, Career assessment, Internships, Regional alumni. At Merrimack College we offer experiential opportunities for students in each major: Traditional 5 year cooperative education program; Full-time paid summer internships; Part-time paid internship opportunities during the academic year; In conjunction with academic departments, unpaid but for-academic credit internships; Service learning volunteer opportunities with local non-profit agencies

FACILITIES

Housing: Coed dorms, special housing for disabled students, apartments for single students, Wellness Housing, Theme Housing. 95% of campus accessible to physically diasbled. **Special Academic Facilities/Equipment:** Observatory, Rogers Center for the Arts. **Computers:** 100% of classrooms, 100% of libraries, 100% of dining areas, 100% of student union, have wireless network access. Students can register for classes online. Administrative functions (other than registration) can be performed online.

CAMPUS LIFE

Environment: Town. **Activities:** Choral groups, dance, drama/theater, jazz band, music ensembles, musical theater, pep band, student government, student newspaper, student-run film society, television station, yearbook, Campus Ministries, Student Organization, Model UN. 47 registered organizations, 3 honor societies, 5 religious organizations. 2 fraternities, 3 sororities. **Athletics (Intercollegiate):** *Men:* baseball, basketball, cross-country, football, ice hockey, lacrosse, soccer, tennis. *Women:* basketball, cross-country, field hockey, lacrosse, soccer, softball, tennis, volleyball. **On-Campus Highlights:** Sakowich Student Center, Rogers Center for the Arts, Santagati Hall, McQuade Library, Volpe Athletic Complex, Campus observatory open one night a week to the public. Rogers Center and the McQuade Library have art gallerys. McQuade Gallery frequently displays student art. **Environmental Initiatives:** Roll-out of the new interdisciplinary Environmental Studies and Sustainability Major in fall 2011. The new major has an integrated curriculum across the College four Schools, Science and Engineering, Liberal Arts, Business, and Education.

ADMISSIONS

Freshman Academic Profile: Average high school GPA 3.1. 73% from public high schools. Minimum internet-based TOEFL 80. **Basis for Candidate Selection:** *Very important factors considered include:* rigor of secondary school record, academic GPA, application essay, extracurricular activities, character/personal qualities, level of applicant's interest. *Important factors considered include:* recommendation(s), interview, talent/ability, volunteer work, work experience. *Other factors considered include:* first generation, alumni/ae relation, geographical residence, racial/ethnic status. **Freshman Admission Requirements:** High school diploma is required and GED is accepted. *Academic units required:* 4 English, 3 math, 2 science, 2 foreign language, 2 history. **Freshman Admission Statistics:** 8,214 applied, 81.91% admitted, 15% enrolled. **Transfer Admission Requirements:** college transcript(s), essay or personal statement, Minimum college GPA of 2.5 required. Lowest grade transferable C. **General Admission Information:** Regular application deadline 2/15. Regular notification 4/15. Nonfall registration accepted. Admission may be deferred for a maximum of 12 months.

COSTS AND FINANCIAL AID

Required Forms and Deadlines: FAFSA. **Notification of Awards:** Applicants will be notified of awards on a rolling basis beginning 3/15. **Types of Aid:** *Need-based scholarships/grants:* Federal Pell, FSEOG, State scholarships/grants, Private scholarships, College/university scholarship or grant aid from institutional funds. *Loans:* Direct Subsidized Stafford Loans, Direct Unsubsidized Stafford Loans, Direct PLUS loans, Federal Perkins Loans, State Loans, College/university loans from institutional funds. *Student Employment:* Federal Work-Study Program available. Institutional employment available. **Financial Aid Statistics:** 100% needy freshmen, 99% needy undergrads receive need-based scholarship or grant aid. 10% freshmen, 11% undergrads receive non-need-based scholarship or grant aid. 86% freshmen, 86% undergrads receive need-based self-help aid. 6% freshmen, 7% undergrads receive athletic scholarships. **Criteria for awarding aid:** *Need-based:* Athletics. *Non-need-based:* Academics, Alumni affiliation, Athletics, Leadership, Music/drama, Religious affiliation.

MESSIAH COLLEGE

One College Avenue, Mechanicsburg, PA 17055
Phone: 717-691-6000 • **Financial Aid Phone:** 717-691-6007
E-mail: admissions@messiah.edu • **CEEB Code:** 2411
Fax: 717-691-2307 • **Website:** www.messiah.edu • **ACT Code:** 3630

This private school was founded in 1909. It has a 471-acre campus.

RATINGS

Admissions Selectivity Rating: 85   **Fire Safety Rating:** 86   **Green Rating:** 84

STUDENTS AND FACULTY

Enrollment: 2,683. **Student Body:** 60% female, 40% male, 36% out-of-state, 5% international (29 countries represented). Asian 2%, African American 2%, Caucasian 81%, Hispanic 4%, Native American <1%, Pacific Islander <1%, Two or more races 4%, Race unknown 1%.
Retention and Graduation: 85% freshmen return for sophomore year. 72% freshmen graduate within 4 years. 76% freshmen graduate within 6 years. 13% grads go on to further study within 1 year. 44% grads pursue arts and sciences degrees. 2% grads pursue law degrees. 5% grads pursue business degrees. 32% grads pursue medical degrees. **Faculty:** Student/faculty ratio 13:1. 189 full-time faculty, 81% hold PhDs, 8% are are members of minority groups, 42% are women. 0% of classes are taught by teaching assistants.

ACADEMICS

Degrees: bachelor's, doctoral/professional, master's, postbachelor's certificate, post-master's certificate. **Classes:** Most classes have 20-29 students. Most lab/discussion sessions have 10-19 students. **Most popular majors:** Engineering; Registered Nursing/Registered Nurse; Psychology. **Special Study Options:** Accelerated program, double major, dual enrollment, English as a Second Language (ESL), exchange student program (domestic), honors program, independent study, internships, student-designed major, study abroad, teacher certification program, Pass/Fail option. **Honors Programs:** The College Honors Program is designed for students who demonstrate high scholarly ability early in their academic career. The program provides a series of interdisciplinary honors courses which satisfy selected general education requirements. In addition, various campus activities are designed each semester for participants in the College Honors Program. Participation in the program culminates in an honors research project, typically during the senior year. Admission to the program is highly competitive and students selected for the College Honors Program receive either full tuition or partial tuition scholarships. **Disability Services:** Special programs offered to physically disabled students, including note-taking services, reader services, tape recorders, tutors. **Career Services:** Alumni network, Alumni services, Career assessment, Internships, Regional alumni, On-campus interviews. Into the City, which is an overnight career immersion trip to a major city. The purpose is to connect students to alumni and to expose students to what it is like to live and work in the city. This is accomplished through employer site visits, alumni lunch panels, and networking receptions.

FACILITIES

Housing: Coed dorms, special housing for disabled students, men's dorms, special housing for international students, women's dorms, apartments for single students. 80% of campus accessible to physically diasbled. **Special Academic Facilities/Equipment:** Boyer Center for Advanced Studies; Brethren in Christ Historical Society and Archives; Oakes Museum of Natural History. **Computers:** 100% of classrooms, 100% of dorms, 100% of libraries, 100% of dining areas, 100% of student union, have wireless network access. Students can register for classes online. Administrative functions (other than registration) can be performed online.

CAMPUS LIFE

Environment: Village. **Activities:** Choral groups, concert band, dance, drama/theater, jazz band, literary magazine, music ensembles, musical theater, pep band, radio station, student government, student newspaper, student-run film society, symphony orchestra, yearbook, Campus Ministries, Student Organization. 71 registered organizations, 7 honor societies, 10 religious organizations. **Athletics (Intercollegiate):** *Men:* baseball, basketball, cross-country, golf, lacrosse, soccer, swimming, tennis, track/field (outdoor), track/field (indoor), ultimate frisbee, wrestling. *Women:* basketball, cross-country, field hockey, lacrosse, soccer, softball, swimming, tennis, track/field (outdoor), track/field (indoor), volleyball. **On-Campus Highlights:** Boyer Hall (Schools of Humanities, Ed. and Soc. Sci., Eisenhower Campus Center/Sollenberger Sports Cent, Oakes Museum of Natural History, Stoner Covered Bridge, Starry Athletic Complex, The scenic Yellow Breeches Creek runs through the 471 acre campus. It is a nationally recognized trout fishing stream, complete with covered bridge and swinging foot bridge.

ADMISSIONS

Freshman Academic Profile: Average high school GPA 3.8. 33% in top 10% of high school class, 62% in top 25% of high school class, 91% in top 50% of high school class. 74% from public high schools. **Reported SAT (pre-2016 redesign) scores:** SAT Math middle 50% range 510-630. SAT Critical Reading middle 50% range 510-630. SAT Writing middle 50% range 490-610. **Concordant SAT scores:** SAT EBRW middle 50% 560-670. SAT Math middle 50% range 540-650. ACT middle 50% range 22-29. Minimum internet-based TOEFL 80. Minimum paper TOEFL 550. **Basis for Candidate Selection:** *Very important factors considered include:* rigor of secondary school record, class rank, academic GPA, standardized test scores, extracurricular activities, talent/ability, character/personal qualities, religious affiliation/commitment. *Important factors considered include:* application essay, volunteer work. *Other factors considered include:* recommendation(s), alumni/ae relation, racial/ethnic status, work experience, level of applicant's interest. **Freshman Admission Requirements:** High school diploma is required and GED is accepted. *Academic units required:* 4 English, 2 math, 2 science, 2 science labs, 2 foreign language, 2 social studies, 4 academic electives. *Academic units recommended:* 4 English, 3 math, 3 science, 3 science labs, 2 foreign language, 2 social studies, 2 history, 4 academic electives. **Freshman Admission Statistics:** 2,596 applied, 79.51% admitted, 33% enrolled. **Transfer Admission Requirements:** college transcript(s), essay or personal statement, statement of good standing from prior institution(s). Minimum college GPA of 2.5 required. Lowest grade transferable C. **General Admission Information:** Application fee $20. Regular notification 9/15. Nonfall registration accepted.

COSTS AND FINANCIAL AID

Required Forms and Deadlines: FAFSA. **Notification of Awards:** Applicants will be notified of awards on a rolling basis beginning 3/15. **Types of Aid:** *Need-based scholarships/grants:* Federal Pell, FSEOG, State scholarships/grants, Private scholarships, College/university scholarship or grant aid from institutional funds, Federal Nursing Scholarships. *Loans:* Direct Subsidized Stafford Loans, Direct Unsubsidized Stafford Loans, Direct PLUS loans, Federal Nursing Loans. *Student Employment:* Federal Work-Study Program available. Institutional employment available. **Financial Aid Statistics:** 99% needy freshmen, 99% needy undergrads receive need-based scholarship or grant aid. 14% freshmen, 12% undergrads receive non-need-based scholarship or grant aid. 79% freshmen, 79% undergrads receive need-based self-help aid. 0% freshmen, 0% undergrads receive athletic scholarships. 100% freshmen, 96% undergrads receive any aid. 70% undergrads borrow to pay for school. Average cumulative indebtedness $39,617. **Criteria for awarding aid:** *Need-based:* Academics. *Non-need-based:* Academics, Art, Leadership, Music/drama, Religious affiliation.

METHODIST UNIVERSITY

5400 Ramsey Street, Fayetteville, NC 28311
Phone: 910-630-7027 • **Financial Aid Phone:** 910-630-7192
E-mail: admissions@methodist.edu • **CEEB Code:** 5426
Fax: 910-630-7285 • **Website:** www.methodist.edu • **ACT Code:** 3127

This private school, affiliated with the Methodist Church, was founded in 1956. It has a 600-acre campus.

RATINGS
Admissions Selectivity Rating: 80 **Fire Safety Rating:** 79 **Green Rating:** 60*

STUDENTS AND FACULTY
Enrollment: 2,226. **Student Body:** 48% female, 52% male, 30% out-of-state, 5% international (53 countries represented). Asian 1%, African American 24%, Caucasian 48%, Hispanic 6%, Native American 1%, Pacific Islander <1%, Two or more races 5%, Race unknown 10%.
Retention and Graduation: 62% freshmen return for sophomore year. 16% freshmen graduate within 4 years. 44% freshmen graduate within 6 years. 38% grads go on to further study within 1 year. 8% grads pursue arts and sciences degrees. 1% grads pursue law degrees. 12% grads pursue business degrees. 7% grads pursue medical degrees. **Faculty:** Student/faculty ratio 13:1. 142 full-time faculty, 69% hold PhDs, 13% are are members of minority groups, 49% are women. 0% of classes are taught by teaching assistants.

ACADEMICS
Degrees: associate, bachelor's, master's, terminal. **Classes:** Most classes have fewer than 10 students. Most lab/discussion sessions have 20-29 students. **Most popular majors:** Secondary Education and Teaching; Cell/Cellular and Molecular Biology; Business/Commerce. **Special Study Options:** cooperative education program, distance learning, double major, dual enrollment, English as a Second Language (ESL), honors program, independent study, internships, liberal arts/career combination, student-designed major, study abroad, teacher certification program, weekend college, distance learning is on-line coursework available. **Honors Programs:** The Methodist College Honors Program is based on the "Great Books" and is an outstanding opportunity for high acheiving students. **Disability Services:** Special programs offered to physically disabled students, including note-taking services, reader services, tape recorders, tutors. **Career Services:** Career/job search classes, Career assessment, Internships.

FACILITIES
Housing: Coed dorms, men's dorms, women's dorms, apartments for single students, first year experience hall. 80% of campus accessible to physically diasbled. **Special Academic Facilities/Equipment:** Art gallery, Nature Trail, 18 hole golf course with practice facilities for PGM students, Academic Developement Center **Computers:** Administrative functions (other than registration) can be performed online.

CAMPUS LIFE
Environment: City. **Activities:** Choral groups, concert band, dance, drama/theater, jazz band, literary magazine, marching band, music ensembles, musical theater, opera, pep band, radio station, student government, student newspaper, symphony orchestra, yearbook, Campus Ministries, Model UN. 72 registered organizations, 15 honor societies, 8 religious organizations. 3 fraternities, 2 sororities. **Athletics (Intercollegiate):** *Men:* baseball, basketball, cheerleading, cross-country, football, golf, soccer, tennis, track/field (outdoor). *Women:* basketball, cheerleading, cross-country, golf, lacrosse, soccer, softball, tennis, track/field (outdoor), volleyball.

ADMISSIONS
Freshman Academic Profile: Average high school GPA 3.3. 9% in top 10% of high school class, 34% in top 25% of high school class, 73% in top 50% of high school class. 86% from public high schools. **Reported SAT (pre-2016 redesign) scores:** SAT Math middle 50% range 450-550. SAT Critical Reading middle 50% range 430-520. SAT Writing middle 50% range 400-490. **Concordant SAT scores:** SAT EBRW middle 50% 460–560. SAT Math middle 50% range 490–570. ACT middle 50% range 17-23. Minimum paper TOEFL 500. **Basis for Candidate Selection:** *Very important factors considered include:* rigor of secondary school record, academic GPA. *Important factors considered include:* class rank, standardized test scores, interview. *Other factors considered include:* application essay, recommendation(s), extracurricular activities, talent/ability, character/personal qualities, first generation, alumni/ae relation. **Freshman Admission Requirements:** High school diploma is required and GED is accepted. *Academic units required:* 4 English, 3 math, 3 science, 1 science lab, 1 social studies, 2 history, 4 academic electives. *Academic units recommended:* 4 English, 4 math, 4 science, 1 science lab, 2 foreign language, 2 social studies, 2 history. **Freshman Admission Statistics:** 3,823 applied, 60.55% admitted, 21% enrolled. **Transfer Admission Requirements:** High school transcript, college transcript(s), statement of good standing from prior institution(s). Minimum college GPA of 2.0 required. Lowest grade transferable C. **General Admission Information:** Application fee $25. Nonfall registration accepted. Admission may be deferred for a maximum of 1 academic year.

COSTS AND FINANCIAL AID
Annual tuition $25,160. Room and board $9,521. Required fees $465. Average book expense $1,200. **Required Forms and Deadlines:** FAFSA. **Notification of Awards:** Applicants will be notified of awards on a rolling basis beginning 3/1. **Types of Aid:** *Need-based scholarships/grants:* Federal Pell, FSEOG, State scholarships/grants, Private scholarships, College/university scholarship or grant aid from institutional funds. *Loans:* Federal Perkins Loans. *Student Employment:* Federal Work-Study Program available. **Financial Aid Statistics:** 96% needy freshmen, 90% needy undergrads receive need-based scholarship or grant aid. 71% freshmen, 79% undergrads receive non-need-based scholarship or grant aid. 92% freshmen, 87% undergrads receive need-based self-help aid. 0% freshmen, 0% undergrads receive athletic scholarships. 90% freshmen, 86% undergrads receive any aid. **Criteria for awarding aid:** *Need-based:* Academics, Alumni affiliation, Leadership, Music/drama, Religious affiliation. *Non-need-based:* Academics, Alumni affiliation, Leadership, Music/drama, Religious affiliation, State/district residency.

METROPOLITAN STATE UNIVERSITY

Website: Http://www.metrostate.edu

This public school was founded in 1971.

RATINGS
Admissions Selectivity Rating: 60* **Fire Safety Rating:** 60* **Green Rating:** 60*

ACADEMICS
Degrees: bachelor's, certificate, master's.

CAMPUS LIFE
Environment: City. **Activities:** student government, student newspaper.

ADMISSIONS
Freshman Admission Requirements: High school diploma is required and GED is accepted. **Transfer Admission Requirements:** High school transcript, college transcript(s), essay or personal statement, standardized test scores, Lowest grade transferable C. **General Admission Information:** Application fee $20.

COSTS AND FINANCIAL AID
Annual in-state tuition $2,918. Annual out-of-state tuition $5,670. *Student Employment:* Federal Work-Study Program available. Institutional employment available.

MIAMI UNIVERSITY

301 S. Campus Ave., Oxford, OH 45056
Phone: 513-529-2531 • **Financial Aid Phone:** 513-529-0001
E-mail: admission@miamioh.edu • **CEEB Code:** 1463
Fax: 513-529-1550 • **Website:** http://www.miamioh.edu/ • **ACT Code:** 3294

This public school was founded in 1809. It has a 2000-acre campus.

RATINGS
Admissions Selectivity Rating: 88 **Fire Safety Rating:** 94 **Green Rating:** 80

STUDENTS AND FACULTY
Enrollment: 16,597. **Student Body:** 51% female, 49% male, 36% out-of-state, 12% international (84 countries represented). Asian 2%, African American 3%, Caucasian 75%, Hispanic 4%, Native American <1%, Pacific Islander <1%, Two or more races 3%, Race unknown <1%.
Retention and Graduation: 92% freshmen return for sophomore year. 66% freshmen graduate within 4 years. 78% freshmen graduate within 6 years. **Faculty:** Student/faculty ratio 17:1. 979 full-time faculty, 85% hold PhDs, 20% are are members of minority groups, 45% are women. 5% of classes are taught by teaching assistants.

ACADEMICS

Degrees: associate, bachelor's, certificate, doctoral/research, doctoral, master's, post-master's certificate, terminal, transfer. **Classes:** Most classes have 20-29 students. Most lab/discussion sessions have 10-19 students. **Most popular majors:** Marketing/Marketing Management; Finance; Biology/Biological Sciences. **Special Study Options:** cooperative education program, cross-registration, distance learning, double major, exchange student program (domestic), honors program, independent study, internships, liberal arts/career combination, student-designed major, study abroad, teacher certification program. **Honors Programs:** Miami has a University Honors Program. Students selected to participate receive a renewable scholarship, priority registration, and other special opportunities. Combined degree programs: BA/MA, 3-1 Arts/Prof. Degree, 3-2 engineering. **Disability Services:** Special programs offered to physically disabled students, including note-taking services, reader services, tape recorders, tutors. **Career Services:** Alumni network, Alumni services, Career/job search classes, Career assessment, Internships, Regional alumni.

FACILITIES

Housing: Coed dorms, special housing for disabled students, men's dorms, special housing for international students, women's dorms, fraternity/sorority housing, apartments for married students, cooperative housing, apartments for single students, Wellness Housing, Theme Housing. 100% of campus accessible to physically disabled. **Special Academic Facilities/Equipment:** Geology, art, anthropology, and zoology museums, performing arts center, herbarium, ecology research center, 400-acre nature preserve, electron microscope center. **Computers:** 100% of classrooms, 100% of dorms, 100% of libraries, 100% of dining areas, 100% of student union, 65% of common outdoor areas have wireless network access. Students can register for classes online. Administrative functions (other than registration) can be performed online.

CAMPUS LIFE

Environment: Village. **Activities:** Choral groups, concert band, dance, drama/theater, jazz band, literary magazine, marching band, music ensembles, musical theater, opera, pep band, radio station, student government, student newspaper, student-run film society, symphony orchestra, television station, yearbook, Campus Ministries, Student Organization, Model UN. 304 registered organizations, 38 honor societies, 22 religious organizations. 32 fraternities, 23 sororities. **Athletics (Intercollegiate):** *Men:* baseball, basketball, cross-country, diving, football, golf, ice hockey, swimming, track/field (outdoor). *Women:* basketball, cross-country, diving, field hockey, soccer, softball, swimming, tennis, track/field (outdoor), volleyball. **On-Campus Highlights:** Farmer School of Business, McGuffey Museum, Center for the Performing Arts, Recreational Sports Center, Peabody Hall (National Historical Landmark), Formal Gardens.

ADMISSIONS

Freshman Academic Profile: Average high school GPA 3.8. 39% in top 10% of high school class, 71% in top 25% of high school class, 95% in top 50% of high school class. 69% from public high schools. **Reported SAT (pre-2016 redesign) scores:** SAT Math middle 50% range 590-690. SAT Critical Reading middle 50% range 540-660. SAT Writing middle 50% range 540-650. **Concordant SAT scores:** SAT EBRW middle 50% 600–700. SAT Math middle 50% range 610–720. ACT middle 50% range 26-31. Minimum internet-based TOEFL 80. Minimum paper TOEFL 550. **Basis for Candidate Selection:** *Very important factors considered include:* rigor of secondary school record, class rank, academic GPA, standardized test scores, application essay, recommendation(s), talent/ability, character/personal qualities. *Other factors considered include:* extracurricular activities, first generation, alumni/ae relation, geographical residence, state residency, volunteer work, work experience. **Freshman Admission Requirements:** High school diploma is required and GED is accepted. *Academic units recommended:* 4 English, 4 math, 3 science, 2 foreign language, 2 social studies, 1 history, 1 visual/performing arts. **Freshman Admission Statistics:** 29,771 applied, 65.38% admitted, 20% enrolled. **Transfer Admission Requirements:** High school transcript, college transcript(s), essay or personal statement, statement of good standing from prior institution(s). Minimum college GPA of 2.0 required. Lowest grade transferable C. **General Admission Information:** Application fee $50. Regular application deadline 2/1. Regular notification 3/15. Nonfall registration accepted. Admission may be deferred for a maximum of 1 year.

COSTS AND FINANCIAL AID

Annual in-state tuition $13,534. Annual out-of-state tuition $30,838. Room and board $12,014. Required fees $754. Average book expense $1,216. **Required Forms and Deadlines:** FAFSA. **Notification of Awards:** Applicants will be notified of awards on a rolling basis beginning 3/20. **Types of Aid:** *Need-based scholarships/grants:* Federal Pell, FSEOG, State scholarships/grants, Private scholarships, College/university scholarship or grant aid from institutional funds. *Loans:* Direct Subsidized Stafford Loans, Direct Unsubsidized Stafford Loans, Direct PLUS loans, Federal Perkins Loans, College/university loans from institutional funds. *Student Employment:* Federal Work-Study Program available. Institutional employment available. **Financial Aid Statistics:** 88% needy freshmen, 85% needy undergrads receive need-based scholarship or grant aid. 21% freshmen, 14% undergrads receive non-need-based scholarship or grant aid. 63% freshmen, 72% undergrads receive need-based self-help aid. 2% freshmen, 2% undergrads receive athletic scholarships. 53% undergrads borrow to pay for school. Average cumulative indebtedness $30,015. **Criteria for awarding aid:** *Need-based:* Academics, Art, Athletics, Leadership, Minority status, Music/drama. *Non-need-based:* Academics, Art, Athletics, Leadership, Minority status, Music/drama, State/district residency.

MICHIGAN STATE UNIVERSITY

250 Administration Building, East Lansing, MI 48824-1046
Phone: 517-355-8332 • **Financial Aid Phone:** 517-353-5940
E-mail: admis@msu.edu • **CEEB Code:** 1465
Fax: 517-353-1647 • **Website:** www.msu.edu • **ACT Code:** 2032

This public school was founded in 1855. It has a 5200-acre campus.

RATINGS

Admissions Selectivity Rating: 86   **Fire Safety Rating:** 60*   **Green Rating:** 95

STUDENTS AND FACULTY

Enrollment: 38,851. **Student Body:** 51% female, 49% male, 14% out-of-state, 12% international (102 countries represented). Asian 5%, African American 7%, Caucasian 67%, Hispanic 4%, Native American <1%, Pacific Islander <1%, Two or more races 3%, Race unknown 1%.
Retention and Graduation: 92% freshmen return for sophomore year. 52% freshmen graduate within 4 years. 79% freshmen graduate within 6 years. 28% grads go on to further study within 1 year. 6% grads pursue law degrees. 33% grads pursue business degrees. 5% grads pursue medical degrees. **Faculty:** Student/faculty ratio 17:1. 2,512 full-time faculty, 90% hold PhDs, 22% are are members of minority groups, 40% are women.

ACADEMICS

Degrees: bachelor's, certificate, doctoral/professional, doctoral/research, master's, post-master's certificate. **Classes:** Most classes have 20-29 students. Most lab/discussion sessions have 20-29 students. **Special Study Options:** Accelerated program, cooperative education program, distance learning, double major, dual enrollment, English as a Second Language (ESL), exchange student program (domestic), honors program, independent study, internships, liberal arts/career combination, student-designed major, study abroad, teacher certification program, weekend college. **Honors Programs:** MSU's Honors College embodies MSU's long-standing commitment to provide programs of study that attract and challenge unusually talented undergraduates utilizing carefully planned, highly individualized programs of study that will meet the needs of academically talented students. Combined degree programs: BA/MA, Computer Science. **Disability Services:** Special programs offered to physically disabled students, including note-taking services, reader services, tape recorders, tutors. **Career Services:** Alumni network, Alumni services, Career/job search classes, Career assessment, Internships, Regional alumni.

FACILITIES

Housing: Coed dorms, special housing for disabled students, special housing for international students, women's dorms, fraternity/sorority housing, apartments for married students, cooperative housing, apartments for single students, Theme Housing. **Special Academic Facilities/Equipment:** Art, natural history, Michigan history and anthropology museums, art center, on-campus preschool and elementary school, biological station, experimental farms, botanical garden, planetarium, two superconducting cyclotrons, observatory. **Computers:** Students can register for classes online. Administrative functions (other than registration) can be performed online. Undergraduates are required to own a computer.

CAMPUS LIFE

Environment: Town. **Activities:** Choral groups, concert band, dance, drama/theater, jazz band, literary magazine, marching band, music ensembles, musical theater, opera, pep band, radio station, student government, student newspaper, student-run film society, symphony orchestra, television station, yearbook, Campus Ministries, Student Organization, Model UN. 500 registered organizations, 47 honor societies, 50 religious organizations. 31 fraternities, 19 sororities. **Athletics (Intercollegiate):** *Men:* baseball, basketball, cheerleading, cross-country, diving, football, golf, ice hockey, soccer, swimming, tennis, track/field (outdoor), track/field (indoor), wrestling. *Women:* basketball, cheerleading, crew/rowing, cross-country, diving, field hockey, golf, gymnastics, soccer, softball, swimming, tennis, track/field (outdoor), track/field (indoor), volleyball. **On-Campus Highlights:** MSU Student Union, Jack Breslin Student Events Center, MSU Main Library and Cyber Caf, The International Center, Wharton Center for the Performing Arts. **Environmental Initiatives:** Chicago Climate Exchange.

ADMISSIONS

Freshman Academic Profile: Average high school GPA 3.7. 30% in top 10% of high school class, 68% in top 25% of high school class, 95% in top 50% of high school class. **Reported SAT (pre-2016 redesign) scores:** SAT Math middle 50% range 540-670. SAT Critical Reading middle 50% range 450-590. SAT Writing middle 50% range 460-580. **Concordant SAT scores:** SAT EBRW middle 50% 510–640. SAT Math middle 50% range 570–700. ACT middle 50% range 24-29. Minimum internet-based TOEFL 79. Minimum paper TOEFL 550. **Basis for Candidate Selection:** *Very important factors considered include:* academic GPA, standardized test scores. *Important factors considered include:* rigor of secondary school record, application essay, extracurricular activities, first generation. *Other factors considered include:* class rank, recommendation(s), interview, talent/ability, character/personal qualities, geographical residence, state residency, volunteer work, work experience, level of applicant's interest. **Freshman Admission Requirements:** High school diploma is required and GED is accepted. *Academic units required:* 4 English, 3 math, 3 science, 1 science lab, 2 foreign language, 3 social studies. *Academic units recommended:* 4 math, 3 science, 1 science lab, 2 foreign language, 3 social studies. **Freshman Admission Statistics:** 37,480 applied, 65.74% admitted, 33% enrolled. **Transfer Admission Requirements:** college transcript(s), essay or personal statement, statement of good standing from prior institution(s). Minimum college GPA of 2.0 required. Lowest grade transferable C. **General Admission Information:** Application fee $50. Nonfall registration accepted.

COSTS AND FINANCIAL AID

Annual in-state tuition $15,698. Annual out-of-state tuition $39,083. Room and board $9,734. Average book expense $1,076. **Required Forms and Deadlines:** FAFSA. **Notification of Awards:** Applicants will be notified of awards on a rolling basis beginning 3/15. **Types of Aid:** *Need-based scholarships/grants:* Federal Pell, FSEOG, State scholarships/grants, Private scholarships, College/university scholarship or grant aid from institutional funds, United Negro College Fund. *Loans:* Direct Subsidized Stafford Loans, Direct Unsubsidized Stafford Loans, Direct PLUS loans, Federal Perkins Loans, College/university loans from institutional funds. *Student Employment:* Federal Work-Study Program available. Institutional employment available. **Financial Aid Statistics:** 71% needy freshmen, 74% needy undergrads receive need-based scholarship or grant aid. 43% freshmen, 29% undergrads receive non-need-based scholarship or grant aid. 79% freshmen, 82% undergrads receive need-based self-help aid. 1% freshmen, 1% undergrads receive athletic scholarships. 48% freshmen, 46% undergrads receive any aid. **Criteria for awarding aid:** *Need-based:* Academics. *Non-need-based:* Academics, Alumni affiliation, Art, Athletics, Leadership, Music/drama, State/district residency.

MICHIGAN TECHNOLOGICAL UNIVERSITY

1400 Townsend Drive, Houghton, MI 49931
Phone: 906-487-2335 • **Financial Aid Phone:** 906-487-2622
E-mail: mtu4u@mtu.edu • **CEEB Code:** 1464
Fax: 906-487-2125 • **Website:** www.mtu.edu • **ACT Code:** 2030

This public school was founded in 1885. It has a 925-acre campus.

RATINGS

Admissions Selectivity Rating: 85   **Fire Safety Rating:** 92   **Green Rating:** 74

STUDENTS AND FACULTY

Enrollment: 5,753. **Student Body:** 27% female, 73% male, 23% out-of-state, 3% international (38 countries represented). Asian 1%, African American 1%, Caucasian 87%, Hispanic 2%, Native American <1%, Pacific Islander <1%, Two or more races 3%, Race unknown 2%.
Retention and Graduation: 83% freshmen return for sophomore year. 28% freshmen graduate within 4 years. 67% freshmen graduate within 6 years. 10% grads go on to further study within 1 year. 34% grads pursue arts and sciences degrees. 1% grads pursue law degrees. 5% grads pursue business degrees. 14% grads pursue medical degrees. **Faculty:** Student/faculty ratio 12:1. 408 full-time faculty, 88% hold PhDs, 20% are are members of minority groups, 29% are women. 11% of classes are taught by teaching assistants.

ACADEMICS

Degrees: associate, bachelor's, certificate, doctoral/research, master's, postbachelor's certificate, terminal. **Classes:** Most classes have fewer than 10 students. Most lab/discussion sessions have 10-19 students. **Most popular**

majors: Mechanical Engineering; Chemical Engineering; Civil Engineering. **Special Study Options:** cooperative education program, distance learning, double major, dual enrollment, English as a Second Language (ESL), exchange student program (domestic), honors program, independent study, internships, study abroad, teacher certification program, Dual degrees with Northwestern MI College, Adrian College, Albion College, Augsburg College (MN), College of St. Scholastica (MN), Mount Senario College, Olivet College, Northland College, University of Wisconsin-Superior, St. Norbert College (WI), Northcentral Technical College (WI), College of Lake County (IL), and Macomb Community College (MI). **Honors Programs:** Qualifying students are invited to apply to Michigan Tech's Honors Institute. Membership focuses on activities and enrichment for top scholars, rather than separate honors courses. More details are at http://honors.mtu.edu/. **Disability Services:** Special programs offered to physically disabled students, including note-taking services, reader services, tape recorders, tutors. **Career Services:** Alumni network, Alumni services, Career/job search classes, Career assessment, Internships, Regional alumni. The programs we are proudest of center around preparing students for their career and successful associated job search. We have labeled this 'Career Fest'. We offer students a personal interest inventory through MyPLAN assessment, helping them discover where their interests lie. From this we have developed a series of 'Industry Days' such as 'Steel Days', 'Petroleum Days', 'Medical Careers Week', 'Railroad Day', with many more to come such as 'Automotive Days', 'Mining Day', 'Aerospace Day', and more. During these days corporations from these industries come on campus to discuss careers in their industry, provide information about their companies' role in the industry, and project what lies in the future for these industrial sectors. This allows students a time to explore where they fit to begin charting their own career path. To support the students choice we offer resume blitz's, mock interviews, and innovative programs that allow students coming off of co-ops/internships to tell the story of their experiential learning experience to fellow students through one-on-one events and short 2 minute videos, the goal being to encourage others to participate in these industry-valued experiences.

FACILITIES

Housing: Coed dorms, special housing for disabled students, special housing for international students, fraternity/sorority housing, apartments for married students, apartments for single students, Wellness Housing, Theme Housing, Alcohol Free, Research Scholar, Honors Housing, ROTC. Learning Communities: Computer Science, First-year Experience, Health Summit, Forest Resources & Environmental Science, International House, Visual & Performing Arts, Leadership. 80% of campus accessible to physically diasbled. **Special Academic Facilities/Equipment:** Mineralogical Museum, 4,700 Acre Research Forest, Scanning Electron Microscope, PUMA Robots, X-ray Fluorescence Spectrometer, Process Simulation and Control Center, Rozsa Center for the Performing Arts, Cleanrooms, MEMS Fabrication Facility, Environmental Scanning Electron Microscope, Transmission Electron Microscope, Radio-frequency Plasma-Assisted Deposition Chamber, Electron Lithography Equipment. **Computers:** 93% of classrooms, 10% of dorms, 100% of libraries, 100% of dining areas, 100% of student union, 10% of common outdoor areas have wireless network access. Students can register for classes online. Administrative functions (other than registration) can be performed online.

CAMPUS LIFE

Environment: Village. **Activities:** Choral groups, concert band, dance, drama/theater, jazz band, literary magazine, music ensembles, musical theater, opera, pep band, radio station, student government, student newspaper, student-run film society, symphony orchestra, Campus Ministries, Student Organization. 210 registered organizations, 16 honor societies, 16 religious organizations. 13 fraternities, 8 sororities. **Athletics (Intercollegiate):** *Men:* basketball, cross-country, football, ice hockey, skiing (nordic/cross-country), tennis, track/field (outdoor). *Women:* basketball, cross-country, skiing (nordic/cross-country), tennis, track/field (outdoor), volleyball. **On-Campus Highlights:** Student Development Complex, Rozsa Center for the Performing Arts, Mont Ripley Ski Hill, Portage Lake Golf Course, Memorial Union Building. **Environmental Initiatives:** Emphasis on multidisciplinary sustainability research (http://www.sfi.mtu.edu/research.php/), education (http://www.sfi.mtu.edu/education.php), and outreach, such as Sustainable Futures Institute, Center for Water and Society, Environmentally Responsible Design and Manufacturing Research Group, National Institute for Climatic Change Research (Midwestern Region), Advanced Power Systems Research Center, Materials in Sustainable Transportation Infrastructure, Power and Energy Research Center, Sustainable Engineering Initiative, IGERT for Sustainable Futures, Graduate Certificate in Sustainability, D80 Center, Peace Corps Masters International Program, Sustainable Development Engineering Certificate, Senior Design Programs, Sustainability Research Experience for Undergraduates, Wood-to-Wheels Graduate Enterprise, sustainability-based undergraduate Enterprise Programs (Challenge X, Clean Snowmobile, Alternative Fuels Group, Aqua Terra Tech, Efficiency Through Engineering and Construction), Undergraduate and Graduate Colloquium in Sustainability, Sustainable Futures 1 and 2 courses.

ADMISSIONS

Freshman Academic Profile: Average high school GPA 3.7. 29% in top 10% of high school class, 62% in top 25% of high school class, 90% in top 50% of high school class. **Reported SAT (pre-2016 redesign) scores:** SAT Math middle 50% range 570–678. SAT Critical Reading middle 50% range 503–645. SAT Writing middle 50% range 470–610. **Concordant SAT scores:** SAT EBRW middle 50% 540–680. SAT Math middle 50% range 590–710. ACT middle 50% range 25-30. Minimum internet-based TOEFL 79. Minimum paper TOEFL 550. **Basis for Candidate Selection:** *Very important factors considered include:* academic GPA, standardized test scores. *Important factors considered include:* rigor of secondary school record. *Other factors considered include:* class rank, application essay, recommendation(s), extracurricular activities, talent/ability, character/personal qualities, volunteer work. **Freshman Admission Requirements:** High school diploma is required and GED is accepted. *Academic units required:* 3 English, 3 math, 2 science. *Academic units recommended:* 4 English, 4 math, 3 science, 2 foreign language, 3 social studies, 2 academic electives, 1 computer science. **Freshman Admission Statistics:** 5,589 applied, 76.44% admitted, 32% enrolled. **Transfer Admission Requirements:** college transcript(s), statement of good standing from prior institution(s). Minimum college GPA of 2.75 required. Lowest grade transferable C. **General Admission Information:** Priority deadline 1/15. Nonfall registration accepted. Admission may be deferred for a maximum of 1 year.

COSTS AND FINANCIAL AID

Required Forms and Deadlines: FAFSA. **Notification of Awards:** Applicants will be notified of awards on a rolling basis beginning 3/15. **Types of Aid:** *Need-based scholarships/grants:* Federal Pell, FSEOG, State scholarships/grants, Private scholarships, College/university scholarship or grant aid from institutional funds. *Loans:* Direct Subsidized Stafford Loans, Direct Unsubsidized Stafford Loans, Direct PLUS loans, Federal Perkins Loans, College/university loans from institutional funds. *Student Employment:* Federal Work-Study Program available. Institutional employment available. **Financial Aid Statistics:** 85% needy freshmen, 79% needy undergrads receive need-based scholarship or grant aid. 82% freshmen, 74% undergrads receive non-need-based scholarship or grant aid. 77% freshmen, 85% undergrads receive need-based self-help aid. 5% freshmen, 5% undergrads receive athletic scholarships. 97% freshmen, 91% undergrads receive any aid. 68% undergrads borrow to pay for school. Average cumulative indebtedness $34,942. **Criteria for awarding aid:** *Need-based:* Academics. *Non-need-based:* Academics, Alumni affiliation, Athletics, Job skills, Leadership, State/district residency.

See page 998.

MIDAMERICA NAZARENE UNIVERSITY

2030 College Way, Olathe, KS 66062
Phone: 913-791-3380 • **Financial Aid Phone:** 913-971-3298
E-mail: admissions@mnu.edu • **CEEB Code:** 6437
Fax: 913-791-3481 • **Website:** www.mnu.edu • **ACT Code:** 1445

This private school, affiliated with the Nazarene Church, was founded in 1966. It has a 105-acre campus.

RATINGS

Admissions Selectivity Rating: 70   **Fire Safety Rating:** 80   **Green Rating:** 60*

STUDENTS AND FACULTY

Student Body: 58% female, 42% male, 41% out-of-state, (12 countries represented).
Retention and Graduation: 74% freshmen return for sophomore year. 42% freshmen graduate within 4 years. 54% freshmen graduate within 6 years.
Faculty: Student/faculty ratio 13:1. 81 full-time faculty, 64% hold PhDs, 0% are are members of minority groups, 48% are women. 0% of classes are taught by teaching assistants.

ACADEMICS

Degrees: associate, bachelor's, master's, postbachelor's certificate, post-master's certificate, terminal. **Classes:** Most classes have 10-19 students. Most lab/discussion sessions have 10-19 students. **Most popular majors:** Elementary Education and Teaching; Business/Commerce. **Special Study Options:** Accelerated program, cross-registration, distance learning, double major, dual enrollment, independent study, internships, student-designed major, study abroad, teacher certification program, weekend college. **Disability Services:** Special programs offered to physically disabled students, including note-taking services, reader services, tape recorders, tutors. **Career Services:** On-campus interviews.

FACILITIES

Housing: special housing for disabled students, men's dorms, women's dorms, apartments for single students. 90% of campus accessible to physically disabled. **Computers:** Students can register for classes online. Administrative functions (other than registration) can be performed online.

CAMPUS LIFE

Environment: City. **Activities:** Choral groups, concert band, drama/theater, jazz band, literary magazine, music ensembles, musical theater, pep band, radio station, student government, student newspaper, television station, yearbook, Campus Ministries, Student Organization. 43 registered organizations, 6 honor societies, 4 religious organizations. **Athletics (Intercollegiate):** *Men:* baseball, basketball, cheerleading, cross-country, football, soccer, track/field (outdoor), track/field (indoor). *Women:* basketball, cheerleading, cross-country, soccer, softball, track/field (outdoor), track/field (indoor), volleyball. **On-Campus Highlights:** Cook Center, Land Memorial Gym, Fitness Center, Campus Center, Bell Cultural Events Center.

ADMISSIONS

Freshman Academic Profile: Average high school GPA 3.4. 88% from public high schools. Minimum paper TOEFL 550. **Basis for Candidate Selection:** *Very important factors considered include:* standardized test scores. *Important factors considered include:* class rank, academic GPA, character/personal qualities, religious affiliation/commitment. *Other factors considered include:* rigor of secondary school record, recommendation(s), extracurricular activities, talent/ability, alumni/ae relation, volunteer work, level of applicant's interest. **Freshman Admission Requirements:** High school diploma is required and GED is accepted. *Academic units recommended:* 4 English, 3 math, 3 science, 1 foreign language, 3 social studies. **Freshman Admission Statistics:** 899 applied, 61.29% admitted. **Transfer Admission Requirements:** college transcript(s), Minimum college GPA of 2.0 required. Lowest grade transferable D. **General Admission Information:** Application fee $25. Priority deadline 3/1. Regular application deadline 8/1. Nonfall registration accepted. Admission may be deferred.

COSTS AND FINANCIAL AID

Annual tuition $27,650. Room and board $7,900. Average book expense $1,490. **Required Forms and Deadlines:** FAFSA. **Notification of Awards:** Applicants will be notified of awards on a rolling basis beginning 2/1. **Types of Aid:** *Need-based scholarships/grants:* Federal Pell, FSEOG, State scholarships/grants, Private scholarships, College/university scholarship or grant aid from institutional funds. *Loans:* Federal Perkins Loans. *Student Employment:* Federal Work-Study Program available. Institutional employment available. **Financial Aid Statistics:** 77% needy freshmen, 94% needy undergrads receive need-based scholarship or grant aid. 53% freshmen, 41% undergrads receive non-need-based scholarship or grant aid. 75% freshmen, 79% undergrads receive need-based self-help aid. 46% freshmen, 36% undergrads receive athletic scholarships. 98% undergrads receive any aid. **Criteria for awarding aid:** *Need-based:* Athletics, Job skills, Leadership, Minority status, Music/drama, Religious affiliation. *Non-need-based:* Academics, Athletics, Leadership, Minority status, Music/drama, Religious affiliation, State/district residency.

MIDDLE TENNESSEE STATE UNIVERSITY

1301 East Main Street, Murfreesboro, TN 37132
Phone: 615-898-2111
E-mail: admissions@mtsu.edu
Fax: 615-898-5478 • **Website:** www.mtsu.edu

This is a public school.

RATINGS

Admissions Selectivity Rating: 76   **Fire Safety Rating:** 60*   **Green Rating:** 60*

STUDENTS AND FACULTY

Enrollment: 18,998. **Student Body:** 54% female, 46% male, 8% out-of-state, 3% international. Asian 3%, African American 21%, Caucasian 64%, Hispanic 5%, Native American <1%, Pacific Islander <1%, Two or more races 3%, Race unknown <1%.
Retention and Graduation: 76% freshmen return for sophomore year.
Faculty: Student/faculty ratio 18:1.

ACADEMICS

Degrees: bachelor's, certificate, doctoral/research, master's, postbachelor's certificate, post-master's certificate. **Classes:** Most classes have 20-29 students. Most lab/discussion sessions have fewer than 10 students. **Special Study Options:** distance learning, double major, dual enrollment, honors program, independent study, internships, study abroad, teacher certification program.

FACILITIES

Housing: Coed dorms, special housing for disabled students, men's dorms, special housing for international students, women's dorms, fraternity/sorority housing, apartments for married students, cooperative housing, apartments for single students, Wellness Housing, Theme Housing.

CAMPUS LIFE

Activities: Choral groups, concert band, dance, drama/theater, jazz band, literary magazine, marching band, music ensembles, musical theater, opera, pep band, radio station, student government, student newspaper, symphony orchestra, television station, Campus Ministries, Student Organization, Model UN.

ADMISSIONS

Freshman Academic Profile: Average high school GPA 3.4. **Reported SAT (pre-2016 redesign) scores:** SAT Math middle 50% range 455-565. SAT Critical Reading middle 50% range 490-590. **Concordant SAT scores:** SAT Math middle 50% range 500–590. ACT middle 50% range 19-25. Minimum paper TOEFL 500. **Basis for Candidate Selection:** *Very important factors considered include:* academic GPA, standardized test scores. *Other factors considered include:* rigor of secondary school record, application essay, recommendation(s), extracurricular activities, talent/ability, character/personal qualities, volunteer work, work experience, level of applicant's interest. **Freshman Admission Requirements:** High school diploma is required and GED is accepted. *Academic units required:* 4 English, 4 math, 3 science, 1 science lab, 2 foreign language, 1 social studies, 1 history, 1 visual/performing arts. **Freshman Admission Statistics:** 8,194 applied, 68.92% admitted, 50% enrolled. **Transfer Admission Requirements:** college transcript(s), Minimum college GPA of 2.0 required. Lowest grade transferable D. **General Admission Information:** Application fee $25. Nonfall registration accepted.

COSTS AND FINANCIAL AID

Required Forms and Deadlines: FAFSA. **Notification of Awards:** Applicants will be notified of awards on a rolling basis beginning 4/1. **Types of Aid:** *Need-based scholarships/grants:* Federal Pell, FSEOG, State scholarships/grants, College/university scholarship or grant aid from institutional funds. *Loans:* Direct Subsidized Stafford Loans, Direct Unsubsidized Stafford Loans, Direct PLUS loans, Federal Perkins Loans. *Student Employment:* Federal Work-Study Program available. Institutional employment available. **Financial Aid Statistics:** 67% needy undergrads receive need-based scholarship or grant aid. 87% freshmen, 59% undergrads receive non-need-based scholarship or grant aid. 59% freshmen, 66% undergrads receive need-based self-help aid. 2% freshmen, 2% undergrads receive athletic scholarships. 64% undergrads borrow to pay for school. Average cumulative indebtedness $25,452. **Criteria for awarding aid:** *Need-based:* Academics, Athletics. *Non-need-based:* Academics, Leadership, Minority status, Music/drama.

MIDDLEBURY COLLEGE

The Emma Willard House, Middlebury, VT 05753-6002
Phone: 802-443-3000 • **Financial Aid Phone:** 802-443-5158
E-mail: admissions@middlebury.edu • **CEEB Code:** 3526
Fax: 802-443-2056 • **Website:** www.middlebury.edu • **ACT Code:** 4306

This private school was founded in 1800. It has a 350-acre campus.

RATINGS

Admissions Selectivity Rating: 97   **Fire Safety Rating:** 95   **Green Rating:** 99

STUDENTS AND FACULTY

Enrollment: 2,513. **Student Body:** 52% female, 48% male, 93% out-of-state, 9% international (74 countries represented). Asian 7%, African American 3%, Caucasian 64%, Hispanic 9%, Native American <1%, Pacific Islander 0%, Two or more races 5%, Race unknown 1%.
Retention and Graduation: 94% freshmen return for sophomore year. 85% freshmen graduate within 4 years. 93% freshmen graduate within 6 years. 12% grads go on to further study within 1 year. **Faculty:** Student/faculty ratio 8:1. 283 full-time faculty, 96% hold PhDs, 19% are are members of minority groups, 46% are women. 0% of classes are taught by teaching assistants.

ACADEMICS

Degrees: bachelor's, doctoral/research, master's. **Classes:** Most classes have 10-19 students. **Most popular majors:** Economics; Environmental Studies; Political Science and Government. **Special Study Options:** Accelerated program, double major, exchange student program (domestic), honors program, independent study, internships, student-designed major, study abroad, teacher certification program, Williams College-Mystic Seaport Program in American Maritime Studies, Oxford University summer Program,independent scholar programs with Berea College and Swarthmore College, 3-year international major. Combined degree programs: http://www.middlebury.edu/about/handbook/academics/. **Disability Services:** Special programs offered to physically disabled students, including note-taking services, reader services, tape recorders, tutors. **Career Services:** Alumni network, Alumni services, Career/job search classes, Career assessment, Internships, Regional alumni.

FACILITIES

Housing: Coed dorms, special housing for disabled students, apartments for single students, Multi-cultural house, environmental house, foreign language house, 5 co-ed social houses. Commons System organizes residence halls into 5 groups,each with its own budget, government, faculty, and staff associates. 65% of campus accessible to physically diasbled. **Special Academic Facilities/Equipment:** Art museum, theatres, language lab, observatory, electron microscope, mountain campus, downhill and cross-country ski areas, golf course, Franklin Environmental Center, organic garden. **Computers:** Students can register for classes online. Administrative functions (other than registration) can be performed online.

CAMPUS LIFE

Environment: Village. **Activities:** Choral groups, dance, drama/theater, jazz band, literary magazine, music ensembles, musical theater, radio station, student government, student newspaper, student-run film society, symphony orchestra, yearbook. 100 registered organizations. **Athletics (Intercollegiate):** *Men:* baseball, basketball, cross-country, diving, football, golf, ice hockey, lacrosse, skiing (downhill/alpine), skiing (nordic/cross-country), soccer, swimming, tennis, track/field (outdoor), track/field (indoor). *Women:* basketball, cross-country, diving, field hockey, golf, ice hockey, lacrosse, skiing (downhill/alpine), skiing (nordic/cross-country), soccer, softball, squash, swimming, tennis, track/field (outdoor), track/field (indoor), volleyball. **On-Campus Highlights:** Science—Bicentennial Hall, The Center for the Arts, Athletic Facilities, The Commons System, Middlebury College Snow Bowl (Ski Area). **Environmental Initiatives:** Student initiated effort that led to Trustees resolution in 2007 charging the entire college community to work together to achieve carbon neutrality by 2016. A similar effort modeled on this one is also in progress with regard to divesting the college endowment from fossil fuel related companies. Thus far, it has led to new proxy voting policies in support of open and transparent governance and environmental and social responsibility, a student member of the Advisory Committee on Socially Responsible Investing has been appointed to the Investment Committee of the Board, and the question of divesting from fossil fuels is currently being given full and open consideration by the Trustees with significant community involvement in the discussion.

ADMISSIONS

Reported SAT (pre-2016 redesign) scores: SAT Math middle 50% range 650-755. SAT Critical Reading middle 50% range 630-740. SAT Writing middle 50% range 645-750. **Concordant SAT scores:** SAT EBRW middle 50% 690–760. SAT Math middle 50% range 670–780. ACT middle 50% range 30-33. **Basis for Candidate Selection:** *Very important factors considered include:* rigor of secondary school record, class rank, academic GPA, extracurricular activities, talent/ability, character/personal qualities. *Important factors considered include:* standardized test scores, application essay, recommendation(s), racial/ethnic status. *Other factors considered include:* interview, first generation, alumni/ae relation, geographical residence, volunteer work, work experience, level of applicant's interest. **Freshman Admission Requirements:** High school diploma or equivalent is not required. *Academic units recommended:* 4 English, 4 math, 3 science, 3 science labs, 4 foreign language, 3 social studies. **Freshman Admission Statistics:** 8,819 applied, 16.14% admitted, 43% enrolled. **Transfer Admission Requirements:** High school transcript, college transcript(s), essay or personal statement, statement of good standing from prior institution(s). Minimum college GPA of 3.0 required. Lowest grade transferable C-. **General Admission Information:** Application fee $65. Regular application deadline 1/1. Nonfall registration accepted. Admission may be deferred.

COSTS AND FINANCIAL AID

Annual tuition $49,648. Room and board $14,269. Required fees $415. Average book expense $1,000. **Required Forms and Deadlines:** FAFSA, Institution's own financial aid form, CSS/Financial Aid PROFILE, Noncustodial PROFILE. **Notification of Awards:** Applicants will be notified of awards on or about 4/1. **Types of Aid:** *Need-based scholarships/grants:* Federal Pell, FSEOG, State scholarships/grants, Private scholarships, College/university scholarship or grant aid from institutional funds. *Loans:* Direct Subsidized Stafford Loans, Direct Unsubsidized Stafford Loans, Direct PLUS loans, College/university loans from institutional funds. *Student Employment:* Federal Work-Study Program available. Institutional employment available. **Financial Aid Statistics:** 100% needy freshmen, 98% needy undergrads receive need-based scholarship or grant aid. 0% undergrads receive non-need-based scholarship or grant aid. 90%

freshmen, 94% undergrads receive need-based self-help aid. 0% freshmen, 0% undergrads receive athletic scholarships. 48% freshmen, 42% undergrads receive any aid. 45% undergrads borrow to pay for school. Average cumulative indebtedness $18,736.

MIDWAY COLLEGE

512 East Stephen Street., Midway, KY 40347-1120
Phone: 859-846-5347 • **Financial Aid Phone:** 859-846-5410
E-mail: admissions@midway.edu • **CEEB Code:** 1975
Fax: 859-846-5787 • **Website:** www.midway.edu • **ACT Code:** 1528

This private school, affiliated with the Disciples of Christ Church, was founded in 1847. It has a 105-acre campus.

RATINGS
Admissions Selectivity Rating: 77   **Fire Safety Rating:** 66   **Green Rating:** 60*

STUDENTS AND FACULTY
Enrollment: 1,123. **Student Body:** 91% female, 9% male, 9% out-of-state, <1% international (1 countries represented). Asian 1%, African American 9%, Caucasian 85%, Hispanic 2%, Native American 1%, Pacific Islander 0%, Two or more races 0%, Race unknown 3%.
Retention and Graduation: 76% freshmen return for sophomore year. 26% freshmen graduate within 4 years. 32% freshmen graduate within 6 years. **Faculty:** Student/faculty ratio 15:1. 41 full-time faculty, 46% hold PhDs, 0% are are members of minority groups, 39% are women. 0% of classes are taught by teaching assistants.

ACADEMICS
Degrees: associate, bachelor's, master's. **Classes:** Most classes have 10-19 students. Most lab/discussion sessions have 10-19 students. **Most popular majors:** Elementary Education and Teaching. **Special Study Options:** Accelerated program, distance learning, double major, dual enrollment, honors program, study abroad, teacher certification program, weekend college. **Honors Programs:** Ruth Slack Roach Leadership, President's Ambassadors, Gamma Beta Phi, Tri Beta. **Disability Services:** Special programs offered to physically disabled students, including note-taking services, reader services, tape recorders, tutors.

FACILITIES
Housing: women's dorms. 75% of campus accessible to physically diasbled.

CAMPUS LIFE
Environment: Rural. **Activities:** Choral groups, music ensembles, student government, student newspaper, yearbook. **Athletics (Intercollegiate):** *Women:* basketball, cross-country, equestrian sports, soccer, softball, tennis, volleyball. **On-Campus Highlights:** Anne Hart Raymond Center, Little Memorial Library, Equestrian Center, McManus Student Center, Piper Dining Hall.

ADMISSIONS
Freshman Academic Profile: Average high school GPA 3.2. 12% in top 10% of high school class, 25% in top 25% of high school class, 64% in top 50% of high school class. **Reported SAT (pre-2016 redesign) scores:** SAT Math middle 50% range 400-560. SAT Critical Reading middle 50% range 420-560. **Concordant SAT scores:** SAT Math middle 50% range 440–580. ACT middle 50% range 18-22. Minimum paper TOEFL 500. **Basis for Candidate Selection:** *Very important factors considered include:* rigor of secondary school record, standardized test scores. *Important factors considered include:* alumni/ae relation. *Other factors considered include:* class rank, application essay, recommendation(s), interview, extracurricular activities, talent/ability, character/personal qualities, volunteer work, work experience. **Freshman Admission Requirements:** High school diploma is required and GED is accepted. *Academic units required:* 4 English. *Academic units recommended:* 3 math, 2 science, 1 foreign language, 1 social studies. **Freshman Admission Statistics:** 399 applied, 76.94% admitted, 66% enrolled. **Transfer Admission Requirements:** High school transcript, college transcript(s), Minimum college GPA of 2.0 required. Lowest grade transferable c. **General Admission Information:** Application fee $25. Priority deadline 4/1. Nonfall registration accepted. Admission may be deferred.

COSTS AND FINANCIAL AID
Annual tuition $15,750. Room and board $6,000. Required fees $150. Average book expense $1,200. **Required Forms and Deadlines:** FAFSA, Institution's own financial aid form. **Types of Aid:** *Need-based scholarships/grants:* Federal Pell, FSEOG, State scholarships/grants, Private scholarships, College/university scholarship or grant aid from institutional funds. *Loans:* Federal Perkins Loans, College/university loans from institutional funds. *Student Employment:* Federal Work-Study Program available. Institutional employment available. **Financial

Aid Statistics: 100% needy freshmen, 93% needy undergrads receive need-based scholarship or grant aid. 8% freshmen, 8% undergrads receive non-need-based scholarship or grant aid. 81% freshmen, 90% undergrads receive need-based self-help aid. 1% freshmen, 1% undergrads receive athletic scholarships. 85% freshmen, 81% undergrads receive any aid. **Criteria for awarding aid:** *Need-based:* Academics, Alumni affiliation, Athletics. *Non-need-based:* Academics, Alumni affiliation, Athletics, Leadership, Religious affiliation.

MILLERSVILLE UNIVERSITY OF PENNSYLVANIA

P.O. Box 1002, Millersville, PA 17551-0302
Phone: 717-871-4625 • **Financial Aid Phone:** 717-871-5100
E-mail: admissions@millersville.edu • **CEEB Code:** 2656
Fax: 717-871-2147 • **Website:** www.millersville.edu • **ACT Code:** 3712

This public school was founded in 1855. It has a 250-acre campus.

RATINGS
Admissions Selectivity Rating: 76   **Fire Safety Rating:** 98   **Green Rating:** 86

STUDENTS AND FACULTY
Enrollment: 6,879. **Student Body:** 56% female, 44% male, 6% out-of-state, 1% international (54 countries represented). Asian 3%, African American 9%, Caucasian 76%, Hispanic 9%, Native American <1%, Pacific Islander <1%, Two or more races 2%, Race unknown 1%.
Retention and Graduation: 77% freshmen return for sophomore year. 38% freshmen graduate within 4 years. 61% freshmen graduate within 6 years. **Faculty:** Student/faculty ratio 19:1. 292 full-time faculty, 98% hold PhDs, 19% are are members of minority groups, 46% are women. 0% of classes are taught by teaching assistants.

ACADEMICS
Degrees: associate, bachelor's, doctoral/research, master's, postbachelor's certificate, post-master's certificate. **Classes:** Most classes have 30-39 students. Most lab/discussion sessions have 20-29 students. **Most popular majors:** Business Administration and Management; Speech Communication and Rhetoric; Psychology. **Special Study Options:** Accelerated program, cooperative education program, cross-registration, distance learning, double major, dual enrollment, honors program, independent study, internships, study abroad, teacher certification program, Academic Remediation; Advanced Placement Credit; Off-Campus Study; Learning Disabilities Services; Adult and Continuing Education (ACE) Program; Internet Courses; Summer Session for credit. **Honors Programs:** Honors College Combined degree programs: BS/Pre-Athletic Training; BS/Pre-Optometry; BS/Pre-Pharmacy; BS/Pre-Podiatry. **Disability Services:** Special programs offered to physically disabled students, including note-taking services, reader services, tape recorders, tutors. **Career Services:** Alumni network, Alumni services, Career/job search classes, Career assessment, Internships. The University's experiential learning program, including internships, co-ops and service-learning experiences, provides high impact learning for students, and associated benefits for employers and the university. Students apply classroom learning in their chosen field and develop professional proficiency, skills, and self-confidence. Employers benefit from the skills of a highly motivated employee for a specific amount of time and the university gains valuable feedback from workplace supervisors regarding our instruction, curriculum, and academic programs.

FACILITIES
Housing: Coed dorms, Wellness Housing, Theme Housing, Academic Interest Housing for several subject areas. 85% of campus accessible to physically diasbled. **Special Academic Facilities/Equipment:** Art galleries, foreign language lab, extensive inventory of scientific & technological instrumentation, weather station, T.V. studio, radio station, teleconferencing center, Distance Learning **Computers:** 100% of classrooms, 100% of dorms, 100% of libraries, 100% of dining areas, 100% of student union, 100% of common outdoor areas have wireless network access. Students can register for classes online. Administrative functions (other than registration) can be performed online.

CAMPUS LIFE
Environment: Village. **Activities:** Choral groups, concert band, dance, drama/theater, jazz band, literary magazine, marching band, music ensembles, musical theater, pep band, radio station, student government, student newspaper, symphony orchestra, television station, yearbook, Campus Ministries. 120 registered organizations, 11 honor societies, 12 religious organizations. 9 fraternities, 10 sororities. **Athletics (Intercollegiate):** *Men:* baseball, basketball, cross-country, football, golf, soccer, tennis, track/field (outdoor), track/field (indoor), wrestling. *Women:* basketball, cheerleading, cross-country, field hockey, lacrosse, soccer, softball, swimming, tennis, track/field (outdoor), track/field (indoor), volleyball. **On-Campus Highlights:** Student Memorial

Center, Ganser Library, Science and Technology Building, Biemesderfer Executive Center, Gordinier Dining Hall. **Environmental Initiatives:** Constructed a Net Zero certified building.

ADMISSIONS

Freshman Academic Profile: 9% in top 10% of high school class, 30% in top 25% of high school class, 64% in top 50% of high school class. **Reported SAT (pre-2016 redesign) scores:** SAT Math middle 50% range 460-560. SAT Critical Reading middle 50% range 470-560. SAT Writing middle 50% range 440-530. **Concordant SAT scores:** SAT EBRW middle 50% 510–600. SAT Math middle 50% range 500–580. ACT middle 50% range 19-25. Minimum internet-based TOEFL 70. Minimum paper TOEFL 550. **Basis for Candidate Selection:** *Very important factors considered include:* rigor of secondary school record, class rank, academic GPA. *Important factors considered include:* standardized test scores, application essay, talent/ability, character/personal qualities. *Other factors considered include:* recommendation(s), extracurricular activities, first generation, racial/ethnic status, volunteer work, work experience, level of applicant's interest. **Freshman Admission Requirements:** High school diploma is required and GED is accepted. *Academic units required:* 4 English, 3 math, 3 science, 2 science labs, 3 social studies, 2 history. *Academic units recommended:* 2 foreign language, 4 academic electives. **Freshman Admission Statistics:** 6,943 applied, 69.05% admitted, 28% enrolled. **Transfer Admission Requirements:** High school transcript, college transcript(s), statement of good standing from prior institution(s). Minimum college GPA of 2.0 required. Lowest grade transferable C. **General Admission Information:** Application fee $50. Nonfall registration accepted. Admission may be deferred for a maximum of 1 year.

COSTS AND FINANCIAL AID

Annual in-state tuition $8,970. Annual out-of-state tuition $18,096. Room and board $12,288. Required fees $2,758. Average book expense $1,000. **Required Forms and Deadlines:** FAFSA. **Notification of Awards:** Applicants will be notified of awards on a rolling basis beginning 3/19. **Types of Aid:** *Need-based scholarships/grants:* Federal Pell, FSEOG, State scholarships/grants, Private scholarships, College/university scholarship or grant aid from institutional funds. *Loans:* Direct Subsidized Stafford Loans, Direct Unsubsidized Stafford Loans, Direct PLUS loans, College/university loans from institutional funds. *Student Employment:* Federal Work-Study Program available. Institutional employment available. **Financial Aid Statistics:** 81% needy freshmen, 71% needy undergrads receive need-based scholarship or grant aid. 15% freshmen, 11% undergrads receive non-need-based scholarship or grant aid. 91% freshmen, 89% undergrads receive need-based self-help aid. 1% freshmen, 1% undergrads receive athletic scholarships. 87% freshmen, 82% undergrads receive any aid. Average cumulative indebtedness $29,481. **Criteria for awarding aid:** *Need-based:* Academics, Art, Minority status. *Non-need-based:* Academics, Athletics, Minority status.

MILLIGAN COLLEGE

P.O. Box 210, Milligan College, TN 37682
Phone: 423-461-8730 • **Financial Aid Phone:** 423-461-8968
E-mail: admissions@milligan.edu • **CEEB Code:** 1469
Fax: 423-461-8982 • **Website:** http://www.milligan.edu/ • **ACT Code:** 3996

This private school was founded in 1866. It has a 181-acre campus.

RATINGS

Admissions Selectivity Rating: 78   **Fire Safety Rating:** 88   **Green Rating:** 71

STUDENTS AND FACULTY

Enrollment: 832. **Student Body:** 63% female, 37% male, 40% out-of-state, 3% international (15 countries represented). Asian 2%, African American 4%, Caucasian 82%, Hispanic 6%, Native American <1%, Pacific Islander <1%, Two or more races 2%, Race unknown <1%.
Retention and Graduation: 78% freshmen return for sophomore year. 54% freshmen graduate within 4 years. 62% freshmen graduate within 6 years. 9% grads pursue arts and sciences degrees. 2% grads pursue law degrees. 2% grads pursue business degrees. 6% grads pursue medical degrees. **Faculty:** Student/faculty ratio 9:1. 79 full-time faculty, 80% hold PhDs, 4% are are members of minority groups, 53% are women. 0% of classes are taught by teaching assistants.

ACADEMICS

Degrees: bachelor's, master's. **Classes:** Most classes have fewer than 10 students. Most lab/discussion sessions have fewer than 10 students. **Most popular majors:** Bible/Biblical Studies; Registered Nursing/Registered Nurse; Business Administration and Management. **Special Study Options:** cross-registration, double major, independent study, internships, study abroad,

teacher certification program. **Disability Services:** Special programs offered to physically disabled students, including note-taking services, tape recorders, tutors. **Career Services:** Alumni network, Career/job search classes, Career assessment, Regional alumni.

FACILITIES

Housing: men's dorms, women's dorms, apartments for married students, apartments for single students. 80% of campus accessible to physically diasbled. **Computers:** 95% of classrooms, 95% of dorms, 100% of libraries, 100% of dining areas, 100% of student union, 25% of common outdoor areas have wireless network access. Students can register for classes online. Administrative functions (other than registration) can be performed online.

CAMPUS LIFE

Environment: Town. **Activities:** Choral groups, concert band, drama/theater, jazz band, literary magazine, music ensembles, musical theater, pep band, radio station, student government, student newspaper, symphony orchestra, yearbook. 36 registered organizations, 5 honor societies, 5 religious organizations. **Athletics (Intercollegiate):** *Men:* baseball, basketball, cross-country, golf, mountain biking, soccer, swimming, tennis, track/field (outdoor), track/field (indoor). *Women:* basketball, cross-country, soccer, softball, swimming, tennis, track/field (outdoor), track/field (indoor), volleyball. **On-Campus Highlights:** The Gregory Center, Student Center, Residence Halls/ Dining Hall, Seeger Chapel, Athletic Facilities. **Environmental Initiatives:** Campuswide Recycling.

ADMISSIONS

Freshman Academic Profile: Average high school GPA 3.8. 80% from public high schools. **Reported SAT (pre-2016 redesign) scores:** SAT Math middle 50% range 503-600. SAT Critical Reading middle 50% range 473-590. SAT Writing middle 50% range 463-588. **Concordant SAT scores:** SAT EBRW middle 50% 530–650. SAT Math middle 50% 530–620. ACT middle 50% range 22-28. Minimum internet-based TOEFL 79. Minimum paper TOEFL 550. **Basis for Candidate Selection:** *Very important factors considered include:* rigor of secondary school record, academic GPA, standardized test scores, application essay, character/personal qualities, religious affiliation/ commitment. *Important factors considered include:* recommendation(s), extracurricular activities. *Other factors considered include:* class rank, interview, talent/ability, alumni/ae relation, racial/ethnic status, volunteer work, work experience. **Freshman Admission Requirements:** High school diploma is required and GED is accepted. *Academic units recommended:* 4 English, 3 math, 3 science, 2 foreign language, 2 social studies, 3 history. **Freshman Admission Statistics:** 603 applied, 65.17% admitted, 48% enrolled. **Transfer Admission Requirements:** college transcript(s), essay or personal statement, Minimum college GPA of 2.0 required. Lowest grade transferable C-. **General Admission Information:** Application fee $30. Priority deadline 4/1. Regular application deadline 8/1. Nonfall registration accepted. Admission may be deferred for a maximum of 1 year.

COSTS AND FINANCIAL AID

Annual tuition $30,250. Room and board $6,700. Required fees $1,200. Average book expense $1,300. **Required Forms and Deadlines:** FAFSA. **Notification of Awards:** Applicants will be notified of awards on a rolling basis beginning 3/15. **Types of Aid:** *Need-based scholarships/grants:* Federal Pell, FSEOG, State scholarships/grants, Private scholarships, College/university scholarship or grant aid from institutional funds. *Loans:* Direct Subsidized Stafford Loans, Direct Unsubsidized Stafford Loans, Direct PLUS loans, Federal Perkins Loans. *Student Employment:* Federal Work-Study Program available. Institutional employment available. **Financial Aid Statistics:** 100% needy freshmen, 99% needy undergrads receive need-based scholarship or grant aid. 31% freshmen, 24% undergrads receive non-need-based scholarship or grant aid. 58% freshmen, 66% undergrads receive need-based self-help aid. 32% freshmen, 20% undergrads receive athletic scholarships. 97% freshmen, 92% undergrads receive any aid. 67% undergrads borrow to pay for school. Average cumulative indebtedness $27,146. **Criteria for awarding aid:** *Need-based:* Alumni affiliation. *Non-need-based:* Academics, Athletics, Job skills, Leadership, Minority status, Music/drama, Religious affiliation, State/district residency.

MILLIKIN UNIVERSITY

1184 West Main Street, Decatur, IL 62522-2084
Phone: 217-424-6210 • **Financial Aid Phone:** 217-424-6317
E-mail: admis@millikin.edu • **CEEB Code:** 1470
Fax: 217-425-4669 • **Website:** www.millikin.edu • **ACT Code:** 1080

This private school, affiliated with the Presbyterian Church, was founded in 1901. It has a 75-acre campus.

RATINGS

Admissions Selectivity Rating: 80   **Fire Safety Rating:** 98   **Green Rating:** 67

STUDENTS AND FACULTY

Enrollment: 1,917. **Student Body:** 58% female, 42% male, 16% out-of-state, 2% international (19 countries represented). Asian 1%, African American 14%, Caucasian 71%, Hispanic 6%, Native American <1%, Pacific Islander 0%, Two or more races 4%, Race unknown 1%.

Retention and Graduation: 72% freshmen return for sophomore year. 49% freshmen graduate within 4 years. 60% freshmen graduate within 6 years. 19% grads go on to further study within 1 year. 13% grads pursue arts and sciences degrees. 1% grads pursue law degrees. 3% grads pursue business degrees. 1% grads pursue medical degrees. **Faculty:** Student/faculty ratio 11:1. 145 full-time faculty, 79% hold PhDs, 6% are are members of minority groups, 50% are women. 0% of classes are taught by teaching assistants.

ACADEMICS

Degrees: bachelor's, doctoral/professional, master's. **Classes:** Most classes have 10-19 students. Most lab/discussion sessions have 10-19 students. **Most popular majors:** Registered Nursing/Registered Nurse; Drama and Dramatics/Theatre Arts; Biology/Biological Sciences. **Special Study Options:** Accelerated program, double major, exchange student program (domestic), honors program, independent study, internships, student-designed major, study abroad, teacher certification program. **Honors Programs:** Presidential Scholars are Millikin's best and brightest students; selection is based upon outstanding academic performance and demonstrated leadership; they receive a full tuition scholarship, renewable for up to four years. Millikin's Honors Program introduces students to college-level scholarship, research, critical thinking, and writing during the freshman and sophomore years; classes are taught as seminars—sessions involving intense discussion and requiring active participation; Millikin's strongest juniors are invited to join the next phase of the Honors Program to become James Millikin Scholars. James Millikin Scholars Program; Honors Program. **Disability Services:** Special programs offered to physically disabled students, including note-taking services, reader services, tape recorders, tutors. **Career Services:** Alumni network, Alumni services, Career/job search classes, Career assessment, Internships. Millikin's Blue Connection, a retail art gallery, serves as the practical laboratory for Millikin's innovative Art of Entrepreneurship curriculum. This gallery sells, original art, produced by Millikin alumni, faculty, staff and students. The Blue Connection retail art store is fully operated by Millikin students, a majority of which are from Art, Business and Music programs. The talents of the various majors are integrated with the concept of business ownership. The success of the venture is in the hands of the Millikin students.

FACILITIES

Housing: Coed dorms, special housing for disabled students, men's dorms, special housing for international students, women's dorms, fraternity/sorority housing, apartments for married students, apartments for single students, Wellness HousingLearning Communities. 66% of campus accessible to physically diasbled. **Special Academic Facilities/Equipment:** Art galleries, art museum, fitness/wellness center, recording studio, indoor sports center, greenhouse, observatory, 2 indoor sports centers, 2000 seat performance center **Computers:** 75% of classrooms, 75% of dorms, 100% of libraries, 100% of dining areas, 100% of student union, 5% of common outdoor areas have wireless network access. Students can register for classes online. Administrative functions (other than registration) can be performed online.

CAMPUS LIFE

Environment: City. **Activities:** Choral groups, concert band, dance, drama/theater, jazz band, literary magazine, music ensembles, musical theater, opera, pep band, radio station, student government, student newspaper, student-run film society, symphony orchestra, Student Organization, Model UN. 96 registered organizations, 7 honor societies, 2 religious organizations. 5 fraternities, 4 sororities. **Athletics (Intercollegiate):** *Men:* baseball, basketball, cheerleading, cross-country, football, golf, soccer, swimming, track/field (outdoor), track/field (indoor). *Women:* basketball, cheerleading, cross-country, golf, soccer, softball, swimming, tennis, track/field (outdoor), track/field (indoor), volleyball. **On-Campus Highlights:** ADM-Scovill Hall, Perkinson Music Center, Albert Taylor Theatre, Decatur Indoor Sports Center, Kirkland Fine Arts Center.

ADMISSIONS

Freshman Academic Profile: Average high school GPA 3.4. 16% in top 10% of high school class, 39% in top 25% of high school class, 67% in top 50% of high school class. 90% from public high schools. **Reported SAT (pre-2016 redesign) scores:** SAT Math middle 50% range 440-500. SAT Critical Reading middle 50% range 470-580. SAT Writing middle 50% range 430-570. **Concordant SAT scores:** SAT EBRW middle 50% 500–630. SAT Math middle 50% range 480–530. ACT middle 50% range 19-26. Minimum internet-based TOEFL 79. Minimum paper TOEFL 550. **Basis for Candidate Selection:** *Very important factors considered include:* rigor of secondary school record. *Important factors considered include:* class rank, academic GPA, standardized test scores, recommendation(s), interview. *Other factors considered include:* extracurricular activities, talent/ability, character/personal qualities, alumni/ae relation, volunteer work, work experience, level of applicant's interest. **Freshman Admission Requirements:** High school diploma is required

and GED is accepted. *Academic units recommended:* 4 English, 3 math, 3 science, 2 foreign language, 2 social studies, 2 history. **Freshman Admission Statistics:** 3,608 applied, 63.80% admitted, 19% enrolled. **Transfer Admission Requirements:** High school transcript, college transcript(s), Minimum college GPA of 2.0 required. Lowest grade transferable C-. **General Admission Information:** Priority deadline 5/1. Nonfall registration accepted. Admission may be deferred for a maximum of 1 year.

COSTS AND FINANCIAL AID

Annual tuition $31,032. Room and board $10,335. Required fees $792. Average book expense $1,000. **Required Forms and Deadlines:** FAFSA. **Notification of Awards:** Applicants will be notified of awards on a rolling basis beginning 3/1. **Types of Aid:** *Need-based scholarships/grants:* Federal Pell, FSEOG, State scholarships/grants, Private scholarships, College/university scholarship or grant aid from institutional funds. *Loans:* Direct Subsidized Stafford Loans, Direct Unsubsidized Stafford Loans, Direct PLUS loans, Federal Perkins Loans. *Student Employment:* Federal Work-Study Program available. Institutional employment available. **Financial Aid Statistics:** 92% needy freshmen, 89% needy undergrads receive need-based scholarship or grant aid. 100% freshmen, 92% undergrads receive non-need-based scholarship or grant aid. 79% freshmen, 81% undergrads receive need-based self-help aid. 0% freshmen, 0% undergrads receive athletic scholarships. 100% freshmen, 99% undergrads receive any aid. 81% undergrads borrow to pay for school. Average cumulative indebtedness $32,924. **Criteria for awarding aid:** *Need-based:* Academics. *Non-need-based:* Academics, Alumni affiliation, Art, Leadership, Minority status, Music/drama.

MILLS COLLEGE

5000 MacArthur Boulevard, Oakland, CA 94613
Phone: 510-430-2135 • **Financial Aid Phone:** 510-430-2000
E-mail: admission@mills.edu • **CEEB Code:** 4485
Fax: 510-430-3314 • **Website:** www.mills.edu • **ACT Code:** 4485

This private school was founded in 1852. It has a 135-acre campus.

RATINGS

Admissions Selectivity Rating: 80   **Fire Safety Rating:** 78   **Green Rating:** 89

STUDENTS AND FACULTY

Enrollment: 806. **Student Body:** 100% female, 0% male, 19% out-of-state, 1% international (6 countries represented). Asian 9%, African American 9%, Caucasian 45%, Hispanic 27%, Native American <1%, Pacific Islander <1%, Two or more races 8%, Race unknown 1%.

Retention and Graduation: 78% freshmen return for sophomore year. 62% freshmen graduate within 4 years. 66 32% grads go on to further study within 1 year. 9% grads pursue arts and sciences degrees. 2% grads pursue business degrees. **Faculty:** Student/faculty ratio 10:1. 91 full-time faculty, 90% hold PhDs, 34% are are members of minority groups, 66% are women.

ACADEMICS

Degrees: bachelor's, certificate, doctoral/research, master's, postbachelor's certifiate. **Classes:** Most classes have 10-19 students. Most lab/discussion sessions have 10-19 students. **Most popular majors:** Psychology; English Language and Literature; Biology/Biological Sciences. **Special Study Options:** cooperative education program, cross-registration, double major, exchange student program (domestic), independent study, internships, liberal arts/career combination, student-designed major, study abroad, teacher certification program. Combined degree programs: BA/MA, BA/MEng, BA/MBA; BA/MPP; BA/MA/Teaching Credential. **Disability Services:** Special programs offered to physically disabled students, including note-taking services, reader services, tape recorders, tutors. **Career Services:** Alumni network, Alumni services, Career/job search classes, Career assessment, Internships, Regional alumni. Career Services is proud of its career development workshops that take place in our new centralized location and a variety of other locations. These workshops range from guiding students in choosing a major to supporting students with the internship and employment process. We also have workshops that educate students around leadership, work etiquette, and graduate school. Networking opportunities with employers and alumnae/i are also offered.

FACILITIES

Housing: Coed dorms, special housing for disabled students, women's dorms, apartments for married students, cooperative housing, apartments for single students, Wellness Housing, Theme Housing, Resumer Student Housing. 100%

of campus accessible to physically diasbled. **Special Academic Facilities/Equipment:** Art Museum, Center for contemporary Music, on-campus elementary school, botanical gardens. **Computers:** 100% of classrooms, 100% of dorms, 100% of libraries, 100% of dining areas, 100% of student union, 100% of common outdoor areas have wireless network access. Students can register for classes online. Administrative functions (other than registration) can be performed online.

CAMPUS LIFE

Environment: Metropolis. **Activities:** Choral groups, dance, drama/theater, literary magazine, music ensembles, musical theater, radio station, student government, student newspaper, student-run film society, yearbook, Campus Ministries, Student Organization, Model UN. 47 registered organizations, 2 honor societies, 4 religious organizations. **Athletics (Intercollegiate):** *Women:* crew/rowing, cross-country, soccer, swimming, tennis, track/field (outdoor), volleyball. **On-Campus Highlights:** The Mills College Art Museum, Haas Pavilion & Trefethen Aquatic Center, Rothwell Student Center, Lorrie Lokey Graduate School of Business, Littlefield Concert Hall. **Environmental Initiatives:** Mills recycles, composts and reuses all consumer materials to the extent possible. www.mills.edu/green/recycling Mills students, staff and faculty participate in Recycle Mania.

ADMISSIONS

Freshman Academic Profile: Average high school GPA 3.6. 11% in top 10% of high school class, 24% in top 25% of high school class, 96% in top 50% of high school class. 81% from public high schools. **Reported SAT (pre-2016 redesign) scores:** SAT Math middle 50% range 440-590. SAT Critical Reading middle 50% range 480-640. SAT Writing middle 50% range 490-630. **Concordant SAT scores:** SAT EBRW middle 50% 540–680. SAT Math middle 50% range 480–610. ACT middle 50% range 23-29. Minimum internet-based TOEFL 80. Minimum paper TOEFL 550. **Basis for Candidate Selection:** *Very important factors considered include:* rigor of secondary school record. *Important factors considered include:* class rank, academic GPA, standardized test scores, application essay, recommendation(s), extracurricular activities, character/personal qualities. *Other factors considered include:* interview, talent/ability, first generation, alumni/ae relation, geographical residence, state residency, racial/ethnic status, volunteer work, work experience. **Freshman Admission Requirements:** High school diploma is required and GED is accepted. *Academic units required:* 4 English, 3 math, 2 science, 2 science labs, 2 foreign language, 2 social studies, 2 history. *Academic units recommended:* 4 English, 4 math, 4 science, 2 science labs, 4 foreign language, 4 social studies, 4 history, 2 visual/performing arts. **Freshman Admission Statistics:** 1,052 applied, 84.41% admitted, 19% enrolled. **Transfer Admission Requirements:** High school transcript, college transcript(s), essay or personal statement, Lowest grade transferable C-. **General Admission Information:** Application fee $50. Priority deadline 1/15. Nonfall registration accepted. Admission may be deferred for a maximum of 1 year.

COSTS AND FINANCIAL AID

Annual tuition $44,765. Room and board $13,614. Required fees $1,471. Average book expense $1,514. **Required Forms and Deadlines:** FAFSA, State aid form. **Notification of Awards:** Applicants will be notified of awards on a rolling basis beginning 3/1. **Types of Aid:** *Need-based scholarships/grants:* Federal Pell, FSEOG, State scholarships/grants, Private scholarships, College/university scholarship or grant aid from institutional funds. *Loans:* Direct Subsidized Stafford Loans, Direct Unsubsidized Stafford Loans, Direct PLUS loans, Federal Perkins Loans, College/university loans from institutional funds. *Student Employment:* Federal Work-Study Program available. Institutional employment available. **Financial Aid Statistics:** 91% needy freshmen, 92% needy undergrads receive need-based scholarship or grant aid. 99% freshmen, 98% undergrads receive non-need-based scholarship or grant aid. 87% freshmen, 85% undergrads receive need-based self-help aid. 0% freshmen, 0% undergrads receive athletic scholarships. 100% freshmen, 95% undergrads receive any aid. 76% undergrads borrow to pay for school. Average cumulative indebtedness $33,327. **Criteria for awarding aid:** *Non-need-based:* Academics, Leadership, Music/drama.

MILLSAPS COLLEGE

1701 North State Street, Jackson, MS 39210
Phone: 601-974-1050 • **Financial Aid Phone:** 800-352-1050
E-mail: admissions@millsaps.edu • **CEEB Code:** 1471
Fax: 601-974-1059 • **Website:** www.millsaps.edu • **ACT Code:** 2212

This private school, affiliated with the Methodist Church, was founded in 1890. It has a 100-acre campus.

RATINGS

Admissions Selectivity Rating: 86   **Fire Safety Rating:** 90   **Green Rating:** 71

STUDENTS AND FACULTY

Enrollment: 760. **Student Body:** 49% female, 51% male, 55% out-of-state, 4% international (16 countries represented). Asian 4%, African American 11%, Caucasian 74%, Hispanic 2%, Native American 1%, Pacific Islander 0%, Two or more races 1%, Race unknown 3%.
Retention and Graduation: 80% freshmen return for sophomore year. 62% freshmen graduate within 4 years. 64 44% grads go on to further study within 1 year. 15% grads pursue arts and sciences degrees. 6% grads pursue law degrees. 9% grads pursue business degrees. 5% grads pursue medical degrees. **Faculty:** Student/faculty ratio 9:1. 82 full-time faculty, 95% hold PhDs, 12% are are members of minority groups, 49% are women. 0% of classes are taught by teaching assistants.

ACADEMICS

Degrees: bachelor's, master's. **Classes:** Most classes have 10-19 students. Most lab/discussion sessions have 10-19 students. **Most popular majors:** Biology/Biological Sciences; Psychology; Business Administration, Management and Operations. **Special Study Options:** Accelerated program, double major, honors program, independent study, internships, liberal arts/career combination, student-designed major, study abroad, teacher certification program, The Millsaps FAITH & WORK INITIATIVE offers an array of curricular and extracurricular programs to help students discern their vocation or call in life and to pursue that call with passion, integrity and an eye toward the needs of the world. Faith & Work options include service-learning courses and the Meaning of Work course, immersion and service experiences, discussion programs with faculty and professionals, leadership and service clubs, internships, and public lecture series. Other Interdisciplinary Programs or concentrations are available in American studies, Christian education, environmental studies, film studies, human services, studies, women's and gender studies, and church music. UUndergraduate Research is available in most academic departments, including field research opportunities in the Pacific Northwest, Yellowstone, the Mexico, and Europe. Millsaps' nonprofit biocultural reserve on 4500 acres in the Yucatan Peninsula of Mexico offers multi-disciplinary options for study, including archaeology, business, ecology, education, geology, history, literature, math and socio-cultural anthropology. Students may also choose among other STUDY ABROAD programs developed by Millsaps faculty–in Albania, Belgium, China, Costa Rica, England, France, Germany, Ghana, Greece, Ireland, Israel, Italy, Japan, Mexico (Yucatan), and Tanzania. Pre-Professional programs include dentistry, engineering, law, medicine, ministry, and social work. Millsaps students may work towards dual degrees in engineering, applied science or nursing through agreements with Auburn University, Columbia University, Vanderbilt University, Washington University, and the University of Mississippi Medical Health Center. Other distinctive programs include the Ford Teaching Fellows program (research and internships for students interested in college teaching), and the Weiner PRE-MEDICAL FELLOWS program (summer research). **Honors Programs:** The Honors Program, Ford Teaching Fellows program (research and internships for students interested in college teaching), Weiner Pre-Medical Fellows Program (summer research), Lilly Fellows Faith and Work Initiative (connecting individual passions with learning, meaning, service, and career) Combined degree programs: BA/MBA-Millsaps; Nursing at Univ. of Miss. and Vanderbilt. **Disability Services:** Special programs offered to physically disabled students, including note-taking services, reader services, tutors. **Career Services:** Alumni network, Alumni services, Career assessment, Internships, Regional alumni. The Millsaps Career Center sponsors an internship-for-credit program designed to assist students with career choices and relate student work experiences to their education. Initially, the Career Center offers orientation and internship search assistance. During the internships, students maintain work logs, write monthly journals of their work experiences, and receive monthly feedback from the Career Center. Interns also obtain written evaluations from their supervisors and write final reports, evaluating their work sites and relating their work experiences to their education and career objectives.

FACILITIES

Housing: Coed dorms, special housing for disabled students, women's dorms, fraternity/sorority housing, Wellness Housing, Theme Housing. Our theme housing is community service housing. 90% of campus accessible to physically diasbled. **Special Academic Facilities/Equipment:** Millsaps' W.M. Keck Center for Instrumental and Biochemical Comparative Archaeology is the only undergraduate facility of its kind in the world. The new multi-disciplinary research laboratory provides undergraduate students with the opportunity to explore complex archeological questions using advanced bioanalytical and biochemical techniques. 4-6 Keck Fellows assist each year in gathering the artifacts studied in the lab from the College''s archaeological field programs in Yucatan, Mexico, and northern Albania. The lab houses an inductively-coupled plasma spectrometer with laser ablation, a gas-chromotography spectrometer, a liquid-chromotography spectrometer, and a portable x-ray fluorescence spectrometer. In addition, the college's other labs include a unique array of spectrometers for measuring atomic absorption, infrared transitional modes, nuclear magnetic resonance, and other forms of energy; high performance chromatographs for separation and identification of compounds; electrophoresis instruments for analyzing biomolecules and other biological materials; and an inert atmosphere reaction chamber. Other facilities include a state-of-the-art molecular biology/functional genomics research laboratory; a fluorescence microscopy suite and imaging facility; a GIS workstation with Rockware and Arcview 9.1 GIS Software; a specially-designed automated 24-hour food monitoring system for rats; a microsurgical lab for animal surgeries; an on-campus hydrogeologic monitoring station to measure the water table and water levels in four on-campus wells; and a computational modeling lab for math, chemistry and physics students which provides numerical and graphical solutions in three dimensions. The College Sorbent and Environmental Laboratory provides undergraduates with opportunities for oil spill and stormwater remediation research. Another unique facility is the college's 4,000-acre biocultural reserve and learning center in the state of Yucatan, Mexico. Here students excavate ancient Mayan archaeological sites, conduct environmental studies of the jungle, research the biology and geology of the area, and live in a sustainable solar-powered facility constructed of materials inspired by the native Mayan architecture. Millsaps' Yucatan program also includes a newly-renovated teaching and living facility for international business studies which is located in the large city of Merida. In addition, Millsaps' newly-renovated digital Language Resource Center has been equipped with 25 network computers and satellite connections for international programming. **Computers:** 100% of classrooms, 100% of dorms, 100% of libraries, 100% of dining areas, 100% of student union, 100% of common outdoor areas have wireless network access. Students can register for classes online. Administrative functions (other than registration) can be performed online.

CAMPUS LIFE

Environment: Metropolis. **Activities:** Choral groups, dance, drama/theater, literary magazine, music ensembles, musical theater, student government, student newspaper, yearbook, Campus Ministries, Student Organization, Model UN. 85 registered organizations, 28 honor societies, 12 religious organizations. 6 fraternities, 6 sororities. **Athletics (Intercollegiate):** *Men:* baseball, basketball, cross-country, football, golf, lacrosse, soccer, tennis, track/field (outdoor). *Women:* basketball, cross-country, golf, lacrosse, soccer, softball, tennis, track/field (outdoor), volleyball. **On-Campus Highlights:** Hall Activities Center (fitness/athletic facility), Campbell College Center (student activities), The Bowl (outdoor green space/campus center), Millsaps Wilson Library (study center), Fraternity Row, The Campbell College Center includes a cafeteria, a coffeehouse, live entertainment and game areas, and a bookstore. The Bowl is a natural, outdoor space in the heart of the campus where students congregate between classes to relax and to participate in outdoor activities. **Environmental Initiatives:** The College supports the Center for Research and Learning at the H. Moyers Biocultural Reserve operated by Kaxil Kiuic, Yucatʔaʔîn, Mexico. The Center is an off the grid facility built using sustainable design and technology. Applied Ecological Design, taught by Millsaps faculty at the Center, focuses on topics critical to planning, designing, and creating a sustainable home including sustainable construction, solar power, energy efficiency, water supply, waste and wastewater management, and agriculture/ permaculture; coursework includes on-site project experimentation, design, and construction.

ADMISSIONS

Freshman Academic Profile: Average high school GPA 3.7. 55% from public high schools. **Reported SAT (pre-2016 redesign) scores:** SAT Math middle 50% range 520-630. SAT Critical Reading middle 50% range 510-640. **Concordant SAT scores:** SAT Math middle 50% range 550–650. ACT middle 50% range 23-29. Minimum internet-based TOEFL 80. Minimum paper TOEFL 550. **Basis for Candidate Selection:** *Very important factors considered include:* rigor of secondary school record, academic GPA, standardized test scores, character/personal qualities. *Important factors considered include:* class rank, application essay, recommendation(s), extracurricular activities, talent/ability. *Other factors considered include:* interview, volunteer work, work experience. **Freshman Admission Requirements:** High school diploma is required and GED is accepted. *Academic units required:* 4 English, 3 math, 3 science, 2 science labs, 1 foreign language, 2 social studies, 2 history, 1 academic elective. *Academic units recommended:* 4 English, 4 math, 4 science, 2 science labs, 2 foreign language, 2 social studies, 2 history, 2 academic electives. **Freshman Admission Statistics:** 2,861 applied, 57.18% admitted, 14% enrolled. **Transfer Admission Requirements:** college transcript(s), essay or personal statement, standardized test scores, statement of good standing from prior institution(s). Minimum college GPA of 2.75 required. Lowest grade transferable C. **General Admission Information:** Priority deadline 2/1. Regular application deadline 7/1. Nonfall registration accepted. Admission may be deferred for a maximum of 1 year.

COSTS AND FINANCIAL AID

Annual tuition $31,872. Room and board $11,878. Required fees $2,110. Average book expense $1,100. **Required Forms and Deadlines:** FAFSA. **Notification of Awards:** Applicants will be notified of awards on a rolling basis beginning 3/15. **Types of Aid:** *Need-based scholarships/grants:* Federal Pell, FSEOG, State scholarships/grants, Private scholarships, College/university scholarship or grant aid from institutional funds. *Loans:* Direct Subsidized Stafford Loans, Direct Unsubsidized Stafford Loans, Direct PLUS loans, Federal Perkins Loans, College/university loans from institutional funds. *Student Employment:* Federal Work-Study Program available. Institutional employment available. **Financial Aid Statistics:** 100% needy freshmen, 100% needy undergrads receive need-based scholarship or grant aid. 26% freshmen, 20% undergrads receive non-need-based scholarship or grant aid. 70% freshmen, 76% undergrads receive need-based self-help aid. 0% freshmen, 0% undergrads receive athletic scholarships. 100% freshmen, 98% undergrads receive any aid. **Criteria for awarding aid:** *Need-based:* Minority status, Religious affiliation. *Non-need-based:* Academics, Art, Leadership, Music/drama, Religious affiliation.

MILWAUKEE SCHOOL OF ENGINEERING

1025 North Broadway, Milwaukee, WI 53202-3109
Phone: 414-277-6763 • **Financial Aid Phone:** 800-778-7223
E-mail: explore@msoe.edu • **CEEB Code:** 1476
Fax: 414-277-7475 • **Website:** www.msoe.edu • **ACT Code:** 4616

This private school was founded in 1903. It has a 15-acre campus.

RATINGS

Admissions Selectivity Rating: 79   **Fire Safety Rating:** 98   **Green Rating:** 73

STUDENTS AND FACULTY

Enrollment: 2,675. **Student Body:** 26% female, 74% male, 33% out-of-state, 11% international (29 countries represented). Asian 4%, African American 2%, Caucasian 67%, Hispanic 5%, Native American <1%, Pacific Islander <1%, Two or more races 2%, Race unknown 8%.
Retention and Graduation: 83% freshmen return for sophomore year. 44% freshmen graduate within 4 years. 64% freshmen graduate within 6 years. 8% grads go on to further study within 1 year. 1% grads pursue law degrees. 3% grads pursue business degrees. 1% grads pursue medical degrees. **Faculty:** Student/faculty ratio 16:1. 139 full-time faculty, 78% hold PhDs, 12% are are members of minority groups, 31% are women. 0% of classes are taught by teaching assistants.

ACADEMICS

Degrees: bachelor's, master's. **Classes:** Most classes have 20-29 students. Most lab/discussion sessions have 10-19 students. **Most popular majors:** Architectural Engineering; Electrical and Electronics Engineering; Mechanical Engineering. **Special Study Options:** Accelerated program, distance learning, double major, dual enrollment, English as a Second Language (ESL), independent study, internships, study abroad, BS in international business and in electrical and mechanical engineering with Fachhochschule Lubeck, Germany. All students may apply to study at Czech Technical University, Prague, Czech Republic. Combined degree programs: BA/MEng, Architectural Eng. and Construction Management; B.S. and M.S. in Civil Engineering. **Disability Services:** Special programs offered to physically disabled students, including note-taking services, reader services, tape recorders, tutors. **Career Services:** Alumni network, Alumni services, Career/job search classes, Career assessment, Internships, Regional alumni. Approximately 85% of graduates have had internship experience.

FACILITIES

Housing: Coed dorms, special housing for disabled students. 95% of campus accessible to physically diasbled. **Special Academic Facilities/Equipment:** Grohmann Museum, Kern Center Health, Wellness and Recreation Facility, Rader School of Business, Johnson Controls Software Engineering Lab, Fluid Power Institute, Rapid Prototyping Center, Applied Technology Center, Center for BioMolecular Modeling, Warren P. Knowles Nursing Lab, Harley Davidson

Design Lab, Johnson Controls Environmental Systems Lab **Computers:** 100% of classrooms, 10% of dorms, 100% of libraries, 100% of dining areas, 100% of student union, 100% of common outdoor areas have wireless network access. Students can register for classes online. Administrative functions (other than registration) can be performed online. Undergraduates are required to own a computer.

CAMPUS LIFE

Environment: Metropolis. **Activities:** dance, drama/theater, jazz band, literary magazine, pep band, radio station, student government, symphony orchestra, Campus Ministries, Student Organization. 61 registered organizations, 6 honor societies, 4 religious organizations. 3 fraternities, 3 sororities. **Athletics (Intercollegiate):** *Men:* baseball, basketball, cheerleading, crew/rowing, cross-country, golf, ice hockey, lacrosse, soccer, tennis, track/field (outdoor), track/field (indoor), volleyball, wrestling. *Women:* basketball, cheerleading, cross-country, golf, soccer, softball, tennis, track/field (outdoor), track/field (indoor), volleyball. **On-Campus Highlights:** Kern Center—Health and Wellness Center, Student Life and Campus Center (dining and game room), The Grohmann Museum, Rapid Prototyping Center, School of Nursing Simulation Lab. **Environmental Initiatives:** In the Fall of 2010, MSOE initiated a compostable service ware program in the school's cafe. It included replacing hot and cold beverage cups, plates and soup bowls. At the time, there was also a dedicated collection stream setup to help divert an estimated 150 cubic yards of waste per year from going into local landfills. Efforts have been made to increase MSOE's recycling rate from 10% in 6/09 to over 60% in 1/11.

ADMISSIONS

Freshman Academic Profile: Average high school GPA 3.6. 92% from public high schools. **Reported SAT (pre-2016 redesign) scores:** SAT Math middle 50% range 580-660. SAT Critical Reading middle 50% range 500-620. **Concordant SAT scores:** SAT Math middle 50% range 600–690. ACT middle 50% range 25-30. Minimum internet-based TOEFL 82. Minimum paper TOEFL 550. **Basis for Candidate Selection:** *Very important factors considered include:* academic GPA, standardized test scores. *Important factors considered include:* rigor of secondary school record, extracurricular activities, talent/ability. *Other factors considered include:* character/personal qualities, alumni/ae relation. **Freshman Admission Requirements:** High school diploma is required and GED is accepted. *Academic units required:* 4 English, 4 math, 4 science. *Academic units recommended:* 3 science labs. **Freshman Admission Statistics:** 2,686 applied, 66.31% admitted, 31% enrolled. **Transfer Admission Requirements:** college transcript(s), Minimum college GPA of 2.5 required. Lowest grade transferable C. **General Admission Information:** Priority deadline 9/1. Nonfall registration accepted. Admission may be deferred for a maximum of 2 year.

COSTS AND FINANCIAL AID

Annual tuition $37,719. Room and board $9,102. Required fees $1,710. Average book expense $1,000. **Required Forms and Deadlines:** FAFSA. **Notification of Awards:** Applicants will be notified of awards on a rolling basis beginning 3/1. **Types of Aid:** *Need-based scholarships/grants:* Federal Pell, FSEOG, State scholarships/grants, Private scholarships, College/university scholarship or grant aid from institutional funds. *Loans:* Direct Subsidized Stafford Loans, Direct Unsubsidized Stafford Loans, Direct PLUS loans, Federal Perkins Loans, State Loans. *Student Employment:* Federal Work-Study Program available. Institutional employment available. **Financial Aid Statistics:** 100% needy freshmen, 100% needy undergrads receive need-based scholarship or grant aid. 18% freshmen, 15% undergrads receive non-need-based scholarship or grant aid. 77% freshmen, 82% undergrads receive need-based self-help aid. 0% freshmen, 0% undergrads receive athletic scholarships. 100% freshmen, 90% undergrads receive any aid. 76% undergrads borrow to pay for school. Average cumulative indebtedness $38,745. **Criteria for awarding aid:** *Non-need-based:* Academics.

MINERVA SCHOOLS AT KGI

1145 Market Street, San Francisco, CA 94103
Phone: 415-649-7658
E-mail: admissions@minerva.kgi.edu
Fax: 415-520-0517 • **Website:** www.minerva.kgi.edu

RATINGS
Admissions Selectivity Rating: 72   **Fire Safety Rating:** 72   **Green Rating:** 60*

STUDENTS AND FACULTY
Enrollment: 111. **Student Body:** 48% female, 52% male, 78% international. Asian 0%, African American 0%, Caucasian 0%, Hispanic 0%, Native American 0%, Pacific Islander 0%, Two or more races 0%, Race unknown 22%. **Retention and Graduation:** 90% freshmen return for sophomore year. **Faculty:** Student/faculty ratio 10 12 full-time faculty, 100% hold PhDs, 17% are

are members of minority groups, 50% are women. 0% of classes are taught by teaching assistants.

ACADEMICS
Degrees: bachelor's. **Career Services:** Career/job search classes, Career assessment, Internships.

ADMISSIONS
Freshman Academic Profile: 0% in top 10% of high school class. **Basis for Candidate Selection:** *Very important factors considered include:* rigor of secondary school record, academic GPA, interview, extracurricular activities, talent/ability, character/personal qualities. *Important factors considered include:* class rank, volunteer work, work experience. **Freshman Admission Statistics:** 9,032 applied, 2.10% admitted, 53% enrolled. **General Admission Information:** Regular application deadline 1/15. Nonfall registration not accepted.

COSTS AND FINANCIAL AID
Annual tuition $10,000. Required fees $1,450. Average book expense $1,000. *Student Employment:* Federal Work-Study Program available. Institutional employment available. **Financial Aid Statistics:** 100% needy undergrads receive need-based scholarship or grant aid. 0% undergrads receive non-need-based scholarship or grant aid. 11% undergrads receive need-based self-help aid. 0% undergrads receive athletic scholarships.

MINNEAPOLIS COLLEGE OF ART AND DESIGN

2501 Stevens Avenue, Minneapolis, MN 55404
Phone: 612-874-3760 • **Financial Aid Phone:** 612-874-3782
E-mail: admissions@mcad.edu • **CEEB Code:** 6411
Fax: 612-874-3701 • **Website:** www.mcad.edu • **ACT Code:** 2130

This private school was founded in 1886. It has a 3-acre campus.

RATINGS
Admissions Selectivity Rating: 77   **Fire Safety Rating:** 60*   **Green Rating:** 60*

STUDENTS AND FACULTY
Enrollment: 623. **Student Body:** 61% female, 39% male, 36% out-of-state, 1% international (10 countries represented). Asian 6%, African American 2%, Caucasian 69%, Hispanic 6%, Native American 1%, Pacific Islander 0%, Two or more races 0%, Race unknown 15%. **Retention and Graduation:** 70% freshmen return for sophomore year. 10% grads go on to further study within 1 year. 10% grads pursue arts and sciences degrees. **Faculty:** Student/faculty ratio 13:1. 42 full-time faculty, 100% hold PhDs, 0% are are members of minority groups, 31% are women. 0% of classes are taught by teaching assistants.

ACADEMICS
Degrees: bachelor's, master's, postbachelor's certificate. **Classes:** Most classes have 10-19 students. **Special Study Options:** cooperative education program, cross-registration, distance learning, independent study, internships, study abroad, Off-Campus Study: Arts Program in New York. Co-Op Programs: Arts. **Disability Services:** Special programs offered to physically disabled students, including note-taking services, reader services, tape recorders, tutors. **Career Services:** Alumni services, Career assessment, Internships, On-campus interviews.

FACILITIES
Housing: Coed dorms, apartments for single students. 95% of campus accessible to physically diasbled. **Special Academic Facilities/Equipment:** Art gallery.

CAMPUS LIFE
Environment: Metropolis. **Activities:** radio station, student government, student-run film society. **On-Campus Highlights:** Main gallery, Student Center.

ADMISSIONS
Freshman Academic Profile: Average high school GPA 3.3. 89% from public high schools. **Reported SAT (pre-2016 redesign) scores:** SAT Math middle 50% range 430-604. SAT Critical Reading middle 50% range 503-680. SAT Writing middle 50% range 467-644. **Concordant SAT scores:** SAT EBRW middle 50% 540–700. SAT Math middle 50% range 470–620. ACT middle 50% range 21-27. Minimum paper TOEFL 550. **Basis for Candidate Selection:** *Very important factors considered include:* academic GPA, standardized test scores, application essay, recommendation(s), talent/ability. *Important factors considered include:* interview, character/personal qualities. *Other factors considered include:* rigor of secondary school record. **Freshman Admission Requirements:** High school diploma is required and GED is accepted. *Academic units recommended:* 4 English, 4 social studies, 4 history, 4 visual/

performing arts. **Freshman Admission Statistics:** 406 applied, 63.55% admitted, 33% enrolled. **Transfer Admission Requirements:** High school transcript, college transcript(s), essay or personal statement, standardized test scores, Minimum college GPA of 2.5 required. Lowest grade transferable C-. **General Admission Information:** Application fee $50. Priority deadline 2/15. Regular application deadline 5/1. Nonfall registration accepted.

COSTS AND FINANCIAL AID

Annual tuition $31,450. Required fees $200. Average book expense $2,724. **Required Forms and Deadlines:** FAFSA. **Notification of Awards:** Applicants will be notified of awards on a rolling basis beginning 3/1. **Types of Aid:** *Need-based scholarships/grants:* Federal Pell, FSEOG, State scholarships/grants, Private scholarships, College/university scholarship or grant aid from institutional funds. *Loans:* Direct Subsidized Stafford Loans, Direct Unsubsidized Stafford Loans, Direct PLUS loans, Federal Perkins Loans, State Loans. *Student Employment:* Federal Work-Study Program available. Institutional employment available. **Financial Aid Statistics:** 99% needy freshmen, 96% needy undergrads receive need-based scholarship or grant aid. 3% freshmen, 4% undergrads receive non-need-based scholarship or grant aid. 97% freshmen, 96% undergrads receive need-based self-help aid. 0% freshmen, 0% undergrads receive athletic scholarships. **Criteria for awarding aid:** *Need-based:* Academics, Art, Leadership, Minority status. *Non-need-based:* Academics, Alumni affiliation, Art, Leadership.

MINNESOTA STATE UNIVERSITY, MANKATO

122 Taylor Center, Mankato, MN 56001
Phone: 507-389-1822 • **Financial Aid Phone:** 507-389-1866
E-mail: admissions@mnsu.edu • **CEEB Code:** 6677
Fax: 507-389-1511 • **Website:** www.mnsu.edu • **ACT Code:** 2126

This public school was founded in 1868. It has a 354-acre campus.

RATINGS

Admissions Selectivity Rating: 75 **Fire Safety Rating:** 73 **Green Rating:** 60*

STUDENTS AND FACULTY

Enrollment: 12,149. **Student Body:** 52% female, 48% male, 7% international (77 countries represented). Asian 4%, African American 5%, Caucasian 75%, Hispanic 4%, Native American <1%, Pacific Islander <1%, Two or more races 3%, Race unknown 1%.
Retention and Graduation: 25% freshmen graduate within 4 years, **Faculty:** Student/faculty ratio 23:1. 487 full-time faculty, 92% hold PhDs, 17% are are members of minority groups, 49% are women.

ACADEMICS

Degrees: associate, bachelor's, certificate, doctoral, master's, postbachelor's certificate, post-master's certificate. **Classes:** Most classes have 20-29 students. Most lab/discussion sessions have 20-29 students. **Most popular majors:** Registered Nursing/Registered Nurse; Psychology; Business Administration and Management. **Special Study Options:** cross-registration, distance learning, double major, dual enrollment, English as a Second Language (ESL), exchange student program (domestic), external degree program, honors program, independent study, internships, student-designed major, study abroad, teacher certification program. **Disability Services:** Special programs offered to physically disabled students, including note-taking services, reader services, tape recorders. **Career Services:** Alumni network, Alumni services, Career/job search classes, Career assessment, Internships, Regional alumni. Career quick stop walk in hours for career advising.

FACILITIES

Housing: Coed dorms, special housing for disabled students. 90% of campus accessible to physically diasbled. **Special Academic Facilities/Equipment:** Two art galleries, day care facility, two astronomy observ- atories, main stage and studio theatres **Computers:** 100% of classrooms, 10% of dorms, 100% of libraries, 100% of dining areas, 100% of student union, 80% of common outdoor areas have wireless network access. Students can register for classes online. Administrative functions (other than registration) can be performed online.

CAMPUS LIFE

Environment: Town. **Activities:** Choral groups, concert band, dance, drama/theater, jazz band, literary magazine, music ensembles, musical theater, pep band, radio station, student government, student newspaper, symphony orchestra, Campus Ministries, Student Organization. 178 registered organizations, 18 honor societies, 15 religious organizations. 7 fraternities, 4 sororities. **Athletics (Intercollegiate):** *Men:* baseball, basketball, cross-country, diving, football, golf, ice hockey, swimming, tennis, track/field (outdoor), track/field (indoor), wrestling. *Women:* basketball, bowling, cross-country, diving,

golf, ice hockey, soccer, softball, swimming, tennis, track/field (outdoor), track/field (indoor), volleyball. **On-Campus Highlights:** Student Union, Myers Field House, Campus Recreation Center, Julia Sears Residence Hall, Memorial Library. **Environmental Initiatives:** Energy retrofit of building for lighting and motors

ADMISSIONS

Freshman Academic Profile: Average high school GPA 3.3. 7% in top 10% of high school class. ACT middle 50% range 20-24. Minimum internet-based TOEFL 61. Minimum paper TOEFL 500. **Basis for Candidate Selection:** *Very important factors considered include:* class rank, standardized test scores. *Other factors considered include:* academic GPA, recommendation(s). **Freshman Admission Requirements:** High school diploma is required and GED is accepted. *Academic units required:* 4 English, 3 math, 3 science, 3 science labs, 2 foreign language, 3 social studies, and 1 unit from above areas or other academic areas. **Freshman Admission Statistics:** 11,428 applied, 62.49% admitted, 34% enrolled. **Transfer Admission Requirements:** college transcript(s), statement of good standing from prior institution(s). Minimum college GPA of 2.0 required. Lowest grade transferable D. **General Admission Information:** Application fee $20. Nonfall registration not accepted. Admission may be deferred.

COSTS AND FINANCIAL AID

Annual in-state tuition $6,905. Annual out-of-state tuition $14,648. Room and board $8,716. Required fees $954. Average book expense $900. **Required Forms and Deadlines:** FAFSA. **Notification of Awards:** Applicants will be notified of awards on a rolling basis beginning 3/30. **Types of Aid:** *Need-based scholarships/grants:* Federal Pell, FSEOG, State scholarships/grants, Private scholarships, College/university scholarship or grant aid from institutional funds. *Loans:* Direct Subsidized Stafford Loans, Direct Unsubsidized Stafford Loans, Direct PLUS loans, Federal Perkins Loans, State Loans. *Student Employment:* Federal Work-Study Program available. Institutional employment available. **Financial Aid Statistics:** 68% needy freshmen, 67% needy undergrads receive need-based scholarship or grant aid. 38% freshmen, 24% undergrads receive non-need-based scholarship or grant aid. 98% freshmen, 96% undergrads receive need-based self-help aid. 1% freshmen, 0% undergrads receive athletic scholarships. 89% freshmen, 80% undergrads receive any aid. 74% undergrads borrow to pay for school. Average cumulative indebtedness $31,117. **Criteria for awarding aid:** *Need-based:* Academics, Minority status. *Non-need-based:* Academics, Art, Athletics, Leadership, Minority status, Music/drama.

MINNESOTA STATE UNIVERSITY MOORHEAD

1104 Seventh Avenue South, Moorhead, MN 56563
Phone: 218-477-2161 • **Financial Aid Phone:** 218-477-2251
E-mail: admissions@mnstate.edu • **CEEB Code:** 6678
Fax: 218-477-4374 • **Website:** www.mnstate.edu • **ACT Code:** 2134

This public school was founded in 1887. It has a 140-acre campus.

RATINGS

Admissions Selectivity Rating: 76 **Fire Safety Rating:** 60* **Green Rating:** 60*

STUDENTS AND FACULTY

Enrollment: 5,037. **Student Body:** 60% female, 40% male, 33% out-of-state, 7% international (56 countries represented). Asian 1%, African American 3%, Caucasian 78%, Hispanic 3%, Native American 1%, Pacific Islander <1%, Two or more races 3%, Race unknown 5%.
Retention and Graduation: 73% freshmen return for sophomore year. 23% freshmen graduate within 4 years. 41% freshmen graduate within 6 years. **Faculty:** Student/faculty ratio 17:1. 274 full-time faculty, 62% hold PhDs, 9% are are members of minority groups, 49% are women.

ACADEMICS

Degrees: associate, bachelor's, certificate, master's, postbachelor's certificate, post-master's certificate. **Classes:** Most classes have 20-29 students. Most lab/discussion sessions have 20-29 students. **Most popular majors:** Elementary Education and Teaching; Mass Communication/Media Studies; Business Administration and Management. **Special Study Options:** cross-registration, distance learning, double major, dual enrollment, exchange student program (domestic), external degree program, honors program, independent study, internships, student-designed major, study abroad, teacher certification program. **Honors Programs:** Honors Program to reward and encourage superior academic achievement. Combined degree programs: Dual degree programs w/University of MN in depts of chemistry & physics. **Disability Services:** Special programs offered to physically disabled students, including note-taking services, reader services, tape recorders, tutors. **Career Services:** Career/job search classes, Career assessment, Internships.

FACILITIES

Housing: Coed dorms, special housing for disabled students, men's dorms, women's dorms, apartments for single students, Theme Housing, Sorority housing. 95% of campus accessible to physically disabled. **Special Academic Facilities/Equipment:** Art and biology museums on-campus, planetarium, regional science center, Center for Business, new Science Building, Center for Business, Wellness Center **Computers:** Students can register for classes online. Administrative functions (other than registration) can be performed online.

CAMPUS LIFE

Environment: City. **Activities:** Choral groups, concert band, dance, drama/theater, jazz band, literary magazine, music ensembles, musical theater, radio station, student government, student newspaper, student-run film society, symphony orchestra, television station, Campus Ministries, Student Organization, Model UN. 109 registered organizations, 6 honor societies, 11 religious organizations. 2 sororities. **Athletics (Intercollegiate):** *Men:* basketball, cross-country, football, track/field (outdoor), track/field (indoor), wrestling. *Women:* basketball, cross-country, golf, soccer, softball, swimming, tennis, track/field (outdoor), track/field (indoor), volleyball. **On-Campus Highlights:** Underground Night Club, Comstock Memorial Student Union, Regional Science Center, Nemzek Athletic Complex, Planetarium, New Science Lab Building, New Wellness Center.

ADMISSIONS

Freshman Academic Profile: 10% in top 10% of high school class, 35% in top 25% of high school class, 74% in top 50% of high school class. **Reported SAT (pre-2016 redesign) scores:** SAT Math middle 50% range 480-570. SAT Critical Reading middle 50% range 445-520. **Concordant SAT scores:** SAT Math middle 50% range 510–590. ACT middle 50% range 20-25. Minimum paper TOEFL 500. **Basis for Candidate Selection:** *Very important factors considered include:* class rank, academic GPA, standardized test scores. *Other factors considered include:* rigor of secondary school record, application essay, recommendation(s). **Freshman Admission Requirements:** High school diploma is required and GED is accepted. *Academic units required:* 4 English, 3 math, 3 science, 1 science lab, 2 foreign language, 3 social studies, and 1 unit from above areas or other academic areas. **Freshman Admission Statistics:** 2,610 applied, 82.11% admitted, 34% enrolled. **Transfer Admission Requirements:** college transcript(s), statement of good standing from prior institution(s). Minimum college GPA of 2.0 required. Lowest grade transferable D. **General Admission Information:** Application fee $20. Regular application deadline 6/15. Nonfall registration accepted. Admission may be deferred for a maximum of one semester.

COSTS AND FINANCIAL AID

Annual in-state tuition $6,898. Annual out-of-state tuition $13,796. Room and board $7,398. Required fees $940. Average book expense $800. **Required Forms and Deadlines:** FAFSA, State aid form. **Types of Aid:** *Need-based scholarships/grants:* State scholarships/grants, Private scholarships, College/university scholarship or grant aid from institutional funds. *Loans:* Direct Subsidized Stafford Loans, Direct Unsubsidized Stafford Loans, Direct PLUS loans, Federal Perkins Loans, State Loans. *Student Employment:* Federal Work-Study Program available. Institutional employment available. **Financial Aid Statistics:** 66% needy freshmen, 67% needy undergrads receive need-based scholarship or grant aid. 58% freshmen, 30% undergrads receive non-need-based scholarship or grant aid. 93% freshmen, 94% undergrads receive need-based self-help aid. 0% freshmen, 0% undergrads receive athletic scholarships. 75% freshmen, 58% undergrads receive any aid. **Criteria for awarding aid:** *Non-need-based:* Academics, Athletics.

MISERICORDIA UNIVERSITY

301 Lake Street, Dallas, PA 18612
Phone: 570-674-6264 • **Financial Aid Phone:** 570-674-6222
E-mail: admiss@misericordia.edu • **CEEB Code:** 2087
Fax: 570-675-2441 • **Website:** www.misericordia.edu • **ACT Code:** 3539

This private school, affiliated with the Roman Catholic Church, was founded in 1924. It has a 120-acre campus.

RATINGS

Admissions Selectivity Rating: 80   **Fire Safety Rating:** 95   **Green Rating:** 60*

STUDENTS AND FACULTY

Enrollment: 2,148. **Student Body:** 67% female, 33% male, 25% out-of-state, <1% international (4 countries represented). Asian 1%, African American 3%, Caucasian 89%, Hispanic 3%, Native American <1%, Pacific Islander <1%, Two or more races 2%, Race unknown 1%.

Retention and Graduation: 82% freshmen return for sophomore year. 68% freshmen graduate within 4 years. 74% freshmen graduate within 6 years. 33% grads go on to further study within 1 year. 25% grads pursue arts and sciences degrees. 8% grads pursue business degrees. **Faculty:** Student/faculty ratio 11:1. 136 full-time faculty, 77% hold PhDs, 10% are are members of minority groups, 57% are women. 0% of classes are taught by teaching assistants.

ACADEMICS

Degrees: bachelor's, certificate, doctoral/professional, master's, postbachelor's certificate, post-master's certificate. **Classes:** Most classes have 10-19 students. Most lab/discussion sessions have 10-19 students. **Most popular majors:** Registered Nursing/Registered Nurse; Business Administration and Management; Health/Health Care Administration/Management. **Special Study Options:** Accelerated program, cross-registration, distance learning, double major, dual enrollment, honors program, independent study, internships, student-designed major, study abroad, teacher certification program, weekend college. **Honors Programs:** The Honors Program is an interdisciplinary community of undergraduate students and faculty working together to create an intellectually stimulating and challenging environment for learning. Honors students take a common sequence of core curriculum courses in place of regular core offerings, participate each semester in our Honors Explorations Seminar, and procuce a professional quality paper or project as part of the Honors Capstone. Combined degree programs: BS/MSOT and BS/MSSLP. **Disability Services:** Special programs offered to physically disabled students, including tape recorders, tutors. **Career Services:** Alumni network, Alumni services, Career/job search classes, Career assessment, Internships, Regional alumni.

FACILITIES

Housing: Coed dorms, Leadership House, Women with Children House. 100% of campus accessible to physically diasbled. **Computers:** 5% of classrooms, 100% of libraries, 100% of dining areas, 100% of student union, 10% of common outdoor areas have wireless network access. Students can register for classes online. Administrative functions (other than registration) can be performed online.

CAMPUS LIFE

Environment: Town. **Activities:** Choral groups, dance, drama/theater, jazz band, literary magazine, music ensembles, radio station, student government, student newspaper, television station, yearbook, Campus Ministries. 27 registered organizations, 1 honor society, 1 religious organization. **Athletics (Intercollegiate):** *Men:* baseball, basketball, cross-country, golf, lacrosse, soccer, swimming, tennis, track/field (outdoor). *Women:* basketball, cheerleading, cross-country, field hockey, lacrosse, soccer, softball, swimming, tennis, track/field (outdoor), volleyball. **On-Campus Highlights:** Anderson Sports and Health Center, Banks Student Life Center, Mangelsdorf Field, Bevevino Library.

ADMISSIONS

Freshman Academic Profile: Average high school GPA 3.3. 18% in top 10% of high school class, 40% in top 25% of high school class, 77% in top 50% of high school class. 82% from public high schools. **Reported SAT (pre-2016 redesign) scores:** SAT Math middle 50% range 480-570. SAT Critical Reading middle 50% range 470-570. **Concordant SAT scores:** SAT Math middle 50% range 510–590. ACT middle 50% range 22-26. Minimum paper TOEFL 500. **Basis for Candidate Selection:** *Very important factors considered include:* rigor of secondary school record, academic GPA, standardized test scores, character/personal qualities. *Important factors considered include:* class rank, extracurricular activities, volunteer work. *Other factors considered include:* application essay, recommendation(s), interview, work experience. **Freshman Admission Requirements:** High school diploma is required and GED is accepted. *Academic units required:* 4 English, 4 math, 4 science, 4 social studies. **Freshman Admission Statistics:** 1,823 applied, 74.44% admitted, 32% enrolled. **Transfer Admission Requirements:** college transcript(s), Minimum college GPA of 2.0 required. Lowest grade transferable C. **General Admission Information:** Application fee $35. Nonfall registration accepted. Admission may be deferred for a maximum of 12 months.

COSTS AND FINANCIAL AID

Annual tuition $30,030. Room and board $13,550. Required fees $1,630. Average book expense $1,250. **Required Forms and Deadlines:** FAFSA, Institution's own financial aid form. **Notification of Awards:** Applicants will be notified of awards on a rolling basis beginning 3/15. **Types of Aid:** *Need-based scholarships/grants:* Federal Pell, FSEOG, State scholarships/grants, Private scholarships, College/university scholarship or grant aid from institutional funds, Federal Nursing Scholarships. *Loans:* Direct Subsidized Stafford Loans, Direct Unsubsidized Stafford Loans, Direct PLUS loans, Federal Perkins Loans, Federal Nursing Loans. *Student Employment:* Federal Work-Study Program available. Institutional employment available. **Financial Aid Statistics:** 99% needy freshmen, 100% needy undergrads receive need-based scholarship or grant aid. 18% freshmen, 17% undergrads receive non-need-based scholarship or grant aid. 80% freshmen, 79% undergrads receive need-based self-help aid. 0% freshmen, 0% undergrads receive athletic scholarships. 99% freshmen, 99%

undergrads receive any aid. 84% undergrads borrow to pay for school. Average cumulative indebtedness $42,686. **Criteria for awarding aid:** *Need-based:* Minority status. *Non-need-based:* Academics, Alumni affiliation, Leadership, Minority status, State/district residency.

MISSISSIPPI COLLEGE

Box 4026, Clinton, MS 39058-0001
Phone: 601-925-3800 • **Financial Aid Phone:** 601-925-3212
E-mail: enrollment-services@mc.edu • **CEEB Code:** 1477
Fax: 601-925-3950 • **Website:** http://www.mc.edu • **ACT Code:** 2214

This private school, affiliated with the Southern Baptist Church, was founded in 1826. It has a 320-acre campus.

RATINGS

Admissions Selectivity Rating: 86   **Fire Safety Rating:** 96   **Green Rating:** 60*

STUDENTS AND FACULTY

Enrollment: 3,030. **Student Body:** 61% female, 39% male, 24% out-of-state, 3% international (21 countries represented). Asian 1%, African American 24%, Caucasian 67%, Hispanic 2%, Native American 1%, Pacific Islander 0%, Two or more races 1%, Race unknown 1%.
Retention and Graduation: 73% freshmen return for sophomore year. 40% freshmen graduate within 4 years. 62% freshmen graduate within 6 years.
Faculty: Student/faculty ratio 15:1. 205 full-time faculty, 78% hold PhDs, 9% are are members of minority groups, 48% are women. 0% of classes are taught by teaching assistants.

ACADEMICS

Degrees: bachelor's, doctoral/professional, doctoral/research, master's, postbachelor's certificate, post-master's certificate. **Classes:** Most classes have 10-19 students. Most lab/discussion sessions have fewer than 10 students.
Most popular majors: Business Administration and Management; Biomedical Sciences; Elementary Education and Teaching. **Special Study Options:** Accelerated program, distance learning, double major, dual enrollment, English as a Second Language (ESL), honors program, independent study, internships, study abroad, teacher certification program, Academic remediation, Advance Placement credit, Work-Study program, Learning disabilities services. **Honors Programs:** Honors programs open to freshmen, sophomores, juniors, and seniors and administered by the Honors Council. Freshmen who have a high ACT score (established each year) are invited to participate in a program of study called Freshman Honors Seminar (IDS161), it is an interdisciplinary study dealing with contemporary issues and interests. Upperclassmen who maintain a high GPA may also participate in Sophomore and Senior Honors Seminars (IDS 261, 461). Successful completion of the Junior-Senior Honors Program leads to a degree "With Honors" or "With High Honors." Combined degree programs: BA/JD. **Disability Services:** Special programs offered to physically disabled students, including note-taking services, reader services, tape recorders, tutors. **Career Services:** Alumni services, Career/job search classes, Career assessment, Internships.

FACILITIES

Housing: special housing for disabled students, men's dorms, women's dorms, apartments for single students. 100% of campus accessible to physically diasbled. **Computers:** 60% of classrooms, 100% of dorms, 100% of libraries, 100% of dining areas, 60% of common outdoor areas have wireless network access. Students can register for classes online. Administrative functions (other than registration) can be performed online.

CAMPUS LIFE

Environment: Metropolis. **Activities:** Choral groups, concert band, dance, drama/theater, jazz band, literary magazine, marching band, music ensembles, musical theater, opera, radio station, student government, student newspaper, yearbook, Campus Ministries, Student Organization. 66 registered organizations, 22 honor societies, 6 religious organizations. 5 fraternities, 4 sororities. **Athletics (Intercollegiate):** *Men:* baseball, basketball, cross-country, football, golf, soccer, tennis, track/field (outdoor). *Women:* basketball, cheerleading, cross-country, equestrian sports, soccer, softball, tennis, track/field (outdoor), volleyball. **On-Campus Highlights:** Gore Gallery, Healthplex, Men's Rotunda and New Women's Residence Hall, Provine Chapel, Anderson Hall in BCR Student Center, Nelson Hall-Administration Building Robinson-Wright Field House.

ADMISSIONS

Freshman Academic Profile: Average high school GPA 3.4. 33% in top 10% of high school class, 57% in top 25% of high school class, 74% in top 50% of high school class. **Reported SAT (pre-2016 redesign) scores:** SAT Math middle 50% range 470-580. SAT Critical Reading middle 50% range 470-

613. **Concordant SAT scores:** SAT Math middle 50% range 510–600. ACT middle 50% range 20-27. Minimum internet-based TOEFL 69. **Basis for Candidate Selection:** *Very important factors considered include:* standardized test scores. *Important factors considered include:* rigor of secondary school record, extracurricular activities, character/personal qualities, level of applicant's interest. *Other factors considered include:* class rank, academic GPA, recommendation(s), interview, talent/ability, alumni/ae relation, volunteer work, work experience. **Freshman Admission Requirements:** High school diploma is required and GED is accepted. *Academic units recommended:* 4 English, 4 math, 4 science, 2 science labs, 1 foreign language, 2 social studies, 2 history, 1 visual/performing arts, and 2 units from above areas or other academic areas. **Freshman Admission Statistics:** 2,178 applied, 58.13% admitted, 38% enrolled. **Transfer Admission Requirements:** college transcript(s), essay or personal statement, statement of good standing from prior institution(s). Minimum college GPA of 2.0 required. Lowest grade transferable C. **General Admission Information:** Application fee $25. Priority deadline 5/1. Nonfall registration accepted. Admission may be deferred for a maximum of 1 year.

COSTS AND FINANCIAL AID

Annual tuition $14,120. Room and board $7,150. Required fees $748. Average book expense $1,100. **Required Forms and Deadlines:** FAFSA, State aid form. **Notification of Awards:** Applicants will be notified of awards on a rolling basis beginning 3/1. **Types of Aid:** *Need-based scholarships/grants:* Federal Pell, FSEOG, State scholarships/grants, Private scholarships, College/ university scholarship or grant aid from institutional funds. *Loans:* Direct Subsidized Stafford Loans, Direct Unsubsidized Stafford Loans, Direct PLUS loans, Federal Perkins Loans, Federal Nursing Loans, College/university loans from institutional funds. *Student Employment:* Federal Work-Study Program available. Institutional employment available. **Financial Aid Statistics:** 89% needy freshmen, 86% needy undergrads receive need-based scholarship or grant aid. 96% freshmen, 86% undergrads receive non-need-based scholarship or grant aid. 81% freshmen, 85% undergrads receive need-based self-help aid. 0% freshmen, 0% undergrads receive athletic scholarships. 98% freshmen, 94% undergrads receive any aid. **Criteria for awarding aid:** *Non-need-based:* Academics, Alumni affiliation, Art, Leadership, Music/drama, Religious affiliation.

MISSISSIPPI STATE UNIVERSITY

P. O. Box 6334, Mississippi State, MS 39762
Phone: 662-325-2224 • **Financial Aid Phone:** 662-325-2450
E-mail: admit@msstate.edu • **CEEB Code:** 1480
Fax: 662-325-1MSU • **Website:** www.msstate.edu • **ACT Code:** 2220

This public school was founded in 1878. It has a 4200-acre campus.

RATINGS

Admissions Selectivity Rating: 84   **Fire Safety Rating:** 91   **Green Rating:** 60*

STUDENTS AND FACULTY

Enrollment: 17,371. **Student Body:** 50% female, 50% male, 30% out-of-state, 1% international (84 countries represented). Asian 1%, African American 20%, Caucasian 72%, Hispanic 3%, Native American <1%, Pacific Islander <1%, Two or more races 2%, Race unknown <1%.
Retention and Graduation: 80% freshmen return for sophomore year.
Faculty: Student/faculty ratio 20:1. 918 full-time faculty, 80% hold PhDs, 17% are are members of minority groups, 40% are women.

ACADEMICS

Degrees: bachelor's, doctoral/professional, doctoral/research, doctoral, master's, post-master's certificate. **Classes:** Most classes have 20-29 students. Most lab/discussion sessions have fewer than 10 students. **Most popular majors:** Physical Education Teaching and Coaching; Business Administration and Management; Geology/Earth Science. **Special Study Options:** cooperative education program, distance learning, double major, dual enrollment, English as a Second Language (ESL), exchange student program (domestic), external degree program, honors program, independent study, internships, liberal arts/ career combination, student-designed major, study abroad, teacher certification program, weekend college. **Honors Programs:** University Honors Program Combined degree programs: DVM-PhD, DVM-MS, BS/MS, BA/MS, Landscape Arch/ Landscape Con. Main. **Disability Services:** Special programs offered to physically disabled students, including note-taking services, reader services, tape recorders, tutors. **Career Services:** Alumni network, Alumni services, Career/job search classes, Career assessment, Internships, Regional alumni. MSU offers a diversified Co-op program. Students are participating from several colleges and schools at the university.

FACILITIES

Housing: special housing for disabled students, men's dorms, women's dorms, fraternity/sorority housing, apartments for married students, apartments for single students, Theme Housing, co-residential. 95% of campus accessible to physically diasbled. **Special Academic Facilities/Equipment:** Geology, archeology, music, entomological museums; art gallery; flight research lab. **Computers:** 100% of classrooms, 100% of dorms, 100% of libraries, 100% of dining areas, 100% of student union, 100% of common outdoor areas have wireless network access. Students can register for classes online. Administrative functions (other than registration) can be performed online.

CAMPUS LIFE

Environment: Town. **Activities:** Choral groups, concert band, dance, drama/theater, jazz band, literary magazine, marching band, music ensembles, musical theater, pep band, radio station, student government, student newspaper, television station, yearbook, Campus Ministries, Student Organization, Model UN. 326 registered organizations, 42 honor societies, 30 religious organizations. 17 fraternities, 11 sororities. **Athletics (Intercollegiate):** *Men:* baseball, basketball, cheerleading, cross-country, football, golf, tennis, track/field (outdoor). *Women:* basketball, cheerleading, cross-country, golf, soccer, softball, tennis, track/field (outdoor), volleyball. **On-Campus Highlights:** Scott Field Stadium, Dudy Noble Field, Humphrey Coliseum, Barnes and Noble Campus Bookstore, Sanderson Student Recreation Center. **Environmental Initiatives:** Recycling.

ADMISSIONS

Freshman Academic Profile: Average high school GPA 3.4. 28% in top 10% of high school class, 56% in top 25% of high school class, 83% in top 50% of high school class. ACT middle 50% range 21-28. Minimum internet-based TOEFL 71. Minimum paper TOEFL 525. **Basis for Candidate Selection:** *Very important factors considered include:* academic GPA, standardized test scores. *Important factors considered include:* class rank. *Other factors considered include:* rigor of secondary school record. **Freshman Admission Requirements:** High school diploma is required and GED is accepted. *Academic units required:* 4 English, 3 math, 3 science, 2 science labs, 1 foreign language, 1 social studies, 2 history, 1 academic elective. *Academic units recommended:* 4 English, 4 math, 4 science, 2 science labs, 1 foreign language, 2 social studies, 2 history, 1 academic elective, 1 visual/performing arts. **Freshman Admission Statistics:** 13,930 applied, 70.83% admitted, 37% enrolled. **Transfer Admission Requirements:** college transcript(s), statement of good standing from prior institution(s). Minimum college GPA of 2.0 required. Lowest grade transferable D. **General Admission Information:** Application fee $40. Nonfall registration accepted.

COSTS AND FINANCIAL AID

Annual in-state tuition $7,780. Annual out-of-state tuition $20,900. Room and board $9,418. Average book expense $1,200. **Required Forms and Deadlines:** FAFSA, State aid form. **Notification of Awards:** Applicants will be notified of awards on a rolling basis beginning 12/1. **Types of Aid:** *Need-based scholarships/grants:* Federal Pell, FSEOG, State scholarships/grants, Private scholarships, College/university scholarship or grant aid from institutional funds, United Negro College Fund. *Loans:* Direct Subsidized Stafford Loans, Direct Unsubsidized Stafford Loans, Direct PLUS loans, Federal Perkins Loans, College/university loans from institutional funds. *Student Employment:* Federal Work-Study Program available. Institutional employment available. **Financial Aid Statistics:** 91% needy freshmen, 87% needy undergrads receive need-based scholarship or grant aid. 14% freshmen, 8% undergrads receive non-need-based scholarship or grant aid. 69% freshmen, 77% undergrads receive need-based self-help aid. 3% freshmen, 3% undergrads receive athletic scholarships. 57% undergrads borrow to pay for school. Average cumulative indebtedness $30,659. **Criteria for awarding aid:** *Need-based:* Academics, Alumni affiliation, Leadership, Minority status, Music/drama. *Non-need-based:* Academics, Alumni affiliation, Art, Athletics, Job skills, Leadership, Minority status, Music/drama, State/district residency.

STUDENTS AND FACULTY

Enrollment: 2,357. **Student Body:** 62% female, 38% male, 11% out-of-state, 0% international (2 countries represented). Asian 0%, African American 93%, Caucasian 4%, Hispanic 1%, Native American <1%, Pacific Islander 0%, Two or more races 0%, Race unknown 2%.
Retention and Graduation: 55% freshmen return for sophomore year. 18% freshmen graduate within 4 years. 35% freshmen graduate within 6 years.
Faculty: Student/faculty ratio 21:1. 133 full-time faculty, 58% hold PhDs, 30% are are members of minority groups, 46% are women. 0% of classes are taught by teaching assistants.

ACADEMICS

Degrees: bachelor's, master's. **Classes:** Most classes have fewer than 10 students. Most lab/discussion sessions have 20-29 students. **Most popular majors:** Kindergarten/Preschool Education and Teaching; Business, Management, Marketing, and Related Support Services; Social Work. **Special Study Options:** cooperative education program, distance learning, double major, honors program, internships, teacher certification program, weekend college, Co-Op Programs: Business, Computer Science, Natural Science, Social/Behavioral Science. **Disability Services:** Special programs offered to physically disabled students, including tape recorders, tutors. **Career Services:** Alumni services, On-campus interviews. Many of our students have received internships with the Environmental Protection Agency in Washington, DC.

FACILITIES

Housing: men's dorms, women's dorms, apartments for married students, apartments for single students. **Computers:** Students can register for classes online.

CAMPUS LIFE

Environment: Rural. **Activities:** Choral groups, concert band, drama/theater, marching band, radio station, student government, student newspaper, yearbook. 35 registered organizations, 19 honor societies, 4 religious organizations. 4 fraternities, 2 sororities. **Athletics (Intercollegiate):** *Men:* baseball, basketball, cross-country, football, golf, tennis, track/field (outdoor). *Women:* basketball, cross-country, golf, soccer, softball, tennis, track/field (outdoor), volleyball. **On-Campus Highlights:** Student Union, Student Pavillion, Administration Building, Library.

ADMISSIONS

Freshman Academic Profile: Average high school GPA 2.6. 0% in top 10% of high school class. 96% from public high schools. ACT middle 50% range 15-19. Minimum paper TOEFL 525. **Basis for Candidate Selection:** *Very important factors considered include:* rigor of secondary school record, class rank, standardized test scores, state residency. *Other factors considered include:* recommendation(s), interview, extracurricular activities, talent/ability. **Freshman Admission Requirements:** High school diploma is required and GED is accepted. *Academic units required:* 4 English, 3 math, 3 science, 2 science labs, 1 foreign language, 3 social studies, 2 academic electives, and 1 unit from above areas or other academic areas. *Academic units recommended:* 1 foreign language. **Freshman Admission Statistics:** 6,086 applied, 29.51% admitted, 23% enrolled. **Transfer Admission Requirements:** college transcript(s), Minimum college GPA of 2.0 required. Lowest grade transferable C. **General Admission Information:** Nonfall registration accepted.

COSTS AND FINANCIAL AID

Annual in-state tuition $4,575. Annual out-of-state tuition $11,410. Room and board $5,081. Required fees $25. Average book expense $1,400. **Required Forms and Deadlines:** FAFSA, Institution's own financial aid form. **Notification of Awards:** Applicants will be notified of awards on or about 7/15. **Types of Aid:** *Need-based scholarships/grants:* Federal Pell, FSEOG, State scholarships/grants, Private scholarships, College/university scholarship or grant aid from institutional funds. *Loans:* Direct Unsubsidized Stafford Loans, Direct PLUS loans. *Student Employment:* Federal Work-Study Program available. **Financial Aid Statistics:** 95% freshmen, 95% undergrads receive any aid.

MISSISSIPPI VALLEY STATE UNIVERSITY

14000 Highway 82 West, Itta Bena, MS 38941-1400
Phone: 662-254-3344 • **Financial Aid Phone:** 662-254-3338
E-mail: nbtaylor@mvsu.edu • **CEEB Code:** 1482
Fax: 662-254-3759 • **Website:** www.mvsu.edu • **ACT Code:** 2224

This public school was founded in 1950. It has a 250-acre campus.

RATINGS

Admissions Selectivity Rating: 76   **Fire Safety Rating:** 81   **Green Rating:** 60*

MISSOURI UNIVERSITY OF SCIENCE AND TECHNOLOGY

106 Parker Hall; 300 W. 13th Street, Rolla, MO 65409-1060
Phone: 573-341-4165 • **Financial Aid Phone:** 573-341-4282
E-mail: admissions@mst.edu • **CEEB Code:** 6876
Fax: 573-341-4082 • **Website:** www.mst.edu • **ACT Code:** 2398

This public school was founded in 1870. It has a 284-acre campus.

RATINGS
Admissions Selectivity Rating: 87   **Fire Safety Rating:** 88   **Green Rating:** 60*

STUDENTS AND FACULTY
Enrollment: 6,857. **Student Body:** 23% female, 77% male, 17% out-of-state, 4% international (60 countries represented). Asian 3%, African American 3%, Caucasian 80%, Hispanic 3%, Native American <1%, Pacific Islander <1%, Two or more races 3%, Race unknown 3%.
Retention and Graduation: 21% freshmen graduate within 4 years. 64% freshmen graduate within 6 years. **Faculty:** Student/faculty ratio 19:1. 374 full-time faculty, 93% hold PhDs, 33% are are members of minority groups, 26% are women. 12% of classes are taught by teaching assistants.

ACADEMICS
Degrees: bachelor's, doctoral/research, master's, postbachelor's certificate. **Classes:** Most classes have 20-29 students. Most lab/discussion sessions have 10-19 students. **Most popular majors:** Civil Engineering; Electrical and Electronics Engineering; Mechanical Engineering. **Special Study Options:** distance learning, double major, dual enrollment, English as a Second Language (ESL), honors program, independent study, internships, liberal arts/career combination, study abroad, teacher certification program. **Honors Programs:** Honors Academy and Master Student Fellowship Programs- http://ugs.mst.edu/honors.html Combined degree programs: BA/MEng. **Disability Services:** Special programs offered to physically disabled students, including note-taking services, reader services, tape recorders, tutors. **Career Services:** Alumni network, Alumni services, Career/job search classes, Career assessment, Internships, Regional alumni. COOPERATIVE EDUCATION AT MISSOURI UNIVERSITY OF SCIENCE AND TECHNOLOGY (S&T) S&T's formal Cooperative Education Program (co-op) has been in existence since 1961. Over the years, thousands of students have participated in co-op, and many have led to full-time job offers. The co-op program, though voluntary, has had record participation in the past two years, with 367 individual students on spring or fall co-op in 2012-2013, and 379 in 2013-2014. Students maintain a full-time student status while on co-op, and have the option to take it for credit through their departments. Studies have shown that approximately 70% of students who have reported full-time career plans to Career Opportunities & Employer Relations upon graduation have participated in a co-op prior to graduation.

FACILITIES
Housing: Coed dorms, special housing for disabled students, fraternity/sorority housing, apartments for married students, cooperative housing, apartments for single students, Wellness Housing, Theme Housing. 95% of campus accessible to physically diasbled. **Special Academic Facilities/Equipment:** Writing Center, Student Design Center, Nuclear Reactor, Observatory, Explosives Testing Lab, Underground Mine, Museum of Rocks, Minerals, and Gemstones, Centers for Environmental Research, Water Resources, Industrial Research, and Rock Mechanics Research, Geophysical Observatory, Computerized Manufacturing System, Millenium Arch, and Stonehenge. **Computers:** 100% of classrooms, 100% of dorms, 100% of libraries, 66% of dining areas, 100% of student union, 80% of common outdoor areas have wireless network access. Students can register for classes online. Administrative functions (other than registration) can be performed online.

CAMPUS LIFE
Environment: Village. **Activities:** Choral groups, concert band, dance, drama/theater, jazz band, literary magazine, marching band, music ensembles, musical theater, pep band, radio station, student government, student newspaper, symphony orchestra, yearbook, Campus Ministries, Student Organization. 202 registered organizations, 29 honor societies, 13 religious organizations. 21 fraternities, 4 sororities. **Athletics (Intercollegiate):** *Men:* baseball, basketball, cross-country, football, soccer, swimming, track/field (outdoor), track/field (indoor). *Women:* basketball, cross-country, soccer, softball, track/field (outdoor), track/field (indoor), volleyball. **On-Campus Highlights:** Havener Student Center, Residential College, Student Design Team Center, Castleman Performing Arts Center, Student Recreation Center. **Environmental Initiatives:** Reducing amount of paper being consumed.

ADMISSIONS
Freshman Academic Profile: Average high school GPA 3.6. 33% in top 10% of high school class, 78% in top 25% of high school class, 97% in top 50% of high school class. 85% from public high schools. **Reported SAT (pre-2016 redesign) scores:** SAT Math middle 50% range 603-698. SAT Critical Reading middle 50% range 583-678. SAT Writing middle 50% range 493-630. **Concordant SAT scores:** SAT EBRW middle 50% 600–700. SAT Math middle 50% range 620–730. ACT middle 50% range 25-31. Minimum internet-based TOEFL 79. Minimum paper TOEFL 550. **Basis for Candidate Selection:** *Very important factors considered include:* rigor of secondary school record, class rank, academic GPA, standardized test scores. *Important factors considered include:* recommendation(s). *Other factors considered include:* application essay, interview, extracurricular activities, talent/ability, character/personal qualities, volunteer work, work experience, level of applicant's interest. **Freshman Admission Requirements:** High school diploma is required and GED is accepted. *Academic units required:* 4 English, 4 math, 3 science, 1 science lab, 2 foreign language, 3 social studies, 1 visual/performing arts. **Freshman Admission Statistics:** 4,166 applied, 79.33% admitted, 45% enrolled. **Transfer Admission Requirements:** college transcript(s), Minimum college GPA of 2.5 required. **General Admission Information:** Application fee $50. Priority deadline 12/1. Regular application deadline 7/1. Nonfall registration accepted. Admission may be deferred for a maximum of 2 year.

COSTS AND FINANCIAL AID
Annual in-state tuition $8,220. Annual out-of-state tuition $23,385. Room and board $9,145. Required fees $1,290. Average book expense $896. **Required Forms and Deadlines:** FAFSA. **Types of Aid:** *Need-based scholarships/grants:* Federal Pell, FSEOG, State scholarships/grants, Private scholarships, College/university scholarship or grant aid from institutional funds. *Loans:* Federal Perkins Loans, State Loans, College/university loans from institutional funds. *Student Employment:* Federal Work-Study Program available. Institutional employment available. **Financial Aid Statistics:** 95% needy freshmen, 92% needy undergrads receive need-based scholarship or grant aid. 33% freshmen, 36% undergrads receive non-need-based scholarship or grant aid. 100% freshmen, 100% undergrads receive need-based self-help aid. 5% freshmen, 5% undergrads receive athletic scholarships. 91% freshmen, 85% undergrads receive any aid. 75% undergrads borrow to pay for school. Average cumulative indebtedness $28,259. **Criteria for awarding aid:** *Need-based:* Job skills, Minority status. *Non-need-based:* Academics, Alumni affiliation, Athletics, Job skills, Leadership, Minority status, Music/drama, Religious affiliation, State/district residency.

MISSOURI VALLEY COLLEGE

500 East College Street, Marshall, MO 65340
Phone: 660-831-4114
E-mail: admissions@moval.edu
Fax: 660-831-4233 • **Website:** www.moval.edu • **ACT Code:** 2330

This private school, affiliated with the Presbyterian Church, was founded in 1889. It has a 150-acre campus.

RATINGS
Admissions Selectivity Rating: 78   **Fire Safety Rating:** 62   **Green Rating:** 60*

STUDENTS AND FACULTY
Enrollment: 1,418. **Student Body:** 42% female, 58% male, 34% out-of-state, 8% international (43 countries represented). Asian 4%, African American 14%, Caucasian 71%, Hispanic 4%, Native American 1%, Pacific Islander 0%, Two or more races 0%, Race unknown 0%.
Retention and Graduation: 45% freshmen return for sophomore year. 11% freshmen graduate within 4 years. 29% freshmen graduate within 6 years. 20% grads go on to further study within 1 year. **Faculty:** Student/faculty ratio 18:1. 66 full-time faculty, 53% hold PhDs, 3% are are members of minority groups, 35% are women. 0% of classes are taught by teaching assistants.

ACADEMICS
Degrees: associate, bachelor's, master's. **Classes:** Most classes have 20-29 students. Most lab/discussion sessions have 20-29 students. **Most popular majors:** Elementary Education and Teaching; Criminal Justice/Law Enforcement Administration; Business/Commerce. **Special Study Options:** double major, dual enrollment, internships, teacher certification program. **Disability Services:** Special programs offered to physically disabled students, including reader services, tutors. **Career Services:** Internships. Many of our majors require the completion of an internship.

FACILITIES

Housing: men's dorms, women's dorms, fraternity/sorority housing, apartments for married students, apartments for single students.

CAMPUS LIFE

Environment: Rural. **Activities:** Choral groups, dance, drama/theater, literary magazine, music ensembles, musical theater, pep band, radio station, student government, student newspaper, television station, yearbook. 28 registered organizations, 8 honor societies, 7 religious organizations. 4 fraternities, 2 sororities. **Athletics (Intercollegiate):** *Men:* baseball, basketball, cheerleading, cross-country, football, golf, rodeo, soccer, tennis, track/field (outdoor), track/field (indoor), volleyball, wrestling. *Women:* basketball, cheerleading, cross-country, golf, rodeo, soccer, softball, tennis, track/field (outdoor), track/field (indoor), volleyball, wrestling. **On-Campus Highlights:** Burns Gym, Eckilson-Mabee Theater, Black Box Theater, Student Lounge (basement of MacDonald Hall), Tech Center Computer Lab.

ADMISSIONS

Freshman Academic Profile: Average high school GPA 2.9. 4% in top 10% of high school class, 38% in top 25% of high school class, 54% in top 50% of high school class. **Reported SAT (pre-2016 redesign) scores:** SAT Math middle 50% range 412-597. SAT Critical Reading middle 50% range 372-537. **Concordant SAT scores:** SAT Math middle 50% range 450–620. ACT middle 50% range 19-27. Minimum paper TOEFL 450. **Basis for Candidate Selection:** *Very important factors considered include:* interview, character/personal qualities. *Important factors considered include:* extracurricular activities, talent/ability, volunteer work. *Other factors considered include:* rigor of secondary school record, class rank, standardized test scores, recommendation(s), alumni/ae relation, work experience. **Freshman Admission Requirements:** High school diploma is required and GED is accepted. *Academic units recommended:* 4 English, 3 math, 2 science, 1 science lab, 2 social studies, 2 history, 3 academic electives. **Freshman Admission Statistics:** 1,345 applied, 66.77% admitted, 45% enrolled. **Transfer Admission Requirements:** High school transcript, college transcript(s), standardized test scores, Minimum college GPA of 2.0 required. Lowest grade transferable C. **General Admission Information:** Application fee $15. Priority deadline 3/1. Regular application deadline 9/1. Nonfall registration accepted.

COSTS AND FINANCIAL AID

Annual tuition $18,500. Room and board $8,400. Required fees $1,250. Average book expense $1,300. **Required Forms and Deadlines:** FAFSA, State aid form. **Types of Aid:** *Need-based scholarships/grants:* Federal Pell, FSEOG, State scholarships/grants, Private scholarships, College/university scholarship or grant aid from institutional funds. *Loans:* Federal Perkins Loans. *Student Employment:* Federal Work-Study Program available. Institutional employment available. **Financial Aid Statistics:** 100% needy freshmen, 100% needy undergrads receive need-based scholarship or grant aid. 100% freshmen, 100% undergrads receive non-need-based scholarship or grant aid. 87% freshmen, 87% undergrads receive need-based self-help aid. 0% freshmen, 0% undergrads receive athletic scholarships. 98% freshmen, 92% undergrads receive any aid.

MITCHELL COLLEGE

437 Pequot Avenue, New London, CT 6320
Phone: 860-701-5011 • **Financial Aid Phone:** 800-443-2811
E-mail: admissions@mitchell.edu • **CEEB Code:** 3528
Fax: 860-444-1209 • **Website:** http://www.mitchell.edu/ • **ACT Code:** 572

This private school was founded in 1938. It has a 68-acre campus.

RATINGS

Admissions Selectivity Rating: 70 **Fire Safety Rating:** 72 **Green Rating:** 60*

STUDENTS AND FACULTY

Enrollment: 785. **Student Body:** 47% female, 53% male, 42% out-of-state, <1% international. Asian 2%, African American 11%, Caucasian 68%, Hispanic 13%, Native American 1%, Pacific Islander 0%, Two or more races 4%, Race unknown 2%.
Retention and Graduation: 57% freshmen return for sophomore year.
Faculty: Student/faculty ratio 14:1. 35 full-time faculty, 74% hold PhDs, 0% are are members of minority groups, 51% are women. 0% of classes are taught by teaching assistants.

ACADEMICS

Degrees: associate, bachelor's. **Special Study Options:** dual enrollment, English as a Second Language (ESL), internships, teacher certification program. **Disability Services:** Special programs offered to physically disabled students, including note-taking services, reader services, tape recorders, tutors. **Career Services:** Career assessment, On-campus interviews.

FACILITIES

Housing: Coed dorms, special housing for disabled students, Four residence halls are Victorian and Colonial houses located on the waterfront. Three other residence halls are of traditional design. 50% of campus accessible to physically diasbled. **Special Academic Facilities/Equipment:** Private dock w/fleet of sailboats, 2 private beaches, 26 acres of woods.

CAMPUS LIFE

Environment: Town. **Activities:** Choral groups, dance, drama/theater, literary magazine, student government, student newspaper, yearbook. 30 registered organizations, 2 honor societies, 2 religious organizations. **Athletics (Intercollegiate):** *Men:* baseball, basketball, cross-country, golf, lacrosse, soccer, tennis. *Women:* basketball, cross-country, golf, soccer, softball, tennis, volleyball.

ADMISSIONS

Freshman Academic Profile: Average high school GPA 2.7. Minimum paper TOEFL 500. **Basis for Candidate Selection:** *Very important factors considered include:* academic GPA, interview. *Important factors considered include:* rigor of secondary school record, application essay, recommendation(s), extracurricular activities, character/personal qualities, volunteer work, level of applicant's interest. *Other factors considered include:* standardized test scores, talent/ability, alumni/ae relation, work experience. **Freshman Admission Requirements:** High school diploma is required and GED is accepted. *Academic units recommended:* 4 English, 3 math, 3 science, 2 social studies, 2 history, 2 academic electives. **Freshman Admission Statistics:** 1,041 applied, 59.65% admitted, 24% enrolled. **Transfer Admission Requirements:** High school transcript, college transcript(s), essay or personal statement, standardized test scores, Minimum college GPA of 2.0 required. Lowest grade transferable C-. **General Admission Information:** Application fee $30. Priority deadline 4/1. Nonfall registration accepted. Admission may be deferred for a maximum of 1 year.

COSTS AND FINANCIAL AID

Annual tuition $26,774. Room and board $12,492. Required fees $1,720. Average book expense $1,500. **Required Forms and Deadlines:** FAFSA. **Notification of Awards:** Applicants will be notified of awards on a rolling basis beginning 3/1. **Types of Aid:** *Need-based scholarships/grants:* Federal Pell, FSEOG, State scholarships/grants, Private scholarships, College/university scholarship or grant aid from institutional funds. *Loans:* Direct Subsidized Stafford Loans, Direct Unsubsidized Stafford Loans, Direct PLUS loans, Federal Perkins Loans. *Student Employment:* Federal Work-Study Program available. Institutional employment available. **Financial Aid Statistics:** 100% needy freshmen, 99% needy undergrads receive need-based scholarship or grant aid. 93% freshmen, 87% undergrads receive non-need-based scholarship or grant aid. 93% freshmen, 95% undergrads receive need-based self-help aid. 0% freshmen, 0% undergrads receive athletic scholarships. **Criteria for awarding aid:** *Non-need-based:* Academics, Alumni affiliation, Art, Leadership.

MOLLOY COLLEGE

1000 Hempstead Avenue, Rockville Centre, NY 11570
Phone: 516-323-4000 • **Financial Aid Phone:** 516-323-4209
E-mail: admissions@molloy.edu • **CEEB Code:** 2415
Website: http://www.molloy.edu/ • **ACT Code:** 2820

This private school, affiliated with the Roman Catholic Church, was founded in 1955. It has a 35-acre campus.

RATINGS

Admissions Selectivity Rating: 79 **Fire Safety Rating:** 99 **Green Rating:** 60*

STUDENTS AND FACULTY

Enrollment: 3,373. **Student Body:** 75% female, 25% male, 3% out-of-state, <1% international (9 countries represented). Asian 7%, African American 12%, Caucasian 60%, Hispanic 15%, Native American <1%, Pacific Islander <1%, Two or more races 1%, Race unknown 3%.
Retention and Graduation: 88% freshmen return for sophomore year. 47% freshmen graduate within 4 years. 71% freshmen graduate within 6 years.
Faculty: Student/faculty ratio 10:1. 186 full-time faculty, 77% hold PhDs, 18% are are members of minority groups, 76% are women. 0% of classes are taught by teaching assistants.

ACADEMICS

Degrees: associate, bachelor's, doctoral/research, master's, post-master's certificate. **Classes:** Most classes have 10-19 students. Most lab/discussion sessions have 10-19 students. **Most popular majors:** Registered Nursing/Registered Nurse; Accounting; Psychology. **Special Study Options:** double major, English as a Second Language (ESL), honors program, independent study, internships, liberal arts/career combination, student-designed major, study abroad, teacher certification program. Combined degree programs: BS/MS. **Disability Services:** Special programs offered to physically disabled students, including note-taking services, reader services, tape recorders, tutors. **Career Services:** Alumni network, Alumni services, Internships, Regional alumni.

FACILITIES

Housing: 100% of campus accessible to physically diasbled. **Special Academic Facilities/Equipment:** Professional Repertory Theatre Company in residence, dance studio, institute of cross-cultural and cross-ethnic studies, institute of gerontology, cablevision studio. **Computers:** 100% of classrooms, 100% of libraries, 100% of dining areas, 100% of student union, 100% of common outdoor areas have wireless network access. Students can register for classes online. Administrative functions (other than registration) can be performed online.

CAMPUS LIFE

Environment: Village. **Activities:** Choral groups, dance, drama/theater, jazz band, literary magazine, music ensembles, student government, student newspaper, yearbook, Campus Ministries. 21 registered organizations, 18 honor societies, 1 religious organization. **Athletics (Intercollegiate):** *Men:* baseball, basketball, cross-country, lacrosse, soccer, track/field (outdoor), track/field (indoor). *Women:* basketball, cross-country, lacrosse, soccer, softball, tennis, track/field (outdoor), track/field (indoor), volleyball. **On-Campus Highlights:** The Anselma Room, The Fitness Center, Center for Social and Ethical Concerns, Media Center **Environmental Initiatives:** The Sustainability Institute at Molloy College http://www.molloy.edu/si/index.asp.

ADMISSIONS

Freshman Academic Profile: Average high school GPA 3.0. 17% in top 10% of high school class, 56% in top 25% of high school class, 83% in top 50% of high school class. 51% from public high schools. **Reported SAT (pre-2016 redesign) scores:** SAT Math middle 50% range 490-580. SAT Critical Reading middle 50% range 480-570. SAT Writing middle 50% range 470-560. **Concordant SAT scores:** SAT EBRW middle 50% range 530–620. SAT Math middle 50% range 520–600. ACT middle 50% range 21-26. Minimum internet-based TOEFL 79. Minimum paper TOEFL 550. **Basis for Candidate Selection:** *Very important factors considered include:* rigor of secondary school record, academic GPA, standardized test scores. *Other factors considered include:* class rank, application essay, recommendation(s), interview, extracurricular activities, talent/ability, volunteer work, work experience. **Freshman Admission Requirements:** High school diploma is required and GED is accepted. *Academic units required:* 4 English, 3 math, 3 science, 3 foreign language, 4 social studies. *Academic units recommended:* 4 English, 4 math, 4 science, 3 foreign language, 4 social studies. **Freshman Admission Statistics:** 3,550 applied, 75.52% admitted, 20% enrolled. **Transfer Admission Requirements:** college transcript(s), Minimum college GPA of 2.0 required. Lowest grade transferable c. **General Admission Information:** Application fee $40. Nonfall registration accepted. Admission may be deferred for a maximum of 1 Year.

COSTS AND FINANCIAL AID

Annual tuition $28,000. Room and board $14,250. Required fees $1,100. Average book expense $1,470. **Required Forms and Deadlines:** FAFSA, State aid form. **Notification of Awards:** Applicants will be notified of awards on a rolling basis beginning 2/1. **Types of Aid:** *Need-based scholarships/grants:* Federal Pell, FSEOG, State scholarships/grants, Private scholarships, College/university scholarship or grant aid from institutional funds, Federal Nursing Scholarships. *Loans:* Direct Subsidized Stafford Loans, Direct Unsubsidized Stafford Loans, Direct PLUS loans, Federal Perkins Loans, Federal Nursing Loans, State Loans. *Student Employment:* Federal Work-Study Program available. **Financial Aid Statistics:** 97% needy freshmen, 93% needy undergrads receive need-based scholarship or grant aid. 7% freshmen, 6% undergrads receive non-need-based scholarship or grant aid. 88% freshmen, 85% undergrads receive need-based self-help aid. 1% freshmen, 2% undergrads receive athletic scholarships. 97% freshmen, 79% undergrads receive any aid. 76% undergrads borrow to pay for school. Average cumulative indebtedness $34,078. **Criteria for awarding aid:** *Non-need-based:* Academics, Alumni affiliation, Art, Athletics, Leadership, Music/drama, Religious affiliation.

MONMOUTH COLLEGE

700 East Broadway, Monmouth, IL 61462
Phone: 309-457-2131 • **Financial Aid Phone:** 309-457-2129
E-mail: admissions@monmouthcollege.edu • **CEEB Code:** 1484
Fax: 309-457-2141 • **Website:** www.monmouthcollege.edu • **ACT Code:** 1084

This private school, affiliated with the Presbyterian Church, was founded in 1853. It has a 80-acre campus.

RATINGS
Admissions Selectivity Rating: 79   **Fire Safety Rating:** 90   **Green Rating:** 82

STUDENTS AND FACULTY
Enrollment: 1,174. **Student Body:** 52% female, 48% male, 9% out-of-state, 6% international (35 countries represented). Asian 2%, African American 10%, Caucasian 63%, Hispanic 12%, Native American 1%, Pacific Islander 0%, Two or more races 2%, Race unknown 5%.
Retention and Graduation: 74% freshmen return for sophomore year. 48% freshmen graduate within 4 years. 58% freshmen graduate within 6 years. 15% grads go on to further study within 1 year. 10% grads pursue arts and sciences degrees. 1% grads pursue law degrees. 1% grads pursue medical degrees.
Faculty: Student/faculty ratio 11:1. 92 full-time faculty, 88% hold PhDs, 5% are are members of minority groups, 42% are women. 0% of classes are taught by teaching assistants.

ACADEMICS
Degrees: bachelor's. **Classes:** Most classes have 20-29 students. Most lab/discussion sessions have 10-19 students. **Most popular majors:** Speech Communication and Rhetoric; Business Administration and Management; Psychology. **Special Study Options:** double major, English as a Second Language (ESL), exchange student program (domestic), honors program, independent study, internships, student-designed major, study abroad, teacher certification program. **Honors Programs:** The Monmouth Coillege Honors Program is intended for a select group of academically well-prepared and intellectually ambitious students. Acceptance into the program is determined competitively,normally occurring at the end of the first semester of the freshman year. The program consists of three levels: exploration of the history of the liberal arts as a field of inquiry, in-depth seminars upon historically significant persons, events, movements and ideas, and a senior capstone course. Combined degree programs: 5- and 6-year agreements in nursing, phys. therapy, med. tech. **Disability Services:** Special programs offered to physically disabled students, including note-taking services, reader services, tape recorders, tutors. **Career Services:** Alumni network, Alumni services, Career/job search classes, Career assessment, Internships, Regional alumni. All Monmouth students are encouraged to add internships to their resumes. Some internships are credit-bearing (when they are closely connected to the student's major). The Career Center provides pre-internship orientation to professional office conduct, placement advising, maintenance of contacts with internship sponsors, and quality-control oversight of internship experiences. The Career Center coordinates closely with academic departments in selecting internships and in assisting students with placement.

FACILITIES
Housing: Coed dorms, special housing for disabled students, men's dorms, special housing for international students, women's dorms, fraternity/sorority housing, apartments for single students, Wellness Housing, Theme Housing. 98% of campus accessible to physically diasbled. **Special Academic Facilities/Equipment:** Shields Art & Antiquities Collection, Wackerle Career & Leadership Center, Mellinger Teaching & Learning Center, MC-TV (student-run television station), WMCR (student-run radio station.) **Computers:** 100% of classrooms, 100% of dorms, 100% of libraries, 100% of dining areas, 100% of student union, 80% of common outdoor areas have wireless network access. Students can register for classes online. Administrative functions (other than registration) can be performed online.

CAMPUS LIFE
Environment: Village. **Activities:** Choral groups, concert band, dance, drama/theater, jazz band, literary magazine, marching band, music ensembles, musical theater, radio station, student government, student newspaper, symphony orchestra, television station, Campus Ministries, Student Organization. 67 registered organizations, 16 honor societies, 6 religious organizations. 4 fraternities, 3 sororities. **Athletics (Intercollegiate):** *Men:* baseball, basketball, cross-country, diving, football, golf, soccer, swimming, tennis, track/field (outdoor), track/field (indoor). *Women:* basketball, cross-country, diving, golf, soccer, softball, swimming, tennis, track/field (outdoor), track/field (indoor), volleyball. **On-Campus Highlights:** Stockdale Student Center, Hewes Library (including coffee shop!), Huff Athletic Center, Mellinger Teaching and Learning Center, Wallace Hall—main floor coffee/study, The nature trail at LeSuer Nature Preserve offers many opportunities for recreation

434   *The Princeton Review's* Complete Book of Colleges

and scientific study. The new Monmouth College athletic fields are available for team practice, of course, but also open to ad hoc student groups and individuals. **Environmental Initiatives:** The College has a comprehensive recycling and waste diversion program. Recycling receptacles are provided for paper, glass, plastic and aluminum in every office and every bedroom in all academic buildings and residence halls, with a recycling center for electronics, flourescent lights and cell phones in the Stockdale Center (the student center). All cardboard generated at the dining service is recycled. A fleet of 5 hybrid cars are used by Monmouth faculty and staff for college purposes.

ADMISSIONS

Freshman Academic Profile: Average high school GPA 3.3. 13% in top 10% of high school class, 36% in top 25% of high school class, 70% in top 50% of high school class. 80% from public high schools. ACT middle 50% range 20-26. Minimum internet-based TOEFL 79. Minimum paper TOEFL 550. **Basis for Candidate Selection:** *Very important factors considered include:* rigor of secondary school record. *Important factors considered include:* class rank, academic GPA, standardized test scores. *Other factors considered include:* application essay, recommendation(s), interview, extracurricular activities, talent/ability, character/personal qualities, alumni/ae relation, volunteer work, level of applicant's interest. **Freshman Admission Requirements:** High school diploma is required and GED is accepted. *Academic units required:* 4 English, 2 math, 2 science, 1 science lab, 1 social studies, 1 history. *Academic units recommended:* 4 English, 4 math, 3 science, 2 science labs, 2 foreign language, 1 social studies, 2 history, 2 academic electives, 2 visual/performing arts. **Freshman Admission Statistics:** 2,657 applied, 62.40% admitted, 16% enrolled. **Transfer Admission Requirements:** college transcript(s), Minimum college GPA of 2.5 required. Lowest grade transferable C-. **General Admission Information:** Nonfall registration accepted. Admission may be deferred for a maximum of 1 year.

COSTS AND FINANCIAL AID

Annual tuition $35,300. Room and board $8,300. Required fees $190. Average book expense $1,200. **Required Forms and Deadlines:** FAFSA. **Notification of Awards:** Applicants will be notified of awards on a rolling basis beginning 2/15. **Types of Aid:** *Need-based scholarships/grants:* Federal Pell, FSEOG, State scholarships/grants, Private scholarships, College/university scholarship or grant aid from institutional funds. *Loans:* Direct Subsidized Stafford Loans, Direct Unsubsidized Stafford Loans, Direct PLUS loans, Federal Perkins Loans. *Student Employment:* Federal Work-Study Program available. Institutional employment available. **Financial Aid Statistics:** 100% needy freshmen, 100% needy undergrads receive need-based scholarship or grant aid. 14% freshmen, 13% undergrads receive non-need-based scholarship or grant aid. 83% freshmen, 80% undergrads receive need-based self-help aid. 0% freshmen, 0% undergrads receive athletic scholarships. 99% freshmen, 99% undergrads receive any aid. 83% undergrads borrow to pay for school. Average cumulative indebtedness $33,646. **Criteria for awarding aid:** *Need-based:* Academics. *Non-need-based:* Academics, Art, Leadership, Music/drama, Religious affiliation.

MONMOUTH UNIVERSITY (NJ)

Admission, Monmouth University, West Long Branch, NJ 07764-1898
Phone: 732-571-3456 • **Financial Aid Phone:** 732-571-3463
E-mail: admission@monmouth.edu • **CEEB Code:** 2416
Fax: 732-263-5166 • **Website:** www.monmouth.edu • **ACT Code:** 2571

This private school was founded in 1933. It has a 156-acre campus.

RATINGS

Admissions Selectivity Rating: 80   **Fire Safety Rating:** 98   **Green Rating:** 78

STUDENTS AND FACULTY

Enrollment: 4,668. **Student Body:** 57% female, 43% male, 14% out-of-state, 1% international (23 countries represented). Asian 3%, African American 5%, Caucasian 72%, Hispanic 12%, Native American <1%, Pacific Islander <1%, Two or more races 2%, Race unknown 4%.
Retention and Graduation: 79% freshmen return for sophomore year. 55% freshmen graduate within 4 years. 70% freshmen graduate within 6 years. 33% grads go on to further study within 1 year. **Faculty:** Student/faculty ratio 13:1. 284 full-time faculty, 80% hold PhDs, 15% are are members of minority groups, 55% are women. 0% of classes are taught by teaching assistants.

ACADEMICS

Degrees: bachelor's, certificate, doctoral/professional, master's, postbachelor's certificate, post-master's certificate. **Classes:** Most classes have 20-29 students. Most lab/discussion sessions have 10-19 students. **Most popular majors:** Business Administration and Management; Education; Speech Communication and Rhetoric. **Special Study Options:** Accelerated program, cooperative education program, cross-registration, distance learning, double major, dual enrollment, honors program, independent study, internships, liberal arts/career combination, student-designed major, study abroad, teacher certification program, Clinical Lab Science Program in collaboration with UMDNJ. Air Force ROTC at Rutgers University. Affiliated with Washington Center providing semester and summer internships and shorter symposia. Monmouth Medical Scholars Program allows five incoming freshmen to complete undergraduate degree at Monmouth, including nine credit clinical requirement at Monmouth Medical Center, and commence medical studies at Drexel University School of Medicine. Study Abroad in London at Regent's College and Sydney, Australia at Macquarie University. **Honors Programs:** The Honors School is committed to providing motivated students with a unique learning environment in a community of scholars. By supporting both disciplinary and interdisciplinary approaches to education, the Honors School seeks to help students develop not only depth within their intended field of study, but also an appreciation for how that knowledge is embedded within a broader context of intellectual inquiry. The Honors School also is dedicated to raising students' level of cultural, ethical, and societal awareness as its participants develop into well-rounded scholars and citizens within a global community. Combined degree programs: BA/MD, BA/MA, 5 yr programs BS/MBA, BS/MS, BA/MA, BSW/MSW, BA/MEd, BA/MSEd. **Disability Services:** Special programs offered to physically disabled students, including note-taking services, reader services, tape recorders, tutors. **Career Services:** Alumni network, Alumni services, Career/job search classes, Career assessment, Internships, Regional alumni. Experiential Education graduation requirement.

FACILITIES

Housing: Coed dorms, apartments for single students, Wellness Housing, Theme Housing, Honor Program Housing, Health & Wellness housing, Community Service housing. 95% of campus accessible to physically diasbled. **Special Academic Facilities/Equipment:** Art gallery, instructional media center with TV and Radio stations, theatre **Computers:** 100% of classrooms, 100% of dorms, 100% of libraries, 100% of dining areas, 100% of student union, 90% of common outdoor areas have wireless network access. Students can register for classes online. Administrative functions (other than registration) can be performed online.

CAMPUS LIFE

Environment: Village. **Activities:** Choral groups, concert band, dance, drama/theater, jazz band, literary magazine, music ensembles, musical theater, pep band, radio station, student government, student newspaper, television station, yearbook, Campus Ministries, Student Organization, Model UN. 67 registered organizations, 19 honor societies, 3 religious organizations. 7 fraternities, 6 sororities. **Athletics (Intercollegiate):** *Men:* baseball, basketball, cross-country, football, golf, soccer, tennis, track/field (outdoor), track/field (indoor). *Women:* basketball, cross-country, field hockey, golf, lacrosse, soccer, softball, tennis, track/field (outdoor), track/field (indoor). **On-Campus Highlights:** Woodrow Wilson Hall, Plangere Center for Communication, Rebecca Stafford Student Center, Multipurpose Activity Center **Environmental Initiatives:** Monmouth University was the first private institution of higher education in New Jersey to enter into a voluntary Memorandum of Understanding (MOU) with the US Environmental Protection Agency (EPA). The MOU documents Monmouth commitment as an environmental steward that has pledged to reduce its carbon footprint and to contribute to a better living environment. Monmouth University uses the EPA environmental stewardship programs to develop policies, practices and specifications for environmental efficiency standards; to increase its stewardship awareness; to remain current with EPA regulations and guidelines; and to increase the involvement and recognition of Monmouth stakeholders in environmental sustainability programs. Monmouth University has pledged to partner with local government on environmental initiatives and addressing environmental concerns swiftly. Monmouth recognizes EPA program requirements for outreach and involvement, data collecting and reporting, and strives to become a recognized leader and a candidate for EPA environmental stewardship awards.

ADMISSIONS

Freshman Academic Profile: Average high school GPA 3.3. 14% in top 10% of high school class, 41% in top 25% of high school class, 75% in top 50% of high school class. 85% from public high schools. **Reported SAT (pre-2016 redesign) scores:** SAT Math middle 50% range 470-570. SAT Critical Reading middle 50% range 460-550. SAT Writing middle 50% range 460-550. **Concordant SAT scores:** SAT EBRW middle 50% 510–610. SAT Math middle 50% range 510–590. ACT middle 50% range 21-25. Minimum internet-based TOEFL 79. Minimum paper TOEFL 550. **Basis for Candidate Selection:** *Very important factors considered include:* rigor of secondary school record, academic GPA, standardized test scores. *Important factors considered include:*

application essay, recommendation(s), extracurricular activities, volunteer work, work experience. *Other factors considered include:* character/personal qualities, alumni/ae relation. **Freshman Admission Requirements:** High school diploma is required and GED is accepted. *Academic units required:* 4 English, 3 math, 2 science, 1 science lab, 2 history, 5 academic electives. *Academic units recommended:* 2 foreign language, 2 social studies. **Freshman Admission Statistics:** 9,097 applied, 77.29% admitted, 16% enrolled. **Transfer Admission Requirements:** college transcript(s), statement of good standing from prior institution(s). Minimum college GPA of 2.25 required. Lowest grade transferable C. **General Admission Information:** Application fee $50. Priority deadline 12/1. Regular application deadline 3/1. Nonfall registration accepted. Admission may be deferred for a maximum of 2 semesters.

COSTS AND FINANCIAL AID

Annual tuition $34,664. Room and board $13,038. Required fees $700. Average book expense $1,234. **Required Forms and Deadlines:** FAFSA. **Notification of Awards:** Applicants will be notified of awards on a rolling basis beginning 2/15. **Types of Aid:** *Need-based scholarships/grants:* Federal Pell, FSEOG, State scholarships/grants, Private scholarships, College/university scholarship or grant aid from institutional funds, Federal Nursing Scholarships. *Loans:* Direct Subsidized Stafford Loans, Direct Unsubsidized Stafford Loans, Direct PLUS loans, Federal Perkins Loans, State Loans, College/university loans from institutional funds. *Student Employment:* Federal Work-Study Program available. Institutional employment available. **Financial Aid Statistics:** 68% needy freshmen, 57% needy undergrads receive need-based scholarship or grant aid. 97% freshmen, 95% undergrads receive non-need-based scholarship or grant aid. 83% freshmen, 84% undergrads receive need-based self-help aid. 8% freshmen, 8% undergrads receive athletic scholarships. 99% freshmen, 96% undergrads receive any aid. 75% undergrads borrow to pay for school. Average cumulative indebtedness $47,794. **Criteria for awarding aid:** *Non-need-based:* Academics, Alumni affiliation, Art, Athletics, State/district residency.

See page 1002.

MONROE COLLEGE

Bronx, NY 10468
Phone: 718-933-6700
E-mail: cpatrick@monroecollege.edu
Fax: 718-364-3552 • **Website:** http://www.monroecollege.edu/

This is a proprietary school.

RATINGS
Admissions Selectivity Rating: 70   **Fire Safety Rating:** 60*   **Green Rating:** 60*

STUDENTS AND FACULTY
Enrollment: 6,673. **Student Body:** 64% female, 36% male, 2% out-of-state, 5% international. Asian 1%, African American 46%, Caucasian 2%, Hispanic 42%, Native American <1%, Pacific Islander 0%, Two or more races 0%, Race unknown 5%.
Retention and Graduation: 75% freshmen return for sophomore year. **Faculty:** Student/faculty ratio 21:1. 70 full-time faculty, 40% hold PhDs, 57% are are members of minority groups, 44% are women.

ACADEMICS
Degrees: associate, bachelor's, certificate, master's. **Classes:** Most classes have 20-29 students. **Special Study Options:** distance learning, honors program, independent study, internships, weekend college.

FACILITIES
Housing: Coed dorms.

CAMPUS LIFE
Activities: literary magazine.

ADMISSIONS
ACT middle 50% range 0-0. **Basis for Candidate Selection:** *Very important factors considered include:* interview. *Important factors considered include:* application essay. *Other factors considered include:* rigor of secondary school record, class rank, standardized test scores, recommendation(s), extracurricular activities, talent/ability, character/personal qualities, alumni/ae relation, geographical residence, state residency, religious affiliation/commitment, racial/ethnic status, volunteer work, work experience. **Freshman Admission Requirements:** High school diploma or equivalent is not required. **Freshman Admission Statistics:** 2,108 applied, 67.46% admitted, 95% enrolled. **General Admission Information:** Application fee $35. Nonfall registration accepted.

COSTS AND FINANCIAL AID
Annual tuition $11,744. Room and board $11,660. Required fees $800. Average book expense $900. **Required Forms and Deadlines:** FAFSA. **Notification**

of Awards: Applicants will be notified of awards on or about 7/1. **Types of Aid:** *Need-based scholarships/grants:* Federal Pell, College/university scholarship or grant aid from institutional funds. *Loans:* Direct Subsidized Stafford Loans, Direct Unsubsidized Stafford Loans, Direct PLUS loans. *Student Employment:* Federal Work-Study Program available. Institutional employment available. **Financial Aid Statistics:** 97% needy freshmen, 100% needy undergrads receive need-based scholarship or grant aid. 1% freshmen, 1% undergrads receive non-need-based scholarship or grant aid. 41% freshmen, 43% undergrads receive need-based self-help aid. 1% freshmen, 0% undergrads receive athletic scholarships. **Criteria for awarding aid:** *Need-based:* Academics.

MONTANA STATE UNIVERSITY

PO Box 172190, 201 Strand Union Bldg, Bozeman, MT 59717-2190
Phone: 406-994-2452 • **Financial Aid Phone:** 406-994-2845
E-mail: admissions@montana.edu • **CEEB Code:** 4488
Fax: 406-994-1923 • **Website:** http://www.montana.edu • **ACT Code:** 2420

This public school was founded in 1893. It has a 1780-acre campus.

RATINGS
Admissions Selectivity Rating: 80   **Fire Safety Rating:** 93   **Green Rating:** 67

STUDENTS AND FACULTY
Enrollment: 13,556. **Student Body:** 45% female, 55% male, 39% out-of-state, 3% international (55 countries represented). Asian 1%, African American 1%, Caucasian 86%, Hispanic 4%, Native American 2%, Pacific Islander <1%, Two or more races 3%, Race unknown 1%.
Retention and Graduation: 77% freshmen return for sophomore year. 22% freshmen graduate within 4 years. 31% grads go on to further study within 1 year. 20% grads pursue business degrees. 9% grads pursue medical degrees. **Faculty:** Student/faculty ratio 19:1. 581 full-time faculty, 82% hold PhDs, 6% are are members of minority groups, 42% are women. 6% of classes are taught by teaching assistants.

ACADEMICS
Degrees: associate, bachelor's, certificate, doctoral/professional, doctoral/research, master's, postbachelor's certificate, post-master's certificate, terminal, transfer. **Classes:** Most classes have 10-19 students. Most lab/discussion sessions have 10-19 students. **Most popular majors:** Liberal Arts and Sciences/Liberal Studies; Marketing/Marketing Management; Registered Nursing/Registered Nurse. **Special Study Options:** cooperative education program, cross-registration, distance learning, double major, English as a Second Language (ESL), exchange student program (domestic), honors program, independent study, internships, student-designed major, study abroad, teacher certification program. **Honors Programs:** http://www.montana.edu/wwwuhp/ Combined degree programs: BA/MEng, BA in Environmental Design/Master of Architecture. **Disability Services:** Special programs offered to physically disabled students, including note-taking services, reader services, tape recorders, tutors. **Career Services:** Alumni network, Alumni services, Career/job search classes, Career assessment, Internships. We've recently launched a new initiative called Professional Advantage which has created a variety of opportunities for students to enhance their professional skills. The most prominent of these is a new professional coaching clinic which provides one-on-one coaching and mentoring.

FACILITIES
Housing: Coed dorms, men's dorms, women's dorms, fraternity/sorority housing, apartments for married students, apartments for single students, Wellness Housing, ThemeHousingWellness floors, non-smoking, older student floors. 90% of campus accessible to physically diasbled. **Special Academic Facilities/Equipment:** • Museum of the Rockies (History & Paleontology Museum) • Planetarium • Studio 1080 (multi-media, interactive learning center) • Subzero Lab • Wind Tunnel • Clean Laboratory • Nano Laboratory • Ion Beam Laboratory • Electron Microscopes • Center for Biofilm Engineering • Plant Growth Center (29 green houses) • Fitness Center ($11.7 million student funded renovation completed in 2008) • Chemistry & Biochemistry Research Facility • Copeland Art Gallery (Art Gallery) • Exit Art Gallery (Student Art Gallery) • Wild Trout Research Laboratory • Burns Telecommunications Center • Plant and Animal Bioscience Research Facilities. **Computers:** Students can register for classes online. Administrative functions (other than registration) can be performed online.

CAMPUS LIFE
Environment: Town. **Activities:** Choral groups, concert band, dance, drama/theater, jazz band, literary magazine, marching band, music ensembles, musical theater, pep band, radio station, student newspaper, student-run film society,

television station, Campus Ministries, Student Organization. 140 registered organizations, 18 honor societies, 12 religious organizations. 9 fraternities, 4 sororities. **Athletics (Intercollegiate):** *Men:* basketball, cheerleading, cross-country, football, rodeo, skiing (downhill/alpine), skiing (nordic/cross-country), tennis, track/field (outdoor), track/field (indoor). *Women:* basketball, cheerleading, cross-country, golf, rodeo, skiing (downhill/alpine), skiing (nordic/cross-country), tennis, track/field (outdoor), track/field (indoor), volleyball. **On-Campus Highlights:** Museum of the Rockies, Planetarium, Fitness Center ($11.7 million student funded renovation completed in 2008, Burns Telecommunications Center, Chemistry & Biochemistry Research Facility, Blackbox Theatre Student Union Building Exit Art Gallery (Student Art Gallery) Copeland Art Gallery (Art Gallery). **Environmental Initiatives:** Building Lighting Retrofit projects.

ADMISSIONS

Freshman Academic Profile: Average high school GPA 3.4. 18% in top 10% of high school class, 42% in top 25% of high school class, 73% in top 50% of high school class. **Reported SAT (pre-2016 redesign) scores:** SAT Math middle 50% range 510-640. SAT Critical Reading middle 50% range 510-630. SAT Writing middle 50% range 490-610. **Concordant SAT scores:** SAT EBRW middle 50% 560–670. SAT Math middle 50% range 540–660. ACT middle 50% range 21-28. Minimum internet-based TOEFL 71. Minimum paper TOEFL 525. **Basis for Candidate Selection:** *Very important factors considered include:* rigor of secondary school record, class rank, academic GPA, standardized test scores. **Freshman Admission Requirements:** High school diploma is required and GED is accepted. *Academic units required:* 4 English, 3 math, 2 science, 2 science labs, 3 social studies, and 2 units from above areas or other academic areas. **Freshman Admission Statistics:** 14,780 applied, 82.92% admitted, 25% enrolled. **Transfer Admission Requirements:** college transcript(s), standardized test scores, statement of good standing from prior institution(s). Minimum college GPA of 2.0 required. Lowest grade transferable D-. **General Admission Information:** Application fee $30. Nonfall registration accepted. Admission may be deferred for a maximum of one year.

COSTS AND FINANCIAL AID

Annual in-state tuition $5,330. Annual out-of-state tuition $20,323. Room and board $8,650. Required fees $1,638. Average book expense $1,250. **Required Forms and Deadlines:** FAFSA. **Notification of Awards:** Applicants will be notified of awards on a rolling basis beginning 4/1. **Types of Aid:** *Need-based scholarships/grants:* Federal Pell, FSEOG, State scholarships/grants, Private scholarships, Federal Nursing Scholarships. *Loans:* Direct Subsidized Stafford Loans, Direct Unsubsidized Stafford Loans, Direct PLUS loans, Federal Perkins Loans, Federal Nursing Loans, College/university loans from institutional funds. *Student Employment:* Institutional employment available. **Financial Aid Statistics:** 75% needy freshmen, 71% needy undergrads receive need-based scholarship or grant aid. 6% freshmen, 3% undergrads receive non-need-based scholarship or grant aid. 77% freshmen, 84% undergrads receive need-based self-help aid. 1% freshmen, 2% undergrads receive athletic scholarships. 76% freshmen, 75% undergrads receive any aid. 57% undergrads borrow to pay for school. Average cumulative indebtedness $27,672. **Criteria for awarding aid:** *Need-based:* Academics, Art, Job skills, Minority status. *Non-need-based:* Academics, Alumni affiliation, Art, Athletics, Job skills, Leadership, Minority status, Music/drama, State/district residency.

MONTANA STATE UNIVERSITY BILLINGS

1500 University Drive, Billings, MT 59101
Phone: 406-657-2158 • **Financial Aid Phone:** 406-657-1617 • **CEEB Code:** 4298
Fax: 406-657-2302 • **Website:** www.msubillings.edu • **ACT Code:** 2416

This public school was founded in 1927. It has a 92-acre campus.

RATINGS

Admissions Selectivity Rating: 73   **Fire Safety Rating:** 82   **Green Rating:** 60*

STUDENTS AND FACULTY

Enrollment: 3,744. **Student Body:** 62% female, 38% male, 10% out-of-state, 3% international (21 countries represented). Asian 1%, African American 1%, Caucasian 82%, Hispanic 5%, Native American 4%, Pacific Islander <1%, Two or more races 3%, Race unknown 1%.
Retention and Graduation: 53% freshmen return for sophomore year. 11% freshmen graduate within 4 years. 24% freshmen graduate within 6 years. 10% grads go on to further study within 1 year. 70% grads pursue arts and sciences degrees. 14% grads pursue business degrees. 1% grads pursue medical degrees. **Faculty:** Student/faculty ratio 17:1. 174 full-time faculty, 59% hold PhDs, 7% are are members of minority groups, 44% are women. 0% of classes are taught by teaching assistants.

ACADEMICS

Degrees: associate, bachelor's, certificate, master's. **Classes:** Most classes have 20-29 students. Most lab/discussion sessions have 10-19 students. **Most popular majors:** Elementary Education and Teaching; Liberal Arts and Sciences/Liberal Studies; Business/Commerce. **Special Study Options:** Accelerated program, cooperative education program, cross-registration, distance learning, double major, dual enrollment, English as a Second Language (ESL), external degree program, honors program, independent study, internships, student-designed major, study abroad, teacher certification program, weekend college, On-line degrees and extensive on-line course offerings. Evening College. **Honors Programs:** The MSU-Billings University Honors Program is designed for curious students who are eager to participate actively in their education. Classes in the University Honors Program tend to be smaller than other classes and emphasize class discussion. Often these classes are interdisciplinary in nature; this helps students study issues from several perspectives. Some classes are team-taught, which also enriches the discussion. **Disability Services:** Special programs offered to physically disabled students, including note-taking services, reader services, tape recorders, tutors. **Career Services:** Career/job search classes, Career assessment, Internships.

FACILITIES

Housing: Coed dorms, special housing for disabled students, men's dorms, women's dorms, apartments for married students, Apartments for students with dependent children. 99% of campus accessible to physically diasbled. **Special Academic Facilities/Equipment:** Montana Center for Disabilities, Business Enterprise, Small Business Institute, Urban Institute, Public Radio, Applied Economic Research, Biological Station, Northern Plains Studies Center, Montana Business Connections, Information Commons, Academic Support Center, Advising Center, TRIO Programs, SOS Programs, Northcutt Steele Gallery, Cisel Recital Hall, Petro Theatre, MSU-Billings Downtown **Computers:** 30% of classrooms, 100% of dorms, 100% of libraries, 100% of dining areas, 100% of student union, have wireless network access. Students can register for classes online. Administrative functions (other than registration) can be performed online.

CAMPUS LIFE

Environment: City. **Activities:** Choral groups, concert band, drama/theater, jazz band, literary magazine, music ensembles, musical theater, pep band, radio station, student government, student newspaper, symphony orchestra, Campus Ministries, Student Organization. 53 registered organizations, 10 honor societies, 8 religious organizations. **Athletics (Intercollegiate):** *Men:* baseball, basketball, cross-country, golf, soccer, tennis, track/field (outdoor), track/field (indoor). *Women:* basketball, cross-country, golf, soccer, softball, tennis, track/field (outdoor), track/field (indoor), volleyball. **On-Campus Highlights:** Alterowitz Gym, MSU Billings Downtown, SUB Coffee Shop, Liberal Arts Coffee Shop, Library.

ADMISSIONS

Freshman Academic Profile: 8% in top 10% of high school class, 31% in top 25% of high school class, 63% in top 50% of high school class. 96% from public high schools. **Reported SAT (pre-2016 redesign) scores:** SAT Math middle 50% range 440-560. SAT Critical Reading middle 50% range 420-540. **Concordant SAT scores:** SAT Math middle 50% range 480–580. ACT middle 50% range 18-24. Minimum internet-based TOEFL 68. Minimum paper TOEFL 515. **Basis for Candidate Selection:** *Very important factors considered include:* rigor of secondary school record, class rank, academic GPA, standardized test scores. *Other factors considered include:* character/personal qualities, work experience. **Freshman Admission Requirements:** High school diploma is required and GED is accepted. *Academic units required:* 4 English, 3 math, 2 science, 2 science labs, 3 social studies, and 2 units from above areas or other academic areas. **Freshman Admission Statistics:** 1,470 applied, 99.52% admitted, 47% enrolled. **Transfer Admission Requirements:** college transcript(s), statement of good standing from prior institution(s). Minimum college GPA of 2.0 required. Lowest grade transferable C-. **General Admission Information:** Application fee $30. Priority deadline 3/1. Regular notification 9/1. Nonfall registration accepted.

COSTS AND FINANCIAL AID

Annual in-state tuition $4,397. Annual out-of-state tuition $16,307. Room and board $7,510. Required fees $1,411. Average book expense $1,460. **Required Forms and Deadlines:** FAFSA. **Notification of Awards:** Applicants will be notified of awards on a rolling basis beginning 3/1. **Types of Aid:** *Need-based scholarships/grants:* Federal Pell, FSEOG, State scholarships/grants, Private scholarships, College/university scholarship or grant aid from institutional funds. *Loans:* Direct Subsidized Stafford Loans, Direct Unsubsidized Stafford Loans, Direct PLUS loans, Federal Perkins Loans, College/university loans from institutional funds. *Student Employment:* Federal Work-Study Program available. Institutional employment available. **Financial Aid Statistics:** 91% needy freshmen, 85% needy undergrads receive need-based scholarship or grant aid. 3% freshmen, 2% undergrads receive non-need-based scholarship or grant aid. 75% freshmen, 83% undergrads receive need-based self-help aid. 4% freshmen, 5% undergrads receive athletic scholarships. 66% undergrads borrow to pay for school. Average cumulative indebtedness $28,546. **Criteria**

for awarding aid: *Need-based:* Academics, Alumni affiliation, Art, Job skills, Leadership, Minority status, Music/drama. *Non-need-based:* Academics, Alumni affiliation, Art, Athletics, Job skills, Leadership, Minority status, Music/drama, State/district residency.

MONTANA TECH OF THE UNIVERSITY OF MONTANA

1300 West Park Street, Butte, MT 59701
Phone: 406-496-4256 • **Financial Aid Phone:** 406-496-4213
E-mail: enrollment@mtech.edu • **CEEB Code:** 4487
Fax: 406-496-4710 • **Website:** www.mtech.edu • **ACT Code:** 24180

This public school was founded in 1893. It has a 113-acre campus.

RATINGS

Admissions Selectivity Rating: 82   **Fire Safety Rating:** 98   **Green Rating:** 60*

STUDENTS AND FACULTY

Enrollment: 2,437. **Student Body:** 37% female, 63% male, 15% out-of-state, 9% international (14 countries represented). Asian 1%, African American 1%, Caucasian 81%, Hispanic 2%, Native American 2%, Pacific Islander 0%, Two or more races <1%, Race unknown 5%.
Retention and Graduation: 71% freshmen return for sophomore year. 17% freshmen graduate within 4 years. 43% freshmen graduate within 6 years. 13% grads go on to further study within 1 year. 11% grads pursue arts and sciences degrees. 1% grads pursue business degrees. 2% grads pursue medical degrees. **Faculty:** Student/faculty ratio 15:1. 148 full-time faculty, 59% hold PhDs, 8% are are members of minority groups, 34% are women.

ACADEMICS

Degrees: associate, bachelor's, certificate, doctoral, master's, postbachelor's certificate. **Classes:** Most classes have 10-19 students. Most lab/discussion sessions have fewer than 10 students. **Most popular majors:** Petroleum Engineering; Engineering; Management Information Systems and Services. **Special Study Options:** cooperative education program, distance learning, double major, dual enrollment, honors program, independent study, internships, teacher certification program. **Honors Programs:** Honors program provided for all programs. Consists of honors seminar and a few extra courses. Combined degree programs: BA/MA. **Disability Services:** Special programs offered to physically disabled students, including note-taking services, reader services, tape recorders, tutors. **Career Services:** Alumni network, Alumni services, Career/job search classes, Career assessment, Internships, Regional alumni. At Montana Tech, students are known for their practical application of their degree. Recruiters often state, student at Montana Tech aren't afraid to get their hands dirty. Student are more successful in their career because they get hands-on experience before they graduate.

FACILITIES

Housing: Coed dorms, special housing for disabled students, special housing for international students, apartments for married students, apartments for single students, Apartments for families (Don't have to be married if have children). 75% of campus accessible to physically diasbled. **Special Academic Facilities/Equipment:** Mineral Museum World Museum of Mining **Computers:** 30% of classrooms, 100% of libraries, 100% of dining areas, 100% of student union, have wireless network access. Students can register for classes online. Administrative functions (other than registration) can be performed online.

CAMPUS LIFE

Environment: Town. **Activities:** concert band, pep band, radio station, student government, student newspaper, yearbook, Campus Ministries. 58 registered organizations, 2 honor societies, 3 religious organizations. **Athletics (Intercollegiate):** *Men:* basketball, football, golf. *Women:* basketball, golf, volleyball. **On-Campus Highlights:** Mineral Museum, Mil Building (which houses Starbucks and, HPER (athletic facility), Student Union, Mall area (outdoor located in the center.

ADMISSIONS

Freshman Academic Profile: Average high school GPA 3.5. 24% in top 10% of high school class, 57% in top 25% of high school class, 85% in top 50% of high school class. **Reported SAT (pre-2016 redesign) scores:** SAT Math middle 50% range 540-630. SAT Critical Reading middle 50%

range 490-590. SAT Writing middle 50% range 450-560. **Concordant SAT scores:** SAT EBRW middle 50% 530–630. SAT Math middle 50% range 570–650. ACT middle 50% range 22-27. Minimum internet-based TOEFL 71. Minimum paper TOEFL 525. **Basis for Candidate Selection:** *Very important factors considered include:* class rank, academic GPA, standardized test scores. **Freshman Admission Requirements:** High school diploma is required and GED is accepted. *Academic units required:* 4 English, 3 math, 2 science, 2 science labs, 3 social studies, and 2 units from above areas or other academic areas. *Academic units recommended:* 4 math. **Freshman Admission Statistics:** 952 applied, 90.44% admitted, 52% enrolled. **Transfer Admission Requirements:** college transcript(s), Minimum college GPA of 2.0 required. Lowest grade transferable C. **General Admission Information:** Application fee $30. Nonfall registration accepted. Admission may be deferred for a maximum of 1 semester.

COSTS AND FINANCIAL AID

Annual in-state tuition $6,881. Annual out-of-state tuition $21,008. Room and board $8,932. Average book expense $1,050. **Required Forms and Deadlines:** FAFSA. **Notification of Awards:** Applicants will be notified of awards on a rolling basis beginning 3/15. **Types of Aid:** *Need-based scholarships/grants:* Federal Pell, FSEOG, State scholarships/grants, Private scholarships, College/university scholarship or grant aid from institutional funds. *Loans:* Direct Subsidized Stafford Loans, Direct Unsubsidized Stafford Loans, Direct PLUS loans, Federal Perkins Loans, College/university loans from institutional funds. *Student Employment:* Federal Work-Study Program available. Institutional employment available. **Financial Aid Statistics:** 90% needy freshmen, 89% needy undergrads receive need-based scholarship or grant aid. 10% freshmen, 5% undergrads receive non-need-based scholarship or grant aid. 73% freshmen, 80% undergrads receive need-based self-help aid. 4% freshmen, 3% undergrads receive athletic scholarships. 72% freshmen, 67% undergrads receive any aid. **Criteria for awarding aid:** *Need-based:* Academics, Athletics, Leadership, Minority status. *Non-need-based:* Academics, Alumni affiliation, Athletics, Leadership, Minority status, Music/drama, Religious affiliation, State/district residency.

MONTCLAIR STATE UNIVERSITY

One Normal Avenue, Montclair, NJ 07043-1624
Phone: 973-655-4444 • **Financial Aid Phone:** 973-655-4461
E-mail: undergraduate.admissions@montclair.edu • **CEEB Code:** 2520
Fax: 973-655-7700 • **Website:** www.montclair.edu/ • **ACT Code:** 2572

This public school was founded in 1908. It has a 275-acre campus.

RATINGS

Admissions Selectivity Rating: 78   **Fire Safety Rating:** 98   **Green Rating:** 83

STUDENTS AND FACULTY

Enrollment: 16,653. **Student Body:** 61% female, 39% male, 3% out-of-state, 1% international (106 countries represented). Asian 6%, African American 12%, Caucasian 43%, Hispanic 27%, Native American <1%, Pacific Islander <1%, Two or more races 3%, Race unknown 9%.
Retention and Graduation: 83% freshmen return for sophomore year. 39% freshmen graduate within 4 years. 65% freshmen graduate within 6 years. 21% grads go on to further study within 1 year. **Faculty:** Student/faculty ratio 17:1. 620 full-time faculty, 92% hold PhDs, 27% are are members of minority groups, 49% are women.

ACADEMICS

Degrees: bachelor's, certificate, doctoral/professional, doctoral/research, doctoral, master's, postbachelor's certificate. **Special Study Options:** cooperative education program, double major, English as a Second Language (ESL), honors program, independent study, internships, study abroad, teacher certification program. Combined degree programs: BA/MA, 5yr BA/MA, 5yr BA/M practical anthropolo. **Disability Services:** Special programs offered to physically disabled students, including note-taking services, reader services, tape recorders, tutors. **Career Services:** Alumni network, Alumni services, Career assessment, Internships, Regional alumni. All of our programs are exceptional.

FACILITIES

Housing: Coed dorms, special housing for disabled students, special housing for international students, women's dorms, apartments for single students, Theme Housing. 90% of campus accessible to physically diasbled. **Special Academic Facilities/Equipment:** The Dumont Television Center, Yogi Berra Museum and Stadium,Floyd Hall Arena **Computers:** 70% of classrooms, 20% of dorms, 100% of libraries, 75% of dining areas, 50% of student union, 10% of common outdoor areas have wireless network access. Students can register for classes online. Administrative functions (other than registration) can be performed online.

CAMPUS LIFE

Environment: Town. **Activities:** Choral groups, concert band, dance, drama/theater, jazz band, literary magazine, marching band, music ensembles, musical theater, opera, pep band, radio station, student government, student newspaper, symphony orchestra, television station, yearbook, Campus Ministries, Student Organization. 121 registered organizations, 28 honor societies, 8 religious organizations. 13 fraternities, 16 sororities. **Athletics (Intercollegiate):** *Men:* baseball, basketball, diving, football, lacrosse, soccer, swimming, track/field (outdoor). *Women:* basketball, diving, field hockey, lacrosse, soccer, softball, swimming, track/field (outdoor), volleyball. **On-Campus Highlights:** Cafe Diem, University Hall, Student Center, Recreation Center, Kasser Theater. **Environmental Initiatives:** Recycling Program—campus-wide, New Cogen Plant.

ADMISSIONS

Freshman Academic Profile: Average high school GPA 3.2. 11% in top 10% of high school class, 35% in top 25% of high school class, 77% in top 50% of high school class. **Reported SAT (pre-2016 redesign) scores:** SAT Math middle 50% range 440-540. SAT Critical Reading middle 50% range 430-530. SAT Writing middle 50% range 430-540. **Concordant SAT scores:** SAT EBRW middle 50% 480–590. SAT Math middle 50% range 480–570. Minimum internet-based TOEFL 80. Minimum paper TOEFL 550. **Basis for Candidate Selection:** *Very important factors considered include:* rigor of secondary school record, academic GPA, recommendation(s). *Important factors considered include:* application essay. *Other factors considered include:* class rank, standardized test scores, extracurricular activities, talent/ability, character/personal qualities, volunteer work, work experience. **Freshman Admission Requirements:** High school diploma is required and GED is accepted. *Academic units required:* 4 English, 3 math, 2 science, 2 science labs, 2 foreign language, 2 social studies, 3 academic electives. **Freshman Admission Statistics:** 12,139 applied, 66.13% admitted, 37% enrolled. **Transfer Admission Requirements:** college transcript(s), statement of good standing from prior institution(s). Minimum college GPA of 2.0 required. Lowest grade transferable C-. **General Admission Information:** Application fee $65. Priority deadline 12/15. Regular application deadline 3/1. Nonfall registration accepted. Admission may be deferred for a maximum of 1 semester.

COSTS AND FINANCIAL AID

Annual in-state tuition $8,768. Annual out-of-state tuition $16,659. Room and board $14,094. Required fees $3,348. Average book expense $1,300. **Required Forms and Deadlines:** FAFSA. **Notification of Awards:** Applicants will be notified of awards on a rolling basis beginning 4/1. **Types of Aid:** *Need-based scholarships/grants:* Federal Pell, FSEOG, State scholarships/grants, Private scholarships, College/university scholarship or grant aid from institutional funds. *Loans:* Direct Subsidized Stafford Loans, Direct Unsubsidized Stafford Loans, Direct PLUS loans, Federal Perkins Loans, State Loans. *Student Employment:* Federal Work-Study Program available. Institutional employment available. **Financial Aid Statistics:** 58% needy freshmen, 62% needy undergrads receive need-based scholarship or grant aid. 7% freshmen, 6% undergrads receive non-need-based scholarship or grant aid. 81% freshmen, 84% undergrads receive need-based self-help aid. 0% freshmen, 0% undergrads receive athletic scholarships. 67% freshmen, 58% undergrads receive any aid. **Criteria for awarding aid:** *Need-based:* Leadership. *Non-need-based:* Academics, Alumni affiliation, Art, Leadership, Minority status, Music/drama, Religious affiliation, State/district residency.

MOORE COLLEGE OF ART AND DESIGN

20th Street and The Parkway, Philadelphia, PA 19103-1179
Phone: 215-965-4017 • **Financial Aid Phone:** 215-965-4042
E-mail: enroll@moore.edu • **CEEB Code:** 2417
Fax: 215-568-3547 • **Website:** www.moore.edu • **ACT Code:** 2417

This private school was founded in 1848.

RATINGS

Admissions Selectivity Rating: 78   **Fire Safety Rating:** 97   **Green Rating:** 60*

STUDENTS AND FACULTY

Enrollment: 482. **Student Body:** 100% female, 0% male, 42% out-of-state, 3% international (15 countries represented). Asian 4%, African American 16%, Caucasian 65%, Hispanic 5%, Native American 1%, Pacific Islander 1%, Two or more races 5%, Race unknown 1%.
Retention and Graduation: 73% freshmen return for sophomore year. 48% freshmen graduate within 4 years. 56% freshmen graduate within 6 years.
Faculty: Student/faculty ratio 9:1. 24 full-time faculty, 50% hold PhDs, 8% are are members of minority groups, 67% are women. 0% of classes are taught by teaching assistants.

ACADEMICS

Degrees: bachelor's, master's, postbachelor's certificate. **Classes:** Most classes have 10-19 students. **Most popular majors:** Fashion/Apparel Design; Fine/Studio Arts; Illustration. **Special Study Options:** double major, independent study, internships, study abroad, teacher certification program, arts, education student travel courses. **Disability Services:** Special programs offered to physically disabled students, including tape recorders, tutors. **Career Services:** Alumni services, Internships, Regional alumni. All majors require an internship before senior year.

FACILITIES

Housing: women's dorms. **Special Academic Facilities/Equipment:** Paley, Graham and Levy Galleries **Computers:** 100% of classrooms, 100% of dorms, 100% of libraries, 100% of dining areas, have wireless network access. Students can register for classes online. Administrative functions (other than registration) can be performed online. Undergraduates are required to own a computer.

CAMPUS LIFE

Environment: Metropolis. **Activities:** student government, yearbook. 8 registered organizations. **On-Campus Highlights:** Three art galleries, Outdoor coffee shop, Internships, Leadership Fellowships, Locks Career Center for Women.

ADMISSIONS

Freshman Academic Profile: Average high school GPA 3.2. **Reported SAT (pre-2016 redesign) scores:** SAT Math middle 50% range 420-520. SAT Critical Reading middle 50% range 450-560. **Concordant SAT scores:** SAT Math middle 50% range 460–550. ACT middle 50% range 17-22. Minimum paper TOEFL 527. **Basis for Candidate Selection:** *Very important factors considered include:* rigor of secondary school record, academic GPA, standardized test scores, interview, talent/ability, character/personal qualities, level of applicant's interest. *Important factors considered include:* application essay, recommendation(s), extracurricular activities. *Other factors considered include:* class rank, volunteer work, work experience. **Freshman Admission Requirements:** High school diploma is required and GED is accepted. *Academic units recommended:* 4 English, 2 math, 2 science, 2 foreign language, 4 social studies, 3 visual/performing arts, and 1 unit from above areas or other academic areas. **Freshman Admission Statistics:** 607 applied, 54.37% admitted, 33% enrolled. **Transfer Admission Requirements:** High school transcript, college transcript(s), essay or personal statement, statement of good standing from prior institution(s). Minimum college GPA of 2.5 required. Lowest grade transferable C. **General Admission Information:** Application fee $40. Priority deadline 3/1. Regular application deadline 8/15. Nonfall registration accepted. Admission may be deferred for a maximum of 1 year.

COSTS AND FINANCIAL AID

Annual tuition $31,654. Room and board $12,298. Required fees $1,084. Average book expense $2,000. **Required Forms and Deadlines:** FAFSA. **Notification of Awards:** Applicants will be notified of awards on a rolling basis beginning 2/15. **Types of Aid:** *Need-based scholarships/grants:* Federal Pell, FSEOG, State scholarships/grants, Private scholarships, College/university scholarship or grant aid from institutional funds. *Loans:* Federal Perkins Loans. *Student Employment:* Federal Work-Study Program available. **Financial Aid Statistics:** 97% undergrads receive any aid. **Criteria for awarding aid:** *Need-based:* Academics, Art, Leadership, Minority status. *Non-need-based:* Academics, Art, Leadership.

MORAVIAN COLLEGE

1200 Main Street, Bethlehem, PA 18018
Phone: 610-861-1320 • **Financial Aid Phone:** 610-861-1330
E-mail: admission@moravian.edu • **CEEB Code:** 3301
Fax: 610-625-7930 • **Website:** www.moravian.edu • **ACT Code:** 3634

This private school, affiliated with the Moravian Church, was founded in 1742. It has a 60-acre campus.

RATINGS

Admissions Selectivity Rating: 80   **Fire Safety Rating:** 87   **Green Rating:** 76

STUDENTS AND FACULTY

Enrollment: 1,926. **Student Body:** 58% female, 42% male, 31% out-of-state, 7% international (7 countries represented). Asian 2%, African American 5%, Caucasian 68%, Hispanic 10%, Native American <1%, Pacific Islander <1%, Two or more races 2%, Race unknown 6%.

Retention and Graduation: 78% freshmen return for sophomore year. 66% freshmen graduate within 4 years. 69 13% grads go on to further study within 1 year. 8% grads pursue arts and sciences degrees. 1% grads pursue law degrees. 1% grads pursue business degrees. 1% grads pursue medical degrees. **Faculty:** Student/faculty ratio 12:1. 137 full-time faculty, 0% hold PhDs, 11% are are members of minority groups, 58% are women. 0% of classes are taught by teaching assistants.

ACADEMICS

Degrees: bachelor's, master's, postbachelor's certificate, post-master's certificate. **Classes:** Most classes have 10-19 students. Most lab/discussion sessions have 10-19 students. **Most popular majors:** Psychology; Business Administration and Management; Registered Nursing/Registered Nurse. **Special Study Options:** cross-registration, double major, honors program, independent study, internships, student-designed major, study abroad, teacher certification program. **Honors Programs:** Students can do honors projects within their selected major Combined degree programs: BA/MBA. **Disability Services:** Special programs offered to physically disabled students, including note-taking services, reader services, tape recorders, tutors. **Career Services:** Alumni network, Alumni services, Career/job search classes, Career assessment, Internships, Regional alumni. The Moravian College Career Center is proud of our engagement of alumni and students. Alumni actively engage with students in person through Student/Alumni Networking events in various cities, an internship and job search preparation program 'Backpack to Briefcase,' a formalized externship program, and through classroom and career development programs. Through our Assistant Director of Career Development and Alumni Relations, students are also connected with alumni based on interests and career goals for informational interviews, job shadowing, internships, job searching advice and mentoring. A LinkedIn 'HoundLinks' group also provides the opportunity for alumni and students to foster mentoring relationships in a digital space.

FACILITIES

Housing: Coed dorms, men's dorms, women's dorms, fraternity/sorority housing, apartments for single students, Wellness Housing, Theme Housing. **Special Academic Facilities/Equipment:** Payne [art] Gallery, Foy [concert] Hall, greenhouse, student art studios, observation room for psychology classes, Leadership Center **Computers:** 80% of classrooms, 100% of libraries, 100% of dining areas, 100% of student union, 25% of common outdoor areas have wireless network access. Administrative functions (other than registration) can be performed online.

CAMPUS LIFE

Environment: City. **Activities:** Choral groups, concert band, dance, drama/theater, jazz band, literary magazine, marching band, music ensembles, musical theater, radio station, student government, student newspaper, symphony orchestra, yearbook, Campus Ministries, Student Organization. 80 registered organizations, 16 honor societies, 4 religious organizations. 3 fraternities, 4 sororities. **Athletics (Intercollegiate):** Men: baseball, basketball, cross-country, football, golf, lacrosse, soccer, tennis, track/field (outdoor), track/field (indoor). Women: basketball, cross-country, field hockey, lacrosse, soccer, softball, tennis, track/field (outdoor), track/field (indoor), volleyball. **On-Campus Highlights:** Alternative (on campus club/hang out), Afterwords Cafe (Library Coffe Shop), Priscilla Payne Hurd Academic Complex, Fitness Center, The Quad. **Environmental Initiatives:** The Sustainability Committee initiated a strategic planning process during 2012 that culminated in the first Campus Sustainability Plan in 2014. The committe hosted three workshops and invited particpants from across the campus community including students, staff and faculty to share current practices, envision a sustainable campus, and create ambitious and measurable goals.

ADMISSIONS

Freshman Academic Profile: Average high school GPA 3.5. 20% in top 10% of high school class, 43% in top 25% of high school class, 77% in top 50% of high school class. 87% from public high schools. **Reported SAT (pre-2016 redesign) scores:** SAT Math middle 50% range 450-560. SAT Critical Reading middle 50% range 450-560. SAT Writing middle 50% range 450-550. **Concordant SAT scores:** SAT EBRW middle 50% 500–610. SAT Math middle 50% range 490–580. ACT middle 50% range 21-25. Minimum internet-based TOEFL 80. Minimum paper TOEFL 550. **Basis for Candidate Selection:** Very important factors considered include: rigor of secondary school record, class rank, academic GPA, character/personal qualities, alumni/ae relation, level of applicant's interest. Important factors considered include: standardized test scores, application essay, recommendation(s), extracurricular activities, talent/ability, first generation, volunteer work. Other factors considered include: interview, geographical residence, work experience. **Freshman Admission Requirements:** High school diploma is required and GED is accepted. Academic units required: 4 English, 3 math, 3 science, 2 science labs, 2 foreign language, 4 social studies. Academic units recommended: 4 math. **Freshman Admission Statistics:** 2,512 applied, 79.82% admitted, 24% enrolled. **Transfer Admission Requirements:** High school transcript, college transcript(s), essay or personal statement, statement of good standing from prior institution(s).

Minimum college GPA of 3.0 required. Lowest grade transferable C. **General Admission Information:** Priority deadline 3/1. Regular application deadline 3/1. Nonfall registration accepted. Admission may be deferred for a maximum of 1 year.

COSTS AND FINANCIAL AID

Annual tuition $40,293. Room and board $12,694. Required fees $1,731. Average book expense $1,200. **Required Forms and Deadlines:** FAFSA, Institution's own financial aid form. **Notification of Awards:** Applicants will be notified of awards on a rolling basis beginning 2/25. **Types of Aid:** Need-based scholarships/grants: Federal Pell, FSEOG, State scholarships/grants, Private scholarships, College/university scholarship or grant aid from institutional funds, United Negro College Fund, Federal Nursing Scholarships. Loans: Direct Subsidized Stafford Loans, Direct Unsubsidized Stafford Loans, Direct PLUS loans, Federal Perkins Loans, Federal Nursing Loans, State Loans. Student Employment: Federal Work-Study Program available. Institutional employment available. **Financial Aid Statistics:** 100% needy freshmen, 100% needy undergrads receive need-based scholarship or grant aid. 12% freshmen, 10% undergrads receive non-need-based scholarship or grant aid. 89% freshmen, 90% undergrads receive need-based self-help aid. 0% freshmen, 0% undergrads receive athletic scholarships. 99% freshmen, 98% undergrads receive any aid. Average cumulative indebtedness $33,377. **Criteria for awarding aid:** Need-based: Academics. Non-need-based: Academics, Alumni affiliation, Art, Leadership, Music/drama, Religious affiliation, State/district residency.

MOREHEAD STATE UNIVERSITY

Admissions Center, Morehead, KY 40351
Phone: 606-783-2000 • **Financial Aid Phone:** 606-783-2011
E-mail: admissions@moreheadstate.edu
Fax: 606-783-5038 • **Website:** http://www.moreheadstate.edu/ • **ACT Code:** 1530

This public school was founded in 1922. It has a 1016-acre campus.

RATINGS

Admissions Selectivity Rating: 78   **Fire Safety Rating:** 88   **Green Rating:** 60*

STUDENTS AND FACULTY

Enrollment: 7,212. **Student Body:** 60% female, 40% male, 14% out-of-state, 1% international (35 countries represented). Asian 0%, African American 4%, Caucasian 90%, Hispanic 1%, Native American <1%, Pacific Islander <1%, Two or more races 1%, Race unknown 1%.
Retention and Graduation: 69% freshmen return for sophomore year.
Faculty: Student/faculty ratio 18:1. 359 full-time faculty, 0% hold PhDs, 7% are are members of minority groups, 48% are women.

ACADEMICS

Degrees: associate, bachelor's, certificate, master's, postbachelor's certifiate, post-master's certificate. **Classes:** Most classes have 20-29 students. Most lab/discussion sessions have 10-19 students. **Most popular majors:** Elementary Education and Teaching; General Studies. **Special Study Options:** Accelerated program, cooperative education program, cross-registration, distance learning, double major, dual enrollment, exchange student program (domestic), honors program, independent study, internships, student-designed major, study abroad, teacher certification program, weekend college. **Disability Services:** Special programs offered to physically disabled students, including note-taking services, reader services, tutors. **Career Services:** Alumni network, Alumni services, Career/job search classes, Career assessment, Internships.

FACILITIES

Housing: Coed dorms, special housing for disabled students, special housing for international students, fraternity/sorority housing, apartments for married students, apartments for single students, Limited housing available at agriculture complex for agriculture science students. Housing for handicapped students and private rooms available. 90% of campus accessible to physically diasbled. **Special Academic Facilities/Equipment:** Ky. Folk Art Center, 320-acre agricultural complex, Space Science Center, Ky. Center for Traditional Music **Computers:** 100% of classrooms, 20% of dorms, 100% of libraries, 100% of dining areas, 100% of student union, 100% of common outdoor areas have wireless network access. Students can register for classes online. Administrative functions (other than registration) can be performed online.

CAMPUS LIFE

Environment: Village. **Activities:** Choral groups, concert band, dance, drama/theater, jazz band, literary magazine, marching band, music ensembles, musical theater, opera, pep band, radio station, student government, student newspaper, symphony orchestra, television station, yearbook. 101 registered organizations, 11 honor societies, 7 religious organizations. 10 fraternities, 9 sororities. **Athletics (Intercollegiate):** Men: baseball, basketball, cheerleading, cross-country, football, golf, riflery, tennis, track/field (outdoor). *Women:* basketball, cheerleading, cross-country, golf, riflery, soccer, softball, tennis, track/field (outdoor), track/field (indoor), volleyball. **On-Campus Highlights:** Adron Doran University Center, Eagle Lake, MSU Wellness Center, Laughlin Health Building. **Environmental Initiatives:** Environmental Education Center: Organizes educational workshops, Earth Day Activities, and community outreach.

ADMISSIONS

Freshman Academic Profile: Average high school GPA 3.3. 17% in top 10% of high school class, 42% in top 25% of high school class, 76% in top 50% of high school class. **Reported SAT (pre-2016 redesign) scores:** SAT Math middle 50% range 450-560. SAT Critical Reading middle 50% range 450-535. SAT Writing middle 50% range 410-530. **Concordant SAT scores:** SAT EBRW middle 50% 480–590. SAT Math middle 50% range 490–580. ACT middle 50% range 19-25. Minimum paper TOEFL 500. **Basis for Candidate Selection:** *Very important factors considered include:* rigor of secondary school record, academic GPA, standardized test scores. *Other factors considered include:* recommendation(s). **Freshman Admission Requirements:** High school diploma is required and GED is accepted. *Academic units required:* 4 English, 3 math, 3 science, 1 science lab, 2 foreign language, 3 social studies, 5 academic electives, 1 visual/performing arts, and 1 unit from above areas or other academic areas. *Academic units recommended:* 1 computer science. **Freshman Admission Statistics:** 5,236 applied, 84.47% admitted, 34% enrolled. **Transfer Admission Requirements:** college transcript(s), statement of good standing from prior institution(s). Minimum college GPA of 2.0 required. Lowest grade transferable C. **General Admission Information:** Application fee $30. Nonfall registration accepted. Admission may be deferred for a maximum of one semester.

COSTS AND FINANCIAL AID

Average book expense $1,200. **Required Forms and Deadlines:** FAFSA, Institution's own financial aid form. **Types of Aid:** *Need-based scholarships/grants:* Federal Pell, FSEOG, State scholarships/grants, Private scholarships, College/university scholarship or grant aid from institutional funds. *Loans:* Direct Subsidized Stafford Loans, Direct Unsubsidized Stafford Loans, Direct PLUS loans, Federal Perkins Loans, College/university loans from institutional funds. *Student Employment:* Federal Work-Study Program available. Institutional employment available. **Financial Aid Statistics:** 67% needy freshmen, 69% needy undergrads receive need-based scholarship or grant aid. 45% freshmen, 63% undergrads receive non-need-based scholarship or grant aid. 66% freshmen, 74% undergrads receive need-based self-help aid. 6% freshmen, 5% undergrads receive athletic scholarships. **Criteria for awarding aid:** *Non-need-based:* Academics, Alumni affiliation, Art, Athletics, Leadership, Minority status, Music/drama, State/district residency.

MORGAN STATE UNIVERSITY

1700 East Cold Spring Lane,
Phone: 800-332-6674
E-mail: tjenness@moac.morgan.edu • **CEEB Code:** 5416
Fax: 410-319-3684 • **Website:** www.morgan.edu • **ACT Code:** 1722

This public school was founded in 1867. It has a 122-acre campus.

RATINGS

Admissions Selectivity Rating: 70   **Fire Safety Rating:** 60*   **Green Rating:** 60*

STUDENTS AND FACULTY

Enrollment: 5,357. **Student Body:** 40% out-of-state, 2% international. Asian 2%, African American 92%, Caucasian 2%, Hispanic 1%, Native American 1%, Pacific Islander 0%, Two or more races 0%, Race unknown 0%.
Retention and Graduation: 76% freshmen return for sophomore year.

ACADEMICS

Degrees: bachelor's, master's. **Special Study Options:** cooperative education program, business, education, engineering, social/behavioral science. Combined degree programs: 3-3 pharmacy, 3-4 predental/premed. **Disability Services:** Special programs offered to physically disabled students, including tutors. **Career Services:** Career/job search classes, Career assessment, Internships.

FACILITIES

Housing: Coed dorms, men's dorms, women's dorms, apartments for single students. **Special Academic Facilities/Equipment:** African-American collection, new science complex and school of engineering.

CAMPUS LIFE

Activities: radio station, student government, student newspaper, television station, yearbook. 250 registered organizations, 1 religious organization. 4

fraternities, 4 sororities. **Athletics (Intercollegiate):** *Men:* basketball, cross-country, football, tennis, track/field (outdoor), volleyball. *Women:* basketball, cross-country, tennis, track/field (outdoor), volleyball. **On-Campus Highlights:** Fine Arts Center, Hughes Stadium, Mitchell Building, Research Facility, University Museum.

ADMISSIONS

Freshman Academic Profile: 10% in top 10% of high school class, 80% in top 25% of high school class, 96% in top 50% of high school class. 77% from public high schools. Minimum internet-based TOEFL 88. Minimum paper TOEFL 570. **Freshman Admission Requirements:** High school diploma is required and GED is accepted. High school diploma is required and GED is not accepted. *Academic units recommended:* 4 English, 3 math, 3 science, 2 foreign language, 3 social studies, 2 history. **Freshman Admission Statistics:** Lowest grade transferable C. **General Admission Information:** Regular application deadline 4/15. Nonfall registration accepted.

COSTS AND FINANCIAL AID

Annual in-state tuition $1,853. Annual out-of-state tuition $4,405. Room and board $5,296. Required fees $762. Average book expense $1,500. **Required Forms and Deadlines:** FAFSA, Institution's own financial aid form, State aid form. **Types of Aid:** *Need-based scholarships/grants:* State scholarships/grants, United Negro College Fund. *Student Employment:* Federal Work-Study Program available. Institutional employment available.

MORNINGSIDE COLLEGE

1501 Morningside Avenue, Sioux City, IA 51106-1751
Phone: 712-274-5511 • **Financial Aid Phone:** 712-274-5159
E-mail: mscadm@morningside.edu • **CEEB Code:** 6415
Fax: 712-274-5101 • **Website:** www.morningside.edu • **ACT Code:** 1338

This private school, affiliated with the Methodist Church, was founded in 1894. It has a 68-acre campus.

RATINGS

Admissions Selectivity Rating: 77   **Fire Safety Rating:** 70   **Green Rating:** 60*

STUDENTS AND FACULTY

Enrollment: 1,180. **Student Body:** 54% female, 46% male, 32% out-of-state, 1% international (4 countries represented). Asian 2%, African American 1%, Caucasian 84%, Hispanic 3%, Native American 1%, Pacific Islander 0%, Two or more races 0%, Race unknown 9%.
Retention and Graduation: 70% freshmen return for sophomore year. 31% freshmen graduate within 4 years. 44% freshmen graduate within 6 years. 11% grads go on to further study within 1 year. 48% grads pursue arts and sciences degrees. 10% grads pursue law degrees. **Faculty:** Student/faculty ratio 17:1. 69 full-time faculty, 77% hold PhDs, 3% are are members of minority groups, 45% are women. 0% of classes are taught by teaching assistants.

ACADEMICS

Degrees: bachelor's, master's. **Classes:** Most classes have 10-19 students. Most lab/discussion sessions have 10-19 students. **Most popular majors:** Biology/Biological Sciences; Elementary Education and Teaching; Business Administration and Management. **Special Study Options:** distance learning, double major, dual enrollment, English as a Second Language (ESL), honors program, independent study, internships, liberal arts/career combination, student-designed major, study abroad, teacher certification program, health professions. Combined degree programs: BA/MA. **Disability Services:** Special programs offered to physically disabled students, including note-taking services, reader services, tape recorders, tutors. **Career Services:** Alumni network, Alumni services, Career/job search classes, Career assessment, Internships, Regional alumni.

FACILITIES

Housing: Coed dorms, fraternity/sorority housing, apartments for married students, apartments for single students. 50% of campus accessible to physically disabled. **Special Academic Facilities/Equipment:** media-enhanced "smart classroom", high-speed campus internet connection, art gallery, theatre, totally renovated science facility. **Computers:** 100% of classrooms, 100% of dorms, 100% of libraries, 100% of dining areas, 100% of student union, 100% of common outdoor areas have wireless network access. Students can register for classes online. Administrative functions (other than registration) can be performed online. Undergraduates are required to own a computer.

CAMPUS LIFE

Environment: City. **Activities:** Choral groups, concert band, dance, drama/theater, jazz band, literary magazine, marching band, music ensembles, musical theater, pep band, radio station, student government, student newspaper, television station, yearbook, Campus Ministries, Student Organization. 40 registered organizations, 15 honor societies, 10 religious organizations. 2 fraternities, 1 sorority. **Athletics (Intercollegiate):** *Men:* baseball, basketball, cheerleading, cross-country, football, golf, soccer, swimming, tennis, track/field (outdoor), track/field (indoor), wrestling. *Women:* basketball, cheerleading, cross-country, golf, soccer, softball, swimming, tennis, track/field (outdoor), track/field (indoor), volleyball. **On-Campus Highlights:** New Student Apartments, Health-Fitness Center, Eppley Auditorium, Olsen Student Center, Walker Science Center.

ADMISSIONS

Freshman Academic Profile: Average high school GPA 3.4. 15% in top 10% of high school class, 42% in top 25% of high school class, 78% in top 50% of high school class. 94% from public high schools. ACT middle 50% range 20-25. Minimum paper TOEFL 450. **Basis for Candidate Selection:** *Very important factors considered include:* rigor of secondary school record, class rank, academic GPA, standardized test scores, recommendation(s). *Important factors considered include:* interview, extracurricular activities, talent/ability. *Other factors considered include:* application essay. **Freshman Admission Requirements:** High school diploma is required and GED is accepted. *Academic units recommended:* 3 English, 2 math, 2 science, 3 social studies. **Freshman Admission Statistics:** 1,240 applied, 89.52% admitted, 30% enrolled. **Transfer Admission Requirements:** High school transcript, college transcript(s), statement of good standing from prior institution(s). Minimum college GPA of 2.25 required. Lowest grade transferable C-. **General Admission Information:** Application fee $25. Priority deadline 8/15. Nonfall registration accepted. Admission may be deferred.

COSTS AND FINANCIAL AID

Annual tuition $21,116. Room and board $6,729. Required fees $1,130. Average book expense $800. **Required Forms and Deadlines:** FAFSA. **Notification of Awards:** Applicants will be notified of awards on a rolling basis beginning 3/31. **Types of Aid:** *Need-based scholarships/grants:* Federal Pell, FSEOG, State scholarships/grants, Private scholarships, College/university scholarship or grant aid from institutional funds. *Loans:* Federal Perkins Loans, State Loans, College/university loans from institutional funds. *Student Employment:* Federal Work-Study Program available. Institutional employment available. **Financial Aid Statistics:** 73% needy freshmen, 76% needy undergrads receive need-based scholarship or grant aid. 83% freshmen, 86% undergrads receive need-based self-help aid. 56% freshmen, 45% undergrads receive athletic scholarships. 100% freshmen, 100% undergrads receive any aid. **Criteria for awarding aid:** *Need-based:* Job skills. *Non-need-based:* Academics, Alumni affiliation, Art, Athletics, Job skills, Leadership, Music/drama, Religious affiliation, State/district residency.

MORRIS COLLEGE

100 West College Street, Sumter, SC 29150
Phone: 803-934-3225 • **Financial Aid Phone:** 803-934-3238
E-mail: gscriven@morris.edu • **CEEB Code:** 5418
Fax: 803-773-8241 • **Website:** http://www.morris.edu/ • **ACT Code:** 3868

This private school, affiliated with the Baptist Church, was founded in 1908. It has a 34-acre campus.

RATINGS

Admissions Selectivity Rating: 63   **Fire Safety Rating:** 85   **Green Rating:** 60*

STUDENTS AND FACULTY

Enrollment: 750. **Student Body:** 59% female, 41% male, 18% out-of-state, 0% international (0 countries represented). Asian 0%, African American 98%, Caucasian 0%, Hispanic 1%, Native American <1%, Pacific Islander 0%, Two or more races 1%, Race unknown 0%.
Retention and Graduation: 55% freshmen return for sophomore year. 6% freshmen graduate within 4 years. 22% freshmen graduate within 6 years. 13% grads go on to further study within 1 year. 7% grads pursue arts and sciences degrees. 1% grads pursue law degrees. 2% grads pursue business degrees. 1% grads pursue medical degrees. **Faculty:** Student/faculty ratio 13:1. 39 full-time faculty, 72% hold PhDs, 64% are are members of minority groups, 49% are women.

ACADEMICS

Degrees: bachelor's. **Classes:** Most classes have 10-19 students. Most lab/discussion sessions have fewer than 10 students. **Most popular majors:** Criminal Justice/Law Enforcement Administration; Business Administration and Management; Biology/Biological Sciences. **Special Study Options:** Accelerated program, cooperative education program, double major, honors program, internships, liberal arts/career combination, study abroad, teacher certification program, Advanced degree program available for adults aged

25 and older with 60 earned credit hours. Combined degree programs: Dual degree, math/engineering with NC A&T State U. **Career Services:** Alumni network, Alumni services, Career/job search classes, Career assessment, Internships. The cooperative education internship program allows students to gain invaluable paid work experience closely related to their chosen field of study while earning their undergraduate degrees. The majority of these students are hired full-time by their co-op employers upon graduation from the college.

FACILITIES

Housing: men's dorms, women's dorms. 90% of campus accessible to physically disabled. **Special Academic Facilities/Equipment:** WMMC-640AM Student Radio Station **Computers:** 100% of classrooms, 100% of dorms, 100% of libraries, 100% of dining areas, 100% of student union, 95% of common outdoor areas have wireless network access. Administrative functions (other than registration) can be performed online.

CAMPUS LIFE

Environment: Town. **Activities:** Choral groups, dance, drama/theater, literary magazine, pep band, radio station, student government, student newspaper, yearbook. 55 registered organizations, 7 honor societies, 2 religious organizations. 4 fraternities, 4 sororities. **Athletics (Intercollegiate):** *Men:* baseball, basketball, cheerleading, cross-country, golf, tennis, track/field (outdoor). *Women:* basketball, cheerleading, cross-country, softball, tennis, track/field (outdoor), volleyball. **On-Campus Highlights:** Student Center, Library, Human Development Center, Outdoor Basketball Court, Auditorium, Computer Labs.

ADMISSIONS

Freshman Academic Profile: Average high school GPA 2.5. 0% in top 10% of high school class, 0% in top 25% of high school class, 31% in top 50% of high school class. 98% from public high schools. Minimum paper TOEFL 500. **Basis for Candidate Selection:** *Very important factors considered include:* academic GPA. *Important factors considered include:* class rank, standardized test scores. **Freshman Admission Requirements:** High school diploma is required and GED is accepted. *Academic units required:* 4 English, 4 math, 3 science, 1 foreign language, 1 social studies, 1 history, 7 academic electives, 1 computer science, and 2 units from above areas or other academic areas. *Academic units recommended:* 2 foreign language. **Freshman Admission Statistics:** 2,551 applied, 78.48% admitted, 11% enrolled. **Transfer Admission Requirements:** High school transcript, college transcript(s), standardized test scores, statement of good standing from prior institution(s). Minimum college GPA of 2.0 required. Lowest grade transferable C. **General Admission Information:** Application fee $20. Priority deadline 7/1. Nonfall registration accepted. Admission may be deferred for a maximum of 1 semester.

COSTS AND FINANCIAL AID

Average book expense $3,000. **Required Forms and Deadlines:** FAFSA, Institution's own financial aid form. **Notification of Awards:** Applicants will be notified of awards on a rolling basis beginning 6/1. **Types of Aid:** *Need-based scholarships/grants:* Federal Pell, FSEOG, State scholarships/grants, Private scholarships, College/university scholarship or grant aid from institutional funds, United Negro College Fund. *Loans:* Direct Subsidized Stafford Loans, Direct Unsubsidized Stafford Loans, Direct PLUS loans, Federal Perkins Loans. *Student Employment:* Federal Work-Study Program available. **Financial Aid Statistics:** 98% needy freshmen, 95% needy undergrads receive need-based scholarship or grant aid. 24% freshmen, 21% undergrads receive non-need-based scholarship or grant aid. 93% freshmen, 96% undergrads receive need-based self-help aid. 7% freshmen, 8% undergrads receive athletic scholarships. 99% freshmen, 98% undergrads receive any aid. 99% undergrads borrow to pay for school. Average cumulative indebtedness $31,500. **Criteria for awarding aid:** *Non-need-based:* Academics, Athletics, State/district residency.

MOUNT ALLISON UNIVERSITY

65 York Street, Sackville, NB E4L1E4
Phone: 506-364-2269 • **Financial Aid Phone:** 506-364-2258
E-mail: admissions@mta.ca
Fax: 506-364-2272 • **Website:** www.mta.ca

This public school was founded in 1839. It has a 25-acre campus.

RATINGS

Admissions Selectivity Rating: 64   **Fire Safety Rating:** 93   **Green Rating:** 60*

STUDENTS AND FACULTY

Student Body: 58% female, 42% male, 43% out-of-state, (40 countries represented).
Retention and Graduation: 82% freshmen return for sophomore year. 60% freshmen graduate within 4 years. 66% freshmen graduate within 6 years. 30%

grads go on to further study within 1 year. 10% grads pursue arts and sciences degrees. 3% grads pursue law degrees. 5% grads pursue business degrees. 12% grads pursue medical degrees. **Faculty:** Student/faculty ratio 15:1. 132 full-time faculty, 92% hold PhDs, 0% are are members of minority groups, 43% are women. 0% of classes are taught by teaching assistants.

ACADEMICS

Degrees: bachelor's, master's. **Classes:** Most classes have fewer than 10 students. **Most popular majors:** Sociology; Business/Commerce. **Special Study Options:** distance learning, double major, English as a Second Language (ESL), exchange student program (domestic), honors program, independent study, internships, student-designed major, study abroad. **Disability Services:** Special programs offered to physically disabled students, including reader services, tutors. **Career Services:** Career/job search classes, On-campus interviews.

FACILITIES

Housing: Coed dorms, special housing for disabled students, special housing for international students, women's dorms, cooperative housing, Zero environment Footprint Housing Pet Friendly Housing. (one residence fosters pets for humane society). 80% of campus accessible to physically diasbled. **Special Academic Facilities/Equipment:** Art gallery **Computers:** 100% of classrooms, 100% of dorms, 100% of libraries, 100% of dining areas, 100% of student union, 85% of common outdoor areas have wireless network access. Students can register for classes online. Administrative functions (other than registration) can be performed online.

CAMPUS LIFE

Environment: Rural. **Activities:** Choral groups, concert band, dance, drama/theater, jazz band, music ensembles, musical theater, radio station, student government, student newspaper, student-run film society, symphony orchestra, yearbook, Student Organization. 106 registered organizations. **Athletics (Intercollegiate):** *Men:* badminton, basketball, football, rugby, soccer, swimming. *Women:* badminton, basketball, rugby, soccer, swimming, volleyball. **On-Campus Highlights:** Ownes Art Gallery, Jenings Dinning Hall, Library, Student Center **Environmental Initiatives:** Residence Climate Change Challenge expanded this year to include academic and administrative buildings—buildings reduced their consumption of utilities during the month of February from 10 to 25%.

ADMISSIONS

Freshman Academic Profile: 99% from public high schools. Minimum paper TOEFL 550. **Basis for Candidate Selection:** *Very important factors considered include:* rigor of secondary school record, academic GPA, interview, extracurricular activities, talent/ability. *Important factors considered include:* recommendation(s), character/personal qualities, volunteer work. *Other factors considered include:* class rank, standardized test scores, application essay, work experience. **Freshman Admission Requirements:** High school diploma is required and GED is accepted. **Freshman Admission Statistics:** 1,789 applied, 84.80% admitted, 49% enrolled. **Transfer Admission Requirements:** High school transcript, college transcript(s), essay or personal statement, statement of good standing from prior institution(s). Lowest grade transferable c-. **General Admission Information:** Application fee $50. Priority deadline 3/15. Nonfall registration accepted. Admission may be deferred.

COSTS AND FINANCIAL AID

Annual in-state tuition $7,465. Annual out-of-state tuition $7,465. Room and board $9,595. Required fees $545. Average book expense $1,200. **Required Forms and Deadlines:** FAFSA, Institution's own financial aid form. **Types of Aid:** *Need-based scholarships/grants:* Private scholarships, College/university scholarship or grant aid from institutional funds. **Financial Aid Statistics:** 100% needy freshmen, 100% needy undergrads receive need-based scholarship or grant aid. 0% undergrads receive non-need-based scholarship or grant aid. 0% freshmen, 0% undergrads receive need-based self-help aid. 0% freshmen, 0% undergrads receive athletic scholarships. **Criteria for awarding aid:** *Need-based:* Academics, Alumni affiliation, Art, Athletics, Job skills, Leadership, Minority status, Music/drama, Religious affiliation. *Non-need-based:* Academics, Alumni affiliation, Art, Athletics, Job skills, Leadership, Minority status, Music/drama, State/district residency.

MOUNT ALOYSIUS COLLEGE

7373 Admiral Peary Highway, Cresson, PA 16630
Phone: 814-886-6383 • **Financial Aid Phone:** 814-886-6463
E-mail: admissions@mtaloy.edu • **CEEB Code:** 2420
Fax: 814-886-6441 • **ACT Code:** 3635

This private school, affiliated with the Roman Catholic Church, was founded in 1939. It has a 125-acre campus.

RATINGS

Admissions Selectivity Rating: 71   **Fire Safety Rating:** 60*   **Green Rating:** 60*

STUDENTS AND FACULTY

Enrollment: 1,310. **Student Body:** 72% female, 28% male, 7% out-of-state, 5% international. Asian 0%, African American 2%, Caucasian 76%, Hispanic 1%, Native American <1%, Pacific Islander 0%, Two or more races 0%, Race unknown 15%.
Faculty: Student/faculty ratio 11:1. 72 full-time faculty, 0% hold PhDs, 3% are are members of minority groups, 74% are women. 0% of classes are taught by teaching assistants.

ACADEMICS

Degrees: associate, bachelor's, certificate, master's, terminal. **Classes:** Most classes have 10-19 students. Most lab/discussion sessions have fewer than 10 students. **Most popular majors:** Medical Radiologic Technology/ Science ; Registered Nursing/Registered Nurse; Business Administration and Management. **Special Study Options:** Accelerated program, distance learning, honors program, independent study, internships, student-designed major, teacher certification program. **Career Services:** Alumni services, Career/job search classes, Career assessment, Internships.

FACILITIES

Housing: Coed dorms. **Computers:** 100% of classrooms, 100% of dorms, 100% of libraries, 100% of dining areas, 100% of student union, 100% of common outdoor areas have wireless network access.

CAMPUS LIFE

Environment: Rural. **Activities:** Choral groups, drama/theater, student government, student newspaper. 16 registered organizations, 2 honor societies, 1 religious organization. **Athletics (Intercollegiate):** *Men:* basketball, golf, soccer. *Women:* basketball, soccer, volleyball.

ADMISSIONS

Freshman Academic Profile: Average high school GPA 3.3. **Reported SAT (pre-2016 redesign) scores:** SAT Math middle 50% range 440-520. SAT Critical Reading middle 50% range 430-510. SAT Writing middle 50% range 400-483. **Concordant SAT scores:** SAT EBRW middle 50% 460-550. SAT Math middle 50% range 480-550. ACT middle 50% range 18-21. **Basis for Candidate Selection:** *Very important factors considered include:* rigor of secondary school record, academic GPA, interview, extracurricular activities, talent/ability, character/personal qualities, first generation, volunteer work. *Important factors considered include:* class rank, standardized test scores, recommendation(s), level of applicant's interest. *Other factors considered include:* application essay. **Freshman Admission Requirements:** High school diploma is required and GED is accepted. *Academic units required:* 4 English, 3 math, 3 science, 3 social studies, 3 academic electives. *Academic units recommended:* 2 foreign language, 3 history. **Transfer Admission Requirements:** High school transcript, college transcript(s), Minimum college GPA of 2.0 required. Lowest grade transferable C. **General Admission Information:** Application fee $30. Nonfall registration accepted. Admission may be deferred for a maximum of 1 year.

COSTS AND FINANCIAL AID

Annual tuition $20,710. Room and board $9,940. Required fees $1,140. Average book expense $2,500. **Required Forms and Deadlines:** FAFSA. **Notification of Awards:** Applicants will be notified of awards on a rolling basis beginning 3/15. **Types of Aid:** *Need-based scholarships/grants:* Federal Pell, FSEOG, State scholarships/grants, Private scholarships. *Loans:* Direct Subsidized Stafford Loans, Direct Unsubsidized Stafford Loans, Direct PLUS loans, Federal Perkins Loans, Federal Nursing Loans. *Student Employment:* Federal Work-Study Program available. Institutional employment available. **Financial Aid Statistics:** 100% needy freshmen, 100% needy undergrads receive need-based scholarship or grant aid. 30% freshmen, 20% undergrads receive non-need-based scholarship or grant aid. 100% freshmen, 100% undergrads receive need-based self-help aid. 0% freshmen, 0% undergrads receive athletic scholarships. **Criteria for awarding aid:** *Non-need-based:* Academics, Art, Leadership, Music/drama, Religious affiliation.

MOUNT HOLYOKE COLLEGE

Best Colleges

Newhall Center, South Hadley, MA 1075
Phone: 413-538-2023 • **Financial Aid Phone:** 413-538-2291
E-mail: admission@mtholyoke.edu • **CEEB Code:** 3529
Fax: 413-538-2409 • **Website:** www.mtholyoke.edu • **ACT Code:** 1866

This private school was founded in 1837. It has a 800-acre campus.

RATINGS
Admissions Selectivity Rating: 90   **Fire Safety Rating:** 88   **Green Rating:** 90

STUDENTS AND FACULTY
Enrollment: 2,179. **Student Body:** 100% female, 0% male, 75% out-of-state, 27% international (69 countries represented). Asian 11%, African American 5%, Caucasian 45%, Hispanic 8%, Native American <1%, Pacific Islander <1%, Two or more races 3%, Race unknown 1%.
Retention and Graduation: 91% freshmen return for sophomore year. 78% freshmen graduate within 4 years. 84% freshmen graduate within 6 years. 16% grads go on to further study within 1 year. 16% grads pursue arts and sciences degrees. 3% grads pursue law degrees. 2% grads pursue medical degrees.
Faculty: Student/faculty ratio 10:1. 200 full-time faculty, 99% hold PhDs, 28% are are members of minority groups, 56% are women. 0% of classes are taught by teaching assistants.

ACADEMICS
Degrees: bachelor's, master's, postbachelor's certificate. **Classes:** Most classes have 10-19 students. Most lab/discussion sessions have 10-19 students. **Most popular majors:** Economics; Psychology; Biology/Biological Sciences. **Special Study Options:** cooperative education program, cross-registration, double major, exchange student program (domestic), independent study, internships, liberal arts/career combination, student-designed major, study abroad, teacher certification program, Community-based learning courses and First-Year seminars. Combined degree programs: 3/2 BA/BEng Pgm with CalTech.
Disability Services: Special programs offered to physically disabled students, including note-taking services, reader services, tape recorders, tutors. **Career Services:** Alumni network, Alumni services, Career/job search classes, Career assessment, Internships, Regional alumni. A central goal of the Mount Holyoke College initiative The Lynk is to ensure that each MHC student has the opportunity to explore her career interests, gain practical experience and begin to develop a professional network through an internship or research project.

FACILITIES
Housing: special housing for disabled students, women's dorms, apartments for single students, Special housing arrangements are available upon request. **Special Academic Facilities/Equipment:** Art and historical museums, bronze-casting foundry, child study center, audio-visual center, language learning center, greenhouse, Japanese meditation garden, equestrian center, observatory, linear accelerator, electron microscope, refracting telescope, nuclear magnetic resonance equipment, MCulloch Center for Global Initiatives, Weissman Center for Leadership and the Liberal Arts, Center for the Environment. **Computers:** 20% of classrooms, 100% of dorms, 100% of libraries, 100% of dining areas, 100% of student union, 4% of common outdoor areas have wireless network access. Students can register for classes online. Administrative functions (other than registration) can be performed online.

CAMPUS LIFE
Environment: Town. **Activities:** Choral groups, dance, drama/theater, jazz band, literary magazine, music ensembles, musical theater, radio station, student government, student newspaper, student-run film society, symphony orchestra, yearbook, Campus Ministries, Student Organization, Model UN. 150 registered organizations, 4 honor societies, 12 religious organizations. **Athletics (Intercollegiate):** *Women:* basketball, crew/rowing, cross-country, diving, equestrian sports, field hockey, golf, horseback riding, lacrosse, soccer, squash, swimming, tennis, track/field (outdoor), track/field (indoor), volleyball. **On-Campus Highlights:** Unified Science Center, Kendall Sports and Dance Complex, The Equestrian Center, Blanchard Campus Center, Williston Memorial Library, The entire campus is an exquisitely maintained botanic garden which includes an arboretum, numerous gardens, and the Talcott Greenhouse. **Environmental Initiatives:** Using the campus as a laboratory, a restoration ecology seminar has designed and is working toward implementing stream, lake and forest restoration projects on campus. https://www.mtholyoke.edu/giving/restoring-world-here

ADMISSIONS
Freshman Academic Profile: Average high school GPA 3.8. 69% from public high schools. **Reported SAT (pre-2016 redesign) scores:** SAT Math middle 50% range 610-740. SAT Critical Reading middle 50% range 610-720. SAT Writing middle 50% range 630-710. **Concordant SAT scores:** SAT EBRW middle 50% 670–740. SAT Math middle 50% range 630–760. ACT middle 50% range 28-32. Minimum internet-based TOEFL 100. **Basis for Candidate Selection:** *Very important factors considered include:* rigor of secondary school record, class rank, academic GPA, application essay, recommendation(s). *Important factors considered include:* interview, extracurricular activities, talent/ability, character/personal qualities, volunteer work, work experience. *Other factors considered include:* standardized test scores, first generation, alumni/ae relation, geographical residence, racial/ethnic status, level of applicant's interest. **Freshman Admission Requirements:** High school diploma is required and GED is accepted. *Academic units recommended:* 4 English, 3 science labs, 3 history, 1 academic elective. **Freshman Admission Statistics:** 3,543 applied, 52.19% admitted, 32% enrolled. **Transfer Admission Requirements:** High school transcript, college transcript(s), essay or personal statement, statement of good standing from prior institution(s). Minimum college GPA of 3.0 required. Lowest grade transferable C-. **General Admission Information:** Application fee $60. Regular application deadline 1/15. Regular notification 4/1. Nonfall registration accepted. Admission may be deferred.

COSTS AND FINANCIAL AID
Annual tuition $45,680. Room and board $13,440. Required fees $186. Average book expense $950. **Required Forms and Deadlines:** FAFSA, CSS/Financial Aid PROFILE, Noncustodial PROFILE. **Notification of Awards:** Applicants will be notified of awards on or about 4/1. **Types of Aid:** *Need-based scholarships/grants:* Federal Pell, FSEOG, State scholarships/grants, Private scholarships, College/university scholarship or grant aid from institutional funds. *Loans:* Direct Subsidized Stafford Loans, Direct Unsubsidized Stafford Loans, Direct PLUS loans, Federal Perkins Loans, State Loans, College/university loans from institutional funds. *Student Employment:* Federal Work-Study Program available. Institutional employment available. **Financial Aid Statistics:** 100% needy freshmen, 99% needy undergrads receive need-based scholarship or grant aid. 23% freshmen, 21% undergrads receive non-need-based scholarship or grant aid. 78% freshmen, 84% undergrads receive need-based self-help aid. 0% freshmen, 0% undergrads receive athletic scholarships. 81% freshmen, 80% undergrads receive any aid. 60% undergrads borrow to pay for school. Average cumulative indebtedness $23,872. **Criteria for awarding aid:** *Non-need-based:* Academics, Leadership.

MOUNT IDA COLLEGE

777 Dedham Street, Newton, MA 2459
Phone: 617-928-4553 • **Financial Aid Phone:** 617-928-4785
E-mail: admissions@mountida.edu • **CEEB Code:** 3530
Fax: 617-928-4507 • **Website:** www.mountida.edu • **ACT Code:** 1868

This private school was founded in 1899. It has a 72-acre campus.

RATINGS
Admissions Selectivity Rating: 74   **Fire Safety Rating:** 60*   **Green Rating:** 60*

STUDENTS AND FACULTY
Enrollment: 884. **Student Body:** 67% female, 33% male, 34% out-of-state, 8% international (32 countries represented). Asian 2%, African American 9%, Caucasian 63%, Hispanic 10%, Native American 0%, Pacific Islander <1%, Two or more races 2%, Race unknown 5%.
Retention and Graduation: 57% freshmen return for sophomore year. 31% freshmen graduate within 4 years. 40 **Faculty:** Student/faculty ratio 14:1. 55 full-time faculty, 0% hold PhDs, 5% are are members of minority groups, 62% are women. 0% of classes are taught by teaching assistants.

ACADEMICS
Degrees: associate, bachelor's, certificate, terminal, transfer. **Classes:** Most classes have 10-19 students. **Special Study Options:** Accelerated program, distance learning, English as a Second Language (ESL), honors program, independent study, internships, student-designed major, study abroad, teacher certification program. **Disability Services:** Special programs offered to physically disabled students, including tape recorders, tutors. **Career Services:** Alumni network, Alumni services, Career assessment, Internships.

FACILITIES
Housing: Coed dorms, special housing for disabled students, men's dorms, women's dorms. **Special Academic Facilities/Equipment:** Mount Ida College Art Gallery.

CAMPUS LIFE

Environment: Village. **Activities:** Choral groups, dance, drama/theater, literary magazine, radio station, student government, student newspaper, yearbook, Student Organization. 22 registered organizations, 6 honor societies. **Athletics (Intercollegiate):** *Men:* basketball, football, lacrosse, soccer, volleyball. *Women:* basketball, cheerleading, cross-country, equestrian sports, soccer, softball, volleyball.

ADMISSIONS

Freshman Academic Profile: Average high school GPA 3.0. **Reported SAT (pre-2016 redesign) scores:** SAT Math middle 50% range 400-500. SAT Critical Reading middle 50% range 400-510. SAT Writing middle 50% range 390-500. **Concordant SAT scores:** SAT EBRW middle 50% 440–560. SAT Math middle 50% range 440–530. ACT middle 50% range 16-22. Minimum internet-based TOEFL 70. Minimum paper TOEFL 525. **Basis for Candidate Selection:** *Very important factors considered include:* academic GPA. *Important factors considered include:* rigor of secondary school record, recommendation(s). *Other factors considered include:* standardized test scores, application essay, interview, extracurricular activities, talent/ability, character/personal qualities, volunteer work, work experience. **Freshman Admission Requirements:** High school diploma is required and GED is accepted. *Academic units recommended:* 4 English, 3 math, 3 science, 2 foreign language, 2 social studies. **Freshman Admission Statistics:** 2,319 applied, 63.26% admitted, 30% enrolled. **Transfer Admission Requirements:** High school transcript, college transcript(s), essay or personal statement, statement of good standing from prior institution(s). Minimum college GPA of 2.0 required. Lowest grade transferable C. **General Admission Information:** Application fee $45. Nonfall registration accepted. Admission may be deferred for a maximum of 1 year.

COSTS AND FINANCIAL AID

Annual tuition $32,300. Room and board $13,000. Required fees $1,520. Average book expense $1,000. **Required Forms and Deadlines:** FAFSA. **Notification of Awards:** Applicants will be notified of awards on a rolling basis beginning 3/1. **Types of Aid:** *Need-based scholarships/grants:* Federal Pell, FSEOG, State scholarships/grants, Private scholarships, College/university scholarship or grant aid from institutional funds. *Loans:* State Loans. *Student Employment:* Federal Work-Study Program available. Institutional employment available. **Financial Aid Statistics:** 99% needy freshmen, 85% needy undergrads receive need-based scholarship or grant aid. 100% freshmen, 99% undergrads receive non-need-based scholarship or grant aid. 90% freshmen, 89% undergrads receive need-based self-help aid. 0% freshmen, 0% undergrads receive athletic scholarships. **Criteria for awarding aid:** *Need-based:* Academics, Art, Leadership. *Non-need-based:* Academics, Art, Leadership.

MOUNT MARY UNIVERSITY

2900 North Menomonee River Parkway, Milwaukee, WI 53222-4597
Phone: 414-930-3024 • **Financial Aid Phone:** 414-930-3163
E-mail: mmu-admiss@mtmary.edu • **CEEB Code:** 1490
Fax: 414-930-3708 • **Website:** http://www.mtmary.edu/ • **ACT Code:** 4620

This private school, affiliated with the Roman Catholic Church, was founded in 1913. It has a 80-acre campus.

RATINGS

Admissions Selectivity Rating: 81   **Fire Safety Rating:** 86   **Green Rating:** 60*

STUDENTS AND FACULTY

Enrollment: 789. **Student Body:** 100% female, 0% male, 7% out-of-state, 2% international (15 countries represented). Asian 8%, African American 17%, Caucasian 52%, Hispanic 16%, Native American <1%, Pacific Islander 0%, Two or more races 4%, Race unknown 4%.
Retention and Graduation: 77% freshmen return for sophomore year. 30% freshmen graduate within 4 years. 46 **Faculty:** Student/faculty ratio 12:1. 61 full-time faculty, 79% hold PhDs, 0% are are members of minority groups, 85% are women. 0% of classes are taught by teaching assistants.

ACADEMICS

Degrees: bachelor's, doctoral/professional, master's, postbachelor's certificate, post-master's certificate. **Classes:** Most classes have 10-19 students. Most lab/discussion sessions have 10-19 students. **Most popular majors:** Occupational Therapy/Therapist; Fashion/Apparel Design; Fashion Merchandising. **Special Study Options:** Accelerated program, double major, honors program, independent study, internships, liberal arts/career combination, student-designed major, study abroad, teacher certification program. **Honors Programs:** The purpose of the Mount Mary College Honors Program is to reward superior scholarly achievement and to provide special challenges to serious students who wish to achieve maximum benefit from their college

education. **Disability Services:** Special programs offered to physically disabled students, including note-taking services, reader services, tape recorders, tutors. **Career Services:** Career/job search classes, Career assessment, Internships.

FACILITIES

Housing: women's dorms. 90% of campus accessible to physically diasbled. **Special Academic Facilities/Equipment:** Hagerty Library, Marian Art Gallery, Walter and Olive Stiemke Memorial Hall and Conference Center. **Computers:** 100% of dorms, have wireless network access. Students can register for classes online. Administrative functions (other than registration) can be performed online.

CAMPUS LIFE

Environment: Metropolis. **Activities:** Choral groups, dance, literary magazine, music ensembles, student government, student newspaper, Campus Ministries, Student Organization, Model UN. 42 registered organizations, 14 honor societies, 1 religious organization. **Athletics (Intercollegiate):** *Women:* basketball, cross-country, soccer, softball, tennis, volleyball. **On-Campus Highlights:** Cyber Cafe, Gerhardinger Science and Technology Center, Haggerty Library, Notre Dame Hall, Bloechl Recreation Center. **Environmental Initiatives:** The university collaborates with our food service provider, FSI, to compost all food preparation materials, plant waste and coffee grounds. The efforts, which began in 2009, produce eight, 18 gallon totes of compost each week during the school year.

ADMISSIONS

Freshman Academic Profile: Average high school GPA 3.2. 23% in top 10% of high school class, 51% in top 25% of high school class, 84% in top 50% of high school class. ACT middle 50% range 18-23. Minimum internet-based TOEFL 61. Minimum paper TOEFL 500. **Basis for Candidate Selection:** *Very important factors considered include:* rigor of secondary school record, academic GPA. *Important factors considered include:* standardized test scores, talent/ability, character/personal qualities. *Other factors considered include:* class rank, application essay, recommendation(s), extracurricular activities, volunteer work, work experience. **Freshman Admission Requirements:** High school diploma is required and GED is accepted. *Academic units required:* 4 English, 2 math, 4 science, 2 science labs, 2 social studies, 2 history, 2 academic electives. *Academic units recommended:* 4 English, 3 math, 5 science, 2 science labs, 2 foreign language, 2 social studies, 2 history, 2 academic electives. **Freshman Admission Statistics:** 689 applied, 56.31% admitted, 30% enrolled. **Transfer Admission Requirements:** High school transcript, college transcript(s), Minimum college GPA of 2.0 required. Lowest grade transferable C. **General Admission Information:** Nonfall registration accepted. Admission may be deferred for a maximum of 1 year.

COSTS AND FINANCIAL AID

Annual tuition $28,940. Room and board $8,530. Required fees $570. Average book expense $1,400. **Required Forms and Deadlines:** FAFSA. **Notification of Awards:** Applicants will be notified of awards on a rolling basis beginning 3/1. **Types of Aid:** *Need-based scholarships/grants:* Federal Pell, FSEOG, State scholarships/grants, Private scholarships, College/university scholarship or grant aid from institutional funds. *Loans:* Direct Subsidized Stafford Loans, Direct Unsubsidized Stafford Loans, Direct PLUS loans, Federal Perkins Loans. *Student Employment:* Federal Work-Study Program available. Institutional employment available. **Financial Aid Statistics:** 100% needy freshmen, 100% needy undergrads receive need-based scholarship or grant aid. 8% freshmen, 7% undergrads receive non-need-based scholarship or grant aid. 86% freshmen, 91% undergrads receive need-based self-help aid. 0% freshmen, 0% undergrads receive athletic scholarships. 100% freshmen, 95% undergrads receive any aid. Average cumulative indebtedness $26,237. **Criteria for awarding aid:** *Non-need-based:* Academics, Alumni affiliation, Art, Leadership, Music/drama.

MOUNT MERCY UNIVERSITY

1330 Elmhurst Drive Northeast, Cedar Rapids, IA 52402-4797
Phone: 319-368-6460 • **Financial Aid Phone:** 319-363-8213
E-mail: admission@mtmercy.edu
Fax: 319-363-5270 • **Website:** www.mtmercy.edu • **ACT Code:** 1340

This is a private school.

RATINGS

Admissions Selectivity Rating: 80   **Fire Safety Rating:** 60*   **Green Rating:** 60*

STUDENTS AND FACULTY

Enrollment: 1,283. **Student Body:** 71% female, 29% male, 6% out-of-state, 3% international (27 countries represented). Asian 1%, African American 4%, Caucasian 84%, Hispanic 2%, Native American <1%, Pacific Islander <1%, Two or more races 2%, Race unknown 4%.

Retention and Graduation: 81% freshmen return for sophomore year. 65% freshmen graduate within 4 years. 72% freshmen graduate within 6 years. 17% grads go on to further study within 1 year. **Faculty:** Student/faculty ratio 14:1. 84 full-time faculty, 54% hold PhDs, 10% are are members of minority groups, 65% are women. 0% of classes are taught by teaching assistants.

ACADEMICS
Degrees: bachelor's, master's. **Classes:** Most classes have 10-19 students. **Most popular majors:** Education; Business/Commerce; Registered Nursing/Registered Nurse. **Special Study Options:** Accelerated program, cooperative education program, cross-registration, double major, dual enrollment, honors program, independent study, internships, liberal arts/career combination, student-designed major, study abroad, teacher certification program, weekend college. Combined degree programs: 2-2 programs with Kirkwood Community College. **Disability Services:** Special programs offered to physically disabled students, including note-taking services, reader services, tape recorders, tutors. **Career Services:** Alumni network, Alumni services, Career/job search classes, Career assessment, Internships, Regional alumni.

FACILITIES
Housing: Coed dorms, apartments for single students. 95% of campus accessible to physically diasbled.

CAMPUS LIFE
Activities: Choral groups, drama/theater, literary magazine, pep band, student government, student newspaper. 35 registered organizations, 16 honor societies, 7 religious organizations. **Athletics (Intercollegiate):** *Men:* baseball, basketball, cross-country, golf, soccer, track/field (outdoor). *Women:* basketball, cross-country, golf, soccer, softball, track/field (outdoor), volleyball. **On-Campus Highlights:** Lundy Commons: Game Room, TV Room, Convenience Store, Bookstore, Lounges, Hilltop Grill and Dining Hall, Busse Library, Andrea's House-144 bed, suite style campus residence, Entire campus is connected by underground tunnels.

ADMISSIONS
Freshman Academic Profile: Average high school GPA 3.4. 10% in top 10% of high school class, 38% in top 25% of high school class, 72% in top 50% of high school class. 83% from public high schools. ACT middle 50% range 19-25. Minimum paper TOEFL 550. **Basis for Candidate Selection:** *Very important factors considered include:* rigor of secondary school record, class rank, standardized test scores. *Important factors considered include:* application essay, recommendation(s), extracurricular activities. *Other factors considered include:* interview, talent/ability, character/personal qualities, volunteer work. **Freshman Admission Requirements:** High school diploma is required and GED is accepted. *Academic units recommended:* 4 English, 4 math, 3 science, 2 foreign language, 2 social studies, 2 history. **Freshman Admission Statistics:** 695 applied, 56.83% admitted, 42% enrolled. **Transfer Admission Requirements:** college transcript(s), statement of good standing from prior institution(s). Minimum college GPA of 2.5 required. Lowest grade transferable D. **General Admission Information:** Application fee $20. Regular application deadline 8/30. Nonfall registration accepted. Admission may be deferred for a maximum of 1 year.

COSTS AND FINANCIAL AID
Annual tuition $28,226. Room and board $8,600. Average book expense $1,200. **Required Forms and Deadlines:** FAFSA. **Notification of Awards:** Applicants will be notified of awards on a rolling basis beginning 3/15. **Types of Aid:** *Need-based scholarships/grants:* Federal Pell, FSEOG, State scholarships/grants, College/university scholarship or grant aid from institutional funds. *Loans:* Direct Subsidized Stafford Loans, Direct Unsubsidized Stafford Loans, Direct PLUS loans, Federal Perkins Loans, State Loans, College/university loans from institutional funds. *Student Employment:* Federal Work-Study Program available. Institutional employment available. **Financial Aid Statistics:** 100% needy freshmen, 99% needy undergrads receive need-based scholarship or grant aid. 14% freshmen, 12% undergrads receive non-need-based scholarship or grant aid. 82% freshmen, 85% undergrads receive need-based self-help aid. 16% freshmen, 9% undergrads receive athletic scholarships. 100% freshmen receive any aid. **Criteria for awarding aid:** *Non-need-based:* Academics, Art, Leadership, Music/drama.

MOUNT OLIVE COLLEGE

634 Henderson Street, Mount Olive, NC 28365
Phone: 919-658-2502
E-mail: admissions@moc.edu • **CEEB Code:** 5435
Fax: 919-658-9816 • **Website:** www.moc.edu • **ACT Code:** 3131

This private school, affiliated with the Baptist Church, was founded in 1951. It has a 138-acre campus.

RATINGS
Admissions Selectivity Rating: 79   **Fire Safety Rating:** 60*   **Green Rating:** 60*

STUDENTS AND FACULTY
Enrollment: 3,248. **Student Body:** 68% female, 32% male, 4% out-of-state, 0% international. Asian 1%, African American 36%, Caucasian 52%, Hispanic 3%, Native American <1%, Pacific Islander 0%, Two or more races 0%, Race unknown 7%.
Retention and Graduation: 68% freshmen return for sophomore year. 20% grads go on to further study within 1 year. **Faculty:** Student/faculty ratio 26:1. 80 full-time faculty, 96% hold PhDs, 15% are are members of minority groups, 35% are women.

ACADEMICS
Degrees: associate, bachelor's, terminal, transfer. **Special Study Options:** Accelerated program, cooperative education program, distance learning, double major, dual enrollment, external degree program, honors program, independent study, internships, liberal arts/career combination, teacher certification program. **Disability Services:** Special programs offered to physically disabled students, including tutors. **Career Services:** Alumni services, Career/job search classes, Career assessment, Internships, On-campus interviews.

FACILITIES
Housing: men's dorms, women's dorms, apartments for single students. 95% of campus accessible to physically diasbled.

CAMPUS LIFE
Environment: Rural. **Activities:** Choral groups, concert band, music ensembles, musical theater, student government, Campus Ministries, Student Organization. 33 registered organizations, 4 honor societies, 6 religious organizations. **Athletics (Intercollegiate):** *Men:* baseball, basketball, cross-country, golf, soccer, tennis. *Women:* basketball, cross-country, soccer, softball, tennis, volleyball.

ADMISSIONS
Freshman Academic Profile: Average high school GPA 3.1. 9% in top 10% of high school class, 26% in top 25% of high school class, 59% in top 50% of high school class. **Reported SAT (pre-2016 redesign) scores:** SAT Math middle 50% range 420-520. SAT Critical Reading middle 50% range 410-490. **Concordant SAT scores:** SAT Math middle 50% range 460–550. ACT middle 50% range 15-20. Minimum paper TOEFL 500. **Basis for Candidate Selection:** *Very important factors considered include:* rigor of secondary school record, academic GPA, character/personal qualities. *Important factors considered include:* class rank, standardized test scores, interview, extracurricular activities, talent/ability, level of applicant's interest. *Other factors considered include:* recommendation(s), alumni/ae relation, geographical residence. **Freshman Admission Requirements:** High school diploma is required and GED is accepted. *Academic units required:* 4 English, 3 math, 3 science, 1 science lab, 3 social studies, 3 academic electives. **Freshman Admission Statistics:** 1,838 applied, 49.84% admitted, 37% enrolled. **Transfer Admission Requirements:** High school transcript, college transcript(s), Minimum college GPA of 2.0 required. **General Admission Information:** Application fee $20. Regular application deadline 8/18. Nonfall registration accepted. Admission may be deferred for a maximum of 1 year.

COSTS AND FINANCIAL AID
Annual tuition $7,223. Room and board $2,775. Required fees $0. Average book expense $656. **Required Forms and Deadlines:** FAFSA, State aid form. **Notification of Awards:** Applicants will be notified of awards on a rolling basis beginning 2/14. **Types of Aid:** *Need-based scholarships/grants:* Federal Pell, FSEOG, State scholarships/grants, Private scholarships, College/university scholarship or grant aid from institutional funds. *Loans:* Direct Subsidized Stafford Loans, Direct Unsubsidized Stafford Loans, Direct PLUS loans, Federal Perkins Loans, Federal Nursing Loans, State Loans. *Student Employment:* Federal Work-Study Program available. **Financial Aid Statistics:** 97% needy freshmen, 93% needy undergrads receive need-based scholarship or grant aid. 5% freshmen, 4% undergrads receive non-need-based scholarship or grant aid. 84% freshmen, 87% undergrads receive need-based self-help aid. 7% freshmen, 2% undergrads receive athletic scholarships. **Criteria for awarding aid:** *Need-based:* Art, Athletics, Music/drama, Religious affiliation. *Non-need-based:* Academics, Art, Athletics, Leadership, Music/drama, Religious affiliation.

MOUNT SAINT MARY COLLEGE

330 Powell Avenue, Newburgh, NY 12550
Phone: 845-569-3488 • **Financial Aid Phone:** 845-569-3298
E-mail: admissions@msmc.edu • **CEEB Code:** 2423
Fax: 845-569-3520 • **Website:** www.msmc.edu • **ACT Code:** 2819

This private school was founded in 1959. It has a 70-acre campus.

RATINGS

Admissions Selectivity Rating: 73　　**Fire Safety Rating:** 97　　**Green Rating:** 60*

STUDENTS AND FACULTY

Enrollment: 2,106. **Student Body:** 72% female, 28% male, 11% out-of-state, <1% international (14 countries represented). Asian 2%, African American 8%, Caucasian 63%, Hispanic 16%, Native American <1%, Pacific Islander <1%, Two or more races 2%, Race unknown 8%.
Retention and Graduation: 77% freshmen return for sophomore year. 43% freshmen graduate within 4 years. 54 31% grads go on to further study within 1 year. 11% grads pursue arts and sciences degrees. 1% grads pursue law degrees. 5% grads pursue business degrees. **Faculty:** Student/faculty ratio 13:1. 89 full-time faculty, 87% hold PhDs, 10% are are members of minority groups, 57% are women. 0% of classes are taught by teaching assistants.

ACADEMICS

Degrees: bachelor's, certificate, master's, post-master's certificate. **Classes:** Most classes have 20-29 students. Most lab/discussion sessions have fewer than 10 students. **Most popular majors:** Registered Nursing/Registered Nurse; Business Administration and Management; Teacher Education and Professional Development, Specific Levels and Methods. **Special Study Options:** Accelerated program, cooperative education program, cross-registration, distance learning, double major, dual enrollment, exchange student program (domestic), honors program, independent study, internships, liberal arts/career combination, student-designed major, study abroad, teacher certification program. **Honors Programs:** The Honors Program comprises academic, cultural, and social activities, each of which complements and reinforces the others. Combined degree programs: BA/MA. **Disability Services:** Special programs offered to physically disabled students, including tape recorders, tutors. **Career Services:** Alumni network, Alumni services, Career/job search classes, Career assessment, Internships. The Career Center offers co-ops and internships, which are educational experiences that promote academic, personal and professional development. These enrichment opportunities add a professional dimension to the traditional college curriculum by enabling students to combine practical work experiences with academic majors and career goals. Students who participate in co-ops and internships gain experience before they graduate that serves to clarify their goals, reinforces their career choice, and gives them a jump start on their careers.

FACILITIES

Housing: Coed dorms, special housing for disabled students, men's dorms, women's dorms. 95% of campus accessible to physically diasbled. **Special Academic Facilities/Equipment:** On-campus elementary school, television studio, and radio station. Multi-media lab. **Computers:** 100% of classrooms, 100% of dorms, 100% of libraries, 100% of dining areas, 100% of student union, 40% of common outdoor areas have wireless network access. Students can register for classes online. Administrative functions (other than registration) can be performed online.

CAMPUS LIFE

Environment: Town. **Activities:** Choral groups, concert band, dance, drama/theater, literary magazine, music ensembles, musical theater, radio station, student government, student newspaper, student-run film society, yearbook, Campus Ministries. 30 registered organizations, 12 honor societies, 1 religious organization. **Athletics (Intercollegiate):** *Men:* baseball, basketball, cross-country, lacrosse, soccer, swimming, tennis. *Women:* basketball, cross-country, lacrosse, soccer, softball, swimming, tennis, volleyball. **On-Campus Highlights:** Athletic Center with indoor pool, cardio/weight rm, Knight Court Cyber Cafe', Library with wireless internet access, Multi-media production laboratory, Theater with student productions/music events. **Environmental Initiatives:** Use of high efficiency boilers.

ADMISSIONS

Freshman Academic Profile: Average high school GPA 3.2. 7% in top 10% of high school class, 34% in top 25% of high school class, 74% in top 50% of high school class. 69% from public high schools. **Reported SAT (pre-2016 redesign) scores:** SAT Math middle 50% range 440-540. SAT Critical Reading middle 50% range 450-530. SAT Writing middle 50% range 440-530. **Concordant SAT scores:** SAT EBRW middle 50% 500–590. SAT Math middle 50% range 480–570. ACT middle 50% range 20-24. Minimum internet-based TOEFL 79. Minimum paper TOEFL 550. **Basis for Candidate Selection:**

Very important factors considered include: rigor of secondary school record, academic GPA. *Important factors considered include:* class rank, standardized test scores, application essay, recommendation(s), interview, talent/ability, character/personal qualities. *Other factors considered include:* extracurricular activities, first generation, alumni/ae relation, volunteer work, work experience, level of applicant's interest. **Freshman Admission Requirements:** High school diploma is required and GED is accepted. *Academic units recommended:* 4 English, 3 math, 3 science, 3 foreign language, 4 social studies. **Freshman Admission Statistics:** 3,747 applied, 89.89% admitted, 11% enrolled. **Transfer Admission Requirements:** High school transcript, college transcript(s), standardized test scores, statement of good standing from prior institution(s). Minimum college GPA of 2.0 required. Lowest grade transferable C. **General Admission Information:** Application fee $45. Regular application deadline 8/15. Nonfall registration accepted. Admission may be deferred for a maximum of 1 year.

COSTS AND FINANCIAL AID

Annual tuition $28,890. Room and board $14,528. Required fees $1,030. Average book expense $1,300. **Required Forms and Deadlines:** FAFSA. **Notification of Awards:** Applicants will be notified of awards on a rolling basis beginning 3/1. **Types of Aid:** *Need-based scholarships/grants:* Federal Pell, FSEOG, State scholarships/grants, Private scholarships, College/university scholarship or grant aid from institutional funds, Federal Nursing Scholarships. *Loans:* Direct Subsidized Stafford Loans, Direct Unsubsidized Stafford Loans, Direct PLUS loans, Federal Perkins Loans, Federal Nursing Loans. *Student Employment:* Federal Work-Study Program available. Institutional employment available. **Financial Aid Statistics:** 100% needy freshmen, 97% needy undergrads receive need-based scholarship or grant aid. 14% freshmen, 10% undergrads receive non-need-based scholarship or grant aid. 86% freshmen, 89% undergrads receive need-based self-help aid. 0% freshmen, 0% undergrads receive athletic scholarships. 99% freshmen, 93% undergrads receive any aid. 80% undergrads borrow to pay for school. Average cumulative indebtedness $26,773. **Criteria for awarding aid:** *Non-need-based:* Academics, Alumni affiliation, Leadership, State/district residency.

MOUNT SAINT MARY'S UNIVERSITY (CA)

12001 Chalon Road, Los Angeles, CA 90049-1597
Financial Aid Phone: 310-954-4190
E-mail: admissions@msmu.edu • **CEEB Code:** 4493
Fax: 310-954-4259 • **Website:** www.msmu.edu • **ACT Code:** 338

This private school, affiliated with the Roman Catholic Church, was founded in 1925. It has a 53-acre campus.

RATINGS

Admissions Selectivity Rating: 74　　**Fire Safety Rating:** 99　　**Green Rating:** 66

STUDENTS AND FACULTY

Enrollment: 2,789. **Student Body:** 94% female, 6% male, 2% out-of-state, 1% international (9 countries represented). Asian 15%, African American 6%, Caucasian 9%, Hispanic 63%, Native American <1%, Pacific Islander 1%, Two or more races 2%, Race unknown 3%.
Retention and Graduation: 79% freshmen return for sophomore year. **Faculty:** Student/faculty ratio 11:1. 126 full-time faculty, 75% hold PhDs, 29% are are members of minority groups, 73% are women. 0% of classes are taught by teaching assistants.

ACADEMICS

Degrees: associate, bachelor's, doctoral/professional, master's, postbachelor's certificate, post-master's certificate. **Classes:** Most classes have 10-19 students. Most lab/discussion sessions have 10-19 students. **Most popular majors:** Registered Nursing/Registered Nurse; Sociology; Business Administration and Management. **Special Study Options:** Accelerated program, cross-registration, double major, exchange student program (domestic), honors program, independent study, internships, student-designed major, study abroad, teacher certification program, weekend college. **Honors Programs:** Honors program is available to qualifying incoming freshmen and college students meeting eligibility requirements. **Disability Services:** Special programs offered to physically disabled students, including note-taking services, reader services, tape recorders, tutors. **Career Services:** Alumni services, Career/job search classes, Career assessment, Internships. Career Services & Internships offers two career courses, one for business majors and one for pre-health majors. The purpose of these courses is to support students in their career development and offer them tools for preparing them in their academic and career pursuits.

FACILITIES

Housing: men's dorms, women's dorms, limited men's housing. 100% of campus accessible to physically diasbled. **Special Academic Facilities/**

Equipment: Drudis-Biada Art Gallery **Computers:** 100% of classrooms, 100% of dorms, 100% of libraries, 100% of dining areas, have wireless network access. Students can register for classes online. Administrative functions (other than registration) can be performed online.

CAMPUS LIFE

Environment: Metropolis. **Activities:** Choral groups, dance, drama/theater, literary magazine, music ensembles, student government, student newspaper, yearbook, Campus Ministries. 29 registered organizations, 3 honor societies, 1 religious organization. 3 sororities. **On-Campus Highlights:** Humanities Building, Chapel, Fitness Center **Environmental Initiatives:** Water Conservation: Bottled water deliveries virtually canceled on both campuses. Activated Carbon Water filters added to bottle-free water dispensers on both campuses.

ADMISSIONS

Freshman Academic Profile: Average high school GPA 3.3. 11% in top 10% of high school class, 35% in top 25% of high school class, 76% in top 50% of high school class. 56% from public high schools. **Reported SAT (pre-2016 redesign) scores:** SAT Math middle 50% range 420-510. SAT Critical Reading middle 50% range 410-510. SAT Writing middle 50% range 400-500. **Concordant SAT scores:** SAT EBRW middle 50% 450–560. SAT Math middle 50% range 460–540. ACT middle 50% range 17-22. Minimum paper TOEFL 530. **Basis for Candidate Selection:** *Very important factors considered include:* rigor of secondary school record, academic GPA, standardized test scores, application essay, recommendation(s). *Other factors considered include:* class rank, interview, extracurricular activities, talent/ability, character/personal qualities, first generation, alumni/ae relation, volunteer work, work experience, level of applicant's interest. **Freshman Admission Requirements:** High school diploma is required and GED is accepted. *Academic units recommended:* 4 English, 3 math, 2 science, 1 science lab, 2 foreign language, 3 social studies, 2 history, 1 academic elective. **Freshman Admission Statistics:** 2,486 applied, 85.92% admitted, 25% enrolled. **Transfer Admission Requirements:** college transcript(s), essay or personal statement, statement of good standing from prior institution(s). Minimum college GPA of 2.4 required. Lowest grade transferable D. **General Admission Information:** Application fee $50. Priority deadline 12/1. Regular application deadline 8/1. Nonfall registration accepted.

COSTS AND FINANCIAL AID

Annual tuition $36,682. Room and board $11,451. Required fees $1,040. Average book expense $1,900. **Required Forms and Deadlines:** FAFSA, Institution's own financial aid form. **Notification of Awards:** Applicants will be notified of awards on a rolling basis beginning 3/1. **Types of Aid:** *Need-based scholarships/grants:* Federal Pell, FSEOG, State scholarships/grants, Private scholarships, College/university scholarship or grant aid from institutional funds. *Loans:* Direct Subsidized Stafford Loans, Direct Unsubsidized Stafford Loans, Direct PLUS loans, Federal Nursing Loans, College/university loans from institutional funds. *Student Employment:* Federal Work-Study Program available. Institutional employment available. **Financial Aid Statistics:** 99% needy freshmen, 80% needy undergrads receive need-based scholarship or grant aid. 98% freshmen, 96% undergrads receive non-need-based scholarship or grant aid. 98% freshmen, 97% undergrads receive need-based self-help aid. 0% freshmen, 0% undergrads receive athletic scholarships. 94% freshmen, 68% undergrads receive any aid. 86% undergrads borrow to pay for school. Average cumulative indebtedness $32,805. **Criteria for awarding aid:** *Non-need-based:* Academics, Alumni affiliation, Music/drama.

MOUNT ST. JOSEPH UNIVERSITY

5701 Delhi Road, Cincinnati, OH 45233
Phone: 513-244-4531 • **Financial Aid Phone:** 513-244-4418
E-mail: admissions@msj.edu • **CEEB Code:** 1129
Fax: 513-244-4629 • **Website:** www.msj.edu • **ACT Code:** 3254

This private school, affiliated with the Roman Catholic Church, was founded in 1920. It has a 92-acre campus.

RATINGS

Admissions Selectivity Rating: 88   **Fire Safety Rating:** 99   **Green Rating:** 60*

STUDENTS AND FACULTY

Enrollment: 1,405. **Student Body:** 57% female, 43% male, 16% out-of-state, <1% international (3 countries represented). Asian 1%, African American 11%, Caucasian 78%, Hispanic 1%, Native American <1%, Pacific Islander <1%, Two or more races 4%, Race unknown 5%.
Retention and Graduation: 67% freshmen return for sophomore year. 51% freshmen graduate within 4 years. 51% freshmen graduate within 6 years. 17% grads go on to further study within 1 year. 12% grads pursue arts and sciences

degrees. 4% grads pursue business degrees. **Faculty:** Student/faculty ratio 12:1. 177 full-time faculty, 14% hold PhDs, 2% are are members of minority groups, 71% are women. 0% of classes are taught by teaching assistants.

ACADEMICS

Degrees: associate, bachelor's, certificate, master's, postbachelor's certificate. **Classes:** Most classes have 10-19 students. Most lab/discussion sessions have 10-19 students. **Most popular majors:** Business Administration and Management; Sport and Fitness Administration/Management; Registered Nursing, Nursing Administration, Nursing Research and Clinical Nursing. **Special Study Options:** Accelerated program, cooperative education program, cross-registration, distance learning, double major, dual enrollment, honors program, independent study, internships, liberal arts/career combination, study abroad, teacher certification program. **Honors Programs:** Honors program– designed to meet the interests of highly motivated students who are able to take responsibility for their own learning under the guidance of experienced faculty members. **Disability Services:** Special programs offered to physically disabled students, including note-taking services, reader services, tape recorders, tutors. **Career Services:** Alumni services, Career/job search classes, Career assessment, Internships. Qualified students have the opportunity to gain career related, paid work experience. Co-ops earn academic credit that will complement classroom training by integrating theory and practice.

FACILITIES

Housing: Coed dorms, special housing for disabled students. 95% of campus accessible to physically disabled. **Special Academic Facilities/Equipment:** Art studio/gallery, Student Scholar Center, Computer Labs, Theatre. **Computers:** 100% of classrooms, 100% of dorms, 100% of libraries, 100% of dining areas, 100% of common outdoor areas have wireless network access. Students can register for classes online. Administrative functions (other than registration) can be performed online.

CAMPUS LIFE

Environment: Metropolis. **Activities:** Choral groups, concert band, dance, drama/theater, jazz band, literary magazine, music ensembles, musical theater, pep band, student government, student newspaper, Campus Ministries, Student Organization. 35 registered organizations, 10 honor societies, 1 religious organization. **Athletics (Intercollegiate):** *Men:* baseball, basketball, cross-country, football, golf, lacrosse, soccer, tennis, track/field (outdoor), track/field (indoor), volleyball, wrestling. *Women:* basketball, cheerleading, cross-country, golf, lacrosse, soccer, softball, tennis, track/field (outdoor), track/field (indoor), volleyball. **On-Campus Highlights:** Harrington Student Center/Sports Complex, Starbucks Gallery, Residential Suites, Computer Learning Center, Project EXCEL. **Environmental Initiatives:** New green roof installed on Library (2008)

ADMISSIONS

Freshman Academic Profile: Average high school GPA 3.3. 9% in top 10% of high school class, 34% in top 25% of high school class, 59% in top 50% of high school class. 70% from public high schools. **Reported SAT (pre-2016 redesign) scores:** SAT Math middle 50% range 420-550. SAT Critical Reading middle 50% range 440-560. **Concordant SAT scores:** SAT Math middle 50% range 460–570. ACT middle 50% range 19-24. Minimum internet-based TOEFL 64. Minimum paper TOEFL 510. **Basis for Candidate Selection:** *Very important factors considered include:* rigor of secondary school record, academic GPA, standardized test scores. *Other factors considered include:* application essay, recommendation(s), interview, extracurricular activities, talent/ability, character/personal qualities, first generation, alumni/ae relation, geographical residence, state residency, religious affiliation/commitment, racial/ethnic status, volunteer work, work experience, level of applicant's interest. **Freshman Admission Requirements:** High school diploma is required and GED is accepted. *Academic units required:* 4 English, 3 math, 3 science, 1 science lab, 2 foreign language, 3 social studies, 3 history, 1 visual/performing arts. *Academic units recommended:* 4 English, 4 math, 4 science, 2 science labs, 2 foreign language, 3 social studies, 3 history, 1 academic elective. **Freshman Admission Statistics:** 2,187 applied, 15.09% admitted, 100% enrolled. **Transfer Admission Requirements:** college transcript(s), Minimum college GPA of 2.0 required. Lowest grade transferable C. **General Admission Information:** Application fee $25. Priority deadline 4/1. Regular application deadline 8/15. Nonfall registration accepted. Admission may be deferred for a maximum of 12 months.

COSTS AND FINANCIAL AID

Annual tuition $25,850. Room and board $8,710. Required fees $1,000. Average book expense $1,000. **Required Forms and Deadlines:** FAFSA. **Notification of Awards:** Applicants will be notified of awards on a rolling basis beginning 1/31. **Types of Aid:** *Need-based scholarships/grants:* Federal Pell, FSEOG, State scholarships/grants, Private scholarships, College/university scholarship or grant aid from institutional funds. *Loans:* Direct Subsidized Stafford Loans, Direct Unsubsidized Stafford Loans, Direct PLUS loans, Federal Perkins Loans, Federal Nursing Loans, State Loans. *Student Employment:* Federal Work-Study Program available. Institutional employment available. **Financial**

Aid Statistics: 100% needy freshmen, 99% needy undergrads receive need-based scholarship or grant aid. 15% freshmen, 13% undergrads receive non-need-based scholarship or grant aid. 90% freshmen, 92% undergrads receive need-based self-help aid. 0% freshmen, 0% undergrads receive athletic scholarships. 99% freshmen, 83% undergrads receive any aid. **Criteria for awarding aid:** *Need-based:* Academics. *Non-need-based:* Academics, Alumni affiliation, Art, Leadership, Music/drama, State/district residency.

MOUNT ST. MARY'S UNIVERSITY

16300 Old Emmitsburg Road, Emmitsburg, MD 21727
Phone: 301-447-5214 • **Financial Aid Phone:** 301-447-5207
E-mail: admissions@msmary.edu • **CEEB Code:** 5421
Fax: 301-447-5860 • **Website:** www.msmary.edu • **ACT Code:** 1726

This private school, affiliated with the Roman Catholic Church, was founded in 1808. It has a 1400-acre campus.

RATINGS
Admissions Selectivity Rating: 82   **Fire Safety Rating:** 90   **Green Rating:** 72

STUDENTS AND FACULTY
Enrollment: 1,717. **Student Body:** 54% female, 46% male, 45% out-of-state, 1% international (12 countries represented). Asian 3%, African American 13%, Caucasian 68%, Hispanic 10%, Native American <1%, Pacific Islander <1%, Two or more races 4%, Race unknown 1%.
Retention and Graduation: 75% freshmen return for sophomore year. 65% freshmen graduate within 4 years. 71 28% grads go on to further study within 1 year. 11% grads pursue arts and sciences degrees. 2% grads pursue law degrees. 8% grads pursue business degrees. 2% grads pursue medical degrees. **Faculty:** Student/faculty ratio 12:1. 125 full-time faculty, 90% hold PhDs, 7% are are members of minority groups, 42% are women. 0% of classes are taught by teaching assistants.

ACADEMICS
Degrees: bachelor's, master's, postbachelor's certificate, post-master's certificate. **Classes:** Most classes have 20-29 students. Most lab/discussion sessions have 10-19 students. **Most popular majors:** Accounting; Business/ Commerce; Criminology. **Special Study Options:** Accelerated program, cross-registration, double major, dual enrollment, honors program, independent study, internships, liberal arts/career combination, student-designed major, study abroad, teacher certification program, weekend college, 3-2 with Johns Hopkins Univ. (BS in Biology; BS in Nursing) 3-3 with Sacred Heart Univ. (BS in Biology; Ph.D in PT) 4-2 with Sacred Heart Univ. (BS in Biology; MS in OT). **Honors Programs:** The Honors Program offers talented and motivated students an educational experience that integrates curricular, co-curricular, and extra-curricular learning in both interdisciplinary and major areas of study. Combined degree programs: 3/2 Nursing Program with Shenandoah Univ., 3/2 Nursing Program with Univ of MD, 4/4 Biology & Osteopathic Medicine with Lake Erie College of Osteopathic Medicine. **Disability Services:** Special programs offered to physically disabled students, including note-taking services, reader services, tape recorders, tutors. **Career Services:** Alumni network, Alumni services, Career/job search classes, Career assessment, Internships, Regional alumni. The Mount's Internship Program provides excellent learning and networking experiences for either credit or non-credit. Internships are tailored to students' majors. 'Mount in Washington' offers full time internships in Washington D.C. The Career Center has also introduced International Internships that coincide with the university's study abroad program in London, Dublin, and Florence.

FACILITIES
Housing: Coed dorms, special housing for disabled students, apartments for single students, Wellness Housing, Theme Housing. 85% of campus accessible to physically diasbled. **Special Academic Facilities/Equipment:** Historical art collection reflecting Catholic history in America and Marylandia. **Computers:** 100% of classrooms, 100% of dorms, 100% of libraries, 100% of dining areas, 100% of student union, 50% of common outdoor areas have wireless network access. Students can register for classes online. Administrative functions (other than registration) can be performed online.

CAMPUS LIFE
Environment: Rural. **Activities:** Choral groups, concert band, dance, drama/ theater, jazz band, literary magazine, music ensembles, musical theater, pep band, radio station, student government, student newspaper, television station, yearbook, Campus Ministries, Student Organization. 68 registered organizations, 19 honor societies, 8 religious organizations. **Athletics (Intercollegiate):** *Men:* baseball, basketball, cross-country, golf, lacrosse, soccer, tennis, track/field (outdoor), track/field (indoor). *Women:* basketball,

cross-country, golf, lacrosse, soccer, softball, swimming, tennis, track/field (outdoor), track/field (indoor). **On-Campus Highlights:** McGowan Student Center—Patriot Hall, Knott Athletic Recreation Convocation Complex, Knott Academic Center, Phillips Library, National Shrine Grotto of Lourdes. **Environmental Initiatives:** Since late 2012 we operate a solar farm on our campus providing for a substantial part of our electricity consumption.

ADMISSIONS
Freshman Academic Profile: Average high school GPA 3.4. 17% in top 10% of high school class, 38% in top 25% of high school class, 68% in top 50% of high school class. 63% from public high schools. **Reported SAT (pre-2016 redesign) scores:** SAT Math middle 50% range 460-580. SAT Critical Reading middle 50% range 480-580. SAT Writing middle 50% range 450-560. **Concordant SAT scores:** SAT EBRW middle 50% 520–630. SAT Math middle 50% range 500–600. ACT middle 50% range 19-24. Minimum internet-based TOEFL 83. Minimum paper TOEFL 550. **Basis for Candidate Selection:** *Very important factors considered include:* academic GPA. *Important factors considered include:* rigor of secondary school record, application essay, recommendation(s), extracurricular activities, talent/ability, character/ personal qualities, level of applicant's interest. *Other factors considered include:* class rank, standardized test scores, interview, volunteer work, work experience. **Freshman Admission Requirements:** High school diploma is required and GED is accepted. *Academic units required:* 4 English, 3 math, 3 science, 2 science labs, 2 foreign language, 3 social studies, 1 academic elective. **Freshman Admission Statistics:** 6,086 applied, 61.53% admitted, 11% enrolled. **Transfer Admission Requirements:** college transcript(s), statement of good standing from prior institution(s). Minimum college GPA of 2.0 required. Lowest grade transferable C. **General Admission Information:** Application fee $45. Priority deadline 12/1. Regular application deadline 3/1. Regular notification 5/1. Nonfall registration accepted. Admission may be deferred for a maximum of 1 yr.

COSTS AND FINANCIAL AID
Annual tuition $39,200. Room and board $12,830. Required fees $1,350. Average book expense $1,300. **Required Forms and Deadlines:** FAFSA. **Notification of Awards:** Applicants will be notified of awards on a rolling basis beginning 2/14. **Types of Aid:** *Need-based scholarships/grants:* Federal Pell, FSEOG, State scholarships/grants, Private scholarships, College/university scholarship or grant aid from institutional funds. *Loans:* Direct Subsidized Stafford Loans, Direct Unsubsidized Stafford Loans, Direct PLUS loans. *Student Employment:* Federal Work-Study Program available. Institutional employment available. **Financial Aid Statistics:** 100% needy freshmen, 99% needy undergrads receive need-based scholarship or grant aid. 24% freshmen, 19% undergrads receive non-need-based scholarship or grant aid. 73% freshmen, 77% undergrads receive need-based self-help aid. 10% freshmen, 8% undergrads receive athletic scholarships. 100% freshmen, 97% undergrads receive any aid. 77% undergrads borrow to pay for school. Average cumulative indebtedness $33,894. **Criteria for awarding aid:** *Need-based:* Job skills. *Non-need-based:* Academics, Art, Athletics, Leadership.

MOUNT VERNON NAZARENE UNIVERSITY

800 Martinsburg Road, Mount Vernon, OH 43050
Phone: 740-392-6868 • **Financial Aid Phone:** 866-686-8243
E-mail: admissions@mvnu.edu • **CEEB Code:** 1531
Fax: 740-393-0511 • **Website:** www.mvnu.edu • **ACT Code:** 3372

This private school, affiliated with the Nazarene Church, was founded in 1964. It has a 401-acre campus.

RATINGS
Admissions Selectivity Rating: 81   **Fire Safety Rating:** 82   **Green Rating:** 60*

STUDENTS AND FACULTY
Enrollment: 865. **Student Body:** 62% female, 38% male, 10% out-of-state, 1% international (16 countries represented). Asian 1%, African American 3%, Caucasian 88%, Hispanic 3%, Native American 0%, Pacific Islander <1%, Two or more races 2%, Race unknown 2%.
Retention and Graduation: 77% freshmen return for sophomore year. 43% freshmen graduate within 4 years. 57% freshmen graduate within 6 years. **Faculty:** Student/faculty ratio 14:1. 55 full-time faculty, 84% hold PhDs, 4% are are members of minority groups, 69% are women. 0% of classes are taught by teaching assistants.

ACADEMICS
Degrees: associate, bachelor's, master's. **Classes:** Most classes have 10-19 students. **Most popular majors:** Registered Nursing/Registered Nurse; Biology/Biological Sciences; Business Administration and Management. **Special Study Options:** cooperative education program, cross-registration, distance

learning, double major, dual enrollment, honors program, independent study, internships, liberal arts/career combination, study abroad, teacher certification program, Cooperative pre-engineering program with Olivet Nazarene University, cooperative pre-occupational therapy/physical therapy/physician's assistant programs with Chatham University, and articulation agreements with Columbus State Community College, Marion Technical College, Zane State College, Central Ohio Technical College, and North Central State College. Several opportunities for students to participate in service learning or mission trips. During the academic year, students may participate in one of the following trips: Germany, Hungary, Venezuela, Costa Rica, Nicaragua, Belize, Benin, Romania, or several out-of-state USA trips. **Honors Programs:** Honors Program for outstandning students is designed to provide rewarding challenges for the academically gifted. Specific courses, seminars, and other out-of-the ordinary experiences, both on and off campus, are offered by the Honors Program. A $250 scholarship the first year, increases to $400 in the fourth year. The Honors Program adds depth to your academic development and allows you to have input in designing your own curiculum by proposing study topics for Honors courses and by developing independent projects. You will work closely with a faculty mentor to complete an Honors Project in your major. There are also opportunities for off-campus culural enrichment and entertainment, including travel to musuems, ballet and music performances, or dinner theater. **Disability Services:** Special programs offered to physically disabled students, including note-taking services, reader services, tape recorders, tutors. **Career Services:** Alumni services, Career/job search classes, Career assessment. Missions and ministry opportunities and study abroad.

FACILITIES

Housing: special housing for disabled students, men's dorms, women's dorms, apartments for single students, Wellness Housing. 95% of campus accessible to physically diasbled. **Special Academic Facilities/Equipment:** Art gallery, nature reserve. **Computers:** 95% of classrooms, 5% of dorms, 100% of libraries, 100% of dining areas, 100% of student union, 10% of common outdoor areas have wireless network access. Administrative functions (other than registration) can be performed online.

CAMPUS LIFE

Environment: Rural. **Activities:** Choral groups, concert band, drama/theater, jazz band, literary magazine, music ensembles, musical theater, opera, pep band, radio station, student government, student newspaper, yearbook, Campus Ministries, Student Organization. 26 registered organizations, 4 honor societies, 16 religious organizations. **Athletics (Intercollegiate):** *Men:* baseball, basketball, cross-country, golf, soccer. *Women:* basketball, cross-country, soccer, softball, volleyball. **On-Campus Highlights:** The Prince Student Union, The Chapel, The Cafeteria, The Quad, The Grove. **Environmental Initiatives:** Campus-wide recycling program.

ADMISSIONS

Freshman Academic Profile: Average high school GPA 3.5. 21% in top 10% of high school class, 51% in top 25% of high school class, 76% in top 50% of high school class. 80% from public high schools. **Reported SAT (pre-2016 redesign) scores:** SAT Math middle 50% range 460-560. SAT Critical Reading middle 50% range 450-550. **Concordant SAT scores:** SAT Math middle 50% range 500–580. ACT middle 50% range 20-25. Minimum internet-based TOEFL 80. **Basis for Candidate Selection:** *Very important factors considered include:* academic GPA, standardized test scores. *Important factors considered include:* rigor of secondary school record, recommendation(s). *Other factors considered include:* application essay, interview. **Freshman Admission Requirements:** High school diploma is required and GED is accepted. *Academic units required:* 2 foreign language. *Academic units recommended:* 4 English, 4 math, 3 science, 3 science labs, 3 foreign language, 3 social studies, 2 academic electives, 1 visual/performing arts, and 1 unit from above areas or other academic areas. **Freshman Admission Statistics:** 1,276 applied, 74.22% admitted, 38% enrolled. **Transfer Admission Requirements:** High school transcript, college transcript(s), essay or personal statement, statement of good standing from prior institution(s). Minimum college GPA of 2.0 required. Lowest grade transferable C-. **General Admission Information:** Application fee $25. Priority deadline 3/15. Regular application deadline 7/15. Nonfall registration accepted. Admission may be deferred for a maximum of 1 year.

COSTS AND FINANCIAL AID

Annual tuition $27,840. Room and board $7,854. Required fees $250. Average book expense $1,400. **Required Forms and Deadlines:** FAFSA. **Notification of Awards:** Applicants will be notified of awards on a rolling basis beginning 3/4. **Types of Aid:** *Need-based scholarships/grants:* Federal Pell, FSEOG, State scholarships/grants, Private scholarships, College/university scholarship or grant aid from institutional funds. *Loans:* Direct Subsidized Stafford Loans, Direct Unsubsidized Stafford Loans, Direct PLUS loans, Federal Perkins Loans, State Loans. *Student Employment:* Federal Work-Study Program available. Institutional employment available. **Financial Aid Statistics:** 98% needy freshmen, 99% needy undergrads receive need-based scholarship or grant aid. 35% freshmen, 42% undergrads receive non-need-based scholarship or grant aid. 75% freshmen, 73% undergrads receive need-based self-help aid.

10% freshmen, 3% undergrads receive athletic scholarships. 82% undergrads borrow to pay for school. Average cumulative indebtedness $21,564. **Criteria for awarding aid:** *Need-based:* Academics. *Non-need-based:* Academics, Art, Athletics, Minority status, Music/drama, Religious affiliation, State/district residency.

MUHLENBERG COLLEGE

2400 West Chew Street, Allentown, PA 18104-5596
Phone: 484-664-3200 • **Financial Aid Phone:** 484-664-3175
E-mail: admissions@muhlenberg.edu • **CEEB Code:** 2424
Fax: 484-664-3032 • **Website:** www.muhlenberg.edu • **ACT Code:** 3640

This private school, affiliated with the Lutheran Church, was founded in 1848. It has a 81-acre campus.

RATINGS

Admissions Selectivity Rating: 90 **Fire Safety Rating:** 96 **Green Rating:** 83

STUDENTS AND FACULTY

Enrollment: 2,375. **Student Body:** 60% female, 40% male, 76% out-of-state, 3% international (18 countries represented). Asian 3%, African American 3%, Caucasian 75%, Hispanic 7%, Native American <1%, Pacific Islander <1%, Two or more races 1%, Race unknown 6%.
Retention and Graduation: 90% freshmen return for sophomore year. 81% freshmen graduate within 4 years. 84% freshmen graduate within 6 years. 22% grads go on to further study within 1 year. 20% grads pursue arts and sciences degrees. 4% grads pursue law degrees. 1% grads pursue business degrees. 5% grads pursue medical degrees. **Faculty:** Student/faculty ratio 11:1. 186 full-time faculty, 89% hold PhDs, 10% are are members of minority groups, 52% are women. 0% of classes are taught by teaching assistants.

ACADEMICS

Degrees: associate, bachelor's, certificate. **Classes:** Most classes have 10-19 students. Most lab/discussion sessions have fewer than 10 students. **Most popular majors:** Business/Commerce; Psychology; Drama and Dramatics/Theatre Arts. **Special Study Options:** Accelerated program, cross-registration, double major, exchange student program (domestic), honors program, independent study, internships, student-designed major, study abroad, teacher certification program. **Honors Programs:** Muhlenberg Scholar, Dana Associate, R.J. Fellow (each provides a $4,000 annual stipend, dedicated freshman seminar, and mentored research) Combined degree programs: BA/MD, BA/DDS, BA/DDS University of Pennsylvania, BS/MD Drexel Un. **Disability Services:** Special programs offered to physically disabled students, including note-taking services, tutors. **Career Services:** Alumni network, Alumni services, Career/job search classes, Career assessment, Internships, Regional alumni. The Muhlenberg Shadow Program matches students with alumni in their field of interest to spend a day on the job over winter break. Students are able to learn first-hand about career options of interest to them, and alumni enjoy the feeling of helping a student and remembering why they enjoy their jobs.

FACILITIES

Housing: Coed dorms, special housing for disabled students, special housing for international students, women's dorms, fraternity/sorority housing, apartments for single students, College-owned houses in the neighborhood surrounding the campus. 95% of campus accessible to physically diasbled. **Special Academic Facilities/Equipment:** Martin art gallery, biology museum, Graver arboretum, greenhouse, mainstage theatre, recital hall, 20-foot boat for marine studies, 40-acre Raker environmental field station, two electron microscopes, dance studios, experimental theatres, proscenium theatres. **Computers:** 10% of classrooms, 20% of dorms, 100% of libraries, 100% of dining areas, 100% of student union, 10% of common outdoor areas have wireless network access. Students can register for classes online. Administrative functions (other than registration) can be performed online.

CAMPUS LIFE

Environment: City. **Activities:** concert band, dance, drama/theater, jazz band, literary magazine, music ensembles, musical theater, pep band, radio station, student government, student newspaper, student-run film society, symphony orchestra, yearbook. 100 registered organizations, 12 honor societies, 7 religious organizations. 4 fraternities, 4 sororities. **Athletics (Intercollegiate):** *Men:* baseball, basketball, cheerleading, cross-country, football, golf, lacrosse, soccer, tennis, track/field (outdoor), track/field (indoor), wrestling. *Women:* basketball, cheerleading, cross-country, field hockey, golf, lacrosse, soccer, softball, tennis, track/field (outdoor), track/field (indoor), volleyball. **On-Campus Highlights:** Seegers Union by fireplace & Java Joe's, The Life Sports Center-Athletic Facility, Parents Plaza-Outdoor Courtyard, GQ, Seegers Union, Trexler Pavilion for Threatre & Dance.

ADMISSIONS

Freshman Academic Profile: Average high school GPA 3.3. 36% in top 10% of high school class, 71% in top 25% of high school class, 93% in top 50% of high school class. 69% from public high schools. **Reported SAT (pre-2016 redesign) scores:** SAT Math middle 50% range 570-660. SAT Critical Reading middle 50% range 560-660. SAT Writing middle 50% range 550-670. **Concordant SAT scores:** SAT EBRW middle 50% 610–710. SAT Math middle 50% range 590–690. ACT middle 50% range 26-30. Minimum internet-based TOEFL 79. Minimum paper TOEFL 550. **Basis for Candidate Selection:** *Very important factors considered include:* rigor of secondary school record, academic GPA, character/personal qualities. *Important factors considered include:* class rank, standardized test scores, application essay, recommendation(s), interview, extracurricular activities, talent/ability, volunteer work, work experience. *Other factors considered include:* first generation, alumni/ae relation, racial/ethnic status, level of applicant's interest. **Freshman Admission Requirements:** High school diploma is required and GED is accepted. *Academic units required:* 4 English, 3 math, 2 science, 2 science labs, 2 foreign language, 2 history, 1 academic elective. *Academic units recommended:* 4 English, 4 math, 3 science, 3 science labs, 4 foreign language, 2 social studies, 2 history, 1 academic elective. **Freshman Admission Statistics:** 4,862 applied, 48.25% admitted, 25% enrolled. **Transfer Admission Requirements:** High school transcript, college transcript(s), essay or personal statement, interview, standardized test scores, statement of good standing from prior institution(s). Minimum college GPA of 2.5 required. Lowest grade transferable C. **General Admission Information:** Application fee $50. Priority deadline 2/15. Regular application deadline 2/15. Regular notification 3/15. Nonfall registration accepted. Admission may be deferred for a maximum of 1 year.

COSTS AND FINANCIAL AID

Annual tuition $47,825. Required fees $485. Average book expense $1,300. **Required Forms and Deadlines:** FAFSA, Institution's own financial aid form, CSS/Financial Aid PROFILE, State aid form, Noncustodial PROFILE, Business/Farm Supplement. **Notification of Awards:** Applicants will be notified of awards on or about 4/1. **Types of Aid:** *Need-based scholarships/grants:* Federal Pell, FSEOG, State scholarships/grants, Private scholarships, College/university scholarship or grant aid from institutional funds. *Loans:* Direct Subsidized Stafford Loans, Direct Unsubsidized Stafford Loans, Direct PLUS loans, Federal Perkins Loans. *Student Employment:* Federal Work-Study Program available. Institutional employment available. **Financial Aid Statistics:** 90% needy freshmen, 97% needy undergrads receive need-based scholarship or grant aid. 24% freshmen, 17% undergrads receive non-need-based scholarship or grant aid. 70% freshmen, 75% undergrads receive need-based self-help aid. 0% freshmen, 0% undergrads receive athletic scholarships. 89% freshmen, 88% undergrads receive any aid. 58% undergrads borrow to pay for school. Average cumulative indebtedness $31,063. **Criteria for awarding aid:** *Non-need-based:* Academics, Art, Leadership, Religious affiliation.

MULTNOMAH UNIVERSITY

8435 NE Glisan Street, Portland, OR 97220-5898
Phone: 503-251-6485 • **Financial Aid Phone:** 503-251-5337
E-mail: admiss@multnomah.edu
Fax: 503-254-1268 • **Website:** http://www.multnomah.edu/

This private school, affiliated with the Christian (Nondenominational) Church, was founded in 1936. It has a 25-acre campus.

RATINGS

Admissions Selectivity Rating: 82　　**Fire Safety Rating:** 63　　**Green Rating:** 60*

STUDENTS AND FACULTY

Enrollment: 341. **Student Body:** 48% female, 52% male, 57% out-of-state, 0% international (2 countries represented). Asian 1%, African American 3%, Caucasian 76%, Hispanic 8%, Native American 1%, Pacific Islander 1%, Two or more races 9%, Race unknown 1%.
Retention and Graduation: 63% freshmen return for sophomore year. 39% freshmen graduate within 4 years. 48% freshmen graduate within 6 years.
Faculty: Student/faculty ratio 12:1. 26 full-time faculty, 77% hold PhDs, 0% are are members of minority groups, 23% are women. 0% of classes are taught by teaching assistants.

ACADEMICS

Degrees: bachelor's, master's. **Classes:** Most classes have fewer than 10 students. Most lab/discussion sessions have 10-19 students. **Most popular majors:** Psychology; Bible/Biblical Studies; Business Administration and Management. **Special Study Options:** cooperative education program, distance learning, double major, internships, liberal arts/career combination, teacher certification program. **Career Services:** Career/job search classes, Career assessment, Internships, On-campus interviews.

FACILITIES

Housing: special housing for disabled students, men's dorms, women's dorms, apartments for married students, apartments for single students, Houses for students with spouses or dependents. 90% of campus accessible to physically diasbled. **Computers:** 100% of classrooms, 100% of dorms, 100% of libraries, 100% of dining areas, 30% of common outdoor areas have wireless network access. Students can register for classes online. Administrative functions (other than registration) can be performed online.

CAMPUS LIFE

Environment: Metropolis. **Activities:** Choral groups, drama/theater, music ensembles, student government, student newspaper. **Athletics (Intercollegiate):** *Men:* basketball. *Women:* volleyball. **On-Campus Highlights:** Solid Rock Cafe, A-Frame Community Lounge, STUGO Game Room, Cafeteria, Commuter Lounge, The Solid Rock Cafe, STUGO Game Room and cafeteria are all centrally located in our JCA Student Center along with a computer lab, post-office, and health center.

ADMISSIONS

Freshman Academic Profile: Average high school GPA 3.2. 24% in top 10% of high school class, 34% in top 25% of high school class, 57% in top 50% of high school class. 53% from public high schools. **Reported SAT (pre-2016 redesign) scores:** SAT Math middle 50% range 450-570. SAT Critical Reading middle 50% range 440-620. SAT Writing middle 50% range 470-580. **Concordant SAT scores:** SAT EBRW middle 50% 510–650. SAT Math middle 50% range 490–590. ACT middle 50% range 20-28. Minimum paper TOEFL 550. **Basis for Candidate Selection:** *Very important factors considered include:* academic GPA, application essay, recommendation(s), character/personal qualities, religious affiliation/commitment. *Important factors considered include:* rigor of secondary school record, standardized test scores. *Other factors considered include:* class rank, interview, extracurricular activities, talent/ability, first generation, alumni/ae relation, geographical residence, volunteer work, work experience, level of applicant's interest. **Freshman Admission Requirements:** High school diploma is required and GED is accepted. *Academic units recommended:* 4 English, 3 math, 2 science, 1 science lab, 3 social studies, 2 academic electives. **Freshman Admission Statistics:** 198 applied, 70.20% admitted, 52% enrolled. **Transfer Admission Requirements:** college transcript(s), essay or personal statement, statement of good standing from prior institution(s). Minimum college GPA of 2.0 required. Lowest grade transferable C-. **General Admission Information:** Application fee $40. Priority deadline 3/1. Nonfall registration accepted. Admission may be deferred for a maximum of one semester.

COSTS AND FINANCIAL AID

Annual tuition $24,100. Room and board $8,560. Required fees $580. Average book expense $1,000. **Required Forms and Deadlines:** FAFSA. **Notification of Awards:** Applicants will be notified of awards on a rolling basis beginning 3/1. **Types of Aid:** *Need-based scholarships/grants:* Federal Pell, FSEOG, Private scholarships, College/university scholarship or grant aid from institutional funds. *Loans:* Direct Subsidized Stafford Loans, Direct Unsubsidized Stafford Loans, Direct PLUS loans. *Student Employment:* Federal Work-Study Program available. Institutional employment available. **Financial Aid Statistics:** 89% needy freshmen, 98% needy undergrads receive need-based scholarship or grant aid. 12% freshmen, 4% undergrads receive non-need-based scholarship or grant aid. 90% freshmen, 97% undergrads receive need-based self-help aid. 10% freshmen, 4% undergrads receive athletic scholarships. 100% freshmen, 93% undergrads receive any aid. Average cumulative indebtedness $14,758. **Criteria for awarding aid:** *Need-based:* Minority status. *Non-need-based:* Academics, Alumni affiliation, Athletics.

MURRAY STATE UNIVERSITY

102 Curris Center, Murray, KY 42071-0009
Phone: 270-809-3741 • **Financial Aid Phone:** 270-809-2546
E-mail: msu.admissions@murraystate.edu • **CEEB Code:** 1494
Fax: 270-809-3780 • **Website:** www.murraystate.edu • **ACT Code:** 1532

This public school was founded in 1922. It has a 350-acre campus.

RATINGS
Admissions Selectivity Rating: 78   **Fire Safety Rating:** 92   **Green Rating:** 71

STUDENTS AND FACULTY
Enrollment: 7,891. **Student Body:** 58% female, 42% male, 26% out-of-state, 4% international (45 countries represented). Asian 1%, African American 8%, Caucasian 81%, Hispanic 2%, Native American <1%, Pacific Islander <1%, Two or more races 2%, Race unknown 2%.
Retention and Graduation: 72% freshmen return for sophomore year. 24% freshmen graduate within 4 years. 49% freshmen graduate within 6 years. 41% grads go on to further study within 1 year. **Faculty:** Student/faculty ratio 15:1. 455 full-time faculty, 77% hold PhDs, 17% are are members of minority groups, 42% are women.

ACADEMICS
Degrees: associate, bachelor's, certificate, doctoral/professional, master's, postbachelor's certifiate, post-master's certificate. **Classes:** Most classes have fewer than 10 students. Most lab/discussion sessions have 10-19 students. **Most popular majors:** Registered Nursing/Registered Nurse; Veterinary/ Animal Health Technology/Technician and Veterinary Assistant; Agriculture, Agriculture Operations, and Related Sciences. **Special Study Options:** Accelerated program, cooperative education program, cross-registration, distance learning, double major, dual enrollment, English as a Second Language (ESL), exchange student program (domestic), external degree program, honors program, independent study, internships, study abroad, teacher certification program, weekend college, agriculture, arts, business/marketing, biological sciences, communications/communication technologies, computer and information sciences, education, engineering/engineering technologies, English, foreign languages, health professions and related sciences, history, home economics, humanities and liberal arts, library sciences, mathematics, natural resources and environmental sciences, natural sciences, parks and recreation, philosophy, physical sciences, protective sciences/public administration, psychology, social/behavioral sciences, technologies, trade and industry, visual and performing arts. **Honors Programs:** The Honors Program offers a unique educational experience designed to teach able students how to learn, how to think critically and creatively, and how to communicate effectively. **Disability Services:** Special programs offered to physically disabled students, including note-taking services, tape recorders, tutors. **Career Services:** Alumni network, Alumni services, Career/job search classes, Career assessment, Internships, Regional alumni. Murray State's Bring Learning to Life program focuses on improving student learning through the implementation of learning experiences in which students apply principles learned in the classroom in a real-world setting. The Bring Learning to Life program includes experience-rich activities specific to each degree program in which all undergraduate students would have the opportunity to participate.

FACILITIES
Housing: Coed dorms, special housing for disabled students, men's dorms, women's dorms, fraternity/sorority housing, apartments for married students, apartments for single studentsAll housing is operated under a Residential College system. **Special Academic Facilities/Equipment:** State-of-the-art 73000 square-foot Student Recreation and Wellness Center nestled in the Residential College housing complex, West Kentucky Museum,8,500 seat Regional Special Events Center **Computers:** 95% of classrooms, 90% of dorms, 100% of libraries, 100% of dining areas, 100% of student union, have wireless network access. Students can register for classes online. Administrative functions (other than registration) can be performed online.

CAMPUS LIFE
Environment: Village. **Activities:** Choral groups, concert band, dance, drama/ theater, jazz band, literary magazine, marching band, music ensembles, musical theater, pep band, radio station, student government, student newspaper, student-run film society, symphony orchestra, television station, yearbook, Campus Ministries, Student Organization. 175 registered organizations, 30 honor societies, 15 religious organizations. 15 fraternities, 7 sororities. **Athletics (Intercollegiate):** *Men:* baseball, basketball, bowling, cheerleading, cross-country, equestrian sports, football, golf, horseback riding, riflery, rodeo, tennis. *Women:* basketball, cheerleading, cross-country, equestrian sports, golf, horseback riding, riflery, rodeo, soccer, softball, tennis, track/field (outdoor), volleyball. **On-Campus Highlights:** New Student Fitness Center, Curris Student Center, Regional Special Events Center, Equine Center, Residential Colleges.

ADMISSIONS
Freshman Academic Profile: Average high school GPA 3.5. 18% in top 10% of high school class, 45% in top 25% of high school class, 75% in top 50% of high school class. **Reported SAT (pre-2016 redesign) scores:** SAT Math middle 50% range 470-570. SAT Critical Reading middle 50% range 480-590. **Concordant SAT scores:** SAT Math middle 50% range 510–590. ACT middle 50% range 20-26. Minimum internet-based TOEFL 71. Minimum paper TOEFL 527. **Basis for Candidate Selection:** *Very important factors considered include:* rigor of secondary school record, class rank, academic GPA, standardized test scores. **Freshman Admission Requirements:** High school diploma is required and GED is accepted. *Academic units required:* 4 English, 3 math, 3 science, 1 science lab, 2 foreign language, 2 social studies, 1 history, 5 academic electives, and 1 unit from above areas or other academic areas. *Academic units recommended:* 4 math, 4 science. **Freshman Admission Statistics:** 4,874 applied, 90.60% admitted, 33% enrolled. **Transfer Admission Requirements:** college transcript(s), statement of good standing from prior institution(s). Minimum college GPA of 2.0 required. Lowest grade transferable d. **General Admission Information:** Application fee $40. Regular application deadline 8/15. Nonfall registration accepted. Admission may be deferred for a maximum of 1 year.

COSTS AND FINANCIAL AID
Annual in-state tuition $6,552. Annual out-of-state tuition $19,656. Room and board $8,206. Required fees $1,056. Average book expense $1,345. **Required Forms and Deadlines:** FAFSA. **Notification of Awards:** Applicants will be notified of awards on a rolling basis beginning 3/15. **Types of Aid:** *Need-based scholarships/grants:* Federal Pell, FSEOG, State scholarships/grants, Private scholarships, College/university scholarship or grant aid from institutional funds. *Loans:* Direct Subsidized Stafford Loans, Direct Unsubsidized Stafford Loans, Direct PLUS loans, Federal Perkins Loans, Federal Nursing Loans, College/ university loans from institutional funds. *Student Employment:* Federal Work-Study Program available. Institutional employment available. **Financial Aid Statistics:** 92% needy freshmen, 86% needy undergrads receive need-based scholarship or grant aid. 10% freshmen, 7% undergrads receive non-need-based scholarship or grant aid. 69% freshmen, 78% undergrads receive need-based self-help aid. 3% freshmen, 3% undergrads receive athletic scholarships. 94% freshmen, 86% undergrads receive any aid. 50% undergrads borrow to pay for school. Average cumulative indebtedness $26,598. **Criteria for awarding aid:** *Need-based:* Academics, Alumni affiliation, Job skills, Minority status, Music/ drama. *Non-need-based:* Academics, Alumni affiliation, Art, Athletics, Job skills, Leadership, Minority status, Music/drama, State/district residency.

MUSKINGUM UNIVERSITY

163 Stormont Street, New Concord, OH 43762
Phone: 740-826-8137 • **Financial Aid Phone:** 740-826-8137
E-mail: jzellers@muskingum.edu • **CEEB Code:** 1496
Fax: 614-826-8100 • **ACT Code:** 3305

This private school, affiliated with the Presbyterian Church, was founded in 1837. It has a 245-acre campus.

RATINGS
Admissions Selectivity Rating: 76   **Fire Safety Rating:** 60*   **Green Rating:** 60*

STUDENTS AND FACULTY
Enrollment: 1,580. **Student Body:** 55% female, 45% male, 8% out-of-state, 3% international (10 countries represented). Asian 1%, African American 5%, Caucasian 78%, Hispanic 2%, Native American <1%, Pacific Islander 0%, Two or more races 3%, Race unknown 7%.
Retention and Graduation: 74% freshmen return for sophomore year. 34% freshmen graduate within 4 years. 52% freshmen graduate within 6 years. 25% grads go on to further study within 1 year. 5% grads pursue arts and sciences degrees. 3% grads pursue law degrees. 4% grads pursue business degrees. 2% grads pursue medical degrees. **Faculty:** Student/faculty ratio 15:1. 92 full-time faculty, 96% hold PhDs, 12% are are members of minority groups, 45% are women. 0% of classes are taught by teaching assistants.

ACADEMICS
Degrees: bachelor's, master's. **Classes:** Most classes have fewer than 10 students. Most lab/discussion sessions have 20-29 students. **Most popular majors:** Early Childhood Education and Teaching; Registered Nursing/ Registered Nurse; Business Administration and Management. **Special Study Options:** Accelerated program, distance learning, double major, dual enrollment, English as a Second Language (ESL), exchange student program (domestic), independent study, internships, liberal arts/career combination, student-designed major, study abroad, teacher certification program, weekend

college. Combined degree programs: BA/MEng, BA,BS,MAE. **Disability Services:** Special programs offered to physically disabled students, including note-taking services, reader services, tape recorders, tutors. **Career Services:** Alumni network, Alumni services, Career assessment, Internships, Regional alumni. Muskingum Leadership Initiative—alumni identify relevant national and regional internships and communicate those opportunities to Muskingum students and faculty.

FACILITIES

Housing: Coed dorms, men's dorms, women's dorms, fraternity/sorority housing, cooperative housing, apartments for single students, Theme Housing. 50% of campus accessible to physically disabled. **Special Academic Facilities/ Equipment:** Art gallery, on-campus nursery school, electron microscope, 57-acre biology field station and mobile biology lab. **Computers:** 15% of classrooms, 100% of libraries, 33% of dining areas, 100% of student union, 10% of common outdoor areas have wireless network access. Students can register for classes online. Administrative functions (other than registration) can be performed online.

CAMPUS LIFE

Environment: Rural. **Activities:** Choral groups, concert band, dance, drama/ theater, jazz band, literary magazine, marching band, music ensembles, musical theater, pep band, radio station, student government, student newspaper, symphony orchestra, television station, yearbook, Campus Ministries, Student Organization, Model UN. 95 registered organizations, 16 honor societies, 4 religious organizations. 5 fraternities, 5 sororities. **Athletics (Intercollegiate):** *Men:* baseball, basketball, cheerleading, cross-country, football, golf, soccer, tennis, track/field (outdoor), track/field (indoor), wrestling. *Women:* basketball, cheerleading, cross-country, golf, soccer, softball, tennis, track/field (outdoor), track/field (indoor), volleyball. **On-Campus Highlights:** Philip and Betsey Caldwell Hall, Boyd Science Center, Rec Center, Patton Dining Center/ Kelly Coffee House, Walter K. Chess Student Center, New music classroom building opening Fall 2010.

ADMISSIONS

Freshman Academic Profile: Average high school GPA 3.1. 12% in top 10% of high school class, 33% in top 25% of high school class, 63% in top 50% of high school class. 92% from public high schools. **Reported SAT (pre-2016 redesign) scores:** SAT Math middle 50% range 400-520. SAT Critical Reading middle 50% range 400-550. SAT Writing middle 50% range 380-480. **Concordant SAT scores:** SAT EBRW middle 50% 440–570. SAT Math middle 50% range 440–550. ACT middle 50% range 18-24. Minimum internet-based TOEFL 79. Minimum paper TOEFL 550. **Basis for Candidate Selection:** *Very important factors considered include:* rigor of secondary school record, academic GPA. *Important factors considered include:* class rank, standardized test scores, recommendation(s). *Other factors considered include:* application essay, interview, extracurricular activities, talent/ability, character/personal qualities, alumni/ae relation, geographical residence, racial/ethnic status, work experience. **Freshman Admission Requirements:** High school diploma is required and GED is accepted. *Academic units required:* 4 English, 2 math, 2 science, 1 science lab, 2 foreign language, 1 social studies, 2 history. *Academic units recommended:* 4 English, 3 math, 3 science, 2 science labs, 2 foreign language, 1 social studies, 2 history. **Freshman Admission Statistics:** 1,977 applied, 73.90% admitted, 25% enrolled. **Transfer Admission Requirements:** High school transcript, college transcript(s), Minimum college GPA of 2.0 required. Lowest grade transferable C. **General Admission Information:** Priority deadline 3/1. Regular application deadline 8/1. Nonfall registration accepted. Admission may be deferred for a maximum of 1 year.

COSTS AND FINANCIAL AID

Annual tuition $26,200. Room and board $10,650. Required fees $978. Average book expense $1,100. **Required Forms and Deadlines:** FAFSA. **Notification of Awards:** Applicants will be notified of awards on a rolling basis beginning 3/1. **Types of Aid:** *Need-based scholarships/grants:* Federal Pell, FSEOG, State scholarships/grants, Private scholarships, College/university scholarship or grant aid from institutional funds, Federal Nursing Scholarships. *Loans:* Direct Subsidized Stafford Loans, Direct Unsubsidized Stafford Loans, Direct PLUS loans, Federal Perkins Loans, Federal Nursing Loans, College/university loans from institutional funds. *Student Employment:* Federal Work-Study Program available. Institutional employment available. **Financial Aid Statistics:** 100% needy freshmen, 99% needy undergrads receive need-based scholarship or grant aid. 89% freshmen, 88% undergrads receive non-need-based scholarship or grant aid. 91% freshmen, 88% undergrads receive need-based self-help aid. 0% freshmen, 0% undergrads receive athletic scholarships. 98% freshmen, 98% undergrads receive any aid. 81% undergrads borrow to pay for school. Average cumulative indebtedness $36,062. **Criteria for awarding aid:** *Need-based:* Academics, Leadership, Minority status. *Non-need-based:* Academics, Alumni affiliation, Art, Leadership, Minority status, Music/drama, Religious affiliation, State/district residency.

NAROPA UNIVERSITY

2130 Araphahoe Avenue, Boulder, CO 80302
Phone: 303-546-3572 • **Financial Aid Phone:** 303-546-3534
E-mail: admissions@naropa.edu • **CEEB Code:** 908
Fax: 303-546-3583 • **Website:** www.naropa.edu/ • **ACT Code:** 4853

This private school was founded in 1974. It has a 12-acre campus.

RATINGS

Admissions Selectivity Rating: 64   **Fire Safety Rating:** 61   **Green Rating:** 85

STUDENTS AND FACULTY

Enrollment: 464. **Student Body:** 61% female, 39% male, 74% out-of-state, 3% international (24 countries represented). Asian 3%, African American 2%, Caucasian 75%, Hispanic 4%, Native American 3%, Pacific Islander 0%, Two or more races 0%, Race unknown 11%.
Retention and Graduation: 64% freshmen return for sophomore year. 19% freshmen graduate within 4 years. 42% freshmen graduate within 6 years. **Faculty:** Student/faculty ratio 9:1. 51 full-time faculty, 51% hold PhDs, 12% are are members of minority groups, 57% are women. 0% of classes are taught by teaching assistants.

ACADEMICS

Degrees: bachelor's, certificate, master's. **Classes:** Most classes have 10-19 students. **Most popular majors:** Psychology; Visual and Performing Arts; English Language and Literature. **Special Study Options:** double major, independent study, internships, student-designed major, study abroad, Some courses available on-line. **Disability Services:** Special programs offered to physically disabled students, including note-taking services, reader services, tape recorders, tutors. **Career Services:** On-campus interviews.

FACILITIES

Housing: apartments for married students, apartments for single students, Themed housing (living and learning concept). 85% of campus accessible to physically disabled. **Special Academic Facilities/Equipment:** Maitri Rooms, meditation halls, Allen Ginsberg library and a preschool **Computers:** 100% of classrooms, 100% of dorms, 100% of libraries, 100% of dining areas, 100% of student union, 100% of common outdoor areas have wireless network access. Students can register for classes online. Administrative functions (other than registration) can be performed online.

CAMPUS LIFE

Environment: City. **Activities:** Choral groups, dance, drama/theater, jazz band, literary magazine, music ensembles, student government 20 registered organizations, 2 religious organizations. **On-Campus Highlights:** Lincoln Building, Nalanda Event Center, Meditation Hall, Naropa Cafe, Visual Arts Studio. **Environmental Initiatives:** We compost all of our paper towels in public restrooms diverting 25% of our landfill waste into compost.

ADMISSIONS

Freshman Academic Profile: Average high school GPA 3.0. Minimum paper TOEFL 550. **Basis for Candidate Selection:** *Very important factors considered include:* rigor of secondary school record, academic GPA, application essay, recommendation(s), interview. *Important factors considered include:* extracurricular activities, talent/ability, character/personal qualities, volunteer work. *Other factors considered include:* first generation, alumni/ae relation, racial/ethnic status, work experience. **Freshman Admission Requirements:** High school diploma is required and GED is accepted. *Academic units recommended:* 4 English, 3 math, 3 science, 2 science labs, 3 foreign language, 3 social studies, 3 history, 2 academic electives, and 2 units from above areas or other academic areas. **Freshman Admission Statistics:** 139 applied, 92.81% admitted, 53% enrolled. **Transfer Admission Requirements:** college transcript(s), essay or personal statement, interview, Lowest grade transferable C. **General Admission Information:** Application fee $50. Priority deadline 1/15. Nonfall registration accepted. Admission may be deferred for a maximum of 1 year.

COSTS AND FINANCIAL AID

Annual tuition $23,420. Room and board $8,478. Required fees $100. Average book expense $1,200. **Required Forms and Deadlines:** FAFSA. **Notification of Awards:** Applicants will be notified of awards on a rolling basis beginning 3/1. **Types of Aid:** *Need-based scholarships/grants:* Federal Pell, FSEOG, Private scholarships, College/university scholarship or grant aid from institutional funds. *Loans:* Federal Perkins Loans. *Student Employment:* Federal Work-Study Program available. **Financial Aid Statistics:** 87% needy freshmen, 88% needy undergrads receive need-based scholarship or grant aid. 0% undergrads receive non-need-based scholarship or grant aid. 94% freshmen, 91% undergrads receive need-based self-help aid. 0% freshmen, 0% undergrads receive athletic scholarships. 71% freshmen, 71% undergrads receive any aid.

Criteria for awarding aid: *Need-based:* Academics, Job skills, Leadership, Minority status, Music/drama, Religious affiliation.

NATIONAL UNIVERSITY OF HEALTH SCIENCES

200 E. Roosevelt Road, Lombard, IL 60148
Phone: 630-889-6566 • **Financial Aid Phone:** 630-889-6700
E-mail: admissions@nuhs.edu
Fax: 630-889-6554 • **Website:** www.nuhs.edu

This private school was founded in 1906. It has a 32-acre campus.

RATINGS

Admissions Selectivity Rating: 62   **Fire Safety Rating:** 60*   **Green Rating:** 60*

STUDENTS AND FACULTY

Enrollment: 165. **Student Body:** 16% female, 84% male, 70% out-of-state, 4% international (9 countries represented). Asian 5%, African American 16%, Caucasian 63%, Hispanic 5%, Native American 0%, Pacific Islander 0%, Two or more races 0%, Race unknown 7%.
Retention and Graduation: 90% freshmen return for sophomore year.
Faculty: Student/faculty ratio 6:1. 46 full-time faculty, 93% hold PhDs, 0% are are members of minority groups, 17% are women.

ACADEMICS

Degrees: bachelor's, certificate, doctoral/professional, master's. **Classes:** Most classes have 40-49 students. Most lab/discussion sessions have 20-29 students. **Most popular majors:** Biomedical Sciences; Massage Therapy/Therapeutic Massage. **Special Study Options:** internships, Accelerated science prerequisite program. Combined degree programs: BS/DC.

FACILITIES

Housing: Coed dorms, men's dorms, women's dorms, apartments for married students, apartments for single students, Studio apartments. **Special Academic Facilities/Equipment:** Museum Fitness Center Learning Resource Center Health Care Clinic **Computers:** 88% of classrooms, 100% of libraries, 100% of common outdoor areas have wireless network access. Students can register for classes online.

CAMPUS LIFE

Environment: Town. **Activities:** student government, student newspaper, yearbook. 24 registered organizations, 1 religious organization. 2 fraternities, 1 sorority. **On-Campus Highlights:** Janse Hall, Student Center, Clinic, Learning Resource Center, Dormitories.

ADMISSIONS

Minimum internet-based TOEFL 79. Minimum paper TOEFL 550.
Freshman Admission Requirements: High school diploma is required and GED is accepted. **Transfer Admission Requirements:** college transcript(s), statement of good standing from prior institution(s). Minimum college GPA of 2.5 required. Lowest grade transferable C. **General Admission Information:** Application fee $55. Nonfall registration accepted. Admission may be deferred.

COSTS AND FINANCIAL AID

Types of Aid: *Need-based scholarships/grants:* Federal Pell, FSEOG, State scholarships/grants, Private scholarships, College/university scholarship or grant aid from institutional funds. *Loans:* Federal Perkins Loans. *Student Employment:* Federal Work-Study Program available. Institutional employment available. **Financial Aid Statistics:** 62% needy undergrads receive need-based scholarship or grant aid. 10% undergrads receive non-need-based scholarship or grant aid. 62% undergrads receive need-based self-help aid.

NAZARETH COLLEGE

4245 East Avenue, Rochester, NY 14618-3790
Phone: 585-389-2860 • **Financial Aid Phone:** 585-389-2310
E-mail: admissions@naz.edu • **CEEB Code:** 2511
Fax: 585-389-2826 • **Website:** www.naz.edu • **ACT Code:** 2826

This private school was founded in 1924. It has a 150-acre campus.

RATINGS

Admissions Selectivity Rating: 83   **Fire Safety Rating:** 93   **Green Rating:** 73

STUDENTS AND FACULTY

Enrollment: 2,125. **Student Body:** 72% female, 28% male, 9% out-of-state, 2% international (34 countries represented). Asian 3%, African American 7%, Caucasian 78%, Hispanic 5%, Native American <1%, Pacific Islander <1%, Two or more races 2%, Race unknown 4%.
Retention and Graduation: 85% freshmen return for sophomore year. 58% freshmen graduate within 4 years. 69 **Faculty:** Student/faculty ratio 9:1. 180 full-time faculty, 82% hold PhDs, 13% are are members of minority groups, 61% are women. 0% of classes are taught by teaching assistants.

ACADEMICS

Degrees: bachelor's, doctoral/professional, master's, postbachelor's certificate, post-master's certificate. **Classes:** Most classes have 10-19 students. Most lab/discussion sessions have 10-19 students. **Most popular majors:** Education; Physical Therapy/Therapist; Business Administration, Management and Operations. **Special Study Options:** cross-registration, distance learning, double major, exchange student program (domestic), honors program, independent study, internships, study abroad, teacher certification program. Combined degree programs: BS/DPT Physical Therapy. **Disability Services:** Special programs offered to physically disabled students, including note-taking services, reader services, tape recorders, tutors. **Career Services:** Alumni network, Alumni services, Career/job search classes, Career assessment, Internships, Regional alumni.

FACILITIES

Housing: Coed dorms, special housing for disabled students, apartments for single students, Substance Free Quiet Floors Language House Honors First-year Experience. 80% of campus accessible to physically diasbled. **Special Academic Facilities/Equipment:** Arts center, speech/hearing/language clinic, reading clinic, psychology center, center for service learning, Center for Teaching Excellence, and Center for International Education. **Computers:** Students can register for classes online.

CAMPUS LIFE

Environment: Village. **Activities:** Choral groups, concert band, dance, drama/theater, jazz band, literary magazine, music ensembles, musical theater, opera, radio station, student government, student newspaper, symphony orchestra, yearbook, Campus Ministries, Student Organization. 50 registered organizations, 19 honor societies, 5 religious organizations. **Athletics (Intercollegiate):** *Men:* basketball, cross-country, diving, equestrian sports, golf, lacrosse, soccer, swimming, tennis, track/field (outdoor), track/field (indoor), volleyball. *Women:* basketball, cross-country, diving, equestrian sports, field hockey, golf, lacrosse, soccer, softball, swimming, tennis, track/field (outdoor), track/field (indoor), volleyball. **On-Campus Highlights:** Cabaret-informal dining/coffee house, Athletic Facilities, Shults Community Center, Colie's Cafe, Library.

ADMISSIONS

Freshman Academic Profile: Average high school GPA 89.8. 24% in top 10% of high school class, 58% in top 25% of high school class, 89% in top 50% of high school class. 90% from public high schools. **Reported SAT (pre-2016 redesign) scores:** SAT Math middle 50% range 490-600. SAT Critical Reading middle 50% range 490-590. SAT Writing middle 50% range 470-570. **Concordant SAT scores:** SAT EBRW middle 50% 540–640. SAT Math middle 50% range 520–620. ACT middle 50% range 23-27. Minimum internet-based TOEFL 79. Minimum paper TOEFL 550. **Basis for Candidate Selection:** *Very important factors considered include:* rigor of secondary school record, class rank, academic GPA, application essay, recommendation(s). *Important factors considered include:* interview, extracurricular activities, talent/ability, character/personal qualities, geographical residence, state residency, racial/ethnic status, volunteer work, work experience, level of applicant's interest. *Other factors considered include:* standardized test scores, first generation, alumni/ae relation. **Freshman Admission Requirements:** High school diploma is required and GED is accepted. *Academic units required:* 4 English, 3 math, 3 science, 2 science labs, 3 foreign language, 3 social studies. *Academic units recommended:* 4 English, 4 math, 4 science, 4 foreign language, 4 social studies. **Freshman Admission Statistics:** 4,118 applied, 72.10% admitted, 17% enrolled. **Transfer Admission Requirements:** college transcript(s), essay or personal statement, Minimum college GPA of 2.5 required. Lowest grade transferable C. **General Admission Information:** Application fee $45. Priority deadline 12/1. Regular application deadline 2/1. Nonfall registration accepted. Admission may be deferred for a maximum of 1 year.

COSTS AND FINANCIAL AID
Annual tuition $31,024. Room and board $13,198. Required fees $1,400. Average book expense $1,100. **Required Forms and Deadlines:** FAFSA, State aid form. **Notification of Awards:** Applicants will be notified of awards on a rolling basis beginning 2/1. **Types of Aid:** *Need-based scholarships/grants:* Federal Pell, FSEOG, State scholarships/grants, Private scholarships, College/university scholarship or grant aid from institutional funds. *Loans:* Direct Subsidized Stafford Loans, Direct Unsubsidized Stafford Loans, Direct PLUS loans, Federal Perkins Loans, Federal Nursing Loans. *Student Employment:* Federal Work-Study Program available. Institutional employment available. **Financial Aid Statistics:** 100% needy freshmen, 100% needy undergrads receive need-based scholarship or grant aid. 49% freshmen, 35% undergrads receive non-need-based scholarship or grant aid. 95% freshmen, 94% undergrads receive need-based self-help aid. 0% freshmen, 0% undergrads receive athletic scholarships. Average cumulative indebtedness $40,567. **Criteria for awarding aid:** *Need-based:* Alumni affiliation. *Non-need-based:* Academics, Art, Minority status, Music/drama.

NEBRASKA METHODIST COLLEGE

720 North 87th Street, Omaha, NE 68114
Phone: 402-354-7200 • **Financial Aid Phone:** 402-354-7225
E-mail: admissions@methodistcollege.edu • **CEEB Code:** 6510
Fax: 402-354-7020 • **ACT Code:** 2465

This private school, affiliated with the Methodist Church, was founded in 1891. It has a 6-acre campus.

RATINGS
Admissions Selectivity Rating: 76   **Fire Safety Rating:** 68   **Green Rating:** 60*

STUDENTS AND FACULTY
Enrollment: 504. **Student Body:** 92% female, 8% male, 35% out-of-state, 0% international (3 countries represented). Asian 3%, African American 3%, Caucasian 87%, Hispanic 1%, Native American 1%, Pacific Islander 0%, Two or more races 0%, Race unknown 5%.
Retention and Graduation: 81% freshmen return for sophomore year. 10% grads go on to further study within 1 year. 10% grads pursue arts and sciences degrees. **Faculty:** Student/faculty ratio 10:1. 43 full-time faculty, 28% hold PhDs, 7% are are members of minority groups, 91% are women. 0% of classes are taught by teaching assistants.

ACADEMICS
Degrees: associate, bachelor's, certificate, master's, post-master's certificate. **Classes:** Most classes have 10-19 students. Most lab/discussion sessions have 10-19 students. **Most popular majors:** Diagnostic Medical Sonography/Sonographer and Ultrasound Technician; Radiologic Technology/Science. **Special Study Options:** Accelerated program, distance learning, independent study. **Disability Services:** Special programs offered to physically disabled students, including note-taking services, reader services, tape recorders, tutors. **Career Services:** Alumni network, Alumni services, Career/job search classes, On-campus interviews.

FACILITIES
Housing: apartments for single students. 90% of campus accessible to physically diasbled. **Computers:** 100% of classrooms, 100% of libraries, 100% of dining areas, 100% of student union, have wireless network access. Students can register for classes online. Administrative functions (other than registration) can be performed online.

CAMPUS LIFE
Environment: City. **Activities:** student government 11 registered organizations, 2 honor societies. **On-Campus Highlights:** Student Center, Library, Human Cadaver Lab, Chapel

ADMISSIONS
Freshman Academic Profile: Average high school GPA 3.3. 11% in top 10% of high school class, 11% in top 25% of high school class, 50% in top 50% of

high school class. 90% from public high schools. ACT middle 50% range 19-23. Minimum internet-based TOEFL 80. Minimum paper TOEFL 550. **Basis for Candidate Selection:** *Very important factors considered include:* rigor of secondary school record, academic GPA, standardized test scores. *Important factors considered include:* class rank, application essay, recommendation(s), interview, character/personal qualities. *Other factors considered include:* first generation, alumni/ae relation, geographical residence, state residency, racial/ethnic status, volunteer work, work experience, level of applicant's interest. **Freshman Admission Requirements:** High school diploma is required and GED is accepted. *Academic units required:* 4 English, 3 math, 2 science, 2 science labs, 2 social studies. **Freshman Admission Statistics:** 64 applied, 60.94% admitted. **Transfer Admission Requirements:** High school transcript, college transcript(s), essay or personal statement, interview, statement of good standing from prior institution(s). Minimum college GPA of 2.5 required. Lowest grade transferable C. **General Admission Information:** Application fee $25. Priority deadline 1/1. Regular application deadline 3/1. Nonfall registration accepted. Admission may be deferred for a maximum of 12 months.

COSTS AND FINANCIAL AID
Annual tuition $12,840. Required fees $600. Average book expense $1,300. **Required Forms and Deadlines:** FAFSA, Institution's own financial aid form. **Notification of Awards:** Applicants will be notified of awards on a rolling basis beginning 3/1. **Types of Aid:** *Need-based scholarships/grants:* Federal Pell, FSEOG, State scholarships/grants, Private scholarships, College/university scholarship or grant aid from institutional funds. *Loans:* Federal Perkins Loans, Federal Nursing Loans, State Loans, College/university loans from institutional funds. *Student Employment:* Federal Work-Study Program available. Institutional employment available. **Financial Aid Statistics:** 38% needy freshmen, 51% needy undergrads receive need-based scholarship or grant aid. 8% freshmen, 7% undergrads receive non-need-based scholarship or grant aid. 92% freshmen, 89% undergrads receive need-based self-help aid. 0% freshmen, 0% undergrads receive athletic scholarships. 85% freshmen, 69% undergrads receive any aid. **Criteria for awarding aid:** *Need-based:* Minority status. *Non-need-based:* Academics, Minority status, Religious affiliation.

NEBRASKA WESLEYAN UNIVERSITY

5000 Saint Paul Ave., Lincoln, NE 68504
Phone: 402-465-2218 • **Financial Aid Phone:** 402-465-2212
E-mail: admissions@nebrwesleyan.edu • **CEEB Code:** 6470
Fax: 402-465-2177 • **Website:** http://www.nebrwesleyan.edu • **ACT Code:** 2474

This private school, affiliated with the Methodist Church, was founded in 1887. It has a 50-acre campus.

RATINGS
Admissions Selectivity Rating: 81   **Fire Safety Rating:** 83   **Green Rating:** 60*

STUDENTS AND FACULTY
Enrollment: 1,788. **Student Body:** 61% female, 39% male, 13% out-of-state, 1% international (20 countries represented). Asian 2%, African American 2%, Caucasian 84%, Hispanic 5%, Native American <1%, Pacific Islander <1%, Two or more races 2%, Race unknown 3%.
Retention and Graduation: 79% freshmen return for sophomore year. 51% freshmen graduate within 4 years. 62% freshmen graduate within 6 years. **Faculty:** Student/faculty ratio 12:1. 106 full-time faculty, 92% hold PhDs, 2% are are members of minority groups, 54% are women. 0% of classes are taught by teaching assistants.

ACADEMICS
Degrees: bachelor's, certificate, master's, postbachelor's certificate, post-master's certificate. **Classes:** Most classes have 20-29 students. Most lab/discussion sessions have 10-19 students. **Most popular majors:** Business Administration and Management; Biology/Biological Sciences; Psychology. **Special Study Options:** double major, dual enrollment, independent study, internships, liberal arts/career combination, study abroad, teacher certification program, weekend college, 3-2 Engineering Program with Washington Univ., Columbia Univ., or Univ. of Nebraska-Lincoln; Capitol Hill Internship Program; Chicago Center for Urban Life & Culture. **Disability Services:** Special programs offered to physically disabled students, including note-taking services, reader services, tape recorders, tutors. **Career Services:** Alumni network, Alumni services, Career/job search classes, Career assessment, Internships, Regional alumni. National and international service learning trips; service learning as part of coursework.

FACILITIES
Housing: Coed dorms, women's dorms, fraternity/sorority housing, apartments for single students, Townhouses; residence hall suites. **Special Academic Facilities/Equipment:** Art galleries, psychology/sleep lab, observatory and

planetarium, green house, laboratory theatre, herbarium, nuclear magnetic resonance laboratory. **Computers:** Students can register for classes online. Administrative functions (other than registration) can be performed online.

CAMPUS LIFE

Environment: City. **Activities:** Choral groups, concert band, drama/theater, jazz band, literary magazine, marching band, music ensembles, musical theater, opera, pep band, radio station, student government, student newspaper, symphony orchestra, Campus Ministries, Student Organization. 80 registered organizations, 18 honor societies, 5 religious organizations. 3 fraternities, 4 sororities. **Athletics (Intercollegiate):** *Men:* baseball, basketball, cross-country, football, golf, soccer, tennis, track/field (outdoor), track/field (indoor). *Women:* basketball, cross-country, golf, soccer, softball, tennis, track/field (outdoor), track/field (indoor), volleyball. **On-Campus Highlights:** Weary Center for Health and Fitness, Wesleyan Coffee House, Old Main, Roy G Story Student Center, Great Hall, Smith-Curtis. **Environmental Initiatives:** Completed light inventory; retrofitted 80% of all lights.

ADMISSIONS

Freshman Academic Profile: Average high school GPA 3.6. 18% in top 10% of high school class, 50% in top 25% of high school class, 84% in top 50% of high school class. **Reported SAT (pre-2016 redesign) scores:** SAT Math middle 50% range 510-600. SAT Critical Reading middle 50% range 430-590. **Concordant SAT scores:** SAT Math middle 50% range 540–620. ACT middle 50% range 22-27. Minimum internet-based TOEFL 71. Minimum paper TOEFL 525. **Basis for Candidate Selection:** *Very important factors considered include:* academic GPA, standardized test scores. *Important factors considered include:* rigor of secondary school record, class rank, extracurricular activities, talent/ability, character/personal qualities. *Other factors considered include:* application essay, recommendation(s), interview, first generation, alumni/ae relation, geographical residence, state residency, racial/ethnic status, volunteer work, level of applicant's interest. **Freshman Admission Requirements:** High school diploma is required and GED is accepted. *Academic units recommended:* 4 English, 4 math, 3 science, 3 science labs, 3 foreign language, 3 social studies. **Freshman Admission Statistics:** 1,689 applied, 78.80% admitted, 33% enrolled. **Transfer Admission Requirements:** college transcript(s), statement of good standing from prior institution(s). Minimum college GPA of 2.0 required. Lowest grade transferable C-. **General Admission Information:** Priority deadline 5/1. Regular application deadline 8/15. Nonfall registration accepted. Admission may be deferred for a maximum of 1 year.

COSTS AND FINANCIAL AID

Annual tuition $29,200. Room and board $8,340. Required fees $600. Average book expense $1,000. **Required Forms and Deadlines:** FAFSA. **Notification of Awards:** Applicants will be notified of awards on a rolling basis beginning 2/1. **Types of Aid:** *Need-based scholarships/grants:* Federal Pell, FSEOG, State scholarships/grants, Private scholarships, College/university scholarship or grant aid from institutional funds. *Loans:* Direct Subsidized Stafford Loans, Direct Unsubsidized Stafford Loans, Direct PLUS loans, Federal Perkins Loans. *Student Employment:* Federal Work-Study Program available. Institutional employment available. **Financial Aid Statistics:** 99% needy freshmen, 98% needy undergrads receive need-based scholarship or grant aid. 19% freshmen, 12% undergrads receive non-need-based scholarship or grant aid. 76% freshmen, 83% undergrads receive need-based self-help aid. 0% freshmen, 0% undergrads receive athletic scholarships. 99% freshmen, 96% undergrads receive any aid. 78% undergrads borrow to pay for school. Average cumulative indebtedness $29,136. **Criteria for awarding aid:** *Need-based:* Academics, Leadership, Minority status, Religious affiliation. *Non-need-based:* Academics, Alumni affiliation, Art, Leadership, Music/drama.

NEUMANN UNIVERSITY

One Neumann Drive, Aston, PA 19014
Phone: 610-558-5616 • **Financial Aid Phone:** 610-558-5521
E-mail: neumann@neumann.edu • **CEEB Code:** 2628
Fax: 610-361-2548 • **Website:** www.neumann.edu • **ACT Code:** 3649

This private school, affiliated with the Roman Catholic Church, was founded in 1965. It has a 55-acre campus.

RATINGS

Admissions Selectivity Rating: 71   **Fire Safety Rating:** 95   **Green Rating:** 67

STUDENTS AND FACULTY

Enrollment: 2,178. **Student Body:** 66% female, 34% male, 31% out-of-state, 1% international (9 countries represented). Asian 1%, African American 23%, Caucasian 53%, Hispanic 5%, Native American <1%, Pacific Islander <1%, Two or more races 2%, Race unknown 14%.

Retention and Graduation: 69% freshmen return for sophomore year. 30% freshmen graduate within 4 years. 53% freshmen graduate within 6 years. **Faculty:** Student/faculty ratio 14:1. 100 full-time faculty, 77% hold PhDs, 0% are are members of minority groups, 63% are women. 0% of classes are taught by teaching assistants.

ACADEMICS

Degrees: associate, bachelor's, doctoral/professional, doctoral/research, doctoral, master's, post-master's certificate. **Classes:** Most classes have 20-29 students. Most lab/discussion sessions have 10-19 students. **Most popular majors:** Registered Nursing, Nursing Administration, Nursing Research and Clinical Nursing; Elementary Education and Teaching; Liberal Arts and Sciences/Liberal Studies. **Special Study Options:** Accelerated program, cooperative education program, distance learning, double major, exchange student program (domestic), honors program, independent study, internships, liberal arts/career combination, student-designed major, study abroad, teacher certification program, weekend college. Combined degree programs: BS/MS. **Disability Services:** Special programs offered to physically disabled students, including note-taking services, reader services, tape recorders, tutors. **Career Services:** Alumni network, Alumni services, Career/job search classes, Career assessment, Internships. At Neumann University, almost every major requires an internship, which is facilitated through the Office of Career and Personal Development.

FACILITIES

Housing: Coed dorms, special housing for disabled students, Off campus housing. 100% of campus accessible to physically diasbled. **Special Academic Facilities/Equipment:** Child development center **Computers:** 100% of classrooms, 100% of libraries, have wireless network access. Administrative functions (other than registration) can be performed online.

CAMPUS LIFE

Environment: Town. **Activities:** Choral groups, dance, drama/theater, jazz band, literary magazine, music ensembles, musical theater, radio station, student government, student newspaper, yearbook, Campus Ministries, Model UN. 14 registered organizations, 4 honor societies, 2 religious organizations. **Athletics (Intercollegiate):** *Men:* baseball, basketball, cross-country, golf, ice hockey, lacrosse, soccer, tennis. *Women:* basketball, cross-country, field hockey, ice hockey, lacrosse, soccer, softball, tennis, volleyball. **On-Campus Highlights:** Life Center, Training room, On campus Chapel, Library, Computer Labs.

ADMISSIONS

Freshman Academic Profile: Average high school GPA 3.1. 70% from public high schools. **Reported SAT (pre-2016 redesign) scores:** SAT Math middle 50% range 400-490. SAT Critical Reading middle 50% range 400-490. SAT Writing middle 50% range 390-480. **Concordant SAT scores:** SAT EBRW middle 50% range 440–540. SAT Math middle 50% range 440–520. ACT middle 50% range 17-19. Minimum internet-based TOEFL 70. Minimum paper TOEFL 550. **Basis for Candidate Selection:** *Very important factors considered include:* rigor of secondary school record, academic GPA, standardized test scores, recommendation(s). *Important factors considered include:* interview. *Other factors considered include:* application essay, extracurricular activities, talent/ability, character/personal qualities, first generation, alumni/ae relation, volunteer work, work experience, level of applicant's interest. **Freshman Admission Requirements:** High school diploma is required and GED is accepted. *Academic units required:* 4 English, 2 math, 2 science, 2 foreign language, 2 social studies, 4 academic electives. *Academic units recommended:* 3 science. **Freshman Admission Statistics:** 1,486 applied, 93.74% admitted, 27% enrolled. **Transfer Admission Requirements:** college transcript(s), Minimum college GPA of 2.0 required. Lowest grade transferable C. **General Admission Information:** Application fee $35. Nonfall registration accepted. Admission may be deferred.

COSTS AND FINANCIAL AID

Annual tuition $27,340. Room and board $12,158. Required fees $1,240. Average book expense $1,488. **Required Forms and Deadlines:** FAFSA. **Notification of Awards:** Applicants will be notified of awards on a rolling basis beginning 3/1. **Types of Aid:** *Need-based scholarships/grants:* Federal Pell, FSEOG, State scholarships/grants, Private scholarships, College/university scholarship or grant aid from institutional funds, United Negro College Fund. *Loans:* Direct Subsidized Stafford Loans, Direct Unsubsidized Stafford Loans, Direct PLUS loans, Federal Nursing Loans. *Student Employment:* Federal Work-Study Program available. **Financial Aid Statistics:** 88% needy freshmen, 83% needy undergrads receive need-based scholarship or grant aid. 100% freshmen, 96% undergrads receive non-need-based scholarship or grant aid. 91% freshmen, 94% undergrads receive need-based self-help aid. 0% freshmen, 0% undergrads receive athletic scholarships. 100% freshmen, 100% undergrads receive any aid. **Criteria for awarding aid:** *Need-based:* Academics. *Non-need-based:* Academics.

NEUMONT UNIVERSITY

143 South Main Street, Salt Lake City, UT 84111
Phone: 888-638-6668 • **Financial Aid Phone:** 801-302-2873
E-mail: admissions@neumont.edu
Fax: 801-302-2811 • **Website:** www.neumont.edu

This proprietary school was founded in 2003.

RATINGS

Admissions Selectivity Rating: 75   **Fire Safety Rating:** 60*   **Green Rating:** 60*

STUDENTS AND FACULTY

Enrollment: 429. **Student Body:** 10% female, 90% male, 88% out-of-state, 0% international. Asian 3%, African American 5%, Caucasian 49%, Hispanic 10%, Native American 1%, Pacific Islander <1%, Two or more races 6%, Race unknown 25%.
Retention and Graduation: 85% freshmen return for sophomore year. 62% freshmen graduate within 4 years. 62% freshmen graduate within 6 years. **Faculty:** Student/faculty ratio 21:1. 15 full-time faculty, 13% hold PhDs, 7% are are members of minority groups, 0% are women.

ACADEMICS

Degrees: bachelor's, master's. **Special Study Options:** Accelerated program, internships. **Disability Services:** Special programs offered to physically disabled students, including note-taking services, reader services, tape recorders, tutors. **Career Services:** Alumni network, Career/job search classes, Career assessment, Internships.

FACILITIES

Housing: apartments for married students, apartments for single students. 100% of campus accessible to physically diasbled. **Computers:** 100% of classrooms, 100% of libraries, 100% of dining areas, 100% of student union, have wireless network access. Students can register for classes online. Undergraduates are required to own a computer.

CAMPUS LIFE

Environment: Metropolis. **Activities:** student government. 8 registered organizations.

ADMISSIONS

Freshman Academic Profile: Average high school GPA 3.2. **Reported SAT (pre-2016 redesign) scores:** SAT Math middle 50% range 455-640. SAT Critical Reading middle 50% range 445-615. SAT Writing middle 50% range 400-570. **Concordant SAT scores:** SAT EBRW middle 50% 480–650. SAT Math middle 50% range 500–660. ACT middle 50% range 20-29. Minimum paper TOEFL 79. **Basis for Candidate Selection:** *Very important factors considered include:* academic GPA, standardized test scores, application essay. *Important factors considered include:* interview, extracurricular activities, talent/ability, character/personal qualities, volunteer work, work experience, level of applicant's interest. *Other factors considered include:* rigor of secondary school record, class rank, recommendation(s). **Freshman Admission Statistics:** 727 applied, 82.94% admitted, 28% enrolled. **General Admission Information:** Application fee $35. Nonfall registration accepted. Admission may be deferred for a maximum of 1 year.

COSTS AND FINANCIAL AID

Annual tuition $22,950. Required fees $1,500. Average book expense $1,200. **Required Forms and Deadlines:** FAFSA, Institution's own financial aid form. **Notification of Awards:** Applicants will be notified of awards on a rolling basis beginning 11/23. **Types of Aid:** *Need-based scholarships/grants:* Federal Pell, FSEOG, Private scholarships, College/university scholarship or grant aid from institutional funds. *Loans:* Direct Subsidized Stafford Loans, Direct Unsubsidized Stafford Loans, Direct PLUS loans, College/university loans from institutional funds. *Student Employment:* Federal Work-Study Program available. Institutional employment available. **Financial Aid Statistics:** 96% needy freshmen, 88% needy undergrads receive need-based scholarship or grant aid. 79% freshmen, 57% undergrads receive non-need-based scholarship or grant aid. 0% freshmen, 0% undergrads receive need-based self-help aid. 0% freshmen, 0% undergrads receive athletic scholarships. 91% undergrads borrow to pay for school. Average cumulative indebtedness $39,623. **Criteria for awarding aid:** *Need-based:* Academics. *Non-need-based:* Academics, Job skills, Leadership, State/district residency.

NEW COLLEGE OF FLORIDA

5800 Bay Shore Rd, Sarasota, FL 34243-2109
Phone: 941-487-5000 • **Financial Aid Phone:** 941-487-5000
E-mail: admissions@ncf.edu • **CEEB Code:** 39574
Fax: 941-487-5001 • **Website:** www.ncf.edu • **ACT Code:** 750

This public school was founded in 1960. It has a 118.6-acre campus.

RATINGS

Admissions Selectivity Rating: 89   **Fire Safety Rating:** 91   **Green Rating:** 71

STUDENTS AND FACULTY

Enrollment: 852. **Student Body:** 61% female, 39% male, 13% out-of-state, 2% international (23 countries represented). Asian 3%, African American 3%, Caucasian 69%, Hispanic 16%, Native American 0%, Pacific Islander 0%, Two or more races 4%, Race unknown 3%.
Retention and Graduation: 81% freshmen return for sophomore year. 63% freshmen graduate within 4 years. 71% freshmen graduate within 6 years. 26% grads go on to further study within 1 year. **Faculty:** Student/faculty ratio 10:1. 77 full-time faculty, 99% hold PhDs, 12% are are members of minority groups, 49% are women. 0% of classes are taught by teaching assistants.

ACADEMICS

Degrees: bachelor's, master's. **Classes:** Most classes have 10-19 students. **Most popular majors:** Psychology; Anthropology; Economics. **Special Study Options:** cross-registration, double major, exchange student program (domestic), honors program, independent study, internships, student-designed major, study abroad, Academic contract, January interterm (independent study), Narrative evaluation/pass-fail, Senior thesis, Tutorials, Undergraduate research. Special or unique academic programs: (1) The New College academic contract whereby each student develops her/his individual academic program of coursework, tutorials, field and lab research, study abroad, and so on, in close consultation with a faculty member. See the General Catalog on the web. http://www.ncf.edu/resources-for-students (2) Non-graded, narrative evaluation which encourages exploration and mastery. (3) Intensive "Independent Study Projects" during January which can be highly individual but can also involve group activities, such as an acting workshop or an ecological tour of Florida. (4) Competitive grants programs to support student research. **Honors Programs:** New College of Florida is the state's officially-designated "honors college for the liberal arts." **Disability Services:** Special programs offered to physically disabled students, including note-taking services, reader services, tape recorders. **Career Services:** Alumni network, Alumni services, Career/job search classes, Career assessment, Internships, Regional alumni. The National Student Exchange program.

FACILITIES

Housing: Coed dorms, special housing for disabled students, apartments for single students, Specialized housing options may be arranged in response to student interest. 80% of campus accessible to physically diasbled. **Special Academic Facilities/Equipment:** Anthropology and psychology labs. Electronic music lab. Individual studio space for senior art students. Marine biology research center with Living Ecosystem Teaching and Research Aquarium, wet lab, and seawater on tap. NMR, scanning electron microscope, inert atmosphere glovebox, transparent fume hoods, greenhouse. **Computers:** 95% of classrooms, 100% of dorms, 100% of libraries, 100% of dining areas, 100% of student union, 20% of common outdoor areas have wireless network access. Students can register for classes online. Administrative functions (other than registration) can be performed online.

CAMPUS LIFE

Environment: Town. **Activities:** Choral groups, dance, drama/theater, literary magazine, music ensembles, musical theater, radio station, student government, student newspaper, student-run film society, Campus Ministries. 90 registered organizations, 5 religious organizations. **Athletics (Intercollegiate):** *Men:* sailing. *Women:* sailing. **On-Campus Highlights:** The R.V. Heiser Natural Sciences Complex, Pritzker Marine Biology Research Center, The Caples Fine Arts Complex, Four Winds Cafe (Student owned and operated), Jane Bancroft Cook Library, Historic bayfront mansions. **Environmental Initiatives:** We've had an environmental studies program since 1972.

ADMISSIONS

Freshman Academic Profile: Average high school GPA 4.0. 43% in top 10% of high school class, 79% in top 25% of high school class, 97% in top 50% of high school class. 79% from public high schools. **Reported SAT (pre-2016 redesign) scores:** SAT Math middle 50% range 560-660. SAT Critical

Reading middle 50% range 610-720. SAT Writing middle 50% range 570-670. **Concordant SAT scores:** SAT EBRW middle 50% 650–730. SAT Math middle 50% range 580–690. ACT middle 50% range 27-31. Minimum internet-based TOEFL 83. Minimum paper TOEFL 560. **Basis for Candidate Selection:** *Very important factors considered include:* rigor of secondary school record, academic GPA, application essay. *Important factors considered include:* class rank, standardized test scores, recommendation(s), extracurricular activities, character/personal qualities, volunteer work, work experience, level of applicant's interest. *Other factors considered include:* talent/ability, first generation, alumni/ae relation, geographical residence, state residency. **Freshman Admission Requirements:** High school diploma is required and GED is accepted. *Academic units required:* 4 English, 4 math, 3 science, 2 science labs, 2 foreign language, 3 social studies, 2 academic electives. *Academic units recommended:* 4 English, 4 math, 4 science, 2 science labs, 4 foreign language, 4 social studies, 4 academic electives. **Freshman Admission Statistics:** 1,655 applied, 60.97% admitted, 26% enrolled. **Transfer Admission Requirements:** college transcript(s), essay or personal statement, Minimum college GPA of 2.0 required. Lowest grade transferable C. **General Admission Information:** Application fee $30. Priority deadline 11/1. Regular application deadline 4/15. Nonfall registration not accepted. Admission may be deferred for a maximum of 1 year.

COSTS AND FINANCIAL AID

Annual in-state tuition $6,916. Annual out-of-state tuition $29,944. Room and board $9,060. Average book expense $1,200. **Required Forms and Deadlines:** FAFSA. **Notification of Awards:** Applicants will be notified of awards on a rolling basis beginning 3/15. **Types of Aid:** *Need-based scholarships/grants:* Federal Pell, FSEOG, State scholarships/grants, Private scholarships, College/university scholarship or grant aid from institutional funds. *Loans:* Direct Subsidized Stafford Loans, Direct Unsubsidized Stafford Loans, Direct PLUS loans. *Student Employment:* Federal Work-Study Program available. Institutional employment available. **Financial Aid Statistics:** 91% needy freshmen, 92% needy undergrads receive need-based scholarship or grant aid. 16% freshmen, 12% undergrads receive non-need-based scholarship or grant aid. 79% freshmen, 84% undergrads receive need-based self-help aid. 0% freshmen, 0% undergrads receive athletic scholarships. 100% freshmen, 98% undergrads receive any aid. 48% undergrads borrow to pay for school. Average cumulative indebtedness $14,929. **Criteria for awarding aid:** *Need-based:* Academics. *Non-need-based:* Academics, State/district residency.

NEW ENGLAND COLLEGE

102 Bridge Street, Henniker, NH 3242
Phone: 603-428-2223 • **Financial Aid Phone:** 603-428-2226
E-mail: admission@nec.edu • **CEEB Code:** 3657
Fax: 603-428-3155 • **Website:** www.nec.edu • **ACT Code:** 2513

This private school was founded in 1946. It has a 225-acre campus.

RATINGS

Admissions Selectivity Rating: 71   **Fire Safety Rating:** 98   **Green Rating:** 74

STUDENTS AND FACULTY

Enrollment: 1,752. **Student Body:** 59% female, 41% male, 82% out-of-state, 4% international. Asian 1%, African American 24%, Caucasian 53%, Hispanic 8%, Native American 1%, Pacific Islander <1%, Two or more races 2%, Race unknown 7%.
Retention and Graduation: 60% freshmen return for sophomore year. 29% freshmen graduate within 4 years. 35% freshmen graduate within 6 years. 22% grads go on to further study within 1 year. 10% grads pursue arts and sciences degrees. 6% grads pursue business degrees. **Faculty:** Student/faculty ratio 16:1. 43 full-time faculty, 79% hold PhDs, 5% are are members of minority groups, 40% are women. 0% of classes are taught by teaching assistants.

ACADEMICS

Degrees: associate, bachelor's, doctoral, master's. **Classes:** Most classes have 10-19 students. Most lab/discussion sessions have 10-19 students. **Most popular majors:** Elementary Education and Teaching; Sport and Fitness Administration/Management; Business/Commerce. **Special Study Options:** Accelerated program, cross-registration, distance learning, double major, dual enrollment, English as a Second Language (ESL), exchange student program (domestic), external degree program, honors program, independent study, internships, liberal arts/career combination, student-designed major, study abroad, teacher certification program. **Honors Programs:** Honors Program for community college honors transfers Combined degree programs: BA/JD, NEC and New York Law 3 + 3 Program. **Disability Services:** Special programs offered to physically disabled students, including note-taking services, tape

recorders, tutors. **Career Services:** Alumni network, Career/job search classes, Career assessment, Internships, Regional alumni, On-campus interviews. Internships and practical experience throughout the curriculum.

FACILITIES

Housing: Coed dorms, fraternity/sorority housing, ThemeHousingResident freshmen and sophomores are required to live in College housing. Quiet study options, special interest housing is available. 75% of campus accessible to physically disabled. **Special Academic Facilities/Equipment:** New England Art Gallery, Graphic Design and Imaging Lab Center for Educational Innovation (High Tech Building) **Computers:** 100% of classrooms, 100% of dorms, 100% of libraries, 100% of dining areas, 100% of student union, 75% of common outdoor areas have wireless network access. Students can register for classes online. Administrative functions (other than registration) can be performed online.

CAMPUS LIFE

Environment: Rural. **Activities:** Choral groups, dance, drama/theater, literary magazine, radio station, student government, student newspaper, yearbook, Student Organization. 26 registered organizations, 2 honor societies, 1 religious organization. 2 fraternities, 2 sororities. **Athletics (Intercollegiate):** *Men:* baseball, basketball, cross-country, ice hockey, lacrosse, soccer. *Women:* basketball, cheerleading, cross-country, field hockey, ice hockey, lacrosse, soccer, softball. **On-Campus Highlights:** Simon Center (Student Center), Center of Education Innovation, Fitness Center, Gilmore Dining Hall, Coffee House. **Environmental Initiatives:** Addition of sustainability to the mission statement. A complete overhaul of lighting at the College for energy efficiency. Completion of a campus wide facilities plan.

ADMISSIONS

Freshman Academic Profile: Average high school GPA 2.6. 1% in top 10% of high school class, 11% in top 25% of high school class, 41% in top 50% of high school class. 90% from public high schools. **Reported SAT (pre-2016 redesign) scores:** SAT Math middle 50% range 400-520. SAT Critical Reading middle 50% range 390-540. SAT Writing middle 50% range 390-400. **Concordant SAT scores:** SAT EBRW middle 50% 440–530. SAT Math middle 50% range 440–550. ACT middle 50% range 17-24. Minimum internet-based TOEFL 13. Minimum paper TOEFL 550. **Basis for Candidate Selection:** *Very important factors considered include:* rigor of secondary school record, application essay, recommendation(s), interview, extracurricular activities, talent/ability, level of applicant's interest. *Important factors considered include:* character/personal qualities, volunteer work. *Other factors considered include:* class rank, academic GPA, standardized test scores, first generation, alumni/ae relation, work experience. **Freshman Admission Requirements:** High school diploma is required and GED is accepted. *Academic units required:* 4 English, 2 math, 2 science, 1 science lab, 2 social studies. *Academic units recommended:* 4 English, 3 math, 3 science, 2 science labs, 2 foreign language, 3 social studies. **Freshman Admission Statistics:** 4,204 applied, 99.02% admitted, 7% enrolled. **Transfer Admission Requirements:** High school transcript, college transcript(s), essay or personal statement, statement of good standing from prior institution(s). Lowest grade transferable C-. **General Admission Information:** Application fee $30. Priority deadline 3/15. Regular application deadline 9/1. Nonfall registration accepted. Admission may be deferred for a maximum of 1 year.

COSTS AND FINANCIAL AID

Annual tuition $35,860. Room and board $13,536. Required fees $992. Average book expense $1,000. **Required Forms and Deadlines:** FAFSA. **Notification of Awards:** Applicants will be notified of awards on a rolling basis beginning 2/1. **Types of Aid:** *Need-based scholarships/grants:* Federal Pell, FSEOG, State scholarships/grants, Private scholarships, College/university scholarship or grant aid from institutional funds. *Loans:* Direct Subsidized Stafford Loans, Direct Unsubsidized Stafford Loans, Direct PLUS loans, Federal Perkins Loans, State Loans. *Student Employment:* Federal Work-Study Program available. Institutional employment available. **Financial Aid Statistics:** 98% needy freshmen, 84% needy undergrads receive need-based scholarship or grant aid. 5% freshmen, 4% undergrads receive non-need-based scholarship or grant aid. 92% freshmen, 92% undergrads receive need-based self-help aid. 0% freshmen, 0% undergrads receive athletic scholarships. 93% freshmen, 86% undergrads receive any aid. 88% undergrads borrow to pay for school. Average cumulative indebtedness $35,230. **Criteria for awarding aid:** *Need-based:* Academics, Alumni affiliation, Art, Job skills, Leadership, Music/drama. *Non-need-based:* Academics, Alumni affiliation, Art, Job skills, Leadership, Music/drama.

NEW ENGLAND INSTITUTE OF TECHNOLOGY

One New England Tech Blvd., East Greenwich, RI 02818
Phone: 401-467-7744
E-mail: NEITAdmissions@neit.edu
Fax: 401-886-0868 • **Website:** www.neit.edu

RATINGS
Admissions Selectivity Rating: 60* **Fire Safety Rating:** 60* **Green Rating:** 75

STUDENTS AND FACULTY
Enrollment: 868. **Student Body:** 47% female, 53% male, 10% international. Asian 1%, African American 4%, Caucasian 81%, Hispanic 2%, Native American <1%, Pacific Islander 0%, Two or more races 2%, Race unknown 1%. **Retention and Graduation:** 86% freshmen return for sophomore year. 0.450805009 freshmen graduate within 4 years. 55 **Faculty:** Student/faculty ratio 13 66 full-time faculty, 67% hold PhDs, 0% are are members of minority groups, 0% are women.

ACADEMICS
Career Services: Alumni services, Career/job search classes, Career assessment, Internships. The Career Services Office maintains close relationships with area employers for internships as well as employment opportunities.

FACILITIES
Housing: 100% of campus accessible to physically diasbled.

ADMISSIONS
Freshman Academic Profile: Average high school GPA 3.4. **Reported SAT (pre-2016 redesign) scores:** SAT Math middle 50% range 440-550. SAT Critical Reading middle 50% range 450-550. SAT Writing middle 50% range 420-520. **Freshman Admission Statistics:** 2,708 applied, 0.71971935 admitted, 10% enrolled.

COSTS AND FINANCIAL AID
Average book expense $2,000. **Financial Aid Statistics:** 45% needy undergrads receive need-based scholarship or grant aid. 0% freshmen, 98% undergrads receive non-need-based scholarship or grant aid. 57% freshmen, 57% undergrads receive need-based self-help aid. 18% freshmen, 12% undergrads receive athletic scholarships. 62% undergrads borrow to pay for school. Average cumulative indebtedness $35,102.

NEW HOPE CHRISTIAN COLLEGE

2155 Bailey Hill Road, Eugene, OR 97405-1194
Phone: 800-322-2638 • **Financial Aid Phone:** 800-322-2638
E-mail: admissions@newhope.edu • **CEEB Code:** 4274
Fax: 541-343-5801 • **Website:** http://www.newhope.edu • **ACT Code:** 3468

This private school was founded in 1925. It has a 33-acre campus.

RATINGS
Admissions Selectivity Rating: 62 **Fire Safety Rating:** 83 **Green Rating:** 60*

STUDENTS AND FACULTY
Enrollment: 162. **Student Body:** 49% female, 51% male, 54% out-of-state, 2% international (5 countries represented). Asian 4%, African American 4%, Caucasian 61%, Hispanic 9%, Native American 1%, Pacific Islander 4%, Two or more races 9%, Race unknown 6%. **Retention and Graduation:** 100% freshmen return for sophomore year. 31% freshmen graduate within 4 years. 41% freshmen graduate within 6 years. 35% grads go on to further study within 1 year. **Faculty:** Student/faculty ratio 10:1. 10 full-time faculty, 30% hold PhDs, 20% are are members of minority groups, 40% are women. 0% of classes are taught by teaching assistants.

ACADEMICS
Degrees: associate, bachelor's, certificate, master's. **Classes:** Most classes have 10-19 students. Most lab/discussion sessions have 10-19 students. **Most popular majors:** Bible/Biblical Studies; Pastoral Studies/Counseling; Youth Ministry. **Special Study Options:** cooperative education program, distance learning, double major, dual enrollment, independent study, internships, liberal arts/career combination, One year Bible Certificate obtainable by external studies program. **Career Services:** On-campus interviews.

FACILITIES
Housing: men's dorms, women's dorms, apartments for married students, apartments for single students. 75% of campus accessible to physically diasbled. **Special Academic Facilities/Equipment:** Music lab, computer lab

CAMPUS LIFE
Environment: City. **Activities:** Choral groups, drama/theater, music ensembles, student government, yearbook. **Athletics (Intercollegiate):** *Men:* basketball, soccer. *Women:* soccer, volleyball. **On-Campus Highlights:** Student Center, Cafeteria, Dorm Lounges, Computer Lab, Workout Room.

ADMISSIONS
Freshman Academic Profile: 90% from public high schools. Minimum paper TOEFL 500. **Basis for Candidate Selection:** *Very important factors considered include:* application essay, recommendation(s), character/personal qualities, religious affiliation/commitment. *Important factors considered include:* rigor of secondary school record, academic GPA. *Other factors considered include:* class rank, standardized test scores, extracurricular activities, talent/ability, volunteer work, work experience, level of applicant's interest. **Freshman Admission Requirements:** High school diploma is required and GED is accepted. **Freshman Admission Statistics:** 92 applied, 100.00% admitted. **Transfer Admission Requirements:** college transcript(s), essay or personal statement, Minimum college GPA of 2.0 required. Lowest grade transferable C. **General Admission Information:** Application fee $50. Regular application deadline 9/1. Nonfall registration accepted. Admission may be deferred for a maximum of 24 months.

COSTS AND FINANCIAL AID
Annual tuition $16,500. Room and board $6,100. Required fees $801. Average book expense $800. **Required Forms and Deadlines:** FAFSA. **Notification of Awards:** Applicants will be notified of awards on a rolling basis beginning 7/15. **Types of Aid:** *Need-based scholarships/grants:* Federal Pell, FSEOG, College/university scholarship or grant aid from institutional funds. *Loans:* Direct Subsidized Stafford Loans, Direct Unsubsidized Stafford Loans, Direct PLUS loans. *Student Employment:* Federal Work-Study Program available. Institutional employment available. **Financial Aid Statistics:** 100% needy freshmen, 100% needy undergrads receive need-based scholarship or grant aid. 16% freshmen, 13% undergrads receive non-need-based scholarship or grant aid. 100% freshmen, 100% undergrads receive need-based self-help aid. 36% freshmen, 49% undergrads receive athletic scholarships. **Criteria for awarding aid:** *Need-based:* Academics, Leadership, Music/drama, Religious affiliation. *Non-need-based:* Academics, Alumni affiliation, Athletics, Leadership, Music/drama.

NEW JERSEY CITY UNIVERSITY

2039 Kennedy Boulevard, Jersey City, NJ 7305
Phone: 888-441-6528 • **Financial Aid Phone:** 201-200-3378
E-mail: admissions@njcu.edu • **CEEB Code:** 2316
Fax: 201-200-2044 • **Website:** www.njcu.edu

This public school was founded in 1927. It has a 17-acre campus.

RATINGS
Admissions Selectivity Rating: 72 **Fire Safety Rating:** 85 **Green Rating:** 65

STUDENTS AND FACULTY
Enrollment: 6,317. **Student Body:** 60% female, 40% male, 1% out-of-state, 3% international (18 countries represented). Asian 7%, African American 21%, Caucasian 23%, Hispanic 35%, Native American <1%, Pacific Islander 1%, Two or more races 2%, Race unknown 2%. **Retention and Graduation:** 74% freshmen return for sophomore year. 5% freshmen graduate within 4 years. 29% freshmen graduate within 6 years. **Faculty:** Student/faculty ratio 14:1. 251 full-time faculty, 0% hold PhDs, 38% are are members of minority groups, 51% are women. 0% of classes are taught by teaching assistants.

ACADEMICS
Degrees: bachelor's, certificate, doctoral/research, master's, postbachelor's certificate, post-master's certificate. **Classes:** Most classes have 20-29 students. **Most popular majors:** Psychology; Corrections and Criminal Justice; Registered Nursing/Registered Nurse. **Special Study Options:** Accelerated program, cooperative education program, cross-registration, distance learning, double major, dual enrollment, English as a Second Language (ESL), honors program, independent study, internships, study abroad, teacher certification program, weekend college. **Honors Programs:** Honors program in the William Maxwell College of Arts and Sciences Combined degree programs: BA/MA. **Disability Services:** Special programs offered to physically disabled students, including reader services, tape recorders, tutors. **Career Services:** Career assessment, Internships. Cooperative education

FACILITIES
Housing: Coed dorms. 90% of campus accessible to physically diasbled. **Special Academic Facilities/Equipment:** Art galleries, lab school for special education, criminal justice institute, electron microscope, Raimondo Center

for Urban Research and Public Policy. **Computers:** Students can register for classes online. Administrative functions (other than registration) can be performed online.

CAMPUS LIFE
Environment: City. **Activities:** Choral groups, concert band, dance, drama/theater, jazz band, literary magazine, music ensembles, musical theater, opera, radio station, student government, student newspaper, symphony orchestra, yearbook, Campus Ministries, Student Organization. 50 registered organizations, 2 religious organizations. 7 fraternities, 5 sororities. **Athletics (Intercollegiate):** *Men:* baseball, basketball, cross-country, soccer, track/field (outdoor), track/field (indoor), volleyball. *Women:* basketball, bowling, cross-country, soccer, softball, track/field (outdoor), track/field (indoor), volleyball. **On-Campus Highlights:** Student Union, Physical fitness center, Library, Cafeteria.

ADMISSIONS
Freshman Academic Profile: Average high school GPA 2.9. 9% in top 10% of high school class, 29% in top 25% of high school class, 61% in top 50% of high school class. **Reported SAT (pre-2016 redesign) scores:** SAT Math middle 50% range 390-500. SAT Critical Reading middle 50% range 370-470. **Concordant SAT scores:** SAT Math middle 50% range 430–530. **Basis for Candidate Selection:** *Very important factors considered include:* rigor of secondary school record, academic GPA, standardized test scores. *Important factors considered include:* class rank. *Other factors considered include:* application essay, recommendation(s), interview, extracurricular activities, talent/ability, character/personal qualities, volunteer work, level of applicant's interest. **Freshman Admission Requirements:** High school diploma is required and GED is accepted. *Academic units required:* 4 English, 4 math, 4 science, 2 science labs, 4 social studies. *Academic units recommended:* 4 English, 4 math, 4 science, 3 science labs, 2 foreign language, 4 social studies. **Freshman Admission Statistics:** 2,789 applied, 86.73% admitted, 34% enrolled. **Transfer Admission Requirements:** college transcript(s), Minimum college GPA of 2.0 required. Lowest grade transferable C. **General Admission Information:** Application fee $50, Nonfall registration accepted. Admission may be deferred.

COSTS AND FINANCIAL AID
Annual in-state tuition $7,936. Annual out-of-state tuition $16,764. Required fees $3,243. Average book expense $1,000. **Required Forms and Deadlines:** FAFSA. **Notification of Awards:** Applicants will be notified of awards on or about 5/15. **Types of Aid:** *Need-based scholarships/grants:* Federal Pell, FSEOG, State scholarships/grants, College/university scholarship or grant aid from institutional funds. *Loans:* Direct Subsidized Stafford Loans, Direct Unsubsidized Stafford Loans, Direct PLUS loans, Federal Perkins Loans, State Loans. *Student Employment:* Federal Work-Study Program available. Institutional employment available. **Financial Aid Statistics:** 84% needy freshmen, 80% needy undergrads receive need-based scholarship or grant aid. 17% freshmen, 13% undergrads receive non-need-based scholarship or grant aid. 46% freshmen, 69% undergrads receive need-based self-help aid. 0% freshmen, 0% undergrads receive athletic scholarships. **Criteria for awarding aid:** *Need-based:* Academics. *Non-need-based:* Academics.

NEW JERSEY INSTITUTE OF TECHNOLOGY

Office of University Admissions, Newark, NJ 7102
Phone: 973-596-3300 • **Financial Aid Phone:** 973-596-3479
E-mail: admissions@njit.edu • **CEEB Code:** 2580
Fax: 973-596-3461 • **Website:** www.njit.edu • **ACT Code:** 2513

This public school was founded in 1881. It has a 48-acre campus.

RATINGS
Admissions Selectivity Rating: 88   **Fire Safety Rating:** 99   **Green Rating:** 60*

STUDENTS AND FACULTY
Enrollment: 7,336. **Student Body:** 22% female, 78% male, 3% out-of-state, 5% international (83 countries represented). Asian 22%, African American 8%, Caucasian 34%, Hispanic 21%, Native American <1%, Pacific Islander <1%, Two or more races 3%, Race unknown 6%.
Retention and Graduation: 88% freshmen return for sophomore year. 25% freshmen graduate within 4 years. 61% freshmen graduate within 6 years. 17% grads go on to further study within 1 year. 1% grads pursue arts and sciences degrees. 1% grads pursue business degrees. **Faculty:** Student/faculty ratio 17:1. 436 full-time faculty, 98% hold PhDs, 32% are are members of minority groups, 20% are women. 0% of classes are taught by teaching assistants.

ACADEMICS
Degrees: bachelor's, doctoral, master's, postbachelor's certificate. **Classes:** Most classes have 20-29 students. **Most popular majors:** Mechanical Engineering; Civil Engineering; Architecture. **Special Study Options:** Accelerated program, cooperative education program, cross-registration, distance learning, double major, English as a Second Language (ESL), honors program, independent study, internships, study abroad. **Honors Programs:** The Albert Dorman Honors College at the New Jersey Institute of Technology (NJIT) enrolls over 500 exceptional students who excel in the fields of engineering, architecture, computing sciences, management, and the sciences. Combined degree programs: BA/MD, BA/MA, BS/MD,BS/DMD, BS/DDS, BS/DPT, BS/OD, BS/JD, BArch/MS Management. **Disability Services:** Special programs offered to physically disabled students, including note-taking services, reader services, tape recorders, tutors. **Career Services:** Alumni network, Alumni services, Career/job search classes, Career assessment, Internships, Regional alumni. Cooperative Education at NJIT is an academically integrated program that gives students the opportunity to gain paid professional work experience before graduation. Although not mandatory, over 400 students choose to participate each year. Most co-op students work fulltime for one or two semesters. The average wage for co-op students exceeds $15.00 per hour. Nearly 2600 different companies have hired NJIT students over the past decade. Employers range from large multinationals to small start-up companies. Students have completed their co-op assignments in New Jersey, ten other states, and four foreign countries.

FACILITIES
Housing: Coed dorms. 100% of campus accessible to physically diasbled. **Special Academic Facilities/Equipment:** New Jersey Literary Hall of Fame and more than 50 research centers and sponsored research laboratories, including computer chip manufacturing center, manufacturing systems center, and many others **Computers:** 100% of classrooms, 100% of dorms, 100% of libraries, 100% of dining areas, 100% of student union, 100% of common outdoor areas have wireless network access. Students can register for classes online. Administrative functions (other than registration) can be performed online. Undergraduates are required to own a computer.

CAMPUS LIFE
Environment: Metropolis. **Activities:** concert band, dance, drama/theater, literary magazine, marching band, musical theater, radio station, student government, student newspaper, yearbook, Student Organization. 70 registered organizations, 10 honor societies, 5 religious organizations. 15 fraternities, 7 sororities. **Athletics (Intercollegiate):** *Men:* baseball, basketball, cheerleading, cross-country, fencing, soccer, swimming, tennis, track/field (outdoor), track/field (indoor), volleyball. *Women:* basketball, cheerleading, cross-country, fencing, soccer, swimming, tennis, track/field (outdoor), track/field (indoor), volleyball. **On-Campus Highlights:** Campus Center, Van Houten Library, Zoom Fleisher Athletic Center, East Building—Admissions, Student Mall. **Environmental Initiatives:** Recycling.

ADMISSIONS
Freshman Academic Profile: Average high school GPA 3.6. 31% in top 10% of high school class, 59% in top 25% of high school class, 87% in top 50% of high school class. 85% from public high schools. **Reported SAT (pre-2016 redesign) scores:** SAT Math middle 50% range 590-680. SAT Critical Reading middle 50% range 520-630. SAT Writing middle 50% range 500-620. **Concordant SAT scores:** SAT EBRW middle 50% 570–680. SAT Math middle 50% range 610–710. ACT middle 50% range 23-29. Minimum internet-based TOEFL 79. Minimum paper TOEFL 550. **Basis for Candidate Selection:** *Very important factors considered include:* rigor of secondary school record, class rank, standardized test scores. *Important factors considered include:* academic GPA. *Other factors considered include:* application essay, recommendation(s), interview, extracurricular activities, talent/ability, character/personal qualities, alumni/ae relation, geographical residence, state residency, religious affiliation/commitment, racial/ethnic status, volunteer work, work experience, level of applicant's interest. **Freshman Admission Requirements:** High school diploma is required and GED is accepted. *Academic units required:* 4 English, 4 math, 2 science, 2 science labs. *Academic units recommended:* 2 foreign language, 1 social studies, 1 history, 2 academic electives. **Freshman Admission Statistics:** 7,222 applied, 59.30% admitted, 26% enrolled. **Transfer Admission Requirements:** college transcript(s), Minimum college GPA of 2.0 required. Lowest grade transferable C. **General Admission Information:** Application fee $75. Regular application deadline 3/1. Nonfall registration accepted. Admission may be deferred for a maximum of 1 year.

COSTS AND FINANCIAL AID
Annual in-state tuition $13,602. Annual out-of-state tuition $28,206. Room and board $13,700. Required fees $2,828. Average book expense $2,600. **Required**

Forms and Deadlines: FAFSA. **Notification of Awards:** Applicants will be notified of awards on a rolling basis beginning 12/15. **Types of Aid:** *Need-based scholarships/grants:* Federal Pell, FSEOG, State scholarships/grants, Private scholarships, College/university scholarship or grant aid from institutional funds, United Negro College Fund. *Loans:* Direct Subsidized Stafford Loans, Direct Unsubsidized Stafford Loans, Direct PLUS loans, Federal Perkins Loans, State Loans. *Student Employment:* Federal Work-Study Program available. Institutional employment available. **Financial Aid Statistics:** 88% needy freshmen, 96% needy undergrads receive need-based scholarship or grant aid. 61% freshmen, 35% undergrads receive non-need-based scholarship or grant aid. 63% freshmen, 76% undergrads receive need-based self-help aid. 2% freshmen, 2% undergrads receive athletic scholarships. 87% freshmen, 72% undergrads receive any aid. 64% undergrads borrow to pay for school. Average cumulative indebtedness $40,967. **Criteria for awarding aid:** *Need-based:* Academics, Alumni affiliation, Art, Athletics, Job skills, Leadership, Minority status, Music/drama, Religious affiliation. *Non-need-based:* Academics, Alumni affiliation, Art, Athletics, Job skills, Leadership, Minority status, Music/drama, Religious affiliation, State/district residency.

NEW MEXICO INSTITUTE OF MINING AND TECHNOLOGY

Campus Station, Socorro, NM 87801
Phone: 575-835-5424 • **Financial Aid Phone:** 575-835-5333
E-mail: admission@nmt.edu • **CEEB Code:** 4533
Fax: 575-835-5989 • **Website:** www.nmt.edu • **ACT Code:** 2642

This public school was founded in 1889. It has a 320-acre campus.

RATINGS
Admissions Selectivity Rating: 92   **Fire Safety Rating:** 60*   **Green Rating:** 60*

STUDENTS AND FACULTY
Enrollment: 1,460. **Student Body:** 27% female, 73% male, 13% out-of-state, 3% international. Asian 3%, African American 2%, Caucasian 51%, Hispanic 31%, Native American 3%, Pacific Islander <1%, Two or more races 5%, Race unknown 2%.
Retention and Graduation: 77% freshmen return for sophomore year. 19% freshmen graduate within 4 years. 49% freshmen graduate within 6 years.
Faculty: Student/faculty ratio 11:1. 137 full-time faculty, 0% hold PhDs, 29% are are members of minority groups, 22% are women.

ACADEMICS
Degrees: bachelor's, doctoral/research, master's, terminal. **Classes:** Most classes have fewer than 10 students. Most lab/discussion sessions have 10-19 students. **Most popular majors:** Computer and Information Sciences; Electrical and Electronics Engineering; Mechanical Engineering. **Special Study Options:** Accelerated program, cooperative education program, distance learning, double major, dual enrollment, exchange student program (domestic), independent study, internships, student-designed major, teacher certification program. Combined degree programs: BS/MS Geology, Hydrology. **Disability Services:** Special programs offered to physically disabled students, including note-taking services, reader services, tape recorders, tutors. **Career Services:** Career/job search classes, Career assessment, Internships.

FACILITIES
Housing: Coed dorms, men's dorms, women's dorms, apartments for married students, apartments for single students. **Special Academic Facilities/Equipment:** Mineral museum, observatory, radio telescope, seismic observatory and library, explosives labs **Computers:** Students can register for classes online. Administrative functions (other than registration) can be performed online.

CAMPUS LIFE
Environment: Village. **Activities:** Choral groups, concert band, dance, drama/theater, jazz band, music ensembles, musical theater, radio station, student government, student newspaper. 60 registered organizations, 7 honor societies, 3 religious organizations. **On-Campus Highlights:** Fidel Student Center, Skeen Library, Workman Center.

ADMISSIONS
Freshman Academic Profile: Average high school GPA 3.7. 36% in top 10% of high school class, 64% in top 25% of high school class, 86% in top 50% of high school class. 80% from public high schools. **Reported SAT (pre-2016 redesign) scores:** SAT Math middle 50% range 540-680. SAT Critical Reading middle 50% range 570-670. **Concordant SAT scores:** SAT Math middle 50% range 570–710. ACT middle 50% range 23-29. Minimum paper TOEFL 540. **Basis for Candidate Selection:** *Very important factors considered include:*

rigor of secondary school record, academic GPA, standardized test scores. *Other factors considered include:* class rank, extracurricular activities, talent/ability. **Freshman Admission Requirements:** High school diploma is required and GED is accepted. *Academic units required:* 4 English, 3 math, 2 science, 2 science labs, 2 social studies, 1 history, 3 academic electives. *Academic units recommended:* 4 English, 4 math, 4 science, 3 science labs, 2 foreign language, 3 social studies, 1 history. **Freshman Admission Statistics:** 1,663 applied, 23.45% admitted, 77% enrolled. **Transfer Admission Requirements:** High school transcript, college transcript(s), statement of good standing from prior institution(s). Minimum college GPA of 2.0 required. Lowest grade transferable D. **General Admission Information:** Application fee $15. Priority deadline 3/1. Regular application deadline 8/1. Nonfall registration accepted. Admission may be deferred for a maximum of 1 year.

COSTS AND FINANCIAL AID
Annual in-state tuition $5,841. Annual out-of-state tuition $18,991. Room and board $7,942. Required fees $1,050. Average book expense $1,078. **Required Forms and Deadlines:** FAFSA. **Notification of Awards:** Applicants will be notified of awards on a rolling basis beginning 5/1. **Types of Aid:** *Need-based scholarships/grants:* Federal Pell, FSEOG, State scholarships/grants, Private scholarships, College/university scholarship or grant aid from institutional funds. *Loans:* Direct Subsidized Stafford Loans, Direct Unsubsidized Stafford Loans, Direct PLUS loans, Federal Perkins Loans. *Student Employment:* Federal Work-Study Program available. Institutional employment available. **Financial Aid Statistics:** 88% needy freshmen, 68% needy undergrads receive need-based scholarship or grant aid. 96% freshmen, 72% undergrads receive non-need-based scholarship or grant aid. 57% freshmen, 64% undergrads receive need-based self-help aid. 0% freshmen, 0% undergrads receive athletic scholarships. 45% undergrads borrow to pay for school. Average cumulative indebtedness $22,355. **Criteria for awarding aid:** *Need-based:* Minority status. *Non-need-based:* Academics, Alumni affiliation, Minority status, State/district residency.

NEW MEXICO STATE UNIVERSITY

Box 30001, Las Cruces, NM 88003-8001
Phone: 575-646-3121
E-mail: admissions@nmsu.edu • **CEEB Code:** 4531
Fax: 575-646-6330 • **Website:** www.nmsu.edu • **ACT Code:** 2638

This public school was founded in 1888. It has a 900-acre campus.

RATINGS
Admissions Selectivity Rating: 83   **Fire Safety Rating:** 60*   **Green Rating:** 60*

STUDENTS AND FACULTY
Enrollment: 11,421. **Student Body:** 53% female, 47% male, 25% out-of-state, 5% international (72 countries represented). Asian 1%, African American 3%, Caucasian 28%, Hispanic 56%, Native American 2%, Pacific Islander <1%, Two or more races 2%, Race unknown 2%.
Retention and Graduation: 72% freshmen return for sophomore year. 17% freshmen graduate within 4 years. 45% freshmen graduate within 6 years.
Faculty: Student/faculty ratio 16:1. 650 full-time faculty, 87% hold PhDs, 32% are are members of minority groups, 44% are women.

ACADEMICS
Degrees: associate, bachelor's, doctoral/professional, doctoral/research, doctoral, master's, postbachelor's certificate, post-master's certificate. **Classes:** Most classes have 20-29 students. Most lab/discussion sessions have 20-29 students. **Most popular majors:** Criminal Justice/Safety Studies; Mechanical Engineering; Kinesiology and Exercise Science. **Special Study Options:** Accelerated program, cooperative education program, cross-registration, distance learning, double major, dual enrollment, English as a Second Language (ESL), exchange student program (domestic), external degree program, honors program, independent study, internships, student-designed major, study abroad, teacher certification program, weekend college. Combined degree programs: BA/MA, BS/MS in Chemical Engineering, Civil Engineering, Computer Science, Electrical Engineering, Industrial Engineering, and Mechanical Engineering, BS/MBA when BS in Engineering. **Disability Services:** Special programs offered to physically disabled students, including note-taking services, reader services, tape recorders, tutors. **Career Services:** Alumni services, Career/job search classes, Career assessment, Internships.

FACILITIES
Housing: Coed dorms, special housing for disabled students, men's dorms, women's dorms, fraternity/sorority housing, apartments for married students, apartments for single students. 95% of campus accessible to physically diasbled. **Special Academic Facilities/Equipment:** University and art department

museums, theatre, horse farm, sports medicine training clinic, observatory, electron microscope, CRAY supercomputer. **Computers:** Students can register for classes online. Administrative functions (other than registration) can be performed online.

CAMPUS LIFE

Environment: City. **Activities:** Choral groups, concert band, dance, drama/theater, jazz band, literary magazine, marching band, music ensembles, musical theater, opera, pep band, radio station, student government, student newspaper, symphony orchestra, television station, Campus Ministries. 263 registered organizations, 24 honor societies, 23 religious organizations. 14 fraternities, 5 sororities. **Athletics (Intercollegiate):** *Men:* baseball, basketball, cross-country, football, golf, tennis. *Women:* basketball, cross-country, golf, softball, swimming, tennis, track/field (outdoor), volleyball.

ADMISSIONS

Freshman Academic Profile: Average high school GPA 3.5. 22% in top 10% of high school class, 51% in top 25% of high school class, 83% in top 50% of high school class. **Reported SAT (pre-2016 redesign) scores:** SAT Math middle 50% range 420-540. SAT Critical Reading middle 50% range 400-530. SAT Writing middle 50% range 390-510. **Concordant SAT scores:** SAT EBRW middle 50% 440–580. SAT Math middle 50% range 460–570. ACT middle 50% range 18-24. Minimum paper TOEFL 500. **Basis for Candidate Selection:** *Important factors considered include:* academic GPA, standardized test scores. *Other factors considered include:* rigor of secondary school record. **Freshman Admission Requirements:** High school diploma is required and GED is accepted. *Academic units required:* 4 English, 4 math, 2 science, 2 science labs, 1 foreign language. **Freshman Admission Statistics:** 7,618 applied, 59.61% admitted, 41% enrolled. **Transfer Admission Requirements:** college transcript(s), Minimum college GPA of 2.0 required. Lowest grade transferable C. **General Admission Information:** Application fee $20. Nonfall registration accepted. Admission may be deferred for a maximum of 1 year.

COSTS AND FINANCIAL AID

Required Forms and Deadlines: FAFSA. **Notification of Awards:** Applicants will be notified of awards on a rolling basis beginning 4/1. **Types of Aid:** *Need-based scholarships/grants:* Federal Pell, FSEOG, State scholarships/grants, Private scholarships, College/university scholarship or grant aid from institutional funds. *Loans:* Direct Subsidized Stafford Loans, Direct Unsubsidized Stafford Loans, Direct PLUS loans, Federal Perkins Loans, State Loans, College/university loans from institutional funds. *Student Employment:* Federal Work-Study Program available. Institutional employment available. **Financial Aid Statistics:** 91% needy freshmen, 95% needy undergrads receive need-based scholarship or grant aid. 9% freshmen, 6% undergrads receive non-need-based scholarship or grant aid. 45% freshmen, 62% undergrads receive need-based self-help aid. 3% freshmen, 2% undergrads receive athletic scholarships. 56% undergrads borrow to pay for school. Average cumulative indebtedness $21,402. **Criteria for awarding aid:** *Need-based:* Academics, Athletics, Minority status, Music/drama. *Non-need-based:* Academics, Alumni affiliation, Athletics, Leadership, Minority status, Music/drama, State/district residency.

NEW YORK SCHOOL OF INTERIOR DESIGN

170 East 70th Street, New York, NY 10021
Phone: 212-472-1500 • **Financial Aid Phone:** 212-472-1500 x212
E-mail: admissions@nysid.edu • **CEEB Code:** 333
Fax: 212-472-1867 • **ACT Code:** 2829

This private school was founded in 1916.

RATINGS

Admissions Selectivity Rating: 71   **Fire Safety Rating:** 60*   **Green Rating:** 60*

STUDENTS AND FACULTY

Enrollment: 353. **Student Body:** 87% female, 13% male, 15% international. Asian 6%, African American 3%, Caucasian 48%, Hispanic 9%, Native American 0%, Pacific Islander 0%, Two or more races 2%, Race unknown 16%. **Retention and Graduation:** 0% grads go on to further study within 1 year. **Faculty:** 8 full-time faculty, 88% hold PhDs, 0% are are members of minority groups, 50% are women. 0% of classes are taught by teaching assistants.

ACADEMICS

Degrees: associate, bachelor's, certificate, master's, transfer. **Classes:** Most classes have 10-19 students. **Most popular majors:** Interior Design. **Special Study Options:** independent study, internships, study abroad. **Disability Services:** Special programs offered to physically disabled students, including tutors. **Career Services:** Alumni network, Alumni services, Internships, On-campus interviews.

FACILITIES

Housing: 100% of campus accessible to physically diasbled. **Special Academic Facilities/Equipment:** Three galleries, lighting laboratory, student atelier.

CAMPUS LIFE

Environment: Metropolis. **Activities:** 1 registered organization.

ADMISSIONS

Minimum internet-based TOEFL 79. Minimum paper TOEFL 550. **Basis for Candidate Selection:** *Very important factors considered include:* rigor of secondary school record, application essay, talent/ability. *Important factors considered include:* academic GPA, recommendation(s), level of applicant's interest. *Other factors considered include:* class rank, standardized test scores, interview, extracurricular activities, character/personal qualities, alumni/ae relation, work experience. **Freshman Admission Requirements:** High school diploma is required and GED is accepted. *Academic units recommended:* 4 English, 2 math, 2 science, 2 foreign language, 2 social studies, 2 history. **Freshman Admission Statistics:** 178 applied, 45.51% admitted, 33% enrolled. **Transfer Admission Requirements:** High school transcript, college transcript(s), essay or personal statement, Minimum college GPA of 3.0 required. Lowest grade transferable C. **General Admission Information:** Application fee $60. Priority deadline 2/1. Regular notification 4/1. Nonfall registration accepted. Admission may be deferred for a maximum of 1 year.

COSTS AND FINANCIAL AID

Annual tuition $30,195. Required fees $570. Average book expense $1,000. **Required Forms and Deadlines:** FAFSA, Institution's own financial aid form, State aid form. **Notification of Awards:** Applicants will be notified of awards on a rolling basis beginning 2/1. **Types of Aid:** *Need-based scholarships/grants:* Federal Pell, FSEOG, State scholarships/grants, College/university scholarship or grant aid from institutional funds. *Student Employment:* Federal Work-Study Program available. **Criteria for awarding aid:** *Need-based:* Academics, Art.

NEW YORK UNIVERSITY

383 Lafayette St, New York, NY 10012
Phone: 212-998-4500 • **Financial Aid Phone:** 212-998-4444
E-mail: admissions@nyu.edu • **CEEB Code:** 2562

Fax: 212-995-4902 • Website: www.nyu.edu • ACT Code: 2838 This private school was founded in 1831.

RATINGS

Admissions Selectivity Rating: 94   **Fire Safety Rating:** 98   **Green Rating:** 83

STUDENTS AND FACULTY

Enrollment: 25,716. **Student Body:** 57% female, 43% male, 62% out-of-state, 18% international (139 countries represented). Asian 20%, African American 6%, Caucasian 32%, Hispanic 13%, Native American <1%, Pacific Islander <1%, Two or more races 4%, Race unknown 7%. **Retention and Graduation:** 93% freshmen return for sophomore year. 82% freshmen graduate within 4 years. 85% freshmen graduate within 6 years. 14% grads go on to further study within 1 year. 1% grads pursue arts and sciences degrees. 2% grads pursue law degrees. 1% grads pursue business degrees. 3% grads pursue medical degrees. **Faculty:** Student/faculty ratio 10:1. 2,981 full-time faculty, 68% hold PhDs, 0% are are members of minority groups, 43% are women.

ACADEMICS

Degrees: associate, bachelor's, certificate, diploma, doctoral/professional, doctoral/research, doctoral, master's, postbachelor's certifiate, post-master's certificate, terminal, transfer. **Classes:** Most classes have 10-19 students. Most lab/discussion sessions have fewer than 10 students. **Most popular majors:** Liberal Arts and Sciences/Liberal Studies; Drama and Dramatics/Theatre Arts; Business/Commerce. **Special Study Options:** cross-registration, distance learning, double major, English as a Second Language (ESL), exchange student program (domestic), honors program, independent study, internships, liberal arts/career combination, student-designed major, study abroad, teacher certification program, Exchange program with several historically black colleges. Combined degree programs: BA/DDS. **Disability Services:** Special programs offered to physically disabled students, including note-taking services, reader services, tape recorders. **Career Services:** Alumni network, Alumni services, Career/job search classes, Career assessment, Internships, Regional alumni. Students have multiple opportunites to advance their entrepreneurial learning through course work, business planning competitions, workshops, mentoring and coaching.

FACILITIES

Housing: Coed dorms, special housing for disabled students, fraternity/sorority housing, apartments for single students, Wellness Housing, Theme Housing Choices: Substance Free Communities; FYRE: First Year Residential Experience; Sophomore Year Residential Experience; Explorations Learning Communities; Mixed Sex Housing. 90% of campus accessible to physically diasbled. **Special Academic Facilities/Equipment:** Bobst Library and study center; Grey Art Gallery and study center; Special academic facilities for arts, business, culture, education, relations, language, law, media, music, public service, research, and social policy, and Skirball Center for Performing Arts. **Computers:** 70% of classrooms, 100% of libraries, 100% of dining areas, 100% of student union, 50% of common outdoor areas have wireless network access. Students can register for classes online. Administrative functions (other than registration) can be performed online.

CAMPUS LIFE

Environment: Metropolis. **Activities:** Choral groups, concert band, dance, drama/theater, jazz band, literary magazine, music ensembles, musical theater, opera, pep band, radio station, student government, student newspaper, student-run film society, symphony orchestra, television station, yearbook, Campus Ministries, Student Organization, Model UN. 407 registered organizations, 3 honor societies, 31 religious organizations. 14 fraternities, 10 sororities. **Athletics (Intercollegiate):** *Men:* basketball, cross-country, diving, fencing, golf, soccer, swimming, tennis, track/field (outdoor), track/field (indoor), volleyball, wrestling. *Women:* basketball, cross-country, diving, fencing, golf, soccer, swimming, tennis, track/field (outdoor), track/field (indoor), volleyball. **On-Campus Highlights:** Kimmel Center for Student Life, Silver Center for Arts and Science, Coles Athletic Center, Palladium Athletic Facility, Skirball Center for the Performing Arts. **Environmental Initiatives:** Reduce Energy Intensity: NYU will reduce the amount of energy used in buildings through conservation, "green" construction and renovation, retrofits and upgrades, and operational innovations to run buildings more effectively. Initial efforts have already resulted in 20% emissions cuts.

ADMISSIONS

Freshman Academic Profile: Average high school GPA 3.3. 59% from public high schools. **Reported SAT (pre-2016 redesign) scores:** SAT Math middle 50% range 630-760. SAT Critical Reading middle 50% range 620-720. **Concordant SAT scores:** SAT Math middle 50% range 650–780. ACT middle 50% range 29-33. Minimum internet-based TOEFL 100. **Basis for Candidate Selection:** *Very important factors considered include:* rigor of secondary school record, class rank, academic GPA, standardized test scores, talent/ability. *Important factors considered include:* application essay, recommendation(s), extracurricular activities, character/personal qualities. *Other factors considered include:* interview, first generation, alumni/ae relation, geographical residence, racial/ethnic status, volunteer work, work experience, level of applicant's interest. **Freshman Admission Requirements:** High school diploma is required and GED is accepted. *Academic units required:* 4 English, 3 math, 3 science, 3 science labs, 3 foreign language, 3 social studies, 3 history. *Academic units recommended:* 4 English, 4 math, 4 science, 4 science labs, 4 foreign language, 4 social studies, 4 history. **Freshman Admission Statistics:** 60,724 applied, 31.87% admitted, 32% enrolled. **Transfer Admission Requirements:** High school transcript, college transcript(s), essay or personal statement, statement of good standing from prior institution(s). Lowest grade transferable C. **General Admission Information:** Application fee $70. Regular application deadline 1/1. Regular notification 4/1. Nonfall registration not accepted. Admission may be deferred for a maximum of 1-3 Years.

COSTS AND FINANCIAL AID

Annual tuition $46,590. Room and board $17,578. Required fees $2,472. Average book expense $1,070. **Required Forms and Deadlines:** FAFSA, CSS/Financial Aid PROFILE, Noncustodial PROFILE. **Notification of Awards:** Applicants will be notified of awards on a rolling basis beginning 4/1. **Types of Aid:** *Need-based scholarships/grants:* Federal Pell, FSEOG, State scholarships/grants, Private scholarships, College/university scholarship or grant aid from institutional funds, Federal Nursing Scholarships. *Loans:* Direct Subsidized Stafford Loans, Direct Unsubsidized Stafford Loans, Direct PLUS loans, Federal Perkins Loans, Federal Nursing Loans, College/university loans from institutional funds. *Student Employment:* Federal Work-Study Program available. Institutional employment available. **Financial Aid Statistics:** 90% needy freshmen, 89% needy undergrads receive need-based scholarship or grant aid. 0% freshmen, 0% undergrads receive non-need-based scholarship or grant aid. 82% freshmen, 84% undergrads receive need-based self-help aid. 0% freshmen, 0% undergrads receive athletic scholarships. 49% undergrads borrow to pay for school. Average cumulative indebtedness $30,480. **Criteria for awarding aid:** *Need-based:* Academics, Art, Leadership, Music/drama. *Non-need-based:* Music/drama.

See page 1006.

NIAGARA UNIVERSITY

Gacioch Family Center, Niagara University, NY 14109
Phone: 716-286-8700 • **Financial Aid Phone:** 716-286-8669
E-mail: vwalker@niagara.edu • **CEEB Code:** 2558
Fax: 716-286-8710 • **Website:** www.niagara.edu • **ACT Code:** 2842

This private school, affiliated with the Roman Catholic Church, was founded in 1856. It has a 160-acre campus.

RATINGS

Admissions Selectivity Rating: 77   **Fire Safety Rating:** 88   **Green Rating:** 90

STUDENTS AND FACULTY

Enrollment: 3,045. **Student Body:** 62% female, 38% male, 9% out-of-state, 12% international (25 countries represented). Asian 1%, African American 5%, Caucasian 72%, Hispanic 4%, Native American 1%, Pacific Islander <1%, Two or more races 2%, Race unknown 2%.
Retention and Graduation: 81% freshmen return for sophomore year. 60% freshmen graduate within 4 years. 67% freshmen graduate within 6 years. 29% grads go on to further study within 1 year. 8% grads pursue arts and sciences degrees. 1% grads pursue law degrees. 10% grads pursue business degrees. 1% grads pursue medical degrees. **Faculty:** Student/faculty ratio 12:1. 165 full-time faculty, 95% hold PhDs, 13% are are members of minority groups, 40% are women. 0% of classes are taught by teaching assistants.

ACADEMICS

Degrees: associate, bachelor's, certificate, doctoral/research, master's, postbachelor's certificate, post-master's certificate. **Classes:** Most classes have 10-19 students. Most lab/discussion sessions have 10-19 students. **Most popular majors:** Teacher Education, Multiple Levels; Business/Commerce. **Special Study Options:** Accelerated program, cooperative education program, cross-registration, double major, dual enrollment, English as a Second Language (ESL), exchange student program (domestic), honors program, independent study, internships, liberal arts/career combination, study abroad, teacher certification program. Combined degree programs: BA/MA, BBA/MBA. **Disability Services:** Special programs offered to physically disabled students, including note-taking services, reader services, tape recorders, tutors. **Career Services:** Alumni network, Alumni services, Career/job search classes, Career assessment, Internships, Regional alumni. A cooperative education experience enables students to explore the world of work firsthand by providing a unique opportunity for them to earn while they learn. Students majoring in liberal arts, business or hospitality are eligible to participate in the co-op program in their junior or senior year, enabling them to gain academic credit as well as paid work experiences in their majors. The cooperative education program increases choices for students, and helps employers to train and hire better qualified personnel.

FACILITIES

Housing: Coed dorms, apartments for single students. 75% of campus accessible to physically diasbled. **Special Academic Facilities/Equipment:** Castellani Art Museum. **Computers:** Students can register for classes online.

CAMPUS LIFE

Environment: Town. **Activities:** Choral groups, dance, drama/theater, musical theater, radio station, student government, student newspaper, yearbook, Campus Ministries, Student Organization. 70 registered organizations, 14 honor societies, 2 religious organizations. 3 fraternities, 2 sororities. **Athletics (Intercollegiate):** *Men:* baseball, basketball, cross-country, diving, golf, ice hockey, soccer, swimming, tennis. *Women:* basketball, cross-country, diving, golf, ice hockey, lacrosse, soccer, softball, swimming, tennis, volleyball. **On-Campus Highlights:** Gallagher Center, St.Vincent's Hall, Castellani Art Museum, Clet Hall, Dwyer Arena, Student Apartments. **Environmental Initiatives:** 50000 sq. ft. science complex opened in Fall 2013 earned LEED Gold Certification.

ADMISSIONS

Freshman Academic Profile: Average high school GPA 89.0. 17% in top 10% of high school class, 42% in top 25% of high school class, 75% in top 50% of high school class. **Reported SAT (pre-2016 redesign) scores:** SAT Math middle 50% range 470-570. SAT Critical Reading middle 50% range 460-560. **Concordant SAT scores:** SAT Math middle 50% range 510–590. ACT middle 50% range 21-25. Minimum internet-based TOEFL 79. Minimum paper TOEFL 550. **Basis for Candidate Selection:** *Very important factors considered include:* academic GPA, standardized test scores. *Important factors considered include:* rigor of secondary school record. *Other factors considered include:* class rank, application essay, recommendation(s), interview, extracurricular activities, alumni/ae relation, volunteer work, level of applicant's interest. **Freshman Admission Requirements:** High school diploma is required and GED is accepted. *Academic units required:* 4 English, 2 math, 2 science, 2 foreign language, 2 social studies, 4 academic electives. **Freshman Admission Statistics:** 3,359 applied, 83.18% admitted, 22% enrolled. **Transfer Admission Requirements:** High school transcript, college transcript(s), Minimum college GPA of 2.0 required. Lowest grade transferable C. **General Admission Information:** Regular application deadline 8/30. Nonfall registration accepted. Admission may be deferred for a maximum of 1 year.

COSTS AND FINANCIAL AID
Annual tuition $29,500. Room and board $12,700. Required fees $1,450. Average book expense $1,050. **Required Forms and Deadlines:** FAFSA, State aid form. **Notification of Awards:** Applicants will be notified of awards on a rolling basis beginning 3/1. **Types of Aid:** *Need-based scholarships/ grants:* Federal Pell, FSEOG, State scholarships/grants, Private scholarships, College/university scholarship or grant aid from institutional funds. *Loans:* Direct Subsidized Stafford Loans, Direct Unsubsidized Stafford Loans, Direct PLUS loans, Federal Perkins Loans, Federal Nursing Loans, College/university loans from institutional funds. *Student Employment:* Federal Work-Study Program available. **Financial Aid Statistics:** 99% needy freshmen, 98% needy undergrads receive need-based scholarship or grant aid. 84% freshmen, 80% undergrads receive non-need-based scholarship or grant aid. 84% freshmen, 79% undergrads receive need-based self-help aid. 7% freshmen, 4% undergrads receive athletic scholarships. 97% freshmen, 94% undergrads receive any aid. 74% undergrads borrow to pay for school. Average cumulative indebtedness $32,251. **Criteria for awarding aid:** *Need-based:* Academics, Athletics, Music/ drama. *Non-need-based:* Academics, Athletics, Music/drama.

See page 1008.

NICHOLLS STATE UNIVERSITY

P.O. Box 2004, Thibodaux, LA 70310
Phone: 985-448-4507 • **Financial Aid Phone:** 985-448-4048
E-mail: nicholls@nicholls.edu • **CEEB Code:** 6221
Fax: 985-448-4929 • **Website:** www.nicholls.edu • **ACT Code:** 1580

This public school was founded in 1948. It has a 210-acre campus.

RATINGS
Admissions Selectivity Rating: 77   **Fire Safety Rating:** 85   **Green Rating:** 60*

STUDENTS AND FACULTY
Enrollment: 6,246. **Student Body:** 61% female, 39% male, 4% out-of-state, 2% international (40 countries represented). Asian 1%, African American 18%, Caucasian 73%, Hispanic 1%, Native American 2%, Pacific Islander 0%, Two or more races 0%, Race unknown 2%.
Retention and Graduation: 66% freshmen return for sophomore year.
Faculty: Student/faculty ratio 20:1. 295 full-time faculty, 54% hold PhDs, 11% are are members of minority groups, 51% are women. 1% of classes are taught by teaching assistants.

ACADEMICS
Degrees: associate, bachelor's, certificate, master's, post-master's certificate. **Classes:** Most classes have 20-29 students. **Most popular majors:** General Studies Business Administration and Management. **Special Study Options:** cooperative education program, cross-registration, distance learning, dual enrollment, honors program, independent study, internships, study abroad, teacher certification program. **Honors Programs:** You can learn advanced material in small classes taught by outstanding professors. You can enrich your college experience through intellectually stimulating courses that allow you to reach your potential. The Honors Program invites all academically talented and intellectually curious students to participate. By joining the program you can become a select member of the campus community and associate with students who share similar goals and interests. The Program is designed to meet students' needs and interests. Therefore, students in the program determine their degree of involvement. You may take as many honors courses as you choose or simply successfully complete one-three hour honors course each year. And because honors classes fit degree requirements for all majors, participants graduate on time. Combined degree programs: BA/MA. **Disability Services:** Special programs offered to physically disabled students, including note-taking services, reader services, tape recorders, tutors. **Career Services:** Alumni network, Alumni services, Career/job search classes, Career assessment, Internships.

FACILITIES
Housing: special housing for disabled students, men's dorms, special housing for international students, women's dorms, apartments for married students, apartments for single students, Wellness Housing. **Special Academic Facilities/Equipment:** Ameen Art Gallery. **Computers:** 100% of classrooms, 100% of dorms, 100% of libraries, 100% of dining areas, 100% of student union,

100% of common outdoor areas have wireless network access. Students can register for classes online. Administrative functions (other than registration) can be performed online.

CAMPUS LIFE
Environment: Village. **Activities:** Choral groups, concert band, dance, drama/ theater, jazz band, literary magazine, marching band, music ensembles, musical theater, radio station, student government, student newspaper, student-run film society, television station, yearbook. 121 registered organizations, 24 honor societies, 6 religious organizations. 10 fraternities, 5 sororities. **Athletics (Intercollegiate):** *Men:* baseball, basketball, cross-country, football, golf, tennis. *Women:* basketball, cross-country, golf, soccer, softball, tennis, track/field (outdoor), track/field (indoor), volleyball. **On-Campus Highlights:** Admissions Office, Student Union, Ellender Memorial Library, Guidry Stadium.

ADMISSIONS
Freshman Academic Profile: Average high school GPA 3.2. 18% in top 10% of high school class, 43% in top 25% of high school class, 73% in top 50% of high school class. 68% from public high schools. ACT middle 50% range 24-20. Minimum internet-based TOEFL 61. Minimum paper TOEFL 500. **Basis for Candidate Selection:** *Very important factors considered include:* rigor of secondary school record. *Important factors considered include:* standardized test scores. *Other factors considered include:* class rank, academic GPA, talent/ability. **Freshman Admission Requirements:** High school diploma is required and GED is accepted. *Academic units required:* 4 English, 3 math, 3 science, 2 foreign language, 1 social studies, 2 history, 2 academic electives. **Freshman Admission Statistics:** 2,075 applied, 87.47% admitted, 70% enrolled. **Transfer Admission Requirements:** college transcript(s), Minimum college GPA of 2.0 required. Lowest grade transferable D. **General Admission Information:** Application fee $20. Priority deadline 8/15. Nonfall registration accepted. Admission may be deferred for a maximum of 1 semester.

COSTS AND FINANCIAL AID
Annual in-state tuition $2,231. Annual out-of-state tuition $7,679. Room and board $4,556. Required fees $1,364. Average book expense $1,200. **Required Forms and Deadlines:** FAFSA, Institution's own financial aid form, State aid form, Noncustodial PROFILE. **Types of Aid:** *Need-based scholarships/ grants:* Federal Pell, FSEOG, State scholarships/grants, Private scholarships, College/university scholarship or grant aid from institutional funds. *Loans:* Federal Perkins Loans. *Student Employment:* Federal Work-Study Program available. Institutional employment available. **Financial Aid Statistics:** 93% needy freshmen, 86% needy undergrads receive need-based scholarship or grant aid. 69% freshmen, 33% undergrads receive non-need-based scholarship or grant aid. 51% freshmen, 70% undergrads receive need-based self-help aid. 3% freshmen, 3% undergrads receive athletic scholarships. 77% freshmen, 74% undergrads receive any aid. **Criteria for awarding aid:** *Need-based:* Academics. *Non-need-based:* Academics, Athletics, State/district residency.

NICHOLS COLLEGE

PO Box 5000, Dudley, MA 01571-5000
Phone: 508-213-2203 • **Financial Aid Phone:** 508-213-2340
E-mail: admissions@nichols.edu • **CEEB Code:** 3666
Fax: 508-943-9885 • **Website:** www.nichols.edu • **ACT Code:** 1878

This private school was founded in 1815. It has a 200-acre campus.

RATINGS
Admissions Selectivity Rating: 72   **Fire Safety Rating:** 97   **Green Rating:** 68

STUDENTS AND FACULTY
Enrollment: 1,256. **Student Body:** 40% female, 60% male, 40% out-of-state, 1% international (12 countries represented). Asian 1%, African American 7%, Caucasian 80%, Hispanic 7%, Native American 0%, Pacific Islander 0%, Two or more races 3%, Race unknown 0%.
Retention and Graduation: 36% freshmen graduate within 4 years. 40% freshmen graduate within 6 years. 9% grads go on to further study within 1 year. 2% grads pursue business degrees. **Faculty:** Student/faculty ratio 19 50 full-time faculty, 56% hold PhDs, 8% are are members of minority groups, 44% are women. 0% of classes are taught by teaching assistants.

ACADEMICS
Degrees: associate, bachelor's, master's. **Classes:** Most classes have 20-29 students. Most lab/discussion sessions have 10-19 students. **Most popular majors:** Sport and Fitness Administration/Management; Criminal Justice/Law Enforcement Administration; Business/Commerce. **Special Study Options:** cooperative education program, distance learning, double major, honors program, independent study, internships, liberal arts/career combination, study abroad, teacher certification program. Combined degree programs: Five year

BSBA/MBA Program; Four year accelerated BSBA/MSA program. **Disability Services:** Special programs offered to physically disabled students, including tutors. **Career Services:** Alumni network, Alumni services, Career/job search classes, Career assessment, Internships. We are most proud of our Professional Development Seminar Program (PDS). Our undergraduate students are required to complete a one credit career focused course each of their four years at Nichols College. Through the PDS program all of our students create resumes and LinkedIn profiles, participate in a series of mock interviews, attend a number of networking events, create personal budgets to use following graduation, and more.

FACILITIES

Housing: Coed dorms, men's dorms, women's dorms, apartments for single students. 80% of campus accessible to physically disabled. **Computers:** 10% of classrooms, 100% of libraries, 100% of dining areas, have wireless network access. Students can register for classes online. Administrative functions (other than registration) can be performed online.

CAMPUS LIFE

Environment: Village. **Activities:** drama/theater, literary magazine, musical theater, radio station, student government, student newspaper, yearbook. 25 registered organizations, 5 honor societies, 1 religious organization. **Athletics (Intercollegiate):** *Men:* baseball, basketball, football, golf, ice hockey, lacrosse, soccer, tennis. *Women:* basketball, field hockey, golf, ice hockey, lacrosse, soccer, softball, tennis. **On-Campus Highlights:** Athletic and Recreation Complex, The Currier Center, Snack Bar in Alumni Hall, Davis Cafe, WNRC Radio Station.

ADMISSIONS

Freshman Academic Profile: Average high school GPA 2.9. 9% in top 10% of high school class, 19% in top 25% of high school class, 54% in top 50% of high school class. 85% from public high schools. **Reported SAT (pre-2016 redesign) scores:** SAT Math middle 50% range 420-530. SAT Critical Reading middle 50% range 410-510. SAT Writing middle 50% range 410-510. **Concordant SAT scores:** SAT EBRW middle 50% 460–570. SAT Math middle 50% range 460–560. ACT middle 50% range 17-23. Minimum paper TOEFL 550. **Basis for Candidate Selection:** *Very important factors considered include:* rigor of secondary school record, academic GPA. *Important factors considered include:* standardized test scores, application essay, recommendation(s), interview, extracurricular activities. *Other factors considered include:* class rank, talent/ability, character/personal qualities, alumni/ae relation, volunteer work, work experience, level of applicant's interest. **Freshman Admission Requirements:** High school diploma is required and GED is accepted. *Academic units required:* 4 English, 3 math, 2 science, 2 science labs, 2 social studies, 5 academic electives. *Academic units recommended:* 4 math, 3 science, 3 science labs, 2 foreign language. **Freshman Admission Statistics:** 2,116 applied, 91.40% admitted, 18% enrolled. **Transfer Admission Requirements:** High school transcript, college transcript(s), essay or personal statement, Minimum college GPA of 2.0 required. Lowest grade transferable C. **General Admission Information:** Nonfall registration accepted. Admission may be deferred for a maximum of 1 year.

COSTS AND FINANCIAL AID

Annual tuition $33,000. Room and board $13,500. Required fees $400. Average book expense $1,400. **Required Forms and Deadlines:** FAFSA. **Types of Aid:** *Need-based scholarships/grants:* Federal Pell, FSEOG, State scholarships/grants, Private scholarships. *Loans:* State Loans. *Student Employment:* Federal Work-Study Program available. Institutional employment available. **Financial Aid Statistics:** 100% needy undergrads receive need-based scholarship or grant aid. 8% freshmen, 13% undergrads receive non-need-based scholarship or grant aid. 96% freshmen, 96% undergrads receive need-based self-help aid. 0% freshmen, 0% undergrads receive athletic scholarships. 87% undergrads borrow to pay for school. Average cumulative indebtedness $35,392. **Criteria for awarding aid:** *Need-based:* Academics. *Non-need-based:* Academics.

2%, Native American <1%, Pacific Islander <1%, Two or more races <1%, Race unknown 3%. **Retention and Graduation:** 74% freshmen return for sophomore year. 17% freshmen graduate within 4 years. **Faculty:** 532 full-time faculty, 77% hold PhDs, 73% are are members of minority groups, 44% are women.

ACADEMICS

Degrees: bachelor's, doctoral/research, master's. **Classes:** Most classes have 20-29 students. **Special Study Options:** cooperative education program, cross-registration, distance learning, double major, external degree program, honors program, independent study, internships, study abroad, teacher certification program.

FACILITIES

Housing: Coed dorms, men's dorms, women's dorms, Theme Housing, Graduate housing.

CAMPUS LIFE

Activities: Choral groups, concert band, dance, drama/theater, jazz band, literary magazine, marching band, music ensembles, musical theater, opera, pep band, radio station, student government, student newspaper, student-run film society, symphony orchestra, television station, yearbook, Student Organization, Model UN.

ADMISSIONS

Freshman Academic Profile: Average high school GPA 3.1. 0% in top 10% of high school class, 6% in top 25% of high school class, 34% in top 50% of high school class. 77% from public high schools. **Reported SAT (pre-2016 redesign) scores:** SAT Math middle 50% range 410-500. SAT Critical Reading middle 50% range 390-480. SAT Writing middle 50% range 370-460. **Concordant SAT scores:** SAT EBRW middle 50% 430–530. SAT Math middle 50% range 450–530. ACT middle 50% range 17-21. Minimum internet-based TOEFL 88. Minimum paper TOEFL 570. **Basis for Candidate Selection:** *Very important factors considered include:* rigor of secondary school record, academic GPA. *Important factors considered include:* class rank, standardized test scores. *Other factors considered include:* extracurricular activities, talent/ability, character/personal qualities, geographical residence, state residency, volunteer work, work experience, level of applicant's interest. **Freshman Admission Requirements:** High school diploma is required and GED is accepted. *Academic units required:* 4 English, 4 math, 3 science, 1 science lab, 2 foreign language, 1 social studies, 1 history, 4 academic electives. **Freshman Admission Statistics:** 6,692 applied, 66.44% admitted, 42% enrolled. **Transfer Admission Requirements:** High school transcript, Minimum college GPA of 2.0 required. Lowest grade transferable C. **General Admission Information:** Application fee $45. Priority deadline 2/15. Nonfall registration accepted. Admission may be deferred for a maximum of 1 year.

COSTS AND FINANCIAL AID

Annual in-state tuition $2,791. Annual out-of-state tuition $12,425. Room and board $7,225. Required fees $1,877. Average book expense $1,400. **Required Forms and Deadlines:** FAFSA. **Notification of Awards:** Applicants will be notified of awards on or about 4/15. **Types of Aid:** *Need-based scholarships/grants:* Federal Pell, FSEOG, State scholarships/grants, Private scholarships, College/university scholarship or grant aid from institutional funds. *Loans:* Direct Subsidized Stafford Loans, Direct Unsubsidized Stafford Loans, Direct PLUS loans. *Student Employment:* Federal Work-Study Program available. Institutional employment available. **Financial Aid Statistics:** 78% needy freshmen, 75% needy undergrads receive need-based scholarship or grant aid. 92% freshmen, 85% undergrads receive non-need-based scholarship or grant aid. 85% freshmen, 86% undergrads receive need-based self-help aid. 3% freshmen, 2% undergrads receive athletic scholarships. **Criteria for awarding aid:** *Non-need-based:* Academics.

NORTH CAROLINA A&T STATE UNIVERSITY

1601 East Market Street, Greensboro, NC 27411
Phone: 336-334-7946
E-mail: uadmit@ncat.edu
Fax: 336-334-7478 • **Website:** www.ncat.edu

This is a public school.

RATINGS

Admissions Selectivity Rating: 74   **Fire Safety Rating:** 60*   **Green Rating:** 60*

STUDENTS AND FACULTY

Enrollment: 8,921. **Student Body:** 54% female, 46% male, 16% out-of-state, 1% international. Asian 1%, African American 89%, Caucasian 4%, Hispanic

---

NORTH CAROLINA STATE UNIVERSITY

Box 7103, Raleigh, NC 27695
Phone: 919-515-2434 • **Financial Aid Phone:** 919-515-2421
E-mail: undergrad-admissions@ncsu.edu • **CEEB Code:** 5496
Fax: 919-515-5039 • **Website:** http://www.ncsu.edu/ • **ACT Code:** 3164

This public school was founded in 1887. It has a 2110-acre campus.

RATINGS

Admissions Selectivity Rating: 90   **Fire Safety Rating:** 98   **Green Rating:** 96

STUDENTS AND FACULTY

Enrollment: 22,423. **Student Body:** 45% female, 55% male, 10% out-of-state, 4% international (107 countries represented). Asian 6%, African American 6%, Caucasian 72%, Hispanic 5%, Native American <1%, Pacific Islander <1%, Two or more races 4%, Race unknown 2%.

Retention and Graduation: 94% freshmen return for sophomore year. 48% freshmen graduate within 4 years. 78% freshmen graduate within 6 years. 17% grads go on to further study within 1 year. 7% grads pursue arts and sciences degrees. 2% grads pursue law degrees. 2% grads pursue business degrees. 5% grads pursue medical degrees. **Faculty:** Student/faculty ratio 13:1. 2,259 full-time faculty, 84% hold PhDs, 16% are are members of minority groups, 37% are women. 16% of classes are taught by teaching assistants.

ACADEMICS

Degrees: associate, bachelor's, certificate, doctoral/professional, doctoral/research, doctoral, master's, postbachelor's certificate, post-master's certificate. **Classes:** Most classes have 10-19 students. Most lab/discussion sessions have 20-29 students. **Most popular majors:** Biology/Biological Sciences; Business Administration and Management; Engineering. **Special Study Options:** Accelerated program, cooperative education program, cross-registration, distance learning, double major, dual enrollment, exchange student program (domestic), honors program, independent study, internships, liberal arts/career combination, student-designed major, study abroad. **Honors Programs:** The University Honors Program recruits and provides programmatic support for a diverse group of nationally outstanding students, ensuring that they benefit fully from the resources of a major land-grant, research university and the Research Triangle by emphasizing inquiry-, creativity-, and discovery-based learning. The program offers interdisciplinary seminars and a variety of credit-earning opportunites for out-of-classroom experiences. The program emphasizes participation in research by students from all disciplines. Entering students may instead choose to participate in the University Scholars program, which emphasizes enrichment activities and leadership development. There are over 30 honors programs located in the colleges or departments that invite students in their sophomore or junior years. These programs include honors sections of courses, honors seminars, and honors research. Some programs require a senior honor thesis. Combined degree programs: We have combined BS/MS programs in a variety of fields, including engineering, sciences, humanities, and social sciences. **Disability Services:** Special programs offered to physically disabled students, including note-taking services, reader services, tape recorders. **Career Services:** Alumni services, Career/job search classes, Career assessment, Internships. All of the services mentioned above are vital, but definitely assisting our students in gaining experiential learning experiences (co-op or internships) are extremely important. They help build the students' credentials and lead to full-time career opportunities.

FACILITIES

Housing: Coed dorms, special housing for disabled students, men's dorms, special housing for international students, women's dorms, fraternity/sorority housing, apartments for married students, apartments for single students, Theme Housing, Living/Learning Dormitories. 81% of campus accessible to physically diasbled. **Special Academic Facilities/Equipment:** Art and arts/crafts galleries, research farms and forest, phytophotron with controlled atmosphere growth chambers. pulp/paper and wood products labs, processing equipment for fiber, fabric, and garment manufacture, electron microscopes, nuclear reactor, stable isotope lab. **Computers:** 94% of classrooms, 100% of libraries, 92% of dining areas, 100% of student union, 52% of common outdoor areas have wireless network access. Students can register for classes online. Administrative functions (other than registration) can be performed online.

CAMPUS LIFE

Environment: Metropolis. **Activities:** Choral groups, concert band, dance, drama/theater, jazz band, literary magazine, marching band, music ensembles, musical theater, pep band, radio station, student government, student newspaper, symphony orchestra, yearbook, Campus Ministries, Student Organization. 560 registered organizations, 26 honor societies, 25 religious organizations. 33 fraternities, 17 sororities. **Athletics (Intercollegiate):** *Men:* baseball, basketball, cheerleading, cross-country, diving, football, golf, riflery, soccer, swimming, tennis, track/field (outdoor), track/field (indoor), wrestling. *Women:* basketball, cheerleading, cross-country, diving, golf, gymnastics, riflery, soccer, softball, swimming, tennis, track/field (outdoor), track/field (indoor), volleyball. **On-Campus Highlights:** RBC Center—Sports Arena, Gallery of Art and Design, Carter Finley Stadium, Talley Student Center, University Theatre. **Environmental Initiatives:** Creation of new leadership in the form of the Sustainability Council, who will lead NC State through development and implementation of the 2017-2022 Sustainability Strategic Plan.

ADMISSIONS

Freshman Academic Profile: Average high school GPA 3.7. 50% in top 10% of high school class, 87% in top 25% of high school class, 100% in top 50% of high school class. 84% from public high schools. **Reported SAT (pre-2016 redesign) scores:** SAT Math middle 50% range 600-690. SAT Critical Reading middle 50% range 570-660. SAT Writing middle 50% range 540-630.

Concordant SAT scores: SAT EBRW middle 50% 610–690. SAT Math middle 50% range 620–720. ACT middle 50% range 27-31. Minimum internet-based TOEFL 85. Minimum paper TOEFL 563. **Basis for Candidate Selection:** *Very important factors considered include:* rigor of secondary school record, class rank, academic GPA, standardized test scores. *Other factors considered include:* application essay, extracurricular activities, talent/ability, character/personal qualities, first generation, alumni/ae relation, geographical residence, state residency, racial/ethnic status, volunteer work, work experience. **Freshman Admission Requirements:** High school diploma is required and GED is not accepted. *Academic units required:* 4 English, 4 math, 3 science, 1 science lab, 2 foreign language, 1 social studies, 1 history. *Academic units recommended:* 4 English, 4 math, 3 science, 1 science lab, 2 foreign language, 1 social studies, 1 history. **Freshman Admission Statistics:** 21,099 applied, 57.04% admitted, 33% enrolled. **Transfer Admission Requirements:** college transcript(s), Minimum college GPA of 2.0 required. Lowest grade transferable C-. **General Admission Information:** Application fee $80. Priority deadline 10/15. Regular application deadline 1/15. Nonfall registration accepted. Admission may be deferred for a maximum of 1 year.

COSTS AND FINANCIAL AID

Annual in-state tuition $6,407. Annual out-of-state tuition $23,926. Room and board $10,635. Required fees $2,473. Average book expense $1,082. **Required Forms and Deadlines:** FAFSA. **Notification of Awards:** Applicants will be notified of awards on a rolling basis beginning 4/1. **Types of Aid:** *Need-based scholarships/grants:* Federal Pell, FSEOG, State scholarships/grants, Private scholarships, College/university scholarship or grant aid from institutional funds, United Negro College Fund. *Loans:* Direct Subsidized Stafford Loans, Direct Unsubsidized Stafford Loans, Direct PLUS loans, Federal Perkins Loans, State Loans, College/university loans from institutional funds. *Student Employment:* Federal Work-Study Program available. Institutional employment available. **Financial Aid Statistics:** 93% needy freshmen, 91% needy undergrads receive need-based scholarship or grant aid. 21% freshmen, 13% undergrads receive non-need-based scholarship or grant aid. 68% freshmen, 73% undergrads receive need-based self-help aid. 2% freshmen, 2% undergrads receive athletic scholarships. 75% freshmen, 68% undergrads receive any aid. 54% undergrads borrow to pay for school. Average cumulative indebtedness $21,509. **Criteria for awarding aid:** *Need-based:* Academics, Alumni affiliation, Leadership. *Non-need-based:* Academics, Alumni affiliation, Athletics, Leadership, State/district residency.

NORTH CENTRAL COLLEGE

Office of Admissions, Naperville, IL 60566-7063
Phone: 630-637-5800 • **Financial Aid Phone:** 630-637-5600
E-mail: admissions@noctrl.edu • **CEEB Code:** 1555
Fax: 630-637-5819 • **Website:** www.northcentralcollege.edu • **ACT Code:** 1096

This private school, affiliated with the Methodist Church, was founded in 1861. It has a 59-acre campus.

RATINGS

Admissions Selectivity Rating: 84   **Fire Safety Rating:** 95   **Green Rating:** 79

STUDENTS AND FACULTY

Enrollment: 2,626. **Student Body:** 53% female, 47% male, 7% out-of-state, 2% international (22 countries represented). Asian 3%, African American 4%, Caucasian 68%, Hispanic 13%, Native American <1%, Pacific Islander <1%, Two or more races 3%, Race unknown 6%.

Retention and Graduation: 78% freshmen return for sophomore year. 56% freshmen graduate within 4 years. 69% freshmen graduate within 6 years. **Faculty:** Student/faculty ratio 15:1. 131 full-time faculty, 98% hold PhDs, 17% are are members of minority groups, 59% are women. 0% of classes are taught by teaching assistants.

ACADEMICS

Degrees: bachelor's, master's, postbachelor's certificate. **Classes:** Most classes have 20-29 students. Most lab/discussion sessions have 20-29 students. **Most popular majors:** Psychology; Kinesiology and Exercise Science; Marketing/Marketing Management. **Special Study Options:** Accelerated program, cross-registration, double major, dual enrollment, English as a Second Language (ESL), exchange student program (domestic), honors program, independent study, internships, student-designed major, study abroad, teacher certification program, 3-2 Engineering program with University of Illinois, University of Minnesota;Integrated 5 year Bachelor's/Master's degree programs. **Honors Programs:** The College Scholars is a comprehensive four year integrative program culminating in a senior honors thesis. The program is open to students from all academic disciplines. Combined degree programs: BA/MA, BA in Acc/MBA; Bachelor's Degree/Masters in Web and Internet Applications; BA or

BS/Master of Leadership Studies;BA or BS/Master of Arts in Liberal Studies. **Disability Services:** Special programs offered to physically disabled students, including note-taking services, reader services, tape recorders, tutors. **Career Services:** Alumni network, Alumni services, Career/job search classes, Career assessment, Internships, Regional alumni. Because career-related experiences support the mission of the college, the Career Development Center actively assists students in developing Internship opportunities. We have found that real hands on experience within the workforce increases graduates marketability following graduation, be it for seeking employment or pursuing graduate school. Today's job market is competitive and we offer a strong resource in helping students get involved in these types of opportunities which ultimately helps them reach their goals.

FACILITIES

Housing: Coed dorms, special housing for disabled students, women's dorms, Substance-free housing. 90% of campus accessible to physically diasbled. **Special Academic Facilities/Equipment:** None **Computers:** 50% of classrooms, 30% of dorms, 100% of libraries, 100% of dining areas, 100% of student union, 100% of common outdoor areas have wireless network access. Students can register for classes online. Administrative functions (other than registration) can be performed online.

CAMPUS LIFE

Environment: City. **Activities:** Choral groups, concert band, dance, drama/theater, jazz band, literary magazine, music ensembles, musical theater, opera, pep band, radio station, student government, student newspaper, Campus Ministries, Student Organization, Model UN. 54 registered organizations, 14 honor societies, 6 religious organizations. **Athletics (Intercollegiate):** *Men:* baseball, basketball, cross-country, football, golf, soccer, swimming, tennis, track/field (outdoor), track/field (indoor), wrestling. *Women:* basketball, cheerleading, cross-country, golf, lacrosse, soccer, softball, swimming, tennis, track/field (outdoor), track/field (indoor), volleyball. **On-Campus Highlights:** Old Main—historic home of North Central College, Benedtti-Wehrli Stadium, Res/Rec Center, Fine Arts Center & Wentz Concert Hall, Oesterle Library, Rolland Boilerhouse Cafe is also a popular on-campus hangout. **Environmental Initiatives:** The College committed to building a one of a kind building with a residence hall wrapped-around a rec center and NCAA regulation sized indoor track. The building was built to LEED silver certification standards with heating and cooling from a geothermal field, occupancy sensors, precast walls made of recycled material, water efficient fixtures, bike storage, and more.

ADMISSIONS

Freshman Academic Profile: Average high school GPA 3.6. 20% in top 10% of high school class, 52% in top 25% of high school class, 83% in top 50% of high school class. 89% from public high schools. ACT middle 50% range 22-27. Minimum internet-based TOEFL 68. Minimum paper TOEFL 520. **Basis for Candidate Selection:** *Very important factors considered include:* rigor of secondary school record, academic GPA, standardized test scores, character/personal qualities. *Important factors considered include:* extracurricular activities, talent/ability, volunteer work. *Other factors considered include:* application essay, recommendation(s), interview, first generation, alumni/ae relation, work experience, level of applicant's interest. **Freshman Admission Requirements:** High school diploma is required and GED is accepted. *Academic units required:* 4 English, 3 math, 3 science, 2 science labs, 2 social studies, 1 history, 3 academic electives. *Academic units recommended:* 4 English, 3 math, 3 science, 3 science labs, 3 foreign language, 2 social studies, 1 history, 3 academic electives. **Freshman Admission Statistics:** 6,860 applied, 59.36% admitted, 7% enrolled. **Transfer Admission Requirements:** college transcript(s), Minimum college GPA of 2.25 required. Lowest grade transferable D. **General Admission Information:** Application fee $25. Priority deadline 4/15. Nonfall registration accepted. Admission may be deferred for a maximum of 1 year.

COSTS AND FINANCIAL AID

Annual tuition $35,241. Room and board $10,089. Required fees $180. Average book expense $1,200. **Required Forms and Deadlines:** FAFSA. **Notification of Awards:** Applicants will be notified of awards on a rolling basis beginning 3/1. **Types of Aid:** *Need-based scholarships/grants:* Federal Pell, FSEOG, State scholarships/grants, Private scholarships, College/university scholarship or grant aid from institutional funds. *Loans:* Direct Subsidized Stafford Loans, Direct Unsubsidized Stafford Loans, Direct PLUS loans, Federal Perkins Loans, College/university loans from institutional funds. *Student Employment:* Federal Work-Study Program available. Institutional employment available. **Financial Aid Statistics:** 100% needy freshmen, 99% needy undergrads receive need-based scholarship or grant aid. 12% freshmen, 11% undergrads receive non-need-based scholarship or grant aid. 82% freshmen, 84% undergrads receive need-based self-help aid. 0% freshmen, 0% undergrads receive athletic scholarships. 100% freshmen, 98% undergrads receive any aid. 99% undergrads borrow to pay for school. Average cumulative indebtedness $34,809. **Criteria for awarding aid:** *Need-based:* Academics, Religious affiliation. *Non-need-based:* Academics, Art, Leadership, Minority status, Music/drama, Religious affiliation, State/district residency.

NORTH DAKOTA STATE UNIVERSITY

PO Box 6050 Dept 2832, Fargo, ND 58108
Phone: 701-231-8643 • **Financial Aid Phone:** 800-726-3188
E-mail: ndsu.admission@ndsu.edu • **CEEB Code:** 6474
Fax: 701-231-8802 • **Website:** www.ndsu.edu • **ACT Code:** 3202

This public school was founded in 1890. It has a 258-acre campus.

RATINGS

Admissions Selectivity Rating: 79   **Fire Safety Rating:** 81   **Green Rating:** 60*

STUDENTS AND FACULTY

Enrollment: 11,609. **Student Body:** 45% female, 55% male, 57% out-of-state, 2% international (39 countries represented). Asian 1%, African American 3%, Caucasian 87%, Hispanic 2%, Native American 1%, Pacific Islander <1%, Two or more races 2%, Race unknown 2%.
Retention and Graduation: 78% freshmen return for sophomore year. 27% freshmen graduate within 4 years. 54% freshmen graduate within 6 years. **Faculty:** Student/faculty ratio 17:1. 712 full-time faculty, 86% hold PhDs, 17% are are members of minority groups, 40% are women.

ACADEMICS

Degrees: bachelor's, certificate, doctoral/professional, doctoral, master's, postbachelor's certifiate, post-master's certificate. **Classes:** Most classes have 20-29 students. Most lab/discussion sessions have 20-29 students. **Most popular majors:** Civil Engineering; Mechanical Engineering; Business, Management, Marketing, and Related Support Services. **Special Study Options:** cooperative education program, cross-registration, distance learning, double major, dual enrollment, English as a Second Language (ESL), honors program, independent study, internships, student-designed major, study abroad, teacher certification program, Tri-College Collaboration and Registration with Minnesota State University and Concordia College. Collaboration with North Dakota University System institutions. **Honors Programs:** Scholars Program. **Disability Services:** Special programs offered to physically disabled students, including note-taking services, reader services, tape recorders, tutors. **Career Services:** Career/job search classes, Internships. Cooperative Education opportunities are available for most majors. Students are paid for their work experience and earn credit.

FACILITIES

Housing: Coed dorms, men's dorms, women's dorms, apartments for married students, apartments for single students, Designated floors for engineering and architecture students. Learning communities. Wellness community. Freshmen under 19 years of age not living with a parent or guardian must live on campus. Housing is guaranteed for freshmen required to live on campus. Handicapped accessible. **Special Academic Facilities/Equipment:** Art gallery, language lab, genetics institute, regional studies institute. **Computers:** Students can register for classes online. Administrative functions (other than registration) can be performed online.

CAMPUS LIFE

Environment: City. **Activities:** Choral groups, concert band, drama/theater, jazz band, marching band, music ensembles, musical theater, pep band, radio station, student government, student newspaper. 218 registered organizations, 22 honor societies, 18 religious organizations. 10 fraternities, 5 sororities. **Athletics (Intercollegiate):** *Men:* baseball, basketball, cross-country, football, golf, track/field (outdoor), track/field (indoor), wrestling. *Women:* basketball, cross-country, golf, soccer, softball, track/field (outdoor), track/field (indoor), volleyball. **On-Campus Highlights:** Wellness Center, Memorial Union, FargoDome, Alumni Center, Industrial Agricultural Communications Center, Residence Halls/Living Learning Center; Newman Outdoor Field; Technology Park.

ADMISSIONS

Freshman Academic Profile: Average high school GPA 3.4. 15% in top 10% of high school class, 41% in top 25% of high school class, 71% in top 50% of high school class. **Reported SAT (pre-2016 redesign) scores:** SAT Math middle 50% range 500-630. SAT Critical Reading middle 50% range 480-630. SAT Writing middle 50% range 460-520. **Concordant SAT scores:** SAT EBRW middle 50% 530–630. SAT Math middle 50% range 530–650. ACT middle 50% range 21-26. Minimum internet-based TOEFL 71. Minimum paper TOEFL 525. **Basis for Candidate Selection:** *Very important factors considered include:* academic GPA, standardized test scores. **Freshman Admission Requirements:** High school diploma is required and GED is accepted. *Academic units required:* 4 English, 3 math, 3 science, 3 science labs, 3 social studies. **Freshman Admission Statistics:** 5,311 applied, 93.65% admitted, 51% enrolled. **Transfer Admission Requirements:** college transcript(s), Minimum college GPA of 2.0 required. Lowest grade transferable D. **General Admission Information:** Application fee $35. Regular application deadline 8/1. Nonfall registration accepted. Admission may be deferred for a maximum of 3 years.

COSTS AND FINANCIAL AID

Annual in-state tuition $6,762. Annual out-of-state tuition $18,056. Room and board $7,502. Required fees $1,216. Average book expense $1,100. **Required Forms and Deadlines:** FAFSA. **Notification of Awards:** Applicants will be notified of awards on a rolling basis beginning 4/1. **Types of Aid:** *Need-based scholarships/grants:* Federal Pell, FSEOG, State scholarships/grants, Private scholarships, College/university scholarship or grant aid from institutional funds. *Loans:* Direct Subsidized Stafford Loans, Direct Unsubsidized Stafford Loans, Direct PLUS loans, Federal Perkins Loans, Federal Nursing Loans. *Student Employment:* Federal Work-Study Program available. Institutional employment available. **Financial Aid Statistics:** 77% needy freshmen, 71% needy undergrads receive need-based scholarship or grant aid. 8% freshmen, 5% undergrads receive non-need-based scholarship or grant aid. 82% freshmen, 83% undergrads receive need-based self-help aid. 2% freshmen, 1% undergrads receive athletic scholarships. 69% undergrads borrow to pay for school. Average cumulative indebtedness $30,740. **Criteria for awarding aid:** *Need-based:* Academics, Alumni affiliation, Art, Athletics, Leadership, Minority status, Music/drama. *Non-need-based:* Academics, Alumni affiliation, Art, Athletics, Leadership, Minority status, Music/drama, State/district residency.

NORTH PARK UNIVERSITY

3225 West Foster Avenue, Chicago, IL 60625-4895
Phone: 773-244-5500 • **Financial Aid Phone:** 773-244-5506
E-mail: admission@northpark.edu • **CEEB Code:** 1556
Fax: 773-244-5243 • **Website:** www.northpark.edu • **ACT Code:** 1098

This private school was founded in 1891. It has a 30-acre campus.

RATINGS

Admissions Selectivity Rating: 80   **Fire Safety Rating:** 75   **Green Rating:** 60*

STUDENTS AND FACULTY

Enrollment: 2,190. **Student Body:** 63% female, 37% male, 31% out-of-state, 4% international (31 countries represented). Asian 7%, African American 9%, Caucasian 60%, Hispanic 10%, Native American <1%, Pacific Islander 0%, Two or more races 0%, Race unknown 0%.
Retention and Graduation: 71% freshmen return for sophomore year. 45% freshmen graduate within 4 years. 55% freshmen graduate within 6 years. 15% grads go on to further study within 1 year. 15% grads pursue arts and sciences degrees. 2% grads pursue law degrees. 10% grads pursue business degrees. 3% grads pursue medical degrees. **Faculty:** Student/faculty ratio 14:1. 125 full-time faculty, 88% hold PhDs, 17% are are members of minority groups, 50% are women. 0% of classes are taught by teaching assistants.

ACADEMICS

Degrees: bachelor's, master's, postbachelor's certificate. **Classes:** Most classes have 10-19 students. Most lab/discussion sessions have 20-29 students. **Most popular majors:** Business Administration and Management; Education; Biology/Biological Sciences. **Special Study Options:** Accelerated program, distance learning, double major, English as a Second Language (ESL), honors program, independent study, internships, liberal arts/career combination, student-designed major, study abroad, teacher certification program. **Honors Programs:** The North Park University Honors Congress brings together students of high academic ability with faculty in a learning community designed to promote academic excellence, rigorous intellectual development, community involvement, service to others, and vocational direction. As Honors Congress Scholars, students of promise are provided opportunities to excel during their first two years of undergraduate study. Honors courses during the second two years are offered in individual departments. We strive to take the words of Jesus, "To whom much is given, much is required," and give them special consideration in the Honors Congress. Our philosophy is simply this: The Honors Congress gives students of high intellectual ability an array of learning experiences from which to choose, places them sideby-side with faculty mentors who care, and offers them guidance and encouragement along the way. Combined degree programs: Gradaute level dual-degrees. **Disability Services:** Special programs offered to physically disabled students, including note-taking services, reader services, tape recorders, tutors. **Career Services:** Alumni network, Career/job search classes, Career assessment, Internships, On-campus interviews. North Park has hundreds of internship opportunities available throughout the Chicago area. Students can decide between public and private, nonprofit and for profit organizations.

FACILITIES

Housing: special housing for disabled students, men's dorms, women's dorms, apartments for single students. **Special Academic Facilities/Equipment:** Art gallery, language lab, Swedish Historical Society Archives. **Computers:** 100% of libraries, 25% of dining areas, have wireless network access. Students can register for classes online. Administrative functions (other than registration) can be performed online.

CAMPUS LIFE

Environment: Metropolis. **Activities:** Choral groups, concert band, drama/theater, jazz band, literary magazine, music ensembles, musical theater, opera, pep band, student government, student newspaper, symphony orchestra, yearbook, Campus Ministries, Student Organization. 4 honor societies, 1 religious organization. **Athletics (Intercollegiate):** *Men:* baseball, basketball, cross-country, football, golf, soccer, track/field (outdoor), track/field (indoor). *Women:* basketball, crew/rowing, cross-country, golf, soccer, softball, track/field (outdoor), track/field (indoor), volleyball. **On-Campus Highlights:** New Student Recreation Center, Brandel Library, New state of the art outdoor athletic facilities, Beautifull New Campus Quadrangle, Diverse neighborhood.

ADMISSIONS

Freshman Academic Profile: Average high school GPA 3.1. 11% in top 10% of high school class, 35% in top 25% of high school class, 66% in top 50% of high school class. 80% from public high schools. **Reported SAT (pre-2016 redesign) scores:** SAT Math middle 50% range 460-590. SAT Critical Reading middle 50% range 470-580. **Concordant SAT scores:** SAT Math middle 50% range 500–610. ACT middle 50% range 19-24. Minimum paper TOEFL 550. **Basis for Candidate Selection:** *Very important factors considered include:* rigor of secondary school record, class rank, academic GPA, standardized test scores, application essay, recommendation(s), talent/ability, character/personal qualities. *Important factors considered include:* interview, extracurricular activities, first generation, racial/ethnic status, volunteer work. *Other factors considered include:* alumni/ae relation, geographical residence, work experience, level of applicant's interest. **Freshman Admission Requirements:** High school diploma is required and GED is accepted. *Academic units recommended:* 4 English, 3 math, 3 science, 2 foreign language, 1 social studies, 1 history. **Freshman Admission Statistics:** 1,304 applied, 69.79% admitted, 46% enrolled. **Transfer Admission Requirements:** college transcript(s), essay or personal statement, statement of good standing from prior institution(s). Minimum college GPA of 2.0 required. Lowest grade transferable D. **General Admission Information:** Application fee $40. Priority deadline 4/1. Regular application deadline 7/1. Nonfall registration accepted. Admission may be deferred for a maximum of 1 year.

COSTS AND FINANCIAL AID

Annual tuition $23,290. Room and board $8,600. Average book expense $1,000. **Required Forms and Deadlines:** FAFSA. **Notification of Awards:** Applicants will be notified of awards on a rolling basis beginning 3/15. **Types of Aid:** *Need-based scholarships/grants:* Federal Pell, FSEOG, State scholarships/grants, Private scholarships, College/university scholarship or grant aid from institutional funds, Federal Nursing Scholarships. *Loans:* Direct Subsidized Stafford Loans, Direct Unsubsidized Stafford Loans, Direct PLUS loans, Federal Perkins Loans, Federal Nursing Loans. *Student Employment:* Federal Work-Study Program available. Institutional employment available. **Financial Aid Statistics:** 70% needy freshmen receive need-based scholarship or grant aid. 42% freshmen, undergrads receive non-need-based scholarship or grant aid. 64% freshmen, undergrads receive need-based self-help aid. 0% freshmen, 0% undergrads receive athletic scholarships. 90% freshmen, 90% undergrads receive any aid. **Criteria for awarding aid:** *Non-need-based:* Academics, Art, Music/drama, Religious affiliation, State/district residency.

NORTHEASTERN ILLINOIS UNIVERSITY

5500 North St. Louis Avenue, Chicago, IL 60625-4699
Phone: 773-442-4000 • **Financial Aid Phone:** 773-442-5009
E-mail: admrec@neiu.edu • **CEEB Code:** 1090
Fax: 773-442-4020 • **Website:** www.neiu.edu • **ACT Code:** 993

This public school was founded in 1961. It has a 63-acre campus.

RATINGS

Admissions Selectivity Rating: 72   **Fire Safety Rating:** 60*   **Green Rating:** 71

STUDENTS AND FACULTY

Enrollment: 7,979. **Student Body:** 56% female, 44% male, 1% out-of-state, 4% international (91 countries represented). Asian 9%, African American 10%, Caucasian 33%, Hispanic 37%, Native American <1%, Pacific Islander <1%, Two or more races 2%, Race unknown 3%.
Retention and Graduation: 61% freshmen return for sophomore year. 5% freshmen graduate within 4 years. **Faculty:** Student/faculty ratio 14:1. 374 full-time faculty, 82% hold PhDs, 30% are are members of minority groups, 53% are women.

ACADEMICS

Degrees: bachelor's, certificate, master's. **Classes:** Most classes have 20-29 students. **Most popular majors:** Psychology; Biology/Biological Sciences; Social Work. **Special Study Options:** cooperative education program, distance learning, double major, dual enrollment, exchange student program (domestic), honors program, independent study, student-designed major, study abroad, teacher certification program. **Disability Services:** Special programs offered to physically disabled students, including note-taking services, reader services, tape recorders, tutors. **Career Services:** Alumni network, Alumni services, Career/job search classes, Career assessment, Internships. We offer a wide variety of career/job search workshops.

FACILITIES

Housing: 98% of campus accessible to physically diasbled. **Special Academic Facilities/Equipment:** Learning center with audiovisual, TV, multimedia, film, photography, graphic arts, and electronic instructional equipment, listening room. **Computers:** 50% of classrooms, n/a% of dorms, 100% of libraries, 80% of dining areas, 100% of student union, 50% of common outdoor areas have wireless network access. Students can register for classes online. Administrative functions (other than registration) can be performed online.

CAMPUS LIFE

Environment: Metropolis. **Activities:** Choral groups, concert band, dance, drama/theater, jazz band, literary magazine, music ensembles, musical theater, radio station, student government, student newspaper. 42 registered organizations, 12 honor societies, 6 religious organizations. 3 fraternities, 3 sororities. **On-Campus Highlights:** International Day, Fine Arst Building/Art Gallery, Ensemble Dance Company, Health and Wellness Center, Library. **Environmental Initiatives:** Recycling.

ADMISSIONS

Freshman Academic Profile: Average high school GPA 2.8. 3% in top 10% of high school class, 13% in top 25% of high school class, 44% in top 50% of high school class. 87% from public high schools. ACT middle 50% range 16-20. Minimum paper TOEFL 500. **Basis for Candidate Selection:** *Very important factors considered include:* class rank, academic GPA, standardized test scores. **Freshman Admission Requirements:** High school diploma is required and GED is accepted. *Academic units required:* 4 English, 3 math, 3 science, 3 social studies, 2 visual/performing arts. *Academic units recommended:* 4 English, 3 math, 3 science, 3 social studies, 2 visual/performing arts. **Freshman Admission Statistics:** 4,499 applied, 67.04% admitted, 25% enrolled. **Transfer Admission Requirements:** college transcript(s), statement of good standing from prior institution(s). Minimum college GPA of 2.0 required. Lowest grade transferable D. **General Admission Information:** Application fee $30. Regular application deadline 7/1. Nonfall registration accepted. Admission may be deferred.

COSTS AND FINANCIAL AID

Annual in-state tuition $7,248. Annual out-of-state tuition $14,596. Room and board $11,100. Required fees $3,322. **Required Forms and Deadlines:** FAFSA. **Notification of Awards:** Applicants will be notified of awards on a rolling basis beginning 3/15. **Types of Aid:** *Need-based scholarships/grants:* Federal Pell, FSEOG, State scholarships/grants, Private scholarships, College/university scholarship or grant aid from institutional funds. *Loans:* Direct Subsidized Stafford Loans, Direct Unsubsidized Stafford Loans, Direct PLUS loans, Federal Perkins Loans. *Student Employment:* Federal Work-Study Program available. Institutional employment available. **Financial Aid Statistics:** 84% needy freshmen, 78% needy undergrads receive need-based scholarship or grant aid. 9% freshmen, 17% undergrads receive non-need-based scholarship or grant aid. 18% freshmen, 41% undergrads receive need-based self-help aid. 0% freshmen, 0% undergrads receive athletic scholarships. 59% freshmen, 55% undergrads receive any aid. Average cumulative indebtedness $15,713. **Criteria for awarding aid:** *Non-need-based:* Academics, Art, Leadership, Music/drama.

NORTHEASTERN STATE UNIVERSITY

Office of Admissions and Recruitment, Tahlequah, OK 74464-2399
Phone: 918-444-2200 • **Financial Aid Phone:** 918-444-3456
E-mail: nsuinfo@nsuok.edu • **CEEB Code:** 6485
Fax: 918-458-2342 • **ACT Code:** 3408

This public school was founded in 1846. It has a 200-acre campus.

RATINGS

Admissions Selectivity Rating: 76   **Fire Safety Rating:** 60*   **Green Rating:** 60*

STUDENTS AND FACULTY

Enrollment: 7,036. **Student Body:** 61% female, 39% male, 6% out-of-state, 2% international (41 countries represented). Asian 2%, African American 4%, Caucasian 49%, Hispanic 5%, Native American 20%, Pacific Islander <1%, Two or more races 17%, Race unknown 2%. **Retention and Graduation:** 62% freshmen return for sophomore year. 12% freshmen graduate within 4 years. 26% freshmen graduate within 6 years. **Faculty:** Student/faculty ratio 17:1. 306 full-time faculty, 77% hold PhDs, 21% are are members of minority groups, 51% are women.

ACADEMICS

Degrees: bachelor's, master's, postbachelor's certificate, post-master's certificate. **Classes:** Most classes have 20-29 students. Most lab/discussion sessions have 10-19 students. **Most popular majors:** Elementary Education and Teaching; Psychology; Accounting. **Special Study Options:** cooperative education program, distance learning, double major, dual enrollment, honors program, independent study, student-designed major, weekend college. **Honors Programs:** NSU Honors Program: The Honors Program at NSU is a challenging educational option for academically talented students who enjoy learning. Honor students work with distinguished faculty members and peers in enhanced courses, pursue independent research, and participate in co-curricular cultural experiences. NSU President's Leadership Class: The President's Leadership Class is a unique scholarship/leadership program designed to identify and cultivate outstanding potential in selected freshmen entering NSU. Membership in the PLC allows students to develop close associations with University administrators, meet scholars and dignitaries who frequently visit campus, take advantage of some of the most talented faculty members at NSU who teach special sections of selected required courses, and receive scholarship assistance which includes a tuition waiver and a stipend. The PLC Scholarship is renewable for four years if members maintain high academic standards while exercising practical leadership in University activities. **Disability Services:** Special programs offered to physically disabled students, including note-taking services, reader services, tape recorders, tutors. **Career Services:** Alumni services, Career/job search classes, Career assessment.

FACILITIES

Housing: Coed dorms, special housing for disabled students, fraternity/sorority housing, apartments for married students, apartments for single students. **Computers:** Administrative functions (other than registration) can be performed online.

CAMPUS LIFE

Environment: Rural. **Activities:** Choral groups, concert band, dance, drama/theater, jazz band, literary magazine, marching band, music ensembles, musical theater, pep band, student government, student newspaper, symphony orchestra, television station 77 registered organizations, 9 honor societies, 5 religious organizations. 7 fraternities, 6 sororities. **Athletics (Intercollegiate):** *Men:* baseball, basketball, football, golf, soccer. *Women:* basketball, golf, soccer, softball, tennis. **On-Campus Highlights:** Seminary Hall, University Center, New Science Lab Building, NET Building, Seminary Suites.

ADMISSIONS

Freshman Academic Profile: Average high school GPA 3.4. 20% in top 10% of high school class, 47% in top 25% of high school class, 83% in top 50% of high school class. 95% from public high schools. ACT middle 50% range 19-23. Minimum paper TOEFL 500. **Basis for Candidate Selection:** *Very important factors considered include:* rigor of secondary school record, class rank, academic GPA, standardized test scores. *Other factors considered include:* interview, extracurricular activities, first generation, geographical residence, state residency, level of applicant's interest. **Freshman Admission Requirements:** High school diploma is required and GED is accepted. *Academic units required:* 4 English, 3 math, 3 science, 3 science labs, 2 social studies, 1 history, and 2 units from above areas or other academic areas. **Freshman Admission Statistics:** 1,512 applied, 91.80% admitted, 58% enrolled. **Transfer Admission Requirements:** college transcript(s), Minimum college GPA of 2.0 required. Lowest grade transferable D. **General Admission Information:** Application fee $25. Nonfall registration accepted. Admission may be deferred.

COSTS AND FINANCIAL AID

Annual in-state tuition $4,425. Annual out-of-state tuition $11,775. Required fees $1,122. Average book expense $1,200. **Required Forms and Deadlines:** FAFSA. **Notification of Awards:** Applicants will be notified of awards on a rolling basis beginning 3/1. **Types of Aid:** *Need-based scholarships/grants:* Federal Pell, FSEOG, State scholarships/grants, Private scholarships, College/university scholarship or grant aid from institutional funds. *Loans:* Direct Subsidized Stafford Loans, Direct Unsubsidized Stafford Loans, Direct PLUS loans, Federal Perkins Loans. *Student Employment:* Federal Work-Study Program available. Institutional employment available. **Financial Aid Statistics:** 94% needy freshmen, 86% needy undergrads receive need-based scholarship or grant aid. 31% freshmen, 15% undergrads receive non-need-based scholarship or grant aid. 80% freshmen, 89% undergrads receive need-based self-help aid. 4% freshmen, 3% undergrads receive athletic scholarships. 63% freshmen, 62% undergrads receive any aid. Average cumulative indebtedness $21,055. **Criteria for awarding aid:** *Non-need-based:* Academics, Alumni affiliation, Art, Athletics, Leadership, Minority status, Music/drama, Religious affiliation, State/district residency.

NORTHEASTERN UNIVERSITY

360 Huntington Avenue, Boston, MA 2115
Phone: 617-373-2200 • **Financial Aid Phone:** 617-373-3190
E-mail: l.bernstein@neu.edu • **CEEB Code:** 3667
Fax: 617-373-8780 • **Website:** www.northeastern.edu • **ACT Code:** 1880

This private school was founded in 1898. It has a 73-acre campus.

RATINGS

Admissions Selectivity Rating: 96   **Fire Safety Rating:** 94   **Green Rating:** 87

STUDENTS AND FACULTY

Enrollment: 17,795. **Student Body:** 51% female, 49% male, 72% out-of-state, 19% international (121 countries represented). Asian 13%, African American 4%, Caucasian 48%, Hispanic 7%, Native American <1%, Pacific Islander <1%, Two or more races 4%, Race unknown 5%.
Retention and Graduation: 97% freshmen return for sophomore year. 86% freshmen graduate within 6 years. **Faculty:** Student/faculty ratio 14:1. 1,259 full-time faculty, 95% hold PhDs, 16% are are members of minority groups, 42% are women.

ACADEMICS

Degrees: bachelor's, doctoral/professional, doctoral/research, master's, post-master's certificate. **Classes:** Most classes have 10-19 students. Most lab/discussion sessions have 10-19 students. **Most popular majors:** Engineering; Health Services/Allied Health/Health Sciences; Business/Commerce. **Special Study Options:** Accelerated program, cooperative education program, cross-registration, distance learning, double major, English as a Second Language (ESL), exchange student program (domestic), honors program, independent study, internships, liberal arts/career combination, student-designed major, study abroad, teacher certification program, ROTC. **Honors Programs:** The University Honors Program offers exceptionally motivated students an undergraduate experience charted by meeting academic challenge. The program includes demanding and challenging academic opportunities, connections to an active community of thinkers committed to making a difference, and Living and Learning in the Honors Program thematic communities. The University Honors Program frames opportunities that are intellectually rigorous; promotes global awareness and civic engagement; and empowers students. Combined degree programs: BA/JD, BA/MA, BA/MEng, BA/MArch, BS/MA, BS/DPT, BS/PharmD, BS/MS, BSN/MS. **Disability Services:** Special programs offered to physically disabled students, including note-taking services, reader services, tape recorders. **Career Services:** Alumni network, Alumni services, Career/job search classes, Career assessment, Internships, Regional alumni. A) "Best Internships/Career Services" (Princeton Review) (Ranked #1 in 2008, 2010 and 2012, as well as #2 in 2011 and 2013) B) We host one of the largest Career Fairs in the region each semester. Among the 5 fairs we offered the past year, over 500 employers participated. New York Life, Peace Corps and Raytheon are among the organizations which have participated in our Employer in Residence program. This fall we launched an Entrepreneur in Residence who provided office hour on a weekly basis. Our Employers in Residence hold regular office hours and advise students on career related topics such as resumes, interviews, job openings, and career paths. C) We also participate in 'Call to Serve' (Partnership for Public Service) which educates a new generation about the importance of strong civil service, helps re-establish links between federal agencies and campus, and provides students with information about federal jobs. In addition, our nuCAUSE (Creating Awareness and Understanding of Social Engagement Careers) initiative is designed to help students learn about social change careers in the non-profit, private and government sectors. Through programs that convene students, faculty, staff, employers and community organizations, nuCAUSE Careers provides information, resources, and connections to help students find work that is personally meaningful and that contributes to the common good. D.)We provide innovative programming that prepares students to be successful when they transition to life after graduation. Our signature Senior Career Conference (SCC) is a day-long conference-style event that offers workshops co-led by staff and employers, to help with the job search and other topics such as financial

planning, handling conflict, managing stress, salary negotiation, business etiquette, personal branding and professionalism. Students can also meet with more than 20 employers throughout the day for resume and cover letter reviews or job search advice. E.) Career Development offers special programming and resources for populations that are traditionally underserved including women, LGBTQ students, arts and sciences students, veterans and students with disabilities.
1. This year we launched sheLEADS, a semester-long series of workshops for women to promote leadership, self-advocacy, and professional development. 2. Additionally, we partnered with nuPRIDE, to ensure all staff receives Safe Zone training, created a vibrant web page, and conducted a workshop for LGBTQ students called 'Assessing your Readiness to Reveal.' The workshop discussed techniques for building a resume, ways to assess workplace fit, and means to critically think about revealing sexual orientation/gender identity at work. 3. For arts and sciences students (CAMD, SSH, COS) we have designed networking events including Non-profit Networking Night, Science Careers Forum, Media and Design Showcase, Global Careers Forum and Music and Creative Careers to connect students and employers in non-traditional ways. 4. For veterans, we have partnered with outside agencies and the Student Veterans Organization to offer Career Fairs, and specialized job search workshops and web resources. 5. Lastly, our nuConnect initiative, developed by Career Development, Coop and the Disability Resource Center, is a model for working with disabled students. Through a wrap-around counseling strategy and employer partners, we work to ensure workplace readiness and increased employment opportunities for our disabled student population.

FACILITIES

Housing: Coed dorms, special housing for disabled students, special housing for international students, apartments for single students, Wellness Housing, Theme Housing. 95% of campus accessible to physically diasbled. **Special Academic Facilities/Equipment:** John D. O'Bryant African American Institute, Egan Science/Engineering Research Center, Behrakis Health Sciences Center, Marine Science Center at Nahant, Center for Subsurfacing Sensing and Imaging Systems (CenSSIS), Center for Complex Network Research, Center for Drug Discovery, Barnett Institute of Chemical and Biological Analysis, Behrakis Health Sciences Center, Center for High Rate Nanomanufacturing, Center for Subsurface Sensing and Imaging Systems (CenSSIS), Egan Science/Engineering Research Center, Institute for Information Assurance, Institute on Urban Health Research, Dukakis Center for Urban and Regional Policy, John D. O'Bryant African-American Institute, Institute on Race and Justice, Institute for Global Innovation Management, Marine Science Center, Marino Recreation Center **Computers:** 100% of classrooms, 20% of dorms, 100% of libraries, 75% of dining areas, 100% of student union, 100% of common outdoor areas have wireless network access. Students can register for classes online. Administrative functions (other than registration) can be performed online.

CAMPUS LIFE

Environment: Metropolis. **Activities:** Choral groups, concert band, dance, drama/theater, jazz band, literary magazine, music ensembles, musical theater, pep band, radio station, student government, student newspaper, symphony orchestra, television station, yearbook, Campus Ministries, Student Organization, Model UN. 225 registered organizations, 15 honor societies, 20 religious organizations. 9 fraternities, 8 sororities. **Athletics (Intercollegiate):** *Men:* baseball, basketball, crew/rowing, cross-country, ice hockey, soccer, track/field (outdoor), track/field (indoor). *Women:* basketball, crew/rowing, cross-country, diving, field hockey, ice hockey, soccer, swimming, track/field (outdoor), track/field (indoor), volleyball. **On-Campus Highlights:** International Village, Curry Student Center, Marino Health and Fitness Center, Levine Marketplace & Stetson West Dining, Cyber Cafe. **Environmental Initiatives:** ACUPCC Presidents Climate Committee.

ADMISSIONS

Freshman Academic Profile: 76% in top 10% of high school class, 94% in top 25% of high school class, 99% in top 50% of high school class. **Reported SAT (pre-2016 redesign) scores:** SAT Math middle 50% range 680-770. SAT Critical Reading middle 50% range 650-740. SAT Writing middle 50% range 630-730. **Concordant SAT scores:** SAT EBRW middle 50% 690–760. SAT Math middle 50% range 710–780. ACT middle 50% range 31-34. Minimum internet-based TOEFL 92. **Basis for Candidate Selection:** *Very important factors considered include:* rigor of secondary school record, academic GPA, standardized test scores, application essay, recommendation(s). *Important factors considered include:* extracurricular activities, talent/ability, character/personal qualities, volunteer work, work experience. *Other factors considered include:* class rank, interview, first generation, geographical residence, racial/ethnic status, level of applicant's interest. **Freshman Admission Requirements:** High school diploma is required and GED is accepted. *Academic units required:* 4 English, 3 math, 3 science, 2 science labs, 2 foreign language, 3 social studies, 2 history. *Academic units recommended:* 4 math, 4 science. **Freshman Admission Statistics:** 51,063 applied, 28.88% admitted, 18% enrolled. **Transfer Admission Requirements:** college transcript(s), essay or personal statement, statement of good standing from prior institution(s).

Minimum college GPA of 2.0 required. Lowest grade transferable C. **General Admission Information:** Application fee $75. Regular application deadline 1/1. Regular notification 4/1. Nonfall registration accepted. Admission may be deferred for a maximum of 2 years.

COSTS AND FINANCIAL AID

Required Forms and Deadlines: FAFSA, CSS/Financial Aid PROFILE, Noncustodial PROFILE. **Notification of Awards:** Applicants will be notified of awards on or about 4/1. **Types of Aid:** *Need-based scholarships/grants:* Federal Pell, FSEOG, State scholarships/grants, Private scholarships, College/university scholarship or grant aid from institutional funds. *Loans:* Direct Subsidized Stafford Loans, Direct Unsubsidized Stafford Loans, Direct PLUS loans, Federal Perkins Loans, Federal Nursing Loans, State Loans. *Student Employment:* Federal Work-Study Program available. Institutional employment available. **Financial Aid Statistics:** 98% needy freshmen, 91% needy undergrads receive need-based scholarship or grant aid. 45% freshmen, 37% undergrads receive non-need-based scholarship or grant aid. 89% freshmen, 88% undergrads receive need-based self-help aid. 2% freshmen, 1% undergrads receive athletic scholarships. **Criteria for awarding aid:** *Non-need-based:* Academics, Athletics, Leadership.

See page 1010.

NORTHERN ARIZONA UNIVERSITY

PO Box 4084, Flagstaff, AZ 86011-4084
Phone: 928-523-5511 • **Financial Aid Phone:** 855-628-6333
E-mail: admissions@nau.edu • **CEEB Code:** 4006
Fax: 928-523-0226 • **Website:** www.nau.edu • **ACT Code:** 86

This public school was founded in 1899. It has a 740-acre campus.

RATINGS
Admissions Selectivity Rating: 80   **Fire Safety Rating:** 88   **Green Rating:** 96

STUDENTS AND FACULTY
Enrollment: 26,400. **Student Body:** 59% female, 41% male, 29% out-of-state, 4% international (72 countries represented). Asian 2%, African American 3%, Caucasian 58%, Hispanic 23%, Native American 3%, Pacific Islander <1%, Two or more races 6%, Race unknown 1%.
Retention and Graduation: 76% freshmen return for sophomore year. 36% freshmen graduate within 4 years. 53% freshmen graduate within 6 years.
Faculty: Student/faculty ratio 18:1. 1,081 full-time faculty, 0% hold PhDs, 16% are are members of minority groups, 50% are women.

ACADEMICS
Degrees: bachelor's, certificate, doctoral/professional, doctoral/research, doctoral, master's, postbachelor's certificate, post-master's certificate. **Classes:** Most classes have 20-29 students. Most lab/discussion sessions have 20-29 students. **Most popular majors:** Registered Nursing/Registered Nurse; Criminology; Biomedical Sciences. **Special Study Options:** Accelerated program, cooperative education program, distance learning, double major, dual enrollment, English as a Second Language (ESL), exchange student program (domestic), honors program, independent study, internships, study abroad, teacher certification program. **Honors Programs:** Honors Program Combined degree programs: BA/JD, BA/MA, BA/MEng, BS/MBS, BS/MS, BA/MS, BS/MEd, BS/MF. **Disability Services:** Special programs offered to physically disabled students, including note-taking services, reader services, tape recorders, tutors. **Career Services:** Alumni services, Career/job search classes, Career assessment, Internships.

FACILITIES
Housing: Coed dorms, men's dorms, special housing for international students, women's dorms, fraternity/sorority housing, apartments for married students, apartments for single students. 90% of campus accessible to physically disabled. **Special Academic Facilities/Equipment:** Art gallery, art and music studios, observatory, multidisciplinary research center, 4,000-acre experimental forest. **Computers:** 100% of classrooms, 100% of dorms, 100% of libraries, 100% of dining areas, 100% of student union, 25% of common outdoor areas have wireless network access. Students can register for classes online. Administrative functions (other than registration) can be performed online.

CAMPUS LIFE
Environment: Town. **Activities:** Choral groups, concert band, dance, drama/theater, jazz band, marching band, music ensembles, musical theater, opera, radio station, student government, student newspaper, symphony orchestra, television station, yearbook, Campus Ministries, Student Organization. 193 registered organizations, 20 honor societies, 7 religious organizations. 14 fraternities, 9 sororities. **Athletics (Intercollegiate):** *Men:* basketball,

cheerleading, cross-country, football, tennis, track/field (outdoor). *Women:* basketball, cheerleading, cross-country, diving, golf, soccer, swimming, tennis, track/field (outdoor), volleyball. **On-Campus Highlights:** University Union, NAU Dome, Wall Aquatic Center, Cline Library, Old Main. **Environmental Initiatives:** Green Building commitment.

ADMISSIONS
Freshman Academic Profile: Average high school GPA 3.6. 21% in top 10% of high school class, 51% in top 25% of high school class, 83% in top 50% of high school class. **Reported SAT (pre-2016 redesign) scores:** SAT Math middle 50% range 470-580. SAT Critical Reading middle 50% range 470-580. SAT Writing middle 50% range 450-560. **Concordant SAT scores:** SAT EBRW middle 50% 510–630. SAT Math middle 50% range 510–600. ACT middle 50% range 20-25. Minimum internet-based TOEFL 70. Minimum paper TOEFL 525. **Basis for Candidate Selection:** *Important factors considered include:* rigor of secondary school record, class rank, academic GPA, standardized test scores. **Freshman Admission Requirements:** High school diploma is required and GED is accepted. *Academic units required:* 4 English, 4 math, 3 science, 3 science labs, 2 foreign language, 1 social studies, 1 history, and 1 unit from above areas or other academic areas. **Freshman Admission Statistics:** 36,511 applied, 78.04% admitted, 20% enrolled. Minimum college GPA of 2.0 required. Lowest grade transferable C. **General Admission Information:** Application fee $25. Priority deadline 3/1. Nonfall registration accepted. Admission may be deferred for a maximum of One Term.

COSTS AND FINANCIAL AID
Average book expense $1,000. **Required Forms and Deadlines:** FAFSA. **Notification of Awards:** Applicants will be notified of awards on a rolling basis beginning 2/1. **Types of Aid:** *Need-based scholarships/grants:* Federal Pell, FSEOG, State scholarships/grants, Private scholarships, College/university scholarship or grant aid from institutional funds, Federal Nursing Scholarships. *Loans:* Direct Subsidized Stafford Loans, Direct Unsubsidized Stafford Loans, Direct PLUS loans, Federal Perkins Loans, Federal Nursing Loans, State Loans, College/university loans from institutional funds. *Student Employment:* Federal Work-Study Program available. Institutional employment available. **Financial Aid Statistics:** 67% needy freshmen, 69% needy undergrads receive need-based scholarship or grant aid. 77% freshmen, 54% undergrads receive non-need-based scholarship or grant aid. 60% freshmen, 67% undergrads receive need-based self-help aid. 1% freshmen, 1% undergrads receive athletic scholarships. 84% freshmen, 75% undergrads receive any aid. 63% undergrads borrow to pay for school. Average cumulative indebtedness $29,311. **Criteria for awarding aid:** *Need-based:* Academics, Art, Leadership, Minority status, Music/drama. *Non-need-based:* Academics, Alumni affiliation, Art, Athletics, Leadership, Minority status, Music/drama, State/district residency.

NORTHERN ILLINOIS UNIVERSITY

Office of Admissions, DeKalb, IL 60115-2857
Phone: 815-753-0446 • **Financial Aid Phone:** 815-753-1395
E-mail: admissions-info@niu.edu • **CEEB Code:** 1559
Fax: 815-753-1783 • **Website:** www.reg.niu.edu • **ACT Code:** 1102

This public school was founded in 1895. It has a 546-acre campus.

RATINGS
Admissions Selectivity Rating: 80   **Fire Safety Rating:** 60*   **Green Rating:** 60*

STUDENTS AND FACULTY
Enrollment: 14,036. **Student Body:** 49% female, 51% male, 3% out-of-state, 2% international. Asian 5%, African American 16%, Caucasian 56%, Hispanic 17%, Native American <1%, Pacific Islander <1%, Two or more races 4%, Race unknown 1%.
Retention and Graduation: 73% freshmen return for sophomore year. 23% freshmen graduate within 4 years. 47% freshmen graduate within 6 years. 16% grads pursue arts and sciences degrees. 3% grads pursue law degrees. 51% grads pursue business degrees. 1% grads pursue medical degrees. **Faculty:** Student/faculty ratio 15:1. 832 full-time faculty, 82% hold PhDs, 14% are are members of minority groups, 46% are women.

ACADEMICS
Degrees: bachelor's, master's. **Classes:** Most classes have 20-29 students. Most lab/discussion sessions have 20-29 students. **Special Study Options:** cooperative education program, distance learning, double major, dual enrollment, external degree program, honors program, independent study, internships, liberal arts/career combination, student-designed major, study abroad, teacher certification program. Combined degree programs: BA/JD. **Disability Services:** Special programs offered to physically disabled students, including note-taking services, tape recorders, tutors. **Career Services:** Alumni

network, Alumni services, Career/job search classes, Internships, Regional alumni. Comprehensive internship and Cooperative ed. program.

FACILITIES
Housing: Coed dorms, special housing for disabled students, special housing for international students, fraternity/sorority housing, apartments for married studentsQuiet and alcohol-free lifestyle floors, 21 and over/graduates student floors, honors floors. Fllors with visitation policies, computer science residential program. 90% of campus accessible to physically diasbled. **Special Academic Facilities/Equipment:** Art and anthropology museums, plant molecular biology center. **Computers:** Students can register for classes online.

CAMPUS LIFE
Environment: Rural. **Activities:** Choral groups, concert band, dance, drama/theater, jazz band, marching band, opera, radio station, student government, student newspaper, student-run film society, symphony orchestra, television station 200 registered organizations, 13 religious organizations. 22 fraternities, 14 sororities. **Athletics (Intercollegiate):** *Men:* baseball, basketball, diving, football, golf, soccer, swimming, tennis, wrestling. *Women:* basketball, cross-country, golf, gymnastics, soccer, softball, swimming, tennis, volleyball. **On-Campus Highlights:** Barsema Hall, Convocation Center, Holmes Student Center, Campus Life Building, Recreation Center.

ADMISSIONS
Freshman Academic Profile: 12% in top 10% of high school class, 36% in top 25% of high school class, 71% in top 50% of high school class. ACT middle 50% range 19-25. Minimum paper TOEFL 525. **Basis for Candidate Selection:** *Very important factors considered include:* rigor of secondary school record, class rank, standardized test scores. *Other factors considered include:* application essay, recommendation(s), interview, extracurricular activities, talent/ability, racial/ethnic status. **Freshman Admission Requirements:** High school diploma is required and GED is accepted. *Academic units required:* 4 English, 2 math, 2 science, 1 science lab, 1 foreign language, 2 social studies, 1 history. *Academic units recommended:* 4 math, 4 science, 2 science labs, 2 foreign language, 3 social studies. **Freshman Admission Statistics:** 14,980 applied, 51.84% admitted, 23% enrolled. **Transfer Admission Requirements:** college transcript(s), Minimum college GPA of 2.0 required. Lowest grade transferable c. **General Admission Information:** Application fee $40. Priority deadline 3/1. Regular application deadline 8/1. Nonfall registration accepted.

COSTS AND FINANCIAL AID
Annual in-state tuition $9,466. Annual out-of-state tuition $18,931. Room and board $9,670. Required fees $2,758. Average book expense $1,400. **Required Forms and Deadlines:** FAFSA, Institution's own financial aid form, Noncustodial PROFILE. **Notification of Awards:** Applicants will be notified of awards on a rolling basis beginning 4/15. **Types of Aid:** *Need-based scholarships/grants:* Federal Pell, FSEOG, State scholarships/grants, Private scholarships, College/university scholarship or grant aid from institutional funds, Federal Nursing Scholarships. *Loans:* Federal Perkins Loans. *Student Employment:* Federal Work-Study Program available. Institutional employment available. **Financial Aid Statistics:** 99% needy freshmen, 83% needy undergrads receive need-based scholarship or grant aid. 6% freshmen, 3% undergrads receive non-need-based scholarship or grant aid. 87% freshmen, 92% undergrads receive need-based self-help aid. 2% freshmen, 2% undergrads receive athletic scholarships. 81% freshmen, 70% undergrads receive any aid. 78% undergrads borrow to pay for school. Average cumulative indebtedness $34,713. **Criteria for awarding aid:** *Need-based:* Academics. *Non-need-based:* Academics, Alumni affiliation, Art, Athletics, Leadership, Music/drama.

NORTHERN KENTUCKY UNIVERSITY

Administrative Center 401, Highland Heights, KY 41099
Financial Aid Phone: 859-572-6437
E-mail: admitnku@nku.edu • **CEEB Code:** 1574
Website: www.nku.edu • **ACT Code:** 1566

This public school was founded in 1968. It has a 397-acre campus.

RATINGS
Admissions Selectivity Rating: 76   **Fire Safety Rating:** 89   **Green Rating:** 76

STUDENTS AND FACULTY
Enrollment: 11,302. **Student Body:** 55% female, 45% male, 31% out-of-state, 3% international (42 countries represented). Asian 1%, African American 7%, Caucasian 82%, Hispanic 3%, Native American <1%, Pacific Islander <1%, Two or more races 2%, Race unknown 1%.
Retention and Graduation: 69% freshmen return for sophomore year. 16% freshmen graduate within 4 years. 40% freshmen graduate within 6 years.

Faculty: Student/faculty ratio 19:1. 583 full-time faculty, 69% hold PhDs, 13% are are members of minority groups, 53% are women. 0% of classes are taught by teaching assistants.

ACADEMICS
Degrees: associate, bachelor's, certificate, doctoral/professional, doctoral, master's, postbachelor's certificate, post-master's certificate. **Classes:** Most classes have 20-29 students. Most lab/discussion sessions have 10-19 students. **Most popular majors:** Business/Commerce; Health Services/Allied Health/Health Sciences; Journalism. **Special Study Options:** cooperative education program, cross-registration, distance learning, double major, dual enrollment, exchange student program (domestic), honors program, independent study, internships, liberal arts/career combination, study abroad, teacher certification program, weekend college, Web-based Programs. **Honors Programs:** The NKU Honors Program provides qualified students a 21-hour minor, which includes 15 semester hours of seminars, each having a maximum enrollment of 15 students, plus 6 semester hours for completing the Honors Thesis. At the core of the Honors experience, the seminars emphasize discussion and discovery of ideas. NKU's Honors Program is university-wide. The program showcases open-ended seminars not conforming to the boundaries traditionally dividing fields of experise. Honors learning affords the intellectual challenges of interdisciplinary education. Combined degree programs: MBA/JD. **Disability Services:** Special programs offered to physically disabled students, including note-taking services, reader services, tape recorders, tutors. **Career Services:** Alumni services, Career/job search classes, Career assessment, Internships. We are proud of all our experiential learning/co-op/internship programs. All these opportunities combine learning with work and offer a unique experience for career exploration. The essential component is that the student is working with structure and intentional objectives to learn about a career field.

FACILITIES
Housing: Coed dorms, special housing for disabled students, men's dorms, women's dorms, cooperative housing, apartments for single studentsOne-Third of all college housing accessible to handicapped. 100% of campus accessible to physically diasbled. **Special Academic Facilities/Equipment:** Art gallery, biology, geology, and anthropology museums, research/technical center, two electron microscopes. **Computers:** Students can register for classes online. Administrative functions (other than registration) can be performed online.

CAMPUS LIFE
Environment: Metropolis. **Activities:** Choral groups, concert band, dance, drama/theater, jazz band, literary magazine, music ensembles, musical theater, opera, pep band, radio station, student government, student newspaper, symphony orchestra, television station 125 registered organizations, 14 honor societies, 9 religious organizations. 8 fraternities, 8 sororities. **Athletics (Intercollegiate):** *Men:* baseball, basketball, cheerleading, cross-country, golf, soccer, tennis. *Women:* basketball, cheerleading, cross-country, golf, soccer, softball, tennis, volleyball. **On-Campus Highlights:** Natural Science Center, University Suites (housing), Starbucks Cafe, Albright Health Center, a full service U.S. Bank Branch. **Environmental Initiatives:** Creation of the Department of Energy Management in 2015 and the sequential hire of the Director of Energy Management and Sustainability Manager in that same year.

ADMISSIONS
Freshman Academic Profile: Average high school GPA 3.3. 11% in top 10% of high school class, 32% in top 25% of high school class, 64% in top 50% of high school class. **Reported SAT (pre-2016 redesign) scores:** SAT Math middle 50% range 460-572.5. SAT Critical Reading middle 50% range 460-590. SAT Writing middle 50% range 440-548. **Concordant SAT scores:** SAT EBRW middle 50% 500–630. SAT Math middle 50% range 500–590. ACT middle 50% range 20-26. Minimum internet-based TOEFL 79. Minimum paper TOEFL 550. **Basis for Candidate Selection:** *Very important factors considered include:* rigor of secondary school record, class rank, academic GPA, standardized test scores. *Other factors considered include:* application essay, recommendation(s), talent/ability, first generation. **Freshman Admission Requirements:** High school diploma is required and GED is accepted. *Academic units required:* 4 English, 3 math, 3 science, 2 foreign language, 3 social studies, 3 history. *Academic units recommended:* 4 English, 4 math, 3 science, 2 foreign language, 3 social studies, 3 history, 1 computer science. **Freshman Admission Statistics:** 7,397 applied, 91.89% admitted, 33% enrolled. **Transfer Admission Requirements:** college transcript(s), Minimum college GPA of 2.0 required. Lowest grade transferable D. **General Admission Information:** Application fee $40. Priority deadline 5/1. Regular application deadline 8/15. Nonfall registration accepted. Admission may be deferred for a maximum of 1 year.

COSTS AND FINANCIAL AID
Required Forms and Deadlines: FAFSA. **Notification of Awards:** Applicants will be notified of awards on a rolling basis beginning 3/15. **Types of Aid:** *Need-based scholarships/grants:* Federal Pell, FSEOG, State scholarships/grants, Private scholarships, College/university scholarship or grant aid from institutional funds. *Loans:* Direct Subsidized Stafford Loans, Direct

Unsubsidized Stafford Loans, Direct PLUS loans, Federal Perkins Loans, Federal Nursing Loans, College/university loans from institutional funds. *Student Employment:* Federal Work-Study Program available. Institutional employment available. **Financial Aid Statistics:** 58% needy freshmen, 59% needy undergrads receive need-based scholarship or grant aid. 75% freshmen, 57% undergrads receive non-need-based scholarship or grant aid. 88% freshmen, 90% undergrads receive need-based self-help aid. 3% freshmen, 3% undergrads receive athletic scholarships. 69% undergrads borrow to pay for school. Average cumulative indebtedness $27,285. **Criteria for awarding aid:** *Non-need-based:* Academics, Alumni affiliation, Art, Athletics, Leadership, Music/drama, State/district residency.

NORTHERN MICHIGAN UNIVERSITY

1401 Presque Isle Avenue, Marquette, MI 49855
Phone: 906-227-2650 • **Financial Aid Phone:** 800-682-9797
E-mail: admiss@nmu.edu • **CEEB Code:** 1560
Fax: 906-227-1747 • **Website:** www.nmu.edu • **ACT Code:** 2038

This public school was founded in 1899. It has a 350-acre campus.

RATINGS
Admissions Selectivity Rating: 73   **Fire Safety Rating:** 75   **Green Rating:** 78

STUDENTS AND FACULTY
Enrollment: 7,977. **Student Body:** 53% female, 47% male, 19% out-of-state, 1% international (30 countries represented). Asian 1%, African American 2%, Caucasian 81%, Hispanic 1%, Native American 2%, Pacific Islander <1%, Two or more races 2%, Race unknown 11%.
Retention and Graduation: 72% freshmen return for sophomore year. 20% freshmen graduate within 4 years. 47% freshmen graduate within 6 years.

ACADEMICS
Degrees: associate, bachelor's, certificate, diploma, master's, postbachelor's certificate, post-master's certificate, terminal, transfer. **Classes:** Most classes have 20-29 students. **Most popular majors:** Art/Art Studies; Criminal Justice/Safety Studies; Nursing Science. **Special Study Options:** distance learning, double major, dual enrollment, English as a Second Language (ESL), honors program, independent study, internships, liberal arts/career combination, student-designed major, study abroad, teacher certification program, weekend college. **Honors Programs:** Honors Program for eligible freshmen and transfer students. **Disability Services:** Special programs offered to physically disabled students, including note-taking services, reader services, tape recorders, tutors. **Career Services:** Alumni network, Career/job search classes, Internships. The offering of internships is specific to each academic department.

FACILITIES
Housing: Coed dorms, special housing for disabled students, apartments for married students, apartments for single students, Wellness Housing, Theme Housing. 100% of campus accessible to physically disabled. **Special Academic Facilities/Equipment:** Seaborg Science Center, New Science facility, new and remodeled Music and Art and Design instructional rooms, DeVos Art Gallery. **Computers:** 100% of classrooms, 100% of dorms, 100% of libraries, 100% of dining areas, 100% of student union, 100% of common outdoor areas have wireless network access. Students can register for classes online. Administrative functions (other than registration) can be performed online.

CAMPUS LIFE
Environment: Village. **Activities:** Choral groups, concert band, dance, drama/theater, jazz band, literary magazine, marching band, music ensembles, musical theater, opera, pep band, radio station, student government, student newspaper, student-run film society, symphony orchestra, television station, Campus Ministries, Student Organization, Model UN. 308 registered organizations, 11 honor societies, 19 religious organizations. 3 fraternities, 4 sororities. **Athletics (Intercollegiate):** *Men:* basketball, football, golf, ice hockey, skiingnordiccrosscountry. *Women:* basketball, cross-country, diving, skiing (nordic/cross-country), soccer, swimming, track/field (outdoor), track/field (indoor), volleyball. **On-Campus Highlights:** Hedgcock Student Service Center, Superior Dome, New Science Facility, Market Place Dining Facility, De Vos Art Galleries, The Starbucks coffee lounge located in the library is a very popular place and doubles as a study lounge. **Environmental Initiatives:** Northern is a member of the Association for the Advancement of Sustainability in Higher Education and USGBC.

ADMISSIONS
Freshman Academic Profile: Average high school GPA 3.1. ACT middle 50% range 19-24. Minimum internet-based TOEFL 61. Minimum paper TOEFL 500. **Basis for Candidate Selection:** *Very important factors considered include:* academic GPA, standardized test scores. **Freshman**

Admission Requirements: High school diploma is required and GED is accepted. *Academic units recommended:* 4 English, 4 math, 4 science, 2 foreign language, 4 social studies. **Freshman Admission Statistics:** 6,841 applied, 67.77% admitted, 36% enrolled. **Transfer Admission Requirements:** college transcript(s), statement of good standing from prior institution(s). Minimum college GPA of 2.0 required. Lowest grade transferable C-. **General Admission Information:** Application fee $30. Nonfall registration accepted. Admission may be deferred for a maximum of 1 year.

COSTS AND FINANCIAL AID
Annual in-state tuition $8,646. Annual out-of-state tuition $13,542. Room and board $8,404. Required fees $64. Average book expense $900. **Required Forms and Deadlines:** FAFSA. **Notification of Awards:** Applicants will be notified of awards on a rolling basis beginning 4/1. **Types of Aid:** *Need-based scholarships/grants:* Federal Pell, FSEOG, State scholarships/grants, Private scholarships, College/university scholarship or grant aid from institutional funds. *Loans:* Direct Subsidized Stafford Loans, Direct Unsubsidized Stafford Loans, Direct PLUS loans, Federal Perkins Loans. *Student Employment:* Federal Work-Study Program available. Institutional employment available. **Financial Aid Statistics:** 60% needy freshmen, 61% needy undergrads receive need-based scholarship or grant aid. 46% freshmen, 37% undergrads receive non-need-based scholarship or grant aid. 79% freshmen, 86% undergrads receive need-based self-help aid. 1% freshmen, 0% undergrads receive athletic scholarships. **Criteria for awarding aid:** *Non-need-based:* Academics, Art, Athletics, Leadership, Minority status, Music/drama, Religious affiliation, State/district residency.

NORTHERN STATE UNIVERSITY

1200 South Jay Street, Aberdeen, SD 57401-7198
Phone: 605-626-2544 • **Financial Aid Phone:** 605-626-2640
E-mail: admission2@northern.edu • **CEEB Code:** 6487
Fax: 605-626-2531 • **Website:** www.northern.edu • **ACT Code:** 3916

This public school was founded in 1901. It has a 72-acre campus.

RATINGS
Admissions Selectivity Rating: 73   **Fire Safety Rating:** 79   **Green Rating:** 60*

STUDENTS AND FACULTY
Enrollment: 1,693. **Student Body:** 57% female, 43% male, 18% out-of-state, 4% international (35 countries represented). Asian 1%, African American 2%, Caucasian 84%, Hispanic 3%, Native American 2%, Pacific Islander <1%, Two or more races 2%, Race unknown <1%.
Retention and Graduation: 67% freshmen return for sophomore year. 20% freshmen graduate within 4 years. 33% grads go on to further study within 1 year. **Faculty:** Student/faculty ratio 21:1. 90 full-time faculty, 86% hold PhDs, 8% are are members of minority groups, 37% are women. 0% of classes are taught by teaching assistants.

ACADEMICS
Degrees: associate, bachelor's, certificate, master's, postbachelor's certificate. **Classes:** Most classes have 10-19 students. **Most popular majors:** Elementary Education and Teaching; Sociology; Business/Commerce. **Special Study Options:** Accelerated program, cooperative education program, cross-registration, distance learning, double major, dual enrollment, English as a Second Language (ESL), exchange student program (domestic), external degree program, honors program, independent study, internships, liberal arts/career combination, student-designed major, study abroad, teacher certification program, weekend college, Business E-Learning Certification. **Honors Programs:** Honors Program Combined degree programs: Accellerated Nursing w/ SDSU; Ag/Banking w/ SDSU. **Disability Services:** Special programs offered to physically disabled students, including note-taking services, reader services, tape recorders, tutors. **Career Services:** Alumni network, Alumni services, Career/job search classes, Career assessment, Internships, Regional alumni, School of Business Programs, School of Education Programs.

FACILITIES
Housing: Coed dorms, men's dorms, women's dorms, apartments for married students, apartments for single students. 90% of campus accessible to physically diasbled. **Special Academic Facilities/Equipment:** State-Wide E-Learning Center; Art galleries. **Computers:** 100% of classrooms, 100% of dorms, 100% of libraries, 100% of dining areas, 100% of student union, have wireless network access. Students can register for classes online. Administrative functions (other than registration) can be performed online.

CAMPUS LIFE
Environment: Rural. **Activities:** Choral groups, concert band, dance, drama/theater, jazz band, marching band, music ensembles, musical theater,

pep band, student government, student newspaper, symphony orchestra, television station, yearbook, Campus Ministries, Student Organization. 100 registered organizations, 5 honor societies, 6 religious organizations. **Athletics (Intercollegiate):** *Men:* baseball, basketball, cheerleading, cross-country, football, golf, track/field (outdoor), track/field (indoor), wrestling. *Women:* basketball, cheerleading, cross-country, golf, soccer, softball, swimming, tennis, track/field (outdoor), track/field (indoor), volleyball. **On-Campus Highlights:** NSU Student Center, NSU State-Wide E-Learning Center, NSU Barnett Athletic Center, NSU Johnson Fine Arts Center, NSU International Center of Excellence.

ADMISSIONS

Freshman Academic Profile: Average high school GPA 3.3. 7% in top 10% of high school class, 20% in top 25% of high school class, 60% in top 50% of high school class. **Reported SAT (pre-2016 redesign) scores:** SAT Math middle 50% range 370-580. SAT Critical Reading middle 50% range 420-540. **Concordant SAT scores:** SAT Math middle 50% range 410–600. ACT middle 50% range 19-25. Minimum internet-based TOEFL 61. Minimum paper TOEFL 525. **Basis for Candidate Selection:** *Very important factors considered include:* rigor of secondary school record, class rank, standardized test scores. *Other factors considered include:* recommendation(s), interview, extracurricular activities, talent/ability, character/personal qualities. **Freshman Admission Requirements:** High school diploma is required and GED is accepted. *Academic units required:* 4 English, 3 math, 3 science, 3 science labs, 3 social studies. **Freshman Admission Statistics:** 1,379 applied, 82.89% admitted, 32% enrolled. **Transfer Admission Requirements:** High school transcript, college transcript(s), statement of good standing from prior institution(s). Minimum college GPA of 2.0 required. Lowest grade transferable C. **General Admission Information:** Application fee $20. Nonfall registration accepted. Admission may be deferred.

COSTS AND FINANCIAL AID

Annual in-state tuition $3,993. Annual out-of-state tuition $5,992. Room and board $6,942. Required fees $4,050. Average book expense $1,200. **Required Forms and Deadlines:** FAFSA. **Notification of Awards:** Applicants will be notified of awards on a rolling basis beginning 4/15. **Types of Aid:** *Need-based scholarships/grants:* Federal Pell, FSEOG, State scholarships/grants. *Loans:* Direct Subsidized Stafford Loans, Direct Unsubsidized Stafford Loans, Direct PLUS loans, Federal Perkins Loans, College/university loans from institutional funds. *Student Employment:* Federal Work-Study Program available. Institutional employment available. **Financial Aid Statistics:** 92% needy freshmen, 83% needy undergrads receive need-based scholarship or grant aid. 8% freshmen, 6% undergrads receive non-need-based scholarship or grant aid. 86% freshmen, 88% undergrads receive need-based self-help aid. 12% freshmen, 9% undergrads receive athletic scholarships. **Criteria for awarding aid:** *Need-based:* Minority status. *Non-need-based:* Academics, Art, Athletics, Leadership, Minority status, Music/drama.

NORTHLAND COLLEGE

1411 Ellis Avenue, Ashland, WI 54806-3999
Phone: 715-682-1224 • **Financial Aid Phone:** 715-682-1254
E-mail: admit@northland.edu • **CEEB Code:** 1561
Fax: 715-682-1258 • **Website:** www.northland.edu • **ACT Code:** 4624

This private school, affiliated with the United Church of Christ Church, was founded in 1892. It has a 130-acre campus.

RATINGS

Admissions Selectivity Rating: 85   **Fire Safety Rating:** 80   **Green Rating:** 95

STUDENTS AND FACULTY

Enrollment: 562. **Student Body:** 51% female, 49% male, 50% out-of-state, 3% international (4 countries represented). Asian 0%, African American 1%, Caucasian 83%, Hispanic 5%, Native American 3%, Pacific Islander 0%, Two or more races 1%, Race unknown 3%.
Retention and Graduation: 77% freshmen return for sophomore year. 45% freshmen graduate within 4 years. 50% freshmen graduate within 6 years.
Faculty: Student/faculty ratio 10:1. 54 full-time faculty, 87% hold PhDs, 2% are are members of minority groups, 37% are women. 0% of classes are taught by teaching assistants.

ACADEMICS

Degrees: bachelor's. **Classes:** Most classes have 10-19 students. Most lab/discussion sessions have 10-19 students. **Most popular majors:** Natural Resources and Conservation; Biology/Biological Sciences; Teacher Education, Multiple Levels. **Special Study Options:** distance learning, double major, dual enrollment, exchange student program (domestic), honors program,

independent study, internships, student-designed major, teacher certification program, 3-2 cooperative programs in Forestry and Engineering with Michigan Technological University and Washington University Eco League consortium with 6 environmental liberal arts colleges around the country (Prescott, Green Mountain, Alaska Pacific University, Antioch College, College of the Atlantic, Northland College)engaging in student semester exchanges. Combined degree programs: 3-2 Pre-engineering. **Disability Services:** Special programs offered to physically disabled students, including note-taking services, reader services, tape recorders, tutors. **Career Services:** Alumni network, Career assessment, Internships.

FACILITIES

Housing: Coed dorms, women's dorms, cooperative housing, apartments for single students, Theme Housing. **Special Academic Facilities/Equipment:** Native American museum, language lab, field stations in nearby national forest, observatory. **Computers:** 20% of classrooms, 20% of dorms, 100% of libraries, 100% of dining areas, 100% of student union, 75% of common outdoor areas have wireless network access. Students can register for classes online. Administrative functions (other than registration) can be performed online.

CAMPUS LIFE

Environment: Village. **Activities:** Choral groups, concert band, drama/theater, jazz band, music ensembles, radio station, student government, student newspaper, symphony orchestra, yearbook, Student Organization. 30 registered organizations, 1 honor society, 2 religious organizations. **Athletics (Intercollegiate):** *Men:* baseball, basketball, cross-country, ice hockey, skiing (nordic/cross-country), soccer. *Women:* basketball, cross-country, skiing (nordic/cross-country), soccer, softball, volleyball. **On-Campus Highlights:** Campus Center, Science Center, The Fire Ring, The Environmental Living and Learning Center, The Ravine. **Environmental Initiatives:** Extensive local food systems work including an 80% local food purchasing goal (at 40% currently); creating a food laboratory that will be used to process and store local fruits and vegetables to help meet this 80% goal, provide work experience to students and community in food processing, and will bolster sustainable food networks for rural communities; and the creation of a sophisticated composting facility to advance our ability to process up to a ton compost a day from a wide variety of community and institutional sources.

ADMISSIONS

Freshman Academic Profile: Average high school GPA 3.3. 17% in top 10% of high school class, 48% in top 25% of high school class, 79% in top 50% of high school class. ACT middle 50% range 21-26. Minimum paper TOEFL 525. **Basis for Candidate Selection:** *Very important factors considered include:* rigor of secondary school record. *Important factors considered include:* class rank, academic GPA, standardized test scores, application essay, recommendation(s). *Other factors considered include:* interview, extracurricular activities, talent/ability, character/personal qualities, first generation, alumni/ae relation, volunteer work, work experience, level of applicant's interest. **Freshman Admission Requirements:** High school diploma is required and GED is accepted. *Academic units required:* 4 English, 3 math, 3 science, 2 science labs, 3 social studies, 3 academic electives. *Academic units recommended:* 2 foreign language, 4 academic electives. **Freshman Admission Statistics:** 1,335 applied, 54.01% admitted, 23% enrolled. **Transfer Admission Requirements:** High school transcript, college transcript(s), essay or personal statement, statement of good standing from prior institution(s). Minimum college GPA of 2.0 required. Lowest grade transferable C-. **General Admission Information:** Priority deadline 12/1. Nonfall registration accepted. Admission may be deferred for a maximum of 2 years.

COSTS AND FINANCIAL AID

Annual tuition $33,640. Room and board $8,886. Required fees $1,517. Average book expense $800. **Required Forms and Deadlines:** FAFSA. **Notification of Awards:** Applicants will be notified of awards on a rolling basis beginning 3/1. **Types of Aid:** *Need-based scholarships/grants:* Federal Pell, FSEOG, State scholarships/grants, Private scholarships, College/university scholarship or grant aid from institutional funds. *Loans:* Direct Subsidized Stafford Loans, Direct Unsubsidized Stafford Loans, Direct PLUS loans, Federal Perkins Loans, State Loans. *Student Employment:* Federal Work-Study Program available. Institutional employment available. **Financial Aid Statistics:** 100% needy freshmen, 96% needy undergrads receive need-based scholarship or grant aid. 15% freshmen, 14% undergrads receive non-need-based scholarship or grant aid. 75% freshmen, 71% undergrads receive need-based self-help aid. 0% freshmen, 0% undergrads receive athletic scholarships. 98% freshmen, 99% undergrads receive any aid. 83% undergrads borrow to pay for school. Average cumulative indebtedness $34,144. **Criteria for awarding aid:** *Need-based:* Academics, Job skills, Minority status, Music/drama. *Non-need-based:* Academics, Alumni affiliation, Art, Job skills, Leadership, Minority status, Music/drama, Religious affiliation, State/district residency.

NORTHWEST NAZARENE UNIVERSITY

623 S. University Blvd., Nampa, ID 83686
Phone: 208-467-8000 • **Financial Aid Phone:** 208-467-8641
E-mail: admissions@nnu.edu • **CEEB Code:** 4544
Fax: 208-467-8645 • **Website:** www.nnu.edu • **ACT Code:** 924

This private school, affiliated with the Nazarene Church, was founded in 1913. It has a 85-acre campus.

RATINGS
Admissions Selectivity Rating: 85   **Fire Safety Rating:** 70   **Green Rating:** 60*

STUDENTS AND FACULTY
Enrollment: 1,145. **Student Body:** 59% female, 41% male, 51% out-of-state, 2% international (20 countries represented). Asian 2%, African American 1%, Caucasian 75%, Hispanic 7%, Native American 1%, Pacific Islander <1%, Two or more races 1%, Race unknown 12%.
Faculty: Student/faculty ratio 14:1. 103 full-time faculty, 73% hold PhDs, 6% are are members of minority groups, 45% are women. 0% of classes are taught by teaching assistants.

ACADEMICS
Degrees: bachelor's, doctoral/professional, master's, post-master's certificate. **Most popular majors:** Education Business/Commerce. **Special Study Options:** cooperative education program, cross-registration, distance learning, double major, English as a Second Language (ESL), exchange student program (domestic), honors program, independent study, internships, liberal arts/career combination, student-designed major, study abroad, teacher certification program, Many service and ministry programs and opportunities. Combined degree programs: 3-2 engineering program with any co-op institution. **Disability Services:** Special programs offered to physically disabled students, including reader services, tape recorders, tutors. **Career Services:** Alumni network, Career/job search classes, Internships, Regional alumni, On-campus interviews.

FACILITIES
Housing: Coed dorms, men's dorms, women's dorms, apartments for married students, apartments for single students, Off-campus housing owned the by University include rental homes and units. 70% of campus accessible to physically diasbled. **Computers:** 100% of classrooms, have wireless network access. Administrative functions (other than registration) can be performed online.

CAMPUS LIFE
Environment: City. **Activities:** Choral groups, concert band, drama/theater, jazz band, literary magazine, music ensembles, musical theater, pep band, student government, student newspaper, symphony orchestra, yearbook, Campus Ministries, Student Organization. 21 registered organizations, 6 honor societies, 8 religious organizations. **Athletics (Intercollegiate):** *Men:* baseball, basketball, cross-country, golf, soccer, track/field (outdoor), track/field (indoor). *Women:* basketball, cross-country, soccer, softball, track/field (outdoor), track/field (indoor), volleyball. **On-Campus Highlights:** Helstrom Business Center, The Brandt Center, Ford Hall, Johnson Sports Center, Student Center.

ADMISSIONS
Freshman Academic Profile: Average high school GPA 3.5. 29% in top 10% of high school class, 52% in top 25% of high school class, 81% in top 50% of high school class. **Reported SAT (pre-2016 redesign) scores:** SAT Math middle 50% range 470-620. SAT Critical Reading middle 50% range 470-600. SAT Writing middle 50% range 470-570. **Concordant SAT scores:** SAT EBRW middle 50% 530-640. SAT Math middle 50% range 510-640. ACT middle 50% range 21-27. Minimum paper TOEFL 500. **Basis for Candidate Selection:** *Very important factors considered include:* class rank, academic GPA, standardized test scores, character/personal qualities. *Other factors considered include:* rigor of secondary school record, recommendation(s), extracurricular activities, talent/ability, alumni/ae relation, religious affiliation/commitment. **Freshman Admission Requirements:** High school diploma is required and GED is accepted. *Academic units recommended:* 4 English, 3 math, 3 science, 2 foreign language, 3 history. **Freshman Admission Statistics:** 984 applied, 69.00% admitted, 41% enrolled. **Transfer Admission Requirements:** college transcript(s), Minimum college GPA of 2.0 required. Lowest grade transferable C-. **General Admission Information:** Application fee $25. Priority deadline 3/1. Regular application deadline 8/15. Nonfall registration accepted. Admission may be deferred.

COSTS AND FINANCIAL AID
Annual tuition $26,150. Room and board $6,400. Required fees $400. Average book expense $1,160. **Required Forms and Deadlines:** FAFSA. **Notification of Awards:** Applicants will be notified of awards on a rolling basis beginning 4/1. **Types of Aid:** *Need-based scholarships/grants:* Federal Pell, FSEOG, State scholarships/grants, Private scholarships, College/university scholarship or grant aid from institutional funds. *Loans:* Direct Subsidized Stafford Loans, Direct Unsubsidized Stafford Loans, Direct PLUS loans, Federal Perkins Loans, College/university loans from institutional funds. *Student Employment:* Federal Work-Study Program available. Institutional employment available. **Financial Aid Statistics:** 100% needy freshmen, 95% needy undergrads receive need-based scholarship or grant aid. 14% freshmen, 8% undergrads receive non-need-based scholarship or grant aid. 72% freshmen, 79% undergrads receive need-based self-help aid. 9% freshmen, 9% undergrads receive athletic scholarships. **Criteria for awarding aid:** *Need-based:* Athletics, Leadership, Religious affiliation. *Non-need-based:* Academics, Alumni affiliation, Art, Athletics, Leadership, Minority status, Music/drama, Religious affiliation.

NORTHWESTERN COLLEGE (IA)

101 7th St SW, Orange City, IA 51041
Phone: 712-707-7130 • **Financial Aid Phone:** 712-707-7131
E-mail: admissions@nwciowa.edu • **CEEB Code:** 6490
Fax: 712-707-7164 • **Website:** www.nwciowa.edu • **ACT Code:** 1346

This private school, affiliated with the Reformed Church Church, was founded in 1882. It has a 100-acre campus.

RATINGS
Admissions Selectivity Rating: 84   **Fire Safety Rating:** 95   **Green Rating:** 60*

STUDENTS AND FACULTY
Enrollment: 1,076. **Student Body:** 56% female, 44% male, 45% out-of-state, 4% international (23 countries represented). Asian 1%, African American 2%, Caucasian 82%, Hispanic 5%, Native American <1%, Pacific Islander 0%, Two or more races 2%, Race unknown 5%.
Retention and Graduation: 82% freshmen return for sophomore year. 56% freshmen graduate within 4 years. 64% freshmen graduate within 6 years. 17% grads go on to further study within 1 year. **Faculty:** Student/faculty ratio 11:1. 82 full-time faculty, 83% hold PhDs, 5% are are members of minority groups, 39% are women. 0% of classes are taught by teaching assistants.

ACADEMICS
Degrees: bachelor's, certificate, master's, postbachelor's certifiate. **Classes:** Most classes have 10-19 students. **Most popular majors:** Education; Registered Nursing/Registered Nurse; Business/Commerce. **Special Study Options:** double major, English as a Second Language (ESL), honors program, independent study, internships, liberal arts/career combination, student-designed major, study abroad, teacher certification program, Off Campus Study Programs: American Studies Program (Washington, D.C.), AuSable Inst of Environmental Studies Program (Michigan), Los Angeles Film Studies Semester, Chicago Metropolitan Studies Program (Chicago), China Studies Program (Xiaman, China), Middle East Studies Program (Cairo, Egypt), Oxford Summer Program (Oxford, England), Romanian Studies Program, Russian Studies Program, Contemporary Music Center (Martha's Vineyard, MA), Latin American Studies Program (Costa Rica), Oxford Honours Programme (England), Trinity Christian College: Semester in Spain, and Creation Care Study Program. **Honors Programs:** Honors Program: Affords students an interdisciplinary approach to understanding perennial and contemporary issues, such as technology, war and peace, gender roles, work and calling, and humor. Affords students th eopportunity to delve more deeply into a topic of their choice, workinh with selected faculty members to complete a project that goes beyond the normal upper-division work at the college. Encourages graduate education by sponsoring trips to regional graduate schools and financially supporting graduate school applications. **Disability Services:** Special programs offered to physically disabled students, including note-taking services, reader services, tape recorders, tutors. **Career Services:** Alumni network, Alumni services, Career/job search classes, Career assessment, Internships. Northwestern's Career Development Center will help you prepare for and find an internship that matches your career interests and talent. Students intern in and around Orange City, as well as in their hometowns or elsewhere in the U.S. through off-campus programs in cities like Chicago, Los Angeles and Washington, D.C.

FACILITIES
Housing: special housing for disabled students, men's dorms, women's dorms, apartments for single students, Theme housing (i.e., Spanish house, etc.). 90% of campus accessible to physically diasbled. **Special Academic Facilities/Equipment:** Thea G Korver Visual Arts Center-Art Gallery; DeWitt Theatre Arts Center-Proscenium Theatre, Black Box Theatre, Costume Shop. **Computers:** 75% of classrooms, 30% of dorms, 100% of libraries, 100% of dining areas, 100% of student union, 30% of common outdoor areas have

wireless network access. Students can register for classes online. Administrative functions (other than registration) can be performed online.

CAMPUS LIFE

Environment: Rural. **Activities:** Choral groups, concert band, dance, drama/theater, jazz band, literary magazine, music ensembles, musical theater, pep band, student government, student newspaper, symphony orchestra, television station, yearbook. 30 registered organizations, 2 honor societies, 5 religious organizations. **Athletics (Intercollegiate):** *Men:* baseball, basketball, cheerleading, cross-country, football, golf, soccer, track/field (outdoor), track/field (indoor), wrestling. *Women:* basketball, cheerleading, cross-country, golf, soccer, softball, track/field (outdoor), track/field (indoor), volleyball. **On-Campus Highlights:** Rowenhorst Student Center, Bultman Center Gym, DeWitt Theatre Arts Center, Korver Visual Arts Center.

ADMISSIONS

Freshman Academic Profile: Average high school GPA 3.6. 24% in top 10% of high school class, 46% in top 25% of high school class, 78% in top 50% of high school class. 75% from public high schools. **Reported SAT (pre-2016 redesign) scores:** SAT Math middle 50% range 475-610. SAT Critical Reading middle 50% range 440-560. **Concordant SAT scores:** SAT Math middle 50% range 510–630. ACT middle 50% range 21-28. Minimum paper TOEFL 475. **Basis for Candidate Selection:** *Very important factors considered include:* rigor of secondary school record, class rank, standardized test scores. *Important factors considered include:* academic GPA, application essay, recommendation(s), interview, talent/ability, character/personal qualities, first generation, level of applicant's interest. *Other factors considered include:* extracurricular activities, religious affiliation/commitment. **Freshman Admission Requirements:** High school diploma is required and GED is accepted. *Academic units recommended:* 4 English, 3 math, 3 science, 3 foreign language, 3 social studies. **Freshman Admission Statistics:** 2,199 applied, 65.53% admitted, 20% enrolled. **Transfer Admission Requirements:** college transcript(s), Minimum college GPA of 2.2 required. Lowest grade transferable C. **General Admission Information:** Application fee $25. Priority deadline 6/1. Nonfall registration accepted. Admission may be deferred for a maximum of 4 years.

COSTS AND FINANCIAL AID

Annual tuition $30,000. Room and board $9,000. Required fees $200. Average book expense $1,350. **Required Forms and Deadlines:** FAFSA. **Notification of Awards:** Applicants will be notified of awards on a rolling basis beginning 3/15. **Types of Aid:** *Need-based scholarships/grants:* Federal Pell, FSEOG, State scholarships/grants, Private scholarships, College/university scholarship or grant aid from institutional funds, United Negro College Fund. *Loans:* Direct Subsidized Stafford Loans, Direct Unsubsidized Stafford Loans, Direct PLUS loans, Federal Perkins Loans, College/university loans from institutional funds. *Student Employment:* Federal Work-Study Program available. Institutional employment available. **Financial Aid Statistics:** 100% needy freshmen, 96% needy undergrads receive need-based scholarship or grant aid. 97% freshmen, 99% undergrads receive non-need-based scholarship or grant aid. 70% freshmen, 76% undergrads receive need-based self-help aid. 20% freshmen, 15% undergrads receive athletic scholarships. 100% freshmen, 99% undergrads receive any aid. 78% undergrads borrow to pay for school. Average cumulative indebtedness $28,501. **Criteria for awarding aid:** *Non-need-based:* Academics, Alumni affiliation, Art, Athletics, Music/drama, Religious affiliation.

NORTHWESTERN STATE UNIVERSITY

South Hall, Natchitoches, LA 71497
Phone: 318-357-4078 • **Financial Aid Phone:** 800-823-3008
E-mail: applications@nsula.edu • **CEEB Code:** 6492
Fax: 318-357-4660 • **Website:** www.nsula.edu • **ACT Code:** 1600

This public school was founded in 1884. It has a 916-acre campus.

RATINGS

Admissions Selectivity Rating: 77　　**Fire Safety Rating:** 88　　**Green Rating:** 60*

STUDENTS AND FACULTY

Enrollment: 7,333. **Student Body:** 68% female, 32% male, 9% out-of-state, 1% international (34 countries represented). Asian 1%, African American 30%, Caucasian 57%, Hispanic 3%, Native American 1%, Pacific Islander <1%, Two or more races 3%, Race unknown 4%.
Retention and Graduation: 71% freshmen return for sophomore year. 17% freshmen graduate within 4 years. 36% freshmen graduate within 6 years.
Faculty: Student/faculty ratio 19:1. 291 full-time faculty, 60% hold PhDs, 8% are are members of minority groups, 55% are women. 1% of classes are taught by teaching assistants.

ACADEMICS

Degrees: associate, bachelor's, master's, postbachelor's certificate, post-master's certificate. **Classes:** Most classes have 10-19 students. Most lab/discussion sessions have fewer than 10 students. **Most popular majors:** General Studies Business Administration and Management. **Special Study Options:** cooperative education program, distance learning, double major, dual enrollment, honors program, independent study, internships, study abroad, teacher certification program. **Honors Programs:** The Louisiana Scholar's College is a special institution at Northwestern that enrolls students in a strong liberal arts program while simultaneously letting them take part in the other great areas of NSU. **Disability Services:** Special programs offered to physically disabled students, including note-taking services, reader services, tape recorders, tutors. **Career Services:** Alumni services, Career/job search classes, Career assessment, Internships.

FACILITIES

Housing: Coed dorms, special housing for disabled students, fraternity/sorority housing, apartments for married students, apartments for single students, Theme Housing. 96% of campus accessible to physically diasbled. **Special Academic Facilities/Equipment:** Cammie G. Henry Research Center; Louisiana Creole Heritage Center; Louisiana Folklife Center; Louisiana Regional Folklife Center; The Space Science Group; Williamson Museum **Computers:** 50% of classrooms, 100% of dorms, 100% of libraries, 50% of dining areas, 100% of student union, 75% of common outdoor areas have wireless network access. Students can register for classes online. Administrative functions (other than registration) can be performed online.

CAMPUS LIFE

Environment: Village. **Activities:** Choral groups, concert band, dance, drama/theater, jazz band, literary magazine, marching band, music ensembles, musical theater, opera, pep band, radio station, student government, student newspaper, symphony orchestra, television station, yearbook, Campus Ministries, Student Organization. 109 registered organizations, 11 honor societies, 6 religious organizations. 10 fraternities, 7 sororities. **Athletics (Intercollegiate):** *Men:* baseball, basketball, cheerleading, cross-country, football, soccer, track/field (outdoor), track/field (indoor). *Women:* basketball, cheerleading, cross-country, soccer, softball, tennis, track/field (outdoor), track/field (indoor), volleyball. **On-Campus Highlights:** Wellness, Recreation, and Activity Center, Student Union, University Place Apartments, University Columns Apartments, BCM/CSO/Wellesley Foundation. **Environmental Initiatives:** NSU student groups and organizations participate in recycling, liter-abatement, campus beautification, and related Green service (and service-learning) activities.

ADMISSIONS

Freshman Academic Profile: Average high school GPA 3.2. 16% in top 10% of high school class, 39% in top 25% of high school class, 72% in top 50% of high school class. **Reported SAT (pre-2016 redesign) scores:** SAT Math middle 50% range 435-555. SAT Critical Reading middle 50% range 435-550. **Concordant SAT scores:** SAT Math middle 50% range 480–580. ACT middle 50% range 19-23. Minimum internet-based TOEFL 61. Minimum paper TOEFL 500. **Basis for Candidate Selection:** *Very important factors considered include:* rigor of secondary school record, standardized test scores. *Important factors considered include:* class rank, academic GPA. *Other factors considered include:* extracurricular activities, talent/ability, alumni/ae relation, geographical residence, state residency. **Freshman Admission Requirements:** High school diploma is required and GED is accepted. *Academic units required:* 4 English, 3 math, 3 science, 3 science labs, 2 foreign language, 1 social studies, 2 history, 1 visual/performing arts, and 1 unit from above areas or other academic areas. **Freshman Admission Statistics:** 2,633 applied, 83.18% admitted, 51% enrolled. **Transfer Admission Requirements:** college transcript(s), statement of good standing from prior institution(s). Minimum college GPA of 2.0 required. Lowest grade transferable D. **General Admission Information:** Application fee $20. Regular application deadline 7/6. Nonfall registration accepted. Admission may be deferred for a maximum of 3 Semesters w/o Fee.

COSTS AND FINANCIAL AID

Required Forms and Deadlines: FAFSA, Institution's own financial aid form. **Notification of Awards:** Applicants will be notified of awards on a rolling basis beginning 5/1. **Types of Aid:** *Need-based scholarships/grants:* Federal Pell, FSEOG, State scholarships/grants, Private scholarships, College/university scholarship or grant aid from institutional funds, United Negro College Fund, Federal Nursing Scholarships. *Loans:* Direct Subsidized Stafford Loans, Direct Unsubsidized Stafford Loans, Direct PLUS loans, Federal Perkins Loans. *Student Employment:* Federal Work-Study Program available. Institutional employment available. **Financial Aid Statistics:** 64% needy freshmen, 65% needy undergrads receive need-based scholarship or grant aid. 68% freshmen, 47% undergrads receive non-need-based scholarship or grant aid. 57% freshmen, 66% undergrads receive need-based self-help aid. 6% freshmen, 5% undergrads receive athletic scholarships. 91% freshmen, 82% undergrads receive any aid. **Criteria for awarding aid:** *Non-need-based:* Academics, Alumni affiliation, Art, Athletics, Job skills, Leadership, Minority status, Music/drama, Religious affiliation, State/district residency.

NORTHWESTERN UNIVERSITY

1801 Hinman Ave, Evanston, IL 60208
Phone: 847-491-7271 • **Financial Aid Phone:** 847-491-7400
E-mail: ug-admission@northwestern.edu • **CEEB Code:** 1565
Website: www.northwestern.edu • **ACT Code:** 1106

This private school was founded in 1851. It has a 240-acre campus.

RATINGS

Admissions Selectivity Rating: 98   **Fire Safety Rating:** 83   **Green Rating:** 96

STUDENTS AND FACULTY

Enrollment: 8,353. **Student Body:** 50% female, 50% male, 10% international (77 countries represented). Asian 17%, African American 6%, Caucasian 48%, Hispanic 12%, Native American <1%, Pacific Islander 0%, Two or more races 5%, Race unknown 2%.
Retention and Graduation: 98% freshmen return for sophomore year. 84% freshmen graduate within 4 years. 94 23% grads go on to further study within 1 year. 7% grads pursue arts and sciences degrees. 3% grads pursue law degrees. 1% grads pursue business degrees. 7% grads pursue medical degrees. **Faculty:** Student/faculty ratio 7:1. 1,479 full-time faculty, 100% hold PhDs, 17% are are members of minority groups, 38% are women. 2% of classes are taught by teaching assistants.

ACADEMICS

Degrees: bachelor's, certificate, doctoral/professional, doctoral/research, doctoral, master's, post-master's certificate. **Classes:** Most classes have fewer than 10 students. Most lab/discussion sessions have 10-19 students. **Most popular majors:** Economics; Engineering; Journalism. **Special Study Options:** Accelerated program, cooperative education program, double major, honors program, independent study, internships, liberal arts/career combination, student-designed major, study abroad, teacher certification program. **Honors Programs:** Honors Program in Medical Education, Integrated Science Program, MENU, MMSS Combined degree programs: BA/MD, BA/MA, BM/MS, BA/BS, BA/BM, BS/BM, BS/MS. **Disability Services:** Special programs offered to physically disabled students, including note-taking services, reader services, tape recorders, tutors. **Career Services:** Alumni network, Alumni services, Career/job search classes, Career assessment, Internships, Regional alumni. At Northwestern, all undergraduates have the opportunity to gain real-world experience through internships, field studies programs, and practicums. These programs place students in corporations, newsrooms, archaeological dig sites, and laboratories throughout Chicago, the United States, and the world.

FACILITIES

Housing: Coed dorms, men's dorms, women's dorms, fraternity/sorority housing, Wellness Housing, Theme Housing. 100% of campus accessible to physically diasbled. **Special Academic Facilities/Equipment:** Art gallery, learning sciences institute, communicative disorders and materials and life sciences buildings, catalysis center, astronomical research center. Ford Motor Compay Engineering Design Center for engineering students. **Computers:** 100% of classrooms, 100% of dorms, 100% of libraries, 100% of dining areas, 100% of student union, 100% of common outdoor areas have wireless network access. Students can register for classes online.

CAMPUS LIFE

Environment: Town. **Activities:** Choral groups, concert band, dance, drama/theater, jazz band, literary magazine, marching band, music ensembles, musical theater, opera, pep band, radio station, student government, student newspaper, student-run film society, symphony orchestra, television station, yearbook, Campus Ministries, Student Organization, Model UN. 415 registered organizations, 23 honor societies, 29 religious organizations. 17 fraternities, 19 sororities. **Athletics (Intercollegiate):** *Men:* baseball, basketball, cheerleading, diving, football, golf, soccer, swimming, tennis, wrestling. *Women:* basketball, cheerleading, cross-country, diving, fencing, field hockey, golf, lacrosse, soccer, softball, swimming, tennis, volleyball. **On-Campus Highlights:** Shakespeare Garden, Dearborn Observatory, Norris Student Center, Henry Crown Sports Pavilion and Acquatic Center, The lakefill on Lake Michigan. **Environmental Initiatives:** The development of a Strategic Plan for sustainability that will detail the long-term sustainability vision and goals for Northwestern University as well as putting in place the governance and accountability for the implementation of that plan and communicating our progress to stakeholders at all levels.

ADMISSIONS

Freshman Academic Profile: 91% in top 10% of high school class, 100% in top 25% of high school class, 100% in top 50% of high school class. 65% from public high schools. **Reported SAT (pre-2016 redesign) scores:** SAT Math middle 50% range 710-800. SAT Critical Reading middle 50% range 690-760. **Concordant SAT scores:** SAT Math middle 50% range 740–800. ACT middle 50% range 32-34. **Basis for Candidate Selection:** *Very important factors considered include:* rigor of secondary school record, class rank, academic GPA, standardized test scores. *Important factors considered include:* application essay, recommendation(s), extracurricular activities, talent/ability, character/personal qualities. *Other factors considered include:* interview, first generation, alumni/ae relation, racial/ethnic status, volunteer work, work experience, level of applicant's interest. **Freshman Admission Requirements:** High school diploma or equivalent is not required. *Academic units recommended:* 4 English, 3 math, 2 science, 2 science labs, 2 foreign language, 2 social studies, 2 history, 1 academic elective. **Freshman Admission Statistics:** 35,100 applied, 10.66% admitted, 53% enrolled. **Transfer Admission Requirements:** High school transcript, college transcript(s), essay or personal statement, standardized test scores, statement of good standing from prior institution(s). Minimum college GPA of 3.0 required. Lowest grade transferable C. **General Admission Information:** Application fee $75. Regular application deadline 1/1. Regular notification 4/1. Nonfall registration accepted. Admission may be deferred for a maximum of 1 year.

COSTS AND FINANCIAL AID

Annual tuition $50,424. Room and board $15,489. Required fees $431. Average book expense $1,620. **Required Forms and Deadlines:** FAFSA, CSS/Financial Aid PROFILE, Noncustodial PROFILE. **Notification of Awards:** Applicants will be notified of awards on or about 4/15. **Types of Aid:** *Need-based scholarships/grants:* Federal Pell, FSEOG, State scholarships/grants, College/university scholarship or grant aid from institutional funds. *Loans:* Direct Subsidized Stafford Loans, Direct Unsubsidized Stafford Loans, Direct PLUS loans, Federal Perkins Loans, College/university loans from institutional funds. *Student Employment:* Federal Work-Study Program available. Institutional employment available. **Financial Aid Statistics:** 98% needy freshmen, 98% needy undergrads receive need-based scholarship or grant aid. 0% undergrads receive non-need-based scholarship or grant aid. 54% freshmen, 65% undergrads receive need-based self-help aid. 4% freshmen, 5% undergrads receive athletic scholarships. 42% undergrads borrow to pay for school. Average cumulative indebtedness $33,369. **Criteria for awarding aid:** *Non-need-based:* Athletics, Music/drama.

NORTHWOOD UNIVERSITY

4000 Whiting Drive, Midland, MI 48640
Phone: 989-837-4273 • **Financial Aid Phone:** 989-837-4320
E-mail: miadmit@northwood.edu • **CEEB Code:** 1568
Fax: 989-837-4273 • **Website:** www.northwood.edu • **ACT Code:** 2041

This private school was founded in 1959. It has a 434-acre campus.

RATINGS

Admissions Selectivity Rating: 75   **Fire Safety Rating:** 85   **Green Rating:** 60*

STUDENTS AND FACULTY

Enrollment: 1,457. **Student Body:** 36% female, 64% male, 13% out-of-state, 6% international (26 countries represented). Asian 0%, African American 7%, Caucasian 78%, Hispanic 3%, Native American <1%, Pacific Islander 1%, Two or more races 2%, Race unknown 3%.
Retention and Graduation: 80% freshmen return for sophomore year. 42% freshmen graduate within 4 years. 57% freshmen graduate within 6 years. **Faculty:** Student/faculty ratio 21:1. 49 full-time faculty, 45% hold PhDs, 22% are are members of minority groups, 49% are women. 0% of classes are taught by teaching assistants.

ACADEMICS

Degrees: associate, bachelor's, master's. **Classes:** Most classes have 10-19 students. **Most popular majors:** Sport and Fitness Administration/Management; Business Administration and Management. **Special Study Options:** Accelerated program, distance learning, double major, dual enrollment, external degree program, honors program, independent study, internships, study abroad, weekend college. **Honors Programs:** An Honors Program began in Fall Term, 1991. In it, honors sections of six critically important courses are offered. The best instructors and the most demanding material and expectations are used. Additionally, special one credit hour seminars, which include outside speakers, are offered to sophomores and juniors. **Disability Services:** Special programs offered to physically disabled students, including tutors. **Career Services:** Alumni network, Alumni services, Career/job search classes, Career assessment, Internships.

FACILITIES

Housing: men's dorms, women's dorms, apartments for single students. **Special Academic Facilities/Equipment:** Hach Student Life Center, Gerstacker Student Union **Computers:** 100% of classrooms, 100% of dorms, 100% of libraries, 100% of dining areas, 100% of student union, have wireless network access. Students can register for classes online. Administrative functions (other than registration) can be performed online.

CAMPUS LIFE

Environment: Town. **Activities:** Choral groups, dance, drama/theater, pep band, student government, student newspaper, yearbook, Student Organization. 42 registered organizations, 2 honor societies, 2 religious organizations. 9 fraternities, 3 sororities. **Athletics (Intercollegiate):** *Men:* baseball, basketball, cheerleading, cross-country, football, golf, soccer, tennis, track/field (outdoor), track/field (indoor). *Women:* basketball, cheerleading, cross-country, golf, soccer, softball, tennis, track/field (outdoor), track/field (indoor), volleyball. **On-Campus Highlights:** Hach Student Life Center, Mid—Caf @ Northwood, Bennett Sports Center.

ADMISSIONS

Freshman Academic Profile: Average high school GPA 3.3. 70% from public high schools. **Reported SAT (pre-2016 redesign) scores:** SAT Math middle 50% range 470-580. SAT Critical Reading middle 50% range 410-540. **Concordant SAT scores:** SAT Math middle 50% range 510–600. ACT middle 50% range 20-25. Minimum paper TOEFL 500. **Basis for Candidate Selection:** *Very important factors considered include:* academic GPA, standardized test scores, level of applicant's interest. *Important factors considered include:* rigor of secondary school record, class rank, application essay, recommendation(s), interview, extracurricular activities. *Other factors considered include:* talent/ability, alumni/ae relation, volunteer work, work experience. **Freshman Admission Requirements:** High school diploma is required and GED is accepted. *Academic units recommended:* 4 English, 3 math, 3 science, 2 science labs, 1 foreign language, 3 social studies, 1 academic elective. **Freshman Admission Statistics:** 1,258 applied, 67.65% admitted, 39% enrolled. **Transfer Admission Requirements:** college transcript(s), Minimum college GPA of 2.0 required. Lowest grade transferable C. **General Admission Information:** Application fee $30. Regular application deadline 8/1. Nonfall registration accepted. Admission may be deferred for a maximum of 1 year.

COSTS AND FINANCIAL AID

Required Forms and Deadlines: FAFSA. **Notification of Awards:** Applicants will be notified of awards on a rolling basis beginning 3/1. **Types of Aid:** *Need-based scholarships/grants:* Federal Pell, FSEOG, State scholarships/grants, Private scholarships, College/university scholarship or grant aid from institutional funds. *Loans:* Direct Subsidized Stafford Loans, Direct Unsubsidized Stafford Loans. *Student Employment:* Federal Work-Study Program available. Institutional employment available. **Financial Aid Statistics:** 82% needy freshmen, 84% needy undergrads receive need-based scholarship or grant aid. 43% freshmen, 41% undergrads receive non-need-based scholarship or grant aid. 86% freshmen, 88% undergrads receive need-based self-help aid. 12% freshmen, 9% undergrads receive athletic scholarships. 75% undergrads borrow to pay for school. Average cumulative indebtedness $26,815. **Criteria for awarding aid:** *Non-need-based:* Academics, Alumni affiliation, Athletics, Leadership, Minority status, State/district residency.

NORTHWOOD UNIVERSITY, FLORIDA CAMPUS

2600 North Military Trail, West Palm Beach, FL 33409-2911
Phone: (561) 478-5500 • **Financial Aid Phone:** 561-478-5590
E-mail: fladmit@northwood.edu • **CEEB Code:** 4072
Fax: 561-681-7901 • **Website:** northwood.edu • **ACT Code:** 6736

This private school was founded in 1982. It has a 90-acre campus.

RATINGS

Admissions Selectivity Rating: 81   **Fire Safety Rating:** 85   **Green Rating:** 60*

STUDENTS AND FACULTY

Enrollment: 496. **Student Body:** 36% female, 64% male, 37% out-of-state, 39% international (40 countries represented). Asian 1%, African American 10%, Caucasian 25%, Hispanic 11%, Native American 1%, Pacific Islander 0%, Two or more races <1%, Race unknown 13%.
Retention and Graduation: 60% freshmen return for sophomore year. 24% freshmen graduate within 4 years. **Faculty:** Student/faculty ratio 20:1. 16 full-time faculty, 38% hold PhDs, 0% are are members of minority groups, 38% are women. 0% of classes are taught by teaching assistants.

ACADEMICS

Degrees: associate, bachelor's, master's. **Classes:** Most classes have 10-19 students. **Most popular majors:** Marketing/Marketing Management; Banking and Financial Support Services. **Special Study Options:** Accelerated program, distance learning, double major, dual enrollment, external degree program, honors program, independent study, internships, study abroad, weekend college. **Honors Programs:** An Honors Program began in fall term 1991. In it, honors sections of a variety of critically important courses are offered. The best instructors and the most demanding material and expectations are used. Additionally, special one-credit-hour seminars, which include outside speakers, are offered to sophomores and juniors. Honor students having completed 17 credit hours in honors courses may apply for honors admission to Term in Europe, Term in Asia, or Term in Northern Europe and are eligible for a partial scholarship to support these travel abroad programs. This also provides a powerful incentive for students to successfully compete in the Honors Program. **Disability Services:** Special programs offered to physically disabled students, including note-taking services. **Career Services:** Alumni network, Alumni services, Career/job search classes, Career assessment, Internships.

FACILITIES

Housing: men's dorms, women's dorms. **Special Academic Facilities/Equipment:** Art Gallery **Computers:** 100% of classrooms, 100% of dorms, 100% of libraries, 100% of dining areas, 100% of student union, have wireless network access. Students can register for classes online. Administrative functions (other than registration) can be performed online.

CAMPUS LIFE

Environment: City. **Activities:** dance, drama/theater, student government, student newspaper, Student Organization. 23 registered organizations, 1 honor society. **Athletics (Intercollegiate):** *Men:* baseball, basketball, golf, soccer, tennis. *Women:* basketball, golf, soccer, softball, tennis, volleyball. **On-Campus Highlights:** Countess de Hoernle Student Life Center **Environmental Initiatives:** We keep use of paper to a minimum (e-mail attachments/files, Blackboard portal).

ADMISSIONS

Freshman Academic Profile: Average high school GPA 3.2. 13% in top 10% of high school class, 27% in top 25% of high school class, 57% in top 50% of high school class. 70% from public high schools. **Reported SAT (pre-2016 redesign) scores:** SAT Math middle 50% range 440-550. SAT Critical Reading middle 50% range 430-510. SAT Writing middle 50% range 390-480. **Concordant SAT scores:** SAT EBRW middle 50% 460–550. SAT Math middle 50% range 480–570. ACT middle 50% range 18-21. Minimum paper TOEFL 500. **Basis for Candidate Selection:** *Very important factors considered include:* rigor of secondary school record, class rank, academic GPA, standardized test scores, application essay, recommendation(s), interview, extracurricular activities, character/personal qualities, level of applicant's interest. *Important factors considered include:* talent/ability, volunteer work, work experience. *Other factors considered include:* first generation, alumni/ae relation. **Freshman Admission Requirements:** High school diploma is required and GED is accepted. *Academic units recommended:* 17 English, 4 math, 3 science. **Freshman Admission Statistics:** 628 applied, 53.98% admitted, 31% enrolled. **Transfer Admission Requirements:** High school transcript, college transcript(s), Minimum college GPA of 2.0 required. Lowest grade transferable C. **General Admission Information:** Application fee $25. Regular application deadline 8/1. Nonfall registration accepted. Admission may be deferred for a maximum of 1 year.

COSTS AND FINANCIAL AID

Required Forms and Deadlines: FAFSA, State aid form. **Notification of Awards:** Applicants will be notified of awards on a rolling basis beginning 3/1. **Types of Aid:** *Need-based scholarships/grants:* Federal Pell, FSEOG, State scholarships/grants, Private scholarships, College/university scholarship or grant aid from institutional funds. *Loans:* Federal Perkins Loans, State Loans. *Student Employment:* Federal Work-Study Program available. Institutional employment available. **Financial Aid Statistics:** 87% needy freshmen, 86% needy undergrads receive need-based scholarship or grant aid. 27% freshmen, 21% undergrads receive non-need-based scholarship or grant aid. 84% freshmen, 90% undergrads receive need-based self-help aid. 20% freshmen, 19% undergrads receive athletic scholarships. **Criteria for awarding aid:** *Non-need-based:* Academics, Athletics, Leadership, Minority status.

NORTHWOOD UNIVERSITY, TEXAS CAMPUS

1114 West FM 1382, Cedar Hill, TX 75104-1204
Financial Aid Phone: 972-293-5430 • **CEEB Code:** 6499
Website: northwood.edu • **ACT Code:** 4135

This private school was founded in 1966. It has a 360-acre campus.

RATINGS
Admissions Selectivity Rating: 78   **Fire Safety Rating:** 71   **Green Rating:** 60*

STUDENTS AND FACULTY
Enrollment: 561. **Student Body:** 42% female, 58% male, 25% international (18 countries represented). Asian 2%, African American 14%, Caucasian 19%, Hispanic 24%, Native American <1%, Pacific Islander 0%, Two or more races <1%, Race unknown 15%.
Retention and Graduation: 31% freshmen graduate within 4 years. **Faculty:** Student/faculty ratio 19:1. 20 full-time faculty, 25% hold PhDs, 15% are are members of minority groups, 45% are women. 0% of classes are taught by teaching assistants.

ACADEMICS
Degrees: associate, bachelor's, master's. **Classes:** Most classes have 10-19 students. **Most popular majors:** Entrepreneurship/Entrepreneurial Studies; International Business/Trade/Commerce; Marketing/Marketing Management. **Special Study Options:** Accelerated program, distance learning, double major, dual enrollment, external degree program, honors program, independent study, internships, study abroad, weekend college. **Honors Programs:** An Honors Program begain in Fall Term, 1991. In it, honors sections of six critically important courses are offered. The best instructors and the most demanding material and expectations are used. Additionally, special one credit hour seminars, which include outside speakers, are offered to sophomores and juniors. **Disability Services:** Special programs offered to physically disabled students, including tutors. **Career Services:** Alumni network, Alumni services, Career assessment, Internships.

FACILITIES
Housing: men's dorms, women's dorms, apartments for single students. **Special Academic Facilities/Equipment:** Butler Gallery, Hopkins Display Cases, Hach Library **Computers:** 100% of classrooms, 100% of dorms, 100% of libraries, 100% of dining areas, 100% of student union, have wireless network access. Students can register for classes online. Administrative functions (other than registration) can be performed online.

CAMPUS LIFE
Environment: Village. **Activities:** Choral groups, dance, drama/theater, student newspaper, Campus Ministries, Student Organization. 17 registered organizations, 1 honor society, 2 religious organizations. 1 fraternity, 1 sorority. **Athletics (Intercollegiate):** *Men:* baseball, cross-country, golf, soccer, track/field (outdoor), track/field (indoor). *Women:* cross-country, golf, soccer, softball, track/field (outdoor), track/field (indoor). **Environmental Initiatives:** Paper recycling. We have two large bins in one of the parking lots. The paper is collected twice a week from offices and common areas.

ADMISSIONS
Freshman Academic Profile: Average high school GPA 3.3. 8% in top 10% of high school class, 27% in top 25% of high school class, 65% in top 50% of high school class. 90% from public high schools. **Reported SAT (pre-2016 redesign) scores:** SAT Math middle 50% range 420-520. SAT Critical Reading middle 50% range 390-500. SAT Writing middle 50% range 390-460. **Concordant SAT scores:** SAT EBRW middle 50% 440–540. SAT Math middle 50% range 460–550. ACT middle 50% range 17-22. Minimum paper TOEFL 500. **Basis for Candidate Selection:** *Very important factors considered include:* rigor of secondary school record, academic GPA, standardized test scores, interview, extracurricular activities, character/personal qualities, level of applicant's interest. *Important factors considered include:* class rank, talent/ability, volunteer work, work experience. *Other factors considered include:* application essay, recommendation(s), first generation, alumni/ae relation. **Freshman Admission Requirements:** High school diploma is required and GED is accepted. *Academic units recommended:* 4 English, 3 math, 3 science, 2 science labs, 1 foreign language, 3 social studies, 1 computer science. **Freshman Admission Statistics:** 452 applied, 58.63% admitted, 65% enrolled. **Transfer Admission Requirements:** High school transcript, college transcript(s), essay or personal statement, Minimum college GPA of 2.0 required. Lowest grade transferable C. **General Admission Information:** Application fee $25. Regular application deadline 8/1. Nonfall registration accepted. Admission may be deferred for a maximum of 1 year.

COSTS AND FINANCIAL AID
Required Forms and Deadlines: FAFSA. **Notification of Awards:** Applicants will be notified of awards on a rolling basis beginning 3/1. **Types**

of Aid: *Need-based scholarships/grants:* Federal Pell, FSEOG, Private scholarships. *Student Employment:* Federal Work-Study Program available. Institutional employment available. **Financial Aid Statistics:** 92% needy freshmen, 89% needy undergrads receive need-based scholarship or grant aid. 24% freshmen, 22% undergrads receive non-need-based scholarship or grant aid. 90% freshmen, 91% undergrads receive need-based self-help aid. 11% freshmen, 12% undergrads receive athletic scholarships. **Criteria for awarding aid:** *Non-need-based:* Academics, Alumni affiliation, Athletics, Leadership, Minority status.

NORWICH UNIVERSITY

Admissions Office, Northfield, VT 5663
Phone: 802-485-2001
E-mail: nuadm@norwich.edu
Fax: 802-485-2032 • **Website:** www.norwich.edu

This private school was founded in 1819. It has a 1125-acre campus.

RATINGS
Admissions Selectivity Rating: 78   **Fire Safety Rating:** 60*   **Green Rating:** 60*

STUDENTS AND FACULTY
Enrollment: 2,246. **Student Body:** 26% female, 74% male, 84% out-of-state, 2% international. Asian 2%, African American 3%, Caucasian 72%, Hispanic 4%, Native American 1%, Pacific Islander <1%, Two or more races 2%, Race unknown 15%.
Retention and Graduation: 85% freshmen return for sophomore year. 45% freshmen graduate within 4 years. 55% freshmen graduate within 6 years. 10% grads go on to further study within 1 year. 2% grads pursue arts and sciences degrees. 2% grads pursue law degrees. 2% grads pursue business degrees. 1% grads pursue medical degrees. **Faculty:** Student/faculty ratio 14:1. 140 full-time faculty, 0% hold PhDs, 9% are are members of minority groups, 36% are women. 0% of classes are taught by teaching assistants.

ACADEMICS
Degrees: bachelor's, master's, postbachelor's certificate. **Classes:** Most classes have 10-19 students. **Special Study Options:** cooperative education program, distance learning, double major, English as a Second Language (ESL), honors program, independent study, internships, study abroad. **Disability Services:** Special programs offered to physically disabled students, including tutors. **Career Services:** Career/job search classes, On-campus interviews.

FACILITIES
Housing: Coed dorms. 95% of campus accessible to physically diasbled. **Special Academic Facilities/Equipment:** museum, architecture and art building w/galery, new library.

CAMPUS LIFE
Environment: Rural. **Activities:** Choral groups, concert band, drama/theater, jazz band, literary magazine, marching band, pep band, radio station, student government, student newspaper, yearbook. 40 registered organizations, 8 honor societies, 4 religious organizations. **Athletics (Intercollegiate):** *Men:* baseball, basketball, cross-country, diving, football, ice hockey, lacrosse, riflery, rugby, soccer, swimming, track/field (outdoor), volleyball, wrestling. *Women:* basketball, cross-country, diving, riflery, rugby, soccer, softball, swimming, track/field (outdoor), volleyball.

ADMISSIONS
Freshman Academic Profile: Average high school GPA 3.1. 11% in top 10% of high school class, 37% in top 25% of high school class, 74% in top 50% of high school class. **Reported SAT (pre-2016 redesign) scores:** SAT Math middle 50% range 500-640. SAT Critical Reading middle 50% range 480-580. SAT Writing middle 50% range 460-620. **Concordant SAT scores:** SAT EBRW middle 50% 530–650. SAT Math middle 50% range 530–660. ACT middle 50% range 21-26. Minimum paper TOEFL 500. **Basis for Candidate Selection:** *Very important factors considered include:* rigor of secondary school record, academic GPA, standardized test scores. *Other factors considered include:* class rank, application essay, recommendation(s), interview, extracurricular activities, talent/ability, character/personal qualities, alumni/ae relation, volunteer work, work experience. **Freshman Admission Requirements:** High school diploma is required and GED is accepted. *Academic units recommended:* 4 English, 4 math, 4 science, 3 science labs, 2 foreign language, 3 social studies, 3 history. **Freshman Admission Statistics:** 1,473 applied, 91.04% admitted, 37% enrolled. **Transfer Admission Requirements:** High school transcript, college transcript(s), Lowest grade transferable c-. **General Admission Information:** Application fee $35. Priority deadline 2/1. Nonfall registration accepted. Admission may be deferred for a maximum of 1 term.

COSTS AND FINANCIAL AID

Annual tuition $30,048. Room and board $10,976. Required fees $1,734. Average book expense $1,000. **Required Forms and Deadlines:** FAFSA. **Notification of Awards:** Applicants will be notified of awards on a rolling basis beginning 2/15. **Types of Aid:** *Need-based scholarships/grants:* Federal Pell, FSEOG, State scholarships/grants, Private scholarships, College/university scholarship or grant aid from institutional funds. *Loans:* Direct Subsidized Stafford Loans, Direct Unsubsidized Stafford Loans, Direct PLUS loans, Federal Perkins Loans. *Student Employment:* Federal Work-Study Program available. Institutional employment available. **Financial Aid Statistics:** 100% needy freshmen, 100% needy undergrads receive need-based scholarship or grant aid. 18% freshmen, 17% undergrads receive non-need-based scholarship or grant aid. 79% freshmen, 79% undergrads receive need-based self-help aid. 0% freshmen, 0% undergrads receive athletic scholarships. **Criteria for awarding aid:** *Need-based:* Academics. *Non-need-based:* Academics.

NOTRE DAME DE NAMUR UNIVERSITY

1500 Ralston Avenue, Belmont, CA 94002-1908
Phone: 650-508-3600 • **Financial Aid Phone:** 650-508-3600
E-mail: admiss@ndnu.edu • **CEEB Code:** 4063
Fax: 650-508-3426 • **Website:** www.ndnu.edu • **ACT Code:** 236

This private school, affiliated with the Roman Catholic Church, was founded in 1851. It has a 80-acre campus.

RATINGS

Admissions Selectivity Rating: 74   **Fire Safety Rating:** 60*   **Green Rating:** 60*

STUDENTS AND FACULTY

Enrollment: 1,177. **Student Body:** 67% female, 33% male, 6% out-of-state, 3% international. Asian 12%, African American 6%, Caucasian 25%, Hispanic 37%, Native American 1%, Pacific Islander 3%, Two or more races 4%, Race unknown 9%.
Retention and Graduation: 75% freshmen return for sophomore year. 43% freshmen graduate within 4 years. 53% freshmen graduate within 6 years.
Faculty: Student/faculty ratio 11:1. 60 full-time faculty, 95% hold PhDs, 22% are are members of minority groups, 55% are women. 0% of classes are taught by teaching assistants.

ACADEMICS

Degrees: bachelor's, doctoral/research, master's, postbachelor's certificate. **Classes:** Most classes have 10-19 students. **Most popular majors:** Psychology; Human Services; Business Administration and Management. **Special Study Options:** Accelerated program, double major, English as a Second Language (ESL), exchange student program (domestic), independent study, internships, liberal arts/career combination, student-designed major, study abroad, teacher certification program. **Disability Services:** Special programs offered to physically disabled students, including note-taking services, reader services. **Career Services:** Alumni network, Career/job search classes, Career assessment, Internships.

FACILITIES

Housing: Coed dorms, 2 or 3 person apartments 4-person suites. **Special Academic Facilities/Equipment:** Student art museum, professional art gallery, archives of modern Christian art, theatre, early learning center for Montessori credential training, on-campus elementary school.

CAMPUS LIFE

Environment: Village. **Activities:** Choral groups, dance, literary magazine, music ensembles, musical theater, student government, student newspaper. 15 registered organizations, 3 honor societies, 1 religious organization. **Athletics (Intercollegiate):** *Men:* basketball, cheerleading, soccer, tennis, track/field (outdoor). *Women:* basketball, cheerleading, cross-country, soccer, softball, tennis, track/field (outdoor), volleyball.

ADMISSIONS

Freshman Academic Profile: Average high school GPA 3.2. 13% in top 10% of high school class, 35% in top 25% of high school class, 76% in top 50% of high school class. 62% from public high schools. **Reported SAT (pre-2016 redesign) scores:** SAT Math middle 50% range 420-520. SAT Critical Reading middle 50% range 430-520. SAT Writing middle 50% range 420-510. **Concordant SAT scores:** SAT EBRW middle 50% 480–570. SAT Math middle 50% range 460–550. ACT middle 50% range 17-21. Minimum internet-based TOEFL 61. Minimum paper TOEFL 500. **Basis for Candidate Selection:** *Very important factors considered include:* rigor of secondary school record, academic GPA. *Important factors considered include:* class rank, standardized test scores, application essay, recommendation(s), extracurricular activities, talent/ability, character/personal qualities, level of applicant's interest. *Other*

factors considered include: interview, first generation, alumni/ae relation, religious affiliation/commitment, racial/ethnic status, volunteer work, work experience. **Freshman Admission Requirements:** High school diploma is required and GED is accepted. *Academic units required:* 4 English, 2 math, 1 science, 1 science lab, 2 foreign language, 2 social studies, 1 history, 3 academic electives. *Academic units recommended:* 4 English, 3 math, 2 science, 1 science lab, 3 foreign language, 2 social studies, 1 history, 3 academic electives. **Freshman Admission Statistics:** 2,167 applied, 77.71% admitted, 11% enrolled. **Transfer Admission Requirements:** college transcript(s), essay or personal statement, statement of good standing from prior institution(s). Minimum college GPA of 2.0 required. Lowest grade transferable C. **General Admission Information:** Application fee $50. Priority deadline 2/1. Nonfall registration accepted. Admission may be deferred for a maximum of 12 months.

COSTS AND FINANCIAL AID

Annual tuition $32,208. Required fees $400. Average book expense $1,790. **Required Forms and Deadlines:** FAFSA. **Notification of Awards:** Applicants will be notified of awards on a rolling basis beginning 2/15. **Types of Aid:** *Need-based scholarships/grants:* Federal Pell, FSEOG, State scholarships/grants, Private scholarships, College/university scholarship or grant aid from institutional funds. *Loans:* Direct Subsidized Stafford Loans, Direct Unsubsidized Stafford Loans, Direct PLUS loans, Federal Perkins Loans. *Student Employment:* Federal Work-Study Program available. Institutional employment available. **Financial Aid Statistics:** 100% needy freshmen, 100% needy undergrads receive need-based scholarship or grant aid. 5% freshmen, 3% undergrads receive non-need-based scholarship or grant aid. 87% freshmen, 80% undergrads receive need-based self-help aid. 3% freshmen, 1% undergrads receive athletic scholarships. **Criteria for awarding aid:** *Need-based:* Academics, Alumni affiliation, Athletics. *Non-need-based:* Academics, Art, Athletics, Leadership, Music/drama, Religious affiliation.

NOVA SOUTHEASTERN UNIVERSITY

3301 College Avenue, Fort Lauderdale, FL 33314
Phone: 954-262-8000 • **Financial Aid Phone:** 954-262-7456
E-mail: admissions@nova.edu • **CEEB Code:** 5514
Fax: 954-262-3811 • **Website:** www.nova.edu • **ACT Code:** 6706

This private school was founded in 1964. It has a 300-acre campus.

RATINGS

Admissions Selectivity Rating: 75   **Fire Safety Rating:** 92   **Green Rating:** 60*

STUDENTS AND FACULTY

Enrollment: 6,246. **Student Body:** 71% female, 29% male, 16% out-of-state, 4% international. Asian 6%, African American 24%, Caucasian 28%, Hispanic 32%, Native American <1%, Pacific Islander <1%, Two or more races 1%, Race unknown 4%.
Retention and Graduation: 70% freshmen return for sophomore year.
Faculty: Student/faculty ratio 20:1. 814 full-time faculty, 88% hold PhDs, 30% are are members of minority groups, 49% are women. 0% of classes are taught by teaching assistants.

ACADEMICS

Degrees: associate, bachelor's, doctoral/professional, doctoral/research, doctoral, master's, postbachelor's certificate, post-master's certificate. **Classes:** Most classes have 10-19 students. **Most popular majors:** Biology/Biological Sciences; Business Administration and Management; Psychology. **Special Study Options:** distance learning, double major, honors program, independent study, internships, study abroad, teacher certification program, Dual admission programs with NSU graduate and professional schools. **Honors Programs:** http://undergrad.nova.edu/honors/index.cfm For the academically motivated student, the NSU Honors program provides a value added experience. Students enjoy greater interaction with faculty through curricular and co-curricular activities, special invitations to events, and enhanced engagement in disciplinary inquiry. Combined degree programs: BA/JD, BA/MA, BA/DDS, www.nova. edu/admissions/academics. **Disability Services:** Special programs offered to physically disabled students, including note-taking services, reader services, tape recorders, tutors. **Career Services:** Alumni services, Career assessment, Internships, Regional alumni. Our comprehensive career development program encompassing career planning, advisement services, employment and career resources, campus relations, and employer recruitment program.

FACILITIES

Housing: Coed dorms, special housing for disabled students, special housing for international students, fraternity/sorority housing, apartments for married students, apartments for single students, Wellness Housing, Theme Housing. **Special Academic Facilities/Equipment:** Institute for Early Childhood Studies, University School for pre-kindergarten to grade 12, Oceanographic

Center and Lab, Biofeedback and Learning Technology Labs, Audiology and Speech Language Pathology, and Psychology Clinics **Computers:** 100% of classrooms, 100% of dorms, 100% of libraries, 80% of dining areas, 100% of student union, 70% of common outdoor areas have wireless network access. Students can register for classes online. Administrative functions (other than registration) can be performed online.

CAMPUS LIFE

Environment: City. **Activities:** Choral groups, dance, drama/theater, jazz band, literary magazine, music ensembles, musical theater, pep band, radio station, student government, student newspaper, Student Organization. 292 registered organizations. **Athletics (Intercollegiate):** *Men:* baseball, basketball, cross-country, golf, soccer, track/field (outdoor). *Women:* basketball, cheerleading, crew/rowing, cross-country, golf, soccer, softball, tennis, track/field (outdoor), volleyball. **On-Campus Highlights:** University Center and Performing Arts Wi, Alvin Sherman Library, Research & Inform, Health Professions Division Museum, Miniaci Performing Arts Center, Law School, University Center includes the sports arena, fitness center, flight deck, shark mural, and mall-style food court. Performing Arts Wing includes multiple theaters, costume and scenery shops, performance practice rooms for music and dance, dressing rooms, and a gallery.

ADMISSIONS

Reported SAT (pre-2016 redesign) scores: SAT Math middle 50% range 470–590. SAT Critical Reading middle 50% range 460-570. **Concordant SAT scores:** SAT Math middle 50% range 510–610. ACT middle 50% range 20-25. Minimum paper TOEFL 550. **Basis for Candidate Selection:** *Very important factors considered include:* academic GPA, standardized test scores. *Important factors considered include:* rigor of secondary school record. *Other factors considered include:* application essay, recommendation(s), interview, extracurricular activities, talent/ability, character/personal qualities, volunteer work. **Freshman Admission Requirements:** High school diploma is required and GED is accepted. *Academic units recommended:* 4 English, 3 math, 3 science, 3 social studies. **Freshman Admission Statistics:** 3,780 applied, 57.67% admitted, 31% enrolled. **Transfer Admission Requirements:** college transcript(s), statement of good standing from prior institution(s). Minimum college GPA of 2.50 required. Lowest grade transferable D. **General Admission Information:** Application fee $50. Regular application deadline 8/1. Nonfall registration accepted. Admission may be deferred for a maximum of 1 year.

COSTS AND FINANCIAL AID

Annual tuition $21,600. Room and board $9,086. Required fees $550. Average book expense $1,500. **Required Forms and Deadlines:** FAFSA, State aid form. **Notification of Awards:** Applicants will be notified of awards on a rolling basis beginning 3/15. **Types of Aid:** *Need-based scholarships/grants:* Federal Pell, FSEOG, State scholarships/grants, Private scholarships, College/university scholarship or grant aid from institutional funds. *Loans:* Direct Subsidized Stafford Loans, Direct Unsubsidized Stafford Loans, Direct PLUS loans, Federal Perkins Loans. *Student Employment:* Federal Work-Study Program available. Institutional employment available. **Financial Aid Statistics:** 97% needy freshmen, 96% needy undergrads receive need-based scholarship or grant aid. 100% freshmen, 100% undergrads receive non-need-based scholarship or grant aid. 83% freshmen, 88% undergrads receive need-based self-help aid. 12% freshmen, 7% undergrads receive athletic scholarships. 92% freshmen, 83% undergrads receive any aid. **Criteria for awarding aid:** *Need-based:* Academics. *Non-need-based:* Academics, Athletics, Leadership, Music/drama.

OAK HILLS CHRISTIAN COLLEGE

1600 Oak Hills Rd SW, Bemidji, MN 56601
Phone: 218-751-8670 • **Financial Aid Phone:** 218-751-8670
E-mail: admissions@oakhills.edu
Fax: 218-751-8825 • **Website:** www.oakhills.edu • **ACT Code:** 2167

This private school was founded in 1946. It has a 180-acre campus.

RATINGS

Admissions Selectivity Rating: 76   **Fire Safety Rating:** 71   **Green Rating:** 60*

STUDENTS AND FACULTY

Enrollment: 109. **Student Body:** 53% female, 47% male, 33% out-of-state, 1% international (1 countries represented). Asian 2%, African American 1%, Caucasian 95%, Hispanic 0%, Native American 1%, Pacific Islander 0%, Two or more races 0%, Race unknown 0%.
Retention and Graduation: 55% freshmen return for sophomore year. 38% freshmen graduate within 6 years. **Faculty:** Student/faculty ratio 13:1. 6 full-time faculty, 67% hold PhDs, 0% are are members of minority groups, 33% are women. 0% of classes are taught by teaching assistants.

ACADEMICS

Degrees: associate, bachelor's, certificate. **Classes:** Most classes have fewer than 10 students. **Most popular majors:** Bible/Biblical Studies; Pastoral Studies/Counseling; Youth Ministry. **Special Study Options:** cooperative education program, double major, independent study, internships. **Disability Services:** Special programs offered to physically disabled students, including note-taking services, reader services, tape recorders, tutors. **Career Services:** Alumni network, Career/job search classes, Career assessment, Internships, On-campus interviews.

FACILITIES

Housing: special housing for disabled students, men's dorms, women's dorms, apartments for married students, apartments for single students. 20% of campus accessible to physically diasbled. **Special Academic Facilities/Equipment:** American Indian Resource Center **Computers:** 50% of classrooms, 100% of dorms, 100% of libraries, 100% of student union, 50% of common outdoor areas have wireless network access. Students can register for classes online. Administrative functions (other than registration) can be performed online.

CAMPUS LIFE

Environment: Village. **Activities:** Choral groups, music ensembles, student government, Campus Ministries. **Athletics (Intercollegiate):** *Men:* basketball. *Women:* basketball, volleyball. **On-Campus Highlights:** The Fellowship Center Lounge, Schreiber Activity Center (SAC) Gym, Library, Chapel, Lake Front.

ADMISSIONS

Freshman Academic Profile: 5% in top 10% of high school class, 5% in top 25% of high school class, 47% in top 50% of high school class. 79% from public high schools. ACT middle 50% range 16-21. Minimum paper TOEFL 500. **Basis for Candidate Selection:** *Important factors considered include:* rigor of secondary school record, class rank, academic GPA, application essay, recommendation(s), character/personal qualities. *Other factors considered include:* standardized test scores, interview, alumni/ae relation, religious affiliation/commitment. **Freshman Admission Requirements:** High school diploma is required and GED is accepted. **Freshman Admission Statistics:** 70 applied, 55.71% admitted, 79% enrolled. **Transfer Admission Requirements:** High school transcript, college transcript(s), essay or personal statement, Minimum college GPA of 2.0 required. Lowest grade transferable C. **General Admission Information:** Application fee $25. Nonfall registration accepted. Admission may be deferred for a maximum of 2 years.

COSTS AND FINANCIAL AID

Annual tuition $14,420. Room and board $5,180. Average book expense $990. **Required Forms and Deadlines:** FAFSA, Institution's own financial aid form. **Notification of Awards:** Applicants will be notified of awards on a rolling basis beginning 3/1. **Types of Aid:** *Need-based scholarships/grants:* Federal Pell, FSEOG, State scholarships/grants, Private scholarships, College/university scholarship or grant aid from institutional funds. *Loans:* State Loans. *Student Employment:* Federal Work-Study Program available. Institutional employment available. **Financial Aid Statistics:** 100% needy freshmen, 100% needy undergrads receive need-based scholarship or grant aid. 0% undergrads receive non-need-based scholarship or grant aid. 75% freshmen, 86% undergrads receive need-based self-help aid. 0% freshmen, 0% undergrads receive athletic scholarships. 100% freshmen, 100% undergrads receive any aid. **Criteria for awarding aid:** *Non-need-based:* Academics, Alumni affiliation.

OAKLAND CITY UNIVERSITY

138 N. Lucretia Street, Oakland City, IN 47660
Phone: 812-749-1221
E-mail: ocuadmit@oak.edu
Fax: 812-749-1433 • **Website:** http://www.oak.edu

This is a private school.

RATINGS

Admissions Selectivity Rating: 80   **Fire Safety Rating:** 60*   **Green Rating:** 60*

STUDENTS AND FACULTY

Enrollment: 1,744. **Student Body:** 53% female, 47% male, 17% out-of-state, 1% international. Asian 1%, African American 11%, Caucasian 84%, Hispanic <1%, Native American <1%, Pacific Islander 0%, Two or more races 0%, Race unknown 3%.
Retention and Graduation: 66% freshmen return for sophomore year. 46% freshmen graduate within 4 years. 64% freshmen graduate within 6 years.
Faculty: Student/faculty ratio 15:1. 58 full-time faculty, 0% hold PhDs, 0% are members of minority groups, 47% are women.

ACADEMICS

Degrees: associate, bachelor's, certificate, doctoral/professional, doctoral, master's. **Classes:** Most classes have 10-19 students. Most lab/discussion sessions have fewer than 10 students. **Special Study Options:** distance learning, double major, dual enrollment, independent study, internships, teacher certification program.

FACILITIES

Housing: men's dorms, women's dorms, apartments for married students, apartments for single students.

CAMPUS LIFE

Activities: Choral groups, drama/theater, pep band, student government, student newspaper, yearbook, Campus Ministries.

ADMISSIONS

Freshman Academic Profile: Average high school GPA 3.2. 9% in top 10% of high school class, 16% in top 25% of high school class, 41% in top 50% of high school class. **Reported SAT (pre-2016 redesign) scores:** SAT Math middle 50% range 420-530. SAT Critical Reading middle 50% range 400-510. SAT Writing middle 50% range 398-500. **Concordant SAT scores:** SAT EBRW middle 50% 450–560. SAT Math middle 50% range 460–560. ACT middle 50% range 17-23. **Basis for Candidate Selection:** *Very important factors considered include:* rigor of secondary school record, academic GPA, standardized test scores. *Other factors considered include:* class rank, interview, character/personal qualities, alumni/ae relation, level of applicant's interest. **Freshman Admission Requirements:** High school diploma is required and GED is accepted. *Academic units recommended:* 4 English, 3 math, 3 science, 2 social studies. **Freshman Admission Statistics:** 620 applied, 56.29% admitted, 100% enrolled. **Transfer Admission Requirements:** High school transcript, college transcript(s), standardized test scores, Minimum college GPA of 2.0 required. Lowest grade transferable C. **General Admission Information:** Application fee $35. Regular application deadline 9/5. Nonfall registration accepted. Admission may be deferred.

COSTS AND FINANCIAL AID

Annual tuition $15,200. Room and board $6,000. Required fees $360. Average book expense $1,500. **Required Forms and Deadlines:** FAFSA. **Notification of Awards:** Applicants will be notified of awards on a rolling basis beginning 5/1. **Types of Aid:** *Need-based scholarships/grants:* Federal Pell, FSEOG, State scholarships/grants, Private scholarships, College/university scholarship or grant aid from institutional funds. *Loans:* Federal Perkins Loans. *Student Employment:* Federal Work-Study Program available. Institutional employment available. **Financial Aid Statistics:** 0% freshmen, 0% undergrads receive athletic scholarships. **Criteria for awarding aid:** *Non-need-based:* Academics, Alumni affiliation, Art, Athletics, Minority status, Music/drama, Religious affiliation.

OAKLAND UNIVERSITY

101 North Foundation Hall, Rochester, MI 48309-4401
Phone: 248-370-3360 • **Financial Aid Phone:** 248-370-2550
E-mail: visit@oakland.edu • **CEEB Code:** 1497
Fax: 248-370-4462 • **Website:** http://www.oakland.edu • **ACT Code:** 2033

This public school was founded in 1957. It has a 1444-acre campus.

RATINGS

Admissions Selectivity Rating: 80   **Fire Safety Rating:** 89   **Green Rating:** 72

STUDENTS AND FACULTY

Enrollment: 16,733. **Student Body:** 57% female, 43% male, 1% out-of-state, 2% international (46 countries represented). Asian 4%, African American 8%, Caucasian 75%, Hispanic 3%, Native American <1%, Pacific Islander <1%, Two or more races 3%, Race unknown 4%.
Retention and Graduation: 16% freshmen graduate within 4 years. **Faculty:** 573 full-time faculty, 91% hold PhDs, 23% are are members of minority groups, 47% are women. 1% of classes are taught by teaching assistants.

ACADEMICS

Degrees: bachelor's, doctoral/professional, doctoral/research, doctoral, master's, postbachelor's certificate, post-master's certificate. **Classes:** Most classes have 20-29 students. Most lab/discussion sessions have 10-19 students. **Most popular majors:** Health Professions and Related Clinical Sciences; Biology/Biological Sciences; Psychology. **Special Study Options:** Accelerated program, cooperative education program, cross-registration, distance learning, double major, English as a Second Language (ESL), honors program, independent study, internships, student-designed major, study abroad, teacher certification program. **Honors Programs:** Honors College Combined degree

programs: 5 year MBA program. **Disability Services:** Special programs offered to physically disabled students, including note-taking services, reader services, tape recorders, tutors. **Career Services:** Alumni network, Alumni services, Career/job search classes, Career assessment, Internships.

FACILITIES

Housing: Coed dorms, special housing for disabled students, special housing for international students, fraternity/sorority housing, apartments for married students, cooperative housing, apartments for single students, Wellness Housing, Theme Housing, Living/Learning Community. 90% of campus accessible to physically disabled. **Special Academic Facilities/Equipment:** Art gallery, robotics lab, Eye Research institute, Professional theater, Meadowbrook Hall, Meadowbrook Music Festival, two golf courses, Pawley Learning center, Lowry Early Childhood Education Center, Jack's Place for Autism at OU **Computers:** Students can register for classes online. Administrative functions (other than registration) can be performed online.

CAMPUS LIFE

Environment: Town. **Activities:** Choral groups, concert band, dance, drama/theater, jazz band, literary magazine, music ensembles, musical theater, pep band, radio station, student government, student newspaper, student-run film society, symphony orchestra, television station, Campus Ministries, Student Organization. 170 registered organizations, 9 honor societies, 12 religious organizations. 6 fraternities, 6 sororities. **Athletics (Intercollegiate):** *Men:* baseball, basketball, cross-country, diving, golf, soccer, swimming, track/field (outdoor). *Women:* basketball, cross-country, diving, golf, soccer, softball, swimming, tennis, track/field (outdoor), volleyball. **On-Campus Highlights:** Recreation Center, Pawley Hall, Oakland Center, Library, Honors College. **Environmental Initiatives:** $8 million Facility upgrade from 1998 to save on energy costs.

ADMISSIONS

Freshman Academic Profile: Average high school GPA 3.4. 15% in top 10% of high school class, 46% in top 25% of high school class, 79% in top 50% of high school class. 90% from public high schools. ACT middle 50% range 20-26. Minimum internet-based TOEFL 79. Minimum paper TOEFL 550. **Basis for Candidate Selection:** *Very important factors considered include:* rigor of secondary school record, academic GPA. *Important factors considered include:* standardized test scores. *Other factors considered include:* class rank, application essay, recommendation(s), interview, extracurricular activities, talent/ability, character/personal qualities, volunteer work, work experience. **Freshman Admission Requirements:** High school diploma is required and GED is accepted. *Academic units required:* 4 English, 4 math, 3 science, 3 social studies. *Academic units recommended:* 2 foreign language. **Freshman Admission Statistics:** 12,579 applied, 64.94% admitted, 33% enrolled. **Transfer Admission Requirements:** college transcript(s), statement of good standing from prior institution(s). Minimum college GPA of 2.50 required. Lowest grade transferable C. **General Admission Information:** Regular application deadline 8/1. Nonfall registration accepted. Admission may be deferred.

COSTS AND FINANCIAL AID

Annual in-state tuition $13,350. Annual out-of-state tuition $25,598. Room and board $9,250. Average book expense $912. **Required Forms and Deadlines:** FAFSA. **Types of Aid:** *Need-based scholarships/grants:* Federal Pell, FSEOG, State scholarships/grants, Private scholarships, College/university scholarship or grant aid from institutional funds. *Loans:* Direct Subsidized Stafford Loans, Direct Unsubsidized Stafford Loans, Direct PLUS loans, Federal Perkins Loans. *Student Employment:* Federal Work-Study Program available. Institutional employment available. **Criteria for awarding aid:** *Need-based:* Academics. *Non-need-based:* Academics, Art, Athletics, Leadership, Music/drama, State/district residency.

OBERLIN COLLEGE

101 North Professor Street, Oberlin, OH 44074
Phone: 440-775-8411 • **Financial Aid Phone:** 440-775-8142
E-mail: college.admissions@oberlin.edu • **CEEB Code:** 1587
Fax: 440-775-6905 • **Website:** www.oberlin.edu • **ACT Code:** 3304

This private school was founded in 1833. It has a 450-acre campus.

RATINGS

Admissions Selectivity Rating: 95   **Fire Safety Rating:** 89   **Green Rating:** 99

STUDENTS AND FACULTY

Enrollment: 2,895. **Student Body:** 57% female, 43% male, 95% out-of-state, 9% international. Asian 4%, African American 5%, Caucasian 66%, Hispanic 8%, Native American 0%, Pacific Islander <1%, Two or more races 7%, Race unknown 1%.
Retention and Graduation: 89% freshmen return for sophomore year. 72% freshmen graduate within 4 years. 85% freshmen graduate within 6 years. 22% grads go on to further study within 1 year. 8% grads pursue arts and sciences degrees. 3% grads pursue law degrees. 2% grads pursue business degrees. 3% grads pursue medical degrees. **Faculty:** Student/faculty ratio 10:1. 331 full-time faculty, 0% hold PhDs, 0% are are members of minority groups, 0% are women. 0% of classes are taught by teaching assistants.

ACADEMICS

Degrees: bachelor's, diploma, master's, postbachelor's certificate. **Classes:** Most classes have 10-19 students. Most lab/discussion sessions have fewer than 10 students. **Most popular majors:** Economics; Political Science and Government; Environmental Studies. **Special Study Options:** cross-registration, double major, dual enrollment, English as a Second Language (ESL), exchange student program (domestic), honors program, independent study, internships, student-designed major, study abroad, teacher certification program, 5 year double degree program with Conservatory of Music and College of Arts and Sciences; 3-2 engineering. Combined degree programs: BA/B.Music. **Disability Services:** Special programs offered to physically disabled students, including note-taking services, reader services, tape recorders, tutors. **Career Services:** Alumni network, Alumni services, Career/job search classes, Career assessment, Internships, Regional alumni. Alumni-Student Mentoring Program: Wisr makes it easy for alumni to guide current students and recentalumni toward fulfilling career paths through automated matching, scheduling, and follow-up communications.

FACILITIES

Housing: Coed dorms, men's dorms, women's dorms, cooperative housing, Theme Housing. 90% of campus accessible to physically diasbled. **Special Academic Facilities/Equipment:** Allen Memorial Art museum, Theaters, music performance halls. **Computers:** Students can register for classes online. Administrative functions (other than registration) can be performed online.

CAMPUS LIFE

Environment: Rural. **Activities:** Choral groups, concert band, dance, drama/theater, jazz band, literary magazine, marching band, music ensembles, musical theater, opera, radio station, student government, student newspaper, student-run film society, symphony orchestra, yearbook, Campus Ministries, Student Organization. 125 registered organizations, 3 honor societies, 10 religious organizations. **Athletics (Intercollegiate):** *Men:* baseball, basketball, cross-country, diving, football, golf, lacrosse, soccer, swimming, tennis, track/field (outdoor), track/field (indoor). *Women:* basketball, cross-country, diving, field hockey, golf, lacrosse, soccer, softball, swimming, tennis, track/field (outdoor), track/field (indoor), volleyball. **On-Campus Highlights:** Allen Art Museum, Oberlin College Science Center, Adam Joseph Lewis Center for Environmental Studies, Mudd Library, Jesse Philips Recreational Center. **Environmental Initiatives:** Development of Campus Resource Monitoring System. oberlin.edu/dormenergy.

ADMISSIONS

Freshman Academic Profile: Average high school GPA 3.6. 61% in top 10% of high school class, 84% in top 25% of high school class, 98% in top 50% of high school class. 66% from public high schools. **Reported SAT (pre-2016 redesign) scores:** SAT Math middle 50% range 620-720. SAT Critical Reading middle 50% range 630-730. SAT Writing middle 50% range 623-720. **Concordant SAT scores:** SAT EBRW middle 50% 680–750. SAT Math middle 50% range 640–750. ACT middle 50% range 29-33. Minimum paper TOEFL 600. **Basis for Candidate Selection:** *Very important factors considered include:* rigor of secondary school record, class rank, academic GPA, standardized test scores. *Important factors considered include:* application essay, recommendation(s), extracurricular activities, talent/ability, character/personal qualities, first generation. *Other factors considered include:* interview, alumni/ae relation, racial/ethnic status, volunteer work, work experience, level of applicant's interest. **Freshman Admission Requirements:** High school diploma is required and GED is accepted. *Academic units required:* 4 English, 3 math, 3 science, 3 foreign language, 3 social studies. *Academic units recommended:* 4 math, 4 science. **Freshman Admission Statistics:** 8,518 applied, 28.03% admitted, 32% enrolled. **Transfer Admission Requirements:** High school transcript, college transcript(s), essay or personal statement, standardized test scores, statement of good standing from prior institution(s). Minimum college GPA of 3.0 required. Lowest grade transferable C-. **General Admission Information:** Regular application deadline 1/15. Regular notification 4/1. Nonfall registration not accepted. Admission may be deferred for a maximum of 1 year.

COSTS AND FINANCIAL AID

Annual tuition $51,324. Room and board $14,010. Required fees $678. Average book expense $930. **Required Forms and Deadlines:** FAFSA, Institution's own financial aid form, CSS/Financial Aid PROFILE, Noncustodial PROFILE. **Notification of Awards:** Applicants will be notified of awards on or about 4/1. **Types of Aid:** *Need-based scholarships/grants:* Federal Pell, FSEOG, State scholarships/grants, Private scholarships, College/university scholarship or grant aid from institutional funds, United Negro College Fund. *Loans:* Direct Subsidized Stafford Loans, Direct Unsubsidized Stafford Loans, Federal Perkins Loans, College/university loans from institutional funds. *Student Employment:* Federal Work-Study Program available. Institutional employment available. **Financial Aid Statistics:** 96% needy freshmen, 99% needy undergrads receive need-based scholarship or grant aid. 81% freshmen, 79% undergrads receive non-need-based scholarship or grant aid. 87% freshmen, 88% undergrads receive need-based self-help aid. 0% freshmen, 0% undergrads receive athletic scholarships. 61% freshmen, 60% undergrads receive any aid. 43% undergrads borrow to pay for school. Average cumulative indebtedness $27,144. **Criteria for awarding aid:** *Non-need-based:* Academics, Music/drama.

OCAD UNIVERSITY

100 McCaul Street Toronto, RI M5T 1W1
Phone: 416-977-6000
E-mail: admissions@ocadu.ca
Fax: 416-977-6006 • **Website:** www.ocadu.ca

RATINGS
Admissions Selectivity Rating: 61   **Fire Safety Rating:** 60*   **Green Rating:** 60*

STUDENTS AND FACULTY

Enrollment: 2,882. **Student Body:** 63% female, 37% male, 8% out-of-state, 8% international. Asian 4%, African American 12%, Caucasian 47%, Hispanic 15%, Native American <1%, Pacific Islander <1%, Two or more races 2%, Race unknown 13%.
Faculty: Student/faculty ratio 16 140 full-time faculty, 88% hold PhDs, 10% are are members of minority groups, are women.

ACADEMICS

Career Services: Alumni network, Alumni services, Career/job search classes, Career assessment, Internships, On-campus interviews.

ADMISSIONS

Freshman Admission Statistics: 46% enrolled.

COSTS AND FINANCIAL AID

Annual tuition $34,352. Annual in-state tuition $6,340. Room and board $3,740. Required fees $800. Average book expense $750. **Financial Aid Statistics:** 98% needy undergrads receive need-based scholarship or grant aid. 100% freshmen, 0% undergrads receive non-need-based scholarship or grant aid. 99% freshmen, 86% undergrads receive need-based self-help aid. 0% freshmen, 0% undergrads receive athletic scholarships.

OCCIDENTAL COLLEGE

1600 Campus Road, Los Angeles, CA 90041-3314
Phone: 800-825-5262 • **Financial Aid Phone:** 323-259-2548
E-mail: admission@oxy.edu • **CEEB Code:** 4581
Fax: 323-341-4875 • **Website:** www.oxy.edu • **ACT Code:** 350

This private school was founded in 1887. It has a 120-acre campus.

RATINGS
Admissions Selectivity Rating: 92   **Fire Safety Rating:** 81   **Green Rating:** 87

STUDENTS AND FACULTY

Enrollment: 2,050. **Student Body:** 57% female, 43% male, 50% out-of-state, 6% international (28 countries represented). Asian 14%, African American 5%, Caucasian 50%, Hispanic 15%, Native American 0%, Pacific Islander <1%, Two or more races 8%, Race unknown 2%.
Retention and Graduation: 91% freshmen return for sophomore year. 76% freshmen graduate within 4 years. 21% grads go on to further study within 1

year. **Faculty:** Student/faculty ratio 10:1. 179 full-time faculty, 97% hold PhDs, 30% are are members of minority groups, 50% are women. 0% of classes are taught by teaching assistants.

ACADEMICS

Degrees: bachelor's, master's. **Classes:** Most classes have 10-19 students. Most lab/discussion sessions have 10-19 students. **Most popular majors:** Economics; International Relations and Affairs; Biology/Biological Sciences. **Special Study Options:** cross-registration, double major, exchange student program (domestic), honors program, independent study, internships, student-designed major, study abroad, Richter fellowships for international research; summer undergraduate research program; endowment investment management program (Blyth Fund). Combined degree programs: BA/JD, law, Columbia; biotech with Keck Grad Institute. **Disability Services:** Special programs offered to physically disabled students, including note-taking services, tape recorders. **Career Services:** Alumni network, Alumni services, Career/job search classes, Internships, Regional alumni. InternLA is Oxy's flagship donor-funded summer internship program. Students obtain transformational summer experiences with employers throughout the Los Angeles area as well as professional development and career readiness preparation.

FACILITIES

Housing: Coed dorms, women's dorms, fraternity/sorority housing, Theme Housing. 65% of campus accessible to physically disabled. **Special Academic Facilities/Equipment:** Keck Theater; Mullin Studio and Art Gallery; Moore Ornithology Collection; Smiley Geological Collection; Morse Collection of Astronomical Instruments; superconducting magnet; vivarium; greenhouses **Computers:** 100% of classrooms, 100% of dorms, 90% of libraries, 100% of dining areas, 80% of student union, 50% of common outdoor areas have wireless network access. Students can register for classes online. Administrative functions (other than registration) can be performed online.

CAMPUS LIFE

Environment: Metropolis. **Activities:** Choral groups, concert band, dance, drama/theater, jazz band, literary magazine, music ensembles, musical theater, radio station, student government, student newspaper, student-run film society, symphony orchestra, yearbook, Student Organization. 8 honor societies, 5 religious organizations. 4 fraternities, 4 sororities. **Athletics (Intercollegiate):** *Men:* baseball, basketball, cross-country, diving, football, golf, soccer, swimming, tennis, track/field (outdoor), water polo. *Women:* basketball, cross-country, diving, golf, lacrosse, soccer, softball, swimming, tennis, track/field (outdoor), volleyball, water polo. **On-Campus Highlights:** Johnson Student Center, Student Quad, Samuelson Pavilion, Clapp Library, Alumni Gymnasium. **Environmental Initiatives:** Sustainability coordinator.

ADMISSIONS

Freshman Academic Profile: Average high school GPA 3.6. 52% in top 10% of high school class, 83% in top 25% of high school class, 98% in top 50% of high school class. 66% from public high schools. **Reported SAT (pre-2016 redesign) scores:** SAT Math middle 50% range 600-720. SAT Critical Reading middle 50% range 600-700. SAT Writing middle 50% range 610-700. **Concordant SAT scores:** SAT EBRW middle 50% 660-730. SAT Math middle 50% range 620-750. ACT middle 50% range 28-31. Minimum paper TOEFL 600. **Basis for Candidate Selection:** *Very important factors considered include:* rigor of secondary school record, academic GPA, application essay, recommendation(s). *Important factors considered include:* class rank, standardized test scores, extracurricular activities, character/personal qualities, volunteer work, work experience. *Other factors considered include:* interview, talent/ability, first generation, alumni/ae relation, geographical residence, racial/ethnic status, level of applicant's interest. **Freshman Admission Requirements:** High school diploma is required and GED is accepted. *Academic units recommended:* 4 English, 3 math, 3 science, 3 foreign language, 2 social studies, 3 history. **Freshman Admission Statistics:** 6,409 applied, 45.81% admitted, 17% enrolled. **Transfer Admission Requirements:** High school transcript, college transcript(s), essay or personal statement, statement of good standing from prior institution(s). Minimum college GPA of 3.0 required. Lowest grade transferable D. **General Admission Information:** Application fee $60. Regular application deadline 1/15. Regular notification 3/25. Nonfall registration not accepted. Admission may be deferred for a maximum of 1 year.

COSTS AND FINANCIAL AID

Annual tuition $50,492. Room and board $14,460. Required fees $578. Average book expense $1,250. **Required Forms and Deadlines:** FAFSA, CSS/Financial Aid PROFILE, State aid form, Noncustodial PROFILE. **Notification of Awards:** Applicants will be notified of awards on or about 4/1. **Types of Aid:** *Need-based scholarships/grants:* Federal Pell, FSEOG, State scholarships/grants, Private scholarships, College/university scholarship or grant aid from institutional funds. *Loans:* Direct Subsidized Stafford Loans, Direct Unsubsidized Stafford Loans, Direct PLUS loans, Federal Perkins Loans, College/university loans from institutional funds. *Student Employment:* Federal Work-Study Program available. Institutional employment available. **Financial Aid Statistics:** 90% needy freshmen, 99% needy undergrads receive

need-based scholarship or grant aid. 56% freshmen, 50% undergrads receive non-need-based scholarship or grant aid. 83% freshmen, 86% undergrads receive need-based self-help aid. 0% freshmen, 0% undergrads receive athletic scholarships. 72% freshmen, 74% undergrads receive any aid. Average cumulative indebtedness $29,940. **Criteria for awarding aid:** *Non-need-based:* Academics, Leadership, Music/drama, State/district residency.

OGLETHORPE UNIVERSITY

4484 Peachtree Road N.E., Atlanta, GA 30319
Phone: 404-364-8307 • **Financial Aid Phone:** 404-364-8356
E-mail: admission@oglethorpe.edu • **CEEB Code:** 5521
Fax: 404-364-8491 • **Website:** www.oglethorpe.edu • **ACT Code:** 850

This private school was founded in 1835. It has a 102-acre campus.

RATINGS

Admissions Selectivity Rating: 75   **Fire Safety Rating:** 83   **Green Rating:** 60*

STUDENTS AND FACULTY

Enrollment: 1,150. **Student Body:** 58% female, 42% male, 23% out-of-state, 7% international (24 countries represented). Asian 3%, African American 18%, Caucasian 33%, Hispanic 10%, Native American <1%, Pacific Islander <1%, Two or more races 3%, Race unknown 26%. **Retention and Graduation:** 73% freshmen return for sophomore year. 44% freshmen graduate within 4 years. 53% freshmen graduate within 6 years. 40% grads go on to further study within 1 year. 19% grads pursue arts and sciences degrees. 9% grads pursue law degrees. 10% grads pursue business degrees. 2% grads pursue medical degrees. **Faculty:** Student/faculty ratio 15:1. 59 full-time faculty, 92% hold PhDs, 15% are are members of minority groups, 39% are women. 0% of classes are taught by teaching assistants.

ACADEMICS

Degrees: bachelor's, master's. **Classes:** Most classes have 10-19 students. **Most popular majors:** English Language and Literature; Psychology; Business/Commerce. **Special Study Options:** Accelerated program, cooperative education program, cross-registration, double major, dual enrollment, exchange student program (domestic), honors program, independent study, internships, liberal arts/career combination, student-designed major, study abroad. **Disability Services:** Special programs offered to physically disabled students, including note-taking services, tutors. **Career Services:** Alumni services, Career/job search classes, Career assessment, Internships.

FACILITIES

Housing: Coed dorms, fraternity/sorority housing. 60% of campus accessible to physically disabled. **Special Academic Facilities/Equipment:** Art museum, scanning electron microscope. **Computers:** 100% of classrooms, 100% of dorms, 100% of libraries, 100% of student union, 25% of common outdoor areas have wireless network access. Administrative functions (other than registration) can be performed online.

CAMPUS LIFE

Environment: Metropolis. **Activities:** Choral groups, dance, drama/theater, jazz band, literary magazine, music ensembles, musical theater, pep band, radio station, student government, student newspaper, student-run film society, yearbook, Campus Ministries, Student Organization. 57 registered organizations, 10 honor societies, 5 religious organizations. 4 fraternities, 3 sororities. **Athletics (Intercollegiate):** *Men:* baseball, basketball, cross-country, golf, lacrosse, soccer, tennis, track/field (outdoor). *Women:* basketball, cheerleading, cross-country, golf, lacrosse, soccer, tennis, track/field (outdoor), volleyball. **On-Campus Highlights:** Oglethorpe University Museum, Phillip Weltner Library, Conant Performing Arts Center, Hermance Stadium, New Residence Halls. **Environmental Initiatives:** New buildings are built according to LEED requirements.

ADMISSIONS

Freshman Academic Profile: Average high school GPA 3.5. 79% from public high schools. **Reported SAT (pre-2016 redesign) scores:** SAT Math middle 50% range 510-610, SAT Critical Reading middle 50% range 530-630. SAT Writing middle 50% range 500-610. **Concordant SAT scores:** SAT EBRW middle 50% 570–670. SAT Math middle 50% range 540–630. ACT middle 50% range 22-28. Minimum paper TOEFL 550. **Basis for Candidate Selection:** *Very important factors considered include:* rigor of secondary school record, academic GPA, standardized test scores. *Important factors considered include:* class rank, application essay, recommendation(s), interview, extracurricular activities, volunteer work, level of applicant's interest. *Other factors considered include:* talent/ability, character/personal qualities, first generation, alumni/ae relation, work experience. **Freshman Admission Requirements:** High school diploma is required and GED is accepted. *Academic units required:* 4 English,

3 math, 2 science, 3 social studies. *Academic units recommended:* 2 foreign language. **Freshman Admission Statistics:** 2,768 applied, 78.47% admitted, 20% enrolled. **Transfer Admission Requirements:** college transcript(s), statement of good standing from prior institution(s). Minimum college GPA of 2.8 required. Lowest grade transferable C. **General Admission Information:** Application fee $50. Priority deadline 11/15. Nonfall registration accepted. Admission may be deferred for a maximum of 1 semester.

COSTS AND FINANCIAL AID

Annual tuition $35,000. Room and board $12,710. Required fees $425. Average book expense $1,100. **Required Forms and Deadlines:** FAFSA. **Notification of Awards:** Applicants will be notified of awards on a rolling basis beginning 3/1. **Types of Aid:** *Need-based scholarships/grants:* Federal Pell, FSEOG, State scholarships/grants, Private scholarships, College/university scholarship or grant aid from institutional funds. *Loans:* Direct Subsidized Stafford Loans, Direct Unsubsidized Stafford Loans, Direct PLUS loans, Federal Perkins Loans, State Loans. *Student Employment:* Federal Work-Study Program available. Institutional employment available. **Financial Aid Statistics:** 100% needy freshmen, 99% needy undergrads receive need-based scholarship or grant aid. 16% freshmen, 13% undergrads receive non-need-based scholarship or grant aid. 75% freshmen, 80% undergrads receive need-based self-help aid. 0% freshmen, 0% undergrads receive athletic scholarships. 95% freshmen, 95% undergrads receive any aid. 68% undergrads borrow to pay for school. Average cumulative indebtedness $23,212. **Criteria for awarding aid:** *Need-based:* Academics, Leadership, Minority status, Music/drama. *Non-need-based:* Academics, Art, Leadership, Minority status, Music/drama, State/district residency.

OHIO DOMINICAN UNIVERSITY

1216 Sunbury Road, Coumbus, OH 42319-2099
Phone: 614-251-4500 • **Financial Aid Phone:** 614-251-4778
E-mail: admissions@ohiodominican.edu • **CEEB Code:** 1131
Fax: 614-251-0156 • **Website:** http://www.ohiodominican.edu • **ACT Code:** 3256

This private school, affiliated with the Roman Catholic Church, was founded in 1911. It has a 75-acre campus.

RATINGS
Admissions Selectivity Rating: 79   **Fire Safety Rating:** 88   **Green Rating:** 69

STUDENTS AND FACULTY
Enrollment: 1,158. **Student Body:** 55% female, 45% male, 5% out-of-state, 2% international (13 countries represented). Asian 1%, African American 21%, Caucasian 58%, Hispanic 3%, Native American <1%, Pacific Islander 0%, Two or more races 5%, Race unknown 9%.
Retention and Graduation: 67% freshmen return for sophomore year. 29% freshmen graduate within 4 years. 37% freshmen graduate within 6 years.
Faculty: Student/faculty ratio 13:1. 69 full-time faculty, 93% hold PhDs, 10% are are members of minority groups, 45% are women. 0% of classes are taught by teaching assistants.

ACADEMICS
Degrees: associate, bachelor's, certificate, master's, postbachelor's certificate.
Classes: Most classes have 10-19 students. **Most popular majors:** Business Administration and Management; Biology/Biological Sciences; Kinesiology and Exercise Science. **Special Study Options:** Accelerated program, cross-registration, distance learning, double major, dual enrollment, exchange student program (domestic), honors program, independent study, internships, study abroad, teacher certification program. **Honors Programs:** The Honors Program is designed for high-ability, motivated students. Honors-designed courses will be offered to specifically challenge and engage students in the program. Combined degree programs: BA/MA, BS/MBA, BS/MS, BS/DO.
Career Services: Alumni network, Alumni services, Career/job search classes, Career assessment, Internships, Regional alumni. Students gain vital practical experience by participating in internships.

FACILITIES
Housing: Coed dorms. **Special Academic Facilities/Equipment:** Wehrle Art Gallery. **Computers:** 90% of classrooms, 100% of libraries, 100% of dining areas, 5% of common outdoor areas have wireless network access. Students can register for classes online. Administrative functions (other than registration) can be performed online.

CAMPUS LIFE
Environment: Metropolis. **Activities:** Choral groups, concert band, dance, drama/theater, literary magazine, marching band, music ensembles, musical theater, pep band, radio station, student government, student newspaper, Campus Ministries, Model UN. 40 registered organizations, 2 honor societies, 1

religious organization. **Athletics (Intercollegiate):** *Men:* baseball, basketball, cross-country, football, golf, soccer, tennis. *Women:* basketball, cross-country, golf, soccer, softball, tennis, volleyball. **On-Campus Highlights:** Student Center opened Fall 2009, Panther Plaza, Alumni Hall, Wehrle Hall, The Underground in Fitzpatrick Hall.

ADMISSIONS
Freshman Academic Profile: Average high school GPA 3.2. 10% in top 10% of high school class, 31% in top 25% of high school class, 79% in top 50% of high school class. **Reported SAT (pre-2016 redesign) scores:** SAT Math middle 50% range 450-520. SAT Critical Reading middle 50% range 420-520. SAT Writing middle 50% range 358-490. **Concordant SAT scores:** SAT EBRW middle 50% 440–560. SAT Math middle 50% range 490–550. ACT middle 50% range 19-24. Minimum internet-based TOEFL 79. Minimum paper TOEFL 550. **Basis for Candidate Selection:** *Very important factors considered include:* rigor of secondary school record, academic GPA, standardized test scores. *Other factors considered include:* class rank, application essay, recommendation(s), interview, extracurricular activities, talent/ability, character/personal qualities, volunteer work, work experience, level of applicant's interest. **Freshman Admission Requirements:** High school diploma is required and GED is accepted. *Academic units recommended:* 4 English, 4 math, 4 science, 3 foreign language, 3 social studies. **Freshman Admission Statistics:** 1,969 applied, 52.16% admitted, 22% enrolled. **Transfer Admission Requirements:** college transcript(s), Lowest grade transferable C. **General Admission Information:** Priority deadline 12/4. Nonfall registration accepted. Admission may be deferred for a maximum of 1 year.

COSTS AND FINANCIAL AID
Annual tuition $30,500. Room and board $10,928. Required fees $580. Average book expense $1,100. **Required Forms and Deadlines:** FAFSA. **Types of Aid:** *Need-based scholarships/grants:* Federal Pell, FSEOG, State scholarships/grants, Private scholarships, College/university scholarship or grant aid from institutional funds. *Loans:* Direct Subsidized Stafford Loans, Direct Unsubsidized Stafford Loans, Direct PLUS loans, Federal Perkins Loans, College/university loans from institutional funds. *Student Employment:* Federal Work-Study Program available. Institutional employment available. **Financial Aid Statistics:** 0% freshmen, 0% undergrads receive athletic scholarships. 100% freshmen, 66% undergrads receive any aid. **Criteria for awarding aid:** *Non-need-based:* Academics, Athletics, Music/drama.

OHIO NORTHERN UNIVERSITY

525 South Main Street, Ada, OH 45810
Phone: 419-772-2260 • **Financial Aid Phone:** 419-772-2272
E-mail: admissions-ug@onu.edu • **CEEB Code:** 1591
Fax: 419-772-2313 • **Website:** www.onu.edu • **ACT Code:** 3310

This private school, affiliated with the Methodist Church, was founded in 1871. It has a 300-acre campus.

RATINGS
Admissions Selectivity Rating: 85   **Fire Safety Rating:** 62   **Green Rating:** 60*

STUDENTS AND FACULTY
Enrollment: 2,116. **Student Body:** 44% female, 56% male, 17% out-of-state, 4% international (17 countries represented). Asian 1%, African American 3%, Caucasian 84%, Hispanic 1%, Native American <1%, Pacific Islander 0%, Two or more races 3%, Race unknown 3%.
Retention and Graduation: 86% freshmen return for sophomore year. 50% freshmen graduate within 4 years. 66% freshmen graduate within 6 years.
Faculty: Student/faculty ratio 11:1. 211 full-time faculty, 84% hold PhDs, 14% are are members of minority groups, 41% are women. 0% of classes are taught by teaching assistants.

ACADEMICS
Degrees: bachelor's, doctoral/professional, postbachelor's certificate. **Classes:** Most classes have 10-19 students. **Most popular majors:** Mechanical Engineering; Biology/Biological Sciences; Registered Nursing/Registered Nurse. **Special Study Options:** cooperative education program, distance learning, double major, dual enrollment, English as a Second Language (ESL), exchange student program (domestic), honors program, independent study, internships, liberal arts/career combination, study abroad, teacher certification program, Washington semester. **Honors Programs:** Honors Program consisits

of a First-Year Honors Seminar and 3 additional Honors Seminars, 2 "contract" courses and a final Honors project. Combined degree programs: BA/JD, Pharm D. **Disability Services:** Special programs offered to physically disabled students, including note-taking services, reader services, tape recorders, tutors. **Career Services:** Alumni network, Alumni services, Career/job search classes, Career assessment, Internships.

FACILITIES

Housing: Coed dorms, special housing for disabled students, men's dorms, special housing for international students, women's dorms, fraternity/sorority housing, apartments for married students, cooperative housing, apartments for single students, Wellness Housing, Theme Housing, Honors Residence Halls. 95% of campus accessible to physically diasbled. **Special Academic Facilities/ Equipment:** Art gallery, performing arts center, language lab, sports center, pharmacy museum. **Computers:** 100% of classrooms, 100% of dorms, 100% of libraries, 100% of dining areas, 100% of student union, have wireless network access. Students can register for classes online. Administrative functions (other than registration) can be performed online.

CAMPUS LIFE

Environment: Village. **Activities:** Choral groups, concert band, dance, drama/ theater, jazz band, literary magazine, marching band, music ensembles, musical theater, opera, pep band, radio station, student government, student newspaper, symphony orchestra, television station, yearbook, Campus Ministries, Student Organization, Model UN. 200 registered organizations, 40 honor societies, 27 religious organizations. 6 fraternities, 4 sororities. **Athletics (Intercollegiate):** *Men:* baseball, basketball, cross-country, diving, football, golf, soccer, swimming, tennis, track/field (outdoor), track/field (indoor), wrestling. *Women:* basketball, cross-country, diving, golf, soccer, softball, swimming, tennis, track/field (outdoor), track/field (indoor), volleyball. **On-Campus Highlights:** ONU Sports Center, Northern on Main Coffee Cafe, Performing Arts Center, New Student Apartments, James F. Dicke Hall.

ADMISSIONS

Freshman Academic Profile: Average high school GPA 3.6. 32% in top 10% of high school class, 60% in top 25% of high school class, 85% in top 50% of high school class. **Reported SAT (pre-2016 redesign) scores:** SAT Math middle 50% range 530-640. SAT Critical Reading middle 50% range 480-600. SAT Writing middle 50% range 508-590. **Concordant SAT scores:** SAT EBRW middle 50% range 550–650. SAT Math middle 50% range 560–660. ACT middle 50% range 23-28. Minimum internet-based TOEFL 54. Minimum paper TOEFL 480. **Basis for Candidate Selection:** *Very important factors considered include:* rigor of secondary school record, academic GPA, standardized test scores. *Important factors considered include:* class rank, application essay, recommendation(s), interview, extracurricular activities. *Other factors considered include:* talent/ability, character/personal qualities, first generation, alumni/ae relation, volunteer work, level of applicant's interest. **Freshman Admission Requirements:** High school diploma is required and GED is accepted. *Academic units required:* 4 English, 2 math, 2 science, 2 science labs, 2 social studies, 2 history, 4 academic electives. *Academic units recommended:* 4 English, 4 math, 3 science, 2 science labs, 2 foreign language, 3 social studies, 2 history, 4 academic electives, 1 computer science, 1 visual/performing arts. **Freshman Admission Statistics:** 3,108 applied, 69.05% admitted, 27% enrolled. **Transfer Admission Requirements:** High school transcript, college transcript(s), statement of good standing from prior institution(s). Minimum college GPA of 2.0 required. Lowest grade transferable C. **General Admission Information:** Priority deadline 12/1. Regular application deadline 8/15. Nonfall registration accepted. Admission may be deferred for a maximum of 1 year.

COSTS AND FINANCIAL AID

Annual tuition $29,240. Room and board $11,050. Required fees $580. Average book expense $1,800. **Required Forms and Deadlines:** FAFSA. **Notification of Awards:** Applicants will be notified of awards on a rolling basis beginning 3/1. **Types of Aid:** *Need-based scholarships/grants:* Federal Pell, FSEOG, State scholarships/grants, Private scholarships, College/university scholarship or grant aid from institutional funds. *Loans:* Direct Subsidized Stafford Loans, Direct Unsubsidized Stafford Loans, Direct PLUS loans, Federal Perkins Loans, State Loans, College/university loans from institutional funds. *Student Employment:* Federal Work-Study Program available. Institutional employment available. **Criteria for awarding aid:** *Non-need-based:* Academics, Alumni affiliation, Art, Leadership, Minority status, Music/drama, State/district residency.

THE OHIO STATE UNIVERSITY AT MANSFIELD

1760 University Drive, Mansfield, OH 44906
Phone: 419-755-4011 • **Financial Aid Phone:** 614-292-0330
E-mail: askabuckeye@osu.edu • **CEEB Code:** 744
Website: www.mansfield.ohio.edu • **ACT Code:** 3312

This public school was founded in 1958. It has a 640-acre campus.

RATINGS

Admissions Selectivity Rating: 72   **Fire Safety Rating:** 76   **Green Rating:** 60*

STUDENTS AND FACULTY

Enrollment: 1,115. **Student Body:** 54% female, 46% male, 0% out-of-state, 0% international (0 countries represented), Asian 2%, African American 11%, Caucasian 78%, Hispanic 3%, Native American <1%, Pacific Islander 0%, Two or more races 3%, Race unknown 2%.
Retention and Graduation: 69% freshmen return for sophomore year. 19% freshmen graduate within 4 years. 43% freshmen graduate within 6 years.
Faculty: Student/faculty ratio 19:1. 38 full-time faculty, 0% hold PhDs, 11% are are members of minority groups, 50% are women.

ACADEMICS

Degrees: associate, bachelor's, master's. **Classes:** Most classes have 10-19 students. Most lab/discussion sessions have 40-49 students. **Special Study Options:** Accelerated program, cooperative education program, cross-registration, distance learning, double major, dual enrollment, English as a Second Language (ESL), exchange student program (domestic), honors program, independent study, internships, liberal arts/career combination, student-designed major, study abroad, teacher certification program, weekend college. **Honors Programs:** The University Honors Program is dedicated to promoting the intellectual and personal development of high-performing students. It strives to promote a more active and enriching relationship between Honors students and the University by connecting them with resources and opportunities that will encourage them to maximize their potential. The University Scholars Program enables talented and motivated students to be part of smaller, selective communnities within the larger university environment. Each of the fourteen programs focuses on a common theme or academic area of interest designed to foster learning and involvement. Scholars live together, attend classes together, and experience diverse opportunities outside the classroom. **Disability Services:** Special programs offered to physically disabled students, including note-taking services, reader services, tape recorders, tutors. **Career Services:** Alumni network, Alumni services.

FACILITIES

Housing: special housing for disabled students, apartments for single students, Wellness Housing. 90% of campus accessible to physically diasbled. **Computers:** 100% of classrooms, 100% of dorms, 100% of libraries, 100% of dining areas, 100% of student union, 50% of common outdoor areas have wireless network access. Students can register for classes online. Administrative functions (other than registration) can be performed online.

CAMPUS LIFE

Environment: Town. **Activities:** Choral groups, dance, drama/theater, student newspaper, student-run film society 16 registered organizations, 2 honor societies, 2 religious organizations. **Athletics (Intercollegiate):** *Men:* baseball, basketball, soccer. *Women:* basketball, cheerleading, volleyball.

ADMISSIONS

Freshman Academic Profile: 6% in top 10% of high school class, 27% in top 25% of high school class, 59% in top 50% of high school class. 90% from public high schools. **Reported SAT (pre-2016 redesign) scores:** SAT Math middle 50% range 465-605. SAT Critical Reading middle 50% range 470-580. SAT Writing middle 50% range 450-565. **Concordant SAT scores:** SAT EBRW middle 50% 510–630. SAT Math middle 50% range 510–630. ACT middle 50% range 20-25. Minimum internet-based TOEFL 79. Minimum paper TOEFL 550. **Basis for Candidate Selection:** *Other factors considered include:* standardized test scores. **Freshman Admission Requirements:** *Academic units required:* 4 English, 3 math, 3 science, 3 science labs, 2 foreign language, 2 social studies, 1 academic elective, 1 visual/performing arts. *Academic units recommended:* 4 English, 4 math, 3 science, 3 science labs, 3 foreign language, 3 social studies, 1 academic elective, 1 visual/performing arts. **Freshman Admission Statistics:** 1,607 applied, 99.25% admitted, 33% enrolled. **Transfer Admission Requirements:** college transcript(s), Minimum college GPA of 2.0 required. Lowest grade transferable C-. **General Admission Information:** Application fee $60. Regular application deadline 6/1. Nonfall registration accepted.

COSTS AND FINANCIAL AID

Annual in-state tuition $7,140. Annual out-of-state tuition $25,332. Average book expense $1,234. **Required Forms and Deadlines:** FAFSA. **Notification** of Awards: Applicants will be notified of awards on or about 3/15. **Types of Aid:** *Need-based scholarships/grants:* Federal Pell, FSEOG, State scholarships/grants, Private scholarships, College/university scholarship or grant aid from institutional funds. *Loans:* Direct Subsidized Stafford Loans, Direct Unsubsidized Stafford Loans, Direct PLUS loans, Federal Perkins Loans, Federal Nursing Loans, College/university loans from institutional funds. *Student Employment:* Federal Work-Study Program available. Institutional employment available. **Financial Aid Statistics:** 83% needy freshmen, 81% needy undergrads receive need-based scholarship or grant aid. 1% freshmen, 1% undergrads receive non-need-based scholarship or grant aid. 93% freshmen, 92% undergrads receive need-based self-help aid. 0% freshmen, 0% undergrads receive athletic scholarships. 93% freshmen, 87% undergrads receive any aid. **Criteria for awarding aid:** *Need-based:* Academics, Alumni affiliation, Art, Athletics, Job skills, Leadership, Minority status, Music/drama. *Non-need-based:* Academics, Alumni affiliation, Art, Athletics, Job skills, Leadership, Minority status, Music/drama, State/district residency.

THE OHIO STATE UNIVERSITY AT MARION

1465 Mount Vernon Avenue, Marion, OH 43302
Phone: 740-725-6337 • **Financial Aid Phone:** 614-292-0300
E-mail: askabuckeye@osu.edu • **CEEB Code:** 752
Website: http://osumarion.osu.edu/ • **ACT Code:** 3312

This public school was founded in 1957. It has a 188-acre campus.

RATINGS
Admissions Selectivity Rating: 73   **Fire Safety Rating:** 60*   **Green Rating:** 60*

STUDENTS AND FACULTY
Enrollment: 1,016. **Student Body:** 52% female, 48% male, 1% out-of-state, <1% international (2 countries represented). Asian 3%, African American 4%, Caucasian 82%, Hispanic 4%, Native American <1%, Pacific Islander <1%, Two or more races 3%, Race unknown 3%.
Retention and Graduation: 64% freshmen return for sophomore year. 17% freshmen graduate within 4 years. 43% freshmen graduate within 6 years.
Faculty: Student/faculty ratio 17:1. 35 full-time faculty, 0% hold PhDs, 11% are are members of minority groups, 46% are women.

ACADEMICS
Degrees: associate, bachelor's, master's. **Classes:** Most classes have 20-29 students. Most lab/discussion sessions have 20-29 students. **Most popular majors:** Elementary and Middle School Administration/Principalship; Elementary Education and Teaching; Junior High/Intermediate/Middle School Education and Teaching. **Special Study Options:** Accelerated program, cooperative education program, cross-registration, distance learning, double major, dual enrollment, English as a Second Language (ESL), exchange student program (domestic), honors program, independent study, internships, liberal arts/career combination, student-designed major, study abroad, teacher certification program, weekend college. **Honors Programs:** The University Honors Program is dedicated to promoting the intellectual and personal development of high-performing students. It strives to promote a more active and enriching relationship between Honors students and the University by connecting them with resources and opportunities that will encourage them to maximize their potential. The University Scholars Program enables talented and motivated students to be part of smaller, selective communnities within the larger university environment. Each of the fourteen programs focuses on a common theme or academic area of interest designed to foster learning and involvement. Scholars live together, attend classes together, and experience diverse opportunities outside the classroom. **Disability Services:** Special programs offered to physically disabled students, including note-taking services, reader services, tape recorders, tutors. **Career Services:** Alumni network, Alumni services, Career/job search classes, Career assessment, Internships, Regional alumni, On-campus interviews.

FACILITIES
Housing: 100% of campus accessible to physically disabled. **Special Academic Facilities/Equipment:** Kuhn Art Gallery **Computers:** 100% of classrooms, 100% of libraries, have wireless network access. Students can register for classes online. Administrative functions (other than registration) can be performed online.

CAMPUS LIFE
Environment: Town. **Activities:** Choral groups, literary magazine, music ensembles, student government, Campus Ministries. 33 registered organizations, 1 honor society, 3 religious organizations. **Athletics (Intercollegiate):** *Men:* basketball, gymnastics, volleyball. *Women:* gymnastics.

ADMISSIONS
Freshman Academic Profile: 10% in top 10% of high school class, 29% in top 25% of high school class, 66% in top 50% of high school class. 98% from public high schools. **Reported SAT (pre-2016 redesign) scores:** SAT Math middle 50% range 490-618. SAT Critical Reading middle 50% range 468-590. SAT Writing middle 50% range 468-563. **Concordant SAT scores:** SAT EBRW middle 50% 530–630. SAT Math middle 50% range 520–640. ACT middle 50% range 19-25. Minimum internet-based TOEFL 79. Minimum paper TOEFL 550. **Basis for Candidate Selection:** *Other factors considered include:* standardized test scores. **Freshman Admission Requirements:** *Academic units required:* 4 English, 3 math, 3 science, 3 science labs, 2 foreign language, 2 social studies, 1 academic elective, 1 visual/performing arts. *Academic units recommended:* 4 English, 4 math, 3 science, 3 science labs, 3 foreign language, 3 social studies, 1 academic elective, 1 visual/performing arts. **Freshman Admission Statistics:** 873 applied, 98.51% admitted, 45% enrolled. **Transfer Admission Requirements:** college transcript(s), Minimum college GPA of 2.0 required. Lowest grade transferable C-. **General Admission Information:** Application fee $60. Regular application deadline 6/1. Regular notification 11/15. Nonfall registration accepted.

COSTS AND FINANCIAL AID
Annual in-state tuition $7,140. Annual out-of-state tuition $25,332. Average book expense $1,234. **Required Forms and Deadlines:** FAFSA. **Notification of Awards:** Applicants will be notified of awards on or about 3/15. **Types of Aid:** *Need-based scholarships/grants:* Federal Pell, FSEOG, State scholarships/grants, Private scholarships, College/university scholarship or grant aid from institutional funds. *Loans:* Direct Subsidized Stafford Loans, Direct Unsubsidized Stafford Loans, Direct PLUS loans, Federal Perkins Loans, Federal Nursing Loans, College/university loans from institutional funds. *Student Employment:* Federal Work-Study Program available. Institutional employment available. **Financial Aid Statistics:** 85% needy freshmen, 83% needy undergrads receive need-based scholarship or grant aid. 2% freshmen, 1% undergrads receive non-need-based scholarship or grant aid. 91% freshmen, 91% undergrads receive need-based self-help aid. 0% freshmen, 0% undergrads receive athletic scholarships. 94% freshmen, 88% undergrads receive any aid. **Criteria for awarding aid:** *Need-based:* Academics, Alumni affiliation, Art, Athletics, Job skills, Leadership, Minority status, Music/drama. *Non-need-based:* Academics, Alumni affiliation, Art, Athletics, Job skills, Leadership, Minority status, Music/drama, State/district residency.

THE OHIO STATE UNIVERSITY—COLUMBUS

Student Academic Services Building, Columbus, OH 43210
Phone: 614-292-3980 • **Financial Aid Phone:** 614-292-0300
E-mail: askabuckeye@osu.edu • **CEEB Code:** 1592
Fax: 614-292-4818 • **Website:** www.osu.edu • **ACT Code:** 3312

This public school was founded in 1870. It has a 3469-acre campus.

RATINGS
Admissions Selectivity Rating: 91   **Fire Safety Rating:** 60*   **Green Rating:** 94

STUDENTS AND FACULTY
Enrollment: 44,131. **Student Body:** 48% female, 52% male, 17% out-of-state, 7% international (112 countries represented). Asian 6%, African American 6%, Caucasian 71%, Hispanic 4%, Native American <1%, Pacific Islander <1%, Two or more races 3%, Race unknown 3%.
Retention and Graduation: 94% freshmen return for sophomore year. 59% freshmen graduate within 4 years. 83% freshmen graduate within 6 years.
Faculty: Student/faculty ratio 19:1. 3,722 full-time faculty, 0% hold PhDs, 24% are are members of minority groups, 38% are women. 13% of classes are taught by teaching assistants.

ACADEMICS
Degrees: associate, bachelor's, certificate, diploma, doctoral/professional, doctoral/research, doctoral, master's, postbachelor's certificate, post-master's certificate. **Classes:** Most classes have 20-29 students. Most lab/discussion sessions have 20-29 students. **Most popular majors:** Psychology; Finance; Communication. **Special Study Options:** Accelerated program, cooperative education program, cross-registration, distance learning, double major, dual enrollment, English as a Second Language (ESL), exchange student program (domestic), honors program, independent study, internships, liberal arts/career combination, student-designed major, study abroad, teacher certification

program, weekend college. **Honors Programs:** The University Honors Program is dedicated to promoting the intellectual and personal development of high-performing students. It strives to promote a more active and enriching relationship between Honors students and the University by connecting them with resources and opportunities that will encourage them to maximize their potential. The University Scholars Program enables talented and motivated students to be part of smaller, selective communnities within the larger university environment. Each of the fourteen programs focuses on a common theme or academic area of interest designed to foster learning and involvement. Scholars live together, attend classes together, and experience diverse opportunities outside the classroom. Combined degree programs: BA/MD, BA/DDS, http://www.gradsch.ohio-state.edu/combined-degrees.html. **Disability Services:** Special programs offered to physically disabled students, including note-taking services, reader services, tape recorders, tutors. **Career Services:** Alumni network, Alumni services, Career/job search classes, Career assessment, Internships, Regional alumni.

FACILITIES

Housing: Coed dorms, special housing for disabled students, special housing for international students, women's dorms, fraternity/sorority housing, apartments for married students, cooperative housing, apartments for single students, Wellness Housing, Theme Housing. 90% of campus accessible to physically diasbled. **Special Academic Facilities/Equipment:** Wexner center for the Arts, zoology museum, geology museum, art and photography galleries, nuclear research reactor, electroscience lab, biomedical engineering center, cartoon art museum. **Computers:** 100% of dorms, 90% of libraries, 100% of dining areas, 100% of student union, 4% of common outdoor areas have wireless network access. Students can register for classes online. Administrative functions (other than registration) can be performed online.

CAMPUS LIFE

Environment: Metropolis. **Activities:** Choral groups, dance, drama/theater, jazz band, literary magazine, marching band, music ensembles, musical theater, opera, pep band, radio station, student government, student newspaper, student-run film society, symphony orchestra, television station, yearbook, Student Organization. 950 registered organizations, 39 honor societies, 93 religious organizations. 42 fraternities, 25 sororities. **Athletics (Intercollegiate):** *Men:* baseball, basketball, cheerleading, cross-country, diving, fencing, football, golf, gymnastics, ice hockey, lacrosse, pistol, riflery, soccer, swimming, tennis, track/field (outdoor), track/field (indoor), volleyball, wrestling. *Women:* baseball, basketball, cheerleading, crew/rowing, cross-country, diving, fencing, field hockey, golf, gymnastics, ice hockey, lacrosse, pistol, riflery, soccer, softball, swimming, synchronized swimming, tennis, track/field (outdoor), track/field (indoor), volleyball. **On-Campus Highlights:** Hale Cultural Center, Chadwick Arboretum, Jack Nicklaus Golf Museum, Schottenstein Center and Value City Arena, Wexner Center for the Arts. **Environmental Initiatives:** Building Energy Auditing Program http://president.osu.edu/sustainability; iee.osu.edu; http://fod.osu.edu/afp/

ADMISSIONS

Freshman Academic Profile: 62% in top 10% of high school class, 95% in top 25% of high school class, 99% in top 50% of high school class. 85% from public high schools. **Reported SAT (pre-2016 redesign) scores:** SAT Math middle 50% range 610-720. SAT Critical Reading middle 50% range 560-670. SAT Writing middle 50% range 560-660. **Concordant SAT scores:** SAT EBRW middle 50% 620–710. SAT Math middle 50% range 630–750. ACT middle 50% range 27-31. Minimum internet-based TOEFL 79. Minimum paper TOEFL 550. **Basis for Candidate Selection:** *Very important factors considered include:* rigor of secondary school record, class rank, academic GPA, standardized test scores. *Important factors considered include:* application essay, extracurricular activities, talent/ability, first generation, volunteer work, work experience. *Other factors considered include:* recommendation(s), character/personal qualities, geographical residence, state residency, racial/ethnic status. **Freshman Admission Requirements:** High school diploma is required and GED is accepted. *Academic units required:* 4 English, 3 math, 3 science, 3 science labs, 2 foreign language, 2 social studies, 1 academic elective, 1 visual/performing arts. *Academic units recommended:* 4 English, 4 math, 3 science, 3 science labs, 3 foreign language, 3 social studies, 1 academic elective, 1 visual/performing arts. **Freshman Admission Statistics:** 40,240 applied, 49.38% admitted, 35% enrolled. **Transfer Admission Requirements:** college transcript(s), Minimum college GPA of 2.0 required. Lowest grade transferable C-. **General Admission Information:** Application fee $60. Regular application deadline 2/1. Regular notification 3/31. Nonfall registration accepted.

COSTS AND FINANCIAL AID

Annual in-state tuition $10,037. Annual out-of-state tuition $28,229. Room and board $11,666. Average book expense $1,234. **Required Forms and Deadlines:** FAFSA. **Notification of Awards:** Applicants will be notified of awards on or about 3/15. **Types of Aid:** *Need-based scholarships/grants:* Federal Pell, FSEOG, State scholarships/grants, Private scholarships, College/university scholarship or grant aid from institutional funds. *Loans:* Direct

Subsidized Stafford Loans, Direct Unsubsidized Stafford Loans, Direct PLUS loans, Federal Perkins Loans, Federal Nursing Loans, State Loans, College/university loans from institutional funds. *Student Employment:* Federal Work-Study Program available. Institutional employment available. **Financial Aid Statistics:** 90% needy freshmen, 83% needy undergrads receive need-based scholarship or grant aid. 9% freshmen, 5% undergrads receive non-need-based scholarship or grant aid. 77% freshmen, 88% undergrads receive need-based self-help aid. 1% freshmen, 1% undergrads receive athletic scholarships. 90% freshmen, 79% undergrads receive any aid. 55% undergrads borrow to pay for school. Average cumulative indebtedness $27,400. **Criteria for awarding aid:** *Need-based:* Academics, Alumni affiliation, Art, Athletics, Job skills, Leadership, Minority status, Music/drama. *Non-need-based:* Academics, Alumni affiliation, Art, Athletics, Job skills, Leadership, Minority status, Music/drama, State/district residency.

THE OHIO STATE UNIVERSITY—LIMA CAMPUS

4240 Campus Drive, Lima, OH 45804-3596
Phone: 419-995-8434 • **Financial Aid Phone:** 614-292-0300
E-mail: askabuckeye@osu.edu • **CEEB Code:** 1541
Fax: 419-995-8483 • **Website:** lima.osu.edu • **ACT Code:** 3312

This public school was founded in 1960. It has a 565-acre campus.

RATINGS

Admissions Selectivity Rating: 72   **Fire Safety Rating:** 60*   **Green Rating:** 60*

STUDENTS AND FACULTY

Enrollment: 928. **Student Body:** 56% female, 44% male, 1% out-of-state, <1% international (1 countries represented). Asian 2%, African American 5%, Caucasian 85%, Hispanic 3%, Native American <1%, Pacific Islander <1%, Two or more races 3%, Race unknown 2%.
Retention and Graduation: 67% freshmen return for sophomore year. 13% freshmen graduate within 4 years. 32% freshmen graduate within 6 years.
Faculty: Student/faculty ratio 18:1. 34 full-time faculty, 0% hold PhDs, 15% are are members of minority groups, 38% are women. 0% of classes are taught by teaching assistants.

ACADEMICS

Degrees: associate, bachelor's, master's. **Classes:** Most classes have 20-29 students. Most lab/discussion sessions have 20-29 students. **Special Study Options:** Accelerated program, cooperative education program, cross-registration, distance learning, double major, dual enrollment, English as a Second Language (ESL), exchange student program (domestic), honors program, independent study, internships, liberal arts/career combination, student-designed major, study abroad, teacher certification program, weekend college. **Honors Programs:** The University Honors Program is dedicated to promoting the intellectual and personal development of high-performing students. It strives to promote a more active and enriching relationship between Honors students and the University by connecting them with resources and opportunities that will encourage them to maximize their potential. The University Scholars Program enables talented and motivated students to be part of smaller, selective communnities within the larger university environment. Each of the fourteen programs focuses on a common theme or academic area of interest designed to foster learning and involvement. Scholars live together, attend classes together, and experience diverse opportunities outside the classroom. **Disability Services:** Special programs offered to physically disabled students, including note-taking services, reader services, tape recorders, tutors. **Career Services:** Alumni network, Alumni services, Career/job search classes, Career assessment, Internships, Regional alumni, On-campus interviews.

FACILITIES

Housing: 100% of campus accessible to physically diasbled. **Special Academic Facilities/Equipment:** OhioSeis seismological network: http://seismic.lima.ohio-state.edu/ Geological Museum Observatory **Computers:** 75% of classrooms, 100% of libraries, 100% of dining areas, 100% of student union, 100% of common outdoor areas have wireless network access. Students can register for classes online. Administrative functions (other than registration) can be performed online.

CAMPUS LIFE

Environment: Rural. **Activities:** Choral groups, dance, drama/theater, musical theater, pep band, student government, student-run film society, Campus Ministries, Student Organization. 32 registered organizations, 1 honor society, 2 religious organizations.

ADMISSIONS

Freshman Academic Profile: 5% in top 10% of high school class, 34% in top 25% of high school class, 70% in top 50% of high school class. 92% from public high schools. **Reported SAT (pre-2016 redesign) scores:** SAT Math middle 50% range 510-618. SAT Critical Reading middle 50% range 425-588. SAT Writing middle 50% range 410-605. **Concordant SAT scores:** SAT EBRW middle 50% 470–650. SAT Math middle 50% range 540–640. ACT middle 50% range 20-25. Minimum internet-based TOEFL 79. Minimum paper TOEFL 550. **Basis for Candidate Selection:** *Other factors considered include:* standardized test scores. **Freshman Admission Requirements:** *Academic units required:* 4 English, 3 math, 3 science, 3 science labs, 2 foreign language, 2 social studies, 1 academic elective, 1 visual/performing arts. *Academic units recommended:* 4 English, 4 math, 3 science, 3 science labs, 3 foreign language, 3 social studies, 1 academic elective, 1 visual/performing arts. **Freshman Admission Statistics:** 1,078 applied, 98.70% admitted, 33% enrolled. **Transfer Admission Requirements:** college transcript(s), Minimum college GPA of 2.0 required. Lowest grade transferable C-. **General Admission Information:** Application fee $60. Regular application deadline 6/1. Nonfall registration accepted.

COSTS AND FINANCIAL AID
Annual in-state tuition $7,140. Annual out-of-state tuition $25,332. Average book expense $1,234. **Required Forms and Deadlines:** FAFSA. **Notification of Awards:** Applicants will be notified of awards on or about 3/15. **Types of Aid:** *Need-based scholarships/grants:* Federal Pell, FSEOG, State scholarships/grants, Private scholarships, College/university scholarship or grant aid from institutional funds. *Loans:* Direct Subsidized Stafford Loans, Direct Unsubsidized Stafford Loans, Direct PLUS loans, Federal Perkins Loans, Federal Nursing Loans, College/university loans from institutional funds. *Student Employment:* Federal Work-Study Program available. Institutional employment available. **Financial Aid Statistics:** 79% needy freshmen, 75% needy undergrads receive need-based scholarship or grant aid. 2% freshmen, 1% undergrads receive non-need-based scholarship or grant aid. 85% freshmen, 90% undergrads receive need-based self-help aid. 0% freshmen, 0% undergrads receive athletic scholarships. 94% freshmen, 87% undergrads receive any aid. **Criteria for awarding aid:** *Need-based:* Academics, Alumni affiliation, Art, Athletics, Job skills, Leadership, Minority status, Music/drama. *Non-need-based:* Academics, Alumni affiliation, Art, Athletics, Job skills, Leadership, Minority status, Music/drama, State/district residency.

THE OHIO STATE UNIVERSITY—NEWARK

1179 University Drive, Newark, OH 43055
Phone: 740-366-9333 • **Financial Aid Phone:** 614-292-0300
E-mail: askabuckeye@osu.edu • **CEEB Code:** 752
Fax: 740-364-9645 • **Website:** http://www.newark.osu.edu/Pages/Index/as
ACT Code: 3312

This public school was founded in 1957. It has a 106-acre campus.

RATINGS
Admissions Selectivity Rating: 72　　**Fire Safety Rating:** 91　　**Green Rating:** 60*

STUDENTS AND FACULTY
Enrollment: 2,362. **Student Body:** 50% female, 50% male, 1% out-of-state, 0% international. Asian 4%, African American 13%, Caucasian 72%, Hispanic 3%, Native American <1%, Pacific Islander <1%, Two or more races 4%, Race unknown 3%.
Retention and Graduation: 63% freshmen return for sophomore year. 11% freshmen graduate within 4 years. 33% freshmen graduate within 6 years.
Faculty: Student/faculty ratio 26:1. 50 full-time faculty, 0% hold PhDs, 20% are are members of minority groups, 34% are women. 0% of classes are taught by teaching assistants.

ACADEMICS
Degrees: associate, bachelor's, master's. **Classes:** Most classes have 20-29 students. Most lab/discussion sessions have 20-29 students. **Most popular majors:** Elementary and Middle School Administration/Principalship; Elementary Education and Teaching; Junior High/Intermediate/Middle School Education and Teaching. **Special Study Options:** Accelerated program, cooperative education program, cross-registration, distance learning, double major, dual enrollment, English as a Second Language (ESL), exchange student program (domestic), honors program, independent study, internships, liberal arts/career combination, student-designed major, study abroad, teacher certification program, weekend college. **Honors Programs:** The University Honors Program is dedicated to promoting the intellectual and personal development of high-performing students. It strives to promote a more active and enriching relationship between Honors students and the University by connecting them with resources and opportunities that will encourage them to maximize their potential. The University Scholars Program enables talented and motivated students to be part of smaller, selective communities within

the larger university environment. Each of the fourteen programs focuses on a common theme or academic area of interest designed to foster learning and involvement. Scholars live together, attend classes together, and experience diverse opportunities outside the classroom. **Disability Services:** Special programs offered to physically disabled students, including note-taking services, reader services, tape recorders, tutors. **Career Services:** Career assessment, Internships, On-campus interviews.

FACILITIES
Housing: Coed dorms, apartments for single students, Wellness Housing. 100% of campus accessible to physically diasbled. **Computers:** 100% of classrooms, 100% of dorms, 100% of libraries, 100% of dining areas, 100% of student union, have wireless network access. Students can register for classes online. Administrative functions (other than registration) can be performed online.

CAMPUS LIFE
Environment: Village. **Activities:** Choral groups, drama/theater, literary magazine, music ensembles, student government, Campus Ministries. 33 registered organizations, 2 honor societies, 2 religious organizations. **Athletics (Intercollegiate):** *Men:* basketball, golf, soccer. *Women:* basketball, soccer, softball, volleyball.

ADMISSIONS
Freshman Academic Profile: 5% in top 10% of high school class, 23% in top 25% of high school class, 58% in top 50% of high school class. 91% from public high schools. **Reported SAT (pre-2016 redesign) scores:** SAT Math middle 50% range 470-570. SAT Critical Reading middle 50% range 440-560. SAT Writing middle 50% range 440-550. **Concordant SAT scores:** SAT EBRW middle 50% range 490–610. SAT Math middle 50% range 510–590. ACT middle 50% range 20-25. **Basis for Candidate Selection:** *Other factors considered include:* standardized test scores. **Freshman Admission Requirements:** High school diploma is required and GED is accepted. *Academic units required:* 4 English, 3 math, 3 science, 3 science labs, 2 foreign language, 2 social studies, 1 academic elective, 1 visual/performing arts. *Academic units recommended:* 4 English, 4 math, 3 science, 3 science labs, 3 foreign language, 3 social studies, 1 academic elective, 1 visual/performing arts. **Freshman Admission Statistics:** 2,831 applied, 98.66% admitted, 44% enrolled. **Transfer Admission Requirements:** college transcript(s), Minimum college GPA of 2.0 required. Lowest grade transferable C-. **General Admission Information:** Application fee $60. Regular application deadline 6/1. Nonfall registration accepted.

COSTS AND FINANCIAL AID
Annual in-state tuition $7,140. Annual out-of-state tuition $25,332. Average book expense $1,234. **Required Forms and Deadlines:** FAFSA. **Notification of Awards:** Applicants will be notified of awards on or about 3/15. **Types of Aid:** *Need-based scholarships/grants:* Federal Pell, FSEOG, State scholarships/grants, Private scholarships, College/university scholarship or grant aid from institutional funds. *Loans:* Direct Subsidized Stafford Loans, Direct Unsubsidized Stafford Loans, Direct PLUS loans, Federal Perkins Loans, Federal Nursing Loans, College/university loans from institutional funds. *Student Employment:* Federal Work-Study Program available. Institutional employment available. **Financial Aid Statistics:** 67% needy freshmen, 69% needy undergrads receive need-based scholarship or grant aid. 1% freshmen, 1% undergrads receive non-need-based scholarship or grant aid. 94% freshmen, 94% undergrads receive need-based self-help aid. 0% freshmen, 0% undergrads receive athletic scholarships. 86% freshmen, 80% undergrads receive any aid. **Criteria for awarding aid:** *Need-based:* Academics, Alumni affiliation, Art, Athletics, Job skills, Leadership, Minority status, Music/drama. *Non-need-based:* Academics, Alumni affiliation, Art, Athletics, Job skills, Leadership, Minority status, Music/drama, State/district residency.

OHIO UNIVERSITY—ATHENS

120 Chubb Hall, Athens, OH 45701
Phone: 740-593-4100 • **Financial Aid Phone:** 740-593-4141
E-mail: admissions@ohio.edu • **CEEB Code:** 1593
Fax: 740-593-0560 • **Website:** www.ohio.edu • **ACT Code:** 3314

This public school was founded in 1804. It has a 1762-acre campus.

RATINGS
Admissions Selectivity Rating: 83　　**Fire Safety Rating:** 88　　**Green Rating:** 92

STUDENTS AND FACULTY

Enrollment: 23,542. **Student Body:** 60% female, 40% male, 15% out-of-state, 2% international (78 countries represented). Asian 1%, African American 5%, Caucasian 84%, Hispanic 3%, Native American <1%, Pacific Islander <1%, Two or more races 3%, Race unknown 1%.

Retention and Graduation: 82% freshmen return for sophomore year. 46% freshmen graduate within 4 years. 64% freshmen graduate within 6 years. 25% grads go on to further study within 1 year. 6% grads pursue arts and sciences degrees. 1% grads pursue law degrees. 1% grads pursue business degrees. 1% grads pursue medical degrees. **Faculty:** Student/faculty ratio 18:1. 939 full-time faculty, 78% hold PhDs, 16% are are members of minority groups, 40% are women. 11% of classes are taught by teaching assistants.

ACADEMICS

Degrees: associate, bachelor's, certificate, doctoral/professional, doctoral/research, master's. **Classes:** Most classes have 20-29 students. Most lab/discussion sessions have 10-19 students. **Most popular majors:** Registered Nursing/Registered Nurse; Liberal Arts and Sciences Studies and Humanities; Speech Communication and Rhetoric. **Special Study Options:** Accelerated program, cooperative education program, cross-registration, distance learning, double major, dual enrollment, English as a Second Language (ESL), external degree program, honors program, independent study, internships, liberal arts/career combination, student-designed major, study abroad, teacher certification program. **Honors Programs:** Honors Tutorial College: The most selective of Ohio University's nine undergraduate colleges the Honor's Tutorial College is the oldest, largest, and most academically diverse degree-only degree-granting college in the country. Based on Oxbridge systems of tutorial education developed in England, it offers highly motivated, talented students the opportunity to receive a substantial part of their education through tutorials (one-on-one classes or small seminars). There are generally 220 students in the Honors Tutorial College spread over 26 programs of study. To preserve the tutorial experience, HTC enrolls about 60 new students each year, and admission is highly competitive. **Disability Services:** Special programs offered to physically disabled students, including reader services, tape recorders, tutors. **Career Services:** Alumni network, Alumni services, Career/job search classes, Career assessment, Internships, Regional alumni. Most internships/co-ops are through college departments as our office focuses on full-time positions.

FACILITIES

Housing: Coed dorms, special housing for disabled students, special housing for international students, women's dorms, apartments for married students. 89% of campus accessible to physically diasbled. **Special Academic Facilities/Equipment:** Museum of American Art, Innovation Center, Nuclear Accelerator, Electron Microscope, Biotech Center, Kennedy Museum of Art, Trisolini Gallery, Art Gallery in Multicultural Programs, Voinovich Center, & Academic & Research Center. **Computers:** 100% of classrooms, 100% of dorms, 100% of libraries, 100% of dining areas, 100% of student union, 100% of common outdoor areas have wireless network access. Students can register for classes online. Administrative functions (other than registration) can be performed online.

CAMPUS LIFE

Environment: Village. **Activities:** Choral groups, concert band, dance, drama/theater, jazz band, literary magazine, marching band, music ensembles, musical theater, opera, pep band, radio station, student government, student newspaper, student-run film society, symphony orchestra, television station, yearbook, Campus Ministries, Student Organization. 323 registered organizations, 16 honor societies, 27 religious organizations. 17 fraternities, 12 sororities. **Athletics (Intercollegiate):** *Men:* baseball, basketball, cheerleading, cross-country, football, golf, wrestling. *Women:* basketball, cheerleading, cross-country, diving, field hockey, golf, soccer, softball, swimming, track/field (outdoor), volleyball. **On-Campus Highlights:** Charles J. Ping Recreation Center, Kennedy Museum of Art, Templeton-Blackburn Memorial Auditorium, Convocation Center, Alden Library, 6. Baker University Center. **Environmental Initiatives:** Ohio University is currently expanding its invessel composting system, already the largest at any college or university in the nation, to handle all organic waste at the university.

ADMISSIONS

Freshman Academic Profile: Average high school GPA 3.5. 15% in top 10% of high school class, 42% in top 25% of high school class, 80% in top 50% of high school class. 82% from public high schools. **Reported SAT (pre-2016 redesign) scores:** SAT Math middle 50% range 500-600. SAT Critical Reading middle 50% range 490-600. SAT Writing middle 50% range 470-580. **Concordant SAT scores:** SAT EBRW middle 50% 540–650. SAT Math middle 50% range 530–620. ACT middle 50% range 21-26. **Basis for Candidate Selection:** *Very important factors considered include:* rigor of secondary school record, academic GPA, standardized test scores. *Important factors considered include:* class rank, application essay, first generation. *Other factors considered include:* recommendation(s), extracurricular activities, talent/ability, character/personal qualities, alumni/ae relation, geographical residence, state residency, volunteer work, work experience. **Freshman Admission Requirements:** High

school diploma is required and GED is accepted. *Academic units required:* 4 English, 4 math, 3 science, 2 foreign language, 3 social studies, 4 academic electives, and 1 unit from above areas or other academic areas. *Academic units recommended:* 4 English, 4 math, 3 science, 2 foreign language, 3 social studies, 4 academic electives, 1 visual/performing arts. **Freshman Admission Statistics:** 20,623 applied, 74.85% admitted, 28% enrolled. **Transfer Admission Requirements:** college transcript(s), Minimum college GPA of 2.0 required. Lowest grade transferable C-. **General Admission Information:** Application fee $50. Priority deadline 2/1. Regular application deadline 2/1. Nonfall registration accepted. Admission may be deferred for a maximum of 12 months.

COSTS AND FINANCIAL AID

Annual in-state tuition $10,602. Annual out-of-state tuition $19,566. Room and board $10,734. Average book expense $1,030. **Required Forms and Deadlines:** FAFSA. **Notification of Awards:** Applicants will be notified of awards on or about 4/1. **Types of Aid:** *Need-based scholarships/grants:* Federal Pell, FSEOG, State scholarships/grants, Private scholarships, College/university scholarship or grant aid from institutional funds. *Loans:* Direct Subsidized Stafford Loans, Direct Unsubsidized Stafford Loans, Direct PLUS loans, Federal Perkins Loans. *Student Employment:* Federal Work-Study Program available. Institutional employment available. **Financial Aid Statistics:** 93% needy freshmen, 77% needy undergrads receive need-based scholarship or grant aid. 13% freshmen, 17% undergrads receive non-need-based scholarship or grant aid. 99% freshmen, 99% undergrads receive need-based self-help aid. 1% freshmen, 1% undergrads receive athletic scholarships. 92% freshmen, 75% undergrads receive any aid. 67% undergrads borrow to pay for school. Average cumulative indebtedness $27,880. **Criteria for awarding aid:** *Non-need-based:* Academics, Art, Athletics, Minority status, Music/drama, Religious affiliation.

OHIO WESLEYAN UNIVERSITY

61 South Sandusky Street, Delaware, OH 43015
Phone: 740-368-3020 • **Financial Aid Phone:** 740-368-3050
E-mail: owuadmit@owu.edu • **CEEB Code:** 1594
Fax: 740-368-3314 • **Website:** www.owu.edu • **ACT Code:** 3316

This private school, affiliated with the Methodist Church, was founded in 1842. It has a 200-acre campus.

RATINGS

Admissions Selectivity Rating: 83   **Fire Safety Rating:** 86   **Green Rating:** 60*

STUDENTS AND FACULTY

Enrollment: 1,629. **Student Body:** 52% female, 48% male, 47% out-of-state, 6% international (41 countries represented). Asian 3%, African American 9%, Caucasian 70%, Hispanic 5%, Native American <1%, Pacific Islander <1%, Two or more races 5%, Race unknown 3%.

Retention and Graduation: 81% freshmen return for sophomore year. 62% freshmen graduate within 4 years. 67% freshmen graduate within 6 years. **Faculty:** Student/faculty ratio 10:1. 134 full-time faculty, 100% hold PhDs, 6% are are members of minority groups, 41% are women. 0% of classes are taught by teaching assistants.

ACADEMICS

Degrees: bachelor's. **Classes:** Most classes have 10-19 students. Most lab/discussion sessions have 10-19 students. **Most popular majors:** Psychology; Economics; Zoology/Animal Biology. **Special Study Options:** double major, dual enrollment, exchange student program (domestic), honors program, independent study, internships, student-designed major, study abroad, teacher certification program. **Honors Programs:** The Leland F. and Helen Schubert Honors Program recognizes the most talented students among Ohio Wesleyan's community of scholars and challenges them through Honors Tutorials, Honors Seminars, and Honors Scholarships. Combined degree programs: BA/MEng. **Disability Services:** Special programs offered to physically disabled students, including note-taking services, tape recorders, tutors. **Career Services:** Alumni network, Alumni services, Career assessment, On-campus interviews.

FACILITIES

Housing: Coed dorms, special housing for international students, women's dorms, fraternity/sorority housing, apartments for single students, Small Living Units (SLUs) offer unique living opportunities to groups of 10-15 OWU students. In these theme houses, students create a small community centered on promoting specific interests and concerns. 60% of campus accessible to physically diasbled. **Special Academic Facilities/Equipment:** Perkins and Student Observatories Scanning electron microscope Woltemade Center for Economics, Business and Entrepreneurship Nine inch refractor telescope Ross Art Museum Newly renovated fine arts facilities Newly renovated 150,000 square foot science center with state-of-the art classrooms and equipment. Wireless Internet in some areas. Fiber optic network **Computers:** 10% of classrooms, 100% of libraries, 10% of dining areas, 10% of common outdoor areas have wireless network access. Administrative functions (other than registration) can be performed online.

CAMPUS LIFE

Environment: Town. **Activities:** Choral groups, dance, drama/theater, jazz band, literary magazine, music ensembles, musical theater, opera, pep band, radio station, student government, student newspaper, symphony orchestra, yearbook, Campus Ministries, Student Organization, Model UN. 86 registered organizations, 26 honor societies, 10 religious organizations. 11 fraternities, 7 sororities. **Athletics (Intercollegiate):** *Men:* baseball, basketball, cross-country, diving, football, golf, lacrosse, sailing, soccer, swimming, tennis, track/field (outdoor), track/field (indoor). *Women:* basketball, cross-country, diving, field hockey, lacrosse, sailing, soccer, softball, swimming, tennis, track/field (outdoor), track/field (indoor), volleyball. **On-Campus Highlights:** Science Center, Hamilton Williams Campus Center, Selby Stadium, R.W. Corns Building, Sanborn Hall (music), Beeghly Library and Ross Museum are additional popular places on campus. **Environmental Initiatives:** Waste reduction.

ADMISSIONS

Freshman Academic Profile: Average high school GPA 3.4. 22% in top 10% of high school class, 45% in top 25% of high school class, 76% in top 50% of high school class. 77% from public high schools. **Reported SAT (pre-2016 redesign) scores:** SAT Math middle 50% range 500-630. SAT Critical Reading middle 50% range 510-640. SAT Writing middle 50% range 480-590. **Concordant SAT scores:** SAT EBRW middle 50% 550–670. SAT Math middle 50% range 530–650. ACT middle 50% range 22-28. Minimum paper TOEFL 550. **Basis for Candidate Selection:** *Very important factors considered include:* rigor of secondary school record, academic GPA, application essay, recommendation(s), interview, character/personal qualities. *Important factors considered include:* class rank, standardized test scores, extracurricular activities, talent/ability. *Other factors considered include:* first generation, alumni/ae relation, geographical residence, racial/ethnic status, volunteer work, work experience, level of applicant's interest. **Freshman Admission Requirements:** High school diploma is required and GED is accepted. *Academic units required:* 4 English, 3 math, 3 science, 2 foreign language, 3 social studies. *Academic units recommended:* 4 English, 4 math, 4 science, 3 foreign language, 4 social studies. **Freshman Admission Statistics:** 4,123 applied, 71.55% admitted, 8% enrolled. **Transfer Admission Requirements:** High school transcript, college transcript(s), essay or personal statement, statement of good standing from prior institution(s). Minimum college GPA of 2.5 required. Lowest grade transferable C-. **General Admission Information:** Priority deadline 1/15. Regular application deadline 3/1. Regular notification 3/1. Nonfall registration accepted. Admission may be deferred for a maximum of 1 year.

COSTS AND FINANCIAL AID

Annual tuition $43,770. Room and board $11,770. Required fees $320. Average book expense $1,300. **Required Forms and Deadlines:** FAFSA. **Types of Aid:** *Need-based scholarships/grants:* Federal Pell, FSEOG, State scholarships/grants, Private scholarships, College/university scholarship or grant aid from institutional funds. *Loans:* Direct Subsidized Stafford Loans, Direct Unsubsidized Stafford Loans, Direct PLUS loans, Federal Perkins Loans, College/university loans from institutional funds. *Student Employment:* Federal Work-Study Program available. Institutional employment available. **Financial Aid Statistics:** 100% needy freshmen, 100% needy undergrads receive need-based scholarship or grant aid. 15% freshmen, 19% undergrads receive non-need-based scholarship or grant aid. 89% freshmen, 85% undergrads receive need-based self-help aid. 0% freshmen, 0% undergrads receive athletic scholarships. 65% undergrads borrow to pay for school. Average cumulative indebtedness $34,666. **Criteria for awarding aid:** *Non-need-based:* Academics, Alumni affiliation, Art, Minority status, Music/drama, Religious affiliation, State/district residency.

500 West University, Shawnee, OK 74804
Phone: 800-654-3285 • **Financial Aid Phone:** 405-878-2016
E-mail: admissions@okbu.edu • **CEEB Code:** 6541
Fax: 405-585-5017 • **Website:** www.okbu.edu • **ACT Code:** 3414

This private school, affiliated with the Southern Baptist Church, was founded in 1910. It has a 200-acre campus.

RATINGS
Admissions Selectivity Rating: 81   **Fire Safety Rating:** 83   **Green Rating:** 60*

STUDENTS AND FACULTY
Enrollment: 1,841. **Student Body:** 60% female, 40% male, 49% out-of-state, 3% international (35 countries represented). Asian 1%, African American 7%, Caucasian 70%, Hispanic 3%, Native American 6%, Pacific Islander <1%, Two or more races 8%, Race unknown 2%.
Retention and Graduation: 75% freshmen return for sophomore year. 44% freshmen graduate within 4 years. 52% freshmen graduate within 6 years. 14% grads go on to further study within 1 year. 8% grads pursue arts and sciences degrees. 1% grads pursue law degrees. 3% grads pursue medical degrees.
Faculty: Student/faculty ratio 13:1. 127 full-time faculty, 71% hold PhDs, 10% are are members of minority groups, 37% are women. 0% of classes are taught by teaching assistants.

ACADEMICS
Degrees: associate, bachelor's, certificate, master's. **Classes:** Most classes have fewer than 10 students. Most lab/discussion sessions have fewer than 10 students. **Most popular majors:** Bible/Biblical Studies; Health Services/Allied Health/Health Sciences; Education. **Special Study Options:** cooperative education program, double major, English as a Second Language (ESL), exchange student program (domestic), honors program, independent study, internships, student-designed major, study abroad, teacher certification program, Semester-away programs available. **Honors Programs:** The OBU Honors Program is a curricular program designed to enhance the undergraduate study experience for certain exceptionally well-qualified students. Students completing all of the requirements for gradulation in the Honors Program earn the designation "with Honors" on their OBU diplomas. Combined degree programs: BA/MA. **Disability Services:** Special programs offered to physically disabled students, including note-taking services, reader services, tape recorders, tutors. **Career Services:** Alumni network, Alumni services, Career/job search classes, Career assessment, Internships. The Office of Career Development Office manages The OBU Internship Program, giving students the opportunity to intern with several on campus offices, currently our Wellness Center, Marketing Department, Intramural Sports, and Athletics Department participate with growing opportunities annually. In just our second year of operation we are able to offer internships to all students eliminating the barriers of travel, status, and time availability.

FACILITIES
Housing: men's dorms, women's dorms, apartments for married students, apartments for single students. 100% of campus accessible to physically diasbled. **Special Academic Facilities/Equipment:** planetarium, Baptist Historical Society Archives, Avery T. Willis Center for Global Outreach **Computers:** Students can register for classes online. Administrative functions (other than registration) can be performed online.

CAMPUS LIFE
Environment: Town. **Activities:** Choral groups, concert band, drama/theater, jazz band, literary magazine, music ensembles, musical theater, opera, pep band, student government, student newspaper, symphony orchestra, television station, yearbook, Campus Ministries. 80 registered organizations, 15 honor societies, 5 religious organizations. 5 fraternities, 5 sororities. **Athletics (Intercollegiate):** *Men:* baseball, basketball, cheerleading, cross-country, golf, soccer, tennis, track/field (outdoor), track/field (indoor). *Women:* basketball, cheerleading, cross-country, golf, soccer, softball, tennis, track/field (outdoor), track/field (indoor), volleyball. **On-Campus Highlights:** Geiger Center (Student Building), Recreation and Wellness Center, Noble Complex (athletics), Mabee Learning Center (Library), Intramural Field.

ADMISSIONS
Freshman Academic Profile: 23% in top 10% of high school class, 49% in top 25% of high school class, 90% in top 50% of high school class. 79% from public high schools. **Reported SAT (pre-2016 redesign) scores:** SAT Math middle 50% range 440-560. SAT Critical Reading middle 50% range 450-580. **Concordant SAT scores:** SAT Math middle 50% range 480–580. ACT middle 50% range 20-25. Minimum paper TOEFL 500. **Basis for Candidate Selection:** *Very important factors considered include:* class rank, academic GPA, application essay. *Important factors considered include:*

rigor of secondary school record, extracurricular activities, level of applicant's interest. *Other factors considered include:* standardized test scores, interview, talent/ability, character/personal qualities, first generation, alumni/ae relation, religious affiliation/commitment, volunteer work, work experience. **Freshman Admission Requirements:** High school diploma is required and GED is accepted. *Academic units recommended:* 4 English, 3 math, 3 science, 2 science labs, 2 foreign language, 2 social studies, 1 history, 2 visual/performing arts. **Freshman Admission Statistics:** 4,785 applied, 75.03% admitted, 15% enrolled. **Transfer Admission Requirements:** college transcript(s), Minimum college GPA of 2.5 required. Lowest grade transferable D. **General Admission Information:** Priority deadline 4/1. Regular application deadline 8/1. Nonfall registration accepted. Admission may be deferred.

COSTS AND FINANCIAL AID

Annual tuition $22,710. Room and board $7,010. Required fees $2,600. Average book expense $1,300. **Required Forms and Deadlines:** FAFSA. **Notification of Awards:** Applicants will be notified of awards on a rolling basis beginning 2/1. **Types of Aid:** *Need-based scholarships/grants:* Federal Pell, FSEOG, State scholarships/grants, Private scholarships, College/university scholarship or grant aid from institutional funds, Federal Nursing Scholarships. *Loans:* Direct Subsidized Stafford Loans, Direct Unsubsidized Stafford Loans, Direct PLUS loans, Federal Perkins Loans, College/university loans from institutional funds. *Student Employment:* Federal Work-Study Program available. Institutional employment available. **Financial Aid Statistics:** 79% needy freshmen, 85% needy undergrads receive need-based scholarship or grant aid. 98% freshmen, 97% undergrads receive non-need-based scholarship or grant aid. 75% freshmen, 76% undergrads receive need-based self-help aid. 22% freshmen, 24% undergrads receive athletic scholarships. 100% freshmen, 98% undergrads receive any aid. 58% undergrads borrow to pay for school. Average cumulative indebtedness $24,451. **Criteria for awarding aid:** *Need-based:* Academics, Leadership, Minority status. *Non-need-based:* Academics, Art, Athletics, Leadership, Minority status, Music/drama, Religious affiliation.

OKLAHOMA CHRISTIAN UNIVERSITY

P.O. Box 11000, Oklahoma City, OK 73136-1100
Phone: 405-425-5050 • **Financial Aid Phone:** 405-425-5190
E-mail: info@oc.edu
Fax: 405-425-5069 • **Website:** www.oc.edu • **ACT Code:** 3415

This private school, affiliated with the Church of Christ Church, was founded in 1950. It has a 240-acre campus.

RATINGS

Admissions Selectivity Rating: 88   **Fire Safety Rating:** 82   **Green Rating:** 60*

STUDENTS AND FACULTY

Enrollment: 1,910. **Student Body:** 49% female, 51% male, 63% out-of-state, 11% international (38 countries represented). Asian 1%, African American 3%, Caucasian 63%, Hispanic 3%, Native American 4%, Pacific Islander 0%, Two or more races 0%, Race unknown 14%.
Retention and Graduation: 73% freshmen return for sophomore year. 31% freshmen graduate within 4 years. 48% freshmen graduate within 6 years.
Faculty: Student/faculty ratio 13:1. 116 full-time faculty, 73% hold PhDs, 0% are are members of minority groups, 30% are women. 0% of classes are taught by teaching assistants.

ACADEMICS

Degrees: bachelor's, master's. **Classes:** Most classes have 10-19 students. **Most popular majors:** Registered Nursing/Registered Nurse; Elementary Education and Teaching; Liberal Arts and Sciences/Liberal Studies. **Special Study Options:** cross-registration, distance learning, double major, English as a Second Language (ESL), honors program, independent study, internships, student-designed major, study abroad, teacher certification program. **Career Services:** Alumni network, Alumni services, Career/job search classes, Career assessment, Internships. They are government sponsored internships with DISA, FBI, CIA, homeland security and more. Also some companies, too many to list.

FACILITIES

Housing: special housing for disabled students, men's dorms, women's dorms, apartments for married students, apartments for single students. **Special Academic Facilities/Equipment:** Art Museum Art Gallery **Computers:** 100% of classrooms, 100% of dorms, 100% of libraries, 100% of dining areas, 100% of student union, 95% of common outdoor areas have wireless network access. Students can register for classes online. Administrative functions (other than registration) can be performed online.

CAMPUS LIFE

Environment: Metropolis. **Activities:** Choral groups, concert band, drama/theater, jazz band, literary magazine, music ensembles, musical theater, opera, pep band, radio station, student government, student newspaper, symphony orchestra, television station, yearbook, Campus Ministries, Student Organization. 20 registered organizations, 5 honor societies, 2 religious organizations. 6 fraternities, 6 sororities. **Athletics (Intercollegiate):** *Men:* baseball, basketball, cross-country, golf, soccer, tennis, track/field (outdoor). *Women:* basketball, cheerleading, cross-country, soccer, softball, tennis, track/field (outdoor). **On-Campus Highlights:** Gaylord University Center, University House Commons, Lawson Commons, Payne Athletic & Fitness Center, Mabee Learning Center. **Environmental Initiatives:** Trayless Cafeteria.

ADMISSIONS

Freshman Academic Profile: Average high school GPA 3.6. 30% in top 10% of high school class, 54% in top 25% of high school class, 80% in top 50% of high school class. **Reported SAT (pre-2016 redesign) scores:** SAT Math middle 50% range 470-640. SAT Critical Reading middle 50% range 440-620. SAT Writing middle 50% range 470-600. **Concordant SAT scores:** SAT EBRW middle 50% 510-660. SAT Math middle 50% range 510-660. ACT middle 50% range 21-28. Minimum internet-based TOEFL 61. Minimum paper TOEFL 500. **Basis for Candidate Selection:** *Very important factors considered include:* character/personal qualities. *Important factors considered include:* academic GPA, standardized test scores. *Other factors considered include:* rigor of secondary school record, class rank, recommendation(s), interview, extracurricular activities, talent/ability, religious affiliation/commitment, volunteer work, work experience, level of applicant's interest. **Freshman Admission Requirements:** High school diploma is required and GED is accepted. *Academic units required:* 4 English, 4 math, 4 science. *Academic units recommended:* 3 science labs, 2 foreign language, 3 social studies. **Freshman Admission Statistics:** 2,156 applied, 44.71% admitted, 47% enrolled. **Transfer Admission Requirements:** High school transcript, college transcript(s), standardized test scores, statement of good standing from prior institution(s). Lowest grade transferable D. **General Admission Information:** Application fee $25. Priority deadline 5/1. Nonfall registration accepted. Admission may be deferred for a maximum of 1 year.

COSTS AND FINANCIAL AID

Annual tuition $18,800. Room and board $6,775. Average book expense $1,000. **Required Forms and Deadlines:** FAFSA. **Notification of Awards:** Applicants will be notified of awards on a rolling basis beginning 2/15. **Types of Aid:** *Need-based scholarships/grants:* Federal Pell, FSEOG, State scholarships/grants, Private scholarships, College/university scholarship or grant aid from institutional funds. *Loans:* Direct Subsidized Stafford Loans, Direct Unsubsidized Stafford Loans, Direct PLUS loans, Federal Perkins Loans. *Student Employment:* Federal Work-Study Program available. Institutional employment available. **Financial Aid Statistics:** 58% needy freshmen, 58% needy undergrads receive need-based scholarship or grant aid. 82% freshmen, 77% undergrads receive non-need-based scholarship or grant aid. 60% freshmen, 42% undergrads receive need-based self-help aid. 9% freshmen, 9% undergrads receive athletic scholarships. 100% freshmen, 98% undergrads receive any aid. **Criteria for awarding aid:** *Need-based:* Academics, Art, Athletics, Music/drama. *Non-need-based:* Religious affiliation.

OKLAHOMA CITY UNIVERSITY

2501 North Blackwelder, Oklahoma City, OK 73106
Phone: 405-208-5055 • **Financial Aid Phone:** 405-208-5848
E-mail: uadmissions@okcu.edu • **CEEB Code:** 6543
Fax: 405-208-5916 • **Website:** www.okcu.edu • **ACT Code:** 3416

This private school, affiliated with the Methodist Church, was founded in 1904. It has a 78-acre campus.

RATINGS

Admissions Selectivity Rating: 85   **Fire Safety Rating:** 92   **Green Rating:** 60*

STUDENTS AND FACULTY

Enrollment: 571. **Student Body:** 66% female, 34% male, 50% out-of-state, 8% international (57 countries represented). Asian 0%, African American 2%, Caucasian 4%, Hispanic 10%, Native American 7%, Pacific Islander 58%, Two or more races 10%, Race unknown <1%.
Retention and Graduation: 80% freshmen return for sophomore year. 46% freshmen graduate within 4 years. 61% freshmen graduate within 6 years.
Faculty: Student/faculty ratio 11:1. 193 full-time faculty, 64% hold PhDs, 18% are are members of minority groups, 49% are women. 0% of classes are taught by teaching assistants.

ACADEMICS

Degrees: bachelor's, doctoral/professional, doctoral/research, doctoral, master's. **Classes:** Most classes have 10-19 students. Most lab/discussion sessions have fewer than 10 students. **Most popular majors:** Business/Commerce; Dance; Nursing Practice. **Special Study Options:** Accelerated program, cooperative education program, distance learning, double major, dual enrollment, English as a Second Language (ESL), exchange student program (domestic), external degree program, honors program, independent study, internships, student-designed major, study abroad, teacher certification program. **Honors Programs:** University Honors Program: The mission of the University Honors program is to provide an enhanced learning environment for academically gifted undergraduate students. Each new class of Honors students at OCU will be a spcial community of scholars. Students will have the opportunity to become acquainted with one another and the Honors program in the Honors Colloquium, a course required for all new honors students during their first semester in the program. Honors students will have the opportunities to meet with visiting scholars and participate in special events. As part of a network of honors programs through the National Collegiate Honors Council and the Great Plains Honors Council, students may present research at national and regional honors conferences and participate in exciting summer and semester programs. Combined degree programs: BA/JD, BA/MA, MBA/JD. **Disability Services:** Special programs offered to physically disabled students, including reader services, tape recorders, tutors. **Career Services:** Alumni network, Alumni services, Career/job search classes, Career assessment, Internships, Regional alumni. Career Fairs hosting over 200+ employers on campus.

FACILITIES

Housing: Coed dorms, special housing for disabled students, men's dorms, women's dorms, fraternity/sorority housing, apartments for married students, apartments for single students, Learning Communities. 98% of campus accessible to physically diasbled. **Special Academic Facilities/Equipment:** Art museum, audiovisual center, language lab. **Computers:** 100% of classrooms, 100% of dorms, 100% of libraries, 100% of dining areas, 100% of student union, 90% of common outdoor areas have wireless network access. Students can register for classes online. Administrative functions (other than registration) can be performed online.

CAMPUS LIFE

Environment: Metropolis. **Activities:** Choral groups, concert band, dance, drama/theater, jazz band, literary magazine, music ensembles, musical theater, opera, pep band, student government, student newspaper, symphony orchestra, television station, yearbook, Campus Ministries, Student Organization. 64 registered organizations, 14 honor societies, 6 religious organizations. 2 fraternities, 4 sororities. **Athletics (Intercollegiate):** *Men:* baseball, basketball, cheerleading, crew/rowing, golf, soccer, track/field (outdoor), wrestling. *Women:* basketball, cheerleading, crew/rowing, golf, soccer, softball, track/field (outdoor), volleyball, wrestling. **On-Campus Highlights:** Tom and Brenda McDaniel Univ Center, Henry J Freede Wellness and Activity Center, Meinders' School of Business, Walker Center for Arts and Sciences, Norick Art Center. **Environmental Initiatives:** Computer recycling program, community garden.

ADMISSIONS

Freshman Academic Profile: Average high school GPA 3.7. 27% in top 10% of high school class, 54% in top 25% of high school class, 85% in top 50% of high school class. 88% from public high schools. **Reported SAT (pre-2016 redesign) scores:** SAT Math middle 50% range 490-597.5. SAT Critical Reading middle 50% range 500-630. SAT Writing middle 50% range 500-610. **Concordant SAT scores:** SAT EBRW middle 50% 560–670. SAT Math middle 50% range 520–620. ACT middle 50% range 22-29. Minimum internet-based TOEFL 80. Minimum paper TOEFL 550. **Basis for Candidate Selection:** *Very important factors considered include:* rigor of secondary school record, talent/ability. *Important factors considered include:* academic GPA, standardized test scores, application essay, character/personal qualities. *Other factors considered include:* class rank, recommendation(s), interview, extracurricular activities, volunteer work, work experience, level of applicant's interest. **Freshman Admission Requirements:** High school diploma is required and GED is accepted. *Academic units required:* 4 English, 3 math, 3 science, 2 science labs, 2 foreign language, 2 social studies, 2 history, 3 academic electives. *Academic units recommended:* 4 English, 4 math, 4 science, 3 science labs, 2 foreign language, 3 social studies, 1 history, 3 academic electives. **Freshman Admission Statistics:** 1,641 applied, 72.15% admitted, 28% enrolled. **Transfer Admission Requirements:** college transcript(s), essay or personal statement, statement of good standing from prior institution(s). Minimum college GPA of 2.0 required. Lowest grade transferable C-. **General Admission Information:** Application fee $55. Priority deadline 3/1. Nonfall registration accepted. Admission may be deferred for a maximum of 1 year.

COSTS AND FINANCIAL AID

Annual tuition $27,276. Room and board $8,624. Required fees $3,450. Average book expense $1,500. **Required Forms and Deadlines:** FAFSA. **Notification of Awards:** Applicants will be notified of awards on a rolling basis beginning 3/1. **Types of Aid:** *Need-based scholarships/grants:* Federal Pell, FSEOG, State scholarships/grants, Private scholarships, College/university scholarship or grant aid from institutional funds. *Loans:* Direct Subsidized Stafford Loans, Direct Unsubsidized Stafford Loans, Direct PLUS loans, Federal Perkins Loans. *Student Employment:* Federal Work-Study Program available. Institutional employment available. **Financial Aid Statistics:** 99% needy freshmen, 93% needy undergrads receive need-based scholarship or grant aid. 16% freshmen, 14% undergrads receive non-need-based scholarship or grant aid. 64% freshmen, 72% undergrads receive need-based self-help aid. 4% freshmen, 3% undergrads receive athletic scholarships. 97% freshmen, 87% undergrads receive any aid. 57% undergrads borrow to pay for school. Average cumulative indebtedness $26,329. **Criteria for awarding aid:** *Non-need-based:* Academics, Art, Athletics, Leadership, Music/drama, Religious affiliation.

OKLAHOMA STATE UNIVERSITY

219 Student Union, Stillwater, OK 74078
Phone: 405-744-5358 • **Financial Aid Phone:** 405-744-6604
E-mail: admissions@okstate.edu • **CEEB Code:** 6546
Fax: 405-744-7092 • **Website:** http://go.okstate.edu • **ACT Code:** 3424

This public school was founded in 1890. It has a 840-acre campus.

RATINGS

Admissions Selectivity Rating: 84 | **Fire Safety Rating:** 92 | **Green Rating:** 90

STUDENTS AND FACULTY

Enrollment: 20,828. **Student Body:** 49% female, 51% male, 27% out-of-state, 4% international (87 countries represented). Asian 2%, African American 5%, Caucasian 69%, Hispanic 7%, Native American 5%, Pacific Islander <1%, Two or more races 9%, Race unknown <1%.
Retention and Graduation: 81% freshmen return for sophomore year. 39% freshmen graduate within 4 years. 63% freshmen graduate within 6 years.
Faculty: Student/faculty ratio 20:1. 1,048 full-time faculty, 92% hold PhDs, 20% are are members of minority groups, 35% are women. 17% of classes are taught by teaching assistants.

ACADEMICS

Degrees: bachelor's, doctoral/professional, doctoral/research, master's, postbachelor's certificate, post-master's certificate. **Classes:** Most classes have 10-19 students. Most lab/discussion sessions have 10-19 students. **Most popular majors:** Mechanical Engineering; Business Administration and Management; Animal Sciences. **Special Study Options:** Accelerated program, cross-registration, distance learning, double major, dual enrollment, English as a Second Language (ESL), exchange student program (domestic), honors program, independent study, internships, student-designed major, study abroad, teacher certification program. Combined degree programs: BA/MA, BS/MS Accounting, Professional Program in Special Education, BS/MS Biochemistry, BS/MS Early Childhood Education. **Disability Services:** Special programs offered to physically disabled students, including note-taking services, reader services, tape recorders, tutors. **Career Services:** Alumni network, Alumni services, Career/job search classes, Career assessment, Internships, Regional alumni. OSU Career Services began a partnership with the OSU Alumni Association that launched in January 2015 to expand career services to alumni members. The program features Career Consulting, experienced job search options on the Hire System, additional job search and networking tools, virtual events, speed networking programs with students, access to career fairs, and programs within chapters in various cities.

FACILITIES

Housing: Coed dorms, special housing for disabled students, men's dorms, women's dorms, fraternity/sorority housing, apartments for married students, apartments for single students, Wellness Housing, Theme Housing. 97% of campus accessible to physically diasbled. **Special Academic Facilities/Equipment:** Art, history, and natural science museums, wellness center, laser research center. **Computers:** 80% of classrooms, 80% of dorms, 100% of libraries, 80% of student union, have wireless network access. Students can register for classes online. Administrative functions (other than registration) can be performed online.

CAMPUS LIFE

Environment: Town. **Activities:** Choral groups, concert band, dance, drama/theater, jazz band, literary magazine, marching band, music ensembles, musical theater, opera, pep band, radio station, student government, student newspaper, symphony orchestra, television station, Campus Ministries, Student Organization. 300 registered organizations. **Athletics (Intercollegiate):** *Men:* baseball, basketball, cross-country, football, golf, tennis, track/field (outdoor), wrestling. *Women:* basketball, cross-country, equestrian sports, golf, soccer, softball, tennis, track/field (outdoor). **On-Campus Highlights:** Colvin Recreational Center, Gallagher/Iba Arena and Museum, Student Union Building, Library, ConocoPhillips Alumni Center. **Environmental Initiatives:** Energy conservation—turning off lights, computers, monitors, speakers, printers, etc when not in use. Reducing thermostat settings during winter and turning it up during summer. This program has saved over $30 million since 2007.

ADMISSIONS

Freshman Academic Profile: Average high school GPA 3.5. 25% in top 10% of high school class, 54% in top 25% of high school class, 84% in top 50% of high school class. **Reported SAT (pre-2016 redesign) scores:** SAT Math middle 50% range 490-610. SAT Critical Reading middle 50% range 480-590. **Concordant SAT scores:** SAT Math middle 50% range 520–630. ACT middle 50% range 21-27. Minimum internet-based TOEFL 61. Minimum paper TOEFL 500. **Basis for Candidate Selection:** *Very important factors considered include:* class rank, academic GPA, standardized test scores. *Important factors considered include:* application essay. *Other factors considered include:* recommendation(s). **Freshman Admission Requirements:** High school diploma is required and GED is accepted. *Academic units required:* 4 English, 3 math, 3 science, 3 science labs, 2 social studies, 1 history. **Freshman Admission Statistics:** 13,055 applied, 74.52% admitted, 43% enrolled. **Transfer Admission Requirements:** college transcript(s), Minimum college GPA of 2.25 required. Lowest grade transferable D. **General Admission Information:** Application fee $40. Nonfall registration accepted. Admission may be deferred.

COSTS AND FINANCIAL AID

Annual in-state tuition $4,943. Annual out-of-state tuition $19,065. Room and board $8,443. Required fees $3,378. Average book expense $1,260. **Required Forms and Deadlines:** FAFSA. **Notification of Awards:** Applicants will be notified of awards on a rolling basis beginning 4/1. **Types of Aid:** *Need-based scholarships/grants:* Federal Pell, FSEOG, State scholarships/grants, Private scholarships, College/university scholarship or grant aid from institutional funds. *Loans:* Direct Subsidized Stafford Loans, Direct Unsubsidized Stafford Loans, Direct PLUS loans, Federal Perkins Loans. *Student Employment:* Federal Work-Study Program available. Institutional employment available. **Financial Aid Statistics:** 80% needy freshmen, 76% needy undergrads receive need-based scholarship or grant aid. 10% freshmen, 6% undergrads receive non-need-based scholarship or grant aid. 55% freshmen, 66% undergrads receive need-based self-help aid. 1% freshmen, 1% undergrads receive athletic scholarships. 88% freshmen, 84% undergrads receive any aid. 50% undergrads borrow to pay for school. Average cumulative indebtedness $24,252. **Criteria for awarding aid:** *Need-based:* Academics, Minority status. *Non-need-based:* Academics, Alumni affiliation, Art, Athletics, Leadership, Minority status, Music/drama, State/district residency.

OLD DOMINION UNIVERSITY

108 Rollins Hall, Norfolk, VA 23529-0050
Phone: 757-683-3685 • **Financial Aid Phone:** 757-683-3683
E-mail: admissions@odu.edu • **CEEB Code:** 5126
Fax: 757-683-3255 • **Website:** www.odu.edu

This public school was founded in 1930. It has a 188-acre campus.

RATINGS

Admissions Selectivity Rating: 75   **Fire Safety Rating:** 90   **Green Rating:** 68

STUDENTS AND FACULTY

Enrollment: 19,606. **Student Body:** 54% female, 46% male, 7% out-of-state, 1% international (95 countries represented). Asian 4%, African American 29%, Caucasian 46%, Hispanic 8%, Native American <1%, Pacific Islander <1%, Two or more races 7%, Race unknown 3%.
Retention and Graduation: 78% freshmen return for sophomore year. 26% freshmen graduate within 4 years. 51% freshmen graduate within 6 years.
Faculty: Student/faculty ratio 18:1. 835 full-time faculty, 81% hold PhDs, 21% are are members of minority groups, 44% are women.

ACADEMICS

Degrees: bachelor's, doctoral/professional, doctoral/research, doctoral, master's, postbachelor's certifiate, post-master's certificate. **Classes:** Most classes have 10-19 students. Most lab/discussion sessions have 20-29 students. **Most popular majors:** Psychology; Criminology; Mental and Social Health Services and Allied Professions. **Special Study Options:** Accelerated program, cooperative education program, cross-registration, distance learning, double major, dual enrollment, English as a Second Language (ESL), exchange student program (domestic), honors program, independent study, internships, liberal arts/career combination, student-designed major, study abroad, teacher

certification program, weekend college, Experiential Learning. **Honors Programs:** Honors College. The Honors College was established to further the University's commitment to excellence in education. With an emphasis on teaching, innovation, and small classes, the college offers the experience of a small liberal arts college within the framework of the large university. The four-year experience offers specially designed, low-enrollment courses to honors students and selected juniors and seniors. Several out-of-class and off-campus experiences are often part of these courses–at no extra cost to students. A one credit honors tutorial is required in the junior year, and a senior honors colloquium is taken in the final year of study. All Honors College students are awarded an annual honors stipend. Combined degree programs: BA/MA, BA/MEng, 5-year Master's degree program in education. **Disability Services:** Special programs offered to physically disabled students, including note-taking services, reader services, tutors. **Career Services:** Alumni network, Alumni services, Career/job search classes, Career assessment, Internships, Regional alumni. Career Development Services begins engagement with prospective students (from first point of contact) and works with individuals throughout college years and beyond, serving alumni free of charge. A new initiative is a strengthened focus on undecided/exploratory students in addition to the key student employment programs including LEAP (a targeted Student Employment program with workplace readiness skills classes).

FACILITIES

Housing: Coed dorms, special housing for disabled students, special housing for international students, apartments for single students. 100% of campus accessible to physically diasbled. **Special Academic Facilities/Equipment:** Centers for urban research/service, economic education, and child study, planetarium, marine science research vessel, random wave pool. **Computers:** 100% of classrooms, 100% of dorms, 100% of libraries, 100% of dining areas, 100% of student union, 20% of common outdoor areas have wireless network access. Students can register for classes online. Administrative functions (other than registration) can be performed online.

CAMPUS LIFE

Environment: City. **Activities:** Choral groups, concert band, dance, drama/theater, jazz band, marching band, music ensembles, musical theater, pep band, radio station, student government, student newspaper, symphony orchestra, television station, Campus Ministries, Student Organization, Model UN. 155 registered organizations, 16 honor societies, 25 religious organizations. 14 fraternities, 10 sororities. **Athletics (Intercollegiate):** *Men:* baseball, basketball, diving, football, golf, sailing, soccer, tennis, wrestling. *Women:* basketball, crew/rowing, diving, field hockey, golf, lacrosse, sailing, soccer, tennis. **On-Campus Highlights:** Webb Student Center, Engineering/Computational Bldg, University Village, Constant Convocation Center, Kaufman Mall. **Environmental Initiatives:** All new contruction and major renovations are designed to LEED Silver standards at a minimum. We completed two projects this year, one new construction and one renovation.

ADMISSIONS

Freshman Academic Profile: Average high school GPA 3.3. 9% in top 10% of high school class, 31% in top 25% of high school class, 69% in top 50% of high school class. 93% from public high schools. **Reported SAT (pre-2016 redesign) scores:** SAT Math middle 50% range 440-570. SAT Critical Reading middle 50% range 450-570. **Concordant SAT scores:** SAT Math middle 50% range 480–590. ACT middle 50% range 18-25. Minimum internet-based TOEFL 79. Minimum paper TOEFL 550. **Basis for Candidate Selection:** *Very important factors considered include:* rigor of secondary school record, academic GPA, standardized test scores. *Important factors considered include:* application essay, recommendation(s), extracurricular activities, volunteer work, work experience. *Other factors considered include:* class rank, talent/ability, character/personal qualities, first generation, alumni/ae relation, level of applicant's interest. **Freshman Admission Requirements:** High school diploma is required and GED is accepted. *Academic units required:* 4 English, 3 math, 3 science, 3 foreign language, 3 social studies. *Academic units recommended:* 4 English, 4 math, 3 science, 3 foreign language, 3 social studies. **Freshman Admission Statistics:** 11,352 applied, 84.64% admitted, 29% enrolled. **Transfer Admission Requirements:** college transcript(s), Minimum college GPA of 2.2 required. Lowest grade transferable c. **General Admission Information:** Application fee $50. Priority deadline 12/1. Regular application deadline 2/1. Nonfall registration accepted. Admission may be deferred for a maximum of 12 months.

COSTS AND FINANCIAL AID

Annual in-state tuition $9,750. Annual out-of-state tuition $26,730. Room and board $10,864. Required fees $296. Average book expense $1,000. **Required Forms and Deadlines:** FAFSA. **Notification of Awards:** Applicants will be notified of awards on a rolling basis beginning 3/15. **Types of Aid:** *Need-based scholarships/grants:* Federal Pell, FSEOG, State scholarships/grants, Private scholarships, College/university scholarship or grant aid from institutional funds, United Negro College Fund, Federal Nursing Scholarships. *Loans:* Direct Subsidized Stafford Loans, Direct Unsubsidized Stafford Loans, Direct PLUS loans, Federal Nursing Loans, College/university loans from institutional funds. *Student Employment:* Federal Work-Study Program available. Institutional employment available. **Financial Aid Statistics:** 75% needy freshmen, 76% needy undergrads receive need-based scholarship or grant aid. 38% freshmen, 21% undergrads receive non-need-based scholarship or grant aid. 80% freshmen, 81% undergrads receive need-based self-help aid. 3% freshmen, 2% undergrads receive athletic scholarships. 85% freshmen, 72% undergrads receive any aid. 70% undergrads borrow to pay for school. Average cumulative indebtedness $30,410. **Criteria for awarding aid:** *Non-need-based:* Academics, Alumni affiliation, Art, Athletics, Leadership, Music/drama, State/district residency.

ORAL ROBERTS UNIVERSITY

7777 S. Lewis Avenue, Tulsa, OK 74171
Phone: 918-495-6518
E-mail: admissions@oru.edu • **CEEB Code:** 6552
Fax: 918-495-6222 • **Website:** www.oru.edu • **ACT Code:** 3427

This is a private school. It has a 500-acre campus.

RATINGS

Admissions Selectivity Rating: 89   **Fire Safety Rating:** 60*   **Green Rating:** 60*

STUDENTS AND FACULTY

Enrollment: 2,979. **Student Body:** 60% female, 40% male, 58% out-of-state, 8% international. Asian 2%, African American 15%, Caucasian 49%, Hispanic 10%, Native American 3%, Pacific Islander 0%, Two or more races 7%, Race unknown 7%.
Retention and Graduation: 80% freshmen return for sophomore year. 46% freshmen graduate within 4 years. 56% freshmen graduate within 6 years. 50% grads go on to further study within 1 year. 25% grads pursue arts and sciences degrees. 1% grads pursue law degrees. 10% grads pursue business degrees. 5% grads pursue medical degrees. **Faculty:** Student/faculty ratio 16:1. 155 full-time faculty, 70% hold PhDs, 21% are are members of minority groups, 43% are women. 0% of classes are taught by teaching assistants.

ACADEMICS

Degrees: bachelor's, certificate, diploma, doctoral/research, master's.
Classes: Most classes have 10-19 students. Most lab/discussion sessions have 20-29 students. **Most popular majors:** Mass Communication/Media Studies; Theology/Theological Studies; Marketing/Marketing Management. **Special Study Options:** Accelerated program, distance learning, double major, dual enrollment, English as a Second Language (ESL), external degree program, honors program, independent study, internships, liberal arts/career combination, student-designed major, study abroad, teacher certification program, weekend college. **Honors Programs:** ORU HOnors Program includes "Scholars" and "Fellows" – Highly selective Includes Beta Gamma Phi and others Combined degree programs: 3-2 bachelor's/ MBA and bachelor's/ MA.Ed. programs. **Disability Services:** Special programs offered to physically disabled students, including note-taking services, reader services, tape recorders, tutors.

FACILITIES

Housing: men's dorms, women's dorms. 100% of campus accessible to physically diasbled. **Special Academic Facilities/Equipment:** Dial Access Information Retrieval System, programmed learning facilities, early learning center, TV production studio.

CAMPUS LIFE

Activities: Choral groups, concert band, dance, drama/theater, jazz band, music ensembles, musical theater, pep band, radio station, student government, student newspaper, television station, yearbook, Campus Ministries, Student Organization, Model UN. **Athletics (Intercollegiate):** *Men:* baseball, basketball, cheerleading, cross-country, soccer, swimming, tennis, track/field (outdoor). *Women:* basketball, cheerleading, cross-country, soccer, swimming, tennis, track/field (outdoor), volleyball. **On-Campus Highlights:** Eagle's Nest, Aerobics Center, Prayer Tower, Mabee Center (Multi-purpose Event Complex), Gabrielle Christian Salem Hall.

ADMISSIONS

Freshman Academic Profile: Average high school GPA 3.4. 13% in top 10% of high school class, 36% in top 25% of high school class, 64% in top 50% of high school class. 75% from public high schools. **Reported SAT (pre-2016 redesign) scores:** SAT Math middle 50% range 440-560. SAT Critical Reading middle 50% range 450-568. **Concordant SAT scores:** SAT Math middle 50% range 480–580. ACT middle 50% range 19-24. Minimum paper TOEFL 500. **Basis for Candidate Selection:** *Very important factors considered include:* academic GPA, standardized test scores. **Freshman Admission Requirements:** High school diploma is required and GED is accepted. *Academic units recommended:* 4 English, 2 math, 2 science, 1 science lab, 2 foreign language, 2 social studies, 4 academic electives. **Freshman Admission**

Statistics: 2,635 applied, 21.37% admitted, 85% enrolled. **Transfer Admission Requirements:** High school transcript, college transcript(s), essay or personal statement, Minimum college GPA of 2.0 required. Lowest grade transferable 2. **General Admission Information:** Application fee $35. Nonfall registration accepted. Admission may be deferred for a maximum of 1 year.

COSTS AND FINANCIAL AID

Annual tuition $25,800. Room and board $8,750. Required fees $992. Average book expense $1,848. **Required Forms and Deadlines:** FAFSA. **Notification of Awards:** Applicants will be notified of awards on a rolling basis beginning 3/15. **Types of Aid:** *Need-based scholarships/grants:* Federal Pell, FSEOG, State scholarships/grants, Private scholarships, College/university scholarship or grant aid from institutional funds. *Loans:* Direct Subsidized Stafford Loans, Direct Unsubsidized Stafford Loans, Direct PLUS loans, Federal Perkins Loans. *Student Employment:* Federal Work-Study Program available. Institutional employment available. **Financial Aid Statistics:** 99% needy freshmen, 98% needy undergrads receive need-based scholarship or grant aid. 28% freshmen, 37% undergrads receive non-need-based scholarship or grant aid. 92% freshmen, 93% undergrads receive need-based self-help aid. 5% freshmen, 4% undergrads receive athletic scholarships. Average cumulative indebtedness $32,970. **Criteria for awarding aid:** *Non-need-based:* Academics, Alumni affiliation, Art, Athletics, Job skills, Leadership, Music/ drama.

See page 1012.

OREGON COLLEGE OF ART AND CRAFT

8245 Southwest Barnes Road, Portland, OR 97225
Phone: 971-255-4192 • **Financial Aid Phone:** 971-255-4224
E-mail: admissions@ocac.edu • **CEEB Code:** 4236
Fax: 503-297-9651 • **Website:** www.ocac.edu • **ACT Code:** 3471

This private school was founded in 1907. It has a 9-acre campus.

RATINGS

Admissions Selectivity Rating: 71   **Fire Safety Rating:** 68   **Green Rating:** 60*

STUDENTS AND FACULTY

Enrollment: 151. **Student Body:** 73% female, 27% male, 18% out-of-state, 0% international (2 countries represented). Asian 2%, African American 0%, Caucasian 70%, Hispanic 5%, Native American 3%, Pacific Islander 2%, Two or more races 8%, Race unknown 11%.
Retention and Graduation: 65% freshmen return for sophomore year. 25% freshmen graduate within 4 years. 38% freshmen graduate within 6 years. 9% grads pursue arts and sciences degrees. **Faculty:** Student/faculty ratio 7:1. 10 full-time faculty, 90% hold PhDs, 10% are are members of minority groups, 50% are women. 0% of classes are taught by teaching assistants.

ACADEMICS

Degrees: bachelor's, certificate, postbachelor's certifiate. **Classes:** Most classes have fewer than 10 students. **Most popular majors:** Fine Arts and Art Studies. **Special Study Options:** cross-registration, exchange student program (domestic), independent study, internships, study abroad. **Career Services:** Alumni network, Career/job search classes, Internships, On-campus interviews.

FACILITIES

Housing: cooperative housing, The college offers a small number of on-campus housing for new students straight from high school. In addition, the college has contract with two apartment complexes across the street from the college. **Special Academic Facilities/Equipment:** Hoffman Gallery, Centrum Gallery, and 7 specialized studios for artmaking.

CAMPUS LIFE

Environment: Metropolis. **Activities:** student government, student newspaper. 1 registered organization. **On-Campus Highlights:** Hands On Cafe, Centrum Art Gallery, Thesis Studios, Library, Computer Lab. **Environmental Initiatives:** Public Transportation.

ADMISSIONS

Freshman Academic Profile: Average high school GPA 3.0. 20% in top 10% of high school class, 20% in top 25% of high school class, 60% in top 50% of high school class. Minimum internet-based TOEFL 80. Minimum paper TOEFL 550. **Basis for Candidate Selection:** *Very important factors considered include:* academic GPA, application essay, talent/ability. *Important factors considered include:* rigor of secondary school record, standardized test scores, recommendation(s), interview. *Other factors considered include:* class rank, extracurricular activities, character/personal qualities, alumni/ae relation, volunteer work, work experience, level of applicant's interest. **Freshman Admission Requirements:** High school diploma is required and GED is accepted. *Academic units recommended:* 4 English, 3 math, 3 science, 2 foreign language, 1 social studies, 3 history, 4 visual/performing arts. **Freshman Admission Statistics:** 60 applied, 75.00% admitted, 58% enrolled. **Transfer Admission Requirements:** High school transcript, college transcript(s), essay or personal statement, Minimum college GPA of 2.0 required. Lowest grade transferable C. **General Admission Information:** Application fee $35. Nonfall registration accepted. Admission may be deferred for a maximum of 1 year.

COSTS AND FINANCIAL AID
Annual tuition $22,614. Required fees $1,657. Average book expense $1,000. **Required Forms and Deadlines:** FAFSA. **Notification of Awards:** Applicants will be notified of awards on a rolling basis beginning 3/15. **Types of Aid:** *Need-based scholarships/grants:* Federal Pell, FSEOG, State scholarships/grants, Private scholarships, College/university scholarship or grant aid from institutional funds. *Loans:* Direct Subsidized Stafford Loans, Direct Unsubsidized Stafford Loans, Direct PLUS loans. *Student Employment:* Federal Work-Study Program available. Institutional employment available. **Financial Aid Statistics:** 100% needy freshmen, 84% needy undergrads receive need-based scholarship or grant aid. 88% freshmen, 82% undergrads receive non-need-based scholarship or grant aid. 94% freshmen, 95% undergrads receive need-based self-help aid. 0% freshmen, 0% undergrads receive athletic scholarships. 90% freshmen, 93% undergrads receive any aid. **Criteria for awarding aid:** *Need-based:* Academics, Art. *Non-need-based:* Academics, Art.

OREGON HEALTH & SCIENCE UNIVERSITY

3181 SW Sam Jackson Park Rd, Portland, OR 97239
Phone: 503-494-2998 • **Financial Aid Phone:** 503-494-7800
E-mail: proginfo@ohsu.edu • **CEEB Code:** 4900
Fax: 503-494-3400 • **Website:** www.ohsu.edu

This public school was founded in 1867. It has a 120-acre campus.

RATINGS
Admissions Selectivity Rating: 61   **Fire Safety Rating:** 60*   **Green Rating:** 60*

STUDENTS AND FACULTY
Enrollment: 591. **Student Body:** 84% female, 16% male, 10% out-of-state, 1% international. Asian 5%, African American 1%, Caucasian 79%, Hispanic 5%, Native American 2%, Pacific Islander 0%, Two or more races 0%, Race unknown 6%.
Faculty: 1,290 full-time faculty, 0% hold PhDs, 0% are are members of minority groups, 0% are women.

ACADEMICS
Degrees: associate, bachelor's, master's, postbachelor's certificate, post-master's certificate. **Special Study Options:** Accelerated program, distance learning. Combined degree programs: MD/PhD, MD/MPH.

FACILITIES
Computers: Students can register for classes online.

CAMPUS LIFE
Environment: Metropolis. **Activities:** student government, student newspaper, yearbook. **On-Campus Highlights:** Portland Aerial Tram, Center for Health and Healing Cafe, Marquam Hill Hiking Trails.

ADMISSIONS
Freshman Admission Requirements: High school diploma is required and GED is accepted. **Transfer Admission Requirements:** college transcript(s), essay or personal statement, standardized test scores, statement of good standing from prior institution(s). Lowest grade transferable C. **General Admission Information:** Application fee $120. Regular application deadline 1/15. Admission may be deferred.

COSTS AND FINANCIAL AID
Annual out-of-state tuition $20,176. **Types of Aid:** *Need-based scholarships/ grants:* Federal Pell, FSEOG, State scholarships/grants, Private scholarships, College/university scholarship or grant aid from institutional funds. *Loans:* Direct Subsidized Stafford Loans, Direct Unsubsidized Stafford Loans, Direct PLUS loans, Federal Perkins Loans, Federal Nursing Loans, College/ university loans from institutional funds. *Student Employment:* Federal Work-Study Program available. Institutional employment available. **Financial Aid Statistics:** 49% needy undergrads receive need-based scholarship or grant aid. 1% undergrads receive non-need-based scholarship or grant aid. 100% undergrads receive need-based self-help aid. 0% undergrads receive athletic scholarships. 70% undergrads receive any aid. **Criteria for awarding aid:** *Need-based:* Academics, Minority status. *Non-need-based:* Academics, Minority status, State/district residency.

OREGON STATE UNIVERSITY

104 Kerr Administration Building, Corvallis, OR 97331-2106
Phone: 541-737-4411 • **Financial Aid Phone:** 541-737-2241
E-mail: osuadmit@oregonstate.edu • **CEEB Code:** 3210
Fax: 541-737-2482 • **Website:** http://oregonstate.edu/ • **ACT Code:** 3482

This public school was founded in 1858. It has a 421-acre campus.

RATINGS
Admissions Selectivity Rating: 84   **Fire Safety Rating:** 92   **Green Rating:** 98

STUDENTS AND FACULTY
Enrollment: 24,350. **Student Body:** 46% female, 54% male, 30% out-of-state, 7% international (78 countries represented). Asian 7%, African American 1%, Caucasian 65%, Hispanic 9%, Native American 1%, Pacific Islander <1%, Two or more races 7%, Race unknown 2%.
Retention and Graduation: 83% freshmen return for sophomore year. 33% freshmen graduate within 4 years. 63% freshmen graduate within 6 years. **Faculty:** Student/faculty ratio 18:1. 1,175 full-time faculty, 86% hold PhDs, 17% are are members of minority groups, 38% are women. 8% of classes are taught by teaching assistants.

ACADEMICS
Degrees: bachelor's, certificate, doctoral/professional, doctoral/research, doctoral, master's, postbachelor's certificate, post-master's certificate. **Classes:** Most classes have 20-29 students. Most lab/discussion sessions have 20-29 students. **Most popular majors:** Computer Science; Business Administration and Management; Mechanical Engineering. **Special Study Options:** Accelerated program, cooperative education program, cross-registration, distance learning, double major, dual enrollment, English as a Second Language (ESL), exchange student program (domestic), external degree program, honors program, independent study, internships, liberal arts/career combination, student-designed major, study abroad, teacher certification program. Combined degree programs: BA/PharmD. **Disability Services:** Special programs offered to physically disabled students, including note-taking services, reader services, tape recorders, tutors. **Career Services:** Alumni network, Alumni services, Career/job search classes, Career assessment, Internships, Regional alumni. Our relationship building efforts are the foundation of our success. As a result of our collaborations and partnerships with faculty/staff, employers, alumni, and parents, we're seeing record high student demand for our services including: presentation requests, career counseling/advising appointments, drop-in sessions, career seminars and events. We've generated high traffic to our website and recently received recognition for having one of the best career resources websites.

FACILITIES
Housing: Coed dorms, special housing for disabled students, special housing for international students, fraternity/sorority housing, apartments for married students, cooperative housing, apartments for single students, Theme Housing. 86% of campus accessible to physically disabled. **Special Academic Facilities/ Equipment:** Museums, galleries, collections, exhibits of cultural and scientific materials, language lab. **Computers:** 100% of classrooms, 2% of dorms, 100% of libraries, 50% of dining areas, 100% of student union, 2% of common outdoor areas have wireless network access. Students can register for classes online. Administrative functions (other than registration) can be performed online.

CAMPUS LIFE
Environment: Town. **Activities:** Choral groups, concert band, dance, drama/ theater, jazz band, literary magazine, marching band, music ensembles, musical theater, opera, pep band, radio station, student government, student newspaper, student-run film society, symphony orchestra, television station, yearbook, Campus Ministries, Student Organization, Model UN. 350 registered organizations, 29 honor societies, 23 religious organizations. 24 fraternities, 13 sororities. **Athletics (Intercollegiate):** *Men:* baseball, basketball, crew/rowing, football, golf, soccer, wrestling. *Women:* basketball, crew/rowing, cross-country, golf, gymnastics, soccer, softball, swimming, track/field (outdoor), volleyball. **On-Campus Highlights:** Memorial Union, Java II, Weatherford Hall, Dixon Recreation Center, Reser Stadium. **Environmental Initiatives:** OSU sustainability related research has impacts state- and nation-wide. Standout research occurs at the Oregon Climate Change Research Institute and within the colleges of Earth, Atmospheric and Oceanic Sciences, Agricultural Sciences and Engineering. More info at http://senergi.oregonstate.edu/home

ADMISSIONS
Freshman Academic Profile: Average high school GPA 3.7. 28% in top 10% of high school class, 60% in top 25% of high school class, 91% in top 50% of high school class. **Reported SAT (pre-2016 redesign) scores:** SAT Math middle 50% range 500-620. SAT Critical Reading middle 50% range 490-620. SAT Writing middle 50% range 470-590. **Concordant SAT scores:** SAT

EBRW middle 50% 540–660. SAT Math middle 50% range 530–640. ACT middle 50% range 22-28. Minimum internet-based TOEFL 80. Minimum paper TOEFL 550. **Basis for Candidate Selection:** *Very important factors considered include:* academic GPA. *Important factors considered include:* rigor of secondary school record, application essay, talent/ability, character/personal qualities, volunteer work, work experience. *Other factors considered include:* class rank, standardized test scores, recommendation(s), extracurricular activities, level of applicant's interest. **Freshman Admission Requirements:** High school diploma is required and GED is accepted. *Academic units required:* 4 English, 3 math, 3 science, 2 science labs, 2 foreign language, 3 social studies. *Academic units recommended:* 3 science labs. **Freshman Admission Statistics:** 14,595 applied, 77.48% admitted, 34% enrolled. **Transfer Admission Requirements:** college transcript(s), essay or personal statement, statement of good standing from prior institution(s). Minimum college GPA of 2.25 required. Lowest grade transferable D. **General Admission Information:** Application fee $60. Priority deadline 2/1. Regular application deadline 9/1. Nonfall registration accepted. Admission may be deferred for a maximum of 12 months.

COSTS AND FINANCIAL AID

Annual in-state tuition $8,715. Annual out-of-state tuition $27,195. Room and board $12,153. Required fees $1,651. Average book expense $1,551. **Required Forms and Deadlines:** FAFSA. **Notification of Awards:** Applicants will be notified of awards on a rolling basis beginning 4/1. **Types of Aid:** *Need-based scholarships/grants:* Federal Pell, FSEOG, State scholarships/grants, Private scholarships, College/university scholarship or grant aid from institutional funds. *Loans:* Direct Subsidized Stafford Loans, Direct Unsubsidized Stafford Loans, Direct PLUS loans, Federal Perkins Loans, College/university loans from institutional funds. *Student Employment:* Federal Work-Study Program available. Institutional employment available. **Financial Aid Statistics:** 81% needy freshmen, 77% needy undergrads receive need-based scholarship or grant aid. 2% freshmen, 2% undergrads receive non-need-based scholarship or grant aid. 96% freshmen, 97% undergrads receive need-based self-help aid. 2% freshmen, 2% undergrads receive athletic scholarships. 74% freshmen, 71% undergrads receive any aid. 61% undergrads borrow to pay for school. Average cumulative indebtedness $26,400. **Criteria for awarding aid:** *Need-based:* Academics, Alumni affiliation, Athletics, Job skills, Leadership, Minority status. *Non-need-based:* Academics, Alumni affiliation, Athletics, Job skills, Leadership, Minority status, State/district residency.

OTIS COLLEGE OF ART AND DESIGN

9045 Lincoln Boulevard, Los Angeles, CA 90045
Phone: 310-665-6820 • **Financial Aid Phone:** 310-665-6880
E-mail: admissions@otis.edu • **CEEB Code:** 4394
Fax: 310-665-6821 • **Website:** www.otis.edu • **ACT Code:** 359

This private school was founded in 1918. It has a 5-acre campus.

RATINGS
Admissions Selectivity Rating: 71 **Fire Safety Rating:** 60* **Green Rating:** 60*

STUDENTS AND FACULTY
Enrollment: 1,090. **Student Body:** 67% female, 33% male, 22% international. Asian 29%, African American 4%, Caucasian 24%, Hispanic 10%, Native American 1%, Pacific Islander <1%, Two or more races 6%, Race unknown 4%. **Retention and Graduation:** 79% freshmen return for sophomore year. 52% freshmen graduate within 4 years. 62% freshmen graduate within 6 years. 80% grads pursue arts and sciences degrees. **Faculty:** Student/faculty ratio 4:1. 55 full-time faculty, 53% hold PhDs, 20% are are members of minority groups, 55% are women. 0% of classes are taught by teaching assistants.

ACADEMICS
Degrees: bachelor's, master's. **Classes:** Most classes have 10-19 students. **Most popular majors:** Animation, Interactive Technology, Video Graphics and Special Effects; Fashion/Apparel Design; Graphic Design. **Special Study Options:** English as a Second Language (ESL), exchange student program (domestic), honors program, independent study, internships, study abroad. **Honors Programs:** We have an honors program for qualified enrolled students. **Disability Services:** Special programs offered to physically disabled students, including tape recorders, tutors. **Career Services:** Alumni network, Alumni services, Career/job search classes, Career assessment, Internships, Regional alumni, On-campus interviews. Strong and growing network for students to experience real world work.

FACILITIES
Housing: apartments for single students. 100% of campus accessible to physically diasbled. **Special Academic Facilities/Equipment:** Art gallery, student gallery, Woodshop, Metal Shop, Photo lab, Digital Media lab,

Printmaking lab, letterpress lab **Computers:** Administrative functions (other than registration) can be performed online.

CAMPUS LIFE
Environment: Metropolis. **Activities:** literary magazine, student government, student newspaper. 7 registered organizations.

ADMISSIONS
Freshman Academic Profile: Average high school GPA 3.2. **Reported SAT (pre-2016 redesign) scores:** SAT Math middle 50% range 440-590. SAT Critical Reading middle 50% range 430-560. **Concordant SAT scores:** SAT Math middle 50% range 480–610. ACT middle 50% range 18-25. Minimum internet-based TOEFL 79. Minimum paper TOEFL 550. **Basis for Candidate Selection:** *Very important factors considered include:* rigor of secondary school record, academic GPA, standardized test scores, talent/ability. *Important factors considered include:* application essay, level of applicant's interest. *Other factors considered include:* interview, extracurricular activities, character/personal qualities, alumni/ae relation, volunteer work, work experience. **Freshman Admission Requirements:** High school diploma is required and GED is accepted. *Academic units required:* 4 English, 3 math, 2 science, 1 science lab, 1 social studies, 2 history. *Academic units recommended:* 4 English, 4 math, 4 science, 4 science labs, 2 foreign language, 2 social studies, 3 history. **Freshman Admission Statistics:** 1,160 applied, 90.78% admitted, 27% enrolled. **Transfer Admission Requirements:** High school transcript, college transcript(s), essay or personal statement, statement of good standing from prior institution(s). Minimum college GPA of 2.5 required. Lowest grade transferable C. **General Admission Information:** Application fee $60. Priority deadline 2/15. Nonfall registration accepted.

COSTS AND FINANCIAL AID
Annual tuition $37,380. Room and board $11,800. Required fees $2,050. Average book expense $1,400. **Required Forms and Deadlines:** FAFSA, State aid form. **Notification of Awards:** Applicants will be notified of awards on a rolling basis beginning 3/1. **Types of Aid:** *Need-based scholarships/grants:* Federal Pell, FSEOG, State scholarships/grants, Private scholarships, College/university scholarship or grant aid from institutional funds. *Loans:* Direct Subsidized Stafford Loans, Direct Unsubsidized Stafford Loans, Direct PLUS loans, Federal Perkins Loans. *Student Employment:* Federal Work-Study Program available. Institutional employment available. **Financial Aid Statistics:** 100% needy freshmen, 99% needy undergrads receive need-based scholarship or grant aid. 38% freshmen, 28% undergrads receive non-need-based scholarship or grant aid. 82% freshmen, 87% undergrads receive need-based self-help aid. 0% freshmen, 0% undergrads receive athletic scholarships. **Criteria for awarding aid:** *Need-based:* Academics, Art, Leadership. *Non-need-based:* Academics, Art.

OTTERBEIN COLLEGE

Office of Admission, Westerville, OH 43081
Phone: 614-823-1500 • **Financial Aid Phone:** 614-823-1502
E-mail: uotterb@otterbein.edu • **CEEB Code:** 1597
Fax: 614-823-1200 • **Website:** www.otterbein.edu • **ACT Code:** 3318

This private school, affiliated with the Methodist Church, was founded in 1847. It has a 140-acre campus.

RATINGS
Admissions Selectivity Rating: 80 **Fire Safety Rating:** 60* **Green Rating:** 60*

STUDENTS AND FACULTY
Enrollment: 2,979. **Student Body:** 10% out-of-state, 2% international (12 countries represented). Asian 1%, African American 6%, Caucasian 83%, Hispanic 1%, Native American <1%, Pacific Islander 0%, Two or more races 0%, Race unknown 5%. **Retention and Graduation:** 92% freshmen return for sophomore year. **Faculty:** Student/faculty ratio 12:1. 161 full-time faculty, 93% hold PhDs, 11% are are members of minority groups, 55% 0% of classes are taught by teaching assistants.

ACADEMICS
Degrees: bachelor's, master's. **Most popular majors:** Education; Business/Commerce. **Special Study Options:** Accelerated program, cooperative education program, cross-registration, double major, dual enrollment, exchange student program (domestic), honors program, independent study, internships, liberal arts/career combination, student-designed major, study abroad, teacher certification program, weekend college. **Honors Programs:** The Honors Program at Otterbein College is designed to provide intellectual stimulation and challenge for students with high academic ability and motivation. The four-year program provides the opportunity to participate in a community of

students and faculty who have shared scholarly and creative interests. As part of that community students develop and complete their own Honors research and creative projects. Through the Honors seminars and Honors project, students develop advanced knowledge in their disciplinary fields and acquire the skills for independent work in their own areas of academic and professional interest. The Honors Program at Otterbein College is designed to provide intellectual stimulation and challenge for students with high academic ability and motivation. The four-year program provides the opportunity to participate in a community of students and faculty who have shared scholarly and creative interests. As part of that community students develop and complete their own Honors research and creative projects. Through the Honors seminars and Honors project, students develop advanced knowledge in their disciplinary fields and acquire the skills for independent work in their own areas of academic and professional interest. **Disability Services:** Special programs offered to physically disabled students, including note-taking services, reader services, tape recorders, tutors. **Career Services:** Alumni network, Alumni services, Career/job search classes, Career assessment, Internships, Regional alumni.

FACILITIES

Housing: Coed dorms, men's dorms, women's dorms, fraternity/sorority housing, apartments for single students, Theme housing. **Special Academic Facilities/Equipment:** Language lab, horse stable, observatory and planetarium, Celestron 8-inch and 14-inch telescopes, 3 art galleries. **Computers:** Students can register for classes online. Administrative functions (other than registration) can be performed online.

CAMPUS LIFE

Environment: Town. **Activities:** Choral groups, concert band, dance, drama/theater, jazz band, literary magazine, marching band, music ensembles, musical theater, opera, pep band, radio station, student government, student newspaper, symphony orchestra, television station, yearbook, Student Organization. 100 registered organizations, 7 fraternities, 6 sororities. **Athletics (Intercollegiate):** *Men:* baseball, basketball, cheerleading, cross-country, equestrian sports, football, golf, soccer, tennis, track/field (outdoor), track/field (indoor). *Women:* basketball, cheerleading, cross-country, equestrian sports, golf, soccer, softball, tennis, track/field (outdoor), track/field (indoor), volleyball. **On-Campus Highlights:** Clements Recreation Center, Cowen Hall- Theatre, Campus Center, Art Galleries/Art Building.

ADMISSIONS

Freshman Academic Profile: Average high school GPA 3.3. 24% in top 10% of high school class, 55% in top 25% of high school class, 85% in top 50% of high school class. **Reported SAT (pre-2016 redesign) scores:** SAT Math middle 50% range 480-590. SAT Critical Reading middle 50% range 470-600. SAT Writing middle 50% range 460-600. **Concordant SAT scores:** SAT EBRW middle 50% 520–650. SAT Math middle 50% range 510–610. ACT middle 50% range 20-25. Minimum paper TOEFL 500. **Basis for Candidate Selection:** *Important factors considered include:* rigor of secondary school record, class rank, standardized test scores. *Other factors considered include:* application essay, recommendation(s), interview, extracurricular activities, talent/ability, character/personal qualities, alumni/ae relation, racial/ethnic status, volunteer work, work experience. **Freshman Admission Requirements:** High school diploma is required and GED is accepted. *Academic units recommended:* 4 English, 3 math, 3 science, 2 foreign language, 3 social studies, and 2 units from above areas or other academic areas. **Freshman Admission Statistics:** 3,381 applied, 82.05% admitted, 24% enrolled. **Transfer Admission Requirements:** college transcript(s), Minimum college GPA of 2.5 required. Lowest grade transferable c-. **General Admission Information:** Application fee $25. Priority deadline 3/1. Nonfall registration accepted. Admission may be deferred.

COSTS AND FINANCIAL AID

Annual tuition $26,319. Room and board $7,461. Average book expense $700. **Required Forms and Deadlines:** FAFSA. **Types of Aid:** *Need-based scholarships/grants:* Federal Pell, FSEOG, State scholarships/grants, Private scholarships, College/university scholarship or grant aid from institutional funds. *Loans:* Direct Subsidized Stafford Loans, Direct Unsubsidized Stafford Loans, Direct PLUS loans, Federal Perkins Loans. *Student Employment:* Federal Work-Study Program available. Institutional employment available. **Criteria for awarding aid:** *Non-need-based:* Academics, Alumni affiliation, Art, Leadership, Minority status, Music/drama, Religious affiliation.

OUACHITA BAPTIST UNIVERSITY

410 Ouachita St, Arkadelphia, AR 71998-0001
Phone: 870-245-5110 • **Financial Aid Phone:** 870-245-5587
E-mail: admissions@alpha.obu.edu • **CEEB Code:** 6549
Fax: 870-245-5500 • **Website:** www.obu.edu • **ACT Code:** 134

This private school, affiliated with the Southern Baptist Church, was founded in 1886. It has a 200-acre campus.

RATINGS

Admissions Selectivity Rating: 86   **Fire Safety Rating:** 94   **Green Rating:** 60*

STUDENTS AND FACULTY

Enrollment: 1,474. **Student Body:** 53% female, 47% male, 33% out-of-state, 2% international (36 countries represented). Asian 1%, African American 8%, Caucasian 84%, Hispanic 4%, Native American 1%, Pacific Islander <1%, Two or more races <1%, Race unknown 0%.
Retention and Graduation: 81% freshmen return for sophomore year. 57% freshmen graduate within 4 years. 69% freshmen graduate within 6 years. 44% grads go on to further study within 1 year. 22% grads pursue arts and sciences degrees. 2% grads pursue law degrees. 2% grads pursue business degrees. 13% grads pursue medical degrees. **Faculty:** Student/faculty ratio 12:1. 104 full-time faculty, 87% hold PhDs, 3% are are members of minority groups, 35% are women. 0% of classes are taught by teaching assistants.

ACADEMICS

Degrees: associate, bachelor's. **Classes:** Most classes have 10-19 students. Most lab/discussion sessions have fewer than 10 students. **Most popular majors:** Business Administration and Management; Biology/Biological Sciences; Mass Communication/Media Studies. **Special Study Options:** cross-registration, distance learning, double major, English as a Second Language (ESL), honors program, independent study, internships, study abroad, teacher certification program. **Disability Services:** Special programs offered to physically disabled students, including note-taking services, reader services, tape recorders, tutors. **Career Services:** Alumni network, Alumni services, Career/job search classes, Career assessment, Internships. Tiger Career Connection (online job postings and resources).

FACILITIES

Housing: special housing for disabled students, men's dorms, women's dorms, apartments for married students, apartments for single students. 95% of campus accessible to physically disabled. **Special Academic Facilities/Equipment:** Historical archives, Senator John McClellan collection, language lab, TV studio. **Computers:** 100% of classrooms, 100% of dorms, 100% of libraries, 100% of dining areas, 100% of student union, 50% of common outdoor areas have wireless network access. Administrative functions (other than registration) can be performed online.

CAMPUS LIFE

Environment: Village. **Activities:** Choral groups, concert band, dance, drama/theater, jazz band, literary magazine, marching band, music ensembles, musical theater, opera, pep band, student government, student newspaper, television station, yearbook, Campus Ministries, Student Organization, Model UN. 60 registered organizations, 8 honor societies, 4 religious organizations. 5 fraternities, 5 sororities. **Athletics (Intercollegiate):** *Men:* baseball, basketball, diving, football, golf, soccer, swimming, tennis, wrestling. *Women:* basketball, cross-country, diving, golf, soccer, softball, swimming, tennis, volleyball. **On-Campus Highlights:** Starbuck's, Chick-fil-A, Commons (dining), Student Center, Sturgis Recreation Center. **Environmental Initiatives:** Employment of Energy Management Director.

ADMISSIONS

Freshman Academic Profile: Average high school GPA 3.6. 34% in top 10% of high school class, 62% in top 25% of high school class, 84% in top 50% of high school class. 86% from public high schools. **Reported SAT (pre-2016 redesign) scores:** SAT Math middle 50% range 480-590. SAT Critical Reading middle 50% range 470-610. **Concordant SAT scores:** SAT Math middle 50% range 510–610. ACT middle 50% range 21-28. Minimum internet-based TOEFL 80. Minimum paper TOEFL 550. **Basis for Candidate Selection:** *Very important factors considered include:* rigor of secondary school record, academic GPA, standardized test scores. *Other factors considered include:* talent/ability, character/personal qualities. **Freshman Admission Requirements:** High school diploma is required and GED is accepted. *Academic units required:* 4 English, 2 math, 2 science, 1 social studies, 2 history, 4 academic electives. *Academic units recommended:* 4 English, 3 math, 3 science, 2 foreign language, 1 social studies, 2 history, 4 academic electives. **Freshman Admission Statistics:** 1,712 applied, 66.88% admitted, 35% enrolled. **Transfer Admission Requirements:** college transcript(s), statement of good standing from prior institution(s). Minimum college GPA of 2.0 required. Lowest grade transferable C. **General Admission Information:**

Priority deadline 1/31. Nonfall registration accepted. Admission may be deferred for a maximum of 1 year.

COSTS AND FINANCIAL AID

Annual tuition $25,300. Room and board $7,630. Required fees $570. Average book expense $1,100. **Required Forms and Deadlines:** FAFSA, State aid form. **Notification of Awards:** Applicants will be notified of awards on a rolling basis beginning 11/1. **Types of Aid:** *Need-based scholarships/grants:* Federal Pell, FSEOG, State scholarships/grants, Private scholarships, College/university scholarship or grant aid from institutional funds. *Loans:* Direct Subsidized Stafford Loans, Direct Unsubsidized Stafford Loans, Direct PLUS loans, Federal Perkins Loans, College/university loans from institutional funds. *Student Employment:* Federal Work-Study Program available. **Financial Aid Statistics:** 99% needy freshmen, 98% needy undergrads receive need-based scholarship or grant aid. 22% freshmen, 23% undergrads receive non-need-based scholarship or grant aid. 83% freshmen, 71% undergrads receive need-based self-help aid. 8% freshmen, 8% undergrads receive athletic scholarships. 98% freshmen, 96% undergrads receive any aid. 51% undergrads borrow to pay for school. Average cumulative indebtedness $26,648. **Criteria for awarding aid:** *Non-need-based:* Academics, Alumni affiliation, Art, Athletics, Job skills, Leadership, Minority status, Music/drama, Religious affiliation, State/district residency.

OUR LADY OF THE LAKE UNIVERSITY (OLLU)

Admissions Office, San Antonio, TX 78207-4689
Phone: 210-431-3961 • **Financial Aid Phone:** 800-324-4310
E-mail: webmaster@ollusa.edu • **CEEB Code:** 6550
Fax: 210-431-4036 • **Website:** www.ollusa.edu • **ACT Code:** 4140

This private school, affiliated with the Roman Catholic Church, was founded in 1895. It has a 75-acre campus.

RATINGS

Admissions Selectivity Rating: 82   Fire Safety Rating: 64   Green Rating: 60*

STUDENTS AND FACULTY

Enrollment: 1,554. **Student Body:** 73% female, 27% male, 2% out-of-state, 1% international. Asian 1%, African American 8%, Caucasian 17%, Hispanic 63%, Native American 1%, Pacific Islander <1%, Two or more races 1%, Race unknown 8%.
Retention and Graduation: 60% freshmen return for sophomore year. 14% freshmen graduate within 4 years. 32% freshmen graduate within 6 years. 30% grads go on to further study within 1 year. **Faculty:** Student/faculty ratio 15:1. 101 full-time faculty, 80% hold PhDs, 35% are are members of minority groups, 60% are women. 0% of classes are taught by teaching assistants.

ACADEMICS

Degrees: bachelor's, doctoral/professional, doctoral/research, master's, postbachelor's certificate, post-master's certificate. **Classes:** Most classes have fewer than 10 students. **Most popular majors:** Biology/Biological Sciences; Psychology; Business Administration and Management. **Special Study Options:** cooperative education program, cross-registration, distance learning, double major, dual enrollment, English as a Second Language (ESL), honors program, independent study, internships, liberal arts/career combination, study abroad, teacher certification program, weekend college, service learning. **Disability Services:** Special programs offered to physically disabled students, including note-taking services, reader services, tape recorders, tutors. **Career Services:** Alumni services, Career assessment, Internships. We have a very successful program where grants fund salaries for interns in nonprofit settings. Also, we launched a Guaranteed Internship program in fall 2010.

FACILITIES

Housing: Coed dorms, special housing for disabled students, men's dorms, women's dorms, Wellness Housing. 99% of campus accessible to physically disabled. **Special Academic Facilities/Equipment:** Lab school for children with language and learning disabilities, elementary demonstration school, intercultural institute for training and research, language lab.

CAMPUS LIFE

Activities: Choral groups, dance, drama/theater, jazz band, music ensembles, musical theater, student government, student newspaper, symphony orchestra, television station, Campus Ministries.

ADMISSIONS

Freshman Academic Profile: Average high school GPA 3.3. 22% in top 10% of high school class, 49% in top 25% of high school class, 82% in top 50% of high school class. **Reported SAT (pre-2016 redesign) scores:** SAT Math middle 50% range 410-513. SAT Critical Reading middle 50%

range 400-500. **Concordant SAT scores:** SAT Math middle 50% range 450–540. ACT middle 50% range 17-21. Minimum internet-based TOEFL 79. Minimum paper TOEFL 650. **Basis for Candidate Selection:** *Other factors considered include:* rigor of secondary school record, class rank, academic GPA, standardized test scores, application essay, recommendation(s), talent/ability, volunteer work, work experience. **Freshman Admission Requirements:** High school diploma is required and GED is accepted. *Academic units required:* 4 English, 3 math, 2 science, 3 social studies, and 2 units from above areas or other academic areas. **Freshman Admission Statistics:** 2,109 applied, 48.55% admitted, 29% enrolled. **Transfer Admission Requirements:** college transcript(s), Minimum college GPA of 2.0 required. Lowest grade transferable D. **General Admission Information:** Application fee $25. Nonfall registration accepted. Admission may be deferred for a maximum of 1 year.

COSTS AND FINANCIAL AID

Annual tuition $22,256. Room and board $7,327. Required fees $456. Average book expense $1,200. **Required Forms and Deadlines:** FAFSA, Institution's own financial aid form. **Notification of Awards:** Applicants will be notified of awards on a rolling basis beginning 3/31. **Types of Aid:** *Need-based scholarships/grants:* Federal Pell, FSEOG, State scholarships/grants, Private scholarships, College/university scholarship or grant aid from institutional funds. *Loans:* Direct Subsidized Stafford Loans, Direct Unsubsidized Stafford Loans, Direct PLUS loans, Federal Perkins Loans, State Loans. *Student Employment:* Federal Work-Study Program available. Institutional employment available. **Financial Aid Statistics:** 99% needy freshmen, 96% needy undergrads receive need-based scholarship or grant aid. 3% freshmen, 6% undergrads receive non-need-based scholarship or grant aid. 71% freshmen, 84% undergrads receive need-based self-help aid. 5% freshmen, 7% undergrads receive athletic scholarships. 91% freshmen, 89% undergrads receive any aid. **Criteria for awarding aid:** *Non-need-based:* Academics, Alumni affiliation, Art, Leadership, Music/drama.

PACE UNIVERSITY

Best Colleges

1 Pace Plaza, New York, NY 10038
Phone: 212-346-1323 • **Financial Aid Phone:** 877-672-1830
E-mail: ugnyc@pace.edu • **CEEB Code:** 2635
Fax: 212-346-1040 • **Website:** www.pace.edu • **ACT Code:** 2852

This private school was founded in 1906. It has a 1-acre campus.

RATINGS

Admissions Selectivity Rating: 78   Fire Safety Rating: 91   Green Rating: 69

STUDENTS AND FACULTY

Enrollment: 8,384. **Student Body:** 60% female, 40% male, 41% out-of-state, 10% international (100 countries represented). Asian 8%, African American 11%, Caucasian 51%, Hispanic 14%, Native American <1%, Pacific Islander <1%, Two or more races 4%, Race unknown 3%.
Retention and Graduation: 77% freshmen return for sophomore year. 39% freshmen graduate within 4 years. 58% freshmen graduate within 6 years. 11% grads go on to further study within 1 year. **Faculty:** Student/faculty ratio 14:1. 509 full-time faculty, 82% hold PhDs, 20% are are members of minority groups, 50% are women. 0% of classes are taught by teaching assistants.

ACADEMICS

Degrees: associate, bachelor's, certificate, doctoral/professional, doctoral/research, doctoral, master's, postbachelor's certificate, post-master's certificate. **Classes:** Most classes have 10-19 students. Most lab/discussion sessions have fewer than 10 students. **Most popular majors:** Finance; Accounting; Registered Nursing/Registered Nurse. **Special Study Options:** Accelerated program, cooperative education program, cross-registration, distance learning, double major, dual enrollment, English as a Second Language (ESL), honors program, independent study, internships, study abroad, teacher certification program, Evening and freshman studies programs, Pre-freshman summer program, Learning Communities and Service Learning. **Honors Programs:** Pforzheimer Honors College for incoming freshmen. Combined degree programs: BA/JD, BA/MA, BBA/MBA; BA/MPA, BA/MSED, MA/MS, BA/MST. **Disability Services:** Special programs offered to physically disabled students, including note-taking services, reader services, tape recorders. **Career Services:** Alumni network, Alumni services, Career/job search classes, Career assessment, Internships, Regional alumni. Career Services, Internship Program.

FACILITIES

Housing: Coed dorms, apartments for single students, Apartment style for 3-4 upperclassmen. 80% of campus accessible to physically diasbled. **Special Academic Facilities/Equipment:** Laboratory Theatre, Communication Center, Language Center, Center for the Arts, Art Gallery, English Language Institute. **Computers:** 20% of classrooms, 10% of dorms, 100% of libraries, 100% of dining areas, 100% of student union, have wireless network access. Students can register for classes online. Administrative functions (other than registration) can be performed online.

CAMPUS LIFE

Environment: Metropolis. **Activities:** Choral groups, dance, drama/theater, literary magazine, musical theater, radio station, student government, student newspaper, student-run film society, television station, yearbook, Student Organization, Model UN. 79 registered organizations, 25 honor societies, 4 religious organizations. 11 fraternities, 9 sororities. **Athletics (Intercollegiate):** *Men:* baseball, basketball, cross-country, football, golf, lacrosse, swimming, tennis, track/field (outdoor), track/field (indoor). *Women:* basketball, cheerleading, cross-country, equestrian sports, soccer, softball, swimming, tennis, track/field (outdoor), track/field (indoor), volleyball. **On-Campus Highlights:** Library, Fitness Center, Theater, Classrooms, Dormitories. **Environmental Initiatives:** Environmental Law Program—Pace Law School

ADMISSIONS

Freshman Academic Profile: Average high school GPA 3.2. 17% in top 10% of high school class, 43% in top 25% of high school class, 75% in top 50% of high school class. 75% from public high schools. **Reported SAT (pre-2016 redesign) scores:** SAT Math middle 50% range 470-580. SAT Critical Reading middle 50% range 470-580. **Concordant SAT scores:** SAT Math middle 50% range 510–600. ACT middle 50% range 21-26. Minimum internet-based TOEFL 80. Minimum paper TOEFL 550. **Basis for Candidate Selection:** *Very important factors considered include:* rigor of secondary school record, standardized test scores, application essay. *Important factors considered include:* class rank, academic GPA, recommendation(s). *Other factors considered include:* interview, extracurricular activities, talent/ability, character/personal qualities, alumni/ae relation, volunteer work, work experience. **Freshman Admission Requirements:** High school diploma is required and GED is accepted. *Academic units required:* 4 English, 3 math, 2 science, 2 science labs, 2 foreign language, 3 history, 2 academic electives. **Freshman Admission Statistics:** 18,462 applied, 83.77% admitted, 13% enrolled. **Transfer Admission Requirements:** college transcript(s), statement of good standing from prior institution(s). Minimum college GPA of 2.5 required. Lowest grade transferable C. **General Admission Information:** Application fee $50. Priority deadline 2/15. Nonfall registration accepted. Admission may be deferred for a maximum of 12 months.

COSTS AND FINANCIAL AID

Annual tuition $41,120. Room and board $18,280. Required fees $1,602. Average book expense $800. **Required Forms and Deadlines:** FAFSA, State aid form. **Notification of Awards:** Applicants will be notified of awards on a rolling basis beginning 3/1. **Types of Aid:** *Need-based scholarships/grants:* Federal Pell, FSEOG, State scholarships/grants, Private scholarships, College/university scholarship or grant aid from institutional funds, Federal Nursing Scholarships. *Loans:* Direct Subsidized Stafford Loans, Direct Unsubsidized Stafford Loans, Direct PLUS loans, Federal Perkins Loans, Federal Nursing Loans. *Student Employment:* Federal Work-Study Program available. Institutional employment available. **Financial Aid Statistics:** 100% needy freshmen, 99% needy undergrads receive need-based scholarship or grant aid. 13% freshmen, 10% undergrads receive non-need-based scholarship or grant aid. 80% freshmen, 80% undergrads receive need-based self-help aid. 0% freshmen, 0% undergrads receive athletic scholarships. 92% freshmen, 85% undergrads receive any aid. 75% undergrads borrow to pay for school. Average cumulative indebtedness $33,749. **Criteria for awarding aid:** *Need-based:* Academics. *Non-need-based:* Academics, Alumni affiliation, Athletics, Music/drama.

PACIFIC LUTHERAN UNIVERSITY

Office of Admission, Tacoma, WA 98447
Phone: 253-535-7151 • **Financial Aid Phone:** 253-535-7134
E-mail: admissions@plu.edu • **CEEB Code:** 4597
Fax: 253-536-5136 • **Website:** www.plu.edu • **ACT Code:** 4597

This private school, affiliated with the Lutheran Church, was founded in 1890. It has a 126-acre campus.

RATINGS

Admissions Selectivity Rating: 75   **Fire Safety Rating:** 93   **Green Rating:** 71

STUDENTS AND FACULTY

Enrollment: 2,743. **Student Body:** 63% female, 37% male, 24% out-of-state, 3% international (21 countries represented). Asian 9%, African American 3%, Caucasian 66%, Hispanic 8%, Native American 1%, Pacific Islander 1%, Two or more races 8%, Race unknown 1%.
Retention and Graduation: 79% freshmen return for sophomore year. 58% freshmen graduate within 4 years. 71% freshmen graduate within 6 years. 14% grads go on to further study within 1 year. **Faculty:** Student/faculty ratio 11:1. 225 full-time faculty, 93% hold PhDs, 13% are are members of minority groups, 53% are women. 0% of classes are taught by teaching assistants.

ACADEMICS

Degrees: bachelor's, certificate, doctoral/professional, master's, post-master's certificate. **Classes:** Most classes have 20-29 students. Most lab/discussion sessions have 10-19 students. **Most popular majors:** Business Administration and Management; Registered Nursing/Registered Nurse; Social Sciences. **Special Study Options:** cooperative education program, cross-registration, double major, dual enrollment, English as a Second Language (ESL), exchange student program (domestic), honors program, independent study, internships, liberal arts/career combination, student-designed major, study abroad, teacher certification program. **Honors Programs:** International Honors Program Combined degree programs: BA/MEng. **Disability Services:** Special programs offered to physically disabled students, including note-taking services, reader services, tape recorders, tutors. **Career Services:** Alumni network, Alumni services, Career/job search classes, Career assessment, Internships, Regional alumni. Our Alumni Network, Lute Link. We currently have 1450 alumni career advisers with 562 connections made.

FACILITIES

Housing: Coed dorms, special housing for disabled students, special housing for international students, women's dorms, apartments for married students, apartments for single students, Foreign Languages Learning Housing. 90% of campus accessible to physically diasbled. **Special Academic Facilities/Equipment:** Mary Baker Russell Music Center Wekell Art Gallery Keck Observatory Rieke Science Center Scandinavian Cultural Center Morken Center for Learning and Technology **Computers:** 25% of classrooms, 25% of dorms, 100% of libraries, 100% of dining areas, 100% of student union, 25% of common outdoor areas have wireless network access. Students can register for classes online.

CAMPUS LIFE

Environment: City. **Activities:** Choral groups, concert band, dance, drama/theater, jazz band, literary magazine, music ensembles, musical theater, opera, pep band, radio station, student government, student newspaper, student-run film society, symphony orchestra, television station, yearbook, Campus Ministries, Student Organization. 67 registered organizations, 6 honor societies, 8 religious organizations. **Athletics (Intercollegiate):** *Men:* baseball, basketball, cheerleading, crew/rowing, cross-country, football, golf, soccer, swimming, tennis, track/field (outdoor), track/field (indoor). *Women:* basketball, cheerleading, crew/rowing, cross-country, golf, soccer, softball, swimming, tennis, track/field (outdoor), track/field (indoor), volleyball. **On-Campus Highlights:** Keck Observatory, Rieke Science Center, Mary Baker Russell Music Center, Wekell Art Gallery, Names Fitness Center, Morken Center for Learning and Technology, Scandinavian Cultural Center. **Environmental Initiatives:** Successfully building a community commitment to sustainability that encompasses students, faculty and staff in part through sustainability fellowships.

ADMISSIONS

Freshman Academic Profile: Average high school GPA 3.7. **Reported SAT (pre-2016 redesign) scores:** SAT Math middle 50% range 490-620. SAT Critical Reading middle 50% range 490-610. SAT Writing middle 50% range 480-580. **Concordant SAT scores:** SAT EBRW middle 50% 540–650. SAT Math middle 50% range 520–640. ACT middle 50% range 22-28. Minimum internet-based TOEFL 79. Minimum paper TOEFL 550. **Basis for Candidate Selection:** *Very important factors considered include:* rigor of secondary school record, application essay. *Important factors considered include:* class rank, academic GPA, standardized test scores, recommendation(s), extracurricular activities, talent/ability, character/personal qualities, volunteer work. *Other factors considered include:* interview, first generation, alumni/ae relation, geographical residence, state residency, religious affiliation/commitment, racial/ethnic status, work experience. **Freshman Admission Requirements:** High school diploma is required and GED is accepted. *Academic units required:* 2 math, 2 foreign language. *Academic units recommended:* 4 English, 3 math, 2 science, 2 science labs, 2 foreign language, 2 social studies, 3 academic electives, 1 visual/performing arts. **Freshman Admission Statistics:** 3,770 applied, 76.82% admitted, 23% enrolled. **Transfer Admission Requirements:** High school transcript, college transcript(s), essay or personal statement, statement of good standing from prior institution(s). Minimum college GPA of 2.5 required. Lowest grade transferable C-. **General Admission Information:** Application fee $40. Priority deadline 2/1. Nonfall registration accepted. Admission may be deferred for a maximum of 2 years.

COSTS AND FINANCIAL AID

Annual tuition $40,352. Room and board $10,520. Required fees $370. Average book expense $840. **Required Forms and Deadlines:** FAFSA. **Notification of Awards:** Applicants will be notified of awards on a rolling basis beginning 2/15. **Types of Aid:** *Need-based scholarships/grants:* Federal Pell, FSEOG, State scholarships/grants, Private scholarships, College/university scholarship or grant aid from institutional funds, Federal Nursing Scholarships. *Loans:* Direct Subsidized Stafford Loans, Direct Unsubsidized Stafford Loans, Direct PLUS loans, Federal Perkins Loans, Federal Nursing Loans, College/university loans from institutional funds. *Student Employment:* Federal Work-Study Program available. Institutional employment available. **Financial Aid Statistics:** 99% needy freshmen, 99% needy undergrads receive need-based scholarship or grant aid. 87% freshmen, 87% undergrads receive non-need-based scholarship or grant aid. 78% freshmen, 85% undergrads receive need-based self-help aid. 0% freshmen, 0% undergrads receive athletic scholarships. 99% freshmen, 97% undergrads receive any aid. 74% undergrads borrow to pay for school. Average cumulative indebtedness $32,862. **Criteria for awarding aid:** *Need-based:* Academics. *Non-need-based:* Academics, Alumni affiliation, Art, Leadership, Music/drama, Religious affiliation, State/district residency.

PACIFIC STATES UNIVERSITY

3450 Wilshire blvd, 5th floor, Los Angeles, CA 90010
Phone: 323-731-2383 EXT:203
E-mail: admissions@psuca.edu
Fax: 323-731-7276 • **Website:** www.psuca.edu

This private school was founded in 1928.

RATINGS

Admissions Selectivity Rating: 71   **Fire Safety Rating:** 60*   **Green Rating:** 60*

STUDENTS AND FACULTY

Enrollment: 14. **Student Body:** 29% female, 71% male, 5% out-of-state, 57% international. Asian 14%, African American 7%, Caucasian 7%, Hispanic 0%, Native American 0%, Pacific Islander 0%, Two or more races 0%, Race unknown 14%.
Retention and Graduation: 100% freshmen return for sophomore year.
Faculty: Student/faculty ratio 6:1. 7 full-time faculty, 43% hold PhDs, 0% are are members of minority groups, 29% are women.

ACADEMICS

Degrees: bachelor's, doctoral/research, master's, postbachelor's certificate. **Special Study Options:** distance learning, double major, English as a Second Language (ESL), independent study. **Career Services:** On-campus interviews.

FACILITIES

Housing: Coed dorms.

CAMPUS LIFE

Environment: Metropolis. **Activities:** television station.

ADMISSIONS

Basis for Candidate Selection: *Important factors considered include:* standardized test scores. *Other factors considered include:* rigor of secondary school record, academic GPA, application essay, level of applicant's interest. **Freshman Admission Requirements:** High school diploma is required and GED is accepted. **Freshman Admission Statistics:** 2 applied, 50.00% admitted, 100% enrolled. **Transfer Admission Requirements:** college transcript(s), Minimum college GPA of 2.5 required. Lowest grade transferable C. **General Admission Information:** Application fee $100. Nonfall registration accepted.

COSTS AND FINANCIAL AID

Annual tuition $14,055. Required fees $540. Average book expense $1,800. **Required Forms and Deadlines:** FAFSA. **Types of Aid:** *Need-based scholarships/grants:* Federal Pell. *Loans:* Direct Subsidized Stafford Loans, Direct Unsubsidized Stafford Loans.

PACIFIC UNION COLLEGE

Enrollment Services, Angwin, CA 94508
Phone: 707-965-6336 • **Financial Aid Phone:** 707-965-7200
E-mail: enroll@puc.edu • **CEEB Code:** 4600
Fax: 707-965-6671 • **Website:** www.puc.edu • **ACT Code:** 362

This private school, affiliated with the Seventh Day Adventist Church, was founded in 1882. It has a 200-acre campus.

RATINGS

Admissions Selectivity Rating: 78   **Fire Safety Rating:** 89   **Green Rating:** 60*

STUDENTS AND FACULTY

Enrollment: 1,508. **Student Body:** 58% female, 42% male, 14% out-of-state, 3% international (21 countries represented). Asian 19%, African American 9%, Caucasian 26%, Hispanic 28%, Native American <1%, Pacific Islander 2%, Two or more races 7%, Race unknown 5%.
Retention and Graduation: 77% freshmen return for sophomore year. 34% freshmen graduate within 4 years. **Faculty:** Student/faculty ratio 14:1. 94 full-time faculty, 52% hold PhDs, 26% are are members of minority groups, 50% are women. 0% of classes are taught by teaching assistants.

ACADEMICS

Degrees: associate, bachelor's, certificate, master's, terminal, transfer. **Classes:** Most classes have fewer than 10 students. Most lab/discussion sessions have fewer than 10 students. **Most popular majors:** Registered Nursing/Registered Nurse; Business/Commerce; Biology/Biological Sciences. **Special Study Options:** cooperative education program, double major, external degree program, honors program, independent study, internships, study abroad, teacher certification program. **Honors Programs:** The Honors Program offers an alternative general-education program for academically motivated students. There are no other general education requirements. Students fulfilling the Honors Program graduate "With Honors.". **Disability Services:** Special programs offered to physically disabled students, including note-taking services, reader services, tape recorders, tutors. **Career Services:** Alumni network, Career/job search classes, Career assessment, Internships.

FACILITIES

Housing: men's dorms, women's dorms, apartments for married students. 80% of campus accessible to physically diasbled. **Special Academic Facilities/ Equipment:** Art gallery, natural history collection, Pitcairn Island studies center, on-campus elementary and high schools, airport, flight training facility, observatory. **Computers:** Students can register for classes online. Administrative functions (other than registration) can be performed online.

CAMPUS LIFE

Environment: Rural. **Activities:** Choral groups, concert band, drama/ theater, jazz band, literary magazine, music ensembles, musical theater, radio station, student government, student newspaper, student-run film society, symphony orchestra, yearbook. 24 registered organizations, 8 honor societies. **Athletics (Intercollegiate):** *Men:* basketball, cross-country, volleyball. *Women:* basketball, cross-country, volleyball. **On-Campus Highlights:** Campus Center, Clark Hall/Museum, Pacific Auditorium (Gym), Paulin Auditorium (Music), 1500 acres of hiking/biking land. **Environmental Initiatives:** Buy Locally (50%).

ADMISSIONS

Freshman Academic Profile: Average high school GPA 3.3. 31% from public high schools. **Reported SAT (pre-2016 redesign) scores:** SAT Math middle 50% range 430-570. SAT Critical Reading middle 50% range 420-560. SAT Writing middle 50% range 420-540. **Concordant SAT scores:** SAT EBRW middle 50% 470–610. SAT Math middle 50% range 470–590. ACT middle 50% range 18-23. Minimum internet-based TOEFL 70. Minimum paper TOEFL 525. **Basis for Candidate Selection:** *Very important factors considered include:* academic GPA, recommendation(s). *Important factors considered include:* rigor of secondary school record, standardized test scores, character/ personal qualities, level of applicant's interest. *Other factors considered include:* class rank, interview, extracurricular activities, talent/ability, religious affiliation/ commitment. **Freshman Admission Requirements:** High school diploma is required and GED is accepted. *Academic units required:* 4 English, 2 math, 2 science, 2 history. *Academic units recommended:* 4 English, 3 math, 3 science, 2 foreign language, 2 history, 1 computer science, and 1 unit from above areas or other academic areas. **Freshman Admission Statistics:** 2,041 applied, 45.22% admitted, 27% enrolled. **Transfer Admission Requirements:** High school transcript, college transcript(s), Minimum college GPA of 2.0 required. Lowest grade transferable C-. **General Admission Information:** Application fee $30. Nonfall registration accepted. Admission may be deferred for a maximum of 1 year.

COSTS AND FINANCIAL AID

Annual tuition $27,999. Room and board $7,695. Required fees $315. Average book expense $1,764. **Required Forms and Deadlines:** FAFSA, Institution's own financial aid form. **Notification of Awards:** Applicants will be notified of awards on a rolling basis beginning 4/1. **Types of Aid:** *Need-based scholarships/grants:* Federal Pell, FSEOG, State scholarships/grants, Private scholarships, College/university scholarship or grant aid from institutional funds. *Loans:* Direct Subsidized Stafford Loans, Direct Unsubsidized Stafford Loans, Direct PLUS loans, Federal Perkins Loans, College/university loans from institutional funds. *Student Employment:* Federal Work-Study Program available. Institutional employment available. **Financial Aid Statistics:** 100% needy freshmen, 100% needy undergrads receive need-based scholarship or grant aid. 39% freshmen, 31% undergrads receive non-need-based scholarship or grant aid. 95% freshmen, 97% undergrads receive need-based self-help aid. 2% freshmen, 0% undergrads receive athletic scholarships. **Criteria for awarding aid:** *Need-based:* Academics. *Non-need-based:* Academics, Art, Athletics, Leadership, Music/drama, Religious affiliation.

PACIFIC UNIVERSITY

2043 College Way, Forest Grove, OR 97116
Phone: 503-352-2218 • **Financial Aid Phone:** 503-352-2222
E-mail: admissions@pacificu.edu • **CEEB Code:** 4601
Fax: 503-352-2975 • **Website:** www.pacificu.edu

This private school was founded in 1849. It has a 60-acre campus.

RATINGS

Admissions Selectivity Rating: 75 **Fire Safety Rating:** 82 **Green Rating:** 60*

STUDENTS AND FACULTY

Enrollment: 1,884. **Student Body:** 60% female, 40% male, 55% out-of-state, 2% international (32 countries represented). Asian 12%, African American 2%, Caucasian 52%, Hispanic 13%, Native American 1%, Pacific Islander 3%, Two or more races 12%, Race unknown 4%.
Retention and Graduation: 77% freshmen return for sophomore year. 64% freshmen graduate within 4 years. 71% freshmen graduate within 6 years. 24% grads go on to further study within 1 year. 11% grads pursue arts and sciences degrees. 4% grads pursue law degrees. 2% grads pursue business degrees. 2% grads pursue medical degrees. **Faculty:** Student/faculty ratio 10:1. 216 full-time faculty, 87% hold PhDs, 13% are are members of minority groups, 51% are women. 0% of classes are taught by teaching assistants.

ACADEMICS

Degrees: bachelor's, doctoral/professional, master's, postbachelor's certificate, post-master's certificate. **Classes:** Most classes have 10-19 students. Most lab/discussion sessions have 10-19 students. **Most popular majors:** Kinesiology and Exercise Science; Business Administration and Management; Biology/Biological Sciences. **Special Study Options:** cross-registration, double major, English as a Second Language (ESL), independent study, internships, liberal arts/career combination, study abroad, teacher certification program. Combined degree programs: 3-2 applied physics program and 4-1 computer scien. **Disability Services:** Special programs offered to physically disabled students, including note-taking services, reader services, tape recorders, tutors. **Career Services:** Alumni network, Alumni services, Career/job search classes, Career assessment, Internships, Regional alumni, Internships.

FACILITIES

Housing: Coed dorms, special housing for disabled students, apartments for single students, ThemeHousing1 wing designated female. **Special Academic Facilities/Equipment:** State history museum, performing arts center, media center, humanitarian center, Holocaust resource center, politics/law forum, Berglund Center for Internet Studies, electron microscopes. **Computers:** 100% of classrooms, 100% of dorms, 100% of libraries, 100% of dining areas, 100% of student union, 90% of common outdoor areas have wireless network access. Administrative functions (other than registration) can be performed online.

CAMPUS LIFE

Environment: Village. **Activities:** Choral groups, concert band, dance, drama/theater, jazz band, literary magazine, music ensembles, pep band, radio station, student government, student newspaper, student-run film society, Campus Ministries, Student Organization. 58 registered organizations, 2 honor societies, 4 religious organizations. 3 fraternities, 4 sororities. **Athletics (Intercollegiate):** Men: baseball, basketball, cross-country, golf, soccer, swimming, tennis, track/field (outdoor), wrestling. Women: basketball, cross-country, golf, lacrosse, soccer, softball, swimming, tennis, track/field (outdoor), volleyball, wrestling. **On-Campus Highlights:** Pacific Athletic Center, Pacific Library (New Library), Marsh Hall, Old College Hall, New Bookstore/Vera's Cafe. **Environmental Initiatives:** Sustainability Committee.

ADMISSIONS

Freshman Academic Profile: Average high school GPA 3.6. 88% from public high schools. **Reported SAT (pre-2016 redesign) scores:** SAT Math middle 50% range 500-600. SAT Critical Reading middle 50% range 490-590. **Concordant SAT scores:** SAT Math middle 50% range 530-620. ACT middle 50% range 21-26. Minimum paper TOEFL 550. **Basis for Candidate Selection:** *Very important factors considered include:* rigor of secondary school record, academic GPA, standardized test scores, recommendation(s), extracurricular activities, character/personal qualities, volunteer work, level of applicant's interest. *Important factors considered include:* class rank, application essay, talent/ability. *Other factors considered include:* first generation, alumni/ae relation, work experience. **Freshman Admission Requirements:** High school diploma is required and GED is accepted. *Academic units recommended:* 4 English, 3 math, 3 science, 1 science lab, 2 foreign language, 3 social studies, 1 history, 4 academic electives. **Freshman Admission Statistics:** 3,004 applied, 79.03% admitted, 20% enrolled. **Transfer Admission Requirements:** college transcript(s), essay or personal statement, statement of good standing from prior institution(s). Minimum college GPA of 2.70 required. Lowest grade transferable C-. **General Admission Information:** Application fee $40. Priority deadline 2/15. Regular application deadline 8/15. Nonfall registration accepted. Admission may be deferred for a maximum of 2 years.

COSTS AND FINANCIAL AID

Annual tuition $40,120. Room and board $11,822. Required fees $934. Average book expense $1,050. **Required Forms and Deadlines:** FAFSA. **Notification of Awards:** Applicants will be notified of awards on a rolling basis beginning 3/1. **Types of Aid:** *Need-based scholarships/grants:* Federal Pell, FSEOG, State scholarships/grants, Private scholarships, College/university scholarship or grant aid from institutional funds. *Loans:* Direct Subsidized Stafford Loans, Direct Unsubsidized Stafford Loans, Direct PLUS loans, Federal Perkins Loans. *Student Employment:* Federal Work-Study Program available. Institutional employment available. **Financial Aid Statistics:** 97% needy freshmen, 72% needy undergrads receive need-based scholarship or grant aid. 97% freshmen, 92% undergrads receive non-need-based scholarship or grant aid. 84% freshmen, 84% undergrads receive need-based self-help aid. 0% freshmen, 0% undergrads receive athletic scholarships. 93% freshmen, 93% undergrads receive any aid. 79% undergrads borrow to pay for school. Average cumulative indebtedness $30,081. **Criteria for awarding aid:** *Need-based:* Academics, Leadership. *Non-need-based:* Academics, Alumni affiliation, Art, Music/drama.

PALM BEACH ATLANTIC UNIVERSITY

PO Box 24708, West Palm Beach, FL 33416-4708
Phone: 561-803-2100 • **Financial Aid Phone:** 561-803-2126
E-mail: admit@pba.edu • **CEEB Code:** 5553
Fax: 561-803-2115 • **Website:** www.pba.edu • **ACT Code:** 739

This private school, affiliated with the Christian (Nondenominational) Church, was founded in 1968. It has a 25-acre campus.

RATINGS

Admissions Selectivity Rating: 73 **Fire Safety Rating:** 60* **Green Rating:** 60*

STUDENTS AND FACULTY

Enrollment: 2,474. **Student Body:** 66% female, 34% male, 34% out-of-state, 4% international (28 countries represented). Asian 2%, African American 12%, Caucasian 62%, Hispanic 16%, Native American 1%, Pacific Islander <1%, Two or more races 3%, Race unknown 3%.
Retention and Graduation: 75% freshmen return for sophomore year. 40% freshmen graduate within 4 years. 51% freshmen graduate within 6 years.
Faculty: Student/faculty ratio 12:1. 174 full-time faculty, 82% hold PhDs, 16% are are members of minority groups, 47% are women. 0% of classes are taught by teaching assistants.

ACADEMICS

Degrees: associate, bachelor's, doctoral/professional, master's. **Classes:** Most classes have 10-19 students. Most lab/discussion sessions have 10-19 students. **Most popular majors:** Psychology; Accounting and Business/Management; Education. **Special Study Options:** Accelerated program, distance learning, double major, dual enrollment, honors program, independent study, internships, student-designed major, study abroad, teacher certification program. **Honors Programs:** The Frederick M. Supper Honors Program exists to establish a community of scholars. The program encourages students to develop a thoughtful and insightful Christian worldview through enduring conversation to enable students to live the examined life and to facilitate character formation. Combined degree programs: PharmD/MBA. **Career Services:** Alumni network, Alumni services, Career/job search classes, Career assessment, Internships, On-campus interviews. The Workship program is a distinctive service program at PBA which enables students to offer a Christian response to human needs by serving in nonprofit agencies, churches, and schools outside the university community.

FACILITIES

Housing: Coed dorms, men's dorms, women's dorms, apartments for married students, Theme Housing. **Special Academic Facilities/ Equipment:** DeSantis Family Chapel; Greene Sports Complex (Cafe); Helen K.Persson Recital Hall **Computers:** Students can register for classes online. Administrative functions (other than registration) can be performed online.

CAMPUS LIFE

Environment: Metropolis. **Activities:** Choral groups, dance, drama/theater, jazz band, literary magazine, music ensembles, musical theater, pep band, radio station, student government, student newspaper, symphony orchestra, television station, yearbook, Campus Ministries, Student Organization. 56 registered organizations, 29 honor societies, 6 religious organizations. **Athletics (Intercollegiate):** *Men:* baseball, basketball, cross-country, soccer, tennis. *Women:* basketball, cross-country, soccer, softball, tennis, volleyball. **On-Campus Highlights:** DeSantis Family Chapel, Greene Complex (athletics, snack shop), Vera Lea Rinker Music Building.

ADMISSIONS

Freshman Academic Profile: Average high school GPA 3.6. **Reported SAT (pre-2016 redesign) scores:** SAT Math middle 50% range 460-570. SAT Critical Reading middle 50% range 470-600. SAT Writing middle 50% range 458-573. **Concordant SAT scores:** SAT EBRW middle 50% 520–640. SAT Math middle 50% range 500–590. ACT middle 50% range 21-27. Minimum paper TOEFL 550. **Basis for Candidate Selection:** *Very important factors considered include:* academic GPA, standardized test scores, application essay, character/personal qualities, religious affiliation/commitment. *Important factors considered include:* rigor of secondary school record, recommendation(s), interview, extracurricular activities, talent/ability. *Other factors considered include:* class rank, alumni/ae relation, volunteer work, level of applicant's interest. **Freshman Admission Requirements:** High school diploma is required and GED is accepted. *Academic units required:* 4 English, 3 math, 3 science, 3 science labs, 5 academic electives. *Academic units recommended:* 4 English, 3 math, 3 science, 1 science lab, 2 foreign language. **Freshman Admission Statistics:** 1,449 applied, 93.37% admitted, 37% enrolled. **Transfer Admission Requirements:** college transcript(s), essay or personal statement, Minimum college GPA of 2.5 required. Lowest grade transferable C. **General Admission Information:** Application fee $50. Nonfall registration accepted. Admission may be deferred for a maximum of 1 year.

COSTS AND FINANCIAL AID

Annual tuition $29,510. Room and board $9,770. Required fees $440. Average book expense $1,030. **Required Forms and Deadlines:** FAFSA, State aid form. **Notification of Awards:** Applicants will be notified of awards on a rolling basis beginning 3/1. **Types of Aid:** *Need-based scholarships/grants:* Federal Pell, FSEOG, State scholarships/grants, Private scholarships, College/university scholarship or grant aid from institutional funds. *Loans:* Direct Subsidized Stafford Loans, Direct Unsubsidized Stafford Loans, Direct PLUS loans, Federal Perkins Loans. *Student Employment:* Federal Work-Study Program available. Institutional employment available. **Financial Aid Statistics:** 100% needy freshmen, 100% needy undergrads receive need-based scholarship or grant aid. 20% freshmen, 15% undergrads receive non-need-based scholarship or grant aid. 61% freshmen, 68% undergrads receive need-based self-help aid. 5% freshmen, 5% undergrads receive athletic scholarships. 100% freshmen, 100% undergrads receive any aid. 63% undergrads borrow to pay for school. Average cumulative indebtedness $28,862. **Criteria for awarding aid:** *Need-based:* Academics, Alumni affiliation. *Non-need-based:* Academics, Alumni affiliation, Art, Athletics, Leadership, Music/drama, State/district residency.

PARK UNIVERSITY

8700 NW River Park Drive, Parkville, MO 64152
Phone: 816-584-6213 • **Financial Aid Phone:** 816-548-6290
E-mail: admissions@mail.park.edu • **CEEB Code:** 6574
Fax: 816-741-4462 • **ACT Code:** 2340

This private school was founded in 1875. It has a 700-acre campus.

RATINGS

Admissions Selectivity Rating: 78   **Fire Safety Rating:** 75   **Green Rating:** 60*

STUDENTS AND FACULTY

Enrollment: 1,672. **Student Body:** 56% female, 44% male, 20% out-of-state, 19% international (93 countries represented). Asian 0%, African American 10%,

Caucasian 61%, Hispanic 5%, Native American 1%, Pacific Islander <1%, Two or more races 3%, Race unknown 0%.
Retention and Graduation: 61% freshmen return for sophomore year. 22% freshmen graduate within 4 years. 39% freshmen graduate within 6 years. 7% grads go on to further study within 1 year. 6% grads pursue arts and sciences degrees. 1% grads pursue business degrees. **Faculty:** Student/faculty ratio 12:1. 82 full-time faculty, 66% hold PhDs, 4% are are members of minority groups, 38% are women. 0% of classes are taught by teaching assistants.

ACADEMICS

Degrees: associate, bachelor's, certificate, master's, postbachelor's certificate. **Most popular majors:** Business Administration and Management; Education; Computer and Information Sciences. **Special Study Options:** Accelerated program, cross-registration, distance learning, double major, dual enrollment, English as a Second Language (ESL), honors program, independent study, internships, student-designed major, study abroad, teacher certification program, weekend college. **Disability Services:** Special programs offered to physically disabled students, including note-taking services, reader services, tape recorders, tutors.

FACILITIES

Housing: Coed dorms, apartments for married students. 90% of campus accessible to physically disabled. **Computers:** Students can register for classes online. Administrative functions (other than registration) can be performed online.

CAMPUS LIFE

Environment: Town. **Activities:** Choral groups, drama/theater, literary magazine, radio station, student government, student newspaper, symphony orchestra, yearbook. 15 registered organizations, 4 honor societies, 13 religious organizations. **Athletics (Intercollegiate):** *Men:* baseball, basketball, cross-country, soccer, track/field (outdoor), track/field (indoor), volleyball. *Women:* basketball, cross-country, golf, soccer, softball, track/field (outdoor), track/field (indoor), volleyball. **On-Campus Highlights:** Gym, Cafeteria, Classrooms (Underground), Library, Bookstore.

ADMISSIONS

Freshman Academic Profile: Average high school GPA 3.3. 14% in top 10% of high school class, 37% in top 25% of high school class, 68% in top 50% of high school class. 80% from public high schools. ACT middle 50% range 17-23. Minimum paper TOEFL 500. **Basis for Candidate Selection:** *Very important factors considered include:* rigor of secondary school record, class rank, standardized test scores. *Other factors considered include:* application essay, recommendation(s). **Freshman Admission Requirements:** High school diploma is required and GED is accepted. *Academic units recommended:* 3 English, 2 math, 2 science, 1 science lab, 2 foreign language, 3 social studies, 1 history, 6 academic electives. **Freshman Admission Statistics:** 778 applied, 69.28% admitted, 39% enrolled. **Transfer Admission Requirements:** High school transcript, college transcript(s), Minimum college GPA of 2.0 required. Lowest grade transferable C. **General Admission Information:** Application fee $25. Priority deadline 4/15. Regular application deadline 7/1. Nonfall registration accepted. Admission may be deferred.

COSTS AND FINANCIAL AID

Annual tuition $10,380. Required fees $100. Average book expense $1,800. **Required Forms and Deadlines:** FAFSA, Institution's own financial aid form. **Notification of Awards:** Applicants will be notified of awards on a rolling basis beginning 2/15. **Types of Aid:** *Need-based scholarships/grants:* Federal Pell, FSEOG, State scholarships/grants, Private scholarships. *Loans:* Direct Subsidized Stafford Loans, Direct Unsubsidized Stafford Loans, Direct PLUS loans, Federal Perkins Loans. *Student Employment:* Federal Work-Study Program available. Institutional employment available. **Financial Aid Statistics:** 78% needy freshmen, 73% needy undergrads receive need-based scholarship or grant aid. 75% freshmen, 53% undergrads receive non-need-based scholarship or grant aid. 56% freshmen, 71% undergrads receive need-based self-help aid. 17% freshmen, 11% undergrads receive athletic scholarships. 78% freshmen receive any aid. **Criteria for awarding aid:** *Non-need-based:* Academics, Alumni affiliation, Art, Athletics, Job skills, State/district residency.

PARSONS SCHOOL OF DESIGN

72 Fifth Avenue, New York, NY 10003
Phone: 212-229-5150 • **Financial Aid Phone:** 212-229-8930
E-mail: admission@newschool.edu • **CEEB Code:** 2638
Website: www.newschool.edu • **ACT Code:** 2854

This private school was founded in 1896.

RATINGS
Admissions Selectivity Rating: 83   **Fire Safety Rating:** 89   **Green Rating:** 87

STUDENTS AND FACULTY
Enrollment: 4,204. **Student Body:** 78% female, 22% male, 78% out-of-state, 44% international (93 countries represented). Asian 13%, African American 5%, Caucasian 25%, Hispanic 9%, Native American <1%, Pacific Islander <1%, Two or more races 2%, Race unknown 2%.
Retention and Graduation: 87% freshmen return for sophomore year. 51% freshmen graduate within 4 years. 62% freshmen graduate within 6 years. 2% grads go on to further study within 1 year. **Faculty:** Student/faculty ratio 11:1. 155 full-time faculty, 61% hold PhDs, 14% are are members of minority groups, 49% are women. 0% of classes are taught by teaching assistants.

ACADEMICS
Degrees: associate, bachelor's, master's, postbachelor's certificate. **Classes:** Most classes have 10-19 students. Most lab/discussion sessions have 20-29 students. **Most popular majors:** Fashion/Apparel Design; Graphic Design; Fine and Studio Arts Management. **Special Study Options:** Accelerated program, cross-registration, distance learning, double major, dual enrollment, English as a Second Language (ESL), exchange student program (domestic), independent study, internships, liberal arts/career combination, student-designed major, study abroad, Five Year combined BA/BFA. Combined degree programs: BA/BFA, MFA/ARC. **Disability Services:** Special programs offered to physically disabled students, including note-taking services, reader services, tape recorders. **Career Services:** Alumni network, Alumni services, Career/job search classes, Career assessment, Internships, Regional alumni. Both programs provide students with unique opportunities to explore future career paths, to learn new skills and to build strong communities.

FACILITIES
Housing: Coed dorms, special housing for disabled students, apartments for single students. 99% of campus accessible to physically diasbled. **Special Academic Facilities/Equipment:** Fashion Education Center in New York's garment district with labs and studios for fashion design students. **Computers:** 95% of classrooms, 100% of libraries, 100% of dining areas, na% of student union, 100% of common outdoor areas have wireless network access. Students can register for classes online. Administrative functions (other than registration) can be performed online.

CAMPUS LIFE
Environment: Metropolis. **Activities:** Choral groups, dance, drama/theater, jazz band, literary magazine, music ensembles, radio station, student government, student newspaper, symphony orchestra, Student Organization. 34 registered organizations. **On-Campus Highlights:** Sheila Johnson Design Center, Schwartz Fashion Center, University Welcome Center **Environmental Initiatives:** Lighting Retrofits: 2W 13th St. and 66 5th Ave are in the midst of an ongoing replacement of all non-LED fixtures. The majority of the building's T8 fluorescent bulbs are being replaced with LED, stairwells are being replaced with dimming-occupancy based bi-level fixtures, and all rooms will be equiped with vacancy sensors. The main lobby and gallery spaces will also recieve significant upgrades as well. These same upgrades are being applied to 2 other large buildings, with a goal of completing the entire campus by early 2017.

ADMISSIONS
Freshman Academic Profile: Average high school GPA 3.3. 14% in top 10% of high school class, 23% in top 25% of high school class, 34% in top 50% of high school class. 63% from public high schools. **Reported SAT (pre-2016 redesign) scores:** SAT Math middle 50% range 500-630. SAT Critical Reading middle 50% range 500-620. SAT Writing middle 50% range 500-620. **Concordant SAT scores:** SAT EBRW middle 50% 560–670. SAT Math middle 50% range 530–650. ACT middle 50% range 22-27. Minimum internet-based TOEFL 92. **Basis for Candidate Selection:** *Very important factors considered include:* academic GPA, application essay, extracurricular activities. *Important factors considered include:* rigor of secondary school record, recommendation(s), character/personal qualities. *Other factors considered include:* class rank, standardized test scores, interview, talent/ability, volunteer work, work experience, level of applicant's interest. **Freshman Admission Requirements:** High school diploma is required and GED is accepted. *Academic units required:* 4 English. *Academic units recommended:* 4 math, 4 science, 4 foreign language, 4 social studies, 4 history. **Freshman Admission Statistics:** 2,947 applied, 64.10% admitted, 39% enrolled. **Transfer Admission**

Requirements: college transcript(s), Minimum college GPA of 2.0 required. Lowest grade transferable C. **General Admission Information:** Application fee $50. Priority deadline 1/15. Regular application deadline 8/1. Nonfall registration accepted. Admission may be deferred for a maximum of 1 year.

COSTS AND FINANCIAL AID
Annual tuition $43,560. Room and board $18,930. Required fees $1,106. Average book expense $2,050. **Required Forms and Deadlines:** FAFSA, State aid form. **Types of Aid:** *Need-based scholarships/grants:* Federal Pell, FSEOG, State scholarships/grants, Private scholarships, College/university scholarship or grant aid from institutional funds. *Loans:* Direct Subsidized Stafford Loans, Direct Unsubsidized Stafford Loans, Direct PLUS loans, Federal Perkins Loans. *Student Employment:* Federal Work-Study Program available. Institutional employment available. **Financial Aid Statistics:** 95% needy freshmen, 98% needy undergrads receive need-based scholarship or grant aid. 71% freshmen, 63% undergrads receive non-need-based scholarship or grant aid. 80% freshmen, 83% undergrads receive need-based self-help aid. 0% freshmen, 0% undergrads receive athletic scholarships. 38% freshmen, 40% undergrads receive any aid. 52% undergrads borrow to pay for school. Average cumulative indebtedness $30,659. **Criteria for awarding aid:** *Need-based:* Academics, Art, Leadership, Minority status, Music/drama. *Non-need-based:* Academics, Art, Leadership, Minority status, Music/drama, State/district residency.

PATRICK HENRY COLLEGE

10 Patrick Henry Circle, Purcellville, VA 20132
Financial Aid Phone: 540-441-8142
E-mail: admissions@phc.edu • **CEEB Code:** 2804
Fax: 540-441-8119 • **Website:** www.phc.edu • **ACT Code:** 4383

This private school, affiliated with the Christian (Nondenominational) Church, was founded in 2000. It has a 106-acre campus.

RATINGS
Admissions Selectivity Rating: 84   **Fire Safety Rating:** 90   **Green Rating:** 60*

STUDENTS AND FACULTY
Enrollment: 263. **Student Body:** 46% female, 54% male, 80% out-of-state, 0% international. Asian 3%, African American <1%, Caucasian 82%, Hispanic 5%, Native American 0%, Pacific Islander <1%, Two or more races 0%, Race unknown 10%.
Retention and Graduation: 83% freshmen return for sophomore year. 64% freshmen graduate within 4 years. 74% freshmen graduate within 6 years. 10% grads go on to further study within 1 year. 23% grads pursue law degrees. **Faculty:** Student/faculty ratio 10:1. 19 full-time faculty, 89% hold PhDs, 0% are are members of minority groups, 5% are women. 0% of classes are taught by teaching assistants.

ACADEMICS
Degrees: bachelor's. **Classes:** Most classes have fewer than 10 students. **Most popular majors:** Political Science and Government; Journalism; Business/Managerial Economics. **Special Study Options:** distance learning, liberal arts/career combination. **Disability Services:** Special programs offered to physically disabled students, including tutors. **Career Services:** Alumni network, Alumni services, Career/job search classes, Career assessment, Internships.

FACILITIES
Housing: men's dorms, women's dorms. 100% of campus accessible to physically diasbled. **Computers:** 100% of classrooms, 100% of dorms, 100% of libraries, 100% of dining areas, 100% of student union, 100% of common outdoor areas have wireless network access. Students can register for classes online. Administrative functions (other than registration) can be performed online. Undergraduates are required to own a computer.

CAMPUS LIFE
Environment: Village. **Activities:** Choral groups, concert band, drama/theater, literary magazine, music ensembles, student government, student newspaper, student-run film society, yearbook, Campus Ministries, Model UN. **Athletics (Intercollegiate):** *Men:* basketball, soccer. *Women:* basketball, soccer. **On-Campus Highlights:** Student Coffee Lounge, Workout facilities, Raquetball courts **Environmental Initiatives:** water conservation

ADMISSIONS
Freshman Academic Profile: Average high school GPA 3.8. 20% from public high schools. **Reported SAT (pre-2016 redesign) scores:** SAT Math middle 50% range 523-625. SAT Critical Reading middle 50% range 593-738. SAT Writing middle 50% range 523-668. **Concordant SAT scores:** SAT EBRW middle 50% 620–740. SAT Math middle 50% range 550–650. ACT

middle 50% range 25-31. **Basis for Candidate Selection:** *Very important factors considered include:* rigor of secondary school record, standardized test scores, application essay, recommendation(s), character/personal qualities, religious affiliation/commitment, level of applicant's interest. *Important factors considered include:* academic GPA, interview, extracurricular activities, talent/ability, volunteer work. *Other factors considered include:* work experience. **Freshman Admission Requirements:** High school diploma is required and GED is accepted. *Academic units required:* 4 English, 3 math, 2 science, 2 science labs, 1 foreign language, 2 history, 3 academic electives. *Academic units recommended:* 4 English, 3 math, 3 science, 3 science labs, 2 foreign language, 2 history, 3 academic electives. **Freshman Admission Statistics:** 244 applied, 52.46% admitted, 40% enrolled. **Transfer Admission Requirements:** High school transcript, college transcript(s), essay or personal statement, interview, standardized test scores, statement of good standing from prior institution(s). Lowest grade transferable C. **General Admission Information:** Application fee $20. Priority deadline 2/1. Regular application deadline 6/15. Nonfall registration accepted. Admission may be deferred for a maximum of one year.

COSTS AND FINANCIAL AID

Annual tuition $27,922. Room and board $10,728. Required fees $200. Average book expense $1,000. **Required Forms and Deadlines:** CSS/Financial Aid PROFILE. **Notification of Awards:** Applicants will be notified of awards on a rolling basis beginning 3/1. **Types of Aid:** *Need-based scholarships/grants:* Private scholarships, College/university scholarship or grant aid from institutional funds. *Loans:* College/university loans from institutional funds. *Student Employment:* Institutional employment available. **Financial Aid Statistics:** 100% needy freshmen, 100% needy undergrads receive need-based scholarship or grant aid. 87% freshmen, 86% undergrads receive non-need-based scholarship or grant aid. 100% freshmen, 100% undergrads receive need-based self-help aid. 0% freshmen, 0% undergrads receive athletic scholarships. 94% freshmen, 94% undergrads receive any aid. 39% undergrads borrow to pay for school. **Criteria for awarding aid:** *Non-need-based:* Academics, Leadership, Music/drama.

THE PENNSYLVANIA ACADEMY OF THE FINE ARTS

128 North Broad Street, Philadelphia, PA 19102
Phone: 215-972-7625 • **Financial Aid Phone:** 215-972-2019
E-mail: admissions@pafa.edu
Fax: 215-972-0839 • **Website:** www.pafa.edu

This private school was founded in 1804.

RATINGS
Admissions Selectivity Rating: 61 **Fire Safety Rating:** 60* **Green Rating:** 60*

STUDENTS AND FACULTY
Enrollment: 169. **Student Body:** 66% female, 34% male, 25% out-of-state, 5% international (19 countries represented). Asian 6%, African American 7%, Caucasian 59%, Hispanic 7%, Native American 1%, Pacific Islander 0%, Two or more races 4%, Race unknown 12%.
Faculty: Student/faculty ratio 13:1. 0% of classes are taught by teaching assistants.

ACADEMICS
Degrees: bachelor's, certificate, master's, postbachelor's certifiate. **Most popular majors:** Painting; Fine/Studio Arts. **Special Study Options:** dual enrollment, exchange student program (domestic), independent study, internships. Combined degree programs: BFA in conjunction wit the University of Pennsylvania.

FACILITIES
Housing: The Pennsylvania Academy has a housing arrangement with International House, Philadelphia. We do not offer our own on-campus housing opportunities.

CAMPUS LIFE
Environment: Metropolis. **Activities:** student government 4 registered organizations. **On-Campus Highlights:** Museum of American Art, World Famous Cast Hall

ADMISSIONS
Minimum internet-based TOEFL 100. Minimum paper TOEFL 600. **Freshman Admission Requirements:** High school diploma is required and GED is accepted. **Transfer Admission Requirements:** High school transcript, essay or personal statement, Lowest grade transferable C. **General Admission Information:** Application fee $60. Priority deadline 12/1. Regular application deadline 2/15.

COSTS AND FINANCIAL AID

Annual tuition $32,960. Room and board $10,815. Required fees $1,450. Average book expense $1,511. **Required Forms and Deadlines:** FAFSA. **Notification of Awards:** Applicants will be notified of awards on a rolling basis beginning 3/1. **Types of Aid:** *Need-based scholarships/grants:* Federal Pell, FSEOG, State scholarships/grants, Private scholarships, College/university scholarship or grant aid from institutional funds. *Loans:* Direct Subsidized Stafford Loans, Direct Unsubsidized Stafford Loans, Direct PLUS loans. *Student Employment:* Federal Work-Study Program available. Institutional employment available. **Financial Aid Statistics:** 80% freshmen, 80% undergrads receive any aid. **Criteria for awarding aid:** *Non-need-based:* Academics, Art.

PENNSYLVANIA COLLEGE OF TECHNOLOGY

One College Avenue, Williamsport, PA 17701
Phone: 570-327-4761 • **Financial Aid Phone:** 570-327-4761
E-mail: admissions@pct.edu
Fax: 570-321-5551 • **Website:** www.pct.edu

This public school was founded in 1989. It has a 984-acre campus.

RATINGS
Admissions Selectivity Rating: 63 **Fire Safety Rating:** 60* **Green Rating:** 60*

STUDENTS AND FACULTY
Student Body: 36% female, 64% male, 10% out-of-state.
Retention and Graduation: 75% freshmen return for sophomore year.
Faculty: Student/faculty ratio 18:1. 293 full-time faculty, 0% hold PhDs, 5% are are members of minority groups, 31% are women. 0% of classes are taught by teaching assistants.

ACADEMICS
Degrees: associate, bachelor's, certificate. **Special Study Options:** Accelerated program, cooperative education program, cross-registration, distance learning, dual enrollment, exchange student program (domestic), honors program, independent study, internships, student-designed major, study abroad, weekend college. **Disability Services:** Special programs offered to physically disabled students, including note-taking services, reader services, tape recorders, tutors. **Career Services:** Alumni services, Career/job search classes, Career assessment.

FACILITIES
Housing: Coed dorms, apartments for single students, Wellness Housing. 100% of campus accessible to physically diasbled. **Computers:** Students can register for classes online. Administrative functions (other than registration) can be performed online.

CAMPUS LIFE
Environment: Town. **Activities:** dance, radio station, student government, Campus Ministries. 50 registered organizations, 3 honor societies, 4 religious organizations. 3 fraternities. **Athletics (Intercollegiate):** *Men:* archery, baseball, basketball, bowling, cross-country, golf, soccer, tennis, volleyball. *Women:* archery, basketball, bowling, cross-country, golf, soccer, softball, tennis, volleyball. **On-Campus Highlights:** Academic Facilities, Madigan Library, Campus Center, Student & Administrative Services Center, Academic Center.

ADMISSIONS
Freshman Academic Profile: 4% in top 10% of high school class, 16% in top 25% of high school class, 48% in top 50% of high school class. Minimum paper TOEFL 500. **Freshman Admission Requirements:** High school diploma is required and GED is accepted. **Freshman Admission Statistics:** 3,144 applied, 84.99% admitted. **Transfer Admission Requirements:** High school transcript, college transcript(s), Minimum college GPA of 2.5 required. Lowest grade transferable C. **General Admission Information:** Application fee $50. Regular application deadline 7/1. Nonfall registration accepted. Admission may be deferred for a maximum of 1 year.

COSTS AND FINANCIAL AID

Annual in-state tuition $13,320. Annual out-of-state tuition $19,980. Room and board $11,108. Required fees $2,490. Average book expense $1,400. **Required Forms and Deadlines:** FAFSA, Institution's own financial aid form. **Notification of Awards:** Applicants will be notified of awards on a rolling basis beginning 6/1. **Types of Aid:** *Need-based scholarships/grants:* Federal Pell, FSEOG, State scholarships/grants, Private scholarships. *Student Employment:* Federal Work-Study Program available. Institutional employment available.

PENNSYLVANIA STATE UNIVERSITY—ABINGTON

106 Sutherland Building, Abington, PA 19001
Phone: 215-881-7600
E-mail: abingtonadmissions@psu.edu
Fax: 215-881-7655 • **Website:** http://www.abington.psu.edu

This public school was founded in 1950. It has a 45-acre campus.

RATINGS
Admissions Selectivity Rating: 74   **Fire Safety Rating:** 60*   **Green Rating:** 60*

STUDENTS AND FACULTY
Enrollment: 3,490. **Student Body:** 51% female, 49% male, 7% out-of-state, 5% international. Asian 17%, African American 13%, Caucasian 50%, Hispanic 10%, Native American <1%, Pacific Islander <1%, Two or more races 2%, Race unknown 3%.
Retention and Graduation: 80% freshmen return for sophomore year. 23% freshmen graduate within 4 years. 48% freshmen graduate within 6 years. **Faculty:** Student/faculty ratio 18:1. 136 full-time faculty, 65% hold PhDs, 17% are are members of minority groups, 50% are women.

ACADEMICS
Degrees: associate, bachelor's, certificate, postbachelor's certifiate. **Classes:** Most classes have 20-29 students. Most lab/discussion sessions have 20-29 students. **Special Study Options:** Accelerated program, cooperative education program, distance learning, double major, dual enrollment, English as a Second Language (ESL), exchange student program (domestic), external degree program, honors program, independent study, internships, liberal arts/career combination, student-designed major, study abroad.

CAMPUS LIFE
Environment: Village. **Activities:** dance, drama/theater, literary magazine, student government, student newspaper, student-run film society, Campus Ministries. **Athletics (Intercollegiate):** *Men:* basketball, soccer, softball, tennis. *Women:* basketball, field hockey, softball, tennis, volleyball.

ADMISSIONS
Freshman Academic Profile: Average high school GPA 3.1. 8% in top 10% of high school class, 27% in top 25% of high school class, 64% in top 50% of high school class. **Reported SAT (pre-2016 redesign) scores:** SAT Math middle 50% range 430-570. SAT Critical Reading middle 50% range 420-520. SAT Writing middle 50% range 410-520. **Concordant SAT scores:** SAT EBRW middle 50% 460–580. SAT Math middle 50% range 470–590. ACT middle 50% range 19-25. Minimum paper TOEFL 550. **Basis for Candidate Selection:** *Very important factors considered include:* academic GPA, standardized test scores. *Important factors considered include:* rigor of secondary school record. *Other factors considered include:* class rank, application essay, extracurricular activities, talent/ability, character/personal qualities, alumni/ae relation, geographical residence, state residency, volunteer work, work experience. **Freshman Admission Requirements:** High school diploma is required and GED is accepted. *Academic units required:* 4 English, 3 math, 3 science, 2 foreign language, 3 social studies. *Academic units recommended:* 3 foreign language. **Freshman Admission Statistics:** 3,946 applied, 82.39% admitted, 27% enrolled. **Transfer Admission Requirements:** High school transcript, college transcript(s), Lowest grade transferable C. **General Admission Information:** Application fee $50. Priority deadline 11/30. Nonfall registration accepted. Admission may be deferred for a maximum of One Year.

COSTS AND FINANCIAL AID
Annual in-state tuition $13,012. Annual out-of-state tuition $20,324. Required fees $942. **Required Forms and Deadlines:** FAFSA. **Types of Aid:** *Need-based scholarships/grants:* Federal Pell, FSEOG, State scholarships/grants, Private scholarships, College/university scholarship or grant aid from institutional funds. *Loans:* Direct Subsidized Stafford Loans, Direct Unsubsidized Stafford Loans, Direct PLUS loans, Federal Perkins Loans, College/university loans from institutional funds. *Student Employment:* Federal Work-Study Program available. Institutional employment available. **Financial Aid Statistics:** 77% needy freshmen, 80% needy undergrads receive need-based scholarship or grant aid. 36% freshmen, 29% undergrads receive non-need-based scholarship or grant aid. 71% freshmen, 81% undergrads receive need-based self-help aid. 0% freshmen, 0% undergrads receive athletic scholarships. 82% undergrads borrow to pay for school. Average cumulative indebtedness $35,013. **Criteria for awarding aid:** *Need-based:* Academics, Alumni affiliation. *Non-need-based:* Academics, Alumni affiliation.

PENNSYLVANIA STATE UNIVERSITY—ALTOONA

E108 Smith Building, Altoona, PA 16601-3760
Phone: 814-949-5466
E-mail: aaadmit@psu.edu
Fax: 814-949-5564 • **Website:** www.altoona.psu.edu

This public school was founded in 1929.

RATINGS
Admissions Selectivity Rating: 72   **Fire Safety Rating:** 60*   **Green Rating:** 60*

STUDENTS AND FACULTY
Enrollment: 3,772. **Student Body:** 44% female, 56% male, 17% out-of-state, 5% international. Asian 3%, African American 7%, Caucasian 77%, Hispanic 6%, Native American <1%, Pacific Islander <1%, Two or more races 2%, Race unknown 1%.
Retention and Graduation: 84% freshmen return for sophomore year. 47% freshmen graduate within 4 years. 69% freshmen graduate within 6 years. **Faculty:** Student/faculty ratio 16:1. 203 full-time faculty, 67% hold PhDs, 12% are are members of minority groups, 50% are women.

ACADEMICS
Degrees: associate, bachelor's, certificate. **Classes:** Most classes have 20-29 students. Most lab/discussion sessions have 20-29 students. **Special Study Options:** cooperative education program, cross-registration, distance learning, double major, dual enrollment, English as a Second Language (ESL), exchange student program (domestic), honors program, independent study, internships, liberal arts/career combination, student-designed major, study abroad, teacher certification program.

FACILITIES
Housing: Coed dorms, special housing for disabled students, Suites, Special Interest Housing.

CAMPUS LIFE
Environment: Village. **Activities:** Choral groups, dance, drama/theater, jazz band, literary magazine, music ensembles, pep band, student government, student newspaper, student-run film society, yearbook, Campus Ministries, Student Organization. **Athletics (Intercollegiate):** *Men:* basketball, diving, skiing (downhill/alpine), soccer, swimming, tennis, volleyball. *Women:* basketball, diving, skiing (downhill/alpine), swimming, tennis, volleyball.

ADMISSIONS
Freshman Academic Profile: Average high school GPA 3.1. 6% in top 10% of high school class, 24% in top 25% of high school class, 67% in top 50% of high school class. **Reported SAT (pre-2016 redesign) scores:** SAT Math middle 50% range 450-550. SAT Critical Reading middle 50% range 440-540. SAT Writing middle 50% range 430-530. **Concordant SAT scores:** SAT EBRW middle 50% 490–590. SAT Math middle 50% range 490–570. ACT middle 50% range 20-24. **Basis for Candidate Selection:** *Very important factors considered include:* academic GPA, standardized test scores. *Important factors considered include:* rigor of secondary school record. *Other factors considered include:* class rank, application essay, extracurricular activities, talent/ability, character/personal qualities, alumni/ae relation, geographical residence, state residency, volunteer work, work experience. **Freshman Admission Requirements:** High school diploma is required and GED is accepted. *Academic units required:* 4 English, 3 math, 3 science, 2 foreign language, 3 social studies. *Academic units recommended:* 3 foreign language. **Freshman Admission Statistics:** 5,738 applied, 89.39% admitted, 27% enrolled. **Transfer Admission Requirements:** High school transcript, college transcript(s), Lowest grade transferable C. **General Admission Information:** Application fee $50. Priority deadline 11/30. Nonfall registration accepted. Admission may be deferred for a maximum of One Year.

COSTS AND FINANCIAL AID
Annual in-state tuition $13,658. Annual out-of-state tuition $21,392. Room and board $10,920. Required fees $952. Average book expense $1,840. **Required Forms and Deadlines:** FAFSA. **Types of Aid:** *Need-based scholarships/grants:* Federal Pell, FSEOG, State scholarships/grants, Private scholarships, College/university scholarship or grant aid from institutional funds. *Loans:* Direct Subsidized Stafford Loans, Direct Unsubsidized Stafford Loans, Direct PLUS loans, Federal Perkins Loans, College/university loans from institutional funds. *Student Employment:* Federal Work-Study Program available. Institutional employment available. **Financial Aid Statistics:** 58% needy freshmen, 62% needy undergrads receive need-based scholarship or grant aid. 51% freshmen, 46% undergrads receive non-need-based scholarship or grant aid. 83% freshmen, 86% undergrads receive need-based self-help aid. 0% freshmen, 0% undergrads receive athletic scholarships. 76% undergrads borrow to pay for school. Average cumulative indebtedness $39,091. **Criteria for awarding aid:** *Need-based:* Academics, Alumni affiliation. *Non-need-based:* Academics, Alumni affiliation.

PENNSYLVANIA STATE UNIVERSITY—BEAVER

100 University Drive, 113 Student Union, Monaca, PA 15061-2799
Phone: 877-564-6778
E-mail: br-admissions@psu.edu
Fax: 724-773-3769 • **Website:** http://beaver.psu.edu

This is a public school.

RATINGS

Admissions Selectivity Rating: 73   Fire Safety Rating: 60*   Green Rating: 60*

STUDENTS AND FACULTY

Enrollment: 639. **Student Body:** 39% female, 61% male, 9% out-of-state, 3% international. Asian 3%, African American 9%, Caucasian 75%, Hispanic 5%, Native American <1%, Pacific Islander <1%, Two or more races 2%, Race unknown 1%.
Retention and Graduation: 78% freshmen return for sophomore year. 24% freshmen graduate within 4 years. 45% freshmen graduate within 6 years.
Faculty: Student/faculty ratio 16:1. 32 full-time faculty, 66% hold PhDs, 22% are are members of minority groups, 59% are women.

ACADEMICS

Degrees: bachelor's, certificate.

ADMISSIONS

Freshman Academic Profile: Average high school GPA 3.1. 7% in top 10% of high school class, 31% in top 25% of high school class, 73% in top 50% of high school class. **Reported SAT (pre-2016 redesign) scores:** SAT Math middle 50% range 450-570. SAT Critical Reading middle 50% range 430-550. SAT Writing middle 50% range 410-530. **Concordant SAT scores:** SAT EBRW middle 50% range 470–600. SAT Math middle 50% range 490–590. ACT middle 50% range 18-24. **Basis for Candidate Selection:** *Very important factors considered include:* academic GPA, standardized test scores. *Important factors considered include:* rigor of secondary school record. *Other factors considered include:* class rank, application essay, extracurricular activities, talent/ability, character/personal qualities, alumni/ae relation, volunteer work, work experience. **Freshman Admission Requirements:** *Academic units required:* 4 English, 3 math, 3 science, 2 foreign language, 3 social studies. *Academic units recommended:* 3 foreign language. **Freshman Admission Statistics:** 653 applied, 94.95% admitted, 34% enrolled. **General Admission Information:** Application fee $50. Priority deadline 11/30. Nonfall registration accepted. Admission may be deferred for a maximum of One Year.

COSTS AND FINANCIAL AID

Annual in-state tuition $12,718. Annual out-of-state tuition $19,404. Room and board $10,920. Required fees $942. Average book expense $1,840. **Required Forms and Deadlines:** FAFSA. **Types of Aid:** *Need-based scholarships/grants:* Federal Pell, FSEOG, State scholarships/grants, Private scholarships, College/university scholarship or grant aid from institutional funds. *Loans:* Direct Subsidized Stafford Loans, Direct Unsubsidized Stafford Loans, Direct PLUS Loans, Federal Perkins Loans, College/university loans from institutional funds. *Student Employment:* Federal Work-Study Program available. Institutional employment available. **Financial Aid Statistics:** 70% needy freshmen, 75% needy undergrads receive need-based scholarship or grant aid. 69% freshmen, 57% undergrads receive non-need-based scholarship or grant aid. 85% freshmen, 87% undergrads receive need-based self-help aid. 0% freshmen, 0% undergrads receive athletic scholarships. 86% undergrads borrow to pay for school. Average cumulative indebtedness $37,485. **Criteria for awarding aid:** *Need-based:* Academics, Alumni affiliation. *Non-need-based:* Academics, Alumni affiliation.

PENNSYLVANIA STATE UNIVERSITY—BERKS

Tulpehocken Road PO Box 7009, Reading, PA 19610-6009
Phone: 610-396-6060
E-mail: admissionsbk@psu.edu
Fax: 610-396-6077 • **Website:** http://berks.psu.edu

This public school was founded in 1924. It has a 241-acre campus.

RATINGS

Admissions Selectivity Rating: 74   Fire Safety Rating: 60*   Green Rating: 60*

STUDENTS AND FACULTY

Enrollment: 2,778. **Student Body:** 43% female, 57% male, 8% out-of-state, 3% international. Asian 5%, African American 9%, Caucasian 68%, Hispanic 11%, Native American <1%, Pacific Islander <1%, Two or more races 2%, Race unknown 1%.
Retention and Graduation: 82% freshmen return for sophomore year. 40% freshmen graduate within 4 years. 82% freshmen graduate within 6 years.
Faculty: Student/faculty ratio 17:1. 136 full-time faculty, 70% hold PhDs, 15% are are members of minority groups, 50% are women.

ACADEMICS

Degrees: associate, bachelor's, certificate, postbachelor's certificate. **Classes:** Most classes have 20-29 students. Most lab/discussion sessions have 10-19 students. **Special Study Options:** Accelerated program, cooperative education program, cross-registration, distance learning, dual enrollment, English as a Second Language (ESL), honors program, independent study, internships, study abroad, teacher certification program.

FACILITIES

Housing: Coed dorms, special housing for disabled students, Honor Students, Suites, Special Interest Houses.

CAMPUS LIFE

Environment: Village. **Activities:** Choral groups, dance, drama/theater, pep band, radio station, student government, student newspaper, student-run film society, yearbook, Campus Ministries, Student Organization. **Athletics (Intercollegiate):** *Men:* baseball, basketball, fencing, soccer, tennis, volleyball. *Women:* fencing, softball, tennis, volleyball.

ADMISSIONS

Freshman Academic Profile: Average high school GPA 3.1. 8% in top 10% of high school class, 29% in top 25% of high school class, 66% in top 50% of high school class. **Reported SAT (pre-2016 redesign) scores:** SAT Math middle 50% range 430-560. SAT Critical Reading middle 50% range 420-540. SAT Writing middle 50% range 410-520. **Concordant SAT scores:** SAT EBRW middle 50% range 460–590. SAT Math middle 50% range 470–580. ACT middle 50% range 18-25. Minimum paper TOEFL 550. **Basis for Candidate Selection:** *Very important factors considered include:* academic GPA, standardized test scores. *Important factors considered include:* rigor of secondary school record. *Other factors considered include:* class rank, application essay, extracurricular activities, talent/ability, character/personal qualities, alumni/ae relation, geographical residence, state residency, volunteer work, work experience. **Freshman Admission Requirements:** High school diploma is required and GED is accepted. *Academic units required:* 4 English, 3 math, 3 science, 2 foreign language, 3 social studies. *Academic units recommended:* 3 foreign language. **Freshman Admission Statistics:** 2,413 applied, 84.87% admitted, 39% enrolled. **Transfer Admission Requirements:** High school transcript, college transcript(s), Lowest grade transferable C. **General Admission Information:** Application fee $50. Priority deadline 11/30. Nonfall registration accepted. Admission may be deferred for a maximum of One Year.

COSTS AND FINANCIAL AID

Annual in-state tuition $13,658. Annual out-of-state tuition $21,392. Room and board $11,950. Required fees $952. Average book expense $1,840. **Required Forms and Deadlines:** FAFSA. **Types of Aid:** *Need-based scholarships/grants:* Federal Pell, FSEOG, State scholarships/grants, Private scholarships, College/university scholarship or grant aid from institutional funds. *Loans:* Direct Subsidized Stafford Loans, Direct Unsubsidized Stafford Loans, Direct PLUS loans, Federal Perkins Loans, College/university loans from institutional funds. *Student Employment:* Federal Work-Study Program available. Institutional employment available. **Financial Aid Statistics:** 66% needy freshmen, 70% needy undergrads receive need-based scholarship or grant aid. 38% freshmen, 33% undergrads receive non-need-based scholarship or grant aid. 85% freshmen, 87% undergrads receive need-based self-help aid. 0% freshmen, 0% undergrads receive athletic scholarships. 80% undergrads borrow to pay for school. Average cumulative indebtedness $35,853. **Criteria for awarding aid:** *Need-based:* Academics, Alumni affiliation. *Non-need-based:* Academics, Alumni affiliation.

PENNSYLVANIA STATE UNIVERSITY— BRANDYWINE

25 Yearsley Mill Road, Media, PA 19063
Phone: 610-892-1200
E-mail: bwadmissions@psu.edu
Fax: 610-892-1320 • **Website:** brandywine.psu.edu

This is a public school.

RATINGS

Admissions Selectivity Rating: 72   Fire Safety Rating: 60*   Green Rating: 60*

STUDENTS AND FACULTY

Enrollment: 1,291. **Student Body:** 44% female, 56% male, 5% out-of-state, 1% international. Asian 11%, African American 15%, Caucasian 63%, Hispanic 5%, Native American <1%, Pacific Islander <1%, Two or more races 2%, Race unknown 2%.
Retention and Graduation: 74% freshmen return for sophomore year. 16% freshmen graduate within 4 years. 41% freshmen graduate within 6 years. **Faculty:** Student/faculty ratio 15:1. 68 full-time faculty, 71% hold PhDs, 15% are are members of minority groups, 53% are women.

ACADEMICS

Degrees: associate, bachelor's, certificate, postbachelor's certificate.

ADMISSIONS

Freshman Academic Profile: Average high school GPA 3.0. 4% in top 10% of high school class, 18% in top 25% of high school class, 56% in top 50% of high school class. **Reported SAT (pre-2016 redesign) scores:** SAT Math middle 50% range 440-550. SAT Critical Reading middle 50% range 420-520. SAT Writing middle 50% range 410-510. **Concordant SAT scores:** SAT EBRW middle 50% 460-570. SAT Math middle 50% range 480-570. ACT middle 50% range 18-26. **Basis for Candidate Selection:** *Very important factors considered include:* academic GPA, standardized test scores. *Important factors considered include:* rigor of secondary school record. *Other factors considered include:* class rank, application essay, extracurricular activities, talent/ability, character/personal qualities, alumni/ae relation, volunteer work, work experience. **Freshman Admission Requirements:** *Academic units required:* 4 English, 3 math, 3 science, 2 foreign language, 3 social studies. *Academic units recommended:* 3 foreign language. **Freshman Admission Statistics:** 1,265 applied, 83.08% admitted, 36% enrolled. **General Admission Information:** Application fee $50. Priority deadline 11/30. Nonfall registration accepted. Admission may be deferred for a maximum of One year.
COSTS AND FINANCIAL AID Annual in-state tuition $13,012. Annual out-of-state tuition $20,206. Required fees $952. **Required Forms and Deadlines:** FAFSA. **Types of Aid:** *Need-based scholarships/grants:* Federal Pell, FSEOG, State scholarships/grants, Private scholarships, College/university scholarship or grant aid from institutional funds. *Loans:* Direct Subsidized Stafford Loans, Direct Unsubsidized Stafford Loans, Direct PLUS loans, Federal Perkins Loans, College/university loans from institutional funds. *Student Employment:* Federal Work-Study Program available. Institutional employment available. **Financial Aid Statistics:** 75% needy freshmen, 76% needy undergrads receive need-based scholarship or grant aid. 41% freshmen, 32% undergrads receive non-need-based scholarship or grant aid. 80% freshmen, 83% undergrads receive need-based self-help aid. 0% freshmen, 0% undergrads receive athletic scholarships. 78% undergrads borrow to pay for school. Average cumulative indebtedness $34,962. **Criteria for awarding aid:** *Need-based:* Academics, Alumni affiliation. *Non-need-based:* Academics, Alumni affiliation.

PENNSYLVANIA STATE UNIVERSITY—DUBOIS

Hochrein House, 1 College Place, DuBois, PA 15801-3199
Phone: 814-375-4720
E-mail: duboisinfo@psu.edu
Fax: 814-375-4784 • **Website:** http://dubois.psu.edu

This is a public school.

RATINGS

Admissions Selectivity Rating: 75   **Fire Safety Rating:** 60*   **Green Rating:** 60*

STUDENTS AND FACULTY

Enrollment: 512. **Student Body:** 44% female, 56% male, 3% out-of-state, <1% international. Asian 1%, African American 2%, Caucasian 94%, Hispanic 2%, Native American 0%, Pacific Islander <1%, Two or more races <1%, Race unknown 1%.
Retention and Graduation: 87% freshmen return for sophomore year. 20% freshmen graduate within 4 years. 41% freshmen graduate within 6 years. **Faculty:** Student/faculty ratio 11:1. 42 full-time faculty, 57% hold PhDs, 19% are are members of minority groups, 60% are women.

ACADEMICS

Degrees: associate, bachelor's, certificate.

ADMISSIONS

Freshman Academic Profile: Average high school GPA 3.1. 9% in top 10% of high school class, 33% in top 25% of high school class, 68% in top 50% of high school class. **Reported SAT (pre-2016 redesign) scores:** SAT Math middle 50% range 420-560. SAT Critical Reading middle 50% range 420-530. SAT Writing middle 50% range 390-490. **Concordant SAT scores:** SAT

EBRW middle 50% 450-570. SAT Math middle 50% range 460-580. ACT middle 50% range 21-25. **Basis for Candidate Selection:** *Very important factors considered include:* academic GPA, standardized test scores. *Important factors considered include:* rigor of secondary school record. *Other factors considered include:* class rank, application essay, extracurricular activities, talent/ability, character/personal qualities, alumni/ae relation, volunteer work, work experience. **Freshman Admission Requirements:** *Academic units required:* 4 English, 3 math, 3 science, 2 foreign language, 3 social studies. *Academic units recommended:* 3 foreign language. **Freshman Admission Statistics:** 394 applied, 85.03% admitted, 49% enrolled. **General Admission Information:** Application fee $50. Priority deadline 11/30. Nonfall registration accepted. Admission may be deferred for a maximum of 1 year.

COSTS AND FINANCIAL AID

Annual in-state tuition $12,718. Annual out-of-state tuition $19,404. Required fees $828. **Required Forms and Deadlines:** FAFSA. **Types of Aid:** *Need-based scholarships/grants:* Federal Pell, FSEOG, State scholarships/grants, Private scholarships, College/university scholarship or grant aid from institutional funds. *Loans:* Direct Subsidized Stafford Loans, Direct Unsubsidized Stafford Loans, Direct PLUS loans, Federal Perkins Loans, College/university loans from institutional funds. *Student Employment:* Federal Work-Study Program available. Institutional employment available. **Financial Aid Statistics:** 87% needy freshmen, 89% needy undergrads receive need-based scholarship or grant aid. 48% freshmen, 37% undergrads receive non-need-based scholarship or grant aid. 81% freshmen, 87% undergrads receive need-based self-help aid. 0% freshmen, 0% undergrads receive athletic scholarships. 88% undergrads borrow to pay for school. Average cumulative indebtedness $43,504. **Criteria for awarding aid:** *Need-based:* Academics, Alumni affiliation. *Non-need-based:* Academics, Alumni affiliation.

PENNSYLVANIA STATE UNIVERSITY— ERIE, THE BEHREND COLLEGE

Metzgar Admissions & Alumnia Ct, Erie, PA 16563-0105
Phone: 814-898-6100
E-mail: behrend.admissions@psu.edu
Fax: 814-898-6044 • **Website:** http://psbehrend.psu.edu/ • **ACT Code:** 3656

This public school was founded in 1948. It has a 732-acre campus.

RATINGS

Admissions Selectivity Rating: 76   **Fire Safety Rating:** 60*   **Green Rating:** 60*

STUDENTS AND FACULTY

Enrollment: 4,092. **Student Body:** 35% female, 65% male, 10% out-of-state, 9% international. Asian 3%, African American 4%, Caucasian 79%, Hispanic 2%, Native American <1%, Pacific Islander <1%, Two or more races 2%, Race unknown 1%.
Retention and Graduation: 85% freshmen return for sophomore year. 47% freshmen graduate within 4 years. 69% freshmen graduate within 6 years. **Faculty:** Student/faculty ratio 15:1. 260 full-time faculty, 67% hold PhDs, 12% are are members of minority groups, 37% are women. 0% of classes are taught by teaching assistants.

ACADEMICS

Degrees: associate, bachelor's, certificate, master's. **Classes:** Most classes have 20-29 students. Most lab/discussion sessions have 10-19 students. **Special Study Options:** Accelerated program, cooperative education program, distance learning, double major, dual enrollment, honors program, independent study, internships, liberal arts/career combination, study abroad, teacher certification program. **Disability Services:** Special programs offered to physically disabled students, including note-taking services, reader services, tape recorders, tutors. **Career Services:** Alumni services, Career/job search classes, Career assessment, Internships.

FACILITIES

Housing: Coed dorms, special housing for disabled students, men's dorms, women's dorms, apartments for single students, Suites, Special Interest Housing. **Special Academic Facilities/Equipment:** Observatory, plastics lab. **Computers:** Students can register for classes online. Administrative functions (other than registration) can be performed online.

CAMPUS LIFE

Environment: Village. **Activities:** Choral groups, concert band, dance, drama/theater, jazz band, literary magazine, music ensembles, pep band, radio station, student government, student newspaper, student-run film society, Campus Ministries, Student Organization. 75 registered organizations, 46 honor societies, 26 religious organizations. 6 fraternities, 4 sororities. **Athletics**

(Intercollegiate): *Men:* baseball, basketball, cheerleading, cross-country, golf, soccer, swimming, tennis, track/field (outdoor), water polo, wrestling. *Women:* basketball, cheerleading, cross-country, golf, soccer, softball, swimming, tennis, track/field (outdoor), volleyball, water polo. **On-Campus Highlights:** Junker Athletic Center, Logan House, Smith Chapel and Carillon, Bruno's Café, Reen Union Building, Historic Behrend Farmhouse.

ADMISSIONS

Freshman Academic Profile: Average high school GPA 3.3. 13% in top 10% of high school class, 42% in top 25% of high school class, 80% in top 50% of high school class. **Reported SAT (pre-2016 redesign) scores:** SAT Math middle 50% range 480-610. SAT Critical Reading middle 50% range 460-560. SAT Writing middle 50% range 440-550. **Concordant SAT scores:** SAT EBRW middle 50% 500–610. SAT Math middle 50% range 510–630. ACT middle 50% range 20-25. Minimum paper TOEFL 550. **Basis for Candidate Selection:** *Very important factors considered include:* academic GPA, standardized test scores. *Important factors considered include:* rigor of secondary school record. *Other factors considered include:* class rank, application essay, extracurricular activities, talent/ability, character/personal qualities, alumni/ae relation, geographical residence, state residency, volunteer work, work experience. **Freshman Admission Requirements:** High school diploma is required and GED is accepted. *Academic units required:* 4 English, 3 math, 3 science, 2 foreign language, 3 social studies. *Academic units recommended:* 3 foreign language. **Freshman Admission Statistics:** 4,079 applied, 87.08% admitted, 33% enrolled. **Transfer Admission Requirements:** High school transcript, college transcript(s), Lowest grade transferable C. **General Admission Information:** Application fee $50. Priority deadline 11/30. Nonfall registration accepted. Admission may be deferred for a maximum of One Year.

COSTS AND FINANCIAL AID

Annual in-state tuition $13,658. Annual out-of-state tuition $21,392. Room and board $10,920. Required fees $952. Average book expense $1,840. **Required Forms and Deadlines:** FAFSA. *Types of Aid: Need-based scholarships/grants:* Federal Pell, FSEOG, State scholarships/grants, Private scholarships, College/university scholarship or grant aid from institutional funds. *Loans:* Direct Subsidized Stafford Loans, Direct Unsubsidized Stafford Loans, Direct PLUS loans, Federal Perkins Loans, College/university loans from institutional funds. *Student Employment:* Federal Work-Study Program available. Institutional employment available. **Financial Aid Statistics:** 63% needy freshmen, 64% needy undergrads receive need-based scholarship or grant aid. 46% freshmen, 39% undergrads receive non-need-based scholarship or grant aid. 87% freshmen, 89% undergrads receive need-based self-help aid. 0% freshmen, 0% undergrads receive athletic scholarships. 81% undergrads borrow to pay for school. Average cumulative indebtedness $39,346. **Criteria for awarding aid:** *Need-based:* Academics, Alumni affiliation. *Non-need-based:* Academics, Alumni affiliation.

PENNSYLVANIA STATE UNIVERSITY— FAYETTE, THE EBERLY CAMPUS

110 Eberly Building, 2201 University Dri, Lemont Furnace, PA 15456
Phone: 724-430-4130
E-mail: feadm@psu.edu
Fax: 724-430-4175 • **Website:** fe.psu.edu

This is a public school.

RATINGS

Admissions Selectivity Rating: 74   **Fire Safety Rating:** 60*   **Green Rating:** 60*

STUDENTS AND FACULTY

Enrollment: 671. **Student Body:** 59% female, 41% male, 5% out-of-state, 2% international. Asian 0%, African American 4%, Caucasian 89%, Hispanic 2%, Native American <1%, Pacific Islander 0%, Two or more races 3%, Race unknown 1%.
Retention and Graduation: 77% freshmen return for sophomore year. 31% freshmen graduate within 4 years. 51% freshmen graduate within 6 years.
Faculty: Student/faculty ratio 12:1. 44 full-time faculty, 48% hold PhDs, 2% are are members of minority groups, 45% are women.

ACADEMICS

Degrees: associate, bachelor's, certificate.

ADMISSIONS

Freshman Academic Profile: Average high school GPA 3.2. 10% in top 10% of high school class, 35% in top 25% of high school class, 73% in top 50% of high school class. **Reported SAT (pre-2016 redesign) scores:** SAT Math

middle 50% range 410-520. SAT Critical Reading middle 50% range 390-510. SAT Writing middle 50% range 370-470. **Concordant SAT scores:** SAT EBRW middle 50% 430–550. SAT Math middle 50% range 450–550. ACT middle 50% range 17-22. **Basis for Candidate Selection:** *Very important factors considered include:* academic GPA, standardized test scores. *Important factors considered include:* rigor of secondary school record. *Other factors considered include:* class rank, application essay, extracurricular activities, talent/ability, character/personal qualities, alumni/ae relation, geographical residence, state residency, volunteer work, work experience. **Freshman Admission Requirements:** *Academic units required:* 4 English, 3 math, 3 science, 2 foreign language, 3 social studies. *Academic units recommended:* 3 foreign language. **Freshman Admission Statistics:** 659 applied, 80.88% admitted, 36% enrolled. **General Admission Information:** Application fee $50. Priority deadline 11/30. Nonfall registration accepted. Admission may be deferred for a maximum of One Year.

COSTS AND FINANCIAL AID

Annual in-state tuition $12,718. Annual out-of-state tuition $19,404. Required fees $890. **Required Forms and Deadlines:** FAFSA. **Types of Aid:** *Need-based scholarships/grants:* Federal Pell, FSEOG, State scholarships/grants, Private scholarships, College/university scholarship or grant aid from institutional funds. *Loans:* Direct Subsidized Stafford Loans, Direct Unsubsidized Stafford Loans, Direct PLUS loans, Federal Perkins Loans, College/university loans from institutional funds. *Student Employment:* Federal Work-Study Program available. Institutional employment available. **Financial Aid Statistics:** 80% needy freshmen, 82% needy undergrads receive need-based scholarship or grant aid. 55% freshmen, 44% undergrads receive non-need-based scholarship or grant aid. 74% freshmen, 81% undergrads receive need-based self-help aid. 0% freshmen, 0% undergrads receive athletic scholarships. 87% undergrads borrow to pay for school. Average cumulative indebtedness $37,338. **Criteria for awarding aid:** *Need-based:* Academics, Alumni affiliation. *Non-need-based:* Academics, Alumni affiliation.

PENNSYLVANIA STATE UNIVERSITY— GREATER ALLEGHENY

123 Frable Bldg., 4000 University Drive, McKeesport, PA 15132-7698
Phone: 412-675-9010
E-mail: psuga@psu.edu
Fax: 412-675-9056 • **Website:** http://ga.psu.edu

This is a public school.

RATINGS

Admissions Selectivity Rating: 74   **Fire Safety Rating:** 60*   **Green Rating:** 60*

STUDENTS AND FACULTY

Enrollment: 532. **Student Body:** 41% female, 59% male, 7% out-of-state, 4% international. Asian 5%, African American 19%, Caucasian 61%, Hispanic 7%, Native American 0%, Pacific Islander 0%, Two or more races 3%, Race unknown 1%.
Retention and Graduation: 80% freshmen return for sophomore year. 20% freshmen graduate within 4 years. 38% freshmen graduate within 6 years.
Faculty: Student/faculty ratio 11:1. 34 full-time faculty, 74% hold PhDs, 29% are are members of minority groups, 59% are women.

ACADEMICS

Degrees: associate, bachelor's, certificate, master's.

ADMISSIONS

Freshman Academic Profile: Average high school GPA 3.1. 6% in top 10% of high school class, 22% in top 25% of high school class, 64% in top 50% of high school class. **Reported SAT (pre-2016 redesign) scores:** SAT Math middle 50% range 400-540. SAT Critical Reading middle 50% range 390-540. SAT Writing middle 50% range 380-510. **Concordant SAT scores:** SAT EBRW middle 50% 430–580. SAT Math middle 50% range 440–570. ACT middle 50% range 20-25. **Basis for Candidate Selection:** *Very important factors considered include:* academic GPA, standardized test scores. *Important factors considered include:* rigor of secondary school record. *Other factors considered include:* class rank, application essay, extracurricular activities, talent/ability, character/personal qualities, alumni/ae relation, geographical residence, state residency, volunteer work, work experience. **Freshman Admission Requirements:** *Academic units required:* 4 English, 3 math, 3 science, 2 foreign language, 3 social studies. *Academic units recommended:* 3 foreign language. **Freshman Admission Statistics:** 594 applied, 78.79% admitted, 34% enrolled. **General Admission Information:** Application fee $50. Priority deadline 11/30. Nonfall registration accepted. Admission may be deferred for a maximum of One Year.

COSTS AND FINANCIAL AID

Annual in-state tuition $12,718. Annual out-of-state tuition $19,404. Room and board $10,920. Required fees $942. Average book expense $1,840. **Required Forms and Deadlines:** FAFSA. **Types of Aid:** *Need-based scholarships/ grants:* Federal Pell, FSEOG, State scholarships/grants, Private scholarships, College/university scholarship or grant aid from institutional funds. *Loans:* Direct Subsidized Stafford Loans, Direct Unsubsidized Stafford Loans, Direct PLUS loans, Federal Perkins Loans, College/university loans from institutional funds. *Student Employment:* Federal Work-Study Program available. Institutional employment available. **Financial Aid Statistics:** 86% needy freshmen, 84% needy undergrads receive need-based scholarship or grant aid. 71% freshmen, 52% undergrads receive non-need-based scholarship or grant aid. 77% freshmen, 84% undergrads receive need-based self-help aid. 0% freshmen, 0% undergrads receive athletic scholarships. 81% undergrads borrow to pay for school. Average cumulative indebtedness $38,931. **Criteria for awarding aid:** *Need-based:* Academics, Alumni affiliation. *Non-need-based:* Academics, Alumni affiliation.

PENNSYLVANIA STATE UNIVERSITY— HARRISBURG

Swatara Bldg., Middletown, PA 17057-4898
Phone: 717-948-6250
E-mail: hbgadmit@psu.edu
Fax: 717-948-6325 • **Website:** www.harrisburg.psu.edu

This public school was founded in 1966.

RATINGS

Admissions Selectivity Rating: 75   **Fire Safety Rating:** 60*   **Green Rating:** 60*

STUDENTS AND FACULTY

Enrollment: 3,740. **Student Body:** 39% female, 61% male, 16% out-of-state, 10% international. Asian 9%, African American 11%, Caucasian 59%, Hispanic 6%, Native American <1%, Pacific Islander <1%, Two or more races 3%, Race unknown 2%.
Retention and Graduation: 87% freshmen return for sophomore year. 41% freshmen graduate within 4 years. 64% freshmen graduate within 6 years.
Faculty: Student/faculty ratio 15:1. 229 full-time faculty, 85% hold PhDs, 20% are are members of minority groups, 41% are women.

ACADEMICS

Degrees: associate, bachelor's, certificate, doctoral/research, master's, postbachelor's certificate. **Classes:** Most classes have 20-29 students. Most lab/ discussion sessions have fewer than 10 students. **Special Study Options:** cooperative education program, cross-registration, distance learning, double major, dual enrollment, honors program, independent study, internships, student-designed major, study abroad, teacher certification program.

FACILITIES

Housing: special housing for disabled students, apartments for single students, Special Interest Housing.

CAMPUS LIFE

Environment: Village. **Activities:** Choral groups, dance, drama/theater, literary magazine, music ensembles, radio station, student government, student newspaper. 2 honor societies, 1 religious organization. **Athletics (Intercollegiate):** *Men:* basketball, skiing (downhill/alpine), soccer, tennis, track/field (outdoor), volleyball. *Women:* skiing (downhill/alpine), soccer, track/ field (outdoor), volleyball.

ADMISSIONS

Freshman Academic Profile: Average high school GPA 3.1. 9% in top 10% of high school class, 33% in top 25% of high school class, 72% in top 50% of high school class. **Reported SAT (pre-2016 redesign) scores:** SAT Math middle 50% range 470-610. SAT Critical Reading middle 50% range 440-560. SAT Writing middle 50% range 430-550. **Concordant SAT scores:** SAT EBRW middle 50% 490–610. SAT Math middle 50% range 510–630. ACT middle 50% range 20-26. **Basis for Candidate Selection:** *Very important factors considered include:* academic GPA, standardized test scores. *Important factors considered include:* rigor of secondary school record. *Other factors considered include:* class rank, application essay, extracurricular activities, talent/ ability, character/personal qualities, alumni/ae relation, geographical residence, state residency, volunteer work, work experience. **Freshman Admission Requirements:** High school diploma is required and GED is accepted. *Academic units required:* 4 English, 3 math, 3 science, 2 foreign language, 3 social studies. *Academic units recommended:* 3 foreign language. **Freshman**

Admission Statistics: 3,938 applied, 84.87% admitted, 26% enrolled. **Transfer Admission Requirements:** High school transcript, college transcript(s), Lowest grade transferable C. **General Admission Information:** Application fee $50. Priority deadline 11/30. Nonfall registration accepted. Admission may be deferred for a maximum of One Year.

COSTS AND FINANCIAL AID

Annual in-state tuition $13,658. Annual out-of-state tuition $21,392. Room and board $12,450. Required fees $952. Average book expense $1,840. **Required Forms and Deadlines:** FAFSA. **Types of Aid:** *Need-based scholarships/ grants:* Federal Pell, FSEOG, State scholarships/grants, Private scholarships, College/university scholarship or grant aid from institutional funds. *Loans:* Direct Subsidized Stafford Loans, Direct Unsubsidized Stafford Loans, Direct PLUS loans, Federal Perkins Loans, College/university loans from institutional funds. *Student Employment:* Institutional employment available. **Financial Aid Statistics:** 62% needy freshmen, 66% needy undergrads receive need-based scholarship or grant aid. 70% freshmen, 46% undergrads receive non-need-based scholarship or grant aid. 77% freshmen, 83% undergrads receive need-based self-help aid. 0% freshmen, 0% undergrads receive athletic scholarships. 76% undergrads borrow to pay for school. Average cumulative indebtedness $40,639. **Criteria for awarding aid:** *Need-based:* Academics, Alumni affiliation. *Non-need-based:* Academics, Alumni affiliation.

PENNSYLVANIA STATE UNIVERSITY— HAZLETON

110 Schiavo Hall, Hazleton, PA 18202-1291
Phone: 570-450-3142
E-mail: hn-admissions@psu.edu
Website: http://hazleton.psu.edu/

This is a public school.

RATINGS

Admissions Selectivity Rating: 75   **Fire Safety Rating:** 60*   **Green Rating:** 60*

STUDENTS AND FACULTY

Enrollment: 753. **Student Body:** 42% female, 58% male, 19% out-of-state, 2% international. Asian 3%, African American 12%, Caucasian 60%, Hispanic 19%, Native American <1%, Pacific Islander <1%, Two or more races 3%, Race unknown 1%.
Retention and Graduation: 79% freshmen return for sophomore year. 33% freshmen graduate within 4 years. 54% freshmen graduate within 6 years.
Faculty: Student/faculty ratio 13:1. 50 full-time faculty, 66% hold PhDs, 12% are are members of minority groups, 38% are women.

ACADEMICS

Degrees: associate, bachelor's, certificate, postbachelor's certificate.

ADMISSIONS

Freshman Academic Profile: Average high school GPA 3.1. 11% in top 10% of high school class, 36% in top 25% of high school class, 77% in top 50% of high school class. **Reported SAT (pre-2016 redesign) scores:** SAT Math middle 50% range 430-540. SAT Critical Reading middle 50% range 410-520. SAT Writing middle 50% range 390-500. **Concordant SAT scores:** SAT EBRW middle 50% 450–570. SAT Math middle 50% range 470–570. ACT middle 50% range 17-25. **Basis for Candidate Selection:** *Very important factors considered include:* academic GPA, standardized test scores. *Important factors considered include:* rigor of secondary school record. *Other factors considered include:* class rank, application essay, extracurricular activities, talent/ ability, character/personal qualities, alumni/ae relation, volunteer work, work experience. **Freshman Admission Requirements:** *Academic units required:* 4 English, 3 math, 3 science, 2 foreign language, 3 social studies. *Academic units recommended:* 3 foreign language. **Freshman Admission Statistics:** 763 applied, 83.88% admitted, 41% enrolled. **General Admission Information:** Application fee $50. Priority deadline 11/30. Nonfall registration accepted. Admission may be deferred for a maximum of One Year.

COSTS AND FINANCIAL AID

Annual in-state tuition $13,012. Annual out-of-state tuition $20,206. Room and board $10,920. Required fees $890. Average book expense $1,840. **Required Forms and Deadlines:** FAFSA. **Types of Aid:** *Need-based scholarships/grants:* Federal Pell, FSEOG, State scholarships/grants, Private scholarships, College/university scholarship or grant aid from institutional funds. *Loans:* Direct Subsidized Stafford Loans, Direct Unsubsidized Stafford Loans, Direct PLUS loans, Federal Perkins Loans, College/university loans from institutional funds. *Student Employment:* Federal Work-Study Program available. Institutional employment available. **Financial Aid Statistics:** 72%

needy freshmen, 76% needy undergrads receive need-based scholarship or grant aid. 60% freshmen, 50% undergrads receive non-need-based scholarship or grant aid. 81% freshmen, 86% undergrads receive need-based self-help aid. 0% freshmen, 0% undergrads receive athletic scholarships. 83% undergrads borrow to pay for school. Average cumulative indebtedness $45,582. **Criteria for awarding aid:** *Need-based:* Academics, Alumni affiliation. *Non-need-based:* Academics, Alumni affiliation.

PENNSYLVANIA STATE UNIVERSITY— LEHIGH VALLEY

2809 Saucon Valley Road, Center Valley, PA 18034-8447
Phone: 610-285-5035
E-mail: admissions-lv@psu.edu
Fax: 610-285-5220 • **Website:** www.lv.psu.edu

This public school was founded in 1912. It has a 42-acre campus.

RATINGS
Admissions Selectivity Rating: 74   **Fire Safety Rating:** 60*   **Green Rating:** 60*

STUDENTS AND FACULTY
Enrollment: 773. **Student Body:** 48% female, 52% male, 3% out-of-state, <1% international. Asian 10%, African American 6%, Caucasian 64%, Hispanic 16%, Native American 0%, Pacific Islander <1%, Two or more races 2%, Race unknown 1%.
Retention and Graduation: 78% freshmen return for sophomore year. 28% freshmen graduate within 4 years. 51% freshmen graduate within 6 years. **Faculty:** Student/faculty ratio 14:1. 43 full-time faculty, 60% hold PhDs, 9% are are members of minority groups, 65% are women.

ACADEMICS
Degrees: associate, bachelor's, certificate, postbachelor's certificate. **Classes:** Most classes have 10-19 students. Most lab/discussion sessions have 10-19 students. **Special Study Options:** Accelerated program, cooperative education program, cross-registration, distance learning, dual enrollment, honors program, independent study, internships, study abroad.

CAMPUS LIFE
Activities: drama/theater, student government, student newspaper. **Athletics (Intercollegiate):** *Men:* basketball, cross-country, golf, soccer, tennis, volleyball. *Women:* basketball, golf, tennis, volleyball.

ADMISSIONS
Freshman Academic Profile: Average high school GPA 3.0. 8% in top 10% of high school class, 33% in top 25% of high school class, 69% in top 50% of high school class. **Reported SAT (pre-2016 redesign) scores:** SAT Math middle 50% range 450-580. SAT Critical Reading middle 50% range 440-560. SAT Writing middle 50% range 420-540. **Concordant SAT scores:** SAT EBRW middle 50% 480–610. SAT Math middle 50% range 490–600. ACT middle 50% range 19-27. Minimum paper TOEFL 550. **Basis for Candidate Selection:** *Very important factors considered include:* academic GPA, standardized test scores. *Important factors considered include:* rigor of secondary school record. *Other factors considered include:* class rank, application essay, extracurricular activities, talent/ability, character/personal qualities, alumni/ae relation, volunteer work, work experience. **Freshman Admission Requirements:** High school diploma is required and GED is accepted. *Academic units required:* 4 English, 3 math, 3 science, 2 foreign language, 3 social studies. *Academic units recommended:* 3 foreign language. **Freshman Admission Statistics:** 843 applied, 86.36% admitted, 29% enrolled. **Transfer Admission Requirements:** High school transcript, college transcript(s), Lowest grade transferable C. **General Admission Information:** Application fee $50. Priority deadline 11/30. Nonfall registration accepted. Admission may be deferred for a maximum of 1 year.

COSTS AND FINANCIAL AID
Annual in-state tuition $13,012. Annual out-of-state tuition $20,206. Required fees $952. **Required Forms and Deadlines:** FAFSA. **Types of Aid:** *Need-based scholarships/grants:* Federal Pell, FSEOG, State scholarships/grants, Private scholarships, College/university scholarship or grant aid from institutional funds. *Loans:* Direct Subsidized Stafford Loans, Direct Unsubsidized Stafford Loans, Direct PLUS loans, Federal Perkins Loans, College/university loans from institutional funds. *Student Employment:* Federal Work-Study Program available. Institutional employment available. **Financial Aid Statistics:** 74% needy freshmen, 80% needy undergrads receive need-based scholarship or grant aid. 46% freshmen, 30% undergrads receive non-need-based scholarship or grant aid. 72% freshmen, 82% undergrads receive need-based self-help aid. 0% freshmen, 0% undergrads receive athletic

scholarships. 79% undergrads borrow to pay for school. Average cumulative indebtedness $35,803. **Criteria for awarding aid:** *Need-based:* Academics, Alumni affiliation. *Non-need-based:* Academics, Alumni affiliation.

PENNSYLVANIA STATE UNIVERSITY— MONT ALTO

1 Campus Drive, Mont Alto, PA 17237-9703
Phone: 717-749-6130
E-mail: psuma@psu.edu
Fax: 717-749-6132 • **Website:** http://www.montalto.psu.edu

This public school was founded in 1929. It has a 62-acre campus.

RATINGS
Admissions Selectivity Rating: 75   **Fire Safety Rating:** 60*   **Green Rating:** 60*

STUDENTS AND FACULTY
Enrollment: 809. **Student Body:** 58% female, 42% male, 12% out-of-state, <1% international. Asian 2%, African American 8%, Caucasian 80%, Hispanic 5%, Native American 0%, Pacific Islander <1%, Two or more races 3%, Race unknown 1%.
Retention and Graduation: 77% freshmen return for sophomore year. 27% freshmen graduate within 4 years. 22% grads go on to further study within 1 year. **Faculty:** Student/faculty ratio 11:1. 56 full-time faculty, 46% hold PhDs, 11% are are members of minority groups, 52% are women.

ACADEMICS
Degrees: associate, bachelor's, certificate. **Classes:** Most classes have 10-19 students. Most lab/discussion sessions have 10-19 students. **Special Study Options:** Accelerated program, cross-registration, distance learning, double major, dual enrollment, honors program, independent study, internships, study abroad. **Honors Programs:** The Schreyer Honors College is widely recognized as one of the best and most comprehensive undergraduate honors programs in the United States. http://www.scholars.psu.edu/index.cfm Combined degree programs: BA/MD, BA/MEng, Science/MBA Program; JD/MBA. **Disability Services:** Special programs offered to physically disabled students, including note-taking services, reader services, tape recorders, tutors.

FACILITIES
Housing: Coed dorms, special housing for disabled students, Suites, Special Interest Housing, Townhouses. 99% of campus accessible to physically diasbled.

CAMPUS LIFE
Environment: Village. **Activities:** dance, drama/theater, jazz band, student government, student newspaper, Campus Ministries. **Athletics (Intercollegiate):** *Men:* basketball, soccer, tennis. *Women:* basketball, tennis.

ADMISSIONS
Freshman Academic Profile: Average high school GPA 3.1. 6% in top 10% of high school class, 36% in top 25% of high school class, 77% in top 50% of high school class. **Reported SAT (pre-2016 redesign) scores:** SAT Math middle 50% range 425-535. SAT Critical Reading middle 50% range 420-530. SAT Writing middle 50% range 410-500. **Concordant SAT scores:** SAT EBRW middle 50% 460–570. SAT Math middle 50% range 470–570. ACT middle 50% range 17-24. **Basis for Candidate Selection:** *Very important factors considered include:* academic GPA, standardized test scores. *Important factors considered include:* rigor of secondary school record. *Other factors considered include:* class rank, application essay, extracurricular activities, talent/ability, character/personal qualities, alumni/ae relation, volunteer work, work experience. **Freshman Admission Requirements:** High school diploma is required and GED is accepted. *Academic units required:* 4 English, 3 math, 3 science, 2 foreign language, 3 social studies. *Academic units recommended:* 3 foreign language. **Freshman Admission Statistics:** 688 applied, 79.36% admitted, 45% enrolled. **Transfer Admission Requirements:** High school transcript, college transcript(s), Lowest grade transferable C. **General Admission Information:** Application fee $50. Priority deadline 11/30. Nonfall registration accepted. Admission may be deferred for a maximum of One Year.

COSTS AND FINANCIAL AID
Annual in-state tuition $12,718. Annual out-of-state tuition $19,404. Room and board $10,920. Required fees $952. Average book expense $1,840. **Required Forms and Deadlines:** FAFSA. **Types of Aid:** *Need-based scholarships/grants:* Federal Pell, FSEOG, State scholarships/grants, Private scholarships, College/university scholarship or grant aid from institutional funds. *Loans:* Direct Subsidized Stafford Loans, Direct Unsubsidized Stafford Loans, Direct PLUS loans, Federal Perkins Loans, College/university loans from institutional funds. *Student Employment:* Federal Work-Study Program

available. Institutional employment available. **Financial Aid Statistics:** 71% needy freshmen, 75% needy undergrads receive need-based scholarship or grant aid. 56% freshmen, 48% undergrads receive non-need-based scholarship or grant aid. 82% freshmen, 86% undergrads receive need-based self-help aid. 0% freshmen, 0% undergrads receive athletic scholarships. 87% undergrads borrow to pay for school. Average cumulative indebtedness $46,030. **Criteria for awarding aid:** *Need-based:* Academics, Alumni affiliation, Minority status. *Non-need-based:* Academics, Alumni affiliation, Minority status.

PENNSYLVANIA STATE UNIVERSITY— NEW KENSINGTON

Office of Admissions, 3550 7th Street Rd, New Kensington, PA 15068-1765
Phone: 724-334-5466
E-mail: nkadmissions@psu.edu
Fax: 724-334-6111 • **Website:** http://nk.psu.edu

RATINGS
Admissions Selectivity Rating: 75   Fire Safety Rating: 60*   Green Rating: 60*

STUDENTS AND FACULTY
Enrollment: 598. **Student Body:** 41% female, 59% male, 2% out-of-state, 2% international. Asian 2%, African American 5%, Caucasian 87%, Hispanic 2%, Native American <1%, Pacific Islander 0%, Two or more races 1%, Race unknown 1%.
Retention and Graduation: 67% freshmen return for sophomore year. 28% freshmen graduate within 4 years. 52% freshmen graduate within 6 years.
Faculty: Student/faculty ratio 12:1. 35 full-time faculty, 63% hold PhDs, 20% are are members of minority groups, 43% are women.

ACADEMICS
Degrees: associate, bachelor's, certificate.

ADMISSIONS
Freshman Academic Profile: Average high school GPA 3.1. 10% in top 10% of high school class, 29% in top 25% of high school class, 68% in top 50% of high school class. **Reported SAT (pre-2016 redesign) scores:** SAT Math middle 50% range 440-550. SAT Critical Reading middle 50% range 440-530. SAT Writing middle 50% range 410-510. **Concordant SAT scores:** SAT EBRW middle 50% 480–580. SAT Math middle 50% range 480–570. ACT middle 50% range 19-23. **Basis for Candidate Selection:** *Very important factors considered include:* academic GPA, standardized test scores. *Important factors considered include:* rigor of secondary school record. *Other factors considered include:* class rank, application essay, extracurricular activities, talent/ability, character/personal qualities, alumni/ae relation, geographical residence, state residency, volunteer work, work experience, level of applicant's interest. **Freshman Admission Requirements:** *Academic units required:* 4 English, 3 math, 3 science, 2 foreign language, 3 social studies. *Academic units recommended:* 3 foreign language. **Freshman Admission Statistics:** 508 applied, 79.13% admitted, 44% enrolled. **General Admission Information:** Application fee $50. Priority deadline 11/30. Nonfall registration accepted. Admission may be deferred for a maximum of One Year.

COSTS AND FINANCIAL AID
Annual in-state tuition $12,718. Annual out-of-state tuition $19,404. Required fees $890. **Required Forms and Deadlines:** FAFSA. **Types of Aid:** *Need-based scholarships/grants:* Federal Pell, FSEOG, State scholarships/grants, Private scholarships, College/university scholarship or grant aid from institutional funds. *Loans:* Direct Subsidized Stafford Loans, Direct Unsubsidized Stafford Loans, Direct PLUS loans, Federal Perkins Loans, College/university loans from institutional funds. *Student Employment:* Federal Work-Study Program available. Institutional employment available. **Financial Aid Statistics:** 81% needy freshmen, 77% needy undergrads receive need-based scholarship or grant aid. 62% freshmen, 40% undergrads receive non-need-based scholarship or grant aid. 65% freshmen, 81% undergrads receive need-based self-help aid. 0% freshmen, 0% undergrads receive athletic scholarships. 93% undergrads borrow to pay for school. Average cumulative indebtedness $33,237. **Criteria for awarding aid:** *Need-based:* Academics, Alumni affiliation. *Non-need-based:* Academics, Alumni affiliation.

PENNSYLVANIA STATE UNIVERSITY— SCHUYLKILL

200 University Drive, Schuykill Haven, PA 17972-2208
Phone: 570-385-6252
E-mail: sl-admissions@psu.edu
Fax: 570-385-3672 • **Website:** http://www.sl.psu.edu

This public school was founded in 1934. It has a 42-acre campus.

RATINGS
Admissions Selectivity Rating: 74   Fire Safety Rating: 60*   Green Rating: 60*

STUDENTS AND FACULTY
Enrollment: 720. **Student Body:** 60% female, 40% male, 12% out-of-state, 1% international. Asian 1%, African American 18%, Caucasian 69%, Hispanic 7%, Native American <1%, Pacific Islander <1%, Two or more races 1%, Race unknown 2%.
Retention and Graduation: 76% freshmen return for sophomore year. 22% freshmen graduate within 4 years. 45% freshmen graduate within 6 years.
Faculty: Student/faculty ratio 13:1. 43 full-time faculty, 77% hold PhDs, 2% are are members of minority groups, 40% are women.

ACADEMICS
Degrees: associate, bachelor's, certificate. **Classes:** Most classes have 20-29 students. Most lab/discussion sessions have 10-19 students. **Special Study Options:** Accelerated program, cooperative education program, distance learning, double major, dual enrollment, honors program, independent study, internships, student-designed major, study abroad.

FACILITIES
Housing: special housing for disabled students, apartments for single students.

CAMPUS LIFE
Activities: Choral groups, dance, drama/theater, musical theater, student government, student newspaper, Campus Ministries. **Athletics (Intercollegiate):** *Men:* basketball, cross-country, softball, tennis, volleyball. *Women:* basketball, cross-country, softball, tennis, volleyball.

ADMISSIONS
Freshman Academic Profile: Average high school GPA 2.9. 5% in top 10% of high school class, 24% in top 25% of high school class, 51% in top 50% of high school class. **Reported SAT (pre-2016 redesign) scores:** SAT Math middle 50% range 420-510. SAT Critical Reading middle 50% range 410-520. SAT Writing middle 50% range 395-500. **Concordant SAT scores:** SAT EBRW middle 50% 450–570. SAT Math middle 50% range 460–540. ACT middle 50% range 16-19. Minimum paper TOEFL 550. **Basis for Candidate Selection:** *Very important factors considered include:* academic GPA, standardized test scores. *Important factors considered include:* rigor of secondary school record. *Other factors considered include:* class rank, application essay, extracurricular activities, talent/ability, character/personal qualities, alumni/ae relation, volunteer work, work experience. **Freshman Admission Requirements:** High school diploma is required and GED is accepted. *Academic units required:* 4 English, 3 math, 3 science, 2 foreign language, 3 social studies. *Academic units recommended:* 3 foreign language. **Freshman Admission Statistics:** 690 applied, 73.04% admitted, 44% enrolled. **Transfer Admission Requirements:** High school transcript, college transcript(s), Lowest grade transferable C. **General Admission Information:** Application fee $50. Priority deadline 11/30. Nonfall registration accepted. Admission may be deferred for a maximum of 1 year.

COSTS AND FINANCIAL AID
Annual in-state tuition $13,012. Annual out-of-state tuition $20,206. Room and board $8,060. Required fees $890. Average book expense $1,840. **Required Forms and Deadlines:** FAFSA. **Types of Aid:** *Need-based scholarships/grants:* Federal Pell, FSEOG, State scholarships/grants, Private scholarships, College/university scholarship or grant aid from institutional funds. *Loans:* Direct Subsidized Stafford Loans, Direct Unsubsidized Stafford Loans, Direct PLUS loans, Federal Perkins Loans, College/university loans from institutional funds. *Student Employment:* Federal Work-Study Program available. Institutional employment available. **Financial Aid Statistics:** 84% needy freshmen, 83% needy undergrads receive need-based scholarship or grant aid. 78% freshmen, 57% undergrads receive non-need-based scholarship or grant aid. 85% freshmen, 89% undergrads receive need-based self-help aid. 0% freshmen, 0% undergrads receive athletic scholarships. 92% undergrads borrow to pay for school. Average cumulative indebtedness $38,822. **Criteria for awarding aid:** *Need-based:* Academics, Alumni affiliation.

PENNSYLVANIA STATE UNIVERSITY— SHENANGO

147 Shenango Ave., Shenango, PA 16146-1597
Phone: 724-983-2803
E-mail: psushenango@psu.edu
Fax: 724-983-2820 • **Website:** http://shenango.psu.edu

RATINGS
Admissions Selectivity Rating: 77   **Fire Safety Rating:** 60*   **Green Rating:** 60*

STUDENTS AND FACULTY
Enrollment: 436. **Student Body:** 73% female, 27% male, 22% out-of-state, 0% international. Asian 1%, African American 7%, Caucasian 85%, Hispanic 2%, Native American 0%, Pacific Islander 0%, Two or more races 3%, Race unknown 3%.
Retention and Graduation: 66% freshmen return for sophomore year. 14% freshmen graduate within 4 years. 33% freshmen graduate within 6 years. **Faculty:** Student/faculty ratio 11:1. 28 full-time faculty, 50% hold PhDs, 7% are are members of minority groups, 68% are women.

ACADEMICS
Degrees: associate, bachelor's, certificate.

ADMISSIONS
Freshman Academic Profile: Average high school GPA 3.0. 1% in top 10% of high school class, 35% in top 25% of high school class, 72% in top 50% of high school class. **Reported SAT (pre-2016 redesign) scores:** SAT Math middle 50% range 410-520. SAT Critical Reading middle 50% range 410-530. SAT Writing middle 50% range 400-500. **Concordant SAT scores:** SAT EBRW middle 50% 450–570. SAT Math middle 50% range 450–550. ACT middle 50% range 19-22. **Basis for Candidate Selection:** *Very important factors considered include:* academic GPA, standardized test scores. *Important factors considered include:* rigor of secondary school record. *Other factors considered include:* class rank, application essay, extracurricular activities, talent/ability, character/personal qualities, alumni/ae relation, volunteer work, work experience. **Freshman Admission Requirements:** *Academic units required:* 4 English, 3 math, 3 science, 2 foreign language, 3 social studies. *Academic units recommended:* 3 foreign language. **Freshman Admission Statistics:** 154 applied, 68.18% admitted, 54% enrolled. **General Admission Information:** Application fee $50. Priority deadline 11/30. Nonfall registration accepted. Admission may be deferred for a maximum of One Year.

COSTS AND FINANCIAL AID
Annual in-state tuition $12,474. Annual out-of-state tuition $19,030. Required fees $880. **Required Forms and Deadlines:** FAFSA. **Types of Aid:** *Need-based scholarships/grants:* Federal Pell, FSEOG, State scholarships/grants, Private scholarships, College/university scholarship or grant aid from institutional funds. *Loans:* Direct Subsidized Stafford Loans, Direct Unsubsidized Stafford Loans, Direct PLUS loans, Federal Perkins Loans, College/university loans from institutional funds. *Student Employment:* Federal Work-Study Program available. Institutional employment available. **Financial Aid Statistics:** 81% needy freshmen, 85% needy undergrads receive need-based scholarship or grant aid. 66% freshmen, 54% undergrads receive non-need-based scholarship or grant aid. 75% freshmen, 87% undergrads receive need-based self-help aid. 0% freshmen, 0% undergrads receive athletic scholarships. 80% undergrads borrow to pay for school. Average cumulative indebtedness $35,187. **Criteria for awarding aid:** *Need-based:* Academics, Alumni affiliation. *Non-need-based:* Academics, Alumni affiliation.

PENNSYLVANIA STATE UNIVERSITY— UNIVERSITY PARK

201 Shields Building, University Park, PA 16802
Phone: 814-865-5471 • **Financial Aid Phone:** 814-865-6301
E-mail: admissions@psu.edu • **CEEB Code:** 2660
Fax: 814-863-7590 • **Website:** www.psu.edu • **ACT Code:** 3656

This public school was founded in 1855. It has a 7264-acre campus.

RATINGS
Admissions Selectivity Rating: 89   **Fire Safety Rating:** 98   **Green Rating:** 93

STUDENTS AND FACULTY
Enrollment: 40,891. **Student Body:** 47% female, 53% male, 33% out-of-state, 12% international (110 countries represented). Asian 6%, African American 4%, Caucasian 67%, Hispanic 6%, Native American <1%, Pacific Islander <1%, Two or more races 3%, Race unknown 2%.
Retention and Graduation: 93% freshmen return for sophomore year. 68% freshmen graduate within 4 years. 86% freshmen graduate within 6 years. 24% grads go on to further study within 1 year. **Faculty:** Student/faculty ratio 16:1. 2,761 full-time faculty, 81% hold PhDs, 18% are are members of minority groups, 38% are women.

ACADEMICS
Degrees: associate, bachelor's, certificate, doctoral/professional, doctoral/research, master's, postbachelor's certificate. **Classes:** Most classes have 20-29 students. Most lab/discussion sessions have 20-29 students. **Most popular majors:** Business, Management, Marketing, and Related Support Services; Engineering; Communication, Journalism, and Related Programs. **Special Study Options:** Accelerated program, cooperative education program, cross-registration, distance learning, double major, dual enrollment, English as a Second Language (ESL), exchange student program (domestic), external degree program, honors program, independent study, internships, liberal arts/career combination, student-designed major, study abroad, teacher certification program, weekend college. **Honors Programs:** The Schreyer Honors College is widely recognized as one of the best and most comprehensive undergraduate honors programs in the United States. http://www.shc.psu.edu/ Combined degree programs: BA/MD, BA/MA, BA/MEng, Science/MBA Program; JD/MBA, MD/MBA; several dual-title degrees available in various programs. **Disability Services:** Special programs offered to physically disabled students, including note-taking services, reader services, tape recorders, tutors. **Career Services:** Alumni network, Alumni services, Career/job search classes, Career assessment, Internships, Regional alumni. Internships are one of the top college experiences that employers value.

FACILITIES
Housing: Coed dorms, special housing for disabled students, men's dorms, special housing for international students, women's dorms, fraternity/sorority housing, apartments for married students, apartments for single students, Suites, Special Interest Housing. 95% of campus accessible to physically diasbled. **Special Academic Facilities/Equipment:** Museums, theatres, language labs, weather station, nuclear reactor. **Computers:** 83% of classrooms, 50% of dorms, 100% of libraries, 100% of dining areas, 100% of student union, 25% of common outdoor areas have wireless network access. Students can register for classes online. Administrative functions (other than registration) can be performed online.

CAMPUS LIFE
Environment: Town. **Activities:** Choral groups, concert band, dance, drama/theater, jazz band, literary magazine, marching band, music ensembles, musical theater, opera, pep band, radio station, student government, student newspaper, student-run film society, symphony orchestra, television station, yearbook, Campus Ministries, Student Organization, Model UN. 784 registered organizations, 34 honor societies, 49 religious organizations. 58 fraternities, 32 sororities. **Athletics (Intercollegiate):** *Men:* baseball, basketball, cheerleading, cross-country, diving, fencing, football, golf, gymnastics, lacrosse, soccer, swimming, tennis, track/field (outdoor), track/field (indoor), volleyball, wrestling. *Women:* basketball, cheerleading, cross-country, diving, fencing, field hockey, golf, gymnastics, lacrosse, soccer, softball, swimming, tennis, track/field (outdoor), track/field (indoor), volleyball. **On-Campus Highlights:** Hetzel Union Building, Pattee Paterno Library, The Creamery, Old Main, The Lion Shrine. **Environmental Initiatives:** To address the issue of climate change, Pennsylvania State University–established the goal of reducing greenhouse gas emissions to 17.5% below FY05/06 levels by 2012. This goal was achieved, and

the university subsequently set a more ambitious goal of reducing emissions by an additional 17.5%, for a total 35% reduction by 2020. In 2014, Pennsylvania State University–joined the U.S. Department of Energy Better Buildings Challenge and pledged to reduce its building portfolio energy use by 20 percent over the next decade. With a commitment of 28 million square feet (all campuses except Hershey Medical & Pennsylvania College of Technology), Pennsylvania State University–becomes the largest university in the program.

ADMISSIONS

Freshman Academic Profile: Average high school GPA 3.6. 36% in top 10% of high school class, 77% in top 25% of high school class, 97% in top 50% of high school class. **Reported SAT (pre-2016 redesign) scores:** SAT Math middle 50% range 560-670. SAT Critical Reading middle 50% range 530-630. **Concordant SAT scores:** SAT Math middle 50% range 580–700. ACT middle 50% range 25-29. Minimum internet-based TOEFL 80. Minimum paper TOEFL 550. **Basis for Candidate Selection:** *Very important factors considered include:* academic GPA, standardized test scores. *Important factors considered include:* rigor of secondary school record. *Other factors considered include:* class rank, application essay, extracurricular activities, talent/ability, character/personal qualities, alumni/ae relation, geographical residence, state residency, volunteer work, work experience. **Freshman Admission Requirements:** High school diploma is required and GED is accepted. *Academic units required:* 4 English, 3 math, 3 science, 2 foreign language, 3 social studies. *Academic units recommended:* 3 foreign language. **Freshman Admission Statistics:** 52,974 applied, 56.40% admitted, 28% enrolled. **Transfer Admission Requirements:** High school transcript, college transcript(s), Lowest grade transferable C. **General Admission Information:** Application fee $50. Priority deadline 11/30. Nonfall registration accepted. Admission may be deferred for a maximum of One Year.

COSTS AND FINANCIAL AID

Annual in-state tuition $16,952. Annual out-of-state tuition $31,434. Room and board $11,860. Required fees $948. Average book expense $1,840. **Required Forms and Deadlines:** FAFSA. **Types of Aid:** *Need-based scholarships/grants:* Federal Pell, FSEOG, State scholarships/grants, Private scholarships, College/university scholarship or grant aid from institutional funds. *Loans:* Direct Subsidized Stafford Loans, Direct Unsubsidized Stafford Loans, Direct PLUS loans, Federal Perkins Loans, College/university loans from institutional funds. *Student Employment:* Federal Work-Study Program available. Institutional employment available. **Financial Aid Statistics:** 43% needy freshmen, 50% needy undergrads receive need-based scholarship or grant aid. 54% freshmen, 40% undergrads receive non-need-based scholarship or grant aid. 77% freshmen, 85% undergrads receive need-based self-help aid. 2% freshmen, 2% undergrads receive athletic scholarships. 66% freshmen, 67% undergrads receive any aid. 54% undergrads borrow to pay for school. Average cumulative indebtedness $37,213. **Criteria for awarding aid:** *Need-based:* Academics, Alumni affiliation, Athletics. *Non-need-based:* Academics, Alumni affiliation, Athletics.

PENNSYLVANIA STATE UNIVERSITY— WILKES-BARRE

Murphy Center 125, Lehman, PA 18627-0217
Phone: 570-675-9238
E-mail: wbadmissions@psu.edu
Fax: 570-675-9113 • **Website:** http://www.wb.psu.edu

This is a public school.

RATINGS
Admissions Selectivity Rating: 73   **Fire Safety Rating:** 60*   **Green Rating:** 60*

STUDENTS AND FACULTY
Enrollment: 460. **Student Body:** 33% female, 67% male, 5% out-of-state, <1% international. Asian 1%, African American 3%, Caucasian 88%, Hispanic 5%, Native American <1%, Pacific Islander 0%, Two or more races 2%, Race unknown 1%.
Retention and Graduation: 84% freshmen return for sophomore year. 28% freshmen graduate within 4 years. 53% freshmen graduate within 6 years.
Faculty: Student/faculty ratio 13:1. 30 full-time faculty, 63% hold PhDs, 23% are are members of minority groups, 33% are women.

ACADEMICS
Degrees: associate, bachelor's, certificate, postbachelor's certificate.

ADMISSIONS
Freshman Academic Profile: Average high school GPA 3.1. 8% in top 10% of high school class, 30% in top 25% of high school class, 74% in top 50% of

high school class. **Reported SAT (pre-2016 redesign) scores:** SAT Math middle 50% range 440-550. SAT Critical Reading middle 50% range 430-540. SAT Writing middle 50% range 420-520. **Concordant SAT scores:** SAT EBRW middle 50% 480–590. SAT Math middle 50% range 480–570. ACT middle 50% range 18-26. **Basis for Candidate Selection:** *Very important factors considered include:* academic GPA, standardized test scores. *Important factors considered include:* rigor of secondary school record. *Other factors considered include:* class rank, application essay, extracurricular activities, talent/ability, character/personal qualities, alumni/ae relation, volunteer work, work experience. **Freshman Admission Requirements:** *Academic units required:* 4 English, 3 math, 3 science, 2 foreign language, 3 social studies. *Academic units recommended:* 3 foreign language. **Freshman Admission Statistics:** 411 applied, 87.59% admitted, 40% enrolled. **General Admission Information:** Application fee $50. Priority deadline 11/30. Nonfall registration accepted. Admission may be deferred for a maximum of 1 year.

COSTS AND FINANCIAL AID
Annual in-state tuition $12,718. Annual out-of-state tuition $19,404. Required fees $880. **Required Forms and Deadlines:** FAFSA. **Types of Aid:** *Need-based scholarships/grants:* Federal Pell, FSEOG, State scholarships/grants, Private scholarships, College/university scholarship or grant aid from institutional funds. *Loans:* Direct Subsidized Stafford Loans, Direct Unsubsidized Stafford Loans, Direct PLUS loans, Federal Perkins Loans, College/university loans from institutional funds. *Student Employment:* Federal Work-Study Program available. Institutional employment available. **Financial Aid Statistics:** 75% needy freshmen, 74% needy undergrads receive need-based scholarship or grant aid. 56% freshmen, 45% undergrads receive non-need-based scholarship or grant aid. 82% freshmen, 81% undergrads receive need-based self-help aid. 0% freshmen, 0% undergrads receive athletic scholarships. 85% undergrads borrow to pay for school. Average cumulative indebtedness $38,387. **Criteria for awarding aid:** *Need-based:* Academics, Alumni affiliation. *Non-need-based:* Academics, Alumni affiliation.

PENNSYLVANIA STATE UNIVERSITY— WORTHINGTON SCRANTON

120 Ridge View Drive, Dawson Building, Dunmore, PA 18512-1602
Phone: 570-963-2500
E-mail: wsadmissions@psu.edu
Fax: 570-963-2524 • **Website:** http://worthingtonscranton.psu.edu/

RATINGS
Admissions Selectivity Rating: 74   **Fire Safety Rating:** 60*   **Green Rating:** 60*

STUDENTS AND FACULTY
Enrollment: 967. **Student Body:** 53% female, 47% male, 1% out-of-state, <1% international. Asian 5%, African American 3%, Caucasian 81%, Hispanic 6%, Native American 0%, Pacific Islander 0%, Two or more races 2%, Race unknown 2%.
Retention and Graduation: 75% freshmen return for sophomore year. 22% freshmen graduate within 4 years. 43% freshmen graduate within 6 years.
Faculty: Student/faculty ratio 14:1. 50 full-time faculty, 64% hold PhDs, 10% are are members of minority groups, 52% are women.

ACADEMICS
Degrees: associate, bachelor's, certificate.

ADMISSIONS
Freshman Academic Profile: Average high school GPA 3.0. 10% in top 10% of high school class, 30% in top 25% of high school class, 70% in top 50% of high school class. **Reported SAT (pre-2016 redesign) scores:** SAT Math middle 50% range 430-540. SAT Critical Reading middle 50% range 420-530. SAT Writing middle 50% range 410-510. **Concordant SAT scores:** SAT EBRW middle 50% 460–580. SAT Math middle 50% range 470–570. ACT middle 50% range 17-21. **Basis for Candidate Selection:** *Very important factors considered include:* academic GPA, standardized test scores. *Important factors considered include:* rigor of secondary school record. *Other factors considered include:* class rank, application essay, extracurricular activities, talent/ability, character/personal qualities, alumni/ae relation, geographical residence, state residency, volunteer work, work experience. **Freshman Admission Requirements:** *Academic units required:* 4 English, 3 math, 3 science, 2 foreign language, 3 social studies. *Academic units recommended:* 3 foreign language. **Freshman Admission Statistics:** 733 applied, 80.63% admitted, 39% enrolled. **General Admission Information:** Application fee $50. Priority deadline 11/30. Nonfall registration accepted. Admission may be deferred for a maximum of One Year.

COSTS AND FINANCIAL AID

Annual in-state tuition $13,012. Annual out-of-state tuition $20,206. Required fees $890. **Required Forms and Deadlines:** FAFSA. **Types of Aid:** *Need-based scholarships/grants:* Federal Pell, FSEOG, State scholarships/grants, Private scholarships, College/university scholarship or grant aid from institutional funds. *Loans:* Direct Subsidized Stafford Loans, Direct Unsubsidized Stafford Loans, Direct PLUS loans, Federal Perkins Loans, College/university loans from institutional funds. *Student Employment:* Federal Work-Study Program available. Institutional employment available. **Financial Aid Statistics:** 76% needy freshmen, 80% needy undergrads receive need-based scholarship or grant aid. 34% freshmen, 25% undergrads receive non-need-based scholarship or grant aid. 80% freshmen, 86% undergrads receive need-based self-help aid. 0% freshmen, 0% undergrads receive athletic scholarships. 76% undergrads borrow to pay for school. Average cumulative indebtedness $42,128. **Criteria for awarding aid:** *Need-based:* Academics, Alumni affiliation. *Non-need-based:* Academics, Alumni affiliation.

PENNSYLVANIA STATE UNIVERSITY—YORK

1031 Edgecomb Avenue, York, PA 17403-3398
Phone: 717-771-4040
E-mail: ykadmission@psu.edu
Fax: 717-771-4005 • **Website:** www.yk.psu.edu

This public school was founded in 1926. It has a 52-acre campus.

RATINGS

Admissions Selectivity Rating: 74   **Fire Safety Rating:** 60*   **Green Rating:** 60*

STUDENTS AND FACULTY

Enrollment: 1,070. **Student Body:** 44% female, 56% male, 5% out-of-state, <1% international. Asian 6%, African American 5%, Caucasian 83%, Hispanic 5%, Native American <1%, Pacific Islander 0%, Two or more races 0%, Race unknown 0%.
Retention and Graduation: 71% freshmen return for sophomore year.
Faculty: Student/faculty ratio 15:1. 59 full-time faculty, 61% hold PhDs, 17% are are members of minority groups, 36% are women.

ACADEMICS

Degrees: bachelor's, terminal, transfer. **Classes:** Most classes have 10-19 students. Most lab/discussion sessions have fewer than 10 students. **Special Study Options:** Accelerated program, cross-registration, distance learning, double major, English as a Second Language (ESL), honors program, independent study, internships, student-designed major, study abroad.

FACILITIES

Housing: Nearby rooms, apartments, house rentals in the local community.

CAMPUS LIFE

Environment: Village. **Activities:** dance, drama/theater, literary magazine, student government, student newspaper, Campus Ministries, Student Organization, Model UN. **Athletics (Intercollegiate):** *Men:* basketball, soccer, tennis. *Women:* tennis, volleyball.

ADMISSIONS

Freshman Academic Profile: Average high school GPA 2.8. 6% in top 10% of high school class, 24% in top 25% of high school class, 55% in top 50% of high school class. **Reported SAT (pre-2016 redesign) scores:** SAT Math middle 50% range 440-550. SAT Critical Reading middle 50% range 410-530. **Concordant SAT scores:** SAT Math middle 50% range 480–570. ACT middle 50% range 0-0. Minimum paper TOEFL 550. **Basis for Candidate Selection:** *Very important factors considered include:* academic GPA, standardized test scores. *Important factors considered include:* rigor of secondary school record. *Other factors considered include:* class rank, application essay, recommendation(s), extracurricular activities, talent/ability, character/personal qualities, alumni/ae relation, volunteer work, work experience. **Freshman Admission Requirements:** High school diploma is required and GED is accepted. *Academic units required:* 4 English, 3 math, 3 science, 2 foreign language, 3 social studies. **Freshman Admission Statistics:** 1,328 applied, 84.19% admitted, 30% enrolled. **Transfer Admission Requirements:** High school transcript, college transcript(s), Lowest grade transferable C. **General Admission Information:** Application fee $50. Priority deadline 11/30. Nonfall registration accepted. Admission may be deferred for a maximum of One year.

COSTS AND FINANCIAL AID

Annual in-state tuition $10,454. Annual out-of-state tuition $15,954. Room and board $3,360. Required fees $532. Average book expense $1,168. **Required Forms and Deadlines:** FAFSA. **Notification of Awards:** Applicants will be notified of awards on or about 3/1. **Types of Aid:** *Need-based scholarships/grants:* Federal Pell, FSEOG, State scholarships/grants, Private scholarships,

College/university scholarship or grant aid from institutional funds. *Loans:* Federal Perkins Loans, College/university loans from institutional funds. *Student Employment:* Federal Work-Study Program available. Institutional employment available. **Financial Aid Statistics:** 66% needy freshmen, 75% needy undergrads receive need-based scholarship or grant aid. 40% freshmen, 36% undergrads receive non-need-based scholarship or grant aid. 80% freshmen, 83% undergrads receive need-based self-help aid. 0% freshmen, 0% undergrads receive athletic scholarships. **Criteria for awarding aid:** *Need-based:* Academics, Alumni affiliation, Athletics, Minority status. *Non-need-based:* Academics, Alumni affiliation, Athletics, Minority status.

PEPPERDINE UNIVERSITY

24255 Pacific Coast Highway, Malibu, CA 90263
Phone: 310-506-4392 • **Financial Aid Phone:** 310-506-4301
E-mail: admission-seaver@pepperdine.edu • **CEEB Code:** 4630
Fax: 310-506-4861 • **Website:** www.pepperdine.edu • **ACT Code:** 373

This private school, affiliated with the Church of Christ Church, was founded in 1937. It has a 830-acre campus.

RATINGS

Admissions Selectivity Rating: 93   **Fire Safety Rating:** 85   **Green Rating:** 75

STUDENTS AND FACULTY

Enrollment: 2,785. **Student Body:** 59% female, 41% male, 42% out-of-state, 11% international (76 countries represented). Asian 12%, African American 5%, Caucasian 47%, Hispanic 16%, Native American <1%, Pacific Islander <1%, Two or more races 5%, Race unknown 4%.
Retention and Graduation: 90% freshmen return for sophomore year. 76% freshmen graduate within 4 years. 87% freshmen graduate within 6 years. 18% grads go on to further study within 1 year. 10% grads pursue arts and sciences degrees. 2% grads pursue law degrees. 2% grads pursue business degrees. 3% grads pursue medical degrees. **Faculty:** Student/faculty ratio 14:1. 377 full-time faculty, 88% hold PhDs, 19% are are members of minority groups, 41% are women. 0% of classes are taught by teaching assistants.

ACADEMICS

Degrees: bachelor's, doctoral/professional, doctoral/research, master's. **Classes:** Most classes have 10-19 students. Most lab/discussion sessions have 10-19 students. **Most popular majors:** Business Administration and Management; Clinical Psychology; Law. **Special Study Options:** double major, honors program, independent study, internships, student-designed major, study abroad, teacher certification program, weekend college, 3-2 programing engineering with University of Southern California, Washington University(MO), Boston University(MA). Combined degree programs: BS/MBA program. **Disability Services:** Special programs offered to physically disabled students, including note-taking services, reader services, tape recorders, tutors. **Career Services:** Alumni network, Alumni services, Career/job search classes, Career assessment, Internships, Regional alumni. Pepperdine has a very active internship program that reaches into the local LA areas, Washington DC, nationally through our participation in the University Career Action Network, and internationally through an internship emphasis at our international campuses. Students at Pepperdine can receive academic credit for internships. Service-learning is employed as a teaching pedagogy by a variety of faculty members. One example the senior capstone business class "Service Leadership" where class members serve on a consulting team for a nonprofit.

FACILITIES

Housing: special housing for disabled students, men's dorms, women's dorms, apartments for married students, cooperative housing, apartments for single students, Freshman and sophomores must live on campus or at home with parent or guardian if single and under age 21. **Special Academic Facilities/Equipment:** Weisman Art Museum **Computers:** 100% of classrooms, 100% of dorms, 100% of libraries, 100% of dining areas, 100% of student union, 100% of common outdoor areas have wireless network access. Students can register for classes online. Administrative functions (other than registration) can be performed online.

CAMPUS LIFE

Environment: City. **Activities:** Choral groups, concert band, dance, drama/theater, jazz band, literary magazine, music ensembles, musical theater, opera, pep band, radio station, student government, student newspaper, student-run film society, symphony orchestra, television station, yearbook, Campus

Ministries, Student Organization, Model UN. 50 registered organizations, 5 honor societies, 8 religious organizations. 5 fraternities, 7 sororities. **Athletics (Intercollegiate):** *Men:* baseball, basketball, cross-country, golf, tennis, volleyball, water polo. *Women:* basketball, cheerleading, cross-country, golf, soccer, swimming, tennis, track/field (outdoor), volleyball. **On-Campus Highlights:** Theme Tower, Smother'sTheatre, The Sandbar, Payson Library, Alumni Park. **Environmental Initiatives:** Pepperdine University has conserved billions of gallons of drinking water annually dating back to 1972. Pepperdine uses recycled water to irrigate over 99% of the University managed grounds. The University carefully monitors irrigation practices and uses an automated irrigation program based upon historical trends and current climactic conditions to conserve water and reduce runoff.

ADMISSIONS

Freshman Academic Profile: Average high school GPA 3.6. 48% in top 10% of high school class, 90% in top 25% of high school class, 98% in top 50% of high school class. **Reported SAT (pre-2016 redesign) scores:** SAT Math middle 50% range 560-680. SAT Critical Reading middle 50% range 550-650. SAT Writing middle 50% range 550-650. **Concordant SAT scores:** SAT EBRW middle 50% 610–700. SAT Math middle 50% range 580–710. ACT middle 50% range 26-31. Minimum internet-based TOEFL 80. Minimum paper TOEFL 550. **Basis for Candidate Selection:** *Very important factors considered include:* rigor of secondary school record, academic GPA, application essay, extracurricular activities, talent/ability, character/personal qualities, religious affiliation/commitment. *Important factors considered include:* standardized test scores, recommendation(s), volunteer work. *Other factors considered include:* first generation, alumni/ae relation, racial/ethnic status, work experience. **Freshman Admission Requirements:** High school diploma is required and GED is accepted. **Freshman Admission Statistics:** 11,111 applied, 36.87% admitted, 18% enrolled. **Transfer Admission Requirements:** High school transcript, college transcript(s), essay or personal statement, Minimum college GPA of 3.00 required. Lowest grade transferable C. **General Admission Information:** Application fee $65. Regular application deadline 1/5. Regular notification 4/1. Nonfall registration accepted.

COSTS AND FINANCIAL AID

Required Forms and Deadlines: FAFSA. **Notification of Awards:** Applicants will be notified of awards on or about 4/15. **Types of Aid:** *Need-based scholarships/grants:* Federal Pell, FSEOG, State scholarships/grants, Private scholarships, College/university scholarship or grant aid from institutional funds, United Negro College Fund. *Loans:* Direct Subsidized Stafford Loans, Direct Unsubsidized Stafford Loans, Direct PLUS loans, Federal Perkins Loans, College/university loans from institutional funds. *Student Employment:* Federal Work-Study Program available. Institutional employment available. **Financial Aid Statistics:** 99% needy freshmen, 98% needy undergrads receive need-based scholarship or grant aid. 0% undergrads receive non-need-based scholarship or grant aid. 70% freshmen, 70% undergrads receive need-based self-help aid. 4% freshmen, 3% undergrads receive athletic scholarships. 94% freshmen, 81% undergrads receive any aid. Average cumulative indebtedness $29,640. **Criteria for awarding aid:** *Need-based:* Alumni affiliation, Job skills, Minority status. *Non-need-based:* Academics, Art, Athletics, Leadership, Music/drama, Religious affiliation.

PHILADELPHIA UNIVERSITY

School House Lane and Henry Avenue, Philadelphia, PA 19144-5497
Phone: 215-951-2800 • **Financial Aid Phone:** 215-951-2940
E-mail: admissions@philau.edu • **CEEB Code:** 2666
Fax: 215-951-2907 • **Website:** www.PhilaU.edu • **ACT Code:** 3668

This private school was founded in 1884. It has a 100-acre campus.

RATINGS

Admissions Selectivity Rating: 83   **Fire Safety Rating:** 60*   **Green Rating:** 60*

STUDENTS AND FACULTY

Enrollment: 2,885. **Student Body:** 66% female, 34% male, 42% out-of-state, 4% international (30 countries represented). Asian 5%, African American 14%, Caucasian 59%, Hispanic 7%, Native American <1%, Pacific Islander <1%, Two or more races 2%, Race unknown 8%.
Retention and Graduation: 79% freshmen return for sophomore year. 49% freshmen graduate within 4 years. 19% grads go on to further study within 1 year. 8% grads pursue arts and sciences degrees. 1% grads pursue law degrees. 10% grads pursue business degrees. 1% grads pursue medical degrees. **Faculty:** Student/faculty ratio 13:1. 123 full-time faculty, 76% hold PhDs, 13% are members of minority groups, 46% are women. 0% of classes are taught by teaching assistants.

ACADEMICS

Degrees: associate, bachelor's, certificate, doctoral/research, master's, postbachelor's certificate, post-master's certificate. **Classes:** Most classes have 10-19 students. Most lab/discussion sessions have 10-19 students. **Most popular majors:** Fashion/Apparel Design; Industrial and Product Design. **Special Study Options:** distance learning, double major, honors program, independent study, internships, liberal arts/career combination, study abroad. **Honors Programs:** University Honors Program Combined degree programs: BS/MS, BS/MBA. **Disability Services:** Special programs offered to physically disabled students, including note-taking services, reader services, tape recorders, tutors. **Career Services:** Alumni services, Career/job search classes, Career assessment, Internships.

FACILITIES

Housing: Coed dorms, special housing for disabled students, women's dorms, apartments for single students, Townhouses. 63% of campus accessible to physically diasbled. **Special Academic Facilities/Equipment:** The Design Center, Industrial Design Studios, Graphic Design Studios, Architecture Design Studios, CAD Labs in fashion design, interior design and architecture. **Computers:** Students can register for classes online. Administrative functions (other than registration) can be performed online.

CAMPUS LIFE

Environment: Metropolis. **Activities:** Choral groups, dance, drama/theater, student government, student newspaper, yearbook. 32 registered organizations, 3 religious organizations. 1 fraternity, 1 sorority. **Athletics (Intercollegiate):** *Men:* baseball, basketball, crew/rowing, cross-country, golf, soccer, tennis. *Women:* basketball, crew/rowing, cross-country, field hockey, lacrosse, soccer, softball, tennis, volleyball. **On-Campus Highlights:** Kanbar Campus Center, Athletic and Recreation Center, Gutman Library, Architecture and Design Building, The Design Center.

ADMISSIONS

Freshman Academic Profile: Average high school GPA 3.5. 17% in top 10% of high school class, 46% in top 25% of high school class, 78% in top 50% of high school class. 80% from public high schools. **Reported SAT (pre-2016 redesign) scores:** SAT Math middle 50% range 490-600. SAT Critical Reading middle 50% range 480-580. SAT Writing middle 50% range 470-580. **Concordant SAT scores:** SAT EBRW middle 50% 530–640. SAT Math middle 50% range 520–620. ACT middle 50% range 20-26. Minimum paper TOEFL 500. **Basis for Candidate Selection:** *Very important factors considered include:* rigor of secondary school record, academic GPA, standardized test scores. *Important factors considered include:* class rank, application essay, recommendation(s). *Other factors considered include:* interview, extracurricular activities. **Freshman Admission Requirements:** High school diploma is required and GED is accepted. *Academic units required:* 4 English, 3 math, 3 science, 2 science labs, 2 social studies, 1 history, 2 academic electives. *Academic units recommended:* 4 English, 4 math, 4 science, 2 foreign language, 3 social studies, 2 history. **Freshman Admission Statistics:** 4,767 applied, 63.94% admitted, 22% enrolled. **Transfer Admission Requirements:** college transcript(s), Minimum college GPA of 2.5 required. Lowest grade transferable C. **General Admission Information:** Application fee $40. Nonfall registration accepted. Admission may be deferred for a maximum of 1 year.

COSTS AND FINANCIAL AID

Average book expense $1,600. **Required Forms and Deadlines:** FAFSA. **Notification of Awards:** Applicants will be notified of awards on a rolling basis beginning 3/1. **Types of Aid:** *Need-based scholarships/grants:* Federal Pell, FSEOG, State scholarships/grants, Private scholarships, College/university scholarship or grant aid from institutional funds. *Loans:* Direct Subsidized Stafford Loans, Direct Unsubsidized Stafford Loans, Direct PLUS loans, Federal Perkins Loans. *Student Employment:* Federal Work-Study Program available. Institutional employment available. **Financial Aid Statistics:** 100% needy freshmen, 100% needy undergrads receive need-based scholarship or grant aid. 24% freshmen, 10% undergrads receive non-need-based scholarship or grant aid. 77% freshmen, 88% undergrads receive need-based self-help aid. 1% freshmen, 3% undergrads receive athletic scholarships. 99% freshmen, 97% undergrads receive any aid. **Criteria for awarding aid:** *Need-based:* Academics. *Non-need-based:* Academics, Athletics.

PIEDMONT COLLEGE

P.O. Box 10, Demorest, GA 30535
Phone: 706-776-0103 • **Financial Aid Phone:** 706-778-3000
E-mail: ugrad@piedmont.edu • **CEEB Code:** 5537
Fax: 706-776-6635 • **Website:** www.piedmont.edu • **ACT Code:** 853

This private school, affiliated with the Congregational Church, was founded in 1897. It has a 115-acre campus.

RATINGS

Admissions Selectivity Rating: 75   **Fire Safety Rating:** 60*   **Green Rating:** 60*

STUDENTS AND FACULTY

Enrollment: 1,284. **Student Body:** 66% female, 34% male, 9% out-of-state, 1% international (4 countries represented). Asian 1%, African American 9%, Caucasian 71%, Hispanic 5%, Native American <1%, Pacific Islander <1%, Two or more races 2%, Race unknown 10%.
Retention and Graduation: 63% freshmen return for sophomore year. 37% freshmen graduate within 4 years. 45% freshmen graduate within 6 years.
Faculty: Student/faculty ratio 11:1. 128 full-time faculty, 74% hold PhDs, 0% are are members of minority groups, 55% are women. 0% of classes are taught by teaching assistants.

ACADEMICS

Degrees: bachelor's, doctoral/research, master's, post-master's certificate.
Classes: Most classes have fewer than 10 students. Most lab/discussion sessions have 10-19 students. **Most popular majors:** Elementary Education and Teaching; Business/Commerce; Nursing Practice. **Special Study Options:** Accelerated program, distance learning, double major, dual enrollment, honors program, independent study, internships, student-designed major, study abroad, teacher certification program. Combined degree programs: BA/MAT (Education). **Disability Services:** Special programs offered to physically disabled students, including note-taking services, reader services, tape recorders, tutors. **Career Services:** Alumni network, Career/job search classes, Career assessment, Regional alumni, On-campus interviews.

FACILITIES

Housing: Coed dorms, special housing for disabled students, men's dorms, women's dorms, apartments for single students. 98% of campus accessible to physically diasbled. **Special Academic Facilities/Equipment:** Art Gallery; 4 NE Georgia Youth and Tech Center; Botanical Center; Fitness Center. **Computers:** Administrative functions (other than registration) can be performed online.

CAMPUS LIFE

Environment: Rural. **Activities:** Choral groups, concert band, drama/theater, music ensembles, opera, radio station, student government, student newspaper, student-run film society, television station, yearbook. 20 registered organizations, 7 honor societies, 1 religious organization. **Athletics (Intercollegiate):** *Men:* baseball, basketball, cross-country, golf, soccer, tennis. *Women:* basketball, cross-country, golf, soccer, softball, tennis, volleyball. **On-Campus Highlights:** Johnny Mize Athletic Center, Lane Student Center, Stewart Hall, Center for Music and Worship, Arrendale Library.

ADMISSIONS

Freshman Academic Profile: Average high school GPA 3.4. **Reported SAT (pre-2016 redesign) scores:** SAT Math middle 50% range 440-550. SAT Critical Reading middle 50% range 430-550. **Concordant SAT scores:** SAT Math middle 50% range 480–570. ACT middle 50% range 19-24. Minimum paper TOEFL 550. **Basis for Candidate Selection:** *Very important factors considered include:* rigor of secondary school record, academic GPA, standardized test scores. *Important factors considered include:* class rank, application essay, recommendation(s), interview, extracurricular activities, talent/ability, character/personal qualities, first generation. *Other factors considered include:* alumni/ae relation, geographical residence, state residency, volunteer work, work experience, level of applicant's interest. **Freshman Admission Requirements:** High school diploma is required and GED is accepted. *Academic units recommended:* 4 English, 4 math, 4 science, 2 foreign language, 1 social studies, 2 history. **Freshman Admission Statistics:** 1,135 applied, 57.00% admitted, 43% enrolled. **Transfer Admission Requirements:** college transcript(s), statement of good standing from prior institution(s). Minimum college GPA of 2.0 required. Lowest grade transferable C.
General Admission Information: Regular application deadline 7/1. Regular notification 7/1. Nonfall registration accepted. Admission may be deferred.

COSTS AND FINANCIAL AID

Annual tuition $21,990. Room and board $9,050. Average book expense $1,400. **Required Forms and Deadlines:** FAFSA, Institution's own financial aid form, State aid form. **Notification of Awards:** Applicants will be notified of awards on a rolling basis beginning 2/1. **Types of Aid:** *Need-based scholarships/grants:* Federal Pell, FSEOG, State scholarships/grants, Private scholarships, College/university scholarship or grant aid from institutional funds. *Loans:* Direct Subsidized Stafford Loans, Direct Unsubsidized Stafford Loans, Direct PLUS loans, State Loans. *Student Employment:* Federal Work-Study Program available. Institutional employment available. **Financial Aid Statistics:** 100% needy freshmen, 100% needy undergrads receive need-based scholarship or grant aid. 19% freshmen, 12% undergrads receive non-need-based scholarship or grant aid. 56% freshmen, 73% undergrads receive need-based self-help aid. 0% freshmen, 0% undergrads receive athletic scholarships. 99% freshmen, 99% undergrads receive any aid. 80% undergrads borrow to pay for school. Average cumulative indebtedness $29,289. **Criteria for awarding aid:** *Need-based:* Academics, Leadership. *Non-need-based:* Academics, Alumni affiliation, Art, Leadership, Music/drama, Religious affiliation, State/district residency.

PITTSBURG STATE UNIVERSITY

1701 South Broadway, Pittsburg, KS 66762
Phone: 620-235-4251 • **Financial Aid Phone:** 800-854-7488 • **CEEB Code:** 6336
Fax: 620-235-6003 • **Website:** www.pittstate.edu • **ACT Code:** 1449

This public school was founded in 1903. It has a 443-acre campus.

RATINGS

Admissions Selectivity Rating: 79   **Fire Safety Rating:** 90   **Green Rating:** 85

STUDENTS AND FACULTY

Enrollment: 5,536. **Student Body:** 47% female, 53% male, 30% out-of-state, 3% international (42 countries represented). Asian 1%, African American 4%, Caucasian 79%, Hispanic 5%, Native American 1%, Pacific Islander <1%, Two or more races 6%, Race unknown <1%.
Retention and Graduation: 74% freshmen return for sophomore year. 27% freshmen graduate within 4 years. 51 **Faculty:** Student/faculty ratio 17:1. 323 full-time faculty, 80% hold PhDs, 10% are are members of minority groups, 43% are women. 2% of classes are taught by teaching assistants.

ACADEMICS

Degrees: associate, bachelor's, certificate, master's, post-master's certificate.
Classes: Most classes have 20-29 students. Most lab/discussion sessions have 10-19 students. **Most popular majors:** Engineering Technology; Business Administration and Management; Education. **Special Study Options:** Accelerated program, distance learning, double major, dual enrollment, English as a Second Language (ESL), honors program, independent study, internships, student-designed major, study abroad, teacher certification program. **Honors Programs:** Honors College. **Disability Services:** Special programs offered to physically disabled students, including note-taking services, reader services, tape recorders, tutors. **Career Services:** Alumni services, Career/job search classes, Career assessment, Internships.

FACILITIES

Housing: Coed dorms, special housing for disabled students, apartments for married students, substance free and academic excellence floors are available. 90% of campus accessible to physically diasbled. **Special Academic Facilities/Equipment:** planetarium, observatory, field biology reserve, nature reach, herbarium, technology center, mammal collection, greenhouse, art gallery, polymer research center, cadaver lab, Veterans Memorial Amphitheater, broadcasting lab, public radio station **Computers:** 100% of classrooms, 100% of dorms, 100% of libraries, 100% of dining areas, 100% of student union, 80% of common outdoor areas have wireless network access. Students can register for classes online. Administrative functions (other than registration) can be performed online.

CAMPUS LIFE

Environment: Village. **Activities:** Choral groups, concert band, dance, drama/theater, jazz band, literary magazine, marching band, music ensembles, pep band, radio station, student government, student newspaper, television station, yearbook, Campus Ministries, Student Organization. 150 registered organizations, 8 fraternities, 3 sororities. **Athletics (Intercollegiate):** *Men:* baseball, basketball, cheerleading, cross-country, football, golf, track/field (outdoor), track/field (indoor). *Women:* basketball, cheerleading, cross-country, softball, track/field (outdoor), track/field (indoor), volleyball. **On-Campus Highlights:** Planetarium, Veterans Memorial Amphitheater, Gorilla Village, Brandenburg Field/Carnie Smith Stadium, Timmons Chapel, Russ Hall, Kansas Technology Center, Nature Reach, Centennial Mural, Centennial Bell Tower, herbarium, art gallery, broadcasting lab, cadaver lab, polymer research lab, mammal collection, ROTC & student fitness center. **Environmental Initiatives:** Addition of Sustainability as a goal in the university strategic plan.

ADMISSIONS

Freshman Academic Profile: Average high school GPA 3.4. 31% in top 10% of high school class, 46% in top 25% of high school class, 74% in top 50% of high school class. ACT middle 50% range 19-24. Minimum internet-based TOEFL 68. Minimum paper TOEFL 520. **Basis for Candidate Selection:** *Very important factors considered include:* rigor of secondary school record, class rank, academic GPA, standardized test scores. **Freshman Admission Requirements:** High school diploma is required and GED is accepted. *Academic units recommended:* 4 English, 4 math, 3 science, 3 social studies, 3 computer science. **Freshman Admission Statistics:** 2,593 applied, 84.30% admitted, 45% enrolled. **Transfer Admission Requirements:** college transcript(s), Minimum college GPA of 2.0 required. Lowest grade transferable D. **General Admission Information:** Application fee $30. Nonfall registration accepted. Admission may be deferred for a maximum of 3 semesters.

COSTS AND FINANCIAL AID

Annual in-state tuition $6,508. Annual out-of-state tuition $16,978. Room and board $6,734. Required fees $1,196. Average book expense $1,000. **Required Forms and Deadlines:** FAFSA, State aid form. **Notification of Awards:** Applicants will be notified of awards on a rolling basis beginning 3/1. **Types of Aid:** *Need-based scholarships/grants:* Federal Pell, FSEOG, State scholarships/grants, Private scholarships, College/university scholarship or grant aid from institutional funds. *Loans:* Direct Subsidized Stafford Loans, Direct Unsubsidized Stafford Loans, Direct PLUS loans, Federal Perkins Loans, Federal Nursing Loans, College/university loans from institutional funds. *Student Employment:* Federal Work-Study Program available. Institutional employment available. **Financial Aid Statistics:** 64% needy freshmen receive need-based scholarship or grant aid. 72% freshmen, 57% undergrads receive non-need-based scholarship or grant aid. 48% freshmen, 55% undergrads receive need-based self-help aid. 0% freshmen, 0% undergrads receive athletic scholarships. 91% freshmen, 85% undergrads receive any aid. 70% undergrads borrow to pay for school. Average cumulative indebtedness $24,384. **Criteria for awarding aid:** *Non-need-based:* Academics, Alumni affiliation, Art, Athletics, Leadership, Minority status, Music/drama.

PITZER COLLEGE

1050 North Mills Avenue, Claremont, CA 91711-6101
Phone: 909-621-8129 • **Financial Aid Phone:** 909-621-8208
E-mail: admission@pitzer.edu • **CEEB Code:** 4619
Fax: 909-621-8770 • **Website:** www.pitzer.edu • **ACT Code:** 363

This private school was founded in 1963. It has a 35-acre campus.

RATINGS

Admissions Selectivity Rating: 97   **Fire Safety Rating:** 60*   **Green Rating:** 91

STUDENTS AND FACULTY

Enrollment: 1,062. **Student Body:** 55% female, 45% male, 52% out-of-state, 9% international (15 countries represented). Asian 9%, African American 5%, Caucasian 46%, Hispanic 15%, Native American <1%, Pacific Islander 0%, Two or more races 10%, Race unknown 6%.
Retention and Graduation: 94% freshmen return for sophomore year. 83% freshmen graduate within 4 years. 88% freshmen graduate within 6 years.
Faculty: Student/faculty ratio 11:1. 82 full-time faculty, 100% hold PhDs, 34% are are members of minority groups, 61% are women. 0% of classes are taught by teaching assistants.

ACADEMICS

Degrees: bachelor's. **Classes:** Most classes have 10-19 students. **Most popular majors:** Psychology; Political Science and Government; Biological and Physical Sciences. **Special Study Options:** cooperative education program, cross-registration, double major, English as a Second Language (ESL), exchange student program (domestic), honors program, independent study, internships, liberal arts/career combination, student-designed major, study abroad. Combined degree programs: BA/MA, B.A./D.O. (Doctor of Osteopathy); BA/MBA. **Disability Services:** Special programs offered to physically disabled students, including note-taking services, reader services, tape recorders, tutors. **Career Services:** Alumni network, Career/job search classes, Career assessment, Internships. Many of our courses have an internship component which provides students with practical experience as well as classroom learning.

FACILITIES

Housing: Coed dorms, special housing for disabled students, ThemeHousingGreen housing. 95% of campus accessible to physically diasbled. **Special Academic Facilities/Equipment:** Theatre arts center, Black, Asian American and Chicano Study centers; film, TV, and videotape studios; arboretum; biological field station; student health services, Gold Student Center. **Computers:** 95% of classrooms, 100% of dorms, 95% of libraries, have wireless network access. Students can register for classes online. Administrative functions (other than registration) can be performed online.

CAMPUS LIFE

Environment: Town. **Activities:** Choral groups, dance, drama/theater, literary magazine, music ensembles, radio station, student government, student newspaper, symphony orchestra, Campus Ministries, Student Organization, Model UN. 120 registered organizations, 1 honor society. **Athletics (Intercollegiate):** *Men:* baseball, basketball, cross-country, diving, football, golf, soccer, swimming, tennis, track/field (outdoor), water polo. *Women:* basketball, cross-country, diving, soccer, softball, swimming, tennis, track/field (outdoor), volleyball, water polo. **On-Campus Highlights:** Grove House, McConnell Center, Gloria and Peter Gold Student Center, Marquis Library, The Mounds, http://www.pitzer.edu/admission/campusvisit.aspThe Claremont Colleges Consortium Pitzer students may cross-register at any of The Claremont Colleges, and may utilize all Claremont facilities, including Honnold Library, the third-largest academic library in the state, with more than 2 million volumes; Huntley Bookstore; Baxter Medical Center; McAlister Center for Religious Activities and Monsour Counseling Center. Pitzer sponsors the Joint Science Program with Claremont McKenna and Scripps colleges, and the five undergraduate colleges offer a wide range of recreational facilities, student gathering places and dining areas. Pitzer combines with Pomona College for NCAA Division III sports. **Environmental Initiatives:** New 'Green' dorms.

ADMISSIONS

Freshman Academic Profile: Average high school GPA 3.8. 54% in top 10% of high school class, 81% in top 25% of high school class, 98% in top 50% of high school class. **Reported SAT (pre-2016 redesign) scores:** SAT Math middle 50% range 650-720. SAT Critical Reading middle 50% range 650-730. **Concordant SAT scores:** SAT Math middle 50% range 670–750. ACT middle 50% range 29-32. Minimum internet-based TOEFL 70. Minimum paper TOEFL 520. **Basis for Candidate Selection:** *Very important factors considered include:* rigor of secondary school record, academic GPA, application essay, character/personal qualities. *Important factors considered include:* recommendation(s), extracurricular activities, talent/ability, volunteer work. *Other factors considered include:* class rank, first generation, alumni/ae relation, geographical residence, racial/ethnic status, work experience, level of applicant's interest. **Freshman Admission Requirements:** High school diploma is required and GED is accepted. *Academic units required:* 4 English, 3 math, 3 science, 3 science labs, 3 foreign language, 3 social studies, 1 history, 1 visual/performing arts. **Freshman Admission Statistics:** 4,142 applied, 13.40% admitted, 47% enrolled. **Transfer Admission Requirements:** college transcript(s), essay or personal statement, statement of good standing from prior institution(s). Minimum college GPA of 2.0 required. Lowest grade transferable C-. **General Admission Information:** Application fee $70. Regular application deadline 1/1. Regular notification 4/1. Nonfall registration not accepted. Admission may be deferred for a maximum of 1 year.

COSTS AND FINANCIAL AID

Required Forms and Deadlines: FAFSA, CSS/Financial Aid PROFILE, State aid form, Noncustodial PROFILE. **Notification of Awards:** Applicants will be notified of awards on or about 4/1. **Types of Aid:** *Need-based scholarships/grants:* Federal Pell, FSEOG, State scholarships/grants, Private scholarships, College/university scholarship or grant aid from institutional funds. *Loans:* Direct Subsidized Stafford Loans, Direct Unsubsidized Stafford Loans, Direct PLUS loans, Federal Perkins Loans, College/university loans from institutional funds. *Student Employment:* Federal Work-Study Program available. Institutional employment available. **Financial Aid Statistics:** 100% needy freshmen, 98% needy undergrads receive need-based scholarship or grant aid. 5% freshmen, 6% undergrads receive non-need-based scholarship or grant aid. 89% freshmen, 89% undergrads receive need-based self-help aid. 0% freshmen, 0% undergrads receive athletic scholarships. 34% freshmen, 40% undergrads receive any aid. 38% undergrads borrow to pay for school. Average cumulative indebtedness $21,569. **Criteria for awarding aid:** *Need-based:* Academics, Art, Leadership, Minority status, Music/drama. *Non-need-based:* Academics, Leadership.

PLYMOUTH STATE UNIVERSITY

17 High Street, Plymouth, NH 3264
Phone: 603-535-2237 • **Financial Aid Phone:** 877-846-5755
E-mail: plymouthadmit@plymouth.edu • **CEEB Code:** 3690
Fax: 603-535-2714 • **Website:** www.plymouth.edu • **ACT Code:** 2518

This public school was founded in 1871. It has a 170-acre campus.

RATINGS

Admissions Selectivity Rating: 75   **Fire Safety Rating:** 99   **Green Rating:** 60*

STUDENTS AND FACULTY

Enrollment: 4,042. **Student Body:** 49% female, 51% male, 44% out-of-state, 2% international (24 countries represented). Asian 2%, African American 2%, Caucasian 81%, Hispanic 2%, Native American <1%, Pacific Islander <1%, Two or more races 2%, Race unknown 10%.
Retention and Graduation: 77% freshmen return for sophomore year. 44% freshmen graduate within 4 years. 58 **Faculty:** Student/faculty ratio 17:1. 188 full-time faculty, 87% hold PhDs, 10% are are members of minority groups, 49% are women. 0% of classes are taught by teaching assistants.

ACADEMICS

Degrees: bachelor's, certificate, doctoral/research, master's, postbachelor's certificate, post-master's certificate. **Classes:** Most classes have 20-29 students. Most lab/discussion sessions have 10-19 students. **Most popular majors:** Business Administration and Management; Criminal Justice/Safety Studies; Marketing/Marketing Management. **Special Study Options:** cross-registration, distance learning, double major, dual enrollment, English as a Second Language (ESL), exchange student program (domestic), external degree program, honors program, independent study, internships, student-designed major, study abroad, teacher certification program. **Honors Programs:** First and Second Year Honors Program, Business Honors, Psychology Honors Combined degree programs: BFA/MAT. **Disability Services:** Special programs offered to physically disabled students, including note-taking services, reader services, tape recorders, tutors. **Career Services:** Alumni network, Alumni services, Career/job search classes, Career assessment, Internships, Regional alumni.

FACILITIES

Housing: Coed dorms, special housing for disabled students, fraternity/sorority housing, apartments for married students, apartments for single students, Wellness Housing, Theme Housing, Non-traditional student apts. Quiet study/Academic. 80% of campus accessible to physically disabled. **Special Academic Facilities/Equipment:** Karl Drerup Art gallery, Silver Cultural Arts Center, Sylvestre Planetarium, Child Development and Family Center (NAEYC accredited lab school for children 2-6 years old), meteorology lab, Geographic Information System lab, psychology lab, graphic design computer lab **Computers:** 75% of classrooms, 5% of dorms, 100% of libraries, 100% of dining areas, 100% of student union, 10% of common outdoor areas have wireless network access. Students can register for classes online. Administrative functions (other than registration) can be performed online.

CAMPUS LIFE

Environment: Village. **Activities:** Choral groups, concert band, dance, drama/theater, jazz band, literary magazine, music ensembles, musical theater, radio station, student government, student newspaper, student-run film society, yearbook, Campus Ministries, Student Organization, Model UN. 80 registered organizations, 13 honor societies, 4 religious organizations. 3 sororities. **Athletics (Intercollegiate):** *Men:* baseball, basketball, football, ice hockey, lacrosse, skiing (downhill/alpine), soccer, wrestling. *Women:* basketball, cheerleading, diving, field hockey, ice hockey, lacrosse, skiing (downhill/alpine), soccer, softball, swimming, tennis, volleyball. **On-Campus Highlights:** Hartman Union Building, Silver Center for the Arts, PE Center-New-Fall '10 Ice Arena & Welcome Center, Prospect Dining Hall, Lamson Library—Information Commons. **Environmental Initiatives:** New degree program.

ADMISSIONS

Freshman Academic Profile: Average high school GPA 3.0. 5% in top 10% of high school class, 21% in top 25% of high school class, 54% in top 50% of high school class. 85% from public high schools. **Reported SAT (pre-2016 redesign) scores:** SAT Math middle 50% range 440-550. SAT Critical Reading middle 50% range 440-530. SAT Writing middle 50% range 430-520. **Concordant SAT scores:** SAT EBRW middle 50% 490–580. SAT Math middle 50% range 480–570. ACT middle 50% range 19-24. Minimum internet-based TOEFL 68. Minimum paper TOEFL 520. **Basis for Candidate Selection:** *Very important factors considered include:* rigor of secondary school record. *Important factors considered include:* class rank, academic GPA, standardized test scores, application essay, recommendation(s), talent/ability, character/personal qualities. *Other factors considered include:* extracurricular activities, alumni/ae relation, racial/ethnic status, volunteer work, work experience, level of applicant's interest. **Freshman Admission Requirements:** High school diploma is required and GED is accepted. *Academic units required:* 4 English, 3 math, 2 science, 1 science lab, 2 social studies, 1 history. *Academic units recommended:* 4 English, 3 math, 3 science, 1 science lab, 2 foreign language, 3 social studies, 2 history. **Freshman Admission Statistics:** 6,626 applied, 73.57% admitted, 28% enrolled. **Transfer Admission Requirements:** High school transcript, college transcript(s), Minimum college GPA of 2.0 required. Lowest grade transferable C. **General Admission Information:** Application fee $50. Regular application deadline 4/1. Nonfall registration accepted. Admission may be deferred for a maximum of 1 year.

COSTS AND FINANCIAL AID

Required Forms and Deadlines: FAFSA. **Notification of Awards:** Applicants will be notified of awards on a rolling basis beginning 3/1. **Types of Aid:** *Need-based scholarships/grants:* Federal Pell, FSEOG, State scholarships/grants, Private scholarships, College/university scholarship or grant aid from institutional funds. *Loans:* Direct Subsidized Stafford Loans, Direct Unsubsidized Stafford Loans, Direct PLUS loans, Federal Perkins Loans. *Student Employment:* Federal Work-Study Program available. Institutional employment available. **Financial Aid Statistics:** 60% needy freshmen, 61% needy undergrads receive need-based scholarship or grant aid. 74% freshmen, 49% undergrads receive non-need-based scholarship or grant aid. 96% freshmen, 97% undergrads receive need-based self-help aid. 0% freshmen, 0% undergrads receive athletic scholarships. 83% freshmen, 78% undergrads receive any aid. 87% undergrads borrow to pay for school. Average cumulative indebtedness $32,592. **Criteria for awarding aid:** *Non-need-based:* Academics, Alumni affiliation, Art, Leadership, Music/drama.

POINT LOMA NAZARENE UNIVERSITY

3900 Lomaland Drive, San Diego, CA 92106
Phone: 619-849-2273 • **Financial Aid Phone:** 619-849-2538
E-mail: admissions@pointloma.edu • **CEEB Code:** 4605
Fax: 619-849-2601 • **ACT Code:** 370

This private school, affiliated with the Nazarene Church, was founded in 1902. It has a 90-acre campus.

RATINGS

Admissions Selectivity Rating: 86   **Fire Safety Rating:** 82   **Green Rating:** 67

STUDENTS AND FACULTY

Enrollment: 2,558. **Student Body:** 64% female, 36% male, 17% out-of-state, 1% international (17 countries represented). Asian 5%, African American 2%, Caucasian 62%, Hispanic 22%, Native American 1%, Pacific Islander 1%, Two or more races 6%, Race unknown 1%.
Retention and Graduation: 85% freshmen return for sophomore year. 59% freshmen graduate within 4 years. 73% freshmen graduate within 6 years. **Faculty:** Student/faculty ratio 14:1. 136 full-time faculty, 82% hold PhDs, 16% are are members of minority groups, 41% are women. 0% of classes are taught by teaching assistants.

ACADEMICS

Degrees: bachelor's, certificate, master's. **Classes:** Most classes have 20-29 students. **Most popular majors:** Business/Commerce; Registered Nursing, Nursing Administration, Nursing Research and Clinical Nursing; Pre-medical Studies. **Special Study Options:** double major, honors program, independent study, internships, study abroad, teacher certification program. **Honors Programs:** Honors Scholars Program. **Career Services:** Alumni network, Alumni services, Career/job search classes, Career assessment, Internships, Regional alumni. Our Offices of Strengths and Vocation exists to help students with their next step, whether that's grad school or employment, when they leave PLNU

FACILITIES

Housing: men's dorms, women's dorms, apartments for married students, apartments for single students. 100% of campus accessible to physically disabled. **Special Academic Facilities/Equipment:** Language lab, on-campus preschool, electron microscope. **Computers:** Students can register for classes online. Administrative functions (other than registration) can be performed online.

CAMPUS LIFE

Environment: Metropolis. **Activities:** Choral groups, concert band, drama/theater, jazz band, literary magazine, music ensembles, musical theater, radio station, student government, student newspaper, television station, yearbook, Campus Ministries, Student Organization. 30 registered organizations, 2 honor societies, 7 religious organizations. 3 fraternities, 3 sororities. **Athletics (Intercollegiate):** *Men:* baseball, basketball, cross-country, golf, soccer, tennis, track/field (outdoor). *Women:* basketball, cross-country, softball, tennis, track/field (outdoor), volleyball. **On-Campus Highlights:** Point Break Cafe, Recreation Center, Ryan Library, Greek Ampitheatre, Golden Gymnasium.

ADMISSIONS

Freshman Academic Profile: Average high school GPA 3.8. 34% in top 10% of high school class, 67% in top 25% of high school class, 91% in top 50% of high school class. **Reported SAT (pre-2016 redesign) scores:** SAT Math middle 50% range 500-620. SAT Critical Reading middle 50% range 510-600. SAT Writing middle 50% range 510-600. **Concordant SAT scores:** SAT EBRW middle 50% 570–650. SAT Math middle 50% range 530–640. ACT middle 50% range 23-28. Minimum paper TOEFL 550. **Basis for Candidate Selection:** *Very important factors considered include:* rigor of secondary school record, academic GPA, standardized test scores, character/personal qualities, religious affiliation/commitment. *Important factors considered include:* class rank, application essay, recommendation(s), interview. *Other factors considered include:* extracurricular activities, talent/ability, first generation, alumni/ae relation, level of applicant's interest. **Freshman Admission Requirements:** High school diploma is required and GED is accepted. *Academic units recommended:* 4 English, 3 math, 2 science, 2 science labs, 2 foreign language, 2 social studies, 2 history, 1 academic elective. **Freshman Admission Statistics:** 3,096 applied, 68.18% admitted, 28% enrolled. **Transfer Admission Requirements:** college transcript(s), essay or personal statement, interview, Minimum college GPA of 2.0 required. Lowest grade transferable D. **General Admission Information:** Application fee $55. Priority deadline 2/15. Regular application deadline 3/1. Regular notification 4/1. Nonfall registration not accepted.

COSTS AND FINANCIAL AID

Annual tuition $31,800. Room and board $9,800. Required fees $624. Average book expense $1,764. **Required Forms and Deadlines:** FAFSA. **Notification of Awards:** Applicants will be notified of awards on a rolling basis beginning 12/20. **Types of Aid:** *Need-based scholarships/grants:* Federal Pell, FSEOG, State scholarships/grants, Private scholarships, College/university scholarship or grant aid from institutional funds, Federal Nursing Scholarships. *Loans:* Direct Subsidized Stafford Loans, Direct Unsubsidized Stafford Loans, Direct PLUS loans, Federal Perkins Loans, Federal Nursing Loans. *Student Employment:* Federal Work-Study Program available. Institutional employment available. **Financial Aid Statistics:** 94% needy freshmen, 93% needy undergrads receive need-based scholarship or grant aid. 10% freshmen, 8% undergrads receive non-need-based scholarship or grant aid. 90% freshmen, 92% undergrads receive need-based self-help aid. 2% freshmen, 3% undergrads receive athletic scholarships. 74% undergrads borrow to pay for school. Average cumulative indebtedness $32,649. **Criteria for awarding aid:** *Need-based:* Academics, Alumni affiliation, Leadership, Minority status, Religious affiliation. *Non-need-based:* Academics, Art, Athletics, Job skills, Music/drama, Religious affiliation.

POINT PARK UNIVERSITY

201 Wood Street, Pittsburgh, PA 15222
Phone: 412-392-3430 • **Financial Aid Phone:** 412-392-3930
E-mail: enroll@pointpark.edu • **CEEB Code:** 2676
Fax: 412-391-1980 • **ACT Code:** 3530

This private school was founded in 1960.

RATINGS
Admissions Selectivity Rating: 76   **Fire Safety Rating:** 97   **Green Rating:** 60*

STUDENTS AND FACULTY
Enrollment: 3,167. **Student Body:** 58% female, 42% male, 21% out-of-state, 2% international (38 countries represented). Asian 1%, African American 17%, Caucasian 73%, Hispanic 3%, Native American <1%, Pacific Islander 0%, Two or more races 3%, Race unknown <1%.
Retention and Graduation: 74% freshmen return for sophomore year. 39% freshmen graduate within 4 years. 50% freshmen graduate within 6 years.
Faculty: Student/faculty ratio 13:1. 133 full-time faculty, 74% hold PhDs, 10% are are members of minority groups, 38% are women. 0% of classes are taught by teaching assistants.

ACADEMICS
Degrees: associate, bachelor's, certificate, master's, postbachelor's certificate. **Classes:** Most classes have 10-19 students. **Most popular majors:** Teacher Education and Professional Development, Specific Subject Areas; Dance; Drama and Dramatics/Theatre Arts. **Special Study Options:** Accelerated program, cooperative education program, cross-registration, distance learning, double major, dual enrollment, English as a Second Language (ESL), exchange student program (domestic), honors program, independent study, internships, liberal arts/career combination, student-designed major, study abroad, teacher certification program, weekend college. **Honors Programs:** The Point Park

Honors Program mission provides the foundation from which honors courses are developed. Honors courses will not be defined by more work but rather by a different kind of learning environment. Students will be introduced to the usual content and objectives of the course, but they will also develop in-depth understandings of topics. Students will be expected to use primary sources when possible and to develop appropriate research skills which should result in major documented papers or projects. Students will be encouraged to become adventurous, independent thinkers. Students should experience a variety of learning activities which may include collaborative learning, field experience, debates, documented projects, interviews, and presentations. Evaluation will be based on performance, creativity, imagination, critical thinking, and risk taking rather than on more assignments and tests. Honors students will be expected to participate in the quest for knowledge by being prepared and willing to contribute to all class activities. Honors students also may join our Honors Student Organization and participate in a variety of community service efforts and projects inside and outside the Point Park community. Students annually are offered the chance to travel for an alternative spring break, and they can present papers and research at national and regional honors conferences. Every effort is made to encourage all of them to assume leadership positions and propose their own activities and endeavors to complement their work in the classroom. Students who complete program requirements will be recognized in the program at graduation and will receive a separate certificate and notation on their transcript. **Disability Services:** Special programs offered to physically disabled students, including note-taking services, reader services, tape recorders, tutors. **Career Services:** Alumni network, Alumni services, Career/job search classes, Career assessment, Internships, Regional alumni, On-campus interviews.

FACILITIES
Housing: Coed dorms, special housing for disabled students, women's dorms, apartments for single students, ThemeHousingLiving & Learning Communities; Suite Style. 95% of campus accessible to physically diasbled. **Special Academic Facilities/Equipment:** Theater, day care center and elementary school, engineering technology labs, television and radio studios, digital film editing suites, dance studios **Computers:** 100% of classrooms, 100% of libraries, 100% of dining areas, 100% of student union, 100% of common outdoor areas have wireless network access. Students can register for classes online. Administrative functions (other than registration) can be performed online.

CAMPUS LIFE
Environment: Metropolis. **Activities:** Choral groups, dance, drama/theater, literary magazine, musical theater, radio station, student government, student newspaper, student-run film society, television station, Student Organization. 25 registered organizations, 3 honor societies, 2 religious organizations. **Athletics (Intercollegiate):** *Men:* baseball, basketball, cross-country, golf, soccer. *Women:* basketball, cross-country, golf, soccer, softball, volleyball. **On-Campus Highlights:** Point Cafe, Atrium Overlook, Recreation Center, Coffee Kiosk, Outdoor Patio. **Environmental Initiatives:** Recycling.

ADMISSIONS
Freshman Academic Profile: Average high school GPA 3.2. 10% in top 10% of high school class, 30% in top 25% of high school class, 66% in top 50% of high school class. **Reported SAT (pre-2016 redesign) scores:** SAT Math middle 50% range 450-560. SAT Critical Reading middle 50% range 460-580. SAT Writing middle 50% range 450-560. **Concordant SAT scores:** SAT EBRW middle 50% 510–630. SAT Math middle 50% range 490–580. ACT middle 50% range 20-26. Minimum paper TOEFL 500. **Basis for Candidate Selection:** *Very important factors considered include:* standardized test scores, talent/ability. *Important factors considered include:* rigor of secondary school record. *Other factors considered include:* academic GPA, recommendation(s). **Freshman Admission Requirements:** High school diploma is required and GED is accepted. *Academic units recommended:* 4 English, 4 math, 3 science, 2 foreign language, 3 social studies, 3 history, 1 academic elective, 1 computer science, 1 visual/performing arts. **Freshman Admission Statistics:** 3,673 applied, 76.20% admitted, 19% enrolled. **Transfer Admission Requirements:** college transcript(s), Minimum college GPA of 2.0 required. Lowest grade transferable C. **General Admission Information:** Application fee $40. Nonfall registration accepted. Admission may be deferred for a maximum of 1 year.

COSTS AND FINANCIAL AID
Annual tuition $24,020. Room and board $9,920. Required fees $1,170. Average book expense $1,000. **Required Forms and Deadlines:** FAFSA. **Notification of Awards:** Applicants will be notified of awards on a rolling basis beginning 2/15. **Types of Aid:** *Need-based scholarships/grants:* Federal Pell, FSEOG, State scholarships/grants, Private scholarships, College/university scholarship or grant aid from institutional funds. *Loans:* Direct Subsidized Stafford Loans, Direct Unsubsidized Stafford Loans, Direct PLUS loans, Federal Perkins Loans. *Student Employment:* Federal Work-Study Program available. Institutional employment available. **Financial Aid Statistics:** 100% needy freshmen, 99% needy undergrads receive need-based scholarship or grant aid.

11% freshmen, 9% undergrads receive non-need-based scholarship or grant aid. 88% freshmen, 88% undergrads receive need-based self-help aid. 1% freshmen, 2% undergrads receive athletic scholarships. 100% freshmen, 93% undergrads receive any aid. **Criteria for awarding aid:** *Non-need-based:* Academics, Athletics, Music/drama.

POINT UNIVERSITY

507 West 10th Street, West Point, GA 31833
Phone: 706-385-1202 • **Financial Aid Phone:** 706-385-1045
E-mail: admissions@point.edu • **CEEB Code:** 5029
Fax: 706-645-9473 • **Website:** www.point.edu • **ACT Code:** 785

This private school, affiliated with the Christian (Nondenominational) Church, was founded in 1937. It has a 52-acre campus.

RATINGS
Admissions Selectivity Rating: 77   **Fire Safety Rating:** 74   **Green Rating:** 60*

STUDENTS AND FACULTY
Enrollment: 1,358. **Student Body:** 50% female, 50% male, 37% out-of-state, 2% international (8 countries represented). Asian 0%, African American 34%, Caucasian 47%, Hispanic 6%, Native American <1%, Pacific Islander <1%, Two or more races 5%, Race unknown 5%.
Retention and Graduation: 68% freshmen return for sophomore year. 21% freshmen graduate within 4 years. 34% freshmen graduate within 6 years. **Faculty:** Student/faculty ratio 18:1. 41 full-time faculty, 63% hold PhDs, 27% are are members of minority groups, 59% are women. 0% of classes are taught by teaching assistants.

ACADEMICS
Degrees: associate, bachelor's, certificate. **Most popular majors:** Business Administration and Management; Bible/Biblical Studies; Kinesiology and Exercise Science. **Special Study Options:** double major, dual enrollment, independent study, internships. **Career Services:** Alumni network, Alumni services, Career/job search classes, Internships, On-campus interviews.

FACILITIES
Housing: men's dorms, women's dorms, apartments for married students, apartments for single students. **Computers:** Students can register for classes online.

CAMPUS LIFE
Environment: Village. **Activities:** Choral groups, music ensembles, student government, yearbook. 2 fraternities, 2 sororities. **Athletics (Intercollegiate):** *Men:* baseball, basketball, golf, soccer. *Women:* basketball, soccer, volleyball.

ADMISSIONS
Freshman Academic Profile: Average high school GPA 3.2. **Reported SAT (pre-2016 redesign) scores:** SAT Math middle 50% range 410-520. SAT Critical Reading middle 50% range 400-490. **Concordant SAT scores:** SAT Math middle 50% range 450–550. ACT middle 50% range 17-22. Minimum internet-based TOEFL 80. Minimum paper TOEFL 550. **Basis for Candidate Selection:** *Very important factors considered include:* academic GPA, standardized test scores, character/personal qualities, religious affiliation/commitment. *Important factors considered include:* rigor of secondary school record, class rank, recommendation(s), extracurricular activities. *Other factors considered include:* application essay, interview, talent/ability, alumni/ae relation, volunteer work, work experience, level of applicant's interest. **Freshman Admission Requirements:** High school diploma is required and GED is accepted. *Academic units recommended:* 4 English, 4 math, 4 science, 2 science labs, 2 foreign language, 3 social studies. **Freshman Admission Statistics:** 1,184 applied, 51.44% admitted, 53% enrolled. **Transfer Admission Requirements:** college transcript(s), statement of good standing from prior institution(s). Minimum college GPA of 2.0 required. Lowest grade transferable C. **General Admission Information:** Priority deadline 7/1. Regular application deadline 8/1. Nonfall registration accepted. Admission may be deferred for a maximum of 1 year.

COSTS AND FINANCIAL AID
Annual tuition $18,100. Room and board $7,700. Required fees $1,100. Average book expense $2,000. *Student Employment:* Federal Work-Study Program available. Institutional employment available. **Financial Aid Statistics:** 99% freshmen, 99% undergrads receive any aid.

POLYTECHNIC INSTITUTE OF NEW YORK UNIVERSITY—BROOKLYN

6 Metrotech Center, Brooklyn, NY 11201-2999
Phone: 718-260-5955 • **Financial Aid Phone:** 718-260-3025
E-mail: uadmit@poly.edu • **CEEB Code:** 2668
Fax: 718-260-3446 • **Website:** www.poly.edu • **ACT Code:** 2860

This private school was founded in 1854. It has a 3-acre campus.

RATINGS
Admissions Selectivity Rating: 88   **Fire Safety Rating:** 82   **Green Rating:** 60*

STUDENTS AND FACULTY
Enrollment: 2,000. **Student Body:** 20% female, 80% male, 19% out-of-state, 10% international (34 countries represented). Asian 35%, African American 6%, Caucasian 30%, Hispanic 10%, Native American <1%, Pacific Islander 0%, Two or more races 0%, Race unknown 9%.
Retention and Graduation: 84% freshmen return for sophomore year. 31% freshmen graduate within 4 years. 54% freshmen graduate within 6 years. 15% grads go on to further study within 1 year. **Faculty:** Student/faculty ratio 14:1. 157 full-time faculty, 91% hold PhDs, 29% are are members of minority groups, 17% are women. 0% of classes are taught by teaching assistants.

ACADEMICS
Degrees: bachelor's, certificate, doctoral/research, doctoral, master's, postbachelor's certificate. **Classes:** Most classes have 10-19 students. Most lab/discussion sessions have 10-19 students. **Most popular majors:** Electrical and Electronics Engineering; Civil Engineering; Mechanical Engineering. **Special Study Options:** Accelerated program, cooperative education program, distance learning, double major, dual enrollment, honors program, independent study, internships. **Honors Programs:** The Honors College serves as a magnet for attracting academically superior Undergraduates to the University. It accepts students of exceptional talent and promise from a variety of backgrounds. It offers outstanding Honors students the opportunity to earn a BS and possibly an MS degree in possibly as few as four years, including summers. Honors College students work one-on-one with faculty mentors, who, among other things, stress interdisciplinary research where appropriate, originality of thought, and active learning. Honors College students form a talented cadre of high-achievers who will become engineers, scientists, managers, and other professionals positioned for leadership roles in our emerging knowledge-based economy. They will also form a highly enthusiastic and supportive part of the University's alumni population and enhance the overall reputation of the University for delivering excellence in education. Combined degree programs: BA/MA, BA/MEng, 2-2 engineering program with CUNY Brooklyn Coll. **Disability Services:** Special programs offered to physically disabled students, including note-taking services, tape recorders, tutors. **Career Services:** Alumni network, Alumni services, Career/job search classes, Career assessment, Internships.

FACILITIES
Housing: Coed dorms, fraternity/sorority housing. 100% of campus accessible to physically diasbled. **Special Academic Facilities/Equipment:** Electron microscope, supersonic wind tunnel. Art Displays in Student Center. **Computers:** 100% of classrooms, 100% of dorms, 100% of libraries, 100% of dining areas, 100% of student union, 100% of common outdoor areas have wireless network access. Students can register for classes online. Administrative functions (other than registration) can be performed online. Undergraduates are required to own a computer.

CAMPUS LIFE
Environment: Metropolis. **Activities:** drama/theater, literary magazine, radio station, student government, student newspaper, student-run film society, yearbook. 36 registered organizations, 8 honor societies, 4 religious organizations. 3 fraternities, 1 sorority. **Athletics (Intercollegiate):** *Men:* baseball, basketball, cross-country, soccer, tennis, track/field (outdoor), volleyball. *Women:* basketball, cross-country, softball, tennis, track/field (outdoor), volleyball. **On-Campus Highlights:** Recreation Center–Wunsch Student Center, Fitness Center–Jacobs Building, Bern Dibner Library for Science and Technology, Jasper H. Kane Dining Hall–Rogers Hall, Gymnasium–Jacobs Building. **Environmental Initiatives:** Enhanced/expanded recycling.

ADMISSIONS
Freshman Academic Profile: Average high school GPA 3.5. 46% in top 10% of high school class, 81% in top 25% of high school class, 95% in top 50% of high school class. 73% from public high schools. **Reported SAT (pre-2016 redesign) scores:** SAT Math middle 50% range 640-720. SAT Critical Reading middle 50% range 550-650. SAT Writing middle 50% range 540-650. **Concordant SAT scores:** SAT EBRW middle 50% 600–700. SAT Math middle 50% range 660–750. ACT middle 50% range 26-30. Minimum internet-based

TOEFL 80. Minimum paper TOEFL 550. **Basis for Candidate Selection:** *Very important factors considered include:* rigor of secondary school record, standardized test scores. *Important factors considered include:* class rank. *Other factors considered include:* application essay, recommendation(s), interview. **Freshman Admission Requirements:** High school diploma is required and GED is accepted. *Academic units required:* 4 English, 4 math, 4 science, 3 social studies, 2 academic electives. *Academic units recommended:* 2 foreign language. **Freshman Admission Statistics:** 3,284 applied, 74.70% admitted, 20% enrolled. **Transfer Admission Requirements:** college transcript(s), Minimum college GPA of 2.5 required. Lowest grade transferable c. **General Admission Information:** Application fee $65. Nonfall registration accepted. Admission may be deferred.

COSTS AND FINANCIAL AID

Annual tuition $40,060. Room and board $13,500. Required fees $1,268. Average book expense $1,500. **Required Forms and Deadlines:** FAFSA, Institution's own financial aid form, CSS/Financial Aid PROFILE, State aid form. **Notification of Awards:** Applicants will be notified of awards on a rolling basis beginning 3/15. **Types of Aid:** *Need-based scholarships/grants:* Federal Pell, FSEOG, State scholarships/grants, Private scholarships, College/university scholarship or grant aid from institutional funds, United Negro College Fund. *Loans:* Direct Subsidized Stafford Loans, Direct Unsubsidized Stafford Loans, Direct PLUS loans, Federal Perkins Loans, College/university loans from institutional funds. *Student Employment:* Federal Work-Study Program available. Institutional employment available. **Financial Aid Statistics:** 93% needy freshmen, 93% needy undergrads receive need-based scholarship or grant aid. 89% freshmen, 60% undergrads receive non-need-based scholarship or grant aid. 86% freshmen, 88% undergrads receive need-based self-help aid. 0% freshmen, 0% undergrads receive athletic scholarships. 97% freshmen, 92% undergrads receive any aid. **Criteria for awarding aid:** *Need-based:* Academics, Leadership, Minority status. *Non-need-based:* Academics, Minority status, State/district residency.

POLYTECHNIC UNIVERSITY OF PUERTO RICO

PO BOX 192017, Hato Rey, PR 00919-2017
Phone: 787-622-8000 • **Financial Aid Phone:** 787-622-8000 • **CEEB Code:** 614
Fax: 787-764-8712 • **Website:** www.pupr.edu

This private school was founded in 1966.

RATINGS

Admissions Selectivity Rating: 64   **Fire Safety Rating:** 68   **Green Rating:** 65

STUDENTS AND FACULTY

Enrollment: 3,334. **Student Body:** 20% female, 80% male, 0% international. Asian 0%, African American <1%, Caucasian <1%, Hispanic 100%, Native American 0%, Pacific Islander 0%, Two or more races 0%, Race unknown <1%. **Retention and Graduation:** 77% freshmen return for sophomore year. 11% freshmen graduate within 4 years. 25% freshmen graduate within 6 years. 73% grads go on to further study within 1 year. 1% grads pursue arts and sciences degrees. 15% grads pursue business degrees. 1% grads pursue medical degrees. **Faculty:** Student/faculty ratio 11:1. 131 full-time faculty, 37% hold PhDs, 0% are are members of minority groups, 34% are women. 0% of classes are taught by teaching assistants.

ACADEMICS

Degrees: associate, bachelor's, doctoral, master's. **Most popular majors:** Civil Engineering; Electrical and Electronics Engineering; Mechanical Engineering. **Special Study Options:** cooperative education program, distance learning, honors program. **Honors Programs:** In a continuing effort to provide educational opportunities consistent with the ability of the individual student, the University invites a select group of students to enroll in and benefit from the Honor Program and corresponding Scholarship. This program consists of honors seminars, special courses, and independent study. The special courses enable students who excel to be challenged to their full intellectual capacity. The program is designed both to broaden and deepen the student's intellectual power. At the advanced level, honor students are encouraged to undertake faculty-guided independent research in their areas of special interest or competencies. These courses are conducted as seminars and involve topics at the forefront of current scientific interest. Students who excel in mathematics and physics, regardless of the major preference, are encouraged to enroll in these courses. The program also offers an opportunity for independent study for honor students whose interests lie beyond the topics ordinarily covered by the university program. **Disability Services:** Special programs offered to physically disabled students, including note-taking services, tutors. **Career Services:** Career/job search classes, Career assessment, Internships. Our University in addition to provide an academic experience to our students, we emphasize the

professional development. Over 50% of our students upon graduation already have work experience or already worked within their area of studies.

FACILITIES

Computers: 100% of classrooms, 100% of libraries, 100% of dining areas, 100% of student union, 100% of common outdoor areas have wireless network access.

CAMPUS LIFE

Environment: Metropolis. **Activities:** Choral groups, student government 20 registered organizations, 1 honor society, 1 religious organization. **Athletics (Intercollegiate):** *Men:* basketball, cross-country, martial arts, table tennis, tennis, track/field (outdoor), volleyball, wrestling. *Women:* cross-country, martial arts, table tennis, tennis, track/field (outdoor), volleyball.

ADMISSIONS

Freshman Academic Profile: Average high school GPA 3.2. 39% from public high schools. **Basis for Candidate Selection:** *Very important factors considered include:* academic GPA. *Other factors considered include:* standardized test scores. **Freshman Admission Requirements:** High school diploma is required and GED is accepted. *Academic units required:* 3 English, 3 math, 3 science, 3 foreign language, 3 social studies. **Freshman Admission Statistics:** 611 applied, 85.27% admitted, 83% enrolled. **Transfer Admission Requirements:** college transcript(s). **General Admission Information:** Application fee $30. Nonfall registration accepted. Admission may be deferred for a maximum of 2 trimesters.

COSTS AND FINANCIAL AID

Annual tuition $7,488. Room and board $11,857. Required fees $840. Average book expense $2,342. **Required Forms and Deadlines:** FAFSA. *Student Employment:* Federal Work-Study Program available. Institutional employment available. **Financial Aid Statistics:** 97% needy freshmen, 97% needy undergrads receive need-based scholarship or grant aid. 53% freshmen, 33% undergrads receive non-need-based scholarship or grant aid. 12% freshmen, 20% undergrads receive need-based self-help aid. 66% freshmen, 41% undergrads receive athletic scholarships. 91% freshmen, 90% undergrads receive any aid.

POMONA COLLEGE

333 N. College Way, Claremont, CA 91711-6312
Phone: 909-621-8134 • **Financial Aid Phone:** 909-621-8205
E-mail: admissions@pomona.edu • **CEEB Code:** 4607
Fax: 909-621-8952 • **Website:** www.pomona.edu • **ACT Code:** 372

This private school was founded in 1887. It has a 140-acre campus.

RATINGS

Admissions Selectivity Rating: 98   **Fire Safety Rating:** 93   **Green Rating:** 98

STUDENTS AND FACULTY

Enrollment: 1,642. **Student Body:** 51% female, 49% male, 69% out-of-state, 11% international (41 countries represented). Asian 14%, African American 8%, Caucasian 38%, Hispanic 15%, Native American <1%, Pacific Islander <1%, Two or more races 7%, Race unknown 5%. **Retention and Graduation:** 97% freshmen return for sophomore year. 92% freshmen graduate within 4 years. 97% freshmen graduate within 6 years. 20% grads go on to further study within 1 year. **Faculty:** Student/faculty ratio 8:1. 188 full-time faculty, 97% hold PhDs, 31% are are members of minority groups, 44% are women. 0% of classes are taught by teaching assistants.

ACADEMICS

Degrees: bachelor's. **Classes:** Most classes have 10-19 students. Most lab/discussion sessions have 10-19 students. **Most popular majors:** Neuroscience; Mathematics; Economics. **Special Study Options:** cross-registration, double major, exchange student program (domestic), independent study, internships, student-designed major, study abroad, The college has a 3-2 combined Bachelors (BA & BS) in Engineering with Washington University in St. Louis and the California Institute of Technology. Combined degree programs: Combined BA/BS in engineering with Caltech, Washington University in St. Louis, and Dartmouth College. **Disability Services:** Special programs offered to physically disabled students, including note-taking services, reader services, tape recorders, tutors. **Career Services:** Alumni network, Alumni services, Career/job search classes, Career assessment, Internships, Regional alumni. Pomona College Internship Program (PCIP): Students receive school credit for having a part-time internship over the course of a semester, totaling at minimum 60 hours. They can choose from a list of local internship options coordinated through our Career Development Office. Students submit a written evaluation at the end of the semester.

FACILITIES

Housing: Coed dorms, Theme Housing, Language Residence Hall. 85% of campus accessible to physically diasbled. **Special Academic Facilities/Equipment:** Oldenborg Center for Foreign Languages, Musuem of Art, Brackett Observatory **Computers:** 75% of classrooms, 50% of dorms, 100% of libraries, 100% of dining areas, 100% of student union, 100% of common outdoor areas have wireless network access. Administrative functions (other than registration) can be performed online.

CAMPUS LIFE

Environment: Town. **Activities:** Choral groups, concert band, dance, drama/theater, jazz band, literary magazine, music ensembles, musical theater, pep band, radio station, student government, student newspaper, student-run film society, symphony orchestra, television station, yearbook, Campus Ministries, Student Organization, Model UN. 280 registered organizations, 3 honor societies, 5 religious organizations. 3 fraternities. **Athletics (Intercollegiate):** *Men:* baseball, basketball, cross-country, diving, football, golf, soccer, swimming, tennis, track/field (outdoor), water polo. *Women:* basketball, cross-country, diving, golf, lacrosse, soccer, softball, swimming, tennis, track/field (outdoor), volleyball, water polo. **On-Campus Highlights:** Smith Campus Center, Sontag Greek Theater, Rains Center for Sports and Recreation, Brackett Observatory **Environmental Initiatives:** Pomona's Environmental Analysis Program incorporates sustainability across the curriculum in a variety of disciplines. The program offers 11 tracks within its major and minor, allowing students to focus on sustainability in a variety of natural science, social science, and humanities subjects. Sustainability is well incorporated across the curriculum.

ADMISSIONS

Freshman Academic Profile: 91% in top 10% of high school class, 99% in top 25% of high school class, 100% in top 50% of high school class. 68% from public high schools. **Reported SAT (pre-2016 redesign) scores:** SAT Math middle 50% range 690-770. SAT Critical Reading middle 50% range 690-770. SAT Writing middle 50% range 690-780. **Concordant SAT scores:** SAT EBRW middle 50% 730–780. SAT Math middle 50% range 720–780. ACT middle 50% range 31-34. Minimum internet-based TOEFL 100. Minimum paper TOEFL 600. **Basis for Candidate Selection:** *Very important factors considered include:* rigor of secondary school record, class rank, academic GPA, standardized test scores, application essay, recommendation(s), extracurricular activities, talent/ability, character/personal qualities. *Important factors considered include:* interview. *Other factors considered include:* first generation, alumni/ae relation, racial/ethnic status, volunteer work, work experience. **Freshman Admission Requirements:** High school diploma or equivalent is not required. *Academic units required:* 4 English, 4 math, 2 science, 2 science labs, 3 foreign language, 2 social studies. *Academic units recommended:* 4 English, 4 math, 4 science, 3 science labs, 4 foreign language, 4 social studies. **Freshman Admission Statistics:** 7,727 applied, 12.19% admitted, 48% enrolled. **Transfer Admission Requirements:** High school transcript, college transcript(s), essay or personal statement, standardized test scores, statement of good standing from prior institution(s). Lowest grade transferable C. **General Admission Information:** Application fee $70. Regular application deadline 1/1. Regular notification 4/1. Nonfall registration not accepted. Admission may be deferred for a maximum of 1 year.

COSTS AND FINANCIAL AID

Annual tuition $47,280. Room and board $15,150. Required fees $340. Average book expense $900. **Required Forms and Deadlines:** FAFSA, CSS/Financial Aid PROFILE, Noncustodial PROFILE, Business/Farm Supplement. **Notification of Awards:** Applicants will be notified of awards on or about 4/1. **Types of Aid:** *Need-based scholarships/grants:* Federal Pell, FSEOG, State scholarships/grants, Private scholarships, College/university scholarship or grant aid from institutional funds. *Loans:* Direct Subsidized Stafford Loans, Direct Unsubsidized Stafford Loans, Direct PLUS loans, College/university loans from institutional funds. *Student Employment:* Federal Work-Study Program available. Institutional employment available. **Financial Aid Statistics:** 100% needy freshmen, 100% needy undergrads receive need-based scholarship or grant aid. 0% undergrads receive non-need-based scholarship or grant aid. 100% freshmen, 100% undergrads receive need-based self-help aid. 0% freshmen, 0% undergrads receive athletic scholarships. 58% freshmen, 54% undergrads receive any aid.

PONTIFICAL COLLEGE JOSEPHINUM

7625 North High Street, Columbus, OH 43235-1498
Phone: 614-885-5585 • **Financial Aid Phone:** 614-885-5585
E-mail: admissions@pcj.edu
Fax: 614-885-2307

This private school, affiliated with the Roman Catholic Church, affiliated with the Seminarian Church, was founded in 1888. It has a 100-acre campus.

RATINGS

Admissions Selectivity Rating: 81   **Fire Safety Rating:** 60*   **Green Rating:** 60*

STUDENTS AND FACULTY

Enrollment: 78. **Student Body:** 0% female, 100% male, 64% out-of-state, 8% international (15 countries represented). Asian 1%, African American 0%, Caucasian 79%, Hispanic 10%, Native American 1%, Pacific Islander 0%, Two or more races 0%, Race unknown 0%.
Retention and Graduation: 92% freshmen return for sophomore year. 63% freshmen graduate within 4 years. 62% freshmen graduate within 6 years. 95% grads go on to further study within 1 year. 5% grads pursue arts and sciences degrees. **Faculty:** Student/faculty ratio 4:1. 17 full-time faculty, 76% hold PhDs, 0% are are members of minority groups, 35% are women. 0% of classes are taught by teaching assistants.

ACADEMICS

Degrees: bachelor's, master's. **Classes:** Most classes have 10-19 students. **Special Study Options:** cross-registration, double major, honors program, independent study. **Career Services:** On-campus interviews.

FACILITIES

Housing: men's dorms.

CAMPUS LIFE

Environment: Metropolis. **Activities:** Choral groups. 1 religious organization.

ADMISSIONS

Freshman Academic Profile: 25% in top 10% of high school class, 35% in top 25% of high school class, 60% in top 50% of high school class. **Reported SAT (pre-2016 redesign) scores:** SAT Math middle 50% range 360-610. SAT Critical Reading middle 50% range 380-600. SAT Writing middle 50% range 350-610. **Concordant SAT scores:** SAT EBRW middle 50% 410–660. SAT Math middle 50% range 400–630. ACT middle 50% range 17-25. Minimum paper TOEFL 550. **Basis for Candidate Selection:** *Very important factors considered include:* rigor of secondary school record, standardized test scores, recommendation(s), religious affiliation/commitment. *Important factors considered include:* academic GPA, application essay, interview. *Other factors considered include:* class rank, extracurricular activities, talent/ability, character/personal qualities, volunteer work. **Freshman Admission Requirements:** High school diploma is required and GED is accepted. *Academic units required:* 4 English, 2 math, 1 science, 1 foreign language, 2 social studies. *Academic units recommended:* 4 math, 4 science, 2 foreign language, 4 social studies. **Freshman Admission Statistics:** 8 applied, 75.00% admitted, 100% enrolled. **Transfer Admission Requirements:** High school transcript, college transcript(s), essay or personal statement, interview, standardized test scores, Lowest grade transferable C. **General Admission Information:** Application fee $25. Priority deadline 7/31. Nonfall registration not accepted.

COSTS AND FINANCIAL AID

Annual tuition $16,701. Room and board $7,908. Required fees $720. Average book expense $1,100. **Required Forms and Deadlines:** FAFSA, Institution's own financial aid form. **Types of Aid:** *Need-based scholarships/grants:* Federal Pell, FSEOG, State scholarships/grants, Private scholarships, College/university scholarship or grant aid from institutional funds. *Loans:* Federal Perkins Loans. *Student Employment:* Federal Work-Study Program available. **Financial Aid Statistics:** 83% needy undergrads receive need-based scholarship or grant aid. 0% undergrads receive non-need-based scholarship or grant aid. 100% freshmen, 33% undergrads receive need-based self-help aid. 0% freshmen, 0% undergrads receive athletic scholarships. **Criteria for awarding aid:** *Need-based:* Academics. *Non-need-based:* Academics.

PORTLAND STATE UNIVERSITY

Best Colleges

Office of Admissions, Portland, OR 97207-0751
Phone: 503-725-3511 • **Financial Aid Phone:** 800-547-8887
E-mail: admissions@pdx.edu • **CEEB Code:** 4610
Fax: 503-725-5525 • **Website:** http://www.pdx.edu/ • **ACT Code:** 3492

This public school was founded in 1946. It has a 49-acre campus.

RATINGS

Admissions Selectivity Rating: 79   **Fire Safety Rating:** 73   **Green Rating:** 98

STUDENTS AND FACULTY

Enrollment: 19,119. **Student Body:** 53% female, 47% male, 17% out-of-state, 5% international (94 countries represented). Asian 9%, African American 4%, Caucasian 57%, Hispanic 13%, Native American 1%, Pacific Islander 1%, Two or more races 6%, Race unknown 4%.
Retention and Graduation: 73% freshmen return for sophomore year. 18% freshmen graduate within 4 years. 47% freshmen graduate within 6 years. **Faculty:** Student/faculty ratio 20:1. 889 full-time faculty, 74% hold PhDs, 18% are are members of minority groups, 47% are women. 5% of classes are taught by teaching assistants.

ACADEMICS

Degrees: bachelor's, certificate, doctoral/research, master's, postbachelor's certificate, post-master's certificate. **Classes:** Most classes have 10-19 students. Most lab/discussion sessions have 10-19 students. **Most popular majors:** Psychology; Business/Commerce; Social Sciences. **Special Study Options:** Accelerated program, cooperative education program, cross-registration, distance learning, double major, English as a Second Language (ESL), exchange student program (domestic), honors program, independent study, internships, study abroad, teacher certification program, Haystack Summer Program in the Arts and Sciences. **Honors Programs:** University Honors Program. **Disability Services:** Special programs offered to physically disabled students, including note-taking services, reader services, tape recorders, tutors. **Career Services:** Alumni network, Alumni services, Career/job search classes, Career assessment, Internships, On-campus interviews. The Senior Capstone's purpose is to further enhance student learning while cultivating crucial life abilities that are important both academically and professionally; establishing connections within the larger community, developing strategies for analyzing and addressing problems, and working with others trained in fields different from one's own. This 6-credit, community-based learning course is designed to provide students with the opportunity to apply, in a team context, what they have learned in the major and in their other University Studies courses to a real challenge emanating from the metropolitan community.

FACILITIES

Housing: Coed dorms, special housing for disabled students, special housing for international students, fraternity/sorority housing, apartments for married students, apartments for single students, Special housing for new students. Apartments for students with dependent children. 95% of campus accessible to physically diasbled. **Special Academic Facilities/Equipment:** Art galleries, audiovisual resources, classroom multimedia computer systems, learning lab, child development center, native american center. **Computers:** 50% of dorms, 100% of libraries, 100% of dining areas, 100% of student union, have wireless network access. Students can register for classes online. Administrative functions (other than registration) can be performed online.

CAMPUS LIFE

Environment: Metropolis. **Activities:** Choral groups, concert band, dance, drama/theater, jazz band, literary magazine, music ensembles, musical theater, opera, pep band, radio station, student government, student newspaper, student-run film society, symphony orchestra, Campus Ministries, Student Organization, Model UN. 200 registered organizations, 10 honor societies, 14 religious organizations. 4 fraternities, 4 sororities. **Athletics (Intercollegiate):** *Men:* basketball, cross-country, football, tennis, track/field (outdoor), track/field (indoor). *Women:* basketball, cross-country, golf, soccer, softball, tennis, track/field (outdoor), track/field (indoor), volleyball. **On-Campus Highlights:** Park Blocks, Student Union Center **Environmental Initiatives:** Since 2002 PSU has focused on designing new buildings and retrofitting and renovating older campus buildings with sustainability in mind. Several PSU buildings serve as models of these kinds of innovative sustainable design and construction projects. These include the new Engineering Building, Broadway Housing Building, Stephen Epler Hall, and Native American Student and Community Center. In all but the latter, the US Green Building Council's LEED certification program was used as the measuring stick and standard for sustainable design and construction.

ADMISSIONS

Freshman Academic Profile: Average high school GPA 3.4. 11% in top 10% of high school class, 39% in top 25% of high school class, 83% in top 50% of high school class. 85% from public high schools. **Reported SAT (pre-2016 redesign) scores:** SAT Math middle 50% range 460-570. SAT Critical Reading middle 50% range 470-590. SAT Writing middle 50% range 440-570. **Concordant SAT scores:** SAT EBRW middle 50% 510–640. SAT Math middle 50% range 500–590. ACT middle 50% range 19-25. Minimum internet-based TOEFL 60. Minimum paper TOEFL 527. **Basis for Candidate Selection:** *Very important factors considered include:* rigor of secondary school record, academic GPA. *Other factors considered include:* standardized test scores, application essay. **Freshman Admission Requirements:** High school diploma is required and GED is accepted. *Academic units required:* 4 English, 3 math, 2 science, 2 foreign language, 2 social studies, 1 history. *Academic units recommended:* 1 science labs. **Freshman Admission Statistics:** 6,373 applied, 89.42% admitted, 32% enrolled. **Transfer Admission Requirements:** college transcript(s), Minimum college GPA of 2.25 required. Lowest grade transferable D-. **General Admission Information:** Application fee $50. Priority deadline 6/1. Nonfall registration accepted. Admission may be deferred for a maximum of One Year.

COSTS AND FINANCIAL AID

Annual in-state tuition $5,616. Annual out-of-state tuition $18,828. Room and board $12,822. Required fees $1,317. Average book expense $1,263. **Required Forms and Deadlines:** FAFSA. **Notification of Awards:** Applicants will be notified of awards on a rolling basis beginning 3/15. **Types of Aid:** *Need-based scholarships/grants:* Federal Pell, FSEOG, State scholarships/grants, Private scholarships, College/university scholarship or grant aid from institutional funds, United Negro College Fund. *Loans:* Direct Subsidized Stafford Loans, Direct Unsubsidized Stafford Loans, Direct PLUS loans, Federal Perkins Loans. *Student Employment:* Federal Work-Study Program available. Institutional employment available. **Financial Aid Statistics:** 73% needy freshmen, 78% needy undergrads receive need-based scholarship or grant aid. 2% freshmen, 1% undergrads receive non-need-based scholarship or grant aid. 73% freshmen, 79% undergrads receive need-based self-help aid. 1% freshmen, 1% undergrads receive athletic scholarships. 75% freshmen, 56% undergrads receive any aid. Average cumulative indebtedness $32,018. **Criteria for awarding aid:** *Need-based:* Academics, Alumni affiliation, Art, Athletics, Leadership, Minority status, Music/drama. *Non-need-based:* Academics, Alumni affiliation, Art, Athletics, Leadership, Minority status, Music/drama, State/district residency.

PRAIRIE VIEW A&M UNIVERSITY

PO Box 519, Prairie View, TX 77446
Phone: 936-261-3500 • **Financial Aid Phone:** 1-877-782-6830
E-mail: admissions@pvamu.edu • **CEEB Code:** 6580
Website: www.pvamu.edu • **ACT Code:** 4202

This public school was founded in 1876. It has a 1388-acre campus.

RATINGS

Admissions Selectivity Rating: 78   **Fire Safety Rating:** 82   **Green Rating:** 60*

STUDENTS AND FACULTY

Enrollment: 6,969. **Student Body:** 58% female, 42% male, 7% out-of-state, 1% international (40 countries represented). Asian 2%, African American 88%, Caucasian 3%, Hispanic 5%, Native American <1%, Pacific Islander 0%, Two or more races 0%, Race unknown 1%.
Retention and Graduation: 71% freshmen return for sophomore year. 12% freshmen graduate within 4 years. 32% freshmen graduate within 6 years. **Faculty:** Student/faculty ratio 17:1. 394 full-time faculty, 67% hold PhDs, 80% are are members of minority groups, 39% are women.

ACADEMICS

Degrees: bachelor's, doctoral, master's. **Most popular majors:** Multi-/Interdisciplinary Studies; Business Administration and Management. **Special Study Options:** Accelerated program, cooperative education program, distance learning, double major, dual enrollment, English as a Second Language (ESL), honors program, independent study, internships, liberal arts/career combination, study abroad, teacher certification program, weekend college. **Disability Services:** Special programs offered to physically disabled students, including tape recorders, tutors. **Career Services:** Alumni network, Alumni services, Career assessment, Internships, Regional alumni, On-campus interviews.

FACILITIES

Housing: Coed dorms, special housing for disabled students, apartments for single students. 90% of campus accessible to physically diasbled. **Computers:** 100% of classrooms, 100% of dorms, 100% of libraries, 75% of dining areas, 75% of student union, 50% of common outdoor areas have wireless network access. Students can register for classes online.

CAMPUS LIFE

Environment: Rural. **Activities:** Choral groups, concert band, dance, drama/theater, jazz band, marching band, music ensembles, radio station, student government, student newspaper, symphony orchestra, television station, yearbook, Campus Ministries, Student Organization. 100 registered organizations, 15 honor societies, 6 religious organizations. 9 fraternities, 9 sororities. **Athletics (Intercollegiate):** *Men:* baseball, basketball, cross-country, football, golf, tennis, track/field (outdoor), track/field (indoor). *Women:* basketball, cheerleading, cross-country, golf, soccer, softball, tennis, track/field (outdoor), track/field (indoor), volleyball. **On-Campus Highlights:** Purple Zone Student Sports Bar, Memorial Student Center, Baby Dome, J.B. Coleman Library, Jazzman Coffee Cafe, University College and University Village.

ADMISSIONS

Freshman Academic Profile: Average high school GPA 2.9. 5% in top 10% of high school class, 21% in top 25% of high school class, 56% in top 50% of high school class. **Reported SAT (pre-2016 redesign) scores:** SAT Math middle 50% range 380-440. SAT Critical Reading middle 50% range 370-450. SAT Writing middle 50% range 360-440. **Concordant SAT scores:** SAT EBRW middle 50% 410–500. SAT Math middle 50% range 420–480. ACT middle 50% range 15-19. Minimum paper TOEFL 500. **Basis for Candidate Selection:** *Very important factors considered include:* academic GPA, standardized test scores. *Important factors considered include:* rigor of secondary school record. *Other factors considered include:* extracurricular activities, character/personal qualities, first generation, volunteer work, work experience. **Freshman Admission Requirements:** High school diploma is required and GED is accepted. *Academic units required:* 4 English, 3 math, 2 science, 1 computer science, 1 visual/performing arts. *Academic units recommended:* 4 English, 4 math, 4 science, 2 foreign language, 1 computer science. **Freshman Admission Statistics:** 7,931 applied, 41.57% admitted, 52% enrolled. **Transfer Admission Requirements:** college transcript(s), statement of good standing from prior institution(s). Minimum college GPA of 2.0 required. Lowest grade transferable C. **General Admission Information:** Application fee $25. Priority deadline 6/1. Regular application deadline 6/1. Nonfall registration accepted. Admission may be deferred.

COSTS AND FINANCIAL AID

Annual in-state tuition $5,076. Annual out-of-state tuition $14,376. Room and board $7,064. Required fees $1,779. Average book expense $1,000. **Required Forms and Deadlines:** FAFSA, Institution's own financial aid form. **Notification of Awards:** Applicants will be notified of awards on or about 6/1. **Types of Aid:** *Need-based scholarships/grants:* Federal Pell, FSEOG, State scholarships/grants, Private scholarships, College/university scholarship or grant aid from institutional funds, United Negro College Fund. *Loans:* Direct Subsidized Stafford Loans, Direct Unsubsidized Stafford Loans, Direct PLUS loans, Federal Perkins Loans, College/university loans from institutional funds. *Student Employment:* Federal Work-Study Program available. Institutional employment available. **Financial Aid Statistics:** 69% needy freshmen, 63% needy undergrads receive need-based scholarship or grant aid. 35% freshmen, 18% undergrads receive non-need-based scholarship or grant aid. 94% freshmen, 90% undergrads receive need-based self-help aid. 1% freshmen, 4% undergrads receive athletic scholarships. 61% freshmen, 53% undergrads receive any aid. **Criteria for awarding aid:** *Need-based:* Academics, Athletics. *Non-need-based:* Academics, Athletics, State/district residency.

PRATT INSTITUTE

200 Willoughby Avenue, Brooklyn, NY 11205
Phone: 718-636-3514 • **Financial Aid Phone:** 718-636-3599
E-mail: admissions@pratt.edu • **CEEB Code:** 2669
Fax: 718-636-3670 • **Website:** http://www.pratt.edu • **ACT Code:** 2862

This private school was founded in 1887. It has a 25-acre campus.

RATINGS

Admissions Selectivity Rating: 83 **Fire Safety Rating:** 76 **Green Rating:** 66

STUDENTS AND FACULTY

Enrollment: 3,271. **Student Body:** 69% female, 31% male, 71% out-of-state, 27% international (78 countries represented). Asian 14%, African American 4%, Caucasian 41%, Hispanic 10%, Native American <1%, Pacific Islander <1%, Two or more races 3%, Race unknown 1%.

Retention and Graduation: 87% freshmen return for sophomore year. **Faculty:** Student/faculty ratio 10:1. 149 full-time faculty, 77% hold PhDs, 19% are are members of minority groups, 46% are women. 0% of classes are taught by teaching assistants.

ACADEMICS

Degrees: associate, bachelor's, master's, post-master's certificate, terminal, transfer. **Classes:** Most classes have 10-19 students. **Most popular majors:** Design and Visual Communications; Architecture; Fine/Studio Arts. **Special Study Options:** English as a Second Language (ESL), exchange student program (domestic), independent study, internships, study abroad, teacher certification program. Combined degree programs: BA/MA, art history/fine art, digital art/library science. **Disability Services:** Special programs offered to physically disabled students, including note-taking services, reader services, tutors. **Career Services:** Alumni network, Alumni services, Career/job search classes, Career assessment, Internships. As part of the internship program, students can become involved with community matters, contributing their design skills to a community program.

FACILITIES

Housing: Coed dorms, special housing for disabled students, special housing for international students, apartments for single students, Wellness HousingGlobal Learning (for international and domestic students), Healthy Choice and Quiet Floors are available. **Special Academic Facilities/Equipment:** Five art galleries, fine arts center, printmaking center, computer graphics lab. **Computers:** Undergraduates are required to own a computer.

CAMPUS LIFE

Environment: Metropolis. **Activities:** literary magazine, music ensembles, radio station, student government, student newspaper, student-run film society, television station, yearbook, Campus Ministries, Student Organization. 50 registered organizations, 4 honor societies, 3 religious organizations. 3 fraternities, 1 sorority. **Athletics (Intercollegiate):** *Men:* basketball, cross-country, soccer, tennis, track/field (outdoor), track/field (indoor). *Women:* basketball, cross-country, soccer, tennis, track/field (outdoor), volleyball. **On-Campus Highlights:** studios, galleries, three cafeterias/coffee shops, athletic center, student union, Pratt is the only East Coast art school with a traditional campus (25 acres). **Environmental Initiatives:** Our new building, Myrtle Hall is LEED gold.

ADMISSIONS

Freshman Academic Profile: Average high school GPA 3.7. 70% from public high schools. **Reported SAT (pre-2016 redesign) scores:** SAT Math middle 50% range 550-670. SAT Critical Reading middle 50% range 540-640. SAT Writing middle 50% range 540-640. **Concordant SAT scores:** SAT EBRW middle 50% 600–690. SAT Math middle 50% range 570–700. ACT middle 50% range 25-30. Minimum paper TOEFL 550. **Basis for Candidate Selection:** *Very important factors considered include:* rigor of secondary school record, academic GPA, standardized test scores, talent/ability. *Important factors considered include:* application essay, character/personal qualities, alumni/ae relation, level of applicant's interest. *Other factors considered include:* class rank, interview, extracurricular activities, volunteer work, work experience. **Freshman Admission Requirements:** High school diploma is required and GED is accepted. *Academic units recommended:* 4 English, 1 social studies. **Freshman Admission Statistics:** 5,711 applied, 51.83% admitted, 24% enrolled. **Transfer Admission Requirements:** High school transcript, college transcript(s), essay or personal statement, statement of good standing from prior institution(s). Lowest grade transferable C. **General Admission Information:** Application fee $50. Regular application deadline 1/5. Regular notification 4/1. Nonfall registration accepted. Admission may be deferred for a maximum of 1 year.

COSTS AND FINANCIAL AID

Annual tuition $47,986. Room and board $12,020. Required fees $2,052. Average book expense $1,750. **Required Forms and Deadlines:** FAFSA, State aid form. **Types of Aid:** *Need-based scholarships/grants:* Federal Pell, FSEOG, State scholarships/grants, College/university scholarship or grant aid from institutional funds. *Loans:* Direct Subsidized Stafford Loans, Direct Unsubsidized Stafford Loans, Direct PLUS loans, Federal Perkins Loans. *Student Employment:* Federal Work-Study Program available. Institutional employment available. **Financial Aid Statistics:** 54% needy undergrads receive need-based scholarship or grant aid. 99% freshmen, 86% undergrads receive non-need-based scholarship or grant aid. 100% freshmen, 60% undergrads receive need-based self-help aid. 0% freshmen, 0% undergrads receive athletic scholarships. 92% freshmen, 83% undergrads receive any aid. Average cumulative indebtedness $7,427. **Criteria for awarding aid:** *Need-based:* Academics. *Non-need-based:* Academics.

PRESBYTERIAN COLLEGE

503 South Broad Street, Clinton, SC 29325
Phone: 864-833-8230 • **Financial Aid Phone:** 864-833-8287
E-mail: admissions@presby.edu • **CEEB Code:** 5540
Fax: 864-833-8195 • **Website:** www.presby.edu • **ACT Code:** 3874

This private school, affiliated with the Presbyterian Church, affiliated with the Presbyterian USA Church, was founded in 1880. It has a 240-acre campus.

RATINGS
Admissions Selectivity Rating: 86 Fire Safety Rating: 97 Green Rating: 60*

STUDENTS AND FACULTY
Enrollment: 963. **Student Body:** 52% female, 48% male, 65% out-of-state, 1% international (23 countries represented). Asian 1%, African American 14%, Caucasian 77%, Hispanic 3%, Native American <1%, Pacific Islander 0%, Two or more races 2%, Race unknown 1%.
Retention and Graduation: 81% freshmen return for sophomore year. 70% freshmen graduate within 6 years. 28% grads go on to further study within 1 year. **Faculty:** Student/faculty ratio 12:1. 77 full-time faculty, 97% hold PhDs, 9% are are members of minority groups, 39% are women. 0% of classes are taught by teaching assistants.

ACADEMICS
Degrees: bachelor's, doctoral/professional. **Classes:** Most classes have 20-29 students. Most lab/discussion sessions have 20-29 students. **Most popular majors:** Business Administration and Management; Biology/Biological Sciences; Psychology. **Special Study Options:** double major, dual enrollment, exchange student program (domestic), honors program, independent study, internships, study abroad, teacher certification program, Program in forestry and environmental science, 3-2 engineering program. **Honors Programs:** A variety of opportunities are available to highly motivated students with above average abilities through the normal programs of the College. These include research, internships, special projects, and directed studies. Presbyterian College also offers a special honors program for students who are chosen on the basis of their demonstrated ability. Students with a 3.20 GPA in all courses and a 3.40 GPA in all courses in the major field may, with the approval of departmental faculty, undertake an honors research program during the junior and/or senior years. Oral and written presentations of the results of the project will be required. Students who successfully complete the departmental honors research program will graduate with honors in the major field. **Disability Services:** Special programs offered to physically disabled students, including tutors. **Career Services:** Alumni network, Alumni services, Career/job search classes, Career assessment, Internships, Regional alumni. Internship Program: Students of all disciplines are coordinated to participate in on-campus seminar sessions at the beginning, middle, and end of the semester to reflect/review, compare/contrast their internship experience as a group.

FACILITIES
Housing: Coed dorms, men's dorms, special housing for international students, women's dorms, fraternity/sorority housing, apartments for single students. Sorority housing is not available. 95% of campus accessible to physically diasbled. **Special Academic Facilities/Equipment:** Art gallery, recital hall, media center, marine/ecological center, scanning and transmission electron microscopes, visible spectrophotometer. **Computers:** 95% of classrooms, 100% of dorms, 100% of libraries, 100% of dining areas, 100% of student union, 50% of common outdoor areas have wireless network access. Students can register for classes online. Administrative functions (other than registration) can be performed online.

CAMPUS LIFE
Environment: Village. **Activities:** Choral groups, concert band, dance, drama/theater, jazz band, literary magazine, music ensembles, musical theater, opera, pep band, radio station, student government, student newspaper, symphony orchestra, yearbook, Campus Ministries. 85 registered organizations, 11 honor societies, 6 religious organizations. 6 fraternities, 3 sororities. **Athletics (Intercollegiate):** Men: baseball, basketball, cheerleading, cross-country, football, golf, lacrosse, soccer, tennis. Women: basketball, cheerleading, cross-country, golf, lacrosse, soccer, softball, tennis, volleyball. **On-Campus Highlights:** Inklings Coffee House, Bailey Stadium, Springs Campus Center, Harrington Peachtree Academic Building, Thompson Library, Inklings—hot spot for open mics and up and coming bands Springs Campus Center—workout facilities, Starbucks, WPCX, ping pong Harrington Peachtree Academic Building—commonly known as H-P it is an ideal study and gathering spot in the late night hours Thompson Library—with the new expansion and renovations to the existing facilities, the library has seen a Renaissance—comfy chairs and cozy corners offer students a relaxing atmosphere for studying and researching. **Environmental Initiatives:** Energy conservation.

ADMISSIONS
Freshman Academic Profile: Average high school GPA 3.5. 27% in top 10% of high school class, 56% in top 25% of high school class, 91% in top 50% of high school class. **Reported SAT (pre-2016 redesign) scores:** SAT Math middle 50% range 490-600. SAT Critical Reading middle 50% range 480-590. **Concordant SAT scores:** SAT Math middle 50% range 520–620. ACT middle 50% range 20-27. Minimum internet-based TOEFL 80. Minimum paper TOEFL 550. **Basis for Candidate Selection:** *Very important factors considered include:* rigor of secondary school record, class rank, academic GPA, application essay. *Important factors considered include:* recommendation(s), extracurricular activities, talent/ability, character/personal qualities. *Other factors considered include:* standardized test scores, interview, first generation, alumni/ae relation, volunteer work, work experience, level of applicant's interest. **Freshman Admission Requirements:** High school diploma is required and GED is accepted. *Academic units required:* 4 English, 4 math, 2 science, 2 science labs, 2 foreign language, 2 social studies, 2 history, 2 academic electives. *Academic units recommended:* 4 science. **Freshman Admission Statistics:** 2,072 applied, 62.31% admitted, 20% enrolled. **Transfer Admission Requirements:** High school transcript, college transcript(s), essay or personal statement, standardized test scores, statement of good standing from prior institution(s). Lowest grade transferable C. **General Admission Information:** Priority deadline 2/1. Regular application deadline 6/30. Regular notification 3/15. Nonfall registration accepted. Admission may be deferred for a maximum of 1 Year.

COSTS AND FINANCIAL AID
Annual tuition $33,200. Room and board $9,750. Required fees $2,930. Average book expense $1,200. **Required Forms and Deadlines:** FAFSA. **Notification of Awards:** Applicants will be notified of awards on a rolling basis beginning 3/1. **Types of Aid:** *Need-based scholarships/grants:* Federal Pell, FSEOG, State scholarships/grants, Private scholarships, College/university scholarship or grant aid from institutional funds. *Loans:* Direct Subsidized Stafford Loans, Direct Unsubsidized Stafford Loans, Direct PLUS loans, Federal Perkins Loans, State Loans, College/university loans from institutional funds. *Student Employment:* Federal Work-Study Program available. **Financial Aid Statistics:** 100% needy freshmen, 100% needy undergrads receive need-based scholarship or grant aid. 52% freshmen, 36% undergrads receive non-need-based scholarship or grant aid. 63% freshmen, 100% undergrads receive need-based self-help aid. 7% freshmen, 8% undergrads receive athletic scholarships. 80% freshmen, 77% undergrads receive any aid. 61% undergrads borrow to pay for school. Average cumulative indebtedness $27,169. **Criteria for awarding aid:** *Need-based:* Alumni affiliation, Art, Job skills, Leadership, Minority status, Music/drama, Religious affiliation. *Non-need-based:* Academics, Alumni affiliation, Athletics, Job skills, Leadership, Minority status, Music/drama, Religious affiliation, State/district residency.

PRESCOTT COLLEGE

220 Grove Avenue, Prescott, AZ 86301
Phone: 928-350-2100 x 2100 • **Financial Aid Phone:** 928-350-1112
E-mail: admissions@prescott.edu • **CEEB Code:** 9295
Fax: 928-776-5242 • **Website:** www.prescott.edu • **ACT Code:** 5022

This private school was founded in 1966. It has a 6-acre campus.

RATINGS
Admissions Selectivity Rating: 84 Fire Safety Rating: 78 Green Rating: 60*

STUDENTS AND FACULTY
Enrollment: 350. **Student Body:** 60% female, 40% male, 72% out-of-state, 1% international (11 countries represented). Asian 1%, African American 1%, Caucasian 71%, Hispanic 7%, Native American 4%, Pacific Islander 0%, Two or more races 7%, Race unknown 8%.
Retention and Graduation: 71% freshmen return for sophomore year. 44% freshmen graduate within 4 years. 49% freshmen graduate within 6 years.
Faculty: Student/faculty ratio 9:1. 66 full-time faculty, 56% hold PhDs, 15% are are members of minority groups, 58% are women. 0% of classes are taught by teaching assistants.

ACADEMICS
Degrees: bachelor's, doctoral/research, master's, postbachelor's certificate, post-master's certificate. **Classes:** Most classes have 10-19 students. **Most popular majors:** Elementary Education and Teaching; Environmental Studies;

Education. **Special Study Options:** cross-registration, double major, exchange student program (domestic), external degree program, independent study, internships, liberal arts/career combination, student-designed major, teacher certification program, Dual Credit. **Disability Services:** Special programs offered to physically disabled students, including note-taking services, tape recorders, tutors. **Career Services:** Alumni network, Alumni services, Career/job search classes, Career assessment, Regional alumni. One on one career development counseling.

FACILITIES

Housing: Coed dorms. 90% of campus accessible to physically disabled. **Special Academic Facilities/Equipment:** Wolfberry Farm: An experimental agroecology farm Kino Bay Center, MX: A field station on the Gulf of CA. Sam Hill Warehouse: Our visual arts center GIS Lab (Geographic Information Systems) Several Computer Labs Multi-Media Center **Computers:** 50% of classrooms, 100% of dorms, 100% of libraries, 100% of dining areas, 75% of common outdoor areas have wireless network access.

CAMPUS LIFE

Environment: Town. **Activities:** dance, drama/theater, literary magazine, radio station, student government, student newspaper, student-run film society, Student Organization. 18 registered organizations. **On-Campus Highlights:** Crossroads Cafe, Crossroads Library, HUB (Helping Understand Bikes), Sam Hill Visual Arts Building. **Environmental Initiatives:** ACUPCC commitment and Climate Action Plan.

ADMISSIONS

Freshman Academic Profile: Average high school GPA 3.2. 0% in top 10% of high school class, 0% in top 50% of high school class. 78% from public high schools. **Reported SAT (pre-2016 redesign) scores:** SAT Math middle 50% range 440-580. SAT Critical Reading middle 50% range 480-620. SAT Writing middle 50% range 460-570. **Concordant SAT scores:** SAT EBRW middle 50% 530–650. SAT Math middle 50% range 480–600. ACT middle 50% range 21-28. Minimum internet-based TOEFL 61. Minimum paper TOEFL 550. **Basis for Candidate Selection:** *Very important factors considered include:* rigor of secondary school record, application essay, recommendation(s). *Important factors considered include:* academic GPA, standardized test scores, interview, extracurricular activities, talent/ability, volunteer work, work experience, level of applicant's interest. *Other factors considered include:* character/personal qualities. **Freshman Admission Requirements:** High school diploma is required and GED is accepted. *Academic units recommended:* 4 English, 3 math, 2 science, 1 foreign language, 3 social studies, 1 visual/performing arts. **Freshman Admission Statistics:** 314 applied, 68.47% admitted, 22% enrolled. **Transfer Admission Requirements:** college transcript(s), essay or personal statement, Lowest grade transferable C. **General Admission Information:** Nonfall registration accepted. Admission may be deferred for a maximum of 2 terms.

COSTS AND FINANCIAL AID

Annual tuition $28,976. Room and board $10,140. Required fees $1,665. Average book expense $982. **Required Forms and Deadlines:** FAFSA. **Types of Aid:** *Need-based scholarships/grants:* Federal Pell, FSEOG, State scholarships/grants, Private scholarships, College/university scholarship or grant aid from institutional funds. *Loans:* Direct Subsidized Stafford Loans, Direct Unsubsidized Stafford Loans, Direct PLUS loans. *Student Employment:* Federal Work-Study Program available. Institutional employment available. **Financial Aid Statistics:** 100% needy freshmen, 100% needy undergrads receive need-based scholarship or grant aid. 4% freshmen, 5% undergrads receive non-need-based scholarship or grant aid. 96% freshmen, 95% undergrads receive need-based self-help aid. 0% freshmen, 0% undergrads receive athletic scholarships. 93% freshmen, 88% undergrads receive any aid. 72% undergrads borrow to pay for school. Average cumulative indebtedness $27,130. **Criteria for awarding aid:** *Non-need-based:* Academics, Leadership.

PRINCETON UNIVERSITY

PO Box 430, Princeton, NJ 08544-0430
Phone: 609-258-3060 • **Financial Aid Phone:** 609-258-3330
E-mail: uaoffice@princeton.edu • **CEEB Code:** 2672
Fax: 609-258-6743 • **Website:** www.princeton.edu • **ACT Code:** 2588

This private school was founded in 1746. It has a 500-acre campus.

RATINGS

Admissions Selectivity Rating: 99   **Fire Safety Rating:** 94   **Green Rating:** 86

STUDENTS AND FACULTY

Enrollment: 5,236. **Student Body:** 48% female, 52% male, 82% out-of-state, 12% international (92 countries represented). Asian 21%, African American 8%, Caucasian 44%, Hispanic 10%, Native American <1%, Pacific Islander <1%, Two or more races 4%, Race unknown 2%.
Retention and Graduation: 98% freshmen return for sophomore year. 89% freshmen graduate within 4 years. 97% freshmen graduate within 6 years.
Faculty: Student/faculty ratio 5:1. 924 full-time faculty, 93% hold PhDs, 23% are members of minority groups, 33% are women. 0% of classes are taught by teaching assistants.

ACADEMICS

Degrees: bachelor's, doctoral/research, master's. **Classes:** Most classes have 10-19 students. Most lab/discussion sessions have 10-19 students. **Most popular majors:** Computer Engineering; Public Administration; Economics. **Special Study Options:** cross-registration, exchange student program (domestic), independent study, student-designed major, study abroad, teacher certification program. **Disability Services:** Special programs offered to physically disabled students, including note-taking services, reader services, tape recorders. **Career Services:** Alumni network, Alumni services, Career/job search classes, Career assessment, Internships, Regional alumni.

FACILITIES

Housing: Coed dorms, special housing for disabled students, apartments for married students. **Special Academic Facilities/Equipment:** Art Museum, Natural history museum, energy and environmental studies center, plasma physics lab, Center for Jewish Life, Center for Human Values, Woodrow Wilson School of Public and International Affairs, etc. **Computers:** 100% of classrooms, 100% of dorms, 70% of libraries, 100% of dining areas, 100% of student union, 20% of common outdoor areas have wireless network access. Students can register for classes online. Administrative functions (other than registration) can be performed online.

CAMPUS LIFE

Environment: Town. **Activities:** Choral groups, concert band, dance, drama/theater, jazz band, literary magazine, marching band, music ensembles, musical theater, opera, pep band, radio station, student government, student newspaper, student-run film society, symphony orchestra, yearbook, Campus Ministries, Student Organization, Model UN. 250 registered organizations, 30 honor societies, 28 religious organizations. **Athletics (Intercollegiate):** *Men:* baseball, basketball, crew/rowing, cross-country, diving, fencing, football, golf, ice hockey, lacrosse, light weight football, soccer, squash, swimming, tennis, track/field (outdoor), track/field (indoor), volleyball, water polo, wrestling. *Women:* basketball, crew/rowing, cross-country, diving, fencing, field hockey, golf, ice hockey, lacrosse, soccer, softball, squash, swimming, tennis, track/field (outdoor), track/field (indoor), volleyball, water polo. **On-Campus Highlights:** Nassau Hall, Firestone Library, McCarter Theater, Princeton U. Art Museum, University Chapel, Frist Campus Center. **Environmental Initiatives:** Greenhouse Gas reduction goal: 1990 levels by 2020 through local verifiable action, while adding more than 1 million gross square feet of built area, and without the purchase of offsets. 5.3 megawatt solar PV installation to be installed on campus property by 2012.

ADMISSIONS

Freshman Academic Profile: Average high school GPA 3.9. 94% in top 10% of high school class, 99% in top 25% of high school class, 100% in top 50% of high school class. 60% from public high schools. **Reported SAT (pre-2016 redesign) scores:** SAT Math middle 50% range 710-800. SAT Critical Reading middle 50% range 690-790. SAT Writing middle 50% range 700-790. **Concordant SAT scores:** SAT EBRW middle 50% 730–800. SAT Math middle 50% range 740–800. ACT middle 50% range 32-35. Minimum paper TOEFL 600. **Basis for Candidate Selection:** *Very important factors considered include:* rigor of secondary school record, class rank, academic GPA, standardized test scores, application essay, recommendation(s), talent/

ability, character/personal qualities. *Important factors considered include:* extracurricular activities. *Other factors considered include:* interview, first generation, alumni/ae relation, geographical residence, racial/ethnic status, volunteer work, work experience, level of applicant's interest. **Freshman Admission Requirements:** High school diploma or equivalent is not required. *Academic units recommended:* 4 English, 4 math, 4 science, 2 science labs, 4 foreign language, 2 social studies, 2 history, 1 visual/performing arts. **Freshman Admission Statistics:** 29,303 applied, 6.52% admitted, 68% enrolled. **General Admission Information:** Application fee $65. Regular application deadline 1/1. Regular notification 3/31. Nonfall registration not accepted. Admission may be deferred for a maximum of 1 year.

COSTS AND FINANCIAL AID

Annual tuition $45,320. Room and board $14,770. Average book expense $1,050. **Required Forms and Deadlines:** FAFSA, Institution's own financial aid form. **Notification of Awards:** Applicants will be notified of awards on or about 4/1. *Types of Aid: Need-based scholarships/grants:* Federal Pell, FSEOG, State scholarships/grants, Private scholarships, College/university scholarship or grant aid from institutional funds. *Loans:* Direct Subsidized Stafford Loans, Direct Unsubsidized Stafford Loans, Direct PLUS loans, Federal Nursing Loans, College/university loans from institutional funds. *Student Employment:* Federal Work-Study Program available. Institutional employment available. **Financial Aid Statistics:** 100% needy freshmen, 100% needy undergrads receive need-based scholarship or grant aid. 0% undergrads receive non-need-based scholarship or grant aid. 100% freshmen, 100% undergrads receive need-based self-help aid. 0% freshmen, 0% undergrads receive athletic scholarships. 59% freshmen, 59% undergrads receive any aid. 18% undergrads borrow to pay for school. Average cumulative indebtedness $8,908.

See page 1014.

PRINCIPIA COLLEGE

1 Maybeck Place, Elsah, IL 62028
Phone: 618-374-5181 • **Financial Aid Phone:** 618-374-5628
E-mail: collegeadmissions@principia.edu • **CEEB Code:** 1630
Fax: 618-374-4000 • **Website:** www.principiacollege.edu • **ACT Code:** 1118

This private school, affiliated with the Christian Science Church, was founded in 1898. It has a 2600-acre campus.

RATINGS

Admissions Selectivity Rating: 83   Fire Safety Rating: 92   Green Rating: 79

STUDENTS AND FACULTY

Enrollment: 447. **Student Body:** 50% female, 50% male, 90% out-of-state, 16% international (28 countries represented). Asian 1%, African American 2%, Caucasian 73%, Hispanic 4%, Native American <1%, Pacific Islander <1%, Two or more races 2%, Race unknown 2%.
Retention and Graduation: 88% freshmen return for sophomore year. 71% freshmen graduate within 4 years. 80% freshmen graduate within 6 years.
Faculty: Student/faculty ratio 8:1. 60 full-time faculty, 65% hold PhDs, 3% are are members of minority groups, 47% are women. 0% of classes are taught by teaching assistants.

ACADEMICS

Degrees: bachelor's. **Classes:** Most classes have 10-19 students. **Most popular majors:** Business Administration and Management; Education; Mass Communication/Media Studies. **Special Study Options:** double major, independent study, internships, liberal arts/career combination, student-designed major, study abroad, teacher certification program, 3-2 Engineering with Washington University (St. Louis, MO), USC (Los Angeles), and Southern Illinois University (SIU) in Edwardsville, IL. **Honors Programs:** One honors program of three courses is taught in conjunction with our First Year Experience Program (FYE). **Career Services:** Alumni network, Career/job search classes, Career assessment, Internships, Regional alumni.

FACILITIES

Housing: men's dorms, women's dorms, apartments for married studentsHouses with single-sex wings (one side for men and one side for women) and a common living room. This is not really considered "coed" because there are no shared bathrooms or men and women living together on the same floor or on alternate floors. Cottages (for 8 people) are available for non-traditionally aged students, special programs, or theme houses. 80% of campus accessible to physically diasbled. **Special Academic Facilities/Equipment:** Science Center with indoor aviary, School of Nations Museum and Classrooms, Voney Art Studio, School of Government, Merrick Wing for Performing Arts.

CAMPUS LIFE

Environment: Rural. **Activities:** Choral groups, dance, drama/theater, jazz band, music ensembles, musical theater, radio station, student government, student newspaper, television station, yearbook. 29 registered organizations, 1 honor society, 1 religious organization. **Athletics (Intercollegiate):** *Men:* baseball, basketball, cross-country, diving, football, soccer, swimming, tennis, track/field (outdoor), track/field (indoor). *Women:* basketball, cross-country, diving, soccer, swimming, tennis, track/field (outdoor), track/field (indoor), volleyball. **On-Campus Highlights:** Piasa Pub, Hay Field House, Planetarium, Science Center, Chapel, By January, 2007 a new 68,000 square foot athletic training center will be built. This includes two regulation-size basketball courts and 200 meter indoor track. Also part of the facility will be a 6-lane 25-meter natatorium with four diving boards and am adjacent well-appointed fitness center. **Environmental Initiatives:** 100% renewable energy (electricity)—recognized as a Gold Partner by the US Environmental Protection Agency's "Green Power Partnership."

ADMISSIONS

Freshman Academic Profile: Average high school GPA 3.4. 21% in top 10% of high school class, 32% in top 25% of high school class, 84% in top 50% of high school class. 53% from public high schools. **Reported SAT (pre-2016 redesign) scores:** SAT Math middle 50% range 470-608. SAT Critical Reading middle 50% range 460-590. SAT Writing middle 50% range 460-568. **Concordant SAT scores:** SAT EBRW middle 50% range 510–640. SAT Math middle 50% range 510–630. ACT middle 50% range 21-27. Minimum internet-based TOEFL 79. **Basis for Candidate Selection:** *Very important factors considered include:* academic GPA, application essay, recommendation(s), character/personal qualities, religious affiliation/commitment. *Important factors considered include:* rigor of secondary school record, standardized test scores, interview, extracurricular activities, talent/ability. *Other factors considered include:* class rank, alumni/ae relation, volunteer work, work experience. **Freshman Admission Requirements:** High school diploma is required and GED is accepted. *Academic units required:* 4 English, 3 math, 3 science, 1 science lab, 2 foreign language, 2 social studies, 1 history, 1 academic elective. *Academic units recommended:* 4 English, 4 math, 4 science, 2 science labs, 3 foreign language, 2 social studies, 2 history, 2 academic electives. **Freshman Admission Statistics:** 159 applied, 75.47% admitted, 66% enrolled. **Transfer Admission Requirements:** High school transcript, college transcript(s), essay or personal statement, Minimum college GPA of 2.0 required. Lowest grade transferable C-. **General Admission Information:** Priority deadline 1/15. Regular application deadline 7/25. Nonfall registration accepted. Admission may be deferred for a maximum of 1 year.

COSTS AND FINANCIAL AID

Annual tuition $26,940. Room and board $10,810. Required fees $500. Average book expense $1,000. **Required Forms and Deadlines:** CSS/Financial Aid PROFILE, Noncustodial PROFILE. **Notification of Awards:** Applicants will be notified of awards on a rolling basis beginning 3/15. **Types of Aid:** *Need-based scholarships/grants:* Private scholarships, College/university scholarship or grant aid from institutional funds. *Loans:* College/university loans from institutional funds. *Student Employment:* Institutional employment available. **Financial Aid Statistics:** 100% needy freshmen, 100% needy undergrads receive need-based scholarship or grant aid. 76% freshmen, 55% undergrads receive non-need-based scholarship or grant aid. 82% freshmen, 69% undergrads receive need-based self-help aid. 0% freshmen, 0% undergrads receive athletic scholarships. 96% freshmen, 96% undergrads receive any aid. 0% undergrads borrow to pay for school. Average cumulative indebtedness $0. **Criteria for awarding aid:** *Non-need-based:* Academics, Alumni affiliation, Leadership.

PROVIDENCE COLLEGE

Harkins Hall 103, Providence, RI 2918
Phone: 401-865-2535 • **Financial Aid Phone:** 401-865-2286
E-mail: pcadmiss@providence.edu • **CEEB Code:** 3693
Fax: 401-865-2826 • **Website:** www.providence.edu • **ACT Code:** 3806

This private school, affiliated with the Roman Catholic Church, was founded in 1917. It has a 105-acre campus.

RATINGS

Admissions Selectivity Rating: 88   Fire Safety Rating: 93   Green Rating: 60*

STUDENTS AND FACULTY

Enrollment: 4,173. **Student Body:** 56% female, 44% male, 90% out-of-state, 2% international (24 countries represented). Asian 1%, African American 4%, Caucasian 77%, Hispanic 9%, Native American <1%, Pacific Islander <1%, Two or more races 2%, Race unknown 5%.

Retention and Graduation: 93% freshmen return for sophomore year. 81% freshmen graduate within 4 years. 83% freshmen graduate within 6 years. 42% grads go on to further study within 1 year. **Faculty:** Student/faculty ratio 12 297 full-time faculty, 93% hold PhDs, 15% are are members of minority groups, 43% are women. 0% of classes are taught by teaching assistants.

ACADEMICS

Degrees: associate, bachelor's, certificate, master's, terminal. **Classes:** Most classes have 20-29 students. Most lab/discussion sessions have 10-19 students. **Most popular majors:** Marketing/Marketing Management; Finance; Biology/Biological Sciences. **Special Study Options:** cross-registration, distance learning, double major, dual enrollment, exchange student program (domestic), honors program, independent study, internships, liberal arts/career combination, student-designed major, study abroad, teacher certification program. **Honors Programs:** Liberal Arts Honors Program Combined degree programs: Comb-plan Bio/Opt w/ NE College of Optometry. **Disability Services:** Special programs offered to physically disabled students, including note-taking services, reader services, tape recorders, tutors. **Career Services:** Alumni network, Career/job search classes, Career assessment, Internships. Fall Career Expo which included a grad school fair, LinkedIn photo booth, "image checks" booth, summer showcase event, and a major/minor fair for all students of all majors and all years. We had over 1,000 students attend.

FACILITIES

Housing: Coed dorms, special housing for disabled students, men's dorms, women's dorms, Wellness Housing. 87% of campus accessible to physically diasbled. **Special Academic Facilities/Equipment:** Hunt-Cavanagh Art Gallery, Blackfriar Theatre, Science Center Complex, Computer and Language Labs, Smith Center for the Arts. **Computers:** 100% of classrooms, 50% of dorms, 100% of libraries, 100% of dining areas, 100% of student union, 20% of common outdoor areas have wireless network access. Students can register for classes online. Administrative functions (other than registration) can be performed online.

CAMPUS LIFE

Environment: City. **Activities:** Choral groups, concert band, dance, drama/theater, jazz band, literary magazine, music ensembles, musical theater, pep band, radio station, student government, student newspaper, television station, yearbook, Campus Ministries, Student Organization. 112 registered organizations, 18 honor societies, 2 religious organizations. **Athletics (Intercollegiate):** *Men:* basketball, cross-country, diving, ice hockey, lacrosse, soccer, swimming, track/field (outdoor), track/field (indoor). *Women:* basketball, cross-country, diving, field hockey, ice hockey, soccer, softball, swimming, tennis, track/field (outdoor), track/field (indoor), volleyball. **On-Campus Highlights:** McPhails- Student Activity Center, Peterson Center- Athletic Facility, Slavin Center- Student Center, Smith Center for the Arts, St. Dominic Chapel, Harkins Hall- Classrooms, Admin Offices; Blackfriars Theatre; Hunt-Cavanagh Art Gallery.

ADMISSIONS

Freshman Academic Profile: Average high school GPA 3.4. 39% in top 10% of high school class, 69% in top 25% of high school class, 92% in top 50% of high school class. 57% from public high schools. **Reported SAT (pre-2016 redesign) scores:** SAT Math middle 50% range 520-630. SAT Critical Reading middle 50% range 510-610. SAT Writing middle 50% range 510-620. **Concordant SAT scores:** SAT EBRW middle 50% 570–670. SAT Math middle 50% range 550–650. ACT middle 50% range 23-28. Minimum internet-based TOEFL 90. **Basis for Candidate Selection:** *Very important factors considered include:* rigor of secondary school record, academic GPA, application essay. *Important factors considered include:* recommendation(s), extracurricular activities, character/personal qualities. *Other factors considered include:* class rank, standardized test scores, talent/ability, first generation, alumni/ae relation, geographical residence, racial/ethnic status, volunteer work, work experience, level of applicant's interest. **Freshman Admission Requirements:** High school diploma is required and GED is not accepted. *Academic units required:* 4 English, 4 math, 3 science, 2 science labs, 3 foreign language, 2 social studies, 2 history. *Academic units recommended:* 4 English, 4 math, 4 science, 2 science labs, 4 foreign language, 2 social studies, 2 history. **Freshman Admission Statistics:** 10,820 applied, 55.03% admitted, 18% enrolled. **Transfer Admission Requirements:** High school transcript, college transcript(s), essay or personal statement, statement of good standing from prior institution(s). Minimum college GPA of 3.0 required. Lowest grade transferable c. **General Admission Information:** Application fee $65. Priority deadline 1/15. Regular application deadline 1/15. Regular notification 4/1. Nonfall registration accepted. Admission may be deferred for a maximum of 1 year.

COSTS AND FINANCIAL AID

Annual tuition $46,080. Room and board $13,790. Required fees $890. Average book expense $940. **Required Forms and Deadlines:** FAFSA, CSS/Financial Aid PROFILE. **Notification of Awards:** Applicants will be notified of awards on or about 3/16. **Types of Aid:** *Need-based scholarships/grants:* Federal Pell, FSEOG, State scholarships/grants, Private scholarships, College/university scholarship or grant aid from institutional funds. *Loans:* Direct Subsidized Stafford Loans, Direct Unsubsidized Stafford Loans, Direct PLUS loans, Federal Perkins Loans, State Loans. *Student Employment:* Federal Work-Study Program available. Institutional employment available. **Financial Aid Statistics:** 94% needy freshmen, 98% needy undergrads receive need-based scholarship or grant aid. 10% freshmen, 8% undergrads receive non-need-based scholarship or grant aid. 87% freshmen, 88% undergrads receive need-based self-help aid. 5% freshmen, 5% undergrads receive athletic scholarships. 84% freshmen, 81% undergrads receive any aid. 70% undergrads borrow to pay for school. Average cumulative indebtedness $39,775. **Criteria for awarding aid:** *Need-based:* Minority status, Music/drama. *Non-need-based:* Academics, Athletics, Leadership, Minority status, Music/drama.

PURDUE UNIVERSITY—CALUMET

Office of Admissions, Hammond, IN 46323-2094
Phone: 219-989-2213 • **Financial Aid Phone:** 219-989-2301
E-mail: adms@purduecal.edu • **CEEB Code:** 1638
Fax: 219-989-2775 • **Website:** http://www.purduecal.edu/ • **ACT Code:** 1233

This public school was founded in 1946. It has a 194-acre campus.

RATINGS

Admissions Selectivity Rating: 75 **Fire Safety Rating:** 95 **Green Rating:** 60*

STUDENTS AND FACULTY

Enrollment: 8,325. **Student Body:** 55% female, 45% male, 11% out-of-state, 3% international (39 countries represented). Asian 1%, African American 19%, Caucasian 61%, Hispanic 15%, Native American <1%, Pacific Islander 0%, Two or more races 0%, Race unknown 0%.

Retention and Graduation: 69% freshmen return for sophomore year. 6% freshmen graduate within 4 years. 26% freshmen graduate within 6 years. **Faculty:** Student/faculty ratio 21:1. 268 full-time faculty, 69% hold PhDs, 21% are are members of minority groups, 48% are women.

ACADEMICS

Degrees: associate, bachelor's, certificate, master's, postbachelor's certificate. **Classes:** Most classes have 20-29 students. Most lab/discussion sessions have 20-29 students. **Most popular majors:** Elementary Education and Teaching; Marketing/Marketing Management; Engineering. **Special Study Options:** Accelerated program, cooperative education program, distance learning, double major, dual enrollment, English as a Second Language (ESL), honors program, independent study, internships, study abroad, teacher certification program, weekend college. **Honors Programs:** Purdue Calumet Honors Program Combined degree programs: 2-2 nursing program. **Disability Services:** Special programs offered to physically disabled students, including note-taking services, reader services, tape recorders, tutors. **Career Services:** Career/job search classes, Career assessment, Internships.

FACILITIES

Housing: apartments for single students. 100% of campus accessible to physically diasbled. **Special Academic Facilities/Equipment:** Audio-visual services, urban development institute. **Computers:** Students can register for classes online. Administrative functions (other than registration) can be performed online.

CAMPUS LIFE

Environment: City. **Activities:** Choral groups, dance, drama/theater, radio station, student government, student newspaper, Campus Ministries, Student Organization. 56 registered organizations, 25 honor societies, 3 religious organizations. 2 fraternities, 3 sororities. **Athletics (Intercollegiate):** *Men:* basketball. *Women:* basketball. **On-Campus Highlights:** Physical Education and Recreation Building, Enrollment Services Center, Challenger Learning Center of Northwest Indiana **Environmental Initiatives:** Campus-wide Recycling.

ADMISSIONS

Freshman Academic Profile: Average high school GPA 2.6. 10% in top 10% of high school class, 28% in top 25% of high school class, 58% in top 50% of high school class. **Reported SAT (pre-2016 redesign) scores:** SAT Math middle 50% range 410-520. SAT Critical Reading middle 50% range 410-510. **Concordant SAT scores:** SAT Math middle 50% range 450–550. ACT middle 50% range 17-23. Minimum paper TOEFL 550. **Basis for Candidate**

Selection: *Important factors considered include:* rigor of secondary school record, class rank, academic GPA, standardized test scores. **Freshman Admission Requirements:** High school diploma is required and GED is accepted. *Academic units required:* 4 English, 2 math, 1 science, 1 science lab, 2 foreign language, 1 social studies, 1 history. *Academic units recommended:* 4 English, 2 math, 2 science, 2 science labs, 2 foreign language, 2 social studies, 1 history. **Freshman Admission Statistics:** 5,884 applied, 69.36% admitted, 33% enrolled. **Transfer Admission Requirements:** High school transcript, Minimum college GPA of 2.0 required. Lowest grade transferable C. **General Admission Information:** Nonfall registration accepted. Admission may be deferred for a maximum of 1 semester.

COSTS AND FINANCIAL AID

Average book expense $1,125. **Required Forms and Deadlines:** FAFSA. **Notification of Awards:** Applicants will be notified of awards on a rolling basis beginning 4/15. **Types of Aid:** *Need-based scholarships/grants:* Federal Pell, FSEOG, State scholarships/grants, College/university scholarship or grant aid from institutional funds. *Loans:* Direct Subsidized Stafford Loans, Direct Unsubsidized Stafford Loans, Direct PLUS loans, Federal Perkins Loans. *Student Employment:* Federal Work-Study Program available. Institutional employment available. **Financial Aid Statistics:** 61% needy freshmen, 65% needy undergrads receive need-based scholarship or grant aid. 27% freshmen, 16% undergrads receive non-need-based scholarship or grant aid. 67% freshmen, 77% undergrads receive need-based self-help aid. 1% freshmen, 0% undergrads receive athletic scholarships. **Criteria for awarding aid:** *Need-based:* Academics, Minority status. *Non-need-based:* Academics, Athletics, Minority status, State/district residency.

PURDUE UNIVERSITY—WEST LAFAYETTE

Best Colleges

475 Stadium Mall Drive, West Lafayette, IN 47907-2050
Phone: 765-494-1776 • **Financial Aid Phone:** 765-494-0998
E-mail: admissions@purdue.edu • **CEEB Code:** 1631
Fax: 765-494-0544 • **Website:** www.purdue.edu • **ACT Code:** 1230

This public school was founded in 1869. It has a 2552-acre campus.

RATINGS

Admissions Selectivity Rating: 90   **Fire Safety Rating:** 96   **Green Rating:** 97

STUDENTS AND FACULTY

Enrollment: 29,866. **Student Body:** 42% female, 58% male, 36% out-of-state, 17% international (123 countries represented). Asian 7%, African American 3%, Caucasian 63%, Hispanic 5%, Native American <1%, Pacific Islander <1%, Two or more races 2%, Race unknown 3%.
Retention and Graduation: 92% freshmen return for sophomore year. 49% freshmen graduate within 4 years. 77% freshmen graduate within 6 years. 21% grads go on to further study within 1 year. **Faculty:** Student/faculty ratio 12:1. 2,316 full-time faculty, 98% hold PhDs, 24% are are members of minority groups, 34% are women. 29% of classes are taught by teaching assistants.

ACADEMICS

Degrees: bachelor's, certificate, doctoral/professional, doctoral/research, doctoral, master's, postbachelor's certifiate, post-master's certificate, terminal. **Classes:** Most classes have 10-19 students. Most lab/discussion sessions have 20-29 students. **Most popular majors:** Mechanical Engineering; Computer Science; Mechanical Engineering/Mechanical Technology/Technician. **Special Study Options:** Accelerated program, cooperative education program, cross-registration, distance learning, double major, dual enrollment, exchange student program (domestic), honors program, independent study, internships, liberal arts/career combination, study abroad, teacher certification program, weekend college. **Honors Programs:** University Honors Program Combined degree programs: BS/MBA, BA/MS, BS/MS, BS/MPH, PharmD/PhD, PharmD, MSIA. **Disability Services:** Special programs offered to physically disabled students, including note-taking services, reader services, tape recorders, tutors. **Career Services:** Alumni network, Alumni services, Career/job search classes, Career assessment, Internships, Regional alumni.

FACILITIES

Housing: Coed dorms, special housing for disabled students, men's dorms, women's dorms, fraternity/sorority housing, apartments for married students, cooperative housing, apartments for single students, Wellness Housing. 93.4%

of campus accessible to physically diasbled. **Special Academic Facilities/Equipment:** Hall of music, child development lab, speech and hearing clinic, small animal veterinary clinic, horticulture park, linear accelerator, tornado simulator, nuclear accelerator. **Computers:** 95% of classrooms, 5% of dorms, 95% of libraries, 90% of dining areas, 95% of student union, 5% of common outdoor areas have wireless network access. Students can register for classes online. Administrative functions (other than registration) can be performed online.

CAMPUS LIFE

Environment: Town. **Activities:** Choral groups, concert band, dance, drama/theater, jazz band, literary magazine, marching band, music ensembles, musical theater, opera, pep band, radio station, student government, student newspaper, student-run film society, symphony orchestra, television station, yearbook, Campus Ministries, Student Organization, Model UN. 850 registered organizations, 25 honor societies, 66 religious organizations. 48 fraternities, 32 sororities. **Athletics (Intercollegiate):** *Men:* baseball, basketball, cross-country, diving, football, golf, swimming, tennis, track/field (outdoor), track/field (indoor), wrestling. *Women:* basketball, cross-country, diving, golf, soccer, softball, swimming, tennis, track/field (outdoor), track/field (indoor), volleyball. **On-Campus Highlights:** Pudue Memorial Union, Recreational Sports Center, Fountain areas, Libraries, Sporting events. **Environmental Initiatives:** Development and implementation of the Sustainability Strategic Plan. The Sustainability Strategic Plan also establishes eight program areas or 'pillars' of sustainability focus on campus. These eight 'pillars' are as follows: 1. Site Considerations 2. Water Resources 3. Energy and Built Environment 4. Materials Management 5. Food Systems 6. Academics and Research 7. Endowment / Development 8. Community Relationships Within this plan, there are 56 short-term goals (to be achieved by 2014) and 85 long-term goals (to be achieved by 2025).

ADMISSIONS

Freshman Academic Profile: Average high school GPA 3.7. 43% in top 10% of high school class, 77% in top 25% of high school class, 97% in top 50% of high school class. **Reported SAT (pre-2016 redesign) scores:** SAT Math middle 50% range 560-690. SAT Critical Reading middle 50% range 520-640. SAT Writing middle 50% range 520-630. **Concordant SAT scores:** SAT EBRW middle 50% 580–680. SAT Math middle 50% range 580–720. ACT middle 50% range 25-31. Minimum internet-based TOEFL 79. Minimum paper TOEFL 550. **Basis for Candidate Selection:** *Very important factors considered include:* rigor of secondary school record, academic GPA, standardized test scores. *Important factors considered include:* application essay, recommendation(s), extracurricular activities, character/personal qualities, first generation. *Other factors considered include:* class rank, talent/ability, alumni/ae relation, geographical residence, state residency, racial/ethnic status, volunteer work, work experience, level of applicant's interest. **Freshman Admission Requirements:** High school diploma is required and GED is accepted. *Academic units required:* 4 English, 3 math, 3 science, 2 science labs, 3 foreign language. **Freshman Admission Statistics:** 48,774 applied, 55.82% admitted, 26% enrolled. **Transfer Admission Requirements:** college transcript(s), essay or personal statement, statement of good standing from prior institution(s). Minimum college GPA of 2.5 required. Lowest grade transferable C. **General Admission Information:** Application fee $60. Priority deadline 2/1. Regular notification 12/12. Nonfall registration accepted.

COSTS AND FINANCIAL AID

Annual in-state tuition $9,208. Annual out-of-state tuition $28,010. Room and board $10,030. Required fees $794. Average book expense $1,220. **Required Forms and Deadlines:** FAFSA. **Notification of Awards:** Applicants will be notified of awards on or about 4/15. **Types of Aid:** *Need-based scholarships/grants:* Federal Pell, FSEOG, State scholarships/grants, Private scholarships, College/university scholarship or grant aid from institutional funds. *Loans:* Direct Subsidized Stafford Loans, Direct Unsubsidized Stafford Loans, Direct PLUS loans, Federal Perkins Loans, College/university loans from institutional funds. *Student Employment:* Federal Work-Study Program available. Institutional employment available. **Financial Aid Statistics:** 62% needy freshmen, 64% needy undergrads receive need-based scholarship or grant aid. 49% freshmen, 43% undergrads receive non-need-based scholarship or grant aid. 73% freshmen, 79% undergrads receive need-based self-help aid. 1% freshmen, 1% undergrads receive athletic scholarships. 74% freshmen, 77% undergrads receive any aid. 46% undergrads borrow to pay for school. Average cumulative indebtedness $27,530. **Criteria for awarding aid:** *Non-need-based:* Academics, Athletics, Leadership, Music/drama, State/district residency.

QUEENS UNIVERSITY OF CHARLOTTE

1900 Selwyn Avenue, Charlotte, NC 28274
Phone: 704-337-2212 • **Financial Aid Phone:** 704-337-2225
E-mail: admissions@queens.edu • **CEEB Code:** 5560
Fax: 704-337-2403 • **Website:** www.queens.edu • **ACT Code:** 3148

This private school, affiliated with the Presbyterian Church, was founded in 1857. It has a 30-acre campus.

RATINGS
Admissions Selectivity Rating: 79   **Fire Safety Rating:** 70   **Green Rating:** 60*

STUDENTS AND FACULTY
Enrollment: 1,911. **Student Body:** 76% female, 24% male, 8% international. Asian 2%, African American 16%, Caucasian 55%, Hispanic 3%, Native American 1%, Pacific Islander 0%, Two or more races 2%, Race unknown 13%. **Retention and Graduation:** 70% freshmen return for sophomore year. 48% freshmen graduate within 4 years. 59% freshmen graduate within 6 years. **Faculty:** Student/faculty ratio 12:1. 123 full-time faculty, 72% hold PhDs, 7% are are members of minority groups, 68% are women. 0% of classes are taught by teaching assistants.

ACADEMICS
Degrees: bachelor's, master's, postbachelor's certificate, terminal. **Classes:** Most classes have 10-19 students. Most lab/discussion sessions have 10-19 students. **Special Study Options:** cross-registration, double major, dual enrollment, honors program, independent study, internships, liberal arts/career combination, student-designed major, study abroad, teacher certification program, weekend college. **Disability Services:** Special programs offered to physically disabled students, including note-taking services, reader services, tape recorders, tutors. **Career Services:** Alumni network, Career/job search classes, Internships. The Internship is a required component of the undergraduate degree here at Queens.

FACILITIES
Housing: Coed dorms, special housing for disabled studentsApartment style 2 bedroom suites for traditional-aged undergraduates 1/2 mile from campus. 63% of campus accessible to physically diasbled. **Special Academic Facilities/Equipment:** Three art galleries, rare books museum.

CAMPUS LIFE
Environment: Metropolis. **Activities:** Choral groups, dance, drama/theater, literary magazine, music ensembles, musical theater, pep band, student government, student newspaper, yearbook, Campus Ministries, Student Organization. 38 registered organizations, 9 honor societies, 2 religious organizations. 2 fraternities, 4 sororities. **Athletics (Intercollegiate):** *Men:* basketball, cheerleading, cross-country, golf, lacrosse, soccer, tennis, track/field (outdoor). *Women:* basketball, cheerleading, cross-country, golf, lacrosse, soccer, softball, tennis, track/field (outdoor), volleyball. **On-Campus Highlights:** Fitness Center, The Lion's Den, Trexler Courtyard, Queens' Off-Campus Athletic Facility.

ADMISSIONS
Freshman Academic Profile: Average high school GPA 3.5. 14% in top 10% of high school class, 39% in top 25% of high school class, 78% in top 50% of high school class. **Reported SAT (pre-2016 redesign) scores:** SAT Math middle 50% range 460-570. SAT Critical Reading middle 50% range 470-580. SAT Writing middle 50% range 460-560. **Concordant SAT scores:** SAT EBRW middle 50% 520–630. SAT Math middle 50% range 500–590. ACT middle 50% range 20-25. Minimum internet-based TOEFL 79. Minimum paper TOEFL 550. **Basis for Candidate Selection:** *Very important factors considered include:* rigor of secondary school record, academic GPA, standardized test scores, extracurricular activities, character/personal qualities. *Important factors considered include:* class rank, interview, volunteer work. *Other factors considered include:* application essay, recommendation(s), talent/ability, first generation, alumni/ae relation, work experience. **Freshman Admission Requirements:** High school diploma is required and GED is accepted. *Academic units required:* 4 English, 3 math, 2 science, 1 science lab, 2 foreign language, 2 social studies. **Freshman Admission Statistics:** 2,199 applied, 73.58% admitted, 22% enrolled. **Transfer Admission Requirements:** High school transcript, college transcript(s), essay or personal statement, statement of good standing from prior institution(s). Minimum college GPA of 2.0 required. Lowest grade transferable C. **General Admission Information:** Application fee $40. Nonfall registration accepted. Admission may be deferred for a maximum of 1 year.

COSTS AND FINANCIAL AID
Required fees $0. **Required Forms and Deadlines:** FAFSA, State aid form. **Notification of Awards:** Applicants will be notified of awards on a rolling basis beginning 3/15. **Types of Aid:** *Need-based scholarships/grants:* Federal Pell, FSEOG, State scholarships/grants, Private scholarships, College/university scholarship or grant aid from institutional funds. *Loans:* Direct Subsidized Stafford Loans, Direct Unsubsidized Stafford Loans, Direct PLUS loans, Federal Perkins Loans, State Loans. *Student Employment:* Federal Work-Study Program available. Institutional employment available. **Financial Aid Statistics:** 100% needy freshmen, 99% needy undergrads receive need-based scholarship or grant aid. 18% freshmen, 15% undergrads receive non-need-based scholarship or grant aid. 79% freshmen, 83% undergrads receive need-based self-help aid. 11% freshmen, 10% undergrads receive athletic scholarships. **Criteria for awarding aid:** *Need-based:* Academics, Leadership, Minority status. *Non-need-based:* Academics, Art, Athletics, Leadership, Minority status, Music/drama, Religious affiliation.

QUINCY UNIVERSITY

1800 College Avenue, Quincy, IL 62301-2699
Phone: 217-228-5210 • **Financial Aid Phone:** 217-228-5260
E-mail: admissions@quincy.edu • **CEEB Code:** 1645
Fax: 217-228-5479 • **Website:** www.quincy.edu • **ACT Code:** 1120

This private school, affiliated with the Roman Catholic Church, was founded in 1860. It has a 70-acre campus.

RATINGS
Admissions Selectivity Rating: 71   **Fire Safety Rating:** 79   **Green Rating:** 60*

STUDENTS AND FACULTY
Student Body: 56% female, 44% male, 28% out-of-state, (6 countries represented). **Retention and Graduation:** 76% freshmen return for sophomore year. 33% freshmen graduate within 4 years. 49% freshmen graduate within 6 years. 22% grads go on to further study within 1 year. 11% grads pursue arts and sciences degrees. 2% grads pursue law degrees. 5% grads pursue business degrees. 2% grads pursue medical degrees. **Faculty:** Student/faculty ratio 14:1. 56 full-time faculty, 71% hold PhDs, 7% are are members of minority groups, 39% are women. 0% of classes are taught by teaching assistants.

ACADEMICS
Degrees: bachelor's, master's, transfer. **Classes:** Most classes have 10-19 students. Most lab/discussion sessions have fewer than 10 students. **Most popular majors:** Elementary Education and Teaching; Registered Nursing/Registered Nurse; Management Science. **Special Study Options:** Accelerated program, distance learning, double major, dual enrollment, honors program, independent study, internships, student-designed major, study abroad, teacher certification program, 3-2 program in engineering with Washington University; 3-1 program in medical technology with various hospitals. **Honors Programs:** The Honors Program provides a challenging course of study which adds an interdisciplinary dimension to a student's major field. The program promotes academic excellence through critical thinking, original research, exceptional writing, and public presentation of scholarship. **Disability Services:** Special programs offered to physically disabled students, including note-taking services, reader services, tape recorders, tutors. **Career Services:** Alumni services, Career/job search classes, Career assessment, Internships. The University, in cooperation with the state of Illinois and local businesses and social service agencies, provides early exploratory internships to first and second year students to aid in the career development/decision-making process.

FACILITIES
Housing: Coed dorms, men's dorms, women's dorms, fraternity/sorority housing, apartments for married students, apartments for single students, Theme Housing, Honors. 75% of campus accessible to physically diasbled. **Special Academic Facilities/Equipment:** Reading center for student teachers, multimedia and graphic design labs, TV broadcast studio, temperature-controlled rare books Library archive, art gallery, 200-seat theater, environmental studies institute, hospital simulation lab, aviation facility with flight simulator, College-operated national public radio station. **Computers:** 100% of classrooms, 100% of dorms, 100% of libraries, 100% of dining areas, 100% of student union, 40% of common outdoor areas have wireless network access. Administrative functions (other than registration) can be performed online.

CAMPUS LIFE
Environment: Town. **Activities:** Choral groups, concert band, dance, drama/theater, jazz band, literary magazine, music ensembles, musical theater, opera, pep band, radio station, student government, student newspaper, symphony orchestra, television station, Campus Ministries. 40 registered organizations, 8 honor societies, 2 religious organizations. 1 fraternity, 2 sororities. **Athletics (Intercollegiate):** *Men:* baseball, basketball, cross-country, football, golf, soccer, tennis, volleyball. *Women:* basketball, cross-country, golf, soccer, softball,

tennis, volleyball. **On-Campus Highlights:** Health and Fitness Center, Newly renovated University Center, QU Chapel, Francis Garden, Brenner Library. **Environmental Initiatives:** Residence hall renovation: Helein Hall renovations included use of recycled furniture and the installation of an energy-efficient VRV hvac system.

ADMISSIONS

Freshman Academic Profile: 76% from public high schools. **Reported SAT (pre-2016 redesign) scores:** SAT Math middle 50% range 410-490. SAT Critical Reading middle 50% range 460-490. **Concordant SAT scores:** SAT Math middle 50% range 450–520. ACT middle 50% range 19-25. Minimum internet-based TOEFL 61. Minimum paper TOEFL 500. **Basis for Candidate Selection:** *Very important factors considered include:* rigor of secondary school record, academic GPA. *Important factors considered include:* class rank, standardized test scores, application essay, recommendation(s), extracurricular activities, character/personal qualities, volunteer work, work experience, level of applicant's interest. *Other factors considered include:* interview, talent/ability. **Freshman Admission Requirements:** High school diploma is required and GED is accepted. *Academic units recommended:* 4 English, 3 math, 3 science, 2 foreign language, 3 social studies. **Freshman Admission Statistics:** 903 applied, 88.93% admitted, 27% enrolled. **Transfer Admission Requirements:** college transcript(s), statement of good standing from prior institution(s). Minimum college GPA of 2.0 required. Lowest grade transferable D. **General Admission Information:** Application fee $25. Priority deadline 4/1. Nonfall registration accepted. Admission may be deferred.

COSTS AND FINANCIAL AID

Annual tuition $25,598. Room and board $11,336. Required fees $974. Average book expense $1,250. **Required Forms and Deadlines:** FAFSA. **Notification of Awards:** Applicants will be notified of awards on a rolling basis beginning 3/1. **Types of Aid:** *Need-based scholarships/grants:* Federal Pell, FSEOG, State scholarships/grants, Private scholarships, College/university scholarship or grant aid from institutional funds. *Loans:* Direct Subsidized Stafford Loans, Direct Unsubsidized Stafford Loans, Direct PLUS loans. *Student Employment:* Federal Work-Study Program available. Institutional employment available. **Financial Aid Statistics:** 98% needy freshmen, 92% needy undergrads receive need-based scholarship or grant aid. 23% freshmen, 17% undergrads receive non-need-based scholarship or grant aid. 69% freshmen, 75% undergrads receive need-based self-help aid. 8% freshmen, 4% undergrads receive athletic scholarships. 100% freshmen, 93% undergrads receive any aid. **Criteria for awarding aid:** *Need-based:* Academics, Alumni affiliation, Art, Leadership, Minority status, Music/drama. *Non-need-based:* Academics, Alumni affiliation, Art, Athletics, Leadership, Music/drama.

QUINNIPIAC UNIVERSITY

275 Mount Carmel Avenue, Hamden, CT 6518
Phone: 203-582-8600 • **Financial Aid Phone:** 203-582-8750
E-mail: admissions@qu.edu • **CEEB Code:** 3712
Fax: 203-582-8906 • **Website:** www.qu.edu • **ACT Code:** 582

This private school was founded in 1929. It has a 600-acre campus.

RATINGS

Admissions Selectivity Rating: 84   **Fire Safety Rating:** 97   **Green Rating:** 75

STUDENTS AND FACULTY

Enrollment: 7,042. **Student Body:** 61% female, 39% male, 75% out-of-state, 2% international (43 countries represented). Asian 3%, African American 5%, Caucasian 76%, Hispanic 9%, Native American <1%, Pacific Islander 0%, Two or more races 2%, Race unknown 3%.
Retention and Graduation: 90% freshmen return for sophomore year. 69% freshmen graduate within 4 years. 77% freshmen graduate within 6 years. 39% grads go on to further study within 1 year. 19% grads pursue arts and sciences degrees. 2% grads pursue law degrees. 10% grads pursue business degrees. 2% grads pursue medical degrees. **Faculty:** Student/faculty ratio 16:1. 398 full-time faculty, 89% hold PhDs, 17% are are members of minority groups, 54% are women. 0% of classes are taught by teaching assistants.

ACADEMICS

Degrees: bachelor's, doctoral/professional, doctoral, master's, postbachelor's certifiate, post-master's certificate. **Classes:** Most classes have 20-29 students.

Most lab/discussion sessions have 10-19 students. **Most popular majors:** Psychology; Business/Commerce; Registered Nursing/Registered Nurse. **Special Study Options:** distance learning, double major, exchange student program (domestic), honors program, independent study, internships, liberal arts/career combination, student-designed major, study abroad, teacher certification program, Online option for summer course offerings Online degrees offered at the graduate level. **Honors Programs:** The University Honors Program, limited to 60-70 freshmen who are selected following their acceptance,provides challenging coursework and opportunities for learning and service. Combined degree programs: BA/JD, BA/MA, BS/MBA, BA/MAT, BA/MS, BS/MOT, BS/DPT, BS/MHS. **Career Services:** Alumni network, Alumni services, Career/job search classes, Career assessment, Internships, Regional alumni. Extensive internship programs in all business and communications fields. Clinical placements in all of the health science fields.

FACILITIES

Housing: Coed dorms, apartments for single students, Wellness Housing. University owned houses provide housing for about 100 seniors/juniors. 100% of campus accessible to physically diasbled. **Special Academic Facilities/Equipment:** Quinnipiac Polling Institute, Financial Technology Center, Motion Analysis Lab, Albert Schweitzer Institute, Critical Care Nursing Lab,Fully digital/high definition TV production studio,editing labs, news technology center. Lender family special collection room in Library on the Irish Famine, "An Gorta Mor". **Computers:** 100% of classrooms, 100% of dorms, 100% of libraries, 100% of dining areas, 100% of student union, 100% of common outdoor areas have wireless network access. Students can register for classes online. Administrative functions (other than registration) can be performed online. Undergraduates are required to own a computer.

CAMPUS LIFE

Environment: Town. **Activities:** Choral groups, dance, drama/theater, literary magazine, pep band, radio station, student government, student newspaper, television station, yearbook, Campus Ministries, Student Organization. 78 registered organizations, 8 honor societies, 3 religious organizations. 2 fraternities, 3 sororities. **Athletics (Intercollegiate):** *Men:* baseball, basketball, cross-country, ice hockey, lacrosse, soccer, tennis. *Women:* basketball, cheerleading, cross-country, field hockey, ice hockey, lacrosse, soccer, softball, tennis, track/field (outdoor), track/field (indoor), volleyball. **On-Campus Highlights:** Arnold Bernhard Library, Recreation Center with suspended banked track, An Gorta Mor, Irish famine literature and art, Cafe Q with Zia/Starbucks, Bobcat Den/Coffee Bar, The nearby 250 acre 'York Hill' campus with the TD Bank Sports Center-twin 3500 seat arenas for ice hockey and basketball, includes residence halls with 1800 beds and a student/recreation center. About 5 miles away is the North Haven campus of 104 acres, home to the graduate programs in the School of Health Sciences. Upper division (juniors and seniors) students in Physical Therapy, Occupational Therapy, Nursing, Diagnostic Imaging and Physician Assistant programs also use this outstanding state-of-the-art facility. **Environmental Initiatives:** 100 percent of Quinnipiac electricity requirements on all three of its campuses have been purchased from renewable energy credits.

ADMISSIONS

Freshman Academic Profile: Average high school GPA 3.4. 27% in top 10% of high school class, 62% in top 25% of high school class, 92% in top 50% of high school class. 70% from public high schools. **Reported SAT (pre-2016 redesign) scores:** SAT Math middle 50% range 490-600. SAT Critical Reading middle 50% range 490-590. SAT Writing middle 50% range 490-580. **Concordant SAT scores:** SAT EBRW middle 50% 550–640. SAT Math middle 50% range 520–620. ACT middle 50% range 22-27. Minimum internet-based TOEFL 80. Minimum paper TOEFL 550. **Basis for Candidate Selection:** *Very important factors considered include:* rigor of secondary school record, academic GPA. *Important factors considered include:* class rank, standardized test scores, application essay, recommendation(s). *Other factors considered include:* interview, extracurricular activities, talent/ability, character/personal qualities, first generation, alumni/ae relation, racial/ethnic status, volunteer work, work experience, level of applicant's interest. **Freshman Admission Requirements:** High school diploma is required and GED is accepted. *Academic units required:* 4 English, 3 math, 3 science, 2 science labs, 2 foreign language, 2 social studies, and 4 units from above areas or other academic areas. *Academic units recommended:* 4 English, 4 math, 4 science, 3 science labs, 2 foreign language, 3 social studies. **Freshman Admission Statistics:** 23,492 applied, 76.44% admitted, 11% enrolled. **Transfer Admission Requirements:** college transcript(s), essay or personal statement, Minimum college GPA of 2.5 required. Lowest grade transferable C. **General Admission Information:** Application fee $65. Priority deadline 2/1. Nonfall registration accepted. Admission may be deferred for a maximum of 12 months.

COSTS AND FINANCIAL AID

Annual tuition $41,990. Room and board $14,200. Required fees $1,650. Average book expense $800. **Required Forms and Deadlines:** FAFSA, CSS/Financial Aid PROFILE, Noncustodial PROFILE. **Notification of Awards:** Applicants will be notified of awards on a rolling basis beginning 2/15.

Types of Aid: *Need-based scholarships/grants:* Federal Pell, FSEOG, State scholarships/grants, Private scholarships, College/university scholarship or grant aid from institutional funds. *Loans:* Direct Subsidized Stafford Loans, Direct Unsubsidized Stafford Loans, Direct PLUS loans, Federal Perkins Loans. *Student Employment:* Federal Work-Study Program available. Institutional employment available. **Financial Aid Statistics:** 98% needy freshmen, 97% needy undergrads receive need-based scholarship or grant aid. 77% freshmen, 67% undergrads receive non-need-based scholarship or grant aid. 76% freshmen, 79% undergrads receive need-based self-help aid. 5% freshmen, 5% undergrads receive athletic scholarships. 88% freshmen, 83% undergrads receive any aid. 71% undergrads borrow to pay for school. Average cumulative indebtedness $47,217. **Criteria for awarding aid:** *Non-need-based:* Academics, Athletics.

See page 1016.

RADFORD UNIVERSITY

PO Box 6903, Radford, VA 24142
Phone: 540-831-5371 • **Financial Aid Phone:** 540-831-5408
E-mail: admissions@radford.edu • **CEEB Code:** 5565
Fax: 540-831-5038 • **Website:** www.radford.edu • **ACT Code:** 4422

This public school was founded in 1910. It has a 191-acre campus.

RATINGS

Admissions Selectivity Rating: 73   **Fire Safety Rating:** 98   **Green Rating:** 90

STUDENTS AND FACULTY

Enrollment: 8,426. **Student Body:** 57% female, 43% male, 5% out-of-state, 1% international (61 countries represented). Asian 1%, African American 15%, Caucasian 69%, Hispanic 7%, Native American <1%, Pacific Islander <1%, Two or more races 5%, Race unknown 1%.

Retention and Graduation: 74% freshmen return for sophomore year. 43% freshmen graduate within 4 years. 58% freshmen graduate within 6 years. 16% grads go on to further study within 1 year. **Faculty:** Student/faculty ratio 16:1. 469 full-time faculty, 83% hold PhDs, 12% are are members of minority groups, 51% are women. 2% of classes are taught by teaching assistants.

ACADEMICS

Degrees: bachelor's, certificate, master's, postbachelor's certificate, post-master's certificate. **Classes:** Most classes have 20-29 students. Most lab/discussion sessions have 20-29 students. **Most popular majors:** Physical Education Teaching and Coaching; Multi-/Interdisciplinary Studies; Business Administration and Management. **Special Study Options:** Accelerated program, cross-registration, distance learning, double major, dual enrollment, honors program, independent study, internships, student-designed major, study abroad, teacher certification program. **Honors Programs:** Student members of Honors Academy work toward graduating as Highlander Scholars. To graduate as a Highlander Scholar, one must complete 27 credit hours of Honors Coursework, present their Honors Capstone Project in a public forum, and have a cumulative GPA of 3.5 at the time of graduation. The 27 hours of honors coursework are completed as follows: 6-12 credits in the Core Curriculum as honors credits (usually earned by taking Honors Classes), 12-15 in one's major as honors credits (usually by contracting the course for honors credit and a 3-6 credit hour honors capstone project in one's major (a piece of scholarship completed under the supervision of a faculty member in one's department). There is also a residential/social component to the Honors Academy. Active members in the Honors Academy enjoy early registration, and their status as a Highlander Scholar Graduate is noted on their diploma and transcript. Students are also supported financially to present the results of their work at professional and undergraduate conferences. Combined degree programs: BA/MA. **Disability Services:** Special programs offered to physically disabled students, including note-taking services, reader services, tape recorders, tutors. **Career Services:** Alumni network, Alumni services, Career/job search classes, Career assessment, Internships, Regional alumni. Radford University creates an innovative community that fosters career and talent development. Students collaborate with career advisors, employers, faculty, and alumni to help discover their career path, gain relevant experience and thrive professionally. One way that we do this is by encouraging all students to develop their talents through leadership, volunteer, research, study abroad and internship experiences. Radford alum can be found applying their knowledge in Fortune 100 companies, educational institutions, on Capitol Hill, non-profit organizations and a variety of other industries. Through their experiences at Radford University our Highlanders are equipped and prepared to make their distinct contributions in the world.

FACILITIES

Housing: Coed dorms, special housing for disabled students, special housing for international students, apartments for single students, Wellness Housing,

Theme Housing. 98% of campus accessible to physically diasbled. **Special Academic Facilities/Equipment:** Language Lab, Art Gallery with Sculpture Garden, Planetarium, Selu Conservancy, and on-campus speech/language/hearing clinic. **Computers:** 100% of classrooms, 100% of dorms, 100% of libraries, 100% of dining areas, 100% of student union, 100% of common outdoor areas have wireless network access. Students can register for classes online. Administrative functions (other than registration) can be performed online.

CAMPUS LIFE

Environment: Village. **Activities:** Choral groups, concert band, dance, drama/theater, jazz band, literary magazine, music ensembles, musical theater, pep band, radio station, student government, student newspaper, television station, yearbook, Campus Ministries, Student Organization. 237 registered organizations, 14 honor societies, 10 religious organizations, 15 fraternities, 10 sororities. **Athletics (Intercollegiate):** *Men:* baseball, basketball, cheerleading, cross-country, golf, soccer, tennis, track/field (outdoor), track/field (indoor). *Women:* basketball, cheerleading, cross-country, diving, field hockey, golf, soccer, softball, swimming, tennis, track/field (outdoor), track/field (indoor), volleyball. **On-Campus Highlights:** Hurlburt Student Center– The Bonnie, Heth Hall- Students Services, Young Hall–High Tech Classrooms, Covington Center for Arts, Muse Hall–New River Grill. **Environmental Initiatives:** Recycling: Radford University is committed to being a more eco-friendly campus through a variety of measures, including a strong commitment to recycling. Initiatives in this area include online recycling bin request, RecycleMania competition, Y-Toss program, and the RU Recycling campaign in our residence halls.

ADMISSIONS

Freshman Academic Profile: Average high school GPA 3.2. 6% in top 10% of high school class, 22% in top 25% of high school class, 56% in top 50% of high school class. 94% from public high schools. **Reported SAT (pre-2016 redesign) scores:** SAT Math middle 50% range 430-520. SAT Critical Reading middle 50% range 430-530. SAT Writing middle 50% range 410-510. **Concordant SAT scores:** SAT EBRW middle 50% 470–580. SAT Math middle 50% range 470–550. ACT middle 50% range 17-22. Minimum internet-based TOEFL 68. Minimum paper TOEFL 520. **Basis for Candidate Selection:** *Very important factors considered include:* rigor of secondary school record. *Important factors considered include:* academic GPA. *Other factors considered include:* class rank, standardized test scores, application essay, recommendation(s), interview, extracurricular activities, talent/ability, character/personal qualities, first generation, alumni/ae relation, volunteer work, work experience, level of applicant's interest. **Freshman Admission Requirements:** High school diploma is required and GED is accepted. *Academic units recommended:* 4 English, 4 math, 4 science, 4 science labs, 4 foreign language, 2 social studies, 2 history. **Freshman Admission Statistics:** 7,447 applied, 81.20% admitted, 29% enrolled. **Transfer Admission Requirements:** college transcript(s), Minimum college GPA of 2.0 required. Lowest grade transferable C. **General Admission Information:** Application fee $50. Priority deadline 2/1. Regular notification 4/1. Nonfall registration accepted. Admission may be deferred for a maximum of 1 year.

COSTS AND FINANCIAL AID

Annual in-state tuition $6,991. Annual out-of-state tuition $18,626. Room and board $8,946. Required fees $3,090. Average book expense $1,200. **Required Forms and Deadlines:** FAFSA. **Notification of Awards:** Applicants will be notified of awards on a rolling basis beginning 4/15. **Types of Aid:** *Need-based scholarships/grants:* Federal Pell, FSEOG, State scholarships/grants, Private scholarships, College/university scholarship or grant aid from institutional funds. *Loans:* Direct Subsidized Stafford Loans, Direct Unsubsidized Stafford Loans, Direct PLUS loans, Federal Perkins Loans, Federal Nursing Loans, State Loans, College/university loans from institutional funds. *Student Employment:* Federal Work-Study Program available. Institutional employment available. **Financial Aid Statistics:** 56% needy freshmen, 60% needy undergrads receive need-based scholarship or grant aid. 27% freshmen, 21% undergrads receive non-need-based scholarship or grant aid. 84% freshmen, 86% undergrads receive need-based self-help aid. 1% freshmen, 1% undergrads receive athletic scholarships. 79% freshmen, 77% undergrads receive any aid. 69% undergrads borrow to pay for school. Average cumulative indebtedness $29,103. **Criteria for awarding aid:** *Need-based:* Academics. *Non-need-based:* Academics, Alumni affiliation, Art, Athletics, Leadership, Music/drama, State/district residency.

RAMAPO COLLEGE OF NEW JERSEY

505 Ramapo Valley Road-Admissions Office, Mahwah, NJ 07430-1680
Phone: 201-684-7300 • **Financial Aid Phone:** 201-684-7550
E-mail: admissions@ramapo.edu • **CEEB Code:** 2884
Fax: 201-684-7964 • **Website:** www.ramapo.edu • **ACT Code:** 2591

This public school was founded in 1971. It has a 300-acre campus.

RATINGS

Admissions Selectivity Rating: 71   **Fire Safety Rating:** 97   **Green Rating:** 60*

STUDENTS AND FACULTY

Enrollment: 5,425. **Student Body:** 54% female, 46% male, 5% out-of-state, 1% international (27 countries represented). Asian 7%, African American 5%, Caucasian 64%, Hispanic 13%, Native American <1%, Pacific Islander <1%, Two or more races 1%, Race unknown 7%.
Retention and Graduation: 86% freshmen return for sophomore year. 60% freshmen graduate within 4 years. 74% freshmen graduate within 6 years. **Faculty:** Student/faculty ratio 18:1. 215 full-time faculty, 91% hold PhDs, 25% are are members of minority groups, 51% are women. 0% of classes are taught by teaching assistants.

ACADEMICS

Degrees: bachelor's, certificate, master's, postbachelor's certifiate, post-master's certificate. **Classes:** Most classes have 20-29 students. Most lab/discussion sessions have 10-19 students. **Most popular majors:** Business Administration and Management; Psychology; Speech Communication and Rhetoric. **Special Study Options:** Accelerated program, cooperative education program, cross-registration, distance learning, double major, dual enrollment, exchange student program (domestic), external degree program, honors program, independent study, internships, liberal arts/career combination, student-designed major, study abroad, teacher certification program, The RCNJ Teacher's Education program is accredited by TEAC. Students with non-Business majors may enroll in courses to earn a Business Essentials Certificate. **Honors Programs:** http://www.ramapo.edu/honors/ The Ramapo College Honors Program is designed for students who desire a scholarly environment and an opportunity to interact with challenging faculty members and like- minded students. The Honors Program provides expanded opportunities for learning and reflection. Other benefits of the College Honors Program include residence hall options, special seminars, and exciting trips. Graduation from the College Honors Program is one indicator of a highly motivated, highly skilled, self-initiating individual. Students may participate in the College Honors Program by completing three H-option courses and receiving an Honors Certificate or by completing three H-option courses and completing a senior project, in which case the student graduates with full college honors. Full college honors is indicated on the diploma. For more information, please log onto http://www.ramapo.edu/academics/honors/ Combined degree programs: BA/MD, BA/MA, BA/DDS, BS/DR- PT, Phys. Ast.,Chiro.,Optom.,Osteo. **Disability Services:** Special programs offered to physically disabled students, including note-taking services, reader services, tape recorders, tutors. **Career Services:** Alumni network, Alumni services, Career/job search classes, Career assessment, Internships. The Career Center provides a full range of career development activities for Ramapo College of New Jersey students and alumni. In addition to individual and group career advising, our staff works with students, faculty and employers to deliver over 100 targeted programs and events each year. Our highly-regarded Cooperative Education program continues to be one of the best ways to prepare students for post-graduation success in employment and graduate school.

FACILITIES

Housing: Coed dorms, special housing for disabled students, special housing for international students, cooperative housing, apartments for single students, Special arrangements are made from time to time. Disabled students. live in same residence halls as non-disabled students. 100% of campus accessible to physically diasbled. **Special Academic Facilities/Equipment:** Art museum, media center, telecommunications center, electron microscope, astronomical observatory, Holocaust Studies Center, new sports/fitness complex. A new Center for Science, Education and Technology is underway, as well as a Sustainability Education Center, and a Spirituality Center. **Computers:** 100% of classrooms, 100% of dorms, 100% of libraries, 100% of dining areas, 100% of student union, 60% of common outdoor areas have wireless network access. Students can register for classes online. Administrative functions (other than registration) can be performed online.

CAMPUS LIFE

Environment: Town. **Activities:** Choral groups, dance, drama/theater, literary magazine, music ensembles, musical theater, radio station, student government, student newspaper, television station, yearbook, Campus Ministries, Student Organization, Model UN. 80 registered organizations, 19 honor societies, 7 religious organizations. 10 fraternities, 11 sororities. **Athletics**

(Intercollegiate): *Men:* baseball, basketball, cross-country, soccer, swimming, tennis, track/field (outdoor), track/field (indoor), volleyball. *Women:* basketball, cross-country, field hockey, lacrosse, soccer, softball, swimming, tennis, track/field (outdoor), track/field (indoor), volleyball. **On-Campus Highlights:** Berrie Center for Performing and Visual Arts, The Pavilion, The Market Place at the Birch Tree Inn, J Lee's in the Student Center, The Bill Bradley Sports and Fitness center. **Environmental Initiatives:** Curriculum (and a new building for the Sustainability Education Center).

ADMISSIONS

Freshman Academic Profile: Average high school GPA 3.3. 10% in top 10% of high school class, 25% in top 25% of high school class, 52% in top 50% of high school class. Minimum internet-based TOEFL 90. Minimum paper TOEFL 550. **Basis for Candidate Selection:** *Very important factors considered include:* rigor of secondary school record, class rank, academic GPA, standardized test scores. *Important factors considered include:* application essay, recommendation(s), extracurricular activities, talent/ability. *Other factors considered include:* character/personal qualities, first generation, alumni/ae relation, geographical residence, state residency, volunteer work, work experience, level of applicant's interest. **Freshman Admission Requirements:** High school diploma is required and GED is accepted. *Academic units required:* 4 English, 3 math, 3 science, 2 science labs, 2 foreign language, 3 social studies, 3 academic electives. **Freshman Admission Statistics:** 7,106 applied, 53.24% admitted, 24% enrolled. **Transfer Admission Requirements:** college transcript(s), essay or personal statement, Minimum college GPA of 2.5 required. Lowest grade transferable C. **General Admission Information:** Application fee $60. Regular application deadline 3/1. Regular notification 4/1. Nonfall registration accepted. Admission may be deferred for a maximum of 1 year.

COSTS AND FINANCIAL AID

Annual in-state tuition $11,600. Annual out-of-state tuition $22,000. Room and board $11,900. Required fees $4,872. Average book expense $1,569. **Required Forms and Deadlines:** FAFSA, State aid form. **Notification of Awards:** Applicants will be notified of awards on a rolling basis beginning 4/1. **Types of Aid:** *Need-based scholarships/grants:* Federal Pell, FSEOG, State scholarships/grants, Private scholarships, College/university scholarship or grant aid from institutional funds, Federal Nursing Scholarships. *Loans:* Direct Subsidized Stafford Loans, Direct Unsubsidized Stafford Loans, Direct PLUS loans, Federal Perkins Loans, State Loans. *Student Employment:* Federal Work-Study Program available. Institutional employment available. **Financial Aid Statistics:** 43% needy freshmen, 50% needy undergrads receive need-based scholarship or grant aid. 30% freshmen, 10% undergrads receive non-need-based scholarship or grant aid. 82% freshmen, 45% undergrads receive need-based self-help aid. 0% freshmen, 0% undergrads receive athletic scholarships. 80% freshmen, 74% undergrads receive any aid. 51% undergrads borrow to pay for school. Average cumulative indebtedness $10,715. **Criteria for awarding aid:** *Non-need-based:* Academics, Leadership, State/district residency.

See page 1018.

RANDOLPH COLLEGE

2500 Rivermont Avenue, Lynchburg, VA 24503-1555
Phone: 434-947-8100 • **Financial Aid Phone:** 434-947-8128
E-mail: admissions@randolphcollege.edu • **CEEB Code:** 5567
Fax: 434-947-8996 • **Website:** www.randolphcollege.com • **ACT Code:** 4388

This private school, affiliated with the Methodist Church, was founded in 1891. It has a 100-acre campus.

RATINGS

Admissions Selectivity Rating: 78   **Fire Safety Rating:** 95   **Green Rating:** 97

STUDENTS AND FACULTY

Enrollment: 649. **Student Body:** 66% female, 34% male, 35% out-of-state, 6% international (20 countries represented). Asian 2%, African American 13%, Caucasian 69%, Hispanic 6%, Native American <1%, Pacific Islander <1%, Two or more races 4%, Race unknown 0%.
Retention and Graduation: 72% freshmen return for sophomore year. 53% freshmen graduate within 4 years. 60% freshmen graduate within 6 years. **Faculty:** Student/faculty ratio 9:1. 70 full-time faculty, 94% hold PhDs, 16% are are members of minority groups, 57% are women. 0% of classes are taught by teaching assistants.

ACADEMICS

Degrees: bachelor's, master's. **Classes:** Most classes have fewer than 10 students. **Most popular majors:** Psychology; Biology/Biological Sciences; English Language and Literature. **Special Study Options:** Accelerated program, cross-registration, double major, dual enrollment, exchange student program (domestic), honors program, independent study, internships, liberal arts/career combination, student-designed major, study abroad, teacher certification program, 7-college exchange with Washington and Lee University, Hollins University, Hampden-Sydney College, Mary Baldwin College, Sweet Briar College, and Randolph-Macon College. Study abroad is encouraged and facilitated. The College currently offers a program for one or two semesters in Reading,England and affiliated programs in Greece, France, Denmark, Japan, Italy, Spain, N. Ireland, Mexico, and Czech Republic. Qualified students may elect to study abroad on a Randolph College or independent program. Endowed funds provide need-based assistance for study abroad to both American and international students. American Culture Program, a 1-Semester program that includes study on-site at key locations in and near Virginia, open to Randolph College students and students from other colleges who are accepted through a special application process. **Honors Programs:** Juniors and seniors who have a cumulative 3.45 in all academic work and a 3.7 in the major are eligible to read for Honors in the Major. The Honors Program encourages students of exceptional ability to engage in independent and intensive study in their fields of interest. Combined degree programs: BA/MA, BA/MEng, BA/MS Nursing; BS/BS Engineering. **Disability Services:** Special programs offered to physically disabled students, including note-taking services, reader services, tape recorders, tutors. **Career Services:** Alumni network, Alumni services, Career assessment, Internships, Regional alumni. We are most proud of our Experiential Learning opportunities made available to our students. The Career Development Center serves as a hub for all experiential activities and is responsible for coordination of those activities including service learning, study abroad, internships, volunteerism, the American Culture Program and the Davenport Leadership Program. The Experiential Learning Center empowers Randolph College students and faculty to creatively combine learning in the classroom with experiential opportunities within our campus and beyond. Through effective communication and collaboration, we help students make meaningful connections between their academic goals and life-long pursuits.

FACILITIES

Housing: Coed dorms, women's dorms, Special housing for non-traditional age students. 65% of campus accessible to physically diasbled. **Special Academic Facilities/Equipment:** Maier Museum of American Art recognized as one of the most outstanding college collections in the nation, computer-equipped classrooms (including wireless computer networks and smart boards), 100-acre equestrian center, language lab, science and math resource center, learning resources center, writing lab, nursery school, nature preserves, observatory, electron microscope. **Computers:** 100% of classrooms, 100% of dorms, 100% of libraries, 100% of dining areas, 100% of student union, 100% of common outdoor areas have wireless network access. Students can register for classes online. Administrative functions (other than registration) can be performed online.

CAMPUS LIFE

Environment: City. **Activities:** Choral groups, dance, drama/theater, literary magazine, music ensembles, pep band, radio station, student government, student newspaper, student-run film society, yearbook, Student Organization, Model UN. 40 registered organizations, 7 honor societies, 6 religious organizations. **Athletics (Intercollegiate):** *Men:* basketball, cross-country, equestrian sports, horseback riding, lacrosse, soccer, tennis. *Women:* basketball, cross-country, equestrian sports, horseback riding, lacrosse, soccer, softball, swimming, tennis, volleyball. **On-Campus Highlights:** The Maier Museum of Art, Macon Bookshop (on Rivermont Avenue), The Whiteside Amphitheater, Botanical Gardens, Main Hall and Main Grounds coffee bar, Randolph College Riding Center Skeller (in Main Hall) Houston Chapel.

ADMISSIONS

Freshman Academic Profile: Average high school GPA 3.5. 16% in top 10% of high school class, 45% in top 25% of high school class, 82% in top 50% of high school class. 82% from public high schools. **Reported SAT (pre-2016 redesign) scores:** SAT Math middle 50% range 440-570. SAT Critical Reading middle 50% range 460-580. SAT Writing middle 50% range 430-550. **Concordant SAT scores:** SAT EBRW middle 50% 500–620. SAT Math middle 50% range 480–590. ACT middle 50% range 20-26. **Basis for Candidate Selection:** *Very important factors considered include:* academic GPA, standardized test scores, recommendation(s). *Important factors considered include:* rigor of secondary school record, application essay, extracurricular activities, alumni/ae relation, level of applicant's interest. *Other factors considered include:* class rank, interview, talent/ability, character/personal qualities, first generation, volunteer work, work experience. **Freshman Admission Requirements:** High school diploma is required and GED is accepted. *Academic units required:* 4 English, 3 math, 3 science, 2 science labs, 2 history, 1 academic elective. *Academic units recommended:* 4 math, 3 foreign language, 3 academic electives. **Freshman Admission Statistics:**

1,214 applied, 83.61% admitted, 18% enrolled. **Transfer Admission Requirements:** High school transcript, college transcript(s), essay or personal statement, Lowest grade transferable C-. **General Admission Information:** Priority deadline 11/15. Regular application deadline 2/15. Nonfall registration accepted. Admission may be deferred for a maximum of 1 year.

COSTS AND FINANCIAL AID

Annual tuition $36,160. Room and board $12,580. Required fees $610. Average book expense $1,100. **Notification of Awards:** Applicants will be notified of awards on a rolling basis beginning 10/1. **Types of Aid:** *Need-based scholarships/grants:* Federal Pell, FSEOG, State scholarships/grants, Private scholarships, College/university scholarship or grant aid from institutional funds, United Negro College Fund. *Loans:* Direct Subsidized Stafford Loans, Direct Unsubsidized Stafford Loans, Direct PLUS loans, College/university loans from institutional funds. *Student Employment:* Federal Work-Study Program available. Institutional employment available. **Financial Aid Statistics:** 100% needy freshmen, 100% needy undergrads receive need-based scholarship or grant aid. 17% freshmen, 17% undergrads receive non-need-based scholarship or grant aid. 82% freshmen, 82% undergrads receive need-based self-help aid. 0% freshmen, 0% undergrads receive athletic scholarships. 99% freshmen, 99% undergrads receive any aid. 65% undergrads borrow to pay for school. Average cumulative indebtedness $35,199. **Criteria for awarding aid:** *Non-need-based:* Academics, Alumni affiliation, Art, Music/drama, Religious affiliation, State/district residency.

RANDOLPH-MACON COLLEGE

P.O. Box 5005, Ashland, VA 23005
Phone: 804-752-7305 • **Financial Aid Phone:** 804-752-7259
E-mail: admissions@rmc.edu • **CEEB Code:** 5566
Fax: 804-752-4707 • **Website:** www.rmc.edu • **ACT Code:** 4386

This private school, affiliated with the Methodist Church, was founded in 1830. It has a 120-acre campus.

RATINGS

Admissions Selectivity Rating: 86   **Fire Safety Rating:** 93   **Green Rating:** 60*

STUDENTS AND FACULTY

Enrollment: 1,429. **Student Body:** 53% female, 47% male, 26% out-of-state, 2% international (20 countries represented). Asian 2%, African American 8%, Caucasian 78%, Hispanic 4%, Native American <1%, Pacific Islander <1%, Two or more races 4%, Race unknown 1%.

Retention and Graduation: 85% freshmen return for sophomore year. 52% freshmen graduate within 4 years. 59% freshmen graduate within 6 years. 16% grads go on to further study within 1 year. 7% grads pursue arts and sciences degrees. 1% grads pursue law degrees. 2% grads pursue business degrees. 4% grads pursue medical degrees. **Faculty:** Student/faculty ratio 12:1. 102 full-time faculty, 99% hold PhDs, 9% are are members of minority groups, 48% are women. 0% of classes are taught by teaching assistants.

ACADEMICS

Degrees: bachelor's. **Classes:** Most classes have 10-19 students. **Most popular majors:** Biology/Biological Sciences; Psychology; Communication. **Special Study Options:** Accelerated program, cross-registration, double major, dual enrollment, exchange student program (domestic), honors program, independent study, internships, liberal arts/career combination, study abroad, teacher certification program, Member of Seven College Consortium, 3-2 program in engineering with Columbia University University of Virginia, 3-2 in forestry with Duke University, 4-1 in accounting with Virginia Commonwealth University. **Honors Programs:** The Honors Program offers qualified students the opportunity to take special honors classes, participate in unique programs and events for honors students, and an Honors House for recreation and socializing. Combined degree programs: BA/MD, BA/MA, BA/MEng, 3:2 Forestry, 4:1 Accounting, 4:1 MBA. **Disability Services:** Special programs offered to physically disabled students, including note-taking services, reader services, tape recorders, tutors. **Career Services:** Alumni network, Alumni services, Career/job search classes, Career assessment, Internships, Regional alumni. Randolph-Macon offers outstanding internship opportunities to students of all class years and majors. The Bassett Internship Program, open to seniors and juniors, offers course credit. There are also opportunities for paid internships.

FACILITIES

Housing: Coed dorms, special housing for disabled students, men's dorms, special housing for international students, women's dorms, fraternity/sorority housing, apartments for single students, Honors House; Substance-free housing; Special Interest Housing. 85% of campus accessible to physically diasbled. **Special Academic Facilities/Equipment:** Language lab, learning center, media center, greenhouse, observatory with telescope, electron microscopes, nuclear magnetic resonator, art gallery, fine arts center. **Computers:** 20% of classrooms, 100% of dorms, 100% of libraries, 100% of dining areas, 100% of student union, 25% of common outdoor areas have wireless network access. Students can register for classes online. Administrative functions (other than registration) can be performed online.

CAMPUS LIFE

Environment: Village. **Activities:** Choral groups, concert band, dance, drama/theater, jazz band, literary magazine, music ensembles, musical theater, pep band, radio station, student government, student newspaper, student-run film society, television station, yearbook, Campus Ministries, Student Organization. 102 registered organizations, 18 honor societies, 4 religious organizations. 6 fraternities, 4 sororities. **Athletics (Intercollegiate):** *Men:* baseball, basketball, football, golf, lacrosse, soccer, tennis. *Women:* basketball, field hockey, lacrosse, soccer, softball, swimming, tennis, volleyball. **On-Campus Highlights:** Randolph-Macon Performing Arts Center, The Brock Sports and Recreation Center, Frank E. Brown Campus Center, Pace-Armistead Hall and Flippo Gallery, Washington and Franklin Hall, Campus is located on 120 acres in the suburban community of Ashland, Virginia. R-MC has six historic landmarks, including three academic buildings listed on the National Historic Register. **Environmental Initiatives:** Designing, Planning, Building and Operating a LEED-certified residence hall incorporating solar power, geothermal heat exchange, rainwater reclamation and other sustainable aspects.

ADMISSIONS

Freshman Academic Profile: Average high school GPA 3.7. 24% in top 10% of high school class, 46% in top 25% of high school class, 84% in top 50% of high school class. 77% from public high schools. **Reported SAT (pre-2016 redesign) scores:** SAT Math middle 50% range 485-590. SAT Critical Reading middle 50% range 490-600. SAT Writing middle 50% range 460-565. **Concordant SAT scores:** SAT EBRW middle 50% 530–640. SAT Math middle 50% range 520–610. ACT middle 50% range 22-26. Minimum internet-based TOEFL 80. Minimum paper TOEFL 550. **Basis for Candidate Selection:** *Very important factors considered include:* rigor of secondary school record, academic GPA. *Important factors considered include:* class rank, standardized test scores, application essay, recommendation(s). *Other factors considered include:* interview, extracurricular activities, talent/ability, character/personal qualities, first generation, alumni/ae relation, racial/ethnic status, volunteer work, work experience, level of applicant's interest. **Freshman Admission Requirements:** High school diploma is required and GED is accepted. *Academic units required:* 4 English, 3 math, 3 science, 2 science labs, 2 social studies, 1 history, 1 academic elective. *Academic units recommended:* 4 English, 4 math, 4 science, 4 science labs, 4 foreign language, 3 social studies, 3 history, 2 academic electives. **Freshman Admission Statistics:** 2,842 applied, 61.40% admitted, 23% enrolled. **Transfer Admission Requirements:** High school transcript, college transcript(s), essay or personal statement, statement of good standing from prior institution(s). Minimum college GPA of 2.0 required. Lowest grade transferable C-. **General Admission Information:** Application fee $30. Priority deadline 2/1. Regular application deadline 3/1. Regular notification 4/1. Nonfall registration accepted. Admission may be deferred for a maximum of 1 year.

COSTS AND FINANCIAL AID

Annual tuition $38,750. Room and board $11,480. Required fees $1,350. Average book expense $1,200. **Required Forms and Deadlines:** FAFSA, State aid form. **Notification of Awards:** Applicants will be notified of awards on or about 3/1. **Types of Aid:** *Need-based scholarships/grants:* Federal Pell, FSEOG, State scholarships/grants, Private scholarships, College/university scholarship or grant aid from institutional funds. *Loans:* Direct Subsidized Stafford Loans, Direct Unsubsidized Stafford Loans, Direct PLUS loans, Federal Perkins Loans. *Student Employment:* Federal Work-Study Program available. Institutional employment available. **Financial Aid Statistics:** 100% needy freshmen, 100% needy undergrads receive need-based scholarship or grant aid. 30% freshmen, 27% undergrads receive non-need-based scholarship or grant aid. 69% freshmen, 72% undergrads receive need-based self-help aid. 0% freshmen, 0% undergrads receive athletic scholarships. 99% freshmen, 99% undergrads receive any aid. 70% undergrads borrow to pay for school. Average cumulative indebtedness $33,015. **Criteria for awarding aid:** *Need-based:* Academics, Religious affiliation. *Non-need-based:* Academics, Alumni affiliation, Minority status, Religious affiliation, State/district residency.

REED COLLEGE

3203 SE Woodstock Boulevard, Portland, OR 97202-8199
Phone: 503-777-7511 • **Financial Aid Phone:** 503-777-7223
E-mail: admission@reed.edu • **CEEB Code:** 4654
Fax: 503-777-7553 • **Website:** www.reed.edu • **ACT Code:** 3494

This private school was founded in 1908. It has a 116-acre campus.

RATINGS

Admissions Selectivity Rating: 95   **Fire Safety Rating:** 96   **Green Rating:** 60*

STUDENTS AND FACULTY

Enrollment: 1,376. **Student Body:** 55% female, 45% male, 92% out-of-state, 8% international (46 countries represented). Asian 6%, African American 2%, Caucasian 59%, Hispanic 12%, Native American <1%, Pacific Islander <1%, Two or more races 8%, Race unknown 4%.
Retention and Graduation: 87% freshmen return for sophomore year. 66% freshmen graduate within 4 years. 78% freshmen graduate within 6 years. 65% grads go on to further study within 1 year. 48% grads pursue arts and sciences degrees. 5% grads pursue law degrees. 3% grads pursue business degrees. 4% grads pursue medical degrees. **Faculty:** Student/faculty ratio 9:1. 147 full-time faculty, 94% hold PhDs, 17% are are members of minority groups, 41% are women. 0% of classes are taught by teaching assistants.

ACADEMICS

Degrees: bachelor's, master's. **Classes:** Most classes have 10-19 students. Most lab/discussion sessions have 10-19 students. **Most popular majors:** English Language and Literature; Anthropology; Psychology. **Special Study Options:** cross-registration, double major, dual enrollment, exchange student program (domestic), independent study, internships, liberal arts/career combination, study abroad. Computer Science: By arrangement with the University of Washington, a student may obtain a bachelor of arts degree from Reed and a bachelor of science degree in computer science from the University of Washington. The program calls for three years at Reed, including completion of the general distribution requirements and major requirements in one department, the passing of the junior qualifying examination, the acquisition of a minimum of 22 Reed units (at least 20 of which, including the distribution requirements, must be earned at Reed), and two years at the University of Washington. The university will admit up to five students per year on the recommendation of Reed College. Recommended students must satisfy the university's GPA requirements for transfer students, which may differ from year to year and which are not necessarily the same for Washington residents and non-residents. Computer science degrees are also available under the engineering programs described later in this section. Course Requirements These vary, depending upon the field of the Reed major -chemistry, mathematics, or physics. Consult the Reed dual degree coordinator for specific information. In special cases, an ad hoc program with the biology or economics department, or with another department, may be approved. Engineering: By arrangement with the California Institute of Technology (Caltech), the Columbia University School of Engineering and Applied Sciences, or Rensselaer Polytechnic Institute, a student may obtain a bachelor's degree in engineering (alternatively, computer science or certain earth and planetary sciences) and a bachelor of arts degree from Reed. The program calls for three years at Reed, including the completion of the general college distribution requirements, completion of major requirements in one department (excluding thesis), the passing of the junior qualifying examination, the acquisition of a minimum of 22 Reed units (at least 20 of which, including all but two units of the distribution requirement, must be earned at Reed), and two years at the engineering school. Transfer students entering these programs should expect to spend no fewer than five semesters at Reed to meet this requirement. The two degrees will be awarded concurrently; all requirements for both degrees must be met before either is awarded. Admission to the engineering school is contingent on the college's recommendation and the student's having met certain course requirements of the engineering school while at Reed. Typical course requirements are two years of physics, one or two years of chemistry, and two years of mathematics, including differential equations. Normally, students with a G.P.A. less than 3.0 should not expect to be recommended. Admission to the specific field of engineering preferred by the student is not guaranteed; the student's academic record can be relevant. Admission to Caltech is not automatic upon recommendation, but is subject to review by Caltech and may depend upon factors that cannot be anticipated. Caltech does not guarantee financial aid to otherwise eligible students. While admission to the other programs is also subject to review by the participating school, admission can usually be expected upon recommendation. Course Requirements During the freshman year: Mathematics 111/112 or 211/212; Physics 100. Consult with the Reed dual degree coordinator for information on other required courses. Forestry-Environmental Sciences: By arrangement with the Nicholas School of the Environment of Duke University, a student may obtain a bachelor of arts degree at Reed and a professional master's degree from Duke (master of forestry or master of environmental management). Work at Duke emphasizes three aspects of study and research in forest and other renewable natural resources: management, science, and policy. The program calls for three years at Reed, including completion of the general college distribution and major requirements (excluding thesis), passing of the junior qualifying examination, the acquisition of a minimum of 22 Reed units (at least 20 of which, including the distribution requirements, must be earned at Reed), and two years at Duke. Students in all academic majors may qualify for the program. Course Requirements l. Biology 101,102; Mathematics 111 or 112, and Mathematics 141; and Economics 201. 2. Successful completion of the junior qualifying exam before the end of the junior year. Students should plan to take the Graduate Record Examination and make formal application for admission to Duke during the third year at Reed. In the summer following the third year, the student should begin work at Duke. Additional information may be obtained from the faculty adviser for the forestry-environmental sciences program. Pre-Medical and Pre-Veterinary Medical schools value the breadth in educational programs offered by liberal arts colleges. Work in the humanities and social sciences, as well as non-academic factors are all very important. Students should choose a major according to their academic interests and include the following laboratory and other courses to fulfill the admission requirements of most medical schools: 1. General biology: Biology 101 and 102 2. General chemistry: Chemistry 101 and 102 3. Organic chemistry: Chemistry 201 and 202 4. General physics: Physics 100, with lab 5. English or humanities: Humanities 110 6. One year of mathematics, including calculus (Mathematics 111) Course prerequisites for veterinary school usually include the courses above plus additional specific courses, such as biochemistry or upper-level biology. Since there are more than 100 domestic medical schools and 30 veterinary schools, the student may encounter variation in the number and character of admission requirements. Students should be acquainted with the specific requirements and programs of the schools to which they apply. To prepare a competitive application portfolio, students considering medical or veterinary school are strongly encouraged to consult with health professions advisers and the career services office early in their undergraduate careers. In addition to offering advising, the career services office maintains a library of resources essential to the medical school planning process, such as Medical School Admission Requirements, a publication by the American Association of Medical Colleges. The guide Preparation for Medical School at Reed is available online, and includes important timelines, health care internship information, insight into letters of evaluation, and useful web links. It is strongly recommended that students take advantage of additional resources by attending informational seminars, seeking assistance with the application process, and using mock interviews. Graduating students who plan to take time off before applying to medical or veterinary school should discuss their plans with a health-profession adviser before graduation. Visual Arts: The college has made arrangements for Reed students to participate in a variety of exchange programs and summer internships at other institutions. They may choose from programs in painting and sculpture, architecture, art history, archaeology, conservation, historic preservation, and museum work. A joint five-year program is also available with the Pacific Northwest College of Art. These programs are described in more detail in the art department section of the catalog. Combined degree programs: Computing: Univ. of Washington; Art: Pacific NW College of Art. **Disability Services:** Special programs offered to physically disabled students, including note-taking services, reader services, tape recorders, tutors. **Career Services:** Alumni network, Alumni services, Career/job search classes, Career assessment, Internships, Regional alumni.

FACILITIES

Housing: Coed dorms, special housing for disabled students, women's dorms, cooperative housing, apartments for single students, Wellness Housing, Theme Housing, Reed language houses accommodate upper-division students studying Chinese, French, German, Russian, and Spanish. First-year students required to live on campus; exceptions granted for unusual situations. 85% of campus accessible to physically diasbled. **Special Academic Facilities/Equipment:** Art gallery, studio art building, language labs, computerized music listening lab, nuclear research reactor, 20 music practice rooms and midi lab, 760 seat auditorium, academic support center (quantitative skills, writing, math support), educational technology center **Computers:** 100% of classrooms, 100% of dorms, 100% of libraries, 100% of dining areas, 100% of student union, 50% of common outdoor areas have wireless network access. Students can register for classes online. Administrative functions (other than registration) can be performed online.

CAMPUS LIFE

Environment: Metropolis. **Activities:** Choral groups, dance, drama/theater, literary magazine, music ensembles, radio station, student government, student newspaper, student-run film society, symphony orchestra, Campus Ministries, Student Organization, Model UN. 130 registered organizations, 1 honor society,

5 religious organizations. **On-Campus Highlights:** Thesis Tower, Nuclear Research Reactor, Crystal Springs Canyon, Cerf Amphitheatre, The Paradox Cafe. **Environmental Initiatives:** LEED construction.

ADMISSIONS

Freshman Academic Profile: Average high school GPA 3.9. 54% in top 10% of high school class, 83% in top 25% of high school class, 97% in top 50% of high school class. 59% from public high schools. **Reported SAT (pre-2016 redesign) scores:** SAT Math middle 50% range 620-730. SAT Critical Reading middle 50% range 660-750. SAT Writing middle 50% range 630-730. **Concordant SAT scores:** SAT EBRW middle 50% 690–760. SAT Math middle 50% range 640–760. ACT middle 50% range 29-33. Minimum internet-based TOEFL 100. Minimum paper TOEFL 600. **Basis for Candidate Selection:** *Very important factors considered include:* rigor of secondary school record, academic GPA, application essay. *Important factors considered include:* class rank, standardized test scores, recommendation(s), interview, level of applicant's interest. *Other factors considered include:* extracurricular activities, talent/ability, character/personal qualities, first generation, alumni/ae relation, geographical residence, racial/ethnic status, volunteer work, work experience. **Freshman Admission Requirements:** High school diploma is required and GED is accepted. *Academic units recommended:* 4 English, 3 science, 3 foreign language. **Freshman Admission Statistics:** 5,705 applied, 31.31% admitted, 20% enrolled. **Transfer Admission Requirements:** High school transcript, college transcript(s), essay or personal statement, standardized test scores, statement of good standing from prior institution(s). Lowest grade transferable C-. **General Admission Information:** Regular application deadline 1/15. Regular notification 4/1. Nonfall registration not accepted. Admission may be deferred for a maximum of 1 year.

COSTS AND FINANCIAL AID

Annual tuition $51,850. Room and board $13,150. Required fees $300. Average book expense $1,050. **Required Forms and Deadlines:** FAFSA, CSS/Financial Aid PROFILE, Noncustodial PROFILE, Business/Farm Supplement. **Notification of Awards:** Applicants will be notified of awards on or about 4/1. **Types of Aid:** *Need-based scholarships/grants:* Federal Pell, FSEOG, State scholarships/grants, Private scholarships, College/university scholarship or grant aid from institutional funds. *Loans:* Direct Subsidized Stafford Loans, Direct Unsubsidized Stafford Loans, Direct PLUS loans, Federal Perkins Loans, College/university loans from institutional funds. *Student Employment:* Federal Work-Study Program available. Institutional employment available. **Financial Aid Statistics:** 98% needy freshmen, 98% needy undergrads receive need-based scholarship or grant aid. 0% undergrads receive non-need-based scholarship or grant aid. 100% freshmen, 100% undergrads receive need-based self-help aid. 0% freshmen, 0% undergrads receive athletic scholarships. 53% freshmen, 54% undergrads receive any aid. 44% undergrads borrow to pay for school. Average cumulative indebtedness $19,627.

See page 1020.

REGENT UNIVERSITY

1000 Regent University Drive, Virginia Beach, VA 23464
Phone: 800-373-5504 • **Financial Aid Phone:** 757-352-4125
E-mail: admissions@regent.edu • **CEEB Code:** 30913
Fax: 757-352-4381 • **Website:** www.regent.edu • **ACT Code:** 6738

This private school, affiliated with the Christian (Nondenominational) Church, was founded in 1978. It has a 70-acre campus.

RATINGS

Admissions Selectivity Rating: 77   **Fire Safety Rating:** 87   **Green Rating:** 65

STUDENTS AND FACULTY

Enrollment: 3,657. **Student Body:** 61% female, 39% male, 54% out-of-state, 1% international (84 countries represented). Asian 2%, African American 28%, Caucasian 54%, Hispanic 7%, Native American 1%, Pacific Islander <1%, Two or more races 5%, Race unknown 1%.
Retention and Graduation: 77% freshmen return for sophomore year. 24% freshmen graduate within 4 years. 46% freshmen graduate within 6 years.
Faculty: Student/faculty ratio 21:1. 153 full-time faculty, 91% hold PhDs, 16% are are members of minority groups, 32% are women. 0% of classes are taught by teaching assistants.

ACADEMICS

Degrees: associate, bachelor's, certificate, doctoral/professional, doctoral/research, doctoral, master's, postbachelor's certificate, post-master's certificate. **Classes:** Most classes have 20-29 students. **Most popular majors:** Religion/Religious Studies; Psychology; Business/Commerce. **Special Study Options:** distance learning, double major, dual enrollment, internships, study abroad, teacher certification program. Combined degree programs: BA/MA. **Disability Services:** Special programs offered to physically disabled students, including note-taking services, reader services, tape recorders, tutors. **Career Services:** Alumni network, Alumni services, Career/job search classes, Career assessment, Internships, Regional alumni. At Regent's Career Services, you will find our programs and resources are a great way to prepare for your career path.

FACILITIES

Housing: apartments for married students, apartments for single students. 100% of campus accessible to physically diasbled. **Special Academic Facilities/Equipment:** The 31,000-square-foot Student Center on Regent's Virginia Beach Campus, opened in 2003, offers a central location for campus and student services. The building houses the University Bookstore, student organizations and meeting rooms, a cafe/coffee shop, computer lab, student lounge and offices for the Registrar, Admissions and Financial Aid. The 135,000-square-foot Communication & Performing Arts Center, opened in 2002, includes film and animation studios, a state-of-the-art main theatre, screening rooms and editing suites in one of the most technologically advanced communication buildings on the east coast. **Computers:** 80% of classrooms, 100% of dorms, 100% of libraries, 100% of student union, 50% of common outdoor areas have wireless network access. Students can register for classes online. Administrative functions (other than registration) can be performed online.

CAMPUS LIFE

Environment: City. **Activities:** Choral groups, concert band, dance, drama/theater, student government, student newspaper, Campus Ministries, Student Organization. 47 registered organizations, 4 honor societies. **On-Campus Highlights:** The Student Center, Communication & Performing Arts, The Ordinary Cafe and Coffee Shop, Robertson Hall, University Library, Robertson Hall is equipped with the latest technology in audio/video equipment and cameras for simultaneous broadcasting. The 132,000-square-foot building also boasts a 380-seat moot court/city council chamber. The 135,000-square-foot Communication & Performing Arts Center features a 750-seat theater and a 150-seat experimental theater, cinema-television production studio, film sound stage, screening theaters, technical studios and teaching labs. A back lot area offers space for sets for indoor and outdoor filming. Just opened in 2002, the 31,000-square-foot Student Center houses the University Bookstore, student organization offices, The Ordinary cafe/coffee shop, a computer lab, student lounge and meeting rooms. **Environmental Initiatives:** Our investments in "cool storage" systems since our beginning in 1978 allows us to shave peak demand when the power company desires. This helps reduce the size of the power plant needed to support this area. This results in a major decrease in greenhouse emissions for this area. This fact is recognized by VA Dominion Power –our supplier of electricity.

ADMISSIONS

Freshman Academic Profile: Average high school GPA 3.5. 10% in top 10% of high school class, 33% in top 25% of high school class, 66% in top 50% of high school class. **Reported SAT (pre-2016 redesign) scores:** SAT Math middle 50% range 440-550. SAT Critical Reading middle 50% range 480-590. SAT Writing middle 50% range 450-570. **Concordant SAT scores:** SAT EBRW middle 50% 520–640. SAT Math middle 50% range 480–570. ACT middle 50% range 19-25. Minimum internet-based TOEFL 90. Minimum paper TOEFL 577. **Basis for Candidate Selection:** *Very important factors considered include:* academic GPA, standardized test scores. *Important factors considered include:* application essay. *Other factors considered include:* rigor of secondary school record, recommendation(s), character/personal qualities. **Freshman Admission Requirements:** High school diploma or equivalent is not required. *Academic units recommended:* 4 English, 3 math, 3 science, 3 foreign language, 3 social studies. **Freshman Admission Statistics:** 1,953 applied, 82.74% admitted, 28% enrolled. **Transfer Admission Requirements:** college transcript(s), Lowest grade transferable c. **General Admission Information:** Application fee $50. Regular application deadline 5/1. Nonfall registration accepted. Admission may be deferred for a maximum of One year.

COSTS AND FINANCIAL AID

Average book expense $1,000. **Required Forms and Deadlines:** FAFSA, Institution's own financial aid form, State aid form. **Notification of Awards:** Applicants will be notified of awards on a rolling basis beginning 12/1. **Types of Aid:** *Need-based scholarships/grants:* Federal Pell, State scholarships/grants, Private scholarships, College/university scholarship or grant aid from institutional funds. *Loans:* Direct Subsidized Stafford Loans, Direct Unsubsidized Stafford Loans, Direct PLUS loans. *Student Employment:* Institutional employment available. **Financial Aid Statistics:** 97% needy freshmen, 91% needy undergrads receive need-based scholarship or grant aid. 16% freshmen, 7% undergrads receive non-need-based scholarship or grant aid. 90% freshmen, 95% undergrads receive need-based self-help aid. 0% freshmen, 0% undergrads receive athletic scholarships. 92% freshmen, 87% undergrads receive any aid. 71% undergrads borrow to pay for school. Average cumulative indebtedness $28,780. **Criteria for awarding aid:** *Non-need-based:* Academics, Alumni affiliation, Leadership.

REGIS COLLEGE

235 Wellesley Street, Weston, MA 02493-1571
Phone: 781-768-7100 • **Financial Aid Phone:** 781-768-7184
E-mail: admission@regiscollege.edu • **CEEB Code:** 3723
Fax: 781-768-7071 • **Website:** www.regiscollege.edu • **ACT Code:** 1886

This private school, affiliated with the Roman Catholic Church, was founded in 1927. It has a 131-acre campus.

RATINGS

Admissions Selectivity Rating: 74   **Fire Safety Rating:** 89   **Green Rating:** 60*

STUDENTS AND FACULTY

Enrollment: 1,235. **Student Body:** 79% female, 21% male, 19% out-of-state, 2% international (17 countries represented). Asian 4%, African American 19%, Caucasian 49%, Hispanic 11%, Native American <1%, Pacific Islander <1%, Two or more races 1%, Race unknown 12%.
Retention and Graduation: 82% freshmen return for sophomore year. 38% freshmen graduate within 4 years. 47% freshmen graduate within 6 years. 28% grads go on to further study within 1 year. 16% grads pursue arts and sciences degrees. 1% grads pursue law degrees. 2% grads pursue business degrees. 2% grads pursue medical degrees. **Faculty:** Student/faculty ratio 11:1. 96 full-time faculty, 70% hold PhDs, 9% are are members of minority groups, 76% are women. 0% of classes are taught by teaching assistants.

ACADEMICS

Degrees: associate, bachelor's, doctoral/professional, master's, post-master's certificate, transfer. **Classes:** Most classes have 10-19 students. **Most popular majors:** Registered Nursing/Registered Nurse; Business/Commerce; Biology/Biological Sciences. **Special Study Options:** Accelerated program, cross-registration, double major, English as a Second Language (ESL), exchange student program (domestic), honors program, independent study, internships, student-designed major, study abroad, teacher certification program. **Honors Programs:** The Honors Program at Regis College offers qualified students a stimulating and challenging learning experience, and opportunities for distinguished scholarship. It prepares students to become leaders committed to the betterment of the human condition and our society, a goal that is central to the Regis College mission. **Disability Services:** Special programs offered to physically disabled students, including note-taking services, tape recorders, tutors. **Career Services:** Alumni network, Alumni services, Career/job search classes, Career assessment, Internships, On-campus interviews. Internships offer students opportunities to apply classroom learning to the world of work while receiving academic credit.

FACILITIES

Housing: Coed dorms, women's dorms. 85% of campus accessible to physically diasbled. **Special Academic Facilities/Equipment:** Fine arts center, philatelic museum. **Computers:** 30% of classrooms, 100% of dorms, 100% of libraries, 100% of dining areas, 100% of student union, 15% of common outdoor areas have wireless network access. Students can register for classes online. Administrative functions (other than registration) can be performed online.

CAMPUS LIFE

Environment: Village. **Activities:** Choral groups, dance, drama/theater, literary magazine, music ensembles, musical theater, radio station, student government, yearbook, Campus Ministries, Model UN. 36 registered organizations, 10 honor societies, 2 religious organizations. **Athletics (Intercollegiate):** *Men:* basketball, diving, soccer, swimming. *Women:* basketball, diving, field hockey, lacrosse, soccer, softball, swimming, tennis, track/field (outdoor), track/field (indoor), volleyball. **On-Campus Highlights:** College Hall, Student Union, Tower, Athletic Complex, Fine Arts Center. **Environmental Initiatives:** Replacement of steam boilers w/high efficiency designs.

ADMISSIONS

Freshman Academic Profile: Average high school GPA 3.1. 10% in top 10% of high school class, 35% in top 25% of high school class, 66% in top 50% of high school class. 75% from public high schools. **Reported SAT (pre-2016 redesign) scores:** SAT Math middle 50% range 420-540. SAT Critical Reading middle 50% range 420-520. SAT Writing middle 50% range 420-520. **Concordant SAT scores:** SAT EBRW middle 50% 470–580. SAT Math middle 50% range 460–570. ACT middle 50% range 19-23. Minimum paper TOEFL 550. **Basis for Candidate Selection:** *Very important factors considered include:* rigor of secondary school record, academic GPA, application essay, recommendation(s), character/personal qualities. *Important factors considered include:* class rank, interview, extracurricular activities, talent/ability, volunteer work, work experience. *Other factors considered include:* standardized test scores, first generation, alumni/ae relation, geographical residence, level of applicant's interest. **Freshman Admission Requirements:** High school diploma is required and GED is accepted. *Academic units required:* 4 English, 3 math, 2 science, 1 science lab, 2 foreign language, 2 social studies, 3 academic electives. *Academic units recommended:* 3 foreign language, 4 social studies. **Freshman Admission Statistics:** 2,023 applied, 84.23% admitted, 16% enrolled. **Transfer Admission Requirements:** High school transcript, college transcript(s), essay or personal statement, Minimum college GPA of 2.0 required. Lowest grade transferable C. **General Admission Information:** Application fee $50. Priority deadline 2/15. Regular application deadline 6/1. Regular notification 12/20. Nonfall registration accepted. Admission may be deferred for a maximum of 1 year.

COSTS AND FINANCIAL AID
Annual tuition $37,540. Room and board $14,380. Average book expense $1,000. **Required Forms and Deadlines:** FAFSA. **Notification of Awards:** Applicants will be notified of awards on a rolling basis beginning 3/15. **Types of Aid:** *Need-based scholarships/grants:* Federal Pell, FSEOG, State scholarships/grants, Private scholarships, College/university scholarship or grant aid from institutional funds. *Loans:* Direct Subsidized Stafford Loans, Direct Unsubsidized Stafford Loans, Direct PLUS loans, Federal Perkins Loans. *Student Employment:* Federal Work-Study Program available. Institutional employment available. **Financial Aid Statistics:** 92% needy freshmen, 91% needy undergrads receive need-based scholarship or grant aid. 49% freshmen, 50% undergrads receive non-need-based scholarship or grant aid. 94% freshmen, 96% undergrads receive need-based self-help aid. 0% freshmen, 0% undergrads receive athletic scholarships. 91% freshmen, 84% undergrads receive any aid. 94% undergrads borrow to pay for school. Average cumulative indebtedness $49,217. **Criteria for awarding aid:** *Need-based:* Leadership, Minority status, Religious affiliation. *Non-need-based:* Academics, Alumni affiliation, Religious affiliation.

See page 1022.

REGIS UNIVERSITY

3333 Regis Boulevard, Denver, CO 80221-1099
Phone: 303-458-4900 • **Financial Aid Phone:** 303-458-4126
E-mail: RUAdmissions@regis.edu • **CEEB Code:** 4656
Fax: 303-964-5534 • **Website:** www.regis.edu • **ACT Code:** 526

This private school, affiliated with the Roman Catholic Church, was founded in 1877. It has a 90-acre campus.

RATINGS
Admissions Selectivity Rating: 83   **Fire Safety Rating:** 65   **Green Rating:** 70

STUDENTS AND FACULTY
Enrollment: 4,414. **Student Body:** 61% female, 39% male, 37% out-of-state, 1% international (8 countries represented). Asian 5%, African American 5%, Caucasian 59%, Hispanic 19%, Native American 1%, Pacific Islander <1%, Two or more races 4%, Race unknown 7%.
Retention and Graduation: 79% freshmen return for sophomore year. 56% freshmen graduate within 4 years. 73% freshmen graduate within 6 years.
Faculty: Student/faculty ratio 14:1. 274 full-time faculty, 82% hold PhDs, 11% are are members of minority groups, 59% are women. 0% of classes are taught by teaching assistants.

ACADEMICS
Degrees: bachelor's, certificate, doctoral/professional, master's, postbachelor's certificate, post-master's certificate. **Classes:** Most classes have fewer than 10 students. Most lab/discussion sessions have 10-19 students. **Most popular majors:** Business Administration and Management; Registered Nursing/ Registered Nurse; Computer Science. **Special Study Options:** Accelerated program, cooperative education program, cross-registration, distance learning, double major, dual enrollment, exchange student program (domestic), honors program, independent study, internships, liberal arts/career combination, student-designed major, study abroad, teacher certification program, weekend college. Combined degree programs: BA/MA, BS/MS; BAS/MS. **Disability Services:** Special programs offered to physically disabled students, including tutors. **Career Services:** Alumni services, Career/job search classes, Career assessment, Internships. Regis is proud of both its experiential learning and internship programs.

FACILITIES
Housing: Coed dorms, special housing for disabled students, apartments for single students. 90% of campus accessible to physically diasbled. Language lab, wellness center. **Computers:** Administrative functions (other than registration) can be performed online.

CAMPUS LIFE
Environment: Metropolis. **Activities:** Choral groups, drama/theater, literary magazine, music ensembles, musical theater, radio station, student government, student newspaper, yearbook. 40 registered organizations, 1 honor society, 1 religious organization. **Athletics (Intercollegiate):** *Men:* baseball, basketball, cross-country, golf, soccer. *Women:* basketball, cross-country, lacrosse, soccer, softball, volleyball.

ADMISSIONS
Freshman Academic Profile: Average high school GPA 3.5. 21% in top 10% of high school class, 50% in top 25% of high school class, 79% in top 50% of high school class. 65% from public high schools. **Reported SAT (pre-2016 redesign) scores:** SAT Math middle 50% range 470-590. SAT Critical Reading middle 50% range 480-580. SAT Writing middle 50% range 480-570. **Concordant SAT scores:** SAT EBRW middle 50% 540–630. SAT Math middle 50% range 510–610. ACT middle 50% range 21-27. Minimum internet-based TOEFL 82. Minimum paper TOEFL 550. **Basis for Candidate Selection:** *Very important factors considered include:* rigor of secondary school record, academic GPA, standardized test scores, character/personal qualities. *Other factors considered include:* class rank, application essay, recommendation(s), interview, extracurricular activities, talent/ability, volunteer work. **Freshman Admission Requirements:** High school diploma is required and GED is accepted. *Academic units recommended:* 4 English, 3 math, 2 science, 1 science lab, 2 foreign language, 2 social studies, 1 academic elective. **Freshman Admission Statistics:** 5,493 applied, 65.70% admitted, 15% enrolled. **Transfer Admission Requirements:** college transcript(s), essay or personal statement, Minimum college GPA of 2.0 required. **General Admission Information:** Priority deadline 4/15. Regular application deadline 8/1. Nonfall registration accepted. Admission may be deferred for a maximum of 1 year.

COSTS AND FINANCIAL AID
Annual tuition $33,110. Room and board $10,040. Required fees $600. Average book expense $1,800. **Required Forms and Deadlines:** FAFSA. **Notification of Awards:** Applicants will be notified of awards on a rolling basis beginning 3/15. **Types of Aid:** *Need-based scholarships/grants:* Federal Pell, FSEOG, State scholarships/grants, Private scholarships, College/university scholarship or grant aid from institutional funds. *Loans:* Direct Subsidized Stafford Loans, Direct Unsubsidized Stafford Loans, Direct PLUS loans, Federal Perkins Loans, Federal Nursing Loans. *Student Employment:* Federal Work-Study Program available. Institutional employment available. **Financial Aid Statistics:** 100% needy freshmen, 86% needy undergrads receive need-based scholarship or grant aid. 14% freshmen, 10% undergrads receive non-need-based scholarship or grant aid. 71% freshmen, 79% undergrads receive need-based self-help aid. 7% freshmen, 5% undergrads receive athletic scholarships. 69% freshmen, 67% undergrads receive any aid. 61% undergrads borrow to pay for school. Average cumulative indebtedness $28,128. **Criteria for awarding aid:** *Need-based:* Academics, Athletics, Leadership, Music/drama, Religious affiliation. *Non-need-based:* Academics, Athletics, Leadership, Music/drama, Religious affiliation, State/district residency.

REINHARDT UNIVERSITY

7300 Reinhardt Circle, Waleska, GA 30183
Phone: 770-720-5526 • **Financial Aid Phone:** 770-720-5667
E-mail: www.reinhardt.edu
Fax: 770-720-5899 • **Website:** www.reinhardt.edu • **ACT Code:** 856

This private school, affiliated with the Methodist Church, was founded in 1883. It has a 600-acre campus.

RATINGS
Admissions Selectivity Rating: 75   **Fire Safety Rating:** 97   **Green Rating:** 60*

STUDENTS AND FACULTY
Enrollment: 980. **Student Body:** 55% female, 45% male, 27% out-of-state, 0% international. Asian 1%, African American 13%, Caucasian 75%, Hispanic 4%, Native American 1%, Pacific Islander 0%, Two or more races 0%, Race unknown 6%.
Retention and Graduation: 23% freshmen graduate within 4 years. 35% grads go on to further study within 1 year. 20% grads pursue arts and sciences degrees. 5% grads pursue law degrees. 45% grads pursue business degrees. 5% grads pursue medical degrees. **Faculty:** Student/faculty ratio 12:1. 62 full-time faculty, 74% hold PhDs, 11% are are members of minority groups, 48% are women. 0% of classes are taught by teaching assistants.

ACADEMICS
Degrees: associate, bachelor's, master's, transfer. **Classes:** Most classes have 10-19 students. **Most popular majors:** Business Administration and

Management; Elementary Education and Teaching; Music. **Special Study Options:** Accelerated program, double major, dual enrollment, external degree program, honors program, independent study, internships, study abroad, teacher certification program. **Honors Programs:** The Honors Program is designed for students who are bright, curious and enjoy being challenged. Entering freshman with High Schjool GPA of at least 3.5 or a combined SAT of 1050 or higher, with verbal score of at least 580, will be invited to apply for admission to Reinhardt College's Honors Program. **Disability Services:** Special programs offered to physically disabled students, including note-taking services, reader services, tape recorders, tutors. **Career Services:** Alumni services, Career/job search classes, Career assessment, Internships, Regional alumni, On-campus interviews, School of Communications.

FACILITIES

Housing: Coed dorms, special housing for disabled students, men's dorms, women's dorms, honors house. 99% of campus accessible to physically diasbled. **Special Academic Facilities/Equipment:** Funk Heritage Center, Falany Performing Arts **Computers:** 100% of classrooms, 100% of dorms, 100% of libraries, 100% of student union, 5% of common outdoor areas have wireless network access. Students can register for classes online. Administrative functions (other than registration) can be performed online.

CAMPUS LIFE

Environment: Rural. **Activities:** Choral groups, concert band, drama/theater, jazz band, music ensembles, student government, student newspaper, student-run film society, television station, yearbook, Campus Ministries, Student Organization. 40 registered organizations, 6 honor societies, 5 religious organizations. **Athletics (Intercollegiate):** *Men:* baseball, basketball, cheerleading, cross-country, golf, soccer, tennis. *Women:* basketball, cheerleading, cross-country, golf, soccer, softball, tennis, volleyball. **On-Campus Highlights:** Falany Performing Arts Center, Funk Heritage Center, Gordy Center, Library, Class room building. **Environmental Initiatives:** Recycle paper, RU Green.

ADMISSIONS

Freshman Academic Profile: Average high school GPA 3.0. 63% in top 50% of high school class. 98% from public high schools. **Reported SAT (pre-2016 redesign) scores:** SAT Math middle 50% range 430-530. SAT Critical Reading middle 50% range 410-540. **Concordant SAT scores:** SAT Math middle 50% range 470–560. ACT middle 50% range 17-22. Minimum paper TOEFL 500. **Basis for Candidate Selection:** *Very important factors considered include:* academic GPA, standardized test scores. *Important factors considered include:* rigor of secondary school record, class rank. **Freshman Admission Requirements:** High school diploma is required and GED is accepted. *Academic units required:* 4 English, 4 math, 3 science, 3 social studies. *Academic units recommended:* 2 foreign language. **Freshman Admission Statistics:** 1,310 applied, 58.70% admitted, 30% enrolled. **Transfer Admission Requirements:** college transcript(s), statement of good standing from prior institution(s). Minimum college GPA of 2.0 required. Lowest grade transferable C. **General Admission Information:** Application fee $25. Nonfall registration accepted. Admission may be deferred.

COSTS AND FINANCIAL AID

Required Forms and Deadlines: FAFSA, State aid form. **Notification of Awards:** Applicants will be notified of awards on a rolling basis beginning 1/1. **Types of Aid:** *Need-based scholarships/grants:* Federal Pell, FSEOG, State scholarships/grants, Private scholarships, College/university scholarship or grant aid from institutional funds. *Loans:* Direct Subsidized Stafford Loans, Direct Unsubsidized Stafford Loans, Direct PLUS loans. *Student Employment:* Federal Work-Study Program available. **Financial Aid Statistics:** 99% needy freshmen, 98% needy undergrads receive need-based scholarship or grant aid. 7% freshmen, 7% undergrads receive non-need-based scholarship or grant aid. 76% freshmen, 75% undergrads receive need-based self-help aid. 9% freshmen, 7% undergrads receive athletic scholarships. **Criteria for awarding aid:** *Need-based:* Academics, Art, Athletics, Leadership, Music/drama, Religious affiliation. *Non-need-based:* Academics, Art, Athletics, Leadership, Music/drama, Religious affiliation, State/district residency.

RENSSELAER POLYTECHNIC INSTITUTE

110 Eighth Street, Troy, NY 12180-3590
Phone: 518-276-6216 • **Financial Aid Phone:** 518-276-6813
E-mail: admissions@rpi.edu • **CEEB Code:** 2757
Fax: 518-276-4072 • **Website:** www.rpi.edu • **ACT Code:** 2866

This private school was founded in 1824. It has a 284-acre campus.

RATINGS
Admissions Selectivity Rating: 92   **Fire Safety Rating:** 93   **Green Rating:** 60*

STUDENTS AND FACULTY
Enrollment: 6,200. **Student Body:** 32% female, 68% male, 66% out-of-state, 11% international (44 countries represented). Asian 11%, African American 3%, Caucasian 57%, Hispanic 9%, Native American <1%, Pacific Islander <1%, Two or more races 7%, Race unknown 2%.
Retention and Graduation: 93% freshmen return for sophomore year. 61% freshmen graduate within 4 years. 83% freshmen graduate within 6 years. 24% grads go on to further study within 1 year. 5% grads pursue arts and sciences degrees. 2% grads pursue business degrees. 2% grads pursue medical degrees.
Faculty: Student/faculty ratio 15:1. 0% of classes are taught by teaching assistants.

ACADEMICS
Degrees: bachelor's, doctoral/research, master's. **Classes:** Most classes have 10-19 students. **Most popular majors:** Computer Engineering; Electrical and Electronics Engineering; Business/Commerce. **Special Study Options:** Accelerated program, cooperative education program, cross-registration, double major, dual enrollment, exchange student program (domestic), honors program, independent study, internships, liberal arts/career combination, student-designed major, study abroad, The accelerated BS-Phd program in the School of Science is possible in all the science departments. Computer Science Physics Applied Physics Biology Biochemistry and Biophysics Geology Hydrogeology. **Honors Programs:** The Rensselaer Medal Program, the Presidential Scholars Program Combined degree programs: BA/MEng, BS/MBA, BS/MS, BS/M. Eng, BS/MD, BS/JD, BS/Ph.D. **Disability Services:** Special programs offered to physically disabled students, including note-taking services, reader services, tape recorders, tutors. **Career Services:** Alumni network, Alumni services, Career/job search classes, Career assessment, Internships, Regional alumni. Rensselaer has actively encouraged the translation of cutting edge academic research into new products and new businesses. Scientific and technological entrepreneurship is a significant part of 'The Rensselaer Plan', a comprehensive strategic plan for the Institute. Historically and consistently, faculty, students, and alumni have successfully developed technologies, created innovations, and formed business ventures to bring ideas into practice to create value. Rensselaer's focus on entrepreneurship iscross-campus, interdisciplinary, and presents multiple perspectives. It involves creative thinking, and is not only ideas, but ideas to enterprise. Entrepreneurship at Rensselaer goes beyond curriculum, with a broad spectrum of technology presentations, lecture series, and mentor programs. It has a global focus, and is further focused as technology commercialization and entrepreneurship. The Lally School at Rensselaer has a strong tradition of developing entrepreneurs who create new ventures or bring their entrepreneurial management skills to established organizations. Theory and practice are combined in the classroom, and students interact with experienced entrepreneurs. The Severino Center for Technological Entrepreneurship is the focal point for both entrepreneurship scholarship and learning, and it serves as a bridge for the Rensselaer Incubator and Technology Park. Students participate in lectures and discussions, and events that include both the entire Rensselaer university community as well as professionals from successful startups and fast growth companies from the Tech Valley Region.

FACILITIES
Housing: Coed dorms, special housing for disabled students, fraternity/sorority housing, apartments for married students, apartments for single students, Theme Housing. 75% of campus accessible to physically diasbled. **Special Academic Facilities/Equipment:** Shelnutt Art Gallery in the Student Union;The George M. Low Gallery (museum); Center for Terahertz Research; Nanoscale Science and Engineering Centers (NSEC); Center for Biotechnology and Interdisciplinary Studies; Gaerttner Linear Accelerator (LINAC) Laboratory; Hirsch Observatory; RPIdeaLab and Incubator Program (supports student business ventures); Rensselaer Technology Park; Darrin Fresh Water Institute at Lake George; Experimental Media and Performing Arts Center (EMPAC—under construction); Lighting Research Center; Social and

Behavioral Research Laboratory; O.T. Swanson Multidisciplinary Laboratory; and other research centers and laboratories as described at www.rpi.edu/research/research_centers.html,Computational Center for Nanotechnology Innovations (CCNI); http://www.rpi.edu/dept/ess/greening/EECbooks.html **Computers:** 75% of classrooms, 75% of dorms, 100% of libraries, 75% of dining areas, 100% of student union, 75% of common outdoor areas have wireless network access. Students can register for classes online. Administrative functions (other than registration) can be performed online. Undergraduates are required to own a computer.

CAMPUS LIFE
Environment: City. **Activities:** Choral groups, concert band, dance, drama/theater, jazz band, literary magazine, music ensembles, musical theater, pep band, radio station, student government, student newspaper, student-run film society, symphony orchestra, television station, yearbook, Campus Ministries, Student Organization. 177 registered organizations, 40 honor societies, 11 religious organizations. 32 fraternities, 5 sororities. **Athletics (Intercollegiate):** *Men:* baseball, basketball, cross-country, diving, football, golf, ice hockey, lacrosse, soccer, swimming, tennis, track/field (outdoor), track/field (indoor). *Women:* basketball, cross-country, diving, field hockey, ice hockey, lacrosse, soccer, softball, swimming, tennis, track/field (outdoor), track/field (indoor). **On-Campus Highlights:** Rensselaer Union, Mueller Fitness Center, Experimental Media & Performing Arts Ctr, Houston Field House (hockey arena), ECAV, Quiet and parklike, yet full of all the conveniences of a self-contained city, Rensselaer's 275-acre campus is a blend of modern style and classic charm. The Institute is in a period of tremendous growth, building new facilities that greatly enhance the lives of our students and faculty. **Environmental Initiatives:** Student Sustainability Task Force

ADMISSIONS
Freshman Academic Profile: 66% in top 10% of high school class, 93% in top 25% of high school class, 99% in top 50% of high school class. 70% from public high schools. **Reported SAT (pre-2016 redesign) scores:** SAT Math middle 50% range 670-770. SAT Critical Reading middle 50% range 610-710. **Concordant SAT scores:** SAT Math middle 50% range 700–780. ACT middle 50% range 28-32. Minimum internet-based TOEFL 88. Minimum paper TOEFL 570. **Basis for Candidate Selection:** *Very important factors considered include:* rigor of secondary school record, class rank, academic GPA, standardized test scores. *Important factors considered include:* application essay, recommendation(s), extracurricular activities, character/personal qualities, level of applicant's interest. *Other factors considered include:* talent/ability, first generation, alumni/ae relation, racial/ethnic status, volunteer work, work experience. **Freshman Admission Requirements:** High school diploma is required and GED is accepted. *Academic units required:* 4 English, 4 math, 3 science, 3 social studies. *Academic units recommended:* 4 science, 3 social studies. **Freshman Admission Statistics:** 18,524 applied, 44.35% admitted, 21% enrolled. **Transfer Admission Requirements:** college transcript(s), statement of good standing from prior institution(s). Minimum college GPA of 3.0 required. Lowest grade transferable C. **General Admission Information:** Application fee $70. Regular application deadline 1/15. Regular notification 3/14. Nonfall registration accepted. Admission may be deferred for a maximum of 1 year.

COSTS AND FINANCIAL AID
Required Forms and Deadlines: FAFSA, CSS/Financial Aid PROFILE. **Notification of Awards:** Applicants will be notified of awards on or about 3/15. **Types of Aid:** *Need-based scholarships/grants:* Federal Pell, FSEOG, State scholarships/grants, Private scholarships, College/university scholarship or grant aid from institutional funds. *Loans:* Direct Subsidized Stafford Loans, Direct Unsubsidized Stafford Loans, Direct PLUS loans, Federal Perkins Loans, State Loans. *Student Employment:* Federal Work-Study Program available. Institutional employment available. **Financial Aid Statistics:** 100% needy freshmen, 100% needy undergrads receive need-based scholarship or grant aid. 18% freshmen, 13% undergrads receive non-need-based scholarship or grant aid. 99% freshmen, 97% undergrads receive need-based self-help aid. 1% freshmen, 1% undergrads receive athletic scholarships. 89% freshmen, 89% undergrads receive any aid. **Criteria for awarding aid:** *Need-based:* Academics, Alumni affiliation, Art, Leadership, Minority status, Music/drama. *Non-need-based:* Academics, Alumni affiliation, Art, Athletics, Leadership, Minority status, Music/drama.

RHODE ISLAND COLLEGE

600 Mount Pleasant Avenue, Providence, RI 2908
Phone: 401-456-8234 • **Financial Aid Phone:** 401-456-8033
E-mail: admissions@ric.edu • **CEEB Code:** 3407
Fax: 401-456-8817 • **Website:** http://www.ric.edu • **ACT Code:** 3810

RATINGS
Admissions Selectivity Rating: 75 **Fire Safety Rating:** 60* **Green Rating:** 72

STUDENTS AND FACULTY
Enrollment: 7,216. **Student Body:** 68% female, 32% male, 14% out-of-state, <1% international. Asian 3%, African American 8%, Caucasian 62%, Hispanic 16%, Native American <1%, Pacific Islander <1%, Two or more races 2%, Race unknown 8%.
Retention and Graduation: 76% freshmen return for sophomore year. 14% freshmen graduate within 4 years. 44% freshmen graduate within 6 years.
Faculty: Student/faculty ratio 14:1. 335 full-time faculty, 89% hold PhDs, 14% are are members of minority groups, 58% are women.

ACADEMICS
Degrees: bachelor's, certificate, doctoral/research, master's, postbachelor's certifiate, post-master's certificate.

CAMPUS LIFE
Environmental Initiatives: 1. The Sustainable Communities Initiative at RIC is an innovative pilot project which works to further inform RIC students and the general public on the local and global issues of sustainability, while providing a vehicle through which to take action for positive change. SCI has already exposed RIC students and community members to some of the region and nation most recognized sustainability thought leaders, trained nearly twenty SCI Community Leaders from twelve Rhode Island communities, established a nine person leadership committee and has begun to collaboratively work on the development of a participatory research tool that will empower community residents to evaluate and improve the sustainability performance of their own town and cities.

ADMISSIONS
Freshman Academic Profile: 11% in top 10% of high school class, 35% in top 25% of high school class, 75% in top 50% of high school class. 75% from public high schools. **Reported SAT (pre-2016 redesign) scores:** SAT Math middle 50% range 400-510. SAT Critical Reading middle 50% range 400-520. SAT Writing middle 50% range 400-500. **Concordant SAT scores:** SAT EBRW middle 50% 450–570. SAT Math middle 50% range 440–540. ACT middle 50% range 16-21. Minimum internet-based TOEFL 80. Minimum paper TOEFL 550. **Basis for Candidate Selection:** *Very important factors considered include:* rigor of secondary school record, class rank, academic GPA. *Important factors considered include:* standardized test scores, application essay, recommendation(s). *Other factors considered include:* interview, extracurricular activities, talent/ability, alumni/ae relation, volunteer work, work experience. **Freshman Admission Requirements:** *Academic units required:* 4 English, 3 math, 2 science, 2 science labs, 2 foreign language, 2 social studies, 5 academic electives. **Freshman Admission Statistics:** 4,732 applied, 71.62% admitted, 33% enrolled. **General Admission Information:** Application fee $50. Regular application deadline 3/15. Nonfall registration accepted.

COSTS AND FINANCIAL AID
Annual in-state tuition $7,118. Annual out-of-state tuition $18,779. Room and board $10,394. Required fees $1,079. Average book expense $1,200. **Required Forms and Deadlines:** FAFSA, Institution's own financial aid form. **Notification of Awards:** Applicants will be notified of awards on a rolling basis beginning 3/15. **Types of Aid:** *Need-based scholarships/grants:* Federal Pell, FSEOG, State scholarships/grants, Private scholarships, College/university scholarship or grant aid from institutional funds. *Loans:* Direct Subsidized Stafford Loans, Direct Unsubsidized Stafford Loans, Direct PLUS loans, Federal Perkins Loans, State Loans. *Student Employment:* Federal Work-Study Program available. Institutional employment available. **Financial Aid Statistics:** 81% needy freshmen, 81% needy undergrads receive need-based scholarship or grant aid. 3% freshmen, 2% undergrads receive non-need-based scholarship or grant aid. 85% freshmen, 83% undergrads receive need-based self-help aid. 0% freshmen, 0% undergrads receive athletic scholarships. 75% undergrads borrow to pay for school. Average cumulative indebtedness $26,624. **Criteria for awarding aid:** *Need-based:* Academics. *Non-need-based:* Academics, Alumni affiliation, Art, Music/drama.

RHODE ISLAND SCHOOL OF DESIGN

2 College Street, Providence, RI 2903
Phone: 401-454-6300 • **Financial Aid Phone:** 401-454-6636
E-mail: admissions@risd.edu • **CEEB Code:** 3726
Fax: 401-454-6309 • **Website:** www.risd.edu • **ACT Code:** 3812

This private school was founded in 1877. It has a 13-acre campus.

RATINGS

Admissions Selectivity Rating: 71　　**Fire Safety Rating:** 92　　**Green Rating:** 60*

STUDENTS AND FACULTY

Enrollment: 2,000. **Student Body:** 69% female, 31% male, 94% out-of-state, 27% international (52 countries represented). Asian 20%, African American 3%, Caucasian 32%, Hispanic 8%, Native American <1%, Pacific Islander 0%, Two or more races 5%, Race unknown 5%.
Retention and Graduation: 93% freshmen return for sophomore year. 68% freshmen graduate within 4 years. 89% freshmen graduate within 6 years. **Faculty:** Student/faculty ratio 10:1. 156 full-time faculty, 77% hold PhDs, 11% are are members of minority groups, 42% are women.

ACADEMICS

Degrees: bachelor's, master's. **Most popular majors:** Illustration; Industrial and Product Design; Graphic Design. **Special Study Options:** cross-registration, exchange student program (domestic), independent study, internships, study abroad, Continuing Education program. 6-week precollege summer program for secondary school students. summer workshops for undergraduate credit. 6 week winter session study abroad courses. **Disability Services:** Special programs offered to physically disabled students, including note-taking services, reader services, tape recorders. **Career Services:** Alumni network, Alumni services, Career/job search classes, Career assessment, Internships, Regional alumni. "ArtWorks" is an exclusive opportunities board for alumni and students that includes, internships, jobs, freelance, grants, residencies, and artist opportunities. Nearly 5,000 opportunities are posted each year and the employer directory has 9,000 active contacts.

FACILITIES

Housing: Coed dorms, apartments for single students. 27% of campus accessible to physically diasbled. **Special Academic Facilities/Equipment:** Art museum with over 45 galleries, extensive facilities for glassblowing, metalsmithing, lithography, sculpture, painting, and other art disciplines, nature lab. **Computers:** Administrative functions (other than registration) can be performed online.

CAMPUS LIFE

Environment: City. **Activities:** drama/theater, literary magazine, student government, student newspaper, student-run film society, yearbook. 35 registered organizations, 5 religious organizations. **On-Campus Highlights:** The RISD Museum, The Edna Lawrence Nature Lab, Metcalf 3 dimensional fine art building, 161 S. Main St.—Industrial Design Building, RISD Works.

ADMISSIONS

Minimum internet-based TOEFL 93. Minimum paper TOEFL 580. **Basis for Candidate Selection:** *Very important factors considered include:* rigor of secondary school record, academic GPA, talent/ability. *Important factors considered include:* standardized test scores, application essay. *Other factors considered include:* recommendation(s), extracurricular activities, character/personal qualities, first generation, alumni/ae relation, geographical residence, racial/ethnic status, volunteer work, work experience. **Freshman Admission Requirements:** High school diploma is required and GED is accepted. **Freshman Admission Statistics:** 2,776 applied, 34.40% admitted, 48% enrolled. **Transfer Admission Requirements:** college transcript(s), essay or personal statement, Lowest grade transferable C. **General Admission Information:** Application fee $60. Regular application deadline 2/1. Regular notification 3/22. Nonfall registration accepted. Admission may be deferred for a maximum of 1 year.

COSTS AND FINANCIAL AID

Annual tuition $46,800. Room and board $12,850. Required fees $310. Average book expense $2,700. **Required Forms and Deadlines:** FAFSA, CSS/Financial Aid PROFILE. **Notification of Awards:** Applicants will be notified of awards on or about 4/1. **Types of Aid:** *Need-based scholarships/grants:* Federal Pell, FSEOG, State scholarships/grants, Private scholarships, College/university scholarship or grant aid from institutional funds. *Loans:* Direct Subsidized Stafford Loans, Direct Unsubsidized Stafford Loans, Direct PLUS loans, Federal Perkins Loans. *Student Employment:* Federal Work-Study Program available. **Financial Aid Statistics:** 88% needy freshmen, 91% needy undergrads receive need-based scholarship or grant aid. 3% undergrads receive non-need-based scholarship or grant aid. 100% freshmen, 91% undergrads receive need-based self-help aid. 0% freshmen, 0% undergrads receive athletic scholarships. 42% freshmen, 41% undergrads receive any aid. 41% undergrads borrow to pay for school. Average cumulative indebtedness $31,037. **Criteria for awarding aid:** *Need-based:* Academics, Art. *Non-need-based:* Academics, Art.

RHODES COLLEGE

2000 North Parkway, Memphis, TN 38112
Phone: 901-843-3700 • **Financial Aid Phone:** 901-843-3810
E-mail: adminfo@rhodes.edu • **CEEB Code:** 1730
Fax: 901-843-3631 • **Website:** http://www.rhodes.edu • **ACT Code:** 4008

This private school, affiliated with the Presbyterian Church, was founded in 1848. It has a 100-acre campus.

RATINGS

Admissions Selectivity Rating: 91　　**Fire Safety Rating:** 87　　**Green Rating:** 75

STUDENTS AND FACULTY

Enrollment: 1,980. **Student Body:** 56% female, 44% male, 73% out-of-state, 3% international (18 countries represented). Asian 6%, African American 8%, Caucasian 72%, Hispanic 5%, Native American <1%, Pacific Islander <1%, Two or more races 4%, Race unknown 2%.
Retention and Graduation: 93% freshmen return for sophomore year. 77% freshmen graduate within 4 years. 80% freshmen graduate within 6 years. 38% grads go on to further study within 1 year. **Faculty:** Student/faculty ratio 10:1. 177 full-time faculty, 98% hold PhDs, 16% are are members of minority groups, 50% are women. 0% of classes are taught by teaching assistants.

ACADEMICS

Degrees: bachelor's, master's. **Classes:** Most classes have 10-19 students. Most lab/discussion sessions have 20-29 students. **Most popular majors:** Biology/Biological Sciences; Business Administration and Management; English Language and Literature. **Special Study Options:** cooperative education program, cross-registration, double major, dual enrollment, exchange student program (domestic), honors program, independent study, internships, liberal arts/career combination, student-designed major, study abroad, duel degree: Master of Education; Master of Science in Nursing; Master of Science in Biomedical Engineering. **Honors Programs:** The Honors program is a culminating experience in the major field, for seniors only. It is the principal means whereby a student may do more independent, intensive, and individual work than can be done in the regular degree programs. The Honors work offers an excellent introduction to graduate study as it employs the full resources of library and laboratory and encourages independent research and study. Honors is available in most majors. Combined degree programs: BA/MEd, BA/MSN, BS/MS Biomed Engineering. **Disability Services:** Special programs offered to physically disabled students, including note-taking services, reader services, tape recorders, tutors. **Career Services:** Alumni network, Alumni services, Career/job search classes, Career assessment, Internships, Regional alumni. The Rhodes St. Jude Summer Plus program typifies the integrated learning philosophy at Rhodes through which students take classroom skills into the community where they connect knowledge with practice and learn effective leadership through service, internships, travel and research. The approach also assures that students return to the classroom with the discoveries, problem-solving skills, contextualization, engagement and motivation gained through their experiences. John Sexton '04 describes his experience this way: "I was able to maintain close personal relationships with Rhodes faculty–the kind of relationships a student would be unlikely to have at a larger, research-oriented school–and also access the world-class facilities and experts at St. Jude–the kinds of resources not generally available to students at small liberal arts colleges." Clearly the Summer Plus program at St. Jude Children's Research Hospital provides the best of both worlds for the Rhodes science major who is ready to commit to two summers and a good deal of the school year working at a research hospital world renowned for its development of treatments for life-threatening diseases of childhood. In this program aspiring physicians and biomedical researchers have a unique opportunity to participate in every phase of the process in which basic research is translated into therapeutic interventions from bench to bedside. The intense and sustained challenge of work in this extraordinary environment fosters both scientific curiosity and humanitarian concern.

FACILITIES

Housing: Coed dorms, men's dorms, women's dorms, apartments for single students, learning communities; Substance free; quiet study; restricted visitation; non-smoking; special interest townhouses. 90% of campus accessible to physically disabled. **Special Academic Facilities/Equipment:** 136,000 square foot library; Art gallery; archaeology lab; astronomy observation domes with 14 and 31.5 inch telescopes; machine and woodworking shops; scanning electron microscopes; cell culture lab; nuclear magnetic resonance instrument; gas chromatography systems; UV, X-ray, infrared, and atomic absorption spectrophotometers. **Computers:** 100% of classrooms, 100% of dorms, 100% of libraries, 100% of dining areas, 50% of common outdoor areas have wireless network access. Students can register for classes online. Administrative functions (other than registration) can be performed online.

CAMPUS LIFE

Environment: Metropolis. **Activities:** Choral groups, dance, drama/theater, jazz band, literary magazine, music ensembles, musical theater, pep band, radio station, student government, student newspaper, student-run film society, symphony orchestra, television station, yearbook, Campus Ministries, Student Organization, Model UN. 115 registered organizations, 14 honor societies, 8 religious organizations. 7 fraternities, 6 sororities. **Athletics (Intercollegiate):** *Men:* baseball, basketball, cross-country, football, golf, soccer, swimming, tennis, track/field (outdoor). *Women:* basketball, cross-country, field hockey, golf, soccer, softball, swimming, tennis, track/field (outdoor), volleyball. **On-Campus Highlights:** Barret Library (includes a Starbucks coffee shop), Burrow Center for Student Opportunity, Bryan Campus Life Center (home to the Ly, East Village (apartment-style dorms), McCoy Theater, The Burrow Center for Student Opportunity opened in Spring, 2008. It consolidates most student services under one roof, including a one-stop transaction center, enrolling and financing, student development and academic support, and out of class experiences. It also includes space for student organizations and is open to students 24x7. **Environmental Initiatives:** $500,000 Andrew W. Mellon Foundation grant to expand Environmental Studies initiatives through community partnerships.

ADMISSIONS

Freshman Academic Profile: Average high school GPA 3.9. 48% in top 10% of high school class, 79% in top 25% of high school class, 94% in top 50% of high school class. 46% from public high schools. **Reported SAT (pre-2016 redesign) scores:** SAT Math middle 50% range 590-690. SAT Critical Reading middle 50% range 580-670. **Concordant SAT scores:** SAT Math middle 50% range 610–720. ACT middle 50% range 27-31. Minimum paper TOEFL 550. **Basis for Candidate Selection:** *Very important factors considered include:* rigor of secondary school record, class rank, academic GPA. *Important factors considered include:* standardized test scores, application essay, recommendation(s), character/personal qualities, alumni/ae relation, racial/ethnic status. *Other factors considered include:* interview, extracurricular activities, talent/ability, first generation, geographical residence, state residency, volunteer work, work experience, level of applicant's interest. **Freshman Admission Requirements:** High school diploma is required and GED is accepted. *Academic units required:* 4 English, 3 math, 2 science, 2 science labs, 2 foreign language, 2 social studies, 3 academic electives. **Freshman Admission Statistics:** 4,481 applied, 54.32% admitted, 21% enrolled. **Transfer Admission Requirements:** High school transcript, college transcript(s), essay or personal statement, standardized test scores, statement of good standing from prior institution(s). Lowest grade transferable C-. **General Admission Information:** Priority deadline 1/15. Regular notification 4/1. Nonfall registration accepted. Admission may be deferred.

COSTS AND FINANCIAL AID

Annual tuition $44,632. Room and board $11,068. Required fees $310. Average book expense $1,125. **Required Forms and Deadlines:** FAFSA, CSS/Financial Aid PROFILE, Noncustodial PROFILE. **Types of Aid:** *Need-based scholarships/grants:* Federal Pell, FSEOG, State scholarships/grants, Private scholarships, College/university scholarship or grant aid from institutional funds. *Loans:* Direct Subsidized Stafford Loans, Direct Unsubsidized Stafford Loans, Direct PLUS loans, Federal Perkins Loans. *Student Employment:* Federal Work-Study Program available. Institutional employment available. **Financial Aid Statistics:** 99% needy freshmen, 100% needy undergrads receive need-based scholarship or grant aid. 48% freshmen, 32% undergrads receive non-need-based scholarship or grant aid. 55% freshmen, 65% undergrads receive need-based self-help aid. 0% freshmen, 0% undergrads receive athletic scholarships. 95% freshmen, 94% undergrads receive any aid. Average cumulative indebtedness $25,859. **Criteria for awarding aid:** *Need-based:* Minority status. *Non-need-based:* Academics, Art, Minority status, Music/drama, Religious affiliation.

RICE UNIVERSITY

Best Colleges

MS 17 PO Box 1892, Houston, TX 77251-1892
Phone: 713-348-7423 • **Financial Aid Phone:** 713-348-4958
E-mail: admi@rice.edu • **CEEB Code:** 6609
Fax: 713-348-5952 • **Website:** www.rice.edu • **ACT Code:** 4152

This private school was founded in 1912. It has a 300-acre campus.

RATINGS

Admissions Selectivity Rating: 97   **Fire Safety Rating:** 95   **Green Rating:** 93

STUDENTS AND FACULTY

Enrollment: 3,879. **Student Body:** 48% female, 52% male, 50% out-of-state, 12% international (46 countries represented). Asian 24%, African American 7%, Caucasian 37%, Hispanic 14%, Native American <1%, Pacific Islander <1%, Two or more races 4%, Race unknown 2%.
Retention and Graduation: 96% freshmen return for sophomore year. 83% freshmen graduate within 4 years. 93% freshmen graduate within 6 years. 54% grads go on to further study within 1 year. **Faculty:** Student/faculty ratio 6:1. 671 full-time faculty, 99% hold PhDs, 21% are are members of minority groups, 33% are women.

ACADEMICS

Degrees: bachelor's, doctoral, master's. **Classes:** Most classes have 10-19 students. **Most popular majors:** Biology/Biological Sciences; Economics; Chemical Engineering. **Special Study Options:** cross-registration, double major, dual enrollment, English as a Second Language (ESL), honors program, independent study, internships, liberal arts/career combination, student-designed major, study abroad, teacher certification program, 8 year guaranteed medical school program with The Baylor College of Medicine. **Honors Programs:** Honors programs through individual departments. Combined degree programs: BA/MD, Guaranteeed med school program with Baylor College of Medicine. **Disability Services:** Special programs offered to physically disabled students, including note-taking services, reader services, tape recorders. **Career Services:** Alumni network, Alumni services, Career/job search classes, Career assessment, Internships, Regional alumni. We are most proud of our relationship with alumni and their support (in terms of professional advice as well as recruitment) of current undergraduate and graduate students.

FACILITIES

Housing: Coed dorms, special housing for disabled students. All undergraduate students are automatically assigned to one of nine (coed) residential colleges and keep affiliation regardless of whether they live on campus or not. 90% of campus accessible to physically disabled. **Special Academic Facilities/Equipment:** Art gallery, museum, media center, language labs, computer labs, civil engineering lab, observatory and NASA equipment for students in space physics courses. **Computers:** 100% of classrooms, 100% of dorms, 1000% of libraries, 100% of dining areas, 100% of student union, 5% of common outdoor areas have wireless network access. Students can register for classes online. Administrative functions (other than registration) can be performed online.

CAMPUS LIFE

Environment: Metropolis. **Activities:** Choral groups, concert band, dance, drama/theater, jazz band, literary magazine, marching band, music ensembles, musical theater, opera, pep band, radio station, student government, student newspaper, student-run film society, symphony orchestra, television station, yearbook, Campus Ministries, Student Organization, Model UN. 215 registered organizations, 11 honor societies, 14 religious organizations. **Athletics (Intercollegiate):** *Men:* baseball, basketball, cross-country, football, golf, tennis, track/field (outdoor), track/field (indoor). *Women:* basketball, cross-country, soccer, swimming, tennis, track/field (outdoor), track/field (indoor), volleyball. **On-Campus Highlights:** Rice Memorial Center, Baker Institute for Public Policy, Brochstein Pavilion (cafe), Shepherd School of Music, Reckling Park—baseball stadium. **Environmental Initiatives:** 1. Green Building. At present, we have roughly 1,000,000 square feet of facilities on campus that are under construction that will receive some level of LEED certification, including the student dormitory Duncan College which is targeted for LEED-Gold. In addition, an off-campus child care center is pursuing LEED certification. Also, an off-campus graduate student apartment complex has been designed to LEED standards although it will not be formally submitted for certification. With this complex, we anticipate savings in energy of about 30% and water savings of 20%. Further, the complex was constructed in an area with excellent pedestrian access, and it includes extensive bicycle storage along with shuttle bus service to campus and to major nearby grocery stores. Our campus standard for on-campus LEED certification for new buildings is LEED-Silver as a minimum. The University has also enjoyed significant successes with construction waste recycling, with many of our largest projects to date logging diversion rates of 85-90% to recycling.

ADMISSIONS

Freshman Academic Profile: 88% in top 10% of high school class, 97% in top 25% of high school class, 99% in top 50% of high school class. **Reported SAT (pre-2016 redesign) scores:** SAT Math middle 50% range 720-800. SAT Critical Reading middle 50% range 690-770. SAT Writing middle 50% range 680-770. **Concordant SAT scores:** SAT EBRW middle 50% 720–780. SAT Math middle 50% range 750–800. ACT middle 50% range 32-35. Minimum internet-based TOEFL 100. Minimum paper TOEFL 600. **Basis for Candidate Selection:** *Very important factors considered include:* rigor of secondary school record, class rank, academic GPA, standardized test scores, application essay, recommendation(s), extracurricular activities, talent/ability, character/personal qualities. *Other factors considered include:* interview, first generation, alumni/ae relation, geographical residence, state residency, racial/ethnic status, volunteer work, work experience, level of applicant's interest. **Freshman Admission Requirements:** High school diploma or equivalent is not required. *Academic units required:* 4 English, 3 math, 2 science, 2 science labs, 2 foreign language, 2 social studies, 3 academic electives. *Academic units recommended:* 4 English, 4 math, 4 science, 3 science labs, 4 foreign language, 3 social studies, 3 academic electives. **Freshman Admission Statistics:** 18,236 applied, 15.27% admitted, 35% enrolled. **Transfer Admission Requirements:** High school transcript, college transcript(s), essay or personal statement, standardized test scores, statement of good standing from prior institution(s). Minimum college GPA of 3.2 required. Lowest grade transferable C-. **General Admission Information:** Application fee $75. Regular application deadline 1/1. Regular notification 4/1. Nonfall registration not accepted. Admission may be deferred for a maximum of 2 years.

COSTS AND FINANCIAL AID

Annual tuition $43,220. Room and board $13,750. Required fees $698. Average book expense $800. **Required Forms and Deadlines:** FAFSA, CSS/Financial Aid PROFILE, Noncustodial PROFILE, Business/Farm Supplement. **Notification of Awards:** Applicants will be notified of awards on or about 4/1. **Types of Aid:** *Need-based scholarships/grants:* Federal Pell, FSEOG, State scholarships/grants, Private scholarships, College/university scholarship or grant aid from institutional funds. *Loans:* Direct Subsidized Stafford Loans, Direct Unsubsidized Stafford Loans, Direct PLUS loans, Federal Perkins Loans, State Loans. *Student Employment:* Federal Work-Study Program available. Institutional employment available. **Financial Aid Statistics:** 97% needy freshmen, 98% needy undergrads receive need-based scholarship or grant aid. 7% freshmen, 4% undergrads receive non-need-based scholarship or grant aid. 61% freshmen, 72% undergrads receive need-based self-help aid. 6% freshmen, 7% undergrads receive athletic scholarships. 41% freshmen, 39% undergrads receive any aid. 27% undergrads borrow to pay for school. Average cumulative indebtedness $22,497. **Criteria for awarding aid:** *Non-need-based:* Academics, Art, Athletics, Leadership, Minority status, Music/drama, State/district residency.

RICHMOND, THE AMERICAN INTERNATIONAL UNIVERSITY IN LONDON

US Office of Admissions, Boston, MA 2210
Phone: 617-450-5617 • **Financial Aid Phone:** 011-44-20-8332-8244
E-mail: us_admissions@richmond.ac.uk • **CEEB Code:** 823
Fax: 617-450-5601 • **ACT Code:** 5244

This private school was founded in 1972. It has a 6-acre campus.

RATINGS

Admissions Selectivity Rating: 85   **Fire Safety Rating:** 72   **Green Rating:** 60*

STUDENTS AND FACULTY

Student Body: 51% female, 49% male, % out-of-state.
Retention and Graduation: 72% freshmen return for sophomore year. 35% grads go on to further study within 1 year. **Faculty:** Student/faculty ratio 12:1. 41 full-time faculty, 85% hold PhDs, 0% are are members of minority groups, 39% are women. 0% of classes are taught by teaching assistants.

ACADEMICS

Degrees: bachelor's, master's. **Classes:** Most classes have 10-19 students. **Most popular majors:** International Relations and Affairs; Business/Commerce. **Special Study Options:** English as a Second Language (ESL), independent

study, internships, liberal arts/career combination, study abroad, Joint Engineering program with George Washington University.

FACILITIES

Housing: Coed dorms, men's dorms, women's dorms. **Computers:** Administrative functions (other than registration) can be performed online.

CAMPUS LIFE

Environment: Metropolis. **Activities:** Choral groups, dance, drama/theater, literary magazine, music ensembles, musical theater, student government, student newspaper, yearbook. 1 honor society. **Athletics (Intercollegiate):** *Men:* rugby, soccer. *Women:* rugby. **On-Campus Highlights:** Caffe del Mondo Gourmet Coffee Shop, Wireless Computer Network, Student Common Room, Student Cafeteria.

ADMISSIONS

Freshman Academic Profile: Average high school GPA 3.3. 29% in top 10% of high school class, 40% in top 25% of high school class, 94% in top 50% of high school class. 60% from public high schools. **Reported SAT (pre-2016 redesign) scores:** SAT Math middle 50% range 488-610. SAT Critical Reading middle 50% range 495-625. **Concordant SAT scores:** SAT Math middle 50% range 520–630. ACT middle 50% range 24-28. Minimum paper TOEFL 550. **Basis for Candidate Selection:** *Very important factors considered include:* rigor of secondary school record, academic GPA, application essay, recommendation(s). *Important factors considered include:* extracurricular activities. *Other factors considered include:* standardized test scores, interview, talent/ability, character/personal qualities, alumni/ae relation. **Freshman Admission Requirements:** High school diploma is required and GED is accepted. *Academic units required:* 4 English, 3 math, 3 science. **Freshman Admission Statistics:** 1,232 applied, 52.19% admitted, 32% enrolled. **Transfer Admission Requirements:** college transcript(s), essay or personal statement, statement of good standing from prior institution(s). Minimum college GPA of 2.5 required. Lowest grade transferable C. **General Admission Information:** Application fee $50. Regular application deadline 3/1. Nonfall registration accepted. Admission may be deferred for a maximum of 1 year.

COSTS AND FINANCIAL AID

Annual tuition $27,000. Room and board $12,900. Required fees $0. Average book expense $1,000. **Required Forms and Deadlines:** FAFSA. **Notification of Awards:** Applicants will be notified of awards on or about 3/15. **Types of Aid:** *Need-based scholarships/grants:* Private scholarships, College/university scholarship or grant aid from institutional funds. *Loans:* College/university loans from institutional funds. *Student Employment:* Federal Work-Study Program available. Institutional employment available. **Financial Aid Statistics:** 80% freshmen, 70% undergrads receive any aid. **Criteria for awarding aid:** *Non-need-based:* Academics.

RIDER UNIVERSITY

2083 Lawrenceville Road, Lawrenceville, NJ 08648-3099
Phone: 609-896-5042 • **Financial Aid Phone:** 609-896-5360
E-mail: admissions@rider.edu • **CEEB Code:** 2758
Fax: 609-895-6645 • **Website:** www.rider.edu • **ACT Code:** 2590

This private school was founded in 1865. It has a 280-acre campus.

RATINGS

Admissions Selectivity Rating: 82   **Fire Safety Rating:** 83   **Green Rating:** 93

STUDENTS AND FACULTY

Enrollment: 3,978. **Student Body:** 58% female, 42% male, 23% out-of-state, 3% international (64 countries represented). Asian 5%, African American 12%, Caucasian 61%, Hispanic 14%, Native American <1%, Pacific Islander <1%, Two or more races 3%, Race unknown 2%.
Retention and Graduation: 78% freshmen return for sophomore year. 60% freshmen graduate within 4 years. 66% freshmen graduate within 6 years. 8% grads go on to further study within 1 year. 4% grads pursue arts and sciences degrees. 2% grads pursue law degrees. 4% grads pursue business degrees. 2% grads pursue medical degrees. **Faculty:** Student/faculty ratio 11:1. 247 full-time faculty, 99% hold PhDs, 17% are are members of minority groups, 49% are women. 0% of classes are taught by teaching assistants.

ACADEMICS

Degrees: associate, bachelor's, master's, post-master's certificate. **Classes:** Most classes have 10-19 students. Most lab/discussion sessions have 10-19 students. **Most popular majors:** Accounting; Business Administration, Management and Operations; Elementary Education and Teaching. **Special Study Options:** cooperative education program, cross-registration, distance learning, double major, honors program, independent study, internships, liberal arts/career combination, study abroad, teacher certification program, weekend college, Learning Communities. **Honors Programs:** The Baccalaureate Honors Program is designed to enrich the educational opportunities for Rider students of proven intellectual capability who choose to become Baccalaureate Scholars. Through a series of team-taught seminars, small classes, personal contact with faculty, colloquia and symposia, as well as independent study opportunities, the scholars extend their ability to think critically, coherently, and systematically about the great themes, ideals and movements of their human heritage. Students may apply, or be invited, as entering freshmen, as currently enrolled freshmen or sophomores, or as transfer freshmen or sophomores. To be considered for the program incoming freshmen must be in the top 10 percent of their high school class. Combined degree programs: BS/BA. **Disability Services:** Special programs offered to physically disabled students, including reader services, tape recorders, tutors. **Career Services:** Alumni network, Alumni services, Internships.

FACILITIES

Housing: Coed dorms, special housing for disabled students, women's dorms, fraternity/sorority housing, apartments for single students, Suites, Special interest areas: Wellness, Quite, First Year Experience, Science, Learning Community. 73% of campus accessible to physically diasbled. **Special Academic Facilities/Equipment:** Art gallery, Holocaust/Genocide Resource Center. **Computers:** Students can register for classes online. Administrative functions (other than registration) can be performed online.

CAMPUS LIFE

Environment: Village. **Activities:** Choral groups, concert band, dance, drama/theater, literary magazine, music ensembles, musical theater, opera, pep band, radio station, student government, student newspaper, student-run film society, television station, yearbook, Campus Ministries, Student Organization, Model UN. 84 registered organizations, 24 honor societies, 6 religious organizations. 4 fraternities, 8 sororities. **Athletics (Intercollegiate):** *Men:* baseball, basketball, cheerleading, cross-country, diving, golf, soccer, swimming, tennis, track/field (outdoor), wrestling. *Women:* basketball, cheerleading, cross-country, diving, field hockey, soccer, softball, swimming, tennis, track/field (outdoor), volleyball. **On-Campus Highlights:** Residence Hall Quad, Alumni Gym, Student Recreation Center, Daly's Dining Hall/Cranberry Cafe, Academic Quad. **Environmental Initiatives:** Signing the American College & University Presidents Climate Commitment and formation of the Energy and Sustainability Steering Committee in 2007 to implement strategic plan establishing sustainability initiatives for the university.

ADMISSIONS

Freshman Academic Profile: Average high school GPA 3.3. 15% in top 10% of high school class, 40% in top 25% of high school class, 75% in top 50% of high school class. **Reported SAT (pre-2016 redesign) scores:** SAT Math middle 50% range 460-560. SAT Critical Reading middle 50% range 456-550. SAT Writing middle 50% range 440-550. **Concordant SAT scores:** SAT EBRW middle 50% 500–610. SAT Math middle 50% range 500–580. ACT middle 50% range 19-24. Minimum internet-based TOEFL 80. Minimum paper TOEFL 550. **Basis for Candidate Selection:** *Very important factors considered include:* rigor of secondary school record, academic GPA, standardized test scores, application essay, recommendation(s). *Important factors considered include:* level of applicant's interest. *Other factors considered include:* class rank, interview, extracurricular activities, talent/ability, character/ personal qualities, alumni/ae relation, geographical residence, state residency, volunteer work, work experience. **Freshman Admission Requirements:** High school diploma is required and GED is accepted. *Academic units required:* 4 English, 3 math. *Academic units recommended:* 4 math, 4 science, 2 science labs, 2 foreign language, 2 social studies, 2 history. **Freshman Admission Statistics:** 9,172 applied, 69.41% admitted, 14% enrolled. **Transfer Admission Requirements:** college transcript(s), essay or personal statement, Minimum college GPA of 2.5 required. Lowest grade transferable C. **General Admission Information:** Application fee $50. Nonfall registration accepted. Admission may be deferred for a maximum of 1 year.

COSTS AND FINANCIAL AID

Annual tuition $39,080. Room and board $14,230. Required fees $740. Average book expense $1,500. **Required Forms and Deadlines:** FAFSA. **Notification of Awards:** Applicants will be notified of awards on a rolling basis beginning 3/1. **Types of Aid:** *Need-based scholarships/grants:* Federal Pell, FSEOG, State scholarships/grants, Private scholarships, College/university scholarship or grant aid from institutional funds. *Loans:* Direct Subsidized Stafford Loans, Direct Unsubsidized Stafford Loans, Direct PLUS loans, Federal Perkins Loans. *Student Employment:* Federal Work-Study Program available. Institutional employment available. **Financial Aid Statistics:** 99% needy freshmen, 98% needy undergrads receive need-based scholarship or grant aid. 14% freshmen, 15% undergrads receive non-need-based scholarship or grant aid. 73%

freshmen, 78% undergrads receive need-based self-help aid. 6% freshmen, 6% undergrads receive athletic scholarships. Average cumulative indebtedness $36,032. **Criteria for awarding aid:** *Need-based:* Academics, Alumni affiliation, Athletics, Leadership, Music/drama. *Non-need-based:* Academics, Leadership.

RINGLING COLLEGE OF ART AND DESIGN

2700 N. Tamiami Trail, Sarasota, FL 34234-5895
Phone: 941-351-5100 • **Financial Aid Phone:** 941-359-7532
E-mail: admissions@ringling.edu • **CEEB Code:** 5573
Fax: 941-359-7517 • **Website:** www.ringling.edu • **ACT Code:** 6724

This private school was founded in 1931. It has a 49-acre campus.

RATINGS
Admissions Selectivity Rating: 65   **Fire Safety Rating:** 86   **Green Rating:** 60*

STUDENTS AND FACULTY
Enrollment: 1,331. **Student Body:** 65% female, 35% male, 46% out-of-state, 16% international (58 countries represented). Asian 8%, African American 3%, Caucasian 47%, Hispanic 16%, Native American 1%, Pacific Islander <1%, Two or more races 3%, Race unknown 6%.
Retention and Graduation: 87% freshmen return for sophomore year. 61% freshmen graduate within 4 years. 69% freshmen graduate within 6 years. 5% grads go on to further study within 1 year. **Faculty:** Student/faculty ratio 11:1. 102 full-time faculty, 61% hold PhDs, 5% are are members of minority groups, 30% are women. 0% of classes are taught by teaching assistants.

ACADEMICS
Degrees: bachelor's. **Classes:** Most classes have 10-19 students. **Most popular majors:** Animation, Interactive Technology, Video Graphics and Special Effects; Illustration; Game and Interactive Media Design. **Special Study Options:** dual enrollment, exchange student program (domestic), independent study, internships, study abroad. **Disability Services:** Special programs offered to physically disabled students, including note-taking services, reader services, tape recorders, tutors. **Career Services:** Alumni network, Alumni services, Career/job search classes, Career assessment, Internships, Regional alumni. Career/job search **Classes:** direct approach to students on areas of interest, review of core approaches and resources. Alumni services: helping those who graduated, who, in turn, help us with recruiting, posting jobs, etc. Regional alumni and alumni network: help us with conference, workshops, visits to classes. Internships: growing opportunities especially in new majors and increasing success as full-time employees by those who interned at the company. Career assessment: help students who need to determine best major for their goals.

FACILITIES
Housing: Coed dorms, men's dorms, women's dorms, apartments for married students, apartments for single students, Wellness Housing. All housing accommodations are ADA compliant. 98% of campus accessible to physically diasbled. **Special Academic Facilities/Equipment:** William G. and Marie Selby Gallery, Crossley Gallery, Verman Kimbrough Memorial Library **Computers:** 60% of classrooms, 100% of dorms, 100% of libraries, 100% of dining areas, 100% of student union, 60% of common outdoor areas have wireless network access. Students can register for classes online. Administrative functions (other than registration) can be performed online.

CAMPUS LIFE
Environment: City. **Activities:** dance, drama/theater, student government, Campus Ministries, Student Organization. 22 registered organizations, 2 religious organizations. **On-Campus Highlights:** Student Center, Selby Gallery, Crossley Gallery, Verman Kimbrough Memorial Library, Hammond Commons. **Environmental Initiatives:** The College has an active sustainability committee comprised of staff, faculty and student members. the charge of the committee is to review current and proposed sustainability practices, provide oversight in the implementation of these practices and to raise awareness of sustainability practices.

ADMISSIONS
Freshman Academic Profile: Average high school GPA 3.3. Minimum internet-based TOEFL 61. Minimum paper TOEFL 500. **Basis for Candidate Selection:** *Very important factors considered include:* rigor of secondary school record, academic GPA, recommendation(s), talent/ability. *Important factors considered include:* application essay. *Other factors considered include:* interview, extracurricular activities, alumni/ae relation, geographical residence, volunteer work, work experience, level of applicant's interest. **Freshman Admission Requirements:** High school diploma is required and GED is accepted. **Freshman Admission Statistics:** 1,752 applied, 78.14% admitted,

26% enrolled. **Transfer Admission Requirements:** High school transcript, college transcript(s), essay or personal statement, Minimum college GPA of 2.0 required. Lowest grade transferable C. **General Admission Information:** Application fee $70. Nonfall registration not accepted. Admission may be deferred for a maximum of 2 years.

COSTS AND FINANCIAL AID
Required Forms and Deadlines: FAFSA. **Notification of Awards:** Applicants will be notified of awards on a rolling basis beginning 4/1. **Types of Aid:** *Need-based scholarships/grants:* Federal Pell, FSEOG, State scholarships/grants, Private scholarships, College/university scholarship or grant aid from institutional funds. *Loans:* Direct Subsidized Stafford Loans, Direct Unsubsidized Stafford Loans, Direct PLUS loans. *Student Employment:* Federal Work-Study Program available. Institutional employment available. **Financial Aid Statistics:** 100% needy freshmen, 100% needy undergrads receive need-based scholarship or grant aid. 5% freshmen, 3% undergrads receive non-need-based scholarship or grant aid. 93% freshmen, 94% undergrads receive need-based self-help aid. 0% freshmen, 0% undergrads receive athletic scholarships. 96% freshmen, 76% undergrads receive any aid. 63% undergrads borrow to pay for school. Average cumulative indebtedness $44,384. **Criteria for awarding aid:** *Need-based:* Academics, Art. *Non-need-based:* Academics, Art.

RIPON COLLEGE

PO Box 248, Ripon, WI 54971
Phone: 920-748-8337 • **Financial Aid Phone:** 920-748-8301
E-mail: adminfo@ripon.edu • **CEEB Code:** 1664
Fax: 920-748-8335 • **Website:** www.ripon.edu • **ACT Code:** 4636

This private school was founded in 1851. It has a 250-acre campus.

RATINGS
Admissions Selectivity Rating: 83   **Fire Safety Rating:** 76   **Green Rating:** 69

STUDENTS AND FACULTY
Enrollment: 778. **Student Body:** 52% female, 48% male, 30% out-of-state, 4% international (12 countries represented). Asian 1%, African American 2%, Caucasian 83%, Hispanic 6%, Native American <1%, Pacific Islander 0%, Two or more races 2%, Race unknown 1%.
Retention and Graduation: 81% freshmen return for sophomore year. 58% freshmen graduate within 4 years. 68% freshmen graduate within 6 years. 29% grads go on to further study within 1 year. 17% grads pursue arts and sciences degrees. 5% grads pursue law degrees. 1% grads pursue business degrees. 2% grads pursue medical degrees. **Faculty:** Student/faculty ratio 12:1. 62 full-time faculty, 95% hold PhDs, 11% are are members of minority groups, 40% are women. 0% of classes are taught by teaching assistants.

ACADEMICS
Degrees: bachelor's. **Classes:** Most classes have 10-19 students. Most lab/discussion sessions have 10-19 students. **Most popular majors:** History; Business/Commerce; Health and Physical Education/Fitness. **Special Study Options:** double major, exchange student program (domestic), internships, student-designed major, study abroad, teacher certification program, Argonne Science Semester (Illinois). Newberry Library Program in the Humanities (Illinois). Urban Studies Program (Chicago). Wilderness Field Station Program (Minnesota). Other semester-away programs. **Disability Services:** Special programs offered to physically disabled students, including tutors. **Career Services:** Alumni network, Career assessment, Internships, Regional alumni.

FACILITIES
Housing: Coed dorms, men's dorms, women's dorms, fraternity/sorority housing, apartments for single students. **Special Academic Facilities/Equipment:** Art gallery, language labs. **Computers:** 2% of classrooms, 30% of libraries, 100% of dining areas, 60% of student union, have wireless network access.

CAMPUS LIFE
Environment: Village. **Activities:** Choral groups, concert band, dance, drama/theater, jazz band, literary magazine, music ensembles, musical theater, radio station, student government, student newspaper, symphony orchestra, yearbook, Campus Ministries, Student Organization. 45 registered organizations, 13 honor societies, 2 religious organizations. 5 fraternities, 3 sororities. **Athletics (Intercollegiate):** *Men:* baseball, basketball, cross-country, cycling, football,

golf, soccer, swimming, tennis, track/field (outdoor), track/field (indoor). *Women:* basketball, cross-country, cycling, golf, soccer, softball, swimming, tennis, track/field (outdoor), track/field (indoor), volleyball. **On-Campus Highlights:** Ceresco Prairie Conservancy, Art Gallery, Storzer Athletic Center, Lane Library.

ADMISSIONS
Freshman Academic Profile: Average high school GPA 3.4. 21% in top 10% of high school class, 47% in top 25% of high school class, 82% in top 50% of high school class. 75% from public high schools. **Reported SAT (pre-2016 redesign) scores:** SAT Math middle 50% range 420-580. SAT Critical Reading middle 50% range 450-580. **Concordant SAT scores:** SAT Math middle 50% range 460–600. ACT middle 50% range 21-26. Minimum internet-based TOEFL 79. Minimum paper TOEFL 550. **Basis for Candidate Selection:** *Very important factors considered include:* rigor of secondary school record, interview. *Important factors considered include:* class rank, academic GPA, standardized test scores, recommendation(s), extracurricular activities, character/personal qualities. *Other factors considered include:* application essay, talent/ability, volunteer work. **Freshman Admission Requirements:** High school diploma is required and GED is accepted. *Academic units required:* 4 English, 2 math, 2 science, 2 social studies. *Academic units recommended:* 4 math, 4 science, 2 foreign language, 4 social studies. **Freshman Admission Statistics:** 2,552 applied, 65.28% admitted, 13% enrolled. **Transfer Admission Requirements:** college transcript(s), essay or personal statement, statement of good standing from prior institution(s). Minimum college GPA of 2.0 required. Lowest grade transferable C. **General Admission Information:** Application fee $30. Priority deadline 3/15. Nonfall registration accepted. Admission may be deferred for a maximum of 1 year.

COSTS AND FINANCIAL AID
Annual tuition $41,535. Room and board $8,156. Required fees $300. Average book expense $750. **Required Forms and Deadlines:** FAFSA. **Notification of Awards:** Applicants will be notified of awards on a rolling basis beginning 3/1. **Types of Aid:** *Need-based scholarships/grants:* Federal Pell, FSEOG, State scholarships/grants, Private scholarships, College/university scholarship or grant aid from institutional funds. *Loans:* Direct Subsidized Stafford Loans, Direct Unsubsidized Stafford Loans, Direct PLUS loans, Federal Perkins Loans. *Student Employment:* Federal Work-Study Program available. Institutional employment available. **Financial Aid Statistics:** 100% needy freshmen, 100% needy undergrads receive need-based scholarship or grant aid. 22% freshmen, 16% undergrads receive non-need-based scholarship or grant aid. 74% freshmen, 81% undergrads receive need-based self-help aid. 0% freshmen, 0% undergrads receive athletic scholarships. 95% freshmen, 96% undergrads receive any aid. 80% undergrads borrow to pay for school. Average cumulative indebtedness $35,213. **Criteria for awarding aid:** *Non-need-based:* Academics, Alumni affiliation, Art, Leadership, Minority status, Music/drama, Religious affiliation, State/district residency.

See page 1024.

RIVIER COLLEGE

420 South Main Street, Nashua, NH 3060
Phone: 603-897-8219 • **Financial Aid Phone:** 603-897-8810
E-mail: rivadmit@rivier.edu • **CEEB Code:** 3728
Fax: 603-891-1799 • **Website:** www.rivier.edu • **ACT Code:** 2520

This private school, affiliated with the Roman Catholic Church, was founded in 1933. It has a 68-acre campus.

RATINGS
Admissions Selectivity Rating: 74   **Fire Safety Rating:** 89   **Green Rating:** 60*

STUDENTS AND FACULTY
Enrollment: 1,370. **Student Body:** 85% female, 15% male, 38% out-of-state, 0% international (12 countries represented). Asian 2%, African American 2%, Caucasian 75%, Hispanic 5%, Native American 1%, Pacific Islander 0%, Two or more races <1%, Race unknown 16%.
Retention and Graduation: 78% freshmen return for sophomore year. 42% freshmen graduate within 4 years. 53% freshmen graduate within 6 years. **Faculty:** Student/faculty ratio 17:1. 68 full-time faculty, 75% hold PhDs, 0% are are members of minority groups, 65% are women. 0% of classes are taught by teaching assistants.

ACADEMICS
Degrees: associate, bachelor's, certificate, doctoral, master's, postbachelor's certificate, post-master's certificate. **Classes:** Most classes have 10-19 students. Most lab/discussion sessions have fewer than 10 students. **Special Study Options:** cross-registration, double major, honors program, independent

study, internships, liberal arts/career combination, student-designed major, teacher certification program. **Disability Services:** Special programs offered to physically disabled students, including note-taking services, reader services, tape recorders, tutors. **Career Services:** Alumni services, Career/job search classes, Career assessment, Internships, On-campus interviews.

FACILITIES

Housing: Coed dorms, Coed wellness dorm (substance free). 75% of campus accessible to physically diasbled. **Special Academic Facilities/Equipment:** Art gallery, Early Childhood Center/Laboratory School, language lab, TV microscope, video/laser disk system, photospectrometer, high-performance liquid chromatograph, digital imaging lab, several art studios including a photography darkroom. **Computers:** 100% of classrooms, 100% of dorms, 100% of libraries, 100% of dining areas, 100% of student union, 100% of common outdoor areas have wireless network access. Administrative functions (other than registration) can be performed online.

CAMPUS LIFE

Environment: City. **Activities:** Choral groups, dance, drama/theater, music ensembles, student government, student newspaper, television station, yearbook. 30 registered organizations, 2 honor societies, 2 religious organizations. **Athletics (Intercollegiate):** *Men:* baseball, basketball, cross-country, soccer, volleyball. *Women:* basketball, cross-country, soccer, softball, volleyball.

ADMISSIONS

Freshman Academic Profile: Average high school GPA 3.0. 6% in top 10% of high school class, 27% in top 25% of high school class, 71% in top 50% of high school class. **Reported SAT (pre-2016 redesign) scores:** SAT Math middle 50% range 410-510. SAT Critical Reading middle 50% range 410-510. SAT Writing middle 50% range 420-520. **Concordant SAT scores:** SAT EBRW middle 50% 460–570. SAT Math middle 50% range 450–540. ACT middle 50% range 17-21. Minimum paper TOEFL 500. **Basis for Candidate Selection:** *Very important factors considered include:* rigor of secondary school record, academic GPA. *Important factors considered include:* class rank, standardized test scores, application essay, extracurricular activities, talent/ability, volunteer work, work experience. *Other factors considered include:* recommendation(s), interview, character/personal qualities. **Freshman Admission Requirements:** High school diploma is required and GED is accepted. *Academic units recommended:* 4 English, 3 math, 1 science, 1 science lab, 2 foreign language, 2 social studies, 1 history, 3 academic electives. **Freshman Admission Statistics:** 665 applied, 81.65% admitted, 36% enrolled. **Transfer Admission Requirements:** essay or personal statement, Minimum college GPA of 2.0 required. Lowest grade transferable C. **General Admission Information:** Application fee $25. Nonfall registration not accepted. Admission may be deferred for a maximum of 1 year.

COSTS AND FINANCIAL AID

Annual tuition $25,410. Room and board $9,798. Required fees $600. Average book expense $1,200. **Required Forms and Deadlines:** FAFSA. **Notification of Awards:** Applicants will be notified of awards on a rolling basis beginning 3/1. **Types of Aid:** *Need-based scholarships/grants:* Federal Pell, FSEOG, State scholarships/grants, Private scholarships, College/university scholarship or grant aid from institutional funds. *Loans:* Direct Subsidized Stafford Loans, Direct Unsubsidized Stafford Loans, Direct PLUS loans, Federal Perkins Loans, College/university loans from institutional funds. *Student Employment:* Federal Work-Study Program available. Institutional employment available. **Financial Aid Statistics:** 100% needy freshmen, 91% needy undergrads receive need-based scholarship or grant aid. 4% freshmen, 4% undergrads receive non-need-based scholarship or grant aid. 91% freshmen, 93% undergrads receive need-based self-help aid. 0% freshmen, 0% undergrads receive athletic scholarships. 82% freshmen, 89% undergrads receive any aid. **Criteria for awarding aid:** *Need-based:* Academics. *Non-need-based:* Academics, Alumni affiliation, Leadership.

ROANOKE BIBLE COLLEGE

715 N. Poindexter St., Elizabeth City, NC 27909-4054
Phone: 252-334-2028 • **Financial Aid Phone:** 252-334-2020
E-mail: admissions@roanokebible.edu
Fax: 252-334-2064 • **ACT Code:** 3153

This private school was founded in 1948. It has a 20-acre campus.

RATINGS

Admissions Selectivity Rating: 77   **Fire Safety Rating:** 76   **Green Rating:** 60*

STUDENTS AND FACULTY

Student Body: (1 countries represented).
Retention and Graduation: 53% freshmen return for sophomore year. 36% freshmen graduate within 4 years. 58% freshmen graduate within 6 years.
Faculty: Student/faculty ratio 10:1. 9 full-time faculty, 56% hold PhDs, 0% are are members of minority groups, 33% are women. 0% of classes are taught by teaching assistants.

ACADEMICS

Degrees: associate, bachelor's, certificate. **Classes:** Most classes have fewer than 10 students. Most lab/discussion sessions have 10-19 students. **Most popular majors:** Bible/Biblical Studies. **Special Study Options:** distance learning, double major, dual enrollment, internships, Cross-cultural semester abroad. **Disability Services:** Special programs offered to physically disabled students, including tape recorders, tutors.

FACILITIES

Housing: special housing for disabled students, men's dorms, women's dorms, apartments for married students, apartments for single students. 90% of campus accessible to physically diasbled. **Computers:** 80% of classrooms, 100% of libraries, have wireless network access.

CAMPUS LIFE

Environment: Village. **Activities:** Choral groups, drama/theater, music ensembles, musical theater, student government, yearbook. 1 honor society. **Athletics (Intercollegiate):** *Men:* basketball. *Women:* basketball, volleyball. **On-Campus Highlights:** On the Pasquotank River, New Married Housing apartments, New student life center **Environmental Initiatives:** Geothermal heating & cooling

ADMISSIONS

Freshman Academic Profile: Average high school GPA 2.8. 2% in top 10% of high school class, 14% in top 25% of high school class, 37% in top 50% of high school class. 87% from public high schools. **Reported SAT (pre-2016 redesign) scores:** SAT Math middle 50% range 420-590. SAT Critical Reading middle 50% range 410-565. **Concordant SAT scores:** SAT Math middle 50% range 460–610. Minimum internet-based TOEFL 80. Minimum paper TOEFL 500. **Basis for Candidate Selection:** *Very important factors considered include:* class rank, academic GPA, standardized test scores, recommendation(s), character/personal qualities, religious affiliation/commitment. *Important factors considered include:* rigor of secondary school record, application essay. *Other factors considered include:* interview, extracurricular activities, talent/ability, volunteer work, work experience, level of applicant's interest. **Freshman Admission Requirements:** High school diploma is required and GED is accepted. *Academic units required:* 4 English, 3 math, 3 science, 2 science labs, 2 social studies, 2 history, 4 academic electives. *Academic units recommended:* 6 foreign language, 1 computer science. **Freshman Admission Statistics:** 127 applied, 55.91% admitted, 58% enrolled. **Transfer Admission Requirements:** college transcript(s), essay or personal statement, statement of good standing from prior institution(s). Minimum college GPA of 2.0 required. Lowest grade transferable C. **General Admission Information:** Application fee $50. Nonfall registration accepted. Admission may be deferred for a maximum of 1 semester.

COSTS AND FINANCIAL AID

Required Forms and Deadlines: FAFSA, Institution's own financial aid form. **Notification of Awards:** Applicants will be notified of awards on a rolling basis beginning 5/1. **Types of Aid:** *Need-based scholarships/grants:* Federal Pell, FSEOG, State scholarships/grants, Private scholarships, College/university scholarship or grant aid from institutional funds. *Student Employment:* Federal Work-Study Program available. Institutional employment available. **Financial Aid Statistics:** 100% needy freshmen, 100% needy undergrads receive need-based scholarship or grant aid. 29% freshmen, 23% undergrads receive non-need-based scholarship or grant aid. 68% freshmen, 82% undergrads receive need-based self-help aid. 0% freshmen, 0% undergrads receive athletic scholarships. 88% freshmen, 90% undergrads receive any aid. **Criteria for awarding aid:** *Non-need-based:* Academics, Alumni affiliation, Art, Athletics, Leadership, Music/drama, Religious affiliation.

ROANOKE COLLEGE

221 College Lane, Salem, VA 24153-3794
Phone: 540-375-2270 • **Financial Aid Phone:** 540-375-2235
E-mail: admissions@roanoke.edu • **CEEB Code:** 5571
Fax: 540-375-2267 • **Website:** www.roanoke.edu • **ACT Code:** 4392

This private school, affiliated with the Lutheran Church, was founded in 1842. It has a 68-acre campus.

RATINGS
Admissions Selectivity Rating: 82   **Fire Safety Rating:** 89   **Green Rating:** 76

STUDENTS AND FACULTY
Enrollment: 1,946. **Student Body:** 58% female, 42% male, 46% out-of-state, 3% international (32 countries represented). Asian 1%, African American 6%, Caucasian 82%, Hispanic 4%, Native American <1%, Pacific Islander <1%, Two or more races 4%, Race unknown <1%.
Retention and Graduation: 83% freshmen return for sophomore year. 57% freshmen graduate within 4 years. 63% freshmen graduate within 6 years. 18% grads go on to further study within 1 year. **Faculty:** Student/faculty ratio 11:1. 164 full-time faculty, 87% hold PhDs, 10% are are members of minority groups, 51% are women. 0% of classes are taught by teaching assistants.

ACADEMICS
Degrees: bachelor's. **Classes:** Most classes have 20-29 students. Most lab/discussion sessions have 10-19 students. **Most popular majors:** Business Administration and Management; Psychology; Biology/Biological Sciences. **Special Study Options:** Accelerated program, cross-registration, double major, dual enrollment, English as a Second Language (ESL), honors program, independent study, internships, liberal arts/career combination, study abroad, teacher certification program. **Honors Programs:** The Honors Program is designed for students with excellent academic performance, broad extracurricular interests, and leadership abilities. The Honors Program substitutes a coordinated sequence of interdisciplinary courses for a portion of the core requirements. A Plenary Enrichment Program of supplemental activities, a special scholarship, and a distinct recognition on the diploma and transcript are provided. **Disability Services:** Special programs offered to physically disabled students, including note-taking services, reader services, tape recorders, tutors. **Career Services:** Alumni network, Alumni services, Career/job search classes, Career assessment, Internships, Regional alumni. Alumni Networking, which is offered to both students and alumni. Roanoke alumni are very open to helping students and fellow graduates in the career development area.

FACILITIES
Housing: Coed dorms, men's dorms, women's dorms, fraternity/sorority housing, apartments for single students, Theme Housing. 60% of campus accessible to physically diasbled. **Special Academic Facilities/Equipment:** Fine arts center, community research center, language lab, church and society center. **Computers:** 100% of classrooms, 100% of libraries, 100% of dining areas, 100% of student union, 50% of common outdoor areas have wireless network access. Students can register for classes online. Administrative functions (other than registration) can be performed online.

CAMPUS LIFE
Environment: City. **Activities:** Choral groups, dance, drama/theater, jazz band, literary magazine, music ensembles, musical theater, pep band, radio station, student government, student newspaper, student-run film society, yearbook, Campus Ministries, Student Organization, Model UN. 85 registered organizations, 30 honor societies, 7 religious organizations. 4 fraternities, 4 sororities. **Athletics (Intercollegiate):** *Men:* baseball, basketball, cross-country, golf, lacrosse, soccer, tennis, track/field (outdoor), track/field (indoor). *Women:* basketball, cross-country, field hockey, lacrosse, soccer, softball, tennis, track/field (outdoor), track/field (indoor), volleyball. **On-Campus Highlights:** Colket Student Center, Belk Fitness Center, Fintel Library, Bast Gymnasium & Kerr Stadium, Olin Hall (performing arts). **Environmental Initiatives:** Within the last five years Lucas Hall was renovated and is LEED-Silver Certified. LEED stands for "Leadership in Energy and Environmental Design" and it means this construction project was environmentally sensitive in many different ways. A new residence hall was also built in this period, to LEED standards, although the college is not seeking formal certification. A new campus community center

is under construction for fall, 2016, and is also using LEED-type standards, but will not be certified.

ADMISSIONS
Freshman Academic Profile: Average high school GPA 3.5. 21% in top 10% of high school class, 47% in top 25% of high school class, 79% in top 50% of high school class. 81% from public high schools. **Reported SAT (pre-2016 redesign) scores:** SAT Math middle 50% range 480-590. SAT Critical Reading middle 50% range 490-610. SAT Writing middle 50% range 463-580. **Concordant SAT scores:** SAT EBRW middle 50% 530–650. SAT Math middle 50% range 510–610. ACT middle 50% range 21-27. Minimum internet-based TOEFL 80. **Basis for Candidate Selection:** *Very important factors considered include:* rigor of secondary school record, academic GPA, character/personal qualities. *Important factors considered include:* class rank, standardized test scores, interview, extracurricular activities, level of applicant's interest. *Other factors considered include:* application essay, recommendation(s), talent/ability, alumni/ae relation, racial/ethnic status, volunteer work, work experience. **Freshman Admission Requirements:** High school diploma is required and GED is accepted. *Academic units required:* 4 English, 3 math, 2 science, 2 science labs, 2 social studies, 5 academic electives. *Academic units recommended:* 4 foreign language. **Freshman Admission Statistics:** 4,459 applied, 73.04% admitted, 16% enrolled. **Transfer Admission Requirements:** High school transcript, college transcript(s), statement of good standing from prior institution(s). Minimum college GPA of 2.2 required. Lowest grade transferable C-. **General Admission Information:** Application fee $30. Regular application deadline 3/15. Nonfall registration accepted. Admission may be deferred for a maximum of 2 years.

COSTS AND FINANCIAL AID
Annual tuition $41,110. Room and board $13,258. Required fees $1,584. Average book expense $1,000. **Required Forms and Deadlines:** FAFSA, State aid form. **Notification of Awards:** Applicants will be notified of awards on a rolling basis beginning 10/15. **Types of Aid:** *Need-based scholarships/grants:* Federal Pell, FSEOG, State scholarships/grants, College/university scholarship or grant aid from institutional funds. *Loans:* Direct Subsidized Stafford Loans, Direct Unsubsidized Stafford Loans, Direct PLUS loans, Federal Perkins Loans, College/university loans from institutional funds. *Student Employment:* Federal Work-Study Program available. Institutional employment available. **Financial Aid Statistics:** 99% needy freshmen, 98% needy undergrads receive need-based scholarship or grant aid. 100% freshmen, 97% undergrads receive non-need-based scholarship or grant aid. 75% freshmen, 77% undergrads receive need-based self-help aid. 0% freshmen, 0% undergrads receive athletic scholarships. 100% freshmen, 99% undergrads receive any aid. 77% undergrads borrow to pay for school. Average cumulative indebtedness $39,175. **Criteria for awarding aid:** *Need-based:* Academics, Minority status, Religious affiliation. *Non-need-based:* Academics, Art, Minority status, Music/drama, Religious affiliation.

ROBERT MORRIS UNIVERSITY

6001 University Boulevard, Moon Township, PA 15108-1189
Phone: 412-397-5200 • **Financial Aid Phone:** 412-397-6250
E-mail: admissionsoffice@rmu.edu • **CEEB Code:** 2769
Fax: 412-397-2425 • **Website:** www.rmu.edu • **ACT Code:** 3674

This private school was founded in 1921. It has a 230-acre campus.

RATINGS
Admissions Selectivity Rating: 78   **Fire Safety Rating:** 93   **Green Rating:** 60*

STUDENTS AND FACULTY
Enrollment: 4,372. **Student Body:** 42% female, 58% male, 14% out-of-state, 12% international (36 countries represented). Asian 1%, African American 6%, Caucasian 73%, Hispanic 2%, Native American <1%, Pacific Islander <1%, Two or more races 3%, Race unknown 2%.
Retention and Graduation: 80% freshmen return for sophomore year. 45% freshmen graduate within 4 years. 61% freshmen graduate within 6 years. 9% grads go on to further study within 1 year. **Faculty:** Student/faculty ratio 15:1. 203 full-time faculty, 92% hold PhDs, 19% are members of minority groups, 44% are women. 0% of classes are taught by teaching assistants.

ACADEMICS
Degrees: bachelor's, certificate, doctoral/professional, doctoral/research, master's, postbachelor's certificate. **Classes:** Most classes have 20-29 students. **Most popular majors:** Accounting; Marketing/Marketing Management; Business Administration and Management. **Special Study Options:** cooperative education program, cross-registration, distance learning, double major, honors program, independent study, internships, study abroad, teacher certification program, weekend college, Evening, weekend and 5 week/8 week

programs. **Honors Programs:** International Honors Program Combined degree programs: BSBA/MS BS/MS. **Disability Services:** Special programs offered to physically disabled students, including note-taking services, reader services, tape recorders, tutors. **Career Services:** Alumni network, Alumni services, Career/job search classes, Career assessment, Internships, Regional alumni. Extensive internship and co-op placement program.

FACILITIES

Housing: Coed dorms, men's dorms, women's dorms, apartments for single students. 85% of campus accessible to physically diasbled. **Computers:** 50% of classrooms, 75% of libraries, 100% of dining areas, 100% of student union, 25% of common outdoor areas have wireless network access. Students can register for classes online. Administrative functions (other than registration) can be performed online.

CAMPUS LIFE

Environment: Metropolis. **Activities:** Choral groups, drama/theater, literary magazine, marching band, musical theater, pep band, radio station, student government, student newspaper, television station, Campus Ministries, Student Organization. 97 registered organizations, 6 honor societies, 5 religious organizations. 4 fraternities, 3 sororities. **Athletics (Intercollegiate):** *Men:* basketball, football, golf, ice hockey, lacrosse, soccer, tennis, track/field (outdoor), track/field (indoor). *Women:* basketball, crew/rowing, field hockey, golf, ice hockey, lacrosse, soccer, softball, tennis, track/field (outdoor), track/field (indoor), volleyball. **On-Campus Highlights:** Student Center, RMU Island Sports Center Complex, Computer Labs, Athletic Center, Health Club. **Environmental Initiatives:** Recycling paper, cardboard, plastic, bottles and cans, and florescent bulbs.

ADMISSIONS

Freshman Academic Profile: Average high school GPA 3.5. 14% in top 10% of high school class, 41% in top 25% of high school class, 75% in top 50% of high school class. 89% from public high schools. **Reported SAT (pre-2016 redesign) scores:** SAT Math middle 50% range 470-580. SAT Critical Reading middle 50% range 470-560. SAT Writing middle 50% range 440-530. **Concordant SAT scores:** SAT EBRW middle 50% 510–600. SAT Math middle 50% range 510–600. ACT middle 50% range 21-26. Minimum internet-based TOEFL 61. Minimum paper TOEFL 500. **Basis for Candidate Selection:** *Very important factors considered include:* academic GPA, standardized test scores. *Important factors considered include:* rigor of secondary school record, interview. *Other factors considered include:* class rank, application essay, recommendation(s), extracurricular activities, character/personal qualities, volunteer work, work experience, level of applicant's interest. **Freshman Admission Requirements:** High school diploma is required and GED is accepted. *Academic units required:* 4 English, 3 math, 2 science, 4 social studies, 3 academic electives. *Academic units recommended:* 2 foreign language. **Freshman Admission Statistics:** 7,164 applied, 79.84% admitted, 16% enrolled. **Transfer Admission Requirements:** college transcript(s), statement of good standing from prior institution(s). Minimum college GPA of 2.0 required. Lowest grade transferable C. **General Admission Information:** Application fee $30. Nonfall registration accepted. Admission may be deferred for a maximum of 12 months.

COSTS AND FINANCIAL AID

Annual tuition $27,320. Room and board $10,910. Required fees $930. Average book expense $1,200. **Required Forms and Deadlines:** FAFSA. **Notification of Awards:** Applicants will be notified of awards on a rolling basis beginning 2/15. **Types of Aid:** *Need-based scholarships/grants:* Federal Pell, FSEOG, State scholarships/grants, Private scholarships, College/university scholarship or grant aid from institutional funds. *Loans:* Direct Subsidized Stafford Loans, Direct Unsubsidized Stafford Loans, Direct PLUS loans, Federal Perkins Loans. *Student Employment:* Federal Work-Study Program available. Institutional employment available. **Financial Aid Statistics:** 99% needy freshmen, 98% needy undergrads receive need-based scholarship or grant aid. 10% freshmen, 10% undergrads receive non-need-based scholarship or grant aid. 88% freshmen, 87% undergrads receive need-based self-help aid. 3% freshmen, 3% undergrads receive athletic scholarships. 80% freshmen, 71% undergrads receive any aid. 82% undergrads borrow to pay for school. Average cumulative indebtedness $39,431. **Criteria for awarding aid:** *Non-need-based:* Academics, Athletics.

ROBERT MORRIS UNIVERSITY (IL)

401 South State Street, Chicago, IL 60605
Phone: 800-762-5960 • **Financial Aid Phone:** 312-935-4077
E-mail: enroll@robertmorris.edu • **CEEB Code:** 1670
Fax: 312-935-4440 • **ACT Code:** 1121

This is a private school.

RATINGS

Admissions Selectivity Rating: 78 **Fire Safety Rating:** 97 **Green Rating:** 72

STUDENTS AND FACULTY

Enrollment: 3,196. **Student Body:** 53% female, 47% male, 8% out-of-state, 1% international (27 countries represented). Asian 3%, African American 33%, Caucasian 38%, Hispanic 23%, Native American <1%, Pacific Islander <1%, Two or more races 1%, Race unknown 1%.
Retention and Graduation: 49% freshmen return for sophomore year. 69% freshmen graduate within 4 years. 73% freshmen graduate within 6 years. 16% grads go on to further study within 1 year. **Faculty:** Student/faculty ratio 20:1. 124 full-time faculty, 27% hold PhDs, 23% are are members of minority groups, 48% are women.

ACADEMICS

Degrees: associate, bachelor's, master's. **Classes:** Most classes have 20-29 students. **Most popular majors:** Business Administration and Management; Graphic Design; Information Technology. **Special Study Options:** Accelerated program, cooperative education program, distance learning, dual enrollment, honors program, internships, study abroad. Combined degree programs: BBA/MBA, BAS/MIS, MBA/MIS. **Career Services:** Alumni network, Alumni services, Career/job search classes, Career assessment, Internships.

FACILITIES

Housing: Coed dorms. 100% of campus accessible to physically diasbled.

CAMPUS LIFE

Activities: Choral groups, dance, drama/theater, literary magazine, student newspaper. **Environmental Initiatives:** The establishment of the RMU Sustainability Council, which is represented on our Academic Council and was issued a Proclamation for its work.

ADMISSIONS

Freshman Academic Profile: Average high school GPA 2.7. 6% in top 10% of high school class, 19% in top 25% of high school class, 46% in top 50% of high school class. ACT middle 50% range 16-22. Minimum internet-based TOEFL 80. Minimum paper TOEFL 550. **Basis for Candidate Selection:** *Very important factors considered include:* rigor of secondary school record, class rank, academic GPA, interview. *Important factors considered include:* level of applicant's interest. *Other factors considered include:* standardized test scores, extracurricular activities, talent/ability, character/personal qualities, volunteer work, work experience. **Freshman Admission Requirements:** High school diploma is required and GED is accepted. *Academic units recommended:* 4 English, 3 math, 2 science, 1 science lab, 2 foreign language, 2 social studies, 3 history. **Freshman Admission Statistics:** 2,786 applied, 33.96% admitted. **General Admission Information:** Application fee $20. Nonfall registration accepted. Admission may be deferred for a maximum of 1 year.

COSTS AND FINANCIAL AID

Annual tuition $22,800. Room and board $11,754. **Required Forms and Deadlines:** FAFSA. **Types of Aid:** *Need-based scholarships/grants:* Federal Pell, FSEOG, State scholarships/grants, Private scholarships, College/university scholarship or grant aid from institutional funds. *Loans:* Federal Perkins Loans. *Student Employment:* Federal Work-Study Program available. **Financial Aid Statistics:** 83% needy freshmen, 80% needy undergrads receive need-based scholarship or grant aid. 43% freshmen, 73% undergrads receive non-need-based scholarship or grant aid. 89% freshmen, 81% undergrads receive need-based self-help aid. 16% freshmen, 17% undergrads receive athletic scholarships. 92% freshmen, 92% undergrads receive any aid. **Criteria for awarding aid:** *Need-based:* Academics, Art, Athletics, Leadership, Music/drama. *Non-need-based:* Academics, Art, Athletics, Leadership, Music/drama, State/district residency.

ROBERTS WESLEYAN COLLEGE

2301 Westside Drive, Rochester, NY 14624-1997
Phone: 585-594-6400 • **Financial Aid Phone:** 585-594-6150
E-mail: admissions@roberts.edu • **CEEB Code:** 2805
Fax: 585-594-6371 • **Website:** www.roberts.edu • **ACT Code:** 2868

This private school was founded in 1866. It has a 75-acre campus.

RATINGS

Admissions Selectivity Rating: 85   **Fire Safety Rating:** 73   **Green Rating:** 60*

STUDENTS AND FACULTY

Enrollment: 1,288. **Student Body:** 69% female, 31% male, 7% out-of-state, 3% international (33 countries represented). Asian 1%, African American 12%, Caucasian 75%, Hispanic 5%, Native American <1%, Pacific Islander <1%, Two or more races 2%, Race unknown 2%.
Retention and Graduation: 80% freshmen return for sophomore year. 48% freshmen graduate within 4 years. 59% freshmen graduate within 6 years. 24% grads go on to further study within 1 year. **Faculty:** 92 full-time faculty, 72% hold PhDs, 7% are are members of minority groups, 52% are women. 0% of classes are taught by teaching assistants.

ACADEMICS

Degrees: bachelor's, master's. **Classes:** Most classes have 10-19 students. Most lab/discussion sessions have 10-19 students. **Most popular majors:** Elementary Education and Teaching; Music Teacher Education. **Special Study Options:** cross-registration, distance learning, double major, English as a Second Language (ESL), honors program, independent study, internships, study abroad, teacher certification program. Combined degree programs: BA/MEng, Pharmacy. **Disability Services:** Special programs offered to physically disabled students, including note-taking services, reader services, tape recorders, tutors. **Career Services:** Alumni network, Alumni services, Career assessment, Internships, Regional alumni. Alumni Networking and shadowing programs, Alumni Career Panels, Alumni Career Services Group on Linkedin.com, Mock Interviews.

FACILITIES

Housing: Coed dorms, special housing for disabled students, men's dorms, women's dorms, apartments for married students, apartments for single students. 71% of campus accessible to physically diasbled. **Special Academic Facilities/Equipment:** Davison Art Gallery **Computers:** 100% of classrooms, 100% of dorms, 100% of libraries, 100% of dining areas, 100% of student union, 70% of common outdoor areas have wireless network access. Students can register for classes online. Administrative functions (other than registration) can be performed online.

CAMPUS LIFE

Environment: City. **Activities:** Choral groups, concert band, dance, drama/theater, jazz band, music ensembles, musical theater, opera, student government, student newspaper, symphony orchestra, yearbook, Campus Ministries, Student Organization, Model UN. 28 registered organizations, 11 religious organizations. **Athletics (Intercollegiate):** *Men:* basketball, cross-country, golf, soccer, tennis, track/field (outdoor), track/field (indoor). *Women:* basketball, cross-country, soccer, tennis, track/field (outdoor), track/field (indoor), volleyball. **On-Campus Highlights:** Voller Athletic Center & Sports Complex, New B. Thomas Golisano Library, Rinker Community Service Center, BT's Cafe, Cultural Life Center.

ADMISSIONS

Freshman Academic Profile: Average high school GPA 3.4. 24% in top 10% of high school class, 49% in top 25% of high school class, 85% in top 50% of high school class. **Reported SAT (pre-2016 redesign) scores:** SAT Math middle 50% range 470-590. SAT Critical Reading middle 50% range 470-600. SAT Writing middle 50% range 440-580. **Concordant SAT scores:** SAT EBRW middle 50% 510–650. SAT Math middle 50% range 510–610. ACT middle 50% range 20-27. Minimum internet-based TOEFL 75. Minimum paper TOEFL 540. **Basis for Candidate Selection:** *Very important factors considered include:* rigor of secondary school record, academic GPA, standardized test scores, interview, character/personal qualities, religious affiliation/commitment. *Important factors considered include:* application essay, recommendation(s), extracurricular activities. *Other factors considered include:* class rank, talent/ability, alumni/ae relation, volunteer work, level of applicant's interest. **Freshman Admission Requirements:** High school diploma is required and GED is accepted. *Academic units required:* 4 English, 3 math, 3 science, 1 science lab, 3 social studies. *Academic units recommended:* 4 math, 4 science, 3 science labs, 3 foreign language. **Freshman Admission Statistics:** 1,928 applied, 46.52% admitted, 24% enrolled. **Transfer Admission Requirements:** college transcript(s), essay or personal statement, Minimum college GPA of 2.70 required. Lowest grade transferable C. **General**

Admission Information: Application fee $35. Priority deadline 2/1. Nonfall registration accepted. Admission may be deferred for a maximum of 1 year.

COSTS AND FINANCIAL AID

Annual tuition $25,350. Room and board $9,264. Required fees $974. Average book expense $1,000. **Required Forms and Deadlines:** FAFSA, State aid form. **Notification of Awards:** Applicants will be notified of awards on a rolling basis beginning 3/1. **Types of Aid:** *Need-based scholarships/grants:* Federal Pell, FSEOG, State scholarships/grants, Private scholarships, College/university scholarship or grant aid from institutional funds. *Loans:* Direct Subsidized Stafford Loans, Direct Unsubsidized Stafford Loans, Direct PLUS loans, Federal Perkins Loans. *Student Employment:* Federal Work-Study Program available. Institutional employment available. **Financial Aid Statistics:** 100% needy freshmen, 98% needy undergrads receive need-based scholarship or grant aid. 12% freshmen, 7% undergrads receive non-need-based scholarship or grant aid. 86% freshmen, 89% undergrads receive need-based self-help aid. 6% freshmen, 3% undergrads receive athletic scholarships. 98% freshmen, 97% undergrads receive any aid. **Criteria for awarding aid:** *Need-based:* Leadership. *Non-need-based:* Academics, Alumni affiliation, Art, Athletics, Music/drama, Religious affiliation.

ROCHESTER COLLEGE

800 West Avon Road, Rochester Hills, MI 48307
Phone: 248-218-2031
E-mail: admissions@rc.edu • **CEEB Code:** 1516
Fax: 248-218-2035 • **Website:** www.rc.edu • **ACT Code:** 2072

This private school, affiliated with the Church of Christ Church, was founded in 1959. It has a 83-acre campus.

RATINGS

Admissions Selectivity Rating: 64   **Fire Safety Rating:** 60*   **Green Rating:** 60*

STUDENTS AND FACULTY

Enrollment: 927. **Student Body:** 14% out-of-state, 3% international (10 countries represented). Asian 1%, African American 11%, Caucasian 83%, Hispanic 1%, Native American 1%, Pacific Islander 0%, Two or more races 0%, Race unknown 1%.
Retention and Graduation: 69% freshmen return for sophomore year. 8% freshmen graduate within 4 years. 12% freshmen graduate within 6 years. **Faculty:** Student/faculty ratio 15:1. 32 full-time faculty, 28% hold PhDs, 0% are are members of minority groups, 34% 0% of classes are taught by teaching assistants.

ACADEMICS

Degrees: associate, bachelor's, master's, transfer. **Special Study Options:** Accelerated program, cross-registration, double major, dual enrollment, independent study, internships, liberal arts/career combination, study abroad, teacher certification program, weekend college. **Disability Services:** Special programs offered to physically disabled students, including note-taking services, reader services. **Career Services:** Alumni network, Alumni services, Career/job search classes, Career assessment, Internships.

FACILITIES

Housing: special housing for disabled students, men's dorms, women's dorms, apartments for married students.

CAMPUS LIFE

Environment: Village. **Activities:** Choral groups, drama/theater, jazz band, music ensembles, student government, student newspaper, yearbook. 19 registered organizations, 3 honor societies, 1 religious organization. **Athletics (Intercollegiate):** *Men:* baseball, basketball, cross-country, soccer, track/field (outdoor). *Women:* basketball, cross-country, softball, track/field (outdoor), volleyball.

ADMISSIONS

Minimum paper TOEFL 500. **Basis for Candidate Selection:** *Important factors considered include:* rigor of secondary school record, standardized test scores. *Other factors considered include:* interview. **Freshman Admission Requirements:** High school diploma is required and GED is accepted. **Freshman Admission Statistics:** 277 applied, 83.39% admitted, 65% enrolled. **Transfer Admission Requirements:** High school transcript, college transcript(s), Minimum college GPA of 2.0 required. Lowest grade transferable C. **General Admission Information:** Application fee $25. Nonfall registration accepted. Admission may be deferred for a maximum of 24 months.

COSTS AND FINANCIAL AID

Annual tuition $9,462. Room and board $5,342. Required fees $600. Average book expense $600. **Required Forms and Deadlines:** FAFSA, Institution's own financial aid form. **Notification of Awards:** Applicants will be notified of awards on a rolling basis beginning 6/1. **Types of Aid:** *Need-based scholarships/ grants:* Federal Pell, FSEOG, State scholarships/grants, Private scholarships, College/university scholarship or grant aid from institutional funds. *Loans:* Direct Subsidized Stafford Loans, Direct Unsubsidized Stafford Loans, Direct PLUS loans, Federal Perkins Loans. *Student Employment:* Federal Work-Study Program available. Institutional employment available. **Financial Aid Statistics:** 87% needy freshmen receive need-based scholarship or grant aid. 79% freshmen, undergrads receive non-need-based scholarship or grant aid. 84% freshmen, undergrads receive need-based self-help aid. 29% freshmen receive athletic scholarships. **Criteria for awarding aid:** *Non-need-based:* Academics, Alumni affiliation, Athletics, Leadership, Music/drama.

ROCHESTER INSTITUTE OF TECHNOLOGY

60 Lomb Memorial Drive, Rochester, NY 14623-5604
Phone: 585-475-6631 • **Financial Aid Phone:** 585-475-5502
E-mail: admissions@rit.edu • **CEEB Code:** 2760
Fax: 585-475-7424 • **Website:** www.rit.edu • **ACT Code:** 2870

This private school was founded in 1829. It has a 1300-acre campus.

RATINGS
Admissions Selectivity Rating: 89   **Fire Safety Rating:** 89   **Green Rating:** 93

STUDENTS AND FACULTY
Enrollment: 12,638. **Student Body:** 33% female, 67% male, 46% out-of-state, 6% international (68 countries represented). Asian 8%, African American 5%, Caucasian 67%, Hispanic 7%, Native American <1%, Pacific Islander <1%, Two or more races 3%, Race unknown 3%.
Retention and Graduation: 87% freshmen return for sophomore year. 29% freshmen graduate within 4 years. 66% freshmen graduate within 6 years. 18% grads go on to further study within 1 year. **Faculty:** Student/faculty ratio 13:1. 1,023 full-time faculty, 70% hold PhDs, 19% are are members of minority groups, 36% are women. 0% of classes are taught by teaching assistants.

ACADEMICS
Degrees: associate, bachelor's, certificate, doctoral, master's, post-master's certificate. **Classes:** Most classes have 10-19 students. Most lab/discussion sessions have 10-19 students. **Most popular majors:** Mechanical Engineering; Computer Science; Modeling, Virtual Environments and Simulation. **Special Study Options:** Accelerated program, cooperative education program, cross-registration, distance learning, double major, English as a Second Language (ESL), exchange student program (domestic), honors program, independent study, internships, liberal arts/career combination, student-designed major, study abroad, weekend college. **Honors Programs:** The RIT Honors Program provides a variety of curricular and extracurricular options, special Honors housing, and Honors scholarships. Combined degree programs: BA/ MEng, BS/MS, 4+1 MBA, BS/ME. **Disability Services:** Special programs offered to physically disabled students, including note-taking services, reader services, tape recorders, tutors. **Career Services:** Alumni network, Alumni services, Career/job search classes, Career assessment, Internships, Regional alumni. Every academic program at RIT offers some form of experiential education opportunity. Experiential education is designed to enrich the learning experience by providing students the opportunity to apply what they are learning in the lab and classroom to real-world problems, projects, and settings. Experiential education takes many forms including cooperative education, internships, study-abroad, undergraduate research, and industry sponsored project work. Experiential education requirements and opportunities vary among academic programs. Notable among these programs at RIT is cooperative education (co-op). The College of Applied Science and Technology, the E. Philip Saunders College of Business, the B. Thomas Golisano College of Computing and Information Sciences, and the Kate Gleason College of Engineering all require co-op for undergraduate students. It is available on an optional basis in other RIT colleges. Co-op students alternate periods of full-time study with periods of full-time paid work experience in business and industry directly related to their field of study and career interests. Last year more than 3,300 students completed work assignments with nearly 1,500 employers earning collectively in excess of $30 million.

FACILITIES
Housing: Coed dorms, special housing for disabled students, special housing for international students, fraternity/sorority housing, apartments for married students, apartments for single students, Special interest floors for selected

majors/ groups. Men's floors Women's floors. 100% of campus accessible to physically disabled. **Special Academic Facilities/Equipment:** Art galleries, microelectronic engineering center, RIT Inn and Conference Center, observatory, student-managed restaurant, packaging testing facility, media resource center, Sunday 2000 printing press, Center for manufacturing studies, two OC3 connections to Internet and Internet2, laser optics laboratory, an observatory, an animal care facility, more than 100 color and black-and-white photography darkrooms, electronic prepress and publishing equipment, ceramic kilns, glass furnaces, a blacksmithing area, and computer graphics and robotic labs **Computers:** 75% of classrooms, 25% of dorms, 100% of libraries, 100% of dining areas, 100% of student union, 100% of common outdoor areas have wireless network access. Students can register for classes online. Administrative functions (other than registration) can be performed online.

CAMPUS LIFE
Environment: City. **Activities:** Choral groups, concert band, dance, drama/ theater, jazz band, literary magazine, music ensembles, musical theater, pep band, radio station, student government, student newspaper, student-run film society, symphony orchestra, yearbook, Campus Ministries, Student Organization. 175 registered organizations, 9 honor societies, 5 religious organizations. 19 fraternities, 10 sororities. **Athletics (Intercollegiate):** *Men:* baseball, basketball, crew/rowing, cross-country, diving, ice hockey, lacrosse, soccer, swimming, tennis, track/field (outdoor), track/field (indoor), wrestling. *Women:* basketball, cheerleading, crew/rowing, cross-country, diving, ice hockey, lacrosse, soccer, softball, swimming, tennis, track/field (outdoor), track/ field (indoor), volleyball. **On-Campus Highlights:** Java Wally's (Wallace Library coffee sho, Student Life Center/Field House/Ice Aren, ESPN Zone @ RIT Student Alumni Union, Ben and Jerry's (RIT Student Alumni Uni, The Cafe and Market at Crossroads. **Environmental Initiatives:** RIT has signed of the American College & University Presidents Climate Commitment (ACUPCC) and established 2030 as the target date for neutrality.

ADMISSIONS
Freshman Academic Profile: Average high school GPA 3.6. 39% in top 10% of high school class, 73% in top 25% of high school class, 94% in top 50% of high school class. 85% from public high schools. **Reported SAT (pre-2016 redesign) scores:** SAT Math middle 50% range 590-680. SAT Critical Reading middle 50% range 550-650. SAT Writing middle 50% range 520-620. **Concordant SAT scores:** SAT EBRW middle 50% 590–680. SAT Math middle 50% range 610–710. ACT middle 50% range 26-31. Minimum internet-based TOEFL 79. Minimum paper TOEFL 550. **Basis for Candidate Selection:** *Very important factors considered include:* rigor of secondary school record, academic GPA. *Important factors considered include:* class rank, standardized test scores. *Other factors considered include:* application essay, recommendation(s), interview, extracurricular activities, talent/ability, character/ personal qualities, first generation, alumni/ae relation, geographical residence, volunteer work, work experience, level of applicant's interest. **Freshman Admission Requirements:** High school diploma is required and GED is accepted. *Academic units required:* 4 English, 2 math, 2 science, 1 science lab, 4 social studies, 10 academic electives. *Academic units recommended:* 4 English, 3 math, 3 science, 2 science labs, 3 foreign language, 4 social studies, 5 academic electives. **Freshman Admission Statistics:** 19,824 applied, 54.93% admitted, 27% enrolled. **Transfer Admission Requirements:** college transcript(s), essay or personal statement, Minimum college GPA of 2.7 required. Lowest grade transferable C-. **General Admission Information:** Application fee $60. Priority deadline 2/1. Regular application deadline 2/1. Nonfall registration accepted. Admission may be deferred for a maximum of 12 months.

COSTS AND FINANCIAL AID
Annual tuition $38,024. Room and board $12,274. Required fees $544. Average book expense $1,050. **Required Forms and Deadlines:** FAFSA, Institution's own financial aid form, State aid form. **Notification of Awards:** Applicants will be notified of awards on a rolling basis beginning 3/15. **Types of Aid:** *Need-based scholarships/grants:* Federal Pell, FSEOG, State scholarships/ grants, Private scholarships, College/university scholarship or grant aid from institutional funds. *Loans:* Direct Subsidized Stafford Loans, Direct Unsubsidized Stafford Loans, Direct PLUS loans, Federal Perkins Loans. *Student Employment:* Federal Work-Study Program available. Institutional employment available. **Financial Aid Statistics:** 95% needy freshmen, 95% needy undergrads receive need-based scholarship or grant aid. 30% freshmen, 34% undergrads receive non-need-based scholarship or grant aid. 90% freshmen, 90% undergrads receive need-based self-help aid. 0% freshmen, 0% undergrads receive athletic scholarships. 87% freshmen, 77% undergrads receive any aid. 76% undergrads borrow to pay for school. Average cumulative indebtedness $38,198. **Criteria for awarding aid:** *Need-based:* Academics. *Non-need-based:* Academics, Art, Leadership.

See page 1026.

ROCKFORD UNIVERSITY

Admission, Rockford, IL 61108-2393
Phone: 815-226-4050 • **Financial Aid Phone:** 815-226-4062
E-mail: RCAdmissions@rockford.edu • **CEEB Code:** 1665
Fax: 815-226-2822 • **Website:** www.rockford.edu • **ACT Code:** 1122

This private school was founded in 1847. It has a 130-acre campus.

RATINGS

Admissions Selectivity Rating: 82   **Fire Safety Rating:** 81   **Green Rating:** 60*

STUDENTS AND FACULTY

Enrollment: 857. **Student Body:** 61% female, 39% male, 10% out-of-state, <1% international. Asian 2%, African American 8%, Caucasian 69%, Hispanic 6%, Native American 0%, Pacific Islander 0%, Two or more races 0%, Race unknown 14%.
Faculty: Student/faculty ratio 9:1. 69 full-time faculty, 68% hold PhDs, 3% are are members of minority groups, 42% are women. 0% of classes are taught by teaching assistants.

ACADEMICS

Degrees: bachelor's, master's. **Classes:** Most classes have 10-19 students. Most lab/discussion sessions have fewer than 10 students. **Most popular majors:** Business/Commerce Education. **Special Study Options:** Accelerated program, distance learning, double major, English as a Second Language (ESL), exchange student program (domestic), honors program, independent study, internships, study abroad, teacher certification program, Community-Based Learning, Tutorial Courses, Special Studies Courses. **Honors Programs:** Honors program in Liberal Arts. **Disability Services:** Special programs offered to physically disabled students, including note-taking services, reader services, tutors. **Career Services:** Career assessment, Internships. Community-Based Learning: Founded at Rockford College in the early 1990s, our community-based learning program is based on the conviction that Rockford College is a citizen of the community and that the community has a stake in Rockford College, as well. The work that the students perform serves the dual function of providing a defined need for the community while also fulfilling a specific learning objective determined by the professor.

FACILITIES

Housing: Coed dorms, special housing for disabled students, Theme Housing, Special housing for first-year students. We offer single rooms, double rooms, and suite style living options. **Special Academic Facilities/Equipment:** Language lab. Art Gallery. Sculpture Garden. **Computers:** Students can register for classes online. Administrative functions (other than registration) can be performed online.

CAMPUS LIFE

Environment: City. **Activities:** Choral groups, dance, drama/theater, literary magazine, music ensembles, musical theater, opera, pep band, student government, Campus Ministries, Student Organization, Model UN. 25 registered organizations, 6 honor societies, 1 religious organization. **Athletics (Intercollegiate):** *Men:* baseball, basketball, cross-country, football, golf, soccer, tennis, track/field (outdoor), track/field (indoor). *Women:* basketball, cross-country, golf, soccer, softball, tennis, track/field (outdoor), track/field (indoor), volleyball. **On-Campus Highlights:** Residence Halls, Seaver Gym, Lion's Den-student gathering place, Football/Soccer Stadium, Clark Arts Center, Tour also highlights classroom buildings. **Environmental Initiatives:** Green Week.

ADMISSIONS

Freshman Academic Profile: Average high school GPA 3.1. 18% in top 10% of high school class, 33% in top 25% of high school class, 65% in top 50% of high school class. ACT middle 50% range 19-24. Minimum internet-based TOEFL 79. Minimum paper TOEFL 550. **Basis for Candidate Selection:** *Very important factors considered include:* academic GPA. *Important factors considered include:* rigor of secondary school record, standardized test scores, application essay. *Other factors considered include:* class rank, recommendation(s). **Freshman Admission Requirements:** High school diploma is required and GED is accepted. *Academic units required:* 4 English, 3 math, 3 science, 3 science labs, 3 social studies, 2 academic electives. *Academic units recommended:* 2 foreign language. **Freshman Admission Statistics:** 967 applied, 41.16% admitted, 23% enrolled. **Transfer Admission Requirements:** college transcript(s), statement of good standing from prior institution(s). Minimum college GPA of 2.3 required. Lowest grade transferable C. **General Admission Information:** Application fee $35. Nonfall registration accepted. Admission may be deferred for a maximum of 1 year.

COSTS AND FINANCIAL AID

Annual tuition $24,750. Room and board $6,950. Average book expense $1,200. **Required Forms and Deadlines:** FAFSA. **Notification of Awards:**

Applicants will be notified of awards on a rolling basis beginning 3/1. **Types of Aid:** *Need-based scholarships/grants:* Federal Pell, FSEOG, State scholarships/grants, Private scholarships, College/university scholarship or grant aid from institutional funds. *Loans:* Federal Perkins Loans. *Student Employment:* Federal Work-Study Program available. Institutional employment available. **Financial Aid Statistics:** 98% needy freshmen, 95% needy undergrads receive need-based scholarship or grant aid. 12% freshmen, 16% undergrads receive non-need-based scholarship or grant aid. 95% freshmen, 98% undergrads receive need-based self-help aid. 0% freshmen, 0% undergrads receive athletic scholarships. 99% freshmen, 99% undergrads receive any aid. **Criteria for awarding aid:** *Need-based:* Academics. *Non-need-based:* Academics, Alumni affiliation, Leadership, Minority status, Music/drama, State/district residency.

ROCKHURST UNIVERSITY

1100 Rockhurst Road, Kansas City, MO 64110
Phone: 816-501-4100 • **Financial Aid Phone:** 816-501-4600
E-mail: admission@rockhurst.edu • **CEEB Code:** 6611
Fax: 816-501-4241 • **Website:** www.rockhurst.edu • **ACT Code:** 2342

This private school, affiliated with the Roman Catholic Church, was founded in 1910. It has a 55-acre campus.

RATINGS

Admissions Selectivity Rating: 85   **Fire Safety Rating:** 80   **Green Rating:** 60*

STUDENTS AND FACULTY

Enrollment: 1,495. **Student Body:** 58% female, 42% male, 43% out-of-state, 1% international (17 countries represented). Asian 3%, African American 4%, Caucasian 72%, Hispanic 8%, Native American <1%, Pacific Islander <1%, Two or more races 4%, Race unknown 7%.
Retention and Graduation: 83% freshmen return for sophomore year. 63% freshmen graduate within 4 years. 72% freshmen graduate within 6 years.
Faculty: Student/faculty ratio 11:1. 127 full-time faculty, 89% hold PhDs, 10% are are members of minority groups, 54% are women. 0% of classes are taught by teaching assistants.

ACADEMICS

Degrees: bachelor's, certificate, doctoral/professional, master's, postbachelor's certificate. **Classes:** Most classes have 20-29 students. Most lab/discussion sessions have 10-19 students. **Most popular majors:** Psychology; Business/Commerce; Kinesiology and Exercise Science. **Special Study Options:** Accelerated program, cooperative education program, cross-registration, double major, dual enrollment, exchange student program (domestic), honors program, independent study, internships, study abroad, teacher certification program. **Honors Programs:** The Rockhurst University Honors Program is for motivated and talented students, regardless of major, who want to be active participants in designing their education. Students find honors courses to be more innovative, personal, and challenging than other courses. The Benefits Beginning in the first year, honors students have specially designed core courses that are usually small in enrollment and are taught by some of the University's most creative faculty. During the sophomore through senior years, honors students may earn honors credit through "honors options"-individually designed projects that allow students to explore areas of their own interest under the mentorship of a professor. An honors option is typically an offshoot of a regular course, but an option can also be arranged as an independent study course. It is through the honors option that honors students shape their curriculum. Combined degree programs: BS/CSD, B/MBA. **Disability Services:** Special programs offered to physically disabled students, including note-taking services, reader services, tape recorders, tutors. **Career Services:** Alumni network, Alumni services, Career/job search classes, Career assessment, Internships, Regional alumni. All three add to the experiential education programs at Rockhurst.

FACILITIES

Housing: Coed dorms, special housing for disabled students, men's dorms, women's dorms, apartments for single students, RU on-campus housing. **Special Academic Facilities/Equipment:** Greenlease Art Gallery, Richardson Science Center. **Computers:** Students can register for classes online. Administrative functions (other than registration) can be performed online.

CAMPUS LIFE

Environment: Metropolis. **Activities:** Choral groups, drama/theater, literary magazine, musical theater, student government, student newspaper, yearbook. 44 registered organizations, 4 honor societies, 6 religious organizations. 3 fraternities, 3 sororities. **Athletics (Intercollegiate):** *Men:* baseball, basketball, golf, soccer, tennis. *Women:* basketball, golf, soccer, softball, tennis, volleyball. **On-Campus Highlights:** New Bell Tower and Fountains, Richardson Science

Center / state-of-art facility, Business School / complete computer lab and classroom renovations, Career and Learning Center, The Old Gym (historic) plus the new.

ADMISSIONS

Freshman Academic Profile: Average high school GPA 3.7. 30% in top 10% of high school class, 60% in top 25% of high school class, 89% in top 50% of high school class. 48% from public high schools. **Reported SAT (pre-2016 redesign) scores:** SAT Math middle 50% range 468-573. SAT Critical Reading middle 50% range 518-593. **Concordant SAT scores:** SAT Math middle 50% range 510–590. ACT middle 50% range 23-28. Minimum internet-based TOEFL 79. Minimum paper TOEFL 550. **Basis for Candidate Selection:** *Very important factors considered include:* rigor of secondary school record, academic GPA. *Important factors considered include:* standardized test scores. *Other factors considered include:* recommendation(s), interview, extracurricular activities, talent/ability, character/personal qualities, alumni/ae relation, volunteer work. **Freshman Admission Requirements:** High school diploma is required and GED is accepted. *Academic units recommended:* 4 English, 3 math, 3 science, 3 science labs, 2 foreign language, 3 social studies, 2 history, 4 academic electives. **Freshman Admission Statistics:** 3,038 applied, 74.06% admitted, 18% enrolled. **Transfer Admission Requirements:** college transcript(s), Minimum college GPA of 2.5 required. Lowest grade transferable C-. **General Admission Information:** Application fee $25. Nonfall registration accepted. Admission may be deferred.

COSTS AND FINANCIAL AID

Annual tuition $34,880. Room and board $9,080. Required fees $790. Average book expense $1,485. **Required Forms and Deadlines:** FAFSA. **Notification of Awards:** Applicants will be notified of awards on a rolling basis beginning 3/1. **Types of Aid:** *Need-based scholarships/grants:* Federal Pell, FSEOG, State scholarships/grants, Private scholarships, College/university scholarship or grant aid from institutional funds, United Negro College Fund. *Loans:* Direct Subsidized Stafford Loans, Direct Unsubsidized Stafford Loans, Direct PLUS loans, Federal Perkins Loans. *Student Employment:* Federal Work-Study Program available. Institutional employment available. **Financial Aid Statistics:** 97% needy freshmen, 100% needy undergrads receive need-based scholarship or grant aid. 52% freshmen, 45% undergrads receive non-need-based scholarship or grant aid. 73% freshmen, 74% undergrads receive need-based self-help aid. 14% freshmen, 14% undergrads receive athletic scholarships. 100% freshmen, 98% undergrads receive any aid. 78% undergrads borrow to pay for school. Average cumulative indebtedness $23,753. **Criteria for awarding aid:** *Need-based:* Minority status, Religious affiliation. *Non-need-based:* Academics, Alumni affiliation, Art, Athletics, Leadership, Music/drama.

ROCKY MOUNTAIN COLLEGE

1511 Poly Drive, Billings, MT 59102-1796
Phone: 406-657-1026 • **Financial Aid Phone:** 406-657-1031
E-mail: admissions@rocky.edu • **CEEB Code:** 4660
Fax: 406-657-1189 • **Website:** www.rocky.edu • **ACT Code:** 2426

This private school was founded in 1878. It has a 60-acre campus.

RATINGS

Admissions Selectivity Rating: 80   **Fire Safety Rating:** 87   **Green Rating:** 67

STUDENTS AND FACULTY

Enrollment: 984. **Student Body:** 49% female, 51% male, 44% out-of-state, 4% international (16 countries represented). Asian 1%, African American 3%, Caucasian 82%, Hispanic 4%, Native American 2%, Pacific Islander 1%, Two or more races 2%, Race unknown 2%.
Retention and Graduation: 67% freshmen return for sophomore year. 26% freshmen graduate within 4 years. 18% grads go on to further study within 1 year. 16% grads pursue arts and sciences degrees. 1% grads pursue law degrees. 1% grads pursue business degrees. **Faculty:** Student/faculty ratio 12:1. 65 full-time faculty, 77% hold PhDs, 0% are are members of minority groups, 40% are women. 0% of classes are taught by teaching assistants.

ACADEMICS

Degrees: associate, bachelor's, master's. **Classes:** Most classes have 10-19 students. Most lab/discussion sessions have fewer than 10 students. **Most popular majors:** Biology/Biological Sciences; Airline/Commercial/Professional Pilot and Flight Crew; Business Administration and Management. **Special Study Options:** Accelerated program, distance learning, double major, dual enrollment, English as a Second Language (ESL), honors program, independent study, internships, student-designed major, study abroad, teacher certification program. **Honors Programs:** Successful honors students find that participation in this program not only brings them closer to professionals in their chosen fields, but also grants them a substantial credential in their applications to graduate schools or employment opportunities. **Disability Services:** Special programs offered to physically disabled students, including note-taking services, reader services, tape recorders, tutors. **Career Services:** Alumni network, Alumni services, Career/job search classes, Career assessment, Internships, Regional alumni.

FACILITIES

Housing: Coed dorms, apartments for married students, apartments for single students, Suites. 75% of campus accessible to physically diasbled. **Special Academic Facilities/Equipment:** Billings Studio Theater, museum, studio, flight simulator/flight school, equestrian facilities, geology collection. **Computers:** Students can register for classes online. Administrative functions (other than registration) can be performed online.

CAMPUS LIFE

Environment: City. **Activities:** Choral groups, concert band, drama/theater, jazz band, literary magazine, music ensembles, musical theater, pep band, student government, student newspaper, yearbook. 28 registered organizations, 1 honor society, 4 religious organizations. **Athletics (Intercollegiate):** *Men:* basketball, cheerleading, football, golf, skiing (downhill/alpine). *Women:* basketball, cheerleading, golf, skiing (downhill/alpine), soccer, volleyball. **On-Campus Highlights:** Bair Family Student Center, Educational Resource Center, Fortin Center-Gymnasium, Herb Klindt Field-Football Stadium, Losekamp Hall-Music Theatre.

ADMISSIONS

Freshman Academic Profile: Average high school GPA 3.4. 10% in top 10% of high school class, 36% in top 25% of high school class, 70% in top 50% of high school class. **Reported SAT (pre-2016 redesign) scores:** SAT Math middle 50% range 450-550. SAT Critical Reading middle 50% range 440-540. SAT Writing middle 50% range 420-510. **Concordant SAT scores:** SAT EBRW middle 50% 480–580. SAT Math middle 50% range 490–570. ACT middle 50% range 20-25. Minimum paper TOEFL 525. **Basis for Candidate Selection:** *Very important factors considered include:* academic GPA, standardized test scores, level of applicant's interest. *Important factors considered include:* rigor of secondary school record, application essay, recommendation(s). *Other factors considered include:* class rank, interview, extracurricular activities, talent/ability, character/personal qualities, first generation, alumni/ae relation, work experience. **Freshman Admission Requirements:** High school diploma is required and GED is accepted. *Academic units required:* 4 English, 4 math, 3 science, 3 social studies, 2 history, 3 academic electives. **Freshman Admission Statistics:** 1,347 applied, 63.55% admitted, 31% enrolled. **Transfer Admission Requirements:** college transcript(s), Minimum college GPA of 2.0 required. Lowest grade transferable C-. **General Admission Information:** Application fee $35. Priority deadline 3/1. Nonfall registration accepted. Admission may be deferred for a maximum of 1 year.

COSTS AND FINANCIAL AID

Annual tuition $22,442. Room and board $7,160. Required fees $450. Average book expense $1,300. **Required Forms and Deadlines:** FAFSA. **Notification of Awards:** Applicants will be notified of awards on a rolling basis beginning 2/15. **Types of Aid:** *Need-based scholarships/grants:* Federal Pell, FSEOG, State scholarships/grants, Private scholarships, College/university scholarship or grant aid from institutional funds. *Loans:* Direct Subsidized Stafford Loans, Direct Unsubsidized Stafford Loans, Direct PLUS loans, Federal Perkins Loans. *Student Employment:* Federal Work-Study Program available. Institutional employment available. **Financial Aid Statistics:** 98% needy freshmen, 97% needy undergrads receive need-based scholarship or grant aid. 96% freshmen, 94% undergrads receive non-need-based scholarship or grant aid. 84% freshmen, 84% undergrads receive need-based self-help aid. 26% freshmen, 27% undergrads receive athletic scholarships. 90% freshmen, 90% undergrads receive any aid. **Criteria for awarding aid:** *Non-need-based:* Academics, Athletics.

ROCKY MOUNTAIN COLLEGE OF ART + DESIGN

1600 Pierce St, Denver, CO 80214
Phone: 303-753-6046 • **Financial Aid Phone:** 303-753-6046
E-mail: admissions@rmcad.edu
Fax: 303-567-7281 • **Website:** www.rmcad.edu • **ACT Code:** 5359

This proprietary school was founded in 1963. It has a 23-acre campus.

RATINGS

Admissions Selectivity Rating: 62   **Fire Safety Rating:** 60*   **Green Rating:** 60*

STUDENTS AND FACULTY

Enrollment: 1,019. **Student Body:** 65% female, 35% male, 53% out-of-state, <1% international. Asian 2%, African American 9%, Caucasian 60%, Hispanic 9%, Native American 4%, Pacific Islander 0%, Two or more races 1%, Race unknown 15%.
Retention and Graduation: 52% freshmen return for sophomore year. 46% freshmen graduate within 6 years. **Faculty:** Student/faculty ratio 9:1. 38 full-time faculty, 34% hold PhDs, 5% are are members of minority groups, 55% are women.

ACADEMICS

Degrees: bachelor's, certificate, master's. **Special Study Options:** independent study, internships, study abroad. **Career Services:** Alumni network, Alumni services, Career/job search classes, Career assessment, Internships.

FACILITIES

Special Academic Facilities/Equipment: Philip Steele Gallery, Fine Arts Exhibit Space, Drive Up Gallery

CAMPUS LIFE

Environment: Metropolis. **Activities:** dance, music ensembles, student government, student newspaper, Campus Ministries.

ADMISSIONS

Basis for Candidate Selection: *Important factors considered include:* academic GPA, interview, extracurricular activities. **Freshman Admission Requirements:** High school diploma is required and GED is accepted. **Transfer Admission Requirements:** college transcript(s), Minimum college GPA of 2.0 required. **General Admission Information:** Application fee $50. Nonfall registration accepted. Admission may be deferred for a maximum of one semester.

COSTS AND FINANCIAL AID

Annual tuition $15,870. Room and board $8,640. Required fees $500. Average book expense $1,045. **Required Forms and Deadlines:** FAFSA, Institution's own financial aid form. **Types of Aid:** *Need-based scholarships/grants:* Federal Pell, FSEOG, State scholarships/grants, Private scholarships, College/university scholarship or grant aid from institutional funds. *Loans:* Direct Subsidized Stafford Loans, Direct Unsubsidized Stafford Loans, Direct PLUS loans, College/university loans from institutional funds. *Student Employment:* Federal Work-Study Program available. **Criteria for awarding aid:** *Need-based:* Academics, Art. *Non-need-based:* Academics, Art.

ROGER WILLIAMS UNIVERSITY

One Old Ferry Road, Bristol, RI 02809-2921
Phone: 401-254-3500 • **Financial Aid Phone:** 401-254-3100
E-mail: admit@rwu.edu • **CEEB Code:** 3729
Fax: 401-254-3557 • **Website:** www.rwu.edu • **ACT Code:** 3814

This private school was founded in 1956. It has a 140-acre campus.

RATINGS

Admissions Selectivity Rating: 75   **Fire Safety Rating:** 88   **Green Rating:** 77

STUDENTS AND FACULTY

Enrollment: 4,586. **Student Body:** 53% female, 47% male, 77% out-of-state, 4% international (56 countries represented). Asian 1%, African American 3%, Caucasian 77%, Hispanic 6%, Native American <1%, Pacific Islander <1%, Two or more races 2%, Race unknown 7%.
Retention and Graduation: 83% freshmen return for sophomore year. 55% freshmen graduate within 4 years. 64% freshmen graduate within 6 years. 7% grads go on to further study within 1 year. **Faculty:** Student/faculty ratio 14:1. 214 full-time faculty, 95% hold PhDs, 13% are are members of minority groups, 43% are women. 0% of classes are taught by teaching assistants.

ACADEMICS

Degrees: associate, bachelor's, certificate, doctoral/professional, master's, postbachelor's certificate, terminal. **Classes:** Most classes have 10-19 students. Most lab/discussion sessions have 10-19 students. **Most popular majors:** Criminal Justice/Law Enforcement Administration; Architecture; Psychology. **Special Study Options:** cooperative education program, distance learning, double major, dual enrollment, English as a Second Language (ESL), exchange student program (domestic), external degree program, honors program, independent study, internships, liberal arts/career combination, student-designed major, study abroad, teacher certification program, weekend college. **Honors Programs:** 1. Alpha Chi Honors Society-University-wide association for Juniors and Seniors; 2. Four-year Honors Program-For full-time students

in any major which includes special sections of general education classes, a unique group service project for juniors and a required senior thesis. The program includes a variety of cultural and co-curricular activities, as well as leadership opportunities; 3. Honors Society Associations-Department-level honors associations within various disciplines Combined degree programs: BA/JD, BA/MA, 3-3 Business Law program. JD/MS Criminal Justice. B.S./PharmD. in Biology/ Pharmacy. **Disability Services:** Special programs offered to physically disabled students, including note-taking services, reader services, tape recorders, tutors.

FACILITIES

Housing: Coed dorms, special housing for disabled students, apartments for single students, Wellness Housing, Theme Housing, Special Interest, Academic Theme Housing, Honors, Wellness, Non-Smoking. **Special Academic Facilities/Equipment:** Marine and Natural Sciences Building, School of Law and Law Library, Main Library, Architecture Building and Architecture Library, Performing Arts Center, Thomas J. Paolino Recreation Center, Global Heritage Hall **Computers:** 100% of classrooms, 100% of dorms, 100% of libraries, 100% of dining areas, 100% of student union, 20% of common outdoor areas have wireless network access. Students can register for classes online. Administrative functions (other than registration) can be performed online.

CAMPUS LIFE

Environment: Village. **Activities:** Choral groups, dance, drama/theater, literary magazine, musical theater, radio station, student government, student newspaper, student-run film society, yearbook, Student Organization, Model UN. 93 registered organizations, 13 honor societies, 4 religious organizations. **Athletics (Intercollegiate):** *Men:* baseball, basketball, cross-country, diving, equestrian sports, lacrosse, sailing, soccer, swimming, tennis, track/field (outdoor), track/field (indoor), wrestling. *Women:* basketball, cross-country, diving, equestrian sports, lacrosse, sailing, soccer, softball, swimming, tennis, track/field (outdoor), track/field (indoor), volleyball. **On-Campus Highlights:** Recreation Center, Library, Dining Commons, Marine Science Wet Lab, Bookstore, Students are taken to any speficic place they would also like to see. Residence Halls are available for viewing with permission from occupants at certain points in the year. **Environmental Initiatives:** All renovation and new construction on campus meets LEED Silver standards.

ADMISSIONS

Freshman Academic Profile: Average high school GPA 3.3. **Reported SAT (pre-2016 redesign) scores:** SAT Math middle 50% range 500-600. SAT Critical Reading middle 50% range 490-580. SAT Writing middle 50% range 480-580. **Concordant SAT scores:** SAT EBRW middle 50% 540–640. SAT Math middle 50% range 530–620. ACT middle 50% range 23-27. Minimum internet-based TOEFL 85. **Basis for Candidate Selection:** *Very important factors considered include:* rigor of secondary school record, academic GPA, application essay, recommendation(s), character/personal qualities. *Important factors considered include:* extracurricular activities, volunteer work, work experience, level of applicant's interest. *Other factors considered include:* class rank, standardized test scores, interview, talent/ability, first generation, alumni/ ae relation. **Freshman Admission Requirements:** High school diploma is required and GED is accepted. *Academic units required:* 4 English, 3 math, 3 science, 2 science labs, 3 social studies, 2 history, 2 academic electives. *Academic units recommended:* 4 math, 4 science, 2 foreign language, 3 social studies, 3 history, 3 academic electives. **Freshman Admission Statistics:** 9,829 applied, 79.26% admitted, 15% enrolled. **Transfer Admission Requirements:** college transcript(s), essay or personal statement, Minimum college GPA of 2.5 required. Lowest grade transferable C. **General Admission Information:** Application fee $50. Priority deadline 2/1. Regular application deadline 2/1. Nonfall registration accepted. Admission may be deferred for a maximum of 1 YEAR.

COSTS AND FINANCIAL AID

Required fees $1,874. Average book expense $900. **Required Forms and Deadlines:** FAFSA, CSS/Financial Aid PROFILE. **Notification of Awards:** Applicants will be notified of awards on or about 3/15. **Types of Aid:** *Need-based scholarships/grants:* Federal Pell, FSEOG, State scholarships/grants, Private scholarships, College/university scholarship or grant aid from institutional funds. *Loans:* Direct Subsidized Stafford Loans, Direct Unsubsidized Stafford Loans, Direct PLUS loans, Federal Perkins Loans, College/university loans from institutional funds. *Student Employment:* Federal Work-Study Program available. Institutional employment available. **Financial Aid Statistics:** 87% needy freshmen, 69% needy undergrads receive need-based scholarship or grant aid. 97% freshmen, 86% undergrads receive non-need-based scholarship or grant aid. 85% freshmen, 70% undergrads receive need-based self-help aid. 0% freshmen, 0% undergrads receive athletic scholarships. 69% freshmen, 57% undergrads receive any aid. 58% undergrads borrow to pay for school. Average cumulative indebtedness $41,632. **Criteria for awarding aid:** *Non-need-based:* Academics, Leadership.

ROLLINS COLLEGE

Best Colleges

1000 Holt Avenue, Winter Park, FL 32789-4499
Phone: 407-646-2161 • **Financial Aid Phone:** 407-646-2395
E-mail: admission@rollins.edu • **CEEB Code:** 5572
Fax: 407-646-1502 • **Website:** http://www.rollins.edu • **ACT Code:** 748

This private school was founded in 1885. It has a 70-acre campus.

RATINGS
Admissions Selectivity Rating: 87   **Fire Safety Rating:** 97   **Green Rating:** 83

STUDENTS AND FACULTY
Enrollment: 1,925. **Student Body:** 60% female, 40% male, 25% out-of-state, 10% international (54 countries represented). Asian 3%, African American 3%, Caucasian 64%, Hispanic 14%, Native American <1%, Pacific Islander 0%, Two or more races 3%, Race unknown 3%.
Retention and Graduation: 83% freshmen return for sophomore year. 64% freshmen graduate within 4 years. 72 **Faculty:** Student/faculty ratio 10:1. 235 full-time faculty, 99% hold PhDs, 15% are are members of minority groups, 49% are women. 0% of classes are taught by teaching assistants.

ACADEMICS
Degrees: bachelor's, doctoral/research, master's. **Classes:** Most classes have 10-19 students. **Most popular majors:** Economics; Communication and Media Studies; International Business/Trade/Commerce. **Special Study Options:** Accelerated program, cross-registration, double major, dual enrollment, exchange student program (domestic), honors program, independent study, internships, student-designed major, study abroad, teacher certification program. Combined degree programs: BA/MBA. **Disability Services:** Special programs offered to physically disabled students, including note-taking services, reader services, tape recorders, tutors. **Career Services:** Alumni network, Alumni services, Career/job search classes, Career assessment, Internships. Rollins Internship Program—Undergraduate students engage in internships during the fall, spring, and summer terms both for credit and not for credit. These occur locally, across the country and overseas. Nearly 60% of our graduating seniors report having completed at least one internship while in college.

FACILITIES
Housing: Coed dorms, special housing for disabled students, fraternity/sorority housing, apartments for single students, Theme Housing. 80% of campus accessible to physically disabled. **Special Academic Facilities/Equipment:** Art museum, theatres, fine arts center, language lab, skills development building, child development center, psychology center, "state-of-the-art" IT classroom. **Computers:** 100% of classrooms, 100% of dorms, 100% of libraries, 100% of dining areas, 100% of student union, have wireless network access. Students can register for classes online. Administrative functions (other than registration) can be performed online.

CAMPUS LIFE
Environment: Town. **Activities:** Choral groups, concert band, dance, drama/theater, jazz band, literary magazine, music ensembles, musical theater, pep band, radio station, student government, student newspaper, student-run film society, symphony orchestra, television station, yearbook, Campus Ministries, Student Organization. 125 registered organizations, 5 honor societies, 5 religious organizations. 5 fraternities, 6 sororities. **Athletics (Intercollegiate):** *Men:* baseball, basketball, crew/rowing, cross-country, golf, lacrosse, sailing, soccer, swimming, tennis, water skiing. *Women:* basketball, crew/rowing, cross-country, golf, lacrosse, sailing, soccer, softball, swimming, tennis, volleyball, water skiing. **On-Campus Highlights:** Cornell Campus Center, Alfond Sports Center, Art Gallery, Cornell Fine Arts Museum, Olin Library, Rice Family Bookstore. **Environmental Initiatives:** Reuse existing buildings, renovating and updating to conform to LEAD principles, but limited to and bound by LEAD criteria

ADMISSIONS
Freshman Academic Profile: Average high school GPA 3.3. 36% in top 10% of high school class, 67% in top 25% of high school class, 88% in top 50% of high school class. 51% from public high schools. **Reported SAT (pre-2016 redesign) scores:** SAT Math middle 50% range 560-640. SAT Critical Reading middle 50% range 560-650. SAT Writing middle 50% range 550-640. **Concordant SAT scores:** SAT EBRW middle 50% 610–690. SAT Math middle 50% range 580–660. ACT middle 50% range 25-30. Minimum internet-based TOEFL 80. Minimum paper TOEFL 550. **Basis for Candidate Selection:**

Very important factors considered include: rigor of secondary school record, academic GPA. *Important factors considered include:* standardized test scores, application essay, recommendation(s), extracurricular activities, talent/ability. *Other factors considered include:* class rank, character/personal qualities, first generation, alumni/ae relation, volunteer work, work experience, level of applicant's interest. **Freshman Admission Requirements:** High school diploma is required and GED is accepted. *Academic units required:* 4 English, 3 math, 2 science, 2 foreign language, 2 social studies, 2 history, 2 academic electives. *Academic units recommended:* 4 English, 4 math, 4 science. **Freshman Admission Statistics:** 5,445 applied, 60.62% admitted, 16% enrolled. **Transfer Admission Requirements:** High school transcript, college transcript(s), essay or personal statement, statement of good standing from prior institution(s). Lowest grade transferable C-. **General Admission Information:** Application fee $50. Regular application deadline 2/15. Regular notification 4/1. Nonfall registration accepted. Admission may be deferred for a maximum of One year.

COSTS AND FINANCIAL AID
Average book expense $1,250. **Required Forms and Deadlines:** FAFSA. **Notification of Awards:** Applicants will be notified of awards on a rolling basis beginning 3/1. **Types of Aid:** *Need-based scholarships/grants:* Federal Pell, FSEOG, State scholarships/grants, Private scholarships, College/university scholarship or grant aid from institutional funds. *Loans:* Direct Subsidized Stafford Loans, Direct Unsubsidized Stafford Loans, Direct PLUS loans, Federal Perkins Loans. *Student Employment:* Federal Work-Study Program available. Institutional employment available. **Financial Aid Statistics:** 99% needy freshmen, 100% needy undergrads receive need-based scholarship or grant aid. 15% freshmen, 15% undergrads receive non-need-based scholarship or grant aid. 75% freshmen, 81% undergrads receive need-based self-help aid. 5% freshmen, 6% undergrads receive athletic scholarships. 88% freshmen, 86% undergrads receive any aid. Average cumulative indebtedness $32,208. **Criteria for awarding aid:** *Non-need-based:* Academics, Art, Athletics, Leadership, Music/drama, State/district residency.

ROOSEVELT UNIVERSITY

430 South Michigan Avenue, Chicago, IL 60605
Phone: 877-277-5978 • **Financial Aid Phone:** 866-421-0935
E-mail: admission@roosevelt.edu • **CEEB Code:** 1666
Fax: 847-619-4216 • **Website:** http://www.roosevelt.edu/Home.aspx
ACT Code: 1124

This private school was founded in 1945. It has a 34-acre campus.

RATINGS
Admissions Selectivity Rating: 77   **Fire Safety Rating:** 95   **Green Rating:** 87

STUDENTS AND FACULTY
Enrollment: 2,710. **Student Body:** 64% female, 36% male, 15% out-of-state, 4% international (63 countries represented). Asian 5%, African American 18%, Caucasian 45%, Hispanic 24%, Native American <1%, Pacific Islander <1%, Two or more races 3%, Race unknown 1%.
Retention and Graduation: 65% freshmen return for sophomore year. 26% freshmen graduate within 4 years. 40% freshmen graduate within 6 years. **Faculty:** Student/faculty ratio 11:1. 242 full-time faculty, 91% hold PhDs, 23% are are members of minority groups, 43% are women. 0% of classes are taught by teaching assistants.

ACADEMICS
Degrees: bachelor's, doctoral/professional, doctoral/research, master's, postbachelor's certificate. **Classes:** Most classes have 10-19 students. **Most popular majors:** Psychology; Biology/Biological Sciences; Accounting. **Special Study Options:** Accelerated program, distance learning, double major, dual enrollment, English as a Second Language (ESL), exchange student program (domestic), honors program, independent study, internships, student-designed major, study abroad, teacher certification program. **Honors Programs:** Roosevelt Scholars program offers an enriched academic program combining the students' area of interest with an interdisciplinary approach that includes internships, and research opportunities. Scholars are eligible to receive a special merit scholarship. The Scholars website is http://www.roosevelt.edu/scholars/default.htm Combined degree programs: BA/JD, BA/MA, MA/JD. **Disability Services:** Special programs offered to physically disabled students, including note-taking services, reader services, tape recorders, tutors. **Career Services:** Alumni network, Alumni services, Career/job search classes, Career assessment, Internships, Regional alumni. Internship opportunities are available for academic credit in several majors. Roosevelt's proximity to major corporations and non-profit organizations provides numerous internship opportunities for students.

FACILITIES

Housing: Coed dorms, apartments for single students. 90% of campus accessible to physically diasbled. **Special Academic Facilities/Equipment:** The Chicago campus is approx. 1 mile from the Museum of Natural History, Aquarium, Planetarium and Contemporary Art museums; and is 2 blocks from the Art Institute of Chicago **Computers:** Students can register for classes online. Administrative functions (other than registration) can be performed online.

CAMPUS LIFE

Environment: Metropolis. **Activities:** dance, literary magazine, radio station, student government, student newspaper, Student Organization. 48 registered organizations, 3 honor societies, 4 religious organizations. 1 fraternity, 2 sororities. **Environmental Initiatives:** Roosevelt has achieved LEED certification for both of its new campus buildings in the heart of downtown Chicago. LEED Gold for Wabash Building and LEED Silver for the Goodman Center. The university has also achieved SERF (Society of Environmentally Responsible Facilities) certification for the Wabash Building.

ADMISSIONS

Freshman Academic Profile: Average high school GPA 3.1. 8% in top 10% of high school class, 46% in top 25% of high school class, 62% in top 50% of high school class. 85% from public high schools. **Reported SAT (pre-2016 redesign) scores:** SAT Math middle 50% range 450-550. SAT Critical Reading middle 50% range 455-595. SAT Writing middle 50% range 450-560. **Concordant SAT scores:** SAT EBRW middle 50% 510–640. SAT Math middle 50% range 490–570. ACT middle 50% range 19-24. Minimum internet-based TOEFL 40. **Basis for Candidate Selection:** *Very important factors considered include:* academic GPA, standardized test scores. *Other factors considered include:* rigor of secondary school record, class rank, application essay, recommendation(s), interview, extracurricular activities, talent/ability, character/personal qualities, first generation, alumni/ae relation, level of applicant's interest. **Freshman Admission Requirements:** High school diploma is required and GED is accepted. *Academic units required:* 4 English, 3 math, 2 science, 2 science labs, 2 social studies. *Academic units recommended:* 4 English, 4 math, 3 science, 3 science labs, 2 foreign language, 3 social studies, 2 history, 2 academic electives. **Freshman Admission Statistics:** 5,996 applied, 73.27% admitted, 8% enrolled. **Transfer Admission Requirements:** college transcript(s), statement of good standing from prior institution(s). Minimum college GPA of 2.0 required. Lowest grade transferable D. **General Admission Information:** Application fee $25. Priority deadline 8/15. Nonfall registration accepted. Admission may be deferred for a maximum of 1 year.

COSTS AND FINANCIAL AID

Annual tuition $28,119. Average book expense $1,200. **Required Forms and Deadlines:** FAFSA, Institution's own financial aid form. **Notification of Awards:** Applicants will be notified of awards on a rolling basis beginning 2/1. **Types of Aid:** *Need-based scholarships/grants:* Federal Pell, FSEOG, State scholarships/grants, Private scholarships, College/university scholarship or grant aid from institutional funds. *Loans:* Direct Subsidized Stafford Loans, Direct Unsubsidized Stafford Loans, Direct PLUS loans. *Student Employment:* Federal Work-Study Program available. Institutional employment available. **Financial Aid Statistics:** 91% needy undergrads receive need-based scholarship or grant aid. 89% freshmen, 90% undergrads receive non-need-based scholarship or grant aid. 69% freshmen, 80% undergrads receive need-based self-help aid. 7% freshmen, 2% undergrads receive athletic scholarships. 94% freshmen, 90% undergrads receive any aid. **Criteria for awarding aid:** *Need-based:* Minority status. *Non-need-based:* Academics, Alumni affiliation, Leadership, Minority status, Music/drama, State/district residency.

ROSE-HULMAN INSTITUTE OF TECHNOLOGY

5500 Wabash Avenue, Terre Haute, IN 47803-3999
Phone: 812-877-8213 • **Financial Aid Phone:** 812-877-8259
E-mail: admissions@rose-hulman.edu • **CEEB Code:** 1668
Fax: 812-877-8941 • **Website:** www.rose-hulman.edu • **ACT Code:** 1232

This private school was founded in 1874. It has a 200-acre campus.

RATINGS

Admissions Selectivity Rating: 93   **Fire Safety Rating:** 96   **Green Rating:** 79

STUDENTS AND FACULTY

Enrollment: 2,186. **Student Body:** 25% female, 75% male, 65% out-of-state, 13% international (15 countries represented). Asian 4%, African American 2%, Caucasian 71%, Hispanic 4%, Native American <1%, Pacific Islander <1%, Two or more races 4%, Race unknown <1%.
Retention and Graduation: 94% freshmen return for sophomore year. 69% freshmen graduate within 4 years. 82% freshmen graduate within 6 years. 19% grads go on to further study within 1 year. 14% grads pursue arts and sciences degrees. 1% grads pursue business degrees. 1% grads pursue medical degrees. **Faculty:** Student/faculty ratio 12:1. 184 full-time faculty, 99% hold PhDs, 14% are are members of minority groups, 23% are women. 0% of classes are taught by teaching assistants.

ACADEMICS

Degrees: bachelor's, master's. **Classes:** Most classes have 20-29 students. Most lab/discussion sessions have 10-19 students. **Most popular majors:** Chemical Engineering; Mechanical Engineering; Electrical and Electronics Engineering; MajorsArray. **Special Study Options:** Accelerated program, cooperative education program, cross-registration, double major, independent study, internships, study abroad. Combined degree programs: MS/MD in Biomedical Engineering. **Disability Services:** Special programs offered to physically disabled students, including reader services, tutors. **Career Services:** Alumni network, Alumni services, Career/job search classes, Career assessment, Internships. For the Rose-Hulman student, experiential learning continually takes place during a student's college career. Whether it is through co-curricular activities, company projects brought to the classroom, or participation in degree related internship/co-op experiences. The Rose-Hulman graduate is fully prepared to enter the workforce running.

FACILITIES

Housing: Coed dorms, men's dorms, fraternity/sorority housing, apartments for single students. 95% of campus accessible to physically diasbled. **Special Academic Facilities/Equipment:** Museums-none officially. Union Bldg-collection of British Watercolors. Moench Hall Section A-Western Sculpture. All Sections-Eclectic Art. Hadley Hall-Hadley Pottery and Salty Seamon Paintings. Other art in various offices. Oakley Observatory **Computers:** 100% of classrooms, 5% of dorms, 100% of libraries, 100% of dining areas, 100% of student union, 25% of common outdoor areas have wireless network access. Students can register for classes online. Administrative functions (other than registration) can be performed online. Undergraduates are required to own a computer.

CAMPUS LIFE

Environment: Town. **Activities:** Choral groups, concert band, dance, drama/theater, jazz band, literary magazine, music ensembles, musical theater, pep band, radio station, student government, student newspaper, Student Organization. 105 registered organizations, 7 honor societies, 2 religious organizations. 8 fraternities, 3 sororities. **Athletics (Intercollegiate):** *Men:* baseball, basketball, cross-country, diving, football, golf, riflery, soccer, swimming, tennis, track/field (outdoor), track/field (indoor). *Women:* basketball, cross-country, diving, golf, riflery, soccer, softball, swimming, tennis, track/field (outdoor), track/field (indoor), volleyball. **On-Campus Highlights:** Sports and Recreation Center, Hatfield Hall, White Chapel, Moench Hall, Chauncey's Place. **Environmental Initiatives:** Signing of the American College & University President's Climate Commitment.

ADMISSIONS

Freshman Academic Profile: Average high school GPA 4.0. 62% in top 10% of high school class, 92% in top 25% of high school class, 99% in top 50% of high school class. 62% from public high schools. **Reported SAT (pre-2016 redesign) scores:** SAT Math middle 50% range 640-760. SAT Critical Reading middle 50% range 560-670. SAT Writing middle 50% range 560-660. **Concordant SAT scores:** SAT EBRW middle 50% 620–710. SAT Math middle 50% range 660–780. ACT middle 50% range 27-32. Minimum internet-based TOEFL 80. Minimum paper TOEFL 550. **Basis for Candidate Selection:** *Very important factors considered include:* rigor of secondary school record, class rank, academic GPA. *Important factors considered include:* standardized test scores, recommendation(s), interview, extracurricular activities, character/personal qualities, volunteer work, work experience. *Other factors considered include:* application essay, talent/ability, alumni/ae relation, geographical residence, racial/ethnic status. **Freshman Admission Requirements:** High school diploma is required and GED is not accepted. *Academic units required:* 4 English, 4 math, 2 science, 2 science labs, 2 social studies, 4 academic electives. *Academic units recommended:* 5 math, 3 science. **Freshman Admission Statistics:** 4,241 applied, 61.07% admitted, 21% enrolled. **Transfer Admission Requirements:** college transcript(s), essay or personal statement, statement of good standing from prior institution(s). Minimum college GPA of 3.0 required. Lowest grade transferable C. **General Admission Information:** Application fee $40. Priority deadline 11/1. Regular application deadline 2/1. Regular notification 12/15. Nonfall registration not accepted. Admission may be deferred for a maximum of 12 months.

COSTS AND FINANCIAL AID

Annual tuition $43,122. Room and board $13,293. Required fees $888. Average book expense $1,500. **Required Forms and Deadlines:** FAFSA. **Notification of Awards:** Applicants will be notified of awards on or about 3/10. **Types of Aid:** *Need-based scholarships/grants:* Federal Pell, FSEOG, State scholarships/grants, College/university scholarship or grant aid from institutional funds. *Loans:* Direct Subsidized Stafford Loans, Direct Unsubsidized Stafford Loans, Direct PLUS loans, Federal Perkins Loans. *Student Employment:* Federal Work-Study Program available. Institutional employment available. **Financial Aid Statistics:** 83% needy freshmen, 85% needy undergrads receive need-based scholarship or grant aid. 100% freshmen, 99% undergrads receive non-need-based scholarship or grant aid. 89% freshmen, 87% undergrads receive need-based self-help aid. 0% freshmen, 0% undergrads receive athletic scholarships. 99% freshmen, 97% undergrads receive any aid. 65% undergrads borrow to pay for school. Average cumulative indebtedness $59,113. **Criteria for awarding aid:** *Need-based:* Academics, Minority status. *Non-need-based:* Academics, Minority status.

ROSEMONT COLLEGE

1400 Montgomery Ave., Rosemont, PA 19010
Phone: 610-526-2966 • **Financial Aid Phone:** 610-527-0200
E-mail: admissions@rosemont.edu • **CEEB Code:** 2763
Fax: 610-520-4399 • **Website:** www.rosemont.edu • **ACT Code:** 3676

This private school, affiliated with the Roman Catholic Church, was founded in 1921. It has a 56-acre campus.

RATINGS

Admissions Selectivity Rating: 73   **Fire Safety Rating:** 83   **Green Rating:** 60*

STUDENTS AND FACULTY

Enrollment: 529. **Student Body:** 65% female, 35% male, 27% out-of-state, 2% international (11 countries represented). Asian 5%, African American 40%, Caucasian 38%, Hispanic 6%, Native American 0%, Pacific Islander 0%, Two or more races 4%, Race unknown 4%.
Retention and Graduation: 69% freshmen return for sophomore year. 34% freshmen graduate within 4 years. 47% freshmen graduate within 6 years. 36% grads go on to further study within 1 year. 35% grads pursue arts and sciences degrees. 2% grads pursue law degrees. 5% grads pursue business degrees. 9% grads pursue medical degrees. **Faculty:** Student/faculty ratio 10:1. 25 full-time faculty, 84% hold PhDs, 4% are are members of minority groups, 48% are women. 0% of classes are taught by teaching assistants.

ACADEMICS

Degrees: bachelor's, master's, postbachelor's certificate. **Classes:** Most classes have 10-19 students. **Most popular majors:** Biology/Biological Sciences; Art/Art Studies; Business/Commerce. **Special Study Options:** Accelerated program, cross-registration, distance learning, double major, honors program, independent study, internships, liberal arts/career combination, student-designed major, study abroad, teacher certification program. Combined degree programs: BA/MA, BSN in conjunction with Drexel Univ. **Disability Services:** Special programs offered to physically disabled students, including note-taking services, tape recorders, tutors. **Career Services:** Alumni services, Career/job search classes, Career assessment, Internships. All students partake of an Internship or a form of Experiential Learning prior to graduation.

FACILITIES

Housing: women's dorms. Cornelia Connelly Hall located in the center of campus is totally redesigned. It is now a state of the art residence hall. Beginning with Fall 2009 Rosemont College welcomes men into the Undergraduate College. 45% of campus accessible to physically disabled. **Special Academic Facilities/Equipment:** McShain Performing Arts Center and Conwell Learning Center. **Computers:** 25% of classrooms, 25% of dorms, 50% of libraries, 15% of dining areas, 15% of student union, 10% of common outdoor areas have wireless network access. Students can register for classes online. Administrative functions (other than registration) can be performed online.

CAMPUS LIFE

Environment: Village. **Activities:** Choral groups, concert band, dance, drama/theater, jazz band, literary magazine, marching band, music ensembles, musical theater, opera, pep band, radio station, student government, student newspaper, yearbook, Campus Ministries. 23 registered organizations, 6 honor societies, 3 religious organizations. **Athletics (Intercollegiate):** *Men:* basketball, softball, tennis. *Women:* basketball, field hockey, lacrosse, softball, tennis, volleyball. **On-Campus Highlights:** Campus Grill, The Grind Coffee Shop, Fitness Center **Environmental Initiatives:** Energy Star Procurement Policy.

ADMISSIONS

Freshman Academic Profile: Average high school GPA 3.3. 70% from public high schools. **Reported SAT (pre-2016 redesign) scores:** SAT Math middle 50% range 380-505. SAT Critical Reading middle 50% range 400-520. SAT Writing middle 50% range 390-505. **Concordant SAT scores:** SAT EBRW middle 50% 440–570. SAT Math middle 50% range 420–540. ACT middle 50% range 15-20. Minimum internet-based TOEFL 61. Minimum paper TOEFL 500. **Basis for Candidate Selection:** *Very important factors considered include:* rigor of secondary school record, academic GPA, standardized test scores, interview, level of applicant's interest. *Important factors considered include:* class rank, application essay, extracurricular activities, talent/ability, volunteer work. *Other factors considered include:* recommendation(s), character/personal qualities, alumni/ae relation, work experience. **Freshman Admission Requirements:** High school diploma is required and GED is accepted. *Academic units required:* 4 English, 3 math, 3 science, 2 science labs, 1 social studies, 1 history, 7 academic electives. *Academic units recommended:* 4 English, 3 math, 3 science, 2 science labs, 2 foreign language, 2 social studies, 2 history, 4 academic electives. **Freshman Admission Statistics:** 875 applied, 70.63% admitted, 22% enrolled. **Transfer Admission Requirements:** college transcript(s), Minimum college GPA of 2.5 required. Lowest grade transferable C. **General Admission Information:** Priority deadline 8/1. Regular application deadline 8/1. Regular notification 3/15. Nonfall registration accepted. Admission may be deferred for a maximum of 1 year.

COSTS AND FINANCIAL AID

Annual tuition $18,500. Room and board $11,500. Required fees $980. Average book expense $1,500. **Required Forms and Deadlines:** FAFSA. **Notification of Awards:** Applicants will be notified of awards on a rolling basis beginning 3/1. **Types of Aid:** *Need-based scholarships/grants:* Federal Pell, FSEOG, State scholarships/grants, Private scholarships, College/university scholarship or grant aid from institutional funds. *Loans:* Federal Perkins Loans. *Student Employment:* Federal Work-Study Program available. Institutional employment available. **Financial Aid Statistics:** 99% needy freshmen, 99% needy undergrads receive need-based scholarship or grant aid. 10% freshmen, 12% undergrads receive non-need-based scholarship or grant aid. 95% freshmen, 99% undergrads receive need-based self-help aid. 0% freshmen, 0% undergrads receive athletic scholarships. 92% freshmen, 92% undergrads receive any aid. 90% undergrads borrow to pay for school. Average cumulative indebtedness $40,792. **Criteria for awarding aid:** *Need-based:* Academics, Art, Leadership. *Non-need-based:* Academics, Alumni affiliation, Art, Leadership, Religious affiliation.

ROWAN UNIVERSITY

Savitz Hall 201 Mullica Hill Road, Glassboro, NJ 08028-1701
Phone: 856-256-4200 • **Financial Aid Phone:** 856-256-5186
E-mail: admissions@rowan.edu • **CEEB Code:** 2515
Fax: 856-256-4430 • **Website:** www.rowan.edu • **ACT Code:** 2560

This public school was founded in 1923. It has a 800-acre campus.

RATINGS

Admissions Selectivity Rating: 76   **Fire Safety Rating:** 97   **Green Rating:** 71

STUDENTS AND FACULTY

Enrollment: 11,819. **Student Body:** 47% female, 53% male, 5% out-of-state, 1% international (44 countries represented). Asian 6%, African American 9%, Caucasian 69%, Hispanic 9%, Native American <1%, Pacific Islander <1%, Two or more races 3%, Race unknown 3%.
Retention and Graduation: 86% freshmen return for sophomore year. 43% freshmen graduate within 4 years. **Faculty:** Student/faculty ratio 17:1. 95 full-time faculty, are women. 0% of classes are taught by teaching assistants.

ACADEMICS

Degrees: bachelor's, certificate, doctoral/professional, doctoral/research, doctoral, master's, postbachelor's certificate, post-master's certificate. **Classes:** Most classes have 20-29 students. **Most popular majors:** Psychology; Elementary Education and Teaching; Biology/Biological Sciences. **Special Study Options:** cooperative education program, distance learning, double major, English as a Second Language (ESL), exchange student program (domestic), external degree program, honors program, independent study, internships, study abroad, teacher certification program, weekend college. **Honors Programs:** The Thomas N. Bantavoglio Honors Concentration offers qualified students access to a variety of academic, enrichment, and service experiences including honors classes, the Honors Student Organization and the 45 activities sponsored by the HSO, as well as travel for cultural and enrichment activities along the eastern seaboard. Combined degree programs: BA/MA, BS/MS in Mathematics; BS/MS in Computer Science. **Disability Services:** Special programs offered to physically disabled students, including note-taking services, reader services, tape recorders, tutors. **Career Services:** Alumni network, Alumni services, Career/job search classes, Career assessment, Internships, Regional alumni. The Rowan University undergraduate Entrepreneurship faculty are proud of our focus on experiential learning and the use of project-based learning in all of our entrepreneurship program courses. Experiential learning provides our B.S. degree in Entrepreneurship graduates with the knowledge and skills to run their own business ventures. Graduates of our program currently run successful businesses based on their work for our Business Plan Competition and their Rowan University entrepreneurship education. For example, the the 1st, 2nd,and 3rd place winners of our first school business plan in 2007 were honored at our fifth annual event in 2011. All three of of our student winners are currently running profitable businesses that they planned in their business plans. Our graduates are earning comfortable incomes with plans for future business growth.

FACILITIES

Housing: Coed dorms, special housing for disabled students, apartments for single students, Wellness Housing, Townhouses. 95% of campus accessible to physically diasbled. **Special Academic Facilities/Equipment:** Concert hall, glass collection, student recreation center, on-campus early childhood demonstration center, greenhouse for biological studies, observatory, art gallery **Computers:** 100% of classrooms, 100% of dorms, 100% of libraries, 100% of dining areas, 100% of student union, 100% of common outdoor areas have wireless network access. Students can register for classes online. Administrative functions (other than registration) can be performed online.

CAMPUS LIFE

Environment: Town. **Activities:** Choral groups, concert band, dance, drama/theater, jazz band, literary magazine, music ensembles, musical theater, opera, pep band, radio station, student government, student newspaper, student-run film society, television station, yearbook, Campus Ministries. 135 registered organizations, 10 honor societies, 6 religious organizations. 10 fraternities, 10 sororities. **Athletics (Intercollegiate):** *Men:* baseball, basketball, cross-country, diving, football, soccer, swimming, track/field (outdoor), track/field (indoor). *Women:* basketball, cross-country, diving, field hockey, lacrosse, soccer, softball, swimming, track/field (outdoor), track/field (indoor), volleyball. **On-Campus Highlights:** Recreation Center, Student Center, Campbell Library, Savitz Hall (Student Services Building), Education Hall. **Environmental Initiatives:** Energy use has decreased 25% from fiscal year 13 to base year 11 because of the operation of the central utility plant and the co-generation. Cut energy usage from 700000 mmbtu's to 510000 mmbtu's over 2 years. Generating electricity in the co-generation plant avoids our purchase of coal generated electricity.

ADMISSIONS

Freshman Academic Profile: Average high school GPA 3.5. **Reported SAT (pre-2016 redesign) scores:** SAT Math middle 50% range 520-630. SAT Critical Reading middle 50% range 490-590. SAT Writing middle 50% range 480-580. **Concordant SAT scores:** SAT EBRW middle 50% 540–640. SAT Math middle 50% range 550–650. Minimum internet-based TOEFL 79. Minimum paper TOEFL 550. **Basis for Candidate Selection:** *Very important factors considered include:* rigor of secondary school record. *Important factors considered include:* academic GPA, standardized test scores, application essay. *Other factors considered include:* class rank, recommendation(s), extracurricular activities, talent/ability, character/personal qualities, racial/ethnic status, volunteer work. **Freshman Admission Requirements:** High school diploma is required and GED is accepted. *Academic units required:* 4 English, 3 math, 2 science, 2 science labs, 2 history, 5 academic electives. *Academic units recommended:* 4 math, 3 science, 3 science labs, 2 foreign language, 2 social studies, 1 visual/performing arts. **Freshman Admission Statistics:** 10,078 applied, 65.49% admitted, 29% enrolled. **Transfer Admission Requirements:** college transcript(s), Minimum college GPA of 2.0 required. Lowest grade transferable D. **General Admission Information:** Application fee $65. Regular application deadline 3/1. Regular notification 4/15. Nonfall registration accepted. Admission may be deferred for a maximum of 1 year.

COSTS AND FINANCIAL AID

Annual in-state tuition $9,076. Annual out-of-state tuition $17,030. Room and board $11,406. Required fees $3,540. Average book expense $1,500. **Required Forms and Deadlines:** FAFSA. **Notification of Awards:** Applicants will be notified of awards on a rolling basis beginning 3/16. **Types of Aid:** *Need-based scholarships/grants:* Federal Pell, FSEOG, State scholarships/grants, Private scholarships. *Loans:* Direct Subsidized Stafford Loans, Direct Unsubsidized Stafford Loans, Direct PLUS loans. *Student Employment:* Federal Work-Study Program available. Institutional employment available. **Financial Aid Statistics:** 45% needy freshmen receive need-based scholarship or grant aid. 50% freshmen, 23% undergrads receive non-need-based scholarship or grant aid. 75% freshmen, 84% undergrads receive need-based self-help aid. 0% freshmen, 0% undergrads receive athletic scholarships. 83% freshmen, 73% undergrads receive any aid. **Criteria for awarding aid:** *Non-need-based:* Academics, Art, Music/drama.

RUSH UNIVERSITY

600 South Paulina, Chicago, IL 60612-3878
Phone: 312-942-7100 • **Financial Aid Phone:** 312-942-6256
E-mail: Rush_Admissions@rush.edu
Fax: 312-942-2219 • **Website:** www.rushu.rush.edu • **ACT Code:** 1617

This private school was founded in 1972. It has a 35-acre campus.

RATINGS

Admissions Selectivity Rating: 61 **Fire Safety Rating:** 79 **Green Rating:** 60*

STUDENTS AND FACULTY

Enrollment: 259. **Student Body:** 87% female, 13% male, 15% out-of-state, 2% international. Asian 18%, African American 7%, Caucasian 69%, Hispanic 3%, Native American <1%, Pacific Islander 0%, Two or more races 0%, Race unknown 2%.
Retention and Graduation: 25% grads go on to further study within 1 year. 5% grads pursue medical degrees. **Faculty:** Student/faculty ratio 8:1. 305 full-time faculty, 0% hold PhDs, 0% are are members of minority groups, 65% are women. 0% of classes are taught by teaching assistants.

ACADEMICS

Degrees: bachelor's, master's. **Classes:** Most classes have 10-19 students. **Most popular majors:** Audiology/Audiologist and Speech; Medicine. **Special Study Options:** distance learning. Combined degree programs: MD/PhD. **Disability Services:** Special programs offered to physically disabled students, including tape recorders, tutors. **Career Services:** Alumni network, Alumni services, Career/job search classes, Career assessment, Internships, Regional alumni, On-campus interviews.

FACILITIES

Housing: apartments for married students, apartments for single students. 85% of campus accessible to physically diasbled.

CAMPUS LIFE

Environment: Metropolis. **Activities:** yearbook. 15 registered organizations, 2 honor societies, 1 religious organization. **On-Campus Highlights:** Student Lounge, Computer lab (100+ stations), Library, Au Bon Pain **Environmental Initiatives:** Launched new recycling commitment and awareness campaign on Earth Day 2008.

ADMISSIONS

Freshman Academic Profile: 100% in top 50% of high school class. Minimum paper TOEFL 550. **Transfer Admission Requirements:** college transcript(s), essay or personal statement, Minimum college GPA of 2.7 required. Lowest grade transferable c. **General Admission Information:** Nonfall registration not accepted.

COSTS AND FINANCIAL AID

Required Forms and Deadlines: FAFSA, Institution's own financial aid form, Business/Farm Supplement. **Types of Aid:** *Need-based scholarships/grants:* Federal Pell, FSEOG, State scholarships/grants, Private scholarships, College/university scholarship or grant aid from institutional funds. *Loans:* Federal Perkins Loans, Federal Nursing Loans, College/university loans from institutional funds. *Student Employment:* Federal Work-Study Program available. Institutional employment available. **Financial Aid Statistics:** 74% needy undergrads receive need-based scholarship or grant aid. 13% undergrads receive non-need-based scholarship or grant aid. 88% undergrads receive need-based self-help aid. 0% undergrads receive athletic scholarships. 0% freshmen, 69% undergrads receive any aid. **Criteria for awarding aid:** *Non-need-based:* Academics, Leadership, Minority status.

RUST COLLEGE

150 Rust Avenue, Holly Springs, MS 38635
Phone: 662-252-8000 • **Financial Aid Phone:** 662-252-8000, x4062
E-mail: jb_mcdonald@rustcollege.edu
Fax: 662-252-8895 • **Website:** www.rustcollege.edu • **ACT Code:** 2240

This private school, affiliated with the Moravian Church, was founded in 1866. It has a 126-acre campus.

RATINGS

Admissions Selectivity Rating: 73 **Fire Safety Rating:** 60* **Green Rating:** 60*

STUDENTS AND FACULTY

Enrollment: 922. **Student Body:** 63% female, 37% male, 5% international. Asian 0%, African American 93%, Caucasian 1%, Hispanic 0%, Native American 0%, Pacific Islander 0%, Two or more races 0%, Race unknown 1%. **Retention and Graduation:** 53% freshmen return for sophomore year. 14% freshmen graduate within 4 years. 28% freshmen graduate within 6 years. **Faculty:** Student/faculty ratio 17:1. 48 full-time faculty, 0% hold PhDs, 90% are are members of minority groups, 40% are women. 0% of classes are taught by teaching assistants.

ACADEMICS

Degrees: associate, bachelor's. **Classes:** Most classes have 10-19 students. Most lab/discussion sessions have 10-19 students. **Most popular majors:** Computer and Information Sciences; Biology/Biological Sciences; Business/Commerce. **Special Study Options:** double major, honors program, independent study, internships, liberal arts/career combination, study abroad, teacher certification program, weekend college, 1)Advanced Placement Program. 2)Adult Pathway Program. Dual enrollment includes three Dual Degree Programs with other institutions and one Cooperative Program with another institution. Combined degree programs: Dual degree with other colleges. **Disability Services:** Special programs offered to physically disabled students, including tutors.

FACILITIES

Housing: men's dorms, women's dorms, Honors. **Special Academic Facilities/Equipment:** Dr. Ron Trojcak collection of African tribal art which includes fabrics, masks and statues used for religious ceremonies, weddings, ritual dance and funerals.

CAMPUS LIFE

Environment: Rural. **Activities:** Choral groups, concert band, dance, drama/theater, marching band, music ensembles, pep band, radio station, student government, student newspaper, television station, yearbook, Student Organization. 35 registered organizations, 7 honor societies, 5 religious organizations. 3 fraternities, 4 sororities. **Athletics (Intercollegiate):** *Men:* baseball, basketball, cheerleading, cross-country, soccer, tennis, track/field (outdoor). *Women:* basketball, cheerleading, cross-country, softball, tennis, track/field (outdoor), volleyball. **On-Campus Highlights:** Leontyne Price Library Exhibits, James Elam Chapel, McDonald Science Building, David Beckley Conference Center, McMillan Multi-Purpose Center.

ADMISSIONS

Freshman Academic Profile: 98% from public high schools. ACT middle 50% range 14-21. Minimum paper TOEFL 540. **Basis for Candidate Selection:** *Very important factors considered include:* first generation. *Important factors considered include:* rigor of secondary school record, class rank, academic GPA, standardized test scores, application essay, recommendation(s), character/personal qualities, alumni/ae relation, level of applicant's interest. *Other factors considered include:* talent/ability, volunteer work. **Freshman Admission Requirements:** High school diploma is required and GED is accepted. *Academic units required:* 4 English, 3 math, 3 science, 3 social studies, 6 academic electives. **Freshman Admission Statistics:** 3,983 applied, 45.62% admitted, 16% enrolled. **Transfer Admission Requirements:** High school transcript, college transcript(s), statement of good standing from prior institution(s). Minimum college GPA of 2.0 required. Lowest grade transferable C. **General Admission Information:** Application fee $10. Priority deadline 7/15. Nonfall registration accepted. Admission may be deferred for a maximum of one year.

COSTS AND FINANCIAL AID

Annual tuition $8,100. Room and board $3,700. Average book expense $250. **Required Forms and Deadlines:** FAFSA, Institution's own financial aid form. **Notification of Awards:** Applicants will be notified of awards on a rolling basis beginning 4/1. **Types of Aid:** *Need-based scholarships/grants:* Federal Pell, FSEOG, Private scholarships, United Negro College Fund. *Student Employment:* Federal Work-Study Program available. Institutional employment available. **Financial Aid Statistics:** 86% needy freshmen, 87% needy undergrads receive need-based scholarship or grant aid. 43% freshmen, 29% undergrads receive non-need-based scholarship or grant aid. 87% freshmen, 89% undergrads receive need-based self-help aid. 0% freshmen, 0% undergrads receive athletic scholarships. **Criteria for awarding aid:** *Non-need-based:* Academics, Leadership, Music/drama, Religious affiliation, State/district residency.

RUTGERS, THE STATE UNIVERSITY OF NEW JERSEY—CAMDEN

406 Penn Street, Camden, NJ 8102
Phone: 856-225-6104 • **Financial Aid Phone:** 732-932-7305
E-mail: admissions@ugadm.rutgers.edu • **CEEB Code:** 2765
Fax: 856-225-6498 • **Website:** Office of Institutional Research • **ACT Code:** 2592

This public school was founded in 1927. It has a 25-acre campus.

RATINGS

Admissions Selectivity Rating: 79   **Fire Safety Rating:** 83   **Green Rating:** 60*

STUDENTS AND FACULTY

Enrollment: 4,978. **Student Body:** 59% female, 41% male, 2% out-of-state, 1% international (20 countries represented). Asian 9%, African American 17%, Caucasian 53%, Hispanic 14%, Native American <1%, Pacific Islander <1%, Two or more races 4%, Race unknown 2%. **Retention and Graduation:** 89% freshmen return for sophomore year. **Faculty:** Student/faculty ratio 10:1. 292 full-time faculty, 98% hold PhDs, 17% are are members of minority groups, 44% are women. 4% of classes are taught by teaching assistants.

ACADEMICS

Degrees: bachelor's, doctoral/research, master's. **Most popular majors:** Psychology Business Administration and Management. **Special Study Options:** Accelerated program, cooperative education program, cross-registration, distance learning, double major, dual enrollment, English as a Second Language (ESL), exchange student program (domestic), honors program, independent study, internships, liberal arts/career combination, student-designed major, study abroad, teacher certification program, weekend college, Cooperative baccalaureate program in engineering with School of Engineering (New Brunswick Campus). Interdisciplinary programs in African-American studies, general science. Cooperative baccalaureate in medical technology with approved hospital. B.A./M.A. in English, history, liberal studies or psychology; B.A./M.S. in biology, chemistry or mathematics (with the Graduate School-Camden). B.A. in economics or political science/Master of Public Administration (with the Graduate School-Camden). Combined degree programs: BA/MD, 2+4 Pharm. D. **Disability Services:** Special programs offered to physically disabled students, including note-taking services, reader services, tape recorders, tutors.

FACILITIES

Housing: Coed dorms, special housing for disabled students, apartments for single students. **Computers:** Students can register for classes online. Administrative functions (other than registration) can be performed online.

CAMPUS LIFE

Environment: City. **Activities:** drama/theater, literary magazine, radio station, student government, yearbook, Student Organization. 50 registered organizations, 11 honor societies, 4 fraternities, 4 sororities. **Athletics (Intercollegiate):** *Men:* baseball, basketball, cross-country, golf, soccer, track/field (outdoor). *Women:* basketball, cross-country, soccer, softball, track/field (outdoor), volleyball.

ADMISSIONS

Freshman Academic Profile: 14% in top 10% of high school class, 44% in top 25% of high school class, 81% in top 50% of high school class. 60% from public high school. **Reported SAT (pre-2016 redesign) scores:** SAT Math middle 50% range 450-570. SAT Critical Reading middle 50% range 440-550. SAT Writing middle 50% range 440-540. **Concordant SAT scores:** SAT EBRW middle 50% 490-600. SAT Math middle 50% range 490-590. Minimum internet-based TOEFL 79. Minimum paper TOEFL 550. **Basis for Candidate Selection:** *Very important factors considered include:* rigor of secondary school record, class rank, academic GPA, standardized test scores. *Other factors considered include:* application essay, recommendation(s), extracurricular activities, first generation, geographical residence, state residency, racial/ethnic status, volunteer work, work experience. **Freshman Admission Requirements:** High school diploma is required and GED is accepted. *Academic units required:* 4 English, 3 math, 2 science, 2 foreign language, 5 academic electives. *Academic units recommended:* 4 math. **Freshman Admission Statistics:** 8,725 applied, 57.49% admitted, 13% enrolled. **Transfer Admission Requirements:** High school transcript, college transcript(s), Minimum college GPA of NA required. **General Admission Information:** Application fee $65. Regular application deadline 12/1. Nonfall registration accepted.

COSTS AND FINANCIAL AID

Annual in-state tuition $11,408. Annual out-of-state tuition $26,551. Room and board $11,908. Required fees $2,830. Average book expense $1,350. **Required**

Forms and Deadlines: FAFSA. **Notification of Awards:** Applicants will be notified of awards on a rolling basis beginning 3/1. **Types of Aid:** *Need-based scholarships/grants:* Federal Pell, FSEOG, State scholarships/grants, Private scholarships, College/university scholarship or grant aid from institutional funds, Federal Nursing Scholarships. *Loans:* Direct Subsidized Stafford Loans, Direct Unsubsidized Stafford Loans, Direct PLUS loans, Federal Perkins Loans, State Loans, College/university loans from institutional funds. *Student Employment:* Federal Work-Study Program available. Institutional employment available. **Financial Aid Statistics:** 68% needy freshmen receive need-based scholarship or grant aid. 70% freshmen, 72% undergrads receive any aid. **Criteria for awarding aid:** *Need-based:* Academics, Alumni affiliation, Art, Leadership, Music/drama. *Non-need-based:* Academics, Alumni affiliation, Art, Athletics, Leadership, Music/drama, State/district residency.

RUTGERS, THE STATE UNIVERSITY OF NEW JERSEY—NEWARK CAMPUS

249 University Avenue, Newark, NJ 07102-1896
Phone: 973-353-5205 • **Financial Aid Phone:** 732-932-7305
E-mail: admissions@ugadm.rutgers.edu • **CEEB Code:** 2765
Fax: 973-353-1440 • **ACT Code:** 2592

This public school was founded in 1930. It has a 36-acre campus.

RATINGS
Admissions Selectivity Rating: 79   **Fire Safety Rating:** 83   **Green Rating:** 60*

STUDENTS AND FACULTY
Enrollment: 7,691. **Student Body:** 54% female, 46% male, 2% out-of-state, 5% international (84 countries represented). Asian 20%, African American 19%, Caucasian 24%, Hispanic 28%, Native American <1%, Pacific Islander <1%, Two or more races 3%, Race unknown 2%.
Retention and Graduation: 84% freshmen return for sophomore year. **Faculty:** Student/faculty ratio 11:1. 515 full-time faculty, 99% hold PhDs, 14% are are members of minority groups, 33% are women. 9% of classes are taught by teaching assistants.

ACADEMICS
Degrees: associate, bachelor's, doctoral/professional, doctoral/research, master's. **Most popular majors:** Biology/Biological Sciences Business Administration and Management. **Special Study Options:** Accelerated program, cooperative education program, cross-registration, distance learning, double major, dual enrollment, English as a Second Language (ESL), exchange student program (domestic), honors program, independent study, internships, liberal arts/career combination, student-designed major, study abroad, teacher certification program, weekend college, 5-year baccalaureate-MBA with Rutgers Business School; Baccalaureate/M.A. in Criminal Justice with the School of Criminal Justice; Baccalaureate/MPA with the School of Public Affairs and Administration; Cooperative baccalaureate program with School of Engineering (New Brunswick campus); Cooperative baccalaureate in medical technology with affiliated hospitals; Interdisciplinary programs in archaeology, affairs, legal studies, women's studies; continuing professional education; The College of Nursing offers a program on the New Brunswick Campus. Students are admitted in the fall semester only; Baccalaureate in Business Major/Master of Human Resource Management (with School of Management and Labor Relations in New Brunswick); Baccalaureate-master's dual degree programs with the School of Criminal Justice and Rutgers Business School. The Honors College of Rutgers University's Newark College of Arts and Sciences is a four-year program, a college within a college, providing its by-invitation-only students with opportunities for enrichment both in and outside of the classroom. Students invited to join the Honors College benefit from small classes with first-rate faculty, co-curricular internships in major corporations and other institutions, and other special options. Reserved dormitory space, a substantial scholarship program, and research assistantships with faculty members combine to make the RU-Newark Honors College experience unique. For additional information, visit the Honors College web site at http://honorsnewark.rutgers.edu or call (973)353-5860. Combined degree programs: BA/MD, BA/MA, BA or BS/MA in Criminal justice, 7 and 8 year BA/MD. **Disability Services:** Special programs offered to physically disabled students, including note-taking services, reader services, tape recorders, tutors.

FACILITIES
Housing: Coed dorms, fraternity/sorority housing, apartments for single students. **Special Academic Facilities/Equipment:** Institute of Jazz Studies, TV/Radio media center, Institute of Animal Behavior, Center for Crime Preventio Studies, Center for Negotiation and Conflict Resolution, Center for Molecular and Behaviorial Neuroscience, Center for Nursing Research.

Computers: Students can register for classes online. Administrative functions (other than registration) can be performed online.

CAMPUS LIFE
Activities: Choral groups, drama/theater, radio station, student government, student newspaper, yearbook, Student Organization. 80 registered organizations, 16 honor societies, 7 fraternities, 7 sororities. **Athletics (Intercollegiate):** *Men:* baseball, basketball, soccer, tennis, volleyball. *Women:* basketball, softball, tennis, volleyball. **On-Campus Highlights:** The Arts at Rutgers Newark, Robeson Campus Center, Athletic Center, Bradley Hall/Bookstore, Dana Library.

ADMISSIONS
Freshman Academic Profile: 20% in top 10% of high school class, 50% in top 25% of high school class, 85% in top 50% of high school class. **Reported SAT (pre-2016 redesign) scores:** SAT Math middle 50% range 470-570. SAT Critical Reading middle 50% range 440-530. SAT Writing middle 50% range 450-540. **Concordant SAT scores:** SAT EBRW middle 50% 500–590. SAT Math middle 50% range 510–590. Minimum paper TOEFL 550. **Basis for Candidate Selection:** *Very important factors considered include:* rigor of secondary school record, class rank, academic GPA, standardized test scores. *Other factors considered include:* application essay, recommendation(s), extracurricular activities, first generation, geographical residence, state residency, racial/ethnic status, volunteer work, work experience. **Freshman Admission Requirements:** High school diploma is required and GED is accepted. *Academic units required:* 4 English, 3 math, 2 science, 2 foreign language, 5 academic electives. *Academic units recommended:* 4 math. **Freshman Admission Statistics:** 13,085 applied, 65.31% admitted, 16% enrolled. **Transfer Admission Requirements:** High school transcript, college transcript(s), Minimum college GPA of na required. **General Admission Information:** Application fee $65. Priority deadline 12/1. Regular notification 2/28. Nonfall registration accepted.

COSTS AND FINANCIAL AID
Annual in-state tuition $11,408. Annual out-of-state tuition $27,059. Room and board $13,459. Required fees $2,421. Average book expense $1,350. **Required Forms and Deadlines:** FAFSA. **Notification of Awards:** Applicants will be notified of awards on a rolling basis beginning 3/1. **Types of Aid:** *Need-based scholarships/grants:* Federal Pell, FSEOG, State scholarships/grants, Private scholarships, College/university scholarship or grant aid from institutional funds, Federal Nursing Scholarships. *Loans:* Direct Subsidized Stafford Loans, Direct Unsubsidized Stafford Loans, Direct PLUS loans, Federal Perkins Loans, State Loans, College/university loans from institutional funds. *Student Employment:* Federal Work-Study Program available. Institutional employment available. **Financial Aid Statistics:** 78% needy freshmen receive need-based scholarship or grant aid. 80% freshmen, 80% undergrads receive any aid. **Criteria for awarding aid:** *Need-based:* Academics, Alumni affiliation, Art, Leadership, Music/drama. *Non-need-based:* Academics, Alumni affiliation, Art, Athletics, Leadership, Music/drama, State/district residency.

RUTGERS, THE STATE UNIVERSITY OF NEW JERSEY—NEW BRUNSWICK

Piscataway, NJ 08854-8097
Phone: 732-932-4636 • **Financial Aid Phone:** 732-932-7305
E-mail: admissions@ugadm.rutgers.edu • **CEEB Code:** 2765
Website: www.newbrunswick.rutgers.edu • **ACT Code:** 2592

This public school was founded in 1766. It has a 2695-acre campus.

RATINGS
Admissions Selectivity Rating: 88   **Fire Safety Rating:** 86   **Green Rating:** 60*

STUDENTS AND FACULTY
Enrollment: 35,782. **Student Body:** 50% female, 50% male, 6% out-of-state, 8% international (117 countries represented). Asian 26%, African American 8%, Caucasian 40%, Hispanic 13%, Native American <1%, Pacific Islander <1%, Two or more races 3%, Race unknown 2%.
Retention and Graduation: 93% freshmen return for sophomore year. 80% freshmen graduate within 6 years. **Faculty:** Student/faculty ratio 12:1. 2,022 full-time faculty, 98% hold PhDs, 18% are are members of minority groups, 46% are women. 20% of classes are taught by teaching assistants.

ACADEMICS

Degrees: associate, bachelor's, certificate, doctoral/professional, doctoral/research, doctoral, master's, postbachelor's certifiate, post-master's certificate. **Classes:** Most classes have 20-29 students. Most lab/discussion sessions have 20-29 students. **Most popular majors:** Engineering; Biology/Biological Sciences. **Special Study Options:** Accelerated program, cooperative education program, cross-registration, distance learning, double major, dual enrollment, English as a Second Language (ESL), exchange student program (domestic), honors program, independent study, internships, liberal arts/career combination, student-designed major, study abroad, teacher certification program, 5-year B.A. or B.S./MBA program in Rutgers Business School; BS in business Discipline/MBA; BA or BS in Science Discipline/MBA; 8-year Bachelor/Medical Dual Degree program with UMDNJ-Robert Wood Johnson Medical School; 5-year BS/BS in Bioenvironmental Engineering with the School of Engineering; 5-year accelerated baccalaureate-M.B.A with Rutgers Business School.; Bureau of Engineering Research, supported by the university, industry, state and federal government, provides research opportunities for students and faculty; Continuing professional education; Exchange program between School of Engineering and the City University of London for qualified students majoring in civil, electrical, or mechanical engineering; 5-year (BA/BS degree) program in liberal arts and engineering; 5-year BA or BS/M.Ed. with the Graduate School of Education; Interdepartmental programs and certificate programs are available; Study Abroad in England, Italy, Ireland, Germany, Greece, Mexico, Israel, Australia, India, Japan, Netherlands, Scotland, South Africa, South Korea and Spain; Alumnae externship program; Language and Cultural House Program; 5-year BA/BS in cooperation with Rutgers Business School.; B.A./Master of communication and information studies (with SCILS); B.A./MLER (with School of Management and Labor Relations); Baccalaureate/M.C.R.P., M.P.H., or M.P.P with EJB School of Planning and Public Policy;Baccalaureate in Business major/Master of Human Resource Management (with School of Management and Labor Relations {SMLR}). Combined degree programs: BA/MD, 5-year BAor BS/MPP, 6-year Pharm.D., 6-year Bach. **Disability Services:** Special programs offered to physically disabled students, including note-taking services, reader services, tape recorders, tutors. **Career Services:** Alumni network, Alumni services, Career/job search classes, Career assessment, Internships, Regional alumni.

FACILITIES

Housing: Coed dorms, men's dorms, special housing for international students, women's dorms, fraternity/sorority housing, apartments for married students, cooperative housing, apartments for single students, Theme Housing, Special interest housing, language and cultural houses, substance-free house, Math/Science Engineering House for women, first-year residence, transfer center, residence for single mothers and children. **Special Academic Facilities/Equipment:** Geology Museum, Zimmerli Museum, Mason Gross Performing Arts Center; NJ Museum of Agriculture; NJ Film Festival/RU Film Co-op; Rutgers Gardens **Computers:** Students can register for classes online. Administrative functions (other than registration) can be performed online.

CAMPUS LIFE

Environment: Town. **Activities:** Choral groups, concert band, dance, drama/theater, jazz band, literary magazine, marching band, music ensembles, musical theater, opera, pep band, radio station, student government, student newspaper, student-run film society, symphony orchestra, television station, yearbook, Campus Ministries, Student Organization. 400 registered organizations, 24 honor societies, 29 fraternities, 15 sororities. **Athletics (Intercollegiate):** *Men:* baseball, basketball, cheerleading, cross-country, diving, football, golf, lacrosse, soccer, track/field (outdoor), track/field (indoor), wrestling. *Women:* basketball, cheerleading, crew/rowing, cross-country, diving, field hockey, golf, gymnastics, lacrosse, soccer, softball, swimming, tennis, track/field (outdoor), track/field (indoor), volleyball. **On-Campus Highlights:** Geology Museum, Jane Voorhees Zimmereli Art Museum, Rutgers Display Gardens and Heylar Woods, Hutchenson Memorial Forest.

ADMISSIONS

Freshman Academic Profile: 38% in top 10% of high school class, 76% in top 25% of high school class, 97% in top 50% of high school class. **Reported SAT (pre-2016 redesign) scores:** SAT Math middle 50% range 580-700. SAT Critical Reading middle 50% range 530-640. SAT Writing middle 50% range 540-660. **Concordant SAT scores:** SAT EBRW middle 50% 590-700. SAT Math middle 50% range 600-730. Minimum paper TOEFL 550. **Basis for Candidate Selection:** *Very important factors considered include:* rigor of secondary school record, class rank, academic GPA, standardized test scores, interview, talent/ability. *Other factors considered include:* application essay, recommendation(s), extracurricular activities, first generation, geographical residence, state residency, racial/ethnic status, volunteer work, work experience. **Freshman Admission Requirements:** High school diploma is required and GED is accepted. *Academic units required:* 4 English, 3 math, 2 science, 2 foreign language, 5 academic electives. *Academic units recommended:* 4 math, 2 foreign language. **Freshman Admission Statistics:** 35,340 applied, 58.45% admitted, 32% enrolled. **Transfer Admission Requirements:** High

school transcript, college transcript(s), Lowest grade transferable C. **General Admission Information:** Application fee $65. Priority deadline 12/1. Regular notification 3/1. Nonfall registration accepted. Admission may be deferred for a maximum of 1 year.

COSTS AND FINANCIAL AID

Annual in-state tuition $11,408. Annual out-of-state tuition $27,059. Room and board $12,260. Required fees $2,964. Average book expense $1,350. **Required Forms and Deadlines:** FAFSA. **Notification of Awards:** Applicants will be notified of awards on a rolling basis beginning 3/1. **Types of Aid:** *Need-based scholarships/grants:* Federal Pell, FSEOG, State scholarships/grants, College/university scholarship or grant aid from institutional funds, Federal Nursing Scholarships. *Loans:* Direct Subsidized Stafford Loans, Direct Unsubsidized Stafford Loans, Direct PLUS loans, Federal Perkins Loans, Federal Nursing Loans, State Loans, College/university loans from institutional funds. *Student Employment:* Federal Work-Study Program available. Institutional employment available. **Financial Aid Statistics:** 67% needy freshmen receive need-based scholarship or grant aid. 67% freshmen, 69% undergrads receive any aid. **Criteria for awarding aid:** *Need-based:* Academics, Alumni affiliation, Art, Leadership, Music/drama. *Non-need-based:* Academics, Alumni affiliation, Art, Athletics, Leadership, Music/drama, State/district residency.

SACRED HEART UNIVERSITY

5151 Park Avenue, Fairfield, CT 6825
Phone: 203-371-7880 • **Financial Aid Phone:** 203-371-7980
E-mail: enroll@sacredheart.edu • **CEEB Code:** 3780
Fax: 203-365-7607 • **Website:** www.sacredheart.edu • **ACT Code:** 589

This private school, affiliated with the Roman Catholic Church, was founded in 1963. It has a 67-acre campus.

RATINGS

Admissions Selectivity Rating: 87   **Fire Safety Rating:** 94   **Green Rating:** 61

STUDENTS AND FACULTY

Enrollment: 5,325. **Student Body:** 64% female, 36% male, 63% out-of-state, 1% international (24 countries represented). Asian 2%, African American 4%, Caucasian 73%, Hispanic 10%, Native American <1%, Pacific Islander <1%, Two or more races 2%, Race unknown 8%.
Retention and Graduation: 81% freshmen return for sophomore year. 54% freshmen graduate within 4 years. 60% freshmen graduate within 6 years. 43% grads go on to further study within 1 year. 54% grads pursue arts and sciences degrees. 22% grads pursue business degrees. **Faculty:** Student/faculty ratio 15:1. 281 full-time faculty, 79% hold PhDs, 9% are are members of minority groups, 54% are women. 0% of classes are taught by teaching assistants.

ACADEMICS

Degrees: associate, bachelor's, doctoral/professional, master's, post-master's certifiate. **Classes:** Most classes have 20-29 students. **Most popular majors:** Business Administration and Management; Psychology; Registered Nursing/Registered Nurse. **Special Study Options:** Accelerated program, cooperative education program, cross-registration, distance learning, double major, English as a Second Language (ESL), exchange student program (domestic), honors program, independent study, internships, liberal arts/career combination, student-designed major, study abroad, teacher certification program, weekend college, Off-campus study: Summer program in Luxembourg, Summer, Winter Intercession, Spring Break, and Semester in Ireland. Sponsored and approved study abroad programs worldwide. Combined degree programs: combined degree programs in physical therapy (doctoral) and occupational therapy (masters). Accelerated 5th year M.B.A. program. Accelerated MSCIS (Computer Information Systems). **Honors Programs:** The Thomas More School of Honors Studies offers a challenging curriculum of Honors-level courses. These studies will provide each student with the quest for the full meaning of our humanity exploring the following three components: (1) the cognitive, (2) the aesthetic and (3) the moral or ethical. The Program also includes advisement, cultural events, dinners with the University President and other events. Combined degree programs: BA/MA, BA/S/MBA; BA/S/DPT; BA/S/MSOT; BA/S/MAT; BS/MSCIS; BA/S/MACJ. **Disability Services:** Special programs offered to physically disabled students, including note-taking services, reader services, tape recorders, tutors. **Career Services:** Alumni network, Alumni services, Career/job search classes, Career assessment, Internships, Regional alumni. The Career Development and Placement Center works diligently to facilitate professional internship opportunities for students in all academic majors and career interests.

FACILITIES

Housing: Coed dorms, special housing for disabled students, apartments for single students, Wellness Housing, Thematic floors; living & learning communities for specific academic programs. **Special Academic Facilities/Equipment:** WHRT student radio station, WSHU National Public Radio, Edgerton Center for the Performing Arts, Gallery of Contemporary Art **Computers:** 100% of classrooms, 100% of dorms, 100% of libraries, 100% of dining areas, 100% of student union, 100% of common outdoor areas have wireless network access. Students can register for classes online. Administrative functions (other than registration) can be performed online. Undergraduates are required to own a computer.

CAMPUS LIFE

Environment: Town. **Activities:** Choral groups, concert band, dance, drama/theater, jazz band, literary magazine, marching band, music ensembles, musical theater, pep band, radio station, student government, student newspaper, student-run film society, television station, yearbook, Campus Ministries, Student Organization. 80 registered organizations, 14 honor societies, 4 religious organizations. 4 fraternities, 6 sororities. **Athletics (Intercollegiate):** *Men:* baseball, basketball, cross-country, fencing, football, golf, ice hockey, lacrosse, soccer, tennis, track/field (outdoor), track/field (indoor), volleyball, wrestling. *Women:* basketball, bowling, crew/rowing, cross-country, diving, equestrian sports, fencing, field hockey, golf, ice hockey, lacrosse, soccer, softball, swimming, tennis, track/field (outdoor), track/field (indoor), volleyball. **On-Campus Highlights:** Pitt Health and Recreation Center, Edgerton Center for Performing Arts, Holy Grounds Cafe, Ryan-Matura Library, Hawley Lounge, New University Chapel (Chapel of the Holy Spirit) opened in Fall 2009.

ADMISSIONS

Freshman Academic Profile: Average high school GPA 3.5. 8% in top 10% of high school class, 31% in top 25% of high school class, 68% in top 50% of high school class. 77% from public high schools. **Reported SAT (pre-2016 redesign) scores:** SAT Math middle 50% range 497-632. SAT Critical Reading middle 50% range 486-622. SAT Writing middle 50% range 473-631. **Concordant SAT scores:** SAT EBRW middle 50% 540–680. SAT Math middle 50% range 530–650. ACT middle 50% range 22-28. Minimum internet-based TOEFL 80. Minimum paper TOEFL 550. **Basis for Candidate Selection:** *Very important factors considered include:* rigor of secondary school record, academic GPA, volunteer work, work experience. *Important factors considered include:* class rank, application essay, recommendation(s), interview, extracurricular activities, talent/ability, character/personal qualities, level of applicant's interest. *Other factors considered include:* standardized test scores, first generation, alumni/ae relation, geographical residence, state residency, religious affiliation/commitment, racial/ethnic status. **Freshman Admission Requirements:** High school diploma is required and GED is accepted. *Academic units required:* 4 English, 3 math, 3 science, 1 science lab, 2 foreign language, 3 social studies, 3 history, 3 academic electives. *Academic units recommended:* 4 English, 4 math, 4 science, 2 science labs, 4 foreign language, 4 social studies, 4 history, 4 academic electives. **Freshman Admission Statistics:** 10,017 applied, 57.21% admitted, 23% enrolled. **Transfer Admission Requirements:** High school transcript, college transcript(s), essay or personal statement, Minimum college GPA of 2.5 required. Lowest grade transferable C-. **General Admission Information:** Application fee $50. Priority deadline 2/5. Nonfall registration accepted. Admission may be deferred for a maximum of 1 year.

COSTS AND FINANCIAL AID

Annual tuition $38,050. Room and board $14,450. Required fees $250. Average book expense $1,200. **Required Forms and Deadlines:** FAFSA, CSS/Financial Aid PROFILE, Noncustodial PROFILE. **Notification of Awards:** Applicants will be notified of awards on a rolling basis beginning 3/1. **Types of Aid:** *Need-based scholarships/grants:* Federal Pell, FSEOG, State scholarships/grants, Private scholarships, College/university scholarship or grant aid from institutional funds. *Loans:* Direct Subsidized Stafford Loans, Direct Unsubsidized Stafford Loans, Direct PLUS loans, Federal Perkins Loans, State Loans. *Student Employment:* Federal Work-Study Program available. Institutional employment available. **Financial Aid Statistics:** 100% needy freshmen, 99% needy undergrads receive need-based scholarship or grant aid. 16% freshmen, 15% undergrads receive non-need-based scholarship or grant aid. 80% freshmen, 79% undergrads receive need-based self-help aid. 4% freshmen, 6% undergrads receive athletic scholarships. 70% freshmen, 63% undergrads receive any aid. 76% undergrads borrow to pay for school. Average cumulative indebtedness $40,240. **Criteria for awarding aid:** *Need-based:* Academics. *Non-need-based:* Academics, Alumni affiliation, Art, Athletics, Leadership, Music/drama, Religious affiliation, State/district residency.

SAGINAW VALLEY STATE UNIVERSITY

7400 Bay Road, University Center, MI 48710
Phone: 989-964-4200 • **Financial Aid Phone:** 989-964-4103
E-mail: admissions@svsu.edu • **CEEB Code:** 1766
Fax: 989-790-0180 • **Website:** www.svsu.edu • **ACT Code:** 2057

This public school was founded in 1963. It has a 782-acre campus.

RATINGS

Admissions Selectivity Rating: 73   **Fire Safety Rating:** 66   **Green Rating:** 60*

STUDENTS AND FACULTY

Enrollment: 8,434. **Student Body:** 57% female, 43% male, 1% out-of-state, 8% international (30 countries represented). Asian 1%, African American 9%, Caucasian 71%, Hispanic 4%, Native American <1%, Pacific Islander <1%, Two or more races 2%, Race unknown 6%.
Retention and Graduation: 72% freshmen return for sophomore year. 10% freshmen graduate within 4 years. 20% grads go on to further study within 1 year. **Faculty:** Student/faculty ratio 18:1. 308 full-time faculty, 83% hold PhDs, 0% are are members of minority groups, 0% are women. 0% of classes are taught by teaching assistants.

ACADEMICS

Degrees: bachelor's, master's, post-master's certificate. **Classes:** Most classes have 20-29 students. Most lab/discussion sessions have 10-19 students. **Most popular majors:** Registered Nursing/Registered Nurse; Social Work; Criminal Justice/Safety Studies. **Special Study Options:** Accelerated program, cooperative education program, distance learning, double major, dual enrollment, English as a Second Language (ESL), honors program, independent study, internships, student-designed major, study abroad, teacher certification program. **Honors Programs:** The University Honors Program allows students to pursue their major and minor degree work, while providing enriched academic experiences in Honors courses, seminars, research projects, and social activities. The Honors experience enables students to work more intensively with active teacher/scholars and to participate in interdisciplinary courses. Honors students will have ample opportunity to develop as critical thinkers, active learners, and problem solvers. **Disability Services:** Special programs offered to physically disabled students, including note-taking services, reader services, tutors. **Career Services:** Career assessment, Internships.

FACILITIES

Housing: Coed dorms, special housing for disabled students, apartments for single students, Wellness Housing, Theme Housing. 95% of campus accessible to physically diasbled. **Special Academic Facilities/Equipment:** Sculpture gallery, fine arts center, center for health and physical education, independent testing lab, center for economic and business research, applied technology research center. **Computers:** Students can register for classes online. Administrative functions (other than registration) can be performed online.

CAMPUS LIFE

Environment: City. **Activities:** Choral groups, concert band, dance, drama/theater, jazz band, literary magazine, marching band, music ensembles, musical theater, pep band, student government, student newspaper, student-run film society, Campus Ministries, Student Organization, Model UN. 110 registered organizations, 8 honor societies, 9 religious organizations. 4 fraternities, 7 sororities. **Athletics (Intercollegiate):** *Men:* baseball, basketball, bowling, cheerleading, cross-country, football, golf, soccer, track/field (outdoor), track/field (indoor). *Women:* basketball, cheerleading, cross-country, soccer, softball, tennis, track/field (outdoor), track/field (indoor), volleyball. **On-Campus Highlights:** Student Center, Student Recreation Center (Ryder), Zahnow Library, Arbury Fine Arts Center, University Village. **Environmental Initiatives:** Building buildings with energy savings in mind for many years.

ADMISSIONS

Freshman Academic Profile: Average high school GPA 3.4. 2% in top 10% of high school class, 7% in top 25% of high school class, 26% in top 50% of high school class. ACT middle 50% range 19-25. Minimum internet-based TOEFL 61. Minimum paper TOEFL 500. **Basis for Candidate Selection:** *Very important factors considered include:* rigor of secondary school record, academic GPA, standardized test scores, extracurricular activities, talent/ability. **Freshman Admission Requirements:** High school diploma is required and GED is accepted. *Academic units recommended:* 4 English, 3 math, 3 science, 2 foreign language, 3 social studies. **Freshman Admission Statistics:** 7,021 applied, 76.17% admitted, 29% enrolled. **Transfer Admission Requirements:** college transcript(s), Minimum college GPA of 2.0 required. Lowest grade transferable C-. **General Admission Information:** Application fee $30. Nonfall registration accepted. Admission may be deferred for a maximum of 1 year.

COSTS AND FINANCIAL AID

Required Forms and Deadlines: FAFSA. **Notification of Awards:** Applicants will be notified of awards on a rolling basis beginning 3/1. **Types of Aid:** *Need-based scholarships/grants:* Federal Pell, FSEOG, State scholarships/ grants, Private scholarships, College/university scholarship or grant aid from institutional funds. *Loans:* Direct Subsidized Stafford Loans, Direct Unsubsidized Stafford Loans, Direct PLUS loans. *Student Employment:* Federal Work-Study Program available. Institutional employment available. **Financial Aid Statistics:** 71% needy freshmen, 71% needy undergrads receive need-based scholarship or grant aid. 0% undergrads receive non-need-based scholarship or grant aid. 94% freshmen, 94% undergrads receive need-based self-help aid. 0% freshmen, 0% undergrads receive athletic scholarships. 94% freshmen, 95% undergrads receive any aid. **Criteria for awarding aid:** *Need-based:* Academics, Leadership, Minority status. *Non-need-based:* Academics, Art, Athletics, Leadership, Minority status, Music/drama.

SAINT ANSELM COLLEGE

100 Saint Anselm Drive, Manchester, NH 03102-1310
Phone: 603-641-7500 • **Financial Aid Phone:** 603-641-7110
E-mail: admission@anselm.edu • **CEEB Code:** 3748
Fax: 603-641-7550 • **Website:** www.anselm.edu • **ACT Code:** 2522

This private school, affiliated with the Roman Catholic Church, was founded in 1889. It has a 404-acre campus.

RATINGS

Admissions Selectivity Rating: 83   **Fire Safety Rating:** 85   **Green Rating:** 60*

STUDENTS AND FACULTY

Enrollment: 1,916. **Student Body:** 62% female, 38% male, 77% out-of-state, 1% international (7 countries represented). Asian 1%, African American 2%, Caucasian 88%, Hispanic 3%, Native American <1%, Pacific Islander 0%, Two or more races 2%, Race unknown 4%.
Retention and Graduation: 85% freshmen return for sophomore year. 69% freshmen graduate within 4 years. 72% freshmen graduate within 6 years. 16% grads go on to further study within 1 year. 11% grads pursue arts and sciences degrees. 3% grads pursue law degrees. 1% grads pursue business degrees. 2% grads pursue medical degrees. **Faculty:** Student/faculty ratio 11:1. 151 full-time faculty, 91% hold PhDs, 9% are are members of minority groups, 54% are women. 0% of classes are taught by teaching assistants.

ACADEMICS

Degrees: bachelor's. **Classes:** Most classes have 10-19 students. Most lab/ discussion sessions have fewer than 10 students. **Most popular majors:** Registered Nursing/Registered Nurse; Biology; Psychology. **Special Study Options:** cross-registration, honors program, independent study, internships, liberal arts/career combination, study abroad, teacher certification program. **Honors Programs:** Honors Program for Presidential Scholars. **Disability Services:** Special programs offered to physically disabled students, including note-taking services, reader services, tape recorders, tutors. **Career Services:** Alumni network, Alumni services, Career/job search classes, Career assessment, Internships, Regional alumni.

FACILITIES

Housing: Coed dorms, special housing for disabled students, men's dorms, women's dorms, apartments for single students, Theme Housing, Substance Free Housing. **Special Academic Facilities/Equipment:** Chapel Art Center, New Hampshire Institute of Politics, Izart Observatory, Koonz Theatre, Comisky Studio (Fine Arts), Poisson Hall **Computers:** 100% of classrooms, 100% of dorms, 100% of libraries, 100% of dining areas, 100% of student union, have wireless network access. Students can register for classes online. Administrative functions (other than registration) can be performed online.

CAMPUS LIFE

Environment: City. **Activities:** Choral groups, dance, drama/theater, jazz band, literary magazine, musical theater, radio station, student government, student newspaper, television station, yearbook, Campus Ministries, Student Organization, Model UN. 120 registered organizations, 11 honor societies, 7 religious organizations. **Athletics (Intercollegiate):** *Men:* baseball, basketball, cross-country, football, golf, ice hockey, lacrosse, skiing (downhill/alpine), soccer, tennis. *Women:* basketball, cross-country, field hockey, golf, ice hockey, lacrosse, skiing (downhill/alpine), soccer, softball, tennis, volleyball. **On-Campus Highlights:** Joseph Hall Academic Building, Chapel Arts Center,

Davidson Hall Dining Hall, Sullivan Ice Arena & Fitness Center, Abbey Church, Coffee Shop and Pub Cushing Student Center.

ADMISSIONS

Freshman Academic Profile: Average high school GPA 3.3. 20% in top 10% of high school class, 57% in top 25% of high school class, 89% in top 50% of high school class. 65% from public high schools. **Reported SAT (pre-2016 redesign) scores:** SAT Math middle 50% range 530-610. SAT Critical Reading middle 50% range 520-610. SAT Writing middle 50% range 510-600. **Concordant SAT scores:** SAT EBRW middle 50% 570-660. SAT Math middle 50% range 560-630. ACT middle 50% range 23-28. Minimum internet-based TOEFL 80. Minimum paper TOEFL 550. **Basis for Candidate Selection:** *Very important factors considered include:* rigor of secondary school record, academic GPA. *Important factors considered include:* application essay, recommendation(s), extracurricular activities, character/personal qualities. *Other factors considered include:* class rank, standardized test scores, talent/ ability, first generation, alumni/ae relation, geographical residence, racial/ ethnic status, volunteer work, work experience. **Freshman Admission Requirements:** High school diploma is required and GED is accepted. *Academic units required:* 4 English, 3 math, 3 science, 2 science labs, 2 foreign language, 2 social studies. *Academic units recommended:* 4 English, 4 math, 4 science, 2 science labs, 4 foreign language, 4 social studies. **Freshman Admission Statistics:** 3,826 applied, 75.90% admitted, 18% enrolled. **Transfer Admission Requirements:** High school transcript, college transcript(s), essay or personal statement, standardized test scores, statement of good standing from prior institution(s). Minimum college GPA of 2.5 required. Lowest grade transferable C. **General Admission Information:** Application fee $50. Regular application deadline 2/1. Regular notification 3/15. Nonfall registration accepted. Admission may be deferred for a maximum of 1 year.

COSTS AND FINANCIAL AID

Annual tuition $37,826. Room and board $13,734. Required fees $1,000. Average book expense $1,000. **Required Forms and Deadlines:** FAFSA, CSS/Financial Aid PROFILE, Noncustodial PROFILE. **Notification of Awards:** Applicants will be notified of awards on a rolling basis beginning 3/1. **Types of Aid:** *Need-based scholarships/grants:* Federal Pell, FSEOG, State scholarships/grants, Private scholarships, College/university scholarship or grant aid from institutional funds. *Loans:* Direct Subsidized Stafford Loans, Direct Unsubsidized Stafford Loans, Direct PLUS loans, Federal Perkins Loans. *Student Employment:* Federal Work-Study Program available. Institutional employment available. **Financial Aid Statistics:** 99% needy freshmen, 100% needy undergrads receive need-based scholarship or grant aid. 25% freshmen, 21% undergrads receive non-need-based scholarship or grant aid. 80% freshmen, 82% undergrads receive need-based self-help aid. 0% freshmen, 5% undergrads receive athletic scholarships. 98% freshmen, 98% undergrads receive any aid. 81% undergrads borrow to pay for school. Average cumulative indebtedness $37,402. **Criteria for awarding aid:** *Need-based:* Academics, Alumni affiliation, Athletics, Leadership, Minority status, Music/drama, Religious affiliation. *Non-need-based:* Academics, Alumni affiliation, Athletics, Leadership, Music/drama, State/district residency.

See page 1028.

SAINT ANTHONY COLLEGE OF NURSING

5658 East State Street, Rockford, IL 61108-2468
Phone: 815-227-2141 • **Financial Aid Phone:** 815-395-5089
E-mail: admissions@sacn.edu
Fax: 815-227-2730 • **Website:** www.sacn.edu

This private school, affiliated with the Roman Catholic Church, was founded in 1915.

RATINGS

Admissions Selectivity Rating: 61   **Fire Safety Rating:** 60*   **Green Rating:** 60*

STUDENTS AND FACULTY

Enrollment: 230. **Student Body:** 89% female, 11% male, 10% out-of-state, 0% international (0 countries represented). Asian 5%, African American 2%, Caucasian 77%, Hispanic 13%, Native American 0%, Pacific Islander <1%, Two or more races 2%, Race unknown <1%.
Retention and Graduation: 100% freshmen return for sophomore year.
Faculty: Student/faculty ratio 7:1. 23 full-time faculty, 22% hold PhDs, 9% are are members of minority groups, 91% are women. 0% of classes are taught by teaching assistants.

ACADEMICS

Degrees: bachelor's, master's, post-master's certificate. **Most popular majors:** Registered Nursing/Registered Nurse. **Special Study Options:** distance learning, independent study.

FACILITIES

Housing: Private apartments, student plan housing, private rooms.

CAMPUS LIFE

Environment: City. **Activities:** student government, student newspaper. 1 registered organization.

ADMISSIONS

Minimum paper TOEFL 550. **Basis for Candidate Selection:** *Important factors considered include:* academic GPA, standardized test scores, application essay, recommendation(s). *Other factors considered include:* extracurricular activities, volunteer work, work experience. **Freshman Admission Requirements:** High school diploma or equivalent is not required. **Transfer Admission Requirements:** college transcript(s), essay or personal statement, interview, Minimum college GPA of 2.5 required. Lowest grade transferable c. **General Admission Information:** Application fee $50. Priority deadline 9/15. Regular application deadline 2/15.

COSTS AND FINANCIAL AID

Annual tuition $22,144. Required fees $481. **Types of Aid:** *Need-based scholarships/grants:* Federal Pell, State scholarships/grants, Private scholarships, College/university scholarship or grant aid from institutional funds. *Loans:* Direct Subsidized Stafford Loans, Direct Unsubsidized Stafford Loans, Direct PLUS loans. **Financial Aid Statistics:** 64% needy undergrads receive need-based scholarship or grant aid. 2% undergrads receive non-need-based scholarship or grant aid. 97% undergrads receive need-based self-help aid. 0% undergrads receive athletic scholarships. 0% freshmen, 86% undergrads receive any aid. **Criteria for awarding aid:** *Need-based:* Academics, Leadership. *Non-need-based:* Academics.

SAINT CHARLES BORROMEO SEMINARY

100 East Wynnewood Road, Wynnewood, PA 19096
Phone: 610-785-6291
Fax: 610-617-9267 • **Website:** www.scs.edu

RATINGS

Admissions Selectivity Rating: 75　　**Fire Safety Rating:** 60*　　**Green Rating:** 60*

STUDENTS AND FACULTY

Enrollment: 47. **Student Body:** 0% female, 100% male, 25% out-of-state, 0% international. Asian 2%, African American 0%, Caucasian 89%, Hispanic 9%, Native American 0%, Pacific Islander 0%, Two or more races 0%, Race unknown 0%.
Retention and Graduation: 77% freshmen return for sophomore year. 70% freshmen graduate within 4 years. 80% freshmen graduate within 6 years.
Faculty: Student/faculty ratio 6:1. 16 full-time faculty, 75% hold PhDs, 0% are are members of minority groups, 13% are women.

ACADEMICS

Degrees: bachelor's, certificate, master's.

ADMISSIONS

Freshman Academic Profile: 33% in top 25% of high school class, 67% in top 50% of high school class. **Reported SAT (pre-2016 redesign) scores:** SAT Math middle 50% range 530-640. SAT Critical Reading middle 50% range 550-690. SAT Writing middle 50% range 490-580. **Concordant SAT scores:** SAT EBRW middle 50% 580–680. SAT Math middle 50% range 560–660. **Basis for Candidate Selection:** *Very important factors considered include:* application essay, recommendation(s), interview, religious affiliation/commitment, level of applicant's interest. *Important factors considered include:* character/personal qualities. *Other factors considered include:* talent/ability. **Freshman Admission Requirements:** *Academic units recommended:* 4 English, 4 math, 3 science, 3 foreign language, 3 social studies. **Freshman Admission Statistics:** 8 applied, 100.00% admitted, 88% enrolled. **General Admission Information:** Priority deadline 3/31. Regular application deadline 7/31. Nonfall registration accepted. Admission may be deferred.

COSTS AND FINANCIAL AID

Annual tuition $17,600. Room and board $11,820. Required fees $1,175. Average book expense $1,100. **Required Forms and Deadlines:** FAFSA, Institution's own financial aid form. **Notification of Awards:** Applicants will be notified of awards on a rolling basis beginning 3/1. **Types of Aid:** *Need-based scholarships/grants:* Federal Pell, FSEOG, State scholarships/grants, College/university scholarship or grant aid from institutional funds. *Loans:* Direct Subsidized Stafford Loans, Direct Unsubsidized Stafford Loans, Direct PLUS loans. *Student Employment:* Federal Work-Study Program available. Institutional employment available. **Financial Aid Statistics:** 57% needy

---

freshmen, 48% needy undergrads receive need-based scholarship or grant aid. 100% freshmen, 100% undergrads receive non-need-based scholarship or grant aid. 100% freshmen, 64% undergrads receive need-based self-help aid. 0% freshmen, 0% undergrads receive athletic scholarships.

SAINT FRANCIS MEDICAL CENTER
COLLEGE OF NURSING

511 NE. Greenleaf Street, Peoria, IL 61603
Phone: 309-624-8980 • **Financial Aid Phone:** 309-655-4119
E-mail: janice.e.farquharson@osfhealthcare.org
Fax: 309-624-8973 • **Website:** http://www.sfmccon.edu/

This is a private school.

RATINGS

Admissions Selectivity Rating: 60*　　**Fire Safety Rating:** 98　　**Green Rating:** 60*

STUDENTS AND FACULTY

Enrollment: 408. **Student Body:** 90% female, 10% male, 1% out-of-state, <1% international (2 countries represented). Asian 4%, African American 2%, Caucasian 91%, Hispanic 2%, Native American 0%, Pacific Islander 0%, Two or more races <1%, Race unknown 1%.
Faculty: Student/faculty ratio 10:1. 36 full-time faculty, 33% hold PhDs, 0% are are members of minority groups, 97% are women. 0% of classes are taught by teaching assistants.

ACADEMICS

Degrees: bachelor's, doctoral, master's, post-master's certificate. **Classes:** Most classes have 40-49 students. Most lab/discussion sessions have fewer than 10 students. **Special Study Options:** Accelerated program, distance learning, independent study.

FACILITIES

Housing: Coed dorms. 1% of campus accessible to physically diasbled.

CAMPUS LIFE

Activities: student government.

ADMISSIONS

Freshman Admission Requirements: High school diploma is required and GED is accepted. **Transfer Admission Requirements:** High school transcript, college transcript(s), essay or personal statement, statement of good standing from prior institution(s). Minimum college GPA of 2.50 required. Lowest grade transferable C. **General Admission Information:** Application fee $50. Priority deadline 9/15.

COSTS AND FINANCIAL AID

Annual tuition $19,140. Required fees $930. Average book expense $1,218. **Required Forms and Deadlines:** FAFSA, Institution's own financial aid form. **Notification of Awards:** Applicants will be notified of awards on a rolling basis beginning 5/15. **Types of Aid:** *Need-based scholarships/grants:* Federal Pell, State scholarships/grants, Private scholarships, College/university scholarship or grant aid from institutional funds. *Loans:* Direct Subsidized Stafford Loans, Direct Unsubsidized Stafford Loans, Direct PLUS loans, College/university loans from institutional funds. **Financial Aid Statistics:** 75% needy undergrads receive need-based scholarship or grant aid. 0% undergrads receive non-need-based scholarship or grant aid. 86% undergrads receive need-based self-help aid. 0% undergrads receive athletic scholarships. **Criteria for awarding aid:** *Non-need-based:* Academics, Alumni affiliation.

SAINT FRANCIS UNIVERSITY (PA)

PO Box 600, Loretto, PA 15940
Phone: 814-472-3000 • **Financial Aid Phone:** 814-472-3010
E-mail: admissions@francis.edu • **CEEB Code:** 2797
Fax: 814-472-3335 • **ACT Code:** 3682

This private school, affiliated with the Roman Catholic Church, was founded in 1847. It has a 600-acre campus.

RATINGS
Admissions Selectivity Rating: 83   **Fire Safety Rating:** 84   **Green Rating:** 60*

STUDENTS AND FACULTY
Enrollment: 1,710. **Student Body:** 63% female, 37% male, 20% out-of-state, 5% international (25 countries represented). Asian 1%, African American 6%, Caucasian 79%, Hispanic 2%, Native American <1%, Pacific Islander <1%, Two or more races 1%, Race unknown 6%.
Retention and Graduation: 86% freshmen return for sophomore year. 62% freshmen graduate within 4 years. 71% freshmen graduate within 6 years. 29% grads go on to further study within 1 year. 5% grads pursue arts and sciences degrees. 3% grads pursue law degrees. 9% grads pursue business degrees. 3% grads pursue medical degrees. **Faculty:** Student/faculty ratio 14:1. 125 full-time faculty, 70% hold PhDs, 7% are are members of minority groups, 56% are women. 0% of classes are taught by teaching assistants.

ACADEMICS
Degrees: associate, bachelor's, doctoral/professional, master's, postbachelor's certificate. **Classes:** Most classes have 10-19 students. Most lab/discussion sessions have 10-19 students. **Most popular majors:** Physician Assistant; Health Professions and Related Clinical Sciences; Business/Commerce. **Special Study Options:** cooperative education program, distance learning, double major, honors program, independent study, internships, liberal arts/career combination, student-designed major, study abroad, teacher certification program. **Honors Programs:** Honors Program Combined degree programs: BA/MD, BA/DDS, BS/MPAS, BS/MOT, BS/DPT, 3-3 BS/PharmD, 2-3 PharmD. **Disability Services:** Special programs offered to physically disabled students, including note-taking services, tape recorders, tutors. **Career Services:** Alumni network, Career/job search classes, Career assessment, Internships.

FACILITIES
Housing: Coed dorms, men's dorms, women's dorms, fraternity/sorority housing, apartments for single students, Special Housing for Honors Students, Special Housing for Campus Ministry. 20% of campus accessible to physically diasbled. **Special Academic Facilities/Equipment:** Art museum, elementary-level library for education majors, physician assistant practice facilities, cadaver lab, physical therapy lab, Center of Excellence for Remote and Medically Underserved Areas. **Computers:** Administrative functions (other than registration) can be performed online. Undergraduates are required to own a computer.

CAMPUS LIFE
Environment: Rural. **Activities:** Choral groups, dance, drama/theater, literary magazine, music ensembles, pep band, radio station, student government, student newspaper, student-run film society, television station, yearbook. 60 registered organizations, 9 honor societies, 10 religious organizations. 3 fraternities, 3 sororities. **Athletics (Intercollegiate):** *Men:* basketball, cross-country, football, golf, soccer, swimming, tennis, track/field (outdoor), track/field (indoor), volleyball. *Women:* basketball, cross-country, field hockey, golf, lacrosse, soccer, softball, swimming, tennis, track/field (outdoor), track/field (indoor), volleyball. **On-Campus Highlights:** Christian Hall—residence hall, JFK Student Center, Immaculate Conception Chapel, Stokes Athletics Facility, Mt. Assisi Gardens.

ADMISSIONS
Freshman Academic Profile: 30% in top 10% of high school class, 50% in top 25% of high school class, 83% in top 50% of high school class. 79% from public high schools. **Reported SAT (pre-2016 redesign) scores:** SAT Math middle 50% range 470-590. SAT Critical Reading middle 50% range 460-570. SAT Writing middle 50% range 450-560. **Concordant SAT scores:** SAT EBRW middle 50% 510–620. SAT Math middle 50% range 510–610. ACT middle 50% range 21-26. Minimum paper TOEFL 500. **Basis for Candidate Selection:** *Very important factors considered include:* rigor of secondary school record, class rank, academic GPA, standardized test scores, extracurricular activities. *Important factors considered include:* application essay, recommendation(s),

interview, talent/ability, character/personal qualities, volunteer work, level of applicant's interest. *Other factors considered include:* alumni/ae relation, work experience. **Freshman Admission Requirements:** High school diploma is required and GED is accepted. *Academic units required:* 4 English, 2 math, 1 science, 2 social studies, 7 academic electives. *Academic units recommended:* 4 English, 4 math, 2 science, 1 science lab, 2 foreign language, 2 social studies, 7 academic electives, and 4 units from above areas or other academic areas. **Freshman Admission Statistics:** 2,045 applied, 70.02% admitted, 28% enrolled. **Transfer Admission Requirements:** High school transcript, college transcript(s), standardized test scores, statement of good standing from prior institution(s). Minimum college GPA of 2.0 required. Lowest grade transferable C. **General Admission Information:** Application fee $30. Priority deadline 4/1. Nonfall registration accepted. Admission may be deferred.

COSTS AND FINANCIAL AID
Annual tuition $30,028. Room and board $11,190. Required fees $1,100. Average book expense $2,000. **Required Forms and Deadlines:** FAFSA. **Notification of Awards:** Applicants will be notified of awards on a rolling basis beginning 3/1. **Types of Aid:** *Need-based scholarships/grants:* Federal Pell, FSEOG, State scholarships/grants, Private scholarships, College/university scholarship or grant aid from institutional funds. *Loans:* Federal Perkins Loans. *Student Employment:* Federal Work-Study Program available. Institutional employment available. **Financial Aid Statistics:** 55% needy freshmen, 59% needy undergrads receive need-based scholarship or grant aid. 100% freshmen, 94% undergrads receive non-need-based scholarship or grant aid. 72% freshmen, 77% undergrads receive need-based self-help aid. 33% freshmen, 27% undergrads receive athletic scholarships. 98% freshmen receive any aid. **Criteria for awarding aid:** *Non-need-based:* Academics, Alumni affiliation, Athletics, Leadership, Music/drama, Religious affiliation.

See page 1030.

SAINT JOSEPH SEMINARY COLLEGE

75376 River Road, St. Benedict, LA 70457
Phone: 985-867-2273 • **Financial Aid Phone:** 985-867-2229
E-mail: registrar@sjasc.edu • **CEEB Code:** 6689
Fax: 985-327-1085 • **ACT Code:** 1604

This private school, affiliated with the Roman Catholic Church, was founded in 1891. It has a 1200-acre campus.

RATINGS
Admissions Selectivity Rating: 63   **Fire Safety Rating:** 60*   **Green Rating:** 60*

STUDENTS AND FACULTY
Enrollment: 100. **Student Body:** 0% female, 100% male, 34% out-of-state, 0% international. Asian 5%, African American 0%, Caucasian 69%, Hispanic 26%, Native American 0%, Pacific Islander 0%, Two or more races 0%, Race unknown 0%.
Faculty: Student/faculty ratio 7:1. 16 full-time faculty, 31% hold PhDs, 0% are are members of minority groups, 44% are women. 0% of classes are taught by teaching assistants.

ACADEMICS
Degrees: bachelor's. **Classes:** Most classes have 10-19 students. **Special Study Options:** distance learning, English as a Second Language (ESL), independent study, study abroad. **Disability Services:** Special programs offered to physically disabled students, including tape recorders, tutors.

FACILITIES
Housing: men's dorms 100% of campus accessible to physically diasbled.

CAMPUS LIFE
Environment: Rural. **Activities:** Choral groups, drama/theater, literary magazine, student government, student newspaper, yearbook. 1 religious organization.

ADMISSIONS
Minimum paper TOEFL 520. **Basis for Candidate Selection:** *Very important factors considered include:* rigor of secondary school record, character/personal qualities, religious affiliation/commitment. *Important factors considered include:* standardized test scores, recommendation(s). *Other factors considered include:* class rank, interview, extracurricular activities, volunteer work. **Freshman Admission Requirements:** High school diploma is required and GED is accepted. *Academic units required:* 3 English, 2 math, 2 science, 2 foreign language, 1 history. *Academic units recommended:* 3 English, 3 math, 2 science, 2 foreign language, 1 history. **Freshman Admission Statistics:** 11 applied, 100.00% admitted, 100% enrolled. **Transfer Admission Requirements:** High school transcript, college transcript(s), standardized

test scores, Lowest grade transferable C. **General Admission Information:** Nonfall registration accepted.

COSTS AND FINANCIAL AID
Annual tuition $13,500. Room and board $13,040. Required fees $1,165. Average book expense $1,000. **Required Forms and Deadlines:** FAFSA, Institution's own financial aid form, State aid form. **Notification of Awards:** Applicants will be notified of awards on a rolling basis beginning 8/3. **Types of Aid:** *Need-based scholarships/grants:* Federal Pell, FSEOG, State scholarships/ grants, Private scholarships, College/university scholarship or grant aid from institutional funds. *Loans:* Federal Perkins Loans. *Student Employment:* Federal Work-Study Program available. Institutional employment available. **Financial Aid Statistics:** 100% needy freshmen, 100% needy undergrads receive need-based scholarship or grant aid. 100% freshmen, 20% undergrads receive non-need-based scholarship or grant aid. 100% freshmen, 100% undergrads receive need-based self-help aid. 0% freshmen, 0% undergrads receive athletic scholarships.

SAINT JOSEPH'S COLLEGE (IN)

P.O. Box 890, Rensselaer, IN 47978
Phone: 219-866-6170 • **Financial Aid Phone:** 219-866-6163
E-mail: admissions@saintjoe.edu • **CEEB Code:** 1697
Fax: 219-866-6122 • **Website:** www.saintjoe.edu • **ACT Code:** 1240

This private school, affiliated with the Roman Catholic Church, was founded in 1889. It has a 180-acre campus.

RATINGS
Admissions Selectivity Rating: 74   **Fire Safety Rating:** 84   **Green Rating:** 60*

STUDENTS AND FACULTY
Enrollment: 948. **Student Body:** 52% female, 48% male, 24% out-of-state, 3% international (3 countries represented). Asian 0%, African American 10%, Caucasian 76%, Hispanic 6%, Native American <1%, Pacific Islander 0%, Two or more races 4%, Race unknown 1%.
Retention and Graduation: 68% freshmen return for sophomore year. 45% freshmen graduate within 4 years. 54% freshmen graduate within 6 years. 15% grads go on to further study within 1 year. 8% grads pursue arts and sciences degrees. 1% grads pursue law degrees. 4% grads pursue business degrees. 1% grads pursue medical degrees. **Faculty:** Student/faculty ratio 10:1. 80 full-time faculty, 69% hold PhDs, 9% are are members of minority groups, 55% are women. 0% of classes are taught by teaching assistants.

ACADEMICS
Degrees: bachelor's, diploma, master's, terminal. **Classes:** Most classes have 10-19 students. Most lab/discussion sessions have 10-19 students. **Most popular majors:** Business/Commerce; Elementary Education and Teaching; Biology/Biological Sciences. **Special Study Options:** Accelerated program, cross-registration, double major, dual enrollment, honors program, independent study, internships, liberal arts/career combination, student-designed major, study abroad, teacher certification program. **Disability Services:** Special programs offered to physically disabled students, including note-taking services, reader services, tape recorders, tutors. **Career Services:** Alumni network, Alumni services, Career assessment, Internships, Regional alumni, Internships.

FACILITIES
Housing: Coed dorms, special housing for disabled students, men's dorms, women's dorms, apartments for single students. 74% of campus accessible to physically diasbled. **Computers:** 100% of dorms, 100% of libraries, 100% of dining areas, have wireless network access.

CAMPUS LIFE
Environment: Village. **Activities:** Choral groups, concert band, dance, drama/ theater, jazz band, literary magazine, marching band, music ensembles, musical theater, pep band, radio station, student government, student newspaper, student-run film society, television station 41 registered organizations, 4 honor societies, 7 religious organizations. **Athletics (Intercollegiate):** *Men:* baseball, basketball, cross-country, football, golf, soccer, tennis, track/field (outdoor), track/field (indoor). *Women:* basketball, cross-country, golf, soccer, softball, tennis, track/field (outdoor), track/field (indoor), volleyball. **On-Campus Highlights:** Rev. Charles Banet, C.PP.S. Core Educati, Saint Joseph's Chapel, Lourdes Grotto, Hanson Recreation Center/Fitness Center, Lake Banet.

ADMISSIONS
Freshman Academic Profile: Average high school GPA 3.1. 8% in top 10% of high school class, 22% in top 25% of high school class, 61% in top 50% of high school class. 85% from public high schools. **Reported SAT (pre-2016 redesign) scores:** SAT Math middle 50% range 530-430. SAT Critical Reading middle 50% range 510-420. SAT Writing middle 50% range 490-410.

Concordant SAT scores: SAT EBRW middle 50% 560–460. SAT Math middle 50% range 560–470. ACT middle 50% range 25-18. Minimum internet-based TOEFL 80. Minimum paper TOEFL 550. **Basis for Candidate Selection:** *Very important factors considered include:* academic GPA, standardized test scores. *Important factors considered include:* rigor of secondary school record. *Other factors considered include:* application essay, recommendation(s). **Freshman Admission Requirements:** High school diploma is required and GED is accepted. *Academic units recommended:* 4 English, 3 math, 3 science, 2 science labs, 2 foreign language, 3 social studies. **Freshman Admission Statistics:** 1,506 applied, 76.83% admitted, 20% enrolled. **Transfer Admission Requirements:** college transcript(s), Minimum college GPA of 2.0 required. Lowest grade transferable C-. **General Admission Information:** Application fee $25. Nonfall registration accepted. Admission may be deferred for a maximum of 1 acad year.

COSTS AND FINANCIAL AID
Annual tuition $28,252. Room and board $9,480. Required fees $430. Average book expense $900. **Required Forms and Deadlines:** FAFSA. **Notification of Awards:** Applicants will be notified of awards on a rolling basis beginning 3/1. **Types of Aid:** *Need-based scholarships/grants:* Federal Pell, FSEOG, State scholarships/grants, Private scholarships, College/university scholarship or grant aid from institutional funds. *Loans:* Direct Subsidized Stafford Loans, Direct Unsubsidized Stafford Loans, Direct PLUS loans, Federal Perkins Loans. *Student Employment:* Federal Work-Study Program available. Institutional employment available. **Financial Aid Statistics:** 99% needy freshmen, 97% needy undergrads receive need-based scholarship or grant aid. 22% freshmen, 30% undergrads receive non-need-based scholarship or grant aid. 71% freshmen, 67% undergrads receive need-based self-help aid. 9% freshmen, 7% undergrads receive athletic scholarships. 99% freshmen, 99% undergrads receive any aid. 83% undergrads borrow to pay for school. Average cumulative indebtedness $28,527. **Criteria for awarding aid:** *Non-need-based:* Academics, Alumni affiliation, Athletics, Music/drama, Religious affiliation.

SAINT JOSEPH'S UNIVERSITY (PA)

5600 City Avenue, Philadelphia, PA 19131
Phone: 888-BE-A-HAWK • **Financial Aid Phone:** 610-660-1556
E-mail: admit@sju.edu • **CEEB Code:** 2801
Fax: 610-660-1314 • **Website:** www.sju.edu • **ACT Code:** 3684

This private school, affiliated with the Roman Catholic-Jesuit Church, affiliated with the Jesuit Church, was founded in 1851. It has a 103-acre campus.

RATINGS
Admissions Selectivity Rating: 82   **Fire Safety Rating:** 90   **Green Rating:** 73

STUDENTS AND FACULTY
Enrollment: 5,238. **Student Body:** 55% female, 45% male, 52% out-of-state, 2% international (35 countries represented). Asian 3%, African American 6%, Caucasian 79%, Hispanic 6%, Native American <1%, Pacific Islander <1%, Two or more races 2%, Race unknown 2%.
Retention and Graduation: 91% freshmen return for sophomore year. 72% freshmen graduate within 4 years. 80% freshmen graduate within 6 years. 21% grads go on to further study within 1 year. 31% grads pursue arts and sciences degrees. 16% grads pursue law degrees. 13% grads pursue business degrees. 18% grads pursue medical degrees. **Faculty:** Student/faculty ratio 13:1. 307 full-time faculty, 91% hold PhDs, 16% are are members of minority groups, 45% are women. 0% of classes are taught by teaching assistants.

ACADEMICS
Degrees: associate, bachelor's, certificate, doctoral/research, master's, postbachelor's certifiate, post-master's certificate, transfer. **Classes:** Most classes have 20-29 students. Most lab/discussion sessions have 10-19 students. **Most popular majors:** Special Products Marketing Operations; Marketing/ Marketing Management; Finance. **Special Study Options:** Accelerated program, cooperative education program, distance learning, double major, dual enrollment, English as a Second Language (ESL), exchange student program (domestic), honors program, independent study, internships, student-designed major, study abroad, teacher certification program, weekend college, off campus study in Jesuit student exchange. **Honors Programs:** There are distinctive benefits attached to belonging to the SJU Honors Program: Team-taught courses allow distinguished faculty members to share their knowledge and expertise with students in a challenging academic environment. Individual honors courses stress a detailed and thorough scholarly exploration of different fields of knowledge. Honors students register ahead of other students in their year. Honors suites in the residence halls allow like-minded students to live together, even as freshmen. Honors students are provided with free tickets and

transportation to concerts and performances by world-renowned institutions such as the Arden Theater Company, the Curtis Institute of Music, the Philadelphia Orchestra, the Pennsylvania Ballet, the Academy of Vocal Arts, the Philadelphia Museum of Art, and the Franklin Science Institute. Receptions, concerts and lectures are regularly sponsored by the Honors Program for Honors Students. Students have access to Claver House, a quiet retreat where honors students can study, work with personal computers and attend receptions. Students have opportunities to present research and creative work at national conferences and seminars; they are also kept informed about scholarship and funding opportunities for graduate and professional work. Combined degree programs: BS/MS in Education; BS/MS in Psychology; 5th yr MA in Writing Studies. **Disability Services:** Special programs offered to physically disabled students, including note-taking services, reader services, tape recorders, tutors. **Career Services:** Alumni network, Alumni services, Career/job search classes, Career assessment, Internships, Regional alumni. Saint Joseph's University's Erivan K. Haub School of Business Cooperative Education (Co-op) Program allows students to engage in real-world applications of their academic pursuits. Through two full-time, professionally engaging and paid experiences (creating one year of full-time work experience within the four-year degree), students discover their professional passions and bring real-world experience back to the classroom. In addition, the Co-op Program offers students substantial earning potential. Employers commonly ask Co-op students to continue working as part-time employees following their formal Co-op assignment, adding to these earnings. Employers, likewise, have expressed significant satisfaction with Saint Joseph's Co-op students. On the categories of dependability, attitude, quality of work and overall performance, the collective employer rating of all Co-op students (since the Program's inception) is a 4.5 on a scale of 5.0, and 93% of employers would hire their Co-op student(s) full-time, if a full-time job were available.

FACILITIES

Housing: Coed dorms, men's dorms, women's dorms, apartments for single students, Theme Housing, Special accommodations upon need for disabled students. 85% of campus accessible to physically diasbled. **Special Academic Facilities/Equipment:** Wall Street Trading Room Claver House—Honors Program Mandeville Hall Moot Board Room University Gallery **Computers:** 100% of classrooms, 100% of dorms, 100% of libraries, 100% of dining areas, 100% of student union, 10% of common outdoor areas have wireless network access. Students can register for classes online. Administrative functions (other than registration) can be performed online.

CAMPUS LIFE

Environment: Metropolis. **Activities:** Choral groups, concert band, dance, drama/theater, jazz band, literary magazine, music ensembles, musical theater, pep band, radio station, student government, student newspaper, student-run film society, yearbook, Campus Ministries, Student Organization. 100 registered organizations, 20 honor societies, 4 fraternities, 4 sororities. **Athletics (Intercollegiate):** *Men:* baseball, basketball, crew/rowing, cross-country, golf, lacrosse, soccer, tennis, track/field (outdoor), track/field (indoor). *Women:* basketball, crew/rowing, cross-country, field hockey, lacrosse, soccer, softball, tennis, track/field (outdoor), track/field (indoor). **On-Campus Highlights:** Campion Student Center, Hagan Arena and Athletics Center, Chapel of St. Joseph, Mandeville Hall, Maguire Sports Complex, 2008 brought the expansion of the SJU campus through the acquisition of 38 acres of property adjacent to the University as well as the construction of a new parking and retail facility. **Environmental Initiatives:** We have a full-time office of Health, Safety and Environmental compliance.

ADMISSIONS

Freshman Academic Profile: Average high school GPA 3.6. 20% in top 10% of high school class, 50% in top 25% of high school class, 84% in top 50% of high school class. 50% from public high schools. **Reported SAT (pre-2016 redesign) scores:** SAT Math middle 50% range 530-620. SAT Critical Reading middle 50% range 520-610. **Concordant SAT scores:** SAT Math middle 50% range 560-640. ACT middle 50% range 23-28. Minimum internet-based TOEFL 79. Minimum paper TOEFL 550. **Basis for Candidate Selection:** *Very important factors considered include:* rigor of secondary school record, class rank, academic GPA. *Important factors considered include:* standardized test scores, application essay, recommendation(s). *Other factors considered include:* interview, extracurricular activities, talent/ability, character/personal qualities, first generation, alumni/ae relation, geographical residence, racial/ethnic status, volunteer work, work experience, level of applicant's interest. **Freshman Admission Requirements:** High school diploma is required and GED is not accepted. *Academic units required:* 4 English, 3 math, 3 science, 2 foreign language, 3 social studies, 5 academic electives. *Academic units recommended:* 4 English, 3 math, 3 science, 1 science lab, 2 foreign language, 3 social studies, 5 academic electives, 1 visual/performing arts. **Freshman Admission Statistics:** 8,876 applied, 78.12% admitted, 18% enrolled. **Transfer Admission Requirements:** High school transcript, college transcript(s), statement of good standing from prior institution(s). Minimum college GPA of 2.5 required. Lowest grade transferable C. **General Admission Information:** Application fee $50. Priority deadline 2/1. Nonfall registration accepted. Admission may be deferred for a maximum of 1 year.

COSTS AND FINANCIAL AID

Annual tuition $42,840. Room and board $14,524. Required fees $180. Average book expense $825. **Required Forms and Deadlines:** FAFSA. **Notification of Awards:** Applicants will be notified of awards on a rolling basis beginning 3/31. **Types of Aid:** *Need-based scholarships/grants:* Federal Pell, FSEOG, State scholarships/grants, Private scholarships, College/university scholarship or grant aid from institutional funds. *Loans:* Direct Subsidized Stafford Loans, Direct Unsubsidized Stafford Loans, Direct PLUS loans, Federal Perkins Loans. *Student Employment:* Federal Work-Study Program available. Institutional employment available. **Financial Aid Statistics:** 97% needy freshmen, 95% needy undergrads receive need-based scholarship or grant aid. 66% freshmen, 69% undergrads receive non-need-based scholarship or grant aid. 72% freshmen, 70% undergrads receive need-based self-help aid. 3% freshmen, 5% undergrads receive athletic scholarships. 98% freshmen, 95% undergrads receive any aid. **Criteria for awarding aid:** *Need-based:* Academics, Athletics, Minority status, Music/drama. *Non-need-based:* Academics, Alumni affiliation, Art, Athletics, Minority status, Music/drama.

SAINT LEO UNIVERSITY

Office of Admission MC2008, Saint Leo, FL 33574-6665
Phone: 352-588-8283 • **Financial Aid Phone:** 800-240-7658
E-mail: admissions@saintleo.edu • **CEEB Code:** 5638
Fax: 352-588-8257 • **Website:** www.saintleo.edu • **ACT Code:** 755

This private school, affiliated with the Roman Catholic Church, was founded in 1889. It has a 186-acre campus.

RATINGS
Admissions Selectivity Rating: 77   **Fire Safety Rating:** 93   **Green Rating:** 60*

STUDENTS AND FACULTY
Enrollment: 2,367. **Student Body:** 54% female, 46% male, 29% out-of-state, 12% international (58 countries represented). Asian 2%, African American 13%, Caucasian 45%, Hispanic 19%, Native American <1%, Pacific Islander 0%, Two or more races 3%, Race unknown 6%.
Retention and Graduation: 71% freshmen return for sophomore year. 31% freshmen graduate within 4 years. 42% freshmen graduate within 6 years. **Faculty:** Student/faculty ratio 15:1. 125 full-time faculty, 82% hold PhDs, 10% are are members of minority groups, 41% are women. 0% of classes are taught by teaching assistants.

ACADEMICS
Degrees: associate, bachelor's, certificate, doctoral/professional, master's, postbachelor's certifiate, transfer. **Classes:** Most classes have 20-29 students. Most lab/discussion sessions have 10-19 students. **Most popular majors:** Criminal Justice/Safety Studies; Business Administration and Management; Computer and Information Sciences. **Special Study Options:** distance learning, double major, honors program, independent study, internships, liberal arts/career combination, study abroad, teacher certification program, weekend college. **Honors Programs:** The Saint Leo University Honors Program consists of an integrated sequence of six interdisciplinary courses, spread over the first three years of college, and an extensive senior honors project carried out under the supervision of a distinguished faculty mentor. Combined degree programs: BA/DDS, BA/DO 3 + DC. **Disability Services:** Special programs offered to physically disabled students, including note-taking services, reader services, tape recorders, tutors. **Career Services:** Alumni network, Alumni services, Career/job search classes, Career assessment, Internships.

FACILITIES
Housing: Coed dorms, special housing for disabled students, men's dorms, women's dorms, apartments for single students, Wellness Housing, Theme Housing, Freshmen only housing. 95% of campus accessible to physically diasbled. **Computers:** 95% of classrooms, 85% of dorms, 100% of libraries, 100% of dining areas, 100% of student union, 90% of common outdoor areas have wireless network access. Students can register for classes online. Administrative functions (other than registration) can be performed online.

CAMPUS LIFE
Environment: Rural. **Activities:** Choral groups, concert band, dance, drama/theater, literary magazine, music ensembles, musical theater, student government, student newspaper, television station, yearbook, Campus Ministries, Student Organization. 58 registered organizations, 12 honor societies, 7 religious organizations. 6 fraternities, 4 sororities. **Athletics (Intercollegiate):** *Men:* baseball, basketball, cross-country, golf, lacrosse, soccer, swimming, tennis. *Women:* basketball, cross-country, golf, soccer, softball, swimming, tennis, volleyball. **On-Campus Highlights:** Student Community Center, Student Activities Building, Marion Bowman Activities Center, Swimming Pool, Lakefront.

ADMISSIONS

Freshman Academic Profile: Average high school GPA 3.5. 10% in top 10% of high school class, 32% in top 25% of high school class, 69% in top 50% of high school class. 76% from public high schools. **Reported SAT (pre-2016 redesign) scores:** SAT Math middle 50% range 450-540. SAT Critical Reading middle 50% range 458-540. SAT Writing middle 50% range 428-530. **Concordant SAT scores:** SAT EBRW middle 50% 500–590. SAT Math middle 50% range 490–570. ACT middle 50% range 20-24. Minimum internet-based TOEFL 78. Minimum paper TOEFL 547. **Basis for Candidate Selection:** *Very important factors considered include:* rigor of secondary school record, academic GPA, standardized test scores, recommendation(s), character/personal qualities. *Important factors considered include:* interview, extracurricular activities, talent/ability, alumni/ae relation, volunteer work, level of applicant's interest. *Other factors considered include:* class rank, application essay, first generation, work experience. **Freshman Admission Requirements:** High school diploma is required and GED is accepted. *Academic units recommended:* 4 English, 3 math, 2 science, 2 foreign language, 3 social studies, 2 academic electives. **Freshman Admission Statistics:** 3,865 applied, 72.52% admitted, 24% enrolled. **Transfer Admission Requirements:** college transcript(s), essay or personal statement, statement of good standing from prior institution(s). Minimum college GPA of 2.0 required. Lowest grade transferable D. **General Admission Information:** Application fee $40. Priority deadline 1/15. Nonfall registration accepted. Admission may be deferred for a maximum of 1 year.

COSTS AND FINANCIAL AID

Annual tuition $20,760. Room and board $10,210. Required fees $370. Average book expense $1,720. **Required Forms and Deadlines:** FAFSA, State aid form. **Notification of Awards:** Applicants will be notified of awards on a rolling basis beginning 1/1. **Types of Aid:** *Need-based scholarships/grants:* Federal Pell, FSEOG, State scholarships/grants, Private scholarships, College/university scholarship or grant aid from institutional funds, United Negro College Fund. *Loans:* Direct Subsidized Stafford Loans, Direct Unsubsidized Stafford Loans, Direct PLUS loans. *Student Employment:* Federal Work-Study Program available. Institutional employment available. **Financial Aid Statistics:** 100% needy freshmen, 100% needy undergrads receive need-based scholarship or grant aid. 7% freshmen, 7% undergrads receive non-need-based scholarship or grant aid. 82% freshmen, 87% undergrads receive need-based self-help aid. 4% freshmen, 5% undergrads receive athletic scholarships. 99% freshmen, 89% undergrads receive any aid. 73% undergrads borrow to pay for school. Average cumulative indebtedness $28,456. **Criteria for awarding aid:** *Non-need-based:* Academics, Alumni affiliation, Athletics, Leadership, Minority status, Religious affiliation, State/district residency.

SAINT LOUIS UNIVERSITY

One North Grand Boulevard, Saint Louis, MO 63103
Phone: 314-977-2500 • **Financial Aid Phone:** 314-977-2350
E-mail: admission@slu.edu • **CEEB Code:** 6629
Fax: 314-977-7136 • **Website:** www.slu.edu • **ACT Code:** 2352

This private school, affiliated with the Roman Catholic Church, was founded in 1818. It has a 235-acre campus.

RATINGS

Admissions Selectivity Rating: 89   **Fire Safety Rating:** 93   **Green Rating:** 83

STUDENTS AND FACULTY

Enrollment: 7,354. **Student Body:** 59% female, 41% male, 58% out-of-state, 5% international (52 countries represented). Asian 9%, African American 6%, Caucasian 68%, Hispanic 5%, Native American <1%, Pacific Islander 0%, Two or more races 4%, Race unknown 1%. **Retention and Graduation:** 92% freshmen return for sophomore year. 66% freshmen graduate within 4 years. 77% freshmen graduate within 6 years. 38% grads go on to further study within 1 year. **Faculty:** Student/faculty ratio 9:1. 732 full-time faculty, 90% hold PhDs, 17% are are members of minority groups, 49% are women. 4% of classes are taught by teaching assistants.

ACADEMICS

Degrees: bachelor's, certificate, doctoral/professional, doctoral/research, doctoral, master's, postbachelor's certificate, post-master's certificate. **Classes:** Most classes have 10-19 students. Most lab/discussion sessions have 10-19 students. **Most popular majors:** Registered Nursing/Registered Nurse;

Biology/Biological Sciences; Business Administration and Management. **Special Study Options:** Accelerated program, cooperative education program, cross-registration, distance learning, double major, dual enrollment, English as a Second Language (ESL), honors program, independent study, internships, liberal arts/career combination, student-designed major, study abroad, teacher certification program. **Honors Programs:** The Honors Program at Saint Louis University offers eligible students the opportunity to develop an individual course of study that complements their undergraduate major, leading to an Honors degree in that discipline. Undergraduates from any of the schools and colleges at Saint Louis University can successfully pursue an honors degree through the University Honors Program. The Saint Louis University Honors Program offers interdisciplinary programs and opportunities with reflective and expressive elements to students in the Honors Program. The Honors Program offers seminar courses with integrated collaborative learning experiences including service learning, internships, and research. The Honors Program offers Honors students study abroad opportunities. The Honors Program offers Honors courses at the Saint Louis University Madrid Campus. The Honors Program offers teaching assistant positions to undergraduate Honors students. The Honors Program offers a residential learning community and several Freshman Interest Groups. The Honors Program provides academic, cultural, and social opportunities. The Honors Program provides peer mentorship programs. Combined degree programs: BA/JD, BA/MA, MHA/MBA, JD/MBA, JD/MHA, JD/PhD, JD/MS, JD/MA, JD/MPA, JD/MPH, JD/MSW, JD/MA, MD/PhD, MD/MBA, MD/MPH, MSPH/PhD, MPH/MS, MPH/MSW, MPA/MS, MPA/MSW, MSW/MAPS, MSW/MDiv, MSW/MATh, MSW/MDeac, MA/MBA, MA/PhD, MA/M. **Disability Services:** Special programs offered to physically disabled students, including note-taking services, reader services, tape recorders, tutors. **Career Services:** Alumni network, Alumni services, Career/job search classes, Career assessment, Internships, Regional alumni. Career Services offered over 5000 individual appointments with students and alumni annually, with free services for alumni.

FACILITIES

Housing: Coed dorms, special housing for disabled students, men's dorms, women's dorms, fraternity/sorority housing, apartments for married students, apartments for single students, ThemeHousingForeign Language Housing. 95% of campus accessible to physically diasbled. **Special Academic Facilities/Equipment:** Saint Louis University Museum of Art (SLUMA), McNamee Gallery of Samuel Cupples House, Museum of Contemporary Religious Art (MOCRA). **Computers:** 100% of classrooms, 100% of dorms, 100% of libraries, 100% of dining areas, 100% of student union, 100% of common outdoor areas have wireless network access. Students can register for classes online. Administrative functions (other than registration) can be performed online.

CAMPUS LIFE

Environment: Metropolis. **Activities:** Choral groups, dance, drama/theater, jazz band, literary magazine, music ensembles, musical theater, pep band, radio station, student government, student newspaper, student-run film society, television station, yearbook, Campus Ministries, Student Organization, Model UN. 170 registered organizations, 25 honor societies, 36 religious organizations. 11 fraternities, 6 sororities. **Athletics (Intercollegiate):** *Men:* baseball, basketball, cross-country, diving, soccer, swimming, tennis, track/field (outdoor), track/field (indoor). *Women:* basketball, cross-country, diving, field hockey, soccer, softball, swimming, tennis, track/field (outdoor), track/field (indoor), volleyball. **On-Campus Highlights:** St. Francis Xavier Church, Busch Student Center, St. Louis University Museum of Art, Simon Recreation Center, Robert R. Hermann Soccer Stadium, Chaifetz Arena.

ADMISSIONS

Freshman Academic Profile: Average high school GPA 3.9. 41% in top 10% of high school class, 75% in top 25% of high school class, 93% in top 50% of high school class. 53% from public high schools. **Reported SAT (pre-2016 redesign) scores:** SAT Math middle 50% range 570-670. SAT Critical Reading middle 50% range 550-660. **Concordant SAT scores:** SAT Math middle 50% range 590–700. ACT middle 50% range 24-30. Minimum internet-based TOEFL 80. Minimum paper TOEFL 550. **Basis for Candidate Selection:** *Very important factors considered include:* academic GPA, standardized test scores, application essay. *Important factors considered include:* rigor of secondary school record, interview, extracurricular activities, talent/ability, character/personal qualities. *Other factors considered include:* recommendation(s), first generation, alumni/ae relation, volunteer work, work experience, level of applicant's interest. **Freshman Admission Requirements:** High school diploma is required and GED is accepted. *Academic units required:* 4 English, 4 math, 3 science, 3 foreign language, 3 social studies, 3 academic electives. *Academic units recommended:* 4 English, 4 math, 3 science, 3 foreign language, 3 social studies, 3 academic electives. **Freshman Admission Statistics:** 12,737 applied, 64.83% admitted, 19% enrolled. **Transfer Admission Requirements:** college transcript(s), Minimum college GPA of 2.0 required. Lowest grade transferable C. **General Admission Information:** Priority deadline 12/1. Regular application deadline 8/20. Regular notification 8/20. Nonfall registration accepted. Admission may be deferred for a maximum of 1 Year.

COSTS AND FINANCIAL AID

Annual tuition $40,100. Room and board $10,640. Required fees $626. Average book expense $1,200. **Required Forms and Deadlines:** FAFSA. **Notification of Awards:** Applicants will be notified of awards on a rolling basis beginning 3/15. **Types of Aid:** *Need-based scholarships/grants:* Federal Pell, FSEOG, State scholarships/grants, Private scholarships, College/university scholarship or grant aid from institutional funds, Federal Nursing Scholarships. *Loans:* Direct Subsidized Stafford Loans, Direct Unsubsidized Stafford Loans, Direct PLUS loans, Federal Perkins Loans, Federal Nursing Loans, State Loans, College/ university loans from institutional funds. *Student Employment:* Federal Work-Study Program available. Institutional employment available. **Financial Aid Statistics:** 98% needy freshmen, 94% needy undergrads receive need-based scholarship or grant aid. 18% freshmen, 13% undergrads receive non-need-based scholarship or grant aid. 62% freshmen, 70% undergrads receive need-based self-help aid. 4% freshmen, 3% undergrads receive athletic scholarships. 97% freshmen, 89% undergrads receive any aid. 58% undergrads borrow to pay for school. Average cumulative indebtedness $33,299. **Criteria for awarding aid:** *Non-need-based:* Academics, Art, Athletics, Leadership, Music/drama, Religious affiliation.

See page 1032.

SAINT MARTIN'S UNIVERSITY

5000 Abbey Way SE, Lacey, WA 98503-7500
Phone: 360-438-4596 • **Financial Aid Phone:** 360-438-4397
E-mail: admissions@stmartin.edu • **CEEB Code:** 4674
Fax: 360-412-6189 • **Website:** www.stmartin.edu • **ACT Code:** 4474

This private school, affiliated with the Roman Catholic Church, was founded in 1895. It has a 320-acre campus.

RATINGS

Admissions Selectivity Rating: 77   **Fire Safety Rating:** 60*   **Green Rating:** 60*

STUDENTS AND FACULTY

Enrollment: 1,178. **Student Body:** 52% female, 48% male, 28% out-of-state, 4% international (14 countries represented). Asian 6%, African American 6%, Caucasian 55%, Hispanic 16%, Native American 1%, Pacific Islander 3%, Two or more races 6%, Race unknown 3%.
Retention and Graduation: 81% freshmen return for sophomore year. 41% freshmen graduate within 4 years. 49% freshmen graduate within 6 years.
Faculty: Student/faculty ratio 12:1. 81 full-time faculty, 90% hold PhDs, 19% are are members of minority groups, 47% are women. 0% of classes are taught by teaching assistants.

ACADEMICS

Degrees: bachelor's, master's, postbachelor's certificate, post-master's certificate. **Classes:** Most classes have fewer than 10 students. Most lab/discussion sessions have fewer than 10 students. **Most popular majors:** Business Administration and Management; Mechanical Engineering; Biology/Biological Sciences. **Special Study Options:** distance learning, double major, English as a Second Language (ESL), exchange student program (domestic), independent study, internships, study abroad, teacher certification program. Combined degree programs: BA/MEng. **Disability Services:** Special programs offered to physically disabled students, including note-taking services, reader services, tape recorders, tutors. **Career Services:** Alumni network, Alumni services, Career/job search classes, Career assessment, Regional alumni. We invite our local alumni to participate in any and all of our career-related workshops and career advising sessions and we have had a great turnout. The alumni have initiated an online mentor profile so that students may contact an alum with a question or ask advice. Many relationships can be formed by their participation in these two new activities.

FACILITIES

Housing: Coed dorms, special housing for disabled students, apartments for single students. 85% of campus accessible to physically diasbled. **Special Academic Facilities/Equipment:** Cap Art Gallery, Waynick Museum **Computers:** 80% of classrooms, 10% of dorms, 100% of libraries, 100% of dining areas, 100% of student union, have wireless network access. Students can register for classes online. Administrative functions (other than registration) can be performed online.

CAMPUS LIFE

Environment: Town. **Activities:** Choral groups, concert band, dance, drama/theater, jazz band, musical theater, pep band, student government, student newspaper, Campus Ministries, Student Organization, Model UN. 23 registered organizations, 3 honor societies, 3 religious organizations. **Athletics (Intercollegiate):** *Men:* baseball, basketball, cross-country, golf, track/

field (outdoor), track/field (indoor). *Women:* basketball, cross-country, golf, softball, track/field (outdoor), track/field (indoor), volleyball. **On-Campus Highlights:** O'Grady Library, Student Union Building, Recreation and Fitness Center, Baran/Burton/Spangler Halls, Abbey Church, Dining Hall renovation completed in December 2009, Spangler Residence Hall opened Fall 2005. New residence hall and new academic building opened Fall 2008. New Recreation and fitness center opened in January 2010.

ADMISSIONS

Freshman Academic Profile: Average high school GPA 3.4. 23% in top 10% of high school class, 51% in top 25% of high school class, 85% in top 50% of high school class. 95% from public high schools. **Reported SAT (pre-2016 redesign) scores:** SAT Math middle 50% range 450-580. SAT Critical Reading middle 50% range 445-570. SAT Writing middle 50% range 440-560. **Concordant SAT scores:** SAT EBRW middle 50% 500–620. SAT Math middle 50% range 490–600. ACT middle 50% range 20-25. Minimum internet-based TOEFL 54. Minimum paper TOEFL 480. **Basis for Candidate Selection:** *Very important factors considered include:* rigor of secondary school record, academic GPA. *Important factors considered include:* standardized test scores, application essay, recommendation(s), extracurricular activities, character/ personal qualities, volunteer work. *Other factors considered include:* class rank, interview, talent/ability, alumni/ae relation, work experience. **Freshman Admission Requirements:** High school diploma is required and GED is accepted. *Academic units recommended:* 4 English, 3 math, 3 science, 1 science lab, 2 foreign language, 2 social studies, 3 academic electives. **Freshman Admission Statistics:** 1,344 applied, 95.31% admitted, 19% enrolled. **Transfer Admission Requirements:** college transcript(s), essay or personal statement, Minimum college GPA of 2.25 required. Lowest grade transferable C-. **General Admission Information:** Priority deadline 11/1. Regular application deadline 7/31. Nonfall registration accepted. Admission may be deferred for a maximum of One year.

COSTS AND FINANCIAL AID

Annual tuition $35,520. Room and board $11,030. Required fees $406. Average book expense $1,000. **Required Forms and Deadlines:** FAFSA. **Notification of Awards:** Applicants will be notified of awards on a rolling basis beginning 2/15. **Types of Aid:** *Need-based scholarships/grants:* Federal Pell, FSEOG, State scholarships/grants, Private scholarships, College/university scholarship or grant aid from institutional funds. *Loans:* Direct Subsidized Stafford Loans, Direct Unsubsidized Stafford Loans, Direct PLUS loans, Federal Perkins Loans, State Loans. *Student Employment:* Federal Work-Study Program available. Institutional employment available. **Financial Aid Statistics:** 99% needy freshmen, 99% needy undergrads receive need-based scholarship or grant aid. 26% freshmen, 19% undergrads receive non-need-based scholarship or grant aid. 58% freshmen, 69% undergrads receive need-based self-help aid. 17% freshmen, 9% undergrads receive athletic scholarships. 78% undergrads borrow to pay for school. Average cumulative indebtedness $27,807. **Criteria for awarding aid:** *Need-based:* Academics, Alumni affiliation, Art, Leadership, Minority status, Music/drama, Religious affiliation. *Non-need-based:* Academics, Alumni affiliation, Art, Athletics, Leadership, Minority status, Music/drama, Religious affiliation, State/district residency.

SAINT MARY-OF-THE-WOODS COLLEGE

Office of Admission, Saint Mary-of-the-Woods, IN 47876-0068
Phone: 812-535-5106 • **Financial Aid Phone:** 812-535-5100
E-mail: smwcadms@smwc.edu • **CEEB Code:** 1704
Fax: 812-535-5010 • **Website:** www.smwc.edu • **ACT Code:** 1242

This private school, affiliated with the Roman Catholic Church, was founded in 1840. It has a 67-acre campus.

RATINGS

Admissions Selectivity Rating: 73   **Fire Safety Rating:** 99   **Green Rating:** 60*

STUDENTS AND FACULTY

Student Body: 97% female, 3% male, 30% out-of-state, (5 countries represented).
Retention and Graduation: 77% freshmen return for sophomore year. 35% freshmen graduate within 4 years. 42% freshmen graduate within 6 years. 18% grads go on to further study within 1 year. 15% grads pursue arts and sciences degrees. 1% grads pursue law degrees. 1% grads pursue business degrees. 1% grads pursue medical degrees. **Faculty:** Student/faculty ratio 8:1. 67 full-time faculty, 54% hold PhDs, 6% are are members of minority groups, 66% are women. 0% of classes are taught by teaching assistants.

ACADEMICS

Degrees: associate, bachelor's, certificate, master's, postbachelor's certificate, post-master's certificate, transfer. **Classes:** Most classes have fewer than 10 students. **Most popular majors:** Elementary Education and Teaching; Biology/Biological Sciences; Equestrian/Equine Studies. **Special Study Options:** Accelerated program, cross-registration, distance learning, double major, external degree program, honors program, independent study, internships, student-designed major, study abroad, teacher certification program. **Disability Services:** Special programs offered to physically disabled students, including tutors. **Career Services:** Alumni network, Alumni services, Career/job search classes, Career assessment, Internships, Regional alumni, On-campus interviews. Experiential Learning: Externship, Supplemental Learning Experience, and Internship programs.

FACILITIES

Housing: special housing for disabled students, women's dorms. 100% of campus accessible to physically disabled. **Special Academic Facilities/Equipment:** Cecilian Auditorium and Conservatory of Music SMWC Art Gallery **Computers:** 100% of classrooms, 100% of dorms, 100% of libraries, 20% of dining areas, 15% of common outdoor areas have wireless network access. Students can register for classes online. Administrative functions (other than registration) can be performed online.

CAMPUS LIFE

Environment: Town. **Activities:** Choral groups, concert band, dance, drama/theater, jazz band, literary magazine, music ensembles, musical theater, student government, student newspaper, yearbook, Campus Ministries, Student Organization. 30 registered organizations, 6 honor societies, 1 religious organization. **Athletics (Intercollegiate):** *Women:* basketball, equestrian sports, golf, soccer, softball, track/field (outdoor). **On-Campus Highlights:** Le Fer Hall (residence hall), Mari Hulman George School of Equine Studies, Softball/Soccer Fields, Cecilian Auditorium, Church of the Immaculate Conception, Saint Mary-of-the-Woods College is a 67-acre wooded campus located five miles northwest of Terre Haute, Indiana. The peaceful and beautiful campus features a fitness trail, lake and stables amid the stately academic buildings. Besides the College, Saint Mary-of-the-Woods is common ground for the Sisters of Providence, Woods Day Care/Pre-School, Providence Center and the White Violet Center for Eco-Justice. **Environmental Initiatives:** Recycling.

ADMISSIONS

Freshman Academic Profile: Average high school GPA 3.3. 85% from public high schools. **Reported SAT (pre-2016 redesign) scores:** SAT Math middle 50% range 410-520. SAT Critical Reading middle 50% range 430-540. SAT Writing middle 50% range 410-550. **Concordant SAT scores:** SAT EBRW middle 50% 470–600. SAT Math middle 50% range 450–550. ACT middle 50% range 18-25. Minimum internet-based TOEFL 62. Minimum paper TOEFL 500. **Basis for Candidate Selection:** *Important factors considered include:* rigor of secondary school record, class rank, academic GPA, standardized test scores, application essay, recommendation(s). *Other factors considered include:* interview, talent/ability, character/personal qualities, level of applicant's interest. **Freshman Admission Requirements:** High school diploma is required and GED is accepted. *Academic units required:* 8 English, 6 math, 6 science, 2 science labs, 4 foreign language, 4 social studies, 2 history, 10 academic electives. *Academic units recommended:* 8 English, 8 math, 8 science, 4 science labs, 6 foreign language, 6 social studies, 4 history, 7 academic electives. **Freshman Admission Statistics:** 268 applied, 77.61% admitted, 62% enrolled. **Transfer Admission Requirements:** college transcript(s), essay or personal statement, Minimum college GPA of 2.0 required. Lowest grade transferable C. **General Admission Information:** Application fee $30. Regular application deadline 8/8. Nonfall registration accepted. Admission may be deferred for a maximum of 1 year.

COSTS AND FINANCIAL AID

Annual tuition $20,900. Room and board $7,890. Required fees $650. Average book expense $900. **Required Forms and Deadlines:** FAFSA. **Notification of Awards:** Applicants will be notified of awards on a rolling basis beginning 12/1. **Types of Aid:** *Need-based scholarships/grants:* Federal Pell, FSEOG, State scholarships/grants, Private scholarships, College/university scholarship or grant aid from institutional funds. *Loans:* Federal Perkins Loans. *Student Employment:* Federal Work-Study Program available. Institutional employment available. **Financial Aid Statistics:** 77% needy freshmen, 92% needy undergrads receive need-based scholarship or grant aid. 76% freshmen, 12% undergrads receive non-need-based scholarship or grant aid. 49% freshmen, 83% undergrads receive need-based self-help aid. 10% freshmen, 4% undergrads receive athletic scholarships. 98% freshmen, 96% undergrads receive any aid. **Criteria for awarding aid:** *Need-based:* Academics, Alumni affiliation, Art, Athletics, Leadership, Music/drama. *Non-need-based:* Academics, Alumni affiliation, Art, Athletics, Leadership, Music/drama.

SAINT MARY'S COLLEGE (CA)

1928 St. Mary's Rd, PMB 4800, Moraga, CA 94575-4800
Phone: 925-631-4224 • **Financial Aid Phone:** 925-631-4370
E-mail: smcadmit@stmarys-ca.edu • **CEEB Code:** 4675
Fax: 925-376-7193 • **Website:** www.stmarys-ca.edu • **ACT Code:** 386

This private school, affiliated with the Roman Catholic Church, was founded in 1863. It has a 420-acre campus.

RATINGS
Admissions Selectivity Rating: 82   **Fire Safety Rating:** 92   **Green Rating:** 91

STUDENTS AND FACULTY
Enrollment: 2,916. **Student Body:** 60% female, 40% male, 11% out-of-state, 2% international (20 countries represented). Asian 10%, African American 4%, Caucasian 46%, Hispanic 25%, Native American <1%, Pacific Islander 1%, Two or more races 7%, Race unknown 4%.
Retention and Graduation: 88% freshmen return for sophomore year. 70% freshmen graduate within 4 years. 71% freshmen graduate within 6 years. 27% grads go on to further study within 1 year. **Faculty:** Student/faculty ratio 11:1. 219 full-time faculty, 0% hold PhDs, 10% are are members of minority groups, 53% are women. 0% of classes are taught by teaching assistants.

ACADEMICS
Degrees: bachelor's, doctoral/professional, master's. **Classes:** Most classes have 20-29 students. **Most popular majors:** Business Administration, Management and Operations; Psychology; Communication and Media Studies. **Special Study Options:** double major, exchange student program (domestic), independent study, student-designed major, study abroad. **Disability Services:** Special programs offered to physically disabled students, including note-taking services, reader services, tape recorders, tutors. **Career Services:** Alumni network, Alumni services, Career/job search classes, Career assessment, Internships. Career Information Night Series plus our Career and Internship Fair.

FACILITIES
Housing: Coed dorms, special housing for disabled students, Theme Housing. 90% of campus accessible to physically disabled. **Special Academic Facilities/Equipment:** Hearst Art gallery Brousseau Hall, Science Building Geissberger Observatory **Computers:** 100% of classrooms, 100% of libraries, 100% of dining areas, 100% of student union, 70% of common outdoor areas have wireless network access. Students can register for classes online. Administrative functions (other than registration) can be performed online.

CAMPUS LIFE
Environment: Village. **Activities:** Choral groups, dance, drama/theater, jazz band, music ensembles, musical theater, pep band, radio station, student government, student newspaper, Campus Ministries, Student Organization. 56 registered organizations, 3 religious organizations. **Athletics (Intercollegiate):** *Men:* baseball, basketball, cheerleading, cross-country, golf, soccer, tennis. *Women:* basketball, cheerleading, crew/rowing, cross-country, lacrosse, soccer, softball, tennis, volleyball. **On-Campus Highlights:** Br. Alfred Brousseau Hall, Cassin Student Union and LeFevre Quad, College Chapel, Hearst Art Gallery, Oliver Dining Hall, Power Plant (exercise facility) McKeon Pavilion, "St. Patty's Cathedral." **Environmental Initiatives:** 2007 Summer reading program for incoming students focuses on global warming.

ADMISSIONS
Freshman Academic Profile: Average high school GPA 3.6. 61% from public high schools. **Reported SAT (pre-2016 redesign) scores:** SAT Math middle 50% range 530-630. SAT Critical Reading middle 50% range 510-620. **Concordant SAT scores:** SAT Math middle 50% range 560–650. ACT middle 50% range 22-27. Minimum internet-based TOEFL 79. Minimum paper TOEFL 550. **Basis for Candidate Selection:** *Very important factors considered include:* rigor of secondary school record, academic GPA. *Important factors considered include:* standardized test scores, application essay, recommendation(s), first generation, racial/ethnic status. *Other factors considered include:* interview, extracurricular activities, talent/ability, character/personal qualities, alumni/ae relation, geographical residence, religious affiliation/commitment, volunteer work, work experience, level of applicant's interest. **Freshman Admission Requirements:** High school diploma is required and GED is accepted. *Academic units required:* 4 English, 3 math, 2 science, 1 science lab, 2 foreign language, 1 social studies, 1 history, 2 academic electives. *Academic units recommended:* 4 English, 4 math, 3 science, 1 science lab, 3 foreign language, 1 social studies, 1 history, 2 academic

electives. **Freshman Admission Statistics:** 4,852 applied, 75.87% admitted, 18% enrolled. **Transfer Admission Requirements:** High school transcript, college transcript(s), essay or personal statement, Minimum college GPA of 2.3 required. Lowest grade transferable C-. **General Admission Information:** Application fee $55. Priority deadline 11/15. Regular application deadline 2/1. Regular notification 3/15. Nonfall registration accepted. Admission may be deferred for a maximum of 12 months.

COSTS AND FINANCIAL AID

Annual tuition $44,210. Room and board $14,880. Required fees $150. Average book expense $1,107. **Required Forms and Deadlines:** FAFSA. **Notification of Awards:** Applicants will be notified of awards on a rolling basis beginning 2/1. **Types of Aid:** *Need-based scholarships/grants:* Federal Pell, FSEOG, State scholarships/grants, Private scholarships, College/university scholarship or grant aid from institutional funds. *Loans:* Direct Subsidized Stafford Loans, Direct Unsubsidized Stafford Loans, Direct PLUS loans, Federal Perkins Loans. *Student Employment:* Federal Work-Study Program available. Institutional employment available. **Financial Aid Statistics:** 100% needy freshmen, 98% needy undergrads receive need-based scholarship or grant aid. 34% freshmen, 25% undergrads receive non-need-based scholarship or grant aid. 88% freshmen, 83% undergrads receive need-based self-help aid. 3% freshmen, 4% undergrads receive athletic scholarships. 77% freshmen, 74% undergrads receive any aid. 77% undergrads borrow to pay for school. Average cumulative indebtedness $31,203. **Criteria for awarding aid:** *Need-based:* Alumni affiliation, Minority status. *Non-need-based:* Academics, Athletics, Leadership, Music/drama, Religious affiliation.

SAINT MARY'S COLLEGE (IN)

Admission office, Notre Dame, IN 46556
Phone: 574-284-4587 • **Financial Aid Phone:** 574-284-4557
E-mail: admission@saintmarys.edu • **CEEB Code:** 1702
Fax: 574-284-4841 • **Website:** www.saintmarys.edu • **ACT Code:** 1244

This private school, affiliated with the Roman Catholic Church, was founded in 1844. It has a 275-acre campus.

RATINGS

Admissions Selectivity Rating: 83   Fire Safety Rating: 90   Green Rating: 73

STUDENTS AND FACULTY

Enrollment: 1,576. **Student Body:** 100% female, 0% male, 73% out-of-state, 2% international (16 countries represented). Asian 2%, African American 2%, Caucasian 77%, Hispanic 11%, Native American <1%, Pacific Islander <1%, Two or more races 3%, Race unknown 3%.
Retention and Graduation: 86% freshmen return for sophomore year. 71% freshmen graduate within 4 years. 77% freshmen graduate within 6 years. 33% grads go on to further study within 1 year. 4% grads pursue arts and sciences degrees. 2% grads pursue law degrees. 1% grads pursue business degrees. 2% grads pursue medical degrees. **Faculty:** Student/faculty ratio 10:1. 140 full-time faculty, 83% hold PhDs, 13% are are members of minority groups, 69% are women. 0% of classes are taught by teaching assistants.

ACADEMICS

Degrees: bachelor's, doctoral/professional, master's. **Classes:** Most classes have 20-29 students. Most lab/discussion sessions have 10-19 students. **Most popular majors:** Biology/Biological Sciences; Business Administration and Management; Registered Nursing/Registered Nurse. **Special Study Options:** Accelerated program, cross-registration, double major, exchange student program (domestic), independent study, internships, liberal arts/ career combination, student-designed major, study abroad, teacher certification program. **Disability Services:** Special programs offered to physically disabled students, including note-taking services, reader services, tape recorders, tutors. **Career Services:** Alumni network, Alumni services, Career/job search classes, Career assessment, Internships, Regional alumni.

FACILITIES

Housing: special housing for disabled students, women's dorms, apartments for single students, Intercultural Living Floor. 100% of campus accessible to physically diasbled. **Special Academic Facilities/Equipment:** Art gallery, early childhood development center, language lab, electron microscope. **Computers:** 80% of classrooms, 60% of dorms, 100% of libraries, 100% of dining areas, 100% of student union, have wireless network access. Students can register for classes online. Administrative functions (other than registration) can be performed online.

CAMPUS LIFE

Environment: City. **Activities:** Choral groups, dance, drama/theater, jazz band, literary magazine, marching band, music ensembles, musical theater,

opera, pep band, radio station, student government, student newspaper, television station, yearbook, Campus Ministries, Student Organization. 78 registered organizations, 14 honor societies, 8 religious organizations. **Athletics (Intercollegiate):** *Women:* basketball, cross-country, diving, golf, soccer, softball, swimming, tennis, volleyball. **On-Campus Highlights:** Student Center/Noble Family Dining hall, Dalloway's Coffee House, Angela Athletic Facility, Spes Unica, Moreau Center for the Arts / O'Laughlin. **Environmental Initiatives:** Campus Recycling Program.

ADMISSIONS

Freshman Academic Profile: Average high school GPA 3.7. 18% in top 10% of high school class, 54% in top 25% of high school class, 89% in top 50% of high school class. 55% from public high schools. **Reported SAT (pre-2016 redesign) scores:** SAT Math middle 50% range 480-570. SAT Critical Reading middle 50% range 500-590. SAT Writing middle 50% range 490-600. **Concordant SAT scores:** SAT EBRW middle 50% 550–650. SAT Math middle 50% range 510–590. ACT middle 50% range 22-28. Minimum internet-based TOEFL 80. Minimum paper TOEFL 550. **Basis for Candidate Selection:** *Important factors considered include:* rigor of secondary school record, academic GPA, standardized test scores. *Other factors considered include:* class rank, application essay, recommendation(s), interview, extracurricular activities, talent/ability, character/personal qualities, first generation, alumni/ae relation, geographical residence, state residency, racial/ethnic status, volunteer work, work experience. **Freshman Admission Requirements:** High school diploma is required and GED is accepted. *Academic units required:* 4 English, 3 math, 2 science, 2 science labs, 2 foreign language, 3 history. *Academic units recommended:* 4 English, 4 math, 4 science, 2 science labs, 4 foreign language, 2 social studies. **Freshman Admission Statistics:** 1,771 applied, 81.65% admitted, 30% enrolled. **Transfer Admission Requirements:** High school transcript, college transcript(s), essay or personal statement, standardized test scores, statement of good standing from prior institution(s). Minimum college GPA of 3.0 required. Lowest grade transferable C. **General Admission Information:** Priority deadline 2/15. Nonfall registration accepted. Admission may be deferred for a maximum of 2 years.

COSTS AND FINANCIAL AID

Annual tuition $39,980. Room and board $12,100. Required fees $820. Average book expense $1,000. **Required Forms and Deadlines:** FAFSA. **Types of Aid:** *Need-based scholarships/grants:* Federal Pell, FSEOG, State scholarships/grants, Private scholarships, College/university scholarship or grant aid from institutional funds. *Loans:* Direct Subsidized Stafford Loans, Direct Unsubsidized Stafford Loans, Direct PLUS loans, Federal Perkins Loans. *Student Employment:* Federal Work-Study Program available. Institutional employment available. **Financial Aid Statistics:** 99% needy freshmen, 100% needy undergrads receive need-based scholarship or grant aid. 95% freshmen, 92% undergrads receive non-need-based scholarship or grant aid. 77% freshmen, 76% undergrads receive need-based self-help aid. 0% freshmen, 0% undergrads receive athletic scholarships. 99% freshmen, 98% undergrads receive any aid. 68% undergrads borrow to pay for school. Average cumulative indebtedness $31,036. **Criteria for awarding aid:** *Need-based:* Academics. *Non-need-based:* Academics, Art, Music/drama.

SAINT MARY'S UNIVERSITY OF MINNESOTA

700 Terrace Heights #2, Winona, MN 55987-1399
Phone: 507-457-1700 • **Financial Aid Phone:** 507-457-1438
E-mail: admission@smumn.edu • **CEEB Code:** 6632
Fax: 507-457-1722 • **Website:** www.smumn.edu • **ACT Code:** 2148

This private school, affiliated with the Roman Catholic Church, was founded in 1912. It has a 400-acre campus.

RATINGS

Admissions Selectivity Rating: 77   Fire Safety Rating: 94   Green Rating: 60*

STUDENTS AND FACULTY

Enrollment: 1,552. **Student Body:** 54% female, 46% male, 29% out-of-state, 3% international (38 countries represented). Asian 2%, African American 6%, Caucasian 58%, Hispanic 5%, Native American <1%, Pacific Islander <1%, Two or more races 1%, Race unknown 24%.
Retention and Graduation: 70% freshmen return for sophomore year. 51% freshmen graduate within 4 years. 61% freshmen graduate within 6 years. 15% grads go on to further study within 1 year. 2% grads pursue arts and sciences degrees. 1% grads pursue law degrees. 1% grads pursue business degrees. 4% grads pursue medical degrees. **Faculty:** Student/faculty ratio 20:1. 99 full-time faculty, 91% hold PhDs, 6% are are members of minority groups, 39% are women. 0% of classes are taught by teaching assistants.

ACADEMICS

Degrees: bachelor's, certificate, diploma, doctoral/professional, doctoral/research, doctoral, master's, postbachelor's certificate, post-master's certificate. **Classes:** Most classes have 20-29 students. Most lab/discussion sessions have 10-19 students. **Most popular majors:** Marketing/Marketing Management; Biology/Biological Sciences; Elementary Education and Teaching. **Special Study Options:** cooperative education program, cross-registration, double major, dual enrollment, English as a Second Language (ESL), honors program, independent study, internships, student-designed major, study abroad, teacher certification program. **Honors Programs:** The Lasallian Honors Program at Saint Mary's University is a general education program for motivated students who wish to engage in "shared inquiry" in small seminar classes. The hallmarks of the program are study of the Great Books, service learning, and participation in a community of learners who desire to grow intellectually and spiritually, together over four years. Great Books, Shared-Inquiry Seminars The Lasallian Honors Program is an interdisciplinary program of learning in the Great Books and other notable texts of Western and Eastern traditions. All of the courses are shared-inquiry seminars: the students and the professor discuss the works together in lively, interactive, and informed conversations about the most important ideas in human history. Working Smarter Honors courses do not necessarily require more work than other general education courses. What differs is the style of learning, in student-centered seminars. You have the opportunity to participate with other motivated students in small classes taught by professors committed to engaged learning and individualized attention. Streamlined General Education A practical advantage of the Honors program is that it streamlines course requirements. Because of our interdisciplinary 4-credit model, honors students take fewer general education courses. That leaves room for a second major, extracurricular activities, an internship, and/or studying abroad. Future Benefits Participation in the Lasallian Honors Program also has rewards after graduation. When it comes time to compete for a job, internship, or acceptance to graduate school, Honors students have a clear advantage. We have an enviable record (98%) of placing our students in some of the best graduate programs in the country. Personal Growth The most important reason to join the Lasallian Honors Program is the desire to extend yourself intellectually, spiritually, and creatively. We can help you do that in a supportive and challenging academic atmosphere. You will be part of a cohort group that shares your talents and interests—and likely will become your closest college friends. **Disability Services:** Special programs offered to physically disabled students, including note-taking services, reader services, tape recorders, tutors. **Career Services:** Alumni network, Alumni services, Career/job search classes, Career assessment, Internships. The Mayo Innovation Scholars Program offers an opportunity for selected undergraduate science and business students to research projects submitted by Mayo Clinic professionals through the Mayo Clinic Office of Intellectual Property. The Washington Center Internship Program combines real-world work experience with academic learning in a unique environment that fosters success and achievement. For one semester, students can work and earn college credits in their chosen academic field in the heart of the nation's capitol, Washington, D.C. Internships can be arranged in government agencies or in private non-profit organizations and are available for all majors.

FACILITIES

Housing: Coed dorms, special housing for disabled students, men's dorms, women's dorms, apartments for single students. 93% of campus accessible to physically diasbled. **Special Academic Facilities/Equipment:** Art gallery, performance center, laboratories, observatory. **Computers:** 100% of dorms, 100% of libraries, 100% of dining areas, 100% of student union, have wireless network access. Students can register for classes online. Administrative functions (other than registration) can be performed online.

CAMPUS LIFE

Environment: Town. **Activities:** Choral groups, concert band, dance, drama/theater, jazz band, literary magazine, music ensembles, musical theater, radio station, student government, student newspaper, yearbook, Campus Ministries, Student Organization. 80 registered organizations, 13 honor societies, 6 religious organizations. **Athletics (Intercollegiate):** *Men:* baseball, basketball, cross-country, diving, golf, ice hockey, skiing (nordic/cross-country), soccer, swimming, tennis, track/field (outdoor), track/field (indoor). *Women:* basketball, cross-country, diving, golf, ice hockey, skiing (nordic/cross-country), soccer, softball, swimming, tennis, track/field (outdoor), track/field (indoor), volleyball. **On-Campus Highlights:** Lillian Hogan Davis Galleries, Gostomski Fieldhouse, Page Theatre, Toner Student Center, Outdoor Track and Field Complex, Saint Mary's also offers an 18 hole disc golf course which runs through the bluffs surrounding the campus. Also, a network of trails run along the bluffs and into wooded valleys allowing for hiking, running, walking, and cross country skiing. **Environmental Initiatives:** ISO 14001 Certified Environmental Management System (EMS)

ADMISSIONS

Freshman Academic Profile: Average high school GPA 3.3. 8% in top 10% of high school class, 38% in top 25% of high school class, 70% in top 50% of high school class. 65% from public high schools. **Reported SAT (pre-**

2016 redesign) scores: SAT Math middle 50% range 440-570. SAT Critical Reading middle 50% range 460-540. SAT Writing middle 50% range 430-520. **Concordant SAT scores:** SAT EBRW middle 50% 500-590. SAT Math middle 50% range 480-590. ACT middle 50% range 20-26. Minimum internet-based TOEFL 79. Minimum paper TOEFL 520. **Basis for Candidate Selection:** *Very important factors considered include:* rigor of secondary school record, academic GPA, standardized test scores. *Important factors considered include:* interview, talent/ability, character/personal qualities. *Other factors considered include:* class rank, application essay, recommendation(s), extracurricular activities, alumni/ae relation, volunteer work, level of applicant's interest. **Freshman Admission Requirements:** High school diploma is required and GED is accepted. *Academic units required:* 4 English, 3 math, 3 science, 2 science labs, 2 social studies, 6 academic electives. *Academic units recommended:* 2 foreign language. **Freshman Admission Statistics:** 1,686 applied, 79.24% admitted, 21% enrolled. **Transfer Admission Requirements:** High school transcript, college transcript(s), statement of good standing from prior institution(s). Minimum college GPA of 2.0 required. Lowest grade transferable C. **General Admission Information:** Application fee $25. Priority deadline 4/1. Regular application deadline 5/1. Regular notification 5/1. Nonfall registration accepted. Admission may be deferred for a maximum of 1 year.

COSTS AND FINANCIAL AID

Annual tuition $33,020. Room and board $8,880. Required fees $540. Average book expense $1,300. **Required Forms and Deadlines:** FAFSA. **Notification of Awards:** Applicants will be notified of awards on a rolling basis beginning 2/1. **Types of Aid:** *Need-based scholarships/grants:* Federal Pell, FSEOG, State scholarships/grants, College/university scholarship or grant aid from institutional funds. *Loans:* Direct Subsidized Stafford Loans, Direct Unsubsidized Stafford Loans, Direct PLUS loans, Federal Perkins Loans, State Loans. *Student Employment:* Federal Work-Study Program available. Institutional employment available. **Financial Aid Statistics:** 100% needy freshmen, 97% needy undergrads receive need-based scholarship or grant aid. 0% undergrads receive non-need-based scholarship or grant aid. 73% freshmen, 77% undergrads receive need-based self-help aid. 0% freshmen, 0% undergrads receive athletic scholarships. 98% freshmen, 96% undergrads receive any aid. 80% undergrads borrow to pay for school. Average cumulative indebtedness $39,196. **Criteria for awarding aid:** *Need-based:* Academics. *Non-need-based:* Academics, Alumni affiliation, Art, Leadership, Music/drama.

SAINT MICHAEL'S COLLEGE

One Winooski Park, Box 7, Colchester, VT 5439
Phone: 802-654-3000 • **Financial Aid Phone:** 802-654-3243
E-mail: admission@smcvt.edu • **CEEB Code:** 3757
Fax: 802-654-2906 • **Website:** www.smcvt.edu • **ACT Code:** 4312

This private school, affiliated with the Roman Catholic Church, was founded in 1904. It has a 440-acre campus.

RATINGS

Admissions Selectivity Rating: 84   **Fire Safety Rating:** 89   **Green Rating:** 96

STUDENTS AND FACULTY

Enrollment: 1,863. **Student Body:** 56% female, 44% male, 84% out-of-state, 4% international (36 countries represented). Asian 2%, African American 2%, Caucasian 85%, Hispanic 4%, Native American <1%, Pacific Islander <1%, Two or more races 2%, Race unknown 1%.
Retention and Graduation: 89% freshmen return for sophomore year. 73% freshmen graduate within 4 years. 79% freshmen graduate within 6 years. 12% grads go on to further study within 1 year. 7% grads pursue arts and sciences degrees. 1% grads pursue law degrees. 1% grads pursue business degrees. 1% grads pursue medical degrees. **Faculty:** Student/faculty ratio 11:1. 148 full-time faculty, 91% hold PhDs, 7% are are members of minority groups, 45% are women. 0% of classes are taught by teaching assistants.

ACADEMICS

Degrees: bachelor's, master's, postbachelor's certificate, post-master's certificate. **Classes:** Most classes have 10-19 students. Most lab/discussion sessions have 10-19 students. **Most popular majors:** Business/Commerce; Biology/Biological Sciences; Psychology. **Special Study Options:** cross-registration, distance learning, double major, dual enrollment, English as a Second Language (ESL), honors program, independent study, internships, liberal arts/career combination, student-designed major, study abroad, teacher certification program, Research for Academic Credit: Many majors require students to complete the equivalent of a senior thesis (sometimes called a Senior Seminar) for which they receive academic credit. Students work closely with an academic advisor on these capstone projects. Independent Research with **Faculty:** Independent research projects with faculty members–which are not-for-credit–often lead to peer-reviewed publications and presentations at major conferences. These projects are an exciting opportunity for students and faculty to work side-by-side, making important discoveries in their fields. For students, these opportunities not only provide excellent resume-building experience, but also the chance to work closely with a mentor. Some students may even qualify for grant-funded research stipends. **Honors Programs:** The Honors Program at Saint Michael's provides additional challenges and opportunities to outstanding students through small group discussion, research and extra-curricular activities. Saint Michael's also has chapters of several national honors societies on campus including Phi Beta Kappa, and Delta Epsilon Sigma. Combined degree programs: BA/JD, BA/MA, 4+1 MBA w/Clarkson, (B.S., + D.Pharm.) with Albany College of Pharmacy. **Disability Services:** Special programs offered to physically disabled students, including note-taking services, reader services, tape recorders, tutors. **Career Services:** Alumni network, Alumni services, Career/job search classes, Career assessment, Internships, Regional alumni. Our Internship Program gives students the opportunity to integrate their academic studies with a supervised work experience. Internships enhance classroom learning by integrating academics with the world of work. This on-the-job experience assists students in their career decision-making process. Internships provide valuable work experiences that increase job opportunities after graduation. Through this process students learn valuable job search and career-defining skills.

FACILITIES

Housing: Coed dorms, special housing for disabled students, men's dorms, special housing for international students, women's dorms, apartments for single students, Theme **Housing:** 1. Honors Housing, 2. Substance Free Housing. 75% of campus accessible to physically diasbled. **Special Academic Facilities/Equipment:** Holcomb Observatory, McCarthy Arts Center Gallary. **Computers:** 90% of classrooms, 100% of dorms, 100% of libraries, 100% of dining areas, 100% of student union, have wireless network access. Students can register for classes online. Administrative functions (other than registration) can be performed online.

CAMPUS LIFE

Environment: City. **Activities:** Choral groups, concert band, dance, drama/ theater, jazz band, literary magazine, music ensembles, musical theater, radio station, student government, student newspaper, yearbook, Campus Ministries, Student Organization. 50 registered organizations, 11 honor societies, 1 religious organization. **Athletics (Intercollegiate):** *Men:* baseball, basketball, cross-country, diving, golf, ice hockey, lacrosse, skiing (downhill/alpine), skiing (nordic/cross-country), soccer, swimming, tennis. *Women:* basketball, cross-country, diving, field hockey, ice hockey, lacrosse, skiing (downhill/alpine), skiing (nordic/cross-country), soccer, softball, swimming, tennis, volleyball. **On-Campus Highlights:** Alliot Student Center, McCarthy Arts Center, Chapel of Saint Michael the Archangel, Vincent C. Ross Sports Center, Tarrant Student Recreational Center. **Environmental Initiatives:** Energy Efficiency Programs: "Three Degree Challenge" to further reduce campus wide building temperatures by turning down thermostats to reduce energy consumption (in addition to reducing energy consumption, all new major appliances must be energy star certified); new building aims for LEED certification; all campus buildings on an Energy Management System to ensure efficient use of energy;

ADMISSIONS

Freshman Academic Profile: Average high school GPA 3.2. 26% in top 10% of high school class, 49% in top 25% of high school class, 75% in top 50% of high school class. 70% from public high schools. **Reported SAT (pre-2016 redesign) scores:** SAT Math middle 50% range 540-630. SAT Critical Reading middle 50% range 560-640. SAT Writing middle 50% range 530-630. **Concordant SAT scores:** SAT EBRW middle 50% 600–680. SAT Math middle 50% range 570–650. ACT middle 50% range 24-29. Minimum paper TOEFL 550. **Basis for Candidate Selection:** *Very important factors considered include:* rigor of secondary school record, class rank, academic GPA. *Important factors considered include:* standardized test scores, application essay, recommendation(s), talent/ability, character/personal qualities. *Other factors considered include:* interview, extracurricular activities, first generation, alumni/ae relation, geographical residence, state residency, racial/ethnic status, volunteer work, work experience, level of applicant's interest. **Freshman Admission Requirements:** High school diploma is required and GED is accepted. *Academic units required:* 4 English, 4 math, 3 science, 2 science labs, 2 foreign language, 3 social studies, 3 history. *Academic units recommended:* 4 English, 4 math, 4 science, 3 science labs, 4 foreign language, 4 social studies, 4 history. **Freshman Admission Statistics:** 5,013 applied, 77.00% admitted, 12% enrolled. **Transfer Admission Requirements:** High school transcript, college transcript(s), essay or personal statement, standardized test scores, Minimum college GPA of 2.8 required. Lowest grade transferable C-. **General**

Admission Information: Application fee $50. Priority deadline 11/1. Regular application deadline 2/1. Regular notification 4/1. Nonfall registration accepted. Admission may be deferred for a maximum of 1 year.

COSTS AND FINANCIAL AID

Annual tuition $41,650. Room and board $11,300. Required fees $325. Average book expense $1,280. **Required Forms and Deadlines:** FAFSA, State aid form. **Notification of Awards:** Applicants will be notified of awards on a rolling basis beginning 3/21. *Types of Aid: Need-based scholarships/ grants:* Federal Pell, FSEOG, State scholarships/grants, Private scholarships, College/university scholarship or grant aid from institutional funds. *Loans:* Direct Subsidized Stafford Loans, Direct Unsubsidized Stafford Loans, Direct PLUS loans. *Student Employment:* Federal Work-Study Program available. Institutional employment available. **Financial Aid Statistics:** 100% needy freshmen, 99% needy undergrads receive need-based scholarship or grant aid. 26% freshmen, 20% undergrads receive non-need-based scholarship or grant aid. 70% freshmen, 77% undergrads receive need-based self-help aid. 1% freshmen, 1% undergrads receive athletic scholarships. 99% freshmen, 98% undergrads receive any aid. 72% undergrads borrow to pay for school. Average cumulative indebtedness $38,226. **Criteria for awarding aid:** *Non-need-based:* Academics, Art, Athletics, Music/drama.

SAINT PETER'S UNIVERSITY

2641 Kennedy Boulevard, Jersey City, NJ 7306
Phone: 201-761-7100 • **Financial Aid Phone:** 201-761-6071
E-mail: admissions@saintpeters.edu • **CEEB Code:** 2806
Fax: 201-761-7105 • **Website:** www.saintpeters.edu • **ACT Code:** 2604

This private school, affiliated with the Roman Catholic Church, was founded in 1872. It has a 10-acre campus.

RATINGS

Admissions Selectivity Rating: 73   Fire Safety Rating: 60*   Green Rating: 86

STUDENTS AND FACULTY

Enrollment: 2,424. **Student Body:** 61% female, 39% male, 11% out-of-state, 2% international (56 countries represented). Asian 7%, African American 25%, Caucasian 18%, Hispanic 37%, Native American 1%, Pacific Islander 1%, Two or more races 2%, Race unknown 8%.
Retention and Graduation: 82% freshmen return for sophomore year. 37% freshmen graduate within 4 years. 55% freshmen graduate within 6 years. 27% grads go on to further study within 1 year. 9% grads pursue arts and sciences degrees. 5% grads pursue law degrees. 6% grads pursue business degrees. 7% grads pursue medical degrees. **Faculty:** Student/faculty ratio 13:1. 113 full-time faculty, 85% hold PhDs, 15% are are members of minority groups, 47% are women. 0% of classes are taught by teaching assistants.

ACADEMICS

Degrees: associate, bachelor's, certificate, doctoral/professional, master's, postbachelor's certificate, post-master's certificate. **Classes:** Most classes have 10-19 students. **Most popular majors:** Business Administration and Management; Biology/Biological Sciences; Registered Nursing/Registered Nurse. **Special Study Options:** Accelerated program, cooperative education program, double major, dual enrollment, exchange student program (domestic), honors program, independent study, internships, liberal arts/career combination, student-designed major, study abroad, teacher certification program, weekend college, Joint degree in clinical and laboratory sciences with the University of Medicine and Dentistry of New Jersey (UMDNJ); Joint degree in Pharmacy with Rutgers University. **Honors Programs:** While Honors provides academic enrichment for highly motivated students, it is not a formal major or minor. Students enrolled in the program must complete a minimum of 30 credits designated as Honors courses, which include Honors core course seminars, Honors advanced electives, and 6 credits of Honors Thesis: research and independent study. Independent study projects must be approved by the Honors Program and the respective chairs of the student's major department. Independent study projects may carry departmental as well as Honors credit. Combined degree programs: BA/MD, BA/JD, Combined-Degree programs at Seton Hall, NJIT, Rutgers. **Disability Services:** Special programs offered to physically disabled students, including note-taking services, reader services, tape recorders, tutors. **Career Services:** Career/job search classes, Internships.

FACILITIES

Housing: Coed dorms, men's dorms, women's dorms, apartments for single students. **Special Academic Facilities/Equipment:** TV production facilities, center for government affairs.

CAMPUS LIFE

Environment: City. **Activities:** Choral groups, drama/theater, literary magazine, radio station, student government, student newspaper, yearbook. 45 registered organizations, 11 honor societies. **Athletics (Intercollegiate):** *Men:* baseball, basketball, cheerleading, cross-country, diving, football, golf, soccer, swimming, tennis, track/field (outdoor). *Women:* basketball, bowling, cheerleading, cross-country, diving, soccer, softball, swimming, tennis, track/field (outdoor), volleyball. **Environmental Initiatives:** Use of solar and wind energy.

ADMISSIONS

Freshman Academic Profile: Average high school GPA 3.2. **Reported SAT (pre-2016 redesign) scores:** SAT Math middle 50% range 410-510. SAT Critical Reading middle 50% range 400-500. SAT Writing middle 50% range 400-490. **Concordant SAT scores:** SAT EBRW middle 50% 450–550. SAT Math middle 50% range 450–540. ACT middle 50% range 16-21. Minimum internet-based TOEFL 79. Minimum paper TOEFL 550. **Basis for Candidate Selection:** *Very important factors considered include:* rigor of secondary school record, academic GPA. *Important factors considered include:* standardized test scores, application essay, recommendation(s). *Other factors considered include:* class rank, interview, extracurricular activities, talent/ability, character/personal qualities, first generation, alumni/ae relation, geographical residence, state residency, volunteer work, work experience. **Freshman Admission Requirements:** High school diploma is required and GED is accepted. *Academic units required:* 4 English, 3 math, 2 science, 1 science lab, 2 foreign language, 2 history, 3 academic electives. **Freshman Admission Statistics:** 4,528 applied, 67.31% admitted, 19% enrolled. **Transfer Admission Requirements:** college transcript(s), essay or personal statement, Minimum college GPA of 2.0 required. Lowest grade transferable C. **General Admission Information:** Priority deadline 12/1. Regular application deadline 8/31. Nonfall registration accepted. Admission may be deferred for a maximum of 1 semester.

COSTS AND FINANCIAL AID

Required Forms and Deadlines: FAFSA, State aid form. **Notification of Awards:** Applicants will be notified of awards on a rolling basis beginning 2/15. **Types of Aid:** *Need-based scholarships/grants:* Federal Pell, FSEOG, State scholarships/grants, Private scholarships, College/university scholarship or grant aid from institutional funds, Federal Nursing Scholarships. *Loans:* Direct Subsidized Stafford Loans, Direct Unsubsidized Stafford Loans, Direct PLUS loans. *Student Employment:* Federal Work-Study Program available. Institutional employment available. **Financial Aid Statistics:** 99% needy freshmen, 97% needy undergrads receive need-based scholarship or grant aid. 7% freshmen, 5% undergrads receive non-need-based scholarship or grant aid. 72% freshmen, 79% undergrads receive need-based self-help aid. 3% freshmen, 3% undergrads receive athletic scholarships. 98% freshmen, 90% undergrads receive any aid. **Criteria for awarding aid:** *Need-based:* Academics, Athletics. *Non-need-based:* Academics, Athletics.

SAINT VINCENT COLLEGE

Office of Admission and Financial Aid, Latrobe, PA 15650-2690
Phone: 724-537-4540 • **Financial Aid Phone:** 800-782-5549
E-mail: admission@stvincent.edu • **CEEB Code:** 2808
Fax: 724-532-5069 • **Website:** www.stvincent.edu • **ACT Code:** 3686

This private school, affiliated with the Roman Catholic Church, was founded in 1846. It has a 200-acre campus.

RATINGS

Admissions Selectivity Rating: 85   Fire Safety Rating: 69   Green Rating: 60*

STUDENTS AND FACULTY

Enrollment: 1,617. **Student Body:** 50% female, 50% male, 12% out-of-state, 1% international (15 countries represented). Asian 1%, African American 3%, Caucasian 90%, Hispanic 2%, Native American <1%, Pacific Islander 0%, Two or more races 0%, Race unknown 3%. **Retention and Graduation:** 84% freshmen return for sophomore year. 60% freshmen graduate within 4 years. 70% freshmen graduate within 6 years. 30% grads go on to further study within 1 year. **Faculty:** Student/faculty ratio 13:1. 91 full-time faculty, 84% hold PhDs, 2% are are members of minority groups, 24% are women. 0% of classes are taught by teaching assistants.

ACADEMICS

Degrees: bachelor's, certificate, master's, postbachelor's certificate. **Classes:** Most classes have 20-29 students. Most lab/discussion sessions have 10-19 students. **Most popular majors:** History; Biology/Biological Sciences; Psychology. **Special Study Options:** Accelerated program, cooperative education program, cross-registration, distance learning, double major, dual

---

enrollment, external degree program, honors program, independent study, internships, liberal arts/career combination, study abroad, teacher certification program. **Honors Programs:** Honors Classes Professors design Honors classes to challenge and reward students who seek substantial intellectual development in college. The quality, not the quantity of work, distinguishes Honors classes from other courses. Portfolio As part of their coursework in Honors classes, all students are required to submit a short reflective essay and sample of their work at the end of each Honors class. Honors Events Dinner and evening discussions based on a reading, or attendance of a play, a film, an art exhibit, etc., on campus provide a special, congenial setting for intellectual exchange as part of a course or an extracurricular event. Off-Campus Explorations All Honors students and faculty are regularly invited to attend a play, film, art exhibit, etc. Extended trips within the U.S. or abroad may be planned during breaks or the summer. Senior Capstone Projects Honors students in majors with a senior research or capstone project will be strongly encouraged to present their work in a special colloquium at Saint Vincent and at professional meetings in their research areas. Combined degree programs: BA/JD, BA/MEng, 3-3 JD, 4-1 MBA w/ Duquesne. **Disability Services:** Special programs offered to physically disabled students, including note-taking services, tutors. **Career Services:** Alumni network, Alumni services, Career assessment, Internships, Regional alumni. Students can take internship program for credit, though this is not required. Students are assisted in looking for internships in their field or industry of interest.

FACILITIES

Housing: Coed dorms, apartments for single students. 95% of campus accessible to physically diasbled. **Special Academic Facilities/Equipment:** Art gallery, life sciences research center, spectrophotometer, spectrometer, physiograph work stations, data acquisition work station, planetarium, observatory, radio telescope, instructional technology resource center. **Computers:** 75% of libraries, 100% of student union, 25% of common outdoor areas have wireless network access. Students can register for classes online. Administrative functions (other than registration) can be performed online.

CAMPUS LIFE

Environment: Village. **Activities:** Choral groups, dance, drama/theater, literary magazine, music ensembles, musical theater, pep band, radio station, student government, student newspaper, television station, yearbook, Campus Ministries, Student Organization. 43 registered organizations, 12 honor societies, 2 religious organizations. **Athletics (Intercollegiate):** *Men:* baseball, basketball, cross-country, football, golf, lacrosse, soccer, swimming, tennis, track/field (outdoor). *Women:* basketball, cross-country, field hockey, golf, lacrosse, soccer, softball, swimming, tennis, volleyball. **On-Campus Highlights:** Library, Carey Student Center, St. Benedict Hall, Basilica, Chuck Noll Field. **Environmental Initiatives:** New construction on campus, including a current building project, will be green

ADMISSIONS

Freshman Academic Profile: Average high school GPA 3.6. 24% in top 10% of high school class, 54% in top 25% of high school class, 84% in top 50% of high school class. 67% from public high schools. **Reported SAT (pre-2016 redesign) scores:** SAT Math middle 50% range 490-600. SAT Critical Reading middle 50% range 480-590. SAT Writing middle 50% range 470-570. **Concordant SAT scores:** SAT EBRW middle 50% 530–640. SAT Math middle 50% range 520–620. ACT middle 50% range 20-26. Minimum paper TOEFL 550. **Basis for Candidate Selection:** *Very important factors considered include:* rigor of secondary school record, class rank, academic GPA. *Important factors considered include:* standardized test scores, application essay, character/personal qualities. *Other factors considered include:* recommendation(s), interview, extracurricular activities, talent/ability, first generation. **Freshman Admission Requirements:** High school diploma is required and GED is accepted. *Academic units required:* 4 English, 3 math, 1 science, 1 science lab, 3 social studies, 5 academic electives. *Academic units recommended:* 4 English, 3 math, 3 science, 1 science lab, 2 foreign language, 3 social studies, 5 academic electives. **Freshman Admission Statistics:** 1,855 applied, 61.78% admitted, 37% enrolled. **Transfer Admission Requirements:** High school transcript, college transcript(s), essay or personal statement, statement of good standing from prior institution(s). Minimum college GPA of 2.5 required. Lowest grade transferable C-. **General Admission Information:** Application fee $25. Priority deadline 2/1. Regular application deadline 5/1. Nonfall registration accepted. Admission may be deferred for a maximum of 1 year.

COSTS AND FINANCIAL AID

Annual tuition $22,350. Room and board $7,242. Required fees $650. Average book expense $650. **Required Forms and Deadlines:** FAFSA, State aid form. **Notification of Awards:** Applicants will be notified of awards on a rolling basis beginning 3/1. **Types of Aid:** *Need-based scholarships/grants:* Federal Pell, FSEOG, State scholarships/grants, Private scholarships, College/university scholarship or grant aid from institutional funds, United Negro College Fund. *Loans:* Federal Perkins Loans. *Student Employment:* Federal Work-Study Program available. Institutional employment available. **Financial Aid Statistics:** 10% needy freshmen, 100% needy undergrads receive need-based scholarship or grant aid. 43% freshmen, 85% undergrads receive non-need-based scholarship or grant aid. 75% freshmen, 80% undergrads receive need-based self-help aid. 0% freshmen, 10% undergrads receive athletic scholarships. 99% freshmen, 96% undergrads receive any aid. **Criteria for awarding aid:** *Need-based:* Alumni affiliation. *Non-need-based:* Academics, Alumni affiliation, Leadership, Minority status, Music/drama.

SAINT XAVIER UNIVERSITY

3700 West 103rd Street., Chicago, IL 60655
Phone: 773-298-3050
E-mail: admissions@sxu.edu • **CEEB Code:** 1708
Fax: 773-298-3076 • **Website:** www.sxu.edu • **ACT Code:** 1134

This private school, affiliated with the Roman Catholic Church, was founded in 1847. It has a 70-acre campus.

RATINGS
Admissions Selectivity Rating: 79   Fire Safety Rating: 60*   Green Rating: 60*

STUDENTS AND FACULTY
Enrollment: 2,897. **Student Body:** 67% female, 33% male, 5% out-of-state, <1% international. Asian 3%, African American 16%, Caucasian 50%, Hispanic 23%, Native American <1%, Pacific Islander 0%, Two or more races 2%, Race unknown 5%.
Retention and Graduation: 75% freshmen return for sophomore year. 30% freshmen graduate within 4 years. 47% freshmen graduate within 6 years. 10% grads go on to further study within 1 year. **Faculty:** Student/faculty ratio 13:1. 168 full-time faculty, 86% hold PhDs, 13% are are members of minority groups, 57% are women. 0% of classes are taught by teaching assistants.

ACADEMICS
Degrees: bachelor's, certificate, master's, postbachelor's certifiate, post-master's certificate. **Classes:** Most classes have 20-29 students. Most lab/discussion sessions have 10-19 students. **Most popular majors:** Elementary Education and Teaching Business/Commerce. **Special Study Options:** Accelerated program, cooperative education program, distance learning, double major, dual enrollment, English as a Second Language (ESL), external degree program, honors program, independent study, internships, liberal arts/career combination, student-designed major, study abroad, teacher certification program, weekend college. Combined degree programs: BS/RN RN/MS BS/LPN. **Disability Services:** Special programs offered to physically disabled students, including note-taking services, reader services, tape recorders, tutors. **Career Services:** Alumni services, Career/job search classes, Career assessment, Internships.

FACILITIES
Housing: Coed dorms, special housing for disabled students, apartments for single students. 98% of campus accessible to physically diasbled. **Computers:** Students can register for classes online. Administrative functions (other than registration) can be performed online.

CAMPUS LIFE
Environment: Metropolis. **Activities:** Choral groups, concert band, jazz band, literary magazine, marching band, music ensembles, pep band, radio station, student government, student newspaper, student-run film society, symphony orchestra, yearbook, Campus Ministries, Student Organization. 41 registered organizations, 2 honor societies, 2 religious organizations. **Athletics (Intercollegiate):** *Men:* baseball, basketball, football, soccer. *Women:* basketball, cross-country, soccer, softball, volleyball. **On-Campus Highlights:** Convocation and Athletic Center, McDonough Chapel and Mercy Ministry Center, McCarthy Hall, Speech language Pathology Clinic, Art Gallery.

ADMISSIONS
Freshman Academic Profile: 25% in top 10% of high school class, 54% in top 25% of high school class, 84% in top 50% of high school class. 55% from public high schools. **Reported SAT (pre-2016 redesign) scores:** SAT Math middle 50% range 440-545. SAT Critical Reading middle 50% range 455-570. SAT Writing middle 50% range 455-540. **Concordant SAT scores:** SAT EBRW middle 50% 510–610. SAT Math middle 50% range 480–570. ACT middle 50% range 19-24. Minimum paper TOEFL 550. **Basis for Candidate Selection:** *Very important factors considered include:* academic GPA, standardized test scores, application essay. *Important factors considered include:* rigor of secondary school record. *Other factors considered include:* recommendation(s), interview, extracurricular activities, talent/ability, character/personal qualities, volunteer work, work experience, level of applicant's interest. **Freshman Admission Requirements:** High school diploma is required and GED is accepted. *Academic units recommended:* 4 English, 3 math, 2 foreign language, 3 academic electives, and 4 units from above areas or other academic areas. **Freshman Admission Statistics:** 6,693 applied, 79.29% admitted, 11%

enrolled. **Transfer Admission Requirements:** college transcript(s), Minimum college GPA of 2.5 required. Lowest grade transferable C. **General Admission Information:** Application fee $25. Nonfall registration accepted. Admission may be deferred.

COSTS AND FINANCIAL AID
Annual tuition $29,990. Room and board $10,320. Required fees $820. Average book expense $1,200. **Required Forms and Deadlines:** FAFSA. **Notification of Awards:** Applicants will be notified of awards on a rolling basis beginning 2/15. **Types of Aid:** *Need-based scholarships/grants:* Federal Pell, FSEOG, State scholarships/grants, Private scholarships, College/university scholarship or grant aid from institutional funds. *Loans:* Federal Perkins Loans. *Student Employment:* Federal Work-Study Program available. Institutional employment available. **Financial Aid Statistics:** 100% needy freshmen, 99% needy undergrads receive need-based scholarship or grant aid. 98% freshmen, 92% undergrads receive non-need-based scholarship or grant aid. 84% freshmen, 87% undergrads receive need-based self-help aid. 12% freshmen, 9% undergrads receive athletic scholarships. **Criteria for awarding aid:** *Non-need-based:* Academics, Athletics, Music/drama.

SALEM COLLEGE

PO Box 10548, Winston-Salem, NC 27108
Phone: 336-721-2621 • **Financial Aid Phone:** 336-721-2808
E-mail: admissions@salem.edu • **CEEB Code:** 5607
Fax: 336-917-5572 • **Website:** www.salem.edu • **ACT Code:** 3156

This private school, affiliated with the Moravian Church, was founded in 1772. It has a 57-acre campus.

RATINGS
Admissions Selectivity Rating: 87   Fire Safety Rating: 86   Green Rating: 60*

STUDENTS AND FACULTY
Enrollment: 741. **Student Body:** 98% female, 2% male, 23% out-of-state, 13% international (22 countries represented). Asian 1%, African American 19%, Caucasian 60%, Hispanic 4%, Native American <1%, Pacific Islander 0%, Two or more races 0%, Race unknown 4%.
Retention and Graduation: 78% freshmen return for sophomore year. 50% freshmen graduate within 4 years. 52% freshmen graduate within 6 years. 30% grads go on to further study within 1 year. 25% grads pursue arts and sciences degrees. 3% grads pursue law degrees. 5% grads pursue business degrees. **Faculty:** Student/faculty ratio 12:1. 57 full-time faculty, 86% hold PhDs, 9% are are members of minority groups, 61% are women. 0% of classes are taught by teaching assistants.

ACADEMICS
Degrees: bachelor's, master's. **Classes:** Most classes have 10-19 students. Most lab/discussion sessions have 10-19 students. **Most popular majors:** Sociology; Business/Commerce. **Special Study Options:** cross-registration, double major, dual enrollment, honors program, independent study, internships, liberal arts/career combination, student-designed major, study abroad, teacher certification program. **Career Services:** Alumni network, Internships.

FACILITIES
Housing: women's dorms, apartments for single students. 75% of campus accessible to physically diasbled. **Special Academic Facilities/Equipment:** Art gallery, fine arts center, Center for Women Writers, videoconferencing center. **Computers:** Administrative functions (other than registration) can be performed online.

CAMPUS LIFE
Environment: City. **Activities:** Choral groups, dance, drama/theater, literary magazine, marching band, music ensembles, musical theater, student government, student newspaper, yearbook. 26 registered organizations, 14 honor societies, 7 religious organizations. **Athletics (Intercollegiate):** *Women:* basketball, cross-country, field hockey, swimming, tennis, volleyball. **On-Campus Highlights:** back porch of Main Hall, Salem Grille/Java City, residence hall basement lounges **Environmental Initiatives:** Recycle committment-all residence halls and academic buildings have paper, plastic and aluminum containers.

ADMISSIONS
Freshman Academic Profile: Average high school GPA 3.7. 39% in top 10% of high school class, 67% in top 25% of high school class, 94% in top 50% of high school class. **Reported SAT (pre-2016 redesign) scores:** SAT Math middle 50% range 480-630. SAT Critical Reading middle 50% range 490-650. **Concordant SAT scores:** SAT Math middle 50% range 510–650. ACT middle 50% range 20-25. Minimum paper TOEFL 550. **Basis for Candidate**

Selection: *Very important factors considered include:* rigor of secondary school record, academic GPA. *Important factors considered include:* class rank, standardized test scores, application essay, recommendation(s), extracurricular activities, talent/ability, character/personal qualities. *Other factors considered include:* interview, first generation, alumni/ae relation, volunteer work, level of applicant's interest. **Freshman Admission Requirements:** High school diploma is required and GED is accepted. *Academic units required:* 4 English, 3 math, 3 science, 2 foreign language, 2 history. **Freshman Admission Statistics:** 435 applied, 69.43% admitted, 51% enrolled. **Transfer Admission Requirements:** High school transcript, college transcript(s), essay or personal statement, statement of good standing from prior institution(s). Minimum college GPA of 2.0 required. Lowest grade transferable C-. **General Admission Information:** Application fee $30. Priority deadline 3/1. Nonfall registration accepted. Admission may be deferred for a maximum of 1 year.

COSTS AND FINANCIAL AID

Annual tuition $18,850. Room and board $10,050. Required fees $340. Average book expense $900. **Required Forms and Deadlines:** FAFSA. **Notification of Awards:** Applicants will be notified of awards on a rolling basis beginning 3/1. **Types of Aid:** *Need-based scholarships/grants:* Federal Pell, FSEOG, State scholarships/grants, Private scholarships, College/university scholarship or grant aid from institutional funds. *Loans:* Federal Perkins Loans. *Student Employment:* Federal Work-Study Program available. Institutional employment available. **Financial Aid Statistics:** 80% needy freshmen, 71% needy undergrads receive need-based scholarship or grant aid. 96% freshmen, 95% undergrads receive non-need-based scholarship or grant aid. 88% freshmen, 83% undergrads receive need-based self-help aid. 0% freshmen, 0% undergrads receive athletic scholarships. **Criteria for awarding aid:** *Non-need-based:* Academics, Alumni affiliation, Leadership, Minority status, Music/drama, State/district residency.

SALEM STATE UNIVERSITY

352 Lafayette Street, Salem, MA 1970
Phone: 978-542-6210 • **Financial Aid Phone:** 978-542-6112
E-mail: admissions@salemstate.edu • **CEEB Code:** 3522
Fax: 978-542-6893 • **Website:** www.salemstate.edu

This public school was founded in 1854. It has a 108-acre campus.

RATINGS

Admissions Selectivity Rating: 74   **Fire Safety Rating:** 78   **Green Rating:** 60*

STUDENTS AND FACULTY

Enrollment: 7,296. **Student Body:** 61% female, 39% male, 3% out-of-state, 3% international. Asian 3%, African American 9%, Caucasian 76%, Hispanic 7%, Native American <1%, Pacific Islander 0%, Two or more races 0%, Race unknown 2%.
Faculty: Student/faculty ratio 14:1. 333 full-time faculty, 0% hold PhDs, 10% are are members of minority groups, 54% are women. 0% of classes are taught by teaching assistants.

ACADEMICS

Degrees: bachelor's, certificate, master's, postbachelor's certificate, post-master's certificate. **Classes:** Most classes have 10-19 students. Most lab/discussion sessions have 10-19 students. **Most popular majors:** Education; Criminal Justice/Law Enforcement Administration; Business/Commerce. **Special Study Options:** distance learning, double major, dual enrollment, English as a Second Language (ESL), honors program, independent study, internships, study abroad, teacher certification program. Combined degree programs: BS/MS Occupational Therapy. **Disability Services:** Special programs offered to physically disabled students, including reader services, tape recorders.

FACILITIES

Housing: Coed dorms, Faculty in Residence. 100% of campus accessible to physically diasbled. **Special Academic Facilities/Equipment:** Aquaculture center, On-campus elementary school, color TV studio, instructional media center.

CAMPUS LIFE

Environment: Village. **Activities:** Choral groups, concert band, dance, drama/theater, jazz band, literary magazine, music ensembles, musical theater, radio station, student government, student newspaper. 149 registered organizations, 13 honor societies, 3 religious organizations. **Athletics (Intercollegiate):** *Men:* baseball, basketball, cross-country, diving, golf, ice hockey, lacrosse, soccer, swimming, tennis, track/field (outdoor). *Women:* basketball, cross-country, diving, field hockey, lacrosse, soccer, softball, swimming, tennis, track/field (outdoor), volleyball.

ADMISSIONS

Reported SAT (pre-2016 redesign) scores: SAT Math middle 50% range 450-540. SAT Critical Reading middle 50% range 440-550. **Concordant SAT scores:** SAT Math middle 50% range 490–570. Minimum paper TOEFL 500. **Basis for Candidate Selection:** *Very important factors considered include:* rigor of secondary school record, academic GPA, standardized test scores. *Other factors considered include:* recommendation(s), interview, extracurricular activities, talent/ability, character/personal qualities, volunteer work, work experience, level of applicant's interest. **Freshman Admission Requirements:** High school diploma is required and GED is accepted. *Academic units required:* 4 English, 3 math, 3 science, 2 science labs, 2 foreign language, 2 social studies, 1 history, 2 academic electives, 1 computer science, 1 visual/performing arts. *Academic units recommended:* 4 English, 3 math, 3 science, 2 science labs, 2 foreign language, 2 social studies, 3 history, 2 academic electives, 1 computer science, 1 visual/performing arts. **Freshman Admission Statistics:** 5,697 applied, 57.36% admitted, 31% enrolled. **Transfer Admission Requirements:** college transcript(s), Minimum college GPA of 2.0 required. Lowest grade transferable C-. **General Admission Information:** Application fee $75. Priority deadline 3/1. Regular application deadline 4/15. Regular notification 5/1. Nonfall registration accepted. Admission may be deferred for a maximum of 1 semester.

COSTS AND FINANCIAL AID

Required Forms and Deadlines: FAFSA. **Notification of Awards:** Applicants will be notified of awards on a rolling basis beginning 6/1. *Student Employment:* Federal Work-Study Program available. Institutional employment available. **Financial Aid Statistics:** 73% freshmen, 75% undergrads receive any aid.

SALISBURY UNIVERSITY

Admissions Office, Salisbury, MD 21801
Phone: 410-543-6161 • **Financial Aid Phone:** 410-543-6165
E-mail: admissions@salisbury.edu • **CEEB Code:** 2091
Fax: 410-546-6016 • **Website:** www.salisbury.edu • **ACT Code:** 1716

This public school was founded in 1925. It has a 155-acre campus.

RATINGS

Admissions Selectivity Rating: 85   **Fire Safety Rating:** 96   **Green Rating:** 96

STUDENTS AND FACULTY

Enrollment: 7,657. **Student Body:** 57% female, 43% male, 14% out-of-state, 2% international (61 countries represented). Asian 3%, African American 14%, Caucasian 70%, Hispanic 4%, Native American 1%, Pacific Islander <1%, Two or more races 3%, Race unknown 3%.
Retention and Graduation: 84% freshmen return for sophomore year. 47% freshmen graduate within 4 years. 68% freshmen graduate within 6 years. 48% grads pursue arts and sciences degrees. 3% grads pursue law degrees. 15% grads pursue business degrees. 19% grads pursue medical degrees. **Faculty:** Student/faculty ratio 16:1. 411 full-time faculty, 84% hold PhDs, 15% are are members of minority groups, 49% are women. 3% of classes are taught by teaching assistants.

ACADEMICS

Degrees: bachelor's, doctoral/professional, master's, postbachelor's certificate. **Classes:** Most classes have 20-29 students. Most lab/discussion sessions have 20-29 students. **Most popular majors:** Registered Nursing/Registered Nurse; Biology/Biological Sciences; Kinesiology and Exercise Science. **Special Study Options:** Accelerated program, cross-registration, distance learning, double major, dual enrollment, English as a Second Language (ESL), honors program, independent study, internships, liberal arts/career combination, student-designed major, study abroad, teacher certification program. **Honors Programs:** The Thomas E. Bellavance Honors Program Combined degree programs: BASW/MSW, BASW/BA Soc., BS/BS Biology/Envirn., Early Childhood/Elem. Educ. **Disability Services:** Special programs offered to physically disabled students, including note-taking services, reader services, tutors. **Career Services:** Alumni network, Alumni services, Career/job search classes, Career assessment, Internships, Regional alumni.

FACILITIES

Housing: Coed dorms, men's dorms, women's dorms, apartments for single students, Wellness Housing, Theme Housing, Affiliated off-campus apartments, quiet/study housing available. World living/learning option-community of

International and American students. 95% of campus accessible to physically diasbled. **Special Academic Facilities/Equipment:** Arboretum, University Galleries, Delmarva History and Culture Research Center, Small Business Development Center, Ward Museum of Wildfowl Art. **Computers:** 100% of classrooms, 100% of dorms, 100% of libraries, 100% of dining areas, 100% of student union, have wireless network access. Students can register for classes online. Administrative functions (other than registration) can be performed online.

CAMPUS LIFE

Environment: Town. **Activities:** Choral groups, concert band, dance, drama/theater, jazz band, literary magazine, music ensembles, musical theater, pep band, radio station, student government, student newspaper, student-run film society, symphony orchestra, television station, Campus Ministries, Student Organization. 126 registered organizations, 23 honor societies, 8 religious organizations. 8 fraternities, 4 sororities. **Athletics (Intercollegiate):** *Men:* baseball, basketball, cross-country, football, lacrosse, soccer, swimming, tennis, track/field (outdoor). *Women:* basketball, cross-country, field hockey, lacrosse, soccer, softball, swimming, tennis, track/field (outdoor), volleyball. **On-Campus Highlights:** Commons (housing our Dining Hall and Bookstore), Cool Beans Cyber Caf, Scarborough Leadership Center, Honors House, Maggs Physical Activities Center. **Environmental Initiatives:** Major renovations and construction of 12 buildings to LEED Silver or Gold certification.

ADMISSIONS

Freshman Academic Profile: Average high school GPA 3.7. 21% in top 10% of high school class, 55% in top 25% of high school class, 86% in top 50% of high school class. **Reported SAT (pre-2016 redesign) scores:** SAT Math middle 50% range 540-620. SAT Critical Reading middle 50% range 540-610. SAT Writing middle 50% range 530-600. **Concordant SAT scores:** SAT EBRW middle 50% 590–660. SAT Math middle 50% range 570–640. ACT middle 50% range 21-25. Minimum internet-based TOEFL 550. Minimum paper TOEFL 79. **Basis for Candidate Selection:** *Very important factors considered include:* rigor of secondary school record, academic GPA. *Important factors considered include:* class rank, standardized test scores. *Other factors considered include:* application essay, recommendation(s), extracurricular activities, talent/ability, character/personal qualities, first generation, alumni/ae relation, geographical residence, state residency, racial/ethnic status, volunteer work, work experience, level of applicant's interest. **Freshman Admission Requirements:** High school diploma is required and GED is accepted. *Academic units required:* 4 English, 4 math, 3 science, 2 science labs, 2 foreign language, 3 social studies. *Academic units recommended:* 4 English, 4 math, 4 science, 3 science labs, 3 foreign language, 3 social studies, 3 academic electives. **Freshman Admission Statistics:** 8,307 applied, 65.93% admitted, 24% enrolled. **Transfer Admission Requirements:** college transcript(s), Minimum college GPA of 2.0 required. Lowest grade transferable C. **General Admission Information:** Application fee $50. Regular application deadline 1/15. Regular notification 3/15. Nonfall registration accepted. Admission may be deferred for a maximum of 1 year.

COSTS AND FINANCIAL AID

Annual in-state tuition $6,846. Annual out-of-state tuition $15,258. Room and board $11,350. Required fees $2,518. Average book expense $1,300. **Required Forms and Deadlines:** FAFSA. **Notification of Awards:** Applicants will be notified of awards on a rolling basis beginning 3/15. **Types of Aid:** *Need-based scholarships/grants:* Federal Pell, FSEOG, State scholarships/grants, Private scholarships, College/university scholarship or grant aid from institutional funds. *Loans:* Direct Subsidized Stafford Loans, Direct Unsubsidized Stafford Loans, Direct PLUS loans, Federal Perkins Loans. *Student Employment:* Federal Work-Study Program available. Institutional employment available. **Financial Aid Statistics:** 83% needy freshmen, 78% needy undergrads receive need-based scholarship or grant aid. 0% undergrads receive non-need-based scholarship or grant aid. 78% freshmen, 82% undergrads receive need-based self-help aid. 0% freshmen, 0% undergrads receive athletic scholarships. 87% freshmen, 76% undergrads receive any aid. 59% undergrads borrow to pay for school. Average cumulative indebtedness $26,940. **Criteria for awarding aid:** *Need-based:* Academics, Job skills. *Non-need-based:* Academics, Alumni affiliation, Art, Leadership, Music/drama, State/district residency.

SALVE REGINA UNIVERSITY

100 Ochre Point Avenue, Newport, RI 02840-4192
Phone: 401-341-2908 • **Financial Aid Phone:** 401-341-2140
E-mail: sruadmis@salve.edu • **CEEB Code:** 3759
Fax: 401-848-2823 • **Website:** www.salve.edu • **ACT Code:** 3816

This private school, affiliated with the Roman Catholic Church, was founded in 1947. It has a 81-acre campus.

RATINGS

Admissions Selectivity Rating: 83   **Fire Safety Rating:** 94   **Green Rating:** 68

STUDENTS AND FACULTY

Enrollment: 2,090. **Student Body:** 70% female, 30% male, 78% out-of-state, 1% international (14 countries represented). Asian 1%, African American 2%, Caucasian 82%, Hispanic 6%, Native American <1%, Pacific Islander <1%, Two or more races 2%, Race unknown 5%.
Retention and Graduation: 82% freshmen return for sophomore year. 64% freshmen graduate within 4 years. 68% freshmen graduate within 6 years. 19% grads go on to further study within 1 year. **Faculty:** Student/faculty ratio 13:1. 125 full-time faculty, 84% hold PhDs, 10% are are members of minority groups, 58% are women. 0% of classes are taught by teaching assistants.

ACADEMICS

Degrees: associate, bachelor's, certificate, doctoral/professional, doctoral/research, master's, postbachelor's certificate, post-master's certificate. **Classes:** Most classes have 10-19 students. Most lab/discussion sessions have 20-29 students. **Most popular majors:** Criminal Justice/Law Enforcement Administration; Elementary Education and Teaching; Registered Nursing/Registered Nurse. **Special Study Options:** Accelerated program, distance learning, double major, dual enrollment, English as a Second Language (ESL), honors program, independent study, internships, liberal arts/career combination, study abroad, teacher certification program, Washington Semester. **Honors Programs:** The Pell Honors Program is open to students from all majors who receive the Dean's, Trustee's, or Presidential Scholarships, or who are nominated by Salve Regina faculty or the Admissions Office. The goal of the Pell Honors Program is to create a learning community of students from different disciplines. The honors education is an enhancement of the core curriculum with a focus in international relations and public policy emphasizing civic responsibility and action. Students are required to take classes together, participate in either an internship or study abroad experience, and write and publicly defend a senior thesis. Combined degree programs: BA/JD, BA/MA, 4-1 MA, 4-1 MS, BA,BS/MBA. **Disability Services:** Special programs offered to physically disabled students, including note-taking services, reader services, tape recorders, tutors. **Career Services:** Alumni network, Alumni services, Career/job search classes, Career assessment, Internships, Regional alumni.

FACILITIES

Housing: Coed dorms, special housing for disabled students, men's dorms, women's dorms, apartments for single students, Wellness HousingBoth historic style housing and conventional style housing options are available on campus. Off-campus housing is available to upper class students. 85% of campus accessible to physically diasbled. **Special Academic Facilities/Equipment:** Art gallery, theater, technology center. **Computers:** 98% of classrooms, 10% of dorms, 100% of libraries, 100% of dining areas, 100% of student union, 25% of common outdoor areas have wireless network access. Students can register for classes online. Administrative functions (other than registration) can be performed online. Undergraduates are required to own a computer.

CAMPUS LIFE

Environment: Town. **Activities:** Choral groups, concert band, dance, drama/theater, jazz band, literary magazine, music ensembles, pep band, radio station, student government, student newspaper, student-run film society, yearbook, Campus Ministries, Student Organization, Model UN. 42 registered organizations, 14 honor societies, 2 religious organizations. **Athletics (Intercollegiate):** *Men:* baseball, basketball, cross-country, football, ice hockey, lacrosse, soccer, tennis. *Women:* basketball, field hockey, ice hockey, lacrosse, soccer, softball, tennis, track/field (outdoor), volleyball. **On-Campus Highlights:** New Residence Hall, Athletic Center, O'Hare Academic & Antone Academic Cntrs, Library and Computer Labs, Historic Mansions on campus. **Environmental Initiatives:** Recycling.

ADMISSIONS

Freshman Academic Profile: Average high school GPA 3.3. 17% in top 10% of high school class, 45% in top 25% of high school class, 81% in top 50% of high school class. 77% from public high schools. **Reported SAT (pre-2016 redesign) scores:** SAT Math middle 50% range 510-590. SAT Critical Reading middle 50% range 510-590. SAT Writing middle 50% range 510-590. **Concordant SAT scores:** SAT EBRW middle 50% 570–650. SAT Math middle 50% range 540–610. ACT middle 50% range 22-26. Minimum internet-based

TOEFL 80. Minimum paper TOEFL 500. **Basis for Candidate Selection:** *Very important factors considered include:* rigor of secondary school record, class rank, academic GPA. *Important factors considered include:* standardized test scores, application essay, recommendation(s). *Other factors considered include:* extracurricular activities, talent/ability, character/personal qualities, alumni/ae relation, racial/ethnic status, volunteer work, work experience, level of applicant's interest. **Freshman Admission Requirements:** High school diploma is required and GED is accepted. *Academic units required:* 4 English, 3 math, 2 science, 2 science labs, 2 foreign language, 1 social studies, 4 academic electives. **Freshman Admission Statistics:** 5,100 applied, 69.16% admitted, 16% enrolled. **Transfer Admission Requirements:** High school transcript, college transcript(s), essay or personal statement, statement of good standing from prior institution(s). Minimum college GPA of 2.7 required. Lowest grade transferable C. **General Admission Information:** Application fee $50. Priority deadline 2/1. Nonfall registration accepted. Admission may be deferred for a maximum of 12 months.

COSTS AND FINANCIAL AID

Annual tuition $37,270. Room and board $13,650. Required fees $550. Average book expense $1,400. **Required Forms and Deadlines:** FAFSA. **Notification of Awards:** Applicants will be notified of awards on a rolling basis beginning 1/3. **Types of Aid:** *Need-based scholarships/grants:* Federal Pell, FSEOG, State scholarships/grants, Private scholarships, College/university scholarship or grant aid from institutional funds. *Loans:* Direct Subsidized Stafford Loans, Direct Unsubsidized Stafford Loans, Direct PLUS loans, Federal Perkins Loans, Federal Nursing Loans. *Student Employment:* Federal Work-Study Program available. Institutional employment available. **Financial Aid Statistics:** 98% needy freshmen, 100% needy undergrads receive need-based scholarship or grant aid. 8% freshmen, 9% undergrads receive non-need-based scholarship or grant aid. 97% freshmen, 89% undergrads receive need-based self-help aid. 0% freshmen, 0% undergrads receive athletic scholarships. 99% freshmen, 84% undergrads receive any aid. 69% undergrads borrow to pay for school. Average cumulative indebtedness $29,192. **Criteria for awarding aid:** *Non-need-based:* Academics, Alumni affiliation, Art.

SAM HOUSTON STATE UNIVERSITY

Box 2418, Huntsville, TX 77341-2418
Phone: 936-294-1828 • **Financial Aid Phone:** 936-294-1774
E-mail: admissions@shsu.edu • **CEEB Code:** 6643
Website: www.shsu.edu • **ACT Code:** 4162

This public school was founded in 1879. It has a 272-acre campus.

RATINGS
Admissions Selectivity Rating: 78   **Fire Safety Rating:** 92   **Green Rating:** 60*

STUDENTS AND FACULTY
Enrollment: 15,611. **Student Body:** 58% female, 42% male, 1% out-of-state, 1% international (59 countries represented). Asian 1%, African American 17%, Caucasian 58%, Hispanic 17%, Native American <1%, Pacific Islander <1%, Two or more races 2%, Race unknown 2%.
Retention and Graduation: 27% freshmen graduate within 4 years. 49% freshmen graduate within 6 years. **Faculty:** Student/faculty ratio 25:1. 620 full-time faculty, 79% hold PhDs, 16% are are members of minority groups, 45% are women. 5% of classes are taught by teaching assistants.

ACADEMICS
Degrees: bachelor's, diploma, doctoral/professional, doctoral/research, master's. **Classes:** Most classes have 20-29 students. Most lab/discussion sessions have 20-29 students. **Most popular majors:** Multi-/Interdisciplinary Studies; Criminal Justice/Safety Studies; Business/Commerce. **Special Study Options:** distance learning, double major, dual enrollment, English as a Second Language (ESL), honors program, independent study, internships, teacher certification program. **Honors Programs:** The Honors student earns Honors credit in a variety of specially designated classes, and works toward the distinction of graduating 'With Honors' or 'With Highest Honors.' To qualify for graduation with honors, a student must have been a participant in the Honors Program and have completed 24 hours of Honors class credit, including participation in two interdisciplinary Honors seminars. To qualify for graduation 'With Highest Honors' a student must, in addition, complete a senior thesis in an approved discipline under the direction of a faculty member of his/her choice. The student will receive 6 credit hours of departmental course credit when completing the senior thesis. **Disability Services:** Special programs offered to physically disabled students, including note-taking services, reader services, tape recorders. **Career Services:** Alumni network, Alumni services, Career/job search classes, Career assessment, Internships, Regional

alumni. We are proud of all our internship programs including Disney, Target Asset Protection, numerous Criminal Justice related agencies and all the major accounting firms.

FACILITIES
Housing: Coed dorms, men's dorms, women's dorms, fraternity/sorority housing, apartments for single students. 85% of campus accessible to physically diasbled. **Special Academic Facilities/Equipment:** Sam Houston Memorial Museum, on-campus elementary school, communications center for photography, radio, TV, and film, agricultural complex and university farm. **Computers:** Students can register for classes online. Administrative functions (other than registration) can be performed online.

CAMPUS LIFE
Environment: Town. **Activities:** Choral groups, concert band, dance, drama/theater, jazz band, marching band, music ensembles, musical theater, pep band, radio station, student government, student newspaper, symphony orchestra, television station, yearbook, Campus Ministries, Student Organization. 185 registered organizations, 12 honor societies, 17 religious organizations. 16 fraternities, 10 sororities. **Athletics (Intercollegiate):** *Men:* baseball, basketball, cheerleading, cross-country, equestrian sports, football, golf, rodeo, soccer, softball, tennis, track/field (outdoor), track/field (indoor). *Women:* basketball, cheerleading, cross-country, equestrian sports, golf, rodeo, soccer, softball, tennis, track/field (outdoor), track/field (indoor), volleyball. **On-Campus Highlights:** Lowman Student Center, Health and Kinesiology Center, Computer Labs, Mall Area, Old Main Pit. **Environmental Initiatives:** Hired an Energy Manager.

ADMISSIONS
Freshman Academic Profile: 13% in top 10% of high school class, 42% in top 25% of high school class, 85% in top 50% of high school class. **Reported SAT (pre-2016 redesign) scores:** SAT Math middle 50% range 470-550. SAT Critical Reading middle 50% range 450-540. **Concordant SAT scores:** SAT Math middle 50% range 510–570. ACT middle 50% range 19-23. Minimum paper TOEFL 550. **Basis for Candidate Selection:** *Very important factors considered include:* class rank, standardized test scores. *Important factors considered include:* academic GPA. *Other factors considered include:* rigor of secondary school record, recommendation(s), extracurricular activities, talent/ability, character/personal qualities, volunteer work. **Freshman Admission Requirements:** High school diploma is required and GED is accepted. *Academic units required:* 4 English, 4 math, 4 science, 12 science labs, 2 foreign language, 2 social studies, 2 history, 6 academic electives, 1 computer science, 1 visual/performing arts, and 2 units from above areas or other academic areas. *Academic units recommended:* 4 English, 4 math, 4 science, 12 science labs, 2 foreign language, 2 social studies, 2 history, 6 academic electives, 1 computer science, 1 visual/performing arts, and 2 units from above areas or other academic areas. **Freshman Admission Statistics:** 9,315 applied, 64.99% admitted, 40% enrolled. **Transfer Admission Requirements:** college transcript(s), statement of good standing from prior institution(s). Minimum college GPA of 2.0 required. Lowest grade transferable D. **General Admission Information:** Application fee $45. Priority deadline 6/15. Regular application deadline 8/1. Nonfall registration accepted.

COSTS AND FINANCIAL AID
Annual in-state tuition $5,850. Annual out-of-state tuition $16,470. Room and board $8,324. Required fees $2,744. Average book expense $1,124. **Required Forms and Deadlines:** FAFSA. **Notification of Awards:** Applicants will be notified of awards on a rolling basis beginning 3/15. **Types of Aid:** *Need-based scholarships/grants:* Federal Pell, FSEOG, State scholarships/grants, College/university scholarship or grant aid from institutional funds. *Loans:* Direct Subsidized Stafford Loans, Direct Unsubsidized Stafford Loans, Direct PLUS loans, Federal Perkins Loans, State Loans, College/university loans from institutional funds. *Student Employment:* Federal Work-Study Program available. Institutional employment available. **Financial Aid Statistics:** 86% needy freshmen, 80% needy undergrads receive need-based scholarship or grant aid. 4% freshmen, 1% undergrads receive non-need-based scholarship or grant aid. 78% freshmen, 84% undergrads receive need-based self-help aid. 2% freshmen, 2% undergrads receive athletic scholarships. 79% freshmen, 71% undergrads receive any aid. **Criteria for awarding aid:** *Need-based:* Academics, Art, Music/drama. *Non-need-based:* Academics, Alumni affiliation, Art, Athletics, Job skills, Leadership, Music/drama, Religious affiliation, State/district residency.

SAMFORD UNIVERSITY

800 Lakeshore Drive, Birmingham, AL 35229
Phone: 205-726-3673 • **Financial Aid Phone:** 205-726-2905
E-mail: admissions@samford.edu • **CEEB Code:** 1302
Fax: 205-726-2171 • **Website:** www.samford.edu • **ACT Code:** 16

This private school, affiliated with the Baptist Church, was founded in 1841. It has a 180-acre campus.

RATINGS

Admissions Selectivity Rating: 83   **Fire Safety Rating:** 96   **Green Rating:** 75

STUDENTS AND FACULTY

Enrollment: 3,324. **Student Body:** 65% female, 35% male, 67% out-of-state, 2% international (21 countries represented). Asian 1%, African American 7%, Caucasian 83%, Hispanic 4%, Native American <1%, Pacific Islander 0%, Two or more races 2%, Race unknown 1%.
Retention and Graduation: 89% freshmen return for sophomore year. 59% freshmen graduate within 4 years. 73% freshmen graduate within 6 years. 34% grads go on to further study within 1 year. **Faculty:** Student/faculty ratio 12:1. 352 full-time faculty, 87% hold PhDs, 11% are are members of minority groups, 51% are women. 0% of classes are taught by teaching assistants.

ACADEMICS

Degrees: bachelor's, certificate, doctoral/professional, doctoral/research, master's, postbachelor's certificate, post-master's certificate. **Classes:** Most classes have 10-19 students. Most lab/discussion sessions have 10-19 students. **Most popular majors:** Journalism; Registered Nursing/Registered Nurse; Teacher Education, Multiple Levels. **Special Study Options:** Accelerated program, cooperative education program, distance learning, double major, dual enrollment, exchange student program (domestic), honors program, independent study, internships, liberal arts/career combination, study abroad, teacher certification program. **Honors Programs:** Samford University Fellows program targets academically gifted high schools students for a highly-competitive program of innovative liberal arts courses, study and undergraduate research. **Disability Services:** Special programs offered to physically disabled students, including note-taking services, reader services, tape recorders. **Career Services:** Alumni network, Alumni services, Career/job search classes, Career assessment, Internships, Regional alumni. The Career Development Center has created a CDC Steering Committee that is composed of employers (some of whom are alumni) and important campus constituents to provide ideas and feedback to the CDC, while also creating potential connections for internships and employment for students and alumni.

FACILITIES

Housing: special housing for disabled students, men's dorms, women's dorms, fraternity/sorority housing, Wellness Housing. 100% of campus accessible to physically diasbled. **Special Academic Facilities/Equipment:** Language lab, reflective telescope, geographic information systems lab, global center, planetarium, conservatory, Pete Hanna Sports Center. **Computers:** 100% of classrooms, 100% of libraries, 100% of dining areas, 100% of student union, have wireless network access. Students can register for classes online. Administrative functions (other than registration) can be performed online.

CAMPUS LIFE

Environment: Town. **Activities:** Choral groups, concert band, dance, drama/theater, jazz band, literary magazine, marching band, music ensembles, musical theater, radio station, student government, student newspaper, symphony orchestra, yearbook, Campus Ministries, Student Organization, Model UN. 119 registered organizations, 25 honor societies, 16 religious organizations. 6 fraternities, 6 sororities. **Athletics (Intercollegiate):** *Men:* baseball, basketball, cross-country, football, golf, tennis, track/field (outdoor). *Women:* basketball, cross-country, golf, soccer, softball, tennis, track/field (outdoor), volleyball. **On-Campus Highlights:** Sciencenter, Pete Hanna Center, University Library, Wright Center Student Center, Beeson University Center, The Quad, Hodges Chapel, Harrison Theatre, and Jane Hollock Brock Recital Hall. **Environmental Initiatives:** The university strategic plan includes "conserve all resources" as one of the 16 goals.

ADMISSIONS

Freshman Academic Profile: Average high school GPA 3.6. 31% in top 10% of high school class, 57% in top 25% of high school class, 84% in top 50% of high school class. 48% from public high schools. **Reported SAT (pre-2016 redesign) scores:** SAT Math middle 50% range 500-618. SAT Critical Reading middle 50% range 520-620. SAT Writing middle 50% range 510-610. **Concordant SAT scores:** SAT EBRW middle 50% range 570–670. SAT Math middle 50% range 530–640. ACT middle 50% range 23-29. Minimum internet-based TOEFL 90. Minimum paper TOEFL 575. **Basis for Candidate Selection:** *Very important factors considered include:* rigor of secondary school record, academic GPA, standardized test scores, application essay, recommendation(s).

Important factors considered include: extracurricular activities, character/personal qualities, level of applicant's interest. *Other factors considered include:* talent/ability. **Freshman Admission Requirements:** High school diploma is required and GED is accepted. *Academic units required:* 4 English, 3 math, 2 science, 2 science labs, 2 foreign language, 2 history. *Academic units recommended:* 4 English, 4 math, 2 science, 2 science labs, 2 foreign language, 4 history. **Freshman Admission Statistics:** 3,446 applied, 91.38% admitted, 29% enrolled. **Transfer Admission Requirements:** college transcript(s), essay or personal statement, statement of good standing from prior institution(s). Minimum college GPA of 2.5 required. Lowest grade transferable C-. **General Admission Information:** Application fee $40. Priority deadline 4/1. Regular application deadline 6/30. Nonfall registration accepted. Admission may be deferred for a maximum of 1 year.

COSTS AND FINANCIAL AID

Annual tuition $28,552. Room and board $9,830. Required fees $850. Average book expense $1,000. **Required Forms and Deadlines:** FAFSA, State aid form. **Notification of Awards:** Applicants will be notified of awards on a rolling basis beginning 3/1. **Types of Aid:** *Need-based scholarships/grants:* Federal Pell, FSEOG, State scholarships/grants, Private scholarships, College/university scholarship or grant aid from institutional funds, United Negro College Fund, Federal Nursing Scholarships. *Loans:* Direct Subsidized Stafford Loans, Direct Unsubsidized Stafford Loans, Direct PLUS loans, Federal Perkins Loans, Federal Nursing Loans, College/university loans from institutional funds. *Student Employment:* Federal Work-Study Program available. Institutional employment available. **Financial Aid Statistics:** 100% needy freshmen, 96% needy undergrads receive need-based scholarship or grant aid. 24% freshmen, 20% undergrads receive non-need-based scholarship or grant aid. 68% freshmen, 75% undergrads receive need-based self-help aid. 3% freshmen, 4% undergrads receive athletic scholarships. 96% freshmen, 89% undergrads receive any aid. Average cumulative indebtedness $29,292. **Criteria for awarding aid:** *Non-need-based:* Academics, Alumni affiliation, Art, Athletics, Leadership, Minority status, Music/drama, Religious affiliation, State/district residency.

SAN DIEGO STATE UNIVERSITY

5500 Campanile Drive, San Diego, CA 92182-7455
Phone: 619-594-6336 • **Financial Aid Phone:** 619-594-6323 • **CEEB Code:** 4682
Website: www.sdsu.edu • **ACT Code:** 398

This public school was founded in 1897. It has a 300-acre campus.

RATINGS

Admissions Selectivity Rating: 91   **Fire Safety Rating:** 89   **Green Rating:** 60*

STUDENTS AND FACULTY

Enrollment: 29,853. **Student Body:** 54% female, 46% male, 9% out-of-state, 7% international (125 countries represented). Asian 14%, African American 4%, Caucasian 33%, Hispanic 31%, Native American <1%, Pacific Islander <1%, Two or more races 7%, Race unknown 4%.
Retention and Graduation: 90% freshmen return for sophomore year. 34% freshmen graduate within 4 years. 74% freshmen graduate within 6 years. **Faculty:** Student/faculty ratio 27:1. 873 full-time faculty, 89% hold PhDs, 27% are are members of minority groups, 45% are women.

ACADEMICS

Degrees: bachelor's, doctoral/research, master's, postbachelor's certificate. **Classes:** Most classes have 20-29 students. Most lab/discussion sessions have 20-29 students. **Most popular majors:** Psychology; Criminal Justice/Safety Studies; Business Administration and Management. **Special Study Options:** distance learning, double major, English as a Second Language (ESL), exchange student program (domestic), external degree program, honors program, independent study, internships, liberal arts/career combination, study abroad, teacher certification program. Combined degree programs: BS/MS, MBA/JD, MSW/JD, MPH/MA, MPH/MSW, MBA/MA, MPA/MA, MS/MS. **Disability Services:** Special programs offered to physically disabled students, including note-taking services, reader services, tape recorders, tutors. **Career Services:** Alumni network, Alumni services, Career assessment, Internships.

FACILITIES

Housing: Coed dorms, special housing for international students, fraternity/sorority housing, apartments for single students, Extended Quiet Study Hours (more quiet study environment), Living/Learning Center Housing Over the

Break. 99% of campus accessible to physically diasbled. **Special Academic Facilities/Equipment:** Art gallery, theatre, recital hall, research bureaus for labor economics, marine studies and social science, audiovisual center, electronic boardroom, multimedia interactive fine arts technology lab, Palomar Observatory (off-campus), field studies stations (off-campus). **Computers:** Students can register for classes online. Administrative functions (other than registration) can be performed online.

CAMPUS LIFE

Environment: City. **Activities:** Choral groups, concert band, dance, drama/theater, jazz band, literary magazine, marching band, music ensembles, musical theater, opera, pep band, radio station, student government, student newspaper, student-run film society, symphony orchestra, television station, Campus Ministries, Student Organization. 264 registered organizations, 6 honor societies, 14 religious organizations. 21 fraternities, 23 sororities. **Athletics (Intercollegiate):** *Men:* baseball, basketball, football, golf, soccer, tennis. *Women:* basketball, crew/rowing, cross-country, diving, golf, soccer, softball, swimming, tennis, track/field (outdoor), track/field (indoor), volleyball, water polo.

ADMISSIONS

Freshman Academic Profile: Average high school GPA 3.7. 31% in top 10% of high school class, 72% in top 25% of high school class, 96% in top 50% of high school class. 92% from public high schools. **Reported SAT (pre-2016 redesign) scores:** SAT Math middle 50% range 510-620. SAT Critical Reading middle 50% range 490-600. SAT Writing middle 50% range 480-590. **Concordant SAT scores:** SAT EBRW middle 50% 540–650. SAT Math middle 50% range 540–640. ACT middle 50% range 23-28. Minimum internet-based TOEFL 80. Minimum paper TOEFL 550. **Basis for Candidate Selection:** *Very important factors considered include:* rigor of secondary school record, academic GPA, standardized test scores. *Important factors considered include:* geographical residence, state residency. **Freshman Admission Requirements:** High school diploma is required and GED is accepted. *Academic units required:* 4 English, 3 math, 2 science, 2 science labs, 2 foreign language, 1 social studies, 1 history, 1 academic elective, 1 visual/performing arts. *Academic units recommended:* 4 math. **Freshman Admission Statistics:** 60,691 applied, 34.51% admitted, 24% enrolled. **Transfer Admission Requirements:** college transcript(s), Lowest grade transferable D-. **General Admission Information:** Application fee $55. Regular application deadline 11/30. Nonfall registration not accepted.

COSTS AND FINANCIAL AID

Annual in-state tuition $5,472. Annual out-of-state tuition $16,632. Room and board $14,812. Required fees $1,612. Average book expense $1,818. **Required Forms and Deadlines:** FAFSA, State aid form. **Notification of Awards:** Applicants will be notified of awards on a rolling basis beginning 3/15. **Types of Aid:** *Need-based scholarships/grants:* Federal Pell, FSEOG, State scholarships/grants, Private scholarships, College/university scholarship or grant aid from institutional funds. *Loans:* Direct Subsidized Stafford Loans, Direct Unsubsidized Stafford Loans, Direct PLUS loans, College/university loans from institutional funds. *Student Employment:* Federal Work-Study Program available. Institutional employment available. **Financial Aid Statistics:** 62% needy freshmen, 80% needy undergrads receive need-based scholarship or grant aid. 54% freshmen, 41% undergrads receive non-need-based scholarship or grant aid. 100% freshmen, 98% undergrads receive need-based self-help aid. 2% freshmen, 1% undergrads receive athletic scholarships. 61% freshmen, 66% undergrads receive any aid. 49% undergrads borrow to pay for school. Average cumulative indebtedness $19,969. **Criteria for awarding aid:** *Need-based:* Academics, Alumni affiliation, Art, Leadership, Music/drama. *Non-need-based:* Academics, Alumni affiliation, Art, Athletics, Leadership, Music/drama, State/district residency.

See page 1034.

SAN FRANCISCO STATE UNIVERSITY

1600 Holloway Avenue, San Francisco, CA 93132
Phone: 415-338-6486 • **Financial Aid Phone:** 415-338-7000
E-mail: ugadmit@sfsu.edu • **CEEB Code:** 4684
Fax: 415-338-3880 • **Website:** www.sfsu.edu

This public school was founded in 1899. It has a 142-acre campus.

RATINGS

Admissions Selectivity Rating: 73   **Fire Safety Rating:** 87   **Green Rating:** 89

STUDENTS AND FACULTY

Enrollment: 24,882. **Student Body:** 56% female, 44% male, 1% out-of-state, 6% international (91 countries represented). Asian 28%, African American 5%, Caucasian 19%, Hispanic 31%, Native American <1%, Pacific Islander <1%, Two or more races 6%, Race unknown 4%.
Retention and Graduation: 80% freshmen return for sophomore year. 18% freshmen graduate within 4 years. 53% freshmen graduate within 6 years.

ACADEMICS

Degrees: bachelor's, certificate, doctoral/professional, doctoral/research, doctoral, master's, postbachelor's certifate, post-master's certificate. **Classes:** Most classes have 20-29 students. Most lab/discussion sessions have 10-19 students. **Most popular majors:** Marketing/Marketing Management; Communication; Computer Science. **Special Study Options:** cooperative education program, cross-registration, distance learning, double major, dual enrollment, English as a Second Language (ESL), honors program, independent study, internships, liberal arts/career combination, student-designed major, study abroad, teacher certification program. **Disability Services:** Special programs offered to physically disabled students, including note-taking services, reader services, tape recorders, tutors. **Career Services:** Alumni services, Career/job search classes, Career assessment, Internships.

FACILITIES

Housing: Coed dorms, special housing for disabled students, special housing for international students, apartments for married students, apartments for single students, Wellness Housing, Theme Housing, Women only floors. **Special Academic Facilities/Equipment:** Treganza Anthropology Museum, Moss Landing Marine Laboratories, Romberg Tiburon Center for Environmental Studies, Sierra Nevada Field Campus, Sutro Egyptian Collection. **Computers:** 100% of classrooms, 100% of dorms, 100% of libraries, 100% of dining areas, 100% of student union, 100% of common outdoor areas have wireless network access. Students can register for classes online. Administrative functions (other than registration) can be performed online.

CAMPUS LIFE

Environment: Metropolis. **Activities:** Choral groups, concert band, dance, drama/theater, jazz band, literary magazine, music ensembles, musical theater, opera, pep band, radio station, student government, student newspaper, student-run film society, symphony orchestra, television station, Campus Ministries, Student Organization. 213 registered organizations, 6 honor societies, 13 religious organizations. 3 fraternities, 4 sororities. **Athletics (Intercollegiate):** *Men:* baseball, basketball, cross-country, soccer, wrestling. *Women:* basketball, cross-country, soccer, softball, track/field (outdoor), track/field (indoor), volleyball. **On-Campus Highlights:** Cesar Chavez Student Center, Cox Stadium, SFSU Fine Arts Gallery, Residential Theme Communities, J. Paul Leonard Library Annex, Malcolm X Plaza, The Village at Centennial Square, and McKenna Theatre. **Environmental Initiatives:** SF State is dedicated to reducing the campus' use of resources and its impact on climate change. Some of the projects that demonstrate that are: the Buy Recycled Campaign, purchasing 20% renewable energy, implementing a green cleaning program, hiring a Sustainability Programs Manager and a Sustainability Coordinator, offering alternative transportation incentives, pursuing LEED Gold for its new Rec and Wellness Center and diverting over 75% of the waste from the landfill.

ADMISSIONS

Freshman Academic Profile: Average high school GPA 3.2. 88% from public high schools. **Reported SAT (pre-2016 redesign) scores:** SAT Math middle 50% range 430-550. SAT Critical Reading middle 50% range 430-540. SAT Writing middle 50% range 420-530. **Concordant SAT scores:** SAT EBRW middle 50% 480–590. SAT Math middle 50% range 470–570. ACT middle 50% range 18-24. Minimum internet-based TOEFL 61. Minimum paper TOEFL 500. **Basis for Candidate Selection:** *Very important factors considered include:* rigor of secondary school record, academic GPA, standardized test scores. *Important factors considered include:* state residency. **Freshman Admission Requirements:** High school diploma is required and GED is accepted. *Academic units required:* 4 English, 3 math, 2 science, 2 science labs, 2 foreign language, 1 social studies, 1 history, 1 academic elective, 1 visual/performing arts. *Academic units recommended:* 4 English, 4 math, 2 science, 2 science labs, 2 foreign language, 1 social studies, 1 history, 1 academic elective, 1 visual/performing arts. **Freshman Admission Statistics:** 36,223 applied, 68.20% admitted, 15% enrolled. **Transfer Admission Requirements:** college transcript(s), statement of good standing from prior institution(s). Minimum college GPA of 2.0 required. Lowest grade transferable D. **General Admission Information:** Application fee $55. Priority deadline 10/1. Regular application deadline 11/30. Nonfall registration accepted.

COSTS AND FINANCIAL AID

Annual in-state tuition $5,472. Annual out-of-state tuition $16,632. Required fees $1,012. Average book expense $1,900. **Required Forms and Deadlines:** FAFSA. **Notification of Awards:** Applicants will be notified of awards on a rolling basis beginning 4/15. **Types of Aid:** *Need-based scholarships/grants:* Federal Pell, FSEOG, State scholarships/grants, Private scholarships, College/university scholarship or grant aid from institutional funds. *Loans:* Direct Subsidized Stafford Loans, Direct Unsubsidized Stafford Loans, Direct PLUS loans, Federal Perkins Loans. *Student Employment:* Federal Work-

The Princeton Review's Complete Book of Colleges

Study Program available. Institutional employment available. **Financial Aid Statistics:** 90% needy freshmen, 89% needy undergrads receive need-based scholarship or grant aid. 24% freshmen, 13% undergrads receive non-need-based scholarship or grant aid. 78% freshmen, 76% undergrads receive need-based self-help aid. 1% freshmen, 1% undergrads receive athletic scholarships. Average cumulative indebtedness $20,716. **Criteria for awarding aid:** *Need-based:* Academics, Athletics. *Non-need-based:* Academics, Athletics.

SAN JOSE STATE UNIVERSITY

One Washington Square, San Jose, CA 95192-0016
Phone: 408-283-7500 • **Financial Aid Phone:** 408-283-7500
E-mail: admissions@sjsu.edu • **CEEB Code:** 4687
Fax: 408-924-2050 • **Website:** www.sjsu.edu

This public school was founded in 1857. It has a 154-acre campus.

RATINGS

Admissions Selectivity Rating: 76   **Fire Safety Rating:** 60*   **Green Rating:** 98

STUDENTS AND FACULTY

Enrollment: 26,432. **Student Body:** 48% female, 52% male, 1% out-of-state, 7% international (139 countries represented). Asian 36%, African American 3%, Caucasian 18%, Hispanic 26%, Native American <1%, Pacific Islander <1%, Two or more races 5%, Race unknown 4%.
Retention and Graduation: 87% freshmen return for sophomore year. 11% freshmen graduate within 4 years. 62% freshmen graduate within 6 years.
Faculty: Student/faculty ratio 26:1. 727 full-time faculty, 0% hold PhDs, 9% are are members of minority groups, 50% are women. 4% of classes are taught by teaching assistants.

ACADEMICS

Degrees: bachelor's, master's. **Classes:** Most classes have 20-29 students. Most lab/discussion sessions have 20-29 students. **Most popular majors:** Electrical and Electronics Engineering; Business Administration and Management; Art/Art Studies. **Special Study Options:** distance learning, double major, dual enrollment, honors program, independent study, internships, student-designed major, study abroad, teacher certification program. **Disability Services:** Special programs offered to physically disabled students, including note-taking services, reader services, tutors. **Career Services:** Alumni services, Career/job search classes, Career assessment, Internships. We are proud of our Neat Ideas Fair program, which was nominated for the 2008 USASBE innovative pedagogy award. The Fair is a venue for students from across the SJSU campus to display and pitch their business ideas and receive feedback from seasoned entrepreneurs, investors, lawyers, professors, and their peers.

FACILITIES

Housing: Coed dorms, special housing for disabled students, men's dorms, special housing for international students, women's dorms, fraternity/sorority housing, cooperative housing, apartments for single students. 100% of campus accessible to physically disabled. **Special Academic Facilities/Equipment:** Martin Luther King, Jr. Library (Joint with City), Child development lab, Chicano resource center, Beethoven studies center, John Steinbeck research center, art metal foundry, natural history living museum (science education), science resource center, deep-sea research ship, electro-acoustical/recording studios, nuclear science and engineering labs. **Computers:** Students can register for classes online. Administrative functions (other than registration) can be performed online.

CAMPUS LIFE

Environment: Metropolis. **Activities:** Choral groups, dance, drama/theater, literary magazine, marching band, music ensembles, musical theater, radio station, student government, student newspaper, student-run film society, symphony orchestra, Campus Ministries, Student Organization. 283 registered organizations, 13 honor societies, 20 religious organizations. 20 fraternities, 15 sororities. **Athletics (Intercollegiate):** *Men:* baseball, basketball, cheerleading, cross-country, diving, football, golf, soccer, softball, swimming, volleyball, water polo. *Women:* basketball, cheerleading, cross-country, diving, golf, gymnastics, soccer, softball, swimming, tennis, volleyball, water polo. **On-Campus Highlights:** Martin Luther King, Jr. Library, Student Union, Art Quad, Market Cafe/Burger King/Sparro, Gym.

ADMISSIONS

Freshman Academic Profile: Average high school GPA 3.4. 77% from public high schools. **Reported SAT (pre-2016 redesign) scores:** SAT Math middle 50% range 470-590. SAT Critical Reading middle 50% range 450-560. SAT Writing middle 50% range 450-550. **Concordant SAT scores:** SAT EBRW middle 50% 500–610. SAT Math middle 50% range 510–610. ACT middle 50% range 20-25. Minimum internet-based TOEFL 80. Minimum paper TOEFL

550. **Basis for Candidate Selection:** *Very important factors considered include:* rigor of secondary school record, academic GPA, standardized test scores. *Important factors considered include:* geographical residence, state residency. **Freshman Admission Requirements:** High school diploma is required and GED is accepted. *Academic units required:* 4 English, 3 math, 2 science, 2 science labs, 2 foreign language, 1 social studies, 1 history, 1 academic elective, 1 visual/performing arts. **Freshman Admission Statistics:** 31,555 applied, 53.44% admitted, 19% enrolled. **Transfer Admission Requirements:** college transcript(s), statement of good standing from prior institution(s). Minimum college GPA of 2.0 required. Lowest grade transferable 2. **General Admission Information:** Application fee $55. Regular application deadline 11/30. Nonfall registration accepted.

COSTS AND FINANCIAL AID

Annual in-state tuition $5,472. Annual out-of-state tuition $14,400. Room and board $15,212. Required fees $1,946. Average book expense $1,899. **Required Forms and Deadlines:** FAFSA. **Notification of Awards:** Applicants will be notified of awards on a rolling basis beginning 4/1. **Types of Aid:** *Need-based scholarships/grants:* Federal Pell, FSEOG, State scholarships/grants, Private scholarships, College/university scholarship or grant aid from institutional funds. *Loans:* Direct Subsidized Stafford Loans, Direct Unsubsidized Stafford Loans, Direct PLUS loans, Federal Perkins Loans. *Student Employment:* Federal Work-Study Program available. Institutional employment available. **Financial Aid Statistics:** 70% needy freshmen, 93% needy undergrads receive need-based scholarship or grant aid. 7% freshmen, 4% undergrads receive non-need-based scholarship or grant aid. 95% freshmen, 96% undergrads receive need-based self-help aid. 3% freshmen, 1% undergrads receive athletic scholarships. 40% freshmen, 39% undergrads receive any aid. 43% undergrads borrow to pay for school. Average cumulative indebtedness $19,797. **Criteria for awarding aid:** *Need-based:* Academics, Art, Athletics, Job skills, Leadership, Music/drama. *Non-need-based:* Academics, Art, Athletics, Job skills, Leadership, Music/drama, State/district residency.

SANTA CLARA UNIVERSITY

500 El Camino Real, Santa Clara, CA 95053
Phone: 408-554-4700 • **Financial Aid Phone:** 408-554-4505
E-mail: Admission@scu.edu • **CEEB Code:** 4851
Fax: 408-554-5255 • **Website:** www.scu.edu

This private school, affiliated with the Roman Catholic Church, was founded in 1851. It has a 106-acre campus.

RATINGS

Admissions Selectivity Rating: 92   **Fire Safety Rating:** 93   **Green Rating:** 98

STUDENTS AND FACULTY

Enrollment: 5,411. **Student Body:** 50% female, 50% male, 28% out-of-state, 4% international (44 countries represented). Asian 17%, African American 3%, Caucasian 49%, Hispanic 17%, Native American <1%, Pacific Islander <1%, Two or more races 7%, Race unknown 3%.
Retention and Graduation: 96% freshmen return for sophomore year. 82% freshmen graduate within 4 years. 89% freshmen graduate within 6 years. 19% grads go on to further study within 1 year. 14% grads pursue arts and sciences degrees. 4% grads pursue law degrees. 1% grads pursue medical degrees.
Faculty: Student/faculty ratio 11:1. 544 full-time faculty, 95% hold PhDs, 27% are are members of minority groups, 45% are women. 0% of classes are taught by teaching assistants.

ACADEMICS

Degrees: bachelor's, doctoral/professional, doctoral/research, doctoral, master's, postbachelor's certificate, post-master's certificate. **Classes:** Most classes have 10-19 students. Most lab/discussion sessions have 10-19 students. **Most popular majors:** Finance; Speech Communication and Rhetoric; Political Science and Government. **Special Study Options:** cooperative education program, double major, honors program, independent study, internships, student-designed major, study abroad, teacher certification program. **Honors Programs:** The University Honors Program provides Santa Clara's most able students with intellectual opportunities based in small, seminar-style classes. With 14 to 17 students each, seminars emphasize analytical rigor, effective expression, and interaction among professors and students. The course of study combines broadly based, liberal learning with depth of specialization in a major field. Honors Program classes are designed to fit within the curricula of the humanities, natural and social sciences, business, and engineering. Possible majors include every undergraduate field in the University. Combined degree programs: BA/MEng. **Disability Services:** Special programs offered to physically disabled students, including note-taking services, reader services, tape recorders, tutors. **Career Services:** Alumni network, Alumni services, Career/job search classes, Career assessment, Internships, Regional alumni. The Career Center at Santa Clara University provides students with access to quality internships on a local, national, and international level. Employers from all sectors recruit students for internships that emphasize intentional learning, professional development, real-world experience, skill-building, and networking. Almost 4,000 internships are posted each year that target our students on Handshake. Almost one-third of these are technical internships, reflecting our location in the heart of Silicon Valley. Students also have access to thousands of internships posted on over 100 internship databases through our online resources. In addition, we provide effective and successful co-curricular internship programming through which students effectively connect with employers; educate students, faculty/staff, and parents about all aspects of internships; offer a Freshmen/Sophomore Internship Fair each February; and educate employer organizations about developing substantive internship programs that are committed to intentional learning and provide quality, engaged supervision for the student. We also provide numerous internship-related workshops for students, clubs and organizations, classes, and parents during Parent Weekend.

FACILITIES

Housing: Coed dorms, apartments for single students, Theme Housing. 95% of campus accessible to physically diasbled. **Special Academic Facilities/Equipment:** Art and history museum (de Saisset), mission church, theatre, media lab, retail management institute, computer design center, engineering labs, Markkula Center for Applied Ethics, Center for Science, Technology, and Society, Ignatian Center for Jesuit Education. **Computers:** 100% of classrooms, 100% of dorms, 100% of libraries, 100% of dining areas, 100% of student union, 90% of common outdoor areas have wireless network access. Students can register for classes online. Administrative functions (other than registration) can be performed online.

CAMPUS LIFE

Environment: City. **Activities:** Choral groups, dance, drama/theater, jazz band, literary magazine, music ensembles, musical theater, opera, pep band, radio station, student government, student newspaper, symphony orchestra, yearbook, Campus Ministries, Student Organization, Model UN. 86 registered organizations, 25 honor societies, 5 religious organizations. **Athletics (Intercollegiate):** *Men:* baseball, basketball, crew/rowing, cross-country, golf, soccer, tennis, track/field (outdoor), water polo. *Women:* basketball, crew/rowing, cross-country, golf, soccer, softball, tennis, track/field (outdoor), volleyball, water polo. **On-Campus Highlights:** Historic Mission Church; Mission gardens, Pat Malley Fitness Center, Harrington Learning Commons and Library, Benson Memorial Student Center, Leavey Activities Center, The palm tree dotted campus is gorgeous, with stunning gardens, walkways, Mission style buildings, and lots of greenery. At the heart of Santa Clara University is the historic Mission Santa Clara de Asis. Founded in 1777, it is the eighth oldest of the original 21 California missions. The current Mission Church was dedicated May 13, 1928. From then until now it has served as the University chapel, and is used by the University community for Masses, baptisms, weddings and funerals. The Mission Church is open to the public and welcomes visitors. The de Saisset Museum at Santa Clara University is the South Bay Area's free Museum of art and history. The 19,210 square foot facility was founded adjacent to the Mission Santa Clara de Asis on the Santa Clara University campus in 1955 and is currently one of only two museums in the South Bay accredited by the American Association of Museums.

ADMISSIONS

Freshman Academic Profile: Average high school GPA 3.7. 51% in top 10% of high school class, 85% in top 25% of high school class, 98% in top 50% of high school class. 45% from public high schools. **Reported SAT (pre-2016 redesign) scores:** SAT Math middle 50% range 610-720. SAT Critical Reading middle 50% range 590-680. **Concordant SAT scores:** SAT Math middle 50% range 630–750. ACT middle 50% range 28-32. Minimum internet-based TOEFL 90. Minimum paper TOEFL 575. **Basis for Candidate Selection:** *Very important factors considered include:* rigor of secondary school record, academic GPA, application essay. *Important factors considered include:* class rank, standardized test scores, recommendation(s), extracurricular activities, talent/ability, character/personal qualities, alumni/ae relation, racial/ethnic status, volunteer work. *Other factors considered include:* first generation, geographical residence, state residency, religious affiliation/commitment, work experience, level of applicant's interest. **Freshman Admission Requirements:** High school diploma is required and GED is not accepted. *Academic units required:* 4 English, 3 math, 2 science, 2 science labs, 2 foreign language, 3 social studies, 1 academic elective. *Academic units recommended:* 4 English, 4 math, 3 science labs, 3 social studies, 1 academic elective, 1 visual/performing arts. **Freshman Admission Statistics:** 15,834 applied, 48.30% admitted, 17% enrolled. **Transfer Admission Requirements:** college transcript(s), essay

or personal statement, Lowest grade transferable C. **General Admission Information:** Application fee $60. Regular application deadline 1/7. Nonfall registration not accepted. Admission may be deferred.

COSTS AND FINANCIAL AID

Required Forms and Deadlines: FAFSA, CSS/Financial Aid PROFILE. **Notification of Awards:** Applicants will be notified of awards on or about 4/1. **Types of Aid:** *Need-based scholarships/grants:* Federal Pell, FSEOG, State scholarships/grants, Private scholarships, College/university scholarship or grant aid from institutional funds. *Loans:* Direct Subsidized Stafford Loans, Direct Unsubsidized Stafford Loans, Direct PLUS loans, Federal Perkins Loans. *Student Employment:* Federal Work-Study Program available. Institutional employment available. **Financial Aid Statistics:** 80% needy freshmen, 71% needy undergrads receive need-based scholarship or grant aid. 53% freshmen, 41% undergrads receive non-need-based scholarship or grant aid. 36% freshmen, 50% undergrads receive need-based self-help aid. 5% freshmen, 4% undergrads receive athletic scholarships. 70% freshmen, 77% undergrads receive any aid. 44% undergrads borrow to pay for school. Average cumulative indebtedness $27,385. **Criteria for awarding aid:** *Need-based:* Academics, Alumni affiliation. *Non-need-based:* Academics, Athletics, Music/drama.

SANTA FE UNIVERSITY OF ART AND DESIGN

1600 St. Michaels Drive, Santa Fe, NM 87505-7634
Phone: 505-473-6937 • **Financial Aid Phone:** 505-473-6318
E-mail: admissions@santafeuniversity.edu
Fax: 505-473-6127 • **Website:** www.santafeuniversity.edu

This private school was founded in 1874. It has a 100-acre campus.

RATINGS

| Admissions Selectivity Rating: 63 | Fire Safety Rating: 98 | Green Rating: 69 |

STUDENTS AND FACULTY

Enrollment: 839. **Student Body:** 52% female, 48% male, 78% out-of-state, 5% international (21 countries represented). Asian 2%, African American 7%, Caucasian 45%, Hispanic 28%, Native American 3%, Pacific Islander 2%, Two or more races 8%, Race unknown 1%.
Retention and Graduation: 64% freshmen return for sophomore year. 17% freshmen graduate within 4 years. 21% freshmen graduate within 6 years.
Faculty: Student/faculty ratio 15:1.

ACADEMICS

Degrees: bachelor's, certificate, master's. **Classes:** Most classes have 10-19 students. Most lab/discussion sessions have 40-49 students. **Most popular majors:** Film/Cinema/Video Studies; Graphic Design; Drama and Dramatics/Theatre Arts. **Special Study Options:** Accelerated program, cooperative education program, distance learning, double major, dual enrollment, exchange student program (domestic), independent study, internships, student-designed major, study abroad, teacher certification program. **Disability Services:** Special programs offered to physically disabled students, including note-taking services, reader services, tape recorders, tutors. **Career Services:** Alumni services, Career assessment, Internships, On-campus interviews.

FACILITIES

Housing: Coed dorms, special housing for disabled students, men's dorms, women's dorms, apartments for single studentsSubstance-free floors, quiet floors, smoking floors. **Special Academic Facilities/Equipment:** Thaw Art History Library, Marion Center Photographic Library, Garson Studios, Visual Art Center, Greer Garson Theatre Centre **Computers:** Administrative functions (other than registration) can be performed online.

CAMPUS LIFE

Environment: Town. **Activities:** Choral groups, dance, drama/theater, literary magazine, music ensembles, musical theater, student government, student newspaper, television station 14 registered organizations, 1 honor society. **Athletics (Intercollegiate):** *Men:* tennis. *Women:* tennis. **On-Campus Highlights:** Visual Arts Center, Garson Studios, Driscoll Fitness Center, Greer Garson Theatre Center, Fogelson Library.

ADMISSIONS

Minimum internet-based TOEFL 79. Minimum paper TOEFL 550. **Basis for Candidate Selection:** *Very important factors considered include:* academic GPA, talent/ability. *Other factors considered include:* application essay, recommendation(s). **Freshman Admission Requirements:** High school diploma is required and GED is accepted. *Academic units required:* 4 English, 2 math, 2 science, 2 science labs, 2 social studies. *Academic units recommended:* 4 English, 2 math, 2 science, 2 science labs, 2 foreign language, 2 social studies, 4 academic electives. **Freshman Admission Statistics:** 608 applied, 100.00%

admitted, 41% enrolled. **Transfer Admission Requirements:** High school transcript, college transcript(s), essay or personal statement, Lowest grade transferable C-. **General Admission Information:** Application fee $50. Nonfall registration accepted. Admission may be deferred for a maximum of 1 year.

COSTS AND FINANCIAL AID

Annual tuition $28,836. Room and board $8,984. Required fees $1,300. Average book expense $1,400. **Required Forms and Deadlines:** FAFSA. **Notification of Awards:** Applicants will be notified of awards on a rolling basis beginning 3/1. **Types of Aid:** *Need-based scholarships/grants:* Federal Pell, FSEOG, Private scholarships, College/university scholarship or grant aid from institutional funds. *Loans:* Direct Subsidized Stafford Loans, Direct Unsubsidized Stafford Loans, Direct PLUS loans, Federal Perkins Loans. *Student Employment:* Federal Work-Study Program available. **Financial Aid Statistics:** 100% needy freshmen, 100% needy undergrads receive need-based scholarship or grant aid. 4% freshmen, 4% undergrads receive non-need-based scholarship or grant aid. 94% freshmen, 91% undergrads receive need-based self-help aid. 0% freshmen, 0% undergrads receive athletic scholarships. 99% freshmen receive any aid. **Criteria for awarding aid:** *Non-need-based:* Academics, Art, Music/drama.

SARAH LAWRENCE COLLEGE

1 Mead Way, Bronxville, NY 10708-5999
Phone: 914-395-2510 • **Financial Aid Phone:** 914-395 2570
E-mail: slcadmit@sarahlawrence.edu • **CEEB Code:** 2810
Fax: 914-395-2515 • **Website:** www.sarahlawrence.edu • **ACT Code:** 2904

This private school was founded in 1926. It has a 44-acre campus.

RATINGS

Admissions Selectivity Rating: 90   **Fire Safety Rating:** 96   **Green Rating:** 71

RATING: 60* STUDENTS AND FACULTY

Enrollment: 1,377. **Student Body:** 71% female, 29% male, 78% out-of-state, 14% international (44 countries represented). Asian 5%, African American 4%, Caucasian 52%, Hispanic 9%, Native American <1%, Pacific Islander <1%, Two or more races 7%, Race unknown 9%.
Retention and Graduation: 89% freshmen return for sophomore year. 76% freshmen graduate within 4 years. 82% freshmen graduate within 6 years. **Faculty:** Student/faculty ratio 10:1. 108 full-time faculty, 84% hold PhDs, 18% are are members of minority groups, 50% are women. 0% of classes are taught by teaching assistants.

ACADEMICS

Degrees: bachelor's, master's. **Classes:** Most classes have 10-19 students. **Most popular majors:** Liberal Arts and Sciences/Liberal Studies. **Special Study Options:** double major, exchange student program (domestic), independent study, internships, student-designed major, study abroad, teacher certification program, Sarah Lawrence College has no formal majors. However students may concentrate in subject areas. All students design their own educational programs (with faculty advisement), so the equivalent of a "double major" is available. We have a 3-2 program where students can get their B.A. degree and M.S.Ed. in The Art of Teaching or M.A. in Women's History. We also have a 3-2 program in which the student receives a B.A. in the Liberal Arts from Sarah Lawrence and a B.S. in Engineering from Columbia. Combined degree programs: BA/MA, BA/MEng, B.A./M.A. Education, MSW/MA with NYU, MA/JD with Pace Law School. **Disability Services:** Special programs offered to physically disabled students, including note-taking services, reader services, tape recorders, tutors. **Career Services:** Alumni network, Alumni services, Career/job search classes, Career assessment, Internships. The Internship Program provides high quality placements in work environments closely related to our students' career, personal, and academic interests. Since Sarah Lawrence College is a 25 minute train ride away from New York City, and NYC is the hub for so many career fields, our office has access to some of the most prestigious organizations available which consistently seek out our students. Our students' stellar performance in the workplace creates future internship opportunities for other students and full-time post-graduation employment. Other programs include senior transitions and employee/alumni site visits. Excellent experiential learning opportunities available through the office of Community Partnerships and Service Learning.

FACILITIES

Housing: Coed dorms, men's dorms, women's dorms, Wellness Housing, Theme Housing. First year students required to live on campus unless living at home. 60% of campus accessible to physically disabled. **Special Academic Facilities/Equipment:** Performing arts center including a concert hall, dance studios,and theatres; visual arts center including studios, gallery, film theatre, sound stage, visual resources library; music building including music library; science center, early childhood center, greenhouse **Computers:** 100% of classrooms, 30% of dorms, 100% of libraries, 100% of dining areas, 100% of common outdoor areas have wireless network access. Administrative functions (other than registration) can be performed online.

CAMPUS LIFE

Environment: Metropolis. **Activities:** Choral groups, dance, drama/theater, jazz band, literary magazine, music ensembles, musical theater, radio station, student government, student newspaper, student-run film society, symphony orchestra, yearbook, Campus Ministries, Student Organization, Model UN. 30 registered organizations, 3 religious organizations. **Athletics (Intercollegiate):** *Men:* basketball, crew/rowing, cross-country, equestrian sports, soccer, tennis. *Women:* crew/rowing, cross-country, equestrian sports, softball, swimming, tennis, volleyball. **On-Campus Highlights:** Campbell Sports Center, Communitea House, Siegel Center, Library, Heimbold Visual Arts Center. **Environmental Initiatives:** A sustainable living residence and a green roof on another dorm.

ADMISSIONS

Freshman Academic Profile: Average high school GPA 3.6. 40% in top 10% of high school class, 57% in top 25% of high school class, 91% in top 50% of high school class. 49% from public high schools. **Reported SAT (pre-2016 redesign) scores:** SAT Math middle 50% range 550-680. SAT Critical Reading middle 50% range 620-720. SAT Writing middle 50% range 610-700. **Concordant SAT scores:** SAT EBRW middle 50% 670–740. SAT Math middle 50% range 570–710. ACT middle 50% range 27-31. Minimum internet-based TOEFL 100. Minimum paper TOEFL 600. **Basis for Candidate Selection:** *Very important factors considered include:* rigor of secondary school record, application essay, recommendation(s). *Important factors considered include:* academic GPA, extracurricular activities, talent/ability, character/personal qualities. *Other factors considered include:* class rank, standardized test scores, interview, first generation, alumni/ae relation, geographical residence, racial/ethnic status, volunteer work, work experience, level of applicant's interest. **Freshman Admission Requirements:** High school diploma is required and GED is accepted. *Academic units required:* 4 English, 2 math, 2 science, 2 foreign language, 2 history. *Academic units recommended:* 4 math, 4 science, 4 foreign language, 4 social studies, 4 history. **Freshman Admission Statistics:** 3,068 applied, 51.79% admitted, 24% enrolled. **Transfer Admission Requirements:** High school transcript, college transcript(s), essay or personal statement, statement of good standing from prior institution(s). Lowest grade transferable C. **General Admission Information:** Application fee $60. Regular application deadline 1/15. Nonfall registration not accepted. Admission may be deferred for a maximum of 1 year.

COSTS AND FINANCIAL AID

Required Forms and Deadlines: FAFSA, CSS/Financial Aid PROFILE, State aid form, Noncustodial PROFILE. **Notification of Awards:** Applicants will be notified of awards on or about 4/1. **Types of Aid:** *Need-based scholarships/grants:* Federal Pell, FSEOG, State scholarships/grants, Private scholarships, College/university scholarship or grant aid from institutional funds. *Loans:* Direct Subsidized Stafford Loans, Direct Unsubsidized Stafford Loans, Direct PLUS loans, Federal Perkins Loans. *Student Employment:* Federal Work-Study Program available. Institutional employment available. **Financial Aid Statistics:** 98% needy freshmen, 97% needy undergrads receive need-based scholarship or grant aid. 16% freshmen, 14% undergrads receive non-need-based scholarship or grant aid. 80% freshmen, 75% undergrads receive need-based self-help aid. 0% freshmen, 0% undergrads receive athletic scholarships. 79% freshmen, 76% undergrads receive any aid. 35% undergrads borrow to pay for school. Average cumulative indebtedness $19,772. **Criteria for awarding aid:** *Need-based:* Academics, Leadership. *Non-need-based:* Academics, Leadership.

SAVANNAH COLLEGE OF ART AND DESIGN

PO Box 3146, Savannah, GA 31402-3146
Phone: 912-525-5100 • **Financial Aid Phone:** 800-869-7223
E-mail: admission@scad.edu • **CEEB Code:** 5631
Fax: 912-525-5986 • **Website:** www.scad.edu • **ACT Code:** 855

This private school was founded in 1978.

RATINGS

Admissions Selectivity Rating: 77   **Fire Safety Rating:** 85   **Green Rating:** 61

STUDENTS AND FACULTY

Enrollment: 10,484. **Student Body:** 67% female, 33% male, 79% out-of-state, 21% international (115 countries represented). Asian 5%, African American 10%, Caucasian 52%, Hispanic 8%, Native American 1%, Pacific Islander <1%, Two or more races <1%, Race unknown 3%.
Retention and Graduation: 85% freshmen return for sophomore year. 52% freshmen graduate within 4 years. 68% freshmen graduate within 6 years.
Faculty: Student/faculty ratio 19:1. 532 full-time faculty, 80% hold PhDs, 18% are are members of minority groups, 40% are women. 0% of classes are taught by teaching assistants.

ACADEMICS

Degrees: bachelor's, certificate, master's, post-master's certificate. **Classes:** Most classes have 10-19 students. **Most popular majors:** Animation, Interactive Technology, Video Graphics and Special Effects; Graphic Design; Fashion/Apparel Design. **Special Study Options:** distance learning, double major, dual enrollment, English as a Second Language (ESL), independent study, internships, study abroad, teacher certification program, Summer quarter programs in New York City and Europe; apprenticeships with artists or designers and internships with museums, agencies, media production companies, architectural firms, and other companies in the U.S. or abroad. **Disability Services:** Special programs offered to physically disabled students, including note-taking services, tape recorders, tutors. **Career Services:** Alumni network, Alumni services, Career/job search classes, Career assessment, Internships, Regional alumni.

FACILITIES

Housing: Coed dorms, women's dorms, apartments for single students, Learning communities. Accommodations for disabled students. are handled on an individual basis. 82% of campus accessible to physically diasbled. **Special Academic Facilities/Equipment:** Art galleries; computer, video, photography, and design labs; SCAD Museum of Art. **Computers:** 80% of classrooms, 100% of dorms, 100% of libraries, 100% of dining areas, 100% of student union, 50% of common outdoor areas have wireless network access. Students can register for classes online. Administrative functions (other than registration) can be performed online.

CAMPUS LIFE

Environment: City. **Activities:** Choral groups, dance, drama/theater, music ensembles, musical theater, radio station, student government, student newspaper, television station, Student Organization. 68 registered organizations, 2 honor societies, 3 religious organizations. **Athletics (Intercollegiate):** *Men:* baseball, basketball, cross-country, equestrian sports, golf, lacrosse, soccer, swimming, tennis. *Women:* basketball, cross-country, equestrian sports, golf, lacrosse, soccer, softball, swimming, tennis, volleyball. **On-Campus Highlights:** SCAD Museum of Art, Club SCAD, Jen Library, Cafe SCAD, Trustees Theatre.

ADMISSIONS

Freshman Academic Profile: Average high school GPA 3.5. **Reported SAT (pre-2016 redesign) scores:** SAT Math middle 50% range 460-580. SAT Critical Reading middle 50% range 490-610. SAT Writing middle 50% range 460-580. **Concordant SAT scores:** SAT EBRW middle 50% 530–650. SAT Math middle 50% range 500–600. ACT middle 50% range 21-27. Minimum internet-based TOEFL 85. Minimum paper TOEFL 550. **Basis for Candidate Selection:** *Important factors considered include:* rigor of secondary school record, academic GPA, standardized test scores, level of applicant's interest. *Other factors considered include:* class rank, application essay, recommendation(s), interview, extracurricular activities, talent/ability, character/personal qualities. **Freshman Admission Requirements:** High school diploma is required and GED is accepted. **Freshman Admission Statistics:** 11,723 applied, 71.05% admitted, 28% enrolled. **Transfer Admission Requirements:** college transcript(s), Minimum college GPA of 2.0 required. Lowest grade transferable C. **General Admission Information:** Application fee $70. Nonfall registration accepted. Admission may be deferred for a maximum of 2 consecutive quarters.

COSTS AND FINANCIAL AID

Annual tuition $35,190. Room and board $13,905. Required fees $500. Average book expense $2,025. **Required Forms and Deadlines:** FAFSA, State aid form. **Notification of Awards:** Applicants will be notified of awards on a rolling basis beginning 3/1. **Types of Aid:** *Need-based scholarships/grants:* Federal Pell, FSEOG, State scholarships/grants, Private scholarships, College/university scholarship or grant aid from institutional funds, United Negro College Fund. *Loans:* Direct Subsidized Stafford Loans, Direct Unsubsidized Stafford Loans, Direct PLUS loans, State Loans. *Student Employment:* Federal Work-Study Program available. Institutional employment available. **Financial Aid Statistics:** 61% needy freshmen, 63% needy undergrads receive need-based scholarship or grant aid. 98% freshmen, 91% undergrads receive non-need-based scholarship or grant aid. 88% freshmen, 92% undergrads receive need-based self-help aid. 1% freshmen, 1% undergrads receive athletic scholarships. 58% undergrads borrow to pay for school. Average cumulative indebtedness $40,718. **Criteria for awarding aid:** *Need-based:* Academics, Art, Music/drama. *Non-need-based:* Academics, Alumni affiliation, Art, Athletics, Job skills, Leadership, Minority status, Music/drama.

SCHOOL OF THE ART INSTITUTE OF CHICAGO

36 South Wabash Avenue, Chicago, IL 60603
Phone: 312-629-6100 • **Financial Aid Phone:** 312-629-6600
E-mail: admiss@saic.edu • **CEEB Code:** 1713
Fax: 312-629-6101 • **Website:** www.saic.edu • **ACT Code:** 1136

This private school was founded in 1866.

RATINGS

Admissions Selectivity Rating: 62   **Fire Safety Rating:** 83   **Green Rating:** 61

STUDENTS AND FACULTY

Student Body: 73% female, 27% male, 70% out-of-state, (68 countries represented).
Retention and Graduation: 81% freshmen return for sophomore year.
Faculty: Student/faculty ratio 10:1. 172 full-time faculty, 63% hold PhDs, 22% are are members of minority groups, 46% are women.

ACADEMICS

Degrees: bachelor's, master's, postbachelor's certificate. **Classes:** Most classes have 10-19 students. **Special Study Options:** cooperative education program, cross-registration, double major, English as a Second Language (ESL), exchange student program (domestic), independent study, internships, student-designed major, study abroad, teacher certification program, credit/no credit grading option; multi-disciplinary curriculum; 6 credit off-campus requirement. **Disability Services:** Special programs offered to physically disabled students, including note-taking services, reader services, tape recorders, tutors. **Career Services:** Alumni network, Alumni services, Career/job search classes, Career assessment, Internships, On-campus interviews. SAIC's Cooperative Education Program is the recipient of the National Society for Experiential Education (NSEE) Experiential Education Higher Education Program of the Year Award. The award recognizes an 'outstanding educational institution that has demonstrated an exceptional commitment to experiential education in their classrooms or on their campuses.'

FACILITIES

Housing: Coed dorms, special housing for disabled students. 99% of campus accessible to physically diasbled. **Special Academic Facilities/Equipment:** The School is directly affiliated with the Art Institute of Chicago. Other resources include: The Gene Siskel Film Center; Fashion Resource Center, John M. Flaxman Library and Screening Room Galleries (Betty Rymer, Sullivan Galleries, Student Union Galleries, project space and Gallery X), Joan Flasch Artists' Book Collection,Poetry Center, Roger Brown Resources, Video Data Bank, The Poetry Center, Visiting Artists' Program, Media Center **Computers:** Students can register for classes online. Administrative functions (other than registration) can be performed online. Undergraduates are required to own a computer.

CAMPUS LIFE

Environment: Metropolis. **Activities:** dance, drama/theater, literary magazine, radio station, student government, student newspaper, student-run film society, television station, Campus Ministries, Student Organization. 43 registered organizations, 2 religious organizations. **On-Campus Highlights:** Studio Classrooms, Residence Halls, The Art Institute of Chicago, Gene Siskel Film Center, Galleries. **Environmental Initiatives:** Incandescent light bulbs in dorm rooms have been replaced with CFLs and new low-flow restrictions have been installed in all dorm room showers and sinks. Expected results are 206 Metric Tons of CO_2 not being release into the atmosphere and 1.7 Million Gallons of Water Saved annually.

ADMISSIONS

Minimum internet-based TOEFL 79. Minimum paper TOEFL 550. **Basis for Candidate Selection:** *Very important factors considered include:* rigor of secondary school record, standardized test scores, application essay, recommendation(s), talent/ability, character/personal qualities, level of applicant's interest. *Important factors considered include:* class rank, academic GPA, extracurricular activities, first generation, racial/ethnic status, volunteer work. *Other factors considered include:* interview, alumni/ae relation, geographical residence, state residency, work experience. **Freshman Admission Requirements:** High school diploma is required and GED is accepted. **Transfer Admission Requirements:** High school transcript, college transcript(s), essay or personal statement, Lowest grade transferable C. **General Admission Information:** Application fee $65. Priority deadline 2/15. Regular application deadline 6/1. Nonfall registration accepted. Admission may be deferred for a maximum of 1 year.

COSTS AND FINANCIAL AID

Annual tuition $44,910. Room and board $13,150. Required fees $840. Average book expense $1,770. **Required Forms and Deadlines:** FAFSA. **Notification of Awards:** Applicants will be notified of awards on a rolling basis beginning 3/1. **Types of Aid:** *Need-based scholarships/grants:* Federal Pell, FSEOG, State scholarships/grants, Private scholarships, College/university scholarship or grant aid from institutional funds. *Loans:* Federal Perkins Loans. *Student Employment:* Federal Work-Study Program available. Institutional employment available. **Financial Aid Statistics:** 99% needy freshmen receive need-based scholarship or grant aid. 98% freshmen, 99% undergrads receive any aid. **Criteria for awarding aid:** *Need-based:* Academics, Art. *Non-need-based:* Academics, Art.

SCHOOL OF THE MUSEUM OF FINE ARTS

230 The Fenway, Boston, MA 2115
Phone: 617-369-3626 • **Financial Aid Phone:** 617-369-3684
E-mail: admissions@smfa.edu • **CEEB Code:** 3794
Fax: 617-369-4264 • **ACT Code:** 1895

This private school was founded in 1876. It has a 14-acre campus.

RATINGS

Admissions Selectivity Rating: 64   **Fire Safety Rating:** 90   **Green Rating:** 65

STUDENTS AND FACULTY

Enrollment: 278. **Student Body:** 73% female, 27% male, 53% out-of-state, 12% international (45 countries represented). Asian 3%, African American 2%, Caucasian 48%, Hispanic 12%, Native American 0%, Pacific Islander 0%, Two or more races 4%, Race unknown 18%.
Retention and Graduation: 78% freshmen return for sophomore year.
Faculty: Student/faculty ratio 8:1. 40 full-time faculty, 85% hold PhDs, 13% are are members of minority groups, 68% are women. 5% of classes are taught by teaching assistants.

ACADEMICS

Degrees: bachelor's, certificate, diploma, master's, postbachelor's certificate. **Classes:** Most classes have 10-19 students. **Most popular majors:** Fine/Studio Arts; Fine Arts and Art Studies. **Special Study Options:** cross-registration, double major, English as a Second Language (ESL), exchange student program (domestic), independent study, internships, liberal arts/career combination, student-designed major, study abroad, teacher certification program, Combined Degree opportunity (BFA + BS or BA). All-studio elective program (Diploma). 5th Year study / Certificate for Diploma recipients. Joint BFA with Northeastern University. Combined degree programs: BA/BFA, BS/BFA. **Disability Services:** Special programs offered to physically disabled students, including reader services, tape recorders. **Career Services:** Alumni network, Alumni services, Career/job search classes, Internships, On-campus interviews. Creative Futures is a program for SMFA students to learn about entrepreneurship, business skills, grant-writing, and more. Creative Futures is composed of a series of lectures and workshops.

FACILITIES

Housing: Coed dorms, Professional off-campus housing assistance. 100% of campus accessible to physically disabled. **Special Academic Facilities/Equipment:** Museum of Fine Arts, Boston; Art galleries; welding equipment; darkrooms; digital equipment; kilns; and more! **Computers:** 100% of classrooms, 100% of dorms, 100% of libraries, 100% of dining areas, 100% of student union, have wireless network access. Students can register for classes online. Administrative functions (other than registration) can be performed online.

CAMPUS LIFE

Environment: Metropolis. **Activities:** student government, student-run film society 10 registered organizations. **On-Campus Highlights:** Classrooms and Studios, Museum of Fine Arts, Boston, Galleries and Exhibition Spaces, Museum and School Libraries, "Art in progress—everywhere you look". **Environmental Initiatives:** Installed a new state of the art HVAC ventilation system, which includes interior vents and hoods customized for specific art making practices.

ADMISSIONS

Freshman Academic Profile: Average high school GPA 3.5. Minimum internet-based TOEFL 79. Minimum paper TOEFL 550. **Basis for Candidate Selection:** *Important factors considered include:* academic GPA, application essay, talent/ability, level of applicant's interest. *Other factors considered include:* rigor of secondary school record, class rank, recommendation(s), interview, extracurricular activities, character/personal qualities, volunteer work, work experience. **Freshman Admission Requirements:** High school diploma is required and GED is accepted. *Academic units recommended:* 4 English, 3 math, 3 science, 2 science labs, 2 foreign language, 2 social studies, 2 history, 2 academic electives, 1 computer science, 2 visual/performing arts. **Freshman Admission Statistics:** 371 applied, 82.75% admitted, 12% enrolled. **Transfer Admission Requirements:** college transcript(s), essay or personal statement, Minimum college GPA of 1.75 required. Lowest grade transferable C-. **General Admission Information:** Application fee $65. Priority deadline 2/17. Nonfall registration accepted. Admission may be deferred for a maximum of 1 year.

COSTS AND FINANCIAL AID

Annual tuition $39,928. Required fees $1,300. Average book expense $1,600. **Required Forms and Deadlines:** FAFSA. **Notification of Awards:** Applicants will be notified of awards on a rolling basis beginning 4/1. **Types of Aid:** *Need-based scholarships/grants:* Federal Pell, FSEOG, State scholarships/grants, Private scholarships, College/university scholarship or grant aid from institutional funds. *Loans:* Direct Subsidized Stafford Loans, Direct Unsubsidized Stafford Loans, Direct PLUS loans, State Loans. *Student Employment:* Federal Work-Study Program available. Institutional employment available. **Financial Aid Statistics:** 95% needy freshmen, 94% needy undergrads receive need-based scholarship or grant aid. 100% freshmen, 99% undergrads receive non-need-based scholarship or grant aid. 95% freshmen, 89% undergrads receive need-based self-help aid. 0% freshmen, 0% undergrads receive athletic scholarships. 94% freshmen, 97% undergrads receive any aid. 69% undergrads borrow to pay for school. Average cumulative indebtedness $33,176. **Criteria for awarding aid:** *Non-need-based:* Art.

SCHOOL OF VISUAL ARTS

209 East 23rd Street, New York, NY 10010
Phone: 212-592-2100 • **Financial Aid Phone:** 212-592-2030
E-mail: admissions@sva.edu • **CEEB Code:** 2835
Fax: 212-592-2116 • **Website:** www.sva.edu • **ACT Code:** 2895

This proprietary school was founded in 1947.

RATINGS

Admissions Selectivity Rating: 76   **Fire Safety Rating:** 98   **Green Rating:** 60*

STUDENTS AND FACULTY

Enrollment: 3,332. **Student Body:** 55% female, 45% male, 57% out-of-state, 15% international (55 countries represented). Asian 13%, African American 3%, Caucasian 49%, Hispanic 10%, Native American 1%, Pacific Islander 0%, Two or more races 0%, Race unknown 9%.
Retention and Graduation: 86% freshmen return for sophomore year. 60% freshmen graduate within 4 years. 67% freshmen graduate within 6 years.
Faculty: Student/faculty ratio 9:1. 163 full-time faculty, 24% hold PhDs, 4% are are members of minority groups, 31% are women.

ACADEMICS

Degrees: bachelor's, master's. **Classes:** Most classes have 10-19 students. **Most popular majors:** Graphic Design; Photography; Film/Video and Photographic Arts. **Special Study Options:** English as a Second Language (ESL), exchange student program (domestic), honors program, internships, liberal arts/career combination, study abroad, teacher certification program. **Honors Programs:** SVA offers an honors program for incoming freshmen; program involves a two year commitment, with an optional third year. **Disability Services:** Special programs offered to physically disabled students, including note-taking services, reader services, tape recorders, tutors. **Career Services:** Alumni network, Alumni services, Internships.

FACILITIES

Housing: Coed dorms, women's dorms. 100% of campus accessible to physically diasbled. **Special Academic Facilities/Equipment:** Visual Art Museum, Milton Glaser Design Study Center and Archives, 8 student galleries. **Computers:** 100% of classrooms, 100% of libraries, 100% of student union, have wireless network access. Students can register for classes online. Administrative functions (other than registration) can be performed online.

CAMPUS LIFE

Environment: Metropolis. **Activities:** literary magazine, radio station, student government, student-run film society, yearbook. 23 registered organizations, 3 religious organizations. **On-Campus Highlights:** Visual Arts Gallery, Westside Gallery, Visual Arts Museum, Visual Arts Student Association, Student Lounge. **Environmental Initiatives:** Yes, we do recycle our trash, but we do it off site. Due to space limitations we don't have an area to collect and sort out recyclables from our trash, nor do we have the space to store the recyclables prior to shipment to an appropriate recycler. To accomplish this we rely on an outside contractor to collect our trash and sort it at their facilities. They ensure that anything that can be recycled from our trash finds its way to the recyclers.

ADMISSIONS

Freshman Academic Profile: Average high school GPA 3.1. 60% from public high schools. **Reported SAT (pre-2016 redesign) scores:** SAT Math middle 50% range 460-590. SAT Critical Reading middle 50% range 450-580. SAT Writing middle 50% range 450-580. **Concordant SAT scores:** SAT EBRW middle 50% 500–640. SAT Math middle 50% range 500–610. ACT middle 50% range 20-25. Minimum paper TOEFL 550. **Basis for Candidate Selection:** *Very important factors considered include:* rigor of secondary school record, academic GPA, application essay, interview, talent/ability, level of applicant's interest. *Other factors considered include:* standardized test scores, recommendation(s), extracurricular activities, alumni/ae relation, volunteer work, work experience. **Freshman Admission Requirements:** High school diploma is required and GED is accepted. *Academic units recommended:* 4 English, 4 social studies, 4 history, 2 visual/performing arts. **Freshman Admission Statistics:** 2,530 applied, 68.97% admitted, 38% enrolled. **Transfer Admission Requirements:** college transcript(s), essay or personal statement, statement of good standing from prior institution(s). Minimum college GPA of 2.0 required. Lowest grade transferable C. **General Admission Information:** Application fee $50. Priority deadline 2/1. Nonfall registration not accepted. Admission may be deferred for a maximum of 1 year.

COSTS AND FINANCIAL AID

Annual tuition $26,800. Average book expense $3,150. **Required Forms and Deadlines:** FAFSA, State aid form. **Notification of Awards:** Applicants will be notified of awards on a rolling basis beginning 2/15. **Types of Aid:** *Need-based scholarships/grants:* Federal Pell, FSEOG, State scholarships/grants, Private scholarships, College/university scholarship or grant aid from institutional funds. *Loans:* Federal Perkins Loans. *Student Employment:* Federal Work-Study Program available. **Financial Aid Statistics:** 68% needy freshmen, 68% needy undergrads receive need-based scholarship or grant aid. 19% freshmen, 19% undergrads receive non-need-based scholarship or grant aid. 96% freshmen, 97% undergrads receive need-based self-help aid. 0% freshmen, 0% undergrads receive athletic scholarships. 60% freshmen, 55% undergrads receive any aid. **Criteria for awarding aid:** *Non-need-based:* Art.

See page 1036.

SCHREINER UNIVERSITY

2100 Memorial Boulevard, Kerrville, TX 78028-5697
Phone: 830-792-7217 • **Financial Aid Phone:** 830-792-7217
E-mail: http://www.schreiner.edu/admission/index • **CEEB Code:** 6647
Fax: 830-792-7226 • **Website:** www.schreiner.edu • **ACT Code:** 4168

This private school, affiliated with the Presbyterian Church, was founded in 1923. It has a 175-acre campus.

RATINGS

Admissions Selectivity Rating: 75   **Fire Safety Rating:** 62   **Green Rating:** 60*

STUDENTS AND FACULTY

Enrollment: 1,126. **Student Body:** 59% female, 41% male, 3% out-of-state, 1% international. Asian 1%, African American 4%, Caucasian 56%, Hispanic 35%, Native American <1%, Pacific Islander 0%, Two or more races 3%, Race unknown <1%.
Retention and Graduation: 70% freshmen return for sophomore year. 34% freshmen graduate within 4 years. 40% freshmen graduate within 6 years. 15% grads go on to further study within 1 year. **Faculty:** Student/faculty ratio 14:1. 60 full-time faculty, 77% hold PhDs, 12% are are members of minority groups, 48% are women. 0% of classes are taught by teaching assistants.

ACADEMICS

Degrees: associate, bachelor's, certificate, master's. **Classes:** Most classes have 20-29 students. Most lab/discussion sessions have 20-29 students. **Most popular majors:** Registered Nursing/Registered Nurse; Kinesiology and Exercise Science; Psychology. **Special Study Options:** Accelerated program, double major, dual enrollment, honors program, independent study, internships, liberal arts/career combination, student-designed major, study abroad, teacher certification program, weekend college. **Disability Services:** Special programs offered to physically disabled students, including note-taking services, reader services, tape recorders, tutors. **Career Services:** Alumni network, Alumni services, Career/job search classes, Career assessment, Internships, Regional alumni.

FACILITIES

Housing: Coed dorms, special housing for disabled students, apartments for married students, apartments for single students. 95% of campus accessible to physically diasbled. **Computers:** 100% of classrooms, 100% of dorms, 100% of libraries, 100% of dining areas, 100% of student union, 30% of common outdoor areas have wireless network access.

CAMPUS LIFE

Environment: Town. **Activities:** Choral groups, dance, drama/theater, literary magazine, music ensembles, musical theater, pep band, student government, student newspaper, symphony orchestra, Campus Ministries. 35 registered organizations, 5 honor societies, 7 religious organizations. 2 fraternities, 2 sororities. **Athletics (Intercollegiate):** *Men:* baseball, basketball, golf, soccer, tennis. *Women:* basketball, cheerleading, golf, soccer, softball, tennis, volleyball. **On-Campus Highlights:** Caillioux Campus Activity Center, Logan Library, Griffin Welcome Center, Deitert Auditorium, Gus Schreiner Student Center.

ADMISSIONS

Freshman Academic Profile: Average high school GPA 3.6. 11% in top 10% of high school class, 36% in top 25% of high school class, 70% in top 50% of high school class. 98% from public high schools. **Reported SAT (pre-2016 redesign) scores:** SAT Math middle 50% range 450-550. SAT Critical Reading middle 50% range 440-540. SAT Writing middle 50% range 420-520. **Concordant SAT scores:** SAT EBRW middle 50% 480–590. SAT Math middle 50% range 490–570. ACT middle 50% range 19-24. Minimum internet-based TOEFL 79. Minimum paper TOEFL 550. **Basis for Candidate Selection:** *Very important factors considered include:* class rank, academic GPA, standardized test scores. *Important factors considered include:* rigor of secondary school record, application essay, character/personal qualities, volunteer work, work experience, level of applicant's interest. *Other factors considered include:* recommendation(s), interview, extracurricular activities, talent/ability. **Freshman Admission Requirements:** High school diploma is required and GED is accepted. *Academic units recommended:* 4 English, 3 math, 3 science, 2 science labs, 2 foreign language, 2 social studies, 2 history, 1 computer science, 1 visual/performing arts. **Freshman Admission Statistics:** 943 applied, 90.14% admitted, 34% enrolled. **Transfer Admission Requirements:** college transcript(s), Minimum college GPA of 2.0 required. Lowest grade transferable D. **General Admission Information:** Application fee $25. Priority deadline 5/1. Regular application deadline 8/1. Nonfall registration accepted. Admission may be deferred for a maximum of 1 semester.

COSTS AND FINANCIAL AID

Annual tuition $24,030. Room and board $9,806. Required fees $1,720. Average book expense $100. **Required Forms and Deadlines:** FAFSA. **Notification of Awards:** Applicants will be notified of awards on a rolling basis beginning 2/15. **Types of Aid:** *Need-based scholarships/grants:* Federal Pell, FSEOG, State scholarships/grants, Private scholarships, College/university scholarship or grant aid from institutional funds. *Loans:* Direct Subsidized Stafford Loans, Direct Unsubsidized Stafford Loans, Direct PLUS loans, State Loans. *Student Employment:* Federal Work-Study Program available. Institutional employment available. **Financial Aid Statistics:** 100% needy freshmen, 100% needy undergrads receive need-based scholarship or grant aid. 14% freshmen, 12% undergrads receive non-need-based scholarship or grant aid. 84% freshmen, 84% undergrads receive need-based self-help aid. 0% freshmen, 0% undergrads receive athletic scholarships. 99% freshmen, 97% undergrads receive any aid. **Criteria for awarding aid:** *Non-need-based:* Academics, Art, Leadership, Music/drama, Religious affiliation.

SCRIPPS COLLEGE

1030 Columbia Avenue, Claremont, CA 91711
Phone: 909-621-8149 • **Financial Aid Phone:** 909-621-8275
E-mail: admission@scrippscollege.edu • **CEEB Code:** 4693
Fax: 909-607-7508 • **Website:** www.scrippscollege.edu • **ACT Code:** 426

This private school was founded in 1926. It has a 37-acre campus.

RATINGS

Admissions Selectivity Rating: 96   **Fire Safety Rating:** 79   **Green Rating:** 79

STUDENTS AND FACULTY

Enrollment: 1,030. **Student Body:** 100% female, 0% male, 53% out-of-state, 5% international (17 countries represented). Asian 15%, African American 4%, Caucasian 52%, Hispanic 11%, Native American 0%, Pacific Islander <1%, Two or more races 6%, Race unknown 6%.
Retention and Graduation: 92% freshmen return for sophomore year. 80% freshmen graduate within 4 years. 84% freshmen graduate within 6 years. 19% grads go on to further study within 1 year. **Faculty:** Student/faculty ratio 11:1. 92 full-time faculty, 98% hold PhDs, 33% are are members of minority groups, 55% are women. 0% of classes are taught by teaching assistants.

ACADEMICS

Degrees: bachelor's, postbachelor's certifiate. **Classes:** Most classes have 10-19 students. **Most popular majors:** Psychology; Biology/Biological Sciences; Economics. **Special Study Options:** Accelerated program, cross-registration, double major, dual enrollment, exchange student program (domestic), independent study, internships, student-designed major, study abroad. **Honors Programs:** Honors programs in all academic majors available. Combined degree programs: BA/MA, BA/MEng, BA/MBA. **Disability Services:** Special programs offered to physically disabled students, including note-taking services, reader services, tape recorders, tutors. **Career Services:** Alumni network, Alumni services, Career/job search classes, Career assessment, Internships, Regional alumni. Career Planning & Resources at Scripps College believes internships are an essential element of a student's career development, and offers a variety of resources to assist students in their internship search including exclusive access to the Nationwide Internship Consortium—a partnership with more than a dozen elite higher ed institutions across the country who share internship listings. Scripps also awards $57,000—$97,000 annually in grants to students in unpaid internships to accommodate travel, housing, and transportation needs for students in unpaid summer internships. The average grant is $3,500 per student and depends to a large extent on annual donations. Currrently, nearly 85% of Scripps graduates have completed at least one internship before commencement.

FACILITIES

Housing: special housing for disabled students, women's dorms, apartments for single students, Small college owned houses. 85% of campus accessible to physically diasbled. **Special Academic Facilities/Equipment:** Art center, music complex, dance studio, humanities museum and institute, science center, biological field station, field house. **Computers:** 100% of classrooms, 100% of dorms, 100% of libraries, 100% of dining areas, 100% of common outdoor areas have wireless network access. Administrative functions (other than registration) can be performed online.

CAMPUS LIFE

Environment: Town. **Activities:** Choral groups, dance, drama/theater, literary magazine, music ensembles, radio station, student government, student newspaper, symphony orchestra, yearbook, Campus Ministries, Student Organization, Model UN. 200 registered organizations, 5 honor societies, 7 religious organizations. **Athletics (Intercollegiate):** *Women:* basketball, cross-country, diving, golf, lacrosse, soccer, softball, swimming, tennis, track/field (outdoor), volleyball, water polo. **On-Campus Highlights:** Williamson Gallery, Rare book room, Denison Library, Margaret Fowler Garden, Malott Commons, Graffitti Wall, Sallie Tiernan Field House. **Environmental Initiatives:** Establishment of a sustainability committee to serve as an advisory counsel to president regarding campus operations.

ADMISSIONS

Freshman Academic Profile: Average high school GPA 4.0. 67% in top 10% of high school class, 90% in top 25% of high school class, 100% in top 50% of high school class. **Reported SAT (pre-2016 redesign) scores:** SAT Math middle 50% range 630-700. SAT Critical Reading middle 50% range 660-740. SAT Writing middle 50% range 660-733. **Concordant SAT scores:** SAT EBRW middle 50% 700–760. SAT Math middle 50% range 650–730. ACT middle 50% range 28-32. Minimum internet-based TOEFL 100. Minimum paper TOEFL 600. **Basis for Candidate Selection:** *Very important factors considered include:* rigor of secondary school record, class rank, academic GPA, standardized test scores, application essay, recommendation(s), extracurricular activities, talent/ability, character/personal qualities. *Other factors considered include:* interview, first generation, alumni/ae relation, geographical residence, racial/ethnic status, volunteer work, work experience. **Freshman Admission Requirements:** High school diploma is required and GED is accepted. *Academic units required:* 4 English, 3 math, 3 science, 3 foreign language, 3 social studies. **Freshman Admission Statistics:** 3,032 applied, 29.78% admitted, 30% enrolled. **Transfer Admission Requirements:** High school transcript, college transcript(s), essay or personal statement, standardized test scores, statement of good standing from prior institution(s). Minimum college GPA of 3.0 required. Lowest grade transferable C. **General Admission Information:** Application fee $60. Regular application deadline 1/1. Regular notification 4/1. Nonfall registration not accepted. Admission may be deferred for a maximum of one year.

COSTS AND FINANCIAL AID

Annual tuition $50,766. Room and board $15,682. Required fees $216. Average book expense $800. **Required Forms and Deadlines:** FAFSA, CSS/Financial Aid PROFILE, State aid form, Noncustodial PROFILE, Business/Farm Supplement. **Notification of Awards:** Applicants will be notified of awards on or about 4/1. **Types of Aid:** *Need-based scholarships/grants:* Federal Pell, FSEOG, State scholarships/grants, Private scholarships, College/university scholarship or grant aid from institutional funds. *Loans:* Direct Subsidized Stafford Loans, Direct Unsubsidized Stafford Loans, Direct PLUS loans, Federal Perkins Loans, College/university loans from institutional funds. *Student Employment:* Federal Work-Study Program available. Institutional employment available. **Financial Aid Statistics:** 100% needy freshmen, 100% needy undergrads receive need-based scholarship or grant aid. 0% undergrads receive non-need-based scholarship or grant aid. 80% freshmen, 87% undergrads receive need-based self-help aid. 0% freshmen, 0% undergrads receive athletic scholarships. 39% undergrads borrow to pay for school. Average cumulative indebtedness $20,205. **Criteria for awarding aid:** *Non-need-based:* Academics, Leadership.

SEATTLE PACIFIC UNIVERSITY

3307 3rd Avenue West, Seattle, WA 98119-1997
Phone: 206-281-2021 • **Financial Aid Phone:** 206-281-2061
E-mail: admissions@spu.edu • **CEEB Code:** 4694
Fax: 206-281-2669 • **Website:** www.spu.edu • **ACT Code:** 4476

This private school, affiliated with the Methodist Church, was founded in 1891. It has a 35-acre campus.

RATINGS

Admissions Selectivity Rating: 74   **Fire Safety Rating:** 60*   **Green Rating:** 60*

STUDENTS AND FACULTY

Enrollment: 3,079. **Student Body:** 67% female, 33% male, 36% out-of-state, 4% international. Asian 11%, African American 4%, Caucasian 59%, Hispanic 10%, Native American <1%, Pacific Islander 1%, Two or more races 9%, Race unknown 2%.
Retention and Graduation: 82% freshmen return for sophomore year. 56% freshmen graduate within 4 years. 71% freshmen graduate within 6 years. **Faculty:** Student/faculty ratio 15:1. 205 full-time faculty, 90% hold PhDs, 14% are are members of minority groups, 45% are women. 0% of classes are taught by teaching assistants.

ACADEMICS

Degrees: bachelor's, doctoral, master's, post-master's certificate. **Classes:** Most classes have 10-19 students. Most lab/discussion sessions have fewer than 10 students. **Most popular majors:** Business/Commerce; Biology/Biological Sciences. **Special Study Options:** distance learning, double major, exchange student program (domestic), external degree program, honors program, independent study, internships, liberal arts/career combination, student-designed major, study abroad, teacher certification program. **Honors Programs:** University Scholars. **Disability Services:** Special programs offered to physically disabled students, including note-taking services, reader services, tape recorders. **Career Services:** Alumni network, Alumni services, Career/job search classes, Career assessment, Internships. Very strong internship program. Also great 1 & 2 credit classes offered as electives.

FACILITIES

Housing: Coed dorms, apartments for married students, apartments for single students, Theme Housing. **Special Academic Facilities/Equipment:** Art gallery, theatre facilities **Computers:** 100% of classrooms, 90% of dorms, 100% of libraries, 100% of dining areas, 100% of student union, 50% of common outdoor areas have wireless network access. Students can register for classes online. Administrative functions (other than registration) can be performed online.

CAMPUS LIFE
Environment: Metropolis. **Activities:** Choral groups, drama/theater, jazz band, literary magazine, music ensembles, musical theater, pep band, radio station, student government, student newspaper, symphony orchestra, yearbook, Campus Ministries. 63 registered organizations, 1 honor society, 7 religious organizations. **Athletics (Intercollegiate):** *Men:* badminton, basketball, bowling, crew/rowing, cross-country, football, soccer, softball, table tennis, tennis, track/field (outdoor), track/field (indoor), volleyball, weight lifting. *Women:* badminton, basketball, bowling, crew/rowing, cross-country, football, gymnastics, soccer, softball, table tennis, tennis, track/field (outdoor), track/field (indoor), volleyball, weight lifting. **On-Campus Highlights:** Pura Vida Coffee Shop, Royal Brougham Pavilion, Weter Lounge, Student Union Building, The Science Building. **Environmental Initiatives:** June 2010 completion of a solar photovoltaic installation atop our physics and engineering building. The installation was conceived as part of a senior honors project and returns to the grid the approximate amount of electricity consumed by our electric maintenance vehicles. A visible production meter in the second floor hallway allows students in the recently created Appropriate and Sustainable Engineering major to monitor its production.

ADMISSIONS
Freshman Academic Profile: Average high school GPA 3.6. **Reported SAT (pre-2016 redesign) scores:** SAT Math middle 50% range 490–610. SAT Critical Reading middle 50% range 500–620. **Concordant SAT scores:** SAT Math middle 50% range 520–630. ACT middle 50% range 21-27. Minimum internet-based TOEFL 79. Minimum paper TOEFL 550. **Basis for Candidate Selection:** *Very important factors considered include:* rigor of secondary school record, academic GPA, standardized test scores, application essay, recommendation(s). *Important factors considered include:* interview, extracurricular activities, talent/ability, character/personal qualities, first generation, religious affiliation/commitment, racial/ethnic status, volunteer work, work experience, level of applicant's interest. *Other factors considered include:* class rank, alumni/ae relation, geographical residence. **Freshman Admission Requirements:** High school diploma is required and GED is accepted. *Academic units recommended:* 4 English, 3 math, 3 science, 3 foreign language, 2 history. **Freshman Admission Statistics:** 4,034 applied, 87.28% admitted, 19% enrolled. **Transfer Admission Requirements:** college transcript(s), essay or personal statement, Minimum college GPA of 2.5 required. Lowest grade transferable C. **General Admission Information:** Application fee $50. Regular application deadline 2/1. Regular notification 3/1. Nonfall registration accepted.

COSTS AND FINANCIAL AID
Annual tuition $38,520. Room and board $10,824. Required fees $420. Average book expense $825. **Required Forms and Deadlines:** FAFSA. **Notification of Awards:** Applicants will be notified of awards on a rolling basis beginning 3/15. **Types of Aid:** *Need-based scholarships/grants:* Federal Pell, FSEOG, State scholarships/grants, Private scholarships, College/university scholarship or grant aid from institutional funds. *Loans:* Federal Perkins Loans, Federal Nursing Loans, College/university loans from institutional funds. *Student Employment:* Federal Work-Study Program available. Institutional employment available. **Financial Aid Statistics:** 100% needy freshmen, 99% needy undergrads receive need-based scholarship or grant aid. 0% undergrads receive non-need-based scholarship or grant aid. 92% freshmen, 93% undergrads receive need-based self-help aid. 1% freshmen, 2% undergrads receive athletic scholarships. 69% undergrads borrow to pay for school. Average cumulative indebtedness $28,880. **Criteria for awarding aid:** *Non-need-based:* Academics, Alumni affiliation, Art, Athletics, Leadership, Minority status, Music/drama, Religious affiliation.

SEATTLE UNIVERSITY

Admissions Office, Seattle, WA 98122-1090
Phone: 206-296-2000 • **Financial Aid Phone:** 206-296-8020
E-mail: admissions@seattleu.edu • **CEEB Code:** 4695
Fax: 206-296-5656 • **Website:** www.seattleu.edu • **ACT Code:** 4478

This private school, affiliated with the Roman Catholic-Jesuit Church, was founded in 1891. It has a 50-acre campus.

RATINGS
Admissions Selectivity Rating: 86   **Fire Safety Rating:** 97   **Green Rating:** 94

STUDENTS AND FACULTY
Enrollment: 4,751. **Student Body:** 61% female, 39% male, 59% out-of-state, 11% international (80 countries represented). Asian 16%, African American 3%, Caucasian 44%, Hispanic 10%, Native American <1%, Pacific Islander 1%, Two or more races 8%, Race unknown 8%.
Retention and Graduation: 87% freshmen return for sophomore year. 64% freshmen graduate within 4 years. 75% freshmen graduate within 6 years. 14% grads go on to further study within 1 year. **Faculty:** Student/faculty ratio 12:1. 508 full-time faculty, 85% hold PhDs, 21% are are members of minority groups, 53% are women. 0% of classes are taught by teaching assistants.

ACADEMICS
Degrees: bachelor's, doctoral/professional, master's, postbachelor's certificate, post-master's certificate. **Classes:** Most classes have 10-19 students. Most lab/discussion sessions have 10-19 students. **Most popular majors:** Liberal Arts and Sciences Studies and Humanities; Registered Nursing/Registered Nurse; Business/Commerce. **Special Study Options:** cooperative education program, cross-registration, double major, English as a Second Language (ESL), honors program, independent study, internships, liberal arts/career combination, student-designed major, study abroad. **Honors Programs:** The University Honors program provides students of high ability and motivation the opportunity to join a small, select, two-year-long learning community. The program is taken in the freshman and sophomore years and fulfills most of the University's Core Curriculum requirements. Honors programs are also offered within majors. Combined degree programs: BA/MBA; MBA/JD. **Disability Services:** Special programs offered to physically disabled students, including note-taking services, reader services, tape recorders, tutors. **Career Services:** Alumni network, Alumni services, Career/job search classes, Career assessment, Internships, Regional alumni.

FACILITIES
Housing: Coed dorms, special housing for disabled students, apartments for single students, Theme Housing. 95% of campus accessible to physically disabled. **Special Academic Facilities/Equipment:** Observatory, electron microscope, St. Ignatius Chapel **Computers:** 100% of classrooms, 20% of dorms, 100% of libraries, 100% of dining areas, 100% of student union, 95% of common outdoor areas have wireless network access. Students can register for classes online. Administrative functions (other than registration) can be performed online.

CAMPUS LIFE
Environment: Metropolis. **Activities:** Choral groups, drama/theater, jazz band, literary magazine, music ensembles, pep band, radio station, student government, student newspaper, Campus Ministries. 130 registered organizations. **Athletics (Intercollegiate):** *Men:* baseball, basketball, cross-country, golf, soccer, swimming, tennis, track/field (outdoor), track/field (indoor). *Women:* basketball, cross-country, golf, soccer, softball, swimming, tennis, track/field (outdoor), track/field (indoor), volleyball. **On-Campus Highlights:** Chapel of Saint Ignatius, Brand new Student Center, Award Winning Grounds and Open Space, Sullivan Hall, home of the School of Law. **Environmental Initiatives:** Plastic bottled water is not sold anywhere on campus including: the bookstore, vending machines, athletics concession stands, restaurants, and catered events. Free, filtered water and bottle fillers are available at over 30 water fountains throughout campus. The Bookstore is selling a 27 ounce, steel water bottle at a discounted price to make owning a bottle affordable.

ADMISSIONS
Freshman Academic Profile: Average high school GPA 3.6. 31% in top 10% of high school class, 64% in top 25% of high school class, 94% in top 50% of high school class. 64% from public high schools. **Reported SAT (pre-2016 redesign) scores:** SAT Math middle 50% range 530–650. SAT Critical

The Princeton Review's Complete Book of Colleges

Reading middle 50% range 540-640. SAT Writing middle 50% range 530-640. **Concordant SAT scores:** SAT EBRW middle 50% 590–690. SAT Math middle 50% range 560–670. ACT middle 50% range 25-30. Minimum internet-based TOEFL 68. Minimum paper TOEFL 520. **Basis for Candidate Selection:** *Very important factors considered include:* rigor of secondary school record, academic GPA, standardized test scores, character/personal qualities. *Important factors considered include:* application essay, recommendation(s), extracurricular activities, level of applicant's interest. *Other factors considered include:* class rank, interview, talent/ability, first generation, alumni/ae relation, geographical residence, state residency, religious affiliation/commitment, racial/ethnic status, volunteer work, work experience. **Freshman Admission Requirements:** High school diploma is required and GED is accepted. *Academic units required:* 4 English, 3 math, 2 science, 2 science labs, 2 foreign language, 3 social studies, 1 history, 2 academic electives. *Academic units recommended:* 4 English, 3 math, 2 science, 2 science labs, 2 foreign language, 3 social studies, 1 history, 2 academic electives. **Freshman Admission Statistics:** 8,149 applied, 73.64% admitted, 16% enrolled. **Transfer Admission Requirements:** college transcript(s), essay or personal statement, statement of good standing from prior institution(s). Minimum college GPA of 2.25 required. Lowest grade transferable C-. **General Admission Information:** Application fee $55. Priority deadline 1/15. Nonfall registration accepted. Admission may be deferred for a maximum of 1 year.

COSTS AND FINANCIAL AID
Required Forms and Deadlines: FAFSA. **Notification of Awards:** Applicants will be notified of awards on a rolling basis beginning 3/1. **Types of Aid:** *Need-based scholarships/grants:* Federal Pell, FSEOG, State scholarships/grants, Private scholarships, College/university scholarship or grant aid from institutional funds, Federal Nursing Scholarships. *Loans:* Direct Subsidized Stafford Loans, Direct Unsubsidized Stafford Loans, Direct PLUS loans, Federal Perkins Loans, Federal Nursing Loans. *Student Employment:* Federal Work-Study Program available. Institutional employment available. **Financial Aid Statistics:** 84% needy freshmen, 91% needy undergrads receive need-based scholarship or grant aid. 58% freshmen, 45% undergrads receive non-need-based scholarship or grant aid. 71% freshmen, 74% undergrads receive need-based self-help aid. 5% freshmen, 5% undergrads receive athletic scholarships. 95% freshmen, 83% undergrads receive any aid. 67% undergrads borrow to pay for school. Average cumulative indebtedness $28,297. **Criteria for awarding aid:** *Need-based:* Academics, Athletics, Leadership, Minority status, Music/drama. *Non-need-based:* Academics, Alumni affiliation, Athletics, Leadership, Minority status, Music/drama, State/district residency.

See page 1038.

SETON HALL UNIVERSITY

Office of Admission, Seton Hall, South Orange, NJ 7079
Phone: 800-THE HALL • **Financial Aid Phone:** 973-761-9332
E-mail: thehall@shu.edu • **CEEB Code:** 2811
Fax: 973-275-2339 • **Website:** http://admissions.shu.edu/ • **ACT Code:** 2606

This private school, affiliated with the Roman Catholic Church, was founded in 1856. It has a 58-acre campus.

RATINGS
Admissions Selectivity Rating: 82   **Fire Safety Rating:** 92   **Green Rating:** 60*

STUDENTS AND FACULTY
Enrollment: 5,295. **Student Body:** 59% female, 41% male, 22% out-of-state, 2% international (71 countries represented). Asian 8%, African American 13%, Caucasian 51%, Hispanic 16%, Native American <1%, Pacific Islander <1%, Two or more races 2%, Race unknown 7%.
Retention and Graduation: 85% freshmen return for sophomore year. 66 30% grads go on to further study within 1 year. 9% grads pursue arts and sciences degrees. 7% grads pursue law degrees. 5% grads pursue business degrees. 9% grads pursue medical degrees. **Faculty:** 4% of classes are taught by teaching assistants.

ACADEMICS
Degrees: bachelor's, doctoral/professional, doctoral/research, master's, post-master's certificate. **Most popular majors:** Speech Communication and Rhetoric; Criminal Justice/Safety Studies; Communication, Journalism, and Related Programs. **Special Study Options:** Accelerated program, cooperative education program, cross-registration, distance learning, double

major, dual enrollment, English as a Second Language (ESL), honors program, independent study, internships, study abroad, teacher certification program. **Honors Programs:** University Honors Program fosters intellectual development through academic challenge. A structured sequence of colloquia and seminars helps to develop critical thinking abilities. Student study the great texts of the past and also have the opportunity to attend operas, theater, museums, concerts and other cultural events. Combined degree programs: BA/MA, BA/MEng, BS/MS Phys Asst or OT or Athl Trng, BS/D Phys Ther. **Disability Services:** Special programs offered to physically disabled students, including note-taking services, reader services, tape recorders, tutors. **Career Services:** Alumni network, Alumni services, Career/job search classes, Career assessment, Internships, Regional alumni, Internships.

FACILITIES
Housing: Coed dorms, special housing for disabled students, apartments for single students. 94% of campus accessible to physically diasbled. **Special Academic Facilities/Equipment:** Art, natural history, museums, theatre-in-the-round, archaeological research center, TV studio, radio station. **Computers:** 100% of classrooms, 100% of dorms, 100% of libraries, 100% of dining areas, 100% of student union, 100% of common outdoor areas have wireless network access. Students can register for classes online. Administrative functions (other than registration) can be performed online. Undergraduates are required to own a computer.

CAMPUS LIFE
Environment: Village. **Activities:** Choral groups, drama/theater, pep band, radio station, student government, television station 100 registered organizations, 13 honor societies, 3 religious organizations. **Athletics (Intercollegiate):** *Men:* baseball, basketball, cross-country, diving, golf, soccer, swimming, track/field (outdoor). *Women:* basketball, cross-country, diving, soccer, softball, swimming, tennis, track/field (outdoor). **On-Campus Highlights:** Jubilee Hall, University Center, Walsh Library, Recreation Center, Chapel.

ADMISSIONS
Freshman Academic Profile: Average high school GPA 3.5. 37% in top 10% of high school class, 61% in top 25% of high school class, 86% in top 50% of high school class. 70% from public high schools. **Reported SAT (pre-2016 redesign) scores:** SAT Math middle 50% range 510-610. SAT Critical Reading middle 50% range 490-590. SAT Writing middle 50% range 490-600. **Concordant SAT scores:** SAT EBRW middle 50% 550–650. SAT Math middle 50% range 540–630. ACT middle 50% range 22-27. Minimum paper TOEFL 550. **Freshman Admission Requirements:** *Academic units required:* 4 English, 3 math, 1 science, 1 science lab, 2 foreign language, 2 social studies, 4 academic electives. **Freshman Admission Statistics:** 10,180 applied, 84.39% admitted, 17% enrolled. **General Admission Information:** Application fee $55. Priority deadline 3/1. Nonfall registration accepted. Admission may be deferred for a maximum of 1 year.

COSTS AND FINANCIAL AID
Annual tuition $35,940. Room and board $11,522. Required fees $1,782. **Required Forms and Deadlines:** FAFSA. *Student Employment:* Federal Work-Study Program available. Institutional employment available. **Financial Aid Statistics:** 97% freshmen, 97% undergrads receive any aid. **Criteria for awarding aid:** *Non-need-based:* Academics, Alumni affiliation, Athletics, Leadership, Music/drama.

See page 1040.

SETON HILL UNIVERSITY

1 Seton Hill Drive, Greensburg, PA 15601
Phone: 724-838-4255 • **Financial Aid Phone:** 724-838-4293
E-mail: admit@setonhill.edu • **CEEB Code:** 2812
Fax: 724-830-1294 • **Website:** www.setonhill.edu • **ACT Code:** 3688

This private school, affiliated with the Roman Catholic Church, was founded in 1883. It has a 200-acre campus.

RATINGS
Admissions Selectivity Rating: 83   **Fire Safety Rating:** 88   **Green Rating:** 60*

STUDENTS AND FACULTY
Enrollment: 1,433. **Student Body:** 65% female, 35% male, 24% out-of-state, 3% international (17 countries represented). Asian 1%, African American 8%, Caucasian 80%, Hispanic 4%, Native American 0%, Pacific Islander <1%, Two or more races 3%, Race unknown 2%.
Retention and Graduation: 79% freshmen return for sophomore year. 43% freshmen graduate within 4 years. 57% freshmen graduate within 6 years. 30% grads go on to further study within 1 year. 20% grads pursue arts and sciences

degrees. 1% grads pursue law degrees. 3% grads pursue business degrees. 1% grads pursue medical degrees. **Faculty:** Student/faculty ratio 12:1. 101 full-time faculty, 85% hold PhDs, 6% are are members of minority groups, 55% are women. 0% of classes are taught by teaching assistants.

ACADEMICS

Degrees: bachelor's, certificate, master's, postbachelor's certificate. **Classes:** Most classes have 10-19 students. **Most popular majors:** Fine/Studio Arts; Business/Commerce; Psychology. **Special Study Options:** Accelerated program, cross-registration, distance learning, double major, dual enrollment, English as a Second Language (ESL), exchange student program (domestic), honors program, independent study, internships, liberal arts/career combination, student-designed major, study abroad, teacher certification program, weekend college. **Honors Programs:** Honors Program has designated curriculum components. Combined degree programs: BA/JD, BS/DO, /DPharm with Lake Erie Coll of Osteopath Med, BA/Law with Duquesne U. **Disability Services:** Special programs offered to physically disabled students, including note-taking services, reader services, tape recorders, tutors. **Career Services:** Alumni network, Alumni services, Career assessment, Internships, Regional alumni. Internships encouraged or required in every major.

FACILITIES

Housing: Coed dorms, men's dorms, women's dorms, Special housing for honors students. 95% of campus accessible to physically diasbled. **Special Academic Facilities/Equipment:** Art gallery, concert hall, theatre, Child Development Center, NEW: Performing Arts Center, Studio 215, smart classrooms. **Computers:** 100% of classrooms, 100% of dorms, 100% of libraries, 100% of dining areas, 100% of common outdoor areas have wireless network access. Students can register for classes online. Administrative functions (other than registration) can be performed online.

CAMPUS LIFE

Environment: Town. **Activities:** Choral groups, concert band, dance, drama/theater, jazz band, literary magazine, marching band, music ensembles, musical theater, pep band, student government, student newspaper, symphony orchestra, Campus Ministries, Student Organization. 53 registered organizations, 4 honor societies, 7 religious organizations. **Athletics (Intercollegiate):** *Men:* baseball, basketball, cross-country, football, lacrosse, soccer, track/field (outdoor), track/field (indoor), wrestling. *Women:* basketball, cross-country, equestrian sports, field hockey, golf, lacrosse, soccer, softball, tennis, track/field (outdoor), track/field (indoor), volleyball. **On-Campus Highlights:** Griffin's Cove, McKenna Recreation Center, Sullivan Lounge, Residence Halls, Lowe Dining Hall, New additions to Seton Hill include the Center for Performing Arts and Visual Arts Center; both of these venues are located in downtown Greensburg within walking distance of campus. **Environmental Initiatives:** Association of Independent Colleges and Universities of Pennsylvania self/peer assessment program.

ADMISSIONS

Freshman Academic Profile: Average high school GPA 3.7. 24% in top 10% of high school class, 56% in top 25% of high school class, 81% in top 50% of high school class. **Reported SAT (pre-2016 redesign) scores:** SAT Math middle 50% range 470-580. SAT Critical Reading middle 50% range 460-590. SAT Writing middle 50% range 450-570. **Concordant SAT scores:** SAT EBRW middle 50% 510–640. SAT Math middle 50% range 510–600. ACT middle 50% range 21-28. Minimum paper TOEFL 550. **Basis for Candidate Selection:** *Very important factors considered include:* rigor of secondary school record, academic GPA, interview. *Important factors considered include:* class rank, standardized test scores, extracurricular activities, talent/ability, character/personal qualities. *Other factors considered include:* application essay, recommendation(s), alumni/ae relation, volunteer work, work experience, level of applicant's interest. **Freshman Admission Requirements:** High school diploma is required and GED is accepted. *Academic units required:* 4 English, 2 math, 1 science, 1 science lab, 2 social studies, 4 academic electives. *Academic units recommended:* 4 English, 2 math, 1 science, 1 science lab, 2 foreign language, 2 social studies, 4 academic electives. **Freshman Admission Statistics:** 2,206 applied, 73.07% admitted, 23% enrolled. **Transfer Admission Requirements:** High school transcript, college transcript(s), statement of good standing from prior institution(s). Minimum college GPA of 2.0 required. Lowest grade transferable C-. **General Admission Information:** Application fee $35. Priority deadline 5/1. Regular application deadline 8/15. Nonfall registration accepted. Admission may be deferred for a maximum of 12 months.

COSTS AND FINANCIAL AID

Required Forms and Deadlines: FAFSA, Institution's own financial aid form, State aid form. **Notification of Awards:** Applicants will be notified of awards on a rolling basis beginning 11/30. **Types of Aid:** *Need-based scholarships/grants:* Federal Pell, FSEOG, State scholarships/grants, Private scholarships, College/university scholarship or grant aid from institutional funds. *Loans:* Direct Subsidized Stafford Loans, Direct Unsubsidized Stafford Loans, Direct PLUS loans, Federal Perkins Loans, College/university loans from institutional funds. *Student Employment:* Federal Work-Study Program

available. Institutional employment available. **Financial Aid Statistics:** 100% needy freshmen, 100% needy undergrads receive need-based scholarship or grant aid. 18% freshmen, 12% undergrads receive non-need-based scholarship or grant aid. 76% freshmen, 82% undergrads receive need-based self-help aid. 10% freshmen, 10% undergrads receive athletic scholarships. 100% freshmen, 82% undergrads receive any aid. **Criteria for awarding aid:** *Need-based:* Job skills, Leadership, Minority status, Religious affiliation. *Non-need-based:* Academics, Alumni affiliation, Art, Athletics, Music/drama.

SEWANEE: THE UNIVERSITY OF THE SOUTH

735 University Avenue, Sewanee, TN 37383-1000
Phone: 931-598-1238 • **Financial Aid Phone:** 931-598-1312
E-mail: admiss@sewanee.edu • **CEEB Code:** 1842
Fax: 931-538-3248 • **Website:** www.sewanee.edu • **ACT Code:** 4924

This private school, affiliated with the Episcopal Church, was founded in 1857. It has a 13000-acre campus.

RATINGS
Admissions Selectivity Rating: 91　　**Fire Safety Rating:** 96　　**Green Rating:** 84

STUDENTS AND FACULTY
Enrollment: 1,714. **Student Body:** 53% female, 47% male, 79% out-of-state, 3% international (26 countries represented). Asian 2%, African American 4%, Caucasian 82%, Hispanic 6%, Native American <1%, Pacific Islander 0%, Two or more races 3%, Race unknown 0%.
Retention and Graduation: 88% freshmen return for sophomore year. 79% freshmen graduate within 4 years. 82% freshmen graduate within 6 years. **Faculty:** 161 full-time faculty, 96% hold PhDs, 15% are are members of minority groups, 45% are women. 0% of classes are taught by teaching assistants.

ACADEMICS
Degrees: bachelor's, doctoral/professional, master's, postbachelor's certificate, post-master's certificate. **Classes:** Most classes have 10-19 students. Most lab/discussion sessions have 10-19 students. **Most popular majors:** English Language and Literature; Economics; Psychology. **Special Study Options:** double major, independent study, internships, student-designed major, study abroad. Combined degree programs: BA/MEng. **Disability Services:** Special programs offered to physically disabled students, including note-taking services, reader services, tape recorders. **Career Services:** Alumni network, Alumni services, Career/job search classes, Career assessment, Internships, Regional alumni. Sewanee's Internship Fund Program- Thanks to the help of alumni and the donors of Sewanee's endowed internship funds, 163 students received $445,000 in stipends or paid internships in 2016. Sewanee students interned in 21 states and 17 countries, and these endowed funds enabled the students to do meaningful internships that would otherwise have been unpaid.

FACILITIES
Housing: Coed dorms, special housing for disabled students, men's dorms, special housing for international students, women's dorms, fraternity/sorority housing, apartments for married students, cooperative housing, apartments for single students, Wellness Housing, Theme Housing, Substance-free housing & Living and Learning Communities. 90% of campus accessible to physically diasbled. **Special Academic Facilities/Equipment:** Art gallery, observatory, keyboard collection, materials analysis lab with electron microscope. **Computers:** 80% of classrooms, 80% of dorms, 100% of libraries, 100% of dining areas, 100% of student union, 25% of common outdoor areas have wireless network access. Students can register for classes online. Administrative functions (other than registration) can be performed online.

CAMPUS LIFE
Environment: Rural. **Activities:** Choral groups, concert band, dance, drama/theater, jazz band, literary magazine, music ensembles, musical theater, radio station, student government, student newspaper, student-run film society, symphony orchestra, yearbook, Campus Ministries, Student Organization, Model UN. 110 registered organizations, 9 honor societies, 11 religious organizations. 12 fraternities, 9 sororities. **Athletics (Intercollegiate):** *Men:* baseball, basketball, cross-country, diving, equestrian sports, football, golf, lacrosse, soccer, swimming, tennis, track/field (outdoor), track/field (indoor). *Women:* basketball, cheerleading, cross-country, diving, equestrian sports, field hockey, golf, lacrosse, soccer, softball, swimming, tennis, track/field (outdoor), track/field (indoor), volleyball. **On-Campus Highlights:** Outdoor recreation on

Sewanee's 10,000 a, All Saints' Chapel, Abbo's Alley Ravine Garden, Memorial Cross and University View, University Golf and Tennis Club. **Environmental Initiatives:** In pursuit of a goal from our 2008 Strategic Planning Addendum, Sewanee's Sustainability Steering Committee developed a Sustainability Master Plan that has been formerly adopted. The plan, the first of its kind at Sewanee, is a blueprint for the institution's commitment to sustainability as we move forward, empowering Sewanee to teach and lead by example.

ADMISSIONS

Freshman Academic Profile: Average high school GPA 3.7. 33% in top 10% of high school class, 63% in top 25% of high school class, 91% in top 50% of high school class. 45% from public high schools. **Reported SAT (pre-2016 redesign) scores:** SAT Math middle 50% range 570-670. SAT Critical Reading middle 50% range 590-670. SAT Writing middle 50% range 570-670. **Concordant SAT scores:** SAT EBRW middle 50% 640–710. SAT Math middle 50% range 590–700. ACT middle 50% range 27-31. Minimum internet-based TOEFL 90. Minimum paper TOEFL 577. **Basis for Candidate Selection:** *Very important factors considered include:* rigor of secondary school record, academic GPA, recommendation(s). *Important factors considered include:* application essay, extracurricular activities, character/personal qualities, volunteer work, work experience. *Other factors considered include:* class rank, standardized test scores, interview, talent/ability, first generation, alumni/ae relation, geographical residence, level of applicant's interest. **Freshman Admission Requirements:** High school diploma is required and GED is not accepted. *Academic units required:* 4 English, 3 math, 2 science, 2 science labs, 2 foreign language, 1 social studies, 1 history. *Academic units recommended:* 4 English, 4 math, 4 science, 3 science labs, 4 foreign language, 2 social studies, 2 history. **Freshman Admission Statistics:** 4,423 applied, 43.64% admitted, 27% enrolled. **Transfer Admission Requirements:** High school transcript, college transcript(s), essay or personal statement, standardized test scores, statement of good standing from prior institution(s). Minimum college GPA of 3.00 required. Lowest grade transferable C. **General Admission Information:** Regular application deadline 2/1. Nonfall registration not accepted. Admission may be deferred for a maximum of one year.

COSTS AND FINANCIAL AID

Required fees $272. Average book expense $1,200. **Required Forms and Deadlines:** FAFSA, CSS/Financial Aid PROFILE. **Notification of Awards:** Applicants will be notified of awards on a rolling basis beginning 3/1. **Types of Aid:** *Need-based scholarships/grants:* Federal Pell, FSEOG, State scholarships/grants, Private scholarships, College/university scholarship or grant aid from institutional funds. *Loans:* Direct Subsidized Stafford Loans, Direct Unsubsidized Stafford Loans, Direct PLUS loans, Federal Perkins Loans. *Student Employment:* Federal Work-Study Program available. Institutional employment available. **Financial Aid Statistics:** 98% needy freshmen, 98% needy undergrads receive need-based scholarship or grant aid. 22% freshmen, 25% undergrads receive non-need-based scholarship or grant aid. 75% freshmen, 74% undergrads receive need-based self-help aid. 0% freshmen, 0% undergrads receive athletic scholarships. 85% freshmen, 80% undergrads receive any aid. 43% undergrads borrow to pay for school. Average cumulative indebtedness $24,431. **Criteria for awarding aid:** *Need-based:* Academics, Religious affiliation. *Non-need-based:* Academics, Art, Religious affiliation, State/district residency.

SHAW UNIVERSITY

118 East South Street, Raleigh, NC 27601
Phone: 919-546-8275 • **Financial Aid Phone:** 919-546-8565
E-mail: admissions@shawu.edu • **CEEB Code:** 5612
Fax: 919-546-8271 • **Website:** www.shawu.edu • **ACT Code:** 3158

This private school, affiliated with the Baptist Church, was founded in 1865. It has a 30-acre campus.

RATINGS

Admissions Selectivity Rating: 73   **Fire Safety Rating:** 60*   **Green Rating:** 60*

STUDENTS AND FACULTY

Enrollment: 2,027. **Student Body:** 58% female, 42% male, 30% out-of-state, 2% international (17 countries represented). Asian 0%, African American 85%, Caucasian 1%, Hispanic <1%, Native American <1%, Pacific Islander 0%, Two or more races 0%, Race unknown 11%.
Retention and Graduation: 13% freshmen graduate within 4 years. **Faculty:** Student/faculty ratio 15:1. 109 full-time faculty, 74% hold PhDs, 76% are are members of minority groups, 44% are women. 0% of classes are taught by teaching assistants.

ACADEMICS

Degrees: associate, bachelor's, master's. **Classes:** Most classes have fewer than 10 students. **Most popular majors:** Business Administration and Management; Social Work; Sociology. **Special Study Options:** Accelerated program, cross-registration, distance learning, double major, dual enrollment, honors program, independent study, internships, student-designed major, study abroad, teacher certification program, weekend college. **Disability Services:** Special programs offered to physically disabled students, including tape recorders, tutors.

FACILITIES

Housing: men's dorms, women's dorms. **Special Academic Facilities/Equipment:** TV and film production facilities. Curriculum and Materials Center. **Computers:** Students can register for classes online. Administrative functions (other than registration) can be performed online.

CAMPUS LIFE

Environment: City. **Activities:** Choral groups, concert band, dance, drama/theater, jazz band, marching band, music ensembles, musical theater, pep band, radio station, student government, student newspaper, yearbook. 4 honor societies, 4 fraternities, 4 sororities. **Athletics (Intercollegiate):** *Men:* baseball, basketball, cross-country, football, golf, tennis, track/field (outdoor), track/field (indoor). *Women:* basketball, bowling, cross-country, softball, tennis, track/field (outdoor), track/field (indoor), volleyball.

ADMISSIONS

Freshman Academic Profile: Average high school GPA 2.3. 1% in top 10% of high school class, 5% in top 25% of high school class, 25% in top 50% of high school class. 90% from public high schools. **Reported SAT (pre-2016 redesign) scores:** SAT Math middle 50% range 330-410. SAT Critical Reading middle 50% range 330-410. SAT Writing middle 50% range 310-390. **Concordant SAT scores:** SAT EBRW middle 50% 370–450. SAT Math middle 50% range 370–450. ACT middle 50% range 13-16. **Basis for Candidate Selection:** *Very important factors considered include:* rigor of secondary school record, academic GPA, recommendation(s), level of applicant's interest. *Important factors considered include:* class rank, standardized test scores, application essay, extracurricular activities, talent/ability, character/personal qualities, alumni/ae relation. *Other factors considered include:* geographical residence, state residency, volunteer work, work experience. **Freshman Admission Requirements:** High school diploma is required and GED is accepted. *Academic units required:* 3 English, 2 math, 2 science, 2 social studies, 9 academic electives. **Freshman Admission Statistics:** 6,207 applied, 54.49% admitted, 15% enrolled. **Transfer Admission Requirements:** college transcript(s), Lowest grade transferable C. **General Admission Information:** Application fee $25. Priority deadline 7/30. Regular application deadline 7/30. Nonfall registration accepted. Admission may be deferred.

COSTS AND FINANCIAL AID

Annual tuition $11,160. Room and board $7,844. Required fees $3,254. Average book expense $1,300. **Required Forms and Deadlines:** FAFSA, Institution's own financial aid form, State aid form. **Notification of Awards:** Applicants will be notified of awards on a rolling basis beginning 2/1. **Types of Aid:** *Need-based scholarships/grants:* Federal Pell, FSEOG, State scholarships/grants, Private scholarships, College/university scholarship or grant aid from institutional funds, United Negro College Fund. *Loans:* Federal Perkins Loans. *Student Employment:* Federal Work-Study Program available. Institutional employment available. **Criteria for awarding aid:** *Need-based:* Alumni affiliation, Religious affiliation. *Non-need-based:* Academics, Alumni affiliation, Art, Athletics, Music/drama, Religious affiliation.

SHAWNEE STATE UNIVERSITY

940 Second Street, Portsmouth, OH 45662
Phone: 740-351-4778 • **Financial Aid Phone:** 740-351-4357
E-mail: to_ssu@shawnee.edu • **CEEB Code:** 1790
Fax: 740-351-3111 • **Website:** www.shawnee.edu • **ACT Code:** 3336

This public school was founded in 1986. It has a 50-acre campus.

RATINGS

Admissions Selectivity Rating: 91   **Fire Safety Rating:** 96   **Green Rating:** 84

STUDENTS AND FACULTY

Enrollment: 3,756. **Student Body:** 56% female, 44% male, 11% out-of-state, 1% international (20 countries represented). Asian 0%, African American 6%, Caucasian 87%, Hispanic 1%, Native American 1%, Pacific Islander <1%, Two or more races 2%, Race unknown 3%.

Retention and Graduation: 57% freshmen return for sophomore year. 13% freshmen graduate within 4 years. 27% freshmen graduate within 6 years. **Faculty:** Student/faculty ratio 18:1. 145 full-time faculty, 59% hold PhDs, 10% are are members of minority groups, 41% are women. 0% of classes are taught by teaching assistants.

ACADEMICS

Degrees: associate, bachelor's, certificate, master's. **Classes:** Most classes have 10-19 students. Most lab/discussion sessions have 20-29 students. **Most popular majors:** Psychology; Business Administration and Management; Biological and Biomedical Sciences. **Special Study Options:** cross-registration, distance learning, double major, dual enrollment, English as a Second Language (ESL), honors program, independent study, internships, student-designed major, study abroad, teacher certification program. **Disability Services:** Special programs offered to physically disabled students, including note-taking services, reader services, tape recorders, tutors. **Career Services:** Alumni services, Career/job search classes, Career assessment, Internships.

FACILITIES

Housing: Coed dorms, list of housing in community available. 100% of campus accessible to physically diasbled. **Special Academic Facilities/Equipment:** Vern Riffe Center for the Arts. **Computers:** Students can register for classes online.

CAMPUS LIFE

Environment: Town. **Activities:** Choral groups, drama/theater, literary magazine, music ensembles, musical theater, student government, student newspaper, Campus Ministries. 36 registered organizations, 2 honor societies, 3 religious organizations. 1 fraternity, 1 sorority. **Athletics (Intercollegiate):** *Men:* baseball, basketball, cross-country, golf, soccer. *Women:* basketball, cross-country, soccer, softball, tennis, volleyball. **On-Campus Highlights:** Vern Riffe Center for the Arts, University Center. **Environmental Initiatives:** geothermal chiller plant for new building.

ADMISSIONS

Freshman Academic Profile: 12% in top 10% of high school class, 33% in top 25% of high school class, 63% in top 50% of high school class. **Reported SAT (pre-2016 redesign) scores:** SAT Math middle 50% range 433-628. SAT Critical Reading middle 50% range 440-588. SAT Writing middle 50% range 405-548. **Concordant SAT scores:** SAT EBRW middle 50% 480–630. SAT Math middle 50% range 470–650. ACT middle 50% range 18-24. Minimum internet-based TOEFL 60. Minimum paper TOEFL 500. **Freshman Admission Requirements:** High school diploma is required and GED is accepted. *Academic units recommended:* 4 English, 3 math, 3 science, 2 foreign language, 3 social studies, 1 visual/performing arts. **Freshman Admission Statistics:** 3,686 applied, 74.15% admitted, 35% enrolled. **Transfer Admission Requirements:** High school transcript, college transcript(s), Minimum college GPA of 1.0 required. Lowest grade transferable D. **General Admission Information:** Nonfall registration accepted. Admission may be deferred.

COSTS AND FINANCIAL AID

Annual in-state tuition $6,251. Annual out-of-state tuition $11,504. Room and board $9,552. Required fees $1,113. Average book expense $1,440. **Required Forms and Deadlines:** FAFSA. **Notification of Awards:** Applicants will be notified of awards on a rolling basis beginning 3/15. **Types of Aid:** *Need-based scholarships/grants:* Federal Pell, FSEOG, State scholarships/grants, Private scholarships, College/university scholarship or grant aid from institutional funds. *Loans:* Direct Subsidized Stafford Loans, Direct Unsubsidized Stafford Loans, Direct PLUS loans. *Student Employment:* Federal Work-Study Program available. Institutional employment available.

SHENANDOAH UNIVERSITY

1460 University Drive, Winchester, VA 22601-5195
Phone: 540-665-4581 • **Financial Aid Phone:** 540-665-4621
E-mail: admit@su.edu • **CEEB Code:** 5613
Fax: 540-665-4627 • **Website:** www.su.edu • **ACT Code:** 4396

This private school, affiliated with the Methodist Church, was founded in 1875. It has a 100-acre campus.

RATINGS

Admissions Selectivity Rating: 72   Fire Safety Rating: 92   Green Rating: 82

STUDENTS AND FACULTY

Enrollment: 2,087. **Student Body:** 60% female, 40% male, 39% out-of-state, 4% international (32 countries represented). Asian 3%, African American 12%, Caucasian 57%, Hispanic 7%, Native American 1%, Pacific Islander <1%, Two or more races 3%, Race unknown 15%.

Retention and Graduation: 82% freshmen return for sophomore year. 40% freshmen graduate within 4 years. 10% grads go on to further study within 1 year. **Faculty:** Student/faculty ratio 10:1. 250 full-time faculty, 79% hold PhDs, 11% are are members of minority groups, 59% are women. 0% of classes are taught by teaching assistants.

ACADEMICS

Degrees: bachelor's, certificate, doctoral/professional, doctoral/research, doctoral, master's, postbachelor's certifiate, post-master's certificate. **Classes:** Most classes have 10-19 students. Most lab/discussion sessions have fewer than 10 students. **Most popular majors:** Registered Nursing/Registered Nurse; Biology/Biological Sciences; Business Administration and Management. **Special Study Options:** Accelerated program, cooperative education program, distance learning, double major, English as a Second Language (ESL), independent study, internships, liberal arts/career combination, student-designed major, study abroad, teacher certification program, weekend college. Combined degree programs: PharmD-MBA; DPT-MSAT. **Disability Services:** Special programs offered to physically disabled students, including note-taking services, reader services, tape recorders, tutors. **Career Services:** Alumni network, Alumni services, Career/job search classes, Career assessment, Internships. Full-service career preparation from interview training, etiquette training, resume assistance. Alumni networking is available for business students through the Byrd School of Business alumni networking program.

FACILITIES

Housing: Coed dorms, special housing for disabled students, special housing for international students. 91% of campus accessible to physically diasbled. **Special Academic Facilities/Equipment:** None **Computers:** 100% of classrooms, 100% of dorms, 100% of libraries, 100% of dining areas, 100% of student union, 25% of common outdoor areas have wireless network access. Students can register for classes online. Administrative functions (other than registration) can be performed online.

CAMPUS LIFE

Environment: Town. **Activities:** Choral groups, concert band, dance, drama/theater, jazz band, music ensembles, musical theater, opera, radio station, student government, student newspaper, symphony orchestra, television station 65 registered organizations, 2 honor societies, 2 religious organizations. 7 fraternities, 1 sorority. **Athletics (Intercollegiate):** *Men:* baseball, basketball, cross-country, football, golf, lacrosse, soccer, tennis. *Women:* basketball, cross-country, field hockey, lacrosse, soccer, softball, tennis, volleyball. **On-Campus Highlights:** Ohrstrom-Bryant Theatre, Aikens Athletic Center, Alson H. Smith, Jr. Library, Health Professions Building, Goodson Chapel/Recital Hall. **Environmental Initiatives:** Continued refitting of lights, from incandescent to CF or LED.

ADMISSIONS

Freshman Academic Profile: Average high school GPA 3.4. **Reported SAT (pre-2016 redesign) scores:** SAT Math middle 50% range 440-550. SAT Critical Reading middle 50% range 440-570. **Concordant SAT scores:** SAT Math middle 50% range 480–570. ACT middle 50% range 19-25. Minimum internet-based TOEFL 79. Minimum paper TOEFL 550. **Basis for Candidate Selection:** *Very important factors considered include:* academic GPA. *Important factors considered include:* rigor of secondary school record, standardized test scores, extracurricular activities, talent/ability. *Other factors considered include:* application essay, recommendation(s), interview, character/personal qualities, first generation, volunteer work, work experience, level of applicant's interest. **Freshman Admission Requirements:** High school diploma is required and GED is accepted. *Academic units required:* 4 English, 3 math, 2 science, 1 science lab. *Academic units recommended:* 2 foreign language. **Freshman Admission Statistics:** 1,911 applied, 88.02% admitted, 27% enrolled. **Transfer Admission Requirements:** college transcript(s), statement of good standing from prior institution(s). Minimum college GPA of 2.0 required. Lowest grade transferable C. **General Admission Information:** Application fee $30. Priority deadline 2/1. Nonfall registration accepted. Admission may be deferred for a maximum of 12 months.

COSTS AND FINANCIAL AID

Annual tuition $30,132. Room and board $9,990. Required fees $1,190. Average book expense $1,500. **Required Forms and Deadlines:** FAFSA, State aid form. **Notification of Awards:** Applicants will be notified of awards on a rolling basis beginning 3/15. **Types of Aid:** *Need-based scholarships/grants:* Federal Pell, FSEOG, State scholarships/grants, College/university scholarship or grant aid from institutional funds. *Loans:* Direct Subsidized Stafford Loans, Direct Unsubsidized Stafford Loans, Direct PLUS loans, Federal Perkins Loans, Federal Nursing Loans. *Student Employment:* Federal Work-Study Program available. Institutional employment available. **Financial Aid Statistics:** 43% needy freshmen, 72% needy undergrads receive need-based scholarship or grant aid. 100% freshmen, 98% undergrads receive non-need-based scholarship or grant aid. 80% freshmen, 81% undergrads receive need-based self-help aid. 0% freshmen, 10% undergrads receive athletic scholarships. 99% freshmen, 98% undergrads receive any aid. 59% undergrads borrow to pay for school.

Average cumulative indebtedness $22,392. **Criteria for awarding aid:** *Non-need-based:* Academics, Music/drama, Religious affiliation.

SHEPHERD UNIVERSITY

Office of Admissions, Shepherdstown, WV 25443-5000
Phone: 304-876-5212 • **Financial Aid Phone:** 304-876-5470
E-mail: admission@shepherd.edu • **CEEB Code:** 5615
Fax: 304-876-5165 • **Website:** www.shepherd.edu • **ACT Code:** 4532

This public school was founded in 1871. It has a 323-acre campus.

RATINGS
Admissions Selectivity Rating: 72   **Fire Safety Rating:** 88   **Green Rating:** 70

STUDENTS AND FACULTY
Enrollment: 3,094. **Student Body:** 60% female, 40% male, 35% out-of-state, <1% international (15 countries represented). Asian 2%, African American 9%, Caucasian 81%, Hispanic 4%, Native American <1%, Pacific Islander <1%, Two or more races 2%, Race unknown 1%.
Retention and Graduation: 60% freshmen return for sophomore year. 25% freshmen graduate within 4 years. 46% freshmen graduate within 6 years. **Faculty:** Student/faculty ratio 15:1. 140 full-time faculty, 88% hold PhDs, 11% are are members of minority groups, 48% are women. 0% of classes are taught by teaching assistants.

ACADEMICS
Degrees: bachelor's, doctoral/professional, master's. **Classes:** Most classes have 20-29 students. Most lab/discussion sessions have 20-29 students. **Most popular majors:** Business Administration and Management; Teacher Education, Multiple Levels; Registered Nursing/Registered Nurse. **Special Study Options:** cooperative education program, double major, dual enrollment, honors program, independent study, internships, study abroad, teacher certification program. **Honors Programs:** See Honors Program on Web site www.shepherd.edu Combined degree programs: B.S.-M.B.A.; MedStep with WVU School of Medicine: B.S. chemistry with WVU School of Pharmacy. **Disability Services:** Special programs offered to physically disabled students, including note-taking services, reader services, tape recorders, tutors. **Career Services:** Alumni network, Alumni services, Career/job search classes, Career assessment, Internships. Shepherd's experiential learning program encourages, assists, and fosters the incorporation of service learning into all areas of academic study.

FACILITIES
Housing: Coed dorms, special housing for disabled students, apartments for single students, Theme Housing, Suites, first-year housing. 90% of campus accessible to physically diasbled. **Special Academic Facilities/Equipment:** Nursery school, elementary education lab, art gallery, theaters, Fazioli Concert Grand Piano, George Tyler Moore Center for the Study of the Civil War, Robert C. Byrd Center for Legislative Studies. **Computers:** 90% of classrooms, 100% of libraries, 100% of dining areas, 100% of student union, 1% of common outdoor areas have wireless network access. Students can register for classes online. Administrative functions (other than registration) can be performed online.

CAMPUS LIFE
Environment: Village. **Activities:** Choral groups, concert band, drama/theater, jazz band, literary magazine, marching band, music ensembles, musical theater, pep band, radio station, student government, student newspaper, symphony orchestra, Campus Ministries, Student Organization. 85 registered organizations, 9 honor societies, 4 religious organizations. 4 fraternities, 3 sororities. **Athletics (Intercollegiate):** *Men:* baseball, basketball, football, golf, soccer, tennis. *Women:* basketball, lacrosse, soccer, softball, tennis, volleyball. **On-Campus Highlights:** Butcher Athletic Center, Center for Contemporary Arts, Scarborough Library, Wellness Center, Student Center. **Environmental Initiatives:** Recycling.

ADMISSIONS
Freshman Academic Profile: Average high school GPA 3.3. 90% from public high schools. **Reported SAT (pre-2016 redesign) scores:** SAT Math middle 50% range 430-530. SAT Critical Reading middle 50% range 440-550. **Concordant SAT scores:** SAT Math middle 50% range 470–560. ACT middle 50% range 19-24. Minimum internet-based TOEFL 79. Minimum paper TOEFL 550. **Basis for Candidate Selection:** *Very important factors considered include:* rigor of secondary school record, academic GPA, standardized test scores. *Important factors considered include:* talent/ability. *Other factors considered include:* class rank, application essay, recommendation(s), interview, extracurricular activities, character/personal qualities, alumni/ae relation, level of applicant's interest. **Freshman Admission**

Requirements: High school diploma is required and GED is accepted. *Academic units required:* 4 English, 4 math, 3 science, 3 science labs, 2 foreign language, 2 social studies, 1 history, 1 visual/performing arts. **Freshman Admission Statistics:** 1,546 applied, 91.91% admitted, 40% enrolled. **Transfer Admission Requirements:** college transcript(s), Minimum college GPA of 2.0 required. Lowest grade transferable D. **General Admission Information:** Application fee $45. Priority deadline 2/1. Regular application deadline 8/16. Nonfall registration accepted. Admission may be deferred for a maximum of 12 months.

COSTS AND FINANCIAL AID
Annual in-state tuition $7,170. Annual out-of-state tuition $17,482. Room and board $10,054. Average book expense $1,000. **Required Forms and Deadlines:** FAFSA, State aid form. **Notification of Awards:** Applicants will be notified of awards on a rolling basis beginning 3/15. **Types of Aid:** *Need-based scholarships/grants:* Federal Pell, FSEOG, State scholarships/grants, Private scholarships, College/university scholarship or grant aid from institutional funds. *Loans:* Direct Subsidized Stafford Loans, Direct Unsubsidized Stafford Loans, Direct PLUS loans, Federal Perkins Loans. *Student Employment:* Federal Work-Study Program available. Institutional employment available. **Financial Aid Statistics:** 66% needy freshmen, 67% needy undergrads receive need-based scholarship or grant aid. 51% freshmen, 37% undergrads receive non-need-based scholarship or grant aid. 63% freshmen, 69% undergrads receive need-based self-help aid. 8% freshmen, 8% undergrads receive athletic scholarships. 91% freshmen, 82% undergrads receive any aid. 72% undergrads borrow to pay for school. Average cumulative indebtedness $30,526. **Criteria for awarding aid:** *Need-based:* Academics. *Non-need-based:* Academics, Art, Athletics, Job skills, Leadership, Minority status, Music/drama, State/district residency.

SHIMER COLLEGE

3424 S. State St, Chicago, IL 60616
Phone: 312-235-3555 • **Financial Aid Phone:** 312-235-3507
E-mail: admission@shimer.edu • **CEEB Code:** 1717
Fax: 888-808-3133 • **Website:** http://www.shimer.edu/ • **ACT Code:** 1142

This private school was founded in 1853. It has a 140-acre campus.

RATINGS
Admissions Selectivity Rating: 77   **Fire Safety Rating:** 60*   **Green Rating:** 60*

STUDENTS AND FACULTY
Enrollment: 74. **Student Body:** 47% female, 53% male, 50% out-of-state, 0% international (4 countries represented). Asian 7%, African American 9%, Caucasian 68%, Hispanic 12%, Native American 0%, Pacific Islander 0%, Two or more races 0%, Race unknown 4%.
Retention and Graduation: 63% freshmen return for sophomore year. 19% freshmen graduate within 4 years. **Faculty:** Student/faculty ratio 7:1. 9 full-time faculty, 100% hold PhDs, 22% are are members of minority groups, 33% are women. 0% of classes are taught by teaching assistants.

ACADEMICS
Degrees: bachelor's. **Classes:** Most classes have fewer than 10 students. Most lab/discussion sessions have 10-19 students. **Most popular majors:** Humanities/Humanistic Studies; Natural Sciences; Social Sciences. **Special Study Options:** cross-registration, double major, independent study, internships, liberal arts/career combination, study abroad, weekend college, one-on-one tutorials with faculty member for in depth study in any area of interest to the student. Combined degree programs: BA/JD. **Career Services:** Alumni network, Alumni services, Career/job search classes, Internships, Regional alumni. Shimer students may intern off campus during their program. Funded internships are available.

FACILITIES
Housing: Coed dorms, women's dorms, apartments for married students, apartments for single students. 100% of campus accessible to physically diasbled. **Special Academic Facilities/Equipment:** The Galvin Library has over one million volumes and 120 digital databases. The MTCC (student center) is an amazing place to eat, play and hang out. **Computers:** 100% of classrooms, 100% of dorms, 100% of libraries, 100% of dining areas, 100% of student union, 100% of common outdoor areas have wireless network access. **CAMPUS LIFE Environment:** Metropolis. **Activities:** Choral groups, concert band, drama/theater, jazz band, literary magazine, music ensembles, radio station, student government, student newspaper, Student Organization. 10 religious organizations. **On-Campus Highlights:** The Shimer College space on the IIT Camp, The Galvin Library/Art Galery, McCormic Tribune Campus Center, Crown Hall, Keating Sports Center, Students are strongly encouraged to visit when classes are in session. The best way to know if Shimer is a good fit for you is if you sit in on a class.

ADMISSIONS

Freshman Academic Profile: Average high school GPA 3.0. 50% from public high schools. **Reported SAT (pre-2016 redesign) scores:** SAT Math middle 50% range 500-640. SAT Critical Reading middle 50% range 620-760. SAT Writing middle 50% range 500-620. **Concordant SAT scores:** SAT EBRW middle 50% 620–730. SAT Math middle 50% range 530–660. Minimum paper TOEFL 625. **Basis for Candidate Selection:** *Very important factors considered include:* application essay, recommendation(s), interview, level of applicant's interest. *Important factors considered include:* rigor of secondary school record, academic GPA, extracurricular activities, talent/ability, character/personal qualities. *Other factors considered include:* standardized test scores, first generation, alumni/ae relation, volunteer work, work experience. **Freshman Admission Requirements:** High school diploma or equivalent is not required. *Academic units recommended:* 4 English, 3 math, 3 science, 2 foreign language, 2 history, 1 visual/performing arts. **Freshman Admission Statistics:** 31 applied, 83.87% admitted, 46% enrolled. **Transfer Admission Requirements:** college transcript(s), essay or personal statement, interview, Lowest grade transferable C. **General Admission Information:** Application fee $25. Priority deadline 5/1. Nonfall registration accepted. Admission may be deferred for a maximum of 1 year.

COSTS AND FINANCIAL AID

Annual tuition $26,510. Room and board $10,626. Required fees $4,720. Average book expense $800. **Required Forms and Deadlines:** FAFSA. **Notification of Awards:** Applicants will be notified of awards on a rolling basis beginning 3/15. **Types of Aid:** *Need-based scholarships/grants:* Federal Pell, FSEOG, State scholarships/grants, Private scholarships, College/university scholarship or grant aid from institutional funds. *Loans:* Direct Subsidized Stafford Loans, Direct Unsubsidized Stafford Loans, Direct PLUS loans, Federal Perkins Loans. *Student Employment:* Federal Work-Study Program available. Institutional employment available. **Financial Aid Statistics:** 71% needy freshmen, 100% needy undergrads receive need-based scholarship or grant aid. 71% freshmen, 75% undergrads receive non-need-based scholarship or grant aid. 71% freshmen, 91% undergrads receive need-based self-help aid. 0% freshmen, 0% undergrads receive athletic scholarships. 74% freshmen, 84% undergrads receive any aid. **Criteria for awarding aid:** *Need-based:* Academics, Alumni affiliation. *Non-need-based:* Academics, Alumni affiliation.

SHIPPENSBURG UNIVERSITY
OF PENNSYLVANIA

Old Main 105, Shippensburg, PA 17257-2299
Phone: 717-477-1231 • **Financial Aid Phone:** 717-477-1131
E-mail: admiss@ship.edu • **CEEB Code:** 2657
Fax: 717-477-4016 • **Website:** www.ship.edu • **ACT Code:** 3714

This public school was founded in 1871. It has a 200-acre campus.

RATINGS

Admissions Selectivity Rating: 73   **Fire Safety Rating:** 98   **Green Rating:** 71

STUDENTS AND FACULTY

Enrollment: 5,853. **Student Body:** 50% female, 50% male, 8% out-of-state, 1% international (29 countries represented). Asian 2%, African American 11%, Caucasian 77%, Hispanic 5%, Native American <1%, Pacific Islander <1%, Two or more races 3%, Race unknown 1%.
Retention and Graduation: 75% freshmen return for sophomore year. 41% freshmen graduate within 4 years. 56% freshmen graduate within 6 years.

ACADEMICS

Degrees: bachelor's, certificate, doctoral/research, master's, postbachelor's certificate, post-master's certificate. **Classes:** Most classes have 20-29 students. Most lab/discussion sessions have 10-19 students. **Most popular majors:** Psychology; Criminal Justice/Safety Studies; Biology/Biological Sciences. **Special Study Options:** Accelerated program, cooperative education program, distance learning, double major, dual enrollment, honors program, independent study, internships, study abroad, teacher certification program, Raider Plan. **Honors Programs:** Program in General Education and Psychology Combined degree programs: 3-2 EngProg/PSU and U of Md; Chem and Bio/Med Tech. **Disability Services:** Special programs offered to physically disabled students, including note-taking services, reader services, tape recorders, tutors. **Career Services:** Alumni network, Alumni services, Career/job search classes, Career assessment, Internships, Regional alumni. Pennsylvania has been working to transform itself from a manufacturing economy to a diversified service-based economy with strength in technology intensive industries. Pennsylvania's workforce development strategy seeks to align education and training to High Priority Occupations (HPOs), which are fields with identified skill needs and job openings. Internships are a vital link between education and employment. Shippensburg University, and each of the 14 Pennsylvania State System of Higher Education (PASSHE) Universities. Student teaching, practicuums, field experiences, and internships are offered by all three colleges at both the undergraduate and graduate levels. Students gain professional experience directly related to their major by working part- or full-time during the fall or spring semesters or during the summer. Students earn credit based upon the number of hours worked; they are supervised by a faculty advisor and are expected to develop a rapport with their employer to fully understand and satisfy the duties and responsibilities of their assignment. Students are expected to complete a variety of academic assignments related to their experience and in a number of programs, also participate in a seminar course associated with their experiential learning placement. Responsibility for assessment rests within the academic departments and is incorporated into departmental five-year program reviews.

FACILITIES

Housing: Coed dorms, Wellness Housing, Theme Housing, Suites, Apartment Complex Off-Campus. 93% of campus accessible to physically diasbled. **Special Academic Facilities/Equipment:** art gallery, vertebrate museum, on-campus elementary school, planetarium, electron microscope, NMR spectrometer, greenhouse, herbarium, Fashion Archives, Women's Center, Closed Circuit TV. **Computers:** 95% of classrooms, 10% of dorms, 100% of libraries, 100% of dining areas, 95% of student union, 75% of common outdoor areas have wireless network access. Students can register for classes online. Administrative functions (other than registration) can be performed online.

CAMPUS LIFE

Environment: Village. **Activities:** Choral groups, concert band, dance, drama/theater, jazz band, literary magazine, marching band, music ensembles, musical theater, radio station, student government, student newspaper, television station, yearbook, Campus Ministries, Student Organization. 200 registered organizations, 23 honor societies, 8 religious organizations. 12 fraternities, 15 sororities. **Athletics (Intercollegiate):** *Men:* baseball, basketball, cross-country, football, soccer, swimming, track/field (outdoor), track/field (indoor), wrestling. *Women:* basketball, cross-country, field hockey, lacrosse, soccer, softball, swimming, tennis, track/field (outdoor), track/field (indoor), volleyball. **On-Campus Highlights:** Ceddia Union Building, Heiges Field House, Student Recreation Center, Ritazza Coffee Shop, Student Fitness Center, Starbucks, Quiznos, Chick-fil-A, Dauphin Humanities Center, Lehman Library, Learning Assistant Center, Reisner Dining Hall.

ADMISSIONS

Freshman Academic Profile: Average high school GPA 3.2. 7% in top 10% of high school class, 25% in top 25% of high school class, 58% in top 50% of high school class. 89% from public high schools. **Reported SAT (pre-2016 redesign) scores:** SAT Math middle 50% range 440-540. SAT Critical Reading middle 50% range 430-530. SAT Writing middle 50% range 410-510. **Concordant SAT scores:** SAT EBRW middle 50% 470–580. SAT Math middle 50% range 480–570. ACT middle 50% range 18-23. Minimum internet-based TOEFL 66. Minimum paper TOEFL 500. **Basis for Candidate Selection:** *Very important factors considered include:* rigor of secondary school record, class rank, academic GPA, standardized test scores. *Other factors considered include:* application essay, recommendation(s), interview, extracurricular activities, talent/ability, character/personal qualities, volunteer work, work experience, level of applicant's interest. **Freshman Admission Requirements:** High school diploma is required and GED is accepted. *Academic units recommended:* 4 English, 3 math, 3 science, 3 science labs, 3 foreign language, and 3 units from above areas or other academic areas. **Freshman Admission Statistics:** 5,799 applied, 88.31% admitted, 27% enrolled. **Transfer Admission Requirements:** college transcript(s), statement of good standing from prior institution(s). Minimum college GPA of 2.2 required. Lowest grade transferable C. **General Admission Information:** Application fee $45. Nonfall registration accepted. Admission may be deferred for a maximum of 1 year.

COSTS AND FINANCIAL AID

Annual in-state tuition $8,430. Annual out-of-state tuition $16,286. Room and board $11,776. Required fees $3,022. Average book expense $1,200. **Required Forms and Deadlines:** FAFSA. **Types of Aid:** *Need-based scholarships/grants:* Federal Pell, FSEOG, State scholarships/grants, Private scholarships, College/university scholarship or grant aid from institutional funds. *Loans:* Direct Subsidized Stafford Loans, Direct Unsubsidized Stafford Loans, Direct PLUS loans, Federal Perkins Loans. *Student Employment:* Federal Work-Study Program available. Institutional employment available. **Financial Aid Statistics:** 74% needy freshmen, 74% needy undergrads receive need-based scholarship or grant aid. 3% freshmen, 4% undergrads receive non-need-based scholarship or grant aid. 95% freshmen, 94% undergrads receive need-based self-help aid. 6% freshmen, 6% undergrads receive athletic scholarships. 92% freshmen, 88% undergrads receive any aid. 80% undergrads borrow to pay for school. Average cumulative indebtedness $33,673. **Criteria for awarding aid:** *Need-based:* Academics. *Non-need-based:* Academics, Athletics.

SHORTER UNIVERSITY

315 Shorter Avenue, Rome, GA 30165
Phone: 706-233-7319 • **Financial Aid Phone:** 706-233-7227
E-mail: admissions@shorter.edu • **CEEB Code:** 5616
Fax: 706-233-7224 • **Website:** www.shorter.edu • **ACT Code:** 860

This private school, affiliated with the Southern Baptist Church, was founded in 1873. It has a 150-acre campus.

RATINGS

Admissions Selectivity Rating: 80   **Fire Safety Rating:** 86   **Green Rating:** 60*

STUDENTS AND FACULTY

Enrollment: 1,581. **Student Body:** 55% female, 45% male, 12% out-of-state, 3% international (22 countries represented). Asian 1%, African American 17%, Caucasian 69%, Hispanic 4%, Native American <1%, Pacific Islander <1%, Two or more races 1%, Race unknown 4%.
Retention and Graduation: 68% freshmen return for sophomore year. 33% freshmen graduate within 4 years. 43% freshmen graduate within 6 years. 30% grads go on to further study within 1 year. **Faculty:** Student/faculty ratio 13:1. 92 full-time faculty, 70% hold PhDs, 9% are are members of minority groups, 50% are women. 0% of classes are taught by teaching assistants.

ACADEMICS

Degrees: associate, bachelor's. **Classes:** Most classes have 10-19 students. Most lab/discussion sessions have 10-19 students. **Most popular majors:** Education; Visual and Performing Arts; Business Administration and Management. **Special Study Options:** cross-registration, double major, dual enrollment, honors program, independent study, internships, student-designed major, study abroad, teacher certification program, weekend college. **Honors Programs:** Academy of Aristaeus: a four-year honors program featuring seminar discussions and a research project. **Disability Services:** Special programs offered to physically disabled students, including note-taking services, reader services, tape recorders, tutors. **Career Services:** Career/job search classes, Career assessment, Internships, On-campus interviews. Most majors include required internships.

FACILITIES

Housing: men's dorms, women's dorms, apartments for single students. 70% of campus accessible to physically diasbled. **Special Academic Facilities/Equipment:** Shorter History Museum **Computers:** Students can register for classes online. Administrative functions (other than registration) can be performed online.

CAMPUS LIFE

Environment: Town. **Activities:** Choral groups, concert band, dance, drama/theater, literary magazine, marching band, music ensembles, musical theater, opera, pep band, radio station, student government, student newspaper, student-run film society, yearbook, Campus Ministries, Student Organization, Model UN. 34 registered organizations, 10 honor societies, 3 religious organizations. 3 fraternities, 3 sororities. **Athletics (Intercollegiate):** *Men:* baseball, basketball, cheerleading, cross-country, football, golf, soccer, tennis, track/field (outdoor). *Women:* basketball, cheerleading, cross-country, golf, lacrosse, soccer, softball, tennis, track/field (outdoor), volleyball. **On-Campus Highlights:** Fitton Student Union, Winthrop-King Activities Center, Brookes Chapel, Ledbetter Baseball Complex

ADMISSIONS

Freshman Academic Profile: Average high school GPA 3.3. 21% in top 10% of high school class, 47% in top 25% of high school class, 77% in top 50% of high school class. 95% from public high schools. **Reported SAT (pre-2016 redesign) scores:** SAT Math middle 50% range 430-550. SAT Critical Reading middle 50% range 420-550. SAT Writing middle 50% range 410-530. **Concordant SAT scores:** SAT EBRW middle 50% 460–600. SAT Math middle 50% range 470–570. ACT middle 50% range 18-24. Minimum paper TOEFL 500. **Basis for Candidate Selection:** *Very important factors considered include:* academic GPA, standardized test scores. *Important factors considered include:* rigor of secondary school record, class rank, application essay, talent/ability. *Other factors considered include:* recommendation(s), interview, extracurricular activities, character/personal qualities, first generation, alumni/ae relation, volunteer work, work experience, level of applicant's interest. **Freshman Admission Requirements:** High school diploma is required and GED is accepted. *Academic units required:* 4 English, 4 math, 3 science, 2 foreign language, 3 history. **Freshman Admission Statistics:** 1,944 applied, 64.97% admitted, 32% enrolled. **Transfer Admission Requirements:** college transcript(s), statement of good standing from prior institution(s). Minimum college GPA of 2.0 required. Lowest grade transferable C. **General Admission Information:** Application fee $25. Nonfall registration accepted. Admission may be deferred for a maximum of 2 years.

COSTS AND FINANCIAL AID

Annual tuition $17,500. Room and board $8,600. Required fees $370. Average book expense $1,200. **Required Forms and Deadlines:** FAFSA, Institution's own financial aid form, State aid form. **Notification of Awards:** Applicants will be notified of awards on a rolling basis beginning 4/1. **Types of Aid:** *Need-based scholarships/grants:* Federal Pell, FSEOG, State scholarships/grants, Private scholarships, College/university scholarship or grant aid from institutional funds. *Loans:* Federal Perkins Loans. *Student Employment:* Federal Work-Study Program available. Institutional employment available. **Financial Aid Statistics:** 99% needy freshmen, 99% needy undergrads receive need-based scholarship or grant aid. 16% freshmen, 15% undergrads receive non-need-based scholarship or grant aid. 79% freshmen, 75% undergrads receive need-based self-help aid. 15% freshmen, 11% undergrads receive athletic scholarships. 99% freshmen, 99% undergrads receive any aid. **Criteria for awarding aid:** *Need-based:* Academics, Art, Athletics, Music/drama, Religious affiliation. *Non-need-based:* Academics, Art, Athletics, Music/drama, Religious affiliation.

SIENA COLLEGE

515 Loudon Road, Loudonville, NY 12211
Phone: 518-783-2423 • **Financial Aid Phone:** 888-287-4362
E-mail: admissions@siena.edu • **CEEB Code:** 2814
Fax: 518-783-2436 • **Website:** www.siena.edu • **ACT Code:** 2878

This private school, affiliated with the Roman Catholic Church, was founded in 1937. It has a 166-acre campus.

RATINGS

Admissions Selectivity Rating: 85   **Fire Safety Rating:** 91   **Green Rating:** 67

STUDENTS AND FACULTY

Enrollment: 3,141. **Student Body:** 52% female, 48% male, 19% out-of-state, 2% international (13 countries represented). Asian 4%, African American 4%, Caucasian 79%, Hispanic 8%, Native American <1%, Pacific Islander <1%, Two or more races 2%, Race unknown 1%.
Retention and Graduation: 87% freshmen return for sophomore year. 69% freshmen graduate within 4 years. 77 32% grads go on to further study within 1 year. 30% grads pursue arts and sciences degrees. 8% grads pursue law degrees. 19% grads pursue business degrees. 9% grads pursue medical degrees. **Faculty:** Student/faculty ratio 12:1. 216 full-time faculty, 88% hold PhDs, 14% are are members of minority groups, 44% are women. 0% of classes are taught by teaching assistants.

ACADEMICS

Degrees: bachelor's, certificate, master's. **Classes:** Most classes have 20-29 students. Most lab/discussion sessions have 10-19 students. **Most popular majors:** Accounting; Psychology; Biology. **Special Study Options:** Accelerated program, cross-registration, double major, English as a Second Language (ESL), honors program, independent study, internships, liberal arts/career combination, study abroad, teacher certification program, Semester in Washington D.C., Gettysburg Semester. **Honors Programs:** College-wide Honors program. Combined degree programs: BA/MD, BA/JD, BA/MA, BA/DDS, BA/MEng. **Disability Services:** Special programs offered to physically disabled students, including note-taking services, reader services, tape recorders, tutors. **Career Services:** Alumni network, Alumni services, Career/job search classes, Career assessment, Internships, Regional alumni. Students at Siena have internship, practicum, or other experiential learning opportunities in almost every field of academic study we offer. We also have several centers that provide students with real life experiences in several areas: Undergraduate Research, Community Engagement, and the Stack Center for Innovation and Entrepreneurship.

FACILITIES

Housing: Coed dorms, special housing for disabled students, special housing for international students, apartments for single students, Quiet Living Area available; on-campus townhouses (men and women). 90% of campus accessible to physically diasbled. **Special Academic Facilities/Equipment:** Hickey Financial Center. **Computers:** 20% of classrooms, 40% of dorms, 100% of libraries, 100% of dining areas, 100% of student union, have wireless network access. Students can register for classes online. Administrative functions (other than registration) can be performed online.

CAMPUS LIFE

Environment: Town. **Activities:** Choral groups, dance, drama/theater, literary magazine, musical theater, opera, pep band, radio station, student government, student newspaper, symphony orchestra, television station, yearbook, Campus Ministries, Model UN. 70 registered organizations, 15 honor societies, 2 religious organizations. **Athletics (Intercollegiate):** *Men:* baseball, basketball, cross-country, golf, lacrosse, soccer, tennis. *Women:* basketball, cross-country, field hockey, golf, lacrosse, soccer, softball, swimming, tennis, volleyball, water polo. **On-Campus Highlights:** Sarazen Student Union, J. Spencer and Patricia Standish Library, MAC/ARC—Athletic Facilities, Siena Hall, Academic Quad, Hickey Financial Technical Center.

ADMISSIONS

Freshman Academic Profile: Average high school GPA 3.5. 25% in top 10% of high school class, 56% in top 25% of high school class, 89% in top 50% of high school class. 77% from public high schools. **Reported SAT (pre-2016 redesign) scores:** SAT Math middle 50% range 500-610. SAT Critical Reading middle 50% range 480-590. SAT Writing middle 50% range 460-580. **Concordant SAT scores:** SAT EBRW middle 50% 530–640. SAT Math middle 50% range 530–630. ACT middle 50% range 22-28. Minimum internet-based TOEFL 79. Minimum paper TOEFL 550. **Basis for Candidate Selection:** *Very important factors considered include:* rigor of secondary school record, academic GPA. *Important factors considered include:* standardized test scores, recommendation(s), interview. *Other factors considered include:* class rank, application essay, extracurricular activities, talent/ability, character/personal qualities, first generation, alumni/ae relation, geographical residence, racial/ethnic status, volunteer work, work experience, level of applicant's interest. **Freshman Admission Requirements:** High school diploma is required and GED is accepted. *Academic units required:* 4 English, 3 math, 3 science, 3 science labs, 2 foreign language, 3 social studies, 3 history. *Academic units recommended:* 4 English, 4 math, 4 science, 4 science labs, 3 foreign language, 4 social studies, 4 history. **Freshman Admission Statistics:** 9,704 applied, 60.13% admitted, 13% enrolled. **Transfer Admission Requirements:** college transcript(s), statement of good standing from prior institution(s). Minimum college GPA of 2.5 required. Lowest grade transferable C+. **General Admission Information:** Application fee $50. Priority deadline 2/15. Regular application deadline 2/15. Regular notification 3/15. Nonfall registration accepted. Admission may be deferred for a maximum of 1 year.

COSTS AND FINANCIAL AID

Annual tuition $35,435. Room and board $14,550. Required fees $400. Average book expense $1,292. **Required Forms and Deadlines:** FAFSA, State aid form. **Notification of Awards:** Applicants will be notified of awards on or about 4/1. **Types of Aid:** *Need-based scholarships/grants:* Federal Pell, FSEOG, State scholarships/grants, Private scholarships, College/university scholarship or grant aid from institutional funds. *Loans:* Direct Subsidized Stafford Loans, Direct Unsubsidized Stafford Loans, Direct PLUS loans, Federal Perkins Loans. *Student Employment:* Federal Work-Study Program available. Institutional employment available. **Financial Aid Statistics:** 100% needy freshmen, 100% needy undergrads receive need-based scholarship or grant aid. 95% freshmen, 93% undergrads receive non-need-based scholarship or grant aid. 77% freshmen, 79% undergrads receive need-based self-help aid. 10% freshmen, 8% undergrads receive athletic scholarships. 98% freshmen, 91% undergrads receive any aid. 77% undergrads borrow to pay for school. Average cumulative indebtedness $35,874. **Criteria for awarding aid:** *Need-based:* Academics, Alumni affiliation, Art, Athletics, Job skills, Leadership, Minority status, Music/drama. *Non-need-based:* Academics, Athletics, Leadership, Minority status, State/district residency.

SIENA HEIGHTS UNIVERSITY

1247 E. Siena Heights Drive, Adrian, MI 49221
Phone: 517-264-7180 • **Financial Aid Phone:** 517-264-7110
E-mail: admissions@sienaheights.edu • **CEEB Code:** 2316
Fax: 517-264-7744 • **Website:** www.sienaheights.edu • **ACT Code:** 2052

This is a private school.

RATINGS

Admissions Selectivity Rating: 76 **Fire Safety Rating:** 67 **Green Rating:** 60*

STUDENTS AND FACULTY

Enrollment: 2,307. **Student Body:** 57% female, 43% male, 12% out-of-state, <1% international (6 countries represented). Asian 1%, African American 13%, Caucasian 76%, Hispanic 5%, Native American 1%, Pacific Islander <1%, Two or more races 2%, Race unknown 2%.
Retention and Graduation: 59% freshmen return for sophomore year. 43% freshmen graduate within 4 years. 43% freshmen graduate within 6 years.
Faculty: 0% of classes are taught by teaching assistants.

ACADEMICS

Degrees: associate, bachelor's, certificate, master's, post-master's certificate. **Most popular majors:** Business Administration and Management; Biology/Biological Sciences; Medical Radiologic Technology/Science. **Career Services:** Alumni network, Alumni services, Career/job search classes, Career assessment, Internships, Regional alumni.

FACILITIES

Housing: 90% of campus accessible to physically diasbled.

ADMISSIONS

Freshman Academic Profile: Average high school GPA 3.2. 8% in top 10% of high school class, 22% in top 25% of high school class, 68% in top 50% of high school class. ACT middle 50% range 19-23. **Basis for Candidate Selection:** *Very important factors considered include:* rigor of secondary school record, academic GPA, standardized test scores. *Important factors considered include:* class rank, application essay. **Freshman Admission Statistics:** 1,422 applied, 67.65% admitted, 31% enrolled. **General Admission Information:** Application fee $25. Nonfall registration accepted.

COSTS AND FINANCIAL AID

Annual tuition $21,250. Room and board $8,710. Required fees $640. **Types of Aid:** *Need-based scholarships/grants:* Federal Pell, FSEOG, State scholarships/grants, Private scholarships, College/university scholarship or grant aid from institutional funds. *Loans:* Direct Subsidized Stafford Loans, Direct Unsubsidized Stafford Loans, Direct PLUS loans. *Student Employment:* Federal Work-Study Program available. Institutional employment available. **Financial Aid Statistics:** 99% freshmen receive any aid.

SIERRA NEVADA COLLEGE

999 Tahoe Blvd., Incline Village, NV 89451
Phone: 775-831-1314 • **Financial Aid Phone:** 775-831-1314 x 7404
E-mail: admissions@sierraneveda.edu • **CEEB Code:** 9192
Fax: 775-831-6223 • **Website:** www.sierraneveda.edu • **ACT Code:** 2497

This private school was founded in 1969. It has a 25-acre campus.

RATINGS

Admissions Selectivity Rating: 74 **Fire Safety Rating:** 96 **Green Rating:** 73

STUDENTS AND FACULTY

Enrollment: 494. **Student Body:** 41% female, 59% male, 84% out-of-state, 7% international (14 countries represented). Asian 1%, African American 1%, Caucasian 72%, Hispanic 1%, Native American 3%, Pacific Islander 1%, Two or more races 0%, Race unknown 15%.
Retention and Graduation: 71% freshmen return for sophomore year. 33% freshmen graduate within 4 years. 45% freshmen graduate within 6 years.
Faculty: Student/faculty ratio 11:1. 36 full-time faculty, 61% hold PhDs, 14% are are members of minority groups, 58% are women. 0% of classes are taught by teaching assistants.

ACADEMICS

Degrees: bachelor's, certificate, diploma, master's. **Most popular majors:** Business, Management, Marketing, and Related Support Services; Multi/Interdisciplinary Studies. **Special Study Options:** double major, honors program, internships, study abroad, teacher certification program. Combined degree programs: BA/MA. **Disability Services:** Special programs offered to physically disabled students, including note-taking services, tutors. **Career Services:** Career/job search classes, Career assessment, Internships, On-campus interviews. Sierra Nevada College prides itself on its focus on experiential learning throughout our curriculum. Students in all of our majors will find themselves learning about their discipline through projects, assignments and co-curricular activities that focus on learning while doing.

FACILITIES

Housing: Coed dorms. 99% of campus accessible to physically diasbled. **Special Academic Facilities/Equipment:** McLean Observatory.

CAMPUS LIFE

Environment: Village. **Activities:** literary magazine, student government, student newspaper. 10 registered organizations, 1 honor society, 2 religious organizations. **Athletics (Intercollegiate):** *Men:* equestrian sports, skiing (downhill/alpine). *Women:* equestrian sports, skiing (downhill/alpine). **Environmental Initiatives:** Sierra Nevada College four Core Themes; Sustainability, Professional Preparedness, Entrepreneurship, Liberal Art.

ADMISSIONS

Freshman Academic Profile: Average high school GPA 3.0. 0% in top 10% of high school class, 20% in top 25% of high school class, 50% in top 50% of

high school class. 80% from public high schools. **Reported SAT (pre-2016 redesign) scores:** SAT Math middle 50% range 430-530. SAT Critical Reading middle 50% range 440-540. **Concordant SAT scores:** SAT Math middle 50% range 470–560. ACT middle 50% range 17-25. Minimum internet-based TOEFL 59. Minimum paper TOEFL 500. **Basis for Candidate Selection:** *Important factors considered include:* academic GPA, application essay, recommendation(s). *Other factors considered include:* rigor of secondary school record, class rank, standardized test scores, interview, extracurricular activities, talent/ability, character/personal qualities, first generation, alumni/ae relation, geographical residence, state residency, religious affiliation/commitment, racial/ethnic status, volunteer work, work experience, level of applicant's interest. **Freshman Admission Requirements:** High school diploma is required and GED is accepted. *Academic units recommended:* 4 English, 3 math, 2 science, 2 science labs, 2 social studies. **Freshman Admission Statistics:** 604 applied, 86.75% admitted, 17% enrolled. **Transfer Admission Requirements:** college transcript(s), essay or personal statement, Lowest grade transferable C. **General Admission Information:** Priority deadline 2/15. Regular application deadline 8/28. Regular notification 8/28. Nonfall registration accepted. Admission may be deferred for a maximum of 1 year.

COSTS AND FINANCIAL AID

Annual tuition $28,170. Room and board $12,066. Required fees $979. Average book expense $1,600. **Required Forms and Deadlines:** FAFSA. **Types of Aid:** *Need-based scholarships/grants:* Federal Pell, FSEOG, State scholarships/grants, Private scholarships, College/university scholarship or grant aid from institutional funds. *Loans:* Direct Subsidized Stafford Loans, Direct Unsubsidized Stafford Loans, Direct PLUS loans. *Student Employment:* Federal Work-Study Program available. Institutional employment available. **Financial Aid Statistics:** 100% needy freshmen, 100% needy undergrads receive need-based scholarship or grant aid. 100% freshmen, 100% undergrads receive non-need-based scholarship or grant aid. 100% freshmen, 100% undergrads receive need-based self-help aid. 0% freshmen, 1% undergrads receive athletic scholarships. 62% freshmen, 65% undergrads receive any aid. **Criteria for awarding aid:** *Non-need-based:* Academics, Alumni affiliation, Athletics, State/district residency.

SIMMONS COLLEGE

300 The Fenway, Boston, MA 2115
Phone: 617-521-2051 • **Financial Aid Phone:** 617-521-2001
E-mail: ugadm@simmons.edu • **CEEB Code:** 3761
Fax: 617-521-3190 • **Website:** www.simmons.edu • **ACT Code:** 1892

This private school was founded in 1899. It has a 12-acre campus.

RATINGS

Admissions Selectivity Rating: 87   **Fire Safety Rating:** 85   **Green Rating:** 67

STUDENTS AND FACULTY

Enrollment: 1,706. **Student Body:** 100% female, 0% male, 41% out-of-state, 3% international (51 countries represented). Asian 9%, African American 7%, Caucasian 67%, Hispanic 6%, Native American <1%, Pacific Islander <1%, Two or more races 4%, Race unknown 4%.
Retention and Graduation: 85% freshmen return for sophomore year. 67% freshmen graduate within 4 years. 74% freshmen graduate within 6 years. 22% grads go on to further study within 1 year. 15% grads pursue arts and sciences degrees. 1% grads pursue law degrees. 2% grads pursue business degrees. 1% grads pursue medical degrees. **Faculty:** Student/faculty ratio 10:1. 218 full-time faculty, 0% hold PhDs, 18% are are members of minority groups, 74% are women.

ACADEMICS

Degrees: bachelor's, certificate, doctoral/professional, doctoral/research, doctoral, master's, postbachelor's certificate, post-master's certificate. **Classes:** Most classes have 10-19 students. Most lab/discussion sessions have 10-19 students. **Most popular majors:** Nursing Practice. **Special Study Options:** Accelerated program, cross-registration, double major, dual enrollment, English as a Second Language (ESL), exchange student program (domestic), honors program, independent study, internships, liberal arts/career combination, student-designed major, study abroad, teacher certification program, Exhange program with Mills College (CA), Spellman College (GA), Fisk University (TN), American University (DC), Colleges of the Fenway exchange program,

double-degree programs with Massachusetts College of Pharmacy and Health Sciences, and with Hebrew College. **Honors Programs:** One Honors Program Combined degree programs: BA/MA, BA/MAT, BA/MBA, BA/MA, BSW/MSW, BS/MS, BS/DPT. **Disability Services:** Special programs offered to physically disabled students, including note-taking services, reader services, tape recorders, tutors. **Career Services:** Alumni network, Alumni services, Career/job search classes, Career assessment, Internships.

FACILITIES

Housing: special housing for disabled students, women's dorms, Wellness Housing, Theme Housing. **Special Academic Facilities/Equipment:** Art gallery, media center, science center with dream/sleep analysis lab, physical therapy clinic areas, sports center with pool **Computers:** 100% of classrooms, 5% of dorms, 100% of libraries, 100% of dining areas, 100% of student union, have wireless network access. Students can register for classes online. Administrative functions (other than registration) can be performed online.

CAMPUS LIFE

Environment: City. **Activities:** Choral groups, dance, drama/theater, literary magazine, radio station, student government, student newspaper, student-run film society, symphony orchestra, yearbook. 91 registered organizations, 4 honor societies, 4 religious organizations. **Athletics (Intercollegiate):** *Women:* basketball, crew/rowing, diving, field hockey, lacrosse, soccer, softball, swimming, tennis, volleyball. **On-Campus Highlights:** Java City, Beatley Library, Park Science Center, Palace Road Building/Pottruck Technology, School of Management. **Environmental Initiatives:** We are committed to maximizing recycling and composting opportunities to minimize landfill waste.

ADMISSIONS

Freshman Academic Profile: 35% in top 10% of high school class, 72% in top 25% of high school class, 97% in top 50% of high school class. **Reported SAT (pre-2016 redesign) scores:** SAT Math middle 50% range 520-610. SAT Critical Reading middle 50% range 540-630. SAT Writing middle 50% range 530-630. **Concordant SAT scores:** SAT EBRW middle 50% 590–680. SAT Math middle 50% range 550–630. ACT middle 50% range 24-29. Minimum internet-based TOEFL 83. Minimum paper TOEFL 83. **Basis for Candidate Selection:** *Very important factors considered include:* rigor of secondary school record, academic GPA, standardized test scores. *Important factors considered include:* application essay, recommendation(s), extracurricular activities. *Other factors considered include:* class rank, interview, talent/ability, character/personal qualities, first generation, alumni/ae relation, volunteer work, work experience, level of applicant's interest. **Freshman Admission Requirements:** High school diploma is required and GED is accepted. *Academic units required:* 4 English, 3 math, 4 science, 3 science labs, 3 foreign language, 3 social studies, 2 history, 3 academic electives. *Academic units recommended:* 4 math, 4 science, 4 foreign language, 3 social studies, 3 history, 4 academic electives. **Freshman Admission Statistics:** 4,575 applied, 57.57% admitted, 18% enrolled. **Transfer Admission Requirements:** High school transcript, college transcript(s), essay or personal statement, statement of good standing from prior institution(s). Minimum college GPA of 2.8 required. Lowest grade transferable C+. **General Admission Information:** Application fee $55. Priority deadline 11/1. Regular application deadline 2/1. Regular notification 3/15. Nonfall registration accepted. Admission may be deferred for a maximum of 1 Year.

COSTS AND FINANCIAL AID

Annual tuition $37,500. Room and board $14,500. Required fees $1,090. Average book expense $1,280. **Required Forms and Deadlines:** FAFSA, Institution's own financial aid form. **Notification of Awards:** Applicants will be notified of awards on a rolling basis beginning 3/15. **Types of Aid:** *Need-based scholarships/grants:* Federal Pell, FSEOG, State scholarships/grants, Private scholarships, College/university scholarship or grant aid from institutional funds. *Loans:* Direct Subsidized Stafford Loans, Direct Unsubsidized Stafford Loans, Direct PLUS loans, Federal Perkins Loans, College/university loans from institutional funds. *Student Employment:* Federal Work-Study Program available. **Financial Aid Statistics:** 100% needy freshmen, 100% needy undergrads receive need-based scholarship or grant aid. 11% freshmen, 6% undergrads receive non-need-based scholarship or grant aid. 84% freshmen, 89% undergrads receive need-based self-help aid. 0% freshmen, 0% undergrads receive athletic scholarships. 99% freshmen, 91% undergrads receive any aid. **Criteria for awarding aid:** *Non-need-based:* Academics, Alumni affiliation.

SKIDMORE COLLEGE

815 North Broadway, Saratoga Springs, NY 12866-1632
Phone: 518-580-5570 • **Financial Aid Phone:** 518-580-5750
E-mail: admissions@skidmore.edu • **CEEB Code:** 2815
Fax: 518-580-5584 • **Website:** www.skidmore.edu • **ACT Code:** 2906

This private school was founded in 1903. It has a 750-acre campus.

RATINGS
Admissions Selectivity Rating: 93   **Fire Safety Rating:** 98   **Green Rating:** 94

STUDENTS AND FACULTY
Enrollment: 2,661. **Student Body:** 60% female, 40% male, 67% out-of-state, 10% international (61 countries represented). Asian 5%, African American 4%, Caucasian 64%, Hispanic 9%, Native American 0%, Pacific Islander 0%, Two or more races 4%, Race unknown 3%.
Retention and Graduation: 91% freshmen return for sophomore year. 85% freshmen graduate within 4 years. 89% freshmen graduate within 6 years. 15% grads go on to further study within 1 year. **Faculty:** Student/faculty ratio 8:1. 279 full-time faculty, 87% hold PhDs, 17% are are members of minority groups, 55% are women. 0% of classes are taught by teaching assistants.

ACADEMICS
Degrees: bachelor's, master's. **Classes:** Most classes have 10-19 students. Most lab/discussion sessions have 10-19 students. **Most popular majors:** Business/Commerce; Social Sciences; Psychology. **Special Study Options:** Accelerated program, cross-registration, double major, dual enrollment, exchange student program (domestic), honors program, independent study, internships, liberal arts/career combination, student-designed major, study abroad, teacher certification program. **Honors Programs:** Honors Forum. **Disability Services:** Special programs offered to physically disabled students, including note-taking services, reader services, tape recorders, tutors. **Career Services:** Alumni network, Alumni services, Career/job search classes, Career assessment, Internships, Regional alumni.

FACILITIES
Housing: Coed dorms, special housing for disabled students, special housing for international students, women's dorms, apartments for single students, gender neutral wing. 75% of campus accessible to physically diasbled. **Special Academic Facilities/Equipment:** Tang Teaching Museum and Art Gallery, center for child study, art, music, dance, and theatre facilities, electron microscope, spectrometer **Computers:** Students can register for classes online. Administrative functions (other than registration) can be performed online.

CAMPUS LIFE
Environment: Town. **Activities:** Choral groups, concert band, dance, drama/theater, jazz band, literary magazine, music ensembles, musical theater, opera, radio station, student government, student newspaper, symphony orchestra, television station, yearbook, Campus Ministries, Student Organization, Model UN. 80 registered organizations, 10 honor societies, 3 religious organizations. **Athletics (Intercollegiate):** *Men:* baseball, basketball, crew/rowing, diving, golf, ice hockey, lacrosse, soccer, swimming, tennis. *Women:* basketball, crew/rowing, diving, equestrian sports, field hockey, lacrosse, soccer, softball, swimming, tennis, volleyball. **On-Campus Highlights:** Tang Teaching Museum, Lucy Scribner Library, Case Student Center, Woodlawn Village Apartments, Murray-Atkins Dining Hall.

ADMISSIONS
Freshman Academic Profile: 32% in top 10% of high school class, 71% in top 25% of high school class, 96% in top 50% of high school class. 58% from public high schools. **Reported SAT (pre-2016 redesign) scores:** SAT Math middle 50% range 560-660. SAT Critical Reading middle 50% range 560-670. SAT Writing middle 50% range 570-670. **Concordant SAT scores:** SAT EBRW middle 50% 620–710. SAT Math middle 50% range 580–690. ACT middle 50% range 26-30. Minimum paper TOEFL 590. **Basis for Candidate Selection:** *Very important factors considered include:* rigor of secondary school record. *Important factors considered include:* class rank, academic GPA, application essay, recommendation(s), extracurricular activities, talent/ability, character/personal qualities, volunteer work, work experience, level of applicant's interest. *Other factors considered include:* standardized test scores, interview, first generation, alumni/ae relation, geographical residence, racial/ethnic status. **Freshman Admission Requirements:** High school diploma is required and GED is accepted. *Academic units recommended:* 4 English, 4 math, 4 science, 3 science labs, 4 foreign language, 4 social studies. **Freshman Admission**

Statistics: 9,181 applied, 29.08% admitted, 27% enrolled. **Transfer Admission Requirements:** High school transcript, college transcript(s), essay or personal statement, standardized test scores, statement of good standing from prior institution(s). Minimum college GPA of 2.7 required. Lowest grade transferable C. **General Admission Information:** Application fee $65. Regular application deadline 1/15. Regular notification 4/1. Nonfall registration not accepted. Admission may be deferred for a maximum of 2 years.

COSTS AND FINANCIAL AID
Annual tuition $49,716. Room and board $13,530. Required fees $968. Average book expense $1,300. **Required Forms and Deadlines:** CSS/Financial Aid PROFILE, Noncustodial PROFILE. **Notification of Awards:** Applicants will be notified of awards on or about 4/1. **Types of Aid:** *Need-based scholarships/grants:* Federal Pell, FSEOG, State scholarships/grants, Private scholarships, College/university scholarship or grant aid from institutional funds. *Loans:* Direct Subsidized Stafford Loans, Direct Unsubsidized Stafford Loans, Direct PLUS loans, Federal Perkins Loans, State Loans. *Student Employment:* Federal Work-Study Program available. Institutional employment available. **Financial Aid Statistics:** 100% needy freshmen, 100% needy undergrads receive need-based scholarship or grant aid. 6% freshmen, 8% undergrads receive non-need-based scholarship or grant aid. 67% freshmen, 73% undergrads receive need-based self-help aid. 0% freshmen, 0% undergrads receive athletic scholarships. 49% freshmen, 51% undergrads receive any aid. 39% undergrads borrow to pay for school. Average cumulative indebtedness $25,001. **Criteria for awarding aid:** *Need-based:* Academics, Leadership. *Non-need-based:* Music/drama.

See page 1042.

SLIPPERY ROCK UNIVERSITY OF PENNSYLVANIA

1 Morrow Way, Slippery Rock, PA 16057
Phone: 724-738-2015 • **Financial Aid Phone:** 724-738-2220
E-mail: asktherock@sru.edu • **CEEB Code:** 2658
Fax: 724-738-2913 • **Website:** http://www.sru.edu • **ACT Code:** 3716

This public school was founded in 1889. It has a 600-acre campus.

RATINGS
Admissions Selectivity Rating: 79   **Fire Safety Rating:** 98   **Green Rating:** 92

STUDENTS AND FACULTY
Enrollment: 7,569. **Student Body:** 57% female, 43% male, 10% out-of-state, 1% international (35 countries represented). Asian 1%, African American 5%, Caucasian 86%, Hispanic 2%, Native American <1%, Pacific Islander <1%, Two or more races 4%, Race unknown 1%.
Retention and Graduation: 83% freshmen return for sophomore year. 51% freshmen graduate within 4 years. 68% freshmen graduate within 6 years. 21% grads go on to further study within 1 year. **Faculty:** Student/faculty ratio 22:1. 336 full-time faculty, 88% hold PhDs, 17% are are members of minority groups, 52% are women. 0% of classes are taught by teaching assistants.

ACADEMICS
Degrees: bachelor's, certificate, doctoral/professional, doctoral/research, master's, postbachelor's certificate. **Classes:** Most classes have 20-29 students. Most lab/discussion sessions have fewer than 10 students. **Most popular majors:** Health and Wellness; Business Administration and Management; Occupational Safety and Health Technology/Technician. **Special Study Options:** distance learning, double major, dual enrollment, exchange student program (domestic), honors program, independent study, internships, liberal arts/career combination, student-designed major, study abroad, teacher certification program. **Honors Programs:** Undergraduate Honors Program Combined degree programs: Pre-Osteo 3+4 and Pre-Pharm 3+3 LECOM; Osteopathic 4+4 LECOM; Pre-Chiro 3+3 Logan; Pre-PT 3+3 SRU; Dental 4+4 WVU; Dental 4+4 LECOM; 3+1 Biology: Cytotechnology FAHC or AMC; 3+2 Physicians Assistant. **Disability Services:** Special programs offered to physically disabled students, including note-taking services, reader services, tape recorders, tutors. **Career Services:** Alumni services, Career/job search classes, Career assessment, Internships, Regional alumni. The Office of Career Education & Development offers students and alumni the opportunity to meet individually with career counselors.

FACILITIES
Housing: Coed dorms, special housing for disabled students, apartments for single students, Theme Housing. 90% of campus accessible to physically diasbled. **Special Academic Facilities/Equipment:** Special education school for student teachers, physical therapy clinic, microvideo system, planetarium, electron microscope. Residence Halls have academic interest floors with special

facilities for specific majors whereby students can interact with faculty and have academically related programs where they live. **Computers:** 80% of classrooms, 100% of dorms, 100% of libraries, 50% of dining areas, 100% of student union, 5% of common outdoor areas have wireless network access. Students can register for classes online. Administrative functions (other than registration) can be performed online.

CAMPUS LIFE

Environment: Rural. **Activities:** Choral groups, concert band, dance, drama/theater, jazz band, literary magazine, marching band, music ensembles, musical theater, radio station, student government, student newspaper, student-run film society, symphony orchestra, television station, Campus Ministries, Student Organization, Model UN. 145 registered organizations, 37 honor societies, 4 religious organizations. 9 fraternities, 8 sororities. **Athletics (Intercollegiate):** *Men:* baseball, basketball, cheerleading, cross-country, football, soccer, track/field (outdoor), track/field (indoor). *Women:* basketball, cheerleading, cross-country, field hockey, lacrosse, soccer, softball, tennis, track/field (outdoor), track/field (indoor), volleyball. **On-Campus Highlights:** Aebersold Recreation Center, New Residential Suite Living Complexes, Bailey Library, Advanced Science and Technology Building, University Union.

ADMISSIONS

Freshman Academic Profile: Average high school GPA 3.5. 13% in top 10% of high school class, 37% in top 25% of high school class, 73% in top 50% of high school class. 92% from public high schools. **Reported SAT (pre-2016 redesign) scores:** SAT Math middle 50% range 460-550. SAT Critical Reading middle 50% range 450-540. SAT Writing middle 50% range 423-520. **Concordant SAT scores:** SAT EBRW middle 50% 490–590. SAT Math middle 50% range 500–570. ACT middle 50% range 19-23. Minimum internet-based TOEFL 61. Minimum paper TOEFL 500. **Basis for Candidate Selection:** *Important factors considered include:* rigor of secondary school record, class rank, academic GPA, standardized test scores. *Other factors considered include:* application essay, recommendation(s), talent/ability. **Freshman Admission Requirements:** High school diploma is required and GED is accepted. *Academic units recommended:* 4 English, 3 math, 3 science, 1 science lab, 2 foreign language. **Freshman Admission Statistics:** 5,889 applied, 69.49% admitted, 38% enrolled. **Transfer Admission Requirements:** college transcript(s), Minimum college GPA of 2.0 required. Lowest grade transferable C. **General Admission Information:** Application fee $30. Nonfall registration accepted. Admission may be deferred for a maximum of 1 year.

COSTS AND FINANCIAL AID

Annual in-state tuition $7,238. Annual out-of-state tuition $10,858. Room and board $10,110. Required fees $2,624. Average book expense $1,550. **Required Forms and Deadlines:** FAFSA. **Notification of Awards:** Applicants will be notified of awards on a rolling basis beginning 3/16. **Types of Aid:** *Need-based scholarships/grants:* Federal Pell, FSEOG, State scholarships/grants, Private scholarships, College/university scholarship or grant aid from institutional funds. *Loans:* Direct Subsidized Stafford Loans, Direct Unsubsidized Stafford Loans, Direct PLUS loans, Federal Perkins Loans. *Student Employment:* Federal Work-Study Program available. Institutional employment available. **Financial Aid Statistics:** 60% needy freshmen, 65% needy undergrads receive need-based scholarship or grant aid. 50% freshmen, 28% undergrads receive non-need-based scholarship or grant aid. 90% undergrads receive need-based self-help aid. 4% freshmen, 3% undergrads receive athletic scholarships. 93% freshmen, 94% undergrads receive any aid. 87% undergrads borrow to pay for school. Average cumulative indebtedness $33,303. **Criteria for awarding aid:** *Need-based:* Academics, Minority status. *Non-need-based:* Academics, Alumni affiliation, Art, Athletics, Job skills, Leadership, Minority status, Music/drama, State/district residency.

SMITH COLLEGE

7 College Lane, Northampton, MA 1063
Phone: 413-585-2500 • **Financial Aid Phone:** 413-585-2530
E-mail: admission@smith.edu • **CEEB Code:** 3762
Fax: 413-585-2527 • **Website:** www.smith.edu • **ACT Code:** 1894

This private school was founded in 1871. It has a 147-acre campus.

RATINGS

Admissions Selectivity Rating: 96   **Fire Safety Rating:** 84   **Green Rating:** 96

STUDENTS AND FACULTY

Enrollment: 2,501. **Student Body:** 100% female, 0% male, 80% out-of-state, 14% international (59 countries represented). Asian 12%, African American 6%, Caucasian 45%, Hispanic 10%, Native American <1%, Pacific Islander <1%, Two or more races 5%, Race unknown 8%.
Retention and Graduation: 94% freshmen return for sophomore year. 86% freshmen graduate within 4 years. 89% freshmen graduate within 6 years.
Faculty: 0% of classes are taught by teaching assistants.

ACADEMICS

Degrees: bachelor's, doctoral/research, master's, postbachelor's certificate, post-master's certificate. **Most popular majors:** Psychology; Political Science and Government; Economics. **Special Study Options:** Accelerated program, cross-registration, double major, exchange student program (domestic), honors program, independent study, internships, study abroad, teacher certification program. **Disability Services:** Special programs offered to physically disabled students, including note-taking services, reader services, tape recorders, tutors. **Career Services:** Alumni network, Alumni services, Career/job search classes, Career assessment, Internships, Regional alumni. Praxis internship program: guaranteed $2000 stipend per student for summer internship

FACILITIES

Housing: women's dorms, cooperative housing, Apartment complex for limited number of juniors and seniors. Also,one senior house, french speaking house, and Ada Comstock (non-traditional age) house. 85% of campus accessible to physically diasbled. **Special Academic Facilities/Equipment:** Art museum, printing, darkroom, and sculpture facilities, dance, electronic music, television, and theatre studios, recital hall, rehearsal rooms, multimedia language lab, early childhood/elementary education campus school, two electronic classrooms, physiology and horticultural labs, animal care facilities, two electron microscopes, greenhouses, observatories. **Computers:** 85% of classrooms, 100% of dorms, 100% of libraries, 100% of dining areas, 100% of student union, 50% of common outdoor areas have wireless network access. Students can register for classes online. Administrative functions (other than registration) can be performed online.

CAMPUS LIFE

Environment: Town. **Activities:** Choral groups, concert band, dance, drama/theater, jazz band, literary magazine, music ensembles, musical theater, radio station, student government, student newspaper, television station, yearbook, Campus Ministries, Student Organization, Model UN. 133 registered organizations, 3 honor societies, 9 religious organizations. **Athletics (Intercollegiate):** *Women:* basketball, crew/rowing, cross-country, diving, equestrian sports, field hockey, lacrosse, skiing (downhill/alpine), soccer, softball, squash, swimming, tennis, track/field (outdoor), track/field (indoor), volleyball. **On-Campus Highlights:** Smith Art Museum, The Botanical Gardens, Campus Center, Mendenhall Center for Performing Arts, Lyman Plant House. **Environmental Initiatives:** A new natural gas fired cogeneration facility went online in October 2008, which generates most campus electric use and achieves 80% efficiency with new absorption chillers.

ADMISSIONS

Freshman Academic Profile: Average high school GPA 4.0. 71% in top 10% of high school class, 93% in top 25% of high school class, 100% in top 50% of high school class. 62% from public high schools. **Reported SAT (pre-2016 redesign) scores:** SAT Math middle 50% range 600-740. SAT Critical Reading middle 50% range 630-740. SAT Writing middle 50% range 640-730. **Concordant SAT scores:** SAT EBRW middle 50% 680–760. SAT Math middle 50% range 620–760. ACT middle 50% range 29-33. Minimum internet-based TOEFL 90. Minimum paper TOEFL 600. **Basis for Candidate Selection:** *Very important factors considered include:* rigor of secondary school record, academic GPA, application essay, recommendation(s), character/personal qualities. *Important factors considered include:* class rank, interview, extracurricular activities, talent/ability. *Other factors considered include:* standardized test scores, first generation, alumni/ae relation, racial/ethnic status, volunteer work, work experience. **Freshman Admission Requirements:** High school diploma or equivalent is not required. *Academic units recommended:* 4 English, 3 math, 3 science, 3 science labs, 3 foreign language, 2 history, 1 academic elective. **Freshman Admission Statistics:** 5,254 applied, 37.23% admitted, 33% enrolled. **Transfer Admission Requirements:** High school transcript, college transcript(s), essay or personal statement, statement of good standing from prior institution(s). Lowest grade transferable C. **General Admission Information:** Regular application deadline 1/15. Nonfall registration not accepted. Admission may be deferred for a maximum of 1 Year.

COSTS AND FINANCIAL AID

Required Forms and Deadlines: FAFSA, Institution's own financial aid form, CSS/Financial Aid PROFILE, Noncustodial PROFILE. **Notification of Awards:** Applicants will be notified of awards on or about 4/1. **Types of Aid:** *Need-based scholarships/grants:* Federal Pell, FSEOG, State scholarships/grants, Private scholarships, College/university scholarship or grant aid from institutional funds. *Loans:* Direct Subsidized Stafford Loans, Direct Unsubsidized Stafford Loans, Direct PLUS loans, Federal Perkins Loans,

College/university loans from institutional funds. *Student Employment:* Federal Work-Study Program available. Institutional employment available. **Financial Aid Statistics:** 97% needy freshmen, 98% needy undergrads receive need-based scholarship or grant aid. 2% freshmen, 1% undergrads receive non-need-based scholarship or grant aid. 94% freshmen, 94% undergrads receive need-based self-help aid. 0% freshmen, 0% undergrads receive athletic scholarships. 70% freshmen, 71% undergrads receive any aid. 62% undergrads borrow to pay for school. Average cumulative indebtedness $23,857. **Criteria for awarding aid:** *Non-need-based:* Academics, State/district residency.

SOKA UNIVERSITY OF AMERICA

1 University Drive, Aliso Viejo, CA 92656-8081
Phone: 949-480-4150 • **Financial Aid Phone:** 949-480-4112
E-mail: admission@soka.edu • **CEEB Code:** 4066
Fax: 949-480-4151 • **Website:** www.soka.edu • **ACT Code:** 467

This private school was founded in 2001. It has a 103-acre campus.

RATINGS
Admissions Selectivity Rating: 91   **Fire Safety Rating:** 96   **Green Rating:** 74

STUDENTS AND FACULTY
Enrollment: 419. **Student Body:** 62% female, 38% male, 46% out-of-state, 43% international (32 countries represented). Asian 15%, African American 4%, Caucasian 20%, Hispanic 10%, Native American <1%, Pacific Islander <1%, Two or more races 5%, Race unknown 4%.
Retention and Graduation: 94% freshmen return for sophomore year. 85% freshmen graduate within 4 years. 90% freshmen graduate within 6 years. 20% grads go on to further study within 1 year. 78% grads pursue arts and sciences degrees. 4% grads pursue law degrees. 7% grads pursue medical degrees.
Faculty: Student/faculty ratio 8:1. 47 full-time faculty, 98% hold PhDs, 38% are are members of minority groups, 43% are women. 0% of classes are taught by teaching assistants.

ACADEMICS
Degrees: bachelor's, master's. **Classes:** Most classes have 10-19 students. Most lab/discussion sessions have 10-19 students. **Most popular majors:** Liberal Arts and Sciences/Liberal Studies. **Special Study Options:** English as a Second Language (ESL), independent study, internships, liberal arts/career combination, study abroad. **Disability Services:** Special programs offered to physically disabled students, including note-taking services, reader services, tape recorders, tutors. **Career Services:** Alumni network, Alumni services, Career/job search classes, Career assessment, Internships, On-campus interviews. Annual Future Expo mentor event. This is an event where professionals and alumni from a variety of relevant industries share their career stories with students. Each panelist summarizes their career path and then students meet in small groups with representative form the areas in which they have interest.

FACILITIES
Housing: Coed dorms, special housing for disabled students. 100% of campus accessible to physically diasbled. **Special Academic Facilities/Equipment:** Art Gallery, Athenaeum (Reception Center) **Computers:** Students can register for classes online. Administrative functions (other than registration) can be performed online. Undergraduates are required to own a computer.

CAMPUS LIFE
Environment: Town. **Activities:** Choral groups, concert band, dance, drama/theater, jazz band, literary magazine, music ensembles, student government, student newspaper, student-run film society, symphony orchestra, yearbook. 38 registered organizations, 1 religious organization. **Athletics (Intercollegiate):** *Men:* cross-country, diving, soccer, swimming, track/field (outdoor). *Women:* cross-country, diving, soccer, swimming, track/field (outdoor). **On-Campus Highlights:** Founders Hall Art Gallery, Student Center Dining Hall, Student Center Bookstore, Recreation Center, Ikeda Library, Hiking trail along canyon rim surrounding campus. **Environmental Initiatives:** Individual building electrical metering.

ADMISSIONS
Freshman Academic Profile: Average high school GPA 3.9. 22% in top 10% of high school class, 73% in top 25% of high school class, 100% in top 50% of high school class. 97% from public high schools. **Reported SAT (pre-2016 redesign) scores:** SAT Math middle 50% range 580-740. SAT Critical Reading middle 50% range 490-630. SAT Writing middle 50% range 550-650. **Concordant SAT scores:** SAT EBRW middle 50% 580–690. SAT Math middle 50% range 600–760. ACT middle 50% range 26-30. **Basis for Candidate Selection:** *Very important factors considered include:* rigor of secondary school record, academic GPA, standardized test scores, application essay,

recommendation(s), extracurricular activities, character/personal qualities. *Important factors considered include:* talent/ability, volunteer work, level of applicant's interest. *Other factors considered include:* class rank, interview, first generation, geographical residence, state residency, work experience. **Freshman Admission Requirements:** High school diploma is required and GED is accepted. *Academic units recommended:* 4 English, 3 math, 2 science, 2 science labs, 2 foreign language, 1 social studies, 2 history. **Freshman Admission Statistics:** 500 applied, 38.40% admitted, 54% enrolled. **General Admission Information:** Application fee $45. Regular application deadline 1/15. Regular notification 3/1. Nonfall registration not accepted. Admission may be deferred for a maximum of 1 year.

COSTS AND FINANCIAL AID
Annual tuition $30,106. Room and board $12,166. Average book expense $1,854. **Required Forms and Deadlines:** FAFSA, State aid form. **Notification of Awards:** Applicants will be notified of awards on or about 3/15. **Types of Aid:** *Need-based scholarships/grants:* Federal Pell, FSEOG, State scholarships/grants, Private scholarships, College/university scholarship or grant aid from institutional funds. *Loans:* Direct Subsidized Stafford Loans, Direct Unsubsidized Stafford Loans, Direct PLUS loans, College/university loans from institutional funds. *Student Employment:* Federal Work-Study Program available. Institutional employment available. **Financial Aid Statistics:** 100% needy freshmen, 100% needy undergrads receive need-based scholarship or grant aid. 100% freshmen, 100% undergrads receive non-need-based scholarship or grant aid. 53% freshmen, 49% undergrads receive need-based self-help aid. 3% freshmen, 3% undergrads receive athletic scholarships. 100% freshmen, 100% undergrads receive any aid. 57% undergrads borrow to pay for school. Average cumulative indebtedness $22,409. **Criteria for awarding aid:** *Need-based:* Academics. *Non-need-based:* Academics, Athletics, Leadership, Minority status.

SONOMA STATE UNIVERSITY

1801 East Cotati Avenue, Rohnert Park, CA 94928
Phone: 707-664-2778 • **Financial Aid Phone:** 707-664-2389
E-mail: student.outreach@sonoma.edu • **CEEB Code:** 4723
Fax: 707-664-2060 • **Website:** www.sonoma.edu • **ACT Code:** 431

This public school was founded in 1960. It has a 269-acre campus.

RATINGS
Admissions Selectivity Rating: 79   **Fire Safety Rating:** 85   **Green Rating:** 74

STUDENTS AND FACULTY
Enrollment: 8,547. **Student Body:** 63% female, 37% male, 2% international. Asian 5%, African American 2%, Caucasian 46%, Hispanic 31%, Native American <1%, Pacific Islander <1%, Two or more races 7%, Race unknown 6%.
Retention and Graduation: 79% freshmen return for sophomore year. 28% freshmen graduate within 4 years. 61% freshmen graduate within 6 years. **Faculty:** Student/faculty ratio 24:1. 238 full-time faculty, 99% hold PhDs, 20% are are members of minority groups, 47% are women. 1% of classes are taught by teaching assistants.

ACADEMICS
Degrees: bachelor's, master's. **Classes:** Most classes have 20-29 students. Most lab/discussion sessions have 20-29 students. **Most popular majors:** Liberal Arts and Sciences Studies and Humanities; Business/Commerce. **Special Study Options:** Accelerated program, cooperative education program, cross-registration, distance learning, double major, dual enrollment, English as a Second Language (ESL), exchange student program (domestic), external degree program, honors program, independent study, internships, liberal arts/career combination, student-designed major, study abroad, teacher certification program, Combined degree programs: bachelors/MBA; bachelors/MPA. Combined degree programs: BA/MA, MBA. **Disability Services:** Special programs offered to physically disabled students, including note-taking services, reader services, tape recorders, tutors. **Career Services:** Career/job search classes, Internships, On-campus interviews.

FACILITIES
Housing: Coed dorms, men's dorms, special housing for international students, women's dorms, apartments for single students, Housing for focused learning communities—freshman seminar dorms, healthy living dorms;

women in math/science dorms. 99% of campus accessible to physically diasbled. **Special Academic Facilities/Equipment:** Performing arts center, observatory, electron microscope, seismograph, information technology center, environmental technology center, high technology high school,nature preserve **Computers:** 95% of classrooms, 90% of dorms, 100% of libraries, 85% of dining areas, 100% of student union, 20% of common outdoor areas have wireless network access. Students can register for classes online. Administrative functions (other than registration) can be performed online. Undergraduates are required to own a computer.

CAMPUS LIFE

Environment: Town. **Activities:** Choral groups, dance, drama/theater, jazz band, literary magazine, music ensembles, musical theater, opera, pep band, radio station, student government, student newspaper, symphony orchestra 109 registered organizations, 2 honor societies, 4 religious organizations. 5 fraternities, 9 sororities. **Athletics (Intercollegiate):** *Men:* baseball, basketball, soccer, tennis. *Women:* basketball, cross-country, soccer, softball, tennis, track/field (outdoor), volleyball. **On-Campus Highlights:** Schultz Information Center, Environmental Technology Center, Charlie Brown's (coffee shop), Observatory, University Recreation Center. **Environmental Initiatives:** Energy efficiency.

ADMISSIONS

Freshman Academic Profile: Average high school GPA 3.2. **Reported SAT (pre-2016 redesign) scores:** SAT Math middle 50% range 440-540. SAT Critical Reading middle 50% range 440-540. **Concordant SAT scores:** SAT Math middle 50% range 480–570. ACT middle 50% range 19-24. Minimum internet-based TOEFL 61. Minimum paper TOEFL 500. **Basis for Candidate Selection:** *Very important factors considered include:* academic GPA, standardized test scores. *Other factors considered include:* geographical residence. **Freshman Admission Requirements:** High school diploma is required and GED is accepted. *Academic units required:* 4 English, 3 math, 2 science, 1 science lab, 2 foreign language, 2 history, 1 academic elective, 1 visual/performing arts, and 1 unit from above areas or other academic areas. **Freshman Admission Statistics:** 16,487 applied, 76.27% admitted, 14% enrolled. **Transfer Admission Requirements:** college transcript(s), Minimum college GPA of 2.0 required. Lowest grade transferable D. **General Admission Information:** Application fee $55. Priority deadline 3/1. Regular application deadline 11/30. Regular notification 3/1. Nonfall registration accepted.

COSTS AND FINANCIAL AID

Annual in-state tuition $5,472. Annual out-of-state tuition $16,632. Room and board $13,146. Required fees $7,330. Average book expense $1,790. **Required Forms and Deadlines:** FAFSA. **Notification of Awards:** Applicants will be notified of awards on a rolling basis beginning 3/25. **Types of Aid:** *Need-based scholarships/grants:* Federal Pell, FSEOG, State scholarships/grants, Private scholarships, College/university scholarship or grant aid from institutional funds. *Loans:* Direct Subsidized Stafford Loans, Direct Unsubsidized Stafford Loans, Direct PLUS loans, Federal Perkins Loans. *Student Employment:* Federal Work-Study Program available. Institutional employment available. **Financial Aid Statistics:** 68% needy freshmen, 65% needy undergrads receive need-based scholarship or grant aid. 41% freshmen, 35% undergrads receive non-need-based scholarship or grant aid. 70% freshmen, 62% undergrads receive need-based self-help aid. 0% freshmen, 0% undergrads receive athletic scholarships. 59% freshmen, 51% undergrads receive any aid. **Criteria for awarding aid:** *Need-based:* Academics, Minority status. *Non-need-based:* Academics, Alumni affiliation, Art, Athletics, Leadership, Minority status, Music/drama.

SOUTH DAKOTA SCHOOL OF MINES AND TECHNOLOGY

501 East St. Joseph Street, Rapid City, SD 57701-3995
Phone: 605-394-2414 • **Financial Aid Phone:** 605-394-2274
E-mail: admissions@sdsmt.edu • **CEEB Code:** 3470
Fax: 605-394-1979 • **Website:** www.sdsmt.edu • **ACT Code:** 3922

This public school was founded in 1885. It has a 118-acre campus.

RATINGS

Admissions Selectivity Rating: 84   **Fire Safety Rating:** 95   **Green Rating:** 76

STUDENTS AND FACULTY

Enrollment: 2,353. **Student Body:** 20% female, 80% male, 53% out-of-state, 3% international (39 countries represented). Asian 1%, African American 2%, Caucasian 84%, Hispanic 5%, Native American 2%, Pacific Islander <1%, Two or more races 3%, Race unknown 1%.

Retention and Graduation: 78% freshmen return for sophomore year. 15% freshmen graduate within 4 years. 47% freshmen graduate within 6 years. 21% grads go on to further study within 1 year. 3% grads pursue arts and sciences degrees. 1% grads pursue law degrees. 1% grads pursue business degrees. 2% grads pursue medical degrees. **Faculty:** Student/faculty ratio 15:1. 151 full-time faculty, 85% hold PhDs, 15% are are members of minority groups, 26% are women.

ACADEMICS

Degrees: associate, bachelor's, certificate, doctoral/research, master's, postbachelor's certificate. **Classes:** Most classes have 20-29 students. **Most popular majors:** Mechanical Engineering; Chemical Engineering; Civil Engineering. **Special Study Options:** cooperative education program, cross-registration, distance learning, dual enrollment, English as a Second Language (ESL), independent study, internships, liberal arts/career combination, study abroad, Distance Education—SDSMT offfers an M.S. degree in Technology Management via the internet. Dual Degrees—We do not offer double majors but students may graduate with more than one degree by completing a minimum of thirty (30) semester hours of credit in residence beyond the credit hours used for the first B.S. degree. **Disability Services:** Special programs offered to physically disabled students, including note-taking services, reader services, tape recorders, tutors. **Career Services:** Alumni network, Alumni services, Career/job search classes, Career assessment, Internships, Regional alumni. Both the cooperative/internship programs are very successful and usually lead to permanent employment for the students after graduation. 75% of graduates have relevant co-op or internship experience when they graduate.

FACILITIES

Housing: Coed dorms, special housing for disabled students, fraternity/sorority housing, apartments for married students, apartments for single students, Wellness Housing. SDSM&T recently acquired apartments which can be rented by single students or groups of students or married students with families. 81% of campus accessible to physically diasbled. **Special Academic Facilities/Equipment:** Museum of geology and paleontology, electron microscope, engineering/mining experiment station, supersonic wind tunnel,3-D visualization lab, polymer processing lab, friction stir welding lab, high-frequency microwave lab, tech development lab, fluid computational dynamics lab, robotics lab, clean manufacturing lab, institute atmospheric science and other research institutes. **Computers:** 100% of classrooms, 100% of dorms, 100% of libraries, 100% of dining areas, 100% of student union, 100% of common outdoor areas have wireless network access. Students can register for classes online. Administrative functions (other than registration) can be performed online.

CAMPUS LIFE

Environment: Town. **Activities:** Choral groups, concert band, dance, drama/theater, jazz band, music ensembles, pep band, radio station, student government, student newspaper, Campus Ministries, Student Organization. 67 registered organizations, 6 honor societies, 9 religious organizations. 4 fraternities, 2 sororities. **Athletics (Intercollegiate):** *Men:* basketball, cross-country, football, golf, track/field (outdoor), track/field (indoor). *Women:* basketball, cross-country, golf, track/field (outdoor), track/field (indoor), volleyball. **On-Campus Highlights:** O'Harra Stadium (football and track), King (Sports) Center—basketball, pool, exercise, Geology and Paleontology Museum, Surbeck Student Center, Apex Gallery. **Environmental Initiatives:** A minimun of LEED Silver is required on all new construction or renovation

ADMISSIONS

Freshman Academic Profile: Average high school GPA 3.6. 24% in top 10% of high school class, 56% in top 25% of high school class, 86% in top 50% of high school class. **Reported SAT (pre-2016 redesign) scores:** SAT Math middle 50% range 550-660. SAT Critical Reading middle 50% range 490-630. SAT Writing middle 50% range 440-590. **Concordant SAT scores:** SAT EBRW middle 50% range 520–660. SAT Math middle 50% range 570–690. ACT middle 50% range 24-29. Minimum internet-based TOEFL 68. Minimum paper TOEFL 520. **Basis for Candidate Selection:** *Very important factors considered include:* rigor of secondary school record, class rank, academic GPA, standardized test scores. *Other factors considered include:* extracurricular activities, talent/ability, character/personal qualities, volunteer work, work experience. **Freshman Admission Requirements:** High school diploma is required and GED is accepted. *Academic units required:* 4 English, 4 math, 4 science, 3 science labs, 2 foreign language, 3 social studies, 1 visual/performing arts. *Academic units recommended:* 4 English, 4 math, 4 science, 3 science labs, 2 foreign language, 3 social studies, 1 visual/performing arts. **Freshman Admission Statistics:** 1,368 applied, 84.50% admitted, 43% enrolled. **Transfer Admission Requirements:** college transcript(s), statement of good standing from prior institution(s). Minimum college GPA of 2.0 required. Lowest grade transferable D. **General Admission Information:** Application fee $20. Nonfall registration accepted. Admission may be deferred for a maximum of 1 Semester.

COSTS AND FINANCIAL AID

Annual in-state tuition $7,340. Annual out-of-state tuition $11,500. Room and board $7,720. Required fees $3,820. Average book expense $2,000. **Required Forms and Deadlines:** FAFSA. **Notification of Awards:** Applicants will be notified of awards on a rolling basis beginning 4/15. **Types of Aid:** *Need-based scholarships/grants:* Federal Pell, FSEOG, State scholarships/grants, Private scholarships, College/university scholarship or grant aid from institutional funds. *Loans:* Direct Subsidized Stafford Loans, Direct Unsubsidized Stafford Loans, Direct PLUS loans, Federal Perkins Loans. *Student Employment:* Federal Work-Study Program available. Institutional employment available. **Financial Aid Statistics:** 77% needy freshmen, 65% needy undergrads receive need-based scholarship or grant aid. 60% freshmen, 38% undergrads receive non-need-based scholarship or grant aid. 79% freshmen, 84% undergrads receive need-based self-help aid. 4% freshmen, 4% undergrads receive athletic scholarships. 90% freshmen, 79% undergrads receive any aid. **Criteria for awarding aid:** *Non-need-based:* Academics, Athletics, Leadership, Minority status.

SOUTH DAKOTA STATE UNIVERSITY

SAD 200, Brookings, SD 57007-0649
Phone: 605-688-4121 • **Financial Aid Phone:** 605-688-4695
E-mail: sdsu.admissions@sdstate.edu • **CEEB Code:** 6653
Fax: 605-688-6891 • **Website:** www.sdstate.edu • **ACT Code:** 3924

This public school was founded in 1881. It has a 272-acre campus.

RATINGS
Admissions Selectivity Rating: 75   **Fire Safety Rating:** 89   **Green Rating:** 72

STUDENTS AND FACULTY
Enrollment: 9,835. **Student Body:** 52% female, 48% male, 4% international. Asian 1%, African American 2%, Caucasian 88%, Hispanic 2%, Native American 1%, Pacific Islander <1%, Two or more races 2%, Race unknown <1%.
Retention and Graduation: 76% freshmen return for sophomore year. **Faculty:** Student/faculty ratio 17:1. 546 full-time faculty, 72% hold PhDs, 13% are are members of minority groups, 46% are women.

ACADEMICS
Degrees: associate, bachelor's, certificate, doctoral/professional, doctoral/research, master's, postbachelor's certificate, post-master's certificate. **Classes:** Most classes have 20-29 students. Most lab/discussion sessions have 20-29 students. **Special Study Options:** Accelerated program, cooperative education program, cross-registration, distance learning, double major, dual enrollment, exchange student program (domestic), honors program, independent study, internships, liberal arts/career combination, study abroad, teacher certification program, We offer help and courses in ESL but it is not an official program. **Honors Programs:** Have an Honors College. See website http://www3. sdstate.edu/Academics/HonorsCollege/ Combined degree programs: BS/MS in Economics. **Disability Services:** Special programs offered to physically disabled students, including note-taking services, reader services, tape recorders, tutors. **Career Services:** Career/job search classes, Career assessment, Internships.

FACILITIES
Housing: Coed dorms, special housing for disabled students, special housing for international students, fraternity/sorority housing, apartments for married students, apartments for single students, Wellness Housing. Limited single rooms with optional meal plan for upperclassmen. Students out of high school less than 2 yrs are required to live in campus housing unless living with family. 99% of campus accessible to physically disabled. **Special Academic Facilities/Equipment:** SD Art Museum, SD Agricultural Heritage Museum, Northern Plains Bio-stress Laboratory, Animal Disease Research and Diagnostic Lab, McCrory Gardens, new Center for Infectious Disease Research and Vaccinology, EROS-SDSU GISc Center of Excellence. **Computers:** 30% of classrooms, 100% of dorms, 100% of libraries, 100% of dining areas, 100% of student union, 20% of common outdoor areas have wireless network access. Students can register for classes online. Administrative functions (other than registration) can be performed online.

CAMPUS LIFE
Environment: Village. **Activities:** Choral groups, concert band, dance, drama/theater, jazz band, literary magazine, marching band, music ensembles, musical theater, pep band, radio station, student government, student newspaper, symphony orchestra, yearbook. 200 registered organizations, 32 honor societies, 14 religious organizations. 6 fraternities, 4 sororities. **Athletics (Intercollegiate):** *Men:* baseball, basketball, cross-country, diving,

football, golf, swimming, tennis, track/field (outdoor), track/field (indoor), wrestling. *Women:* basketball, cross-country, diving, equestrian sports, golf, soccer, softball, swimming, tennis, track/field (outdoor), track/field (indoor), volleyball. **On-Campus Highlights:** Performing Arts Center, Dairy Bar, University Student Union, Frost Arena, South Dakota Art Museum, Northern Plains Bio-Stress Laboratory Enterprise Institute SD Ag Heritage Museum. **Environmental Initiatives:** Establishment of environmental stewardship and sustainability shared governance committee.

ADMISSIONS
Freshman Academic Profile: Average high school GPA 3.4. 14% in top 10% of high school class, 36% in top 25% of high school class, 68% in top 50% of high school class. **Reported SAT (pre-2016 redesign) scores:** SAT Math middle 50% range 470-600. SAT Critical Reading middle 50% range 430-560. **Concordant SAT scores:** SAT Math middle 50% range 510–620. ACT middle 50% range 20-26. Minimum internet-based TOEFL 61. Minimum paper TOEFL 500. **Basis for Candidate Selection:** *Important factors considered include:* rigor of secondary school record, class rank, academic GPA, standardized test scores. *Other factors considered include:* recommendation(s). **Freshman Admission Requirements:** High school diploma is required and GED is accepted. *Academic units required:* 4 English, 3 math, 3 science, 3 science labs, 3 social studies, 1 visual/performing arts. **Freshman Admission Statistics:** 5,060 applied, 91.70% admitted, 48% enrolled. **Transfer Admission Requirements:** High school transcript, college transcript(s), statement of good standing from prior institution(s). Minimum college GPA of 2.0 required. Lowest grade transferable D. **General Admission Information:** Application fee $20. Nonfall registration accepted.

COSTS AND FINANCIAL AID
Annual in-state tuition $4,341. Annual out-of-state tuition $6,512. Room and board $7,462. Required fees $3,831. Average book expense $1,500. **Required Forms and Deadlines:** FAFSA. **Notification of Awards:** Applicants will be notified of awards on a rolling basis beginning 4/1. **Types of Aid:** *Need-based scholarships/grants:* Federal Pell, FSEOG, State scholarships/grants, Private scholarships, College/university scholarship or grant aid from institutional funds, United Negro College Fund. *Loans:* Direct Subsidized Stafford Loans, Direct Unsubsidized Stafford Loans, Direct PLUS loans, Federal Perkins Loans, Federal Nursing Loans. *Student Employment:* Federal Work-Study Program available. Institutional employment available. **Financial Aid Statistics:** 50% needy freshmen, 50% needy undergrads receive need-based scholarship or grant aid. 20% freshmen, 14% undergrads receive non-need-based scholarship or grant aid. 89% freshmen, 92% undergrads receive need-based self-help aid. 4% freshmen, 5% undergrads receive athletic scholarships. 75% undergrads borrow to pay for school. Average cumulative indebtedness $28,796. **Criteria for awarding aid:** *Non-need-based:* Academics, Alumni affiliation, Art, Athletics, Leadership, Minority status, Music/drama, State/district residency.

SOUTHEAST MISSOURI STATE UNIVERSITY

One University Plaza, Cape Girardeau, MO 63701
Phone: 573-651-2590 • **Financial Aid Phone:** 573-651-2253
E-mail: admissions@semo.edu • **CEEB Code:** 6655
Fax: 573-651-5936 • **Website:** www.semo.edu • **ACT Code:** 2366

This public school was founded in 1873. It has a 400-acre campus.

RATINGS
Admissions Selectivity Rating: 79   **Fire Safety Rating:** 93   **Green Rating:** 73

STUDENTS AND FACULTY
Enrollment: 9,028. **Student Body:** 56% female, 44% male, 19% out-of-state, 7% international (39 countries represented). Asian 1%, African American 10%, Caucasian 78%, Hispanic 2%, Native American <1%, Pacific Islander <1%, Two or more races 1%, Race unknown 1%.
Retention and Graduation: 74% freshmen return for sophomore year. 29% freshmen graduate within 4 years. 49% freshmen graduate within 6 years. **Faculty:** Student/faculty ratio 21:1. 403 full-time faculty, 74% hold PhDs, 16% are are members of minority groups, 52% are women. 3% of classes are taught by teaching assistants.

ACADEMICS
Degrees: associate, bachelor's, certificate, master's, postbachelor's certificate, post-master's certificate. **Classes:** Most classes have 20-29 students. **Most popular majors:** General Studies; Registered Nursing/Registered Nurse; Business Administration and Management. **Special Study Options:** Accelerated program, distance learning, double major, dual enrollment, English as a Second Language (ESL), honors program, independent study, internships, liberal arts/career combination, student-designed major, study abroad, teacher

certification program. **Honors Programs:** The Honors Program encourages intellectual perspective, addresses special needs of outstanding students and contributes to the general advancement of learning. **Disability Services:** Special programs offered to physically disabled students, including note-taking services, reader services, tape recorders, tutors. **Career Services:** Alumni services, Career/job search classes, Career assessment, Internships. The CLs (CL 001-004) are four career proficiency checks required for graduation for all students. These proficiencies were implemented to insure that all students graduate with appropriate career planning knowledge. Following the completion of these courses every student will have a resume and cover letter tailored to a career in their major field or graduate school.

FACILITIES

Housing: Coed dorms, fraternity/sorority housing, Wellness HousingApartments for students with dependents. 100% of campus accessible to physically diasbled. **Special Academic Facilities/Equipment:** River Campus at Southeast; Crisp Museum;Bedell Performance Hall; Center for Faulkner Studies; Center for Scholarship in Teaching and Learning; Missouri Statewide Early Literacy Intervention Program (MSELIP); Writing Center; University Demonstration Farm; 4 corporate video studios, 2 radio stations; Southeast Explorer; SHOW (Southeast Health on Wheels); Linda Godwin Center for Science and Math Education; **Computers:** 15% of dorms, 90% of libraries, 90% of dining areas, 90% of student union, 10% of common outdoor areas have wireless network access. Students can register for classes online. Administrative functions (other than registration) can be performed online.

CAMPUS LIFE

Environment: Town. **Activities:** Choral groups, concert band, dance, drama/theater, jazz band, literary magazine, marching band, music ensembles, musical theater, opera, pep band, radio station, student government, student newspaper, symphony orchestra, Campus Ministries, Student Organization, Model UN. 136 registered organizations, 8 honor societies, 14 religious organizations. 11 fraternities, 7 sororities. **Athletics (Intercollegiate):** *Men:* baseball, basketball, cheerleading, cross-country, football, track/field (outdoor), track/field (indoor). *Women:* basketball, cheerleading, cross-country, gymnastics, soccer, softball, tennis, track/field (outdoor), track/field (indoor), volleyball. **On-Campus Highlights:** River Campus at Southeast, Recreation Center & Aquatic Center, Kent Library Information Commons, Otto and Della Seabaugh Polytechnic Bldg, Robert A. Dempster Hall, River Campus: Holland School of Visual adn Performing Arts,Bedell Performance Hall, Crisp Regional Museum, Rust Flexible Theatre, Glenn Convocation Center, Shuck Music Recital Hall.

ADMISSIONS

Freshman Academic Profile: Average high school GPA 3.4. 18% in top 10% of high school class, 44% in top 25% of high school class, 77% in top 50% of high school class. **Reported SAT (pre-2016 redesign) scores:** SAT Math middle 50% range 457.5-582.5. SAT Critical Reading middle 50% range 420-552.5. **Concordant SAT scores:** SAT Math middle 50% range 500–600. ACT middle 50% range 20-25. Minimum internet-based TOEFL 61. Minimum paper TOEFL 500. **Basis for Candidate Selection:** *Very important factors considered include:* rigor of secondary school record, academic GPA, standardized test scores. *Other factors considered include:* class rank. **Freshman Admission Requirements:** High school diploma is required and GED is accepted. *Academic units required:* 4 English, 3 math, 3 science, 1 science lab, 2 social studies, 1 history, 3 academic electives, 1 visual/performing arts. **Freshman Admission Statistics:** 5,184 applied, 82.81% admitted, 43% enrolled. **Transfer Admission Requirements:** college transcript(s), Minimum college GPA of 2.0 required. Lowest grade transferable D. **General Admission Information:** Application fee $30. Priority deadline 12/1. Regular application deadline 7/1. Nonfall registration accepted.

COSTS AND FINANCIAL AID

Annual in-state tuition $5,979. Annual out-of-state tuition $11,364. Room and board $8,508. Required fees $1,011. Average book expense $502. **Required Forms and Deadlines:** FAFSA. **Notification of Awards:** Applicants will be notified of awards on a rolling basis beginning 4/1. **Types of Aid:** *Need-based scholarships/grants:* Federal Pell, FSEOG, State scholarships/grants, Private scholarships, College/university scholarship or grant aid from institutional funds. *Loans:* Direct Subsidized Stafford Loans, Direct Unsubsidized Stafford Loans, Direct PLUS loans, Federal Perkins Loans. *Student Employment:* Federal Work-Study Program available. Institutional employment available. **Financial Aid Statistics:** 94% needy freshmen, 88% needy undergrads receive need-based scholarship or grant aid. 13% freshmen, 7% undergrads receive non-need-based scholarship or grant aid. 59% freshmen, 72% undergrads receive need-based self-help aid. 2% freshmen, 2% undergrads receive athletic scholarships. 85% freshmen, 83% undergrads receive any aid. 64% undergrads borrow to pay for school. Average cumulative indebtedness $27,991. **Criteria for awarding aid:** *Need-based:* Academics, Minority status. *Non-need-based:* Academics, Alumni affiliation, Art, Athletics, Job skills, Leadership, Minority status, Music/drama, State/district residency.

SOUTHEASTERN BIBLE COLLEGE

2545 Valleydale Road, Birmingham, AL 35244
Phone: 205-970-9211
E-mail: info@sebc.edu
Fax: 205-970-9207 • **Website:** www.sebc.edu

This private school was founded in 1935. It has a 10-acre campus.

RATINGS

Admissions Selectivity Rating: 71   **Fire Safety Rating:** 60*   **Green Rating:** 60*

STUDENTS AND FACULTY

Student Body: 12% out-of-state.
Retention and Graduation: 67% freshmen return for sophomore year. 20% freshmen graduate within 4 years. 36% freshmen graduate within 6 years. **Faculty:** Student/faculty ratio 8:1. 8 full-time faculty, 75% hold PhDs, 0% are are members of minority groups, 25% 0% of classes are taught by teaching assistants.

ACADEMICS

Degrees: associate, bachelor's, diploma. **Classes:** Most classes have fewer than 10 students. **Most popular majors:** Bible/Biblical Studies. **Special Study Options:** independent study, internships. **Disability Services:** Special programs offered to physically disabled students, including note-taking services, tape recorders. **Career Services:** On-campus interviews.

FACILITIES

Housing: men's dorms, women's dorms, apartments for married students. 100% of campus accessible to physically diasbled.

CAMPUS LIFE

Environment: Metropolis. **Activities:** Choral groups, music ensembles, student government. **On-Campus Highlights:** Gannett-Estes Library

ADMISSIONS

ACT middle 50% range 18-23. **Basis for Candidate Selection:** *Very important factors considered include:* recommendation(s), character/personal qualities, religious affiliation/commitment. *Important factors considered include:* application essay. *Other factors considered include:* academic GPA, standardized test scores. **Freshman Admission Requirements:** High school diploma is required and GED is accepted. *Academic units recommended:* 4 English, 4 math, 4 science, 4 social studies, 8 academic electives. **Freshman Admission Statistics:** 18 applied, 100.00% admitted, 83% enrolled. **Transfer Admission Requirements:** High school transcript, college transcript(s), essay or personal statement, Minimum college GPA of 2.0 required. Lowest grade transferable C. **General Admission Information:** Application fee $30. Priority deadline 8/1. Nonfall registration accepted. Admission may be deferred for a maximum of 1 year.

COSTS AND FINANCIAL AID

Required Forms and Deadlines: FAFSA, Institution's own financial aid form. **Notification of Awards:** Applicants will be notified of awards on or about 5/1. **Types of Aid:** *Need-based scholarships/grants:* Federal Pell, FSEOG, College/university scholarship or grant aid from institutional funds. *Loans:* Direct Subsidized Stafford Loans, Direct Unsubsidized Stafford Loans, Direct PLUS loans. *Student Employment:* Federal Work-Study Program available. **Criteria for awarding aid:** *Need-based:* Academics, Leadership. *Non-need-based:* Academics, Leadership.

SOUTHEASTERN LOUISIANA UNIVERSITY

SLU 10752, Hammond, LA 70402
Phone: 985-549-2066 • **Financial Aid Phone:** 985-549-2030
E-mail: admissions@southeastern.edu • **CEEB Code:** 6656
Fax: 985-549-5632 • **Website:** www.southeastern.edu • **ACT Code:** 1608

This public school was founded in 1925. It has a 365-acre campus.

RATINGS

Admissions Selectivity Rating: 76   **Fire Safety Rating:** 95   **Green Rating:** 74

STUDENTS AND FACULTY

Enrollment: 10,836. **Student Body:** 62% female, 38% male, 5% out-of-state, 2% international (54 countries represented). Asian 1%, African American 20%, Caucasian 63%, Hispanic 8%, Native American <1%, Pacific Islander <1%, Two or more races 6%, Race unknown 1%.

Retention and Graduation: 63% freshmen return for sophomore year. **Faculty:** Student/faculty ratio 20:1. 472 full-time faculty, 66% hold PhDs, 13% are are members of minority groups, 57% are women. 0% of classes are taught by teaching assistants.

ACADEMICS
Degrees: associate, bachelor's, doctoral/professional, doctoral/research, master's, post-master's certificate. **Classes:** Most classes have 20-29 students. Most lab/discussion sessions have 20-29 students. **Most popular majors:** Registered Nursing/Registered Nurse; Biology/Biological Sciences; Sport and Fitness Administration/Management. **Special Study Options:** Accelerated program, cross-registration, distance learning, double major, dual enrollment, English as a Second Language (ESL), honors program, independent study, internships, liberal arts/career combination, study abroad, teacher certification program. **Honors Programs:** reduced size classes, scholarships, honors residence hall, achievement awards, and honor academic credit shown on the transcript. **Disability Services:** Special programs offered to physically disabled students, including note-taking services, tape recorders, tutors. **Career Services:** Alumni services, Career assessment, Internships. The University offers a wide range of courses and curricula that address emerging regional, national and international priorities. The University embraces active partnerships that benefit students, faculty and the region we serve. Programs enable students to understand themselves and the world around them in a broad intellectual perspective. Such a perspective provides students the opportunity to live full, rich, balanced lives and to assume positions of leadership in the public and private sector. Graduates are prepared to think critically, communicate effectively and become lifelong learners. Emphasis is placed on preparation for careers or graduate study through undergraduate research in collaboration with faculty, "hands-on" internships, field experiences, work-study placements, cooperative education, service-learning, and opportunities to study abroad. Many of these opportunities earn college credit. Southeastern also has honors tracks in place for all degree programs. Undergraduate research programs such as Undergraduate Research and Creative Activities Grants Programs in the College of Arts, Humanities and Social Sciences, PROFIT (Preferred Research Option for Intensive Training) in the College of Business, SOAR (Student Opportunities for Achievement and Research) in the College of Nursing and Health Sciences, SURE (Student Undergraduate Research in Education) in the College of Education and Human Development, and STAR (Science and Technology Awards for Research) in the College of Science and Technology provide opportunities for undergraduate students to conduct research and engage in creative ventures with Southeastern faculty members.

FACILITIES
Housing: Coed dorms, women's dorms, fraternity/sorority housing, apartments for single students. 95% of campus accessible to physically diasbled. **Special Academic Facilities/Equipment:** Contemporary Art Gallery, Radio Station, Television Station, Columbia Theatre, Maritime Museum **Computers:** 5% of classrooms, 100% of dorms, 100% of libraries, 50% of dining areas, 25% of student union, 25% of common outdoor areas have wireless network access. Students can register for classes online. Administrative functions (other than registration) can be performed online.

CAMPUS LIFE
Environment: Village. **Activities:** Choral groups, concert band, dance, drama/theater, jazz band, literary magazine, marching band, music ensembles, musical theater, opera, pep band, radio station, student government, student newspaper, student-run film society, symphony orchestra, television station, yearbook, Campus Ministries, Student Organization. 105 registered organizations, 11 honor societies, 12 religious organizations. 7 fraternities, 8 sororities. **Athletics (Intercollegiate):** *Men:* baseball, basketball, cross-country, football, golf, track/field (outdoor), track/field (indoor). *Women:* basketball, cross-country, soccer, softball, tennis, track/field (outdoor), track/field (indoor), volleyball. **On-Campus Highlights:** Student Union, Student Recreation Center, Library, Bookstore, Campus Dining Complex. **Environmental Initiatives:** Renewable Energy: investment in solar power, on site waste oil biodiesel fuel production, proactive energy usage reduction management. The university has focused on these areas to reduce both waste and the need for grid power.

ADMISSIONS
Freshman Academic Profile: Average high school GPA 3.2. 14% in top 10% of high school class, 38% in top 25% of high school class, 71% in top 50% of high school class. ACT middle 50% range 20-24. Minimum internet-based TOEFL 61. Minimum paper TOEFL 500. **Basis for Candidate Selection:** *Very important factors considered include:* rigor of secondary school record, academic GPA, standardized test scores. **Freshman Admission Requirements:** High school diploma is required and GED is accepted. *Academic units required:* 4 English, 4 math, 4 science, 2 foreign language, 4 social studies, 1 visual/performing arts. **Freshman Admission Statistics:** 4,226 applied, 88.07% admitted, 70% enrolled. **Transfer Admission Requirements:** college transcript(s), statement of good standing from prior institution(s). Minimum college GPA of 2.0 required. Lowest grade transferable D. **General**

Admission Information: Application fee $20. Priority deadline 7/15. Regular application deadline 8/1. Nonfall registration accepted. Admission may be deferred for a maximum of 1 Year.

COSTS AND FINANCIAL AID
Annual in-state tuition $5,652. Annual out-of-state tuition $18,130. Room and board $7,510. Required fees $2,121. Average book expense $1,220. **Required Forms and Deadlines:** FAFSA. **Notification of Awards:** Applicants will be notified of awards on a rolling basis beginning 4/1. **Types of Aid:** *Need-based scholarships/grants:* Federal Pell, FSEOG, State scholarships/grants, Private scholarships, College/university scholarship or grant aid from institutional funds. *Loans:* Direct Subsidized Stafford Loans, Direct Unsubsidized Stafford Loans, Direct PLUS loans, Federal Perkins Loans, College/university loans from institutional funds. *Student Employment:* Federal Work-Study Program available. Institutional employment available. **Financial Aid Statistics:** 65% needy freshmen, 66% needy undergrads receive need-based scholarship or grant aid. 68% freshmen, 52% undergrads receive non-need-based scholarship or grant aid. 56% freshmen, 62% undergrads receive need-based self-help aid. 3% freshmen, 3% undergrads receive athletic scholarships. 59% undergrads borrow to pay for school. Average cumulative indebtedness $21,517. **Criteria for awarding aid:** *Need-based:* Academics, Job skills, Leadership. *Non-need-based:* Academics, Athletics, Job skills, Leadership, Music/drama, State/district residency.

SOUTHEASTERN OKLAHOMA STATE UNIVERSITY

1405 North 4th Avenue, Durant, OK 74701-0609
Phone: 580-745-2060 • **Financial Aid Phone:** 580-745-2186
E-mail: admissions@se.edu • **CEEB Code:** 6657
Fax: 580-745-4502 • **ACT Code:** 3438

This public school was founded in 1909. It has a 268-acre campus.

RATINGS
Admissions Selectivity Rating: 76   **Fire Safety Rating:** 88   **Green Rating:** 60*

STUDENTS AND FACULTY
Enrollment: 3,465. **Student Body:** 55% female, 45% male, 22% out-of-state, 1% international (28 countries represented). Asian 1%, African American 5%, Caucasian 59%, Hispanic 3%, Native American 31%, Pacific Islander 0%, Two or more races 0%, Race unknown 0%.
Retention and Graduation: 58% freshmen return for sophomore year. 19% freshmen graduate within 4 years. **Faculty:** Student/faculty ratio 18:1. 143 full-time faculty, 74% hold PhDs, 17% are are members of minority groups, 41% are women. 0% of classes are taught by teaching assistants.

ACADEMICS
Degrees: bachelor's, master's, post-master's certificate. **Classes:** Most classes have 20-29 students. Most lab/discussion sessions have 20-29 students. **Most popular majors:** Elementary Education and Teaching; Occupational Safety and Health Technology/Technician; Psychology. **Special Study Options:** distance learning, double major, honors program, independent study, internships, teacher certification program. **Honors Programs:** Our Honors program offers six different scholarships ranging in value from $6,400 to $26,400 over four years. **Disability Services:** Special programs offered to physically disabled students, including note-taking services, reader services, tape recorders, tutors. **Career Services:** Alumni network, Career/job search classes, Career assessment, Internships.

FACILITIES
Housing: Coed dorms, apartments for single students. 100% of campus accessible to physically diasbled. **Special Academic Facilities/Equipment:** Visual and Performing Arts Gallery **Computers:** 65% of classrooms, 50% of dorms, 100% of libraries, 100% of dining areas, 100% of student union, 50% of common outdoor areas have wireless network access. Students can register for classes online. Administrative functions (other than registration) can be performed online.

CAMPUS LIFE
Environment: Village. **Activities:** Choral groups, concert band, dance, drama/theater, jazz band, literary magazine, marching band, music ensembles, musical theater, opera, pep band, radio station, student government, student newspaper, yearbook, Campus Ministries, Student Organization. 70 registered organizations, 12 honor societies, 8 religious organizations. 2 fraternities, 2 sororities. **Athletics (Intercollegiate):** *Men:* baseball, basketball, football, golf, tennis. *Women:* basketball, cross-country, softball, tennis, volleyball. **On-Campus Highlights:** Shearer Hall and Suites (New Apartments), New Student

Union, Newly Renovated Football Stadium, New Basketball Arena, "Campus of a Thousand Magnolias".

ADMISSIONS

Freshman Academic Profile: Average high school GPA 3.3. 16% in top 10% of high school class, 40% in top 25% of high school class, 77% in top 50% of high school class. 99% from public high schools. ACT middle 50% range 18-23. Minimum paper TOEFL 500. **Basis for Candidate Selection:** *Very important factors considered include:* class rank, academic GPA, standardized test scores. *Other factors considered include:* rigor of secondary school record, recommendation(s), interview, talent/ability, character/personal qualities, state residency, level of applicant's interest. **Freshman Admission Requirements:** High school diploma is required and GED is accepted. *Academic units required:* 4 English, 3 math, 2 science, 2 science labs, 3 history, 2 academic electives. *Academic units recommended:* 1 foreign language, 1 social studies, 1 computer science. **Freshman Admission Statistics:** 922 applied, 87.96% admitted, 76% enrolled. **Transfer Admission Requirements:** college transcript(s), Minimum college GPA of 2.0 required. Lowest grade transferable D. **General Admission Information:** Application fee $20. Nonfall registration accepted.

COSTS AND FINANCIAL AID

Annual in-state tuition $3,639. Annual out-of-state tuition $10,010. Room and board $2,005. Required fees $677. Average book expense $800. **Required Forms and Deadlines:** FAFSA, Institution's own financial aid form. **Notification of Awards:** Applicants will be notified of awards on a rolling basis beginning 4/15. **Types of Aid:** *Need-based scholarships/grants:* Federal Pell, FSEOG, State scholarships/grants, Private scholarships, College/university scholarship or grant aid from institutional funds. *Loans:* Federal Perkins Loans. *Student Employment:* Federal Work-Study Program available. Institutional employment available. **Financial Aid Statistics:** 71% needy freshmen, 81% needy undergrads receive need-based scholarship or grant aid. 45% freshmen, 33% undergrads receive non-need-based scholarship or grant aid. 37% freshmen, 59% undergrads receive need-based self-help aid. 10% freshmen, 7% undergrads receive athletic scholarships. 66% freshmen, 65% undergrads receive any aid. **Criteria for awarding aid:** *Non-need-based:* Academics, Alumni affiliation, Art, Athletics, Leadership, Minority status, Music/drama, State/district residency.

SOUTHEASTERN UNIVERSITY

1000 Longfellow Blvd., Lakeland, FL 33801
Phone: 863-667-5018 • **Financial Aid Phone:** 800-500-8760
E-mail: admission@seu.edu
Fax: 863-667-5200 • **Website:** http://www.seu.edu/

RATINGS

Admissions Selectivity Rating: 78   **Fire Safety Rating:** 99   **Green Rating:** 60*

STUDENTS AND FACULTY

Enrollment: 2,946. **Student Body:** 55% female, 45% male, 32% out-of-state, 2% international. Asian 1%, African American 15%, Caucasian 61%, Hispanic 17%, Native American <1%, Pacific Islander <1%, Two or more races 1%, Race unknown 4%.
Retention and Graduation: 66% freshmen return for sophomore year. 31% freshmen graduate within 4 years. **Faculty:** Student/faculty ratio 19:1. 118 full-time faculty, 72% hold PhDs, 16% are are members of minority groups, 37% are women.

ACADEMICS

Degrees: associate, bachelor's, certificate, doctoral, master's, postbachelor's certifiate. **Most popular majors:** Theology and Religious Vocations; Psychology; Elementary Education and Teaching. **Career Services:** Career assessment, Internships.

FACILITIES

Housing: 100% of campus accessible to physically disabled.

ADMISSIONS

Freshman Academic Profile: 77% from public high schools. **Reported SAT (pre-2016 redesign) scores:** SAT Math middle 50% range 410-520. SAT Critical Reading middle 50% range 430-560. SAT Writing middle 50% range 420-540. **Concordant SAT scores:** SAT EBRW middle 50% 480–610. SAT Math middle 50% range 450–550. ACT middle 50% range 18-23. Minimum internet-based TOEFL 88. Minimum paper TOEFL 570. **Basis for Candidate Selection:** *Very important factors considered include:* character/personal qualities, religious affiliation/commitment. *Important factors considered include:* academic GPA, standardized test scores, application essay, recommendation(s), level of applicant's interest. *Other factors considered*

include: rigor of secondary school record, class rank, interview, extracurricular activities, talent/ability, first generation, alumni/ae relation, volunteer work, work experience. **Freshman Admission Requirements:** *Academic units recommended:* 4 English, 4 math, 4 science, 1 science lab, 2 foreign language, 4 social studies. **Freshman Admission Statistics:** 3,402 applied, 43.94% admitted, 61% enrolled. **General Admission Information:** Application fee $40. Regular application deadline 5/1. Nonfall registration accepted. Admission may be deferred.

COSTS AND FINANCIAL AID

Required Forms and Deadlines: FAFSA, Institution's own financial aid form, State aid form. **Notification of Awards:** Applicants will be notified of awards on a rolling basis beginning 1/1. **Types of Aid:** *Need-based scholarships/grants:* Federal Pell, FSEOG, State scholarships/grants, Private scholarships, College/university scholarship or grant aid from institutional funds. *Loans:* Federal Perkins Loans. *Student Employment:* Federal Work-Study Program available. Institutional employment available. **Financial Aid Statistics:** 95% needy freshmen, 96% needy undergrads receive need-based scholarship or grant aid. 10% freshmen, 9% undergrads receive non-need-based scholarship or grant aid. 85% freshmen, 87% undergrads receive need-based self-help aid. 4% freshmen, 3% undergrads receive athletic scholarships. 90% freshmen receive any aid. **Criteria for awarding aid:** *Non-need-based:* Academics, Athletics, Leadership, Music/drama, State/district residency.

SOUTHERN ADVENTIST UNIVERSITY

P.O. Box 370, Collegedale, TN 37315
Phone: 423-236-2835 • **Financial Aid Phone:** 423-236-2894
E-mail: admissions@southern.edu • **CEEB Code:** 3518
Fax: 423-236-1835 • **ACT Code:** 4006

This private school, affiliated with the Seventh Day Adventist Church, was founded in 1892. It has a 1000-acre campus.

RATINGS

Admissions Selectivity Rating: 75   **Fire Safety Rating:** 90   **Green Rating:** 60*

STUDENTS AND FACULTY

Enrollment: 2,585. **Student Body:** 55% female, 45% male, 69% out-of-state, 5% international. Asian 6%, African American 12%, Caucasian 58%, Hispanic 19%, Native American <1%, Pacific Islander 1%, Two or more races <1%, Race unknown 0%.
Retention and Graduation: 72% freshmen return for sophomore year. 23% freshmen graduate within 4 years. 48% freshmen graduate within 6 years. 15% grads go on to further study within 1 year. 10% grads pursue arts and sciences degrees. 1% grads pursue business degrees. 3% grads pursue medical degrees. **Faculty:** Student/faculty ratio 15:1. 146 full-time faculty, 64% hold PhDs, 12% are are members of minority groups, 42% are women. 0% of classes are taught by teaching assistants.

ACADEMICS

Degrees: associate, bachelor's, certificate, master's, post-master's certificate. **Most popular majors:** Business/Commerce; Biology/Biological Sciences. **Special Study Options:** double major, dual enrollment, English as a Second Language (ESL), honors program, independent study, internships, study abroad, teacher certification program. **Honors Programs:** Southern Scholars program includes special projects, inter-disciplinary studies, and designated honors courses to provide a challenging and intellectually stimulating educational experience. Combined degree programs: BA/MA, Nursing. **Disability Services:** Special programs offered to physically disabled students, including note-taking services, reader services, tape recorders, tutors.

FACILITIES

Housing: men's dorms, women's dorms, apartments for married students, apartments for single students. 70% of campus accessible to physically disabled. **Special Academic Facilities/Equipment:** Near-Eastern archaeology teaching collection **Computers:** 100% of classrooms, 5% of dorms, 100% of libraries, 80% of dining areas, 10% of common outdoor areas have wireless network access. Students can register for classes online. Administrative functions (other than registration) can be performed online.

CAMPUS LIFE

Environment: Rural. **Activities:** Choral groups, concert band, drama/theater, jazz band, music ensembles, radio station, student government, student newspaper, student-run film society, symphony orchestra, television station, yearbook, Campus Ministries, Student Organization. 30 registered organizations, 8 honor societies, 3 religious organizations. **On-Campus Highlights:** Student Center, Wellness Center, The Village Market, KRs Place, Library. **Environmental Initiatives:** Establishing environmental sustainability committee.

ADMISSIONS

Freshman Academic Profile: Average high school GPA 3.4. 18% from public high schools. **Reported SAT (pre-2016 redesign) scores:** SAT Math middle 50% range 430-560. SAT Critical Reading middle 50% range 460-580. **Concordant SAT scores:** SAT Math middle 50% range 470–580. ACT middle 50% range 19-25. Minimum paper TOEFL 550. **Basis for Candidate Selection:** *Very important factors considered include:* rigor of secondary school record, academic GPA, standardized test scores. **Freshman Admission Requirements:** High school diploma is required and GED is accepted. *Academic units required:* 3 English, 2 math, 2 science, 1 social studies, 1 history, 9 academic electives. *Academic units recommended:* 4 English, 3 math, 3 science, 2 foreign language, 1 social studies, 2 history, 9 academic electives, and 1 unit from above areas or other academic areas. **Freshman Admission Statistics:** 1,452 applied, 80.37% admitted, 54% enrolled. **Transfer Admission Requirements:** college transcript(s), Minimum college GPA of 2 required. Lowest grade transferable D. **General Admission Information:** Application fee $40. Regular application deadline 9/8. Nonfall registration accepted. Admission may be deferred for a maximum of 1 year.

COSTS AND FINANCIAL AID

Annual tuition $17,534. Room and board $5,786. Required fees $790. Average book expense $1,100. **Required Forms and Deadlines:** FAFSA. **Notification of Awards:** Applicants will be notified of awards on a rolling basis beginning 2/15. **Types of Aid:** *Need-based scholarships/grants:* Federal Pell, FSEOG, State scholarships/grants, Private scholarships, College/university scholarship or grant aid from institutional funds. *Loans:* Federal Perkins Loans, Federal Nursing Loans, College/university loans from institutional funds. *Student Employment:* Federal Work-Study Program available. Institutional employment available. **Financial Aid Statistics:** 99% needy freshmen, 98% needy undergrads receive need-based scholarship or grant aid. 82% freshmen, 55% undergrads receive non-need-based scholarship or grant aid. 83% freshmen, 86% undergrads receive need-based self-help aid. 0% freshmen, 0% undergrads receive athletic scholarships. 95% undergrads receive any aid. **Criteria for awarding aid:** *Need-based:* Academics, Art. *Non-need-based:* Academics, Alumni affiliation, Art, Leadership, Music/drama.

SOUTHERN CALIFORNIA INSTITUTE OF ARCHITECTURE

SCI-Arc Admissions Office, Los Angeles, CA 90013-1822
Phone: 213.356.5320 • **Financial Aid Phone:** 213-356-5346
E-mail: admissions@sciarc.edu
Fax: 213-613-2260 • **Website:** www.sciarc.edu

This private school was founded in 1972.

RATINGS
Admissions Selectivity Rating: 63   **Fire Safety Rating:** 60*   **Green Rating:** 60*

STUDENTS AND FACULTY
Enrollment: 245. **Student Body:** 27% female, 73% male, 40% out-of-state, 20% international (45 countries represented). Asian 24%, African American 1%, Caucasian 30%, Hispanic 18%, Native American 0%, Pacific Islander 0%, Two or more races 0%, Race unknown 7%.
Retention and Graduation: 93% freshmen return for sophomore year. **Faculty:** Student/faculty ratio 11:1. 33 full-time faculty, 0% are are members of minority groups, 33% are women.

ACADEMICS
Degrees: bachelor's, master's. **Special Study Options:** internships, study abroad. **Career Services:** Alumni network, Internships.

FACILITIES
Special Academic Facilities/Equipment: SCI-Arc gallery, Wood/Metal Shop, Digital Fabrication shop **Computers:** Students can register for classes online.

CAMPUS LIFE
Environment: Metropolis. **Activities:** student government. **On-Campus Highlights:** SCI-Arc Gallery, Kappe Library, Wood/Metal Shop, Studios.

ADMISSIONS
Minimum internet-based TOEFL 83. Minimum paper TOEFL 560. **Basis for Candidate Selection:** *Very important factors considered include:* academic GPA, application essay, recommendation(s), talent/ability, character/personal qualities, level of applicant's interest. *Important factors considered include:* rigor of secondary school record. *Other factors considered include:* standardized test scores, extracurricular activities, racial/ethnic status, volunteer work, work experience. **Freshman Admission Requirements:** High school diploma is

required and GED is accepted. **Freshman Admission Statistics:** 70 applied, 91.43% admitted, 41% enrolled. **Transfer Admission Requirements:** college transcript(s), essay or personal statement, Lowest grade transferable C. **General Admission Information:** Application fee $75. Regular application deadline 2/1. Regular notification 4/1. Nonfall registration not accepted. Admission may be deferred for a maximum of 1 year.

COSTS AND FINANCIAL AID
Annual tuition $27,500. Required fees $350. **Required Forms and Deadlines:** FAFSA, Institution's own financial aid form. **Types of Aid:** *Need-based scholarships/grants:* Federal Pell, FSEOG, State scholarships/grants, College/university scholarship or grant aid from institutional funds. *Student Employment:* Federal Work-Study Program available. Institutional employment available. **Criteria for awarding aid:** *Need-based:* Academics. *Non-need-based:* Academics, State/district residency.

SOUTHERN CONNECTICUT STATE UNIVERSITY

SCSU-Admissions House, New Haven, CT 06515-1202
Phone: 203-392-5644 • **CEEB Code:** 3662
Fax: 203-392-5727 • **Website:** www.southernct.edu

This public school was founded in 1893. It has a 168-acre campus.

RATINGS
Admissions Selectivity Rating: 73   **Fire Safety Rating:** 60*   **Green Rating:** 87

STUDENTS AND FACULTY
Enrollment: 8,520. **Student Body:** 60% female, 40% male, 4% out-of-state, <1% international (39 countries represented). Asian 3%, African American 16%, Caucasian 62%, Hispanic 10%, Native American <1%, Pacific Islander 0%, Two or more races 2%, Race unknown 6%.
Retention and Graduation: 12% freshmen graduate within 4 years. 44% freshmen graduate within 6 years. 27% grads go on to further study within 1 year. **Faculty:** Student/faculty ratio 17:1. 403 full-time faculty, 90% hold PhDs, 14% are are members of minority groups, 45% are women.

ACADEMICS
Degrees: bachelor's, master's, post-master's certificate. **Classes:** Most classes have 20-29 students. Most lab/discussion sessions have 10-19 students. **Special Study Options:** Accelerated program, cooperative education program, cross-registration, distance learning, double major, exchange student program (domestic), external degree program, honors program, independent study, internships, liberal arts/career combination, student-designed major, study abroad, teacher certification program, Undergrads may take grad level classes Cooperative Education Programs: Arts, Business, Computer Science, Education, Health Professions, Humanities, Natural Science, Social/Behavioral Science, Technologies. Domestic Exchange Program(s): Exchange programs with other members of state university system. Foreign Exchange Program(s): Study abroad in England, France, and Spain. Evening division. **Disability Services:** Special programs offered to physically disabled students, including note-taking services, reader services, tape recorders, tutors. **Career Services:** Career/job search classes, Internships.

FACILITIES
Housing: Coed dorms, special housing for disabled students, apartments for single students, Freshmen have their own residence halls. Students must be 19 or older to live in upper-classman residence halls. 95% of campus accessible to physically diasbled. **Special Academic Facilities/Equipment:** Art gallery, language lab, child development center, communication disorders center, planetarium and observatory, closed-circuit TV center.

CAMPUS LIFE
Environment: Village. **Activities:** Choral groups, concert band, drama/theater, literary magazine, marching band, music ensembles, pep band, radio station, student government, student newspaper, yearbook. 63 registered organizations, 3 religious organizations. 2 fraternities, 4 sororities. **Athletics (Intercollegiate):** *Men:* baseball, basketball, cross-country, football, golf, gymnastics, ice hockey, rugby, soccer, softball, swimming, track/field (outdoor), track/field (indoor), volleyball, wrestling. *Women:* basketball, cheerleading, cross-country, field hockey, golf, gymnastics, rugby, soccer, softball, swimming, track/field (outdoor), track/field (indoor), volleyball.

ADMISSIONS
Freshman Academic Profile: 5% in top 10% of high school class, 21% in top 25% of high school class, 60% in top 50% of high school class. 88% from public high schools. **Reported SAT (pre-2016 redesign) scores:** SAT Math middle 50% range 410-530. SAT Critical Reading middle 50% range 420-520. SAT

Writing middle 50% range 420-530. **Concordant SAT scores:** SAT EBRW middle 50% range 470–580. SAT Math middle 50% range 450–560. ACT middle 50% range 17-22. Minimum paper TOEFL 525. **Basis for Candidate Selection:** *Very important factors considered include:* rigor of secondary school record, academic GPA. *Important factors considered include:* class rank, standardized test scores, application essay, recommendation(s). *Other factors considered include:* extracurricular activities, talent/ability, character/personal qualities, first generation, volunteer work, work experience. **Freshman Admission Requirements:** High school diploma is required and GED is accepted. *Academic units required:* 4 English, 3 math, 2 science, 1 science lab, 2 foreign language, 2 social studies, 2 history. *Academic units recommended:* 4 English, 4 math, 3 science, 4 foreign language, 3 social studies, 3 history. **Freshman Admission Statistics:** 4,978 applied, 75.45% admitted, 37% enrolled. **Transfer Admission Requirements:** college transcript(s), essay or personal statement, statement of good standing from prior institution(s). Minimum college GPA of 2.0 required. Lowest grade transferable C-. **General Admission Information:** Application fee $50. Regular application deadline 4/1. Nonfall registration accepted. Admission may be deferred for a maximum of 2 years.

COSTS AND FINANCIAL AID

Annual in-state tuition $4,285. Annual out-of-state tuition $15,137. Room and board $10,687. Required fees $4,256. Average book expense $1,400. **Required Forms and Deadlines:** FAFSA. **Types of Aid:** *Need-based scholarships/grants:* Federal Pell, FSEOG, State scholarships/grants, College/university scholarship or grant aid from institutional funds. *Loans:* Federal Perkins Loans. *Student Employment:* Federal Work-Study Program available. Institutional employment available. **Financial Aid Statistics:** 75% needy freshmen, 76% needy undergrads receive need-based scholarship or grant aid. 25% freshmen, 15% undergrads receive non-need-based scholarship or grant aid. 79% freshmen, 88% undergrads receive need-based self-help aid. 1% freshmen, 2% undergrads receive athletic scholarships. **Criteria for awarding aid:** *Non-need-based:* Academics, Alumni affiliation, Athletics.

SOUTHERN ILLINOIS UNIVERSITY CARBONDALE

Undergraduate Admissions, Mailcode 4710, Carbondale, IL 62901
Phone: 618-536-4405 • **Financial Aid Phone:** 618-453-4334
E-mail: admissions@siu.edu • **CEEB Code:** 1726
Fax: 618-453-4609 • **Website:** www.siu.edu • **ACT Code:** 1144

This public school was founded in 1869. It has a 1136-acre campus.

RATINGS

Admissions Selectivity Rating: 76   **Fire Safety Rating:** 93   **Green Rating:** 84

STUDENTS AND FACULTY

Enrollment: 12,858. **Student Body:** 46% female, 54% male, 16% out-of-state, 4% international (58 countries represented). Asian 2%, African American 19%, Caucasian 64%, Hispanic 8%, Native American <1%, Pacific Islander <1%, Two or more races 3%, Race unknown <1%.
Retention and Graduation: 68% freshmen return for sophomore year. 26% freshmen graduate within 4 years. 45% freshmen graduate within 6 years.
Faculty: Student/faculty ratio 15:1. 812 full-time faculty, 79% hold PhDs, 23% are are members of minority groups, 37% are women. 14% of classes are taught by teaching assistants.

ACADEMICS

Degrees: associate, bachelor's, certificate, doctoral/professional, doctoral/research, master's, postbachelor's certificate. **Classes:** Most classes have 10-19 students. Most lab/discussion sessions have 20-29 students. **Most popular majors:** Biology/Biological Sciences; Accounting; Psychology. **Special Study Options:** cooperative education program, distance learning, double major, English as a Second Language (ESL), honors program, independent study, internships, student-designed major, study abroad, teacher certification program, ROTC: Army; Air Force. **Honors Programs:** University Honors Program—to reward its best undergraduates for their high academic achievement, intended to give the Honors Student a taste of the private-college experience at a state-university price. Classes are small, unique in character, and specially designed for University Honors Students by outstanding SIUC faculty. Combined degree programs: JD/MD, MA/MBA, MS/MBA, MBA/JD, MBA/MS, MSW/JD. **Disability Services:** Special programs offered to physically disabled students, including note-taking services, reader services, tape recorders, tutors. **Career Services:** Alumni services, Career/job search classes, Career assessment, Internships. Extern Program—a job shadowing program. Business students typically comprise the largest number of participants of this campus-wide program, resulting in a 53+% job/internship offer rate.

FACILITIES

Housing: Coed dorms, special housing for disabled students, men's dorms, women's dorms, fraternity/sorority housing, apartments for married students, apartments for single students, Living Learning Communities; Residential College; General Living Learning; Freshman Interest Groups. 98% of campus accessible to physically diasbled. **Special Academic Facilities/Equipment:** Art, natural history, and science museums, outdoor education center, center for crime studies, advertising and public relations agencies, child development lab, community human services center, airport training facility, archaeological research center, fisheries and wildlife research labs, coal research center, electron microscopy center. SIUC's two newest additions: Troutt-Wittmann Academic and Training Center; Student Health Center. **Computers:** 15% of classrooms, 100% of libraries, 95% of dining areas, 100% of student union, 70% of common outdoor areas have wireless network access. Students can register for classes online. Administrative functions (other than registration) can be performed online.

CAMPUS LIFE

Environment: Town. **Activities:** Choral groups, concert band, dance, drama/theater, jazz band, literary magazine, marching band, music ensembles, musical theater, opera, pep band, radio station, student government, student newspaper, student-run film society, symphony orchestra, television station, yearbook, Campus Ministries, Student Organization. 408 registered organizations, 26 honor societies, 25 religious organizations. 20 fraternities, 8 sororities. **Athletics (Intercollegiate):** *Men:* baseball, basketball, cheerleading, cross-country, diving, football, golf, swimming, tennis, track/field (outdoor), track/field (indoor). *Women:* basketball, cheerleading, cross-country, diving, golf, softball, swimming, tennis, track/field (outdoor), track/field (indoor), volleyball. **On-Campus Highlights:** Morris Library, Student Center, Recreation Center, Campus Lake, Faner Museum. **Environmental Initiatives:** $4.0M campus-wide energy efficiency and conservation project to reduce purchased utilities.

ADMISSIONS

Freshman Academic Profile: Average high school GPA 3.1. 10% in top 10% of high school class, 32% in top 25% of high school class, 61% in top 50% of high school class. **Reported SAT (pre-2016 redesign) scores:** SAT Math middle 50% range 470-600. SAT Critical Reading middle 50% range 460-610. **Concordant SAT scores:** SAT Math middle 50% range 510–620. ACT middle 50% range 19-25. Minimum internet-based TOEFL 68. Minimum paper TOEFL 520. **Basis for Candidate Selection:** *Very important factors considered include:* rigor of secondary school record, class rank, academic GPA, standardized test scores, extracurricular activities. *Important factors considered include:* talent/ability, volunteer work, work experience. *Other factors considered include:* application essay, recommendation(s), interview, character/personal qualities, first generation. **Freshman Admission Requirements:** High school diploma is required and GED is accepted. *Academic units required:* 4 English, 3 math, 3 science, 3 science labs, 3 social studies, 2 academic electives. *Academic units recommended:* 4 English, 4 math, 3 science, 3 science labs, 3 social studies, 2 academic electives. **Freshman Admission Statistics:** 10,645 applied, 80.81% admitted, 25% enrolled. **Transfer Admission Requirements:** college transcript(s), statement of good standing from prior institution(s). Minimum college GPA of 2.0 required. Lowest grade transferable D. **General Admission Information:** Application fee $40. Regular application deadline 5/1. Nonfall registration accepted. Admission may be deferred for a maximum of 1 year.

COSTS AND FINANCIAL AID

Annual in-state tuition $8,835. Annual out-of-state tuition $22,088. Room and board $10,186. Required fees $4,382. Average book expense $1,100. **Required Forms and Deadlines:** FAFSA. **Notification of Awards:** Applicants will be notified of awards on a rolling basis beginning 3/15. **Types of Aid:** *Need-based scholarships/grants:* Federal Pell, FSEOG, State scholarships/grants, Private scholarships, College/university scholarship or grant aid from institutional funds. *Loans:* Direct Subsidized Stafford Loans, Direct Unsubsidized Stafford Loans, Direct PLUS loans, Federal Perkins Loans. *Student Employment:* Federal Work-Study Program available. Institutional employment available. **Financial Aid Statistics:** 68% needy freshmen, 66% needy undergrads receive need-based scholarship or grant aid. 34% freshmen, 28% undergrads receive non-need-based scholarship or grant aid. 89% freshmen, 88% undergrads receive need-based self-help aid. 2% freshmen, 2% undergrads receive athletic scholarships. 69% undergrads borrow to pay for school. Average cumulative indebtedness $33,288. **Criteria for awarding aid:** *Need-based:* Academics. *Non-need-based:* Academics, Alumni affiliation, Art, Athletics, Leadership, Minority status, Music/drama, State/district residency.

See page 1044.

SOUTHERN ILLINOIS UNIVERSITY— EDWARDSVILLE

SIUE Office of Admissions, Edwardsville, IL 62026-1047
Phone: 618-650-3705 • **Financial Aid Phone:** 618-650-3880
E-mail: admissions@siue.edu • **CEEB Code:** 1759
Fax: 618-650-5013 • **Website:** www.siue.edu • **ACT Code:** 1147

This public school was founded in 1957. It has a 2660-acre campus.

RATINGS
Admissions Selectivity Rating: 76   **Fire Safety Rating:** 93   **Green Rating:** 88

STUDENTS AND FACULTY
Enrollment: 11,652. **Student Body:** 53% female, 47% male, 12% out-of-state, 1% international (36 countries represented). Asian 2%, African American 14%, Caucasian 73%, Hispanic 4%, Native American <1%, Pacific Islander <1%, Two or more races 3%, Race unknown 1%.
Retention and Graduation: 72% freshmen return for sophomore year. 26% freshmen graduate within 4 years. 47% freshmen graduate within 6 years. 31% grads go on to further study within 1 year. **Faculty:** Student/faculty ratio 20:1. 592 full-time faculty, 30% hold PhDs, 20% are are members of minority groups, 48% are women. 3% of classes are taught by teaching assistants.

ACADEMICS
Degrees: bachelor's, doctoral/professional, doctoral/research, doctoral, master's, postbachelor's certifiate, post-master's certificate. **Classes:** Most classes have 10-19 students. Most lab/discussion sessions have 10-19 students. **Most popular majors:** Registered Nursing/Registered Nurse; Business Administration and Management; Psychology. **Special Study Options:** Accelerated program, cooperative education program, cross-registration, distance learning, double major, English as a Second Language (ESL), honors program, independent study, internships, student-designed major, study abroad, teacher certification program, Independent Study; elementary and secondary teacher certificate programs in art, music, social studies, English,kinesiology, biology, chemistry, foreign languages, history, math, physics, speech communication. Combined degree programs: DNP/MBA, PharmD/MBA. **Disability Services:** Special programs offered to physically disabled students, including note-taking services, reader services, tape recorders, tutors. **Career Services:** Alumni network, Alumni services, Career/job search classes, Career assessment, Internships, Regional alumni. Through the SIUE Co-op program, students work in professional assignments for employers throughout the U.S. and globally

FACILITIES
Housing: Coed dorms, special housing for disabled students, fraternity/sorority housing, apartments for married students, apartments for single students, Focused Interest Communities. 100% of campus accessible to physically disabled. **Special Academic Facilities/Equipment:** Art gallery, anthropology museum, language lab, center for advanced manufacturing and production, technology commercialization center, electron microscope, psychomotorskills lab, new engineering building and lab. **Computers:** Administrative functions (other than registration) can be performed online.

CAMPUS LIFE
Environment: Village. **Activities:** Choral groups, concert band, dance, drama/theater, jazz band, literary magazine, music ensembles, musical theater, opera, pep band, radio station, student government, student newspaper, symphony orchestra, Campus Ministries. 140 registered organizations, 15 honor societies, 9 religious organizations. 10 fraternities, 7 sororities. **Athletics (Intercollegiate):** *Men:* baseball, basketball, cross-country, golf, soccer, tennis, track/field (outdoor), track/field (indoor), wrestling. *Women:* basketball, cross-country, golf, soccer, softball, tennis, track/field (outdoor), track/field (indoor), volleyball. **On-Campus Highlights:** Morris University Center, Starbucks Coffee, Auntie Anne's Pretzels, New School of Engineering Building, New School of Pharmacy Building, The SIUE campus sits on 2,660 acres of beautiful woodlands and lakes just 25 minutes from St. Louis, Missouri. Also, SIUE residence halls are among the newest in the state.

ADMISSIONS
Freshman Academic Profile: Average high school GPA 3.4. 17% in top 10% of high school class, 40% in top 25% of high school class, 73% in top 50% of high school class. ACT middle 50% range 20-26. Minimum internet-based TOEFL 79. Minimum paper TOEFL 550. **Basis for Candidate Selection:** *Very important factors considered include:* rigor of secondary school record, academic GPA, standardized test scores. *Important factors considered include:* class rank. **Freshman Admission Requirements:** High school diploma is required and GED is accepted. *Academic units required:* 4 English, 3 math, 3 science, 3 science labs, 3 social studies, 2 academic electives. *Academic units*

recommended: 2 foreign language. **Freshman Admission Statistics:** 7,274 applied, 89.30% admitted, 30% enrolled. **Transfer Admission Requirements:** college transcript(s), Minimum college GPA of 2 required. Lowest grade transferable D. **General Admission Information:** Application fee $30. Priority deadline 12/1. Regular application deadline 5/1. Nonfall registration accepted. Admission may be deferred.

COSTS AND FINANCIAL AID
Annual in-state tuition $8,199. Annual out-of-state tuition $20,498. Room and board $9,211. Required fees $2,656. Average book expense $840. **Required Forms and Deadlines:** FAFSA. **Notification of Awards:** Applicants will be notified of awards on a rolling basis beginning 3/15. **Types of Aid:** *Need-based scholarships/grants:* Federal Pell, FSEOG, State scholarships/grants, Private scholarships, College/university scholarship or grant aid from institutional funds, Federal Nursing Scholarships. *Loans:* Direct Subsidized Stafford Loans, Direct Unsubsidized Stafford Loans, Direct PLUS loans, Federal Perkins Loans, College/university loans from institutional funds. *Student Employment:* Federal Work-Study Program available. Institutional employment available. **Financial Aid Statistics:** 80% needy freshmen, 75% needy undergrads receive need-based scholarship or grant aid. 71% freshmen, 34% undergrads receive non-need-based scholarship or grant aid. 78% freshmen, 82% undergrads receive need-based self-help aid. 1% freshmen, 1% undergrads receive athletic scholarships. 75% freshmen, 67% undergrads receive any aid. **Criteria for awarding aid:** *Non-need-based:* Academics, Art, Athletics, Leadership, Minority status, Music/drama.

SOUTHERN METHODIST UNIVERSITY

PO Box 750181, Dallas, TX 75275-0181
Phone: 214-768-2058 • **Financial Aid Phone:** 214-768-3417
E-mail: ugadmission@smu.edu • **CEEB Code:** 6660
Fax: 214-768-0103 • **Website:** www.smu.edu • **ACT Code:** 4171

This private school, affiliated with the Methodist Church, was founded in 1911. It has a 210-acre campus.

RATINGS
Admissions Selectivity Rating: 92   **Fire Safety Rating:** 97   **Green Rating:** 60*

STUDENTS AND FACULTY
Enrollment: 6,487. **Student Body:** 50% female, 50% male, 54% out-of-state, 8% international (65 countries represented). Asian 6%, African American 5%, Caucasian 65%, Hispanic 11%, Native American <1%, Pacific Islander <1%, Two or more races 4%, Race unknown <1%.
Retention and Graduation: 91% freshmen return for sophomore year. 68% freshmen graduate within 4 years. 79% freshmen graduate within 6 years. **Faculty:** Student/faculty ratio 11:1. 748 full-time faculty, 82% hold PhDs, 19% are are members of minority groups, 39% are women.

ACADEMICS
Degrees: bachelor's, doctoral/professional, doctoral/research, doctoral, master's, postbachelor's certifiate, post-master's certificate. **Classes:** Most classes have 10-19 students. Most lab/discussion sessions have 20-29 students. **Most popular majors:** Finance; Economics; Accounting. **Special Study Options:** Accelerated program, cooperative education program, distance learning, double major, English as a Second Language (ESL), exchange student program (domestic), honors program, independent study, internships, student-designed major, study abroad, teacher certification program. **Honors Programs:** The University Honors Program is designed to prepare Honors students for a new millennium to ensure that they can cope with the challenges of rapid change while taking advantage of the possibilities such a volatile and versatile world presents. The BBA Honors Program, which is separate from the University Honors Program, is composed of special sections of courses in accounting, finance, statistics, operations management, marketing, and management. Advertising Honors Program: A student may apply for the Temerlin Advertising Institute Honors program after completion of his or her first semester as a declared Advertising major. Combined degree programs: BA/MEng, BS/BA in Comp. Sci. and Music; 3-2 Bachelor's MBA; B.F.A. in Art/M.I.T. in Digital Game Development. **Disability Services:** Special programs offered to physically disabled students, including note-taking services, reader services, tape recorders, tutors. **Career Services:** Alumni network, Alumni services, Career/job search classes, Career assessment, Internships, Regional alumni. Our office prides itself in focusing on the developmental

aspect of students, transitioning them into our engaged student model. Through these enhanced relationships, we are able to assist students with meaningful connections through some of our exploratory programs. Our SMU Connection Externship Program connects SMU students with SMU Alumni across the country and for some students, has resulted in internship and mentorship opportunities.

FACILITIES

Housing: Coed dorms, fraternity/sorority housing, apartments for married students, apartments for single students, Wellness Housing, Theme Housing. 95% of campus accessible to physically diasbled. **Special Academic Facilities/ Equipment:** Art, natural history, and paleontology museums, southwest film/ video archives, sculpture garden, performing arts theatres, pollen analysis and geothermal labs, electron microbe lab, microscopy lab, seismological observatory, institute of technology services, TV studio. **Computers:** 30% of classrooms, 100% of dorms, 100% of libraries, 100% of dining areas, 100% of student union, 10% of common outdoor areas have wireless network access. Students can register for classes online. Administrative functions (other than registration) can be performed online.

CAMPUS LIFE

Environment: Metropolis. **Activities:** Choral groups, concert band, dance, drama/theater, jazz band, literary magazine, marching band, music ensembles, musical theater, opera, pep band, radio station, student government, student newspaper, student-run film society, symphony orchestra, yearbook, Campus Ministries, Student Organization. 180 registered organizations, 15 honor societies, 27 religious organizations. 15 fraternities, 13 sororities. **Athletics (Intercollegiate):** *Men:* basketball, diving, football, golf, soccer, swimming, tennis, volleyball, water polo. *Women:* basketball, crew/rowing, cross-country, diving, equestrian sports, golf, soccer, swimming, tennis, track/field (outdoor), volleyball, water polo. **On-Campus Highlights:** Gerald J Ford Stadium, Meadows Museum, Hughes Trigg Student Center, Dallas Hall, Fondren Library. **Environmental Initiatives:** Broad academic commitment: research from Geothermal Energy Lab has revealed widespread availability of green energy source. Geothermal Lab partnership with Google.org has resulted in sophisticated mapping of geothermal resources across North America. Lab hosts annual geothermal conference attended by the international community. Undergraduate and Graduate environmental degrees available through three portals: the Environmental Studies and Environmental Science programs in Dedman College of Science and Humanities, and the Environmental and Civil Engineering Department of the Lyle School of Engineering.

ADMISSIONS

Freshman Academic Profile: Average high school GPA 3.7. 49% in top 10% of high school class, 77% in top 25% of high school class, 93% in top 50% of high school class. 43% from public high schools. **Reported SAT (pre-2016 redesign) scores:** SAT Math middle 50% range 620-710. SAT Critical Reading middle 50% range 600-700. SAT Writing middle 50% range 590-690. **Concordant SAT scores:** SAT EBRW middle 50% 650–730. SAT Math middle 50% range 640–740. ACT middle 50% range 28-32. Minimum internet-based TOEFL 80. Minimum paper TOEFL 550. **Basis for Candidate Selection:** *Very important factors considered include:* rigor of secondary school record, academic GPA, standardized test scores, application essay, recommendation(s). *Important factors considered include:* class rank, extracurricular activities, talent/ability, character/personal qualities. *Other factors considered include:* first generation, alumni/ae relation, racial/ethnic status, volunteer work, work experience, level of applicant's interest. **Freshman Admission Requirements:** High school diploma is required and GED is not accepted. *Academic units required:* 4 English, 3 math, 3 science, 2 science labs, 2 foreign language, 3 social studies. *Academic units recommended:* 4 English, 4 math, 3 science, 2 science labs, 3 foreign language, 3 history, 3 academic electives. **Freshman Admission Statistics:** 13,250 applied, 48.92% admitted, 23% enrolled. **Transfer Admission Requirements:** college transcript(s), essay or personal statement, Minimum college GPA of 2.7 required. Lowest grade transferable C-. **General Admission Information:** Application fee $60. Priority deadline 1/15. Regular application deadline 1/15. Regular notification 4/1. Nonfall registration accepted. Admission may be deferred for a maximum of 1 year.

COSTS AND FINANCIAL AID

Annual tuition $44,694. Room and board $16,125. Required fees $5,664. Average book expense $800. **Required Forms and Deadlines:** FAFSA, CSS/Financial Aid PROFILE, Noncustodial PROFILE. **Notification of Awards:** Applicants will be notified of awards on a rolling basis beginning 4/1. **Types of Aid:** *Need-based scholarships/grants:* Federal Pell, FSEOG, State scholarships/grants, Private scholarships, College/university scholarship or grant aid from institutional funds. *Loans:* Direct Subsidized Stafford Loans, Direct Unsubsidized Stafford Loans, Direct PLUS loans, Federal Perkins Loans, State Loans, College/university loans from institutional funds. *Student Employment:* Federal Work-Study Program available. Institutional employment available. **Financial Aid Statistics:** 64% needy freshmen, 73% needy undergrads receive need-based scholarship or grant aid. 78% freshmen, 68% undergrads receive non-need-based scholarship or grant aid. 74% freshmen, 80% undergrads

receive need-based self-help aid. 5% freshmen, 5% undergrads receive athletic scholarships. 73% freshmen, 70% undergrads receive any aid. Average cumulative indebtedness $29,601. **Criteria for awarding aid:** *Need-based:* Religious affiliation. *Non-need-based:* Academics, Alumni affiliation, Art, Athletics, Leadership, Music/drama.

SOUTHERN NEW HAMPSHIRE UNIVERSITY

2500 North River Road, Manchester, NH 03106-1045
Phone: 603-645-9611 • **Financial Aid Phone:** 603-645-9645
E-mail: admission@snhu.edu • **CEEB Code:** 3649
Fax: 603-645-9693 • **Website:** www.snhu.edu • **ACT Code:** 2514

This private school was founded in 1932. It has a 300-acre campus.

RATINGS

Admissions Selectivity Rating: 72   **Fire Safety Rating:** 97   **Green Rating:** 60*

STUDENTS AND FACULTY

Enrollment: 1,929. **Student Body:** 52% female, 48% male, 55% out-of-state, 5% international (79 countries represented). Asian 1%, African American 1%, Caucasian 75%, Hispanic 2%, Native American <1%, Pacific Islander 0%, Two or more races 0%, Race unknown 15%.
Retention and Graduation: 49% freshmen graduate within 4 years. 12% grads go on to further study within 1 year. **Faculty:** Student/faculty ratio 16:1. 120 full-time faculty, 76% hold PhDs, 12% are are members of minority groups, 38% are women. 0% of classes are taught by teaching assistants.

ACADEMICS

Degrees: associate, bachelor's, certificate, master's, postbachelor's certificate, post-master's certificate. **Classes:** Most classes have 10-19 students. **Most popular majors:** Culinary Arts/Chef Training; Psychology; Business Administration and Management. **Special Study Options:** Accelerated program, cooperative education program, distance learning, double major, dual enrollment, English as a Second Language (ESL), honors program, independent study, internships, student-designed major, study abroad, teacher certification program, weekend college. **Honors Programs:** Three-Year Honors Program (B.S. in Business Administration) and our traditional four-year honors program (available in conjunction with most majors) Combined degree programs: Three-Year Bachelor's Degree + 1-Year M.B.A. **Disability Services:** Special programs offered to physically disabled students, including note-taking services, reader services, tape recorders, tutors. **Career Services:** Alumni network, Alumni services, Career/job search classes, Career assessment, Internships. Active internship program at the undergraduate and graduate level.

FACILITIES

Housing: Coed dorms, special housing for disabled students, apartments for single students, Wellness Housing, Theme Housing. 85% of campus accessible to physically diasbled. **Special Academic Facilities/Equipment:** Art Gallery **Computers:** 100% of classrooms, 40% of dorms, 100% of libraries, 100% of dining areas, 100% of student union, have wireless network access. Students can register for classes online. Undergraduates are required to own a computer.

CAMPUS LIFE

Environment: City. **Activities:** Choral groups, concert band, dance, drama/ theater, jazz band, literary magazine, musical theater, radio station, student government, student newspaper, television station, yearbook, Campus Ministries, Student Organization, Model UN. 58 registered organizations, 7 honor societies, 1 religious organization. 3 fraternities, 3 sororities. **Athletics (Intercollegiate):** *Men:* baseball, basketball, cheerleading, cross-country, golf, ice hockey, lacrosse, soccer, tennis. *Women:* basketball, cheerleading, cross-country, lacrosse, soccer, softball, tennis, volleyball. **On-Campus Highlights:** Center for Financial Studies, Fitness Center / Athletic Complex, Robert Frost Hall (Academic Building), McIninch Art Gallery, Last Chapter Pub, In addition to our five most popular places on campus, we also have a gourmet restaurant on campus run by our culinary and hospitality students, a bakery and coffee shop. **Environmental Initiatives:** Renewable Energy Hedge from 2007-2022 based on 17,500 megawatt hours of wind power output with PPM Energy Inc. By a financial swap, the hedge will flat line SNHU energy budget, and 100% offset energy green house gas use in the voluntary market with RECs, and provide the wind developer a consistent stream of income to facilitate more wind construction. This represents a new sustainable model of utility cost control based on long-term agreements between energy users and renewable developers.

ADMISSIONS

Freshman Academic Profile: Average high school GPA 3.0. 88% from public high schools. **Reported SAT (pre-2016 redesign) scores:** SAT Math middle 50% range 440-540. SAT Critical Reading middle 50% range 440-520. SAT

Writing middle 50% range 430-520. **Concordant SAT scores:** SAT EBRW middle 50% 490–580. SAT Math middle 50% range 480–570. ACT middle 50% range 18-24. Minimum internet-based TOEFL 71. Minimum paper TOEFL 530. **Basis for Candidate Selection:** *Very important factors considered include:* rigor of secondary school record, academic GPA. *Important factors considered include:* application essay, recommendation(s), extracurricular activities, character/personal qualities, first generation, level of applicant's interest. *Other factors considered include:* class rank, standardized test scores, interview, talent/ability, alumni/ae relation, volunteer work, work experience. **Freshman Admission Requirements:** High school diploma is required and GED is accepted. *Academic units required:* 4 English, 2 science labs. **Freshman Admission Statistics:** 3,124 applied, 84.22% admitted, 18% enrolled. **Transfer Admission Requirements:** High school transcript, college transcript(s), essay or personal statement, Minimum college GPA of 2.50 required. Lowest grade transferable C-. **General Admission Information:** Application fee $40. Priority deadline 3/15. Nonfall registration accepted. Admission may be deferred for a maximum of 1 year.

COSTS AND FINANCIAL AID
Required Forms and Deadlines: FAFSA. **Notification of Awards:** Applicants will be notified of awards on a rolling basis beginning 3/1. **Types of Aid:** *Need-based scholarships/grants:* Federal Pell, FSEOG, State scholarships/grants, Private scholarships, College/university scholarship or grant aid from institutional funds. *Loans:* Direct Subsidized Stafford Loans, Direct Unsubsidized Stafford Loans, Direct PLUS loans. *Student Employment:* Federal Work-Study Program available. Institutional employment available. **Financial Aid Statistics:** 94% freshmen, 93% undergrads receive any aid. **Criteria for awarding aid:** *Need-based:* Academics. *Non-need-based:* Academics, Alumni affiliation, Athletics, Leadership, State/district residency.

SOUTHERN OREGON UNIVERSITY

Office of Admissions, Ashland, OR 97520-5032
Phone: 541-552-6411 • **Financial Aid Phone:** 541-552-6600
E-mail: admissions@sou.edu • **CEEB Code:** 4702
Fax: 541-552-8403 • **Website:** www.sou.edu • **ACT Code:** 3496

This public school was founded in 1926. It has a 175-acre campus.

RATINGS
Admissions Selectivity Rating: 73   **Fire Safety Rating:** 88   **Green Rating:** 97

STUDENTS AND FACULTY
Enrollment: 4,088. **Student Body:** 59% female, 41% male, 40% out-of-state, 3% international (12 countries represented). Asian 2%, African American 2%, Caucasian 59%, Hispanic 12%, Native American 1%, Pacific Islander 1%, Two or more races 10%, Race unknown 10%.
Retention and Graduation: 68% freshmen return for sophomore year. 24% freshmen graduate within 4 years. 40% freshmen graduate within 6 years. **Faculty:** Student/faculty ratio 21:1. 167 full-time faculty, 67% hold PhDs, 17% are are members of minority groups, 44% are women. 0% of classes are taught by teaching assistants.

ACADEMICS
Degrees: bachelor's, certificate, master's, postbachelor's certificate. **Most popular majors:** Business Administration and Management; Psychology; Visual and Performing Arts. **Special Study Options:** Accelerated program, cooperative education program, cross-registration, distance learning, double major, dual enrollment, English as a Second Language (ESL), exchange student program (domestic), external degree program, honors program, independent study, internships, liberal arts/career combination, student-designed major, study abroad, teacher certification program, Undergrads may take grad level classes. Nursing programs with Oregon Health Sciences U. Exchange programs with Coll of the Redwoods, Coll of the Siskiyous, and Shasta Coll. Member of National Student Exchange(NSE). Exchange programs abroad in Korea(Dankook U) and Mexico(U of Guanajuato). Study abroad also in Asian, European, and South American countries. Concurrent enrollment with Rogue Community College. **Disability Services:** Special programs offered to physically disabled students, including note-taking services, reader services, tape recorders, tutors. **Career Services:** Alumni network, Alumni services, Career/job search classes, Career assessment, Internships, Regional alumni. Community-based Learning (CBL) allows students the opportunity to work and learn in a community environment, and to apply what they learn in the classroom to real-world situations. Community-based Learning is a broad term that encompasses a variety of teaching and learning strategies, including the following: 1) Experiential learning 2) Service learning Apprenticeships and internships that enhance and reinforce learning 3) Practicum and capstone projects that connects learning with activity in the community 4) Civic Engagement

FACILITIES
Housing: Coed dorms, special housing for disabled students, special housing for international students, apartments for married students, apartments for single students, Special quiet, substance free, nonsmoking, older students or freshman only residence halls. 80% of campus accessible to physically diasbled. **Special Academic Facilities/Equipment:** Art and history museums, art galleries, on-campus preschool and kindergarten, National Guard armory, United States Wildlife Forensics Lab. **Computers:** Students can register for classes online. Administrative functions (other than registration) can be performed online.

CAMPUS LIFE
Environment: Village. **Activities:** Choral groups, concert band, dance, drama/theater, jazz band, literary magazine, music ensembles, musical theater, opera, pep band, radio station, student government, student newspaper, student-run film society, symphony orchestra, television station, Student Organization. 52 registered organizations, 13 honor societies, 5 religious organizations. **Athletics (Intercollegiate):** *Men:* basketball, cross-country, football, track/field (outdoor), wrestling. *Women:* basketball, cross-country, soccer, softball, tennis, track/field (outdoor), volleyball. **On-Campus Highlights:** Hannon Library, Center for the Visual Arts, Student Union, Theatre Building, Music Building. **Environmental Initiatives:** Through the student-initiated Green Energy Fee, SOU purchases Renewable Energy Certificates (RECs) to offset 100% of its electricity consumption and carbon offsets to offset 100% of its natural gas consumption. Among the 54 colleges and universities that are U. S. EPA Green Power Partners, SOU ranked #12 on the EPA's April 6, 2010 Top 20 College & University list.

ADMISSIONS
Freshman Academic Profile: Average high school GPA 3.3. 90% from public high schools. **Reported SAT (pre-2016 redesign) scores:** SAT Math middle 50% range 440-550. SAT Critical Reading middle 50% range 460-580. SAT Writing middle 50% range 430-550. **Concordant SAT scores:** SAT EBRW middle 50% 500–620. SAT Math middle 50% range 480–570. ACT middle 50% range 19-25. Minimum paper TOEFL 520. **Basis for Candidate Selection:** *Very important factors considered include:* academic GPA, standardized test scores. *Other factors considered include:* rigor of secondary school record, application essay, recommendation(s), interview, extracurricular activities, geographical residence, state residency, volunteer work. **Freshman Admission Requirements:** High school diploma is required and GED is accepted. *Academic units required:* 4 English, 3 math, 2 science, 1 science lab, 2 foreign language, 3 social studies. **Freshman Admission Statistics:** 2,766 applied, 78.20% admitted, 31% enrolled. **Transfer Admission Requirements:** college transcript(s), Minimum college GPA of 2.2 required. Lowest grade transferable D-. **General Admission Information:** Application fee $60. Priority deadline 2/15. Nonfall registration accepted. Admission may be deferred for a maximum of 1 year.

COSTS AND FINANCIAL AID
Annual in-state tuition $6,813. Annual out-of-state tuition $21,460. Room and board $11,610. Required fees $1,710. Average book expense $999. **Required Forms and Deadlines:** FAFSA. **Notification of Awards:** Applicants will be notified of awards on a rolling basis beginning 3/2. **Types of Aid:** *Need-based scholarships/grants:* Federal Pell, FSEOG, State scholarships/grants, Private scholarships, College/university scholarship or grant aid from institutional funds. *Loans:* Direct Subsidized Stafford Loans, Direct Unsubsidized Stafford Loans, Direct PLUS loans, Federal Perkins Loans. *Student Employment:* Federal Work-Study Program available. Institutional employment available. **Financial Aid Statistics:** 77% needy freshmen, 43% needy undergrads receive need-based scholarship or grant aid. 59% freshmen, 45% undergrads receive non-need-based scholarship or grant aid. 73% freshmen, 41% undergrads receive need-based self-help aid. 7% freshmen, 5% undergrads receive athletic scholarships. 70% freshmen, 81% undergrads receive any aid. 89% undergrads borrow to pay for school. Average cumulative indebtedness $24,179. **Criteria for awarding aid:** *Need-based:* Academics. *Non-need-based:* Academics, Athletics, State/district residency.

SOUTHERN UNIVERSITY AND A&M COLLEGE

P.O. Box 9901, Baton Rouge, LA 70813
Phone: 225-771-2430 • **Financial Aid Phone:** 225-771-2790
E-mail: admit@subr.edu • **CEEB Code:** 6663
Fax: 225-771-2500 • **Website:** subr.edu • **ACT Code:** 1610

This public school was founded in 1880. It has a 884-acre campus.

RATINGS
Admissions Selectivity Rating: 75   **Fire Safety Rating:** 79   **Green Rating:** 60*

610

STUDENTS AND FACULTY

Enrollment: 6,892. **Student Body:** 61% female, 39% male, 19% out-of-state, 2% international (48 countries represented). Asian 0%, African American 95%, Caucasian 3%, Hispanic <1%, Native American <1%, Pacific Islander 0%, Two or more races 0%, Race unknown 0%.

Retention and Graduation: 65% freshmen return for sophomore year. 7% freshmen graduate within 4 years. 29% freshmen graduate within 6 years. 16% grads go on to further study within 1 year. 15% grads pursue arts and sciences degrees. 1% grads pursue law degrees. **Faculty:** Student/faculty ratio 16:1. 405 full-time faculty, 66% hold PhDs, 85% are are members of minority groups, 47% are women. 0% of classes are taught by teaching assistants.

ACADEMICS

Degrees: associate, bachelor's, master's, post-master's certificate. **Classes:** Most classes have 20-29 students. Most lab/discussion sessions have 10-19 students. **Most popular majors:** Biology/Biological Sciences Business Administration and Management. **Special Study Options:** cooperative education program, cross-registration, distance learning, double major, dual enrollment, exchange student program (domestic), honors program, independent study, internships, study abroad, teacher certification program, weekend college, Undergrads may take grad level classes. Cooperative Education Programs: Engineering Combined Degree Programs: Dual degree programs with Jackson State U and Xavier U. **Honors Programs:** The Honors College provides an enhances educational experience for students who have a history of strong academic achievement and who have demonstrated exceptional creativity or talent. The College also provides cultural and intellectual opportunities that are designed to motivae students to perform at the highest level of excellence that they are capable of and through which they may become knowledgeable and effective leaders. **Disability Services:** Special programs offered to physically disabled students, including note-taking services, tape recorders, tutors. **Career Services:** Career/job search classes, Internships. The 3.0 credit hour co-op education course.

FACILITIES

Housing: special housing for disabled students, men's dorms, women's dorms. 100% of campus accessible to physically diasbled. **Special Academic Facilities/Equipment:** Jazz institute Southern Museum of Art **Computers:** 100% of classrooms, 20% of dorms, 100% of libraries, 50% of dining areas, 90% of student union, 25% of common outdoor areas have wireless network access. Students can register for classes online. Administrative functions (other than registration) can be performed online.

CAMPUS LIFE

Environment: Metropolis. **Activities:** Choral groups, concert band, dance, drama/theater, jazz band, literary magazine, marching band, music ensembles, musical theater, pep band, student government, student newspaper, yearbook. 88 registered organizations, 11 honor societies, 6 religious organizations. 4 fraternities, 4 sororities. **Athletics (Intercollegiate):** *Men:* baseball, basketball, cross-country, football, golf, tennis, track/field (outdoor). *Women:* basketball, cross-country, golf, softball, tennis, track/field (outdoor), volleyball. **On-Campus Highlights:** SUBR Museum of Art, Smith—Brown Student Union, Site of the original Red Stick for Baton, Bluff over the Mississippi River. **Environmental Initiatives:** MS4-Stormwater Permit with the Parish of East Baton Rouge.

ADMISSIONS

Freshman Academic Profile: Average high school GPA 2.8. 3% in top 10% of high school class, 13% in top 25% of high school class, 40% in top 50% of high school class. **Reported SAT (pre-2016 redesign) scores:** SAT Math middle 50% range 380-460. **Concordant SAT scores:** SAT Math middle 50% range 420–500. ACT middle 50% range 15-18. **Basis for Candidate Selection:** *Very important factors considered include:* rigor of secondary school record, class rank, academic GPA, standardized test scores. *Other factors considered include:* talent/ability. **Freshman Admission Requirements:** High school diploma is required and GED is accepted. *Academic units required:* 4 English, 3 math, 3 science, 2 foreign language, 2 social studies, 1 history, and 1 unit from above areas or other academic areas. **Freshman Admission Statistics:** 4,703 applied, 52.71% admitted, 60% enrolled. **Transfer Admission Requirements:** High school transcript, college transcript(s), standardized test scores, statement of good standing from prior institution(s). Minimum college GPA of 2.0 required. Lowest grade transferable C. **General Admission Information:** Application fee $20. Regular application deadline 7/1. Nonfall registration accepted. Admission may be deferred for a maximum of 2 semesters.

COSTS AND FINANCIAL AID

Annual in-state tuition $3,666. Annual out-of-state tuition $9,458. Room and board $5,784. Required fees $0. Average book expense $1,200. **Required Forms and Deadlines:** FAFSA, Institution's own financial aid form. **Notification of Awards:** Applicants will be notified of awards on a rolling basis beginning 6/30. **Types of Aid:** *Need-based scholarships/grants:* Federal Pell, FSEOG, State scholarships/grants, Private scholarships, College/university scholarship or grant aid from institutional funds. *Loans:* Direct Subsidized

Stafford Loans, Direct Unsubsidized Stafford Loans, Direct PLUS loans, College/university loans from institutional funds. *Student Employment:* Federal Work-Study Program available. Institutional employment available. **Financial Aid Statistics:** 80% needy freshmen, 77% needy undergrads receive need-based scholarship or grant aid. 21% freshmen, 18% undergrads receive non-need-based scholarship or grant aid. 79% freshmen, 89% undergrads receive need-based self-help aid. 5% freshmen, 3% undergrads receive athletic scholarships. 89% freshmen, 85% undergrads receive any aid. **Criteria for awarding aid:** *Need-based:* Academics, Alumni affiliation, Athletics, Music/drama. *Non-need-based:* Academics, Athletics.

SOUTHERN UTAH UNIVERSITY

351 W University Bvd, Cedar City, UT 84720
Phone: 435-586-7740 • **Financial Aid Phone:** 435-586-7735
E-mail: adminfo@suu.edu • **CEEB Code:** 4092
Fax: 435-865-8223 • **Website:** www.suu.edu • **ACT Code:** 4271

This public school was founded in 1897. It has a 113-acre campus.

RATINGS

Admissions Selectivity Rating: 80   **Fire Safety Rating:** 60*   **Green Rating:** 60*

STUDENTS AND FACULTY

Enrollment: 6,353. **Student Body:** 54% female, 46% male, 23% out-of-state, 4% international (31 countries represented). Asian 1%, African American 2%, Caucasian 76%, Hispanic 6%, Native American 1%, Pacific Islander 2%, Two or more races 1%, Race unknown 6%.

Retention and Graduation: 69% freshmen return for sophomore year. 22% freshmen graduate within 4 years. 39% freshmen graduate within 6 years. **Faculty:** Student/faculty ratio 19:1. 282 full-time faculty, 66% hold PhDs, 7% are are members of minority groups, 35% are women. 0% of classes are taught by teaching assistants.

ACADEMICS

Degrees: associate, bachelor's, certificate, diploma, master's, terminal, transfer. **Classes:** Most classes have 20-29 students. Most lab/discussion sessions have 20-29 students. **Most popular majors:** Biology/Biological Sciences; General Studies; Psychology. **Special Study Options:** cooperative education program, distance learning, double major, English as a Second Language (ESL), honors program, independent study, internships, liberal arts/career combination, teacher certification program, weekend college. **Disability Services:** Special programs offered to physically disabled students, including reader services, tape recorders, tutors. **Career Services:** Alumni services, Career/job search classes, Career assessment, Internships.

FACILITIES

Housing: Coed dorms, special housing for disabled students, men's dorms, special housing for international students, women's dorms, fraternity/sorority housing, apartments for single students.

CAMPUS LIFE

Environment: Village. **Activities:** Choral groups, concert band, dance, drama/theater, jazz band, literary magazine, marching band, music ensembles, musical theater, opera, pep band, radio station, student government, student newspaper, symphony orchestra, television station, yearbook. **Athletics (Intercollegiate):** *Men:* baseball, basketball, cross-country, football, golf, track/field (outdoor). *Women:* basketball, cross-country, gymnastics, softball, tennis, track/field (outdoor).

ADMISSIONS

Freshman Academic Profile: Average high school GPA 3.5. 19% in top 10% of high school class, 48% in top 25% of high school class, 77% in top 50% of high school class. **Reported SAT (pre-2016 redesign) scores:** SAT Math middle 50% range 440-570. SAT Critical Reading middle 50% range 450-580. SAT Writing middle 50% range 440-550. **Concordant SAT scores:** SAT EBRW middle 50% 500–620. SAT Math middle 50% range 480–590. ACT middle 50% range 20-26. Minimum internet-based TOEFL 71. Minimum paper TOEFL 525. **Basis for Candidate Selection:** *Very important factors considered include:* academic GPA, standardized test scores. **Freshman Admission Requirements:** High school diploma is required and GED is accepted. *Academic units recommended:* 4 English, 4 math, 3 science, 1 science lab, 2 foreign language, 3 social studies. **Freshman Admission Statistics:** 10,573 applied, 72.28% admitted, 20% enrolled. **Transfer Admission Requirements:** college transcript(s), Minimum college GPA of 2.25 required. Lowest grade transferable D. **General Admission Information:** Application fee $50. Priority deadline 12/1. Regular application deadline 5/1. Nonfall registration accepted. Admission may be deferred for a maximum of 5 semesters.

COSTS AND FINANCIAL AID

Annual in-state tuition $5,774. Annual out-of-state tuition $19,054. Room and board $7,067. Required fees $756. Average book expense $1,600. **Required Forms and Deadlines:** FAFSA. **Notification of Awards:** Applicants will be notified of awards on a rolling basis beginning 11/1. **Types of Aid:** *Need-based scholarships/grants:* Federal Pell, FSEOG, State scholarships/grants, Private scholarships, College/university scholarship or grant aid from institutional funds. *Loans:* Direct Subsidized Stafford Loans, Direct Unsubsidized Stafford Loans, Direct PLUS loans, Federal Perkins Loans. *Student Employment:* Federal Work-Study Program available. Institutional employment available. **Financial Aid Statistics:** 62% needy freshmen, 72% needy undergrads receive need-based scholarship or grant aid. 60% freshmen, 33% undergrads receive non-need-based scholarship or grant aid. 91% freshmen, 93% undergrads receive need-based self-help aid. 5% freshmen, 5% undergrads receive athletic scholarships. 51% undergrads borrow to pay for school. Average cumulative indebtedness $16,892. **Criteria for awarding aid:** *Non-need-based:* Academics, Alumni affiliation, Art, Athletics, Job skills, Leadership, Minority status, Music/drama, State/district residency.

SOUTHERN WESLEYAN UNIVERSITY

Wesleyan Drive, Central, SC 29630-1020
Phone: 864-644-5550 • **Financial Aid Phone:** 864-644-5500
E-mail: admissions@swu.edu • **CEEB Code:** 5896
Fax: 864-644-5972 • **Website:** www.swu.edu • **ACT Code:** 3837

This private school, affiliated with the Wesleyan Church, was founded in 1906. It has a 330-acre campus.

RATINGS

Admissions Selectivity Rating: 75   **Fire Safety Rating:** 77   **Green Rating:** 60*

STUDENTS AND FACULTY

Enrollment: 1,444. **Student Body:** 60% female, 40% male, 28% out-of-state, 1% international (9 countries represented). Asian 0%, African American 27%, Caucasian 61%, Hispanic 2%, Native American 1%, Pacific Islander 0%, Two or more races 0%, Race unknown 8%.
Retention and Graduation: 70% freshmen return for sophomore year. 33% freshmen graduate within 4 years. 39% freshmen graduate within 6 years.
Faculty: Student/faculty ratio 18:1. 58 full-time faculty, 72% hold PhDs, 12% are are members of minority groups, 31% are women. 0% of classes are taught by teaching assistants.

ACADEMICS

Degrees: associate, bachelor's, master's. **Classes:** Most classes have 10-19 students. Most lab/discussion sessions have 20-29 students. **Most popular majors:** Elementary Education and Teaching; Religion/Religious Studies; Business/Commerce. **Special Study Options:** cross-registration, double major, dual enrollment, English as a Second Language (ESL), honors program, independent study, internships, student-designed major, study abroad, teacher certification program. **Honors Programs:** The honors program consists of specialized coursework, non-credit academic experiences, and service opportunities. Honors students must complete a research-based Honors Major Project in their Junior or Senior years. **Disability Services:** Special programs offered to physically disabled students, including note-taking services, reader services, tape recorders, tutors. **Career Services:** Career/job search classes, Career assessment, Internships.

FACILITIES

Housing: Coed dorms, special housing for disabled students, women's dorms, apartments for single students. 90% of campus accessible to physically disabled. **Special Academic Facilities/Equipment:** Freedom's Hill Historic Site, Clayton Genealogical Research library, Electron Microscope lab **Computers:** 100% of classrooms, 50% of dorms, 100% of libraries, 100% of dining areas, 100% of student union, 25% of common outdoor areas have wireless network access. Students can register for classes online. Administrative functions (other than registration) can be performed online.

CAMPUS LIFE

Environment: Town. **Activities:** Choral groups, concert band, drama/theater, jazz band, literary magazine, music ensembles, musical theater, student government, yearbook, Campus Ministries. 12 registered organizations, 2 honor societies, 3 religious organizations. **Athletics (Intercollegiate):** *Men:* baseball, basketball, cross-country, golf, soccer. *Women:* basketball, cross-country, soccer, softball, volleyball. **On-Campus Highlights:** Jennings Campus Center, Java City Coffee Shop, Historic Tysinger Gymnasium, Student Apartment Complex **Environmental Initiatives:** Voluntary recycling of paper and plastic in residence halls and academic buildings. Materials are collected by the city.

ADMISSIONS

Freshman Academic Profile: Average high school GPA 3.5. 13% in top 10% of high school class, 34% in top 25% of high school class, 75% in top 50% of high school class. **Reported SAT (pre-2016 redesign) scores:** SAT Math middle 50% range 445-550. SAT Critical Reading middle 50% range 430-540. SAT Writing middle 50% range 420-520. **Concordant SAT scores:** SAT EBRW middle 50% 480-590. SAT Math middle 50% range 490-570. ACT middle 50% range 18-22. Minimum paper TOEFL 500. **Basis for Candidate Selection:** *Very important factors considered include:* academic GPA, standardized test scores. *Important factors considered include:* rigor of secondary school record, class rank, talent/ability, character/personal qualities. *Other factors considered include:* recommendation(s). **Freshman Admission Requirements:** High school diploma is required and GED is accepted. *Academic units recommended:* 4 English, 2 math, 2 science, 2 social studies. **Freshman Admission Statistics:** 575 applied, 93.91% admitted, 31% enrolled. **Transfer Admission Requirements:** college transcript(s), Minimum college GPA of 2.0 required. Lowest grade transferable C. **General Admission Information:** Application fee $25. Regular application deadline 8/1. Nonfall registration accepted. Admission may be deferred for a maximum of 1 semester.

COSTS AND FINANCIAL AID

Annual tuition $19,950. Room and board $8,410. Required fees $600. Average book expense $1,020. **Required Forms and Deadlines:** FAFSA, Institution's own financial aid form. **Notification of Awards:** Applicants will be notified of awards on a rolling basis beginning 2/1. **Types of Aid:** *Need-based scholarships/grants:* Federal Pell, FSEOG, State scholarships/grants, Private scholarships, College/university scholarship or grant aid from institutional funds. *Loans:* Direct Subsidized Stafford Loans, Direct Unsubsidized Stafford Loans, Direct PLUS loans, Federal Perkins Loans, State Loans. *Student Employment:* Federal Work-Study Program available. Institutional employment available. **Financial Aid Statistics:** 100% needy freshmen, 91% needy undergrads receive need-based scholarship or grant aid. 16% freshmen, 8% undergrads receive non-need-based scholarship or grant aid. 73% freshmen, 80% undergrads receive need-based self-help aid. 5% freshmen, 2% undergrads receive athletic scholarships. 100% freshmen, 99% undergrads receive any aid. **Criteria for awarding aid:** *Non-need-based:* Academics, Athletics, Music/drama, Religious affiliation.

SOUTHWEST BAPTIST UNIVERSITY

1600 University Avenue, Bolivar, MO 65613-2597
Phone: 417-328-1810 • **Financial Aid Phone:** 417-328-1823
E-mail: admitme@sbuniv.edu • **CEEB Code:** 6664
Fax: 417-328-1808 • **ACT Code:** 2368

This private school, affiliated with the Southern Baptist Church, was founded in 1878. It has a 180-acre campus.

RATINGS

Admissions Selectivity Rating: 78   **Fire Safety Rating:** 77   **Green Rating:** 60*

STUDENTS AND FACULTY

Enrollment: 2,646. **Student Body:** 66% female, 34% male, 29% out-of-state, 1% international (16 countries represented). Asian 1%, African American 4%, Caucasian 86%, Hispanic 1%, Native American 1%, Pacific Islander 0%, Two or more races 0%, Race unknown 6%.
Retention and Graduation: 70% freshmen return for sophomore year. 38% freshmen graduate within 4 years. 48% freshmen graduate within 6 years.
Faculty: Student/faculty ratio 13:1. 116 full-time faculty, 59% hold PhDs, 2% are are members of minority groups, 41% are women. 0% of classes are taught by teaching assistants.

ACADEMICS

Degrees: associate, bachelor's, certificate, doctoral/professional, master's, post-master's certificate. **Classes:** Most classes have fewer than 10 students. Most lab/discussion sessions have 10-19 students. **Most popular majors:** Elementary Education and Teaching; Psychology; Business Administration and Management. **Special Study Options:** cooperative education program, distance learning, double major, dual enrollment, exchange student program (domestic), honors program, independent study, internships, student-designed major, study abroad, teacher certification program. **Honors Programs:** Our academic honors program consists of the following components: academics, servant leadership, intercultural experiences, spiritual growth, and enrichment opportunities. **Disability Services:** Special programs offered to physically disabled students, including note-taking services, reader services, tutors. **Career Services:** Career/job search classes, Career assessment.

FACILITIES

Housing: special housing for disabled students, men's dorms, women's dorms, apartments for single students. 95% of campus accessible to physically diasbled. **Special Academic Facilities/Equipment:** The Driskell Art Gallery, Jester Learning and Performance Center, Meyer Wellness and Sports Center. **Computers:** 100% of classrooms, 100% of dorms, 100% of libraries, 100% of dining areas, 100% of student union, 40% of common outdoor areas have wireless network access. Administrative functions (other than registration) can be performed online.

CAMPUS LIFE

Environment: Village. **Activities:** Choral groups, concert band, drama/ theater, jazz band, music ensembles, musical theater, opera, pep band, student government, student newspaper, symphony orchestra, yearbook, Campus Ministries. 34 registered organizations, 8 honor societies, 10 religious organizations. **Athletics (Intercollegiate):** *Men:* baseball, basketball, cheerleading, cross-country, football, golf, tennis, track/field (outdoor), track/field (indoor). *Women:* basketball, cheerleading, cross-country, soccer, softball, tennis, track/field (outdoor), track/field (indoor), volleyball. **On-Campus Highlights:** Meyer Wellness and Sports Center, Jester Learning and Performance Center, Felix Goodson Student Union, Harriet K. Hutchens Library, Plaster Stadium.

ADMISSIONS

Freshman Academic Profile: Average high school GPA 3.5. 22% in top 10% of high school class, 41% in top 25% of high school class, 67% in top 50% of high school class. **Reported SAT (pre-2016 redesign) scores:** SAT Math middle 50% range 450-600. SAT Critical Reading middle 50% range 410-560. **Concordant SAT scores:** SAT Math middle 50% range 490–620. ACT middle 50% range 20-26. Minimum paper TOEFL 550. **Basis for Candidate Selection:** *Very important factors considered include:* class rank, academic GPA, standardized test scores. *Important factors considered include:* rigor of secondary school record, application essay, recommendation(s). *Other factors considered include:* interview, talent/ability, character/personal qualities. **Freshman Admission Requirements:** High school diploma is required and GED is accepted. *Academic units recommended:* 4 English, 3 math, 2 science, 2 social studies, and 2 units from above areas or other academic areas. **Freshman Admission Statistics:** 1,617 applied, 92.33% admitted, 31% enrolled. **Transfer Admission Requirements:** High school transcript, college transcript(s), standardized test scores, Minimum college GPA of 2.0 required. Lowest grade transferable D. **General Admission Information:** Application fee $30. Nonfall registration accepted. Admission may be deferred for a maximum of 1 year.

COSTS AND FINANCIAL AID

Annual tuition $16,500. Room and board $5,720. Required fees $780. Average book expense $1,000. **Required Forms and Deadlines:** FAFSA, Institution's own financial aid form. **Notification of Awards:** Applicants will be notified of awards on a rolling basis beginning 3/1. **Types of Aid:** *Need-based scholarships/ grants:* Federal Pell, FSEOG, State scholarships/grants, Private scholarships, College/university scholarship or grant aid from institutional funds. *Loans:* Federal Perkins Loans, Federal Nursing Loans. *Student Employment:* Federal Work-Study Program available. Institutional employment available. **Financial Aid Statistics:** 66% needy freshmen, 68% needy undergrads receive need-based scholarship or grant aid. 93% freshmen, 80% undergrads receive non-need-based scholarship or grant aid. 80% freshmen, 84% undergrads receive need-based self-help aid. 16% freshmen, 12% undergrads receive athletic scholarships. 88% freshmen, 71% undergrads receive any aid. **Criteria for awarding aid:** *Non-need-based:* Academics, Alumni affiliation, Art, Athletics, Job skills, Leadership, Minority status, Music/drama, Religious affiliation, State/ district residency.

SOUTHWESTERN COLLEGE (KS)

100 College Street, Winfield, KS 67156
Phone: 620-229-6236 • **Financial Aid Phone:** 620-229-6215
E-mail: scadmit@sckans.edu • **CEEB Code:** 6670
Fax: 620-229-6344 • **Website:** www.sckans.edu • **ACT Code:** 1464

This private school, affiliated with the Methodist Church, was founded in 1885. It has a 85-acre campus.

RATINGS

Admissions Selectivity Rating: 76   **Fire Safety Rating:** 85   **Green Rating:** 60*

STUDENTS AND FACULTY

Enrollment: 1,471. **Student Body:** 48% female, 52% male, 34% out-of-state, 1% international (12 countries represented). Asian 2%, African American 8%, Caucasian 63%, Hispanic 6%, Native American 2%, Pacific Islander 0%, Two or more races 0%, Race unknown 18%.
Retention and Graduation: 70% freshmen return for sophomore year. 29% freshmen graduate within 4 years. 45% freshmen graduate within 6 years.
Faculty: Student/faculty ratio 12:1. 47 full-time faculty, 60% hold PhDs, 6% are are members of minority groups, 38% are women. 0% of classes are taught by teaching assistants.

ACADEMICS

Degrees: bachelor's, master's, postbachelor's certificate, post-master's certificate. **Classes:** Most classes have fewer than 10 students. Most lab/discussion sessions have fewer than 10 students. **Most popular majors:** Elementary Education and Teaching; Business Administration and Management. **Special Study Options:** Accelerated program, distance learning, double major, honors program, independent study, internships, student-designed major, teacher certification program. **Disability Services:** Special programs offered to physically disabled students, including reader services, tape recorders, tutors.

FACILITIES

Housing: Coed dorms, men's dorms, women's dorms, apartments for married students, apartments for single students. 90% of campus accessible to physically diasbled. **Special Academic Facilities/Equipment:** Ruth Warren Abbott Horticulture Lab Floyd and Ethel Moore Biological Field Station Norman E. Hege Education Center **Computers:** 100% of classrooms, 100% of dorms, 100% of libraries, 100% of dining areas, 100% of student union, 100% of common outdoor areas have wireless network access. Students can register for classes online. Administrative functions (other than registration) can be performed online.

CAMPUS LIFE

Environment: Village. **Activities:** Choral groups, concert band, dance, drama/ theater, jazz band, music ensembles, musical theater, pep band, radio station, student government, student newspaper, symphony orchestra, television station, yearbook, Campus Ministries, Student Organization. 25 registered organizations, 2 honor societies, 7 religious organizations. 2 fraternities. **Athletics (Intercollegiate):** *Men:* basketball, cheerleading, cross-country, football, golf, soccer, tennis, track/field (outdoor), track/field (indoor). *Women:* basketball, cheerleading, cross-country, golf, soccer, softball, tennis, track/field (outdoor), track/field (indoor), volleyball. **On-Campus Highlights:** Brand new Women's residence hall, Beech Science Center, Historic Stewart Field House, Christy Administration Building, Roy L. Smith Student Center (Newly re-modeled Cafeteria and bookstore). **Environmental Initiatives:** Kansas Envirothon

ADMISSIONS

Freshman Academic Profile: Average high school GPA 3.3. 16% in top 10% of high school class, 44% in top 25% of high school class, 73% in top 50% of high school class. 95% from public high schools. **Reported SAT (pre-2016 redesign) scores:** SAT Math middle 50% range 430-550. SAT Critical Reading middle 50% range 380-540. SAT Writing middle 50% range 390-560. **Concordant SAT scores:** SAT EBRW middle 50% 430–610. SAT Math middle 50% range 470–570. ACT middle 50% range 19-24. Minimum internet-based TOEFL 80. Minimum paper TOEFL 550. **Basis for Candidate Selection:** *Very important factors considered include:* rigor of secondary school record, academic GPA, standardized test scores. *Important factors considered include:* application essay. *Other factors considered include:* class rank, recommendation(s), interview, extracurricular activities, talent/ability, character/ personal qualities, alumni/ae relation. **Freshman Admission Requirements:** High school diploma is required and GED is accepted. *Academic units required:* 4 English, 3 math, 2 science, 1 science lab, 1 history. **Freshman Admission Statistics:** 293 applied, 90.10% admitted, 45% enrolled. **Transfer Admission Requirements:** college transcript(s), essay or personal statement, Minimum college GPA of 2.25 required. Lowest grade transferable C. **General Admission Information:** Application fee $25. Regular application deadline 8/25. Nonfall registration accepted.

COSTS AND FINANCIAL AID

Annual tuition $19,530. Room and board $5,750. Required fees $150. Average book expense $600. **Required Forms and Deadlines:** FAFSA. **Types of Aid:** *Need-based scholarships/grants:* Federal Pell, FSEOG, State scholarships/ grants, College/university scholarship or grant aid from institutional funds. *Loans:* Direct Subsidized Stafford Loans, Direct Unsubsidized Stafford Loans, Direct PLUS loans, Federal Perkins Loans. *Student Employment:* Federal Work-Study Program available. Institutional employment available. **Financial Aid Statistics:** 100% needy freshmen, 98% needy undergrads receive need-based scholarship or grant aid. 9% freshmen, 7% undergrads receive non-need-based scholarship or grant aid. 82% freshmen, 85% undergrads receive need-based self-help aid. 25% freshmen, 25% undergrads receive athletic scholarships. 100% freshmen, 99% undergrads receive any aid. **Criteria for awarding aid:** *Non-need-based:* Academics, Athletics, Leadership, Minority status, Music/drama.

SOUTHWESTERN UNIVERSITY

Admission Office, Georgetown, TX 78627-0770
Phone: 512-863-1200 • **Financial Aid Phone:** 512-863-1259
E-mail: admission@southwestern.edu • **CEEB Code:** 6674
Fax: 512-863-9601 • **Website:** http://www.southwestern.edu/ • **ACT Code:** 4186

This private school, affiliated with the Methodist Church, was founded in 1840. It has a 703-acre campus.

RATINGS
Admissions Selectivity Rating: 89   **Fire Safety Rating:** 90   **Green Rating:** 93

STUDENTS AND FACULTY
Enrollment: 1,477. **Student Body:** 57% female, 43% male, 10% out-of-state, 2% international (6 countries represented). Asian 4%, African American 6%, Caucasian 62%, Hispanic 21%, Native American <1%, Pacific Islander <1%, Two or more races 4%, Race unknown 1%.
Retention and Graduation: 85% freshmen return for sophomore year. 66% freshmen graduate within 4 years. 72 22% grads go on to further study within 1 year. 17% grads pursue arts and sciences degrees. 3% grads pursue law degrees. 3% grads pursue medical degrees. **Faculty:** Student/faculty ratio 12:1. 110 full-time faculty, 99% hold PhDs, 16% are are members of minority groups, 50% are women. 0% of classes are taught by teaching assistants.

ACADEMICS
Degrees: bachelor's. **Classes:** Most classes have 10-19 students. Most lab/discussion sessions have 10-19 students. **Most popular majors:** Business/Commerce; Psychology; Speech Communication and Rhetoric. **Special Study Options:** double major, honors program, independent study, internships, liberal arts/career combination, student-designed major, study abroad, teacher certification program. **Disability Services:** Special programs offered to physically disabled students, including note-taking services, reader services, tape recorders, tutors. **Career Services:** Alumni network, Alumni services, Career assessment, Internships, Regional alumni. Internships; 62% of 2015 graduates completed at least one internship.

FACILITIES
Housing: Coed dorms, special housing for disabled students, men's dorms, special housing for international students, women's dorms, fraternity/sorority housing, apartments for married students, apartments for single students. 100% of campus accessible to physically diasbled. **Special Academic Facilities/Equipment:** Alma Thomas Fine Arts Center Red and Charline McCombs Campus Center Corbin J. Robertson Center for Fitness and Wellness Fountainwood Astronomical Observatory **Computers:** 100% of classrooms, 100% of dorms, 100% of libraries, 100% of dining areas, 100% of student union, 50% of common outdoor areas have wireless network access. Students can register for classes online. Administrative functions (other than registration) can be performed online.

CAMPUS LIFE
Environment: Town. **Activities:** Choral groups, concert band, dance, drama/theater, jazz band, literary magazine, music ensembles, musical theater, radio station, student government, student newspaper, student-run film society 99 registered organizations, 14 honor societies, 10 religious organizations. 4 fraternities, 4 sororities. **Athletics (Intercollegiate):** Men: baseball, basketball, cross-country, diving, golf, lacrosse, soccer, swimming, tennis, track/field (outdoor). Women: basketball, cross-country, diving, golf, soccer, softball, swimming, tennis, track/field (outdoor), volleyball. **On-Campus Highlights:** Robertson Center-indoor olympic size pool, McCombs Center-Student Center, Fountainwood Observatory, Korovva Milkbar-student run coffee house, Academic Mall-grassy area in the middle of campus. **Environmental Initiatives:** 100% Green (wind) power.

ADMISSIONS
Freshman Academic Profile: 36% in top 10% of high school class, 73% in top 25% of high school class, 93% in top 50% of high school class. 73% from public high schools. **Reported SAT (pre-2016 redesign) scores:** SAT Math middle 50% range 520-630. SAT Critical Reading middle 50% range 530-650. **Concordant SAT scores:** SAT Math middle 50% range 550-650. ACT middle 50% range 23-28. Minimum internet-based TOEFL 88. Minimum paper TOEFL 570. **Basis for Candidate Selection:** *Very important factors considered include:* rigor of secondary school record, class rank, academic GPA, standardized test scores, application essay, recommendation(s). *Important factors considered include:* interview, extracurricular activities, talent/ability, character/personal qualities, first generation, alumni/ae relation, geographical

residence, state residency, racial/ethnic status, volunteer work. *Other factors considered include:* religious affiliation/commitment, work experience, level of applicant's interest. **Freshman Admission Requirements:** High school diploma is required and GED is accepted. *Academic units required:* 4 English, 4 math, 3 science, 2 science labs, 2 foreign language, 2 social studies, 1 history, 1 academic elective. *Academic units recommended:* 4 English, 4 math, 4 science, 3 science labs, 3 foreign language, 3 social studies, 2 history, 1 academic elective. **Freshman Admission Statistics:** 3,774 applied, 45.02% admitted, 22% enrolled. **Transfer Admission Requirements:** High school transcript, college transcript(s), essay or personal statement, statement of good standing from prior institution(s). Minimum college GPA of 3.0 required. Lowest grade transferable C. **General Admission Information:** Priority deadline 2/1. Regular notification 4/1. Nonfall registration not accepted. Admission may be deferred for a maximum of 1 year.

COSTS AND FINANCIAL AID
Annual tuition $40,560. Room and board $11,810. Average book expense $1,300. **Required Forms and Deadlines:** FAFSA. **Notification of Awards:** Applicants will be notified of awards on a rolling basis beginning 3/1. **Types of Aid:** *Need-based scholarships/grants:* Federal Pell, FSEOG, State scholarships/grants, Private scholarships, College/university scholarship or grant aid from institutional funds. *Loans:* Direct Subsidized Stafford Loans, Direct Unsubsidized Stafford Loans, Direct PLUS loans, Federal Perkins Loans, State Loans, College/university loans from institutional funds. *Student Employment:* Federal Work-Study Program available. Institutional employment available. **Financial Aid Statistics:** 100% needy freshmen, 99% needy undergrads receive need-based scholarship or grant aid. 96% freshmen, 96% undergrads receive non-need-based scholarship or grant aid. 75% freshmen, 80% undergrads receive need-based self-help aid. 0% freshmen, 0% undergrads receive athletic scholarships. 99% freshmen, 97% undergrads receive any aid. Average cumulative indebtedness $32,801. **Criteria for awarding aid:** *Need-based:* Academics. *Non-need-based:* Academics, Alumni affiliation, Art, Leadership, Minority status, Music/drama, Religious affiliation.

See page 1046.

SPELMAN COLLEGE

350 Spelman Lane, Atlanta, GA 30314-4399
Phone: 404-270-5193 • **Financial Aid Phone:** 404-270-5212
E-mail: admiss@spelman.edu • **CEEB Code:** 5628
Fax: 404-270-5201 • **Website:** www.spelman.edu • **ACT Code:** 794

This private school was founded in 1881. It has a 32-acre campus.

RATINGS
Admissions Selectivity Rating: 90   **Fire Safety Rating:** 95   **Green Rating:** 83

STUDENTS AND FACULTY
Enrollment: 1,586. **Student Body:** 100% female, 0% male, 72% out-of-state, 1% international (10 countries represented). Asian 0%, African American 96%, Caucasian <1%, Hispanic <1%, Native American 1%, Pacific Islander 0%, Two or more races 2%, Race unknown 0%.
Retention and Graduation: 83% freshmen return for sophomore year. 71% freshmen graduate within 4 years. 77% freshmen graduate within 6 years. 24% grads go on to further study within 1 year. **Faculty:** Student/faculty ratio 9:1. 171 full-time faculty, 91% hold PhDs, 86% are are members of minority groups, 71% are women. 0% of classes are taught by teaching assistants.

ACADEMICS
Degrees: bachelor's. **Classes:** Most classes have 10-19 students. Most lab/discussion sessions have 10-19 students. **Most popular majors:** Political Science and Government; Psychology; Biology. **Special Study Options:** cross-registration, double major, exchange student program (domestic), honors program, independent study, internships, liberal arts/career combination, student-designed major, study abroad, teacher certification program. **Honors Programs:** Ethel Waddell Githii Honors Program. **Disability Services:** Special programs offered to physically disabled students, including note-taking services, reader services, tape recorders, tutors. **Career Services:** Career/job search classes, Career assessment, Internships. The College has incorporated as part of the strategic plan a goal of every student having an internship or research opportunity prior to graduation. This goal is effective in generating an applicant pool large enough to meet the growing demands of employers seeking our students for internship opportunities within their organizations.

FACILITIES

Housing: women's dorms, apartments for single students. 85% of campus accessible to physically disabled. **Special Academic Facilities/Equipment:** Nursery-elementary school for child development majors, language lab, electron microscope. **Computers:** Students can register for classes online. Administrative functions (other than registration) can be performed online.

CAMPUS LIFE

Environment: Metropolis. **Activities:** Choral groups, dance, drama/theater, jazz band, student government, student newspaper, yearbook, Campus Ministries, Student Organization. 17 registered organizations, 18 honor societies, 9 religious organizations. 4 sororities. **Athletics (Intercollegiate):** *Women:* basketball, cross-country, golf, soccer, softball, tennis, volleyball. **On-Campus Highlights:** Sister's Chapel, The Spelman College Art Museum, Camille Olivia Hanks-Cosby Academic Center, Albro, Falconer, Manley Science Center, The Oval and Alumni Arch.

ADMISSIONS

Freshman Academic Profile: Average high school GPA 3.5. 38% in top 10% of high school class, 73% in top 25% of high school class, 93% in top 50% of high school class. **Reported SAT (pre-2016 redesign) scores:** SAT Math middle 50% range 480-580. SAT Critical Reading middle 50% range 500-590. SAT Writing middle 50% range 490-585. **Concordant SAT scores:** SAT EBRW middle 50% 550–650. SAT Math middle 50% range 510–600. ACT middle 50% range 22-26. Minimum internet-based TOEFL 120. Minimum paper TOEFL 550. **Basis for Candidate Selection:** *Very important factors considered include:* rigor of secondary school record, academic GPA, standardized test scores, application essay, recommendation(s), character/personal qualities. *Important factors considered include:* class rank, extracurricular activities, volunteer work. *Other factors considered include:* talent/ability, alumni/ae relation, geographical residence, work experience, level of applicant's interest. **Freshman Admission Requirements:** High school diploma is required and GED is accepted. *Academic units required:* 4 English, 2 math, 2 science, 1 science lab, 2 foreign language, 6 academic electives. *Academic units recommended:* 4 English, 4 math, 3 science, 2 science labs, 3 foreign language, 2 social studies, 1 history, 3 academic electives. **Freshman Admission Statistics:** 7,864 applied, 35.73% admitted, 19% enrolled. **Transfer Admission Requirements:** High school transcript, college transcript(s), Minimum college GPA of 2.0 required. Lowest grade transferable C. **General Admission Information:** Application fee $35. Regular application deadline 2/1. Regular notification 4/1. Nonfall registration accepted. Admission may be deferred for a maximum of one year.

COSTS AND FINANCIAL AID

Annual tuition $23,626. Room and board $12,795. Required fees $3,688. Average book expense $2,000. **Required Forms and Deadlines:** FAFSA, Institution's own financial aid form, State aid form, Noncustodial PROFILE. **Notification of Awards:** Applicants will be notified of awards on a rolling basis beginning 2/15. **Types of Aid:** *Need-based scholarships/grants:* Federal Pell, FSEOG, State scholarships/grants, Private scholarships, College/university scholarship or grant aid from institutional funds, United Negro College Fund. *Loans:* Direct Subsidized Stafford Loans, Direct Unsubsidized Stafford Loans, Direct PLUS loans, Federal Perkins Loans, State Loans. *Student Employment:* Federal Work-Study Program available. Institutional employment available. **Financial Aid Statistics:** 85% needy freshmen, 79% needy undergrads receive need-based scholarship or grant aid. 0% undergrads receive non-need-based scholarship or grant aid. 96% freshmen, 96% undergrads receive need-based self-help aid. 0% freshmen, 0% undergrads receive athletic scholarships. 84% freshmen, 90% undergrads receive any aid. 73% undergrads borrow to pay for school. Average cumulative indebtedness $38,430. **Criteria for awarding aid:** *Need-based:* Academics, Alumni affiliation, Leadership, Music/drama, Religious affiliation. *Non-need-based:* Academics, Alumni affiliation, Music/drama, State/district residency.

SPRING ARBOR UNIVERSITY

---

106 East Main Street, Spring Arbor, MI 49283-9799
Phone: 517-750-6458 • **Financial Aid Phone:** 800-968-0011
E-mail: admissions@admin.arbor.edu • **CEEB Code:** 1732
Fax: 517-750-6620 • **Website:** www.arbor.edu • **ACT Code:** 2056

This private school was founded in 1873. It has a 100-acre campus.

RATINGS

Admissions Selectivity Rating: 82   **Fire Safety Rating:** 84   **Green Rating:** 60*

STUDENTS AND FACULTY

Student Body: 69% female, 31% male, 12% out-of-state, (10 countries represented).

Retention and Graduation: 78% freshmen return for sophomore year. 33% freshmen graduate within 4 years. 54% freshmen graduate within 6 years. 22% grads go on to further study within 1 year. 8% grads pursue arts and sciences degrees. 3% grads pursue business degrees. 8% grads pursue medical degrees. **Faculty:** Student/faculty ratio 15:1. 81 full-time faculty, 72% hold PhDs, 11% are members of minority groups, 32% are women. 0% of classes are taught by teaching assistants.

ACADEMICS

Degrees: associate, bachelor's, master's, postbachelor's certificate. **Classes:** Most classes have 10-19 students. Most lab/discussion sessions have 10-19 students. **Most popular majors:** Elementary Education and Teaching; Psychology; Secondary Education and Teaching. **Special Study Options:** Accelerated program, cross-registration, distance learning, double major, dual enrollment, English as a Second Language (ESL), honors program, independent study, internships, student-designed major, study abroad, teacher certification program, weekend college, Off-Campus Study: Washington Journalism semester, Los Angeles Film Studies program, AuSable Inst of Environmental Studies Program (Michigan). Study abroad programs available: China, Latin America Middle East, Oxford Honors, Russian, Japan, Jerusalem Univ., Russia @ St. Petersburg, People's Republic of China @ Sichuan College. Other programs/destinations are available through petition. Combined degree programs: BA/MEng. **Disability Services:** Special programs offered to physically disabled students, including note-taking services, reader services, tape recorders, tutors. **Career Services:** Alumni network, Alumni services, Career/job search classes, Career assessment, Internships, Regional alumni, On-campus interviews.

FACILITIES

Housing: special housing for disabled students, men's dorms, special housing for international students, women's dorms, apartments for married students, apartments for single students. 80% of campus accessible to physically disabled. **Special Academic Facilities/Equipment:** State-of-the-art academic building (Poling Center); the Poling Center features the CP Federal Credit Union Trading Center and is equipped with some of the same technology that is used daily on Wall Street including: An electronic wrap-around ticker, large light emitting diode (LED) financial data board, Bloomberg terminal, and continuous financial news feeds. Radio and TV studios, commercial writing/computer graphics lab, science center, art gallery. **Computers:** 90% of classrooms, 100% of dorms, 100% of libraries, 100% of dining areas, 75% of common outdoor areas have wireless network access. Students can register for classes online. Administrative functions (other than registration) can be performed online.

CAMPUS LIFE

Environment: Rural. **Activities:** Choral groups, concert band, drama/theater, jazz band, literary magazine, music ensembles, musical theater, pep band, radio station, student government, student newspaper, student-run film society, symphony orchestra, television station, yearbook, Campus Ministries, Student Organization. 50 registered organizations. **Athletics (Intercollegiate):** *Men:* baseball, basketball, cross-country, golf, soccer, tennis, track/field (outdoor), track/field (indoor). *Women:* basketball, cross-country, soccer, softball, tennis, track/field (outdoor), track/field (indoor), volleyball. **On-Campus Highlights:** Sacred Grounds (Starbucks), Ganton Art Gallery, Poling Center, University Plaza, McKenna Carillon Tower, State-of-the-Art Academic Building (Poling Center) houses a trading center that is equipped with some of the same technology used on Wall Street.

ADMISSIONS

Freshman Academic Profile: Average high school GPA 3.4. 22% in top 10% of high school class, 48% in top 25% of high school class, 77% in top 50% of high school class. 80% from public high schools. **Reported SAT (pre-2016 redesign) scores:** SAT Math middle 50% range 460-580. SAT Critical Reading middle 50% range 480-585. SAT Writing middle 50% range 480-550. **Concordant SAT scores:** SAT EBRW middle 50% 540–630. SAT Math middle 50% range 500–600. ACT middle 50% range 20-26. Minimum paper TOEFL 525. **Basis for Candidate Selection:** *Very important factors considered include:* rigor of secondary school record, standardized test scores, character/personal qualities. *Important factors considered include:* academic GPA. *Other factors considered include:* class rank, application essay, recommendation(s), interview, extracurricular activities, talent/ability, religious affiliation/commitment. **Freshman Admission Requirements:** High school diploma is required and GED is accepted. *Academic units required:* 4 English, 3 math, 3 science, 3 science labs, 3 history, and 1 unit from above areas or other academic areas. *Academic units recommended:* 2 foreign language, 1 computer science. **Freshman Admission Statistics:** 2,698 applied, 65.05% admitted, 21% enrolled. **Transfer Admission Requirements:** High school transcript, college transcript(s), essay or personal statement, Minimum college GPA of 2.0 required. Lowest grade transferable C. **General Admission Information:** Application fee $30. Priority deadline 2/15. Regular application deadline 8/1. Nonfall registration accepted. Admission may be deferred.

COSTS AND FINANCIAL AID

Annual tuition $21,998. Room and board $7,900. Required fees $540. Average book expense $800. **Required Forms and Deadlines:** FAFSA. **Notification**

of Awards: Applicants will be notified of awards on a rolling basis beginning 3/1. **Types of Aid:** *Need-based scholarships/grants:* Federal Pell, FSEOG, Private scholarships, College/university scholarship or grant aid from institutional funds. *Loans:* Direct Subsidized Stafford Loans, Direct Unsubsidized Stafford Loans, Direct PLUS loans, Federal Perkins Loans. *Student Employment:* Federal Work-Study Program available. Institutional employment available. **Financial Aid Statistics:** 100% needy freshmen, 99% needy undergrads receive need-based scholarship or grant aid. 10% freshmen, 10% undergrads receive non-need-based scholarship or grant aid. 83% freshmen, 84% undergrads receive need-based self-help aid. 22% freshmen, 19% undergrads receive athletic scholarships. 97% freshmen, 93% undergrads receive any aid. **Criteria for awarding aid:** *Non-need-based:* Academics, Art, Athletics, Minority status, Religious affiliation.

SPRING HILL COLLEGE

4000 Dauphin Street, Mobile, AL 36608
Phone: 251-380-3030 • **Financial Aid Phone:** 251-380-3097
E-mail: admit@shc.edu • **CEEB Code:** 1733
Fax: 251-460-2186 • **Website:** www.shc.edu • **ACT Code:** 42

This private school, affiliated with the Roman Catholic Church, was founded in 1830. It has a 450-acre campus.

RATINGS

Admissions Selectivity Rating: 88   **Fire Safety Rating:** 84   **Green Rating:** 60*

STUDENTS AND FACULTY

Enrollment: 1,379. **Student Body:** 63% female, 37% male, 61% out-of-state, 3% international (23 countries represented). Asian 1%, African American 15%, Caucasian 69%, Hispanic 3%, Native American 1%, Pacific Islander <1%, Two or more races 3%, Race unknown 5%.
Retention and Graduation: 76% freshmen return for sophomore year. 46% freshmen graduate within 4 years. 53% freshmen graduate within 6 years.
Faculty: Student/faculty ratio 14:1. 99 full-time faculty, 82% hold PhDs, 9% are are members of minority groups, 44% are women. 0% of classes are taught by teaching assistants.

ACADEMICS

Degrees: bachelor's, certificate, master's, postbachelor's certificate, post-master's certificate. **Classes:** Most classes have 10-19 students. Most lab/discussion sessions have 20-29 students. **Most popular majors:** Business Administration and Management; Psychology; Speech Communication and Rhetoric. **Special Study Options:** Accelerated program, distance learning, double major, dual enrollment, honors program, independent study, internships, student-designed major, study abroad, teacher certification program, 3-2 engineering with Auburn University, University of Alabama Birmingham, Marquette University, University of Florida, and Texas A&M University. Marine biology classes at Dauphin Island Sea Lab in conjunction with the Marine Environmental Sciences Consortium. **Honors Programs:** SHC's 4-year Honors Program offers a challenging and rewarding course of study to academically gifted and motivated students. It is comprised of academic courses; seminar experiences; and additional opportunities for service, leadership, cultural exploration, and social interaction both on and off campus. Honors courses cover material in greater depth, use primary materials when possible, stress student participation and responsibility, and encourage high individual achievement. Combined degree programs: Dual Degree program BS/BE continued—Univ of South Ala. **Disability Services:** Special programs offered to physically disabled students, including tutors. **Career Services:** Alumni network, Alumni services, Career/job search classes, Career assessment, Internships, Regional alumni.

FACILITIES

Housing: Coed dorms, men's dorms, women's dorms, apartments for single students. 90% of campus accessible to physically disabled. **Special Academic Facilities/Equipment:** Public radio broadcasting station, theater **Computers:** 50% of classrooms, 15% of dorms, 100% of libraries, 100% of dining areas, 100% of student union, 25% of common outdoor areas have wireless network access. Students can register for classes online. Administrative functions (other than registration) can be performed online.

CAMPUS LIFE

Environment: Metropolis. **Activities:** Choral groups, dance, drama/theater, literary magazine, student government, student newspaper, yearbook, Campus Ministries. 66 registered organizations, 16 honor societies, 5 religious organizations. 3 fraternities, 5 sororities. **Athletics (Intercollegiate):** *Men:* baseball, basketball, cross-country, golf, soccer, tennis. *Women:* basketball, cross-country, golf, soccer, softball, tennis, volleyball. **On-Campus Highlights:** Arthur Outlaw Recreation Center, Golf Course, Burke Library, Java City Coffee Shop, Dorn Field.

ADMISSIONS

Freshman Academic Profile: Average high school GPA 3.6. 27% in top 10% of high school class, 60% in top 25% of high school class, 90% in top 50% of high school class. **Reported SAT (pre-2016 redesign) scores:** SAT Math middle 50% range 500-590. SAT Critical Reading middle 50% range 500-600. **Concordant SAT scores:** SAT Math middle 50% range 530–610. ACT middle 50% range 22-27. Minimum internet-based TOEFL 80. Minimum paper TOEFL 550. **Basis for Candidate Selection:** *Very important factors considered include:* rigor of secondary school record, academic GPA, standardized test scores. *Important factors considered include:* class rank, recommendation(s), interview. *Other factors considered include:* application essay, extracurricular activities, talent/ability, character/personal qualities, alumni/ae relation, volunteer work. **Freshman Admission Requirements:** High school diploma is required and GED is accepted. *Academic units recommended:* 4 English, 3 math, 3 science, 1 science lab, 2 foreign language, 2 social studies, 1 history, 1 academic elective. **Freshman Admission Statistics:** 8,534 applied, 43.53% admitted, 11% enrolled. **Transfer Admission Requirements:** college transcript(s), statement of good standing from prior institution(s). Minimum college GPA of 2.5 required. Lowest grade transferable C-. **General Admission Information:** Application fee $25. Priority deadline 1/15. Regular application deadline 7/15. Nonfall registration accepted. Admission may be deferred for a maximum of 1 year.

COSTS AND FINANCIAL AID

Required Forms and Deadlines: FAFSA, State aid form. **Notification of Awards:** Applicants will be notified of awards on a rolling basis beginning 2/15. **Types of Aid:** *Need-based scholarships/grants:* Federal Pell, FSEOG, State scholarships/grants, Private scholarships, College/university scholarship or grant aid from institutional funds. *Loans:* Direct Subsidized Stafford Loans, Direct Unsubsidized Stafford Loans, Direct PLUS loans, Federal Perkins Loans. *Student Employment:* Federal Work-Study Program available. Institutional employment available. **Financial Aid Statistics:** 100% needy freshmen receive need-based scholarship or grant aid. **Criteria for awarding aid:** *Need-based:* Academics, Alumni affiliation, Athletics, Job skills, Leadership, Minority status. *Non-need-based:* Academics, Alumni affiliation, Art, Athletics, Job skills, Leadership, Minority status, State/district residency.

ST. AMBROSE UNIVERSITY

518 West Locust Street, Davenport, IA 52803-2898
Phone: 563-333-6300 • **Financial Aid Phone:** 563-333-6314
E-mail: admit@sau.edu • **CEEB Code:** 6617
Fax: 563-333-6038 • **Website:** www.sau.edu • **ACT Code:** 1352

This private school, affiliated with the Roman Catholic Church, was founded in 1882. It has a 118-acre campus.

RATINGS

Admissions Selectivity Rating: 76   **Fire Safety Rating:** 60*   **Green Rating:** 60*

STUDENTS AND FACULTY

Enrollment: 2,381. **Student Body:** 57% female, 43% male, 60% out-of-state, 3% international (14 countries represented). Asian 1%, African American 4%, Caucasian 78%, Hispanic 7%, Native American <1%, Pacific Islander <1%, Two or more races 2%, Race unknown 4%.
Retention and Graduation: 77% freshmen return for sophomore year. 53% freshmen graduate within 4 years. 63% freshmen graduate within 6 years. 19% grads go on to further study within 1 year. **Faculty:** Student/faculty ratio 12:1. 182 full-time faculty, 83% hold PhDs, 10% are are members of minority groups, 37% are women. 0% of classes are taught by teaching assistants.

ACADEMICS

Degrees: bachelor's, certificate, doctoral/professional, doctoral/research, master's, post-master's certificate. **Classes:** Most classes have 10-19 students. Most lab/discussion sessions have 20-29 students. **Most popular majors:** Business/Commerce; Nursing Science; Psychology. **Special Study Options:** Accelerated program, cooperative education program, distance learning, double major, independent study, internships, liberal arts/career combination, student-designed major, study abroad, teacher certification program, weekend college, We have overseas academic experiences in England, Ireland, Lithuania, and Ecuador. Our students can, also, take advantage of the overseas experiences thru Central College in Iowa. Combined degree programs: BA/MA, BA-DPT, BA-MSW, BA-MCJ. **Disability Services:** Special programs offered to physically disabled students, including note-taking services, reader services, tape recorders, tutors. **Career Services:** Alumni network, Alumni services, Career/job search classes, Career assessment, Internships, Regional alumni.

FACILITIES

Housing: Coed dorms, special housing for disabled students, men's dorms, women's dorms, apartments for single students, The University owns several houses next to campus and will rent them out to graduate or married studens. 95% of campus accessible to physically diasbled. **Special Academic Facilities/Equipment:** Art gallery, observatory, language lab, and distance learning classrooms (5). **Computers:** 1% of classrooms, 27% of dorms, 100% of libraries, 100% of student union, have wireless network access. Students can register for classes online. Administrative functions (other than registration) can be performed online.

CAMPUS LIFE

Environment: City. **Activities:** Choral groups, concert band, dance, drama/theater, jazz band, literary magazine, music ensembles, musical theater, opera, pep band, radio station, student government, student newspaper, symphony orchestra, television station, Campus Ministries, Student Organization. 26 registered organizations, 12 honor societies, 3 religious organizations. **Athletics (Intercollegiate):** *Men:* baseball, basketball, bowling, cheerleading, cross-country, football, golf, soccer, tennis, track/field (outdoor), track/field (indoor), volleyball. *Women:* basketball, bowling, cheerleading, cross-country, golf, soccer, softball, tennis, track/field (outdoor), track/field (indoor), volleyball. **On-Campus Highlights:** Rogalski Center (Student Union), Cafeteria, Coffee Shop and Bookstore, Chapel, Galvin Fine Arts Building. **Environmental Initiatives:** STORM WATER DETENTION In order to minimize storm water flow into underground storm sewers, the following areas have been developed to detain water during storm events and allow a slower release into the ground.— Townhouse west 2,154 gallons—University Center parking lot islands 9,694 gallons—University Center west grounds 71,808 gallons—Lombard Street at University Center 10,771 gallons—LINK east entry 1,212 gallons—Rohlman north 2,100 gallons—Cosgrove north grounds 8,617 gallons TOTAL: 106,356 gallons of detention

ADMISSIONS

Freshman Academic Profile: Average high school GPA 3.3. 71% from public high schools. ACT middle 50% range 20-25. Minimum paper TOEFL 500. **Basis for Candidate Selection:** *Very important factors considered include:* rigor of secondary school record, class rank, academic GPA, standardized test scores. *Other factors considered include:* application essay, recommendation(s), interview, extracurricular activities, talent/ability, character/personal qualities, first generation, alumni/ae relation, geographical residence, racial/ethnic status, volunteer work. **Freshman Admission Requirements:** High school diploma is required and GED is accepted. *Academic units recommended:* 4 English, 3 math, 2 science, 2 science labs, 1 foreign language, 1 social studies, 1 history, 4 academic electives. **Freshman Admission Statistics:** 4,426 applied, 63.58% admitted, 16% enrolled. **Transfer Admission Requirements:** High school transcript, college transcript(s), standardized test scores. Statement of good standing from prior institution(s). Minimum college GPA of 2.0 required. Lowest grade transferable D. **General Admission Information:** Application fee $25. Nonfall registration accepted. Admission may be deferred for a maximum of 1 semester.

COSTS AND FINANCIAL AID

Annual tuition $29,736. Room and board $10,164. Required fees $280. Average book expense $1,320. **Required Forms and Deadlines:** FAFSA. **Notification of Awards:** Applicants will be notified of awards on a rolling basis beginning 2/15. **Types of Aid:** *Need-based scholarships/grants:* Federal Pell, FSEOG, State scholarships/grants, Private scholarships, College/university scholarship or grant aid from institutional funds. *Loans:* Direct Subsidized Stafford Loans, Direct Unsubsidized Stafford Loans, Direct PLUS loans, Federal Perkins Loans. *Student Employment:* Federal Work-Study Program available. Institutional employment available. **Financial Aid Statistics:** 99% needy freshmen, 99% needy undergrads receive need-based scholarship or grant aid. 41% freshmen, 26% undergrads receive non-need-based scholarship or grant aid. 71% freshmen, 78% undergrads receive need-based self-help aid. 10% freshmen, 8% undergrads receive athletic scholarships. 99% freshmen, 88% undergrads receive any aid. **Criteria for awarding aid:** *Need-based:* Academics, Minority status. *Non-need-based:* Academics, Alumni affiliation, Art, Athletics, Music/drama.

ST. ANDREWS UNIVERSITY

1700 Dogwood Mile, Laurinburg, NC 28352
Phone: 910-277-5555 • **Financial Aid Phone:** 910-277-5560
E-mail: admissions@sapc.edu • **CEEB Code:** 5214
Fax: 910-277-5020 • **Website:** sapc.edu • **ACT Code:** 3146

This private school, affiliated with the Presbyterian Church, was founded in 1958. It has a 600-acre campus.

RATINGS

Admissions Selectivity Rating: 76   **Fire Safety Rating:** 60*   **Green Rating:** 60*

STUDENTS AND FACULTY

Enrollment: 580. **Student Body:** 54% female, 46% male, 59% out-of-state, 12% international (8 countries represented). Asian 0%, African American 12%, Caucasian 61%, Hispanic 0%, Native American 0%, Pacific Islander 0%, Two or more races 2%, Race unknown 14%.
Retention and Graduation: 59% freshmen return for sophomore year. 26% freshmen graduate within 4 years. 28% freshmen graduate within 6 years. 40% grads go on to further study within 1 year. **Faculty:** Student/faculty ratio 15:1. 30 full-time faculty, 73% hold PhDs, 3% are are members of minority groups, 47% are women. 0% of classes are taught by teaching assistants.

ACADEMICS

Degrees: bachelor's, diploma, master's. **Classes:** Most classes have fewer than 10 students. Most lab/discussion sessions have 10-19 students. **Most popular majors:** Elementary Education and Teaching; English Language and Literature; Business/Commerce. **Special Study Options:** double major, honors program, independent study, internships, student-designed major, study abroad, teacher certification program, weekend college, online classes. **Disability Services:** Special programs offered to physically disabled students, including note-taking services, reader services, tape recorders, tutors. **Career Services:** Alumni network, Alumni services, Career/job search classes, Career assessment, Internships, Regional alumni.

FACILITIES

Housing: Coed dorms, men's dorms, women's dorms. 90% of campus accessible to physically diasbled. **Special Academic Facilities/Equipment:** Art gallery, anthropology museum, science lab, electron microscopy center with three electron microscopes, psychology lab, artronics graphics computer, Scottish Heritage Foundation. **Computers:** 100% of libraries, 50% of dining areas, 100% of student union, have wireless network access. Administrative functions (other than registration) can be performed online.

CAMPUS LIFE

Environment: Rural. **Activities:** Choral groups, drama/theater, literary magazine, student government, student newspaper, yearbook, Campus Ministries. 30 registered organizations, 3 honor societies, 1 religious organization. **Athletics (Intercollegiate):** *Men:* baseball, basketball, cross-country, equestrian sports, golf, horseback riding, lacrosse, soccer, track/field (outdoor), wrestling. *Women:* basketball, cross-country, equestrian sports, horseback riding, lacrosse, soccer, softball, track/field (outdoor), volleyball, wrestling. **On-Campus Highlights:** Equesterian Center, Morgan Jones Science Labs, Electronic and Fine Arts Center, Athletic Facilities, Art Studios.

ADMISSIONS

Freshman Academic Profile: Average high school GPA 3.2. 7% in top 10% of high school class, 30% in top 25% of high school class, 66% in top 50% of high school class. **Reported SAT (pre-2016 redesign) scores:** SAT Math middle 50% range 355-605. SAT Writing middle 50% range 330-590. **Concordant SAT scores:** SAT EBRW middle 50% –350. SAT Math middle 50% range 400–630. Minimum paper TOEFL 550. **Basis for Candidate Selection:** *Important factors considered include:* academic GPA, standardized test scores, extracurricular activities, character/personal qualities. *Other factors considered include:* rigor of secondary school record, class rank, application essay, recommendation(s), interview, talent/ability, first generation, volunteer work, work experience. **Freshman Admission Requirements:** High school diploma is required and GED is accepted. *Academic units required:* 3 English, 3 math, 3 science, 1 foreign language, 3 social studies. **Freshman Admission Statistics:** 926 applied, 57.13% admitted, 29% enrolled. **Transfer Admission Requirements:** High school transcript, college transcript(s), statement of good standing from prior institution(s). Minimum college GPA of 2.5 required. Lowest grade transferable C-. **General Admission Information:** Application fee $35. Nonfall registration accepted.

COSTS AND FINANCIAL AID

Annual tuition $23,682. Average book expense $1,800. **Types of Aid:** *Need-based scholarships/grants:* Federal Pell, FSEOG, State scholarships/grants, Private scholarships, College/university scholarship or grant aid from institutional funds. *Loans:* Direct Subsidized Stafford Loans, Direct Unsubsidized Stafford Loans, Direct PLUS loans. *Student Employment:*

Federal Work-Study Program available. Institutional employment available. **Financial Aid Statistics:** 99% needy freshmen, 98% needy undergrads receive need-based scholarship or grant aid. 9% freshmen, 8% undergrads receive non-need-based scholarship or grant aid. 85% freshmen, 84% undergrads receive need-based self-help aid. 17% freshmen, 17% undergrads receive athletic scholarships. 99% freshmen, 98% undergrads receive any aid. **Criteria for awarding aid:** *Non-need-based:* Academics, Alumni affiliation, Art, Athletics, Job skills, Leadership, Music/drama, Religious affiliation.

ST. BONAVENTURE UNIVERSITY

3261 West State Road, St. Bonaventure, NY 14778
Phone: 716-375-2434 • **Financial Aid Phone:** 716-375-2528
E-mail: admissions@sbu.edu • **CEEB Code:** 2793
Fax: 716-375-4005 • **Website:** www.sbu.edu • **ACT Code:** 2882

This private school, affiliated with the Roman Catholic Church, was founded in 1858. It has a 500-acre campus.

RATINGS

Admissions Selectivity Rating: 84   **Fire Safety Rating:** 83   **Green Rating:** 60*

STUDENTS AND FACULTY

Enrollment: 1,609. **Student Body:** 50% female, 50% male, 28% out-of-state, 3% international (15 countries represented). Asian 4%, African American 6%, Caucasian 69%, Hispanic 8%, Native American <1%, Pacific Islander <1%, Two or more races 3%, Race unknown 8%.
Retention and Graduation: 82% freshmen return for sophomore year. 52% freshmen graduate within 4 years. 64% freshmen graduate within 6 years. 46% grads go on to further study within 1 year. **Faculty:** Student/faculty ratio 11:1. 127 full-time faculty, 76% hold PhDs, 6% are are members of minority groups, 38% are women.

ACADEMICS

Degrees: bachelor's, master's, postbachelor's certificate, post-master's certificate. **Classes:** Most classes have 10-19 students. Most lab/discussion sessions have 10-19 students. **Most popular majors:** Journalism; Biology/Biological Sciences; Business Administration and Management. **Special Study Options:** Accelerated program, cross-registration, distance learning, double major, dual enrollment, exchange student program (domestic), honors program, independent study, internships, liberal arts/career combination, student-designed major, study abroad, teacher certification program, weekend college. **Disability Services:** Special programs offered to physically disabled students, including note-taking services, reader services, tutors. **Career Services:** Alumni network, Alumni services, Career/job search classes, Career assessment, Internships, Regional alumni.

FACILITIES

Housing: special housing for disabled students, men's dorms, women's dorms, apartments for single students. 54% of campus accessible to physically diasbled. **Special Academic Facilities/Equipment:** Quick Center for the Arts, Digital Conferencing and Media Center, Franciscan Center for Social Concern, Franciscan Institute. **Computers:** 100% of classrooms, have wireless network access. Students can register for classes online.

CAMPUS LIFE

Environment: Village. **Activities:** Choral groups, concert band, dance, drama/theater, jazz band, literary magazine, music ensembles, pep band, radio station, student government, student newspaper, television station, yearbook. 47 registered organizations, 7 honor societies, 6 religious organizations. **Athletics (Intercollegiate):** *Men:* baseball, basketball, cross-country, diving, golf, soccer, swimming, tennis. *Women:* basketball, cross-country, diving, lacrosse, soccer, softball, swimming, tennis. **On-Campus Highlights:** Reilly Center, Richter Center, Quick Arts Center, Allegany River Trail, Golf Course and Clubhouse, Several major construction projects are taking place between 2006 and 2008, including renovation and addition to Hickey Dining Hall, renovation of Shay-Loughlen Residence Hall and addition of rare books wing to Friedsam Library. **Environmental Initiatives:** New campus construction: St. Bonaventure's William F. Walsh Science Center and the Friedsam Memorial Library Rare Books addition use underground water for cooling systems, reducing the release of carbon dioxide.

ADMISSIONS

Freshman Academic Profile: Average high school GPA 3.4. 19% in top 10% of high school class, 46% in top 25% of high school class, 77% in top 50% of

high school class. **Reported SAT (pre-2016 redesign) scores:** SAT Math middle 50% range 470-585. SAT Critical Reading middle 50% range 460-580. SAT Writing middle 50% range 440-570. **Concordant SAT scores:** SAT EBRW middle 50% 500–630. SAT Math middle 50% range 510–610. ACT middle 50% range 19-26. Minimum paper TOEFL 550. **Basis for Candidate Selection:** *Very important factors considered include:* rigor of secondary school record, academic GPA, recommendation(s), character/personal qualities. *Important factors considered include:* standardized test scores, application essay, extracurricular activities, talent/ability, volunteer work, work experience, level of applicant's interest. *Other factors considered include:* class rank, interview, first generation, alumni/ae relation, geographical residence, state residency. **Freshman Admission Requirements:** High school diploma is required and GED is accepted. *Academic units recommended:* 4 English, 3 math, 3 science, 3 science labs, 2 foreign language, 4 social studies. **Freshman Admission Statistics:** 2,871 applied, 65.90% admitted, 23% enrolled. **Transfer Admission Requirements:** High school transcript, college transcript(s), statement of good standing from prior institution(s). Minimum college GPA of 2.0 required. Lowest grade transferable C. **General Admission Information:** Priority deadline 2/15. Regular application deadline 7/1. Nonfall registration accepted. Admission may be deferred for a maximum of 1 year.

COSTS AND FINANCIAL AID

Annual tuition $31,366. Room and board $11,906. Required fees $965. Average book expense $800. **Required Forms and Deadlines:** FAFSA, State aid form. **Notification of Awards:** Applicants will be notified of awards on a rolling basis beginning 3/1. **Types of Aid:** *Need-based scholarships/grants:* Federal Pell, FSEOG, State scholarships/grants, Private scholarships, College/university scholarship or grant aid from institutional funds. *Loans:* Direct Subsidized Stafford Loans, Direct Unsubsidized Stafford Loans, Direct PLUS loans, Federal Perkins Loans. *Student Employment:* Federal Work-Study Program available. Institutional employment available. **Financial Aid Statistics:** 100% needy freshmen, 100% needy undergrads receive need-based scholarship or grant aid. 89% freshmen, 86% undergrads receive non-need-based scholarship or grant aid. 78% freshmen, 77% undergrads receive need-based self-help aid. 13% freshmen, 12% undergrads receive athletic scholarships. 99% freshmen, 97% undergrads receive any aid. **Criteria for awarding aid:** *Need-based:* Job skills. *Non-need-based:* Academics, Athletics, Minority status, Music/drama, Religious affiliation, State/district residency.

ST. CATHERINE UNIVERSITY

2004 Randolph Avenue, Saint Paul, MN 55105
Phone: 651-690-8850 • **Financial Aid Phone:** 651-690-6540
E-mail: admissions@stkate.edu • **CEEB Code:** 6105
Fax: 651-690-8868 • **Website:** www.stkate.edu • **ACT Code:** 2096

This private school, affiliated with the Roman Catholic Church, was founded in 1905. It has a 110-acre campus.

RATINGS

Admissions Selectivity Rating: 85   **Fire Safety Rating:** 88   **Green Rating:** 60*

STUDENTS AND FACULTY

Enrollment: 3,265. **Student Body:** 97% female, 3% male, 11% out-of-state, 1% international (34 countries represented). Asian 12%, African American 9%, Caucasian 64%, Hispanic 7%, Native American 1%, Pacific Islander <1%, Two or more races 3%, Race unknown 4%.
Retention and Graduation: 86% freshmen return for sophomore year. 40% freshmen graduate within 4 years. 64% freshmen graduate within 6 years. 28% grads go on to further study within 1 year. 2% grads pursue arts and sciences degrees. 4% grads pursue law degrees. 10% grads pursue business degrees. 2% grads pursue medical degrees. **Faculty:** Student/faculty ratio 10:1. 293 full-time faculty, 79% hold PhDs, 10% are are members of minority groups, 82% are women. 0% of classes are taught by teaching assistants.

ACADEMICS

Degrees: associate, bachelor's, certificate, doctoral/professional, master's, postbachelor's certificate, terminal. **Classes:** Most classes have 10-19 students. Most lab/discussion sessions have 10-19 students. **Most popular majors:** Elementary Education and Teaching; Registered Nursing, Nursing Administration, Nursing Research and Clinical Nursing; Social Work. **Special Study Options:** cross-registration, double major, dual enrollment, exchange student program (domestic), honors program, independent study, internships, student-designed major, study abroad, weekend college. **Honors Programs:** Antonian Scholars are students who exhibit exceptional academic performance in the University and who show promise as learners, researchers, writers, performers, campus or community leaders, and/or creative thinkers. Scholars possess both creativity and love of learning. Scholars are inquisitive and hard working. They love challenges. Scholars are also students who want to take an active role in "tailoring" their college experiences to their needs, interests and passions. Scholars complete a five-component program that includes interdisciplinary seminars, as well as optional honors sections of TRW and/ or GSJ, optional study abroad experiences, and a required Senior Honors Project. Scholars participate in at least two and up to four Honors seminars specifically designed for their learning needs and offered in an interdisciplinary format with two professors. All scholars as seniors are required to enroll in a four-credit independent study course in which they develop a senior project based on an interest, curiosity, or passion. Senior projects are completed with a faculty advisor and an interdisciplinary faculty committee who provide guidance and feedback on the project. Other privileges of membership in the Antonian Scholars Honors Program includes priority registration for courses each semester, special diplomas and commencement recognition, and leadership opportunities in the Honors Program Student Organization. Scholars also have opportunities on a regular basis to socialize, network, and converse with others in the Honors Program. Scholars have access to the Honor's Hub in Coeur de Catherine. The Hub is a quiet place to study when you need one and also a place where Scholars may gather for special activities or conversation. Combined degree programs: BA/DPT, BA/MA (Occupational Therapy). **Disability Services:** Special programs offered to physically disabled students, including note-taking services, reader services, tape recorders, tutors. **Career Services:** Alumni network, Alumni services, Career/job search classes, Career assessment, Internships.

FACILITIES

Housing: women's dorms, apartments for single students, Theme Housing, Housing for student-parents. 90% of campus accessible to physically disabled. **Special Academic Facilities/Equipment:** Art gallery, theatre, recital hall, experimental psychology lab, language lab, observatory. **Computers:** Students can register for classes online. Administrative functions (other than registration) can be performed online.

CAMPUS LIFE

Environment: Metropolis. **Activities:** Choral groups, drama/theater, literary magazine, music ensembles, musical theater, student government, student newspaper, Campus Ministries. 40 registered organizations, 24 honor societies, 4 religious organizations. 1 sororities. **Athletics (Intercollegiate):** *Women:* basketball, cross-country, diving, ice hockey, soccer, softball, swimming, tennis, track/field (outdoor), track/field (indoor), volleyball. **On-Campus Highlights:** Coeur de Catherine, English garden, Butler Center, Dew Drop Pond, Art Gallery. **Environmental Initiatives:** Retrofitted older building with green roof

ADMISSIONS

Freshman Academic Profile: Average high school GPA 3.6. 25% in top 10% of high school class, 68% in top 25% of high school class, 93% in top 50% of high school class. 86% from public high schools. **Reported SAT (pre-2016 redesign) scores:** SAT Math middle 50% range 490-550. SAT Critical Reading middle 50% range 510-610. **Concordant SAT scores:** SAT Math middle 50% range 520–570. ACT middle 50% range 21-26. Minimum paper TOEFL 500. **Basis for Candidate Selection:** *Very important factors considered include:* rigor of secondary school record. *Important factors considered include:* class rank, academic GPA, standardized test scores, application essay, recommendation(s). *Other factors considered include:* interview, first generation, level of applicant's interest. **Freshman Admission Requirements:** High school diploma is required and GED is accepted. *Academic units recommended:* 4 English, 3 math, 2 science, 4 foreign language, 2 social studies. **Freshman Admission Statistics:** 2,999 applied, 67.39% admitted, 21% enrolled. **Transfer Admission Requirements:** High school transcript, college transcript(s), statement of good standing from prior institution(s). Minimum college GPA of 2.0 required. Lowest grade transferable C-. **General Admission Information:** Nonfall registration accepted. Admission may be deferred for a maximum of 1 year.

COSTS AND FINANCIAL AID

Annual tuition $36,240. Room and board $8,390. Required fees $644. Average book expense $1,000. **Required Forms and Deadlines:** FAFSA, Institution's own financial aid form. **Types of Aid:** *Need-based scholarships/grants:* Federal Pell, FSEOG, State scholarships/grants, Private scholarships, College/ university scholarship or grant aid from institutional funds. *Loans:* Direct Subsidized Stafford Loans, Direct Unsubsidized Stafford Loans, Direct PLUS loans, Federal Perkins Loans, Federal Nursing Loans, State Loans. *Student Employment:* Federal Work-Study Program available. Institutional employment available. **Financial Aid Statistics:** 86% needy freshmen, 78% needy undergrads receive need-based scholarship or grant aid. 100% freshmen, 94% undergrads receive non-need-based scholarship or grant aid. 78% freshmen, 82% undergrads receive need-based self-help aid. 0% freshmen, 0% undergrads receive athletic scholarships. 94% freshmen, 93% undergrads receive any aid. 85% undergrads borrow to pay for school. Average cumulative indebtedness $39,150. **Criteria for awarding aid:** *Non-need-based:* Academics, Alumni affiliation, Leadership, State/district residency.

ST. EDWARD'S UNIVERSITY

3001 South Congress Avenue, Austin, TX 78704-6489
Phone: 512-448-8500 • **Financial Aid Phone:** 512-448-8523
E-mail: admit@stedwards.edu • **CEEB Code:** 6619
Fax: 512-464-8877 • **Website:** https://www.stedwards.edu • **ACT Code:** 4156

This private school, affiliated with the Roman Catholic Church, was founded in 1885. It has a 160-acre campus.

RATINGS

Admissions Selectivity Rating: 80   **Fire Safety Rating:** 92   **Green Rating:** 80

STUDENTS AND FACULTY

Enrollment: 4,050. **Student Body:** 61% female, 39% male, 14% out-of-state, 8% international (57 countries represented). Asian 3%, African American 4%, Caucasian 37%, Hispanic 41%, Native American <1%, Pacific Islander <1%, Two or more races 3%, Race unknown 2%. **Retention and Graduation:** 74% freshmen return for sophomore year. 52% freshmen graduate within 4 years. 64% freshmen graduate within 6 years. **Faculty:** Student/faculty ratio 14:1. 196 full-time faculty, 90% hold PhDs, 14% are are members of minority groups, 53% are women. 0% of classes are taught by teaching assistants.

ACADEMICS

Degrees: bachelor's, master's, postbachelor's certificate. **Classes:** Most classes have 20-29 students. **Most popular majors:** Psychology; Communication; Biology/Biological Sciences. **Special Study Options:** double major, honors program, internships, study abroad, teacher certification program. **Honors Programs:** Honors Program Combined degree programs: We offer a BS Math/ BS Engineering degree with Carroll College. **Disability Services:** Special programs offered to physically disabled students, including note-taking services, reader services, tutors. **Career Services:** Alumni network, Alumni services, Career/job search classes, Career assessment, Internships, Regional alumni. We offer internship advising and administer internship programs with nonprofit organizations with funding from private donors.

FACILITIES

Housing: Coed dorms, special housing for disabled students, women's dorms, apartments for single students, Community-style living (casas, casitas) and two living-learning communities: Global Understanding and Social Justice. 93% of campus accessible to physically disabled. **Special Academic Facilities/ Equipment:** Fine arts facility with digital photography lab; natural sciences center including state-of-the-art labs, classrooms and seminar rooms; interdisciplinary research lab at Wild Basin Wilderness Preserve. **Computers:** 100% of classrooms, 100% of dorms, 100% of libraries, 100% of dining areas, 100% of student union, 100% of common outdoor areas have wireless network access. Students can register for classes online. Administrative functions (other than registration) can be performed online.

CAMPUS LIFE

Environment: Metropolis. **Activities:** Choral groups, dance, drama/theater, literary magazine, music ensembles, musical theater, student government, student newspaper, student-run film society, symphony orchestra, television station, Campus Ministries, Student Organization. 95 registered organizations, 10 honor societies, 3 religious organizations. **Athletics (Intercollegiate):** *Men:* baseball, basketball, golf, soccer, tennis. *Women:* basketball, golf, soccer, softball, tennis, volleyball. **On-Campus Highlights:** Historic Main Building (view of Austin), Meadows Coffee House, New 119,000 sq ft residential villa 2009, John Brooks Williams Natural Sciences Center, Meditation and Prayer Grotto/Sorin Oak, Sorin Oak is the largest oak tree in Austin at 14.6 feet in circumference. **Environmental Initiatives:** Performance contract to reduce utility consumption across campus: lighting retrofit, thermal storage tank for chilled water supply, replaced steam system with individual building hot water boilers, installed low flow plumbing fixtures (toilets, urinals, showerheads, faucet aerators). John Brooks Williams South, our new science facility, is an Austin Green Energy Building 3-star facility and the UFCU Alumni Gym is in its final stages of being certified as a Three Star rated facility.

ADMISSIONS

Freshman Academic Profile: 24% in top 10% of high school class, 60% in top 25% of high school class, 88% in top 50% of high school class. 74% from public high schools. **Reported SAT (pre-2016 redesign) scores:** SAT Math middle 50% range 500-590. SAT Critical Reading middle 50% range 510-610. SAT Writing middle 50% range 490-590. **Concordant SAT scores:** SAT EBRW middle 50% 560–650. SAT Math middle 50% range 530–610. ACT middle 50% range 22-27. Minimum internet-based TOEFL 61. Minimum paper TOEFL 500. **Basis for Candidate Selection:** *Very important factors considered include:* rigor of secondary school record, academic GPA, standardized test scores, application essay. *Important factors considered include:* class rank, recommendation(s), extracurricular activities, volunteer work. *Other factors* *considered include:* interview, talent/ability, character/personal qualities, first generation, alumni/ae relation, geographical residence, state residency, religious affiliation/commitment, racial/ethnic status, work experience, level of applicant's interest. **Freshman Admission Requirements:** High school diploma is required and GED is accepted. *Academic units required:* 4 English, 3 math, 2 science, 2 science labs, 2 foreign language, 1 social studies, 2 history. *Academic units recommended:* 4 English, 4 math, 3 science, 3 science labs, 3 foreign language, 1 social studies, 3 history, 1 academic elective, 1 computer science. **Freshman Admission Statistics:** 6,046 applied, 73.90% admitted, 19% enrolled. **Transfer Admission Requirements:** High school transcript, college transcript(s), essay or personal statement, Minimum college GPA of 2.50 required. Lowest grade transferable C. **General Admission Information:** Application fee $50. Priority deadline 2/1. Regular application deadline 5/1. Nonfall registration accepted. Admission may be deferred for a maximum of One Year.

COSTS AND FINANCIAL AID
Annual tuition $42,550. Room and board $12,940. Required fees $500. Average book expense $900. **Required Forms and Deadlines:** FAFSA. **Notification of Awards:** Applicants will be notified of awards on a rolling basis beginning 2/1. **Types of Aid:** *Need-based scholarships/grants:* Federal Pell, FSEOG, State scholarships/grants, Private scholarships, College/university scholarship or grant aid from institutional funds. *Loans:* Direct Subsidized Stafford Loans, Direct Unsubsidized Stafford Loans, Direct PLUS loans, Federal Perkins Loans, State Loans. *Student Employment:* Federal Work-Study Program available. Institutional employment available. **Financial Aid Statistics:** 92% needy freshmen, 90% needy undergrads receive need-based scholarship or grant aid. 72% freshmen, 69% undergrads receive non-need-based scholarship or grant aid. 73% freshmen, 74% undergrads receive need-based self-help aid. 6% freshmen, 5% undergrads receive athletic scholarships. 89% freshmen, 84% undergrads receive any aid. Average cumulative indebtedness $36,123. **Criteria for awarding aid:** *Need-based:* Academics. *Non-need-based:* Academics, Athletics, Music/drama, State/district residency.

ST. JOHN FISHER COLLEGE

3690 East Avenue, Rochester, NY 14618-3597
Phone: 585-385-8064 • **Financial Aid Phone:** 585-385-8042
E-mail: admissions@sjfc.edu • **CEEB Code:** 2798
Fax: 585-385-8386 • **Website:** http://www.sjfc.edu/ • **ACT Code:** 2798

This private school, affiliated with the Roman Catholic Church, affiliated with the The College is guided by its Catholic heritage. Church, was founded in 1948. It has a 154-acre campus.

RATINGS
Admissions Selectivity Rating: 83   **Fire Safety Rating:** 92   **Green Rating:** 67

STUDENTS AND FACULTY
Enrollment: 2,757. **Student Body:** 60% female, 40% male, 3% out-of-state, <1% international (14 countries represented). Asian 4%, African American 4%, Caucasian 84%, Hispanic 4%, Native American <1%, Pacific Islander <1%, Two or more races 2%, Race unknown 2%.
Retention and Graduation: 84% freshmen return for sophomore year. 65% freshmen graduate within 4 years. 73% freshmen graduate within 6 years. **Faculty:** Student/faculty ratio 11:1. 237 full-time faculty, 90% hold PhDs, 17% are are members of minority groups, 54% are women. 0% of classes are taught by teaching assistants.

ACADEMICS
Degrees: bachelor's, certificate, doctoral/professional, doctoral/research, master's, postbachelor's certificate, post-master's certificate. **Classes:** Most classes have 20-29 students. Most lab/discussion sessions have 10-19 students. **Most popular majors:** Biology/Biological Sciences; Registered Nursing/Registered Nurse; Business Administration and Management. **Special Study Options:** Accelerated program, cross-registration, distance learning, double major, exchange student program (domestic), honors program, independent study, internships, liberal arts/career combination, student-designed major, study abroad, teacher certification program, weekend college. **Honors Programs:** St John Fisher College Honors Program; Science Scholars Program. **Disability Services:** Special programs offered to physically disabled students, including note-taking services, reader services, tape recorders, tutors. **Career Services:** Alumni network, Career/job search classes, Career assessment, Internships, Regional alumni.

FACILITIES
Housing: Coed dorms, special housing for disabled students, women's dorms. 100% of campus accessible to physically diasbled. **Special Academic**

Facilities/Equipment: Student Campus Center, State-of-the-Art Laboratories, Two Electron Microscopes, Multimedia Computer Lab, TV Studio Childcare Center (for observation and development), Cyber Cafe, Skalny Welcome Center Art Gallery **Computers:** 25% of classrooms, 100% of libraries, 50% of dining areas, 100% of student union, 10% of common outdoor areas have wireless network access. Students can register for classes online. Administrative functions (other than registration) can be performed online.

CAMPUS LIFE
Environment: City. **Activities:** Choral groups, dance, drama/theater, literary magazine, musical theater, student government, student newspaper, television station, yearbook, Campus Ministries. 70 registered organizations, 10 honor societies, 4 religious organizations. **Athletics (Intercollegiate):** *Men:* baseball, basketball, football, golf, lacrosse, soccer, tennis. *Women:* basketball, golf, lacrosse, soccer, softball, tennis, volleyball. **On-Campus Highlights:** Campus Center, Cyber Cafe, Golisano Gateway, Growney Stadium, Student Life Center. **Environmental Initiatives:** Commitment to buying local, fresh, organic produce and foods—http://www.sjfc.edu/student-life/dining/about/green.dot

ADMISSIONS
Freshman Academic Profile: Average high school GPA 3.6. 25% in top 10% of high school class, 53% in top 25% of high school class, 88% in top 50% of high school class. 92% from public high schools. **Reported SAT (pre-2016 redesign) scores:** SAT Math middle 50% range 490-590. SAT Critical Reading middle 50% range 480-560. SAT Writing middle 50% range 460-540. **Concordant SAT scores:** SAT EBRW middle 50% 530–610. SAT Math middle 50% range 520–610. ACT middle 50% range 22-26. Minimum internet-based TOEFL 80. Minimum paper TOEFL 550. **Basis for Candidate Selection:** *Very important factors considered include:* rigor of secondary school record, academic GPA, recommendation(s), character/personal qualities, alumni/ ae relation. *Important factors considered include:* class rank, standardized test scores, application essay, interview, extracurricular activities, talent/ ability, volunteer work, work experience, level of applicant's interest. *Other factors considered include:* first generation, geographical residence, state residency. **Freshman Admission Requirements:** High school diploma is required and GED is not accepted. *Academic units recommended:* 4 English, 4 math, 4 science, 3 foreign language, 4 social studies. **Freshman Admission Statistics:** 4,551 applied, 64.54% admitted, 20% enrolled. **Transfer Admission Requirements:** college transcript(s), statement of good standing from prior institution(s). Minimum college GPA of 2.0 required. Lowest grade transferable C. **General Admission Information:** Nonfall registration not accepted. Admission may be deferred for a maximum of 2 semesters.

COSTS AND FINANCIAL AID
Annual tuition $31,300. Room and board $11,740. Required fees $580. Average book expense $1,100. **Required Forms and Deadlines:** FAFSA, State aid form. **Notification of Awards:** Applicants will be notified of awards on a rolling basis beginning 3/15. **Types of Aid:** *Need-based scholarships/grants:* Federal Pell, FSEOG, State scholarships/grants, Private scholarships, College/university scholarship or grant aid from institutional funds, Federal Nursing Scholarships. *Loans:* Direct Subsidized Stafford Loans, Direct Unsubsidized Stafford Loans, Direct PLUS loans, Federal Perkins Loans. *Student Employment:* Federal Work-Study Program available. Institutional employment available. **Financial Aid Statistics:** 100% needy freshmen, 99% needy undergrads receive need-based scholarship or grant aid. 74% freshmen, 72% undergrads receive non-need-based scholarship or grant aid. 92% freshmen, 93% undergrads receive need-based self-help aid. 0% freshmen, 0% undergrads receive athletic scholarships. 99% freshmen, 99% undergrads receive any aid. 85% undergrads borrow to pay for school. Average cumulative indebtedness $35,925. **Criteria for awarding aid:** *Need-based:* Academics. *Non-need-based:* Academics, Leadership.

ST. JOHN'S COLLEGE

1160 Camino Cruz Blanca, Santa Fe, NM 87505
Phone: 505-984-6060 • **Financial Aid Phone:** 505-984-6058
E-mail: SantaFe.Admissions@sjc.edu • **CEEB Code:** 4737
Fax: 505-984-6162 • **Website:** www.sjc.edu • **ACT Code:** 2649

This private school was founded in 1696. It has a 250-acre campus.

RATINGS
Admissions Selectivity Rating: 87   **Fire Safety Rating:** 66   **Green Rating:** 73

STUDENTS AND FACULTY

Enrollment: 294. **Student Body:** 43% female, 57% male, 92% out-of-state, 22% international (27 countries represented). Asian 3%, African American <1%, Caucasian 66%, Hispanic 3%, Native American <1%, Pacific Islander 0%, Two or more races 4%, Race unknown 1%.

Retention and Graduation: 82% freshmen return for sophomore year. 42% freshmen graduate within 4 years. 47 12% grads go on to further study within 1 year. 12% grads pursue arts and sciences degrees. **Faculty:** Student/faculty ratio 8:1. 44 full-time faculty, 80% hold PhDs, 2% are are members of minority groups, 23% are women. 0% of classes are taught by teaching assistants.

ACADEMICS

Degrees: bachelor's, master's. **Classes:** Most classes have 10-19 students. **Special Study Options:** Accelerated program, internships. **Career Services:** Alumni network, Alumni services, Career/job search classes, Internships, Regional alumni. The Ariel Internship Program enables Santa Fe students to gain practical experience while exploring possible career fields. Internships have ranged from apprenticing with a custom guitar maker, to training in legal mediation, to teaching students aspiring to be the first in their families to attend college. Internship stipends are also available to students interested in medicine or biomedical careers. The Pathways Fellowships help St. John's students transition into graduate study or careers that call for special or prerequisite courses. Pathways Fellowships are available for summer study abroad (Global Pathways) and for summer study or attendance at professional conferences in the United States (General Pathways). With Pathways Fellowships students are able to enroll, for example, in teacher education courses for the pursuit of public school teaching, art classes in preparation of a portfolio, pre-medical or biomedical courses, or global education programs.

FACILITIES

Housing: Coed dorms, special housing for disabled students, men's dorms, women's dorms, apartments for married students, apartments for single students, Wellness Housing, Single-sex suites are available. 70% of campus accessible to physically disabled. **Special Academic Facilities/Equipment:** Art gallery. **Computers:** 75% of classrooms, 10% of dorms, 100% of dining areas, 100% of student union, 10% of common outdoor areas have wireless network access. Administrative functions (other than registration) can be performed online.

CAMPUS LIFE

Environment: City. **Activities:** Choral groups, concert band, dance, drama/theater, jazz band, literary magazine, music ensembles, musical theater, student government, student newspaper, student-run film society 27 registered organizations. **On-Campus Highlights:** Placita/Fish Pond, Student Activities Center, Great Hall, Coffee Shop, Levan Hall (new building). **Environmental Initiatives:** Paper, glass, plastic, cardboard recycling.

ADMISSIONS

Freshman Academic Profile: 26% in top 10% of high school class, 57% in top 25% of high school class, 88% in top 50% of high school class. 50% from public high schools. **Reported SAT (pre-2016 redesign) scores:** SAT Math middle 50% range 560-690. SAT Critical Reading middle 50% range 600-730. SAT Writing middle 50% range 570-680. **Concordant SAT scores:** SAT EBRW middle 50% 640–740. SAT Math middle 50% range 580–720. ACT middle 50% range 26-31. Minimum internet-based TOEFL 79. Minimum paper TOEFL 550. **Basis for Candidate Selection:** *Very important factors considered include:* application essay. *Important factors considered include:* rigor of secondary school record, recommendation(s), character/personal qualities, level of applicant's interest. *Other factors considered include:* class rank, academic GPA, standardized test scores, interview, extracurricular activities, talent/ability, first generation, alumni/ae relation, racial/ethnic status, volunteer work, work experience. **Freshman Admission Requirements:** High school diploma is required and GED is accepted. *Academic units required:* 3 math, 2 foreign language. *Academic units recommended:* 4 English, 4 math, 3 science, 3 science labs, 4 foreign language, 2 history. **Freshman Admission Statistics:** 177 applied, 81.36% admitted, 53% enrolled. **Transfer Admission Requirements:** High school transcript, college transcript(s), essay or personal statement. **General Admission Information:** Priority deadline 11/15. Nonfall registration accepted. Admission may be deferred for a maximum of 2 semesters.

COSTS AND FINANCIAL AID

Annual tuition $48,544. Room and board $11,162. Required fees $1,390. Average book expense $630. **Required Forms and Deadlines:** FAFSA. **Notification of Awards:** Applicants will be notified of awards on a rolling basis beginning 2/15. **Types of Aid:** *Need-based scholarships/grants:* Federal Pell, FSEOG, State scholarships/grants, Private scholarships, College/university scholarship or grant aid from institutional funds. *Loans:* Direct Subsidized Stafford Loans, Direct Unsubsidized Stafford Loans, Direct PLUS loans, Federal Perkins Loans, College/university loans from institutional funds. *Student Employment:* Federal Work-Study Program available. Institutional employment available. **Financial Aid Statistics:** 100% needy freshmen, 99% needy undergrads receive need-based scholarship or grant aid. 18% freshmen,

9% undergrads receive non-need-based scholarship or grant aid. 100% freshmen, 99% undergrads receive need-based self-help aid. 16% freshmen, 8% undergrads receive athletic scholarships. 100% freshmen, 81% undergrads receive any aid. 76% undergrads borrow to pay for school. Average cumulative indebtedness $26,195. **Criteria for awarding aid:** *Need-based:* Academics. *Non-need-based:* Academics.

ST. JOHN'S COLLEGE (MD)

60 College Avenue, Annapolis, MD 21401
Phone: 410-626-2522 • **Financial Aid Phone:** 410-295-6932
E-mail: Annapolis.Admissions@sjc.edu • **CEEB Code:** 5598
Fax: 410-269-7916 • **Website:** www.sjc.edu • **ACT Code:** 1732

This private school was founded in 1696. It has a 36-acre campus.

RATINGS

Admissions Selectivity Rating: 90   **Fire Safety Rating:** 97   **Green Rating:** 60*

STUDENTS AND FACULTY

Enrollment: 434. **Student Body:** 45% female, 55% male, 78% out-of-state, 18% international (14 countries represented). Asian 4%, African American 1%, Caucasian 69%, Hispanic 5%, Native American <1%, Pacific Islander 0%, Two or more races 2%, Race unknown <1%.

Retention and Graduation: 79% freshmen return for sophomore year. 70% freshmen graduate within 4 years. 76% freshmen graduate within 6 years. 14% grads go on to further study within 1 year. 12% grads pursue arts and sciences degrees. 1% grads pursue law degrees. **Faculty:** Student/faculty ratio 6:1. 73 full-time faculty, 88% hold PhDs, 8% are are members of minority groups, 30% are women. 0% of classes are taught by teaching assistants.

ACADEMICS

Degrees: bachelor's, master's. **Most popular majors:** Liberal Arts and Sciences/Liberal Studies. **Special Study Options:** internships, Students may spend one or more years at the college's Santa Fe, N.Mex., campus. **Disability Services:** Special programs offered to physically disabled students, including reader services, tape recorders. **Career Services:** Alumni network, Alumni services, Career/job search classes, Career assessment, Internships, Regional alumni. Hodson Internship is a competitive funding program that allows students to receive a stipend for internships which offer them a substantial opportunity to explore a career and learn related skills.

FACILITIES

Housing: Coed dorms, special housing for disabled students. 80% of campus accessible to physically disabled. **Special Academic Facilities/Equipment:** Art gallery, planetarium, pendulum, Ptolemy stone, Faraday cage, laboratories. **Computers:** 20% of dorms, 30% of common outdoor areas have wireless network access. Administrative functions (other than registration) can be performed online.

CAMPUS LIFE

Environment: Town. **Activities:** Choral groups, dance, drama/theater, literary magazine, music ensembles, student government, student newspaper, student-run film society, yearbook. 64 registered organizations, 3 religious organizations. **On-Campus Highlights:** Mitchell Art Gallery, Greenfiled Library, McDowell Hall, Caroll Barrister House, French Monument, The entire campus is a registered national landmark. **Environmental Initiatives:** purchasing renewable energy credits for 100% of our electric consumption

ADMISSIONS

Freshman Academic Profile: Average high school GPA 3.5. 33% in top 10% of high school class, 64% in top 25% of high school class, 88% in top 50% of high school class. 47% from public high schools. **Reported SAT (pre-2016 redesign) scores:** SAT Math middle 50% range 570-710. SAT Critical Reading middle 50% range 610-730. SAT Writing middle 50% range 600-700. **Concordant SAT scores:** SAT EBRW middle 50% 660–740. SAT Math middle 50% range 590–740. ACT middle 50% range 27-33. **Basis for Candidate Selection:** *Very important factors considered include:* application essay. *Important factors considered include:* rigor of secondary school record, recommendation(s), character/personal qualities, level of applicant's interest. *Other factors considered include:* class rank, academic GPA, standardized test scores, interview, extracurricular activities, talent/ability, first generation, alumni/ae relation, geographical residence, racial/ethnic status, volunteer work, work experience. **Freshman Admission Requirements:** High school diploma is required and GED is accepted. *Academic units recommended:* 4 English, 3 science, 3 social studies. **Freshman Admission Statistics:** 612 applied, 53.27% admitted, 39% enrolled. **Transfer Admission Requirements:** High school transcript, college transcript(s), essay or personal statement. **General Admission Information:** Priority deadline 11/15. Nonfall registration not accepted. Admission may be deferred for a maximum of 1 year.

COSTS AND FINANCIAL AID

Annual tuition $51,200. Room and board $12,233. Required fees $470. Average book expense $630. **Required Forms and Deadlines:** FAFSA, State aid form. **Notification of Awards:** Applicants will be notified of awards on a rolling basis beginning 12/15. **Types of Aid:** *Need-based scholarships/grants:* Federal Pell, FSEOG, State scholarships/grants, Private scholarships, College/university scholarship or grant aid from institutional funds. *Loans:* Direct Subsidized Stafford Loans, Direct Unsubsidized Stafford Loans, Direct PLUS loans, Federal Perkins Loans, College/university loans from institutional funds. *Student Employment:* Federal Work-Study Program available. Institutional employment available. **Financial Aid Statistics:** 99% needy freshmen, 98% needy undergrads receive need-based scholarship or grant aid. 27% freshmen, 19% undergrads receive non-need-based scholarship or grant aid. 96% freshmen, 97% undergrads receive need-based self-help aid. 0% freshmen, 0% undergrads receive athletic scholarships. 82% freshmen, 71% undergrads receive any aid. 83% undergrads borrow to pay for school. Average cumulative indebtedness $18,165. **Criteria for awarding aid:** *Non-need-based:* Academics.

ST. JOHN'S UNIVERSITY

Best Colleges

8000 Utopia Parkway, Queens, NY 11439
Phone: 718-990-2000 • **Financial Aid Phone:** 718-990-2000
E-mail: admhelp@stjohns.edu • **CEEB Code:** 2799
Fax: 718-990-2096 • **Website:** www.stjohns.edu • **ACT Code:** 2888

This private school, affiliated with the Roman Catholic Church, was founded in 1870. It has a 122-acre campus.

RATINGS

Admissions Selectivity Rating: 85   **Fire Safety Rating:** 94   **Green Rating:** 95

STUDENTS AND FACULTY

Enrollment: 11,768. **Student Body:** 56% female, 44% male, 27% out-of-state, 6% international (106 countries represented). Asian 17%, African American 17%, Caucasian 37%, Hispanic 10%, Native American <1%, Pacific Islander <1%, Two or more races 5%, Race unknown 8%.
Retention and Graduation: 84% freshmen return for sophomore year. 37% freshmen graduate within 4 years. 58% freshmen graduate within 6 years. 19% grads go on to further study within 1 year. 33% grads pursue arts and sciences degrees. 7% grads pursue law degrees. 27% grads pursue business degrees. 13% grads pursue medical degrees. **Faculty:** Student/faculty ratio 17:1. 627 full-time faculty, 93% hold PhDs, 26% are are members of minority groups, 44% are women. 0% of classes are taught by teaching assistants.

ACADEMICS

Degrees: associate, bachelor's, certificate, doctoral/professional, doctoral/research, master's, postbachelor's certificate, post-master's certificate.
Classes: Most classes have 20-29 students. Most lab/discussion sessions have 20-29 students. **Most popular majors:** Pharmacy; Biology/Biological Sciences. **Special Study Options:** Accelerated program, cross-registration, distance learning, double major, dual enrollment, English as a Second Language (ESL), honors program, independent study, internships, liberal arts/career combination, study abroad, teacher certification program, weekend college.
Honors Programs: The University Honors Program is available to qualified incoming freshmen. The program primarily comprises honors versions of the courses which are part of the core curriculum. Honors students must complete 30 credits of honors-designated courses to complete the program. Additional options for obtaining honors credits are also available. The program also features a range of special activities and events. Combined degree programs: BA/JD, BA/MA, BS/MA; BS/MS; BS/MBA; BS/OD; BS/JD; MBA/JD.
Disability Services: Special programs offered to physically disabled students, including note-taking services, reader services, tape recorders, tutors. **Career Services:** Alumni network, Alumni services, Career/job search classes, Career assessment, Internships. University Career Services prides itself on efforts to provide access and opportunity to connect with alumni and employers

mentors through a comprehensive and developmentally appropriate offering of programs. The C3: Creating Career Connections program includes three opportunities for students to explore careers with intent to equip them the knowledge necessary to make informed major/career choices. From Career Conversations (informational interviews via phone/skype) to Job Shadowing and Career Immersion which match students for on-site experiences for 1-3 days, the program focuses on first and second year students. Further, Career Services provides third-year students with an opportunity to be matched one-on-one with a successful young alumni mentor within their aspirant industry through the ASPIRE Mentor Program. This year-long commitment provides virtual, in-person and group opportunities for achievement-oriented career mentorship and professional development and is aimed at developing in-demand skills and competencies within our students.

FACILITIES

Housing: Coed dorms, apartments for single students, ThemeHousingSome off-campus apartments are available on a limited basis. 90% of campus accessible to physically diasbled. **Special Academic Facilities/Equipment:** University Gallery; Instuctional Media Center; Institute of Asian Studies; Health Education Resource Center; Center for Psychological Services; TV Center; Speech and Hearing Center and Reading and Writing Education Center. **Computers:** 100% of classrooms, 90% of dorms, 100% of libraries, 100% of dining areas, 100% of student union, 100% of common outdoor areas have wireless network access. Students can register for classes online. Administrative functions (other than registration) can be performed online. Undergraduates are required to own a computer.

CAMPUS LIFE

Environment: Metropolis. **Activities:** Choral groups, dance, drama/theater, jazz band, literary magazine, music ensembles, musical theater, pep band, radio station, student government, student newspaper, television station, yearbook, Campus Ministries. 180 registered organizations. **Athletics (Intercollegiate):** *Men:* baseball, basketball, fencing, golf, lacrosse, soccer, softball, table tennis, tennis, volleyball, weight lifting. *Women:* basketball, cross-country, fencing, soccer, softball, table tennis, tennis, track/field (outdoor), track/field (indoor), volleyball, weight lifting. **On-Campus Highlights:** The Great Lawn, D'Angelo Center, The University Library. **Environmental Initiatives:** Senior management signed the NYC Mayoral Challenge committing to 30% reduction in carbon emissions by the year 2017.

ADMISSIONS

Freshman Academic Profile: 18% in top 10% of high school class, 45% in top 25% of high school class, 77% in top 50% of high school class. 52% from public high schools. **Reported SAT (pre-2016 redesign) scores:** SAT Math middle 50% range 490-600. SAT Critical Reading middle 50% range 480-580. **Concordant SAT scores:** SAT Math middle 50% range 520–620. ACT middle 50% range 22-28. Minimum internet-based TOEFL 80. Minimum paper TOEFL 550. **Basis for Candidate Selection:** *Very important factors considered include:* academic GPA, standardized test scores. *Important factors considered include:* rigor of secondary school record. *Other factors considered include:* class rank, application essay, recommendation(s), extracurricular activities, talent/ability, character/personal qualities, first generation, alumni/ae relation, geographical residence, state residency, volunteer work, work experience. **Freshman Admission Requirements:** High school diploma is required and GED is accepted. *Academic units required:* 4 English, 1 science, 1 history. *Academic units recommended:* 4 English, 1 science, 1 history. **Freshman Admission Statistics:** 28,590 applied, 63.36% admitted, 18% enrolled. **Transfer Admission Requirements:** college transcript(s), Lowest grade transferable C. **General Admission Information:** Application fee $50. Nonfall registration accepted. Admission may be deferred for a maximum of 1 year.

COSTS AND FINANCIAL AID

Annual tuition $38,630. Room and board $16,760. Required fees $830. Average book expense $615. **Required Forms and Deadlines:** FAFSA. **Notification of Awards:** Applicants will be notified of awards on a rolling basis beginning 3/1. **Types of Aid:** *Need-based scholarships/grants:* Federal Pell, FSEOG, State scholarships/grants, Private scholarships, College/university scholarship or grant aid from institutional funds. *Loans:* Direct Subsidized Stafford Loans, Direct Unsubsidized Stafford Loans, Direct PLUS loans, Federal Perkins Loans. *Student Employment:* Federal Work-Study Program available. Institutional employment available. **Financial Aid Statistics:** 80% needy freshmen, 78% needy undergrads receive need-based scholarship or grant aid. 94% undergrads receive non-need-based scholarship or grant aid. 70% freshmen, 71% undergrads receive need-based self-help aid. 2% freshmen, 2% undergrads receive athletic scholarships. 98% freshmen, 96% undergrads receive any aid. 74% undergrads borrow to pay for school. Average cumulative indebtedness $34,234. **Criteria for awarding aid:** *Non-need-based:* Academics, Alumni affiliation, Art, Athletics, Leadership, Music/drama, Religious affiliation.

ST. JOSEPH'S COLLEGE

245 Clinton Avenue, Brooklyn, NY 11205
Phone: 718-940-5800 • **Financial Aid Phone:** 631-687-2611
E-mail: brooklynas@sjcny.edu
Fax: 718-636-8303 • **Website:** www.sjcny.edu • **ACT Code:** 2923

This is a private school.

RATINGS
Admissions Selectivity Rating: 74   **Fire Safety Rating:** 60*   **Green Rating:** 60*

STUDENTS AND FACULTY
Enrollment: 953. **Student Body:** 67% female, 33% male, 4% out-of-state, 0% international (22 countries represented). Asian 7%, African American 24%, Caucasian 39%, Hispanic 20%, Native American <1%, Pacific Islander <1%, Two or more races 2%, Race unknown 9%.
Retention and Graduation: 81% freshmen return for sophomore year. 55% freshmen graduate within 4 years. 67% freshmen graduate within 6 years. **Faculty:** Student/faculty ratio 11:1. 58 full-time faculty, 81% hold PhDs, 19% are are members of minority groups, 41% are women. 0% of classes are taught by teaching assistants.

ACADEMICS
Degrees: bachelor's, certificate, master's. **Classes:** Most classes have fewer than 10 students. Most lab/discussion sessions have fewer than 10 students. **Most popular majors:** Business Administration and Management; Special Education and Teaching; Psychology. **Special Study Options:** Accelerated program, honors program, independent study, internships, teacher certification program, weekend college, Biomedical Program with New York College of Podiatric medicine. **Honors Programs:** Freshman Honors Program provides enriched inter-disciplinary courses. Capstone course includes a travel or global studies component. Honors indicated on transcript. Combined degree programs: BS/MS; BS/MBA. **Disability Services:** Special programs offered to physically disabled students, including note-taking services, reader services, tape recorders. **Career Services:** Alumni network, Alumni services, Career assessment, Internships.

FACILITIES
Housing: 40% of campus accessible to physically diasbled. **Special Academic Facilities/Equipment:** Clare Rose Playhouse. **Computers:** Students can register for classes online.

CAMPUS LIFE
Activities: Choral groups, dance, drama/theater, literary magazine, musical theater, student government, student newspaper, yearbook, Campus Ministries. 34 registered organizations, 8 honor societies, 2 religious organizations. 2 fraternities, 2 sororities. **On-Campus Highlights:** Athletic Center with pool, Eagles Nest Cafeteria, Student Lounge, Quad Area, Clare Rose Playhouse.

ADMISSIONS
Freshman Academic Profile: Average high school GPA 3.3. 60% from public high schools. **Reported SAT (pre-2016 redesign) scores:** SAT Math middle 50% range 433-520. SAT Critical Reading middle 50% range 413-510. SAT Writing middle 50% range 420-520. **Concordant SAT scores:** SAT EBRW middle 50% 460–570. SAT Math middle 50% range 470–550. ACT middle 50% range 19-24. Minimum internet-based TOEFL 79. Minimum paper TOEFL 550. **Basis for Candidate Selection:** *Very important factors considered include:* academic GPA, standardized test scores. *Important factors considered include:* rigor of secondary school record, class rank, application essay, recommendation(s), character/personal qualities. *Other factors considered include:* interview, extracurricular activities, talent/ability, alumni/ae relation, volunteer work, work experience, level of applicant's interest. **Freshman Admission Requirements:** High school diploma is required and GED is accepted. *Academic units required:* 4 English, 3 math, 3 science, 2 foreign language, 4 social studies, 2 academic electives. *Academic units recommended:* 3 foreign language. **Freshman Admission Statistics:** 1,903 applied, 62.06% admitted, 17% enrolled. **Transfer Admission Requirements:** college transcript(s), interview, statement of good standing from prior institution(s). Minimum college GPA of 2.0 required. **General Admission Information:** Application fee $25. Nonfall registration accepted. Admission may be deferred for a maximum of 1 year.

COSTS AND FINANCIAL AID
Annual tuition $25,930. Required fees $614. **Required Forms and Deadlines:** FAFSA, Institution's own financial aid form, State aid form. **Notification of Awards:** Applicants will be notified of awards on a rolling basis beginning 3/15. **Types of Aid:** *Need-based scholarships/grants:* Federal Pell, FSEOG, State scholarships/grants, Private scholarships, College/university scholarship or grant aid from institutional funds. *Loans:* Direct Subsidized Stafford Loans, Direct Unsubsidized Stafford Loans, Direct PLUS loans, Federal Perkins Loans. *Student Employment:* Federal Work-Study Program available. Institutional employment available. **Financial Aid Statistics:** 100% needy freshmen, 99% needy undergrads receive need-based scholarship or grant aid. 99% freshmen, 89% undergrads receive non-need-based scholarship or grant aid. 59% freshmen, 57% undergrads receive need-based self-help aid. 0% freshmen, 0% undergrads receive athletic scholarships. 62% freshmen, 63% undergrads receive any aid. 45% undergrads borrow to pay for school. Average cumulative indebtedness $23,124. **Criteria for awarding aid:** *Non-need-based:* Academics, Alumni affiliation.

ST. JOSEPH'S COLLEGE, NEW YORK (PATCHOGUE)

155 West Roe Blvd, Patchogue, NY 11772
Phone: 631-687-4500 • **Financial Aid Phone:** 631-687-2611
E-mail: longislandas@sjcny.edu • **CEEB Code:** 2802
Fax: 631-447-3601 • **Website:** www.sjcny.edu • **ACT Code:** 2923

This private school was founded in 1916. It has a 30-acre campus.

RATINGS
Admissions Selectivity Rating: 75   **Fire Safety Rating:** 60*   **Green Rating:** 67

STUDENTS AND FACULTY
Enrollment: 3,031. **Student Body:** 66% female, 34% male, 1% out-of-state, 0% international (22 countries represented). Asian 2%, African American 5%, Caucasian 68%, Hispanic 11%, Native American <1%, Pacific Islander <1%, Two or more races 2%, Race unknown 12%.
Retention and Graduation: 87% freshmen return for sophomore year. 59% freshmen graduate within 4 years. 75% freshmen graduate within 6 years. **Faculty:** Student/faculty ratio 15:1. 107 full-time faculty, 79% hold PhDs, 5% are are members of minority groups, 60% are women. 0% of classes are taught by teaching assistants.

ACADEMICS
Degrees: bachelor's, certificate, master's. **Classes:** Most classes have 10-19 students. **Most popular majors:** Special Education and Teaching; Business Administration and Management; Accounting. **Special Study Options:** Accelerated program, cross-registration, double major, honors program, internships, liberal arts/career combination, study abroad, teacher certification program, weekend college. **Honors Programs:** Freshman Honors Program provides enriched inter-disciplinary courses. Capstone course includes a travel or global studies component. Honors indicated on transcript. Combined degree programs: BA/MA; BS/MBA; BS/MS; BS/MA. **Disability Services:** Special programs offered to physically disabled students, including note-taking services, reader services, tape recorders. **Career Services:** Alumni network, Alumni services, Career/job search classes, Career assessment, Internships. Both are run through the Academic Departments and Experiential Learning.

FACILITIES
Housing: 100% of campus accessible to physically diasbled. **Special Academic Facilities/Equipment:** Clare Rose Playhouse **Computers:** Students can register for classes online.

CAMPUS LIFE
Environment: Town. **Activities:** Choral groups, dance, drama/theater, jazz band, literary magazine, music ensembles, musical theater, student government, student newspaper, yearbook, Campus Ministries. 34 registered organizations, 8 honor societies, 2 religious organizations. 2 fraternities, 2 sororities. **Athletics (Intercollegiate):** *Men:* baseball, basketball, cross-country, golf, soccer, tennis, track/field (outdoor). *Women:* basketball, cross-country, equestrian sports, soccer, softball, swimming, tennis, track/field (outdoor), volleyball. **On-Campus Highlights:** Athletic Center with pool, Eagles Nest Cafeteria, Student Lounge, Quad Area, Clare Rose Playhouse.

ADMISSIONS
Freshman Academic Profile: Average high school GPA 3.6. 91% from public high schools. **Reported SAT (pre-2016 redesign) scores:** SAT Math middle 50% range 480-580. SAT Critical Reading middle 50% range 470-560. SAT Writing middle 50% range 450-560. **Concordant SAT scores:** SAT EBRW middle 50% 510–620. SAT Math middle 50% range 510–600. ACT middle 50% range 21-25. Minimum internet-based TOEFL 79. Minimum paper TOEFL 550. **Basis for Candidate Selection:** *Very important factors considered include:* rigor of secondary school record, class rank, academic GPA. *Important factors considered include:* standardized test scores, application essay, recommendation(s), interview, extracurricular activities, character/personal qualities. *Other factors considered include:* talent/ability, first generation, alumni/ae relation, volunteer work, work experience, level of applicant's

interest. **Freshman Admission Requirements:** High school diploma is required and GED is accepted. *Academic units required:* 4 English, 3 math, 3 science, 3 science labs, 2 foreign language, 4 social studies, 3 academic electives, 2 visual/performing arts. *Academic units recommended:* 4 English, 4 math, 4 science, 4 science labs, 3 foreign language, 4 social studies, 4 academic electives, 2 visual/performing arts. **Freshman Admission Statistics:** 1,770 applied, 71.86% admitted, 34% enrolled. **Transfer Admission Requirements:** college transcript(s), Minimum college GPA of 2.0 required. **General Admission Information:** Application fee $25. Nonfall registration accepted. Admission may be deferred for a maximum of 1 years.

COSTS AND FINANCIAL AID

Annual tuition $25,930. Required fees $624. **Required Forms and Deadlines:** FAFSA, Institution's own financial aid form, State aid form. **Notification of Awards:** Applicants will be notified of awards on or about 3/15. **Types of Aid:** *Need-based scholarships/grants:* Federal Pell, FSEOG, State scholarships/grants, Private scholarships, College/university scholarship or grant aid from institutional funds. *Loans:* Direct Subsidized Stafford Loans, Direct Unsubsidized Stafford Loans, Direct PLUS loans, Federal Perkins Loans. *Student Employment:* Federal Work-Study Program available. Institutional employment available. **Financial Aid Statistics:** 78% needy freshmen, 96% needy undergrads receive need-based scholarship or grant aid. 98% freshmen, 87% undergrads receive non-need-based scholarship or grant aid. 63% freshmen, 67% undergrads receive need-based self-help aid. 0% freshmen, 0% undergrads receive athletic scholarships. 62% freshmen, 63% undergrads receive any aid. 66% undergrads borrow to pay for school. Average cumulative indebtedness $27,364. **Criteria for awarding aid:** *Non-need-based:* Academics, Alumni affiliation.

See page 1048.

ST. LAWRENCE UNIVERSITY

23 Romoda Drive, Canton, NY 13617
Phone: 315-229-5261 • **Financial Aid Phone:** 315-229-5265
E-mail: admissions@stlawu.edu • **CEEB Code:** 2805
Fax: 315-229-5818 • **Website:** www.stlawu.edu • **ACT Code:** 2896

This private school was founded in 1856. It has a 1000-acre campus.

RATINGS

Admissions Selectivity Rating: 91 **Fire Safety Rating:** 81 **Green Rating:** 68

STUDENTS AND FACULTY

Enrollment: 2,344. **Student Body:** 55% female, 45% male, 59% out-of-state, 8% international (62 countries represented). Asian 2%, African American 3%, Caucasian 79%, Hispanic 4%, Native American <1%, Pacific Islander <1%, Two or more races 2%, Race unknown 1%.
Retention and Graduation: 90% freshmen return for sophomore year. 81% freshmen graduate within 4 years. 84% freshmen graduate within 6 years. 18% grads go on to further study within 1 year. 6% grads pursue arts and sciences degrees. 1% grads pursue law degrees. 2% grads pursue business degrees. 3% grads pursue medical degrees. **Faculty:** Student/faculty ratio 11:1. 176 full-time faculty, 99% hold PhDs, 15% are are members of minority groups, 49% are women. 0% of classes are taught by teaching assistants.

ACADEMICS

Degrees: bachelor's, master's, post-master's certificate. **Classes:** Most classes have 10-19 students. Most lab/discussion sessions have 10-19 students. **Most popular majors:** Biology/Biological Sciences; Psychology; Economics. **Special Study Options:** cross-registration, double major, exchange student program (domestic), independent study, internships, student-designed major, study abroad, teacher certification program, Community-based learning. **Honors Programs:** The University Fellows program offers a $3500 stipend plus room for summer research on campus. This is a competitive program for students who wish to undertake a serious, independent academic project as their summer employment. Combined degree programs: 4+1 Business Program; 3+2 Nursing; 3+4 doctor of Pharmacy; 4+2 Physicians Assistant; 4+4, doctor of physical therapy. **Disability Services:** Special programs offered to physically disabled students, including note-taking services, reader services, tape recorders, tutors. **Career Services:** Alumni network, Alumni services, Career/job search classes, Career assessment, Internships.

FACILITIES

Housing: Coed dorms, special housing for disabled students, special housing for international students, women's dorms, fraternity/sorority housing, apartments for single students, Theme Housing. 60% of campus accessible to physically diasbled. **Special Academic Facilities/Equipment:** Art gallery, arts technology center, language lab, center for international education, environmental research facility, 76-acre forest preserve, two electron microscopes, microscopy and sleep labs, Neuroscience lab, sustainability lab **Computers:** 100% of classrooms, 100% of dorms, 100% of libraries, 100% of dining areas, 100% of student union, 100% of common outdoor areas have wireless network access. Students can register for classes online. Administrative functions (other than registration) can be performed online.

CAMPUS LIFE

Environment: Village. **Activities:** Choral groups, concert band, dance, drama/theater, jazz band, literary magazine, music ensembles, radio station, student government, student newspaper, student-run film society, yearbook, Campus Ministries, Student Organization, Model UN. 117 registered organizations, 22 honor societies, 4 religious organizations. 2 fraternities, 4 sororities. **Athletics (Intercollegiate):** *Men:* baseball, basketball, crew/rowing, cross-country, equestrian sports, football, golf, ice hockey, lacrosse, skiing (downhill/alpine), skiing (nordic/cross-country), soccer, squash, swimming, tennis, track/field (outdoor), track/field (indoor). *Women:* basketball, crew/rowing, cross-country, equestrian sports, field hockey, golf, ice hockey, lacrosse, skiing (downhill/alpine), skiing (nordic/cross-country), soccer, softball, squash, swimming, tennis, track/field (outdoor), track/field (indoor), volleyball. **On-Campus Highlights:** Newell Field House, Brewer Bookstore, Johnson Hall of Science, Owen D. Young Library, Student Center, Student Center opened January 2004, Newell Center for Arts Technology opened 2007, LEED Gold Johnson Hall of Science opened fall 2007. **Environmental Initiatives:** Pledge of climate neutrality.

ADMISSIONS

Freshman Academic Profile: Average high school GPA 3.5. 45% in top 10% of high school class, 77% in top 25% of high school class, 92% in top 50% of high school class. 67% from public high schools. **Reported SAT (pre-2016 redesign) scores:** SAT Math middle 50% range 560-650. SAT Critical Reading middle 50% range 550-650. SAT Writing middle 50% range 540-650. **Concordant SAT scores:** SAT EBRW middle 50% 600–700. SAT Math middle 50% range 580–670. ACT middle 50% range 25-30. Minimum internet-based TOEFL 82. Minimum paper TOEFL 600. **Basis for Candidate Selection:** *Very important factors considered include:* rigor of secondary school record, academic GPA, application essay, recommendation(s), character/personal qualities. *Important factors considered include:* class rank, interview, extracurricular activities, racial/ethnic status. *Other factors considered include:* standardized test scores, talent/ability, first generation, alumni/ae relation, geographical residence, volunteer work, work experience, level of applicant's interest. **Freshman Admission Requirements:** High school diploma is required and GED is accepted. *Academic units recommended:* 4 English, 4 math, 4 science, 4 foreign language, 2 social studies, 2 history. **Freshman Admission Statistics:** 5,874 applied, 42.88% admitted, 22% enrolled. **Transfer Admission Requirements:** High school transcript, college transcript(s), essay or personal statement, statement of good standing from prior institution(s). Lowest grade transferable C. **General Admission Information:** Application fee $60. Regular application deadline 2/1. Nonfall registration accepted. Admission may be deferred for a maximum of 1 year.

COSTS AND FINANCIAL AID

Annual tuition $50,830. Room and board $13,190. Required fees $370. Average book expense $750. **Required Forms and Deadlines:** FAFSA, Noncustodial PROFILE. **Notification of Awards:** Applicants will be notified of awards on or about 3/30. **Types of Aid:** *Need-based scholarships/grants:* Federal Pell, FSEOG, State scholarships/grants, Private scholarships, College/university scholarship or grant aid from institutional funds. *Loans:* Direct Subsidized Stafford Loans, Direct Unsubsidized Stafford Loans, Direct PLUS loans, Federal Perkins Loans, College/university loans from institutional funds. *Student Employment:* Federal Work-Study Program available. Institutional employment available. **Financial Aid Statistics:** 100% needy freshmen, 100% needy undergrads receive need-based scholarship or grant aid. 74% freshmen, 70% undergrads receive non-need-based scholarship or grant aid. 70% freshmen, 74% undergrads receive need-based self-help aid. 2% freshmen, 2% undergrads receive athletic scholarships. 100% freshmen, 96% undergrads receive any aid. 58% undergrads borrow to pay for school. Average cumulative indebtedness $37,919. **Criteria for awarding aid:** *Need-based:* Academics, Minority status. *Non-need-based:* Academics, Alumni affiliation, Leadership, Minority status.

See page 1050.

ST. LOUIS COLLEGE OF PHARMACY

4588 Parkview Place, St. Louis, MO 63110
Phone: 314-367-8700
E-mail: connie.horrall@stlcop.edu • **CEEB Code:** 6626
Fax: 314-446-8310 • **Website:** www.stlcop.edu • **ACT Code:** 2346

This private school was founded in 1864. It has a 7-acre campus.

RATINGS

Admissions Selectivity Rating: 87   **Fire Safety Rating:** 77   **Green Rating:** 60*

STUDENTS AND FACULTY

Enrollment: 477. **Student Body:** 60% female, 40% male, 53% out-of-state, 1% international. Asian 22%, African American 5%, Caucasian 66%, Hispanic 1%, Native American <1%, Pacific Islander <1%, Two or more races 1%, Race unknown 4%.
Retention and Graduation: 92% freshmen return for sophomore year. 65% freshmen graduate within 6 years. **Faculty:** Student/faculty ratio 13:1. 91 full-time faculty, 100% hold PhDs, 9% are are members of minority groups, 47% are women.

ACADEMICS

Degrees: doctoral/professional. **Career Services:** Alumni services, Internships.

FACILITIES

Housing: Coed dorms, fraternity/sorority housing, apartments for single students.

CAMPUS LIFE

Activities: Choral groups, concert band, drama/theater, literary magazine, musical theater, student government, student newspaper, Campus Ministries. 2 honor societies, 6 religious organizations. 5 fraternities. **Athletics (Intercollegiate):** *Men:* basketball, cheerleading, cross-country. *Women:* cheerleading, cross-country, volleyball.

ADMISSIONS

Freshman Academic Profile: Average high school GPA 3.7. 50% in top 10% of high school class, 33% in top 25% of high school class, 17% in top 50% of high school class. **Reported SAT (pre-2016 redesign) scores:** SAT Math middle 50% range 640-730. SAT Critical Reading middle 50% range 570-660. **Concordant SAT scores:** SAT Math middle 50% range 660–760. ACT middle 50% range 25-29. Minimum paper TOEFL 550. **Basis for Candidate Selection:** *Very important factors considered include:* rigor of secondary school record, academic GPA, standardized test scores, application essay, recommendation(s), level of applicant's interest. *Other factors considered include:* class rank, extracurricular activities, character/personal qualities, alumni/ae relation, volunteer work, work experience. **Freshman Admission Requirements:** High school diploma is required and GED is accepted. *Academic units required:* 4 English, 4 math, 3 science, 2 science labs. *Academic units recommended:* 3 science. **Freshman Admission Statistics:** 555 applied, 62.70% admitted, 71% enrolled. **Transfer Admission Requirements:** college transcript(s), essay or personal statement, standardized test scores, Minimum college GPA of 3.0 required. Lowest grade transferable C. **General Admission Information:** Application fee $50. Priority deadline 12/15. Regular application deadline 2/1. Regular notification 3/1. Nonfall registration not accepted.

COSTS AND FINANCIAL AID

Annual tuition $26,736. Room and board $9,555. Required fees $325. Average book expense $1,500. **Required Forms and Deadlines:** FAFSA. **Notification of Awards:** Applicants will be notified of awards on a rolling basis beginning 2/19. **Types of Aid:** *Need-based scholarships/grants:* Federal Pell, FSEOG, State scholarships/grants, Private scholarships, College/university scholarship or grant aid from institutional funds. *Loans:* Direct Subsidized Stafford Loans, Direct Unsubsidized Stafford Loans, Direct PLUS loans, Federal Perkins Loans. *Student Employment:* Federal Work-Study Program available. Institutional employment available. **Financial Aid Statistics:** 99% needy freshmen, 90% needy undergrads receive need-based scholarship or grant aid. 9% freshmen, 5% undergrads receive non-need-based scholarship or grant aid. 83% freshmen, 91% undergrads receive need-based self-help aid. 4% freshmen, 2% undergrads receive athletic scholarships. **Criteria for awarding aid:** *Need-based:* Academics, Athletics, Job skills, Minority status. *Non-need-based:* Academics, Athletics, Job skills, State/district residency.

ST. MARY'S COLLEGE OF MARYLAND

47645 College Drive, St. Marys City, MD 20686-3001
Phone: 240-895-5000 • **Financial Aid Phone:** 240-895-3000
E-mail: admissions@smcm.edu • **CEEB Code:** 5601
Fax: 240-895-5001 • **Website:** www.smcm.edu • **ACT Code:** 1736

This public school was founded in 1840. It has a 319-acre campus.

RATINGS

Admissions Selectivity Rating: 81   **Fire Safety Rating:** 88   **Green Rating:** 97

STUDENTS AND FACULTY

Enrollment: 1,618. **Student Body:** 57% female, 43% male, 7% out-of-state, <1% international (12 countries represented). Asian 4%, African American 9%, Caucasian 69%, Hispanic 9%, Native American <1%, Pacific Islander 0%, Two or more races 5%, Race unknown 4%.
Retention and Graduation: 87% freshmen return for sophomore year. 65% freshmen graduate within 4 years. 73% freshmen graduate within 6 years. 46% grads go on to further study within 1 year. **Faculty:** Student/faculty ratio 10:1. 141 full-time faculty, 98% hold PhDs, 14% are are members of minority groups, 48% are women. 0% of classes are taught by teaching assistants.

ACADEMICS

Degrees: bachelor's, master's. **Classes:** Most classes have 10-19 students. Most lab/discussion sessions have 10-19 students. **Most popular majors:** Biology/Biological Sciences; Psychology; Economics. **Special Study Options:** double major, dual enrollment, exchange student program (domestic), honors program, independent study, internships, student-designed major, study abroad, teacher certification program. **Honors Programs:** Nitze Scholars Program. **Disability Services:** Special programs offered to physically disabled students, including note-taking services, reader services, tape recorders, tutors. **Career Services:** Alumni network, Alumni services, Career/job search classes, Career assessment, Internships, Regional alumni. The MicroInternship program is a career exploration program that pairs students with alumni and community members for 1-2 days of hands on experience.

FACILITIES

Housing: Coed dorms, special housing for disabled students, men's dorms, women's dorms, apartments for single students, Wellness Housing, ThemeHousingThere are a variety of different housing options at SMCM. Townhouses for upper-class students as well as suites are offered. There is also special interest housing (ex. SAFE house which is substance and alcohol free housing) and living learning centers (ex. international house, Women in Science House (WiSH), eco-house). 80% of campus accessible to physically diasbled. **Special Academic Facilities/Equipment:** Art gallery, archaeological sites, Historic St. Mary's City, historic state house of early Maryland settlers, electron microscope, freshwater and saltwater research facilities, research boat. **Computers:** 100% of classrooms, 20% of dorms, 100% of libraries, 100% of dining areas, 100% of student union, 100% of common outdoor areas have wireless network access. Students can register for classes online. Administrative functions (other than registration) can be performed online.

CAMPUS LIFE

Environment: Rural. **Activities:** Choral groups, dance, drama/theater, jazz band, literary magazine, music ensembles, musical theater, radio station, student government, student newspaper, symphony orchestra, television station, yearbook, Campus Ministries, Student Organization. 117 registered organizations, 8 honor societies, 4 religious organizations. **Athletics (Intercollegiate):** *Men:* baseball, basketball, cross-country, lacrosse, sailing, soccer, swimming, tennis. *Women:* basketball, cross-country, field hockey, lacrosse, sailing, soccer, swimming, tennis, volleyball. **On-Campus Highlights:** Student Center, Library, Athletics and Recreation Center (ARC), Waterfront, Garden of Remembrance. **Environmental Initiatives:** In 2007, students voted overwhelmingly (94%) to increase student fees $25 to purchase renewable energy credits (RECs) to offset 100% of the College annual purchased electrical consumption. In the last two years the College has been able to increase its purchase of renewable energy credits by 15% allowing the school to offset over 85% of GHG emissions from campus buildings. Last year, students also voted to begin "Meatless Mondays," a schoolwide effort to reduce carbon usage of students by encouraging vegetarianism and minimizing meat options on Mondays.

ADMISSIONS

Freshman Academic Profile: Average high school GPA 3.3. 75% from public high schools. **Reported SAT (pre-2016 redesign) scores:** SAT Math middle

50% range 490-610. SAT Critical Reading middle 50% range 510-640. SAT Writing middle 50% range 490-600. **Concordant SAT scores:** SAT EBRW middle 50% 560–670. SAT Math middle 50% range 520–630. ACT middle 50% range 23-29. Minimum internet-based TOEFL 90. Minimum paper TOEFL 550. **Basis for Candidate Selection:** *Very important factors considered include:* rigor of secondary school record, academic GPA, standardized test scores, application essay, recommendation(s). *Important factors considered include:* class rank, extracurricular activities, talent/ability, character/personal qualities, volunteer work. *Other factors considered include:* interview, first generation, alumni/ae relation, geographical residence, state residency, racial/ethnic status, work experience, level of applicant's interest. **Freshman Admission Requirements:** High school diploma is required and GED is accepted. *Academic units required:* 4 English, 3 math, 3 science, 2 science labs, 2 social studies, 1 history. *Academic units recommended:* 4 math, 4 foreign language, 3 social studies. **Freshman Admission Statistics:** 1,767 applied, 79.97% admitted, 24% enrolled. **Transfer Admission Requirements:** college transcript(s), essay or personal statement, Minimum college GPA of 3.0 required. Lowest grade transferable C-. **General Admission Information:** Application fee $50. Priority deadline 11/1. Regular application deadline 2/15. Regular notification 1/1. Nonfall registration accepted. Admission may be deferred for a maximum of 1.5 Years.

COSTS AND FINANCIAL AID

Annual in-state tuition $11,418. Annual out-of-state tuition $26,566. Room and board $12,442. Required fees $2,774. Average book expense $1,200. **Required Forms and Deadlines:** FAFSA. **Notification of Awards:** Applicants will be notified of awards on or about 3/15. **Types of Aid:** *Need-based scholarships/ grants:* Federal Pell, FSEOG, State scholarships/grants, Private scholarships, College/university scholarship or grant aid from institutional funds. *Loans:* Direct Subsidized Stafford Loans, Direct Unsubsidized Stafford Loans, Direct PLUS loans. *Student Employment:* Federal Work-Study Program available. Institutional employment available. **Financial Aid Statistics:** 89% needy freshmen, 73% needy undergrads receive need-based scholarship or grant aid. 55% freshmen, 61% undergrads receive non-need-based scholarship or grant aid. 67% freshmen, 68% undergrads receive need-based self-help aid. 0% freshmen, 0% undergrads receive any athletic scholarships. 72% freshmen, 74% undergrads receive any aid. 53% undergrads borrow to pay for school. Average cumulative indebtedness $24,213. **Criteria for awarding aid:** *Non-need-based:* Academics, Leadership.

ST. MARY'S UNIVERSITY

One Camino Santa Maria, San Antonio, TX 78228-8503
Phone: 210.436.3126 • **Financial Aid Phone:** 210-436-3141
E-mail: uadm@stmarytx.edu • **CEEB Code:** 6637
Fax: 210.431.6742 • **Website:** http://www.stmarytx.edu/ • **ACT Code:** 4158

This private school, affiliated with the Roman Catholic Church, was founded in 1852. It has a 135-acre campus.

RATINGS
Admissions Selectivity Rating: 81   **Fire Safety Rating:** 87   **Green Rating:** 72

STUDENTS AND FACULTY
Enrollment: 2,274. **Student Body:** 53% female, 47% male, 9% out-of-state, 9% international (35 countries represented). Asian 2%, African American 3%, Caucasian 14%, Hispanic 68%, Native American <1%, Pacific Islander <1%, Two or more races 1%, Race unknown 3%. **Retention and Graduation:** 76% freshmen return for sophomore year. 41% freshmen graduate within 4 years. 55% freshmen graduate within 6 years. 25% grads go on to further study within 1 year. 69% grads pursue arts and sciences degrees. 10% grads pursue law degrees. 8% grads pursue business degrees. 10% grads pursue medical degrees. **Faculty:** Student/faculty ratio 11:1. 210 full-time faculty, 93% hold PhDs, 24% are are members of minority groups, 37% are women. 0% of classes are taught by teaching assistants.

ACADEMICS
Degrees: bachelor's, doctoral/professional, doctoral/research, doctoral, master's, postbachelor's certificate. **Classes:** Most classes have 20-29 students. Most lab/discussion sessions have 20-29 students. **Most popular majors:** Biology/Biological Sciences; Kinesiology and Exercise Science; Accounting. **Special Study Options:** cross-registration, distance learning, double major, dual enrollment, English as a Second Language (ESL), exchange student program (domestic), honors program, independent study, internships, liberal arts/career combination, study abroad, teacher certification program, Evening Studies Program. **Honors Programs:** The Honors Program offers an academically challenging and personally enriching course of study designed to cultivate critical analysis, clear oral and written expression, aesthetic awareness and ethical judgment. In and out of the classroom we seek to prepare our future graduates for lives of leadership and service to their communities. Combined degree programs: BA/JD, BA/MA. **Disability Services:** Special programs offered to physically disabled students, including note-taking services, reader services, tape recorders, tutors. **Career Services:** Alumni network, Alumni services, Career/job search classes, Career assessment, Internships, Regional alumni.

FACILITIES
Housing: Coed dorms, Science Learning, Living Community; Residence hall for students 22 yrs. old or above/non traditional. 80% of campus accessible to physically disabled. **Computers:** 100% of classrooms, 100% of dorms, 100% of libraries, 100% of dining areas, 100% of student union, 80% of common outdoor areas have wireless network access. Students can register for classes online. Administrative functions (other than registration) can be performed online. Undergraduates are required to own a computer.

CAMPUS LIFE
Environment: Metropolis. **Activities:** Choral groups, concert band, dance, drama/theater, jazz band, literary magazine, music ensembles, musical theater, pep band, student government, student newspaper, Campus Ministries, Student Organization. 91 registered organizations, 1 religious organization. 4 fraternities, 4 sororities. **Athletics (Intercollegiate):** *Men:* baseball, basketball, cheerleading, golf, soccer, tennis. *Women:* basketball, cheerleading, cross-country, golf, soccer, softball, tennis, volleyball. **On-Campus Highlights:** Alumni Athletics and Convocation Center, University Center, Java City Coffee Shop, The Quad, Barrett Memorial Bell Tower, Pecan Grove and the new 278-bed Founders Hall round out the list of popular campus spots. Founders Hall opened in fall 2009. Designed for freshmen, it provides spacious rooms, welcoming indoor and outdoor common spaces, and a cyber cafe. **Environmental Initiatives:** Energy efficiency electric motors, chillers, lighting, Demand Energy Limiting.

ADMISSIONS
Freshman Academic Profile: Average high school GPA 3.5. 27% in top 10% of high school class, 55% in top 25% of high school class, 81% in top 50% of high school class. 69% from public high schools. **Reported SAT (pre-2016 redesign) scores:** SAT Math middle 50% range 480-570. SAT Critical Reading middle 50% range 470-560. SAT Writing middle 50% range 450-540. **Concordant SAT scores:** SAT EBRW middle 50% 510–610. SAT Math middle 50% range 510–590. ACT middle 50% range 19-25. Minimum internet-based TOEFL 80. Minimum paper TOEFL 550. **Basis for Candidate Selection:** *Very important factors considered include:* rigor of secondary school record, academic GPA. *Important factors considered include:* class rank, standardized test scores. *Other factors considered include:* application essay, recommendation(s), interview, extracurricular activities, talent/ability, character/ personal qualities, volunteer work. **Freshman Admission Requirements:** High school diploma is required and GED is accepted. *Academic units required:* 4 English, 3 math, 3 science, 2 foreign language, 3 social studies, 1 academic elective. *Academic units recommended:* 4 English, 4 math, 4 science, 3 foreign language, 4 social studies. **Freshman Admission Statistics:** 4,346 applied, 77.66% admitted, 17% enrolled. **Transfer Admission Requirements:** college transcript(s), Minimum college GPA of 2.5 required. Lowest grade transferable C-. **General Admission Information:** Priority deadline 1/15. Nonfall registration accepted. Admission may be deferred for a maximum of 1 year.

COSTS AND FINANCIAL AID
Annual tuition $27,520. Room and board $9,300. Required fees $680. Average book expense $1,300. **Required Forms and Deadlines:** FAFSA. **Notification of Awards:** Applicants will be notified of awards on a rolling basis beginning 3/1. **Types of Aid:** *Need-based scholarships/grants:* Federal Pell, FSEOG, State scholarships/grants, Private scholarships, College/university scholarship or grant aid from institutional funds. *Loans:* Direct Subsidized Stafford Loans, Direct Unsubsidized Stafford Loans, Direct PLUS loans, Federal Perkins Loans, State Loans. *Student Employment:* Federal Work-Study Program available. Institutional employment available. **Financial Aid Statistics:** 100% needy freshmen, 98% needy undergrads receive need-based scholarship or grant aid. 9% freshmen, 7% undergrads receive non-need-based scholarship or grant aid. 80% freshmen, 84% undergrads receive need-based self-help aid. 4% freshmen, 6% undergrads receive athletic scholarships. 95% freshmen, 92% undergrads receive any aid. 77% undergrads borrow to pay for school. Average cumulative indebtedness $39,883. **Criteria for awarding aid:** *Need-based:* Academics. *Non-need-based:* Academics, Alumni affiliation, Athletics, Music/drama, Religious affiliation, State/district residency.

ST. NORBERT COLLEGE

100 Grant Street, De Pere, WI 54115-2099
Phone: 920-403-3005 • **Financial Aid Phone:** 920-403-3071
E-mail: admit@snc.edu • **CEEB Code:** 1706
Fax: 920-403-4072 • **Website:** www.snc.edu • **ACT Code:** 4644

This private school, affiliated with the Roman Catholic Church, was founded in 1898. It has a 93-acre campus.

RATINGS
Admissions Selectivity Rating: 81   **Fire Safety Rating:** 90   **Green Rating:** 72

STUDENTS AND FACULTY
Enrollment: 2,064. **Student Body:** 57% female, 43% male, 21% out-of-state, 3% international (16 countries represented). Asian 1%, African American 1%, Caucasian 88%, Hispanic 4%, Native American 1%, Pacific Islander <1%, Two or more races 2%, Race unknown <1%.
Retention and Graduation: 86% freshmen return for sophomore year. 68% freshmen graduate within 4 years. 73% freshmen graduate within 6 years. 17% grads go on to further study within 1 year. **Faculty:** Student/faculty ratio 13:1. 140 full-time faculty, 91% hold PhDs, 10% are are members of minority groups, 46% are women. 0% of classes are taught by teaching assistants.

ACADEMICS
Degrees: bachelor's, master's. **Classes:** Most classes have 10-19 students. Most lab/discussion sessions have 10-19 students. **Most popular majors:** Elementary Education and Teaching; Business/Commerce; Speech Communication and Rhetoric. **Special Study Options:** distance learning, double major, English as a Second Language (ESL), honors program, independent study, internships, student-designed major, study abroad, teacher certification program, Foundation for International Education (London)Internships; Washington Semester. **Honors Programs:** The Honors Program at St. Norbert College offers a sophisticated and demanding program of studies and readings to provide the most academically talented students with an enriched academic curriculum that is stimulating and challenging. **Disability Services:** Special programs offered to physically disabled students, including note-taking services, reader services, tape recorders, tutors. **Career Services:** Alumni network, Alumni services, Career assessment, Internships, Regional alumni. Students can begin internships on campus or off campus after their freshmen year. Strong emphasis is placed on learning contracts.

FACILITIES
Housing: Coed dorms, special housing for disabled students, special housing for international students, women's dorms, fraternity/sorority housing, apartments for single students, Townhouses Off-campus college owned housing. 82% of campus accessible to physically diasbled. **Special Academic Facilities/Equipment:** New state-of-the-art Mulva Library, Center for leadership and service, Bush Art Center with three art galleries, scanning electron microscope, visual and performing arts center, center for international education, riverfront campus center with marina, peace and justice center, career services, children's center in cooperation with early childhood education, center of economic education,survey center, Kress Inn, conference services, academic support services, St. Joseph Church, chapels in residence halls, women's center and Journey-Men (men's center). **Computers:** 100% of classrooms, 60% of dorms, 100% of libraries, 100% of dining areas, 100% of student union, have wireless network access. Students can register for classes online. Administrative functions (other than registration) can be performed online.

CAMPUS LIFE
Environment: Village. **Activities:** Choral groups, concert band, drama/theater, jazz band, literary magazine, music ensembles, musical theater, pep band, radio station, student government, student newspaper, student-run film society, television station, Campus Ministries, Student Organization. 63 registered organizations, 10 honor societies, 3 religious organizations. 3 fraternities, 4 sororities. **Athletics (Intercollegiate):** *Men:* baseball, basketball, cross-country, football, golf, ice hockey, soccer, tennis, track/field (outdoor), track/field (indoor). *Women:* basketball, cross-country, golf, ice hockey, soccer, softball, tennis, track/field (outdoor), track/field (indoor), volleyball. **On-Campus Highlights:** The Ray Van Den Heuvel Campus Center, The Bush Fine Arts Center, The F.K. Bemis International Center, Austin E Cofrin Hall, New Mulva Library with Coffee Shop. **Environmental Initiatives:** Designed new Mulva Library with solar water heating system.

ADMISSIONS
Freshman Academic Profile: Average high school GPA 3.5. 24% in top 10% of high school class, 54% in top 25% of high school class, 85% in top 50% of high school class. 75% from public high schools. ACT middle 50% range 22-27. Minimum internet-based TOEFL 80. Minimum paper TOEFL 550. **Basis for Candidate Selection:** *Very important factors considered include:* rigor of secondary school record, academic GPA, standardized test scores. *Other*

factors considered include: class rank, application essay, recommendation(s), interview, extracurricular activities, talent/ability, character/personal qualities, first generation, alumni/ae relation, geographical residence, state residency, religious affiliation/commitment, racial/ethnic status, volunteer work, work experience, level of applicant's interest. **Freshman Admission Requirements:** High school diploma is required and GED is accepted. *Academic units recommended:* 4 English, 3 math, 3 science, 3 science labs, 2 foreign language, 2 social studies, 2 history. **Freshman Admission Statistics:** 3,605 applied, 81.39% admitted, 20% enrolled. **Transfer Admission Requirements:** High school transcript, college transcript(s), essay or personal statement, standardized test scores, Minimum college GPA of 2.5 required. Lowest grade transferable C. **General Admission Information:** Application fee $10. Priority deadline 4/1. Nonfall registration accepted. Admission may be deferred for a maximum of 2 years.

COSTS AND FINANCIAL AID
Annual tuition $35,878. Room and board $9,467. Required fees $715. Average book expense $950. **Required Forms and Deadlines:** FAFSA. **Notification of Awards:** Applicants will be notified of awards on a rolling basis beginning 3/15. **Types of Aid:** *Need-based scholarships/grants:* Federal Pell, FSEOG, State scholarships/grants, Private scholarships, College/university scholarship or grant aid from institutional funds. *Loans:* Direct Subsidized Stafford Loans, Direct Unsubsidized Stafford Loans, Direct PLUS loans, Federal Perkins Loans, State Loans, College/university loans from institutional funds. *Student Employment:* Federal Work-Study Program available. Institutional employment available. **Financial Aid Statistics:** 99% needy freshmen, 97% needy undergrads receive need-based scholarship or grant aid. 2% freshmen, 3% undergrads receive non-need-based scholarship or grant aid. 77% freshmen, 79% undergrads receive need-based self-help aid. 0% freshmen, 0% undergrads receive athletic scholarships. 95% freshmen, 96% undergrads receive any aid. 74% undergrads borrow to pay for school. Average cumulative indebtedness $33,948. **Criteria for awarding aid:** *Need-based:* Academics, Art, Leadership, Minority status, Music/drama. *Non-need-based:* Academics, Art, Leadership, Minority status, Music/drama, State/district residency.

See page 1052.

ST. OLAF COLLEGE

1520 St. Olaf Avenue, Northfield, MN 55057
Phone: 507-786-3025 • **Financial Aid Phone:** 507-786-3019
E-mail: admissions@stolaf.edu • **CEEB Code:** 6638
Fax: 507-786-3832 • **Website:** http://wp.stolaf.edu • **ACT Code:** 2150

This private school, affiliated with the Lutheran Church, was founded in 1874. It has a 300-acre campus.

RATINGS
Admissions Selectivity Rating: 91   **Fire Safety Rating:** 82   **Green Rating:** 60*

STUDENTS AND FACULTY
Enrollment: 2,991. **Student Body:** 56% female, 44% male, 55% out-of-state, 8% international (80 countries represented). Asian 6%, African American 2%, Caucasian 73%, Hispanic 6%, Native American <1%, Pacific Islander <1%, Two or more races 3%, Race unknown 1%.
Retention and Graduation: 92% freshmen return for sophomore year. 85% freshmen graduate within 4 years. 88% freshmen graduate within 6 years. 23% grads go on to further study within 1 year. 13% grads pursue arts and sciences degrees. 1% grads pursue law degrees. 3% grads pursue medical degrees. **Faculty:** Student/faculty ratio 12:1. 213 full-time faculty, 94% hold PhDs, 12% are are members of minority groups, 46% are women. 0% of classes are taught by teaching assistants.

ACADEMICS
Degrees: bachelor's. **Classes:** Most classes have 10-19 students. Most lab/discussion sessions have 10-19 students. **Most popular majors:** Biology/Biological Sciences; Economics; Mathematics. **Special Study Options:** cross-registration, double major, dual enrollment, independent study, internships, student-designed major, study abroad, teacher certification program. **Disability Services:** Special programs offered to physically disabled students, including note-taking services, reader services, tape recorders, tutors. **Career Services:** Alumni network, Alumni services, Career/job search classes, Career assessment, Internships, Regional alumni. The Piper Center for Vocation and Career provides resources and experiences designed to help students leverage their

liberal arts education to achieve their full potential. We are proud of programs that help students build professional skills, interact with alumni, and begin to discern their vocation: Last year students received $460,000 in financial support for internships, research, and shadowing experiences. These experiences helped students clarify their academic and professional goals. More than half of all first-year students participated in a event that included both small-group reflection and a fair that showcased student employment, internship, research, and leadership opportunities. About a quarter of the sophomore class participated in our off-campus leadership development and vocational exploration retreat, where students gained valuable insight from alumni and faculty about taking the first steps toward a meaningful career. More than 90 employers, graduate schools, and post-graduate service programs visited St. Olaf to recruit students for internships, jobs, continuing education, and gap year programs. Selected seniors received job offers more than five months prior to graduation. Seventy-five sophomores, juniors and seniors traveled to New York City, Seattle and Denver to network with over 300 alumni and parents. Students were hosted by dozens of employers in fields such as business, journalism, publishing, performing arts, social services, technology, bioscience, engineering, environment, health care, and marketing. On alternating years, students travel to Chicago, Madison, San Francisco, and Washington, D.C. We also intend to add programs in Atlanta, Boston and Los Angeles during the 2017-18 academic year.

FACILITIES

Housing: Coed dorms, special housing for disabled students, ThemeHousingHonor houses, language houses, quiet halls, first-year only dorms. Disabled students. accommodated in dorm of their choice. 76% of campus accessible to physically diasbled. **Special Academic Facilities/ Equipment:** Finstad Program for Entrepreneurial Studies, Kierkegaard Library, Flaten Art Museum, Norwegian American Historical Association archives. **Computers:** 100% of classrooms, 100% of dorms, 100% of libraries, 100% of dining areas, 100% of student union, 100% of common outdoor areas have wireless network access. Students can register for classes online. Administrative functions (other than registration) can be performed online.

CAMPUS LIFE

Environment: Village. **Activities:** Choral groups, concert band, dance, drama/ theater, jazz band, literary magazine, music ensembles, musical theater, opera, pep band, radio station, student government, student newspaper, student-run film society, symphony orchestra, television station, Campus Ministries, Student Organization, Model UN. 193 registered organizations, 18 honor societies, 16 religious organizations. **Athletics (Intercollegiate):** *Men:* baseball, basketball, cross-country, diving, football, golf, ice hockey, skiing (downhill/alpine), skiing (nordic/cross-country), soccer, swimming, tennis, track/field (outdoor), track/ field (indoor), wrestling. *Women:* basketball, cross-country, diving, golf, ice hockey, skiing (downhill/alpine), skiing (nordic/cross-country), soccer, softball, swimming, tennis, track/field (outdoor), track/field (indoor), volleyball. **On-Campus Highlights:** Regents Hall of Natural Science & Math, Buntrock Commons, Tostrud Recreation Center, The Lion's Pause, Dittman Art Museum, Beautiful 300 acre campus.

ADMISSIONS

Freshman Academic Profile: Average high school GPA 3.6. 44% in top 10% of high school class, 77% in top 25% of high school class, 94% in top 50% of high school class. 74% from public high schools. **Reported SAT (pre-2016 redesign) scores:** SAT Math middle 50% range 570-700. SAT Critical Reading middle 50% range 550-700. **Concordant SAT scores:** SAT Math middle 50% range 590–730. ACT middle 50% range 26-31. Minimum internet-based TOEFL 90. **Basis for Candidate Selection:** *Very important factors considered include:* rigor of secondary school record, academic GPA, application essay. *Important factors considered include:* class rank, standardized test scores, recommendation(s), interview, extracurricular activities, talent/ability, character/personal qualities. *Other factors considered include:* first generation, alumni/ae relation, geographical residence, state residency, religious affiliation/ commitment, racial/ethnic status, volunteer work, work experience, level of applicant's interest. **Freshman Admission Requirements:** High school diploma is required and GED is accepted. *Academic units recommended:* 4 English, 4 math, 4 science, 2 science labs, 4 foreign language, 4 social studies. **Freshman Admission Statistics:** 6,041 applied, 44.76% admitted, 30% enrolled. **Transfer Admission Requirements:** High school transcript, college transcript(s), essay or personal statement, standardized test scores, statement of good standing from prior institution(s). Minimum college GPA of 2.50 required. Lowest grade transferable C. **General Admission Information:** Regular application deadline 1/15. Regular notification 3/20. Nonfall registration accepted. Admission may be deferred for a maximum of 1 year.

COSTS AND FINANCIAL AID

Annual tuition $44,180. Room and board $10,080. Average book expense $100. **Required Forms and Deadlines:** FAFSA, CSS/Financial Aid PROFILE, Noncustodial PROFILE. **Notification of Awards:** Applicants will be notified of awards on or about 4/1. **Types of Aid:** *Need-based scholarships/grants:* Federal Pell, FSEOG, State scholarships/grants, Private scholarships, College/

university scholarship or grant aid from institutional funds. *Loans:* Direct Subsidized Stafford Loans, Direct Unsubsidized Stafford Loans, Direct PLUS loans, Federal Nursing Loans, State Loans, College/university loans from institutional funds. *Student Employment:* Federal Work-Study Program available. Institutional employment available. **Financial Aid Statistics:** 100% needy freshmen, 100% needy undergrads receive need-based scholarship or grant aid. 53% freshmen, 37% undergrads receive non-need-based scholarship or grant aid. 100% freshmen, 99% undergrads receive need-based self-help aid. 0% freshmen, 0% undergrads receive athletic scholarships. 92% freshmen, 93% undergrads receive any aid. Average cumulative indebtedness $27,945. **Criteria for awarding aid:** *Non-need-based:* Academics, Art, Leadership, Music/drama.

ST. THOMAS AQUINAS COLLEGE

125 Route 340, Sparkill, NY 10976
Phone: 845-398-4100 • **Financial Aid Phone:** 845-398-4106
E-mail: admissions@stac.edu • **CEEB Code:** 2807
Fax: 845-398-4372 • **Website:** www.stac.edu • **ACT Code:** 2897

This private school was founded in 1952. It has a 47-acre campus.

RATINGS
Admissions Selectivity Rating: 73　　**Fire Safety Rating:** 97　　**Green Rating:** 60*

STUDENTS AND FACULTY
Enrollment: 1,152. **Student Body:** 53% female, 47% male, 20% out-of-state, 3% international (10 countries represented). Asian 3%, African American 11%, Caucasian 50%, Hispanic 24%, Native American <1%, Pacific Islander <1%, Two or more races 1%, Race unknown 8%.
Retention and Graduation: 74% freshmen return for sophomore year.
Faculty: Student/faculty ratio 13:1. 61 full-time faculty, 75% hold PhDs, 7% are are members of minority groups, 57% are women. 0% of classes are taught by teaching assistants.

ACADEMICS
Degrees: associate, bachelor's, master's, postbachelor's certificate, post-master's certificate. **Classes:** Most classes have 20-29 students. **Most popular majors:** Criminal Justice/Law Enforcement Administration; Psychology; Special Education and Teaching. **Special Study Options:** Accelerated program, cooperative education program, cross-registration, double major, dual enrollment, exchange student program (domestic), honors program, independent study, internships, liberal arts/career combination, study abroad, teacher certification program, Undergrads may take grad level classes–e.g. cooperative education programs: combined BS/MSW in social work in partnership with NYU; engineering combined degree programs: 3-2 engineering programs with George Washington U and Manhattan Coll foreign exchange program(s): study abroad in England. **Honors Programs:** Highly selective honors program with maximum 20 student each class. Honor students receive full scholarship. Combined degree programs: BA/MA. **Disability Services:** Special programs offered to physically disabled students, including note-taking services, tape recorders, tutors. **Career Services:** Alumni network, Alumni services, Career/job search classes, Career assessment, Internships, Regional alumni.

FACILITIES
Housing: men's dorms, women's dorms, apartments for single students. 80% of campus accessible to physically diasbled. **Special Academic Facilities/ Equipment:** Azarian-McCullough Art Gallery, Sullivan Theatre, Spellman Technology Corridor, Costello Hall Science and Technology Center. **Computers:** Students can register for classes online.

CAMPUS LIFE
Environment: Village. **Activities:** Choral groups, dance, drama/theater, literary magazine, musical theater, opera, radio station, student government, student newspaper, yearbook. 35 registered organizations, 8 honor societies, 1 religious organization. **Athletics (Intercollegiate):** *Men:* baseball, basketball, cross-country, golf, soccer, tennis, track/field (outdoor), track/field (indoor). *Women:* basketball, cross-country, lacrosse, soccer, softball, tennis, track/field (outdoor). **On-Campus Highlights:** The College Commons, The Fitness Center, The Romano Alumni Center, The Art Gallery, The Techonology Corridor.

ADMISSIONS
Freshman Academic Profile: Average high school GPA 3.0. 5% in top 10% of high school class, 18% in top 25% of high school class, 68% in top 50% of high school class. 70% from public high schools. **Reported SAT (pre-2016 redesign) scores:** SAT Math middle 50% range 412-530. SAT Critical Reading middle 50% range 420-527. SAT Writing middle 50% range 410-510. **Concordant SAT scores:** SAT EBRW middle 50% 460–580. SAT Math middle 50% range 450–560. ACT middle 50% range 17-22. Minimum

paper TOEFL 530. **Basis for Candidate Selection:** *Very important factors considered include:* rigor of secondary school record, academic GPA. *Important factors considered include:* standardized test scores, application essay, recommendation(s), interview, extracurricular activities, talent/ability. *Other factors considered include:* alumni/ae relation, volunteer work, work experience, level of applicant's interest. **Freshman Admission Requirements:** High school diploma is required and GED is accepted. *Academic units required:* 4 English, 3 math, 3 science, 2 science labs, 2 foreign language, 4 social studies. *Academic units recommended:* 4 math, 3 foreign language. **Freshman Admission Statistics:** 1,953 applied, 79.16% admitted, 17% enrolled. **Transfer Admission Requirements:** college transcript(s), statement of good standing from prior institution(s). Minimum college GPA of 2.0 required. Lowest grade transferable C. **General Admission Information:** Application fee $25. Nonfall registration accepted. Admission may be deferred for a maximum of one year.

COSTS AND FINANCIAL AID

Annual tuition $28,800. Room and board $13,100. Required fees $800. Average book expense $1,250. **Required Forms and Deadlines:** FAFSA. **Notification of Awards:** Applicants will be notified of awards on a rolling basis beginning 11/1. **Types of Aid:** *Need-based scholarships/grants:* Federal Pell, FSEOG, State scholarships/grants, Private scholarships, College/university scholarship or grant aid from institutional funds. *Loans:* Direct Subsidized Stafford Loans, Direct Unsubsidized Stafford Loans, Direct PLUS loans, Federal Perkins Loans. *Student Employment:* Federal Work-Study Program available. Institutional employment available. **Financial Aid Statistics:** 90% needy freshmen, 92% needy undergrads receive need-based scholarship or grant aid. 63% freshmen, 71% undergrads receive non-need-based scholarship or grant aid. 69% freshmen, 93% undergrads receive need-based self-help aid. 9% freshmen, 5% undergrads receive athletic scholarships. Average cumulative indebtedness $29,500. **Criteria for awarding aid:** *Need-based:* Academics, Athletics, Job skills, Minority status. *Non-need-based:* Academics, Alumni affiliation, Art, Athletics, Leadership, Minority status, Music/drama, Religious affiliation.

ST. THOMAS UNIVERSITY

16401 Northwest 37th Avenue, Miami Gardens, FL 33054
Phone: 305-628-6546 • **Financial Aid Phone:** 305-628-6547
E-mail: signup@stu.edu • **CEEB Code:** 5076
Fax: 305-628-6591 • **Website:** www.stu.edu • **ACT Code:** 719

This private school, affiliated with the Roman Catholic Church, was founded in 1961. It has a 140-acre campus.

RATINGS

Admissions Selectivity Rating: 81 **Fire Safety Rating:** 77 **Green Rating:** 60*

STUDENTS AND FACULTY

Enrollment: 882. **Student Body:** 55% female, 45% male, 92% out-of-state, 15% international (57 countries represented). Asian 1%, African American 23%, Caucasian 12%, Hispanic 40%, Native American <1%, Pacific Islander 0%, Two or more races 1%, Race unknown 8%.
Retention and Graduation: 70% freshmen return for sophomore year. 22% freshmen graduate within 4 years. **Faculty:** Student/faculty ratio 14:1. 105 full-time faculty, 89% hold PhDs, 30% are are members of minority groups, 47% are women. 0% of classes are taught by teaching assistants.

ACADEMICS

Degrees: bachelor's, certificate, doctoral/professional, doctoral/research, master's, postbachelor's certificate, post-master's certificate. **Classes:** Most classes have 10-19 students. Most lab/discussion sessions have 10-19 students. **Most popular majors:** Psychology; Organizational Behavior Studies; Business Administration and Management. **Special Study Options:** distance learning, double major, dual enrollment, honors program, independent study, internships, liberal arts/career combination, teacher certification program. **Honors Programs:** The St. Thomas University Honors Program is designed to provide an intensive and stimulating alternative for students who wish to enhance their college academic experience. Qualified students are offered the opportunity to take Honors courses in the subjects of their choice, and, if they desire, to work for an Honors degree. Combined degree programs: BA/JD. **Disability Services:** Special programs offered to physically disabled students, including note-taking services, reader services, tape recorders, tutors. **Career Services:** Career/job search classes, Career assessment, Internships, On-campus interviews.

FACILITIES

Housing: men's dorms, women's dorms. 80% of campus accessible to physically diasbled. **Special Academic Facilities/Equipment:** Multimedia computer equipment, TV studio, Art Atrium Gallery. **Computers:** 100% of libraries,

100% of dining areas, have wireless network access. Students can register for classes online. Administrative functions (other than registration) can be performed online.

CAMPUS LIFE

Environment: Metropolis. **Activities:** Choral groups, literary magazine, music ensembles, student government, television station, yearbook, Campus Ministries, Student Organization. 26 registered organizations, 4 honor societies, 2 religious organizations. **Athletics (Intercollegiate):** *Men:* baseball, basketball, cross-country, golf, soccer, tennis. *Women:* basketball, cross-country, soccer, softball, tennis, volleyball. **On-Campus Highlights:** Campus Chapel, Library, Fernandez Family Center, Kennedy Hall.

ADMISSIONS

Freshman Academic Profile: Average high school GPA 3.0. 6% in top 10% of high school class, 17% in top 25% of high school class, 53% in top 50% of high school class. **Reported SAT (pre-2016 redesign) scores:** SAT Math middle 50% range 408-500. SAT Critical Reading middle 50% range 410-510. SAT Writing middle 50% range 400-490. **Concordant SAT scores:** SAT EBRW middle 50% 450–560. SAT Math middle 50% range 450–530. ACT middle 50% range 16.25-20.75. Minimum paper TOEFL 525. **Basis for Candidate Selection:** *Very important factors considered include:* class rank, academic GPA, standardized test scores. *Important factors considered include:* rigor of secondary school record, application essay, recommendation(s), alumni/ae relation, level of applicant's interest. *Other factors considered include:* extracurricular activities, talent/ability, character/personal qualities, volunteer work, work experience. **Freshman Admission Requirements:** High school diploma is required and GED is accepted. *Academic units required:* 4 English, 3 math, 2 science, 3 social studies, 6 academic electives. **Freshman Admission Statistics:** 727 applied, 45.67% admitted, 63% enrolled. **Transfer Admission Requirements:** college transcript(s), essay or personal statement, statement of good standing from prior institution(s). Minimum college GPA of 2.0 required. Lowest grade transferable C-. **General Admission Information:** Application fee $40. Nonfall registration accepted. Admission may be deferred for a maximum of One year.

COSTS AND FINANCIAL AID

Required Forms and Deadlines: FAFSA. **Notification of Awards:** Applicants will be notified of awards on a rolling basis beginning 3/1. **Types of Aid:** *Need-based scholarships/grants:* Federal Pell, FSEOG, State scholarships/grants, Private scholarships, College/university scholarship or grant aid from institutional funds. *Loans:* Direct Subsidized Stafford Loans, Direct Unsubsidized Stafford Loans, Direct PLUS loans, Federal Perkins Loans. *Student Employment:* Federal Work-Study Program available. Institutional employment available. **Financial Aid Statistics:** 77% needy freshmen, 76% needy undergrads receive need-based scholarship or grant aid. 100% freshmen, 99% undergrads receive non-need-based scholarship or grant aid. 56% freshmen, 55% undergrads receive need-based self-help aid. 12% freshmen, 15% undergrads receive athletic scholarships. **Criteria for awarding aid:** *Need-based:* Academics. *Non-need-based:* Academics, Athletics, Leadership.

ST. THOMAS UNIVERSITY

Admissions Office, St. Thomas University, Fredericton, NB E3B 5G3
Phone: 506-452-0532
E-mail: admissions@stu.ca
Fax: 506-452-0617 • **Website:** http://www.stu.ca

This private school, affiliated with the Roman Catholic Church, was founded in 1910. It has a 21-acre campus.

RATINGS

Admissions Selectivity Rating: 65 **Fire Safety Rating:** 95 **Green Rating:** 60*

STUDENTS AND FACULTY

Enrollment: 2,475. **Student Body:** 66% female, 34% male, 27% out-of-state, 5% international (42 countries represented). Asian 0%, African American 0%, Caucasian 0%, Hispanic 0%, Native American 0%, Pacific Islander 0%, Two or more races 0%, Race unknown 95%.
Retention and Graduation: 69% freshmen return for sophomore year. 41% freshmen graduate within 4 years. 54% freshmen graduate within 6 years. **Faculty:** Student/faculty ratio 19:1. 109 full-time faculty, 95% hold PhDs, 0% are are members of minority groups, 39% are women. 0% of classes are taught by teaching assistants.

ACADEMICS

Degrees: bachelor's, certificate, postbachelor's certificate. **Classes:** Most classes have 10-19 students. **Most popular majors:** English Language and Literature; Psychology; Criminology. **Special Study Options:** Accelerated program, cross-registration, double major, English as a Second Language (ESL), exchange student program (domestic), honors program, independent study, student-designed major, study abroad, teacher certification program, Aquinas Program: Thematically linked courses from various disciplines. **Disability Services:** Special programs offered to physically disabled students, including note-taking services, reader services, tape recorders, tutors. **Career Services:** Career/job search classes, Career assessment, Internships.

FACILITIES

Housing: Coed dorms, women's dorms. 80% of campus accessible to physically diasbled. **Computers:** 100% of dorms, 100% of libraries, 100% of dining areas, have wireless network access. Students can register for classes online. Administrative functions (other than registration) can be performed online.

CAMPUS LIFE

Environment: Town. **Activities:** Choral groups, drama/theater, jazz band, music ensembles, musical theater, radio station, student government, student newspaper, student-run film society, yearbook, Campus Ministries, Student Organization, Model UN. 5 religious organizations. **Athletics (Intercollegiate):** *Men:* basketball, cross-country, golf, ice hockey, rugby, soccer, volleyball. *Women:* basketball, cross-country, golf, ice hockey, rugby, soccer, volleyball. **On-Campus Highlights:** Margaret Norrie McCain Hall, Lower courtyard, J.B. O'Keefe Fitness Centre, Sir James Dunn Hall, The Black Box Theatre. **Environmental Initiatives:** Recycle bins in all areas.

ADMISSIONS

Freshman Academic Profile: Average high school GPA 3.3. Minimum internet-based TOEFL 88. Minimum paper TOEFL 570. **Basis for Candidate Selection:** *Very important factors considered include:* academic GPA. *Other factors considered include:* standardized test scores, application essay, recommendation(s). **Freshman Admission Requirements:** High school diploma is required and GED is not accepted. **Freshman Admission Statistics:** 1,345 applied, 80.67% admitted, 58% enrolled. **Transfer Admission Requirements:** college transcript(s), statement of good standing from prior institution(s). Lowest grade transferable D. **General Admission Information:** Application fee $35. Regular application deadline 8/31. Nonfall registration accepted. Admission may be deferred for a maximum of 1 year.

COSTS AND FINANCIAL AID

Average book expense $1,000. *Student Employment:* Federal Work-Study Program available. Institutional employment available.

STANFORD UNIVERSITY

Undergraduate Admission, Stanford, CA 94305-6106
Phone: 650-723-2091 • **Financial Aid Phone:** 650-723-3058
E-mail: admission@stanford.edu • **CEEB Code:** 4704
Fax: 650-725-2846 • **Website:** www.stanford.edu • **ACT Code:** 434

This private school was founded in 1885. It has a 8180-acre campus.

RATINGS

Admissions Selectivity Rating: 99   **Fire Safety Rating:** 89   **Green Rating:** 99

STUDENTS AND FACULTY

Enrollment: 6,994. **Student Body:** 48% female, 52% male, 61% out-of-state, 9% international (90 countries represented). Asian 20%, African American 6%, Caucasian 37%, Hispanic 15%, Native American 1%, Pacific Islander <1%, Two or more races 10%, Race unknown <1%.
Retention and Graduation: 98% freshmen return for sophomore year. 75% freshmen graduate within 4 years. 93% freshmen graduate within 6 years. 25% grads go on to further study within 1 year. **Faculty:** Student/faculty ratio 4:1. 1,589 full-time faculty, 99% hold PhDs, 23% are are members of minority groups, 26% are women. 6% of classes are taught by teaching assistants.

ACADEMICS

Degrees: bachelor's, doctoral/professional, doctoral/research, master's. **Classes:** Most classes have 10-19 students. Most lab/discussion sessions have fewer than 10 students. **Most popular majors:** Computer Science; Human Biology; Engineering. **Special Study Options:** distance learning, double major, exchange student program (domestic), honors program, independent study, internships, student-designed major, study abroad, Marine research center, Bing Stanford in Washington program, exchange programs with Dartmouth, Howard, Morehouse and Spelman, undergraduate research opportunities, Bing Honors College, overseas study. **Honors Programs:** About 100 student

annually participate in Bing Honors College. About 25 percent of each graduating class earn departmental honors. Combined degree programs: BA/MA, Many bachelors/masters coterminal degree. **Disability Services:** Special programs offered to physically disabled students, including note-taking services, reader services, tape recorders, tutors. **Career Services:** Alumni network, Alumni services, Career/job search classes, Career assessment, Internships, Regional alumni. The Haas Center for Public Service at Stanford connects academic study with public service to strengthen communities and develop effective public leaders.

FACILITIES

Housing: Coed dorms, special housing for disabled students, women's dorms, fraternity/sorority housing, apartments for married students, cooperative housing, apartments for single students, Theme Housing, Academic, cross-cultural, language theme and ethnic theme houses. 98% of campus accessible to physically diasbled. **Special Academic Facilities/Equipment:** Art museum, marine station, observatory, biological preserve, linear accelerator. **Computers:** 100% of classrooms, 100% of dorms, 100% of libraries, 100% of dining areas, 100% of student union, 75% of common outdoor areas have wireless network access. Students can register for classes online. Administrative functions (other than registration) can be performed online.

CAMPUS LIFE

Environment: City. **Activities:** Choral groups, concert band, dance, drama/theater, jazz band, literary magazine, marching band, music ensembles, musical theater, opera, pep band, radio station, student government, student newspaper, student-run film society, symphony orchestra, television station, yearbook, Campus Ministries, Student Organization, Model UN. 600 registered organizations, 40 religious organizations. 17 fraternities, 11 sororities. **Athletics (Intercollegiate):** *Men:* baseball, basketball, crew/rowing, cross-country, diving, fencing, football, golf, gymnastics, sailing, soccer, swimming, tennis, track/field (outdoor), volleyball, water polo, wrestling. *Women:* basketball, crew/rowing, cross-country, diving, fencing, field hockey, golf, gymnastics, lacrosse, sailing, soccer, softball, squash, swimming, synchronized swimming, tennis, track/field (outdoor), volleyball, water polo. **On-Campus Highlights:** Cantor Center for the Visual Arts, Rodin Sculpture Garden, Memorial Church, Observation Deck at Hoover Tower, athletic facilities, The Stanford campus is among the most beautiful anywhere and is a popular destination for tourists and other visitors. **Environmental Initiatives:** (a) SIGNIFICANT COMMITMENT TO SUSTAINABILITY PROJECT IMPLEMENTATION: (1) The Stanford Energy System Innovations (SESI) project is a $438 million major transformation of the campus district energy system from gas-fired combined heat and power with steam distribution to electrically-powered combined heat and cooling with hot water distribution. When completed, the new heat recovery system will be 52% more efficient than the existing cogeneration system; immediately cut Stanford greenhouse gas emissions in half; save 18% of Stanford drinking water supply; and save $303 million over the next 35 years compared to the existing system. Project additions with conceptual approval that are now under final feasibility study include the installation of 4 to 7 MW of on-site behind-the-meter photovoltaic (PV) power generation; installation of a Ground Source Heat Exchange system to augment the base heat recovery scheme; and the installation of a new 60kV high voltage transmission line connecting SLAC, Stanford, and the City of Palo Alto to strengthen the local transmission grid. http://sesi.stanford.edu (2) $433 million for the Initiative on Environment and Sustainability (research and teaching), a component of the Stanford Challenge http://thestanfordchallenge.stanford.edu/highlights-by-initiative/environment-sustainability/ (3) $70 million over the past ten years on energy retrofits, recommissioning, energy efficiency projects large and small, and water conservation measuresince 2002, energy retrofits of older building shave resulted in an estimated savings of 176 million kilowatt‐hours of electricity, about 8 months of Stanford current electricity use. Water consumption has been reduced from 2.7 million gallons per day to 2.15 million since 2001. New constructions and major renovations have energy and water standards comparable to LEED-NC GOLD. http://sustainable.stanford.edu/climate_action http://sustainable.stanford.edu/energy_initiatives http://sustainable.stanford.edu/water_initiatives http://sustainable.stanford.edu/guidelines

ADMISSIONS

Freshman Academic Profile: Average high school GPA 4.0. 96% in top 10% of high school class, 99% in top 25% of high school class, 100% in top 50% of high school class. 57% from public high schools. **Reported SAT (pre-2016 redesign) scores:** SAT Math middle 50% range 700-800. SAT Critical Reading middle 50% range 690-780. SAT Writing middle 50% range 690-780. **Concordant SAT scores:** SAT EBRW middle 50% 730–790. SAT Math middle 50% range 730–800. ACT middle 50% range 31-35. **Basis for Candidate Selection:** *Very important factors considered include:* rigor of secondary school record, class rank, academic GPA, standardized test scores, application essay, recommendation(s), extracurricular activities, talent/ability, character/personal qualities. *Other factors considered include:* interview, first generation, alumni/ae relation, geographical residence, racial/ethnic status, volunteer work, work experience. **Freshman Admission Requirements:** High school diploma is required and GED is accepted. *Academic units recommended:* 4 English, 4 math, 3 science, 3 science labs, 3 foreign language, 3 social studies, 3 history. **Freshman Admission Statistics:** 42,167 applied, 5.09% admitted, 78% enrolled. **Transfer Admission Requirements:** High school transcript, college transcript(s), essay or personal statement, standardized test scores, statement of good standing from prior institution(s). Lowest grade transferable C-. **General Admission Information:** Application fee $90. Regular application deadline 1/3. Regular notification 4/1. Nonfall registration not accepted. Admission may be deferred for a maximum of 2 years.

COSTS AND FINANCIAL AID

Annual tuition $47,331. Room and board $14,601. Required fees $609. Average book expense $1,425. **Required Forms and Deadlines:** FAFSA, CSS/Financial Aid PROFILE, Noncustodial PROFILE. **Notification of Awards:** Applicants will be notified of awards on a rolling basis beginning 4/1. **Types of Aid:** *Need-based scholarships/grants:* Federal Pell, FSEOG, State scholarships/grants, Private scholarships, College/university scholarship or grant aid from institutional funds. *Loans:* Direct Subsidized Stafford Loans, Direct Unsubsidized Stafford Loans, Direct PLUS loans, Federal Perkins Loans. *Student Employment:* Federal Work-Study Program available. Institutional employment available. **Financial Aid Statistics:** 95% needy freshmen, 100% needy undergrads receive need-based scholarship or grant aid. 3% freshmen, 3% undergrads receive non-need-based scholarship or grant aid. 59% freshmen, 76% undergrads receive need-based self-help aid. 7% freshmen, 7% undergrads receive athletic scholarships. 86% freshmen, 85% undergrads receive any aid. 22% undergrads borrow to pay for school. Average cumulative indebtedness $21,238. **Criteria for awarding aid:** *Non-need-based:* Athletics.

STATE UNIVERSITY OF NEW YORK— ALFRED STATE COLLEGE

Huntington Administration Bldg., Alfred, NY 14802
Phone: 607-587-4215 • **Financial Aid Phone:** 607-587-4253
E-mail: admissions@alfredstate.edu • **CEEB Code:** 2522
Fax: 607-587-4299 • **Website:** www.alfredstate.edu • **ACT Code:** 2910

This public school was founded in 1908. It has a 840-acre campus.

RATINGS

Admissions Selectivity Rating: 75 **Fire Safety Rating:** 90 **Green Rating:** 60*

STUDENTS AND FACULTY

Enrollment: 3,669. **Student Body:** 38% female, 62% male, 4% out-of-state, 2% international (13 countries represented). Asian 1%, African American 10%, Caucasian 76%, Hispanic 7%, Native American <1%, Pacific Islander <1%, Two or more races 2%, Race unknown 1%.
Retention and Graduation: 88% freshmen return for sophomore year. 53% freshmen graduate within 4 years. 60% freshmen graduate within 6 years. 38% grads go on to further study within 1 year. **Faculty:** Student/faculty ratio 18:1. 175 full-time faculty, 33% hold PhDs, 6% are are members of minority groups, 30% are women. 0% of classes are taught by teaching assistants.

ACADEMICS

Degrees: associate, bachelor's, certificate, terminal, transfer. **Classes:** Most classes have 10-19 students. Most lab/discussion sessions have 10-19 students. **Most popular majors:** Business, Management, Marketing, and Related Support Services; Mechanical Engineering/Mechanical Technology/Technician; Architectural Engineering Technology/Technician. **Special Study Options:** cooperative education program, cross-registration, distance learning, honors program, independent study, internships, student-designed major, study abroad, Internet courses. **Honors Programs:** Participants complete a series of seminars, as well as a substantial honors project and 10 hours of volunteer community service. **Disability Services:** Special programs offered to physically disabled students, including note-taking services, reader services, tape recorders, tutors. **Career Services:** Alumni network, Career/job search classes.

FACILITIES

Housing: Coed dorms, special housing for disabled students, Suite, corridor, singles, smoke-free, over 21 yrs, over 24 yrs, wellness living, quiet study, same curriculum housing, baccalaureate, single room options, and computer life style New upperclassmen apartment suite complex. 100% of campus accessible to physically diasbled. **Computers:** 100% of classrooms, 100% of dorms, 100% of libraries, 100% of dining areas, 100% of common outdoor areas have wireless network access. Students can register for classes online. Administrative functions (other than registration) can be performed online.

CAMPUS LIFE

Environment: Rural. **Activities:** Choral groups, concert band, drama/theater, jazz band, literary magazine, music ensembles, musical theater, radio station, student government, student newspaper, symphony orchestra, yearbook. 60 registered organizations, 4 honor societies, 3 fraternities, 2 sororities. **Athletics (Intercollegiate):** *Men:* baseball, basketball, cheerleading, cross-country, football, lacrosse, soccer, swimming, track/field (outdoor), wrestling. *Women:* basketball, cheerleading, cross-country, soccer, softball, swimming, track/field (outdoor), volleyball. **On-Campus Highlights:** Pioneer Center, Orvis (Athletic Center), Peach Pit, Central Dining Hall, Upperclassmen Apartment Suite Complex. **Environmental Initiatives:** Energy conservation, greenhouse gas inventory and shrinking our carbon footprint through renewable energy.

ADMISSIONS

Freshman Academic Profile: Average high school GPA 3.0. **Reported SAT (pre-2016 redesign) scores:** SAT Math middle 50% range 430-550. SAT Critical Reading middle 50% range 410-530. **Concordant SAT scores:** SAT Math middle 50% range 470–570. ACT middle 50% range 18-24. Minimum internet-based TOEFL 61. Minimum paper TOEFL 500. **Basis for Candidate Selection:** *Very important factors considered include:* rigor of secondary school record, academic GPA, standardized test scores. *Other factors considered include:* application essay, recommendation(s), interview, extracurricular activities, talent/ability, character/personal qualities, volunteer work, work experience, level of applicant's interest. **Freshman Admission Requirements:** High school diploma is required and GED is accepted. *Academic units recommended:* 4 English, 4 math, 4 science, 4 social studies. **Freshman Admission Statistics:** 4,912 applied, 56.80% admitted, 38% enrolled. **Transfer Admission Requirements:** High school transcript, college transcript(s), statement of good standing from prior institution(s). Minimum college GPA of 2.4 required. Lowest grade transferable C. **General Admission Information:** Application fee $50. Nonfall registration accepted. Admission may be deferred for a maximum of 1 semester.

COSTS AND FINANCIAL AID

Annual in-state tuition $6,470. Annual out-of-state tuition $9,740. Room and board $12,010. Required fees $1,587. Average book expense $1,200. **Required Forms and Deadlines:** FAFSA, State aid form. **Notification of Awards:** Applicants will be notified of awards on a rolling basis beginning 3/1. **Types of Aid:** *Need-based scholarships/grants:* Federal Pell, FSEOG, State scholarships/grants, Private scholarships, College/university scholarship or grant aid from institutional funds. *Loans:* Direct Subsidized Stafford Loans, Direct Unsubsidized Stafford Loans, Direct PLUS loans, Federal Perkins Loans, Federal Nursing Loans, State Loans. *Student Employment:* Federal Work-Study Program available. Institutional employment available. **Financial Aid Statistics:** 83% needy freshmen, 79% needy undergrads receive need-based scholarship or grant aid. 34% freshmen, 29% undergrads receive non-need-based scholarship or grant aid. 87% freshmen, 86% undergrads receive need-based self-help aid. 0% freshmen, 0% undergrads receive athletic scholarships. 83% freshmen, 79% undergrads receive any aid. 88% undergrads borrow to pay for school. Average cumulative indebtedness $30,200. **Criteria for awarding aid:** *Non-need-based:* Academics, Alumni affiliation, Job skills, Music/drama, State/district residency.

STATE UNIVERSITY OF NEW YORK AT BINGHAMTON (BINGHAMTON UNIVERSITY)

PO Box 6001, Binghamton, NY 13902-6001
Phone: 607-777-2171 • **Financial Aid Phone:** 607-777-2428
E-mail: admit@binghamton.edu • **CEEB Code:** 2535
Fax: 607-777-4445 • **Website:** www.binghamton.edu • **ACT Code:** 2956

This public school was founded in 1946. It has a 930-acre campus.

RATINGS

Admissions Selectivity Rating: 91 **Fire Safety Rating:** 94 **Green Rating:** 95

STUDENTS AND FACULTY

Enrollment: 13,578. **Student Body:** 48% female, 52% male, 7% out-of-state, 9% international (115 countries represented). Asian 14%, African American 5%, Caucasian 57%, Hispanic 11%, Native American <1%, Pacific Islander <1%, Two or more races 2%, Race unknown 2%.

Retention and Graduation: 92% freshmen return for sophomore year. 71% freshmen graduate within 4 years. 83% freshmen graduate within 6 years. 57% grads go on to further study within 1 year. 2% grads pursue law degrees. 9% grads pursue business degrees. 6% grads pursue medical degrees. **Faculty:** Student/faculty ratio 19:1. 725 full-time faculty, 92% hold PhDs, 30% are are members of minority groups, 42% are women. 9% of classes are taught by teaching assistants.

ACADEMICS

Degrees: bachelor's, doctoral/professional, doctoral/research, master's, post-master's certificate. **Classes:** Most classes have 10-19 students. Most lab/discussion sessions have 20-29 students. **Most popular majors:** Business Administration and Management; Engineering; Psychology. **Special Study Options:** Accelerated program, cross-registration, distance learning, double major, dual enrollment, English as a Second Language (ESL), exchange student program (domestic), honors program, independent study, internships, liberal arts/career combination, student-designed major, study abroad, teacher certification program, Teacher Certification Program is graduate only. **Honors Programs:** Binghamton University Scholars Program–See http://scholars.binghamton.edu Each academic department offers an honors program. Binghamton also has a PricewaterhouseCoopers Scholars program for students in the School of Management. Combined degree programs: BA/MA, Nearly 100 different bachelors/masters combinations. **Disability Services:** Special programs offered to physically disabled students, including note-taking services, reader services, tape recorders. **Career Services:** Alumni network, Alumni services, Career/job search classes, Career assessment, Internships, Regional alumni. Binghamton University transformed their career center last year in terms of space, structure, and offerings. Thanks to a significant donation from a Binghamton alumnus, a brand new state-of-the art career center was opened in the heart of campus, now named the Fleishman Center for Career and Professional Development. Staff now serve students through a 'career community' approach. Career Communities are tailored to the unique career development needs/interests of our students, including 'entrepreneurship' for example, and staff are responsible for collaborating with student organizations, faculty, and departments across campus to connect students with alumni and employers within their assigned community. With more than 117,000 alumni spread across the globe, a great emphasis is placed on connecting students with alumni through cutting-edge programs. For example, Bearcats in the City is a week long program during January in New York City where students learn about different careers through nearly 50 employer site visits and network with alumni to receive guidance on achieving professional success through "Metro Career Night". Additionally, a collaborative program with the Alumni Association allows for interactive, virtual connections with alumni around the world in a variety of career fields. Binghamton also encourages student participation in high-impact internships, as demonstrated by Binghamton students participating in academic internships at a significantly higher rate than the national average. The CDCI internship program facilitates the annual placement of 1000+ students in local, regional and national credit-bearing internships.

FACILITIES

Housing: Coed dorms, special housing for disabled students, apartments for single students, Wellness Housing, Theme Housing. 95% of campus accessible to physically diasbled. **Special Academic Facilities/Equipment:** Art gallery, performing arts center, indoor/outdoor theater, multi-climate and teaching greenhouse, sculpture foundry, 8,000-seat Events Center, Analytical and Diagnostics Laboratory, Electron Microscopy Facility, Public Archaeology Facility, 930-acre Nature Preserve. **Computers:** 95% of classrooms, 100% of dorms, 100% of libraries, 100% of dining areas, 100% of student union, 60% of common outdoor areas have wireless network access. Students can register for classes online. Administrative functions (other than registration) can be performed online.

CAMPUS LIFE

Environment: City. **Activities:** Choral groups, concert band, dance, drama/theater, jazz band, literary magazine, music ensembles, musical theater, opera, pep band, radio station, student government, student newspaper, student-run film society, symphony orchestra, television station, yearbook, Campus Ministries, Student Organization, Model UN. 23 honor societies, 15 religious organizations. 23 fraternities, 23 sororities. **Athletics (Intercollegiate):** *Men:* baseball, basketball, cross-country, diving, golf, lacrosse, soccer, swimming, tennis, track/field (outdoor), track/field (indoor), wrestling. *Women:* basketball, cross-country, diving, lacrosse, soccer, softball, swimming, tennis, track/field (outdoor), track/field (indoor), volleyball. **On-Campus Highlights:** University Union, Fitspace, Nature Preserve, Events Center, Anderson Center for the Arts, Rosefsky Art Gallery, Libraries. **Environmental Initiatives:** Binghamton University designs, constructs, operates and maintains all new buildings following guidelines set forth by the U.S. Green Building Council's LEED rating system. Since 2004, Binghamton has obtained multiple LEED certifications under the New Construction program including 2 LEED, 3 LEED Silver, 7 LEED Gold, and 1 LEED Platinum for a total of 1,690,183 square feet of building space. This represents 27% of total building space owned by Binghamton University.

ADMISSIONS

Freshman Academic Profile: Average high school GPA 3.7. 90% from public high schools. **Reported SAT (pre-2016 redesign) scores:** SAT Math middle 50% range 630-710. SAT Critical Reading middle 50% range 600-690. SAT Writing middle 50% range 580-670. **Concordant SAT scores:** SAT EBRW middle 50% 650–720. SAT Math middle 50% range 650–740. ACT middle 50% range 28-31. Minimum internet-based TOEFL 83. Minimum paper TOEFL 560. **Basis for Candidate Selection:** *Very important factors considered include:* rigor of secondary school record, academic GPA, standardized test scores. *Important factors considered include:* class rank, application essay, recommendation(s), extracurricular activities. *Other factors considered include:* talent/ability, character/personal qualities, first generation, alumni/ae relation, geographical residence, state residency, racial/ethnic status, volunteer work, work experience, level of applicant's interest. **Freshman Admission Requirements:** High school diploma is required and GED is accepted. *Academic units required:* 4 English, 3 math, 2 science, 3 foreign language, 2 social studies. *Academic units recommended:* 4 math, 4 science, 4 social studies, 4 history. **Freshman Admission Statistics:** 32,139 applied, 40.62% admitted, 21% enrolled. **Transfer Admission Requirements:** college transcript(s), Lowest grade transferable C-. **General Admission Information:** Application fee $50. Priority deadline 1/15. Nonfall registration accepted. Admission may be deferred.

COSTS AND FINANCIAL AID

Annual in-state tuition $6,470. Annual out-of-state tuition $21,550. Room and board $13,590. Required fees $2,801. Average book expense $1,000. **Required Forms and Deadlines:** FAFSA, State aid form. **Notification of Awards:** Applicants will be notified of awards on a rolling basis beginning 3/4. **Types of Aid:** *Need-based scholarships/grants:* Federal Pell, FSEOG, State scholarships/grants, Private scholarships, College/university scholarship or grant aid from institutional funds. *Loans:* Direct Subsidized Stafford Loans, Direct Unsubsidized Stafford Loans, Direct PLUS loans, Federal Perkins Loans, Federal Nursing Loans, College/university loans from institutional funds. *Student Employment:* Federal Work-Study Program available. Institutional employment available. **Financial Aid Statistics:** 80% needy freshmen, 83% needy undergrads receive need-based scholarship or grant aid. 13% freshmen, 7% undergrads receive non-need-based scholarship or grant aid. 96% freshmen, 97% undergrads receive need-based self-help aid. 4% freshmen, 3% undergrads receive athletic scholarships. 81% freshmen, 70% undergrads receive any aid. 50% undergrads borrow to pay for school. Average cumulative indebtedness $25,718. **Criteria for awarding aid:** *Need-based:* Academics, Art, Athletics, Leadership, Minority status, Music/drama. *Non-need-based:* Academics, Art, Athletics, Leadership, Minority status, Music/drama, State/district residency.

STATE UNIVERSITY OF NEW YORK AT COBLESKILL

Knapp Hall, Cobleskill, NY 12043
Phone: 518-255-5525 • **Financial Aid Phone:** 518-255-5623
E-mail: admissions@cobleskill.edu • **CEEB Code:** 2524
Fax: 518-255-6769 • **Website:** www.cobleskill.edu • **ACT Code:** 2914

This public school was founded in 1916. It has a 750-acre campus.

RATINGS

Admissions Selectivity Rating: 74   **Fire Safety Rating:** 83   **Green Rating:** 72

STUDENTS AND FACULTY

Enrollment: 2,421. **Student Body:** 52% female, 48% male, 10% out-of-state, 1% international (11 countries represented). Asian 1%, African American 12%, Caucasian 74%, Hispanic 7%, Native American <1%, Pacific Islander 0%, Two or more races 0%, Race unknown 5%.
Retention and Graduation: 74% freshmen return for sophomore year. 29% freshmen graduate within 4 years. 44% freshmen graduate within 6 years. 63% grads go on to further study within 1 year. **Faculty:** Student/faculty ratio 18:1. 100 full-time faculty, 46% hold PhDs, 7% are are members of minority groups, 33% are women. 0% of classes are taught by teaching assistants.

ACADEMICS

Degrees: associate, bachelor's, certificate, terminal, transfer. **Classes:** Most classes have 10-19 students. Most lab/discussion sessions have 10-19 students. **Most popular majors:** Animal Sciences; Business Administration and Management; Wildlife, Fish and Wildlands Science and Management. **Special Study Options:** cross-registration, distance learning, English as a Second Language (ESL), honors program, internships, study abroad, weekend college. **Disability Services:** Special programs offered to physically disabled students, including note-taking services, reader services, tape recorders, tutors. **Career**

Services: Alumni services, Career/job search classes, Career assessment, Internships. A 15 week internship is required for nearly all of the baccalaureate programs. It is the capstone ot our 4-year degrees

FACILITIES

Housing: Coed dorms, special housing for disabled students, men's dorms, women's dorms, LIfestyle floors: designated quiet study lifestyle, wellness lifestyle, sustainability lifestyle, sophomore experience, upper class experience. **Special Academic Facilities/Equipment:** Art museum, 650 acre agricultural campus, distance learning classrooms, ski area, adult study center. **Computers:** Students can register for classes online. Administrative functions (other than registration) can be performed online.

CAMPUS LIFE

Environment: Rural. **Activities:** drama/theater, student government, student newspaper, Campus Ministries, Student Organization. 40 registered organizations, 1 honor society, 1 religious organization. **Athletics (Intercollegiate):** *Men:* baseball, basketball, cross-country, diving, equestrian sports, golf, lacrosse, soccer, swimming, tennis, track/field (outdoor), volleyball. *Women:* basketball, cross-country, diving, equestrian sports, golf, soccer, softball, swimming, tennis, track/field (outdoor), volleyball. **On-Campus Highlights:** Bouck Hall/Student Union, Brickyard Point, American Heritage, Foundation Equestrian Center, Grosvenor Art Gallery. **Environmental Initiatives:** recycling—paper, plastics, metals, galss and cardboard boxes.

ADMISSIONS

Freshman Academic Profile: Average high school GPA 82.0. 6% in top 10% of high school class, 22% in top 25% of high school class, 56% in top 50% of high school class. 98% from public high schools. **Reported SAT (pre-2016 redesign) scores:** SAT Math middle 50% range 380-500. SAT Critical Reading middle 50% range 380-500. **Concordant SAT scores:** SAT Math middle 50% range 420–530. ACT middle 50% range 17-22. Minimum paper TOEFL 500. **Basis for Candidate Selection:** *Very important factors considered include:* rigor of secondary school record, academic GPA, standardized test scores, level of applicant's interest. *Other factors considered include:* class rank, application essay, recommendation(s), interview, extracurricular activities, talent/ability, character/personal qualities, first generation, alumni/ae relation, geographical residence, state residency, volunteer work, work experience. **Freshman Admission Requirements:** High school diploma is required and GED is accepted. *Academic units recommended:* 3 English, 3 math, 3 science, 3 science labs, 1 foreign language, 3 social studies, 3 history, 3 academic electives. **Freshman Admission Statistics:** 2,765 applied, 73.09% admitted, 39% enrolled. **Transfer Admission Requirements:** college transcript(s), Minimum college GPA of 2.25 required. Lowest grade transferable D. **General Admission Information:** Application fee $50. Nonfall registration accepted. Admission may be deferred for a maximum of 1 year.

COSTS AND FINANCIAL AID

Annual in-state tuition $5,870. Annual out-of-state tuition $15,320. Room and board $11,720. Required fees $1,279. Average book expense $1,200. **Required Forms and Deadlines:** FAFSA, State aid form. **Notification of Awards:** Applicants will be notified of awards on a rolling basis beginning 3/15. **Types of Aid:** *Need-based scholarships/grants:* Federal Pell, FSEOG, State scholarships/grants, Private scholarships, College/university scholarship or grant aid from institutional funds. *Loans:* Direct Subsidized Stafford Loans, Direct Unsubsidized Stafford Loans, Direct PLUS loans, Federal Perkins Loans. *Student Employment:* Federal Work-Study Program available. Institutional employment available. **Financial Aid Statistics:** 100% needy freshmen, 99% needy undergrads receive need-based scholarship or grant aid. 33% freshmen, 22% undergrads receive non-need-based scholarship or grant aid. 84% freshmen, 80% undergrads receive need-based self-help aid. 0% freshmen, 0% undergrads receive athletic scholarships. 81% freshmen, 75% undergrads receive any aid. **Criteria for awarding aid:** *Non-need-based:* Academics, Alumni affiliation, Leadership, State/district residency.

STATE UNIVERSITY OF NEW YORK AT CORTLAND

PO Box 2000, Cortland, NY 13045-0900
Phone: 607-753-4712 • **Financial Aid Phone:** 607-753-4717
E-mail: admissions@cortland.edu • **CEEB Code:** 2538
Fax: 607-753-5998 • **Website:** http://www2.cortland.edu/home/ • **ACT Code:** 2932

This public school was founded in 1868. It has a 191-acre campus.

RATINGS

Admissions Selectivity Rating: 81   **Fire Safety Rating:** 65   **Green Rating:** 97

STUDENTS AND FACULTY

Enrollment: 6,276. **Student Body:** 57% female, 43% male, 4% out-of-state, 1% international (14 countries represented). Asian 1%, African American 6%, Caucasian 74%, Hispanic 11%, Native American <1%, Pacific Islander <1%, Two or more races 2%, Race unknown 5%. **Retention and Graduation:** 78% freshmen return for sophomore year. 53% freshmen graduate within 4 years. **Faculty:** Student/faculty ratio 17:1. 293 full-time faculty, 78% hold PhDs, 13% are members of minority groups, 53% are women. 0% of classes are taught by teaching assistants.

ACADEMICS

Degrees: bachelor's, master's, postbachelor's certificate, post-master's certificate. **Classes:** Most classes have 20-29 students. Most lab/discussion sessions have 20-29 students. **Special Study Options:** cooperative education program, cross-registration, distance learning, double major, dual enrollment, exchange student program (domestic), honors program, independent study, internships, liberal arts/career combination, student-designed major, study abroad, teacher certification program. **Disability Services:** Special programs offered to physically disabled students, including note-taking services, reader services, tape recorders, tutors.

FACILITIES

Housing: Coed dorms, special housing for disabled students, special housing for international students, cooperative housing, apartments for single students, Wellness HousingLeadership House, Transfer Floor, Quiet Atmosphere. 75% of campus accessible to physically disabled. **Special Academic Facilities/Equipment:** Natural science museum, greenhouse, center for speech and hearing disorders, classrooms with integrated technologies, specialized labs to support various program offerings. **Computers:** Students can register for classes online. Administrative functions (other than registration) can be performed online.

CAMPUS LIFE

Environment: Village. **Activities:** Choral groups, dance, drama/theater, literary magazine, music ensembles, musical theater, radio station, student government, student newspaper, student-run film society, symphony orchestra, television station, yearbook, Campus Ministries, Student Organization, Model UN. 100 registered organizations, 16 honor societies, 3 religious organizations. 2 fraternities, 5 sororities. **Athletics (Intercollegiate):** *Men:* baseball, basketball, cheerleading, cross-country, diving, football, gymnastics, ice hockey, lacrosse, soccer, swimming, track/field (outdoor), track/field (indoor), wrestling. *Women:* basketball, cheerleading, cross-country, diving, field hockey, golf, gymnastics, ice hockey, lacrosse, soccer, softball, swimming, tennis, track/field (outdoor), track/field (indoor), volleyball. **On-Campus Highlights:** Corey Union, Stadium Complex, Fitness Facilities, Dining Halls, Library.

ADMISSIONS

Freshman Academic Profile: Average high school GPA 88.9. 10% in top 10% of high school class, 39% in top 25% of high school class, 50% in top 50% of high school class. 91% from public high schools. **Reported SAT (pre-2016 redesign) scores:** SAT Math middle 50% range 490-560. SAT Critical Reading middle 50% range 470-550. **Concordant SAT scores:** SAT Math middle 50% range 520–580. ACT middle 50% range 22-25. Minimum paper TOEFL 550. **Basis for Candidate Selection:** *Very important factors considered include:* rigor of secondary school record, academic GPA, standardized test scores. *Important factors considered include:* application essay, recommendation(s), extracurricular activities, talent/ability. *Other factors considered include:* class rank, interview, alumni/ae relation, geographical residence, state residency, racial/ethnic status, volunteer work, work experience. **Freshman Admission Requirements:** High school diploma is required and GED is accepted. *Academic units required:* 4 English, 3 math, 3 science, 3 science labs, 3 foreign language, 4 social studies. *Academic units recommended:* 4 English, 4 math, 4 science, 4 science labs, 4 foreign language, 4 social studies. **Freshman Admission Statistics:** 11,060 applied, 50.84% admitted, 22% enrolled. **Transfer Admission Requirements:** High school transcript, college transcript(s), Minimum college GPA of 2.5 required. Lowest grade transferable C-. **General Admission Information:** Application fee $50. Priority deadline 12/1. Nonfall registration accepted. Admission may be deferred for a maximum of 1 year.

COSTS AND FINANCIAL AID

Annual in-state tuition $6,470. Annual out-of-state tuition $16,320. Room and board $12,200. Required fees $1,636. Average book expense $1,000. **Required Forms and Deadlines:** FAFSA, State aid form. **Notification of Awards:** Applicants will be notified of awards on a rolling basis beginning 3/15. **Types of Aid:** *Need-based scholarships/grants:* Federal Pell, FSEOG, State scholarships/grants, Private scholarships, College/university scholarship or grant aid from institutional funds. *Loans:* Direct Subsidized Stafford Loans, Direct Unsubsidized Stafford Loans, Direct PLUS loans, Federal Perkins Loans. *Student Employment:* Federal Work-Study Program available. Institutional employment available. **Financial Aid Statistics:** 71% needy freshmen, 72% needy undergrads receive need-based scholarship or grant aid. 37% freshmen, 24% undergrads receive non-need-based scholarship or grant aid. 87%

freshmen, 87% undergrads receive need-based self-help aid. 0% freshmen, 0% undergrads receive athletic scholarships. 74% undergrads borrow to pay for school. Average cumulative indebtedness $28,070. **Criteria for awarding aid:** *Need-based:* Academics, Art, Leadership, Music/drama. *Non-need-based:* Academics, Art, Leadership, Minority status, Music/drama, State/district residency.

STATE UNIVERSITY OF NEW YORK AT GENESEO

1 College Circle, Geneseo, NY 14454
Phone: 585-245-5571 • **Financial Aid Phone:** 585-245-5731
E-mail: admissions@geneseo.edu • **CEEB Code:** 2540
Fax: 585-245-5550 • **Website:** www.geneseo.edu • **ACT Code:** 2936

This public school was founded in 1871. It has a 220-acre campus.

RATINGS

Admissions Selectivity Rating: 87   Fire Safety Rating: 98   Green Rating: 87

STUDENTS AND FACULTY

Enrollment: 5,405. **Student Body:** 59% female, 41% male, 2% out-of-state, 2% international (26 countries represented). Asian 6%, African American 3%, Caucasian 75%, Hispanic 8%, Native American <1%, Pacific Islander <1%, Two or more races 3%, Race unknown 3%.
Retention and Graduation: 87% freshmen return for sophomore year. 71% freshmen graduate within 4 years. 81% freshmen graduate within 6 years. 33% grads go on to further study within 1 year. 36% grads pursue arts and sciences degrees. 8% grads pursue law degrees. 8% grads pursue business degrees. 22% grads pursue medical degrees. **Faculty:** Student/faculty ratio 19:1. 251 full-time faculty, 88% hold PhDs, 17% are are members of minority groups, 45% are women. 0% of classes are taught by teaching assistants.

ACADEMICS

Degrees: bachelor's, master's. **Classes:** Most classes have 20-29 students. Most lab/discussion sessions have 10-19 students. **Most popular majors:** Business Administration and Management; Biology; Psychology. **Special Study Options:** cross-registration, double major, dual enrollment, English as a Second Language (ESL), honors program, independent study, internships, study abroad, teacher certification program, Albany semester, Washington semester, 3/2 Engineering, 3-3 Engineering, 4/1 MBA, 3/4 Dentistry, 3/4 Optometry, 3/4 Osteopathic Medicine, 3/2 or 3/1 nursing, 3/3 physical therapy, pre-med and pre-law advisory program. Combined degree programs: BA/MA, BA/DDS, BA/DO; BA/OD. **Disability Services:** Special programs offered to physically disabled students, including note-taking services, reader services, tape recorders. **Career Services:** Alumni network, Alumni services, Career/job search classes, Career assessment, Internships.

FACILITIES

Housing: Coed dorms, special housing for disabled students, special housing for international students, Town houses and special interest housing is available. Some fraternities and sororities have housing independent of college. 95% of campus accessible to physically diasbled. **Special Academic Facilities/ Equipment:** Four theatres, electron microscopes. Integrated Science Center **Computers:** 100% of classrooms, 60% of dorms, 100% of libraries, 100% of dining areas, 100% of student union, 10% of common outdoor areas have wireless network access. Students can register for classes online. Administrative functions (other than registration) can be performed online. Undergraduates are required to own a computer.

CAMPUS LIFE

Environment: Village. **Activities:** Choral groups, dance, drama/theater, jazz band, literary magazine, music ensembles, musical theater, pep band, radio station, student government, student newspaper, symphony orchestra, television station, Campus Ministries, Student Organization, Model UN. 175 registered organizations, 12 honor societies, 7 religious organizations. 8 fraternities, 11 sororities. **Athletics (Intercollegiate):** *Men:* basketball, cross-country, diving, ice hockey, lacrosse, soccer, swimming, track/field (outdoor), track/ field (indoor). *Women:* basketball, cross-country, diving, equestrian sports, field hockey, lacrosse, soccer, softball, swimming, tennis, track/field (outdoor), track/field (indoor), volleyball. **On-Campus Highlights:** MacVittie College Union, The Gazebo, Milne Library, Alumni Fieldhouse (Workout Center), College Green. **Environmental Initiatives:** Signing of the Presidents Climate Commitment. A final draft of the Climate Action Plan was released on July 2010.

ADMISSIONS

Freshman Academic Profile: Average high school GPA 3.7. 38% in top 10% of high school class, 74% in top 25% of high school class, 95% in top 50% of high school class. **Reported SAT (pre-2016 redesign) scores:** SAT Math middle 50% range 550-650. SAT Critical Reading middle 50% range 540-650. **Concordant SAT scores:** SAT Math middle 50% range 570–670. ACT middle 50% range 25-29. Minimum internet-based TOEFL 71. Minimum paper TOEFL 525. **Basis for Candidate Selection:** *Very important factors considered include:* rigor of secondary school record, standardized test scores. *Important factors considered include:* class rank, academic GPA, application essay, recommendation(s), extracurricular activities, talent/ability, racial/ ethnic status. *Other factors considered include:* character/personal qualities, first generation, alumni/ae relation, state residency, volunteer work, work experience, level of applicant's interest. **Freshman Admission Requirements:** High school diploma is required and GED is accepted. *Academic units recommended:* 4 English, 4 math, 4 science, 4 foreign language, 4 social studies. **Freshman Admission Statistics:** 8,892 applied, 66.85% admitted, 21% enrolled. **Transfer Admission Requirements:** High school transcript, college transcript(s), Minimum college GPA of 3.0 required. Lowest grade transferable D. **General Admission Information:** Application fee $50. Regular application deadline 1/1. Regular notification 3/1. Nonfall registration accepted. Admission may be deferred for a maximum of 1 year.

COSTS AND FINANCIAL AID

Annual in-state tuition $6,470. Annual out-of-state tuition $16,320. Room and board $12,264. Required fees $1,706. Average book expense $1,000. **Required Forms and Deadlines:** FAFSA, State aid form. **Notification of Awards:** Applicants will be notified of awards on a rolling basis beginning 3/15. **Types of Aid:** *Need-based scholarships/grants:* Federal Pell, FSEOG, State scholarships/ grants. *Loans:* Direct Subsidized Stafford Loans, Direct Unsubsidized Stafford Loans, Direct PLUS loans, Federal Perkins Loans. *Student Employment:* Federal Work-Study Program available. Institutional employment available. **Financial Aid Statistics:** 51% needy freshmen, 79% needy undergrads receive need-based scholarship or grant aid. 29% freshmen, 24% undergrads receive non-need-based scholarship or grant aid. 84% freshmen, 83% undergrads receive need-based self-help aid. 0% freshmen, 0% undergrads receive athletic scholarships. 71% freshmen, 66% undergrads receive any aid. 55% undergrads borrow to pay for school. Average cumulative indebtedness $24,784. **Criteria for awarding aid:** *Need-based:* Academics. *Non-need-based:* Academics, Art, Leadership, Minority status, Music/drama, Religious affiliation, State/district residency.

STATE UNIVERSITY OF NEW YORK AT NEW PALTZ

100 Hawk Drive, New Paltz, NY 12561
Phone: 845-257-3200 • **Financial Aid Phone:** 845-257-3250
E-mail: admissions@newpaltz.edu • **CEEB Code:** 2541
Fax: 845-257-3209 • **Website:** www.newpaltz.edu • **ACT Code:** 2938

This public school was founded in 1828. It has a 216-acre campus.

RATINGS

Admissions Selectivity Rating: 86   Fire Safety Rating: 93   Green Rating: 89

STUDENTS AND FACULTY

Enrollment: 6,582. **Student Body:** 62% female, 38% male, 3% out-of-state, 2% international. Asian 6%, African American 6%, Caucasian 63%, Hispanic 18%, Native American <1%, Pacific Islander <1%, Two or more races 2%, Race unknown 3%.
Retention and Graduation: 87% freshmen return for sophomore year. 54% freshmen graduate within 4 years. 72% freshmen graduate within 6 years. 19% grads go on to further study within 1 year. **Faculty:** Student/faculty ratio 15:1. 372 full-time faculty, 83% hold PhDs, 19% are are members of minority groups, 52% are women. 1% of classes are taught by teaching assistants.

ACADEMICS

Degrees: bachelor's, master's, postbachelor's certifiate, post-master's certificate. **Classes:** Most classes have 20-29 students. **Most popular majors:** Psychology; Elementary Education and Teaching; Sociology. **Special Study Options:** cooperative education program, cross-registration, distance learning, double major, dual enrollment, English as a Second Language (ESL), exchange student program (domestic), honors program, independent study, internships, liberal arts/career combination, student-designed major, study abroad, teacher certification program. **Honors Programs:** The Honors Program exists to challenge New Paltz Students beyond what is usually expected of them. It was designed around the philosophy that intense and rigorous courses, taught by outstanding instructors and filled with motivated, focused students would create the optimal learning environment. The Honors Program is small, consisting of around 100 students. Once admitted to the Program, students take special Honors seminars, which are interdisciplinary and small in size (usually around 10 students). Unlike traditional lecture courses, Honors seminars emphasize dialogue and non-lecture based learning; students are expected to come to class with something to say and to actively participate in debate and discussion. Combined degree programs: BS/DO BS/MS BA/MAT. **Disability Services:** Special programs offered to physically disabled students, including note-taking services, reader services, tape recorders, tutors. **Career Services:** Alumni services, Career/job search classes, Career assessment, Internships. Internship stipend program provides SUNY New Paltz students with scholarship stipends. These funds allow students to participate in career related experiences regardless of financial constraints

FACILITIES

Housing: Coed dorms, special housing for disabled students, men's dorms, special housing for international students, women's dorms, The First-Year Initiative, Honors Housing, Art Program Housing. 90% of campus accessible to physically diasbled. **Special Academic Facilities/Equipment:** Samuel Dorsky Museum of Art, Resnick Engineering Hall, Coykendall Media Center, Communication Disorders Training Center and Clinic; Music Therapy Training Center and Clinic; Shepherd Recital Hall, Honors Center; Martin Luther King, Jr. Study Center; Fournier Mass Spectrometer; Raymond Kurdt Theatre Collection. **Computers:** 70% of classrooms, 45% of dorms, 100% of libraries, 90% of dining areas, 90% of student union, 10% of common outdoor areas have wireless network access. Students can register for classes online. Administrative functions (other than registration) can be performed online.

CAMPUS LIFE

Environment: Village. **Activities:** Choral groups, concert band, dance, drama/theater, jazz band, literary magazine, music ensembles, musical theater, radio station, student government, student newspaper, symphony orchestra, television station, Campus Ministries, Student Organization, Model UN. 196 registered organizations, 12 honor societies, 10 religious organizations. 11 fraternities, 17 sororities. **Athletics (Intercollegiate):** *Men:* baseball, basketball, cross-country, diving, soccer, swimming, tennis, volleyball. *Women:* basketball, cross-country, diving, field hockey, lacrosse, soccer, softball, swimming, tennis, volleyball. **On-Campus Highlights:** Samuel Dorsky Museum of Art, Lenape and Esopus Residence Halls, Athletic and Wellness Center, Student Union, Hasbrouck Dining Hall. **Environmental Initiatives:** Investing $2 million in a campus wide submetering system for electricity, natural gas, high temp hot water, and domestic water.

ADMISSIONS

Freshman Academic Profile: Average high school GPA 3.6. 20% in top 10% of high school class, 58% in top 25% of high school class, 91% in top 50% of high school class. 92% from public high schools. **Reported SAT (pre-2016 redesign) scores:** SAT Math middle 50% range 510-600. SAT Critical Reading middle 50% range 500-600. SAT Writing middle 50% range 500-590. **Concordant SAT scores:** SAT EBRW middle 50% 560–650. SAT Math middle 50% range 540–620. ACT middle 50% range 23-27. Minimum internet-based TOEFL 80. Minimum paper TOEFL 550. **Basis for Candidate Selection:** *Very important factors considered include:* rigor of secondary school record, academic GPA, standardized test scores. *Important factors considered include:* application essay, recommendation(s). *Other factors considered include:* extracurricular activities, talent/ability, volunteer work, work experience, level of applicant's interest. **Freshman Admission Requirements:** High school diploma is required and GED is accepted. *Academic units required:* 4 English, 3 math, 3 science, 3 science labs, 2 foreign language, 4 social studies, 1 history. *Academic units recommended:* 4 English, 4 math, 4 science, 4 science labs, 4 foreign language, 4 social studies, 1 history. **Freshman Admission Statistics:** 14,042 applied, 42.94% admitted, 18% enrolled. **Transfer Admission Requirements:** college transcript(s), statement of good standing from prior institution(s). Minimum college GPA of 2.75 required. Lowest grade transferable C-. **General Admission Information:** Application fee $50. Regular application deadline 4/1. Nonfall registration not accepted.

COSTS AND FINANCIAL AID

Average book expense $1,600. **Required Forms and Deadlines:** FAFSA, State aid form. **Notification of Awards:** Applicants will be notified of awards on a rolling basis beginning 4/1. **Types of Aid:** *Need-based scholarships/ grants:* Federal Pell, FSEOG, State scholarships/grants, Private scholarships, College/university scholarship or grant aid from institutional funds. *Loans:* Direct Subsidized Stafford Loans, Direct Unsubsidized Stafford Loans, Direct PLUS loans, Federal Perkins Loans. *Student Employment:* Federal Work-Study Program available. Institutional employment available. **Financial Aid Statistics:** 54% needy freshmen, 59% needy undergrads receive need-based scholarship or grant aid. 10% freshmen, 8% undergrads receive non-need-based scholarship or grant aid. 87% freshmen, 89% undergrads receive need-based self-help aid. 0% freshmen, 0% undergrads receive athletic scholarships. Average cumulative indebtedness $26,283. **Criteria for awarding aid:** *Need-*

based: Academics, Alumni affiliation, Art. *Non-need-based:* Academics, Alumni affiliation, Art, Music/drama.

STATE UNIVERSITY OF NEW YORK AT PURCHASE COLLEGE

Phone: 914-251-6300
E-mail: admissions@purchase.edu • **CEEB Code:** 2878
Fax: 914-251-6314 • **Website:** www.purchase.edu • **ACT Code:** 2931

This public school was founded in 1967. It has a 550-acre campus.

RATINGS

Admissions Selectivity Rating: 88   **Fire Safety Rating:** 60*   **Green Rating:** 60*

STUDENTS AND FACULTY

Enrollment: 3,944. **Student Body:** 57% female, 43% male, 15% out-of-state, 2% international (39 countries represented). Asian 4%, African American 11%, Caucasian 53%, Hispanic 19%, Native American <1%, Pacific Islander <1%, Two or more races 5%, Race unknown 6%.
Retention and Graduation: 81% freshmen return for sophomore year. 54% freshmen graduate within 4 years. 63% freshmen graduate within 6 years.
Faculty: Student/faculty ratio 14:1. 167 full-time faculty, 49% hold PhDs, 20% are are members of minority groups, 55% are women. 1% of classes are taught by teaching assistants.

ACADEMICS

Degrees: bachelor's, certificate, master's, postbachelor's certifiate, post-master's certificate. **Classes:** Most classes have 10-19 students. Most lab/discussion sessions have 10-19 students. **Most popular majors:** Visual and Performing Arts; Liberal Arts and Sciences/Liberal Studies. **Special Study Options:** cross-registration, distance learning, double major, English as a Second Language (ESL), independent study, internships, liberal arts/career combination, student-designed major, study abroad. **Disability Services:** Special programs offered to physically disabled students, including note-taking services, reader services, tape recorders, tutors. **Career Services:** Alumni services, Career/job search classes, Career assessment, Internships.

FACILITIES

Housing: Coed dorms, special housing for disabled students, special housing for international students, apartments for married students, apartments for single students, Wellness Housing, Theme Housing. 100% of campus accessible to physically diasbled. **Special Academic Facilities/Equipment:** Museum, four-theatre performing arts center, visual arts facility, children's center, recording studio, electron microscopes. **Computers:** Students can register for classes online. Administrative functions (other than registration) can be performed online.

CAMPUS LIFE

Environment: Town. **Activities:** Choral groups, dance, drama/theater, jazz band, literary magazine, music ensembles, musical theater, radio station, student government, student newspaper, student-run film society, television station 30 registered organizations. **Athletics (Intercollegiate):** *Men:* baseball, basketball, cross-country, golf, soccer, tennis, volleyball. *Women:* basketball, cross-country, soccer, softball, tennis, volleyball. **On-Campus Highlights:** The Performing Arts Center, The Neuberger Museum, State-of-the-Art Athletic Complex, Starbucks, Fort Awesome, New Student Services building. **Environmental Initiatives:** Commited to reduce GHG emissions by 80% by 2050 (Presidents Climate Commitment).

ADMISSIONS

Freshman Academic Profile: Average high school GPA 3.2. **Reported SAT (pre-2016 redesign) scores:** SAT Math middle 50% range 470-570. SAT Critical Reading middle 50% range 500-610. **Concordant SAT scores:** SAT Math middle 50% range 510–590. ACT middle 50% range 20-27. Minimum paper TOEFL 550. **Basis for Candidate Selection:** *Very important factors considered include:* academic GPA, application essay, talent/ability. *Important factors considered include:* standardized test scores. *Other factors considered include:* rigor of secondary school record, class rank, recommendation(s), interview, extracurricular activities, character/personal qualities. **Freshman Admission Requirements:** High school diploma is required and GED is accepted. *Academic units recommended:* 4 English, 4 math, 3 science, 3 foreign language, 4 social studies, 2 academic electives. **Freshman Admission**

Statistics: 6,762 applied, 43.51% admitted, 25% enrolled. **Transfer Admission Requirements:** college transcript(s), Minimum college GPA of 3.0 required. Lowest grade transferable D. **General Admission Information:** Application fee $50. Priority deadline 3/1. Regular application deadline 7/15. Nonfall registration accepted. Admission may be deferred.

COSTS AND FINANCIAL AID

Annual in-state tuition $6,470. Annual out-of-state tuition $16,320. Room and board $12,952. Required fees $1,828. Average book expense $1,298. **Required Forms and Deadlines:** FAFSA, State aid form. **Notification of Awards:** Applicants will be notified of awards on a rolling basis beginning 3/1. **Types of Aid:** *Need-based scholarships/grants:* Federal Pell, FSEOG, State scholarships/grants, Private scholarships, College/university scholarship or grant aid from institutional funds. *Loans:* Direct Subsidized Stafford Loans, Direct Unsubsidized Stafford Loans, Direct PLUS loans, Federal Perkins Loans. *Student Employment:* Federal Work-Study Program available. Institutional employment available. **Financial Aid Statistics:** 98% needy freshmen, 98% needy undergrads receive need-based scholarship or grant aid. 14% freshmen, 17% undergrads receive non-need-based scholarship or grant aid. 93% freshmen, 92% undergrads receive need-based self-help aid. 0% freshmen, 0% undergrads receive athletic scholarships. 68% undergrads borrow to pay for school. Average cumulative indebtedness $31,188. **Criteria for awarding aid:** *Need-based:* Academics, Art, Minority status, Music/drama. *Non-need-based:* Academics, Art, Minority status, Music/drama.

STATE UNIVERSITY OF NEW YORK— BUFFALO STATE

1300 Elmwood Avenue, Buffalo, NY 14222
Phone: 716-878-4017 • **Financial Aid Phone:** 716-878-4902
E-mail: admissions@buffalostate.edu • **CEEB Code:** 2533
Fax: 716-878-6100 • **ACT Code:** 2930

This public school was founded in 1871. It has a 115-acre campus.

RATINGS

Admissions Selectivity Rating: 86   Fire Safety Rating: 62   Green Rating: 98

STUDENTS AND FACULTY

Enrollment: 8,360. **Student Body:** 57% female, 43% male, 1% out-of-state, 1% international (44 countries represented). Asian 3%, African American 31%, Caucasian 47%, Hispanic 13%, Native American 1%, Pacific Islander <1%, Two or more races 4%, Race unknown <1%.
Retention and Graduation: 68% freshmen return for sophomore year. 29% freshmen graduate within 4 years. 50% freshmen graduate within 6 years. 25% grads go on to further study within 1 year. 24% grads pursue arts and sciences degrees. 1% grads pursue law degrees. 3% grads pursue business degrees.
Faculty: Student/faculty ratio 16 382 full-time faculty, 86% hold PhDs, 21% are are members of minority groups, 53% are women. 0% of classes are taught by teaching assistants.

ACADEMICS

Degrees: bachelor's, master's, post-master's certificate. **Most popular majors:** Elementary Education and Teaching; Business/Commerce. **Special Study Options:** cooperative education program, cross-registration, distance learning, double major, dual enrollment, English as a Second Language (ESL), exchange student program (domestic), honors program, independent study, internships, liberal arts/career combination, study abroad, teacher certification program. **Disability Services:** Special programs offered to physically disabled students, including note-taking services, reader services, tape recorders, tutors. **Career Services:** Alumni network, Alumni services, Career/job search classes, Career assessment, Internships.

FACILITIES

Housing: Coed dorms, special housing for international students, Apartments for students with dependent children. 100% of campus accessible to physically diasbled. **Special Academic Facilities/Equipment:** Burchfield Penney Art center, anthropology museum, concert hall with pipe organ, nature preserve. **Computers:** 10% of classrooms, 30% of libraries, 100% of dining areas, 50% of student union, 10% of common outdoor areas have wireless network access. Students can register for classes online. Administrative functions (other than registration) can be performed online.

CAMPUS LIFE

Environment: City. **Activities:** Choral groups, concert band, dance, drama/theater, jazz band, literary magazine, music ensembles, radio station, student government, student newspaper, student-run film society, television station, yearbook, Student Organization. 75 registered organizations, 5 religious

organizations. 10 fraternities, 10 sororities. **Athletics (Intercollegiate):** *Men:* basketball, cross-country, diving, football, ice hockey, soccer, swimming, track/field (outdoor), track/field (indoor). *Women:* basketball, cheerleading, cross-country, diving, ice hockey, lacrosse, soccer, softball, swimming, tennis, track/field (outdoor), track/field (indoor), volleyball. **On-Campus Highlights:** Burchfield Penny Art Center, Sports Arena, Houston Gymnasium/Fitness Center, Rockwell Hall/Performing Arts Center, Campus House. **Environmental Initiatives:** 1) Creation of a campus wide recycling program for plastic, glass, metal, paper, cardboard, light bulbs, electronics, electronic media (printer cartridges, dvds, cds, VHS, cassettes, etc), batteries, shrink wrap, bubble wrap, and many other misc items! This was applied to every building on campus including the residential halls.

ADMISSIONS

Freshman Academic Profile: Average high school GPA 3.1. 3% in top 10% of high school class, 32% in top 25% of high school class, 74% in top 50% of high school class. **Reported SAT (pre-2016 redesign) scores:** SAT Math middle 50% range 380-490. SAT Critical Reading middle 50% range 390-490. SAT Writing middle 50% range 380-470. **Concordant SAT scores:** SAT EBRW middle 50% 430–540. SAT Math middle 50% range 420–520. ACT middle 50% range 19-22. Minimum paper TOEFL 500. **Basis for Candidate Selection:** *Very important factors considered include:* rigor of secondary school record, academic GPA, standardized test scores. *Important factors considered include:* class rank. *Other factors considered include:* application essay, recommendation(s), interview, extracurricular activities, talent/ability, character/personal qualities, first generation, volunteer work, work experience. **Freshman Admission Requirements:** High school diploma is required and GED is accepted. *Academic units required:* 2 math, 2 science. *Academic units recommended:* 4 English, 3 math, 3 science, 3 foreign language, 4 history. **Freshman Admission Statistics:** 13,715 applied, 64.07% admitted, 19% enrolled. **Transfer Admission Requirements:** college transcript(s), statement of good standing from prior institution(s). Minimum college GPA of 2.0 required. Lowest grade transferable C. **General Admission Information:** Application fee $50. Nonfall registration accepted. Admission may be deferred for a maximum of 1 year.

COSTS AND FINANCIAL AID

Annual in-state tuition $6,770. Annual out-of-state tuition $16,320. Room and board $12,614. Required fees $1,199. Average book expense $1,037. **Required Forms and Deadlines:** FAFSA. **Notification of Awards:** Applicants will be notified of awards on a rolling basis beginning 5/1. **Types of Aid:** *Need-based scholarships/grants:* Federal Pell, FSEOG, State scholarships/grants. *Loans:* Federal Perkins Loans. *Student Employment:* Federal Work-Study Program available. Institutional employment available. **Financial Aid Statistics:** 81% needy freshmen, 76% needy undergrads receive need-based scholarship or grant aid. 19% freshmen, 13% undergrads receive non-need-based scholarship or grant aid. 72% freshmen, 69% undergrads receive need-based self-help aid. 0% freshmen, 0% undergrads receive athletic scholarships. 78% undergrads receive any aid. **Criteria for awarding aid:** *Non-need-based:* Academics, Minority status.

STATE UNIVERSITY OF NEW YORK— THE COLLEGE AT BROCKPORT

350 New Campus Drive, Brockport, NY 14420
Phone: 585-395-2751 • **Financial Aid Phone:** 585-395-2501
E-mail: admit@brockport.edu • **CEEB Code:** 2537
Fax: 585-395-5452 • **Website:** www.brockport.edu • **ACT Code:** 2928

This public school was founded in 1835. It has a 464-acre campus.

RATINGS

Admissions Selectivity Rating: 75   Fire Safety Rating: 90   Green Rating: 84

STUDENTS AND FACULTY

Enrollment: 7,062. **Student Body:** 56% female, 44% male, 2% out-of-state, 1% international (18 countries represented). Asian 2%, African American 11%, Caucasian 69%, Hispanic 7%, Native American <1%, Pacific Islander <1%, Two or more races 5%, Race unknown 5%.
Retention and Graduation: 82% freshmen return for sophomore year. 48% freshmen graduate within 4 years. 68% freshmen graduate within 6 years.
Faculty: Student/faculty ratio 17:1. 345 full-time faculty, 77% hold PhDs, 15% are are members of minority groups, 54% are women.

ACADEMICS

Degrees: bachelor's, master's, postbachelor's certificate, post-master's certificate. **Classes:** Most classes have 20-29 students. Most lab/discussion sessions have 10-19 students. **Most popular majors:** Registered Nursing/Registered Nurse;

Kinesiology and Exercise Science; Business Administration and Management. **Special Study Options:** Accelerated program, cross-registration, distance learning, double major, dual enrollment, honors program, independent study, internships, student-designed major, study abroad, teacher certification program. **Honors Programs:** 1)College Honors Program, which designs to let students complete general education requirements in small classes; 2) Delta College, which is a time-variable degree program for highly-motivated students. Combined degree programs: BS/MS Environmental Sci & Bio; BA/MA or BS/MA in History; BS/MS Biology; BS/PharmD Bio; BS/MA Mathematics; BA/MPA or BS/MPA in Political Science; BS/MA Psych; BA/MPA or BS/MPA Sociology/Public Admin. **Disability Services:** Special programs offered to physically disabled students, including note-taking services, reader services, tape recorders, tutors. **Career Services:** Alumni network, Alumni services, Career/job search classes, Career assessment, Internships, Regional alumni. Brockport has a 94% placement rate for recent Bachelor's graduates.

FACILITIES

Housing: Coed dorms, special housing for international students, apartments for single students, Wellness Housing, Extended housing (open during college breaks-excludes summer). 95% of campus accessible to physically diasbled. **Special Academic Facilities/Equipment:** aquaculture ponds, weather information system, high-resolution germanium detector, research vessel on Lake Ontario, electron microscope, low- temperature physics lab, vacuum deposition lab, computational; physics lab, 2 supercomputers, Doppler Radar system, ultramodern dance facilities including green room, hydrotherapy room, student learning center, academic computing center, and two theaters. **Computers:** 100% of classrooms, 100% of dorms, 100% of libraries, 100% of dining areas, 100% of student union, 80% of common outdoor areas have wireless network access. Students can register for classes online. Administrative functions (other than registration) can be performed online.

CAMPUS LIFE

Environment: Village. **Activities:** Choral groups, dance, drama/theater, literary magazine, music ensembles, musical theater, radio station, student government, student newspaper, television station, Campus Ministries, Student Organization, Model UN. 71 registered organizations, 20 honor societies, 8 religious organizations. 6 fraternities, 3 sororities. **Athletics (Intercollegiate):** *Men:* baseball, basketball, cross-country, diving, football, ice hockey, lacrosse, soccer, swimming, track/field (outdoor), track/field (indoor), wrestling. *Women:* basketball, cross-country, diving, field hockey, gymnastics, lacrosse, soccer, softball, swimming, tennis, track/field (outdoor), track/field (indoor), volleyball. **On-Campus Highlights:** Seymour College Union, Drake Memorial Library, Hartwell Performance Center, Harrison Dining Hall, Tuttle Athletic Complex, Smith Hall Science Center Dailey Hall Computing Center Tower Fine Arts Center. **Environmental Initiatives:** We received the 2010 Pollution Prevention Award from the Rochester Business Journal for our comprehensive programs and continuing efforts to improve our sustainability performance.

ADMISSIONS

Freshman Academic Profile: 0% in top 10% of high school class, 4% in top 25% of high school class, 24% in top 50% of high school class. **Reported SAT (pre-2016 redesign) scores:** SAT Math middle 50% range 470-570. SAT Critical Reading middle 50% range 450-550. **Concordant SAT scores:** SAT Math middle 50% range 510–590. ACT middle 50% range 20-26. Minimum internet-based TOEFL 76. Minimum paper TOEFL 530. **Basis for Candidate Selection:** *Very important factors considered include:* rigor of secondary school record, academic GPA. *Important factors considered include:* class rank, standardized test scores, application essay, recommendation(s), extracurricular activities, talent/ability, character/personal qualities, volunteer work. *Other factors considered include:* interview, first generation, work experience, level of applicant's interest. **Freshman Admission Requirements:** High school diploma is required and GED is accepted. *Academic units required:* 4 English, 3 math, 3 science, 1 science lab, 4 social studies, 3 history. *Academic units recommended:* 3 foreign language. **Freshman Admission Statistics:** 9,211 applied, 55.33% admitted, 24% enrolled. **Transfer Admission Requirements:** college transcript(s), Minimum college GPA of 2.5 required. Lowest grade transferable D-. **General Admission Information:** Application fee $50. Priority deadline 3/1. Regular application deadline 8/1. Nonfall registration accepted. Admission may be deferred for a maximum of 1 year.

COSTS AND FINANCIAL AID

Annual in-state tuition $6,470. Annual out-of-state tuition $16,320. Room and board $12,418. Required fees $1,458. Average book expense $1,330. **Required Forms and Deadlines:** FAFSA, State aid form. **Notification of Awards:** Applicants will be notified of awards on a rolling basis beginning 3/1. **Types of Aid:** *Need-based scholarships/grants:* Federal Pell, FSEOG, State scholarships/grants, Private scholarships, College/university scholarship or grant aid from institutional funds. *Loans:* Direct Subsidized Stafford Loans, Direct Unsubsidized Stafford Loans, Direct PLUS loans, Federal Perkins Loans, Federal Nursing Loans. *Student Employment:* Federal Work-Study Program available. Institutional employment available. **Financial Aid Statistics:** 76% needy freshmen, 81% needy undergrads receive need-based scholarship or

grant aid. 37% freshmen, 21% undergrads receive non-need-based scholarship or grant aid. 84% freshmen, 85% undergrads receive need-based self-help aid. 90% freshmen, 85% undergrads receive any aid. Average cumulative indebtedness $29,748. **Criteria for awarding aid:** *Non-need-based:* Academics, Alumni affiliation, Art, Leadership, Minority status, Music/drama.

STATE UNIVERSITY OF NEW YORK— THE COLLEGE AT OLD WESTBURY

PO Box 307, Old Westbury, NY 11568-0307
Phone: 516-876-3073 • **Financial Aid Phone:** 516-876-3247
E-mail: enroll@oldwestbury.edu • **CEEB Code:** 2866
Fax: 516-876-3307 • **Website:** www.oldwestbury.edu • **ACT Code:** 2939

This public school was founded in 1968. It has a 605-acre campus.

RATINGS

Admissions Selectivity Rating: 79 **Fire Safety Rating:** 88 **Green Rating:** 60*

STUDENTS AND FACULTY

Enrollment: 4,084. **Student Body:** 59% female, 41% male, 1% out-of-state, <1% international (58 countries represented). Asian 11%, African American 28%, Caucasian 31%, Hispanic 25%, Native American <1%, Pacific Islander <1%, Two or more races 3%, Race unknown 2%. **Retention and Graduation:** 81% freshmen return for sophomore year. 22% freshmen graduate within 4 years. 43% freshmen graduate within 6 years. **Faculty:** Student/faculty ratio 18:1. 166 full-time faculty, 87% hold PhDs, 40% are are members of minority groups, 57% are women. 0% of classes are taught by teaching assistants.

ACADEMICS

Degrees: bachelor's, certificate, master's, post-master's certificate. **Classes:** Most classes have 20-29 students. Most lab/discussion sessions have 20-29 students. **Most popular majors:** Accounting; Psychology; Biology/Biological Sciences. **Special Study Options:** cross-registration, distance learning, double major, English as a Second Language (ESL), exchange student program (domestic), honors program, independent study, internships, liberal arts/career combination, study abroad, teacher certification program, Disabled Student Services; Minority Access to Research Centers; Minority Biomedical Research. **Honors Programs:** The Honors College teaches students to integrate learning methods by using in-depth primary source material and complex and intellectually challenging secondary sources. The program emphasizes critical thinking and experiential learning. Combined degree programs: BS/DO. **Disability Services:** Special programs offered to physically disabled students, including note-taking services, reader services, tape recorders, tutors. **Career Services:** Alumni network, Alumni services, Career/job search classes, Career assessment, Internships, Regional alumni. The Community Engagement and Partnership Center founded in 2006, and its First-Year Experience Program, Old Westbury shares its resources to support the programmatic efforts of non-profit organizations and to address issues of shared concern within various communities. The college, as a whole, is using its influential role as a regional employer and developer to contribute directly and tangibly to community revitalization efforts. Critical to this effort is the student community engagement component. Implemented by CEPC and the FYE, the College has initiated a voluntary course-embedded community-based learning and action program in which students engage in community service in areas related to their course of study.

FACILITIES

Housing: Coed dorms, Honors College residence. 90% of campus accessible to physically diasbled. **Special Academic Facilities/Equipment:** Art gallery, language lab, TV studio, radio station, recital hall, physical recreation center and Maguire Theatre. **Computers:** 100% of classrooms, 60% of dorms, 100% of libraries, 100% of dining areas, 100% of student union, 30% of common outdoor areas have wireless network access. Students can register for classes online. Administrative functions (other than registration) can be performed online.

CAMPUS LIFE

Environment: Village. **Activities:** Choral groups, dance, drama/theater, radio station, student government, student newspaper, student-run film society, yearbook, Campus Ministries, Student Organization. 55 registered organizations, 5 honor societies, 2 religious organizations. 6 fraternities, 4 sororities. **Athletics (Intercollegiate):** *Men:* baseball, basketball, cross-country, golf, soccer, swimming, ultimate frisbee, volleyball. *Women:* basketball, cross-country, soccer, softball, swimming, ultimate frisbee, volleyball. **On-Campus Highlights:** Student Union, Clark Center (athletic facility), Library, Theatre, Art Gallery. **Environmental Initiatives:** SEMPRA Energy Contract; One (1) solar installation; Gas consortium.

ADMISSIONS

Freshman Academic Profile: Average high school GPA 3.1. 85% from public high schools. **Reported SAT (pre-2016 redesign) scores:** SAT Math middle 50% range 440-540. SAT Critical Reading middle 50% range 440-520. SAT Writing middle 50% range 425-510. **Concordant SAT scores:** SAT EBRW middle 50% 490–570. SAT Math middle 50% range 480–570. Minimum internet-based TOEFL 65. Minimum paper TOEFL 513. **Basis for Candidate Selection:** *Very important factors considered include:* academic GPA, standardized test scores, application essay, recommendation(s). *Other factors considered include:* interview, character/personal qualities, alumni/ ae relation. **Freshman Admission Requirements:** High school diploma is required and GED is accepted. *Academic units required:* 4 English, 3 math, 3 science, 2 science labs, 1 foreign language, 3 social studies, 1 visual/performing arts. *Academic units recommended:* 4 English, 3 math, 3 science, 3 science labs, 3 foreign language, 4 social studies, 3 academic electives, 1 computer science. **Freshman Admission Statistics:** 3,545 applied, 40.51% admitted, 71% enrolled. **Transfer Admission Requirements:** college transcript(s), essay or personal statement, Minimum college GPA of 2.0 required. Lowest grade transferable C. **General Admission Information:** Application fee $50. Priority deadline 12/1. Nonfall registration accepted. Admission may be deferred for a maximum of one year.

COSTS AND FINANCIAL AID

Annual in-state tuition $6,470. Annual out-of-state tuition $16,320. Room and board $11,020. Required fees $1,213. Average book expense $2,500. **Required Forms and Deadlines:** FAFSA, Institution's own financial aid form, State aid form. **Notification of Awards:** Applicants will be notified of awards on or about 4/15. **Types of Aid:** *Need-based scholarships/grants:* Federal Pell, FSEOG, State scholarships/grants, Private scholarships, College/university scholarship or grant aid from institutional funds. *Loans:* Direct Subsidized Stafford Loans, Direct Unsubsidized Stafford Loans, Direct PLUS loans, Federal Perkins Loans. *Student Employment:* Federal Work-Study Program available. Institutional employment available. **Financial Aid Statistics:** 83% needy freshmen, 85% needy undergrads receive need-based scholarship or grant aid. 8% freshmen, 3% undergrads receive non-need-based scholarship or grant aid. 61% freshmen, 62% undergrads receive need-based self-help aid. 0% freshmen, 0% undergrads receive athletic scholarships. 72% freshmen, 67% undergrads receive any aid. 60% undergrads borrow to pay for school. Average cumulative indebtedness $19,141. **Criteria for awarding aid:** *Need-based:* Academics. *Non-need-based:* Academics, State/district residency.

STATE UNIVERSITY OF NEW YORK— COLLEGE AT ONEONTA

116 Alumni Hall, Oneonta, NY 13820
Phone: 607-436-2524 • **Financial Aid Phone:** 607-436-2532
E-mail: admissions@oneonta.edu • **CEEB Code:** 2542
Fax: 607-436-3074 • **Website:** www.oneonta.edu • **ACT Code:** 2940

This public school was founded in 1889. It has a 250-acre campus.

RATINGS

Admissions Selectivity Rating: 80   **Fire Safety Rating:** 91   **Green Rating:** 60*

STUDENTS AND FACULTY

Enrollment: 5,804. **Student Body:** 60% female, 40% male, 1% out-of-state, 2% international (18 countries represented). Asian 1%, African American 3%, Caucasian 81%, Hispanic 4%, Native American <1%, Pacific Islander 0%, Two or more races 7%, Race unknown 2%.
Retention and Graduation: 84% freshmen return for sophomore year. 50% freshmen graduate within 4 years. 64% freshmen graduate within 6 years.
Faculty: Student/faculty ratio 18:1. 259 full-time faculty, 86% hold PhDs, 17% are are members of minority groups, 43% are women. 0% of classes are taught by teaching assistants.

ACADEMICS

Degrees: bachelor's, master's, postbachelor's certificate, post-master's certificate. **Classes:** Most classes have 10-19 students. **Most popular majors:** Elementary Education and Teaching; Family and Consumer Sciences/Home Economics Teacher Education; Secondary Education and Teaching. **Special Study Options:** cross-registration, distance learning, double major, English as a Second Language (ESL), honors program, independent study, internships, liberal arts/career combination, study abroad, teacher certification program, Variety of 3-1, 3-2, and 2-2 programs with other colleges and universities.
Honors Programs: Oneonta Honors Program Combined degree programs: BA/MA, BA/MEng, 4-1 MBA, 3-4 Optometry, 3-3 Physical Therapy. **Disability**

Services: Special programs offered to physically disabled students, including note-taking services, reader services, tape recorders, tutors. **Career Services:** Alumni network, Alumni services, Career/job search classes, Career assessment, Internships, Regional alumni. New York City Internship Fair during winter break

FACILITIES

Housing: Coed dorms, Special interest wings in residence halls; apartment-style suites in new hall. **Special Academic Facilities/Equipment:** Science Discovery Center, Biological Field Station, digital planetarium, observatory, College Camp, children's center **Computers:** 100% of classrooms, 100% of dorms, 100% of libraries, 100% of dining areas, 100% of student union, 100% of common outdoor areas have wireless network access. Students can register for classes online. Administrative functions (other than registration) can be performed online.

CAMPUS LIFE

Environment: Village. **Activities:** Choral groups, concert band, dance, drama/theater, jazz band, literary magazine, music ensembles, musical theater, opera, pep band, radio station, student government, student newspaper, student-run film society, symphony orchestra, television station, yearbook, Campus Ministries, Student Organization, Model UN. 70 registered organizations, 14 honor societies, 4 religious organizations. 4 fraternities, 6 sororities.
Athletics (Intercollegiate): *Men:* baseball, basketball, cross-country, diving, lacrosse, soccer, swimming, tennis, track/field (outdoor), track/field (indoor), wrestling. *Women:* basketball, cross-country, diving, field hockey, lacrosse, soccer, softball, swimming, tennis, track/field (outdoor), track/field (indoor), volleyball. **On-Campus Highlights:** Alumni Field House, Center for Multicultural Experiences, Hunt College Union, College Camp, Center for Social Responsibility and Community, Newly remodeled Science Building with state-of-the-art Digital Planetarium. **Environmental Initiatives:** Recycling program.

ADMISSIONS

Freshman Academic Profile: Average high school GPA 90.6. **Reported SAT (pre-2016 redesign) scores:** SAT Math middle 50% range 520-600. SAT Critical Reading middle 50% range 500-580. **Concordant SAT scores:** SAT Math middle 50% range 550–620. ACT middle 50% range 22-26. Minimum internet-based TOEFL 61. Minimum paper TOEFL 500. **Basis for Candidate Selection:** *Very important factors considered include:* rigor of secondary school record, academic GPA, standardized test scores. *Important factors considered include:* application essay, recommendation(s), talent/ability, character/personal qualities, volunteer work, work experience. *Other factors considered include:* class rank, interview, extracurricular activities, first generation, racial/ethnic status, level of applicant's interest. **Freshman Admission Requirements:** High school diploma is required and GED is accepted. *Academic units required:* 4 English, 4 math, 4 science, 3 foreign language, 4 social studies. *Academic units recommended:* 4 foreign language. **Freshman Admission Statistics:** 12,031 applied, 43.14% admitted, 22% enrolled. **Transfer Admission Requirements:** college transcript(s), Minimum college GPA of 2.5 required. Lowest grade transferable C-. **General Admission Information:** Application fee $50. Nonfall registration accepted. Admission may be deferred for a maximum of 12 months.

COSTS AND FINANCIAL AID

Required Forms and Deadlines: FAFSA, Noncustodial PROFILE. **Notification of Awards:** Applicants will be notified of awards on a rolling basis beginning 3/1. **Types of Aid:** *Need-based scholarships/grants:* Federal Pell, FSEOG, State scholarships/grants, Private scholarships, College/university scholarship or grant aid from institutional funds. *Loans:* Direct Subsidized Stafford Loans, Direct Unsubsidized Stafford Loans, Direct PLUS loans, Federal Perkins Loans. *Student Employment:* Federal Work-Study Program available. Institutional employment available. **Financial Aid Statistics:** 73% needy freshmen, 95% needy undergrads receive need-based scholarship or grant aid. 26% freshmen, 0% undergrads receive non-need-based scholarship or grant aid. 84% freshmen, 85% undergrads receive need-based self-help aid. 0% freshmen, 0% undergrads receive athletic scholarships. 83% freshmen, 66% undergrads receive any aid. **Criteria for awarding aid:** *Need-based:* Academics, Leadership, Minority status, Music/drama. *Non-need-based:* Academics, Leadership, Minority status, Music/drama, State/district residency.

STATE UNIVERSITY OF NEW YORK—COLLEGE OF ENVIRONMENTAL SCIENCE AND FORESTRY

Office of Undergraduate Admissions, Syracuse, NY 13210
Phone: 315-470-6600 • **Financial Aid Phone:** 315-470-6706
E-mail: esfinfo@esf.edu • **CEEB Code:** 2530
Fax: 315-470-6933 • **Website:** www.esf.edu • **ACT Code:** 2948

This public school was founded in 1911. It has a 25000-acre campus.

RATINGS
Admissions Selectivity Rating: 89   **Fire Safety Rating:** 98   **Green Rating:** 99

STUDENTS AND FACULTY
Enrollment: 1,751. **Student Body:** 47% female, 53% male, 18% out-of-state, 2% international (11 countries represented). Asian 4%, African American 2%, Caucasian 80%, Hispanic 6%, Native American <1%, Pacific Islander 0%, Two or more races 3%, Race unknown 5%.
Retention and Graduation: 83% freshmen return for sophomore year. 60% freshmen graduate within 4 years. 68% freshmen graduate within 6 years. 25% grads go on to further study within 1 year. **Faculty:** Student/faculty ratio 13:1. 116 full-time faculty, 85% hold PhDs, 14% are are members of minority groups, 28% are women. 0% of classes are taught by teaching assistants.

ACADEMICS
Degrees: associate, bachelor's, certificate, doctoral/research, doctoral, master's, postbachelor's certificate. **Classes:** Most classes have 10-19 students. Most lab/discussion sessions have 10-19 students. **Most popular majors:** Environmental Science; Environmental Biology; Landscape Architecture. **Special Study Options:** cooperative education program, cross-registration, distance learning, double major, English as a Second Language (ESL), honors program, independent study, internships, study abroad, teacher certification program, Associate degrees in forest technology & land surveying technology are offered at The Ranger School campus. Graduates of these degrees may then continue their studies at the Syracuse campus to complete bachelor degrees, usually in forest resources management or natural resources management. **Honors Programs:** Lower Division Honors Program: freshmen & sophomores, all academic programs, highly selective, associated scholarship, mentoring, honors seminar, honors writing course. Upper Division Thesis Honors Program: juniors and seniors, 16 of 20 academic programs eligible, intensive research or creative projects guided by faculty mentors, thesis exploration seminar, related course work, Honors Thesis/Project course. Combined degree programs: BS/Doctor of Physical Therapy. **Disability Services:** Special programs offered to physically disabled students, including note-taking services, reader services, tape recorders, tutors. **Career Services:** Alumni network, Alumni services, Career/job search classes, Career assessment, Internships, Regional alumni. Experiential learning is "built into" all aspects of learning at ESF. Service Learning is an integral part of an ESF education. Required and voluntary undergraduate research, internships and field experiences are components of every degree program.

FACILITIES
Housing: Coed dorms, special housing for disabled students, special housing for international students, fraternity/sorority housing, apartments for married students, apartments for single students, Theme Housing. 95% of campus accessible to physically diasbled. **Special Academic Facilities/Equipment:** Museums, art galleries, plant growth and animal environmental simulation chambers, wildlife collection, electron microscope, paper making facility, photogrammetric and geodetic facilities, hydrology flumes. **Computers:** 50% of classrooms, 100% of dorms, 100% of libraries, 100% of dining areas, 100% of student union, 10% of common outdoor areas have wireless network access. Students can register for classes online. Administrative functions (other than registration) can be performed online.

CAMPUS LIFE
Environment: City. **Activities:** Choral groups, concert band, dance, drama/theater, jazz band, literary magazine, marching band, music ensembles, musical theater, pep band, radio station, student government, student newspaper, student-run film society, symphony orchestra, television station, yearbook, Campus Ministries, Student Organization. 300 registered organizations, 1 honor society, 13 religious organizations. 26 fraternities, 21 sororities. **Athletics (Intercollegiate):** *Men:* cross-country, golf, soccer. *Women:* cross-country, golf, soccer. **On-Campus Highlights:** Library, Green houses, Wildlife collection, Labratories & Studios, Student lounge, snack bar, student store, SUNY-ESF is on the campus of Syracuse University. The most popular sites on that campus are the Carrier Dome, Crouse College (a historic building), Schine Student Center, Hendricks Chapel. **Environmental Initiatives:** (1)Biomass fueled power plant in Student Center provides up to 65% of campus heating and 20% of electricity (2)photovoltaic arrays/green roof (3) College owns and manages 25,000 acres of forest (providing carbon offsets).

ADMISSIONS
Freshman Academic Profile: Average high school GPA 3.8. 36% in top 10% of high school class, 72% in top 25% of high school class, 95% in top 50% of high school class. 90% from public high schools. **Reported SAT (pre-2016 redesign) scores:** SAT Math middle 50% range 550-630. SAT Critical Reading middle 50% range 520-630. **Concordant SAT scores:** SAT Math middle 50% range 570–650. ACT middle 50% range 23-27. Minimum internet-based TOEFL 79. Minimum paper TOEFL 550. **Basis for Candidate Selection:** *Very important factors considered include:* rigor of secondary school record, academic GPA, standardized test scores, application essay, level of applicant's interest. *Important factors considered include:* class rank, recommendation(s), interview, extracurricular activities, talent/ability, character/personal qualities, volunteer work, work experience. *Other factors considered include:* first generation, alumni/ae relation, geographical residence, state residency, racial/ethnic status. **Freshman Admission Requirements:** High school diploma is required and GED is accepted. *Academic units required:* 4 English, 3 math, 3 science, 3 science labs, 3 social studies. *Academic units recommended:* 4 math, 4 science, 2 foreign language, 3 social studies, 1 history. **Freshman Admission Statistics:** 1,651 applied, 54.21% admitted, 37% enrolled. **Transfer Admission Requirements:** High school transcript, college transcript(s), Minimum college GPA of 2.25 required. Lowest grade transferable C. **General Admission Information:** Application fee $50. Priority deadline 2/1. Nonfall registration accepted. Admission may be deferred for a maximum of 1 year.

COSTS AND FINANCIAL AID
Annual in-state tuition $6,470. Annual out-of-state tuition $16,320. Room and board $15,040. Required fees $1,633. Average book expense $1,200. **Required Forms and Deadlines:** FAFSA, State aid form. **Notification of Awards:** Applicants will be notified of awards on a rolling basis beginning 3/15. **Types of Aid:** *Need-based scholarships/grants:* Federal Pell, FSEOG, State scholarships/grants, Private scholarships, College/university scholarship or grant aid from institutional funds. *Loans:* Direct Subsidized Stafford Loans, Direct Unsubsidized Stafford Loans, Direct PLUS loans, Federal Perkins Loans. *Student Employment:* Federal Work-Study Program available. Institutional employment available. **Financial Aid Statistics:** 89% needy freshmen, 99% needy undergrads receive need-based scholarship or grant aid. 67% freshmen, 57% undergrads receive non-need-based scholarship or grant aid. 67% freshmen, 95% undergrads receive need-based self-help aid. 0% freshmen, 0% undergrads receive athletic scholarships. 91% freshmen, 93% undergrads receive any aid. 64% undergrads borrow to pay for school. Average cumulative indebtedness $24,269. **Criteria for awarding aid:** *Need-based:* Academics, Alumni affiliation, Leadership, Minority status. *Non-need-based:* Academics, Alumni affiliation, Leadership, Minority status, State/district residency.

See page 1054.

STATE UNIVERSITY OF NEW YORK— EMPIRE STATE COLLEGE

Two Union Avenue, Saratoga, NY 12866
Phone: 518-587-2100 • **Financial Aid Phone:** 518-587-2100
E-mail: admissions@esc.edu • **CEEB Code:** 2214
Fax: 518-587-9759 • **Website:** esc.edu • **ACT Code:** 2737

This public school was founded in 1971.

RATINGS
Admissions Selectivity Rating: 64   **Fire Safety Rating:** 60*   **Green Rating:** 60*

STUDENTS AND FACULTY
Enrollment: 10,128. **Student Body:** 62% female, 38% male, 8% out-of-state, 0% international. Asian 2%, African American 18%, Caucasian 66%, Hispanic 5%, Native American 1%, Pacific Islander 0%, Two or more races 1%, Race unknown 7%.
Faculty: Student/faculty ratio 9:1. 202 full-time faculty, 96% hold PhDs, 19% are are members of minority groups, 64% are women. 0% of classes are taught by teaching assistants.

ACADEMICS
Degrees: associate, bachelor's, certificate, master's, postbachelor's certificate. **Most popular majors:** Business/Commerce; Community Organization and Advocacy; Physical Sciences. **Special Study Options:** cross-registration, distance learning, double major, dual enrollment, external degree program,

independent study, internships, student-designed major, Student-designed courses of study. Combined degree programs: BA/MA, BS/MA ; B.P.S./MA.

FACILITIES
Computers: Students can register for classes online. Administrative functions (other than registration) can be performed online.

CAMPUS LIFE
Environment: Village. **Activities:** literary magazine.

ADMISSIONS
Minimum paper TOEFL 550. **Basis for Candidate Selection:** *Very important factors considered include:* application essay, character/personal qualities. *Other factors considered include:* rigor of secondary school record, recommendation(s), talent/ability. **Freshman Admission Requirements:** High school diploma is required and GED is accepted. **Freshman Admission Statistics:** 1,536 applied, 79.49% admitted, 72% enrolled. **Transfer Admission Requirements:** High school transcript, essay or personal statement, Lowest grade transferable C. **General Admission Information:** Priority deadline 6/1. Nonfall registration accepted. Admission may be deferred for a maximum of 3 years.

COSTS AND FINANCIAL AID
Annual in-state tuition $5,570. Annual out-of-state tuition $14,820. Required fees $395. **Required Forms and Deadlines:** FAFSA, State aid form. **Types of Aid:** *Need-based scholarships/grants:* Federal Pell, FSEOG, State scholarships/grants, Private scholarships, College/university scholarship or grant aid from institutional funds. *Loans:* Direct Subsidized Stafford Loans, Direct Unsubsidized Stafford Loans, Direct PLUS loans, Federal Perkins Loans, State Loans, College/university loans from institutional funds. *Student Employment:* Federal Work-Study Program available. **Financial Aid Statistics:** 63% undergrads receive any aid. **Criteria for awarding aid:** *Need-based:* Academics, Minority status.

STATE UNIVERSITY OF NEW YORK— FASHION INSTITUTE OF TECHNOLOGY

227 West 27th Street, New York, NY 10001-5992
Phone: 212-217-3760
E-mail: fitinfo@fitsuny.edu
Fax: 212-217-3761 • **Website:** fitnyc.edu

This public school was founded in 1944.

RATINGS
Admissions Selectivity Rating: 60*   **Fire Safety Rating:** 91   **Green Rating:** 60*

STUDENTS AND FACULTY
Enrollment: 8,229. **Student Body:** 86% female, 14% male, 14% international. Asian 10%, African American 9%, Caucasian 47%, Hispanic 17%, Native American <1%, Pacific Islander <1%, Two or more races 4%, Race unknown <1%.
Faculty: Student/faculty ratio 17:1.

ACADEMICS
Degrees: bachelor's, master's. **Career Services:** Alumni services, Career/job search classes, Career assessment, Internships.

FACILITIES
Housing: Coed dorms, men's dorms, women's dorms, apartments for single students.

CAMPUS LIFE
Activities: literary magazine, radio station, student government, student newspaper, yearbook. 70 registered organizations, 7 honor societies, 1 religious organization.

ADMISSIONS
General Admission Information: Regular application deadline 1/15.

COSTS AND FINANCIAL AID
Required Forms and Deadlines: FAFSA, Institution's own financial aid form, State aid form. *Student Employment:* Federal Work-Study Program available.

See page 956.

STATE UNIVERSITY OF NEW YORK—FREDONIA

178 Central Avenue, Fredonia, NY 14063
Phone: 716-673-3251 • **Financial Aid Phone:** 716-673-3253
E-mail: admissions@fredonia.edu • **CEEB Code:** 2539
Fax: 716-673-3249 • **Website:** www.fredonia.edu • **ACT Code:** 2934

This public school was founded in 1826. It has a 249-acre campus.

RATINGS
Admissions Selectivity Rating: 80   **Fire Safety Rating:** 86   **Green Rating:** 85

STUDENTS AND FACULTY
Enrollment: 4,359. **Student Body:** 57% female, 43% male, 4% out-of-state, 2% international (8 countries represented). Asian 2%, African American 7%, Caucasian 77%, Hispanic 8%, Native American 1%, Pacific Islander <1%, Two or more races 3%, Race unknown 2%.
Retention and Graduation: 79% freshmen return for sophomore year. 47% freshmen graduate within 4 years. 62% freshmen graduate within 6 years. 44% grads go on to further study within 1 year. **Faculty:** Student/faculty ratio 14:1. 257 full-time faculty, 86% hold PhDs, 10% are are members of minority groups, 44% are women. 2% of classes are taught by teaching assistants.

ACADEMICS
Degrees: bachelor's, master's, post-master's certificate. **Classes:** Most classes have 10-19 students. Most lab/discussion sessions have 20-29 students. **Most popular majors:** Elementary Education and Teaching; Music; Business/Commerce. **Special Study Options:** Accelerated program, distance learning, double major, honors program, independent study, internships, student-designed major, study abroad, teacher certification program. Combined degree programs: BA/DDS, 3+4 Optometry with SUNY State College of Optometry. **Disability Services:** Special programs offered to physically disabled students, including note-taking services, reader services, tape recorders, tutors. **Career Services:** Alumni network, Alumni services, Career/job search classes, Career assessment, Internships. Over 900 Internships per year.

FACILITIES
Housing: Coed dorms, special housing for disabled students, men's dorms, women's dorms, apartments for single students. 85% of campus accessible to physically disabled. **Special Academic Facilities/Equipment:** Art center, education and local history museums, teacher education research center, developmental reading center, Sheldon Communications Lab, SMART classrooms, greenhouse. **Computers:** 100% of classrooms, 100% of libraries, 100% of dining areas, 100% of student union, 85% of common outdoor areas have wireless network access. Students can register for classes online. Administrative functions (other than registration) can be performed online.

CAMPUS LIFE
Environment: Village. **Activities:** Choral groups, concert band, dance, drama/theater, jazz band, literary magazine, music ensembles, musical theater, opera, pep band, radio station, student government, student newspaper, symphony orchestra, television station, Campus Ministries, Student Organization. 152 registered organizations, 22 honor societies, 5 religious organizations. 3 fraternities, 3 sororities. **Athletics (Intercollegiate):** *Men:* baseball, basketball, cross-country, diving, ice hockey, soccer, swimming, track/field (outdoor), track/field (indoor). *Women:* basketball, cheerleading, cross-country, diving, lacrosse, soccer, softball, swimming, tennis, track/field (outdoor), track/field (indoor), volleyball. **On-Campus Highlights:** University Commons, Michael C. Rockefeller Arts Center, Library, Natatorium-Swimming pool and diving area, Rosch Recital Hall. **Environmental Initiatives:** Campus owned gas well.

ADMISSIONS
Freshman Academic Profile: Average high school GPA 3.3. 14% in top 10% of high school class, 38% in top 25% of high school class, 72% in top 50% of high school class. 95% from public high schools. **Reported SAT (pre-2016 redesign) scores:** SAT Math middle 50% range 450-550. SAT Critical Reading middle 50% range 450-570. **Concordant SAT scores:** SAT Math middle 50% range 490–570. ACT middle 50% range 22-27. Minimum internet-based TOEFL 62. Minimum paper TOEFL 500. **Basis for Candidate Selection:** *Very important factors considered include:* rigor of secondary school record, academic GPA. *Important factors considered include:* class rank, standardized test scores, application essay, recommendation(s). *Other factors considered include:* extracurricular activities, talent/ability, character/personal qualities, alumni/ae relation, work experience. **Freshman Admission Requirements:** High school diploma is required and GED is accepted. *Academic units required:* 4 English, 3 math, 3 science, 3 science labs, 3 foreign language, 4 social studies. *Academic units recommended:* 4 English, 4 math, 4 science, 4 science labs, 3 foreign language, 4 social studies, 1 academic elective. **Freshman Admission Statistics:** 5,381 applied, 62.35% admitted, 28% enrolled. **Transfer Admission Requirements:** college transcript(s), Minimum

college GPA of 2.0 required. Lowest grade transferable D. **General Admission Information:** Application fee $50. Nonfall registration accepted. Admission may be deferred for a maximum of 1 year.

COSTS AND FINANCIAL AID

Annual in-state tuition $6,470. Annual out-of-state tuition $16,320. Room and board $12,730. Required fees $1,618. Average book expense $1,000. **Required Forms and Deadlines:** FAFSA, State aid form. **Notification of Awards:** Applicants will be notified of awards on a rolling basis beginning 3/1. **Types of Aid:** *Need-based scholarships/grants:* Federal Pell, FSEOG, State scholarships/grants, Private scholarships, College/university scholarship or grant aid from institutional funds. *Loans:* Direct Subsidized Stafford Loans, Direct Unsubsidized Stafford Loans, Direct PLUS loans, Federal Perkins Loans. *Student Employment:* Federal Work-Study Program available. Institutional employment available. **Financial Aid Statistics:** 76% needy freshmen, 74% needy undergrads receive need-based scholarship or grant aid. 63% freshmen, 33% undergrads receive non-need-based scholarship or grant aid. 84% freshmen, 82% undergrads receive need-based self-help aid. 0% freshmen, 0% undergrads receive athletic scholarships. 81% freshmen, 85% undergrads receive any aid. 82% undergrads borrow to pay for school. Average cumulative indebtedness $32,083. **Criteria for awarding aid:** *Non-need-based:* Academics, Alumni affiliation, Art, Leadership, Minority status, Music/drama, State/district residency.

STATE UNIVERSITY OF NEW YORK— MARITIME COLLEGE

6 Pennyfield Ave, Throggs Neck, NY 10465
Phone: 718-409-7200 • **Financial Aid Phone:** 718-409-7227
E-mail: admissions@sunymaritime.edu
Fax: 718-409-7465 • **Website:** www.sunymaritime.edu • **ACT Code:** 2954

This public school was founded in 1874. It has a 56-acre campus.

RATINGS

Admissions Selectivity Rating: 85   **Fire Safety Rating:** 89   **Green Rating:** 67

STUDENTS AND FACULTY

Enrollment: 1,626. **Student Body:** 12% female, 88% male, 24% out-of-state, 2% international (14 countries represented). Asian 5%, African American 4%, Caucasian 71%, Hispanic 13%, Native American <1%, Pacific Islander 0%, Two or more races 2%, Race unknown 4%.
Retention and Graduation: 85% freshmen return for sophomore year. 34% freshmen graduate within 4 years. 56% freshmen graduate within 6 years. 5% grads go on to further study within 1 year. **Faculty:** Student/faculty ratio 16:1. 92 full-time faculty, 48% hold PhDs, 10% are are members of minority groups, 22% are women. 0% of classes are taught by teaching assistants.

ACADEMICS

Degrees: associate, bachelor's, certificate, master's. **Classes:** Most classes have 20-29 students. Most lab/discussion sessions have 20-29 students. **Most popular majors:** Marine Science/Merchant Marine Officer; Mechanical Engineering; Business, Management, Marketing, and Related Support Services. **Special Study Options:** cooperative education program, distance learning, double major, dual enrollment, English as a Second Language (ESL), honors program, independent study, internships, United States Coast Guard-issued deck and engine license program. **Honors Programs:** Honors Program Combined degree programs: BS/MS. **Disability Services:** Special programs offered to physically disabled students, including note-taking services, reader services, tape recorders, tutors. **Career Services:** Alumni network, Alumni services, Career/job search classes, Career assessment, Internships, Regional alumni. The most unique component of the Maritime experience is the opportunity to travel across the world on the College's 565-foot Training Ship Empire State VI, while getting hands-on experience in leadership and the maritime industry.

FACILITIES

Housing: Coed dorms, special housing for disabled studentsMost undergraduates required to live in on-campus housing. 81% of campus accessible to physically disabled. **Special Academic Facilities/Equipment:** Maritime Industry Museum, Fort Schuyler(National Historic Landmark), Bridge Simulator, Liquid Cargo Simulator, 565 ft. Training Ship Empire State VI, Diesel Simulator, 2 Research Ships, State-of-the-Art Electrical Engineering Lab, NY State Strategic Center for Port and Maritime Security (224 ft USS Stalwart), Computerized Weather Station, Maritime College Waterfront Sailboat Fleet:20 Vanguard 420's, 6 Vanguard FJ's, 1 Laser, J-105, J-35, J-24, Colgate 26 **Computers:** 75% of classrooms, 30% of dorms, 100% of libraries,

50% of student union, have wireless network access. Students can register for classes online.

CAMPUS LIFE

Environment: Metropolis. **Activities:** Choral groups, jazz band, marching band, music ensembles, pep band, student government, yearbook, Campus Ministries, Student Organization. 30 registered organizations, 4 religious organizations. **Athletics (Intercollegiate):** *Men:* baseball, basketball, cross-country, football, ice hockey, lacrosse, riflery, soccer, swimming. *Women:* basketball, crew/rowing, cross-country, lacrosse, riflery, soccer, softball, swimming, volleyball. **On-Campus Highlights:** Fort Schuyler, Empire State VI. **Environmental Initiatives:** Energy Reduction Programs with NYPA.

ADMISSIONS

Freshman Academic Profile: Average high school GPA 89.0. 25% in top 10% of high school class, 50% in top 25% of high school class, 100% in top 50% of high school class. **Reported SAT (pre-2016 redesign) scores:** SAT Math middle 50% range 530-620. SAT Critical Reading middle 50% range 500-590. SAT Writing middle 50% range 460-570. **Concordant SAT scores:** SAT EBRW middle 50% 540–640. SAT Math middle 50% range 560–640. ACT middle 50% range 23-27. Minimum internet-based TOEFL 79. Minimum paper TOEFL 550. **Basis for Candidate Selection:** *Very important factors considered include:* rigor of secondary school record, academic GPA, standardized test scores. *Important factors considered include:* recommendation(s). *Other factors considered include:* class rank, application essay, interview, extracurricular activities, talent/ability, character/personal qualities, first generation, alumni/ae relation, geographical residence, volunteer work, work experience, level of applicant's interest. **Freshman Admission Requirements:** High school diploma is required and GED is accepted. *Academic units required:* 3 English, 3 math, 3 science, 1 science lab, 1 foreign language, 3 social studies, 3 history. *Academic units recommended:* 4 English, 4 math, 4 science, 3 foreign language. **Freshman Admission Statistics:** 1,449 applied, 58.04% admitted, 37% enrolled. **Transfer Admission Requirements:** High school transcript, college transcript(s), Minimum college GPA of 2.5 required. Lowest grade transferable 2. **General Admission Information:** Application fee $50. Regular application deadline 1/31. Nonfall registration accepted. Admission may be deferred.

COSTS AND FINANCIAL AID

Annual in-state tuition $6,470. Annual out-of-state tuition $16,320. Room and board $11,948. Required fees $1,364. Average book expense $1,500. **Required Forms and Deadlines:** FAFSA. **Notification of Awards:** Applicants will be notified of awards on a rolling basis beginning 3/15. **Types of Aid:** *Need-based scholarships/grants:* Federal Pell, FSEOG, State scholarships/grants, Private scholarships, College/university scholarship or grant aid from institutional funds. *Loans:* Federal Perkins Loans, State Loans. *Student Employment:* Federal Work-Study Program available. Institutional employment available. **Financial Aid Statistics:** 54% needy freshmen, 65% needy undergrads receive need-based scholarship or grant aid. 42% freshmen, 33% undergrads receive non-need-based scholarship or grant aid. 80% freshmen, 82% undergrads receive need-based self-help aid. 0% freshmen, 0% undergrads receive athletic scholarships. 83% freshmen, 78% undergrads receive any aid. **Criteria for awarding aid:** *Need-based:* Academics, Leadership. *Non-need-based:* Academics, Leadership, Minority status, State/district residency.

STATE UNIVERSITY OF NEW YORK—OSWEGO

229 Sheldon Hall, Oswego, NY 13126-3599
Phone: 315-312-2250 • **Financial Aid Phone:** 315-312-2248
E-mail: admiss@oswego.edu • **CEEB Code:** 2543
Fax: 315-312-3260 • **Website:** www.oswego.edu • **ACT Code:** 2942

This public school was founded in 1861. It has a 696-acre campus.

RATINGS

Admissions Selectivity Rating: 84   **Fire Safety Rating:** 81   **Green Rating:** 88

STUDENTS AND FACULTY

Enrollment: 7,113. **Student Body:** 50% female, 50% male, 3% out-of-state, 2% international (23 countries represented). Asian 3%, African American 8%, Caucasian 72%, Hispanic 11%, Native American <1%, Pacific Islander <1%, Two or more races 3%, Race unknown <1%.
Retention and Graduation: 81% freshmen return for sophomore year. 49% freshmen graduate within 4 years. 66% freshmen graduate within 6 years. 19% grads go on to further study within 1 year. 22% grads pursue arts and sciences degrees. 4% grads pursue law degrees. 6% grads pursue business degrees. 5% grads pursue medical degrees. **Faculty:** Student/faculty ratio 17:1. 354 full-time faculty, 88% hold PhDs, 18% are are members of minority groups, 48% are women. 0% of classes are taught by teaching assistants.

ACADEMICS

Degrees: bachelor's, master's, postbachelor's certificate, post-master's certificate. **Classes:** Most classes have 10-19 students. Most lab/discussion sessions have 20-29 students. **Most popular majors:** Business Administration and Management; Mass Communication/Media Studies; Accounting. **Special Study Options:** Accelerated program, cross-registration, distance learning, double major, dual enrollment, English as a Second Language (ESL), exchange student program (domestic), external degree program, honors program, independent study, internships, liberal arts/career combination, study abroad, teacher certification program. **Honors Programs:** Over 275 students participate in our campus wide Honors Program. Students will take smaller courses based on the program's core multidisciplinary courses in the social sciences, the natural sciences, the humanities, and philosophy, as well as several other courses in math, English, and a foreign language. The courses emphasize the interrelatedness of the disciplines, their historical and intellectual origins, their roles in modern society, and their impact on life in the future. Combined degree programs: BA/MA, BS/MBA—5 year accounting BS/MBA program. **Disability Services:** Special programs offered to physically disabled students, including note-taking services, reader services, tape recorders, tutors. **Career Services:** Alumni network, Alumni services, Career/job search classes, Career assessment, Internships, Regional alumni. We have developed an innovative industry-centric model that provides optimal support for our to our students, faculty, employers, and alumni.

FACILITIES

Housing: Coed dorms, Wellness Housing, Theme Housing, Global living and learning center, suites for upperclassmen, nontraditional student housing, first-year experience residence hall for incoming freshmen only, housing for 21 and over single suites, several rooms equipped with special equipment to meet needs of disabled students. available. 95% of campus accessible to physically diasbled. **Special Academic Facilities/Equipment:** Tyler Hall Art Galleries, Rice Creek Biological Field Station, curriculum materials center, electron microscopy lab, planetarium. **Computers:** 80% of classrooms, 10% of dorms, 100% of libraries, 100% of dining areas, 100% of student union, have wireless network access. Students can register for classes online. Administrative functions (other than registration) can be performed online.

CAMPUS LIFE

Environment: Village. **Activities:** Choral groups, concert band, dance, drama/theater, jazz band, literary magazine, music ensembles, musical theater, radio station, student government, student newspaper, student-run film society, symphony orchestra, television station, yearbook, Student Organization. 148 registered organizations, 21 honor societies, 6 religious organizations. 13 fraternities, 10 sororities. **Athletics (Intercollegiate):** *Men:* baseball, basketball, cross-country, diving, golf, ice hockey, lacrosse, soccer, swimming, tennis, track/field (outdoor), track/field (indoor), wrestling. *Women:* basketball, cross-country, diving, field hockey, ice hockey, lacrosse, soccer, softball, swimming, tennis, track/field (outdoor), track/field (indoor), volleyball. **On-Campus Highlights:** Romney Fieldhouse/ Campus Ctr(Hockey and Conference), Hewitt Union; The Student Union, Rich Hall; The School of Business, Tyler Hall; The Fine Arts Building, Penfield Library and Cafe, Rice Creek Biological field station; The Sweete Shoppe in the Hewitt Union; Laker Hall (Field House); Johnson Hall (1st Year Residence Hall). **Environmental Initiatives:** Commitment to LEED Gold for construction projects.

ADMISSIONS

Freshman Academic Profile: Average high school GPA 3.5. 13% in top 10% of high school class, 50% in top 25% of high school class, 85% in top 50% of high school class. **Reported SAT (pre-2016 redesign) scores:** SAT Math middle 50% range 510-590. SAT Critical Reading middle 50% range 500-590. **Concordant SAT scores:** SAT Math middle 50% range 540–610. ACT middle 50% range 22-27. **Basis for Candidate Selection:** *Very important factors considered include:* rigor of secondary school record, academic GPA. *Important factors considered include:* standardized test scores. *Other factors considered include:* class rank, application essay, recommendation(s), interview, extracurricular activities, talent/ability, character/personal qualities, first generation, alumni/ae relation, geographical residence, racial/ethnic status, volunteer work, work experience, level of applicant's interest. **Freshman Admission Requirements:** High school diploma is required and GED is accepted. *Academic units required:* 4 English, 3 math, 3 science, 2 science labs, 2 foreign language, 4 social studies. *Academic units recommended:* 4 English, 4 math, 4 science, 3 science labs, 4 foreign language, 4 social studies. **Freshman Admission Statistics:** 10,715 applied, 54.35% admitted, 25% enrolled. **Transfer Admission Requirements:** college transcript(s), Minimum college GPA of 2.5 required. Lowest grade transferable D. **General Admission Information:** Application fee $50. Priority deadline 1/15. Nonfall registration accepted. Admission may be deferred for a maximum of 12 months.

COSTS AND FINANCIAL AID

Annual in-state tuition $6,470. Annual out-of-state tuition $16,320. Room and board $13,390. Required fees $1,491. Average book expense $800. **Required Forms and Deadlines:** FAFSA, State aid form. **Notification of Awards:** Applicants will be notified of awards on a rolling basis beginning 2/15.

Types of Aid: *Need-based scholarships/grants:* Federal Pell, FSEOG, State scholarships/grants, Private scholarships, College/university scholarship or grant aid from institutional funds. *Loans:* Direct Subsidized Stafford Loans, Direct Unsubsidized Stafford Loans, Direct PLUS loans, Federal Perkins Loans. *Student Employment:* Federal Work-Study Program available. Institutional employment available. **Financial Aid Statistics:** 95% needy freshmen, 87% needy undergrads receive need-based scholarship or grant aid. 68% freshmen, 36% undergrads receive non-need-based scholarship or grant aid. 95% freshmen, 95% undergrads receive need-based self-help aid. 0% freshmen, 0% undergrads receive athletic scholarships. 93% freshmen, 85% undergrads receive any aid. 81% undergrads borrow to pay for school. Average cumulative indebtedness $28,810. **Criteria for awarding aid:** *Need-based:* Academics. *Non-need-based:* Academics, State/district residency.

STATE UNIVERSITY OF NEW YORK POLYTECHNIC INSTITUTE

PO Box 3050, Utica, NY 13504
Phone: 315-792-7500 • **Financial Aid Phone:** 315-792-7210
E-mail: admissions@sunyit.edu • **CEEB Code:** 2896
Fax: 315-792-7837 • **Website:** www.sunyit.edu • **ACT Code:** 2953

This public school was founded in 1966. It has a 850-acre campus.

RATINGS

Admissions Selectivity Rating: 83   **Fire Safety Rating:** 60*   **Green Rating:** 60*

STUDENTS AND FACULTY

Enrollment: 1,892. **Student Body:** 38% female, 62% male, 1% out-of-state, 1% international (13 countries represented). Asian 3%, African American 8%, Caucasian 79%, Hispanic 7%, Native American <1%, Pacific Islander <1%, Two or more races 2%, Race unknown <1%.
Retention and Graduation: 84% freshmen return for sophomore year. 24% freshmen graduate within 4 years. 43% freshmen graduate within 6 years.
Faculty: Student/faculty ratio 18:1. 131 full-time faculty, 87% hold PhDs, 22% are are members of minority groups, 32% are women.

ACADEMICS

Degrees: bachelor's, master's, postbachelor's certificate, post-master's certificate. **Classes:** Most classes have 10-19 students. Most lab/discussion sessions have 10-19 students. **Most popular majors:** Computer and Information Sciences; Business Administration and Management; Mechanical Engineering/Mechanical Technology/Technician. **Special Study Options:** Accelerated program, cross-registration, distance learning, double major, dual enrollment, English as a Second Language (ESL), independent study, internships, study abroad. Combined degree programs: Computer/Info Science—BS/MS, Nursing—BS/MS, Network and Computer Security—BS/MS. **Disability Services:** Special programs offered to physically disabled students, including note-taking services, reader services, tape recorders, tutors. **Career Services:** Alumni network, Alumni services, Career/job search classes, Career assessment, Internships, Regional alumni.

FACILITIES

Housing: Coed dorms, special housing for disabled students. 98% of campus accessible to physically diasbled. **Special Academic Facilities/Equipment:** Gannett Gallery, New York State Telecommunications Museum **Computers:** Students can register for classes online. Administrative functions (other than registration) can be performed online.

CAMPUS LIFE

Environment: Village. **Activities:** drama/theater, jazz band, music ensembles, radio station, student government, student newspaper, television station, yearbook, Student Organization. 30 registered organizations, 4 honor societies, 1 religious organization. **Athletics (Intercollegiate):** *Men:* baseball, basketball, golf, lacrosse, soccer. *Women:* basketball, cross-country, golf, soccer, softball, volleyball.

ADMISSIONS

Freshman Academic Profile: Average high school GPA 89.0. 17% in top 10% of high school class, 43% in top 25% of high school class, 83% in top 50% of high school class. 98% from public high schools. **Reported SAT (pre-2016 redesign) scores:** SAT Math middle 50% range 460-650. SAT Critical Reading middle 50% range 460-610. **Concordant SAT scores:** SAT Math middle 50% range 500–670. ACT middle 50% range 22-28. Minimum internet-based TOEFL 79. Minimum paper TOEFL 550. **Basis for Candidate Selection:** *Very important factors considered include:* rigor of secondary school record, academic GPA, standardized test scores, recommendation(s). *Important factors* considered include: class rank, application essay, interview, extracurricular activities. *Other factors considered include:* talent/ability, character/personal qualities, first generation, volunteer work, work experience. **Freshman Admission Requirements:** High school diploma is required and GED is accepted. *Academic units required:* 4 English, 3 math, 3 science, 3 science labs, 2 social studies, 2 history. *Academic units recommended:* 4 math, 4 science, 4 science labs, 3 foreign language, 2 academic electives. **Freshman Admission Statistics:** 2,233 applied, 56.56% admitted, 27% enrolled. **Transfer Admission Requirements:** college transcript(s), statement of good standing from prior institution(s). Minimum college GPA of 2.5 required. Lowest grade transferable D. **General Admission Information:** Application fee $50. Priority deadline 3/1. Regular application deadline 7/15. Nonfall registration accepted. Admission may be deferred for a maximum of 1 year.

COSTS AND FINANCIAL AID

Annual in-state tuition $6,170. Annual out-of-state tuition $15,820. Room and board $12,250. Required fees $1,270. Average book expense $1,500. **Required Forms and Deadlines:** FAFSA, State aid form. **Notification of Awards:** Applicants will be notified of awards on a rolling basis beginning 3/15. **Types of Aid:** *Need-based scholarships/grants:* Federal Pell, FSEOG, State scholarships/grants, Private scholarships, College/university scholarship or grant aid from institutional funds. *Loans:* Direct Subsidized Stafford Loans, Direct Unsubsidized Stafford Loans, Direct PLUS loans, Federal Perkins Loans, Federal Nursing Loans. *Student Employment:* Federal Work-Study Program available. Institutional employment available. **Financial Aid Statistics:** 90% needy freshmen, 87% needy undergrads receive need-based scholarship or grant aid. 63% freshmen, 30% undergrads receive non-need-based scholarship or grant aid. 98% freshmen, 99% undergrads receive need-based self-help aid. 0% freshmen, 0% undergrads receive athletic scholarships. **Criteria for awarding aid:** *Non-need-based:* Academics.

STATE UNIVERSITY OF NEW YORK—POTSDAM

44 Pierrepont Avenue, Potsdam, NY 13676
Phone: 315-267-2180 • **Financial Aid Phone:** 315-267-2162
E-mail: admissions@potsdam.edu • **CEEB Code:** 2545
Fax: 315-267-2163 • **Website:** www.potsdam.edu • **ACT Code:** 2946

This public school was founded in 1816. It has a 240-acre campus.

RATINGS
Admissions Selectivity Rating: 77   **Fire Safety Rating:** 89   **Green Rating:** 81

STUDENTS AND FACULTY
Enrollment: 3,406. **Student Body:** 57% female, 43% male, 4% out-of-state, 1% international (40 countries represented). Asian 2%, African American 11%, Caucasian 62%, Hispanic 14%, Native American 2%, Pacific Islander <1%, Two or more races 3%, Race unknown 5%.
Retention and Graduation: 75% freshmen return for sophomore year. 35% freshmen graduate within 4 years. 52% freshmen graduate within 6 years. 41% grads go on to further study within 1 year. 23% grads pursue arts and sciences degrees. 1% grads pursue law degrees. 3% grads pursue business degrees. 1% grads pursue medical degrees. **Faculty:** Student/faculty ratio 11:1. 260 full-time faculty, 85% hold PhDs, 13% are are members of minority groups, 45% are women.

ACADEMICS
Degrees: bachelor's, master's, post-master's certificate. **Classes:** Most classes have 10-19 students. Most lab/discussion sessions have 10-19 students. **Most popular majors:** Business Administration and Management; Psychology; Elementary Education and Teaching. **Special Study Options:** cross-registration, distance learning, double major, dual enrollment, exchange student program (domestic), honors program, independent study, internships, liberal arts/career combination, student-designed major, study abroad, teacher certification program, First-year students may enroll in interdisciplinary program to study art, literature, science, and sociology of the Adirondacks. Extension offers undergraduate and graduate courses with emphasis on teacher education. Combined degree options in engineering with Clarkson University and SUNY Binghamton; accounting, engineering or management with SUNY Institute of Technology. **Honors Programs:** The Honors Program is designed to offer special curricular, co-curricular, and extra curricular opportunities for our college's most academically talented students. Benefits include priority registration, honors courses, field trips, mentoring, housing, and select study abroad options. Combined degree programs: BA/MA, BA/MST. **Disability Services:** Special programs offered to physically disabled students, including note-taking services, reader services, tape recorders, tutors. **Career Services:** Alumni network, Alumni services, Career/job search classes, Career assessment.

FACILITIES
Housing: Coed dorms, special housing for disabled students, special housing for international students, apartments for single students, Wellness Housing, ThemeHousingFirst year experience, Quiet study, House, Transfer student housing, Sustainability. 95% of campus accessible to physically diasbled.
Special Academic Facilities/Equipment: Art gallery, anthropology museum, ecology museum, three performance halls, theatre, synthesizer music studios, planetarium, electron microscope, nuclear magnetic resonator, seismograph.
Computers: 20% of classrooms, 100% of dorms, 100% of libraries, 100% of dining areas, 100% of student union, 40% of common outdoor areas have wireless network access. Students can register for classes online. Administrative functions (other than registration) can be performed online.

CAMPUS LIFE
Environment: Village. **Activities:** Choral groups, concert band, dance, drama/theater, jazz band, literary magazine, music ensembles, musical theater, opera, radio station, student government, student newspaper, symphony orchestra, yearbook, Campus Ministries, Student Organization. 100 registered organizations, 17 honor societies, 3 religious organizations. 4 fraternities, 7 sororities. **Athletics (Intercollegiate):** *Men:* basketball, cross-country, diving, equestrian sports, golf, ice hockey, lacrosse, soccer, swimming. *Women:* basketball, cross-country, diving, equestrian sports, ice hockey, lacrosse, soccer, softball, swimming, tennis, volleyball. **On-Campus Highlights:** Hosmer Concert Hall, Maxcy Athletic Complex, Townhouses, Gibson Art Gallery, Barrrington Student Union, Becky's Place (new dining facility) Minerva's Cafe. **Environmental Initiatives:** Promote sustainability education through eco rep program.

ADMISSIONS
Freshman Academic Profile: Average high school GPA 87.1. 14% in top 10% of high school class, 14% in top 25% of high school class, 62% in top 50% of high school class. 94% from public high schools. **Reported SAT (pre-2016 redesign) scores:** SAT Math middle 50% range 490-600. SAT Critical Reading middle 50% range 500-610. **Concordant SAT scores:** SAT Math middle 50% range 520–620. ACT middle 50% range 21-27. Minimum internet-based TOEFL 79. Minimum paper TOEFL 550. **Basis for Candidate Selection:** *Very important factors considered include:* rigor of secondary school record, academic GPA. *Important factors considered include:* application essay, recommendation(s), interview, extracurricular activities, talent/ability, character/personal qualities. *Other factors considered include:* class rank, standardized test scores, alumni/ae relation, volunteer work, work experience, level of applicant's interest. **Freshman Admission Requirements:** High school diploma is required and GED is accepted. *Academic units required:* 4 English, 2 math, 2 science, 1 science lab, 4 social studies, 1 visual/performing arts. *Academic units recommended:* 4 English, 3 math, 3 science, 1 science lab, 3 foreign language, 4 social studies, 1 visual/performing arts. **Freshman Admission Statistics:** 5,454 applied, 71.78% admitted, 20% enrolled. **Transfer Admission Requirements:** college transcript(s), Minimum college GPA of 2.0 required. Lowest grade transferable D. **General Admission Information:** Application fee $50. Nonfall registration accepted. Admission may be deferred for a maximum of 1 year.

COSTS AND FINANCIAL AID
Average book expense $810. **Required Forms and Deadlines:** FAFSA, State aid form. **Notification of Awards:** Applicants will be notified of awards on a rolling basis beginning 2/1. **Types of Aid:** *Need-based scholarships/grants:* Federal Pell, FSEOG, State scholarships/grants, Private scholarships, College/university scholarship or grant aid from institutional funds. *Loans:* Direct Subsidized Stafford Loans, Direct Unsubsidized Stafford Loans, Direct PLUS loans, Federal Perkins Loans, College/university loans from institutional funds. *Student Employment:* Federal Work-Study Program available. Institutional employment available. **Financial Aid Statistics:** 91% needy freshmen, 83% needy undergrads receive need-based scholarship or grant aid. 40% freshmen, 36% undergrads receive non-need-based scholarship or grant aid. 89% freshmen, 87% undergrads receive need-based self-help aid. 0% freshmen, 0% undergrads receive athletic scholarships. 97% freshmen, 81% undergrads receive any aid. 79% undergrads borrow to pay for school. Average cumulative indebtedness $28,582. **Criteria for awarding aid:** *Non-need-based:* Academics, Art, Leadership, Music/drama.

STATE UNIVERSITY OF NEW YORK— STONY BROOK UNIVERSITY

Office of Admissions, Stony Brook, NY 11794-1901
Phone: 631-632-6868 • **Financial Aid Phone:** 631-632-6840
E-mail: enroll@stonybrook.edu • **CEEB Code:** 2548
Fax: 631-632-9898 • **Website:** www.stonybrook.edu/ • **ACT Code:** 2952

This public school was founded in 1957. It has a 1450-acre campus.

RATINGS

Admissions Selectivity Rating: 91   **Fire Safety Rating:** 88   **Green Rating:** 96

STUDENTS AND FACULTY

Enrollment: 16,863. **Student Body:** 46% female, 54% male, 7% out-of-state, 14% international (90 countries represented). Asian 24%, African American 7%, Caucasian 35%, Hispanic 12%, Native American <1%, Pacific Islander <1%, Two or more races 2%, Race unknown 6%.
Retention and Graduation: 89% freshmen return for sophomore year. 52% freshmen graduate within 4 years. 72% freshmen graduate within 6 years. 31% grads go on to further study within 1 year. 18% grads pursue arts and sciences degrees. 2% grads pursue law degrees. 1% grads pursue business degrees. 7% grads pursue medical degrees. **Faculty:** Student/faculty ratio 17:1. 1,086 full-time faculty, 90% hold PhDs, 21% are are members of minority groups, 37% are women.

ACADEMICS

Degrees: bachelor's, doctoral/professional, doctoral/research, doctoral, master's, postbachelor's certificate, post-master's certificate. **Classes:** Most classes have 10-19 students. Most lab/discussion sessions have 20-29 students. **Most popular majors:** Biology/Biological Sciences; Health Services/Allied Health/Health Sciences; Business Administration and Management. **Special Study Options:** cross-registration, distance learning, double major, English as a Second Language (ESL), exchange student program (domestic), honors program, independent study, internships, student-designed major, study abroad, teacher certification program, Albany Semester, Undergrads may take grad level courses BS/MS programs, BE/MS, BS/MA—Living Learning Centers in residence halls, Honors College, undergraduate research and creative activities program where undergraduates work with faculty on research projects, university learning communities and (WISE) Women in Science and Engineering. **Honors Programs:** BA/MD Combined degree programs: BA/MA, MD/PhD. **Disability Services:** Special programs offered to physically disabled students, including note-taking services, reader services, tape recorders, tutors. **Career Services:** Alumni network, Alumni services, Career/job search classes, Career assessment, Internships, Regional alumni. Career services internship program modeled after successful corporate internship programs. Includes career counseling, marketing, graphics, human resources, and technology.

FACILITIES

Housing: Coed dorms, special housing for disabled students, apartments for married students, apartments for single students. Single sex floors in Coed dorms. Living Learning Centers. First year resident members of each College are housed together in the same residential Quadrangle. 75% of campus accessible to physically diasbled. **Special Academic Facilities/Equipment:** SAC Gallery, Staller Gallery, Wang Center, Tabler Center for the Arts **Computers:** 50% of classrooms, 50% of dorms, 50% of libraries, 50% of dining areas, 50% of student union, 50% of common outdoor areas have wireless network access. Students can register for classes online. Administrative functions (other than registration) can be performed online.

CAMPUS LIFE

Environment: Town. **Activities:** Choral groups, concert band, dance, drama/theater, jazz band, literary magazine, marching band, music ensembles, musical theater, opera, pep band, radio station, student government, student newspaper, student-run film society, symphony orchestra, yearbook, Campus Ministries. 292 registered organizations, 6 honor societies, 25 religious organizations. 17 fraternities, 16 sororities. **Athletics (Intercollegiate):** *Men:* baseball, basketball, cross-country, diving, football, lacrosse, soccer, swimming, tennis, track/field (outdoor), track/field (indoor). *Women:* basketball, cross-country, diving, lacrosse, soccer, softball, swimming, tennis, track/field (outdoor), track/field (indoor), volleyball. **On-Campus Highlights:** Staller Center for the Arts, Sports Complex and Stadium, Student Activities Center, University Hospital, The Charles B. Wang Center, Building and Grounds: Main campus. 1,100 acres.

Research and Development Campus, 246 acres adjacent to the main campus. Stony Brook Southampton, 82 acres. Stony Brook Manhattan. New buildings: Humanities Building, undergraduate apartments; Center for Excellence in Wireless and Information Technology under construction. **Environmental Initiatives:** Signing of ACUPCC. Commitment to obtain carbon nuetrality by 2050.

ADMISSIONS

Freshman Academic Profile: Average high school GPA 3.8. 48% in top 10% of high school class, 80% in top 25% of high school class, 96% in top 50% of high school class. 90% from public high schools. **Reported SAT (pre-2016 redesign) scores:** SAT Math middle 50% range 600-710. SAT Critical Reading middle 50% range 550-660. SAT Writing middle 50% range 540-660. **Concordant SAT scores:** SAT EBRW middle 50% 600–700. SAT Math middle 50% range 620–740. ACT middle 50% range 26-31. Minimum internet-based TOEFL 80. Minimum paper TOEFL 550. **Basis for Candidate Selection:** *Very important factors considered include:* rigor of secondary school record, academic GPA, standardized test scores. *Important factors considered include:* application essay, recommendation(s). *Other factors considered include:* class rank, interview, extracurricular activities, talent/ability, character/personal qualities, first generation, alumni/ae relation, geographical residence, state residency, volunteer work, work experience, level of applicant's interest. **Freshman Admission Requirements:** High school diploma is required and GED is accepted. *Academic units required:* 4 English, 3 math, 3 science, 2 foreign language, 4 social studies. *Academic units recommended:* 4 math, 4 science, 3 foreign language. **Freshman Admission Statistics:** 34,999 applied, 40.67% admitted, 21% enrolled. **Transfer Admission Requirements:** college transcript(s), Minimum college GPA of 3.0 required. Lowest grade transferable C. **General Admission Information:** Application fee $50. Priority deadline 1/15. Regular notification 4/1. Nonfall registration accepted. Admission may be deferred for a maximum of 2 semesters.

COSTS AND FINANCIAL AID

Annual in-state tuition $6,470. Annual out-of-state tuition $23,710. Room and board $12,882. Required fees $2,529. Average book expense $900. **Required Forms and Deadlines:** FAFSA, State aid form. **Notification of Awards:** Applicants will be notified of awards on a rolling basis beginning 4/1. **Types of Aid:** *Need-based scholarships/grants:* Federal Pell, FSEOG, State scholarships/grants, Private scholarships, College/university scholarship or grant aid from institutional funds. *Loans:* Direct Subsidized Stafford Loans, Direct Unsubsidized Stafford Loans, Direct PLUS loans, Federal Perkins Loans. *Student Employment:* Federal Work-Study Program available. Institutional employment available. **Financial Aid Statistics:** 89% needy freshmen, 84% needy undergrads receive need-based scholarship or grant aid. 12% freshmen, 5% undergrads receive non-need-based scholarship or grant aid. 89% freshmen, 91% undergrads receive need-based self-help aid. 2% freshmen, 1% undergrads receive athletic scholarships. 76% freshmen, 69% undergrads receive any aid. 55% undergrads borrow to pay for school. Average cumulative indebtedness $24,656. **Criteria for awarding aid:** *Need-based:* Academics, Leadership, Minority status. *Non-need-based:* Academics, Alumni affiliation, Art, Athletics, Job skills, Leadership, Music/drama.

STATE UNIVERSITY OF NEW YORK— UNIVERSITY AT ALBANY

Office of Undergraduate Admissions, Albany, NY 12222
Phone: 518-442-5435 • **Financial Aid Phone:** 518-442-3202
E-mail: ugadmissions@albany.edu • **CEEB Code:** 2532
Fax: 518-442-5383 • **Website:** www.albany.edu • **ACT Code:** 2926

This public school was founded in 1844. It has a 795-acre campus.

RATINGS

Admissions Selectivity Rating: 87   **Fire Safety Rating:** 89   **Green Rating:** 93

STUDENTS AND FACULTY

Enrollment: 12,955. **Student Body:** 49% female, 51% male, 5% out-of-state, 6% international (84 countries represented). Asian 9%, African American 17%, Caucasian 47%, Hispanic 16%, Native American <1%, Pacific Islander <1%, Two or more races 3%, Race unknown 2%.
Retention and Graduation: 80% freshmen return for sophomore year. 56% freshmen graduate within 4 years. 66 **Faculty:** Student/faculty ratio 18:1. 684 full-time faculty, 95% hold PhDs, 23% are are members of minority groups, 39% are women. 10% of classes are taught by teaching assistants.

ACADEMICS

Degrees: bachelor's, master's, postbachelor's certificate, post-master's certificate. **Classes:** Most classes have 20-29 students. Most lab/discussion sessions have

10-19 students. **Most popular majors:** English Language and Literature; Psychology; Business Administration and Management. **Special Study Options:** Accelerated program, cross-registration, distance learning, double major, dual enrollment, English as a Second Language (ESL), honors program, independent study, internships, liberal arts/career combination, student-designed major, study abroad, Accelerated 5 year Bachelors/Masters programs in 40 fields; Internships with New York State Legislature; Combined Bachelors/Law degree with Albany Law school; 3+2 Engineering Program with RPI, Clarkson, and others; Biology/Dental Program with Boston University Goldman School of Dental Medicine, Bachelors/Doctor of Optometry with SUNY State College; Early Assurance Program with Albany Medical College and SUNY Upstate Medical College. **Honors Programs:** Our Presidential Scholars program combines merit scholarships, honors courses, priority registration, special housing, and faculty mentor opportunities. Combined degree programs: BA/JD, BA/MA, BA/MEng, Accelerated 5 yr Bachelors/Masters in 40 fields. **Disability Services:** Special programs offered to physically disabled students, including note-taking services, reader services, tape recorders, tutors. **Career Services:** Alumni network, Alumni services, Career/job search classes, Career assessment, Internships, Regional alumni. Internships with New York State Legislature; On-Campus Recruiting for graduates and those seeking internships.

FACILITIES

Housing: Coed dorms, special housing for international students, apartments for married students, apartments for single students, Wellness Housing, Theme Housing. Disabled Student Services provides individualized services including information on accessible housing. 99% of campus accessible to physically diasbled. **Special Academic Facilities/Equipment:** Performing Arts Center, Art Museum, art and dance studios, sculpture foundry, nuclear accelerator and advanced materials facilities, a peptide synthesis facility, recombinatnt DNA sequencing laboratories, and atmospheric science's Whiteface Mountain observational facility. **Computers:** 75% of classrooms, 100% of dorms, 100% of libraries, 75% of dining areas, 100% of student union, 75% of common outdoor areas have wireless network access. Students can register for classes online. Administrative functions (other than registration) can be performed online.

CAMPUS LIFE

Environment: City. **Activities:** Choral groups, concert band, dance, drama/theater, jazz band, literary magazine, music ensembles, musical theater, pep band, radio station, student government, student newspaper, student-run film society, symphony orchestra, television station, yearbook, Campus Ministries, Student Organization. 200 registered organizations, 20 honor societies, 17 religious organizations. 11 fraternities, 18 sororities. **Athletics (Intercollegiate):** *Men:* baseball, basketball, cross-country, football, lacrosse, soccer, track/field (outdoor), track/field (indoor). *Women:* basketball, cross-country, field hockey, golf, lacrosse, soccer, softball, tennis, track/field (outdoor), track/field (indoor), volleyball. **On-Campus Highlights:** Campus Center with bookstore, cafes, and lounges, SEFCU Arena, Science Library /Main Library, Performing Arts Center, University Art Museum, Students often find that a visit to the University at Albany helps them decide whether this is the university for them. Visitors can attend an information session and join a student-led tour during the academic year or the summer. The tour visits classrooms, academic and other facilities, a residence hall and a dining area. Information Sessions begin at 10:00 a.m. and 12:00 p.m. Your visit includes a QandA session and campus tour. Please allow two hours for your visit. **Environmental Initiatives:** energy conservation.

ADMISSIONS

Freshman Academic Profile: Average high school GPA 3.2. 16% in top 10% of high school class, 32% in top 25% of high school class, 83% in top 50% of high school class. **Reported SAT (pre-2016 redesign) scores:** SAT Math middle 50% range 500-590. SAT Critical Reading middle 50% range 490-580. **Concordant SAT scores:** SAT Math middle 50% range 530–610. ACT middle 50% range 22-26. Minimum internet-based TOEFL 79. Minimum paper TOEFL 550. **Basis for Candidate Selection:** *Very important factors considered include:* rigor of secondary school record, class rank, academic GPA, standardized test scores, recommendation(s), character/personal qualities. *Important factors considered include:* application essay. *Other factors considered include:* extracurricular activities, talent/ability, first generation, alumni/ae relation, geographical residence, volunteer work, work experience. **Freshman Admission Requirements:** High school diploma is required and GED is accepted. *Academic units required:* 4 English, 2 math, 2 science, 2 science labs, 1 foreign language, 3 social studies, 2 history, 4 academic electives. *Academic units recommended:* 4 math, 3 science, 3 science labs, 3 foreign language. **Freshman Admission Statistics:** 23,799 applied, 54.39% admitted, 21% enrolled. **Transfer Admission Requirements:** college transcript(s), essay or personal statement, statement of good standing from prior institution(s). Minimum college GPA of 2.5 required. Lowest grade transferable C. **General Admission Information:** Application fee $50. Priority deadline 3/1. Regular application deadline 3/1. Nonfall registration accepted. Admission may be deferred for a maximum of 1 year.

COSTS AND FINANCIAL AID

Annual in-state tuition $6,470. Annual out-of-state tuition $21,550. Room and board $12,942. Required fees $2,753. Average book expense $1,200. **Required Forms and Deadlines:** FAFSA. **Notification of Awards:** Applicants will be notified of awards on a rolling basis beginning 3/20. **Types of Aid:** *Need-based scholarships/grants:* Federal Pell, FSEOG, State scholarships/grants, Private scholarships, College/university scholarship or grant aid from institutional funds. *Loans:* Direct Subsidized Stafford Loans, Direct Unsubsidized Stafford Loans, Direct PLUS loans, Federal Perkins Loans. *Student Employment:* Federal Work-Study Program available. Institutional employment available. **Financial Aid Statistics:** 84% needy freshmen, 84% needy undergrads receive need-based scholarship or grant aid. 3% freshmen, 2% undergrads receive non-need-based scholarship or grant aid. 79% freshmen, 81% undergrads receive need-based self-help aid. 2% freshmen, 2% undergrads receive athletic scholarships. 64% freshmen, 57% undergrads receive any aid. **Criteria for awarding aid:** *Non-need-based:* Academics, Athletics, State/district residency.

STATE UNIVERSITY OF NEW YORK—
UNIVERSITY AT BUFFALO

12 Capen Hall, Buffalo, NY 14260-1660
Phone: 716-645-6900 • **Financial Aid Phone:** 716-645-2450
E-mail: ub-admissions@buffalo.edu • **CEEB Code:** 2925
Fax: 716-645-6411 • **Website:** www.buffalo.edu • **ACT Code:** 2978

This public school was founded in 1846. It has a 1346-acre campus.

RATINGS
Admissions Selectivity Rating: 75   **Fire Safety Rating:** 81   **Green Rating:** 65

STUDENTS AND FACULTY
Enrollment: 20,102. **Student Body:** 43% female, 57% male, 3% out-of-state, 16% international (87 countries represented). Asian 14%, African American 7%, Caucasian 48%, Hispanic 7%, Native American <1%, Pacific Islander <1%, Two or more races 2%, Race unknown 3%.
Retention and Graduation: 86% freshmen return for sophomore year. 58% freshmen graduate within 4 years. 74% freshmen graduate within 6 years. 29% grads go on to further study within 1 year. 28% grads pursue arts and sciences degrees. 8% grads pursue law degrees. 10% grads pursue business degrees. 7% grads pursue medical degrees. **Faculty:** Student/faculty ratio 13:1. 1,255 full-time faculty, 98% hold PhDs, 27% are are members of minority groups, 38% are women. 11% of classes are taught by teaching assistants.

ACADEMICS
Degrees: bachelor's, certificate, doctoral/professional, doctoral/research, doctoral, master's, post-master's certificate. **Classes:** Most classes have 20-29 students. Most lab/discussion sessions have 20-29 students. **Most popular majors:** Social Sciences; Business Administration and Management; Engineering. **Special Study Options:** Accelerated program, cooperative education program, cross-registration, distance learning, double major, dual enrollment, English as a Second Language (ESL), exchange student program (domestic), honors program, independent study, internships, liberal arts/career combination, student-designed major, study abroad, teacher certification program, Certificate programs, Combined Degree Programs, Early Assurance Program with School of Medicine & Dentistry, Honors College & Learning Communities. **Honors Programs:** There is a University Honors College as well as honors programs within the majors. Undergraduate research is an option in a variety of disciplines and often affords the student an opportunity to participate in cutting-edge research activities. See • **Website:** http://honors.buffalo.edu Combined degree programs: BA/MA, BA/MS, BS/MS, BA/MBA, BS/MBA, BA/MA, BA/MSW, BS/DDS, BA/EDM, BA/MFA. **Disability Services:** Special programs offered to physically disabled students, including note-taking services, reader services, tape recorders, tutors. **Career Services:** Alumni network, Alumni services, Career/job search classes, Internships.

FACILITIES
Housing: Coed dorms, special housing for disabled students, special housing for international students, apartments for married students, apartments for single students, Theme Housing, Honors Housing, Academic Interest Housing, Freshman Housing. See • **Website:** http://www.ub-housing.buffalo.edu/special. 90% of campus accessible to physically diasbled. **Special Academic Facilities/Equipment:** UB Center for the Arts, Slee Concert Hall, Anthropology Research Museum, Multidisciplinary Center for Earthquake Engineering Research (MCEER), New York State Center of Excellence in Bioinformatics and Life Sciences, Center for Computational Research (CCR), Poetry and Rare Books Collection, Center of Excellence for Document Analysis and Recognition Center, New York State Center for Engineering Design and Industrial Innova-

tion, Pharmacy Museum, The Virtual Site Museum, Electronic Poetry Center, Archeological Survey Center, Anderson Gallery, Alfiero Center and numerous research centers **Computers:** Students can register for classes online. Administrative functions (other than registration) can be performed online.

CAMPUS LIFE

Environment: City. **Activities:** Choral groups, concert band, dance, drama/theater, jazz band, literary magazine, marching band, music ensembles, musical theater, pep band, radio station, student government, student newspaper, student-run film society, symphony orchestra, television station, Campus Ministries, Student Organization. 215 registered organizations, 29 honor societies, 35 religious organizations. 22 fraternities, 17 sororities. **Athletics (Intercollegiate):** *Men:* baseball, basketball, cross-country, football, soccer, swimming, tennis, track/field (outdoor), wrestling. *Women:* basketball, crew/rowing, cross-country, soccer, softball, swimming, tennis, track/field (outdoor), volleyball. **On-Campus Highlights:** Center for the Arts, Alumni Arena and Athletic Stadium, Center for Computational Research, Apartment style student housing, The Commons (on-campus shopping).

ADMISSIONS

Freshman Academic Profile: Average high school GPA 3.6. 27% in top 10% of high school class, 59% in top 25% of high school class, 90% in top 50% of high school class. **Reported SAT (pre-2016 redesign) scores:** SAT Math middle 50% range 550-660. SAT Critical Reading middle 50% range 520-610. **Concordant SAT scores:** SAT Math middle 50% range 570–690. ACT middle 50% range 24-29. Minimum internet-based TOEFL 79. Minimum paper TOEFL 550. **Basis for Candidate Selection:** *Very important factors considered include:* rigor of secondary school record, academic GPA, standardized test scores. *Important factors considered include:* class rank, recommendation(s), interview. *Other factors considered include:* application essay, extracurricular activities, talent/ability, character/personal qualities, first generation, geographical residence, racial/ethnic status, volunteer work, work experience. **Freshman Admission Requirements:** High school diploma is required and GED is accepted. *Academic units recommended:* 4 English, 3 math, 3 science, 3 foreign language, 4 social studies. **Freshman Admission Statistics:** 26,001 applied, 59.38% admitted, 27% enrolled. **Transfer Admission Requirements:** High school transcript, college transcript(s), essay or personal statement, Minimum college GPA of 2.5 required. Lowest grade transferable D. **General Admission Information:** Application fee $50. Priority deadline 11/15. Nonfall registration accepted.

COSTS AND FINANCIAL AID

Annual in-state tuition $6,470. Annual out-of-state tuition $23,710. Room and board $13,548. Required fees $3,104. Average book expense $1,196. **Required Forms and Deadlines:** FAFSA. **Notification of Awards:** Applicants will be notified of awards on a rolling basis beginning 2/1. **Types of Aid:** *Need-based scholarships/grants:* Federal Pell, FSEOG, State scholarships/grants, Private scholarships, College/university scholarship or grant aid from institutional funds, Federal Nursing Scholarships. *Loans:* Direct Subsidized Stafford Loans, Direct Unsubsidized Stafford Loans, Direct PLUS loans, Federal Perkins Loans, Federal Nursing Loans. *Student Employment:* Federal Work-Study Program available. Institutional employment available. **Financial Aid Statistics:** 85% needy freshmen, 76% needy undergrads receive need-based scholarship or grant aid. 36% freshmen, 22% undergrads receive non-need-based scholarship or grant aid. 72% freshmen, 79% undergrads receive need-based self-help aid. 0% freshmen, 0% undergrads receive athletic scholarships. 65% freshmen, 64% undergrads receive any aid. **Criteria for awarding aid:** *Need-based:* Academics, Minority status, Music/drama. *Non-need-based:* Academics, Art, Athletics, Minority status, Music/drama, State/district residency.

STATE UNIVERSITY OF NEW YORK— UPSTATE MEDICAL UNIVERSITY

766 Irving Avenue, Syracuse, NY 13210
Phone: 315-464-4570 • **Financial Aid Phone:** 315-464-4329
E-mail: admiss@upstate.edu • **CEEB Code:** 2547
Fax: 315-464-8867 • **ACT Code:** 2981

This public school was founded in 1850. It has a 25-acre campus.

RATINGS

Admissions Selectivity Rating: 61 **Fire Safety Rating:** 81 **Green Rating:** 60*

STUDENTS AND FACULTY

Student Body: 75% female, 25% male, 9% out-of-state.
Faculty: 43 full-time faculty, 60% hold PhDs, 2% are are members of minority groups, 70% are women. 0% of classes are taught by teaching assistants.

ACADEMICS

Degrees: bachelor's, doctoral/professional, doctoral/research, doctoral, master's, post-master's certificate. **Classes:** Most classes have fewer than 10 students. **Disability Services:** Special programs offered to physically disabled students, including note-taking services, reader services, tape recorders, tutors. **Career Services:** Alumni network, Regional alumni, On-campus interviews.

FACILITIES

Housing: Coed dorms, apartments for married students, apartments for single students. 100% of campus accessible to physically diasbled. **Special Academic Facilities/Equipment:** 350 bed Tertiary Care Hospital **Computers:** Administrative functions (other than registration) can be performed online.

CAMPUS LIFE

Environment: City. **Activities:** student government, Student Organization. 51 registered organizations, 3 religious organizations. **On-Campus Highlights:** Weiskotten Hall, Silverman Hall, University Hospital, Institute for Human Performance, Campus Activities Building.

ADMISSIONS

Minimum paper TOEFL 550. **Freshman Admission Requirements:** High school diploma is required and GED is accepted. **Transfer Admission Requirements:** High school transcript, college transcript(s), essay or personal statement, interview, Minimum college GPA of 2.0 required. Lowest grade transferable C-. **General Admission Information:** Application fee $50. Nonfall registration not accepted. Admission may be deferred for a maximum of 1 Year.

COSTS AND FINANCIAL AID

Annual in-state tuition $4,970. Annual out-of-state tuition $13,380. Room and board $10,422. Required fees $575. Average book expense $1,070. **Required Forms and Deadlines:** FAFSA. **Types of Aid:** *Need-based scholarships/grants:* Federal Pell, FSEOG, State scholarships/grants, Private scholarships, College/university scholarship or grant aid from institutional funds. *Loans:* Direct Subsidized Stafford Loans, Direct Unsubsidized Stafford Loans, Direct PLUS loans, Federal Perkins Loans. *Student Employment:* Federal Work-Study Program available. Institutional employment available. **Financial Aid Statistics:** 18% needy undergrads receive need-based scholarship or grant aid. 27% undergrads receive non-need-based scholarship or grant aid. 13% undergrads receive need-based self-help aid. 78% freshmen receive any aid. **Criteria for awarding aid:** *Need-based:* Academics.

STEPHENS COLLEGE

1200 East Broadway, Columbia, MO 65215
Phone: 573-876-7207 • **Financial Aid Phone:** 573-876-7106
E-mail: apply@stephens.edu • **CEEB Code:** 6683
Fax: 573-876-7237 • **Website:** http://www.stephens.edu/ • **ACT Code:** 2374

This private school was founded in 1833. It has a 86-acre campus.

RATINGS

Admissions Selectivity Rating: 85 **Fire Safety Rating:** 84 **Green Rating:** 60*

STUDENTS AND FACULTY

Enrollment: 724. **Student Body:** 99% female, 1% male, 37% out-of-state, <1% international (2 countries represented). Asian 2%, African American 13%, Caucasian 69%, Hispanic 4%, Native American 1%, Pacific Islander <1%, Two or more races 6%, Race unknown 4%.
Retention and Graduation: 69% freshmen return for sophomore year. 46% freshmen graduate within 4 years. 50% freshmen graduate within 6 years.
Faculty: Student/faculty ratio 9:1. 54 full-time faculty, 57% hold PhDs, 9% are are members of minority groups, 74% are women. 0% of classes are taught by teaching assistants.

ACADEMICS

Degrees: associate, bachelor's, master's, postbachelor's certificate, post-master's certificate. **Classes:** Most classes have fewer than 10 students. Most lab/discussion sessions have 10-19 students. **Most popular majors:** Fashion/Apparel Design; Biology/Biological Sciences; Health Services/Allied Health/Health Sciences. **Special Study Options:** cross-registration, distance learning, double major, dual enrollment, external degree program, independent study, internships, liberal arts/career combination, student-designed major, study abroad, teacher certification program. Combined degree programs: BA/JD, BA/MA, Occupational Therapy with Washington University. **Disability Services:**

Special programs offered to physically disabled students, including note-taking services, tutors. **Career Services:** Alumni network, Alumni services, Career/job search classes, Career assessment, Internships, Regional alumni. The Center for Career and Profession Development (CCPD) offers a full range of services to assist with career planning. The CCPD partners with faculty, advisers, alumnae and employers on a wide range of student success initiatives. A 20,000 strong nationwide (and international) alumnae network partners with students to help them find and take advantage of opportunities.

FACILITIES

Housing: special housing for disabled students, women's dorms, fraternity/sorority housing, apartments for single students, Pet Friendly Residence. 80% of campus accessible to physically diasbled. **Special Academic Facilities/Equipment:** Art gallery and historical costume collections, on-campus preschool, kindergarten, and elementary school, language lab. **Computers:** 100% of classrooms, 100% of dorms, 100% of libraries, 100% of dining areas, 100% of student union, have wireless network access. Students can register for classes online. Administrative functions (other than registration) can be performed online.

CAMPUS LIFE

Environment: City. **Activities:** Choral groups, dance, drama/theater, literary magazine, music ensembles, musical theater, radio station, student government, student newspaper, student-run film society, television station 28 registered organizations, 11 honor societies, 3 religious organizations. 2 sororities. **Athletics (Intercollegiate):** *Women:* basketball, cross-country, softball, swimming, tennis, volleyball. **On-Campus Highlights:** Equestrian Stables, The Commons, Senior Hall, The Quad, Residence Halls. **Environmental Initiatives:** Recycling.

ADMISSIONS

Freshman Academic Profile: Average high school GPA 3.3. 14% in top 10% of high school class, 44% in top 25% of high school class, 79% in top 50% of high school class. 80% from public high schools. **Reported SAT (pre-2016 redesign) scores:** SAT Math middle 50% range 440-570. SAT Critical Reading middle 50% range 450-620. SAT Writing middle 50% range 430-620. **Concordant SAT scores:** SAT EBRW middle 50% 490-670. SAT Math middle 50% range 480-590. ACT middle 50% range 20-25. Minimum paper TOEFL 550. **Basis for Candidate Selection:** *Very important factors considered include:* rigor of secondary school record, academic GPA, standardized test scores, application essay. *Important factors considered include:* recommendation(s), extracurricular activities. *Other factors considered include:* class rank, interview, talent/ability, character/personal qualities, volunteer work, work experience, level of applicant's interest. **Freshman Admission Requirements:** High school diploma is required and GED is accepted. *Academic units recommended:* 4 English, 3 math, 2 science, 2 foreign language, 1 social studies. **Freshman Admission Statistics:** 1,168 applied, 61.04% admitted, 22% enrolled. **Transfer Admission Requirements:** High school transcript, college transcript(s), essay or personal statement, Minimum college GPA of 2.0 required. Lowest grade transferable C-. **General Admission Information:** Application fee $50. Priority deadline 1/1. Nonfall registration accepted. Admission may be deferred for a maximum of 1 year.

COSTS AND FINANCIAL AID

Annual tuition $30,144. Room and board $10,424. Required fees $200. Average book expense $1,000. **Required Forms and Deadlines:** FAFSA. **Notification of Awards:** Applicants will be notified of awards on a rolling basis beginning 3/1. **Types of Aid:** *Need-based scholarships/grants:* Federal Pell, FSEOG, State scholarships/grants, Private scholarships, College/university scholarship or grant aid from institutional funds. *Loans:* Federal Perkins Loans. *Student Employment:* Federal Work-Study Program available. Institutional employment available. **Financial Aid Statistics:** 100% needy freshmen, 100% needy undergrads receive need-based scholarship or grant aid. 84% freshmen, 93% undergrads receive non-need-based scholarship or grant aid. 100% freshmen, 100% undergrads receive need-based self-help aid. 1% freshmen, 2% undergrads receive athletic scholarships. 100% freshmen, 99% undergrads receive any aid. 93% undergrads borrow to pay for school. Average cumulative indebtedness $9,238. **Criteria for awarding aid:** *Non-need-based:* Academics, Alumni affiliation, Athletics, Leadership, Music/drama, State/district residency.

See page 1056.

STERLING COLLEGE

125 W. Cooper, Sterling, KS 67579
Phone: 620-278-4275 • **Financial Aid Phone:** 620-278-4207
E-mail: admissions@sterling.edu • **CEEB Code:** 6684
Fax: 620-869-9021 • **Website:** www.sterling.edu • **ACT Code:** 1466

This private school, affiliated with the Presbyterian Church, was founded in 1887. It has a 42-acre campus.

RATINGS

Admissions Selectivity Rating: 82   **Fire Safety Rating:** 71   **Green Rating:** 99

STUDENTS AND FACULTY

Enrollment: 611. **Student Body:** 47% female, 53% male, 63% out-of-state, 0% international (6 countries represented). Asian 2%, African American 12%, Caucasian 66%, Hispanic 15%, Native American 3%, Pacific Islander 0%, Two or more races 0%, Race unknown 3%.
Retention and Graduation: 62% freshmen return for sophomore year. 35% freshmen graduate within 4 years. 41% freshmen graduate within 6 years.
Faculty: Student/faculty ratio 12:1. 40 full-time faculty, 45% hold PhDs, 15% are are members of minority groups, 35% are women. 0% of classes are taught by teaching assistants.

ACADEMICS

Degrees: bachelor's. **Classes:** Most classes have fewer than 10 students. Most lab/discussion sessions have 20-29 students. **Most popular majors:** Elementary Education and Teaching; Health and Physical Education/Fitness; Business/Commerce. **Special Study Options:** distance learning, double major, dual enrollment, external degree program, honors program, independent study, internships, student-designed major, study abroad, teacher certification program. **Honors Programs:** The honors program is still being developed. At this point honors level general education classes are offered in interdisciplinary history and literature. **Disability Services:** Special programs offered to physically disabled students, including tutors. **Career Services:** Alumni network, Alumni services, Career assessment, Internships.

FACILITIES

Housing: men's dorms, women's dorms. 80% of campus accessible to physically diasbled. **Special Academic Facilities/Equipment:** History/cultural museum. **Computers:** Administrative functions (other than registration) can be performed online.

CAMPUS LIFE

Environment: Rural. **Activities:** Choral groups, concert band, drama/theater, jazz band, literary magazine, music ensembles, musical theater, radio station, student government, student newspaper, television station, yearbook, Campus Ministries. 16 registered organizations, 4 honor societies, 2 religious organizations. **Athletics (Intercollegiate):** *Men:* baseball, basketball, cross-country, football, golf, soccer, track/field (outdoor). *Women:* basketball, cheerleading, cross-country, golf, soccer, softball, track/field (outdoor), volleyball. **On-Campus Highlights:** Gleason Phy. Educ. Center, Student Union, Cooper Hall, Evan's Hall, Campbell Hall.

ADMISSIONS

Freshman Academic Profile: Average high school GPA 3.3. 8% in top 10% of high school class, 17% in top 25% of high school class, 45% in top 50% of high school class. 80% from public high schools. **Reported SAT (pre-2016 redesign) scores:** SAT Math middle 50% range 420-510. SAT Critical Reading middle 50% range 400-520. SAT Writing middle 50% range 380-460. **Concordant SAT scores:** SAT EBRW middle 50% 440-550. SAT Math middle 50% range 460-540. ACT middle 50% range 19-24. Minimum internet-based TOEFL 70. Minimum paper TOEFL 525. **Basis for Candidate Selection:** *Very important factors considered include:* rigor of secondary school record, standardized test scores, character/personal qualities. *Important factors considered include:* academic GPA, application essay, recommendation(s), interview, extracurricular activities, religious affiliation/commitment, volunteer work, level of applicant's interest. *Other factors considered include:* class rank, talent/ability, first generation, alumni/ae relation, work experience. **Freshman Admission Requirements:** High school diploma is required and GED is accepted. *Academic units recommended:* 4 English, 3 math, 3 science, 2 science labs, 2 foreign language, 1 social studies, 2 history, 1 academic elective, 1 computer science, and 1 unit from above areas or other academic areas. **Freshman Admission Statistics:** 1,118 applied, 41.41% admitted, 30% enrolled. **Transfer Admission Requirements:** college transcript(s), essay or personal statement, Minimum college GPA of 2.2 required. Lowest grade transferable C-. **General Admission Information:** Application fee $25. Priority deadline 3/1. Nonfall registration accepted. Admission may be deferred for a maximum of 1 semester.

COSTS AND FINANCIAL AID

Annual tuition $23,400. Room and board $8,580. Average book expense $700. **Required Forms and Deadlines:** FAFSA. **Notification of Awards:** Applicants will be notified of awards on a rolling basis beginning 1/1. **Types of Aid:** *Need-based scholarships/grants:* Federal Pell, FSEOG, State scholarships/grants, Private scholarships, College/university scholarship or grant aid from institutional funds. *Loans:* Federal Perkins Loans. *Student Employment:* Federal Work-Study Program available. Institutional employment available. **Financial Aid Statistics:** 0% freshmen, 0% undergrads receive athletic scholarships. 100% freshmen, 96% undergrads receive any aid. **Criteria for awarding aid:** *Non-need-based:* Academics, Art, Athletics, Leadership, Music/drama.

STERLING COLLEGE (VT)

PO Box 72, Craftsbury Common, VT 5827
Phone: 802-586-7711 • **Financial Aid Phone:** 802-586-7711 x 103
E-mail: admission@sterlingcollege.edu • **CEEB Code:** 3752
Fax: 802-586-2596 • **Website:** www.sterlingcollege.edu • **ACT Code:** 6946

This private school was founded in 1958. It has a 430-acre campus.

RATINGS

Admissions Selectivity Rating: 71   **Fire Safety Rating:** 94   **Green Rating:** 90

STUDENTS AND FACULTY

Enrollment: 119. **Student Body:** 49% female, 51% male, 80% out-of-state, 3% international (4 countries represented). Asian 1%, African American 4%, Caucasian 83%, Hispanic 2%, Native American 0%, Pacific Islander 0%, Two or more races 2%, Race unknown 6%.
Retention and Graduation: 52% freshmen return for sophomore year. 33% freshmen graduate within 4 years. 52% freshmen graduate within 6 years. 3% grads go on to further study within 1 year. **Faculty:** Student/faculty ratio 6:1. 18 full-time faculty, 22% hold PhDs, 0% are are members of minority groups, 50% are women. 0% of classes are taught by teaching assistants.

ACADEMICS

Degrees: bachelor's. **Classes:** Most classes have 10-19 students. **Most popular majors:** Agroecology and Sustainable Agriculture. **Special Study Options:** double major, dual enrollment, exchange student program (domestic), independent study, internships, student-designed major, study abroad, Global Field Studies to Japan, Scandinavia, Belize, Alaska, Sierra Nevada, Newfoundland, Iceland, James Bay, and more. **Disability Services:** Special programs offered to physically disabled students, including tutors. **Career Services:** Alumni network, Alumni services, Career/job search classes, Career assessment, Internships, Regional alumni. The Internship is a ten-week experience (working full time) and two courses prior and post to the experience. It is a total of 8 credits and a requirement of all second year students. Past Internship sites have included: 58 federal agencies, including National Forests, National Parks, and National Wildlife Refuges, 18 state agencies, 94 educational organizations including environmental, outdoor adventure, classroom, and interpretative centers,112 agricultural producers, 24 environmental advocacy organizations, 21 wildlife rehabilitation, veterinary medicine, and animal shelter organizations, 30 for-profit green businesses, 36 research institutions, and several national organizations including The Sierra Club, National Audubon Society, PETA, Heifer Project International, The Nature Conservancy, Outward Bound, and NOLS.

FACILITIES

Housing: Coed dorms, Wellness Housing. **Special Academic Facilities/Equipment:** Library serves as art gallery. There is a 6—8 week rotation of Vermont artist displays. Campus also includes wind and solar-powered barns that serves as an instructional facility and lab, a greenhouse provides a working lab for plant and soil studies. Other facilities include: a woodshop, logging shop, sugarhouse, root cellar, darkroom, certified organic gardens, and a 32' tall climbing wall provides students with the ability to develop leadership and technical rock-climbing skills. The Center for Northern Studies at Sterling College includes a 300 acre boreal forest. **Computers:** 100% of classrooms, 100% of dorms, 100% of libraries, 100% of dining areas, 100% of student union, 100% of common outdoor areas have wireless network access. Administrative functions (other than registration) can be performed online.

CAMPUS LIFE

Environment: Rural. **Activities:** Choral groups, dance, drama/theater, music ensembles, student government, student-run film society, yearbook. **On-Campus Highlights:** Challenge Course and Climbing Wall, Organic Gardens and Livestock Farm, Dining Hall serves local, organic food, 300-acre Boreal Forest, Wind and Solar Powered Barns, Student Lounge, Dancing Goat Cafe,

Recreation Room, Lean-toos, XC ski trails, nature trails, Computer labs, common areas in dorms, front porch. **Environmental Initiatives:** Curriculum is completely devoted to environmental stewardship.

ADMISSIONS

Freshman Academic Profile: Average high school GPA 3.2. 20% in top 10% of high school class, 33% in top 25% of high school class, 74% in top 50% of high school class. 64% from public high schools. Minimum internet-based TOEFL 61. Minimum paper TOEFL 500. **Basis for Candidate Selection:** *Very important factors considered include:* rigor of secondary school record, academic GPA, application essay, recommendation(s), interview, level of applicant's interest. *Important factors considered include:* class rank, extracurricular activities, talent/ability, character/personal qualities, volunteer work. *Other factors considered include:* alumni/ae relation, geographical residence, work experience. **Freshman Admission Requirements:** High school diploma is required and GED is accepted. *Academic units required:* 4 English, 3 math, 2 science, 2 science labs, 2 social studies, 2 history. *Academic units recommended:* 4 English, 4 math, 3 science, 3 science labs, 2 foreign language, 2 social studies, 2 history. **Freshman Admission Statistics:** 101 applied, 72.28% admitted, 55% enrolled. **Transfer Admission Requirements:** High school transcript, college transcript(s), essay or personal statement, Minimum college GPA of 2.0 required. Lowest grade transferable C. **General Admission Information:** Application fee $35. Regular application deadline 4/1. Regular notification 4/15. Nonfall registration accepted. Admission may be deferred for a maximum of One year.

COSTS AND FINANCIAL AID

Annual tuition $32,592. Room and board $8,796. Required fees $3,700. Average book expense $900. **Required Forms and Deadlines:** FAFSA, Institution's own financial aid form, State aid form. **Notification of Awards:** Applicants will be notified of awards on a rolling basis beginning 2/1. **Types of Aid:** *Need-based scholarships/grants:* Federal Pell, FSEOG, State scholarships/grants, Private scholarships, College/university scholarship or grant aid from institutional funds. *Loans:* Direct Subsidized Stafford Loans, Direct Unsubsidized Stafford Loans, Direct PLUS loans. *Student Employment:* Federal Work-Study Program available. Institutional employment available. **Financial Aid Statistics:** 100% needy freshmen, 100% needy undergrads receive need-based scholarship or grant aid. 22% undergrads receive non-need-based scholarship or grant aid. 100% freshmen, 100% undergrads receive need-based self-help aid. 0% freshmen, 0% undergrads receive athletic scholarships. 100% freshmen, 100% undergrads receive any aid. **Criteria for awarding aid:** *Need-based:* Academics, Leadership. *Non-need-based:* Academics, Leadership, State/district residency.

STETSON UNIVERSITY

421 N. Woodland Blvd, DeLand, FL 32723
Phone: 386-822-7100 • **Financial Aid Phone:** 800-688-7120
E-mail: admissions@stetson.edu • **CEEB Code:** 5630
Fax: 386-822-7112 • **Website:** stetson.edu • **ACT Code:** 756

This private school was founded in 1883. It has a 175-acre campus.

RATINGS

Admissions Selectivity Rating: 85   **Fire Safety Rating:** 81   **Green Rating:** 78

STUDENTS AND FACULTY

Enrollment: 3,052. **Student Body:** 58% female, 42% male, 32% out-of-state, 5% international (50 countries represented). Asian 2%, African American 8%, Caucasian 64%, Hispanic 15%, Native American <1%, Pacific Islander <1%, Two or more races 3%, Race unknown 1%.
Retention and Graduation: 79% freshmen return for sophomore year. 56% freshmen graduate within 4 years. 64% freshmen graduate within 6 years. 38% grads go on to further study within 1 year. 25% grads pursue arts and sciences degrees. 5% grads pursue law degrees. 18% grads pursue business degrees. 6% grads pursue medical degrees. **Faculty:** Student/faculty ratio 13:1. 271 full-time faculty, 95% hold PhDs, 18% are are members of minority groups, 47% are women. 0% of classes are taught by teaching assistants.

ACADEMICS

Degrees: bachelor's, doctoral/professional, master's, post-master's certificate. **Classes:** Most classes have 10-19 students. Most lab/discussion sessions have 20-29 students. **Most popular majors:** Business Administration and Management; Psychology; Health Services/Allied Health/Health Sciences.

Special Study Options: Accelerated program, double major, honors program, independent study, internships, liberal arts/career combination, student-designed major, study abroad, teacher certification program, weekend college. Combined degree programs: BA/JD, Cooperative Program in Forestry and Environ. Studies w/ Duke Univ. **Disability Services:** Special programs offered to physically disabled students, including note-taking services, reader services, tape recorders, tutors. **Career Services:** Alumni network, Alumni services, Career/job search classes, Career assessment, Internships, Regional alumni. Select employers and alumni who come typically give an hour presentation on many campuses are asked to spend one to two days at Stetson infused in multiple classrooms, with student groups and meeting with faculty and staff. Our relationships with employers and alumni are built on this deep engagement which creates strong ties and pipelines for our interns and graduates.

FACILITIES

Housing: Coed dorms, men's dorms, women's dorms, fraternity/sorority housing, apartments for single students, Wellness Housing, Theme Housing, "Pet" Dorm (pets allowed), Foreign Language House, French House, The Service Station (community service house). 77% of campus accessible to physically diasbled. **Special Academic Facilities/Equipment:** Language lab, art gallery, greenhouse with growth chambers, mineral museum, electron microscopes. **Computers:** 90% of classrooms, 100% of dorms, 100% of libraries, 95% of dining areas, 100% of student union, 30% of common outdoor areas have wireless network access. Students can register for classes online. Administrative functions (other than registration) can be performed online.

CAMPUS LIFE

Environment: Town. **Activities:** Choral groups, concert band, dance, drama/theater, jazz band, literary magazine, music ensembles, musical theater, opera, pep band, radio station, student government, student newspaper, student-run film society, symphony orchestra, Campus Ministries, Student Organization, Model UN. 125 registered organizations, 24 honor societies, 8 religious organizations. 6 fraternities, 5 sororities. **Athletics (Intercollegiate):** *Men:* baseball, basketball, crew/rowing, cross-country, golf, soccer, tennis. *Women:* basketball, crew/rowing, cross-country, golf, soccer, softball, tennis, volleyball. **On-Campus Highlights:** Lynn Business Center, DuPont-Ball Library, Homer and Dolly Hand Art Center, Hollis Center, Sage Hall. **Environmental Initiatives:** The Stetson College of Law is home to the Institute for Biodiversity Law and Policy. The Institute serves as an interdisciplinary focal point for education, research and service activities related to biodiversity issues, and is committed to environmental education and service from the local to the global scale. Each semester, the Institute sponsors several biodiversity lectures.

ADMISSIONS

Freshman Academic Profile: Average high school GPA 3.9. 24% in top 10% of high school class, 59% in top 25% of high school class, 86% in top 50% of high school class. **Reported SAT (pre-2016 redesign) scores:** SAT Math middle 50% range 510-620. SAT Critical Reading middle 50% range 530-630. SAT Writing middle 50% range 500-600. **Concordant SAT scores:** SAT EBRW middle 50% 570–670. SAT Math middle 50% range 540–640. ACT middle 50% range 23-28. Minimum internet-based TOEFL 79. Minimum paper TOEFL 550. **Basis for Candidate Selection:** *Very important factors considered include:* rigor of secondary school record, academic GPA. *Important factors considered include:* class rank, standardized test scores, application essay, recommendation(s), interview, extracurricular activities, talent/ability, character/personal qualities, volunteer work, work experience. *Other factors considered include:* alumni/ae relation, geographical residence, state residency, racial/ethnic status. **Freshman Admission Requirements:** High school diploma is required and GED is accepted. *Academic units required:* 4 English, 3 math, 3 science, 2 foreign language, 2 social studies. **Freshman Admission Statistics:** 12,130 applied, 65.60% admitted, 10% enrolled. **Transfer Admission Requirements:** High school transcript, college transcript(s), essay or personal statement, standardized test scores, statement of good standing from prior institution(s). Minimum college GPA of 2.0 required. Lowest grade transferable C. **General Admission Information:** Application fee $50. Priority deadline 12/1. Nonfall registration accepted. Admission may be deferred.

COSTS AND FINANCIAL AID

Annual tuition $44,130. Room and board $12,684. Required fees $350. Average book expense $1,200. **Required Forms and Deadlines:** FAFSA. **Notification of Awards:** Applicants will be notified of awards on a rolling basis beginning 3/1. **Types of Aid:** *Need-based scholarships/grants:* Federal Pell, FSEOG, State scholarships/grants, Private scholarships, College/university scholarship or grant aid from institutional funds. *Loans:* Direct Subsidized Stafford Loans, Direct Unsubsidized Stafford Loans, Direct PLUS loans, Federal Perkins Loans. *Student Employment:* Federal Work-Study Program available. Institutional employment available. **Financial Aid Statistics:** 100% needy freshmen, 99% needy undergrads receive need-based scholarship or grant aid. 19% freshmen, 16% undergrads receive non-need-based scholarship or grant aid. 74% freshmen, 75% undergrads receive need-based self-help aid. 3% freshmen, 4% undergrads receive athletic scholarships. 100% freshmen, 99% undergrads receive any aid. 70% undergrads borrow to pay for school. Average cumulative

indebtedness $31,457. **Criteria for awarding aid:** *Need-based:* Academics, Alumni affiliation, Art, Athletics, Leadership, Minority status, Music/drama, Religious affiliation. *Non-need-based:* Academics, Alumni affiliation, Art, Athletics, Leadership, Minority status, Music/drama, Religious affiliation, State/district residency.

STEVENS INSTITUTE OF TECHNOLOGY

One Castle Point Terrace, Hoboken, NJ 7030
Phone: 201-216-5194 • **Financial Aid Phone:** 201-216-8142
E-mail: admissions@stevens.edu • **CEEB Code:** 2819
Fax: 201-216-8348 • **Website:** http://www.stevens.edu/princetonreview • **ACT Code:** 2610

This private school was founded in 1870. It has a 55-acre campus.

RATINGS

Admissions Selectivity Rating: 94   **Fire Safety Rating:** 98   **Green Rating:** 84

STUDENTS AND FACULTY

Enrollment: 3,109. **Student Body:** 29% female, 71% male, 38% out-of-state, 5% international (29 countries represented). Asian 11%, African American 2%, Caucasian 67%, Hispanic 10%, Native American <1%, Pacific Islander 0%, Two or more races 0%, Race unknown 6%.
Retention and Graduation: 95% freshmen return for sophomore year. 39% freshmen graduate within 4 years. 83% freshmen graduate within 6 years. 24% grads go on to further study within 1 year. 5% grads pursue arts and sciences degrees. 2% grads pursue law degrees. 1% grads pursue business degrees. 4% grads pursue medical degrees. **Faculty:** Student/faculty ratio 10:1. 262 full-time faculty, 95% hold PhDs, 27% are are members of minority groups, 26% are women. 0% of classes are taught by teaching assistants.

ACADEMICS

Degrees: bachelor's, doctoral, master's, postbachelor's certificate. **Classes:** Most classes have 20-29 students. Most lab/discussion sessions have 20-29 students. **Most popular majors:** Mechanical Engineering; Engineering; Computer Science. **Special Study Options:** Accelerated program, cooperative education program, cross-registration, distance learning, double major, dual enrollment, honors program, independent study, internships, study abroad, Dual enrollment program with NYU. **Honors Programs:** The Scholars Program allows high-achieving students to participate in research over the summer or take up to four tuition-free courses each summer. Scholars students may also complete their Bachelor's in three years or a combined bachelor's and Master's in four years at no extra cost. Combined degree programs: BA/MD, BA/JD, BA/DDS, BS/MS; BS/DMD; BS/JD; BS/MD. **Disability Services:** Special programs offered to physically disabled students, including note-taking services, tutors. **Career Services:** Alumni network, Alumni services, Career/job search classes, Career assessment, Internships, Regional alumni. Our educational philosophy encourages experience with real-world practitioners in business, science and engineering, therefore, 100% of Stevens students participate in coop, research or internships; 40% of students participate in coop. Our programs are hands-on and we work with each student to develop a career outline. Stevens begins this process in the student's freshman year resulting in multiple work experiences and enhanced career options.

FACILITIES

Housing: Coed dorms, women's dorms, fraternity/sorority housing, apartments for married students, apartments for single studentsFreshmen not living at home must live on campus. 100% of campus accessible to physically diasbled. **Special Academic Facilities/Equipment:** Art museum, electron microscope, ocean engineering lab, HDTV research facility, advanced telecommunications institute, environmental lab, design/manufacturing institute, wind tunnel, robotics lab, product management center, polymer processing institute. DeBaun Theater, a multi-media facility, wireless campus network **Computers:** 95% of classrooms, 100% of dorms, 100% of libraries, 100% of dining areas, 100% of student union, 99% of common outdoor areas have wireless network access. Students can register for classes online. Administrative functions (other than registration) can be performed online. Undergraduates are required to own a computer.

CAMPUS LIFE

Environment: Town. **Activities:** Choral groups, concert band, dance, drama/theater, jazz band, literary magazine, music ensembles, musical theater, pep band, radio station, student government, student newspaper, student-run film society, symphony orchestra, television station, yearbook, Campus Ministries, Student Organization. 120 registered organizations, 12 honor societies, 6 religious organizations. 10 fraternities, 3 sororities. **Athletics (Intercollegiate):** *Men:* baseball, basketball, cross-country, fencing, lacrosse, soccer, swimming, tennis, track/field (outdoor), track/field (indoor), volleyball, wrestling. *Women:* basketball, cross-country, equestrian sports, fencing, field hockey, lacrosse, soccer, swimming, tennis, track/field (outdoor), track/field (indoor), volleyball. **On-Campus Highlights:** Schaefer Athletic Center, DeBaun Auditorium, Castle Point, overlooking Manhattan, Babbio Center, Wesley J. Howe Center. **Environmental Initiatives:** Green minor.

ADMISSIONS

Freshman Academic Profile: Average high school GPA 3.8. 66% in top 10% of high school class, 91% in top 25% of high school class, 100% in top 50% of high school class. **Reported SAT (pre-2016 redesign) scores:** SAT Math middle 50% range 660-750. SAT Critical Reading middle 50% range 600-690. **Concordant SAT scores:** SAT Math middle 50% range 690–770. ACT middle 50% range 29-33. Minimum internet-based TOEFL 82. Minimum paper TOEFL 550. **Basis for Candidate Selection:** *Very important factors considered include:* rigor of secondary school record, academic GPA, standardized test scores. *Important factors considered include:* talent/ability, character/personal qualities. *Other factors considered include:* class rank, application essay, recommendation(s), interview, extracurricular activities, first generation, alumni/ae relation, geographical residence, state residency, racial/ethnic status, volunteer work, work experience, level of applicant's interest. **Freshman Admission Requirements:** High school diploma is required and GED is not accepted. *Academic units required:* 4 English, 4 math, 3 science, 3 science labs. *Academic units recommended:* 4 science, 4 science labs, 2 foreign language, 2 social studies, 2 history, 4 academic electives. **Freshman Admission Statistics:** 7,409 applied, 39.11% admitted, 25% enrolled. **Transfer Admission Requirements:** High school transcript, college transcript(s), essay or personal statement, interview, Minimum college GPA of 3.0 required. Lowest grade transferable C. **General Admission Information:** Application fee $60. Regular application deadline 2/1. Regular notification 4/1. Nonfall registration not accepted. Admission may be deferred for a maximum of 1 year.

COSTS AND FINANCIAL AID

Annual tuition $48,784. Required fees $1,770. Average book expense $1,200. **Required Forms and Deadlines:** FAFSA, CSS/Financial Aid PROFILE. **Types of Aid:** *Need-based scholarships/grants:* Federal Pell, FSEOG, State scholarships/grants, Private scholarships, College/university scholarship or grant aid from institutional funds, United Negro College Fund. *Loans:* Direct Subsidized Stafford Loans, Direct Unsubsidized Stafford Loans, Direct PLUS loans, Federal Perkins Loans, State Loans. *Student Employment:* Federal Work-Study Program available. Institutional employment available. **Financial Aid Statistics:** 43% needy freshmen, 61% needy undergrads receive need-based scholarship or grant aid. 97% freshmen, 94% undergrads receive non-need-based scholarship or grant aid. 62% freshmen, 73% undergrads receive need-based self-help aid. 0% freshmen, 0% undergrads receive athletic scholarships. 99% freshmen, 91% undergrads receive any aid. 75% undergrads borrow to pay for school. Average cumulative indebtedness $48,244. **Criteria for awarding aid:** *Non-need-based:* Academics, Leadership, Minority status, Music/drama.

See page 1058.

STEVENSON UNIVERSITY

1525 Greenspring Valley Road, Stevenson, MD 21153-0641
Phone: 410-486-7001 • **Financial Aid Phone:** 443-352-4369
E-mail: admissions@stevenson.edu • **CEEB Code:** 2107
Fax: 443-352-4440 • **Website:** http://www.stevenson.edu • **ACT Code:** 1753

This private school was founded in 1947. It has a 150-acre campus.

RATINGS

Admissions Selectivity Rating: 79   **Fire Safety Rating:** 79   **Green Rating:** 60*

STUDENTS AND FACULTY

Enrollment: 3,835. **Student Body:** 65% female, 35% male, 21% out-of-state, 0% international (7 countries represented). Asian 3%, African American 29%, Caucasian 57%, Hispanic 4%, Native American <1%, Pacific Islander <1%, Two or more races 2%, Race unknown 4%.
Retention and Graduation: 17% grads go on to further study within 1 year. **Faculty:** Student/faculty ratio 15:1. 130 full-time faculty, 74% hold PhDs, 15% are members of minority groups, 54% are women. 0% of classes are taught by teaching assistants.

ACADEMICS

Degrees: bachelor's, master's. **Classes:** Most classes have 10-19 students. **Most popular majors:** Legal Assistant/Paralegal; Business Administration and Management; Registered Nursing/Registered Nurse. **Special Study Options:** Accelerated program, cooperative education program, cross-registration, distance learning, double major, dual enrollment, honors program, independent study, internships, liberal arts/career combination, student-designed major, study abroad, teacher certification program. **Honors Programs:** Consistent with its mission, the Stevenson University Honors Program seeks to admit academically outstanding students who are interested in challenging themselves through a unique and stimulating curriculum that extends beyond traditional academic boundaries. **Disability Services:** Special programs offered to physically disabled students, including note-taking services, reader services, tape recorders, tutors. **Career Services:** Alumni network, Alumni services, Career assessment, Internships, Regional alumni. Career Architecture.

FACILITIES

Housing: apartments for single students, suite style (2 bedrooms share 1 bath); accommodations made for students with disabilities. 100% of campus accessible to physically diasbled. **Special Academic Facilities/Equipment:** Art gallery and theatre. **Computers:** Students can register for classes online. Administrative functions (other than registration) can be performed online.

CAMPUS LIFE

Environment: Village. **Activities:** Choral groups, dance, drama/theater, jazz band, literary magazine, music ensembles, pep band, student government, student newspaper, symphony orchestra, Campus Ministries, Student Organization. 40 registered organizations, 10 honor societies, 4 religious organizations. 2 sororities. **Athletics (Intercollegiate):** *Men:* baseball, basketball, cheerleading, cross-country, golf, lacrosse, soccer, tennis, track/field (indoor), volleyball. *Women:* basketball, cheerleading, cross-country, field hockey, lacrosse, soccer, softball, tennis, track/field (indoor), volleyball. **On-Campus Highlights:** Rockland Center (Dining Hall/Student Ce), Avalon Community Center, The Wellness Center/Caves, Garrison Hall, Theater.

ADMISSIONS

Freshman Academic Profile: Average high school GPA 3.2. 11% in top 10% of high school class, 31% in top 25% of high school class, 58% in top 50% of high school class. 70% from public high schools. **Reported SAT (pre-2016 redesign) scores:** SAT Math middle 50% range 450-560. SAT Critical Reading middle 50% range 440-540. SAT Writing middle 50% range 450-540. **Concordant SAT scores:** SAT EBRW middle 50% 500–600. SAT Math middle 50% range 490–580. ACT middle 50% range 18-23. Minimum paper TOEFL 550. **Basis for Candidate Selection:** *Very important factors considered include:* rigor of secondary school record, academic GPA. *Important factors considered include:* standardized test scores, application essay, recommendation(s), extracurricular activities, talent/ability, character/personal qualities. *Other factors considered include:* class rank, interview, first generation, alumni/ae relation, geographical residence, volunteer work, work experience, level of applicant's interest. **Freshman Admission Requirements:** High school diploma is required and GED is accepted. *Academic units required:* 4 English, 3 math, 3 science, 2 science labs, 2 social studies, 1 history, 4 academic electives. *Academic units recommended:* 4 English, 3 math, 3 science, 2 science labs, 2 foreign language, 2 social studies, 1 history, 4 academic electives. **Freshman Admission Statistics:** 5,318 applied, 59.59% admitted, 24% enrolled. **Transfer Admission Requirements:** college transcript(s), statement of good standing from prior institution(s). Minimum college GPA of 2.5 required. Lowest grade transferable C. **General Admission Information:** Application fee $40. Priority deadline 3/1. Nonfall registration accepted. Admission may be deferred.

COSTS AND FINANCIAL AID

Annual tuition $25,210. Room and board $11,894. Required fees $1,872. Average book expense $1,250. **Required Forms and Deadlines:** FAFSA. **Notification of Awards:** Applicants will be notified of awards on a rolling basis beginning 3/15. **Types of Aid:** *Need-based scholarships/grants:* Federal Pell, FSEOG, State scholarships/grants, Private scholarships, College/university scholarship or grant aid from institutional funds. *Loans:* Direct Subsidized Stafford Loans, Direct Unsubsidized Stafford Loans, Direct PLUS loans, Federal Perkins Loans. *Student Employment:* Federal Work-Study Program available. Institutional employment available. **Financial Aid Statistics:** 99% needy freshmen, 96% needy undergrads receive need-based scholarship or grant aid. 9% freshmen, 8% undergrads receive non-need-based scholarship or grant aid. 79% freshmen, 79% undergrads receive need-based self-help aid. 0% freshmen, 0% undergrads receive athletic scholarships. **Criteria for awarding aid:** *Need-based:* Leadership, Minority status. *Non-need-based:* Academics, Art, Leadership, Music/drama.

STOCKTON UNIVERSITY

101 Vera King Farris Drive, Galloway, NJ 8205
Phone: 609-652-4261 • **Financial Aid Phone:** 609-652-4203
E-mail: admissions@stockton.edu • **CEEB Code:** 2889
Fax: 609-748-5541 • **Website:** www.stockton.edu

This public school was founded in 1969. It has a 1600-acre campus.

RATINGS

Admissions Selectivity Rating: 82   **Fire Safety Rating:** 96   **Green Rating:** 95

STUDENTS AND FACULTY

Enrollment: 7,772. **Student Body:** 59% female, 41% male, 1% out-of-state, <1% international (11 countries represented). Asian 5%, African American 7%, Caucasian 72%, Hispanic 11%, Native American <1%, Pacific Islander <1%, Two or more races 3%, Race unknown 1%.
Retention and Graduation: 87% freshmen return for sophomore year. 53% freshmen graduate within 4 years. 73% freshmen graduate within 6 years. 33% grads go on to further study within 1 year. 71% grads pursue arts and sciences degrees. 5% grads pursue law degrees. 6% grads pursue business degrees. 4% grads pursue medical degrees. **Faculty:** Student/faculty ratio 17:1. 315 full-time faculty, 95% hold PhDs, 23% are are members of minority groups, 55% are women. 0% of classes are taught by teaching assistants.

ACADEMICS

Degrees: bachelor's, doctoral/professional, master's. **Classes:** Most classes have 30-39 students. Most lab/discussion sessions have 10-19 students. **Most popular majors:** Psychology; Business Administration and Management; Biology/Biological Sciences. **Special Study Options:** Accelerated program, distance learning, double major, English as a Second Language (ESL), honors program, independent study, internships, liberal arts/career combination, study abroad, teacher certification program, Dual degree bachelor's program in engineering with Rutger's University and New Jersey Institute of Technology, preceptorial advising, opportunities for specialized research, Washington Internship available, and Service-Learning. **Honors Programs:** Stockton Honors Program Combined degree programs: BA/MD, BA/MA, BA/DDS, BA/MACJ, BS/PSM Envl Sc., BS/DPT, BS/MS Computational Sc. BA or BS/MBA. **Disability Services:** Special programs offered to physically disabled students, including note-taking services, reader services, tape recorders, tutors. **Career Services:** Alumni network, Alumni services, Career/job search classes, Career assessment, Internships, Regional alumni. We are proud of all of our programs, but we are proudest of our internship and experiential learning opportunities.

FACILITIES

Housing: Coed dorms, special housing for disabled students, apartments for single students, Wellness Housing, Theme Housing, Academic units. Living/Learning Communities include themes of Diversity, Global Citizenship, Sustainability, and Wellness. 100% of campus accessible to physically diasbled. **Special Academic Facilities/Equipment:** Observatory, Nacote Creek field station, Holocaust Resource Center. **Computers:** 100% of classrooms, 5% of dorms, 100% of libraries, 100% of dining areas, n/a% of student union, 10% of common outdoor areas have wireless network access. Students can register for classes online. Administrative functions (other than registration) can be performed online.

CAMPUS LIFE

Environment: Town. **Activities:** Choral groups, concert band, dance, drama/theater, literary magazine, music ensembles, musical theater, radio station, student government, student newspaper, television station, yearbook, Campus Ministries, Student Organization. 130 registered organizations, 6 honor societies, 5 religious organizations. 11 fraternities, 9 sororities. **Athletics (Intercollegiate):** *Men:* baseball, basketball, cheerleading, cross-country, lacrosse, soccer, track/field (outdoor), track/field (indoor). *Women:* basketball, cheerleading, crew/rowing, cross-country, field hockey, soccer, softball, tennis, track/field (outdoor), track/field (indoor), volleyball. **On-Campus Highlights:** Performing Arts Center, Library, Housing options, Osprey's Nest, Marine Field Station. **Environmental Initiatives:** Alternative Energy: A. Solar electrical generation: 1200 KW capacity arrays operating on campus. This includes rooftop installations and shade canopies over parking lots. An additional 700 KW is under construction, expected to be operational in June of 2012. B. The GEOTHERMAL PROJECT provides up to 1650 tons of cooling capacity and allows portions of the building to be heated and cooled using the same equipment. C. Solar hot water heating has been installed on the roof of the newest residential facility, which accommodates 390 students.

ADMISSIONS

Freshman Academic Profile: 23% in top 10% of high school class, 54% in top 25% of high school class, 91% in top 50% of high school class. 88% from public high schools. **Reported SAT (pre-2016 redesign) scores:** SAT Math middle

50% range 500-600. SAT Critical Reading middle 50% range 480-580. SAT Writing middle 50% range 470-560. **Concordant SAT scores:** SAT EBRW middle 50% 530–630. SAT Math middle 50% range 530–620. ACT middle 50% range 19-25. Minimum internet-based TOEFL 80. Minimum paper TOEFL 550. **Basis for Candidate Selection:** *Very important factors considered include:* rigor of secondary school record, class rank, academic GPA. *Important factors considered include:* standardized test scores. *Other factors considered include:* application essay, recommendation(s), extracurricular activities, talent/ability, character/personal qualities, alumni/ae relation, volunteer work, work experience, level of applicant's interest. **Freshman Admission Requirements:** High school diploma is required and GED is accepted. *Academic units required:* 4 English, 3 math, 2 science, 2 science labs, 2 social studies, 5 academic electives. *Academic units recommended:* 2 foreign language. **Freshman Admission Statistics:** 5,483 applied, 64.42% admitted, 33% enrolled. Minimum college GPA of 2.5 required. Lowest grade transferable C. **General Admission Information:** Application fee $50. Priority deadline 2/1. Regular application deadline 5/1. Nonfall registration accepted. Admission may be deferred for a maximum of 1 Year.

COSTS AND FINANCIAL AID

Annual in-state tuition $8,269. Annual out-of-state tuition $14,921. Required fees $4,551. Average book expense $1,587. **Required Forms and Deadlines:** FAFSA, State aid form. **Notification of Awards:** Applicants will be notified of awards on a rolling basis beginning 4/1. **Types of Aid:** *Need-based scholarships/grants:* Federal Pell, FSEOG, State scholarships/grants, Private scholarships, College/university scholarship or grant aid from institutional funds. *Loans:* Direct Subsidized Stafford Loans, Direct Unsubsidized Stafford Loans, Direct PLUS loans, Federal Perkins Loans, State Loans. *Student Employment:* Federal Work-Study Program available. Institutional employment available. **Financial Aid Statistics:** 68% needy freshmen, 59% needy undergrads receive need-based scholarship or grant aid. 36% freshmen, 27% undergrads receive non-need-based scholarship or grant aid. 79% undergrads receive need-based self-help aid. 0% freshmen, 0% undergrads receive athletic scholarships. 86% freshmen, 84% undergrads receive any aid. Average cumulative indebtedness $33,201. **Criteria for awarding aid:** *Non-need-based:* Academics, Art, Leadership, Minority status, Music/drama, State/district residency.

STONEHILL COLLEGE

320 Washington Street, Easton, MA 02357-5610
Phone: 508-565-1373 • **Financial Aid Phone:** 508-565-1088
E-mail: admission@stonehill.edu • **CEEB Code:** 3770
Fax: 508-565-1545 • **Website:** www.stonehill.edu • **ACT Code:** 1918

This private school, affiliated with the Roman Catholic Church, was founded in 1948. It has a 375-acre campus.

RATINGS

Admissions Selectivity Rating: 83   **Fire Safety Rating:** 96   **Green Rating:** 84

STUDENTS AND FACULTY

Enrollment: 2,472. **Student Body:** 60% female, 40% male, 40% out-of-state, 1% international (15 countries represented). Asian 2%, African American 5%, Caucasian 83%, Hispanic 5%, Native American <1%, Pacific Islander <1%, Two or more races 2%, Race unknown 2%.
Retention and Graduation: 92% freshmen return for sophomore year. 76% freshmen graduate within 4 years. 80 14% grads go on to further study within 1 year. 11% grads pursue arts and sciences degrees. 2% grads pursue law degrees. 2% grads pursue business degrees. 2% grads pursue medical degrees. **Faculty:** Student/faculty ratio 12:1. 166 full-time faculty, 80% hold PhDs, 11% are are members of minority groups, 43% are women. 0% of classes are taught by teaching assistants.

ACADEMICS

Degrees: bachelor's. **Classes:** Most classes have 20-29 students. Most lab/discussion sessions have 10-19 students. **Most popular majors:** Psychology; Biology/Biological Sciences; Accounting. **Special Study Options:** cross-registration, double major, dual enrollment, honors program, independent study, internships, liberal arts/career combination, student-designed major, study abroad, teacher certification program. **Honors Programs:** The Honors Program, which requires 5 honors courses and a Senior Honors Experience. **Disability Services:** Special programs offered to physically disabled students, including note-taking services, reader services, tape recorders, tutors. **Career

Services: Alumni network, Alumni services, Career/job search classes, Career assessment, Internships. We are very proud of the fact that 82% of our senior class has completed an internship-related experience.

FACILITIES

Housing: Coed dorms, special housing for disabled students, women's dorms, Wellness HousingSpecial interest housing. 100% of campus accessible to physically diasbled. **Special Academic Facilities/Equipment:** Institute for law and society, observatory, Stonehill Industrial History Center, shovel museum **Computers:** 30% of classrooms, 80% of dorms, 100% of libraries, 100% of dining areas, 50% of student union, 20% of common outdoor areas have wireless network access. Students can register for classes online. Administrative functions (other than registration) can be performed online.

CAMPUS LIFE

Environment: Village. **Activities:** Choral groups, dance, drama/theater, literary magazine, music ensembles, musical theater, pep band, radio station, student government, student newspaper, student-run film society, yearbook, Campus Ministries. 76 registered organizations, 19 honor societies, 3 religious organizations. **Athletics (Intercollegiate):** *Men:* baseball, basketball, cross-country, football, ice hockey, soccer, tennis, track/field (outdoor), track/field (indoor). *Women:* basketball, cross-country, equestrian sports, field hockey, lacrosse, soccer, softball, tennis, track/field (outdoor), track/field (indoor), volleyball. **On-Campus Highlights:** The Hill (entertainment/dining social space), The MacPhaidin Library, The Roche Dining Commons, The Residence Courts (housing/social space), The Sally Blair Ames Sports Complex. **Environmental Initiatives:** Joined AASHE (Association for the Advancement of Sustainability in Higher Education) and will participate in the STARS survey.

ADMISSIONS

Freshman Academic Profile: Average high school GPA 3.3. 20% in top 10% of high school class, 58% in top 25% of high school class, 90% in top 50% of high school class. 67% from public high schools. **Reported SAT (pre-2016 redesign) scores:** SAT Math middle 50% range 500-640. SAT Critical Reading middle 50% range 500-600. SAT Writing middle 50% range 500-600. **Concordant SAT scores:** SAT EBRW middle 50% 560–650. SAT Math middle 50% range 530–660. ACT middle 50% range 22-28. Minimum internet-based TOEFL 90. Minimum paper TOEFL 575. **Basis for Candidate Selection:** *Very important factors considered include:* rigor of secondary school record, class rank, academic GPA, talent/ability. *Important factors considered include:* application essay, recommendation(s), extracurricular activities. *Other factors considered include:* standardized test scores, interview, character/personal qualities, first generation, alumni/ae relation, geographical residence, religious affiliation/commitment, racial/ethnic status, volunteer work, work experience, level of applicant's interest. **Freshman Admission Requirements:** High school diploma is required and GED is accepted. *Academic units required:* 4 English, 3 math, 3 science, 3 science labs, 3 foreign language, 3 history. *Academic units recommended:* 4 English, 4 math, 4 science, 3 science labs, 4 foreign language, 4 history. **Freshman Admission Statistics:** 6,362 applied, 72.92% admitted, 16% enrolled. **Transfer Admission Requirements:** High school transcript, college transcript(s), essay or personal statement, statement of good standing from prior institution(s). Minimum college GPA of 2.0 required. Lowest grade transferable C. **General Admission Information:** Application fee $60. Regular application deadline 1/15. Regular notification 3/15. Nonfall registration accepted. Admission may be deferred for a maximum of 1 year.

COSTS AND FINANCIAL AID

Annual tuition $39,900. Room and board $15,230. Average book expense $893. **Required Forms and Deadlines:** FAFSA, CSS/Financial Aid PROFILE, Noncustodial PROFILE. **Notification of Awards:** Applicants will be notified of awards on or about 4/1. **Types of Aid:** *Need-based scholarships/grants:* Federal Pell, FSEOG, State scholarships/grants, Private scholarships, College/university scholarship or grant aid from institutional funds. *Loans:* Direct Subsidized Stafford Loans, Direct Unsubsidized Stafford Loans, Direct PLUS loans, Federal Perkins Loans, State Loans. *Student Employment:* Federal Work-Study Program available. Institutional employment available. **Financial Aid Statistics:** 99% needy freshmen, 97% needy undergrads receive need-based scholarship or grant aid. 28% freshmen, 21% undergrads receive non-need-based scholarship or grant aid. 70% freshmen, 77% undergrads receive need-based self-help aid. 3% freshmen, 4% undergrads receive athletic scholarships. 99% freshmen, 95% undergrads receive any aid. Average cumulative indebtedness $35,462. **Criteria for awarding aid:** *Need-based:* Academics, Leadership. *Non-need-based:* Academics, Athletics, Leadership.

SUFFOLK UNIVERSITY

8 Ashburton Place, Boston, MA 2108
Phone: 617-573-8480 • **Financial Aid Phone:** 617-573-8470
E-mail: admission@suffolk.edu • **CEEB Code:** 3771
Fax: 617-573-1574 • **Website:** www.suffolk.edu • **ACT Code:** 1920

This private school was founded in 1906.

RATINGS

Admissions Selectivity Rating: 79   **Fire Safety Rating:** 98   **Green Rating:** 72

STUDENTS AND FACULTY

Enrollment: 5,454. **Student Body:** 54% female, 46% male, 32% out-of-state, 23% international (108 countries represented). Asian 8%, African American 6%, Caucasian 40%, Hispanic 12%, Native American <1%, Pacific Islander <1%, Two or more races 2%, Race unknown 9%. **Retention and Graduation:** 74% freshmen return for sophomore year. 41% freshmen graduate within 4 years. 56% freshmen graduate within 6 years. 30% grads go on to further study within 1 year. 4% grads pursue arts and sciences degrees. 4% grads pursue law degrees. 7% grads pursue business degrees. 1% grads pursue medical degrees. **Faculty:** Student/faculty ratio 13:1. 331 full-time faculty, 91% hold PhDs, 18% are are members of minority groups, 44% are women.

ACADEMICS

Degrees: associate, bachelor's, certificate, diploma, doctoral/professional, doctoral/research, master's, postbachelor's certificate, post-master's certificate. **Classes:** Most classes have 10-19 students. Most lab/discussion sessions have 10-19 students. **Special Study Options:** Accelerated program, cooperative education program, cross-registration, distance learning, double major, English as a Second Language (ESL), honors program, independent study, internships, liberal arts/career combination, study abroad, weekend college. **Honors Programs:** A Community of Scholars Suffolk University honors students work in collaboration with their school's program director and advisory committee to plan events that bring the honors community together on a regular basis outside of the classroom. Lectures by Suffolk University scholars or by noted intellectuals outside of the University, a variety of social events, visits to cultural and historical sites, and public service projects offer intellectual challenge, promote leadership, and develop networking skills with faculty, alumni, community, business, and government leaders. The program provides honors scholars with a broader context for their academic pursuits, while strengthening their sense of community. Special Benefits and Recognition for Honors Scholars: Honors scholars are eligible for a full tuition scholarship. In addition, honors scholars enjoy the following benefits and recognition: Guaranteed housing in University residence halls through the sophomore year; Priority course registration; Special honors program advisors; Application assistance, when applicable, for Fulbright, Marshall, Rhodes, and other post-graduate academic and scholarship programs; Honors Program designation on official academic transcript; and Special listing in commencement program. http://www.suffolk.edu/admission/gchonors.htm Combined degree programs: BA/JD, BA/MA. **Disability Services:** Special programs offered to physically disabled students, including note-taking services, reader services, tape recorders, tutors. **Career Services:** Alumni network, Alumni services, Career/job search classes, Career assessment, Internships, Regional alumni. The Co-op Program offers both part-time and full-time work options and is available to full-time undergraduate and graduate students. By combining relevant work experience with academic studies, students have the best opportunity for personal, professional and career development. Additionally, students are able to subsidize their education costs while building their resumes in preparation for their professional lives. Students can work either part-time (the most popular option) or full-time. Part-time co-ops usually involve working 15-25 hours per week while continuing to take a full load of courses. Students working full-time must have completed a full load of courses the previous semester and then must return to school for the semester after their co-op placement. Co-ops are available for all majors. Most positions are located in businesses and organizations within easy commuting distance of campus, so that students can balance their work and academic schedules. Some of the employers who have participated in the Suffolk Co-op Program include: 96.9 FM, Biogen, Boston Globe, Cape Cod Potato Chips, Commonwealth of Massachusetts, EF Education, Ernst and Young, LLP, Fidelity Investments Greater Boston Convention and Visitors Bureau, Investors Bank and Trust Mass General Hospital, Massport, North Suffolk Mental Health Association, PricewaterhouseCoopers. Eligibility for participation in Co-op Program: Undergraduates must have a minimum 2.5 GPA, Undergraduates have completed their freshman year, Transfer students must have completed one semester at Suffolk University, Full-time graduate students are eligible upon enrollment in their degree program. Student interested in Co-op must call the office at 617-573-8480 to schedule an appointment with a counselor

FACILITIES

Housing: Coed dorms, apartments for single students. **Special Academic Facilities/Equipment:** Marine biology field station in Maine, NESAD art gallery, Adams art gallery, C. Walsh Theatre and 10 West Street Theatre **Computers:** 100% of classrooms, 100% of dorms, 100% of libraries, 100% of dining areas, 100% of student union, 20% of common outdoor areas have wireless network access. Students can register for classes online. Administrative functions (other than registration) can be performed online.

CAMPUS LIFE

Environment: Metropolis. **Activities:** Choral groups, dance, drama/theater, literary magazine, music ensembles, musical theater, radio station, student government, student newspaper, television station, yearbook, Campus Ministries, Student Organization. 75 registered organizations, 11 honor societies, 3 religious organizations. 1 fraternity, 1 sorority **Athletics (Intercollegiate):** *Men:* baseball, basketball, cross-country, golf, ice hockey, soccer, tennis. *Women:* basketball, cross-country, softball, tennis, volleyball. **On-Campus Highlights:** Donahue Student Lounge, Donahue Cafe, Sawyer Library, NESAD Gallery, Alumni Park, Sawyer Computer Lab,Donahue Computer Lab, Sawyer Lounge, 150 Tremont St Dining Room. **Environmental Initiatives:** Energy efficiency and conservation.

ADMISSIONS

Freshman Academic Profile: Average high school GPA 3.2. 11% in top 10% of high school class, 40% in top 25% of high school class, 73% in top 50% of high school class. 61% from public high schools. **Reported SAT (pre-2016 redesign) scores:** SAT Math middle 50% range 460-560. SAT Critical Reading middle 50% range 450-560. SAT Writing middle 50% range 450-560. **Concordant SAT scores:** SAT EBRW middle 50% 500–620. SAT Math middle 50% range 500–580. ACT middle 50% range 20-25. Minimum internet-based TOEFL 77. Minimum paper TOEFL 550. **Basis for Candidate Selection:** *Very important factors considered include:* rigor of secondary school record, academic GPA. *Important factors considered include:* class rank. *Other factors considered include:* standardized test scores, application essay, recommendation(s), interview, extracurricular activities, talent/ability, character/personal qualities, first generation, volunteer work, work experience, level of applicant's interest. **Freshman Admission Requirements:** High school diploma is required and GED is accepted. *Academic units required:* 4 English, 3 math, 2 science, 1 science lab, 2 foreign language, 1 social studies, 1 history, 3 computer science. *Academic units recommended:* 4 English, 4 math, 4 science, 4 foreign language, 2 social studies, 3 history, 3 computer science. **Freshman Admission Statistics:** 8,650 applied, 82.39% admitted, 19% enrolled. **Transfer Admission Requirements:** High school transcript, college transcript(s), essay or personal statement, Minimum college GPA of 2.5 required. Lowest grade transferable C. **General Admission Information:** Application fee $50. Nonfall registration accepted. Admission may be deferred for a maximum of 2 years.

COSTS AND FINANCIAL AID

Annual tuition $33,800. Room and board $14,648. Required fees $134. Average book expense $1,200. **Required Forms and Deadlines:** FAFSA. **Notification of Awards:** Applicants will be notified of awards on a rolling basis beginning 2/5. **Types of Aid:** *Need-based scholarships/grants:* Federal Pell, FSEOG, State scholarships/grants, Private scholarships, College/university scholarship or grant aid from institutional funds. *Loans:* Direct Subsidized Stafford Loans, Direct Unsubsidized Stafford Loans, Direct PLUS loans, Federal Perkins Loans, State Loans, College/university loans from institutional funds. *Student Employment:* Federal Work-Study Program available. Institutional employment available. **Financial Aid Statistics:** 81% needy freshmen, 83% needy undergrads receive need-based scholarship or grant aid. 99% freshmen, 72% undergrads receive non-need-based scholarship or grant aid. 83% freshmen, 85% undergrads receive need-based self-help aid. 0% freshmen, 0% undergrads receive athletic scholarships. 94% freshmen, 73% undergrads receive any aid. 75% undergrads borrow to pay for school. Average cumulative indebtedness $42,584. **Criteria for awarding aid:** *Need-based:* Academics. *Non-need-based:* Academics, Alumni affiliation.

SUMMIT UNIVERSITY OF PENNSYLVANIA

Phone: 570-586-2400 • **Financial Aid Phone:** 570-585-9206
E-mail: admissions@SummitU.edu • **CEEB Code:** 2036
Fax: 570-585-9299 • **Website:** www.SummitU.edu • **ACT Code:** 3523

This private school, affiliated with the Baptist Church, was founded in 1932. It has a 121-acre campus.

RATINGS

Admissions Selectivity Rating: 76   **Fire Safety Rating:** 67   **Green Rating:** 60*

STUDENTS AND FACULTY

Enrollment: 667. **Student Body:** 59% female, 41% male, 68% out-of-state, 2% international (13 countries represented). Asian 1%, African American 1%, Caucasian 94%, Hispanic 2%, Native American <1%, Pacific Islander 0%, Two or more races 0%, Race unknown 1%.
Retention and Graduation: 69% freshmen return for sophomore year. **Faculty:** 35 full-time faculty, 57% hold PhDs, 3% are are members of minority groups, 29% are women. 0% of classes are taught by teaching assistants.

ACADEMICS

Degrees: associate, bachelor's, certificate, doctoral/professional, doctoral, master's. **Classes:** Most classes have fewer than 10 students. **Most popular majors:** Elementary Education and Teaching; Theology and Religious Vocations. **Special Study Options:** distance learning, double major, dual enrollment, independent study, internships, study abroad, teacher certification program. **Career Services:** Alumni services, Internships.

FACILITIES

Housing: men's dorms, women's dorms. **Computers:** 100% of classrooms, 100% of libraries, 100% of dining areas, 100% of student union, 100% of common outdoor areas have wireless network access. Students can register for classes online. Administrative functions (other than registration) can be performed online.

CAMPUS LIFE

Environment: Town. **Activities:** Choral groups, concert band, drama/theater, music ensembles, student government, yearbook, Campus Ministries. **Athletics (Intercollegiate):** *Men:* baseball, basketball, cross-country, golf, soccer. *Women:* basketball, cross-country, soccer, softball, tennis, volleyball. **On-Campus Highlights:** Underground Cafe, Dorm, Student Center, Classroom building.

ADMISSIONS

Freshman Academic Profile: 40% from public high schools. **Reported SAT (pre-2016 redesign) scores:** SAT Math middle 50% range 430-560. SAT Critical Reading middle 50% range 460-570. **Concordant SAT scores:** SAT Math middle 50% range 470–580. ACT middle 50% range 20-24. Minimum paper TOEFL 500. **Basis for Candidate Selection:** *Very important factors considered include:* rigor of secondary school record, standardized test scores, application essay, recommendation(s), character/personal qualities, religious affiliation/commitment. *Important factors considered include:* academic GPA. *Other factors considered include:* interview, extracurricular activities, talent/ability, volunteer work, work experience, level of applicant's interest. **Freshman Admission Requirements:** High school diploma is required and GED is accepted. **Freshman Admission Statistics:** 452 applied, 76.11% admitted, 48% enrolled. **Transfer Admission Requirements:** High school transcript, college transcript(s), essay or personal statement, Minimum college GPA of 2 required. Lowest grade transferable 2. **General Admission Information:** Application fee $30. Priority deadline 5/1. Regular application deadline 8/15. Nonfall registration accepted. Admission may be deferred.

COSTS AND FINANCIAL AID

Annual tuition $6,840. Room and board $5,900. Required fees $468. **Required Forms and Deadlines:** FAFSA, Institution's own financial aid form. **Notification of Awards:** Applicants will be notified of awards on a rolling basis beginning 10/1. **Types of Aid:** *Need-based scholarships/grants:* Federal Pell, State scholarships/grants, College/university scholarship or grant aid from institutional funds. *Loans:* Direct Unsubsidized Stafford Loans, State Loans. *Student Employment:* Federal Work-Study Program available. Institutional employment available. **Financial Aid Statistics:** 100% freshmen, 96% undergrads receive any aid. **Criteria for awarding aid:** *Need-based:* Academics. *Non-need-based:* Academics, Leadership.

SUSQUEHANNA UNIVERSITY

514 University Avenue, Selinsgrove, PA 17870
Phone: 570-372-4260 • **Financial Aid Phone:** 570-372-4450
E-mail: suadmiss@susqu.edu • **CEEB Code:** 2820
Fax: 570-372-2722 • **Website:** www.susqu.edu • **ACT Code:** 3720

This private school, affiliated with the Lutheran Church, was founded in 1858. It has a 306-acre campus.

RATINGS
Admissions Selectivity Rating: 83   **Fire Safety Rating:** 95   **Green Rating:** 75

STUDENTS AND FACULTY
Enrollment: 2,136. **Student Body:** 56% female, 44% male, 51% out-of-state, 2% international (20 countries represented). Asian 2%, African American 7%, Caucasian 80%, Hispanic 6%, Native American <1%, Pacific Islander 0%, Two or more races 3%, Race unknown <1%.
Retention and Graduation: 83% freshmen return for sophomore year. 70% freshmen graduate within 4 years. 74% freshmen graduate within 6 years. 19% grads go on to further study within 1 year. **Faculty:** Student/faculty ratio 13:1. 133 full-time faculty, 90% hold PhDs, 18% are are members of minority groups, 46% are women. 0% of classes are taught by teaching assistants.

ACADEMICS
Degrees: bachelor's. **Classes:** Most classes have 10-19 students. Most lab/discussion sessions have 10-19 students. **Most popular majors:** Biology/Biological Sciences; Business/Commerce; Communication. **Special Study Options:** Accelerated program, cross-registration, distance learning, double major, dual enrollment, exchange student program (domestic), honors program, independent study, internships, student-designed major, study abroad, teacher certification program. **Honors Programs:** Recognized as a model for similar programs throughout the country, the Honors Program at Susquehanna offers a challenging curriculum to students interested in a more self-directed and interdisciplinary approach at the undergraduate level. The program is well suited to the aggressively curious, active learner who values breadth of study and multiple perspectives. Discussion groups, lectures, off-campus visits and residential programs complement Honors Program courses. Combined degree programs: BA/DDS, BS/MS in OT at Thomas Jefferson University. **Disability Services:** Special programs offered to physically disabled students, including note-taking services, reader services, tape recorders, tutors. **Career Services:** Alumni network, Alumni services, Career/job search classes, Career assessment, Internships, Regional alumni. Susquehanna University and the Career Development Center support and encourage student participation in credit internships. Gundaker Enrichment Fund Grants provide qualifying students with supplemental support for internships or volunteer activities. Awards from the funds are intended to provide a range of experiential learning opportunities for students. In addition, Susquehanna University has partnerships with several programs offering students opportunities to combine internships and academic coursework for university credit.

FACILITIES
Housing: Coed dorms, special housing for disabled students, special housing for international students, fraternity/sorority housing, apartments for single students, Theme Housing. 90% of campus accessible to physically diasbled.
Special Academic Facilities/Equipment: Art gallery,electronic music lab, child development center, foreign language broadcast system, teaching theatre, greenhouse, rare book room, ecological field station, electron microscope, reflecting telescope, fluorescent microscopes, video conference center, and the new Business and Communications Building featuring three multimedia classrooms, three computer laboratories/classrooms, conference and seminar rooms, student team study rooms and alcoves, two video studios, seminar/observation rooms and a room for faculty instructional development. The building facilitates use of laptop computers by offering informational technology dataports for every seat in the classrooms, team study areas and student lounges and faculty offices **Computers:** 90% of classrooms, 10% of dorms, 100% of libraries, 100% of dining areas, 100% of student union, 30% of common outdoor areas have wireless network access. Students can register for classes online. Administrative functions (other than registration) can be performed online.

CAMPUS LIFE
Environment: Town. **Activities:** Choral groups, concert band, dance, drama/theater, jazz band, literary magazine, music ensembles, musical theater, opera, pep band, radio station, student government, student newspaper, student-run film society, symphony orchestra, television station, yearbook, Campus Ministries, Student Organizaton. 120 registered organizations, 24 honor societies, 12 religious organizations. 4 fraternities, 5 sororities. **Athletics (Intercollegiate): Men:** baseball, basketball, crew/rowing, cross-country, football, golf, lacrosse, soccer, swimming, tennis, track/field (outdoor), track/field (indoor). *Women:* basketball, crew/rowing, cross-country, field hockey, golf, lacrosse, soccer, softball, swimming, tennis, track/field (outdoor), track/field (indoor), volleyball. **On-Campus Highlights:** Sports and Fitness Complex, Business and Communications Center, Blough-Weis Library, Trax (campus nightclub), Java City in the Campus Center. **Environmental Initiatives:** New science facility and new student housing are LEED certified. This housing and two units built in 2010 utilize geo-thermal energy for heating and cooling.

ADMISSIONS
Freshman Academic Profile: Average high school GPA 3.5. 23% in top 10% of high school class, 51% in top 25% of high school class, 86% in top 50% of high school class. 83% from public high schools. **Reported SAT (pre-2016 redesign) scores:** SAT Math middle 50% range 510-600. SAT Critical Reading middle 50% range 500-610. SAT Writing middle 50% range 480-600. **Concordant SAT scores:** SAT EBRW middle 50% 550–660. SAT Math middle 50% range 540–620. ACT middle 50% range 23-27. Minimum internet-based TOEFL 81. Minimum paper TOEFL 550. **Basis for Candidate Selection:** *Very important factors considered include:* rigor of secondary school record, academic GPA. *Important factors considered include:* class rank, standardized test scores, application essay, recommendation(s), interview, extracurricular activities, talent/ability, character/personal qualities, alumni/ae relation, racial/ethnic status, volunteer work, work experience, level of applicant's interest. *Other factors considered include:* first generation, geographical residence, state residency. **Freshman Admission Requirements:** High school diploma is required and GED is accepted. *Academic units required:* 4 English, 3 math, 2 science, 2 science labs, 2 foreign language, 2 social studies, 2 history, 2 academic electives. *Academic units recommended:* 4 English, 4 math, 3 science, 3 science labs, 4 foreign language, 4 social studies, 2 history, 3 academic electives. **Freshman Admission Statistics:** 6,629 applied, 67.70% admitted, 14% enrolled. **Transfer Admission Requirements:** High school transcript, college transcript(s), essay or personal statement, statement of good standing from prior institution(s). Minimum college GPA of 2.0 required. Lowest grade transferable C-. **General Admission Information:** Nonfall registration accepted. Admission may be deferred for a maximum of one year.

COSTS AND FINANCIAL AID
Annual tuition $44,890. Room and board $12,090. Required fees $580. Average book expense $900. **Required Forms and Deadlines:** FAFSA, CSS/Financial Aid PROFILE, Business/Farm Supplement. **Notification of Awards:** Applicants will be notified of awards on a rolling basis beginning 3/15. **Types of Aid:** *Need-based scholarships/grants:* Federal Pell, FSEOG, State scholarships/grants, Private scholarships, College/university scholarship or grant aid from institutional funds. *Loans:* Direct Subsidized Stafford Loans, Direct Unsubsidized Stafford Loans, Direct PLUS loans, Federal Perkins Loans, College/university loans from institutional funds. *Student Employment:* Federal Work-Study Program available. Institutional employment available. **Financial Aid Statistics:** 100% needy freshmen, 100% needy undergrads receive need-based scholarship or grant aid. 19% freshmen, 15% undergrads receive non-need-based scholarship or grant aid. 79% freshmen, 83% undergrads receive need-based self-help aid. 0% freshmen, 0% undergrads receive athletic scholarships. 99% freshmen, 99% undergrads receive any aid. 81% undergrads borrow to pay for school. Average cumulative indebtedness $36,882. **Criteria for awarding aid:** *Non-need-based:* Academics, Alumni affiliation, Leadership, Minority status, Music/drama.

SWARTHMORE COLLEGE

500 College Avenue, Swarthmore, PA 19081
Phone: 610-328-8300 • **Financial Aid Phone:** 610-328-8358
E-mail: admissions@swarthmore.edu • **CEEB Code:** 2821
Fax: 610-328-8580 • **Website:** www.swarthmore.edu • **ACT Code:** 3722

This private school was founded in 1864. It has a 399-acre campus.

RATINGS
Admissions Selectivity Rating: 98   **Fire Safety Rating:** 90   **Green Rating:** 85

STUDENTS AND FACULTY

Enrollment: 1,617. **Student Body:** 51% female, 49% male, 88% out-of-state, 12% international (64 countries represented). Asian 16%, African American 7%, Caucasian 42%, Hispanic 13%, Native American <1%, Pacific Islander <1%, Two or more races 7%, Race unknown 3%.

Retention and Graduation: 98% freshmen return for sophomore year. 88% freshmen graduate within 4 years. 94% freshmen graduate within 6 years. 26% grads go on to further study within 1 year. 10% grads pursue arts and sciences degrees. 2% grads pursue law degrees. 1% grads pursue business degrees. 2% grads pursue medical degrees. **Faculty:** Student/faculty ratio 8:1. 187 full-time faculty, 99% hold PhDs, 22% are are members of minority groups, 46% are women. 0% of classes are taught by teaching assistants.

ACADEMICS

Degrees: bachelor's. **Classes:** Most classes have 10-19 students. Most lab/discussion sessions have 10-19 students. **Most popular majors:** Economics; Biology/Biological Sciences; Political Science and Government. **Special Study Options:** Accelerated program, cross-registration, double major, exchange student program (domestic), honors program, independent study, internships, student-designed major, study abroad, teacher certification program, Swarthmore offers cooperative exchange programs with Rice and Tufts universities and Harvey Mudd, Pomona, Mills and Middlebury colleges. **Honors Programs:** Swarthmore"s Honors Program features faculty working with small groups of dedicated and accomplished students; an emphasis on independent learning; students entering into a dialogue with peers, teachers, and examiners; a demanding program of study in major and minor fields; and an examination at the end of two years' study by outside scholars. Combined degree programs: BA/BS in engineering and another major. **Disability Services:** Special programs offered to physically disabled students, including note-taking services, reader services, tape recorders, tutors. **Career Services:** Alumni network, Alumni services, Career/job search classes, Career assessment, Internships. Swarthmore's innovative externship program allows students to explore a field of interest by shadowing an alum in their professional environment for a week between semesters. Each year, this hands-on and real-time program matches 200 students with more than 300 alumni sponsors—leaders of industries and agents of change who are as invested in their alma mater and the success of its students as they are in making a difference in their careers and communities. Whether it's a national park in California, a Wall Street investment bank, a microbiology lab in Europe, or a nonprofit in Philly, students collect invaluable insights and memories and better understand the career opportunities in front of them.

FACILITIES

Housing: Coed dorms, men's dorms, women's dorms, Gender Neutral housing (students of any gender may share rooms and/or share bathrooms). 90% of campus accessible to physically disabled. **Special Academic Facilities/Equipment:** The Campus is a 399-acre, nationally registered arboretum. The Lang Performing Arts Center's resources include an art gallery, dance studios, cinema, and theater performance space. Highlights of Swarthmore's library facilities include the Friends Historical Library and the Peace Collection. The athletics facilities include a lighted stadium complex, a 400-meter dual durometer track, and synthetic grass playing field, state-of-the-art fitness center and three indoor tennis courts with Rebound Ace surface. The Science Center has been recognized by the U.S. Green Building Council for "leadership in energy and environmental design." The College's two newest residence halls feature loft-style rooms and environmentally friendly green roofs. **Computers:** 100% of classrooms, 100% of dorms, 100% of libraries, 100% of dining areas, 100% of student union, 100% of common outdoor areas have wireless network access. Students can register for classes online. Administrative functions (other than registration) can be performed online.

CAMPUS LIFE

Environment: Village. **Activities:** Choral groups, dance, drama/theater, jazz band, literary magazine, music ensembles, opera, student government, student newspaper, student-run film society, symphony orchestra, yearbook, Campus Ministries, Student Organization. 138 registered organizations, 3 honor societies, 12 religious organizations. 2 fraternities. **Athletics (Intercollegiate):** *Men:* baseball, basketball, cross-country, golf, lacrosse, soccer, swimming, tennis, track/field (outdoor), track/field (indoor). *Women:* badminton, basketball, cross-country, field hockey, lacrosse, soccer, softball, swimming, tennis, track/field (outdoor), track/field (indoor), volleyball. **On-Campus Highlights:** Kohlberg & Eldridge Commons Coffee Bars, Parrish Beach (the central campus lawn), Scott Outdoor Amphitheater, Mullan Tennis & Fitness Center, Paces (student-run cafe), Recent years have seen an exciting array of student projects and student spaces develop at Swarthmore. Among them: The acclaimed War News Radio (www.warnewsradio.org), the nation's only student-run national radio program focusing on the wars in Iraq and Afghanistan, now carried by more than 60 stations worldwide; the Genocide Intervention Network (www.genocideintervention.net), a student-founded group that is raising hundreds of thousands of dollars to support peace-keeping in Darfur; two new dormitories, whose student-influenced integrative design features loft-style doubles, wide halls, generous lounge and community kitchens—all aimed at promoting

robust hall social life; and the Lang Center for Civic and Social Responsibility (www.swarthmore.edu/langcenter) which prepares students for leadership in civic engagement, public service, advocacy, and social action. **Environmental Initiatives:** 100% of the College electrical demands are met by renewable energy credits and the College has made the decision to burn natural gas as it's primary fuel and convert the heat plant from #6 fuel oil to #2 fuel oil as it's back-up reserve.

ADMISSIONS

Freshman Academic Profile: 91% in top 10% of high school class, 96% in top 25% of high school class, 100% in top 50% of high school class. 59% from public high schools. **Reported SAT (pre-2016 redesign) scores:** SAT Math middle 50% range 660-770. SAT Critical Reading middle 50% range 645-760. **Concordant SAT scores:** SAT Math middle 50% range 690–780. ACT middle 50% range 30-34. **Basis for Candidate Selection:** *Very important factors considered include:* rigor of secondary school record, class rank, academic GPA, application essay, recommendation(s), character/personal qualities. *Important factors considered include:* standardized test scores, extracurricular activities. *Other factors considered include:* interview, talent/ability, first generation, alumni/ae relation, geographical residence, state residency, religious affiliation/commitment, racial/ethnic status, volunteer work, work experience, level of applicant's interest. **Freshman Admission Requirements:** High school diploma or equivalent is not required. *Academic units recommended:* 4 English, 3 math, 3 science, 3 foreign language, 3 social studies, 3 history. **Freshman Admission Statistics:** 7,717 applied, 12.80% admitted, 42% enrolled. **Transfer Admission Requirements:** High school transcript, college transcript(s), essay or personal statement, standardized test scores, statement of good standing from prior institution(s). Lowest grade transferable C. **General Admission Information:** Application fee $60. Regular application deadline 1/1. Regular notification 4/1. Nonfall registration not accepted. Admission may be deferred for a maximum of 1 Year.

COSTS AND FINANCIAL AID

Annual tuition $48,720. Room and board $14,446. Required fees $384. Average book expense $1,315. **Required Forms and Deadlines:** FAFSA, CSS/Financial Aid PROFILE, State aid form, Noncustodial PROFILE, Business/Farm Supplement. **Notification of Awards:** Applicants will be notified of awards on or about 4/1. **Types of Aid:** *Need-based scholarships/grants:* Federal Pell, FSEOG, State scholarships/grants, Private scholarships, College/university scholarship or grant aid from institutional funds. *Loans:* Direct Subsidized Stafford Loans, Direct Unsubsidized Stafford Loans, Direct PLUS loans, Federal Perkins Loans, State Loans, College/university loans from institutional funds. *Student Employment:* Federal Work-Study Program available. Institutional employment available. **Financial Aid Statistics:** 100% needy freshmen, 100% needy undergrads receive need-based scholarship or grant aid. 0% undergrads receive non-need-based scholarship or grant aid. 99% freshmen, 98% undergrads receive need-based self-help aid. 0% freshmen, 0% undergrads receive athletic scholarships. 52% freshmen, 50% undergrads receive any aid. 31% undergrads borrow to pay for school. Average cumulative indebtedness $22,957. **Criteria for awarding aid:** *Non-need-based:* Academics, Leadership, State/district residency.

See page 1060.

SWEET BRIAR COLLEGE

P. O. Box 1052, Sweet Briar, VA 24595
Phone: 434-381-6142 • **Financial Aid Phone:** 434-381-6156
E-mail: admissions@sbc.edu • **CEEB Code:** 5634
Fax: 434-381-6152 • **Website:** www.sbc.edu • **ACT Code:** 4406

This private school was founded in 1901. It has a 3250-acre campus.

RATINGS

Admissions Selectivity Rating: 76   **Fire Safety Rating:** 91   **Green Rating:** 60*

STUDENTS AND FACULTY

Enrollment: 320. **Student Body:** 100% female, 0% male, 49% out-of-state, 2% international (1 countries represented). Asian 2%, African American 10%, Caucasian 71%, Hispanic 10%, Native American <1%, Pacific Islander <1%, Two or more races 4%, Race unknown 1%.

Retention and Graduation: 50% freshmen return for sophomore year. 55% freshmen graduate within 4 years. 61% freshmen graduate within 6 years. 25% grads go on to further study within 1 year. **Faculty:** Student/faculty ratio 5:1. 59 full-time faculty, 86% hold PhDs, 12% are are members of minority groups, 53% are women. 0% of classes are taught by teaching assistants.

ACADEMICS

Degrees: bachelor's, master's. **Classes:** Most classes have 10-19 students. Most lab/discussion sessions have fewer than 10 students. **Most popular**

majors: Biology/Biological Sciences; Psychology; Business/Commerce.
Special Study Options: Accelerated program, cross-registration, double
major, dual enrollment, exchange student program (domestic), honors
program, independent study, internships, liberal arts/career combination,
student-designed major, study abroad, teacher certification program. **Honors
Programs:** The Honors Program was established and continues to evolve
in response to the needs of students who demonstrate exceptional initiative,
ability, and creativity. The program consists of challenging courses, Summer
Research Fellowships, opportunities for independent work, and a series
of extracurricular activities. The program also brings advanced graduate
degree candidates to campus, providing role models for students considering
graduate studies. Combined degree programs: BA/MEng, BA/BS Eng. with
Columbia, VaTech, Wash. Univ. **Disability Services:** Special programs offered
to physically disabled students, including tutors. **Career Services:** Alumni
network, Alumni services, Career/job search classes, Career assessment,
Internships, Regional alumni. The program of which we are the proudest is
the Field/Major Specific Careers Event Program. This series of rotating career
development events involve faculty, alumnae, current employers, professionals,
and students. The events are developed after assessing the largest majors
in the college and through perceived need. For example, there may be a
Commerce/Business Careers Event, a Natural/Sciences/Environment Event,
a Government/International Affairs event, and a Careers in Humanities event.
Each of these programs allow for active and substantive interactions from all of
the Career Service's Center's major constituencies. Students are able to garner
internship opportunities, full-time opportunities and learn much about the
various fields and employment sectors. These programs which regularly involve
the faculty and alumnae of Sweet Briar have greatly contributed to our Center's
strong reputation both on and off campus as evidenced by varying assessment
metrics and yearly national rankings of several types.

FACILITIES

Housing: women's dorms, Substance-free, Eco Floor, Academic House,
Corridor. **Special Academic Facilities/Equipment:** Art museum and
galleries, college and local history museums, environmental education/nature
center, kindergarten/nursery school, riding center, electron microscope, DNA
sequencing equipment, 400MHz nuclear magnetic resonance spectrometer.
Computers: 60% of classrooms, 50% of dorms, 100% of libraries, 100% of
dining areas, 100% of student union, 30% of common outdoor areas have
wireless network access. Students can register for classes online. Administrative
functions (other than registration) can be performed online.

CAMPUS LIFE

Environment: Rural. **Activities:** Choral groups, dance, drama/theater, literary
magazine, music ensembles, musical theater, radio station, student government,
student newspaper, student-run film society, symphony orchestra, television
station, yearbook, Campus Ministries. 61 registered organizations, 11 honor
societies, 3 religious organizations. **Athletics (Intercollegiate):** *Women:* field
hockey, horseback riding, lacrosse, soccer, softball, swimming, tennis, volleyball.
On-Campus Highlights: Bistro, Riding Center, Boathouse, Book Shop, Art
Barn. **Environmental Initiatives:** Collegiate Clean Energy coalition: http://
sbc.edu/news/uncategorized/virginia-private-colleges-announce-sustainability-
initiative/

ADMISSIONS

Freshman Academic Profile: Average high school GPA 3.5. 15% in top 10%
of high school class, 38% in top 25% of high school class, 68% in top 50% of
high school class. **Reported SAT (pre-2016 redesign) scores:** SAT Math
middle 50% range 420-560. SAT Critical Reading middle 50% range 460-620.
SAT Writing middle 50% range 440-580. **Concordant SAT scores:** SAT
EBRW middle 50% 500–650. SAT Math middle 50% range 460–580. ACT
middle 50% range 18-27. Minimum internet-based TOEFL 79. Minimum
paper TOEFL 550. **Basis for Candidate Selection:** *Very important
factors considered include:* rigor of secondary school record, academic GPA.
Important factors considered include: standardized test scores, application
essay, recommendation(s), interview. *Other factors considered include:* class
rank, extracurricular activities, talent/ability, character/personal qualities,
first generation, alumni/ae relation, racial/ethnic status, volunteer work, work
experience. **Freshman Admission Requirements:** High school diploma is
required and GED is accepted. *Academic units required:* 4 English, 3 math, 3
science, 2 science labs, 2 foreign language, 3 social studies, 3 history. *Academic
units recommended:* 4 English, 4 math, 4 science, 3 science labs, 4 foreign
language, 4 social studies, 4 history. **Freshman Admission Statistics:** 950
applied, 93.05% admitted, 15% enrolled. **Transfer Admission Requirements:**
High school transcript, college transcript(s), essay or personal statement,
standardized test scores, statement of good standing from prior institution(s).
Minimum college GPA of 2.5 required. Lowest grade transferable C-. **General
Admission Information:** Application fee $40. Priority deadline 2/1. Nonfall
registration accepted. Admission may be deferred for a maximum of one year.

COSTS AND FINANCIAL AID

Annual tuition $36,520. Room and board $12,900. Required fees $640.
Average book expense $1,250. **Required Forms and Deadlines:** FAFSA,

---

Noncustodial PROFILE. **Notification of Awards:** Applicants will be
notified of awards on a rolling basis beginning 3/1. **Types of Aid:** *Need-based
scholarships/grants:* Federal Pell, FSEOG, State scholarships/grants, Private
scholarships, College/university scholarship or grant aid from institutional funds,
United Negro College Fund. *Loans:* Direct Subsidized Stafford Loans, Direct
Unsubsidized Stafford Loans, Direct PLUS loans, Federal Perkins Loans,
College/university loans from institutional funds. *Student Employment:* Federal
Work-Study Program available. Institutional employment available. **Financial
Aid Statistics:** 100% needy freshmen, 99% needy undergrads receive
need-based scholarship or grant aid. 22% freshmen, 26% undergrads receive
non-need-based scholarship or grant aid. 65% freshmen, 69% undergrads
receive need-based self-help aid. 0% freshmen, 0% undergrads receive athletic
scholarships. 100% freshmen, 99% undergrads receive any aid. 70% undergrads
borrow to pay for school. Average cumulative indebtedness $33,026. **Criteria
for awarding aid:** *Need-based:* Alumni affiliation. *Non-need-based:* Academics,
Art, Leadership, Music/drama, State/district residency.

SYRACUSE UNIVERSITY

100 Crouse-Hinds Hall, Syracuse, NY 13244-2130
Phone: 315-443-3611 • **Financial Aid Phone:** 315-443-1513
E-mail: orange@syr.edu • **CEEB Code:** 2823
Fax: 315-443-4226 • **Website:** www.syracuse.edu • **ACT Code:** 2968

This private school was founded in 1870. It has a 200-acre campus.

RATINGS

Admissions Selectivity Rating: 89   **Fire Safety Rating:** 95   **Green Rating:** 96

STUDENTS AND FACULTY

Enrollment: 14,777. **Student Body:** 54% female, 46% male, 59% out-of-state,
12% international (93 countries represented). Asian 7%, African American 8%,
Caucasian 56%, Hispanic 10%, Native American 1%, Pacific Islander <1%, Two
or more races 3%, Race unknown 2%.
Retention and Graduation: 91% freshmen return for sophomore year.
69% freshmen graduate within 4 years. 82 1% grads pursue arts and sciences
degrees. 2% grads pursue law degrees. 2% grads pursue business degrees. 1%
grads pursue medical degrees. **Faculty:** Student/faculty ratio 15:1. 1,090 full-
time faculty, 90% hold PhDs, 20% are are members of minority groups, 41%
are women.

ACADEMICS

Degrees: associate, bachelor's, certificate, doctoral/professional, doctoral/
research, master's, postbachelor's certificate, post-master's certificate. **Classes:**
Most classes have 10-19 students. Most lab/discussion sessions have 20-29
students. **Most popular majors:** Information Science/Studies; Architecture;
Speech Communication and Rhetoric. **Special Study Options:** Accelerated
program, cooperative education program, distance learning, double major,
dual enrollment, English as a Second Language (ESL), honors program,
independent study, internships, liberal arts/career combination, student-
designed major, study abroad, teacher certification program, SU offers many
undergraduate research opportunities, pre-professional programs, and minors.
Honors Programs: The University Honors program combines the benefits of
a small intimate community with the advantages of diversity and opportunity
found only at larger institutions. Students enjoy provocative coursework in small
classes taught by some of the University's most able and experienced faculty,
as well as some of the nation's leading research scholars. In the Honors Thesis
Project upper class students are closely guided by faculty to pursue intensive
research on a topic of their choice. Combined degree programs: BA/MEng,
Arts and Sciences/Education (BA/MS 5-year teacher preparation programs);
Engineering and Computer Science/Management (BS/MBA). **Disability
Services:** Special programs offered to physically disabled students, including
note-taking services, reader services, tape recorders, tutors. **Career Services:**
Alumni network, Alumni services, Career/job search classes, Career assessment,
Internships, Regional alumni. Syracuse's diverse student body represents all 50
states and more than 120 countries. About 25 percent are students of color and
17 percent are first-generation college students. This reflects the University's
longstanding commitment to diversity and tradition of welcoming students with
different experiences and backgrounds. During its earliest years, the University
admitted women and people of color at a time when most other institutions of
higher learning closed their doors to them. In 1945, following World War II,
the University welcomed thousands of military veterans under the GI Bill of

Rights, tripling its enrollment with a 'can-do' spirit that would come to define the 'Greatest Generation.' Since that time, the University has built on this foundation with nationally recognized programs for veterans, their families, and those who serve our country.

FACILITIES

Housing: Coed dorms, special housing for disabled students, special housing for international students, fraternity/sorority housing, apartments for married students, apartments for single students, Wellness Housing, ThemeHousingInternational living center, single-sex floors and wings of residence halls, numerous learning communities, and interest housing available. 95% of campus accessible to physically diasbled. **Special Academic Facilities/Equipment:** SUArt Galleries; The Warehouse Gallery; digital media convergence center; Syracuse Center of Excellence in Environmental and Energy Systems; Fidelity MOTUS 622i flight simulator for aerospace engineering; Ballentine Investment Institute; community darkrooms; Syracuse Stage professional equity theater; Bernice M. Wright Child Development Laboratory School; Belfer Audio Laboratory and Archive; Gebbie Speech, Language, and Hearing Clinic; Life Sciences Complex; SU Library Special Collections Research Center; UPSTATE: A Center for Design, Research and Real Estate at the SU School of Architecture; Center on Human Policy; Center for Emerging Network Technologies; JPMorgan Chase Technology Center **Computers:** 75% of classrooms, 100% of dorms, 100% of libraries, 100% of dining areas, 100% of student union, 75% of common outdoor areas have wireless network access. Students can register for classes online. Administrative functions (other than registration) can be performed online.

CAMPUS LIFE

Environment: Metropolis. **Activities:** Choral groups, concert band, dance, drama/theater, jazz band, literary magazine, marching band, music ensembles, musical theater, pep band, radio station, student government, student newspaper, student-run film society, symphony orchestra, television station, yearbook, Campus Ministries, Student Organization. 347 registered organizations, 43 honor societies, 30 religious organizations. 29 fraternities, 19 sororities. **Athletics (Intercollegiate):** *Men:* basketball, cheerleading, crew/rowing, cross-country, diving, football, lacrosse, soccer, swimming, track/field (outdoor). *Women:* basketball, cheerleading, crew/rowing, cross-country, diving, field hockey, ice hockey, lacrosse, soccer, softball, swimming, tennis, track/field (outdoor), volleyball. **On-Campus Highlights:** Schine Student Center, Bird Library Cafe, Hendricks Chapel, Whitman School, Archbold Athletic Complex. **Environmental Initiatives:** SU has established a target date of 2040 for carbon neutrality, at least a decade earlier than most ACUPCC signatories. At present, we are ahead of schedule for attaining that target.

ADMISSIONS

Freshman Academic Profile: Average high school GPA 3.6. 36% in top 10% of high school class, 71% in top 25% of high school class, 94% in top 50% of high school class. 66% from public high schools. **Reported SAT (pre-2016 redesign) scores:** SAT Math middle 50% range 560-660. SAT Critical Reading middle 50% range 530-630. SAT Writing middle 50% range 540-640. **Concordant SAT scores:** SAT EBRW middle 50% 590–680. SAT Math middle 50% range 580–690. ACT middle 50% range 25-29. Minimum internet-based TOEFL 85. Minimum paper TOEFL 550. **Basis for Candidate Selection:** *Very important factors considered include:* rigor of secondary school record, class rank, academic GPA, standardized test scores, application essay, recommendation(s), interview, extracurricular activities, talent/ability, character/personal qualities, volunteer work, level of applicant's interest. *Other factors considered include:* first generation, alumni/ae relation, geographical residence, state residency, racial/ethnic status, work experience. **Freshman Admission Requirements:** High school diploma is required and GED is accepted. *Academic units recommended:* 4 English, 4 math, 4 science, 3 foreign language, 4 social studies, 4 history. **Freshman Admission Statistics:** 30,923 applied, 52.32% admitted, 23% enrolled. **Transfer Admission Requirements:** college transcript(s), essay or personal statement, statement of good standing from prior institution(s). Lowest grade transferable C. **General Admission Information:** Application fee $75. Priority deadline 1/1. Regular application deadline 1/1. Nonfall registration accepted. Admission may be deferred for a maximum of 1 year.

COSTS AND FINANCIAL AID

Required Forms and Deadlines: FAFSA, CSS/Financial Aid PROFILE, Noncustodial PROFILE. **Notification of Awards:** Applicants will be notified of awards on or about 3/15. **Types of Aid:** *Need-based scholarships/grants:* Federal Pell, FSEOG, State scholarships/grants, Private scholarships, College/university scholarship or grant aid from institutional funds. *Loans:* Direct Subsidized Stafford Loans, Direct Unsubsidized Stafford Loans, Direct PLUS loans, Federal Perkins Loans. *Student Employment:* Federal Work-Study Program available. Institutional employment available. **Financial Aid Statistics:** 93% needy freshmen, 92% needy undergrads receive need-based scholarship or grant aid. 13% freshmen, 7% undergrads receive non-need-based scholarship or grant aid. 89% freshmen, 92% undergrads receive need-based self-help aid. 2% freshmen, 2% undergrads receive athletic scholarships. 71%

freshmen, 73% undergrads receive any aid. Average cumulative indebtedness $37,753. **Criteria for awarding aid:** *Need-based:* Academics, Athletics. *Non-need-based:* Academics, Art, Athletics, Music/drama.

TALLADEGA COLLEGE

627 West Battle Street, Talladega, AL 35160
Phone: 205-761-6235 • **Financial Aid Phone:** 256-761-6341
E-mail: admissions@talladega.edu
Fax: 205-362-0274 • **Website:** www.talladega.edu • **ACT Code:** 26

This private school, affiliated with the United Church of Christ Church, was founded in 1867. It has a 50-acre campus.

RATINGS

Admissions Selectivity Rating: 77   **Fire Safety Rating:** 91   **Green Rating:** 60*

STUDENTS AND FACULTY

Enrollment: 601. **Student Body:** 58% female, 42% male, 48% out-of-state, 0% international. Asian 0%, African American 95%, Caucasian <1%, Hispanic 4%, Native American 0%, Pacific Islander 0%, Two or more races 0%, Race unknown 0%.
Retention and Graduation: 43% freshmen return for sophomore year. 27% freshmen graduate within 4 years. 41% freshmen graduate within 6 years. 25% grads go on to further study within 1 year. 25% grads pursue arts and sciences degrees. 25% grads pursue law degrees. 25% grads pursue business degrees. 25% grads pursue medical degrees. **Faculty:** Student/faculty ratio 16:1. 29 full-time faculty, 62% hold PhDs, 66% are are members of minority groups, 45% are women. 0% of classes are taught by teaching assistants.

ACADEMICS

Degrees: bachelor's. **Classes:** Most classes have fewer than 10 students. Most lab/discussion sessions have more than 10 students. **Most popular majors:** Biology/Biological Sciences; Psychology; Business/Commerce. **Special Study Options:** double major, dual enrollment, independent study, internships, teacher certification program. **Disability Services:** Special programs offered to physically disabled students, including note-taking services, tape recorders, tutors. **Career Services:** Alumni network, Alumni services, Career assessment, Internships.

FACILITIES

Housing: men's dorms, women's dorms. 100% of campus accessible to physically diasbled. **Special Academic Facilities/Equipment:** Savery Library, Home of the famous Amistad Murals, historic Swayne Hall, which is listed on the National Register; DeForest Chapel, which has the stained glass windows by famous artist, David Driskell; Goodnow Art Building **Computers:** 100% of libraries, 50% of common outdoor areas have wireless network access. Administrative functions (other than registration) can be performed online.

CAMPUS LIFE

Environment: Rural. **Activities:** Choral groups, concert band, dance, drama/theater, jazz band, student government, student newspaper, yearbook. 40 registered organizations, 8 honor societies, 1 religious organization. 4 fraternities, 4 sororities. **Athletics (Intercollegiate):** *Men:* baseball, basketball, golf. *Women:* basketball, cheerleading, volleyball. **On-Campus Highlights:** Savery Library, DeForest Chapel, Swayne Hall, Callanan Hall, Fanning Hall.

ADMISSIONS

Freshman Academic Profile: Average high school GPA 2.7. 90% from public high schools. **Reported SAT (pre-2016 redesign) scores:** SAT Math middle 50% range 340-410. SAT Critical Reading middle 50% range 320-460. **Concordant SAT scores:** SAT Math middle 50% range 380–450. ACT middle 50% range 16-19. Minimum paper TOEFL 500. **Basis for Candidate Selection:** *Very important factors considered include:* rigor of secondary school record, standardized test scores, application essay, recommendation(s), extracurricular activities, talent/ability, character/personal qualities, volunteer work, work experience. *Important factors considered include:* class rank. *Other factors considered include:* interview. **Freshman Admission Requirements:** High school diploma is required and GED is accepted. *Academic units required:* 4 English, 2 math, 2 science, 3 social studies, and 2 units from above areas or other academic areas. **Freshman Admission Statistics:** 1,960 applied, 37.96% admitted, 40% enrolled. **Transfer Admission Requirements:** High school transcript, college transcript(s), essay or personal statement, standardized test scores, statement of good standing from prior institution(s). Minimum college GPA of 2.0 required. Lowest grade transferable C. **General Admission Information:** Application fee $25. Nonfall registration accepted. Admission may be deferred for a maximum of 2 years.

COSTS AND FINANCIAL AID

Annual tuition $6,720. Room and board $4,290. Required fees $408. Average book expense $1,000. **Required Forms and Deadlines:** FAFSA, Institution's own financial aid form, CSS/Financial Aid PROFILE, State aid form. **Notification of Awards:** Applicants will be notified of awards on or about 4/1. **Types of Aid:** *Need-based scholarships/grants:* Federal Pell, FSEOG, State scholarships/grants, Private scholarships, College/university scholarship or grant aid from institutional funds, United Negro College Fund. *Loans:* Federal Perkins Loans. *Student Employment:* Federal Work-Study Program available. Institutional employment available. **Financial Aid Statistics:** 45% needy freshmen, 26% needy undergrads receive need-based scholarship or grant aid. 45% freshmen, 26% undergrads receive non-need-based scholarship or grant aid. 0% freshmen, 0% undergrads receive need-based self-help aid. 0% freshmen, 0% undergrads receive athletic scholarships. 90% freshmen, 90% undergrads receive any aid. **Criteria for awarding aid:** *Need-based:* Leadership, Minority status, Religious affiliation. *Non-need-based:* Academics, Alumni affiliation, Art, Athletics, Music/drama.

TARLETON STATE UNIVERSITY

PO Box T-0030, Stephenville, TX 76402
Phone: 254-968-9125 • **Financial Aid Phone:** 254-968-9070
E-mail: uadm@tarleton.edu • **CEEB Code:** 6817
Fax: 254-968-9951 • **ACT Code:** 4204

This public school was founded in 1899. It has a 125-acre campus.

RATINGS

Admissions Selectivity Rating: 76   **Fire Safety Rating:** 94   **Green Rating:** 60*

STUDENTS AND FACULTY

Enrollment: 10,749. **Student Body:** 61% female, 39% male, 2% out-of-state, <1% international (22 countries represented). Asian 1%, African American 8%, Caucasian 68%, Hispanic 18%, Native American 1%, Pacific Islander <1%, Two or more races 3%, Race unknown 1%.
Retention and Graduation: 66% freshmen return for sophomore year. 24% freshmen graduate within 4 years. 44% freshmen graduate within 6 years.
Faculty: Student/faculty ratio 19:1. 383 full-time faculty, 0% hold PhDs, 17% are are members of minority groups, 52% are women. 2% of classes are taught by teaching assistants.

ACADEMICS

Degrees: associate, bachelor's, doctoral, master's. **Classes:** Most classes have 20-29 students. Most lab/discussion sessions have 10-19 students. **Most popular majors:** Multi-/Interdisciplinary Studies; Kinesiology and Exercise Science; Psychology. **Special Study Options:** Accelerated program, distance learning, double major, dual enrollment, honors program, internships, study abroad, teacher certification program, Undergrads may take grad level classes. **Honors Programs:** Offer honors classes in core curriculum subjects, including English, history, political science, chemistry, biology, geology, and speech. Courses offer intellectually challenging material, innovative approaches to the subject, increased opportunities for honing critical thinking and writing skills, and the opportunity to interact closely with similarly motivated students and with outstanding faculty. **Disability Services:** Special programs offered to physically disabled students, including note-taking services, reader services, tutors. **Career Services:** Career/job search classes, Career assessment, Internships. Education Department and Student Teaching opportunities.

FACILITIES

Housing: Coed dorms, special housing for disabled students, men's dorms, special housing for international students, women's dorms, fraternity/sorority housing, apartments for married students, cooperative housing, apartments for single students. **Special Academic Facilities/Equipment:** Planetarium in Science Bldg. W.K. Gordon Center for Industrial History of Texas **Computers:** 100% of classrooms, 100% of dorms, 100% of libraries, 100% of student union, have wireless network access. Students can register for classes online. Administrative functions (other than registration) can be performed online.

CAMPUS LIFE

Environment: Village. **Activities:** Choral groups, concert band, dance, drama/theater, jazz band, literary magazine, marching band, music ensembles, musical theater, opera, pep band, radio station, student government, student newspaper, student-run film society, symphony orchestra, television station, yearbook, Campus Ministries, Student Organization. 117 registered organizations, 13 honor societies, 13 religious organizations. 7 fraternities, 8 sororities. **Athletics (Intercollegiate):** *Men:* baseball, basketball, cheerleading, cross-country, football, rodeo, track/field (outdoor). *Women:* basketball, cheerleading, cross-country, golf, rodeo, softball, tennis, track/field (outdoor), volleyball. **On-Campus Highlights:** Barry B. Thompson Student Center, New Recreational

Sports Facility, Dick Smith Library, Wisdom Gym, Science Bldg with Planetarium. **Environmental Initiatives:** 15% Electric from wind.

ADMISSIONS

Freshman Academic Profile: 9% in top 10% of high school class, 37% in top 25% of high school class, 87% in top 50% of high school class. 97% from public high schools. **Reported SAT (pre-2016 redesign) scores:** SAT Math middle 50% range 430-530. SAT Critical Reading middle 50% range 420-520. SAT Writing middle 50% range 400-500. **Concordant SAT scores:** SAT EBRW middle 50% 460–570. SAT Math middle 50% range 470–560. ACT middle 50% range 18-23. Minimum internet-based TOEFL 190. Minimum paper TOEFL 520. **Basis for Candidate Selection:** *Very important factors considered include:* rigor of secondary school record, academic GPA, standardized test scores. *Important factors considered include:* class rank. **Freshman Admission Requirements:** High school diploma is required and GED is accepted. *Academic units required:* 4 English, 3 math, 2 science, 2 social studies, 1 history, 2 academic electives. *Academic units recommended:* 3 science, 2 foreign language, 4 academic electives. **Freshman Admission Statistics:** 6,288 applied, 71.28% admitted, 44% enrolled. **Transfer Admission Requirements:** college transcript(s), Minimum college GPA of 2.0 required. Lowest grade transferable D. **General Admission Information:** Application fee $45. Priority deadline 3/1. Regular application deadline 7/21. Nonfall registration accepted.

COSTS AND FINANCIAL AID

Required Forms and Deadlines: FAFSA. **Notification of Awards:** Applicants will be notified of awards on a rolling basis beginning 5/1. **Types of Aid:** *Need-based scholarships/grants:* Federal Pell, FSEOG, State scholarships/grants, College/university scholarship or grant aid from institutional funds. *Loans:* Direct Subsidized Stafford Loans, Direct Unsubsidized Stafford Loans, Direct PLUS loans, State Loans. *Student Employment:* Federal Work-Study Program available. Institutional employment available. **Financial Aid Statistics:** 94% needy freshmen, 89% needy undergrads receive need-based scholarship or grant aid. 6% freshmen, 2% undergrads receive non-need-based scholarship or grant aid. 71% freshmen, 77% undergrads receive need-based self-help aid. 0% freshmen, 0% undergrads receive athletic scholarships. 57% freshmen, 37% undergrads receive any aid. 68% undergrads borrow to pay for school. Average cumulative indebtedness $26,507. **Criteria for awarding aid:** *Non-need-based:* Academics, Alumni affiliation, Athletics, Leadership, Music/drama.

TAYLOR UNIVERSITY

236 West Reade Avenue, Upland, IN 46989-1001
Phone: 765-998-5134 • **Financial Aid Phone:** 765-998-5358
E-mail: admissions@tayloru.edu • **CEEB Code:** 1802
Fax: 765-998-4925 • **Website:** www.taylor.edu • **ACT Code:** 1248

This private school was founded in 1846. It has a 952-acre campus.

RATINGS

Admissions Selectivity Rating: 86   **Fire Safety Rating:** 95   **Green Rating:** 60*

STUDENTS AND FACULTY

Enrollment: 1,806. **Student Body:** 56% female, 44% male, 59% out-of-state, 6% international (33 countries represented). Asian 3%, African American 3%, Caucasian 83%, Hispanic 4%, Native American 1%, Pacific Islander <1%, Two or more races <1%, Race unknown 0%.
Retention and Graduation: 85% freshmen return for sophomore year. 66% freshmen graduate within 4 years. 76% freshmen graduate within 6 years. 30% grads go on to further study within 1 year. 4% grads pursue arts and sciences degrees. 1% grads pursue law degrees. 2% grads pursue business degrees. 1% grads pursue medical degrees. **Faculty:** Student/faculty ratio 13:1. 131 full-time faculty, 85% hold PhDs, 7% are are members of minority groups, 27% are women. 0% of classes are taught by teaching assistants.

ACADEMICS

Degrees: associate, bachelor's, diploma, master's. **Classes:** Most classes have 10-19 students. Most lab/discussion sessions have 10-19 students. **Most popular majors:** Biology/Biological Sciences; Elementary Education and Teaching; Kinesiology and Exercise Science. **Special Study Options:** cooperative education program, distance learning, double major, dual enrollment, exchange student program (domestic), honors program, independent study, internships, student-designed major, study abroad, teacher certification program. **Honors Programs:** Honors Program emphasizes to a greater extent than the general curriculum, integration of faith and learning, ideas and values in content and discussion and student initiative in format. Also offer Freshmen Irish Studies Program in Ireland. **Disability Services:** Special programs offered to physically disabled students, including note-taking services, reader services, tape recorders, tutors. **Career Services:** Alumni network, Alumni services, Career assessment, Internships, Regional alumni.

FACILITIES

Housing: men's dorms, women's dorms, apartments for married students, apartments for single students, Some off-campus apartments available to upperclassmen with special permission. 95% of campus accessible to physically diasbled. **Special Academic Facilities/Equipment:** Compton Art Gallery, Edwin W. Brown Collection/CS Lewis and Friends. **Computers:** 100% of classrooms, 100% of dorms, 100% of libraries, 100% of dining areas, 100% of student union, 50% of common outdoor areas have wireless network access. Students can register for classes online. Administrative functions (other than registration) can be performed online.

CAMPUS LIFE

Environment: Rural. **Activities:** Choral groups, concert band, drama/theater, jazz band, literary magazine, music ensembles, musical theater, opera, pep band, radio station, student government, student newspaper, student-run film society, symphony orchestra, television station, yearbook, Campus Ministries, Student Organization, Model UN. 87 registered organizations, 7 honor societies, 23 religious organizations. **Athletics (Intercollegiate):** *Men:* baseball, basketball, cross-country, football, golf, soccer, tennis, track/field (outdoor), track/field (indoor). *Women:* basketball, cross-country, soccer, softball, tennis, track/field (outdoor), track/field (indoor), volleyball. **On-Campus Highlights:** The Jumping Bean (Student coffee shop), Kesler Student Activities Center, Modelle Metcalf Visual Arts Center, Rediger Chapel and Auditorium, Mitchell Theater. **Environmental Initiatives:** The 127,000 sq. ft. Euler Science Complex, was completed in the summer of 2012, and subsequently obtained LEED status. This facility includes innovative sustainability features. This includes two 50kW wind turbines and a 10kW photovoltaic system.

ADMISSIONS

Freshman Academic Profile: Average high school GPA 3.7. 38% in top 10% of high school class, 64% in top 25% of high school class, 88% in top 50% of high school class. 80% from public high schools. **Reported SAT (pre-2016 redesign) scores:** SAT Math middle 50% range 480-620. SAT Critical Reading middle 50% range 470-630. SAT Writing middle 50% range 480-610. **Concordant SAT scores:** SAT EBRW middle 50% 530–670. SAT Math middle 50% range 510–640. ACT middle 50% range 22-29. Minimum internet-based TOEFL 80. **Basis for Candidate Selection:** *Very important factors considered include:* rigor of secondary school record, academic GPA, standardized test scores, application essay, recommendation(s), character/personal qualities, religious affiliation/commitment. *Important factors considered include:* class rank, interview, extracurricular activities, volunteer work. *Other factors considered include:* talent/ability, first generation, alumni/ae relation, geographical residence, state residency, racial/ethnic status, work experience. **Freshman Admission Requirements:** High school diploma is required and GED is accepted. *Academic units required:* 4 English, 3 math, 3 science, 3 science labs, 2 social studies, 3 academic electives. *Academic units recommended:* 4 math, 4 science, 4 science labs, 2 foreign language, 3 social studies, 1 computer science, 1 visual/performing arts. **Freshman Admission Statistics:** 1,775 applied, 79.61% admitted, 33% enrolled. **Transfer Admission Requirements:** High school transcript, college transcript(s), essay or personal statement, standardized test scores, statement of good standing from prior institution(s). Minimum college GPA of 2.5 required. Lowest grade transferable C+. **General Admission Information:** Application fee $25. Priority deadline 2/1. Regular application deadline 8/1. Nonfall registration accepted. Admission may be deferred for a maximum of 2 years.

COSTS AND FINANCIAL AID

Annual tuition $31,232. Required fees $240. Average book expense $3,400. **Required Forms and Deadlines:** FAFSA. **Notification of Awards:** Applicants will be notified of awards on a rolling basis beginning 3/1. **Types of Aid:** *Need-based scholarships/grants:* Federal Pell, FSEOG, State scholarships/grants, Private scholarships, College/university scholarship or grant aid from institutional funds. *Loans:* Direct Subsidized Stafford Loans, Direct Unsubsidized Stafford Loans, Direct PLUS loans, Federal Perkins Loans, College/university loans from institutional funds. *Student Employment:* Federal Work-Study Program available. Institutional employment available. **Financial Aid Statistics:** 100% needy freshmen, 100% needy undergrads receive need-based scholarship or grant aid. 19% freshmen, 18% undergrads receive non-need-based scholarship or grant aid. 81% freshmen, 82% undergrads receive need-based self-help aid. 6% freshmen, 7% undergrads receive athletic scholarships. 99% freshmen, 96% undergrads receive any aid. 62% undergrads borrow to pay for school. Average cumulative indebtedness $29,411. **Criteria for awarding aid:** *Need-based:* Art, Athletics, Leadership, Minority status, Music/drama, Religious affiliation. *Non-need-based:* Academics, Alumni affiliation, Art, Athletics, Leadership, Minority status, Music/drama, Religious affiliation, State/district residency.

TECNOLÓGICO DE MONTERREY

Monterrey, Mexico
Phone: +52 (81) 8158-2269
E-mail: admisiones.mty@itesm.mx
Website: www.itesm.mx

RATINGS

Admissions Selectivity Rating: 64   **Fire Safety Rating:** 60*   **Green Rating:** 60*

STUDENTS AND FACULTY

Student Body: 43% female, 57% male, 22% out-of-state. **Retention and Graduation:** 90% freshmen return for sophomore year. 29% freshmen graduate within 4 years. 74% freshmen graduate within 6 years. **Faculty:** Student/faculty ratio 15:1. 1,609 full-time faculty, 57% hold PhDs, 0% are are members of minority groups, 38% are women.

ACADEMICS

Degrees: bachelor's, doctoral/research, master's.

ADMISSIONS

Freshman Admission Statistics: 15,717 applied, 85.93% admitted, 74% enrolled.

COSTS AND FINANCIAL AID

Student Employment: Federal Work-Study Program available. Institutional employment available.

TEMPLE UNIVERSITY

Best Colleges

1801 North Broad Street (041-09), Philadelphia, PA 19122-6096
Phone: 215-204-7200 • **Financial Aid Phone:** 215-204-2244
E-mail: TUADM@TEMPLE.EDU • **CEEB Code:** 2906
Fax: 215-204-5694 • **Website:** www.temple.edu • **ACT Code:** 3724

This public school was founded in 1888. It has a 330-acre campus.

RATINGS

Admissions Selectivity Rating: 89   **Fire Safety Rating:** 98   **Green Rating:** 91

STUDENTS AND FACULTY

Enrollment: 28,709. **Student Body:** 52% female, 48% male, 20% out-of-state, 6% international (118 countries represented). Asian 11%, African American 13%, Caucasian 56%, Hispanic 6%, Native American <1%, Pacific Islander <1%, Two or more races 3%, Race unknown 4%. **Retention and Graduation:** 90% freshmen return for sophomore year. 44% freshmen graduate within 4 years. 70% freshmen graduate within 6 years. 36% grads go on to further study within 1 year. **Faculty:** Student/faculty ratio 15:1. 1,454 full-time faculty, 88% hold PhDs, 20% are are members of minority groups, 42% are women.

ACADEMICS

Degrees: associate, bachelor's, certificate, diploma, doctoral/professional, doctoral/research, doctoral, master's, postbachelor's certifiate, post-master's certificate, terminal, transfer. **Classes:** Most classes have 10-19 students. Most lab/discussion sessions have 20-29 students. **Most popular majors:** Biology/Biological Sciences; Psychology; Business/Commerce. **Special Study Options:** cooperative education program, cross-registration, distance learning, double major, dual enrollment, English as a Second Language (ESL), exchange student program (domestic), honors program, independent study, internships, liberal arts/career combination, study abroad, teacher certification program, Programs are offered in a number of foreign countries: Japan, Italy, Costa Rica, France,Germany, Ghana, India, Spain, Turkey, United Kingdom and Brazil. **Honors Programs:** 1) Honors Certificate Program 2) Honors Scholars Program Combined degree programs: BA/MA, B.S/M.A., B.S./M.S., B.A./M.S., M.B.A./M.A, M.B.A./M.S., Ph.d,and B.F.A. with Teaching Certification. **Disability Services:** Special programs offered to physically disabled students, including note-taking services, reader services, tape recorders, tutors. **Career Services:** Alumni network, Career/job search classes, Career assessment, Internships, Regional alumni. Our office provides opportunities through internship postings and on campus recruiting events. Specific programs are managed by individual schools and colleges within the university.

FACILITIES

Housing: Coed dorms, special housing for disabled students, apartments for single students, Living/Learning Centers are available. 100% of campus accessible to physically diasbled. **Special Academic Facilities/Equipment:** Blockson Collection, Urban Archieves, observatory **Computers:** 40% of classrooms, 30% of dorms, 80% of libraries, 90% of dining areas, 100% of student union, 40% of common outdoor areas have wireless network access. Students can register for classes online. Administrative functions (other than registration) can be performed online.

CAMPUS LIFE

Environment: Metropolis. **Activities:** Choral groups, concert band, dance, drama/theater, jazz band, literary magazine, marching band, music ensembles, musical theater, opera, pep band, radio station, student government, student newspaper, student-run film society, symphony orchestra, television station, yearbook, Campus Ministries, Student Organization. 232 registered organizations, 12 honor societies, 24 religious organizations. 11 fraternities, 9 sororities. **Athletics (Intercollegiate):** *Men:* baseball, basketball, cheerleading, crew/rowing, cross-country, football, golf, gymnastics, soccer, table tennis, tennis, track/field (outdoor), track/field (indoor). *Women:* basketball, cheerleading, crew/rowing, cross-country, fencing, field hockey, gymnastics, lacrosse, soccer, softball, table tennis, tennis, track/field (outdoor), track/field (indoor), volleyball. **On-Campus Highlights:** The Tech Center, Howard Gittis Student Center, Liacouras Center (athletic/convocation center), The Shops at Liacouras Walk, Bell Tower, 6. Independence Blue Cross Student Recreation Center 7. Alumni Circle 8. Rock Hall 9. Student Pavilion 10. Campus mall. **Environmental Initiatives:** President Hart signed the American College and University Presidents Climate Commitment in April 2008.

ADMISSIONS

Freshman Academic Profile: Average high school GPA 3.6. 24% in top 10% of high school class, 58% in top 25% of high school class, 92% in top 50% of high school class. **Reported SAT (pre-2016 redesign) scores:** SAT Math middle 50% range 530-650. SAT Critical Reading middle 50% range 520-630. SAT Writing middle 50% range 510-620. **Concordant SAT scores:** SAT EBRW middle 50% 570–680. SAT Math middle 50% range 560–670. ACT middle 50% range 24-30. Minimum internet-based TOEFL 79. Minimum paper TOEFL 550. **Basis for Candidate Selection:** *Very important factors considered include:* rigor of secondary school record, academic GPA. *Important factors considered include:* class rank, standardized test scores. *Other factors considered include:* application essay, recommendation(s), extracurricular activities, talent/ability, character/personal qualities, alumni/ae relation, geographical residence, state residency, volunteer work, work experience, level of applicant's interest. **Freshman Admission Requirements:** High school diploma is required and GED is accepted. *Academic units required:* 4 English, 3 math, 2 science, 1 science lab, 2 foreign language, 2 social studies, 1 history, 1 academic elective. *Academic units recommended:* 4 English, 4 math, 3 science, 2 science labs, 2 foreign language, 2 social studies, 1 history, 3 academic electives. **Freshman Admission Statistics:** 33,139 applied, 52.19% admitted, 30% enrolled. **Transfer Admission Requirements:** High school transcript, college transcript(s), essay or personal statement, Minimum college GPA of 2.50 required. Lowest grade transferable C. **General Admission Information:** Application fee $55. Regular application deadline 3/1. Nonfall registration accepted. Admission may be deferred for a maximum of 1 year.

COSTS AND FINANCIAL AID

Annual in-state tuition $15,384. Annual out-of-state tuition $26,376. Room and board $11,478. Required fees $890. Average book expense $1,000. **Required Forms and Deadlines:** FAFSA. **Notification of Awards:** Applicants will be notified of awards on a rolling basis beginning 2/15. **Types of Aid:** *Need-based scholarships/grants:* Federal Pell, FSEOG, State scholarships/grants, Private scholarships, College/university scholarship or grant aid from institutional funds, Federal Nursing Scholarships. *Loans:* Direct Subsidized Stafford Loans, Direct Unsubsidized Stafford Loans, Direct PLUS loans, Federal Perkins Loans, Federal Nursing Loans, State Loans, College/university loans from institutional funds. *Student Employment:* Federal Work-Study Program available. Institutional employment available. **Financial Aid Statistics:** 85% needy freshmen, 84% needy undergrads receive need-based scholarship or grant aid. 58% freshmen, 45% undergrads receive non-need-based scholarship or grant aid. 77% freshmen, 83% undergrads receive need-based self-help aid. 2% freshmen, 2% undergrads receive athletic scholarships. 90% freshmen, 83% undergrads receive any aid. 77% undergrads borrow to pay for school. Average cumulative indebtedness $37,708. **Criteria for awarding aid:** *Non-need-based:* Academics, Art, Athletics, Music/drama.

See page 1062.

TENNESSEE STATE UNIVERSITY

3500 John Merritt Boulevard, Nashville, 37209-1561
Phone: 615-963-3101
E-mail: jcade@tnstate.edu
Fax: 615-963-5108 • **Website:** www.tnstate.edu

This is a public school.

RATINGS

Admissions Selectivity Rating: 80 **Fire Safety Rating:** 60* **Green Rating:** 60*

STUDENTS AND FACULTY

Enrollment: 7,000. **Student Body:** 63% female, 37% male, 49% out-of-state, 1% international. Asian 1%, African American 83%, Caucasian 15%, Hispanic 1%, Native American 0%, Pacific Islander 0%, Two or more races 0%, Race unknown 0%.
Retention and Graduation: 77% freshmen return for sophomore year.
Faculty: Student/faculty ratio 22:1. 383 full-time faculty, 74% hold PhDs, 37% are are members of minority groups, 42% are women.

ACADEMICS

Degrees: associate, bachelor's, master's. **Classes:** Most classes have fewer than 10 students. Most lab/discussion sessions have 10-19 students. **Special Study Options:** cooperative education program, cross-registration, double major, exchange student program (domestic), honors program, independent study, internships, liberal arts/career combination, teacher certification program, On-line Degree (courses offered via computer approved by Tennessee Board of Regents).

FACILITIES

Housing: Coed dorms, men's dorms, women's dorms, apartments for single students.

CAMPUS LIFE

Activities: Choral groups, drama/theater, jazz band, marching band, music ensembles, radio station, student government, student newspaper, yearbook.

ADMISSIONS

Freshman Academic Profile: Average high school GPA 3.0. 90% from public high schools. **Reported SAT (pre-2016 redesign) scores:** SAT Math middle 50% range 430-510. SAT Critical Reading middle 50% range 430-510. **Concordant SAT scores:** SAT Math middle 50% range 470–540. ACT middle 50% range 18-21. Minimum paper TOEFL 500. **Basis for Candidate Selection:** *Very important factors considered include:* standardized test scores, state residency. *Important factors considered include:* rigor of secondary school record, class rank, recommendation(s), geographical residence. *Other factors considered include:* extracurricular activities, talent/ability, character/personal qualities, alumni/ae relation. **Freshman Admission Requirements:** High school diploma is required and GED is accepted. *Academic units required:* 4 English, 3 math, 2 science, 1 science lab, 2 foreign language, 1 social studies, 1 history, 1 academic elective. **Freshman Admission Statistics:** 6,344 applied, 34.68% admitted, 59% enrolled. **Transfer Admission Requirements:** college transcript(s), Minimum college GPA of 2.9 required. Lowest grade transferable C. **General Admission Information:** Application fee $15. Regular application deadline 8/1.

COSTS AND FINANCIAL AID

Annual in-state tuition $3,272. Annual out-of-state tuition $10,230. Room and board $3,060. Required fees $150. Average book expense $850. **Required Forms and Deadlines:** FAFSA, CSS/Financial Aid PROFILE, Noncustodial PROFILE. **Types of Aid:** *Need-based scholarships/grants:* Federal Pell, FSEOG. *Loans:* Direct Subsidized Stafford Loans, Direct Unsubsidized Stafford Loans, Direct PLUS loans, Federal Perkins Loans. *Student Employment:* Federal Work-Study Program available. Institutional employment available. **Financial Aid Statistics:** 66% needy freshmen, 64% needy undergrads receive need-based scholarship or grant aid. 25% freshmen, 24% undergrads receive non-need-based scholarship or grant aid. 77% freshmen, 76% undergrads receive need-based self-help aid. 1% freshmen receive athletic scholarships. **Criteria for awarding aid:** *Need-based:* Academics, Athletics.

TENNESSEE TECHNOLOGICAL UNIVERSITY

PO Box 5006, Cookeville, TN 38505
Phone: 931-372-3888 • **Financial Aid Phone:** 931-372-3073
E-mail: admissions@tntech.edu • **CEEB Code:** 1804
Fax: 931-372-6250 • **Website:** www.tntech.edu • **ACT Code:** 4012

This public school was founded in 1915. It has a 235-acre campus.

RATINGS
Admissions Selectivity Rating: 78   **Fire Safety Rating:** 80   **Green Rating:** 77

STUDENTS AND FACULTY
Enrollment: 9,647. **Student Body:** 45% female, 55% male, 3% out-of-state, 6% international. Asian 1%, African American 4%, Caucasian 84%, Hispanic 2%, Native American <1%, Pacific Islander <1%, Two or more races 2%, Race unknown <1%.
Retention and Graduation: 70% freshmen return for sophomore year. 20% freshmen graduate within 4 years. **Faculty:** Student/faculty ratio 21:1. 389 full-time faculty, 72% hold PhDs, 13% are are members of minority groups, 40% are women. 1% of classes are taught by teaching assistants.

ACADEMICS
Degrees: bachelor's, doctoral, master's, post-master's certificate. **Classes:** Most classes have 20-29 students. Most lab/discussion sessions have 20-29 students. **Most popular majors:** Elementary Education and Teaching; Mechanical Engineering; Business/Commerce. **Special Study Options:** cooperative education program, distance learning, double major, dual enrollment, honors program, internships, study abroad, teacher certification program. **Disability Services:** Special programs offered to physically disabled students, including note-taking services, reader services, tape recorders, tutors. **Career Services:** Alumni network, Alumni services, Career/job search classes, Internships, Regional alumni.

FACILITIES
Housing: Coed dorms, special housing for disabled students, men's dorms, special housing for international students, women's dorms, apartments for married students, apartments for single students. 99% of campus accessible to physically diasbled. **Special Academic Facilities/Equipment:** 300-acre farm lab, electric power center, water resources center, manufacturing center. **Computers:** Students can register for classes online. Administrative functions (other than registration) can be performed online.

CAMPUS LIFE
Environment: Rural. **Activities:** Choral groups, concert band, dance, drama/theater, jazz band, literary magazine, marching band, music ensembles, musical theater, opera, pep band, radio station, student government, student newspaper, symphony orchestra, television station, yearbook. 182 registered organizations, 26 honor societies, 16 religious organizations. 12 fraternities, 8 sororities. **Athletics (Intercollegiate):** *Men:* baseball, basketball, cheerleading, cross-country, football, golf, riflery, tennis. *Women:* basketball, cheerleading, cross-country, golf, riflery, soccer, softball, tennis, track/field (outdoor), track/field (indoor), volleyball. **On-Campus Highlights:** Recreation/ Fitness Center, Barnes and Noble Bookstore, Joan Derryberry Art Gallery, New Residence Halls, Bryan Fine Arts Music Auditorium.

ADMISSIONS
Freshman Academic Profile: Average high school GPA 3.4. 24% in top 10% of high school class, 50% in top 25% of high school class, 82% in top 50% of high school class. 80% from public high schools. **Reported SAT (pre-2016 redesign) scores:** SAT Math middle 50% range 490-640. SAT Critical Reading middle 50% range 480-600. **Concordant SAT scores:** SAT Math middle 50% range 520–660. ACT middle 50% range 20-26. Minimum paper TOEFL 500. **Basis for Candidate Selection:** *Very important factors considered include:* rigor of secondary school record, academic GPA, standardized test scores. *Other factors considered include:* application essay, recommendation(s), interview, extracurricular activities, character/personal qualities, alumni/ae relation. **Freshman Admission Requirements:** High school diploma is required and GED is accepted. *Academic units required:* 4 English, 3 math, 2 science, 1 science lab, 2 foreign language, 1 social studies, 1 history, and 1 unit from above areas or other academic areas. **Freshman Admission Statistics:** 4,553 applied, 93.94% admitted, 45% enrolled. **Transfer Admission Requirements:** college transcript(s), Minimum college GPA of 2.0 required. Lowest grade transferable D. **General Admission Information:** Application fee $25. Priority deadline 12/15. Regular application deadline 8/1. Nonfall registration accepted. Admission may be deferred for a maximum of 1 semester.

COSTS AND FINANCIAL AID
Annual in-state tuition $5,004. Annual out-of-state tuition $18,000. Room and board $7,382. Required fees $1,034. Average book expense $1,500. **Required Forms and Deadlines:** FAFSA. **Notification of Awards:** Applicants will be notified of awards on a rolling basis beginning 3/15. **Types of Aid:** *Need-based scholarships/grants:* Federal Pell, FSEOG, State scholarships/grants, Private scholarships, College/university scholarship or grant aid from institutional funds, United Negro College Fund. *Loans:* Direct Subsidized Stafford Loans, Direct Unsubsidized Stafford Loans, Direct PLUS loans, Federal Perkins Loans, College/university loans from institutional funds. *Student Employment:* Federal Work-Study Program available. Institutional employment available. **Financial Aid Statistics:** 61% needy freshmen, 63% needy undergrads receive need-based scholarship or grant aid. 91% freshmen, 68% undergrads receive non-need-based scholarship or grant aid. 50% freshmen, 59% undergrads receive need-based self-help aid. 2% freshmen, 2% undergrads receive athletic scholarships. 91% freshmen, 89% undergrads receive any aid. **Criteria for awarding aid:** *Need-based:* Academics, Athletics. *Non-need-based:* Academics, Alumni affiliation, Art, Athletics, Leadership, Minority status, Music/drama.

TEXAS A&M UNIVERSITY AT GALVESTON

Admissions Office, Galveston, TX 77553
Phone: 409-740-4414 • **Financial Aid Phone:** 409-740-4418
E-mail: seaaggie@tamug.edu • **CEEB Code:** 6835
Fax: 409-740-4731 • **Website:** www.tamug.edu • **ACT Code:** 6592

This public school was founded in 1963. It has a 150-acre campus.

RATINGS
Admissions Selectivity Rating: 89   **Fire Safety Rating:** 92   **Green Rating:** 72

STUDENTS AND FACULTY
Enrollment: 50,415. **Student Body:** 49% female, 51% male, 13% out-of-state, 1% international (19 countries represented). Asian 6%, African American 3%, Caucasian 63%, Hispanic 23%, Native American <1%, Pacific Islander <1%, Two or more races 3%, Race unknown <1%.
Retention and Graduation: 91% freshmen return for sophomore year. 52% freshmen graduate within 4 years. 80% freshmen graduate within 6 years. **Faculty:** Student/faculty ratio 15:1. 105 full-time faculty, 61% hold PhDs, 21% are are members of minority groups, 33% are women. 3% of classes are taught by teaching assistants.

ACADEMICS
Degrees: bachelor's, doctoral, master's. **Classes:** Most classes have 10-19 students. **Most popular majors:** Naval Architecture and Marine Engineering; Marine Biology and Biological Oceanography. **Special Study Options:** Accelerated program, cooperative education program, double major, dual enrollment, independent study, internships, study abroad, teacher certification program, Merchant Marine Certification NROTC Naval Sciences. Combined degree programs: BS Ocean and Coastal Resources/MS Marine Resources Management. **Disability Services:** Special programs offered to physically disabled students, including note-taking services, reader services, tutors. **Career Services:** Alumni network, Career assessment, Internships, Regional alumni.

FACILITIES
Housing: Coed dorms, special housing for disabled students, women's dorms, Privatized apartment housing available next to campus. 90% of campus accessible to physically diasbled. **Special Academic Facilities/Equipment:** USTS Texas Clipper II, Radar School/Ship Bridge Simulator, Engineering Laboratory Building, Sea Camp, Center for Bioacoustics, Center for Marine Training and Safety/TEEX, Laboratory for Oceanographic and Environmental Research, Galveston Bay Information Center, Center for Ports and Waterways, Coastal Zone Laboratory, GulfCet, Marine Mammal Research Program, Naval Science, Texas State Maritime Academy, Texas Institute of Oceanography, Texas Marine Mammal Stranding Network, Sea Turtle/Fisheries Ecology Lab. **Computers:** Students can register for classes online. Administrative functions (other than registration) can be performed online.

CAMPUS LIFE
Environment: Town. **Activities:** Choral groups, dance, drama/theater, literary magazine, student government, student newspaper, television station, yearbook. 45 registered organizations, 16 honor societies, 4 religious organizations. **Athletics (Intercollegiate):** *Men:* crew/rowing, sailing. *Women:* crew/rowing, sailing. **On-Campus Highlights:** Mary Moody Northen Student Center, P.E. Facility, Small Boat Basin, Training Ship—Sirius, Jack K. Williams Library.

ADMISSIONS
Freshman Academic Profile: 66% in top 10% of high school class, 90% in top 25% of high school class, 99% in top 50% of high school class. 81% from public high schools. **Reported SAT (pre-2016 redesign) scores:** SAT Math middle 50% range 550-670. SAT Critical Reading middle 50% range 520-640. SAT Writing middle 50% range 490-610. **Concordant SAT scores:** SAT EBRW

middle 50% 560–680. SAT Math middle 50% range 570–700. ACT middle 50% range 24-30. Minimum internet-based TOEFL 80. Minimum paper TOEFL 550. **Basis for Candidate Selection:** *Very important factors considered include:* rigor of secondary school record, class rank, standardized test scores. *Important factors considered include:* academic GPA, application essay, recommendation(s), extracurricular activities, talent/ability, character/personal qualities, volunteer work, work experience. *Other factors considered include:* interview, first generation, alumni/ae relation, level of applicant's interest. **Freshman Admission Requirements:** High school diploma is required and GED is accepted. *Academic units required:* 4 English, 3 math, 3 science, 2 science labs, 3 social studies, and 1 unit from above areas or other academic areas. *Academic units recommended:* 4 English, 4 math, 4 science, 3 foreign language, 3 social studies, and 1 unit from above areas or other academic areas. **Freshman Admission Statistics:** 34,780 applied, 67.17% admitted, 43% enrolled. **Transfer Admission Requirements:** High school transcript, college transcript(s), essay or personal statement, Minimum college GPA of 2.5 required. Lowest grade transferable C. **General Admission Information:** Application fee $75. Priority deadline 3/1. Nonfall registration accepted. Admission may be deferred for a maximum of 1 Semester.

COSTS AND FINANCIAL AID
Average book expense $1,246. **Required Forms and Deadlines:** FAFSA. **Notification of Awards:** Applicants will be notified of awards on or about 3/15. **Types of Aid:** *Need-based scholarships/grants:* Federal Pell, FSEOG, State scholarships/grants, Private scholarships, College/university scholarship or grant aid from institutional funds. *Loans:* Direct Subsidized Stafford Loans, Direct Unsubsidized Stafford Loans, Direct PLUS loans, Federal Perkins Loans, State Loans, College/university loans from institutional funds. *Student Employment:* Federal Work-Study Program available. Institutional employment available. **Financial Aid Statistics:** 75% needy freshmen, 74% needy undergrads receive need-based scholarship or grant aid. 37% freshmen, 30% undergrads receive non-need-based scholarship or grant aid. 76% freshmen, 80% undergrads receive need-based self-help aid. 0% freshmen, 0% undergrads receive athletic scholarships. 45% freshmen, 56% undergrads receive any aid. **Criteria for awarding aid:** *Need-based:* Academics, Leadership. *Non-need-based:* Academics, Leadership, State/district residency.

TEXAS A&M UNIVERSITY—COLLEGE STATION

P.O. Box 30014, College Station, TX 77843-3014
Phone: 979-845-1060 • **Financial Aid Phone:** 979-845-3236
E-mail: admissions@tamu.edu • **CEEB Code:** 6003
Fax: 979-458-1808 • **Website:** www.tamu.edu • **ACT Code:** 4198

This public school was founded in 1876. It has a 5200-acre campus.

RATINGS
Admissions Selectivity Rating: 89 **Fire Safety Rating:** 95 **Green Rating:** 91

STUDENTS AND FACULTY
Enrollment: 50,415. **Student Body:** 49% female, 51% male, 4% out-of-state, 1% international (77 countries represented). Asian 6%, African American 3%, Caucasian 63%, Hispanic 23%, Native American <1%, Pacific Islander <1%, Two or more races 3%, Race unknown <1%.
Retention and Graduation: 91% freshmen return for sophomore year. 52% freshmen graduate within 4 years. 80% freshmen graduate within 6 years. **Faculty:** Student/faculty ratio 21:1. 3,048 full-time faculty, 89% hold PhDs, 28% are are members of minority groups, 34% are women. 17% of classes are taught by teaching assistants.

ACADEMICS
Degrees: bachelor's, doctoral/professional, doctoral/research, master's, postbachelor's certifiate, post-master's certificate. **Classes:** Most classes have 20-29 students. Most lab/discussion sessions have 20-29 students. **Most popular majors:** Engineering; Biomedical Sciences; Business Administration and Management. **Special Study Options:** Accelerated program, cooperative education program, cross-registration, distance learning, double major, dual enrollment, English as a Second Language (ESL), exchange student program (domestic), honors program, independent study, internships, study abroad, teacher certification program. **Disability Services:** Special programs offered to physically disabled students, including note-taking services, reader services, tape recorders, tutors. **Career Services:** Alumni network, Alumni services, Career/job search classes, Career assessment, Internships, Regional alumni.

Students receive personalized career assistance tailored to their majors by career consultants who have both career experience and education related to the disciplines they serve. Combined, these staff members have over 200 years of professional experience in industry and education. The Career Consultants help students gain career clarity through in-depth advising, valuable networking contacts, and expert job search assistance. To further ensure that students are successful upon graduation, Texas A&M University is dedicating staff to assist freshmen and sophomores in their career development process. As parents and students are concerned about the costs of a college education, it is critical that students optimize their use of resources available to them to achieve post-graduation goals. Students can participate in various hands-on learning experiences as early as their freshmen year. Options are available that will both meet student interests and develop key professional skills, including externships, one-day shadowing experiences at corporate sites; internships; and Cooperative Education. Texas A&M University is a highly recruited university. More than 5,000 employers representing business entities, non-profit organizations, and government agencies posted jobs, interviewed students, or attended Career Fairs in 2014-15.

FACILITIES
Housing: Coed dorms, special housing for disabled students, men's dorms, women's dorms, fraternity/sorority housing, apartments for married students, cooperative housing, apartments for single students, Theme Housing, Honors Dorm. 85% of campus accessible to physically diasbled. **Special Academic Facilities/Equipment:** Bush Library/Museum; Jordan International Collection; Corps of Cadets Center/Museum; Forsyth Center Gallary; MSC Visual Arts Gallary; J.Wayne Stark University Center Gallaries Oran W. Nicks Low Speed Wind Tunnel Astronomical Observatory Ocean Drilling Program Building **Computers:** 100% of classrooms, 10% of dorms, 100% of libraries, 100% of dining areas, 100% of student union, have wireless network access. Students can register for classes online. Administrative functions (other than registration) can be performed online.

CAMPUS LIFE
Environment: City. **Activities:** Choral groups, concert band, dance, drama/theater, jazz band, literary magazine, marching band, music ensembles, musical theater, radio station, student government, student newspaper, student-run film society, symphony orchestra, television station, yearbook, Campus Ministries, Student Organization. 725 registered organizations, 34 honor societies, 77 religious organizations. 33 fraternities, 23 sororities. **Athletics (Intercollegiate):** *Men:* baseball, basketball, cross-country, diving, football, golf, riflery, swimming, tennis, track/field (outdoor), track/field (indoor). *Women:* basketball, cross-country, diving, equestrian sports, golf, riflery, soccer, softball, swimming, tennis, track/field (outdoor), track/field (indoor), volleyball. **On-Campus Highlights:** Student Recreation Center, Kyle Field, Corps of Cadets, George Bush Presidential Library/Museum, Research Park. **Environmental Initiatives:** Energy Stewardship Program.

ADMISSIONS
Freshman Academic Profile: 66% in top 10% of high school class, 90% in top 25% of high school class, 99% in top 50% of high school class. **Reported SAT (pre-2016 redesign) scores:** SAT Math middle 50% range 550-670. SAT Critical Reading middle 50% range 520-640. SAT Writing middle 50% range 490-610. **Concordant SAT scores:** SAT EBRW middle 50% 560–680. SAT Math middle 50% range 570–700. ACT middle 50% range 24-30. Minimum internet-based TOEFL 80. Minimum paper TOEFL 550. **Basis for Candidate Selection:** *Very important factors considered include:* rigor of secondary school record, class rank, academic GPA, standardized test scores, extracurricular activities, talent/ability. *Important factors considered include:* application essay, first generation, geographical residence, state residency, volunteer work, work experience. *Other factors considered include:* recommendation(s), character/personal qualities, level of applicant's interest. **Freshman Admission Requirements:** High school diploma is required and GED is accepted. *Academic units required:* 4 English, 3 math, 3 science, 1 science lab, 2 foreign language, 3 social studies, 5 academic electives, 1 visual/performing arts, and 1 unit from above areas or other academic areas. *Academic units recommended:* 4 English, 4 math, 4 science, 2 science labs, 2 foreign language, 4 social studies, 7 academic electives, 1 visual/performing arts, and 1 unit from above areas or other academic areas. **Freshman Admission Statistics:** 35,494 applied, 66.47% admitted, 43% enrolled. **Transfer Admission Requirements:** High school transcript, college transcript(s), Minimum college GPA of 2.5 required. Lowest grade transferable D. **General Admission Information:** Application fee $75. Regular application deadline 12/1. Nonfall registration accepted.

COSTS AND FINANCIAL AID
Annual in-state tuition $6,679. Annual out-of-state tuition $26,857. Room and board $10,368. Required fees $3,351. Average book expense $1,054. **Required Forms and Deadlines:** FAFSA. **Notification of Awards:** Applicants will be notified of awards on a rolling basis beginning 4/1. **Types of Aid:** *Need-based scholarships/grants:* Federal Pell, FSEOG, State scholarships/grants, Private scholarships, College/university scholarship or grant aid from institutional funds. *Loans:* Direct Subsidized Stafford Loans, Direct Unsubsidized Stafford Loans, Direct PLUS loans, Federal Perkins Loans, State Loans, College/

university loans from institutional funds. *Student Employment:* Federal Work-Study Program available. Institutional employment available. **Financial Aid Statistics:** 94% needy freshmen, 82% needy undergrads receive need-based scholarship or grant aid. 12% freshmen, 7% undergrads receive non-need-based scholarship or grant aid. 54% freshmen, 60% undergrads receive need-based self-help aid. 0% freshmen, 1% undergrads receive athletic scholarships. 75% freshmen, 70% undergrads receive any aid. Average cumulative indebtedness $24,072. **Criteria for awarding aid:** *Need-based:* Academics. *Non-need-based:* Academics, Alumni affiliation, Art, Athletics, Job skills, Leadership, Music/drama, Religious affiliation, State/district residency.

TEXAS A&M UNIVERSITY—KINGSVILLE

MSC 105, Kingsville, TX 78363
Phone: 361-593-2315
E-mail: ksossrx@tamuk.edu
Fax: 361-593-2195 • **Website:** www.tamuk.edu

This is a public school.

RATINGS
Admissions Selectivity Rating: 61   **Fire Safety Rating:** 60*   **Green Rating:** 60*

STUDENTS AND FACULTY
Enrollment: 4,377. **Student Body:** 47% female, 53% male, 2% out-of-state, 1% international. Asian 1%, African American 5%, Caucasian 27%, Hispanic 66%, Native American <1%, Pacific Islander 0%, Two or more races 0%, Race unknown <1%.
Retention and Graduation: 59% freshmen return for sophomore year.
Faculty: Student/faculty ratio 15:1. 276 full-time faculty, 70% hold PhDs, 24% are are members of minority groups, 35% are women.

ACADEMICS
Degrees: bachelor's, master's, postbachelor's certificate, post-master's certificate. **Classes:** Most classes have 10-19 students. Most lab/discussion sessions have 20-29 students. **Special Study Options:** Accelerated program, cooperative education program, distance learning, double major, English as a Second Language (ESL), honors program, internships, study abroad, teacher certification program.

FACILITIES
Housing: Coed dorms, men's dorms, women's dorms, apartments for married students.

CAMPUS LIFE
Activities: Choral groups, concert band, dance, drama/theater, jazz band, marching band, music ensembles, musical theater, pep band, radio station, student government, student newspaper, television station.

ADMISSIONS
Basis for Candidate Selection: *Important factors considered include:* rigor of secondary school record, class rank, standardized test scores. **Freshman Admission Requirements:** *Academic units recommended:* 4 English, 3 math, 3 science, 3 foreign language, 4 social studies, 3 history, 3 academic electives. **Freshman Admission Statistics:** 2,105 applied, 99.38% admitted, 43% enrolled. Minimum college GPA of 2.0 required. **General Admission Information:** Application fee $15. Nonfall registration not accepted. Admission may be deferred.

COSTS AND FINANCIAL AID
Annual in-state tuition $1,380. Annual out-of-state tuition $7,590. Room and board $3,966. Required fees $1,602. Average book expense $614. **Required Forms and Deadlines:** FAFSA. *Student Employment:* Federal Work-Study Program available. Institutional employment available. **Financial Aid Statistics:** 92% needy freshmen, 100% needy undergrads receive need-based scholarship or grant aid. 31% freshmen, 71% undergrads receive non-need-based scholarship or grant aid. 87% freshmen, 82% undergrads receive need-based self-help aid. 0% freshmen, 0% undergrads receive athletic scholarships.

TEXAS A&M UNIVERSITY—TEXARKANA

P.O. Box 5518, Texarkana, TX 75505
Phone: 903-223-3069
E-mail: admissions@tamut.edu
Fax: 903-223-3140

This public school was founded in 1971. It has a 1-acre campus.

RATINGS
Admissions Selectivity Rating: 60*   **Fire Safety Rating:** 60*   **Green Rating:** 60*

STUDENTS AND FACULTY
Enrollment: 1,046. **Student Body:** 71% female, 29% male, <1% international. Asian 1%, African American 15%, Caucasian 76%, Hispanic 6%, Native American 1%, Pacific Islander 0%, Two or more races 0%, Race unknown <1%.
Faculty: Student/faculty ratio 13:1. 59 full-time faculty, 0% hold PhDs, 15% are are members of minority groups, 41% are women.

ACADEMICS
Degrees: bachelor's, master's. **Most popular majors:** General Studies; Multi-/Interdisciplinary Studies; Accounting. **Special Study Options:** cross-registration, distance learning, independent study, internships, liberal arts/career combination, study abroad, teacher certification program. **Disability Services:** Special programs offered to physically disabled students, including note-taking services, tape recorders. **Career Services:** Career/job search classes.

FACILITIES
Housing: 100% of campus accessible to physically disabled. **Computers:** Students can register for classes online. Administrative functions (other than registration) can be performed online.

CAMPUS LIFE
Environment: Village. **Activities:** student government, student newspaper. 20 registered organizations, 5 honor societies, 1 religious organization.

ADMISSIONS
Minimum paper TOEFL 550. **Transfer Admission Requirements:** college transcript(s), Minimum college GPA of 2.0 required. Lowest grade transferable D. **General Admission Information:** Nonfall registration not accepted.

COSTS AND FINANCIAL AID
Average book expense $0. **Required Forms and Deadlines:** FAFSA, Institution's own financial aid form. **Notification of Awards:** Applicants will be notified of awards on or about 6/1. **Types of Aid:** *Need-based scholarships/grants:* Federal Pell, FSEOG, State scholarships/grants, Private scholarships, College/university scholarship or grant aid from institutional funds. *Loans:* College/university loans from institutional funds. *Student Employment:* Federal Work-Study Program available. **Financial Aid Statistics:** freshmen, 0% undergrads receive non-need-based scholarship or grant aid. 0% undergrads receive need-based self-help aid. 0% undergrads receive athletic scholarships. **Criteria for awarding aid:** *Need-based:* Academics. *Non-need-based:* Academics, Alumni affiliation, Leadership, State/district residency.

TEXAS CHRISTIAN UNIVERSITY

Office of Admissions, Fort Worth, TX 76129
Phone: 817-257-7490 • **Financial Aid Phone:** 817-257-7858
E-mail: frogmail@tcu.edu • **CEEB Code:** 6820
Fax: 817-257-7268 • **Website:** www.tcu.edu • **ACT Code:** 4206

This private school, affiliated with the Disciples of Christ Church, was founded in 1873. It has a 300-acre campus.

RATINGS
Admissions Selectivity Rating: 91   **Fire Safety Rating:** 92   **Green Rating:** 77

STUDENTS AND FACULTY
Enrollment: 8,852. **Student Body:** 60% female, 40% male, 46% out-of-state, 5% international (70 countries represented). Asian 3%, African American 5%, Caucasian 72%, Hispanic 12%, Native American 1%, Pacific Islander <1%, Two or more races <1%, Race unknown 2%.

Retention and Graduation: 91% freshmen return for sophomore year. 63% freshmen graduate within 4 years. 77% freshmen graduate within 6 years. 21% grads go on to further study within 1 year. **Faculty:** Student/faculty ratio 13:1. 641 full-time faculty, 85% hold PhDs, 16% are are members of minority groups, 47% are women. 1% of classes are taught by teaching assistants.

ACADEMICS

Degrees: bachelor's, certificate, master's, postbachelor's certificate. **Classes:** Most classes have 10-19 students. Most lab/discussion sessions have 20-29 students. **Most popular majors:** Registered Nursing/Registered Nurse; Finance; Speech Communication and Rhetoric. **Special Study Options:** Accelerated program, cross-registration, distance learning, double major, dual enrollment, English as a Second Language (ESL), honors program, independent study, internships, liberal arts/career combination, study abroad, teacher certification program. **Honors Programs:** John V. Roach Honors College The Honors College offers programs for students of all majors and complements all areas of study on campus. Entering freshmen who complete the Honors College requirements will graduate with a John V. Roach Honors College Diploma, as well as a specialized degree from the college of their chosen major(s). Combined degree programs: BSE/MED. **Disability Services:** Special programs offered to physically disabled students, including note-taking services. **Career Services:** Alumni network, Alumni services, Career/job search classes, Career assessment, Internships, Regional alumni. Career development/job search classes enable us to reach more students in an educational setting which adds credibility to our message. We have 3 dedicated career courses, 2 for credit; make an average of 150 class and club presentations a year; provide over 20 workshop and networking events for individual colleges and the athletic program per year. We have established two intern scholarship funds that provide students scholarships for unpaid internships; one fund is dedicated to non-profit organization internships and the other to general and international internships.

FACILITIES

Housing: Coed dorms, men's dorms, women's dorms, fraternity/sorority housing, apartments for married students, apartments for single students, Wellness Housing, ThemeHousingDesignated rooms available for ADA needs. 99% of campus accessible to physically disabled. **Special Academic Facilities/Equipment:** Art exhibition hall, Tandy film library, speech/hearing clinic, TV studios, computer labs, observatory, Moncrief Meteorite, special collections, alumni and visitors center, cable TV, radio station, performance hall, variety of athletic facilities. **Computers:** 100% of classrooms, 100% of dorms, 100% of libraries, 100% of dining areas, 100% of student union, 100% of common outdoor areas have wireless network access. Students can register for classes online. Administrative functions (other than registration) can be performed online.

CAMPUS LIFE

Environment: Metropolis. **Activities:** Choral groups, concert band, dance, drama/theater, jazz band, literary magazine, marching band, music ensembles, musical theater, opera, pep band, radio station, student government, student newspaper, television station, yearbook, Campus Ministries, Student Organization, Model UN. 200 registered organizations, 29 honor societies, 17 religious organizations. 15 fraternities, 18 sororities. **Athletics (Intercollegiate):** *Men:* baseball, basketball, cross-country, diving, football, golf, swimming, tennis, track/field (outdoor), track/field (indoor). *Women:* basketball, cross-country, diving, equestrian sports, golf, riflery, soccer, swimming, tennis, track/field (outdoor), track/field (indoor), volleyball. **On-Campus Highlights:** Amon Carter Stadium, University Recreation Center, Monnig Meteorite Collection, Brown-Lupton University Union, Campus Commons/Frog Fountain. **Environmental Initiatives:** American Colleges and Universities President's Climate Commitment.

ADMISSIONS

Freshman Academic Profile: 44% in top 10% of high school class, 74% in top 25% of high school class, 93% in top 50% of high school class. 58% from public high schools. **Reported SAT (pre-2016 redesign) scores:** SAT Math middle 50% range 540-650. SAT Critical Reading middle 50% range 530-630. SAT Writing middle 50% range 520-650. **Concordant SAT scores:** SAT EBRW middle 50% 580–690. SAT Math middle 50% range 570–670. ACT middle 50% range 25-30. Minimum internet-based TOEFL 80. Minimum paper TOEFL 550. **Basis for Candidate Selection:** *Very important factors considered include:* rigor of secondary school record, class rank, academic GPA. *Important factors considered include:* standardized test scores, application essay, recommendation(s), extracurricular activities, character/personal qualities, first generation, alumni/ae relation, racial/ethnic status. *Other factors considered include:* interview, talent/ability, geographical residence, state residency, religious affiliation/commitment, volunteer work, work experience, level of applicant's interest. **Freshman Admission Requirements:** High school diploma is required and GED is not accepted. *Academic units required:* 4 English, 3 math, 3 science, 1 science lab, 2 foreign language, 3 social studies, 2 academic electives. *Academic units recommended:* 4 English, 4 math, 4 science, 1 science lab, 4 foreign language, 4 social studies. **Freshman Admission**

Statistics: 19,972 applied, 37.58% admitted, 25% enrolled. **Transfer Admission Requirements:** college transcript(s), essay or personal statement, Minimum college GPA of 2.0 required. Lowest grade transferable C. **General Admission Information:** Application fee $40. Regular application deadline 2/15. Regular notification 4/1. Nonfall registration accepted. Admission may be deferred for a maximum of 1 year (with exceptions).

COSTS AND FINANCIAL AID

Required Forms and Deadlines: FAFSA, CSS/Financial Aid PROFILE, Noncustodial PROFILE. **Notification of Awards:** Applicants will be notified of awards on a rolling basis beginning 3/15. **Types of Aid:** *Need-based scholarships/grants:* Federal Pell, FSEOG, State scholarships/grants, Private scholarships, College/university scholarship or grant aid from institutional funds. *Loans:* Direct Subsidized Stafford Loans, Direct Unsubsidized Stafford Loans, Direct PLUS loans, Federal Perkins Loans, Federal Nursing Loans, State Loans. *Student Employment:* Federal Work-Study Program available. Institutional employment available. **Financial Aid Statistics:** 94% needy freshmen, 93% needy undergrads receive need-based scholarship or grant aid. 68% freshmen, 62% undergrads receive non-need-based scholarship or grant aid. 72% freshmen, 76% undergrads receive need-based self-help aid. 4% freshmen, 4% undergrads receive athletic scholarships. 77% freshmen, 76% undergrads receive any aid. 37% undergrads borrow to pay for school. Average cumulative indebtedness $36,550. **Criteria for awarding aid:** *Non-need-based:* Academics, Alumni affiliation, Art, Minority status, Music/drama, Religious affiliation, State/district residency.

TEXAS LUTHERAN UNIVERSITY

1000 West Court Street, Seguin, TX 78155
Phone: 830-372-8050 • **Financial Aid Phone:** 830-372-8078
E-mail: admissions@tlu.edu
Fax: 830-372-8096 • **Website:** www.tlu.edu

This private school, affiliated with the Lutheran Church, was founded in 1891. It has a 184-acre campus.

RATINGS

Admissions Selectivity Rating: 85   **Fire Safety Rating:** 87   **Green Rating:** 60*

STUDENTS AND FACULTY

Enrollment: 1,252. **Student Body:** 51% female, 49% male, 2% out-of-state, <1% international (12 countries represented). Asian 1%, African American 10%, Caucasian 54%, Hispanic 32%, Native American <1%, Pacific Islander 0%, Two or more races 1%, Race unknown 2%.
Retention and Graduation: 68% freshmen return for sophomore year. 30% freshmen graduate within 4 years. 52% freshmen graduate within 6 years. **Faculty:** Student/faculty ratio 16:1. 82 full-time faculty, 84% hold PhDs, 18% are are members of minority groups, 52% are women. 0% of classes are taught by teaching assistants.

ACADEMICS

Degrees: bachelor's, master's. **Classes:** Most classes have 10-19 students. **Most popular majors:** Education; Business/Commerce; Kinesiology and Exercise Science. **Special Study Options:** double major, dual enrollment, exchange student program (domestic), honors program, independent study, internships, study abroad, teacher certification program, senior seminars. Combined degree programs: BBA/MACCY. **Disability Services:** Special programs offered to physically disabled students, including note-taking services, reader services, tutors. **Career Services:** Alumni network, Alumni services, Career/job search classes, Internships.

FACILITIES

Housing: Coed dorms, men's dorms, women's dorms, apartments for married students, apartments for single students. 95% of campus accessible to physically disabled. **Special Academic Facilities/Equipment:** Mexican-American studies center, geological museum. **Computers:** 100% of classrooms, 100% of dorms, 100% of libraries, 100% of dining areas, 100% of student union, 100% of common outdoor areas have wireless network access. Students can register for classes online. Administrative functions (other than registration) can be performed online.

CAMPUS LIFE

Environment: Town. **Activities:** Choral groups, concert band, dance, drama/theater, jazz band, literary magazine, music ensembles, musical theater, pep band, student government, student newspaper, symphony orchestra, Campus Ministries, Student Organization. 53 registered organizations, 10 honor societies, 3 religious organizations. 5 fraternities, 4 sororities. **Athletics (Intercollegiate):** *Men:* baseball, basketball, football, golf, soccer, tennis. *Women:* basketball, cross-country, golf, soccer, softball, tennis, track/field (outdoor), track/field (indoor), volleyball. **On-Campus Highlights:** Lucky's Snack Shack, Fitness Center, Alumni Student Center, Residence Halls, Hein Dining Hall. **Environmental Initiatives:** Installation of more efficient HVAC system campus wide.

ADMISSIONS

Freshman Academic Profile: Average high school GPA 3.6. 20% in top 10% of high school class, 51% in top 25% of high school class, 85% in top 50% of high school class. 94% from public high schools. **Reported SAT (pre-2016 redesign) scores:** SAT Math middle 50% range 450-540. SAT Critical Reading middle 50% range 430-540. SAT Writing middle 50% range 410-510. **Concordant SAT scores:** SAT EBRW middle 50% 470–580. SAT Math middle 50% range 490–570. ACT middle 50% range 18-23. Minimum internet-based TOEFL 80. Minimum paper TOEFL 550. **Basis for Candidate Selection:** *Very important factors considered include:* rigor of secondary school record, class rank, academic GPA, standardized test scores, application essay, recommendation(s). *Important factors considered include:* interview, talent/ability, character/personal qualities, volunteer work. *Other factors considered include:* extracurricular activities, work experience, level of applicant's interest. **Freshman Admission Requirements:** High school diploma is required and GED is accepted. *Academic units required:* 4 English, 3 math, 3 science, 2 science labs, 2 foreign language, 3 social studies, 1 academic elective. *Academic units recommended:* 4 English, 4 math, 4 science, 2 science labs, 3 foreign language, 4 social studies, 1 computer science, and 1 unit from above areas or other academic areas. **Freshman Admission Statistics:** 2,131 applied, 42.61% admitted, 42% enrolled. **Transfer Admission Requirements:** High school transcript, college transcript(s), essay or personal statement, statement of good standing from prior institution(s). Minimum college GPA of 2.25 required. Lowest grade transferable C. **General Admission Information:** Priority deadline 12/15. Regular application deadline 2/1. Nonfall registration accepted. Admission may be deferred for a maximum of 1 year.

COSTS AND FINANCIAL AID

Annual tuition $28,600. Room and board $9,720. Required fees $400. Average book expense $950. **Required Forms and Deadlines:** FAFSA, State aid form. **Notification of Awards:** Applicants will be notified of awards on a rolling basis beginning 3/1. **Types of Aid:** *Need-based scholarships/grants:* Federal Pell, FSEOG, State scholarships/grants, Private scholarships, College/university scholarship or grant aid from institutional funds. *Loans:* Direct Subsidized Stafford Loans, Direct Unsubsidized Stafford Loans, Direct PLUS loans, Federal Perkins Loans, State Loans. *Student Employment:* Federal Work-Study Program available. Institutional employment available. **Financial Aid Statistics:** 100% needy freshmen, 99% needy undergrads receive need-based scholarship or grant aid. 5% freshmen, 2% undergrads receive non-need-based scholarship or grant aid. 80% freshmen, 79% undergrads receive need-based self-help aid. 0% freshmen, 0% undergrads receive athletic scholarships. 100% freshmen, 95% undergrads receive any aid. 73% undergrads borrow to pay for school. Average cumulative indebtedness $37,337. **Criteria for awarding aid:** *Non-need-based:* Academics, Alumni affiliation, Art, Leadership, Minority status, Music/drama, Religious affiliation.

TEXAS STATE UNIVERSITY

429 North Guadalupe St., San Marcos, TX 78666
Phone: 512-245-2364 • **Financial Aid Phone:** 512-245 2315
E-mail: admissions@txstate.edu • **CEEB Code:** 6667
Fax: 512-245-8044 • **Website:** www.txstate.edu • **ACT Code:** 4178

This public school was founded in 1899. It has a 455-acre campus.

RATINGS

Admissions Selectivity Rating: 78   **Fire Safety Rating:** 87   **Green Rating:** 79

STUDENTS AND FACULTY

Enrollment: 34,244. **Student Body:** 57% female, 43% male, 2% out-of-state, 1% international (66 countries represented). Asian 2%, African American 10%, Caucasian 47%, Hispanic 36%, Native American <1%, Pacific Islander <1%, Two or more races 3%, Race unknown <1%.
Retention and Graduation: 77% freshmen return for sophomore year. 27% freshmen graduate within 4 years. 54% freshmen graduate within 6 years. 14% grads go on to further study within 1 year. 9% grads pursue arts and sciences degrees. 1% grads pursue law degrees. 2% grads pursue business degrees. 1% grads pursue medical degrees. **Faculty:** Student/faculty ratio 19:1. 1,382 full-time faculty, 77% hold PhDs, 23% are are members of minority groups, 49% are women. 4% of classes are taught by teaching assistants.

ACADEMICS

Degrees: bachelor's, doctoral/professional, doctoral, master's, postbachelor's certificate. **Classes:** Most classes have 20-29 students. Most lab/discussion

sessions have 20-29 students. **Most popular majors:** Kinesiology and Exercise Science; Psychology; Multi-/Interdisciplinary Studies. **Special Study Options:** Accelerated program, distance learning, double major, dual enrollment, English as a Second Language (ESL), exchange student program (domestic), honors program, independent study, internships, study abroad, teacher certification program, weekend college, English as a Second Language is offered to international students or any students for that matter, who wish to improve their command of the English language. But it is not offered as a degree program. **Honors Programs:** To graduate in the University Honors Program, a student must complete at least five Honors Classes (which includes the Honors Thesis course) and maintain a minimum GPA of 3.25. Honors courses substitute for certain general education core curriculum and inidividual departmental requirements and thus become integral parts of the degree program. Combined degree programs: BA/MD, BA/DDS, See 2014-2016 undgrad catalog page 40. **Disability Services:** Special programs offered to physically disabled students, including note-taking services, reader services, tape recorders, tutors. **Career Services:** Alumni network, Alumni services, Career/job search classes, Career assessment, Internships. Experiential learning through the College of Education. All teacher education majors participate on practice teaching with a supervising teacher mentoring.

FACILITIES

Housing: Coed dorms, special housing for disabled students, men's dorms, women's dorms, fraternity/sorority housing, apartments for married students, apartments for single students, Non-smoking, honors, access for the disabled, but not separate housing. 90% of campus accessible to physically diasbled. **Special Academic Facilities/Equipment:** Child development center, aquifer research center, two demonstration farms, physical anthropology and archaeology laboratories. Southwestern Writer's Collection. Observatory with a 17 inch telescope. **Computers:** 100% of classrooms, 100% of dorms, 100% of libraries, 100% of dining areas, 100% of student union, 100% of common outdoor areas have wireless network access. Students can register for classes online. Administrative functions (other than registration) can be performed online.

CAMPUS LIFE

Environment: Town. **Activities:** Choral groups, concert band, dance, drama/theater, jazz band, literary magazine, marching band, music ensembles, musical theater, opera, pep band, radio station, student government, student newspaper, student-run film society, symphony orchestra, yearbook, Campus Ministries, Student Organization, Model UN. 254 registered organizations, 16 honor societies, 27 religious organizations. 18 fraternities, 14 sororities. **Athletics (Intercollegiate):** *Men:* baseball, basketball, cheerleading, cross-country, football, golf, track/field (outdoor). *Women:* basketball, cheerleading, cross-country, golf, soccer, softball, tennis, track/field (outdoor), volleyball. **On-Campus Highlights:** LBJ Student Center, Alkek Library, Student Recreation Center, The Quad, Sewell Park, The Quad is a walk way that runs the length of the campus which most academic buildings open on to. Student gather here to socialize between classes. Sewell Park is a general recreational park where students gather to swim, sun bathe, throw frisbees, and play ball. The San Marcos river runs through the park. **Environmental Initiatives:** Established the Texas Rivers Systems Institute. Our programs and projects demonstrate our deep commitment to the careful stewardship of the world's freshwater resources. Through collaborative research, public advocacy, and education on river systems, the Institute affirms the unique role of water in our lives. As one of the earth's most remarkable resources, we are dedicated to preserving and protecting this irreplaceable gift—water.

ADMISSIONS

Freshman Academic Profile: 14% in top 10% of high school class, 52% in top 25% of high school class, 93% in top 50% of high school class. 98% from public high schools. **Reported SAT (pre-2016 redesign) scores:** SAT Math middle 50% range 470-560. SAT Critical Reading middle 50% range 460-560. SAT Writing middle 50% range 440-530. **Concordant SAT scores:** SAT EBRW middle 50% 500–600. SAT Math middle 50% range 510–580. ACT middle 50% range 20-25. Minimum internet-based TOEFL 78. Minimum paper TOEFL 550. **Basis for Candidate Selection:** *Very important factors considered include:* class rank, standardized test scores. *Other factors considered include:* rigor of secondary school record, application essay, extracurricular activities, talent/ability, first generation. **Freshman Admission Requirements:** High school diploma is required and GED is accepted. *Academic units required:* 4 English, 4 math, 4 science, 2 science labs, 2 foreign language, 2 social studies, 2 history, 7 academic electives, 1 visual/performing arts, and 1 unit from above areas or other academic areas. *Academic units recommended:* 4 English, 4 math, 4 science, 2 science labs, 2 foreign language, 2 social studies, 2 history, 6 academic electives, 1 visual/performing arts, and 1 unit from above areas or other academic areas. **Freshman Admission Statistics:** 21,524 applied, 70.80% admitted, 38% enrolled. **Transfer Admission Requirements:** college transcript(s), statement of good standing from prior institution(s). Minimum college GPA of 2.2 required. Lowest grade transferable D. **General Admission Information:** Application fee $75. Priority deadline 3/1. Regular application deadline 5/1. Nonfall registration accepted. Admission may be deferred.

COSTS AND FINANCIAL AID

Annual in-state tuition $7,750. Annual out-of-state tuition $19,990. Room and board $9,132. Required fees $2,468. Average book expense $820. **Required Forms and Deadlines:** FAFSA. **Notification of Awards:** Applicants will be notified of awards on a rolling basis beginning 5/1. **Types of Aid:** *Need-based scholarships/grants:* Federal Pell, FSEOG, State scholarships/grants, Private scholarships, College/university scholarship or grant aid from institutional funds. *Loans:* Direct Subsidized Stafford Loans, Direct Unsubsidized Stafford Loans, Direct PLUS loans, Federal Perkins Loans, State Loans, College/university loans from institutional funds. *Student Employment:* Federal Work-Study Program available. Institutional employment available. **Financial Aid Statistics:** 80% needy freshmen, 80% needy undergrads receive need-based scholarship or grant aid. 13% freshmen, 7% undergrads receive non-need-based scholarship or grant aid. 76% freshmen, 78% undergrads receive need-based self-help aid. 0% freshmen, 1% undergrads receive athletic scholarships. 81% freshmen, 71% undergrads receive any aid. Average cumulative indebtedness $25,246. **Criteria for awarding aid:** *Need-based:* Academics, Art, Leadership, Minority status, Music/drama. *Non-need-based:* Academics, Art, Athletics, Leadership, Minority status, Music/drama, State/district residency.

TEXAS TECH UNIVERSITY

Box 45005, Lubbock, TX 79409-5005
Phone: 806-742-1480 • **Financial Aid Phone:** 806-742-3681
E-mail: admissions@ttu.edu • **CEEB Code:** 6827
Fax: 806-742-0062 • **Website:** www.ttu.edu • **ACT Code:** 4220

This public school was founded in 1923. It has a 1839-acre campus.

RATINGS

Admissions Selectivity Rating: 84   **Fire Safety Rating:** 97   **Green Rating:** 78

STUDENTS AND FACULTY

Enrollment: 29,587. **Student Body:** 45% female, 55% male, 6% out-of-state, 5% international (88 countries represented). Asian 3%, African American 6%, Caucasian 59%, Hispanic 24%, Native American <1%, Pacific Islander <1%, Two or more races 2%, Race unknown <1%.
Retention and Graduation: 84% freshmen return for sophomore year. 34% freshmen graduate within 4 years. 60% freshmen graduate within 6 years. **Faculty:** Student/faculty ratio 21 1,526 full-time faculty, 0% hold PhDs, 14% are are members of minority groups, 40% are women. 13% of classes are taught by teaching assistants.

ACADEMICS

Degrees: bachelor's, certificate, doctoral/professional, doctoral/research, master's, postbachelor's certificate. **Classes:** Most classes have 10-19 students. Most lab/discussion sessions have 20-29 students. **Most popular majors:** Kinesiology and Exercise Science; Marketing/Marketing Management; Multi-/Interdisciplinary Studies. **Special Study Options:** Accelerated program, cooperative education program, distance learning, double major, dual enrollment, English as a Second Language (ESL), external degree program, honors program, independent study, internships, liberal arts/career combination, student-designed major, study abroad, teacher certification program. **Honors Programs:** Honors Studies is a special program under our Honors College for highly motivated and academically talented students who want to maximize their college education. It is designed to provide such students with a unique and broadly integrated intellectual experience that is complementary to virtually every major and career path. Combined degree programs: BA/MA, BA/MA; BA/MPA; BS/BS; BS/MAB; BS/MS; BS/MSA; BBA/BS; B.Arch/M.Arch; BM/MMEd. **Disability Services:** Special programs offered to physically disabled students, including note-taking services, reader services, tape recorders, tutors. **Career Services:** Alumni network, Alumni services, Career/job search classes, Career assessment, Internships, Regional alumni. Texas Tech students have actively engaged in internship programs as a vehicle to reinforce the academic subjects with real world exposure. These programs allow a student to apply what they have learned in the classroom, gain new job-related skills, and receive valuable feedback from the management team of the organization that they work with.

FACILITIES

Housing: Coed dorms, special housing for disabled students, men's dorms, women's dorms, apartments for single students. 100% of campus accessible to physically disabled. **Special Academic Facilities/Equipment:** Museum, child development center, textile research center, agricultural research center, planetarium, ranching heritage center, semi-arid land studies center, ranching heritage center, seismological observatory. **Computers:** Students can register for classes online. Administrative functions (other than registration) can be performed online.

CAMPUS LIFE

Environment: City. **Activities:** Choral groups, concert band, dance, drama/theater, jazz band, marching band, music ensembles, musical theater, pep band, radio station, student government, student newspaper, symphony orchestra, television station, yearbook, Campus Ministries, Student Organization. 399 registered organizations, 33 honor societies, 35 religious organizations. 25 fraternities, 18 sororities. **Athletics (Intercollegiate):** *Men:* baseball, basketball, cross-country, football, golf, tennis, track/field (outdoor), track/field (indoor). *Women:* basketball, cross-country, golf, soccer, softball, tennis, track/field (outdoor), track/field (indoor), volleyball. **On-Campus Highlights:** Student Union Building, Student Recreation Center, Library, Classrooms, United Spirit Arena, Jones AT&T Stadium, Museums, National Ranching and Heritage Center.

ADMISSIONS

Freshman Academic Profile: Average high school GPA 3.5. 21% in top 10% of high school class, 53% in top 25% of high school class, 87% in top 50% of high school class. 86% from public high schools. **Reported SAT (pre-2016 redesign) scores:** SAT Math middle 50% range 520-610. SAT Critical Reading middle 50% range 500-590. SAT Writing middle 50% range 470-560. **Concordant SAT scores:** SAT EBRW middle 50% 540–630. SAT Math middle 50% range 550–630. ACT middle 50% range 22-27. Minimum internet-based TOEFL 79. Minimum paper TOEFL 550. **Basis for Candidate Selection:** *Very important factors considered include:* rigor of secondary school record, class rank, academic GPA, standardized test scores. *Important factors considered include:* application essay, recommendation(s), extracurricular activities, talent/ability, character/personal qualities, volunteer work, work experience. *Other factors considered include:* first generation, geographical residence, level of applicant's interest. **Freshman Admission Requirements:** High school diploma is required and GED is accepted. *Academic units required:* 4 English, 3 math, 3 science, 3 science labs, 2 foreign language, 3 social studies, 5 academic electives, 1 visual/performing arts, and 1 unit from above areas or other academic areas. *Academic units recommended:* 4 English, 4 math, 4 science, 4 science labs, 2 foreign language, 6 academic electives, 1 visual/performing arts, and 2 units from above areas or other academic areas. **Freshman Admission Statistics:** 23,311 applied, 62.60% admitted, 33% enrolled. **Transfer Admission Requirements:** college transcript(s), statement of good standing from prior institution(s). Minimum college GPA of 2.25 required. Lowest grade transferable D-. **General Admission Information:** Application fee $60. Priority deadline 2/1. Regular application deadline 8/1. Nonfall registration accepted.

COSTS AND FINANCIAL AID

Required Forms and Deadlines: FAFSA. **Types of Aid:** *Need-based scholarships/grants:* Federal Pell, FSEOG, State scholarships/grants, Private scholarships, College/university scholarship or grant aid from institutional funds. *Loans:* Direct Subsidized Stafford Loans, Direct Unsubsidized Stafford Loans, Direct PLUS loans, Federal Perkins Loans, State Loans, College/university loans from institutional funds. *Student Employment:* Federal Work-Study Program available. Institutional employment available. **Financial Aid Statistics:** 86% needy undergrads receive need-based scholarship or grant aid. 54% freshmen, 29% undergrads receive non-need-based scholarship or grant aid. 70% freshmen, 83% undergrads receive need-based self-help aid. 1% freshmen, 0% undergrads receive athletic scholarships. 47% freshmen, 61% undergrads receive any aid. **Criteria for awarding aid:** *Need-based:* Academics, Leadership, Music/drama. *Non-need-based:* Academics, Art, Athletics, Job skills, Leadership, Music/drama.

TEXAS WOMAN'S UNIVERSITY

P.O. Box 425589, Denton, TX 76204-5589
Phone: 940-898-3188 • **Financial Aid Phone:** 940-898-3050
E-mail: admissions@twu.edu • **CEEB Code:** 6826
Fax: 940-898-3081 • **Website:** www.twu.edu • **ACT Code:** 4224

This public school was founded in 1901. It has a 270-acre campus.

RATINGS

Admissions Selectivity Rating: 73   **Fire Safety Rating:** 99   **Green Rating:** 60*

STUDENTS AND FACULTY

Enrollment: 8,668. **Student Body:** 90% female, 10% male, 0% out-of-state, 1% international (62 countries represented). Asian 8%, African American 21%, Caucasian 40%, Hispanic 25%, Native American <1%, Pacific Islander <1%, Two or more races 4%, Race unknown 1%.
Retention and Graduation: 73% freshmen return for sophomore year. 24% freshmen graduate within 4 years. 47% freshmen graduate within 6 years. 4% grads go on to further study within 1 year. **Faculty:** Student/faculty ratio 14:1.

413 full-time faculty, 0% hold PhDs, 17% are are members of minority groups, 76% are women.

ACADEMICS

Degrees: bachelor's, doctoral/professional, doctoral/research, doctoral, master's, postbachelor's certificate, post-master's certificate. **Classes:** Most classes have 10-19 students. **Special Study Options:** cross-registration, distance learning, double major, dual enrollment, honors program, independent study, internships, study abroad, teacher certification program. **Honors Programs:** Honors Scholars Program www.twu.edu/honors/index.html Combined degree programs: BA/MEng, 3-2 program with UNT. **Disability Services:** Special programs offered to physically disabled students, including note-taking services, reader services, tape recorders, tutors. **Career Services:** Internships, On-campus interviews.

FACILITIES

Housing: Coed dorms, special housing for disabled students, special housing for international students, women's dorms, apartments for married students, apartments for single students, Wellness Housing, Theme Housing. 100% of campus accessible to physically diasbled. **Special Academic Facilities/ Equipment:** Museum, radiation lab, language lab, Texas First Ladies Gown Collection, Texas Women's Hall of Fame. **Computers:** Students can register for classes online. Administrative functions (other than registration) can be performed online.

CAMPUS LIFE

Environment: City. **Activities:** Choral groups, dance, drama/theater, jazz band, music ensembles, musical theater, opera, student government, student newspaper, television station, Student Organization. 94 registered organizations, 16 honor societies, 10 religious organizations. 9 sororities. **Athletics (Intercollegiate):** *Women:* basketball, gymnastics, soccer, softball, volleyball. **On-Campus Highlights:** Student Union, Pioneer Hall, Mega Computer Lab, Guinn/Stark High Rise Resident Halls, Little Chapel-in-the-Woods, TWU has four campuses—two in Dallas, one in Houston and the 270 acre main campus in Denton. The Denton Campus houses the Texas Women's Hall of Fame and the Gowns of Texas First Ladies Collection; The Houston Campus is located in the Houston Medical Center and recently opened the new facility; The Dallas campuses have begun construction on a new multi-million dollar facility.

ADMISSIONS

Freshman Academic Profile: Average high school GPA 3.1. 14% in top 10% of high school class, 29% in top 25% of high school class, 79% in top 50% of high school class. 93% from public high schools. **Reported SAT (pre-2016 redesign) scores:** SAT Math middle 50% range 430-530. SAT Critical Reading middle 50% range 410-530. **Concordant SAT scores:** SAT Math middle 50% range 470–560. ACT middle 50% range 17-17. Minimum paper TOEFL 550. **Basis for Candidate Selection:** *Very important factors considered include:* rigor of secondary school record, class rank, academic GPA. *Important factors considered include:* standardized test scores. *Other factors considered include:* recommendation(s), first generation. **Freshman Admission Requirements:** High school diploma is required and GED is accepted. *Academic units required:* 4 English, 3 math, 3 science, 3 social studies, 1 academic elective. *Academic units recommended:* 4 English, 4 math, 4 science, 2 foreign language, 1 computer science, 1 visual/performing arts, and 1 unit from above areas or other academic areas. **Freshman Admission Statistics:** 4,582 applied, 85.31% admitted, 29% enrolled. **Transfer Admission Requirements:** college transcript(s), Minimum college GPA of 2.0 required. Lowest grade transferable D. **General Admission Information:** Application fee $50. Priority deadline 3/1. Regular application deadline 7/15. Nonfall registration accepted. Admission may be deferred for a maximum of 2 years.

COSTS AND FINANCIAL AID

Annual in-state tuition $5,650. Annual out-of-state tuition $16,510. Room and board $6,780. Required fees $2,345. Average book expense $1,050. **Required Forms and Deadlines:** FAFSA, Institution's own financial aid form. **Notification of Awards:** Applicants will be notified of awards on a rolling basis beginning 3/1. **Types of Aid:** *Need-based scholarships/grants:* Federal Pell, FSEOG, State scholarships/grants, Private scholarships, College/university scholarship or grant aid from institutional funds, United Negro College Fund, Federal Nursing Scholarships. *Loans:* Federal Perkins Loans, Federal Nursing Loans, State Loans. *Student Employment:* Federal Work-Study Program available. Institutional employment available. **Financial Aid Statistics:** 94% needy freshmen, 91% needy undergrads receive need-based scholarship or grant aid. 30% freshmen, 25% undergrads receive non-need-based scholarship or grant aid. 69% freshmen, 83% undergrads receive need-based self-help aid. 0% freshmen, 0% undergrads receive athletic scholarships. 77% freshmen, 85% undergrads receive any aid. **Criteria for awarding aid:** *Need-based:* Academics, Art, Athletics, Music/drama.

THIEL COLLEGE

75 College Avenue, Greenville, PA 16125
Phone: 724-589-2345 • **Financial Aid Phone:** 724-589-2178
E-mail: admissions@thiel.edu • **CEEB Code:** 2910
Fax: 724-589-2013 • **Website:** www.thiel.edu • **ACT Code:** 3730

This private school, affiliated with the Lutheran Church, was founded in 1866. It has a 135-acre campus.

RATINGS

Admissions Selectivity Rating: 77   **Fire Safety Rating:** 88   **Green Rating:** 60*

STUDENTS AND FACULTY

Enrollment: 1,019. **Student Body:** 43% female, 57% male, 37% out-of-state, 3% international (14 countries represented). Asian 0%, African American 6%, Caucasian 69%, Hispanic 2%, Native American <1%, Pacific Islander 0%, Two or more races 1%, Race unknown 18%.
Retention and Graduation: 67% freshmen return for sophomore year. 30% freshmen graduate within 4 years. 13% grads go on to further study within 1 year. 86% grads pursue arts and sciences degrees. 1% grads pursue law degrees. 12% grads pursue business degrees. 1% grads pursue medical degrees. **Faculty:** Student/faculty ratio 13:1. 64 full-time faculty, 73% hold PhDs, 8% are are members of minority groups, 41% are women. 0% of classes are taught by teaching assistants.

ACADEMICS

Degrees: associate, bachelor's. **Classes:** Most classes have 10-19 students. Most lab/discussion sessions have 20-29 students. **Most popular majors:** Elementary Education and Teaching; Biology/Biological Sciences; Business/ Commerce. **Special Study Options:** cooperative education program, distance learning, double major, dual enrollment, English as a Second Language (ESL), honors program, independent study, internships, liberal arts/career combination, study abroad, teacher certification program. **Honors Programs:** Four year Honors Program with special courses for honors students. **Disability Services:** Special programs offered to physically disabled students, including note-taking services, reader services, tape recorders, tutors. **Career Services:** Alumni network, Career/job search classes, Career assessment, Internships.

FACILITIES

Housing: Coed dorms, fraternity/sorority housing, apartments for single students. 90% of campus accessible to physically diasbled. **Special Academic Facilities/Equipment:** Art Gallery, Blackbox Theater,Star Bucks Bistro **Computers:** Students can register for classes online. Undergraduates are required to own a computer.

CAMPUS LIFE

Environment: Rural. **Activities:** Choral groups, concert band, dance, drama/ theater, literary magazine, musical theater, pep band, radio station, student government, student newspaper, symphony orchestra, television station, yearbook, Campus Ministries. 40 registered organizations, 8 honor societies, 4 religious organizations. 3 fraternities, 4 sororities. **Athletics (Intercollegiate):** *Men:* baseball, basketball, cheerleading, cross-country, football, golf, soccer, track/field (outdoor), track/field (indoor), wrestling. *Women:* basketball, cheerleading, cross-country, soccer, softball, track/field (outdoor), track/field (indoor), volleyball. **On-Campus Highlights:** Howard Miller Student Center, Robinson Black Box Theater, New Student Apartments, Alumni Stadium, Paul Bush Memorial Fitness Center.

ADMISSIONS

Freshman Academic Profile: Average high school GPA 3.0. 12% in top 10% of high school class, 25% in top 25% of high school class, 46% in top 50% of high school class. 88% from public high schools. **Reported SAT (pre-2016 redesign) scores:** SAT Math middle 50% range 420-520. SAT Critical Reading middle 50% range 410-510. **Concordant SAT scores:** SAT Math middle 50% range 460–550. ACT middle 50% range 18-23. Minimum paper TOEFL 450. **Basis for Candidate Selection:** *Very important factors considered include:* rigor of secondary school record, academic GPA, standardized test scores, application essay, recommendation(s), level of applicant's interest. *Important factors considered include:* class rank, character/personal qualities. *Other factors considered include:* interview, extracurricular activities, talent/ability, volunteer work, work experience. **Freshman Admission Requirements:** High school diploma is required and GED is accepted. *Academic units recommended:* 4 English, 2 math, 2 science, 2 science labs, 2 foreign language, 3 social studies, 1 academic elective. **Freshman Admission Statistics:** 1,856 applied, 67.62% admitted, 28% enrolled. **Transfer Admission Requirements:** High school transcript, college transcript(s), essay or personal statement, interview, standardized test scores, statement of good standing from prior institution(s). Minimum college GPA of 2.0 required. Lowest grade transferable C. **General Admission Information:** Application fee $35. Priority deadline 4/1. Regular application deadline 7/1. Nonfall registration accepted. Admission may be deferred for a maximum of 1 year.

COSTS AND FINANCIAL AID

Required Forms and Deadlines: FAFSA, State aid form. **Notification of Awards:** Applicants will be notified of awards on a rolling basis beginning 2/15. **Types of Aid:** *Need-based scholarships/grants:* Federal Pell, FSEOG, State scholarships/grants, Private scholarships, College/university scholarship or grant aid from institutional funds. *Loans:* Direct Subsidized Stafford Loans, Direct Unsubsidized Stafford Loans, Direct PLUS loans, Federal Perkins Loans, College/university loans from institutional funds. *Student Employment:* Federal Work-Study Program available. Institutional employment available. **Financial Aid Statistics:** 100% needy undergrads receive need-based scholarship or grant aid. 0% undergrads receive non-need-based scholarship or grant aid. 100% undergrads receive need-based self-help aid. 0% freshmen, 0% undergrads receive athletic scholarships. **Criteria for awarding aid:** *Need-based:* Academics, Alumni affiliation, Leadership, Religious affiliation. *Non-need-based:* Academics, Alumni affiliation, Leadership, Religious affiliation, State/district residency.

THOMAS AQUINAS COLLEGE

10000 Ojai Road, Santa Paula, CA 93060
Phone: 805-525-4417 • **Financial Aid Phone:** 800-634-9797
E-mail: admissions@thomasaquinas.edu • **CEEB Code:** 4828
Fax: 805-421-5905 • **Website:** www.thomasaquinas.edu • **ACT Code:** 425

This private school, affiliated with the Roman Catholic Church, was founded in 1971. It has a 131-acre campus.

RATINGS

Admissions Selectivity Rating: 88   **Fire Safety Rating:** 94   **Green Rating:** 60*

STUDENTS AND FACULTY

Enrollment: 389. **Student Body:** 49% female, 51% male, 62% out-of-state, 3% international (8 countries represented). Asian 2%, African American <1%, Caucasian 71%, Hispanic 15%, Native American 0%, Pacific Islander 0%, Two or more races 7%, Race unknown 2%.
Retention and Graduation: 92% freshmen return for sophomore year. 76% freshmen graduate within 4 years. 83% freshmen graduate within 6 years. 22% grads go on to further study within 1 year. 7% grads pursue arts and sciences degrees. 1% grads pursue law degrees. **Faculty:** Student/faculty ratio 11:1. 33 full-time faculty, 91% hold PhDs, 0% are are members of minority groups, 9% are women. 0% of classes are taught by teaching assistants.

ACADEMICS

Degrees: bachelor's. **Classes:** Most classes have 10-19 students. **Most popular majors:** Liberal Arts and Sciences/Liberal Studies. **Special Study Options:**, The sole academic program offered: a "cross-disciplinary" curriculum of liberal education through reading and analyzing the "Great Books," with special emphasis on philosophy, theology, mathematics, science, and literature. **Career Services:** Alumni network, Alumni services, Career/job search classes, Career assessment, Internships, Regional alumni. Career Advising & Alumni networking: We work directly with our students, one on one, in order to help them determine their strengths and introduce options and opportunities best suited to their talents and aspirations. The College's alumni are well networked and are an excellent resource. The College also welcomes guest speakers (alumni and others) to aid students in their career discernment as they reach the end of the College's program.

FACILITIES

Housing: men's dorms, women's dorms, Students living with their families may live off campus. 100% of campus accessible to physically diasbled. **Special Academic Facilities/Equipment:** St. Bernardine Library.

CAMPUS LIFE

Environment: Rural. **Activities:** Choral groups, dance, drama/theater, music ensembles, musical theater 2 registered organizations, 4 religious organizations. **On-Campus Highlights:** St. Joseph Commons, The Dumb Ox Coffee Shop, Dorm Commons, St. Bernardine Library, Student Lounge.

ADMISSIONS

Freshman Academic Profile: Average high school GPA 3.8. 25% in top 10% of high school class, 50% in top 25% of high school class, 75% in top 50% of high school class. 11% from public high schools. **Reported SAT (pre-2016 redesign) scores:** SAT Math middle 50% range 540-650. SAT

Critical Reading middle 50% range 600-710. SAT Writing middle 50% range 570-680. **Concordant SAT scores:** SAT EBRW middle 50% 640–730. SAT Math middle 50% range 570–670. ACT middle 50% range 25-30. Minimum paper TOEFL 570. **Basis for Candidate Selection:** *Very important factors considered include:* rigor of secondary school record, standardized test scores, application essay, recommendation(s), character/personal qualities, level of applicant's interest. *Important factors considered include:* academic GPA. *Other factors considered include:* class rank, interview, extracurricular activities, talent/ability, religious affiliation/commitment, volunteer work, work experience. **Freshman Admission Requirements:** High school diploma is required and GED is accepted. *Academic units required:* 4 English, 3 math, 2 science, 2 foreign language, 2 history. *Academic units recommended:* 4 English, 4 math, 3 science, 2 science labs, 2 history, 3 academic electives. **Freshman Admission Statistics:** 193 applied, 74.61% admitted, 62% enrolled. **General Admission Information:** Nonfall registration not accepted. Admission may be deferred for a maximum of 1 year.

COSTS AND FINANCIAL AID

Annual tuition $24,500. Room and board $7,950. Required fees $0. Average book expense $50. **Required Forms and Deadlines:** FAFSA, Institution's own financial aid form, State aid form. **Notification of Awards:** Applicants will be notified of awards on a rolling basis beginning 2/1. **Types of Aid:** *Need-based scholarships/grants:* Federal Pell, State scholarships/grants, Private scholarships, College/university scholarship or grant aid from institutional funds. *Loans:* Direct Subsidized Stafford Loans, Direct Unsubsidized Stafford Loans, Direct PLUS loans, College/university loans from institutional funds. *Student Employment:* Institutional employment available. **Financial Aid Statistics:** 94% needy freshmen, 86% needy undergrads receive need-based scholarship or grant aid. 0% undergrads receive non-need-based scholarship or grant aid. 100% freshmen, 100% undergrads receive need-based self-help aid. 0% freshmen, 0% undergrads receive athletic scholarships. 82% freshmen, 81% undergrads receive any aid. 85% undergrads borrow to pay for school. Average cumulative indebtedness $16,986.

THOMAS COLLEGE

180 West River Road, Waterville, ME 4901
Phone: 207-859-1101 • **Financial Aid Phone:** 207-859-1105
E-mail: admiss@thomas.edu • **CEEB Code:** 2052
Fax: 207-859-1114 • **Website:** www.thomas.edu • **ACT Code:** 1663

This private school was founded in 1894. It has a 120-acre campus.

RATINGS

Admissions Selectivity Rating: 73   **Fire Safety Rating:** 95   **Green Rating:** 60*

STUDENTS AND FACULTY

Enrollment: 739. **Student Body:** 49% female, 51% male, 20% out-of-state, <1% international. Asian 1%, African American 2%, Caucasian 88%, Hispanic 1%, Native American <1%, Pacific Islander 0%, Two or more races 0%, Race unknown 9%.
Retention and Graduation: 63% freshmen return for sophomore year. 51% freshmen graduate within 6 years. 7% grads go on to further study within 1 year. 7% grads pursue business degrees. **Faculty:** Student/faculty ratio 18:1. 21 full-time faculty, 48% hold PhDs, 0% are are members of minority groups, 38% are women. 0% of classes are taught by teaching assistants.

ACADEMICS

Degrees: associate, bachelor's, master's, terminal, transfer. **Classes:** Most classes have 20-29 students. **Most popular majors:** Accounting; Accounting and Business/Management; Sport and Fitness Administration/Management. **Special Study Options:** cross-registration, distance learning, double major, internships, study abroad, teacher certification program. Combined degree programs: BS/MBA. **Career Services:** Career assessment, Internships.

FACILITIES

Housing: Coed dormsResidence halls are designated coed–male or female by floor or suite, not by building. 71% of campus accessible to physically diasbled. **Computers:** Students can register for classes online. Administrative functions (other than registration) can be performed online.

CAMPUS LIFE

Environment: Rural. **Activities:** Choral groups, dance, drama/theater, student government, student newspaper, yearbook. 26 registered organizations, 3 honor societies, 1 fraternity, 1 sorority. **Athletics (Intercollegiate):** *Men:* baseball, basketball, golf, lacrosse, soccer, tennis. *Women:* basketball, field hockey, lacrosse, soccer, softball, volleyball.

ADMISSIONS

Freshman Academic Profile: Average high school GPA 2.7. 7% in top 10% of high school class, 19% in top 25% of high school class, 54% in top 50% of high school class. **Reported SAT (pre-2016 redesign) scores:** SAT Math middle 50% range 390-510. SAT Critical Reading middle 50% range 400-500. SAT Writing middle 50% range 380-500. **Concordant SAT scores:** SAT EBRW middle 50% 440–560. SAT Math middle 50% range 430–540. ACT middle 50% range 13-22. Minimum paper TOEFL 530. **Basis for Candidate Selection:** *Very important factors considered include:* rigor of secondary school record, class rank, academic GPA, standardized test scores, application essay, recommendation(s). *Important factors considered include:* interview, extracurricular activities, character/personal qualities. *Other factors considered include:* talent/ability, first generation, alumni/ae relation, volunteer work, work experience, level of applicant's interest. **Freshman Admission Requirements:** High school diploma is required and GED is accepted. *Academic units recommended:* 4 English, 3 math, 3 science, 2 foreign language, 2 social studies, 2 history. **Freshman Admission Statistics:** 483 applied, 82.82% admitted, 62% enrolled. **Transfer Admission Requirements:** High school transcript, college transcript(s), essay or personal statement, Minimum college GPA of 2.0 required. Lowest grade transferable C. **General Admission Information:** Application fee $50. Nonfall registration accepted. Admission may be deferred for a maximum of 2 years.

COSTS AND FINANCIAL AID

Annual tuition $17,280. Required fees $450. Average book expense $800. **Required Forms and Deadlines:** FAFSA. **Notification of Awards:** Applicants will be notified of awards on a rolling basis beginning 3/15. **Types of Aid:** *Need-based scholarships/grants:* Federal Pell, FSEOG, State scholarships/grants, Private scholarships, College/university scholarship or grant aid from institutional funds. *Loans:* Direct Subsidized Stafford Loans, Direct Unsubsidized Stafford Loans, Direct PLUS loans, Federal Perkins Loans. *Student Employment:* Federal Work-Study Program available. Institutional employment available. **Financial Aid Statistics:** 100% needy freshmen, 98% needy undergrads receive need-based scholarship or grant aid. 31% freshmen, 19% undergrads receive non-need-based scholarship or grant aid. 90% freshmen, 90% undergrads receive need-based self-help aid. 0% freshmen, 0% undergrads receive athletic scholarships. 95% freshmen, 90% undergrads receive any aid. **Criteria for awarding aid:** *Need-based:* Academics. *Non-need-based:* Academics.

THOMAS EDISON STATE UNIVERSITY

111 West State Street, Trenton, NJ 08608-1176
Phone: 888-442-8372 • **Financial Aid Phone:** 609-633-9658
E-mail: admissions@tesu.edu • **CEEB Code:** 2612
Fax: 609-984-8447 • **Website:** www.tesu.edu • **ACT Code:** 274872

This public school was founded in 1972. It has a 2-acre campus.

RATINGS

Admissions Selectivity Rating: 60*   **Fire Safety Rating:** 60*   **Green Rating:** 60*

STUDENTS AND FACULTY

Enrollment: 16,506. **Student Body:** 44% female, 56% male, 1% international (68 countries represented). Asian 4%, African American 15%, Caucasian 51%, Hispanic 9%, Native American 1%, Pacific Islander 1%, Two or more races 2%, Race unknown 16%.

ACADEMICS

Degrees: associate, bachelor's, certificate, master's, postbachelor's certificate, post-master's certificate. **Special Study Options:** distance learning, dual enrollment, external degree program, independent study, Joint degree program with the University of Medicine and Dentistry of New Jersey for Bachelor of Science in Health Sciences. Graduates of associate degree and diploma programs of nursing may enroll for a BSN degree only (RN-BSN program), or both a BSN and a MSN degree (RN-BSN/MSN program) with preparation as a Nurse Educator at the Master's level. Combined degree programs: BSN/MSN. **Career Services:** Alumni network.

FACILITIES

Housing: Thomas Edison State College serves adult students at a distance. The College doesn't own/operate any housing units and/or dorms. **Computers:** Students can register for classes online. Administrative functions (other than registration) can be performed online.

CAMPUS LIFE

Environment: City. **Activities:** 3 honor societies. **On-Campus Highlights:** Prudence Townsend Kelsey Memorial Roo **Environmental Initiatives:** Solar panels installed on 2 facilities.

ADMISSIONS

Minimum internet-based TOEFL 79. Minimum paper TOEFL 550. **Basis for Candidate Selection:** *Other factors considered include:* state residency. **Freshman Admission Requirements:** High school diploma is required and GED is accepted. **Transfer Admission Requirements:** college transcript(s), Lowest grade transferable D. **General Admission Information:** Application fee $75. Admission may be deferred for a maximum of 6 months.

COSTS AND FINANCIAL AID

Annual in-state tuition $6,350. Annual out-of-state tuition $9,352. **Required Forms and Deadlines:** FAFSA, Institution's own financial aid form. **Notification of Awards:** Applicants will be notified of awards on a rolling basis beginning 3/1. **Types of Aid:** *Need-based scholarships/grants:* Federal Pell, State scholarships/grants, Private scholarships. *Loans:* State Loans. **Financial Aid Statistics:** 17% undergrads receive any aid.

THOMAS JEFFERSON UNIVERSITY

130 South 9th Street, Philadelphia, PA 19107
Phone: 215-503-8890 • **Financial Aid Phone:** 215-955-2867
E-mail: jchp@jefferson.edu • **CEEB Code:** 2903
Fax: 215-503-7241 • **Website:** www.jefferson.edu/jchp

This private school was founded in 1967.

RATINGS

Admissions Selectivity Rating: 61   **Fire Safety Rating:** 79   **Green Rating:** 60*

STUDENTS AND FACULTY

Enrollment: 827. **Student Body:** 83% female, 17% male, 27% out-of-state, 1% international. Asian 8%, African American 9%, Caucasian 71%, Hispanic 3%, Native American <1%, Pacific Islander 0%, Two or more races 0%, Race unknown 7%.
Faculty: Student/faculty ratio 14:1. 82 full-time faculty, 43% hold PhDs, 12% are are members of minority groups, 85% are women.

ACADEMICS

Degrees: associate, bachelor's, master's, postbachelor's certificate, post-master's certificate, transfer. **Special Study Options:** Accelerated program, distance learning, double major, independent study, internships, study abroad. **Disability Services:** Special programs offered to physically disabled students, including note-taking services, reader services, tutors. **Career Services:** Alumni network, Alumni services, Career/job search classes, Career assessment, Regional alumni.

FACILITIES

Housing: Coed dorms, special housing for disabled students, apartments for married students, apartments for single students. 80% of campus accessible to physically diasbled. **Special Academic Facilities/Equipment:** Copy of the famous Gross Clinic, New building with simulation labs. Located in the heart of Center City close to all historical sights as well as cultural events and museums. **Computers:** 100% of classrooms, 100% of dorms, 100% of libraries, have wireless network access. Students can register for classes online. Administrative functions (other than registration) can be performed online.

CAMPUS LIFE

Environment: Metropolis. **Activities:** Choral groups, student government, yearbook, Student Organization. **On-Campus Highlights:** New Education and Research Building, Famous painting called the Gross Clinic, Close to Historic Sites, Close to famous museums, Many fine restaurants and theaters, Jefferson is located in Center City Philadelphia, near the Convention Center with many fine restaurants, shops and other cultural sights.

ADMISSIONS

Freshman Admission Requirements: High school diploma is required and GED is accepted. **Transfer Admission Requirements:** college transcript(s), essay or personal statement, statement of good standing from prior institution(s). Minimum college GPA of 2.5 required. Lowest grade transferable C. **General Admission Information:** Application fee $50. Priority deadline 3/1. Nonfall registration accepted. Admission may be deferred.

COSTS AND FINANCIAL AID

Annual tuition $23,685. Required fees $400. Average book expense $1,495. **Required Forms and Deadlines:** FAFSA, Institution's own financial aid form. **Types of Aid:** *Need-based scholarships/grants:* Federal Pell, FSEOG, State scholarships/grants, Private scholarships, College/university scholarship or grant aid from institutional funds, Federal Nursing Scholarships. *Loans:* Direct Subsidized Stafford Loans, Direct Unsubsidized Stafford Loans, Federal Perkins Loans, Federal Nursing Loans, State Loans, College/university loans from institutional funds. *Student Employment:* Federal Work-Study Program available. Institutional employment available. **Criteria for awarding aid:** *Need-based:* Academics. *Non-need-based:* Academics, Leadership, State/district residency.

THOMAS MORE COLLEGE OF LIBERAL ARTS

6 Manchester Street, Merrimack, NH 03054-4818
Phone: 603-880-8308
E-mail: admissions@thomasmorecollege.edu
Fax: 603-880-9280 • **Website:** www.thomasmorecollege.edu • **ACT Code:** 3892

This private school, affiliated with the Roman Catholic Church, was founded in 1978. It has a 13-acre campus.

RATINGS
Admissions Selectivity Rating: 71   **Fire Safety Rating:** 60*   **Green Rating:** 60*

STUDENTS AND FACULTY
Enrollment: 67. **Student Body:** 48% female, 52% male, 84% out-of-state, 6% international. Asian 0%, African American 0%, Caucasian 72%, Hispanic 1%, Native American 0%, Pacific Islander 0%, Two or more races 0%, Race unknown 21%.
Retention and Graduation: 60% freshmen return for sophomore year. 52% grads go on to further study within 1 year. 48% grads pursue arts and sciences degrees. 8% grads pursue law degrees. 2% grads pursue business degrees. 2% grads pursue medical degrees. **Faculty:** Student/faculty ratio 12:1. 5 full-time faculty, 100% hold PhDs, 0% are are members of minority groups, 20% are women. 0% of classes are taught by teaching assistants.

ACADEMICS
Degrees: bachelor's. **Classes:** Most classes have 10-19 students. **Most popular majors:** Computer and Information Sciences Business/Commerce. **Special Study Options:** internships, study abroad, Spring semester in Rome for all sophomores. **Career Services:** On-campus interviews.

FACILITIES
Housing: men's dorms, women's dorms. 70% of campus accessible to physically diasbled.

CAMPUS LIFE
Environment: Village. **Activities:** Choral groups, drama/theater.

ADMISSIONS
Freshman Academic Profile: 12% from public high schools. **Basis for Candidate Selection:** *Very important factors considered include:* application essay, recommendation(s), interview, character/personal qualities. *Important factors considered include:* talent/ability. *Other factors considered include:* rigor of secondary school record, class rank, academic GPA, standardized test scores, extracurricular activities, religious affiliation/commitment, level of applicant's interest. **Freshman Admission Requirements:** High school diploma is required and GED is accepted. *Academic units required:* 4 English, 3 math, 2 science, 2 science labs, 2 foreign language, 2 social studies, 2 history. *Academic units recommended:* 2 units from above areas or other academic areas. **Freshman Admission Statistics:** 75 applied, 54.67% admitted, 68% enrolled. **Transfer Admission Requirements:** college transcript(s), essay or personal statement, Lowest grade transferable C. **General Admission Information:** Nonfall registration accepted. Admission may be deferred.

COSTS AND FINANCIAL AID
Annual tuition $11,100. Room and board $8,000. Average book expense $525. **Required Forms and Deadlines:** FAFSA. **Notification of Awards:** Applicants will be notified of awards on a rolling basis beginning 3/15. **Types of Aid:** *Need-based scholarships/grants:* Federal Pell, FSEOG, State scholarships/grants, Private scholarships, College/university scholarship or grant aid from institutional funds. **Financial Aid Statistics:** 100% needy freshmen, 100% needy undergrads receive need-based scholarship or grant aid. 70% freshmen, 62% undergrads receive need-based self-help aid. 0% freshmen, 0% undergrads receive athletic scholarships. **Criteria for awarding aid:** *Non-need-based:* Academics.

TIFFIN UNIVERSITY

155 Miami Street, Tiffin, OH 44883
Phone: 419-448-3423 • **Financial Aid Phone:** 419-448-3415
E-mail: admiss@tiffin.edu • **CEEB Code:** 1817
Fax: 419-443-5006 • **Website:** www.tiffin.edu/ • **ACT Code:** 3334

This private school was founded in 1888. It has a 110-acre campus.

RATINGS
Admissions Selectivity Rating: 75   **Fire Safety Rating:** 87   **Green Rating:** 60*

STUDENTS AND FACULTY
Enrollment: 2,597. **Student Body:** 53% female, 47% male, 34% out-of-state, 7% international (34 countries represented). Asian 0%, African American 17%, Caucasian 44%, Hispanic 3%, Native American <1%, Pacific Islander <1%, Two or more races 2%, Race unknown 26%.
Retention and Graduation: 62% freshmen return for sophomore year. 34% freshmen graduate within 4 years. 25% grads go on to further study within 1 year. **Faculty:** Student/faculty ratio 15:1. 72 full-time faculty, 61% hold PhDs, 4% are are members of minority groups, 46% are women. 0% of classes are taught by teaching assistants.

ACADEMICS
Degrees: associate, bachelor's, certificate, master's, postbachelor's certificate, post-master's certificate. **Classes:** Most classes have fewer than 10 students. Most lab/discussion sessions have fewer than 10 students. **Most popular majors:** Marketing/Marketing Management; Business Administration and Management; Forensic Science and Technology. **Special Study Options:** Accelerated program, cross-registration, distance learning, double major, dual enrollment, English as a Second Language (ESL), honors program, independent study, internships, study abroad, teacher certification program. **Honors Programs:** We offer a Freshman Honors Program. **Career Services:** Alumni network, Alumni services, Career/job search classes, Career assessment, Internships, Regional alumni.

FACILITIES
Housing: Coed dorms, special housing for disabled students, men's dorms, special housing for international students, women's dorms, fraternity/sorority housing, apartments for married students, Theme Housing. 85% of campus accessible to physically diasbled. **Special Academic Facilities/Equipment:** University Art Gallery Multi-Media Lab **Computers:** 100% of classrooms, 25% of dorms, 100% of libraries, 100% of dining areas, 100% of student union, have wireless network access. Students can register for classes online. Administrative functions (other than registration) can be performed online.

CAMPUS LIFE
Environment: Village. **Activities:** Choral groups, concert band, dance, drama/theater, jazz band, literary magazine, marching band, music ensembles, musical theater, pep band, student government, student newspaper, Campus Ministries, Student Organization. 32 registered organizations, 1 honor society, 2 religious organizations. 3 fraternities, 3 sororities. **Athletics (Intercollegiate):** *Men:* baseball, basketball, cheerleading, cross-country, equestrian sports, football, golf, soccer, tennis, track/field (outdoor), track/field (indoor). *Women:* basketball, cheerleading, cross-country, equestrian sports, golf, lacrosse, soccer, softball, tennis, track/field (outdoor), track/field (indoor), volleyball.
On-Campus Highlights: Gillmor Student Center, Hayes Center for the Arts, Hertzer Technology Center, Main Classroom Building, Franks Hall. **Environmental Initiatives:** Establishment of a Green Committee and formation of a Green Technologies Minor and Concentration.

ADMISSIONS
Freshman Academic Profile: Average high school GPA 3.0. 75% from public high schools. **Reported SAT (pre-2016 redesign) scores:** SAT Math middle 50% range 400-500. SAT Critical Reading middle 50% range 420-500. **Concordant SAT scores:** SAT Math middle 50% range 440–530. ACT middle 50% range 17-22. Minimum internet-based TOEFL 61. Minimum paper TOEFL 500. **Basis for Candidate Selection:** *Very important factors considered include:* rigor of secondary school record, academic GPA, standardized test scores. *Other factors considered include:* application essay, recommendation(s), interview, extracurricular activities, talent/ability, character/personal qualities, alumni/ae relation, volunteer work, work experience, level of applicant's interest. **Freshman Admission Requirements:** High school diploma is required and GED is accepted. *Academic units recommended:* 4 English, 4 math, 3 science, 1 science lab, 3 social studies, 5 academic electives, 1 visual/performing arts. **Freshman Admission Statistics:** 4,384 applied, 53.99% admitted, 21% enrolled. **Transfer Admission Requirements:** High school transcript, college transcript(s), Minimum college GPA of 2.0 required. Lowest grade transferable C. **General Admission Information:** Application fee $20. Nonfall registration accepted. Admission may be deferred for a maximum of 1 year.

COSTS AND FINANCIAL AID

Annual tuition $21,510. Room and board $9,870. Average book expense $2,000. **Required Forms and Deadlines:** FAFSA. **Notification of Awards:** Applicants will be notified of awards on a rolling basis beginning 2/1. **Types of Aid:** *Need-based scholarships/grants:* Federal Pell, FSEOG, State scholarships/grants, Private scholarships, College/university scholarship or grant aid from institutional funds. *Loans:* Direct Subsidized Stafford Loans, Direct Unsubsidized Stafford Loans, Direct PLUS loans. *Student Employment:* Federal Work-Study Program available. Institutional employment available. **Financial Aid Statistics:** 100% needy freshmen, 97% needy undergrads receive need-based scholarship or grant aid. 7% freshmen, 8% undergrads receive non-need-based scholarship or grant aid. 93% freshmen, 91% undergrads receive need-based self-help aid. 4% freshmen, 4% undergrads receive athletic scholarships. 95% freshmen, 95% undergrads receive any aid. **Criteria for awarding aid:** *Non-need-based:* Academics, Art, Athletics, Leadership, Music/drama, State/district residency.

TOCCOA FALLS COLLEGE

107 Kincaid Drive, Toccoa Falls, GA 30598
Phone: 888-785-5624 • **Financial Aid Phone:** 706-886-6831
E-mail: admissions@tfc.edu
Fax: 706-282-6012 • **Website:** www.tfc.edu • **ACT Code:** 868

This private school, affiliated with the Christian & Missionary Allianc Church, was founded in 1907. It has a 1100-acre campus.

RATINGS

Admissions Selectivity Rating: 80   **Fire Safety Rating:** 70   **Green Rating:** 60*

STUDENTS AND FACULTY

Enrollment: 796. **Student Body:** 53% female, 47% male, 23% out-of-state, 1% international. Asian 8%, African American 7%, Caucasian 72%, Hispanic 4%, Native American <1%, Pacific Islander <1%, Two or more races 2%, Race unknown 6%.
Retention and Graduation: 72% freshmen return for sophomore year. 36% freshmen graduate within 4 years. 47% freshmen graduate within 6 years. **Faculty:** Student/faculty ratio 14:1. 42 full-time faculty, 60% hold PhDs, 12% are are members of minority groups, 31% are women. 0% of classes are taught by teaching assistants.

ACADEMICS

Degrees: associate, bachelor's, certificate. **Classes:** Most classes have fewer than 10 students. **Most popular majors:** Missions/Missionary Studies and Missiology; Elementary Education and Teaching; Counseling Psychology. **Special Study Options:** distance learning, double major, dual enrollment, independent study, internships, teacher certification program. **Disability Services:** Special programs offered to physically disabled students, including note-taking services, reader services, tutors. **Career Services:** Career assessment.

FACILITIES

Housing: men's dorms, special housing for international students, women's dorms, apartments for married students, Mobile home court living available for married students. 70% of campus accessible to physically diasbled. **Computers:** 40% of classrooms, 50% of dorms, 100% of libraries, 100% of dining areas, 50% of student union, 1% of common outdoor areas have wireless network access. Students can register for classes online. Administrative functions (other than registration) can be performed online.

CAMPUS LIFE

Environment: Rural. **Activities:** Choral groups, concert band, drama/theater, jazz band, music ensembles, radio station, student government, student newspaper, yearbook, Campus Ministries. **Athletics (Intercollegiate):** Men: baseball, basketball, cross-country, golf, soccer, tennis. Women: basketball, cheerleading, cross-country, golf, soccer, tennis, volleyball. **On-Campus Highlights:** The Waterfall, Student Center, Gymnatorium, Eagle's Nest, Grace Chapel & Performing Arts Center.

ADMISSIONS

Freshman Academic Profile: Average high school GPA 3.4. 10% in top 10% of high school class, 28% in top 25% of high school class, 63% in top 50% of high school class. 60% from public high schools. **Reported SAT (pre-2016 redesign) scores:** SAT Math middle 50% range 410-550. SAT Critical Reading middle 50% range 410-560. **Concordant SAT scores:** SAT Math middle 50% range 450–570. ACT middle 50% range 17-24. Minimum paper TOEFL 500. **Basis for Candidate Selection:** *Very important factors considered include:* rigor of secondary school record, academic GPA, standardized test scores, application essay, recommendation(s), character/personal qualities,

religious affiliation/commitment. *Other factors considered include:* interview, extracurricular activities, talent/ability, volunteer work, work experience, level of applicant's interest. **Freshman Admission Requirements:** High school diploma is required and GED is accepted. *Academic units recommended:* 4 English, 3 math, 3 science, 2 science labs, 3 social studies, 6 academic electives. **Freshman Admission Statistics:** 879 applied, 53.81% admitted, 42% enrolled. **Transfer Admission Requirements:** college transcript(s), essay or personal statement, Minimum college GPA of 2.0 required. Lowest grade transferable C-. **General Admission Information:** Application fee $20. Regular application deadline 8/1. Regular notification 3/1. Nonfall registration accepted. Admission may be deferred for a maximum of 2 years.

COSTS AND FINANCIAL AID

Annual tuition $21,334. Room and board $7,934. Required fees $700. Average book expense $1,000. **Required Forms and Deadlines:** FAFSA, Institution's own financial aid form, State aid form. **Notification of Awards:** Applicants will be notified of awards on a rolling basis beginning 3/1. **Types of Aid:** *Need-based scholarships/grants:* Federal Pell, FSEOG, State scholarships/grants, Private scholarships, College/university scholarship or grant aid from institutional funds. *Loans:* Federal Perkins Loans, State Loans, College/university loans from institutional funds. *Student Employment:* Federal Work-Study Program available. Institutional employment available. **Financial Aid Statistics:** 44% needy freshmen, 100% needy undergrads receive need-based scholarship or grant aid. 9% freshmen, 8% undergrads receive non-need-based scholarship or grant aid. 83% freshmen, 82% undergrads receive need-based self-help aid. 0% freshmen, 0% undergrads receive athletic scholarships. 100% freshmen, 98% undergrads receive any aid. Average cumulative indebtedness $29,977. **Criteria for awarding aid:** *Need-based:* Academics, Leadership. *Non-need-based:* Academics, Alumni affiliation, Leadership, Music/drama, Religious affiliation, State/district residency.

TOWSON UNIVERSITY

8000 York Road, Towson, MD 21252-0001
Phone: 410-704-2113 • **Financial Aid Phone:** 410-704-4236
E-mail: admissions@towson.edu • **CEEB Code:** 5404
Fax: 410-704-3030 • **Website:** www.towson.edu • **ACT Code:** 1718

This public school was founded in 1866. It has a 328-acre campus.

RATINGS

Admissions Selectivity Rating: 80   **Fire Safety Rating:** 84   **Green Rating:** 60*

STUDENTS AND FACULTY

Enrollment: 18,968. **Student Body:** 60% female, 40% male, 14% out-of-state, 2% international (70 countries represented). Asian 6%, African American 19%, Caucasian 59%, Hispanic 7%, Native American <1%, Pacific Islander <1%, Two or more races 5%, Race unknown 2%.
Retention and Graduation: 85% freshmen return for sophomore year. 46% freshmen graduate within 4 years. 71% freshmen graduate within 6 years. 30% grads go on to further study within 1 year. **Faculty:** Student/faculty ratio 17:1. 905 full-time faculty, 78% hold PhDs, 20% are are members of minority groups, 57% are women. 0% of classes are taught by teaching assistants.

ACADEMICS

Degrees: bachelor's, doctoral/professional, doctoral/research, master's, postbachelor's certificate, post-master's certificate. **Classes:** Most classes have 20-29 students. Most lab/discussion sessions have 10-19 students. **Most popular majors:** Psychology; Biology/Biological Sciences; Business Administration and Management. **Special Study Options:** cooperative education program, cross-registration, distance learning, double major, dual enrollment, English as a Second Language (ESL), exchange student program (domestic), honors program, independent study, internships, liberal arts/career combination, student-designed major, study abroad, teacher certification program. **Honors Programs:** Honors College Combined degree programs: BA/MA, BS/MS. **Disability Services:** Special programs offered to physically disabled students, including note-taking services, reader services. **Career Services:** Alumni network, Alumni services, Career/job search classes, Career assessment, Internships, Regional alumni. Towson University now hosts the largest career fair in the state of Maryland with around 200 employers attending both the 2016 Spring Mega Job & Internship Fair.

FACILITIES

Housing: Coed dorms, special housing for disabled students, special housing for international students, apartments for single students, 80% of campus accessible to physically diasbled. **Special Academic Facilities/Equipment:** Art galleries, animal museum, Asian art collection, elementary school, media center, speech/language clinic, planetarium/observatory, herbarium, electron microscope, argon laser. **Computers:** 100% of classrooms, 100% of dorms,

100% of libraries, 100% of dining areas, 100% of student union, 100% of common outdoor areas have wireless network access. Students can register for classes online. Administrative functions (other than registration) can be performed online.

CAMPUS LIFE

Environment: Metropolis. **Activities:** Choral groups, concert band, dance, drama/theater, jazz band, literary magazine, marching band, music ensembles, musical theater, pep band, radio station, student government, student newspaper, symphony orchestra, television station, yearbook, Campus Ministries, Student Organization. 198 registered organizations, 15 honor societies, 12 religious organizations. 12 fraternities, 10 sororities. **Athletics (Intercollegiate):** *Men:* baseball, basketball, cheerleading, cross-country, diving, football, golf, lacrosse, soccer, swimming, tennis. *Women:* basketball, cheerleading, cross-country, diving, field hockey, gymnastics, lacrosse, soccer, softball, swimming, tennis, track/field (outdoor), volleyball. **On-Campus Highlights:** Johnny Unitas Stadium, University Union, Burdick Hall-athletic facilities, The Den, Towson Center-events. **Environmental Initiatives:** Sign the American College and University President's Climate Committment (ACUPCC) in 2007 pledging to become/achieve climate neutrality

ADMISSIONS

Freshman Academic Profile: Average high school GPA 3.6. 17% in top 10% of high school class, 42% in top 25% of high school class, 78% in top 50% of high school class. **Reported SAT (pre-2016 redesign) scores:** SAT Math middle 50% range 490-580. SAT Critical Reading middle 50% range 490-580. SAT Writing middle 50% range 490-570. **Concordant SAT scores:** SAT EBRW middle 50% 550–630. SAT Math middle 50% range 520–600. ACT middle 50% range 21-25. Minimum internet-based TOEFL 61. Minimum paper TOEFL 500. **Basis for Candidate Selection:** *Very important factors considered include:* academic GPA. *Important factors considered include:* rigor of secondary school record, standardized test scores. *Other factors considered include:* class rank, application essay, recommendation(s), talent/ability, first generation. **Freshman Admission Requirements:** High school diploma is required and GED is accepted. *Academic units required:* 4 English, 4 math, 3 science, 2 science labs, 2 foreign language, 3 social studies, 6 academic electives. **Freshman Admission Statistics:** 11,897 applied, 73.74% admitted, 31% enrolled. **Transfer Admission Requirements:** college transcript(s), Minimum college GPA of 2.0 required. Lowest grade transferable D. **General Admission Information:** Application fee $45. Priority deadline 12/1. Regular application deadline 1/15. Nonfall registration accepted. Admission may be deferred for a maximum of 1 year.

COSTS AND FINANCIAL AID

Annual in-state tuition $6,560. Annual out-of-state tuition $18,228. Room and board $12,100. Required fees $2,848. Average book expense $1,080. **Required Forms and Deadlines:** FAFSA, State aid form. **Notification of Awards:** Applicants will be notified of awards on a rolling basis beginning 3/21. **Types of Aid:** *Need-based scholarships/grants:* Federal Pell, FSEOG, State scholarships/grants, Private scholarships, College/university scholarship or grant aid from institutional funds. *Loans:* Direct Subsidized Stafford Loans, Direct Unsubsidized Stafford Loans, Direct PLUS loans, Federal Perkins Loans. *Student Employment:* Federal Work-Study Program available. Institutional employment available. **Financial Aid Statistics:** 56% needy freshmen, 62% needy undergrads receive need-based scholarship or grant aid. 39% freshmen, 27% undergrads receive non-need-based scholarship or grant aid. 78% freshmen, 76% undergrads receive need-based self-help aid. 2% freshmen, 1% undergrads receive athletic scholarships. 75% freshmen, 73% undergrads receive any aid. 61% undergrads borrow to pay for school. Average cumulative indebtedness $25,483. **Criteria for awarding aid:** *Non-need-based:* Academics, Alumni affiliation, Art, Athletics, Leadership, Music/drama, State/district residency.

TRANSYLVANIA UNIVERSITY

300 North Broadway, Lexington, KY 40508-1797
Phone: 859-233-8242 • **Financial Aid Phone:** 859-233-8239
E-mail: admissions@transy.edu • **CEEB Code:** 1808
Fax: 859-281-3649 • **Website:** www.transy.edu • **ACT Code:** 1550

This private school, affiliated with the Christian (Nondenominational) Church, was founded in 1780. It has a 36-acre campus.

RATINGS

Admissions Selectivity Rating: 84   **Fire Safety Rating:** 90   **Green Rating:** 60*

STUDENTS AND FACULTY

Enrollment: 960. **Student Body:** 59% female, 41% male, 26% out-of-state, 4% international (7 countries represented). Asian 1%, African American 4%, Caucasian 79%, Hispanic 6%, Native American <1%, Pacific Islander 0%, Two or more races 3%, Race unknown 2%.
Retention and Graduation: 86% freshmen return for sophomore year. 71% freshmen graduate within 4 years. 75% freshmen graduate within 6 years. 45% grads go on to further study within 1 year. 55% grads pursue arts and sciences degrees. 23% grads pursue law degrees. 7% grads pursue medical degrees. **Faculty:** Student/faculty ratio 11:1. 84 full-time faculty, 96% hold PhDs, 7% are are members of minority groups, 45% are women. 0% of classes are taught by teaching assistants.

ACADEMICS

Degrees: bachelor's. **Classes:** Most classes have 10-19 students. Most lab/discussion sessions have 10-19 students. **Most popular majors:** Business/Commerce; Accounting; Psychology. **Special Study Options:** double major, independent study, internships, liberal arts/career combination, student-designed major, study abroad, teacher certification program. **Disability Services:** Special programs offered to physically disabled students, including note-taking services, reader services, tape recorders, tutors. **Career Services:** Alumni network, Alumni services, Career/job search classes, Career assessment, Internships, Regional alumni. Internship Programs

FACILITIES

Housing: Coed dorms, special housing for disabled students, men's dorms, women's dorms, apartments for single students, ThemeHousingEfficiency apartment option for upperclassmen. Units with facilities for disabled students. 90% of campus accessible to physically diasbled. **Special Academic Facilities/Equipment:** Art gallery, museum of early scientific apparatus, medical museum, language lab, transmission electron microscope. **Computers:** 20% of classrooms, 20% of dorms, 75% of libraries, 20% of dining areas, 100% of student union, 10% of common outdoor areas have wireless network access. Administrative functions (other than registration) can be performed online.

CAMPUS LIFE

Environment: City. **Activities:** Choral groups, concert band, dance, drama/theater, jazz band, literary magazine, music ensembles, musical theater, opera, pep band, radio station, student government, student newspaper, yearbook. 55 registered organizations, 10 honor societies, 7 religious organizations. 4 fraternities, 4 sororities. **Athletics (Intercollegiate):** *Men:* baseball, basketball, cheerleading, cross-country, diving, golf, soccer, swimming, tennis, track/field (outdoor). *Women:* basketball, cheerleading, cross-country, diving, field hockey, golf, soccer, softball, swimming, tennis, track/field (outdoor), volleyball. **On-Campus Highlights:** Beck Athletic and Recreation Center, William T. Young Campus Center, Mitchell Fine Arts Center, Little Theater, 1780 Cafe. **Environmental Initiatives:** Developing a comprehensive sustainability master plan.

ADMISSIONS

Freshman Academic Profile: Average high school GPA 3.7. 36% in top 10% of high school class, 64% in top 25% of high school class, 92% in top 50% of high school class. 78% from public high schools. **Reported SAT (pre-2016 redesign) scores:** SAT Math middle 50% range 460-640. SAT Critical Reading middle 50% range 520-610. **Concordant SAT scores:** SAT Math middle 50% range 500–660. ACT middle 50% range 25-30. Minimum internet-based TOEFL 80. Minimum paper TOEFL 550. **Basis for Candidate Selection:** *Very important factors considered include:* rigor of secondary school record, academic GPA, standardized test scores, application essay. *Important factors considered include:* recommendation(s), extracurricular activities, talent/ability, character/personal qualities. *Other factors considered include:* class rank, interview, first generation, alumni/ae relation, geographical residence, racial/ethnic status, volunteer work, work experience. **Freshman Admission Requirements:** High school diploma is required and GED is accepted. *Academic units required:* 4 English, 3 math, 3 science, 2 science labs, 2 foreign language, 2 social studies, 2 academic electives. *Academic units recommended:* 4 English, 4 math, 4 science, 3 science labs, 2 foreign language, 2 social studies, 1 history, 2 academic electives. **Freshman Admission Statistics:** 1,216 applied, 94.82% admitted, 21% enrolled. **Transfer Admission Requirements:** High school transcript, college transcript(s), essay or personal statement, Minimum college GPA of 2.75 required. Lowest grade transferable C-. **General Admission Information:** Priority deadline 12/1. Nonfall registration accepted. Admission may be deferred for a maximum of 12 months.

COSTS AND FINANCIAL AID

Annual tuition $35,770. Room and board $10,160. Required fees $1,520. Average book expense $1,000. **Required Forms and Deadlines:** FAFSA. **Notification of Awards:** Applicants will be notified of awards on or about 3/15. **Types of Aid:** *Need-based scholarships/grants:* Federal Pell, FSEOG, State scholarships/grants, Private scholarships, College/university scholarship or grant aid from institutional funds. *Loans:* Direct Subsidized Stafford Loans, Direct Unsubsidized Stafford Loans, Direct PLUS loans, Federal Perkins Loans. *Student Employment:* Federal Work-Study Program available. Institutional employment available. **Financial Aid Statistics:** 100% needy freshmen, 100% needy undergrads receive need-based scholarship or grant aid. 21% freshmen, 14% undergrads receive non-need-based scholarship or grant aid. 76% freshmen, 75% undergrads receive need-based self-help aid. 0% freshmen, 0% undergrads receive athletic scholarships. 99% freshmen, 98% undergrads receive any aid. 63% undergrads borrow to pay for school. Average cumulative indebtedness $30,514. **Criteria for awarding aid:** *Need-based:* Academics, Minority status, Religious affiliation. *Non-need-based:* Academics, Art, Minority status, Music/drama, Religious affiliation, State/district residency.

TREVECCA NAZARENE UNIVERSITY

333 Murfreesboro Road, Nashville, TN 37210
Phone: 615-248-1320 • **Financial Aid Phone:** 615-248-1242
E-mail: admissions_und@trevecca.edu
Fax: 615-248-7406 • **Website:** www.trevecca.edu • **ACT Code:** 4016

This private school, affiliated with the Nazarene Church, was founded in 1901. It has a 65-acre campus.

RATINGS

Admissions Selectivity Rating: 75   **Fire Safety Rating:** 60*   **Green Rating:** 60*

STUDENTS AND FACULTY

Enrollment: 1,762. **Student Body:** 57% female, 43% male, 36% out-of-state, 1% international (16 countries represented). Asian 1%, African American 11%, Caucasian 69%, Hispanic 9%, Native American <1%, Pacific Islander <1%, Two or more races 3%, Race unknown 6%.
Retention and Graduation: 77% freshmen return for sophomore year. 40% freshmen graduate within 4 years. 51% freshmen graduate within 6 years.
Faculty: Student/faculty ratio 17:1. 81 full-time faculty, 86% hold PhDs, 9% are are members of minority groups, 35% are women.

ACADEMICS

Degrees: associate, bachelor's, certificate, doctoral/research, master's, postbachelor's certificate. **Classes:** Most classes have 10-19 students. **Most popular majors:** Biology/Biological Sciences; Psychology; Registered Nursing/Registered Nurse. **Special Study Options:** double major, internships, study abroad, teacher certification program, Four adult degree-completion programs offer non-traditional class schedules (night/on-line). **Disability Services:** Special programs offered to physically disabled students, including note-taking services, reader services, tutors. **Career Services:** Internships.

FACILITIES

Housing: men's dorms, women's dorms, apartments for married students, apartments for single students. **Computers:** 100% of classrooms, 100% of dorms, 100% of libraries, 100% of dining areas, 100% of student union, 100% of common outdoor areas have wireless network access. Administrative functions (other than registration) can be performed online.

CAMPUS LIFE

Environment: Metropolis. **Activities:** Choral groups, concert band, drama/theater, jazz band, literary magazine, marching band, music ensembles, musical theater, pep band, radio station, student government, student newspaper, symphony orchestra, television station, yearbook, Campus Ministries, Student Organization. **Athletics (Intercollegiate):** *Men:* baseball, basketball, golf, soccer. *Women:* basketball, golf, soccer, softball, volleyball. **On-Campus Highlights:** Library, Student Center.

ADMISSIONS

Freshman Academic Profile: Average high school GPA 3.4. **Reported SAT (pre-2016 redesign) scores:** SAT Math middle 50% range 440-570. SAT Critical Reading middle 50% range 450-560. **Concordant SAT scores:** SAT Math middle 50% range 480–590. ACT middle 50% range 19-25. Minimum internet-based TOEFL 173. Minimum paper TOEFL 500. **Basis for Candidate Selection:** *Very important factors considered include:* academic GPA, standardized test scores, character/personal qualities. *Important factors considered include:* level of applicant's interest. *Other factors considered include:* rigor of secondary school record, class rank, application essay, recommendation(s), extracurricular activities, talent/ability. **Freshman Admission Requirements:** High school diploma is required and GED is accepted. *Academic units recommended:* 4 English, 2 math, 1 science, 2 foreign language, 1 social studies, 1 history, 4 academic electives. **Freshman Admission Statistics:** 1,212 applied, 72.52% admitted, 42% enrolled. **Transfer Admission Requirements:** college transcript(s), Lowest grade transferable D. **General Admission Information:** Application fee $25. Priority deadline 4/1. Regular application deadline 8/1. Nonfall registration accepted. Admission may be deferred for a maximum of 1 year.

COSTS AND FINANCIAL AID

Notification of Awards: Applicants will be notified of awards on a rolling basis beginning 3/1. **Types of Aid:** *Need-based scholarships/grants:* Federal Pell, FSEOG, State scholarships/grants, Private scholarships, College/university scholarship or grant aid from institutional funds, United Negro College Fund, Federal Nursing Scholarships. *Loans:* Direct Subsidized Stafford Loans, Direct Unsubsidized Stafford Loans, Direct PLUS loans, Federal Perkins Loans. *Student Employment:* Federal Work-Study Program available. Institutional employment available. **Financial Aid Statistics:** 96% undergrads receive any aid. 64% undergrads borrow to pay for school. Average cumulative indebtedness $30,667. **Criteria for awarding aid:** *Non-need-based:* Academics, Alumni affiliation, Athletics, Leadership, Minority status, Music/drama, Religious affiliation.

TRINE UNIVERSITY

1 University Avenue, Angola, IN 46703
Phone: 260-665-4100 • **Financial Aid Phone:** 260-664-4158
E-mail: admit@trine.edu • **CEEB Code:** 1811
Fax: 260-665-4578 • **Website:** www.trine.edu • **ACT Code:** 1250

This private school was founded in 1884. It has a 400-acre campus.

RATINGS

Admissions Selectivity Rating: 80   **Fire Safety Rating:** 93   **Green Rating:** 61

STUDENTS AND FACULTY

Student Body: 28% female, 72% male, 39% out-of-state, (13 countries represented).
Retention and Graduation: 76% freshmen return for sophomore year. 46% freshmen graduate within 4 years. 57% freshmen graduate within 6 years. 25% grads go on to further study within 1 year. 10% grads pursue arts and sciences degrees. 5% grads pursue law degrees. 10% grads pursue business degrees.
Faculty: Student/faculty ratio 13:1. 116 full-time faculty, 64% hold PhDs, 11% are are members of minority groups, 38% are women. 0% of classes are taught by teaching assistants.

ACADEMICS

Degrees: associate, bachelor's, doctoral/professional, master's. **Classes:** Most classes have 20-29 students. Most lab/discussion sessions have 10-19 students. **Most popular majors:** Civil Engineering; Mechanical Engineering; Criminal Justice/Safety Studies. **Special Study Options:** cooperative education program, distance learning, double major, dual enrollment, English as a Second Language (ESL), honors program, internships, liberal arts/career combination, study abroad, teacher certification program. **Honors Programs:** Honors program began with Fall 2006 entering class of freshmen. Combined degree programs: BA/MEng. **Disability Services:** Special programs offered to physically disabled students, including tutors. **Career Services:** Alumni network, Alumni services, Career/job search classes, Career assessment, Internships, Regional alumni. Students may elect to incorporate cooperative education (Co-op) as a part of their academic curriculum. Co-op students alternate semesters of employment with semesters of full-time study, that provides both academic knowledge,relevant work experience, and a salary or stipend. A Co-op background is highly regarded by prospective employers; seniors seeking full-time employment with the cooperative education credential are consistently selected over candidates without this major-related experience.

FACILITIES

Housing: Coed dorms, men's dorms, women's dorms, apartments for single students, Honors housing. 95% of campus accessible to physically diasbled. **Special Academic Facilities/Equipment:** Lewis Hershey Museum; Wells Gallery of Engravings; Zollner Golf Course **Computers:** 100% of classrooms, 100% of dorms, 100% of libraries, 100% of dining areas, 100% of student union, have wireless network access. Students can register for classes online. Administrative functions (other than registration) can be performed online.

CAMPUS LIFE

Environment: Village. **Activities:** Choral groups, dance, drama/theater, music ensembles, pep band, radio station, student government, student newspaper, yearbook. 35 registered organizations, 13 honor societies, 3 religious organizations. 8 fraternities, 6 sororities. **Athletics (Intercollegiate):** *Men:* baseball, basketball, cross-country, football, golf, lacrosse, soccer, tennis, track/field (outdoor), track/field (indoor), wrestling. *Women:* basketball, cross-country, golf, lacrosse, soccer, softball, tennis, track/field (outdoor), track/field (indoor), volleyball. **On-Campus Highlights:** University Center/Ctr for online Technol, Fawick Hall of Engineering, Taylor Hall of Humanities, Zollner Golf Course (on campus), Hershey Hall (Recreational Facilities). **Environmental Initiatives:** IDEM—MS4 Storm Water Program– Erosion control best management practices, public outreach, World Wide Water Sampling Day, Water retention projects, water gardens, storm water inlet identification.

ADMISSIONS

Freshman Academic Profile: Average high school GPA 3.5. 15% in top 10% of high school class, 46% in top 25% of high school class, 82% in top 50% of high school class. 85% from public high schools. **Reported SAT (pre-2016 redesign) scores:** SAT Math middle 50% range 490-620. SAT Critical Reading middle 50% range 450-580. **Concordant SAT scores:** SAT Math middle 50% range 520–640. ACT middle 50% range 19.5-26.5. Minimum internet-based TOEFL 80. Minimum paper TOEFL 550. **Basis for Candidate Selection:** *Very important factors considered include:* rigor of secondary school record, class rank, academic GPA, standardized test scores. *Important factors considered include:* recommendation(s), interview, extracurricular activities. *Other factors considered include:* application essay, talent/ability, character/personal qualities, alumni/ae relation, volunteer work, work experience. **Freshman Admission Requirements:** High school diploma is required and GED is accepted. *Academic units required:* 4 English, 3 math, 3 science, 2 science labs, 3 social studies, 2 history, 3 academic electives. **Freshman Admission Statistics:** 2,890 applied, 76.71% admitted, 21% enrolled. **Transfer Admission Requirements:** High school transcript, college transcript(s), statement of good standing from prior institution(s). Minimum college GPA of 2.0 required. Lowest grade transferable C. **General Admission Information:** Priority deadline 6/1. Regular application deadline 8/1. Regular notification 8/1. Nonfall registration accepted. Admission may be deferred for a maximum of 12 months.

COSTS AND FINANCIAL AID

Annual tuition $30,500. Room and board $10,350. Required fees $460. Average book expense $1,200. **Required Forms and Deadlines:** FAFSA. **Notification of Awards:** Applicants will be notified of awards on a rolling basis beginning 3/15. **Types of Aid:** *Need-based scholarships/grants:* Federal Pell, FSEOG, State scholarships/grants, Private scholarships, College/university scholarship or grant aid from institutional funds. *Loans:* Direct Subsidized Stafford Loans, Direct Unsubsidized Stafford Loans, Direct PLUS loans. *Student Employment:* Federal Work-Study Program available. **Financial Aid Statistics:** 100% needy freshmen, 99% needy undergrads receive need-based scholarship or grant aid. 100% freshmen, 100% undergrads receive non-need-based scholarship or grant aid. 94% freshmen, 90% undergrads receive need-based self-help aid. 0% freshmen, 0% undergrads receive athletic scholarships. 99% freshmen, 98% undergrads receive any aid. **Criteria for awarding aid:** *Non-need-based:* Academics, Alumni affiliation, Minority status, Music/drama.

TRINITY CHRISTIAN COLLEGE

6601 West College Drive, Palos Heights, IL 60463
Phone: 708-239-4708 • **Financial Aid Phone:** 708-239-4872
E-mail: admissions@trnty.edu • **CEEB Code:** 1820
Fax: 708-239-4826 • **Website:** www.trnty.edu • **ACT Code:** 1165

This private school was founded in 1959. It has a 60-acre campus.

RATINGS

Admissions Selectivity Rating: 78   **Fire Safety Rating:** 88   **Green Rating:** 60*

STUDENTS AND FACULTY

Enrollment: 1,085. **Student Body:** 67% female, 33% male, 30% out-of-state, 2% international (12 countries represented). Asian 2%, African American 9%, Caucasian 68%, Hispanic 14%, Native American <1%, Pacific Islander <1%, Two or more races 2%, Race unknown 4%.
Retention and Graduation: 83% freshmen return for sophomore year. 57% freshmen graduate within 4 years. 58% freshmen graduate within 6 years. 12% grads go on to further study within 1 year. 4% grads pursue arts and sciences degrees. 1% grads pursue law degrees. 1% grads pursue business degrees. 2% grads pursue medical degrees. **Faculty:** Student/faculty ratio 10:1. 70 full-time faculty, 70% hold PhDs, 10% are are members of minority groups, 59% are women. 0% of classes are taught by teaching assistants.

ACADEMICS

Degrees: bachelor's, master's. **Classes:** Most classes have 10-19 students. Most lab/discussion sessions have 10-19 students. **Most popular majors:** Elementary Education and Teaching; Business/Commerce; Registered Nursing/Registered Nurse. **Special Study Options:** cooperative education program, double major, English as a Second Language (ESL), honors program, independent study, internships, liberal arts/career combination, study abroad, teacher certification program. **Honors Programs:** The Trinity Honors Program challenges and academically supports gifted students through seminars, unique opportunities within the major program, and participation in co-curricular activities. **Disability Services:** Special programs offered to physically disabled students, including reader services, tape recorders, tutors. **Career Services:** Alumni network, Alumni services, Career assessment, Internships, Regional alumni. Chicago Semester Internships.

FACILITIES

Housing: Coed dorms, apartments for married students, apartments for single students. 98% of campus accessible to physically diasbled. **Special Academic Facilities/Equipment:** Dutch Heritage Center. **Computers:** 100% of classrooms, 100% of dorms, 100% of libraries, 100% of dining areas, 100% of student union, 15% of common outdoor areas have wireless network access. Students can register for classes online. Administrative functions (other than registration) can be performed online.

CAMPUS LIFE

Environment: Metropolis. **Activities:** Choral groups, concert band, dance, drama/theater, jazz band, music ensembles, musical theater, student government, student newspaper, yearbook, Campus Ministries. 15 registered organizations, 2 honor societies, 1 religious organization. **Athletics (Intercollegiate):** *Men:* baseball, basketball, cross-country, soccer, track/field (outdoor), track/field (indoor). *Women:* basketball, cross-country, soccer, softball, track/field (outdoor), track/field (indoor), volleyball. **On-Campus Highlights:** Bootsma Bookstore/Cafe, West Hall Rec, Chapel, South Hall Lobby. **Environmental Initiatives:** Recycling of paper, aluminum, and glass.

ADMISSIONS

Freshman Academic Profile: Average high school GPA 3.5. 6% in top 10% of high school class, 24% in top 25% of high school class, 49% in top 50% of high school class. 54% from public high schools. **Reported SAT (pre-2016 redesign) scores:** SAT Math middle 50% range 450-600. SAT Critical Reading middle 50% range 418-618. **Concordant SAT scores:** SAT Math middle 50% range 490–620. ACT middle 50% range 20-27. Minimum internet-based TOEFL 79. Minimum paper TOEFL 550. **Basis for Candidate Selection:** *Very important factors considered include:* rigor of secondary school record, academic GPA, standardized test scores. *Important factors considered include:* application essay, recommendation(s), interview, extracurricular activities, talent/ability, character/personal qualities, religious affiliation/commitment. *Other factors considered include:* class rank, first generation, alumni/ae relation, geographical residence, state residency, volunteer work, work experience, level of applicant's interest. **Freshman Admission Requirements:** High school diploma is required and GED is accepted. *Academic units required:* 3 English, 3 math, 2 science, 2 social studies. *Academic units recommended:* 4 English, 4 math, 3 science, 2 foreign language, 3 social studies, 2 history. **Freshman Admission Statistics:** 884 applied, 70.02% admitted, 26% enrolled. **Transfer Admission Requirements:** college transcript(s), essay or personal statement, interview, statement of good standing from prior institution(s). Minimum college GPA of 2.0 required. Lowest grade transferable C. **General Admission Information:** Application fee $30. Priority deadline 1/15. Nonfall registration accepted. Admission may be deferred for a maximum of 1 semester.

COSTS AND FINANCIAL AID

Annual tuition $17,920. Room and board $7,010. Average book expense $925. **Required Forms and Deadlines:** FAFSA. **Notification of Awards:** Applicants will be notified of awards on a rolling basis beginning 3/1. **Types of Aid:** *Need-based scholarships/grants:* Federal Pell, FSEOG, State scholarships/grants, Private scholarships, College/university scholarship or grant aid from institutional funds, Federal Nursing Scholarships. *Loans:* Direct Subsidized Stafford Loans, Direct Unsubsidized Stafford Loans, Direct PLUS loans, Federal Perkins Loans, Federal Nursing Loans. *Student Employment:* Federal Work-Study Program available. Institutional employment available. **Financial Aid Statistics:** 100% needy freshmen, 98% needy undergrads receive need-based scholarship or grant aid. 17% freshmen, 10% undergrads receive non-need-based scholarship or grant aid. 81% freshmen, 82% undergrads receive need-based self-help aid. 8% freshmen, 5% undergrads receive athletic scholarships. 100% freshmen, 98% undergrads receive any aid. 80% undergrads borrow to pay for school. Average cumulative indebtedness $31,321. **Criteria for awarding aid:** *Need-based:* Leadership. *Non-need-based:* Academics, Alumni affiliation, Art, Athletics, Leadership, Minority status, Music/drama, Religious affiliation.

TRINITY COLLEGE (CT)

300 Summit Street, Hartford, CT 6016
Phone: 860-297-2180 • **Financial Aid Phone:** 860-297-2047
E-mail: admissions.office@trincoll.edu • **CEEB Code:** 3899
Fax: 860-297-2287 • **Website:** www.trincoll.edu • **ACT Code:** 598

This private school was founded in 1823. It has a 100-acre campus.

RATINGS

Admissions Selectivity Rating: 92 **Fire Safety Rating:** 94 **Green Rating:** 78

STUDENTS AND FACULTY

Enrollment: 2,205. **Student Body:** 47% female, 53% male, 83% out-of-state, 10% international (62 countries represented). Asian 4%, African American 6%, Caucasian 65%, Hispanic 7%, Native American <1%, Pacific Islander 0%, Two or more races 3%, Race unknown 5%.
Retention and Graduation: 89% freshmen return for sophomore year. 79% freshmen graduate within 4 years. 84% freshmen graduate within 6 years. 19% grads go on to further study within 1 year. 10% grads pursue arts and sciences degrees. 4% grads pursue law degrees. 1% grads pursue business degrees. 1% grads pursue medical degrees. **Faculty:** Student/faculty ratio 10:1. 193 full-time faculty, 93% hold PhDs, 21% are are members of minority groups, 48% are women. 0% of classes are taught by teaching assistants.

ACADEMICS

Degrees: bachelor's, master's. **Classes:** Most classes have 10-19 students. Most lab/discussion sessions have 10-19 students. **Most popular majors:** Economics; Political Science and Government; English Language and Literature. **Special Study Options:** Accelerated program, cross-registration, double major, exchange student program (domestic), honors program, independent study, internships, liberal arts/career combination, student-designed major, study abroad, teacher certification program, 5-year BS/MS in Electrical Engineering or Mechanical Engineering with Rensselaer Polytechnic Institute, Community Learning Initiative. Combined degree programs: BA/MEng, BA/MS in Elect, Engg,or Mech Engg. with RPI. **Disability Services:** Special programs offered to physically disabled students, including note-taking services, reader services, tape recorders, tutors. **Career Services:** Alumni network, Alumni services, Career/job search classes, Career assessment, Internships, Regional alumni. Our academic internships provide real-life experiences within the framework of an academic analysis. They range from internships in for-profit governmental to non-profit organizations. Over half of our students take courses with a community-based experiential component also linking community engagement with an academic course.

FACILITIES

Housing: Coed dorms, special housing for disabled students, fraternity/sorority housing, Community service dorm, quiet dorm, wellness and substance-free, 21+ only, cooking. All dorms are non-smoking. 60% of campus accessible to physically diasbled. **Special Academic Facilities/Equipment:** Watkinson Library; Austin Arts Center **Computers:** 95% of classrooms, 85% of dorms, 100% of libraries, 100% of dining areas, 100% of student union, 90% of common outdoor areas have wireless network access. Students can register for classes online. Administrative functions (other than registration) can be performed online.

CAMPUS LIFE

Environment: Metropolis. **Activities:** Choral groups, dance, drama/theater, jazz band, literary magazine, music ensembles, musical theater, radio station, student government, student newspaper, student-run film society, yearbook, Campus Ministries, Student Organization, Model UN. 105 registered organizations, 5 honor societies, 5 religious organizations. 7 fraternities, 3 sororities. **Athletics (Intercollegiate):** *Men:* baseball, basketball, crew/rowing, cross-country, diving, football, golf, ice hockey, lacrosse, soccer, squash, swimming, tennis, track/field (outdoor), track/field (indoor), wrestling. *Women:* basketball, crew/rowing, cross-country, diving, field hockey, ice hockey, lacrosse, soccer, softball, squash, swimming, tennis, track/field (outdoor), track/field

(indoor), volleyball. **On-Campus Highlights:** The Learning Corridor, Library, The Science/Engineering Labs, Summit Suites (newest residence hall), The Chapel. **Environmental Initiatives:** Reduced energy consumption in the dining halls through automated lighting and low-draw fume hoods as well as a new Building Automation System to increase control of temperatures on campus.

ADMISSIONS

Freshman Academic Profile: 43% in top 10% of high school class, 80% in top 25% of high school class, 97% in top 50% of high school class. 42% from public high schools. **Reported SAT (pre-2016 redesign) scores:** SAT Math middle 50% range 580-680. SAT Critical Reading middle 50% range 570-660. SAT Writing middle 50% range 580-680. **Concordant SAT scores:** SAT EBRW middle 50% 630–710. SAT Math middle 50% range 600–710. ACT middle 50% range 26-30. Minimum internet-based TOEFL 95. Minimum paper TOEFL 550. **Basis for Candidate Selection:** *Very important factors considered include:* rigor of secondary school record. *Important factors considered include:* class rank, academic GPA, application essay, recommendation(s), interview, extracurricular activities, talent/ability, character/personal qualities, racial/ ethnic status. *Other factors considered include:* first generation, alumni/ ae relation, geographical residence, volunteer work, work experience, level of applicant's interest. **Freshman Admission Requirements:** High school diploma is required and GED is accepted. *Academic units required:* 4 English, 3 math, 2 science, 2 science labs, 3 foreign language, 2 history. **Freshman Admission Statistics:** 7,507 applied, 33.04% admitted, 25% enrolled. **Transfer Admission Requirements:** High school transcript, college transcript(s), essay or personal statement, standardized test scores, statement of good standing from prior institution(s). Minimum college GPA of 3.0 required. Lowest grade transferable C-. **General Admission Information:** Application fee $60. Regular application deadline 1/1. Regular notification 4/1. Nonfall registration not accepted. Admission may be deferred for a maximum of 12 months.

COSTS AND FINANCIAL AID

Annual tuition $48,446. Room and board $13,144. Required fees $2,330. Average book expense $1,000. **Required Forms and Deadlines:** FAFSA, CSS/Financial Aid PROFILE, Noncustodial PROFILE, Business/Farm Supplement. **Notification of Awards:** Applicants will be notified of awards on or about 4/1. **Types of Aid:** *Need-based scholarships/grants:* Federal Pell, FSEOG, State scholarships/grants, Private scholarships, College/university scholarship or grant aid from institutional funds. *Loans:* Direct Subsidized Stafford Loans, Direct Unsubsidized Stafford Loans, Direct PLUS loans, Federal Perkins Loans, College/university loans from institutional funds. *Student Employment:* Federal Work-Study Program available. Institutional employment available. **Financial Aid Statistics:** 95% needy freshmen, 95% needy undergrads receive need-based scholarship or grant aid. 14% freshmen, 7% undergrads receive non-need-based scholarship or grant aid. 73% freshmen, 76% undergrads receive need-based self-help aid. 0% freshmen, 0% undergrads receive athletic scholarships. 49% freshmen, 45% undergrads receive any aid. **Criteria for awarding aid:** *Non-need-based:* Academics, Leadership.

TRINITY COLLEGE DUBLIN

Academic Registry, Watts Building, Dublin, IR
Phone: 353 18 964 500
E-mail: academic.registry@tcd.ie
Website: www.tcd.ie

This is a public school.

RATINGS

Admissions Selectivity Rating: 87 **Fire Safety Rating:** 90 **Green Rating:** 74

STUDENTS AND FACULTY

Student Body: 60% female, 40% male, 15% out-of-state, (122 countries represented).
Retention and Graduation: 91% freshmen return for sophomore year.
Faculty: Student/faculty ratio 17:1. 864 full-time faculty, 0% hold PhDs, 0% are are members of minority groups, 0% are women. 10% of classes are taught by teaching assistants.

ACADEMICS

Degrees: bachelor's, doctoral/professional, doctoral/research, doctoral, master's, post-master's certificate. Combined degree programs: Two Subject Moderatorship (http://www.tcd.ie/TSM/about-tsm/). **Career Services:** Alumni network, Alumni services, Career/job search classes, Career assessment, Internships, Regional alumni.

ADMISSIONS

Basis for Candidate Selection: *Very important factors considered include:* rigor of secondary school record, academic GPA, standardized test scores.

Important factors considered include: application essay, recommendation(s). Other factors considered include: extracurricular activities, character/personal qualities, volunteer work, work experience, level of applicant's interest. **Freshman Admission Statistics:** 18,995 applied, 15.84% admitted, 93% enrolled. **General Admission Information:** Priority deadline 2/1. Regular application deadline 6/1. Nonfall registration not accepted. Admission may be deferred for a maximum of 1 year.

COSTS AND FINANCIAL AID
Annual in-state tuition $19,000. **Required Forms and Deadlines:** FAFSA. **Types of Aid:** *Need-based scholarships/grants:* State scholarships/grants, Private scholarships. *Loans:* Direct Subsidized Stafford Loans, Direct Unsubsidized Stafford Loans, Direct PLUS loans, Federal Perkins Loans, Federal Nursing Loans, State Loans. *Student Employment:* Federal Work-Study Program available. **Criteria for awarding aid:** *Non-need-based:* Academics, Leadership.

TRINITY COLLEGE OF FLORIDA

2430 Welbilt Boulevard, Trinity, FL 34655
Phone: 727-569-1411 • **Financial Aid Phone:** 727-569-1413
E-mail: admissions@trinitycollege.edu
Fax: 727-569-1410 • **Website:** www.trinitycollege.edu • **ACT Code:** 4876

This private school was founded in 1932. It has a 40-acre campus.

RATINGS
Admissions Selectivity Rating: 72   Fire Safety Rating: 86   Green Rating: 60*

STUDENTS AND FACULTY
Enrollment: 210. **Student Body:** 39% female, 61% male, 28% out-of-state, 1% international (2 countries represented). Asian 0%, African American 18%, Caucasian 64%, Hispanic 16%, Native American <1%, Pacific Islander 0%, Two or more races 0%, Race unknown 0%.
Retention and Graduation: 67% freshmen return for sophomore year. 30% freshmen graduate within 4 years. 14% grads go on to further study within 1 year. **Faculty:** Student/faculty ratio 14:1. 6 full-time faculty, 83% hold PhDs, 0% are are members of minority groups, 17% are women. 0% of classes are taught by teaching assistants.

ACADEMICS
Degrees: associate, bachelor's, certificate, terminal. **Classes:** Most classes have fewer than 10 students. **Most popular majors:** Pastoral Studies/Counseling; Youth Ministry; Pre-Theology/Pre-Ministerial Studies. **Special Study Options:** Accelerated program, double major, dual enrollment, honors program, independent study, internships, weekend college. **Honors Programs:** Our honors program consists of 4 Great Books Seminars. **Disability Services:** Special programs offered to physically disabled students, including tutors. **Career Services:** Career assessment, Internships, On-campus interviews.

FACILITIES
Housing: special housing for disabled students, men's dorms, women's dorms, Apartments available for double occupancy or more. 100% of campus accessible to physically disabled. **Computers:** 100% of classrooms, 100% of dorms, 100% of libraries, 100% of dining areas, 100% of student union, have wireless network access.

CAMPUS LIFE
Environment: City. **Activities:** Choral groups, drama/theater, student government, yearbook, Campus Ministries. 4 religious organizations. **Athletics (Intercollegiate):** *Men:* basketball. *Women:* volleyball. **On-Campus Highlights:** Epiphanies Coffee Shop, Library, Lounge Areas, Outdoor Gazebo, Horseshoe Pits.

ADMISSIONS
Freshman Academic Profile: Average high school GPA 2.8. **Reported SAT (pre-2016 redesign) scores:** SAT Math middle 50% range 370-480. SAT Critical Reading middle 50% range 460-550. **Concordant SAT scores:** SAT Math middle 50% range 410–510. ACT middle 50% range 19-23. Minimum paper TOEFL 500. **Basis for Candidate Selection:** *Very important factors considered include:* academic GPA, standardized test scores, application essay, recommendation(s), religious affiliation/commitment. *Important factors considered include:* character/personal qualities. *Other factors considered include:* extracurricular activities. **Freshman Admission Requirements:** High school diploma is required and GED is accepted. *Academic units required:* 4 English, 4 math, 4 science, 2 foreign language, 2 social studies, 2 history. **Freshman Admission Statistics:** 79 applied, 84.81% admitted, 49% enrolled. **Transfer Admission Requirements:** High school transcript, college transcript(s), essay or personal statement, Minimum college GPA of 2.0

required. Lowest grade transferable C. **General Admission Information:** Application fee $25. Regular application deadline 8/2. Nonfall registration accepted. Admission may be deferred for a maximum of 1 year.

COSTS AND FINANCIAL AID
Annual tuition $11,024. Room and board $6,656. Required fees $800. Average book expense $1,185. **Required Forms and Deadlines:** FAFSA, Institution's own financial aid form. **Types of Aid:** *Need-based scholarships/grants:* Federal Pell, FSEOG, State scholarships/grants, Private scholarships, College/university scholarship or grant aid from institutional funds. *Student Employment:* Federal Work-Study Program available. Institutional employment available. **Financial Aid Statistics:** 100% needy freshmen, 86% needy undergrads receive need-based scholarship or grant aid. 100% freshmen, 74% undergrads receive non-need-based scholarship or grant aid. 75% freshmen, 79% undergrads receive need-based self-help aid. 0% freshmen, 0% undergrads receive athletic scholarships. 99% freshmen, 99% undergrads receive any aid. **Criteria for awarding aid:** *Need-based:* Academics. *Non-need-based:* Academics, Music/drama.

TRINITY INTERNATIONAL UNIVERSITY

2065 Half Day Road, Deerfield, IL 60015
Phone: 847-317-7000 • **Financial Aid Phone:** 847-317-7033
E-mail: tcadmissions@tiu.edu • **CEEB Code:** 1810
Fax: 847-317-8097 • **Website:** www.tiu.edu • **ACT Code:** 1150

This private school was founded in 1897. It has a 111-acre campus.

RATINGS
Admissions Selectivity Rating: 82   Fire Safety Rating: 82   Green Rating: 60*

STUDENTS AND FACULTY
Enrollment: 950. **Student Body:** 57% female, 43% male, 41% out-of-state, 1% international (38 countries represented). Asian 5%, African American 17%, Caucasian 63%, Hispanic 4%, Native American <1%, Pacific Islander 0%, Two or more races 0%, Race unknown 10%.
Retention and Graduation: 66% freshmen return for sophomore year. 40% freshmen graduate within 4 years. 52% freshmen graduate within 6 years. 32% grads go on to further study within 1 year. **Faculty:** Student/faculty ratio 12:1. 43 full-time faculty, 84% hold PhDs, 14% are are members of minority groups, 42% are women. 0% of classes are taught by teaching assistants.

ACADEMICS
Degrees: bachelor's, certificate, master's, postbachelor's certificate. **Classes:** Most classes have 20-29 students. Most lab/discussion sessions have 10-19 students. **Most popular majors:** Elementary Education and Teaching; Theology and Religious Vocations; Business/Commerce. **Special Study Options:** cross-registration, double major, dual enrollment, honors program, independent study, internships, study abroad, teacher certification program, REACH (for nontraditional students with previous college credit), Graduate courses. **Honors Programs:** Trinity has adopted a model for an Honors Program that is intended to enhance the breadth and depth of your liberal-arts learning, but without the burden of many additional requirements. Hence, you will do honors work in the areas of your disciplinary major, general education, and special interdisciplinary classes, but virtually all of your honors work will also fulfill regular Trinity requirements. Combined degree programs: BA/MA. **Disability Services:** Special programs offered to physically disabled students, including note-taking services, reader services, tape recorders, tutors. **Career Services:** Alumni services, Career/job search classes, Career assessment, Internships, On-campus interviews. Students in Trinity International University's Athletic Training Education Program have benefited through Trinity's partnership with Condell Health Network in Libertyville, Illinois. Condell's internship opportunities provide our students with necessary clinical experience while they work under the supervision of certified athletic trainers.

FACILITIES
Housing: special housing for disabled students, men's dorms, women's dorms, apartments for married students, apartments for single students. 75% of campus accessible to physically disabled. **Special Academic Facilities/Equipment:** None **Computers:** 100% of classrooms, 50% of dorms, 100% of libraries, 100% of student union, have wireless network access. Students can register for classes online. Administrative functions (other than registration) can be performed online.

CAMPUS LIFE
Environment: Village. **Activities:** Choral groups, concert band, drama/theater, jazz band, music ensembles, musical theater, pep band, student government, student newspaper, symphony orchestra, yearbook, Campus Ministries. 33 registered organizations, 2 honor societies. **Athletics (Intercollegiate):**

Men: baseball, basketball, football, soccer. *Women:* basketball, soccer, softball, volleyball. **On-Campus Highlights:** Lew Student Center, Trinity Hall, McLennan Academic Building, Rodine Global Ministry Building, Melton Dining Hall.

ADMISSIONS

Freshman Academic Profile: Average high school GPA 3.3. 37% in top 10% of high school class, 43% in top 25% of high school class, 68% in top 50% of high school class. 69% from public high schools. **Reported SAT (pre-2016 redesign) scores:** SAT Math middle 50% range 440-600. SAT Critical Reading middle 50% range 445-610. **Concordant SAT scores:** SAT Math middle 50% range 480-620. ACT middle 50% range 19-26. Minimum paper TOEFL 530. **Basis for Candidate Selection:** *Very important factors considered include:* class rank, academic GPA, standardized test scores, application essay, recommendation(s), character/personal qualities, religious affiliation/commitment. *Other factors considered include:* rigor of secondary school record, extracurricular activities, talent/ability, first generation. **Freshman Admission Requirements:** High school diploma is required and GED is accepted. *Academic units required:* 4 English, 2 math, 2 science, 1 science lab, 2 foreign language, 2 social studies, 2 history, 2 visual/performing arts. **Freshman Admission Statistics:** 466 applied, 80.47% admitted, 44% enrolled. **Transfer Admission Requirements:** High school transcript, college transcript(s), essay or personal statement, statement of good standing from prior institution(s). Minimum college GPA of 2.0 required. Lowest grade transferable C-. **General Admission Information:** Application fee $25. Nonfall registration accepted. Admission may be deferred for a maximum of 12 months.

COSTS AND FINANCIAL AID

Annual tuition $21,980. Room and board $7,430. Required fees $390. **Required Forms and Deadlines:** FAFSA. **Notification of Awards:** Applicants will be notified of awards on a rolling basis beginning 2/15. **Types of Aid:** *Need-based scholarships/grants:* Federal Pell, FSEOG, State scholarships/grants, Private scholarships, College/university scholarship or grant aid from institutional funds. *Loans:* Federal Perkins Loans. *Student Employment:* Federal Work-Study Program available. Institutional employment available. **Financial Aid Statistics:** 95% needy freshmen, 95% needy undergrads receive need-based scholarship or grant aid. 95% freshmen, 95% undergrads receive non-need-based scholarship or grant aid. 82% freshmen, 78% undergrads receive need-based self-help aid. 0% freshmen, 0% undergrads receive athletic scholarships. 90% freshmen, 86% undergrads receive any aid. **Criteria for awarding aid:** *Non-need-based:* Academics, Alumni affiliation, Athletics, Minority status, Music/drama, Religious affiliation.

TRINITY LUTHERAN COLLEGE

4221 228th Avenue SE, Issaquah, WA 98029
Phone: 425-961-5510 • **Financial Aid Phone:** 425-961-5514
E-mail: admission@tlc.edu
Fax: 425-392-0404 • **Website:** www.tlc.edu

This private school, affiliated with the Lutheran Church, was founded in 1944.

RATINGS

Admissions Selectivity Rating: 71   **Fire Safety Rating:** 82   **Green Rating:** 60*

STUDENTS AND FACULTY

Enrollment: 114. **Student Body:** 53% female, 47% male, 35% out-of-state, 0% international. Asian 4%, African American 1%, Caucasian 89%, Hispanic 4%, Native American 1%, Pacific Islander 0%, Two or more races 0%, Race unknown 2%.
Retention and Graduation: 78% freshmen return for sophomore year. **Faculty:** 13 full-time faculty, 0% hold PhDs, 0% are are members of minority groups, 0% are women.

ACADEMICS

Degrees: associate, bachelor's, diploma, postbachelor's certificate, terminal, transfer. **Most popular majors:** Bible/Biblical Studies; Youth Ministry; Music. **Special Study Options:** double major, independent study, internships, liberal arts/career combination, student-designed major, study abroad, teacher certification program. **Disability Services:** Special programs offered to physically disabled students, including note-taking services, reader services, tape recorders, tutors. **Career Services:** Alumni network, Alumni services, Career assessment, Internships, Regional alumni, On-campus interviews. 10 week internships are a graduation requirement for all students

FACILITIES

Housing: Coed dorms, special housing for disabled students, men's dorms, women's dorms, apartments for married students, apartments for single

students, Special housing for married students and non-traditional age students. **Computers:** Administrative functions (other than registration) can be performed online.

CAMPUS LIFE

Environment: Village. **Activities:** Choral groups, drama/theater, music ensembles, musical theater, student government, student newspaper, yearbook. **Athletics (Intercollegiate):** *Men:* basketball, softball. *Women:* softball. **On-Campus Highlights:** Student Center, The Running Cup, Chapel, YMCA, Bookstore.

ADMISSIONS

Freshman Academic Profile: 0% in top 10% of high school class, 33% in top 25% of high school class, 60% in top 50% of high school class. Minimum paper TOEFL 525. **Basis for Candidate Selection:** *Very important factors considered include:* recommendation(s), character/personal qualities. *Important factors considered include:* rigor of secondary school record, academic GPA, standardized test scores, religious affiliation/commitment, volunteer work. *Other factors considered include:* extracurricular activities, talent/ability, first generation, alumni/ae relation, work experience, level of applicant's interest. **Freshman Admission Requirements:** High school diploma is required and GED is accepted. **Freshman Admission Statistics:** 113 applied, 59.29% admitted, 72% enrolled. **Transfer Admission Requirements:** college transcript(s), Minimum college GPA of 2.0 required. Lowest grade transferable C-. **General Admission Information:** Application fee $30. Priority deadline 6/15. Regular application deadline 8/15. Nonfall registration accepted. Admission may be deferred for a maximum of 2 years.

COSTS AND FINANCIAL AID

Annual tuition $13,714. Room and board $6,078. Required fees $450. Average book expense $500. **Required Forms and Deadlines:** FAFSA, Institution's own financial aid form. **Notification of Awards:** Applicants will be notified of awards on a rolling basis beginning 1/1. **Types of Aid:** *Need-based scholarships/grants:* Federal Pell, FSEOG, Private scholarships, College/university scholarship or grant aid from institutional funds. *Loans:* Direct Subsidized Stafford Loans, Direct Unsubsidized Stafford Loans, Direct PLUS loans. *Student Employment:* Federal Work-Study Program available. Institutional employment available. **Criteria for awarding aid:** *Need-based:* Academics. *Non-need-based:* Academics, Alumni affiliation, Art, Leadership, Music/drama, Religious affiliation.

TRINITY UNIVERSITY

One Trinity Place, San Antonio, TX 78212-7200
Phone: 210-999-7207 • **Financial Aid Phone:** 210-999-8898
E-mail: admissions@trinity.edu • **CEEB Code:** 6831
Fax: 210-999-8164 • **Website:** www.trinity.edu • **ACT Code:** 4226

This private school was founded in 1869. It has a 117-acre campus.

RATINGS

Admissions Selectivity Rating: 91   **Fire Safety Rating:** 94   **Green Rating:** 60*

STUDENTS AND FACULTY

Enrollment: 2,334. **Student Body:** 53% female, 47% male, 23% out-of-state, 7% international (66 countries represented). Asian 6%, African American 4%, Caucasian 55%, Hispanic 21%, Native American <1%, Pacific Islander 0%, Two or more races 5%, Race unknown 2%.
Retention and Graduation: 89% freshmen return for sophomore year. 68% freshmen graduate within 4 years. 77% freshmen graduate within 6 years. 33% grads go on to further study within 1 year. 3% grads pursue law degrees. 4% grads pursue medical degrees. **Faculty:** Student/faculty ratio 8:1. 236 full-time faculty, 98% hold PhDs, 23% are are members of minority groups, 43% are women. 0% of classes are taught by teaching assistants.

ACADEMICS

Degrees: bachelor's, master's. **Classes:** Most classes have 10-19 students. Most lab/discussion sessions have 20-29 students. **Most popular majors:** Engineering Science; Communication; Business Administration and Management. **Special Study Options:** Accelerated program, double major, honors program, independent study, internships, liberal arts/career combination, student-designed major, study abroad, teacher certification program. **Honors Programs:** Honors Program Combined degree programs: BA/MA, BA/MA-education; BS/MS-accounting. **Disability Services:** Special programs offered to physically disabled students, including note-taking services, reader services, tutors. **Career Services:** Alumni network, Alumni services, Career/job search classes, Career assessment, Internships, Regional alumni.

FACILITIES

Housing: Coed dorms, Wellness Housing, Theme Housing. 99% of campus accessible to physically diasbled. **Special Academic Facilities/Equipment:** Steiren Theatre, Richardson Communication Center, Ruth Taylor Arts Complex including art gallery, Laurie Auditorium. **Computers:** 100% of classrooms, 100% of dorms, 100% of libraries, 100% of dining areas, 100% of student union, 100% of common outdoor areas have wireless network access. Students can register for classes online. Administrative functions (other than registration) can be performed online.

CAMPUS LIFE

Environment: Metropolis. **Activities:** Choral groups, concert band, dance, drama/theater, jazz band, literary magazine, music ensembles, musical theater, opera, pep band, radio station, student government, student newspaper, student-run film society, symphony orchestra, television station, yearbook, Campus Ministries, Student Organization, Model UN. 130 registered organizations, 24 honor societies, 4 religious organizations. 7 fraternities, 6 sororities. **Athletics (Intercollegiate):** *Men:* baseball, basketball, cross-country, diving, football, golf, soccer, swimming, tennis, track/field (outdoor). *Women:* basketball, cross-country, diving, golf, soccer, softball, swimming, tennis, track/field (outdoor), volleyball. **On-Campus Highlights:** Stieren Theatre, Laurie Auditorium, Coates Library, Bell Athletic Center, Coates University Center, Northrup Hall.

ADMISSIONS

Freshman Academic Profile: Average high school GPA 3.6. 41% in top 10% of high school class, 75% in top 25% of high school class, 93% in top 50% of high school class. 76% from public high schools. **Reported SAT (pre-2016 redesign) scores:** SAT Math middle 50% range 580-680. SAT Critical Reading middle 50% range 580-690. SAT Writing middle 50% range 560-670. **Concordant SAT scores:** SAT EBRW middle 50% 630–720. SAT Math middle 50% range 600–710. ACT middle 50% range 27-31. **Basis for Candidate Selection:** *Very important factors considered include:* rigor of secondary school record, class rank, academic GPA, standardized test scores. *Important factors considered include:* application essay, recommendation(s), interview, extracurricular activities, talent/ability, character/personal qualities. *Other factors considered include:* first generation, alumni/ae relation, geographical residence, volunteer work, work experience, level of applicant's interest. **Freshman Admission Requirements:** High school diploma is required and GED is accepted. *Academic units required:* 4 English, 3 math, 3 science, 2 science labs, 2 foreign language, 3 social studies. *Academic units recommended:* 4 English, 3 math, 3 science, 2 science labs, 2 foreign language, 3 social studies. **Freshman Admission Statistics:** 7,255 applied, 40.66% admitted, 22% enrolled. **Transfer Admission Requirements:** High school transcript, college transcript(s), essay or personal statement, statement of good standing from prior institution(s). Minimum college GPA of 3.0 required. Lowest grade transferable C-. **General Admission Information:** Regular application deadline 2/1. Regular notification 4/1. Nonfall registration accepted. Admission may be deferred.

COSTS AND FINANCIAL AID

Annual tuition $38,974. Room and board $12,754. Required fees $586. Average book expense $1,000. **Required Forms and Deadlines:** FAFSA, CSS/Financial Aid PROFILE. **Notification of Awards:** Applicants will be notified of awards on or about 3/15. **Types of Aid:** *Need-based scholarships/grants:* Federal Pell, FSEOG, State scholarships/grants, Private scholarships, College/university scholarship or grant aid from institutional funds. *Loans:* Direct Subsidized Stafford Loans, Direct Unsubsidized Stafford Loans, Direct PLUS loans, Federal Perkins Loans, State Loans, College/university loans from institutional funds. *Student Employment:* Federal Work-Study Program available. Institutional employment available. **Financial Aid Statistics:** 100% needy freshmen, 98% needy undergrads receive need-based scholarship or grant aid. 39% freshmen, 24% undergrads receive non-need-based scholarship or grant aid. 53% freshmen, 62% undergrads receive need-based self-help aid. 0% freshmen, 0% undergrads receive athletic scholarships. 98% freshmen, 93% undergrads receive any aid. 45% undergrads borrow to pay for school. Average cumulative indebtedness $38,605. **Criteria for awarding aid:** *Need-based:* Academics. *Non-need-based:* Academics, Art, Leadership, Music/drama.

TROY UNIVERSITY—TROY
(FORMERLY TROY STATE UNIVERSITY)

111 Adams Administration, Troy, AL 36082
Phone: 334-670-3179 • **Financial Aid Phone:** 334-670-3186
E-mail: admit@troy.edu • **CEEB Code:** 1738
Fax: 334-670-3733 • **Website:** www.troy.edu • **ACT Code:** 48

This public school was founded in 1887. It has a 512-acre campus.

RATINGS

Admissions Selectivity Rating: 72   **Fire Safety Rating:** 94   **Green Rating:** 60*

STUDENTS AND FACULTY

Enrollment: 14,149. **Student Body:** 60% female, 40% male, 33% out-of-state, 5% international. Asian 3%, African American 30%, Caucasian 51%, Hispanic 3%, Native American 1%, Pacific Islander <1%, Two or more races 3%, Race unknown 4%.
Retention and Graduation: 74% freshmen return for sophomore year. 15% freshmen graduate within 4 years. 39% freshmen graduate within 6 years. **Faculty:** Student/faculty ratio 15:1. 523 full-time faculty, 0% hold PhDs, 19% are are members of minority groups, 49% are women. 1% of classes are taught by teaching assistants.

ACADEMICS

Degrees: associate, bachelor's, doctoral/professional, master's, post-master's certificate. **Classes:** Most classes have 10-19 students. Most lab/discussion sessions have 20-29 students. **Most popular majors:** Accounting; Business Administration and Management; Psychology. **Special Study Options:** Accelerated program, cross-registration, distance learning, double major, dual enrollment, English as a Second Language (ESL), external degree program, honors program, independent study, internships, study abroad, teacher certification program, weekend college. **Honors Programs:** The University Honors Program, open to students in all undergraduate divisions of the university, is administered by the Honors Council and the director of university honors. The purpose of the University Honors Program is to offer the academically superior student a specially designed program, within a supportive community, that fosters critical thinking, intellectual development and social responsibility. This enhanced program is designed to provide a balance of common experience and flexibility addressed to individual achievement as well as a comprehensive framework on which to build disciplinary studies. The Honors Program also has an honors house on campus which houses both male and female students. Students should consult with the director of the University Honors Program and the director of University Housing for availabilities and stipulations. The house serves as a residence and a focal point for meetings and activities with the Honors Alliance, faculty and staff in the Honors Program. The official student voice within the program is the University Honors Alliance. Membership to the University Honors Alliance is offered to any student with a 3.3 grade point average or higher. There is an annual membership fee of $5. **Disability Services:** Special programs offered to physically disabled students, including note-taking services, reader services, tape recorders, tutors.

FACILITIES

Housing: Coed dorms, men's dorms, special housing for international students, women's dorms, fraternity/sorority housing, apartments for married students, apartments for single students, Substance Free Housing Honor Student Housing. 95% of campus accessible to physically diasbled. **Special Academic Facilities/Equipment:** Art museum, recording studio. **Computers:** Students can register for classes online.

CAMPUS LIFE

Environment: Town. **Activities:** Choral groups, concert band, dance, drama/theater, jazz band, marching band, music ensembles, musical theater, opera, pep band, radio station, student government, student newspaper, symphony orchestra, television station, yearbook. 125 registered organizations, 22 honor societies, 7 religious organizations. 12 fraternities, 9 sororities. **Athletics (Intercollegiate):** *Men:* baseball, basketball, cheerleading, cross-country, football, golf, rodeo, tennis, track/field (outdoor). *Women:* basketball, cheerleading, cross-country, golf, rodeo, soccer, softball, tennis, track/field (outdoor), volleyball. **On-Campus Highlights:** Movie Gallery Veterans Stadium, Malone Art Gallery, Hall of Honor/National Band Hall of Fame, Trojan Center, Rosa Parks Museum—Montgomery Campus. **Environmental Initiatives:** Recycling.

ADMISSIONS

Freshman Academic Profile: Average high school GPA 3.4. **Reported SAT (pre-2016 redesign) scores:** SAT Math middle 50% range 430-550. SAT Critical Reading middle 50% range 433-528. SAT Writing middle 50% range 440-585. **Concordant SAT scores:** SAT EBRW middle 50% 490–610. SAT

Math middle 50% range 470–570. ACT middle 50% range 19-26. Minimum internet-based TOEFL 80. Minimum paper TOEFL 500. **Basis for Candidate Selection:** *Very important factors considered include:* rigor of secondary school record, academic GPA, standardized test scores. *Other factors considered include:* application essay, recommendation(s), interview, extracurricular activities, talent/ability, character/personal qualities, alumni/ae relation. **Freshman Admission Requirements:** High school diploma is required and GED is accepted. *Academic units required:* 4 English, 4 math, 4 science, 4 social studies. *Academic units recommended:* 2 foreign language. **Freshman Admission Statistics:** 6,565 applied, 90.45% admitted, 36% enrolled. **Transfer Admission Requirements:** college transcript(s), Minimum college GPA of 2.0 required. Lowest grade transferable D. **General Admission Information:** Application fee $30. Nonfall registration accepted. Admission may be deferred for a maximum of 2 years.

COSTS AND FINANCIAL AID

Annual in-state tuition $9,632. Annual out-of-state tuition $19,264. Room and board $7,853. Required fees $1,567. Average book expense $1,129. **Required Forms and Deadlines:** FAFSA, Institution's own financial aid form. **Notification of Awards:** Applicants will be notified of awards on a rolling basis beginning 5/1. **Types of Aid:** *Need-based scholarships/grants:* Federal Pell, FSEOG, State scholarships/grants, Private scholarships, College/university scholarship or grant aid from institutional funds. *Loans:* Federal Perkins Loans. *Student Employment:* Federal Work-Study Program available. Institutional employment available. **Financial Aid Statistics:** 54% needy freshmen, 62% needy undergrads receive need-based scholarship or grant aid. 58% freshmen, 47% undergrads receive non-need-based scholarship or grant aid. 100% freshmen, 99% undergrads receive need-based self-help aid. 2% freshmen, 33% undergrads receive athletic scholarships. **Criteria for awarding aid:** *Need-based:* Academics. *Non-need-based:* Academics, Athletics, Leadership, Music/drama.

See page 1064.

TRUMAN STATE UNIVERSITY

100 E. Normal Ave., Kirksville, MO 63501
Phone: 660-785-4114 • **Financial Aid Phone:** 660-785-4130
E-mail: admissions@truman.edu • **CEEB Code:** 6483
Fax: 660-785-7456 • **Website:** http://www.truman.edu • **ACT Code:** 2336

This public school was founded in 1867. It has a 140-acre campus.

RATINGS

Admissions Selectivity Rating: 89   **Fire Safety Rating:** 98   **Green Rating:** 60*

STUDENTS AND FACULTY

Enrollment: 5,302. **Student Body:** 58% female, 42% male, 19% out-of-state, 7% international (50 countries represented). Asian 3%, African American 4%, Caucasian 79%, Hispanic 3%, Native American <1%, Pacific Islander <1%, Two or more races 3%, Race unknown 1%.
Retention and Graduation: 87% freshmen return for sophomore year. 57% freshmen graduate within 4 years. 72% freshmen graduate within 6 years. 40% grads go on to further study within 1 year. **Faculty:** Student/faculty ratio 16:1. 332 full-time faculty, 84% hold PhDs, 12% are are members of minority groups, 42% are women. 1% of classes are taught by teaching assistants.

ACADEMICS

Degrees: bachelor's, master's, postbachelor's certificate. **Classes:** Most classes have 20-29 students. Most lab/discussion sessions have fewer than 10 students. **Most popular majors:** Business Administration, Management and Operations; Biology/Biological Sciences; Psychology. **Special Study Options:** double major, dual enrollment, honors program, independent study, internships, student-designed major, study abroad, teacher certification program. **Honors Programs:** General Honors Program: Students must complete five upper-level courses in math, social science, science and humanities with a 3.5 GPA in these 5 courses. Departmental honors are also available in some disciplines. Combined degree programs: Bach. in subject area/Master of Arts in Education. **Disability Services:** Special programs offered to physically disabled students, including note-taking services, reader services, tape recorders, tutors. **Career Services:** Alumni network, Alumni services, Career/job search classes, Career assessment, Internships, Regional alumni. One of the most developed partnerships that Truman offers is through the Washington Center in D.C. A wide variety of experiential internships through the "Truman in Washington" liaison program offered on our campus gives support to students interested in internship opportunities in D.C. Included are work-experience opportunities in such areas as foreign affairs/diplomacy, government affairs, criminal justice, relations, health and human services, and communications as well as other areas.

FACILITIES

Housing: Coed dorms, special housing for disabled students, special housing for international students, apartments for married students, apartments for single students, Theme Housing, Sorority housing, French language housing, and Spanish language housing. 99% of campus accessible to physically diasbled. **Special Academic Facilities/Equipment:** Art gallery, local history and artifacts museum, human performance lab, greenhouse, observatory, IR and NMR instrumentation, and convergent media center (TV studio, newspaper, and radio station). **Computers:** 100% of classrooms, 100% of dorms, 100% of libraries, 75% of dining areas, 100% of student union, 90% of common outdoor areas have wireless network access. Students can register for classes online. Administrative functions (other than registration) can be performed online.

CAMPUS LIFE

Environment: Village. **Activities:** Choral groups, concert band, dance, drama/theater, jazz band, literary magazine, marching band, music ensembles, musical theater, opera, pep band, radio station, student government, student newspaper, student-run film society, symphony orchestra, television station, Campus Ministries, Student Organization, Model UN. 282 registered organizations, 18 honor societies, 16 religious organizations. 16 fraternities, 11 sororities. **Athletics (Intercollegiate):** *Men:* baseball, basketball, cross-country, football, golf, soccer, swimming, tennis, track/field (outdoor), track/field (indoor), wrestling. *Women:* basketball, cross-country, golf, soccer, softball, swimming, tennis, track/field (outdoor), track/field (indoor), volleyball. **On-Campus Highlights:** Student Recreation Center, Pickler Memorial Library, Student Union Building, The Quadrangle, Jazzman's Coffee Shop.

ADMISSIONS

Freshman Academic Profile: Average high school GPA 3.8. 52% in top 10% of high school class, 83% in top 25% of high school class, 97% in top 50% of high school class. 86% from public high schools. **Reported SAT (pre-2016 redesign) scores:** SAT Math middle 50% range 520-650. SAT Critical Reading middle 50% range 550-680. **Concordant SAT scores:** SAT Math middle 50% range 550–670. ACT middle 50% range 24-30. Minimum internet-based TOEFL 79. Minimum paper TOEFL 550. **Basis for Candidate Selection:** *Very important factors considered include:* rigor of secondary school record, class rank, academic GPA, standardized test scores. *Important factors considered include:* application essay. *Other factors considered include:* recommendation(s), extracurricular activities, talent/ability, character/personal qualities, first generation, alumni/ae relation, geographical residence, state residency, racial/ethnic status, volunteer work, work experience, level of applicant's interest. **Freshman Admission Requirements:** High school diploma is required and GED is accepted. *Academic units required:* 4 English, 3 math, 3 science, 2 science labs, 2 foreign language, 2 social studies, 1 history, 5 academic electives, 1 visual/performing arts, and 3 units from above areas or other academic areas. *Academic units recommended:* 4 English, 4 math, 3 science, 2 science labs, 2 foreign language, 2 social studies, 1 history, 5 academic electives, 1 visual/performing arts, and 3 units from above areas or other academic areas. **Freshman Admission Statistics:** 5,178 applied, 67.69% admitted, 36% enrolled. **Transfer Admission Requirements:** college transcript(s), essay or personal statement. **General Admission Information:** Priority deadline 12/1. Nonfall registration accepted. Admission may be deferred.

COSTS AND FINANCIAL AID

Annual in-state tuition $7,152. Annual out-of-state tuition $13,636. Room and board $8,558. Required fees $304. Average book expense $1,000. **Required Forms and Deadlines:** FAFSA. **Notification of Awards:** Applicants will be notified of awards on a rolling basis beginning 3/1. **Types of Aid:** *Need-based scholarships/grants:* Federal Pell, FSEOG, State scholarships/grants, Private scholarships, College/university scholarship or grant aid from institutional funds. *Loans:* Direct Subsidized Stafford Loans, Direct Unsubsidized Stafford Loans, Direct PLUS loans, Federal Perkins Loans, Federal Nursing Loans, College/university loans from institutional funds. *Student Employment:* Federal Work-Study Program available. Institutional employment available. **Financial Aid Statistics:** 99% needy freshmen, 94% needy undergrads receive need-based scholarship or grant aid. 99% freshmen, 79% undergrads receive non-need-based scholarship or grant aid. 70% freshmen, 78% undergrads receive need-based self-help aid. 6% freshmen, 6% undergrads receive athletic scholarships. 99% freshmen, 86% undergrads receive any aid. 56% undergrads borrow to pay for school. Average cumulative indebtedness $24,811. **Criteria for awarding aid:** *Need-based:* Academics. *Non-need-based:* Academics, Alumni affiliation, Art, Athletics, Leadership, Minority status, Music/drama, State/district residency.

See page 1066.

TUFTS UNIVERSITY

Bendetson Hall, Medford, MA 2155
Phone: 617-627-3170 • **Financial Aid Phone:** 617-627-2000
E-mail: undergraduate.admissions@tufts.edu • **CEEB Code:** 3901
Fax: 617-627-3860 • **Website:** www.tufts.edu • **ACT Code:** 1922

This private school was founded in 1852. It has a 150-acre campus.

RATINGS

Admissions Selectivity Rating: 98   **Fire Safety Rating:** 98   **Green Rating:** 89

STUDENTS AND FACULTY

Enrollment: 5,459. **Student Body:** 50% female, 50% male, 74% out-of-state, 10% international (74 countries represented). Asian 12%, African American 4%, Caucasian 56%, Hispanic 7%, Native American 0%, Pacific Islander 0%, Two or more races 5%, Race unknown 6%.
Retention and Graduation: 96% freshmen return for sophomore year. 87% freshmen graduate within 4 years. 92% freshmen graduate within 6 years. 14% grads go on to further study within 1 year. **Faculty:** Student/faculty ratio 8:1. 674 full-time faculty, 93% hold PhDs, 0% are are members of minority groups, 44% are women. 1% of classes are taught by teaching assistants.

ACADEMICS

Degrees: bachelor's, doctoral/professional, doctoral/research, doctoral, master's, postbachelor's certificate, post-master's certificate. **Classes:** Most classes have 10-19 students. Most lab/discussion sessions have 10-19 students. **Most popular majors:** International Relations and Affairs; Economics; Computer Science. **Special Study Options:** cross-registration, double major, exchange student program (domestic), honors program, independent study, internships, liberal arts/career combination, student-designed major, study abroad, teacher certification program. Combined degree programs: BA/MD, BA/MA, BA/DDS, BA/MEng, 5-yr BA/BFA with SMFA; 5-yr BA/BFA with NEC. **Disability Services:** Special programs offered to physically disabled students, including note-taking services, reader services, tape recorders, tutors. **Career Services:** Alumni network, Alumni services, Career/job search classes, Career assessment, Internships, Regional alumni. Thanks to our proximity to Boston, most of our students are able to pursue an internship during their 4 years, many for academic credit. Tufts also has a program geared at providing a stipend to students who pursue an internship with non-profit or public sector organizations.

FACILITIES

Housing: Coed dorms, special housing for disabled students, women's dorms, fraternity/sorority housing, cooperative housing, Special Interest Housing. **Special Academic Facilities/Equipment:** Language lab, nutrition institute, research lab for physical electronics, bioelectrical and biochemical labs, computer-aided design (CAD) facility, electro-optics technology and environmental management centers. **Computers:** 50% of classrooms, 20% of dorms, 100% of libraries, 75% of dining areas, 100% of student union, 75% of common outdoor areas have wireless network access. Students can register for classes online. Administrative functions (other than registration) can be performed online.

CAMPUS LIFE

Environment: Town. **Activities:** Choral groups, concert band, dance, drama/theater, jazz band, literary magazine, marching band, music ensembles, musical theater, opera, pep band, radio station, student government, student newspaper, student-run film society, symphony orchestra, television station, yearbook, Campus Ministries, Student Organization, Model UN. 160 registered organizations, 4 honor societies, 6 religious organizations. 11 fraternities, 3 sororities. **Athletics (Intercollegiate):** *Men:* baseball, basketball, crew/rowing, cross-country, diving, football, golf, ice hockey, lacrosse, sailing, soccer, squash, swimming, tennis, track/field (outdoor), track/field (indoor). *Women:* basketball, cheerleading, crew/rowing, cross-country, diving, fencing, field hockey, golf, lacrosse, sailing, soccer, softball, squash, swimming, tennis, track/field (outdoor), track/field (indoor), volleyball. **On-Campus Highlights:** The Aidekman Arts Center, Tisch Library, Edwin Ginn Library, Cousens Gymnasium, Ellis Oval, Meyer Campus Center. **Environmental Initiatives:** Reduced green house gas emissions to below 1998 levels, working to further that with the creation of a new power plant that will decrease energy usage.

ADMISSIONS

Freshman Academic Profile: 59% from public high schools. **Reported SAT (pre-2016 redesign) scores:** SAT Math middle 50% range 690-770.

SAT Critical Reading middle 50% range 680-750. SAT Writing middle 50% range 680-760. **Concordant SAT scores:** SAT EBRW middle 50% 720–770. SAT Math middle 50% range 720–780. ACT middle 50% range 31-34. Minimum internet-based TOEFL 100. Minimum paper TOEFL 600. **Basis for Candidate Selection:** *Very important factors considered include:* rigor of secondary school record, class rank, academic GPA, standardized test scores, application essay, recommendation(s), character/personal qualities. *Important factors considered include:* extracurricular activities, talent/ability, volunteer work, work experience. *Other factors considered include:* interview, first generation, alumni/ae relation, geographical residence, racial/ethnic status, level of applicant's interest. **Freshman Admission Requirements:** High school diploma is required and GED is accepted. *Academic units required:* 4 English, 4 math, 4 science, 3 foreign language, 4 social studies. *Academic units recommended:* 4 foreign language. **Freshman Admission Statistics:** 20,223 applied, 14.29% admitted, 46% enrolled. **Transfer Admission Requirements:** High school transcript, college transcript(s), essay or personal statement, standardized test scores, statement of good standing from prior institution(s). Lowest grade transferable C. **General Admission Information:** Application fee $70. Regular application deadline 1/1. Regular notification 4/1. Nonfall registration not accepted. Admission may be deferred for a maximum of 1 year.

COSTS AND FINANCIAL AID

Required Forms and Deadlines: FAFSA, CSS/Financial Aid PROFILE, Noncustodial PROFILE. **Notification of Awards:** Applicants will be notified of awards on or about 4/1. **Types of Aid:** *Need-based scholarships/grants:* Federal Pell, FSEOG, State scholarships/grants, Private scholarships, College/university scholarship or grant aid from institutional funds. *Loans:* Direct Subsidized Stafford Loans, Direct Unsubsidized Stafford Loans, Direct PLUS loans, Federal Perkins Loans, College/university loans from institutional funds. *Student Employment:* Federal Work-Study Program available. Institutional employment available. **Financial Aid Statistics:** 92% needy freshmen, 93% needy undergrads receive need-based scholarship or grant aid. 5% freshmen, 4% undergrads receive non-need-based scholarship or grant aid. 90% freshmen, 91% undergrads receive need-based self-help aid. 0% freshmen, 0% undergrads receive athletic scholarships. 37% freshmen, 38% undergrads receive any aid. Average cumulative indebtedness $24,267. **Criteria for awarding aid:** *Non-need-based:* Academics.

TULANE UNIVERSITY

6823 St. Charles Avenue, New Orleans, LA 70118
Phone: 504-865-5731 • **Financial Aid Phone:** 504-865-5723
E-mail: undergrad.admission@tulane.edu • **CEEB Code:** 6832
Fax: 504-862-8715 • **Website:** www.tulane.edu • **ACT Code:** 1614

This private school was founded in 1834. It has a 110-acre campus.

RATINGS

Admissions Selectivity Rating: 95   **Fire Safety Rating:** 95   **Green Rating:** 89

STUDENTS AND FACULTY

Enrollment: 6,821. **Student Body:** 59% female, 41% male, 76% out-of-state, 3% international (37 countries represented). Asian 4%, African American 4%, Caucasian 77%, Hispanic 6%, Native American <1%, Pacific Islander <1%, Two or more races 4%, Race unknown 2%.
Retention and Graduation: 92% freshmen return for sophomore year. 72% freshmen graduate within 4 years. 83% freshmen graduate within 6 years. **Faculty:** Student/faculty ratio 9:1. 707 full-time faculty, 96% hold PhDs, 17% are are members of minority groups, 40% are women.

ACADEMICS

Degrees: associate, bachelor's, certificate, doctoral/professional, doctoral/research, doctoral, master's, postbachelor's certifiate. **Classes:** Most classes have 10-19 students. Most lab/discussion sessions have 10-19 students. **Special Study Options:** Accelerated program, cross-registration, distance learning, double major, English as a Second Language (ESL), exchange student program (domestic), honors program, independent study, internships, liberal arts/career combination, student-designed major, study abroad, teacher certification program. **Honors Programs:** Tulane Honors Program Combined degree programs: BA/MD, BA/JD, BA/MA, Integrated Graduate Studies 4+1 programs. **Disability Services:** Special programs offered to physically disabled students, including note-taking services, reader services, tape recorders, tutors. **Career Services:** Alumni network, Alumni services, Career/job search classes, Career assessment, Internships, Regional alumni.

FACILITIES

Housing: Coed dorms, special housing for disabled students, special housing for international students, women's dorms, apartments for married students, apartments for single students, Wellness Housing. 60% of campus accessible to physically diasbled. **Special Academic Facilities/Equipment:** Newcomb Art Gallery, Amistad Research Center, Latin American Library, Maxwell Music Library, Hogan Jazz Archives, Louisiana Special Collection, Manuscripts Department, Koch Herbarium, Tulane Museum of Natural History, Government Documents. **Computers:** 100% of classrooms, 100% of dorms, 100% of libraries, 100% of dining areas, 100% of student union, 100% of common outdoor areas have wireless network access. Students can register for classes online. Administrative functions (other than registration) can be performed online.

CAMPUS LIFE

Environment: City. **Activities:** Choral groups, concert band, dance, drama/theater, jazz band, literary magazine, marching band, music ensembles, musical theater, pep band, radio station, student government, student newspaper, student-run film society, television station, yearbook. 250 registered organizations, 43 honor societies, 16 religious organizations. 15 fraternities, 11 sororities. **Athletics (Intercollegiate):** *Men:* baseball, basketball, cross-country, football, tennis, track/field (outdoor). *Women:* basketball, cross-country, diving, golf, swimming, tennis, track/field (outdoor), track/field (indoor), volleyball. **On-Campus Highlights:** Amistad Research Center, Newcomb Art Gallery, Reily Recreation Center, Howard Tilton Memorial Library, PJ's Coffee Shop.

ADMISSIONS

Freshman Academic Profile: Average high school GPA 3.5. 61% in top 10% of high school class, 87% in top 25% of high school class, 96% in top 50% of high school class. 60% from public high schools. **Reported SAT (pre-2016 redesign) scores:** SAT Math middle 50% range 630-710. SAT Critical Reading middle 50% range 620-710. SAT Writing middle 50% range 640-720. **Concordant SAT scores:** SAT EBRW middle 50% 680–740. SAT Math middle 50% range 650–740. ACT middle 50% range 29-33. Minimum paper TOEFL 550. **Basis for Candidate Selection:** *Very important factors considered include:* rigor of secondary school record, class rank, academic GPA, standardized test scores. *Important factors considered include:* application essay, recommendation(s), character/personal qualities. *Other factors considered include:* interview, extracurricular activities, talent/ability, first generation, alumni/ae relation, volunteer work, work experience, level of applicant's interest. **Freshman Admission Requirements:** High school diploma is required and GED is accepted. *Academic units recommended:* 4 English, 4 math, 4 science, 4 science labs, 3 foreign language, 3 social studies, 3 academic electives. **Freshman Admission Statistics:** 32,006 applied, 25.50% admitted, 23% enrolled. **Transfer Admission Requirements:** High school transcript, college transcript(s), essay or personal statement, Minimum college GPA of 2.5 required. Lowest grade transferable C. **General Admission Information:** Regular application deadline 1/15. Regular notification 4/1. Nonfall registration accepted. Admission may be deferred for a maximum of 1 year.

COSTS AND FINANCIAL AID

Annual tuition $45,758. Room and board $14,446. Required fees $3,880. Average book expense $1,200. **Required Forms and Deadlines:** FAFSA, CSS/Financial Aid PROFILE, Noncustodial PROFILE, Business/Farm Supplement. **Notification of Awards:** Applicants will be notified of awards on a rolling basis beginning 3/15. **Types of Aid:** *Need-based scholarships/grants:* Federal Pell, FSEOG, State scholarships/grants, Private scholarships, College/university scholarship or grant aid from institutional funds. *Loans:* Direct Subsidized Stafford Loans, Direct Unsubsidized Stafford Loans, Direct PLUS loans, Federal Perkins Loans. *Student Employment:* Federal Work-Study Program available. Institutional employment available. **Financial Aid Statistics:** 97% needy freshmen, 97% needy undergrads receive need-based scholarship or grant aid. 39% freshmen, 28% undergrads receive non-need-based scholarship or grant aid. 71% freshmen, 78% undergrads receive need-based self-help aid. 2% freshmen, 3% undergrads receive athletic scholarships. 38% undergrads borrow to pay for school. Average cumulative indebtedness $31,642. **Criteria for awarding aid:** *Non-need-based:* Academics, Athletics, Leadership, Music/drama, State/district residency.

TUSKEGEE UNIVERSITY

Best Colleges

Margaret Murray Washington Hall, Tuskegee, AL 36088
Phone: 334-727-8500 • **Financial Aid Phone:** 334-727-8088
E-mail: admissions@mytu.tuskegee.edu • **CEEB Code:** 1813
Fax: 334-727-5750 • **Website:** www.tuskegee.edu • **ACT Code:** 50

This private school was founded in 1881. It has a 5200-acre campus.

RATINGS

Admissions Selectivity Rating: 88   **Fire Safety Rating:** 97   **Green Rating:** 60*

STUDENTS AND FACULTY

Enrollment: 2,485. **Student Body:** 61% female, 39% male, 70% out-of-state, <1% international (19 countries represented). Asian 0%, African American 78%, Caucasian <1%, Hispanic <1%, Native American <1%, Pacific Islander 0%, Two or more races 0%, Race unknown 21%.
Retention and Graduation: 73% freshmen return for sophomore year. 21% freshmen graduate within 4 years. 47 23% grads go on to further study within 1 year. 11% grads pursue arts and sciences degrees. 2% grads pursue law degrees. 4% grads pursue business degrees. 3% grads pursue medical degrees. **Faculty:** Student/faculty ratio 14:1. 194 full-time faculty, 87% hold PhDs, 84% are are members of minority groups, 32% are women. 0% of classes are taught by teaching assistants.

ACADEMICS

Degrees: bachelor's, doctoral/professional, doctoral/research, master's. **Classes:** Most classes have 10-19 students. **Most popular majors:** Electrical and Electronics Engineering; Veterinary Medicine. **Special Study Options:** cooperative education program, double major, dual enrollment, honors program, independent study, internships, teacher certification program. **Career Services:** Alumni network, Career/job search classes, Career assessment, Internships, Regional alumni.

FACILITIES

Housing: Coed dorms, men's dorms, women's dorms, apartments for married students, apartments for single students. 33% of campus accessible to physically diasbled. **Special Academic Facilities/Equipment:** Agricultural and natural history museum, electron microscopes, two nursery schools. **Computers:** 100% of classrooms, 100% of dorms, 100% of libraries, 100% of dining areas, 100% of student union, 100% of common outdoor areas have wireless network access. Students can register for classes online.

CAMPUS LIFE

Environment: Rural. **Activities:** Choral groups, drama/theater, marching band, student government, student newspaper, yearbook, Campus Ministries, Student Organization. 36 registered organizations, 22 honor societies, 6 religious organizations. 5 fraternities, 6 sororities. **Athletics (Intercollegiate):** *Men:* baseball, basketball, cheerleading, cross-country, diving, fencing, football, golf, gymnastics, riflery, soccer, swimming, tennis, track/field (outdoor), track/field (indoor), volleyball. *Women:* basketball, cheerleading, cross-country, diving, fencing, golf, gymnastics, riflery, soccer, swimming, tennis, track/field (outdoor), track/field (indoor), volleyball. **On-Campus Highlights:** George Washington Carver Museum, Kellogg Conference Center, Tuskegee Chapel, The Tuskegee Cemetery, General Daniel.

ADMISSIONS

Freshman Academic Profile: Average high school GPA 3.2. 20% in top 10% of high school class, 60% in top 25% of high school class, 100% in top 50% of high school class. 88% from public high schools. **Reported SAT (pre-2016 redesign) scores:** SAT Math middle 50% range 420-520. SAT Critical Reading middle 50% range 440-510. **Concordant SAT scores:** SAT Math middle 50% range 460–550. ACT middle 50% range 18-23. Minimum internet-based TOEFL 62. Minimum paper TOEFL 500. **Basis for Candidate Selection:** *Very important factors considered include:* rigor of secondary school record, class rank, academic GPA, standardized test scores, recommendation(s), talent/ability. *Important factors considered include:* character/personal qualities, alumni/ae relation. *Other factors considered include:* application essay, interview, extracurricular activities, first generation, geographical residence, state residency, volunteer work, work experience. **Freshman Admission Requirements:** High school diploma is required and GED is accepted. *Academic units required:* 4 English, 3 math, 2 science, 3 social studies, 4 academic electives. **Freshman Admission Statistics:** 9,582 applied, 35.66% admitted, 17% enrolled. **Transfer Admission Requirements:** college transcript(s), Minimum college GPA of 2.0 required. Lowest grade transferable C. **General Admission Information:** Application fee $25. Priority deadline

3/31. Regular application deadline 7/15. Regular notification 3/15. Nonfall registration accepted. Admission may be deferred for a maximum of 12 months.

COSTS AND FINANCIAL AID

Annual tuition $18,100. Room and board $8,510. Required fees $3,525. Average book expense $1,282. **Required Forms and Deadlines:** FAFSA, Institution's own financial aid form, CSS/Financial Aid PROFILE. **Types of Aid:** *Need-based scholarships/grants:* Federal Pell, FSEOG, State scholarships/grants, Private scholarships, College/university scholarship or grant aid from institutional funds, United Negro College Fund, Federal Nursing Scholarships. *Loans:* Direct Subsidized Stafford Loans, Direct Unsubsidized Stafford Loans, Direct PLUS loans, Federal Perkins Loans, Federal Nursing Loans, State Loans, College/university loans from institutional funds. *Student Employment:* Federal Work-Study Program available. Institutional employment available. **Financial Aid Statistics:** 100% needy freshmen, 100% needy undergrads receive need-based scholarship or grant aid. 17% freshmen, 22% undergrads receive non-need-based scholarship or grant aid. 100% freshmen, 68% undergrads receive need-based self-help aid. 7% freshmen, 9% undergrads receive athletic scholarships. 90% freshmen, 92% undergrads receive any aid. 49% undergrads borrow to pay for school. Average cumulative indebtedness $18,100. **Criteria for awarding aid:** *Need-based:* Academics, Athletics. *Non-need-based:* Academics, Athletics, State/district residency.

UNION COLLEGE

310 College Street, Barbourville, KY 40906
Phone: 606-546-1229 • **Financial Aid Phone:** 606-546-1224
E-mail: enrollme@unionky.edu
Fax: 606-546-1667 • **Website:** www.unionky.edu • **ACT Code:** 15520

This private school, affiliated with the Methodist Church, was founded in 1879.

RATINGS

Admissions Selectivity Rating: 74 **Fire Safety Rating:** 65 **Green Rating:** 60*

STUDENTS AND FACULTY

Enrollment: 794. **Student Body:** 47% female, 53% male, 26% out-of-state, 8% international (19 countries represented). Asian 1%, African American 12%, Caucasian 72%, Hispanic 2%, Native American <1%, Pacific Islander <1%, Two or more races 5%, Race unknown 1%.
Retention and Graduation: 56% freshmen return for sophomore year. 16% freshmen graduate within 4 years. 32% freshmen graduate within 6 years.
Faculty: Student/faculty ratio 12:1. 56 full-time faculty, 45% hold PhDs, 11% are are members of minority groups, 45% are women. 0% of classes are taught by teaching assistants.

ACADEMICS

Degrees: bachelor's, master's, postbachelor's certificate. **Classes:** Most classes have 10-19 students. Most lab/discussion sessions have 10-19 students. **Most popular majors:** Business Administration and Management; Psychology; Special Education and Teaching. **Special Study Options:** distance learning, double major, honors program, independent study, internships, liberal arts/career combination, student-designed major, study abroad, teacher certification program. Combined degree programs: BA/MA. **Disability Services:** Special programs offered to physically disabled students, including reader services, tape recorders, tutors. **Career Services:** Alumni network, Career/job search classes, Career assessment, Internships, Regional alumni.

FACILITIES

Housing: men's dorms, women's dorms, apartments for married students, apartments for single students. 50% of campus accessible to physically disabled. **Computers:** 100% of classrooms, 100% of dorms, 100% of libraries, 100% of dining areas, 100% of student union, 50% of common outdoor areas have wireless network access. Students can register for classes online. Administrative functions (other than registration) can be performed online.

CAMPUS LIFE

Environment: Rural. **Activities:** Choral groups, drama/theater, literary magazine, pep band, student government, television station, yearbook. 23 registered organizations, 2 honor societies, 2 religious organizations. **Athletics (Intercollegiate):** *Men:* baseball, basketball, bowling, cheerleading, cross-country, cycling, football, golf, soccer, swimming, tennis, track/field (outdoor). *Women:* basketball, bowling, cheerleading, cross-country, cycling, golf, soccer, softball, swimming, tennis, track/field (outdoor), volleyball. **On-Campus Highlights:** Student Center, Sharp Center Coffee Shop, Fitness Center.

ADMISSIONS

Reported SAT (pre-2016 redesign) scores: SAT Math middle 50% range 453-553. SAT Critical Reading middle 50% range 433-508. **Concordant**

SAT scores: SAT Math middle 50% range 490–570. ACT middle 50% range 18-23. Minimum paper TOEFL 550. **Basis for Candidate Selection:** *Important factors considered include:* rigor of secondary school record, class rank, academic GPA, standardized test scores, level of applicant's interest. *Other factors considered include:* recommendation(s), extracurricular activities, talent/ability, character/personal qualities, first generation, alumni/ae relation, geographical residence, volunteer work. **Freshman Admission Requirements:** High school diploma is required and GED is accepted. *Academic units recommended:* 4 English, 3 math, 2 science, 2 science labs, 1 foreign language, 2 social studies. **Freshman Admission Statistics:** 1,332 applied, 69.07% admitted, 23% enrolled. **Transfer Admission Requirements:** college transcript(s), Minimum college GPA of 2.0 required. Lowest grade transferable 2. **General Admission Information:** Application fee $10. Nonfall registration accepted. Admission may be deferred.

COSTS AND FINANCIAL AID

Annual tuition $22,720. Room and board $7,000. Required fees $640. **Required Forms and Deadlines:** FAFSA. **Notification of Awards:** Applicants will be notified of awards on a rolling basis beginning 3/1. **Types of Aid:** *Need-based scholarships/grants:* Federal Pell, FSEOG, State scholarships/grants, Private scholarships, College/university scholarship or grant aid from institutional funds. *Loans:* Direct Subsidized Stafford Loans, Direct Unsubsidized Stafford Loans, Direct PLUS loans, College/university loans from institutional funds. *Student Employment:* Federal Work-Study Program available. Institutional employment available. **Financial Aid Statistics:** 98% needy freshmen, 95% needy undergrads receive need-based scholarship or grant aid. 7% freshmen, 11% undergrads receive non-need-based scholarship or grant aid. 89% freshmen, 82% undergrads receive need-based self-help aid. 0% freshmen, 0% undergrads receive athletic scholarships. 100% freshmen, 100% undergrads receive any aid. **Criteria for awarding aid:** *Need-based:* Academics, Alumni affiliation, Athletics, Job skills. *Non-need-based:* Academics, Athletics, Job skills, Religious affiliation, State/district residency.

UNION COLLEGE

Grant Hall, Schenectady, NY 12308
Phone: 518-388-6112 • **Financial Aid Phone:** 518-388-6123
E-mail: admissions@union.edu • **CEEB Code:** 2920
Fax: 518-388-6986 • **Website:** www.union.edu • **ACT Code:** 2970

This private school was founded in 1795. It has a 100-acre campus.

RATINGS

Admissions Selectivity Rating: 94 **Fire Safety Rating:** 92 **Green Rating:** 93

STUDENTS AND FACULTY

Enrollment: 2,119. **Student Body:** 46% female, 54% male, 67% out-of-state, 8% international (33 countries represented). Asian 6%, African American 4%, Caucasian 72%, Hispanic 7%, Native American 0%, Pacific Islander 0%, Two or more races 3%, Race unknown <1%.
Retention and Graduation: 91% freshmen return for sophomore year. 80% freshmen graduate within 4 years. 86% freshmen graduate within 6 years. 20% grads go on to further study within 1 year. **Faculty:** Student/faculty ratio 10:1. 211 full-time faculty, 98% hold PhDs, 12% are are members of minority groups, 44% are women. 0% of classes are taught by teaching assistants.

ACADEMICS

Degrees: bachelor's. **Classes:** Most classes have 10-19 students. Most lab/discussion sessions have 10-19 students. **Most popular majors:** Economics; Psychology; Mechanical Engineering. **Special Study Options:** Accelerated program, cross-registration, double major, dual enrollment, honors program, independent study, internships, liberal arts/career combination, student-designed major, study abroad, teacher certification program. **Honors Programs:** The Union Scholars program offers selected students the opportunity to take full advantage of the diverse intellectual experiences at Union. Specific features of the program are an enriched two-term version of First-Year Preceptorial; a sophomore independent study project with a professor of the student's choosing; the option to participate as a junior in a program in which students take a leadership role in the College's intellectual and social life; and a Scholars Colloquium run by students for presenting faculty and student research, in the senior year. Union Scholars use their extra courses to create an enriched program that meets their specific needs and interests. Combined degree programs: BA/JD, BS/MS or MBA/MD; BS/MS;BA or BS/MBA(joint pgms). **Disability Services:** Special programs offered to physically disabled students, including note-taking services, reader services, tape recorders. **Career Services:** Alumni network, Alumni services, Career/job search classes, Career assessment, Internships, Regional alumni. The Career Center is well integrated within the campus community (esp. academic, athletic, and admissions departments) and is frequently called upon to speak to students/recruits, and conduct programs.

FACILITIES

Housing: Coed dorms, fraternity/sorority housing, apartments for single students, Theme Housing, Minerva Houses. Up to 45 students live in each. All students and faculty members have (Minerva) house affiliations. Each house contributes intellectual, cultural, and social events to the campus. 80% of campus accessible to physically disabled. **Special Academic Facilities/Equipment:** The Nott Memorial and its Mandeville Gallery; Yulman Theater; Burns Arts Atrium; Taylor Music Center and its Emerson Auditorium; Special Collections at Schaffer Library; Memorial Chapel; Jackson''s Garden, an eight-acre formal garden and woodland. Academic facilities include the F.W. Olin Center, with high technology classrooms and laboratories, a multi-media auditorium, collaborative computer classrooms, and a 20-inch remote-controlled telescope. Science and engineering facilities include superconducting nuclear magnetic resonance spectrometer, two electron microscopes, tandem pelletron positive ion accelerator, a fully accessible machine lab, and Aerogel fabrication and analysis lab. **Computers:** 100% of classrooms, 75% of dorms, 100% of libraries, 100% of dining areas, 100% of student union, 100% of common outdoor areas have wireless network access. Students can register for classes online. Administrative functions (other than registration) can be performed online.

CAMPUS LIFE

Environment: Town. **Activities:** Choral groups, concert band, dance, drama/theater, jazz band, literary magazine, music ensembles, radio station, student government, student newspaper, student-run film society, symphony orchestra, television station, yearbook, Campus Ministries, Student Organization, Model UN. 100 registered organizations, 13 honor societies, 7 religious organizations. 12 fraternities, 5 sororities. **Athletics (Intercollegiate):** *Men:* baseball, basketball, crew/rowing, cross-country, diving, football, ice hockey, lacrosse, soccer, swimming, tennis, track/field (outdoor), track/field (indoor). *Women:* basketball, crew/rowing, cross-country, diving, field hockey, ice hockey, lacrosse, soccer, softball, swimming, tennis, track/field (outdoor), track/field (indoor), volleyball. **On-Campus Highlights:** The Nott Memorial, Schaffer Library, Reamer Campus Center, Jackson's Garden, Memorial Chapel. **Environmental Initiatives:** Incorporation of Sustainability into Union College's Mission, Presidential Priority & Strategic Plan.

ADMISSIONS

Freshman Academic Profile: Average high school GPA 3.4. 67% in top 10% of high school class, 86% in top 25% of high school class, 98% in top 50% of high school class. 65% from public high schools. **Reported SAT (pre-2016 redesign) scores:** SAT Math middle 50% range 710-610. SAT Critical Reading middle 50% range 680-590. SAT Writing middle 50% range 680-570. **Concordant SAT scores:** SAT EBRW middle 50% 720–640. SAT Math middle 50% range 740–630. ACT middle 50% range 31-28. Minimum internet-based TOEFL 90. Minimum paper TOEFL 600. **Basis for Candidate Selection:** *Very important factors considered include:* rigor of secondary school record, class rank, academic GPA, standardized test scores. *Important factors considered include:* application essay, recommendation(s), extracurricular activities, talent/ability, character/personal qualities, volunteer work, work experience. *Other factors considered include:* interview, first generation, alumni/ae relation, geographical residence, state residency, racial/ethnic status, level of applicant's interest. **Freshman Admission Requirements:** High school diploma is required and GED is not accepted. *Academic units required:* 4 English, 3 math, 2 science, 2 science labs, 2 foreign language, 1 social studies, 1 history. *Academic units recommended:* 4 English, 4 math, 4 science, 4 science labs, 4 foreign language, 2 social studies, 2 history. **Freshman Admission Statistics:** 6,648 applied, 36.90% admitted, 23% enrolled. **Transfer Admission Requirements:** High school transcript, college transcript(s), essay or personal statement, statement of good standing from prior institution(s). Minimum college GPA of 3.0 required. Lowest grade transferable C. **General Admission Information:** Regular application deadline 1/15. Regular notification 4/1. Nonfall registration accepted. Admission may be deferred for a maximum of 2 years.

COSTS AND FINANCIAL AID

Annual tuition $51,225. Room and board $12,678. Required fees $471. Average book expense $1,500. **Required Forms and Deadlines:** FAFSA, CSS/Financial Aid PROFILE, State aid form, Noncustodial PROFILE. **Notification of Awards:** Applicants will be notified of awards on or about 3/25. **Types of Aid:** *Need-based scholarships/grants:* Federal Pell, FSEOG, State scholarships/grants, Private scholarships, College/university scholarship or grant aid from institutional funds. *Loans:* Direct Subsidized Stafford Loans,

Direct Unsubsidized Stafford Loans, Direct PLUS loans, Federal Perkins Loans, College/university loans from institutional funds. *Student Employment:* Federal Work-Study Program available. Institutional employment available. **Financial Aid Statistics:** 98% needy freshmen, 94% needy undergrads receive need-based scholarship or grant aid. 9% freshmen, 11% undergrads receive non-need-based scholarship or grant aid. 93% freshmen, 94% undergrads receive need-based self-help aid. 0% freshmen, 0% undergrads receive athletic scholarships. 84% freshmen, 80% undergrads receive any aid. 54% undergrads borrow to pay for school. Average cumulative indebtedness $33,045. **Criteria for awarding aid:** *Need-based:* Academics. *Non-need-based:* Academics.

See page 1068.

UNION INSTITUTE & UNIVERSITY

440 East McMillan Street, Cincinnati, OH 45206
Phone: 513-861-6400 • **Financial Aid Phone:** 800-486-3116
E-mail: admissions@myunion.edu
Fax: 513-861-3238 • **Website:** www.myunion.edu

This private school was founded in 1964.

RATINGS
Admissions Selectivity Rating: 61   **Fire Safety Rating:** 60*   **Green Rating:** 60*

STUDENTS AND FACULTY
Enrollment: 1,146. **Student Body:** 53% female, 47% male, 16% out-of-state, 0% international (24 countries represented). Asian 1%, African American 26%, Caucasian 33%, Hispanic 13%, Native American 1%, Pacific Islander <1%, Two or more races 2%, Race unknown 24%.
Retention and Graduation: 90% freshmen return for sophomore year. 9% freshmen graduate within 4 years. 9% freshmen graduate within 6 years.
Faculty: Student/faculty ratio 9:1. 31 full-time faculty, 84% hold PhDs, 19% are are members of minority groups, 52% are women. 0% of classes are taught by teaching assistants.

ACADEMICS
Degrees: bachelor's, doctoral/research, doctoral, master's. **Most popular majors:** Criminal Justice/Law Enforcement Administration; Liberal Arts and Sciences Studies and Humanities; Child Development. **Special Study Options:** cross-registration, distance learning, external degree program, independent study, internships, teacher certification program. **Career Services:** Alumni services, Career assessment, On-campus interviews.

FACILITIES
Housing: Housing (not university-owned) available for learners participating in brief on-campus residencies at Montpelier, Vermont center (applicable to BA and MEd programs only). 100% of campus accessible to physically disabled. **Computers:** Students can register for classes online. Administrative functions (other than registration) can be performed online.

CAMPUS LIFE
Environment: Metropolis.

ADMISSIONS
Basis for Candidate Selection: *Important factors considered include:* application essay, recommendation(s), interview, level of applicant's interest. *Other factors considered include:* extracurricular activities, talent/ability, character/personal qualities, volunteer work, work experience. **Freshman Admission Requirements:** High school diploma is required and GED is accepted. **Transfer Admission Requirements:** college transcript(s), essay or personal statement, interview, Lowest grade transferable D. **General Admission Information:** Nonfall registration accepted. Admission may be deferred for a maximum of 12 months.

COSTS AND FINANCIAL AID
Required Forms and Deadlines: FAFSA, Institution's own financial aid form. **Notification of Awards:** Applicants will be notified of awards on a rolling basis beginning 5/1. **Types of Aid:** *Need-based scholarships/grants:* Federal Pell, FSEOG, State scholarships/grants, Private scholarships, College/university scholarship or grant aid from institutional funds. *Loans:* Federal Perkins Loans. *Student Employment:* Federal Work-Study Program available. **Criteria for awarding aid:** *Need-based:* Academics. *Non-need-based:* Academics, State/district residency.

UNION UNIVERSITY

1050 Union University Drive, Jackson, TN 38305-3697
Phone: 731-661-5000 • **Financial Aid Phone:** 731-661-5015
E-mail: rgrimm@uu.edu • **CEEB Code:** 1826
Fax: 731-661-5017 • **ACT Code:** 4020

This private school, affiliated with the Southern Baptist Church, was founded in 1823. It has a 360-acre campus.

RATINGS

Admissions Selectivity Rating: 86   **Fire Safety Rating:** 86   **Green Rating:** 68

STUDENTS AND FACULTY

Enrollment: 2,171. **Student Body:** 62% female, 38% male, 31% out-of-state, 2% international (36 countries represented). Asian 1%, African American 14%, Caucasian 77%, Hispanic 2%, Native American <1%, Pacific Islander <1%, Two or more races 2%, Race unknown 2%.
Retention and Graduation: 93% freshmen return for sophomore year. 51% freshmen graduate within 4 years. 40% grads go on to further study within 1 year. **Faculty:** Student/faculty ratio 11:1. 229 full-time faculty, 83% hold PhDs, 10% are are members of minority groups, 49% are women. 0% of classes are taught by teaching assistants.

ACADEMICS

Degrees: associate, bachelor's, diploma, doctoral/professional, doctoral/research, doctoral, master's, post-master's certificate, transfer. **Classes:** Most classes have 10-19 students. Most lab/discussion sessions have 10-19 students. **Most popular majors:** Elementary Education and Teaching; Christian Studies. **Special Study Options:** Accelerated program, cross-registration, distance learning, double major, dual enrollment, English as a Second Language (ESL), exchange student program (domestic), honors program, independent study, internships, study abroad, teacher certification program. Combined degree programs: Digital Media Studies. **Disability Services:** Special programs offered to physically disabled students, including note-taking services, reader services, tape recorders, tutors. **Career Services:** Alumni network, Alumni services, Career/job search classes, Career assessment, Internships, Regional alumni. Our department is proudest of the career development and recruitment opportunities that are discipline-specific which include capstone life calling and career development workshops geared towards individual majors and the workshop series entitled: What Can I Do With a Major In...? as well as our recruitment-specific offerings(Backpack to Briefcase, professional development and prep for internships recruitment; College to Career, professional development and prep for full-time career opportunities; internship and majors fair; and Teacher Expo, education recruitment). We are also excited about our Five-Star Aspiring Pre-professionals Program or Five-Star App which carries select students with competitive GPAs, quality experience, leadership/community service, life calling and career focus, competitive skills (discipline-specific and soft), exceptional character and who are recommended by our faculty through a Five-Star Life Calling and Career Development process. The five areas of development include professional resume, cover letter, and portfolio development, interview training, job search strategies/career coaching, personality assessment and interpretation, and graduate school preparation and test prep guidance.

FACILITIES

Housing: special housing for disabled students, men's dorms, women's dorms, apartments for married students. 98% of campus accessible to physically diasbled. **Special Academic Facilities/Equipment:** Elementary education lab, 21st-century classroom, TV communications truck, nursing/health assessment labs, health and wellness center, art gallery. **Computers:** 75% of classrooms, 100% of dorms, 100% of libraries, 50% of dining areas, 100% of student union, have wireless network access. Administrative functions (other than registration) can be performed online.

CAMPUS LIFE

Environment: City. **Activities:** Choral groups, concert band, drama/theater, jazz band, literary magazine, music ensembles, pep band, student government, student newspaper, student-run film society, yearbook, Campus Ministries, Student Organization. 67 registered organizations, 12 honor societies, 4 religious organizations. 3 fraternities, 3 sororities. **Athletics (Intercollegiate):** *Men:* baseball, basketball, cheerleading, cross-country, golf, soccer. *Women:* basketball, cheerleading, cross-country, soccer, softball, volleyball. **On-Campus Highlights:** Bowld Commons, New Residence Life Complexes, Pharmacy Building, White Hall, Jennings Hall, Athletic Facility, Penick Academic Complex, Barefoot's Joe Coffee Shop. **Environmental Initiatives:** Campus-wide recycling campaign for aluminum, plastics and paper. This includes pick up from all student residential areas as well as all buildings/offices.

ADMISSIONS

Freshman Academic Profile: Average high school GPA 3.7. 33% in top 10% of high school class, 62% in top 25% of high school class, 85% in top 50% of high school class. 57% from public high schools. **Reported SAT (pre-2016 redesign) scores:** SAT Math middle 50% range 520-670. SAT Critical Reading middle 50% range 500-680. **Concordant SAT scores:** SAT Math middle 50% range 550–700. ACT middle 50% range 22-29. Minimum internet-based TOEFL 80. Minimum paper TOEFL 550. **Basis for Candidate Selection:** *Very important factors considered include:* rigor of secondary school record, academic GPA, character/personal qualities, level of applicant's interest. *Important factors considered include:* class rank, standardized test scores, interview, extracurricular activities, talent/ability, religious affiliation/commitment. *Other factors considered include:* application essay, recommendation(s), first generation, alumni/ae relation, volunteer work, work experience. **Freshman Admission Requirements:** High school diploma is required and GED is accepted. *Academic units required:* 4 English, 3 math, 3 science, 2 science labs, 1 foreign language, 2 social studies, 1 history, 1 academic elective. *Academic units recommended:* 4 English, 4 math, 4 science, 2 science labs, 2 foreign language, 2 social studies, 2 history, 4 academic electives, 1 computer science, 1 visual/performing arts. **Freshman Admission Statistics:** 1,930 applied, 74.20% admitted, 32% enrolled. **Transfer Admission Requirements:** college transcript(s), statement of good standing from prior institution(s). Minimum college GPA of 2.3 required. Lowest grade transferable C. **General Admission Information:** Application fee $35. Priority deadline 12/1. Regular application deadline 8/1. Nonfall registration accepted. Admission may be deferred for a maximum of 1 year.

COSTS AND FINANCIAL AID

Annual tuition $26,160. Room and board $8,430. Required fees $720. Average book expense $1,220. **Required Forms and Deadlines:** FAFSA, Institution's own financial aid form. **Notification of Awards:** Applicants will be notified of awards on a rolling basis beginning 12/1. **Types of Aid:** *Need-based scholarships/grants:* Federal Pell, FSEOG, State scholarships/grants, Private scholarships, College/university scholarship or grant aid from institutional funds, Federal Nursing Scholarships. *Loans:* Direct Subsidized Stafford Loans, Direct Unsubsidized Stafford Loans, Direct PLUS loans, Federal Perkins Loans. *Student Employment:* Federal Work-Study Program available. Institutional employment available. **Financial Aid Statistics:** 76% needy freshmen, 70% needy undergrads receive need-based scholarship or grant aid. 99% freshmen, 77% undergrads receive non-need-based scholarship or grant aid. 58% freshmen, 69% undergrads receive need-based self-help aid. 7% freshmen, 7% undergrads receive athletic scholarships. 99% freshmen, 99% undergrads receive any aid. **Criteria for awarding aid:** *Need-based:* Job skills, Minority status. *Non-need-based:* Academics, Alumni affiliation, Art, Athletics, Job skills, Leadership, Minority status, Music/drama, Religious affiliation.

UNITED STATES AIR FORCE ACADEMY

HQ USAFA/ RRS, USAF Academy, CO 80840-5025
Phone: 719-333-2520
E-mail: rr_webmail@usafa.edu
Fax: 719-333-3012 • **Website:** www.academyadmissions.com • **ACT Code:** 530

This public school was founded in 1954. It has a 18000-acre campus.

RATINGS

Admissions Selectivity Rating: 98   **Fire Safety Rating:** 99   **Green Rating:** 70

STUDENTS AND FACULTY

Enrollment: 4,237. **Student Body:** 25% female, 75% male, 85% out-of-state, 1% international (25 countries represented). Asian 5%, African American 6%, Caucasian 62%, Hispanic 11%, Native American <1%, Pacific Islander 1%, Two or more races 7%, Race unknown 7%.
Retention and Graduation: 88% freshmen return for sophomore year. 79% freshmen graduate within 4 years. 81% freshmen graduate within 6 years. 10% grads pursue arts and sciences degrees. 2% grads pursue medical degrees. **Faculty:** Student/faculty ratio 9:1. 501 full-time faculty, 60% hold PhDs, 6% are are members of minority groups, 20% are women. 0% of classes are taught by teaching assistants.

ACADEMICS

Degrees: bachelor's. **Classes:** Most classes have 10-19 students. Most lab/discussion sessions have 10-19 students. **Most popular majors:** Aerospace,

Aeronautical and Astronautical/Space Engineering; Systems Engineering; Business Administration and Management. **Special Study Options:** double major, English as a Second Language (ESL), exchange student program (domestic), honors program, independent study, internships, student-designed major, study abroad, Academically At-Risk Program Hospital Instruction Program Extra Instruction Program Summer Programs. **Career Services:** Alumni network, Alumni services, Regional alumni, On-campus interviews. Majors' Night—Each Department, ability to recruit freshman cadets into various majors. Display tables (demos, experiments, studies from each department) and Faculty to meet with cadets to answer questions about a major in their department. Faculty and Students enthusiastic about this evening of discussion.

FACILITIES

Housing: Coed dorms. All students are required to live on campus all four years. 0% of campus accessible to physically diasbled. **Special Academic Facilities/Equipment:** Language learning center, laser and optics research center, USAFA observatory, Dept. of Engineering Mechanics Lab, US Air Force Academy visitor's center, consolidated educational training facility, Air Force Academy cadet chapel, American Legion Memorial Tower, Clune area athletic and speaking events (seats 6,000), air garden, Falcon Stadium, Aeronautics Lab, Meterology Lab, Arnold Hall Broadway Theater, ballroom and conference rooms, and historical displays. **Computers:** 100% of classrooms, 100% of libraries, 100% of student union, have wireless network access. Students can register for classes online. Administrative functions (other than registration) can be performed online. Undergraduates are required to own a computer.

CAMPUS LIFE

Environment: Metropolis. **Activities:** Choral groups, dance, drama/theater, marching band, musical theater, pep band, radio station, yearbook, Campus Ministries, Model UN. 77 registered organizations, 2 honor societies, 14 religious organizations. **Athletics (Intercollegiate):** *Men:* baseball, basketball, boxing, cheerleading, cross-country, diving, fencing, football, golf, gymnastics, ice hockey, lacrosse, riflery, soccer, swimming, tennis, track/field (outdoor), track/field (indoor), water polo, wrestling. *Women:* basketball, cheerleading, cross-country, diving, fencing, gymnastics, riflery, soccer, swimming, tennis, track/field (outdoor), track/field (indoor), volleyball. **On-Campus Highlights:** USAF Academy Chapel, Thunderbird Lookout and Air Field, Falcon Stadium, Cadet Sports Complex, Visitor Center. **Environmental Initiatives:** Solar

ADMISSIONS

Freshman Academic Profile: Average high school GPA 3.9. 52% in top 10% of high school class, 81% in top 25% of high school class, 97% in top 50% of high school class. **Reported SAT (pre-2016 redesign) scores:** SAT Math middle 50% range 620-720. SAT Critical Reading middle 50% range 600-690. **Concordant SAT scores:** SAT Math middle 50% range 640–750. ACT middle 50% range 27-33. **Basis for Candidate Selection:** *Very important factors considered include:* rigor of secondary school record, class rank, academic GPA, standardized test scores, application essay, recommendation(s), interview, extracurricular activities, character/personal qualities, level of applicant's interest. *Important factors considered include:* talent/ability, volunteer work, work experience. *Other factors considered include:* first generation, alumni/ae relation, geographical residence, racial/ethnic status. **Freshman Admission Requirements:** High school diploma is required and GED is accepted. *Academic units recommended:* 4 English, 4 math, 4 science, 4 science labs, 2 foreign language, 3 social studies, 3 history, 1 computer science. **Freshman Admission Statistics:** 9,894 applied, 15.08% admitted, 75% enrolled. **Transfer Admission Requirements:** High school transcript, college transcript(s), essay or personal statement, interview, standardized test scores, Minimum college GPA of 2.0 required. **General Admission Information:** Regular application deadline 12/31. Nonfall registration not accepted.

COSTS AND FINANCIAL AID

Annual in-state tuition $0. Annual out-of-state tuition $0. Required fees $0. Average book expense $0. *Student Employment:* Federal Work-Study Program available. Institutional employment available. **Financial Aid Statistics:** 0% undergrads borrow to pay for school. Average cumulative indebtedness $0.

UNITED STATES COAST GUARD ACADEMY

31 Mohegan Avenue, New London, CT 06320-8103
Phone: 860-444-8500
E-mail: USCGA.Admissions@uscga.edu • **CEEB Code:** 5807
Fax: 860-701-6700 • **Website:** www.uscga.edu • **ACT Code:** 600

This public school was founded in 1876. It has a 120-acre campus.

RATINGS

Admissions Selectivity Rating: 97   **Fire Safety Rating:** 91   **Green Rating:** 65

STUDENTS AND FACULTY

Enrollment: 898. **Student Body:** 35% female, 65% male, 95% out-of-state, 2% international (12 countries represented). Asian 7%, African American 4%, Caucasian 67%, Hispanic 10%, Native American <1%, Pacific Islander <1%, Two or more races 8%, Race unknown 2%.
Retention and Graduation: 90% freshmen return for sophomore year. 84% freshmen graduate within 4 years. 85 **Faculty:** Student/faculty ratio 8:1. 115 full-time faculty, 56% hold PhDs, 12% are are members of minority groups, 28% are women. 0% of classes are taught by teaching assistants.

ACADEMICS

Degrees: bachelor's. **Classes:** Most classes have 10-19 students. Most lab/discussion sessions have 10-19 students. **Most popular majors:** Oceanography, Chemical and Physical; Political Science and Government; Business Administration and Management. **Special Study Options:** double major, exchange student program (domestic), honors program, independent study, internships. **Career Services:** Alumni network, Career assessment, Regional alumni, On-campus interviews. All graduates are "employed" and assigned to operational field units upon graduation.

FACILITIES

Housing: Coed dorms. 95% of campus accessible to physically diasbled. **Special Academic Facilities/Equipment:** CG Museum; Library; Visitors Center; Alumni Center **Computers:** 100% of classrooms, 65% of dorms, 100% of libraries, 50% of dining areas, 100% of student union, 50% of common outdoor areas have wireless network access. Students can register for classes online. Administrative functions (other than registration) can be performed online. Undergraduates are required to own a computer.

CAMPUS LIFE

Environment: City. **Activities:** Choral groups, concert band, dance, drama/theater, jazz band, marching band, pep band, yearbook, Campus Ministries. 2 honor societies, 7 religious organizations. **Athletics (Intercollegiate):** *Men:* baseball, basketball, crew/rowing, cross-country, diving, football, pistol, riflery, sailing, soccer, swimming, tennis, track/field (outdoor), track/field (indoor), wrestling. *Women:* basketball, cheerleading, crew/rowing, cross-country, diving, pistol, riflery, sailing, soccer, softball, swimming, track/field (outdoor), track/field (indoor), volleyball. **On-Campus Highlights:** Coast Guard Barque EAGLE, Coast Guard Museum, Sailing Center and Waterfront, Souvenier Shop (Military Exchange), Coast Guard Academy Chapel and Crown Park. **Environmental Initiatives:** Federal Electronic Recycling Challenge Participant and winner 2008 and 2009.

ADMISSIONS

Freshman Academic Profile: Average high school GPA 3.8. 45% in top 10% of high school class, 79% in top 25% of high school class, 96% in top 50% of high school class. 76% from public high schools. **Reported SAT (pre-2016 redesign) scores:** SAT Math middle 50% range 610-690. SAT Critical Reading middle 50% range 570-660. SAT Writing middle 50% range 560-650. **Concordant SAT scores:** SAT EBRW middle 50% 620–700. SAT Math middle 50% range 630–720. ACT middle 50% range 26-31. Minimum internet-based TOEFL 90. Minimum paper TOEFL 560. **Basis for Candidate Selection:** *Very important factors considered include:* rigor of secondary school record, class rank, academic GPA, standardized test scores, extracurricular activities, character/personal qualities. *Important factors considered include:* application essay, recommendation(s), talent/ability. *Other factors considered include:* interview, first generation, alumni/ae relation, geographical residence, state residency, religious affiliation/commitment, racial/ethnic status, volunteer work, work experience, level of applicant's interest. **Freshman Admission Requirements:** High school diploma is required and GED is accepted. *Academic units required:* 4 English, 4 math, 3 science, 3 science labs. *Academic units recommended:* 4 English, 4 math, 4 science, 3 science labs. **Freshman Admission Statistics:** 2,214 applied, 17.52% admitted, 75% enrolled.

Transfer Admission Requirements: High school transcript, essay or personal statement, standardized test scores, statement of good standing from prior institution(s). **General Admission Information:** Priority deadline 11/15. Regular application deadline 2/1. Regular notification 4/15. Nonfall registration not accepted. Admission may be deferred for a maximum of 1 year.

COSTS AND FINANCIAL AID

Annual in-state tuition $0. Annual out-of-state tuition $0. Required fees $978. Average book expense $2,199. **Financial Aid Statistics:** 0% freshmen, 0% undergrads receive athletic scholarships. 0% freshmen, 0% undergrads receive any aid.

UNITED STATES MERCHANT MARINE ACADEMY

Office of Admissions, Kings Point, NY 11024-1699
Phone: 516-773-5391 • **Financial Aid Phone:** 516-773-5295
E-mail: admissions@usmma.edu • **CEEB Code:** 2923
Fax: 516-773-5390 • **Website:** www.usmma.edu • **ACT Code:** 2974

This public school was founded in 1943. It has a 82-acre campus.

RATINGS

Admissions Selectivity Rating: 97   **Fire Safety Rating:** 98   **Green Rating:** 67

STUDENTS AND FACULTY

Enrollment: 904. **Student Body:** 17% female, 83% male, 87% out-of-state, 1% international (4 countries represented). Asian 7%, African American 3%, Caucasian 75%, Hispanic 10%, Native American 2%, Pacific Islander 0%, Two or more races 0%, Race unknown 2%.
Retention and Graduation: 98% freshmen return for sophomore year. 63% freshmen graduate within 4 years. 68% freshmen graduate within 6 years. **Faculty:** Student/faculty ratio 15:1. 120 full-time faculty, 34% hold PhDs, 8% are are members of minority groups, 13% are women.

ACADEMICS

Degrees: bachelor's, master's. **Classes:** Most classes have 10-19 students. **Most popular majors:** Engineering; Naval Architecture and Marine Engineering; Transportation and Materials Moving. **Special Study Options:** honors program, independent study, internships. **Career Services:** Alumni network, Alumni services, Career/job search classes, Career assessment, Internships. Sea Year Experience.

FACILITIES

Housing: Coed dormsAll students required to live on campus in dormitories provided. **Special Academic Facilities/Equipment:** American Merchant Marine Museum **Computers:** Students can register for classes online. Administrative functions (other than registration) can be performed online. Undergraduates are required to own a computer.

CAMPUS LIFE

Environment: Village. **Activities:** Choral groups, concert band, drama/theater, marching band, student government, student newspaper, yearbook, Campus Ministries. 3 religious organizations. **Athletics (Intercollegiate):** *Men:* baseball, basketball, crew/rowing, cross-country, diving, football, golf, lacrosse, riflery, sailing, soccer, swimming, tennis, track/field (outdoor), volleyball, water polo, wrestling. *Women:* basketball, crew/rowing, cross-country, diving, golf, riflery, sailing, softball, swimming, tennis, track/field (outdoor), volleyball.

ADMISSIONS

Freshman Academic Profile: Average high school GPA 3.6. 33% in top 10% of high school class, 57% in top 25% of high school class, 92% in top 50% of high school class. 75% from public high schools. **Reported SAT (pre-2016 redesign) scores:** SAT Math middle 50% range 620-690. SAT Critical Reading middle 50% range 570-660. **Concordant SAT scores:** SAT Math middle 50% range 640–720. ACT middle 50% range 26-30. Minimum internet-based TOEFL 83. Minimum paper TOEFL 540. **Basis for Candidate Selection:** *Very important factors considered include:* rigor of secondary school record, standardized test scores, character/personal qualities. *Important factors considered include:* class rank, academic GPA, application essay, recommendation(s), extracurricular activities, talent/ability, level of applicant's interest. *Other factors considered include:* interview, first generation, geographical residence, state residency, racial/ethnic status, volunteer work,

---

work experience. **Freshman Admission Requirements:** High school diploma is required and GED is accepted. *Academic units required:* 4 English, 3 math, 3 science, 1 science lab, 8 academic electives. *Academic units recommended:* 4 math, 4 science, 2 science labs, 2 foreign language, 4 social studies. **Freshman Admission Statistics:** 1,662 applied, 21.72% admitted, 71% enrolled. **Transfer Admission Requirements:** High school transcript, college transcript(s), essay or personal statement, standardized test scores, statement of good standing from prior institution(s). Minimum college GPA of 2.5 required. **General Admission Information:** Regular application deadline 3/1. Nonfall registration not accepted.

COSTS AND FINANCIAL AID

Annual in-state tuition $0. Annual out-of-state tuition $0. Required fees $1,167. Average book expense $1,000. **Required Forms and Deadlines:** FAFSA, Institution's own financial aid form. **Notification of Awards:** Applicants will be notified of awards on a rolling basis beginning 5/1. **Types of Aid:** *Need-based scholarships/grants:* Federal Pell, State scholarships/grants, Private scholarships. *Loans:* Direct Subsidized Stafford Loans, Direct Unsubsidized Stafford Loans, Direct PLUS loans. **Financial Aid Statistics:** 100% needy freshmen, 100% needy undergrads receive need-based scholarship or grant aid. 100% freshmen, 100% undergrads receive non-need-based scholarship or grant aid. 100% freshmen, 100% undergrads receive need-based self-help aid. 0% freshmen, 0% undergrads receive athletic scholarships. 33% freshmen, 30% undergrads receive any aid. Average cumulative indebtedness $7,500.

UNITED STATES MILITARY ACADEMY

646 Swift Road, West Point, NY 10996-1905
Phone: 845-938-4041
E-mail: admissions@usma.edu • **CEEB Code:** 2924
Fax: 845-938-3021 • **Website:** www.westpoint.edu • **ACT Code:** 2976

This public school was founded in 1802. It has a 16080-acre campus.

RATINGS

Admissions Selectivity Rating: 98   **Fire Safety Rating:** 91   **Green Rating:** 60*

STUDENTS AND FACULTY

Enrollment: 4,389. **Student Body:** 20% female, 80% male, 94% out-of-state, 1% international (33 countries represented). Asian 6%, African American 11%, Caucasian 64%, Hispanic 12%, Native American 1%, Pacific Islander 1%, Two or more races 4%, Race unknown 1%.
Retention and Graduation: 94% freshmen return for sophomore year. 83% freshmen graduate within 4 years. 85% freshmen graduate within 6 years. 38% grads go on to further study within 1 year. 1% grads pursue arts and sciences degrees. 2% grads pursue medical degrees. **Faculty:** Student/faculty ratio 7:1. 630 full-time faculty, 51% hold PhDs, 11% are are members of minority groups, 17% are women. 0% of classes are taught by teaching assistants.

ACADEMICS

Degrees: bachelor's. **Classes:** Most classes have 10-19 students. Most lab/discussion sessions have 10-19 students. **Most popular majors:** Economics; Business Administration and Management; Engineering/Industrial Management. **Special Study Options:** double major, exchange student program (domestic), honors program, independent study, internships, study abroad, Opportunities to attend Army Schools (Airborne, Air Assault, etc.) to learn special skills. **Career Services:** During the summer cadets participate in Individual Advanced Development (IADs). Some military IADs include Airborne School (parachuting), Air Assault School (rappelling out of helicopters), Combat Engineering Sapper School, Mountain Warfare School, and Special Forces Scuba School. There are physical IADs such as training at the U.S. Olympic Center and Outward Bound.

FACILITIES

Housing: Coed dorms, Coed dorms. are called barracks. 0% of campus accessible to physically diasbled. **Special Academic Facilities/Equipment:** West Point Museum.(oldest of U.S. army museums. The athletic facilities rate as highly as the academic plant. Arvin gymnasium, featuring swimming pools, wrestling, squash, racquetball, handball, and volleyball courts has undergone a major renovation to modernize and improve its contribution to the physical development of the corps of cadets. Michie Stadium, home of the Army football team, is considered one of America's most picturesque stadiums to watch a college football game. Holleder Center houses Tate Rink for the Army hockey team and Christl Arena is the home of the Army men and women's basketball teams. Additionally, the Shea Stadium outdoor track facility and Gillis Field House indoor practice facility are newly renovated to include an all-weather track, an astroturf football field and new lighting. There is also a redesigned 18-hole golf course and a new indoor tennis facility. Eisenhower Hall, the modern "student union," contains a 4,500- seat auditorium, a 1,000-seat snack bar and cafeteria, a large ballroom, and other social and recreational rooms. About 60 major productions, to include Broadway shows, musicals, popular rock, jazz, country/western, and alternative music concerts are staged annually in the theater. The new cadet library, Jefferson Hall opened this year. **Computers:** 100% of classrooms, 100% of libraries, 100% of student union, have wireless network access. Students can register for classes online. Administrative functions (other than registration) can be performed online. Undergraduates are required to own a computer.

CAMPUS LIFE

Environment: Village. **Activities:** Choral groups, drama/theater, jazz band, music ensembles, pep band, radio station, student government, student newspaper, television station, yearbook, Campus Ministries, Student Organization, Model UN. 105 registered organizations, 7 honor societies, 13 religious organizations. **Athletics (Intercollegiate):** *Men:* baseball, basketball, cross-country, football, golf, gymnastics, ice hockey, lacrosse, riflery, soccer, swimming, tennis, track/field (outdoor), track/field (indoor), wrestling. *Women:* basketball, cross-country, riflery, soccer, softball, swimming, tennis, track/field (outdoor), track/field (indoor), volleyball. **On-Campus Highlights:** Cadet Chapel, West Point Museum, Eisenhower Hall, Michie Stadium, Trophy Point, Fort Putnam, West Point Cemetery.

ADMISSIONS

Freshman Academic Profile: 48% in top 10% of high school class, 75% in top 25% of high school class, 95% in top 50% of high school class. 80% from public high schools. **Reported SAT (pre-2016 redesign) scores:** SAT Math middle 50% range 600-700. SAT Critical Reading middle 50% range 580-690. SAT Writing middle 50% range 550-660. **Concordant SAT scores:** SAT EBRW middle 50% 620–710. SAT Math middle 50% range 620–730. ACT middle 50% range 26-31. Minimum internet-based TOEFL 75. Minimum paper TOEFL 500. **Basis for Candidate Selection:** *Very important factors considered include:* rigor of secondary school record, class rank, academic GPA, standardized test scores, extracurricular activities, character/personal qualities. *Important factors considered include:* application essay, recommendation(s), talent/ability, level of applicant's interest. *Other factors considered include:* interview, first generation, racial/ethnic status, volunteer work, work experience. **Freshman Admission Requirements:** High school diploma is required and GED is accepted. *Academic units recommended:* 4 English, 4 math, 4 science, 2 science labs, 2 foreign language, 3 social studies, 1 history, 3 academic electives. **Freshman Admission Statistics:** 14,829 applied, 9.66% admitted, 88% enrolled. **General Admission Information:** Regular application deadline 2/28. Nonfall registration not accepted.

COSTS AND FINANCIAL AID

Annual in-state tuition $0. Annual out-of-state tuition $0. Required fees $0. Average book expense $0. **Financial Aid Statistics:** 0% freshmen, 0% undergrads receive any aid.

UNITED STATES NAVAL ACADEMY

52 King George Street, Annapolis, MD 21402
Phone: 410-293-1858
E-mail: webmail@usna.edu • **CEEB Code:** 5809
Fax: 410-293-4348 • **Website:** www.usna.edu • **ACT Code:** 1742

This public school was founded in 1845. It has a 330-acre campus.

RATINGS
Admissions Selectivity Rating: 98   **Fire Safety Rating:** 77   **Green Rating:** 60*

STUDENTS AND FACULTY
Enrollment: 4,526. **Student Body:** 26% female, 74% male, 94% out-of-state, 1% international (28 countries represented). Asian 7%, African American 7%, Caucasian 64%, Hispanic 11%, Native American <1%, Pacific Islander <1%, Two or more races 8%, Race unknown 1%.
Retention and Graduation: 97% freshmen return for sophomore year. 86% freshmen graduate within 4 years. 86% freshmen graduate within 6 years. 6% grads go on to further study within 1 year. 1% grads pursue medical degrees.
Faculty: Student/faculty ratio 8:1. 554 full-time faculty, 66% hold PhDs, 12%

are are members of minority groups, 29% are women. 0% of classes are taught by teaching assistants.

ACADEMICS
Degrees: bachelor's. **Classes:** Most classes have 10-19 students. **Most popular majors:** Economics; Political Science and Government; Systems Engineering. **Special Study Options:** double major, exchange student program (domestic), honors program, independent study, Voluntary Graduate Education Program. **Honors Programs:** Voluntary Graduate Education Program—second semester seniors may enroll in graduate school at a nearby college or university. **Career Services:** Alumni network, Alumni services. The United States Navy and the United States Marine Corps hire all our graduates. Upon graduation, each new officer is obligated to a 5 year military service commitment.

FACILITIES
Housing: Coed dormsNo options. All midshipmen live in same dormitory. **Special Academic Facilities/Equipment:** Naval history museum, Naval Institute Proceedings, propulsion lab, wind tunnels, flight simulator, ship tow tanks, satellite dish, coastal chamber facilities, fleet of small training craft (power and sail), oceanographic research vessel. **Computers:** Students can register for classes online. Administrative functions (other than registration) can be performed online. Undergraduates are required to own a computer.

CAMPUS LIFE
Environment: Town. **Activities:** Choral groups, concert band, drama/theater, jazz band, literary magazine, marching band, musical theater, pep band, radio station, student government, yearbook, Campus Ministries, Student Organization. 70 registered organizations, 10 honor societies, 8 religious organizations. **Athletics (Intercollegiate):** *Men:* baseball, basketball, crew/rowing, cross-country, diving, football, golf, gymnastics, lacrosse, light weight football, riflery, sailing, soccer, squash, swimming, tennis, track/field (outdoor), track/field (indoor), water polo, wrestling. *Women:* basketball, crew/rowing, cross-country, diving, lacrosse, riflery, sailing, soccer, swimming, tennis, track/field (outdoor), track/field (indoor), volleyball. **On-Campus Highlights:** Bancroft Hall, U.S. Naval Academy Museum, Armel-Leftwich Visitor Center, U.S. Naval Academy Chapel, Lejeune Hall.

ADMISSIONS
Freshman Academic Profile: Average high school GPA 4.2. 59% in top 10% of high school class, 83% in top 25% of high school class, 95% in top 50% of high school class. 60% from public high schools. **Reported SAT (pre-2016 redesign) scores:** SAT Math middle 50% range 600-710. SAT Critical Reading middle 50% range 570-680. **Concordant SAT scores:** SAT Math middle 50% range 620–740. **Basis for Candidate Selection:** *Very important factors considered include:* rigor of secondary school record, class rank, academic GPA, application essay, recommendation(s), interview, extracurricular activities, character/personal qualities, level of applicant's interest. *Important factors considered include:* standardized test scores, talent/ability. *Other factors considered include:* first generation, alumni/ae relation, geographical residence, state residency, racial/ethnic status, volunteer work, work experience. **Freshman Admission Requirements:** High school diploma or equivalent is not required. *Academic units recommended:* 4 English, 4 math, 2 science, 1 science lab, 2 foreign language, 2 history, and 1 unit from above areas or other academic areas. **Freshman Admission Statistics:** 17,043 applied, 7.95% admitted, 87% enrolled. **General Admission Information:** Regular application deadline 1/31. Regular notification 4/15. Nonfall registration not accepted.

COSTS AND FINANCIAL AID
Annual in-state tuition $0. Annual out-of-state tuition $0. Required fees $0. Average book expense $0. **Financial Aid Statistics:** 0% freshmen, 0% undergrads receive athletic scholarships. 0% freshmen, 0% undergrads receive any aid. 0% undergrads borrow to pay for school. Average cumulative indebtedness $0.

UNITY COLLEGE

PO Box 532, Unity, ME 4988
Phone: 800.624.1024 • **Financial Aid Phone:** 207-948-3131 ext 235
E-mail: admissions@unity.edu • **CEEB Code:** 6858
Fax: 207.948.9776 • **Website:** www.unity.edu • **ACT Code:** 3925

This is a private school.

RATINGS
Admissions Selectivity Rating: 83   **Fire Safety Rating:** 94   **Green Rating:** 93

STUDENTS AND FACULTY
Enrollment: 574. **Student Body:** 55% female, 45% male, 75% out-of-state, 0% international. Asian 1%, African American 1%, Caucasian 93%, Hispanic

2%, Native American 2%, Pacific Islander 0%, Two or more races 1%, Race unknown 0%.

Retention and Graduation: 83% freshmen return for sophomore year. 37% freshmen graduate within 4 years. 46% freshmen graduate within 6 years. 24% grads go on to further study within 1 year. 22% grads pursue arts and sciences degrees. 1% grads pursue law degrees. **Faculty:** Student/faculty ratio 12:1. 37 full-time faculty, 89% hold PhDs, 0% are are members of minority groups, 54% are women.

ACADEMICS

Degrees: associate, bachelor's. **Most popular majors:** Natural Resources Law Enforcement and Protective Services; Wildlife Biology; Wildlife, Fish and Wildlands Science and Management. **Career Services:** Alumni network, Alumni services, Career assessment, Internships.

CAMPUS LIFE

Environmental Initiatives: We only offer environmental degree programs and every student studies sustainability through our Environmental Stewardship Core curriculum. Campus sustainability efforts are an outgrowth of our academic focus.

ADMISSIONS

Freshman Academic Profile: Average high school GPA 3.3. 14% in top 10% of high school class, 33% in top 25% of high school class, 55% in top 50% of high school class. 97% from public high schools. **Reported SAT (pre-2016 redesign) scores:** SAT Math middle 50% range 490-560. SAT Critical Reading middle 50% range 480-560. SAT Writing middle 50% range 450-520. **Concordant SAT scores:** SAT EBRW middle 50% 520–600. SAT Math middle 50% range 520–580. ACT middle 50% range 22-25. Minimum paper TOEFL 550. **Basis for Candidate Selection:** *Very important factors considered include:* rigor of secondary school record, academic GPA, application essay, level of applicant's interest. *Important factors considered include:* recommendation(s), extracurricular activities, talent/ability, character/personal qualities. *Other factors considered include:* class rank, standardized test scores, interview. **Freshman Admission Requirements:** *Academic units required:* 4 English, 3 math, 2 science, 2 science labs, 3 social studies, 3 history. *Academic units recommended:* 4 math, 3 science, 3 science labs, 2 foreign language. **Freshman Admission Statistics:** 737 applied, 61.47% admitted, 38% enrolled. **General Admission Information:** Application fee $25. Priority deadline 12/15. Regular application deadline 2/15. Regular notification 3/15. Nonfall registration accepted. Admission may be deferred for a maximum of 3 years.

COSTS AND FINANCIAL AID

Annual tuition $22,440. Room and board $8,380. Required fees $800. Average book expense $500. **Required Forms and Deadlines:** FAFSA. **Types of Aid:** *Need-based scholarships/grants:* Federal Pell, FSEOG, State scholarships/grants, Private scholarships, College/university scholarship or grant aid from institutional funds. *Loans:* Direct Subsidized Stafford Loans, Direct Unsubsidized Stafford Loans, Direct PLUS loans, Federal Perkins Loans. *Student Employment:* Federal Work-Study Program available. Institutional employment available. **Financial Aid Statistics:** 100% needy freshmen, 100% needy undergrads receive need-based scholarship or grant aid. 8% freshmen, 3% undergrads receive non-need-based scholarship or grant aid. 91% freshmen, 95% undergrads receive need-based self-help aid. 0% freshmen, 0% undergrads receive athletic scholarships. 98% freshmen, 98% undergrads receive any aid. **Criteria for awarding aid:** *Non-need-based:* Academics, Leadership, Minority status.

UNIVERSITÉ LAVAL—FACULTÉ DES SCIENCES DE L'ADMINISTRATION

2345 Allée des bibliothéques, local 2440, Québec, Qc G1V 0A6
Phone: 418-656-3080 • **Financial Aid Phone:** 418-656-3332
E-mail: reg@reg.ulaval.ca
Fax: 418-656-5216 • **Website:** www.fsa.ulaval.ca

This public school was founded in 1924.

RATINGS

Admissions Selectivity Rating: 65   **Fire Safety Rating:** 60*   **Green Rating:** 60*

STUDENTS AND FACULTY

Enrollment: 2,009. **Student Body:** 43% female, 57% male, 3% international. Asian 0%, African American 0%, Caucasian 0%, Hispanic 0%, Native American 0%, Pacific Islander 0%, Two or more races 0%, Race unknown 97%.
Retention and Graduation: 75% freshmen return for sophomore year. 65% freshmen graduate within 4 years. 68% freshmen graduate within 6 years.

ACADEMICS

Degrees: bachelor's, certificate, diploma, master's, postbachelor's certifiate.
Special Study Options: cooperative education program, exchange student program (domestic), internships, student-designed major, study abroad.
Disability Services: Special programs offered to physically disabled students, including note-taking services, reader services, tape recorders. **Career Services:** Alumni network, Alumni services, Career/job search classes, Internships.

FACILITIES

Housing: Coed dorms, men's dorms, women's dorms. 100% of campus accessible to physically diasbled. **Computers:** 100% of classrooms, 100% of dorms, 100% of libraries, 100% of dining areas, 100% of student union, 100% of common outdoor areas have wireless network access. Students can register for classes online. Administrative functions (other than registration) can be performed online. Undergraduates are required to own a computer.

CAMPUS LIFE

Environment: Metropolis. **Activities:** Choral groups, concert band, dance, drama/theater, jazz band, literary magazine, music ensembles, radio station, student government, student newspaper, Student Organization, Model UN. 200 registered organizations. **Athletics (Intercollegiate):** *Men:* badminton, basketball, diving, golf, rugby, skiing (downhill/alpine), skiing (nordic/cross-country), soccer, swimming, track/field (outdoor), track/field (indoor), volleyball. *Women:* badminton, basketball, diving, golf, rugby, skiing (downhill/alpine), skiing (nordic/cross-country), soccer, swimming, track/field (outdoor), track/field (indoor), volleyball. **Environmental Initiatives:** Table de concertation sur le d?â'veloppement durabla See http://www.developpementdurable.ulaval.ca/agir/la_table_de_concertation_sur_le_developpement_durable/

ADMISSIONS

Basis for Candidate Selection: *Very important factors considered include:* rigor of secondary school record, academic GPA. *Other factors considered include:* standardized test scores, extracurricular activities, work experience. **Freshman Admission Requirements:** High school diploma is required and GED is not accepted. **Freshman Admission Statistics:** 1,377 applied, 71.02% admitted, 57% enrolled. **General Admission Information:** Application fee $30. Nonfall registration accepted.

COSTS AND FINANCIAL AID

Annual in-state tuition $2,500. Annual out-of-state tuition $5,956. Average book expense $2,000.

UNIVERSITY OF ADVANCING TECHNOLOGY (UAT)

2625 W. Baseline Rd., Tempe, AZ 85283-1056
Phone: 602-383-8228 • **Financial Aid Phone:** 602-383-8228
E-mail: admissions@uat.edu
Fax: 602-383-8222 • **Website:** www.uat.edu

This proprietary school was founded in 1983.

RATINGS

Admissions Selectivity Rating: 61   **Fire Safety Rating:** 60*   **Green Rating:** 60*

STUDENTS AND FACULTY

Enrollment: 1,090. **Student Body:** 10% female, 90% male, 6% out-of-state, <1% international. Asian 4%, African American 7%, Caucasian 61%, Hispanic 6%, Native American 1%, Pacific Islander 0%, Two or more races 0%, Race unknown 21%.
Faculty: Student/faculty ratio 12:1. 31 full-time faculty, 16% hold PhDs, 0% are are members of minority groups, 35% are women. 0% of classes are taught by teaching assistants.

ACADEMICS

Degrees: associate, bachelor's, master's. **Classes:** Most classes have 20-29 students. **Special Study Options:** Accelerated program, cooperative education program, distance learning, double major, independent study, internships, student-designed major. **Career Services:** Alumni network, Alumni services, Career/job search classes, Career assessment, Internships, Regional alumni. UAT expends its resources on seeking out internship opportunities for all of our majors. For example, many of our game design students are currently interns at Rainbow Studios, Buena Vista Games and many other prominent game development companies. Internships are also a graduation requirements for all UAT students.

FACILITIES

Housing: 100% of campus accessible to physically diasbled. **Computers:** Administrative functions (other than registration) can be performed online.

CAMPUS LIFE

Environment: Metropolis. **Activities:** student government 1 religious organization. **On-Campus Highlights:** Cuban Pete's Cafe, UAT Library, Computer Commons, Campus Game Stations.

ADMISSIONS

Minimum paper TOEFL 550. **Basis for Candidate Selection:** *Very important factors considered include:* interview, talent/ability, character/personal qualities, level of applicant's interest. *Important factors considered include:* rigor of secondary school record. *Other factors considered include:* academic GPA, standardized test scores, volunteer work. **Freshman Admission Requirements:** High school diploma is required and GED is accepted. **Transfer Admission Requirements:** High school transcript, college transcript(s), Minimum college GPA of 2.0 required. Lowest grade transferable C. **General Admission Information:** Nonfall registration accepted. Admission may be deferred for a maximum of 1 year.

COSTS AND FINANCIAL AID

Annual tuition $19,400. Average book expense $1,000. **Required Forms and Deadlines:** FAFSA. **Types of Aid:** *Need-based scholarships/grants:* Federal Pell, FSEOG, Private scholarships, College/university scholarship or grant aid from institutional funds. *Student Employment:* Federal Work-Study Program available. Institutional employment available.

THE UNIVERSITY OF AKRON

The University of Akron, Akron, OH 44325-2001
Phone: 330-972-7100 • **Financial Aid Phone:** 800-621-3847
E-mail: admissions@uakron.edu • **CEEB Code:** 1829
Fax: 330-972-7022 • **Website:** www.uakron.edu • **ACT Code:** 3338

This public school was founded in 1870. It has a 223-acre campus.

RATINGS

Admissions Selectivity Rating: 76   **Fire Safety Rating:** 91   **Green Rating:** 60*

STUDENTS AND FACULTY

Enrollment: 18,137. **Student Body:** 47% female, 53% male, 4% out-of-state, 2% international (61 countries represented). Asian 2%, African American 13%, Caucasian 74%, Hispanic 2%, Native American <1%, Pacific Islander <1%, Two or more races 3%, Race unknown 3%.
Retention and Graduation: 74% freshmen return for sophomore year. 14% freshmen graduate within 4 years. 41% freshmen graduate within 6 years.
Faculty: Student/faculty ratio 19:1. 792 full-time faculty, 79% hold PhDs, 21% are are members of minority groups, 42% are women. 4% of classes are taught by teaching assistants.

ACADEMICS

Degrees: associate, bachelor's, certificate, doctoral/professional, doctoral/research, doctoral, master's, postbachelor's certifiate, post-master's certificate.
Classes: Most classes have 20-29 students. Most lab/discussion sessions have 10-19 students. **Most popular majors:** Mechanical Engineering; Biology/Biological Sciences; Marketing/Marketing Management. **Special Study Options:** Accelerated program, cooperative education program, distance learning, double major, English as a Second Language (ESL), external degree program, honors program, independent study, internships, student-designed major, study abroad, teacher certification program, weekend college, Undergraduates may take graduate level courses. Co-Op Programs: Arts, Business, Computer Science, Engineering, Family and Consumer Sciences, Humanities, Natural Science, Technologies. Dual Enrollment offered for select graduate level programs. **Honors Programs:** Honors Delegates, Engineering Program, Emerging Leaders Program Combined degree programs: BA/MD, RN/MSN in Nursing, BS/MS in Accounting and Math. **Disability Services:** Special programs offered to physically disabled students, including note-taking services, reader services, tape recorders, tutors. **Career Services:** Alumni services, Career/job search classes, Career assessment, Internships. One of two finalists for the "Most innovative Pedagogy for Entrepreneurship Education Award" at the United States Assocatiation for Small Business and Entrepreneurship (USASBE) annual conference, 2009.

FACILITIES

Housing: Coed dorms, special housing for disabled students, men's dorms, special housing for international students, women's dorms, fraternity/sorority housing, Honors student dormitory. 90% of campus accessible to physically diasbled. Performing arts hall, nursery center, language lab, speech and

hearing center, nursing learning resource labs, institute of polymer science and engineering, chemical lab, institute for health and social policy, Bliss Institute of Applied Politics, **Computers:** 100% of classrooms, 100% of dorms, 100% of libraries, 100% of dining areas, 100% of student union, 100% of common outdoor areas have wireless network access. Students can register for classes online. Administrative functions (other than registration) can be performed online.

CAMPUS LIFE

Environment: City. **Activities:** Choral groups, concert band, dance, drama/theater, jazz band, marching band, music ensembles, musical theater, pep band, radio station, student government, student newspaper, symphony orchestra, television station, yearbook, Campus Ministries, Student Organization. 216 registered organizations, 30 honor societies, 12 religious organizations. 15 fraternities, 8 sororities. **Athletics (Intercollegiate):** *Men:* baseball, basketball, cheerleading, cross-country, football, golf, riflery, soccer, track/field (outdoor), track/field (indoor). *Women:* basketball, cheerleading, cross-country, diving, riflery, soccer, softball, swimming, tennis, track/field (outdoor), track/field (indoor), volleyball. **On-Campus Highlights:** Recreation Center, Student Union (includes food court, Starbucks), E.J. Thomas Performing Arts Hall, James A. Rhodes Arena, Robertson Cafe, Student Recreation and Wellness Center, which features a 56-foot rock-climbing wall, recreation pool, "lazy river", spa, ball courts and fitness facilities; Student Union with a movie theatre, bowling and billiards, a food court and a Starbucks Cafe.

ADMISSIONS

Freshman Academic Profile: Average high school GPA 3.2. 13% in top 10% of high school class, 38% in top 25% of high school class, 66% in top 50% of high school class. **Reported SAT (pre-2016 redesign) scores:** SAT Math middle 50% range 450-620. SAT Critical Reading middle 50% range 450-580. **Concordant SAT scores:** SAT Math middle 50% range 490–640. ACT middle 50% range 19-26. Minimum internet-based TOEFL 79. Minimum paper TOEFL 550. **Basis for Candidate Selection:** *Very important factors considered include:* rigor of secondary school record, class rank, academic GPA, standardized test scores. *Other factors considered include:* application essay, recommendation(s), extracurricular activities, talent/ability, volunteer work, level of applicant's interest. **Freshman Admission Requirements:** High school diploma is required and GED is accepted. *Academic units recommended:* 4 English, 3 math, 3 science, 2 foreign language, 3 social studies. **Freshman Admission Statistics:** 13,109 applied, 86.86% admitted, 32% enrolled. **Transfer Admission Requirements:** college transcript(s), statement of good standing from prior institution(s). Lowest grade transferable D-. **General Admission Information:** Application fee $45. Regular application deadline 7/1. Nonfall registration accepted. Admission may be deferred for a maximum of 2 Semesters.

COSTS AND FINANCIAL AID

Annual in-state tuition $8,618. Annual out-of-state tuition $17,149. Room and board $11,322. Required fees $1,891. Average book expense $1,000. **Required Forms and Deadlines:** FAFSA, Institution's own financial aid form. **Notification of Awards:** Applicants will be notified of awards on a rolling basis beginning 4/1. **Types of Aid:** *Need-based scholarships/grants:* Federal Pell, FSEOG. *Loans:* Direct Subsidized Stafford Loans, Direct Unsubsidized Stafford Loans, Direct PLUS loans, Federal Perkins Loans, Federal Nursing Loans, College/university loans from institutional funds. *Student Employment:* Federal Work-Study Program available. Institutional employment available. **Financial Aid Statistics:** 55% needy freshmen, 53% needy undergrads receive need-based scholarship or grant aid. 62% freshmen, 52% undergrads receive non-need-based scholarship or grant aid. 74% freshmen, 72% undergrads receive need-based self-help aid. 0% freshmen, 0% undergrads receive athletic scholarships. 78% freshmen, 81% undergrads receive any aid. **Criteria for awarding aid:** *Non-need-based:* Academics, Art, Athletics, Leadership, Music/drama, State/district residency.

THE UNIVERSITY OF ALABAMA AT BIRMINGHAM

Office of Undergraduate Admissions, Birmingham, AL 35294-4412
Phone: 205-934-8221 • **Financial Aid Phone:** 205-934-8223
E-mail: chooseuab@uab.edu • **CEEB Code:** 1856
Fax: 205-975-7114 • **Website:** www.uab.edu • **ACT Code:** 56

This public school was founded in 1969. It has a 183-acre campus.

RATINGS
Admissions Selectivity Rating: 81   **Fire Safety Rating:** 92   **Green Rating:** 81

STUDENTS AND FACULTY
Enrollment: 12,087. **Student Body:** 59% female, 41% male, 11% out-of-state, 2% international (53 countries represented). Asian 6%, African American 26%, Caucasian 58%, Hispanic 3%, Native American <1%, Pacific Islander <1%, Two or more races 4%, Race unknown 1%.
Retention and Graduation: 82% freshmen return for sophomore year. 30% freshmen graduate within 4 years. 53% freshmen graduate within 6 years.
Faculty: Student/faculty ratio 18:1. 858 full-time faculty, 86% hold PhDs, 22% are are members of minority groups, 47% are women.

ACADEMICS
Degrees: bachelor's, certificate, doctoral/professional, doctoral/research, doctoral, master's, postbachelor's certificate, post-master's certificate. **Classes:** Most classes have 10-19 students. Most lab/discussion sessions have 20-29 students. **Most popular majors:** Biology/Biological Sciences; Psychology; Speech Communication and Rhetoric. **Special Study Options:** Accelerated program, cooperative education program, cross-registration, distance learning, double major, dual enrollment, English as a Second Language (ESL), honors program, independent study, internships, student-designed major, study abroad, teacher certification program. **Honors Programs:** The University Honors Program is designed for students who want to satisfy their intellectual curiosity both inside and outside the classroom. The program is limited in size to 200 students who represent a wide variety of disciplines, backgrounds and interests. Without delaying progress toward a degree, the Honors Program provides students an opportunity to participate in a community of committed scholars, to form close relationships with faculty, to explore new ideas, and to share their ideas, interests, and lives on a daily basis in the Honors House. Students have opportunities to work on independent projects, to travel, and to participate in special extracurricular activities. Those who complete the program are recognized with the designation "With University Honors" on their transcripts and in the graduation program. Please visit our Univeristy Honors website for more information: http://main.uab.edu/show.asp?durki=80738 Combined degree programs: BA/MD, BA/MA, Fifth Year BS/MS in Biology Program; EMSAP; BS/MS in BioMedical Engineering; BS/MS in Civil Engineering; BS/MS in Electrical Engineering; BS/MS in Materials Engineering; BS/MS in Mechanical Engineeri. **Disability Services:** Special programs offered to physically disabled students, including note-taking services, reader services, tape recorders. **Career Services:** Alumni network, Alumni services, Career/job search classes, Career assessment, Internships, Regional alumni.

FACILITIES
Housing: Coed dorms, special housing for disabled students, special housing for international students, apartments for married students, apartments for single students, Theme Housing. 100% of campus accessible to physically diasbled. **Special Academic Facilities/Equipment:** Museum of health sciences. **Computers:** Students can register for classes online. Administrative functions (other than registration) can be performed online.

CAMPUS LIFE
Environment: Metropolis. **Activities:** Choral groups, concert band, dance, drama/theater, jazz band, literary magazine, marching band, music ensembles, musical theater, opera, pep band, radio station, student government, student newspaper, Campus Ministries, Student Organization. 150 registered organizations, 45 honor societies, 9 religious organizations, 9 fraternities, 8 sororities. **Athletics (Intercollegiate):** *Men:* baseball, basketball, football, golf, soccer, tennis. *Women:* basketball, cross-country, golf, riflery, soccer, softball, synchronized swimming, tennis, track/field (outdoor), track/field (indoor), volleyball. **On-Campus Highlights:** Student Rec Center, Commons Dining Hall, Hill University Center, Blazer Hall, Heritage Hall. **Environmental Initiatives:** Recycling.

ADMISSIONS
Freshman Academic Profile: Average high school GPA 3.7. 28% in top 10% of high school class, 55% in top 25% of high school class, 83% in top 50% of high school class. ACT middle 50% range 21-28. Minimum internet-based TOEFL 77. **Basis for Candidate Selection:** *Very important factors considered include:* rigor of secondary school record, academic GPA, standardized test scores. **Freshman Admission Requirements:** High school diploma is required and GED is accepted. *Academic units required:* 4 English, 4 math, 3 science, 2 science labs, 1 foreign language, 3 social studies, 3 academic electives. **Freshman Admission Statistics:** 5,838 applied, 89.28% admitted, 39% enrolled. **Transfer Admission Requirements:** college transcript(s), Minimum college GPA of 2.0 required. **General Admission Information:** Application fee $30. Priority deadline 6/1. Nonfall registration accepted. Admission may be deferred for a maximum of 1 year.

COSTS AND FINANCIAL AID
Annual in-state tuition $9,936. Annual out-of-state tuition $22,844. Required fees $0. Average book expense $1,200. **Required Forms and Deadlines:** FAFSA. **Notification of Awards:** Applicants will be notified of awards on a rolling basis beginning 3/15. **Types of Aid:** *Need-based scholarships/grants:* Federal Pell, FSEOG, State scholarships/grants, Private scholarships, College/university scholarship or grant aid from institutional funds, United Negro College Fund. *Loans:* Direct Subsidized Stafford Loans, Direct Unsubsidized Stafford Loans, Direct PLUS loans, Federal Perkins Loans, State Loans, College/university loans from institutional funds. *Student Employment:* Federal Work-Study Program available. Institutional employment available. **Financial Aid Statistics:** 61% needy freshmen, 89% needy undergrads receive need-based scholarship or grant aid. 71% freshmen, 45% undergrads receive non-need-based scholarship or grant aid. 70% freshmen, 76% undergrads receive need-based self-help aid. 4% freshmen, 4% undergrads receive athletic scholarships. 63% undergrads borrow to pay for school. Average cumulative indebtedness $31,610. **Criteria for awarding aid:** *Need-based:* Academics, Alumni affiliation, Minority status. *Non-need-based:* Academics, Alumni affiliation, Art, Athletics, Leadership, Minority status, Music/drama.

THE UNIVERSITY OF ALABAMA IN HUNTSVILLE

UAH Office of Admissions, Huntsville, AL 35899
Phone: 256-824-2773 • **Financial Aid Phone:** 256-824-2761
E-mail: uahadmissions@uah.edu • **CEEB Code:** 1854
Fax: 256-824-4539 • **Website:** www.uah.edu • **ACT Code:** 53

This public school was founded in 1950. It has a 400-acre campus.

RATINGS
Admissions Selectivity Rating: 85   **Fire Safety Rating:** 96   **Green Rating:** 73

STUDENTS AND FACULTY
Enrollment: 6,338. **Student Body:** 42% female, 58% male, 16% out-of-state, 3% international (75 countries represented). Asian 4%, African American 11%, Caucasian 72%, Hispanic 4%, Native American 1%, Pacific Islander 0%, Two or more races 2%, Race unknown 3%.
Retention and Graduation: 83% freshmen return for sophomore year. 15% freshmen graduate within 4 years. 49% freshmen graduate within 6 years.
Faculty: Student/faculty ratio 17:1. 326 full-time faculty, 79% hold PhDs, 25% are are members of minority groups, 43% are women. 3% of classes are taught by teaching assistants.

ACADEMICS
Degrees: bachelor's, certificate, doctoral/professional, doctoral/research, doctoral, master's, postbachelor's certificate, post-master's certificate. **Classes:** Most classes have 20-29 students. Most lab/discussion sessions have fewer than 10 students. **Most popular majors:** Mechanical Engineering; Biology/Biological Sciences; Registered Nursing/Registered Nurse. **Special Study Options:** cooperative education program, cross-registration, distance learning, double major, dual enrollment, English as a Second Language (ESL), honors program, independent study, internships, study abroad, teacher certification program, Intensive English Program. **Honors Programs:** The Honors Program at UAH provides academically talented undergraduate students with opportunities to develop their special talents and skills within an expanded and enriched version of the curriculum leading to an Honors Diploma. Honors coursework parallels regular offerings in all majors and programs. The courses include special interdisciplinary seminars, and opportunities for independent study and research/creative work, including the opportunity to work closely with faculty on special student projects. Students may participate in an Honors internship that offers active involvement in a business enterprise, professional organization, or government agency that has particular interest and relevance to the student"s course of study. Participating students also benefit from

the interaction the Honors Program affords with other talented and highly motivated students. See honors.uah.edu for more information. Combined degree programs: BA/MA, BA/MEng, Atmospheric Science, Biological Sciences, Business, Chemistry, Computer Science, Math, Physics. **Disability Services:** Special programs offered to physically disabled students, including note-taking services, reader services, tape recorders, tutors. **Career Services:** Alumni services, Career/job search classes, Career assessment, Internships. Coop program is one of the largest in the state of Alabama and is accredited by the Accreditation Council for Cooperative Education.

FACILITIES

Housing: Coed dorms, special housing for disabled students, fraternity/sorority housing, apartments for married students, cooperative housing, apartments for single students, Theme Housing, Athletic Teammates. 98% of campus accessible to physically diasbled. **Special Academic Facilities/Equipment:** Art museum and galleries, observatory with a Solar Magnetometer, optics building, centers for applied optics, micro-gravity research, robotics, solar research, space plasma, and aeronomic research. **Computers:** 25% of classrooms, 30% of dorms, 100% of libraries, 100% of dining areas, 100% of student union, 90% of common outdoor areas have wireless network access. Students can register for classes online. Administrative functions (other than registration) can be performed online.

CAMPUS LIFE

Environment: City. **Activities:** Choral groups, concert band, dance, drama/theater, jazz band, literary magazine, music ensembles, pep band, student government, student newspaper, Campus Ministries, Student Organization. 52 registered organizations, 24 honor societies, 5 religious organizations. 7 fraternities, 4 sororities. **Athletics (Intercollegiate):** *Men:* baseball, basketball, cheerleading, cross-country, ice hockey, soccer, tennis, track/field (outdoor), track/field (indoor). *Women:* basketball, cheerleading, cross-country, soccer, softball, tennis, track/field (outdoor), track/field (indoor), volleyball. **On-Campus Highlights:** University Fitness Center, Shelby Center, Salmon Library, University Center, Central Campus Residence Hall. **Environmental Initiatives:** A hazard chemical waste and waste minimization program has been in effect for over 15 years. Improved environmental awareness communications and training/learning opportunities will soon be available on the OEHS web site.

ADMISSIONS

Freshman Academic Profile: Average high school GPA 3.8. 29% in top 10% of high school class, 56% in top 25% of high school class, 85% in top 50% of high school class. 90% from public high schools. **Reported SAT (pre-2016 redesign) scores:** SAT Math middle 50% range 540-680. SAT Critical Reading middle 50% range 520-650. **Concordant SAT scores:** SAT Math middle 50% range 570–710. ACT middle 50% range 25-31. Minimum internet-based TOEFL 62. Minimum paper TOEFL 500. **Basis for Candidate Selection:** *Very important factors considered include:* rigor of secondary school record, academic GPA, standardized test scores. *Other factors considered include:* class rank, application essay, level of applicant's interest. **Freshman Admission Requirements:** High school diploma is required and GED is accepted. *Academic units required:* 4 English, 3 math, 3 science, 4 social studies, 6 academic electives. *Academic units recommended:* 4 English, 4 math, 4 science, 2 science labs, 2 foreign language, 4 social studies, 6 academic electives. **Freshman Admission Statistics:** 4,545 applied, 76.28% admitted, 35% enrolled. **Transfer Admission Requirements:** college transcript(s), statement of good standing from prior institution(s). Minimum college GPA of 2.0 required. Lowest grade transferable D. **General Admission Information:** Application fee $30. Regular application deadline 8/20. Nonfall registration accepted. Admission may be deferred for a maximum of 1 year.

COSTS AND FINANCIAL AID

Annual in-state tuition $8,996. Annual out-of-state tuition $19,766. Room and board $9,603. Required fees $846. Average book expense $1,688. **Required Forms and Deadlines:** FAFSA. **Notification of Awards:** Applicants will be notified of awards on a rolling basis beginning 4/1. **Types of Aid:** *Need-based scholarships/grants:* Federal Pell, FSEOG, State scholarships/grants, Private scholarships, College/university scholarship or grant aid from institutional funds, Federal Nursing Scholarships. *Loans:* Direct Subsidized Stafford Loans, Direct Unsubsidized Stafford Loans, Direct PLUS loans. *Student Employment:* Federal Work-Study Program available. Institutional employment available. **Financial Aid Statistics:** 87% needy freshmen, 84% needy undergrads receive need-based scholarship or grant aid. 26% freshmen, 10% undergrads receive non-need-based scholarship or grant aid. 67% freshmen, 80% undergrads receive need-based self-help aid. 6% freshmen, 4% undergrads receive athletic scholarships. 88% freshmen, 78% undergrads receive any aid. 54% undergrads borrow to pay for school. Average cumulative indebtedness $35,009. **Criteria for awarding aid:** *Non-need-based:* Academics, Art, Athletics, Leadership, Minority status, Music/drama.

THE UNIVERSITY OF ALABAMA—TUSCALOOSA

Box 870132, Tuscaloosa, AL 35487-0132
Phone: 205-348-5666 • **Financial Aid Phone:** 205-348-7949
E-mail: admissions@ua.edu • **CEEB Code:** 1830
Fax: 205-348-9046 • **Website:** www.ua.edu • **ACT Code:** 52

This public school was founded in 1831. It has a 1000-acre campus.

RATINGS

Admissions Selectivity Rating: 89   **Fire Safety Rating:** 81   **Green Rating:** 60*

STUDENTS AND FACULTY

Enrollment: 31,663. **Student Body:** 55% female, 45% male, 57% out-of-state, 2% international (56 countries represented). Asian 1%, African American 10%, Caucasian 78%, Hispanic 4%, Native American <1%, Pacific Islander <1%, Two or more races 3%, Race unknown <1%.
Retention and Graduation: 86% freshmen return for sophomore year. 44% freshmen graduate within 4 years. 69% freshmen graduate within 6 years. 26% grads go on to further study within 1 year. 5% grads pursue arts and sciences degrees. 3% grads pursue law degrees. 7% grads pursue business degrees. 3% grads pursue medical degrees. **Faculty:** Student/faculty ratio 23:1. 1,329 full-time faculty, 80% hold PhDs, 24% are are members of minority groups, 44% are women. 11% of classes are taught by teaching assistants.

ACADEMICS

Degrees: bachelor's, doctoral/professional, doctoral/research, doctoral, master's, post-master's certificate. **Classes:** Most classes have 10-19 students. Most lab/discussion sessions have 20-29 students. **Most popular majors:** Registered Nursing/Registered Nurse; Mechanical Engineering; Finance. **Special Study Options:** Accelerated program, cooperative education program, cross-registration, distance learning, double major, dual enrollment, English as a Second Language (ESL), exchange student program (domestic), external degree program, honors program, independent study, internships, liberal arts/career combination, student-designed major, study abroad, teacher certification program, weekend college. **Honors Programs:** University Honors College is composed of the University Honors Program, Computer-Based Honors Program and the International Honors Program. There is also a program called the University Fellows Experience. Combined degree programs: BA/MA, BA/MEng, BS-MBA. **Disability Services:** Special programs offered to physically disabled students, including note-taking services, reader services, tape recorders, tutors. **Career Services:** Alumni network, Alumni services, Career/job search classes, Career assessment, Internships, Regional alumni, On-campus interviews. The University of Alabama's Career Center at Culverhouse serves University of Alabama business students. The Career Center in partnership with the Culverhouse College of Commerce manages a program called "Culverhouse Connections." The program is unique in that it offers comprehensive mentoring, job shadowing and professional development programming. A key facet of the program is connecting current Culverhouse students with alumni through mentoring relationships.

FACILITIES

Housing: Coed dorms, special housing for disabled students, men's dorms, special housing for international students, women's dorms, fraternity/sorority housing, apartments for married students, apartments for single students, ThemeHousingApartments for visiting scholars. 99% of campus accessible to physically diasbled. **Special Academic Facilities/Equipment:** Art gallery, natural history museum, concert hall, archaeologic site and museum, arboretum, observatory, simulated coal mine, robotics lab, wind tunnel, artificial intelligence lab, jet propulsion engine mini-lab, special collections building. **Computers:** 55% of classrooms, 100% of dorms, 100% of libraries, 75% of dining areas, 100% of student union, 22% of common outdoor areas have wireless network access. Students can register for classes online. Administrative functions (other than registration) can be performed online.

CAMPUS LIFE

Environment: City. **Activities:** Choral groups, concert band, dance, drama/theater, jazz band, literary magazine, marching band, music ensembles, musical theater, opera, pep band, radio station, student government, student newspaper, student-run film society, symphony orchestra, television station, yearbook, Campus Ministries, Student Organization, Model UN. 294 registered organizations, 66 honor societies, 30 religious organizations. 31 fraternities, 23 sororities. **Athletics (Intercollegiate):** *Men:* baseball, basketball, cross-country, diving, football, golf, swimming, tennis, track/field (outdoor), track/field (indoor). *Women:* basketball, crew/rowing, cross-country, diving, golf, gymnastics, soccer, softball, swimming, tennis, track/field (outdoor), track/field (indoor), volleyball. **On-Campus Highlights:** University of Alabama Museum of Natural History, Amelia Gayle Gorgas Library, Bryant-Denny Stadium, The Gorgas House Museum (built in 1829), Paul W. Bryant Museum, Located right on campus is a wonderful blend of cultures and ethnic foods. Interesting shops, a new shopping center, great coffee shops, local and visiting musical talent– all located on University Blvd. **Environmental Initiatives:** Recycling has increased by 181% over fiscal year 2008. Currently we are recycling over 1,300 tons of recyclable material.

ADMISSIONS
Freshman Academic Profile: Average high school GPA 3.7. 27% in top 10% of high school class, 51% in top 25% of high school class, 79% in top 50% of high school class. **Reported SAT (pre-2016 redesign) scores:** SAT Math middle 50% range 490-620. SAT Critical Reading middle 50% range 490-610. SAT Writing middle 50% range 470-590. **Concordant SAT scores:** SAT EBRW middle 50% 540–650. SAT Math middle 50% range 520–640. ACT middle 50% range 23-31. Minimum internet-based TOEFL 79. Minimum paper TOEFL 550. **Basis for Candidate Selection:** *Very important factors considered include:* rigor of secondary school record, academic GPA, standardized test scores. *Important factors considered include:* class rank. *Other factors considered include:* application essay, recommendation(s), interview, extracurricular activities, talent/ability, character/personal qualities, first generation, alumni/ae relation, volunteer work, work experience. **Freshman Admission Requirements:** High school diploma is required and GED is accepted. *Academic units required:* 4 English, 3 math, 3 science, 2 science labs, 1 foreign language, 4 social studies, 5 academic electives. *Academic units recommended:* 4 English, 3 math, 3 science, 2 science labs, 2 foreign language, 4 social studies, 5 academic electives. **Freshman Admission Statistics:** 38,237 applied, 52.58% admitted, 38% enrolled. **Transfer Admission Requirements:** college transcript(s), Minimum college GPA of 2.0 required. Lowest grade transferable D. **General Admission Information:** Application fee $40. Priority deadline 2/1. Nonfall registration accepted. Admission may be deferred for a maximum of one year.

COSTS AND FINANCIAL AID
Annual in-state tuition $10,470. Annual out-of-state tuition $26,950. Room and board $9,550. Required fees $0. Average book expense $1,200. **Required Forms and Deadlines:** FAFSA, Institution's own financial aid form, CSS/Financial Aid PROFILE, State aid form, Noncustodial PROFILE, Business/Farm Supplement. **Notification of Awards:** Applicants will be notified of awards on a rolling basis beginning 4/1. **Types of Aid:** *Need-based scholarships/grants:* Federal Pell, FSEOG, State scholarships/grants, Private scholarships, College/university scholarship or grant aid from institutional funds, Federal Nursing Scholarships. *Loans:* Direct Subsidized Stafford Loans, Direct Unsubsidized Stafford Loans, Direct PLUS loans, Federal Perkins Loans, College/university loans from institutional funds. *Student Employment:* Federal Work-Study Program available. Institutional employment available. **Financial Aid Statistics:** 79% needy freshmen, 75% needy undergrads receive need-based scholarship or grant aid. 66% freshmen, 51% undergrads receive non-need-based scholarship or grant aid. 68% freshmen, 78% undergrads receive need-based self-help aid. 2% freshmen, 2% undergrads receive athletic scholarships. 81% freshmen, 73% undergrads receive any aid. 47% undergrads borrow to pay for school. Average cumulative indebtedness $33,816. **Criteria for awarding aid:** *Need-based:* Academics. *Non-need-based:* Academics, Alumni affiliation, Art, Athletics, Leadership, Minority status, Music/drama, State/district residency.

UNIVERSITY OF ALASKA ANCHORAGE

3211 Providence Drive, Anchorage, AK 99508-8046
Phone: 907-786-1480
E-mail: enroll@uaa.alaska.edu • **CEEB Code:** 4896
Fax: 907-786-4888 • **Website:** www.uaa.alaska.edu/ • **ACT Code:** 137

This public school was founded in 1954. It has a 384-acre campus.

RATINGS
Admissions Selectivity Rating: 74   **Fire Safety Rating:** 75   **Green Rating:** 60*

STUDENTS AND FACULTY
Enrollment: 13,380. **Student Body:** 58% female, 42% male, 10% out-of-state, <1% international (35 countries represented). Asian 7%, African American 4%, Caucasian 58%, Hispanic 7%, Native American 12%, Pacific Islander 1%, Two or more races 3%, Race unknown 6%.
Retention and Graduation: 73% freshmen return for sophomore year.
Faculty: Student/faculty ratio 12:1. 680 full-time faculty, 53% hold PhDs, 12% are are members of minority groups, 52% are women. 0% of classes are taught by teaching assistants.

ACADEMICS
Degrees: associate, bachelor's, certificate, master's, postbachelor's certificate, post-master's certificate. **Classes:** Most classes have fewer than 10 students. Most lab/discussion sessions have 10-19 students. **Special Study Options:** cooperative education program, cross-registration, distance learning, double major, dual enrollment, English as a Second Language (ESL), exchange student program (domestic), honors program, independent study, internships, liberal arts/career combination, student-designed major, study abroad, teacher certification program. **Honors Programs:** University Honors Program. **Disability Services:** Special programs offered to physically disabled students, including note-taking services, reader services, tape recorders. **Career Services:** Alumni services, Career/job search classes, Career assessment, Internships, On-campus interviews.

FACILITIES
Housing: Coed dorms, special housing for disabled students, special housing for international students, apartments for single students, Wellness HousingSeparate floors for: Alaska natives studying engineering, nursing students, honor students, language and cultures, first-year students under age 20, healthy lifestyle, quiet lifestyle, WWAMI program, Far East exchange program. 95% of campus accessible to physically diasbled. **Special Academic Facilities/Equipment:** Kimura and student Center Galleries. **Computers:** Students can register for classes online. Administrative functions (other than registration) can be performed online.

CAMPUS LIFE
Environment: City. **Activities:** Choral groups, dance, drama/theater, jazz band, literary magazine, music ensembles, musical theater, opera, radio station, student government, student newspaper, student-run film society, Campus Ministries, Student Organization, Model UN. 70 registered organizations, 5 honor societies, 5 religious organizations. 1 fraternity, 2 sororities. **Athletics (Intercollegiate):** *Men:* basketball, cross-country, ice hockey, skiing (downhill/alpine), skiingnordiccross-country. *Women:* basketball, cross-country, gymnastics, skiing (downhill/alpine), skiing (nordic/cross-country), volleyball. **On-Campus Highlights:** Campus Center, Wells Fargo Sports Center, Creakside Eatery, Cuddy Center, Student Health Center, The University of Alaska Anchorage campus has covered walkways across much of the campus as well as bike trails that connect the camus to the town's bike trail system. Student Housing is adjacent to the campus with shuttle buses running every 15 minutes throughout the main campus and University Center area of campus.

ADMISSIONS
Freshman Academic Profile: 13% in top 10% of high school class, 32% in top 25% of high school class, 62% in top 50% of high school class. 95% from public high schools. **Reported SAT (pre-2016 redesign) scores:** SAT Math middle 50% range 440-570. SAT Critical Reading middle 50% range 430-580. **Concordant SAT scores:** SAT Math middle 50% range 480–590. Minimum paper TOEFL 450. **Basis for Candidate Selection:** *Very important factors considered include:* rigor of secondary school record. *Other factors considered include:* class rank, standardized test scores, talent/ability. **Freshman Admission Requirements:** High school diploma is required and GED is accepted. **Freshman Admission Statistics:** 2,976 applied, 100.00% admitted, 61% enrolled. **Transfer Admission Requirements:** college transcript(s), statement of good standing from prior institution(s). Minimum college GPA of 2.0 required. Lowest grade transferable C. **General Admission Information:** Application fee $50. Regular application deadline 7/1. Nonfall registration accepted. Admission may be deferred for a maximum of 1 years.

COSTS AND FINANCIAL AID
Annual in-state tuition $4,950. Annual out-of-state tuition $17,400. Room and board $9,827. Required fees $832. Average book expense $1,575. **Required Forms and Deadlines:** FAFSA, Institution's own financial aid form. **Notification of Awards:** Applicants will be notified of awards on a rolling basis beginning 3/15. **Types of Aid:** *Need-based scholarships/grants:* Federal Pell, FSEOG, State scholarships/grants, Private scholarships, College/university scholarship or grant aid from institutional funds. *Loans:* State Loans. *Student Employment:* Federal Work-Study Program available. Institutional employment available. **Financial Aid Statistics:** 84% needy freshmen, 74% needy undergrads receive need-based scholarship or grant aid. 11% freshmen, 3% undergrads receive non-need-based scholarship or grant aid. 66% freshmen, 75% undergrads receive need-based self-help aid. 2% freshmen, 1% undergrads receive athletic scholarships. **Criteria for awarding aid:** *Need-based:* Academics, Leadership, Minority status. *Non-need-based:* Academics, Athletics.

UNIVERSITY OF ALASKA FAIRBANKS

PO Box 757480, Fairbanks, AK 99775-7480
Phone: 907-474-7500 • **Financial Aid Phone:** 888-474-7256
E-mail: admissions@uaf.edu • **CEEB Code:** 4866
Fax: 907-474-5379 • **Website:** www.uaf.edu • **ACT Code:** 64

This public school was founded in 1917. It has a 2250-acre campus.

RATINGS
Admissions Selectivity Rating: 81   **Fire Safety Rating:** 93   **Green Rating:** 60*

STUDENTS AND FACULTY
Enrollment: 5,445. **Student Body:** 55% female, 45% male, 14% out-of-state, 1% international (29 countries represented). Asian 1%, African American 2%, Caucasian 42%, Hispanic 6%, Native American 14%, Pacific Islander <1%, Two or more races 4%, Race unknown 29%.
Retention and Graduation: 75% freshmen return for sophomore year. 15% freshmen graduate within 4 years. 42% freshmen graduate within 6 years.
Faculty: Student/faculty ratio 11:1. 357 full-time faculty, 76% hold PhDs, 20% are are members of minority groups, 43% are women.

ACADEMICS
Degrees: associate, bachelor's, certificate, doctoral/research, master's, postbachelor's certificate, terminal, transfer. **Most popular majors:** Biology/Biological Sciences; Business Administration and Management; Mechanical Engineering. **Special Study Options:** Accelerated program, cooperative education program, distance learning, double major, dual enrollment, exchange student program (domestic), external degree program, honors program, independent study, internships, student-designed major, study abroad, teacher certification program, Legislative Aide Intern Program; Undergraduate Research Opportunities. **Honors Programs:** The Honors Program at UAF provides superior undergraduate students with intellectual opportunities greater than those generally found in university lecture halls. Honors students experience small classes, direct contact with top faculty members, a flexible curriculum and great encouragement to pursue their own intellectual interests. Combined degree programs: BS/MS Computer Science, BS/MS Mechanical Engineering. **Disability Services:** Special programs offered to physically disabled students, including note-taking services, reader services, tape recorders, tutors. **Career Services:** Alumni network, Alumni services, Career/job search classes, Career assessment, Internships, On-campus interviews.

FACILITIES
Housing: Coed dorms, special housing for disabled students, apartments for married students, apartments for single students, Wellness HousingAlaska Native cultural housing. 90% of campus accessible to physically diasbled. **Special Academic Facilities/Equipment:** Museum of natural/cultural history of Alaska and the North, Cray Super Computer, extensive telecommunication network, Geophysical Institute, NASA earth station, Poker Flat Research Range, electron microscope, microprobe, Arctic Research Center, Institute of Arctic Biology, Institute of Northern Engineering, Arctic Region Supercomputing Center, Institute of Marine Biology, Agriculture and Forestry Experiment Station, Office of Electronic Miniaturization, Alaska Native Language Center, Georgeson Botanical Gardens, Cold Climate Housing Research Center,Large Animal Research Station **Computers:** 100% of classrooms, 100% of dorms, 100% of libraries, 100% of dining areas, 100% of student union, 50% of common outdoor areas have wireless network access. Students can register for classes online. Administrative functions (other than registration) can be performed online.

CAMPUS LIFE
Environment: City. **Activities:** Choral groups, concert band, dance, drama/theater, jazz band, literary magazine, music ensembles, pep band, radio station, student government, student newspaper, symphony orchestra, television station, Campus Ministries, Student Organization, Model UN. 122 registered organizations, 11 honor societies, 10 religious organizations. 1 fraternity, 1 sorority. **Athletics (Intercollegiate):** *Men:* basketball, cross-country, ice hockey, riflery, skiingnordiccross-country. *Women:* basketball, cross-country, riflery, skiing (nordic/cross-country), volleyball. **On-Campus Highlights:** Wood Center (includes food court), Student Recreation Center (SRC), Rasmuson Library, Groomed cross-country ski trails on campus, Hess Recreation Center, Wood Center (includes food court, coffee shop, bowling alley and pool tables, Outdoor Adventures, the Pub and various spaces for groups to gather or hold meetings) The 2,250 acre Fairbanks campus includes two lakes and 17 miles of ski and hiking trails as well as a major student recreation complex. We often refer to UAF as having a 360-million-acre campus because research and field work might take you anywhere in Alaska.

ADMISSIONS
Freshman Academic Profile: Average high school GPA 3.3. 18% in top 10% of high school class, 38% in top 25% of high school class, 69% in top 50% of

high school class. **Reported SAT (pre-2016 redesign) scores:** SAT Math middle 50% range 480-610. SAT Critical Reading middle 50% range 480-610. SAT Writing middle 50% range 450-570. **Concordant SAT scores:** SAT EBRW middle 50% 520–650. SAT Math middle 50% range 510–630. ACT middle 50% range 18-26. Minimum internet-based TOEFL 79. **Basis for Candidate Selection:** *Very important factors considered include:* academic GPA, standardized test scores. **Freshman Admission Requirements:** High school diploma is required and GED is not accepted. *Academic units required:* 4 English, 3 math, 3 science, 1 science lab, 3 social studies. *Academic units recommended:* 2 foreign language. **Freshman Admission Statistics:** 1,554 applied, 73.10% admitted, 70% enrolled. **Transfer Admission Requirements:** college transcript(s), Minimum college GPA of 2.0 required. Lowest grade transferable C. **General Admission Information:** Application fee $50. Priority deadline 2/15. Regular application deadline 6/15. Regular notification 9/1. Nonfall registration accepted. Admission may be deferred for a maximum of 1 year.

COSTS AND FINANCIAL AID
Annual in-state tuition $6,360. Annual out-of-state tuition $21,030. Room and board $8,380. Required fees $1,439. Average book expense $1,400.
Required Forms and Deadlines: FAFSA, Institution's own financial aid form. **Notification of Awards:** Applicants will be notified of awards on a rolling basis beginning 3/1. **Types of Aid:** *Need-based scholarships/grants:* Federal Pell, FSEOG, State scholarships/grants, Private scholarships, College/university scholarship or grant aid from institutional funds. *Loans:* Direct Subsidized Stafford Loans, Direct Unsubsidized Stafford Loans, Direct PLUS loans, State Loans. *Student Employment:* Federal Work-Study Program available. Institutional employment available. **Financial Aid Statistics:** 89% needy freshmen, 87% needy undergrads receive need-based scholarship or grant aid. 14% freshmen, 9% undergrads receive non-need-based scholarship or grant aid. 44% freshmen, 59% undergrads receive need-based self-help aid. 2% freshmen, 3% undergrads receive athletic scholarships. 79% freshmen, 68% undergrads receive any aid. 48% undergrads borrow to pay for school. Average cumulative indebtedness $27,805. **Criteria for awarding aid:** *Need-based:* Academics. *Non-need-based:* Academics, Art, Athletics, Music/drama, State/district residency.

UNIVERSITY OF ARIZONA

PO Box 210073, Tucson, AZ 85721-0073
Phone: 520-621-3237 • **Financial Aid Phone:** 520-626-6809
E-mail: admissions@arizona.edu • **CEEB Code:** 4832
Fax: 520-621-9799 • **Website:** http://www.arizona.edu • **ACT Code:** 96

This public school was founded in 1885. It has a 378-acre campus.

RATINGS
Admissions Selectivity Rating: 82   **Fire Safety Rating:** 91   **Green Rating:** 94

STUDENTS AND FACULTY
Enrollment: 33,780. **Student Body:** 52% female, 48% male, 32% out-of-state, 7% international (112 countries represented). Asian 5%, African American 4%, Caucasian 51%, Hispanic 26%, Native American 1%, Pacific Islander <1%, Two or more races 4%, Race unknown 1%.
Retention and Graduation: 80% freshmen return for sophomore year. 42% freshmen graduate within 4 years. 60% freshmen graduate within 6 years.
Faculty: Student/faculty ratio 22 1,654 full-time faculty, 89% hold PhDs, 20% are are members of minority groups, 40% are women.

ACADEMICS
Degrees: bachelor's, doctoral/professional, doctoral/research, doctoral, master's, postbachelor's certificate, post-master's certificate. **Classes:** Most classes have 20-29 students. Most lab/discussion sessions have 20-29 students. **Most popular majors:** Psychology; Political Science and Government; Cell/Cellular and Molecular Biology. **Special Study Options:** Accelerated program, cooperative education program, cross-registration, distance learning, double major, dual enrollment, English as a Second Language (ESL), exchange student program (domestic), external degree program, independent study, internships, liberal arts/career combination, study abroad, teacher certification program, weekend college. **Honors Programs:** For information on our Honors College, visit: http://www.honors.arizona.edu/. **Disability Services:** Special programs offered to physically disabled students, including note-taking services, reader services, tape recorders, tutors. **Career Services:** Alumni network, Alumni

services, Career/job search classes, Career assessment, Internships, Regional alumni.

FACILITIES

Housing: Coed dorms, special housing for disabled students, special housing for international students, women's dorms, fraternity/sorority housing, apartments for single students. 100% of campus accessible to physically disasbled. **Special Academic Facilities/Equipment:** Art, photography, and natural history museums, tree-ring lab, planetarium, optical sciences center, nuclear reactor. **Computers:** 100% of classrooms, 100% of dorms, 100% of libraries, 100% of dining areas, 100% of student union, 75% of common outdoor areas have wireless network access. Students can register for classes online. Administrative functions (other than registration) can be performed online.

CAMPUS LIFE

Environment: Metropolis. **Activities:** Choral groups, concert band, dance, drama/theater, jazz band, literary magazine, marching band, music ensembles, musical theater, opera, pep band, radio station, student government, student newspaper, symphony orchestra, television station, yearbook, Campus Ministries, Student Organization, Model UN. 504 registered organizations, 13 honor societies, 13 religious organizations. 25 fraternities, 20 sororities. **Athletics (Intercollegiate):** *Men:* baseball, basketball, cross-country, diving, football, golf, swimming, tennis, track/field (outdoor). *Women:* basketball, cross-country, diving, golf, gymnastics, soccer, softball, swimming, tennis, track/field (outdoor), track/field (indoor), volleyball. **On-Campus Highlights:** Flandrau Science Center, Center for Creative Photography, UA Museum of Art, Athletics Events, Arizona State Museum. **Environmental Initiatives:** The University of Arizona top environmental commitments are conducting comprehensive research on environmental issues ranging from biodiversity, management, and global change.

ADMISSIONS

Freshman Academic Profile: Average high school GPA 3.5. 29% in top 10% of high school class, 57% in top 25% of high school class, 84% in top 50% of high school class. 90% from public high schools. **Reported SAT (pre-2016 redesign) scores:** SAT Math middle 50% range 490-620. SAT Critical Reading middle 50% range 480-600. SAT Writing middle 50% range 470-580. **Concordant SAT scores:** SAT EBRW middle 50% 530–650. SAT Math middle 50% range 520–640. ACT middle 50% range 21-27. Minimum internet-based TOEFL 70. **Basis for Candidate Selection:** *Very important factors considered include:* rigor of secondary school record, academic GPA, standardized test scores, application essay. *Important factors considered include:* extracurricular activities, talent/ability, character/personal qualities, level of applicant's interest. *Other factors considered include:* class rank, recommendation(s), first generation, volunteer work, work experience. **Freshman Admission Requirements:** High school diploma is required and GED is accepted. *Academic units required:* 4 English, 4 math, 3 science, 3 science labs, 2 foreign language, 2 social studies, 1 visual/performing arts. *Academic units recommended:* 4 English, 4 math, 3 science, 3 science labs, 2 foreign language, 2 social studies, 1 visual/performing arts. **Freshman Admission Statistics:** 36,166 applied, 78.62% admitted, 27% enrolled. **Transfer Admission Requirements:** college transcript(s), Lowest grade transferable C. **General Admission Information:** Application fee $50. Priority deadline 5/1. Regular application deadline 5/1. Nonfall registration accepted.

COSTS AND FINANCIAL AID

Annual in-state tuition $11,171. Annual out-of-state tuition $31,770. Room and board $11,300. Required fees $1,011. Average book expense $800. **Required Forms and Deadlines:** FAFSA. **Types of Aid:** *Need-based scholarships/grants:* Federal Pell, FSEOG, State scholarships/grants, Private scholarships, College/university scholarship or grant aid from institutional funds, Federal Nursing Scholarships. *Loans:* Direct Subsidized Stafford Loans, Direct Unsubsidized Stafford Loans, Direct PLUS loans, Federal Perkins Loans, Federal Nursing Loans, College/university loans from institutional funds. *Student Employment:* Federal Work-Study Program available. Institutional employment available. **Financial Aid Statistics:** 94% needy freshmen, 89% needy undergrads receive need-based scholarship or grant aid. 12% freshmen, 9% undergrads receive non-need-based scholarship or grant aid. 58% freshmen, 66% undergrads receive need-based self-help aid. 1% freshmen, 1% undergrads receive athletic scholarships. 46% undergrads borrow to pay for school. Average cumulative indebtedness $23,273. **Criteria for awarding aid:** *Need-based:* Academics. *Non-need-based:* Academics, Art, Athletics, Music/drama.

232 Silas H. Hunt Hall, Fayetteville, AR 72701
Phone: 479-575-5346 • **Financial Aid Phone:** 479-575-3806
E-mail: uofa@uark.edu • **CEEB Code:** 6866
Fax: 479-575-7515 • **Website:** http://www.uark.edu • **ACT Code:** 144

This public school was founded in 1871. It has a 410-acre campus.

RATINGS

Admissions Selectivity Rating: 87   **Fire Safety Rating:** 90   **Green Rating:** 90

STUDENTS AND FACULTY

Enrollment: 22,243. **Student Body:** 53% female, 47% male, 44% out-of-state, 3% international (85 countries represented). Asian 2%, African American 5%, Caucasian 77%, Hispanic 8%, Native American 1%, Pacific Islander <1%, Two or more races 3%, Race unknown 1%.
Retention and Graduation: 82% freshmen return for sophomore year. 42% freshmen graduate within 4 years. 64% freshmen graduate within 6 years. 31% grads go on to further study within 1 year. 10% grads pursue arts and sciences degrees. 3% grads pursue law degrees. 1% grads pursue business degrees. 8% grads pursue medical degrees. **Faculty:** Student/faculty ratio 19:1. 1,177 full-time faculty, 84% hold PhDs, 18% are are members of minority groups, 39% are women. 18% of classes are taught by teaching assistants.

ACADEMICS

Degrees: bachelor's, certificate, doctoral/professional, doctoral/research, doctoral, master's, postbachelor's certifiate, post-master's certificate. **Classes:** Most classes have 10-19 students. Most lab/discussion sessions have 20-29 students. **Most popular majors:** Registered Nursing/Registered Nurse; Marketing/Marketing Management; Finance. **Special Study Options:** Accelerated program, cooperative education program, distance learning, double major, dual enrollment, English as a Second Language (ESL), honors program, independent study, internships, liberal arts/career combination, student-designed major, study abroad, teacher certification program. **Honors Programs:** The Honors College provides exceptional opportunities for outstanding undergraduates. The College incorporates 4 areas of responsiblity: recruitment, administration of honors fellowships, coordination of honors program and curricula, and coordination of related services. Combined degree programs: BA/MD, BA/JD, BA/DDS, MBA/JD, BS/MD, BS/JD, BS/DDS, BSBA/M.Acc. **Disability Services:** Special programs offered to physically disabled students, including note-taking services, reader services, tape recorders, tutors. **Career Services:** Alumni network, Alumni services, Career/job search classes, Career assessment, Internships. Career/job search classes.

FACILITIES

Housing: Coed dorms, women's dorms, fraternity/sorority housing, apartments for single students, Suites with private bedrooms. Special interest floors. Enhanced learning centers. First year experience program area. Adaptable housing for disabled students. Several residences remain open over holiday and winter breaks. Honors housing. Sophmore and beyond program area. 100% of campus accessible to physically diasbled. **Special Academic Facilities/Equipment:** Public Radio-KUAF, High Density Electronics Center,Reynolds Center for Enterprise Development, Center for Excellence in Poultry Science, Genesis Small Business Incubation Center, Chemical Hazards Research Center (NEW), Honors College. **Computers:** Students can register for classes online. Administrative functions (other than registration) can be performed online.

CAMPUS LIFE

Environment: Town. **Activities:** Choral groups, concert band, dance, drama/theater, jazz band, literary magazine, marching band, music ensembles, musical theater, opera, pep band, radio station, student government, student newspaper, student-run film society, symphony orchestra, television station, yearbook, Campus Ministries, Student Organization. 340 registered organizations, 39 honor societies, 32 religious organizations. 16 fraternities, 11 sororities. **Athletics (Intercollegiate):** *Men:* baseball, basketball, cross-country, football, golf, tennis, track/field (outdoor), track/field (indoor). *Women:* basketball, cross-country, diving, golf, gymnastics, soccer, softball, swimming, tennis, track/field (outdoor), track/field (indoor), volleyball. **On-Campus Highlights:** Bud Walton Arena, Old Main, Reynolds Razorback Stadium, Greek AmphiTheater, Senior Walk (every graduate's name engraved). **Environmental Initiatives:** ACUPCC Signatory, GHG inventory, climate action plan.

ADMISSIONS

Freshman Academic Profile: Average high school GPA 3.7. 25% in top 10% of high school class, 54% in top 25% of high school class, 85% in top 50% of high school class. 82% from public high schools. **Reported SAT (pre-2016 redesign) scores:** SAT Math middle 50% range 510-620. SAT Critical Reading middle 50% range 500-600. **Concordant SAT scores:** SAT Math middle 50% range 540–640. ACT middle 50% range 23-29. Minimum internet-based TOEFL 79. Minimum paper TOEFL 550. **Basis for Candidate Selection:** *Very important factors considered include:* academic GPA, standardized test scores. *Other factors considered include:* rigor of secondary school record, class rank, application essay, recommendation(s), extracurricular activities, talent/ability, character/personal qualities, first generation, alumni/ae relation, geographical residence, state residency, volunteer work, work experience. **Freshman Admission Requirements:** High school diploma is required and GED is accepted. *Academic units required:* 4 English, 4 math, 3 science, 1 science lab, 1 social studies, 2 history, 2 academic electives. *Academic units recommended:* 2 foreign language. **Freshman Admission Statistics:** 21,539 applied, 63.20% admitted, 36% enrolled. **Transfer Admission Requirements:** college transcript(s), Minimum college GPA of 2.0 required. Lowest grade transferable C-. **General Admission Information:** Application fee $40. Priority deadline 11/1. Regular application deadline 8/1. Nonfall registration accepted.

COSTS AND FINANCIAL AID

Annual in-state tuition $7,204. Annual out-of-state tuition $21,552. Room and board $10,332. Required fees $1,616. Average book expense $1,046. **Required Forms and Deadlines:** FAFSA. **Notification of Awards:** Applicants will be notified of awards on or about 4/1. **Types of Aid:** *Need-based scholarships/ grants:* Federal Pell, FSEOG, State scholarships/grants, Private scholarships, College/university scholarship or grant aid from institutional funds. *Loans:* Direct Subsidized Stafford Loans, Direct Unsubsidized Stafford Loans, Direct PLUS loans, Federal Perkins Loans, State Loans, College/university loans from institutional funds. *Student Employment:* Federal Work-Study Program available. Institutional employment available. **Financial Aid Statistics:** 82% needy freshmen, 78% needy undergrads receive need-based scholarship or grant aid. 11% freshmen, 9% undergrads receive non-need-based scholarship or grant aid. 70% freshmen, 73% undergrads receive need-based self-help aid. 2% freshmen, 2% undergrads receive athletic scholarships. 79% freshmen, 72% undergrads receive any aid. 48% undergrads borrow to pay for school. Average cumulative indebtedness $24,768. **Criteria for awarding aid:** *Need-based:* Academics, Alumni affiliation, Leadership, Minority status. *Non-need-based:* Academics, Alumni affiliation, Art, Athletics, Leadership, Minority status, Music/drama, State/district residency.

UNIVERSITY OF ARKANSAS AT PINE BLUFF

1200 N. University Drive, Pine Bluff, AR 71601
Phone: 870-575-8492
E-mail: fultone@uapb.edu
Fax: 870-575-4608 • **Website:** http://www.uapb.edu

This is a public school.

RATINGS

Admissions Selectivity Rating: 73   **Fire Safety Rating:** 60*   **Green Rating:** 60*

STUDENTS AND FACULTY

Enrollment: 3,048. **Student Body:** 58% female, 42% male, 33% out-of-state, <1% international. Asian 0%, African American 96%, Caucasian 3%, Hispanic <1%, Native American 0%, Pacific Islander 0%, Two or more races 0%, Race unknown <1%.
Retention and Graduation: 57% freshmen return for sophomore year. 14% freshmen graduate within 4 years. 32% freshmen graduate within 6 years.
Faculty: Student/faculty ratio 18:1. 164 full-time faculty, 0% hold PhDs, 46% are are members of minority groups, 54% are women.

ACADEMICS

Degrees: associate, bachelor's, certificate, master's. **Classes:** Most classes have fewer than 10 students. **Special Study Options:** cooperative education program, distance learning, double major, dual enrollment, honors program, internships, study abroad, teacher certification program.

FACILITIES

Housing: men's dorms, women's dorms.

CAMPUS LIFE

Activities: Choral groups, concert band, drama/theater, jazz band, marching band, radio station, student government, student newspaper, television station, yearbook.

ADMISSIONS

Freshman Academic Profile: 93% from public high schools. **Reported SAT (pre-2016 redesign) scores:** SAT Math middle 50% range 350-450. SAT Critical Reading middle 50% range 350-440. **Concordant SAT scores:** SAT Math middle 50% range 390–490. ACT middle 50% range 14-18. Minimum internet-based TOEFL 61. Minimum paper TOEFL 500. **Basis for Candidate Selection:** *Very important factors considered include:* rigor of secondary school record, standardized test scores. *Important factors considered include:* academic GPA. **Freshman Admission Requirements:** High school diploma is required and GED is accepted. *Academic units required:* 4 English, 3 math, 3 science, 2 science labs, 2 foreign language, 1 social studies, 2 history, 4 academic electives. **Freshman Admission Statistics:** 2,169 applied, 64.27% admitted, 59% enrolled. **Transfer Admission Requirements:** High school transcript, college transcript(s). **General Admission Information:** Priority deadline 8/1. Nonfall registration accepted. Admission may be deferred.

COSTS AND FINANCIAL AID

Annual in-state tuition $3,300. Annual out-of-state tuition $7,710. Room and board $6,070. Required fees $1,199. Average book expense $1,000. **Required Forms and Deadlines:** FAFSA. **Types of Aid:** *Need-based scholarships/ grants:* Federal Pell, FSEOG, State scholarships/grants, Private scholarships, College/university scholarship or grant aid from institutional funds. *Loans:* Federal Perkins Loans. *Student Employment:* Federal Work-Study Program available. Institutional employment available.

UNIVERSITY OF THE ARTS

320 South Broad Street, Philadelphia, PA 19102
Phone: 215-717-6049 • **Financial Aid Phone:** 215-717-6170
E-mail: admissions@uarts.edu • **CEEB Code:** 2664
Fax: 215-717-6045 • **Website:** www.uarts.edu • **ACT Code:** 3664

This private school was founded in 1876. It has a 18-acre campus.

RATINGS

Admissions Selectivity Rating: 74   **Fire Safety Rating:** 60*   **Green Rating:** 60*

STUDENTS AND FACULTY

Enrollment: 1,865. **Student Body:** 58% female, 42% male, 62% out-of-state, 5% international (19 countries represented). Asian 3%, African American 13%, Caucasian 62%, Hispanic 9%, Native American <1%, Pacific Islander 1%, Two or more races 4%, Race unknown 4%.
Retention and Graduation: 82% freshmen return for sophomore year. 57% freshmen graduate within 4 years. **Faculty:** Student/faculty ratio 8:1. 113 full-time faculty, 0% hold PhDs, 0% are are members of minority groups, 0% are women. 0% of classes are taught by teaching assistants.

ACADEMICS

Degrees: bachelor's, diploma, master's, postbachelor's certificate. **Classes:** Most classes have 10-19 students. **Most popular majors:** Graphic Design; Dance; Illustration. **Special Study Options:** Accelerated program, cross-registration, double major, dual enrollment, English as a Second Language (ESL), exchange student program (domestic), independent study, internships, study abroad, teacher certification program. Combined degree programs: 5-year BFA/MAT. **Disability Services:** Special programs offered to physically disabled students, including note-taking services, reader services, tape recorders, tutors. **Career Services:** Alumni network, Alumni services, Career/job search classes, Career assessment, Internships, On-campus interviews. Our Summer Fellows Program provides opportunities for high-achieving University of the Arts students to gain meaningful experience in a creative field during summer break. Fellows are matched with a UArts alumni host, who invites them into his or her workplace to observe, engage and participate in unique projects and programs. The program offers students an exceptional opportunity to work one-on-one with alumni who are working artists. Students selected to be UArts Summer Fellows go through a rigorous application process, including an interview, and are motivated to demonstrate their classroom skills in the working world. The University of the Arts provides Summer Fellows with a stipend and alumni hosts provide a summer internship that can be one, four or eight weeks in duration.

FACILITIES

Housing: Coed dorms, apartments for single students. 85% of campus accessible to physically diasbled. **Special Academic Facilities/Equipment:** Rosenwald-Wolf Gallery, Merriam Theater, Arts Bank, Borowsky Center for Publication arts, Gershman Y.

CAMPUS LIFE

Environment: Metropolis. **Activities:** Choral groups, concert band, dance, drama/theater, jazz band, music ensembles, musical theater, radio station, student government 5 registered organizations, 1 religious organization.

ADMISSIONS

Reported SAT (pre-2016 redesign) scores: SAT Math middle 50% range 440-550. SAT Critical Reading middle 50% range 450-580. SAT Writing middle 50% range 440-560. **Concordant SAT scores:** SAT EBRW middle 50% 500–630. SAT Math middle 50% range 480–570. ACT middle 50% range 18-25. Minimum internet-based TOEFL 80. Minimum paper TOEFL 550. **Basis for Candidate Selection:** *Very important factors considered include:* rigor of secondary school record, interview, talent/ability. *Important factors considered include:* class rank, academic GPA, standardized test scores, application essay, extracurricular activities, level of applicant's interest. *Other factors considered include:* recommendation(s), alumni/ae relation, racial/ethnic status, volunteer work, work experience. **Freshman Admission Requirements:** High school diploma is required and GED is accepted. *Academic units required:* 4 English. *Academic units recommended:* 3 math, 2 science, 2 foreign language, 2 social studies, 2 history, and 2 units from above areas or other academic areas. **Freshman Admission Statistics:** 1,479 applied, 75.39% admitted, 41% enrolled. **Transfer Admission Requirements:** High school transcript, college transcript(s), essay or personal statement, standardized test scores, Minimum college GPA of 2.0 required. Lowest grade transferable C. **General Admission Information:** Application fee $60. Priority deadline 3/15. Nonfall registration accepted. Admission may be deferred for a maximum of 12 months.

COSTS AND FINANCIAL AID

Annual tuition $39,908. Room and board $14,552. **Required Forms and Deadlines:** FAFSA. **Notification of Awards:** Applicants will be notified of awards on a rolling basis beginning 3/15. **Types of Aid:** *Need-based scholarships/grants:* Federal Pell, FSEOG, State scholarships/grants, Private scholarships, College/university scholarship or grant aid from institutional funds. *Loans:* Direct Subsidized Stafford Loans, Direct Unsubsidized Stafford Loans, Direct PLUS loans, Federal Perkins Loans. *Student Employment:* Federal Work-Study Program available. Institutional employment available. **Financial Aid Statistics:** 95% needy freshmen, 94% needy undergrads receive need-based scholarship or grant aid. 10% freshmen, 5% undergrads receive non-need-based scholarship or grant aid. 99% freshmen, 98% undergrads receive need-based self-help aid. 0% freshmen, 0% undergrads receive athletic scholarships. 80% undergrads receive any aid. **Criteria for awarding aid:** *Non-need-based:* Academics, Art, Music/drama.

UNIVERSITY OF BALTIMORE

1420 North Charles Street, Baltimore, MD 21201
Phone: 410-837-4777 • **Financial Aid Phone:** 410-837-4763
E-mail: admissions@ubmall.ubalt.edu • **CEEB Code:** 5810
Fax: 410-837-4793 • **Website:** http://www.ubalt.edu/admission/

This public school was founded in 1925. It has a 47-acre campus.

RATINGS

Admissions Selectivity Rating: 74   **Fire Safety Rating:** 60*   **Green Rating:** 60*

STUDENTS AND FACULTY

Enrollment: 6,526. **Student Body:** 57% female, 43% male, 4% out-of-state, 3% international. Asian 4%, African American 38%, Caucasian 42%, Hispanic 4%, Native American <1%, Pacific Islander <1%, Two or more races 3%, Race unknown 5%.
Retention and Graduation: 18% grads go on to further study within 1 year. 10% grads pursue arts and sciences degrees. 2% grads pursue law degrees. 9% grads pursue business degrees. **Faculty:** Student/faculty ratio 16:1. 182 full-time faculty, 85% hold PhDs, 23% are are members of minority groups, 45% are women. 0% of classes are taught by teaching assistants.

ACADEMICS

Degrees: bachelor's, certificate, doctoral, master's, postbachelor's certificate, post-master's certificate. **Classes:** Most classes have 20-29 students. **Most popular majors:** Criminal Justice/Law Enforcement Administration; Business Administration and Management; Digital Communication and Media/Multimedia. **Special Study Options:** Accelerated program, cooperative education program, distance learning, honors program, independent study, internships, student-designed major, study abroad. Combined degree programs: BA/JD, BA/MA, MBA/JD. **Disability Services:** Special programs offered to physically disabled students, including note-taking services, reader services, tape recorders, tutors. **Career Services:** Alumni network, Alumni services, Career/job search classes, Career assessment, Internships, Regional alumni. The internship program serves students who do not have experimental learning built into their academic units.

FACILITIES

Housing: The University works with sevearl apartment complexes in the area to provide direct leases to students. 100% of campus accessible to physically disabled. **Computers:** Students can register for classes online. Administrative functions (other than registration) can be performed online.

CAMPUS LIFE

Environment: Metropolis. **Activities:** drama/theater, literary magazine, student government, student newspaper, Student Organization. 26 registered organizations, 11 honor societies, 2 religious organizations. **On-Campus Highlights:** Student Union **Environmental Initiatives:** 30% energy reduction contract with En, Energy Systems Group

ADMISSIONS

Freshman Academic Profile: Average high school GPA 3.0. **Reported SAT (pre-2016 redesign) scores:** SAT Math middle 50% range 410-540. SAT Critical Reading middle 50% range 420-560. SAT Writing middle 50% range 420-530. **Concordant SAT scores:** SAT EBRW middle 50% 470–600. SAT Math middle 50% range 450–570. ACT middle 50% range 17-21. Minimum paper TOEFL 550. **Basis for Candidate Selection:** *Important factors considered include:* rigor of secondary school record, class rank, academic GPA, standardized test scores. *Other factors considered include:* application essay, recommendation(s), extracurricular activities, talent/ability, character/personal qualities, first generation, alumni/ae relation, volunteer work, work experience. **Freshman Admission Requirements:** High school diploma is required and GED is accepted. *Academic units required:* 4 English, 3 math, 3 science, 2 science labs, 3 social studies, 6 academic electives. **Freshman Admission Statistics:** 730 applied, 64.38% admitted, 51% enrolled. **Transfer Admission Requirements:** college transcript(s), Minimum college GPA of 2.0 required. Lowest grade transferable D. **General Admission Information:** Application fee $30. Priority deadline 2/15. Nonfall registration accepted. Admission may be deferred for a maximum of 1 year.

COSTS AND FINANCIAL AID

Annual in-state tuition $5,992. Annual out-of-state tuition $16,550. Required fees $1,846. **Required Forms and Deadlines:** FAFSA. **Types of Aid:** *Need-based scholarships/grants:* Federal Pell, FSEOG, State scholarships/grants, Private scholarships, College/university scholarship or grant aid from institutional funds. *Loans:* Direct Subsidized Stafford Loans, Direct Unsubsidized Stafford Loans, Direct PLUS loans, Federal Perkins Loans. *Student Employment:* Federal Work-Study Program available. Institutional employment available. **Financial Aid Statistics:** 90% needy freshmen, 91% needy undergrads receive need-based scholarship or grant aid. 0% undergrads receive non-need-based scholarship or grant aid. 65% freshmen, 72% undergrads receive need-based self-help aid. 0% freshmen, 0% undergrads receive athletic scholarships. 97% freshmen, 86% undergrads receive any aid. **Criteria for awarding aid:** *Need-based:* Academics. *Non-need-based:* Academics, State/district residency.

UNIVERSITY OF BRIDGEPORT

126 Park Avenue, Bridgeport, CT 6604
Phone: 203-576-4552 • **Financial Aid Phone:** 203-576-4568
E-mail: admit@.bridgeport.edu • **CEEB Code:** 3914
Fax: 203-576-4941 • **ACT Code:** 602

This private school was founded in 1927. It has a 86-acre campus.

RATINGS

Admissions Selectivity Rating: 76   **Fire Safety Rating:** 91   **Green Rating:** 60*

STUDENTS AND FACULTY

Enrollment: 2,688. **Student Body:** 68% female, 32% male, 38% out-of-state, 11% international (74 countries represented). Asian 3%, African American 37%, Caucasian 27%, Hispanic 18%, Native American 1%, Pacific Islander <1%, Two or more races 3%, Race unknown 0%.
Retention and Graduation: 62% freshmen return for sophomore year. 23% freshmen graduate within 4 years. 32% freshmen graduate within 6 years. 15% grads go on to further study within 1 year. 5% grads pursue arts and sciences degrees. 10% grads pursue law degrees. 10% grads pursue business degrees. 5% grads pursue medical degrees. **Faculty:** Student/faculty ratio 17:1. 121 full-time faculty, 79% hold PhDs, 19% are are members of minority groups, 38% are women. 0% of classes are taught by teaching assistants.

ACADEMICS

Degrees: associate, bachelor's, certificate, doctoral/professional, doctoral/research, master's, postbachelor's certificate, post-master's certificate. **Classes:** Most classes have 10-19 students. **Most popular majors:** Dental Hygiene/Hygienist; Business/Commerce; Psychology. **Special Study Options:** Accelerated program, cooperative education program, cross-registration, distance learning, double major, English as a Second Language (ESL), honors program, independent study, internships, liberal arts/career combination, student-designed major, study abroad, teacher certification program, weekend college. Combined degree programs: BS/DC, BS/MBA. **Disability Services:** Special programs offered to physically disabled students, including note-taking services, reader services, tape recorders, tutors. **Career Services:** Alumni network, Alumni services, Career/job search classes, Career assessment, Internships, Regional alumni.

FACILITIES

Housing: Coed dorms, Mens, Womens floors. 80% of campus accessible to physically diasbled. **Computers:** 80% of classrooms, 100% of dorms, 100% of libraries, 30% of dining areas, 50% of student union, have wireless network access. Students can register for classes online. Administrative functions (other than registration) can be performed online.

CAMPUS LIFE

Environment: City. **Activities:** Choral groups, dance, literary magazine, music ensembles, student government, student newspaper, yearbook, Student Organization. 30 registered organizations, 11 honor societies, 6 religious organizations. 2 fraternities, 4 sororities. **Athletics (Intercollegiate):** *Men:* baseball, basketball, cross-country, soccer, swimming. *Women:* basketball, cross-country, gymnastics, lacrosse, soccer, softball, swimming, volleyball. **On-Campus Highlights:** Arnold Bernhard Center, Wheeler Recreation Center, John J. Cox Student Center, The University Gallery, Hubbell Gymnasium.

ADMISSIONS

Freshman Academic Profile: Average high school GPA 3.0. 1% in top 10% of high school class, 32% in top 25% of high school class, 69% in top 50% of high school class. 90% from public high schools. **Reported SAT (pre-2016 redesign) scores:** SAT Math middle 50% range 410-500. SAT Critical Reading middle 50% range 410-490. SAT Writing middle 50% range 410-490. **Concordant SAT scores:** SAT EBRW middle 50% 460–550. SAT Math middle 50% range 450–530. ACT middle 50% range 18-21. Minimum internet-based TOEFL 61. Minimum paper TOEFL 500. **Basis for Candidate Selection:** *Very important factors considered include:* rigor of secondary school record, academic GPA, standardized test scores. *Important factors considered include:* class rank, application essay, recommendation(s), talent/ability, character/personal qualities, level of applicant's interest. *Other factors considered include:* interview, extracurricular activities, volunteer work, work experience. **Freshman Admission Requirements:** High school diploma is required and GED is accepted. *Academic units required:* 4 English, 3 math, 2 science, 2 science labs, 2 social studies, 5 academic electives. *Academic units recommended:* 4 English, 3 math, 2 science, 2 science labs, 2 social studies, 5 academic electives. **Freshman Admission Statistics:** 5,736 applied, 63.46% admitted, 16% enrolled. **Transfer Admission Requirements:** college transcript(s), essay or personal statement, Minimum college GPA of 2.0 required. Lowest grade transferable C-. **General Admission Information:** Application fee $25. Priority deadline 4/1. Nonfall registration accepted. Admission may be deferred for a maximum of 1 year.

COSTS AND FINANCIAL AID

Annual tuition $25,950. Room and board $12,050. Required fees $2,190. Average book expense $1,500. **Required Forms and Deadlines:** FAFSA. **Notification of Awards:** Applicants will be notified of awards on a rolling basis beginning 3/1. **Types of Aid:** *Need-based scholarships/grants:* Federal Pell, FSEOG, State scholarships/grants, Private scholarships, College/university scholarship or grant aid from institutional funds. *Loans:* Direct Subsidized Stafford Loans, Direct Unsubsidized Stafford Loans, Direct PLUS loans, Federal Perkins Loans. *Student Employment:* Federal Work-Study Program available. Institutional employment available. **Financial Aid Statistics:** 85% needy freshmen, 87% needy undergrads receive need-based scholarship or grant aid. 96% freshmen, 89% undergrads receive non-need-based scholarship or grant aid. 86% freshmen, 88% undergrads receive need-based self-help aid. 3% freshmen, 8% undergrads receive athletic scholarships. 98% freshmen, 98% undergrads receive any aid. **Criteria for awarding aid:** *Non-need-based:* Academics, Art, Athletics, Leadership, Music/drama, State/district residency.

THE UNIVERSITY OF BRITISH COLUMBIA

Room 2016, Vancouver, BC V6T 1Z1
Phone: 1-604-822-3014 • **Financial Aid Phone:** 604-822-5111
E-mail: askme@interchange.ubc.ca
Fax: 604-822-3599 • **Website:** www.ubc.ca

This public school was founded in 1908. It has a 1000-acre campus.

RATINGS

Admissions Selectivity Rating: 71   **Fire Safety Rating:** 79   **Green Rating:** 91

STUDENTS AND FACULTY

Student Body: 54% female, 46% male, (144 countries represented). **Retention and Graduation:** 91% freshmen return for sophomore year. 31% freshmen graduate within 4 years. 50% grads go on to further study within 1 year. **Faculty:** Student/faculty ratio 15:1.

ACADEMICS

Degrees: bachelor's, certificate, diploma, doctoral/professional, doctoral, master's. **Classes:** Most classes have 50-59 students. Most lab/discussion sessions have 20-29 students. **Most popular majors:** Computer and Information Sciences; Biological and Physical Sciences; Psychology. **Special Study Options:** cooperative education program, distance learning, double major, dual enrollment, English as a Second Language (ESL), exchange student program (domestic), honors program, internships, liberal arts/career combination, student-designed major, study abroad, teacher certification program, Cross-disciplinary first year options. **Honors Programs:** UBC offers many honours programs for academically strong undergraduates. Combined degree programs: BA/BSc. **Disability Services:** Special programs offered to physically disabled students, including note-taking services, reader services, tape recorders, tutors. **Career Services:** Alumni network, Alumni services, Career/job search classes, Career assessment, Internships, Regional alumni. Outstanding Coop (Work Learn) programs in six major Faculties.

FACILITIES

Housing: Coed dorms, special housing for disabled students, men's dorms, special housing for international students, women's dorms, fraternity/sorority housing, apartments for married students, apartments for single students, Theme **Housing:** National theme housing in association with partner universities in Japan, Mexico, Korea, and Hong Kong SAR. 90% of campus accessible to physically diasbled. **Special Academic Facilities/Equipment:** Museum of Anthropology Barber Learning Centre Beaty Biodiversity Museum Geological Museum TRIUMF, sub-atomic particle research Botanical Gardens Nitobe Garden Belkin Art Gallery Chan Centre for Performing Arts Liu International Studies Centre St.John's College (Graduate College) Pulp and Paper Centre Centre for Intergrated Systems Research Wall Centre for Interdisciplinary Studies **Computers:** 100% of classrooms, 100% of dorms, 100% of libraries, 100% of dining areas, 100% of student union, 100% of common outdoor areas have wireless network access. Students can register for classes online. Administrative functions (other than registration) can be performed online.

CAMPUS LIFE

Environment: Metropolis. **Activities:** Choral groups, concert band, dance, drama/theater, literary magazine, music ensembles, musical theater, opera, radio station, student government, student newspaper, student-run film society, symphony orchestra, Student Organization. 250 registered organizations, 1 honor society, 7 religious organizations. 9 fraternities, 8 sororities. **Athletics (Intercollegiate):** *Men:* baseball, basketball, crew/rowing, cross-country, field hockey, football, golf, ice hockey, rugby, soccer, swimming, track/field (outdoor), volleyball. *Women:* basketball, crew/rowing, cross-country, field hockey, golf, ice hockey, rugby, soccer, swimming, track/field (outdoor), volleyball. **On-Campus Highlights:** Koerner Library, Museum of Anthropology, Chan Centre, Student Union Building, Barber Learning Centre. **Environmental Initiatives:** UBC is a signatory to the Talloires Declaration. It has integrated sustainability into its vision statement and strategic plan and formed a President Advisory Council on Sustainability. The UBC Sustainability Office opened in 1998, the first of its kind in a Canadian university. UBC has created an advisory committee of faculty, staff, students and alumni on socially responsible investing. The committee advises the Board of Governors on issues of transparency, proxy votes, and socially responsible investment practices.

ADMISSIONS

Basis for Candidate Selection: *Very important factors considered include:* rigor of secondary school record, academic GPA. *Important factors considered include:* application essay. *Other factors considered include:* standardized test scores, recommendation(s), extracurricular activities, talent/ability, character/personal qualities, volunteer work, work experience, level of applicant's interest. **Freshman Admission Requirements:** High school diploma is required and GED is not accepted. *Academic units required:* 4 English, 3 math, 12 academic electives. **Freshman Admission Statistics:** 27,134 applied, 48.52% admitted, 48% enrolled. **Transfer Admission Requirements:** college transcript(s), statement of good standing from prior institution(s). **General Admission Information:** Application fee $102. Priority deadline 1/31. Regular application deadline 1/31. Nonfall registration accepted. Admission may be deferred.

COSTS AND FINANCIAL AID

Required Forms and Deadlines: Institution's own financial aid form. **Types of Aid:** *Loans:* Direct Subsidized Stafford Loans, Direct Unsubsidized Stafford Loans, Direct PLUS loans. *Student Employment:* Federal Work-Study Program available. Institutional employment available. **Criteria for awarding aid:** *Need-based:* Academics, Athletics, Leadership. *Non-need-based:* Academics, Athletics, Leadership.

UNIVERSITY OF CALIFORNIA, BERKELEY

110 Sproul Hall, Berkeley, CA 94720-5800
CEEB Code: 4833
Website: www.berkeley.edu • **ACT Code:** 444

This public school was founded in 1868. It has a 1232-acre campus.

RATINGS

Admissions Selectivity Rating: 98   **Fire Safety Rating:** 91   **Green Rating:** 97

STUDENTS AND FACULTY

Enrollment: 27,496. **Student Body:** 52% female, 48% male, 15% out-of-state, 14% international. Asian 35%, African American 2%, Caucasian 27%, Hispanic 14%, Native American <1%, Pacific Islander <1%, Two or more races 5%, Race unknown 3%.
Retention and Graduation: 97% freshmen return for sophomore year. 73% freshmen graduate within 4 years. 91% freshmen graduate within 6 years.
Faculty: Student/faculty ratio 17:1. 1,623 full-time faculty, 99% hold PhDs, 21% are are members of minority groups, 35% are women. 0% of classes are taught by teaching assistants.

ACADEMICS

Degrees: bachelor's, doctoral/professional, doctoral/research, master's, postbachelor's certificate. **Classes:** Most classes have 20-29 students. Most lab/discussion sessions have 20-29 students. **Most popular majors:** Computer Engineering; English Language and Literature; Political Science and Government. **Special Study Options:** Accelerated program, cross-registration, double major, dual enrollment, English as a Second Language (ESL), exchange student program (domestic), honors program, independent study, internships, student-designed major, study abroad, teacher certification program. Combined degree programs: 10 Engineering Double Majors BS Degree. **Disability Services:** Special programs offered to physically disabled students, including note-taking services, reader services, tape recorders, tutors. **Career Services:** Alumni services, Career/job search classes, Career assessment, Internships.

FACILITIES

Housing: Coed dorms, special housing for disabled students, men's dorms, special housing for international students, women's dorms, fraternity/sorority housing, apartments for married students, cooperative housing, apartments for single students, Theme Housing. 95% of campus accessible to physically diasbled. **Special Academic Facilities/Equipment:** Lawrence Berkeley National Lab, Pacific Film Archive, Earthquake Data Center, Museums of art, anthropology, natural history, paleontology, Botanical Garden **Computers:** Students can register for classes online. Administrative functions (other than registration) can be performed online.

CAMPUS LIFE

Activities: Choral groups, concert band, dance, drama/theater, jazz band, literary magazine, marching band, music ensembles, musical theater, pep band, radio station, student government, student newspaper, student-run film society, symphony orchestra, television station, yearbook, Student Organization, Model UN. 300 registered organizations, 6 honor societies, 28 religious organizations. 38 fraternities, 19 sororities. **Athletics (Intercollegiate):** *Men:* baseball, basketball, crew/rowing, cross-country, diving, football, golf, gymnastics, rugby, sailing, soccer, swimming, tennis, track/field (outdoor), water polo. *Women:* basketball, crew/rowing, cross-country, diving, field hockey, golf, gymnastics, lacrosse, sailing, soccer, softball, swimming, tennis, track/field (outdoor), volleyball, water polo. **On-Campus Highlights:** Botanical Gardens, Lawrence Hall of Science, Museum of Anthropology, Museum of Art **Environmental Initiatives:** Climate and Energy: Six years ago the campus set out to reduce its carbon footprint by one-third Pé?Çô to bring Berkeley greenhouse gas emissions from campus operations back to the levels they were in 1990. Our most recent emissions inventory reveals that Berkeley has met this target, two years ahead of schedule. Ambitious at the outset, this voluntary target to reduce greenhouse gas emissions (GHG) to 1990 levels by 2014 puts Berkeley ahead of UC Policy and State of California guidelines which call for this level of reduction by the year 2020. We have reduced our emissions and met our first target by: Investing in energy efficiency and sustainable transportation practices. Since 2006, the campus has saved 20 million kWh of electricity through building retrofits and reduced fuel use by more than 1 million gallons by increasing the number of bicycle, pedestrian and mass-transit commuters. Buying Greener Power. The campus is using electricity that includes more solar and wind energy and less coal through purchases from Pacific Gas & Electric, a utility that is required by state law to provide power that by 2020 will include 33 percent renewable energy. Improving Data and Methods. UC Berkeley has improved the accuracy of its emissions inventory profile by using the best data available about campus energy use and by staying current with the best reporting methods.

ADMISSIONS

Freshman Academic Profile: Average high school GPA 3.9. 98% in top 10% of high school class, 100% in top 25% of high school class, 100% in top 50% of high school class. **Reported SAT (pre-2016 redesign) scores:** SAT Math middle 50% range 640-770. SAT Critical Reading middle 50% range 610-730. SAT Writing middle 50% range 620-750. **Concordant SAT scores:** SAT EBRW middle 50% 670–760. SAT Math middle 50% range 660–780. ACT middle 50% range 29-34. Minimum internet-based TOEFL 80. Minimum paper TOEFL 550. **Basis for Candidate Selection:** *Very important factors considered include:* rigor of secondary school record, academic GPA, standardized test scores, application essay. *Important factors considered include:* extracurricular activities, character/personal qualities, volunteer work, work experience. *Other factors considered include:* first generation, state residency. **Freshman Admission Requirements:** High school diploma is required and GED is accepted. *Academic units required:* 4 English, 3 math, 2 science, 2 science labs, 2 foreign language, 2 history, 1 academic elective, 1 visual/performing arts. *Academic units recommended:* 4 English, 4 math, 3 science, 3 science labs, 3 foreign language, 2 history, 1 academic elective, 1 visual/performing arts. **Freshman Admission Statistics:** 78,924 applied, 15.27% admitted, 46% enrolled. **Transfer Admission Requirements:** essay or personal statement, Minimum college GPA of 2.4 required. Lowest grade transferable D. **General Admission Information:** Application fee $70. Regular application deadline 11/30. Nonfall registration accepted.

COSTS AND FINANCIAL AID

Annual in-state tuition $11,220. Annual out-of-state tuition $37,902. Room and board $16,042. Required fees $2,289. Average book expense $1,262. **Required Forms and Deadlines:** FAFSA, State aid form. **Notification of Awards:** Applicants will be notified of awards on or about 3/31. **Types of Aid:** *Need-based scholarships/grants:* Federal Pell, FSEOG, State scholarships/grants, Private scholarships, College/university scholarship or grant aid from institutional funds. *Loans:* Direct Subsidized Stafford Loans, Direct Unsubsidized Stafford Loans, Direct PLUS loans, Federal Perkins Loans. *Student Employment:* Federal Work-Study Program available. Institutional employment available. **Financial Aid Statistics:** 99% needy freshmen, 98% needy undergrads receive need-based scholarship or grant aid. 5% freshmen, 3% undergrads receive non-need-based scholarship or grant aid. 50% freshmen, 55% undergrads receive need-based self-help aid. 1% freshmen, 1% undergrads receive athletic scholarships. 38% undergrads borrow to pay for school. Average cumulative indebtedness $17,869. **Criteria for awarding aid:** *Need-based:* Academics. *Non-need-based:* Academics, Athletics, Leadership.

UNIVERSITY OF CALIFORNIA, DAVIS

178 Mrak Hall, One Shields Ave, Davis, CA 95616
Phone: 530-752-2971 • **Financial Aid Phone:** 530-752-2396
E-mail: undergraduateadmissions@ucdavis.edu • **CEEB Code:** 4834
Fax: 530-752-1280 • **Website:** www.ucdavis.edu • **ACT Code:** 454

This public school was founded in 1908. It has a 5200-acre campus.

RATINGS

Admissions Selectivity Rating: 90   **Fire Safety Rating:** 94   **Green Rating:** 98

STUDENTS AND FACULTY

Enrollment: 29,358. **Student Body:** 59% female, 41% male, 5% out-of-state, 13% international (121 countries represented). Asian 30%, African American 2%, Caucasian 27%, Hispanic 20%, Native American <1%, Pacific Islander <1%, Two or more races 5%, Race unknown 2%.
Retention and Graduation: 92% freshmen return for sophomore year. 55% freshmen graduate within 4 years. 85% freshmen graduate within 6 years. 40% grads go on to further study within 1 year. 23% grads pursue arts and sciences degrees. 4% grads pursue law degrees. 1% grads pursue business degrees. 12% grads pursue medical degrees. **Faculty:** Student/faculty ratio 19:1. 1,702 full-time faculty, 98% hold PhDs, 25% are are members of minority groups, 39% are women.

ACADEMICS

Degrees: bachelor's, doctoral/professional, doctoral/research, doctoral, master's, postbachelor's certificate, post-master's certificate. **Classes:** Most classes have 20-29 students. Most lab/discussion sessions have 20-29 students. **Most popular majors:** Biology/Biological Sciences; Psychology; Economics. **Special Study Options:** Accelerated program, cross-registration, double major, dual enrollment, English as a Second Language (ESL), honors program, independent study, internships, student-designed major, study abroad, teacher certification program, Washington DC Center. **Honors Programs:** The Davis Honors Challenge (DHC) is an innovative, open-application, campuswide honors program for highly motivated students. In addition to a mentor program and a residential living-learning option for first-year students, DHC offers students the opportunity to participate in an honors program for four years. Integrated Studies Honors Program (ISHP), the oldest continuous residential learning community in the UC system, is an invitational, residential honors program for first-year students. ISHP provides an academic residential community similar to those of the best small colleges and helps students integrate knowledge from the arts and humanities, natural sciences and engineering, and social sciences. **Disability Services:** Special programs offered to physically disabled students, including note-taking services, reader services, tape recorders, tutors.

FACILITIES

Housing: Coed dorms, special housing for disabled students, women's dorms, apartments for married students, cooperative housing, apartments for single students, Wellness Housing, Theme Housing, Special Interest Communities: Davis Honors Challenge, Hammarskjöld International Relations Integrated Studies Multiethnic Program, Music, Arts & Performance, Quiet Program, Rainbow House, Women's Community. **Special Academic Facilities/Equipment:** Art galleries, 150-acre university arboretum, equestrian center, craft center, student experimental farm, nuclear lab, human performance lab, natural reserves, early childhood lab, raptor center, primate research center. **Computers:** Students can register for classes online. Administrative functions (other than registration) can be performed online.

CAMPUS LIFE

Environment: Town. **Activities:** Choral groups, concert band, dance, drama/theater, jazz band, literary magazine, marching band, music ensembles, musical theater, pep band, radio station, student government, student newspaper, student-run film society, symphony orchestra, television station, yearbook, Campus Ministries, Student Organization, Model UN. 364 registered organizations, 1 honor society, 50 religious organizations. 28 fraternities, 21 sororities. **Athletics (Intercollegiate):** *Men:* baseball, basketball, cross-country, diving, football, golf, soccer, swimming, tennis, track/field (outdoor), track/field (indoor), water polo, wrestling. *Women:* basketball, crew/rowing, cross-country, diving, field hockey, golf, gymnastics, lacrosse, soccer, softball, swimming, tennis, track/field (outdoor), track/field (indoor), volleyball, water polo. **On-Campus Highlights:** Mondavi Center for the Performing Arts, Memorial Union/Coffee House, Activities and Recreation Center (The ARC), Sciences Laboratory Building, The UC Davis Arboretum, http://daviswiki.org/. **Environmental Initiatives:** UC Davis is taking action to reduce greenhouse gas emissions and energy use on campus through programs like the Strategic Energy Partnership Program, which is improving energy conservation and energy efficiency on campus and has identified retrofit and recommissioning projects that will save more than 28 million kilowatt-hours and 2 million therms. The campus installed a 756kW solar photovoltaic system, which generates over 1 million kilowatt-hours a year. UC Davis has also embarked on an ambitious initiative to reduce lighting energy use by 60% in five years, which will reduce energy use and greenhouse gas emissions (www.sustainability.ucdavis.edu/news/2010/november/smart_lighting.html) and is pursuing a project to build an on-campus anaerobic biodigester that will generate about 2 million kilowatt-hours a year of clean, renewable electricity from campus organic wastes (news.ucdavis.edu/search/news_detail.lasso?id=10202). Work on climate issues at UC Davis includes everything from studying pollution in the Arctic atmosphere and building global climate models to the campus Climate Action Plan (CAP) and energy use reduction. UC Davis faculty and student research on climate change spans a wide range of investigation from basic inquiry to solution-based engineering work (climatechange.ucdavis.edu/). The CAP analyzes campus issues around greenhouse gas emissions reductions, energy use and energy sourcing (www.sustainability.ucdavis.edu/progress/climate/index.html).

ADMISSIONS

Freshman Academic Profile: Average high school GPA 4.0. 84% from public high schools. **Reported SAT (pre-2016 redesign) scores:** SAT Math middle 50% range 540-700. SAT Critical Reading middle 50% range 510-630. SAT Writing middle 50% range 520-650. **Concordant SAT scores:** SAT EBRW middle 50% 570–690. SAT Math middle 50% range 570–730. ACT middle 50% range 24-30. Minimum internet-based TOEFL 60. Minimum paper TOEFL 550. **Basis for Candidate Selection:** *Very important factors considered include:* rigor of secondary school record, academic GPA, standardized test scores, application essay. *Important factors considered include:* extracurricular activities, talent/ability, character/personal qualities, volunteer work. *Other factors considered include:* first generation, state residency, work experience. **Freshman Admission Requirements:** High school diploma is required and GED is accepted. *Academic units required:* 4 English, 3 math, 2 science, 2

science labs, 2 foreign language, 1 social studies, 1 history, 1 academic elective, 1 visual/performing arts. *Academic units recommended:* 4 English, 4 math, 3 science, 3 science labs, 3 foreign language, 1 social studies, 1 history, 1 academic elective, 1 visual/performing arts. **Freshman Admission Statistics:** 67,472 applied, 42.41% admitted, 20% enrolled. **Transfer Admission Requirements:** High school transcript, college transcript(s), essay or personal statement, statement of good standing from prior institution(s). Lowest grade transferable D-. **General Admission Information:** Application fee $70. Regular application deadline 11/30. Regular notification 3/31. Nonfall registration not accepted.

COSTS AND FINANCIAL AID

Annual in-state tuition $11,220. Annual out-of-state tuition $37,902. Room and board $14,838. Required fees $2,826. Average book expense $1,601. **Required Forms and Deadlines:** FAFSA, State aid form. **Notification of Awards:** Applicants will be notified of awards on or about 3/16. **Types of Aid:** *Need-based scholarships/grants:* Federal Pell, FSEOG, State scholarships/grants, Private scholarships, College/university scholarship or grant aid from institutional funds. *Loans:* Direct Subsidized Stafford Loans, Direct Unsubsidized Stafford Loans, Direct PLUS loans, Federal Perkins Loans, College/university loans from institutional funds. *Student Employment:* Federal Work-Study Program available. Institutional employment available. **Financial Aid Statistics:** 97% needy freshmen, 96% needy undergrads receive need-based scholarship or grant aid. 2% freshmen, 1% undergrads receive non-need-based scholarship or grant aid. 62% freshmen, 57% undergrads receive need-based self-help aid. 1% freshmen, 1% undergrads receive athletic scholarships. 55% undergrads receive any aid. 56% undergrads borrow to pay for school. Average cumulative indebtedness $19,588. **Criteria for awarding aid:** *Need-based:* Academics, Athletics. *Non-need-based:* Academics, Athletics.

UNIVERSITY OF CALIFORNIA, IRVINE

Office of Admissions and Relations with Schools, Irvine, CA 92697-1075
Phone: 949-824-6703 • **Financial Aid Phone:** 949-824-2004
E-mail: admissions@uci.edu • **CEEB Code:** 4859
Fax: 949-824-2951 • **Website:** www.uci.edu

This public school was founded in 1965. It has a 1500-acre campus.

RATINGS

Admissions Selectivity Rating: 95   **Fire Safety Rating:** 88   **Green Rating:** 99

STUDENTS AND FACULTY

Enrollment: 25,256. **Student Body:** 54% female, 46% male, 3% out-of-state, 16% international (70 countries represented). Asian 37%, African American 2%, Caucasian 12%, Hispanic 25%, Native American <1%, Pacific Islander <1%, Two or more races 4%, Race unknown 4%.
Retention and Graduation: 93% freshmen return for sophomore year. 72% freshmen graduate within 4 years. 88% freshmen graduate within 6 years. **Faculty:** Student/faculty ratio 19:1. 1,203 full-time faculty, 98% hold PhDs, 28% are are members of minority groups, 36% are women.

ACADEMICS

Degrees: bachelor's, doctoral/professional, doctoral/research, master's, postbachelor's certificate. **Classes:** Most classes have 20-29 students. Most lab/discussion sessions have fewer than 10 students. **Most popular majors:** Biology/Biological Sciences; Social Psychology; Business/Managerial Economics. **Special Study Options:** Accelerated program, distance learning, double major, dual enrollment, English as a Second Language (ESL), honors program, independent study, internships, liberal arts/career combination, study abroad, teacher certification program. **Honors Programs:** Campuswide Honors Program (CHP). **Disability Services:** Special programs offered to physically disabled students, including note-taking services, reader services, tape recorders. **Career Services:** Alumni network, Alumni services, Career/job search classes, Career assessment, Internships.

FACILITIES

Housing: Coed dorms, special housing for disabled students, men's dorms, special housing for international students, women's dorms, fraternity/sorority housing, apartments for married students, cooperative housing, apartments for single students, Theme Housing. 95% of campus accessible to physically diasbled. **Special Academic Facilities/Equipment:** Museum of systemic biology, freshwater marsh reserve, electron microscope, nuclear reactor, laser institute, research facilities. **Computers:** 90% of classrooms, 100% of libraries, 100% of dining areas, 100% of student union, have wireless network access. Students can register for classes online. Administrative functions (other than registration) can be performed online.

CAMPUS LIFE

Environment: City. **Activities:** Choral groups, concert band, dance, drama/ theater, jazz band, literary magazine, music ensembles, musical theater, opera, pep band, radio station, student government, student newspaper, student-run film society, symphony orchestra, yearbook, Student Organization, Model UN. 484 registered organizations, 18 honor societies, 51 religious organizations. 21 fraternities, 23 sororities. **Athletics (Intercollegiate): Men:** baseball, basketball, cross-country, golf, sailing, soccer, tennis, track/field (outdoor), volleyball, water polo. **Women:** basketball, cross-country, golf, sailing, soccer, tennis, track/field (outdoor), volleyball, water polo. **On-Campus Highlights:** Anteater Recreation Center, Bren Events Center, Cross-Cultural Center, Beall Center for Art and Technology, Arts Plaza. **Environmental Initiatives:** 1. Water The University of California is a leader in water conservation and water efficiency. Every UC campus, including UCI, has committed to reducing per capita potable water consumption by 20 percent by 2020 and has developed a Water Action Plan that establishes a baseline against which the 20 percent reduction is measured and identifies strategies to achieve the goal. The UCI Water Resources Working Group assembled the campus Water Action Plan in 2013. The campus is currently on track to exceed the original systemwide goal. UC Policy on Sustainable Practices was revised in 2015 to include a reduction of 36 percent per capita by 2025, and UCI Water Action Plan is currently being revised to reflect this policy change. Since 2007, UCI main campus has reduced potable water use by retrofitting old plumbing fixtures in the campus core and student housing. Building on past water conservation projects that have resulted in annual savings of approximately 30 percent per capita, the UCI Water Resources Working Group has identified more than 50 initiatives with the potential to reduce water use by an additional 25 percent. For more information, see: http://sustainability.uci.edu/sustainablecampus/ water/ UCI strong performance in water-wise operations is more than matched by the campus academic expertise on this front. In addition to individual faculty research, a number of research centers are focused on water issues and/or host water-focused seminars throughout the year. These include: The Center for Environmental Biology; The Center for Hydrometeorology and Remote Sensing; The Center for Land, Environment, and Natural Resources in UCI School of Law; The Center for Unconventional Security Affairs; The Newkirk Center for Science and Society; The UCI Water Energy Nexus Center Additionally, examples of campuswide initiatives include: Water UCI—This initiative coordinates collaboration across schools, departments, and existing research centers around questions of fundamental and applied water science, technology, management, and policy; Salton Sea Initiative—This initiative mobilizes UCI research, teaching, and service resources to address myriad sustainability challenges facing the Salton Sea region. The California Natural Resources Agency recently named UCI biologist Tim Bradley, director of the Salton Sea Initiative, to the science advisory committee for the state effort to preserve its largest inland body of water; FloodRISE—This National Science Foundation (NSF)-funded project seeks to understand what factors and conditions allow parcel-level prediction of urban flooding to catalyze behavioral change in flood vulnerable communities; UCI Water-Partnerships for International Research & Education—This NSF-funded project catalyzes, through research and education, the development and deployment of low-energy options for improving water productivity while protecting human and ecosystem health; Borrego Springs Water Sustainability and Climate—This project evaluates the integrated water infrastructure of the arid, closed-basin Borrego Springs Aquifer System using a participatory science framework.

ADMISSIONS

Freshman Academic Profile: Average high school GPA 3.9. 96% in top 10% of high school class, 100% in top 25% of high school class, 100% in top 50% of high school class. 69% from public high schools. **Reported SAT (pre-2016 redesign) scores:** SAT Math middle 50% range 550-690. SAT Critical Reading middle 50% range 490-620. SAT Writing middle 50% range 510-620. **Concordant SAT scores:** SAT EBRW middle 50% 560–670. SAT Math middle 50% range 570–720. Minimum internet-based TOEFL 80. Minimum paper TOEFL 550. **Basis for Candidate Selection:** *Very important factors considered include:* rigor of secondary school record, academic GPA, standardized test scores, application essay, extracurricular activities, talent/ ability, volunteer work, work experience, level of applicant's interest. *Important factors considered include:* class rank, character/personal qualities. *Other factors considered include:* first generation, geographical residence, state residency. **Freshman Admission Requirements:** High school diploma is required and GED is accepted. *Academic units required:* 4 English, 3 math, 2 science, 2 science labs, 2 foreign language, 2 social studies, 1 academic elective, 1 visual/ performing arts. *Academic units recommended:* 4 English, 4 math, 3 science, 3 science labs, 3 foreign language, 2 social studies, 1 academic elective, 1 visual/ performing arts. **Freshman Admission Statistics:** 71,768 applied, 38.69% admitted, 21% enrolled. **Transfer Admission Requirements:** High school transcript, college transcript(s), essay or personal statement, Minimum college GPA of 2.0 required. Lowest grade transferable C. **General Admission Information:** Application fee $70. Regular application deadline 11/30. Regular notification 3/31. Nonfall registration not accepted.

COSTS AND FINANCIAL AID

Annual in-state tuition $11,220. Annual out-of-state tuition $37,902. Room and board $13,661. Required fees $3,806. Average book expense $1,772. **Required Forms and Deadlines:** FAFSA, State aid form. **Notification of Awards:** Applicants will be notified of awards on a rolling basis beginning 4/1. **Types of Aid:** *Need-based scholarships/grants:* Federal Pell, FSEOG, State scholarships/grants, Private scholarships, College/university scholarship or grant aid from institutional funds. *Loans:* Direct Subsidized Stafford Loans, Direct Unsubsidized Stafford Loans, Direct PLUS loans, Federal Perkins Loans, College/university loans from institutional funds. *Student Employment:* Federal Work-Study Program available. Institutional employment available. **Financial Aid Statistics:** 97% needy freshmen, 93% needy undergrads receive need-based scholarship or grant aid. 1% freshmen, 1% undergrads receive non-need-based scholarship or grant aid. 76% freshmen, 66% undergrads receive need-based self-help aid. 0% freshmen, 0% undergrads receive athletic scholarships. Average cumulative indebtedness $20,628.

UNIVERSITY OF CALIFORNIA, LOS ANGELES

1147 Murphy Hall, Los Angeles, CA 90095-1436
Phone: 310-825-3101 • **Financial Aid Phone:** 310-206-0400
E-mail: ugadm@saonet.ucla.edu • **CEEB Code:** 4837
Fax: 310-206-1206 • **Website:** www.ucla.edu • **ACT Code:** 448

This public school was founded in 1919. It has a 419-acre campus.

RATINGS

Admissions Selectivity Rating: 97   **Fire Safety Rating:** 92   **Green Rating:** 93

STUDENTS AND FACULTY

Enrollment: 30,856. **Student Body:** 57% female, 43% male, 11% out-of-state, 12% international (138 countries represented). Asian 29%, African American 3%, Caucasian 27%, Hispanic 22%, Native American <1%, Pacific Islander <1%, Two or more races 5%, Race unknown 2%.
Retention and Graduation: 97% freshmen return for sophomore year. 74% freshmen graduate within 4 years. 91% freshmen graduate within 6 years.
Faculty: Student/faculty ratio 17:1. 1,570 full-time faculty, 95% hold PhDs, 30% are are members of minority groups, 34% are women. 0% of classes are taught by teaching assistants.

ACADEMICS

Degrees: bachelor's, doctoral/professional, doctoral/research, master's. **Classes:** Most classes have 10-19 students. Most lab/discussion sessions have 20-29 students. **Most popular majors:** Biology/Biological Sciences; Psychology; Business/Managerial Economics. **Special Study Options:** Accelerated program, double major, English as a Second Language (ESL), honors program, independent study, internships, liberal arts/career combination, student-designed major, study abroad. **Honors Programs:** The College Honors Program. **Disability Services:** Special programs offered to physically disabled students, including note-taking services, reader services, tape recorders, tutors. **Career Services:** Alumni network, Alumni services, Career/job search classes, Career assessment, Internships, Regional alumni. Based at the UC Washington Center, CAPPP students carry out a research project on a topic of their own choosing, and complete a challenging, substantive internship at one of DC's hundreds of government agencies, think tanks, NGOs, non-profits, media outlets, advocacy, trade, and business organizations. Program participants earn up to 16 upper division units while remaining full-time UCLA students.

FACILITIES

Housing: Coed dorms, special housing for disabled students, fraternity/sorority housing, apartments for married students, apartments for single students, Wellness Housing, Theme Housing. 100% of campus accessible to physically diasbled. **Special Academic Facilities/Equipment:** Art gallery, cultural history museum, sculpture garden, graphic arts center, numerous study centers, research institutes, UCLA Armand Hammer Museum of Art and Cultural Center, Murphy Sculpture Garden, Fowler Museum of Cultural History **Computers:** Students can register for classes online. Administrative functions (other than registration) can be performed online.

CAMPUS LIFE

Environment: Metropolis. **Activities:** Choral groups, concert band, dance, drama/theater, jazz band, literary magazine, marching band, music ensembles, musical theater, opera, pep band, radio station, student government, student newspaper, student-run film society, symphony orchestra, television station, yearbook, Campus Ministries, Student Organization, Model UN. 870 registered organizations, 21 honor societies, 38 religious organizations. 36 fraternities, 28 sororities. **Athletics (Intercollegiate):** *Men:* baseball, basketball, cross-country, football, golf, soccer, tennis, track/field (outdoor), track/field (indoor), volleyball, water polo. *Women:* basketball, crew/rowing, cross-country, diving, golf, gymnastics, soccer, softball, swimming, tennis, track/field (outdoor), track/field (indoor), volleyball, water polo. **On-Campus Highlights:** The UCLA Library, UCLA Fowler Museum of Cultural History, UCLA Book Store, DeNeve Plaza, Kerckhoff Coffee House. **Environmental Initiatives:** The University of California and state legislation set a target of reducing greenhouse gas emissions to 1990 levels by 2020. UCLA comprehensive Climate Action Plan lays out a plan for the university to achieve that goal by 2012, eight years ahead. The plan catalogues the steps the university has taken in the past and contains a detailed financial feasibility analysis for the initiatives that the university will undertake in energy and transportation to reduce greenhouse gas emissions. The initiatives outlined in the Climate Action Plan, in addition to addressing a critical environmental issue, will also conserve university resources and result in significant cost reductions. The energy initiatives have an average payback period of less than 5 years, with some lighting initiatives paying back through cost savings in less than a year. By demonstrating that it is possible to address climate change through concrete verifiable emissions reductions even in the toughest budget situation, UCLA is setting an example for the rest of California and the nation. The plan also catalogues academic and research initiatives at UCLA focused on climate change and sustainability. UCLA is a living laboratory for climate and sustainability research. Undergraduate and graduate students engage with staff and faculty to pilot new technologies and policies on the university campus. With over 25 research centers focused on climate and sustainability, UCLA is creating the technology and training the leaders of tomorrow, while leading by example in our own operations.

ADMISSIONS

Freshman Academic Profile: Average high school GPA 4.3. 97% in top 10% of high school class, 100% in top 25% of high school class, 100% in top 50% of high school class. 68% from public high schools. **Reported SAT (pre-2016 redesign) scores:** SAT Math middle 50% range 580-740. SAT Critical Reading middle 50% range 570-700. SAT Writing middle 50% range 570-720. **Concordant SAT scores:** SAT EBRW middle 50% 630–740. SAT Math middle 50% range 600–760. ACT middle 50% range 25-33. Minimum internet-based TOEFL 83. Minimum paper TOEFL 550. **Basis for Candidate Selection:** *Very important factors considered include:* rigor of secondary school record, academic GPA, standardized test scores, application essay. *Important factors considered include:* extracurricular activities, talent/ability, character/personal qualities, volunteer work, work experience. *Other factors considered include:* first generation, geographical residence. **Freshman Admission Requirements:** High school diploma is required and GED is accepted. *Academic units required:* 4 English, 3 math, 2 science, 2 science labs, 2 foreign language, 2 history, 1 academic elective, 1 visual/performing arts. *Academic units recommended:* 4 English, 4 math, 3 science, 3 science labs, 3 foreign language, 2 history, 1 academic elective, 1 visual/performing arts. **Freshman Admission Statistics:** 97,121 applied, 17.99% admitted, 37% enrolled. **Transfer Admission Requirements:** college transcript(s), essay or personal statement, statement of good standing from prior institution(s). Minimum college GPA of 2.4 required. Lowest grade transferable D. **General Admission Information:** Application fee $70. Regular application deadline 11/30. Nonfall registration not accepted.

COSTS AND FINANCIAL AID

Annual in-state tuition $11,220. Annual out-of-state tuition $37,902. Room and board $14,029. Required fees $2,024. Average book expense $1,635. **Required Forms and Deadlines:** FAFSA. **Notification of Awards:** Applicants will be notified of awards on a rolling basis beginning 3/15. **Types of Aid:** *Need-based scholarships/grants:* Federal Pell, FSEOG, State scholarships/grants, Private scholarships, College/university scholarship or grant aid from institutional funds, United Negro College Fund. *Loans:* Direct Subsidized Stafford Loans, Direct Unsubsidized Stafford Loans, Direct PLUS loans, Federal Perkins Loans, Federal Nursing Loans, College/university loans from institutional funds. *Student Employment:* Federal Work-Study Program available. Institutional employment available. **Financial Aid Statistics:** 97% needy freshmen, 96% needy undergrads receive need-based scholarship or grant aid. 2% freshmen, 1% undergrads receive non-need-based scholarship or grant aid. 57% freshmen, 62% undergrads receive need-based self-help aid. 1% freshmen, 1% undergrads receive athletic scholarships. 54% freshmen, 55% undergrads receive any aid. 46% undergrads borrow to pay for school. Average cumulative indebtedness $21,596. **Criteria for awarding aid:** *Non-need-based:* Academics, Art, Job skills.

UNIVERSITY OF CALIFORNIA—MERCED

5200 North Lake Raod, Merced, CA 95343
Phone: 209-228-7178
E-mail: admissions@ucmerced.edu
Fax: 209-228-4244 • **Website:** www.ucmerced.edu

RATINGS

Admissions Selectivity Rating: 73   **Fire Safety Rating:** 60*   **Green Rating:** 95

STUDENTS AND FACULTY

Student Body: 9% out-of-state.
Retention and Graduation: 74% freshmen return for sophomore year. 0.273364486 freshmen graduate within 4 years. 46 **Faculty:** 42%

ADMISSIONS

Freshman Academic Profile: Average high school GPA 3.5. **Reported SAT (pre-2016 redesign) scores:** SAT Math middle 50% range 470-570. SAT Critical Reading middle 50% range 470-580. SAT Writing middle 50% range 460-590. **Concordant SAT scores:** SAT EBRW middle 50% 470–580. SAT Math middle 50% range 480–570. ACT middle 50% range 18-23. **Freshman Admission Statistics:** 20,888 applied, 74% admitted.

UNIVERSITY OF CALIFORNIA, RIVERSIDE

3106 Student Services Building, Riverside, CA 92521
Phone: 951-827-3411 • **Financial Aid Phone:** 951-827-7249
E-mail: admissions@ucr.edu • **CEEB Code:** 4839
Fax: 951-827-6344 • **Website:** www.ucr.edu

This public school was founded in 1954. It has a 1200-acre campus.

RATINGS

Admissions Selectivity Rating: 91   **Fire Safety Rating:** 94   **Green Rating:** 98

STUDENTS AND FACULTY

Enrollment: 19,786. **Student Body:** 54% female, 46% male, 1% out-of-state, 2% international (100 countries represented). Asian 34%, African American 4%, Caucasian 12%, Hispanic 41%, Native American <1%, Pacific Islander <1%, Two or more races 6%, Race unknown 1%.
Retention and Graduation: 91% freshmen return for sophomore year. 47% freshmen graduate within 4 years. 73% freshmen graduate within 6 years.
Faculty: 0% of classes are taught by teaching assistants.

ACADEMICS

Degrees: bachelor's, doctoral, master's, postbachelor's certificate. **Classes:** Most classes have 20-29 students. Most lab/discussion sessions have 20-29 students. **Most popular majors:** Psychology; Business Administration and Management; Biological and Biomedical Sciences. **Special Study Options:** Accelerated program, cross-registration, double major, English as a Second Language (ESL), honors program, independent study, internships, student-designed major, study abroad, teacher certification program. Combined degree programs: BA/MA. **Disability Services:** Special programs offered to physically disabled students, including note-taking services, reader services, tape recorders, tutors. **Career Services:** Alumni services, Career/job search classes, Career assessment, Internships. Today's students do not always have the time to come to the brick and mortar home of the traditional Career Center. The UCR Career Center has responded by developing state-of-the-art best practices to deliver services. These new alternatives and virtual services range from a highly interactive website using podcasts, Skype, Webinars and YouTube features to providing workshops. Information on resume writing, interviewing techniques, job search strategies and/or plans for graduate school give students virtual opportunities to gather important information. We still offer an array of workshops, information sessions and industry panels in the traditional face-to-face format, but this new venues offers students more flexibility.

FACILITIES

Housing: Coed dorms, special housing for disabled students, special housing for international students, apartments for married students, apartments for single students, Theme Housing. **Special Academic Facilities/Equipment:** Art gallery, photography museum, botanical gardens, audio-visual resource center/studios, media resource center, statistical consulting center, citrus research center and agricultural experiment station, air pollution research center, center for environmental research and technology, water resources center, geophysics and planetary physics institute, center for bibliographical studies, center for family studies, center for crime and justice studies, natural reserve system, water resources center, salinity lab. **Computers:** 100% of classrooms, 15% of dorms, 100% of libraries, 100% of dining areas, 100% of student union, 100% of common outdoor areas have wireless network access. Students can register for classes online. Administrative functions (other than registration) can be performed online.

CAMPUS LIFE

Environment: City. **Activities:** Choral groups, concert band, dance, drama/ theater, jazz band, literary magazine, music ensembles, musical theater, pep band, radio station, student government, student newspaper, student-run film society, Student Organization. 264 registered organizations, 9 honor societies, 27 religious organizations. 20 fraternities, 20 sororities. **Athletics (Intercollegiate):** *Men:* baseball, basketball, cross-country, golf, soccer, tennis, track/field (outdoor), track/field (indoor). *Women:* basketball, cross-country, golf, soccer, softball, tennis, track/field (outdoor), track/field (indoor), volleyball. **On-Campus Highlights:** Basketball Games, Student Recreation Center and intramural sports, The Barn (music and comedy acts), Coffee Bean and Tea Leaf, The Highlander Union Building (HUB). **Environmental Initiatives:** UCR has a funded non-restrictive Office of Sustainability charged with coordinating sustainability initiatives throughout the campus supported by the Chancellor's Committee on Sustainability with the Chancellor serving as chair.

ADMISSIONS

Freshman Academic Profile: Average high school GPA 3.7. 94% in top 10% of high school class, 100% in top 25% of high school class, 100% in top 50% of high school class. 90% from public high schools. **Reported SAT (pre-2016 redesign) scores:** SAT Math middle 50% range 480-610. SAT Critical Reading middle 50% range 460-580. SAT Writing middle 50% range 470-580. **Concordant SAT scores:** SAT EBRW middle 50% 520–640. SAT Math middle 50% range 510–630. ACT middle 50% range 21-27. Minimum internet-based TOEFL 80. Minimum paper TOEFL 550. **Basis for Candidate Selection:** *Very important factors considered include:* rigor of secondary school record, academic GPA, standardized test scores, application essay. *Other factors considered include:* extracurricular activities, talent/ability, character/personal qualities, first generation, state residency, volunteer work, work experience. **Freshman Admission Requirements:** High school diploma is required and GED is accepted. *Academic units required:* 4 English, 3 math, 2 science, 2 science labs, 2 foreign language, 2 history, 1 academic elective, 1 visual/ performing arts. *Academic units recommended:* 4 math, 3 science, 3 science labs, 3 foreign language. **Freshman Admission Statistics:** 42,629 applied, 66.34% admitted, 19% enrolled. **Transfer Admission Requirements:** college transcript(s), essay or personal statement, statement of good standing from prior institution(s). Minimum college GPA of 2.4 required. Lowest grade transferable D-. **General Admission Information:** Application fee $70. Regular application deadline 11/30. Regular notification 3/31. Nonfall registration not accepted.

COSTS AND FINANCIAL AID

Required Forms and Deadlines: FAFSA, State aid form. **Notification of Awards:** Applicants will be notified of awards on a rolling basis beginning 3/1. **Types of Aid:** *Need-based scholarships/grants:* Federal Pell, FSEOG, State scholarships/grants, Private scholarships, College/university scholarship or grant aid from institutional funds. *Loans:* Direct Subsidized Stafford Loans, Direct Unsubsidized Stafford Loans, Direct PLUS loans, Federal Perkins Loans, College/university loans from institutional funds. *Student Employment:* Federal Work-Study Program available. Institutional employment available. **Financial Aid Statistics:** 97% needy freshmen, 96% needy undergrads receive need-based scholarship or grant aid. 1% freshmen, 1% undergrads receive non-need-based scholarship or grant aid. 78% freshmen, 68% undergrads receive need-based self-help aid. 0% freshmen, 0% undergrads receive athletic scholarships. 89% freshmen, 85% undergrads receive any aid. Average cumulative indebtedness $21,838. **Criteria for awarding aid:** *Need-based:* Academics. *Non-need-based:* Academics, Alumni affiliation, Art, Athletics, Leadership.

UNIVERSITY OF CALIFORNIA, SAN DIEGO

9500 Gilman Drive, La Jolla, CA 92093-0021
Phone: 858-534-4831 • **Financial Aid Phone:** 858-534-4480
E-mail: admissionsinfo@ucsd.edu • **CEEB Code:** 4836
Fax: 858-534-5723 • **Website:** www.ucsd.edu

This public school was founded in 1960. It has a 1976-acre campus.

RATINGS

Admissions Selectivity Rating: 97   **Fire Safety Rating:** 92   **Green Rating:** 90

STUDENTS AND FACULTY

Enrollment: 26,590. **Student Body:** 48% female, 52% male, 6% out-of-state, 23% international (92 countries represented). Asian 34%, African American 2%, Caucasian 19%, Hispanic 15%, Native American <1%, Pacific Islander <1%, Two or more races 0%, Race unknown 7%.
Retention and Graduation: 95% freshmen return for sophomore year. 58% freshmen graduate within 4 years. 87% freshmen graduate within 6 years. 42% grads go on to further study within 1 year. 34% grads pursue arts and sciences degrees. 15% grads pursue law degrees. 8% grads pursue business degrees. 16% grads pursue medical degrees. **Faculty:** Student/faculty ratio 19:1. 1,011 full-time faculty, 98% hold PhDs, 25% are are members of minority groups, 28% are women. 0% of classes are taught by teaching assistants.

ACADEMICS

Degrees: bachelor's, doctoral/professional, doctoral/research, doctoral, master's. **Classes:** Most classes have 10-19 students. Most lab/discussion sessions have 10-19 students. **Most popular majors:** Economics; Biology/ Biological Sciences. **Special Study Options:** Accelerated program, cooperative education program, cross-registration, double major, English as a Second Language (ESL), exchange student program (domestic), honors program, independent study, internships, liberal arts/career combination, student-designed major, study abroad, teacher certification program, Summer sessions for credit; special services for students with learning disabilities; Research programs, freshman honors program, in-depth academic assignments working in small groups or one-to-one with faculty. **Honors Programs:** Each of UCSD"s six colleges offers an honors program. Honors programs differ from college to college and year to year. Combined degree programs: BA/ MD, BA/MA, BA/MEng, Psychology, Experimental Psychology, Chemistry, Biochemistry, Cognitive Sci. **Disability Services:** Special programs offered to physically disabled students, including note-taking services, reader services, tape recorders, tutors. **Career Services:** Alumni network, Alumni services, Career/job search classes, Career assessment, Internships, Regional alumni. The UC San Diego quarterly Triton Job & Internship Fairs draw over 350 employers annually and are attended by over 1500 students/alumni at each fair. The fall event is targeted to our technology-focused students while the other quarterly fairs are more broad-based attracting employers from not only science and engineering but also business, finance, government, and nonprofits.

FACILITIES

Housing: Coed dorms, special housing for disabled students, men's dorms, special housing for international students, women's dorms, fraternity/sorority housing, apartments for married students, cooperative housing, apartments for single students, House for international students and others interested in international living. 100% of campus accessible to physically disabled. **Special Academic Facilities/Equipment:** Art galleries, center for U.S.-Mexican studies, music recording studio, audiovisual center, center for music experimentation, aquarium, structural lab, San Diego supercomputer center,electron microscopes lab, the UC San Diego Medical Center, Scripps Institution of Oceanography, California Institute for Telecommunications and Information Technology (Calit2), Institute on Global Conflict and Cooperation; Institute of the Americas. **Computers:** 100% of classrooms, 100% of dorms, 100% of libraries, 100% of dining areas, 100% of student union, 30% of common outdoor areas have wireless network access. Students can register for classes online. Administrative functions (other than registration) can be performed online.

CAMPUS LIFE

Environment: Metropolis. **Activities:** Choral groups, concert band, dance, drama/theater, jazz band, literary magazine, marching band, music ensembles, musical theater, opera, pep band, radio station, student government, student newspaper, student-run film society, symphony orchestra, television station, yearbook, Campus Ministries, Student Organization, Model UN. 406 registered organizations, 5 honor societies, 46 religious organizations. 19 fraternities,

14 sororities. **Athletics (Intercollegiate):** *Men:* baseball, basketball, crew/rowing, cross-country, diving, fencing, golf, soccer, swimming, tennis, track/field (outdoor), volleyball, water polo. *Women:* basketball, crew/rowing, cross-country, diving, fencing, soccer, softball, swimming, tennis, track/field (outdoor), volleyball, water polo. **On-Campus Highlights:** Geisel Library, Stuart Art (sculpture) Gallery, Sun God Statue, Ocean Cliffs, Stephen Birch Aquarium and Museum, Price Center Expansion. **Environmental Initiatives:** The LEED Gold Certified Sustainability Resource Center (SRC), completed November 20, 2009 was constructed to provide a centralized, collaborative space in which to realize the common goals of maximizing campus environmental, social, and economic stewardship and sustainability; reducing the campus impact on the environment; maximizing campus and local outreach and participation; and, establishing a model for contributing to local, national, and global sustainability.

ADMISSIONS

Freshman Academic Profile: Average high school GPA 4.0. 100% in top 10% of high school class, 100% in top 25% of high school class, 100% in top 50% of high school class. **Reported SAT (pre-2016 redesign) scores:** SAT Math middle 50% range 630-770. SAT Critical Reading middle 50% range 580-680. SAT Writing middle 50% range 590-700. **Concordant SAT scores:** SAT EBRW middle 50% 640-730. SAT Math middle 50% range 650-780. ACT middle 50% range 27-32. Minimum paper TOEFL 550. **Basis for Candidate Selection:** *Very important factors considered include:* rigor of secondary school record, academic GPA, standardized test scores, application essay. *Important factors considered include:* extracurricular activities, talent/ability, character/personal qualities, state residency, volunteer work. *Other factors considered include:* first generation, geographical residence, work experience. **Freshman Admission Requirements:** High school diploma is required and GED is accepted. *Academic units required:* 4 English, 3 math, 2 science, 2 science labs, 2 foreign language, 2 history, 1 visual/performing arts. *Academic units recommended:* 4 English, 4 math, 3 science, 3 science labs, 3 foreign language, 2 history, 1 academic elective, 1 visual/performing arts. **Freshman Admission Statistics:** 78,056 applied, 33.96% admitted, 20% enrolled. **Transfer Admission Requirements:** college transcript(s), essay or personal statement, statement of good standing from prior institution(s). Minimum college GPA of 2.4 required. Lowest grade transferable D. **General Admission Information:** Application fee $60. Regular application deadline 11/30. Regular notification 3/31. Nonfall registration accepted.

COSTS AND FINANCIAL AID

Annual in-state tuition $13,672. Annual out-of-state tuition $40,354. Room and board $12,477. Required fees $1,378. Average book expense $1,521. **Required Forms and Deadlines:** FAFSA, State aid form. **Notification of Awards:** Applicants will be notified of awards on a rolling basis beginning 3/15. **Types of Aid:** *Need-based scholarships/grants:* Federal Pell, FSEOG, State scholarships/grants, Private scholarships, College/university scholarship or grant aid from institutional funds. *Loans:* Direct Subsidized Stafford Loans, Direct Unsubsidized Stafford Loans, Direct PLUS loans, Federal Perkins Loans, College/university loans from institutional funds. *Student Employment:* Federal Work-Study Program available. Institutional employment available. **Financial Aid Statistics:** 92% needy freshmen, 94% needy undergrads receive need-based scholarship or grant aid. 2% freshmen, 1% undergrads receive non-need-based scholarship or grant aid. 78% freshmen, 76% undergrads receive need-based self-help aid. 0% freshmen, 0% undergrads receive athletic scholarships. 77% freshmen, 63% undergrads receive any aid. 60% undergrads borrow to pay for school. Average cumulative indebtedness $21,660. **Criteria for awarding aid:** *Need-based:* Academics, Art, Leadership, Minority status, Music/drama. *Non-need-based:* Academics, Art, Athletics, Leadership, Minority status, Music/drama.

UNIVERSITY OF CALIFORNIA, SANTA BARBARA

Office of Admissions, Santa Barbara, CA 93106-2014
Phone: 805-893-2881 • **Financial Aid Phone:** 805-893-2432
E-mail: admissions@sa.ucsb.edu • **CEEB Code:** 4835
Fax: 805-893-2676 • **Website:** www.ucsb.edu

This public school was founded in 1909. It has a 989-acre campus.

RATINGS

Admissions Selectivity Rating: 96   **Fire Safety Rating:** 95   **Green Rating:** 96

STUDENTS AND FACULTY

Enrollment: 21,574. **Student Body:** 53% female, 47% male, 5% out-of-state, 8% international (82 countries represented). Asian 21%, African American 2%, Caucasian 34%, Hispanic 26%, Native American <1%, Pacific Islander <1%, Two or more races 6%, Race unknown 1%.
Retention and Graduation: 92% freshmen return for sophomore year. 69% freshmen graduate within 4 years. 82% freshmen graduate within 6 years.
Faculty: Student/faculty ratio 18:1. 922 full-time faculty, 100% hold PhDs, 20% are members of minority groups, 38% are women.

ACADEMICS

Degrees: bachelor's, doctoral/research, master's, postbachelor's certificate, post-master's certificate. **Classes:** Most classes have fewer than 10 students. Most lab/discussion sessions have 20-29 students. **Most popular majors:** Biology/Biological Sciences; Economics; Psychology. **Special Study Options:** Accelerated program, cross-registration, double major, dual enrollment, English as a Second Language (ESL), exchange student program (domestic), honors program, independent study, internships, student-designed major, study abroad, teacher certification program, Undergrads may take grad level classes. Off-Campus Study: Washington, DC. Freshman Seminars, pre-professional programs and advising, academic minors, and undergraduate research. **Honors Programs:** The College Honors Program is designed to give students in the College of Letters and Science the opportunity to pursue their interests as part of a small community of scholars. The program connects such students to the resources of a large university, while providing an intimate collegiate atmosphere where students work closely with peers and professors in small classes, research laboratories, and special program and activities. Combined degree programs: BA/MA, BS/MS. **Disability Services:** Special programs offered to physically disabled students, including note-taking services, reader services, tape recorders, tutors. **Career Services:** Career/job search classes, Career assessment, Internships.

FACILITIES

Housing: Coed dorms, fraternity/sorority housing, apartments for married students, cooperative housing, apartments for single students, Wellness Housing, Theme Housing. 100% of campus accessible to physically diasbled. **Special Academic Facilities/Equipment:** Art museum, centers for black studies, Chicano studies, and study of developing nations, institutes for applied behavioral sciences, community/organizational research, marine science, and theoretical physics, Channel Islands field station. **Computers:** 100% of dorms, 100% of dining areas, 100% of student union, have wireless network access. Students can register for classes online. Administrative functions (other than registration) can be performed online.

CAMPUS LIFE

Environment: City. **Activities:** Choral groups, concert band, dance, drama/theater, jazz band, literary magazine, music ensembles, musical theater, opera, pep band, radio station, student government, student newspaper, student-run film society, symphony orchestra, television station, yearbook, Campus Ministries, Student Organization, Model UN. 508 registered organizations, 5 honor societies, 19 religious organizations. 17 fraternities, 18 sororities. **Athletics (Intercollegiate):** *Men:* baseball, basketball, cross-country, diving, golf, gymnastics, soccer, swimming, tennis, track/field (outdoor), volleyball, water polo. *Women:* basketball, cross-country, diving, gymnastics, soccer, softball, swimming, tennis, track/field (outdoor), volleyball, water polo. **On-Campus Highlights:** Storke Tower Plaza/University Center, University Art Museum, UCSB Davidson Library, Recreation Center, Career and Counseling Services Center. **Environmental Initiatives:** 1) Green buildings: minimum silver and strive for gold LEED certification; six buildings are currently certified, including San Clemente Villages Graduate Housing—one of the largest Gold certified housing projects in the US—and Bren Hall—the first building in the US to receive two Platinum ratings for new construction and existing buildings. Plus, 24 additional existing buildings scheduled to be certified in the next couple years through the USGBC Portfolio Program. UCSB has the most LEED EB buildings in the UC System. We created Low Environmental Impact Cleaning Policy for the campus custodial services. All cleaning products and soaps used by the custodial staff are Green Seal certified. Plus toilet tissue, seat covers, and brown paper towels have 100% recycled content. Housing & Residential Services, supports solar water heating providing hot water for dorms, recycling used cooking oil from dining commons for biofuel, extensive recycling program including composting of food waste, purchasing local and/or organic foods for dining commons, using Green Seal cleaning products for custodial duties.

ADMISSIONS

Freshman Academic Profile: Average high school GPA 4.0. 100% in top 10% of high school class, 100% in top 25% of high school class, 100% in top 50% of high school class. 80% from public high schools. **Reported SAT (pre-2016 redesign) scores:** SAT Math middle 50% range 580-720. SAT Critical Reading middle 50% range 560-670. SAT Writing middle 50% range 570-680. **Concordant SAT scores:** SAT EBRW middle 50% 620-710. SAT Math middle 50% range 600-750. ACT middle 50% range 25-31. Minimum internet-based

TOEFL 80. Minimum paper TOEFL 550. **Basis for Candidate Selection:** *Very important factors considered include:* rigor of secondary school record, academic GPA, standardized test scores, application essay. *Other factors considered include:* class rank, extracurricular activities, talent/ability, character/ personal qualities, first generation, state residency, volunteer work, work experience, level of applicant's interest. **Freshman Admission Requirements:** High school diploma is required and GED is accepted. *Academic units required:* 4 English, 3 math, 2 science labs, 2 foreign language, 2 history, 1 academic elective, 1 visual/performing arts. *Academic units recommended:* 4 math, 3 science labs, 3 foreign language. **Freshman Admission Statistics:** 77,098 applied, 35.77% admitted, 18% enrolled. **Transfer Admission Requirements:** High school transcript, college transcript(s), essay or personal statement, Minimum college GPA of 2.4 required. Lowest grade transferable D. **General Admission Information:** Application fee $70. Regular application deadline 11/30. Regular notification 3/1. Nonfall registration not accepted.

COSTS AND FINANCIAL AID
Annual in-state tuition $12,294. Annual out-of-state tuition $38,976. Room and board $15,186. Required fees $1,779. Average book expense $1,428. **Required Forms and Deadlines:** FAFSA. **Types of Aid:** *Need-based scholarships/ grants:* Federal Pell, FSEOG, State scholarships/grants, College/university scholarship or grant aid from institutional funds. *Loans:* Direct Subsidized Stafford Loans, Direct Unsubsidized Stafford Loans, Direct PLUS loans, Federal Perkins Loans. *Student Employment:* Federal Work-Study Program available. Institutional employment available. **Financial Aid Statistics:** 95% needy freshmen, 93% needy undergrads receive need-based scholarship or grant aid. 1% freshmen, 1% undergrads receive non-need-based scholarship or grant aid. 64% freshmen, 62% undergrads receive need-based self-help aid. 1% freshmen, 1% undergrads receive athletic scholarships. 60% undergrads receive any aid. 56% undergrads borrow to pay for school. Average cumulative indebtedness $20,978. **Criteria for awarding aid:** *Need-based:* Academics, Alumni affiliation, Art, Athletics, Music/drama. *Non-need-based:* Academics, Alumni affiliation, Athletics.

UNIVERSITY OF CALIFORNIA, SANTA CRUZ

Office of Admissions, Cook House, Santa Cruz, CA 95064
Phone: 831-459-4008 • **Financial Aid Phone:** 831-459-2963
E-mail: admissions@ucsc.edu • **CEEB Code:** 4860
Fax: 831-459-4452 • **Website:** www.ucsc.edu

This public school was founded in 1965. It has a 2000-acre campus.

RATINGS
Admissions Selectivity Rating: 92   **Fire Safety Rating:** 80   **Green Rating:** 98

STUDENTS AND FACULTY
Enrollment: 16,962. **Student Body:** 51% female, 49% male, 3% out-of-state, 4% international. Asian 22%, African American 2%, Caucasian 32%, Hispanic 30%, Native American <1%, Pacific Islander <1%, Two or more races 8%, Race unknown 2%.
Retention and Graduation: 90% freshmen return for sophomore year. 52% freshmen graduate within 4 years. 77 **Faculty:** Student/faculty ratio 19:1. 567 full-time faculty, 0% hold PhDs, 30% are are members of minority groups, 39% are women. 0% of classes are taught by teaching assistants.

ACADEMICS
Degrees: bachelor's, doctoral/research, doctoral, master's, postbachelor's certificate. **Classes:** Most classes have 10-19 students. Most lab/discussion sessions have 20-29 students. **Most popular majors:** Business/Managerial Economics; Psychology; Sociology. **Special Study Options:** cooperative education program, cross-registration, double major, exchange student program (domestic), independent study, internships, student-designed major, study abroad, teacher certification program. Combined degree programs: BA/JD, BA/MA, Economics/Applied Economics, Business Management Economics, Global Economics,Linguistics. **Disability Services:** Special programs offered to physically disabled students, including note-taking services, reader services, tape recorders, tutors. **Career Services:** Alumni network, Alumni services, Career/job search classes, Career assessment, Internships. Chancellor's Undergraduate Internship Program (CUIP)- CUIP provides professional level on-campus internships in administrative departments throughout campus. Interns work with a mentor to develop personal and professional skills and take a lead role in producing a product or result in thir one-year internship.

Interns receive a scholarship equivalent to their registration fees for a year in exchange for 450 hours of work. Students attend a 2-unit leadership seminar led by the Dean of Undergraduate Education during both Fall and Spring quarters. This program places an average of 35 students per year. Professions Training Program and Bonner Leaders (PTP/BL)- The PTP/BL service-learning program provides internships in local non-profit organizations along with an academic component focused on leadership development. Students receive a $1000 scholarship for 300 hours of work. This program is a partnership with the Bonner Foundation and AmeriCorps and places 15-20 students each year.

FACILITIES
Housing: Coed dorms, men's dorms, special housing for international students, women's dorms, apartments for married students, apartments for single students, Theme Housing, University-sponsored off-campus housing, RV Park, University Inn and Conference Center. 100% of campus accessible to physically diasbled. **Special Academic Facilities/Equipment:** Eloise Pickard Smith Gallery, Mary Porter Sesnon Gallery, Center for Agroecology, Wellness Center, Long Marine Laboratory. **Computers:** 100% of classrooms, 100% of dorms, 100% of libraries, 100% of dining areas, 100% of student union, have wireless network access. Students can register for classes online. Administrative functions (other than registration) can be performed online.

CAMPUS LIFE
Environment: City. **Activities:** Choral groups, dance, drama/theater, jazz band, literary magazine, music ensembles, musical theater, opera, radio station, student government, student newspaper, student-run film society, symphony orchestra, television station, Campus Ministries, Student Organization, Model UN. 138 registered organizations, 3 honor societies, 19 religious organizations. 9 fraternities, 11 sororities. **Athletics (Intercollegiate):** *Men:* basketball, diving, soccer, swimming, tennis, volleyball. *Women:* basketball, cross-country, diving, golf, soccer, swimming, tennis, volleyball. **On-Campus Highlights:** Arboretum, Farm and Garden, East Field House, Bay Tree Bookstore/Grad Student Commons, Pogonip Open Area Reserve. **Environmental Initiatives:** Climate Action Plan: Achieve 2000 levels of emissions by 2014.

ADMISSIONS
Freshman Academic Profile: Average high school GPA 3.5. 96% in top 10% of high school class, 100% in top 25% of high school class, 100% in top 50% of high school class. 87% from public high schools. **Reported SAT (pre-2016 redesign) scores:** SAT Math middle 50% range 540-660. SAT Critical Reading middle 50% range 520-640. SAT Writing middle 50% range 520-630. **Concordant SAT scores:** SAT EBRW middle 50% 580–680. SAT Math middle 50% range 570–690. ACT middle 50% range 23-29. Minimum internet-based TOEFL 80. Minimum paper TOEFL 550. **Basis for Candidate Selection:** *Very important factors considered include:* rigor of secondary school record, academic GPA, standardized test scores, application essay, state residency. *Important factors considered include:* extracurricular activities, talent/ability, character/personal qualities, first generation, geographical residence. *Other factors considered include:* volunteer work, work experience. **Freshman Admission Requirements:** High school diploma is required and GED is accepted. *Academic units required:* 4 English, 3 math, 2 science, 2 science labs, 2 foreign language, 1 social studies, 1 history, 1 academic elective, 1 visual/ performing arts. *Academic units recommended:* 4 English, 4 math, 3 science, 3 science labs, 3 foreign language, 1 social studies, 1 history, 1 academic elective, 1 visual/performing arts. **Freshman Admission Statistics:** 47,553 applied, 58.47% admitted, 15% enrolled. **Transfer Admission Requirements:** college transcript(s), essay or personal statement, statement of good standing from prior institution(s). Minimum college GPA of 2.4 required. Lowest grade transferable D. **General Admission Information:** Application fee $70. Regular application deadline 11/30. Regular notification 3/31. Nonfall registration not accepted.

COSTS AND FINANCIAL AID
Average book expense $1,470. **Required Forms and Deadlines:** FAFSA, State aid form. **Notification of Awards:** Applicants will be notified of awards on a rolling basis beginning 4/1. **Types of Aid:** *Need-based scholarships/ grants:* Federal Pell, FSEOG, State scholarships/grants, Private scholarships, College/university scholarship or grant aid from institutional funds. *Loans:* Direct Subsidized Stafford Loans, Direct Unsubsidized Stafford Loans, Direct PLUS loans, Federal Perkins Loans. *Student Employment:* Federal Work-Study Program available. Institutional employment available. **Financial Aid Statistics:** 95% needy freshmen, 95% needy undergrads receive need-based scholarship or grant aid. 1% freshmen, 1% undergrads receive non-need-based scholarship or grant aid. 78% freshmen, 76% undergrads receive need-based self-help aid. 0% freshmen, 0% undergrads receive athletic scholarships. 67% freshmen, 68% undergrads receive any aid. 64% undergrads borrow to pay for school. Average cumulative indebtedness $22,580. **Criteria for awarding aid:** *Need-based:* Academics, Alumni affiliation, Art, Leadership, Music/drama. *Non-need-based:* Academics, Alumni affiliation, Art, Leadership, Music/drama.

UNIVERSITY OF CENTRAL ARKANSAS

201 Donaghey Avenue, Conway, AR 72035
Phone: 501-450-3128 • **Financial Aid Phone:** 501-450-3140
E-mail: admissions@uca.edu • **CEEB Code:** 6012
Fax: 501-450-5228 • **Website:** www.uca.edu/ • **ACT Code:** 118

This public school was founded in 1907. It has a 262-acre campus.

RATINGS
Admissions Selectivity Rating: 78   **Fire Safety Rating:** 62   **Green Rating:** 65

STUDENTS AND FACULTY
Enrollment: 9,081. **Student Body:** 59% female, 41% male, 8% out-of-state, 5% international (72 countries represented). Asian 2%, African American 17%, Caucasian 66%, Hispanic 5%, Native American 1%, Pacific Islander <1%, Two or more races 4%, Race unknown 1%.
Retention and Graduation: 73% freshmen return for sophomore year.
Faculty: 0% of classes are taught by teaching assistants.

ACADEMICS
Degrees: associate, bachelor's, doctoral/professional, doctoral/research, doctoral, master's, postbachelor's certificate, post-master's certificate. **Classes:** Most classes have 20-29 students. **Special Study Options:** Accelerated program, cooperative education program, distance learning, double major, dual enrollment, English as a Second Language (ESL), honors program, independent study, internships, liberal arts/career combination, study abroad, teacher certification program, 5 year professional program in Physical and Occupational Therapy. **Disability Services:** Special programs offered to physically disabled students, including note-taking services, reader services, tape recorders. **Career Services:** Alumni network, Career/job search classes, Internships, Regional alumni.

FACILITIES
Housing: Coed dorms, special housing for disabled students, men's dorms, special housing for international students, women's dorms, fraternity/sorority housing, apartments for married students, apartments for single students, Residential colleges are offered, as well as Honors housing. **Special Academic Facilities/Equipment:** Greenhouse, Baum Gellery, HPER Center, Planetarium, Technology Plaza, Smartboards, H.L. Minton Center for Geospatial Analysis and Research **Computers:** 100% of classrooms, 100% of dorms, 100% of libraries, 100% of dining areas, 100% of student union, 100% of common outdoor areas have wireless network access. Students can register for classes online. Administrative functions (other than registration) can be performed online.

CAMPUS LIFE
Environment: Town. **Activities:** Choral groups, concert band, dance, drama/theater, jazz band, literary magazine, marching band, music ensembles, pep band, radio station, student government, student newspaper, student-run film society, symphony orchestra, television station, yearbook, Campus Ministries, Student Organization, Model UN. 158 registered organizations, 11 honor societies, 16 religious organizations. 12 fraternities, 8 sororities. **Athletics (Intercollegiate):** *Men:* baseball, basketball, cheerleading, cross-country, football, golf, soccer, tennis, track/field (outdoor), track/field (indoor). *Women:* basketball, cheerleading, cross-country, golf, soccer, softball, tennis, track/field (outdoor), track/field (indoor), volleyball. **On-Campus Highlights:** Student Center, HPER Center, Baum Gallery, Estes Stadium, Farris Center.

ADMISSIONS
Freshman Academic Profile: Average high school GPA 3.5. 18% in top 10% of high school class, 47% in top 25% of high school class, 79% in top 50% of high school class. **Reported SAT (pre-2016 redesign) scores:** SAT Math middle 50% range 460-540. SAT Critical Reading middle 50% range 410-520. SAT Writing middle 50% range 400-510. **Concordant SAT scores:** SAT EBRW middle 50% 450–570. SAT Math middle 50% range 500–570. ACT middle 50% range 20-27. Minimum internet-based TOEFL 61. Minimum paper TOEFL 500. **Basis for Candidate Selection:** *Very important factors considered include:* academic GPA, standardized test scores. *Important factors considered include:* class rank. **Freshman Admission Requirements:** High school diploma is required and GED is accepted. *Academic units recommended:* 4 English, 4 math, 3 science, 1 social studies, 2 history, 10 academic electives. **Freshman Admission Statistics:** 4,922 applied, 89.78% admitted, 43% enrolled. **Transfer Admission Requirements:** college transcript(s), statement of good standing from prior institution(s). Minimum college GPA of 2.0 required. Lowest grade transferable C. **General Admission Information:** Application fee $25. Nonfall registration accepted. Admission may be deferred.

COSTS AND FINANCIAL AID
Student Employment: Federal Work-Study Program available. Institutional employment available.

UNIVERSITY OF CENTRAL FLORIDA

P.O. Box 160111, Orlando, FL 32816-0111
Phone: 407-823-3000 • **Financial Aid Phone:** 407-823-2827
E-mail: admission@ucf.edu • **CEEB Code:** 5233
Fax: 407-823-5625 • **Website:** www.ucf.edu • **ACT Code:** 735

This public school was founded in 1963. It has a 1415-acre campus.

RATINGS
Admissions Selectivity Rating: 89   **Fire Safety Rating:** 96   **Green Rating:** 93

STUDENTS AND FACULTY
Enrollment: 55,292. **Student Body:** 55% female, 45% male, 6% out-of-state, 1% international (140 countries represented). Asian 6%, African American 11%, Caucasian 51%, Hispanic 25%, Native American <1%, Pacific Islander <1%, Two or more races 4%, Race unknown 1%.
Retention and Graduation: 89% freshmen return for sophomore year. 40% freshmen graduate within 4 years. 69% freshmen graduate within 6 years. **Faculty:** Student/faculty ratio 30:1. 1,514 full-time faculty, 81% hold PhDs, 26% are are members of minority groups, 43% are women. 5% of classes are taught by teaching assistants.

ACADEMICS
Degrees: associate, bachelor's, certificate, doctoral/professional, doctoral/research, master's, postbachelor's certificate. **Classes:** Most classes have 20-29 students. Most lab/discussion sessions have 30-39 students. **Most popular majors:** Marketing/Marketing Management; Psychology; Health Services/Allied Health/Health Sciences. **Special Study Options:** cooperative education program, distance learning, double major, dual enrollment, English as a Second Language (ESL), honors program, internships, study abroad, teacher certification program. **Honors Programs:** The Burnett Honors College combines the intimacy of a small liberal arts college with the benefits of a large, metropolitan research university. The college fosters an atmosphere of intellectual excitement and a passion for learning; offers cutting-edge courses and innovative teaching methods; provides academic and professional advisement, mentoring, select co-curricular activities to Honors students; and develops sound values of social responsibility, inclusiveness, and good citizenship. The Burnett Honors College offers two main tracks, University Honors and Honors in the Major, and a special accelerated Medical School program in partnership with University of South Florida. University Honors targets primarily incoming freshmen and comprises a special freshman symposium, General Education Program (GEP) courses, and upper-division seminars and disciplinary core courses. Honors GEP courses are taught across the curriculum and are limited to enrollments of 20 students for all courses except English Composition, which is limited to 15 students. Honors English Composition also differs from regular Composition offerings that follow a standardized curriculum in that each Honors section is "themed." Upper division University Honors students take 9-15 hours of special interdisciplinary, team-taught seminars or, in the case of the professional colleges, a combination of core courses in their fields and interdisciplinary seminars. In addition, students participating in University Honors enroll in a well-respected and established first-year experience course, the Honors Symposium. lt;brgt;lt;brgt; Honors in the Major is a senior thesis Honors program. Honors in the Major students engage in a two-semester course of study consisting of preparing a research proposal, conducting original research, and writing a thesis. The student selects a three-member faculty committee to oversee the thesis process that culminates in the thesis defense. Early Acceptance/Accelerated Medical Program: This unique program offers qualified UCF Honors students the opportunity to complete the baccalaureate and Doctor in Medicine degrees in seven years. Through a special partnership with the College of Medicine at the University of South Florida, UCF Honors students are guaranteed admission to the USF medical school once they have successfully completed the program requirements. Combined degree programs: BA/JD, BA/MA, BA/MEng, BS/MS; BSN/MSN. **Disability Services:** Special programs offered to physically disabled students, including note-taking services, reader services, tape recorders, tutors. **Career Services:** Alumni services, Career/job search classes, Career assessment. I am very proud of our operation. Some of our most outstanding programs would include: Career Planning Services, Career Peer Advisor Program, Career Events, Externship, and OCR.

FACILITIES
Housing: Coed dorms, men's dorms, women's dorms, fraternity/sorority housing, apartments for single students, Wellness Housing, Theme Housing. Affiliated student residences available across street from campus with university

705

resident assistants. On-campus: Honors Center; Living Learning Communities, Lead Scholars Center. 97% of campus accessible to physically disabled.
Special Academic Facilities/Equipment: Center for research and education in optics and lasers, arboretum, observatory, New student union, student recreation center. **Computers:** 100% of classrooms, 100% of dorms, 100% of libraries, 90% of dining areas, 100% of student union, 90% of common outdoor areas have wireless network access. Students can register for classes online. Administrative functions (other than registration) can be performed online.

CAMPUS LIFE
Environment: City. **Activities:** Choral groups, concert band, drama/theater, jazz band, literary magazine, marching band, music ensembles, musical theater, pep band, radio station, student government, student newspaper, student-run film society, symphony orchestra, Campus Ministries, Student Organization, Model UN. 361 registered organizations, 36 honor societies, 29 religious organizations. 21 fraternities, 18 sororities. **Athletics (Intercollegiate):** *Men:* baseball, basketball, cheerleading, cross-country, football, golf, soccer, tennis. *Women:* basketball, cheerleading, crew/rowing, cross-country, golf, soccer, softball, tennis, track/field (outdoor), track/field (indoor), volleyball.
On-Campus Highlights: Student Union, Recreation and Wellness Center, Bookstore (Barnes and Noble café), Reflecting Pond, New Arena and Football Stadium.

ADMISSIONS
Freshman Academic Profile: Average high school GPA 3.9. 33% in top 10% of high school class, 71% in top 25% of high school class, 97% in top 50% of high school class. **Reported SAT (pre-2016 redesign) scores:** SAT Math middle 50% range 540-640. SAT Critical Reading middle 50% range 540-630. SAT Writing middle 50% range 510-600. **Concordant SAT scores:** SAT EBRW middle 50% 580–670. SAT Math middle 50% range 570–660. ACT middle 50% range 24-28. Minimum internet-based TOEFL 80. Minimum paper TOEFL 550. **Basis for Candidate Selection:** *Very important factors considered include:* rigor of secondary school record, academic GPA, standardized test scores. *Important factors considered include:* application essay, recommendation(s). *Other factors considered include:* class rank, extracurricular activities, talent/ability, character/personal qualities, first generation, alumni/ae relation, geographical residence, state residency, volunteer work, work experience, level of applicant's interest. **Freshman Admission Requirements:** High school diploma is required and GED is accepted. *Academic units required:* 4 English, 4 math, 3 science, 2 science labs, 2 foreign language, 3 social studies, 2 academic electives. **Freshman Admission Statistics:** 34,886 applied, 49.99% admitted, 38% enrolled. **Transfer Admission Requirements:** college transcript(s), Minimum college GPA of 2.0 required. Lowest grade transferable D. **General Admission Information:** Application fee $30. Regular application deadline 5/1. Nonfall registration accepted.

COSTS AND FINANCIAL AID
Annual in-state tuition $6,368. Annual out-of-state tuition $22,467. Room and board $9,554. Required fees $0. Average book expense $1,152. **Required Forms and Deadlines:** FAFSA. **Notification of Awards:** Applicants will be notified of awards on a rolling basis beginning 3/15. **Types of Aid:** *Need-based scholarships/grants:* Federal Pell, FSEOG, State scholarships/grants, Private scholarships, College/university scholarship or grant aid from institutional funds. *Loans:* Direct Subsidized Stafford Loans, Direct Unsubsidized Stafford Loans, Direct PLUS loans, Federal Perkins Loans. *Student Employment:* Federal Work-Study Program available. Institutional employment available.
Financial Aid Statistics: 66% needy freshmen, 71% needy undergrads receive need-based scholarship or grant aid. 65% freshmen, 45% undergrads receive non-need-based scholarship or grant aid. 54% freshmen, 62% undergrads receive need-based self-help aid. 1% freshmen, 1% undergrads receive athletic scholarships. 86% freshmen, 78% undergrads receive any aid. 52% undergrads borrow to pay for school. Average cumulative indebtedness $21,911. **Criteria for awarding aid:** *Need-based:* Academics, Athletics, Leadership, Minority status, Music/drama. *Non-need-based:* Academics, Alumni affiliation, Athletics, Leadership, State/district residency.

See page 1070.

UNIVERSITY OF CENTRAL MISSOURI

Office of Admissions, Warrensburg, MO 64093
Phone: 660-543-4290 • **Financial Aid Phone:** 660-543-4040
E-mail: admit@ucmovmb.edu • **CEEB Code:** 6090
Fax: 660-543-8517 • **Website:** www.cmsu.edu • **ACT Code:** 2272

This public school was founded in 1871. It has a 1561-acre campus.

RATINGS
Admissions Selectivity Rating: 76   **Fire Safety Rating:** 81   **Green Rating:** 60*

STUDENTS AND FACULTY
Enrollment: 9,013. **Student Body:** 55% female, 45% male, 10% out-of-state, 3% international (53 countries represented). Asian 1%, African American 8%, Caucasian 65%, Hispanic 3%, Native American <1%, Pacific Islander <1%, Two or more races 3%, Race unknown 17%.
Retention and Graduation: 70% freshmen return for sophomore year. 29% freshmen graduate within 4 years. 52% freshmen graduate within 6 years.
Faculty: Student/faculty ratio 20:1. 486 full-time faculty, 71% hold PhDs, 12% are are members of minority groups, 47% are women. 4% of classes are taught by teaching assistants.

ACADEMICS
Degrees: bachelor's, certificate, master's, postbachelor's certificate, post-master's certificate. **Classes:** Most classes have 20-29 students. **Most popular majors:** Education; Criminal Justice/Law Enforcement Administration; Marketing/Marketing Management. **Special Study Options:** Accelerated program, cooperative education program, cross-registration, distance learning, double major, dual enrollment, English as a Second Language (ESL), honors program, internships, student-designed major, study abroad, teacher certification program, weekend college. **Disability Services:** Special programs offered to physically disabled students, including note-taking services, reader services, tape recorders, tutors.

FACILITIES
Housing: Coed dorms, special housing for disabled students, special housing for international students, women's dorms, fraternity/sorority housing, apartments for married students, apartments for single students, Economy Suites and Townhouses. 95% of campus accessible to physically disabled.
Special Academic Facilities/Equipment: Art gallery,Nance Museum and Library of Antiquities, natural history museum, English language center, child development lab, speech and hearing lab, 260-acre farm, Missouri Safety center, National Police Institute, driving/safety range, center for technology and business research,airport for aviation program.Extended campus,Lee's Summit,MO.KCMW-FM,KMOS-TV, Public Broadcasting Stations
Computers: Students can register for classes online. Administrative functions (other than registration) can be performed online.

CAMPUS LIFE
Environment: Rural. **Activities:** Choral groups, concert band, dance, drama/theater, jazz band, literary magazine, marching band, music ensembles, musical theater, opera, pep band, radio station, student government, student newspaper, student-run film society, symphony orchestra, television station, yearbook. 150 registered organizations, 24 honor societies, 14 religious organizations. 9 fraternities, 10 sororities. **Athletics (Intercollegiate):** *Men:* baseball, basketball, bowling, cross-country, football, golf, soccer, track/field (outdoor), wrestling. *Women:* basketball, bowling, cross-country, soccer, softball, track/field (outdoor), volleyball. **On-Campus Highlights:** Union Commons, Library, Pertle Springs, Multi-purpose building.

ADMISSIONS
Freshman Academic Profile: Average high school GPA 3.3. 11% in top 10% of high school class, 32% in top 25% of high school class, 67% in top 50% of high school class. 90% from public high schools. ACT middle 50% range 19-24. Minimum paper TOEFL 500. **Basis for Candidate Selection:** *Very important factors considered include:* class rank, academic GPA, standardized test scores. *Other factors considered include:* rigor of secondary school record, application essay. **Freshman Admission Requirements:** High school diploma is required and GED is accepted. *Academic units required:* 4 English, 3 math, 2 science, 1 science lab, 3 social studies, 3 academic electives, 1 visual/performing arts. *Academic units recommended:* 2 foreign language. **Freshman Admission Statistics:** 4,612 applied, 77.95% admitted, 48% enrolled. **Transfer Admission Requirements:** college transcript(s), Minimum college GPA of 2.0 required. Lowest grade transferable C. **General Admission Information:** Application fee $30. Priority deadline 6/19. Nonfall registration accepted. Admission may be deferred for a maximum of 3 semesters.

COSTS AND FINANCIAL AID
Annual in-state tuition $6,446. Annual out-of-state tuition $12,891. Room and board $8,102. Required fees $876. Average book expense $800. **Required Forms and Deadlines:** FAFSA, Institution's own financial aid form. **Notification of Awards:** Applicants will be notified of awards on or about 3/1. **Types of Aid:** *Need-based scholarships/grants:* Federal Pell, FSEOG, State scholarships/grants, Private scholarships, College/university scholarship or grant aid from institutional funds. *Loans:* Direct Subsidized Stafford Loans, Direct Unsubsidized Stafford Loans, Direct PLUS loans, Federal Perkins Loans, State Loans, College/university loans from institutional funds. *Student Employment:* Federal Work-Study Program available. Institutional employment available.
Financial Aid Statistics: 61% needy freshmen, 63% needy undergrads receive need-based scholarship or grant aid. 99% freshmen, 96% undergrads receive non-need-based scholarship or grant aid. 82% freshmen, 82% undergrads receive need-based self-help aid. 5% freshmen, 4% undergrads receive athletic scholarships. 51% freshmen, 61% undergrads receive any aid. **Criteria for**

awarding aid: *Non-need-based:* Academics, Alumni affiliation, Art, Athletics, Leadership, Minority status, Music/drama, Religious affiliation, State/district residency.

UNIVERSITY OF CENTRAL OKLAHOMA

100 North University Drive, Edmond, OK 73034
Phone: 405-974-2727 • **Financial Aid Phone:** 405-974-2727
E-mail: onestop@uco.edu • **CEEB Code:** 6091
Fax: 405-974-3841 • **Website:** http://www.uco.edu • **ACT Code:** 3390

This public school was founded in 1890. It has a 200-acre campus.

RATINGS
Admissions Selectivity Rating: 78   **Fire Safety Rating:** 84   **Green Rating:** 60*

STUDENTS AND FACULTY
Enrollment: 14,788. **Student Body:** 58% female, 42% male, 3% out-of-state, 7% international (67 countries represented). Asian 3%, African American 9%, Caucasian 58%, Hispanic 9%, Native American 4%, Pacific Islander <1%, Two or more races 9%, Race unknown 1%.
Retention and Graduation: 62% freshmen return for sophomore year. 13% freshmen graduate within 4 years. 39% freshmen graduate within 6 years.
Faculty: Student/faculty ratio 19:1. 513 full-time faculty, 78% hold PhDs, 13% are are members of minority groups, 50% are women. 1% of classes are taught by teaching assistants.

ACADEMICS
Degrees: associate, bachelor's, certificate, master's. **Classes:** Most classes have 20-29 students. Most lab/discussion sessions have 10-19 students. **Most popular majors:** Psychology. **Special Study Options:** Accelerated program, distance-learning, double major, dual enrollment, English as a Second Language (ESL), honors program, independent study, internships, teacher certification program. **Disability Services:** Special programs offered to physically disabled students, including note-taking services, reader services, tape recorders, tutors. **Career Services:** Alumni services, Career/job search classes, Career assessment, Internships.

FACILITIES
Housing: Coed dorms, men's dorms, women's dorms, fraternity/sorority housing, apartments for married students, apartments for single students. 95% of campus accessible to physically diasbled. **Special Academic Facilities/Equipment:** Art and history museums, archives. **Computers:** 100% of classrooms, 100% of dorms, 100% of libraries, 100% of dining areas, 100% of student union, 50% of common outdoor areas have wireless network access. Students can register for classes online. Administrative functions (other than registration) can be performed online.

CAMPUS LIFE
Environment: Metropolis. **Activities:** Choral groups, concert band, dance, drama/theater, jazz band, marching band, music ensembles, musical theater, pep band, radio station, student government, student newspaper, symphony orchestra, television station, yearbook. 150 registered organizations, 27 honor societies, 16 religious organizations. 9 fraternities, 10 sororities. **Athletics (Intercollegiate):** *Men:* baseball, basketball, football, golf, wrestling. *Women:* basketball, cross-country, golf, soccer, softball, tennis, volleyball. **On-Campus Highlights:** Starbucks, Wellness Center, University Center. **Environmental Initiatives:** Use 100% wind power.

ADMISSIONS
Freshman Academic Profile: Average high school GPA 3.3. 11% in top 10% of high school class, 35% in top 25% of high school class, 68% in top 50% of high school class. 91% from public high schools. ACT middle 50% range 19-24. Minimum internet-based TOEFL 83. Minimum paper TOEFL 560.
Basis for Candidate Selection: *Very important factors considered include:* rigor of secondary school record, class rank, academic GPA, standardized test scores. *Other factors considered include:* extracurricular activities, talent/ability.
Freshman Admission Requirements: High school diploma is required and GED is accepted. *Academic units required:* 4 English, 3 math, 3 science, 3 science labs, 1 social studies, 2 history. *Academic units recommended:* 4 English, 4 math, 3 science, 3 science labs, 2 foreign language, 1 social studies, 3 history, 1 computer science. **Freshman Admission Statistics:** 5,122 applied, 69.91% admitted, 69% enrolled. **Transfer Admission Requirements:** college transcript(s), statement of good standing from prior institution(s). Minimum college GPA of 2.0 required. Lowest grade transferable D. **General Admission Information:** Application fee $90. Nonfall registration accepted. Admission may be deferred for a maximum of 1 semester.

COSTS AND FINANCIAL AID
Annual in-state tuition $5,157. Annual out-of-state tuition $14,033. Room and board $7,130. Required fees $939. Average book expense $1,200.
Required Forms and Deadlines: FAFSA, Institution's own financial aid form. **Notification of Awards:** Applicants will be notified of awards on a rolling basis beginning 5/1. **Types of Aid:** *Need-based scholarships/grants:* Federal Pell, FSEOG, State scholarships/grants, Private scholarships, College/university scholarship or grant aid from institutional funds. *Loans:* Federal Perkins Loans. *Student Employment:* Federal Work-Study Program available. Institutional employment available. **Financial Aid Statistics:** 66% freshmen, 75% undergrads receive any aid. **Criteria for awarding aid:** *Need-based:* Academics, Alumni affiliation, Art, Athletics, Leadership, Minority status, Music/drama. *Non-need-based:* Academics, Alumni affiliation, Art, Athletics, Leadership, Minority status, Music/drama, State/district residency.

UNIVERSITY OF CHARLESTON

2300 MacCorkle Ave SE, Charleston, WV 25304
Phone: 304-357-4750 • **Financial Aid Phone:** 304-357-4950
E-mail: admissions@ucwv.edu • **CEEB Code:** 5419
Fax: 304-357-4781 • **Website:** http://www.ucwv.edu/ • **ACT Code:** 4528

This private school was founded in 1888. It has a 24-acre campus.

RATINGS
Admissions Selectivity Rating: 78   **Fire Safety Rating:** 85   **Green Rating:** 65

STUDENTS AND FACULTY
Student Body: 45% female, 55% male, 43% out-of-state, (40 countries represented).
Retention and Graduation: 66% freshmen return for sophomore year. 34% freshmen graduate within 4 years. 40% freshmen graduate within 6 years.
Faculty: Student/faculty ratio 15:1. 116 full-time faculty, 0% hold PhDs, 9% are are members of minority groups, 67% are women.

ACADEMICS
Degrees: associate, bachelor's, doctoral/professional, master's. **Classes:** Most classes have 10-19 students. Most lab/discussion sessions have fewer than 10 students. **Most popular majors:** Business Administration and Management; Biology/Biological Sciences; Registered Nursing/Registered Nurse. **Special Study Options:** double major, English as a Second Language (ESL), independent study, internships, liberal arts/career combination, study abroad. **Disability Services:** Special programs offered to physically disabled students, including note-taking services, reader services, tape recorders, tutors. **Career Services:** Alumni network, Alumni services, Career assessment, Internships, Regional alumni.

FACILITIES
Housing: Coed dorms, special housing for disabled students, apartments for single students. **Special Academic Facilities/Equipment:** Erma Byrd Art Gallery **Computers:** 75% of classrooms, 100% of dorms, 100% of libraries, 100% of dining areas, 100% of student union, 50% of common outdoor areas have wireless network access. Students can register for classes online. Administrative functions (other than registration) can be performed online.

CAMPUS LIFE
Environment: City. **Activities:** Choral groups, dance, drama/theater, music ensembles, pep band, student government, student newspaper, yearbook, Campus Ministries, Student Organization, Model UN. 39 registered organizations, 7 honor societies, 2 religious organizations. 2 fraternities, 3 sororities. **Athletics (Intercollegiate):** *Men:* baseball, basketball, football, golf, soccer, tennis. *Women:* basketball, crew/rowing, cross-country, golf, soccer, softball, tennis, track/field (outdoor), volleyball. **On-Campus Highlights:** New Fitness Center, School of Pharmacy, Coffee Tavern, University of Charleston Stadium, Graduate School of Business. **Environmental Initiatives:** Recycling on campus.

ADMISSIONS
Freshman Academic Profile: Average high school GPA 3.3. **Reported SAT (pre-2016 redesign) scores:** SAT Math middle 50% range 422.5-517.5. SAT Critical Reading middle 50% range 420-500. **Concordant SAT scores:** SAT Math middle 50% range 460–550. ACT middle 50% range 18-24. Minimum internet-based TOEFL 61. Minimum paper TOEFL 500.
Basis for Candidate Selection: *Very important factors considered include:* academic GPA. *Important factors considered include:* rigor of secondary school record, standardized test scores. *Other factors considered include:* class rank, recommendation(s), alumni/ae relation. **Freshman Admission Requirements:** High school diploma is required and GED is accepted. *Academic units required:* 4 English, 4 math, 2 science, 2 science labs, 1 social

studies, 1 history, 1 computer science. *Academic units recommended:* 1 foreign language, 1 visual/performing arts. **Freshman Admission Statistics:** 1,801 applied, 51.86% admitted, 33% enrolled. **Transfer Admission Requirements:** college transcript(s), Minimum college GPA of 2.25 required. Lowest grade transferable C. **General Admission Information:** Application fee $25. Priority deadline 5/1. Nonfall registration accepted. Admission may be deferred.

COSTS AND FINANCIAL AID

Annual tuition $28,900. Room and board $9,100. Required fees $1,000. Average book expense $1,800. **Required Forms and Deadlines:** FAFSA, Institution's own financial aid form, State aid form. **Notification of Awards:** Applicants will be notified of awards on a rolling basis beginning 3/1. **Types of Aid:** *Need-based scholarships/grants:* Federal Pell, FSEOG, State scholarships/grants, Private scholarships, College/university scholarship or grant aid from institutional funds. *Loans:* Direct Subsidized Stafford Loans, Direct Unsubsidized Stafford Loans, Federal Perkins Loans, Federal Nursing Loans. *Student Employment:* Federal Work-Study Program available. Institutional employment available. **Financial Aid Statistics:** 81% needy undergrads receive need-based scholarship or grant aid. 100% freshmen, 100% undergrads receive non-need-based scholarship or grant aid. 100% freshmen, 81% undergrads receive need-based self-help aid. 49% freshmen, 34% undergrads receive athletic scholarships. 100% freshmen receive any aid. **Criteria for awarding aid:** *Need-based:* Minority status. *Non-need-based:* Academics, Alumni affiliation, Art, Athletics, Leadership, Music/drama.

THE UNIVERSITY OF CHICAGO

1101 E 58th Street, Chicago, IL 60637
Phone: 773-702-8650 • **Financial Aid Phone:** 773-702-8666
E-mail: collegeadmissions@uchicago.edu • **CEEB Code:** 1832
Fax: 773-702-4199 • **Website:** collegeadmissions@uchicago.edu
ACT Code: 1152

This private school was founded in 1890. It has a 211-acre campus.

RATINGS

Admissions Selectivity Rating: 99   **Fire Safety Rating:** 95   **Green Rating:** 94

STUDENTS AND FACULTY

Enrollment: 5,930. **Student Body:** 48% female, 52% male, 81% out-of-state, 12% international (70 countries represented). Asian 18%, African American 5%, Caucasian 44%, Hispanic 11%, Native American <1%, Pacific Islander <1%, Two or more races 4%, Race unknown 6%.
Retention and Graduation: 99% freshmen return for sophomore year. 89% freshmen graduate within 4 years. 94% freshmen graduate within 6 years.
Faculty: Student/faculty ratio 5:1. 1,323 full-time faculty, 100% hold PhDs, 20% are are members of minority groups, 31% are women.

ACADEMICS

Degrees: bachelor's, doctoral/professional, doctoral/research, doctoral, master's. **Classes:** Most classes have 10-19 students. Most lab/discussion sessions have 10-19 students. **Most popular majors:** Biology/Biological Sciences; Economics; Mathematics. **Special Study Options:** Accelerated program, cross-registration, double major, dual enrollment, English as a Second Language (ESL), exchange student program (domestic), honors program, independent study, internships, student-designed major, study abroad, teacher certification program. Combined degree programs: BA/MD, BA/MA. **Career Services:** Alumni network, Alumni services, Career/job search classes, Career assessment, Internships, Regional alumni. The Jeff Metcalf Internship Program provides paid, substantive internships to UChicago undergraduates during the summer and the academic year. Nearly 5,000 students and over 1,500 employer partners, both within the United States and abroad, have benefited from the program since its inception in 1997. In 2015-16, the program will offer 1,600 opportunities to UChicago students.

FACILITIES

Housing: Coed dorms, special housing for disabled students, special housing for international students, fraternity/sorority housing, apartments for married students, cooperative housing **Special Academic Facilities/Equipment:** Smart Museum, Renaissance Society, Oriental Institute, Business and Economics Resource Center, D'Angelo Law Library, Echhart Library, John Crerar Library, Joseph Regenstein Library, Special Collections Research Center, Social Services Administration Library, Yerkes Obsevatory Library,

On Campus Lab School(PreK-12),Argonne National Laboratory, Enrico Fermi Institute, Court Theater, Observatory, Two Telescopes, Fermi National Accelerator Laboratory. **Computers:** 100% of classrooms, 100% of dorms, 100% of libraries, 100% of dining areas, 100% of student union, 100% of common outdoor areas have wireless network access. Students can register for classes online.

CAMPUS LIFE

Environment: Metropolis. **Activities:** Choral groups, concert band, dance, drama/theater, jazz band, literary magazine, music ensembles, musical theater, pep band, radio station, student government, student newspaper, student-run film society, symphony orchestra, yearbook, Campus Ministries, Student Organization, Model UN. 400 registered organizations, 5 honor societies, 36 religious organizations. 10 fraternities, 3 sororities. **Athletics (Intercollegiate):** *Men:* baseball, basketball, cross-country, diving, football, soccer, swimming, tennis, track/field (outdoor), track/field (indoor), volleyball, wrestling. *Women:* basketball, cross-country, diving, soccer, softball, swimming, tennis, track/field (outdoor), track/field (indoor), volleyball. **On-Campus Highlights:** Gerald Ratner Athletics Center, Joseph Regenstein Library, Robie House, Court Theatre, Rockefeller Memorial Chapel, Food on Campus UChicago boasts over a dozen on-campus coffee shops and three residential dining halls, as well as a host of delis and snack shops. Of note, Bartlett Dining Commons, once an athletic field house, is a large dining hall that offers excellent a la carte options and a kosher deli and Hallowed Grounds, a student-run lounge that offers international food from neighborhood restaurants, two pool tables, and popular open-mic nights. Books on Campus Seminary Co-op Bookstore (58th Street and University Avenue) One of the best academic bookstores in the world, the Co-Op also has a veritable maze of fiction, poetry, drama, and everything in-between. It also carries the textbooks for most social sciences and humanities courses. University of Chicago Bookstore (Barnes and Noble) (58th Street and Ellis Ave) University t-shirts, pennants, and math and science textbooks. Also contains a Starbucks. O'Gara and Wilson, Chicago's 'oldest' bookstore, specializing in rare and used books. Arts and Music on campus Professional companies and artists in residence include Court Theatre, one of the top reparatory theater companies in the city; the critically acclaimed (and Grammy award winning) Pacifica Quartet; the Newberry Consort, famed for their performances of medieval and Renaissance music on period instruments; the Saint Paul Chamber Orchestra; and the modern ensemble 'eighth blackbird.' The University of Chicago Presents series brings musicians from all over the world to Mandel Hall in the Reynolds Club (the main student center). **Environmental Initiatives:** Formation of the Program on the Global Environment.

ADMISSIONS

Freshman Academic Profile: Average high school GPA 4.2. 98% in top 10% of high school class, 100% in top 25% of high school class, 100% in top 50% of high school class. **Reported SAT (pre-2016 redesign) scores:** SAT Math middle 50% range 730-800. SAT Critical Reading middle 50% range 720-800. SAT Writing middle 50% range 700-780. **Concordant SAT scores:** SAT EBRW middle 50% 740–800. SAT Math middle 50% range 760–800. ACT middle 50% range 32-35. Minimum internet-based TOEFL 104. Minimum paper TOEFL 600. **Basis for Candidate Selection:** *Very important factors considered include:* rigor of secondary school record, class rank, academic GPA, standardized test scores, application essay, recommendation(s), talent/ability, character/personal qualities. *Important factors considered include:* extracurricular activities, volunteer work. *Other factors considered include:* interview, first generation, alumni/ae relation, racial/ethnic status, work experience, level of applicant's interest. **Freshman Admission Requirements:** High school diploma or equivalent is not required. *Academic units recommended:* 4 English, 4 math, 4 science, 3 foreign language, 2 social studies, 2 history. **Freshman Admission Statistics:** 31,484 applied, 7.94% admitted, 64% enrolled. **Transfer Admission Requirements:** High school transcript, college transcript(s), essay or personal statement, standardized test scores, statement of good standing from prior institution(s). Minimum college GPA of 3.0 required. Lowest grade transferable 2. **General Admission Information:** Application fee $75. Regular application deadline 1/1. Regular notification 4/1. Nonfall registration not accepted. Admission may be deferred for a maximum of 2 years.

COSTS AND FINANCIAL AID

Annual tuition $50,997. Room and board $15,093. Required fees $1,494. Average book expense $1,800. **Required Forms and Deadlines:** FAFSA, Institution's own financial aid form, CSS/Financial Aid PROFILE. **Notification of Awards:** Applicants will be notified of awards on or about 4/1. **Types of Aid:** *Need-based scholarships/grants:* Federal Pell, FSEOG, State scholarships/grants, Private scholarships, College/university scholarship or grant aid from institutional funds. *Loans:* Direct Subsidized Stafford Loans, Direct Unsubsidized Stafford Loans, Direct PLUS loans, Federal Perkins Loans. *Student Employment:* Federal Work-Study Program available. Institutional employment available. **Financial Aid Statistics:** 98% needy freshmen, 98% needy undergrads receive need-based scholarship or grant aid. 0% undergrads receive non-need-based scholarship or grant aid. 41% freshmen, 51%

undergrads receive need-based self-help aid. 0% freshmen, 0% undergrads receive athletic scholarships. 64% freshmen, 62% undergrads receive any aid. 33% undergrads borrow to pay for school. Average cumulative indebtedness $23,852. **Criteria for awarding aid:** *Non-need-based:* Academics, Leadership.

UNIVERSITY OF CINCINNATI

P.O. Box 210091, Cincinnati, OH 45221-0091
Phone: 513-556-1100 • **Financial Aid Phone:** 513-556-1000
E-mail: admissions@uc.edu • **CEEB Code:** 1833
Fax: 513-556-1105 • **Website:** www.uc.edu • **ACT Code:** 3340

This public school was founded in 1819. It has a 392-acre campus.

RATINGS
Admissions Selectivity Rating: 85   **Fire Safety Rating:** 96   **Green Rating:** 88

STUDENTS AND FACULTY
Enrollment: 24,890. **Student Body:** 50% female, 50% male, 15% out-of-state, 4% international (109 countries represented). Asian 3%, African American 7%, Caucasian 75%, Hispanic 3%, Native American <1%, Pacific Islander <1%, Two or more races 3%, Race unknown 4%.
Retention and Graduation: 88% freshmen return for sophomore year. 31% freshmen graduate within 4 years. 67 2% grads pursue arts and sciences degrees. 1% grads pursue law degrees. 3% grads pursue business degrees. 3% grads pursue medical degrees. **Faculty:** 5% of classes are taught by teaching assistants.

ACADEMICS
Degrees: associate, bachelor's, certificate, doctoral/professional, doctoral/research, master's, postbachelor's certifiate, post-master's certificate, terminal, transfer. **Classes:** Most classes have 20-29 students. **Most popular majors:** Marketing/Marketing Management; Psychology; Criminal Justice/Safety Studies. **Special Study Options:** Accelerated program, cooperative education program, distance learning, double major, English as a Second Language (ESL), honors program, independent study, internships, liberal arts/career combination, study abroad, teacher certification program, weekend college. **Honors Programs:** www.uc.edu/honors Combined degree programs: BA/MA. **Disability Services:** Special programs offered to physically disabled students, including note-taking services, reader services, tape recorders, tutors. **Career Services:** Alumni network, Alumni services, Career/job search classes, Career assessment, Internships, Regional alumni. While Cooperative Education is certainly to be recognized as a leader in its field for over 100 years, it is Experiential Learning that we can take greatest pride in over the past 10 years. In the national Case of the Year Competition sponsored by the Small Business Institute', UC students in the College of Business have taken 5 First Place, 2 Second Place, 2 Third Place, and 1 Honorable Mention. Quite an impressive track record!

FACILITIES
Housing: Coed dorms, men's dorms, women's dorms, fraternity/sorority housing, apartments for married students, apartments for single students. 100% of campus accessible to physically diasbled. **Special Academic Facilities/Equipment:** Art museum, language lab, observatory. **Computers:** 50% of classrooms, 75% of libraries, 75% of dining areas, 55% of student union, 75% of common outdoor areas have wireless network access. Students can register for classes online. Administrative functions (other than registration) can be performed online.

CAMPUS LIFE
Environment: Metropolis. **Activities:** Choral groups, concert band, dance, drama/theater, jazz band, marching band, music ensembles, musical theater, opera, pep band, radio station, student government, student newspaper, student-run film society, symphony orchestra, yearbook. 250 registered organizations, 16 honor societies, 23 religious organizations. 23 fraternities, 10 sororities. **Athletics (Intercollegiate):** *Men:* baseball, basketball, cheerleading, cross-country, diving, football, golf, soccer, swimming, track/field (outdoor). *Women:* basketball, cheerleading, cross-country, diving, golf, lacrosse, soccer, swimming, tennis, track/field (outdoor), track/field (indoor), volleyball. **Environmental Initiatives:** UC has commited to a policy that all new construction and major renovations on campus will be built to LEED standards, striving for at least Silver certification levels.

ADMISSIONS
Freshman Academic Profile: Average high school GPA 3.6. **Reported SAT (pre-2016 redesign) scores:** SAT Math middle 50% range 520-650. SAT Critical Reading middle 50% range 510-640. SAT Writing middle 50% range 490-610. **Concordant SAT scores:** SAT EBRW middle 50% 560–680. SAT Math middle 50% range 550–670. ACT middle 50% range 23-28. Minimum internet-based TOEFL 66. Minimum paper TOEFL 517. **Basis for Candidate Selection:** *Very important factors considered include:* rigor of secondary school record, academic GPA, standardized test scores. *Important factors considered include:* class rank, application essay, recommendation(s), talent/ability. *Other factors considered include:* extracurricular activities, character/personal qualities, volunteer work, work experience. **Freshman Admission Requirements:** High school diploma is required and GED is accepted. *Academic units required:* 4 English, 4 math, 3 science, 3 social studies, and 3 units from above areas or other academic areas. *Academic units recommended:* 2 foreign language. **Freshman Admission Statistics:** 19,370 applied, 76.42% admitted, 34% enrolled. **General Admission Information:** Application fee $50. Priority deadline 12/1. Regular application deadline 3/1. Nonfall registration accepted. Admission may be deferred for a maximum of 1 year.

COSTS AND FINANCIAL AID
Annual in-state tuition $9,322. Annual out-of-state tuition $24,656. Room and board $10,964. Required fees $1,678. Average book expense $1,500. **Required Forms and Deadlines:** FAFSA. **Notification of Awards:** Applicants will be notified of awards on a rolling basis beginning 3/15. **Types of Aid:** *Need-based scholarships/grants:* Federal Pell, FSEOG, State scholarships/grants, Private scholarships, College/university scholarship or grant aid from institutional funds, United Negro College Fund, Federal Nursing Scholarships. *Loans:* Direct Subsidized Stafford Loans, Direct Unsubsidized Stafford Loans, Direct PLUS loans, Federal Perkins Loans, Federal Nursing Loans, State Loans, College/university loans from institutional funds. *Student Employment:* Federal Work-Study Program available. Institutional employment available. **Financial Aid Statistics:** 38% needy freshmen, 42% needy undergrads receive need-based scholarship or grant aid. 53% freshmen, 39% undergrads receive non-need-based scholarship or grant aid. 77% freshmen, 79% undergrads receive need-based self-help aid. 0% freshmen, 1% undergrads receive athletic scholarships. 84% freshmen, 77% undergrads receive any aid. 65% undergrads borrow to pay for school. Average cumulative indebtedness $28,970. **Criteria for awarding aid:** *Non-need-based:* Academics, Alumni affiliation, Art, Athletics, Leadership, Minority status, Music/drama, State/district residency.

UNIVERSITY OF COLORADO
AT COLORADO SPRINGS

1420 Austin Bluffs Parkway, Colorado Springs, CO 80918
Phone: 719-255-3084 • **Financial Aid Phone:** 719-262-3460
E-mail: go@uccs.edu • **CEEB Code:** 4874
Website: www.uccs.edu • **ACT Code:** 535

This public school was founded in 1965. It has a 504-acre campus.

RATINGS
Admissions Selectivity Rating: 76   **Fire Safety Rating:** 60*   **Green Rating:** 96

STUDENTS AND FACULTY
Enrollment: 8,868. **Student Body:** 53% female, 47% male, 11% out-of-state, 1% international (35 countries represented). Asian 3%, African American 4%, Caucasian 69%, Hispanic 14%, Native American 1%, Pacific Islander <1%, Two or more races 6%, Race unknown 3%.
Retention and Graduation: 71% freshmen return for sophomore year. 26% freshmen graduate within 4 years. **Faculty:** Student/faculty ratio 17:1. 371 full-time faculty, 73% hold PhDs, 14% are are members of minority groups, 51% are women.

ACADEMICS
Degrees: bachelor's, doctoral/professional, doctoral/research, master's. **Classes:** Most classes have 10-19 students. Most lab/discussion sessions have 20-29 students. **Special Study Options:** Accelerated program, cooperative education program, cross-registration, distance learning, double major, dual enrollment, English as a Second Language (ESL), exchange student program (domestic), independent study, internships, liberal arts/career combination, student-designed major, study abroad, teacher certification program. Combined degree programs: BA/MA. **Disability Services:** Special programs offered to physically disabled students, including note-taking services, reader services, tape recorders, tutors. **Career Services:** Alumni network, Alumni services, Career/job search classes, Career assessment.

FACILITIES

Housing: Coed dorms, special housing for disabled students, men's dorms, women's dorms, apartments for single students. **Special Academic Facilities/Equipment:** Gallery of contemporary art. **Computers:** Students can register for classes online.

CAMPUS LIFE

Environment: Metropolis. **Activities:** Choral groups, dance, drama/theater, jazz band, literary magazine, music ensembles, musical theater, radio station, student government, student newspaper, student-run film society 55 registered organizations, 7 religious organizations. 1 sororities. **Athletics (Intercollegiate):** *Men:* basketball, cross-country, golf, soccer, tennis, track/field (outdoor). *Women:* basketball, cross-country, softball, tennis, track/field (outdoor), volleyball. **On-Campus Highlights:** El Pomar Center (Kramer family Library), University Center, The Lodge, Gallery of Contemporary Art.

ADMISSIONS

Freshman Academic Profile: Average high school GPA 3.3. 13% in top 10% of high school class, 36% in top 25% of high school class, 70% in top 50% of high school class. **Reported SAT (pre-2016 redesign) scores:** SAT Math middle 50% range 472-600. SAT Critical Reading middle 50% range 470-590. SAT Writing middle 50% range 450-560. **Concordant SAT scores:** SAT EBRW middle 50% 510–630. SAT Math middle 50% range 510–620. ACT middle 50% range 21-25. Minimum paper TOEFL 550. **Basis for Candidate Selection:** *Very important factors considered include:* rigor of secondary school record, class rank, academic GPA, standardized test scores. *Other factors considered include:* application essay, recommendation(s). **Freshman Admission Requirements:** High school diploma is required and GED is accepted. *Academic units required:* 4 English, 4 math, 3 science, 2 science labs, 1 foreign language, 3 social studies, 1 history, 2 academic electives. *Academic units recommended:* 4 English, 4 math, 3 science, 2 science labs, 1 foreign language, 3 social studies, 1 history, 2 academic electives. **Freshman Admission Statistics:** 7,352 applied, 89.05% admitted, 25% enrolled. **Transfer Admission Requirements:** High school transcript, college transcript(s), Minimum college GPA of 2.0 required. Lowest grade transferable C. **General Admission Information:** Application fee $50. Nonfall registration accepted. Admission may be deferred for a maximum of 3 terms.

COSTS AND FINANCIAL AID

Average book expense $1,800. **Required Forms and Deadlines:** FAFSA. **Notification of Awards:** Applicants will be notified of awards on a rolling basis beginning 4/15. **Types of Aid:** *Need-based scholarships/grants:* Federal Pell, FSEOG, State scholarships/grants, Private scholarships, College/university scholarship or grant aid from institutional funds. *Loans:* Direct Subsidized Stafford Loans, Direct Unsubsidized Stafford Loans, Direct PLUS loans, Federal Perkins Loans. *Student Employment:* Federal Work-Study Program available. Institutional employment available. **Financial Aid Statistics:** 58% needy freshmen, 65% needy undergrads receive need-based scholarship or grant aid. 39% freshmen, 24% undergrads receive non-need-based scholarship or grant aid. 79% freshmen, 84% undergrads receive need-based self-help aid. 2% freshmen, 2% undergrads receive athletic scholarships. **Criteria for awarding aid:** *Need-based:* Academics, Alumni affiliation, Athletics. *Non-need-based:* Academics, Alumni affiliation, Athletics, Leadership, State/district residency.

UNIVERSITY OF COLORADO AT DENVER

P.O. Box 173364, Denver, CO 80217
Phone: 303-556-2704 • **Financial Aid Phone:** 303-556-2886
E-mail: admissions@cudenver.edu • **CEEB Code:** 4875
Fax: 303-556-4838 • **Website:** www.cudenver.edu • **ACT Code:** 533

This public school was founded in 1912. It has a 127-acre campus.

RATINGS

Admissions Selectivity Rating: 81   **Fire Safety Rating:** 60*   **Green Rating:** 60*

STUDENTS AND FACULTY

Enrollment: 8,248. **Student Body:** 55% female, 45% male, 4% out-of-state, 1% international (57 countries represented). Asian 10%, African American 5%, Caucasian 64%, Hispanic 12%, Native American 1%, Pacific Islander 0%, Two or more races 0%, Race unknown 8%.
Retention and Graduation: 71% freshmen return for sophomore year. 7% grads go on to further study within 1 year. 19% grads pursue arts and sciences degrees. 8% grads pursue business degrees. **Faculty:** Student/faculty ratio 15:1. 2,186 full-time faculty, 81% hold PhDs, 11% are are members of minority groups, 47% are women.

ACADEMICS

Degrees: bachelor's, master's, post-master's certificate. **Classes:** Most classes have 20-29 students. Most lab/discussion sessions have 20-29 students. **Most popular majors:** Biology/Biological Sciences; Psychology; Business/Commerce. **Special Study Options:** Accelerated program, cooperative education program, cross-registration, distance learning, double major, English as a Second Language (ESL), honors program, independent study, internships, student-designed major, study abroad, teacher certification program, weekend college. Combined degree programs: BS/MBA. **Disability Services:** Special programs offered to physically disabled students, including note-taking services, reader services, tape recorders, tutors. **Career Services:** Alumni services, Career assessment, Internships.

FACILITIES

Housing: Coed dorms. 100% of campus accessible to physically diasbled. **Special Academic Facilities/Equipment:** Emmanual Gallery **Computers:** Students can register for classes online. Administrative functions (other than registration) can be performed online.

CAMPUS LIFE

Environment: Metropolis. **Activities:** Choral groups, dance, drama/theater, jazz band, music ensembles, musical theater, student government, student newspaper. 77 registered organizations, 5 honor societies, 4 religious organizations. **On-Campus Highlights:** PE/Events Center and Emmanuel Gallery, The Auraria Library, Tivoli Student Union, St. Elizabeth's Church, King Academic and Performing Arts Center.

ADMISSIONS

Freshman Academic Profile: Average high school GPA 3.3. 17% in top 10% of high school class, 43% in top 25% of high school class, 78% in top 50% of high school class. **Reported SAT (pre-2016 redesign) scores:** SAT Math middle 50% range 490-590. SAT Critical Reading middle 50% range 490-600. **Concordant SAT scores:** SAT Math middle 50% range 520–610. ACT middle 50% range 19-25. Minimum internet-based TOEFL 71. Minimum paper TOEFL 525. **Basis for Candidate Selection:** *Very important factors considered include:* rigor of secondary school record, class rank, academic GPA, standardized test scores. *Important factors considered include:* application essay, recommendation(s), level of applicant's interest. *Other factors considered include:* extracurricular activities, talent/ability, character/personal qualities. **Freshman Admission Requirements:** High school diploma is required and GED is accepted. *Academic units required:* 4 English, 3 math, 3 science, 2 foreign language, 2 social studies, 1 academic elective. *Academic units recommended:* 4 English, 3 math, 3 science, 2 science labs, 2 foreign language, 2 social studies, 1 history, 1 academic elective. **Freshman Admission Statistics:** 2,968 applied, 68.90% admitted, 52% enrolled. **Transfer Admission Requirements:** college transcript(s), statement of good standing from prior institution(s). Minimum college GPA of 2.4 required. Lowest grade transferable C-. **General Admission Information:** Application fee $50. Priority deadline 7/22. Nonfall registration accepted. Admission may be deferred for a maximum of 12 mos.

COSTS AND FINANCIAL AID

Annual in-state tuition $5,054. Annual out-of-state tuition $17,010. Room and board $9,990. Required fees $878. Average book expense $1,700. **Required Forms and Deadlines:** FAFSA, Institution's own financial aid form. **Notification of Awards:** Applicants will be notified of awards on a rolling basis beginning 5/1. **Types of Aid:** *Need-based scholarships/grants:* Federal Pell, FSEOG, State scholarships/grants, Private scholarships, College/university scholarship or grant aid from institutional funds, Federal Nursing Scholarships. *Loans:* Direct Subsidized Stafford Loans, Direct Unsubsidized Stafford Loans, Direct PLUS loans, Federal Perkins Loans, Federal Nursing Loans. *Student Employment:* Federal Work-Study Program available. **Financial Aid Statistics:** 97% needy freshmen, 86% needy undergrads receive need-based scholarship or grant aid. 12% freshmen, 5% undergrads receive non-need-based scholarship or grant aid. 73% freshmen, 87% undergrads receive need-based self-help aid. 0% freshmen, 0% undergrads receive athletic scholarships. **Criteria for awarding aid:** *Need-based:* Academics, Minority status. *Non-need-based:* Academics, Art, Leadership, Music/drama.

UNIVERSITY OF COLORADO BOULDER

552 UCB, Boulder, CO 80309-0552
Phone: 303-492-6301
Fax: 303-735-2501 • **Website:** www.colorado.edu/

This public school was founded in 1876. It has a 600-acre campus.

RATINGS

Admissions Selectivity Rating: 86   **Fire Safety Rating:** 87   **Green Rating:** 95

STUDENTS AND FACULTY

Enrollment: 27,418. **Student Body:** 44% female, 56% male, 41% out-of-state, 7% international (113 countries represented). Asian 5%, African American 2%, Caucasian 69%, Hispanic 11%, Native American <1%, Pacific Islander <1%, Two or more races 5%, Race unknown 1%.
Retention and Graduation: 86% freshmen return for sophomore year. 47% freshmen graduate within 4 years. 70% freshmen graduate within 6 years. 5% grads pursue arts and sciences degrees. 2% grads pursue law degrees. 2% grads pursue business degrees. 1% grads pursue medical degrees. **Faculty:** Student/faculty ratio 17:1. 1,590 full-time faculty, 0% hold PhDs, 17% are are members of minority groups, 37% are women. 13% of classes are taught by teaching assistants.

ACADEMICS

Degrees: bachelor's, doctoral/professional, doctoral/research, master's, post-master's certificate. **Classes:** Most classes have 10-19 students. Most lab/discussion sessions have 20-29 students. **Most popular majors:** Physiology; Psychology; Speech Communication and Rhetoric. **Special Study Options:** Accelerated program, cooperative education program, cross-registration, distance learning, double major, dual enrollment, English as a Second Language (ESL), exchange student program (domestic), honors program, independent study, internships, liberal arts/career combination, student-designed major, study abroad, teacher certification program, °Research and combined BA/MA include Undergraduate Research Opportunities and Concurrent Bachelor's/Master's Programs. °°Small Group Academic Programs include Residence Hall Academic Programs, FallFEST, and Presidents Leadership Class. **Honors Programs:** The CU Honors Program provides special educational opportunities for academically prepared, highly motivated undergraduate students. The Honors Program offers a wide-ranging curriculum supported by thoughtful advising and close contact with faculty. The program aspires to provide the best education possible for the leaders of the future. The Honors Residential Academic Program (HRAP) is a residential academic program within the general Honors Program. Qualified first-year students who are invited to participate in the Honors Program may elect to live in an honors part of the Kittredge residence hall complex. In this living and learning environment, students experience all of the advantages of a small liberal arts college while also enjoying the diverse resources of a major university. We offer incoming students the opportunity to associate with other bright, highly motivated students and to become part of a special community of peers and faculty. The Norlin Scholars Program is a community of students with a broad, synthetic view of education that embraces active learning, creativity, and interdisciplinary scholarship. Norlin Scholars participate in small, specialized courses and other small-group experiences emphasizing critical thinking, collaboration, and written and oral communications skills. They also engage in research or creative work with faculty mentors. The Presidents Leadership Class (PLC) offers a unique opportunity to those students who want to make a difference for themselves and their community. The core of PLC is an academic program focusing on leadership, service, ethics, American communities, and global challenges. PLC scholars receive a four-year scholarship. Combined degree programs: BA/MA, BS/MS. **Disability Services:** Special programs offered to physically disabled students, including note-taking services, reader services, tape recorders, tutors. **Career Services:** Alumni network, Alumni services, Career/job search classes, Career assessment, Internships, Regional alumni. International and National Voluntary Service Training (INVST) Based on service learning principles, INVST is a two-year leadership-training program in community service. It offers a unique educational experience to all majors in the College of Arts and Sciences. Aspects of the program include small innovative classes, a community-building experience in the mountains, two summer programs of service in the US and abroad, and supervised community service positions during the fall and spring semesters. Issues of global development, nonviolent social change, interpersonal conflict and conflict resolution, community development, and solving community problems are all addressed, with focus on poverty, racism, and other manifestations of social inequality and injustice.

FACILITIES

Housing: Coed dorms, special housing for disabled students, fraternity/sorority housing, apartments for married students, apartments for single students, Wellness Housing, Theme Housing, Residential academic programs within specific dorms. 87% of campus accessible to physically diasbled. **Special Academic Facilities/Equipment:** Art galleries, natural history museum, heritage center, observatory, planetarium and science center, electron microscopes, outdoor theater, video interactive foreign language laboratory, mountain research station, centrifuge, hands-on teaching and learning laboratory for engineering, multipurpose cultural/athletics/educational events and conference center, a premier concert hall, and an innovative multi-disciplinary Information Technology center. **Computers:** 100% of classrooms, 65% of dorms, 100% of libraries, 100% of dining areas, 100% of student union, 50% of common outdoor areas have wireless network access. Students can register for classes online. Administrative functions (other than registration) can be performed online.

CAMPUS LIFE

Environment: City. **Activities:** Choral groups, concert band, dance, drama/theater, jazz band, literary magazine, marching band, music ensembles, musical theater, opera, pep band, radio station, student government, student newspaper, student-run film society, symphony orchestra, television station, Campus Ministries, Student Organization, Model UN. 300 registered organizations, 26 honor societies, 35 religious organizations. 20 fraternities, 19 sororities. **Athletics (Intercollegiate):** *Men:* basketball, cross-country, football, golf, skiing (downhill/alpine), skiing (nordic/cross-country), track/field (outdoor), track/field (indoor). *Women:* basketball, cross-country, golf, skiing (downhill/alpine), skiing (nordic/cross-country), soccer, tennis, track/field (outdoor), track/field (indoor), volleyball. **On-Campus Highlights:** University Memorial Center (UMC), Student Recreation Center, Norlin Library, ATLAS Building, Farrand Field, CU-Boulder's Outdoor Program, at the Recreation Center, offers many opportunities to explore the wonderful backcountry regions of Colorado and other unique locations. The program provides recreational experiences emphasizing adventure, skill acquisition, environmental awareness, safety, challenge, a sense of community, and fun. **Environmental Initiatives:** EDUCATION AND RESEARCH: Campus commitment to environmental education and research has helped CU-Boulder become one of the nation top environmental research universities. CU-Boulder reputation and performance as a national leader in environmental issues and sustainability helps recruit and retain faculty with the recognized expertise to win leading-edge research awards, to contribute to the global sustainability knowledge base, and to enhance an already respected environmental studies department–one with integrated environmental content across the campus. Environmental Studies is an interdisciplinary program that draws from curricula in the earth and natural sciences as well as the social sciences. Undergraduate students have the opportunity to participate in three residential academic programs (RAPs) that emphasize environmental studies and sustainability. All offer smaller courses in the residences halls. The Baker RAP consists of a cohort of students with interest in the environment and in future careers in working on environmental problems, such as sustainable use of our resources. The Sustainable by Design RAP includes students with an interest in resource-efficient design, renewable energy, and environmental and social impacts of community development. The Sustainability and Social Innovation RAP guides students in developing innovative, self-sustaining solutions for addressing critical social and environmental issues around the globe.

ADMISSIONS

Freshman Academic Profile: Average high school GPA 3.7. 29% in top 10% of high school class, 60% in top 25% of high school class, 90% in top 50% of high school class. 88% from public high schools. **Reported SAT (pre-2016 redesign) scores:** SAT Math middle 50% range 550-670. SAT Critical Reading middle 50% range 520-640. **Concordant SAT scores:** SAT Math middle 50% range 570–700. ACT middle 50% range 25-30. Minimum internet-based TOEFL 1023685|1023692|. Minimum paper TOEFL Colorado. **Basis for Candidate Selection:** *Very important factors considered include:* rigor of secondary school record, class rank, academic GPA, standardized test scores. *Important factors considered include:* application essay, recommendation(s), extracurricular activities, talent/ability, character/personal qualities, first generation. *Other factors considered include:* alumni/ae relation, geographical residence, state residency, racial/ethnic status, volunteer work, work experience, level of applicant's interest. **Freshman Admission Requirements:** High school diploma is required and GED is accepted. *Academic units required:* 4 English, 4 math, 3 science, 2 science labs, 3 foreign language, 3 social studies, 1 history, and 1 unit from above areas or other academic areas. **Freshman Admission Statistics:** 34,047 applied, 76.62% admitted, 49% enrolled. **Transfer Admission Requirements:** High school transcript, college transcript(s), essay or personal statement, Lowest grade transferable C-. **General Admission Information:** Application fee $50. Priority deadline 11/15. Regular application deadline 1/15. Regular notification 4/1. Nonfall registration accepted. Admission may be deferred for a maximum of 12 months.

COSTS AND FINANCIAL AID

Annual in-state tuition $9,768. Annual out-of-state tuition $32,346. Room and board $13,590. Required fees $1,763. Average book expense $1,800. **Required Forms and Deadlines:** FAFSA. **Notification of Awards:** Applicants will be notified of awards on a rolling basis beginning 3/15. **Types of Aid:** *Need-based scholarships/grants:* Federal Pell, FSEOG, State scholarships/grants, Private scholarships, College/university scholarship or grant aid from institutional funds. *Loans:* Direct Subsidized Stafford Loans, Direct Unsubsidized Stafford Loans, Direct PLUS loans, Federal Perkins Loans, College/university loans from institutional funds. *Student Employment:* Federal Work-Study Program available. Institutional employment available. **Financial Aid Statistics:** 76% needy freshmen, 76% needy undergrads receive need-based scholarship or grant aid. 6% freshmen, 4% undergrads receive non-need-based scholarship or grant aid. 86% freshmen, 88% undergrads receive need-based self-help aid. 1% freshmen, 1% undergrads receive athletic scholarships. 43% undergrads borrow to pay for school. Average cumulative indebtedness $27,405. **Criteria for awarding aid:** *Need-based:* Academics, Alumni affiliation, Art, Athletics, Leadership, Music/drama. *Non-need-based:* Academics, Alumni affiliation, Art, Athletics, Leadership, Music/drama, State/district residency.

UNIVERSITY OF CONNECTICUT

2131 Hillside Road, Storrs, CT 06268-3088
Phone: 860-486-3137 • **Financial Aid Phone:** 860-486-2819
E-mail: beahusky@uconn.edu • **CEEB Code:** 3915
Fax: 860-486-1476 • **Website:** www.uconn.edu • **ACT Code:** 604

This public school was founded in 1881. It has a 4104-acre campus.

RATINGS

Admissions Selectivity Rating: 89   **Fire Safety Rating:** 90   **Green Rating:** 99

STUDENTS AND FACULTY

Enrollment: 18,451. **Student Body:** 50% female, 50% male, 23% out-of-state, 5% international (113 countries represented). Asian 10%, African American 5%, Caucasian 61%, Hispanic 9%, Native American <1%, Pacific Islander <1%, Two or more races 3%, Race unknown 7%.
Retention and Graduation: 92% freshmen return for sophomore year. 70% freshmen graduate within 4 years. 83% freshmen graduate within 6 years. 32% grads go on to further study within 1 year. 19% grads pursue arts and sciences degrees. 2% grads pursue law degrees. 3% grads pursue business degrees. 1% grads pursue medical degrees. **Faculty:** Student/faculty ratio 17:1. 1,209 full-time faculty, 93% hold PhDs, 24% are are members of minority groups, 40% are women. 20% of classes are taught by teaching assistants.

ACADEMICS

Degrees: associate, bachelor's, doctoral/professional, doctoral/research, doctoral, master's, postbachelor's certificate, post-master's certificate, terminal, transfer. **Classes:** Most classes have 10-19 students. Most lab/discussion sessions have 10-19 students. **Most popular majors:** Psychology; Biology/Biological Sciences; Economics. **Special Study Options:** Accelerated program, cooperative education program, distance learning, double major, dual enrollment, English as a Second Language (ESL), exchange student program (domestic), honors program, independent study, internships, liberal arts/career combination, student-designed major, study abroad, teacher certification program, Winter inter-session, summer session, and urban semester. **Honors Programs:** Honors Scholar Program for all Undergraduates Combined degree programs: BA/MD, BA/MA, BA/DDS, Pharm.D. **Disability Services:** Special programs offered to physically disabled students, including note-taking services, reader services, tape recorders, tutors. **Career Services:** Alumni services, Career assessment, Internships.

FACILITIES

Housing: Coed dorms, special housing for disabled students, men's dorms, special housing for international students, women's dorms, fraternity/sorority housing, apartments for married students, apartments for single students, Wellness Housing, Theme Housing, Special Interests, Honors, Foreign Languages, Older-Student Housing, Freshman Year Experience Housing, "Global House," Women in Math, Science, and Engineering, Other learning communities. 90% of campus accessible to physically diasbled. **Special Academic Facilities/Equipment:** Art and natural history museums, child

development labs, national undersea research center, arboretum, institute for social inquiry, institute of materials science, electron microscope labs. **Computers:** 90% of libraries, 5% of dining areas, 25% of student union, have wireless network access. Students can register for classes online. Administrative functions (other than registration) can be performed online.

CAMPUS LIFE

Environment: Town. **Activities:** Choral groups, concert band, dance, drama/theater, jazz band, literary magazine, marching band, music ensembles, musical theater, opera, pep band, radio station, student government, student newspaper, student-run film society, symphony orchestra, television station, yearbook, Campus Ministries, Student Organization, Model UN. 303 registered organizations, 29 honor societies, 17 religious organizations. 14 fraternities, 12 sororities. **Athletics (Intercollegiate):** *Men:* baseball, basketball, cross-country, diving, football, golf, ice hockey, soccer, swimming, tennis, track/field (outdoor), track/field (indoor). *Women:* basketball, crew/rowing, cross-country, diving, field hockey, ice hockey, lacrosse, soccer, softball, swimming, tennis, track/field (outdoor), track/field (indoor), volleyball. **On-Campus Highlights:** William Benton Museum of Art, Dairy Product Salesroom, Puppetry Museum, Green Houses, Jorgensen Auditorium and Connecticut Repertory Theater. **Environmental Initiatives:** Signed ACUPCC and began developing Climate Action Plan and, in 2010, began implementing several of its more than 200 strategies related to energy, transportation, sustainable development and environmental literacy.

ADMISSIONS

Freshman Academic Profile: 50% in top 10% of high school class, 85% in top 25% of high school class, 97% in top 50% of high school class. 88% from public high schools. **Reported SAT (pre-2016 redesign) scores:** SAT Math middle 50% range 580-690. SAT Critical Reading middle 50% range 550-650. SAT Writing middle 50% range 550-650. **Concordant SAT scores:** SAT EBRW middle 50% 610–700. SAT Math middle 50% range 600–720. ACT middle 50% range 26-31. Minimum internet-based TOEFL 79. Minimum paper TOEFL 550. **Basis for Candidate Selection:** *Very important factors considered include:* rigor of secondary school record, class rank, academic GPA, standardized test scores. *Important factors considered include:* application essay, recommendation(s), extracurricular activities, talent/ability, character/personal qualities, first generation, racial/ethnic status, volunteer work. *Other factors considered include:* alumni/ae relation, geographical residence, state residency, work experience, level of applicant's interest. **Freshman Admission Requirements:** High school diploma is required and GED is accepted. *Academic units required:* 4 English, 3 math, 2 science, 2 science labs, 2 foreign language, 2 social studies, 3 academic electives. *Academic units recommended:* 3 foreign language. **Freshman Admission Statistics:** 34,978 applied, 53.17% admitted, 20% enrolled. **Transfer Admission Requirements:** High school transcript, college transcript(s), essay or personal statement, Minimum college GPA of 2.7 required. Lowest grade transferable C. **General Admission Information:** Application fee $70. Regular application deadline 1/15. Nonfall registration accepted. Admission may be deferred for a maximum of 1 semester.

COSTS AND FINANCIAL AID

Annual in-state tuition $11,224. Annual out-of-state tuition $33,016. Room and board $12,436. Required fees $2,842. Average book expense $850. **Required Forms and Deadlines:** FAFSA. **Notification of Awards:** Applicants will be notified of awards on a rolling basis beginning 3/1. **Types of Aid:** *Need-based scholarships/grants:* Federal Pell, FSEOG, State scholarships/grants, Private scholarships, College/university scholarship or grant aid from institutional funds. *Loans:* Direct Subsidized Stafford Loans, Direct Unsubsidized Stafford Loans, Direct PLUS loans, Federal Perkins Loans, Federal Nursing Loans. *Student Employment:* Federal Work-Study Program available. Institutional employment available. **Financial Aid Statistics:** 68% needy freshmen, 72% needy undergrads receive need-based scholarship or grant aid. 44% freshmen, 30% undergrads receive non-need-based scholarship or grant aid. 68% freshmen, 73% undergrads receive need-based self-help aid. 3% freshmen, 2% undergrads receive athletic scholarships. 49% freshmen, 48% undergrads receive any aid. 64% undergrads borrow to pay for school. Average cumulative indebtedness $24,999. **Criteria for awarding aid:** *Non-need-based:* Academics, Art, Athletics, Leadership, Minority status, Music/drama.

UNIVERSITY OF DALLAS

1845 East Northgate Drive, Irving, TX 75062
Phone: 972-721-5266 • **Financial Aid Phone:** 972-721-5266
E-mail: crusader@udallas.edu • **CEEB Code:** 6868
Fax: 972-721-5017 • **Website:** www.udallas.edu • **ACT Code:** 4234

This private school, affiliated with the Roman Catholic Church, was founded in 1956. It has a 450-acre campus.

RATINGS

Admissions Selectivity Rating: 85   **Fire Safety Rating:** 87   **Green Rating:** 60*

STUDENTS AND FACULTY

Enrollment: 1,393. **Student Body:** 55% female, 45% male, 53% out-of-state, 3% international (19 countries represented). Asian 6%, African American 2%, Caucasian 63%, Hispanic 22%, Native American 1%, Pacific Islander <1%, Two or more races 3%, Race unknown 1%.
Retention and Graduation: 83% freshmen return for sophomore year. 63% freshmen graduate within 4 years. 70% freshmen graduate within 6 years. **Faculty:** Student/faculty ratio 7:1. 152 full-time faculty, 0% hold PhDs, 12% are are members of minority groups, 39% are women. 0% of classes are taught by teaching assistants.

ACADEMICS

Degrees: bachelor's, doctoral, master's, postbachelor's certificate. **Classes:** Most classes have 10-19 students. Most lab/discussion sessions have 10-19 students. **Most popular majors:** English Language and Literature; Biology/Biological Sciences; History. **Special Study Options:** double major, dual enrollment, independent study, internships, liberal arts/career combination, student-designed major, study abroad, teacher certification program. Combined degree programs: BA/MA, BA/MBA BA/M-Psy. **Disability Services:** Special programs offered to physically disabled students, including note-taking services, reader services, tape recorders, tutors. **Career Services:** Alumni network, Alumni services, Career/job search classes, Career assessment, Internships. Professional Viewpoints Series-employer and alumni recruitment week

FACILITIES

Housing: Coed dorms, men's dorms, women's dorms, apartments for single students. **Special Academic Facilities/Equipment:** Art gallery, theater, language science, and computer labs, observatory. **Computers:** 50% of classrooms, 100% of dorms, 100% of libraries, 20% of dining areas, 100% of student union, 50% of common outdoor areas have wireless network access. Students can register for classes online. Administrative functions (other than registration) can be performed online.

CAMPUS LIFE

Environment: City. **Activities:** Choral groups, dance, drama/theater, literary magazine, music ensembles, musical theater, radio station, student government, student newspaper, student-run film society, yearbook, Campus Ministries, Student Organization. 35 registered organizations, 4 honor societies, 5 religious organizations. **Athletics (Intercollegiate):** *Men:* baseball, basketball, cross-country, golf, lacrosse, soccer, track/field (outdoor). *Women:* basketball, cross-country, lacrosse, soccer, softball, track/field (outdoor), volleyball. **On-Campus Highlights:** Church of the Incarnation, Capp Bar, The Mall, The Rathskeller, Art Village. **Environmental Initiatives:** Student Government recycling committee and Environmental Alliance Club. SG provides recycling receptacles for cans and papers.

ADMISSIONS

Freshman Academic Profile: Average high school GPA 3.8. 34% in top 10% of high school class, 61% in top 25% of high school class, 90% in top 50% of high school class. 50% from public high schools. **Reported SAT (pre-2016 redesign) scores:** SAT Math middle 50% range 520-630. SAT Critical Reading middle 50% range 520-660. SAT Writing middle 50% range 510-630. **Concordant SAT scores:** SAT EBRW middle 50% range 570–690. SAT Math middle 50% range 550–650. ACT middle 50% range 23-30. Minimum internet-based TOEFL 79. **Basis for Candidate Selection:** *Very important factors considered include:* rigor of secondary school record, academic GPA, standardized test scores, application essay, recommendation(s), character/personal qualities. *Important factors considered include:* talent/ability. *Other factors considered include:* class rank, interview, extracurricular activities, first generation, alumni/ae relation, volunteer work, work experience, level of applicant's interest. **Freshman Admission Requirements:** High school diploma is required and GED is accepted. *Academic units required:* 4 English, 3 math, 3 science, 2 foreign language, 3 social studies, 3 history, 4 academic electives, 2 visual/performing arts. *Academic units recommended:* 4 English, 4 math, 3 science, 3 science labs, 3 foreign language, 4 social studies, 4 history, 4 academic electives, 2 visual/performing arts. **Freshman Admission Statistics:** 2,135 applied, 80.47% admitted, 22% enrolled. **Transfer Admission Requirements:** college transcript(s), essay or personal statement, statement of good standing from prior institution(s). Minimum college GPA of 2.5 required. Lowest grade transferable C-. **General Admission Information:** Application fee $50. Priority deadline 1/15. Regular application deadline 8/1. Nonfall registration accepted. Admission may be deferred for a maximum of 2 years.

COSTS AND FINANCIAL AID

Annual tuition $36,000. Room and board $11,960. Required fees $2,716. Average book expense $1,000. **Required Forms and Deadlines:** FAFSA. **Notification of Awards:** Applicants will be notified of awards on a rolling basis beginning 3/1. **Types of Aid:** *Need-based scholarships/grants:* Federal Pell, FSEOG, State scholarships/grants, Private scholarships, College/university scholarship or grant aid from institutional funds. *Loans:* Direct Subsidized Stafford Loans, Direct Unsubsidized Stafford Loans, Direct PLUS loans, Federal Perkins Loans, State Loans. *Student Employment:* Federal Work-Study Program available. Institutional employment available. **Financial Aid Statistics:** 99% needy freshmen, 98% needy undergrads receive need-based scholarship or grant aid. 0% undergrads receive non-need-based scholarship or grant aid. 63% freshmen, 70% undergrads receive need-based self-help aid. 0% freshmen, 0% undergrads receive athletic scholarships. 96% freshmen, 94% undergrads receive any aid. Average cumulative indebtedness $32,921. **Criteria for awarding aid:** *Non-need-based:* Academics, Alumni affiliation, Art, Leadership, Minority status, Music/drama, Religious affiliation, State/district residency.

UNIVERSITY OF DAYTON

300 College Park, Dayton, OH 45469-1669
Phone: 937-229-4411 • **Financial Aid Phone:** 800-427-5029
E-mail: admission@udayton.edu • **CEEB Code:** 1834
Fax: 937-229-4729 • **Website:** www.udayton.edu • **ACT Code:** 3342

This private school, affiliated with the Roman Catholic Church, was founded in 1850. It has a 259-acre campus.

RATINGS

Admissions Selectivity Rating: 86   **Fire Safety Rating:** 81   **Green Rating:** 88

STUDENTS AND FACULTY

Enrollment: 8,261. **Student Body:** 47% female, 53% male, 51% out-of-state, 9% international (70 countries represented). Asian 1%, African American 3%, Caucasian 79%, Hispanic 4%, Native American <1%, Pacific Islander <1%, Two or more races 2%, Race unknown 1%.
Retention and Graduation: 89% freshmen return for sophomore year. 58% freshmen graduate within 4 years. 75% freshmen graduate within 6 years. 26% grads go on to further study within 1 year. **Faculty:** Student/faculty ratio 16:1. 535 full-time faculty, 87% hold PhDs, 16% are are members of minority groups, 41% are women. 3% of classes are taught by teaching assistants.

ACADEMICS

Degrees: bachelor's, doctoral/professional, doctoral/research, master's. **Classes:** Most classes have 20-29 students. Most lab/discussion sessions have 10-19 students. **Most popular majors:** Mechanical Engineering; Marketing/Marketing Management; Speech Communication and Rhetoric. **Special Study Options:** Accelerated program, cooperative education program, cross-registration, distance learning, double major, dual enrollment, English as a Second Language (ESL), exchange student program (domestic), honors program, independent study, internships, liberal arts/career combination, student-designed major, study abroad, teacher certification program, Distance learning courses are offered, but not programs; domestic exchange only among other Marianist institutions; student-designed major is general studies. **Honors Programs:** The University Honors Program offers courses, programming, fellowship advising, funding, guidance and benefits to undergraduates who have superior academic records, culminating in an Honors-designated diploma. Through the Honors Program, students can develop their academic talents, explore the world, undertake extensive, self-directed research, and apply their knowledge for the benefit of others. Combined degree programs: BA/MA, ACC/MBA, JD/MBA. **Disability Services:** Special programs offered to physically disabled students, including note-taking services, reader services, tape recorders, tutors. **Career Services:** Alumni network, Alumni services, Career/job search classes, Career assessment, Internships, Regional alumni.

FACILITIES
Housing: Coed dorms, special housing for disabled students, men's dorms, special housing for international students, women's dorms, fraternity/sorority housing, apartments for single students, Wellness Housing, Theme Housing, University-owned houses. 95% of campus accessible to physically diasbled. **Special Academic Facilities/Equipment:** UD Research Institute, Bombeck Family Learning Center, Learning Teaching Center, Davis Center for Portfolio Management, Marian Library, ArtStreet living-learning complex, RecPlex. **Computers:** 100% of classrooms, 100% of dorms, 100% of libraries, 100% of dining areas, 100% of student union, 100% of common outdoor areas have wireless network access. Students can register for classes online. Administrative functions (other than registration) can be performed online. Undergraduates are required to own a computer.

CAMPUS LIFE
Environment: City. **Activities:** Choral groups, concert band, dance, drama/theater, jazz band, literary magazine, marching band, music ensembles, musical theater, opera, pep band, radio station, student government, student newspaper, symphony orchestra, television station, yearbook, Campus Ministries, Student Organization, Model UN. 200 registered organizations, 14 honor societies, 30 religious organizations, 13 fraternities, 9 sororities. **Athletics (Intercollegiate):** *Men:* baseball, basketball, cheerleading, cross-country, football, golf, soccer, tennis. *Women:* basketball, cheerleading, crew/rowing, cross-country, golf, soccer, softball, tennis, track/field (outdoor), track/field (indoor), volleyball. **On-Campus Highlights:** John F. Kennedy Memorial Union, Ryan C. Harris Learning-Teaching Center, University of Dayton Arena, University of Dayton Science Center, Kettering Laboratories; UDRI, ArtStreet, an innovative living-learning complex, combines student residential quarters with performance and visual arts spaces, a recording studio, radio station and cafe. Marianst Hall, a multifunctional facility consisting of student housing, a book store, post office, credit union, food emporium, worship space and learning center, was completed in fall 2004. A $22 million addition to and renovation of Sherman and Wohlleben Halls, home to UD science programs, connects them and provides close to 55,000 square feet for new laboratories, classrooms, offices and gathering spaces. A fitness and recreation complex, or RecPlex, opened in January 2006. It consists of three levels and totals 129,540 square feet. **Environmental Initiatives:** Composting program that has eliminated ~90% of waste from all campus dining halls complete with a total conversion to compostable disposable products for takeout and washable service ware for dine-in customers.

ADMISSIONS
Freshman Academic Profile: Average high school GPA 3.7. 27% in top 10% of high school class, 56% in top 25% of high school class, 87% in top 50% of high school class. 43% from public high schools. **Reported SAT (pre-2016 redesign) scores:** SAT Math middle 50% range 520-630. SAT Writing middle 50% range 500-600. **Concordant SAT scores:** SAT Math middle 50% range 550–650. ACT middle 50% range 24-29. Minimum internet-based TOEFL 70. Minimum paper TOEFL 523. **Basis for Candidate Selection:** *Very important factors considered include:* rigor of secondary school record, academic GPA, standardized test scores, application essay. *Important factors considered include:* recommendation(s), extracurricular activities, character/personal qualities, alumni/ae relation, level of applicant's interest. *Other factors considered include:* class rank, talent/ability, first generation, racial/ethnic status, volunteer work, work experience. **Freshman Admission Requirements:** High school diploma is required and GED is accepted. *Academic units recommended:* 4 English, 4 math, 4 science, 1 science lab, 2 foreign language, 4 social studies, 4 history, 4 computer science, 4 visual/performing arts. **Freshman Admission Statistics:** 17,477 applied, 60.35% admitted, 18% enrolled. **Transfer Admission Requirements:** High school transcript, college transcript(s), essay or personal statement, Minimum college GPA of 2.0 required. Lowest grade transferable C-. **General Admission Information:** Application fee $50. Priority deadline 12/15. Regular application deadline 3/1. Regular notification 2/15. Nonfall registration accepted. Admission may be deferred for a maximum of 1 semester.

COSTS AND FINANCIAL AID
Required Forms and Deadlines: FAFSA. **Notification of Awards:** Applicants will be notified of awards on a rolling basis beginning 3/20. **Types of Aid:** *Need-based scholarships/grants:* Federal Pell, FSEOG, State scholarships/grants, Private scholarships, College/university scholarship or grant aid from institutional funds. *Loans:* Direct Subsidized Stafford Loans, Direct Unsubsidized Stafford Loans, Direct PLUS loans, Federal Perkins Loans. *Student Employment:* Federal Work-Study Program available. Institutional employment available. **Financial Aid Statistics:** 100% needy freshmen, 99% needy undergrads receive need-based scholarship or grant aid. 19% freshmen, 22% undergrads receive non-need-based scholarship or grant aid. 70% freshmen, 81% undergrads receive need-based self-help aid. 2% freshmen, 2% undergrads receive athletic scholarships. 98% freshmen, 94% undergrads receive any aid. 62% undergrads borrow to pay for school. Average cumulative

indebtedness $35,740. **Criteria for awarding aid:** *Need-based:* Academics, Alumni affiliation, Art, Athletics, Leadership, Minority status, Music/drama, Religious affiliation. *Non-need-based:* Academics, Alumni affiliation, Art, Athletics, Leadership, Minority status, Music/drama, Religious affiliation, State/district residency.

UNIVERSITY OF DELAWARE

Best Colleges

210 South College Ave., Newark, DE 19716
Phone: 302-831-8123 • **Financial Aid Phone:** 302-831-0520
E-mail: admissions@udel.edu • **CEEB Code:** 5811
Fax: 302-831-6905 • **Website:** http://www.udel.edu • **ACT Code:** 634

This public school was founded in 1743. It has a 1000-acre campus.

RATINGS
Admissions Selectivity Rating: 88   **Fire Safety Rating:** 98   **Green Rating:** 72

STUDENTS AND FACULTY
Enrollment: 17,575. **Student Body:** 58% female, 42% male, 61% out-of-state, 4% international (55 countries represented). Asian 5%, African American 5%, Caucasian 75%, Hispanic 7%, Native American <1%, Pacific Islander <1%, Two or more races 3%, Race unknown 1%.
Retention and Graduation: 92% freshmen return for sophomore year. 68% freshmen graduate within 4 years. 81% freshmen graduate within 6 years. 28% grads go on to further study within 1 year. 19% grads pursue arts and sciences degrees. 9% grads pursue law degrees. 6% grads pursue business degrees. 9% grads pursue medical degrees. **Faculty:** Student/faculty ratio 13:1. 1,181 full-time faculty, 91% hold PhDs, 20% are are members of minority groups, 41% are women. 5% of classes are taught by teaching assistants.

ACADEMICS
Degrees: associate, bachelor's, doctoral/professional, doctoral/research, master's. **Classes:** Most classes have 20-29 students. Most lab/discussion sessions have 10-19 students. **Most popular majors:** Registered Nursing/Registered Nurse; Finance; Biology/Biological Sciences. **Special Study Options:** Accelerated program, cooperative education program, distance learning, double major, dual enrollment, English as a Second Language (ESL), honors program, independent study, internships, liberal arts/career combination, student-designed major, study abroad, teacher certification program. **Honors Programs:** University Honors Program, http://honors.udel.edu/ Combined degree programs: 4+1 BS Hotel Restaurant and Inst. Mgmt./MBA. **Disability Services:** Special programs offered to physically disabled students, including note-taking services, reader services, tape recorders, tutors. **Career Services:** Alumni network, Alumni services, Career/job search classes, Career assessment, Internships, Regional alumni. Extensive web-based career workshop series. Strong relationships with academic departments and colleges to deliver services to students. Discovery Learning: internships, study abroad, undergraduate research, and service learning.

FACILITIES
Housing: Coed dorms, special housing for disabled students, women's dorms, fraternity/sorority housing, apartments for married students, apartments for single students, Theme Housing, Special-interest housing. 95% of campus accessible to physically diasbled. **Special Academic Facilities/Equipment:** $20 million Lammont du Pont Laboratory, $11 million Biotechnology Center, $1,8 million Fischer Greenhouse Laboratory, 23,000-seat Delaware Football Stadium, 350-acre Agricultural Teachning and Research Complex, 35-acre Woodlot harboring numerous wild species of animals and birds, 28 micro-computing sites, 6-acre Morris Library containing pver 2.8 million books and over 270 networked databases, 2 student/University centers, art coservation laboratories at Winterthur Museum and Gardens, Bob Carpenter Sports/Convocation Center, livestock arena and working farm, composites manufacturing science laboratory, Delaware Field House, Fred P. Rullo Stadium, Gerald Culley foreign language media center, historic costume and textile collection, laboratory for the analysis of cultural materials, medical technology laboratories, the mineralogical museum, nursing practice practice laboratories, orthopedic and biomechanical engineering center, Rust and Gold ice skating arenas, textiles, botanical gardens, the University gallery, University honors center, University laboratory preschool, Vita Nova, 40+ research centers and institutes, Center for the Arts. **Computers:** 100% of classrooms, 100% of dorms, 100% of libraries, 100% of dining areas, 100% of student union, 50% of common outdoor areas have wireless network access. Students can register

for classes online. Administrative functions (other than registration) can be performed online.

CAMPUS LIFE

Environment: Town. **Activities:** Choral groups, concert band, dance, drama/theater, jazz band, literary magazine, marching band, music ensembles, musical theater, opera, pep band, radio station, student government, student newspaper, student-run film society, symphony orchestra, television station, Campus Ministries, Student Organization, Model UN. 250 registered organizations, 23 honor societies, 24 religious organizations. 22 fraternities, 15 sororities. **Athletics (Intercollegiate):** *Men:* baseball, basketball, cross-country, diving, football, golf, lacrosse, soccer, swimming, tennis, track/field (outdoor). *Women:* basketball, crew/rowing, cross-country, diving, field hockey, lacrosse, soccer, softball, swimming, tennis, track/field (outdoor), track/field (indoor), volleyball. **On-Campus Highlights:** Trabant University Center, Gore Hall, Memorial Hall, Morris Library, Delaware Stadium/Bob Carpenter Center. **Environmental Initiatives:** The University of Delaware is launching a revolving energy loan fund dedicated to increase energy efficiency of campus buildings.

ADMISSIONS

Freshman Academic Profile: Average high school GPA 3.7. 33% in top 10% of high school class, 68% in top 25% of high school class, 94% in top 50% of high school class. 80% from public high schools. **Reported SAT (pre-2016 redesign) scores:** SAT Math middle 50% range 560-660. SAT Critical Reading middle 50% range 550-650. SAT Writing middle 50% range 550-650. **Concordant SAT scores:** SAT EBRW middle 50% 610–700. SAT Math middle 50% range 580–690. ACT middle 50% range 25-29. Minimum internet-based TOEFL 90. Minimum paper TOEFL 570. **Basis for Candidate Selection:** *Very important factors considered include:* rigor of secondary school record, academic GPA, state residency. *Important factors considered include:* standardized test scores, application essay, recommendation(s), extracurricular activities, talent/ability, character/personal qualities, volunteer work, work experience. *Other factors considered include:* class rank, interview, first generation, alumni/ae relation, geographical residence, racial/ethnic status, level of applicant's interest. **Freshman Admission Requirements:** High school diploma is required and GED is accepted. *Academic units required:* 4 English, 3 math, 3 science, 2 science labs, 2 foreign language, 2 social studies, 2 history, 2 academic electives. *Academic units recommended:* 4 English, 4 math, 4 science, 3 science labs, 4 foreign language, 2 social studies, 2 history. **Freshman Admission Statistics:** 24,881 applied, 62.57% admitted, 26% enrolled. **Transfer Admission Requirements:** High school transcript, college transcript(s), essay or personal statement, statement of good standing from prior institution(s). Minimum college GPA of 2.5 required. Lowest grade transferable C. **General Admission Information:** Application fee $75. Regular application deadline 1/15. Nonfall registration accepted. Admission may be deferred for a maximum of 1 year.

COSTS AND FINANCIAL AID

Annual in-state tuition $11,540. Annual out-of-state tuition $30,960. Room and board $12,068. Required fees $1,290. Average book expense $800. **Required Forms and Deadlines:** FAFSA. **Notification of Awards:** Applicants will be notified of awards on a rolling basis beginning 3/15. **Types of Aid:** *Need-based scholarships/grants:* Federal Pell, FSEOG, State scholarships/grants, Private scholarships, College/university scholarship or grant aid from institutional funds. *Loans:* Direct Subsidized Stafford Loans, Direct Unsubsidized Stafford Loans, Direct PLUS loans, Federal Perkins Loans, Federal Nursing Loans. *Student Employment:* Federal Work-Study Program available. Institutional employment available. **Financial Aid Statistics:** 92% needy freshmen, 81% needy undergrads receive need-based scholarship or grant aid. 9% freshmen, 7% undergrads receive non-need-based scholarship or grant aid. 75% freshmen, 82% undergrads receive need-based self-help aid. 2% freshmen, 2% undergrads receive athletic scholarships. 56% freshmen, 49% undergrads receive any aid. 61% undergrads borrow to pay for school. Average cumulative indebtedness $34,101. **Criteria for awarding aid:** *Need-based:* Academics, Art. *Non-need-based:* Academics, Alumni affiliation, Art, Athletics, Leadership, Minority status, Music/drama, State/district residency.

See page 1072.

UNIVERSITY OF DENVER

Office of Admission, Denver, CO 80208
Phone: (303) 871-2036 • **Financial Aid Phone:** 303-871-4020
E-mail: admission@du.edu • **CEEB Code:** 4842
Fax: 303-871-3301 • **Website:** http://www.du.edu • **ACT Code:** 534

This private school was founded in 1864. It has a 125-acre campus.

RATINGS

Admissions Selectivity Rating: 90   **Fire Safety Rating:** 82   **Green Rating:** 86

STUDENTS AND FACULTY

Enrollment: 5,738. **Student Body:** 54% female, 46% male, 62% out-of-state, 8% international (43 countries represented). Asian 4%, African American 2%, Caucasian 69%, Hispanic 10%, Native American <1%, Pacific Islander <1%, Two or more races 4%, Race unknown 2%.
Retention and Graduation: 87% freshmen return for sophomore year. 66% freshmen graduate within 4 years. 79 19% grads go on to further study within 1 year. **Faculty:** Student/faculty ratio 11:1. 723 full-time faculty, 90% hold PhDs, 18% are are members of minority groups, 44% are women. 2% of classes are taught by teaching assistants.

ACADEMICS

Degrees: bachelor's, certificate, doctoral/professional, doctoral/research, doctoral, master's, postbachelor's certificate, post-master's certificate. **Classes:** Most classes have 10-19 students. Most lab/discussion sessions have 10-19 students. **Most popular majors:** Finance; Psychology; Speech Communication and Rhetoric. **Special Study Options:** Accelerated program, cooperative education program, distance learning, double major, dual enrollment, English as a Second Language (ESL), honors program, independent study, internships, student-designed major, study abroad, teacher certification program, weekend college, Learning disabilities services. **Honors Programs:** The University of Denver offers a challenging Honors Program for talented students who seek an advanced liberal education, lively dialogue with their peers and faculty on important issues, study abroad in first-rate universities, and inspiring in-depth work in their majors. The aim of the program is to challenge students to cultivate strong habits of critical thinking, creativity, and scholarship and to offer close support for advanced work. Students in the Honors Program have the best of both worlds: the small classes and close community of a liberal arts college and the opportunities and resources of a research university. Combined degree programs: BA/JD, BA/MA, BA/MPP, BA or BS and MBA, BA or BS and MSW, BA or BS and JD, others. **Disability Services:** Special programs offered to physically disabled students, including note-taking services, reader services, tape recorders, tutors. **Career Services:** Alumni network, Alumni services, Career/job search classes, Career assessment, Internships, Regional alumni. Employers expect recent graduates to have at least one, preferably two internships by the time they graduate. For students who find a rewarding and skill-building internship that is unpaid over the summer, they may not have the monetary means to support themselves and complete an unpaid internship. Through the Summer Internship Award Program, students may apply for a monetary award to help cover their living expenses and other expenses incurred by working in the internship. Sample award winners have taught English in Zanibar, helped save the manatees in Florida, worked for the Mayor of Chicago, built and promoted an urban garden program and worked as a guide and leader in an animal assistance therapy program.

FACILITIES

Housing: Coed dorms, fraternity/sorority housing, apartments for married students, apartments for single students, Wellness Housing, Theme Housing. 85% of campus accessible to physically diasbled. **Special Academic Facilities/Equipment:** Art gallery, performing arts center, centers for Judaic and Latin American studies, Anthropology Museum, center for child study, center for gifted and talented children, regional conservation center, high altitude research lab, law enforcement technology center, observatory. **Computers:** 75% of classrooms, 10% of dorms, 100% of libraries, 100% of dining areas, 100% of student union, 50% of common outdoor areas have wireless network access. Students can register for classes online. Administrative functions (other than registration) can be performed online. Undergraduates are required to own a computer.

CAMPUS LIFE

Environment: Metropolis. **Activities:** Choral groups, concert band, dance, drama/theater, jazz band, literary magazine, music ensembles, musical theater, opera, pep band, radio station, student government, student newspaper, student-run film society, symphony orchestra, Campus Ministries, Student Organization, Model UN. 160 registered organizations, 19 honor societies, 14 religious organizations. 9 fraternities, 6 sororities. **Athletics (Intercollegiate):** *Men:* basketball, diving, golf, ice hockey, lacrosse, skiing (downhill/alpine), skiing (nordic/cross-country), soccer, swimming, tennis. *Women:* basketball, diving, golf, gymnastics, lacrosse, skiing (downhill/alpine), skiing (nordic/cross-country), soccer, swimming, tennis, volleyball. **On-Campus Highlights:** Campus Green (Driscoll Lawn), Ritchie Center (athletic facility), Newman Center (performing arts), Daniels College of Business building, Jazzman's Cafe (located inside Driscoll Center). **Environmental Initiatives:** The University of Denver expanded from single stream recycling to outdoor bins and composting in two campus dining halls.

ADMISSIONS
Freshman Academic Profile: Average high school GPA 3.7. 42% in top 10% of high school class, 74% in top 25% of high school class, 96% in top 50% of high school class. **Reported SAT (pre-2016 redesign) scores:** SAT Math middle 50% range 560-650. SAT Critical Reading middle 50% range 550-660. SAT Writing middle 50% range 520-570. **Concordant SAT scores:** SAT EBRW middle 50% 590–670. SAT Math middle 50% range 580–670. ACT middle 50% range 26-31. Minimum internet-based TOEFL 80. Minimum paper TOEFL 550. **Basis for Candidate Selection:** *Very important factors considered include:* rigor of secondary school record, academic GPA, standardized test scores. *Important factors considered include:* application essay, recommendation(s), extracurricular activities, talent/ability, character/personal qualities. *Other factors considered include:* first generation, alumni/ae relation, geographical residence, racial/ethnic status, volunteer work, work experience, level of applicant's interest. **Freshman Admission Requirements:** High school diploma is required and GED is accepted. *Academic units recommended:* 4 English, 2 science labs. **Freshman Admission Statistics:** 20,322 applied, 53.47% admitted, 13% enrolled. **Transfer Admission Requirements:** college transcript(s), essay or personal statement, statement of good standing from prior institution(s). Lowest grade transferable C. **General Admission Information:** Application fee $60. Regular application deadline 1/15. Regular notification 3/15. Nonfall registration accepted. Admission may be deferred for a maximum of 12 months.

COSTS AND FINANCIAL AID
Annual tuition $47,520. Room and board $12,612. Required fees $1,149. Average book expense $1,200. **Required Forms and Deadlines:** FAFSA, CSS/Financial Aid PROFILE, Noncustodial PROFILE. **Notification of Awards:** Applicants will be notified of awards on or about 3/20. **Types of Aid:** *Need-based scholarships/grants:* Federal Pell, FSEOG, State scholarships/grants, Private scholarships, College/university scholarship or grant aid from institutional funds. *Loans:* Direct Subsidized Stafford Loans, Direct Unsubsidized Stafford Loans, Direct PLUS loans, Federal Perkins Loans, College/university loans from institutional funds. *Student Employment:* Federal Work-Study Program available. Institutional employment available. **Financial Aid Statistics:** 98% needy freshmen, 98% needy undergrads receive need-based scholarship or grant aid. 25% freshmen, 26% undergrads receive non-need-based scholarship or grant aid. 67% freshmen, 69% undergrads receive need-based self-help aid. 4% freshmen, 4% undergrads receive athletic scholarships. 85% freshmen, 83% undergrads receive any aid. 44% undergrads borrow to pay for school. Average cumulative indebtedness $31,077. **Criteria for awarding aid:** *Need-based:* Academics, Art, Athletics, Leadership, Music/drama. *Non-need-based:* Academics, Art, Athletics, Leadership, Music/drama.

UNIVERSITY OF DUBUQUE

2000 University Avenue, Dubuque, IA 52001-5050
Phone: 319-589-3200 • **Financial Aid Phone:** 563-589-3396
E-mail: admssns@dbq.edu • **CEEB Code:** 6869
Fax: 319-589-3690 • **Website:** www.dbq.edu • **ACT Code:** 1358

This private school, affiliated with the Presbyterian Church, was founded in 1852. It has a 56-acre campus.

RATINGS
Admissions Selectivity Rating: 76   **Fire Safety Rating:** 96   **Green Rating:** 60*

STUDENTS AND FACULTY
Enrollment: 1,548. **Student Body:** 44% female, 56% male, 53% out-of-state, 1% international. Asian 2%, African American 12%, Caucasian 73%, Hispanic 3%, Native American 1%, Pacific Islander <1%, Two or more races 0%, Race unknown 8%.
Retention and Graduation: 68% freshmen return for sophomore year. 21% freshmen graduate within 4 years. 38% freshmen graduate within 6 years. 20% grads go on to further study within 1 year. 10% grads pursue arts and sciences degrees. 2% grads pursue law degrees. 3% grads pursue business degrees. 2%

grads pursue medical degrees. **Faculty:** Student/faculty ratio 14:1. 87 full-time faculty, 56% hold PhDs, 6% are members of minority groups, 39% are women. 0% of classes are taught by teaching assistants.

ACADEMICS
Degrees: bachelor's, doctoral/professional, master's. **Classes:** Most classes have 10-19 students. Most lab/discussion sessions have fewer than 10 students. **Most popular majors:** Animation, Interactive Technology, Video Graphics and Special Effects; Airline/Commercial/Professional Pilot and Flight Crew; Business/Commerce. **Special Study Options:** cooperative education program, cross-registration, distance learning, double major, dual enrollment, independent study, internships, liberal arts/career combination, student-designed major, study abroad, teacher certification program, Undergrads may take grad level classes. Off-Campus Study: Semester-away programs. Combined degree programs: BA/MA, 3-3. M.Div. program, BBA/MBA (4+1). **Disability Services:** Special programs offered to physically disabled students, including note-taking services, reader services, tape recorders, tutors. **Career Services:** Alumni network, Alumni services, Career/job search classes, Career assessment, Internships, Regional alumni.

FACILITIES
Housing: Coed dorms, special housing for disabled students, apartments for married students, apartments for single students, Houses and Townhouses and Suites. 50% of campus accessible to physically diasbled. **Special Academic Facilities/Equipment:** Art gallery, language labs, electron microscope, gas chromatograph/mass spectrometer, floating science lab on the Mississippi River, computer graphics/interactive media stduios, multimedia project production studio in the new Charles C. Myers Library **Computers:** 20% of classrooms, 100% of libraries, 100% of student union, have wireless network access. Students can register for classes online. Administrative functions (other than registration) can be performed online.

CAMPUS LIFE
Environment: Town. **Activities:** Choral groups, dance, drama/theater, jazz band, literary magazine, music ensembles, musical theater, pep band, student government, student newspaper, student-run film society, yearbook, Campus Ministries, Student Organization. 50 registered organizations, 2 honor societies, 3 religious organizations. 7 fraternities, 4 sororities. **Athletics (Intercollegiate):** *Men:* baseball, basketball, cross-country, football, golf, soccer, tennis, track/field (outdoor), track/field (indoor), wrestling. *Women:* basketball, cross-country, golf, soccer, softball, tennis, track/field (outdoor), track/field (indoor), volleyball. **On-Campus Highlights:** Coffee Shop, Stoltz Sports Center, Library, Student Union, Chlapaty Recreation & Wellness Center. **Environmental Initiatives:** Campus-wide Recycling.

ADMISSIONS
Freshman Academic Profile: Average high school GPA 3.0. 7% in top 10% of high school class, 24% in top 25% of high school class, 54% in top 50% of high school class. 85% from public high schools. **Reported SAT (pre-2016 redesign) scores:** SAT Math middle 50% range 420-550. SAT Critical Reading middle 50% range 440-550. **Concordant SAT scores:** SAT Math middle 50% range 460–570. ACT middle 50% range 18-23. Minimum paper TOEFL 500. **Basis for Candidate Selection:** *Very important factors considered include:* rigor of secondary school record, class rank, standardized test scores, application essay, recommendation(s), character/personal qualities. *Other factors considered include:* interview, extracurricular activities, talent/ability, alumni/ae relation, volunteer work, work experience. **Freshman Admission Requirements:** High school diploma is required and GED is accepted. *Academic units required:* 4 English, 3 math, 3 science, 3 social studies, 3 academic electives. *Academic units recommended:* 4 English, 3 math, 3 science, 3 social studies, 3 academic electives. **Freshman Admission Statistics:** 1,288 applied, 75.78% admitted, 42% enrolled. **Transfer Admission Requirements:** college transcript(s), Minimum college GPA of 2.0 required. Lowest grade transferable C. **General Admission Information:** Application fee $25. Nonfall registration accepted. Admission may be deferred for a maximum of 1 year.

COSTS AND FINANCIAL AID
Annual tuition $21,000. Room and board $7,370. Required fees $590. Average book expense $950. **Required Forms and Deadlines:** FAFSA. **Notification of Awards:** Applicants will be notified of awards on a rolling basis beginning 3/1. **Types of Aid:** *Need-based scholarships/grants:* Federal Pell, FSEOG, State scholarships/grants, Private scholarships, College/university scholarship or grant aid from institutional funds. *Loans:* Direct Subsidized Stafford Loans, Direct Unsubsidized Stafford Loans, Direct PLUS loans, Federal Perkins Loans, State Loans, College/university loans from institutional funds. *Student Employment:* Federal Work-Study Program available. Institutional employment available. **Financial Aid Statistics:** 99% needy freshmen, 98% needy undergrads receive need-based scholarship or grant aid. 16% freshmen, 12% undergrads receive non-need-based scholarship or grant aid. 80% freshmen, 83% undergrads receive need-based self-help aid. 0% freshmen, 0% undergrads receive athletic scholarships. 85% freshmen, 85% undergrads receive any aid. **Criteria for awarding aid:** *Need-based:* Academics, Alumni affiliation, Minority status,

Music/drama, Religious affiliation. *Non-need-based:* Academics, Alumni affiliation, Leadership, Music/drama, State/district residency.

UNIVERSITY OF EVANSVILLE

1800 Lincoln Avenue, Evansville, IN 47722
Phone: 812-488-2468 • **Financial Aid Phone:** 812-488-2364
E-mail: admission@evansville.edu • **CEEB Code:** 1208
Fax: 812-488-4076 • **Website:** www.evansville.edu • **ACT Code:** 1188

This private school, affiliated with the Methodist Church, was founded in 1854. It has a 75-acre campus.

RATINGS
Admissions Selectivity Rating: 86   **Fire Safety Rating:** 64   **Green Rating:** 60*

STUDENTS AND FACULTY
Enrollment: 2,164. **Student Body:** 54% female, 46% male, 39% out-of-state, 15% international (52 countries represented). Asian 2%, African American 3%, Caucasian 71%, Hispanic 4%, Native American <1%, Pacific Islander 0%, Two or more races 2%, Race unknown 3%.
Retention and Graduation: 89% freshmen return for sophomore year. 59% freshmen graduate within 4 years. 69% freshmen graduate within 6 years. 18% grads go on to further study within 1 year. **Faculty:** Student/faculty ratio 12:1. 169 full-time faculty, 86% hold PhDs, 12% are are members of minority groups, 41% are women. 0% of classes are taught by teaching assistants.

ACADEMICS
Degrees: associate, bachelor's, doctoral/professional, master's. **Classes:** Most classes have 10-19 students. Most lab/discussion sessions have 20-29 students. **Most popular majors:** Drama and Dramatics/Theatre Arts; Kinesiology and Exercise Science; Registered Nursing/Registered Nurse. **Special Study Options:** Accelerated program, cooperative education program, double major, dual enrollment, English as a Second Language (ESL), external degree program, honors program, independent study, internships, student-designed major, study abroad, teacher certification program. **Honors Programs:** The Honors Program incorporates unique courses with distinct learning environments to provide enhanced educational learning experiences for exceptional students. Students openly discuss different viewpoints in small, seminar-style classes offered in various academic disciplines. Intellectually curious students who desire academic challenges will enjoy the collaborative learning atmosphere of the Honors Program, as well as the opportunity to engage in advanced independent study, a senior project, and special social programs. Combined degree programs: BS/MS in health services administration. **Disability Services:** Special programs offered to physically disabled students, including note-taking services, tutors. **Career Services:** Alumni network, Alumni services, Career/job search classes, Career assessment, Internships, Regional alumni.

FACILITIES
Housing: Coed dorms, men's dorms, women's dorms, fraternity/sorority housing, apartments for single students, Theme Housing. 87% of campus accessible to physically diasbled. **Computers:** 100% of classrooms, 100% of dorms, 100% of libraries, 100% of dining areas, 100% of student union, 100% of common outdoor areas have wireless network access. Students can register for classes online. Administrative functions (other than registration) can be performed online.

CAMPUS LIFE
Environment: City. **Activities:** Choral groups, concert band, dance, drama/theater, jazz band, literary magazine, music ensembles, musical theater, opera, pep band, radio station, student government, student newspaper, student-run film society, symphony orchestra, yearbook, Campus Ministries, Student Organization, Model UN. 154 registered organizations, 11 honor societies, 10 religious organizations. 6 fraternities, 5 sororities. **Athletics (Intercollegiate):** *Men:* baseball, basketball, cross-country, diving, golf, soccer, swimming. *Women:* basketball, cross-country, diving, golf, soccer, softball, swimming, tennis, volleyball. **On-Campus Highlights:** Koch Center, Fitness Center, School of Business Administration, Ridgway Student Center, Jazzman's Cafe, The library and Memorial Plaza are also popular places on campus.

ADMISSIONS
Freshman Academic Profile: Average high school GPA 3.7. 34% in top 10% of high school class, 68% in top 25% of high school class, 90% in top 50% of high school class. **Reported SAT (pre-2016 redesign) scores:** SAT Math middle 50% range 500-620. SAT Critical Reading middle 50% range 490-600. SAT Writing middle 50% range 480-600. **Concordant SAT scores:** SAT EBRW middle 50% range 540–650. SAT Math middle 50% range 530–640. ACT middle 50% range 23-29. Minimum internet-based TOEFL

61. Minimum paper TOEFL 500. **Basis for Candidate Selection:** *Very important factors considered include:* rigor of secondary school record, academic GPA, standardized test scores, character/personal qualities. *Important factors considered include:* application essay, extracurricular activities, talent/ability, volunteer work, work experience. *Other factors considered include:* class rank, recommendation(s), interview, first generation, alumni/ae relation, geographical residence, state residency, level of applicant's interest. **Freshman Admission Requirements:** High school diploma is required and GED is accepted. *Academic units required:* 4 English, 3 math, 3 science, 3 science labs, 3 social studies. *Academic units recommended:* 4 English, 4 math, 4 science, 4 science labs, 2 foreign language, 4 social studies. **Freshman Admission Statistics:** 4,033 applied, 70.89% admitted, 19% enrolled. **Transfer Admission Requirements:** High school transcript, college transcript(s), statement of good standing from prior institution(s). Minimum college GPA of 2.0 required. Lowest grade transferable C. **General Admission Information:** Nonfall registration accepted. Admission may be deferred for a maximum of 1 year.

COSTS AND FINANCIAL AID
Annual tuition $32,900. Room and board $11,690. Required fees $1,066. Average book expense $1,200. **Required Forms and Deadlines:** FAFSA. **Notification of Awards:** Applicants will be notified of awards on a rolling basis beginning 3/1. **Types of Aid:** *Need-based scholarships/grants:* Federal Pell, FSEOG, State scholarships/grants, Private scholarships, College/university scholarship or grant aid from institutional funds. *Loans:* Direct Subsidized Stafford Loans, Direct Unsubsidized Stafford Loans, Direct PLUS loans, Federal Perkins Loans, Federal Nursing Loans, College/university loans from institutional funds. *Student Employment:* Federal Work-Study Program available. Institutional employment available. **Financial Aid Statistics:** 100% needy freshmen, 96% needy undergrads receive need-based scholarship or grant aid. 24% freshmen, 21% undergrads receive non-need-based scholarship or grant aid. 66% freshmen, 68% undergrads receive need-based self-help aid. 5% freshmen, 6% undergrads receive athletic scholarships. 95% freshmen, 94% undergrads receive any aid. 65% undergrads borrow to pay for school. Average cumulative indebtedness $35,346. **Criteria for awarding aid:** *Need-based:* Job skills. *Non-need-based:* Academics, Alumni affiliation, Art, Athletics, Job skills, Music/drama, Religious affiliation.

THE UNIVERSITY OF FINDLAY

1140 College Drive, Pineville, OH 45840
Phone: 516-299-2900
E-mail: admissions@findlay.edu
Fax: 419-434-4898 • **Website:** www.findlay.edu

RATINGS
Admissions Selectivity Rating: 82   **Fire Safety Rating:** 60*   **Green Rating:** 60*

STUDENTS AND FACULTY
Enrollment: 3,133. **Student Body:** 60% female, 40% male, 3% international. Asian 2%, African American 5%, Caucasian 62%, Hispanic 12%, Native American 1%, Pacific Islander <1%, Two or more races 2%, Race unknown 12%.
Retention and Graduation: 18% grads go on to further study within 1 year. **Faculty:** 203 full-time faculty, 21% hold PhDs, 12% are are members of minority groups, 48% are women.

ACADEMICS
Degrees: Combined degree programs: 3-1 medical technology and nuclear medicine tech. **Career Services:** Alumni services, Career/job search classes, Career assessment, Internships.

FACILITIES
Housing: 90% of campus accessible to physically diasbled.

ADMISSIONS
Freshman Academic Profile: 26% in top 10% of high school class, 54% in top 25% of high school class, 80% in top 50% of high school class. 92% from public high schools. **Concordant SAT scores:** SAT EBRW middle 50% 520–640. SAT Math middle 50% range 510–600. ACT middle 50% range 20-25. **Freshman Admission Statistics:** 37% enrolled.

COSTS AND FINANCIAL AID
Annual tuition $30,564. Room and board $9,442. Required fees $959. **Financial Aid Statistics:** 86% needy undergrads receive need-based scholarship or grant aid. 88% freshmen, 23% undergrads receive non-need-based scholarship or grant aid. 0.679471033 freshmen, 0.682744903 undergrads receive need-based self-help aid. 0% freshmen, 0% undergrads receive athletic scholarships. 75% undergrads borrow to pay for school. Average cumulative indebtedness $20,180.

See page 1074.

UNIVERSITY OF FLORIDA

201 Criser Hall, Gainesville, FL 32611-4000
Phone: 352-392-1365 • **Financial Aid Phone:** 352-392-1271
E-mail: webrequests@admissions.ufl.edu • **CEEB Code:** 5812
Fax: 352-392-2115 • **Website:** www.ufl.edu

This public school was founded in 1853. It has a 2000-acre campus.

RATINGS

Admissions Selectivity Rating: 94   **Fire Safety Rating:** 80   **Green Rating:** 93

STUDENTS AND FACULTY

Enrollment: 33,972. **Student Body:** 55% female, 45% male, 3% out-of-state, 1% international (157 countries represented). Asian 8%, African American 6%, Caucasian 57%, Hispanic 21%, Native American <1%, Pacific Islander 1%, Two or more races 3%, Race unknown 3%.
Retention and Graduation: 96% freshmen return for sophomore year. 66% freshmen graduate within 4 years. 87 **Faculty:** Student/faculty ratio 21:1. 3,543 full-time faculty, 85% hold PhDs, 26% are are members of minority groups, 36% are women. 34% of classes are taught by teaching assistants.

ACADEMICS

Degrees: associate, bachelor's, certificate, doctoral/professional, doctoral/research, master's, postbachelor's certifiate, post-master's certificate. **Classes:** Most classes have 10-19 students. Most lab/discussion sessions have 20-29 students. **Most popular majors:** Psychology; Finance; Biology/Biological Sciences. **Special Study Options:** Accelerated program, cooperative education program, cross-registration, distance learning, double major, dual enrollment, English as a Second Language (ESL), exchange student program (domestic), external degree program, honors program, independent study, internships, liberal arts/career combination, student-designed major, study abroad, teacher certification program, weekend college, Adult/Continuing Education, TV-delivered credit-bearing courses, Honors Program, and distance learning courses. **Honors Programs:** The University of Florida Honors Program blends the vast resources of a research university with the individualized attention often available only at small liberal arts colleges. With small classes taught by the top faculty at the university, the program offers students the opportunity to make the most of their education al experience. Close interaction with faculty often leads to undergraduate research projects, and students are encouraged to pursue such activities. Students in the Honors Program have the opportunity to live in the Honors Residential College at Hume Hall, the university"s newest and most modern dormitory, where they will be surrounded by like-minded individuals and engage in a unique living-learning community. Combined degree programs: https://catalog.ufl.edu/ugrad/current/pages/combined-degree-programs.aspx. **Disability Services:** Special programs offered to physically disabled students, including note-taking services, reader services, tape recorders. **Career Services:** Alumni services, Career/job search classes, Career assessment, Internships, Regional alumni. Major Career Showcase conducted each semester—one of the largest fairs of its type nationally. Number one Career Center in U.S. for 2010 and 2012.

FACILITIES

Housing: Coed dorms, special housing for disabled students, special housing for international students, fraternity/sorority housing, apartments for married students, apartments for single students, Honors Residential College at Hume Hall, House at Weaver Hall, Career Exploration Community at Graham Hall, Wellness Communities at Springs and Beaty Towers, Faculty-In-Residence Program, First-Year Experience Program, No-Visitation by Opposite Sex Floor available by request, East Hall Engineering Community, Community Service Floor in Fletcher, Fine Arts Living Learning Community in Reid hall, Global Learning Community in Yulee. 90% of campus accessible to physically diasbled. **Special Academic Facilities/Equipment:** Natural history museum, art museum, art gallery, center for the performing arts, Aeolian Skinner organ, cast-bell carillon, citrus research center, coastal engineering wave tank, 100-kilowatt training and research reactor, academic computing center, microkelvin lab, self-contained intensive care hyperbaric chamber. **Computers:** 80% of classrooms, 100% of dorms, 100% of libraries, 100% of dining areas, 100% of student union, 100% of common outdoor areas have wireless network access. Students can register for classes online. Administrative functions (other than registration) can be performed online.

CAMPUS LIFE

Environment: City. **Activities:** Choral groups, concert band, dance, drama/theater, jazz band, literary magazine, marching band, music ensembles, musical theater, pep band, radio station, student government, student newspaper, student-run film society, symphony orchestra, television station, yearbook. 853 registered organizations. **Athletics (Intercollegiate):** *Men:* baseball, basketball, cross-country, diving, football, golf, swimming, tennis, track/field (outdoor), track/field (indoor). *Women:* basketball, cross-country, diving, golf, gymnastics, lacrosse, soccer, softball, swimming, tennis, track/field (outdoor), track/field (indoor), volleyball. **On-Campus Highlights:** Center for Performing Arts, Florida Museum of Natural History, Cancer & Genetic Research Complex, Brain Institute, Lake Alice Wildlife Reserve. **Environmental Initiatives:** Zero Waste by 2015: As a result of Dr. Machen goal for Zero Waste by 2015, UF now recycles over 6,500 tons of material annually, approximately 43% of the waste stream. Additionally, UF strives to recycle at least 75% of its deconstruction debris and has instituted an Electronics Reuse/Recycling Policy and accompanying step-by-step guide for disposal and recycling. Indoor collection of paper, cans & bottles is institution-wide. UF initiated a Tail-gator recycling program for home game days in 2006 and the program has diverted more than 350,000 pounds of recyclables from the landfill since then. This program continues to grow through self-service stations and other outreach on campus and within the stadium. In 2013, UF began composting efforts on campus by taking the stadium "zero waste" through the football season-diverting an additional 50,000 pounds of organic waste from the landfill. UF researchers recycle Helium on campus and the Veterinary Medical Center repurposes animal waste through a composting partnership with the Forestry Service.

ADMISSIONS

Freshman Academic Profile: 72% in top 10% of high school class, 96% in top 25% of high school class, 100% in top 50% of high school class. 70% from public high schools. **Reported SAT (pre-2016 redesign) scores:** SAT Math middle 50% range 590-680. SAT Critical Reading middle 50% range 580-670. SAT Writing middle 50% range 570-670. **Concordant SAT scores:** SAT EBRW middle 50% 630–710. SAT Math middle 50% range 610–710. ACT middle 50% range 27-31. **Basis for Candidate Selection:** *Very important factors considered include:* rigor of secondary school record, academic GPA, application essay, extracurricular activities, talent/ability, character/personal qualities, volunteer work. *Important factors considered include:* standardized test scores, first generation, geographical residence, work experience. *Other factors considered include:* class rank, alumni/ae relation, state residency, level of applicant's interest. **Freshman Admission Requirements:** High school diploma is required and GED is accepted. *Academic units required:* 4 English, 4 math, 3 science, 2 science labs, 2 foreign language, 3 social studies. **Freshman Admission Statistics:** 29,237 applied, 48.70% admitted, 51% enrolled. **Transfer Admission Requirements:** High school transcript, college transcript(s), standardized test scores, Minimum college GPA of 2.0 required. **General Admission Information:** Application fee $30. Regular application deadline 11/1. Nonfall registration accepted.

COSTS AND FINANCIAL AID

Annual in-state tuition $6,381. Annual out-of-state tuition $28,658. Room and board $9,910. Average book expense $1,290. **Required Forms and Deadlines:** FAFSA. **Notification of Awards:** Applicants will be notified of awards on a rolling basis beginning 4/15. **Types of Aid:** *Need-based scholarships/grants:* Federal Pell, FSEOG, State scholarships/grants, Private scholarships, College/university scholarship or grant aid from institutional funds. *Loans:* Direct Subsidized Stafford Loans, Direct Unsubsidized Stafford Loans, Direct PLUS loans, Federal Perkins Loans, College/university loans from institutional funds. *Student Employment:* Federal Work-Study Program available. Institutional employment available. **Financial Aid Statistics:** 62% needy freshmen, 65% needy undergrads receive need-based scholarship or grant aid. 87% freshmen, 77% undergrads receive non-need-based scholarship or grant aid. 41% freshmen, 50% undergrads receive need-based self-help aid. 1% freshmen, 1% undergrads receive athletic scholarships. 94% freshmen, 91% undergrads receive any aid. 43% undergrads borrow to pay for school. Average cumulative indebtedness $21,028. **Criteria for awarding aid:** *Need-based:* Academics. *Non-need-based:* Academics, Alumni affiliation, Art, Athletics, Leadership, Minority status, Music/drama, State/district residency.

UNIVERSITY OF GEORGIA

Terrell Hall, 210 South Jackson Street, Athens, GA 30602-1633
Phone: 706-542-8776 • **Financial Aid Phone:** 706-542-6147
E-mail: adm-info@uga.edu • **CEEB Code:** 5813
Website: www.uga.edu • **ACT Code:** 872

This public school was founded in 1785. It has a 324-acre campus.

RATINGS
Admissions Selectivity Rating: 92   **Fire Safety Rating:** 86   **Green Rating:** 94

STUDENTS AND FACULTY
Enrollment: 27,828. **Student Body:** 57% female, 43% male, 8% out-of-state, 2% international (125 countries represented). Asian 10%, African American 8%, Caucasian 70%, Hispanic 6%, Native American <1%, Pacific Islander <1%, Two or more races 4%, Race unknown 1%.
Retention and Graduation: 95% freshmen return for sophomore year. 63% freshmen graduate within 4 years. 85% freshmen graduate within 6 years. 19% grads go on to further study within 1 year. **Faculty:** Student/faculty ratio 18 2,012 full-time faculty, 95% hold PhDs, 19% are are members of minority groups, 39% are women. 17% of classes are taught by teaching assistants.

ACADEMICS
Degrees: bachelor's, certificate, doctoral/professional, doctoral/research, doctoral, master's, postbachelor's certifiate, post-master's certificate. **Most popular majors:** Biology/Biological Sciences; Psychology; Finance. **Special Study Options:** Accelerated program, cooperative education program, cross-registration, distance learning, double major, dual enrollment, exchange student program (domestic), external degree program, honors program, independent study, internships, liberal arts/career combination, student-designed major, study abroad, teacher certification program. **Honors Programs:** General Honors Program (university-wide), Foundation Fellows, Center for Undergraduate Research Summer Research Fellows, CURO Apprentice Program. **Disability Services:** Special programs offered to physically disabled students, including note-taking services, reader services, tape recorders, tutors. **Career Services:** Alumni network, Alumni services, Career/job search classes, Career assessment, Internships, Regional alumni. The University of Georgia Career Boot Camp is a one-day, intensive career program that jump starts the career skills of participating students so that they can immediately launch a successful job search campaign. During the event, students hear from employers and alumni representing Fortune 100 companies regarding Career Fair Preparation, Resume Creation, Mock Interviews, and Career Paths. The Career Center has the 2nd largest Twitter following among all Career Centers nationwide.

FACILITIES
Housing: Coed dorms, special housing for disabled students, special housing for international students, women's dorms, fraternity/sorority housing, apartments for married students, apartments for single students, Theme Housing. Honors and Language focused dorms are available. 90% of campus accessible to physically diasbled. **Special Academic Facilities/Equipment:** Miller Learning Center, Georgia Museum of Art, Georgia Museum of Natural History, Ramsey Student Center for Physical Activities, Performing Arts Center, Tate Student Center **Computers:** 90% of classrooms, 15% of dorms, 100% of libraries, 100% of dining areas, 100% of student union, 100% of common outdoor areas have wireless network access. Students can register for classes online. Administrative functions (other than registration) can be performed online.

CAMPUS LIFE
Environment: City. **Activities:** Choral groups, concert band, dance, drama/theater, jazz band, literary magazine, marching band, music ensembles, musical theater, opera, pep band, radio station, student government, student newspaper, student-run film society, symphony orchestra, television station, yearbook, Campus Ministries, Student Organization, Model UN. 597 registered organizations, 22 honor societies, 35 religious organizations. 34 fraternities, 25 sororities. **Athletics (Intercollegiate):** *Men:* baseball, basketball, cross-country, diving, football, golf, swimming, tennis, track/field (outdoor), track/field (indoor). *Women:* basketball, cross-country, diving, equestrian sports, golf, gymnastics, soccer, softball, swimming, tennis, track/field (outdoor), track/field (indoor), volleyball. **On-Campus Highlights:** Zell B. Miller Learning Center, Sanford Stadium, Ramsey Student Center for Physical Activ, Performing and Visual Arts Complex, Tate Student Center. **Environmental Initiatives:** Inclusion of sustainability as a hallmark of the 2020 Strategic Plan, campus

sustainability specifically included in Strategic Direction VII, and woven through all other strategic directions. Hallmarks of the 2020 Strategic Plan: "Two other themes emerge in the 2020 Plan: sustainability and diversity. First, a comprehensive set of recommendations will allow UGA, which was after all the home of the pioneering ecologist Gene Odum, to emerge as a model institution and national leader in research and implementation in this important area. These, then, are the hallmarks of the UGA 2020 Strategic Plan: a clarion call to improving research and graduate education, while preserving and enhancing recent gains in undergraduate education; increasing interdisciplinary efforts across campus as well as local-to-global education and outreach experiences as keys to expanding opportunities for both research and education; establishing a leadership position in sustainability as a major theme for research, education, and service; and ensuring the future relevance of our missions by diversifying the UGA community to better reflect the demographics of Georgia." Strategic Direction 7—Improving Stewardship of Natural Resources and Advancing Campus Sustainability Because the University of Georgia is committed by its land- and sea-grant mission to serve people living and working in Georgia along with our vision to be a leading university internationally, it is incumbent upon the University to provide leadership concerning unprecedented environmental challenges. It is equally important for the University to manage financial and human resources with the greatest of care and respect and to the maximum benefit of the state. A sustainable university is one that meets the needs of the present without compromising the ability of future generations to meet their needs. It also creates opportunities for students, faculty, and staff to enhance the quality of life throughout their communities (Working Group on Sustainability, 2009; World Commission on Environment and Development). A sustainable university acts as a living laboratory where sustainability is researched, taught, tested, and constantly refined. UGA must demonstrate and promote leadership in sustainable living and learning, contextualizing the local as part of the global in sustainability. Over the next decade, the University campuses should be examples to others in reducing their environmental footprints to the greatest extent possible. This includes efforts to reduce energy use significantly, and intelligently, and carefully use and reuse scarce water resources, improve air and water quality, provide sustainable food and transportation options, purchase environmentally responsible products and equipment, increase recycling, and drastically reduce waste. Second, in the effort to prepare students for effective leadership on campus and beyond, sustainability should be infused into formal and informal educational opportunities throughout the University. Campus buildings and landscapes should be incorporated as teaching opportunities, which through design and functional interpretation will reveal innovative practices with the potential to enlighten and inform students and citizens about sound approaches to sustainable living. Third, research generated by UGA faculty and students as well as advances from the global community will be used to reduce dependency on fossil fuels, increase the reuse of materials, and continue the search for other methods that will reduce human impacts on the environment. A priority for the University at large is to design and construct buildings, plaza spaces, hardscapes, and other landscapes that embody the latest in environmental advances and to incorporate the increasing social nature of learning today by creating ample spaces for people to interact. To accomplish these goals, the University should establish a formal coordinating body to work with the UGA Office of Sustainability to develop and implement a comprehensive sustainability plan for the University. a. Strategic Priority: Annually evaluate and update the University sustainability performance in instruction, research, public service, campus development, and operations activities. Benchmark: Stages for developing a systematic evaluation of the University sustainability performance in instruction, research, public service, campus development, and operations activities. Goal: An annual report on the status of and progress in sustainability performance in instruction, research, public service, campus development, and operations activities by 2020. b. Strategic Priority: Demonstrate a commitment to reducing fossil fuel use, thereby reducing the University carbon emissions. Pre-benchmark Activity: Calculate the University carbon footprint. Benchmark: The University carbon footprint when calculated. Goals: By 2020: Reduce carbon emissions by 20 percent. Reduce University consumption of energy by 25 percent. Increase purchase of energy from renewable sources by 10 percent. Increase generation of energy from renewable sources by 10 percent. c. Strategic Priority: Update UGA Guidelines for Design and Construction to incorporate, implement, and monitor current sustainable design strategies, including Leadership in Energy and Environmental Design (LEED) and Sustainable Sites Initiative standards when appropriate. Benchmark: Stages of completion of drafting, gaining support for, and implementing the guidelines. Goal: Updated Guidelines for Design and Construction by 2020. d. Strategic Priority: Integrate sustainability into the student experience through curricular and co-curricular activities both in the classroom and beyond. Pre-benchmark Activity: Develop a system for identifying and designating courses with a curricular sustainability component. Benchmark: The number of courses with curricular sustainability component when system is implemented. Goal: Increase number of courses with curricular sustainability component by10 percent by 2020. Pre-benchmark Activity: Develop a system for identifying and designating co-curricular experiences with a sustainability component. Benchmark: The number of available co-curricular experiences with sustainability components when system is implemented. Goal: Increase number of available co-curricular experiences with sustainability components by 10 percent by 2020. e. Strategic Priority: Enhance the coordination, support, and awareness of the University sustainability efforts by establishing a coordinating body to lead efforts, increasing endowments for sustainable activities and promoting campus sustainability efforts. Benchmark: Stages for establishing and charging a coordinating body to oversee sustainability efforts. Goal: A functioning coordinating body to oversee sustainability efforts by 2020. Benchmark: The level of endowment funds for sustainable activities in 2010-2011. Goal: Increase the endowment for sustainable activities by 25 percent by 2020. Benchmark: Stages of action to identify, develop, fund, and install interpretive signs for key campus sustainability efforts. Goal: Interpretive signs installed by 2020. f. Strategic Priority: Encourage the further development and use of mass transportation to and on campus. Benchmark: The number of campus bus passengers in 2010-2011. Goal: Increase the number of campus bus passengers by 2020. Benchmark: The number of faculty, staff, and students who commute to campus who use alternate modes of transportation such as mass transit, bicycles, or walking in 2010-2011. Goal: Increase by 20 percent the number of faculty, staff, and students who commute to campus using alternate modes of transportation such as mass transit, bicycles, or walking by 2020. Benchmark: The number of Alternative Transportation Permits in 2010-2011 (2,100). Goal: Increase the number of Alternative Transportation options.

ADMISSIONS

Freshman Academic Profile: Average high school GPA 4.0. 55% in top 10% of high school class, 91% in top 25% of high school class, 99% in top 50% of high school class. 71% from public high schools. **Reported SAT (pre-2016 redesign) scores:** SAT Math middle 50% range 570-670. SAT Critical Reading middle 50% range 570-670. SAT Writing middle 50% range 560-660. **Concordant SAT scores:** SAT EBRW middle 50% 620–710. SAT Math middle 50% range 590–700. ACT middle 50% range 26-31. Minimum internet-based TOEFL 80. Minimum paper TOEFL 550. **Basis for Candidate Selection:** *Very important factors considered include:* rigor of secondary school record, academic GPA. *Important factors considered include:* standardized test scores. *Other factors considered include:* application essay, recommendation(s), extracurricular activities, talent/ability, character/personal qualities, first generation, volunteer work, work experience. **Freshman Admission Requirements:** High school diploma is required and GED is accepted. *Academic units required:* 4 English, 4 math, 4 science, 2 science labs, 2 foreign language, 3 social studies. *Academic units recommended:* 4 English, 4 math, 4 science, 2 science labs, 3 foreign language, 1 social studies, 2 history, 1 academic elective. **Freshman Admission Statistics:** 22,694 applied, 53.90% admitted, 44% enrolled. **Transfer Admission Requirements:** college transcript(s), Lowest grade transferable D. **General Admission Information:** Application fee $60. Priority deadline 10/15. Regular application deadline 1/15. Nonfall registration accepted. Admission may be deferred for a maximum of one year.

COSTS AND FINANCIAL AID

Average book expense $840. **Required Forms and Deadlines:** FAFSA. **Notification of Awards:** Applicants will be notified of awards on a rolling basis beginning 5/1. **Types of Aid:** *Need-based scholarships/grants:* Federal Pell, FSEOG, State scholarships/grants, Private scholarships, College/university scholarship or grant aid from institutional funds. *Loans:* Direct Subsidized Stafford Loans, Direct Unsubsidized Stafford Loans, Direct PLUS loans, Federal Perkins Loans, State Loans, College/university loans from institutional funds. *Student Employment:* Federal Work-Study Program available. Institutional employment available. **Financial Aid Statistics:** 98% needy freshmen, 92% needy undergrads receive need-based scholarship or grant aid. 25% freshmen, 17% undergrads receive non-need-based scholarship or grant aid. 48% freshmen, 57% undergrads receive need-based self-help aid. 2% freshmen, 2% undergrads receive athletic scholarships. 47% freshmen, 48% undergrads receive any aid. 47% undergrads borrow to pay for school. Average cumulative indebtedness $21,730. **Criteria for awarding aid:** *Non-need-based:* Academics, Athletics, State/district residency.

UNIVERSITY OF GREAT FALLS

1301 20th Street South, Great Falls, MT 59405
Phone: 406-791-5200 • **Financial Aid Phone:** 406-791-5235
E-mail: enroll@ugf.edu • **CEEB Code:** 4058
Fax: 406-791-5209 • **Website:** www.ugf.edu • **ACT Code:** 2410

This private school, affiliated with the Roman Catholic Church, was founded in 1932. It has a 44-acre campus.

RATINGS

Admissions Selectivity Rating: 74   **Fire Safety Rating:** 60*   **Green Rating:** 60*

STUDENTS AND FACULTY

Student Body: 63% female, 37% male, 20% out-of-state. **Retention and Graduation:** 59% freshmen return for sophomore year. 20% grads pursue arts and sciences degrees. 100% grads pursue medical degrees. **Faculty:** Student/faculty ratio 12:1. 33 full-time faculty, 61% hold PhDs, 6% are are members of minority groups, 33% are women. 0% of classes are taught by teaching assistants.

ACADEMICS

Degrees: associate, bachelor's, master's, terminal, transfer. **Classes:** Most classes have fewer than 10 students. **Most popular majors:** Elementary Education and Teaching; Psychology; Criminal Justice/Safety Studies. **Special Study Options:** cooperative education program, distance learning, double major, independent study, internships, liberal arts/career combination, teacher certification program. **Disability Services:** Special programs offered to physically disabled students, including note-taking services, reader services, tape recorders, tutors. **Career Services:** Alumni network, Alumni services, Career/job search classes, Internships.

FACILITIES

Housing: Coed dorms, apartments for married students, apartments for single students. 85% of campus accessible to physically diasbled. **Special Academic Facilities/Equipment:** Art museum; Dr. Hong Herbarium. **Computers:** 70% of classrooms, 100% of dorms, 100% of libraries, 100% of student union, have wireless network access. Students can register for classes online.

CAMPUS LIFE

Environment: Town. **Activities:** Choral groups, concert band, dance, drama/theater, jazz band, music ensembles, musical theater, pep band, radio station, student government, student newspaper, symphony orchestra, Campus Ministries. 10 registered organizations, 2 honor societies, 1 religious organization. **Athletics (Intercollegiate):** *Men:* basketball, cheerleading, cross-country, golf, track/field (outdoor), wrestling. *Women:* basketball, cheerleading, cross-country, golf, soccer, softball, track/field (outdoor), volleyball. **On-Campus Highlights:** Student Center, Wellness Center, Athletic Facility, Art Gallery.

ADMISSIONS

Freshman Academic Profile: Average high school GPA 3.4. 87% from public high schools. **Reported SAT (pre-2016 redesign) scores:** SAT Math middle 50% range 360-490. SAT Critical Reading middle 50% range 330-430. **Concordant SAT scores:** SAT Math middle 50% range 400–520. ACT middle 50% range 18-24. Minimum paper TOEFL 500. **Basis for Candidate Selection:** *Important factors considered include:* rigor of secondary school record, academic GPA, standardized test scores, application essay, interview, character/personal qualities, religious affiliation/commitment, level of applicant's interest. *Other factors considered include:* class rank, recommendation(s), extracurricular activities, talent/ability, first generation, racial/ethnic status, volunteer work, work experience. **Freshman Admission Requirements:** High school diploma is required and GED is accepted. *Academic units required:* 4 English, 3 math, 3 science, 1 science lab, 1 social studies, 3 history, 5 academic electives. *Academic units recommended:* 4 English, 3 math, 3 science, 1 science lab, 2 foreign language, 2 social studies, 3 history, 3 academic electives. **Freshman Admission Statistics:** 278 applied, 73.38% admitted, 73% enrolled. **Transfer Admission Requirements:** college transcript(s), essay or personal statement, Minimum college GPA of 2.0 required. Lowest grade transferable C. **General Admission Information:** Application fee $35. Priority deadline 6/1. Regular application deadline 8/30. Nonfall registration accepted. Admission may be deferred for a maximum of 2 Semesters.

COSTS AND FINANCIAL AID

Annual tuition $15,500. Room and board $6,490. Required fees $900. Average book expense $500. **Required Forms and Deadlines:** FAFSA. **Notification of Awards:** Applicants will be notified of awards on a rolling basis beginning 3/1. **Types of Aid:** *Need-based scholarships/grants:* Federal Pell, FSEOG, State scholarships/grants, Private scholarships, College/university scholarship or grant aid from institutional funds. *Loans:* Federal Perkins Loans. *Student Employment:* Federal Work-Study Program available. Institutional employment available. **Financial Aid Statistics:** 69% needy freshmen, 73% needy undergrads receive need-based scholarship or grant aid. 92% freshmen, 92% undergrads receive non-need-based scholarship or grant aid. 90% freshmen, 93% undergrads receive need-based self-help aid. 47% freshmen, 38% undergrads receive athletic scholarships. 46% freshmen, 50% undergrads receive any aid. **Criteria for awarding aid:** *Need-based:* Job skills, Minority status, Religious affiliation. *Non-need-based:* Academics, Alumni affiliation, Art, Athletics, Job skills, Leadership, Minority status, Music/drama, Religious affiliation, State/district residency.

UNIVERSITY OF HARTFORD

200 Bloomfield Avenue, West Hartford, CT 6117
Phone: 860-768-4296 • **Financial Aid Phone:** 800-947-4303
E-mail: admissions@mail.hartford.edu • **CEEB Code:** 3436
Fax: 860-768-4961 • **Website:** www.hartford.edu • **ACT Code:** 606

This private school was founded in 1877. It has a 320-acre campus.

RATINGS

Admissions Selectivity Rating: 75   **Fire Safety Rating:** 78   **Green Rating:** 60*

STUDENTS AND FACULTY

Enrollment: 5,028. **Student Body:** 51% female, 49% male, 51% out-of-state, 6% international (65 countries represented). Asian 3%, African American 16%, Caucasian 56%, Hispanic 12%, Native American <1%, Pacific Islander <1%, Two or more races 3%, Race unknown 4%.
Retention and Graduation: 74% freshmen return for sophomore year. 49% freshmen graduate within 4 years. 60% freshmen graduate within 6 years. 22% grads go on to further study within 1 year. 39% grads pursue arts and sciences degrees. 2% grads pursue law degrees. 14% grads pursue business degrees. 2% grads pursue medical degrees. **Faculty:** Student/faculty ratio 9:1. 354 full-time faculty, 0% hold PhDs, 16% are are members of minority groups, 40% are women. 0% of classes are taught by teaching assistants.

ACADEMICS

Degrees: associate, bachelor's, certificate, diploma, doctoral/professional, doctoral/research, doctoral, master's, postbachelor's certificate, post-master's certificate. **Classes:** Most classes have 10-19 students. Most lab/discussion sessions have fewer than 10 students. **Most popular majors:** Speech Communication and Rhetoric; Architectural Engineering Technology/ Technician; Psychology. **Special Study Options:** cooperative education program, cross-registration, distance learning, double major, dual enrollment, English as a Second Language (ESL), exchange student program (domestic), honors program, independent study, internships, liberal arts/career combination, student-designed major, study abroad, teacher certification program. Combined degree programs: BS Health Science/MS Physical Therapy. **Disability Services:** Special programs offered to physically disabled students, including note-taking services, reader services, tutors.

FACILITIES

Housing: Coed dorms, special housing for disabled students, women's dorms, apartments for single students, Honors Housing. **Special Academic Facilities/ Equipment:** Museum of presidential memorabilia, Art Gallery, off-campus child care center for student teaching, learning skills and language lab, audio-visual aids center, 8,000-acre environmental center. **Computers:** Students can register for classes online. Administrative functions (other than registration) can be performed online.

CAMPUS LIFE

Environment: Metropolis. **Activities:** Choral groups, concert band, dance, drama/theater, jazz band, literary magazine, music ensembles, musical theater, opera, pep band, radio station, student government, student newspaper, symphony orchestra, television station, yearbook. 93 registered organizations, 22 honor societies, 7 religious organizations. 16 fraternities, 14 sororities. **Athletics (Intercollegiate):** *Men:* baseball, basketball, cross-country, golf, lacrosse, soccer, tennis, track/field (outdoor), track/field (indoor). *Women:* basketball, cross-country, golf, soccer, softball, tennis, track/field (outdoor), track/field (indoor), volleyball. **On-Campus Highlights:** Museum of American Political Life, Art Gallery, Sports Center, Java City Coffee House, Hawk's Nest.

ADMISSIONS

Freshman Academic Profile: 76% from public high schools. **Reported SAT (pre-2016 redesign) scores:** SAT Math middle 50% range 470-580. SAT Critical Reading middle 50% range 470-580. **Concordant SAT scores:** SAT Math middle 50% range 510–600. ACT middle 50% range 20-25. Minimum paper TOEFL 550. **Basis for Candidate Selection:** *Very important factors considered include:* rigor of secondary school record. *Important factors considered include:* class rank, academic GPA, standardized test scores. *Other factors considered include:* application essay, recommendation(s), interview, extracurricular activities, talent/ability, character/personal qualities. **Freshman Admission Requirements:** High school diploma is required and GED is accepted. *Academic units required:* 4 English, 2 math, 2 science, 2 social studies, 2 history, 4 academic electives. *Academic units recommended:* 3 math, 3 science, 2 foreign language. **Freshman Admission Statistics:** 15,093 applied, 63.51% admitted, 15% enrolled. **Transfer Admission Requirements:** college transcript(s), Minimum college GPA of 2.2 required. Lowest grade transferable C-. **General Admission Information:** Application fee $35. Nonfall registration accepted. Admission may be deferred for a maximum of 1 year.

COSTS AND FINANCIAL AID

Annual tuition $35,036. Room and board $11,986. Required fees $2,754. Average book expense $800. **Required Forms and Deadlines:** FAFSA. **Notification of Awards:** Applicants will be notified of awards on a rolling basis beginning 3/1. **Types of Aid:** *Need-based scholarships/grants:* Federal Pell, FSEOG, State scholarships/grants, Private scholarships, College/university scholarship or grant aid from institutional funds. *Loans:* Direct Subsidized Stafford Loans, Direct Unsubsidized Stafford Loans, Direct PLUS loans, Federal Perkins Loans. *Student Employment:* Federal Work-Study Program available. Institutional employment available. **Financial Aid Statistics:** 97% freshmen, 95% undergrads receive any aid. **Criteria for awarding aid:** *Non-need-based:* Academics, Art, Athletics, Music/drama, State/district residency.

UNIVERSITY OF HAWAII AT HILO

200 West Kawili Street, Hilo, HI 96720-4091
Phone: 808-974-7414 • **Financial Aid Phone:** 808-974-7323
E-mail: uhhadm@hawaii.edu
Fax: 808-933-0861 • **ACT Code:** 904

This public school was founded in 1970. It has a 225-acre campus.

RATINGS

Admissions Selectivity Rating: 81   **Fire Safety Rating:** 60*   **Green Rating:** 60*

STUDENTS AND FACULTY

Enrollment: 3,385. **Student Body:** 59% female, 41% male, 35% out-of-state, 5% international. Asian 19%, African American 1%, Caucasian 24%, Hispanic 10%, Native American 1%, Pacific Islander 12%, Two or more races 27%, Race unknown <1%.
Retention and Graduation: 69% freshmen return for sophomore year. 12% freshmen graduate within 4 years. 36% freshmen graduate within 6 years. **Faculty:** Student/faculty ratio 14:1. 227 full-time faculty, 0% hold PhDs, 0% are are members of minority groups, 44% are women. 0% of classes are taught by teaching assistants.

ACADEMICS

Degrees: bachelor's, certificate, master's, postbachelor's certificate. **Classes:** Most classes have 10-19 students. **Most popular majors:** Psychology; Business, Management, Marketing, and Related Support Services. **Special Study Options:** cross-registration, distance learning, double major, dual enrollment, English as a Second Language (ESL), exchange student program (domestic), honors program, independent study, internships, student-designed major, study abroad, teacher certification program. **Disability Services:** Special programs offered to physically disabled students, including note-taking services, reader services, tape recorders, tutors. **Career Services:** Alumni network, Alumni services, Career assessment, Internships, Service Learning opportunities.

FACILITIES

Housing: Coed dorms, special housing for disabled students, apartments for married students, apartments for single students. 90% of campus accessible to physically diasbled. **Computers:** Students can register for classes online. Administrative functions (other than registration) can be performed online.

CAMPUS LIFE

Environment: Town. **Activities:** Choral groups, dance, drama/theater, jazz band, literary magazine, music ensembles, radio station, student government, student newspaper. 43 registered organizations, 4 religious organizations. **Athletics (Intercollegiate):** *Men:* baseball, basketball, cross-country, golf, tennis. *Women:* cross-country, softball, tennis, volleyball. **On-Campus Highlights:** University Classroom Building (opened Fall '02), University Campus Center Plaza (opening Sp '04), University Lava Landing (Student Cyber Lounge), University Mo'okini Library, University Theatre, Student Life Center Facilities (Opening Spr 08).

ADMISSIONS

Freshman Academic Profile: Average high school GPA 3.3. 17% in top 10% of high school class, 47% in top 25% of high school class, 82% in top 50% of high school class. **Reported SAT (pre-2016 redesign) scores:** SAT Math middle 50% range 440-600. SAT Critical Reading middle 50% range 440-560. **Concordant SAT scores:** SAT Math middle 50% range 480–620. ACT middle 50% range 17-24. Minimum paper TOEFL 500. **Basis for Candidate Selection:** *Very important factors considered include:* rigor of secondary school record. *Important factors considered include:* class rank, academic GPA, standardized test scores. *Other factors considered include:* application essay, recommendation(s), extracurricular activities, talent/ability. **Freshman Admission Requirements:** High school diploma is required and GED is accepted. *Academic units required:* 4 English, 3 math, 3 science, 3 science labs, 7 academic electives. *Academic units recommended:* 4 English, 4 math, 4 science, 3 science labs, 2 foreign language, 2 social studies, 2 history. **Freshman Admission Statistics:** 1,500 applied, 72.27% admitted, 44% enrolled. **Transfer Admission Requirements:** college transcript(s), Minimum college GPA of 2.0 required. Lowest grade transferable C. **General Admission Information:** Application fee $50. Priority deadline 3/1. Regular application deadline 7/1. Nonfall registration accepted. Admission may be deferred for a maximum of 1 semester.

COSTS AND FINANCIAL AID

Annual in-state tuition $5,640. Annual out-of-state tuition $17. Room and board $7,134. Required fees $304. Average book expense $1,017. **Required Forms and Deadlines:** FAFSA. **Notification of Awards:** Applicants will be notified of awards on a rolling basis beginning 4/12. **Types of Aid:** *Need-based scholarships/grants:* Federal Pell, FSEOG, State scholarships/grants, Private scholarships, College/university scholarship or grant aid from institutional funds. *Loans:* Federal Perkins Loans, State Loans. *Student Employment:* Federal Work-Study Program available. Institutional employment available. **Financial Aid Statistics:** 78% needy freshmen, 79% needy undergrads receive need-based scholarship or grant aid. 15% freshmen, 17% undergrads receive non-need-based scholarship or grant aid. 56% freshmen, 65% undergrads receive need-based self-help aid. 3% freshmen, 3% undergrads receive athletic scholarships. **Criteria for awarding aid:** *Need-based:* Academics. *Non-need-based:* Academics, Art, Athletics, Leadership, Minority status, Music/drama.

UNIVERSITY OF HAWAII AT MANOA

2600 Campus Road, Honolulu, HI 96822
Phone: 808-956-8975 • **Financial Aid Phone:** 808-956-7251
E-mail: manoa.admissions@hawaii.edu • **CEEB Code:** 4867
Fax: 808-956-4148 • **Website:** http://manoa.hawaii.edu • **ACT Code:** 902

This public school was founded in 1907. It has a 320-acre campus.

RATINGS

Admissions Selectivity Rating: 82   **Fire Safety Rating:** 89   **Green Rating:** 60*

STUDENTS AND FACULTY

Enrollment: 12,767. **Student Body:** 55% female, 45% male, 26% out-of-state, 3% international (67 countries represented). Asian 41%, African American 2%, Caucasian 19%, Hispanic 2%, Native American <1%, Pacific Islander 17%, Two or more races 16%, Race unknown <1%.
Retention and Graduation: 77% freshmen return for sophomore year. 25% freshmen graduate within 4 years. 58% freshmen graduate within 6 years. **Faculty:** Student/faculty ratio 10:1. 1,148 full-time faculty, 90% hold PhDs, 44% are are members of minority groups, 45% are women.

ACADEMICS

Degrees: bachelor's, doctoral/professional, doctoral/research, master's, postbachelor's certificate. **Classes:** Most classes have 10-19 students. Most lab/discussion sessions have 10-19 students. **Most popular majors:** Biology/Biological Sciences; Psychology; Registered Nursing/Registered Nurse. **Special Study Options:** cooperative education program, distance learning, double major, English as a Second Language (ESL), exchange student program (domestic), honors program, independent study, internships, student-designed major, study abroad, teacher certification program. **Honors Programs:** Selected Studies Program Combined degree programs: Architecture. **Disability Services:** Special programs offered to physically disabled students, including note-taking services, reader services, tape recorders. **Career Services:** Alumni services, Career/job search classes, Career assessment, Internships. Cooperative Education and internships Research has shown that out of classroom experiences are positively linked to academic persistence and educational attainment. Early career work-based experiences helps students with career clarification and academic pursuits.

FACILITIES

Housing: Coed dorms, special housing for disabled students, apartments for married students, apartments for single students. 40% of campus accessible to physically diasbled. **Special Academic Facilities/Equipment:** UH Art and Commons Galleries, John Young Museum, John F. Kennedy Theatre, Lyon Arboretum, Waikiki Aquarium, Sunset (travel industry) Library, Chuck Gee Technology Learning Center, Advanced Computing Research Laboratory, Environmental Engineering Lab, Hawaii Center for Advanced Communications, Coral Reef Science Laboratory, traditionally designed Korean Studies Building, Coconut Island marine biology labs, Wong Audio-Visual Center, language lab, speech and hearing and dental hygiene clinics, law library, Hawaiian lo'i(garden), electron microscope and laser laboratories, ship and submersible research fleet, and Maui Super Computer, Jakuan Tea House. **Computers:** Students can register for classes online. Administrative functions (other than registration) can be performed online.

CAMPUS LIFE

Environment: Metropolis. **Activities:** Choral groups, concert band, dance, drama/theater, jazz band, literary magazine, marching band, music ensembles, musical theater, pep band, radio station, student government, student newspaper, student-run film society, symphony orchestra, Campus Ministries, Student Organization. 161 registered organizations, 7 honor societies, 24 religious organizations. 3 fraternities, 2 sororities **Athletics (Intercollegiate):** *Men:* baseball, basketball, cheerleading, diving, football, golf, sailing, swimming, tennis, volleyball. *Women:* basketball, cheerleading, cross-country, diving, golf, sailing, soccer, softball, swimming, tennis, track/field (outdoor), track/field (indoor), volleyball, water polo. **On-Campus Highlights:** Campus Center, Queen Lili'uokalani Ctr for Student Svcs, Quad Courtyard, Sinclair Library, Hamilton Library. **Environmental Initiatives:** Creation & convening of Manoa Sustainability Corps.

ADMISSIONS

Freshman Academic Profile: Average high school GPA 3.5. 26% in top 10% of high school class, 55% in top 25% of high school class, 87% in top 50% of high school class. **Reported SAT (pre-2016 redesign) scores:** SAT Math middle 50% range 490-610. SAT Critical Reading middle 50% range 480-580. SAT Writing middle 50% range 470-570. **Concordant SAT scores:** SAT EBRW middle 50% 530–630. SAT Math middle 50% range 520–630. ACT middle 50% range 21-26. Minimum internet-based TOEFL 61. Minimum paper TOEFL 500. **Basis for Candidate Selection:** *Very important factors considered include:* rigor of secondary school record, academic GPA, standardized test scores. *Important factors considered include:* class rank, state residency. *Other factors considered include:* application essay, recommendation(s), interview, extracurricular activities, talent/ability, geographical residence. **Freshman Admission Requirements:** High school diploma is required and GED is accepted. *Academic units required:* 4 English, 3 math, 3 science, 3 social studies, 5 academic electives. **Freshman Admission Statistics:** 7,861 applied, 80.09% admitted, 31% enrolled. **Transfer Admission Requirements:** college transcript(s), Minimum college GPA of 2.5 required. Lowest grade transferable D. **General Admission Information:** Application fee $70. Priority deadline 1/5. Regular application deadline 3/1. Nonfall registration accepted.

COSTS AND FINANCIAL AID

Annual in-state tuition $10,872. Annual out-of-state tuition $32,904. Required fees $860. Average book expense $1,012. **Required Forms and Deadlines:** FAFSA. **Notification of Awards:** Applicants will be notified of awards on a rolling basis beginning 4/1. **Types of Aid:** *Need-based scholarships/grants:* Federal Pell, FSEOG, State scholarships/grants, Private scholarships, College/university scholarship or grant aid from institutional funds. *Loans:* Direct Subsidized Stafford Loans, Direct Unsubsidized Stafford Loans, Direct PLUS loans, Federal Perkins Loans, State Loans. *Student Employment:* Federal Work-Study Program available. Institutional employment available. **Financial Aid Statistics:** 98% needy freshmen, 93% needy undergrads receive need-based scholarship or grant aid. 25% freshmen, 23% undergrads receive non-need-based scholarship or grant aid. 53% freshmen, 63% undergrads receive need-based self-help aid. 2% freshmen, 2% undergrads receive athletic scholarships. 62% freshmen, 59% undergrads receive any aid. Average cumulative indebtedness $24,225. **Criteria for awarding aid:** *Need-based:* Academics. *Non-need-based:* Academics, Alumni affiliation, Art, Athletics, Leadership, Music/drama, State/district residency.

UNIVERSITY OF HAWAII—WEST OAHU

91-1001 Farrington Hwy, Kapolei, HI 96707
Phone: 808-689-2900 • **Financial Aid Phone:** 808-454-4700
E-mail: uhwo.admissions@hawaii.edu • **CEEB Code:** 1042
Fax: 808-689-2901 • **Website:** www.uhwo.hawaii.edu • **ACT Code:** 6465

This public school was founded in 1976.

RATINGS

Admissions Selectivity Rating: 71   **Fire Safety Rating:** 60*   **Green Rating:** 60*

STUDENTS AND FACULTY

Enrollment: 1,950. **Student Body:** 67% female, 33% male, 2% out-of-state, <1% international (16 countries represented). Asian 41%, African American

1%, Caucasian 14%, Hispanic 1%, Native American <1%, Pacific Islander 27%, Two or more races 14%, Race unknown <1%.
Retention and Graduation: 67% freshmen return for sophomore year.
Faculty: Student/faculty ratio 18:1. 51 full-time faculty, 92% hold PhDs, 51% are are members of minority groups, 41% are women. 0% of classes are taught by teaching assistants.

ACADEMICS

Degrees: bachelor's, certificate. **Classes:** Most classes have 10-19 students. Most lab/discussion sessions have 20-29 students. **Most popular majors:** Psychology; Business/Commerce; Elementary Education and Teaching. **Special Study Options:** distance learning, double major, teacher certification program. **Disability Services:** Special programs offered to physically disabled students, including note-taking services, reader services. **Career Services:** The Senior Practicum is an internship course which students complete in their senior year. It serves as a culminating experience through on-the-job learning and is an excellent opportunity to develop a network of contacts for future work or research.

FACILITIES

Housing: 100% of campus accessible to physically diasbled. **Computers:** 10% of classrooms, 30% of common outdoor areas have wireless network access. Students can register for classes online.

CAMPUS LIFE

Environment: Town. **Activities:** student government 12 registered organizations, 1 honor society. **Environmental Initiatives:** All buildings being constructed at new campus are LEED Silver Certified or above.

ADMISSIONS

Freshman Academic Profile: 74% from public high schools. Minimum internet-based TOEFL 79. Minimum paper TOEFL 550. **Basis for Candidate Selection:** *Very important factors considered include:* academic GPA. *Important factors considered include:* rigor of secondary school record. *Other factors considered include:* standardized test scores, application essay, recommendation(s), interview, extracurricular activities, first generation, geographical residence, state residency. **Freshman Admission Requirements:** High school diploma is required and GED is accepted. *Academic units required:* 4 English, 3 math, 3 science, 3 social studies, 5 academic electives, and 4 units from above areas or other academic areas. **Freshman Admission Statistics:** 908 applied, 51.43% admitted, 64% enrolled. Minimum college GPA of 2.0 required. Lowest grade transferable D. **General Admission Information:** Application fee $50. Priority deadline 3/1. Regular application deadline 8/1. Nonfall registration accepted. Admission may be deferred for a maximum of 1 semester.

COSTS AND FINANCIAL AID

Annual in-state tuition $5,592. Annual out-of-state tuition $16,656. **Required Forms and Deadlines:** FAFSA. **Notification of Awards:** Applicants will be notified of awards on a rolling basis beginning 4/15. **Types of Aid:** *Need-based scholarships/grants:* Federal Pell, FSEOG, State scholarships/grants, Private scholarships. *Loans:* Direct Subsidized Stafford Loans, Direct Unsubsidized Stafford Loans, Direct PLUS loans. *Student Employment:* Federal Work-Study Program available. Institutional employment available. **Financial Aid Statistics:** 40% needy freshmen, 69% needy undergrads receive need-based scholarship or grant aid. 70% freshmen, 10% undergrads receive non-need-based scholarship or grant aid. 20% freshmen, 62% undergrads receive need-based self-help aid. 0% freshmen, 0% undergrads receive athletic scholarships. **Criteria for awarding aid:** *Need-based:* Academics. *Non-need-based:* Academics.

UNIVERSITY OF HOUSTON

Office of Admissions, Houston, TX 77204-2023
Phone: 713-743-1010 • **Financial Aid Phone:** 713-743-1010
E-mail: admissions@uh.edu • **CEEB Code:** 6870
Fax: 713-743-7542 • **Website:** www.uh.edu • **ACT Code:** 4236

This public school was founded in 1927. It has a 551-acre campus.

RATINGS

Admissions Selectivity Rating: 88   **Fire Safety Rating:** 93   **Green Rating:** 87

STUDENTS AND FACULTY

Enrollment: 34,688. **Student Body:** 49% female, 51% male, 2% out-of-state, 4% international (117 countries represented). Asian 22%, African American 10%, Caucasian 25%, Hispanic 33%, Native American <1%, Pacific Islander <1%, Two or more races 3%, Race unknown 1%.
Retention and Graduation: 85% freshmen return for sophomore year. 23% freshmen graduate within 4 years. 51% freshmen graduate within 6 years.
Faculty: Student/faculty ratio 21:1. 1,524 full-time faculty, 85% hold PhDs, 28% are are members of minority groups, 40% are women. 1% of classes are taught by teaching assistants.

ACADEMICS

Degrees: bachelor's, doctoral/professional, doctoral/research, master's. **Classes:** Most classes have 20-29 students. Most lab/discussion sessions have 20-29 students. **Most popular majors:** Business Administration and Management; Biology/Biological Sciences; Psychology. **Special Study Options:** Accelerated program, cooperative education program, cross-registration, distance learning, double major, dual enrollment, English as a Second Language (ESL), exchange student program (domestic), honors program, independent study, internships, study abroad, teacher certification program, weekend college, Academic Enrichment programs, certification programs, affiliated studies, and continuing education. **Honors Programs:** The Honors College at the University of Houston is a nationally recognized, intellectually stimulating learning community. As a vibrant, leading presence within the university, The Honors College attracts highly talented and motivated students and educators to a collegial environment where tradition is honored and possibilities are both realized and created. Combined degree programs: JD/MBA, MBA/MA, MBA/MIE, MBA/MSW. **Disability Services:** Special programs offered to physically disabled students, including note-taking services, reader services, tape recorders, tutors. **Career Services:** Alumni network, Alumni services, Career/job search classes, Career assessment, Internships. The Campus Recruitment program is the one we are most proud of. **FACILITIES**
Housing: Coed dorms, special housing for disabled students, fraternity/sorority housing, apartments for married students, apartments for single students, Special housing for honors students, upper level and graduate students. Cambridge Oaks and Cullen Oaks Apartments. 98% of campus accessible to physically diasbled. **Special Academic Facilities/Equipment:** Art gallery, language lab, human development lab school, University Hilton (staffed in part by students in Coll. of Hotel and Restaurant Management), opera studio. **Computers:** 100% of classrooms, 25% of dorms, 100% of libraries, 25% of dining areas, 100% of student union, 25% of common outdoor areas have wireless network access. Students can register for classes online. Administrative functions (other than registration) can be performed online.

CAMPUS LIFE

Environment: Metropolis. **Activities:** Choral groups, concert band, dance, drama/theater, jazz band, literary magazine, marching band, music ensembles, musical theater, opera, pep band, radio station, student government, student newspaper, student-run film society, symphony orchestra, television station, yearbook, Campus Ministries, Student Organization. 350 registered organizations, 25 honor societies, 39 religious organizations. 21 fraternities, 19 sororities. **Athletics (Intercollegiate):** *Men:* baseball, basketball, cross-country, football, golf, track/field (outdoor), track/field (indoor). *Women:* basketball, cross-country, diving, soccer, softball, swimming, tennis, track/field (outdoor), track/field (indoor), volleyball. **On-Campus Highlights:** University Center, Campus Recreation and Wellness Center, University Center Satellite, Blaffer Gallery, Campus Activities. **Environmental Initiatives:** Education through communications, events, campus as a living laboratory.

ADMISSIONS

Freshman Academic Profile: 32% in top 10% of high school class, 66% in top 25% of high school class, 89% in top 50% of high school class. 92% from public high schools. **Reported SAT (pre-2016 redesign) scores:** SAT Math middle 50% range 530-640. SAT Critical Reading middle 50% range 510-610. **Concordant SAT scores:** SAT Math middle 50% range 560–660. ACT middle 50% range 23-28. Minimum internet-based TOEFL 79. Minimum paper TOEFL 550. **Basis for Candidate Selection:** *Very important factors considered include:* rigor of secondary school record, class rank, standardized test scores. *Important factors considered include:* academic GPA. *Other factors considered include:* application essay, recommendation(s), extracurricular activities, talent/ability, first generation, volunteer work, work experience, level of applicant's interest. **Freshman Admission Requirements:** High school diploma is required and GED is accepted. *Academic units required:* 4 English, 4 math, 4 science, 4 social studies. *Academic units recommended:* 2 science labs, 2 foreign language, 1 computer science, 1 visual/performing arts. **Freshman Admission Statistics:** 19,860 applied, 58.54% admitted, 38% enrolled. **Transfer Admission Requirements:** college transcript(s), Minimum college GPA of 2.0 required. Lowest grade transferable C-. **General Admission Information:** Application fee $50. Priority deadline 12/1. Regular application deadline 7/1. Regular notification 4/15. Nonfall registration accepted.

COSTS AND FINANCIAL AID

Annual in-state tuition $10,671. Annual out-of-state tuition $25,911. Room and board $9,830. Required fees $982. Average book expense $1,300. **Required Forms and Deadlines:** FAFSA. **Notification of Awards:** Applicants will be notified of awards on a rolling basis beginning 5/1. **Types of Aid:** *Need-based scholarships/grants:* Federal Pell, FSEOG, State scholarships/grants, Private scholarships, College/university scholarship or grant aid from institutional funds. *Loans:* Direct Subsidized Stafford Loans, Direct Unsubsidized Stafford Loans, Direct PLUS loans, Federal Perkins Loans, State Loans. *Student Employment:* Federal Work-Study Program available. Institutional employment available. **Financial Aid Statistics:** 90% needy freshmen, 78% needy undergrads receive need-based scholarship or grant aid. 7% freshmen, 4% undergrads receive non-need-based scholarship or grant aid. 52% freshmen, 64% undergrads receive need-based self-help aid. 1% freshmen, 1% undergrads receive athletic scholarships. 87% freshmen, 77% undergrads receive any aid. 51% undergrads borrow to pay for school. Average cumulative indebtedness $23,665. **Criteria for awarding aid:** *Need-based:* Academics, Leadership. *Non-need-based:* Academics, Alumni affiliation, Art, Athletics, Job skills, Leadership, Music/drama, State/district residency.

UNIVERSITY OF HOUSTON—CLEAR LAKE

2700 Bay Area Boulevard, Houston, TX 77058-1098
Phone: 281-283-2500 • **Financial Aid Phone:** 281-283-2480
E-mail: admissions@uhcl.edu • **CEEB Code:** 6916
Fax: 281-283-2522

This public school was founded in 1974. It has a 524-acre campus.

RATINGS

Admissions Selectivity Rating: 60*   **Fire Safety Rating:** 60*   **Green Rating:** 60*

STUDENTS AND FACULTY

Enrollment: 4,689. **Student Body:** 68% female, 32% male, 0% out-of-state, 2% international (45 countries represented). Asian 6%, African American 9%, Caucasian 49%, Hispanic 32%, Native American <1%, Pacific Islander <1%, Two or more races <1%, Race unknown 1%.
Faculty: Student/faculty ratio 17:1. 247 full-time faculty, 86% hold PhDs, 27% are are members of minority groups, 46% are women.

ACADEMICS

Degrees: bachelor's, certificate, doctoral, master's, postbachelor's certificate, post-master's certificate. **Classes:** Most classes have 10-19 students. **Most popular majors:** Accounting; Psychology; Multi-/Interdisciplinary Studies. **Special Study Options:** cooperative education program, distance learning, double major, dual enrollment, independent study, internships, student-designed major, study abroad, teacher certification program, weekend college. Combined degree programs: BS/MS in Professional Accounting. **Disability Services:** Special programs offered to physically disabled students, including note-taking services, reader services, tape recorders, tutors. **Career Services:** Alumni network, Alumni services, Career/job search classes, Career assessment, Internships.

FACILITIES

Housing: Privatized Housing Apartments. 100% of campus accessible to physically diasbled. **Special Academic Facilities/Equipment:** Student Art Gallery, Fitness Center/Fitness Zone. **Computers:** 100% of classrooms, 100% of libraries, 100% of dining areas, 100% of student union, 100% of common outdoor areas have wireless network access. Students can register for classes online. Administrative functions (other than registration) can be performed online.

CAMPUS LIFE

Environment: Metropolis. **Activities:** literary magazine, student government, student newspaper, student-run film society, Student Organization. 70 registered organizations, 16 honor societies, 5 religious organizations. **On-Campus Highlights:** Student Serivce Building, Bayou Building, Library, Delta Building, Computer Labs.

ADMISSIONS

Minimum internet-based TOEFL 79. Minimum paper TOEFL 550. **Transfer Admission Requirements:** college transcript(s), standardized test scores, statement of good standing from prior institution(s). Minimum college GPA of 2.0 required. Lowest grade transferable D-. **General Admission Information:** Application fee $45. Regular application deadline 6/1. Nonfall registration accepted. Admission may be deferred for a maximum of 1 year.

COSTS AND FINANCIAL AID

Annual in-state tuition $5,142. Annual out-of-state tuition $16,992. Required fees $1,372. **Types of Aid:** *Need-based scholarships/grants:* Federal Pell,

FSEOG, State scholarships/grants, College/university scholarship or grant aid from institutional funds. *Loans:* Direct Subsidized Stafford Loans, Direct Unsubsidized Stafford Loans, Direct PLUS loans, Federal Perkins Loans, State Loans. *Student Employment:* Federal Work-Study Program available. Institutional employment available. **Financial Aid Statistics:** 41% undergrads receive any aid. **Criteria for awarding aid:** *Need-based:* Academics, Art, Leadership, Minority status.

UNIVERSITY OF HOUSTON—DOWNTOWN

One Main Street, Office of Admissions, Houston, TX 77002-1001
Phone: 713-221-8522 • **Financial Aid Phone:** 713-221-8041
E-mail: uhdadmit@uhd.edu
Fax: 713-221-8157 • **Website:** www.uhd.edu

This public school was founded in 1974.

RATINGS

Admissions Selectivity Rating: 73   **Fire Safety Rating:** 60*   **Green Rating:** 61

STUDENTS AND FACULTY

Enrollment: 13,101. **Student Body:** 60% female, 40% male, 1% out-of-state, 5% international (65 countries represented). Asian 9%, African American 23%, Caucasian 17%, Hispanic 43%, Native American <1%, Pacific Islander <1%, Two or more races 1%, Race unknown 1%.
Retention and Graduation: 66% freshmen return for sophomore year. 1% freshmen graduate within 4 years. 13% freshmen graduate within 6 years.
Faculty: Student/faculty ratio 20:1. 352 full-time faculty, 84% hold PhDs, 35% are are members of minority groups, 49% are women. 0% of classes are taught by teaching assistants.

ACADEMICS

Degrees: bachelor's, master's, postbachelor's certificate. **Classes:** Most classes have 20-29 students. Most lab/discussion sessions have 20-29 students. **Most popular majors:** Psychology; Multi-/Interdisciplinary Studies; Accounting. **Special Study Options:** cooperative education program, distance learning, double major, dual enrollment, English as a Second Language (ESL), honors program, independent study, internships, study abroad, teacher certification program, weekend college. **Career Services:** Alumni services, Career/job search classes, Career assessment, Internships.

FACILITIES

Housing: 95% of campus accessible to physically diasbled. **Computers:** Students can register for classes online. Administrative functions (other than registration) can be performed online.

CAMPUS LIFE

Environment: Metropolis. **Activities:** drama/theater, jazz band, literary magazine, student government, student newspaper. 52 registered organizations, 3 honor societies, 2 religious organizations. 4 fraternities, 4 sororities. **Athletics (Intercollegiate):** *Men:* badminton, basketball, bowling, football, soccer, softball, tennis, volleyball, weight lifting. *Women:* badminton, basketball, bowling, soccer, softball, tennis, volleyball, weight lifting. **On-Campus Highlights:** Special Events Center, O' Kane Gallery, Food court and adjoining Coffee House, Jesse H. Jones Student Life Center, O' Kane Theatre.

ADMISSIONS

Freshman Academic Profile: 6% in top 10% of high school class, 29% in top 25% of high school class, 74% in top 50% of high school class. 86% from public high schools. **Reported SAT (pre-2016 redesign) scores:** SAT Math middle 50% range 408-540. SAT Critical Reading middle 50% range 390-480. SAT Writing middle 50% range 390-470. **Concordant SAT scores:** SAT EBRW middle 50% 440-530. SAT Math middle 50% range 450-570. ACT middle 50% range 16-20. Minimum internet-based TOEFL 80. Minimum paper TOEFL 550. **Basis for Candidate Selection:** *Very important factors considered include:* class rank, academic GPA, standardized test scores. *Important factors considered include:* rigor of secondary school record. **Freshman Admission Requirements:** High school diploma is required and GED is accepted. *Academic units required:* 4 English, 4 math, 4 science, 2 foreign language, 2 social studies, 2 history, 1 visual/performing arts. **Freshman Admission Statistics:** 3,460 applied, 77.63% admitted, 33% enrolled. **Transfer Admission Requirements:** college transcript(s), Lowest grade transferable C. **General Admission Information:** Application fee $35. Regular application deadline 7/1. Nonfall registration accepted. Admission may be deferred.

COSTS AND FINANCIAL AID

Annual in-state tuition $5,790. Annual out-of-state tuition $17,490. Required fees $1,148. **Required Forms and Deadlines:** FAFSA. **Notification of Awards:** Applicants will be notified of awards on a rolling basis beginning 2/1. **Types of Aid:** *Need-based scholarships/grants:* Federal Pell, FSEOG,

State scholarships/grants, Private scholarships, College/university scholarship or grant aid from institutional funds. *Loans:* Direct Subsidized Stafford Loans, Direct Unsubsidized Stafford Loans, Direct PLUS loans, State Loans. *Student Employment:* Federal Work-Study Program available. Institutional employment available. **Financial Aid Statistics:** 85% needy freshmen, 75% needy undergrads receive need-based scholarship or grant aid. 0% freshmen, 5% undergrads receive non-need-based scholarship or grant aid. 2% freshmen, 3% undergrads receive need-based self-help aid. 0% freshmen, 0% undergrads receive athletic scholarships. 81% freshmen, 78% undergrads receive any aid. 52% undergrads borrow to pay for school. Average cumulative indebtedness $22,812. **Criteria for awarding aid:** *Need-based:* Academics, Leadership. *Non-need-based:* Leadership.

UNIVERSITY OF HOUSTON—VICTORIA

Admissions and Records, Victoria, TX 77901-4450
Phone: 361-570-4110 • **Financial Aid Phone:** 316-570-4131
E-mail: admissions@uhv.edu
Fax: 361-580-5500 • **Website:** www.uhv.edu

This public school was founded in 1973.

RATINGS
Admissions Selectivity Rating: 73   **Fire Safety Rating:** 60*   **Green Rating:** 60*

STUDENTS AND FACULTY
Enrollment: 2,991. **Student Body:** 66% female, 34% male, 2% international (39 countries represented). Asian 8%, African American 16%, Caucasian 37%, Hispanic 34%, Native American <1%, Pacific Islander <1%, Two or more races 2%, Race unknown 1%.
Retention and Graduation: 55% freshmen return for sophomore year.
Faculty: Student/faculty ratio 18:1. 136 full-time faculty, 87% hold PhDs, 32% are are members of minority groups, 49% are women. 0% of classes are taught by teaching assistants.

ACADEMICS
Degrees: bachelor's, master's, postbachelor's certificate, post-master's certificate. **Classes:** Most classes have 20-29 students. **Most popular majors:** Education; Multi-/Interdisciplinary Studies; Business/Commerce. **Special Study Options:** distance learning, double major, honors program, independent study, internships, study abroad, teacher certification program. **Disability Services:** Special programs offered to physically disabled students, including note-taking services, tutors. **Career Services:** Alumni services, Career/job search classes, Career assessment, Internships.

FACILITIES
Housing: Coed dorms. 100% of campus accessible to physically diasbled. **Special Academic Facilities/Equipment:** Museum of Coastal Bend. **Computers:** Students can register for classes online. Administrative functions (other than registration) can be performed online.

CAMPUS LIFE
Environment: City. **Activities:** student government, Student Organization. **Athletics (Intercollegiate):** *Men:* baseball. *Women:* softball.

ADMISSIONS
Reported SAT (pre-2016 redesign) scores: SAT Math middle 50% range 390-480. SAT Critical Reading middle 50% range 380-460. **Concordant SAT scores:** SAT Math middle 50% range 430–510. ACT middle 50% range 15-19. Minimum paper TOEFL 79. **Basis for Candidate Selection:** *Very important factors considered include:* rigor of secondary school record. *Important factors considered include:* class rank, academic GPA, standardized test scores. *Other factors considered include:* application essay, recommendation(s), interview, extracurricular activities, talent/ability, character/personal qualities, first generation, alumni/ae relation, geographical residence, state residency, level of applicant's interest. **Freshman Admission Requirements:** High school diploma is required and GED is accepted. **Freshman Admission Statistics:** 3,950 applied, 55.62% admitted, 16% enrolled. **Transfer Admission Requirements:** college transcript(s), standardized test scores, Minimum college GPA of 2.0 required. Lowest grade transferable C. **General Admission Information:** Regular notification 4/15. Nonfall registration accepted. Admission may be deferred.

COSTS AND FINANCIAL AID
Annual in-state tuition $9,632. Annual out-of-state tuition $19,264. Room and board $7,853. Required fees $1,567. Average book expense $1,129. **Required Forms and Deadlines:** FAFSA, Institution's own financial aid form. **Notification of Awards:** Applicants will be notified of awards on a rolling basis beginning 3/30. **Types of Aid:** *Need-based scholarships/grants:* Federal Pell, FSEOG, State scholarships/grants, Private scholarships, College/university

---

scholarship or grant aid from institutional funds. *Loans:* Direct Subsidized Stafford Loans, Direct Unsubsidized Stafford Loans, Direct PLUS loans, State Loans. *Student Employment:* Federal Work-Study Program available. Institutional employment available. **Financial Aid Statistics:** 73% undergrads receive any aid. **Criteria for awarding aid:** *Need-based:* Academics. *Non-need-based:* Academics, Athletics, Leadership, State/district residency.

UNIVERSITY OF IDAHO

UI Admissions Office, Moscow, ID 83844-4264
Phone: 208-885-6326 • **Financial Aid Phone:** 208-885-6312
E-mail: admappl@uidaho.edu • **CEEB Code:** 4843
Fax: 208-885-9119 • **Website:** http://www.uidaho.edu/ • **ACT Code:** 928

This public school was founded in 1889. It has a 12500-acre campus.

RATINGS
Admissions Selectivity Rating: 83   **Fire Safety Rating:** 89   **Green Rating:** 76

STUDENTS AND FACULTY
Enrollment: 5,479. **Student Body:** 46% female, 54% male, 22% out-of-state, 6% international (77 countries represented). Asian 1%, African American 2%, Caucasian 75%, Hispanic 10%, Native American 1%, Pacific Islander <1%, Two or more races 4%, Race unknown 2%.
Retention and Graduation: 77% freshmen return for sophomore year. 30% freshmen graduate within 4 years. 56 13% grads go on to further study within 1 year. **Faculty:** Student/faculty ratio 16:1. 596 full-time faculty, 84% hold PhDs, 14% are are members of minority groups, 36% are women. 9% of classes are taught by teaching assistants.

ACADEMICS
Degrees: bachelor's, certificate, doctoral/professional, doctoral/research, master's, postbachelor's certificate, post-master's certificate. **Classes:** Most classes have 10-19 students. Most lab/discussion sessions have 10-19 students. **Most popular majors:** Psychology; Mechanical Engineering; General Studies. **Special Study Options:** Accelerated program, cooperative education program, cross-registration, distance learning, double major, dual enrollment, English as a Second Language (ESL), exchange student program (domestic), honors program, independent study, internships, student-designed major, study abroad, teacher certification program. **Honors Programs:** Established in 1983, the University Honors Program offers a stimulating course of study and the advantages of an enriched learning community for over 500 students from all colleges and majors. The UHP's diverse curriculum, including special topic courses and innovative seminars, serves a variety of needs and interests. Beyond the classroom, the program's extracurricular opportunities include concerts, plays, films, lectures and other off-campus excursions that foster cultural enrichment, friendship, and learning. Honors classes offer opportunities to explore subjects and methods in significant depth– students find that their education and their academic performance are enhanced by strong mentoring relationships with faculty devoted to enabling each student to fulfill his or her potential, and by the lively, participation-based modes of learning in small classes. Lower-division honors core courses enable students to learn with their peers in small classes taught by honors faculty. Moreover, each year the program offers innovative upper-division seminars, with each class limited to fifteen students. Honors students are frequently interested in and encouraged to apply for exchanges to other American universities or to universities abroad. As part of a dynamic, broad-based education, members are also encouraged to participate in domestic or international exchange programs, and to take advantage of opportunities to engage in laboratory or field-based research programs as well as internships and other forms of cooperative education. Combined degree programs: BA/MA, Architecture. **Disability Services:** Special programs offered to physically disabled students, including note-taking services, reader services, tape recorders, tutors. **Career Services:** Alumni network, Alumni services, Career/job search classes, Career assessment, Internships, Regional alumni, Experiential learning.

FACILITIES
Housing: Coed dorms, special housing for disabled students, men's dorms, special housing for international students, women's dorms, fraternity/sorority housing, apartments for married students, apartments for single students. 87% of campus accessible to physically diasbled. **Special Academic Facilities/ Equipment:** On-campus preschool, experimental forest, electron microscope. **Computers:** 100% of classrooms, 100% of dorms, 100% of libraries, 100% of

dining areas, 100% of student union, have wireless network access. Students can register for classes online. Administrative functions (other than registration) can be performed online.

CAMPUS LIFE

Environment: Town. **Activities:** Choral groups, concert band, dance, drama/theater, jazz band, marching band, music ensembles, musical theater, opera, pep band, radio station, student government, student newspaper, student-run film society, symphony orchestra, television station, Campus Ministries, Student Organization. 190 registered organizations, 13 honor societies, 20 religious organizations. 18 fraternities, 9 sororities. **Athletics (Intercollegiate):** *Men:* basketball, cross-country, football, golf, track/field (outdoor), track/field (indoor). *Women:* basketball, cross-country, golf, soccer, swimming, track/field (outdoor), track/field (indoor), volleyball. **On-Campus Highlights:** Idaho Commons—food and meeting rooms, 18 hole golf course, Kibbie Dome—athletics, Student Recreation Center, Borah Theater, 6. Rec Center/Outdoors Program 7. Frisbee Golf Course 8. Religious Centers See our campus live with web cams at http://www.uidaho.edu/webcams. **Environmental Initiatives:** $35 mil ESCO for energy conservation projects currently underway.

ADMISSIONS

Freshman Academic Profile: Average high school GPA 3.4. 19% in top 10% of high school class, 44% in top 25% of high school class, 73% in top 50% of high school class. 90% from public high schools. **Reported SAT (pre-2016 redesign) scores:** SAT Math middle 50% range 460-580. SAT Critical Reading middle 50% range 470-590. SAT Writing middle 50% range 450-560. **Concordant SAT scores:** SAT EBRW middle 50% 510–630. SAT Math middle 50% range 500–600. ACT middle 50% range 21-27. Minimum internet-based TOEFL 70. Minimum paper TOEFL 525. **Basis for Candidate Selection:** *Very important factors considered include:* academic GPA, standardized test scores. **Freshman Admission Requirements:** High school diploma is required and GED is accepted. *Academic units required:* 4 English, 3 math, 3 science, 1 science lab, and 1 unit from above areas or other academic areas. **Freshman Admission Statistics:** 5,953 applied, 75.89% admitted, 37% enrolled. **Transfer Admission Requirements:** college transcript(s), Minimum college GPA of 2.0 required. Lowest grade transferable D. **General Admission Information:** Application fee $60. Priority deadline 2/15. Regular application deadline 8/1. Nonfall registration accepted. Admission may be deferred.

COSTS AND FINANCIAL AID

Annual in-state tuition $5,162. Annual out-of-state tuition $19,970. Room and board $8,354. Required fees $2,070. Average book expense $1,214. **Required Forms and Deadlines:** FAFSA. **Notification of Awards:** Applicants will be notified of awards on a rolling basis beginning 3/30. **Types of Aid:** *Need-based scholarships/grants:* Federal Pell, FSEOG, State scholarships/grants, Private scholarships, College/university scholarship or grant aid from institutional funds. *Loans:* Direct Subsidized Stafford Loans, Direct Unsubsidized Stafford Loans, Direct PLUS loans, Federal Perkins Loans, College/university loans from institutional funds. *Student Employment:* Federal Work-Study Program available. Institutional employment available. **Financial Aid Statistics:** 73% needy freshmen, 73% needy undergrads receive need-based scholarship or grant aid. 86% freshmen, 59% undergrads receive non-need-based scholarship or grant aid. 74% freshmen, 78% undergrads receive need-based self-help aid. 4% freshmen, 3% undergrads receive athletic scholarships. 90% freshmen, 80% undergrads receive any aid. 64% undergrads borrow to pay for school. Average cumulative indebtedness $26,539. **Criteria for awarding aid:** *Need-based:* Academics. *Non-need-based:* Academics, Alumni affiliation, Art, Athletics, Leadership, Minority status, Music/drama, State/district residency.

UNIVERSITY OF ILLINOIS AT CHICAGO

Suite 100, SSB, 1200 W. Harrison St., Chicago, IL 60607-7161
Phone: 312-996-4350 • **Financial Aid Phone:** 312-996-5563
E-mail: uicadmit@uic.edu • **CEEB Code:** 1851
Fax: 312-413-7628 • **Website:** http://www.uic.edu • **ACT Code:** 1155

This public school was founded in 1965. It has a 218-acre campus.

RATINGS

Admissions Selectivity Rating: 82   **Fire Safety Rating:** 98   **Green Rating:** 92

STUDENTS AND FACULTY

Enrollment: 17,804. **Student Body:** 50% female, 50% male, 3% out-of-state, 3% international (64 countries represented). Asian 22%, African American 8%, Caucasian 32%, Hispanic 31%, Native American <1%, Pacific Islander <1%, Two or more races 3%, Race unknown 1%.
Retention and Graduation: 80% freshmen return for sophomore year. 31% freshmen graduate within 4 years.

ACADEMICS

Degrees: bachelor's, doctoral/professional, doctoral/research, doctoral, master's, postbachelor's certificate, post-master's certificate. **Classes:** Most classes have 20-29 students. Most lab/discussion sessions have 20-29 students. **Most popular majors:** Psychology; Biology/Biological Sciences; Registered Nursing/Registered Nurse. **Special Study Options:** Accelerated program, cooperative education program, distance learning, double major, dual enrollment, exchange student program (domestic), honors program, independent study, internships, student-designed major, study abroad, teacher certification program. Combined degree programs: BA/MD, BA/DDS, MD/Phd, MD/MBA, MD/MPH, PharmD/Phd. **Disability Services:** Special programs offered to physically disabled students, including note-taking services, reader services, tape recorders, tutors. **Career Services:** Alumni network, Alumni services, Career/job search classes, Career assessment, Internships, Regional alumni.

FACILITIES

Housing: Coed dorms, special housing for disabled students, apartments for single students, honors floor, Presidential Awards House. 80% of campus accessible to physically diasbled. **Computers:** 95% of classrooms, 100% of dorms, 100% of libraries, 100% of dining areas, 100% of student union, have wireless network access. Students can register for classes online. Administrative functions (other than registration) can be performed online.

CAMPUS LIFE

Environment: Metropolis. **Activities:** Choral groups, concert band, drama/theater, jazz band, literary magazine, music ensembles, pep band, radio station, student government, student newspaper, Student Organization. 370 registered organizations, 10 honor societies, 33 religious organizations. 13 fraternities, 15 sororities. **Athletics (Intercollegiate):** *Men:* baseball, basketball, cross-country, diving, gymnastics, soccer, swimming, tennis, track/field (outdoor). *Women:* basketball, cross-country, diving, gymnastics, softball, swimming, tennis, track/field (outdoor), volleyball. **On-Campus Highlights:** Student Center East, Student Center West, UIC Pavilion, Student Services Building, Student Recreation Facility. **Environmental Initiatives:** establishment of Office of Sustainability.

ADMISSIONS

Freshman Academic Profile: Average high school GPA 3.3. 27% in top 10% of high school class, 60% in top 25% of high school class, 91% in top 50% of high school class. 60% from public high schools. **Reported SAT (pre-2016 redesign) scores:** SAT Math middle 50% range 510-650. SAT Critical Reading middle 50% range 480-580. SAT Writing middle 50% range 450-580. **Concordant SAT scores:** SAT EBRW middle 50% 520–640. SAT Math middle 50% range 540–670. ACT middle 50% range 21-27. Minimum internet-based TOEFL 80. Minimum paper TOEFL 550. **Basis for Candidate Selection:** *Very important factors considered include:* rigor of secondary school record, class rank, academic GPA, standardized test scores. *Important factors considered include:* application essay. *Other factors considered include:* recommendation(s), extracurricular activities, level of applicant's interest. **Freshman Admission Requirements:** High school diploma is required and GED is accepted. *Academic units required:* 4 English, 3 math, 3 science, 2 foreign language, 3 social studies. *Academic units recommended:* 4 math. **Freshman Admission Statistics:** 17,931 applied, 73.59% admitted, 25% enrolled. **Transfer Admission Requirements:** college transcript(s), Minimum college GPA of 2.5 required. **General Admission Information:** Application fee $50. Regular application deadline 1/15. Nonfall registration not accepted.

COSTS AND FINANCIAL AID

Annual in-state tuition $11,696. Annual out-of-state tuition $21,982. Room and board $11,342. Required fees $3,080. Average book expense $1,400. **Required Forms and Deadlines:** FAFSA. **Notification of Awards:** Applicants will be notified of awards on a rolling basis beginning 3/15. **Types of Aid:** *Need-based scholarships/grants:* Federal Pell, FSEOG, State scholarships/grants, Private scholarships, College/university scholarship or grant aid from institutional funds. *Loans:* Direct Subsidized Stafford Loans, Direct Unsubsidized Stafford Loans, Direct PLUS loans, Federal Perkins Loans, Federal Nursing Loans, College/university loans from institutional funds. *Student Employment:* Federal Work-Study Program available. Institutional employment available. **Financial Aid Statistics:** 84% needy freshmen, 81% needy undergrads receive need-based scholarship or grant aid. 5% freshmen, 3% undergrads receive non-need-based scholarship or grant aid. 70% freshmen, 77% undergrads receive need-based self-help aid. 1% freshmen, 1% undergrads receive athletic scholarships. 62% freshmen, 60% undergrads receive any aid. Average cumulative indebtedness $23,669. **Criteria for awarding aid:** *Need-based:* Music/drama. *Non-need-based:* Academics, Art, Athletics.

UNIVERSITY OF ILLINOIS AT URBANA-CHAMPAIGN

901 West Illinois Street, Urbana, IL 61801-3028
Phone: 217-333-0302 • **Financial Aid Phone:** 217-333-0100
E-mail: http://admissions.illinois.edu/contact_u • **CEEB Code:** 4607
Fax: 217-244-4614 • **Website:** illinois.edu • **ACT Code:** 1154

This public school was founded in 1867. It has a 4724-acre campus.

RATINGS

Admissions Selectivity Rating: 90   **Fire Safety Rating:** 60*   **Green Rating:** 97

STUDENTS AND FACULTY

Enrollment: 31,875. **Student Body:** 44% female, 56% male, 9% out-of-state, 15% international (114 countries represented). Asian 16%, African American 5%, Caucasian 51%, Hispanic 9%, Native American <1%, Pacific Islander <1%, Two or more races 3%, Race unknown 1%.
Retention and Graduation: 93% freshmen return for sophomore year. 69% freshmen graduate within 4 years. 84 **Faculty:** Student/faculty ratio 18:1. 1,928 full-time faculty, 93% hold PhDs, 26% are are members of minority groups, 34% are women.

ACADEMICS

Degrees: bachelor's, certificate, doctoral/professional, doctoral/research, master's, postbachelor's certificate, post-master's certificate. **Classes:** Most classes have 10-19 students. Most lab/discussion sessions have 20-29 students. **Special Study Options:** Accelerated program, cooperative education program, cross-registration, distance learning, double major, dual enrollment, English as a Second Language (ESL), exchange student program (domestic), honors program, independent study, internships, liberal arts/career combination, student-designed major, study abroad, teacher certification program, Jonathan Baldwin Turner Honors program, Campus Honors, Illinois Leadership & Entrepreneurial Programs. **Honors Programs:** Campus Honors Program, James Scholars Program. **Disability Services:** Special programs offered to physically disabled students, including note-taking services, reader services, tape recorders, tutors. **Career Services:** Alumni network, Alumni services, Career/job search classes, Career assessment, Internships, Regional alumni.

FACILITIES

Housing: Coed dorms, special housing for disabled students, men's dorms, special housing for international students, women's dorms, fraternity/sorority housing, apartments for married students, cooperative housing, apartments for single students, Living and Learning Communities housed within the residence halls; Private Certified Housing. 100% of campus accessible to physically diasbled. **Special Academic Facilities/Equipment:** Art, cultural and natural history museums, performing arts center, National Center for Supercomputing Applications, Beckman Institute, Siebel Computer Science Center, University Library (37 separate libraries and centers on campus), Japan House and Gardens, Assembly Hall for large concerts, Allerton Park and Conference Center, Arboretum, and the Illini Student Union. **Computers:** 85% of classrooms, 100% of dorms, 100% of libraries, 100% of dining areas, 100% of student union, 1% of common outdoor areas have wireless network access. Students can register for classes online. Administrative functions (other than registration) can be performed online.

CAMPUS LIFE

Environment: City. **Activities:** Choral groups, concert band, dance, drama/theater, jazz band, literary magazine, marching band, music ensembles, musical theater, opera, pep band, radio station, student government, student newspaper, student-run film society, symphony orchestra, television station, yearbook, Campus Ministries, Student Organization, Model UN. 1000 registered organizations, 30 honor societies, 95 religious organizations. 60 fraternities, 36 sororities. **Athletics (Intercollegiate): Men:** baseball, basketball, cheerleading, cross-country, football, golf, gymnastics, tennis, track/field (outdoor), wrestling. **Women:** basketball, cheerleading, cross-country, diving, golf, gymnastics, soccer, softball, swimming, tennis, track/field (outdoor), volleyball. **On-Campus Highlights:** Campus Town restaurants and shops, Krannert Center for Performing Arts, Assembly Hall, Multiple Campus Recreation Centers, Illini Student Union, On-campus Arboretum; The Japan House; extensive athletic facilities; historic round barns; Siebel Computer Science Center; spacious green space at the Central and Bardeen Quads; Papa Dels Pizza and Za's Italian Cafe. **Environmental Initiatives:** The state-of-the-art Business Instructional Facility at the University of Illinois has earned the world highest honor for sustainable, environmentally friendly construction and design. The year-old building is the first business facility at a public university anywhere in the world to earn platinum certification.

ADMISSIONS

Freshman Academic Profile: 59% in top 10% of high school class, 90% in top 25% of high school class, 99% in top 50% of high school class. **Reported SAT (pre-2016 redesign) scores:** SAT Math middle 50% range 700-790. SAT Critical Reading middle 50% range 590-690. SAT Writing middle 50% range 600-690. **Concordant SAT scores:** SAT EBRW middle 50% 650–730. SAT Math middle 50% range 730–800. ACT middle 50% range 26-32. Minimum internet-based TOEFL 80. **Basis for Candidate Selection:** *Very important factors considered include:* rigor of secondary school record, academic GPA. *Important factors considered include:* standardized test scores, application essay, extracurricular activities, talent/ability. *Other factors considered include:* class rank, character/personal qualities, first generation, geographical residence, state residency, racial/ethnic status, volunteer work, work experience. **Freshman Admission Requirements:** High school diploma is required and GED is accepted. *Academic units required:* 4 English, 2 science labs, 2 foreign language, 2 social studies, 2 academic electives. *Academic units recommended:* 4 English, 4 math, 4 science labs, 4 foreign language, 4 social studies, 4 academic electives. **Freshman Admission Statistics:** 3 applied, admitted, 33% enrolled. **Transfer Admission Requirements:** college transcript(s), essay or personal statement, Lowest grade transferable D. **General Admission Information:** Application fee $50. Priority deadline 11/1. Regular application deadline 12/1. Regular notification 2/13. Nonfall registration not accepted. Admission may be deferred for a maximum of 1 year.

COSTS AND FINANCIAL AID

Annual in-state tuition $12,036. Annual out-of-state tuition $27,196. Room and board $11,010. Required fees $3,662. Average book expense $1,200. **Required Forms and Deadlines:** FAFSA. **Notification of Awards:** Applicants will be notified of awards on a rolling basis beginning 3/15. **Types of Aid:** *Need-based scholarships/grants:* Federal Pell, FSEOG, State scholarships/grants, Private scholarships, College/university scholarship or grant aid from institutional funds, United Negro College Fund. *Loans:* Direct Subsidized Stafford Loans, Direct Unsubsidized Stafford Loans, Direct PLUS loans, Federal Perkins Loans, College/university loans from institutional funds. *Student Employment:* Federal Work-Study Program available. Institutional employment available. **Financial Aid Statistics:** 80% needy freshmen, 83% needy undergrads receive need-based scholarship or grant aid. 20% freshmen, 11% undergrads receive non-need-based scholarship or grant aid. 80% freshmen, 82% undergrads receive need-based self-help aid. 1% freshmen, 1% undergrads receive athletic scholarships. 50% undergrads borrow to pay for school. Average cumulative indebtedness $25,448. **Criteria for awarding aid:** *Need-based:* Academics, Art, Athletics, Leadership, Minority status, Music/drama. *Non-need-based:* Academics, Alumni affiliation, Art, Athletics, Leadership, Minority status, Music/drama, State/district residency.

UNIVERSITY OF ILLINOIS SPRINGFIELD

One University Plaza, Springfield, IL 62703-5407
Phone: 217-206-4847 • **Financial Aid Phone:** 217-206-6724
E-mail: admissions@uis.edu • **CEEB Code:** 834
Fax: 217-206-6620 • **Website:** www.uis.edu • **ACT Code:** 1137

This public school was founded in 1969. It has a 746-acre campus.

RATINGS

Admissions Selectivity Rating: 80   **Fire Safety Rating:** 89   **Green Rating:** 92

STUDENTS AND FACULTY

Enrollment: 2,877. **Student Body:** 51% female, 49% male, 13% out-of-state, 5% international (28 countries represented). Asian 4%, African American 15%, Caucasian 64%, Hispanic 8%, Native American <1%, Pacific Islander <1%, Two or more races 3%, Race unknown 2%.
Retention and Graduation: 74% freshmen return for sophomore year. 37% freshmen graduate within 4 years. 50% freshmen graduate within 6 years. **Faculty:** Student/faculty ratio 14:1. 220 full-time faculty, 83% hold PhDs, 15% are are members of minority groups, 45% are women.

ACADEMICS

Degrees: bachelor's, doctoral/research, master's, postbachelor's certificate, post-master's certificate. **Classes:** Most classes have 20-29 students. Most lab/discussion sessions have 10-19 students. **Most popular majors:** Business Administration and Management; Computer Science; Psychology. **Special Study Options:** distance learning, double major, English as a Second Language (ESL), honors program, independent study, internships, study abroad, teacher certification program. **Honors Programs:** Interdisciplinary four-year baccalaureate experience for highly qualified freshman. **Disability Services:** Special programs offered to physically disabled students, including note-taking services, reader services, tape recorders. **Career Services:** Alumni network, Alumni services, Career/job search classes, Career assessment, Internships, Regional alumni.

FACILITIES

Housing: Coed dorms, special housing for disabled students, special housing for international students, apartments for married students, apartments for single students, Wellness Housing, ThemeHousingFamily Housing. 99% of campus accessible to physically diasbled. **Special Academic Facilities/Equipment:** Norris L. Brookens Library, Sangamon Auditorium, Observatory **Computers:** 100% of classrooms, 100% of dorms, 100% of libraries, 100% of dining areas, 100% of student union, 100% of common outdoor areas have wireless network access. Students can register for classes online. Administrative functions (other than registration) can be performed online.

CAMPUS LIFE

Environment: City. **Activities:** Choral groups, concert band, dance, drama/theater, jazz band, music ensembles, pep band, student government, student newspaper, student-run film society, Campus Ministries, Student Organization, Model UN. 76 registered organizations. **Athletics (Intercollegiate):** *Men:* basketball, golf, soccer, tennis. *Women:* basketball, cheerleading, golf, soccer, softball, tennis, volleyball. **On-Campus Highlights:** University Hall, Public Affairs Center **Environmental Initiatives:** New student union is being designed to LEED Gold standards.

ADMISSIONS

Freshman Academic Profile: Average high school GPA 3.4. 17% in top 10% of high school class, 43% in top 25% of high school class, 80% in top 50% of high school class. 90% from public high schools. ACT middle 50% range 20-26. Minimum paper TOEFL 500. **Basis for Candidate Selection:** *Very important factors considered include:* academic GPA, standardized test scores. *Important factors considered include:* rigor of secondary school record, class rank, application essay. *Other factors considered include:* recommendation(s). **Freshman Admission Requirements:** High school diploma is required and GED is accepted. *Academic units required:* 4 English, 3 math, 3 science, 2 science labs, 2 foreign language, 3 social studies. **Freshman Admission Statistics:** 1,467 applied, 65.30% admitted, 31% enrolled. **Transfer Admission Requirements:** college transcript(s), Minimum college GPA of 2.0 required. Lowest grade transferable D. **General Admission Information:** Application fee $50. Nonfall registration accepted. Admission may be deferred for a maximum of 1 term.

COSTS AND FINANCIAL AID

Average book expense $1,200. **Required Forms and Deadlines:** FAFSA. **Notification of Awards:** Applicants will be notified of awards on a rolling basis beginning 1/1. **Types of Aid:** *Need-based scholarships/grants:* Federal Pell, FSEOG, State scholarships/grants, Private scholarships, College/university scholarship or grant aid from institutional funds. *Loans:* Direct Subsidized Stafford Loans, Direct Unsubsidized Stafford Loans, Direct PLUS loans, Federal Perkins Loans, College/university loans from institutional funds. *Student Employment:* Federal Work-Study Program available. Institutional employment available. **Financial Aid Statistics:** 98% needy freshmen, 89% needy undergrads receive need-based scholarship or grant aid. 19% freshmen, 15% undergrads receive non-need-based scholarship or grant aid. 72% freshmen, 81% undergrads receive need-based self-help aid. 8% freshmen, 3% undergrads receive athletic scholarships. 80% freshmen, 71% undergrads receive any aid. 69% undergrads borrow to pay for school. Average cumulative indebtedness $24,652. **Criteria for awarding aid:** *Need-based:* Academics, Alumni affiliation, Art, Athletics, Job skills, Leadership, Minority status, Music/drama. *Non-need-based:* Academics, Alumni affiliation, Art, Athletics, Job skills, Leadership, Minority status, Music/drama, State/district residency.

UNIVERSITY OF THE INCARNATE WORD

4301 Broadway, San Antonio, TX 78209-6397
Phone: 210-829-6005 • **Financial Aid Phone:** 210-829-6008
E-mail: admis@uiwtx.edu • **CEEB Code:** 6303
Fax: 210-829-3921 • **Website:** www.uiw.edu • **ACT Code:** 4106

This private school, affiliated with the Roman Catholic Church, was founded in 1881. It has a 154-acre campus.

RATINGS

Admissions Selectivity Rating: 72   Fire Safety Rating: 93   Green Rating: 68

STUDENTS AND FACULTY

Enrollment: 6,249. **Student Body:** 60% female, 40% male, 6% out-of-state, 5% international (41 countries represented). Asian 2%, African American 7%, Caucasian 19%, Hispanic 59%, Native American <1%, Pacific Islander <1%, Two or more races 1%, Race unknown 6%.
Retention and Graduation: 76% freshmen return for sophomore year. 31% freshmen graduate within 4 years. 54% freshmen graduate within 6 years. **Faculty:** Student/faculty ratio 13:1. 286 full-time faculty, 62% hold PhDs, 30% are are members of minority groups, 55% are women.

ACADEMICS

Degrees: associate, bachelor's, certificate, doctoral/professional, doctoral/research, master's. **Classes:** Most classes have 20-29 students. Most lab/discussion sessions have 10-19 students. **Most popular majors:** Biology/Biological Sciences; Registered Nursing/Registered Nurse; Business Administration and Management. **Special Study Options:** Accelerated program, cross-registration, distance learning, double major, dual enrollment, English as a Second Language (ESL), honors program, independent study, internships, student-designed major, study abroad, teacher certification program, weekend college. **Honors Programs:** UIW Honors Program Combined degree programs: BA/MA, BBA/MS—Accounting. **Disability Services:** Special programs offered to physically disabled students, including note-taking services, reader services, tape recorders, tutors. **Career Services:** Alumni services, Career/job search classes, Career assessment, Internships.

FACILITIES

Housing: Coed dorms, special housing for disabled students, men's dorms, women's dorms, apartments for single students. 95% of campus accessible to physically diasbled. **Computers:** 100% of classrooms, 100% of dorms, 100% of libraries, 100% of dining areas, 100% of student union, 100% of common outdoor areas have wireless network access. Students can register for classes online. Administrative functions (other than registration) can be performed online. Undergraduates are required to own a computer.

CAMPUS LIFE

Environment: Metropolis. **Activities:** Choral groups, dance, drama/theater, jazz band, literary magazine, music ensembles, musical theater, radio station, student government, student newspaper, symphony orchestra, Campus Ministries, Student Organization. 58 registered organizations, 8 honor societies, 2 religious organizations. 2 fraternities, 4 sororities. **Athletics (Intercollegiate):** *Men:* baseball, basketball, cross-country, football, golf, soccer, swimming, tennis, track/field (outdoor). *Women:* basketball, cross-country, golf, soccer, softball, swimming, synchronized swimming, tennis, track/field (outdoor), volleyball. **On-Campus Highlights:** Student Center, Chick-Fil-A, Library, Wellness Center, Dubuis Lawn.

ADMISSIONS

Freshman Academic Profile: Average high school GPA 3.5. **Reported SAT (pre-2016 redesign) scores:** SAT Math middle 50% range 430-530. SAT Critical Reading middle 50% range 430-530. SAT Writing middle 50% range 410-510. **Concordant SAT scores:** SAT EBRW middle 50% 470–580. SAT Math middle 50% range 470–560. ACT middle 50% range 18-23. Minimum internet-based TOEFL 79. Minimum paper TOEFL 650. **Basis for Candidate Selection:** *Very important factors considered include:* rigor of secondary school record, academic GPA, standardized test scores. *Important factors considered include:* class rank. *Other factors considered include:* application essay, recommendation(s), interview, extracurricular activities, talent/ability, character/personal qualities, alumni/ae relation, geographical residence, volunteer work, work experience, level of applicant's interest. **Freshman Admission Requirements:** High school diploma is required and GED is accepted. *Academic units required:* 4 English, 3 math, 3 science, 2 foreign language, 3 social studies, 1 visual/performing arts. *Academic units recommended:* 4 English, 4 math, 3 science, 2 foreign language, 4 social studies, 1 visual/performing arts. **Freshman Admission Statistics:** 4,050 applied, 92.22% admitted, 24% enrolled. **Transfer Admission Requirements:** college transcript(s), Minimum college GPA of 2.50 required. Lowest grade transferable C. **General Admission Information:** Application fee $20. Priority deadline 2/1. Nonfall registration accepted. Admission may be deferred for a maximum of 1 term.

COSTS AND FINANCIAL AID

Annual tuition $27,000. Room and board $11,880. Required fees $1,898. Average book expense $1,200. **Required Forms and Deadlines:** FAFSA. **Notification of Awards:** Applicants will be notified of awards on a rolling basis beginning 2/15. **Types of Aid:** *Need-based scholarships/grants:* Federal Pell, FSEOG, State scholarships/grants, Private scholarships, College/university scholarship or grant aid from institutional funds, United Negro College Fund, Federal Nursing Scholarships. *Loans:* Direct Subsidized Stafford Loans, Direct Unsubsidized Stafford Loans, Direct PLUS loans, Federal Perkins Loans, Federal Nursing Loans, State Loans. *Student Employment:* Federal Work-Study Program available. Institutional employment available. **Financial Aid Statistics:** 96% needy freshmen, 99% needy undergrads receive need-based scholarship or grant aid. 0% freshmen, 0% undergrads receive non-need-based scholarship or grant aid. 74% freshmen, 80% undergrads receive need-based self-help aid. 4% freshmen, 4% undergrads receive athletic scholarships. 99% freshmen receive any aid. 76% undergrads borrow to pay for school. Average cumulative indebtedness $43,998. **Criteria for awarding aid:** *Non-need-based:* Academics, Alumni affiliation, Art, Athletics, Leadership, Music/drama, Religious affiliation, State/district residency.

UNIVERSITY OF INDIANAPOLIS

1400 East Hanna Avenue, Indianapolis, IN 46227-3697
Phone: 317-788-3216 • **Financial Aid Phone:** 317-788-3217
E-mail: admissions@uindy.edu • **CEEB Code:** 1321
Fax: 317-788-3300 • **Website:** www.uindy.edu • **ACT Code:** 1204

This private school, affiliated with the Methodist Church, was founded in 1902. It has a 65-acre campus.

RATINGS

Admissions Selectivity Rating: 80   **Fire Safety Rating:** 72   **Green Rating:** 60*

STUDENTS AND FACULTY

Enrollment: 4,138. **Student Body:** 68% female, 32% male, 9% out-of-state, 5% international (47 countries represented). Asian 1%, African American 13%, Caucasian 73%, Hispanic 2%, Native American <1%, Pacific Islander <1%, Two or more races 2%, Race unknown 4%.
Retention and Graduation: 74% freshmen return for sophomore year. 36% freshmen graduate within 4 years. 52% freshmen graduate within 6 years.
Faculty: Student/faculty ratio 15:1. 218 full-time faculty, 76% hold PhDs, 6% are are members of minority groups, 57% are women. 0% of classes are taught by teaching assistants.

ACADEMICS

Degrees: associate, bachelor's, doctoral/professional, doctoral/research, master's. **Classes:** Most classes have 10-19 students. Most lab/discussion sessions have 20-29 students. **Most popular majors:** Business/Commerce; Registered Nursing/Registered Nurse; Psychology. **Special Study Options:** Accelerated program, cross-registration, double major, dual enrollment, English as a Second Language (ESL), honors program, independent study, internships, liberal arts/career combination, student-designed major, study abroad, teacher certification program, Spring Term Session (4-4-1). **Disability Services:** Special programs offered to physically disabled students, including note-taking services, reader services, tape recorders, tutors. **Career Services:** Internships, Regional alumni.

FACILITIES

Housing: Coed dorms, women's dorms, apartments for married students, apartments for single students. 90% of campus accessible to physically diasbled. **Special Academic Facilities/Equipment:** Developmental preschool, art gallery, observatory. **Computers:** 100% of classrooms, 100% of dorms, 100% of libraries, 100% of dining areas, 100% of student union, 100% of common outdoor areas have wireless network access.

CAMPUS LIFE

Environment: Metropolis. **Activities:** Choral groups, concert band, dance, drama/theater, jazz band, literary magazine, music ensembles, musical theater, opera, pep band, radio station, student government, student newspaper, television station, yearbook, Campus Ministries, Student Organization. 53 registered organizations, 14 honor societies, 4 religious organizations. **Athletics (Intercollegiate):** *Men:* baseball, basketball, cross-country, diving, football, golf, soccer, swimming, tennis, track/field (outdoor), wrestling. *Women:* basketball, cross-country, diving, golf, soccer, softball, swimming, tennis, track/field (outdoor), volleyball. **On-Campus Highlights:** Ruth Lilly Fitness Center, Schwitzer Center, Krannert Memorial Library, Christel Dehaan Fine Arts Center, Martin Hall.

ADMISSIONS

Freshman Academic Profile: Average high school GPA 3.4. 27% in top 10% of high school class, 56% in top 25% of high school class, 88% in top 50% of high school class. **Reported SAT (pre-2016 redesign) scores:** SAT Math middle 50% range 460-570. SAT Critical Reading middle 50% range 450-560. SAT Writing middle 50% range 440-550. **Concordant SAT scores:** SAT EBRW middle 50% 500–610. SAT Math middle 50% range 500–590. ACT middle 50% range 19-25. Minimum paper TOEFL 500. **Basis for Candidate Selection:** *Very important factors considered include:* rigor of secondary school record, academic GPA. *Important factors considered include:* standardized test scores. *Other factors considered include:* class rank, recommendation(s), interview, talent/ability. **Freshman Admission Requirements:** High school diploma is required and GED is accepted. *Academic units required:* 4 English, 3 math, 2 science, 1 science lab, 2 foreign language, 2 social studies, 1 history,

3 academic electives, 1 computer science, 2 visual/performing arts. *Academic units recommended:* 4 English, 3 math, 3 science, 2 science labs, 3 foreign language, 2 social studies, 1 history, 3 academic electives, 1 computer science, 2 visual/performing arts. **Freshman Admission Statistics:** 5,396 applied, 78.67% admitted, 19% enrolled. **Transfer Admission Requirements:** High school transcript, college transcript(s), standardized test scores, statement of good standing from prior institution(s). Minimum college GPA of 2.0 required. Lowest grade transferable C-. **General Admission Information:** Application fee $25. Regular application deadline 8/20. Nonfall registration accepted. Admission may be deferred.

COSTS AND FINANCIAL AID

Annual tuition $23,590. Room and board $9,090. Required fees $240. Average book expense $1,076. **Required Forms and Deadlines:** FAFSA, Institution's own financial aid form. **Notification of Awards:** Applicants will be notified of awards on a rolling basis beginning 3/1. **Types of Aid:** *Need-based scholarships/grants:* Federal Pell, FSEOG, State scholarships/grants, Private scholarships, College/university scholarship or grant aid from institutional funds. *Loans:* Direct Subsidized Stafford Loans, Direct Unsubsidized Stafford Loans, Direct PLUS loans, Federal Perkins Loans. *Student Employment:* Federal Work-Study Program available. Institutional employment available. **Financial Aid Statistics:** 57% needy freshmen, 68% needy undergrads receive need-based scholarship or grant aid. 99% freshmen, 70% undergrads receive non-need-based scholarship or grant aid. 78% freshmen, 79% undergrads receive need-based self-help aid. 8% freshmen, 8% undergrads receive athletic scholarships. 99% freshmen, 98% undergrads receive any aid. **Criteria for awarding aid:** *Non-need-based:* Academics, Alumni affiliation, Art, Athletics, Job skills, Music/drama, Religious affiliation, State/district residency.

UNIVERSITY OF IOWA

107 Calvin Hall, Iowa City, IA 52242
Phone: 319-335-3847 • **Financial Aid Phone:** 319-335-1450
E-mail: admissions@uiowa.edu • **CEEB Code:** 6681
Fax: 319-333-1535 • **Website:** www.uiowa.edu • **ACT Code:** 1356

This public school was founded in 1847. It has a 1900-acre campus.

RATINGS

Admissions Selectivity Rating: 84   **Fire Safety Rating:** 92   **Green Rating:** 60*

STUDENTS AND FACULTY

Enrollment: 22,990. **Student Body:** 52% female, 48% male, 39% out-of-state, 11% international (63 countries represented). Asian 4%, African American 3%, Caucasian 69%, Hispanic 8%, Native American <1%, Pacific Islander <1%, Two or more races 3%, Race unknown 3%.
Retention and Graduation: 87% freshmen return for sophomore year. 51% freshmen graduate within 4 years. 72% freshmen graduate within 6 years.
Faculty: Student/faculty ratio 16:1. 1,398 full-time faculty, 98% hold PhDs, 19% are are members of minority groups, 32% are women. 11% of classes are taught by teaching assistants.

ACADEMICS

Degrees: bachelor's, doctoral/professional, doctoral/research, doctoral, master's, postbachelor's certificate, post-master's certificate. **Classes:** Most classes have 10-19 students. Most lab/discussion sessions have 20-29 students. **Most popular majors:** Business/Commerce; Engineering; Pre-Medicine/Pre-Medical Studies. **Special Study Options:** Accelerated program, cooperative education program, distance learning, double major, dual enrollment, English as a Second Language (ESL), exchange student program (domestic), external degree program, honors program, independent study, internships, liberal arts/career combination, student-designed major, study abroad, teacher certification program. **Honors Programs:** The University of Iowa Honors Program is dedicated to the academic and personal enrichment of its students. This enrichment is accomplished through special academic opportunities and programs that are sponsored by the Honors Program and open to all Honors students. Combined degree programs: BA/MA, BA/DDS, BA/MEng, BBA/BA,BS; BSE/BA, BS; BSN/BA,BS; BA/MCS; BS/MS; BS/MA; BA/MA; BA/MS. **Disability Services:** Special programs offered to physically disabled students, including note-taking services, reader services, tape recorders, tutors. **Career Services:** Career/job search classes, Career assessment, Internships, Regional alumni. The John Pappajohn Entrepreneurial Center offers all UI students a broad range of experiential learning programs and activities to enhance their academic foundation. Students gain valuable, real-world experience through: Bedell Business Incubator, Field Study Consulting Projects, Okoboji Entrepreneurial Institute, Entrepreneurial Management Institute, Business Plan & Elevator Pitch Competitions, First Year Seminar in Entrepreneurship, Student Entrepreneurship Organization, Experience Iowa Internships, Learning Community in Business and Entrepreneurship.

FACILITIES

Housing: Coed dorms, special housing for disabled students, fraternity/sorority housing, apartments for married students, apartments for single students, Wellness Housing, Theme Housing, quiet Houses available. Living-Learning Communities for the following interests: Honors; Iowa Writers; Health Sciences; Business and Entrepreneurship, Women in Science and Engineering; Men in Engineering; performing arts; international interests; citizenship and service; Law Study and Legal Careers, Sustainability, Career Leadership Academy, Healthy Living Network, Hispanic Culture and Language. 99% of campus accessible to physically disabled. **Special Academic Facilities/Equipment:** National Advanced Driving Simulator, electron microscope, laser facility, Oakdale Research park, UI Hygienic Lab, UI Center for Biocatalysis & Bioprocessing, UI Research Foundation, survey research facilities natural history museum, Medical Museum, Old Capitol Museum, Main Library and 10 departmental libraries, information arcade, newspaper production lab, TV lab, UI Technology Innovation Center, and Project Art. **Computers:** 100% of classrooms, 25% of dorms, 100% of libraries, 25% of dining areas, 90% of student union, 15% of common outdoor areas have wireless network access. Students can register for classes online. Administrative functions (other than registration) can be performed online.

CAMPUS LIFE

Environment: City. **Activities:** Choral groups, concert band, dance, drama/theater, jazz band, literary magazine, marching band, music ensembles, musical theater, opera, pep band, radio station, student government, student newspaper, student-run film society, symphony orchestra, television station, Campus Ministries, Student Organization. 488 registered organizations, 21 honor societies, 24 religious organizations. 18 fraternities, 18 sororities. **Athletics (Intercollegiate):** *Men:* baseball, basketball, cheerleading, cross-country, diving, football, golf, gymnastics, swimming, tennis, track/field (outdoor), track/field (indoor), wrestling. *Women:* basketball, cheerleading, crew/rowing, cross-country, diving, field hockey, golf, gymnastics, soccer, softball, swimming, tennis, track/field (outdoor), track/field (indoor), volleyball. **On-Campus Highlights:** Kinnick Stadium/Carver Hawkeye Arena, The University of Iowa Museum of Natural History, UI Recreational Services, Hawkeye Hall of Fame, UIHC Project Art. **Environmental Initiatives:** The University of Iowa has established seven 2020 Sustainability Targets that include goals for energy conservation, renewable energy, waste diversion, reduced carbon impact of transportation, increasing student opportunities to learn and practice sustainability principles, support sustainability research and develop partnerships to advance collaborative initiatives. The UI was the first certified Tree Campus in Iowa. The number of LEED-Accredited Professionals on staff in Facilities Management tripled to total 17.

ADMISSIONS

Freshman Academic Profile: Average high school GPA 3.6. 28% in top 10% of high school class, 59% in top 25% of high school class, 91% in top 50% of high school class. 90% from public high schools. **Reported SAT (pre-2016 redesign) scores:** SAT Math middle 50% range 540-680. SAT Critical Reading middle 50% range 480-640. **Concordant SAT scores:** SAT Math middle 50% range 570–710. ACT middle 50% range 23-28. Minimum internet-based TOEFL 80. Minimum paper TOEFL 530. **Basis for Candidate Selection:** *Very important factors considered include:* rigor of secondary school record, class rank, academic GPA, standardized test scores. *Other factors considered include:* recommendation(s), talent/ability, character/personal qualities, state residency. **Freshman Admission Requirements:** High school diploma is required and GED is accepted. *Academic units required:* 4 English, 3 math, 3 science, 2 foreign language, 3 social studies. *Academic units recommended:* 4 math, 4 foreign language. **Freshman Admission Statistics:** 28,494 applied, 84.11% admitted, 24% enrolled. **Transfer Admission Requirements:** High school transcript, college transcript(s), Minimum college GPA of 2.5 required. Lowest grade transferable D. **General Admission Information:** Application fee $40. Regular application deadline 4/1. Nonfall registration accepted. Admission may be deferred.

COSTS AND FINANCIAL AID

Annual in-state tuition $7,128. Annual out-of-state tuition $26,966. Room and board $10,108. Required fees $1,447. Average book expense $950. **Required Forms and Deadlines:** FAFSA, Institution's own financial aid form. **Notification of Awards:** Applicants will be notified of awards on a rolling basis beginning 3/15. **Types of Aid:** *Need-based scholarships/grants:* Federal Pell, FSEOG, State scholarships/grants, Private scholarships, College/university scholarship or grant aid from institutional funds. *Loans:* Direct Subsidized Stafford Loans, Direct Unsubsidized Stafford Loans, Direct PLUS loans, Federal Perkins Loans, Federal Nursing Loans, College/university loans

from institutional funds. *Student Employment:* Federal Work-Study Program available. Institutional employment available. **Financial Aid Statistics:** 77% needy freshmen, 73% needy undergrads receive need-based scholarship or grant aid. 75% freshmen, 52% undergrads receive non-need-based scholarship or grant aid. 85% freshmen, 90% undergrads receive need-based self-help aid. 2% freshmen, 2% undergrads receive athletic scholarships. 79% freshmen, 72% undergrads receive any aid. 53% undergrads borrow to pay for school. Average cumulative indebtedness $27,715. **Criteria for awarding aid:** *Need-based:* Academics. *Non-need-based:* Academics, Alumni affiliation, Art, Athletics, Leadership, Music/drama, State/district residency.

UNIVERSITY OF JAMESTOWN

6081 College Lane, Jamestown, ND 58405-0001
Phone: 701-252-3467 • **Financial Aid Phone:** 701-252-3467
E-mail: admissions@uj.edu
Fax: 701-253-4318 • **Website:** www.uj.edu • **ACT Code:** 3200

This private school, affiliated with the Presbyterian Church, was founded in 1883. It has a 110-acre campus.

RATINGS

Admissions Selectivity Rating: 83   **Fire Safety Rating:** 80   **Green Rating:** 60*

STUDENTS AND FACULTY

Enrollment: 934. **Student Body:** 50% female, 50% male, 50% out-of-state, 10% international (15 countries represented). Asian 1%, African American 5%, Caucasian 74%, Hispanic 7%, Native American 1%, Pacific Islander 1%, Two or more races 0%, Race unknown <1%.
Retention and Graduation: 77% freshmen return for sophomore year. 36% freshmen graduate within 4 years. 49% freshmen graduate within 6 years. 12% grads go on to further study within 1 year. 9% grads pursue arts and sciences degrees. 2% grads pursue law degrees. 2% grads pursue medical degrees.
Faculty: Student/faculty ratio 13:1. 73 full-time faculty, 58% hold PhDs, 5% are are members of minority groups, 56% are women. 0% of classes are taught by teaching assistants.

ACADEMICS

Degrees: bachelor's, doctoral/professional, master's. **Classes:** Most classes have 10-19 students. Most lab/discussion sessions have fewer than 10 students. **Most popular majors:** Elementary Education and Teaching; Business/Commerce; Registered Nursing/Registered Nurse. **Special Study Options:** cooperative education program, double major, dual enrollment, English as a Second Language (ESL), exchange student program (domestic), honors program, independent study, internships, liberal arts/career combination, student-designed major, study abroad, teacher certification program. **Honors Programs:** Character and Leadership Program. The heart of the Character in Leadership program is its academic core. Each student who participates will receive a minor in leadership. Jamestown College values its reputation for quality education and therefore is committed through its Character in Leadership Program to providing a broad and sound intellectual foundation that will enable its students to provide ethical leadership in an ever-changing world. **Disability Services:** Special programs offered to physically disabled students, including note-taking services, reader services, tape recorders, tutors. **Career Services:** Alumni network, Alumni services, Career/job search classes, Career assessment, Internships—campus wide program. All students are encouraged to complete at least one.

FACILITIES

Housing: Coed dorms, special housing for disabled students, apartments for married students, apartments for single students. 80% of campus accessible to physically disabled. **Computers:** 95% of classrooms, 100% of dorms, 100% of libraries, 100% of dining areas, 100% of student union, 50% of common outdoor areas have wireless network access. Students can register for classes online. Administrative functions (other than registration) can be performed online.

CAMPUS LIFE

Environment: Village. **Activities:** Choral groups, concert band, dance, drama/theater, jazz band, literary magazine, music ensembles, musical theater, pep band, student government, student newspaper, television station, Campus Ministries, Student Organization. 35 registered organizations, 6 honor societies, 5 religious organizations. **Athletics (Intercollegiate):** *Men:* baseball, basketball, cross-country, football, golf, track/field (outdoor), track/field (indoor), wrestling. *Women:* basketball, cross-country, golf, soccer, softball, track/field (outdoor), track/field (indoor), volleyball, wrestling. **On-Campus Highlights:** Library lobby, Lounge/tv room outside of cafeteria, Larson Center (athletic center)/Foss Wellness Center, Residence Hall lounges, Level 2 (campus nightclub).

ADMISSIONS

Freshman Academic Profile: Average high school GPA 3.4. 13% in top 10% of high school class, 39% in top 25% of high school class, 74% in top 50% of high school class. **Reported SAT (pre-2016 redesign) scores:** SAT Math middle 50% range 440-580. SAT Critical Reading middle 50% range 450-560. **Concordant SAT scores:** SAT Math middle 50% range 480–600. ACT middle 50% range 20-25. Minimum internet-based TOEFL 70. Minimum paper TOEFL 525. **Basis for Candidate Selection:** *Very important factors considered include:* academic GPA, standardized test scores. *Other factors considered include:* rigor of secondary school record, class rank, application essay, recommendation(s), interview, extracurricular activities, talent/ability, character/personal qualities, first generation, alumni/ae relation, level of applicant's interest. **Freshman Admission Requirements:** High school diploma is required and GED is accepted. *Academic units recommended:* 4 English, 3 math, 4 science, 2 foreign language, 3 social studies. **Freshman Admission Statistics:** 1,560 applied, 57.31% admitted, 29% enrolled. **Transfer Admission Requirements:** High school transcript, college transcript(s), statement of good standing from prior institution(s). Minimum college GPA of 2.5 required. Lowest grade transferable c. **General Admission Information:** Priority deadline 5/1. Nonfall registration accepted. Admission may be deferred.

COSTS AND FINANCIAL AID

Annual tuition $20,578. Room and board $7,656. Required fees $580. Average book expense $1,000. **Required Forms and Deadlines:** FAFSA. **Notification of Awards:** Applicants will be notified of awards on a rolling basis beginning 2/1. **Types of Aid:** *Need-based scholarships/grants:* Federal Pell, FSEOG, State scholarships/grants, Private scholarships. *Loans:* Direct Subsidized Stafford Loans, Direct Unsubsidized Stafford Loans, Direct PLUS loans, Federal Perkins Loans. *Student Employment:* Federal Work-Study Program available. Institutional employment available. **Financial Aid Statistics:** 100% needy freshmen, 100% needy undergrads receive need-based scholarship or grant aid. 22% freshmen, 19% undergrads receive non-need-based scholarship or grant aid. 74% freshmen, 75% undergrads receive need-based self-help aid. 32% freshmen, 27% undergrads receive athletic scholarships. 100% freshmen, 98% undergrads receive any aid. 70% undergrads borrow to pay for school. Average cumulative indebtedness $25,368. **Criteria for awarding aid:** *Non-need-based:* Academics, Alumni affiliation, Art, Athletics, Job skills, Leadership, Music/drama, Religious affiliation.

UNIVERSITY OF KANSAS

Office of Admissions, Lawrence, KS 66045-7576

Phone: 785-864-3911 • **Financial Aid Phone:** 785-864-4700

E-mail: adm@ku.edu • **CEEB Code:** 6871

Fax: 785-864-5017 • **Website:** www.ku.edu • **ACT Code:** 1470

This public school was founded in 1866. It has a 1100-acre campus.

RATINGS

Admissions Selectivity Rating: 81   **Fire Safety Rating:** 96   **Green Rating:** 82

STUDENTS AND FACULTY

Enrollment: 18,845. **Student Body:** 51% female, 49% male, 27% out-of-state, 6% international (75 countries represented). Asian 5%, African American 4%, Caucasian 72%, Hispanic 8%, Native American <1%, Pacific Islander <1%, Two or more races 5%, Race unknown 1%.
Retention and Graduation: 81% freshmen return for sophomore year. 41% freshmen graduate within 4 years. 63% freshmen graduate within 6 years. 29% grads go on to further study within 1 year. **Faculty:** Student/faculty ratio 16:1. 1,431 full-time faculty, 90% hold PhDs, 20% are are members of minority groups, 40% are women. 20% of classes are taught by teaching assistants.

ACADEMICS

Degrees: bachelor's, certificate, doctoral/professional, doctoral/research, master's, postbachelor's certificate. **Classes:** Most classes have 10-19 students. Most lab/discussion sessions have 10-19 students. **Most popular majors:** Biology/Biological Sciences; Business/Commerce; Journalism. **Special Study Options:** Accelerated program, cooperative education program, distance learning, double major, dual enrollment, English as a Second Language (ESL), honors program, independent study, internships, liberal arts/career combination, study abroad, teacher certification program, Off Campus Study: Washington DC semester; Study abroad in over 60 countries. **Honors Programs:** The University Honors Program gives outstanding and creative

students opportunities for intellectual growth and achievement through its small, challenging classes. web site at www.honors.ku.edu. **Disability Services:** Special programs offered to physically disabled students, including note-taking services, reader services, tape recorders, tutors. **Career Services:** Career/job search classes, Career assessment, Internships.

FACILITIES

Housing: Coed dorms, women's dorms, fraternity/sorority housing, apartments for married students, cooperative housing, apartments for single students. 95% of campus accessible to physically diasbled. **Special Academic Facilities/Equipment:** 12 libraries (including art and architecture, engineering, law, medical, music and dance, rare research materials, special collections, and science), performing arts center, organ recital hall, museums (art, anthropology, classical, entomology, invertebrate paleontology, and natural history), film studio, student operated radio and television stations, public radio station, herbarium, space technology center, observatory, Robert J. Dole Institute for Politics, Hall Center for the Humanities, Center for International Business Education and Research, ecological reserves, Biological Survey, Geological Survey, Information and Telecommunication Technology Center, energy research center, flight research lab, Transportation Research Center, 400+ bed hospital for clinical learning, Hoglund Brain Imaging Center, Center on Aging.

CAMPUS LIFE

Environment: City. **Activities:** Choral groups, concert band, dance, drama/theater, jazz band, literary magazine, marching band, music ensembles, musical theater, opera, pep band, radio station, student government, student newspaper, symphony orchestra, television station, Student Organization. 476 registered organizations, 14 honor societies, 39 religious organizations. 27 fraternities, 16 sororities. **Athletics (Intercollegiate):** *Men:* baseball, basketball, cross-country, football, golf, track/field (outdoor), track/field (indoor). *Women:* basketball, crew/rowing, cross-country, diving, golf, soccer, softball, swimming, tennis, track/field (outdoor), track/field (indoor), volleyball. **On-Campus Highlights:** Spencer Museum of Art, Kansas Union and Bookstore, Natural History Museum, Athletic Hall of Fame, Robert J. Dole Institute of Politics, Beautiful campus to walk around. **Environmental Initiatives:** In fall 2011, the University of Kansas released its campus sustainability plan, Building Sustainable Traditions, which establishes a vision for a more sustainable campus and outlines specific strategies for achieving the goals of the plan. Action steps are focused in 9 key areas: administration, research & curriculum, student life, energy, built environment, campus grounds, procurement, waste, and transportation. (http://www.sustainability.ku.edu/Plan/)

ADMISSIONS

Freshman Academic Profile: Average high school GPA 3.6. 26% in top 10% of high school class, 57% in top 25% of high school class, 88% in top 50% of high school class. ACT middle 50% range 23-29. **Basis for Candidate Selection:** *Very important factors considered include:* academic GPA, standardized test scores. **Freshman Admission Requirements:** High school diploma is required and GED is accepted. *Academic units required:* 4 English, 3 math, 3 science, 1 science lab, 3 social studies, 3 academic electives. *Academic units recommended:* 4 English, 4 math, 3 science, 3 social studies, 3 academic electives. **Freshman Admission Statistics:** 15,015 applied, 93.01% admitted, 30% enrolled. **Transfer Admission Requirements:** college transcript(s), Minimum college GPA of 2.5 required. Lowest grade transferable C. **General Admission Information:** Application fee $30. Priority deadline 11/1. Nonfall registration accepted.

COSTS AND FINANCIAL AID

Annual in-state tuition $9,579. Annual out-of-state tuition $24,962. Room and board $9,586. Required fees $970. Average book expense $1,080. **Required Forms and Deadlines:** FAFSA. **Notification of Awards:** Applicants will be notified of awards on a rolling basis beginning 4/1. **Types of Aid:** *Need-based scholarships/grants:* Federal Pell, FSEOG, State scholarships/grants, Private scholarships, College/university scholarship or grant aid from institutional funds. *Loans:* Direct Subsidized Stafford Loans, Direct Unsubsidized Stafford Loans, Direct PLUS loans, Federal Perkins Loans, Federal Nursing Loans, College/university loans from institutional funds. *Student Employment:* Federal Work-Study Program available. Institutional employment available. **Financial Aid Statistics:** 84% needy freshmen, 76% needy undergrads receive need-based scholarship or grant aid. 10% freshmen, 7% undergrads receive non-need-based scholarship or grant aid. 69% freshmen, 76% undergrads receive need-based self-help aid. 2% freshmen, 2% undergrads receive athletic scholarships. 77% freshmen, 65% undergrads receive any aid. 52% undergrads borrow to pay for school. Average cumulative indebtedness $27,479. **Criteria for awarding aid:** *Need-based:* Academics, Alumni affiliation, Art, Job skills, Leadership, Minority status, Music/drama. *Non-need-based:* Academics, Alumni affiliation, Art, Athletics, Leadership, Minority status, Music/drama, State/district residency.

UNIVERSITY OF KENTUCKY

100 Funkhouser Building, Lexington, KY 40506
Phone: 859-257-2000 • **Financial Aid Phone:** 859-257-3172
E-mail: admissions@uky.edu • **CEEB Code:** 1837
Fax: 859-257-3823 • **Website:** www.uky.edu • **ACT Code:** 1554

This public school was founded in 1865. It has a 687-acre campus.

RATINGS
Admissions Selectivity Rating: 81   **Fire Safety Rating:** 90   **Green Rating:** 60*

STUDENTS AND FACULTY
Enrollment: 22,247. **Student Body:** 53% female, 47% male, 30% out-of-state, 3% international (117 countries represented). Asian 2%, African American 8%, Caucasian 76%, Hispanic 4%, Native American <1%, Pacific Islander <1%, Two or more races 3%, Race unknown 3%.
Retention and Graduation: 83% freshmen return for sophomore year. 35% freshmen graduate within 4 years. 61% freshmen graduate within 6 years.
Faculty: Student/faculty ratio 17:1. 1,397 full-time faculty, 92% hold PhDs, 19% are are members of minority groups, 39% are women. 20% of classes are taught by teaching assistants.

ACADEMICS
Degrees: bachelor's, certificate, doctoral/professional, doctoral/research, master's, postbachelor's certifiate, post-master's certificate. **Classes:** Most classes have 20-29 students. **Special Study Options:** Accelerated program, cooperative education program, distance learning, double major, English as a Second Language (ESL), exchange student program (domestic), honors program, independent study, internships, study abroad, teacher certification program, weekend college. Combined degree programs: BA/MA, JD/MBA.
Disability Services: Special programs offered to physically disabled students, including note-taking services, reader services.

FACILITIES
Housing: Coed dorms, special housing for disabled students, men's dorms, special housing for international students, women's dorms, fraternity/sorority housing, apartments for married students, apartments for single students. 95% of campus accessible to physically diasbled. **Special Academic Facilities/ Equipment:** Anthropology and art museums, center for the humanities, centers for equine research, cancer research, and robotics, pharmacy manufacturing lab. **Computers:** 30% of classrooms, 10% of dorms, 100% of libraries, 80% of dining areas, 70% of student union, 50% of common outdoor areas have wireless network access. Students can register for classes online. Administrative functions (other than registration) can be performed online.

CAMPUS LIFE
Environment: City. **Activities:** Choral groups, concert band, dance, drama/ theater, jazz band, literary magazine, marching band, music ensembles, musical theater, opera, pep band, radio station, student government, student newspaper, symphony orchestra, yearbook, Student Organization. 348 registered organizations, 28 honor societies, 20 religious organizations. 19 fraternities, 16 sororities. **Athletics (Intercollegiate):** *Men:* baseball, basketball, cheerleading, cross-country, diving, football, golf, riflery, soccer, swimming, tennis, track/field (outdoor), track/field (indoor). *Women:* basketball, cheerleading, cross-country, diving, golf, gymnastics, riflery, soccer, softball, swimming, tennis, track/field (outdoor), track/field (indoor), volleyball. **On-Campus Highlights:** W.T. Young Library, Johnson Fitness Center, Memorial Coliseum, Arboretum, Memorial Hall.

ADMISSIONS
Freshman Academic Profile: Average high school GPA 3.7. 30% in top 10% of high school class, 58% in top 25% of high school class, 86% in top 50% of high school class. **Reported SAT (pre-2016 redesign) scores:** SAT Math middle 50% range 510-630. SAT Critical Reading middle 50% range 500-620. SAT Writing middle 50% range 490-610. **Concordant SAT scores:** SAT EBRW middle 50% 550–670. SAT Math middle 50% range 540–650. ACT middle 50% range 22-28. Minimum paper TOEFL 527. **Basis for Candidate Selection:** *Very important factors considered include:* rigor of secondary school record, academic GPA, standardized test scores. *Other factors considered include:* class rank, application essay, recommendation(s), interview, extracurricular activities, talent/ability, character/personal qualities, alumni/ae relation, geographical residence, racial/ethnic status, volunteer work. **Freshman Admission Requirements:** High school diploma is required and GED is accepted. *Academic units required:* 4 English, 3 math, 3 science,

1 science lab, 2 foreign language, 3 social studies, 7 academic electives, 1 visual/performing arts, and 1 unit from above areas or other academic areas. **Freshman Admission Statistics:** 18,432 applied, 90.52% admitted, 31% enrolled. **Transfer Admission Requirements:** college transcript(s), Minimum college GPA of 2.0 required. Lowest grade transferable D. **General Admission Information:** Application fee $50. Priority deadline 2/15. Regular application deadline 2/15. Regular notification 8/15. Nonfall registration accepted. Admission may be deferred for a maximum of 1 year.

COSTS AND FINANCIAL AID
Annual in-state tuition $10,172. Annual out-of-state tuition $24,845. Room and board $12,184. Required fees $1,311. Average book expense $1,000. **Required Forms and Deadlines:** FAFSA. **Notification of Awards:** Applicants will be notified of awards on a rolling basis beginning 4/1. **Types of Aid:** *Need-based scholarships/grants:* Federal Pell, FSEOG, State scholarships/grants, Private scholarships, College/university scholarship or grant aid from institutional funds. *Loans:* Direct Subsidized Stafford Loans, Direct Unsubsidized Stafford Loans, Direct PLUS loans, Federal Perkins Loans, State Loans, College/ university loans from institutional funds. *Student Employment:* Federal Work-Study Program available. Institutional employment available. **Financial Aid Statistics:** 46% needy freshmen, 49% needy undergrads receive need-based scholarship or grant aid. 90% freshmen, 73% undergrads receive non-need-based scholarship or grant aid. 60% freshmen, 70% undergrads receive need-based self-help aid. 3% freshmen, 3% undergrads receive athletic scholarships. 40% freshmen, 38% undergrads receive any aid. **Criteria for awarding aid:** *Need-based:* Academics, Alumni affiliation, Minority status. *Non-need-based:* Academics, Alumni affiliation, Art, Athletics, Job skills, Leadership, Minority status, Music/drama, State/district residency.

UNIVERSITY OF KING'S COLLEGE

Registrars Office, Halifax, NS B3H 2A1
Phone: 902-422-1271
E-mail: admissions@ukings.ns.ca
Fax: 902-423-3357 • **Website:** www.ukings.ca

This public school was founded in 1789. It has a 3-acre campus.

RATINGS
Admissions Selectivity Rating: 71   **Fire Safety Rating:** 60*   **Green Rating:** 60*

STUDENTS AND FACULTY
Student Body: 57% female, 43% male, 53% out-of-state, (6 countries represented).
Faculty: Student/faculty ratio 25:1. 51 full-time faculty, 71% hold PhDs, 0% are are members of minority groups, 31% are women. 0% of classes are taught by teaching assistants.

ACADEMICS
Degrees: bachelor's. **Most popular majors:** Sociology; English Language and Literature; Psychology. **Special Study Options:** cooperative education program, double major, honors program, internships, study abroad. **Career Services:** Career/job search classes, Career assessment.

FACILITIES
Housing: Coed dorms, men's dorms, women's dorms. **Computers:** Students can register for classes online. Administrative functions (other than registration) can be performed online.

CAMPUS LIFE
Environment: Metropolis. **Activities:** Choral groups, dance, drama/theater, literary magazine, radio station, student government, student newspaper, student-run film society, yearbook. **Athletics (Intercollegiate):** *Men:* badminton, basketball, soccer, volleyball. *Women:* badminton, basketball, soccer, volleyball. **On-Campus Highlights:** The Pit, The Wardroom, The Manning Room, The Library, The Quad.

ADMISSIONS
Minimum paper TOEFL 580. **Basis for Candidate Selection:** *Very important factors considered include:* rigor of secondary school record, standardized test scores. **Freshman Admission Requirements:** High school diploma is required and GED is not accepted. **Freshman Admission Statistics:** 904 applied, 46.68% admitted, 83% enrolled. **Transfer Admission Requirements:** college transcript(s), Lowest grade transferable C. **General Admission Information:** Application fee $45. Priority deadline 3/1. Regular application deadline 6/1. Nonfall registration not accepted. Admission may be deferred for a maximum of One year.

COSTS AND FINANCIAL AID
Average book expense $1,000.

UNIVERSITY OF LA VERNE

1950 Third Street, La Verne, CA 91750
Phone: 800-876-4858 • **Financial Aid Phone:** 1-800-649-0160
E-mail: admission@laverne.edu • **CEEB Code:** 4381
Fax: 909-392-2714 • **Website:** www.laverne.edu • **ACT Code:** 295

This private school was founded in 1891. It has a 38-acre campus.

RATINGS

Admissions Selectivity Rating: 85   **Fire Safety Rating:** 93   **Green Rating:** 98

STUDENTS AND FACULTY

Enrollment: 2,859. **Student Body:** 59% female, 41% male, 4% out-of-state, 5% international (24 countries represented). Asian 6%, African American 5%, Caucasian 25%, Hispanic 51%, Native American <1%, Pacific Islander 1%, Two or more races 5%, Race unknown 2%.
Retention and Graduation: 85% freshmen return for sophomore year. 45% freshmen graduate within 4 years. 64% freshmen graduate within 6 years.
Faculty: Student/faculty ratio 13:1. 233 full-time faculty, 0% hold PhDs, 0% are are members of minority groups, 0% are women. 0% of classes are taught by teaching assistants.

ACADEMICS

Degrees: bachelor's, certificate, doctoral/professional, doctoral/research, master's, postbachelor's certificate. **Classes:** Most classes have 10-19 students. Most lab/discussion sessions have fewer than 10 students. **Most popular majors:** Business Administration and Management; Psychology; Biology/Biological Sciences. **Special Study Options:** distance learning, double major, English as a Second Language (ESL), exchange student program (domestic), honors program, independent study, internships, liberal arts/career combination, student-designed major, study abroad, teacher certification program, weekend college. **Honors Programs:** For students who have demonstrated exceptional academic achievement and motivation, the ULV Honors Program offers increased opportunities for intellectual and personal growth. Participants in the Honors Program can enrich their undergraduate experience through a special Honors curriculum that emphasizes critical thinking skills and the integration of knowledge from various disciplines, through individualized attention from faculty mentors, and through community outreach activities and cultural programs. All eligible undergraduate students, regardless of major, are invited to apply, but participation in the program is completely voluntary. Students who complete the entire program receive the designation "Honors Program Graduate" on their diplomas and transcripts. Students who complete a minimum of two Interdisciplinary Seminars and a total of at least 10 units in Honors receive the designation "Honors Program Participant" on their transcripts. Besides these benefits, students in the program also receive specialized academic advising, greater opportunities for original research and study, and additional enrichment activities, including guest lectures. They may also be eligible for Honors Scholarships. The Honors Center, available to Honors Program students, offers a study lounge, computer laboratory, and a seminar room. Combined degree programs: JD/MBA.
Disability Services: Special programs offered to physically disabled students, including note-taking services, reader services, tape recorders, tutors. **Career Services:** Alumni services, Career/job search classes, Career assessment, Internships, Regional alumni, On-campus interviews. Career Services has numerous internship listings in all career fields.

FACILITIES

Housing: Coed dorms, special housing for disabled students, women's dorms. **Special Academic Facilities/Equipment:** Greenhouse and Animal Care Facility; Montana Field Station–Magpie Ranch; Jeagar science specimen Museum; Photography and Art galleries **Computers:** 100% of classrooms, 100% of dorms, 100% of libraries, 100% of dining areas, 100% of student union, 100% of common outdoor areas have wireless network access. Students can register for classes online. Administrative functions (other than registration) can be performed online.

CAMPUS LIFE

Environment: Town. **Activities:** Choral groups, dance, drama/theater, literary magazine, music ensembles, musical theater, radio station, student government, student newspaper, student-run film society, television station, Campus Ministries, Student Organization, Model UN. 40 registered organizations, 2 honor societies, 1 religious organization. 3 fraternities, 6 sororities. **Athletics (Intercollegiate):** *Men:* baseball, basketball, cross-country, diving, football, golf, soccer, swimming, tennis, track/field (outdoor), water polo. *Women:* basketball, cross-country, diving, soccer, softball, swimming, tennis, track/field (outdoor), volleyball, water polo. **On-Campus Highlights:** Campus Center, Sneaky Park (outdoor events), Davenport Dining Hall, Dailey Theater (Fine Arts Performances), University Quad. **Environmental Initiatives:** Total Recycling Program.

ADMISSIONS

Freshman Academic Profile: Average high school GPA 3.5. 18% in top 10% of high school class, 54% in top 25% of high school class, 86% in top 50% of high school class. **Reported SAT (pre-2016 redesign) scores:** SAT Math middle 50% range 470-570. SAT Critical Reading middle 50% range 470-560. SAT Writing middle 50% range 460-560. **Concordant SAT scores:** SAT EBRW middle 50% 520–620. SAT Math middle 50% range 510–590. ACT middle 50% range 20-24. Minimum internet-based TOEFL 80. Minimum paper TOEFL 550. **Basis for Candidate Selection:** *Very important factors considered include:* rigor of secondary school record, academic GPA, standardized test scores, application essay, recommendation(s), extracurricular activities, character/personal qualities. *Important factors considered include:* class rank. *Other factors considered include:* interview, talent/ability, first generation, alumni/ae relation, geographical residence, volunteer work, work experience, level of applicant's interest. **Freshman Admission Requirements:** High school diploma is required and GED is accepted. *Academic units required:* 4 English, 3 math, 2 science, 1 science lab, 2 social studies, 3 history. *Academic units recommended:* 4 English, 4 math, 2 science, 2 science labs, 2 foreign language, 2 social studies, 3 history, 2 academic electives. **Freshman Admission Statistics:** 8,179 applied, 47.18% admitted, 19% enrolled. **Transfer Admission Requirements:** college transcript(s), essay or personal statement, Minimum college GPA of 2.7 required. Lowest grade transferable C-. **General Admission Information:** Application fee $50. Priority deadline 2/1. Nonfall registration accepted. Admission may be deferred for a maximum of 1 Year.

COSTS AND FINANCIAL AID

Annual tuition $37,100. Room and board $12,510. Required fees $1,460. Average book expense $1,746. **Required Forms and Deadlines:** FAFSA, State aid form. **Types of Aid:** *Need-based scholarships/grants:* Federal Pell, FSEOG, State scholarships/grants, Private scholarships, College/university scholarship or grant aid from institutional funds. *Loans:* Direct Subsidized Stafford Loans, Direct Unsubsidized Stafford Loans, Direct PLUS loans, Federal Perkins Loans, College/university loans from institutional funds. *Student Employment:* Federal Work-Study Program available. Institutional employment available. **Financial Aid Statistics:** 70% needy freshmen, 67% needy undergrads receive need-based scholarship or grant aid. 99% freshmen, 99% undergrads receive non-need-based scholarship or grant aid. 93% freshmen, 93% undergrads receive need-based self-help aid. 0% freshmen, 0% undergrads receive athletic scholarships. 87% freshmen, 83% undergrads receive any aid. 82% undergrads borrow to pay for school. Average cumulative indebtedness $30,844. **Criteria for awarding aid:** *Need-based:* Academics. *Non-need-based:* Academics, Alumni affiliation, Art, Leadership, Minority status, Music/drama, Religious affiliation.

THE UNIVERSITY OF LETHBRIDGE

4401 University Drive, Lethbridge, AB T1K 3M4
Phone: 403-382-7134 • **Financial Aid Phone:** 403-329-2585
E-mail: admissions@uleth.ca
Fax: 403-329-5159 • **Website:** www.uleth.ca • **ACT Code:** 5202

This public school was founded in 1967. It has a 568-acre campus.

RATINGS

Admissions Selectivity Rating: 63   **Fire Safety Rating:** 60*   **Green Rating:** 60*

STUDENTS AND FACULTY

Student Body: 10% out-of-state, (56 countries represented).
Retention and Graduation: 81% freshmen return for sophomore year.

ACADEMICS

Degrees: bachelor's, certificate, diploma, doctoral, master's, postbachelor's certifiate, post-master's certificate. **Classes:** Most classes have 10-19 students. Most lab/discussion sessions have 10-19 students. **Most popular majors:** Business Administration and Management; Accounting; Registered Nursing/Registered Nurse. **Special Study Options:** Accelerated program, cooperative education program, double major, English as a Second Language (ESL), exchange student program (domestic), honors program, independent study, internships, student-designed major, study abroad, teacher certification program, Applied Studies. Combined degree programs: B.A.or B.Sc./B. Ed., B.A.or B.Sc./B.Mgt., B.Mgt./B.Ed., B.F.A.-Art or -Dramatic Arts/B. Ed., B.Mus./B.Ed., B.F.A.-New Media/B.Mgt., B.H.Sc./B.Mgt., B.F.A.-New Media/B.Ed. **Disability Services:** Special programs offered to physically disabled students, including note-taking services, reader services, tape recorders, tutors. **Career Services:** Alumni services, Career/job search classes, Career assessment, Internships.

FACILITIES

Housing: Coed dorms, special housing for disabled students, apartments for married students, apartments for single students, Townhouses for single and married students and students with families. 100% of campus accessible to physically diasbled. **Special Academic Facilities/Equipment:** Art Gallery, Theatres. **Computers:** 100% of classrooms, 100% of libraries, 100% of dining areas, 100% of student union, have wireless network access. Students can register for classes online. Administrative functions (other than registration) can be performed online.

CAMPUS LIFE

Environment: City. **Activities:** Choral groups, dance, drama/theater, jazz band, literary magazine, music ensembles, musical theater, radio station, student government, student newspaper, student-run film society, symphony orchestra, Student Organization. 1 fraternity, 1 sorority. **Athletics (Intercollegiate):** *Men:* basketball, ice hockey, soccer, swimming, track/field (outdoor). *Women:* basketball, ice hockey, rugby, soccer, swimming, track/field (outdoor).

ADMISSIONS

Minimum internet-based TOEFL 80. Minimum paper TOEFL 550. **Basis for Candidate Selection:** *Very important factors considered include:* rigor of secondary school record. *Other factors considered include:* class rank, standardized test scores. **Freshman Admission Requirements:** High school diploma is required and GED is not accepted. **Freshman Admission Statistics:** 2,997 applied, 84.25% admitted, 49% enrolled. **Transfer Admission Requirements:** college transcript(s). **General Admission Information:** Application fee $100. Priority deadline 3/1. Regular application deadline 6/30. Nonfall registration accepted. Admission may be deferred for a maximum of 1 semester.

COSTS AND FINANCIAL AID

Annual in-state tuition $4,974. Annual out-of-state tuition $4,974. Room and board $6,268. Required fees $1,015. **Required Forms and Deadlines:** Institution's own financial aid form. *Student Employment:* Institutional employment available. **Criteria for awarding aid:** *Non-need-based:* Academics, Athletics, Leadership.

UNIVERSITY OF LOUISIANA AT LAFAYETTE

P.O. Drawer 41210, Lafayette, LA 70504
Phone: 337-482-6553 • **Financial Aid Phone:** 337-482-6506
E-mail: enroll@louisiana.edu • **CEEB Code:** 6672
Fax: 337-482-1112 • **Website:** www.louisiana.edu • **ACT Code:** 1612

This public school was founded in 1898. It has a 1375-acre campus.

RATINGS

Admissions Selectivity Rating: 88   **Fire Safety Rating:** 93   **Green Rating:** 60*

STUDENTS AND FACULTY

Enrollment: 14,667. **Student Body:** 56% female, 44% male, 8% out-of-state, 2% international (101 countries represented). Asian 2%, African American 21%, Caucasian 68%, Hispanic 3%, Native American <1%, Pacific Islander <1%, Two or more races 2%, Race unknown 1%.
Retention and Graduation: 76% freshmen return for sophomore year. 15% freshmen graduate within 4 years. 48% freshmen graduate within 6 years.
Faculty: Student/faculty ratio 23:1. 598 full-time faculty, 62% hold PhDs, 20% are are members of minority groups, 45% are women.

ACADEMICS

Degrees: bachelor's, doctoral, master's, postbachelor's certifiate, post-master's certificate. **Classes:** Most classes have 20-29 students. **Most popular majors:** Business Administration and Management Biology/Biological Sciences. **Special Study Options:** Accelerated program, cooperative education program, cross-registration, distance learning, double major, dual enrollment, exchange student program (domestic), honors program, independent study, internships, student-designed major, study abroad, teacher certification program. **Honors Programs:** Honors Baccalaureate degree is available. **Disability Services:** Special programs offered to physically disabled students, including note-taking services, reader services, tape recorders, tutors. **Career Services:** Career/job search classes, Career assessment.

FACILITIES

Housing: men's dorms, women's dorms, fraternity/sorority housing, apartments for married students, apartments for single students. 85% of campus accessible to physically diasbled. **Special Academic Facilities/Equipment:** Art museum, experimental farm, primate center, CAD/CAM laboratory, marine research facility, on campus restaurant and hotel with instructional facilities, 2 nuclear accelerators, 2 electron microscopes, radio station and television production studio, nursery school laboratory, Louisiana Emersive Technologies Enterprise **Computers:** Students can register for classes online. Administrative functions (other than registration) can be performed online.

CAMPUS LIFE

Environment: City. **Activities:** Choral groups, concert band, dance, drama/theater, jazz band, literary magazine, marching band, music ensembles, musical theater, opera, radio station, student government, student newspaper, symphony orchestra, yearbook, Campus Ministries, Student Organization. 155 registered organizations, 14 honor societies, 8 religious organizations. 11 fraternities, 9 sororities. **Athletics (Intercollegiate):** *Men:* baseball, basketball, cheerleading, cross-country, football, golf, tennis, track/field (outdoor), track/field (indoor). *Women:* basketball, cheerleading, cross-country, soccer, softball, tennis, track/field (outdoor), track/field (indoor), volleyball. **On-Campus Highlights:** University Museum, Student Center, Cajun Field, Cajundome, Dupre Library.

ADMISSIONS

Freshman Academic Profile: Average high school GPA 3.3. 19% in top 10% of high school class, 43% in top 25% of high school class, 74% in top 50% of high school class. **Reported SAT (pre-2016 redesign) scores:** SAT Math middle 50% range 490-590. SAT Critical Reading middle 50% range 470-590. **Concordant SAT scores:** SAT Math middle 50% range 520–610. ACT middle 50% range 21-25. Minimum paper TOEFL 525. **Basis for Candidate Selection:** *Very important factors considered include:* rigor of secondary school record, class rank, academic GPA, standardized test scores. *Other factors considered include:* state residency. **Freshman Admission Requirements:** High school diploma is required and GED is accepted. *Academic units required:* 4 English, 4 math, 3 science, 2 foreign language, 1 social studies, 2 history, 1 visual/performing arts, and 1 unit from above areas or other academic areas. **Freshman Admission Statistics:** 9,386 applied, 55.80% admitted, 56% enrolled. **Transfer Admission Requirements:** college transcript(s), Lowest grade transferable D. **General Admission Information:** Application fee $25. Priority deadline 7/20. Nonfall registration accepted. Admission may be deferred for a maximum of 1 semester.

COSTS AND FINANCIAL AID

Annual in-state tuition $4,916. Annual out-of-state tuition $17,316. Room and board $8,566. Required fees $2,033. Average book expense $1,200, **Required Forms and Deadlines:** FAFSA. **Notification of Awards:** Applicants will be notified of awards on a rolling basis beginning 4/1. **Types of Aid:** *Need-based scholarships/grants:* Federal Pell, FSEOG, State scholarships/grants, Private scholarships, College/university scholarship or grant aid from institutional funds, Federal Nursing Scholarships. *Loans:* Federal Perkins Loans, Federal Nursing Loans. *Student Employment:* Federal Work-Study Program available. Institutional employment available. **Financial Aid Statistics:** 96% needy freshmen, 88% needy undergrads receive need-based scholarship or grant aid. 15% freshmen, 9% undergrads receive non-need-based scholarship or grant aid. 49% freshmen, 60% undergrads receive need-based self-help aid. 2% freshmen, 3% undergrads receive athletic scholarships. 87% freshmen, 72% undergrads receive any aid. **Criteria for awarding aid:** *Need-based:* Job skills.

UNIVERSITY OF LOUISVILLE

Admissions Office, Louisville, KY 40292
Phone: 502-852-6531 • **Financial Aid Phone:** 502-852-5511
E-mail: admitme@louisville.edu
Fax: 502-852-4776 • **Website:** www.louisville.edu • **ACT Code:** 1556

This public school was founded in 1798. It has a 274-acre campus.

RATINGS

Admissions Selectivity Rating: 86   **Fire Safety Rating:** 93   **Green Rating:** 93

STUDENTS AND FACULTY

Enrollment: 14,844. **Student Body:** 50% female, 50% male, 16% out-of-state, 1% international (94 countries represented). Asian 3%, African American 11%,

Caucasian 76%, Hispanic 4%, Native American <1%, Pacific Islander <1%, Two or more races 4%, Race unknown <1%.
Retention and Graduation: 79% freshmen return for sophomore year. 25% freshmen graduate within 4 years. 53 33% grads go on to further study within 1 year. 36% grads pursue arts and sciences degrees. 5% grads pursue law degrees. 16% grads pursue business degrees. 17% grads pursue medical degrees.
Faculty: Student/faculty ratio 16:1. 824 full-time faculty, 87% hold PhDs, 20% are are members of minority groups, 45% are women. 9% of classes are taught by teaching assistants.

ACADEMICS

Degrees: associate, bachelor's, certificate, doctoral/professional, doctoral/research, master's, postbachelor's certificate, post-master's certificate. **Classes:** Most classes have 20-29 students. **Most popular majors:** Registered Nursing/Registered Nurse; Biology/Biological Sciences; Speech Communication and Rhetoric. **Special Study Options:** Accelerated program, cooperative education program, cross-registration, distance learning, double major, dual enrollment, English as a Second Language (ESL), honors program, independent study, internships, student-designed major, study abroad, teacher certification program. Combined degree programs: BA/MA, BS-BA/MBA, BS/MENG.
Disability Services: Special programs offered to physically disabled students, including note-taking services, reader services, tape recorders, tutors. **Career Services:** Alumni services, Career/job search classes, Career assessment, On-campus interviews. The University of Louisville offers a strong Career Services program. Operating 5 career services offices across campus, all schools and colleges of the University deliver a custom selection of career services designed to serve the unique career development needs of its' academic programs from Freshman year to employment.
Freshmen Year
Starting at orientation all first year undecided and pre-major students are required to take Cards Career Navigator, an on-line assessment that links their individual interests, skills and values to matching occupations and majors. In addition, all Undecided majors are then required to meet with their career coach to further explore their interests and work toward choosing a major.
Sophomore/Junior Year
Once clear on what major best suits their career goals each student can work on-line or with their career coach to further define their goals and design a career and academic plan that best prepares them for an experiential education opportunity. Through our academic departments UofL offers more internship and cooperative education opportunities than any other school in Kentucky.
Senior Year
As graduation nears, students have the opportunity to participate in a wide variety of workshops and training seminars on topics like, 'Righting your Resume', 'Award Winning Cover-letters', 'Dress for Success', 'How to Make the Most of a Career Fair', 'Networking for Dummies', 'Job Search 101', 'Social Media and Your Job Search: Everything you Need to Know' and 'Grad School: Your Next Step'? in preparation for entering the job market or heading off to Graduate School. Competitive knowledge and skills in hand our students then have the opportunity to meet on campus through presentations, on-campus recruiting and career fairs with over 600 employers and graduate schools a year. In addition, through our on-line job boards students have access to 500-600 new job postings a month and a wide selection of alumni willing to mentor and/or network with our new grads.
UofL is embracing the fact that career development is key to student persistence, graduation and successful career management. That is why at each step in the students' academic process our students are introduced to career development and the reality that a successful job search begins freshmen year and lasts for a lifetime.

FACILITIES

Housing: Coed dorms, special housing for disabled students, fraternity/sorority housing, apartments for married students, cooperative housing, apartments for single students, Theme Housing. 95% of campus accessible to physically diasbled. **Special Academic Facilities/Equipment:** Natural history and art museums, planetarium, numerous institutes and centers. **Computers:** Administrative functions (other than registration) can be performed online.

CAMPUS LIFE

Environment: Metropolis. **Activities:** Choral groups, concert band, dance, drama/theater, jazz band, literary magazine, marching band, music ensembles, musical theater, opera, pep band, radio station, student government, student newspaper, symphony orchestra, Campus Ministries, Student Organization. 237 registered organizations, 7 honor societies, 18 religious organizations. 13 fraternities, 10 sororities. **Athletics (Intercollegiate):** *Men:* baseball, basketball, cheerleading, cross-country, diving, football, golf, soccer, swimming, tennis, track/field (outdoor). *Women:* basketball, cheerleading, crew/rowing, cross-country, diving, field hockey, golf, lacrosse, soccer, softball, swimming, tennis, track/field (outdoor), volleyball. **On-Campus Highlights:** Student Activity Center, J.B. Speed Art Museum **Environmental Initiatives:** Unlimited free public transit ride contract for all UofL students, staff and faculty and Commute Green campaign: http://louisville.edu/parking/commute-green.html

ADMISSIONS

Freshman Academic Profile: Average high school GPA 3.6. 82% from public high schools. **Reported SAT (pre-2016 redesign) scores:** SAT Math middle 50% range 510-620. SAT Critical Reading middle 50% range 490-620. **Concordant SAT scores:** SAT Math middle 50% range 540–640. ACT middle 50% range 22-29. Minimum paper TOEFL 550. **Basis for Candidate Selection:** *Very important factors considered include:* rigor of secondary school record, academic GPA, standardized test scores. *Other factors considered include:* class rank, recommendation(s), extracurricular activities, talent/ability, state residency, racial/ethnic status, volunteer work, work experience.
Freshman Admission Requirements: High school diploma is required and GED is accepted. *Academic units required:* 4 English, 3 math, 3 science, 1 science lab, 2 foreign language, 3 social studies, 5 academic electives, 1 visual/performing arts, and 5 units from above areas or other academic areas. *Academic units recommended:* 4 math, 4 science, 3 foreign language.
Freshman Admission Statistics: 9,430 applied, 71.66% admitted, 41% enrolled. **Transfer Admission Requirements:** college transcript(s), Minimum college GPA of 2.0 required. Lowest grade transferable D. **General Admission Information:** Application fee $50. Priority deadline 2/15. Nonfall registration accepted. Admission may be deferred.

COSTS AND FINANCIAL AID

Annual in-state tuition $10,542. Annual out-of-state tuition $24,848. Room and board $7,942. Average book expense $1,000. **Required Forms and Deadlines:** FAFSA. **Notification of Awards:** Applicants will be notified of awards on a rolling basis beginning 4/1. **Types of Aid:** *Need-based scholarships/grants:* Federal Pell, FSEOG, State scholarships/grants, Private scholarships, College/university scholarship or grant aid from institutional funds. *Loans:* Direct Subsidized Stafford Loans, Direct Unsubsidized Stafford Loans, Direct PLUS loans, Federal Perkins Loans, Federal Nursing Loans. *Student Employment:* Federal Work-Study Program available. Institutional employment available. **Financial Aid Statistics:** 96% needy freshmen, 89% needy undergrads receive need-based scholarship or grant aid. 20% freshmen, 13% undergrads receive non-need-based scholarship or grant aid. 54% freshmen, 63% undergrads receive need-based self-help aid. 4% freshmen, 3% undergrads receive athletic scholarships. 97% freshmen, 79% undergrads receive any aid. **Criteria for awarding aid:** *Non-need-based:* Academics, Art, Athletics, Leadership, Minority status, Music/drama, State/district residency.

UNIVERSITY OF MAINE

5713 Chadbourne Hall, Orono, ME 04469-5713
Phone: 207-581-1561 • **Financial Aid Phone:** 207-581-1324
E-mail: umaineadmissions@maine.edu • **CEEB Code:** 3916
Fax: 207-581-1213 • **Website:** www.umaine.edu • **ACT Code:** 1664

This public school was founded in 1865. It has a 660-acre campus.

RATINGS

Admissions Selectivity Rating: 77   Fire Safety Rating: 98   Green Rating: 98

STUDENTS AND FACULTY

Enrollment: 8,757. **Student Body:** 47% female, 53% male, 30% out-of-state, 2% international (35 countries represented). Asian 2%, African American 2%, Caucasian 84%, Hispanic 3%, Native American 1%, Pacific Islander 0%, Two or more races 3%, Race unknown 4%.
Retention and Graduation: 76% freshmen return for sophomore year. 36% freshmen graduate within 4 years. 59% freshmen graduate within 6 years.
Faculty: Student/faculty ratio 16:1. 502 full-time faculty, 85% hold PhDs, 9% are are members of minority groups, 38% are women. 8% of classes are taught by teaching assistants.

ACADEMICS

Degrees: bachelor's, doctoral/research, doctoral, master's, postbachelor's certificate, post-master's certificate. **Classes:** Most classes have 10-19 students. Most lab/discussion sessions have 10-19 students. **Most popular majors:** Psychology; Registered Nursing/Registered Nurse; Business Administration and Management. **Special Study Options:** Accelerated program, cooperative education program, distance learning, double major, dual enrollment, English as a Second Language (ESL), honors program, independent study, internships, liberal arts/career combination, study abroad, teacher certification program.
Honors Programs: The Honors College at The University of Maine provides

a unique opportunity for a community of five hundred motivated students to investigate diverse academic areas of the University, to be challenged in a supportive intellectual environment, and to critically engage fellow students and enthusiastic, distinguished faculty in thoughtful, provocative discussion. The benefits and rewards are substantial, and the program is flexible enough to be tailored precisely to the individual student's needs and interests. Combined degree programs: BA or BS/MBA; BA/BS; BA or BS liberal arts/MA in teaching. **Disability Services:** Special programs offered to physically disabled students, including note-taking services, reader services, tape recorders, tutors. **Career Services:** Alumni network, Alumni services, Career/job search classes, Career assessment, Internships, Regional alumni. The College of Engineering offers an exceptional co-op program, which provides students real-world experience that often leads directly to job placements after graduation.

FACILITIES

Housing: Coed dorms, special housing for disabled students, special housing for international students, fraternity/sorority housing, apartments for married students, apartments for single students, Wellness Housing, ThemeHousingHonor's College Housing; Graduate Student Housing; Smoke free; chem free; clusters for engineering and science majors. First Year Residential Experience (FYRE). 90% of campus accessible to physically diasbled. **Special Academic Facilities/Equipment:** Laboratory for Advanced Surface Science and Technology (LASST), Advanced Manufacturing Center, Anthropology museum, Digital Media Lab, folklore and oral history museum, art museum, Canadian-American center, social sciences research institute, exceptional child research lab, preschool, experimental farms, land/water resources center, center for marine studies, planetarium/observatory, electron microscopes, farm museum, paper-making machine, aquaculture production facility, woodland preserve, botanical garden, arts center, Franco-American Center **Computers:** 100% of classrooms, 10% of dorms, 100% of libraries, 100% of dining areas, 100% of student union, 50% of common outdoor areas have wireless network access. Students can register for classes online. Administrative functions (other than registration) can be performed online.

CAMPUS LIFE

Environment: Village. **Activities:** Choral groups, concert band, dance, drama/theater, jazz band, literary magazine, marching band, music ensembles, musical theater, opera, pep band, radio station, student government, student newspaper, student-run film society, symphony orchestra, television station, yearbook, Campus Ministries, Student Organization. 224 registered organizations, 42 honor societies, 7 religious organizations. 13 fraternities, 6 sororities. **Athletics (Intercollegiate):** *Men:* baseball, basketball, cross-country, diving, football, ice hockey, soccer, swimming, track/field (outdoor), track/field (indoor). *Women:* basketball, cross-country, diving, field hockey, ice hockey, soccer, softball, swimming, track/field (outdoor), track/field (indoor), volleyball. **On-Campus Highlights:** Collins Center for the Arts, Alfond Arena, Market Place—Memorial Union, Student Recreation Center, The Mall. **Environmental Initiatives:** UMaine has developed a master plan centered on sustainability, restoring habitat, avoiding sprawl, maximizing solar orientation, and reducing carbon emissions.

ADMISSIONS

Freshman Academic Profile: Average high school GPA 3.2. 18% in top 10% of high school class, 42% in top 25% of high school class, 76% in top 50% of high school class. **Reported SAT (pre-2016 redesign) scores:** SAT Math middle 50% range 480-600. SAT Critical Reading middle 50% range 470-590. SAT Writing middle 50% range 460-570. **Concordant SAT scores:** SAT EBRW middle 50% 520–640. SAT Math middle 50% range 510–620. ACT middle 50% range 21-26. Minimum internet-based TOEFL 79. Minimum paper TOEFL 550. **Basis for Candidate Selection:** *Very important factors considered include:* rigor of secondary school record, class rank, academic GPA, standardized test scores. *Important factors considered include:* application essay, recommendation(s). *Other factors considered include:* interview, extracurricular activities, talent/ability, character/personal qualities, volunteer work, work experience. **Freshman Admission Requirements:** High school diploma is required and GED is accepted. *Academic units required:* 4 English, 3 math, 2 science, 2 science labs, 2 foreign language, 2 social studies, 4 academic electives, and 1 unit from above areas or other academic areas. *Academic units recommended:* 4 English, 4 math, 4 science, 3 science labs, 2 foreign language, 2 social studies, 1 history, 4 academic electives, and 1 unit from above areas or other academic areas. **Freshman Admission Statistics:** 12,952 applied, 89.75% admitted, 19% enrolled. **Transfer Admission Requirements:** High school transcript, college transcript(s), essay or personal statement, Minimum college GPA of 2.0 required. Lowest grade transferable C-. **General Admission Information:** Application fee $40. Priority deadline 2/1. Nonfall registration accepted. Admission may be deferred for a maximum of 2 semesters.

COSTS AND FINANCIAL AID

Annual in-state tuition $8,370. Annual out-of-state tuition $27,240. Room and board $10,164. Required fees $2,258. Average book expense $1,000. **Required Forms and Deadlines:** FAFSA. **Notification of Awards:** Applicants will be notified of awards on a rolling basis beginning 3/15. **Types of Aid:** *Need-based scholarships/grants:* Federal Pell, FSEOG, State scholarships/grants, Private scholarships, College/university scholarship or grant aid from institutional funds, Federal Nursing Scholarships. *Loans:* Direct Subsidized Stafford Loans, Direct Unsubsidized Stafford Loans, Direct PLUS loans, Federal Perkins Loans, State Loans, College/university loans from institutional funds. *Student Employment:* Federal Work-Study Program available. Institutional employment available. **Financial Aid Statistics:** 94% needy freshmen, 87% needy undergrads receive need-based scholarship or grant aid. 12% freshmen, 7% undergrads receive non-need-based scholarship or grant aid. 79% freshmen, 84% undergrads receive need-based self-help aid. 2% freshmen, 2% undergrads receive athletic scholarships. 93% freshmen, 83% undergrads receive any aid. Average cumulative indebtedness $34,923. **Criteria for awarding aid:** *Need-based:* Academics, Alumni affiliation, Art, Athletics, Job skills, Leadership, Minority status, Music/drama, Religious affiliation. *Non-need-based:* Academics, Alumni affiliation, Art, Athletics, Job skills, Leadership, Minority status, Music/drama, Religious affiliation, State/district residency.

See page 1076.

UNIVERSITY OF MAINE AT FARMINGTON

246 Main Street, Farmington, ME 4938
Phone: 207-778-7050 • **Financial Aid Phone:** 207-778-7100
E-mail: umfadmit@maine.edu • **CEEB Code:** 3506
Fax: 207-778-8182 • **Website:** www.umf.maine.edu • **ACT Code:** 1640

This public school was founded in 1863. It has a 55-acre campus.

RATINGS

Admissions Selectivity Rating: 77   **Fire Safety Rating:** 91   **Green Rating:** 84

STUDENTS AND FACULTY

Enrollment: 1,753. **Student Body:** 65% female, 35% male, 16% out-of-state, <1% international (9 countries represented). Asian 1%, African American 2%, Caucasian 88%, Hispanic 2%, Native American <1%, Pacific Islander <1%, Two or more races 2%, Race unknown 4%.
Retention and Graduation: 74% freshmen return for sophomore year. 44% freshmen graduate within 4 years. 56 **Faculty:** Student/faculty ratio 13:1. 717 full-time faculty, 14% hold PhDs, 1% are are members of minority groups, 10% are women. 0% of classes are taught by teaching assistants.

ACADEMICS

Degrees: bachelor's, master's, postbachelor's certificate. **Classes:** Most classes have 10-19 students. Most lab/discussion sessions have 10-19 students. **Most popular majors:** Elementary Education and Teaching; Secondary Education and Teaching; Psychology. **Special Study Options:** cooperative education program, cross-registration, double major, dual enrollment, exchange student program (domestic), honors program, independent study, internships, liberal arts/career combination, student-designed major, study abroad, teacher certification program, SALT, Documentary Field Study in Portland,ME, National Student Exchange, Service Learning. **Honors Programs:** UMF Honors Program. **Disability Services:** Special programs offered to physically disabled students, including note-taking services, reader services. **Career Services:** Alumni network, Alumni services, Career/job search classes, Career assessment, Internships, Regional alumni. The growth of our experiential learning opportunities for all UMF students.

FACILITIES

Housing: Coed dorms, special housing for international students, women's dorms, Wellness Housing, Theme Housing, Housing for students maintaining a certain GPA, medical rooms, quiet floors, wellness community, community, independent living environment housing available. 95% of campus accessible to physically diasbled. **Special Academic Facilities/Equipment:** Art gallery, health and fitness center, computer center, Mantor Library, Alumni theater, Nordica Auditorium, observatory **Computers:** 100% of classrooms, 100% of dorms, 100% of libraries, 100% of dining areas, 100% of student union, 100% of common outdoor areas have wireless network access. Students can register for classes online. Administrative functions (other than registration) can be performed online.

CAMPUS LIFE

Environment: Village. **Activities:** Choral groups, concert band, dance, drama/theater, literary magazine, music ensembles, musical theater, radio station, student government, student newspaper, yearbook, Student Organization. 52 registered organizations, 3 honor societies, 3 religious organizations. **Athletics (Intercollegiate):** *Men:* baseball, basketball, cross-country, golf, soccer. *Women:* basketball, cross-country, field hockey, soccer, softball, volleyball. **On-Campus Highlights:** Recreation and Fitness Center, Landing, Computer

Center, Education Center, Student Center. **Environmental Initiatives:** Completion of two LEED-certified buildings and commitment to new construction and major renovations at the LEED silver level.

ADMISSIONS

Freshman Academic Profile: Average high school GPA 3.1. 13% in top 10% of high school class, 42% in top 25% of high school class, 79% in top 50% of high school class. 89% from public high schools. **Reported SAT (pre-2016 redesign) scores:** SAT Math middle 50% range 430-548. SAT Critical Reading middle 50% range 440-580. SAT Writing middle 50% range 440-540. **Concordant SAT scores:** SAT EBRW middle 50% 490-620. SAT Math middle 50% range 470-570. ACT middle 50% range 18-25. Minimum internet-based TOEFL 79. Minimum paper TOEFL 550. **Basis for Candidate Selection:** *Very important factors considered include:* rigor of secondary school record, academic GPA. *Important factors considered include:* class rank, application essay, recommendation(s). *Other factors considered include:* standardized test scores, interview, extracurricular activities, talent/ability, character/personal qualities, first generation, alumni/ae relation, geographical residence, state residency, volunteer work, work experience, level of applicant's interest. **Freshman Admission Requirements:** High school diploma is required and GED is accepted. *Academic units required:* 4 English, 3 math, 3 science, 2 science labs, 3 social studies. *Academic units recommended:* 2 foreign language. **Freshman Admission Statistics:** 1,880 applied, 80.43% admitted, 29% enrolled. **Transfer Admission Requirements:** High school transcript, college transcript(s), essay or personal statement, Minimum college GPA of 2.5 required. Lowest grade transferable c. **General Admission Information:** Nonfall registration accepted. Admission may be deferred for a maximum of one year.

COSTS AND FINANCIAL AID

Required Forms and Deadlines: FAFSA. **Notification of Awards:** Applicants will be notified of awards on a rolling basis beginning 3/15. **Types of Aid:** *Need-based scholarships/grants:* Federal Pell, FSEOG, State scholarships/grants, Private scholarships, College/university scholarship or grant aid from institutional funds. *Loans:* Direct Subsidized Stafford Loans, Direct Unsubsidized Stafford Loans, Direct PLUS loans, Federal Perkins Loans, State Loans, College/university loans from institutional funds. *Student Employment:* Federal Work-Study Program available. Institutional employment available. **Financial Aid Statistics:** 96% needy freshmen, 93% needy undergrads receive need-based scholarship or grant aid. 7% freshmen, 4% undergrads receive non-need-based scholarship or grant aid. 86% freshmen, 90% undergrads receive need-based self-help aid. 0% freshmen, 0% undergrads receive athletic scholarships. 98% freshmen, 93% undergrads receive any aid. 89% undergrads borrow to pay for school. Average cumulative indebtedness $30,648. **Criteria for awarding aid:** *Non-need-based:* Academics, Leadership, Minority status, Music/drama, State/district residency.

UNIVERSITY OF MAINE AT MACHIAS

Office of Admissions, Machias, ME 4654
Phone: 207-255-1318 • **Financial Aid Phone:** 207-255-1203
E-mail: ummadmissions@maine.edu • **CEEB Code:** 3956
Fax: 207-255-1363 • **Website:** www.umm.maine.edu • **ACT Code:** 1666

This public school was founded in 1909. It has a 42-acre campus.

RATINGS

Admissions Selectivity Rating: 73   **Fire Safety Rating:** 76   **Green Rating:** 60*

STUDENTS AND FACULTY

Enrollment: 554. **Student Body:** 65% female, 35% male, 24% out-of-state, 4% international (18 countries represented). Asian 1%, African American 1%, Caucasian 88%, Hispanic 2%, Native American 4%, Pacific Islander 0%, Two or more races 0%, Race unknown 0%. **Retention and Graduation:** 73% freshmen return for sophomore year. 12% freshmen graduate within 4 years. 42% freshmen graduate within 6 years. **Faculty:** Student/faculty ratio 15:1. 30 full-time faculty, 73% hold PhDs, 3% are are members of minority groups, 33% are women. 0% of classes are taught by teaching assistants.

ACADEMICS

Degrees: bachelor's. **Classes:** Most classes have 10-19 students. Most lab/discussion sessions have 10-19 students. **Most popular majors:** Marine Biology and Biological Oceanography; Parks, Recreation and Leisure Facilities Management; Elementary Education and Teaching. **Special Study Options:** cooperative education program, distance learning, double major, dual enrollment, honors program, independent study, internships, student-designed major, study abroad, teacher certification program. **Disability Services:** Special

programs offered to physically disabled students, including reader services, tape recorders, tutors. **Career Services:** Career assessment, Internships.

FACILITIES

Housing: Coed dorms. 85% of campus accessible to physically diasbled. **Special Academic Facilities/Equipment:** Art Gallery Book Arts Print Shop Geographic Information Systems Laboratory and Service Center **Computers:** 100% of classrooms, 100% of dorms, 100% of libraries, 100% of dining areas, 100% of student union, 100% of common outdoor areas have wireless network access. Students can register for classes online. Administrative functions (other than registration) can be performed online.

CAMPUS LIFE

Environment: Rural. **Activities:** Choral groups, dance, drama/theater, literary magazine, music ensembles, musical theater, pep band, radio station, student government, Campus Ministries. 38 registered organizations, 2 religious organizations. 5 fraternities, 4 sororities. **Athletics (Intercollegiate):** *Men:* basketball, soccer. *Women:* basketball, soccer, volleyball. **On-Campus Highlights:** Aquatics/Fitness Center/Gymnasium, Residence Halls, Wireless Computer Lab/Classroom, Performing Arts Center, Early Care and Education Center, The Portal—multi-media center, Marine Biology lab facilities, Campus Radio Station, Art Studios and Gallery, Bookstore, Book Arts Print Shop, Kilburn Commons, The Galley. **Environmental Initiatives:** Green Council.

ADMISSIONS

Freshman Academic Profile: 13% in top 10% of high school class, 24% in top 25% of high school class, 63% in top 50% of high school class. **Reported SAT (pre-2016 redesign) scores:** SAT Math middle 50% range 400-530. SAT Critical Reading middle 50% range 440-530. **Concordant SAT scores:** SAT Math middle 50% range 440-560. ACT middle 50% range 15-25. Minimum paper TOEFL 500. **Basis for Candidate Selection:** *Very important factors considered include:* rigor of secondary school record, application essay, recommendation(s), interview. *Important factors considered include:* class rank, standardized test scores, extracurricular activities. *Other factors considered include:* talent/ability, character/personal qualities, volunteer work, work experience. **Freshman Admission Requirements:** High school diploma is required and GED is accepted. *Academic units required:* 4 English, 3 math, 2 science, 2 science labs, 2 social studies. *Academic units recommended:* 2 foreign language, 3 academic electives. **Freshman Admission Statistics:** 381 applied, 91.60% admitted, 32% enrolled. **Transfer Admission Requirements:** High school transcript, college transcript(s), statement of good standing from prior institution(s). Minimum college GPA of 2.0 required. Lowest grade transferable C-. **General Admission Information:** Application fee $40. Regular application deadline 8/15. Nonfall registration accepted. Admission may be deferred for a maximum of 1 year.

COSTS AND FINANCIAL AID

Annual in-state tuition $6,410. Annual out-of-state tuition $16,550. Room and board $6,574. Average book expense $650. **Required Forms and Deadlines:** FAFSA. **Notification of Awards:** Applicants will be notified of awards on a rolling basis beginning 3/1. **Types of Aid:** *Need-based scholarships/grants:* Federal Pell, FSEOG, State scholarships/grants, Private scholarships, College/university scholarship or grant aid from institutional funds. *Loans:* Federal Perkins Loans. *Student Employment:* Federal Work-Study Program available. Institutional employment available. **Financial Aid Statistics:** 97% needy freshmen, 87% needy undergrads receive need-based scholarship or grant aid. 9% freshmen, 6% undergrads receive non-need-based scholarship or grant aid. 81% freshmen, 81% undergrads receive need-based self-help aid. 0% freshmen, 0% undergrads receive athletic scholarships. 82% freshmen, 74% undergrads receive any aid. **Criteria for awarding aid:** *Need-based:* Academics, Art, Leadership. *Non-need-based:* Academics, Alumni affiliation, Art, Leadership, Minority status, Music/drama, State/district residency.

UNIVERSITY OF MAINE—AUGUSTA

46 University Drive, Augusta, ME 4330
Phone: 207-621-3465 • **Financial Aid Phone:** 207-621-3455
E-mail: umaadm@maine.edu • **CEEB Code:** 3929
Fax: 207-621-3333 • **Website:** www.uma.edu • **ACT Code:** 1641

This public school was founded in 1965. It has a 159-acre campus.

RATINGS

Admissions Selectivity Rating: 62   **Fire Safety Rating:** 60*   **Green Rating:** 60*

STUDENTS AND FACULTY

Enrollment: 4,523. **Student Body:** 73% female, 27% male, 3% out-of-state, <1% international (5 countries represented). Asian 1%, African American 1%, Caucasian 85%, Hispanic 1%, Native American 2%, Pacific Islander <1%, Two or more races 2%, Race unknown 8%.

Retention and Graduation: 53% freshmen return for sophomore year. 4% freshmen graduate within 4 years. 40% grads go on to further study within 1 year. **Faculty:** Student/faculty ratio 18:1. 103 full-time faculty, 56% hold PhDs, 0% are are members of minority groups, 58% are women. 0% of classes are taught by teaching assistants.

ACADEMICS

Degrees: associate, bachelor's, certificate, terminal, transfer. **Classes:** Most classes have 10-19 students. Most lab/discussion sessions have 10-19 students. **Most popular majors:** Social Sciences; Health Services/Allied Health/Health Sciences; Business/Commerce. **Special Study Options:** cross-registration, distance learning, double major, dual enrollment, honors program, independent study, internships, liberal arts/career combination, student-designed major, study abroad. **Honors Programs:** UMA Honors Program—augments a student's academic and co-curricular experience Combined degree programs: BA/M. Architecture with Boston Architectural College. **Disability Services:** Special programs offered to physically disabled students, including note-taking services. **Career Services:** Career/job search classes, Career assessment, On-campus interviews.

FACILITIES

Housing: 99% of campus accessible to physically diasbled. **Special Academic Facilities/Equipment:** Jewett Gallery, Katz Library, Student Center **Computers:** 100% of classrooms, 100% of libraries, 100% of dining areas, 100% of student union, 100% of common outdoor areas have wireless network access. Students can register for classes online. Administrative functions (other than registration) can be performed online.

CAMPUS LIFE

Environment: Village. **Activities:** drama/theater, jazz band, music ensembles, pep band, student government, student newspaper, Student Organization. 23 registered organizations, 1 honor society, 1 religious organization. **Athletics (Intercollegiate):** *Men:* basketball, golf. *Women:* basketball, golf, soccer. **On-Campus Highlights:** Katz Library, Student Center, Campus Center at UCB, Huskins Lounge at UCB. **Environmental Initiatives:** Reduce—Reuse—Recycle program in place since 1990.

ADMISSIONS

Freshman Academic Profile: 95% from public high schools. Minimum paper TOEFL 500. **Basis for Candidate Selection:** *Important factors considered include:* rigor of secondary school record, academic GPA. *Other factors considered include:* class rank, standardized test scores, application essay, recommendation(s), interview, extracurricular activities, talent/ability, character/personal qualities, first generation. **Freshman Admission Requirements:** High school diploma is required and GED is accepted. *Academic units required:* 4 English, 2 math, 2 science, 2 science labs, 2 social studies, 2 history. *Academic units recommended:* 3 math, 3 science. **Freshman Admission Statistics:** 875 applied, 93.37% admitted, 63% enrolled. **Transfer Admission Requirements:** college transcript(s), Minimum college GPA of 2.0 required. Lowest grade transferable C. **General Admission Information:** Application fee $40. Priority deadline 6/15. Regular application deadline 8/15. Nonfall registration accepted. Admission may be deferred for a maximum of 12 months.

COSTS AND FINANCIAL AID

Annual in-state tuition $6,510. Annual out-of-state tuition $15,750. Required fees $938. **Required Forms and Deadlines:** FAFSA. **Notification of Awards:** Applicants will be notified of awards on a rolling basis beginning 3/15. **Types of Aid:** *Need-based scholarships/grants:* Federal Pell, FSEOG, State scholarships/grants, Private scholarships, College/university scholarship or grant aid from institutional funds. *Loans:* Direct Subsidized Stafford Loans, Direct Unsubsidized Stafford Loans, Direct PLUS loans, Federal Perkins Loans, Federal Nursing Loans. *Student Employment:* Federal Work-Study Program available. Institutional employment available. **Financial Aid Statistics:** 87% needy freshmen, 86% needy undergrads receive need-based scholarship or grant aid. 0% freshmen, 1% undergrads receive non-need-based scholarship or grant aid. 81% freshmen, 90% undergrads receive need-based self-help aid. 0% freshmen, 0% undergrads receive athletic scholarships. 64% freshmen, 72% undergrads receive any aid. **Criteria for awarding aid:** *Non-need-based:* Academics, Athletics, Leadership, Music/drama, State/district residency.

UNIVERSITY OF MAINE—FORT KENT

23 University Drive, Fort Kent, ME 4774
Phone: 888-879-8635 • **Financial Aid Phone:** 207-834-7607
E-mail: umfkadm@maine.maine.edu • **CEEB Code:** 3393
Fax: 207-834-7609 • **Website:** www.umfk.maine.edu • **ACT Code:** 1642

This public school was founded in 1878. It has a 52-acre campus.

RATINGS

Admissions Selectivity Rating: 72   **Fire Safety Rating:** 99   **Green Rating:** 67

STUDENTS AND FACULTY

Enrollment: 990. **Student Body:** 72% female, 28% male, 13% out-of-state, 11% international. Asian 1%, African American 4%, Caucasian 75%, Hispanic 2%, Native American 1%, Pacific Islander <1%, Two or more races 2%, Race unknown 5%.

Retention and Graduation: 70% freshmen return for sophomore year. 24% freshmen graduate within 4 years. 39% freshmen graduate within 6 years. 5% grads go on to further study within 1 year. 3% grads pursue arts and sciences degrees. **Faculty:** Student/faculty ratio 15:1. 33 full-time faculty, 58% hold PhDs, 9% are are members of minority groups, 39% are women. 0% of classes are taught by teaching assistants.

ACADEMICS

Degrees: associate, bachelor's, certificate. **Classes:** Most classes have 10-19 students. Most lab/discussion sessions have fewer than 10 students. **Most popular majors:** Elementary Education and Teaching; Business/Commerce; Registered Nursing, Nursing Administration, Nursing Research and Clinical Nursing. **Special Study Options:** cross-registration, distance learning, double major, English as a Second Language (ESL), honors program, independent study, internships, liberal arts/career combination, student-designed major, teacher certification program, Distance learning within entire UMaine system. **Disability Services:** Special programs offered to physically disabled students, including note-taking services, reader services, tape recorders, tutors. **Career Services:** Alumni services, Career/job search classes, Career assessment, Internships, On-campus interviews.

FACILITIES

Housing: Coed dorms, special housing for disabled students, men's dorms, women's dorms. 90% of campus accessible to physically diasbled. **Computers:** 100% of classrooms, 100% of dorms, 100% of libraries, 100% of dining areas, 100% of student union, 100% of common outdoor areas have wireless network access. Students can register for classes online. Administrative functions (other than registration) can be performed online.

CAMPUS LIFE

Environment: Rural. **Activities:** Choral groups, drama/theater, student government 25 registered organizations, 1 honor society, 1 religious organization. 1 sororities. **Athletics (Intercollegiate):** *Men:* basketball, cross-country, golf, skiing (downhill/alpine), skiing (nordic/cross-country), soccer. *Women:* basketball, cross-country, golf, skiing (downhill/alpine), skiing (nordic/cross-country), soccer, volleyball. **On-Campus Highlights:** Bengal's Lair, The Lodge (res hall), Library.

ADMISSIONS

Freshman Academic Profile: Average high school GPA 3.0. 1% in top 10% of high school class, 7% in top 25% of high school class, 39% in top 50% of high school class. 96% from public high schools. **Reported SAT (pre-2016 redesign) scores:** SAT Math middle 50% range 400-500. SAT Critical Reading middle 50% range 400-480. SAT Writing middle 50% range 380-480. **Concordant SAT scores:** SAT EBRW middle 50% 440–540. SAT Math middle 50% range 440–530. ACT middle 50% range 15-19. Minimum paper TOEFL 500. **Basis for Candidate Selection:** *Very important factors considered include:* level of applicant's interest. *Important factors considered include:* rigor of secondary school record, class rank, academic GPA, application essay, recommendation(s), talent/ability, character/personal qualities, first generation, geographical residence, state residency, volunteer work. *Other factors considered include:* standardized test scores, interview, extracurricular activities, alumni/ae relation, work experience. **Freshman Admission Requirements:** High school diploma is required and GED is accepted. *Academic units required:* 4 English, 2 math, 2 science, 2 science labs. *Academic units recommended:* 2 foreign language. **Freshman Admission Statistics:** 215 applied, 89.30% admitted, 65% enrolled. **Transfer Admission Requirements:** High school transcript, college transcript(s), essay or personal statement, Lowest grade transferable C-. **General Admission Information:** Application fee $40. Regular application deadline 8/15. Nonfall registration accepted. Admission may be deferred.

COSTS AND FINANCIAL AID

Annual in-state tuition $6,600. Annual out-of-state tuition $9,900. Room and board $7,910. Required fees $975. Average book expense $500. **Required Forms and Deadlines:** FAFSA, Institution's own financial aid form, CSS/Financial Aid PROFILE, State aid form. **Notification of Awards:** Applicants will be notified of awards on a rolling basis beginning 3/15. **Types of Aid:** *Need-based scholarships/grants:* Federal Pell, FSEOG, State scholarships/grants, Private scholarships, College/university scholarship or grant aid from institutional funds, Federal Nursing Scholarships. *Loans:* Direct Subsidized Stafford Loans, Direct Unsubsidized Stafford Loans, Direct PLUS loans, Federal Perkins Loans, Federal Nursing Loans, State Loans, College/university loans from institutional funds. *Student Employment:* Federal Work-Study Program available. Institutional employment available. **Financial Aid Statistics:** 100% needy freshmen, 94% needy undergrads receive need-based scholarship or grant aid. 4% freshmen, 4% undergrads receive non-need-based scholarship or grant aid. 77% freshmen, 84% undergrads receive need-based self-help aid. 0% freshmen, 0% undergrads receive athletic scholarships. 78% freshmen, 578% undergrads receive any aid. 66% undergrads borrow to pay for school. Average cumulative indebtedness $29,910. **Criteria for awarding aid:** *Need-based:* Academics, Leadership. *Non-need-based:* Academics, Alumni affiliation, Job skills, Leadership, State/district residency.

UNIVERSITY OF MAINE—PRESQUE ISLE

Office of Admissions, Presque Isle, ME 4769
Phone: 207-768-9532 • **Financial Aid Phone:** 207-768-9510
E-mail: admissions@umpi.edu • **CEEB Code:** 3008
Fax: 207-768-9777 • **Website:** www.umpi.edu

This public school was founded in 1903. It has a 150-acre campus.

RATINGS

Admissions Selectivity Rating: 73   **Fire Safety Rating:** 84   **Green Rating:** 67

STUDENTS AND FACULTY

Enrollment: 833. **Student Body:** 62% female, 38% male, 4% out-of-state, 8% international (3 countries represented). Asian 0%, African American 3%, Caucasian 79%, Hispanic 2%, Native American 3%, Pacific Islander 0%, Two or more races 3%, Race unknown 4%.
Retention and Graduation: 65% freshmen return for sophomore year. 23% freshmen graduate within 4 years. 45% freshmen graduate within 6 years.
Faculty: Student/faculty ratio 15:1. 42 full-time faculty, 64% hold PhDs, 5% are are members of minority groups, 48% are women. 0% of classes are taught by teaching assistants.

ACADEMICS

Degrees: associate, bachelor's, certificate. **Classes:** Most classes have 10-19 students. Most lab/discussion sessions have 10-19 students. **Most popular majors:** Elementary Education and Teaching; Liberal Arts and Sciences/Liberal Studies; Business/Commerce. **Special Study Options:** Accelerated program, cooperative education program, cross-registration, distance learning, double major, exchange student program (domestic), honors program, independent study, internships, student-designed major, study abroad, teacher certification program. **Honors Programs:** HON 300 Honors Seminar HON/HTY 401 Oral History HON 421 Honors Senior Year Project. **Disability Services:** Special programs offered to physically disabled students, including note-taking services, reader services, tape recorders, tutors. **Career Services:** Alumni services, Career/job search classes, Career assessment, Internships.

FACILITIES

Housing: Coed dorms, apartments for married students. 100% of campus accessible to physically diasbled. **Special Academic Facilities/Equipment:** Museumn and Art Gallery, Gentile Hall **Computers:** Students can register for classes online. Administrative functions (other than registration) can be performed online.

CAMPUS LIFE

Environment: Village. **Activities:** drama/theater, radio station, student government, student newspaper. 27 registered organizations, 1 honor society, 1 religious organization. 1 fraternity, 1 sorority. **Athletics (Intercollegiate):** *Men:* baseball, basketball, cross-country, golf, skiing (nordic/cross-country), soccer. *Women:* basketball, cross-country, skiing (nordic/cross-country), soccer, softball, volleyball. **On-Campus Highlights:** Caroline D. Gentile Hall, Campus Center, Library, Fitness Center, Owl's Nest, Caroline D. Gentile Hall, the newest building at the University of Maine at Presque Isle, will officially open to the public on January 21, 2006. Named in honor of the University's longest serving faculty member, Gentile Hall features a large multipurpose court, fitness center, pool, elevated track, and climbing wall. The facility will support the University's

academic programs and student body, but the community will also be welcomed and encouraged to use its resources.

ADMISSIONS

Freshman Academic Profile: Average high school GPA 3.0. 3% in top 10% of high school class, 15% in top 25% of high school class, 45% in top 50% of high school class. **Reported SAT (pre-2016 redesign) scores:** SAT Math middle 50% range 397-532. SAT Critical Reading middle 50% range 394-528. SAT Writing middle 50% range 379-507. **Concordant SAT scores:** SAT EBRW middle 50% 430–580. SAT Math middle 50% range 440–560. ACT middle 50% range 18-23. Minimum internet-based TOEFL 71. Minimum paper TOEFL 530. **Basis for Candidate Selection:** *Very important factors considered include:* rigor of secondary school record. *Important factors considered include:* academic GPA, application essay, recommendation(s). *Other factors considered include:* class rank, standardized test scores, interview, extracurricular activities, talent/ability, character/personal qualities, first generation, alumni/ae relation, volunteer work, work experience, level of applicant's interest. **Freshman Admission Requirements:** High school diploma is required and GED is accepted. *Academic units recommended:* 4 English, 3 math, 2 science, 2 science labs, 2 foreign language, 3 social studies, 2 academic electives. **Freshman Admission Statistics:** 1,442 applied, 77.12% admitted, 18% enrolled. **Transfer Admission Requirements:** High school transcript, college transcript(s), essay or personal statement, statement of good standing from prior institution(s). Minimum college GPA of 2.0 required. Lowest grade transferable c-. **General Admission Information:** Application fee $40. Nonfall registration accepted. Admission may be deferred.

COSTS AND FINANCIAL AID

Annual in-state tuition $6,600. Annual out-of-state tuition $9,900. Room and board $8,044. Required fees $700. Average book expense $900. **Required Forms and Deadlines:** FAFSA. **Notification of Awards:** Applicants will be notified of awards on a rolling basis beginning 3/1. **Types of Aid:** *Need-based scholarships/grants:* Federal Pell, FSEOG, State scholarships/grants, Private scholarships, College/university scholarship or grant aid from institutional funds. *Loans:* Direct Subsidized Stafford Loans, Direct Unsubsidized Stafford Loans, Direct PLUS loans, Federal Perkins Loans. *Student Employment:* Federal Work-Study Program available. Institutional employment available. **Financial Aid Statistics:** 99% needy freshmen, 98% needy undergrads receive need-based scholarship or grant aid. 7% freshmen, 5% undergrads receive non-need-based scholarship or grant aid. 74% freshmen, 77% undergrads receive need-based self-help aid. 0% freshmen, 0% undergrads receive athletic scholarships. 83% freshmen, 76% undergrads receive any aid. 84% undergrads borrow to pay for school. Average cumulative indebtedness $25,713. **Criteria for awarding aid:** *Non-need-based:* Academics.

UNIVERSITY OF MARY HARDIN—BAYLOR

UMHB Box 8004, Belton, TX 76513
Phone: 254-295-4520 • **Financial Aid Phone:** 254-295-4517
E-mail: admissions@umhb.edu • **CEEB Code:** 3588
Fax: 254-295-5049 • **Website:** www.umhb.edu • **ACT Code:** 4128

This private school, affiliated with the Baptist Church, was founded in 1845. It has a 170-acre campus.

RATINGS

Admissions Selectivity Rating: 78   **Fire Safety Rating:** 78   **Green Rating:** 60*

STUDENTS AND FACULTY

Enrollment: 3,173. **Student Body:** 63% female, 37% male, 2% out-of-state, 2% international (12 countries represented). Asian 2%, African American 15%, Caucasian 57%, Hispanic 20%, Native American 1%, Pacific Islander <1%, Two or more races 3%, Race unknown 1%.
Retention and Graduation: 69% freshmen return for sophomore year. 28% freshmen graduate within 4 years. 43% freshmen graduate within 6 years.
Faculty: Student/faculty ratio 19:1. 167 full-time faculty, 74% hold PhDs, 14% are are members of minority groups, 55% are women. 0% of classes are taught by teaching assistants.

ACADEMICS

Degrees: bachelor's, doctoral/professional, doctoral/research, master's, post-master's certificate. **Classes:** Most classes have 10-19 students. Most lab/discussion sessions have 10-19 students. **Most popular majors:** Elementary Education and Teaching; Registered Nursing/Registered Nurse. **Special Study Options:** Accelerated program, double major, dual enrollment, English as a Second Language (ESL), honors program, independent study, internships, student-designed major, study abroad, teacher certification program, Tuition exchange program with other participating universities. Undergrads may take grad level classes. Military degree completion programs. Servicemember

Opportunity Colleges (SOCS) programs. **Honors Programs:** Lower Level Honors Program–approximately the top 10% of UMHB's entering freshman class. Freshman year offerings include English and religion, and sophomore year offerings are interdisciplinary courses in the humanities and social sciences. Upper Level Honors Program–Minimum requirements for completion of this program is the completion of three upper level courses designated as honors level and the completion of HNRS 3110 "Great Books and Ideas" and HNRS 3120 "living Issues". Successful completion of these requirements will allow the student to graduate with the cum laude designation. To receive the higher designations of magna cum laude or summa cum laude, the student must also successfully complete an Honors Research Project. This project must include original research and both written and oral presentations of that research to the Honors Committee. Combined degree programs: BBA/MBA; 3-1 Clinical Lab Science with local hospital. **Disability Services:** Special programs offered to physically disabled students, including note-taking services, reader services, tape recorders, tutors. **Career Services:** Alumni network, Alumni services, Career/job search classes, Career assessment, Internships, Regional alumni. The UMHB Career Development Center offers an array of self assessments, exploration, document preparation, and career planning opportunities. The most used and results-generated career program is the one on one Resume Clinic which involves an interactive session with our students drafting a successful career document. Many times this is their first resume, and the new confidence that is reflective by the student after completing this document is most exciting. Additional popular programs and workshops include, Show Me the Money: salary negotiations; Facebook, My Space and My Future Employer; and the President's Senior Etiquette Dinner Program.

FACILITIES

Housing: special housing for disabled students, men's dorms, women's dorms, apartments for single students. 85% of campus accessible to physically disabled. **Special Academic Facilities/Equipment:** Language lab **Computers:** 100% of classrooms, 100% of dorms, 100% of libraries, 100% of dining areas, 100% of student union, 80% of common outdoor areas have wireless network access. Students can register for classes online. Administrative functions (other than registration) can be performed online.

CAMPUS LIFE

Environment: City. **Activities:** Choral groups, concert band, drama/theater, jazz band, literary magazine, marching band, music ensembles, musical theater, opera, pep band, student government, student newspaper, symphony orchestra, yearbook, Campus Ministries, Student Organization. 51 registered organizations, 5 honor societies, 7 religious organizations. **Athletics (Intercollegiate):** *Men:* baseball, basketball, football, golf, soccer, tennis. *Women:* basketball, golf, soccer, softball, tennis, volleyball. **On-Campus Highlights:** SUB (Student Union Building), Sportsplex or ANY sporting event, Millennium Oaks Park (gazebo, pond), Mayborn Center exercise/fitness facilities, Quad area.

ADMISSIONS

Freshman Academic Profile: Average high school GPA 3.6. 20% in top 10% of high school class, 50% in top 25% of high school class, 84% in top 50% of high school class. **Reported SAT (pre-2016 redesign) scores:** SAT Math middle 50% range 470-570. SAT Critical Reading middle 50% range 460-560. SAT Writing middle 50% range 430-530. **Concordant SAT scores:** SAT EBRW middle 50% 500–600. SAT Math middle 50% range 510–590. ACT middle 50% range 20-26. **Basis for Candidate Selection:** *Very important factors considered include:* class rank, standardized test scores. *Important factors considered include:* academic GPA. *Other factors considered include:* rigor of secondary school record, application essay, recommendation(s), interview, extracurricular activities, talent/ability, character/personal qualities, first generation, alumni/ae relation, geographical residence, state residency, religious affiliation/commitment, racial/ethnic status, volunteer work, work experience, level of applicant's interest. **Freshman Admission Requirements:** High school diploma is required and GED is accepted. *Academic units required:* 4 English, 3 math, 3 science, 2 foreign language. **Freshman Admission Statistics:** 7,504 applied, 80.40% admitted, 12% enrolled. **Transfer Admission Requirements:** college transcript(s), Minimum college GPA of 2.0 required. Lowest grade transferable C. **General Admission Information:** Application fee $35. Nonfall registration accepted. Admission may be deferred for a maximum of 1 semester.

COSTS AND FINANCIAL AID

Required Forms and Deadlines: FAFSA. **Notification of Awards:** Applicants will be notified of awards on a rolling basis beginning 2/15. **Types of Aid:** *Need-based scholarships/grants:* Federal Pell, FSEOG, State scholarships/grants, Private scholarships, College/university scholarship or grant aid from institutional funds, Federal Nursing Scholarships. *Loans:* Direct Subsidized Stafford Loans, Direct Unsubsidized Stafford Loans, Direct PLUS loans, Federal Nursing Loans, State Loans. *Student Employment:* Federal Work-Study Program available. Institutional employment available. **Financial Aid Statistics:** 100% needy freshmen, 99% needy undergrads receive need-based scholarship or grant aid. 7% freshmen, 5% undergrads receive non-need-based

scholarship or grant aid. 83% freshmen, 84% undergrads receive need-based self-help aid. 0% freshmen, 0% undergrads receive athletic scholarships. 84% freshmen, 87% undergrads receive any aid. 78% undergrads borrow to pay for school. Average cumulative indebtedness $35,011. **Criteria for awarding aid:** *Need-based:* Academics, Alumni affiliation, Art, Job skills, Leadership, Music/drama, Religious affiliation.

UNIVERSITY OF MARY WASHINGTON

1301 College Avenue, Fredericksburg, VA 22401
Phone: 540-654-2000 • **Financial Aid Phone:** 540-654-2468
E-mail: admit@umw.edu • **CEEB Code:** 5398
Fax: 540-654-1857 • **Website:** www.umw.edu • **ACT Code:** 4414

This public school was founded in 1908. It has a 176-acre campus.

RATINGS

Admissions Selectivity Rating: 83   **Fire Safety Rating:** 93   **Green Rating:** 83

STUDENTS AND FACULTY

Enrollment: 4,318. **Student Body:** 64% female, 36% male, 11% out-of-state, 1% international (23 countries represented). Asian 4%, African American 7%, Caucasian 70%, Hispanic 8%, Native American <1%, Pacific Islander <1%, Two or more races 5%, Race unknown 4%.
Retention and Graduation: 83% freshmen return for sophomore year. 62% freshmen graduate within 4 years. 72% freshmen graduate within 6 years. 17% grads go on to further study within 1 year. 10% grads pursue arts and sciences degrees. 1% grads pursue law degrees. 1% grads pursue business degrees. 1% grads pursue medical degrees. **Faculty:** Student/faculty ratio 14:1. 250 full-time faculty, 86% hold PhDs, 19% are are members of minority groups, 48% are women. 0% of classes are taught by teaching assistants.

ACADEMICS

Degrees: bachelor's, certificate, master's, postbachelor's certificate. **Classes:** Most classes have 20-29 students. Most lab/discussion sessions have 20-29 students. **Most popular majors:** Biology/Biological Sciences; Business Administration and Management; Psychology. **Special Study Options:** Accelerated program, distance learning, double major, independent study, internships, student-designed major, study abroad, teacher certification program. Combined degree programs: BA/BS & M.S. elementary education, BSN-APP, Bachelor of Science in Nursing combined with Associate of Applied Science degree in nursing from Germanna Community College. **Disability Services:** Special programs offered to physically disabled students, including note-taking services, reader services, tape recorders. **Career Services:** Alumni network, Alumni services, Career/job search classes, Career assessment, Internships, Regional alumni. The Center for Career and Professional Development at UMW has a renewed focus on career development. We recently adopted career courses and are working on creating in-depth, four year career plans for students. We have recently relocated to the bustling student center on campus.

FACILITIES

Housing: Coed dorms, special housing for disabled students, men's dorms, special housing for international students, women's dorms, apartments for single students, Wellness Housing, Theme Housing, Substance-Free. 75% of campus accessible to physically disabled. **Special Academic Facilities/Equipment:** Two art galleries, Center for Historic Preservation, language labs, Leidecker Center for Asian Studies, cartography lab, greenhouse. **Computers:** 100% of classrooms, 100% of dorms, 100% of libraries, 100% of dining areas, 100% of student union, 5% of common outdoor areas have wireless network access. Students can register for classes online. Administrative functions (other than registration) can be performed online.

CAMPUS LIFE

Environment: City. **Activities:** Choral groups, concert band, dance, drama/theater, jazz band, literary magazine, music ensembles, musical theater, opera, radio station, student government, student newspaper, student-run film society, symphony orchestra, yearbook, Campus Ministries, Student Organization, Model UN. 120 registered organizations, 23 honor societies, 10 religious organizations. **Athletics (Intercollegiate):** *Men:* baseball, basketball, crew/rowing, cross-country, equestrian sports, lacrosse, soccer, swimming, tennis, track/field (outdoor), track/field (indoor). *Women:* basketball, crew/rowing, cross-country, equestrian sports, field hockey, lacrosse, soccer, softball,

swimming, tennis, track/field (outdoor), track/field (indoor), volleyball.
On-Campus Highlights: Woodard Campus Center, Battleground Athletic facilities/Fitness Center, Palmieri Plaza Fountain, Ball Circle, Lee Hall.
Environmental Initiatives: In July 2010, UMW adopted sustainability policies and practices committing to reducing solid waste, conserving energy and water,encouraging the purchasing of products to promote sustainability and promote alternative methods of transportation.

ADMISSIONS

Freshman Academic Profile: Average high school GPA 3.6. 15% in top 10% of high school class, 46% in top 25% of high school class, 85% in top 50% of high school class. 77% from public high schools. **Reported SAT (pre-2016 redesign) scores:** SAT Math middle 50% range 500-590. SAT Critical Reading middle 50% range 510-620. SAT Writing middle 50% range 490-590. **Concordant SAT scores:** SAT EBRW middle 50% 560–660. SAT Math middle 50% range 530–610. ACT middle 50% range 22-27. Minimum internet-based TOEFL 88. Minimum paper TOEFL 570. **Basis for Candidate Selection:** *Very important factors considered include:* rigor of secondary school record, academic GPA. *Important factors considered include:* class rank, standardized test scores, application essay, recommendation(s), extracurricular activities. *Other factors considered include:* talent/ability, character/personal qualities, first generation, alumni/ae relation, geographical residence, state residency, racial/ethnic status, volunteer work, work experience. **Freshman Admission Requirements:** High school diploma is required and GED is accepted. *Academic units required:* 4 English, 3 math, 3 science, 3 science labs, 2 foreign language, 2 social studies, 1 history. *Academic units recommended:* 4 English, 4 math, 4 science, 4 science labs, 4 foreign language, 2 social studies, 2 history. **Freshman Admission Statistics:** 6,270 applied, 74.45% admitted, 21% enrolled. **Transfer Admission Requirements:** High school transcript, college transcript(s), essay or personal statement, statement of good standing from prior institution(s). Minimum college GPA of 2.0 required. Lowest grade transferable C. **General Admission Information:** Application fee $50. Priority deadline 2/1. Regular notification 4/1. Nonfall registration accepted. Admission may be deferred for a maximum of one year.

COSTS AND FINANCIAL AID

Annual in-state tuition $5,772. Annual out-of-state tuition $20,362. Room and board $11,118. Required fees $5,798. Average book expense $1,200. **Required Forms and Deadlines:** FAFSA. **Notification of Awards:** Applicants will be notified of awards on a rolling basis beginning 3/15. **Types of Aid:** *Need-based scholarships/grants:* Federal Pell, FSEOG, State scholarships/grants, Private scholarships, College/university scholarship or grant aid from institutional funds. *Loans:* Direct Subsidized Stafford Loans, Direct Unsubsidized Stafford Loans, Direct PLUS loans, Federal Perkins Loans. *Student Employment:* Federal Work-Study Program available. Institutional employment available. **Financial Aid Statistics:** 66% needy freshmen, 64% needy undergrads receive need-based scholarship or grant aid. 70% freshmen, 41% undergrads receive non-need-based scholarship or grant aid. 74% freshmen, 81% undergrads receive need-based self-help aid. 0% freshmen, 0% undergrads receive athletic scholarships. 67% freshmen, 63% undergrads receive any aid. 51% undergrads borrow to pay for school. Average cumulative indebtedness $19,444. **Criteria for awarding aid:** *Need-based:* Academics, Art, Music/drama. *Non-need-based:* Academics, Alumni affiliation, Art, Leadership, Music/drama, State/district residency.

UNIVERSITY OF MARYLAND, BALTIMORE COUNTY

1000 Hilltop Circle, Baltimore, MD 21250
Phone: 410-455-2291 • **Financial Aid Phone:** 410-455-2387
E-mail: admissions@umbc.edu • **CEEB Code:** 5835
Fax: 410-455-1094 • **Website:** www.umbc.edu • **ACT Code:** 1751

This public school was founded in 1966. It has a 530-acre campus.

RATINGS

Admissions Selectivity Rating: 88   **Fire Safety Rating:** 98   **Green Rating:** 74

STUDENTS AND FACULTY

Enrollment: 11,025. **Student Body:** 45% female, 55% male, 6% out-of-state, 4% international (96 countries represented). Asian 21%, African American 18%, Caucasian 43%, Hispanic 7%, Native American <1%, Pacific Islander <1%, Two or more races 4%, Race unknown 4%.

Retention and Graduation: 87% freshmen return for sophomore year. 63 49% grads go on to further study within 1 year. 30% grads pursue arts and sciences degrees. 1% grads pursue law degrees. 2% grads pursue business degrees. 5% grads pursue medical degrees. **Faculty:** Student/faculty ratio 19:1. 527 full-time faculty, 86% hold PhDs, 24% are are members of minority groups, 47% are women. 2% of classes are taught by teaching assistants.

ACADEMICS

Degrees: bachelor's, certificate, doctoral/research, doctoral, master's, postbachelor's certificate. **Classes:** Most classes have 20-29 students. Most lab/discussion sessions have 20-29 students. **Most popular majors:** Computer and Information Sciences; Biology/Biological Sciences; Psychology. **Special Study Options:** Accelerated program, cooperative education program, cross-registration, double major, dual enrollment, English as a Second Language (ESL), exchange student program (domestic), honors program, independent study, internships, student-designed major, study abroad, teacher certification program. **Honors Programs:** UMBC Honors College, Merehoff (Science, Technology, Engineering, and Mathematics), Scholars Program, Sherman Teacher Education Scholars Program, Sondheim Scholars Programs, Center for Women and Information Technology (CWIT) Scholars Program, Humanities Scholars Program, Lineman Scholars Program. Combined degree programs: BA/MA, BA/MEng, biochemistry, chemistry, economics, info. systems. **Disability Services:** Special programs offered to physically disabled students, including note-taking services, reader services, tape recorders, tutors. **Career Services:** Alumni network, Alumni services, Career/job search classes, Career assessment, Internships, Regional alumni. UMBC Career Services is proud of many of the programs and stellar customer service that it delivers to multiple constituents. Collaboration is high with internal and external partners and a primary example of this type of collaboration is demonstrated by the development of Career Path, a website that is intended to help students understand what they can do with their major within a variety of industries, access current jobs and hear the stories of UMBC alumni. We are also extremely proud of consistent and continual employer recruitment activities and presence on campus despite a downturn in the economy. Our graduates continue to report very good job offers.

FACILITIES

Housing: Coed dorms, special housing for disabled students, apartments for single students, Theme Housing, Same sex floors, honors floors, quiet lifestyle, Substance-free, and living-learning communities: Center for Women and Information Technology, Emergency Health Services, Exploratory Majors, Honors College, Humanities Floor, Intercultural Living Exchange, Shriver Living Learning Center, Visual and Performing Arts Floor, and Women Involved in Learning and Leadership, gender neutral. 95% of campus accessible to physically diasbled. **Special Academic Facilities/Equipment:** Albin O. Kuhn Library and Gallery, Center for Art and Visual Culture, Women's Center, Center for Environmental Science, Center for Photonics Technology, Center for Women and Information Technology, Center on Research and Teaching in Social Work, Howard Hughes Medical Institute at UMBC, Imaging Research Center, Institute for Global Electronic Commerce, Joint Center for Earth Systems Technology, Laboratory for Healthcare Informatics, Maryland Center for Telecommunications Research, Maryland Institute for Policy Analysis and Research, bwtech@umbc Research and Technology Park and Incubator and Accelerator, Shriver Center, UMBC Technology Center, Goddard Earth Science and Technology Center. **Computers:** 100% of classrooms, 80% of dorms, 100% of libraries, 100% of dining areas, 100% of student union, 40% of common outdoor areas have wireless network access. Students can register for classes online. Administrative functions (other than registration) can be performed online.

CAMPUS LIFE

Environment: Metropolis. **Activities:** Choral groups, dance, drama/theater, jazz band, literary magazine, music ensembles, musical theater, pep band, radio station, student government, student newspaper, student-run film society, symphony orchestra, Campus Ministries, Student Organization, Model UN. 230 registered organizations, 8 honor societies, 20 religious organizations. 11 fraternities, 12 sororities. **Athletics (Intercollegiate):** *Men:* baseball, basketball, cheerleading, cross-country, diving, lacrosse, soccer, swimming, tennis, track/field (outdoor), track/field (indoor). *Women:* basketball, cheerleading, cross-country, diving, lacrosse, soccer, softball, swimming, tennis, track/field (outdoor), track/field (indoor), volleyball. **On-Campus Highlights:** Albin O. Kuhn Library and Gallery, The Commons (Student Center), Center for Art, Design and Visual Cultu, Howard Hughes Medical Institute Lab, Retriever Activities Center, Students attend, and take part in, a world of excellent theatre, music and dance performances on campus. They go to art openings and lectures, start clubs and exchange ideas through the campus paper and literary magazines. **Environmental Initiatives:** Climate Commitment Task Force (students, faculty, staff) will commence implementation of its Climate Action Plan and reduce our carbon footprint.

ADMISSIONS

Freshman Academic Profile: Average high school GPA 3.7. 27% in top 10% of high school class, 56% in top 25% of high school class, 83% in top 50% of

high school class. **Reported SAT (pre-2016 redesign) scores:** SAT Math middle 50% range 570-670. SAT Critical Reading middle 50% range 540-640. SAT Writing middle 50% range 530-640. **Concordant SAT scores:** SAT EBRW middle 50% 590–690. SAT Math middle 50% range 590–700. ACT middle 50% range 24-29. Minimum internet-based TOEFL 48. Minimum paper TOEFL 460. **Basis for Candidate Selection:** *Very important factors considered include:* rigor of secondary school record, academic GPA, standardized test scores, application essay, recommendation(s). *Important factors considered include:* class rank, talent/ability. *Other factors considered include:* extracurricular activities, character/personal qualities, volunteer work, work experience. **Freshman Admission Requirements:** High school diploma is required and GED is accepted. *Academic units required:* 4 English, 4 math, 3 science, 2 foreign language, and 3 units from above areas or other academic areas. *Academic units recommended:* 4 English, 4 math, 3 science, 2 foreign language, and 3 units from above areas or other academic areas. **Freshman Admission Statistics:** 10,646 applied, 59.33% admitted, 25% enrolled. **Transfer Admission Requirements:** college transcript(s), statement of good standing from prior institution(s). Minimum college GPA of 2.5 required. Lowest grade transferable D. **General Admission Information:** Application fee $50. Priority deadline 11/1. Regular application deadline 2/1. Nonfall registration accepted. Admission may be deferred for a maximum of 1 year.

COSTS AND FINANCIAL AID

Annual in-state tuition $11,264. Annual out-of-state tuition $24,492. Room and board $11,568. Required fees $1,530. Average book expense $1,200. **Required Forms and Deadlines:** FAFSA. **Notification of Awards:** Applicants will be notified of awards on a rolling basis beginning 3/25. **Types of Aid:** *Need-based scholarships/grants:* Federal Pell, FSEOG, State scholarships/grants, Private scholarships, College/university scholarship or grant aid from institutional funds, United Negro College Fund. *Loans:* Direct Subsidized Stafford Loans, Direct Unsubsidized Stafford Loans, Direct PLUS loans, Federal Perkins Loans. *Student Employment:* Federal Work-Study Program available. Institutional employment available. **Financial Aid Statistics:** 76% needy freshmen, 77% needy undergrads receive need-based scholarship or grant aid. 30% freshmen, 11% undergrads receive non-need-based scholarship or grant aid. 60% freshmen, 70% undergrads receive need-based self-help aid. 3% freshmen, 2% undergrads receive athletic scholarships. 74% freshmen, 70% undergrads receive any aid. 51% undergrads borrow to pay for school. Average cumulative indebtedness $26,391. **Criteria for awarding aid:** *Non-need-based:* Academics, Alumni affiliation, Art, Athletics, Music/drama.

See page 1078.

UNIVERSITY OF MARYLAND, COLLEGE PARK

Mitchell Building, College Park, MD 20742-5235
Phone: 301-314-8385 • **Financial Aid Phone:** 301-314-9000
E-mail: um-admit@umd.edu • **CEEB Code:** 5814
Fax: 301-314-9693 • **Website:** http://www.umd.edu • **ACT Code:** 1746

This public school was founded in 1856. It has a 1382-acre campus.

RATINGS

Admissions Selectivity Rating: 94   **Fire Safety Rating:** 90   **Green Rating:** 98

STUDENTS AND FACULTY

Enrollment: 27,864. **Student Body:** 47% female, 53% male, 21% out-of-state, 4% international (65 countries represented). Asian 16%, African American 13%, Caucasian 51%, Hispanic 10%, Native American <1%, Pacific Islander <1%, Two or more races 4%, Race unknown 1%.
Retention and Graduation: 95% freshmen return for sophomore year. 69% freshmen graduate within 4 years. 87% freshmen graduate within 6 years. 21% grads go on to further study within 1 year. 2% grads pursue law degrees. 11% grads pursue business degrees. 4% grads pursue medical degrees. **Faculty:** Student/faculty ratio 17:1. 1,803 full-time faculty, 91% hold PhDs, 23% are members of minority groups, 38% are women. 12% of classes are taught by teaching assistants.

ACADEMICS

Degrees: bachelor's, certificate, doctoral/professional, doctoral/research, master's, postbachelor's certificate, post-master's certificate. **Classes:** Most classes have 10-19 students. Most lab/discussion sessions have 20-29 students.
Most popular majors: Biology/Biological Sciences; Criminology; Economics.

Special Study Options: Accelerated program, cooperative education program, cross-registration, distance learning, double major, dual enrollment, English as a Second Language (ESL), exchange student program (domestic), external degree program, honors program, independent study, internships, liberal arts/career combination, student-designed major, study abroad, teacher certification program, Living-Learning programs including Gemstone Program, Honors, First-Year Focus, Jiminez-Porter Writers House, Civicus, College Park Scholars, and others. **Honors Programs:** Gemstones, Honors, Honors Humanities Combined degree programs: BA/JD, BA/MA, BA/MEng, BA/MBA. **Disability Services:** Special programs offered to physically disabled students, including note-taking services, reader services, tape recorders, tutors. **Career Services:** Alumni network, Alumni services, Career/job search classes, Career assessment, Internships, Regional alumni.

FACILITIES

Housing: Coed dorms, special housing for disabled students, special housing for international students, women's dorms, fraternity/sorority housing, cooperative housing, apartments for single students, Wellness Housing, Theme Housing, Living/Learning program housing includes Gemstone program, College Park Scholars, Language House, Beyond the Classroom, Civicus, Hinman CEOs, Global Communities, Jimenz-Porter Writer's House, Honors, House, Honors Humanities, SmokFree/Alcohol-Free. **Special Academic Facilities/Equipment:** Aerospace buoyancy lab, art gallery, piano archives, center for architectural design and research, model nuclear reactor, wind tunnel. **Computers:** 100% of classrooms, 100% of dorms, 100% of libraries, 100% of dining areas, 100% of student union, 100% of common outdoor areas have wireless network access. Students can register for classes online. Administrative functions (other than registration) can be performed online.

CAMPUS LIFE

Environment: Metropolis. **Activities:** Choral groups, concert band, dance, drama/theater, jazz band, literary magazine, marching band, music ensembles, musical theater, opera, pep band, radio station, student government, student newspaper, student-run film society, symphony orchestra, television station, yearbook, Campus Ministries, Student Organization, Model UN. 574 registered organizations, 53 honor societies, 55 religious organizations. 36 fraternities, 27 sororities. **Athletics (Intercollegiate):** *Men:* baseball, basketball, cross-country, football, golf, lacrosse, soccer, swimming, tennis, track/field (outdoor), track/field (indoor), wrestling. *Women:* basketball, cheerleading, cross-country, field hockey, golf, gymnastics, lacrosse, soccer, softball, swimming, tennis, track/field (outdoor), track/field (indoor), volleyball, water polo. **On-Campus Highlights:** Clarice Smith Performing Arts Center, Adele H. Stamp Student Union, Eppley Recreation Center, Chevy Chase Bank Field at Byrd Stadium, Comcast Center, 6. Memorial Chapel 7. Riggs Alumni Center. **Environmental Initiatives:** The Green Office Program engages staff, faculty and students in a voluntary, self-guided initiative that promotes best environmental practices at the University of Maryland. The program supports and promotes offices that are taking steps toward reducing their environmental footprint. Learn more at http://www.sustainability.umd.edu/content/culture/green_offices.php

ADMISSIONS

Freshman Academic Profile: Average high school GPA 4.2. 71% in top 10% of high school class, 89% in top 25% of high school class, 98% in top 50% of high school class. **Reported SAT (pre-2016 redesign) scores:** SAT Math middle 50% range 620-730. SAT Critical Reading middle 50% range 590-690. **Concordant SAT scores:** SAT Math middle 50% range 640–760. ACT middle 50% range 28-33. Minimum internet-based TOEFL 100. **Basis for Candidate Selection:** *Very important factors considered include:* rigor of secondary school record, academic GPA, standardized test scores. *Important factors considered include:* class rank, application essay, recommendation(s), talent/ability, first generation, state residency. *Other factors considered include:* extracurricular activities, character/personal qualities, alumni/ae relation, geographical residence, racial/ethnic status, volunteer work, work experience. **Freshman Admission Requirements:** High school diploma is required and GED is accepted. *Academic units required:* 4 English, 4 math, 3 science, 2 science labs, 2 foreign language, 3 social studies, 3 history. *Academic units recommended:* 4 English, 4 math, 3 science, 2 science labs, 2 foreign language, 3 social studies, 3 history. **Freshman Admission Statistics:** 30,272 applied, 48.02% admitted, 31% enrolled. **Transfer Admission Requirements:** college transcript(s), essay or personal statement, statement of good standing from prior institution(s). Lowest grade transferable C. **General Admission Information:** Application fee $65. Priority deadline 11/1. Regular application deadline 1/20. Nonfall registration accepted. Admission may be deferred for a maximum of 1 year.

COSTS AND FINANCIAL AID

Annual in-state tuition $8,315. Annual out-of-state tuition $30,179. Room and board $11,758. Required fees $1,866. Average book expense $1,200. **Required Forms and Deadlines:** FAFSA. **Notification of Awards:** Applicants will be notified of awards on a rolling basis beginning 4/1. **Types of Aid:** *Need-based scholarships/grants:* Federal Pell, FSEOG, State scholarships/grants, Private scholarships, College/university scholarship or grant aid from institutional funds. *Loans:* Direct Subsidized Stafford Loans, Direct Unsubsidized Stafford Loans, Direct PLUS loans, Federal Perkins Loans. *Student Employment:*

Federal Work-Study Program available. Institutional employment available. **Financial Aid Statistics:** 85% needy freshmen, 80% needy undergrads receive need-based scholarship or grant aid. 12% freshmen, 6% undergrads receive non-need-based scholarship or grant aid. 84% freshmen, 92% undergrads receive need-based self-help aid. 1% freshmen, 1% undergrads receive athletic scholarships. 86% freshmen, 72% undergrads receive any aid. Average cumulative indebtedness $26,818. **Criteria for awarding aid:** *Need-based:* Academics. *Non-need-based:* Academics, Art, Athletics, Leadership, Music/drama, State/district residency.

UNIVERSITY OF MASSACHUSETTS—AMHERST

University Admissions Center, Amherst, MA 01003-9291
Phone: 413-545-0222 • **Financial Aid Phone:** 413-545-0801
E-mail: mail@admissions.umass.edu • **CEEB Code:** 3917
Fax: 413-545-4312 • **Website:** www.umass.edu • **ACT Code:** 1924

This public school was founded in 1863. It has a 1463-acre campus.

RATINGS

Admissions Selectivity Rating: 88   **Fire Safety Rating:** 92   **Green Rating:** 96

STUDENTS AND FACULTY

Enrollment: 22,958. **Student Body:** 49% female, 51% male, 19% out-of-state, 5% international (69 countries represented). Asian 10%, African American 4%, Caucasian 66%, Hispanic 6%, Native American <1%, Pacific Islander <1%, Two or more races 3%, Race unknown 7%.
Retention and Graduation: 91% freshmen return for sophomore year. 67% freshmen graduate within 4 years. 76% freshmen graduate within 6 years. 18% grads go on to further study within 1 year. 1% grads pursue law degrees. 3% grads pursue business degrees. 2% grads pursue medical degrees. **Faculty:** Student/faculty ratio 18:1. 1,288 full-time faculty, 95% hold PhDs, 23% are are members of minority groups, 43% are women.

ACADEMICS

Degrees: associate, bachelor's, certificate, doctoral/professional, doctoral/research, master's, postbachelor's certifiate, post-master's certificate. **Classes:** Most classes have 10-19 students. Most lab/discussion sessions have 20-29 students. **Most popular majors:** Psychology; Biology/Biological Sciences; Computer Science. **Special Study Options:** cooperative education program, cross-registration, distance learning, double major, dual enrollment, English as a Second Language (ESL), exchange student program (domestic), honors program, independent study, internships, liberal arts/career combination, student-designed major, study abroad, teacher certification program. **Honors Programs:** Commonwealth Honors College offers the advantages of a small honors college, but also the wide-ranging opportunities of a nationally recognized research university. There are approximately 2,800 academically talented students in the Commonwealth College, all experiencing the challenges of a dynamic curriculum that includes interdisciplinary seminars, enriched honors courses, colloquia, independent study, service learning, a "culminating experience" and an honors thesis or project, as well as the option of special living-learning accommodations. Combined degree programs: BA/MA, Economics (BA—MA); -Linguistics (BA—MA); Political Science (BA—MA); Public Policy (BA/BS—MPP); Architecture (BFA—MArch); Animal Biotech&Biomed Sci (BS—MS); Biochem. & Molecular Biol. **Disability Services:** Special programs offered to physically disabled students, including note-taking services, reader services, tape recorders, tutors. **Career Services:** Alumni network, Alumni services, Career/job search classes, Career assessment, Internships. We are very proud of the comprehensive career planning services we provide to the students at the University. There is no program that we feel is better than the others.

FACILITIES

Housing: Coed dorms, special housing for disabled students, men's dorms, special housing for international students, women's dorms, fraternity/sorority housing, apartments for married students, apartments for single students, Wellness Housing, Theme Housing, first year housing. **Special Academic Facilities/Equipment:** Computer Science Complex, Polymer Research Institute, Herter (Art) Gallery, University Art Gallery, Natural History Museum, Fine Arts Center, Mullins Center (sports and entertainment arena, Learning Commons. **Computers:** 97% of classrooms, 10% of dorms, 100% of libraries, 100% of dining areas, 100% of student union, 20% of common outdoor

areas have wireless network access. Students can register for classes online. Administrative functions (other than registration) can be performed online.

CAMPUS LIFE

Environment: Town. **Activities:** Choral groups, concert band, dance, drama/theater, jazz band, literary magazine, marching band, music ensembles, musical theater, opera, pep band, radio station, student government, student newspaper, student-run film society, symphony orchestra, television station, Campus Ministries, Student Organization, Model UN. 291 registered organizations, 30 honor societies, 14 religious organizations. 21 fraternities, 15 sororities. **Athletics (Intercollegiate):** *Men:* baseball, basketball, cross-country, diving, football, ice hockey, lacrosse, soccer, swimming, track/field (outdoor), track/field (indoor). *Women:* basketball, crew/rowing, cross-country, diving, field hockey, lacrosse, soccer, softball, swimming, tennis, track/field (outdoor), track/field (indoor). **On-Campus Highlights:** The Campus Center / Student Union, The Learning Commons, Recreation Center, The Mullins Center, The Fine Arts Center, http://www.umass.edu/umhome/visit_campus/. **Environmental Initiatives:** Central Heating Plant: Our new Central Heating Plant now allows us to produce roughly 70% of our campus' energy through co-generation. The Central Heating Plant is fueled by mostly natural gas with some oil in the winter time and has won national awards.

ADMISSIONS

Freshman Academic Profile: Average high school GPA 3.8. 34% in top 10% of high school class, 74% in top 25% of high school class, 97% in top 50% of high school class. **Reported SAT (pre-2016 redesign) scores:** SAT Math middle 50% range 580-680. SAT Critical Reading middle 50% range 550-650. **Concordant SAT scores:** SAT Math middle 50% range 600–710. ACT middle 50% range 25-30. Minimum internet-based TOEFL 80. **Basis for Candidate Selection:** *Very important factors considered include:* rigor of secondary school record, academic GPA, standardized test scores. *Important factors considered include:* class rank, application essay, recommendation(s), extracurricular activities, talent/ability, character/personal qualities, first generation, work experience, level of applicant's interest. *Other factors considered include:* alumni/ae relation, geographical residence, state residency, racial/ethnic status, volunteer work. **Freshman Admission Requirements:** High school diploma is required and GED is accepted. *Academic units required:* 4 English, 3 math, 3 science, 2 science labs, 2 foreign language, 2 social studies, 2 academic electives. **Freshman Admission Statistics:** 40,703 applied, 59.64% admitted, 19% enrolled. **Transfer Admission Requirements:** college transcript(s), essay or personal statement, Minimum college GPA of 2.5 required. Lowest grade transferable C-. **General Admission Information:** Application fee $75. Priority deadline 1/15. Nonfall registration accepted. Admission may be deferred for a maximum of 1 year.

COSTS AND FINANCIAL AID

Annual in-state tuition $13,790. Annual out-of-state tuition $30,123. Room and board $12,028. Required fees $381. Average book expense $1,000. **Required Forms and Deadlines:** FAFSA. **Notification of Awards:** Applicants will be notified of awards on a rolling basis beginning 4/1. **Types of Aid:** *Need-based scholarships/grants:* Federal Pell, FSEOG, State scholarships/grants, Private scholarships, College/university scholarship or grant aid from institutional funds. *Loans:* Direct Subsidized Stafford Loans, Direct Unsubsidized Stafford Loans, Direct PLUS loans, Federal Perkins Loans, Federal Nursing Loans. *Student Employment:* Federal Work-Study Program available. Institutional employment available. **Financial Aid Statistics:** 91% needy freshmen, 87% needy undergrads receive need-based scholarship or grant aid. 11% freshmen, 7% undergrads receive non-need-based scholarship or grant aid. 85% freshmen, 90% undergrads receive need-based self-help aid. 1% freshmen, 1% undergrads receive athletic scholarships. 90% freshmen, 85% undergrads receive any aid. 68% undergrads borrow to pay for school. Average cumulative indebtedness $31,397. **Criteria for awarding aid:** *Non-need-based:* Academics, Art, Athletics, Music/drama, State/district residency.

UNIVERSITY OF MASSACHUSETTS—BOSTON

100 Morrissey Boulevard, Boston, MA 02125-3393
Phone: 617-287-6100 • **Financial Aid Phone:** 617-287-6300
E-mail: undergrad.admissions@umb.edu • **CEEB Code:** 3924
Fax: 617-287-5999 • **Website:** www.umb.edu

This public school was founded in 1964. It has a 177-acre campus.

RATINGS

Admissions Selectivity Rating: 74   **Fire Safety Rating:** 60*   **Green Rating:** 91

STUDENTS AND FACULTY

Enrollment: 11,196. **Student Body:** 54% female, 46% male, 5% out-of-state, 12% international (150 countries represented). Asian 12%, African American

16%, Caucasian 34%, Hispanic 14%, Native American <1%, Pacific Islander <1%, Two or more races 3%, Race unknown 9%.

Retention and Graduation: 80% freshmen return for sophomore year. 18% freshmen graduate within 4 years. 45 **Faculty:** Student/faculty ratio 16:1. 714 full-time faculty, 98% hold PhDs, 22% are are members of minority groups, 51% are women. 0% of classes are taught by teaching assistants.

ACADEMICS

Degrees: bachelor's, certificate, doctoral/professional, doctoral/research, doctoral, master's, postbachelor's certificate, post-master's certificate. **Classes:** Most classes have 20-29 students. Most lab/discussion sessions have fewer than 10 students. **Most popular majors:** Management Science. **Special Study Options:** cooperative education program, cross-registration, distance learning, double major, dual enrollment, English as a Second Language (ESL), exchange student program (domestic), honors program, independent study, internships, liberal arts/career combination, student-designed major, study abroad, teacher certification program. **Honors Programs:** The University Honors Program seeks to meet the needs of students who thrive on intellectual challenge by offering special interdisciplinary academic opportunities outside the major. Combined degree programs: BA/MA, BA/MA Economics BA/MA Sociology. **Disability Services:** Special programs offered to physically disabled students, including note-taking services, reader services, tape recorders, tutors. **Career Services:** Alumni network, Alumni services, Career/job search classes, Career assessment, Internships, Regional alumni.

FACILITIES

Housing: University housing referral service. 100% of campus accessible to physically diasbled. **Special Academic Facilities/Equipment:** Art gallery, tropical greenhouse, observatory, adaptive computer lab. **Computers:** 100% of classrooms, 100% of libraries, 100% of dining areas, 100% of student union, have wireless network access. Students can register for classes online. Administrative functions (other than registration) can be performed online.

CAMPUS LIFE

Environment: Metropolis. **Activities:** Choral groups, concert band, dance, drama/theater, jazz band, literary magazine, music ensembles, radio station, student government, student newspaper, student-run film society, symphony orchestra, yearbook, Campus Ministries, Student Organization, Model UN. 75 registered organizations, 1 honor society. **Athletics (Intercollegiate):** *Men:* baseball, basketball, cross-country, ice hockey, lacrosse, soccer, tennis, track/field (outdoor), track/field (indoor). *Women:* basketball, cross-country, ice hockey, soccer, softball, tennis, track/field (outdoor), track/field (indoor), volleyball. **On-Campus Highlights:** New Campus Center, Clark Athletic Center, Waterfront area and weekly boat tours, Greenhouse, Healey Library. **Environmental Initiatives:** 1.Comprehensive sustainability program, toxics use reduction program, energy conservation and management efforts, master planning. UMB awarded MA Sustainable Campus of the Year in 2004 and 2015.

ADMISSIONS

Freshman Academic Profile: Average high school GPA 3.3. **Reported SAT (pre-2016 redesign) scores:** SAT Math middle 50% range 490-600. SAT Critical Reading middle 50% range 470-580. **Concordant SAT scores:** SAT Math middle 50% range 520–620. ACT middle 50% range 21-26. Minimum internet-based TOEFL 79. **Basis for Candidate Selection:** *Very important factors considered include:* rigor of secondary school record, academic GPA, standardized test scores, character/personal qualities. *Important factors considered include:* application essay, recommendation(s). *Other factors considered include:* extracurricular activities, talent/ability, first generation, volunteer work, work experience. **Freshman Admission Requirements:** High school diploma is required and GED is accepted. *Academic units required:* 4 English, 4 math, 3 science, 2 science labs, 2 foreign language, 1 social studies, 1 history, 2 academic electives. **Freshman Admission Statistics:** 9,886 applied, 68.52% admitted, 24% enrolled. **Transfer Admission Requirements:** college transcript(s), essay or personal statement, statement of good standing from prior institution(s). Minimum college GPA of 2.5 required. Lowest grade transferable C-. **General Admission Information:** Application fee $60. Priority deadline 3/1. Regular application deadline 3/1. Regular notification 4/30. Nonfall registration accepted. Admission may be deferred for a maximum of 1 year.

COSTS AND FINANCIAL AID

Annual in-state tuition $13,110. Required fees $325. **Required Forms and Deadlines:** FAFSA. **Notification of Awards:** Applicants will be notified of awards on a rolling basis beginning 3/6. **Types of Aid:** *Need-based scholarships/grants:* Federal Pell, FSEOG, State scholarships/grants, Private scholarships, College/university scholarship or grant aid from institutional funds. *Loans:* Direct Subsidized Stafford Loans, Direct Unsubsidized Stafford Loans, Direct PLUS loans, Federal Perkins Loans. *Student Employment:* Federal Work-Study Program available. Institutional employment available. **Financial Aid Statistics:** 93% needy freshmen, 91% needy undergrads receive need-based scholarship or grant aid. 5% freshmen, 2% undergrads receive non-need-based scholarship or grant aid. 92% freshmen, 96% undergrads receive need-based self-help aid. 0% freshmen, 0% undergrads receive athletic scholarships.

Criteria for awarding aid: *Need-based:* Academics. *Non-need-based:* Academics, Leadership, State/district residency.

UNIVERSITY OF MASSACHUSETTS— DARTMOUTH

285 Old Westport Road, North Dartmouth, MA 02747-2300
Phone: 508-999-8605 • **Financial Aid Phone:** 508-999-8643
E-mail: admissions@umassd.edu • **CEEB Code:** 3786
Fax: 508-999-8755 • **Website:** http://www.umassd.edu/ • **ACT Code:** 1906

This public school was founded in 1895. It has a 710-acre campus.

RATINGS

Admissions Selectivity Rating: 73   **Fire Safety Rating:** 85   **Green Rating:** 87

STUDENTS AND FACULTY

Enrollment: 6,758. **Student Body:** 49% female, 51% male, 6% out-of-state, 2% international (52 countries represented). Asian 4%, African American 15%, Caucasian 62%, Hispanic 9%, Native American <1%, Pacific Islander <1%, Two or more races 4%, Race unknown 5%.

Retention and Graduation: 73% freshmen return for sophomore year. 4% freshmen graduate within 4 years. 48 **Faculty:** Student/faculty ratio 16:1. 399 full-time faculty, 88% hold PhDs, 20% are are members of minority groups, 45% are women. 3% of classes are taught by teaching assistants.

ACADEMICS

Degrees: bachelor's, certificate, doctoral/professional, doctoral/research, master's, postbachelor's certificate, post-master's certificate. **Classes:** Most classes have 20-29 students. Most lab/discussion sessions have 20-29 students. **Most popular majors:** Psychology; Liberal Arts and Sciences Studies and Humanities; Registered Nursing, Nursing Administration, Nursing Research and Clinical Nursing. **Special Study Options:** cooperative education program, cross-registration, distance learning, double major, dual enrollment, exchange student program (domestic), honors program, independent study, internships, student-designed major, study abroad, teacher certification program. **Honors Programs:** Honors Program Combined degree programs: BA/JD, BA/MA, BS/MS in Chemistry, Biology, Engineering, Nursing; BS/MAT, BA/MAT; BA/PRW in English; BA/MA in Psychology. **Disability Services:** Special programs offered to physically disabled students, including note-taking services, reader services, tape recorders, tutors. **Career Services:** Alumni network, Career/job search classes, Internships.

FACILITIES

Housing: Coed dorms, special housing for disabled students, apartments for single students, Apartments for upperclassmen and graduate students. Program dedicated suites. 97% of campus accessible to physically diasbled. **Special Academic Facilities/Equipment:** Art gallery, language center, center for Jewish culture, Robert F. Kennedy assassination archives, electron microscope, observatory, marine research vessels, Advanced Manufacturing and Technology Center, School of Marine Science and Technology **Computers:** 100% of classrooms, 100% of dorms, 100% of libraries, 100% of dining areas, 100% of student union, 100% of common outdoor areas have wireless network access. Students can register for classes online. Administrative functions (other than registration) can be performed online.

CAMPUS LIFE

Environment: Town. **Activities:** Choral groups, concert band, dance, drama/theater, jazz band, literary magazine, music ensembles, musical theater, pep band, radio station, student government, student newspaper, symphony orchestra, yearbook, Student Organization. 103 registered organizations, 5 honor societies, 6 religious organizations. 5 fraternities, 3 sororities. **Athletics (Intercollegiate):** *Men:* baseball, basketball, cross-country, diving, football, golf, ice hockey, lacrosse, soccer, swimming, tennis, track/field (outdoor), track/field (indoor). *Women:* basketball, cheerleading, cross-country, diving, equestrian sports, field hockey, golf, lacrosse, soccer, softball, swimming, tennis, track/field (outdoor), track/field (indoor), volleyball. **On-Campus Highlights:** Underground Cafe, Tripp Athletic Center, Woodlawn Commons, MacLean Campus Center, Observatory. **Environmental Initiatives:** Large scale energy performance. Lighting,heating, AC, water, sewer.

ADMISSIONS

Freshman Academic Profile: Average high school GPA 3.2. 89% from public high schools. **Reported SAT (pre-2016 redesign) scores:** SAT Math middle 50% range 460-570. SAT Critical Reading middle 50% range 450-560. **Concordant SAT scores:** SAT Math middle 50% range 500–590. ACT middle 50% range 19.5-26. Minimum internet-based TOEFL 68. Minimum paper TOEFL 520. **Basis for Candidate Selection:** *Very important* *factors considered include:* rigor of secondary school record, academic GPA, standardized test scores. *Other factors considered include:* application essay, recommendation(s), extracurricular activities, talent/ability, character/personal qualities, first generation, alumni/ae relation, volunteer work, work experience. **Freshman Admission Requirements:** High school diploma is required and GED is accepted. *Academic units required:* 4 English, 4 math, 3 science, 2 science labs, 2 foreign language, 1 social studies, 1 history, 1 academic elective. **Freshman Admission Statistics:** 8,211 applied, 76.02% admitted, 22% enrolled. **Transfer Admission Requirements:** college transcript(s), essay or personal statement, Minimum college GPA of 2.5 required. Lowest grade transferable C-. **General Admission Information:** Application fee $60. Priority deadline 3/1. Nonfall registration accepted. Admission may be deferred for a maximum of 2 semesters.

COSTS AND FINANCIAL AID

Required Forms and Deadlines: FAFSA. **Types of Aid:** *Need-based scholarships/grants:* Federal Pell, FSEOG, State scholarships/grants, Private scholarships, College/university scholarship or grant aid from institutional funds. *Loans:* Direct Subsidized Stafford Loans, Direct Unsubsidized Stafford Loans, Direct PLUS loans, Federal Perkins Loans, Federal Nursing Loans, State Loans. *Student Employment:* Federal Work-Study Program available. Institutional employment available. **Financial Aid Statistics:** 77% freshmen, 73% undergrads receive any aid. **Criteria for awarding aid:** *Non-need-based:* Academics, Minority status, State/district residency.

UNIVERSITY OF MASSACHUSETTS—LOWELL

University Crossing Suite 420, Lowell, MA 01854-2874
Phone: 978-934-3931 • **Financial Aid Phone:** 978-934-4220
E-mail: admissions@uml.edu • **CEEB Code:** 3911
Fax: 978-934-3086 • **Website:** www.uml.edu • **ACT Code:** 1854

This public school was founded in 1894. It has a 150-acre campus.

RATINGS

Admissions Selectivity Rating: 85   **Fire Safety Rating:** 96   **Green Rating:** 92

STUDENTS AND FACULTY

Enrollment: 12,494. **Student Body:** 38% female, 62% male, 9% out-of-state, 3% international (61 countries represented). Asian 9%, African American 6%, Caucasian 64%, Hispanic 10%, Native American <1%, Pacific Islander <1%, Two or more races 3%, Race unknown 5%.
Retention and Graduation: 86% freshmen return for sophomore year. 31% freshmen graduate within 4 years. 56% freshmen graduate within 6 years. **Faculty:** Student/faculty ratio 17:1. 565 full-time faculty, 91% hold PhDs, 24% are are members of minority groups, 43% are women. 0% of classes are taught by teaching assistants.

ACADEMICS

Degrees: associate, bachelor's, certificate, doctoral/professional, doctoral/research, master's, postbachelor's certifiate, post-master's certificate. **Classes:** Most classes have 20-29 students. Most lab/discussion sessions have 10-19 students. **Most popular majors:** Criminal Justice/Law Enforcement Administration; Business Administration and Management; Mechanical Engineering Related Technologies/Technicians. **Special Study Options:** Accelerated program, cooperative education program, cross-registration, distance learning, double major, dual enrollment, honors program, internships, liberal arts/career combination, study abroad, teacher certification program, Teacher Certification program for Education is Graduate only. **Honors Programs:** The Honors Program at UMass Lowell offers high-achieving students individualized instruction in small groups, often in seminar format; opportunities for undergraduate research; special "Commonwealth Honors Program Scholar" designation on transcripts and diplomas—upon completion of program requirements; opportunity to live on one of the Honors floors in the residence halls; and Honors Program social events. **LEARN PROGRAM—** With the Fall 2004 entering class, all first year students will participate in the LEARN Program. LEARN, which stands for Living Education and Resource Networking, links academic, residential and personal development experiences by clustering offices, labs and classrooms among residence hall rooms, and offering a year-long schedule of programs that address a range of pertinent social and personal issues. Combined degree programs: BA/MA, BA/MEng, BA/BS-MM; BA/BS-MS; MA/BS-DPT; BA/BS-MPH; BA/BS-MBA. **Disability Services:** Special programs offered to physically disabled students, including note-taking services, reader services, tape recorders, tutors. **Career Services:** Alumni network, Alumni services, Career/job search classes, Career assessment, Internships, Regional alumni. UMass Lowell redesigned its 4-year career planning model, called ProPath. Through class-year-specific career activities, students are guided and supported in exploring careers, gaining experience, and transitioning to the workplace as a new professional. Our expanding cooperative education (co-op) program and internship opportunities are designed to help students apply their knowledge in work settings. Our active recruiting program attracts hundreds of employers to recruit UMass Lowell students and recent graduates. Over 180 employers come to each of our career fairs. Plus, employers host company nights, interview on-campus and post jobs to CareerLink, our online recruiting system.

FACILITIES

Housing: Coed dorms, special housing for disabled students, apartments for married students, cooperative housing, apartments for single students. 90% of campus accessible to physically diasbled. **Special Academic Facilities/Equipment:** Language lab, media center, audio-visual department, Centers for Learning, Center for field studies, Center for Performing and Visual Arts, Center for Health Promotion, Research Nuclear Reactor. New $19.5 million recreation center which includes multi court gymnasium, 1/8 mile indoor elevated track, aerobics room, game rooms, locker rooms, and a sauna. Also included are meeting rooms and an indoor/outdoor food court. **Computers:** 50% of classrooms, 90% of dorms, 100% of libraries, 100% of dining areas, 100% of student union, 75% of common outdoor areas have wireless network access. Students can register for classes online. Administrative functions (other than registration) can be performed online.

CAMPUS LIFE

Environment: City. **Activities:** Choral groups, concert band, dance, drama/theater, jazz band, literary magazine, marching band, music ensembles, pep band, radio station, student government, student newspaper, student-run film society, symphony orchestra, yearbook, Student Organization. 100 registered organizations, 16 honor societies, 4 religious organizations. **Athletics (Intercollegiate):** *Men:* baseball, basketball, crew/rowing, cross-country, golf, ice hockey, soccer, track/field (outdoor), track/field (indoor). *Women:* basketball, crew/rowing, cross-country, field hockey, soccer, softball, track/field (outdoor), track/field (indoor), volleyball. **On-Campus Highlights:** Campus Recreation Center, South Campus Quad, McGauvran Student Center, Fox Multi-purpose Room, Southwick Lounge, New updated state of the art dining facility in the Southwick Lounge. **Environmental Initiatives:** Development of the Office of Sustainability.

ADMISSIONS

Freshman Academic Profile: Average high school GPA 3.5. 20% in top 10% of high school class, 49% in top 25% of high school class, 85% in top 50% of high school class. 83% from public high schools. **Reported SAT (pre-2016 redesign) scores:** SAT Math middle 50% range 550-650. SAT Critical Reading middle 50% range 520-620. SAT Writing middle 50% range 500-600. **Concordant SAT scores:** SAT EBRW middle 50% 570–660. SAT Math middle 50% range 570–670. ACT middle 50% range 23-29. Minimum internet-based TOEFL 213. Minimum paper TOEFL 550. **Basis for Candidate Selection:** *Very important factors considered include:* rigor of secondary school record, academic GPA, standardized test scores. *Important factors considered include:* application essay, recommendation(s). *Other factors considered include:* class rank, extracurricular activities, talent/ability, character/personal qualities, first generation, alumni/ae relation, geographical residence, state residency, volunteer work, work experience, level of applicant's interest. **Freshman Admission Requirements:** High school diploma is required and GED is accepted. *Academic units required:* 4 English, 3 math, 3 science, 2 science labs, 2 foreign language, 2 social studies, 2 academic electives. *Academic units recommended:* 4 math, 4 science. **Freshman Admission Statistics:** 10,638 applied, 56.59% admitted, 27% enrolled. **Transfer Admission Requirements:** college transcript(s), Minimum college GPA of 2.0 required. Lowest grade transferable c-. **General Admission Information:** Application fee $60. Priority deadline 11/15. Regular application deadline 2/15. Nonfall registration accepted. Admission may be deferred for a maximum of 12 months.

COSTS AND FINANCIAL AID

Required Forms and Deadlines: FAFSA. **Notification of Awards:** Applicants will be notified of awards on a rolling basis beginning 3/20. **Types of Aid:** *Need-based scholarships/grants:* Federal Pell, FSEOG, State scholarships/grants, Private scholarships, College/university scholarship or grant aid from institutional funds. *Loans:* Direct Subsidized Stafford Loans, Direct Unsubsidized Stafford Loans, Direct PLUS loans, Federal Perkins Loans, Federal Nursing Loans. *Student Employment:* Federal Work-Study Program available. Institutional employment available. **Financial Aid Statistics:** 93% needy freshmen, 87% needy undergrads receive need-based scholarship or grant aid. 7% freshmen, 4% undergrads receive non-need-based scholarship or grant aid. 90% freshmen, 93% undergrads receive need-based self-help aid. 4% freshmen, 3% undergrads receive athletic scholarships. 89% freshmen, 82% undergrads receive any aid. 81% undergrads borrow to pay for school. Average cumulative indebtedness $30,915. **Criteria for awarding aid:** *Need-based:* Academics. *Non-need-based:* Academics, Alumni affiliation, Art, Athletics, Leadership, Minority status, Music/drama, State/district residency.

See page 1080.

THE UNIVERSITY OF MEMPHIS

101 Wilder Tower, Memphis, TN 38152
Phone: 901-678-2111 • **Financial Aid Phone:** 901-678-4825
E-mail: recruitment@memphis.edu • **CEEB Code:** 1459
Fax: 901-678-3053 • **Website:** www.memphis.edu • **ACT Code:** 3992

This public school was founded in 1912. It has a 1160-acre campus.

RATINGS
Admissions Selectivity Rating: 79   **Fire Safety Rating:** 88   **Green Rating:** 60*

STUDENTS AND FACULTY
Enrollment: 16,741. **Student Body:** 61% female, 39% male, 10% out-of-state, 1% international (53 countries represented). Asian 3%, African American 40%, Caucasian 49%, Hispanic 3%, Native American <1%, Pacific Islander <1%, Two or more races 3%, Race unknown 1%.
Retention and Graduation: 76% freshmen return for sophomore year. 13% freshmen graduate within 4 years. **Faculty:** Student/faculty ratio 14:1. 136 full-time faculty, 59% hold PhDs, 14% are are members of minority groups, 57% are women.

ACADEMICS
Degrees: bachelor's, doctoral/professional, doctoral/research, master's, postbachelor's certificate, post-master's certificate. **Classes:** Most classes have 20-29 students. Most lab/discussion sessions have 10-19 students. **Most popular majors:** General Studies; Psychology; Biology/Biological Sciences. **Special Study Options:** Accelerated program, cooperative education program, cross-registration, distance learning, double major, dual enrollment, English as a Second Language (ESL), exchange student program (domestic), external degree program, honors program, independent study, internships, liberal arts/career combination, student-designed major, study abroad, teacher certification program. **Honors Programs:** The Honors Program offers students the opportunity to take small classes and interdisciplinary seminars with the University's most outstanding faculty. The program also includes many wonderful opportunities beyond the classroom such as study abroad, independent research, and co-curricular activities. Honors students also have the chance to participate in nationally recognized undergraduate research conferences and extend their learning through internships and public service. **Disability Services:** Special programs offered to physically disabled students, including note-taking services, reader services, tape recorders. **Career Services:** Alumni network, Alumni services, Career/job search classes, Career assessment, Internships, Regional alumni. Fresh Connections are learning communities that use clusters of courses to connect different disciplines to a common theme. Students in the Learning Communitites take these courses together to develop a deeper understanding of the material.

FACILITIES
Housing: Coed dorms, special housing for disabled students, men's dorms, women's dorms, fraternity/sorority housing, apartments for married students, apartments for single students, Living-Learning communities. 95% of campus accessible to physically diasbled. **Special Academic Facilities/Equipment:** Center for Earthquake Research & Information Institute of Egyptian Art & Archaeology Bureau of Business and Economic Research **Computers:** 100% of classrooms, 55% of dorms, 100% of libraries, 100% of dining areas, 100% of student union, 10% of common outdoor areas have wireless network access. Students can register for classes online. Administrative functions (other than registration) can be performed online.

CAMPUS LIFE
Environment: Metropolis. **Activities:** Choral groups, concert band, dance, drama/theater, jazz band, literary magazine, marching band, music ensembles, musical theater, opera, pep band, radio station, student government, student newspaper, symphony orchestra, Campus Ministries, Student Organization. 140 registered organizations, 20 honor societies, 12 religious organizations. 14 fraternities, 11 sororities. **Athletics (Intercollegiate):** *Men:* baseball, basketball, cross-country, football, golf, riflery, soccer, tennis, track/field (outdoor). *Women:* basketball, cross-country, golf, riflery, soccer, softball, tennis, track/field (outdoor), volleyball. **On-Campus Highlights:** Rose Theater Lecture Hall, FedEx Institute of Technology, Finch Recreation Facility, Harris Concert Hall, Institute of Egyptian Art & Archaeology. **Environmental Initiatives:** Energy Conservation.

ADMISSIONS
Freshman Academic Profile: Average high school GPA 3.3. 1% in top 10% of high school class, 42% in top 25% of high school class, 79% in top 50% of high school class. **Reported SAT (pre-2016 redesign) scores:** SAT Math middle 50% range 440-590. SAT Critical Reading middle 50% range 440-570. SAT Writing middle 50% range 410-560. **Concordant SAT scores:** SAT EBRW middle 50% 480–620. SAT Math middle 50% range 480–610. ACT middle 50% range 20-25. Minimum paper TOEFL 550. **Basis for Candidate Selection:**

Very important factors considered include: rigor of secondary school record, academic GPA, standardized test scores. *Other factors considered include:* application essay, recommendation(s), talent/ability, character/personal qualities, first generation, work experience. **Freshman Admission Requirements:** High school diploma is required and GED is accepted. *Academic units required:* 4 English, 3 math, 2 science, 1 science lab, 2 foreign language, 1 social studies, 1 history, 1 visual/performing arts. **Freshman Admission Statistics:** 6,798 applied, 62.42% admitted, 53% enrolled. **Transfer Admission Requirements:** college transcript(s), standardized test scores, Lowest grade transferable C. **General Admission Information:** Application fee $25. Regular application deadline 7/1. Nonfall registration accepted.

COSTS AND FINANCIAL AID
Required Forms and Deadlines: FAFSA. **Notification of Awards:** Applicants will be notified of awards on a rolling basis beginning 3/15. **Types of Aid:** *Need-based scholarships/grants:* Federal Pell, FSEOG, State scholarships/grants, Private scholarships, College/university scholarship or grant aid from institutional funds. *Loans:* Direct Subsidized Stafford Loans, Direct Unsubsidized Stafford Loans, Direct PLUS loans, Federal Perkins Loans, State Loans. *Student Employment:* Federal Work-Study Program available. Institutional employment available. **Financial Aid Statistics:** 67% needy freshmen, 71% needy undergrads receive need-based scholarship or grant aid. 49% freshmen, 62% undergrads receive non-need-based scholarship or grant aid. 59% freshmen, 81% undergrads receive need-based self-help aid. 3% freshmen, 2% undergrads receive athletic scholarships. 95% freshmen, 91% undergrads receive any aid. **Criteria for awarding aid:** *Need-based:* Academics, Leadership, Minority status. *Non-need-based:* Academics, Alumni affiliation, Art, Athletics, Leadership, Music/drama, State/district residency.

UNIVERSITY OF MIAMI

P.O. Box 248025, Coral Gables, FL 33124-4616
Phone: 305-284-4323 • **Financial Aid Phone:** 305-284-5212
E-mail: admission@miami.edu • **CEEB Code:** 5815
Fax: 305-284-2507 • **Website:** www.miami.edu • **ACT Code:** 760

This private school was founded in 1925. It has a 260-acre campus.

RATINGS
Admissions Selectivity Rating: 93   **Fire Safety Rating:** 91   **Green Rating:** 96

STUDENTS AND FACULTY
Enrollment: 10,615. **Student Body:** 52% female, 48% male, 58% out-of-state, 14% international (106 countries represented). Asian 5%, African American 8%, Caucasian 43%, Hispanic 23%, Native American <1%, Pacific Islander <1%, Two or more races 3%, Race unknown 4%.
Retention and Graduation: 91% freshmen return for sophomore year. 70% freshmen graduate within 4 years. 82% freshmen graduate within 6 years. 33% grads go on to further study within 1 year. 10% grads pursue arts and sciences degrees. 6% grads pursue law degrees. 1% grads pursue business degrees. 7% grads pursue medical degrees. **Faculty:** Student/faculty ratio 12:1. 1,108 full-time faculty, 88% hold PhDs, 34% are are members of minority groups, 41% are women. 7% of classes are taught by teaching assistants.

ACADEMICS
Degrees: bachelor's, certificate, doctoral/professional, doctoral/research, master's, postbachelor's certificate, post-master's certificate. **Classes:** Most classes have 10-19 students. Most lab/discussion sessions have fewer than 10 students. **Most popular majors:** Biology/Biological Sciences; Psychology; Finance. **Special Study Options:** Accelerated program, distance learning, double major, dual enrollment, English as a Second Language (ESL), honors program, independent study, internships, liberal arts/career combination, student-designed major, study abroad, teacher certification program, weekend college. **Honors Programs:** Honors Program in Medicine (HPM) Combined degree programs: BA/MD, BA/JD. **Disability Services:** Special programs offered to physically disabled students, including note-taking services, reader services, tutors. **Career Services:** Alumni services, Career/job search classes, Career assessment, Internships. The Toppel Internship Program (TIP) is a 0-1 credit transcript notation program that was created in 2007. The goal was to help students participate in internships for academic credit (most often unpaid) without being penalized with having to pay for the credit. Since its inception, the program has exploded in popularity, with about 2,400 participants to date.

FACILITIES

Housing: Coed dorms, special housing for disabled students, fraternity/sorority housing, apartments for single students, Theme Housing. **Special Academic Facilities/Equipment:** Lowe Art Museum, Gusman Concert Hall, Jerry Herman Ring Theatre, Bill Cosford Cinema, Convocation Center, Wellness Center. **Computers:** 100% of classrooms, 100% of dorms, 100% of libraries, 100% of dining areas, 100% of student union, 100% of common outdoor areas have wireless network access. Students can register for classes online. Administrative functions (other than registration) can be performed online.

CAMPUS LIFE

Environment: Town. **Activities:** Choral groups, concert band, dance, drama/theater, jazz band, literary magazine, marching band, music ensembles, musical theater, opera, pep band, radio station, student government, student newspaper, student-run film society, symphony orchestra, television station, yearbook, Campus Ministries, Student Organization, Model UN. **Athletics (Intercollegiate):** *Men:* baseball, basketball, cheerleading, cross-country, football, tennis, track/field (outdoor), track/field (indoor). *Women:* basketball, cheerleading, crew/rowing, cross-country, diving, golf, soccer, swimming, tennis, track/field (outdoor), track/field (indoor), volleyball. **On-Campus Highlights:** Lowe Art Museum, Jerry Herman Ring Theater, Bank United Center, Mark Light Stadium (Baseball), Gusman Concert Hall & Recording Studio, University Center Breezeway/ Student Union, The Rock (free speech area). **Environmental Initiatives:** The President signed the ACUPCC. The University also hired a sustainability coordinator.

ADMISSIONS

Freshman Academic Profile: Average high school GPA 3.6. 60% in top 10% of high school class, 85% in top 25% of high school class, 95% in top 50% of high school class. 62% from public high schools. **Reported SAT (pre-2016 redesign) scores:** SAT Math middle 50% range 610-710. SAT Critical Reading middle 50% range 600-680. SAT Writing middle 50% range 590-680. **Concordant SAT scores:** SAT EBRW middle 50% 650–720. SAT Math middle 50% range 630–740. ACT middle 50% range 28-32. Minimum internet-based TOEFL 80. Minimum paper TOEFL 550. **Basis for Candidate Selection:** *Very important factors considered include:* rigor of secondary school record, class rank, academic GPA, standardized test scores, application essay, recommendation(s), extracurricular activities, character/personal qualities. *Important factors considered include:* talent/ability, volunteer work, work experience. *Other factors considered include:* first generation, alumni/ae relation, geographical residence, racial/ethnic status, level of applicant's interest. **Freshman Admission Requirements:** High school diploma is required and GED is accepted. *Academic units recommended:* 4 English, 4 math, 3 science, 2 science labs, 2 foreign language, 3 social studies, 2 history, 1 computer science, 1 visual/performing arts. **Freshman Admission Statistics:** 32,525 applied, 46.88% admitted, 14% enrolled. **Transfer Admission Requirements:** college transcript(s), statement of good standing from prior institution(s). Lowest grade transferable C. **General Admission Information:** Application fee $70. Regular application deadline 1/1. Regular notification 4/15. Nonfall registration accepted. Admission may be deferred for a maximum of 1 year.

COSTS AND FINANCIAL AID

Annual tuition $45,600. Room and board $13,310. Required fees $1,404. Average book expense $930. **Required Forms and Deadlines:** FAFSA, CSS/Financial Aid PROFILE, Noncustodial PROFILE, Business/Farm Supplement. **Notification of Awards:** Applicants will be notified of awards on a rolling basis beginning 1/20. **Types of Aid:** *Need-based scholarships/grants:* Federal Pell, FSEOG, State scholarships/grants, Private scholarships, College/university scholarship or grant aid from institutional funds. *Loans:* Direct Subsidized Stafford Loans, Direct Unsubsidized Stafford Loans, Direct PLUS loans, Federal Perkins Loans, Federal Nursing Loans, College/university loans from institutional funds. *Student Employment:* Federal Work-Study Program available. Institutional employment available. **Financial Aid Statistics:** 30% needy freshmen, 51% needy undergrads receive need-based scholarship or grant aid. 96% freshmen, 92% undergrads receive non-need-based scholarship or grant aid. 63% freshmen, 66% undergrads receive need-based self-help aid. 0% freshmen, 0% undergrads receive athletic scholarships. 85% freshmen, 74% undergrads receive any aid. 37% undergrads borrow to pay for school. Average cumulative indebtedness $21,500. **Criteria for awarding aid:** *Need-based:* Alumni affiliation, Art, Job skills, Leadership, Minority status. *Non-need-based:* Academics, Athletics, Music/drama, State/district residency.

UNIVERSITY OF MICHIGAN—ANN ARBOR

515 E. Jefferson St, Ann Arbor, MI 48109-1316
Phone: 734-764-7433 • **Financial Aid Phone:** 734-763-6600 • **CEEB Code:** 1839
Fax: 734-936-0740 • **Website:** umich.edu • **ACT Code:** 2062

This public school was founded in 1817. It has a 3177-acre campus.

RATINGS

Admissions Selectivity Rating: 95   **Fire Safety Rating:** 88   **Green Rating:** 90

STUDENTS AND FACULTY

Enrollment: 28,761. **Student Body:** 50% female, 50% male, 40% out-of-state, 7% international (89 countries represented). Asian 14%, African American 4%, Caucasian 61%, Hispanic 4%, Native American <1%, Pacific Islander <1%, Two or more races 4%, Race unknown 5%.
Retention and Graduation: 97% freshmen return for sophomore year. 76% freshmen graduate within 4 years. 91% freshmen graduate within 6 years.
Faculty: Student/faculty ratio 15:1. 2,791 full-time faculty, 89% hold PhDs, 23% are are members of minority groups, 41% are women. 35% of classes are taught by teaching assistants.

ACADEMICS

Degrees: bachelor's, doctoral/professional, doctoral/research, doctoral, master's, postbachelor's certificate, post-master's certificate. **Classes:** Most classes have 10-19 students. Most lab/discussion sessions have 20-29 students. **Most popular majors:** Experimental Psychology; Economics; Business Administration and Management. **Special Study Options:** Accelerated program, cooperative education program, cross-registration, distance learning, double major, dual enrollment, English as a Second Language (ESL), exchange student program (domestic), external degree program, honors program, independent study, internships, liberal arts/career combination, student-designed major, study abroad, teacher certification program, weekend college. **Honors Programs:** LSA Honors Program; departmental honors programs Combined degree programs: BA/MA, BA/MEng, BA-BA/BArch; BA-BS/BFA; BA-BS/BSE; BBA/BFA; BBA/BSE; BBA/BFA; BBA/B Sport Mgm); BBA/BA-BS; BFA/BSE; BFA/BEd; BFA/BArch; BFA/BSN; BFA//BKines; BFA-Art&Design and Music; BFA/BSE. **Disability Services:** Special programs offered to physically disabled students, including note-taking services, reader services, tape recorders, tutors. **Career Services:** Alumni network, Alumni services, Career/job search classes, Career assessment, Internships. The University of Michigan is equally proud of all its cooperative, experiential, and internship learning opportunities.

FACILITIES

Housing: Coed dorms, special housing for disabled students, women's dorms, fraternity/sorority housing, apartments for married students, cooperative housing, apartments for single students, Wellness Housing, Theme Housing, Living/learning communities; substance free dorms. 95% of campus accessible to physically diasbled. **Special Academic Facilities/Equipment:** Anthropology, archaeology, art, natural science, paleontology, and zoology museums; audiovisual center, planetarium, electron microscope, biology station, geology camp, athletic campus, medical center, nuclear lab, botanical garden, herbarium, arboretum. **Computers:** 85% of classrooms, 40% of dorms, 80% of libraries, 95% of dining areas, 80% of student union, 10% of common outdoor areas have wireless network access. Students can register for classes online. Administrative functions (other than registration) can be performed online.

CAMPUS LIFE

Environment: City. **Activities:** Choral groups, concert band, dance, drama/theater, jazz band, literary magazine, marching band, music ensembles, musical theater, opera, pep band, radio station, student government, student newspaper, student-run film society, symphony orchestra, television station, yearbook, Campus Ministries, Student Organization, Model UN. 1000 registered organizations, 13 honor societies, 67 religious organizations. 39 fraternities, 27 sororities. **Athletics (Intercollegiate):** *Men:* baseball, basketball, cheerleading, cross-country, diving, football, golf, gymnastics, ice hockey, swimming, tennis, track/field (outdoor), track/field (indoor), wrestling. *Women:* basketball, cheerleading, crew/rowing, cross-country, diving, field hockey, golf, gymnastics, soccer, softball, swimming, tennis, track/field (outdoor), track/field (indoor), volleyball, water polo. **On-Campus Highlights:** Michigan Stadium, Museum of Natural History, Museum of Art, Margaret Dow Towsley Sports Museum **Environmental Initiatives:** Formal announcement of Campus Sustainability goals. http://sustainability.umich.edu/news/leadership-voice-president-colemans-speech-about-going-green-staying-blue-sustainability-michig

ADMISSIONS

Freshman Academic Profile: Average high school GPA 3.8. **Reported SAT (pre-2016 redesign) scores:** SAT Math middle 50% range 670-770. SAT Critical Reading middle 50% range 640-730. SAT Writing middle 50% range 650-740. **Concordant SAT scores:** SAT EBRW middle 50% 690–760. SAT Math middle 50% range 700–780. ACT middle 50% range 29-33. Minimum internet-based TOEFL 100. Minimum paper TOEFL 600. **Basis for Candidate Selection:** *Very important factors considered include:* rigor of secondary school record, academic GPA. *Important factors considered include:* standardized test scores, application essay, recommendation(s), character/personal qualities, first generation. *Other factors considered include:* extracurricular activities, talent/ability, alumni/ae relation, geographical residence, state residency, volunteer work, work experience, level of applicant's interest. **Freshman Admission Requirements:** High school diploma is required and GED is accepted. *Academic units required:* 4 English, 1 science lab. *Academic units recommended:* 4 English, 4 math, 4 science, 1 science lab, 4 foreign language, 4 social studies, 4 history, 1 computer science, 2 visual/performing arts. **Freshman Admission Statistics:** 55,504 applied, 28.59% admitted, 42% enrolled. **Transfer Admission Requirements:** High school transcript, college transcript(s), essay or personal statement, statement of good standing from prior institution(s). Minimum college GPA of 3.0 required. Lowest grade transferable C. **General Admission Information:** Application fee $75. Priority deadline 11/1. Regular application deadline 2/1. Nonfall registration accepted. Admission may be deferred for a maximum of 1 year.

COSTS AND FINANCIAL AID

Annual in-state tuition $14,982. Annual out-of-state tuition $46,676. Room and board $10,872. Required fees $328. Average book expense $1,048. **Required Forms and Deadlines:** FAFSA, CSS/Financial Aid PROFILE. **Notification of Awards:** Applicants will be notified of awards on a rolling basis beginning 3/15. **Types of Aid:** *Need-based scholarships/grants:* Federal Pell, FSEOG, State scholarships/grants, Private scholarships, College/university scholarship or grant aid from institutional funds. *Loans:* Direct Subsidized Stafford Loans, Direct Unsubsidized Stafford Loans, Direct PLUS loans, Federal Perkins Loans, Federal Nursing Loans, College/university loans from institutional funds. *Student Employment:* Federal Work-Study Program available. Institutional employment available. **Financial Aid Statistics:** 83% needy freshmen, 82% needy undergrads receive need-based scholarship or grant aid. 71% freshmen, 63% undergrads receive non-need-based scholarship or grant aid. 70% freshmen, 78% undergrads receive need-based self-help aid. 2% freshmen, 3% undergrads receive athletic scholarships. 68% freshmen, 61% undergrads receive any aid. 44% undergrads borrow to pay for school. Average cumulative indebtedness $25,712. **Criteria for awarding aid:** *Need-based:* Academics. *Non-need-based:* Academics, Alumni affiliation, Art, Athletics, Leadership, Music/drama, Religious affiliation, State/district residency.

liberal arts/career combination, student-designed major, study abroad, teacher certification program,

FACILITIES

Housing: fraternity/sorority housing. 100% of campus accessible to physically disabled.

CAMPUS LIFE

Activities: drama/theater, literary magazine, radio station, student government, student newspaper, student-run film society, television station.

ADMISSIONS

Freshman Academic Profile: Average high school GPA 4.0. 28% in top 10% of high school class, 59% in top 25% of high school class, 90% in top 50% of high school class. ACT middle 50% range 21-27. Minimum internet-based TOEFL 80. Minimum paper TOEFL 550. **Basis for Candidate Selection:** *Very important factors considered include:* academic GPA, standardized test scores. *Other factors considered include:* application essay, interview, alumni/ae relation. **Freshman Admission Requirements:** High school diploma is required and GED is accepted. *Academic units recommended:* 4 English, 4 math, 2 science, 1 science lab, 2 foreign language, 4 social studies, 4 history. **Freshman Admission Statistics:** 5,312 applied, 62.46% admitted, 29% enrolled. **Transfer Admission Requirements:** High school transcript, college transcript(s), Lowest grade transferable C. **General Admission Information:** Application fee $30. Regular application deadline 5/1. Nonfall registration accepted. Admission may be deferred for a maximum of 1 year.

COSTS AND FINANCIAL AID

Annual in-state tuition $14,982. Annual out-of-state tuition $46,676. Room and board $10,872. Required fees $328. Average book expense $1,048. **Required Forms and Deadlines:** FAFSA. **Notification of Awards:** Applicants will be notified of awards on a rolling basis beginning 3/15. **Types of Aid:** *Need-based scholarships/grants:* Federal Pell, FSEOG, State scholarships/grants, Private scholarships, College/university scholarship or grant aid from institutional funds. *Loans:* Direct Subsidized Stafford Loans, Direct Unsubsidized Stafford Loans, Direct PLUS loans, Federal Perkins Loans. *Student Employment:* Federal Work-Study Program available. Institutional employment available. **Financial Aid Statistics:** 90% needy freshmen, 84% needy undergrads receive need-based scholarship or grant aid. 50% freshmen, 34% undergrads receive non-need-based scholarship or grant aid. 86% freshmen, 92% undergrads receive need-based self-help aid. 2% freshmen, 2% undergrads receive athletic scholarships. 68% freshmen, 61% undergrads receive any aid. 65% undergrads borrow to pay for school. Average cumulative indebtedness $27,346. **Criteria for awarding aid:** *Need-based:* Leadership. *Non-need-based:* Academics, Alumni affiliation, Art, Athletics, Job skills, Leadership, Minority status, Music/drama, State/district residency.

UNIVERSITY OF MICHIGAN—DEARBORN

4901 Evergreen Road, Dearborn, MI 48128-1491
Phone: 313-593-5100 • **Financial Aid Phone:** 734-763-6600
E-mail: admissions@umd.umich.edu • **CEEB Code:** 1861
Fax: 313-436-9167 • **Website:** umdearborn.edu • **ACT Code:** 2074

This is a public school.

RATINGS

Admissions Selectivity Rating: 84   **Fire Safety Rating:** 60*   **Green Rating:** 60*

STUDENTS AND FACULTY

Enrollment: 6,865. **Student Body:** 48% female, 52% male, 4% out-of-state, 2% international (27 countries represented). Asian 7%, African American 10%, Caucasian 69%, Hispanic 6%, Native American <1%, Pacific Islander <1%, Two or more races 3%, Race unknown 3%. **Retention and Graduation:** 81% freshmen return for sophomore year. 16% freshmen graduate within 4 years. 53% freshmen graduate within 6 years. 27% grads go on to further study within 1 year. 10% grads pursue arts and sciences degrees. 3% grads pursue law degrees. 4% grads pursue business degrees. 1% grads pursue medical degrees. **Faculty:** Student/faculty ratio 15:1. 322 full-time faculty, 87% hold PhDs, 34% are are members of minority groups, 41% are women. 0% of classes are taught by teaching assistants.

ACADEMICS

Degrees: bachelor's, doctoral/professional, master's, postbachelor's certificate. **Classes:** Most classes have 20-29 students. Most lab/discussion sessions have 10-19 students. **Most popular majors:** Psychology; Mechanical Engineering; Biology/Biological Sciences. **Special Study Options:** Accelerated program, cooperative education program, cross-registration, distance learning, double major, dual enrollment, honors program, independent study, internships,

---

UNIVERSITY OF MICHIGAN—FLINT

303 E. Kearsley St., Flint, MI 48502
Phone: 810-762-3300 • **Financial Aid Phone:** 810-762-3444
E-mail: admissions@umflint.edu • **CEEB Code:** 1853
Fax: 810-762-3272 • **Website:** www.umflint.edu • **ACT Code:** 2063

This public school was founded in 1956. It has a 72-acre campus.

RATINGS

Admissions Selectivity Rating: 80   **Fire Safety Rating:** 96   **Green Rating:** 73

STUDENTS AND FACULTY

Enrollment: 5,827. **Student Body:** 60% female, 40% male, 2% out-of-state, 5% international (34 countries represented). Asian 2%, African American 14%, Caucasian 68%, Hispanic 4%, Native American 1%, Pacific Islander <1%, Two or more races 3%, Race unknown 3%. **Retention and Graduation:** 68% freshmen return for sophomore year. 13% freshmen graduate within 4 years. 37% freshmen graduate within 6 years. **Faculty:** Student/faculty ratio 14:1. 316 full-time faculty, 76% hold PhDs, 20% are are members of minority groups, 52% are women. 0% of classes are taught by teaching assistants.

ACADEMICS

Degrees: bachelor's, doctoral/professional, doctoral/research, master's, postbachelor's certificate, post-master's certificate. **Classes:** Most classes have 20-29 students. Most lab/discussion sessions have 20-29 students. **Most popular majors:** Registered Nursing/Registered Nurse; Pre-nursing studies; Health/Health Care Administration/Management. **Special Study Options:** cooperative education program, distance learning, double major, dual enrollment, English as a Second Language (ESL), honors program, independent study, internships, student-designed major, study abroad, teacher certification program. **Honors Programs:** 4-yr University Honors Scholar Program 2-yr Junior/Senior University Honors Scholar Program Combined degree programs: MBA/MSCSIS, MBA/MSA, DrAP/MBA, DPT/MBA, DNP/MBA. **Disability Services:** Special programs offered to physically disabled students, including note-taking services, reader services, tape recorders, tutors. **Career Services:** Alumni services, Career/job search classes, Career assessment, Internships.

FACILITIES

Housing: Coed dorms. 97% of campus accessible to physically diasbled. **Special Academic Facilities/Equipment:** Frances Willson Thompson Library **Computers:** 100% of classrooms, 100% of dorms, 100% of libraries, 100% of dining areas, 100% of student union, have wireless network access. Students can register for classes online. Administrative functions (other than registration) can be performed online.

CAMPUS LIFE

Environment: City. **Activities:** Choral groups, concert band, dance, drama/theater, jazz band, literary magazine, music ensembles, musical theater, student government, student newspaper, television station, Student Organization. 99 registered organizations, 7 honor societies, 6 religious organizations. 4 fraternities, 5 sororities. **On-Campus Highlights:** Recreation Center, University Center/Student Union, University Pavilion/Food Court/Bookstore, Resident's Hall, Frances Willson Thompson Library. **Environmental Initiatives:** Recycling and Waste Minimization.

ADMISSIONS

Freshman Academic Profile: Average high school GPA 3.4. 16% in top 10% of high school class, 42% in top 25% of high school class, 76% in top 50% of high school class. 92% from public high schools. **Reported SAT (pre-2016 redesign) scores:** SAT Math middle 50% range 485-598. SAT Critical Reading middle 50% range 493-575. SAT Writing middle 50% range 433-560. **Concordant SAT scores:** SAT EBRW middle 50% 520–630. SAT Math middle 50% range 520–620. ACT middle 50% range 19-26. Minimum internet-based TOEFL 61. Minimum paper TOEFL 500. **Basis for Candidate Selection:** *Very important factors considered include:* academic GPA, standardized test scores. *Important factors considered include:* extracurricular activities. *Other factors considered include:* class rank, application essay, recommendation(s), interview, talent/ability, first generation. **Freshman Admission Requirements:** High school diploma is required and GED is accepted. *Academic units recommended:* 4 English, 4 math, 3 science, 3 foreign language, 3 history. **Freshman Admission Statistics:** 4,033 applied, 65.14% admitted, 24% enrolled. **Transfer Admission Requirements:** High school transcript, college transcript(s), Minimum college GPA of 2.0 required. Lowest grade transferable 2. **General Admission Information:** Application fee $30. Regular application deadline 8/1. Nonfall registration accepted. Admission may be deferred for a maximum of 1 Year.

COSTS AND FINANCIAL AID

Annual in-state tuition $10,452. Annual out-of-state tuition $20,370. Room and board $8,178. Required fees $432. Average book expense $1,000. **Required Forms and Deadlines:** FAFSA, Institution's own financial aid form. **Notification of Awards:** Applicants will be notified of awards on a rolling basis beginning 3/15. **Types of Aid:** *Need-based scholarships/grants:* Federal Pell, FSEOG, State scholarships/grants, Private scholarships, College/university scholarship or grant aid from institutional funds. *Loans:* Direct Subsidized Stafford Loans, Direct Unsubsidized Stafford Loans, Direct PLUS loans, Federal Perkins Loans. *Student Employment:* Federal Work-Study Program available. Institutional employment available. **Financial Aid Statistics:** 74% needy freshmen, 75% needy undergrads receive need-based scholarship or grant aid. 33% freshmen, 22% undergrads receive non-need-based scholarship or grant aid. 80% freshmen, 83% undergrads receive need-based self-help aid. 0% freshmen, 0% undergrads receive athletic scholarships. 72% freshmen, 70% undergrads receive any aid. 64% undergrads borrow to pay for school. Average cumulative indebtedness $27,358. **Criteria for awarding aid:** *Need-based:* Academics, Art. *Non-need-based:* Academics, Art, Leadership, Music/drama.

UNIVERSITY OF MINNESOTA, CROOKSTON

University of Minnesota, Crookston, Crookston, MN 56716-5001
Phone: 218-281-8569 • **Financial Aid Phone:** 218-281-8563
E-mail: UMCinfo@umn.edu • **CEEB Code:** 6893
Fax: 218-281-8575 • **Website:** http://www1.crk.umn.edu/ • **ACT Code:** 2129

This public school was founded in 1966. It has a 237-acre campus.

RATINGS

Admissions Selectivity Rating: 78   Fire Safety Rating: 99   Green Rating: 75

STUDENTS AND FACULTY

Enrollment: 1,876. **Student Body:** 50% female, 50% male, 28% out-of-state, 4% international (35 countries represented). Asian 2%, African American 7%, Caucasian 80%, Hispanic 3%, Native American <1%, Pacific Islander <1%, Two or more races 1%, Race unknown 2%. **Retention and Graduation:** 66% freshmen return for sophomore year. 33% freshmen graduate within 4 years. 48% freshmen graduate within 6 years. 12% grads go on to further study within 1 year. **Faculty:** Student/faculty ratio 20:1. 66 full-time faculty, 53% hold PhDs, 6% are are members of minority groups, 41% are women. 0% of classes are taught by teaching assistants.

ACADEMICS

Degrees: bachelor's, certificate. **Classes:** Most classes have 10-19 students. Most lab/discussion sessions have 10-19 students. **Most popular majors:** Business Administration and Management; Natural Resources/Conservation; Animal Sciences. **Special Study Options:** cross-registration, distance learning, double major, dual enrollment, English as a Second Language (ESL), honors program, independent study, internships, student-designed major, study abroad, teacher certification program. **Honors Programs:** The University of Minnesota, Crookston Honor's Program was developed to inspire and transform the students' writing, discussion and critical thinking skills that reflect high expectations for academically successful students. Students will be nurtured and challenged to explore ideas, assess values and develop leadership skills. Honors coursework will address the diverse and global atmosphere in which we live. In addition, students in the Honors Program will have the opportunity for various social outings outside of the normal campus experience. ° Designed for academically highly-motivated students who want more than a degree. ° Small class sizes ensure one-on-one time with faculty, who invest in your success. ° Flexible curriculum helps you meet career goals while meeting discipline and honors specific requirements. ° Innovative program structure involves honor courses, student led discussion groups and individual studies in discipline specific courses. ° You will develop and conduct an original scholarly project as a senior to satisfy final program requirements. ° Exposure to culturally-rich experiences will enable you to develop a global perspective and leadership skills. **Disability Services:** Special programs offered to physically disabled students, including note-taking services, reader services, tape recorders, tutors. **Career Services:** Alumni services, Career/job search classes, Career assessment, Internships. Internships that provide experiential learning and on-the-job training for all students.

FACILITIES

Housing: Coed dorms, special housing for disabled students, apartments for single students, Theme Housing. 90% of campus accessible to physically diasbled. **Special Academic Facilities/Equipment:** Red River Valley Natural History Area; Northwest Research and Outreach Center; UMC Horse Riding Arena; Valley Technology Park **Computers:** 20% of classrooms, 100% of dorms, 100% of libraries, 75% of dining areas, 100% of student union, 25% of common outdoor areas have wireless network access. Students can register for classes online. Administrative functions (other than registration) can be performed online.

CAMPUS LIFE

Environment: Village. **Activities:** Choral groups, drama/theater, pep band, radio station, student government, Campus Ministries, Student Organization. 38 registered organizations, 1 honor society, 2 religious organizations. 1 fraternity, 1 sorority. **Athletics (Intercollegiate):** *Men:* baseball, basketball, football, golf, ice hockey. *Women:* basketball, equestrian sports, golf, soccer, softball, tennis, volleyball. **On-Campus Highlights:** Sargeant Student Center, University Teaching and Outreach Center, Sports Center, Bergland Laboratory, Centennial Hall Student Apartments, Campus Mall Dairy Barns Kiehle Auditorium. **Environmental Initiatives:** 1. Evaluate the reduction of coal as a primary feedstock for the campus energy and supplement with renewable fuels.

ADMISSIONS

Freshman Academic Profile: Average high school GPA 3.2. 12% in top 10% of high school class, 31% in top 25% of high school class, 65% in top 50% of high school class. **Reported SAT (pre-2016 redesign) scores:** SAT Math middle 50% range 470-510. SAT Critical Reading middle 50% range 430-480. SAT Writing middle 50% range 390-470. **Concordant SAT scores:** SAT EBRW middle 50% 460–530. SAT Math middle 50% range 510–540. ACT middle 50% range 19-24. Minimum internet-based TOEFL 68. Minimum paper TOEFL 520. **Basis for Candidate Selection:** *Very important factors considered include:* rigor of secondary school record, class rank, academic GPA, standardized test scores. *Other factors considered include:* application essay, recommendation(s). **Freshman Admission Requirements:** High school diploma is required and GED is accepted. *Academic units required:* 4 English, 3 math, 3 science, 2 science labs, 3 social studies. *Academic units recommended:* 2 foreign language. **Freshman Admission Statistics:** 927 applied, 71.41% admitted, 41% enrolled. **Transfer Admission Requirements:** college transcript(s), Minimum college GPA of 2.0 required. Lowest grade transferable D. **General Admission Information:** Application fee $30. Nonfall registration accepted. Admission may be deferred for a maximum of 1 semester.

COSTS AND FINANCIAL AID

Annual in-state tuition $10,180. Annual out-of-state tuition $10,180. Room and board $8,418. Required fees $1,520. Average book expense $1,200. **Required Forms and Deadlines:** FAFSA. **Notification of Awards:** Applicants will be notified of awards on a rolling basis beginning 3/1. **Types of Aid:** *Need-based scholarships/grants:* Federal Pell, FSEOG, State scholarships/grants, Private scholarships, College/university scholarship or grant aid from institutional funds. *Loans:* Direct Subsidized Stafford Loans, Direct Unsubsidized Stafford Loans, Direct PLUS loans, Federal Perkins Loans, State Loans. *Student Employment:* Federal Work-Study Program available. Institutional employment available. **Financial Aid Statistics:** 96% needy freshmen, 90% needy undergrads receive need-based scholarship or grant aid. 11% freshmen, 8% undergrads receive non-need-based scholarship or grant aid. 74% freshmen, 78% undergrads receive need-based self-help aid. 9% freshmen, 4% undergrads receive athletic scholarships. 88% freshmen, 48% undergrads receive any aid. 80% undergrads borrow to pay for school. Average cumulative indebtedness $28,309. **Criteria for awarding aid:** *Non-need-based:* Academics, Alumni affiliation, Athletics, Leadership, Minority status, Music/drama, State/district residency.

UNIVERSITY OF MINNESOTA, DULUTH

25 Solon Campus Center, Duluth, MN 55812-3000
Phone: 218-726-7171 • **Financial Aid Phone:** 218-726-8000
E-mail: umdadmis@d.umn.edu • **CEEB Code:** 6873
Fax: 218-726-7040 • **Website:** www.d.umn.edu • **ACT Code:** 2157

This public school was founded in 1947. It has a 247-acre campus.

RATINGS

Admissions Selectivity Rating: 79   **Fire Safety Rating:** 93   **Green Rating:** 95

STUDENTS AND FACULTY

Enrollment: 9,422. **Student Body:** 47% female, 53% male, 11% out-of-state, 1% international (42 countries represented). Asian 3%, African American 1%, Caucasian 90%, Hispanic 1%, Native American 1%, Pacific Islander 0%, Two or more races 0%, Race unknown 1%.
Retention and Graduation: 81% freshmen return for sophomore year. 16% grads go on to further study within 1 year. **Faculty:** Student/faculty ratio 21:1. 463 full-time faculty, 75% hold PhDs, 19% are are members of minority groups, 43% are women.

ACADEMICS

Degrees: bachelor's, doctoral/professional, master's, postbachelor's certificate. **Classes:** Most classes have 20-29 students. Most lab/discussion sessions have 10-19 students. **Most popular majors:** Business Administration and Management; Elementary Education and Teaching; Biology/Biological Sciences. **Special Study Options:** Accelerated program, cross-registration, distance learning, double major, dual enrollment, exchange student program (domestic), honors program, independent study, internships, liberal arts/career combination, study abroad, teacher certification program, weekend college. **Honors Programs:** The Honors Program offers motivated students who are serious about their intellectual and personal growth a variety of special classes enhanced by cultural events and activities, as well as leadership and research opportunities. **Disability Services:** Special programs offered to physically disabled students, including note-taking services, reader services, tape recorders, tutors. **Career Services:** Alumni services, Career/job search classes, Career assessment, Internships.

FACILITIES

Housing: Coed dorms, special housing for disabled students, men's dorms, women's dorms. 100% of campus accessible to physically diasbled. **Special Academic Facilities/Equipment:** Art museum, planetarium, music performance hall, theatre. **Computers:** 100% of classrooms, 100% of libraries, 100% of dining areas, 100% of student union, have wireless network access. Students can register for classes online. Administrative functions (other than registration) can be performed online.

CAMPUS LIFE

Environment: Village. **Activities:** Choral groups, concert band, dance, drama/theater, jazz band, literary magazine, marching band, music ensembles, musical theater, opera, pep band, radio station, student government, student newspaper, student-run film society, symphony orchestra, Campus Ministries, Student Organization, Model UN. 150 registered organizations, 10 honor societies, 7 religious organizations. 2 fraternities, 2 sororities. **Athletics (Intercollegiate):** *Men:* baseball, basketball, cross-country, football, ice hockey, track/field (outdoor), track/field (indoor). *Women:* basketball, cross-country, ice hockey, soccer, softball, tennis, track/field (outdoor), track/field (indoor), volleyball. **On-Campus Highlights:** Solon Campus Center, Library, Residence Halls,

Kirby Student Center Food Court, Sports and Health Center. **Environmental Initiatives:** LEED.

ADMISSIONS

Freshman Academic Profile: 16% in top 10% of high school class, 42% in top 25% of high school class, 85% in top 50% of high school class. 94% from public high schools. **Reported SAT (pre-2016 redesign) scores:** SAT Math middle 50% range 480-620. SAT Critical Reading middle 50% range 480-590. SAT Writing middle 50% range 460-580. **Concordant SAT scores:** SAT EBRW middle 50% 530–640. SAT Math middle 50% range 510–640. ACT middle 50% range 20-26. Minimum internet-based TOEFL 80. Minimum paper TOEFL 550. **Basis for Candidate Selection:** *Very important factors considered include:* class rank, standardized test scores. *Important factors considered include:* rigor of secondary school record. *Other factors considered include:* academic GPA, application essay, recommendation(s), extracurricular activities, talent/ability, first generation, alumni/ae relation, geographical residence, state residency, racial/ethnic status. **Freshman Admission Requirements:** High school diploma is required and GED is accepted. *Academic units required:* 4 English, 3 math, 3 science, 2 foreign language, 2 social studies, 1 history. *Academic units recommended:* 1 computer science, 1 visual/performing arts. **Freshman Admission Statistics:** 7,936 applied, 71.43% admitted, 37% enrolled. **Transfer Admission Requirements:** High school transcript, college transcript(s), Minimum college GPA of 2.0 required. Lowest grade transferable D. **General Admission Information:** Application fee $35. Priority deadline 12/15. Regular application deadline 8/1. Nonfall registration accepted. Admission may be deferred for a maximum of 3 semesters.

COSTS AND FINANCIAL AID

Annual in-state tuition $8,230. Annual out-of-state tuition $10,230. Room and board $6,078. Required fees $2,030. Average book expense $1,248. **Required Forms and Deadlines:** FAFSA. **Notification of Awards:** Applicants will be notified of awards on or about 3/1. **Types of Aid:** *Need-based scholarships/grants:* Federal Pell, FSEOG, State scholarships/grants, Private scholarships, College/university scholarship or grant aid from institutional funds. *Loans:* Direct Subsidized Stafford Loans, Direct Unsubsidized Stafford Loans, Direct PLUS loans, Federal Perkins Loans, State Loans, College/university loans from institutional funds. *Student Employment:* Federal Work-Study Program available. Institutional employment available. **Financial Aid Statistics:** 100% needy freshmen, 97% needy undergrads receive need-based scholarship or grant aid. 25% freshmen, 27% undergrads receive non-need-based scholarship or grant aid. 84% freshmen, 87% undergrads receive need-based self-help aid. 0% freshmen, 0% undergrads receive athletic scholarships. 85% freshmen, 81% undergrads receive any aid. **Criteria for awarding aid:** *Need-based:* Alumni affiliation, Athletics, Minority status. *Non-need-based:* Academics, Alumni affiliation, Art, Athletics, Leadership, Minority status, Music/drama, State/district residency.

UNIVERSITY OF MINNESOTA, MORRIS

600 E 4th St, Morris, MN 56267
Phone: 320-589-6035 • **Financial Aid Phone:** 800-992-8863
E-mail: http://admissions.morris.umn.edu/contact • **CEEB Code:** 6890
Fax: 320-589-6051 • **Website:** www.morris.umn.edu • **ACT Code:** 2155

This public school was founded in 1959. It has a 130-acre campus.

RATINGS

Admissions Selectivity Rating: 85   **Fire Safety Rating:** 98   **Green Rating:** 97

STUDENTS AND FACULTY

Enrollment: 1,680. **Student Body:** 56% female, 44% male, 13% out-of-state, 11% international (20 countries represented). Asian 3%, African American 2%, Caucasian 60%, Hispanic 5%, Native American 6%, Pacific Islander 0%, Two or more races 12%, Race unknown <1%.
Retention and Graduation: 78% freshmen return for sophomore year. 50% freshmen graduate within 4 years. 20% grads go on to further study within 1 year. 66% grads pursue arts and sciences degrees. 5% grads pursue law degrees. 2% grads pursue business degrees. 10% grads pursue medical degrees. **Faculty:** Student/faculty ratio 12:1. 118 full-time faculty, 92% hold PhDs, 11% are are members of minority groups, 42% are women. 0% of classes are taught by teaching assistants.

ACADEMICS

Degrees: bachelor's. **Classes:** Most classes have 10-19 students. Most lab/discussion sessions have 10-19 students. **Most popular majors:** Biology/Biological Sciences; Psychology; Economics. **Special Study Options:** Accelerated program, cooperative education program, distance learning, double major, exchange student program (domestic), honors program, independent study, internships, student-designed major, study abroad, teacher certification program. **Honors Programs:** The purpose of the Honors Program is to provide a distinctive, academically challenging, intellectual experience that amplifies and complements the liberal arts mission of UMM for motivated and high-achieving students. It does this by relying upon an interdisciplinary curriculum that is team-taught by UMM's finest faculty. The program consists of a core course, "Traditions in Human Thought." This course explores significant works from history, literature, philosophy, and science from an interdisciplinary perspective. Following the core course, students choose from a variety of interdisciplinary honors courses, participate in service learning and volunteer programs, and complete a senior honors project. **Disability Services:** Special programs offered to physically disabled students, including note-taking services, reader services, tape recorders, tutors. **Career Services:** Alumni network, Alumni services, Career/job search classes, Career assessment, Internships. The Undergraduate Research Opportunities Program (UROP) is a competitive, merit-based program that provides student stipends and expense allowances for students to partner with a faculty member on research, scholarly, or creative projects in laboratories, studios, libraries, and field sites. Students develop detailed knowledge of research methods and may choose to work with faculty members from Morris or from other University of Minnesota campuses, thus giving students access to the University's wide range of faculty and research facilities.

FACILITIES

Housing: Coed dorms, special housing for disabled students, men's dorms, women's dorms, apartments for single students. 70% of campus accessible to physically disabled. **Special Academic Facilities/Equipment:** HFA Art Gallery, conservatory, observatory **Computers:** Students can register for classes online. Administrative functions (other than registration) can be performed online.

CAMPUS LIFE

Environment: Rural. **Activities:** Choral groups, concert band, dance, drama/theater, jazz band, literary magazine, music ensembles, musical theater, radio station, student government, student newspaper, symphony orchestra, television station 90 registered organizations, 5 honor societies, 12 religious organizations. **Athletics (Intercollegiate):** *Men:* baseball, basketball, football, golf, tennis, track/field (outdoor), track/field (indoor). *Women:* basketball, cross-country, diving, golf, soccer, softball, swimming, tennis, track/field (outdoor), track/field (indoor), volleyball. **On-Campus Highlights:** Student Center – KUMM, cafe, Louis' Lower Level, Regional Fitness Center – Outdoor Center, pools, Science Center – completed '02, Humanities Fine Arts Center – gallery, recitals, The Mall – outdoor recreation area. **Environmental Initiatives:** 1. Morris is actively working to become a sustainable and low-carbon community, and renewable energy research and demonstration is a big part of that effort. Morris receives power from two 1.65 MW University of Minnesota wind turbines. We receive power 60% of our annual electricity from wind. We have an on-campus biomass gasification research and demonstration platform. We have solar thermal and solar PV projects on campus. And we have completed a multi-million dollar energy service contract to retrofit the campus for conservation.

ADMISSIONS

Freshman Academic Profile: Average high school GPA 3.6. 20% in top 10% of high school class, 52% in top 25% of high school class, 88% in top 50% of high school class. 95% from public high schools. **Reported SAT (pre-2016 redesign) scores:** SAT Math middle 50% range 530-690. SAT Critical Reading middle 50% range 490-580. SAT Writing middle 50% range 460-610. **Concordant SAT scores:** SAT EBRW middle 50% 530–650. SAT Math middle 50% range 560–720. ACT middle 50% range 22-28. Minimum internet-based TOEFL 79. Minimum paper TOEFL 550. **Basis for Candidate Selection:** *Very important factors considered include:* rigor of secondary school record, class rank, academic GPA, standardized test scores. *Important factors considered include:* extracurricular activities, talent/ability, character/personal qualities, volunteer work, work experience. *Other factors considered include:* application essay, recommendation(s), interview, first generation. **Freshman Admission Requirements:** High school diploma is required and GED is accepted. *Academic units required:* 4 English, 4 math, 3 science, 2 foreign language, 3 social studies. **Freshman Admission Statistics:** 3,414 applied, 58.06% admitted, 19% enrolled. **Transfer Admission Requirements:** college transcript(s), essay or personal statement, statement of good standing from prior institution(s). Minimum college GPA of 2.5 required. Lowest grade transferable D. **General Admission Information:** Application fee $35. Priority deadline 12/15. Regular application deadline 3/15. Nonfall registration accepted. Admission may be deferred for a maximum of 1 year.

COSTS AND FINANCIAL AID

Required Forms and Deadlines: FAFSA. **Notification of Awards:** Applicants will be notified of awards on a rolling basis beginning 4/1. **Types of Aid:** *Need-based scholarships/grants:* Federal Pell, FSEOG, State scholarships/grants, Private scholarships, College/university scholarship or grant aid from institutional funds. *Loans:* Direct Subsidized Stafford Loans, Direct Unsubsidized Stafford Loans, Direct PLUS loans, Federal Perkins Loans.

Student Employment: Federal Work-Study Program available. Institutional employment available. **Financial Aid Statistics:** 97% needy freshmen, 96% needy undergrads receive need-based scholarship or grant aid. 9% freshmen, 9% undergrads receive non-need-based scholarship or grant aid. 63% freshmen, 63% undergrads receive need-based self-help aid. 0% freshmen, 0% undergrads receive athletic scholarships. 93% freshmen, 89% undergrads receive any aid. Average cumulative indebtedness $25,732. **Criteria for awarding aid:** *Non-need-based:* Academics.

UNIVERSITY OF MINNESOTA— TWIN CITIES CAMPUS

240 Williamson Hall, Minneapolis, MN 55455-0213
Phone: 612-625-2008 • **Financial Aid Phone:** 612-624-1111 • **CEEB Code:** 6874
Fax: 612-626-1693 • **Website:** www.umn.edu • **ACT Code:** 2156

This public school was founded in 1851. It has a 2000-acre campus.

RATINGS

Admissions Selectivity Rating: 91   **Fire Safety Rating:** 88   **Green Rating:** 94

STUDENTS AND FACULTY

Enrollment: 30,511. **Student Body:** 51% female, 49% male, 27% out-of-state, 9% international (134 countries represented). Asian 9%, African American 4%, Caucasian 70%, Hispanic 4%, Native American <1%, Pacific Islander <1%, Two or more races 4%, Race unknown 1%.
Retention and Graduation: 93% freshmen return for sophomore year. 59% freshmen graduate within 4 years. 77% freshmen graduate within 6 years.
Faculty: Student/faculty ratio 17:1. 2,589 full-time faculty, 78% hold PhDs, 17% are are members of minority groups, 42% are women.

ACADEMICS

Degrees: bachelor's, certificate, diploma, doctoral/professional, doctoral/research, doctoral, master's, postbachelor's certificate, post-master's certificate. **Classes:** Most classes have 20-29 students. Most lab/discussion sessions have 20-29 students. **Most popular majors:** Psychology; Rhetoric and Composition; Journalism. **Special Study Options:** Accelerated program, cooperative education program, cross-registration, distance learning, double major, dual enrollment, English as a Second Language (ESL), exchange student program (domestic), external degree program, honors program, independent study, internships, liberal arts/career combination, student-designed major, study abroad, teacher certification program, Minors offered in most majors. Students may register in the College of Continuing Education and take courses in any division for B.A. or B.S. degrees. Programs in Foreign Service and pre-social work. Phi Beta Kappa. Pass/fail grading option. Internships. Qualified undergraduates may take graduate level classes. Pre-professional programs in law, medicine, veterinary science, pharmacy, dentistry, architecture, biology, education, journalism, landscape architecture, management, medical technology, mortuary science, nursing, and occupational/physical therapy. **Honors Programs:** Honors, Undergraduate Research Opportunities Program. **Disability Services:** Special programs offered to physically disabled students, including note-taking services, reader services, tape recorders, tutors. **Career Services:** Alumni network, Alumni services, Career/job search classes, Career assessment, Internships, Regional alumni. New business hatchery in which 25 undergraduate students receive pro bono legal support, advice from entrepreneurs-in-residence and access to $17,000 of seed funding each year.

FACILITIES

Housing: Coed dorms, special housing for disabled students, special housing for international students, fraternity/sorority housing, apartments for married students, cooperative housing, apartments for single students, Honors housing, residential college (academic programs in residence). Eight conventional residence halls, plus three new apartment style residence halls. Housing application, $25 non-refundable residence hall application fee, and $100 residence hall advance payment (refundable), required by May 1 for guaranteed freshman housing. Off-campus housing office provides off-campus housing listings. **Special Academic Facilities/Equipment:** Frederick R. Weisman Art Museum, Bell Museum of Natural History, Ted Mann Concert Hall, Recreational Sports Center, Civil Engineering Building, Basic Sciences/Biomedical Engineering Building, Coffman Memorial Union, West Bank Arts Quarter, Goldstein Gallery, Arboretum. **Computers:** Students can register for classes online. Administrative functions (other than registration) can be performed online.

CAMPUS LIFE

Environment: Metropolis. **Activities:** Choral groups, concert band, dance, drama/theater, jazz band, literary magazine, marching band, music ensembles, musical theater, opera, pep band, radio station, student government, student newspaper, student-run film society, symphony orchestra, television station, Student Organization. 600 registered organizations, 10 religious organizations. 22 fraternities, 12 sororities. **Athletics (Intercollegiate):** *Men:* baseball, basketball, cross-country, diving, football, golf, gymnastics, ice hockey, swimming, tennis, track/field (outdoor), track/field (indoor), wrestling. *Women:* basketball, cheerleading, cross-country, diving, golf, gymnastics, ice hockey, soccer, softball, swimming, tennis, track/field (outdoor), track/field (indoor), volleyball. **On-Campus Highlights:** Weisman Art Museum, McNamara Alumni Center, TCF Bank Stadium, Goldstein Gallery, Northrup Memorial Auditorium, Coffman Memorial Union, Mariucci Arena, University Theater, Rarig Center. **Environmental Initiatives:** The University of Minnesota adopted a systemwide sustainability and energy efficiency policy in 2004 founded on earlier waste abatement and energy policies. The University established goals to implement the policy, including one of the most important undertakings as a systemwide signatory of the American College and University Presidents' Climate Commitment (2008). The commitment and Climate Action Plan (CAP) include reducing our carbon footprint but also integrating climate science into the fiber of the university—curriculum, research, outreach and engagement. The University of Minnesota engages its students and faculty in various ways. The It All Adds Up campaign strives to raise awareness within the campus community about energy use and to encourage the community to use energy more efficiently. It All Adds Up has resulted in over 14,000 individual pledges campus wide to conserve energy. When combined with other energy conservation efforts, they helped the University avoid more than $6.8 million (cumulatively about $15 Million) in energy costs, and resulted in the release of nearly 112,000 fewer tons of CO2 into the atmosphere annually. Greenhouse gas emissions from energy sources dropped by 22% compared to the 2008 baseline. The University also received the Xcel Energy Platinum award in 2013 for its long term commitment to energy conservation. In collaboration between It All Adds Up and Housing and Residential Life, the Live Green Games Program was created with the ultimate goal of encouraging students to participate in energy conservation to help the University meet it's goals. In 2013, a new gaming feature was piloted in order to make sustainability fun and effortless. A list of green acts was promoted among students, showing how they could help create a more sustainable campus, community and world. The pilot resulted in over 7000 acts of green, saving 125 tons of carbon, over 97,000 gallons of water and 252,000kWh electricity. The University Services Sustainability Office collaborates with faculty to raise awareness of the campus CAP. For example, the Sustainability Director presented on the CAP, which was featured in Architecture 5750—Planning and Design of the University, a course offered through College of Design. The Sustainability Office participated on the steering committee and work teams to update the City of Minneapolis Climate Action Plan, which provides a roadmap to guide Minneapolis towards greenhouse gas emissions reduction targets. The Twin Cities and Morris campuses, Twin Cities Sustainability Education program and Institute on the Environmental provided space and some support for the Next Generation Congress—a group of students who developed long term environmental policy recommendations and delivered them to the Governor Environmental Congress. The recommendations included addressing climate impacts by supporting renewable energy and sustainable energy and building practices. Some of these students connected through programs and education the University offered to raised awareness about energy and climate, such as It All Adds Up and the Sustainability Minor. The student leaders who helped organize the efforts received the Assn. for the Advancement of Sustainability in Higher Education (AASHE) Student Leadership Award. Links: http://italladdsup.umn.edu/news/platinum.award_03132013.php http://ow.ly/tDUAt http://ow.ly/tDUWF

ADMISSIONS

Freshman Academic Profile: 49% in top 10% of high school class, 85% in top 25% of high school class, 99% in top 50% of high school class. **Reported SAT (pre-2016 redesign) scores:** SAT Math middle 50% range 620-740. SAT Critical Reading middle 50% range 560-700. SAT Writing middle 50% range 570-690. **Concordant SAT scores:** SAT EBRW middle 50% 620-730. SAT Math middle 50% range 640-760. ACT middle 50% range 26-31. Minimum paper TOEFL 550. **Basis for Candidate Selection:** *Very important factors considered include:* rigor of secondary school record, class rank, academic GPA, standardized test scores. *Other factors considered include:* extracurricular activities, talent/ability, character/personal qualities, first generation, alumni/ae relation, geographical residence, racial/ethnic status, volunteer work, work experience. **Freshman Admission Requirements:** High school diploma is required and GED is accepted. *Academic units required:* 4 English, 4 math, 3 science, 1 science lab, 2 foreign language, 3 social studies, 1 visual/performing arts. *Academic units recommended:* 4 English, 4 math, 4 science, 1 science lab, 2 foreign language, 3 social studies, 1 visual/performing arts. **Freshman Admission Statistics:** 46,165 applied, 44.58% admitted, 32% enrolled. **Transfer Admission Requirements:** college transcript(s), Minimum college

GPA of 2.0 required. Lowest grade transferable D. **General Admission Information:** Application fee $55. Priority deadline 12/15. Nonfall registration accepted. Admission may be deferred.

COSTS AND FINANCIAL AID

Annual in-state tuition $12,546. Annual out-of-state tuition $22,210. Room and board $9,377. Required fees $1,596. Average book expense $1,000. **Required Forms and Deadlines:** FAFSA, Institution's own financial aid form. **Notification of Awards:** Applicants will be notified of awards on a rolling basis beginning 2/15. **Types of Aid:** *Need-based scholarships/grants:* Federal Pell, FSEOG, State scholarships/grants, Private scholarships, College/university scholarship or grant aid from institutional funds, Federal Nursing Scholarships. *Loans:* Direct Subsidized Stafford Loans, Direct Unsubsidized Stafford Loans, Direct PLUS loans, Federal Perkins Loans, Federal Nursing Loans, State Loans, College/university loans from institutional funds. *Student Employment:* Federal Work-Study Program available. Institutional employment available. **Financial Aid Statistics:** 84% needy freshmen, 83% needy undergrads receive need-based scholarship or grant aid. 10% freshmen, 7% undergrads receive non-need-based scholarship or grant aid. 81% freshmen, 82% undergrads receive need-based self-help aid. 1% freshmen, 0% undergrads receive athletic scholarships. 59% undergrads borrow to pay for school. Average cumulative indebtedness $26,006. **Criteria for awarding aid:** *Non-need-based:* Academics, Art, Athletics, Job skills, Leadership, Minority status, Music/drama, State/district residency.

UNIVERSITY OF MISSISSIPPI

145 Martindale, University, MS 38677
Phone: 662-915-7226 • **Financial Aid Phone:** 800-891-4596
E-mail: admissions@olemiss.edu • **CEEB Code:** 1840
Fax: 662-915-5869 • **Website:** www.olemiss.edu • **ACT Code:** 2250

This public school was founded in 1844. It has a 2500-acre campus.

RATINGS

Admissions Selectivity Rating: 83   **Fire Safety Rating:** 97   **Green Rating:** 60*

STUDENTS AND FACULTY

Enrollment: 18,472. **Student Body:** 57% female, 43% male, 42% out-of-state, 1% international. Asian 2%, African American 14%, Caucasian 78%, Hispanic 3%, Native American <1%, Pacific Islander <1%, Two or more races 2%, Race unknown <1%.
Retention and Graduation: 87% freshmen return for sophomore year. 39% freshmen graduate within 4 years. 61% freshmen graduate within 6 years.
Faculty: 1,007 full-time faculty, 79% hold PhDs, 19% are are members of minority groups, 47% are women.

ACADEMICS

Degrees: bachelor's, doctoral/professional, doctoral/research, doctoral, master's, postbachelor's certifiate, post-master's certificate. **Classes:** Most classes have 10-19 students. Most lab/discussion sessions have 20-29 students. **Most popular majors:** Elementary Education and Teaching; Accounting; Marketing/Marketing Management. **Special Study Options:** Accelerated program, cooperative education program, distance learning, double major, dual enrollment, English as a Second Language (ESL), honors program, independent study, internships, study abroad, teacher certification program. **Honors Programs:** Sally McDonnell-Barksdale Honors College. **Disability Services:** Special programs offered to physically disabled students, including note-taking services, reader services, tape recorders.

FACILITIES

Housing: men's dorms, special housing for international students, women's dorms, fraternity/sorority housing, apartments for married students, apartments for single students, Graduate/Older Students, intensive study floors, special interest, substance free, environmental interest housing available. **Special Academic Facilities/Equipment:** Sally McDonnell-Barksdale Honors College, Croft Institute for International Studies, National Food Service Management Institute, Mississippi Center for Supercomputing Research,Art and archaeology museums, women's studies center, Center for Study of Southern Culture,William Faulkner home, Marine Minerals Research Institute, National Center for Physical Acoustics, National Center for Natural Products Research, Biological Field Station, Barksdale Reading Institute, Ford Center for the Performing Arts, William Winter Institutue for Racial Reconciliation, Paris-Yates Chapel, Trent Lott Leadership Institute, Living Blues Archive,

Student Media Center **Computers:** 30% of classrooms, 100% of dorms, 100% of libraries, 80% of dining areas, 100% of student union, 30% of common outdoor areas have wireless network access. Students can register for classes online. Administrative functions (other than registration) can be performed online.

CAMPUS LIFE

Environment: Village. **Activities:** Choral groups, concert band, dance, drama/theater, jazz band, marching band, music ensembles, musical theater, opera, pep band, radio station, student government, student newspaper, symphony orchestra, television station, yearbook, Campus Ministries, Student Organization. 250 registered organizations, 25 honor societies, 21 religious organizations. 18 fraternities, 13 sororities. **Athletics (Intercollegiate):** *Men:* baseball, basketball, cheerleading, cross-country, football, golf, tennis, track/field (outdoor), track/field (indoor). *Women:* basketball, cheerleading, cross-country, golf, riflery, soccer, softball, tennis, track/field (outdoor), track/field (indoor), volleyball. **On-Campus Highlights:** Lyceum, Gertrude C. Ford Center for the Performing Arts, Intramural Sports Practice Facility, Student Union, Business School, INFORMATION SESSIONS at 9 am, 11 am, 1pm, 2 pm; TOURS-10 am, and 3 pm (Please register by phone, email, or online); RED/BLUE PREVIEWS-select Saturdays 8:30-1:00 pm (Register online); Fall and Spring Visit Days-8 am to noon (No advanced registration required). **Environmental Initiatives:** UM is installing SmartMeters on the majority of campus buildings.

ADMISSIONS

Freshman Academic Profile: 25% in top 10% of high school class, 50% in top 25% of high school class, 80% in top 50% of high school class. **Reported SAT (pre-2016 redesign) scores:** SAT Math middle 50% range 500-620. SAT Critical Reading middle 50% range 500-610. **Concordant SAT scores:** SAT Math middle 50% range 530–640. ACT middle 50% range 22-29. Minimum paper TOEFL 550. **Basis for Candidate Selection:** *Important factors considered include:* academic GPA, standardized test scores. *Other factors considered include:* rigor of secondary school record, class rank. **Freshman Admission Requirements:** High school diploma is required and GED is accepted. *Academic units required:* 4 English, 3 math, 3 science, 2 science labs, 3 social studies, 1 visual/performing arts. *Academic units recommended:* 4 English, 4 math, 4 science, 2 science labs, 2 foreign language, 4 social studies, and 2 units from above areas or other academic areas. **Freshman Admission Statistics:** 17,918 applied, 78.30% admitted, 28% enrolled. **Transfer Admission Requirements:** college transcript(s), Minimum college GPA of 2.0 required. Lowest grade transferable D. **General Admission Information:** Priority deadline 4/1. Regular application deadline 9/1. Nonfall registration accepted. Admission may be deferred for a maximum of 1 year.

COSTS AND FINANCIAL AID

Required Forms and Deadlines: FAFSA. **Notification of Awards:** Applicants will be notified of awards on a rolling basis beginning 4/1. **Types of Aid:** *Need-based scholarships/grants:* Federal Pell, FSEOG, State scholarships/grants, Private scholarships, College/university scholarship or grant aid from institutional funds. *Loans:* Direct Subsidized Stafford Loans, Direct Unsubsidized Stafford Loans, Direct PLUS loans, Federal Perkins Loans, College/university loans from institutional funds. *Student Employment:* Federal Work-Study Program available. Institutional employment available. **Financial Aid Statistics:** 88% needy freshmen, 84% needy undergrads receive need-based scholarship or grant aid. 16% freshmen, 10% undergrads receive non-need-based scholarship or grant aid. 70% freshmen, 75% undergrads receive need-based self-help aid. 1% freshmen, 1% undergrads receive athletic scholarships. 87% freshmen, 81% undergrads receive any aid. 50% undergrads borrow to pay for school. Average cumulative indebtedness $27,535. **Criteria for awarding aid:** *Need-based:* Academics, Leadership. *Non-need-based:* Academics, Alumni affiliation, Art, Athletics, Leadership, Music/drama, State/district residency.

UNIVERSITY OF MISSOURI

230 Jesse Hall, Columbia, MO 65211
Phone: 573-882-7786 • **Financial Aid Phone:** 573-882-7506
E-mail: MU4U@missouri.edu • **CEEB Code:** 260735
Fax: 573-882-7887 • **Website:** www.missouri.edu • **ACT Code:** 2382

This public school was founded in 1839. It has a 1372-acre campus.

RATINGS
Admissions Selectivity Rating: 84   **Fire Safety Rating:** 95   **Green Rating:** 87

STUDENTS AND FACULTY
Enrollment: 27,393. **Student Body:** 52% female, 48% male, 25% out-of-state, 4% international (120 countries represented). Asian 2%, African American 8%, Caucasian 79%, Hispanic 4%, Native American <1%, Pacific Islander <1%, Two or more races 3%, Race unknown <1%.
Retention and Graduation: 87% freshmen return for sophomore year. 69% freshmen graduate within 6 years. **Faculty:** Student/faculty ratio 20:1. 1,270 full-time faculty, 91% hold PhDs, 21% are are members of minority groups, 40% are women.

ACADEMICS
Degrees: bachelor's, doctoral/professional, doctoral/research, doctoral, master's, post-master's certificate. **Classes:** Most classes have 10-19 students. Most lab/discussion sessions have 20-29 students. **Most popular majors:** Business/Commerce; Biological and Biomedical Sciences; Journalism. **Special Study Options:** Accelerated program, cooperative education program, cross-registration, distance learning, double major, dual enrollment, English as a Second Language (ESL), exchange student program (domestic), external degree program, honors program, independent study, internships, student-designed major, study abroad, teacher certification program, Evening College, MU Direct. **Honors Programs:** Honors College Combined degree programs: BA/MA, Accounting. **Disability Services:** Special programs offered to physically disabled students, including note-taking services, reader services, tape recorders, tutors. **Career Services:** Alumni network, Alumni services, Career/job search classes, Career assessment, Internships, Regional alumni.

FACILITIES
Housing: Coed dorms, men's dorms, women's dorms, fraternity/sorority housing, apartments for married students, Freshmen Interest Groups and unique learning communities allow students to live in coed residence halls and share in exploring the same academic area of interest. 100% of campus accessible to physically diasbled. **Special Academic Facilities/Equipment:** Life Sciences Center for Research, TigerPlace- licensed care facility, Department of Nursing, James B Nutter Family Information Commons—Ellis Library, Museum of Anthropology, Museum of Art and Archeology, World's most powerful univesity research reactor for Nuclear Medicine, one of 15 European Union Centers on college campuses. **Computers:** 100% of classrooms, 10% of dorms, 100% of libraries, 100% of dining areas, 100% of student union, 10% of common outdoor areas have wireless network access. Students can register for classes online. Administrative functions (other than registration) can be performed online.

CAMPUS LIFE
Environment: City. **Activities:** Choral groups, concert band, dance, drama/theater, jazz band, literary magazine, marching band, music ensembles, musical theater, opera, pep band, radio station, student government, student newspaper, student-run film society, symphony orchestra, television station, yearbook, Campus Ministries, Student Organization, Model UN. 598 registered organizations, 25 honor societies, 47 religious organizations. 32 fraternities, 19 sororities. **Athletics (Intercollegiate):** *Men:* baseball, basketball, cross-country, diving, football, golf, swimming, track/field (outdoor), track/field (indoor), wrestling. *Women:* basketball, cheerleading, cross-country, diving, golf, gymnastics, soccer, softball, swimming, tennis, track/field (outdoor), track/field (indoor), volleyball. **On-Campus Highlights:** Student Recreation Center—amazing recr, Mizzou Arena—home of Tiger Basketball, Memorial Stadium—home of Tiger Football, Jesse Hall—home to administ and various concerts, Life Sciences Center—home of research a, Renovation and construction on campus, Life Sciences Center, Mizzou Arena, James B Nutter Family Infomration Center in Ellis Library, Virginia Avenue Housing and Dining Expansion. **Environmental Initiatives:** Signatory to ACUPCC climate change commitment.

ADMISSIONS

Freshman Academic Profile: 28% in top 10% of high school class, 58% in top 25% of high school class, 87% in top 50% of high school class. **Reported SAT (pre-2016 redesign) scores:** SAT Math middle 50% range 530-650. SAT Critical Reading middle 50% range 530-650. **Concordant SAT scores:** SAT Math middle 50% range 560–670. ACT middle 50% range 24-29. Minimum internet-based TOEFL 61. Minimum paper TOEFL 500. **Basis for Candidate Selection:** *Very important factors considered include:* class rank, academic GPA, standardized test scores. *Important factors considered include:* rigor of secondary school record. *Other factors considered include:* application essay, recommendation(s), talent/ability, first generation, racial/ethnic status, volunteer work, work experience, level of applicant's interest. **Freshman Admission Requirements:** High school diploma is required and GED is accepted. *Academic units required:* 4 English, 4 math, 3 science, 1 science lab, 2 foreign language, 3 social studies, and 1 unit from above areas or other academic areas. **Freshman Admission Statistics:** 21,988 applied, 78.13% admitted, 36% enrolled. **Transfer Admission Requirements:** college transcript(s), Minimum college GPA of 2.5 required. **General Admission Information:** Application fee $50. Priority deadline 5/1. Nonfall registration accepted. Admission may be deferred.

COSTS AND FINANCIAL AID

Annual in-state tuition $8,286. Annual out-of-state tuition $23,943. Room and board $9,808. Required fees $1,223. Average book expense $1,124. **Required Forms and Deadlines:** FAFSA. **Notification of Awards:** Applicants will be notified of awards on a rolling basis beginning 4/1. **Types of Aid:** *Need-based scholarships/grants:* Federal Pell, FSEOG, State scholarships/grants, Private scholarships, College/university scholarship or grant aid from institutional funds, Federal Nursing Scholarships. *Loans:* Direct Subsidized Stafford Loans, Direct Unsubsidized Stafford Loans, Direct PLUS loans, Federal Perkins Loans, Federal Nursing Loans, State Loans, College/university loans from institutional funds. *Student Employment:* Federal Work-Study Program available. Institutional employment available. **Financial Aid Statistics:** 84% needy freshmen, 80% needy undergrads receive need-based scholarship or grant aid. 8% freshmen, 5% undergrads receive non-need-based scholarship or grant aid. 72% freshmen, 76% undergrads receive need-based self-help aid. 1% freshmen, 1% undergrads receive athletic scholarships. **Criteria for awarding aid:** *Need-based:* Academics, Alumni affiliation, Art, Athletics, Leadership, Minority status, Music/drama. *Non-need-based:* Academics, Alumni affiliation, Art, Athletics, Leadership, Minority status, Music/drama, State/district residency.

UNIVERSITY OF MISSOURI—KANSAS CITY

5100 Rockhill Road, Kansas City, mo 64114
Phone: 816-235-1111 • **Financial Aid Phone:** 816-235-1154
E-mail: admit@umkc.edu • **CEEB Code:** 6872
Fax: 816-235-5544 • **Website:** www.umkc.edu • **ACT Code:** 2380

This private school was founded in 1929. It has a 191-acre campus.

RATINGS

Admissions Selectivity Rating: 86   **Fire Safety Rating:** 82   **Green Rating:** 97

STUDENTS AND FACULTY

Enrollment: 7,904. **Student Body:** 57% female, 43% male, 19% out-of-state, 5% international (68 countries represented). Asian 7%, African American 15%, Caucasian 57%, Hispanic 9%, Native American <1%, Pacific Islander <1%, Two or more races 4%, Race unknown 4%.
Retention and Graduation: 75% freshmen return for sophomore year. 22% freshmen graduate within 4 years. 53% freshmen graduate within 6 years.
Faculty: Student/faculty ratio 14:1. 745 full-time faculty, 82% hold PhDs, 22% are are members of minority groups, 48% are women. 0% of classes are taught by teaching assistants.

ACADEMICS

Degrees: bachelor's, doctoral/professional, doctoral/research, doctoral, master's, postbachelor's certificate, post-master's certificate. **Classes:** Most classes have 10-19 students. Most lab/discussion sessions have 10-19 students. **Most popular majors:** Business/Commerce; Health Services/Allied Health/Health Sciences; Liberal Arts and Sciences/Liberal Studies. **Special Study Options:** Accelerated program, distance learning, double major, dual enrollment, English as a Second Language (ESL), honors program, independent study, internships, liberal arts/career combination, student-designed major, study abroad, teacher certification program. **Honors Programs:** UMKC Honors Program Combined degree programs: BA/MD, BA/JD, BLA/MD, BA/MPA, BBA/MBA. **Disability Services:** Special programs

offered to physically disabled students, including note-taking services, reader services, tape recorders, tutors. **Career Services:** Alumni network, Alumni services, Career/job search classes, Career assessment, Internships. Cooperative Learning Programs.

FACILITIES

Housing: Coed dorms, special housing for disabled students, fraternity/sorority housing, apartments for married students, apartments for single students, University owned houses. 98% of campus accessible to physically diasbled. **Special Academic Facilities/Equipment:** Art gallery, professional theater, geosciences museums, language lab, observatory. **Computers:** 90% of classrooms, 100% of dorms, 100% of libraries, 100% of dining areas, 100% of student union, have wireless network access. Students can register for classes online. Administrative functions (other than registration) can be performed online.

CAMPUS LIFE

Environment: Metropolis. **Activities:** Choral groups, concert band, dance, drama/theater, jazz band, literary magazine, music ensembles, musical theater, opera, pep band, student government, student newspaper, symphony orchestra, Campus Ministries, Student Organization, Model UN. 200 registered organizations, 32 honor societies, 13 religious organizations. 6 fraternities, 7 sororities. **Athletics (Intercollegiate):** *Men:* basketball, cheerleading, cross-country, golf, riflery, soccer, tennis, track/field (outdoor). *Women:* basketball, cheerleading, cross-country, golf, riflery, softball, tennis, track/field (outdoor), volleyball. **On-Campus Highlights:** Muddy's Coffee Shop, Nelson Atkins Museum, Sweeney Recreation Center, Minsky's restaurant, Planet Sub restaurant. **Environmental Initiatives:** Recycling.

ADMISSIONS

Freshman Academic Profile: Average high school GPA 3.4. 31% in top 10% of high school class, 56% in top 25% of high school class, 84% in top 50% of high school class. **Reported SAT (pre-2016 redesign) scores:** SAT Math middle 50% range 480-640. SAT Critical Reading middle 50% range 500-660. **Concordant SAT scores:** SAT Math middle 50% range 510–660. ACT middle 50% range 21-28. Minimum internet-based TOEFL 61. Minimum paper TOEFL 500. **Basis for Candidate Selection:** *Very important factors considered include:* rigor of secondary school record, class rank, academic GPA, standardized test scores. *Other factors considered include:* application essay, recommendation(s), interview, extracurricular activities, talent/ability, character/personal qualities, first generation, volunteer work, work experience. **Freshman Admission Requirements:** High school diploma is required and GED is accepted. *Academic units required:* 4 English, 4 math, 3 science, 1 science lab, 2 foreign language, 3 social studies, 1 visual/performing arts. **Freshman Admission Statistics:** 5,138 applied, 61.87% admitted, 38% enrolled. **Transfer Admission Requirements:** college transcript(s), Minimum college GPA of 2.0 required. Lowest grade transferable D. **General Admission Information:** Application fee $45. Priority deadline 4/1. Nonfall registration accepted. Admission may be deferred for a maximum of 2 semesters.

COSTS AND FINANCIAL AID

Annual in-state tuition $8,169. Annual out-of-state tuition $21,330. Room and board $10,010. Required fees $1,384. Average book expense $884. **Required Forms and Deadlines:** FAFSA. **Notification of Awards:** Applicants will be notified of awards on a rolling basis beginning 4/15. **Types of Aid:** *Need-based scholarships/grants:* Federal Pell, FSEOG, State scholarships/grants, Private scholarships, College/university scholarship or grant aid from institutional funds, United Negro College Fund, Federal Nursing Scholarships. *Loans:* Direct Subsidized Stafford Loans, Direct Unsubsidized Stafford Loans, Direct PLUS loans, Federal Perkins Loans, Federal Nursing Loans, College/university loans from institutional funds. *Student Employment:* Federal Work-Study Program available. Institutional employment available. **Financial Aid Statistics:** 92% needy freshmen, 80% needy undergrads receive need-based scholarship or grant aid. 5% freshmen, 2% undergrads receive non-need-based scholarship or grant aid. 69% freshmen, 76% undergrads receive need-based self-help aid. 2% freshmen, 2% undergrads receive athletic scholarships. 92% freshmen, 79% undergrads receive any aid. 61% undergrads borrow to pay for school. Average cumulative indebtedness $25,912. **Criteria for awarding aid:** *Need-based:* Academics, Alumni affiliation, Art, Athletics, Leadership, Minority status, Music/drama. *Non-need-based:* Academics, Alumni affiliation, Art, Athletics, Leadership, Minority status, Music/drama, State/district residency.

UNIVERSITY OF MISSOURI—ST. LOUIS

351 Millenium Student Center, St. Louis, MO 63121-4400
Phone: 314-516-5451 • **Financial Aid Phone:** 314-516-5526
E-mail: admissions@umsl.edu • **CEEB Code:** 6889
Fax: 314-516-5310 • **Website:** www.umsl.edu • **ACT Code:** 2383

This public school was founded in 1963. It has a 475-acre campus.

RATINGS

Admissions Selectivity Rating: 82   **Fire Safety Rating:** 81   **Green Rating:** 79

STUDENTS AND FACULTY

Enrollment: 7,737. **Student Body:** 55% female, 45% male, 11% out-of-state, 3% international (47 countries represented). Asian 5%, African American 18%, Caucasian 63%, Hispanic 3%, Native American <1%, Pacific Islander <1%, Two or more races 3%, Race unknown 4%.
Retention and Graduation: 78% freshmen return for sophomore year. 29% freshmen graduate within 4 years. 53% freshmen graduate within 6 years. 15% grads go on to further study within 1 year. 36% grads pursue arts and sciences degrees. 4% grads pursue law degrees. 29% grads pursue business degrees. 1% grads pursue medical degrees. **Faculty:** Student/faculty ratio 18:1. 438 full-time faculty, 76% hold PhDs, 20% are are members of minority groups, 53% are women. 9% of classes are taught by teaching assistants.

ACADEMICS

Degrees: bachelor's, certificate, doctoral/professional, doctoral/research, doctoral, master's, postbachelor's certificate, post-master's certificate. **Classes:** Most classes have 10-19 students. Most lab/discussion sessions have 10-19 students. **Most popular majors:** Business/Commerce; Registered Nursing/Registered Nurse; Psychology. **Special Study Options:** Accelerated program, cooperative education program, cross-registration, distance learning, double major, dual enrollment, English as a Second Language (ESL), exchange student program (domestic), honors program, independent study, internships, student-designed major, study abroad, teacher certification program, Engineering UMSL/WU, 2+3 B.S./M.A. Program in Economics, 2+3 B.A./B.S.-Ed and M.A. Program in History, 2+3 B.A./M.A. Program in Philosophy, 2+3 B.A./M.A. Program in Political Science, 2+3 B.A. in Psychology and M.S. in Gerontology Program, 2+3 B.A./M.A. Program in Sociology, Art and Art History 3+4 Program for School of Architecture at Washington University, Biology 3+4 Program for UMSL College of Optometry, Physics and Astronomy 3+4 Program for UMSL College of Optometry, Biology 3+3 Program for Logan Chiropractic College. **Honors Programs:** Pierre Laclede Honors College offers a four-year (for freshmen) and a two-year (for internal and external transfers) honors program through which students can meet their General Education and some other graduation requirements (e.g., advanced composition, global awareness, cultural diversity). Most instruction is in small seminars (average enrollment is 13). There is a six-hour independent study requirement, and a writing program engages all students. Combined degree programs: BA/MD; BA/MA; BS/MA; BA/BSED/MA; BA/MA; BA/MS; BA/DOPT; BS/DOPT; Biology Prog for Logan Chiropractic,Kansas City Univ of Medicine & Bioscience, Kent State Clg of Podiatric Med, U of MO Clg of Veterinary Med, Occ & Phys Ther. **Disability Services:** Special programs offered to physically disabled students, including note-taking services, reader services, tape recorders. **Career Services:** Alumni services, Career assessment, Internships. Experiential learning-as it includes our Internship and Cooperative Education programs.

FACILITIES

Housing: Coed dorms, special housing for disabled students, special housing for international students, fraternity/sorority housing, apartments for married students, apartments for single students, Theme Housing, Housing for graduate students and students over 21 in apartments; other themed communities. 100% of campus accessible to physically disabled. **Special Academic Facilities/ Equipment:** Art galleries, language, writing labs,math labs Mercantile Library, and observatory,radio station **Computers:** 68% of classrooms, 90% of dorms, 90% of libraries, 100% of dining areas, 90% of student union, 60% of common outdoor areas have wireless network access. Students can register for classes online. Administrative functions (other than registration) can be performed online.

CAMPUS LIFE

Environment: Metropolis. **Activities:** Choral groups, dance, drama/theater, jazz band, literary magazine, music ensembles, musical theater, opera, pep band, radio station, student government, student newspaper, student-run film society, Campus Ministries, Student Organization, Model UN. 125 registered organizations, 24 honor societies, 9 religious organizations. 3 fraternities, 3 sororities. **Athletics (Intercollegiate):** *Men:* baseball, basketball, golf, soccer, tennis. *Women:* basketball, golf, soccer, softball, tennis, volleyball. **On-Campus Highlights:** Millennium Student Center, Touhill Performing Arts Center, Mark Twain Athletic Complex, Gallery 210, Pilot House. **Environmental Initiatives:** Energy Conservation.

ADMISSIONS

Freshman Academic Profile: Average high school GPA 3.4. 26% in top 10% of high school class, 53% in top 25% of high school class, 84% in top 50% of high school class. 80% from public high schools. **Reported SAT (pre-2016 redesign) scores:** SAT Math middle 50% range 470-560. SAT Critical Reading middle 50% range 470-520. SAT Writing middle 50% range 460-590. **Concordant SAT scores:** SAT EBRW middle 50% 520-610. SAT Math middle 50% range 510-580. ACT middle 50% range 21-27. Minimum paper TOEFL 500. **Basis for Candidate Selection:** *Very important factors considered include:* rigor of secondary school record, class rank, academic GPA, standardized test scores. *Other factors considered include:* application essay, recommendation(s). **Freshman Admission Requirements:** High school diploma is required and GED is accepted. *Academic units required:* 4 English, 4 math, 3 science, 1 science lab, 2 foreign language, 3 social studies, and 1 unit from above areas or other academic areas. **Freshman Admission Statistics:** 1,947 applied, 70.62% admitted, 32% enrolled. **Transfer Admission Requirements:** college transcript(s), Minimum college GPA of 2.0 required. Lowest grade transferable D. **General Admission Information:** Application fee $35. Regular application deadline 9/16. Nonfall registration accepted. Admission may be deferred for a maximum of 1 Acad Year.

COSTS AND FINANCIAL AID

Required Forms and Deadlines: FAFSA. **Notification of Awards:** Applicants will be notified of awards on a rolling basis beginning 4/1. **Types of Aid:** *Need-based scholarships/grants:* Federal Pell, FSEOG, State scholarships/ grants, Private scholarships, College/university scholarship or grant aid from institutional funds, United Negro College Fund, Federal Nursing Scholarships. *Loans:* Direct Subsidized Stafford Loans, Direct Unsubsidized Stafford Loans, Direct PLUS loans, Federal Perkins Loans, Federal Nursing Loans, State Loans. *Student Employment:* Federal Work-Study Program available. Institutional employment available. **Financial Aid Statistics:** 90% needy freshmen, 82% needy undergrads receive need-based scholarship or grant aid. 19% freshmen, 11% undergrads receive non-need-based scholarship or grant aid. 66% freshmen, 83% undergrads receive need-based self-help aid. 4% freshmen, 2% undergrads receive athletic scholarships. 91% freshmen, 78% undergrads receive any aid. 61% undergrads borrow to pay for school. Average cumulative indebtedness $24,186. **Criteria for awarding aid:** *Need-based:* Academics, Alumni affiliation, Art, Leadership, Minority status, Music/drama. *Non-need-based:* Academics, Alumni affiliation, Art, Athletics, Music/drama, State/district residency.

UNIVERSITY OF MOBILE

5735 College Parkway, Mobile, AL 36613-2842
Phone: 251-442-2222 • **Financial Aid Phone:** 251-442-2222
E-mail: enrollmentservices@umobile.edu • **CEEB Code:** 1515
Website: www.umobile.edu • **ACT Code:** 29

This private school, affiliated with the Southern Baptist Church, was founded in 1961. It has a 830-acre campus.

RATINGS

Admissions Selectivity Rating: 83   **Fire Safety Rating:** 60*   **Green Rating:** 60*

STUDENTS AND FACULTY

Enrollment: 1,362. **Student Body:** 63% female, 37% male, 18% out-of-state, 4% international (28 countries represented). Asian 1%, African American 19%, Caucasian 54%, Hispanic 3%, Native American 1%, Pacific Islander <1%, Two or more races 3%, Race unknown 16%.
Retention and Graduation: 71% freshmen return for sophomore year. 26% freshmen graduate within 4 years. 48 17% grads go on to further study within 1 year. **Faculty:** Student/faculty ratio 13:1. 79 full-time faculty, 71% hold PhDs, 8% are are members of minority groups, 61% are women. 0% of classes are taught by teaching assistants.

ACADEMICS

Degrees: associate, bachelor's, master's. **Classes:** Most classes have 10-19 students. Most lab/discussion sessions have 10-19 students. **Most popular majors:** Elementary Education and Teaching; Business Administration and Management; Registered Nursing/Registered Nurse. **Special Study Options:** Accelerated program, double major, honors program, independent study, internships, teacher certification program. **Honors Programs:** Exploring the great books and the enduring questions; join a community of enthusiastic students like yourself; take courses designed not to make you do more work, but do the kind of work that will help you become a thinking leader; earn the "Honors Scholar" designation and seal on your diploma and transcript; participate in special events, such as an annual honor dinner hosted by President Foley; have frequent access to honors faculty; benefit from honors roundtable designed to help students prepare for and apply to graduate school, seek grants and scholarships, and pursue post-graduate career opportunities. Combined degree programs: BA/MA, BS/MBA. **Disability Services:** Special programs offered to physically disabled students, including tutors. **Career Services:** Alumni services, Career/job search classes, Career assessment, Internships.

FACILITIES

Housing: men's dorms, women's dorms. 100% of campus accessible to physically diasbled. **Special Academic Facilities/Equipment:** Art gallery, forest learning center **Computers:** 10% of classrooms, 100% of dorms, 100% of libraries, 50% of dining areas, 100% of student union, 20% of common outdoor areas have wireless network access. Students can register for classes online. Administrative functions (other than registration) can be performed online.

CAMPUS LIFE

Environment: City. **Activities:** Choral groups, concert band, jazz band, music ensembles, musical theater, opera, pep band, student government, Campus Ministries. 52 registered organizations, 12 honor societies, 3 religious organizations. **Athletics (Intercollegiate):** *Men:* baseball, basketball, cross-country, golf, soccer, tennis. *Women:* basketball, cheerleading, cross-country, golf, soccer, softball, tennis, volleyball. **On-Campus Highlights:** Ram Hall- State of the Art Auditorium, Newly renovated dining hall, Martin Hall, Donald Art Gallery, New Dorms–Faulkner and Samford Halls, Baseball Field/ Swimming Pool. **Environmental Initiatives:** Recycling.

ADMISSIONS

Freshman Academic Profile: Average high school GPA 3.5. 23% in top 10% of high school class, 53% in top 25% of high school class, 80% in top 50% of high school class. **Reported SAT (pre-2016 redesign) scores:** SAT Math middle 50% range 430-580. SAT Critical Reading middle 50% range 420-540. **Concordant SAT scores:** SAT Math middle 50% range 470–600. ACT middle 50% range 19-25. Minimum internet-based TOEFL 61. Minimum paper TOEFL 500. **Basis for Candidate Selection:** *Very important factors considered include:* academic GPA, standardized test scores. **Freshman Admission Requirements:** High school diploma is required and GED is accepted. *Academic units recommended:* 4 English, 3 math, 3 science, 2 foreign language, 3 social studies, 3 history. **Freshman Admission Statistics:** 935 applied, 61.93% admitted, 39% enrolled. **Transfer Admission Requirements:** college transcript(s), Minimum college GPA of 2.75 required. Lowest grade transferable C. **General Admission Information:** Application fee $25. Nonfall registration accepted. Admission may be deferred for a maximum of 1 year.

COSTS AND FINANCIAL AID

Required Forms and Deadlines: FAFSA, Institution's own financial aid form, State aid form. **Notification of Awards:** Applicants will be notified of awards on a rolling basis beginning 2/1. **Types of Aid:** *Need-based scholarships/grants:* Federal Pell, FSEOG, State scholarships/grants, Private scholarships, College/ university scholarship or grant aid from institutional funds, Federal Nursing Scholarships. *Loans:* Direct Subsidized Stafford Loans, Direct Unsubsidized Stafford Loans, Direct PLUS loans, Federal Perkins Loans, College/university loans from institutional funds. *Student Employment:* Federal Work-Study Program available. Institutional employment available. **Financial Aid Statistics:** 77% needy freshmen, 63% needy undergrads receive need-based scholarship or grant aid. 100% freshmen, 88% undergrads receive non-need-based scholarship or grant aid. 44% freshmen, 6% undergrads receive need-based self-help aid. 3% freshmen, 2% undergrads receive athletic scholarships. 73% undergrads borrow to pay for school. Average cumulative indebtedness $31,266. **Criteria for awarding aid:** *Non-need-based:* Academics, Alumni affiliation, Athletics, Music/drama, Religious affiliation.

THE UNIVERSITY OF MONTANA

Lommasson Center 103, Missoula, MT 59812
Phone: 243-6266 • **Financial Aid Phone:** 406-243-5373
E-mail: admiss@umontana.edu • **CEEB Code:** 4489
Fax: 406-243-5711 • **Website:** www.umt.edu • **ACT Code:** 2422

This public school was founded in 1893. It has a 220-acre campus.

RATINGS

Admissions Selectivity Rating: 79   **Fire Safety Rating:** 90   **Green Rating:** 60*

STUDENTS AND FACULTY

Enrollment: 10,175. **Student Body:** 54% female, 46% male, 26% out-of-state, 2% international (68 countries represented). Asian 1%, African American 1%, Caucasian 79%, Hispanic 4%, Native American 3%, Pacific Islander <1%, Two or more races 4%, Race unknown 5%.
Retention and Graduation: 73% freshmen return for sophomore year. 24% freshmen graduate within 4 years. 46% freshmen graduate within 6 years. 26% grads go on to further study within 1 year. **Faculty:** Student/faculty ratio 18:1. 569 full-time faculty, 78% hold PhDs, 10% are are members of minority groups, 39% are women. 9% of classes are taught by teaching assistants.

ACADEMICS

Degrees: associate, bachelor's, certificate, doctoral/professional, doctoral/ research, master's, postbachelor's certifiate, post-master's certificate, terminal, transfer. **Classes:** Most classes have 10-19 students. Most lab/discussion sessions have 20-29 students. **Most popular majors:** Business Administration and Management; Psychology; Forest Management/Forest Resources Management. **Special Study Options:** cooperative education program, cross-registration, distance learning, double major, English as a Second Language (ESL), exchange student program (domestic), external degree program, honors program, independent study, internships, study abroad, teacher certification program, Bachelor of Nursing in Missoula in cooperation with Montana State Univeristy-Bozeman. **Honors Programs:** The Davidson Honors College offers talented and motivated students an academic and social community as an important part of their undergraduate experience at The University of Montana, regardless of their major disciplines. Honors courses are taught by many of the best scholars on campus and are generally limited to twenty students. The Honors College encourages its students to participate in community service activities, educational experiences and undergraduate research. Combined degree programs: BA/JD, JD/MBA, MBA/PharmD, JD/MPA. **Disability Services:** Special programs offered to physically disabled students, including note-taking services, reader services, tape recorders, tutors. **Career Services:** Alumni network, Alumni services, Career/job search classes, Career assessment, Internships, Regional alumni.

FACILITIES

Housing: Coed dorms, special housing for disabled students, men's dorms, special housing for international students, women's dorms, fraternity/sorority housing, apartments for married students, apartments for single students, ThemeHousingApartments for students and families; Honors floors, floors, and quiet floors in dorms; activity dorms; personal development housing. 87% of campus accessible to physically diasbled. **Special Academic Facilities/ Equipment:** On main campus: clinical psychology center; environmental studies lab; geology field camp; several biological, biomedical, kinesiology, physiology, forestry-related, and other research labs or centers; art galleries; broadcast media center (public radio and television) and performing arts-radio-television building; practical ethics center; extensive presentation technology equipment and services, and others. Other locations: biological station, experimental forest, two-year college of technology (two locations), Fort Missoula field research center, and others. **Computers:** 20% of classrooms, 100% of libraries, 60% of dining areas, 100% of student union, 5% of common outdoor areas have wireless network access. Students can register for classes online. Administrative functions (other than registration) can be performed online.

CAMPUS LIFE

Environment: City. **Activities:** Choral groups, concert band, dance, drama/ theater, jazz band, literary magazine, marching band, music ensembles, musical theater, opera, pep band, radio station, student government, student newspaper, symphony orchestra, television station 150 registered organizations, 5 fraternities, 4 sororities. **Athletics (Intercollegiate):** *Men:* basketball, cheerleading, cross-country, football, tennis, track/field (outdoor), track/field (indoor). *Women:* basketball, cheerleading, cross-country, golf, soccer, tennis, track/field (outdoor), track/field (indoor), volleyball. **On-Campus Highlights:** Adams Event Center (basketball, shows, etc.), Washington-Grizzly Stadium (football, other), Campus Recreation Center (student recreation), University Center (student center, movie theater), Performing Arts-RadioTV Center (public radio-TV), 2. Washington-Grizzly Stadium also used for MAJOR events, like Pearl Jam concert a few years ago (kicking off their annual tour), the Rolling Stones concert Oct 2006, and Elton John concerts (2007 and 2008). **Environmental Initiatives:** Climate Action Plan to reach carbon neutrality by 2020 and biannual Greenhouse Gas Inventories are completed by a full-time Sustainability Coordinator and the Sustainable Campus Committee.

ADMISSIONS

Freshman Academic Profile: Average high school GPA 3.3. 18% in top 10% of high school class, 39% in top 25% of high school class, 72% in top 50% of high school class. **Reported SAT (pre-2016 redesign) scores:** SAT Math middle 50% range 490-600. SAT Critical Reading middle 50% range 490-620. SAT Writing middle 50% range 480-600. **Concordant SAT scores:** SAT EBRW middle 50% 540–660. SAT Math middle 50% range 520–620. ACT middle 50% range 20-27. Minimum internet-based TOEFL 70. Minimum paper TOEFL 525. **Basis for Candidate Selection:** *Very important factors*

The Princeton Review's Complete Book of Colleges

considered include: rigor of secondary school record, class rank, academic GPA, standardized test scores. *Important factors considered include:* extracurricular activities, talent/ability. *Other factors considered include:* application essay, recommendation(s). **Freshman Admission Requirements:** High school diploma is required and GED is accepted. *Academic units required:* 4 English, 3 math, 2 science, 2 science labs, 3 social studies, 2 history. *Academic units recommended:* 2 foreign language, 2 computer science, 2 visual/performing arts, and 2 units from above areas or other academic areas. **Freshman Admission Statistics:** 5,600 applied, 91.02% admitted, 34% enrolled. **Transfer Admission Requirements:** college transcript(s), Minimum college GPA of 2.0 required. Lowest grade transferable D. **General Admission Information:** Application fee $36. Priority deadline 3/1. Nonfall registration accepted. Admission may be deferred for a maximum of 1 year.

COSTS AND FINANCIAL AID

Annual in-state tuition $4,604. Annual out-of-state tuition $22,720. Room and board $8,826. Required fees $1,842. Average book expense $1,400. **Required Forms and Deadlines:** FAFSA. **Notification of Awards:** Applicants will be notified of awards on a rolling basis beginning 4/1. **Types of Aid:** *Need-based scholarships/grants:* Federal Pell, FSEOG, State scholarships/grants, Private scholarships, College/university scholarship or grant aid from institutional funds. *Loans:* Federal Perkins Loans. *Student Employment:* Federal Work-Study Program available. Institutional employment available. **Financial Aid Statistics:** 68% needy freshmen, 65% needy undergrads receive need-based scholarship or grant aid. 84% freshmen, 56% undergrads receive non-need-based scholarship or grant aid. 79% freshmen, 82% undergrads receive need-based self-help aid. 1% freshmen, 1% undergrads receive athletic scholarships. 62% freshmen, 56% undergrads receive any aid. 57% undergrads borrow to pay for school. Average cumulative indebtedness $23,927. **Criteria for awarding aid:** *Need-based:* Academics, Minority status. *Non-need-based:* Academics, Athletics, Leadership, Music/drama, State/district residency.

THE UNIVERSITY OF MONTANA—WESTERN

710 South Atlantic, Dillon, MT 59725
Phone: 406-683-7331
E-mail: admissions@umwestern.edu • **CEEB Code:** 4945
Fax: 406-683-7493 • **Website:** www.umwestern.edu • **ACT Code:** 2428

This public school was founded in 1893. It has a 34-acre campus.

RATINGS
Admissions Selectivity Rating: 75   **Fire Safety Rating:** 60*   **Green Rating:** 60*

STUDENTS AND FACULTY
Enrollment: 1,410. **Student Body:** 61% female, 39% male, 24% out-of-state, 0% international (5 countries represented). Asian 1%, African American 1%, Caucasian 85%, Hispanic 3%, Native American 2%, Pacific Islander <1%, Two or more races 1%, Race unknown 7%.
Retention and Graduation: 69% freshmen return for sophomore year. 11% freshmen graduate within 4 years. 41% freshmen graduate within 6 years. 50% grads go on to further study within 1 year. **Faculty:** Student/faculty ratio 15:1. 70 full-time faculty, 77% hold PhDs, 0% are are members of minority groups, 44% are women. 0% of classes are taught by teaching assistants.

ACADEMICS
Degrees: associate, bachelor's, certificate. **Classes:** Most classes have 10-19 students. **Most popular majors:** Environmental Studies; Elementary Education and Teaching; Business/Commerce. **Special Study Options:** cooperative education program, distance learning, double major, dual enrollment, honors program, independent study, internships, teacher certification program. **Disability Services:** Special programs offered to physically disabled students, including note-taking services, reader services, tape recorders, tutors. **Career Services:** Alumni services, Career/job search classes, Career assessment, Internships.

FACILITIES
Housing: Coed dorms, special housing for disabled students, men's dorms, women's dorms, apartments for married students, apartments for single students, Students with fewer than 30 credits not living w/ family required to live in dorm. Transfer students under 21 w/ less than 30 credits not living with parents must live in dorm. 90% of campus accessible to physically disabled. **Special Academic Facilities/Equipment:** Art gallery, outdoor education center, learning center. **Computers:** Students can register for classes online. Administrative functions (other than registration) can be performed online.

CAMPUS LIFE
Environment: Rural. **Activities:** Choral groups, concert band, drama/theater, jazz band, literary magazine, music ensembles, radio station, student

government, student newspaper, yearbook. 25 registered organizations, 2 honor societies, 2 religious organizations. **Athletics (Intercollegiate):** *Men:* basketball, cheerleading, football, golf, rodeo. *Women:* basketball, cheerleading, golf, rodeo, volleyball. **On-Campus Highlights:** SUB (Sudent Union Building), Straugh Arena, The Cup, STC Tech Building, Bark'n Bite.

ADMISSIONS
Freshman Academic Profile: Average high school GPA 3.1. 4% in top 10% of high school class, 21% in top 25% of high school class, 49% in top 50% of high school class. 96% from public high schools. **Reported SAT (pre-2016 redesign) scores:** SAT Math middle 50% range 390-530. SAT Critical Reading middle 50% range 410-520. **Concordant SAT scores:** SAT Math middle 50% range 430–560. ACT middle 50% range 17-22. Minimum paper TOEFL 500. **Basis for Candidate Selection:** *Very important factors considered include:* rigor of secondary school record, class rank, academic GPA, standardized test scores. **Freshman Admission Requirements:** High school diploma is required and GED is accepted. *Academic units required:* 4 English, 3 math, 2 science, 2 science labs, 3 social studies, 2 academic electives. **Freshman Admission Statistics:** 721 applied, 73.79% admitted, 65% enrolled. **Transfer Admission Requirements:** college transcript(s), Minimum college GPA of 2.0 required. Lowest grade transferable c. **General Admission Information:** Application fee $30. Priority deadline 7/1. Nonfall registration accepted. Admission may be deferred for a maximum of 1 year.

COSTS AND FINANCIAL AID
Annual in-state tuition $3,699. Annual out-of-state tuition $14,788. Room and board $6,994. Required fees $1,194. Average book expense $850. **Required Forms and Deadlines:** FAFSA. **Notification of Awards:** Applicants will be notified of awards on a rolling basis beginning 3/1. **Types of Aid:** *Need-based scholarships/grants:* Federal Pell, FSEOG, State scholarships/grants, Private scholarships, College/university scholarship or grant aid from institutional funds. *Loans:* Direct Subsidized Stafford Loans, Direct Unsubsidized Stafford Loans, Direct PLUS loans, Federal Perkins Loans, College/university loans from institutional funds. *Student Employment:* Federal Work-Study Program available. Institutional employment available. **Financial Aid Statistics:** 93% needy freshmen, 78% needy undergrads receive need-based scholarship or grant aid. 34% freshmen, 26% undergrads receive non-need-based scholarship or grant aid. 82% freshmen, 72% undergrads receive need-based self-help aid. 10% freshmen, 3% undergrads receive athletic scholarships. 67% undergrads borrow to pay for school. Average cumulative indebtedness $20,669. **Criteria for awarding aid:** *Need-based:* Academics, Alumni affiliation, Art, Leadership, Minority status. *Non-need-based:* Academics, Alumni affiliation, Art, Athletics, Leadership, State/district residency.

UNIVERSITY OF MONTEVALLO

Station 6030, Montevallo, AL 35115
Phone: 205-665-6030 • **Financial Aid Phone:** 205-665-6050
E-mail: admissions@montevallo.edu • **CEEB Code:** 1004
Fax: 205-665-6032 • **Website:** http://www.montevallo.edu/ • **ACT Code:** 4

This public school was founded in 1896. It has a 160-acre campus.

RATINGS
Admissions Selectivity Rating: 73   **Fire Safety Rating:** 82   **Green Rating:** 60*

STUDENTS AND FACULTY
Enrollment: 2,399. **Student Body:** 68% female, 32% male, 9% out-of-state, 1% international (23 countries represented). Asian 1%, African American 15%, Caucasian 71%, Hispanic 4%, Native American <1%, Pacific Islander 0%, Two or more races 3%, Race unknown 4%.
Retention and Graduation: 73% freshmen return for sophomore year. **Faculty:** Student/faculty ratio 16:1. 141 full-time faculty, 96% hold PhDs, 8% are are members of minority groups, 50% are women. 0% of classes are taught by teaching assistants.

ACADEMICS
Degrees: bachelor's, master's, post-master's certificate. **Classes:** Most classes have 10-19 students. Most lab/discussion sessions have 20-29 students. **Most popular majors:** Elementary Education and Teaching; Business Administration and Management; Health and Physical Education/Fitness. **Special Study Options:** Accelerated program, cross-registration, double major, dual enrollment, exchange student program (domestic), honors program, independent study, internships, study abroad, teacher certification program, Advanced placement credit; Academic remediation; and Learning disabilities services. **Honors Programs:** Honors History; Honors Composition; Honors Literature; Honors Thesis. Combined degree programs: 3-2 engineering program with U of Alabama at Birmi. **Disability Services:** Special programs offered to physically disabled students, including note-taking services, reader

services, tape recorders, tutors. **Career Services:** Alumni services, Career assessment. The Career Center assists students through all aspects of the career-planning process. Career counseling, including career assessments is available to all enrolled students. Other services include employability skills training, job postings, internship information, on-campus interviewing, career events and seminars and graduate school information.

FACILITIES

Housing: Coed dorms, men's dorms, women's dorms, fraternity/sorority housing, apartments for married students. **Special Academic Facilities/Equipment:** Art gallery, child development, speech and hearing, traffic safety, and undergraduate liberal studies centers, mass communications center with cable TV broadcasting capabilities. **Computers:** 98% of classrooms, 85% of dorms, 100% of libraries, 100% of dining areas, 100% of student union, 75% of common outdoor areas have wireless network access. Students can register for classes online. Administrative functions (other than registration) can be performed online.

CAMPUS LIFE

Environment: Rural. **Activities:** Choral groups, concert band, dance, drama/theater, jazz band, literary magazine, music ensembles, musical theater, student government, student newspaper, television station, yearbook. 93 registered organizations, 26 honor societies, 8 religious organizations, 7 fraternities, 8 sororities. **Athletics (Intercollegiate):** *Men:* baseball, basketball, golf, soccer. *Women:* basketball, cross-country, golf, soccer, tennis, volleyball. **On-Campus Highlights:** Cafeteria, Student Activity Center, Main Quad, University of Montevallo Student Lake, Intramural Fields. **Environmental Initiatives:** Campus lighting retrofit to energy saving bulbs.

ADMISSIONS

Freshman Academic Profile: Average high school GPA 3.4. 90% from public high schools. **Reported SAT (pre-2016 redesign) scores:** SAT Math middle 50% range 475-580. SAT Critical Reading middle 50% range 455-595. SAT Writing middle 50% range 470-585. **Concordant SAT scores:** SAT EBRW middle 50% 520–650. SAT Math middle 50% range 510–600. ACT middle 50% range 20-26. Minimum internet-based TOEFL 71. Minimum paper TOEFL 525. **Freshman Admission Requirements:** High school diploma is required and GED is accepted. **Freshman Admission Statistics:** 2,024 applied, 70.01% admitted, 36% enrolled. **Transfer Admission Requirements:** college transcript(s), Minimum college GPA of 2.0 required. Lowest grade transferable D. **General Admission Information:** Application fee $30. Regular application deadline 8/1. Nonfall registration accepted. Admission may be deferred.

COSTS AND FINANCIAL AID

Annual in-state tuition $9,990. Annual out-of-state tuition $20,550. Room and board $6,400. Required fees $670. Average book expense $2,050. **Required Forms and Deadlines:** FAFSA. **Notification of Awards:** Applicants will be notified of awards on a rolling basis beginning 3/25. **Types of Aid:** *Need-based scholarships/grants:* Federal Pell, FSEOG, State scholarships/grants, Private scholarships, College/university scholarship or grant aid from institutional funds. *Loans:* Direct Subsidized Stafford Loans, Direct Unsubsidized Stafford Loans, Direct PLUS loans, Federal Perkins Loans. *Student Employment:* Federal Work-Study Program available. Institutional employment available. **Financial Aid Statistics:** 85% needy freshmen, 84% needy undergrads receive need-based scholarship or grant aid. 18% freshmen, 10% undergrads receive non-need-based scholarship or grant aid. 79% freshmen, 85% undergrads receive need-based self-help aid. 4% freshmen, 4% undergrads receive athletic scholarships. 87% freshmen, 77% undergrads receive any aid. **Criteria for awarding aid:** *Need-based:* Academics. *Non-need-based:* Academics, Alumni affiliation, Art, Athletics, Leadership, Minority status, Music/drama.

UNIVERSITY OF MOUNT UNION

1972 Clark Avenue, Alliance, OH 44601-3993
Phone: 330-823-2590 • **Financial Aid Phone:** 877-543-9185
E-mail: admission@mountunion.edu • **CEEB Code:** 1492
Fax: 330-823-5097 • **Website:** www.mountunion.edu

This private school, affiliated with the Methodist Church, was founded in 1846. It has a 115-acre campus.

RATINGS

Admissions Selectivity Rating: 80   **Fire Safety Rating:** 90   **Green Rating:** 83

STUDENTS AND FACULTY

Enrollment: 2,110. **Student Body:** 48% female, 52% male, 18% out-of-state, <1% international (16 countries represented). Asian 1%, African American 7%, Caucasian 79%, Hispanic 3%, Native American 1%, Pacific Islander <1%, Two or more races 3%, Race unknown 6%.

Retention and Graduation: 79% freshmen return for sophomore year. 53% freshmen graduate within 4 years. 59% freshmen graduate within 6 years. 27% grads go on to further study within 1 year. 14% grads pursue arts and sciences degrees. 7% grads pursue law degrees. 9% grads pursue business degrees. 34% grads pursue medical degrees. **Faculty:** Student/faculty ratio 13:1. 134 full-time faculty, 90% hold PhDs, 15% are are members of minority groups, 44% are women. 0% of classes are taught by teaching assistants.

ACADEMICS

Degrees: bachelor's, master's. **Classes:** Most classes have 10-19 students. Most lab/discussion sessions have fewer than 10 students. **Most popular majors:** Business Administration and Management; Early Childhood Education and Teaching; Sport and Fitness Administration/Management. **Special Study Options:** cooperative education program, double major, dual enrollment, English as a Second Language (ESL), honors program, independent study, internships, liberal arts/career combination, student-designed major, study abroad, teacher certification program. **Honors Programs:** Four honors programs are offered. Honors in Liberal Arts, Honors in the Major, First Year in Honors and Latin Honors. A qualified student may participate in any program and may discontinue honors study without penalty. Students must declare their intent to participate in an honors program no later than the first semester of their junior year. **Disability Services:** Special programs offered to physically disabled students, including note-taking services, reader services, tape recorders, tutors. **Career Services:** Alumni network, Alumni services, Career/job search classes, Career assessment, Internships, Regional alumni. Employment success results/report.

FACILITIES

Housing: Coed dorms, special housing for disabled students, men's dorms, special housing for international students, women's dorms, fraternity/sorority housing, apartments for single students, ThemeHousingSmall, single-sex, college-owned residential homes converted to college housing. 95% of campus accessible to physically disabled. **Special Academic Facilities/Equipment:** Art gallery, ecological center, observatory, educational media center. **Computers:** 100% of classrooms, 90% of dorms, 100% of libraries, 100% of dining areas, 100% of student union, 50% of common outdoor areas have wireless network access. Students can register for classes online. Administrative functions (other than registration) can be performed online.

CAMPUS LIFE

Environment: Village. **Activities:** Choral groups, concert band, dance, drama/theater, jazz band, literary magazine, marching band, music ensembles, musical theater, pep band, radio station, student government, student newspaper, television station, yearbook, Campus Ministries, Student Organization, Model UN. 80 registered organizations, 16 honor societies, 10 religious organizations. 4 fraternities, 4 sororities. **Athletics (Intercollegiate):** *Men:* baseball, basketball, cross-country, diving, football, golf, soccer, swimming, tennis, track/field (outdoor), track/field (indoor), wrestling. *Women:* basketball, cheerleading, cross-country, diving, golf, soccer, softball, swimming, tennis, track/field (outdoor), track/field (indoor), volleyball. **On-Campus Highlights:** Hoover Price Campus Center, Kolenbrander Harter Information Center, McPherson Athletic Building, Dewald Chapel, Bracy Hall Science Building, Welcome Center. **Environmental Initiatives:** Sustainability (Climate Action) Plan

ADMISSIONS

Freshman Academic Profile: Average high school GPA 3.4. 20% in top 10% of high school class, 50% in top 25% of high school class, 81% in top 50% of high school class. 75% from public high schools. **Reported SAT (pre-2016 redesign) scores:** SAT Math middle 50% range 450-570. SAT Critical Reading middle 50% range 430-540. **Concordant SAT scores:** SAT Math middle 50% range 490–590. ACT middle 50% range 20-26. Minimum internet-based TOEFL 80. Minimum paper TOEFL 550. **Basis for Candidate Selection:** *Very important factors considered include:* rigor of secondary school record, class rank, academic GPA, standardized test scores. *Important factors considered include:* recommendation(s). *Other factors considered include:* application essay, extracurricular activities, talent/ability, character/personal qualities, alumni/ae relation, racial/ethnic status, volunteer work, work experience. **Freshman Admission Requirements:** High school diploma is required and GED is accepted. *Academic units recommended:* 4 English, 3 math, 3 science, 2 science labs, 2 foreign language, 3 social studies, and 1 unit from above areas or other academic areas. **Freshman Admission Statistics:** 2,525 applied, 76.99% admitted, 34% enrolled. **Transfer Admission Requirements:** High school transcript, college transcript(s), essay or personal statement, statement of good standing from prior institution(s). Minimum college GPA of 2.0 required. Lowest grade transferable C. **General Admission Information:** Priority deadline 3/1. Nonfall registration accepted. Admission may be deferred for a maximum of one semester.

COSTS AND FINANCIAL AID

Annual tuition $29,560. Required fees $330. Average book expense $1,100. **Required Forms and Deadlines:** FAFSA. **Types of Aid:** *Need-based scholarships/grants:* Federal Pell, FSEOG, State scholarships/grants, College/

university scholarship or grant aid from institutional funds. *Loans:* Direct Subsidized Stafford Loans, Direct Unsubsidized Stafford Loans, Direct PLUS loans, Federal Perkins Loans, State Loans, College/university loans from institutional funds. *Student Employment:* Federal Work-Study Program available. Institutional employment available. **Financial Aid Statistics:** 100% needy freshmen, 100% needy undergrads receive need-based scholarship or grant aid. 10% freshmen, 11% undergrads receive non-need-based scholarship or grant aid. 90% freshmen, 88% undergrads receive need-based self-help aid. 0% freshmen, 0% undergrads receive athletic scholarships. 88% freshmen, 90% undergrads receive any aid. 68% undergrads borrow to pay for school. Average cumulative indebtedness $37,800. **Criteria for awarding aid:** *Need-based:* Religious affiliation. *Non-need-based:* Academics, Alumni affiliation, Art, Job skills, Leadership, Minority status, Music/drama, Religious affiliation, State/district residency.

UNIVERSITY OF NEBRASKA AT OMAHA

Office of Admissions, Omaha, NE 68182
Phone: 402-554-2393 • **Financial Aid Phone:** 402-554-2327
E-mail: unoadmissions@unomaha.edu • **CEEB Code:** 6420
Fax: 402-554-3472 • **Website:** www.unomaha.edu • **ACT Code:** 2464

This public school was founded in 1908. It has a 472-acre campus.

RATINGS
Admissions Selectivity Rating: 80   **Fire Safety Rating:** 97   **Green Rating:** 93

STUDENTS AND FACULTY
Enrollment: 12,153. **Student Body:** 52% female, 48% male, 7% out-of-state, 3% international (62 countries represented). Asian 3%, African American 7%, Caucasian 72%, Hispanic 9%, Native American <1%, Pacific Islander <1%, Two or more races 3%, Race unknown 3%.
Retention and Graduation: 75% freshmen return for sophomore year. 14% freshmen graduate within 4 years. 42% freshmen graduate within 6 years. 21% grads go on to further study within 1 year. **Faculty:** Student/faculty ratio 17:1. 520 full-time faculty, 83% hold PhDs, 18% are are members of minority groups, 44% are women. 4% of classes are taught by teaching assistants.

ACADEMICS
Degrees: bachelor's, master's, postbachelor's certificate, post-master's certificate. **Classes:** Most classes have 20-29 students. Most lab/discussion sessions have 20-29 students. **Most popular majors:** Business Administration and Management; Criminal Justice/Safety Studies. **Special Study Options:** cooperative education program, cross-registration, distance learning, double major, dual enrollment, English as a Second Language (ESL), exchange student program (domestic), honors program, independent study, internships, student-designed major, study abroad, teacher certification program, Business, Engineering. **Honors Programs:** UNO Honors Program includes many opportunities such as Early Registration, Honors-only courses, Honors-priority Housing, Honors domestic and international semesters, Honors internships, and a Washington Center affiliation. Combined degree programs: MPA/MSW in Public Administration and Social Work. **Disability Services:** Special programs offered to physically disabled students, including note-taking services, reader services, tape recorders, tutors. **Career Services:** Career/job search classes, Career assessment, Internships. The Internships are a UNO strength.

FACILITIES
Housing: Coed dormsLeased Apartment dwellings. 99% of campus accessible to physically diasbled. **Special Academic Facilities/Equipment:** Center for Afghanistan studies, physical education facility, Strauss Performing Arts Center, Speech Center, Writing Center, Math/Science Center, Peter Kiewit Information Technology Building, and Career Center. **Computers:** 100% of classrooms, 100% of dorms, 100% of libraries, 100% of dining areas, 100% of student union, 85% of common outdoor areas have wireless network access. Students can register for classes online. Administrative functions (other than registration) can be performed online.

CAMPUS LIFE
Environment: Metropolis. **Activities:** Choral groups, concert band, dance, drama/theater, jazz band, literary magazine, marching band, music ensembles, musical theater, opera, pep band, radio station, student government, student newspaper, student-run film society, symphony orchestra, television station, Campus Ministries, Student Organization, Model UN. 127 registered organizations, 23 honor societies, 14 religious organizations. 6 fraternities, 8 sororities. **Athletics (Intercollegiate):** *Men:* baseball, basketball, football, ice hockey, wrestling. *Women:* basketball, cross-country, diving, golf, soccer, softball, swimming, tennis, track/field (outdoor), track/field (indoor), volleyball. **On-Campus Highlights:** University Library, Strauss Performing Arts Center,

Milo Bail Student Center, Durham Science Center, Peter Kiewit Institute.
Environmental Initiatives: To identify sustainability opportunities and to develop a recommended action plan for each.

ADMISSIONS
Freshman Academic Profile: Average high school GPA 3.4. 15% in top 10% of high school class, 40% in top 25% of high school class, 75% in top 50% of high school class. 90% from public high schools. ACT middle 50% range 20-26. Minimum internet-based TOEFL 61. Minimum paper TOEFL 500. **Basis for Candidate Selection:** *Very important factors considered include:* rigor of secondary school record, class rank, standardized test scores. *Other factors considered include:* character/personal qualities. **Freshman Admission Requirements:** High school diploma is required and GED is accepted. *Academic units required:* 4 English, 3 math, 3 science, 1 science lab, 2 foreign language, 1 social studies, 2 history, 1 academic elective. **Freshman Admission Statistics:** 4,955 applied, 70.78% admitted, 54% enrolled. **Transfer Admission Requirements:** college transcript(s), statement of good standing from prior institution(s). Minimum college GPA of 2.0 required. Lowest grade transferable C-. **General Admission Information:** Application fee $45. Regular application deadline 8/1. Nonfall registration accepted.

COSTS AND FINANCIAL AID
Annual in-state tuition $5,180. Annual out-of-state tuition $15,520. Room and board $8,090. Required fees $1,370. Average book expense $1,000. **Required Forms and Deadlines:** FAFSA. **Notification of Awards:** Applicants will be notified of awards on a rolling basis beginning 4/15. **Types of Aid:** *Need-based scholarships/grants:* Federal Pell, FSEOG, State scholarships/grants, Private scholarships, College/university scholarship or grant aid from institutional funds. *Loans:* Direct Subsidized Stafford Loans, Direct Unsubsidized Stafford Loans, Direct PLUS loans, Federal Perkins Loans, College/university loans from institutional funds. *Student Employment:* Federal Work-Study Program available. Institutional employment available. **Financial Aid Statistics:** 60% needy freshmen, 64% needy undergrads receive need-based scholarship or grant aid. 13% freshmen, 14% undergrads receive non-need-based scholarship or grant aid. 54% freshmen, 68% undergrads receive need-based self-help aid. 3% freshmen, 2% undergrads receive athletic scholarships. 80% freshmen, 81% undergrads receive any aid. **Criteria for awarding aid:** *Need-based:* Academics, Leadership. *Non-need-based:* Academics, Alumni affiliation, Art, Athletics, Leadership, Music/drama, State/district residency.

UNIVERSITY OF NEBRASKA—LINCOLN

1410 Q Street, Lincoln, NE 68588-0417
Phone: 402-472-2023 • **Financial Aid Phone:** 402-472-2030
E-mail: admissions@unl.edu • **CEEB Code:** 6877
Fax: 402-472-0670 • **Website:** http://www.unl.edu • **ACT Code:** 2482

This public school was founded in 1869. It has a 617-acre campus.

RATINGS
Admissions Selectivity Rating: 86   **Fire Safety Rating:** 84   **Green Rating:** 69

STUDENTS AND FACULTY
Enrollment: 20,833. **Student Body:** 48% female, 52% male, 23% out-of-state, 8% international (107 countries represented). Asian 3%, African American 3%, Caucasian 76%, Hispanic 6%, Native American <1%, Pacific Islander <1%, Two or more races 3%, Race unknown 1%.
Retention and Graduation: 82% freshmen return for sophomore year. 36% freshmen graduate within 4 years. 67 22% grads go on to further study within 1 year. **Faculty:** Student/faculty ratio 21:1. 1,123 full-time faculty, 92% hold PhDs, 21% are are members of minority groups, 32% are women.

ACADEMICS
Degrees: bachelor's, doctoral/professional, doctoral/research, doctoral, master's, postbachelor's certificate, post-master's certificate. **Classes:** Most classes have 20-29 students. Most lab/discussion sessions have 20-29 students. **Most popular majors:** Business Administration and Management; Psychology; Public Relations, Advertising, and Applied Communication. **Special Study Options:** Accelerated program, cooperative education program, cross-registration, distance learning, double major, dual enrollment, English as a Second Language (ESL), exchange student program (domestic), honors program, independent study, internships, liberal arts/career combination, student-designed major, study abroad, teacher certification program. **Honors**

Programs: University Honors Program: Acceptance into the program is based on a comprehensive evaluation of student's potential by the Honors Program Faculty Committee. A special notation is made on the transcript and diploma upon graduation. J.D. Edwards Honors Program: Purpose is to produce top quality graduates who combine business knowledge and computing fundamentals for enterprise information and software systems. Combined degree programs: BA/MD, BA/JD, BA/DDS, BA/MEng, BS/D.Pharm. **Disability Services:** Special programs offered to physically disabled students, including note-taking services, reader services, tape recorders, tutors. **Career Services:** Alumni network, Alumni services, Career/job search classes, Career assessment, Internships. Targeted Career Fairs and Events that reflect various employment sectors.

FACILITIES

Housing: Coed dorms, special housing for disabled students, men's dorms, special housing for international students, women's dorms, fraternity/sorority housing, apartments for married students, cooperative housing, apartments for single students. 100% of campus accessible to physically diasbled. **Special Academic Facilities/Equipment:** Art gallery, performing arts center, food industries complex, planetarium, center for mass spectrometry, natural science museum, animal science complex, veterinary animal research/diagnosis center.

CAMPUS LIFE

Environment: City. **Activities:** Choral groups, concert band, dance, drama/theater, jazz band, literary magazine, marching band, music ensembles, musical theater, opera, pep band, radio station, student government, student newspaper, student-run film society, symphony orchestra, television station, yearbook, Campus Ministries, Student Organization, Model UN. 335 registered organizations, 57 honor societies, 25 religious organizations. 27 fraternities, 18 sororities. **Athletics (Intercollegiate):** *Men:* baseball, basketball, cross-country, football, golf, gymnastics, rodeo, tennis, track/field (outdoor), track/field (indoor), wrestling. *Women:* basketball, bowling, cross-country, diving, golf, gymnastics, riflery, rodeo, soccer, softball, swimming, tennis, track/field (outdoor), track/field (indoor), volleyball. **On-Campus Highlights:** Student Union, Student Recreation, Library, Memorial Stadium and Hewitt Center, Residence Halls. **Environmental Initiatives:** Recycling of paper, plastic, aluminum and many other materials A student government initiative has resulted in UNL eliminating the use of polystyrene, also known as Styrofoam, for food packaging in 2016.

ADMISSIONS

Freshman Academic Profile: Average high school GPA 3.5. 24% in top 10% of high school class, 49% in top 25% of high school class, 83% in top 50% of high school class. **Reported SAT (pre-2016 redesign) scores:** SAT Math middle 50% range 510-650. SAT Critical Reading middle 50% range 480-630. **Concordant SAT scores:** SAT Math middle 50% range 540–670. ACT middle 50% range 22-28. Minimum internet-based TOEFL 70. **Basis for Candidate Selection:** *Very important factors considered include:* class rank, standardized test scores. *Important factors considered include:* rigor of secondary school record. *Other factors considered include:* academic GPA. **Freshman Admission Requirements:** High school diploma is required and GED is accepted. *Academic units required:* 4 English, 4 math, 3 science, 1 science lab, 2 foreign language, 2 social studies, 1 history. **Freshman Admission Statistics:** 11,193 applied, 75.27% admitted, 58% enrolled. **Transfer Admission Requirements:** High school transcript, college transcript(s), Minimum college GPA of 2.0 required. Lowest grade transferable D. **General Admission Information:** Application fee $45. Priority deadline 1/15. Regular application deadline 5/1. Nonfall registration accepted.

COSTS AND FINANCIAL AID

Annual in-state tuition $6,758. Annual out-of-state tuition $21,278. Room and board $10,310. Required fees $1,780. Average book expense $1,012. **Required Forms and Deadlines:** FAFSA. **Notification of Awards:** Applicants will be notified of awards on a rolling basis beginning 4/1. **Types of Aid:** *Need-based scholarships/grants:* Federal Pell, FSEOG, State scholarships/grants, Private scholarships, College/university scholarship or grant aid from institutional funds. *Loans:* Direct Subsidized Stafford Loans, Direct Unsubsidized Stafford Loans, Direct PLUS loans, Federal Perkins Loans. *Student Employment:* Federal Work-Study Program available. Institutional employment available. **Financial Aid Statistics:** 81% needy freshmen, 76% needy undergrads receive need-based scholarship or grant aid. 9% freshmen, 7% undergrads receive non-need-based scholarship or grant aid. 71% freshmen, 71% undergrads receive need-based self-help aid. 3% freshmen, 3% undergrads receive athletic scholarships. 90% freshmen, 78% undergrads receive any aid. 55% undergrads borrow to pay for school. Average cumulative indebtedness $23,231. **Criteria for awarding aid:** *Need-based:* Music/drama. *Non-need-based:* Academics, Alumni affiliation, Art, Athletics, Leadership, Music/drama, State/district residency.

UNIVERSITY OF NEBRASKA MEDICAL CENTER

984230 Nebr Med Ctr, Omaha, NE 68198-4230
Phone: 402-559-6864 • **Financial Aid Phone:** 402-559-4109
E-mail: ttonjes@unmc.edu
Fax: 402-559-6796 • **Website:** http://www.unmc.edu/

This public school was founded in 1902.

RATINGS

Admissions Selectivity Rating: 61   **Fire Safety Rating:** 60*   **Green Rating:** 60*

STUDENTS AND FACULTY

Enrollment: 811. **Student Body:** 88% female, 12% male, 12% out-of-state, 1% international. Asian 1%, African American 1%, Caucasian 93%, Hispanic 3%, Native American 1%, Pacific Islander 0%, Two or more races 0%, Race unknown 0%.
Faculty: 768 full-time faculty, 90% hold PhDs, 14% are are members of minority groups, 39% are women.

ACADEMICS

Degrees: bachelor's, master's, postbachelor's certificate, post-master's certificate. **Most popular majors:** Medicine Pharmacy. **Special Study Options:** Accelerated program, distance learning, honors program, independent study. **Disability Services:** Special programs offered to physically disabled students, including note-taking services, tutors.

CAMPUS LIFE

Environment: Metropolis. **Activities:** student government, student newspaper.

ADMISSIONS

Minimum paper TOEFL 551. **Transfer Admission Requirements:** college transcript(s), Lowest grade transferable c. **General Admission Information:** Nonfall registration not accepted.

COSTS AND FINANCIAL AID

Annual in-state tuition $6,450. Annual out-of-state tuition $18,900. Required fees $310. Average book expense $950. **Required Forms and Deadlines:** FAFSA, Institution's own financial aid form. **Notification of Awards:** Applicants will be notified of awards on or about 4/1. **Types of Aid:** *Need-based scholarships/grants:* Federal Pell, FSEOG, State scholarships/grants, Private scholarships, College/university scholarship or grant aid from institutional funds. *Loans:* Federal Perkins Loans, Federal Nursing Loans, State Loans. *Student Employment:* Federal Work-Study Program available. Institutional employment available. **Financial Aid Statistics:** 79% needy undergrads receive need-based scholarship or grant aid. 4% undergrads receive non-need-based scholarship or grant aid. 90% undergrads receive need-based self-help aid. 0% undergrads receive athletic scholarships. **Criteria for awarding aid:** *Non-need-based:* Academics, Leadership, Minority status.

UNIVERSITY OF NEVADA, LAS VEGAS

4505 Maryland Parkway, Las Vegas, NV 89154-1021
Phone: 702-774-8658
E-mail: admissions@unlv.edu • **CEEB Code:** 4861
Fax: 702-774-8008 • **Website:** www.unlv.edu • **ACT Code:** 2496

This public school was founded in 1957. It has a 337-acre campus.

RATINGS

Admissions Selectivity Rating: 78   **Fire Safety Rating:** 60*   **Green Rating:** 60*

STUDENTS AND FACULTY

Enrollment: 23,329. **Student Body:** 56% female, 44% male, 11% out-of-state, 4% international (84 countries represented). Asian 15%, African American 8%, Caucasian 35%, Hispanic 26%, Native American <1%, Pacific Islander 1%, Two or more races 9%, Race unknown 1%.
Retention and Graduation: 74% freshmen return for sophomore year. 13% freshmen graduate within 4 years. 41% freshmen graduate within 6 years.
Faculty: Student/faculty ratio 20:1. 776 full-time faculty, 90% hold PhDs, 18% are are members of minority groups, 33% are women. 11% of classes are taught by teaching assistants.

ACADEMICS

Degrees: bachelor's, certificate, doctoral/professional, doctoral/research, master's, postbachelor's certificate, post-master's certificate. **Classes:** Most classes have 20-29 students. Most lab/discussion sessions have 20-29 students.

Most popular majors: Elementary Education and Teaching; Psychology; Hospitality Administration/Management. **Special Study Options:** Accelerated program, cooperative education program, cross-registration, distance learning, double major, dual enrollment, English as a Second Language (ESL), exchange student program (domestic), honors program, independent study, internships, student-designed major, study abroad, teacher certification program. Combined degree programs: interdisciplinary program in environmental science. **Disability Services:** Special programs offered to physically disabled students, including note-taking services, reader services, tape recorders, tutors. **Career Services:** Alumni network, Alumni services, Career/job search classes, Career assessment, Internships, Regional alumni.

FACILITIES

Housing: Coed dorms. **Special Academic Facilities/Equipment:** Art galleries, national supercomputing center for energy and environment, natural history museum, arboretum, 3 theaters, concert hall, law school, dental school, gaming institute, professional practice school for teachers. **Computers:** Students can register for classes online. Administrative functions (other than registration) can be performed online.

CAMPUS LIFE

Environment: Metropolis. **Activities:** Choral groups, concert band, dance, drama/theater, jazz band, literary magazine, marching band, music ensembles, musical theater, opera, pep band, radio station, student government, student newspaper, student-run film society, symphony orchestra, television station 24 honor societies, 14 religious organizations. 8 fraternities, 6 sororities. **Athletics (Intercollegiate):** *Men:* baseball, basketball, football, golf, soccer, swimming, tennis. *Women:* basketball, cross-country, equestrian sports, golf, soccer, softball, swimming, tennis, track/field (outdoor), volleyball. **On-Campus Highlights:** Lied Library, Artemus W. Ham Concert Hall, Moyer Student Union, Judy Bailey Theatre, Student Services Complex, Thomas and Mack and Cox Pavilion Event Centers, Lied Athletic Complex, Tonopah Residence Complex.

ADMISSIONS

Freshman Academic Profile: Average high school GPA 3.3. 23% in top 10% of high school class, 52% in top 25% of high school class, 82% in top 50% of high school class. **Reported SAT (pre-2016 redesign) scores:** SAT Math middle 50% range 450-560. SAT Critical Reading middle 50% range 440-560. SAT Writing middle 50% range 420-530. **Concordant SAT scores:** SAT EBRW middle 50% 480–600. SAT Math middle 50% range 490–580. ACT middle 50% range 18-25. Minimum paper TOEFL 500. **Basis for Candidate Selection:** *Very important factors considered include:* rigor of secondary school record, academic GPA. *Important factors considered include:* standardized test scores. **Freshman Admission Requirements:** High school diploma is required and GED is accepted. *Academic units required:* 4 English, 3 math, 3 science, 2 science labs, 3 social studies. **Freshman Admission Statistics:** 7,666 applied, 88.46% admitted, 56% enrolled. **Transfer Admission Requirements:** college transcript(s), Minimum college GPA of 2.0 required. Lowest grade transferable D-. **General Admission Information:** Priority deadline 2/1. Regular application deadline 7/1. Regular notification 7/1. Nonfall registration accepted. Admission may be deferred for a maximum of 1 year.

COSTS AND FINANCIAL AID

Average book expense $1,224. **Required Forms and Deadlines:** FAFSA. **Types of Aid:** *Need-based scholarships/grants:* Federal Pell, FSEOG, State scholarships/grants, Private scholarships, College/university scholarship or grant aid from institutional funds. *Loans:* Direct Subsidized Stafford Loans, Direct Unsubsidized Stafford Loans, Direct PLUS loans, Federal Nursing Loans, College/university loans from institutional funds. *Student Employment:* Federal Work-Study Program available. Institutional employment available. **Financial Aid Statistics:** 64% needy freshmen, 67% needy undergrads receive need-based scholarship or grant aid. 77% freshmen, 48% undergrads receive non-need-based scholarship or grant aid. 84% freshmen, 90% undergrads receive need-based self-help aid. 2% freshmen, 2% undergrads receive athletic scholarships. 41% undergrads borrow to pay for school. Average cumulative indebtedness $24,891. **Criteria for awarding aid:** *Need-based:* Academics, Alumni affiliation. *Non-need-based:* Academics, Alumni affiliation, Athletics, Music/drama.

UNIVERSITY OF NEW ENGLAND

11 Hills Beach Road, Biddeford, ME 04005-9599
Phone: 207-602-2297 • **Financial Aid Phone:** 207-602-2342
E-mail: admissions@une.edu • **CEEB Code:** 3751
Fax: 207-602-5900 • **Website:** www.une.edu • **ACT Code:** 3751

This private school was founded in 1831. It has a 550-acre campus.

RATINGS

Admissions Selectivity Rating: 78   **Fire Safety Rating:** 89   **Green Rating:** 92

STUDENTS AND FACULTY

Enrollment: 2,374. **Student Body:** 73% female, 27% male, 70% out-of-state, 1% international (8 countries represented). Asian 4%, African American 1%, Caucasian 83%, Hispanic <1%, Native American <1%, Pacific Islander 0%, Two or more races 1%, Race unknown 10%.
Retention and Graduation: 81% freshmen return for sophomore year. 53% freshmen graduate within 4 years. 59% freshmen graduate within 6 years.
Faculty: Student/faculty ratio 13:1. 271 full-time faculty, 73% hold PhDs, 8% are members of minority groups, 54% are women. 0% of classes are taught by teaching assistants.

ACADEMICS

Degrees: bachelor's, certificate, diploma, doctoral/professional, doctoral/research, master's, postbachelor's certifiate, post-master's certificate. **Classes:** Most classes have 10-19 students. Most lab/discussion sessions have 20-29 students. **Most popular majors:** Biomedical Sciences; Registered Nursing/Registered Nurse; Kinesiology and Exercise Science. **Special Study Options:** cross-registration, distance learning, double major, English as a Second Language (ESL), honors program, independent study, internships, student-designed major, study abroad, teacher certification program, Advanced standing options are available for qualified undergraduates to both our Physician Assistant and Doctor of Osteopathic Medicine graduate programs. **Honors Programs:** The College of Arts and Sciences offers and honors program to qualified applicants. **Disability Services:** Special programs offered to physically disabled students, including note-taking services, reader services, tutors. **Career Services:** Alumni network, Alumni services, Career/job search classes, Career assessment, Internships. National Clinical Placements. Speciality Career Fairs—Dental Medicine, Pharmacy Health Professions.

FACILITIES

Housing: Coed dorms, women's dorms. **Special Academic Facilities/Equipment:** Payson Art Gallery; Maine Women Writers Collection; Marine Science Education and Research Center; Marine Animal Rehabilitation Center (MARC); Performance Enhancement and Evaluation Center for health sciences (PEEC); Center for Health Ethics, Law and Policy; Center for Transcultural Health; and New England Institute of Cognitive Science and Evolutionary Psychology. **Computers:** Students can register for classes online.

CAMPUS LIFE

Environment: Village. **Activities:** Choral groups, dance, literary magazine, music ensembles, student government, student newspaper, yearbook. 36 registered organizations, 3 honor societies, 1 religious organization. **Athletics (Intercollegiate):** *Men:* basketball, cross-country, golf, lacrosse, soccer. *Women:* basketball, cross-country, field hockey, golf, lacrosse, soccer, softball, swimming, volleyball. **On-Campus Highlights:** Marine Science and Research Center, Alfond Health Science Center, UNE Beach (on Atlantic Ocean and Saco River), The Point Picnic Area, Campus Center.

ADMISSIONS

Freshman Academic Profile: Average high school GPA 3.3. **Reported SAT (pre-2016 redesign) scores:** SAT Math middle 50% range 470-580. SAT Critical Reading middle 50% range 470-570. **Concordant SAT scores:** SAT Math middle 50% range 510–600. Minimum paper TOEFL 550. **Basis for Candidate Selection:** *Very important factors considered include:* rigor of secondary school record, academic GPA. *Important factors considered include:* class rank. *Other factors considered include:* standardized test scores, application essay, recommendation(s), extracurricular activities, talent/ability, character/personal qualities, alumni/ae relation, geographical residence, volunteer work, work experience, level of applicant's interest. **Freshman Admission Requirements:** High school diploma is required and GED is accepted. *Academic units required:* 4 English, 3 math, 3 science, 2 science labs, 2 social studies, 2 history. *Academic units recommended:* 4 math, 4 science, 3 science labs, 2 foreign language, 4 social studies, 4 history, 4 academic electives. **Freshman Admission Statistics:** 4,883 applied, 83.06% admitted,

18% enrolled. **Transfer Admission Requirements:** college transcript(s), Minimum college GPA of 2.0 required. Lowest grade transferable C-. **General Admission Information:** Application fee $40. Priority deadline 12/1. Nonfall registration accepted. Admission may be deferred.

COSTS AND FINANCIAL AID
Annual tuition $34,380. Room and board $13,250. Required fees $1,250. Average book expense $1,400. **Required Forms and Deadlines:** FAFSA. **Notification of Awards:** Applicants will be notified of awards on a rolling basis beginning 3/15. *Student Employment:* Federal Work-Study Program available. Institutional employment available. **Financial Aid Statistics:** 98% freshmen, 98% undergrads receive any aid.

See page 1082.

UNIVERSITY OF NEW HAMPSHIRE

Best Colleges

UNH Office of Admissions, Durham, NH 3824
Phone: 603-862-1360 • **Financial Aid Phone:** 603-862-3600
E-mail: admissions@unh.edu • **CEEB Code:** 3918
Fax: 603-862-0077 • **Website:** www.unh.edu • **ACT Code:** 2524

This public school was founded in 1866. It has a 2600-acre campus.

RATINGS
Admissions Selectivity Rating: 81   **Fire Safety Rating:** 98   **Green Rating:** 99

STUDENTS AND FACULTY
Enrollment: 12,653. **Student Body:** 55% female, 45% male, 52% out-of-state, 3% international (34 countries represented). Asian 2%, African American 1%, Caucasian 81%, Hispanic 3%, Native American <1%, Pacific Islander <1%, Two or more races 2%, Race unknown 6%.
Retention and Graduation: 86% freshmen return for sophomore year. 66% freshmen graduate within 4 years. 77% freshmen graduate within 6 years. 21% grads go on to further study within 1 year. 31% grads pursue arts and sciences degrees. 1% grads pursue law degrees. 6% grads pursue business degrees. 1% grads pursue medical degrees. **Faculty:** Student/faculty ratio 18:1. 644 full-time faculty, 88% hold PhDs, 15% are are members of minority groups, 44% are women. 1% of classes are taught by teaching assistants.

ACADEMICS
Degrees: associate, bachelor's, doctoral/professional, doctoral/research, doctoral, master's, postbachelor's certificate, post-master's certificate, terminal. **Classes:** Most classes have 10-19 students. Most lab/discussion sessions have 20-29 students. **Most popular majors:** Psychology; Business Administration and Management; Biomedical Sciences. **Special Study Options:** Accelerated program, cooperative education program, cross-registration, distance learning, double major, English as a Second Language (ESL), exchange student program (domestic), honors program, independent study, internships, student-designed major, study abroad, teacher certification program, weekend college, Research/Creative Projects, Learning Communities, Experiential Learning, Senior Capstone, Service Learning, Work Study, Honors. **Honors Programs:** The UNH honors program offers small and dynamic classes, opportunities for research and study overseas, individualized advising and a close and supportive community. Combined degree programs: BA/MA, BS/MS OT, BS/MBA, BS/MS Accounting, BA/BS/MEd, BS/MS Biochemistry, BSW/MSW, MSKin/MSW, MBA/JD, JD/MSW, BA/JD. **Disability Services:** Special programs offered to physically disabled students, including note-taking services, reader services, tape recorders, tutors. **Career Services:** Alumni network, Alumni services, Career/job search classes, Career assessment, Internships, Regional alumni. Variety of internship and job shadowing experiences; UNH Pathways Program. UNH's Washington Internship Program through the Washington Internship Program allows UNH students to earn academic credit while working and living in Washington, DC. Recent internships for UNH students have included the US Senate, State Department, US Attorney Generals Office, Environmental Protection Agency, Smithsonian Museum, public interest law firms, lobbyists, and non-profit organizations.

FACILITIES
Housing: Coed dorms, special housing for international students, fraternity/sorority housing, apartments for married students, apartments for single students, Theme Housing. There are 11 theme dorms for only freshman and 11 others for all students. Four "small halls" of 45 to 50 people in mostly single rooms are also available. 88% of campus accessible to physically diasbled. **Special Academic Facilities/Equipment:** Journalism laboratory, Milne

Special Collections Archives and Museum, optical observatory, marine research laboratory, experiential learning center, child development center,language lab, art gallery, agricultural and equine facilities, electron microscope, sawmill, nature preserves and trails, survey center, radio station **Computers:** 5% of classrooms, 100% of dorms, 100% of libraries, 100% of student union, 2% of common outdoor areas have wireless network access. Students can register for classes online. Administrative functions (other than registration) can be performed online.

CAMPUS LIFE
Environment: Village. **Activities:** Choral groups, concert band, dance, drama/theater, jazz band, literary magazine, marching band, music ensembles, musical theater, pep band, radio station, student government, student newspaper, student-run film society, symphony orchestra, television station, yearbook, Campus Ministries, Student Organization, Model UN. 187 registered organizations, 18 honor societies, 10 religious organizations. 10 fraternities, 7 sororities. **Athletics (Intercollegiate):** *Men:* basketball, cross-country, football, ice hockey, skiing (downhill/alpine), skiing (nordic/cross-country), soccer, track/field (outdoor), track/field (indoor). *Women:* basketball, cross-country, diving, field hockey, gymnastics, ice hockey, lacrosse, skiing (downhill/alpine), skiing (nordic/cross-country), soccer, swimming, track/field (outdoor), track/field (indoor), volleyball. **On-Campus Highlights:** Dimond Library, Whittemore Center, Hamel Recreation Center, Student Union/Holloway Commons, College Woods, Other spots include Dairy Bar/Train Station, Art Gallery, Thompson Hall, Morse Hall. **Environmental Initiatives:** 1. The UNH USustainability Academy (UNHSA) is the oldest endowed sustainability program in higher education in the U.S. and has worked with the larger campus community over nearly 15 years to develop UNH unique sustainable learning community model and to foster sustainability locally, statewide, and regionally. www. sustainableunh.unh.edu

ADMISSIONS
Freshman Academic Profile: Average high school GPA 3.5. 19% in top 10% of high school class, 50% in top 25% of high school class, 88% in top 50% of high school class. 80% from public high schools. **Reported SAT (pre-2016 redesign) scores:** SAT Math middle 50% range 500-610. SAT Critical Reading middle 50% range 490-590. SAT Writing middle 50% range 490-590. **Concordant SAT scores:** SAT EBRW middle 50% 550–650. SAT Math middle 50% range 530–630. ACT middle 50% range 22-27. Minimum internet-based TOEFL 80. Minimum paper TOEFL 550. **Basis for Candidate Selection:** *Very important factors considered include:* rigor of secondary school record, class rank, academic GPA. *Important factors considered include:* recommendation(s). *Other factors considered include:* standardized test scores, application essay, extracurricular activities, talent/ability, character/personal qualities, first generation, alumni/ae relation, geographical residence, state residency, racial/ethnic status, volunteer work, work experience. **Freshman Admission Requirements:** High school diploma is required and GED is accepted. *Academic units required:* 4 English, 3 math, 3 science, 2 science labs, 2 foreign language, 3 social studies. *Academic units recommended:* 4 English, 4 math, 4 science, 3 science labs, 3 foreign language, 3 social studies, 1 visual/performing arts. **Freshman Admission Statistics:** 20,173 applied, 75.97% admitted, 19% enrolled. **Transfer Admission Requirements:** High school transcript, college transcript(s), essay or personal statement, interview, standardized test scores, Minimum college GPA of 2.8 required. Lowest grade transferable C. **General Admission Information:** Application fee $50. Regular application deadline 2/1. Nonfall registration accepted. Admission may be deferred for a maximum of 1 year.

COSTS AND FINANCIAL AID
Annual in-state tuition $14,410. Annual out-of-state tuition $28,210. Room and board $10,938. Required fees $3,214. Average book expense $1,200. **Required Forms and Deadlines:** FAFSA. **Notification of Awards:** Applicants will be notified of awards on a rolling basis beginning 3/1. **Types of Aid:** *Need-based scholarships/grants:* Federal Pell, FSEOG, State scholarships/grants, Private scholarships, College/university scholarship or grant aid from institutional funds. *Loans:* Direct Subsidized Stafford Loans, Direct Unsubsidized Stafford Loans, Direct PLUS loans, Federal Perkins Loans. *Student Employment:* Federal Work-Study Program available. Institutional employment available. **Financial Aid Statistics:** 75% needy freshmen, 71% needy undergrads receive need-based scholarship or grant aid. 8% freshmen, 6% undergrads receive non-need-based scholarship or grant aid. 95% freshmen, 96% undergrads receive need-based self-help aid. 1% freshmen, 2% undergrads receive athletic scholarships. 88% freshmen, 80% undergrads receive any aid. 79% undergrads borrow to pay for school. Average cumulative indebtedness $38,799. **Criteria for awarding aid:** *Need-based:* Academics, Alumni affiliation, Art, Athletics, Minority status. *Non-need-based:* Academics, Art, Athletics, Leadership, Music/drama.

UNIVERSITY OF NEW HAVEN

300 Boston Post Road, West Haven, CT 6516
Phone: 203-932-7319 • **Financial Aid Phone:** 203-932-7315
E-mail: admissions@newhaven.edu • **CEEB Code:** 3663
Fax: 203-931-6093 • **Website:** www.newhaven.edu • **ACT Code:** 576

This private school was founded in 1920. It has a 78-acre campus.

RATINGS

Admissions Selectivity Rating: 78   **Fire Safety Rating:** 60*   **Green Rating:** 60*

STUDENTS AND FACULTY

Enrollment: 4,850. **Student Body:** 50% female, 50% male, 57% out-of-state, 8% international (25 countries represented). Asian 3%, African American 11%, Caucasian 62%, Hispanic 10%, Native American <1%, Pacific Islander <1%, Two or more races 2%, Race unknown 5%.
Retention and Graduation: 80% freshmen return for sophomore year. 45% freshmen graduate within 4 years. 56% freshmen graduate within 6 years.
Faculty: Student/faculty ratio 16:1. 262 full-time faculty, 82% hold PhDs, 23% are are members of minority groups, 34% are women.

ACADEMICS

Degrees: associate, bachelor's, certificate, doctoral/research, master's, postbachelor's certificate, post-master's certificate. **Classes:** Most classes have 10-19 students. Most lab/discussion sessions have 10-19 students. **Most popular majors:** Criminal Justice/Law Enforcement Administration; Forensic Science and Technology; Psychology. **Special Study Options:** Accelerated program, cooperative education program, cross-registration, double major, dual enrollment, English as a Second Language (ESL), honors program, independent study, internships, student-designed major, study abroad. Combined degree programs: BS/MS in Environmental Science. **Disability Services:** Special programs offered to physically disabled students, including note-taking services, reader services, tape recorders, tutors. **Career Services:** Alumni network, Alumni services, Career/job search classes, Career assessment, Internships. Each graduating student must complete at least one Experiential Education opportunity as part of his or her academic program. Experiential Education allows students to relate academic learning to practical experience. The Experiential Education requirement allows students the opportunity to explore career options through work-integrated learning, contribute to original research through faculty- mentored research opportunities, impact the community while advancing learning objectives through academic service learning, or broaden their understanding of our global society through study abroad opportunities.

FACILITIES

Housing: Coed dorms, apartments for single students. **Special Academic Facilities/Equipment:** Art gallery, forensic science lab,radio station, tv station, theater Orchestra New England, music and sound recording studio.

CAMPUS LIFE

Environment: Village. **Activities:** Choral groups, dance, drama/theater, music ensembles, musical theater, pep band, radio station, student government, student newspaper, television station, yearbook. 50 registered organizations, 5 honor societies, 1 religious organization. 2 fraternities, 3 sororities. **Athletics (Intercollegiate):** *Men:* baseball, basketball, cross-country, golf, lacrosse, soccer, track/field (outdoor), track/field (indoor), volleyball. *Women:* basketball, cheerleading, cross-country, lacrosse, soccer, softball, tennis, volleyball. **On-Campus Highlights:** Bartel's Student Union, Student Run Dance Hall, Coffe Shop.

ADMISSIONS

Freshman Academic Profile: Average high school GPA 3.4. 14% in top 10% of high school class, 41% in top 25% of high school class, 76% in top 50% of high school class. **Reported SAT (pre-2016 redesign) scores:** SAT Math middle 50% range 460-570. SAT Critical Reading middle 50% range 470-570. SAT Writing middle 50% range 450-560. **Concordant SAT scores:** SAT EBRW middle 50% 510–620. SAT Math middle 50% range 500–590. ACT middle 50% range 20-26. Minimum internet-based TOEFL 80. **Basis for Candidate Selection:** *Very important factors considered include:* academic GPA, standardized test scores. *Important factors considered include:* application essay, recommendation(s). *Other factors considered include:* rigor of secondary school record, interview, extracurricular activities, character/personal qualities, volunteer work, work experience, level of applicant's interest. **Freshman Admission Requirements:** High school diploma is required and GED is

accepted. *Academic units recommended:* 4 English, 3 math, 3 science, 2 science labs, 2 foreign language, 3 social studies. **Freshman Admission Statistics:** 10,720 applied, 80.53% admitted, 13% enrolled. **Transfer Admission Requirements:** High school transcript, college transcript(s), Minimum college GPA of 2.5 required. Lowest grade transferable C. **General Admission Information:** Application fee $50. Priority deadline 3/1. Nonfall registration accepted.

COSTS AND FINANCIAL AID

Annual tuition $35,700. Room and board $15,130. Required fees $1,360. Average book expense $1,000. **Required Forms and Deadlines:** FAFSA. **Notification of Awards:** Applicants will be notified of awards on a rolling basis beginning 3/1. **Types of Aid:** *Need-based scholarships/grants:* Federal Pell, FSEOG, State scholarships/grants, Private scholarships, College/university scholarship or grant aid from institutional funds. *Loans:* Direct Subsidized Stafford Loans, Direct Unsubsidized Stafford Loans, Direct PLUS loans, Federal Perkins Loans. *Student Employment:* Federal Work-Study Program available. Institutional employment available. **Financial Aid Statistics:** 100% needy freshmen, 100% needy undergrads receive need-based scholarship or grant aid. 12% freshmen, 12% undergrads receive non-need-based scholarship or grant aid. 82% freshmen, 81% undergrads receive need-based self-help aid. 1% freshmen, 1% undergrads receive athletic scholarships. 80% undergrads borrow to pay for school. Average cumulative indebtedness $46,449. **Criteria for awarding aid:** *Non-need-based:* Academics, Art, Athletics.

See page 1084.

UNIVERSITY OF NEW MEXICO

Office of Admissions, Albuquerque, NM 86131
Phone: 505-277-2446 • **Financial Aid Phone:** 505-277-8900
E-mail: apply@unm.edu • **CEEB Code:** 4845
Fax: 505-277-6686 • **Website:** www.unm.edu • **ACT Code:** 2650

This public school was founded in 1889. It has a 769-acre campus.

RATINGS

Admissions Selectivity Rating: 90   **Fire Safety Rating:** 80   **Green Rating:** 60*

STUDENTS AND FACULTY

Enrollment: 19,648. **Student Body:** 55% female, 45% male, 7% out-of-state, 2% international (92 countries represented). Asian 4%, African American 2%, Caucasian 34%, Hispanic 47%, Native American 6%, Pacific Islander <1%, Two or more races 3%, Race unknown 1%.
Retention and Graduation: 80% freshmen return for sophomore year. 17% freshmen graduate within 4 years. 44% freshmen graduate within 6 years.
Faculty: Student/faculty ratio 20:1. 1,033 full-time faculty, 73% hold PhDs, 26% are are members of minority groups, 48% are women.

ACADEMICS

Degrees: associate, bachelor's, certificate, doctoral/professional, doctoral/research, master's, postbachelor's certificate, post-master's certificate. **Classes:** Most classes have 10-19 students. Most lab/discussion sessions have 10-19 students. **Most popular majors:** Biology/Biological Sciences; Psychology; Business Administration and Management. **Special Study Options:** Accelerated program, cooperative education program, distance learning, double major, dual enrollment, English as a Second Language (ESL), exchange student program (domestic), honors program, independent study, internships, student-designed major, study abroad, teacher certification program, weekend college. **Honors Programs:** The University Honors Program offers the chance to explore major contemporary ideas and values in small interdisciplinary seminars with the additional benefits of personal interaction with outstanding UNM faculty, opportunities for upper-division independent research, social and cultural events, lecture series, and opportunities to participate in regional and national honors conferences. UHP students do not major in University Honors. They graduate with a degree from one of UNM's degree-granting colleges or schools. Combined degree programs: BA/MD, 3-2 Latin American Studies/ mba. **Disability Services:** Special programs offered to physically disabled students, including note-taking services, reader services, tape recorders, tutors. **Career Services:** Alumni network, Alumni services, Career/job search classes, Career assessment, Internships, Regional alumni.

FACILITIES

Housing: Coed dorms, fraternity/sorority housing, apartments for married students, apartments for single students, Special living options include graduate and senior housing,academic floors,scholars wing,and outdoor/wellness units. Computer Science and Engineering unit also available. 100% of campus accessible to physically diasbled. **Special Academic Facilities/Equipment:** Museums of art, anthropology, geology, and Southwestern biology, lithography institute, meteoritics institute, electron and electron scanning microscopes, nuclear reactor, robotics lab, observatory, planetarium, Science and Technology Park. **Computers:** 100% of classrooms, 100% of dorms, 100% of libraries, 100% of dining areas, 100% of student union, 85% of common outdoor areas have wireless network access. Students can register for classes online. Administrative functions (other than registration) can be performed online.

CAMPUS LIFE

Environment: Metropolis. **Activities:** Choral groups, concert band, dance, drama/theater, jazz band, literary magazine, marching band, music ensembles, musical theater, opera, pep band, radio station, student government, student newspaper, student-run film society, symphony orchestra, television station 375 registered organizations, 20 honor societies, 23 religious organizations. 9 fraternities, 10 sororities. **Athletics (Intercollegiate):** *Men:* baseball, basketball, cross-country, football, golf, skiing (downhill/alpine), skiing (nordic/cross-country), soccer, tennis, track/field (outdoor), track/field (indoor). *Women:* basketball, cross-country, diving, golf, skiing (downhill/alpine), skiing (nordic/cross-country), soccer, softball, swimming, tennis, track/field (outdoor), track/field (indoor), volleyball. **On-Campus Highlights:** SUB (Student Union Building), Duck Pond, Zimmerman Library, Popejoy Hall—Performing Arts Center, Residency Halls, Maxwell Museum, Trolly Tour of Campus for new and prospective students. **Environmental Initiatives:** In November 2009 UNM submitted its first Climate Action Plan to the American College and University Presidents Climate Commitment website and set a climate neutrality target date of year 2050. UNM will use a multi-tiered approach to reducing our greenhouse gas emissions. The tiers are behavior-based energy conservation, technological improvements in utilities production and consumption, renewable energy, and alternative transportation.

ADMISSIONS

Freshman Academic Profile: Average high school GPA 3.4. **Reported SAT (pre-2016 redesign) scores:** SAT Math middle 50% range 470-600. SAT Critical Reading middle 50% range 480-610. **Concordant SAT scores:** SAT Math middle 50% range 510–620. ACT middle 50% range 19-25. Minimum internet-based TOEFL 68. Minimum paper TOEFL 520. **Basis for Candidate Selection:** *Very important factors considered include:* rigor of secondary school record, academic GPA. *Important factors considered include:* standardized test scores. *Other factors considered include:* application essay, extracurricular activities, talent/ability, character/personal qualities, volunteer work, work experience. **Freshman Admission Requirements:** High school diploma is required and GED is accepted. *Academic units required:* 4 English, 4 math, 3 science, 2 science labs, 2 foreign language, 2 social studies, 1 history. **Freshman Admission Statistics:** 15,266 applied, 46.84% admitted, 48% enrolled. **Transfer Admission Requirements:** college transcript(s), Minimum college GPA of 2.0 required. Lowest grade transferable C. **General Admission Information:** Application fee $20. Priority deadline 5/1. Nonfall registration accepted. Admission may be deferred.

COSTS AND FINANCIAL AID

Annual in-state tuition $5,157. Annual out-of-state tuition $20,048. Room and board $8,690. Required fees $1,507. Average book expense $1,064. **Required Forms and Deadlines:** FAFSA. **Notification of Awards:** Applicants will be notified of awards on a rolling basis beginning 4/15. **Types of Aid:** *Need-based scholarships/grants:* Federal Pell, FSEOG, State scholarships/grants, Private scholarships, College/university scholarship or grant aid from institutional funds, United Negro College Fund, Federal Nursing Scholarships. *Loans:* Direct Subsidized Stafford Loans, Direct Unsubsidized Stafford Loans, Direct PLUS loans, Federal Perkins Loans, Federal Nursing Loans, State Loans, College/university loans from institutional funds. *Student Employment:* Federal Work-Study Program available. Institutional employment available. **Criteria for awarding aid:** *Need-based:* Minority status. *Non-need-based:* Academics, Alumni affiliation, Art, Athletics, Job skills, Leadership, Minority status, Music/drama, Religious affiliation, State/district residency.

UNIVERSITY OF NEW ORLEANS

University of New Orleans PEC, New Orleans, LA 70148
Phone: 504-280-6595 • **Financial Aid Phone:** 504-280-6603
E-mail: pec@uno.edu • **CEEB Code:** 6379
Fax: 504-280-3973 • **Website:** www.uno.edu • **ACT Code:** 1591

This public school was founded in 1956. It has a 195-acre campus.

RATINGS

Admissions Selectivity Rating: 87   **Fire Safety Rating:** 89   **Green Rating:** 60*

STUDENTS AND FACULTY

Enrollment: 6,185. **Student Body:** 50% female, 50% male, 6% out-of-state, 4% international (60 countries represented). Asian 8%, African American 16%, Caucasian 54%, Hispanic 12%, Native American <1%, Pacific Islander <1%, Two or more races 4%, Race unknown 2%.
Retention and Graduation: 62% freshmen return for sophomore year. 15% freshmen graduate within 4 years. 35% freshmen graduate within 6 years.
Faculty: Student/faculty ratio 20:1. 270 full-time faculty, 66% hold PhDs, 21% are are members of minority groups, 36% are women.

ACADEMICS

Degrees: bachelor's, doctoral/research, master's, postbachelor's certificate, post-master's certificate. **Classes:** Most classes have 20-29 students. **Most popular majors:** Business Administration and Management; Multi-/Interdisciplinary Studies; Biology/Biological Sciences. **Special Study Options:** cooperative education program, cross-registration, distance learning, double major, dual enrollment, English as a Second Language (ESL), exchange student program (domestic), honors program, independent study, internships, student-designed major, study abroad, teacher certification program, weekend college. **Disability Services:** Special programs offered to physically disabled students, including note-taking services, reader services, tape recorders, tutors. **Career Services:** Alumni network, Alumni services, Career/job search classes, Career assessment, Internships, Regional alumni. Career Services is most proud of the Cooperative Learning and Internships. We offer the Disney College Program, Inroads and other Internship and Cooperative Learning experiences that have afforded our students life changing opportunities in the professional realm.

FACILITIES

Housing: Coed dorms, special housing for disabled students, apartments for married students, apartments for single students. 100% of campus accessible to physically diasbled. **Special Academic Facilities/Equipment:** Performing arts center, audiovisual center, TV studio, Eisenhower leadership studies center, child care center, Louisiana collection. **Computers:** 100% of libraries, 100% of student union, have wireless network access. Students can register for classes online. Administrative functions (other than registration) can be performed online.

CAMPUS LIFE

Environment: Metropolis. **Activities:** Choral groups, concert band, dance, drama/theater, jazz band, literary magazine, music ensembles, musical theater, opera, pep band, radio station, student government, student newspaper, student-run film society, Campus Ministries, Student Organization. 120 registered organizations, 7 religious organizations. 9 fraternities, 8 sororities. **Athletics (Intercollegiate):** *Men:* baseball, basketball, diving, golf, swimming, tennis. *Women:* basketball, diving, swimming, tennis, volleyball. **On-Campus Highlights:** Recreation and Fitness Center, The University Center, The Homer L. Hitt Alumni and Visitors Ce, Earl K. Long Library

ADMISSIONS

Freshman Academic Profile: Average high school GPA 3.1. 14% in top 10% of high school class, 32% in top 25% of high school class, 60% in top 50% of high school class. **Reported SAT (pre-2016 redesign) scores:** SAT Math middle 50% range 480-630. SAT Critical Reading middle 50% range 460-600. **Concordant SAT scores:** SAT Math middle 50% range 510–650. ACT middle 50% range 20-24. Minimum internet-based TOEFL 213. Minimum paper TOEFL 550. **Basis for Candidate Selection:** *Very important factors considered include:* rigor of secondary school record, academic GPA, standardized test scores. *Other factors considered include:* geographical residence, state residency. **Freshman Admission Requirements:** High school diploma is required and GED is accepted. *Academic units required:* 4 English, 4 math, 4 science, 2 foreign language, 4 social studies, 1 visual/performing arts. **Freshman Admission Statistics:** 3,932 applied, 57.66% admitted, 41% enrolled. **Transfer Admission Requirements:** college transcript(s), Minimum college GPA of 2.25 required. Lowest grade transferable D. **General**

Admission Information: Application fee $20. Priority deadline 1/15. Regular application deadline 7/25. Nonfall registration accepted.

COSTS AND FINANCIAL AID

Annual in-state tuition $6,090. Annual out-of-state tuition $6,090. Required fees $2,604. Average book expense $1,220. **Required Forms and Deadlines:** FAFSA. **Notification of Awards:** Applicants will be notified of awards on a rolling basis beginning 3/15. **Types of Aid:** *Need-based scholarships/grants:* Federal Pell, FSEOG, State scholarships/grants, Private scholarships, College/university scholarship or grant aid from institutional funds. *Loans:* Direct Subsidized Stafford Loans, Direct Unsubsidized Stafford Loans, Direct PLUS loans, Federal Perkins Loans. *Student Employment:* Federal Work-Study Program available. Institutional employment available. **Financial Aid Statistics:** 76% needy freshmen, 61% needy undergrads receive need-based scholarship or grant aid. 72% freshmen, 50% undergrads receive non-need-based scholarship or grant aid. 43% freshmen, 46% undergrads receive need-based self-help aid. 2% freshmen, 2% undergrads receive athletic scholarships. 68% freshmen, 64% undergrads receive any aid. 55% undergrads borrow to pay for school. Average cumulative indebtedness $19,861. **Criteria for awarding aid:** *Need-based:* Academics, Alumni affiliation, Art, Athletics, Job skills, Leadership, Minority status, Music/drama. *Non-need-based:* Academics, Athletics, Music/drama.

UNIVERSITY OF NORTH CAROLINA AT ASHEVILLE

CPO #1320, Asheville, NC 28804-8502
Phone: 828-251-6481 • **Financial Aid Phone:** 828-251-6481
E-mail: admissions@unca.edu • **CEEB Code:** 5013
Fax: 828-251-6482 • **Website:** www.unca.edu • **ACT Code:** 3064

This public school was founded in 1927. It has a 265-acre campus.

RATINGS
Admissions Selectivity Rating: 85   **Fire Safety Rating:** 97   **Green Rating:** 88

STUDENTS AND FACULTY

Enrollment: 3,466. **Student Body:** 57% female, 43% male, 11% out-of-state, 1% international (28 countries represented). Asian 2%, African American 4%, Caucasian 78%, Hispanic 6%, Native American <1%, Pacific Islander <1%, Two or more races 4%, Race unknown 4%.
Retention and Graduation: 78% freshmen return for sophomore year. 39% freshmen graduate within 4 years. 62% freshmen graduate within 6 years. 13% grads go on to further study within 1 year. **Faculty:** Student/faculty ratio 13:1. 224 full-time faculty, 88% hold PhDs, 17% are are members of minority groups, 46% are women. 0% of classes are taught by teaching assistants.

ACADEMICS

Degrees: bachelor's, master's, postbachelor's certificate. **Classes:** Most classes have 20-29 students. Most lab/discussion sessions have 10-19 students. **Most popular majors:** Psychology; Biology/Biological Sciences; Business Administration and Management. **Special Study Options:** cross-registration, distance learning, double major, dual enrollment, exchange student program (domestic), honors program, independent study, internships, liberal arts/career combination, student-designed major, study abroad, teacher certification program. **Honors Programs:** University Honors Program—Designed for talented and motivated students, the Honors curriculum complements the General Education and major curricula. Successful completion of the Honors Program enables the student to graduate with Distinction as a University Scholar. (See http://www.unca.edu/honors/ for further information.) Undergraduate Research Program—The Undergraduate Research Program at UNCA seeks to encourage the establishment of faculty/student research pairs who work together on a project of mutual interest. Research may be performed in any discipline on campus. Students who have made oral presentations at symposia and have had their work reviewed and published can receive recognition as University Research Scholars. (See http://www.unca.edu/urp/ for more information.) Combined degree programs: 2-2 B.S. Engineering with North Carolina State University; 3-1 B.S. Engineering in Mechatronics with North Carolina State University. **Disability Services:** Special programs offered to physically disabled students, including note-taking services, reader services, tape recorders, tutors. **Career Services:** Alumni network, Alumni services, Career/job search classes, Career assessment, Internships, Regional

alumni. The majority of our students participate in undergraduate research or an internship in their field of study before they graduate.

FACILITIES

Housing: Coed dorms, special housing for disabled students, men's dorms, women's dorms, substance-free dorms, 24 hour quiet dorms. 95% of campus accessible to physically disabled. **Special Academic Facilities/Equipment:** Undergraduate Research Center, Steelcase Teleconference Center, Music Recording Center, Asheville Botanical Gardens, NC Arboretum, Center for Creative Retirement **Computers:** 1% of classrooms, 100% of libraries, 100% of dining areas, 90% of student union, have wireless network access. Students can register for classes online. Administrative functions (other than registration) can be performed online.

CAMPUS LIFE

Environment: Town. **Activities:** Choral groups, concert band, dance, drama/theater, jazz band, literary magazine, music ensembles, musical theater, pep band, radio station, student government, student newspaper, Campus Ministries, Student Organization. 82 registered organizations, 14 honor societies, 10 religious organizations. 1 fraternity, 2 sororities. **Athletics (Intercollegiate):** *Men:* baseball, basketball, cheerleading, cross-country, soccer, tennis, track/field (outdoor). *Women:* basketball, cheerleading, cross-country, soccer, tennis, track/field (outdoor), volleyball. **On-Campus Highlights:** Health and Fitness Center, Main Campus Quadrangle, Highsmith University Union, Asheville Botanical Gardens, Cafe Ramsey in Ramsey Library. **Environmental Initiatives:** Sustainability is the priority in all campus renovation and new construction: Between 2004 and 2012, the university added four different geothermal systems for heating and cooling which serve three classroom and office buildings and the newest residence hall, while contributing to the needs of six older nearby residence halls. A ground-source heat pump system has been installed to serve another building. A solar thermal system now serves the heating/cooling and hot water systems in one office building, and the university is awaiting approval of funding to add solar panels that will serve two residence halls. Rainwater harvesting is now taking place on three locations, serving campus gardens, and toilets in three buildings. To reduce energy use in its new buildings, UNC Asheville employed designs that maximize natural light, and also installed occupancy sensors and daylighting controls. UNC Asheville follows the University of Buffalo Green Design Guidelines, with new construction stressing a high-performance building envelope and use of high-recycled-content materials. The university has opted to renovate rather than replace older buildings wherever possible, conserving embedded energy, maximizing reuse and recycling of building materials, and adding energy efficiency design features. The university has designed new buildings and renovation to LEED standards, but has not sought certification.

ADMISSIONS

Freshman Academic Profile: Average high school GPA 3.5. 20% in top 10% of high school class, 54% in top 25% of high school class, 92% in top 50% of high school class. 88% from public high schools. **Reported SAT (pre-2016 redesign) scores:** SAT Math middle 50% range 510-610. SAT Critical Reading middle 50% range 520-640. SAT Writing middle 50% range 490-590. **Concordant SAT scores:** SAT EBRW middle 50% 560–780. SAT Math middle 50% range 540–630. ACT middle 50% range 23-28. Minimum internet-based TOEFL 79. Minimum paper TOEFL 550. **Basis for Candidate Selection:** *Very important factors considered include:* rigor of secondary school record, academic GPA. *Important factors considered include:* class rank, standardized test scores, application essay, recommendation(s). *Other factors considered include:* interview, extracurricular activities, talent/ability, first generation, alumni/ae relation, geographical residence, state residency, racial/ethnic status, volunteer work, work experience, level of applicant's interest. **Freshman Admission Requirements:** High school diploma is required and GED is not accepted. *Academic units required:* 4 English, 4 math, 3 science, 1 science lab, 2 foreign language, 1 social studies, 1 history. *Academic units recommended:* 4 academic electives. **Freshman Admission Statistics:** 3,433 applied, 77.95% admitted, 25% enrolled. **Transfer Admission Requirements:** college transcript(s), Minimum college GPA of 2.50 required. Lowest grade transferable C. **General Admission Information:** Application fee $75. Priority deadline 11/15. Regular application deadline 2/15. Nonfall registration accepted. Admission may be deferred for a maximum of One Year.

COSTS AND FINANCIAL AID

Annual in-state tuition $4,041. Annual out-of-state tuition $20,436. Room and board $8,746. Required fees $2,936. Average book expense $1,200. **Required Forms and Deadlines:** FAFSA. **Notification of Awards:** Applicants will be notified of awards on a rolling basis beginning 3/1. **Types of Aid:** *Need-based scholarships/grants:* Federal Pell, FSEOG, State scholarships/grants, Private scholarships, College/university scholarship or grant aid from institutional funds. *Loans:* Direct Subsidized Stafford Loans, Direct Unsubsidized Stafford Loans, Direct PLUS loans, Federal Perkins Loans, State Loans, College/university loans from institutional funds. *Student Employment:* Federal Work-Study Program available. Institutional employment available. **Financial Aid Statistics:** 92% needy freshmen, 94% needy undergrads receive need-based scholarship or grant aid. 11% freshmen, 12% undergrads receive non-need-based scholarship or grant aid. 68% freshmen, 72% undergrads receive need-based self-help aid. 3% freshmen, 3% undergrads receive athletic scholarships. 71% freshmen, 71% undergrads receive any aid. 53% undergrads borrow to pay for school. Average cumulative indebtedness $22,026. **Criteria for awarding aid:** *Need-based:* Academics, Job skills, Leadership, Music/drama. *Non-need-based:* Academics, Alumni affiliation, Art, Athletics, Job skills, Leadership, Music/drama, State/district residency.

THE UNIVERSITY OF NORTH CAROLINA AT CHAPEL HILL

Jackson Hall, Chapel Hill, NC 27599-2200
Phone: 919-966-3621 • **Financial Aid Phone:** 919-962-8396
E-mail: unchelp@admissions.unc.edu • **CEEB Code:** 5816
Fax: 919-962-3045 • **Website:** www.unc.edu • **ACT Code:** 3162

This public school was founded in 1789. It has a 729-acre campus.

RATINGS

Admissions Selectivity Rating: 96   **Fire Safety Rating:** 97   **Green Rating:** 97

STUDENTS AND FACULTY

Enrollment: 18,207. **Student Body:** 58% female, 42% male, 17% out-of-state, 2% international (94 countries represented), Asian 10%, African American 8%, Caucasian 63%, Hispanic 8%, Native American 1%, Pacific Islander <1%, Two or more races 4%, Race unknown 4%.

Retention and Graduation: 97% freshmen return for sophomore year. 84% freshmen graduate within 4 years. 91% freshmen graduate within 6 years. 24% grads go on to further study within 1 year. 15% grads pursue arts and sciences degrees. 4% grads pursue law degrees. 2% grads pursue business degrees. 3% grads pursue medical degrees. **Faculty:** Student/faculty ratio 13:1. 1,669 full-time faculty, 86% hold PhDs, 20% are are members of minority groups, 45% are women. 20% of classes are taught by teaching assistants.

ACADEMICS

Degrees: bachelor's, certificate, doctoral/professional, doctoral/research, doctoral, master's, postbachelor's certifiate, post-master's certificate. **Classes:** Most classes have 10-19 students. Most lab/discussion sessions have 10-19 students. **Most popular majors:** Biology/Biological Sciences; Psychology; Economics. **Special Study Options:** cross-registration, distance learning, double major, dual enrollment, honors program, independent study, internships, student-designed major, study abroad, teacher certification program. **Honors Programs:** see http://www.honors.unc.edu/ Combined degree programs: BS/MSIS, BS/MSLS,BS/MSPH, BS/PharmD,BS MDS/MS Ops Research. **Disability Services:** Special programs offered to physically disabled students, including note-taking services, reader services, tape recorders. **Career Services:** Alumni network, Alumni services, Career/job search classes, Career assessment, Internships, Regional alumni. We offer eight 'meet ups' each year. During these events we bring in 20-30 professionals from a specific career interest area. We focus on fields that are difficult to break into for internships and full-time jobs. This gives students multiple opportunities to make contacts that they can follow up with to gain a 'foot in the door' in fields/industries where it is hard to find an internship/job like environmental careers, advertising, the arts, etc. We have also done these events virtually, where we have used Skype to connect students with alumni who are not local to UNC.

FACILITIES

Housing: Coed dorms, special housing for disabled students, men's dorms, special housing for international students, women's dorms, fraternity/sorority housing, apartments for married students, apartments for single students, Wellness Housing, Theme Housing, Special Options in Housing—Learning Communities such as RELIC—Religion as Explorative Learning Integrated in our Community, Language Houses, The Carolina Experience, Men@Carolina, W.E.L.L.—Women's Experiences: Learning and Leadership, Connected Learning Program, Service and Leadership, Substance Free Environments, Sustainability, UNITAS. 97% of campus accessible to physically diasbled. **Special Academic Facilities/Equipment:** Art museum, Folklore council, Institute of Folk Music, communications center, Basketball Museum, Institute of Latin American Studies, Institute of fisheries research, Sitterson Hall Computer Museum, Institute of Natural Science, Research Laboratory of Anthropology, Hayden Planetarium, Paul Green Theatre, Playmakers Theater,

Memorial Hall. **Computers:** 75% of classrooms, 15% of dorms, 100% of libraries, 100% of dining areas, 100% of student union, 50% of common outdoor areas have wireless network access. Students can register for classes online. Administrative functions (other than registration) can be performed online. Undergraduates are required to own a computer.

CAMPUS LIFE

Environment: Town. **Activities:** Choral groups, concert band, dance, drama/theater, jazz band, literary magazine, marching band, music ensembles, musical theater, opera, pep band, radio station, student government, student newspaper, student-run film society, symphony orchestra, television station, yearbook, Campus Ministries, Student Organization, Model UN. 635 registered organizations, 19 honor societies, 42 religious organizations. 35 fraternities, 23 sororities. **Athletics (Intercollegiate):** *Men:* baseball, basketball, cross-country, diving, fencing, football, golf, lacrosse, soccer, swimming, tennis, track/field (outdoor), track/field (indoor), wrestling. *Women:* basketball, crew/rowing, cross-country, diving, fencing, field hockey, golf, gymnastics, lacrosse, soccer, softball, swimming, tennis, track/field (outdoor), track/field (indoor), volleyball. **On-Campus Highlights:** The Pit, McCorkle Place, Polk Place, Dean Smith Center, Student Union, Old Well, Coker Arboretum, Morehead Planetarium, Ackland Art Museum, Kenan Stadium. **Environmental Initiatives:** Partnered with Orange (County) Water and Sewer Authority (OWASA) to install a water reclamation and reuse system that replaced 180 million gallons of potable water in FY 2015. This system reduces total daily water demand in the OWASA service territory by apx. 10%. Started in summer 2009, the system provides makeup water at campus cooling towers, irrigates athletic fields and grounds, and flushes toilets in new buildings adjacent to the distribution network.

ADMISSIONS

Freshman Academic Profile: Average high school GPA 4.7. 73% in top 10% of high school class, 91% in top 25% of high school class, 94% in top 50% of high school class. 82% from public high schools. **Reported SAT (pre-2016 redesign) scores:** SAT Math middle 50% range 600-710. SAT Critical Reading middle 50% range 590-700. SAT Writing middle 50% range 580-690. **Concordant SAT scores:** SAT EBRW middle 50% 640–730. SAT Math middle 50% range 620–740. ACT middle 50% range 27-32. Minimum internet-based TOEFL 100. Minimum paper TOEFL 600. **Basis for Candidate Selection:** *Very important factors considered include:* rigor of secondary school record, standardized test scores, application essay, recommendation(s), extracurricular activities, talent/ability, character/personal qualities, state residency. *Important factors considered include:* class rank, academic GPA, volunteer work, work experience. *Other factors considered include:* first generation, alumni/ae relation, racial/ethnic status. **Freshman Admission Requirements:** High school diploma is required and GED is not accepted. *Academic units required:* 4 English, 4 math, 3 science, 1 science lab, 2 foreign language, 1 social studies, 1 history, 1 academic elective. **Freshman Admission Statistics:** 34,889 applied, 26.94% admitted, 45% enrolled. **Transfer Admission Requirements:** High school transcript, college transcript(s), essay or personal statement, statement of good standing from prior institution(s). Minimum college GPA of 2.0 required. Lowest grade transferable C. **General Admission Information:** Application fee $80. Priority deadline 10/15. Regular application deadline 1/15. Nonfall registration not accepted. Admission may be deferred for a maximum of 1 year.

COSTS AND FINANCIAL AID

Annual in-state tuition $6,881. Annual out-of-state tuition $32,602. Room and board $11,556. Required fees $1,986. Average book expense $1,604. **Required Forms and Deadlines:** FAFSA, CSS/Financial Aid PROFILE. **Notification of Awards:** Applicants will be notified of awards on a rolling basis beginning 3/15. **Types of Aid:** *Need-based scholarships/grants:* Federal Pell, FSEOG, State scholarships/grants, Private scholarships, College/university scholarship or grant aid from institutional funds. *Loans:* Direct Subsidized Stafford Loans, Direct Unsubsidized Stafford Loans, Direct PLUS loans, Federal Perkins Loans, State Loans, College/university loans from institutional funds. *Student Employment:* Federal Work-Study Program available. Institutional employment available. **Financial Aid Statistics:** 93% needy freshmen, 91% needy undergrads receive need-based scholarship or grant aid. 6% freshmen, 4% undergrads receive non-need-based scholarship or grant aid. 66% freshmen, 73% undergrads receive need-based self-help aid. 2% freshmen, 2% undergrads receive athletic scholarships. 67% freshmen, 63% undergrads receive any aid. Average cumulative indebtedness $20,127. **Criteria for awarding aid:** *Need-based:* Academics, Leadership. *Non-need-based:* Academics, Alumni affiliation, Art, Athletics, Leadership, Music/drama, Religious affiliation, State/district residency.

UNIVERSITY OF NORTH CAROLINA AT CHARLOTTE

9201 University City Boulevard, Charlotte, NC 28223-0001
Phone: 704-687-5507 • **Financial Aid Phone:** 704-687-5504
E-mail: admissions@uncc.edu • **CEEB Code:** 5105
Fax: 704-687-6483 • **Website:** www.uncc.edu • **ACT Code:** 3163

This public school was founded in 1946. It has a 1000-acre campus.

RATINGS

Admissions Selectivity Rating: 85 **Fire Safety Rating:** 94 **Green Rating:** 86

STUDENTS AND FACULTY

Enrollment: 23,246. **Student Body:** 47% female, 53% male, 5% out-of-state, 2% international (85 countries represented). Asian 6%, African American 16%, Caucasian 59%, Hispanic 9%, Native American <1%, Pacific Islander <1%, Two or more races 4%, Race unknown 3%.
Retention and Graduation: 82% freshmen return for sophomore year. 28% freshmen graduate within 4 years. 57% freshmen graduate within 6 years.
Faculty: Student/faculty ratio 19:1. 1,149 full-time faculty, 84% hold PhDs, 18% are are members of minority groups, 47% are women. 2% of classes are taught by teaching assistants.

ACADEMICS

Degrees: bachelor's, doctoral/professional, doctoral/research, doctoral, master's, postbachelor's certificate, post-master's certificate. **Classes:** Most classes have 20-29 students. Most lab/discussion sessions have 10-19 students. **Most popular majors:** Business Administration and Management; Psychology; Speech Communication and Rhetoric. **Special Study Options:** Accelerated program, cooperative education program, cross-registration, distance learning, double major, dual enrollment, English as a Second Language (ESL), honors program, independent study, internships, study abroad, teacher certification program, weekend college, Wilderness Exploration Program. **Disability Services:** Special programs offered to physically disabled students, including note-taking services, reader services, tape recorders, tutors. **Career Services:** Alumni network, Alumni services, Career/job search classes, Career assessment, Internships, Regional alumni. We are most proud of the co-op program. Co-op provides the richest experience for students since they get more long-term exposure to a company and, for College of Engineering students specifically, they have the added benefit of earning time towards their Professional Engineering license, if they choose. It also provides up to 3 credits with the seminar course after each rotation which is a nice incentive that the 49ership program (non-academic credit internships) does not offer. There is more accountability for the co-op program since the students must work with a co-op advisor for their major. We also think that hiring managers value co-op experience more than internship experience since co-ops allow the student to gain more responsibility and a lengthier experience.

FACILITIES

Housing: Coed dorms, special housing for disabled students, special housing for international students, women's dorms, fraternity/sorority housing, apartments for single students, Rooms for students with disabilities limited, apply early. Graduate and older non-traditional student housing and substance free housing available upon request. 90% of campus accessible to physically disabled. **Special Academic Facilities/Equipment:** Urban studies and community service institute, mock court room, applied research center, language lab, 63-acre ecological reserve, botanical and horticultural complex, tropical rainforest conservatory. **Computers:** 10% of classrooms, 10% of dorms, 30% of libraries, 70% of dining areas, 30% of student union, 10% of common outdoor areas have wireless network access. Students can register for classes online. Administrative functions (other than registration) can be performed online.

CAMPUS LIFE

Environment: Metropolis. **Activities:** Choral groups, concert band, dance, drama/theater, jazz band, literary magazine, music ensembles, musical theater, opera, pep band, student government, student newspaper, television station, yearbook, Campus Ministries. 222 registered organizations, 25 honor societies, 22 religious organizations. 14 fraternities, 10 sororities. **Athletics (Intercollegiate):** *Men:* baseball, basketball, cross-country, golf, soccer, tennis, track/field (outdoor). *Women:* basketball, cross-country, soccer, softball, tennis, track/field (outdoor), volleyball. **On-Campus Highlights:** Bonnie E. Cone University Center, James H. Barnhardt Student Activity Center, J. Murrey Atkins Library, UNCC Botanical Gardens and Greenhouse, Ritazza Coffee Shop, After Hours at the Rathskeller, Robinson Hall Theatre. **Environmental Initiatives:** Energy and Water Conservation initiatives led by a full-time Energy Manager.

ADMISSIONS

Freshman Academic Profile: Average high school GPA 4.0. 22% in top 10% of high school class, 59% in top 25% of high school class, 90% in top 50% of high school class. 86% from public high schools. **Reported SAT (pre-2016 redesign) scores:** SAT Math middle 50% range 520-610. SAT Critical Reading middle 50% range 510-590. SAT Writing middle 50% range 490-570. **Concordant SAT scores:** SAT EBRW middle 50% 560–640. SAT Math middle 50% range 550–630. ACT middle 50% range 22-26. Minimum internet-based TOEFL 70. Minimum paper TOEFL 523. **Basis for Candidate Selection:** *Very important factors considered include:* rigor of secondary school record, academic GPA, standardized test scores. *Other factors considered include:* extracurricular activities, talent/ability, character/personal qualities, geographical residence, state residency, work experience. **Freshman Admission Requirements:** High school diploma is required and GED is accepted. *Academic units required:* 4 English, 4 math, 3 science, 1 science lab, 2 foreign language, 1 social studies, 1 history. *Academic units recommended:* 3 foreign language. **Freshman Admission Statistics:** 17,475 applied, 62.19% admitted, 32% enrolled. **Transfer Admission Requirements:** High school transcript, college transcript(s), statement of good standing from prior institution(s). Minimum college GPA of 2.0 required. Lowest grade transferable C. **General Admission Information:** Application fee $60. Regular application deadline 6/1. Nonfall registration accepted.

COSTS AND FINANCIAL AID

Annual in-state tuition $3,737. Annual out-of-state tuition $16,908. Room and board $10,470. Required fees $3,026. Average book expense $1,200. **Required Forms and Deadlines:** FAFSA. **Notification of Awards:** Applicants will be notified of awards on a rolling basis beginning 3/1. **Types of Aid:** *Need-based scholarships/grants:* Federal Pell, FSEOG, State scholarships/grants, Private scholarships, College/university scholarship or grant aid from institutional funds, United Negro College Fund. *Loans:* Direct Subsidized Stafford Loans, Direct Unsubsidized Stafford Loans, Direct PLUS loans, Federal Perkins Loans, State Loans, College/university loans from institutional funds. *Student Employment:* Federal Work-Study Program available. Institutional employment available. **Financial Aid Statistics:** 72% needy freshmen, 77% needy undergrads receive need-based scholarship or grant aid. 23% freshmen, 14% undergrads receive non-need-based scholarship or grant aid. 80% freshmen, 79% undergrads receive need-based self-help aid. 0% freshmen, 0% undergrads receive athletic scholarships. 73% freshmen, 79% undergrads receive any aid. 67% undergrads borrow to pay for school. Average cumulative indebtedness $27,397. **Criteria for awarding aid:** *Non-need-based:* Academics, Alumni affiliation, Art, Athletics, Job skills, Leadership, Minority status, Music/drama, Religious affiliation, State/district residency.

THE UNIVERSITY OF NORTH CAROLINA AT GREENSBORO

1400 Spring Garden Street, Greensboro, NC 27402-6170
Phone: 336-334-5243 • **Financial Aid Phone:** 336-334-5702
E-mail: admissions@uncg.edu • **CEEB Code:** 5913
Fax: 336-334-4180 • **Website:** www.uncg.edu • **ACT Code:** 3166

This public school was founded in 1891. It has a 357-acre campus.

RATINGS

Admissions Selectivity Rating: 84 **Fire Safety Rating:** 91 **Green Rating:** 91

STUDENTS AND FACULTY

Enrollment: 15,783. **Student Body:** 66% female, 34% male, 6% out-of-state, 2% international (47 countries represented). Asian 5%, African American 28%, Caucasian 51%, Hispanic 8%, Native American <1%, Pacific Islander <1%, Two or more races 5%, Race unknown 1%.
Retention and Graduation: 76% freshmen return for sophomore year. 31% freshmen graduate within 4 years. 57 **Faculty:** Student/faculty ratio 18:1. 773 full-time faculty, 80% hold PhDs, 23% are are members of minority groups, 55% are women.

ACADEMICS

Degrees: bachelor's, doctoral/research, master's, postbachelor's certificate, post-master's certificate. **Classes:** Most classes have 20-29 students. Most lab/discussion sessions have 20-29 students. **Most popular majors:** Business Administration and Management; Biology/Biological Sciences; Psychology.

Special Study Options: Accelerated program, cross-registration, distance learning, double major, dual enrollment, honors program, independent study, internships, study abroad, teacher certification program, Evening University. Combined degree programs: BA/MA, Accounting, Mathematics, Chemistry, various BA and MBA. **Disability Services:** Special programs offered to physically disabled students, including note-taking services, reader services, tape recorders, tutors. **Career Services:** Alumni services, Career/job search classes, Career assessment, Internships.

FACILITIES

Housing: Coed dorms, special housing for international students, women's dorms, apartments for single students. 85% of campus accessible to physically disabled. **Special Academic Facilities/Equipment:** 42-acre recreational site, art gallery, 45,000 sq.ft. Student Center, New Music Building, New Science Building. **Computers:** 90% of dorms, 35% of libraries, have wireless network access. Students can register for classes online. Administrative functions (other than registration) can be performed online.

CAMPUS LIFE

Environment: City. **Activities:** Choral groups, concert band, dance, drama/theater, jazz band, literary magazine, music ensembles, musical theater, opera, pep band, radio station, student government, student newspaper, student-run film society, symphony orchestra, Student Organization. 200 registered organizations, 23 honor societies, 13 religious organizations. 11 fraternities, 11 sororities. **Athletics (Intercollegiate):** *Men:* baseball, basketball, cross-country, golf, soccer, tennis, wrestling. *Women:* basketball, cross-country, golf, soccer, softball, tennis, volleyball. **On-Campus Highlights:** Elliott University Center, Student Rec Center, Weatherspoon Art Museum, Peabody Park, UNCG Theatre.

ADMISSIONS

Freshman Academic Profile: Average high school GPA 3.8. 0% in top 10% of high school class, 4% in top 25% of high school class, 23% in top 50% of high school class. 95% from public high schools. **Reported SAT (pre-2016 redesign) scores:** SAT Math middle 50% range 430-530. SAT Critical Reading middle 50% range 480-570. SAT Writing middle 50% range 440-540. **Concordant SAT scores:** SAT EBRW middle 50% 510–610. SAT Math middle 50% range 470–560. ACT middle 50% range 21-25. Minimum internet-based TOEFL 79. Minimum paper TOEFL 550. **Basis for Candidate Selection:** *Very important factors considered include:* rigor of secondary school record, academic GPA. *Important factors considered include:* standardized test scores. *Other factors considered include:* application essay, recommendation(s). **Freshman Admission Requirements:** High school diploma is required and GED is not accepted. *Academic units required:* 4 English, 4 math, 3 science, 1 science lab, 2 foreign language, 2 social studies. **Freshman Admission Statistics:** 9,035 applied, 73.93% admitted, 43% enrolled. **Transfer Admission Requirements:** High school transcript, college transcript(s), standardized test scores, statement of good standing from prior institution(s). Minimum college GPA of 2.0 required. Lowest grade transferable 2. **General Admission Information:** Application fee $55. Priority deadline 11/1. Regular application deadline 3/1. Nonfall registration accepted.

COSTS AND FINANCIAL AID

Annual in-state tuition $4,336. Annual out-of-state tuition $19,198. Required fees $2,706. Average book expense $956. **Required Forms and Deadlines:** FAFSA. **Notification of Awards:** Applicants will be notified of awards on a rolling basis beginning 3/15. **Types of Aid:** *Need-based scholarships/grants:* Federal Pell, FSEOG, State scholarships/grants, Private scholarships, College/university scholarship or grant aid from institutional funds. *Loans:* Direct Subsidized Stafford Loans, Direct Unsubsidized Stafford Loans, Direct PLUS loans, Federal Perkins Loans, State Loans, College/university loans from institutional funds. *Student Employment:* Federal Work-Study Program available. Institutional employment available. **Financial Aid Statistics:** 75% needy freshmen, 67% needy undergrads receive need-based scholarship or grant aid. 71% freshmen, 65% undergrads receive non-need-based scholarship or grant aid. 63% freshmen, 69% undergrads receive need-based self-help aid. 1% freshmen, 1% undergrads receive athletic scholarships. 87% freshmen, 81% undergrads receive any aid. 89% undergrads borrow to pay for school. Average cumulative indebtedness $27,073. **Criteria for awarding aid:** *Need-based:* Academics. *Non-need-based:* Academics, Athletics, Music/drama, Religious affiliation, State/district residency.

UNIVERSITY OF NORTH CAROLINA—PEMBROKE

One University Drive, Pembroke, NC 28372
Phone: 910-521-6262 • **Financial Aid Phone:** 910-521-6255
E-mail: admissions@uncp.edu • **CEEB Code:** 5534
Fax: 910-521-6497 • **Website:** www.uncp.edu • **ACT Code:** 3138

This public school was founded in 1887. It has a 161-acre campus.

RATINGS

Admissions Selectivity Rating: 75   **Fire Safety Rating:** 97   **Green Rating:** 89

STUDENTS AND FACULTY

Enrollment: 5,508. **Student Body:** 60% female, 40% male, 2% out-of-state, 1% international (20 countries represented). Asian 2%, African American 36%, Caucasian 37%, Hispanic 6%, Native American 15%, Pacific Islander <1%, Two or more races 2%, Race unknown 2%.
Retention and Graduation: 67% freshmen return for sophomore year. 18% freshmen graduate within 4 years. **Faculty:** Student/faculty ratio 16:1. 295 full-time faculty, 79% hold PhDs, 25% are are members of minority groups, 51% are women. 0% of classes are taught by teaching assistants.

ACADEMICS

Degrees: bachelor's, master's. **Classes:** Most classes have 20-29 students. Most lab/discussion sessions have fewer than 10 students. **Most popular majors:** Criminal Justice/Safety Studies; Business Administration and Management; Sociology. **Special Study Options:** Accelerated program, cooperative education program, cross-registration, distance learning, double major, dual enrollment, English as a Second Language (ESL), exchange student program (domestic), external degree program, honors program, independent study, internships, study abroad, teacher certification program. **Honors Programs:** The Esther G. Maynor Honors College began in 2001 to attract top scholars to UNCP, and provide an environment that stimulates academic and personal growth. Combined degree programs: BA/MA. **Disability Services:** Special programs offered to physically disabled students, including note-taking services, reader services, tape recorders, tutors. **Career Services:** Alumni network, Alumni services, Career/job search classes, Career assessment, Internships. We are very proud of the opportunities for experiential learning/internships that we offer. This is something we believe is very important and we encourage students to seek out these opportunities.

FACILITIES

Housing: Coed dorms, special housing for disabled students, men's dorms, women's dorms, apartments for single students. 99% of campus accessible to physically disabled. **Special Academic Facilities/Equipment:** Native American Resources Center and Museum **Computers:** 100% of classrooms, 50% of dorms, 100% of libraries, 100% of dining areas, 100% of student union, 30% of common outdoor areas have wireless network access. Students can register for classes online. Administrative functions (other than registration) can be performed online. Undergraduates are required to own a computer.

CAMPUS LIFE

Environment: Rural. **Activities:** Choral groups, concert band, dance, drama/theater, jazz band, literary magazine, marching band, music ensembles, musical theater, pep band, student government, student newspaper, student-run film society, television station, yearbook, Campus Ministries, Student Organization, Model UN. 70 registered organizations, 11 honor societies, 5 religious organizations. 10 fraternities, 11 sororities. **Athletics (Intercollegiate):** *Men:* baseball, basketball, cheerleading, cross-country, football, golf, soccer, track/field (outdoor), wrestling. *Women:* basketball, cheerleading, cross-country, golf, soccer, softball, tennis, track/field (outdoor), volleyball. **On-Campus Highlights:** Newly renovated athletic facility, Native American Resource Center/Museum, Givens Performing Arts Center, Newly renovated Bookstore, Higher Ground Ropes Course. **Environmental Initiatives:** Planning & Construction Dept. mandates all new facilities to be LEED certified.

ADMISSIONS

Freshman Academic Profile: Average high school GPA 3.4. 11% in top 10% of high school class, 34% in top 25% of high school class, 73% in top 50% of high school class. 95% from public high schools. **Reported SAT (pre-2016 redesign) scores:** SAT Math middle 50% range 420-500. SAT Critical Reading middle 50% range 410-490. SAT Writing middle 50% range 390-470. **Concordant SAT scores:** SAT EBRW middle 50% 450–540. SAT Math middle 50% range 460–530. ACT middle 50% range 18-22. Minimum internet-based TOEFL 68. Minimum paper TOEFL 520. **Basis for Candidate Selection:** *Very important factors considered include:* rigor of secondary school record, academic GPA, standardized test scores. *Other factors considered include:* class rank, geographical residence, state residency. **Freshman Admission Requirements:** High school diploma is required and GED is accepted.

Academic units required: 4 English, 4 math, 3 science, 1 science lab, 2 foreign language, 1 social studies, 1 history. **Freshman Admission Statistics:** 4,596 applied, 74.37% admitted. **Transfer Admission Requirements:** High school transcript, college transcript(s), statement of good standing from prior institution(s). Minimum college GPA of 2.0 required. Lowest grade transferable C. **General Admission Information:** Application fee $45. Priority deadline 7/15. Regular application deadline 7/31. Nonfall registration accepted. Admission may be deferred for a maximum of 1 year.

COSTS AND FINANCIAL AID

Annual in-state tuition $3,531. Annual out-of-state tuition $14,475. Room and board $8,572. Required fees $2,285. Average book expense $1,505. **Required Forms and Deadlines:** FAFSA. **Notification of Awards:** Applicants will be notified of awards on a rolling basis beginning 4/15. **Types of Aid:** *Need-based scholarships/grants:* Federal Pell, FSEOG, State scholarships/grants, College/university scholarship or grant aid from institutional funds. *Loans:* Direct Subsidized Stafford Loans, Direct Unsubsidized Stafford Loans, Direct PLUS loans, Federal Perkins Loans. *Student Employment:* Federal Work-Study Program available. **Financial Aid Statistics:** 86% needy freshmen, 84% needy undergrads receive need-based scholarship or grant aid. 15% freshmen, 13% undergrads receive non-need-based scholarship or grant aid. 87% freshmen, 86% undergrads receive need-based self-help aid. 1% freshmen, 1% undergrads receive athletic scholarships. 79% freshmen, 75% undergrads receive any aid. Average cumulative indebtedness $24,169. **Criteria for awarding aid:** *Need-based:* Academics, Alumni affiliation, Art, Athletics, Music/drama. *Non-need-based:* Academics, Alumni affiliation, Art, Athletics, Minority status, Music/drama.

UNIVERSITY OF NORTH CAROLINA— WILMINGTON

601 South College Rd, Wilmington, NC 28403-5904
Phone: 910-962-3243 • **Financial Aid Phone:** 910-962-3177
E-mail: admissions@uncw.edu • **CEEB Code:** 5907
Fax: 910-962-3038 • **Website:** www.uncw.edu • **ACT Code:** 3174

This public school was founded in 1947. It has a 656-acre campus.

RATINGS

Admissions Selectivity Rating: 85   **Fire Safety Rating:** 97   **Green Rating:** 94

STUDENTS AND FACULTY

Enrollment: 13,609. **Student Body:** 62% female, 38% male, 13% out-of-state, 1% international (53 countries represented). Asian 2%, African American 5%, Caucasian 78%, Hispanic 7%, Native American <1%, Pacific Islander <1%, Two or more races 4%, Race unknown 3%.
Retention and Graduation: 85% freshmen return for sophomore year. 53% freshmen graduate within 4 years. 72% freshmen graduate within 6 years. 20% grads go on to further study within 1 year. **Faculty:** Student/faculty ratio 18:1. 618 full-time faculty, 84% hold PhDs, 19% are are members of minority groups, 52% are women. 1% of classes are taught by teaching assistants.

ACADEMICS

Degrees: bachelor's, doctoral/research, master's, postbachelor's certificate, post-master's certificate. **Classes:** Most classes have 20-29 students. Most lab/discussion sessions have 20-29 students. **Most popular majors:** Business Administration and Management; Registered Nursing/Registered Nurse; Biology/Biological Sciences. **Special Study Options:** Accelerated program, cooperative education program, cross-registration, distance learning, double major, dual enrollment, English as a Second Language (ESL), exchange student program (domestic), honors program, independent study, internships, study abroad, teacher certification program, 2+2 Pre-Engineering Program. **Honors Programs:** The HONORS SCHOLARS PROGRAM at UNCW is designed to offer academically talented students challenging and exciting experiences both in and out of the classroom. A student may begin with general honors in the first two years, and then go on to departmental honors in their major. In their freshman and sophomore years, students take special interdisciplinary honors seminars and honors sections of basic studies courses. Honors classes are small–generally not over 20 students–to encourage discussion and faculty-student interaction. In any given semester, an honors scholar will enroll in both honors and other university classes, enhancing his or her experiences in many academic areas with a wide variety of students. In their junior and senior years, honors students will propose and carry out an honors "capstone" experience"–a scholarly project in the student's major. This involves independent work and close interaction with a faculty sponsor. Many of these have led to publication and presentations at professional conferences. Overall, the program encourages

curiosity, critical thinking, and independent work skills by offering exciting academic and cultural activities as well as the opportunity for close working and social relationships with the faculty. Combined degree programs: BA/MA. **Disability Services:** Special programs offered to physically disabled students, including note-taking services, reader services, tape recorders, tutors. **Career Services:** Alumni network, Alumni services, Career/job search classes, Career assessment, Internships. We are very proud of the opportunities for experiential learning/internships that we offer. This is something we believe is very important and we encourage students to seek out these opportunities.

FACILITIES

Housing: Coed dorms, special housing for disabled students, men's dorms, women's dorms, apartments for single students. 99% of campus accessible to physically disabled. **Special Academic Facilities/Equipment:** Native American Resources Center and Museum **Computers:** 100% of classrooms, 50% of dorms, 100% of libraries, 100% of dining areas, 100% of student union, 30% of common outdoor areas have wireless network access. Students can register for classes online. Administrative functions (other than registration) can be performed online. Undergraduates are required to own a computer.

CAMPUS LIFE

Environment: Rural. **Activities:** Choral groups, concert band, dance, drama/theater, jazz band, literary magazine, marching band, music ensembles, musical theater, pep band, student government, student newspaper, student-run film society, television station, yearbook, Campus Ministries, Student Organization, Model UN. 70 registered organizations, 11 honor societies, 5 religious organizations. 10 fraternities, 11 sororities. **Athletics (Intercollegiate):** *Men:* baseball, basketball, cheerleading, cross-country, football, golf, soccer, track/field (outdoor), wrestling. *Women:* basketball, cheerleading, cross-country, golf, soccer, softball, tennis, track/field (outdoor), volleyball. **On-Campus Highlights:** Newly renovated athletic facility, Native American Resource Center/Museum, Givens Performing Arts Center, Newly renovated Bookstore, Higher Ground Ropes Course. **Environmental Initiatives:** Planning & Construction Dept. mandates all new facilities to be LEED certified.

ADMISSIONS

Freshman Academic Profile: Average high school GPA 4.1. 20% in top 10% of high school class, 61% in top 25% of high school class, 94% in top 50% of high school class. 95% from public high schools. **Reported SAT (pre-2016 redesign) scores:** SAT Math middle 50% range 570-630. SAT Critical Reading middle 50% range 560-630. SAT Writing middle 50% range 520-610. **Concordant SAT scores:** SAT EBRW middle 50% 450–540. SAT Math middle 50% range 460–530. ACT middle 50% range 22-26. Minimum internet-based TOEFL 68. Minimum paper TOEFL 520. **Basis for Candidate Selection:** *Very important factors considered include:* rigor of secondary school record, academic GPA, standardized test scores. *Other factors considered include:* class rank, geographical residence, state residency. **Freshman Admission Requirements:** High school diploma is required and GED is accepted. *Academic units required:* 4 English, 4 math, 3 science, 1 science lab, 2 foreign language, 1 social studies, 1 history. **Freshman Admission Statistics:** 10,436 applied, 71.74% admitted, 30% enrolled. **Transfer Admission Requirements:** High school transcript, college transcript(s), statement of good standing from prior institution(s). Minimum college GPA of 2.0 required. Lowest grade transferable C. **General Admission Information:** Application fee $45. Priority deadline 7/15. Regular application deadline 7/31. Nonfall registration accepted. Admission may be deferred for a maximum of 1 year.

COSTS AND FINANCIAL AID

Annual in-state tuition $3,531. Annual out-of-state tuition $14,475. Room and board $8,572. Required fees $2,285. Average book expense $1,505. **Required Forms and Deadlines:** FAFSA. **Notification of Awards:** Applicants will be notified of awards on a rolling basis beginning 4/15. **Types of Aid:** *Need-based scholarships/grants:* Federal Pell, FSEOG, State scholarships/grants, College/university scholarship or grant aid from institutional funds. *Loans:* Direct Subsidized Stafford Loans, Direct Unsubsidized Stafford Loans, Direct PLUS loans, Federal Perkins Loans. *Student Employment:* Federal Work-Study Program available. **Financial Aid Statistics:** 86% needy freshmen, 84% needy undergrads receive need-based scholarship or grant aid. 15% freshmen, 13% undergrads receive non-need-based scholarship or grant aid. 87% freshmen, 86% undergrads receive need-based self-help aid. 1% freshmen, 1% undergrads receive athletic scholarships. 79% freshmen, 75% undergrads receive any aid. Average cumulative indebtedness $24,169. **Criteria for awarding aid:** *Need-based:* Academics, Alumni affiliation, Art, Athletics, Music/drama. *Non-need-based:* Academics, Alumni affiliation, Art, Athletics, Minority status, Music/drama.

UNIVERSITY OF NORTH DAKOTA

3501 University Avenue Stop 8357, Grand Forks, ND 58202
Phone: 701-777-3000 • **Financial Aid Phone:** 701-777-3121
E-mail: admissions@UND.edu • **CEEB Code:** 6878
Fax: 701-777-2721 • **Website:** http://und.edu • **ACT Code:** 3218

This public school was founded in 1883. It has a 549-acre campus.

RATINGS
Admissions Selectivity Rating: 83   **Fire Safety Rating:** 86   **Green Rating:** 60*

STUDENTS AND FACULTY
Enrollment: 10,809. **Student Body:** 44% female, 56% male, 60% out-of-state, 4% international (72 countries represented). Asian 2%, African American 2%, Caucasian 83%, Hispanic 3%, Native American 1%, Pacific Islander <1%, Two or more races 3%, Race unknown 2%.
Retention and Graduation: 81% freshmen return for sophomore year. 24% freshmen graduate within 4 years. 53% freshmen graduate within 6 years. 13% grads go on to further study within 1 year. 1% grads pursue law degrees. 2% grads pursue medical degrees. **Faculty:** Student/faculty ratio 18:1. 683 full-time faculty, 75% hold PhDs, 15% are are members of minority groups, 43% are women.

ACADEMICS
Degrees: bachelor's, certificate, doctoral/professional, doctoral/research, master's, postbachelor's certifiate, post-master's certificate. **Classes:** Most classes have 20-29 students. Most lab/discussion sessions have 10-19 students. **Most popular majors:** Registered Nursing/Registered Nurse; Psychology; Mechanical Engineering. **Special Study Options:** Accelerated program, cooperative education program, cross-registration, distance learning, double major, dual enrollment, English as a Second Language (ESL), exchange student program (domestic), external degree program, honors program, independent study, internships, liberal arts/career combination, student-designed major, study abroad, teacher certification program, weekend college. **Honors Programs:** Students may participate in the Honors Program throughout their undergraduate career.Students in any college of the University may enroll in the Honors Program.Most students graduate from the Program as "Scholars in the Honors Program" while also fulfilling a major in the Colleges, but the Honors Program also offers the option of creating an individually designed program of study through Honors.This option may result in either a B.A. or a B.S. degree earned through the College of Arts and Sciences. Combined degree programs: http://und.edu/dept/registrar/catalogs/catalog. **Disability Services:** Special programs offered to physically disabled students, including note-taking services, reader services, tape recorders. **Career Services:** Alumni network, Alumni services, Career/job search classes, Career assessment, Internships. Cooperative Learning. Internships. Students work closely with entrepreneur practitioners.

FACILITIES
Housing: Coed dorms, special housing for disabled students, men's dorms, women's dorms, fraternity/sorority housing, apartments for married students, apartments for single students, Wellness Housing, Theme Housing. 99% of campus accessible to physically diasbled. **Special Academic Facilities/Equipment:** Hughes Fine Arts Center, Burtness Theatre, North Dakota Museum of Art, Chester Fritz Auditorium, mining/mineral resources research institute/energy research center, remote sensing institute, aviation facilities, meteorology data center,Ralph Engelstad Arena. **Computers:** 70% of classrooms, 100% of dorms, 100% of libraries, 50% of dining areas, 100% of student union, have wireless network access. Students can register for classes online. Administrative functions (other than registration) can be performed online.

CAMPUS LIFE
Environment: Town. **Activities:** Choral groups, concert band, dance, drama/theater, jazz band, literary magazine, marching band, music ensembles, musical theater, opera, pep band, radio station, student government, student newspaper, student-run film society, symphony orchestra, television station, Campus Ministries, Student Organization. 230 registered organizations, 42 honor societies, 3 religious organizations. 13 fraternities, 7 sororities. **Athletics (Intercollegiate):** *Men:* baseball, basketball, cross-country, diving, football, golf, ice hockey, swimming, track/field (outdoor), track/field (indoor). *Women:* basketball, cross-country, diving, golf, ice hockey, soccer, softball, swimming, tennis, track/field (outdoor), track/field (indoor), volleyball. **On-Campus Highlights:** Engelstad Arena, Memorial Union, Archives Coffee shop,

Centre, North Dakota Museum of Art. **Environmental Initiatives:** Energy Conservation Programs.

ADMISSIONS
Freshman Academic Profile: Average high school GPA 3.4. 17% in top 10% of high school class, 41% in top 25% of high school class, 77% in top 50% of high school class. 92% from public high schools. ACT middle 50% range 21-26. Minimum internet-based TOEFL 76. Minimum paper TOEFL 550. **Basis for Candidate Selection:** *Very important factors considered include:* rigor of secondary school record, academic GPA, standardized test scores, application essay. *Other factors considered include:* recommendation(s). **Freshman Admission Requirements:** High school diploma is required and GED is accepted. *Academic units required:* 4 English, 3 math, 3 science, 3 science labs, 3 social studies. *Academic units recommended:* 1 foreign language. **Freshman Admission Statistics:** 4,920 applied, 81.89% admitted, 47% enrolled. **Transfer Admission Requirements:** college transcript(s), Minimum college GPA of 2.0 required. **General Admission Information:** Application fee $35. Priority deadline 3/1. Nonfall registration accepted. Admission may be deferred.

COSTS AND FINANCIAL AID
Annual in-state tuition $6,679. Annual out-of-state tuition $17,833. Room and board $7,630. Required fees $1,458. Average book expense $1,000. *Student Employment:* Federal Work-Study Program available. Institutional employment available.

UNIVERSITY OF NORTH FLORIDA

1 UNF Drive, Jacksonville, FL 32224-7699
Phone: 904-620-5555 • **Financial Aid Phone:** 904-620-2698
E-mail: admissions@unf.edu • **CEEB Code:** 9841
Fax: 904-620-2414 • **Website:** www.unf.edu • **ACT Code:** 5490

This public school was founded in 1965. It has a 1300-acre campus.

RATINGS
Admissions Selectivity Rating: 82   **Fire Safety Rating:** 80   **Green Rating:** 60*

STUDENTS AND FACULTY
Enrollment: 13,585. **Student Body:** 56% female, 44% male, 4% out-of-state, 1% international (112 countries represented). Asian 4%, African American 10%, Caucasian 67%, Hispanic 11%, Native American <1%, Pacific Islander <1%, Two or more races 5%, Race unknown <1%.
Retention and Graduation: 80% freshmen return for sophomore year. **Faculty:** Student/faculty ratio 19:1. 547 full-time faculty, 80% hold PhDs, 15% are are members of minority groups, 50% are women. 0% of classes are taught by teaching assistants.

ACADEMICS
Degrees: associate, bachelor's, doctoral/professional, doctoral/research, master's, postbachelor's certifiate, post-master's certificate. **Classes:** Most classes have 20-29 students. Most lab/discussion sessions have 20-29 students. **Most popular majors:** Psychology; Mass Communication/Media Studies; Registered Nursing/Registered Nurse. **Special Study Options:** Accelerated program, cooperative education program, distance learning, double major, dual enrollment, English as a Second Language (ESL), exchange student program (domestic), honors program, independent study, internships, student-designed major, study abroad, teacher certification program, weekend college, Learning Communities. **Honors Programs:** The Honors Program at the University of North Florida offers talented and ambitious students a unique approach to higher education. Honors Classes are limited to 20 students, combining active and experiential learning in an interdisciplinary setting. The goal is to build a community of learners who have the ability to take their learning outside the classroom and into the real world helping to bridge the gap between education and experience. The honors program is a limited access program and spaces are filled on a first-come-first-serve basis. Combined degree programs: Accelerated BS/MS Computer Science Program. **Disability Services:** Special programs offered to physically disabled students, including note-taking services, reader services, tape recorders. **Career Services:** Alumni network, Alumni services, Career/job search classes, Career assessment, Internships. Empowered: Empowered is a program that teaches homeless women in Jacksonville how to become successful in the business world. we taught these women resume writing skills, how to fill out an application, what to wear to an interview, how to give a good interview, and provided them with the resources to find jobs. This year, we would like to spread this program to not only homeless women by also families and disabled veterans. SIFE works very closely with SHRM for this project.

FACILITIES

Housing: Coed dorms, special housing for disabled students, apartments for single students, Suite style housing. **Special Academic Facilities/Equipment:** Art gallery, bird sanctuary, Fine Arts Center **Computers:** 100% of classrooms, 50% of dorms, 100% of libraries, 50% of dining areas, 100% of student union, 100% of common outdoor areas have wireless network access. Students can register for classes online. Administrative functions (other than registration) can be performed online.

CAMPUS LIFE

Environment: Metropolis. **Activities;** Choral groups, concert band, dance, drama/theater, jazz band, literary magazine, music ensembles, pep band, radio station, student government, student newspaper, television station, Campus Ministries, Student Organization. 140 registered organizations, 8 honor societies, 29 religious organizations. 14 fraternities, 10 sororities. **Athletics (Intercollegiate):** *Men:* baseball, basketball, cheerleading, cross-country, golf, soccer, tennis, track/field (outdoor), track/field (indoor). *Women:* basketball, cheerleading, cross-country, diving, soccer, softball, swimming, tennis, track/field (outdoor), track/field (indoor), volleyball. **On-Campus Highlights:** Student Union, Bookstore, Art Gallery, Nature Trails, Campus skate park, Greek Affairs, Earth Music Festival, Athletics NCAA I, Free movies on Campus, Jazz Program (nationally recognized), Division I sports. **Environmental Initiatives:** Requiring LEED Silver or comparable compliance

ADMISSIONS

Freshman Academic Profile: Average high school GPA 3.8. 14% in top 10% of high school class, 40% in top 25% of high school class, 74% in top 50% of high school class. 80% from public high schools. **Reported SAT (pre-2016 redesign) scores:** SAT Math middle 50% range 520-600. SAT Critical Reading middle 50% range 520-620. SAT Writing middle 50% range 490-580. **Concordant SAT scores:** SAT EBRW middle 50% 560–650. SAT Math middle 50% range 550–620. ACT middle 50% range 21-26. Minimum internet-based TOEFL 61. Minimum paper TOEFL 500. **Basis for Candidate Selection:** *Very important factors considered include:* rigor of secondary school record, academic GPA, standardized test scores. *Other factors considered include:* class rank, application essay, recommendation(s), extracurricular activities, talent/ability, volunteer work, work experience, level of applicant's interest. **Freshman Admission Requirements:** High school diploma is required and GED is accepted. *Academic units required:* 4 English, 4 math, 3 science, 1 science lab, 2 foreign language, 3 social studies, 2 academic electives. **Freshman Admission Statistics:** 11,346 applied, 64.53% admitted, 27% enrolled. **Transfer Admission Requirements:** college transcript(s), Minimum college GPA of 2.0 required. Lowest grade transferable D. **General Admission Information:** Application fee $30. Priority deadline 11/16. Nonfall registration accepted. Admission may be deferred for a maximum of 2 Semesters.

COSTS AND FINANCIAL AID

Required Forms and Deadlines: FAFSA. **Notification of Awards:** Applicants will be notified of awards on a rolling basis beginning 3/15. **Types of Aid:** *Need-based scholarships/grants:* Federal Pell, FSEOG, State scholarships/grants, Private scholarships, College/university scholarship or grant aid from institutional funds. *Loans:* Direct Subsidized Stafford Loans, Direct Unsubsidized Stafford Loans, Direct PLUS loans. *Student Employment:* Federal Work-Study Program available. Institutional employment available. **Financial Aid Statistics:** 68% needy freshmen, 64% needy undergrads receive need-based scholarship or grant aid. 55% freshmen, 35% undergrads receive non-need-based scholarship or grant aid. 62% freshmen, 60% undergrads receive need-based self-help aid. 2% freshmen, 2% undergrads receive athletic scholarships. 76% freshmen, 71% undergrads receive any aid. 50% undergrads borrow to pay for school. Average cumulative indebtedness $18,685. **Criteria for awarding aid:** *Need-based:* Academics. *Non-need-based:* Academics, Athletics, Leadership, Minority status, Music/drama, State/district residency.

UNIVERSITY OF NORTH GEORGIA

Office of Undergraduate Admissions, Dahlonega, GA 30597
Phone: 706-864-1800 • **Financial Aid Phone:** 706-864-1412
E-mail: admissions@ung.edu • **CEEB Code:** 5497
Fax: 706-864-1478 • **Website:** www.ung.edu • **ACT Code:** 848

This public school was founded in 1873. It has a 120-acre campus.

RATINGS

Admissions Selectivity Rating: 84   **Fire Safety Rating:** 95   **Green Rating:** 60*

STUDENTS AND FACULTY

Enrollment: 17,674. **Student Body:** 56% female, 44% male, 5% out-of-state, 2% international (94 countries represented). Asian 3%, African American 4%, Caucasian 75%, Hispanic 11%, Native American <1%, Pacific Islander <1%, Two or more races 3%, Race unknown 1%. **Retention and Graduation:** 79% freshmen return for sophomore year. 28% freshmen graduate within 4 years. 54% freshmen graduate within 6 years. **Faculty:** Student/faculty ratio 21:1. 636 full-time faculty, 65% hold PhDs, 6% are are members of minority groups, 51% are women. 0% of classes are taught by teaching assistants.

ACADEMICS

Degrees: associate, bachelor's, certificate, doctoral/professional, master's, postbachelor's certificate, post-master's certificate. **Classes:** Most classes have 20-29 students. Most lab/discussion sessions have fewer than 10 students. **Most popular majors:** Biology/Biological Sciences; Business Administration and Management. **Special Study Options:** cooperative education program, distance learning, double major, dual enrollment, external degree program, honors program, independent study, internships, study abroad, teacher certification program, Dual degree in Engineering with GA Institute of Technology and Clemson University. **Disability Services:** Special programs offered to physically disabled students, including note-taking services, reader services, tape recorders, tutors. **Career Services:** Alumni network, Alumni services, Career/job search classes, Career assessment, Internships, Regional alumni.

FACILITIES

Housing: Coed dorms, men's dorms, women's dorms, apartments for single students. **Special Academic Facilities/Equipment:** Planetarium; 2 Art galleries; Hall of fame; NGCSU museum **Computers:** Students can register for classes online. Administrative functions (other than registration) can be performed online.

CAMPUS LIFE

Environment: Rural. **Activities:** Choral groups, drama/theater, jazz band, literary magazine, marching band, music ensembles, pep band, student government, student newspaper, symphony orchestra, yearbook. 60 registered organizations, 8 honor societies, 5 religious organizations. 6 fraternities, 4 sororities. **Athletics (Intercollegiate):** *Men:* baseball, basketball, cross-country, football, golf, riflery, soccer, table tennis, tennis, track/field (outdoor), volleyball, water polo. *Women:* basketball, cheerleading, cross-country, golf, riflery, soccer, softball, table tennis, tennis, track/field (outdoor), volleyball, water polo. **On-Campus Highlights:** Canteen, Commuter Lounge, Game Room, Uniform Store, Lounge Areas.

ADMISSIONS

Freshman Academic Profile: Average high school GPA 3.6. 25% in top 10% of high school class, 54% in top 25% of high school class, 72% in top 50% of high school class. **Reported SAT (pre-2016 redesign) scores:** SAT Math middle 50% range 490-590. SAT Critical Reading middle 50% range 510-600. SAT Writing middle 50% range 480-570. **Concordant SAT scores:** SAT EBRW middle 50% 550–640. SAT Math middle 50% range 520–610. ACT middle 50% range 22-26. Minimum internet-based TOEFL 79. Minimum paper TOEFL 550. **Basis for Candidate Selection:** *Very important factors considered include:* rigor of secondary school record, academic GPA, standardized test scores. **Freshman Admission Requirements:** High school diploma is required and GED is accepted. *Academic units required:* 4 English, 4 math, 4 science, 2 science labs, 2 foreign language, 3 social studies. *Academic units recommended:* 4 English, 4 math, 4 science, 2 science labs, 2 foreign language, 3 social studies. **Freshman Admission Statistics:** 4,536 applied, 61.82% admitted. **Transfer Admission Requirements:** college transcript(s), statement of good standing from prior institution(s). Minimum college GPA of 2.0 required. Lowest grade transferable C. **General Admission Information:** Application fee $30. Regular application deadline 2/15. Nonfall registration accepted. Admission may be deferred.

COSTS AND FINANCIAL AID

Annual in-state tuition $5,352. Annual out-of-state tuition $18,894. Room and board $10,138. Required fees $1,826. Average book expense $1,364. **Required Forms and Deadlines:** FAFSA. **Notification of Awards:** Applicants will be notified of awards on a rolling basis beginning 4/1. **Types of Aid:** *Need-based scholarships/grants:* Federal Pell, FSEOG, State scholarships/grants, Private scholarships, College/university scholarship or grant aid from institutional funds. *Loans:* Direct Subsidized Stafford Loans, Direct Unsubsidized Stafford Loans, Direct PLUS loans, Federal Perkins Loans, State Loans, College/university loans from institutional funds. *Student Employment:* Federal Work-Study Program available. Institutional employment available. **Financial Aid Statistics:** 59% needy freshmen, 58% needy undergrads receive need-based scholarship or grant aid. 68% undergrads receive non-need-based scholarship or grant aid. 88% freshmen, 92% undergrads receive need-based self-help aid. 2% freshmen, 2% undergrads receive athletic scholarships. **Criteria for awarding aid:** *Need-based:* Academics, Leadership, Religious affiliation. *Non-need-based:* Academics, Alumni affiliation, Art, Athletics, Leadership, Music/drama, State/district residency.

UNIVERSITY OF NORTH TEXAS

1155 Union Circle #311277, Denton, TX 76203-5017
Phone: 940-565-2681 • **Financial Aid Phone:** 940-565-3901
E-mail: undergrad@unt.edu • **CEEB Code:** 6481
Fax: 940-565-2408 • **Website:** www.unt.edu • **ACT Code:** 4136

This public school was founded in 1890. It has a 850-acre campus.

RATINGS
Admissions Selectivity Rating: 82   **Fire Safety Rating:** 93   **Green Rating:** 94

STUDENTS AND FACULTY
Enrollment: 29,481. **Student Body:** 52% female, 48% male, 4% out-of-state, 3% international (164 countries represented). Asian 6%, African American 13%, Caucasian 53%, Hispanic 20%, Native American 1%, Pacific Islander <1%, Two or more races 3%, Race unknown 1%.
Retention and Graduation: 76% freshmen return for sophomore year. 23% freshmen graduate within 4 years. **Faculty:** Student/faculty ratio 23:1. 963 full-time faculty, 81% hold PhDs, 30% are are members of minority groups, 40% are women. 11% of classes are taught by teaching assistants.

ACADEMICS
Degrees: bachelor's, doctoral/professional, doctoral/research, doctoral, master's, postbachelor's certificate. **Classes:** Most classes have 20-29 students. Most lab/discussion sessions have 20-29 students. **Most popular majors:** Business/Commerce; Multi-/Interdisciplinary Studies; Biology/Biological Sciences. **Special Study Options:** Accelerated program, cooperative education program, cross-registration, distance learning, double major, dual enrollment, English as a Second Language (ESL), honors program, independent study, internships, study abroad, teacher certification program, weekend college. **Honors Programs:** University of North Texas Honors College Combined degree programs: BA/MA. **Disability Services:** Special programs offered to physically disabled students, including note-taking services, reader services, tape recorders, tutors. **Career Services:** Alumni network, Alumni services, Career/job search classes, Career assessment, Internships, Regional alumni. We offer our Alumni Services to our alums at no cost (very important in these times especially), and have developed some very strong programs for the alumni to help them in their transition.

FACILITIES
Housing: Coed dorms, special housing for disabled students, women's dorms, fraternity/sorority housing, apartments for married students, cooperative housing, apartments for single students, Theme Housing. 90% of campus accessible to physically diasbled. **Special Academic Facilities/Equipment:** laser, observatory, accelerators, recreational facility, music facilities, environmental sciences, planetarium, art galleries **Computers:** 75% of classrooms, 30% of dorms, 100% of libraries, 100% of dining areas, 100% of student union, 10% of common outdoor areas have wireless network access. Students can register for classes online. Administrative functions (other than registration) can be performed online.

CAMPUS LIFE
Environment: City. **Activities:** Choral groups, concert band, dance, drama/theater, jazz band, literary magazine, marching band, music ensembles, musical theater, opera, pep band, radio station, student government, student newspaper, student-run film society, symphony orchestra, television station, Campus Ministries, Student Organization. 330 registered organizations, 40 honor societies, 34 religious organizations. 23 fraternities, 16 sororities. **Athletics (Intercollegiate):** *Men:* basketball, cross-country, football, golf, softball, track/field (indoor). *Women:* basketball, cross-country, diving, golf, soccer, softball, swimming, tennis, track/field (indoor), volleyball. **On-Campus Highlights:** University Union, Student Recreation Center, Library Mall and pavilion, Murchison Performing Arts Center, Eagle Student Services Center, Chestnut Hall. **Environmental Initiatives:** In 2011 UNT completed construction on three community sized wind turbine located at the university Eagle Point. The project was funded through a 2.2 million dollar grant awarded by the State Energy Conservation Office. Since their completion the wind turbines have generated 284,182 kWh of energy.

ADMISSIONS
Freshman Academic Profile: 20% in top 10% of high school class, 52% in top 25% of high school class, 90% in top 50% of high school class. 95% from public high schools. **Reported SAT (pre-2016 redesign) scores:** SAT Math middle 50% range 510-610. SAT Critical Reading middle 50% range 490-600. SAT Writing middle 50% range 460-570. **Concordant SAT scores:** SAT EBRW middle 50% range 530–640. SAT Math middle 50% range 540–630. ACT middle 50% range 20-26. Minimum internet-based TOEFL 79. Minimum paper TOEFL 550. **Basis for Candidate Selection:** *Very important factors considered include:* rigor of secondary school record, class rank, academic GPA,

standardized test scores. *Important factors considered include:* application essay, recommendation(s). *Other factors considered include:* extracurricular activities, talent/ability, character/personal qualities, first generation, geographical residence, volunteer work, work experience, level of applicant's interest. **Freshman Admission Requirements:** High school diploma is required and GED is accepted. *Academic units required:* 4 English, 4 math, 4 science, 4 science labs, 2 foreign language, 2 social studies, 2 history, 1 computer science, 1 visual/performing arts. **Freshman Admission Statistics:** 16,326 applied, 61.48% admitted, 44% enrolled. **Transfer Admission Requirements:** college transcript(s), statement of good standing from prior institution(s). Minimum college GPA of 2.5 required. Lowest grade transferable D. **General Admission Information:** Application fee $60. Priority deadline 3/1. Regular application deadline 8/1. Nonfall registration accepted. Admission may be deferred.

COSTS AND FINANCIAL AID
Annual in-state tuition $6,834. Annual out-of-state tuition $17,364. Room and board $7,356. Required fees $2,590. Average book expense $1,000. **Required Forms and Deadlines:** FAFSA. **Notification of Awards:** Applicants will be notified of awards on a rolling basis beginning 4/1. **Types of Aid:** *Need-based scholarships/grants:* Federal Pell, FSEOG, State scholarships/grants, Private scholarships, College/university scholarship or grant aid from institutional funds. *Loans:* Direct Subsidized Stafford Loans, Direct Unsubsidized Stafford Loans, Direct PLUS loans, Federal Perkins Loans, State Loans. *Student Employment:* Federal Work-Study Program available. Institutional employment available. **Financial Aid Statistics:** 82% needy freshmen, 74% needy undergrads receive need-based scholarship or grant aid. 50% freshmen, 27% undergrads receive non-need-based scholarship or grant aid. 80% freshmen, 84% undergrads receive need-based self-help aid. 0% freshmen, 1% undergrads receive athletic scholarships. 88% freshmen, 71% undergrads receive any aid.

UNIVERSITY OF NORTHERN COLORADO

UNC Admissions Office, Greeley, CO 80639
Phone: 970-351-2881 • **Financial Aid Phone:** 970-351-2502
E-mail: admissions@unco.edu • **CEEB Code:** 4074
Fax: 970-351-2984 • **Website:** www.unco.edu • **ACT Code:** 502

This public school was founded in 1890. It has a 243-acre campus.

RATINGS
Admissions Selectivity Rating: 75   **Fire Safety Rating:** 96   **Green Rating:** 67

STUDENTS AND FACULTY
Enrollment: 9,095. **Student Body:** 64% female, 36% male, 15% out-of-state, 1% international (36 countries represented). Asian 2%, African American 4%, Caucasian 58%, Hispanic 19%, Native American <1%, Pacific Islander <1%, Two or more races 4%, Race unknown 10%.
Retention and Graduation: 70% freshmen return for sophomore year. 29% freshmen graduate within 4 years. 48% freshmen graduate within 6 years. **Faculty:** Student/faculty ratio 18:1. 490 full-time faculty, 0% hold PhDs, 13% are are members of minority groups, 52% are women.

ACADEMICS
Degrees: bachelor's, doctoral/research, master's. **Classes:** Most classes have 20-29 students. Most lab/discussion sessions have 20-29 students. **Most popular majors:** Multi-/Interdisciplinary Studies; Business Administration and Management; Psychology. **Special Study Options:** cooperative education program, cross-registration, distance learning, double major, English as a Second Language (ESL), exchange student program (domestic), external degree program, honors program, independent study, internships, student-designed major, study abroad, teacher certification program. **Honors Programs:** The University Honors Program is designed to offer exceptional students both the resources of a comprehensive university and the individual attention traditionally associated with a small college. It asks that they be alive to the life of the mind and pushes them to raise the expectations they have for themselves and their education. It seeks to involve them in learning, heighten their critical awareness, and encourage their independent thinking and research. **Disability Services:** Special programs offered to physically disabled students, including note-taking services, reader services, tape recorders, tutors. **Career Services:** Alumni network, Alumni services, Career/job search classes, Career assessment, Internships, Regional alumni.

FACILITIES
Housing: Coed dorms, special housing for disabled students, women's dorms, fraternity/sorority housing, apartments for married students, apartments for single students. 100% of campus accessible to physically diasbled. **Special Academic Facilities/Equipment:** Art Museum, Music Library, James A. Michener Collection **Computers:** 100% of classrooms, 100% of dorms, 100%

of libraries, 100% of dining areas, 100% of student union, 5% of common outdoor areas have wireless network access. Students can register for classes online. Administrative functions (other than registration) can be performed online.

CAMPUS LIFE

Environment: City. **Activities:** Choral groups, concert band, dance, drama/theater, jazz band, literary magazine, marching band, music ensembles, musical theater, opera, pep band, radio station, student government, student newspaper, student-run film society, symphony orchestra, television station, Campus Ministries, Student Organization. 137 registered organizations, 9 honor societies, 18 religious organizations. 9 fraternities, 8 sororities. **Athletics (Intercollegiate):** *Men:* baseball, basketball, football, golf, tennis, track/field (outdoor), wrestling. *Women:* basketball, cross-country, diving, golf, soccer, softball, swimming, tennis, track/field (outdoor), volleyball. **On-Campus Highlights:** University Center, James Michener Library, Recreation Center, Cultural Centers

ADMISSIONS

Freshman Academic Profile: Average high school GPA 3.3. 13% in top 10% of high school class, 38% in top 25% of high school class, 73% in top 50% of high school class. **Reported SAT (pre-2016 redesign) scores:** SAT Math middle 50% range 460-570. SAT Critical Reading middle 50% range 470-580. **Concordant SAT scores:** SAT Math middle 50% range 500–590. ACT middle 50% range 19-25. **Basis for Candidate Selection:** *Very important factors considered include:* class rank, academic GPA, standardized test scores. *Other factors considered include:* rigor of secondary school record, application essay, recommendation(s), interview, extracurricular activities, talent/ability, character/personal qualities, first generation, alumni/ae relation, geographical residence, state residency, racial/ethnic status, volunteer work, work experience, level of applicant's interest. **Freshman Admission Requirements:** High school diploma is required and GED is accepted. *Academic units recommended:* 4 English, 4 math, 3 science, 2 science labs, 1 foreign language, 2 social studies, 1 history, 2 academic electives. **Freshman Admission Statistics:** 6,784 applied, 90.27% admitted, 35% enrolled. **Transfer Admission Requirements:** college transcript(s), statement of good standing from prior institution(s). Minimum college GPA of 2.4 required. Lowest grade transferable C. **General Admission Information:** Application fee $45. Priority deadline 3/1. Regular application deadline 8/1. Nonfall registration accepted. Admission may be deferred for a maximum of 1 year.

COSTS AND FINANCIAL AID

Annual in-state tuition $6,906. Annual out-of-state tuition $18,492. Room and board $10,770. Required fees $1,982. Average book expense $1,350. **Required Forms and Deadlines:** FAFSA. **Notification of Awards:** Applicants will be notified of awards on a rolling basis beginning 4/1. **Types of Aid:** *Need-based scholarships/grants:* Federal Pell, FSEOG, State scholarships/grants, Private scholarships, College/university scholarship or grant aid from institutional funds. *Loans:* Direct Subsidized Stafford Loans, Direct Unsubsidized Stafford Loans, Direct PLUS loans, Federal Perkins Loans, Federal Nursing Loans. *Student Employment:* Federal Work-Study Program available. Institutional employment available. **Financial Aid Statistics:** 88% needy freshmen, 83% needy undergrads receive need-based scholarship or grant aid. 71% freshmen, 55% undergrads receive non-need-based scholarship or grant aid. 78% freshmen, 81% undergrads receive need-based self-help aid. 3% freshmen, 3% undergrads receive athletic scholarships. 67% freshmen, 68% undergrads receive any aid. 60% undergrads borrow to pay for school. Average cumulative indebtedness $27,393. **Criteria for awarding aid:** *Need-based:* Academics. *Non-need-based:* Academics, Athletics, Music/drama.

UNIVERSITY OF NORTHERN IOWA

1227 West 27th Street, Cedar Falls, IA 50614-0018
Phone: 319-273-2281 • **Financial Aid Phone:** 319-273-2701
E-mail: admissions@uni.edu • **CEEB Code:** 6307
Fax: 319-273-2885 • **Website:** www.uni.edu • **ACT Code:** 1322

This public school was founded in 1876. It has a 910-acre campus.

RATINGS

Admissions Selectivity Rating: 79   **Fire Safety Rating:** 89   **Green Rating:** 99

STUDENTS AND FACULTY

Enrollment: 9,934. **Student Body:** 57% female, 43% male, 6% out-of-state, 4% international (65 countries represented). Asian 1%, African American 3%, Caucasian 83%, Hispanic 3%, Native American <1%, Pacific Islander <1%, Two or more races 2%, Race unknown 3%.

Retention and Graduation: 80% freshmen return for sophomore year. 38% freshmen graduate within 4 years. 68% freshmen graduate within 6 years. 16% grads go on to further study within 1 year. 8% grads pursue arts and sciences degrees. 2% grads pursue business degrees. 2% grads pursue medical degrees. **Faculty:** Student/faculty ratio 17:1. 556 full-time faculty, 78% hold PhDs, 15% are are members of minority groups, 48% are women. 2% of classes are taught by teaching assistants.

ACADEMICS

Degrees: bachelor's, certificate, master's, post-master's certificate. **Classes:** Most classes have 20-29 students. Most lab/discussion sessions have 10-19 students. **Most popular majors:** Elementary Education and Teaching; Biology/Biological Sciences; Psychology. **Special Study Options:** Accelerated program, cooperative education program, distance learning, double major, dual enrollment, English as a Second Language (ESL), exchange student program (domestic), external degree program, honors program, independent study, internships, liberal arts/career combination, student-designed major, study abroad, teacher certification program, weekend college, Combined Bachelors/Masters degree programs (BA/MA, BS/MS, BA/MS); undergraduate Dual Degree Majors; 2+2 Programs; undergraduate and graduate certificates. **Honors Programs:** University Honors Program—includes all 5 colleges and is open to all majors. www.uni.edu/honors Combined degree programs: BA/MS Biology; BA/MS Technology; BS/MS Biology; BS/MS Technology; BA/MAcc. **Disability Services:** Special programs offered to physically disabled students, including note-taking services, reader services, tape recorders, tutors. **Career Services:** Alumni network, Alumni services, Career/job search classes, Career assessment, Internships. UNI has had over 10,000 students conduct internships for credit over the past 30 years, with thousands more participating in an internship for no credit.

FACILITIES

Housing: Coed dorms, men's dorms, women's dorms, fraternity/sorority housing, apartments for married students, apartments for single students, Facilities accessible by persons with disabilities. 95% of campus accessible to physically diasbled. **Special Academic Facilities/Equipment:** Natural history museum, art gallery, greenhouse and biological preserves, Lakeside biology lab and field lab for conservation problems, Tallgrass Prairie Center, Educational Technology Center, curriculum lab, on-campus school for student teachers, NASA Regional Teacher Resource Center, speech and hearing clinic, Small Business Development Center, Iowa Waste Reduction Center, Center for Applied Research in Metal Casting. Iowa Communications Network provides two-way audio/video link between classrooms across the state. Satellite video production truck with three cameras. Performing Arts Center. **Computers:** 80% of classrooms, 75% of libraries, 100% of dining areas, 100% of student union, have wireless network access. Students can register for classes online. Administrative functions (other than registration) can be performed online.

CAMPUS LIFE

Environment: Town. **Activities:** Choral groups, concert band, dance, drama/theater, jazz band, literary magazine, marching band, music ensembles, musical theater, opera, pep band, radio station, student government, student newspaper, symphony orchestra, yearbook, Campus Ministries, Student Organization, Model UN. 278 registered organizations, 18 honor societies, 21 religious organizations. 5 fraternities, 4 sororities. **Athletics (Intercollegiate):** *Men:* basketball, cross-country, football, golf, track/field (outdoor), track/field (indoor), wrestling. *Women:* basketball, cross-country, diving, golf, soccer, softball, swimming, tennis, track/field (outdoor), track/field (indoor), volleyball. **On-Campus Highlights:** Wellness Recreation Center, Gallagher-Bluedorn Performing Arts Center, Piazza and Rialto Dining Centers, Maucker University Union, UNI-DOME and McLeod Center. **Environmental Initiatives:** During the last year, UNI has had a theme for the year of "Food Matters". This theme has focused on many things related to sustainable food systems and a more sustainable campus.

ADMISSIONS

Freshman Academic Profile: Average high school GPA 3.5. 18% in top 10% of high school class, 48% in top 25% of high school class, 84% in top 50% of high school class. 93% from public high schools. ACT middle 50% range 20-25. Minimum internet-based TOEFL 79. Minimum paper TOEFL 550. **Basis for Candidate Selection:** *Very important factors considered include:* rigor of secondary school record, class rank, academic GPA, standardized test scores. *Other factors considered include:* application essay, recommendation(s), interview, talent/ability, first generation. **Freshman Admission Requirements:** High school diploma is required and GED is accepted. *Academic units required:* 4 English, 3 math, 3 science, 3 social studies, 2 academic electives. *Academic units recommended:* 1 science labs, 2 foreign language. **Freshman Admission Statistics:** 5,374 applied, 79.48% admitted, 45% enrolled. **Transfer Admission Requirements:** college transcript(s), Lowest grade transferable D. **General Admission Information:** Application fee $40. Regular application deadline 8/15. Nonfall registration accepted. Admission may be deferred.

COSTS AND FINANCIAL AID

Annual in-state tuition $7,098. Annual out-of-state tuition $17,640. Room and board $8,629. Required fees $1,211. Average book expense $900. **Required Forms and Deadlines:** FAFSA. **Notification of Awards:** Applicants will be notified of awards on a rolling basis beginning 3/15. **Types of Aid:** *Need-based scholarships/grants:* Federal Pell, FSEOG, State scholarships/grants, Private scholarships, College/university scholarship or grant aid from institutional funds. *Loans:* Direct Subsidized Stafford Loans, Direct Unsubsidized Stafford Loans, Direct PLUS loans, Federal Perkins Loans. *Student Employment:* Federal Work-Study Program available. Institutional employment available. **Financial Aid Statistics:** 60% needy freshmen, 58% needy undergrads receive need-based scholarship or grant aid. 75% freshmen, 47% undergrads receive non-need-based scholarship or grant aid. 72% freshmen, 76% undergrads receive need-based self-help aid. 2% freshmen, 2% undergrads receive athletic scholarships. 95% freshmen, 91% undergrads receive any aid. 72% undergrads borrow to pay for school. Average cumulative indebtedness $23,391. **Criteria for awarding aid:** *Need-based:* Academics, Minority status. *Non-need-based:* Academics, Alumni affiliation, Art, Athletics, Leadership, Minority status, Music/drama, State/district residency.

UNIVERSITY OF NOTRE DAME

220 Main Building, Notre Dame, IN 46556
Phone: 574-631-7505 • **Financial Aid Phone:** 574-631-6436
E-mail: admissions@nd.edu • **CEEB Code:** 1841
Fax: 574-631-8865 • **Website:** www.nd.edu • **ACT Code:** 1252

This private school, affiliated with the Roman Catholic Church, was founded in 1842. It has a 1250-acre campus.

RATINGS

Admissions Selectivity Rating: 98   **Fire Safety Rating:** 98   **Green Rating:** 95

STUDENTS AND FACULTY

Enrollment: 8,496. **Student Body:** 47% female, 53% male, 92% out-of-state, 6% international (87 countries represented). Asian 5%, African American 4%, Caucasian 69%, Hispanic 11%, Native American <1%, Pacific Islander <1%, Two or more races 5%, Race unknown <1%.
Retention and Graduation: 98% freshmen return for sophomore year. 90% freshmen graduate within 4 years. 95% freshmen graduate within 6 years. 26% grads go on to further study within 1 year. **Faculty:** Student/faculty ratio 10:1. 1,157 full-time faculty, 91% hold PhDs, 18% are are members of minority groups, 31% are women. 9% of classes are taught by teaching assistants.

ACADEMICS

Degrees: bachelor's, doctoral/professional, doctoral/research, master's. **Classes:** Most classes have 10-19 students. **Most popular majors:** Finance; Psychology; Political Science and Government. **Special Study Options:** Accelerated program, cross-registration, double major, dual enrollment, exchange student program (domestic), honors program, independent study, internships, liberal arts/career combination, student-designed major, study abroad, teacher certification program, Teacher Certification only available through Cross Registration with St. Mary's College. Combined degree programs: B.S. Engr./MBA. **Disability Services:** Special programs offered to physically disabled students, including note-taking services, reader services, tape recorders. **Career Services:** Alumni network, Alumni services, Career/job search classes, Career assessment, Internships. We are proudest of our Employer Development and Alumni Networking: To continue forming and growing relationships with employers during difficult economic times, The Career Center has increased it efforts and outreach to employers to identify career opportunities for students. The importance of networking continues to grow given the current state of the economy. Also recognizing that building and maintaining professional networking relationships will be critical to the hiring process this year. The Career Center has several programs planned for the spring semester that will help students network. The Career Center sent emails to 24,000 alumni in select industries to identify opportunities for Notre Dame students. As a result, employers including IBM, Skanska USA, SwitchFast, Radio Flyer, Fidelity, Bristol Myers Squibb, Lockheed Martin, Draftfcb, and Societe Generale registered for the Winter Career Fair and/or posted job opportunities for our students. Career Counselors have received additional training on searching for jobs within the federal government and public service, a key sector of employment opportunities. The Career Center has successfully developed recruiting relationships with small, mid-sized, and

family-owned companies to post jobs and internships. The Career Center will host a special program in NYC with ND alumni working in private equity and banking, to expand placement opportunities and internships on Wall Street. Also arranging two-week unpaid externships on Wall Street to help students gain experience in a very tough job market. The Career Center has added DirectEmployers Association to its Employer Advisory Board and gained instant access to 420 Fortune 500 employers. The Career Center is working with Alumni Clubs to help seniors find jobs in or near their hometowns. The Career Center is networking with GradStaff.com, CityStaff.com, Adecco and other professional organizations to help students connect to short-term, paid, professional jobs to gain experience with Fortune 500 companies. The Career Center has also implemented distance interviewing with Skype, and Polycam technology as an additional service for employers who cannot travel to campus to interview. A Notre Dame Alumni Group has been established on LinkedIn and currently has over 8,200 members. The Career Center launched a Job Shadow Program in Fall 2008 with over 1,200 alumni volunteering to host students at their companies for a one day networking visit. The Career Center also has an agreement with the ND Alumni Association to grant seniors access to Irish Online, the online community of the Notre Dame Alumni Association. Senior students can create an account on this website before graduation and find alumni contacts. Additionally, networking workshops are being offered, providing students with access to Irish Online that will enable them to find key contacts for career development. Additional programs and information: Confirmed 1,475 internships for ND students documented in the Intern Survey for the Summer of 2008. Raised funding to reimburse students $200 for travel to the Big East Career Fair in March 2008 and March 2009

FACILITIES

Housing: men's dorms, women's dorms. 95% of campus accessible to physically diasbled. **Special Academic Facilities/Equipment:** Art Museum Theater Germ-free research facility Radiation laboratory **Computers:** Students can register for classes online. Administrative functions (other than registration) can be performed online.

CAMPUS LIFE

Environment: City. **Activities:** Choral groups, concert band, dance, drama/theater, jazz band, literary magazine, marching band, music ensembles, musical theater, opera, pep band, radio station, student government, student newspaper, student-run film society, symphony orchestra, yearbook, Campus Ministries, Student Organization, Model UN. 299 registered organizations, 10 honor societies, 11 religious organizations. **Athletics (Intercollegiate):** *Men:* baseball, basketball, cross-country, diving, fencing, football, golf, ice hockey, lacrosse, soccer, swimming, tennis, track/field (outdoor). *Women:* basketball, crew/rowing, cross-country, diving, fencing, golf, lacrosse, soccer, softball, swimming, tennis, track/field (outdoor), volleyball. **On-Campus Highlights:** Grotto, The Dome (Main Building), Basilica of the Sacred Heart, Notre Dame Stadium, Eck Center. **Environmental Initiatives:** Expansion of Office of Sustainability to include 3 full time staff and 7 interns; development of metrics and quantitative goals in 7 key sustainability areas

ADMISSIONS

Freshman Academic Profile: 91% in top 10% of high school class, 98% in top 25% of high school class, 100% in top 50% of high school class. 42% from public high schools. **Reported SAT (pre-2016 redesign) scores:** SAT Math middle 50% range 680-780. SAT Critical Reading middle 50% range 670-760. SAT Writing middle 50% range 650-750. **Concordant SAT scores:** SAT EBRW middle 50% 700–770. SAT Math middle 50% range 710–790. ACT middle 50% range 32-35. Minimum internet-based TOEFL 100. Minimum paper TOEFL 560. **Basis for Candidate Selection:** *Very important factors considered include:* rigor of secondary school record. *Important factors considered include:* class rank, academic GPA, standardized test scores, application essay, recommendation(s), extracurricular activities, talent/ability, character/personal qualities, alumni/ae relation, volunteer work. *Other factors considered include:* first generation, religious affiliation/commitment, racial/ethnic status, work experience, level of applicant's interest. **Freshman Admission Requirements:** High school diploma is required and GED is not accepted. *Academic units required:* 4 English, 3 math, 2 science, 2 science labs, 2 foreign language, 2 history, 3 academic electives. *Academic units recommended:* 4 English, 4 math, 4 science, 2 science labs, 4 foreign language, 4 history. **Freshman Admission Statistics:** 19,505 applied, 18.73% admitted, 56% enrolled. **Transfer Admission Requirements:** High school transcript, college transcript(s), essay or personal statement, standardized test scores, statement of good standing from prior institution(s). Minimum college GPA of 3.0 required. Lowest grade transferable C. **General Admission Information:** Application fee $75. Regular application deadline 1/1. Regular notification 4/10. Nonfall registration accepted. Admission may be deferred for a maximum of 12 months.

COSTS AND FINANCIAL AID

Required fees $507. Average book expense $1,050. **Required Forms and Deadlines:** FAFSA, CSS/Financial Aid PROFILE, Noncustodial PROFILE, Business/Farm Supplement. **Notification of Awards:** Applicants will be notified of awards on a rolling basis beginning 3/28. **Types of Aid:** *Need-based*

UNIVERSITY OF OKLAHOMA

1000 Asp Aveune, Norman, OK 73019
Phone: 405-325-2252 • **Financial Aid Phone:** 405-325-5505
E-mail: admrec@ou.edu • **CEEB Code:** 6879
Fax: 405-325-7124 • **Website:** www.ou.edu • **ACT Code:** 3442

This public school was founded in 1890. It has a 3914-acre campus.

RATINGS

Admissions Selectivity Rating: 87   **Fire Safety Rating:** 90   **Green Rating:** 88

STUDENTS AND FACULTY

Enrollment: 21,909. **Student Body:** 50% female, 50% male, 33% out-of-state, 4% international (111 countries represented). Asian 6%, African American 5%, Caucasian 61%, Hispanic 9%, Native American 4%, Pacific Islander <1%, Two or more races 7%, Race unknown 2%.
Retention and Graduation: 90% freshmen return for sophomore year. 40% freshmen graduate within 4 years. 68% freshmen graduate within 6 years.
Faculty: Student/faculty ratio 17:1. 1,508 full-time faculty, 85% hold PhDs, 21% are are members of minority groups, 43% are women. 7% of classes are taught by teaching assistants.

ACADEMICS

Degrees: bachelor's, doctoral/professional, doctoral/research, doctoral, master's, postbachelor's certificate, post-master's certificate. **Classes:** Most classes have 10-19 students. Most lab/discussion sessions have 20-29 students. **Most popular majors:** Registered Nursing/Registered Nurse; Finance; Accounting. **Special Study Options:** Accelerated program, cooperative education program, distance learning, double major, dual enrollment, English as a Second Language (ESL), external degree program, honors program, independent study, internships, liberal arts/career combination, student-designed major, study abroad, teacher certification program, weekend college. **Honors Programs:** Honors at Oxford: This summer program enables students to study at Oxford (while living at Brasenose College). While there, students work in private tutorials with distinguished Oxford dons. Students can earn up to 6 hours of honors credit in one of our four classes that are offered. Honors in Italy: Honors in Italy is built around a three-hours course called "Imagining Italy" which is taught in the Tuscan town of Arezzo and includes side trips to Florence, Venice, and Rome where students are led on walking tours of the art and history of Italy. The focus is on how Italian culture has influenced writers, filmmakers, and artists from John Adams to Henry James and from Mark Twain to Martin Scorsese. Honors in Germany (new for summer 2010): Honors students and other OU students travel to Leipzig, Germany in June, live at the University of Leipzig, study German, and take a course on German-American literary relations (American writers who wrote in Germany about German culture.) Additionally, students focus on experiencing and exploring major sites for the history and memory of WWII in Germany by taking day trips from Leipzig to major WWII-related sites in Germany. The course will be for six hours credit and will be offered each summer. Honors Undergraduate Research Assistant Program: Honors Undergraduate Research Assistant Program provides undergraduates the opportunity to work with professors as research assistants on specific projects. Student assistants are expected to work 10 hours a week for 10 weeks for $6 an hour. Honors College students with at least 15 hours of college credit and a 3.4+ GPA are eligible to apply. Medical Humanities Scholars Program: The Honors College and the University of Oklahoma College of Medicine have created a special pathway (through a bachelor of arts degree leading to a medical doctorate) for up to five high school students each year who wish to study the humanistic aspects of medicine as

undergraduates. Through a special admissions process, the Medical Humanities Scholars are accepted at the medical school as part of their application to OU's undergraduate honors program. The Honors College has also created a Medical Humanities Minor open to all honors students wishing to study medicine from the perspectives of history, sociology, anthropology, bioethics, literature, and economics. Honors Undergraduate Writing Assistant Program: The Honors Undergraduate Writing Assistant Program includes assistants who receive a stipend to work as writing assistants for the required freshman American Perspectives courses. Students who wish to be writing assistants apply to the program and, if they are selected, participate in a required upper-division preparatory course that focuses on composition pedagogy, research and writing skills, and strategies for commenting and conferencing on students writing. Honors Undergraduate Research Opportunities Program: The Undergraduate Research Opportunities Program is open to all undergraduates at OU. Each semester the Honors College awards more than $12,500 to undergraduate students and their faculty mentors for research and creative activity. Undergraduate Research Day: Each spring the college hosts an Undergraduate Research Day, in which scholars, Honors students or not, share their research with the peers. The Honors College, Phi Beta Kappa and Phi Kappa Phi give cash awards to the best presentations in various categories. Conversations with the Dean: Each week the Dean of the Honors College has in a distinguished professor, author, diplomat, politician, or some other important community or intellectual figure to discuss world events. With the Dean as moderator, students are encouraged to participate in vibrant discussion with the week"s important guest. Honors College Reading Groups: The Dean and Honors College faculty assign a book of their individual choosing to students who voluntarily join an Honors College Reading Group. Limited to 15 students per group, the books are provided free of charge to participants who then meet as a group, one hour a week, to discuss the assigned pages with the professor. There is no charge for this activity, there are no grades, and students may come and go as they please. The aim is to encourage students to read, think, and discuss with other Honors College students important topics of mutual interest, whether fiction or non-fiction. The Honors Undergraduate Research Journal: The Honors Undergraduate Research Journal is a forum in which Honors students of all majors have the opportunity to have their work published. A panel of Honors College professors who annually appoint an editorial board of about eight Honors students advises THURJ. The board accepts research papers, poetry, and short stories of which the top submissions are published every spring. Freshman Summer Reading Series: Each summer all incoming freshmen receive a free, theme-based book chosen by the faculty. The students are encouraged to actively engage the material (the book arrives at the student"s home in late June), which provides the incoming class with a common intellectual experience that the faculty and students can build on during their first semester in order to develop and nurture a collective intellectual community. Combined degree programs: BA/MA, BA/MEng, BAC/MAC. **Disability Services:** Special programs offered to physically disabled students, including note-taking services, reader services, tutors. **Career Services:** Alumni network, Alumni services, Career/job search classes, Career assessment, Internships. Alumni Network- Alumni provide career mentoring to currently enrolled students.

FACILITIES

Housing: Coed dorms, special housing for disabled students, men's dorms, special housing for international students, women's dorms, fraternity/sorority housing, apartments for married students, apartments for single students, Honors House, Cultural Housing, National Merit, and Scholastics floors. 95% of campus accessible to physically diasbled. **Special Academic Facilities/ Equipment:** Fred Jones Museum of Art, Sam Noble Museum of Natural History, National Weather Center, National Severe Storms Library, OU Biological Station, History of Science Collection, Western History Collection, Oklahoma Geological Survey **Computers:** 60% of classrooms, 80% of dorms, 100% of libraries, 75% of dining areas, 100% of student union, 80% of common outdoor areas have wireless network access. Students can register for classes online. Administrative functions (other than registration) can be performed online.

CAMPUS LIFE

Environment: City. **Activities:** Choral groups, concert band, dance, drama/ theater, jazz band, literary magazine, marching band, music ensembles, musical theater, opera, pep band, radio station, student government, student newspaper, student-run film society, symphony orchestra, television station, yearbook, Campus Ministries, Student Organization, Model UN. 388 registered organizations, 17 honor societies, 39 religious organizations. 30 fraternities, 20 sororities. **Athletics (Intercollegiate):** *Men:* baseball, basketball, cross-country, football, golf, gymnastics, tennis, track/field (outdoor), track/field (indoor), wrestling. *Women:* basketball, crew/rowing, cross-country, golf, gymnastics, soccer, softball, tennis, track/field (outdoor), track/field (indoor), volleyball. **On-Campus Highlights:** Fred Jones Jr. Museum of Art, The Gaylord Family Oklahoma Memorial Sta, Sam Noble Ok. Museum of Natural History, Oklahoma Memorial Union, Lloyd Noble Center. **Environmental Initiatives:** American College and University Presidents Climate Commitment (ACUPCC): In April of 2007, the University became a charter signatory to the American

College and University Presidents Climate Commitment. As part of our commitment to create tangible actions to assist in decreasing our greenhouse gas emissions, OU has offered free access to Cleveland Area Rapid Transit (CART) Norman routes to all students, faculty, and staff and has also committed to purchasing 100% of our electricity from renewable energy. In 2016, the American College and University Presidents' Climate Commitment transitioned to Second Nature Carbon commitment.

ADMISSIONS

Freshman Academic Profile: Average high school GPA 3.6. 36% in top 10% of high school class, 66% in top 25% of high school class, 92% in top 50% of high school class. **Reported SAT (pre-2016 redesign) scores:** SAT Math middle 50% range 540-680. SAT Critical Reading middle 50% range 520-665. **Concordant SAT scores:** SAT Math middle 50% range 570–710. ACT middle 50% range 23-29. Minimum internet-based TOEFL 79. Minimum paper TOEFL 550. **Basis for Candidate Selection:** *Very important factors considered include:* rigor of secondary school record, class rank, academic GPA, standardized test scores. *Important factors considered include:* application essay, recommendation(s). *Other factors considered include:* interview, extracurricular activities, talent/ability, character/personal qualities, alumni/ae relation, volunteer work, work experience, level of applicant's interest. **Freshman Admission Requirements:** High school diploma is required and GED is accepted. *Academic units required:* 4 English, 3 math, 3 science, 3 science labs, 1 social studies, 2 history, 2 academic electives. *Academic units recommended:* 4 math, 4 science, 2 foreign language, 1 computer science. **Freshman Admission Statistics:** 14,395 applied, 70.83% admitted, 41% enrolled. **Transfer Admission Requirements:** college transcript(s), Lowest grade transferable D. **General Admission Information:** Application fee $40. Regular application deadline 2/1. Nonfall registration accepted. Admission may be deferred.

COSTS AND FINANCIAL AID

Required Forms and Deadlines: FAFSA. **Notification of Awards:** Applicants will be notified of awards on a rolling basis beginning 3/15. **Types of Aid:** *Need-based scholarships/grants:* Federal Pell, FSEOG, State scholarships/grants, Private scholarships, College/university scholarship or grant aid from institutional funds, United Negro College Fund. *Loans:* Direct Subsidized Stafford Loans, Direct Unsubsidized Stafford Loans, Direct PLUS loans, Federal Perkins Loans, College/university loans from institutional funds. *Student Employment:* Federal Work-Study Program available. Institutional employment available. **Financial Aid Statistics:** 48% needy freshmen, 57% needy undergrads receive need-based scholarship or grant aid. 70% freshmen, 52% undergrads receive non-need-based scholarship or grant aid. 65% freshmen, 71% undergrads receive need-based self-help aid. 1% freshmen, 1% undergrads receive athletic scholarships. 88% freshmen, 86% undergrads receive any aid. 44% undergrads borrow to pay for school. Average cumulative indebtedness $28,444. **Criteria for awarding aid:** *Need-based:* Academics. *Non-need-based:* Academics, Alumni affiliation, Art, Athletics, Leadership, Music/drama, Religious affiliation.

UNIVERSITY OF OREGON

Best Colleges

1217 University of Oregon, Eugene, OR 97403-1217
Phone: 541-346-3201 • **Financial Aid Phone:** 800-760-6953
E-mail: uoadmit@uoregon.edu • **CEEB Code:** 4846
Fax: 541-346-5815 • **Website:** www.uoregon.edu

This public school was founded in 1876. It has a 295-acre campus.

RATINGS

Admissions Selectivity Rating: 83   **Fire Safety Rating:** 85   **Green Rating:** 97

STUDENTS AND FACULTY

Enrollment: 19,773. **Student Body:** 54% female, 46% male, 42% out-of-state, 13% international (80 countries represented). Asian 6%, African American 2%, Caucasian 59%, Hispanic 11%, Native American 1%, Pacific Islander <1%, Two or more races 7%, Race unknown 1%.
Retention and Graduation: 87% freshmen return for sophomore year. 50% freshmen graduate within 4 years. 72% freshmen graduate within 6 years.
Faculty: Student/faculty ratio 17:1. 1,146 full-time faculty, 97% hold PhDs, 17% are are members of minority groups, 45% are women. 17% of classes are taught by teaching assistants.

ACADEMICS

Degrees: bachelor's, doctoral/professional, doctoral/research, master's, postbachelor's certificate, post-master's certificate. **Classes:** Most classes have 10-19 students. Most lab/discussion sessions have 20-29 students. **Most popular majors:** Business/Commerce; Social Sciences; Economics. **Special Study Options:** cross-registration, distance learning, double major, English as a Second Language (ESL), exchange student program (domestic), honors program, independent study, internships, liberal arts/career combination, student-designed major, study abroad, teacher certification program, Semester at Sea program; Professional distinctions program, a certificate program in which students gain direct professional preparation through internships, special courses, a professional mentor program, and the development of an electronic resume and portfolio. There is also a dual enrollment program that allows you to enroll in both UO and Lane Community College or UO and Southwestern Oregon Community College (differs from CDS definition in that it is not a high school dual enrollment program). **Honors Programs:** Robert D. Clark Honors College, College of Arts and Sciences Society of College Scholars, Professional Distinctions program, Dean's List, Junior Scholars. **Disability Services:** Special programs offered to physically disabled students, including note-taking services, reader services, tape recorders, tutors. **Career Services:** Alumni network, Alumni services, Career/job search classes, Career assessment, Internships, Regional alumni. Career Assessment Program: This is a free opportunity available to all students that assists them in assessing values, interests, preferences and strengths. Through this process students gain confidence and self direction which helps them gain insight in major selection and career direction.

FACILITIES

Housing: Coed dorms, fraternity/sorority housing, apartments for married students, cooperative housing, apartments for single students, Wellness Housing, ThemeHousingMost residence halls have separate men's and women's floors; Graduate Student Housing. 95% of campus accessible to physically diasbled. **Special Academic Facilities/Equipment:** Jordan Schnitzer Museum of Art; Museum of Natural and Cultural History; James Warsaw Sports Marketing Center; Lundquist Center for Entrepreneurship; University of Oregon Many Nations Longhouse; Green Chemistry Laboratory and Alice C. Tyler Instrumentation Center; Future Music Oregon, a computer music center in the School of Music; Pine Mountain Observatory (Bend, Oregon); Oregon Institute of Marine Biology (Oregon Coast); Central Oregon programs affiliated with the Oregon University System Cascades Campus (Bend, Oregon); Urban Architecture program and BetterBricks Daylighting Laboratory at the University of Oregon Portland Center (Portland, Oregon). **Computers:** 95% of classrooms, 35% of dorms, 100% of libraries, 100% of dining areas, 100% of student union, 30% of common outdoor areas have wireless network access. Students can register for classes online. Administrative functions (other than registration) can be performed online.

CAMPUS LIFE

Environment: City. **Activities:** Choral groups, concert band, dance, drama/theater, jazz band, literary magazine, marching band, music ensembles, musical theater, opera, pep band, radio station, student government, student newspaper, student-run film society, symphony orchestra, Campus Ministries, Student Organization. 250 registered organizations, 22 honor societies, 20 religious organizations. 12 fraternities, 10 sororities. **Athletics (Intercollegiate):** *Men:* baseball, basketball, cross-country, football, golf, tennis, track/field (outdoor). *Women:* basketball, cross-country, golf, gymnastics, lacrosse, soccer, softball, tennis, track/field (outdoor), volleyball. **On-Campus Highlights:** University of Oregon Duckstore, Knight Library, Erb Memorial Union, Laverne Krauss Gallery in Lawrence Hall, Watch sports at Autzen, Hayward, or Mac Court, The University of Oregon's 295-acre, park-like campus is home to more than 500 varieties of trees, various private spots to study or simply stare at the sky, and tons of quick stops where you can grab a bite between classes. With a wealth of campus resources to make your life as a student easier, the UO campus feeds the mind, body, and spirit. On average, each course you take at the UO will have a person from another country, six people from different states, and several people with religious, cultural, and ethnic heritage different from your own. You'll thrive because this diversity pushes you to see the world differently. You'll listen to new ideas, and maybe even change the world because you changed your mind. **Environmental Initiatives:** Created the Oregon Model for Sustainable Development which puts a cap on building energy consumption.

ADMISSIONS

Freshman Academic Profile: Average high school GPA 3.6. 25% in top 10% of high school class, 60% in top 25% of high school class, 91% in top 50% of high school class. **Reported SAT (pre-2016 redesign) scores:** SAT Math middle 50% range 490-610. SAT Critical Reading middle 50% range 490-610. SAT Writing middle 50% range 480-600. **Concordant SAT scores:** SAT EBRW middle 50% 540–660. SAT Math middle 50% range 520–630. ACT middle 50% range 22-27. Minimum internet-based TOEFL 61. Minimum paper TOEFL 500. **Basis for Candidate Selection:** *Very important factors considered include:* rigor of secondary school record, academic GPA. *Important* *factors considered include:* standardized test scores, application essay. *Other factors considered include:* class rank, extracurricular activities, talent/ability, character/personal qualities, first generation, geographical residence, state residency, racial/ethnic status, volunteer work, work experience. **Freshman Admission Requirements:** High school diploma is required and GED is accepted. *Academic units required:* 4 English, 3 math, 3 science, 2 foreign language, 3 social studies. *Academic units recommended:* 1 science labs. **Freshman Admission Statistics:** 21,821 applied, 77.87% admitted, 24% enrolled. **Transfer Admission Requirements:** college transcript(s), Minimum college GPA of 2.25 required. Lowest grade transferable D-. **General Admission Information:** Application fee $65. Regular application deadline 1/15. Nonfall registration accepted.

COSTS AND FINANCIAL AID

Annual in-state tuition $8,910. Annual out-of-state tuition $31,590. Room and board $12,210. Required fees $1,852. Average book expense $1,122. **Required Forms and Deadlines:** FAFSA. **Notification of Awards:** Applicants will be notified of awards on a rolling basis beginning 4/1. **Types of Aid:** *Need-based scholarships/grants:* Federal Pell, FSEOG, State scholarships/grants, Private scholarships, College/university scholarship or grant aid from institutional funds. *Loans:* Direct Subsidized Stafford Loans, Direct Unsubsidized Stafford Loans, Direct PLUS loans, Federal Perkins Loans, College/university loans from institutional funds. *Student Employment:* Federal Work-Study Program available. Institutional employment available. **Financial Aid Statistics:** 72% needy freshmen, 73% needy undergrads receive need-based scholarship or grant aid. 6% freshmen, 3% undergrads receive non-need-based scholarship or grant aid. 76% freshmen, 80% undergrads receive need-based self-help aid. 2% freshmen, 2% undergrads receive athletic scholarships. 85% freshmen, 91% undergrads receive any aid. 47% undergrads borrow to pay for school. Average cumulative indebtedness $25,542. **Criteria for awarding aid:** *Need-based:* Academics, Athletics, Leadership, Minority status, Music/drama. *Non-need-based:* Academics, Athletics, Leadership, Minority status, Music/drama, State/district residency.

UNIVERSITY OF THE OZARKS

415 N College Avenue, Clarksville, AR 72830
Phone: 479-979-1227 • **Financial Aid Phone:** 479-979-1221
E-mail: admiss@ozarks.edu • **CEEB Code:** 6111
Fax: 479-979-1417 • **Website:** www.ozarks.edu • **ACT Code:** 120

This private school, affiliated with the Presbyterian Church, was founded in 1834. It has a 56-acre campus.

RATINGS

Admissions Selectivity Rating: 83   **Fire Safety Rating:** 93   **Green Rating:** 60*

STUDENTS AND FACULTY

Enrollment: 615. **Student Body:** 55% female, 45% male, 29% out-of-state, 14% international (13 countries represented). Asian 1%, African American 4%, Caucasian 71%, Hispanic 6%, Native American 2%, Pacific Islander 0%, Two or more races 1%, Race unknown 1%.
Retention and Graduation: 64% freshmen return for sophomore year. 33% freshmen graduate within 4 years. 53% freshmen graduate within 6 years.
Faculty: Student/faculty ratio 11:1. 49 full-time faculty, 69% hold PhDs, 8% are are members of minority groups, 37% are women. 0% of classes are taught by teaching assistants.

ACADEMICS

Degrees: bachelor's. **Most popular majors:** Business Administration and Management; Biology/Biological Sciences; Physical Education Teaching and Coaching. **Special Study Options:** cooperative education program, double major, dual enrollment, independent study, internships, liberal arts/career combination, study abroad, teacher certification program. **Disability Services:** Special programs offered to physically disabled students, including note-taking services, reader services, tape recorders, tutors. **Career Services:** Alumni network, Alumni services, Career/job search classes, Career assessment, Internships, Regional alumni. Our goal is to have one-on-one working relationships with students to provide them with the necessary skills needed to be productive members of the workforce and society as a whole.

FACILITIES

Housing: Coed dorms, men's dorms, women's dorms, apartments for married students, apartments for single students, University owned housing. 100% of campus accessible to physically diasbled. **Special Academic Facilities/Equipment:** Walton Fine Arts Center; Stephens Gallery; Smith-Broyles Science Center; Walker Hall Teacher Education and Communications Center. **Computers:** 100% of libraries, have wireless network access.

CAMPUS LIFE

Environment: Village. **Activities:** Choral groups, drama/theater, literary magazine, music ensembles, radio station, student government, student-run film society, television station, yearbook, Campus Ministries, Student Organization. 40 registered organizations, 5 honor societies, 6 religious organizations. **Athletics (Intercollegiate):** *Men:* baseball, basketball, cheerleading, cross-country, soccer, tennis. *Women:* basketball, cheerleading, cross-country, soccer, softball, tennis. **On-Campus Highlights:** Seay Student Center, Walton Fine Arts Center, Walker Education and Communications Buil, Robson Library, Gilbert's Park.

ADMISSIONS

Freshman Academic Profile: Average high school GPA 3.3. 18% in top 10% of high school class, 44% in top 25% of high school class, 76% in top 50% of high school class. 92% from public high schools. **Reported SAT (pre-2016 redesign) scores:** SAT Math middle 50% range 443-560. SAT Critical Reading middle 50% range 450-570. **Concordant SAT scores:** SAT Math middle 50% range 480–580. ACT middle 50% range 19-25. Minimum paper TOEFL 500. **Basis for Candidate Selection:** *Important factors considered include:* standardized test scores. *Other factors considered include:* rigor of secondary school record, academic GPA, application essay, recommendation(s), interview, extracurricular activities, talent/ability, character/personal qualities, alumni/ae relation, volunteer work, work experience, level of applicant's interest. **Freshman Admission Requirements:** High school diploma is required and GED is accepted. *Academic units recommended:* 4 English, 4 math, 3 science, 2 science labs, 2 foreign language, 1 social studies, 2 history. **Freshman Admission Statistics:** 1,372 applied, 59.33% admitted, 25% enrolled. **Transfer Admission Requirements:** college transcript(s), Minimum college GPA of 2.0 required. Lowest grade transferable C. **General Admission Information:** Application fee $30. Priority deadline 4/1. Nonfall registration accepted. Admission may be deferred.

COSTS AND FINANCIAL AID

Annual tuition $21,450. Room and board $6,500. Required fees $600. Average book expense $800. **Required Forms and Deadlines:** FAFSA. **Notification of Awards:** Applicants will be notified of awards on a rolling basis beginning 3/1. **Types of Aid:** *Need-based scholarships/grants:* Federal Pell, FSEOG, State scholarships/grants, Private scholarships, College/university scholarship or grant aid from institutional funds, United Negro College Fund, Federal Nursing Scholarships. *Loans:* Federal Perkins Loans, College/university loans from institutional funds. *Student Employment:* Federal Work-Study Program available. Institutional employment available. **Financial Aid Statistics:** 97% needy freshmen, 97% needy undergrads receive need-based scholarship or grant aid. 0% undergrads receive non-need-based scholarship or grant aid. 82% freshmen, 85% undergrads receive need-based self-help aid. 0% freshmen, 0% undergrads receive athletic scholarships. 100% freshmen, 98% undergrads receive any aid. **Criteria for awarding aid:** *Need-based:* Academics, Alumni affiliation, Art, Leadership, Minority status, Music/drama, Religious affiliation. *Non-need-based:* Academics, Alumni affiliation, Art, Leadership, Minority status, Music/drama, Religious affiliation, State/district residency.

UNIVERSITY OF THE PACIFIC

3601 Pacific Avenue, Stockton, CA 95211
Phone: 209-946-2211 • **Financial Aid Phone:** 209-946-2421
E-mail: admissions@pacific.edu • **CEEB Code:** 4065
Fax: 209-946-4213 • **Website:** www.pacific.edu • **ACT Code:** 240

This private school was founded in 1851. It has a 175-acre campus.

RATINGS

Admissions Selectivity Rating: 85   **Fire Safety Rating:** 93   **Green Rating:** 96

STUDENTS AND FACULTY

Enrollment: 3,474. **Student Body:** 53% female, 47% male, 7% out-of-state, 6% international (66 countries represented). Asian 37%, African American 3%, Caucasian 24%, Hispanic 19%, Native American <1%, Pacific Islander <1%, Two or more races 6%, Race unknown 4%.
Retention and Graduation: 82% freshmen return for sophomore year. 50% freshmen graduate within 4 years. 68% freshmen graduate within 6 years.
Faculty: Student/faculty ratio 13:1. 429 full-time faculty, 92% hold PhDs, 23% are are members of minority groups, 44% are women.

ACADEMICS

Degrees: bachelor's, doctoral/professional, doctoral/research, master's.
Classes: Most classes have 10-19 students. Most lab/discussion sessions have 10-19 students. **Most popular majors:** Engineering; Biology/Biological Sciences; Business/Commerce. **Special Study Options:** Accelerated program, double major, dual enrollment, English as a Second Language (ESL), exchange student program (domestic), honors program, independent study, internships, liberal arts/career combination, student-designed major, study abroad, teacher certification program, minors, practicum, thematic minors, undergraduate research, ethnic studies, envirnomental science, gender studies, service learning. Combined degree programs: BA/DDS, BA or BS/MBA, BA or BS/DDS, BS/Pharm.D. **Disability Services:** Special programs offered to physically disabled students, including note-taking services, reader services, tape recorders, tutors.

FACILITIES

Housing: Coed dorms, fraternity/sorority housing, apartments for single students. 90% of campus accessible to physically diasbled. **Special Academic Facilities/Equipment:** John Muir Collection, Dave and Iola Brubeck Collection, Brubeck Institute for Jazz Studies, Reynolds Art Gallery. **Computers:** 100% of classrooms, 90% of dorms, 100% of libraries, 100% of dining areas, 100% of student union, 30% of common outdoor areas have wireless network access. Students can register for classes online. Administrative functions (other than registration) can be performed online.

CAMPUS LIFE

Environment: City. **Activities:** Choral groups, concert band, dance, drama/theater, jazz band, literary magazine, music ensembles, musical theater, opera, pep band, radio station, student government, student newspaper, student-run film society, symphony orchestra, yearbook, Campus Ministries, Student Organization, Model UN. 100 registered organizations, 14 honor societies, 10 religious organizations. 8 fraternities, 7 sororities. **Athletics (Intercollegiate):** *Men:* baseball, basketball, golf, swimming, tennis, volleyball, water polo. *Women:* basketball, cross-country, field hockey, soccer, softball, swimming, tennis, volleyball, water polo. **On-Campus Highlights:** Brubeck Istitute for Jazz Studies, John Muir Collection and Center, Alex Spanos Center, Reynolds Art Gallery, Pharmacy and Health Sciences Bldg. **Environmental Initiatives:** Natural Resource Institute.

ADMISSIONS

Freshman Academic Profile: Average high school GPA 3.5. 37% in top 10% of high school class, 40% in top 25% of high school class, 92% in top 50% of high school class. 82% from public high schools. **Reported SAT (pre-2016 redesign) scores:** SAT Math middle 50% range 530-670. SAT Critical Reading middle 50% range 500-630. SAT Writing middle 50% range 490-640. **Concordant SAT scores:** SAT EBRW middle 50% 550–680. SAT Math middle 50% range 560–700. ACT middle 50% range 23-30. Minimum internet-based TOEFL 52. Minimum paper TOEFL 475. **Basis for Candidate Selection:** *Very important factors considered include:* rigor of secondary school record. *Important factors considered include:* academic GPA, standardized test scores, application essay, recommendation(s), extracurricular activities, first generation. *Other factors considered include:* class rank, talent/ability, character/personal qualities, alumni/ae relation, geographical residence, volunteer work, work experience. **Freshman Admission Requirements:** High school diploma is required and GED is accepted. *Academic units recommended:* 4 English, 2 foreign language, 2 social studies, 1 history, 1 academic elective, 1 visual/performing arts. **Freshman Admission Statistics:** 8,870 applied, 65.99% admitted, 12% enrolled. **Transfer Admission Requirements:** college transcript(s), statement of good standing from prior institution(s). Minimum college GPA of 3.0 required. Lowest grade transferable C. **General Admission Information:** Application fee $35. Priority deadline 11/15. Regular application deadline 1/15. Nonfall registration accepted. Admission may be deferred for a maximum of 1 year.

COSTS AND FINANCIAL AID

Annual tuition $44,068. Room and board $12,858. Required fees $520. Average book expense $1,791. **Required Forms and Deadlines:** FAFSA. **Notification of Awards:** Applicants will be notified of awards on a rolling basis beginning 3/1. **Types of Aid:** *Need-based scholarships/grants:* Federal Pell, FSEOG, State scholarships/grants, Private scholarships, College/university scholarship or grant aid from institutional funds. *Loans:* Direct Subsidized Stafford Loans, Direct Unsubsidized Stafford Loans, Direct PLUS loans, Federal Perkins Loans. *Student Employment:* Federal Work-Study Program available. Institutional employment available. **Financial Aid Statistics:** 99% needy freshmen, 97% needy undergrads receive need-based scholarship or grant aid. 0% undergrads receive non-need-based scholarship or grant aid. 89% freshmen, 95% undergrads receive need-based self-help aid. 4% freshmen, 4% undergrads receive athletic scholarships. 91% freshmen, 83% undergrads receive any aid. 67% undergrads borrow to pay for school. Average cumulative indebtedness $28,810. **Criteria for awarding aid:** *Need-based:* Academics. *Non-need-based:* Academics, Athletics, Leadership, Music/drama, Religious affiliation.

UNIVERSITY OF PENNSYLVANIA

1 College Hall, Philadelphia, PA 19104
Phone: 215-898-7507 • **Financial Aid Phone:** 215-898-1988
E-mail: info@admissions.upenn.edu • **CEEB Code:** 2926
Fax: 215-898-7507 • **Website:** www.upenn.edu • **ACT Code:** 3732

This private school was founded in 1740. It has a 279-acre campus.

RATINGS

Admissions Selectivity Rating: 99   **Fire Safety Rating:** 83   **Green Rating:** 93

STUDENTS AND FACULTY

Enrollment: 9,726. **Student Body:** 50% female, 50% male, 81% out-of-state, 12% international (126 countries represented). Asian 20%, African American 7%, Caucasian 44%, Hispanic 10%, Native American <1%, Pacific Islander <1%, Two or more races 4%, Race unknown 3%.
Retention and Graduation: 98% freshmen return for sophomore year. 87% freshmen graduate within 4 years. 95% freshmen graduate within 6 years. 20% grads go on to further study within 1 year. 5% grads pursue arts and sciences degrees. 4% grads pursue law degrees. 1% grads pursue business degrees. 5% grads pursue medical degrees. **Faculty:** Student/faculty ratio 6:1. 1,458 full-time faculty, 100% hold PhDs, 21% are are members of minority groups, 38% are women. 5% of classes are taught by teaching assistants.

ACADEMICS

Degrees: associate, bachelor's, certificate, doctoral/professional, doctoral/research, doctoral, master's, postbachelor's certifiate, post-master's certificate, terminal. **Classes:** Most classes have 10-19 students. **Most popular majors:** Finance; Economics; Registered Nursing/Registered Nurse. **Special Study Options:** Accelerated program, cross-registration, double major, dual enrollment, English as a Second Language (ESL), exchange student program (domestic), honors program, independent study, internships, liberal arts/career combination, student-designed major, study abroad, teacher certification program, Joint degree programs among schools. Accelerated degree programs. Opportunities for preprofessional programs in predentistry, prelaw, premedicine, and preveterinary studies (not actual majors). Washington semester. **Honors Programs:** Penn's general honors program is called the Benjamin Franklin Scholars program, although the honors program for students in business is called Joseph Wharton Scholars. There are specialized honors programs including Fisher Program in Management and Technology, the Huntsman Program in International Studies and Business, the Vagelos Scholars Program in Molecular Life Sciences, and the Civic Scholars Program which offers opportunities to integrate community service and academics. The University Scholars Program is open to already matriculated students who are interested in engaging in high-level research. Combined degree programs: BA/JD, BA/MA, BA/DDS, BA/MEng, 4-yr. BSE/BS, BSE/MBA, BA/MS Ed., BAS/MS Ed. **Disability Services:** Special programs offered to physically disabled students, including note-taking services, reader services, tape recorders, tutors. **Career Services:** Alumni network, Alumni services, Career assessment, Internships, Regional alumni. In addition to a full on-campus recruiting program (over 14,000 interviews conducted last year) and nine career fairs, Career Services is extremely active online, with robust Twitter feeds, Facebook and LinkedIn presence, a blog, dozens of videos, and a web site that receives several million hits annually.

FACILITIES

Housing: Coed dorms, special housing for disabled students, fraternity/sorority housing, apartments for married students, apartments for single students, Wellness Housing, private off-campus. 92% of campus accessible to physically diasbled. **Special Academic Facilities/Equipment:** Art gallery, anthropology museum, institute for contemporary art, language lab, large animal research center, primate research center, arboretum, observatory, wind tunnel, electron microscope. **Computers:** 85% of classrooms, 100% of dorms, 100% of libraries, 85% of dining areas, 100% of student union, 25% of common outdoor areas have wireless network access. Students can register for classes online. Administrative functions (other than registration) can be performed online.

CAMPUS LIFE

Environment: Metropolis. **Activities:** Choral groups, concert band, dance, drama/theater, jazz band, literary magazine, marching band, music ensembles, musical theater, opera, pep band, radio station, student government, student newspaper, student-run film society, symphony orchestra, television station, yearbook, Campus Ministries, Student Organization, Model UN. 350 registered organizations, 9 honor societies, 29 religious organizations. 35 fraternities, 13 sororities. **Athletics (Intercollegiate):** *Men:* baseball, basketball, crew/rowing, cross-country, diving, fencing, football, golf, lacrosse, light weight football, soccer, squash, swimming, tennis, track/field (outdoor), track/field (indoor), wrestling. *Women:* basketball, crew/rowing, cross-country, diving, fencing, field hockey, golf, gymnastics, lacrosse, soccer, softball, squash, swimming, tennis, track/field (outdoor), track/field (indoor), volleyball. **On-Campus Highlights:** University of Pennsylvania Museum, Institute of Contemporary Art, Walnut Street shops and restuarants, Annenberg Center, Franklin Field. **Environmental Initiatives:** Building optimization implementation, a program to optimize building systems in high-energy-use buildings to reduce their utility use and carbon footprint. This effort is enhanced by Penn's comprehensive building metering program.

ADMISSIONS

Freshman Academic Profile: Average high school GPA 3.9. 95% in top 10% of high school class, 99% in top 25% of high school class, 100% in top 50% of high school class. 60% from public high schools. **Reported SAT (pre-2016 redesign) scores:** SAT Math middle 50% range 700-790. SAT Critical Reading middle 50% range 680-760. SAT Writing middle 50% range 690-780. **Concordant SAT scores:** SAT EBRW middle 50% 720–780. SAT Math middle 50% range 730–800. ACT middle 50% range 31-34. **Basis for Candidate Selection:** *Very important factors considered include:* rigor of secondary school record, academic GPA, standardized test scores, application essay, recommendation(s), character/personal qualities. *Important factors considered include:* class rank, extracurricular activities, talent/ability. *Other factors considered include:* interview, first generation, alumni/ae relation, geographical residence, state residency, racial/ethnic status, volunteer work, work experience, level of applicant's interest. **Freshman Admission Requirements:** High school diploma or equivalent is not required. *Academic units recommended:* 4 English, 4 math, 3 science, 3 science labs, 4 foreign language, 2 social studies, 3 history. **Freshman Admission Statistics:** 37,268 applied, 10.16% admitted, 64% enrolled. **Transfer Admission Requirements:** High school transcript, college transcript(s), essay or personal statement, standardized test scores, statement of good standing from prior institution(s). Lowest grade transferable C. **General Admission Information:** Application fee $75. Regular application deadline 1/1. Regular notification 4/1. Nonfall registration not accepted. Admission may be deferred for a maximum of 1 year.

COSTS AND FINANCIAL AID

Annual tuition $45,556. Room and board $14,536. Required fees $5,698. Average book expense $1,280. **Required Forms and Deadlines:** FAFSA, Institution's own financial aid form, CSS/Financial Aid PROFILE, Noncustodial PROFILE, Business/Farm Supplement. **Notification of Awards:** Applicants will be notified of awards on or about 4/1. **Types of Aid:** *Need-based scholarships/grants:* Federal Pell, FSEOG, State scholarships/grants, Private scholarships, College/university scholarship or grant aid from institutional funds. *Loans:* Direct Subsidized Stafford Loans, Direct Unsubsidized Stafford Loans, Direct PLUS loans, Federal Perkins Loans, Federal Nursing Loans, College/university loans from institutional funds. *Student Employment:* Federal Work-Study Program available. Institutional employment available. **Financial Aid Statistics:** 99% needy freshmen, 99% needy undergrads receive need-based scholarship or grant aid. 0% undergrads receive non-need-based scholarship or grant aid. 100% freshmen, 100% undergrads receive need-based self-help aid. 0% freshmen, 0% undergrads receive athletic scholarships. 47% freshmen, 45% undergrads receive any aid. 28% undergrads borrow to pay for school. Average cumulative indebtedness $26,157.

UNIVERSITY OF PHOENIX

4035 S. Riverpoint Parkway, Phoenix, AZ 85040
Phone: 480-446-4600 • **Financial Aid Phone:** 1-800-921-1904
Website: www.phoenix.edu

This proprietary school was founded in 1976.

RATINGS
Admissions Selectivity Rating: 60*   **Fire Safety Rating:** 60*   **Green Rating:** 60*

STUDENTS AND FACULTY
Enrollment: 310,170. **Student Body:** 69% female, 31% male, 3% international. Asian 2%, African American 18%, Caucasian 39%, Hispanic 9%, Native American 1%, Pacific Islander 0%, Two or more races 0%, Race unknown 28%.
Retention and Graduation: 39% freshmen return for sophomore year. 1% freshmen graduate within 4 years. 9% freshmen graduate within 6 years. **Faculty:** Student/faculty ratio 43:1. 1,410 full-time faculty, 23% hold PhDs, 19% are are members of minority groups, 46% are women. 0% of classes are taught by teaching assistants.

ACADEMICS

Degrees: associate, bachelor's, certificate, doctoral, master's, postbachelor's certificate, post-master's certificate, transfer. **Most popular majors:** Health/Health Care Administration/Management; Business Administration and Management; Accounting. **Special Study Options:** Accelerated program, distance learning, independent study, Evening courses meeting 4 hours per night, one night per week for 5 weeks at the bachelor level and 6 weeks at the master level. **Disability Services:** Special programs offered to physically disabled students, including tape recorders. **Career Services:** Alumni network, On-campus interviews.

FACILITIES

Housing: 100% of campus accessible to physically diasbled. **Computers:** Students can register for classes online. Administrative functions (other than registration) can be performed online.

CAMPUS LIFE

Environment: Metropolis. **Activities:** 2 honor societies.

ADMISSIONS

Minimum paper TOEFL 550. **Basis for Candidate Selection:** *Very important factors considered include:* work experience. *Other factors considered include:* recommendation(s). **Freshman Admission Requirements:** High school diploma is required and GED is accepted. **Transfer Admission Requirements:** college transcript(s). **General Admission Information:** Nonfall registration accepted.

UNIVERSITY OF PIKEVILE

Admissions Office, Pikeville, KY 41501
Phone: 606-218-5251 • **Financial Aid Phone:** 606-218-5247
E-mail: wewantyou@upike.edu • **CEEB Code:** 1980
Fax: 606-218-5255 • **Website:** http://www.upike.edu/ • **ACT Code:** 1540

This private school, affiliated with the Presbyterian Church, was founded in 1889. It has a 25-acre campus.

RATINGS
Admissions Selectivity Rating: 72   **Fire Safety Rating:** 87   **Green Rating:** 60*

STUDENTS AND FACULTY
Enrollment: 1,244. **Student Body:** 51% female, 49% male, 20% out-of-state, 4% international (22 countries represented). Asian 1%, African American 12%, Caucasian 81%, Hispanic 2%, Native American <1%, Pacific Islander <1%, Two or more races 0%, Race unknown 0%.
Retention and Graduation: 58% freshmen return for sophomore year. 22% freshmen graduate within 4 years. 36% freshmen graduate within 6 years. 32% grads go on to further study within 1 year. 75% grads pursue business degrees. **Faculty:** Student/faculty ratio 15:1. 69 full-time faculty, 59% hold PhDs, 4% are are members of minority groups, 57% are women. 0% of classes are taught by teaching assistants.

ACADEMICS

Degrees: associate, bachelor's, doctoral/professional, master's, terminal. **Classes:** Most classes have 10-19 students. **Most popular majors:** Business/Commerce; Biology; Criminal Justice/Safety Studies. **Special Study Options:** double major, dual enrollment, independent study, internships, liberal arts/career combination, student-designed major, study abroad, teacher certification program. Combined degree programs: BS/DO. **Disability Services:** Special programs offered to physically disabled students, including tape recorders, tutors. **Career Services:** Career/job search classes, On-campus interviews. The University of Pikeville sends students to one-week and two-week seminars in Washington, D.C. The focus of these seminars may be presidential elections, presidential inaugurations, Congress, the media and politics, and national security. The Washington Center seminars are intense academic experiences constituting course credit. The program also gives students the opportunity to live in our nation's capital and experience all it has to offer.

FACILITIES

Housing: Coed dorms, men's dorms, women's dorms. 97% of campus accessible to physically diasbled.

CAMPUS LIFE

Environment: Village. **Activities:** Choral groups, dance, literary magazine, pep band, student government, student newspaper, yearbook, Campus Ministries. 40 registered organizations, 6 honor societies, 2 religious organizations. **Athletics (Intercollegiate):** *Men:* baseball, basketball, bowling, cheerleading, cross-country, football, golf, soccer, tennis. *Women:* basketball, bowling, cheerleading, cross-country, golf, soccer, softball, tennis, volleyball. **On-**

Campus Highlights: Administration Building, Armington Hall, Allara Library, Record Hall, Kinzer Hall.

ADMISSIONS

Freshman Academic Profile: Average high school GPA 3.1. 14% in top 10% of high school class, 27% in top 25% of high school class, 61% in top 50% of high school class. 99% from public high schools. **Reported SAT (pre-2016 redesign) scores:** SAT Math middle 50% range 400-470. SAT Critical Reading middle 50% range 410-460. **Concordant SAT scores:** SAT Math middle 50% range 440–510. ACT middle 50% range 18-23. Minimum internet-based TOEFL 78. **Freshman Admission Requirements:** High school diploma is required and GED is accepted. *Academic units recommended:* 4 English, 3 math, 3 science, 2 social studies, 1 history. **Freshman Admission Statistics:** 2,408 applied, 100.00% admitted, 13% enrolled. **Transfer Admission Requirements:** High school transcript, college transcript(s), standardized test scores, statement of good standing from prior institution(s). Lowest grade transferable C. **General Admission Information:** Regular application deadline 8/15. Nonfall registration accepted. Admission may be deferred.

COSTS AND FINANCIAL AID

Annual tuition $19,600. Room and board $8,376. Required fees $0. Average book expense $2,500. **Required Forms and Deadlines:** FAFSA. **Notification of Awards:** Applicants will be notified of awards on a rolling basis beginning 2/1. **Types of Aid:** *Need-based scholarships/grants:* Federal Pell, FSEOG, State scholarships/grants, Private scholarships, College/university scholarship or grant aid from institutional funds. *Loans:* Direct Subsidized Stafford Loans, Direct Unsubsidized Stafford Loans, Direct PLUS loans, Federal Perkins Loans, College/university loans from institutional funds. *Student Employment:* Federal Work-Study Program available. **Financial Aid Statistics:** 100% needy freshmen, 100% needy undergrads receive need-based scholarship or grant aid. 58% freshmen, 48% undergrads receive non-need-based scholarship or grant aid. 86% freshmen, 84% undergrads receive need-based self-help aid. 0% freshmen, 0% undergrads receive athletic scholarships. 100% freshmen, 97% undergrads receive any aid. 76% undergrads borrow to pay for school. Average cumulative indebtedness $27,645. **Criteria for awarding aid:** *Need-based:* Academics, Alumni affiliation, Athletics, Music/drama.

UNIVERSITY OF PITTSBURGH AT BRADFORD

Office of Admissions–Hanley Library, Bradford, PA 16701
Phone: 814-362-7555 • **Financial Aid Phone:** 814-362-7550
E-mail: Admissions@upb.pitt.edu • **CEEB Code:** 2935
Fax: 814-362-5150 • **Website:** www.upb.pitt.edu • **ACT Code:** 3731

This public school was founded in 1963. It has a 317-acre campus.

RATINGS

Admissions Selectivity Rating: 80   **Fire Safety Rating:** 93   **Green Rating:** 77

STUDENTS AND FACULTY

Enrollment: 1,449. **Student Body:** 54% female, 46% male, 22% out-of-state, 3% international (9 countries represented). Asian 2%, African American 12%, Caucasian 68%, Hispanic 5%, Native American <1%, Pacific Islander <1%, Two or more races 2%, Race unknown 6%.
Retention and Graduation: 65% freshmen return for sophomore year. 33% freshmen graduate within 4 years. 50% freshmen graduate within 6 years. 25% grads go on to further study within 1 year. 18% grads pursue arts and sciences degrees. 2% grads pursue law degrees. 1% grads pursue business degrees. 2% grads pursue medical degrees. **Faculty:** Student/faculty ratio 17:1. 75 full-time faculty, 72% hold PhDs, 19% are are members of minority groups, 39% are women. 0% of classes are taught by teaching assistants.

ACADEMICS

Degrees: associate, bachelor's, terminal, transfer. **Classes:** Most classes have 20-29 students. Most lab/discussion sessions have 10-19 students. **Most popular majors:** Business/Commerce; Biology/Biological Sciences; Criminal Justice/Law Enforcement Administration. **Special Study Options:** cross-registration, distance learning, double major, dual enrollment, external degree program, honors program, independent study, internships, study abroad, teacher certification program. **Honors Programs:** The University of Pittsburgh at Bradford offers the Scholars Program which is designed to create a learning community for outstanding students at Pitt-Bradford. **Disability Services:** Special programs offered to physically disabled students, including note-taking services, reader services, tape recorders, tutors. **Career Services:** Alumni network, Alumni services, Career assessment, Internships, Regional alumni. From Backpack to Briefcase, an annual day long career/leadership development conference sponsored by Career Services and Pitt-Bradford Alumni Association, held the last Saturday in January.

FACILITIES

Housing: Coed dorms, special housing for disabled students, apartments for single students. 99% of campus accessible to physically diasbled. **Special Academic Facilities/Equipment:** Ceramics Studio, Biodiesal Lab, Television and Radio Broadcast Labs **Computers:** 100% of classrooms, 100% of dorms, 90% of libraries, 90% of dining areas, 100% of student union, 50% of common outdoor areas have wireless network access. Students can register for classes online. Administrative functions (other than registration) can be performed online.

CAMPUS LIFE

Environment: Village. **Activities:** Choral groups, dance, drama/theater, literary magazine, radio station, student government, student newspaper, Campus Ministries. 54 registered organizations, 8 honor societies, 1 religious organization. 3 fraternities, 3 sororities. **Athletics (Intercollegiate):** *Men:* baseball, basketball, cross-country, golf, soccer, swimming, tennis. *Women:* basketball, cross-country, golf, soccer, softball, swimming, tennis, volleyball. **On-Campus Highlights:** Sport and Fitness Center, The Commons, Student apartments, Blaisdell Hall (Fine Arts Building), Smart classrooms. **Environmental Initiatives:** Installation of a 2.6 kW solar array to power a sustainability information center in the student commons which connects to energy monitors that were installed on every building on campus.

ADMISSIONS

Freshman Academic Profile: Average high school GPA 3.2. 10% in top 10% of high school class, 33% in top 25% of high school class, 65% in top 50% of high school class. 86% from public high schools. **Reported SAT (pre-2016 redesign) scores:** SAT Math middle 50% range 440-550. SAT Critical Reading middle 50% range 420-520. SAT Writing middle 50% range 400-500. **Concordant SAT scores:** SAT EBRW middle 50% 460–570. SAT Math middle 50% range 480–570. ACT middle 50% range 19-23. Minimum paper TOEFL 550. **Basis for Candidate Selection:** *Very important factors considered include:* level of applicant's interest. *Important factors considered include:* rigor of secondary school record, academic GPA, standardized test scores, interview. *Other factors considered include:* class rank, application essay, recommendation(s), extracurricular activities, talent/ability, character/personal qualities, volunteer work, work experience. **Freshman Admission Requirements:** High school diploma is required and GED is accepted. *Academic units required:* 4 English, 2 math, 1 science, 1 science lab, 2 foreign language, 1 history, 5 academic electives. *Academic units recommended:* 4 English, 2 science, 2 science labs, 2 foreign language, 1 history, 5 academic electives. **Freshman Admission Statistics:** 2,955 applied, 52.99% admitted, 25% enrolled. **Transfer Admission Requirements:** college transcript(s), statement of good standing from prior institution(s). Minimum college GPA of 2.0 required. Lowest grade transferable C-. **General Admission Information:** Application fee $45. Priority deadline 5/1. Nonfall registration accepted. Admission may be deferred for a maximum of 1 year.

COSTS AND FINANCIAL AID

Annual in-state tuition $12,688. Annual out-of-state tuition $23,710. Room and board $8,794. Required fees $920. Average book expense $1,000. **Required Forms and Deadlines:** FAFSA. **Notification of Awards:** Applicants will be notified of awards on a rolling basis beginning 4/1. **Types of Aid:** *Need-based scholarships/grants:* Federal Pell, FSEOG, State scholarships/grants, Private scholarships, College/university scholarship or grant aid from institutional funds. *Loans:* Direct Subsidized Stafford Loans, Direct Unsubsidized Stafford Loans, Direct PLUS loans, Federal Perkins Loans. *Student Employment:* Federal Work-Study Program available. Institutional employment available. **Financial Aid Statistics:** 94% needy freshmen, 98% needy undergrads receive need-based scholarship or grant aid. 8% freshmen, 7% undergrads receive non-need-based scholarship or grant aid. 91% freshmen, 91% undergrads receive need-based self-help aid. 0% freshmen, 0% undergrads receive athletic scholarships. 83% freshmen, 85% undergrads receive any aid. Average cumulative indebtedness $34,020. **Criteria for awarding aid:** *Need-based:* Minority status. *Non-need-based:* Academics, Alumni affiliation, State/district residency.

UNIVERSITY OF PITTSBURGH AT JOHNSTOWN

157 Blackington Hall, Johnstown, PA 15904
Phone: 814-269-7050 • **Financial Aid Phone:** 814-269-7045
E-mail: upjadmit@pitt.edu • **CEEB Code:** 2934
Fax: 814-269-7044 • **Website:** www.upj.pitt.edu

This public school was founded in 1927. It has a 650-acre campus.

RATINGS

Admissions Selectivity Rating: 77   **Fire Safety Rating:** 88   **Green Rating:** 60*

STUDENTS AND FACULTY

Enrollment: 2,814. **Student Body:** 45% female, 55% male, 2% out-of-state, 2% international (20 countries represented). Asian 1%, African American 3%, Caucasian 87%, Hispanic 1%, Native American <1%, Pacific Islander <1%, Two or more races 2%, Race unknown 3%.

Retention and Graduation: 82% freshmen return for sophomore year. 28% freshmen graduate within 4 years. 55% freshmen graduate within 6 years. 8% grads pursue arts and sciences degrees. 1% grads pursue law degrees. 1% grads pursue business degrees. 2% grads pursue medical degrees. **Faculty:** 0% of classes are taught by teaching assistants.

ACADEMICS

Degrees: associate, bachelor's, certificate. **Classes:** Most classes have 20-29 students. Most lab/discussion sessions have 10-19 students. **Most popular majors:** Computer Engineering; Civil Engineering Technology/Technician; Electrical, Electronic and Communications Engineering Technology/Technician. **Special Study Options:** Accelerated program, cooperative education program, cross-registration, distance learning, double major, dual enrollment, independent study, internships, liberal arts/career combination, student-designed major, study abroad, teacher certification program. **Honors Programs:** President's Scholars Program. **Disability Services:** Special programs offered to physically disabled students, including tutors. **Career Services:** Alumni network, Alumni services, Career/job search classes, Internships, Regional alumni.

FACILITIES

Housing: Coed dorms, special housing for disabled students, fraternity/sorority housing, apartments for single students, ThemeHousingTownhouses,Lodges, Single-sex residence upon request. 100% of campus accessible to physically diasbled. **Special Academic Facilities/Equipment:** Art museum, performing arts center, language lab. **Computers:** 75% of classrooms, 100% of libraries, 50% of dining areas, 100% of student union, 50% of common outdoor areas have wireless network access. Administrative functions (other than registration) can be performed online.

CAMPUS LIFE

Environment: City. **Activities:** Choral groups, concert band, dance, drama/theater, literary magazine, music ensembles, musical theater, pep band, radio station, student government, student newspaper, television station, yearbook, Campus Ministries, Model UN. 70 registered organizations, 11 honor societies, 3 religious organizations. 5 fraternities, 3 sororities. **Athletics (Intercollegiate):** *Men:* baseball, basketball, golf, soccer, wrestling. *Women:* basketball, cheerleading, cross-country, golf, soccer, track/field (outdoor), volleyball. **On-Campus Highlights:** Student Union Building, Sports Center, Cafeteria, Living/Learning Center, Performing Arts Center.

ADMISSIONS

Freshman Academic Profile: Average high school GPA 3.5. 14% in top 10% of high school class, 40% in top 25% of high school class, 72% in top 50% of high school class. **Reported SAT (pre-2016 redesign) scores:** SAT Math middle 50% range 460-570. SAT Critical Reading middle 50% range 450-550. SAT Writing middle 50% range 420-530. **Concordant SAT scores:** SAT EBRW middle 50% 490–600. SAT Math middle 50% range 500–590. ACT middle 50% range 20-25. Minimum internet-based TOEFL 80. Minimum paper TOEFL 550. **Basis for Candidate Selection:** *Very important factors considered include:* rigor of secondary school record, class rank, academic GPA. *Important factors considered include:* standardized test scores, interview, extracurricular activities, talent/ability, volunteer work, level of applicant's interest. *Other factors considered include:* application essay, recommendation(s), character/personal qualities, racial/ethnic status, work experience. **Freshman Admission Requirements:** High school diploma is required and GED is accepted. *Academic units required:* 4 English, 2 math, 2 science, 1 science lab, 2 foreign language, 4 social studies. **Freshman Admission Statistics:** 3,456 applied, 81.02% admitted, 26% enrolled. **Transfer Admission Requirements:** High school transcript, college transcript(s), Minimum college GPA of 2.0 required. Lowest grade transferable C. **General Admission Information:** Regular application deadline 5/1. Nonfall registration accepted. Admission may be deferred for a maximum of 12 months.

COSTS AND FINANCIAL AID

Required Forms and Deadlines: FAFSA. **Notification of Awards:** Applicants will be notified of awards on a rolling basis beginning 3/1. **Types of Aid:** *Need-based scholarships/grants:* Federal Pell, FSEOG, State scholarships/grants, Private scholarships, College/university scholarship or grant aid from institutional funds. *Loans:* Direct Subsidized Stafford Loans, Direct Unsubsidized Stafford Loans, Direct PLUS loans, Federal Perkins Loans. *Student Employment:* Federal Work-Study Program available. Institutional employment available. **Financial Aid Statistics:** 85% needy freshmen, 77% needy undergrads receive need-based scholarship or grant aid. 6% freshmen, 4% undergrads receive non-need-based scholarship or grant aid. 84% freshmen, 87% undergrads receive need-based self-help aid. 3% freshmen, 2% undergrads receive athletic scholarships. 80% freshmen, 80% undergrads receive any aid.

85% undergrads borrow to pay for school. Average cumulative indebtedness $34,127. **Criteria for awarding aid:** *Need-based:* Academics, Athletics, Minority status, Music/drama. *Non-need-based:* Academics, Alumni affiliation, Athletics, Leadership, State/district residency.

UNIVERSITY OF PITTSBURGH—GREENSBURG

150 Finoli Drive, Greensburg, PA 15601
Phone: 724-836-9880 • **Financial Aid Phone:** 724-836-9881
E-mail: upgadmit@pitt.edu • **CEEB Code:** 2936
Fax: 724-836-7471 • **Website:** www.greensburg.pitt.edu • **ACT Code:** 3733

This public school was founded in 1963. It has a 217-acre campus.

RATINGS

Admissions Selectivity Rating: 78   **Fire Safety Rating:** 60*   **Green Rating:** 60*

STUDENTS AND FACULTY

Enrollment: 1,578. **Student Body:** 52% female, 48% male, 2% out-of-state, 1% international. Asian 4%, African American 6%, Caucasian 79%, Hispanic 4%, Native American <1%, Pacific Islander <1%, Two or more races 3%, Race unknown 3%.

Retention and Graduation: 76% freshmen return for sophomore year. 33% freshmen graduate within 4 years. 53% freshmen graduate within 6 years. 26% grads go on to further study within 1 year. 11% grads pursue arts and sciences degrees. 1% grads pursue law degrees. 2% grads pursue business degrees. 1% grads pursue medical degrees. **Faculty:** Student/faculty ratio 20:1. 76 full-time faculty, 83% hold PhDs, 13% are are members of minority groups, 57% are women. 0% of classes are taught by teaching assistants.

ACADEMICS

Degrees: bachelor's, certificate. **Classes:** Most classes have 30-39 students. Most lab/discussion sessions have 20-29 students. **Most popular majors:** Management Information Systems; Biology/Biological Sciences; Psychology. **Special Study Options:** cross-registration, double major, dual enrollment, exchange student program (domestic), independent study, internships, liberal arts/career combination, student-designed major, study abroad. **Disability Services:** Special programs offered to physically disabled students, including note-taking services, reader services, tape recorders, tutors. **Career Services:** Alumni network, Alumni services, Career/job search classes, Career assessment, Internships, Regional alumni.

FACILITIES

Housing: Coed dorms, Theme Housing. 95% of campus accessible to physically diasbled. **Computers:** 100% of libraries, 100% of dining areas, 100% of student union, have wireless network access. Students can register for classes online. Administrative functions (other than registration) can be performed online.

CAMPUS LIFE

Environment: Village. **Activities:** Choral groups, dance, drama/theater, literary magazine, musical theater, radio station, student government, student newspaper, Campus Ministries, Student Organization. 25 registered organizations, 8 honor societies, 3 religious organizations. **Athletics (Intercollegiate):** *Men:* baseball, basketball, cross-country, golf, soccer, tennis. *Women:* basketball, cross-country, golf, soccer, softball, volleyball. **On-Campus Highlights:** Academic Villages, Exchange—Coffee House, Fireside Lounge, Wagner Dining Hall, Ferguson Theater.

ADMISSIONS

Freshman Academic Profile: Average high school GPA 3.5. 15% in top 10% of high school class, 47% in top 25% of high school class, 84% in top 50% of high school class. 95% from public high schools. **Reported SAT (pre-2016 redesign) scores:** SAT Math middle 50% range 460-560. SAT Critical Reading middle 50% range 460-550. SAT Writing middle 50% range 440-540. **Concordant SAT scores:** SAT EBRW middle 50% 500–600. SAT Math middle 50% range 500–580. ACT middle 50% range 18-24. Minimum internet-based TOEFL 80. Minimum paper TOEFL 550. **Basis for Candidate Selection:** *Very important factors considered include:* rigor of secondary school record, class rank, academic GPA, standardized test scores. *Other factors considered include:* application essay, recommendation(s), interview, extracurricular activities, talent/ability, character/personal qualities, volunteer work, level of applicant's interest. **Freshman Admission Requirements:** High school diploma is required and GED is accepted. *Academic units required:* 4 English, 2 math, 1 science, 1 science lab, 4 foreign language, 2 social studies, 2 history, 1 academic elective. *Academic units recommended:* 4 English, 4 math, 2 science, 4 foreign language, 2 social studies, 2 history, 3 academic electives, 1 computer science. **Freshman Admission Statistics:** 1,538 applied, 80.69% admitted, 35% enrolled. **Transfer Admission Requirements:** High school transcript, college transcript(s), statement of good standing from prior institution(s). Minimum college GPA of 2.0 required. Lowest grade transferable C. **General Admission Information:** Application fee $45. Nonfall registration accepted. Admission may be deferred for a maximum of 12 months.

COSTS AND FINANCIAL AID
Annual in-state tuition $12,452. Annual out-of-state tuition $23,268. Room and board $9,490. Required fees $920. **Required Forms and Deadlines:** FAFSA, State aid form. **Notification of Awards:** Applicants will be notified of awards on a rolling basis beginning 3/15. **Types of Aid:** *Need-based scholarships/grants:* Federal Pell, FSEOG, State scholarships/grants, Private scholarships, College/university scholarship or grant aid from institutional funds, United Negro College Fund. *Loans:* Direct Subsidized Stafford Loans, Direct Unsubsidized Stafford Loans, Direct PLUS loans, Federal Perkins Loans. *Student Employment:* Federal Work-Study Program available. Institutional employment available. **Financial Aid Statistics:** 83% needy freshmen, 79% needy undergrads receive need-based scholarship or grant aid. 8% freshmen, 4% undergrads receive non-need-based scholarship or grant aid. 83% freshmen, 87% undergrads receive need-based self-help aid. 0% freshmen, 0% undergrads receive athletic scholarships. **Criteria for awarding aid:** *Non-need-based:* Academics, Leadership, Minority status.

UNIVERSITY OF PITTSBURGH— PITTSBURGH CAMPUS

4227 Fifth Avenue, Pittsburgh, PA 15260
Phone: 412-624-7488 • **Financial Aid Phone:** 412-624-7488
E-mail: oafa@pitt.edu • **CEEB Code:** 2927
Fax: 412-648-8815 • **Website:** www.pitt.edu • **ACT Code:** 3734

This public school was founded in 1787. It has a 132-acre campus.

RATINGS
Admissions Selectivity Rating: 91   **Fire Safety Rating:** 90   **Green Rating:** 89

STUDENTS AND FACULTY
Enrollment: 18,920. **Student Body:** 52% female, 48% male, 28% out-of-state, 4% international (48 countries represented). Asian 10%, African American 5%, Caucasian 73%, Hispanic 3%, Native American <1%, Pacific Islander <1%, Two or more races 4%, Race unknown 1%.
Retention and Graduation: 92% freshmen return for sophomore year. 64% freshmen graduate within 4 years. 81% freshmen graduate within 6 years. 33% grads go on to further study within 1 year. 44% grads pursue arts and sciences degrees. 9% grads pursue law degrees. 6% grads pursue business degrees. 14% grads pursue medical degrees. **Faculty:** Student/faculty ratio 14:1. 1,748 full-time faculty, 94% hold PhDs, 19% are are members of minority groups, 44% are women.

ACADEMICS
Degrees: bachelor's, certificate, doctoral/professional, doctoral/research, doctoral, master's, postbachelor's certifiate, post-master's certificate. **Classes:** Most classes have 10-19 students. Most lab/discussion sessions have 20-29 students. **Most popular majors:** Psychology; Finance; Registered Nursing/Registered Nurse. **Special Study Options:** Accelerated program, cooperative education program, cross-registration, distance learning, double major, dual enrollment, English as a Second Language (ESL), exchange student program (domestic), external degree program, honors program, independent study, internships, liberal arts/career combination, student-designed major, study abroad, teacher certification program, weekend college. **Honors Programs:** University Honors College Combined degree programs: BA/MD, BA/JD, BA/DDS, BA/DMD. **Disability Services:** Special programs offered to physically disabled students, including note-taking services, reader services, tape recorders. **Career Services:** Alumni network, Alumni services, Career/job search classes, Career assessment, Internships, Regional alumni. This past year, the Office of Career Development and Placement Assistance (CDPA) introduced for the first time a three day Spring Career Fair. The first two days focused on STEM majors and the third day focused on Business, Humanities and Social Sciences majors. A record 2,356 students attended the fair over three days.

FACILITIES
Housing: Coed dorms, special housing for disabled students, women's dorms, fraternity/sorority housing, apartments for single students, Wellness Housing,

Theme Housing. 90% of campus accessible to physically diasbled. **Special Academic Facilities/Equipment:** Stephen Foster Memorial, observatory. **Computers:** 100% of classrooms, 25% of dorms, 100% of libraries, 100% of dining areas, 100% of student union, 50% of common outdoor areas have wireless network access. Students can register for classes online. Administrative functions (other than registration) can be performed online.

CAMPUS LIFE
Environment: Metropolis. **Activities:** Choral groups, concert band, dance, drama/theater, jazz band, literary magazine, marching band, music ensembles, pep band, radio station, student government, student newspaper, student-run film society, television station, yearbook, Campus Ministries, Student Organization, Model UN. 395 registered organizations, 17 honor societies, 20 fraternities, 16 sororities. **Athletics (Intercollegiate):** *Men:* baseball, basketball, cross-country, diving, football, soccer, swimming, track/field (outdoor), wrestling. *Women:* basketball, cross-country, diving, gymnastics, soccer, softball, swimming, tennis, track/field (outdoor), volleyball. **On-Campus Highlights:** Cathedral of Learning, William Pitt Union, Heinz Chapel, Peterson Event Center, Sennott Square. **Environmental Initiatives:** ENERGY CENTER: The Facilities Management Division recently consolidated all energy-related operations to a single location. The newly constructed Energy Center space is designed to increase collaboration among energy managers, engineers, utility analysts, and energy management system personnel. These personnel will use new and existing controls and diagnostic tools to place an even greater focus on ensuring optimal building operations and incorporating new technologies into building system designs to further energy conservation on campus. A new command center provides technicians and managers with consolidated access to the building automation system and other diagnostic tools.

ADMISSIONS
Freshman Academic Profile: Average high school GPA 4.1. 52% in top 10% of high school class, 86% in top 25% of high school class, 99% in top 50% of high school class. **Reported SAT (pre-2016 redesign) scores:** SAT Math middle 50% range 600-700. SAT Critical Reading middle 50% range 590-680. SAT Writing middle 50% range 570-670. **Concordant SAT scores:** SAT EBRW middle 50% 640–710. SAT Math middle 50% range 620–730. ACT middle 50% range 27-32. Minimum internet-based TOEFL 100. Minimum paper TOEFL 600. **Basis for Candidate Selection:** *Very important factors considered include:* rigor of secondary school record, academic GPA, standardized test scores. *Important factors considered include:* application essay. *Other factors considered include:* class rank, recommendation(s), extracurricular activities, talent/ability, character/personal qualities, first generation, alumni/ae relation, geographical residence, state residency, racial/ethnic status, volunteer work, work experience, level of applicant's interest. **Freshman Admission Requirements:** High school diploma is required and GED is not accepted. *Academic units required:* 4 English, 3 math, 3 science, 3 science labs, 2 foreign language, 2 social studies, 3 academic electives. *Academic units recommended:* 4 English, 4 math, 4 science, 4 science labs, 3 foreign language, 3 social studies, 5 academic electives. **Freshman Admission Statistics:** 29,175 applied, 55.41% admitted, 24% enrolled. **Transfer Admission Requirements:** High school transcript, college transcript(s), essay or personal statement, Lowest grade transferable C. **General Admission Information:** Application fee $45. Nonfall registration accepted.

COSTS AND FINANCIAL AID
Annual in-state tuition $17,688. Annual out-of-state tuition $28,828. Room and board $10,950. Required fees $930. Average book expense $680. **Required Forms and Deadlines:** FAFSA. **Notification of Awards:** Applicants will be notified of awards on a rolling basis beginning 3/15. **Types of Aid:** *Need-based scholarships/grants:* Federal Pell, FSEOG, State scholarships/grants, Private scholarships, College/university scholarship or grant aid from institutional funds, Federal Nursing Scholarships. *Loans:* Direct Subsidized Stafford Loans, Direct Unsubsidized Stafford Loans, Direct PLUS loans, Federal Perkins Loans, Federal Nursing Loans, State Loans, College/university loans from institutional funds. *Student Employment:* Federal Work-Study Program available. Institutional employment available. **Financial Aid Statistics:** 80% needy freshmen, 70% needy undergrads receive need-based scholarship or grant aid. 8% freshmen, 5% undergrads receive non-need-based scholarship or grant aid. 83% freshmen, 88% undergrads receive need-based self-help aid. 3% freshmen, 2% undergrads receive athletic scholarships. 63% freshmen, 58% undergrads receive any aid. 63% undergrads borrow to pay for school. Average cumulative indebtedness $38,045. **Criteria for awarding aid:** *Non-need-based:* Academics, Athletics, Minority status.

UNIVERSITY OF PORTLAND

5000 N. Willamette Blvd., Portland, OR 97203-5798
Phone: 503-943-7147 • **Financial Aid Phone:** 503-943-7311
E-mail: admissions@up.edu • **CEEB Code:** 4847
Fax: 503-943-7315 • **Website:** www.up.edu • **ACT Code:** 3500

This private school, affiliated with the Roman Catholic Church, was founded in 1901. It has a 130-acre campus.

RATINGS

Admissions Selectivity Rating: 89   **Fire Safety Rating:** 92   **Green Rating:** 60*

STUDENTS AND FACULTY

Enrollment: 3,815. **Student Body:** 60% female, 40% male, 73% out-of-state, 3% international (38 countries represented). Asian 12%, African American 1%, Caucasian 58%, Hispanic 12%, Native American <1%, Pacific Islander 2%, Two or more races 9%, Race unknown 3%.
Retention and Graduation: 91% freshmen return for sophomore year. 75% freshmen graduate within 4 years. 82% freshmen graduate within 6 years. 15% grads go on to further study within 1 year. **Faculty:** Student/faculty ratio 13:1. 240 full-time faculty, 64% hold PhDs, 8% are are members of minority groups, 52% are women. 0% of classes are taught by teaching assistants.

ACADEMICS

Degrees: bachelor's, doctoral/professional, master's, post-master's certificate. **Classes:** Most classes have 20-29 students. Most lab/discussion sessions have 10-19 students. **Most popular majors:** Registered Nursing, Nursing Administration, Nursing Research and Clinical Nursing; Biology/Biological Sciences; Mechanical Engineering. **Special Study Options:** cross-registration, double major, honors program, independent study, internships, liberal arts/career combination, study abroad, teacher certification program. **Honors Programs:** The honors program provides an exciting intellectual challenge for highly motivated students whit above average high school records. The program is designed to facilitate learning through special small classes which permit a high level of student-faculty interaction. Honors students may be enrolled in any major. **Disability Services:** Special programs offered to physically disabled students, including note-taking services, reader services, tutors. **Career Services:** Alumni network, Alumni services, Career/job search classes, Career assessment, Internships, Experiential learning.

FACILITIES

Housing: Coed dorms, men's dorms, women's dorms, Theme Housing, Rental housing. 80% of campus accessible to physically diasbled. **Special Academic Facilities/Equipment:** Art gallery, observatory. **Computers:** 100% of classrooms, 100% of dorms, 100% of libraries, 100% of dining areas, 100% of student union, 100% of common outdoor areas have wireless network access. Students can register for classes online. Administrative functions (other than registration) can be performed online.

CAMPUS LIFE

Environment: Metropolis. **Activities:** Choral groups, concert band, dance, drama/theater, jazz band, literary magazine, music ensembles, musical theater, pep band, radio station, student government, student newspaper, student-run film society, symphony orchestra, yearbook, Campus Ministries, Student Organization. 40 registered organizations, 15 honor societies, 9 religious organizations. **Athletics (Intercollegiate):** *Men:* baseball, basketball, cross-country, golf, soccer, tennis, track/field (outdoor). *Women:* basketball, cross-country, golf, soccer, tennis, track/field (outdoor), volleyball. **On-Campus Highlights:** The Cove, St. Mary's Lounge, Howard Recreation Hall **Environmental Initiatives:** Food for Thought (with Michael Pollan), April 2011; Confluences, Water and Justice (with Maude Barlow), May 2010;Portland host and active participant of Focus the Nation, January 30, 2008.

ADMISSIONS

Freshman Academic Profile: Average high school GPA 3.7. 44% in top 10% of high school class, 75% in top 25% of high school class, 97% in top 50% of high school class. 60% from public high schools. **Reported SAT (pre-2016 redesign) scores:** SAT Math middle 50% range 540-640. SAT Critical Reading middle 50% range 540-660. **Concordant SAT scores:** SAT Math middle 50% range 570-660. Minimum internet-based TOEFL 71. Minimum paper TOEFL 525. **Basis for Candidate Selection:** *Very important factors considered include:* rigor of secondary school record, academic GPA, standardized test scores. *Important factors considered include:* class rank, application essay, recommendation(s), extracurricular activities, talent/ability, work experience. *Other factors considered include:* interview, character/personal qualities, first generation, alumni/ae relation, geographical residence, religious affiliation/commitment, racial/ethnic status, level of applicant's interest. **Freshman Admission Requirements:** High school diploma is required and GED is accepted. *Academic units required:* 3 English, 2 math, 2 science, 2 social studies, 2 history, 7 academic electives. *Academic units recommended:* 4 English, 3 math, 2 science, 2 social studies, 2 history, 7 academic electives. **Freshman Admission Statistics:** 11,911 applied, 61.01% admitted, 13% enrolled. **Transfer Admission Requirements:** college transcript(s), essay or personal statement, Minimum college GPA of 2.5 required. Lowest grade transferable C. **General Admission Information:** Application fee $50. Priority deadline 2/1. Regular application deadline 2/1. Nonfall registration accepted.

COSTS AND FINANCIAL AID

Annual tuition $41,844. Room and board $12,394. Required fees $170. Average book expense $864. **Required Forms and Deadlines:** FAFSA. **Notification of Awards:** Applicants will be notified of awards on a rolling basis beginning 3/1. **Types of Aid:** *Need-based scholarships/grants:* Federal Pell, FSEOG, State scholarships/grants, Private scholarships, College/university scholarship or grant aid from institutional funds, United Negro College Fund, Federal Nursing Scholarships. *Loans:* Direct Subsidized Stafford Loans, Direct Unsubsidized Stafford Loans, Direct PLUS loans, Federal Perkins Loans, Federal Nursing Loans, College/university loans from institutional funds. *Student Employment:* Federal Work-Study Program available. **Financial Aid Statistics:** 76% needy freshmen, 78% needy undergrads receive need-based scholarship or grant aid. 96% freshmen, 93% undergrads receive non-need-based scholarship or grant aid. 71% freshmen, 75% undergrads receive need-based self-help aid. 1% freshmen, 3% undergrads receive athletic scholarships. 98% freshmen, 95% undergrads receive any aid. Average cumulative indebtedness $28,249. **Criteria for awarding aid:** *Need-based:* Academics, Minority status. *Non-need-based:* Academics, Athletics, Leadership, Minority status, Music/drama.

UNIVERSITY OF PUGET SOUND

1500 North Warner Street CMB 1062, Tacoma, WA 98416-1062
Phone: 253-879-3211 • **Financial Aid Phone:** 253-879-3214
E-mail: admission@pugetsound.edu • **CEEB Code:** 4067
Fax: 253-879-3993 • **Website:** www.pugetsound.edu • **ACT Code:** 4450

This private school was founded in 1888. It has a 97-acre campus.

RATINGS

Admissions Selectivity Rating: 86   **Fire Safety Rating:** 85   **Green Rating:** 73

STUDENTS AND FACULTY

Enrollment: 2,476. **Student Body:** 59% female, 41% male, 79% out-of-state, <1% international (9 countries represented). Asian 6%, African American 1%, Caucasian 74%, Hispanic 7%, Native American <1%, Pacific Islander <1%, Two or more races 8%, Race unknown 2%.
Retention and Graduation: 86% freshmen return for sophomore year. 72% freshmen graduate within 4 years. 78 **Faculty:** Student/faculty ratio 11:1. 237 full-time faculty, 92% hold PhDs, 9% are are members of minority groups, 49% are women. 0% of classes are taught by teaching assistants.

ACADEMICS

Degrees: bachelor's, doctoral/professional, master's. **Classes:** Most classes have 10-19 students. Most lab/discussion sessions have 10-19 students. **Most popular majors:** Psychology; Business/Commerce; Biology/Biological Sciences. **Special Study Options:** cooperative education program, double major, honors program, independent study, internships, student-designed major, study abroad, teacher certification program, 1 year of study in Asia, 3-2 engineering program, Business Leadership Program. **Honors Programs:** Business Leadership Program; Honors Program. **Disability Services:** Special programs offered to physically disabled students, including note-taking services, reader services, tape recorders, tutors. **Career Services:** Alumni network, Alumni services, Career/job search classes, Career assessment, Internships, Regional alumni. Typically, students begin college focused on part-time employment rather than career-related pursuits. At Puget Sound, we bridge that gap in a single office integrating all internship, job, and career planning resources–part-time, full-time, on-campus, off-campus, summer, and work-study–for new students to seniors planning their first career move. Students gain early exposure to the people and resources that will be vital contacts for their post-graduation plans. All related programs in a one-stop-shop!

FACILITIES

Housing: Coed dorms, special housing for disabled students, women's dorms, fraternity/sorority housing, Small residential houses, theme floors in halls. 80%

of campus accessible to physically disabled. **Special Academic Facilities/ Equipment:** Art gallery, natural history museum, concert hall, transmission and scanning electron microscopes, spectrometers, exercise science lab, observatory, paleomagnetic and X-ray lab, physiology labs, and DNA Sequencer **Computers:** 30% of classrooms, 30% of dorms, 95% of libraries, 95% of dining areas, 85% of student union, 10% of common outdoor areas have wireless network access. Students can register for classes online. Administrative functions (other than registration) can be performed online.

CAMPUS LIFE

Environment: City. **Activities:** Choral groups, concert band, dance, drama/ theater, jazz band, literary magazine, music ensembles, musical theater, opera, radio station, student government, student newspaper, student-run film society, symphony orchestra, yearbook. 77 registered organizations, 2 honor societies, 12 religious organizations. 4 fraternities, 4 sororities. **Athletics (Intercollegiate):** *Men:* baseball, basketball, crew/rowing, cross-country, football, golf, soccer, swimming, tennis, track/field (outdoor), track/field (indoor). *Women:* basketball, crew/rowing, cross-country, golf, lacrosse, soccer, softball, swimming, tennis, track/field (outdoor), track/field (indoor), volleyball. **On-Campus Highlights:** 3-story Dale Chihuly glass sculpture in Wyatt Hall, Harned Hall, new state-of-the-art science facility, Diversions Caf, 97 acres of rolling lawns, native fir groves, and Tudor Gothic architecture, Music and theater productions directed by faculty and students on campus. **Environmental Initiatives:** In 2005, President Thomas established the Sustainability Advisory Committee (SAC), which reports to the president through the Vice President of Student Affairs and the Vice President for Finance and Administration. The president empowered the committee to advise on and implement sustainability policies and programs on campus and collaboratively with our regional community. The committee addresses sustainability across the institution and in partnership with external organizations. It also uniquely engages students, faculty, and staff in comprehensive, collaborative, and strategic sustainability endeavors.

ADMISSIONS

Freshman Academic Profile: Average high school GPA 3.5. 37% in top 10% of high school class, 68% in top 25% of high school class, 94% in top 50% of high school class. 73% from public high schools. **Reported SAT (pre-2016 redesign) scores:** SAT Math middle 50% range 540-660. SAT Critical Reading middle 50% range 560-680. SAT Writing middle 50% range 550-660. **Concordant SAT scores:** SAT EBRW middle 50% 610–710. SAT Math middle 50% range 570–690. ACT middle 50% range 25-30. Minimum internet-based TOEFL 79. Minimum paper TOEFL 550. **Basis for Candidate Selection:** *Very important factors considered include:* rigor of secondary school record, academic GPA, application essay, character/personal qualities. *Important factors considered include:* recommendation(s), extracurricular activities, talent/ability, alumni/ae relation, volunteer work, work experience. *Other factors considered include:* class rank, standardized test scores, interview, first generation, racial/ethnic status, level of applicant's interest. **Freshman Admission Requirements:** High school diploma is required and GED is accepted. *Academic units recommended:* 4 English, 3 social studies, 3 history, 1 visual/performing arts. **Freshman Admission Statistics:** 5,827 applied, 79.22% admitted, 14% enrolled. **Transfer Admission Requirements:** college transcript(s), essay or personal statement, statement of good standing from prior institution(s). Minimum college GPA of 2.0 required. Lowest grade transferable D. **General Admission Information:** Application fee $50. Priority deadline 1/15. Regular application deadline 1/15. Regular notification 4/1. Nonfall registration accepted. Admission may be deferred for a maximum of 1 year.

COSTS AND FINANCIAL AID

Annual tuition $46,310. Room and board $11,800. Required fees $242. Average book expense $1,000. **Required Forms and Deadlines:** FAFSA. **Notification of Awards:** Applicants will be notified of awards on a rolling basis beginning 3/15. **Types of Aid:** *Need-based scholarships/grants:* Federal Pell, FSEOG, State scholarships/grants, Private scholarships, College/university scholarship or grant aid from institutional funds. *Loans:* Direct Subsidized Stafford Loans, Direct Unsubsidized Stafford Loans, Direct PLUS loans, Federal Perkins Loans. *Student Employment:* Federal Work-Study Program available. Institutional employment available. **Financial Aid Statistics:** 98% needy freshmen, 96% needy undergrads receive need-based scholarship or grant aid. 16% freshmen, 13% undergrads receive non-need-based scholarship or grant aid. 76% freshmen, 78% undergrads receive need-based self-help aid. 0% freshmen, 0% undergrads receive athletic scholarships. 96% freshmen, 94% undergrads receive any aid. 58% undergrads borrow to pay for school. Average cumulative indebtedness $33,130. **Criteria for awarding aid:** *Need-based:* Academics, Minority status, Religious affiliation. *Non-need-based:* Academics, Alumni affiliation, Art, Leadership, Music/drama, Religious affiliation.

UNIVERSITY OF REDLANDS

1200 E. Colton Avenue, Redlands, CA 92373
Phone: 909-748-8074 • **Financial Aid Phone:** 909-748-8047
E-mail: admissions@redlands.edu • **CEEB Code:** 4848
Fax: 909-335-4089 • **Website:** www.redlands.edu • **ACT Code:** 464

This private school was founded in 1907. It has a 160-acre campus.

RATINGS

Admissions Selectivity Rating: 86   **Fire Safety Rating:** 86   **Green Rating:** 60*

STUDENTS AND FACULTY

Enrollment: 3,452. **Student Body:** 56% female, 44% male, 24% out-of-state, 1% international (17 countries represented). Asian 6%, African American 5%, Caucasian 48%, Hispanic 27%, Native American 1%, Pacific Islander 1%, Two or more races 5%, Race unknown 8%.
Retention and Graduation: 85% freshmen return for sophomore year. 65% freshmen graduate within 4 years. 72% freshmen graduate within 6 years. 19% grads go on to further study within 1 year. 5% grads pursue law degrees. 20% grads pursue business degrees. 2% grads pursue medical degrees. **Faculty:** Student/faculty ratio 14:1. 161 full-time faculty, 88% hold PhDs, 16% are members of minority groups, 51% are women. 0% of classes are taught by teaching assistants.

ACADEMICS

Degrees: associate, bachelor's, certificate, doctoral/research, master's, postbachelor's certificate, post-master's certificate. **Classes:** Most classes have 10-19 students. **Most popular majors:** Business/Commerce; Psychology; Liberal Arts and Sciences/Liberal Studies. **Special Study Options:** cross-registration, double major, dual enrollment, exchange student program (domestic), honors program, independent study, internships, liberal arts/ career combination, student-designed major, study abroad, teacher certification program. **Honors Programs:** The Johnston Center for Integrative Studies allows students to design their own majors in consultation with faculty advisors. Students write contracts for their courses and receive narrative evaluations in lieu of traditional grades. The center has received national acclaim for its innovative approaches to education. **Disability Services:** Special programs offered to physically disabled students, including note-taking services, reader services, tutors. **Career Services:** Alumni services, Career/job search classes, Regional alumni.

FACILITIES

Housing: Coed dorms, special housing for disabled students, men's dorms, women's dorms, fraternity/sorority housing, apartments for single students, Abroad Programming. Apartments for students with dependent children. 75% of campus accessible to physically disabled. **Special Academic Facilities/ Equipment:** Art gallery, Far East art collection, Southwest collection, center for communicative disorders, language lab, Helen and Vernon Farquar Anthropology Lab, Physics Laser Photonics Lab, Irvine Map Library, Geographic Information System lab. **Computers:** 100% of classrooms, 100% of dorms, 100% of libraries, 100% of dining areas, 100% of student union, 100% of common outdoor areas have wireless network access. Students can register for classes online. Administrative functions (other than registration) can be performed online.

CAMPUS LIFE

Environment: Town. **Activities:** Choral groups, concert band, dance, drama/ theater, jazz band, literary magazine, music ensembles, musical theater, opera, radio station, student government, student newspaper, student-run film society, symphony orchestra, yearbook. 105 registered organizations, 8 honor societies, 8 religious organizations. 5 fraternities, 5 sororities. **Athletics (Intercollegiate):** *Men:* baseball, basketball, cross-country, diving, football, golf, soccer, swimming, tennis, track/field (outdoor), water polo. *Women:* basketball, cross-country, diving, golf, lacrosse, soccer, softball, swimming, tennis, track/field (outdoor), volleyball, water polo. **On-Campus Highlights:** Armacost Library, Peppers Art Center, Currier Gymnasium/Fitness Center, Chapel, Post Office, Other popular places on campus: Math and Physics Building, Aquatic Center, Football Stadium, Jasper's Corner, and Plaza Cafe. **Environmental Initiatives:** Co-Generation facility to provide power to much of the campus.

ADMISSIONS

Freshman Academic Profile: Average high school GPA 3.6. 38% in top 10% of high school class, 68% in top 25% of high school class, 90% in top 50% of high school class. **Reported SAT (pre-2016 redesign) scores:** SAT Math middle 50% range 510-610. SAT Critical Reading middle 50% range 510-610. **Concordant SAT scores:** SAT Math middle 50% range 540–630. ACT middle 50% range 22-28. Minimum paper TOEFL 550. **Basis for Candidate Selection:** *Very important factors considered include:* rigor of secondary school record, academic GPA, recommendation(s), talent/ability, character/personal qualities. *Important factors considered include:* standardized test scores, application essay. *Other factors considered include:* interview, extracurricular activities, first generation, alumni/ae relation, geographical residence, state residency, racial/ethnic status, volunteer work, work experience. **Freshman Admission Requirements:** High school diploma is required and GED is accepted. *Academic units required:* 4 English, 3 math, 2 science, 1 science lab, 2 foreign language, 2 social studies. *Academic units recommended:* 4 English, 4 math, 3 science, 1 science lab, 3 foreign language, 2 social studies, 1 history. **Freshman Admission Statistics:** 4,790 applied, 67.52% admitted, 16% enrolled. **Transfer Admission Requirements:** High school transcript, college transcript(s), essay or personal statement, Minimum college GPA of 2.5 required. Lowest grade transferable C. **General Admission Information:** Application fee $30. Priority deadline 1/15. Nonfall registration accepted. Admission may be deferred for a maximum of 12 months.

COSTS AND FINANCIAL AID

Annual tuition $44,550. Room and board $13,090. Required fees $350. Average book expense $1,764. **Required Forms and Deadlines:** FAFSA, State aid form. **Notification of Awards:** Applicants will be notified of awards on a rolling basis beginning 2/28. **Types of Aid:** *Need-based scholarships/grants:* Federal Pell, FSEOG, State scholarships/grants, Private scholarships, College/university scholarship or grant aid from institutional funds. *Loans:* Federal Perkins Loans, College/university loans from institutional funds. *Student Employment:* Federal Work-Study Program available. **Financial Aid Statistics:** 100% needy freshmen, 99% needy undergrads receive need-based scholarship or grant aid. 74% freshmen, 57% undergrads receive non-need-based scholarship or grant aid. 84% freshmen, 91% undergrads receive need-based self-help aid. 0% freshmen, 0% undergrads receive athletic scholarships. 94% freshmen, 94% undergrads receive any aid. **Criteria for awarding aid:** *Non-need-based:* Academics, Art, Music/drama.

UNIVERSITY OF RHODE ISLAND

Newman Hall, Kingston, RI 2881
Phone: 401-874-7100 • **Financial Aid Phone:** 401-874-7530
E-mail: admission@uri.edu • **CEEB Code:** 3919
Fax: 401-874-5523 • **Website:** www.uri.edu • **ACT Code:** 3818

This public school was founded in 1892. It has a 1300-acre campus.

RATINGS

Admissions Selectivity Rating: 83   **Fire Safety Rating:** 89   **Green Rating:** 91

STUDENTS AND FACULTY

Enrollment: 13,777. **Student Body:** 56% female, 44% male, 46% out-of-state, 1% international (49 countries represented). Asian 3%, African American 5%, Caucasian 72%, Hispanic 10%, Native American <1%, Pacific Islander <1%, Two or more races 2%, Race unknown 6%.
Retention and Graduation: 83% freshmen return for sophomore year. 42% freshmen graduate within 4 years. 63% freshmen graduate within 6 years.
Faculty: Student/faculty ratio 16:1. 699 full-time faculty, 83% hold PhDs, 17% are are members of minority groups, 46% are women.

ACADEMICS

Degrees: bachelor's, doctoral/professional, doctoral/research, master's, postbachelor's certificate. **Classes:** Most classes have 20-29 students. Most lab/discussion sessions have 10-19 students. **Most popular majors:** Speech Communication and Rhetoric; Psychology. **Special Study Options:** distance learning, double major, dual enrollment, exchange student program (domestic), honors program, independent study, internships, study abroad, teacher certification program, weekend college. **Honors Programs:** The Honors Program at URI features small classes, a nationally renowned Honors Colloquium, National Scholarship for upper class students, advising and honors housing for upper class students. Combined degree programs: BA/MA, BA/MEng, MCP/JD, MPA/MDS, PH.D/MMA, MS/JD, MA/MLIS, MMA/JD, PharmD/MBA, MPA/MLIS, MP. **Disability Services:** Special programs offered to physically disabled students, including note-taking services, tape recorders. **Career Services:** Alumni network, Alumni services, Career

assessment, Internships, Regional alumni. Career assessments and job search assistance, full range of alumni services.

FACILITIES

Housing: Coed dorms, special housing for disabled students, fraternity/sorority housing, apartments for married students, cooperative housing, apartments for single students, Wellness Housing, Theme Housing, Learning communities for undecided majors, honor program, health sciences, engineering, college environment and health sciences majors, and nursing. 90% of campus accessible to physically diasbled. **Special Academic Facilities/Equipment:** Center for robotic research, animal science farm, planetarium, Watson House Museum, Narragansett Bay Campus for Marine Sciences, American historic textiles museum, aquaculture center, fisheries and marine technology laboratory, center for biotechnology and life sciences, human performance laboratory. **Computers:** 50% of classrooms, 100% of dorms, 100% of libraries, 75% of dining areas, 100% of student union, 25% of common outdoor areas have wireless network access. Students can register for classes online. Administrative functions (other than registration) can be performed online.

CAMPUS LIFE

Environment: Village. **Activities:** Choral groups, concert band, dance, drama/theater, jazz band, literary magazine, marching band, music ensembles, musical theater, pep band, radio station, student government, student newspaper, student-run film society, television station, yearbook, Campus Ministries, Student Organization. 100 registered organizations, 40 honor societies, 5 religious organizations. 11 fraternities, 9 sororities. **Athletics (Intercollegiate):** *Men:* baseball, basketball, cheerleading, cross-country, football, golf, soccer, track/field (outdoor), track/field (indoor). *Women:* basketball, cheerleading, crew/rowing, cross-country, diving, soccer, softball, swimming, tennis, track/field (outdoor), track/field (indoor), volleyball. **On-Campus Highlights:** Ryan Center and Boss Ice Arena, Ballentine Hall (Business building), Memorial Student Union, Multi-Cultural Center in heart of campus, Hope Dining Commons, Center for Biotechnology and Life Sciences—LEED certified and the focal point of a statewide effort to build a new, knowledge-based economy for Rhode Island. Green Hall—historic building houses Registrar, Financial Aid and Bursar, as well as Administrative Offices. **Environmental Initiatives:** Development of a sustainability component to the general education requirements for all undergraduate students

ADMISSIONS

Freshman Academic Profile: Average high school GPA 3.5. 18% in top 10% of high school class, 47% in top 25% of high school class, 85% in top 50% of high school class. **Reported SAT (pre-2016 redesign) scores:** SAT Math middle 50% range 500-600. SAT Critical Reading middle 50% range 490-590. SAT Writing middle 50% range 490-580. **Concordant SAT scores:** SAT EBRW middle 50% 550–640. SAT Math middle 50% range 530–620. ACT middle 50% range 22-27. Minimum internet-based TOEFL 79. **Basis for Candidate Selection:** *Very important factors considered include:* rigor of secondary school record, academic GPA. *Important factors considered include:* class rank, standardized test scores, application essay. *Other factors considered include:* recommendation(s), extracurricular activities, talent/ability, character/personal qualities, first generation, alumni/ae relation, geographical residence, state residency, racial/ethnic status, volunteer work, work experience, level of applicant's interest. **Freshman Admission Requirements:** High school diploma is required and GED is accepted. *Academic units required:* 4 English, 3 math, 2 science, 1 science lab, 2 foreign language, 2 social studies, 5 academic electives. **Freshman Admission Statistics:** 21,797 applied, 71.04% admitted, 23% enrolled. **Transfer Admission Requirements:** college transcript(s), essay or personal statement, statement of good standing from prior institution(s). Minimum college GPA of 2.5 required. Lowest grade transferable C. **General Admission Information:** Application fee $65. Regular application deadline 2/1. Regular notification 3/31. Nonfall registration accepted. Admission may be deferred for a maximum of 1 semester.

COSTS AND FINANCIAL AID

Annual in-state tuition $11,128. Annual out-of-state tuition $27,118. Room and board $12,022. Required fees $1,734. Average book expense $1,200. **Required Forms and Deadlines:** FAFSA. **Notification of Awards:** Applicants will be notified of awards on a rolling basis beginning 3/15. **Types of Aid:** *Need-based scholarships/grants:* Federal Pell, FSEOG, State scholarships/grants, Private scholarships, College/university scholarship or grant aid from institutional funds. *Loans:* Direct Subsidized Stafford Loans, Direct Unsubsidized Stafford Loans, Direct PLUS loans, Federal Perkins Loans, Federal Nursing Loans, College/university loans from institutional funds. *Student Employment:* Federal Work-Study Program available. Institutional employment available. **Financial Aid Statistics:** 83% needy freshmen, 86% needy undergrads receive need-based scholarship or grant aid. 20% freshmen, 12% undergrads receive non-need-based scholarship or grant aid. 82% freshmen, 77% undergrads receive need-based self-help aid. 0% freshmen, 0% undergrads receive athletic scholarships. 89% freshmen, 85% undergrads receive any aid. 77% undergrads borrow to pay for school. Average cumulative indebtedness $32,750. **Criteria for awarding aid:** *Need-based:* Alumni affiliation, Art, Minority status, Music/drama. *Non-need-based:* Academics, Alumni affiliation, Art, Athletics, Music/drama.

UNIVERSITY OF RICHMOND

Queally Center: 30 UR Drive, University of Richmond, VA 23173
Phone: 804-289-8640 • **Financial Aid Phone:** 804-289-8438
E-mail: admission@richmond.edu • **CEEB Code:** 5569
Fax: 804-287-6003 • **Website:** www.richmond.edu • **ACT Code:** 4410

This private school was founded in 1830. It has a 350-acre campus.

RATINGS

Admissions Selectivity Rating: 93   **Fire Safety Rating:** 93   **Green Rating:** 92

STUDENTS AND FACULTY

Enrollment: 2,950. **Student Body:** 51% female, 49% male, 81% out-of-state, 9% international (61 countries represented). Asian 8%, African American 6%, Caucasian 59%, Hispanic 8%, Native American <1%, Pacific Islander 0%, Two or more races 4%, Race unknown 6%.
Retention and Graduation: 93% freshmen return for sophomore year. 84% freshmen graduate within 4 years. 88% freshmen graduate within 6 years. 21% grads go on to further study within 1 year. 5% grads pursue arts and sciences degrees. 2% grads pursue law degrees. 1% grads pursue business degrees. 3% grads pursue medical degrees. **Faculty:** Student/faculty ratio 8:1. 337 full-time faculty, 94% hold PhDs, 13% are are members of minority groups, 44% are women. 0% of classes are taught by teaching assistants.

ACADEMICS

Degrees: bachelor's, doctoral/professional, master's. **Classes:** Most classes have 10-19 students. Most lab/discussion sessions have 10-19 students. **Most popular majors:** Business Administration and Management; Organizational Behavior Studies; Biology/Biological Sciences. **Special Study Options:** Accelerated program, cross-registration, distance learning, double major, English as a Second Language (ESL), exchange student program (domestic), honors program, independent study, internships, student-designed major, study abroad, teacher certification program, Notes on above: Summer English Language Institute is for accepted International Students only. Distance Learning offered through School of Continuing Studies. **Career Services:** Alumni network, Alumni services, Career/job search classes, Career assessment, Internships, Regional alumni. Provide one-on-one career advising and a number of programs to explore careers and enhance skill development. Signature programs include industry-specific career expos, student-alumni networking events, and six-week career courses. Additionally, there are numerous online resources available. Spider Road Trips are another popular career program. During these trips, students hit the road with career services staff to learn about industries and opportunities in other cities. Spider Road Trips give students in all majors the opportunity to meet with professionals in fields that interest them. Through a set itinerary, student participants get to visit businesses and organizations in major metropolitan areas. Every traditional undergraduate student is guaranteed funding of up to $4,000 for one summer research or internship experience before they graduate. Through eight different programs, UR Summer Fellowships offer students the opportunity to pursue the research or internship experience that best complements their academic pursuits in any field of endeavor, and in any part of the world. UR Summer Fellowships offer students powerful experiences that complement Richmond's rigorous academics. Through faculty-mentored research experiences, students pursue original intellectual discovery while also gaining the laboratory, field, or archival experience needed to secure admission and fellowships to top graduate programs. Summer internships challenge students to apply what they've learned in new settings while obtaining the experience necessary to pursue their professional goals.

FACILITIES

Housing: Coed dorms, special housing for disabled students, men's dorms, women's dorms, apartments for single students, ThemeHousing°Global House, Outdoor House, and Civic Engagement represent co-ed housing. Other housing options include: Spinning your Web (for first-year males) and Ready for Moore (for first-year females). 93% of campus accessible to physically diasbled. **Special Academic Facilities/Equipment:** Art gallery, mineral museum, Virginia Baptist archives, language lab, Neuroscience lab, Speech Center, Music Technology lab, Jepson School of Leadership, Center for Civic Engagement **Computers:** 100% of classrooms, 100% of dorms, 100% of libraries, 100% of dining areas, 100% of student union, 100% of common outdoor areas have wireless network access. Students can register for classes online. Administrative functions (other than registration) can be performed online.

CAMPUS LIFE

Environment: Metropolis. **Activities:** Choral groups, concert band, dance, drama/theater, jazz band, literary magazine, music ensembles, musical theater, pep band, radio station, student government, student newspaper, student-run film society, symphony orchestra, Campus Ministries, Student Organization, Model UN. 208 registered organizations, 28 honor societies, 17 religious organizations. 6 fraternities, 8 sororities. **Athletics (Intercollegiate):** *Men:* baseball, basketball, cross-country, football, golf, soccer, tennis, track/field (outdoor), track/field (indoor). *Women:* basketball, cross-country, diving, field hockey, golf, lacrosse, soccer, swimming, tennis, track/field (outdoor), track/field (indoor). **On-Campus Highlights:** Tyler Haynes Commons, Robins Center (Athletic Center), Boatwright Memorial Library and Coffee Shop, Stern Plaza (Weinstein Hall, Jepson Hall, etc.), Westhampton Green (Modlin Center for the Arts). **Environmental Initiatives:** The University of Richmond has a commitment to carbon neutrality. We have reduced our greenhouse gas emissions 17 percent, despite increasing our total building square footage by 9 percent. We accomplished this by transitioning from coal to natural gas, completing dozens of energy efficiency upgrades, and setting a LEED Silver minimum requirement on all new construction. In 2016, we are installing a 204 kWh solar array on the roof of our recreation and wellness building and are hosting a conversation on clean power with students from across the Commonwealth of Virginia. In support of the agreement reached at the Paris climate conference (COP 21) in December 2015, President Crutcher reaffirmed the University of Richmond commitment to leadership on climate action by signing the American Campuses Act on Climate.

ADMISSIONS

Freshman Academic Profile: 61% in top 10% of high school class, 85% in top 25% of high school class, 98% in top 50% of high school class. 59% from public high schools. **Reported SAT (pre-2016 redesign) scores:** SAT Math middle 50% range 620-720. SAT Critical Reading middle 50% range 600-700. SAT Writing middle 50% range 610-700. **Concordant SAT scores:** SAT EBRW middle 50% 660-730. SAT Math middle 50% range 640-750. ACT middle 50% range 29-32. Minimum internet-based TOEFL 80. Minimum paper TOEFL 550. **Basis for Candidate Selection:** *Very important factors considered include:* rigor of secondary school record, academic GPA. *Important factors considered include:* class rank, standardized test scores, application essay, recommendation(s), extracurricular activities, talent/ability, character/ personal qualities. *Other factors considered include:* first generation, alumni/ae relation, geographical residence, state residency, racial/ethnic status, volunteer work, work experience, level of applicant's interest. **Freshman Admission Requirements:** High school diploma is required and GED is accepted. *Academic units required:* 4 English, 3 math, 2 science, 2 science labs, 2 foreign language, 2 history. *Academic units recommended:* 4 English, 4 math, 4 science, 4 science labs, 4 foreign language, 4 history. **Freshman Admission Statistics:** 10,422 applied, 32.48% admitted, 24% enrolled. **Transfer Admission Requirements:** High school transcript, college transcript(s), essay or personal statement, statement of good standing from prior institution(s). Minimum college GPA of 2.0 required. Lowest grade transferable C. **General Admission Information:** Application fee $50. Regular application deadline 1/15. Regular notification 4/1. Nonfall registration not accepted. Admission may be deferred for a maximum of 1 Year.

COSTS AND FINANCIAL AID

Annual tuition $50,910. Room and board $11,820. Required fees $0. Average book expense $1,100. **Required Forms and Deadlines:** FAFSA, CSS/ Financial Aid PROFILE, Noncustodial PROFILE. **Notification of Awards:** Applicants will be notified of awards on or about 4/1. **Types of Aid:** *Need-based scholarships/grants:* Federal Pell, FSEOG, State scholarships/grants, Private scholarships, College/university scholarship or grant aid from institutional funds. *Loans:* Direct Subsidized Stafford Loans, Direct Unsubsidized Stafford Loans, Direct PLUS loans, Federal Perkins Loans. *Student Employment:* Federal Work-Study Program available. Institutional employment available. **Financial Aid Statistics:** 99% needy freshmen, 98% needy undergrads receive need-based scholarship or grant aid. 27% freshmen, 18% undergrads receive non-need-based scholarship or grant aid. 72% freshmen, 80% undergrads receive need-based self-help aid. 8% freshmen, 8% undergrads receive athletic scholarships. 59% freshmen, 67% undergrads receive any aid. 40% undergrads borrow to pay for school. Average cumulative indebtedness $27,670. **Criteria for awarding aid:** *Non-need-based:* Academics, Art, Athletics, Leadership, Music/drama.

UNIVERSITY OF RIO GRANDE

218 North College Avenue, Rio Grande, OH 45774
Phone: 740-245-7206 • **Financial Aid Phone:** 740-245-7219
E-mail: admissions@rio.edu • **CEEB Code:** 1663
Fax: 740-245-7260 • **Website:** rio.edu • **ACT Code:** 3324

This private school was founded in 1876. It has a 68-acre campus.

RATINGS
Admissions Selectivity Rating: 74   **Fire Safety Rating:** 87   **Green Rating:** 60*

STUDENTS AND FACULTY
Enrollment: 1,165. **Student Body:** 65% female, 35% male, 4% out-of-state, 2% international. Asian 0%, African American 5%, Caucasian 81%, Hispanic 1%, Native American <1%, Pacific Islander <1%, Two or more races <1%, Race unknown 10%.
Retention and Graduation: 50% freshmen return for sophomore year. 27% freshmen graduate within 4 years. 39% freshmen graduate within 6 years. 0% grads go on to further study within 1 year. **Faculty:** Student/faculty ratio 20:1. 77 full-time faculty, 45% hold PhDs, 4% are are members of minority groups, 44% are women. 0% of classes are taught by teaching assistants.

ACADEMICS
Degrees: associate, bachelor's, certificate, master's. **Classes:** Most classes have fewer than 10 students. Most lab/discussion sessions have 20-29 students. **Most popular majors:** Elementary Education and Teaching; Business/Office Automation/Technology/Data Entry. **Special Study Options:** Accelerated program, cooperative education program, distance learning, double major, dual enrollment, English as a Second Language (ESL), honors program, independent study, internships, liberal arts/career combination, student-designed major, study abroad, teacher certification program. Combined degree programs: 2+2 programs: nursing, business, industrial tech. **Disability Services:** Special programs offered to physically disabled students, including note-taking services, reader services, tape recorders, tutors. **Career Services:** Alumni services, Career assessment, Internships.

FACILITIES
Housing: Coed dorms, special housing for disabled students, men's dorms, women's dorms, Wellness Housing, Private housing owned and operated by university available to responsible students. 75% of campus accessible to physically diasbled. **Special Academic Facilities/Equipment:** Archives of local and college history, art museum, fine woodworking, theater, art annex. **Computers:** 75% of classrooms, 100% of dorms, 100% of libraries, 100% of dining areas, 100% of student union, 25% of common outdoor areas have wireless network access. Students can register for classes online. Administrative functions (other than registration) can be performed online.

CAMPUS LIFE
Environment: Rural. **Activities:** Choral groups, concert band, dance, drama/theater, jazz band, literary magazine, music ensembles, musical theater, pep band, radio station, student government, student newspaper, television station 34 registered organizations, 4 honor societies, 3 religious organizations. 4 fraternities, 5 sororities. **Athletics (Intercollegiate):** *Men:* baseball, basketball, cross-country, soccer, track/field (outdoor), track/field (indoor). *Women:* basketball, cheerleading, cross-country, soccer, softball, track/field (outdoor), track/field (indoor), volleyball. **On-Campus Highlights:** Food Court, Red Zone, Basketball Court **Environmental Initiatives:** Recycling program, some solar powered equipment, energy usage reduction program, trayless Tuesdays in the cafeteria.

ADMISSIONS
Freshman Academic Profile: Average high school GPA 2.9. 5% in top 10% of high school class, 20% in top 25% of high school class, 49% in top 50% of high school class. 95% from public high schools. ACT middle 50% range 17-22. Minimum paper TOEFL 400. **Basis for Candidate Selection:** *Other factors considered include:* class rank, academic GPA, standardized test scores. **Freshman Admission Requirements:** High school diploma is required and GED is accepted. *Academic units required:* 4 English, 3 math, 3 science, 1 science lab, 3 social studies, 7 academic electives. *Academic units recommended:* 2 science labs, 2 foreign language, 2 history, 9 academic electives. **Freshman Admission Statistics:** 1,909 applied, 69.41% admitted, 44% enrolled. **Transfer Admission Requirements:** High school transcript, college transcript(s), statement of good standing from prior institution(s). Minimum college GPA of 0 required. Lowest grade transferable D. **General Admission Information:** Application fee $25. Nonfall registration accepted. Admission may be deferred.

COSTS AND FINANCIAL AID
Annual tuitionin-state tuition $23,260$3,900. Room and board $9,920. Required fees $600. Average book expense $1,200. **Required Forms and Deadlines:** FAFSA, Institution's own financial aid form. **Notification of**

Awards: Applicants will be notified of awards on a rolling basis beginning 1/15. **Types of Aid:** *Need-based scholarships/grants:* Federal Pell, FSEOG, State scholarships/grants, Private scholarships, College/university scholarship or grant aid from institutional funds. *Loans:* Direct Subsidized Stafford Loans, Direct Unsubsidized Stafford Loans, Direct PLUS loans, Federal Nursing Loans, College/university loans from institutional funds. *Student Employment:* Federal Work-Study Program available. Institutional employment available. **Financial Aid Statistics:** 69% needy freshmen, 68% needy undergrads receive need-based scholarship or grant aid. 72% freshmen, 71% undergrads receive non-need-based scholarship or grant aid. 59% freshmen, 61% undergrads receive need-based self-help aid. 79% freshmen, 28% undergrads receive athletic scholarships. 78% freshmen, 77% undergrads receive any aid. 74% undergrads borrow to pay for school. Average cumulative indebtedness $32,722. **Criteria for awarding aid:** *Need-based:* Academics. *Non-need-based:* Academics, Alumni affiliation, Athletics, Leadership, Music/drama, State/district residency.

UNIVERSITY OF ROCHESTER

300 Wilson Blvd, Rochester, NY 14627
Phone: 585-275-3221 • **Financial Aid Phone:** 585-275-3226
E-mail: admit@admissions.rochester.edu • **CEEB Code:** 2928
Fax: 585-461-4595 • **Website:** www.rochester.edu • **ACT Code:** 2980

This private school was founded in 1850. It has a 655-acre campus.

RATINGS
Admissions Selectivity Rating: 94   **Fire Safety Rating:** 93   **Green Rating:** 79

STUDENTS AND FACULTY
Enrollment: 6,011. **Student Body:** 49% female, 51% male, 59% out-of-state, 18% international (114 countries represented). Asian 11%, African American 5%, Caucasian 48%, Hispanic 7%, Native American <1%, Pacific Islander <1%, Two or more races 3%, Race unknown 7%.
Retention and Graduation: 96% freshmen return for sophomore year. 74% freshmen graduate within 4 years. 88% freshmen graduate within 6 years. 34% grads go on to further study within 1 year. **Faculty:** Student/faculty ratio 10:1. 606 full-time faculty, 94% hold PhDs, 0% are are members of minority groups, 0% are women.

ACADEMICS
Degrees: bachelor's, doctoral/professional, doctoral/research, doctoral, master's, postbachelor's certificate, post-master's certificate. **Classes:** Most classes have 10-19 students. **Most popular majors:** Economics; Biology/Biological Sciences; Psychology. **Special Study Options:** Accelerated program, cooperative education program, cross-registration, double major, dual enrollment, English as a Second Language (ESL), honors program, independent study, internships, liberal arts/career combination, student-designed major, study abroad, teacher certification program, "Take 5" a fifth year tuition free to supplement regular requirements; Washington Semester Program; Rochester Curriculum (clusters); Quest Courses. Combined degree programs: BA/MD, BA/MA, Medicine, Education, Engineering. **Disability Services:** Special programs offered to physically disabled students, including note-taking services, reader services, tape recorders, tutors. **Career Services:** Alumni network, Alumni services, Career assessment, Internships. Rochester students pursue internship, externship, research and volunteer experiences at a high rate. Many are involved in programs directed by other organizations, including 65+ study abroad programs in which the University is a partner. The campus career center guides individualized plans for student career development and enjoys extraordinary success. A partial listing of the programs the University has created and manages on its own: internships at the Parliament in London, or the European Parliament in Brussels; 'Art New York,' a semester spent living in New York City working at galleries or museums; REU programs at Rochester in chemistry, engineering, and medicine; similar programs at Fermilab in Chicago, at NIH and NASA in the DC area; the Urban Scholars summer program in Rochester; Kaufmann Entrepreneurial Year; a guided summer investigation of Italian architecture, archaeology and engineering; intensive in-country immersion language programs for several foreign languages; earth sciences research expeditions in the Arctic and South Africa; numerous developmental programs in music and in clinical medical research; the Mt. Hope Family Clinic in developmental and social psychology; engineering industry practicum opportunities with Google, Apple, Microsoft, Kodak, Xerox, IBM etc.; cognitive research with the use of an academic MRI facility; undergraduate research programs at Rochester's Laboratory for Laser

Energetics, home of the Omega EP laser system, one of the world's most powerful.

FACILITIES

Housing: Coed dorms, special housing for disabled students, men's dorms, special housing for international students, women's dorms, fraternity/sorority housing, apartments for married students, apartments for single students, Wellness Housing, ThemeHousingFreshman housing; Special interest housing; Suite style living. 90% of campus accessible to physically diasbled. **Special Academic Facilities/Equipment:** Art center and gallery, African and African-American studies institute, center for women's studies, visual science and space science centers, institute of optics, observatory, laser energetics and nuclear structure research labs, electron microscopes. Judaic studies center, political economy institute, sign language research center, biomedical ultrasound center, Polish and central European studies center, electronic imaging systems center, center for future health. **Computers:** 100% of classrooms, 30% of dorms, 100% of libraries, 100% of dining areas, 100% of student union, have wireless network access. Students can register for classes online. Administrative functions (other than registration) can be performed online.

CAMPUS LIFE

Environment: Metropolis. **Activities:** Choral groups, concert band, dance, drama/theater, jazz band, literary magazine, music ensembles, musical theater, opera, pep band, radio station, student government, student newspaper, student-run film society, symphony orchestra, television station, Student Organization, Model UN. 224 registered organizations, 6 honor societies, 14 religious organizations. 17 fraternities, 13 sororities. **Athletics (Intercollegiate):** *Men:* baseball, basketball, cross-country, diving, football, golf, soccer, squash, swimming, tennis, track/field (outdoor), track/field (indoor). *Women:* basketball, crew/rowing, cross-country, diving, field hockey, golf, lacrosse, soccer, softball, swimming, tennis, track/field (outdoor), track/field (indoor), volleyball. **On-Campus Highlights:** Eastman Theater, Memorial Art Gallery, Rush Rhees Library, Interfaith Chapel, Robert B. Goergen Athletic Center, Recent New Buildings on Campus: ° Robert B. Goergen Hall for Biomedical Engineering and Optics—A five-story facility that pairs biomedical engineering and optics in an environment of teaching laboratories, high-tech demonstration areas, and gathering spaces for collaboration. ° The Gleason Library—A collaborative study space, designed with student input, which features an open floor plan and lightweight furniture that students are encouraged to reconfigure. ° Riverview Student Apartments—A five-building, 120-unit dormitory complex. The waterfront building features fully furnished apartments and offers amenities not found in other on-campus housing, including air conditioning, kitchens and separate living rooms. Each of the three- and four-story buildings is equipped with laundry and vending facilities. ° University Health Services Building -The new facility brings together UHS medical care services, physical therapy, health promotion, administrative offices, and the University Counseling Center. The UHS building is the primary health-care stop for Arts, Sciences & Engineering students, as well as faculty, staff, and other members of the University community. **Environmental Initiatives:** For the fourth year in a row, the University of Rochester has been recognized as a Tree Campus USA by the Arbor Day Foundation. The program recognizes college campuses that have made a commitment to effective urban forest management by planting, preserving, and protecting tree resources and that engage staff, students, and the community in conservation goals. To become a Tree Campus, the University must maintain five standards ?é?Çô have a campus tree advisory committee, a campus tree care plan, dedicated annual expenditures, Arbor Day observance, and a service learning project. This past year, Dan Schied, manager of Horticulture and Grounds, gave several tree tours around campus, as well as lead two new tree planting ceremonies with students on campus in celebration of Earth Day and Arbor Day.

ADMISSIONS

Freshman Academic Profile: Average high school GPA 3.8. 66% in top 10% of high school class, 92% in top 25% of high school class, 100% in top 50% of high school class. 74% from public high schools. **Reported SAT (pre-2016 redesign) scores:** SAT Math middle 50% range 640-760. SAT Critical Reading middle 50% range 600-710. SAT Writing middle 50% range 610-710. **Concordant SAT scores:** SAT EBRW middle 50% 660–740. SAT Math middle 50% range 660–780. ACT middle 50% range 29-33. Minimum internet-based TOEFL 100. Minimum paper TOEFL 600. **Basis for Candidate Selection:** *Very important factors considered include:* rigor of secondary school record, recommendation(s), character/personal qualities. *Important factors considered include:* academic GPA, standardized test scores, application essay, interview, extracurricular activities, talent/ability. *Other factors considered include:* class rank, first generation, alumni/ae relation, geographical residence, racial/ethnic status, volunteer work, work experience, level of applicant's interest. **Freshman Admission Requirements:** High school diploma is required and GED is accepted. **Freshman Admission Statistics:** 17,932 applied, 33.78% admitted, 23% enrolled. **Transfer Admission Requirements:** college transcript(s), essay or personal statement, Lowest grade transferable C. **General Admission Information:** Application fee $50. Regular application deadline 1/5. Regular notification 4/1. Nonfall registration accepted. Admission may be deferred.

COSTS AND FINANCIAL AID

Annual tuition $49,260. Room and board $14,890. Required fees $882. Average book expense $1,310. **Required Forms and Deadlines:** FAFSA, CSS/Financial Aid PROFILE, State aid form, Noncustodial PROFILE. **Notification of Awards:** Applicants will be notified of awards on or about 4/1. **Types of Aid:** *Need-based scholarships/grants:* Federal Pell, FSEOG, State scholarships/grants, Private scholarships, College/university scholarship or grant aid from institutional funds. *Loans:* Direct Subsidized Stafford Loans, Direct Unsubsidized Stafford Loans, Direct PLUS loans, Federal Perkins Loans. *Student Employment:* Federal Work-Study Program available. Institutional employment available. **Financial Aid Statistics:** 100% needy freshmen, 99% needy undergrads receive need-based scholarship or grant aid. 15% freshmen, 14% undergrads receive non-need-based scholarship or grant aid. 81% freshmen, 83% undergrads receive need-based self-help aid. 0% freshmen, 0% undergrads receive athletic scholarships. 85% freshmen receive any aid. 58% undergrads borrow to pay for school. Average cumulative indebtedness $30,873. **Criteria for awarding aid:** *Need-based:* Academics, Music/drama. *Non-need-based:* Academics, Alumni affiliation, Art, Leadership, Music/drama.

UNIVERSITY OF SAINT FRANCIS

2701 Spring Street, Fort Wayne, IN 46808
Phone: 260-399-8000 • **Financial Aid Phone:** 260-399-8003
E-mail: admis@sf.edu • **CEEB Code:** 1693
Fax: 260-399-8152 • **Website:** www.sf.edu • **ACT Code:** 1238

RATINGS

Admissions Selectivity Rating: 75   **Fire Safety Rating:** 97   **Green Rating:** 60*

STUDENTS AND FACULTY

Enrollment: 1,758. **Student Body:** 72% female, 28% male, 9% out-of-state, 1% international (13 countries represented). Asian 1%, African American 7%, Caucasian 80%, Hispanic 8%, Native American <1%, Pacific Islander <1%, Two or more races 2%, Race unknown 1%.
Retention and Graduation: 71% freshmen return for sophomore year. 39% freshmen graduate within 4 years. 55% freshmen graduate within 6 years. 16% grads go on to further study within 1 year. 1% grads pursue arts and sciences degrees. 2% grads pursue business degrees. 2% grads pursue medical degrees. **Faculty:** Student/faculty ratio 11:1. 122 full-time faculty, 50% hold PhDs, 2% are are members of minority groups, 64% are women. 0% of classes are taught by teaching assistants.

ACADEMICS

Degrees: associate, bachelor's, certificate, master's, postbachelor's certificate, post-master's certificate. **Most popular majors:** Registered Nursing/Registered Nurse; Business Administration and Management; Health and Wellness. **Career Services:** Alumni services, Career assessment, Internships. The internships program encompasses course registration, orientation, support and assessment to students, faculty and organizations.

ADMISSIONS

Freshman Academic Profile: Average high school GPA 3.3. 18% in top 10% of high school class, 43% in top 25% of high school class, 76% in top 50% of high school class. 82% from public high schools. **Reported SAT (pre-2016 redesign) scores:** SAT Math middle 50% range 450-550. SAT Critical Reading middle 50% range 450-540. SAT Writing middle 50% range 430-540. **Concordant SAT scores:** SAT EBRW middle 50% 490–600. SAT Math middle 50% range 490–570. ACT middle 50% range 19-24. Minimum internet-based TOEFL 80. Minimum paper TOEFL 550. **Basis for Candidate Selection:** *Very important factors considered include:* rigor of secondary school record, academic GPA, standardized test scores. *Important factors considered include:* class rank. *Other factors considered include:* application essay, recommendation(s), interview, work experience, level of applicant's interest. **Freshman Admission Requirements:** *Academic units required:* 4 English, 3 math, 2 science, 2 social studies, 1 history, 1 academic elective. *Academic units recommended:* 4 English, 4 math, 3 science, 3 social studies, 1 history, 4 academic electives. **Freshman Admission Statistics:** 977 applied, 96.72% admitted, 36% enrolled. **General Admission Information:** Nonfall registration accepted. Admission may be deferred for a maximum of one semester.

COSTS AND FINANCIAL AID

Annual tuition $28,390. Required fees $1,040. Average book expense $1,200. **Required Forms and Deadlines:** FAFSA. **Notification of Awards:** Applicants will be notified of awards on a rolling basis beginning 3/1. **Types of Aid:** *Need-based scholarships/grants:* Federal Pell, FSEOG, State scholarships/grants, Private scholarships, College/university scholarship or grant aid from institutional funds. *Loans:* Direct Subsidized Stafford Loans, Direct Unsubsidized Stafford Loans, Direct PLUS loans, Federal Perkins Loans.

Student Employment: Federal Work-Study Program available. Institutional employment available. **Financial Aid Statistics:** 100% needy freshmen, 99% needy undergrads receive need-based scholarship or grant aid. 14% freshmen, 11% undergrads receive non-need-based scholarship or grant aid. 85% freshmen, 88% undergrads receive need-based self-help aid. 12% freshmen, 9% undergrads receive athletic scholarships. 100% freshmen, 98% undergrads receive any aid. 87% undergrads borrow to pay for school. Average cumulative indebtedness $37,167. **Criteria for awarding aid:** *Need-based:* Academics, Art, Athletics, Music/drama. *Non-need-based:* Academics, Art, Athletics, Music/drama, State/district residency.

UNIVERSITY OF SAINT JOSEPH

1678 Asylum Avenue, West Hartford, CT 6117
Phone: 860-231-5216 • **Financial Aid Phone:** 860-231-5223
E-mail: admissions@usj.edu
Fax: 860-231-5744 • **Website:** www.usj.edu

This private school, affiliated with the Roman Catholic Church, was founded in 1932. It has a 84-acre campus.

RATINGS
Admissions Selectivity Rating: 77   **Fire Safety Rating:** 99   **Green Rating:** 60*

STUDENTS AND FACULTY
Enrollment: 843. **Student Body:** 98% female, 2% male, 4% out-of-state, 1% international. Asian 5%, African American 16%, Caucasian 55%, Hispanic 16%, Native American <1%, Pacific Islander <1%, Two or more races 1%, Race unknown 6%.
Retention and Graduation: 75% freshmen return for sophomore year. 57% freshmen graduate within 4 years. 63% freshmen graduate within 6 years. **Faculty:** Student/faculty ratio 10:1. 134 full-time faculty, 84% hold PhDs, 22% are are members of minority groups, 69% are women. 0% of classes are taught by teaching assistants.

ACADEMICS
Degrees: bachelor's, certificate, doctoral/professional, master's, postbachelor's certificate, post-master's certificate. **Classes:** Most classes have 10-19 students. Most lab/discussion sessions have 10-19 students. **Most popular majors:** Social Work; Registered Nursing/Registered Nurse; Psychology. **Special Study Options:** Accelerated program, cross-registration, distance learning, double major, honors program, independent study, internships, liberal arts/career combination, student-designed major, study abroad, teacher certification program, weekend college. Combined degree programs: BA/MA. **Career Services:** Alumni services, Career/job search classes, Career assessment, Internships, Regional alumni.

FACILITIES
Housing: special housing for disabled students, women's dorms, Suite living (double rooms with shared common area and kitchen). **Computers:** Students can register for classes online.

CAMPUS LIFE
Environment: Town. **Activities:** Choral groups, dance, drama/theater, music ensembles, student government, student newspaper, yearbook, Campus Ministries, Student Organization. **Athletics (Intercollegiate):** *Women:* basketball, cross-country, diving, lacrosse, soccer, softball, swimming, tennis, volleyball.

ADMISSIONS
Freshman Academic Profile: Average high school GPA 3.4. 21% in top 10% of high school class, 53% in top 25% of high school class, 93% in top 50% of high school class. **Reported SAT (pre-2016 redesign) scores:** SAT Math middle 50% range 400-540. SAT Critical Reading middle 50% range 430-560. SAT Writing middle 50% range 440-540. **Concordant SAT scores:** SAT EBRW middle 50% 490–610. SAT Math middle 50% range 440–570. ACT middle 50% range 20-24. Minimum paper TOEFL 550. **Basis for Candidate Selection:** *Very important factors considered include:* rigor of secondary school record, academic GPA, standardized test scores. *Important factors considered include:* application essay, recommendation(s), interview. *Other factors considered include:* class rank, extracurricular activities, talent/ability, character/personal qualities, first generation, alumni/ae relation, geographical residence, state residency, religious affiliation/commitment, racial/ethnic status, volunteer work, work experience, level of applicant's interest. **Freshman Admission Requirements:** High school diploma is required and GED is accepted. *Academic units required:* 4 English. *Academic units recommended:* 4 math, 3 science, 2 foreign language, 3 social studies. **Freshman Admission Statistics:** 743 applied, 87.08% admitted, 19% enrolled. **Transfer Admission Requirements:** High school transcript, college transcript(s), Lowest grade transferable C. **General Admission Information:** Application fee $50. Nonfall registration accepted. Admission may be deferred.

COSTS AND FINANCIAL AID
Annual tuition $35,220. Room and board $11,095. Required fees $1,710. Average book expense $1,000. **Required Forms and Deadlines:** FAFSA. **Notification of Awards:** Applicants will be notified of awards on a rolling basis beginning 2/15. **Types of Aid:** *Need-based scholarships/grants:* Federal Pell, FSEOG, State scholarships/grants, Private scholarships, College/university scholarship or grant aid from institutional funds. *Loans:* Direct Subsidized Stafford Loans, Direct Unsubsidized Stafford Loans, Direct PLUS loans, Federal Perkins Loans. *Student Employment:* Federal Work-Study Program available. Institutional employment available. **Financial Aid Statistics:** 99% needy freshmen, 96% needy undergrads receive need-based scholarship or grant aid. 7% freshmen, 6% undergrads receive non-need-based scholarship or grant aid. 92% freshmen, 95% undergrads receive need-based self-help aid. 0% freshmen, 0% undergrads receive athletic scholarships. 76% undergrads borrow to pay for school. Average cumulative indebtedness $35,144. **Criteria for awarding aid:** *Non-need-based:* Academics, Leadership, Minority status.

UNIVERSITY OF SAINT MARY (KS)

4100 South Fourth Street Trafficway, Leavenworth, KS 66048
Phone: 913-758-6118
E-mail: admissions@stmary.edu • **CEEB Code:** 6630
Fax: 913-758-6140 • **Website:** www.stmary.edu • **ACT Code:** 1455

This private school, affiliated with the Roman Catholic Church, was founded in 1923. It has a 240-acre campus.

RATINGS
Admissions Selectivity Rating: 83   **Fire Safety Rating:** 60*   **Green Rating:** 60*

STUDENTS AND FACULTY
Enrollment: 765. **Student Body:** 58% female, 42% male, 49% out-of-state, 1% international. Asian 1%, African American 9%, Caucasian 58%, Hispanic 20%, Native American <1%, Pacific Islander 1%, Two or more races 4%, Race unknown 5%.
Retention and Graduation: 71% freshmen return for sophomore year. 28% freshmen graduate within 4 years. 34% freshmen graduate within 6 years. **Faculty:** Student/faculty ratio 11:1. 65 full-time faculty, 72% hold PhDs, 14% are are members of minority groups, 62% are women. 0% of classes are taught by teaching assistants.

ACADEMICS
Degrees: associate, bachelor's, doctoral, master's, transfer. **Classes:** Most classes have fewer than 10 students. **Most popular majors:** Registered Nursing/Registered Nurse; Biology/Biological Sciences; Sport and Fitness Administration/Management. **Special Study Options:** Accelerated program, distance learning, double major, dual enrollment, honors program, independent study, internships, student-designed major, study abroad, teacher certification program, Semester-away programs available. **Disability Services:** Special programs offered to physically disabled students, including note-taking services, tutors.

FACILITIES
Housing: Coed dorms. **Special Academic Facilities/Equipment:** Lincoln Library Collection Art Gallery Bible Collection **Computers:** Students can register for classes online. Administrative functions (other than registration) can be performed online.

CAMPUS LIFE
Environment: Town. **Activities:** Choral groups, concert band, drama/theater, literary magazine, music ensembles, musical theater, pep band, student government, Campus Ministries. 22 registered organizations, 2 honor societies, 2 religious organizations. **Athletics (Intercollegiate):** *Men:* baseball, basketball, football, soccer. *Women:* basketball, soccer, softball, volleyball.

ADMISSIONS
Freshman Academic Profile: Average high school GPA 3.3. 16% in top 10% of high school class, 31% in top 25% of high school class, 71% in top 50% of high school class. 80% from public high schools. **Reported SAT (pre-2016 redesign) scores:** SAT Math middle 50% range 440-550. SAT Critical Reading middle 50% range 430-540. **Concordant SAT scores:** SAT Math middle 50% range 480–570. ACT middle 50% range 19-24. Minimum paper TOEFL 500. **Basis for Candidate Selection:** *Very important factors considered include:* rigor of secondary school record, academic GPA, character/personal qualities. *Important factors considered include:* standardized test scores, interview, extracurricular activities, talent/ability, volunteer work. *Other factors considered include:* class rank, application essay, recommendation(s), alumni/ae relation, work experience. **Freshman Admission Requirements:** High school diploma is required and GED is accepted. *Academic units required:* 4 English, 2 math, 2

science, 2 history. *Academic units recommended:* 4 English, 4 math, 4 science, 2 science labs, 2 foreign language, 2 social studies, 4 history, 2 academic electives, and 2 units from above areas or other academic areas. **Freshman Admission Statistics:** 888 applied, 49.44% admitted, 28% enrolled. **Transfer Admission Requirements:** college transcript(s), Minimum college GPA of 2.0 required. Lowest grade transferable C. **General Admission Information:** Application fee $25. Nonfall registration accepted.

COSTS AND FINANCIAL AID

Annual tuition $26,940. Required fees $780. Average book expense $2,547. **Required Forms and Deadlines:** FAFSA, State aid form. **Notification of Awards:** Applicants will be notified of awards on a rolling basis beginning 2/15. **Types of Aid:** *Need-based scholarships/grants:* Federal Pell, FSEOG, State scholarships/grants, Private scholarships, College/university scholarship or grant aid from institutional funds. *Loans:* Direct Subsidized Stafford Loans, Direct Unsubsidized Stafford Loans, Direct PLUS loans, Federal Perkins Loans. *Student Employment:* Federal Work-Study Program available. Institutional employment available. **Financial Aid Statistics:** 78% needy freshmen, 81% needy undergrads receive need-based scholarship or grant aid. 100% freshmen, 91% undergrads receive non-need-based scholarship or grant aid. 81% freshmen, 83% undergrads receive need-based self-help aid. 74% freshmen, 44% undergrads receive athletic scholarships. 84% undergrads borrow to pay for school. Average cumulative indebtedness $28,460. **Criteria for awarding aid:** *Non-need-based:* Academics, Alumni affiliation, Art, Athletics, Leadership, Music/drama, Religious affiliation.

UNIVERSITY OF SAINT THOMAS (MN)

2115 Summit Avenue, St. Paul, MN 55105
Phone: (651) 962-6150 • **Financial Aid Phone:** 651-962-6550
E-mail: admissions@stthomas.edu • **CEEB Code:** 6110
Fax: (651) 962-6160 • **Website:** www.stthomas.edu • **ACT Code:** 2102

This private school, affiliated with the Roman Catholic Church, was founded in 1885. It has a 78-acre campus.

RATINGS

Admissions Selectivity Rating: 82   **Fire Safety Rating:** 95   **Green Rating:** 60*

STUDENTS AND FACULTY

Enrollment: 6,026. **Student Body:** 45% female, 55% male, 21% out-of-state, 1% international. Asian 3%, African American 3%, Caucasian 83%, Hispanic 5%, Native American <1%, Pacific Islander 0%, Two or more races 3%, Race unknown 1%.
Retention and Graduation: 89% freshmen return for sophomore year. 60% freshmen graduate within 4 years. 76% freshmen graduate within 6 years.
Faculty: Student/faculty ratio 14:1. 0% of classes are taught by teaching assistants.

ACADEMICS

Degrees: bachelor's, certificate, doctoral/professional, doctoral/research, master's, postbachelor's certifiate, post-master's certificate. **Classes:** Most classes have 20-29 students. Most lab/discussion sessions have 10-19 students. **Special Study Options:** cross-registration, double major, English as a Second Language (ESL), exchange student program (domestic), honors program, independent study, internships, student-designed major, study abroad, teacher certification program. **Honors Programs:** The Aquinas Scholars Program is the undergraduate honors program. Its purpose is to provide opportunities for motivated and curious students to deepen and enrich their undergraduate education. Combined degree programs: BA/MEng. **Disability Services:** Special programs offered to physically disabled students, including note-taking services, reader services, tape recorders, tutors. **Career Services:** Alumni network, Alumni services, Career assessment, Internships, Regional alumni. 58% of our graduates do at least one internship while they are enrolled here compared to the national average of 50%.

FACILITIES

Housing: men's dorms, special housing for international students, women's dorms, apartments for single studentsChemical-free lifestyle, women in science house, first year experience houses, Catholic women's and Catholic men's communities. **Special Academic Facilities/Equipment:** Seminary **Computers:** 100% of classrooms, 100% of dorms, 100% of libraries, 100% of dining areas, 100% of student union, 100% of common outdoor areas have wireless network access. Students can register for classes online. Administrative functions (other than registration) can be performed online.

CAMPUS LIFE

Environment: Metropolis. **Activities:** Choral groups, concert band, dance, drama/theater, jazz band, literary magazine, music ensembles, pep band,

radio station, student government, student newspaper, television station, yearbook, Campus Ministries, Student Organization, Model UN. 114 registered organizations, 7 religious organizations.1 fraternity. **Athletics (Intercollegiate):** *Men:* baseball, basketball, cross-country, diving, football, golf, ice hockey, soccer, swimming, tennis, track/field (outdoor), track/field (indoor). *Women:* basketball, cross-country, diving, golf, ice hockey, soccer, softball, swimming, tennis, track/field (outdoor), track/field (indoor), volleyball. **On-Campus Highlights:** O'Shaughnessy—Frey Library, Scooters non-alcoholic pub and restaurant, Koch Commons (workout facility residence hall area), Frey Science and Engineering Center, Chapel of St. Thomas Aquinas. **Environmental Initiatives:** Climate Action Plan approved by President's Staff June 24, 2010

ADMISSIONS

Freshman Academic Profile: Average high school GPA 3.6. 24% in top 10% of high school class, 56% in top 25% of high school class, 89% in top 50% of high school class. 66% from public high schools. **Reported SAT (pre-2016 redesign) scores:** SAT Math middle 50% range 510-620. SAT Critical Reading middle 50% range 520-630. **Concordant SAT scores:** SAT Math middle 50% range 540–640. ACT middle 50% range 24-29. Minimum internet-based TOEFL 80. Minimum paper TOEFL 550. **Basis for Candidate Selection:** *Very important factors considered include:* rigor of secondary school record, academic GPA, standardized test scores. *Important factors considered include:* class rank, application essay. *Other factors considered include:* recommendation(s), extracurricular activities, talent/ability, character/personal qualities, alumni/ae relation, geographical residence, racial/ethnic status, volunteer work. **Freshman Admission Requirements:** High school diploma is required and GED is accepted. *Academic units required:* 3 math. *Academic units recommended:* 4 English, 4 math, 2 science, 4 foreign language, 2 social studies. **Freshman Admission Statistics:** 5,436 applied, 83.96% admitted, 31% enrolled. **Transfer Admission Requirements:** High school transcript, college transcript(s), essay or personal statement, statement of good standing from prior institution(s). Minimum college GPA of 2.3 required. Lowest grade transferable C-. **General Admission Information:** Nonfall registration accepted. Admission may be deferred for a maximum of 1 year.

COSTS AND FINANCIAL AID

Annual tuition $37,264. Room and board $9,420. Required fees $841. Average book expense $1,000. **Required Forms and Deadlines:** FAFSA. **Notification of Awards:** Applicants will be notified of awards on a rolling basis beginning 3/1. **Types of Aid:** *Need-based scholarships/grants:* Federal Pell, FSEOG, State scholarships/grants, Private scholarships, College/university scholarship or grant aid from institutional funds. *Loans:* Direct Subsidized Stafford Loans, Direct Unsubsidized Stafford Loans, Direct PLUS loans, Federal Perkins Loans, State Loans. *Student Employment:* Federal Work-Study Program available. Institutional employment available. **Financial Aid Statistics:** 98% needy freshmen, 98% needy undergrads receive need-based scholarship or grant aid. 19% freshmen, 15% undergrads receive non-need-based scholarship or grant aid. 76% freshmen, 80% undergrads receive need-based self-help aid. 0% freshmen, 0% undergrads receive athletic scholarships. 99% freshmen, 94% undergrads receive any aid. 65% undergrads borrow to pay for school. Average cumulative indebtedness $40,403. **Criteria for awarding aid:** *Non-need-based:* Academics, Music/drama.

UNIVERSITY OF SAN DIEGO

5998 Alcala Park, San Diego, CA 92110-2492
Phone: 619-260-4506 • **Financial Aid Phone:** 619-260-4514
E-mail: admissions@sandiego.edu • **CEEB Code:** 4849
Fax: 619-260-6836 • **Website:** www.sandiego.edu • **ACT Code:** 394

This private school, affiliated with the Roman Catholic Church, was founded in 1949. It has a 180-acre campus.

RATINGS

Admissions Selectivity Rating: 90   **Fire Safety Rating:** 91   **Green Rating:** 99

STUDENTS AND FACULTY

Enrollment: 5,604. **Student Body:** 54% female, 46% male, 38% out-of-state, 8% international (58 countries represented). Asian 7%, African American 3%, Caucasian 52%, Hispanic 19%, Native American <1%, Pacific Islander <1%, Two or more races 6%, Race unknown 3%.

Retention and Graduation: 87% freshmen return for sophomore year. 66% freshmen graduate within 4 years. 78% freshmen graduate within 6 years. 11% grads go on to further study within 1 year. 36% grads pursue arts and sciences degrees. 28% grads pursue law degrees. 22% grads pursue business degrees. 9% grads pursue medical degrees. **Faculty:** Student/faculty ratio 14:1. 440 full-time faculty, 95% hold PhDs, 23% are are members of minority groups, 45% are women. 0% of classes are taught by teaching assistants.

ACADEMICS

Degrees: bachelor's, doctoral/professional, doctoral/research, master's, postbachelor's certificate, post-master's certificate. **Classes:** Most classes have 20-29 students. Most lab/discussion sessions have 10-19 students. **Most popular majors:** Finance; Business Administration and Management; Communication. **Special Study Options:** double major, English as a Second Language (ESL), honors program, independent study, internships, liberal arts/career combination, study abroad, teacher certification program. **Honors Programs:** Phi Beta Kappa, Honors Program Combined degree programs: JD/MBA, JD/MA. **Career Services:** Alumni network, Alumni services, Career/job search classes, Career assessment, Internships, Regional alumni.

FACILITIES

Housing: Coed dorms, special housing for disabled students, men's dorms, women's dorms, apartments for married students, apartments for single students, Wellness Housing, Theme Housing. 85% of campus accessible to physically disabled. **Special Academic Facilities/Equipment:** Art gallery, peace and justice institute, child development center, language labs. **Computers:** 100% of classrooms, 100% of dorms, 100% of libraries, 100% of dining areas, 100% of student union, 100% of common outdoor areas have wireless network access. Students can register for classes online. Administrative functions (other than registration) can be performed online.

CAMPUS LIFE

Environment: Metropolis. **Activities:** Choral groups, dance, drama/theater, jazz band, literary magazine, music ensembles, musical theater, pep band, radio station, student government, student newspaper, symphony orchestra, television station, yearbook, Campus Ministries, Student Organization, Model UN. 129 registered organizations, 20 honor societies, 2 religious organizations. 5 fraternities, 6 sororities. **Athletics (Intercollegiate):** *Men:* baseball, basketball, crew/rowing, cross-country, football, golf, soccer, tennis. *Women:* basketball, cheerleading, crew/rowing, cross-country, diving, soccer, softball, swimming, tennis, track/field (outdoor), volleyball. **On-Campus Highlights:** Aromas Coffee House, Donald P. Shiley Center for Science and Technology, Jenny Craig Pavilion (Sporting/concert venue), Joan B. Kroc Institute for Peace and Justice, Student Life Pavilion.

ADMISSIONS

Freshman Academic Profile: Average high school GPA 3.9. 39% in top 10% of high school class, 77% in top 25% of high school class, 97% in top 50% of high school class. 56% from public high schools. **Reported SAT (pre-2016 redesign) scores:** SAT Math middle 50% range 560-660. SAT Critical Reading middle 50% range 540-650. SAT Writing middle 50% range 550-650. **Concordant SAT scores:** SAT EBRW middle 50% 600–700. SAT Math middle 50% range 580–690. ACT middle 50% range 26-30. Minimum internet-based TOEFL 80. Minimum paper TOEFL 550. **Basis for Candidate Selection:** *Very important factors considered include:* rigor of secondary school record, academic GPA, standardized test scores. *Important factors considered include:* class rank, application essay, recommendation(s), extracurricular activities, talent/ability, character/personal qualities, alumni/ae relation, religious affiliation/commitment, volunteer work. *Other factors considered include:* interview, first generation, geographical residence, racial/ethnic status, work experience, level of applicant's interest. **Freshman Admission Requirements:** High school diploma is required and GED is accepted. *Academic units required:* 4 English, 3 math, 3 science, 2 science labs, 3 foreign language, 2 social studies. *Academic units recommended:* 4 English, 4 math, 4 science, 3 science labs, 4 foreign language, 3 social studies. **Freshman Admission Statistics:** 14,413 applied, 51.38% admitted, 15% enrolled. **Transfer Admission Requirements:** High school transcript, college transcript(s), essay or personal statement, Minimum college GPA of 3.0 required. Lowest grade transferable C. **General Admission Information:** Application fee $55. Regular application deadline 12/15. Nonfall registration accepted. Admission may be deferred for a maximum of one year.

COSTS AND FINANCIAL AID

Required Forms and Deadlines: FAFSA. **Notification of Awards:** Applicants will be notified of awards on a rolling basis beginning 3/1. **Types of Aid:** *Need-based scholarships/grants:* Federal Pell, FSEOG, State scholarships/grants, Private scholarships, College/university scholarship or grant aid from institutional funds, Federal Nursing Scholarships. *Loans:* Direct Subsidized Stafford Loans, Direct Unsubsidized Stafford Loans, Direct PLUS loans, Federal Perkins Loans, College/university loans from institutional funds. *Student Employment:* Federal Work-Study Program available. Institutional employment available. **Financial Aid Statistics:** 96% needy freshmen, 95% needy undergrads receive need-based scholarship or grant aid. 71% freshmen,

51% undergrads receive non-need-based scholarship or grant aid. 70% freshmen, 77% undergrads receive need-based self-help aid. 2% freshmen, 2% undergrads receive athletic scholarships. 84% freshmen, 73% undergrads receive any aid. 53% undergrads borrow to pay for school. Average cumulative indebtedness $29,646. **Criteria for awarding aid:** *Need-based:* Academics, Leadership, Religious affiliation. *Non-need-based:* Academics, Athletics, Leadership, Music/drama, Religious affiliation.

UNIVERSITY OF SAN FRANCISCO

2130 Fulton Street, San Francisco, CA 94117
Phone: 415-422-6563 • **Financial Aid Phone:** 415-422-2020
E-mail: admission@usfca.edu • **CEEB Code:** 1325
Fax: 415-422-2217 • **Website:** www.usfca.edu • **ACT Code:** 466

This private school, affiliated with the Roman Catholic Church, affiliated with the Jesuit Church, was founded in 1855. It has a 55-acre campus.

RATINGS

Admissions Selectivity Rating: 83   **Fire Safety Rating:** 60*   **Green Rating:** 75

STUDENTS AND FACULTY

Enrollment: 6,664. **Student Body:** 62% female, 38% male, 23% out-of-state, 18% international (63 countries represented). Asian 22%, African American 3%, Caucasian 26%, Hispanic 21%, Native American <1%, Pacific Islander 1%, Two or more races 7%, Race unknown 2%.
Retention and Graduation: 86% freshmen return for sophomore year. 61% freshmen graduate within 4 years. 72% freshmen graduate within 6 years.
Faculty: 0% of classes are taught by teaching assistants.

ACADEMICS

Degrees: bachelor's, doctoral/professional, doctoral/research, master's, postbachelor's certifiate, post-master's certificate. **Classes:** Most classes have 10-19 students. Most lab/discussion sessions have 10-19 students. **Most popular majors:** Psychology Business/Commerce. **Special Study Options:** Accelerated program, cross-registration, distance learning, double major, English as a Second Language (ESL), exchange student program (domestic), external degree program, honors program, independent study, internships, liberal arts/career combination, student-designed major, study abroad, teacher certification program. Combined degree programs: BA/JD, BA/MA, BA/MEng, MBA and MA/MS across disciplines. **Disability Services:** Special programs offered to physically disabled students, including note-taking services, reader services, tape recorders, tutors. **Career Services:** Career/job search classes, Career assessment, Internships.

FACILITIES

Housing: Coed dorms, women's dorms, apartments for single students, Several off campus buildings with flats have been purchased and converted into multiple student housing units. 100% of campus accessible to physically disabled. **Special Academic Facilities/Equipment:** Rare Book Room, Ricci Institute for Chinese-Western Cultural History **Computers:** 25% of classrooms, 25% of dorms, 25% of dining areas, 75% of student union, 25% of common outdoor areas have wireless network access. Students can register for classes online. Administrative functions (other than registration) can be performed online.

CAMPUS LIFE

Environment: Metropolis. **Activities:** Choral groups, dance, drama/theater, literary magazine, music ensembles, musical theater, pep band, radio station, student government, student newspaper, television station, yearbook. 90 registered organizations, 14 honor societies, 4 fraternities, 4 sororities. **Athletics (Intercollegiate):** *Men:* baseball, basketball, cross-country, golf, riflery, soccer, tennis, track/field (outdoor). *Women:* basketball, cross-country, golf, riflery, soccer, tennis, track/field (outdoor), volleyball. **On-Campus Highlights:** Koret Health and Recreation Center, War Memorial Gym, St. Ignatius Church, Geschke Learning Resourse Center, Loan Mountain Campus. **Environmental Initiatives:** Sustainability. Placed 5th in National competition in Recyclemania. Currently, USF's co-generation plant produces about half of lower campus' peak energy needs. Located in the basement of Gleeson Library, the plant converts natural gas into electricity. Although the conversion of natural gas to energy does produce some emissions, natural gas is considered the cleanest of the fossil fuels. The plant gets its co-generation designation because it also captures heat lost during the conversion process and uses that to provide some of the heat lower campus uses. The plant provides about 38 percent of lower campus' heating needs. Additionally, the university uses thermal panels on top of Phelan, Gillson, and Hayes-Healy halls. The panels differ from solar panels in that they heat water directly rather than producing electricity, providing some of the hot water needed in those halls.

ADMISSIONS

Freshman Academic Profile: Average high school GPA 3.5. 31% from public high schools. **Reported SAT (pre-2016 redesign) scores:** SAT Math middle 50% range 520-630. SAT Critical Reading middle 50% range 510-620. SAT Writing middle 50% range 510-620. **Concordant SAT scores:** SAT EBRW middle 50% 570–670. SAT Math middle 50% range 550–650. ACT middle 50% range 23-28. Minimum internet-based TOEFL 79. **Basis for Candidate Selection:** *Very important factors considered include:* rigor of secondary school record, academic GPA, standardized test scores, application essay. *Important factors considered include:* class rank, recommendation(s), extracurricular activities, character/personal qualities, volunteer work. *Other factors considered include:* interview, talent/ability, first generation, alumni/ae relation, racial/ethnic status, work experience. **Freshman Admission Requirements:** High school diploma is required and GED is accepted. *Academic units required:* 4 English, 3 math, 2 science, 2 foreign language, 3 social studies, 6 academic electives, and 2 units from above areas or other academic areas. **Freshman Admission Statistics:** 15,441 applied, 70.64% admitted, 15% enrolled. **Transfer Admission Requirements:** college transcript(s), essay or personal statement, Minimum college GPA of 2.5 required. Lowest grade transferable C. **General Admission Information:** Application fee $65. Priority deadline 11/15. Regular application deadline 1/15. Nonfall registration accepted. Admission may be deferred for a maximum of 1 semester.

COSTS AND FINANCIAL AID

Annual tuition $44,040. Room and board $13,990. Required fees $454. Average book expense $1,600. **Required Forms and Deadlines:** FAFSA, CSS/Financial Aid PROFILE. **Notification of Awards:** Applicants will be notified of awards on a rolling basis beginning 4/1. **Types of Aid:** *Need-based scholarships/grants:* Federal Pell, FSEOG, State scholarships/grants, Private scholarships, College/university scholarship or grant aid from institutional funds, Federal Nursing Scholarships. *Loans:* Direct Subsidized Stafford Loans, Direct Unsubsidized Stafford Loans, Direct PLUS loans, Federal Perkins Loans, Federal Nursing Loans, College/university loans from institutional funds. *Student Employment:* Federal Work-Study Program available. Institutional employment available. **Financial Aid Statistics:** 76% needy freshmen, 84% needy undergrads receive need-based scholarship or grant aid. 76% freshmen, 62% undergrads receive non-need-based scholarship or grant aid. 98% freshmen, 98% undergrads receive need-based self-help aid. 1% freshmen, 2% undergrads receive athletic scholarships. 87% freshmen, 81% undergrads receive any aid. 55% undergrads borrow to pay for school. Average cumulative indebtedness $34,114. **Criteria for awarding aid:** *Need-based:* Academics, Alumni affiliation, Athletics, Minority status. *Non-need-based:* Academics, Athletics, Minority status.

See page 1086.

UNIVERSITY OF SCIENCE & ARTS OF OKLAHOMA

1727 West Alabama, Chickasha, OK 73018
Phone: 405-574-1357 • **Financial Aid Phone:** 405-574-1240
E-mail: usao-admissions@usao.edu • **CEEB Code:** 6544
Fax: 405-574-1220 • **Website:** www.usao.edu • **ACT Code:** 3418

This public school was founded in 1908. It has a 75-acre campus.

RATINGS
Admissions Selectivity Rating: 81   **Fire Safety Rating:** 96   **Green Rating:** 60*

STUDENTS AND FACULTY
Enrollment: 848. **Student Body:** 66% female, 34% male, 14% out-of-state, 8% international (22 countries represented). Asian 1%, African American 5%, Caucasian 63%, Hispanic 7%, Native American 14%, Pacific Islander 0%, Two or more races 0%, Race unknown 2%.
Retention and Graduation: 78% freshmen return for sophomore year. 29% freshmen graduate within 4 years. 42% freshmen graduate within 6 years. **Faculty:** Student/faculty ratio 12:1. 54 full-time faculty, 87% hold PhDs, 11% are are members of minority groups, 52% are women. 0% of classes are taught by teaching assistants.

ACADEMICS
Degrees: bachelor's. **Classes:** Most classes have 10-19 students. Most lab/discussion sessions have 10-19 students. **Most popular majors:** Business Administration and Management; Psychology; Elementary Education and

Teaching. **Special Study Options:** Accelerated program, double major, dual enrollment, honors program, independent study, internships, student-designed major, study abroad, teacher certification program. **Disability Services:** Special programs offered to physically disabled students, including note-taking services, tutors. **Career Services:** Career/job search classes, Career assessment, Internships.

FACILITIES
Housing: Coed dorms, apartments for single students. 100% of campus accessible to physically diasbled. **Special Academic Facilities/Equipment:** Language labs, speech and hearing clinic, multiple computer labs, herbarium **Computers:** 100% of classrooms, 85% of dorms, 100% of libraries, 100% of dining areas, 100% of student union, 100% of common outdoor areas have wireless network access.

CAMPUS LIFE
Environment: Village. **Activities:** Choral groups, concert band, drama/theater, jazz band, literary magazine, music ensembles, musical theater, pep band, student government, student newspaper, television station, Campus Ministries. 24 registered organizations, 7 honor societies, 4 religious organizations. 1 fraternity, 1 sorority. **Athletics (Intercollegiate):** *Men:* baseball, basketball, cheerleading, soccer. *Women:* basketball, cheerleading, soccer, softball. **On-Campus Highlights:** Lawson Court, Nash Library, Student Center, Bill Smith Ballpark, Scooter's Grill.

ADMISSIONS
Freshman Academic Profile: Average high school GPA 3.4. 25% in top 10% of high school class, 47% in top 25% of high school class, 78% in top 50% of high school class. 90% from public high schools. **Reported SAT (pre-2016 redesign) scores:** SAT Math middle 50% range 410-510. SAT Critical Reading middle 50% range 390-490. **Concordant SAT scores:** SAT Math middle 50% range 450–540. ACT middle 50% range 19-24. Minimum internet-based TOEFL 61. Minimum paper TOEFL 500. **Basis for Candidate Selection:** *Very important factors considered include:* class rank, academic GPA, standardized test scores. *Other factors considered include:* recommendation(s), talent/ability. **Freshman Admission Requirements:** High school diploma is required and GED is accepted. *Academic units required:* 4 English, 3 math, 3 science, 3 science labs, 2 social studies, 1 history, 2 academic electives. *Academic units recommended:* 4 English, 4 math, 4 science, 4 science labs, 2 foreign language, 2 social studies, 1 history, 2 academic electives, 1 computer science, 2 visual/performing arts. **Freshman Admission Statistics:** 706 applied, 66.01% admitted, 48% enrolled. **Transfer Admission Requirements:** college transcript(s), Minimum college GPA of 2.0 required. Lowest grade transferable D. **General Admission Information:** Application fee $40. Regular application deadline 9/2. Nonfall registration accepted. Admission may be deferred for a maximum of 1 year.

COSTS AND FINANCIAL AID
Required Forms and Deadlines: FAFSA. **Notification of Awards:** Applicants will be notified of awards on a rolling basis beginning 3/1. **Types of Aid:** *Need-based scholarships/grants:* Federal Pell, FSEOG, State scholarships/grants, Private scholarships, College/university scholarship or grant aid from institutional funds. *Loans:* Direct Subsidized Stafford Loans, Direct Unsubsidized Stafford Loans, Direct PLUS loans, Federal Perkins Loans, College/university loans from institutional funds. *Student Employment:* Federal Work-Study Program available. Institutional employment available. **Financial Aid Statistics:** 93% needy freshmen, 92% needy undergrads receive need-based scholarship or grant aid. 13% freshmen, 11% undergrads receive non-need-based scholarship or grant aid. 63% freshmen, 69% undergrads receive need-based self-help aid. 12% freshmen, 11% undergrads receive athletic scholarships. 93% freshmen, 89% undergrads receive any aid. 52% undergrads borrow to pay for school. Average cumulative indebtedness $24,460. **Criteria for awarding aid:** *Need-based:* Academics, Art, Athletics, Leadership, Music/drama. *Non-need-based:* Academics, Art, Athletics, Leadership, Music/drama, State/district residency.

UNIVERSITY OF THE SCIENCES IN PHILADELPHIA

600 South 43rd Street, Philadelphia, PA 19104-4495
Phone: 215-596-8810 • **Financial Aid Phone:** 215-596-8894
E-mail: admit@usciences.edu • **CEEB Code:** 2663
Fax: 215-596-8821 • **ACT Code:** 3671

This private school was founded in 1821. It has a 35-acre campus.

RATINGS
Admissions Selectivity Rating: 89   **Fire Safety Rating:** 80   **Green Rating:** 61

STUDENTS AND FACULTY

Enrollment: 2,427. **Student Body:** 61% female, 39% male, 59% out-of-state, 2% international (20 countries represented). Asian 36%, African American 5%, Caucasian 46%, Hispanic 2%, Native American <1%, Pacific Islander <1%, Two or more races 2%, Race unknown 7%.

Retention and Graduation: 88% freshmen return for sophomore year. 67% freshmen graduate within 4 years. 72% freshmen graduate within 6 years. **Faculty:** Student/faculty ratio 10:1. 191 full-time faculty, 82% hold PhDs, 20% are are members of minority groups, 52% are women. 0% of classes are taught by teaching assistants.

ACADEMICS

Degrees: bachelor's, certificate, doctoral/professional, doctoral/research, doctoral, master's. **Classes:** Most classes have 20-29 students. Most lab/discussion sessions have 20-29 students. **Most popular majors:** Biology/Biological Sciences; Pharmacy; Physical Therapy/Therapist. **Special Study Options:** distance learning, double major, English as a Second Language (ESL), honors program, internships, liberal arts/career combination, teacher certification program, academic remediation, advanced placement credit, learning disabilities services, off-campus study. **Honors Programs:** The Honors Program at University of the Sciences offers exceptional students the opportunity for specialized, intensive learning experiences both inside and outside the classroom. As an honors student, you will take part in special honors classes and recitations. The workload for these classes is not harder than others at University of the Sciences, but different. For example you may do smaller, more advanced experiments in a lab course. You may tour historic sites for a history class, or meet with a visiting author in your writing class. You will work in smaller classes and have more independent and group projects. Combined degree programs: PharmD/MBA; BSHS/MOT; BSHS/MPT; BSHS/DPT. **Disability Services:** Special programs offered to physically disabled students, including note-taking services, reader services, tape recorders, tutors. **Career Services:** Alumni services, Career/job search classes, Career assessment, Internships. USciences Alumni Career Panels.

FACILITIES

Housing: Coed dorms, fraternity/sorority housing, apartments for single students, Wellness Housing, honor halls in certain dormitories, upper level floor for upper level students. 90% of campus accessible to physically diasbled. **Special Academic Facilities/Equipment:** Pharmacy museum, electron microscope. **Computers:** 80% of classrooms, 100% of dorms, 100% of libraries, 100% of dining areas, 40% of common outdoor areas have wireless network access. Students can register for classes online. Administrative functions (other than registration) can be performed online.

CAMPUS LIFE

Environment: Metropolis. **Activities:** Choral groups, concert band, dance, drama/theater, literary magazine, musical theater, student government, student newspaper, yearbook. 66 registered organizations, 6 honor societies, 6 religious organizations. 2 fraternities, 2 sororities. **Athletics (Intercollegiate):** *Men:* baseball, basketball, cross-country, golf, riflery, tennis. *Women:* basketball, cross-country, golf, riflery, softball, tennis, volleyball. **On-Campus Highlights:** McNeil Science and Technology Center, Athletic Recreation Center, Wilson Hall, Marvin Sampson Museum, Griffith Hall, More than 80 state-of-the-art laboratories, including the Center for Advanced Pharmacy Studies (CAPS), the first laboratory of its kind at any college of pharmacy nationwide. In September 2003, USP opened a new 78,000-square-foot athletic/recreation center that provides exercise and practice space for varsity and intramural sports as well as general recreational facilities. The new building, part of a $30 million campus expansion and beautification project, contains a 3,500-square-foot, three-lane swimming pool; additional classrooms and faculty offices; and space for student organizations to meet and for students to gather informally. In August 2006, USP opened the McNeil Science and Technology Center, a three-story, 77,000-square-foot leading edge facility that reflects the University's commitment to its innovative curriculum. The Center's research laboratories and state-of-the-art-equipped support spaces will accommodate more undergraduate, graduate, post-doctoral, and faculty researchers in biology, microbiology, physics, and other scientific fields. The Center features a 400-seat auditorium, classrooms, computer workrooms and other flexible space that supports innovative teaching and learning through multi-media technology. The Center's two-story, light-filled commons provides a comfortable space for students to relax and study. **Environmental Initiatives:** All "On the Go" containers are fully recyclable.

ADMISSIONS

Freshman Academic Profile: Average high school GPA 3.6. 45% in top 10% of high school class, 80% in top 25% of high school class, 98% in top 50% of high school class. **Reported SAT (pre-2016 redesign) scores:** SAT Math middle 50% range 550-650. SAT Critical Reading middle 50% range 520-590. SAT Writing middle 50% range 520-610. **Concordant SAT scores:** SAT EBRW middle 50% range 580–650. SAT Math middle 50% range 570–670. ACT middle 50% range 22-27. Minimum paper TOEFL 550. **Basis for Candidate Selection:** *Very important factors considered include:* rigor of secondary school record, class rank, academic GPA, standardized test scores. *Other factors considered include:* application essay, recommendation(s), interview, extracurricular activities, character/personal qualities, alumni/ae relation, volunteer work, work experience, level of applicant's interest. **Freshman Admission Requirements:** High school diploma is required and GED is accepted. *Academic units required:* 4 English, 3 math, 3 science, 2 science labs, 1 social studies, 1 history, 4 academic electives. *Academic units recommended:* 4 English, 4 math, 3 science, 3 science labs, 1 social studies, 1 history, 4 academic electives. **Freshman Admission Statistics:** 4,099 applied, 61.33% admitted, 18% enrolled. **Transfer Admission Requirements:** college transcript(s), standardized test scores, Minimum college GPA of 3.0 required. Lowest grade transferable C. **General Admission Information:** Application fee $45. Nonfall registration not accepted. Admission may be deferred for a maximum of 12 months.

COSTS AND FINANCIAL AID

Annual tuition $34,336. Required fees $1,760. Average book expense $1,050. **Required Forms and Deadlines:** FAFSA. **Notification of Awards:** Applicants will be notified of awards on a rolling basis beginning 2/15. **Types of Aid:** *Need-based scholarships/grants:* Federal Pell, FSEOG, State scholarships/grants, Private scholarships, College/university scholarship or grant aid from institutional funds. *Loans:* Direct Subsidized Stafford Loans, Direct Unsubsidized Stafford Loans, Direct PLUS loans, Federal Perkins Loans, College/university loans from institutional funds. *Student Employment:* Federal Work-Study Program available. Institutional employment available. **Financial Aid Statistics:** 81% needy freshmen, 82% needy undergrads receive need-based scholarship or grant aid. 97% freshmen, 88% undergrads receive non-need-based scholarship or grant aid. 77% freshmen, 84% undergrads receive need-based self-help aid. 1% freshmen, 7% undergrads receive athletic scholarships. 100% freshmen, 89% undergrads receive any aid. **Criteria for awarding aid:** *Need-based:* Academics, Athletics. *Non-need-based:* Academics, Athletics.

THE UNIVERSITY OF SCRANTON

800 Linden Street, Scranton, PA 18510
Phone: 570-941-7540 • **Financial Aid Phone:** 570-941-7701
E-mail: admissions@scranton.edu • **CEEB Code:** 2929
Fax: 570-941-5928 • **Website:** www.scranton.edu • **ACT Code:** 3736

This private school, affiliated with the Roman Catholic-Jesuit Church, was founded in 1888. It has a 50-acre campus.

RATINGS

Admissions Selectivity Rating: 85   **Fire Safety Rating:** 95   **Green Rating:** 81

STUDENTS AND FACULTY

Enrollment: 3,757. **Student Body:** 59% female, 41% male, 60% out-of-state, 1% international (11 countries represented). Asian 3%, African American 2%, Caucasian 81%, Hispanic 9%, Native American <1%, Pacific Islander <1%, Two or more races 2%, Race unknown 2%.

Retention and Graduation: 87% freshmen return for sophomore year. 72% freshmen graduate within 4 years. 79% freshmen graduate within 6 years. 38% grads go on to further study within 1 year. 15% grads pursue arts and sciences degrees. 2% grads pursue law degrees. 3% grads pursue business degrees. 6% grads pursue medical degrees. **Faculty:** Student/faculty ratio 12:1. 290 full-time faculty, 88% hold PhDs, 7% are are members of minority groups, 41% are women. 0% of classes are taught by teaching assistants.

ACADEMICS

Degrees: associate, bachelor's, certificate, doctoral/professional, master's, postbachelor's certificate, post-master's certificate. **Classes:** Most classes have 10-19 students. Most lab/discussion sessions have 10-19 students. **Most popular majors:** Biology/Biological Sciences; Registered Nursing/Registered Nurse; Kinesiology and Exercise Science. **Special Study Options:** Accelerated program, cross-registration, distance learning, double major, dual enrollment, English as a Second Language (ESL), exchange student program (domestic), honors program, independent study, internships, study abroad, teacher certification program, Baccalaureate/masters degree program. Combined degree programs: BA/MA, BS/MBA, BA/MBA, BS/MHA, BS/MS, BS/MA, BS/MSN, BS/MS, BS/MACC. **Disability Services:** Special programs offered to physically disabled students, including note-taking services, reader services, tape recorders, tutors. **Career Services:** Alumni network, Alumni services,

Career/job search classes, Career assessment, Internships, Regional alumni. The comprehensive set of career planning and development services we provide to all constituent groups (i.e.—prospective and current students, their parents, their families, alumni, etc.).

FACILITIES

Housing: Coed dorms, men's dorms, women's dorms, apartments for single students, Theme Housing. 100% of campus accessible to physically diasbled. **Special Academic Facilities/Equipment:** Art gallery, fine arts facility, theatre, center for music groups, language lab, microbiology institute, electron microscope, greenhouse. **Computers:** 40% of classrooms, 100% of dorms, 100% of libraries, 100% of dining areas, 100% of student union, 90% of common outdoor areas have wireless network access. Students can register for classes online. Administrative functions (other than registration) can be performed online.

CAMPUS LIFE

Environment: City. **Activities:** Choral groups, concert band, dance, drama/theater, jazz band, literary magazine, music ensembles, radio station, student government, student newspaper, television station, yearbook, Campus Ministries, Student Organization. 50 registered organizations, 32 honor societies, 14 religious organizations. **Athletics (Intercollegiate):** *Men:* baseball, basketball, cross-country, golf, ice hockey, lacrosse, soccer, swimming, tennis, wrestling. *Women:* basketball, cross-country, field hockey, lacrosse, soccer, softball, swimming, tennis, volleyball. **On-Campus Highlights:** Brennan Hall (Home of the Kania School of Management), DeNaples Campus Center, The Harry and Jeanette Weiberg Memorial Library, The Murray Room (workout facility) **Environmental Initiatives:** We have incorporated energy efficient technology in our new construction and renovations over the past 20 years. We have one LEED Silver building, one LEED Gold building, and the recently opened 117,421 GSF Leahy Hall has been submitted for LEED certification.

ADMISSIONS

Freshman Academic Profile: Average high school GPA 3.5. 30% in top 10% of high school class, 62% in top 25% of high school class, 90% in top 50% of high school class. **Reported SAT (pre-2016 redesign) scores:** SAT Math middle 50% range 520-620. SAT Critical Reading middle 50% range 510-600. **Concordant SAT scores:** SAT Math middle 50% range 550–640. ACT middle 50% range 23-28. Minimum internet-based TOEFL 80. **Basis for Candidate Selection:** *Very important factors considered include:* rigor of secondary school record, class rank, academic GPA, standardized test scores. *Important factors considered include:* extracurricular activities. *Other factors considered include:* application essay, recommendation(s), interview, talent/ability, character/personal qualities, alumni/ae relation, volunteer work, work experience, level of applicant's interest. **Freshman Admission Requirements:** High school diploma is required and GED is accepted. *Academic units required:* 4 English, 3 math, 1 science, 2 foreign language, 2 history, and 4 units from above areas or other academic areas. *Academic units recommended:* 4 English, 4 math, 2 science, 2 foreign language, 3 history, and 4 units from above areas or other academic areas. **Freshman Admission Statistics:** 10,128 applied, 74.45% admitted, 13% enrolled. **Transfer Admission Requirements:** High school transcript, college transcript(s), Minimum college GPA of 2.75 required. Lowest grade transferable C. **General Admission Information:** Regular application deadline 3/1. Nonfall registration accepted. Admission may be deferred for a maximum of 1 year.

COSTS AND FINANCIAL AID

Annual tuition $41,762. Required fees $400. Average book expense $1,300. **Required Forms and Deadlines:** FAFSA. **Notification of Awards:** Applicants will be notified of awards on a rolling basis beginning 3/15. **Types of Aid:** *Need-based scholarships/grants:* Federal Pell, FSEOG, State scholarships/grants, Private scholarships, College/university scholarship or grant aid from institutional funds. *Loans:* Direct Subsidized Stafford Loans, Direct Unsubsidized Stafford Loans, Direct PLUS loans, Federal Perkins Loans. *Student Employment:* Federal Work-Study Program available. Institutional employment available. **Financial Aid Statistics:** 96% needy freshmen, 96% needy undergrads receive need-based scholarship or grant aid. 11% freshmen, 8% undergrads receive non-need-based scholarship or grant aid. 81% freshmen, 85% undergrads receive need-based self-help aid. 0% freshmen, 0% undergrads receive athletic scholarships. 96% freshmen, 96% undergrads receive any aid. 73% undergrads borrow to pay for school. Average cumulative indebtedness $42,423. **Criteria for awarding aid:** *Need-based:* Minority status. *Non-need-based:* Academics, Minority status.

UNIVERSITY OF SOUTH ALABAMA

University of South Alabama Meisler Hall, Mobile, AL 36688-0002
Phone: 251-460-6141 • **Financial Aid Phone:** 800-305-6828
E-mail: recruitment@southalabama.edu • **CEEB Code:** 1880
Fax: 251-460-7876 • **Website:** www.southalabama.edu • **ACT Code:** 59

This public school was founded in 1963. It has a 1215-acre campus.

RATINGS

Admissions Selectivity Rating: 74   **Fire Safety Rating:** 65   **Green Rating:** 69

STUDENTS AND FACULTY

Enrollment: 11,483. **Student Body:** 54% female, 46% male, 18% out-of-state, 9% international (72 countries represented). Asian 3%, African American 22%, Caucasian 57%, Hispanic 3%, Native American 1%, Pacific Islander <1%, Two or more races 3%, Race unknown 2%.
Retention and Graduation: 73% freshmen return for sophomore year. 16% freshmen graduate within 4 years. 38 **Faculty:** Student/faculty ratio 20:1. 590 full-time faculty, 76% hold PhDs, 15% are are members of minority groups, 49% are women.

ACADEMICS

Degrees: bachelor's, certificate, doctoral/professional, doctoral/research, master's, postbachelor's certifiate, post-master's certificate. **Most popular majors:** Registered Nursing/Registered Nurse; Health/Medical Preparatory Programs; Multi-/Interdisciplinary Studies. **Special Study Options:** Accelerated program, cooperative education program, distance learning, double major, dual enrollment, English as a Second Language (ESL), honors program, independent study, internships, student-designed major, study abroad, teacher certification program, weekend college. **Honors Programs:** Honor Program. **Disability Services:** Special programs offered to physically disabled students, including note-taking services, reader services, tape recorders, tutors. **Career Services:** Career/job search classes, Career assessment, Internships.

FACILITIES

Housing: Coed dorms, special housing for disabled students, men's dorms, women's dorms, fraternity/sorority housing, apartments for married students, apartments for single students. **Special Academic Facilities/Equipment:** Museum/gallery complex, three hospitals, center for clinical education in health programs, engineering labs. **Computers:** Students can register for classes online. Administrative functions (other than registration) can be performed online. Undergraduates are required to own a computer.

CAMPUS LIFE

Environment: City. **Activities:** Choral groups, concert band, dance, drama/theater, jazz band, literary magazine, marching band, music ensembles, musical theater, opera, student government, student newspaper, student-run film society, symphony orchestra, television station, Campus Ministries. 185 registered organizations, 2 honor societies, 1 religious organization. 8 fraternities, 8 sororities. **Athletics (Intercollegiate):** *Men:* baseball, basketball, cross-country, football, golf, tennis, track/field (outdoor), *Women:* basketball, cross-country, golf, soccer, softball, tennis, track/field (outdoor), volleyball. **On-Campus Highlights:** Mitchell Center (arena), Stanky Field, John W. Laidlaw Performing Arts Center, Intramural Field Complex.

ADMISSIONS

Freshman Academic Profile: Average high school GPA 3.5. 86% from public high schools. **Reported SAT (pre-2016 redesign) scores:** SAT Math middle 50% range 430-560. SAT Critical Reading middle 50% range 445-570. SAT Writing middle 50% range 450-570. **Concordant SAT scores:** SAT EBRW middle 50% 500–630. SAT Math middle 50% range 470–580. ACT middle 50% range 20-26. Minimum internet-based TOEFL 61. Minimum paper TOEFL 500. **Basis for Candidate Selection:** *Very important factors considered include:* academic GPA, standardized test scores. **Freshman Admission Requirements:** High school diploma is required and GED is accepted. *Academic units recommended:* 4 English, 3 math, 3 science, 2 science labs, 3 social studies, 3 academic electives. **Freshman Admission Statistics:** 6,401 applied, 79.63% admitted, 39% enrolled. **Transfer Admission Requirements:** college transcript(s), Minimum college GPA of 2.0 required. Lowest grade transferable D. **General Admission Information:** Application fee $45. Regular application deadline 7/15. Nonfall registration accepted. Admission may be deferred.

COSTS AND FINANCIAL AID

Annual in-state tuition $9,060. Annual out-of-state tuition $18,120. Room and board $7,340. Average book expense $1,260. **Required Forms and Deadlines:** FAFSA, Institution's own financial aid form. **Types of Aid:** *Need-based scholarships/grants:* Federal Pell, FSEOG, State scholarships/grants, Private scholarships, College/university scholarship or grant aid from institutional funds. *Loans:* Direct Subsidized Stafford Loans, Direct

Unsubsidized Stafford Loans, Direct PLUS loans, Federal Perkins Loans, College/university loans from institutional funds. *Student Employment:* Federal Work-Study Program available. Institutional employment available. **Financial Aid Statistics:** 91% needy freshmen, 84% needy undergrads receive need-based scholarship or grant aid. 92% freshmen, 84% undergrads receive non-need-based scholarship or grant aid. 93% freshmen, 93% undergrads receive need-based self-help aid. 3% freshmen, 3% undergrads receive athletic scholarships. 83% freshmen, 61% undergrads receive any aid. **Criteria for awarding aid:** *Non-need-based:* Academics, Alumni affiliation, Art, Athletics, Job skills, Leadership, Minority status, Music/drama, State/district residency.

UNIVERSITY OF SOUTH CAROLINA—AIKEN

471 University Parkway, Aiken, SC 29801
Phone: 803-641-3366 • **Financial Aid Phone:** 803-641-3476
E-mail: admit@usca.edu • **CEEB Code:** 5840
Fax: 803-641-3727 • **Website:** www.usca.edu • **ACT Code:** 3879

This public school was founded in 1961. It has a 453-acre campus.

RATINGS

Admissions Selectivity Rating: 81   **Fire Safety Rating:** 94   **Green Rating:** 76

STUDENTS AND FACULTY

Enrollment: 3,131. **Student Body:** 64% female, 36% male, 11% out-of-state, 4% international (24 countries represented). Asian 1%, African American 27%, Caucasian 58%, Hispanic 4%, Native American 1%, Pacific Islander <1%, Two or more races 4%, Race unknown 1%.
Retention and Graduation: 72% freshmen return for sophomore year. 23% freshmen graduate within 4 years. 43% freshmen graduate within 6 years.
Faculty: Student/faculty ratio 15:1. 152 full-time faculty, 79% hold PhDs, 16% are are members of minority groups, 48% are women. 0% of classes are taught by teaching assistants.

ACADEMICS

Degrees: bachelor's, master's. **Classes:** Most classes have 20-29 students. Most lab/discussion sessions have 20-29 students. **Most popular majors:** Business Administration and Management; Registered Nursing/Registered Nurse; Kinesiology and Exercise Science. **Special Study Options:** cooperative education program, distance learning, double major, dual enrollment, English as a Second Language (ESL), honors program, independent study, internships, student-designed major, study abroad, teacher certification program. **Honors Programs:** The USCA Honors Program is designed to increase the educational opportunities for the academically well qualified and highly motivated student. Designed in accordance with the principles of the National Collegiate Honors Council, the USC Aiken Honors Program provides an enriched academic experience, both in and out of the classroom, for outstanding students committed to reaching their highest potential as scholars and creative thinkers. For details on our Honors Program or the other high quality academic opportunities awaiting you at USC Aiken, please call on our Office of Admissions toll free at 888.WOW.USCA or locally at 803.641.3366. The Honors Director may be reached at 803.641.3226. **Disability Services:** Special programs offered to physically disabled students, including note-taking services, reader services, tape recorders. **Career Services:** Alumni network, Alumni services, Career/job search classes, Career assessment, Internships, Regional alumni.

FACILITIES

Housing: Coed dorms, special housing for disabled students, apartments for single students, Wellness Housing, Theme Housing. 100% of campus accessible to physically diasbled. **Special Academic Facilities/Equipment:** Ruth Patrick Science Education Center Etherredge Center (Fine Arts Center) Wellness Center Planetarium **Computers:** 100% of classrooms, 100% of dorms, 100% of libraries, 100% of dining areas, 100% of student union, 100% of common outdoor areas have wireless network access. Students can register for classes online. Administrative functions (other than registration) can be performed online.

CAMPUS LIFE

Environment: Town. **Activities:** concert band, dance, drama/theater, music ensembles, musical theater, pep band, student government, student newspaper, symphony orchestra, yearbook, Campus Ministries, Student Organization. 89 registered organizations, 12 honor societies, 7 religious organizations. 5 fraternities, 7 sororities. **Athletics (Intercollegiate):** *Men:* baseball, basketball, cheerleading, golf, soccer, tennis. *Women:* basketball, cheerleading, cross-country, soccer, softball, tennis, volleyball. **On-Campus Highlights:** DuPont Planetarium in the Ruth Patrick Science Education Center, The Etherredge Center for Visual and Performing Arts, The Wellness Center and Natatorium,

The Alan B. Miller Nursing Building, Pacer Commons Student Housing, Roberto Hernandez Baseball Stadium USC Aiken Convocation Center. **Environmental Initiatives:** Obtain State Energy Department stimulus funding approval to 'jump start' significant energy conservation actions. The energy conservation projects will reduce each building's energy use (kWh) by 18%—reducing the carbon footprint from purchased electricity by at least 20%.

ADMISSIONS

Freshman Academic Profile: Average high school GPA 3.8. 15% in top 10% of high school class, 40% in top 25% of high school class, 80% in top 50% of high school class. 92% from public high schools. **Reported SAT (pre-2016 redesign) scores:** SAT Math middle 50% range 420-530. SAT Critical Reading middle 50% range 430-530. SAT Writing middle 50% range 400-510. **Concordant SAT scores:** SAT EBRW middle 50% 460–580. SAT Math middle 50% range 460–560. ACT middle 50% range 18-23. Minimum internet-based TOEFL 80. Minimum paper TOEFL 550. **Basis for Candidate Selection:** *Very important factors considered include:* rigor of secondary school record, class rank, academic GPA, standardized test scores. **Freshman Admission Requirements:** High school diploma is required and GED is accepted. *Academic units required:* 4 English, 4 math, 3 science, 3 science labs, 2 foreign language, 2 social studies, 1 history, 4 academic electives, and 1 unit from above areas or other academic areas. *Academic units recommended:* 1 computer science, 1 visual/performing arts. **Freshman Admission Statistics:** 2,177 applied, 60.54% admitted, 47% enrolled. **Transfer Admission Requirements:** college transcript(s), statement of good standing from prior institution(s). Minimum college GPA of 2.0 required. Lowest grade transferable C. **General Admission Information:** Application fee $45. Priority deadline 6/1. Regular application deadline 8/1. Nonfall registration accepted. Admission may be deferred for a maximum of 1 year.

COSTS AND FINANCIAL AID

Annual in-state tuition $9,882. Annual out-of-state tuition $19,788. Room and board $7,466. Required fees $314. Average book expense $1,656. **Required Forms and Deadlines:** FAFSA. **Notification of Awards:** Applicants will be notified of awards on a rolling basis beginning 4/20. **Types of Aid:** *Need-based scholarships/grants:* Federal Pell, FSEOG, State scholarships/grants, Private scholarships, College/university scholarship or grant aid from institutional funds. *Loans:* Direct Subsidized Stafford Loans, Direct Unsubsidized Stafford Loans, Direct PLUS loans, Federal Perkins Loans, State Loans. *Student Employment:* Federal Work-Study Program available. Institutional employment available. **Financial Aid Statistics:** 95% needy freshmen, 83% needy undergrads receive need-based scholarship or grant aid. 10% freshmen, 9% undergrads receive non-need-based scholarship or grant aid. 70% freshmen, 78% undergrads receive need-based self-help aid. 4% freshmen, 4% undergrads receive athletic scholarships. 72% freshmen, 69% undergrads receive any aid. 75% undergrads borrow to pay for school. Average cumulative indebtedness $31,289. **Criteria for awarding aid:** *Need-based:* Leadership. *Non-need-based:* Academics, Alumni affiliation, Art, Athletics, Leadership, Minority status, Music/drama, State/district residency.

UNIVERSITY OF SOUTH CAROLINA—BEAUFORT

1 University Boulevard, Bluffton, SC 29909
Phone: 843-208-8000 • **Financial Aid Phone:** 843-521-3104
E-mail: admissions@uscb.edu • **CEEB Code:** 5845
Fax: 843-208-8290 • **Website:** www.uscb.edu • **ACT Code:** 3835

This public school was founded in 1959. It has a 213-acre campus.

RATINGS

Admissions Selectivity Rating: 64   **Fire Safety Rating:** 60*   **Green Rating:** 60*

STUDENTS AND FACULTY

Student Body: 63% female, 37% male, 22% out-of-state, (14 countries represented).
Retention and Graduation: 54% freshmen return for sophomore year.
Faculty: Student/faculty ratio 18:1. 59 full-time faculty, 76% hold PhDs, 15% are are members of minority groups, 47% are women.

ACADEMICS

Degrees: associate, bachelor's. **Classes:** Most classes have 10-19 students. **Most popular majors:** Business Administration and Management; Hospitality Administration/Management; Registered Nursing, Nursing Administration, Nursing Research and Clinical Nursing. **Special Study Options:** cooperative education program, cross-registration, distance learning, dual enrollment, independent study, internships, study abroad, teacher certification program, weekend college. **Disability Services:** Special programs offered to physically disabled students, including note-taking services, reader services, tape recorders, tutors. **Career Services:** Career/job search classes, Internships.

FACILITIES

Housing: Coed dorms, special housing for disabled students, apartments for single students. **Computers:** Students can register for classes online. Administrative functions (other than registration) can be performed online.

CAMPUS LIFE

Environment: Village. **Activities:** Choral groups, drama/theater, literary magazine, musical theater, student government, student newspaper. 11 registered organizations. **Athletics (Intercollegiate):** *Men:* baseball, cross-country, golf, track/field (outdoor). **On-Campus Highlights:** Sandbar Cafe, Campus Center Gym, Library.

ADMISSIONS

Minimum paper TOEFL 550. **Basis for Candidate Selection:** *Very important factors considered include:* rigor of secondary school record, academic GPA, standardized test scores. *Important factors considered include:* class rank. **Freshman Admission Requirements:** High school diploma is required and GED is accepted. *Academic units required:* 4 English, 4 math, 3 science, 3 science labs, 2 foreign language, 2 social studies, 1 history, 1 academic elective, 1 visual/performing arts, and 1 unit from above areas or other academic areas. *Academic units recommended:* 1 computer science. **Freshman Admission Statistics:** 1,434 applied, 74.62% admitted, 40% enrolled. **Transfer Admission Requirements:** college transcript(s), Minimum college GPA of 2.0 required. Lowest grade transferable C-. **General Admission Information:** Application fee $40. Nonfall registration accepted.

COSTS AND FINANCIAL AID

Required Forms and Deadlines: FAFSA. **Notification of Awards:** Applicants will be notified of awards on a rolling basis beginning 5/31. **Types of Aid:** *Need-based scholarships/grants:* Federal Pell, FSEOG, State scholarships/grants, Private scholarships, College/university scholarship or grant aid from institutional funds. *Loans:* State Loans. *Student Employment:* Federal Work-Study Program available. **Financial Aid Statistics:** 35% freshmen, 65% undergrads receive any aid. **Criteria for awarding aid:** *Need-based:* Academics. *Non-need-based:* Academics, State/district residency.

UNIVERSITY OF SOUTH CAROLINA—COLUMBIA

Office of Undergraduate Admissions, Columbia, SC 29208
Phone: 803-777-7700 • **Financial Aid Phone:** 803-777-8134
E-mail: admissions-ugrad@sc.edu • **CEEB Code:** 5818
Fax: 803-777-0101 • **Website:** www.sc.edu • **ACT Code:** 3880

This public school was founded in 1801. It has a 384-acre campus.

RATINGS

Admissions Selectivity Rating: 87   **Fire Safety Rating:** 96   **Green Rating:** 89

STUDENTS AND FACULTY

Enrollment: 25,121. **Student Body:** 54% female, 46% male, 39% out-of-state, 2% international (115 countries represented). Asian 3%, African American 9%, Caucasian 76%, Hispanic 4%, Native American <1%, Pacific Islander <1%, Two or more races 4%, Race unknown 1%.
Retention and Graduation: 88% freshmen return for sophomore year. 55% freshmen graduate within 4 years. 72% freshmen graduate within 6 years. **Faculty:** Student/faculty ratio 19:1. 1,506 full-time faculty, 83% hold PhDs, 16% are are members of minority groups, 43% are women.

ACADEMICS

Degrees: associate, bachelor's, doctoral/professional, doctoral/research, doctoral, master's, postbachelor's certificate, post-master's certificate. **Classes:** Most classes have 20-29 students. Most lab/discussion sessions have 20-29 students. **Most popular majors:** Experimental Psychology; Registered Nursing, Nursing Administration, Nursing Research and Clinical Nursing; Criminal Justice/Law Enforcement Administration. **Special Study Options:** Accelerated program, cooperative education program, cross-registration, distance learning, double major, dual enrollment, English as a Second Language (ESL), exchange student program (domestic), external degree program, honors program, independent study, internships, student-designed major, study abroad, teacher certification program, weekend college, Alternative Spring Break, Dobson Internship Program, Volunteer Service Program, Program for Students, Undergraduate Research. **Honors Programs:** The Honors College is a small college of about 1,000 students, all of whom excel in academics. What makes the Honors College different is its ability to weave engaging,

exciting course offerings into any undergraduate major. You choose your major and set up your course schedule just like any other student at the University. But your choices include classes especially for Honors College students over 100 courses each semester. **Disability Services:** Special programs offered to physically disabled students, including note-taking services, reader services, tape recorders. **Career Services:** Alumni services, Career/job search classes, Career assessment, Internships. The experiential learning program, Community Internship Program (CIP) has a dedicated staff to help employers connect with talented USC students. In addition to serving as their campus contact, CIP Program staff members assist employers through the development of internship opportunities. This partnership helps maintain quality internship positions and successful outcomes for each participating organization.

FACILITIES

Housing: Coed dorms, special housing for disabled students, men's dorms, special housing for international students, women's dorms, fraternity/sorority housing, apartments for married students, apartments for single students, Wellness Housing, Honors housing (first year freshman and upperclass), Preston Residential College, Pre-Medical (first year and upperclass), Pre-Law, Engineering and Computing Community, Athletic, Greek, Teaching Fellows, Global, Green, Magellan Explorers, Capstone Scholars, Bridge Community, Journalism, Music, French House, Spanish Language, other Special Interest. 85% of campus accessible to physically disabled. **Special Academic Facilities/Equipment:** Art gallery, movie theater, McKissick Museum, South Caroliniana Library, Melton Observatory, Gibbes Planetarium, Melton Observatory, Filtration Research Engineering Demonstration Unit, Belser Arboretum, A.C. Moore Gardens. **Computers:** Students can register for classes online. Administrative functions (other than registration) can be performed online.

CAMPUS LIFE

Environment: City. **Activities:** Choral groups, concert band, dance, drama/theater, jazz band, literary magazine, marching band, music ensembles, musical theater, opera, pep band, radio station, student government, student newspaper, symphony orchestra 300 registered organizations, 25 honor societies, 32 religious organizations. 20 fraternities, 14 sororities. **Athletics (Intercollegiate):** *Men:* baseball, basketball, diving, football, golf, racquetball, soccer, softball, swimming, tennis, track/field (outdoor). *Women:* basketball, cross-country, diving, equestrian sports, golf, racquetball, soccer, softball, swimming, tennis, track/field (outdoor), volleyball. **On-Campus Highlights:** Strom Thurmond Wellness & Fitness Center, Russell House, Greek Village, Williams Brice Stadium, Historic Horseshoe. **Environmental Initiatives:** Sustainable Carolina represents all the sustainability efforts on campus and utilizes over 40 student interns to implement the campus sustainability plan. The program is based on leadership development and allows students to apply sustainability practices on campus. Last year students put in nearly 20,000 hours working, learning and training on sustainability issues.

ADMISSIONS

Freshman Academic Profile: Average high school GPA 4.1. 30% in top 10% of high school class, 65% in top 25% of high school class, 94% in top 50% of high school class. **Reported SAT (pre-2016 redesign) scores:** SAT Math middle 50% range 560-650. SAT Critical Reading middle 50% range 550-640. **Concordant SAT scores:** SAT Math middle 50% range 580–670. ACT middle 50% range 25-30. Minimum internet-based TOEFL 77. Minimum paper TOEFL 550. **Basis for Candidate Selection:** *Very important factors considered include:* academic GPA, application essay. *Important factors considered include:* rigor of secondary school record. *Other factors considered include:* class rank, standardized test scores, recommendation(s), extracurricular activities, talent/ability, character/personal qualities, first generation, alumni/ae relation, state residency, racial/ethnic status, volunteer work, work experience. **Freshman Admission Requirements:** High school diploma is required and GED is accepted. *Academic units required:* 4 English, 4 math, 3 science, 3 science labs, 2 foreign language, 2 social studies, 1 history, 1 academic elective, 1 visual/performing arts, and 1 unit from above areas or other academic areas. **Freshman Admission Statistics:** 25,736 applied, 64.54% admitted, 31% enrolled. **Transfer Admission Requirements:** college transcript(s), Minimum college GPA of 2.25 required. Lowest grade transferable C-. **General Admission Information:** Application fee $50. Priority deadline 12/1. Regular application deadline 12/1. Regular notification 3/15. Nonfall registration accepted. Admission may be deferred for a maximum of 1 Year.

COSTS AND FINANCIAL AID

Annual in-state tuition $11,082. Annual out-of-state tuition $29,898. Room and board $9,248. Required fees $400. Average book expense $1,008. **Required Forms and Deadlines:** FAFSA. **Notification of Awards:** Applicants will be notified of awards on a rolling basis beginning 4/1. **Types of Aid:** *Need-based scholarships/grants:* Federal Pell, FSEOG, State scholarships/grants, Private scholarships, College/university scholarship or grant aid from institutional funds, United Negro College Fund, Federal Nursing Scholarships. *Loans:* Direct Subsidized Stafford Loans, Direct Unsubsidized Stafford Loans, Direct PLUS loans, Federal Perkins Loans, Federal Nursing Loans. *Student Employment:* Federal Work-Study Program available. Institutional employment available. **Financial Aid Statistics:** 42% needy freshmen, 55% needy undergrads receive need-based scholarship or grant aid. 90% freshmen, 63% undergrads receive non-need-based scholarship or grant aid. 71% freshmen, 80% undergrads receive need-based self-help aid. 2% freshmen, 2% undergrads receive athletic scholarships. 96% freshmen, 87% undergrads receive any aid. Average cumulative indebtedness $28,518. **Criteria for awarding aid:** *Non-need-based:* Academics, Alumni affiliation, Art, Athletics, Job skills, Leadership, Minority status, Music/drama, Religious affiliation, State/district residency.

THE UNIVERSITY OF SOUTH DAKOTA

414 East Clark, Vermillion, SD 57069
Phone: 605-677-5434 • **Financial Aid Phone:** 605-677-5446
E-mail: admissions@usd.edu • **CEEB Code:** 6881
Fax: 605-677-6323 • **Website:** www.usd.edu • **ACT Code:** 3928

This public school was founded in 1862. It has a 273-acre campus.

RATINGS

Admissions Selectivity Rating: 84 **Fire Safety Rating:** 98 **Green Rating:** 68

STUDENTS AND FACULTY

Student Body: 62% female, 38% male, 30% out-of-state, (46 countries represented).
Retention and Graduation: 77% freshmen return for sophomore year. 33% freshmen graduate within 4 years. 52% freshmen graduate within 6 years. 48% grads go on to further study within 1 year. 26% grads pursue arts and sciences degrees. 9% grads pursue law degrees. 9% grads pursue business degrees. 9% grads pursue medical degrees. **Faculty:** Student/faculty ratio 17:1. 432 full-time faculty, 67% hold PhDs, 17% are are members of minority groups, 47% are women. 8% of classes are taught by teaching assistants.

ACADEMICS

Degrees: associate, bachelor's, certificate, doctoral/professional, doctoral/research, doctoral, master's, postbachelor's certificate, post-master's certificate. **Classes:** Most classes have 10-19 students. Most lab/discussion sessions have 20-29 students. **Most popular majors:** Psychology; Business/Commerce; Education. **Special Study Options:** Accelerated program, cross-registration, distance learning, double major, dual enrollment, English as a Second Language (ESL), exchange student program (domestic), external degree program, honors program, independent study, internships, liberal arts/career combination, student-designed major, study abroad, teacher certification program. **Honors Programs:** University Honors Program. The program has its own core curriculum that replaces the University's general education requirements. Thesis Scholars Program, Alumni Student Scholars Program, Law Honors Scholars Program Combined degree programs: BA/MA. **Disability Services:** Special programs offered to physically disabled students, including note-taking services, reader services, tape recorders, tutors. **Career Services:** Alumni network, Alumni services, Career/job search classes, Career assessment, Internships. USD, as the flagship liberal arts institution in the state, provides the framework for an extraordinary education and includes the Interdisciplinary Education & Action or "IdEA" Program. The U. has purposefully designed a contemporary liberal arts education that includes a solid foundation of knowledge, exposure to many different academic disciplines, immersion in interdisciplinary and divserse ways of thinkingt, and understanding of service and citizenship.

FACILITIES

Housing: Coed dorms, special housing for disabled students, fraternity/sorority housing, apartments for married students, apartments for single students, Apartments for students with dependent children. Brand new state of the art apartment style housing currently under construction with a new wellness center being constructed due to open in 2010. 96% of campus accessible to physically diasbled. **Special Academic Facilities/Equipment:** W.H. Over Museum, The National Music Museum, Oscar Howe Art Gallery, Center for Instructional Design and Delivery, Institute of American Indian Studies, Native American Cultural Center, Disaster Mental Health Institute, Neuharth Center for Excellence in Journalism, Missouri Rive Institute. **Computers:** 60% of classrooms, 100% of libraries, 100% of dining areas, 100% of student union, have wireless network access. Students can register for classes online. Administrative functions (other than registration) can be performed online.

CAMPUS LIFE

Environment: Village. **Activities:** Choral groups, concert band, dance, drama/theater, jazz band, literary magazine, marching band, music ensembles, musical theater, opera, pep band, radio station, student government, student newspaper, symphony orchestra, television station, Campus Ministries, Student Organization. 120 registered organizations, 6 honor societies, 6 religious organizations. 8 fraternities, 3 sororities. **Athletics (Intercollegiate):** *Men:* basketball, cross-country, diving, football, golf, swimming, track/field (outdoor), track/field (indoor). *Women:* basketball, cross-country, diving, golf, soccer, softball, swimming, tennis, track/field (outdoor), track/field (indoor), volleyball. **On-Campus Highlights:** Al Neuharth Media Center, The National Music Museum, The Dakota Dome, Belbus Student Service Center, Coyote Student Center. **Environmental Initiatives:** Creation of the Sustainability Task Force for evaluation, monitoring and policy creation.

ADMISSIONS

Freshman Academic Profile: 21% in top 10% of high school class, 42% in top 25% of high school class, 72% in top 50% of high school class. 75% from public high schools. **Reported SAT (pre-2016 redesign) scores:** SAT Math middle 50% range 460-610. SAT Critical Reading middle 50% range 440-520. SAT Writing middle 50% range 450-590. **Concordant SAT scores:** SAT EBRW middle 50% 500–610. SAT Math middle 50% range 500–630. ACT middle 50% range 20-25. Minimum internet-based TOEFL 81. Minimum paper TOEFL 550. **Basis for Candidate Selection:** *Very important factors considered include:* rigor of secondary school record, class rank, academic GPA, standardized test scores. *Important factors considered include:* alumni/ae relation. *Other factors considered include:* application essay, recommendation(s), extracurricular activities, talent/ability, character/personal qualities, geographical residence, state residency, racial/ethnic status, volunteer work, work experience. **Freshman Admission Requirements:** High school diploma is required and GED is accepted. *Academic units required:* 4 English, 3 math, 3 science labs, 3 social studies. *Academic units recommended:* 4 math, 4 science, 2 foreign language, and 1 unit from above areas or other academic areas. **Freshman Admission Statistics:** 4,218 applied, 73.54% admitted, 41% enrolled. **Transfer Admission Requirements:** High school transcript, college transcript(s), Minimum college GPA of 2.0 required. Lowest grade transferable D. **General Admission Information:** Application fee $20. Nonfall registration accepted. Admission may be deferred for a maximum of One Semester.

COSTS AND FINANCIAL AID

Annual in-state tuition $4,341. Annual out-of-state tuition $6,512. Room and board $7,172. Required fees $4,826. Average book expense $1,200. **Required Forms and Deadlines:** FAFSA. **Notification of Awards:** Applicants will be notified of awards on a rolling basis beginning 3/1. **Types of Aid:** *Need-based scholarships/grants:* Federal Pell, FSEOG, Private scholarships, College/university scholarship or grant aid from institutional funds, Federal Nursing Scholarships. *Loans:* Federal Perkins Loans, Federal Nursing Loans, College/university loans from institutional funds. *Student Employment:* Federal Work-Study Program available. Institutional employment available. **Financial Aid Statistics:** 47% needy freshmen receive need-based scholarship or grant aid. 94% freshmen, 81% undergrads receive any aid. **Criteria for awarding aid:** *Non-need-based:* Academics, Art, Athletics, Leadership, Minority status, Music/drama.

UNIVERSITY OF SOUTH FLORIDA

4202 East Fowler Avenue, Tampa, FL 33620-9951
Phone: 813-974-3350 • **Financial Aid Phone:** 813-974-4700
E-mail: admissions@usf.edu • **CEEB Code:** 5828
Fax: 813-974-9689 • **Website:** www.usf.edu • **ACT Code:** 761

This public school was founded in 1956. It has a 1797-acre campus.

RATINGS

Admissions Selectivity Rating: 90 **Fire Safety Rating:** 88 **Green Rating:** 98

STUDENTS AND FACULTY

Enrollment: 32,553. **Student Body:** 54% female, 46% male, 6% out-of-state, 6% international (140 countries represented). Asian 6%, African American 10%, Caucasian 47%, Hispanic 26%, Native American <1%, Pacific Islander <1%, Two or more races 4%, Race unknown 2%.
Retention and Graduation: 88% freshmen return for sophomore year. 68 25% grads go on to further study within 1 year. **Faculty:** Student/faculty ratio

24:1. 1,289 full-time faculty, 81% hold PhDs, 30% are are members of minority groups, 45% are women. 15% of classes are taught by teaching assistants.

ACADEMICS

Degrees: associate, bachelor's, doctoral/professional, doctoral/research, master's. **Classes:** Most classes have 20-29 students. Most lab/discussion sessions have 20-29 students. **Most popular majors:** Health Services/Allied Health/Health Sciences; Psychology; Biomedical Sciences. **Special Study Options:** Accelerated program, cooperative education program, cross-registration, distance learning, double major, dual enrollment, exchange student program (domestic), honors program, internships, study abroad, teacher certification program, weekend college, Honors undergraduate research majors. **Honors Programs:** Honors College: http://honors.usf.edu/ Combined degree programs: BA/MD, BA/MA, BA/MEng. **Disability Services:** Special programs offered to physically disabled students, including note-taking services, reader services, tutors. **Career Services:** Alumni services, Career/job search classes, Career assessment, Internships. Our intern for a day program impacts the most students and gives students an early look into one of their areas of occupational interest.

FACILITIES

Housing: Coed dorms, special housing for disabled students, men's dorms, special housing for international students, women's dorms, fraternity/sorority housing, apartments for married students, cooperative housing, apartments for single students, Grad students only; Medical students only. 100% of campus accessible to physically disabled. **Special Academic Facilities/ Equipment:** Art museum and galleries, contemporary art museum, graphic studio,anthropology museum, fitness center, par course. **Computers:** 80% of classrooms, 35% of dorms, 100% of libraries, 50% of dining areas, 100% of student union, 50% of common outdoor areas have wireless network access. Students can register for classes online. Administrative functions (other than registration) can be performed online.

CAMPUS LIFE

Environment: Metropolis. **Activities:** Choral groups, concert band, dance, drama/theater, jazz band, literary magazine, marching band, music ensembles, musical theater, opera, pep band, radio station, student government, student newspaper, student-run film society, symphony orchestra, television station 507 registered organizations, 33 honor societies, 42 religious organizations. 16 fraternities, 22 sororities. **Athletics (Intercollegiate):** *Men:* baseball, basketball, cheerleading, cross-country, football, golf, sailing, soccer, tennis, track/field (outdoor), track/field (indoor). *Women:* basketball, cheerleading, cross-country, golf, sailing, soccer, softball, tennis, track/field (outdoor), track/field (indoor), volleyball. **On-Campus Highlights:** Marshall Center, The Tampa Campus Library, Contemporary Art Museum, Botanical Gardens, Sun Dome. **Environmental Initiatives:** USF 2008 Going Green Tampa Bay sustainability EXPO, which drew over 3,000 visitors.

ADMISSIONS

Freshman Academic Profile: Average high school GPA 3.9. **Reported SAT (pre-2016 redesign) scores:** SAT Math middle 50% range 540-630. SAT Critical Reading middle 50% range 530-620. SAT Writing middle 50% range 510-600. **Concordant SAT scores:** SAT EBRW middle 50% 580–660. SAT Math middle 50% range 570–650. ACT middle 50% range 24-28. Minimum internet-based TOEFL 79. Minimum paper TOEFL 550. **Basis for Candidate Selection:** *Very important factors considered include:* rigor of secondary school record, academic GPA. *Important factors considered include:* standardized test scores, first generation. *Other factors considered include:* application essay, recommendation(s), extracurricular activities, talent/ability, character/personal qualities, geographical residence, state residency, volunteer work, work experience. **Freshman Admission Requirements:** High school diploma is required and GED is accepted. *Academic units required:* 4 English, 4 math, 3 science, 2 science labs, 2 foreign language, 3 social studies, 3 academic electives. *Academic units recommended:* 4 English, 4 math, 4 science, 3 science labs, 4 foreign language, 3 social studies, 3 academic electives. **Freshman Admission Statistics:** 28,623 applied, 46.64% admitted, 30% enrolled. **Transfer Admission Requirements:** college transcript(s), statement of good standing from prior institution(s). Minimum college GPA of 2.3 required. Lowest grade transferable D. **General Admission Information:** Application fee $30. Priority deadline 3/1. Regular application deadline 3/1. Regular notification 4/15. Nonfall registration accepted. Admission may be deferred for a maximum of 1 semester.

COSTS AND FINANCIAL AID

Annual in-state tuition $6,336. Annual out-of-state tuition $17,250. Room and board $9,700. Required fees $74. Average book expense $1,200. **Required Forms and Deadlines:** FAFSA. **Notification of Awards:** Applicants will be notified of awards on a rolling basis beginning 3/1. **Types of Aid:** *Need-based scholarships/grants:* Federal Pell, FSEOG, State scholarships/grants, Private scholarships, College/university scholarship or grant aid from institutional funds. *Loans:* Direct Subsidized Stafford Loans, Direct Unsubsidized Stafford Loans, Direct PLUS loans, Federal Perkins Loans, College/university loans from institutional funds. *Student Employment:* Federal Work-Study Program

available. Institutional employment available. **Financial Aid Statistics:** 88% needy freshmen, 84% needy undergrads receive need-based scholarship or grant aid. 7% freshmen, 4% undergrads receive non-need-based scholarship or grant aid. 56% freshmen, 66% undergrads receive need-based self-help aid. 1% freshmen, 1% undergrads receive athletic scholarships. 70% freshmen, 66% undergrads receive any aid. 57% undergrads borrow to pay for school. Average cumulative indebtedness $22,337. **Criteria for awarding aid:** *Need-based:* Academics. *Non-need-based:* Academics, Art, Athletics, Leadership, Music/drama, State/district residency.

UNIVERSITY OF SOUTH FLORIDA— ST. PETERSBURG

Financial Aid Phone: 727-873-4128
ACT Code: 761

RATINGS

Admissions Selectivity Rating: 60*　　　**Fire Safety Rating:** 60*　　　**Green Rating:** 95

STUDENTS AND FACULTY

Faculty: 0% of classes are taught by teaching assistants.

ACADEMICS

Degrees: associate, bachelor's, certificate, master's.

ADMISSIONS

Minimum internet-based TOEFL 79. Minimum paper TOEFL 550. **Basis for Candidate Selection:** *Other factors considered include:* rigor of secondary school record, academic GPA, standardized test scores, volunteer work. **Freshman Admission Requirements:** *Academic units required:* 4 English, 4 math, 3 science, 2 science labs, 2 foreign language, 3 social studies, 2 academic electives. **General Admission Information:** Application fee $30. Priority deadline 1/2. Regular application deadline 4/15. Nonfall registration accepted.

COSTS AND FINANCIAL AID

Required Forms and Deadlines: FAFSA. *Student Employment:* Federal Work-Study Program available. Institutional employment available. **Financial Aid Statistics:** 70% freshmen, 62% undergrads receive any aid.

UNIVERSITY OF SOUTHERN CALIFORNIA

Office of Admission/ John Hubbard Hall, Los Angeles, CA 90089-0911
Phone: 213-740-1111 • **Financial Aid Phone:** 213-740-4444
E-mail: admitusc@usc.edu • **CEEB Code:** 4852
Fax: 213-821-0200 • **Website:** www.usc.edu • **ACT Code:** 470

This private school was founded in 1880. It has a 155-acre campus.

RATINGS

Admissions Selectivity Rating: 98　　　**Fire Safety Rating:** 97　　　**Green Rating:** 84

STUDENTS AND FACULTY

Enrollment: 18,557. **Student Body:** 52% female, 48% male, 33% out-of-state, 14% international (114 countries represented). Asian 21%, African American 4%, Caucasian 40%, Hispanic 14%, Native American <1%, Pacific Islander <1%, Two or more races 5%, Race unknown 1%.
Retention and Graduation: 96% freshmen return for sophomore year. 77% freshmen graduate within 4 years. 92% freshmen graduate within 6 years. **Faculty:** Student/faculty ratio 12:1. 2,062 full-time faculty, 91% hold PhDs, 28% are are members of minority groups, 40% are women.

ACADEMICS

Degrees: bachelor's, doctoral/professional, doctoral/research, doctoral, master's, postbachelor's certificate, post-master's certificate. **Classes:** Most classes have 10-19 students. Most lab/discussion sessions have 20-29 students. **Most popular majors:** Social Sciences; Visual and Performing Arts; Business Administration and Management. **Special Study Options:** cooperative education program, distance learning, double major, English as a Second Language (ESL), exchange student program (domestic), honors program, independent study, internships, liberal arts/career combination, student-designed major, study abroad, Learning communities, Thematic Option, Undergraduate Research, and Freshman Seminars. **Honors Programs:** Thematic Option Program Multimedia Scholarship Combined degree programs: BA/MA, BA/MEng, BS/MA, BS/MS. **Disability Services:** Special programs offered to physically disabled students, including note-taking services, reader services, tape recorders, tutors. **Career Services:** Alumni network, Alumni services, Career assessment, Internships, Regional alumni. Joint Educational Project, a service learning program that provides an interface between USC and the local community.

FACILITIES

Housing: Coed dorms, special housing for disabled students, special housing for international students, fraternity/sorority housing, apartments for married students, apartments for single students, Wellness Housing, Theme Housing, Special interest floors. 97% of campus accessible to physically diasbled. **Special Academic Facilities/Equipment:** USC Fisher Museum of Art; Hancock Memorial Museum; specialized architecture and fine arts galleries, studios and labs; media labs; cinema scoring sound stage; recording studios; theatres and recital halls; exercise physiology lab; specialized engineering laboratories; biomedical imaging labs; Center for Electron Microscopy and Microanalysis; genomic research facilities; GIS research lab; USC Shoah Foundation Institute visual history archive; Archival Research Center; High-Performance Computing Center; public computing centers and labs; extensive wireless access to the USC network; classrooms outfitted with multiple webcams and microphones **Computers:** 15% of classrooms, 10% of dorms, 100% of libraries, 100% of dining areas, 100% of student union, 90% of common outdoor areas have wireless network access. Students can register for classes online. Administrative functions (other than registration) can be performed online.

CAMPUS LIFE

Environment: Metropolis. **Activities:** Choral groups, concert band, dance, drama/theater, jazz band, literary magazine, marching band, music ensembles, musical theater, opera, pep band, radio station, student government, student newspaper, student-run film society, symphony orchestra, television station, yearbook, Campus Ministries, Student Organization, Model UN. 676 registered organizations, 49 honor societies, 74 religious organizations. 41 fraternities, 23 sororities. **Athletics (Intercollegiate):** *Men:* baseball, basketball, diving, football, golf, swimming, tennis, track/field (outdoor), volleyball, water polo. *Women:* basketball, crew/rowing, cross-country, diving, golf, soccer, swimming, tennis, track/field (outdoor), volleyball, water polo. **On-Campus Highlights:** USC Fisher Museum of Art, Galen Center (event & training pavilion), Leavey Library (open 24 hours), Heritage Hall (athletic awards), Tutor Campus Center (opens fall 2010), USC's University Park campus—located three miles south of downtown Los Angeles, adjacent to the museums and recreational facilities of historic Exposition Park—is an urban oasis, offering a park-like atmosphere and rich architectural history. **Environmental Initiatives:** Energy Efficiency & Innovation: USC employs a full time Director of Energy Services to manage energy programs including lighting retrofits, equipment upgrades, and a recent retrofit of chillers, cooling towers, and pumps throughout the University, including a three million gallon centralized thermal energy storage tank installed below ground. The 3 million-gallon thermal energy water storage (TES) system was built 40 feet below ground. It is estimated that the new system conserves about 4,500 megawatt-hours of electricity a year by circulating chilled water to air conditioning systems throughout the University Park Campus, significantly expanding the capacity of the campus' existing chilled-water system while reducing utility use. The warmer water coming back through pipes has a chance to chill overnight before it is recirculated which allows USC to shift much of the kilowatt-hour usage to off-peak hours when electricity is more available. The entire system was conceived in 2001 and completed in 2005.

ADMISSIONS

Freshman Academic Profile: Average high school GPA 3.7. 88% in top 10% of high school class, 96% in top 25% of high school class, 100% in top 50% of high school class. 54% from public high schools. **Reported SAT (pre-2016 redesign) scores:** SAT Math middle 50% range 650-770. SAT Critical Reading middle 50% range 630-730. SAT Writing middle 50% range 650-750. **Concordant SAT scores:** SAT EBRW middle 50% 690–760. SAT Math middle 50% range 670–780. ACT middle 50% range 30-33. **Basis for Candidate Selection:** *Very important factors considered include:* rigor of secondary school record, academic GPA, standardized test scores, application essay, recommendation(s). *Important factors considered include:* extracurricular activities, talent/ability. *Other factors considered include:* class rank, interview, character/personal qualities, first generation, alumni/ae relation, racial/ethnic status, volunteer work, work experience. **Freshman Admission Requirements:** High school diploma is required and GED is not accepted. *Academic units required:* 4 English, 3 math, 2 science, 2 science labs, 2 foreign language, 2 social studies, 3 academic electives. *Academic units recommended:* 4 English, 4 math, 3 science, 3 science labs, 3 foreign language, 3 social studies, 3 academic electives. **Freshman Admission Statistics:** 54,280 applied, 16.62% admitted, 34% enrolled. **Transfer Admission Requirements:** High school transcript, college transcript(s), essay or personal statement, Lowest

grade transferable C-. **General Admission Information:** Application fee $80. Priority deadline 12/1. Regular application deadline 1/15. Regular notification 4/1. Nonfall registration accepted. Admission may be deferred for a maximum of one year.

COSTS AND FINANCIAL AID

Annual tuition $51,442. Room and board $14,348. Required fees $746. Average book expense $1,200. **Required Forms and Deadlines:** FAFSA, CSS/Financial Aid PROFILE, Noncustodial PROFILE, Business/Farm Supplement. **Notification of Awards:** Applicants will be notified of awards on or about 4/1. **Types of Aid:** *Need-based scholarships/grants:* Federal Pell, FSEOG, State scholarships/grants, Private scholarships, College/university scholarship or grant aid from institutional funds. *Loans:* Direct Subsidized Stafford Loans, Direct Unsubsidized Stafford Loans, Direct PLUS loans, Federal Perkins Loans, College/university loans from institutional funds. *Student Employment:* Federal Work-Study Program available. Institutional employment available. **Financial Aid Statistics:** 86% needy freshmen, 91% needy undergrads receive need-based scholarship or grant aid. 66% freshmen, 47% undergrads receive non-need-based scholarship or grant aid. 89% freshmen, 94% undergrads receive need-based self-help aid. 3% freshmen, 2% undergrads receive athletic scholarships. 68% freshmen, 65% undergrads receive any aid. 41% undergrads borrow to pay for school. Average cumulative indebtedness $27,882. **Criteria for awarding aid:** *Non-need-based:* Academics, Alumni affiliation, Art, Athletics, Leadership, Music/drama.

UNIVERSITY OF SOUTHERN INDIANA

8600 University Boulevard, Evansville, IN 47712
Phone: 812-464-1765 • **Financial Aid Phone:** 812-464-1767
E-mail: enroll@usi.edu • **CEEB Code:** 1335
Fax: 812-465-7154 • **Website:** www.usi.edu • **ACT Code:** 1207

This public school was founded in 1965. It has a 330-acre campus.

RATINGS

Admissions Selectivity Rating: 75   **Fire Safety Rating:** 80   **Green Rating:** 77

STUDENTS AND FACULTY

Enrollment: 7,894. **Student Body:** 62% female, 38% male, 12% out-of-state, 2% international (36 countries represented). Asian 1%, African American 4%, Caucasian 87%, Hispanic 3%, Native American <1%, Pacific Islander <1%, Two or more races 2%, Race unknown <1%.
Retention and Graduation: 70% freshmen return for sophomore year. 19% freshmen graduate within 4 years. 38% freshmen graduate within 6 years. 15% grads go on to further study within 1 year. **Faculty:** Student/faculty ratio 17:1. 355 full-time faculty, 72% hold PhDs, 10% are are members of minority groups, 54% are women. 0% of classes are taught by teaching assistants.

ACADEMICS

Degrees: associate, bachelor's, certificate, doctoral/professional, master's, postbachelor's certificate, terminal, transfer. **Classes:** Most classes have 20-29 students. Most lab/discussion sessions have 20-29 students. **Most popular majors:** Registered Nursing/Registered Nurse; Business Administration and Management; Psychology. **Special Study Options:** cooperative education program, distance learning, double major, dual enrollment, English as a Second Language (ESL), honors program, independent study, internships, study abroad, teacher certification program. Combined degree programs: RN/MSN. **Disability Services:** Special programs offered to physically disabled students, including note-taking services, reader services, tape recorders, tutors. **Career Services:** Alumni network, Alumni services, Career/job search classes, Career assessment, Internships.

FACILITIES

Housing: Coed dorms, special housing for disabled students, fraternity/sorority housing, apartments for married students, apartments for single students, Wellness Housing, Theme Housing. 95% of campus accessible to physically diasbled. **Computers:** 100% of classrooms, 100% of dorms, 100% of libraries, 100% of dining areas, 100% of student union, 100% of common outdoor areas have wireless network access. Students can register for classes online. Administrative functions (other than registration) can be performed online.

CAMPUS LIFE

Environment: City. **Activities:** Choral groups, dance, drama/theater, jazz band, literary magazine, pep band, radio station, student government, student newspaper, Campus Ministries, Student Organization, Model UN. 102 registered organizations, 6 honor societies, 7 religious organizations. 7 fraternities, 4 sororities. **Athletics (Intercollegiate):** *Men:* baseball, basketball, cross-country, golf, soccer, tennis, track/field (outdoor), track/field (indoor). *Women:* basketball, cross-country, golf, soccer, softball, tennis, track/field (outdoor), track/field (indoor), volleyball. **On-Campus Highlights:** Eagle's Nest, The Loft, Recreation and Fitness Center, Rice Library **Environmental Initiatives:** Established environmental stewardship committee.

ADMISSIONS

Freshman Academic Profile: Average high school GPA 3.3. 14% in top 10% of high school class, 37% in top 25% of high school class, 75% in top 50% of high school class. **Reported SAT (pre-2016 redesign) scores:** SAT Math middle 50% range 440-540. SAT Critical Reading middle 50% range 450-540. SAT Writing middle 50% range 420-520. **Concordant SAT scores:** SAT EBRW middle 50% 490–590. SAT Math middle 50% range 480–570. ACT middle 50% range 19-25. Minimum internet-based TOEFL 71. Minimum paper TOEFL 525. **Basis for Candidate Selection:** *Very important factors considered include:* academic GPA, standardized test scores. *Important factors considered include:* class rank. *Other factors considered include:* rigor of secondary school record, application essay, recommendation(s), interview, extracurricular activities, talent/ability, character/personal qualities, work experience. **Freshman Admission Requirements:** High school diploma is required and GED is accepted. *Academic units recommended:* 4 English, 4 math, 2 science, 2 foreign language, 2 social studies, 2 history, 2 academic electives. **Freshman Admission Statistics:** 4,552 applied, 91.89% admitted, 40% enrolled. **Transfer Admission Requirements:** High school transcript, college transcript(s), Minimum college GPA of 2.0 required. Lowest grade transferable C-. **General Admission Information:** Application fee $40. Regular application deadline 8/15. Nonfall registration accepted.

COSTS AND FINANCIAL AID

Annual in-state tuition $7,105. Annual out-of-state tuition $17,347. Room and board $8,896. Required fees $500. Average book expense $1,140. **Required Forms and Deadlines:** FAFSA. **Notification of Awards:** Applicants will be notified of awards on a rolling basis beginning 4/1. **Types of Aid:** *Need-based scholarships/grants:* Federal Pell, FSEOG, State scholarships/grants, Private scholarships, College/university scholarship or grant aid from institutional funds, United Negro College Fund, Federal Nursing Scholarships. *Loans:* Direct Subsidized Stafford Loans, Direct Unsubsidized Stafford Loans, Direct PLUS loans. *Student Employment:* Federal Work-Study Program available. Institutional employment available. **Financial Aid Statistics:** 65% needy freshmen, 81% needy undergrads receive need-based scholarship or grant aid. 44% freshmen, 45% undergrads receive non-need-based scholarship or grant aid. 84% freshmen, 85% undergrads receive need-based self-help aid. 2% freshmen, 4% undergrads receive athletic scholarships. 91% undergrads receive any aid. 69% undergrads borrow to pay for school. Average cumulative indebtedness $24,762. **Criteria for awarding aid:** *Need-based:* Academics. *Non-need-based:* Academics, Art, Athletics, Leadership, Music/drama, State/district residency.

UNIVERSITY OF SOUTHERN MAINE

PO Box 9300, Portland, ME 4104
Phone: 207-780-5670 • **Financial Aid Phone:** 207-780-5250
E-mail: usmadm@usm.maine.edu • **CEEB Code:** 9762
Fax: 207-780-5640 • **Website:** www.usm.maine.edu • **ACT Code:** 1644

This public school was founded in 1878. It has a 144-acre campus.

RATINGS

Admissions Selectivity Rating: 72   Fire Safety Rating: 85   Green Rating: 60*

STUDENTS AND FACULTY

Enrollment: 5,359. **Student Body:** 57% female, 43% male, 11% out-of-state, 1% international (19 countries represented). Asian 2%, African American 4%, Caucasian 82%, Hispanic 2%, Native American 1%, Pacific Islander <1%, Two or more races 3%, Race unknown 5%.
Retention and Graduation: 63% freshmen return for sophomore year. 13% freshmen graduate within 4 years. 33% freshmen graduate within 6 years. **Faculty:** Student/faculty ratio 16:1. 248 full-time faculty, 84% hold PhDs, 7% are are members of minority groups, 48% are women. 0% of classes are taught by teaching assistants.

ACADEMICS

Degrees: bachelor's, certificate, doctoral/professional, doctoral/research, doctoral, master's, postbachelor's certifiate, post-master's certificate. **Most popular majors:** Registered Nursing/Registered Nurse; Biology/Biological Sciences; Business Administration and Management. **Special Study Options:** Accelerated program, cooperative education program, cross-registration, distance learning, double major, English as a Second Language (ESL), exchange student program (domestic), honors program, independent study, internships, liberal arts/career combination, student-designed major, study abroad, teacher certification program, weekend college, Preengineering

program with University of Maine at Orono, living/learning scholars program, Greater Portland Alliance—cross registration with University of New England, St. Joseph's (Maine), Southern Maine Technical College, and Maine College of Art. **Honors Programs:** Russell Scholars—living/learning community, USM honors program Combined degree programs: BS/MBA. **Disability Services:** Special programs offered to physically disabled students, including note-taking services, tape recorders, tutors. **Career Services:** Alumni network, Alumni services, Career/job search classes, Internships.

FACILITIES

Housing: Coed dorms, special housing for disabled students, fraternity/sorority housing, apartments for married students, apartments for single students, Fine Arts House, Russell Scholars (living/learning), Chemical Free Floor 24 Hour Quiet Floor, Community Living program. 90% of campus accessible to physically diasbled. **Special Academic Facilities/Equipment:** Southworth Planetarium, Osher Map Collection and Smith Center for Cartographic Education, WMPG (radio station), GTV (cable t.v. station), Free Press (campus newspaper), various art galleries on all three campuses, and **Computers:** Students can register for classes online. Administrative functions (other than registration) can be performed online.

CAMPUS LIFE

Environment: Town. **Activities:** Choral groups, concert band, dance, drama/theater, jazz band, literary magazine, music ensembles, musical theater, opera, radio station, student government, student newspaper, symphony orchestra, television station, yearbook, Student Organization. 100 registered organizations, 2 honor societies, 3 religious organizations. 4 fraternities, 4 sororities. **Athletics (Intercollegiate):** *Men:* baseball, basketball, cheerleading, cross-country, golf, ice hockey, lacrosse, soccer, tennis, track/field (outdoor), track/field (indoor), wrestling. *Women:* basketball, cheerleading, cross-country, field hockey, golf, ice hockey, lacrosse, soccer, softball, tennis, track/field (outdoor), track/field (indoor), volleyball. **On-Campus Highlights:** Art Gallery, Costello Sports Complex, Russell Theater and Concert Hall, Southworth Planetarium, TV/Radio Station.

ADMISSIONS

Freshman Academic Profile: Average high school GPA 3.0. 5% in top 10% of high school class, 26% in top 25% of high school class, 61% in top 50% of high school class. **Reported SAT (pre-2016 redesign) scores:** SAT Math middle 50% range 440-550. SAT Critical Reading middle 50% range 420-550. SAT Writing middle 50% range 430-540. **Concordant SAT scores:** SAT EBRW middle 50% 480–600. SAT Math middle 50% range 480–570. ACT middle 50% range 19-25. Minimum internet-based TOEFL 80. **Basis for Candidate Selection:** *Very important factors considered include:* rigor of secondary school record, class rank, academic GPA. *Important factors considered include:* standardized test scores, application essay. *Other factors considered include:* recommendation(s), interview, extracurricular activities, talent/ability, character/personal qualities, first generation, alumni/ae relation, geographical residence, state residency, racial/ethnic status, volunteer work, work experience, level of applicant's interest. **Freshman Admission Requirements:** High school diploma is required and GED is accepted. *Academic units required:* 4 English, 3 math, 2 science, 2 science labs, 2 social studies, 1 history. *Academic units recommended:* 3 science, 3 science labs, 3 social studies, 1 history. **Freshman Admission Statistics:** 3,402 applied, 87.77% admitted, 24% enrolled. **Transfer Admission Requirements:** High school transcript, college transcript(s), essay or personal statement, Minimum college GPA of 2.0 required. Lowest grade transferable C-. **General Admission Information:** Application fee $40. Nonfall registration accepted. Admission may be deferred.

COSTS AND FINANCIAL AID

Annual in-state tuition $7,590. Annual out-of-state tuition $19,950. Room and board $9,400. Required fees $1,330. Average book expense $1,220. **Required Forms and Deadlines:** FAFSA. **Notification of Awards:** Applicants will be notified of awards on a rolling basis beginning 3/15. **Types of Aid:** *Need-based scholarships/grants:* Federal Pell, FSEOG, State scholarships/grants, Private scholarships, College/university scholarship or grant aid from institutional funds. *Loans:* Federal Perkins Loans, Federal Nursing Loans, College/university loans from institutional funds. *Student Employment:* Federal Work-Study Program available. Institutional employment available. **Financial Aid Statistics:** 75% needy freshmen, 84% needy undergrads receive need-based scholarship or grant aid. 5% freshmen, 3% undergrads receive non-need-based scholarship or grant aid. 79% freshmen, 87% undergrads receive need-based self-help aid. 0% freshmen, 0% undergrads receive athletic scholarships. **Criteria for awarding aid:** *Need-based:* Academics, Music/drama. *Non-need-based:* Academics, Music/drama, State/district residency.

UNIVERSITY OF SOUTHERN MISSISSIPPI

118 College Drive #5166, Hattiesburg, MS 39406
Phone: 601-266-5000 • **Financial Aid Phone:** 601-266-4774
E-mail: admissions@usm.edu • **CEEB Code:** 1479
Fax: 601-266-5148 • **Website:** www.usm.edu • **ACT Code:** 2218

This public school was founded in 1910. It has a 1090-acre campus.

RATINGS

Admissions Selectivity Rating: 80   **Fire Safety Rating:** 90   **Green Rating:** 60*

STUDENTS AND FACULTY

Enrollment: 11,689. **Student Body:** 63% female, 37% male, 16% out-of-state, 2% international. Asian 1%, African American 29%, Caucasian 61%, Hispanic 3%, Native American <1%, Pacific Islander <1%, Two or more races 2%, Race unknown 1%.
Retention and Graduation: 74% freshmen return for sophomore year. 23% freshmen graduate within 4 years. 45% freshmen graduate within 6 years.
Faculty: Student/faculty ratio 17:1. 687 full-time faculty, 79% hold PhDs, 16% are are members of minority groups, 48% are women.

ACADEMICS

Degrees: bachelor's, certificate, doctoral, master's, postbachelor's certificate, post-master's certificate. **Classes:** Most classes have 10-19 students. Most lab/discussion sessions have 10-19 students. **Most popular majors:** Elementary Education and Teaching; Psychology. **Special Study Options:** distance learning, double major, dual enrollment, honors program, independent study, internships, study abroad, teacher certification program. **Disability Services:** Special programs offered to physically disabled students, including note-taking services, reader services, tape recorders, tutors. **Career Services:** Alumni services, Career/job search classes, Career assessment, Internships. Career Assesment Individualized counselors and 24/7 online career Center.

FACILITIES

Housing: special housing for disabled students, men's dorms, women's dorms, fraternity/sorority housing, apartments for married students, Theme Housing. **Special Academic Facilities/Equipment:** Museum of Art **Computers:** 100% of classrooms, 100% of dorms, 100% of libraries, 100% of dining areas, 100% of student union, 30% of common outdoor areas have wireless network access. Students can register for classes online. Administrative functions (other than registration) can be performed online.

CAMPUS LIFE

Environment: City. **Activities:** Choral groups, concert band, dance, drama/theater, jazz band, literary magazine, marching band, music ensembles, musical theater, opera, pep band, radio station, student government, student newspaper, student-run film society, symphony orchestra, yearbook, Campus Ministries, Student Organization. 8 honor societies, 20 religious organizations. 15 fraternities, 11 sororities. **Athletics (Intercollegiate):** *Men:* baseball, basketball, football, golf, tennis, track/field (outdoor), track/field (indoor). *Women:* basketball, cross-country, golf, soccer, softball, tennis, track/field (outdoor), track/field (indoor), volleyball. **On-Campus Highlights:** Starbucks, Thad Cochran Center, Barnes & Nobles Bookstore. **Environmental Initiatives:** Recycling (12+ years).

ADMISSIONS

Freshman Academic Profile: Average high school GPA 3.3. 88% from public high schools. **Reported SAT (pre-2016 redesign) scores:** SAT Math middle 50% range 510-650. SAT Critical Reading middle 50% range 430-540. **Concordant SAT scores:** SAT Math middle 50% range 540–670. ACT middle 50% range 20-26. Minimum internet-based TOEFL 71. Minimum paper TOEFL 525. **Basis for Candidate Selection:** *Very important factors considered include:* academic GPA, standardized test scores. *Important factors considered include:* class rank. **Freshman Admission Requirements:** High school diploma is required and GED is accepted. *Academic units required:* 4 English, 3 math, 3 science, 3 science labs, 1 foreign language, 3 social studies, 2 academic electives. *Academic units recommended:* 4 English, 4 math, 4 science, 3 science labs, 1 foreign language, 4 social studies, 2 academic electives, 1 visual/performing arts. **Freshman Admission Statistics:** 6,607 applied, 45.69% admitted, 52% enrolled. **Transfer Admission Requirements:** college transcript(s), statement of good standing from prior institution(s). Minimum college GPA of 2.0 required. Lowest grade transferable D. **General Admission Information:** Application fee $40. Nonfall registration accepted.

COSTS AND FINANCIAL AID

Annual in-state tuition $7,854. Annual out-of-state tuition $9,854. Room and board $9,012. Average book expense $1,200. **Required Forms and Deadlines:** FAFSA. **Notification of Awards:** Applicants will be notified of awards on a rolling basis beginning 3/15. **Types of Aid:** *Need-based scholarships/grants:* Federal Pell, FSEOG, State scholarships/grants, Private

scholarships, College/university scholarship or grant aid from institutional funds. *Loans:* Direct Subsidized Stafford Loans, Direct Unsubsidized Stafford Loans, Direct PLUS loans, Federal Perkins Loans. *Student Employment:* Federal Work-Study Program available. Institutional employment available. **Financial Aid Statistics:** 69% needy freshmen, 68% needy undergrads receive need-based scholarship or grant aid. 69% freshmen, 57% undergrads receive non-need-based scholarship or grant aid. 69% freshmen, 75% undergrads receive need-based self-help aid. 6% freshmen, 4% undergrads receive athletic scholarships. 62% freshmen, 63% undergrads receive any aid. 68% undergrads borrow to pay for school. Average cumulative indebtedness $28,700. **Criteria for awarding aid:** *Need-based:* Academics. *Non-need-based:* Academics, Alumni affiliation, Art, Athletics, Leadership, Music/drama, State/district residency.

UNIVERSITY OF ST. FRANCIS

500 Wilcox Street, Joliet, IL 60435
Phone: 815-740-2270 • **Financial Aid Phone:** 866-890-8331
E-mail: admissions@stfrancis.edu • **CEEB Code:** 1130
Fax: 815-740-5078 • **Website:** www.stfrancis.edu • **ACT Code:** 1000

This private school, affiliated with the Roman Catholic Church, was founded in 1920. It has a 22-acre campus.

RATINGS

Admissions Selectivity Rating: 83   **Fire Safety Rating:** 99   **Green Rating:** 77

STUDENTS AND FACULTY

Enrollment: 1,343. **Student Body:** 62% female, 38% male, 5% out-of-state, 3% international (10 countries represented). Asian 2%, African American 8%, Caucasian 63%, Hispanic 20%, Native American <1%, Pacific Islander <1%, Two or more races 3%, Race unknown <1%.
Retention and Graduation: 82% freshmen return for sophomore year. 44% freshmen graduate within 4 years. 63% freshmen graduate within 6 years. 15% grads go on to further study within 1 year. **Faculty:** Student/faculty ratio 12:1. 97 full-time faculty, 71% hold PhDs, 16% are are members of minority groups, 61% are women. 0% of classes are taught by teaching assistants.

ACADEMICS

Degrees: bachelor's, certificate, doctoral/research, doctoral, master's, postbachelor's certificate, post-master's certificate. **Classes:** Most classes have 10-19 students. Most lab/discussion sessions have 10-19 students. **Most popular majors:** Registered Nursing/Registered Nurse; Biology/Biological Sciences; Business/Commerce. **Special Study Options:** cross-registration, distance learning, double major, honors program, independent study, internships, student-designed major, study abroad, teacher certification program. **Honors Programs:** Duns Scotus Fellow/Scholars Program is designed to create a learning community of motivated students who are challenged to excel academically. Combined degree programs: BBA/MBA. **Disability Services:** Special programs offered to physically disabled students, including note-taking services, reader services, tape recorders, tutors. **Career Services:** Alumni network, Alumni services, Career/job search classes, Career assessment, Internships, Regional alumni.

FACILITIES

Housing: Coed dorms, apartments for single students, Wellness Housing. 100% of campus accessible to physically diasbled. **Special Academic Facilities/Equipment:** Rialto City Center Campus, new home of the Art & Design Department; Student Center/Bistro in the Motherhouse; Abbey in Marian Residence Hall; Moser Performing Arts Center **Computers:** 100% of classrooms, 100% of dorms, 100% of libraries, 100% of dining areas, 100% of student union, 100% of common outdoor areas have wireless network access. Students can register for classes online. Administrative functions (other than registration) can be performed online.

CAMPUS LIFE

Environment: City. **Activities:** Choral groups, dance, drama/theater, literary magazine, music ensembles, musical theater, opera, radio station, student government, student newspaper, symphony orchestra, television station, Campus Ministries, Student Organization. 29 registered organizations, 13 honor societies, 1 religious organization. **Athletics (Intercollegiate):** *Men:* baseball, basketball, cross-country, football, golf, soccer, tennis, track/field (outdoor), track/field (indoor). *Women:* basketball, cheerleading, cross-country, golf, soccer, softball, tennis, track/field (outdoor), track/field (indoor), volleyball. **On-Campus Highlights:** Rialto City Center Campus, Student Center/Bistro in Motherhouse, Abbey (in Marian Residence Hall), Moser Performing Arts Center. **Environmental Initiatives:** Campus-wide Recycling.

ADMISSIONS

Freshman Academic Profile: Average high school GPA 3.4. 16% in top 10% of high school class, 40% in top 25% of high school class, 76% in top 50% of high school class. 84% from public high schools. **Reported SAT (pre-2016 redesign) scores:** SAT Math middle 50% range 470-580. SAT Critical Reading middle 50% range 440-530. SAT Writing middle 50% range 450-580. **Concordant SAT scores:** SAT EBRW middle 50% 500–610. SAT Math middle 50% range 510–600. ACT middle 50% range 20-26. Minimum internet-based TOEFL 79. Minimum paper TOEFL 550. **Basis for Candidate Selection:** *Very important factors considered include:* rigor of secondary school record, class rank, academic GPA, standardized test scores. *Other factors considered include:* application essay, recommendation(s), interview. **Freshman Admission Requirements:** High school diploma is required and GED is accepted. *Academic units required:* 4 English, 3 math, 2 science, 1 science lab, 2 social studies, 3 academic electives, and 3 units from above areas or other academic areas. **Freshman Admission Statistics:** 1,560 applied, 49.23% admitted, 28% enrolled. **Transfer Admission Requirements:** college transcript(s), statement of good standing from prior institution(s). Minimum college GPA of 2.5 required. **General Admission Information:** Priority deadline 5/1. Regular application deadline 8/1. Nonfall registration accepted. Admission may be deferred for a maximum of 1 year.

COSTS AND FINANCIAL AID

Annual tuition $28,390. Required fees $1,040. Average book expense $1,200. **Required Forms and Deadlines:** FAFSA, Institution's own financial aid form. **Notification of Awards:** Applicants will be notified of awards on a rolling basis beginning 2/15. **Types of Aid:** *Need-based scholarships/grants:* Federal Pell, FSEOG, State scholarships/grants, Private scholarships, College/university scholarship or grant aid from institutional funds, Federal Nursing Scholarships. *Loans:* Direct Subsidized Stafford Loans, Direct Unsubsidized Stafford Loans, Direct PLUS loans, Federal Perkins Loans. *Student Employment:* Federal Work-Study Program available. Institutional employment available. **Financial Aid Statistics:** 63% needy freshmen, 99% needy undergrads receive need-based scholarship or grant aid. 24% freshmen, 15% undergrads receive non-need-based scholarship or grant aid. 71% freshmen, 77% undergrads receive need-based self-help aid. 5% freshmen, 6% undergrads receive athletic scholarships. 100% freshmen, 93% undergrads receive any aid. 79% undergrads borrow to pay for school. Average cumulative indebtedness $31,506. **Criteria for awarding aid:** *Need-based:* Academics, Art, Athletics, Leadership, Minority status, Music/drama, Religious affiliation. *Non-need-based:* Academics, Alumni affiliation, Art, Athletics, Leadership, Minority status, Music/drama, Religious affiliation, State/district residency.

UNIVERSITY OF ST. THOMAS

3800 Montrose Boulevard, Houston, TX 77006-4696
Phone: 713-525-3500 • **Financial Aid Phone:** 713-525-2151
E-mail: admissions@stthom.edu • **CEEB Code:** 6880
Fax: 713-525-3558 • **Website:** www.stthom.edu • **ACT Code:** 4238

This private school, affiliated with the Roman Catholic Church, was founded in 1947. It has a 20-acre campus.

RATINGS

Admissions Selectivity Rating: 83   **Fire Safety Rating:** 95   **Green Rating:** 60*

STUDENTS AND FACULTY

Enrollment: 1,750. **Student Body:** 60% female, 40% male, 3% out-of-state, 9% international (50 countries represented). Asian 12%, African American 7%, Caucasian 24%, Hispanic 44%, Native American <1%, Pacific Islander <1%, Two or more races 3%, Race unknown 2%.
Retention and Graduation: 82% freshmen return for sophomore year. 33% freshmen graduate within 4 years. 60% freshmen graduate within 6 years.
Faculty: Student/faculty ratio 10:1. 179 full-time faculty, 91% hold PhDs, 22% are are members of minority groups, 45% are women. 0% of classes are taught by teaching assistants.

ACADEMICS

Degrees: bachelor's, diploma, doctoral/research, master's. **Classes:** Most classes have 10-19 students. Most lab/discussion sessions have 10-19 students. **Most popular majors:** Psychology; Biology/Biological Sciences; Finance. **Special Study Options:** Accelerated program, distance learning, double major, dual enrollment, honors program, independent study, internships, liberal arts/career combination, student-designed major, study abroad, teacher certification program, weekend college. **Honors Programs:** The Honors Program at the University of St. Thomas is a four-year interdisciplinary program for students of exceptional intellectual ability, motivation, and curiosity. It is designed not simply to provoke students to master specific disciplines such as philosophy,

history, mathematics, and natural science but to offer an experience which integrates, on the deepest and most profound level, the intellectual, cultural and spiritual foundations of a liberal arts education. Combined degree programs: BA/MA, BBA/MBA. **Disability Services:** Special programs offered to physically disabled students, including note-taking services, reader services, tape recorders, tutors. **Career Services:** Alumni network, Alumni services, Career assessment, Internships.

FACILITIES

Housing: Coed dorms, apartments for single students. 90% of campus accessible to physically diasbled. **Special Academic Facilities/Equipment:** Learning and Writing Center, Chapel of St. Basil, Doherty Library **Computers:** 100% of classrooms, 100% of libraries, 100% of dining areas, 100% of common outdoor areas have wireless network access. Students can register for classes online. Administrative functions (other than registration) can be performed online.

CAMPUS LIFE

Environment: Metropolis. **Activities:** Choral groups, dance, drama/theater, jazz band, literary magazine, music ensembles, musical theater, student government, student newspaper, Campus Ministries, Student Organization. 69 registered organizations, 22 honor societies, 5 religious organizations. **Athletics (Intercollegiate):** *Men:* basketball, soccer. *Women:* volleyball. **On-Campus Highlights:** Jerabeck Activity and Athletic Center, Crooker Student Center, Chapel of St. Basil, The Lounge, Academic Mall. **Environmental Initiatives:** Campus Recycling of glass, aluminum, plastic & paper.

ADMISSIONS

Freshman Academic Profile: Average high school GPA 3.6. 31% in top 10% of high school class, 57% in top 25% of high school class, 85% in top 50% of high school class. 65% from public high schools. **Reported SAT (pre-2016 redesign) scores:** SAT Math middle 50% range 500-590. SAT Critical Reading middle 50% range 490-585. SAT Writing middle 50% range 480-570. **Concordant SAT scores:** SAT EBRW middle 50% 540–640. SAT Math middle 50% range 530–610. ACT middle 50% range 21-26. Minimum internet-based TOEFL 79. Minimum paper TOEFL 550. **Basis for Candidate Selection:** *Very important factors considered include:* academic GPA, standardized test scores. *Important factors considered include:* rigor of secondary school record, application essay. *Other factors considered include:* recommendation(s), interview, extracurricular activities, talent/ability, character/personal qualities, first generation, alumni/ae relation, volunteer work, work experience, level of applicant's interest. **Freshman Admission Requirements:** High school diploma is required and GED is accepted. *Academic units required:* 4 English, 3 math, 3 science, 2 science labs, 2 foreign language, 2 social studies, 1 history, and 3 units from above areas or other academic areas. *Academic units recommended:* 4 English, 3 math, 3 science, 2 science labs, 2 foreign language, 2 social studies, 1 history, and 3 units from above areas or other academic areas. **Freshman Admission Statistics:** 942 applied, 77.39% admitted, 38% enrolled. **Transfer Admission Requirements:** college transcript(s), Minimum college GPA of 2.50 required. Lowest grade transferable C. **General Admission Information:** Priority deadline 2/1. Regular application deadline 5/1. Nonfall registration accepted. Admission may be deferred for a maximum of 1 year.

COSTS AND FINANCIAL AID

Annual tuition $32,100. Room and board $8,850. Required fees $560. Average book expense $1,094. **Required Forms and Deadlines:** FAFSA. **Notification of Awards:** Applicants will be notified of awards on a rolling basis beginning 2/15. **Types of Aid:** *Need-based scholarships/grants:* Federal Pell, FSEOG, State scholarships/grants, Private scholarships, College/university scholarship or grant aid from institutional funds. *Loans:* Direct Subsidized Stafford Loans, Direct Unsubsidized Stafford Loans, Direct PLUS loans, Federal Perkins Loans, State Loans. *Student Employment:* Federal Work-Study Program available. Institutional employment available. **Financial Aid Statistics:** 97% needy freshmen, 98% needy undergrads receive need-based scholarship or grant aid. 8% freshmen, 6% undergrads receive non-need-based scholarship or grant aid. 51% freshmen, 61% undergrads receive need-based self-help aid. 1% freshmen, 3% undergrads receive athletic scholarships. 90% freshmen, 74% undergrads receive any aid. 50% undergrads borrow to pay for school. Average cumulative indebtedness $26,455. **Criteria for awarding aid:** *Non-need-based:* Academics, Athletics, Music/drama, Religious affiliation.

UNIVERSITY OF TAMPA

401 West Kennedy Boulevard, Tampa, FL 33606-1490
Phone: 813-253-6211 • **Financial Aid Phone:** 813-253-6219
E-mail: admissions@ut.edu • **CEEB Code:** 5819
Fax: 813-258-7398 • **Website:** www.ut.edu • **ACT Code:** 762

This private school was founded in 1931. It has a 100-acre campus.

RATINGS

Admissions Selectivity Rating: 88   **Fire Safety Rating:** 98   **Green Rating:** 66

STUDENTS AND FACULTY

Enrollment: 7,363. **Student Body:** 58% female, 42% male, 66% out-of-state, 11% international (114 countries represented). Asian 2%, African American 5%, Caucasian 60%, Hispanic 12%, Native American <1%, Pacific Islander <1%, Two or more races 3%, Race unknown 7%. **Retention and Graduation:** 75% freshmen return for sophomore year. 48% freshmen graduate within 4 years. 59% freshmen graduate within 6 years. 12% grads go on to further study within 1 year. 2% grads pursue arts and sciences degrees. 3% grads pursue law degrees. 8% grads pursue business degrees. 2% grads pursue medical degrees. **Faculty:** Student/faculty ratio 17:1. 311 full-time faculty, 93% hold PhDs, 11% are are members of minority groups, 44% are women. 0% of classes are taught by teaching assistants.

ACADEMICS

Degrees: bachelor's, certificate, master's, post-master's certificate. **Classes:** Most classes have 20-29 students. Most lab/discussion sessions have 10-19 students. **Most popular majors:** Finance; Marketing/Marketing Management; Criminology. **Special Study Options:** double major, dual enrollment, exchange student program (domestic), honors program, independent study, internships, liberal arts/career combination, study abroad, teacher certification program, Certificate in International Studies program. **Honors Programs:** UT's Honors Program offers special classes that are developed to enhance creative thinking processes while meeting general distribution requirements. Combined degree programs: MSN-MBA; BS Chemistry/Biochemistry-MBA; RN-MSN. **Disability Services:** Special programs offered to physically disabled students, including note-taking services, reader services, tutors. **Career Services:** Alumni network, Alumni services, Career/job search classes, Career assessment, Internships. From their first day on campus, students are supported and involved. They are rewarded with an unlimited array of opportunities that take them to the edge of their imaginations and beyond. All students have opportunities to balance "learning by thinking" with "learning by doing." Both in-class hands on projects and out-of-classroom learning activities help students integrate classroom theory with real world practices. Interactive learning activities such as case studies, behavioral and computer simulations, internships, performances, exhibitions, research, service learning, study abroad, etc., are offered across the curriculum.

FACILITIES

Housing: Coed dorms, special housing for disabled students, apartments for single students, Theme Housing. 100% of campus accessible to physically diasbled. **Special Academic Facilities/Equipment:** Victorian art and furniture museum, theatres, studios, music center, language lab, fully equipped research vessel for marine science, H.B.Plant Museum, marine science research center on Tampa Bay. **Computers:** 50% of classrooms, 25% of dorms, 100% of libraries, 80% of dining areas, 100% of student union, 80% of common outdoor areas have wireless network access. Students can register for classes online. Administrative functions (other than registration) can be performed online.

CAMPUS LIFE

Environment: Metropolis. **Activities:** Choral groups, concert band, dance, drama/theater, jazz band, literary magazine, music ensembles, musical theater, pep band, radio station, student government, student newspaper, student-run film society, symphony orchestra, television station, yearbook, Campus Ministries, Student Organization, Model UN. 145 registered organizations, 13 honor societies, 8 religious organizations. 9 fraternities, 10 sororities. **Athletics (Intercollegiate):** *Men:* baseball, basketball, cross-country, golf, soccer, swimming. *Women:* basketball, crew/rowing, cross-country, soccer, softball, swimming, tennis, volleyball. **On-Campus Highlights:** Vaughn Student Center, Plant Hall, Stadium Center, Vaughn Center Courtyard, Martinez Sports Center.

ADMISSIONS

Freshman Academic Profile: Average high school GPA 3.4. 16% in top 10% of high school class, 46% in top 25% of high school class, 84% in top 50% of high school class. 78% from public high schools. **Reported SAT (pre-2016 redesign) scores:** SAT Math middle 50% range 500-580. SAT Critical Reading middle 50% range 490-580. SAT Writing middle 50% range 480-570. **Concordant SAT scores:** SAT EBRW middle 50% 540–630. SAT Math middle 50% range 530–600. ACT middle 50% range 22-27. Minimum internet-based TOEFL 79. Minimum paper TOEFL 550. **Basis for Candidate Selection:** *Very important factors considered include:* rigor of secondary school record, academic GPA, standardized test scores. *Important factors considered include:* application essay, recommendation(s), talent/ability. *Other factors considered include:* class rank, interview, extracurricular activities, character/personal qualities, first generation, alumni/ae relation, volunteer work, work experience, level of applicant's interest. **Freshman Admission Requirements:** High school diploma is required and GED is accepted. *Academic units required:* 4 English, 3 math, 3 science, 2 science labs, 2 foreign language, 3 social studies, 3 academic electives. **Freshman Admission Statistics:** 19,947 applied, 48.30% admitted, 20% enrolled. **Transfer Admission Requirements:** college transcript(s), Minimum college GPA of 2.2 required. Lowest grade transferable C. **General Admission Information:** Application fee $40. Priority deadline 11/15. Nonfall registration accepted. Admission may be deferred for a maximum of 1 term.

COSTS AND FINANCIAL AID

Required Forms and Deadlines: FAFSA. **Notification of Awards:** Applicants will be notified of awards on a rolling basis beginning 3/1. **Types of Aid:** *Need-based scholarships/grants:* Federal Pell, FSEOG, State scholarships/grants, Private scholarships, College/university scholarship or grant aid from institutional funds, Federal Nursing Scholarships. *Loans:* Direct Subsidized Stafford Loans, Direct Unsubsidized Stafford Loans, Direct PLUS loans, Federal Perkins Loans, College/university loans from institutional funds. *Student Employment:* Federal Work-Study Program available. Institutional employment available. **Financial Aid Statistics:** 100% needy freshmen, 98% needy undergrads receive need-based scholarship or grant aid. 95% freshmen, 96% undergrads receive non-need-based scholarship or grant aid. 84% freshmen, 85% undergrads receive need-based self-help aid. 3% freshmen, 4% undergrads receive athletic scholarships. 93% freshmen, 89% undergrads receive any aid. 60% undergrads borrow to pay for school. Average cumulative indebtedness $31,464. **Criteria for awarding aid:** *Non-need-based:* Academics, Art, Athletics, Leadership, Music/drama.

See page 1088.

UNIVERSITY OF TENNESSEE AT MARTIN

200 Hall-Moody, Martin, TN 38238
Phone: 731-881-7020 • **Financial Aid Phone:** 731-881-7031
E-mail: admitme@utm.edu
Fax: 731-881-7029 • **Website:** www.utm.edu • **ACT Code:** 4032

This public school was founded in 1900. It has a 930-acre campus.

RATINGS

Admissions Selectivity Rating: 81   **Fire Safety Rating:** 91   **Green Rating:** 67

STUDENTS AND FACULTY

Enrollment: 5,576. **Student Body:** 57% female, 43% male, 7% out-of-state, 3% international (20 countries represented). Asian 1%, African American 14%, Caucasian 77%, Hispanic 2%, Native American <1%, Pacific Islander 0%, Two or more races 2%, Race unknown 0%.
Retention and Graduation: 75% freshmen return for sophomore year. 24% freshmen graduate within 4 years. 50% freshmen graduate within 6 years. 18% grads go on to further study within 1 year. **Faculty:** Student/faculty ratio 15:1. 292 full-time faculty, 71% hold PhDs, 11% are are members of minority groups, 46% are women. 0% of classes are taught by teaching assistants.

ACADEMICS

Degrees: bachelor's, master's. **Classes:** Most classes have 10-19 students. Most lab/discussion sessions have 10-19 students. **Most popular major**s: Agricultural Business and Management; Management Information Sy_, Registered Nursing/Registered Nurse. **Special Study Options:** A_, program, cooperative education program, cross-registration, dis_, double major, dual enrollment, English as a Second Language_, student program (domestic), honors program, independen_, student-designed major, study abroad, teacher certificati_, programs in pharmacy, veterinary medicine, dentistr_, podiatry and chiropractory. **Honors Programs:** U_

Seminar. **Disability Services:** Special programs offered to physically disabled students, including note-taking services, reader services, tape recorders, tutors. **Career Services:** Alumni network, Alumni services, Career/job search classes, Career assessment, Internships, Regional alumni. Word Press allows our office to post jobs and internship opportunities for students. Hobsons Retain is used to communicate job postings to students.

FACILITIES

Housing: Coed dorms, special housing for disabled students, men's dorms, special housing for international students, women's dorms, fraternity/sorority housing, apartments for married students, apartments for single students, Theme Housing. 100% of campus accessible to physically diasbled. **Special Academic Facilities/Equipment:** Paul Meek Library contains Houston Gordon University Museum **Computers:** 100% of classrooms, 50% of dorms, 100% of libraries, 100% of dining areas, 100% of student union, 100% of common outdoor areas have wireless network access. Students can register for classes online. Administrative functions (other than registration) can be performed online.

CAMPUS LIFE

Environment: Rural. **Activities:** Choral groups, concert band, dance, drama/theater, jazz band, literary magazine, marching band, music ensembles, opera, pep band, radio station, student government, student newspaper, television station, yearbook, Campus Ministries, Student Organization. 100 registered organizations, 27 honor societies, 11 religious organizations. 12 fraternities, 8 sororities. **Athletics (Intercollegiate):** *Men:* baseball, basketball, cross-country, football, golf, riflery, rodeo. *Women:* basketball, cheerleading, cross-country, equestrian sports, riflery, rodeo, soccer, softball, tennis, volleyball. **On-Campus Highlights:** Boling University Center, Paul Meek Library, Fitness Center, Elam Center and Intramural facilities, Quad, Captain's Coffee in Paul Meek Library Student Life Center. **Environmental Initiatives:** Establishing a Recycling Facility to collect campus and community recyclables. The campus recycles its paper, cardboard, cans and plastic bottles.

ADMISSIONS

Freshman Academic Profile: Average high school GPA 3.6. 17% in top 10% of high school class, 48% in top 25% of high school class, 84% in top 50% of high school class. 93% from public high schools. ACT middle 50% range 20-25. Minimum internet-based TOEFL 61. Minimum paper TOEFL 500. **Basis for Candidate Selection:** *Very important factors considered include:* rigor of secondary school record, academic GPA, standardized test scores. **Freshman Admission Requirements:** High school diploma is required and GED is accepted. *Academic units required:* 4 English, 4 math, 3 science, 1 science lab, 2 foreign language, 1 social studies, 1 history, 1 visual/performing arts. **Freshman Admission Statistics:** 3,547 applied, 66.70% admitted, 40% enrolled. **Transfer Admission Requirements:** High school transcript, college transcript(s), Minimum college GPA of 2.0 required. Lowest grade transferable D. **General Admission Information:** Application fee $30. Priority deadline 8/1. Nonfall registration accepted. Admission may be deferred.

COSTS AND FINANCIAL AID

Annual in-state tuition $7,070. Annual out-of-state tuition $12,830. Room and board $5,788. Required fees $1,408. Average book expense $1,400. **Required Forms and Deadlines:** FAFSA. **Notification of Awards:** Applicants will be notified of awards on a rolling basis beginning 3/15. **Types of Aid:** *Need-based scholarships/grants:* Federal Pell, FSEOG, State scholarships/grants, College/university scholarship or grant aid from institutional funds. *Loans:* Direct Subsidized Stafford Loans, Direct Unsubsidized Stafford Loans, Direct PLUS loans, Federal Perkins Loans. *Student Employment:* Federal Work-Study Program available. Institutional employment available. **Financial Aid Statistics:** 68% needy freshmen, 68% needy undergrads receive need-based scholarship or grant aid. 100% freshmen, 100% undergrads receive non-need-based scholarship or grant aid. 54% freshmen, 66% undergrads receive need-based self-help aid. 8% freshmen, 6% undergrads receive athletic scholarships. 72% freshmen, 72% undergrads receive any aid. 657% undergrads borrow to pay for school. Average cumulative indebtedness $28,077. **Criteria for awarding aid:** *Need-based:* Academics. *Non-need-based:* Academics, Alumni affiliation, Art, Athletics, Leadership, Minority status, Music/drama, State/district residency.

UNIVERSITY OF TENNESSEE—CHATTANOOGA

615 McCallie Avenue, Chattanooga, TN 37403
Phone: 423-425-4662 • **Financial Aid Phone:** 423-425-4677
E-mail: utcmocs@utc.edu • **CEEB Code:** 1831
Fax: 423-425-4157 • **Website:** www.utc.edu • **ACT Code:** 4022

This public school was founded in 1886. It has a 120-acre campus.

RATINGS

Admissions Selectivity Rating: 74   **Fire Safety Rating:** 95   **Green Rating:** 78

STUDENTS AND FACULTY

Enrollment: 10,058. **Student Body:** 56% female, 44% male, 5% out-of-state, 1% international (37 countries represented). Asian 2%, African American 11%, Caucasian 77%, Hispanic 4%, Native American <1%, Pacific Islander <1%, Two or more races 5%, Race unknown 1%.
Retention and Graduation: 74% freshmen return for sophomore year. 21% freshmen graduate within 4 years. **Faculty:** 5% of classes are taught by teaching assistants.

ACADEMICS

Degrees: certificate, doctoral/professional, doctoral/research, master's, postbachelor's certificate, post-master's certificate. **Classes:** Most classes have 20-29 students. Most lab/discussion sessions have 20-29 students. **Most popular majors:** Business Administration and Management; Biology/Biological Sciences; Health and Physical Education/Fitness. **Special Study Options:** cooperative education program, cross-registration, distance learning, double major, dual enrollment, English as a Second Language (ESL), honors program, independent study, internships, study abroad, teacher certification program.
Honors Programs: The University Honors curriculum is a 37-hour sequence of specially designed and enhanced seminar courses in the humanities, the fine arts, cultural perspectives, the history of science, and the social sciences, culminating in a senior-year departmental honors project. These seminars fulfill all of the student's general education course requirements except mathematics and laboratory science. http://www.utc.edu/Academic/UniversityHonors/.
Disability Services: Special programs offered to physically disabled students, including note-taking services, reader services, tape recorders, tutors. **Career Services:** Alumni services, Career/job search classes, Internships. Career Day at UTC.

FACILITIES

Housing: Coed dorms, fraternity/sorority housing, apartments for married students, apartments for single students. 95% of campus accessible to physically diasbled. **Special Academic Facilities/Equipment:** Walker Teaching Resource Center; Jones Observatory; Institute of Archaeology; Odor Research Center; SIM Center; Challenger Center; Center for Applied Social Research; The Ochs Center for Metropolitan Studies. **Computers:** 90% of classrooms, 100% of libraries, 100% of dining areas, 100% of student union, 60% of common outdoor areas have wireless network access. Students can register for classes online. Administrative functions (other than registration) can be performed online.

CAMPUS LIFE

Environment: City. **Activities:** Choral groups, concert band, dance, drama/theater, jazz band, literary magazine, marching band, music ensembles, opera, pep band, radio station, student government, student newspaper, student-run film society, symphony orchestra, television station, Campus Ministries, Student Organization, Model UN. 130 registered organizations, 34 honor societies, 8 religious organizations. 7 fraternities, 7 sororities. **Athletics (Intercollegiate):** *Men:* basketball, cross-country, football, golf, tennis, track/field (outdoor), wrestling. *Women:* basketball, cross-country, golf, soccer, softball, tennis, track/field (outdoor), volleyball. **On-Campus Highlights:** Challenger Center, University Center, The Aquatic and Recreation Center (ARC), The Crossroads **Environmental Initiatives:** Central Plan Improvements.

ADMISSIONS

Freshman Academic Profile: Average high school GPA 3.5. 75% from public high schools. **Reported SAT (pre-2016 redesign) scores:** SAT Math middle 50% range 450-590. SAT Critical Reading middle 50% range 470-600. **Concordant SAT scores:** SAT Math middle 50% range 490–610. ACT middle 50% range 21-26. Minimum internet-based TOEFL 61. Minimum paper TOEFL 500. **Basis for Candidate Selection:** *Very important factors considered include:* rigor of secondary school record, academic GPA, standardized test scores. *Important factors considered include:* character/personal qualities. *Other factors considered include:* application essay, recommendation(s), extracurricular activities, talent/ability, volunteer work, work experience. **Freshman Admission Requirements:** High school diploma is required and GED is accepted. *Academic units required:* 4 English, 4 math,

3 science, 3 science labs, 2 foreign language, 2 history, 1 visual/performing arts. **Freshman Admission Statistics:** 7,628 applied, 78.26% admitted, 35% enrolled. **Transfer Admission Requirements:** college transcript(s), Minimum college GPA of 2.0 required. Lowest grade transferable D. **General Admission Information:** Application fee $30. Regular application deadline 5/1. Nonfall registration accepted. Admission may be deferred for a maximum of 1 semester.

COSTS AND FINANCIAL AID
Annual in-state tuition $6,768. Annual out-of-state tuition $22,886. Room and board $8,676. Required fees $1,776. Average book expense $1,400. **Required Forms and Deadlines:** FAFSA. **Notification of Awards:** Applicants will be notified of awards on a rolling basis beginning 3/1. **Types of Aid:** *Need-based scholarships/grants:* Federal Pell, FSEOG, State scholarships/grants, Private scholarships, College/university scholarship or grant aid from institutional funds. *Loans:* Direct Subsidized Stafford Loans, Direct Unsubsidized Stafford Loans, Direct PLUS loans, Federal Perkins Loans. *Student Employment:* Federal Work-Study Program available. Institutional employment available. **Financial Aid Statistics:** 96% needy freshmen, 85% needy undergrads receive need-based scholarship or grant aid. 4% freshmen, 3% undergrads receive non-need-based scholarship or grant aid. 74% freshmen, 77% undergrads receive need-based self-help aid. 2% freshmen, 2% undergrads receive athletic scholarships. 65% freshmen, 63% undergrads receive any aid. 58% undergrads borrow to pay for school. Average cumulative indebtedness $22,917. **Criteria for awarding aid:** *Need-based:* Academics. *Non-need-based:* Academics, Alumni affiliation, Art, Athletics, Leadership, Music/drama, State/district residency.

UNIVERSITY OF TENNESSEE, KNOXVILLE

320 Student Service Building, Knoxville, TN 37996-0230
Phone: 865-974-1111 • **Financial Aid Phone:** 865-974-1111
E-mail: admissions@utk.edu • **CEEB Code:** 1843
Website: http://www.utk.edu • **ACT Code:** 4026

This public school was founded in 1794. It has a 520-acre campus.

RATINGS
Admissions Selectivity Rating: 88   **Fire Safety Rating:** 92   **Green Rating:** 91

STUDENTS AND FACULTY
Enrollment: 21,984. **Student Body:** 49% female, 51% male, 11% out-of-state, 2% international (63 countries represented). Asian 4%, African American 7%, Caucasian 79%, Hispanic 4%, Native American <1%, Pacific Islander 0%, Two or more races 3%, Race unknown 3%.
Retention and Graduation: 86% freshmen return for sophomore year. 43% freshmen graduate within 4 years. 69% freshmen graduate within 6 years. **Faculty:** Student/faculty ratio 17:1. 1,531 full-time faculty, 87% hold PhDs, 19% are are members of minority groups, 43% are women.

ACADEMICS
Degrees: bachelor's, doctoral/professional, doctoral/research, doctoral, master's, postbachelor's certificate. **Classes:** Most classes have 20-29 students. **Most popular majors:** Kinesiology and Exercise Science; Biology/Biological Sciences; Logistics, Materials, and Supply Chain Management. **Special Study Options:** Accelerated program, cooperative education program, cross-registration, distance learning, double major, dual enrollment, English as a Second Language (ESL), exchange student program (domestic), external degree program, honors program, independent study, internships, liberal arts/career combination, student-designed major, study abroad, teacher certification program. **Honors Programs:** 1. Chancellor's Honors Program 2. Haslam Scholars Program 3. College Scholars Program 4. Global Leadership Scholars Program 5. College of Engineering Honors Program 6. College of Agricultural and Natural Resources Honors Program 7. College of Social Work Honors Program 8. Howard H. Baker Jr. Center for Public Policy's Baker Scholars Program 9. The Math Honors Program 10. Additional departmental honors programs. Combined degree programs: JD/MBA, JD/MPA. **Disability Services:** Special programs offered to physically disabled students, including note-taking services, reader services, tape recorders, tutors. **Career Services:** Alumni network, Alumni services, Career/job search classes, Career assessment, Internships, Regional alumni. The Center for Career Development has partnered with Alumni Affairs to offer a database of alumni Career Guides. Career Guides provide opportunities for students to network with alumni through informational interviews, shadowing, internships and career coaching.

These experiential learning offerings help students of all years to both solidify and implement their career goals.

FACILITIES
Housing: Coed dorms, special housing for disabled students, men's dorms, special housing for international students, women's dorms, fraternity/sorority housing, apartments for married students, apartments for single students, Theme Housing, Transfer student floors. 95% of campus accessible to physically diasbled. **Special Academic Facilities/Equipment:** Comprehensive museum of anthropology, archaeology, art, geology, natural history, and medicine, theatre-in-the-round, livestock farms, robotics research center, electron microscope, McClung Museum **Computers:** 100% of classrooms, 100% of dorms, 100% of libraries, 100% of dining areas, 100% of student union, 25% of common outdoor areas have wireless network access. Students can register for classes online.

CAMPUS LIFE
Environment: City. **Activities:** Choral groups, concert band, dance, drama/theater, jazz band, literary magazine, marching band, music ensembles, musical theater, opera, pep band, radio station, student government, student newspaper, student-run film society, symphony orchestra, television station, yearbook, Campus Ministries, Student Organization, Model UN. 450 registered organizations, 90 honor societies, 30 religious organizations. 23 fraternities, 18 sororities. **Athletics (Intercollegiate):** *Men:* baseball, basketball, cheerleading, cross-country, diving, football, golf, swimming, tennis, track/field (outdoor), track/field (indoor). *Women:* basketball, cheerleading, crew/rowing, cross-country, diving, golf, soccer, softball, swimming, tennis, track/field (outdoor), track/field (indoor), volleyball. **On-Campus Highlights:** Ayres Hall and the Hill, Neyland Stadium, Hodges Library, Rec Sports Center, Howard Baker, Jr. Ctr. for Public Policy, McClung Museum, Alumni Memorial Building and Cox Auditorium, Thompson-Boling Arena. **Environmental Initiatives:** Climate Action Plan.

ADMISSIONS
Freshman Academic Profile: Average high school GPA 3.9. 55% in top 10% of high school class, 89% in top 25% of high school class, 100% in top 50% of high school class. **Reported SAT (pre-2016 redesign) scores:** SAT Math middle 50% range 520-630. SAT Critical Reading middle 50% range 520-620. **Concordant SAT scores:** SAT Math middle 50% range 550–650. ACT middle 50% range 24-30. Minimum internet-based TOEFL 70. Minimum paper TOEFL 523. **Basis for Candidate Selection:** *Very important factors considered include:* rigor of secondary school record, academic GPA, standardized test scores, application essay. *Important factors considered include:* extracurricular activities, talent/ability, volunteer work, work experience, level of applicant's interest. *Other factors considered include:* class rank, recommendation(s), first generation, alumni/ae relation, geographical residence, state residency, racial/ethnic status. **Freshman Admission Requirements:** High school diploma is required and GED is accepted. *Academic units required:* 4 English, 4 math, 3 science, 3 science labs, 2 foreign language, 1 social studies, 1 history, 1 visual/performing arts. **Freshman Admission Statistics:** 17,583 applied, 77.22% admitted, 36% enrolled. **Transfer Admission Requirements:** High school transcript, college transcript(s), statement of good standing from prior institution(s). Minimum college GPA of 2.0 required. Lowest grade transferable C. **General Admission Information:** Application fee $50. Priority deadline 11/1. Regular application deadline 12/1. Nonfall registration accepted.

COSTS AND FINANCIAL AID
Annual in-state tuition $10,858. Annual out-of-state tuition $29,048. Room and board $10,238. Required fees $1,810. Average book expense $1,598. **Required Forms and Deadlines:** FAFSA. **Notification of Awards:** Applicants will be notified of awards on a rolling basis beginning 3/15. **Types of Aid:** *Need-based scholarships/grants:* Federal Pell, FSEOG, State scholarships/grants, Private scholarships, College/university scholarship or grant aid from institutional funds. *Loans:* Direct Subsidized Stafford Loans, Direct Unsubsidized Stafford Loans, Direct PLUS loans, Federal Perkins Loans, State Loans, College/university loans from institutional funds. *Student Employment:* Federal Work-Study Program available. **Financial Aid Statistics:** 95% needy freshmen, 88% needy undergrads receive need-based scholarship or grant aid. 0% undergrads receive non-need-based scholarship or grant aid. 100% freshmen, 99% undergrads receive need-based self-help aid. 2% freshmen, 2% undergrads receive athletic scholarships. 89% freshmen, 93% undergrads receive any aid. 51% undergrads borrow to pay for school. Average cumulative indebtedness $24,420. **Criteria for awarding aid:** *Need-based:* Academics, Minority status. *Non-need-based:* Academics, Art, Athletics, Leadership, Minority status, Music/drama, State/district residency.

THE UNIVERSITY OF TEXAS AT ARLINGTON

Office of Admissions, Arlington, TX 76019-0111
Phone: 817-272-6287 • **Financial Aid Phone:** 817-272-3561
E-mail: admissions@uta.edu • **CEEB Code:** 6013
Fax: 817-272-3435 • **Website:** www.uta.edu • **ACT Code:** 4200

This public school was founded in 1895. It has a 394-acre campus.

RATINGS

Admissions Selectivity Rating: 85   **Fire Safety Rating:** 96   **Green Rating:** 79

STUDENTS AND FACULTY

Enrollment: 25,414. **Student Body:** 56% female, 44% male, 3% out-of-state, 4% international (123 countries represented). Asian 12%, African American 15%, Caucasian 40%, Hispanic 26%, Native American <1%, Pacific Islander <1%, Two or more races 3%, Race unknown 1%.
Retention and Graduation: 74% freshmen return for sophomore year. 18% freshmen graduate within 4 years. 44% freshmen graduate within 6 years. **Faculty:** Student/faculty ratio 22:1. 941 full-time faculty, 0% hold PhDs, 28% are are members of minority groups, 42% are women. 16% of classes are taught by teaching assistants.

ACADEMICS

Degrees: bachelor's, doctoral/professional, doctoral/research, doctoral, master's, postbachelor's certificate, post-master's certificate. **Classes:** Most classes have 20-29 students. **Most popular majors:** Business Administration and Management; Registered Nursing/Registered Nurse. **Special Study Options:** cross-registration, distance learning, double major, dual enrollment, English as a Second Language (ESL), honors program, independent study, internships, student-designed major, study abroad, teacher certification program. **Honors Programs:** We have the only Honors College in N. Texas. Freshmen interest groups, honors study abroad. Combined degree programs: BA/MD, BS/MBA. **Disability Services:** Special programs offered to physically disabled students, including note-taking services, reader services, tape recorders, tutors. **Career Services:** Alumni services, Career/job search classes, Career assessment, Internships.

FACILITIES

Housing: Coed dorms, men's dorms, women's dorms, fraternity/sorority housing, apartments for married students, apartments for single students, Family housing (priority given to students with dependent children). 95% of campus accessible to physically disabled. **Special Academic Facilities/Equipment:** Cartographic history library, maps collection, minority cultures collection, library of Texana and Mexican war. Continuing Education Work Force Development Center. material, planetarium, Automation and Robotics Research institute, Wave Scattering Research Center **Computers:** Students can register for classes online. Administrative functions (other than registration) can be performed online.

CAMPUS LIFE

Environment: Metropolis. **Activities:** Choral groups, concert band, dance, drama/theater, jazz band, literary magazine, marching band, music ensembles, opera, radio station, student government, student newspaper, student-run film society, symphony orchestra, Campus Ministries, Student Organization. 459 registered organizations, 30 honor societies, 27 religious organizations. 12 fraternities, 13 sororities. **Athletics (Intercollegiate):** *Men:* baseball, basketball, cross-country, golf, tennis, track/field (outdoor). *Women:* basketball, cross-country, softball, tennis, track/field (outdoor), volleyball. **On-Campus Highlights:** Click Cafe in Library, E. H. Herford University Center, Activities Bldg., Library Mall/Free speech area, Architectue courtyard. **Environmental Initiatives:** Transportation programs like car sharing, ride share, bike program.

ADMISSIONS

Freshman Academic Profile: 28% in top 10% of high school class, 75% in top 25% of high school class, 98% in top 50% of high school class. **Reported SAT (pre-2016 redesign) scores:** SAT Math middle 50% range 500-620. SAT Critical Reading middle 50% range 460-580. SAT Writing middle 50% range 450-560. **Concordant SAT scores:** SAT EBRW middle 50% 510–630. SAT Math middle 50% range 530–640. ACT middle 50% range 20-26. Minimum internet-based TOEFL 79. Minimum paper TOEFL 550. **Basis for Candidate Selection:** *Very important factors considered include:* class rank, academic GPA, standardized test scores. *Important factors considered include:* rigor of secondary school record. *Other factors considered include:* application essay, recommendation(s), extracurricular activities, talent/ability, character/personal qualities, first generation, volunteer work, work experience, level of applicant's interest. **Freshman Admission Requirements:** High school diploma is required and GED is not accepted. *Academic units required:* 4 English, 3 math, 3 science, 2 foreign language, 3 social studies, 5 academic electives, and 5 units from above areas or other academic areas. *Academic units*

recommended: 4 English, 4 math, 3 science, 3 foreign language, 4 social studies, 5 academic electives. **Freshman Admission Statistics:** 10,679 applied, 59.98% admitted, 42% enrolled. **Transfer Admission Requirements:** High school transcript, college transcript(s), Minimum college GPA of 2.25 required. Lowest grade transferable C. **General Admission Information:** Application fee $50. Priority deadline 6/1. Nonfall registration accepted. Admission may be deferred for a maximum of 1 year.

COSTS AND FINANCIAL AID

Annual in-state tuition $8,878. Annual out-of-state tuition $19,497. Room and board $7,864. Average book expense $1,160. **Required Forms and Deadlines:** FAFSA. **Notification of Awards:** Applicants will be notified of awards on a rolling basis beginning 4/1. **Types of Aid:** *Need-based scholarships/ grants:* Federal Pell, FSEOG, State scholarships/grants, Private scholarships, College/university scholarship or grant aid from institutional funds, United Negro College Fund. *Loans:* Direct Subsidized Stafford Loans, Direct Unsubsidized Stafford Loans, Direct PLUS loans, Federal Perkins Loans, State Loans. *Student Employment:* Federal Work-Study Program available. Institutional employment available. **Financial Aid Statistics:** 74% needy freshmen, 80% needy undergrads receive need-based scholarship or grant aid. 50% freshmen, 31% undergrads receive non-need-based scholarship or grant aid. 94% freshmen, 95% undergrads receive need-based self-help aid. 0% freshmen, 0% undergrads receive athletic scholarships. 65% freshmen, 68% undergrads receive any aid. **Criteria for awarding aid:** *Need-based:* Academics, Athletics. *Non-need-based:* Academics, Art, Athletics, Leadership, Music/drama.

THE UNIVERSITY OF TEXAS AT AUSTIN

P.O. Box 8058, Austin, TX 78713-8058
Phone: 512-475-7399 • **Financial Aid Phone:** 512-475-6203 • **CEEB Code:** 6882
Fax: 512-475-7478 • **Website:** http://www.utexas.edu • **ACT Code:** 4240

This public school was founded in 1883. It has a 350-acre campus.

RATINGS

Admissions Selectivity Rating: 93   **Fire Safety Rating:** 84   **Green Rating:** 89

STUDENTS AND FACULTY

Enrollment: 39,676. **Student Body:** 53% female, 47% male, 5% out-of-state, 5% international (95 countries represented). Asian 21%, African American 4%, Caucasian 42%, Hispanic 23%, Native American <1%, Pacific Islander <1%, Two or more races 4%, Race unknown 1%.
Retention and Graduation: 95% freshmen return for sophomore year. 55% freshmen graduate within 4 years. 81% freshmen graduate within 6 years. **Faculty:** Student/faculty ratio 18:1. 2,562 full-time faculty, 89% hold PhDs, 21% are are members of minority groups, 39% are women.

ACADEMICS

Degrees: bachelor's, certificate, doctoral/professional, doctoral/research, master's, postbachelor's certificate. **Classes:** Most classes have 10-19 students. Most lab/discussion sessions have 10-19 students. **Most popular majors:** Biology/Biological Sciences; Economics; Computer and Information Sciences. **Special Study Options:** Accelerated program, cooperative education program, distance learning, double major, dual enrollment, English as a Second Language (ESL), honors program, independent study, internships, liberal arts/career combination, student-designed major, study abroad, teacher certification program. Combined degree programs: BBA/MPA, BS/MS in Computer Science, Pharm. D/Ph.D., B.Arch./BSArchEng, BA/BEng. **Disability Services:** Special programs offered to physically disabled students, including note-taking services, reader services. **Career Services:** Alumni network, Alumni services, Career assessment, Internships, Regional alumni.

FACILITIES

Housing: Coed dorms, men's dorms, women's dorms, apartments for married students, apartments for single students, Honors Residence, Living Learning Centers (First-time Freshmen). **Special Academic Facilities/Equipment:** Blanton Museum of Art, Lyndon Baines Johnson Presidential Library/Museum, Performing Arts Center, Texas Memorial Museum, Harry Ransom Humanities Research Center. **Computers:** Students can register for classes online. Administrative functions (other than registration) can be performed online.

CAMPUS LIFE

Environment: Metropolis. **Activities:** Choral groups, concert band, dance, drama/theater, jazz band, literary magazine, marching band, music ensembles, musical theater, opera, pep band, radio station, student government, student newspaper, student-run film society, symphony orchestra, television station, yearbook, Campus Ministries, Student Organization. 900 registered organizations, 15 honor societies, 95 religious organizations. 26 fraternities, 22 sororities. **Athletics (Intercollegiate):** *Men:* baseball, basketball, cross-country, diving, football, golf, swimming, tennis, track/field (outdoor). *Women:* basketball, crew/rowing, cross-country, diving, golf, soccer, softball, swimming, tennis, track/field (outdoor), volleyball. **On-Campus Highlights:** Texas Union, Frank Erwin Special Events Center, Performing Arts Center, Harry Ransom Humanities Research Center, Blanton Museum of Art. **Environmental Initiatives:** Incorporation of sustainability principles throughout the institution's approved Campus Master Plan (May 2013).

ADMISSIONS

Freshman Academic Profile: 70% in top 10% of high school class, 92% in top 25% of high school class, 99% in top 50% of high school class. **Reported SAT (pre-2016 redesign) scores:** SAT Math middle 50% range 580-730. SAT Critical Reading middle 50% range 560-680. SAT Writing middle 50% range 550-680. **Concordant SAT scores:** SAT EBRW middle 50% 610–720. SAT Math middle 50% range 600–760. ACT middle 50% range 26-32. Minimum internet-based TOEFL 79. Minimum paper TOEFL 550. **Basis for Candidate Selection:** *Very important factors considered include:* rigor of secondary school record, class rank. *Important factors considered include:* standardized test scores, application essay, extracurricular activities, talent/ability, volunteer work, work experience. *Other factors considered include:* recommendation(s), character/personal qualities, first generation, state residency, racial/ethnic status, level of applicant's interest. **Freshman Admission Requirements:** High school diploma is required and GED is accepted. *Academic units required:* 4 English, 4 math, 4 science, 2 foreign language, 4 social studies, 6 academic electives, and 2 units from above areas or other academic areas. **Freshman Admission Statistics:** 47,511 applied, 40.37% admitted, 45% enrolled. **Transfer Admission Requirements:** college transcript(s), essay or personal statement, Minimum college GPA of 3.0 required. Lowest grade transferable C. **General Admission Information:** Application fee $75. Regular application deadline 12/1. Nonfall registration accepted.

COSTS AND FINANCIAL AID

Annual in-state tuition $10,136. Annual out-of-state tuition $35,766. Room and board $10,070. Required fees $0. Average book expense $662. **Required Forms and Deadlines:** FAFSA, Institution's own financial aid form. **Notification of Awards:** Applicants will be notified of awards on a rolling basis beginning 3/15. **Types of Aid:** *Need-based scholarships/grants:* Federal Pell, FSEOG, State scholarships/grants, Private scholarships, College/university scholarship or grant aid from institutional funds. *Loans:* Direct Subsidized Stafford Loans, Direct Unsubsidized Stafford Loans, Direct PLUS loans, Federal Perkins Loans, State Loans. *Student Employment:* Federal Work-Study Program available. Institutional employment available. **Financial Aid Statistics:** 75% needy freshmen, 80% needy undergrads receive need-based scholarship or grant aid. 39% freshmen, 23% undergrads receive non-need-based scholarship or grant aid. 71% freshmen, 69% undergrads receive need-based self-help aid. 2% freshmen, 4% undergrads receive athletic scholarships. 42% undergrads receive any aid. 45% undergrads borrow to pay for school. Average cumulative indebtedness $25,338. **Criteria for awarding aid:** *Need-based:* Academics, Art, Leadership, Music/drama. *Non-need-based:* Academics, Art, Athletics, Leadership, Music/drama, State/district residency.

UNIVERSITY OF TEXAS AT BROWNSVILLE

80 Fort Brown, Brownsville, TX 78520
Phone: 956-882-8295 • **Financial Aid Phone:** 956-882-8814
E-mail: admissions@utb.edu • **CEEB Code:** 6825
Fax: 956-882-7810 • **Website:** www.utb.edu

This public school was founded in 1926.

RATINGS

Admissions Selectivity Rating: 64   **Fire Safety Rating:** 60*   **Green Rating:** 60*

STUDENTS AND FACULTY

Enrollment: 10,145. **Student Body:** 60% female, 40% male, 4% out-of-state, 4% international (21 countries represented). Asian 0%, African American <1%, Caucasian 5%, Hispanic 90%, Native American <1%, Pacific Islander 0%, Two or more races 0%, Race unknown 1%.
Faculty: 366 full-time faculty, 59% hold PhDs, 46% are are members of minority groups, 43% are women. 0% of classes are taught by teaching assistants.

ACADEMICS

Degrees: associate, bachelor's, certificate, master's, terminal, transfer. **Most popular majors:** Multi-/Interdisciplinary Studies; Psychology; Business/Commerce. **Special Study Options:** cooperative education program, distance learning, double major, dual enrollment, English as a Second Language (ESL), independent study, internships, teacher certification program. **Disability Services:** Special programs offered to physically disabled students, including note-taking services, reader services, tape recorders, tutors.

FACILITIES

Housing: Coed dorms, special housing for disabled students, men's dorms, women's dorms, apartments for single students. **Computers:** Students can register for classes online. Administrative functions (other than registration) can be performed online.

CAMPUS LIFE

Environment: City. **Activities:** Choral groups, concert band, dance, drama/theater, jazz band, music ensembles, opera, radio station, student government, student newspaper. 56 registered organizations, 6 honor societies. **Athletics (Intercollegiate):** *Men:* baseball, golf. *Women:* golf, volleyball.

ADMISSIONS

Freshman Academic Profile: Average high school GPA 2.6. 10% in top 10% of high school class, 27% in top 25% of high school class, 57% in top 50% of high school class. 95% from public high schools. **Freshman Admission Requirements:** High school diploma or equivalent is not required. *Academic units required:* 4 English, 2 math, 2 science, 2 science labs, 2 foreign language, 4 social studies, 2 history, 1 academic elective, and 3 units from above areas or other academic areas. *Academic units recommended:* 4 English, 4 math, 3 science, 3 science labs, 3 foreign language, 4 social studies, 2 history, 4 academic electives, and 3 units from above areas or other academic areas. **Freshman Admission Statistics:** 3,594 applied, 100.00% admitted, 50% enrolled. **Transfer Admission Requirements:** High school transcript, college transcript(s), Minimum college GPA of 2.0 required. Lowest grade transferable C. **General Admission Information:** Priority deadline 4/1. Regular application deadline 7/1. Nonfall registration accepted. Admission may be deferred for a maximum of 1 year.

COSTS AND FINANCIAL AID

Average book expense $615. **Required Forms and Deadlines:** FAFSA. **Notification of Awards:** Applicants will be notified of awards on or about 5/1. **Types of Aid:** *Need-based scholarships/grants:* Federal Pell, FSEOG, State scholarships/grants, Private scholarships, College/university scholarship or grant aid from institutional funds. *Loans:* College/university loans from institutional funds. *Student Employment:* Federal Work-Study Program available. Institutional employment available. **Criteria for awarding aid:** *Need-based:* Academics. *Non-need-based:* Academics, Art, Athletics, Leadership, Music/drama.

THE UNIVERSITY OF TEXAS AT DALLAS

Admission & Enrollment, Richardson, TX 75080-3021
Phone: 972-883-2270 • **Financial Aid Phone:** 972-883-2941
E-mail: interest@utdallas.edu • **CEEB Code:** 6897
Fax: 972-883-2599 • **Website:** www.utdallas.edu • **ACT Code:** 4243

This public school was founded in 1969. It has a 500-acre campus.

RATINGS

Admissions Selectivity Rating: 87   **Fire Safety Rating:** 93   **Green Rating:** 77

STUDENTS AND FACULTY

Enrollment: 17,058. **Student Body:** 43% female, 57% male, 4% out-of-state, 4% international (70 countries represented). Asian 30%, African American 6%, Caucasian 36%, Hispanic 18%, Native American <1%, Pacific Islander <1%, Two or more races 4%, Race unknown 2%.
Retention and Graduation: 87% freshmen return for sophomore year. 51% freshmen graduate within 4 years. 68% freshmen graduate within 6 years.
Faculty: Student/faculty ratio 23:1. 857 full-time faculty, 92% hold PhDs, 27% are are members of minority groups, 32% are women. 4% of classes are taught by teaching assistants.

ACADEMICS

Degrees: bachelor's, doctoral/professional, doctoral/research, master's, postbachelor's certificate. **Classes:** Most classes have 10-19 students. Most lab/

discussion sessions have 20-29 students. **Most popular majors:** Computer and Information Sciences; Biology/Biological Sciences; Mechanical Engineering. **Special Study Options:** Accelerated program, cooperative education program, cross-registration, distance learning, double major, dual enrollment, English as a Second Language (ESL), honors program, independent study, internships, liberal arts/career combination, student-designed major, study abroad, teacher certification program, 3-2 Engineering programs, 2-2 Transfer programs. **Honors Programs:** Collegium V offers small classes, innovative instruction, world class faculty, bright and inquisitive colleagues, and an array of extracurricular events to provide special opportunities for professional and personal growth. Combined degree programs: BA/MA, BS/MS, BA/MPA, BS/MPA, MS/PhD. **Disability Services:** Special programs offered to physically disabled students, including note-taking services, reader services, tape recorders, tutors. **Career Services:** Alumni network, Alumni services, Career/job search classes, Career assessment, Internships.

FACILITIES

Housing: Coed dorms, apartments for married students, apartments for single students, Living Learning communities for freshmen. 100% of campus accessible to physically diasbled. **Special Academic Facilities/Equipment:** McDermott Library Special Collections which includes History of Aviation Collection, Wineburgh Philatelic Research Library and Louise B. Belsterling Botanical Library. **Computers:** 80% of classrooms, 100% of dorms, 100% of libraries, 100% of student union, 5% of common outdoor areas have wireless network access. Students can register for classes online.

CAMPUS LIFE

Environment: Metropolis. **Activities:** Choral groups, concert band, dance, drama/theater, jazz band, literary magazine, music ensembles, musical theater, pep band, radio station, student government, student newspaper, student-run film society, symphony orchestra, television station, Student Organization. 142 registered organizations, 8 honor societies, 9 religious organizations. 9 fraternities, 6 sororities. **Athletics (Intercollegiate):** *Men:* baseball, basketball, cross-country, golf, soccer, tennis. *Women:* basketball, cross-country, golf, soccer, softball, tennis, volleyball. **On-Campus Highlights:** The Pub (coffeehouse), Comet Cafe, Student Union, Activity Center, University Village clubhouses. **Environmental Initiatives:** Campus recycling program.

ADMISSIONS

Freshman Academic Profile: 32% in top 10% of high school class, 61% in top 25% of high school class, 88% in top 50% of high school class. 93% from public high schools. **Reported SAT (pre-2016 redesign) scores:** SAT Math middle 50% range 590-710. SAT Critical Reading middle 50% range 550-670. SAT Writing middle 50% range 520-650. **Concordant SAT scores:** SAT EBRW middle 50% 590–700. SAT Math middle 50% range 610–740. ACT middle 50% range 25-31. Minimum internet-based TOEFL 80. Minimum paper TOEFL 550. **Basis for Candidate Selection:** *Very important factors considered include:* rigor of secondary school record, class rank, academic GPA, standardized test scores. *Important factors considered include:* application essay. *Other factors considered include:* recommendation(s), extracurricular activities, state residency, volunteer work, work experience, level of applicant's interest. **Freshman Admission Requirements:** High school diploma is required and GED is accepted. *Academic units required:* 4 English, 4 math, 3 science, 3 science labs, 2 foreign language, 3 social studies. *Academic units recommended:* 4 English, 4 math, 3 science, 3 science labs, 3 foreign language, 4 social studies, 1 computer science, 1 visual/performing arts, and 2 units from above areas or other academic areas. **Freshman Admission Statistics:** 12,686 applied, 67.99% admitted, 37% enrolled. **Transfer Admission Requirements:** college transcript(s), Minimum college GPA of 2.5 required. Lowest grade transferable C. **General Admission Information:** Application fee $50. Regular application deadline 7/1. Nonfall registration accepted. Admission may be deferred for a maximum of One year.

COSTS AND FINANCIAL AID

Annual in-state tuition $12,162. Annual out-of-state tuition $33,654. Room and board $10,668. Average book expense $1,200. **Required Forms and Deadlines:** FAFSA. **Notification of Awards:** Applicants will be notified of awards on a rolling basis beginning 3/1. **Types of Aid:** *Need-based scholarships/grants:* Federal Pell, FSEOG, State scholarships/grants, Private scholarships, College/university scholarship or grant aid from institutional funds. *Loans:* Direct Subsidized Stafford Loans, Direct Unsubsidized Stafford Loans, Direct PLUS loans, Federal Perkins Loans, State Loans, College/university loans from institutional funds. *Student Employment:* Federal Work-Study Program available. Institutional employment available. **Financial Aid Statistics:** 91% needy freshmen, 89% needy undergrads receive need-based scholarship or grant aid. 13% freshmen, 7% undergrads receive non-need-based scholarship or grant aid. 85% freshmen, 90% undergrads receive need-based self-help aid. 0% freshmen, 0% undergrads receive athletic scholarships. 78% freshmen, 71% undergrads receive any aid. 35% undergrads borrow to pay for school. Average cumulative indebtedness $20,432. **Criteria for awarding aid:** *Need-based:* Academics. *Non-need-based:* Academics.

THE UNIVERSITY OF TEXAS AT SAN ANTONIO

One UTSA Circle, San Antonio, TX 78249-0617
Phone: (210) 458-8000 • **Financial Aid Phone:** 210-458-8000
E-mail: prospects@utsa.edu • **CEEB Code:** 6919
Fax: 210-458-7857 • **Website:** http://www.utsa.edu/ • **ACT Code:** 4239

This public school was founded in 1969. It has a 600-acre campus.

RATINGS
Admissions Selectivity Rating: 79   **Fire Safety Rating:** 84   **Green Rating:** 60*

STUDENTS AND FACULTY
Enrollment: 24,036. **Student Body:** 50% female, 50% male, 2% out-of-state, 2% international (63 countries represented). Asian 5%, African American 9%, Caucasian 24%, Hispanic 54%, Native American <1%, Pacific Islander <1%, Two or more races 3%, Race unknown 1%.
Retention and Graduation: 71% freshmen return for sophomore year. 13% freshmen graduate within 4 years. 35 **Faculty:** Student/faculty ratio 23:1. 922 full-time faculty, 84% hold PhDs, 35% are are members of minority groups, 36% are women.

ACADEMICS
Degrees: bachelor's, doctoral/research, master's. **Classes:** Most classes have 20-29 students. Most lab/discussion sessions have 10-19 students. **Most popular majors:** Psychology; Criminal Justice/Safety Studies; Kinesiology and Exercise Science. **Special Study Options:** Accelerated program, cooperative education program, distance learning, double major, dual enrollment, English as a Second Language (ESL), exchange student program (domestic), honors program, independent study, internships, study abroad, teacher certification program. **Honors Programs:** The mission of the Honors College is to provide enhanced educational opportunities for selected, motivated, enthusiastic, diverse, and inquisitive students and to foster the pursuit of excellence in undergraduate, higher education. The underlying philosophy of the program is that well-educated individuals should understand broad, interdisciplinary perspectives while demonstrating expertise in their chosen field. The Honors College is open to students from all academic disciplines. Members of the Honors College pursue a rigorous academic program which satisfies all requirements of their academic departments and Colleges and goes beyond those requirements to provide the basis for outstanding achievement and appropriate recognition for that achievement. The Honors College offers small classes with greater opportunities for student participation, increased student-faculty contact, greater individual attention, lively discussions of important issues, special interdisciplinary seminars, community service opportunities, and supervised research experiences, all designed to challenge talented students. Combined degree programs: BBA-Accounting/MACY; BS-Dietetics/MDS. **Disability Services:** Special programs offered to physically disabled students, including note-taking services, reader services, tape recorders. **Career Services:** Alumni network, Alumni services, Career/job search classes, Career assessment, Internships, Regional alumni. Neither. We are working hard to improve the one that we have and are currently redesigning it.

FACILITIES
Housing: Coed dorms, special housing for disabled students, apartments for married students, apartments for single students. 85% of campus accessible to physically diasbled. **Special Academic Facilities/Equipment:** Art gallery, audiovisual center, Institute of Texan Cultures Museum. **Computers:** Students can register for classes online. Administrative functions (other than registration) can be performed online.

CAMPUS LIFE
Environment: Metropolis. **Activities:** Choral groups, concert band, dance, drama/theater, jazz band, literary magazine, music ensembles, opera, pep band, student government, student newspaper, symphony orchestra, yearbook, Campus Ministries, Student Organization. 140 registered organizations, 40 honor societies, 9 religious organizations. 10 fraternities, 9 sororities. **Athletics (Intercollegiate):** *Men:* baseball, basketball, cross-country, golf, tennis, track/field (outdoor), track/field (indoor). *Women:* basketball, cross-country, soccer, softball, tennis, track/field (outdoor), track/field (indoor), volleyball.

ADMISSIONS
Freshman Academic Profile: 18% in top 10% of high school class, 60% in top 25% of high school class, 91% in top 50% of high school class. **Reported SAT (pre-2016 redesign) scores:** SAT Math middle 50% range 470-570. SAT Critical Reading middle 50% range 450-560. SAT Writing middle 50% range 430-530. **Concordant SAT scores:** SAT EBRW middle 50% 490–600. SAT Math middle 50% range 510–590. ACT middle 50% range 20-25. Minimum internet-based TOEFL 79. Minimum paper TOEFL 550. **Basis for Candidate Selection:** *Very important factors considered include:* class rank, standardized test scores. *Important factors considered include:* extracurricular

activities, talent/ability, character/personal qualities, volunteer work, work experience. *Other factors considered include:* rigor of secondary school record, academic GPA, application essay, recommendation(s). **Freshman Admission Requirements:** High school diploma is required and GED is accepted. *Academic units required:* 4 English, 3 math, 3 science, 2 foreign language, 3 social studies, 1 history, 5 academic electives, 1 visual/performing arts, and 1 unit from above areas or other academic areas. **Freshman Admission Statistics:** 15,500 applied, 76.41% admitted, 37% enrolled. **Transfer Admission Requirements:** college transcript(s), Minimum college GPA of 2.0 required. Lowest grade transferable D. **General Admission Information:** Application fee $60. Priority deadline 3/1. Regular application deadline 6/1. Nonfall registration accepted.

COSTS AND FINANCIAL AID

Annual in-state tuition $6,299. Annual out-of-state tuition $19,545. Room and board $8,074. Required fees $2,745. Average book expense $1,000. **Required Forms and Deadlines:** FAFSA. **Notification of Awards:** Applicants will be notified of awards on a rolling basis beginning 4/1. **Types of Aid:** *Need-based scholarships/grants:* Federal Pell, FSEOG, State scholarships/grants, Private scholarships, College/university scholarship or grant aid from institutional funds. *Loans:* Direct Subsidized Stafford Loans, Direct Unsubsidized Stafford Loans, Direct PLUS loans, Federal Perkins Loans, State Loans, College/university loans from institutional funds. *Student Employment:* Federal Work-Study Program available. Institutional employment available. **Financial Aid Statistics:** 86% needy freshmen, 84% needy undergrads receive need-based scholarship or grant aid. 2% freshmen, 2% undergrads receive non-need-based scholarship or grant aid. 67% freshmen, 71% undergrads receive need-based self-help aid. 1% freshmen, 1% undergrads receive athletic scholarships. 63% undergrads borrow to pay for school. Average cumulative indebtedness $26,763. **Criteria for awarding aid:** *Non-need-based:* Academics, Alumni affiliation, Art, Athletics, Job skills, Leadership, Music/drama, State/district residency.

THE UNIVERSITY OF TEXAS AT TYLER

3900 University Blvd., Tyler, TX 75799
Phone: 903-566-7203 • **Financial Aid Phone:** 903-566-7180
E-mail: admrequest@uttyler.edu
Fax: 903-566-7068 • **Website:** www.uttyler.edu

This public school was founded in 1971. It has a 204-acre campus.

RATINGS

Admissions Selectivity Rating: 80   **Fire Safety Rating:** 93   **Green Rating:** 60*

STUDENTS AND FACULTY

Enrollment: 6,059. **Student Body:** 57% female, 43% male, 1% out-of-state, 2% international (45 countries represented). Asian 3%, African American 9%, Caucasian 58%, Hispanic 16%, Native American <1%, Pacific Islander <1%, Two or more races 8%, Race unknown 3%.
Retention and Graduation: 62% freshmen return for sophomore year. 25% freshmen graduate within 4 years. 41% freshmen graduate within 6 years. 14% grads go on to further study within 1 year.

ACADEMICS

Degrees: bachelor's, doctoral/professional, doctoral/research, master's, post-master's certificate. **Classes:** Most classes have 20-29 students. **Most popular majors:** Multi Business/Managerial Economics. **Special Study Options:** cooperative education program, distance learning, double major, English as a Second Language (ESL), exchange student program (domestic), independent study, internships, student-designed major, study abroad, teacher certification program, weekend college. **Disability Services:** Special programs offered to physically disabled students, including note-taking services, reader services. **Career Services:** Career/job search classes, Career assessment.

FACILITIES

Housing: Coed dorms, apartments for married students, apartments for single students, Univ Pines Apts-384 beds, Patriot Village Apts—200 beds. Residence Hall Project underway, will be five stories with 268 beds, expected to open in fall 2006. http://www.uttyler.edu/housing. **Computers:** Students can register for classes online. Administrative functions (other than registration) can be performed online.

CAMPUS LIFE

Environment: City. **Activities:** Choral groups, concert band, drama/theater, jazz band, literary magazine, music ensembles, musical theater, opera, pep band, student government, student newspaper, student-run film society 73 registered organizations, 6 honor societies, 4 fraternities, 4 sororities. **Athletics (Intercollegiate):** *Men:* baseball, basketball, cheerleading, cross-country, golf, soccer, tennis. *Women:* basketball, cheerleading, cross-country, golf,

soccer, tennis, volleyball. **On-Campus Highlights:** Herrington Patriot Center, Riter Tower and Plaza, Cowan Fine and Performing Art Center, Bill Ratliff Engineering and Science Complex, University Center.

ADMISSIONS

Freshman Academic Profile: Average high school GPA 3.4. 10% in top 10% of high school class, 35% in top 25% of high school class, 64% in top 50% of high school class. **Reported SAT (pre-2016 redesign) scores:** SAT Math middle 50% range 490-590. SAT Critical Reading middle 50% range 480-570. SAT Writing middle 50% range 450-560. **Concordant SAT scores:** SAT EBRW middle 50% 520–620. SAT Math middle 50% range 520–610. ACT middle 50% range 20-25, Minimum paper TOEFL 550. **Basis for Candidate Selection:** *Very important factors considered include:* rigor of secondary school record, class rank, academic GPA, standardized test scores, level of applicant's interest. *Important factors considered include:* extracurricular activities, talent/ability, character/personal qualities, first generation, volunteer work. *Other factors considered include:* work experience. **Freshman Admission Requirements:** High school diploma is required and GED is accepted. *Academic units required:* 4 English, 3 math, 3 science, 2 foreign language, 3 social studies. *Academic units recommended:* 4 math, 4 science, 3 science labs, 4 social studies, 4 history. **Freshman Admission Statistics:** 2,468 applied, 64.47% admitted, 49% enrolled. **Transfer Admission Requirements:** college transcript(s), Minimum college GPA of 2.0 required. Lowest grade transferable C. **General Admission Information:** Regular application deadline 8/24. Nonfall registration accepted. Admission may be deferred for a maximum of 1 year.

COSTS AND FINANCIAL AID

Required Forms and Deadlines: FAFSA, Institution's own financial aid form. **Types of Aid:** *Need-based scholarships/grants:* Federal Pell, FSEOG, State scholarships/grants, Private scholarships, College/university scholarship or grant aid from institutional funds. *Loans:* Federal Perkins Loans, State Loans. *Student Employment:* Federal Work-Study Program available. Institutional employment available. **Criteria for awarding aid:** *Non-need-based:* Academics, Art, Music/drama.

UNIVERSITY OF TEXAS—EL PASO

Mike Loya Academic Services Bldg., #102, El Paso, TX 79968-0510
Phone: 915-747-5890
E-mail: www.academics.utep.edu • **CEEB Code:** 6829
Fax: 915-747-8893 • **Website:** http://www.utep.edu/ • **ACT Code:** 4223

This public school was founded in 1913. It has a 330-acre campus.

RATINGS

Admissions Selectivity Rating: 74   **Fire Safety Rating:** 75   **Green Rating:** 60*

STUDENTS AND FACULTY

Enrollment: 19,078. **Student Body:** 54% female, 46% male, 3% out-of-state, 5% international (65 countries represented). Asian 1%, African American 3%, Caucasian 8%, Hispanic 81%, Native American <1%, Pacific Islander <1%, Two or more races <1%, Race unknown 2%.
Retention and Graduation: 72% freshmen return for sophomore year. **Faculty:** Student/faculty ratio 21:1. 2% of classes are taught by teaching assistants.

ACADEMICS

Degrees: bachelor's, doctoral/professional, doctoral/research, master's, postbachelor's certificate, post-master's certificate. **Classes:** Most classes have 20-29 students. Most lab/discussion sessions have 10-19 students. **Most popular majors:** Multi-/Interdisciplinary Studies; Psychology; Criminal Justice/Safety Studies. **Special Study Options:** Accelerated program, cooperative education program, cross-registration, distance learning, double major, dual enrollment, English as a Second Language (ESL), exchange student program (domestic), honors program, independent study, internships, study abroad, teacher certification program, weekend college. Combined degree programs: BA/MA. **Disability Services:** Special programs offered to physically disabled students, including note-taking services, reader services, tape recorders. **Career Services:** Alumni services, Career assessment, Internships.

FACILITIES

Housing: special housing for disabled students, apartments for single students. 90% of campus accessible to physically diasbled. **Special Academic Facilities/Equipment:** Cross-cultural ethnic study center, natural history and cultural museum, solar pond and solar house, electron microscope, atmospheric and acoustic research lab, seismic observatory. **Computers:** Students can register for classes online. Administrative functions (other than registration) can be performed online.

CAMPUS LIFE

Environment: Metropolis. **Activities:** Choral groups, concert band, dance, drama/theater, jazz band, literary magazine, marching band, music ensembles, musical theater, opera, pep band, radio station, student government, student newspaper, student-run film society, symphony orchestra 1 honor society, 1 religious organization. 6 fraternities, 4 sororities. **Athletics (Intercollegiate):** *Men:* basketball, cross-country, football, golf, track/field (outdoor), track/field (indoor). *Women:* basketball, cross-country, golf, riflery, soccer, softball, tennis, track/field (outdoor), track/field (indoor), volleyball.

ADMISSIONS

Freshman Academic Profile: Average high school GPA 3.2. 17% in top 10% of high school class, 40% in top 25% of high school class, 69% in top 50% of high school class. 94% from public high schools. **Reported SAT (pre-2016 redesign) scores:** SAT Math middle 50% range 420-530. SAT Critical Reading middle 50% range 390-500. **Concordant SAT scores:** SAT Math middle 50% range 460–560. ACT middle 50% range 17-22. **Basis for Candidate Selection:** *Important factors considered include:* rigor of secondary school record, class rank, academic GPA, standardized test scores. **Freshman Admission Requirements:** High school diploma is required and GED is accepted. *Academic units required:* 4 English, 4 math, 4 science, 4 science labs, 2 social studies, 4 history, 6 computer science, 1 visual/performing arts. **Freshman Admission Statistics:** 6,240 applied, 99.81% admitted, 70% enrolled. **Transfer Admission Requirements:** college transcript(s), Minimum college GPA of 2.0 required. Lowest grade transferable D. **General Admission Information:** Nonfall registration accepted. Admission may be deferred for a maximum of 1 semester.

COSTS AND FINANCIAL AID

Annual in-state tuition $5,565. Annual out-of-state tuition $16,095. Room and board $8,924. Required fees $1,649. Average book expense $1,160. *Student Employment:* Federal Work-Study Program available. Institutional employment available. **Financial Aid Statistics:** 88% needy freshmen, 88% needy undergrads receive need-based scholarship or grant aid. 26% freshmen, 14% undergrads receive non-need-based scholarship or grant aid. 82% freshmen, 86% undergrads receive need-based self-help aid. 1% freshmen, 1% undergrads receive athletic scholarships. 77% freshmen, 65% undergrads receive any aid.

THE UNIVERSITY OF TEXAS— MEDICAL BRANCH

301 University Boulevard, Galveston, TX 77555-1305
Phone: 409-772-1215 • **Financial Aid Phone:** 409-772-1215
E-mail: enrollment.services@utmb.edu • **CEEB Code:** 6887
Fax: 409-772-4466 • **Website:** www.utmb.edu

This public school was founded in 1891. It has a 85-acre campus.

RATINGS
Admissions Selectivity Rating: 60*   **Fire Safety Rating:** 60*   **Green Rating:** 60*

STUDENTS AND FACULTY

Enrollment: 492. **Student Body:** 80% female, 20% male, 1% out-of-state, 2% international (34 countries represented). Asian 18%, African American 18%, Caucasian 42%, Hispanic 14%, Native American 1%, Pacific Islander 0%, Two or more races 0%, Race unknown 5%.

ACADEMICS

Degrees: bachelor's, doctoral/professional, doctoral/research, master's, post-master's certificate. **Special Study Options:** distance learning, independent study, internships. Combined degree programs: MD/PhD. **Disability Services:** Special programs offered to physically disabled students, including note-taking services, reader services, tape recorders, tutors. **Career Services:** Alumni network, Alumni services, Internships.

FACILITIES

Housing: Coed dorms, fraternity/sorority housing, apartments for married students, apartments for single students. 100% of campus accessible to physically disabled. **Special Academic Facilities/Equipment:** Moody Medical Library **Computers:** Students can register for classes online. Administrative functions (other than registration) can be performed online.

CAMPUS LIFE

Environment: Town. **Activities:** student government, student newspaper, yearbook. 94 registered organizations, 4 honor societies, 7 religious organizations. 5 fraternities. **On-Campus Highlights:** Joe Jamail Student Center, Rosenberg House, Ashbel Smith Building, Alumni Field House, Moody Medical Library.

ADMISSIONS

Minimum paper TOEFL 550. **Transfer Admission Requirements:** college transcript(s), Minimum college GPA of 2.0 required. Lowest grade transferable C.

COSTS AND FINANCIAL AID

Required Forms and Deadlines: FAFSA. **Types of Aid:** *Need-based scholarships/grants:* Federal Pell, FSEOG, State scholarships/grants, Private scholarships, College/university scholarship or grant aid from institutional funds. *Loans:* Direct Subsidized Stafford Loans, Direct Unsubsidized Stafford Loans, Direct PLUS loans, Federal Perkins Loans, Federal Nursing Loans, College/university loans from institutional funds. *Student Employment:* Federal Work-Study Program available. Institutional employment available. **Criteria for awarding aid:** *Need-based:* Academics, Minority status. *Non-need-based:* Academics, Minority status, State/district residency.

THE UNIVERSITY OF TEXAS—PAN AMERICAN

1201 West University Drive, Edinburg, TX 78539-2999
Phone: 956-665-2999 • **Financial Aid Phone:** 956-665-2501
E-mail: admissions@utrgv.edu • **CEEB Code:** 6570
Fax: 956-665-2687 • **Website:** www.utrgv.edu • **ACT Code:** 4142

This public school was founded in 1927. It has a 330-acre campus.

RATINGS
Admissions Selectivity Rating: 76   **Fire Safety Rating:** 79   **Green Rating:** 85

STUDENTS AND FACULTY

Enrollment: 260. **Student Body:** 56% female, 44% male, 0% out-of-state, 0% international (25 countries represented). Asian 1%, African American 2%, Caucasian 13%, Hispanic 67%, Native American <1%, Pacific Islander 0%, Two or more races 0%, Race unknown 16%.
Retention and Graduation: 76% freshmen return for sophomore year.
Faculty: 1,041 full-time faculty, 0% hold PhDs, 54% are are members of minority groups, 41% are women.

ACADEMICS

Degrees: bachelor's, doctoral/research, master's, postbachelor's certificate. **Classes:** Most classes have 30-39 students. Most lab/discussion sessions have 20-29 students. **Most popular majors:** Multi-/Interdisciplinary Studies; Business Administration and Management; Biology/Biological Sciences. **Special Study Options:** Accelerated program, cooperative education program, distance learning, double major, dual enrollment, English as a Second Language (ESL), exchange student program (domestic), honors program, independent study, internships, study abroad, teacher certification program, weekend college. **Honors Programs:** Pre-Medical Honors College with Baylor College of Medicine. Combined degree programs: BA/MA. **Disability Services:** Special programs offered to physically disabled students, including note-taking services, reader services, tape recorders, tutors. **Career Services:** Alumni services, Career assessment, Internships.

FACILITIES

Housing: Coed dorms, men's dorms, women's dorms, apartments for married students, apartments for single students. 95% of campus accessible to physically disabled. **Computers:** Students can register for classes online. Administrative functions (other than registration) can be performed online.

CAMPUS LIFE

Environment: Town. **Activities:** Choral groups, concert band, dance, drama/theater, jazz band, music ensembles, musical theater, pep band, student government, student newspaper, symphony orchestra, Campus Ministries, Student Organization. 80 registered organizations, 9 honor societies, 7 religious organizations. 4 fraternities, 1 sorority. **Athletics (Intercollegiate):** *Men:* baseball, basketball, cross-country, golf, tennis, track/field (outdoor). *Women:* basketball, cross-country, golf, tennis, track/field (outdoor), volleyball. **On-Campus Highlights:** Visitors Center, Science Courtyard, Residence Halls, Student Union **Environmental Initiatives:** The direction of disposal of hazardous waste streams toward recycling or reuse.

ADMISSIONS

Freshman Academic Profile: 17% in top 10% of high school class, 47% in top 25% of high school class, 80% in top 50% of high school class. 99% from public high schools. **Reported SAT (pre-2016 redesign) scores:** SAT Math middle 50% range 430-530. SAT Critical Reading middle 50% range 410-520. SAT Writing middle 50% range 400-500. **Concordant SAT scores:** SAT EBRW middle 50% 450–570. SAT Math middle 50% range 470–560. ACT middle 50% range 17-21. Minimum internet-based TOEFL 63. Minimum paper TOEFL 500. **Basis for Candidate Selection:** *Very important factors considered* include: standardized test scores. *Important factors considered include:* rigor of secondary school record, class rank, academic GPA, level of applicant's interest. **Freshman Admission Requirements:** High school diploma is required and GED is accepted. *Academic units required:* 4 English, 4 math, 4 science, 2 foreign language, and 3 units from above areas or other academic areas. **Freshman Admission Statistics:** 9,055 applied, 82.24% admitted, 56% enrolled. **Transfer Admission Requirements:** college transcript(s), Minimum college GPA of 2.0 required. Lowest grade transferable D. **General Admission Information:** Priority deadline 2/1. Regular application deadline 7/31. Nonfall registration accepted.

COSTS AND FINANCIAL AID

Average book expense $1,194. **Required Forms and Deadlines:** FAFSA. **Notification of Awards:** Applicants will be notified of awards on a rolling basis beginning 3/15. **Types of Aid:** *Need-based scholarships/grants:* Federal Pell, FSEOG, State scholarships/grants, Private scholarships, College/university scholarship or grant aid from institutional funds. *Loans:* Direct Subsidized Stafford Loans, Direct Unsubsidized Stafford Loans, Direct PLUS loans, Federal Perkins Loans, State Loans. *Student Employment:* Federal Work-Study Program available. Institutional employment available. **Financial Aid Statistics:** 98% needy freshmen, 96% needy undergrads receive need-based scholarship or grant aid. 2% freshmen, 11% undergrads receive non-need-based scholarship or grant aid. 29% freshmen, 46% undergrads receive need-based self-help aid. 1% freshmen, 1% undergrads receive athletic scholarships. 62% undergrads borrow to pay for school. Average cumulative indebtedness $16,178. **Criteria for awarding aid:** *Need-based:* Academics, Athletics. *Non-need-based:* Academics, Alumni affiliation, Art, Athletics.

UNIVERSITY OF TORONTO

172 St. George Street, Toronto, ON M5R 0A3
Phone: 416-978-2190
E-mail: admissions.help@utoronto.ca • **CEEB Code:** 982
Fax: 416-978-7022 • **Website:** www.utoronto.ca

This public school was founded in 1827. It has a 1767-acre campus.

RATINGS

Admissions Selectivity Rating: 71   **Fire Safety Rating:** 79   **Green Rating:** 60*

STUDENTS AND FACULTY

Student Body: 55% female, 45% male, 8% out-of-state, (166 countries represented).
Retention and Graduation: 82% freshmen graduate within 6 years. **Faculty:** 5,854 full-time faculty, 0% hold PhDs, 0% are are members of minority groups, 0% are women.

ACADEMICS

Degrees: bachelor's, certificate, diploma, doctoral/professional, doctoral, master's, postbachelor's certificate, post-master's certificate. **Special Study Options:** cooperative education program, double major, English as a Second Language (ESL), exchange student program (domestic), honors program, internships, study abroad, teacher certification program. Combined degree programs: JD/MBA, JD/MA, JD/PhD/, JD/MISt, JD/MSW. **Disability Services:** Special programs offered to physically disabled students, including note-taking services, reader services, tape recorders, tutors. **Career Services:** Career/job search classes.

FACILITIES

Housing: Coed dorms, men's dorms, women's dorms, apartments for married students, cooperative housing **Computers:** Students can register for classes online. Administrative functions (other than registration) can be performed online.

CAMPUS LIFE

Environment: Metropolis. **Activities:** Choral groups, concert band, dance, drama/theater, jazz band, literary magazine, music ensembles, opera, radio station, student government, student newspaper, student-run film society, symphony orchestra 200 registered organizations, 49 religious organizations. **Athletics (Intercollegiate):** *Men:* badminton, baseball, basketball, crew/rowing, cross-country, curling, fencing, football, golf, ice hockey, lacrosse, mountain biking, rugby, skiing (nordic/cross-country), soccer, squash, swimming, tennis, track/field (outdoor), track/field (indoor), volleyball, water polo, wrestling. *Women:* badminton, basketball, crew/rowing, cross-country,

curling, fencing, field hockey, ice hockey, lacrosse, mountain biking, rugby, skiing (nordic/cross-country), soccer, squash, swimming, tennis, track/field (outdoor), track/field (indoor), volleyball, water polo, wrestling. **On-Campus Highlights:** Hart House, The Athletic Centre, Justine Barnike Gallery, Thomas Fisher Rare Book Library, Convocation Hall.

ADMISSIONS

Minimum paper TOEFL 600. **Basis for Candidate Selection:** *Very important factors considered include:* academic GPA, standardized test scores. **Freshman Admission Requirements:** High school diploma is required and GED is accepted. **Freshman Admission Statistics:** 100% enrolled. **Transfer Admission Requirements:** High school transcript, college transcript(s), standardized test scores. **General Admission Information:** Application fee $225. Regular application deadline 3/1. Nonfall registration not accepted.

COSTS AND FINANCIAL AID

Student Employment: Federal Work-Study Program available. Institutional employment available.

THE UNIVERSITY OF TULSA

800 South Tucker Drive, Tulsa, OK 74104
Phone: 918-631-2307 • **Financial Aid Phone:** 918-631-2526
E-mail: admission@utulsa.edu • **CEEB Code:** 6883
Fax: 918-631-5003 • **Website:** utulsa.edu • **ACT Code:** 3444

This private school, affiliated with the Presbyterian Church, was founded in 1894. It has a 209-acre campus.

RATINGS

Admissions Selectivity Rating: 94   **Fire Safety Rating:** 95   **Green Rating:** 83

STUDENTS AND FACULTY

Enrollment: 3,362. **Student Body:** 43% female, 57% male, 42% out-of-state, 24% international (59 countries represented). Asian 4%, African American 5%, Caucasian 57%, Hispanic 5%, Native American 3%, Pacific Islander <1%, Two or more races 1%, Race unknown 2%.
Retention and Graduation: 91% freshmen return for sophomore year. 58% freshmen graduate within 4 years. 73% freshmen graduate within 6 years. 39% grads go on to further study within 1 year. 29% grads pursue arts and sciences degrees. 1% grads pursue law degrees. 16% grads pursue business degrees. 8% grads pursue medical degrees. **Faculty:** Student/faculty ratio 11:1. 348 full-time faculty, 95% hold PhDs, 17% are are members of minority groups, 33% are women. 4% of classes are taught by teaching assistants.

ACADEMICS

Degrees: bachelor's, doctoral/professional, doctoral/research, doctoral, master's, postbachelor's certificate. **Classes:** Most classes have 10-19 students. Most lab/discussion sessions have 20-29 students. **Most popular majors:** Psychology; Finance; Computer Science. **Special Study Options:** Accelerated program, double major, English as a Second Language (ESL), honors program, independent study, internships, liberal arts/career combination, student-designed major, study abroad, teacher certification program. **Honors Programs:** The Honors Program is a four-year course of study consisting of 21 hours of academic credit. In small classes and individual tutorials, students pursue a critical examination of the moral and political commitments, scientific achievments, and artistic sensibilities that have shaped the modern world. The program culminates in the senior year with students designing and executing individual research projects. The Tulsa Undergraduate Research Challenge (TURC) is an innovative program that enables undergraduates to take challenging courses and conduct advanced research with the guidance of top professors. Its aim is to create leaders in scholarship, research, and public life. The centerpiece of the program is research; the goal of such research may be to deliver papers at academic conferences, to produce publishable articles, or to initiate meaningful community projects. Combined degree programs: BA/JD, BA/MA, BA/MEng, Mathematics, Biochemistry, Biology, Chemistry, Geosciences, History, Physics, Women's Studies, Athletic Training, Business, Computer Science, Cyber Security. **Disability Services:** Special programs offered to physically disabled students, including note-taking services, reader services, tape recorders, tutors. **Career Services:** Alumni network, Alumni services, Career/job search classes, Career assessment, Internships, Regional alumni. Internships provide students with the opportunity to supplement classroom training with real-world experience in a position related to their major or career goals. Students may be paid or may receive academic credit or a combination of pay and credit.

FACILITIES

Housing: Coed dorms, special housing for disabled students, men's dorms, women's dorms, fraternity/sorority housing, apartments for married students, apartments for single students, Honors House. 97% of campus accessible to physically disabled. **Special Academic Facilities/Equipment:** Alexandre Hogue Art Gallery, Biotechnology Institute, Center for Communicative Disorders, Charge-Coupled Camera Microscope, Donald W. Reynolds Center (site of a state-of-the-art athletic training program), Education Technology Lab, Electron Microscopes, Kendall Theatre, McFarlin Library Special Collections (focus on American, British, and Irish Literature of the late 19th and early 20th centuries, and on Native American History and Law), Multimedia "board-room" style classrooms (3), ONEOK Multimedia Auditorium, Sadie Adwan Communication Lab, Sidney Born Technical Library (contains an outstanding collection concerning energy, most notably petroleum), Sun Computer Work Stations, World's largest research flow-loop in Petroleum Engr. **Computers:** 100% of classrooms, 100% of dorms, 100% of libraries, 100% of dining areas, 100% of student union, 100% of common outdoor areas have wireless network access. Students can register for classes online. Administrative functions (other than registration) can be performed online.

CAMPUS LIFE

Environment: Metropolis. **Activities:** Choral groups, concert band, dance, drama/theater, jazz band, literary magazine, marching band, music ensembles, musical theater, opera, pep band, radio station, student government, student newspaper, symphony orchestra, television station, yearbook, Campus Ministries, Student Organization. 245 registered organizations, 40 honor societies, 21 religious organizations. 7 fraternities, 9 sororities. **Athletics (Intercollegiate):** *Men:* basketball, cheerleading, cross-country, football, golf, soccer, tennis, track/field (outdoor), track/field (indoor). *Women:* basketball, cheerleading, crew/rowing, cross-country, golf, soccer, softball, tennis, track/field (outdoor), track/field (indoor), volleyball. **On-Campus Highlights:** Collins Fitness Center, Reynolds Center, McFarlin Library, Allen Chapman Activity Center, Fraternity/Sorority Row, Collins College of Business, The College of Engineering and Natural Sciences, Chapman Hall—The College of Arts and Sciences, Phillips Hall—School of Art, Kendall Hall Theatre, Collins Hall—Visitors Center and Office of Admission, H.A. Chapman Stadium. **Environmental Initiatives:** Terracycling: Resident students were looking for a way to recycle items that were not recycled in our campus Single Stream program. They researched for alternatives and found a program called "Terracyling" that they could sign up for and recycle pens, snack bags, tooth paste and floss packaging, as well as other hard to recycle items. They set up "Terracycling Centers" in some of the dorm halls and the fitness center, and the idea quickly spread to the sorority houses.

ADMISSIONS

Freshman Academic Profile: Average high school GPA 3.9. 76% in top 10% of high school class, 93% in top 25% of high school class, 99% in top 50% of high school class. 74% from public high schools. **Reported SAT (pre-2016 redesign) scores:** SAT Math middle 50% range 550-700. SAT Critical Reading middle 50% range 550-690. SAT Writing middle 50% range 520-670. **Concordant SAT scores:** SAT EBRW middle 50% 590-720. SAT Math middle 50% range 570-730. ACT middle 50% range 26-33. Minimum internet-based TOEFL 80. Minimum paper TOEFL 550. **Basis for Candidate Selection:** *Very important factors considered include:* rigor of secondary school record, academic GPA, standardized test scores. *Important factors considered include:* class rank, application essay, recommendation(s), interview, level of applicant's interest. *Other factors considered include:* extracurricular activities, talent/ability, character/personal qualities, first generation, alumni/ae relation, racial/ethnic status, volunteer work, work experience. **Freshman Admission Requirements:** High school diploma is required and GED is accepted. *Academic units recommended:* 4 English, 4 math, 3 science, 3 science labs, 2 foreign language, 3 social studies, 1 computer science, 1 visual/performing arts. **Freshman Admission Statistics:** 8,089 applied, 36.96% admitted, 24% enrolled. **Transfer Admission Requirements:** college transcript(s), essay or personal statement, statement of good standing from prior institution(s). Minimum college GPA of 2.5 required. Lowest grade transferable c. **General Admission Information:** Application fee $50. Priority deadline 2/1. Nonfall registration accepted. Admission may be deferred for a maximum of 1 year.

COSTS AND FINANCIAL AID

Annual tuition $37,580. Room and board $11,116. Required fees $540. Average book expense $1,200. **Required Forms and Deadlines:** FAFSA. **Notification of Awards:** Applicants will be notified of awards on a rolling basis beginning 3/15. **Types of Aid:** *Need-based scholarships/grants:* Federal Pell, FSEOG, State scholarships/grants, Private scholarships, College/university scholarship or grant aid from institutional funds. *Loans:* Direct Subsidized Stafford Loans, Direct Unsubsidized Stafford Loans, Direct PLUS loans, Federal Perkins Loans. *Student Employment:* Federal Work-Study Program available. Institutional employment available. **Financial Aid Statistics:** 33% needy

freshmen, 36% needy undergrads receive need-based scholarship or grant aid. 96% freshmen, 94% undergrads receive non-need-based scholarship or grant aid. 50% freshmen, 54% undergrads receive need-based self-help aid. 12% freshmen, 10% undergrads receive athletic scholarships. 91% freshmen, 86% undergrads receive any aid. 48% undergrads borrow to pay for school. Average cumulative indebtedness $34,136. **Criteria for awarding aid:** *Need-based:* Minority status. *Non-need-based:* Academics, Alumni affiliation, Art, Athletics, Leadership, Minority status, Music/drama, Religious affiliation.

See page 1090.

UNIVERSITY OF UTAH

201 South 1460 East, Salt Lake City, UT 84112
Phone: 801-581-8761 • **Financial Aid Phone:** 801-581-6211
E-mail: admissions@utah.edu • **CEEB Code:** 4853
Fax: 801-585-7864 • **Website:** www.utah.edu • **ACT Code:** 4274

This public school was founded in 1850. It has a 1535-acre campus.

RATINGS

Admissions Selectivity Rating: 85   **Fire Safety Rating:** 89   **Green Rating:** 94

STUDENTS AND FACULTY

Enrollment: 22,748. **Student Body:** 45% female, 55% male, 20% out-of-state, 5% international (93 countries represented). Asian 6%, African American 1%, Caucasian 70%, Hispanic 12%, Native American <1%, Pacific Islander <1%, Two or more races 5%, Race unknown 1%.
Retention and Graduation: 90% freshmen return for sophomore year. 29% freshmen graduate within 4 years. 65% freshmen graduate within 6 years. 26% grads go on to further study within 1 year. **Faculty:** Student/faculty ratio 16:1. 1,500 full-time faculty, 84% hold PhDs, 14% are are members of minority groups, 39% are women. 28% of classes are taught by teaching assistants.

ACADEMICS

Degrees: bachelor's, doctoral/professional, doctoral/research, doctoral, master's, postbachelor's certificate, post-master's certificate. **Classes:** Most classes have 10-19 students. Most lab/discussion sessions have 10-19 students. **Most popular majors:** Psychology; Economics; Communication. **Special Study Options:** Accelerated program, cooperative education program, cross-registration, distance learning, double major, dual enrollment, English as a Second Language (ESL), exchange student program (domestic), honors program, independent study, internships, liberal arts/career combination, student-designed major, study abroad, teacher certification program. **Honors Programs:** The Honors Program promotes an enriched academic environment for talented and highly motivated students. We foster values of social responsibility, inclusiveness and academic quality—in short a community of excellence. The Honors Program provides talented students with an enhanced undergraduate experience through a number of opportunities. Honors students typically enroll in one or two Honors classes each semester during their first two years. This will put students in contact with other students who set high goals for themselves, like to be challenged and are highly motivated. Rather than the large auditorium classes so many freshmen or sophomore students take, honors classes will be small and students will get to know their professors well. Students will have personal, intense advising at key moments in the next four years that will help them plan for graduation with the Honors degree at each step along the way. Combined degree programs: BA/MEng, Mechanical Engineering BS/MS, Computer Science BS/MS, Math BS/MS, Chemistry BS/MS, Economics BS/MPP, Political Science BS/MPP, Nursing BS/MS. **Disability Services:** Special programs offered to physically disabled students, including note-taking services, reader services, tape recorders, tutors. **Career Services:** Alumni network, Alumni services, Career/job search classes, Career assessment, Internships. We have used our Alumni network to develop specific programming to help students explore possible career paths. Specifically, we've hosted "Career Pathways" where we invite alumni from targeted industries to serve on a panel & network with students. Also, we've put on "Career Treks" in which we take groups of students into the community to site visits with employers in given industries.

FACILITIES

Housing: Coed dorms, special housing for disabled students, special housing for international students, fraternity/sorority housing, apartments for married students, Theme Housing, Limited Visitation, 24-hour Quiet, First Year Students only. 90% of campus accessible to physically disabled.

Special Academic Facilities/Equipment: Museums of natural history and fine arts, government institute, environmental biological research facilities, human genetics lab. **Computers:** 100% of classrooms, 100% of dorms, 100% of libraries, 100% of dining areas, 100% of student union, 60% of common outdoor areas have wireless network access. Students can register for classes online. Administrative functions (other than registration) can be performed online.

CAMPUS LIFE

Environment: Metropolis. **Activities:** Choral groups, concert band, dance, drama/theater, jazz band, literary magazine, marching band, music ensembles, musical theater, opera, pep band, radio station, student government, student newspaper, student-run film society, symphony orchestra, television station, Campus Ministries, Student Organization, Model UN. 238 registered organizations, 41 honor societies, 9 religious organizations. 7 fraternities, 6 sororities. **Athletics (Intercollegiate):** *Men:* baseball, basketball, cheerleading, diving, football, golf, skiing (downhill/alpine), skiing (nordic/cross-country), swimming, tennis. *Women:* basketball, cheerleading, cross-country, diving, gymnastics, skiing (downhill/alpine), skiing (nordic/cross-country), soccer, softball, swimming, tennis, track/field (outdoor), track/field (indoor), volleyball. **On-Campus Highlights:** Rice Eccles Stadium, Jon M. Huntsman Center, Huntsman Cancer Institute, Utah Museum of Fine Arts, Utah Museum of Natural History, Marriott Library Red Butte Gardens Olympic Cauldron Park Fort Douglas Museum and Cemetery Kingsbury Hall/Gardner Hall. **Environmental Initiatives:** Transportation: Free public transportation (Ed-Pass) for all students, staff and faculty; gas-electric hybrid, biodiesel, and natural gas-powered campus vehicles.

ADMISSIONS

Freshman Academic Profile: Average high school GPA 3.6. 35% in top 10% of high school class, 62% in top 25% of high school class, 85% in top 50% of high school class. 91% from public high schools. **Reported SAT (pre-2016 redesign) scores:** SAT Math middle 50% range 530-660. SAT Critical Reading middle 50% range 520-640. SAT Writing middle 50% range 500-620. **Concordant SAT scores:** SAT EBRW middle 50% 570-680. SAT Math middle 50% range 560–690. ACT middle 50% range 21-27. Minimum internet-based TOEFL 80. Minimum paper TOEFL 550. **Basis for Candidate Selection:** *Very important factors considered include:* rigor of secondary school record. *Important factors considered include:* academic GPA, standardized test scores, extracurricular activities, talent/ability, character/personal qualities. *Other factors considered include:* class rank, first generation, alumni/ae relation, geographical residence, state residency, racial/ethnic status, volunteer work, work experience, level of applicant's interest. **Freshman Admission Requirements:** High school diploma is required and GED is accepted. *Academic units required:* 4 English, 2 math, 3 science, 1 science lab, 2 foreign language, 1 history, 4 academic electives. *Academic units recommended:* 4 English, 4 math, 3 science, 2 science labs, 3 foreign language, 1 social studies, 2 history, 4 academic electives. **Freshman Admission Statistics:** 14,308 applied, 76.42% admitted, 33% enrolled. **Transfer Admission Requirements:** college transcript(s), statement of good standing from prior institution(s). Minimum college GPA of 2.6 required. Lowest grade transferable D-. **General Admission Information:** Application fee $45. Priority deadline 12/1. Regular application deadline 4/1. Nonfall registration accepted. Admission may be deferred for a maximum of 7 semesters.

COSTS AND FINANCIAL AID

Required Forms and Deadlines: FAFSA. **Notification of Awards:** Applicants will be notified of awards on a rolling basis beginning 4/1. **Types of Aid:** *Need-based scholarships/grants:* Federal Pell, FSEOG, State scholarships/grants, Private scholarships, College/university scholarship or grant aid from institutional funds, Federal Nursing Scholarships. *Loans:* Direct Subsidized Stafford Loans, Direct Unsubsidized Stafford Loans, Direct PLUS loans, Federal Perkins Loans, Federal Nursing Loans, State Loans, College/university loans from institutional funds. *Student Employment:* Federal Work-Study Program available. Institutional employment available. **Financial Aid Statistics:** 88% needy freshmen, 82% needy undergrads receive need-based scholarship or grant aid. 16% freshmen, 7% undergrads receive non-need-based scholarship or grant aid. 79% freshmen, 90% undergrads receive need-based self-help aid. 2% freshmen, 2% undergrads receive athletic scholarships. 75% freshmen, 64% undergrads receive any aid. 39% undergrads borrow to pay for school. Average cumulative indebtedness $21,081. **Criteria for awarding aid:** *Non-need-based:* Academics, Alumni affiliation, Art, Athletics, Leadership, Minority status, Music/drama, State/district residency.

UNIVERSITY OF VERMONT

University of Vermont Admissions, Burlington, VT 05401-3596
Phone: 802-656-3370 • **Financial Aid Phone:** 802-656-5700
E-mail: admissions@uvm.edu • **CEEB Code:** 3920
Fax: 802-656-8611 • **Website:** www.uvm.edu • **ACT Code:** 4322

This public school was founded in 1791. It has a 460-acre campus.

RATINGS
Admissions Selectivity Rating: 87   **Fire Safety Rating:** 97   **Green Rating:** 99

STUDENTS AND FACULTY

Enrollment: 10,081. **Student Body:** 56% female, 44% male, 71% out-of-state, 4% international (40 countries represented). Asian 3%, African American 1%, Caucasian 82%, Hispanic 4%, Native American <1%, Pacific Islander <1%, Two or more races 3%, Race unknown 3%.
Retention and Graduation: 86% freshmen return for sophomore year. 68% freshmen graduate within 4 years. 77% freshmen graduate within 6 years. 24% grads go on to further study within 1 year. 6% grads pursue arts and sciences degrees. 2% grads pursue law degrees. 1% grads pursue business degrees. 1% grads pursue medical degrees. **Faculty:** Student/faculty ratio 17:1. 609 full-time faculty, 86% hold PhDs, 15% are are members of minority groups, 47% are women. 2% of classes are taught by teaching assistants.

ACADEMICS

Degrees: bachelor's, doctoral/professional, doctoral/research, master's, postbachelor's certificate, post-master's certificate. **Classes:** Most classes have 10-19 students. Most lab/discussion sessions have 10-19 students. **Most popular majors:** Business Administration and Management; Environmental Studies; Mechanical Engineering. **Special Study Options:** cooperative education program, distance learning, double major, dual enrollment, exchange student program (domestic), honors program, independent study, internships, liberal arts/career combination, student-designed major, study abroad, teacher certification program, Evening University option in several programs. **Honors Programs:** University wide Honors College, a residential learning community where students live together and take classes in one of UVM's newest residence halls. Honors College students are simultaneously enrolled in one of seven other UVM undergraduate colleges or schools. Honors College courses comprise approximately 20% of a students overall coursework and include a year-long common first year seminar, a choice of a variety of sophomore seminars, a junior year thesis prep course, and a senior year thesis, creative project or practicum. Upon graduation program completers are designated as Honors College Scholars. Combined degree programs: BA/JD, BS/DVM with Tufts University, BA/BS-DPT,BS/BVetSCI with Massey U, NZ. **Disability Services:** Special programs offered to physically disabled students, including note-taking services, reader services, tape recorders, tutors. **Career Services:** Alumni network, Alumni services, Career/job search classes, Career assessment, Internships, Regional alumni. Dollar Enterprise, an award winning service learning activity in which students are provided with $1 of working capital and develop and run a campus based entrepreneurial activity for one week. The activity is done for one week. All profits are donated to a charity of the group's choice.

FACILITIES

Housing: Coed dorms, fraternity/sorority housing, apartments for married students, apartments for single students, Wellness Housing, Theme Housing. 90% of campus accessible to physically diasbled. **Special Academic Facilities/ Equipment:** Art/ethnography museum, chemistry/physics library, medical library, on-campus preschool, government research and world affairs centers, agricultural experiment station, horse farm, multinuclear magnetic resonance spectrometers, mass spectrometer. **Computers:** 10% of classrooms, 15% of dorms, 100% of libraries, 100% of dining areas, 100% of student union, 5% of common outdoor areas have wireless network access. Students can register for classes online. Administrative functions (other than registration) can be performed online.

CAMPUS LIFE

Environment: Town. **Activities:** Choral groups, concert band, dance, drama/theater, jazz band, literary magazine, music ensembles, musical theater, pep band, radio station, student government, student newspaper, student-run film society, symphony orchestra, television station, Campus Ministries, Student Organization. 140 registered organizations, 30 honor societies, 10 religious organizations. 9 fraternities, 6 sororities. **Athletics (Intercollegiate):** *Men:* basketball, cross-country, ice hockey, lacrosse, skiing (downhill/alpine), skiing (nordic/cross-country), soccer, track/field (outdoor), track/field (indoor). *Women:* basketball, cross-country, diving, field hockey, ice hockey, lacrosse, skiing (downhill/alpine), skiing (nordic/cross-country), soccer, swimming, track/field (outdoor), track/field (indoor). **On-Campus Highlights:** Davis Student Center, Fleming Museum, Campus Green, Athletic Complex/Fitness Center, Spear Street Research Farm and Equine Center. **Environmental Initiatives:** Reporting jointly to the Associate Vice Provost for Teaching & Learning and the VP for Financen, the Office of Sustainability supports the infusion of sustainability into operations, student life, curriculum, and communications, managing University commitments for energy, food, and sustainability education.

ADMISSIONS

Freshman Academic Profile: Average high school GPA 3.5. 32% in top 10% of high school class, 74% in top 25% of high school class, 96% in top 50% of high school class. 70% from public high schools. **Reported SAT (pre-2016 redesign) scores:** SAT Math middle 50% range 550-640. SAT Critical Reading middle 50% range 550-650. SAT Writing middle 50% range 540-650. **Concordant SAT scores:** SAT EBRW middle 50% 600–700. SAT Math middle 50% range 570–660. ACT middle 50% range 25-30. Minimum internet-based TOEFL 79. Minimum paper TOEFL 550. **Basis for Candidate Selection:** *Very important factors considered include:* rigor of secondary school record. *Important factors considered include:* class rank, academic GPA, standardized test scores, application essay, character/personal qualities, state residency. *Other factors considered include:* extracurricular activities, talent/ability, first generation, alumni/ae relation, geographical residence, racial/ethnic status, volunteer work, work experience, level of applicant's interest. **Freshman Admission Requirements:** High school diploma is required and GED is accepted. *Academic units required:* 4 English, 3 math, 2 science, 1 science lab, 2 foreign language, 3 social studies. **Freshman Admission Statistics:** 25,274 applied, 70.85% admitted, 13% enrolled. **Transfer Admission Requirements:** High school transcript, college transcript(s), essay or personal statement, Minimum college GPA of 2.5 required. Lowest grade transferable C. **General Admission Information:** Application fee $55. Regular application deadline 1/15. Regular notification 3/31. Nonfall registration accepted. Admission may be deferred for a maximum of 12 months.

COSTS AND FINANCIAL AID

Annual in-state tuition $14,664. Annual out-of-state tuition $37,056. Room and board $11,150. Required fees $2,104. Average book expense $1,200. **Required Forms and Deadlines:** FAFSA. **Notification of Awards:** Applicants will be notified of awards on a rolling basis beginning 3/31. **Types of Aid:** *Need-based scholarships/grants:* Federal Pell, FSEOG, State scholarships/grants, Private scholarships, College/university scholarship or grant aid from institutional funds, Federal Nursing Scholarships. *Loans:* Direct Subsidized Stafford Loans, Direct Unsubsidized Stafford Loans, Direct PLUS loans, Federal Perkins Loans, Federal Nursing Loans, College/university loans from institutional funds. *Student Employment:* Federal Work-Study Program available. Institutional employment available. **Financial Aid Statistics:** 99% needy freshmen, 97% needy undergrads receive need-based scholarship or grant aid. 12% freshmen, 8% undergrads receive non-need-based scholarship or grant aid. 69% freshmen, 74% undergrads receive need-based self-help aid. 2% freshmen, 2% undergrads receive athletic scholarships. 93% freshmen, 83% undergrads receive any aid. 61% undergrads borrow to pay for school. Average cumulative indebtedness $27,006. **Criteria for awarding aid:** *Need-based:* Academics, Athletics, Leadership, Minority status, Music/drama. *Non-need-based:* Academics, Alumni affiliation, Athletics, Leadership, Minority status, Music/drama, State/district residency.

UNIVERSITY OF VIRGINIA

Office of Admission, Charlottesville, VA 22906
Phone: 434-982-3200 • **Financial Aid Phone:** 434-982-4757
E-mail: undergradadmission@virginia.edu • **CEEB Code:** 5820
Fax: 434-924-3587 • **Website:** www.virginia.edu • **ACT Code:** 4412

This public school was founded in 1819. It has a 1167-acre campus.

RATINGS

Admissions Selectivity Rating: 97   **Fire Safety Rating:** 88   **Green Rating:** 97

STUDENTS AND FACULTY

Enrollment: 15,844. **Student Body:** 54% female, 46% male, 27% out-of-state, 5% international (118 countries represented). Asian 13%, African American 7%,

Caucasian 59%, Hispanic 6%, Native American <1%, Pacific Islander <1%, Two or more races 4%, Race unknown 6%.
Retention and Graduation: 96% freshmen return for sophomore year. 88% freshmen graduate within 4 years. 94% freshmen graduate within 6 years.
Faculty: Student/faculty ratio 15:1. 1,438 full-time faculty, 91% hold PhDs, 17% are are members of minority groups, 38% are women. 7% of classes are taught by teaching assistants.

ACADEMICS

Degrees: bachelor's, doctoral/professional, doctoral/research, master's, post-master's certificate. **Classes:** Most classes have 10-19 students. Most lab/discussion sessions have 20-29 students. **Most popular majors:** Business/Commerce; Biology/Biological Sciences; Economics. **Special Study Options:** Accelerated program, cooperative education program, double major, English as a Second Language (ESL), exchange student program (domestic), honors program, independent study, internships, liberal arts/career combination, student-designed major, study abroad, teacher certification program, Special January term (during Winter Break) where students can take one course. Semester at Sea option of spending an academic semester on board a ship travelling to multiple countries. **Honors Programs:** Jefferson Scholars: Full scholarship given to approximately 30 students per year. Special lectures and discussions with distinguished University faculty; all first year Jefferson Scholars take part in an outdoor leadership experience; all rising-second year Jefferson Scholars, prior to the beginning of school, participate in a two-week Institute for Leadership and Citizenship designed to foster a deeper understanding of the art of leadership and the importance of citizenship. Additionally, all Jefferson Scholars are granted an opportunity to travel and study abroad between their second and third year. Scholars may elect to spend three weeks of study at either Regent's College in England or the Erasmus Institute in Tuscany, Italy. Following the structured tutorial, each Scholar designs and completes two weeks of travel and independent inquiry. Echols Scholars-School of Arts and Sciences. Separate dormitory, with Rodman Scholars, for first-year students. Flexible degree requirements; exemption from some requirements; preference for courses. Rodman Scholars-School of Engineering and Applied Sciences. Separate dormitory, with Echols Scholars, for first-year students. Special courses designed only for Rodman Scholars in first two years. Combined degree programs: 5-year B.A./M.Teaching. **Disability Services:** Special programs offered to physically disabled students, including note-taking services, reader services, tape recorders, tutors. **Career Services:** Alumni network, Alumni services, Career/job search classes, Career assessment, Internships, Regional alumni. (a tie) (1) on-grounds interviewing because, for our size school, we not only have an exceedingly robust program (6,000 to 10,000 individual student interviews per year; and most of the top tier organizations you'd find listed in the Fortune 100), but also because student interviews here are very often evenly distributed among the College, Commerce, and SEAS (Engineering School); and, (2) the dramatic growth and popularity of our internship programs among our students—not only corporate internships, but also non-profit/public policy/community service internships, an initiative you rarely find on a large public university campus.

FACILITIES

Housing: Coed dorms, special housing for international students, fraternity/sorority housing, apartments for married students, apartments for single students, Theme Housing, French, German, Spanish and Russian houses, a multi-lingual house, and three residential colleges. 100% of campus accessible to physically diasbled. **Special Academic Facilities/Equipment:** 15 libraries, art museum, experimental farm, biological station, observatory/planetarium, nuclear information center, media center (multimedia editing). **Computers:** 100% of classrooms, 100% of dorms, 100% of libraries, 100% of dining areas, 100% of student union, 26-50% of common outdoor areas have wireless network access. Students can register for classes online. Administrative functions (other than registration) can be performed online.

CAMPUS LIFE

Environment: City. **Activities:** Choral groups, concert band, dance, drama/theater, jazz band, literary magazine, marching band, music ensembles, musical theater, opera, pep band, radio station, student government, student newspaper, student-run film society, symphony orchestra, television station, Campus Ministries, Student Organization, Model UN. 7 honor societies, 44 religious organizations. 28 fraternities, 15 sororities. **Athletics (Intercollegiate):** *Men:* baseball, basketball, cross-country, diving, football, golf, lacrosse, soccer, swimming, tennis, track/field (outdoor), track/field (indoor), wrestling. *Women:* basketball, crew/rowing, cross-country, diving, field hockey, golf, lacrosse, soccer, softball, swimming, tennis, track/field (outdoor), track/field (indoor), volleyball. **On-Campus Highlights:** Rotunda/Academical Village (orig campus), Alderman and Clemons Libraries, John Paul Jones Arena, Football and Soccer Stadiums, Aquatic and Fitness Center, Location of the future "arts precinct;" new library housing original rare and early American manuscripts; Birdwood Golf Course; Observatory; Old Cabell Hall (music performances); Culbreth Theatre (drama); Newcomb Hall (student services building); University of Virginia Bookstore. **Environmental Initiatives:** Academics: The University of Virginia offers 70+ courses in 8 different schools with significant focus on sustainability, including a global sustainability course, a new course model cross listed and taught jointly by faculty from Engineering, Architecture, and Commerce. In Spring 2011, the University created the interdisciplinary Global Sustainability minor.

ADMISSIONS

Freshman Academic Profile: Average high school GPA 4.2. 88% in top 10% of high school class, 98% in top 25% of high school class, 100% in top 50% of high school class. 70% from public high schools. **Reported SAT (pre-2016 redesign) scores:** SAT Math middle 50% range 620-740. SAT Critical Reading middle 50% range 620-720. SAT Writing middle 50% range 610-730. **Concordant SAT scores:** SAT EBRW middle 50% 670–750. SAT Math middle 50% range 640–760. ACT middle 50% range 29-33. **Basis for Candidate Selection:** *Very important factors considered include:* rigor of secondary school record, class rank, academic GPA, recommendation(s), first generation, alumni/ae relation, state residency, racial/ethnic status. *Important factors considered include:* standardized test scores, application essay, extracurricular activities, talent/ability, character/personal qualities. *Other factors considered include:* geographical residence, volunteer work, work experience. **Freshman Admission Requirements:** High school diploma is required and GED is accepted. *Academic units required:* 4 English, 4 math, 2 science, 2 foreign language, 1 social studies. *Academic units recommended:* 5 math, 4 science, 5 foreign language, 4 social studies. **Freshman Admission Statistics:** 32,377 applied, 29.86% admitted, 38% enrolled. **Transfer Admission Requirements:** High school transcript, college transcript(s), essay or personal statement, standardized test scores, statement of good standing from prior institution(s). Minimum college GPA of 2.0 required. Lowest grade transferable C. **General Admission Information:** Application fee $60. Regular application deadline 1/1. Regular notification 4/1. Nonfall registration not accepted. Admission may be deferred for a maximum of 1 year.

COSTS AND FINANCIAL AID

Annual in-state tuition $12,496. Annual out-of-state tuition $42,643. Room and board $10,726. Required fees $3,354. Average book expense $1,294. **Required Forms and Deadlines:** FAFSA, CSS/Financial Aid PROFILE. **Notification of Awards:** Applicants will be notified of awards on or about 4/5. **Types of Aid:** *Need-based scholarships/grants:* Federal Pell, FSEOG, State scholarships/grants, Private scholarships, College/university scholarship or grant aid from institutional funds, Federal Nursing Scholarships. *Loans:* Direct Subsidized Stafford Loans, Direct Unsubsidized Stafford Loans, Direct PLUS loans, Federal Perkins Loans, Federal Nursing Loans, College/university loans from institutional funds. *Student Employment:* Federal Work-Study Program available. Institutional employment available. **Financial Aid Statistics:** 85% needy freshmen, 84% needy undergrads receive need-based scholarship or grant aid. 7% freshmen, 7% undergrads receive non-need-based scholarship or grant aid. 62% freshmen, 64% undergrads receive need-based self-help aid. 3% freshmen, 3% undergrads receive athletic scholarships. 55% freshmen, 50% undergrads receive any aid. 33% undergrads borrow to pay for school. Average cumulative indebtedness $24,598. **Criteria for awarding aid:** *Need-based:* Academics, Leadership, Minority status. *Non-need-based:* Academics, Athletics, Leadership, Minority status, Music/drama, State/district residency.

UNIVERSITY OF VIRGINIA'S COLLEGE AT WISE

1 College Avenue, Wise, VA 24293
Phone: 276-328-0102
E-mail: admissions@uvawise.edu • **CEEB Code:** 5124
Fax: 276-328-0251 • **Website:** www.uvawise.edu • **ACT Code:** 4343

This public school was founded in 1954. It has a 367-acre campus.

RATINGS

Admissions Selectivity Rating: 78   **Fire Safety Rating:** 60*   **Green Rating:** 60*

STUDENTS AND FACULTY

Enrollment: 1,629. **Student Body:** 52% female, 48% male, 5% out-of-state, <1% international. Asian 1%, African American 7%, Caucasian 90%, Hispanic 2%, Native American <1%, Pacific Islander 0%, Two or more races 0%, Race unknown 0%.
Retention and Graduation: 73% freshmen return for sophomore year. 25% freshmen graduate within 4 years. 44% freshmen graduate within 6 years. 14% grads go on to further study within 1 year. 7% grads pursue arts and sciences degrees. 6% grads pursue law degrees. 4% grads pursue business degrees. 1% grads pursue medical degrees. **Faculty:** Student/faculty ratio 16:1. 91 full-time faculty, 29% hold PhDs, 13% are are members of minority groups, 41% are women. 0% of classes are taught by teaching assistants.

ACADEMICS

Degrees: bachelor's. **Classes:** Most classes have 10-19 students. Most lab/discussion sessions have 10-19 students. **Special Study Options:** Accelerated program, cooperative education program, distance learning, double major, dual enrollment, honors program, independent study, internships, student-designed major, study abroad, teacher certification program. **Disability Services:** Special programs offered to physically disabled students, including note-taking services, reader services, tape recorders, tutors. **Career Services:** Alumni services, Career/job search classes, Career assessment, Internships.

FACILITIES

Housing: Coed dorms, special housing for disabled students, men's dorms, women's dorms, apartments for single students. 95% of campus accessible to physically diasbled. **Computers:** Administrative functions (other than registration) can be performed online.

CAMPUS LIFE

Environment: Rural. **Activities:** Choral groups, concert band, dance, drama/theater, literary magazine, music ensembles, musical theater, pep band, radio station, student government, student newspaper, television station, yearbook. 40 registered organizations, 3 honor societies, 3 religious organizations. 3 fraternities, 2 sororities. **Athletics (Intercollegiate):** *Men:* baseball, basketball, cross-country, football, golf, tennis, track/field (outdoor). *Women:* basketball, cross-country, softball, tennis, track/field (outdoor), volleyball.

ADMISSIONS

Freshman Academic Profile: Average high school GPA 3.3. 18% in top 10% of high school class, 40% in top 25% of high school class, 78% in top 50% of high school class. 99% from public high schools. **Reported SAT (pre-2016 redesign) scores:** SAT Math middle 50% range 430-530. SAT Critical Reading middle 50% range 420-530. **Concordant SAT scores:** SAT Math middle 50% range 470–560. ACT middle 50% range 16-21. Minimum paper TOEFL 550. **Basis for Candidate Selection:** *Very important factors considered include:* rigor of secondary school record, class rank. *Important factors considered include:* standardized test scores, talent/ability. *Other factors considered include:* application essay, recommendation(s), interview, extracurricular activities, character/personal qualities, racial/ethnic status, volunteer work, work experience. **Freshman Admission Requirements:** High school diploma is required and GED is accepted. *Academic units required:* 4 English, 3 math, 2 science, 2 science labs, 2 foreign language, 1 social studies, 1 history, 5 academic electives. **Freshman Admission Statistics:** 987 applied, 77.61% admitted, 52% enrolled. **Transfer Admission Requirements:** college transcript(s), Minimum college GPA of 2.3 required. Lowest grade transferable C-. **General Admission Information:** Application fee $25. Priority deadline 4/1. Regular application deadline 8/1. Nonfall registration accepted. Admission may be deferred for a maximum of 1 year.

COSTS AND FINANCIAL AID

Required Forms and Deadlines: FAFSA. **Notification of Awards:** Applicants will be notified of awards on a rolling basis beginning 4/1. **Types of Aid:** *Need-based scholarships/grants:* Federal Pell, FSEOG, State scholarships/grants, Private scholarships, College/university scholarship or grant aid from institutional funds. *Loans:* Federal Perkins Loans, State Loans, College/university loans from institutional funds. *Student Employment:* Federal Work-Study Program available. Institutional employment available. **Criteria for awarding aid:** *Need-based:* Academics, Alumni affiliation, Athletics, Leadership, Minority status. *Non-need-based:* Academics, Alumni affiliation, Art, Athletics, Job skills, Leadership, Music/drama, State/district residency.

UNIVERSITY OF WASHINGTON

1410 NE Campus Parkway, Seattle, WA 98195-5852
Phone: 206-543-9686 • **Financial Aid Phone:** 206-543-6101 • **CEEB Code:** 4854
Fax: 206-685-3655 • **Website:** www.washington.edu • **ACT Code:** 4484

This public school was founded in 1861. It has a 700-acre campus.

RATINGS

Admissions Selectivity Rating: 91   **Fire Safety Rating:** 95   **Green Rating:** 99

STUDENTS AND FACULTY

Enrollment: 29,990. **Student Body:** 52% female, 48% male, 17% out-of-state, 15% international (83 countries represented). Asian 25%, African American 3%,

Caucasian 41%, Hispanic 8%, Native American <1%, Pacific Islander <1%, Two or more races 7%, Race unknown 1%.
Retention and Graduation: 94% freshmen return for sophomore year. 65% freshmen graduate within 4 years. 84% freshmen graduate within 6 years.
Faculty: Student/faculty ratio 11:1. 3,307 full-time faculty, 90% hold PhDs, 23% are are members of minority groups, 41% are women.

ACADEMICS
Degrees: bachelor's, doctoral/professional, doctoral/research, doctoral, master's, post-master's certificate. **Classes:** Most classes have 20-29 students. Most lab/discussion sessions have 20-29 students. **Most popular majors:** Business Administration and Management; Computer Science; Engineering. **Special Study Options:** cooperative education program, distance learning, double major, English as a Second Language (ESL), exchange student program (domestic), honors program, independent study, internships, student-designed major, study abroad, teacher certification program, Friday Harbor Labs. **Honors Programs:** We have a University Honors Program, as well as departmental honors options. Combined degree programs: Both Pharmacy and Architecture offer combined-degree programs. **Disability Services:** Special programs offered to physically disabled students, including note-taking services, reader services, tape recorders, tutors. **Career Services:** Alumni network, Alumni services, Career/job search classes, Career assessment, Internships, Regional alumni.

FACILITIES
Housing: Coed dorms, special housing for disabled students, special housing for international students, fraternity/sorority housing, apartments for married students, apartments for single students, Theme Housing. 100% of campus accessible to physically diasbled. **Special Academic Facilities/Equipment:** Multiple art galleries, an anthropology and natural history museum, arboretum, closed-circuit TV studio. **Computers:** 100% of dorms, 100% of libraries, 100% of student union, have wireless network access. Students can register for classes online. Administrative functions (other than registration) can be performed online.

CAMPUS LIFE
Environment: Metropolis. **Activities:** Choral groups, concert band, dance, drama/theater, jazz band, literary magazine, marching band, music ensembles, musical theater, opera, pep band, radio station, student government, student newspaper, student-run film society, symphony orchestra, television station, Campus Ministries, Student Organization, Model UN. 711 registered organizations, 13 honor societies, 52 religious organizations. 31 fraternities, 16 sororities. **Athletics (Intercollegiate):** *Men:* baseball, basketball, crew/rowing, cross-country, football, golf, soccer, tennis, track/field (outdoor). *Women:* basketball, crew/rowing, cross-country, golf, gymnastics, soccer, softball, tennis, track/field (outdoor), volleyball. **On-Campus Highlights:** Henry Art Gallery, Burke Museum, Meany Hall for Performing Arts, football games at Husky Stadium, Waterfront Activities Center (WAC). **Environmental Initiatives:** College of the Environment http://coenv.washington.edu/

ADMISSIONS
Freshman Academic Profile: Average high school GPA 3.8. **Reported SAT (pre-2016 redesign) scores:** SAT Math middle 50% range 580-710. SAT Critical Reading middle 50% range 540-660. SAT Writing middle 50% range 540-660. **Concordant SAT scores:** SAT EBRW middle 50% 600–700. SAT Math middle 50% range 600–740. ACT middle 50% range 26-32. Minimum internet-based TOEFL 76. Minimum paper TOEFL 540. **Basis for Candidate Selection:** *Very important factors considered include:* rigor of secondary school record, academic GPA, application essay. *Important factors considered include:* standardized test scores, extracurricular activities, talent/ability, first generation, volunteer work, work experience. *Other factors considered include:* character/personal qualities, state residency. **Freshman Admission Requirements:** High school diploma or equivalent is not required. **Freshman Admission Statistics:** 43,517 applied, 45.35% admitted, 33% enrolled. **Transfer Admission Requirements:** High school transcript, college transcript(s), essay or personal statement, Minimum college GPA of 2.5 required. Lowest grade transferable.7. **General Admission Information:** Nonfall registration accepted.

COSTS AND FINANCIAL AID
Annual in-state tuition $9,694. Annual out-of-state tuition $33,732. Room and board $11,691. Required fees $1,059. Average book expense $825. **Required Forms and Deadlines:** FAFSA. **Notification of Awards:** Applicants will be notified of awards on or about 4/1. **Types of Aid:** *Need-based scholarships/grants:* Federal Pell, FSEOG, State scholarships/grants, Private scholarships, College/university scholarship or grant aid from institutional funds. *Loans:* Direct Subsidized Stafford Loans, Direct Unsubsidized Stafford Loans, Direct PLUS loans, Federal Perkins Loans, Federal Nursing Loans. *Student Employment:* Federal Work-Study Program available. Institutional employment available. **Financial Aid Statistics:** 74% needy freshmen, 77% needy undergrads receive need-based scholarship or grant aid. 15% freshmen, 6% undergrads receive non-need-based scholarship or grant aid. 79% freshmen,

81% undergrads receive need-based self-help aid. 1% freshmen, 1% undergrads receive athletic scholarships. 60% freshmen, 60% undergrads receive any aid. 40% undergrads borrow to pay for school. Average cumulative indebtedness $21,900. **Criteria for awarding aid:** *Need-based:* Academics, Art, Leadership, Music/drama. *Non-need-based:* Academics, Alumni affiliation, Art, Athletics, Leadership, Music/drama, State/district residency.

UNIVERSITY OF WASHINGTON—BOTHELL

Office of Admissions, Bothell, WA 98011
Phone: 425-352-5000 • **Financial Aid Phone:** 425-352-5240
E-mail: uwbinfo@uw.edu • **CEEB Code:** 4467
Fax: 425-352-5455 • **Website:** www.uwb.edu • **ACT Code:** 4497

RATINGS
Admissions Selectivity Rating: 73 **Fire Safety Rating:** 60* **Green Rating:** 60*

STUDENTS AND FACULTY
Enrollment: 4,660. **Student Body:** 50% female, 50% male, 2% out-of-state, 8% international. Asian 26%, African American 6%, Caucasian 42%, Hispanic 9%, Native American <1%, Pacific Islander 1%, Two or more races 6%, Race unknown 1%.
Retention and Graduation: 84% freshmen return for sophomore year. 41% freshmen graduate within 4 years. 70% freshmen graduate within 6 years.

ACADEMICS
Degrees: bachelor's, master's. **Career Services:** Alumni network, Alumni services, Career/job search classes, Career assessment, Internships, Regional alumni. career/job search classes.

ADMISSIONS
Freshman Academic Profile: Average high school GPA 3.3. **Reported SAT (pre-2016 redesign) scores:** SAT Math middle 50% range 470-590. SAT Critical Reading middle 50% range 450-570. SAT Writing middle 50% range 430-550. **Concordant SAT scores:** SAT EBRW middle 50% 490–620. SAT Math middle 50% range 510–610. ACT middle 50% range 19-25. **Basis for Candidate Selection:** *Very important factors considered include:* rigor of secondary school record, academic GPA, standardized test scores, application essay, character/personal qualities. *Important factors considered include:* extracurricular activities, volunteer work, work experience, level of applicant's interest. *Other factors considered include:* recommendation(s), talent/ability. **Freshman Admission Requirements:** *Academic units required:* 4 English, 4 math, 2 science, 2 science labs, 2 foreign language, 3 social studies. *Academic units recommended:* 4 English, 4 math, 4 science, 3 science labs, 2 foreign language, 4 social studies, 1 visual/performing arts. **Freshman Admission Statistics:** 2,840 applied, 78.73% admitted, 31% enrolled. **General Admission Information:** Application fee $60. Nonfall registration accepted. Admission may be deferred.

COSTS AND FINANCIAL AID
Annual in-state tuition $10,690. Annual out-of-state tuition $34,728. Room and board $10,833. Average book expense $825. **Required Forms and Deadlines:** FAFSA. **Notification of Awards:** Applicants will be notified of awards on or about 4/1. **Types of Aid:** *Need-based scholarships/grants:* Federal Pell, FSEOG, State scholarships/grants, Private scholarships, College/university scholarship or grant aid from institutional funds. *Loans:* Direct Subsidized Stafford Loans, Direct Unsubsidized Stafford Loans, Direct PLUS loans, Federal Perkins Loans, Federal Nursing Loans. *Student Employment:* Federal Work-Study Program available. Institutional employment available. **Financial Aid Statistics:** 87% needy freshmen, 96% needy undergrads receive need-based scholarship or grant aid. 3% freshmen, 1% undergrads receive non-need-based scholarship or grant aid. 61% freshmen, 68% undergrads receive need-based self-help aid. 0% freshmen, 0% undergrads receive athletic scholarships. 52% undergrads borrow to pay for school. Average cumulative indebtedness $19,900. **Criteria for awarding aid:** *Need-based:* Academics, Art, Leadership, Music/drama. *Non-need-based:* Academics, Alumni affiliation, Art, Athletics, Leadership, Music/drama, State/district residency.

UNIVERSITY OF WASHINGTON—TACOMA

1900 Commerce Campus, Tacoma, WA, 98402-3100
Phone: 253-692-4742 • **Financial Aid Phone:** 253-692-4374
E-mail: uwtinfo@uw.edu • **Website:** http://www.tacoma.uw.edu/

RATINGS

Admissions Selectivity Rating: 60*   **Fire Safety Rating:** 60*   **Green Rating:** 60*

STUDENTS AND FACULTY

Faculty:

ACADEMICS

Degrees: bachelor's, master's.

ADMISSIONS

Basis for Candidate Selection: *Very important factors considered include:* rigor of secondary school record, academic GPA. *Important factors considered include:* standardized test scores, application essay. *Other factors considered include:* extracurricular activities, talent/ability, character/personal qualities, first generation, volunteer work, work experience, level of applicant's interest. **Freshman Admission Requirements:** *Academic units required:* 4 English, 3 math, 2 science, 2 science labs, 2 foreign language, 3 social studies, and 1 unit from above areas or other academic areas. **General Admission Information:** Application fee $60. Priority deadline 1/15. Regular application deadline 6/30. Nonfall registration accepted. Admission may be deferred for a maximum of 4 quarters.

COSTS AND FINANCIAL AID

Required Forms and Deadlines: FAFSA. **Notification of Awards:** Applicants will be notified of awards on or about 4/1. **Types of Aid:** *Need-based scholarships/grants:* Federal Pell, FSEOG, State scholarships/grants, Private scholarships, College/university scholarship or grant aid from institutional funds. *Loans:* Direct Subsidized Stafford Loans, Direct Unsubsidized Stafford Loans, Direct PLUS loans, Federal Perkins Loans, Federal Nursing Loans. *Student Employment:* Federal Work-Study Program available. Institutional employment available. **Financial Aid Statistics:** 87% needy freshmen receive need-based scholarship or grant aid. **Criteria for awarding aid:** *Need-based:* Academics, Art, Leadership, Music/drama. *Non-need-based:* Academics, Alumni affiliation, Art, Athletics, Leadership, Music/drama, State/district residency.

UNIVERSITY OF WEST ALABAMA

Station 4, Livingston, AL 35470
Phone: 205-652-3578 • **Financial Aid Phone:** 205-652-3576
E-mail: admissions@uwa.edu
Fax: 205-652-3522 • **Website:** http://www.uwa.edu/ • **ACT Code:** 24

This public school was founded in 1835. It has a 600-acre campus.

RATINGS

Admissions Selectivity Rating: 72   **Fire Safety Rating:** 88   **Green Rating:** 69

STUDENTS AND FACULTY

Enrollment: 1,913. **Student Body:** 55% female, 45% male, 19% out-of-state, 6% international (20 countries represented). Asian 0%, African American 40%, Caucasian 45%, Hispanic 2%, Native American <1%, Pacific Islander <1%, Two or more races 2%, Race unknown 4%.
Retention and Graduation: 64% freshmen return for sophomore year. 15% freshmen graduate within 4 years. 28% freshmen graduate within 6 years.
Faculty: Student/faculty ratio 13:1. 126 full-time faculty, 78% hold PhDs, 17% are are members of minority groups, 56% are women. 0% of classes are taught by teaching assistants.

ACADEMICS

Degrees: associate, bachelor's, certificate, master's, post-master's certificate. **Classes:** Most classes have fewer than 10 students. Most lab/discussion sessions have 10-19 students. **Most popular majors:** Physical Education Teaching and Coaching; Registered Nursing/Registered Nurse; Business Administration and Management. **Special Study Options:** Accelerated program, cooperative education program, distance learning, double major, dual enrollment, exchange student program (domestic), honors program, independent study, internships, teacher certification program. Combined degree programs: BA/MEng, 2-yr transfer program in forestry and wildlife sciences with Auburn University. **Disability Services:** Special programs offered to physically disabled students, including tutors. **Career Services:** Alumni services, Career assessment.

FACILITIES

Housing: Coed dorms, men's dorms, women's dorms, apartments for married students, apartments for single students. 100% of campus accessible to physically disabled. **Computers:** Administrative functions (other than registration) can be performed online.

CAMPUS LIFE

Environment: Rural. **Activities:** Choral groups, concert band, dance, drama/theater, marching band, student government, student newspaper, television station, yearbook, Campus Ministries, Student Organization. 30 registered organizations, 8 honor societies, 5 religious organizations. 7 fraternities, 6 sororities. **Athletics (Intercollegiate):** *Men:* baseball, basketball, cheerleading, cross-country, football, rodeo. *Women:* basketball, cheerleading, cross-country, rodeo, softball, volleyball.

ADMISSIONS

Freshman Academic Profile: 85% from public high schools. ACT middle 50% range 18-21. Minimum internet-based TOEFL 61. Minimum paper TOEFL 500. **Basis for Candidate Selection:** *Very important factors considered include:* rigor of secondary school record, academic GPA, standardized test scores. **Freshman Admission Requirements:** High school diploma is required and GED is accepted. *Academic units required:* 3 English, 3 math, 3 science, 3 social studies, 3 academic electives. **Freshman Admission Statistics:** 1,195 applied, 73.47% admitted, 48% enrolled. **Transfer Admission Requirements:** college transcript(s), statement of good standing from prior institution(s). Minimum college GPA of 2.0 required. Lowest grade transferable C. **General Admission Information:** Application fee $40. Nonfall registration accepted. Admission may be deferred for a maximum of 1 year.

COSTS AND FINANCIAL AID

Annual in-state tuition $7,144. Annual out-of-state tuition $14,288. Room and board $6,460. Required fees $1,590. Average book expense $1,200. **Required Forms and Deadlines:** FAFSA. **Notification of Awards:** Applicants will be notified of awards on a rolling basis beginning 4/15. **Types of Aid:** *Need-based scholarships/grants:* Federal Pell, FSEOG, State scholarships/grants, Private scholarships, College/university scholarship or grant aid from institutional funds, United Negro College Fund. *Loans:* Direct Subsidized Stafford Loans, Direct Unsubsidized Stafford Loans, Direct PLUS loans, Federal Perkins Loans. *Student Employment:* Federal Work-Study Program available. Institutional employment available. **Financial Aid Statistics:** 64% needy freshmen, 75% needy undergrads receive need-based scholarship or grant aid. 65% freshmen, 40% undergrads receive non-need-based scholarship or grant aid. 12% freshmen, 15% undergrads receive need-based self-help aid. 13% freshmen, 15% undergrads receive athletic scholarships. 87% freshmen, 73% undergrads receive any aid. 70% undergrads borrow to pay for school. Average cumulative indebtedness $19,843. **Criteria for awarding aid:** *Non-need-based:* Academics, Alumni affiliation, Art, Athletics, Leadership, Music/drama, State/district residency.

UNIVERSITY OF WEST FLORIDA

11000 University Parkway, Pensacola, FL 32514-5750
Phone: 850-474-2230 • **Financial Aid Phone:** 850-474-2400
E-mail: admissions@uwf.edu • **CEEB Code:** 5833
Fax: 850-474-3360 • **Website:** http://uwf.edu • **ACT Code:** 771

This public school was founded in 1963. It has a 1600-acre campus.

RATINGS

Admissions Selectivity Rating: 84   **Fire Safety Rating:** 89   **Green Rating:** 60*

STUDENTS AND FACULTY

Enrollment: 9,786. **Student Body:** 57% female, 43% male, 9% out-of-state, 2% international (71 countries represented). Asian 3%, African American 13%, Caucasian 65%, Hispanic 9%, Native American <1%, Pacific Islander <1%, Two or more races 5%, Race unknown 2%.
Retention and Graduation: 72% freshmen return for sophomore year. 26% freshmen graduate within 4 years. 47% freshmen graduate within 6 years.
Faculty: Student/faculty ratio 22:1. 338 full-time faculty, 0% hold PhDs, 17% are are members of minority groups, 44% are women.

ACADEMICS

Degrees: associate, bachelor's, certificate, doctoral, master's, post-master's certificate. **Classes:** Most classes have 20-29 students. Most lab/discussion sessions have 20-29 students. **Most popular majors:** Psychology; Biology/Biological Sciences; Accounting. **Special Study Options:** cooperative education program, distance learning, dual enrollment, exchange student program (domestic), honors program, independent study, internships, study abroad, teacher certification program, Learning disability services. Combined degree programs: BS/MS Biology,Chemistry—called Fast Track. **Disability Services:** Special programs offered to physically disabled students, including note-taking services, reader services, tape recorders, tutors. **Career Services:** Alumni services, Career/job search classes, Career assessment, Internships. UWF is an accredited cooperative education school. We offer the Myers Briggs Type Indicator and Strong Interest Inventory as career assessments.

FACILITIES

Housing: Coed dorms, fraternity/sorority housing, apartments for married students, apartments for single students, Special dorm rooms for disabled students. 80% of campus accessible to physically diasbled. **Special Academic Facilities/Equipment:** Archeology museum,instructional media center, biology, chemistry, physics, and psychology labs, property on the Gulf of Mexico for marine and ecology research. **Computers:** 100% of classrooms, 100% of libraries, 100% of dining areas, 100% of student union, 100% of common outdoor areas have wireless network access. Students can register for classes online. Administrative functions (other than registration) can be performed online.

CAMPUS LIFE

Environment: City. **Activities:** Choral groups, concert band, dance, drama/ theater, jazz band, music ensembles, musical theater, radio station, student government, student newspaper, symphony orchestra, television station. 157 registered organizations, 15 honor societies, 17 religious organizations. 10 fraternities, 7 sororities. **Athletics (Intercollegiate):** *Men:* baseball, basketball, cross-country, golf, soccer, tennis. *Women:* basketball, cross-country, golf, soccer, softball, tennis, volleyball. **On-Campus Highlights:** The Commons (has cafeteria and bookstore), Fitness Facilities, Center for Fine and Performing Arts, Nature Trails, Library, Archeology Institute Artifact Display. **Environmental Initiatives:** All new buildings must be at least L.E.E.D Silver Certified.

ADMISSIONS

Freshman Academic Profile: Average high school GPA 3.6. 14% in top 10% of high school class, 38% in top 25% of high school class, 74% in top 50% of high school class. **Reported SAT (pre-2016 redesign) scores:** SAT Math middle 50% range 460-550. SAT Critical Reading middle 50% range 470-570. SAT Writing middle 50% range 450-540. **Concordant SAT scores:** SAT EBRW middle 50% 510–610. SAT Math middle 50% range 500–570. ACT middle 50% range 20-26. Minimum paper TOEFL 550. **Basis for Candidate Selection:** *Very important factors considered include:* rigor of secondary school record, academic GPA, standardized test scores. *Other factors considered include:* application essay, recommendation(s), extracurricular activities, talent/ability, character/personal qualities, first generation, alumni/ae relation, geographical residence, state residency, volunteer work, work experience. **Freshman Admission Requirements:** High school diploma is required and GED is accepted. *Academic units required:* 4 English, 3 math, 3 science, 2 science labs, 2 foreign language, 3 social studies, 4 academic electives. **Freshman Admission Statistics:** 7,104 applied, 41.54% admitted, 44% enrolled. **Transfer Admission Requirements:** college transcript(s), Minimum college GPA of 2.0 required. Lowest grade transferable D. **General Admission Information:** Application fee $30. Regular application deadline 6/30. Nonfall registration accepted. Admission may be deferred for a maximum of one year.

COSTS AND FINANCIAL AID

Annual in-state tuition $6,360. Annual out-of-state tuition $19,241. Room and board $9,912. Average book expense $1,200. **Required Forms and Deadlines:** FAFSA. **Notification of Awards:** Applicants will be notified of awards on a rolling basis beginning 3/1. **Types of Aid:** *Need-based scholarships/ grants:* Federal Pell, FSEOG, State scholarships/grants, Private scholarships, College/university scholarship or grant aid from institutional funds. *Loans:* Direct Subsidized Stafford Loans, Direct Unsubsidized Stafford Loans, Direct PLUS loans, Federal Perkins Loans. *Student Employment:* Federal Work-Study Program available. Institutional employment available. **Financial Aid Statistics:** 92% needy freshmen, 85% needy undergrads receive need-based scholarship or grant aid. 3% freshmen, 3% undergrads receive non-need-based scholarship or grant aid. 63% freshmen, 68% undergrads receive need-based self-help aid. 2% freshmen, 2% undergrads receive athletic scholarships. **Criteria for awarding aid:** *Need-based:* Academics, Leadership. *Non-need-based:* Academics, Alumni affiliation, Art, Athletics, Leadership, Minority status, Music/drama.

See page 1092.

UNIVERSITY OF WEST GEORGIA

1601 Maple Street, Carrollton, GA 30118
Phone: 678-839-5600 • **Financial Aid Phone:** 678-839-6421
E-mail: admiss@westga.edu • **CEEB Code:** 5900
Fax: 678-839-4747 • **Website:** www.westga.edu • **ACT Code:** 878

This public school was founded in 1906. It has a 645-acre campus.

RATINGS

Admissions Selectivity Rating: 75 **Fire Safety Rating:** 60* **Green Rating:** 67

STUDENTS AND FACULTY

Enrollment: 11,155. **Student Body:** 64% female, 36% male, 4% out-of-state, 1% international (62 countries represented). Asian 1%, African American 38%, Caucasian 49%, Hispanic 5%, Native American <1%, Pacific Islander <1%, Two or more races 4%, Race unknown 1%. **Retention and Graduation:** 72% freshmen return for sophomore year. 17% freshmen graduate within 4 years. 41% freshmen graduate within 6 years. **Faculty:** Student/faculty ratio 21:1. 424 full-time faculty, 76% hold PhDs, 21% are are members of minority groups, 58% are women. 1% of classes are taught by teaching assistants.

ACADEMICS

Degrees: bachelor's, doctoral/research, master's, postbachelor's certificate, post-master's certificate. **Classes:** Most classes have 20-29 students. Most lab/ discussion sessions have 20-29 students. **Special Study Options:** Accelerated program, cooperative education program, distance learning, double major, dual enrollment, external degree program, honors program, independent study, internships, study abroad, teacher certification program. **Disability Services:** Special programs offered to physically disabled students, including note-taking services, reader services, tape recorders, tutors.

FACILITIES

Housing: Coed dorms, special housing for disabled students, women's dorms, fraternity/sorority housing. of campus accessible to physically diasbled. **Special Academic Facilities/Equipment:** Archaelolgical laboratory, art gallery, electron microscope, observatory, preschool, performing arts center, TV studio. **Computers:** 20% of classrooms, 10% of dorms, 100% of libraries, 100% of dining areas, 100% of student union, 80% of common outdoor areas have wireless network access. Students can register for classes online. Administrative functions (other than registration) can be performed online.

CAMPUS LIFE

Environment: City. **Activities:** Choral groups, concert band, dance, drama/ theater, jazz band, literary magazine, marching band, music ensembles, musical theater, opera, pep band, radio station, student government, student newspaper, television station, Campus Ministries, Student Organization. 131 registered organizations, 32 honor societies, 17 religious organizations. 14 fraternities, 8 sororities. **Athletics (Intercollegiate):** *Men:* baseball, basketball, cheerleading, cross-country, football, golf. *Women:* basketball, cheerleading, cross-country, golf, soccer, softball, volleyball. **On-Campus Highlights:** Technology Learning Center (TLC), Bookstore, Ingram Library, Football Stadium, Campus Recreation Center, University Community Center, Coliseum, and Campus Visitor's Center.

ADMISSIONS

Freshman Academic Profile: Average high school GPA 3.2. **Reported SAT (pre-2016 redesign) scores:** SAT Math middle 50% range 430-500. SAT Critical Reading middle 50% range 440-520. SAT Writing middle 50% range 410-500. **Concordant SAT scores:** SAT EBRW middle 50% 480–570. SAT Math middle 50% range 470–530. ACT middle 50% range 18-22. Minimum internet-based TOEFL 69. Minimum paper TOEFL 523. **Basis for Candidate Selection:** *Very important factors considered include:* academic GPA, standardized test scores. **Freshman Admission Requirements:** High school diploma is required and GED is not accepted. *Academic units required:* 4 English, 4 math, 4 science, 2 science labs, 2 foreign language, 1 social studies, 2 history. **Freshman Admission Statistics:** 8,131 applied, 59.05% admitted, 52% enrolled. **Transfer Admission Requirements:** college transcript(s), Minimum college GPA of 2.0 required. Lowest grade transferable D. **General Admission Information:** Application fee $40. Priority deadline 2/1. Regular application deadline 6/1. Nonfall registration accepted. Admission may be deferred for a maximum of 1 year.

COSTS AND FINANCIAL AID

Annual in-state tuition $5,226. Annual out-of-state tuition $18,444. Room and board $9,652. Required fees $1,962. Average book expense $1,500. **Required Forms and Deadlines:** FAFSA. **Notification of Awards:** Applicants will be notified of awards on a rolling basis beginning 5/1. **Types of Aid:** *Need-based scholarships/grants:* Federal Pell, FSEOG, State scholarships/grants, Private scholarships, College/university scholarship or grant aid from institutional funds, United Negro College Fund, Federal Nursing Scholarships. *Loans:* Direct Subsidized Stafford Loans, Direct Unsubsidized Stafford Loans, Direct PLUS loans, Federal Perkins Loans, Federal Nursing Loans, State Loans. *Student Employment:* Federal Work-Study Program available. Institutional employment available. **Financial Aid Statistics:** 64% needy freshmen, 67% needy undergrads receive need-based scholarship or grant aid. 18% freshmen, 13% undergrads receive non-need-based scholarship or grant aid. 90% freshmen, 90% undergrads receive need-based self-help aid. 2% freshmen, 2% undergrads receive athletic scholarships. 76% undergrads borrow to pay for school. Average cumulative indebtedness $26,874. **Criteria for awarding aid:** *Need-based:* Academics, Alumni affiliation, Art, Job skills, Leadership, Minority status, Music/drama, Religious affiliation. *Non-need-based:* Academics, Alumni affiliation, Art, Athletics, Job skills, Leadership, Minority status, Music/drama, Religious affiliation.

UNIVERSITY OF WINDSOR

Office of the Registrar, Windsor, ON N9B3P4
Phone: 519-253-3000 • **Financial Aid Phone:** 519-253-3000
E-mail: registrar@uwindsor.ca • **CEEB Code:** 0
Fax: 519-971-3653 • **Website:** www.uwindsor.ca • **ACT Code:** 0

This public school was founded in 1857. It has a 125-acre campus.

RATINGS

Admissions Selectivity Rating: 64   **Fire Safety Rating:** 88   **Green Rating:** 83

STUDENTS AND FACULTY
Student Body: 52% female, 48% male, (83 countries represented).
Faculty: Student/faculty ratio 23:1. 573 full-time faculty, 84% hold PhDs, 0% are are members of minority groups, 39% are women.

ACADEMICS
Degrees: bachelor's, certificate, doctoral, master's. **Most popular majors:** Social Sciences; Engineering; Registered Nursing, Nursing Administration, Nursing Research and Clinical Nursing. **Special Study Options:** cooperative education program, distance learning, double major, English as a Second Language (ESL), exchange student program (domestic), honors program, independent study, internships, study abroad, teacher certification program, MBA for Managers and Professionals, which is offered on weekends (Centre for Executive Education). **Honors Programs:** As a comprehensive university we have distinguished ourselves at many levels. Combined degree programs: Dual JD, MBA/JD, MSW/JD. **Disability Services:** Special programs offered to physically disabled students, including note-taking services, reader services, tape recorders, tutors. **Career Services:** Alumni network, Alumni services, Career/job search classes, Career assessment, Internships. Our Volunteer Internship Program (VIP) provides students with the opportunity to gain career related transferable skills and explore potential career paths while getting involved in our community. Each term, approximately 100 VIP students spend 40+ hours as an intern with a local non-profit or publicly funded organization while our centre supports learning through the facilitation of related professional development and reflective activities.

FACILITIES
Housing: Coed dorms, special housing for disabled students, special housing for international students, fraternity/sorority housing, apartments for married students, cooperative housing, apartments for single students, off campus housing lists for tenants and landlords. 85% of campus accessible to physically disabled. **Special Academic Facilities/Equipment:** Centre for Engineering Innovation (completion date 2011), C.A.R.E. (Centre for Automotive Research and Education), GLIER (Great Lakes Institute for Environemntal Research), Jackman Dramatic Art Centre (Theatrical space), Bio-Learning Centre (BLC) Biotechnology Laboratory. **Computers:** 100% of classrooms, 100% of dorms, 100% of libraries, 100% of dining areas, 100% of student union, 100% of common outdoor areas have wireless network access. Students can register for classes online. Administrative functions (other than registration) can be performed online.

CAMPUS LIFE
Environment: City. **Activities:** Choral groups, dance, drama/theater, jazz band, literary magazine, music ensembles, musical theater, radio station, student government, student newspaper, student-run film society, Campus Ministries, Student Organization. 116 registered organizations, 1 honor society, 13 religious organizations. 3 fraternities, 3 sororities. **Athletics (Intercollegiate):** *Men:* basketball, cross-country, football, ice hockey, soccer, track/field (outdoor), track/field (indoor), volleyball. *Women:* basketball, cross-country, ice hockey, soccer, track/field (outdoor), track/field (indoor), volleyball. **On-Campus Highlights:** CAW Student Centre, Forge Fitness

facility, The Basement Pub, St. Denis Athletic Centre/University Sta, Leddy Library, Odette Sculpture Garden which includes a scenic 5km waterfront trail. Many students will exercise or study/relax by the water. **Environmental Initiatives:** In January 2013, the Environmental Advocate was appointed, the University of Windsor Joined AASHE, and the sustainability website was created. The Environmental Advocate is also a member of the Ontario College and University Sustainability Professionals.

ADMISSIONS
Basis for Candidate Selection: *Very important factors considered include:* rigor of secondary school record, academic GPA. *Other factors considered include:* standardized test scores, recommendation(s), interview, extracurricular activities, geographical residence. **Freshman Admission Requirements:** High school diploma is required and GED is not accepted. **Freshman Admission Statistics:** 9,470 applied, 74.09% admitted, 33% enrolled. **Transfer Admission Requirements:** college transcript(s). **General Admission Information:** Application fee $120. Nonfall registration accepted.

COSTS AND FINANCIAL AID
Annual in-state tuition $7,197. Room and board $10,604. **Required Forms and Deadlines:** FAFSA, Institution's own financial aid form. **Notification of Awards:** Applicants will be notified of awards on a rolling basis beginning 8/1. **Types of Aid:** *Loans:* Direct Subsidized Stafford Loans, Direct Unsubsidized Stafford Loans, Direct PLUS loans. *Student Employment:* Federal Work-Study Program available. Institutional employment available. **Criteria for awarding aid:** *Need-based:* Academics, Athletics, Leadership. *Non-need-based:* Academics, Athletics, Leadership.

UNIVERSITY OF WISCONSIN—EAU CLAIRE

105 Garfield Avenue, Eau Claire, WI 54701
Phone: 715-836-5415 • **Financial Aid Phone:** 715-836-3373
E-mail: admissions@uwec.edu • **CEEB Code:** 1913
Fax: 715-836-2409 • **Website:** www.uwec.edu • **ACT Code:** 4670

This public school was founded in 1916. It has a 333-acre campus.

RATINGS

Admissions Selectivity Rating: 78   **Fire Safety Rating:** 90   **Green Rating:** 77

STUDENTS AND FACULTY
Enrollment: 7,496. **Student Body:** 62% female, 38% male, 29% out-of-state, 2% international (28 countries represented). Asian 4%, African American 1%, Caucasian 89%, Hispanic 2%, Native American <1%, Pacific Islander <1%, Two or more races 2%, Race unknown <1%.
Retention and Graduation: 84% freshmen return for sophomore year. 30% freshmen graduate within 4 years. 68% freshmen graduate within 6 years. 18% grads go on to further study within 1 year. 35% grads pursue arts and sciences degrees. 6% grads pursue law degrees. 3% grads pursue business degrees. 6% grads pursue medical degrees. **Faculty:** Student/faculty ratio 22:1. 387 full-time faculty, 83% hold PhDs, 19% are are members of minority groups, 50% are women. 0% of classes are taught by teaching assistants.

ACADEMICS
Degrees: associate, bachelor's, certificate, doctoral/professional, master's, postbachelor's certifiate, post-master's certificate, transfer. **Classes:** Most classes have 20-29 students. Most lab/discussion sessions have 20-29 students. **Most popular majors:** Registered Nursing/Registered Nurse; Biology/Biological Sciences; Kinesiology and Exercise Science. **Special Study Options:** Accelerated program, cooperative education program, cross-registration, distance learning, double major, dual enrollment, English as a Second Language (ESL), exchange student program (domestic), external degree program, honors program, independent study, internships, student-designed major, study abroad, teacher certification program, Collaborative programs in Early Childhood Education. **Disability Services:** Special programs offered to physically disabled students, including note-taking services, reader services, tutors. **Career Services:** Alumni network, Alumni services, Career/job search classes, Career assessment, Internships, Regional alumni. Over 58% of our students report completing at least one internship while a student at UWEC.

FACILITIES
Housing: Coed dorms, men's dorms, women's dorms, apartments for single students. 90% of campus accessible to physically disabled. **Special Academic Facilities/Equipment:** Art gallery, human development center, bird museum, field station, planetarium. **Computers:** 50% of classrooms, 10% of dorms, 100% of libraries, 100% of dining areas, 100% of student union, 100% of common outdoor areas have wireless network access. Students can register for classes online. Administrative functions (other than registration) can be performed online.

CAMPUS LIFE

Environment: Town. **Activities:** Choral groups, concert band, dance, drama/theater, jazz band, literary magazine, marching band, music ensembles, musical theater, opera, pep band, radio station, student government, student newspaper, student-run film society, symphony orchestra, television station, Campus Ministries, Student Organization, Model UN. 240 registered organizations, 30 honor societies, 16 religious organizations. 2 fraternities, 3 sororities. **Athletics (Intercollegiate):** *Men:* basketball, cross-country, diving, football, golf, ice hockey, swimming, tennis, track/field (outdoor), track/field (indoor), wrestling. *Women:* basketball, cross-country, diving, golf, gymnastics, ice hockey, soccer, softball, swimming, tennis, track/field (outdoor), track/field (indoor), volleyball. **On-Campus Highlights:** Chippewa River Footbridge, Davies Center (Student Center/Union), McPhee Center (Athletic Facility), Hass Fine Arts Center, Higher Ground (Recreational Facility). **Environmental Initiatives:** Creation of an energy performance contract to provide $3.4 million in energy conservation measures across campus, including heating and ventilation, lighting, water conservation, etc.

ADMISSIONS

Freshman Academic Profile: 17% in top 10% of high school class, 47% in top 25% of high school class, 90% in top 50% of high school class. **Reported SAT (pre-2016 redesign) scores:** SAT Math middle 50% range 530-600. SAT Critical Reading middle 50% range 530-650. **Concordant SAT scores:** SAT Math middle 50% range 560–620. ACT middle 50% range 22-26. Minimum internet-based TOEFL 79. Minimum paper TOEFL 550. **Basis for Candidate Selection:** *Very important factors considered include:* rigor of secondary school record, class rank, academic GPA. *Important factors considered include:* standardized test scores, application essay. *Other factors considered include:* recommendation(s), interview, extracurricular activities, talent/ability, character/personal qualities, first generation, geographical residence, state residency, racial/ethnic status, volunteer work, work experience, level of applicant's interest. **Freshman Admission Requirements:** High school diploma is required and GED is accepted. *Academic units required:* 4 English, 3 math, 3 science, 3 social studies, 4 academic electives. **Freshman Admission Statistics:** 5,706 applied, 89.01% admitted, 45% enrolled. **Transfer Admission Requirements:** High school transcript, college transcript(s), statement of good standing from prior institution(s). Minimum college GPA of 2.0 required. Lowest grade transferable D-. **General Admission Information:** Application fee $44. Priority deadline 12/1. Regular application deadline 8/25. Nonfall registration accepted.

COSTS AND FINANCIAL AID

Annual in-state tuition $7,361. Annual out-of-state tuition $14,934. Room and board $6,984. Required fees $1,452. Average book expense $400. **Required Forms and Deadlines:** FAFSA. **Notification of Awards:** Applicants will be notified of awards on a rolling basis beginning 4/15. **Types of Aid:** *Need-based scholarships/grants:* Federal Pell, FSEOG, State scholarships/grants, Private scholarships, College/university scholarship or grant aid from institutional funds, Federal Nursing Scholarships. *Loans:* Direct Subsidized Stafford Loans, Direct Unsubsidized Stafford Loans, Direct PLUS loans, Federal Perkins Loans, State Loans, College/university loans from institutional funds. *Student Employment:* Federal Work-Study Program available. Institutional employment available. **Financial Aid Statistics:** 83% needy freshmen, 82% needy undergrads receive need-based scholarship or grant aid. 4% freshmen, 3% undergrads receive non-need-based scholarship or grant aid. 94% freshmen, 94% undergrads receive need-based self-help aid. 0% freshmen, 0% undergrads receive athletic scholarships. 84% freshmen, 74% undergrads receive any aid. 72% undergrads borrow to pay for school. Average cumulative indebtedness $26,295. **Criteria for awarding aid:** *Need-based:* Academics, Minority status. *Non-need-based:* Academics, Art, Leadership, Minority status, Music/drama, State/district residency.

UNIVERSITY OF WISCONSIN—GREEN BAY

2420 Nicolet Drive, Green Bay, WI 53411-7001
Phone: 920-465-2111 • **Financial Aid Phone:** 920-465-2075
E-mail: admissions@uwgb.edu • **CEEB Code:** 1859
Fax: 920-465-5754 • **Website:** http://www.uwgb.edu/ • **ACT Code:** 4688

This public school was founded in 1965. It has a 700-acre campus.

RATINGS

Admissions Selectivity Rating: 72   **Fire Safety Rating:** 82   **Green Rating:** 87

STUDENTS AND FACULTY

Enrollment: 5,502. **Student Body:** 67% female, 33% male, 8% out-of-state, 1% international (24 countries represented). Asian 3%, African American 2%, Caucasian 85%, Hispanic 4%, Native American 1%, Pacific Islander <1%, Two or more races 3%, Race unknown <1%.
Retention and Graduation: 74% freshmen return for sophomore year. 24% freshmen graduate within 4 years. 50% freshmen graduate within 6 years. 15% grads go on to further study within 1 year. 7% grads pursue arts and sciences degrees. 1% grads pursue law degrees. 3% grads pursue business degrees. 1% grads pursue medical degrees. **Faculty:** Student/faculty ratio 22:1. 185 full-time faculty, 87% hold PhDs, 23% are are members of minority groups, 48% are women. 0% of classes are taught by teaching assistants.

ACADEMICS

Degrees: associate, bachelor's, master's. **Classes:** Most classes have 20-29 students. Most lab/discussion sessions have 20-29 students. **Most popular majors:** Psychology; Business Administration and Management; Multi-/Interdisciplinary Studies. **Special Study Options:** cross-registration, distance learning, double major, exchange student program (domestic), external degree program, independent study, internships, liberal arts/career combination, student-designed major, study abroad, teacher certification program. Combined degree programs: BS/MS Environmental Science/Env Science & Policy. **Disability Services:** Special programs offered to physically disabled students, including note-taking services, reader services, tape recorders. **Career Services:** Alumni network, Alumni services, Career/job search classes, Internships.

FACILITIES

Housing: Coed dorms, apartments for single students, Suites w/ private bedrooms. 99% of campus accessible to physically diasbled. **Special Academic Facilities/Equipment:** 290-acre arboretum, Herbarium, regional Performing Arts Center **Computers:** 75% of classrooms, 100% of dorms, 100% of libraries, 100% of dining areas, 100% of student union, 10% of common outdoor areas have wireless network access. Students can register for classes online. Administrative functions (other than registration) can be performed online.

CAMPUS LIFE

Environment: City. **Activities:** Choral groups, concert band, dance, drama/theater, jazz band, literary magazine, music ensembles, musical theater, pep band, radio station, student government, student newspaper, student-run film society, television station, Campus Ministries, Student Organization. 100 registered organizations, 7 honor societies, 5 religious organizations. 2 fraternities, 2 sororities. **Athletics (Intercollegiate):** *Men:* basketball, cheerleading, cross-country, diving, golf, skiing (nordic/cross-country), soccer, swimming, tennis. *Women:* basketball, cheerleading, cross-country, diving, golf, skiing (nordic/cross-country), soccer, softball, swimming, tennis, volleyball. **On-Campus Highlights:** Mary Ann Cofrin Hall—State-of-the-art academic bldg., Kress Event Center -recently remodeled, Weidner Center for Performing Arts, Lambeau Cottage on the shores of Green B, Student Union-recently remodeled. **Environmental Initiatives:** Building integrated photovoltaics in Mary Ann Cofrin Hall (http://www.buildingsolar.com/index.html).

ADMISSIONS

Freshman Academic Profile: Average high school GPA 3.3. 95% from public high schools. **Reported SAT (pre-2016 redesign) scores:** SAT Math middle 50% range 465-555. SAT Critical Reading middle 50% range 450-595. SAT Writing middle 50% range 435-600. **Concordant SAT scores:** SAT EBRW middle 50% 500–650. SAT Math middle 50% range 510–580. ACT middle 50% range 20-25. Minimum internet-based TOEFL 61. Minimum paper TOEFL 500. **Basis for Candidate Selection:** *Very important factors considered include:* rigor of secondary school record, academic GPA, standardized test scores, extracurricular activities. *Important factors considered include:* application essay, volunteer work, work experience, level of applicant's interest. *Other factors considered include:* recommendation(s), interview, talent/ability, character/personal qualities, geographical residence, state residency, racial/ethnic status. **Freshman Admission Requirements:** High school diploma is required and GED is accepted. *Academic units required:* 4 English, 3 math, 3 science, 1 science lab, 3 social studies, 4 academic electives. *Academic units recommended:* 4 English, 3 math, 3 science, 1 science lab, 2 foreign language, 3 social studies, 4 academic electives. **Freshman Admission Statistics:** 2,126 applied, 92.47% admitted, 44% enrolled. **Transfer Admission Requirements:** college transcript(s), Minimum college GPA of 2.0 required. Lowest grade transferable D. **General Admission Information:** Application fee $44. Priority deadline 4/15. Nonfall registration accepted. Admission may be deferred for a maximum of 1 year.

COSTS AND FINANCIAL AID

Annual in-state tuition $6,298. Annual out-of-state tuition $13,871. Room and board $7,286. Required fees $1,580. Average book expense $800. **Required Forms and Deadlines:** FAFSA. **Notification of Awards:** Applicants will be notified of awards on a rolling basis beginning 1/1. **Types of Aid:** *Need-based scholarships/grants:* Federal Pell, FSEOG, State scholarships/grants, Private scholarships, College/university scholarship or grant aid from institutional funds. *Loans:* Direct Subsidized Stafford Loans, Direct Unsubsidized Stafford Loans, Direct PLUS loans, Federal Perkins Loans. *Student Employment:*

Federal Work-Study Program available. Institutional employment available. **Financial Aid Statistics:** 73% needy freshmen, 75% needy undergrads receive need-based scholarship or grant aid. 4% freshmen, 3% undergrads receive non-need-based scholarship or grant aid. 74% freshmen, 74% undergrads receive need-based self-help aid. 1% freshmen, 1% undergrads receive athletic scholarships. 88% freshmen, 80% undergrads receive any aid. 77% undergrads borrow to pay for school. Average cumulative indebtedness $28,940. **Criteria for awarding aid:** *Non-need-based:* Academics, Art, Athletics, Leadership, Minority status, Music/drama.

UNIVERSITY OF WISCONSIN—LA CROSSE

1725 State Street, La Crosse, WI 54601-3742
Phone: 608-785-8939 • **Financial Aid Phone:** 608-785-8604
E-mail: admissions@uwlax.edu • **CEEB Code:** 1914
Fax: 608-785-8940 • **Website:** www.uwlax.edu • **ACT Code:** 4672

This public school was founded in 1909. It has a 120-acre campus.

RATINGS
Admissions Selectivity Rating: 81   **Fire Safety Rating:** 62   **Green Rating:** 60*

STUDENTS AND FACULTY
Enrollment: 9,486. **Student Body:** 56% female, 44% male, 22% out-of-state, 1% international (23 countries represented). Asian 2%, African American 1%, Caucasian 89%, Hispanic 4%, Native American <1%, Pacific Islander <1%, Two or more races 3%, Race unknown <1%.
Retention and Graduation: 86% freshmen return for sophomore year. 36% freshmen graduate within 4 years. 68 **Faculty:** Student/faculty ratio 19:1. 463 full-time faculty, 82% hold PhDs, 16% are are members of minority groups, 49% are women.

ACADEMICS
Degrees: associate, bachelor's, certificate, master's, postbachelor's certificate. **Classes:** Most classes have 20-29 students. Most lab/discussion sessions have 20-29 students. **Most popular majors:** Biology/Biological Sciences; Kinesiology and Exercise Science; Psychology. **Special Study Options:** cooperative education program, cross-registration, distance learning, double major, dual enrollment, English as a Second Language (ESL), honors program, independent study, internships, liberal arts/career combination, study abroad, teacher certification program, Weekend college: grad only. **Honors Programs:** University Honors Program lt;http://www.uwlax.edu/honors/gt;. **Disability Services:** Special programs offered to physically disabled students, including note-taking services, reader services, tape recorders, tutors. **Career Services:** Alumni services, Career/job search classes, Career assessment, Internships. The Cooperative Education and Internship Program is a available to all undergraduate majors and works to help students find internship and coop experiences with employers in business, government and non-profit organizations.

FACILITIES
Housing: Coed dorms, special housing for international students, Wellness HousingFirst Year Experience. 98% of campus accessible to physically diasbled. **Special Academic Facilities/Equipment:** Greenhouse, planetarium, Health Science Center,Mississippi Valley Archaeology Center, River Studies center, Business Development Center, La Crosse Exercise and Health Program. **Computers:** Students can register for classes online. Administrative functions (other than registration) can be performed online.

CAMPUS LIFE
Environment: City. **Activities:** Choral groups, concert band, drama/theater, jazz band, marching band, music ensembles, pep band, radio station, student government, student newspaper, symphony orchestra, Student Organization. 180 registered organizations, 13 honor societies, 10 religious organizations. 4 fraternities, 2 sororities. **Athletics (Intercollegiate):** *Men:* baseball, basketball, cross-country, diving, football, swimming, tennis, track/field (outdoor), track/field (indoor), wrestling. *Women:* basketball, cross-country, diving, gymnastics, soccer, softball, swimming, tennis, track/field (outdoor), track/field (indoor), volleyball. **On-Campus Highlights:** Recreation Eagle Center, Cyber Cafe, Archaeology Museum, Murphy Library, Wing Technology Computer Lab, The 119 acre campus has 32 buildings, including 19 used for instruction, academic support and administrative purposes; 10 residence halls and three student centers.

ADMISSIONS
Freshman Academic Profile: 22% in top 10% of high school class, 59% in top 25% of high school class, 95% in top 50% of high school class. **Reported SAT (pre-2016 redesign) scores:** SAT Math middle 50% range 545-637.5. SAT Critical Reading middle 50% range 550-627.5. SAT Writing middle 50% range

518-603. **Concordant SAT scores:** SAT EBRW middle 50% 590–670. SAT Math middle 50% range 570–660. ACT middle 50% range 23-27. Minimum internet-based TOEFL 73. Minimum paper TOEFL 550. **Basis for Candidate Selection:** *Very important factors considered include:* rigor of secondary school record, class rank, academic GPA, standardized test scores. *Important factors considered include:* application essay, extracurricular activities, volunteer work, level of applicant's interest. *Other factors considered include:* recommendation(s), interview, talent/ability, character/personal qualities, first generation, alumni/ae relation, geographical residence, state residency, racial/ethnic status, work experience. **Freshman Admission Requirements:** High school diploma is required and GED is accepted. *Academic units required:* 4 English, 3 math, 3 science, 2 science labs, 3 social studies, 4 academic electives. *Academic units recommended:* 4 English, 4 math, 4 science, 3 science labs, 3 foreign language, 4 social studies, 4 academic electives. **Freshman Admission Statistics:** 5,801 applied, 82.43% admitted, 44% enrolled. **Transfer Admission Requirements:** college transcript(s), statement of good standing from prior institution(s). Minimum college GPA of 3.0 required. Lowest grade transferable D-. **General Admission Information:** Application fee $44. Priority deadline 2/1. Nonfall registration accepted.

COSTS AND FINANCIAL AID
Annual in-state tuition $7,585. Annual out-of-state tuition $16,106. Room and board $6,156. Required fees $1,506. Average book expense $120. **Required Forms and Deadlines:** FAFSA. **Types of Aid:** *Need-based scholarships/grants:* Federal Pell, FSEOG, State scholarships/grants, Private scholarships, College/university scholarship or grant aid from institutional funds. *Loans:* Direct Subsidized Stafford Loans, Direct Unsubsidized Stafford Loans, Direct PLUS loans, Federal Perkins Loans. *Student Employment:* Federal Work-Study Program available. Institutional employment available. **Financial Aid Statistics:** 41% needy freshmen, 63% needy undergrads receive need-based scholarship or grant aid. 57% freshmen, 32% undergrads receive non-need-based scholarship or grant aid. 77% freshmen, 83% undergrads receive need-based self-help aid. 0% freshmen, 0% undergrads receive athletic scholarships. 88% freshmen, 77% undergrads receive any aid. 69% undergrads borrow to pay for school. Average cumulative indebtedness $26,487. **Criteria for awarding aid:** *Non-need-based:* Academics, Alumni affiliation, Art, Leadership, Minority status, Music/drama.

UNIVERSITY OF WISCONSIN,MADISON

702 West Johnson Street, Suite 101, Madison, WI 53715-1007
Phone: 608-262-3961 • **Financial Aid Phone:** 608-262-3060
E-mail: onwisconsin@admissions.wisc.edu • **CEEB Code:** 1846
Fax: 608-262-7706 • **Website:** www.wisc.edu • **ACT Code:** 4656

This public school was founded in 1848. It has a 933-acre campus.

RATINGS
Admissions Selectivity Rating: 92   **Fire Safety Rating:** 82   **Green Rating:** 60*

STUDENTS AND FACULTY
Enrollment: 29,536. **Student Body:** 51% female, 49% male, 33% out-of-state, 8% international (108 countries represented). Asian 6%, African American 2%, Caucasian 75%, Hispanic 5%, Native American <1%, Pacific Islander <1%, Two or more races 3%, Race unknown <1%.
Retention and Graduation: 95% freshmen return for sophomore year. 57% freshmen graduate within 4 years. 85% freshmen graduate within 6 years. **Faculty:** Student/faculty ratio 18:1. 2,381 full-time faculty, 91% hold PhDs, 19% are are members of minority groups, 40% are women.

ACADEMICS
Degrees: bachelor's, doctoral/professional, doctoral/research, doctoral, master's, postbachelor's certificate. **Classes:** Most classes have 10-19 students. Most lab/discussion sessions have 20-29 students. **Most popular majors:** Political Science and Government; Biology/Biological Sciences; Economics. **Special Study Options:** Accelerated program, cooperative education program, distance learning, double major, dual enrollment, English as a Second Language (ESL), exchange student program (domestic), honors program, independent study, internships, liberal arts/career combination, student-designed major, study abroad, teacher certification program. Combined degree programs: BBA/MACC. **Disability Services:** Special programs offered to physically disabled students, including note-taking services, reader services, tape recorders, tutors. **Career Services:** Alumni network, Career/job search classes, Career

assessment, Internships. This question is difficult to answer. We have multiple career placement centers for different schools and colleges. Futhermore, we have all of the services above, but they are not all offered through a career placement center. For example, internships are generally organized through academic departments and alumni services are provided through our alumni association.

FACILITIES

Housing: Coed dorms, men's dorms, special housing for international students, women's dorms, fraternity/sorority housing, apartments for married students, cooperative housing, apartments for single students, Theme Housing, Residential Learning Communities. 80% of campus accessible to physically diasbled. **Special Academic Facilities/Equipment:** Art, physics, and geology museums, nuclear reactor, arboretum, botanical gardens, observatory, campus dairy store (campus-made ice cream and cheese), American Indian burial mounds **Computers:** 100% of classrooms, 25% of dorms, 100% of libraries, 100% of dining areas, 100% of student union, 100% of common outdoor areas have wireless network access. Students can register for classes online. Administrative functions (other than registration) can be performed online.

CAMPUS LIFE

Environment: City. **Activities:** Choral groups, concert band, dance, drama/theater, jazz band, literary magazine, marching band, music ensembles, musical theater, opera, pep band, radio station, student government, student newspaper, student-run film society, symphony orchestra, television station, yearbook, Student Organization. 685 registered organizations, 27 honor societies, 26 fraternities, 11 sororities. **Athletics (Intercollegiate):** *Men:* basketball, cheerleading, crew/rowing, cross-country, football, golf, ice hockey, soccer, swimming, tennis, track/field (outdoor), wrestling. *Women:* basketball, cheerleading, crew/rowing, cross-country, golf, ice hockey, soccer, softball, swimming, tennis, track/field (outdoor), volleyball. **On-Campus Highlights:** Allen Centennial Gardens, Kohl Center, Memorial Union Terrace, Chazen Museum of Art, Babcock Hall Dairy Plant and Store, http://www.visit.wisc.edu/todo.html. **Environmental Initiatives:** Our conservation efforts in the last four years have reduced campus energy consumption by over 1 trillion BTUs and water consumption by 178,000,000 gallons annually.

ADMISSIONS

Freshman Academic Profile: Average high school GPA 3.8. 54% in top 10% of high school class, 89% in top 25% of high school class, 100% in top 50% of high school class. **Reported SAT (pre-2016 redesign) scores:** SAT Math middle 50% range 640-760. SAT Critical Reading middle 50% range 570-660. **Concordant SAT scores:** SAT Math middle 50% range 660-780. ACT middle 50% range 27-31. **Basis for Candidate Selection:** *Very important factors considered include:* rigor of secondary school record, class rank, academic GPA. *Important factors considered include:* standardized test scores, application essay, state residency. *Other factors considered include:* recommendation(s), extracurricular activities, talent/ability, character/personal qualities, first generation, alumni/ae relation, racial/ethnic status, volunteer work, work experience, level of applicant's interest. **Freshman Admission Requirements:** High school diploma is required and GED is accepted. *Academic units required:* 4 English, 4 math, 3 science, 3 foreign language, 3 social studies, 2 academic electives. *Academic units recommended:* 4 English, 4 math, 4 science, 4 foreign language, 4 social studies, 3 academic electives. **Freshman Admission Statistics:** 32,887 applied, 52.62% admitted, 37% enrolled. **Transfer Admission Requirements:** High school transcript, college transcript(s), essay or personal statement, Lowest grade transferable D. **General Admission Information:** Application fee $50. Regular application deadline 2/1. Nonfall registration accepted. Admission may be deferred for a maximum of 1 year.

COSTS AND FINANCIAL AID

Annual in-state tuition $9,273. Annual out-of-state tuition $31,523. Room and board $10,446. Required fees $1,215. Average book expense $1,200. **Required Forms and Deadlines:** FAFSA. **Notification of Awards:** Applicants will be notified of awards on a rolling basis beginning 4/1. **Types of Aid:** *Need-based scholarships/grants:* Federal Pell, FSEOG, State scholarships/grants, Private scholarships, College/university scholarship or grant aid from institutional funds. *Loans:* Direct Subsidized Stafford Loans, Direct Unsubsidized Stafford Loans, Direct PLUS loans, Federal Perkins Loans, Federal Nursing Loans. *Student Employment:* Federal Work-Study Program available. Institutional employment available. **Financial Aid Statistics:** 94% needy freshmen, 77% needy undergrads receive need-based scholarship or grant aid. 11% freshmen, 9% undergrads receive non-need-based scholarship or grant aid. 80% freshmen, 82% undergrads receive need-based self-help aid. 1% freshmen, 1% undergrads receive athletic scholarships. 46% undergrads borrow to pay for school. Average cumulative indebtedness $27,831. **Criteria for awarding aid:** *Need-based:* Academics, Alumni affiliation, Minority status. *Non-need-based:* Academics, Alumni affiliation, Art, Athletics, Leadership, Minority status, Music/drama, State/district residency.

UNIVERSITY OF WISCONSIN—MILWAUKEE

Department of Admissions and Recruitment, Milwaukee, WI 53211
Phone: 414-229-2222 • **Financial Aid Phone:** 414-229-4541
E-mail: uwmlook@uwm.edu • **CEEB Code:** 1473
Fax: 414-229-6940 • **Website:** www4.uwm.edu • **ACT Code:** 4658

This public school was founded in 1956. It has a 93-acre campus.

RATINGS
Admissions Selectivity Rating: 70   **Fire Safety Rating:** 94   **Green Rating:** 95

STUDENTS AND FACULTY

Enrollment: 20,000. **Student Body:** 51% female, 49% male, 11% out-of-state, 4% international (81 countries represented). Asian 7%, African American 8%, Caucasian 67%, Hispanic 10%, Native American <1%, Pacific Islander <1%, Two or more races 4%, Race unknown <1%.
Retention and Graduation: 72% freshmen return for sophomore year. 14% freshmen graduate within 4 years. **Faculty:** Student/faculty ratio 19:1. 1,010 full-time faculty, 73% hold PhDs, 22% are are members of minority groups, 46% are women.

ACADEMICS

Degrees: bachelor's, certificate, doctoral/professional, doctoral/research, doctoral, master's, postbachelor's certifiate, post-master's certificate. **Classes:** Most classes have 20-29 students. Most lab/discussion sessions have 20-29 students. **Most popular majors:** Marketing/Marketing Management; Education; Psychology. **Special Study Options:** Accelerated program, cooperative education program, cross-registration, distance learning, double major, dual enrollment, English as a Second Language (ESL), external degree program, honors program, independent study, internships, liberal arts/career combination, student-designed major, study abroad, teacher certification program. Combined degree programs: BA/MA, BA/MEng. **Disability Services:** Special programs offered to physically disabled students, including note-taking services, reader services, tape recorders, tutors. **Career Services:** Alumni network, Alumni services, Career/job search classes, Career assessment, Internships. Career Counseling Internship Program.

FACILITIES

Housing: Coed dorms, special housing for disabled students, apartments for single students. **Special Academic Facilities/Equipment:** Art and geology museums, childhood education center, foreign language resource center, Great Lakes research facility and environmental studies field station, planetarium.

CAMPUS LIFE

Activities: Choral groups, concert band, dance, drama/theater, jazz band, literary magazine, marching band, music ensembles, musical theater, pep band, radio station, student government, student newspaper, student-run film society, symphony orchestra, Campus Ministries, Student Organization, Model UN. 250 registered organizations, 1 honor society, 4 religious organizations. 8 fraternities, 4 sororities. **Athletics (Intercollegiate):** *Men:* baseball, basketball, cross-country, diving, soccer, swimming, track/field (outdoor). *Women:* basketball, cross-country, soccer, swimming, tennis, track/field (outdoor), volleyball.
Environmental Initiatives: Performance Contracting--Energy Matters is UWM's energy efficiency project with a goal to achieve an energy reduction of 25% by 2013, reduce campus use of fossil fuels, and provide comfortable study and work space. With more than 50% of the project complete, results are showing an even faster rate of return with a 42% savings.

ADMISSIONS

Freshman Academic Profile: Average high school GPA 3.1. 9% in top 10% of high school class, 19% in top 25% of high school class, 67% in top 50% of high school class. Minimum internet-based TOEFL 68. Minimum paper TOEFL 520. **Basis for Candidate Selection:** *Very important factors considered include:* rigor of secondary school record, academic GPA. *Important factors considered include:* class rank, standardized test scores, application essay, talent/ability. *Other factors considered include:* recommendation(s), interview, extracurricular activities, character/personal qualities, first generation, geographical residence, state residency, racial/ethnic status, volunteer work, work experience, level of applicant's interest. **Freshman Admission Requirements:** High school diploma is required and GED is accepted. *Academic units required:* 4 English, 3 math, 3 science, 1 science lab, 3 social studies, 2 academic electives, and 2 units from above areas or other academic areas. *Academic units recommended:* 4 English, 4 math, 3 science, 1 science lab, 2 foreign language, 3 social studies, 2 academic electives, and 2 units from above areas or other academic areas. **Freshman Admission Statistics:** 9,834 applied, 72.44% admitted, 44% enrolled. **Transfer Admission Requirements:** High school transcript, college transcript(s), Minimum college GPA of 2.0 required. Lowest grade transferable D-. **General Admission Information:** Application fee $44. Priority deadline 3/1. Nonfall registration accepted. Admission may be deferred for a maximum of 1 year.

COSTS AND FINANCIAL AID

Annual in-state tuition $8,090. Annual out-of-state tuition $9,685. Room and board $10,560. Required fees $1,444. Average book expense $800. **Required Forms and Deadlines:** FAFSA. **Notification of Awards:** Applicants will be notified of awards on a rolling basis beginning 3/10. **Types of Aid:** *Need-based scholarships/grants:* Federal Pell, FSEOG, State scholarships/grants, Private scholarships, College/university scholarship or grant aid from institutional funds, Federal Nursing Scholarships. *Loans:* Direct Subsidized Stafford Loans, Direct Unsubsidized Stafford Loans, Direct PLUS loans, Federal Perkins Loans, Federal Nursing Loans, State Loans. *Student Employment:* Federal Work-Study Program available. Institutional employment available. **Financial Aid Statistics:** 59% needy freshmen, 57% needy undergrads receive need-based scholarship or grant aid. 29% freshmen, 20% undergrads receive non-need-based scholarship or grant aid. 79% freshmen, 78% undergrads receive need-based self-help aid. 1% freshmen, 4% undergrads receive athletic scholarships. 76% undergrads borrow to pay for school. Average cumulative indebtedness $36,945. **Criteria for awarding aid:** *Need-based:* Academics, Music/drama. *Non-need-based:* Academics, Art, Athletics, Leadership.

UNIVERSITY OF WISCONSIN—OSHKOSH

Dempsey Hall 135, Oshkosh, WI 54901
Phone: 920-424-0202 • **Financial Aid Phone:** 920-424-4025
E-mail: oshadmuw@uwosh.edu • **CEEB Code:** 1916
Fax: 920-424-1098 • **Website:** http://www.uwosh.edu/home • **ACT Code:** 4674

This public school was founded in 1871. It has a 192-acre campus.

RATINGS

Admissions Selectivity Rating: 78   **Fire Safety Rating:** 60*   **Green Rating:** 97

STUDENTS AND FACULTY

Enrollment: 10,771. **Student Body:** 57% female, 43% male, 3% out-of-state, 1% international (32 countries represented). Asian 4%, African American 2%, Caucasian 88%, Hispanic 3%, Native American 1%, Pacific Islander <1%, Two or more races 1%, Race unknown <1%.
Retention and Graduation: 75% freshmen return for sophomore year. 13% freshmen graduate within 4 years. **Faculty:** Student/faculty ratio 22:1. 416 full-time faculty, 84% hold PhDs, 12% are are members of minority groups, 47% are women. 0% of classes are taught by teaching assistants.

ACADEMICS

Degrees: associate, bachelor's, certificate, master's. **Classes:** Most classes have 20-29 students. Most lab/discussion sessions have 20-29 students. **Most popular majors:** Elementary Education and Teaching; Business/Commerce; Registered Nursing, Nursing Administration, Nursing Research and Clinical Nursing. **Special Study Options:** Accelerated program, cooperative education program, cross-registration, distance learning, double major, dual enrollment, English as a Second Language (ESL), exchange student program (domestic), honors program, independent study, internships, liberal arts/career combination, student-designed major, study abroad, teacher certification program, weekend college. **Disability Services:** Special programs offered to physically disabled students, including note-taking services, reader services, tape recorders, tutors. **Career Services:** Alumni network, Career/job search classes, Career assessment, Internships. Local businesses recruit and mentor undergraduates.

FACILITIES

Housing: Coed dorms, special housing for disabled students, men's dorms, women's dorms, fraternity/sorority housing. **Special Academic Facilities/Equipment:** Art gallery, ceramics lab, electron microscope. **Computers:** Students can register for classes online.

CAMPUS LIFE

Environment: Village. **Activities:** Choral groups, concert band, dance, drama/theater, jazz band, literary magazine, music ensembles, pep band, radio station, student government, student newspaper, student-run film society, television station, Campus Ministries, Student Organization, Model UN. 175 registered organizations, 15 honor societies, 6 religious organizations. 8 fraternities, 5 sororities. **Athletics (Intercollegiate):** *Men:* baseball, basketball, cross-country, diving, football, soccer, swimming, tennis, track/field (outdoor), track/field (indoor), wrestling. *Women:* basketball, cross-country, diving, golf, gymnastics, soccer, softball, swimming, tennis, track/field (outdoor), track/field (indoor), volleyball. **Environmental Initiatives:** Leadership in adopting renewable energy, from 2003 as the largest purchaser of renewable electricity in the State of Wisconsin to the recent construction of the first commercial-scale dry anerobic biodigester in the Western Hemisphere.

ADMISSIONS

Freshman Academic Profile: Average high school GPA 3.3. 10% in top 10% of high school class, 37% in top 25% of high school class, 84% in top 50% of high school class. 90% from public high schools. ACT middle 50% range 20-24. Minimum internet-based TOEFL 70. Minimum paper TOEFL 525. **Basis for Candidate Selection:** *Very important factors considered include:* rigor of secondary school record, class rank, academic GPA, standardized test scores. *Important factors considered include:* application essay, recommendation(s), first generation. *Other factors considered include:* interview, extracurricular activities, talent/ability, character/personal qualities, alumni/ae relation, volunteer work, work experience. **Freshman Admission Requirements:** High school diploma is required and GED is accepted. *Academic units required:* 4 English, 3 math, 3 science, 3 science labs, 3 social studies, 2 history, 4 academic electives. *Academic units recommended:* 4 math, 4 science, 4 science labs, 2 foreign language, 4 social studies, 1 history, 1 visual/performing arts. **Freshman Admission Statistics:** 6,052 applied, 68.47% admitted, 44% enrolled. **Transfer Admission Requirements:** college transcript(s), Minimum college GPA of 2.50 required. Lowest grade transferable D. **General Admission Information:** Application fee $44. Nonfall registration accepted. Admission may be deferred.

COSTS AND FINANCIAL AID

Annual in-state tuition $7,360. Annual out-of-state tuition $14,934. Room and board $6,926. Average book expense $1,000. **Required Forms and Deadlines:** FAFSA. **Notification of Awards:** Applicants will be notified of awards on or about 4/15. **Types of Aid:** *Need-based scholarships/grants:* Federal Pell, FSEOG, State scholarships/grants, Private scholarships, College/university scholarship or grant aid from institutional funds, United Negro College Fund, Federal Nursing Scholarships. *Loans:* Direct Subsidized Stafford Loans, Direct Unsubsidized Stafford Loans, Direct PLUS loans, Federal Perkins Loans, Federal Nursing Loans, State Loans, College/university loans from institutional funds. *Student Employment:* Federal Work-Study Program available. Institutional employment available. **Financial Aid Statistics:** 53% needy freshmen, 55% needy undergrads receive need-based scholarship or grant aid. 35% freshmen, 20% undergrads receive non-need-based scholarship or grant aid. 29% freshmen, 20% undergrads receive need-based self-help aid. 0% freshmen, 0% undergrads receive athletic scholarships. **Criteria for awarding aid:** *Need-based:* Academics, Art, Job skills, Leadership, Minority status, Music/drama. *Non-need-based:* Academics, Art, Job skills, Leadership, Minority status, Music/drama, State/district residency.

UNIVERSITY OF WISCONSIN—RIVER FALLS

410 South Third Street, River Falls, WI 54022
Phone: 715-425-3500 • **Financial Aid Phone:** 715-425-3141
E-mail: admit@uwrf.edu • **CEEB Code:** 3923
Website: www.uwrf.edu • **ACT Code:** 1918

This public school was founded in 1874. It has a 225-acre campus.

RATINGS

Admissions Selectivity Rating: 82   **Fire Safety Rating:** 83   **Green Rating:** 95

STUDENTS AND FACULTY

Enrollment: 5,346. **Student Body:** 61% female, 39% male, 51% out-of-state, 3% international (24 countries represented). Asian 3%, African American 2%, Caucasian 88%, Hispanic 3%, Native American 1%, Pacific Islander <1%, Two or more races 0%, Race unknown <1%.
Retention and Graduation: 74% freshmen return for sophomore year. 26% grads go on to further study within 1 year. 22% grads pursue arts and sciences degrees. 12% grads pursue business degrees. **Faculty:** Student/faculty ratio 18:1. 252 full-time faculty, 0% hold PhDs, 10% are are members of minority groups, 46% are women. 0% of classes are taught by teaching assistants.

ACADEMICS

Degrees: bachelor's, master's, postbachelor's certificate, post-master's certificate. **Classes:** Most classes have 20-29 students. Most lab/discussion sessions have 10-19 students. **Most popular majors:** Elementary Education and Teaching; Business Administration and Management; Animal Sciences. **Special Study Options:** Accelerated program, cooperative education program, distance learning, double major, dual enrollment, exchange student program (domestic), honors program, independent study, internships, student-designed major, study abroad, teacher certification program. **Honors Programs:** The UW-River Falls Honors Program is designed to meet the educational needs of students who have an outstanding record of academic achievement and a true sense of intellectual adventure. It allows students to experience a variety of course types and educationally related experiences while gaining academic credit. Students enrolled in the program may choose Honors sections of many general education classes, take introductory and advanced Honors seminars, participate in Honors colloquia, complete an Honors thesis/project, enroll in a service-learning experience for credit and receive credits for participation in the intellectual and creative life of the UW-RF community and elsewhere. All of these experiences are gained while still keeping within the major and minor requirements of an Honors student's academic program. **Disability Services:** Special programs offered to physically disabled students, including note-taking services, reader services, tape recorders, tutors. **Career Services:** Alumni network, Alumni services, Career/job search classes, Career assessment, Internships, Regional alumni. Professional staff are available for one hour appointments to help you with placement, resume writing, portfolio help, licensing, etc.

FACILITIES

Housing: Coed dorms, women's dorms, fraternity/sorority housing, apartments for single students. 100% of campus accessible to physically diasbled. **Special Academic Facilities/Equipment:** Local history museum, 20-inch reflecting telescope, observatory, electron microscope, greenhouse, lab farms, educational technology center. **Computers:** Students can register for classes online. Administrative functions (other than registration) can be performed online.

CAMPUS LIFE

Environment: Village. **Activities:** Choral groups, concert band, dance, drama/theater, jazz band, literary magazine, music ensembles, musical theater, pep band, radio station, student government, student newspaper, symphony orchestra, television station 120 registered organizations, 9 honor societies, 12 religious organizations. 5 fraternities, 4 sororities. **Athletics (Intercollegiate):** *Men:* basketball, cross-country, football, ice hockey, swimming, track/field (outdoor), track/field (indoor). *Women:* basketball, cross-country, golf, ice hockey, soccer, softball, swimming, tennis, track/field (outdoor), track/field (indoor), volleyball. **On-Campus Highlights:** University Student Center, Leadership Center, Knowles/Hunt Recreation Complex, Chalmer Davee Library, Educational Technology Center, Swenson Sundial (world's largest), Carillon, Fine Arts performing complex, Two campus laboratory farms, and Kansas City Chiefs summer camp.

ADMISSIONS

Freshman Academic Profile: Average high school GPA 3.3. 12% in top 10% of high school class, 36% in top 25% of high school class, 72% in top 50% of high school class. 93% from public high schools. **Reported SAT (pre-2016 redesign) scores:** SAT Math middle 50% range 480-580. SAT Critical Reading middle 50% range 500-680. SAT Writing middle 50% range 480-580. **Concordant SAT scores:** SAT EBRW middle 50% 550–680. SAT Math middle 50% range 510–600. ACT middle 50% range 20-25. Minimum paper TOEFL 500. **Basis for Candidate Selection:** *Very important factors considered include:* rigor of secondary school record, class rank, standardized test scores. *Important factors considered include:* academic GPA, application essay. *Other factors considered include:* recommendation(s), extracurricular activities, talent/ability, character/personal qualities, first generation, racial/ethnic status, volunteer work, work experience. **Freshman Admission Requirements:** High school diploma is required and GED is accepted. *Academic units required:* 4 English, 3 math, 3 science, 3 social studies, 4 academic electives. *Academic units recommended:* 4 English, 4 math, 4 science, 1 science lab, 2 foreign language, 4 social studies, 4 academic electives. **Freshman Admission Statistics:** 3,236 applied, 72.00% admitted, 52% enrolled. **Transfer Admission Requirements:** college transcript(s), statement of good standing from prior institution(s). Minimum college GPA of 2.6 required. Lowest grade transferable D. **General Admission Information:** Application fee $44. Priority deadline 2/1. Nonfall registration accepted. Admission may be deferred for a maximum of 1 Year.

COSTS AND FINANCIAL AID

Annual in-state tuition $6,428. Annual out-of-state tuition $14,001. Room and board $6,576. Required fees $1,553. Average book expense $370. **Required Forms and Deadlines:** FAFSA. **Notification of Awards:** Applicants will be notified of awards on a rolling basis beginning 4/15. **Types of Aid:** *Need-based scholarships/grants:* Federal Pell, FSEOG, State scholarships/grants, Private scholarships, College/university scholarship or grant aid from institutional funds. *Loans:* Direct Subsidized Stafford Loans, Direct Unsubsidized Stafford Loans, Direct PLUS loans, Federal Perkins Loans. *Student Employment:* Federal Work-Study Program available. Institutional employment available. **Financial Aid Statistics:** 55% needy freshmen, 57% needy undergrads receive need-based scholarship or grant aid. 18% freshmen, 24% undergrads receive non-need-based scholarship or grant aid. 85% freshmen, 82% undergrads receive need-based self-help aid. 0% freshmen, 0% undergrads receive athletic scholarships. 77% freshmen, 68% undergrads receive any aid. 77% undergrads borrow to pay for school. Average cumulative indebtedness $27,232. **Criteria for awarding aid:** *Need-based:* Academics, Art, Leadership, Minority status, Music/drama. *Non-need-based:* Academics, Art, Leadership, Minority status, Music/drama, State/district residency.

UNIVERSITY OF WISCONSIN—STEVENS POINT

1108 Fremont St., Stevens Point, WI 54481
Phone: 715-346-2441 • **Financial Aid Phone:** 715-346-4771
E-mail: admiss@uwsp.edu • **CEEB Code:** 1919
Fax: 715-346-3296 • **Website:** www.uwsp.edu • **ACT Code:** 4680

This public school was founded in 1894. It has a 335-acre campus.

RATINGS

Admissions Selectivity Rating: 78   **Fire Safety Rating:** 79   **Green Rating:** 99

STUDENTS AND FACULTY

Enrollment: 8,684. **Student Body:** 52% female, 48% male, 11% out-of-state, 2% international (37 countries represented). Asian 3%, African American 2%, Caucasian 87%, Hispanic 4%, Native American 1%, Pacific Islander 0%, Two or more races 2%, Race unknown <1%.
Retention and Graduation: 27% freshmen graduate within 4 years. 65% freshmen graduate within 6 years. 14% grads go on to further study within 1 year. 20% grads pursue arts and sciences degrees. 1% grads pursue business degrees. **Faculty:** Student/faculty ratio 21:1. 369 full-time faculty, 89% hold PhDs, 10% are are members of minority groups, 43% are women. 0% of classes are taught by teaching assistants.

ACADEMICS

Degrees: associate, bachelor's, doctoral/professional, master's. **Classes:** Most classes have 20-29 students. Most lab/discussion sessions have 20-29 students. **Most popular majors:** Business/Commerce; Biological and Physical Sciences; Natural Resources/Conservation. **Special Study Options:** Accelerated program, distance learning, double major, dual enrollment, English as a Second Language (ESL), independent study, internships, student-designed major, study abroad, teacher certification program. **Disability Services:** Special programs offered to physically disabled students, including note-taking services, reader services, tape recorders, tutors. **Career Services:** Alumni network, Alumni services, Career/job search classes, Career assessment, Internships, Regional alumni, On-campus interviews. All students in UWSP's College of Natural Resources enroll in a six week summer field experience.

FACILITIES

Housing: Coed dorms, men's dorms, women's dorms, Wellness Housing, Theme Housing, Freshman Interest Groups. 100% of campus accessible to physically diasbled. **Special Academic Facilities/Equipment:** Art galleries, costume and goblet collections, museum of natural history, early childhood study institute, communicative disorders center, map center, observatory, planetarium, Foucault pendulum, nature preserve, environmental station, groundwater center, herbarium, aviary, wellness institute. **Computers:** 100% of classrooms, 10% of dorms, 100% of libraries, 100% of dining areas, 100% of student union, have wireless network access. Students can register for classes online. Administrative functions (other than registration) can be performed online.

CAMPUS LIFE

Environment: Town. **Activities:** Choral groups, concert band, dance, drama/theater, jazz band, literary magazine, music ensembles, musical theater, opera, pep band, radio station, student government, student newspaper, student-run film society, symphony orchestra, television station, Campus Ministries, Student Organization, Model UN. 185 registered organizations, 12 honor societies, 9 religious organizations. 4 fraternities, 3 sororities. **Athletics (Intercollegiate):** *Men:* baseball, basketball, cross-country, diving, football, ice hockey, swimming, track/field (outdoor), wrestling. *Women:* basketball, cross-country, diving, golf, ice hockey, soccer, softball, swimming, tennis, track/field (outdoor), volleyball. **On-Campus Highlights:** University Center/Brewhouse, Schmeeckle Reserve/Wisconsin Conservation Hall of, Health Enhancement Center, Allen Recreation Center, Fine Arts Building. The University Center houses the Information Center, Student Activities and Involvement Center, the university bookstore, meeting rooms, study lounges, Multicultural Center, and several dining options. The Schmeeckle Reserve is a 265-acre reserve available for educational and recreational use by students and community alike. The reserve includes a 24-acre lake and a 2 1/2 mile trail system used for recreational purposes. The Health Enhancement Center houses athletics, facilities for physical education programs, an Olympic-sized swimming pool, 7,500 square foot weight room, state-of-the-art training room, 8-lane indoor track with an infield for 6 tennis courts or 4 full-sized basketball courts, a fieldhouse and the Berg Gym. Allen Recreation Center provides a cardio-fitness facility, massage rooms, and a recreation center with rental equipment available for students. The Fine Arts Center houses the departments of Art and Design, Music, and Theatre and Dance. Concerts and drama productions are scheduled throughout the year in its two theatres. The Carlsten Art Gallery is also located here. Other highlights on campus include a huge mosaic on the outer, south wall of the College of Natural Resources building; a plenetarium located in the Science Building; the Learning Resources Center which contains Instructional Media Services, the library, and the Museum of Natural History; and the Communication Arts Center which houses the student radio station, student newspaper. and several television studios. **Environmental Initiatives:** In December 2012, UWSP hired an energy service company (ESCO) through the WI Performance Contracting Program. The ESCO will audit, identify and evaluate energy savings opportunities. Web-based building dashboards will be included in the project to display energy, water, and other environmental variables on kiosks.

ADMISSIONS

Freshman Academic Profile: Average high school GPA 3.1. 11% in top 10% of high school class, 33% in top 25% of high school class, 73% in top 50% of high school class. **Reported SAT (pre-2016 redesign) scores:** SAT Math middle 50% range 410-523. SAT Critical Reading middle 50% range 405-565. SAT Writing middle 50% range 390-530. **Concordant SAT scores:** SAT EBRW middle 50% 450–610. SAT Math middle 50% range 450–550. ACT middle 50% range 20-25. Minimum internet-based TOEFL 70. **Basis for Candidate Selection:** *Very important factors considered include:* rigor of secondary school record, class rank, academic GPA, standardized test scores. *Important factors considered include:* application essay, recommendation(s), talent/ability, first generation. *Other factors considered include:* interview, extracurricular activities, character/personal qualities, alumni/ae relation, geographical residence, state residency, racial/ethnic status, volunteer work, work experience. **Freshman Admission Requirements:** High school diploma is required and GED is accepted. *Academic units required:* 4 English, 3 math, 3 science, 3 social studies, 4 academic electives. *Academic units recommended:* 4 English, 4 math, 4 science, 4 social studies, 4 academic electives. **Freshman Admission Statistics:** 4,901 applied, 74.45% admitted, 49% enrolled. **Transfer Admission Requirements:** High school transcript, college transcript(s), statement of good standing from prior institution(s). Minimum college GPA of 2.25 required. Lowest grade transferable D. **General Admission Information:** Nonfall registration accepted.

COSTS AND FINANCIAL AID

Annual in-state tuition $7,674. Annual out-of-state tuition $15,940. Room and board $3,414. Required fees $1,374. Average book expense $500. **Required Forms and Deadlines:** FAFSA. **Notification of Awards:** Applicants will be notified of awards on a rolling basis beginning 3/1. **Types of Aid:** *Need-based scholarships/grants:* Federal Pell, FSEOG, State scholarships/grants, Private scholarships, College/university scholarship or grant aid from institutional funds. *Loans:* Direct Subsidized Stafford Loans, Direct Unsubsidized Stafford Loans, Direct PLUS Loans, Federal Perkins Loans. *Student Employment:* Federal Work-Study Program available. Institutional employment available. **Financial Aid Statistics:** 71% needy freshmen, 71% needy undergrads receive need-based scholarship or grant aid. 61% freshmen, 62% undergrads receive non-need-based scholarship or grant aid. 90% freshmen, 90% undergrads receive need-based self-help aid. 0% freshmen, 0% undergrads receive athletic scholarships. 65% freshmen, 68% undergrads receive any aid. Average cumulative indebtedness $25,030. **Criteria for awarding aid:** *Non-need-based:* Academics, Alumni affiliation, Art, Music/drama.

UNIVERSITY OF WISCONSIN—STOUT

Admissions UW-Stout, Menomonie, WI 54751
Phone: 715-232-1411 • **Financial Aid Phone:** 715-232-1363
E-mail: admissions@uwstout.edu • **CEEB Code:** 1740
Fax: 715-232-1667 • **Website:** www.uwstout.edu • **ACT Code:** 4652

This public school was founded in 1891. It has a 110-acre campus.

RATINGS

Admissions Selectivity Rating: 74 **Fire Safety Rating:** 62 **Green Rating:** 86

STUDENTS AND FACULTY

Enrollment: 8,178. **Student Body:** 45% female, 55% male, 33% out-of-state, 2% international (28 countries represented). Asian 3%, African American 2%, Caucasian 87%, Hispanic 1%, Native American <1%, Pacific Islander <1%, Two or more races 4%, Race unknown <1%.
Retention and Graduation: 73% freshmen return for sophomore year. 21% freshmen graduate within 4 years. 9% grads go on to further study within 1 year. **Faculty:** Student/faculty ratio 19:1. 401 full-time faculty, 77% hold PhDs, 14% are members of minority groups, 46% are women. 0% of classes are taught by teaching assistants.

ACADEMICS

Degrees: bachelor's, certificate, doctoral/professional, master's, postbachelor's certifiate, post-master's certificate. **Classes:** Most classes have 20-29 students. Most lab/discussion sessions have 20-29 students. **Most popular majors:**

Design and Applied Arts; Business/Commerce; Hospitality Administration/ Management. **Special Study Options:** Accelerated program, cooperative education program, cross-registration, distance learning, double major, dual enrollment, exchange student program (domestic), external degree program, honors program, independent study, internships, study abroad, teacher certification program. **Honors Programs:** The University Honors Program (UHP) is designed to enhance the education of students challenging them to think in more depth and detail and to provide the opportunity to meet other students while doing so. **Disability Services:** Special programs offered to physically disabled students, including note-taking services, reader services, tutors. **Career Services:** Alumni services, Career/job search classes, Internships. Our Co-op Program now exceeds 676 co-op students per year.

FACILITIES

Housing: Coed dorms, special housing for disabled students, apartments for single students, freshmen housing, smoke-free housing, upperclass/graduate housing, alcohol-free housing. 100% of campus accessible to physically diasbled. **Special Academic Facilities/Equipment:** Specialized labs support degree programs throughout the campus. Furlong Art Gallery in Micheal's Hall. **Computers:** Students can register for classes online. Administrative functions (other than registration) can be performed online. Undergraduates are required to own a computer.

CAMPUS LIFE

Environment: Village. **Activities:** Choral groups, concert band, dance, drama/ theater, jazz band, literary magazine, marching band, music ensembles, musical theater, pep band, radio station, student government, student newspaper, student-run film society, Campus Ministries, Student Organization, Model UN. 120 registered organizations, 1 honor society, 12 religious organizations. 5 fraternities, 3 sororities. **Athletics (Intercollegiate):** *Men:* baseball, basketball, cross-country, football, ice hockey, track/field (outdoor). *Women:* basketball, cross-country, gymnastics, soccer, softball, tennis, track/field (outdoor), volleyball. **On-Campus Highlights:** Millenium Hall, Athletic Complex, Ropes Course- Climbing Wall- In-line Skating, Student Center, Micheels Hall.

ADMISSIONS

Freshman Academic Profile: Average high school GPA 3.2. 8% in top 10% of high school class, 28% in top 25% of high school class, 64% in top 50% of high school class. ACT middle 50% range 19-25. Minimum paper TOEFL 500. **Basis for Candidate Selection:** *Very important factors considered include:* class rank, academic GPA, standardized test scores. *Important factors considered include:* rigor of secondary school record, application essay. *Other factors considered include:* recommendation(s), interview, extracurricular activities, talent/ability, character/personal qualities, first generation, alumni/ ae relation, racial/ethnic status, volunteer work, work experience, level of applicant's interest. **Freshman Admission Requirements:** High school diploma is required and GED is accepted. *Academic units required:* 4 English, 3 math, 3 science, 3 social studies, 4 academic electives. *Academic units recommended:* 2 foreign language. **Freshman Admission Statistics:** 3,445 applied, 87.75% admitted, 53% enrolled. **Transfer Admission Requirements:** college transcript(s), statement of good standing from prior institution(s). Minimum college GPA of 2.5 required. Lowest grade transferable D-. **General Admission Information:** Application fee $44. Priority deadline 1/1. Nonfall registration accepted.

COSTS AND FINANCIAL AID

Annual in-state tuition $7,014. Annual out-of-state tuition $14,760. Room and board $6,624. Required fees $2,380. Average book expense $402. **Required Forms and Deadlines:** FAFSA. **Notification of Awards:** Applicants will be notified of awards on a rolling basis beginning 3/21. **Types of Aid:** *Need-based scholarships/grants:* Federal Pell, FSEOG, State scholarships/grants, Private scholarships, College/university scholarship or grant aid from institutional funds. *Loans:* Direct Subsidized Stafford Loans, Direct Unsubsidized Stafford Loans, Direct PLUS loans, Federal Perkins Loans. *Student Employment:* Federal Work-Study Program available. Institutional employment available. **Financial Aid Statistics:** 49% needy freshmen, 72% needy undergrads receive need-based scholarship or grant aid. 36% freshmen, 27% undergrads receive non-need-based scholarship or grant aid. 92% freshmen, 92% undergrads receive need-based self-help aid. 0% freshmen, 0% undergrads receive athletic scholarships. 71% freshmen, 74% undergrads receive any aid. 79% undergrads borrow to pay for school. Average cumulative indebtedness $30,563. **Criteria for awarding aid:** *Non-need-based:* Academics.

UNIVERSITY OF WISCONSIN—SUPERIOR

Belknap and Catlin, P.O. Box 2000, Superior, WI 54880-4500
Phone: 715-394-8230 • **Financial Aid Phone:** 715-394-8200
E-mail: admissions@uwsuper.edu • **CEEB Code:** 1920
Fax: 715-394-8407 • **Website:** www.uwsuper.edu • **ACT Code:** 4682

This public school was founded in 1893. It has a 230-acre campus.

RATINGS
Admissions Selectivity Rating: 77   **Fire Safety Rating:** 84   **Green Rating:** 60*

STUDENTS AND FACULTY
Enrollment: 2,254. **Student Body:** 61% female, 39% male, 40% out-of-state, 8% international (44 countries represented). Asian 1%, African American 2%, Caucasian 81%, Hispanic 2%, Native American 2%, Pacific Islander <1%, Two or more races 3%, Race unknown <1%.
Retention and Graduation: 67% freshmen return for sophomore year. 16% freshmen graduate within 4 years. 40% freshmen graduate within 6 years. **Faculty:** Student/faculty ratio 14:1. 123 full-time faculty, 76% hold PhDs, 10% are are members of minority groups, 52% are women. 0% of classes are taught by teaching assistants.

ACADEMICS
Degrees: associate, bachelor's, certificate, master's, postbachelor's certifate, post-master's certificate. **Classes:** Most classes have 10-19 students. Most lab/discussion sessions have 10-19 students. **Most popular majors:** Business Administration and Management; Elementary Education and Teaching; Communication. **Special Study Options:** cooperative education program, cross-registration, distance learning, double major, dual enrollment, English as a Second Language (ESL), exchange student program (domestic), external degree program, independent study, internships, liberal arts/career combination, student-designed major, study abroad, teacher certification program. **Disability Services:** Special programs offered to physically disabled students, including note-taking services, tape recorders, tutors. **Career Services:** Alumni network, Alumni services, Career/job search classes, Career assessment, Internships, Regional alumni. Our web-based recruiting system, Jacket Jobs, links students with hundreds of positions throughout our region.

FACILITIES
Housing: Coed dorms, special housing for disabled students, women's dorms, apartments for married students, apartments for single students, 90% of campus accessible to physically diasbled. **Special Academic Facilities/Equipment:** TV, radio, and film facilities, observatory, greenhouse, two art galleries, recital hall, four theaters, modern health and wellness center. Major Library renovations to be completed and major student center renovation in works. **Computers:** 40% of classrooms, 100% of libraries, 100% of dining areas, 100% of student union, 20% of common outdoor areas have wireless network access. Students can register for classes online. Administrative functions (other than registration) can be performed online.

CAMPUS LIFE
Environment: City. **Activities:** Choral groups, concert band, dance, drama/theater, jazz band, literary magazine, music ensembles, musical theater, pep band, radio station, student government, student newspaper, student-run film society, symphony orchestra, television station, Campus Ministries, Student Organization. 70 registered organizations, 1 honor society, 5 religious organizations. 1 sororities. **Athletics (Intercollegiate):** *Men:* baseball, basketball, cross-country, ice hockey, soccer, track/field (outdoor), track/field (indoor). *Women:* basketball, cross-country, golf, ice hockey, soccer, softball, track/field (outdoor), track/field (indoor), volleyball. **On-Campus Highlights:** New Health and Wellness Center, Coffee Nook, Snack Bar, Rothwell Student Center Student Lounge, Multicultural Center, Health and Wellness Center is a new $17 million facility complete with running track, climbing wall, raquetball courts and much more. Library renovations underway, new student center renovations starting soon. **Environmental Initiatives:** LEED certification for new buildings.

ADMISSIONS
Freshman Academic Profile: Average high school GPA 3.1. 10% in top 10% of high school class, 21% in top 25% of high school class, 59% in top 50% of high school class. ACT middle 50% range 19-23. Minimum internet-based TOEFL 61. Minimum paper TOEFL 500. **Basis for Candidate Selection:** *Very important factors considered include:* rigor of secondary school record. *Important factors considered include:* class rank, academic GPA, standardized test scores. *Other factors considered include:* application essay, recommendation(s), interview, extracurricular activities, talent/ability, character/personal qualities, first generation, racial/ethnic status, volunteer work, work experience. **Freshman Admission Requirements:** High school diploma is required and GED is accepted. *Academic units required:* 4 English, 3 math, 3

science, 3 social studies, 4 academic electives. *Academic units recommended:* 4 math, 4 science, 2 foreign language, 4 social studies. **Freshman Admission Statistics:** 995 applied, 71.66% admitted, 51% enrolled. **Transfer Admission Requirements:** college transcript(s), Minimum college GPA of 2.0 required. Lowest grade transferable D. **General Admission Information:** Application fee $44. Priority deadline 4/1. Regular application deadline 8/1. Nonfall registration accepted. Admission may be deferred for a maximum of 1 semester.

COSTS AND FINANCIAL AID
Annual in-state tuition $6,535. Annual out-of-state tuition $14,108. Room and board $6,410. Required fees $1,501. Average book expense $900. **Required Forms and Deadlines:** FAFSA. **Notification of Awards:** Applicants will be notified of awards on a rolling basis beginning 4/1. **Types of Aid:** *Need-based scholarships/grants:* Federal Pell, FSEOG, State scholarships/grants, Private scholarships, College/university scholarship or grant aid from institutional funds. *Loans:* Direct Subsidized Stafford Loans, Direct Unsubsidized Stafford Loans, Direct PLUS loans, Federal Perkins Loans, State Loans, College/university loans from institutional funds. *Student Employment:* Federal Work-Study Program available. Institutional employment available. **Financial Aid Statistics:** 58% needy freshmen, 67% needy undergrads receive need-based scholarship or grant aid. 51% freshmen, 28% undergrads receive non-need-based scholarship or grant aid. 81% freshmen, 87% undergrads receive need-based self-help aid. 0% freshmen, 0% undergrads receive athletic scholarships. 54% freshmen, 64% undergrads receive any aid. 76% undergrads borrow to pay for school. Average cumulative indebtedness $29,139. **Criteria for awarding aid:** *Need-based:* Academics, Art, Minority status, Music/drama. *Non-need-based:* Academics, Alumni affiliation, Art, Leadership, Minority status, Music/drama, State/district residency.

UNIVERSITY OF WISCONSIN—WHITEWATER

800 West Main Street, Whitewater, WI 53190-1791
Phone: 262-472-1440 • **Financial Aid Phone:** 262-472-1130
E-mail: uwwadmit@uww.edu • **CEEB Code:** 1921
Fax: 262-472-1515 • **Website:** http://www.uww.edu/ • **ACT Code:** 4684

This public school was founded in 1868. It has a 385-acre campus.

RATINGS
Admissions Selectivity Rating: 76   **Fire Safety Rating:** 84   **Green Rating:** 78

STUDENTS AND FACULTY
Enrollment: 8,999. **Student Body:** 50% female, 50% male, 4% out-of-state, <1% international (69 countries represented). Asian 2%, African American 4%, Caucasian 90%, Hispanic 2%, Native American <1%, Pacific Islander 0%, Two or more races 0%, Race unknown <1%.
Retention and Graduation: 74% freshmen return for sophomore year. 21% freshmen graduate within 4 years. **Faculty:** Student/faculty ratio 22:1. 392 full-time faculty, 85% hold PhDs, 18% are are members of minority groups, 44% are women. 0% of classes are taught by teaching assistants.

ACADEMICS
Degrees: associate, bachelor's, master's. **Classes:** Most classes have 30-39 students. **Most popular majors:** Journalism; Elementary Education and Teaching; Physical Education Teaching and Coaching. **Special Study Options:** Accelerated program, cooperative education program, cross-registration, distance learning, double major, dual enrollment, English as a Second Language (ESL), exchange student program (domestic), external degree program, honors program, independent study, internships, liberal arts/career combination, student-designed major, study abroad, teacher certification program, weekend college. **Honors Programs:** General academic honors program. **Disability Services:** Special programs offered to physically disabled students, including note-taking services, reader services, tape recorders, tutors. **Career Services:** Career/job search classes, Career assessment, Internships.

FACILITIES
Housing: Coed dorms, special housing for disabled students, special housing for international students, women's dorms. 100% of campus accessible to physically diasbled. **Special Academic Facilities/Equipment:** Two electron microscopes, State of the Art Theater/Auditorium. **Computers:** Students can register for classes online. Administrative functions (other than registration) can be performed online.

CAMPUS LIFE
Environment: Village. **Activities:** Choral groups, concert band, dance, drama/theater, jazz band, literary magazine, marching band, music ensembles, musical theater, opera, radio station, student government, student newspaper, symphony orchestra, television station 130 registered organizations, 4 honor societies, 8 religious organizations. 9 fraternities, 8 sororities. **Athletics (Intercollegiate):**

Men: baseball, basketball, cross-country, diving, football, soccer, swimming, tennis, track/field (outdoor), track/field (indoor), wrestling. *Women:* basketball, bowling, cross-country, diving, golf, gymnastics, soccer, softball, swimming, tennis, track/field (outdoor), track/field (indoor), volleyball. **On-Campus Highlights:** New Kachel Field House, University Center, Underground Dance Club, Ritazza Coffee Shop, Warhawk Room.

ADMISSIONS

Freshman Academic Profile: 9% in top 10% of high school class, 32% in top 25% of high school class, 77% in top 50% of high school class. 90% from public high schools. **Reported SAT (pre-2016 redesign) scores:** SAT Math middle 50% range 480-600. SAT Writing middle 50% range 470-610. **Concordant SAT scores:** SAT Math middle 50% range 510–620. ACT middle 50% range 20-24. Minimum paper TOEFL 500. **Basis for Candidate Selection:** *Very important factors considered include:* rigor of secondary school record, class rank, standardized test scores. *Other factors considered include:* academic GPA, application essay, recommendation(s), interview, extracurricular activities, talent/ability, character/personal qualities, first generation, geographical residence, state residency, racial/ethnic status, volunteer work, work experience, level of applicant's interest. **Freshman Admission Requirements:** High school diploma is required and GED is accepted. *Academic units required:* 4 English, 3 math, 3 science, 1 science lab, 3 social studies, 4 academic electives. *Academic units recommended:* 4 math, 4 science, 2 foreign language, 4 social studies. **Freshman Admission Statistics:** 5,570 applied, 75.64% admitted, 43% enrolled. **Transfer Admission Requirements:** High school transcript, college transcript(s), Minimum college GPA of 2.0 required. Lowest grade transferable D-. **General Admission Information:** Application fee $35. Priority deadline 1/1. Nonfall registration accepted. Admission may be deferred for a maximum of 3 terms or 1.

COSTS AND FINANCIAL AID

Annual in-state tuition $5,568. Annual out-of-state tuition $13,042. Room and board $4,322. Required fees $710. Average book expense $170. **Required Forms and Deadlines:** FAFSA. **Notification of Awards:** Applicants will be notified of awards on a rolling basis beginning 4/1. **Types of Aid:** *Need-based scholarships/grants:* Federal Pell, FSEOG, State scholarships/grants, Private scholarships, College/university scholarship or grant aid from institutional funds. *Loans:* Direct Subsidized Stafford Loans, Direct Unsubsidized Stafford Loans, Direct PLUS loans, Federal Perkins Loans, College/university loans from institutional funds. *Student Employment:* Federal Work-Study Program available. Institutional employment available. **Financial Aid Statistics:** 38% needy freshmen, 44% needy undergrads receive need-based scholarship or grant aid. 28% freshmen, 14% undergrads receive non-need-based scholarship or grant aid. 90% freshmen, 89% undergrads receive need-based self-help aid. 0% freshmen, 0% undergrads receive athletic scholarships. 52% freshmen, 42% undergrads receive any aid. **Criteria for awarding aid:** *Need-based:* Academics, Leadership, Minority status. *Non-need-based:* Academics, Alumni affiliation, Art, Leadership, Minority status, Music/drama, State/district residency.

UNIVERSITY OF WYOMING

Dept 3435, Laramie, WY 82071
Phone: 307-766-5160 • **Financial Aid Phone:** 307-766-2116
E-mail: admissions@uwyo.edu • **CEEB Code:** 4855
Fax: 307-766-4042 • **Website:** www.uwyo.edu • **ACT Code:** 5006

This public school was founded in 1886. It has a 785-acre campus.

RATINGS

Admissions Selectivity Rating: 78   **Fire Safety Rating:** 91   **Green Rating:** 76

STUDENTS AND FACULTY

Enrollment: 9,622. **Student Body:** 51% female, 49% male, 38% out-of-state, 4% international (91 countries represented). Asian 1%, African American 1%, Caucasian 73%, Hispanic 7%, Native American 1%, Pacific Islander <1%, Two or more races 3%, Race unknown 9%.
Retention and Graduation: 76% freshmen return for sophomore year. 55% freshmen graduate within 6 years. **Faculty:** Student/faculty ratio 14:1. 764 full-time faculty, 77% hold PhDs, 9% are are members of minority groups, 40% are women. 10% of classes are taught by teaching assistants.

ACADEMICS

Degrees: bachelor's, certificate, doctoral/professional, doctoral/research, master's, postbachelor's certificate, post-master's certificate. **Classes:** Most classes have 20-29 students. Most lab/discussion sessions have 20-29 students. **Most popular majors:** Mechanical Engineering; Psychology; Registered Nursing/Registered Nurse. **Special Study Options:** Accelerated program, distance learning, double major, English as a Second Language (ESL), exchange student program (domestic), external degree program, honors program, independent study, internships, student-designed major, study abroad. **Honors Programs:** The University Honors Program provides highly motivated students a series of curricular and extracurricular opportunities. Most students are selected for the program prior to their freshman year, although the program welcomes UW and transfer students up to the beginning of the junior year. Each year the Honors Program awards scholarships to qualifying students who are beginning their undergraduate education or who are entering the University as transfer students. The honors students organize extracurricular activities, have a student lounge and computers for their use, and have the option of living on one of the honors floors in the residence halls or in the Honors House. Courses offered in the honors program are restricted to honors program students; exceptions must be approved by the Honors program office. Combined degree programs: BA/MEng. **Disability Services:** Special programs offered to physically disabled students, including note-taking services, reader services, tape recorders, tutors. **Career Services:** Alumni network, Alumni services, Career/job search classes, Career assessment, Internships, Regional alumni.

FACILITIES

Housing: Coed dorms, special housing for disabled students, fraternity/sorority housing, apartments for married students, apartments for single students, Floor specific living plans in the residence halls; Health Sciences Living house. 95% of campus accessible to physically diasbled. **Special Academic Facilities/ Equipment:** Art gallery, Geology museum, American Heritage Center, Rocky Mountain Herbarium, Solheim Mycology Herbarium, art museum, planetarium, environmental biology lab, anthropology museum, on-site elementary school, state veterinary lab, infrared telescope observatory, lysimeter lab, insect museum and gallery room, Wyoming Geographic Information Science Center, Writing Center, Wyoming Cooperative Fishery and Wildlife Research Unit. **Computers:** 75% of classrooms, 20% of dorms, 100% of libraries, 5% of dining areas, 100% of student union, 10% of common outdoor areas have wireless network access. Students can register for classes online. Administrative functions (other than registration) can be performed online.

CAMPUS LIFE

Environment: Town. **Activities:** Choral groups, concert band, dance, drama/theater, jazz band, literary magazine, marching band, music ensembles, musical theater, opera, pep band, radio station, student government, student newspaper, symphony orchestra, television station, Campus Ministries, Student Organization, Model UN. 223 registered organizations, 41 honor societies, 17 religious organizations. 8 fraternities, 6 sororities. **Athletics (Intercollegiate):** *Men:* basketball, cheerleading, cross-country, diving, football, golf, swimming, track/field (outdoor), track/field (indoor), wrestling. *Women:* basketball, cheerleading, cross-country, diving, golf, soccer, swimming, tennis, track/field (outdoor), track/field (indoor), volleyball. **On-Campus Highlights:** Student Union, American Heritage Center and Art Museum, Geology Museum, Fine Arts Center, Half-Acre Gym. **Environmental Initiatives:** Campus Sustainability Committee.

ADMISSIONS

Freshman Academic Profile: Average high school GPA 3.5. 22% in top 10% of high school class, 48% in top 25% of high school class, 79% in top 50% of high school class. **Reported SAT (pre-2016 redesign) scores:** SAT Math middle 50% range 490-610. SAT Critical Reading middle 50% range 470-600. **Concordant SAT scores:** SAT Math middle 50% range 520–630. ACT middle 50% range 21-27. Minimum internet-based TOEFL 76. Minimum paper TOEFL 540. **Basis for Candidate Selection:** *Very important factors considered include:* rigor of secondary school record, academic GPA, standardized test scores. *Other factors considered include:* application essay. **Freshman Admission Requirements:** High school diploma is required and GED is accepted. *Academic units required:* 4 English, 4 math, 4 science, 3 science labs, 2 foreign language, 3 social studies, 2 academic electives, and 2 units from above areas or other academic areas. *Academic units recommended:* 4 English, 4 math, 4 science, 3 science labs, 2 foreign language, 3 social studies, 2 academic electives, and 2 units from above areas or other academic areas. **Freshman Admission Statistics:** 4,883 applied, 95.08% admitted, 33% enrolled. **Transfer Admission Requirements:** college transcript(s), Minimum college GPA of 2.0 required. Lowest grade transferable D. **General Admission Information:** Application fee $40. Priority deadline 3/1. Regular application deadline 8/10. Nonfall registration accepted. Admission may be deferred for a maximum of 1 year.

COSTS AND FINANCIAL AID

Annual in-state tuition $3,720. Annual out-of-state tuition $14,880. Room and board $10,320. Required fees $1,335. Average book expense $1,200. **Required Forms and Deadlines:** FAFSA. **Notification of Awards:** Applicants will be notified of awards on a rolling basis beginning 3/28. **Types of Aid:** *Need-based scholarships/grants:* Federal Pell, FSEOG, State scholarships/grants, Private scholarships, College/university scholarship or grant aid from institutional funds. *Loans:* Direct Subsidized Stafford Loans, Direct Unsubsidized Stafford Loans, Direct PLUS loans, Federal Perkins Loans. *Student Employment:* Federal Work-Study Program available. Institutional employment available. **Financial Aid Statistics:** 60% needy freshmen, 66% needy undergrads receive need-based scholarship or grant aid. 90% freshmen, 70% undergrads receive non-need-based scholarship or grant aid. 51% freshmen, 61% undergrads receive need-based self-help aid. 6% freshmen, 4% undergrads receive athletic scholarships. 45% undergrads borrow to pay for school. Average cumulative indebtedness $25,378. **Criteria for awarding aid:** *Need-based:* Academics, Athletics, Job skills, Minority status. *Non-need-based:* Academics, Alumni affiliation, Art, Athletics, Leadership, Minority status, Music/drama, State/district residency.

UPPER IOWA UNIVERSITY

Parker Fox Hall Box 1859, Fayette, IA 52142-1859
Phone: 800-553-4150 • **Financial Aid Phone:** 563-425-5276
E-mail: admission@uiu.edu
Fax: 563-425-5277 • **ACT Code:** 1360

This private school was founded in 1857. It has a 80-acre campus.

RATINGS

Admissions Selectivity Rating: 74   **Fire Safety Rating:** 84   **Green Rating:** 70

STUDENTS AND FACULTY

Enrollment: 3,859. **Student Body:** 62% female, 38% male, 55% out-of-state, 2% international (30 countries represented). Asian 1%, African American 20%, Caucasian 66%, Hispanic 6%, Native American <1%, Pacific Islander <1%, Two or more races 2%, Race unknown 3%.
Retention and Graduation: 63% freshmen return for sophomore year. 28% freshmen graduate within 4 years. 44% freshmen graduate within 6 years. 25% grads go on to further study within 1 year. 29% grads pursue arts and sciences degrees. 1% grads pursue law degrees. 17% grads pursue business degrees. 5% grads pursue medical degrees. **Faculty:** Student/faculty ratio 17:1. 78 full-time faculty, 59% hold PhDs, 3% are are members of minority groups, 55% are women. 0% of classes are taught by teaching assistants.

ACADEMICS

Degrees: associate, bachelor's, certificate, master's, terminal, transfer. **Classes:** Most classes have 10-19 students. Most lab/discussion sessions have 10-19 students. **Most popular majors:** Psychology; Human Services; Human Resources Management/Personnel Administration. **Special Study Options:** Accelerated program, distance learning, double major, dual enrollment, English as a Second Language (ESL), external degree program, independent study, internships, liberal arts/career combination, student-designed major, study abroad, teacher certification program. **Disability Services:** Special programs offered to physically disabled students, including reader services, tape recorders, tutors. **Career Services:** Alumni services, Career/job search classes, Career assessment, Internships, Regional alumni. Our office provides a wide variety of services via our website so that our off-campus center students and alumni have access to the same services as our on campus students; we provide individual career-related (e.g. choosing a major, resume and cover letter, internship/job search, career change) appointments in person, via phone and electronically.

FACILITIES

Housing: Coed dorms, men's dorms, women's dorms, Apartment-style housing. 70% of campus accessible to physically diasbled. **Computers:** 100% of classrooms, 100% of dorms, 100% of libraries, 100% of dining areas, 100% of student union, 33% of common outdoor areas have wireless network access. Students can register for classes online. Administrative functions (other than registration) can be performed online.

CAMPUS LIFE

Environment: Rural. **Activities:** Choral groups, pep band, student government, student newspaper, Campus Ministries, Student Organization. 40 registered organizations, 1 honor society, 1 religious organization. 4 fraternities, 5 sororities. **Athletics (Intercollegiate)** *Men:* baseball, basketball, cross-country, football, golf, soccer, wrestling. *Women:* basketball, cross-country, golf, soccer, softball, tennis, volleyball. **On-Campus Highlights:** Rec Center, Grill

151, Dorman Gym, Andres Center for Business and Education, Cafeteria, We have 3 new buildings that will be opening in 2010. A new student center, liberal arts building and new housing unit. **Environmental Initiatives:** Geothermal Heating/Cooling.

ADMISSIONS

Freshman Academic Profile: Average high school GPA 3.1. 22% in top 10% of high school class, 27% in top 25% of high school class, 57% in top 50% of high school class. ACT middle 50% range 17-24. Minimum internet-based TOEFL 61. Minimum paper TOEFL 500. **Basis for Candidate Selection:** *Very important factors considered include:* academic GPA, standardized test scores. *Other factors considered include:* rigor of secondary school record, class rank, recommendation(s). **Freshman Admission Requirements:** High school diploma is required and GED is accepted. **Freshman Admission Statistics:** 1,121 applied, 94.20% admitted, 20% enrolled. **Transfer Admission Requirements:** High school transcript, college transcript(s), Lowest grade transferable D-. **General Admission Information:** Nonfall registration accepted. Admission may be deferred.

COSTS AND FINANCIAL AID

Annual tuition $28,850. Room and board $8,370. Required fees $750. Average book expense $1,500. **Required Forms and Deadlines:** FAFSA. **Notification of Awards:** Applicants will be notified of awards on a rolling basis beginning 3/1. **Types of Aid:** *Need-based scholarships/grants:* Federal Pell, FSEOG, State scholarships/grants, Private scholarships, College/university scholarship or grant aid from institutional funds. *Loans:* Direct Subsidized Stafford Loans, Direct Unsubsidized Stafford Loans, Direct PLUS loans, Federal Perkins Loans. *Student Employment:* Federal Work-Study Program available. **Financial Aid Statistics:** 45% needy freshmen, 85% needy undergrads receive need-based scholarship or grant aid. 3% freshmen, 7% undergrads receive non-need-based scholarship or grant aid. 97% freshmen, 95% undergrads receive need-based self-help aid. 0% freshmen, 0% undergrads receive athletic scholarships. 100% freshmen, 90% undergrads receive any aid. 96% undergrads borrow to pay for school. Average cumulative indebtedness $18,863. **Criteria for awarding aid:** *Need-based:* Academics, Alumni affiliation. *Non-need-based:* Academics, Alumni affiliation, Athletics.

URSINUS COLLEGE

Best Colleges

Ursinus College, Collegeville, PA 19426
Phone: 610-409-3200 • **Financial Aid Phone:** 610-409-3600
E-mail: admission@ursinus.edu • **CEEB Code:** 2931
Fax: 610-409-3197 • **Website:** www.ursinus.edu • **ACT Code:** 3738

This private school was founded in 1869. It has a 170-acre campus.

RATINGS

Admissions Selectivity Rating: 82   **Fire Safety Rating:** 96   **Green Rating:** 85

STUDENTS AND FACULTY

Enrollment: 1,540. **Student Body:** 53% female, 47% male, 44% out-of-state, 2% international (25 countries represented). Asian 4%, African American 6%, Caucasian 74%, Hispanic 7%, Native American <1%, Pacific Islander 0%, Two or more races 4%, Race unknown 2%.
Retention and Graduation: 84% freshmen return for sophomore year. 73% freshmen graduate within 4 years. 78% freshmen graduate within 6 years. 21% grads go on to further study within 1 year. 67% grads pursue arts and sciences degrees. 7% grads pursue law degrees. 1% grads pursue business degrees. 22% grads pursue medical degrees. **Faculty:** Student/faculty ratio 11:1. 121 full-time faculty, 93% hold PhDs, 16% are are members of minority groups, 55% are women. 0% of classes are taught by teaching assistants.

ACADEMICS

Degrees: bachelor's. **Classes:** Most classes have fewer than 10 students. Most lab/discussion sessions have 10-19 students. **Most popular majors:** Economics; Biology/Biological Sciences; Psychology. **Special Study Options:** double major, dual enrollment, English as a Second Language (ESL), honors program, independent study, internships, student-designed major, study abroad, teacher certification program, Howard University Semester. **Honors Programs:** The Ursinus Summer Fellows program provides stipends to rising juniors and seniors to live on campus and do faculty-mentored research over the summer months. Fellows' projects often lead to senior honors projects. Combined degree programs: BA/MD, BA/MEng, Early Assurance-Drexel Univ. College of

Medicine. **Disability Services:** Special programs offered to physically disabled students, including note-taking services, reader services, tape recorders, tutors. **Career Services:** Alumni network, Alumni services, Career/job search classes, Career assessment, Internships, Regional alumni. Our internship opportunities are exceptional and numerous and have taken our students on all sorts of adventures: to nearby pharmaceutical labs, to U.S. embassies overseas, to the summer stock stages of the Berkshires, and to a marine mammal rescue station at the Jersey Shore. Internships are available to students in every major, and even to those studying abroad. With a full range of staffing and Internet resources to find, match and place students in internships that are right for them, Ursinus has a high percentage of students who participate in these experiences.

FACILITIES

Housing: Coed dorms, men's dorms, special housing for international students, women's dorms, Ursinus features the Residential Village, a cluster of 25 restored Victorian-era houses. Theme houses include: Musser International, Unity, Wellness, Language, Biology, Service, Zwingli Literary House and Wicks Honors House. 40 percent of Ursinus students reside in these houses. **Special Academic Facilities/Equipment:** The Kaleidoscope (performing arts center) lt;brgt; New field house lt;brgt;new 143-bed dormitorylt;brgt; Berman Museum of Artlt;brgt;6 new telescopeslt;brgt; scanning electron microscopelt;brgt;Bruker 300 MHz NMRlt;brgt; Perkin Elmer Spectrum 1000 FTIRlt;brgt; LKB Isothermal Calorimeterlt;brgt; an assortment of spectrometers and an HPLClt;brgt; recently-renovated Pfahler Hall of Science. **Computers:** 100% of classrooms, 100% of libraries, 100% of dining areas, 100% of student union, 50% of common outdoor areas have wireless network access. Students can register for classes online. Administrative functions (other than registration) can be performed online. Undergraduates are required to own a computer.

CAMPUS LIFE

Environment: City. **Activities:** Choral groups, concert band, dance, drama/theater, jazz band, literary magazine, music ensembles, musical theater, pep band, radio station, student government, student newspaper, student-run film society, television station, yearbook. 88 registered organizations, 27 honor societies, 4 religious organizations. 7 fraternities, 7 sororities. **Athletics (Intercollegiate):** *Men:* baseball, basketball, cross-country, football, golf, lacrosse, soccer, swimming, tennis, track/field (outdoor), track/field (indoor), wrestling. *Women:* basketball, cross-country, field hockey, golf, gymnastics, lacrosse, soccer, softball, swimming, tennis, track/field (outdoor), track/field (indoor), volleyball. **On-Campus Highlights:** The Kaleidoscope Performing Arts Centerl, Berman Museum of Art, Pfahler Hall of Science, Richter-North Hall (new dormitory), Bakes Center (field house and fitness ce, Wismer Center houses campus bookstore and dining facilities. Victorian dormitories along Main Street and traditional campus buildings give Ursinus a classic college ambience. **Environmental Initiatives:** Environmental education, both academic and co-curricular, through our ENV department and our Office of Sustainability.

ADMISSIONS

Freshman Academic Profile: Average high school GPA 3.2. 24% in top 10% of high school class, 51% in top 25% of high school class, 82% in top 50% of high school class. 67% from public high schools. **Reported SAT (pre-2016 redesign) scores:** SAT Math middle 50% range 520-650. SAT Critical Reading middle 50% range 513-640. SAT Writing middle 50% range 520-610. **Concordant SAT scores:** SAT EBRW middle 50% 570–680. SAT Math middle 50% range 550–670. ACT middle 50% range 23-29. Minimum internet-based TOEFL 80. **Basis for Candidate Selection:** *Very important factors considered include:* rigor of secondary school record, academic GPA, character/personal qualities. *Important factors considered include:* class rank, application essay, recommendation(s), interview, extracurricular activities, talent/ability. *Other factors considered include:* standardized test scores, first generation, alumni/ae relation, geographical residence, state residency, racial/ethnic status, volunteer work, work experience, level of applicant's interest. **Freshman Admission Requirements:** High school diploma is required and GED is accepted. *Academic units required:* 4 English, 3 math, 2 science, 2 science labs, 2 foreign language, 2 social studies. *Academic units recommended:* 4 English, 4 math, 4 science, 3 foreign language, 4 social studies. **Freshman Admission Statistics:** 2,491 applied, 82.42% admitted, 19% enrolled. **Transfer Admission Requirements:** High school transcript, college transcript(s), essay or personal statement, standardized test scores, Minimum college GPA of 3.0 required. Lowest grade transferable C. **General Admission Information:** Priority deadline 2/1. Nonfall registration accepted. Admission may be deferred for a maximum of 1 year.

COSTS AND FINANCIAL AID

Annual tuition $49,370. Room and board $12,320. Required fees $0. Average book expense $1,000. **Required Forms and Deadlines:** FAFSA, CSS/Financial Aid PROFILE. **Notification of Awards:** Applicants will be notified of awards on or about 3/15. **Types of Aid:** *Need-based scholarships/grants:* Federal Pell, FSEOG, State scholarships/grants, Private scholarships, College/university scholarship or grant aid from institutional funds. *Loans:* Direct Subsidized Stafford Loans, Direct Unsubsidized Stafford Loans, Direct

PLUS loans, Federal Perkins Loans. *Student Employment:* Federal Work-Study Program available. Institutional employment available. **Financial Aid Statistics:** 100% needy freshmen, 100% needy undergrads receive need-based scholarship or grant aid. 25% freshmen, 20% undergrads receive non-need-based scholarship or grant aid. 78% freshmen, 74% undergrads receive need-based self-help aid. 0% freshmen, 0% undergrads receive athletic scholarships. 99% freshmen, 97% undergrads receive any aid. 74% undergrads borrow to pay for school. Average cumulative indebtedness $38,537. **Criteria for awarding aid:** *Need-based:* Academics. *Non-need-based:* Academics, Alumni affiliation, Leadership, Minority status, Music/drama, State/district residency.

URSULINE COLLEGE

2550 Lander Road, Pepper Pike, OH 44124-4398
Phone: 440-449-4203 • **Financial Aid Phone:** 440-646-8309
E-mail: admission@ursuline.edu • **CEEB Code:** 1848
Fax: 440-684-6138 • **Website:** www.ursuline.edu

This private school, affiliated with the Roman Catholic Church, was founded in 1871. It has a 110-acre campus.

RATINGS

Admissions Selectivity Rating: 75 **Fire Safety Rating:** 88 **Green Rating:** 60*

STUDENTS AND FACULTY

Enrollment: 641. **Student Body:** 93% female, 7% male, 8% out-of-state, 2% international (6 countries represented). Asian 1%, African American 26%, Caucasian 62%, Hispanic 3%, Native American 0%, Pacific Islander 0%, Two or more races 3%, Race unknown 4%.

Retention and Graduation: 59% freshmen return for sophomore year. 31% freshmen graduate within 4 years. 44% freshmen graduate within 6 years. 5% grads go on to further study within 1 year. **Faculty:** Student/faculty ratio 7:1. 66 full-time faculty, 68% hold PhDs, 9% are are members of minority groups, 85% are women. 0% of classes are taught by teaching assistants.

ACADEMICS

Degrees: bachelor's, certificate, doctoral/professional, master's, postbachelor's certificate, post-master's certificate. **Classes:** Most classes have 10-19 students. Most lab/discussion sessions have 10-19 students. **Most popular majors:** Health Services/Allied Health/Health Sciences; Business Administration, Management and Operations; Psychology. **Special Study Options:** Accelerated program, cooperative education program, cross-registration, double major, independent study, internships, teacher certification program. **Disability Services:** Special programs offered to physically disabled students, including note-taking services, reader services, tape recorders, tutors. **Career Services:** Career assessment, Internships. We are most proud of our e-recruiting program that assists students in their search

FACILITIES

Housing: Coed dorms, women's dorms. 98% of campus accessible to physically diasbled. **Special Academic Facilities/Equipment:** Fritsche Gallery (Art) Fitness Center Swimming Pool **Computers:** 100% of classrooms, 100% of libraries, 100% of dining areas, have wireless network access.

CAMPUS LIFE

Environment: City. **Activities:** Choral groups, drama/theater, literary magazine, student government, Campus Ministries. 21 registered organizations, 4 honor societies. **Athletics (Intercollegiate):** *Women:* basketball, bowling, cross-country, golf, soccer, softball, swimming, tennis, track/field (outdoor), volleyball. **On-Campus Highlights:** Bishop Anthony M. Pilla Student Learning Center, Florence O'Donnell Wasmer Gallery, Matthew J. O'Brien Campus Center, Joseph J. Mullen Academic Center, Ralph M. Besse Library. **Environmental Initiatives:** Increased Recycling, Energy Conservation, Renewable Energy.

ADMISSIONS

Freshman Academic Profile: Average high school GPA 3.3. 16% in top 10% of high school class, 45% in top 25% of high school class, 74% in top 50% of high school class. 94% from public high schools. **Reported SAT (pre-2016 redesign) scores:** SAT Math middle 50% range 440-535. SAT Critical Reading middle 50% range 425-590. SAT Writing middle 50% range 415-565. **Concordant SAT scores:** SAT EBRW middle 50% 470–640. SAT Math middle 50% range 480–570. ACT middle 50% range 19-24. Minimum internet-based TOEFL 60. Minimum paper TOEFL 500. **Basis for Candidate Selection:** *Very important factors considered include:* academic GPA, standardized test scores. *Other factors considered include:* rigor of secondary school record, class rank, application essay, recommendation(s), interview, alumni/ae relation. **Freshman Admission Requirements:** High school diploma is required and GED is accepted. *Academic units recommended:* 4 English, 3 math, 3 science, 2 science labs, 2 foreign language, 3 social studies, 1 visual/performing arts, and 1 unit from above areas or other academic areas. **Freshman Admission Statistics:** 723 applied, 87.97% admitted, 18% enrolled. **Transfer Admission Requirements:** college transcript(s), essay or personal statement, Minimum college GPA of 2.5 required. Lowest grade transferable c. **General Admission Information:** Regular application deadline 2/1. Nonfall registration accepted. Admission may be deferred for a maximum of 1 year.

COSTS AND FINANCIAL AID

Required Forms and Deadlines: FAFSA. **Notification of Awards:** Applicants will be notified of awards on a rolling basis beginning 2/15. **Types of Aid:** *Need-based scholarships/grants:* Federal Pell, FSEOG, State scholarships/grants, Private scholarships, College/university scholarship or grant aid from institutional funds, Federal Nursing Scholarships. *Loans:* Direct Subsidized Stafford Loans, Direct Unsubsidized Stafford Loans, Direct PLUS loans, Federal Perkins Loans, Federal Nursing Loans, State Loans, College/university loans from institutional funds. *Student Employment:* Federal Work-Study Program available. **Financial Aid Statistics:** 100% needy freshmen, 96% needy undergrads receive need-based scholarship or grant aid. 20% freshmen, 13% undergrads receive non-need-based scholarship or grant aid. 84% freshmen, 88% undergrads receive need-based self-help aid. 17% freshmen, 12% undergrads receive athletic scholarships. 100% freshmen, 80% undergrads receive any aid. 98% undergrads borrow to pay for school. Average cumulative indebtedness $37,900. **Criteria for awarding aid:** *Need-based:* Athletics, Minority status. *Non-need-based:* Academics, Alumni affiliation, Art, Athletics, Job skills, Minority status.

UTAH STATE UNIVERSITY

0160 Old Main Hill, Logan, UT 84322-0160
Phone: 435-797-1079 • **Financial Aid Phone:** 435-797-0173
E-mail: admit@usu.edu
Fax: 435-797-3708 • **Website:** www.usu.edu • **ACT Code:** 4276

This public school was founded in 1888. It has a 400-acre campus.

RATINGS

Admissions Selectivity Rating: 78   **Fire Safety Rating:** 82   **Green Rating:** 91

STUDENTS AND FACULTY

Enrollment: 21,833. **Student Body:** 52% female, 48% male, 26% out-of-state, 1% international (50 countries represented). Asian 1%, African American 1%, Caucasian 82%, Hispanic 6%, Native American 2%, Pacific Islander <1%, Two or more races 2%, Race unknown 4%.
Retention and Graduation: 32% grads go on to further study within 1 year. **Faculty:** 927 full-time faculty, 81% hold PhDs, 11% are are members of minority groups, 37% are women. 7% of classes are taught by teaching assistants.

ACADEMICS

Degrees: associate, bachelor's, certificate, doctoral/professional, doctoral/research, master's, postbachelor's certifiate, terminal, transfer. **Classes:** Most classes have 20-29 students. Most lab/discussion sessions have 10-19 students. **Most popular majors:** Communication Sciences and Disorders; Economics; Physical Education Teaching and Coaching. **Special Study Options:** Accelerated program, cooperative education program, cross-registration, distance learning, double major, dual enrollment, English as a Second Language (ESL), exchange student program (domestic), honors program, independent study, internships, liberal arts/career combination, student-designed major, study abroad, teacher certification program, weekend college. **Honors Programs:** The Honors Program is a community of scholars whose curiosity, creativity, and enthusiasm for learning foster educational achievement and personal growth. Our students are going places–graduate school, professional school, terrific jobs. Honors offers undergraduate students intensive seminars, experimental and interdisciplinary courses, writing projects, leadership opportunities, artistic and social activities. Our classes are smaller, allowing students to get to know professors and encouraging classroom interaction and discussion. We allow students to define their own interests and pursue them through "contracts" with professors, fostering close contact with professors. Other advantages include priority registration, an Honors-only computer lab, the Honors lounge and study areas. Starting in Fall 2005, Honors expects to offer housing. **Disability Services:** Special programs offered to physically disabled students, including reader services, tape recorders. **Career Services:** Alumni network, Alumni services, Career/job search classes, Career assessment, Internships, Regional alumni. The Student Alumni Mentor Network, provided through Career Services, is a network of over 1500 alumni who share their unique paths with current students. These alumni reveal their own real-world success stories as well as provide job shadowing and networking opportunities for current students.

FACILITIES

Housing: Coed dorms, special housing for disabled students, men's dorms, special housing for international students, women's dorms, fraternity/sorority housing, apartments for married students, apartments for single students, Theme Housing, Mobile Home Park. 96% of campus accessible to physically diasbled. **Special Academic Facilities/Equipment:** Art gallery, agricultural and engineering experiment station, water research lab, wildlife and fishery research unit, on-campus school, intermountain herbarium, electron microscope, space dynamics lab. **Computers:** 99% of classrooms, 95% of dorms, 99% of libraries, 99% of dining areas, 99% of student union, 50% of common outdoor areas have wireless network access. Students can register for classes online. Administrative functions (other than registration) can be performed online.

CAMPUS LIFE

Environment: Town. **Activities:** Choral groups, concert band, dance, drama/theater, jazz band, marching band, music ensembles, musical theater, opera, pep band, radio station, student government, student newspaper, student-run film society, symphony orchestra, television station, Campus Ministries, Student Organization. 194 registered organizations, 32 honor societies, 8 religious organizations. 5 fraternities, 3 sororities. **Athletics (Intercollegiate):** *Men:* basketball, cross-country, football, golf, tennis, track/field (outdoor), track/field (indoor). *Women:* basketball, cross-country, gymnastics, soccer, softball, tennis, track/field (outdoor), track/field (indoor), volleyball. **On-Campus Highlights:** Outdoor Recreation Center, Nora Eccles Jones Art Museum, Fieldhouse athletic facility, Taggart Student Center, The quad. **Environmental Initiatives:** Increased efficiency All the new buildings on campus on USU campus are LEED Silver or higher, and projects must achieve EA Credit 3, enhanced commissioning. According to LEED, this can result in improvements in energy efficiency, ensure personnel know how to operate key building systems, and catch mistakes like incorrectly installed equipment. Many buildings have been retro-commisioned to ensure existing buildings are operating efficiently. Non-potable water is used for irrigation. Irrigation systems use central computer controls to maximize efficiency, and water lines are regularly inspected for leaks. Campus housing has installed 6500 LEDs and water efficienct shower heads.

ADMISSIONS

Freshman Academic Profile: Average high school GPA 3.5. 21% in top 10% of high school class, 44% in top 25% of high school class, 75% in top 50% of high school class. **Reported SAT (pre-2016 redesign) scores:** SAT Math middle 50% range 490-610. SAT Critical Reading middle 50% range 490-610. **Concordant SAT scores:** SAT Math middle 50% range 520–630. ACT middle 50% range 20-27. Minimum internet-based TOEFL 71. **Basis for Candidate Selection:** *Very important factors considered include:* academic GPA, standardized test scores. *Other factors considered include:* rigor of secondary school record, class rank, recommendation(s). **Freshman Admission Requirements:** High school diploma is required and GED is accepted. *Academic units required:* 4 English, 3 math, 3 science, 1 science lab, 1 history, 4 academic electives. *Academic units recommended:* 2 foreign language. **Freshman Admission Statistics:** 16,158 applied, 96.67% admitted, 30% enrolled. **Transfer Admission Requirements:** college transcript(s), Minimum college GPA of 2.2 required. Lowest grade transferable D. **General Admission Information:** Application fee $50. Nonfall registration accepted. Admission may be deferred for a maximum of 2 years plus one semester.

COSTS AND FINANCIAL AID

Annual in-state tuition $5,814. Annual out-of-state tuition $18,720. Room and board $5,870. Required fees $1,052. Average book expense $810. **Required Forms and Deadlines:** FAFSA. **Notification of Awards:** Applicants will be notified of awards on a rolling basis beginning 4/1. **Types of Aid:** *Need-based scholarships/grants:* Federal Pell, FSEOG, State scholarships/grants, Private scholarships, College/university scholarship or grant aid from institutional funds. *Loans:* Direct Subsidized Stafford Loans, Direct Unsubsidized Stafford Loans, Direct PLUS loans, Federal Perkins Loans, College/university loans from institutional funds. *Student Employment:* Federal Work-Study Program available. Institutional employment available. **Financial Aid Statistics:** 74% needy undergrads receive need-based scholarship or grant aid. 64% freshmen, 43% undergrads receive non-need-based scholarship or grant aid. 49% freshmen, 54% undergrads receive need-based self-help aid. 2% freshmen, 1% undergrads receive athletic scholarships. 81% freshmen, 80% undergrads receive any aid. 47% undergrads borrow to pay for school. Average cumulative indebtedness $19,172. **Criteria for awarding aid:** *Non-need-based:* Academics, Alumni affiliation, Art, Athletics, Leadership, Minority status, Music/drama, Religious affiliation, State/district residency.

UTICA COLLEGE

1600 Burrstone Road, Utica, NY 13502-4892
Phone: 315-792-3006 • **Financial Aid Phone:** 315-792-3179
E-mail: admiss@utica.edu • **CEEB Code:** 2932
Fax: 315-792-3003 • **Website:** www.utica.edu • **ACT Code:** 2932

This private school was founded in 1946. It has a 128-acre campus.

RATINGS
Admissions Selectivity Rating: 75   **Fire Safety Rating:** 88   **Green Rating:** 71

STUDENTS AND FACULTY
Enrollment: 3,433. **Student Body:** 61% female, 39% male, 19% out-of-state, 1% international (40 countries represented). Asian 3%, African American 12%, Caucasian 67%, Hispanic 10%, Native American <1%, Pacific Islander <1%, Two or more races 2%, Race unknown 3%.
Retention and Graduation: 75% freshmen return for sophomore year. 34% freshmen graduate within 4 years. 45% freshmen graduate within 6 years. 46% grads go on to further study within 1 year. 1% grads pursue medical degrees. **Faculty:** Student/faculty ratio 12:1. 145 full-time faculty, 70% hold PhDs, 11% are are members of minority groups, 48% are women. 0% of classes are taught by teaching assistants.

ACADEMICS
Degrees: bachelor's, certificate, doctoral/professional, master's, postbachelor's certificate. **Classes:** Most classes have 10-19 students. Most lab/discussion sessions have 10-19 students. **Most popular majors:** Corrections and Criminal Justice; Health Services/Allied Health/Health Sciences; Business/Commerce. **Special Study Options:** Accelerated program, cooperative education program, cross-registration, distance learning, double major, dual enrollment, exchange student program (domestic), honors program, independent study, internships, liberal arts/career combination, study abroad, teacher certification program, weekend college, BS Health Studies/ MS OT weekend program; ECI online program for undergraduate transfer students. **Honors Programs:** http://www.utica.edu/academic/opportunities/honors.cfm Combined degree programs: BS(Health Studies)/MS OT; BS(Health Stud). **Disability Services:** Special programs offered to physically disabled students, including note-taking services, reader services, tape recorders, tutors. **Career Services:** Alumni network, Alumni services, Career/job search classes, Career assessment, Internships.

FACILITIES
Housing: Coed dorms, special housing for disabled students, apartments for single students, Women's floors, Men's floors. 85% of campus accessible to physically diasbled. **Special Academic Facilities/Equipment:** Edith Langley Barrett Art Gallery. **Computers:** 95% of classrooms, 10% of dorms, 100% of libraries, 100% of dining areas, 100% of student union, have wireless network access. Students can register for classes online. Administrative functions (other than registration) can be performed online.

CAMPUS LIFE
Environment: City. **Activities:** Choral groups, concert band, dance, drama/theater, literary magazine, radio station, student government, student newspaper, student-run film society, yearbook. 80 registered organizations, 8 honor societies, 4 religious organizations. 5 fraternities, 4 sororities. **Athletics (Intercollegiate):** *Men:* baseball, basketball, cross-country, diving, football, golf, ice hockey, lacrosse, soccer, swimming, tennis, track/field (outdoor). *Women:* basketball, cross-country, diving, field hockey, ice hockey, lacrosse, soccer, softball, swimming, tennis, track/field (outdoor), volleyball, water polo. **On-Campus Highlights:** Strebel Student Center and Lounge, Pioneer Cafe, Clark Athletic Center, Romano Hall Lounge, Library Cafe. **Environmental Initiatives:** Committee on sustainability formed in 2007.

ADMISSIONS
Freshman Academic Profile: Average high school GPA 3.1. 11% in top 10% of high school class, 31% in top 25% of high school class, 68% in top 50% of high school class. **Reported SAT (pre-2016 redesign) scores:** SAT Math middle 50% range 460-570. SAT Critical Reading middle 50% range 450-550. SAT Writing middle 50% range 430-530. **Concordant SAT scores:** SAT EBRW middle 50% 490–600. SAT Math middle 50% range 500–590. ACT middle 50% range 20-25. Minimum paper TOEFL 525. **Basis for Candidate Selection:** *Very important factors considered include:* rigor of secondary school record, academic GPA. *Important factors considered include:* standardized test scores, application essay, level of applicant's interest. *Other factors considered include:* class rank, recommendation(s), interview, extracurricular activities, talent/ability, character/personal qualities, first generation, alumni/ae relation, volunteer work, work experience. **Freshman Admission Requirements:** High school diploma is required and GED is accepted. *Academic units required:* 4 English, 3 math, 3 science, 1 foreign language, 4 social studies, 1 visual/performing arts. **Freshman Admission Statistics:** 5,419 applied,

81.95% admitted, 15% enrolled. **Transfer Admission Requirements:** college transcript(s), essay or personal statement, Minimum college GPA of 2.50 required. Lowest grade transferable C. **General Admission Information:** Application fee $40. Priority deadline 3/1. Nonfall registration accepted. Admission may be deferred for a maximum of one year.

COSTS AND FINANCIAL AID
Annual tuition $19,446. Room and board $10,434. Required fees $550. Average book expense $1,400. **Required Forms and Deadlines:** FAFSA, State aid form. **Notification of Awards:** Applicants will be notified of awards on a rolling basis beginning 2/1. **Types of Aid:** *Need-based scholarships/grants:* Federal Pell, FSEOG, State scholarships/grants, Private scholarships, College/university scholarship or grant aid from institutional funds. *Loans:* Direct Subsidized Stafford Loans, Direct Unsubsidized Stafford Loans, Direct PLUS loans, Federal Perkins Loans. *Student Employment:* Federal Work-Study Program available. Institutional employment available. **Financial Aid Statistics:** 100% needy freshmen, 87% needy undergrads receive need-based scholarship or grant aid. 10% freshmen, 8% undergrads receive non-need-based scholarship or grant aid. 97% freshmen, 94% undergrads receive need-based self-help aid. 0% freshmen, 0% undergrads receive athletic scholarships. 96% freshmen, 95% undergrads receive any aid. 85% undergrads borrow to pay for school. Average cumulative indebtedness $33,336. **Criteria for awarding aid:** *Non-need-based:* Academics, Alumni affiliation, Minority status.

VALDOSTA STATE UNIVERSITY

1500 North Patterson Street, Valdosta, GA 31698
Phone: 229-333-5791 • **Financial Aid Phone:** 229-333-5935
E-mail: admissions@valdosta.edu • **CEEB Code:** 5855
Fax: 229-333-5482 • **Website:** http://www.valdosta.edu/ • **ACT Code:** 874

This public school was founded in 1906. It has a 178-acre campus.

RATINGS
Admissions Selectivity Rating: 76   **Fire Safety Rating:** 63   **Green Rating:** 60*

STUDENTS AND FACULTY
Enrollment: 10,638. **Student Body:** 60% female, 40% male, 4% out-of-state, 1% international (73 countries represented). Asian 1%, African American 34%, Caucasian 54%, Hispanic 4%, Native American <1%, Pacific Islander <1%, Two or more races 3%, Race unknown 2%.
Retention and Graduation: 67% freshmen return for sophomore year. 17% freshmen graduate within 4 years. 43% freshmen graduate within 6 years. **Faculty:** Student/faculty ratio 23:1. 489 full-time faculty, 77% hold PhDs, 15% are are members of minority groups, 48% are women. 2% of classes are taught by teaching assistants.

ACADEMICS
Degrees: associate, bachelor's, doctoral, master's, post-master's certificate. **Classes:** Most classes have 20-29 students. Most lab/discussion sessions have 20-29 students. **Most popular majors:** Biology/Biological Sciences; Registered Nursing/Registered Nurse; Psychology. **Special Study Options:** cooperative education program, distance learning, double major, dual enrollment, English as a Second Language (ESL), external degree program, honors program, independent study, internships, study abroad, teacher certification program, weekend college. **Honors Programs:** Honors Program. **Disability Services:** Special programs offered to physically disabled students, including note-taking services, reader services, tape recorders, tutors. **Career Services:** Alumni services, Career/job search classes, Career assessment, Internships.

FACILITIES
Housing: Coed dorms, special housing for disabled students, men's dorms, special housing for international students, women's dorms, apartments for married students, apartments for single studentsWellness floors and honors floors. 100% of campus accessible to physically diasbled. **Special Academic Facilities/Equipment:** Planetarium; Herbarium; Art Gallery; VSU Archives **Computers:** Students can register for classes online. Administrative functions (other than registration) can be performed online.

CAMPUS LIFE
Environment: City. **Activities:** Choral groups, concert band, dance, drama/theater, jazz band, literary magazine, marching band, music ensembles, pep band, radio station, student government, student newspaper, symphony orchestra, television station 140 registered organizations, 22 honor societies, 11 religious organizations. 12 fraternities, 10 sororities. **Athletics (Intercollegiate):** *Men:* baseball, basketball, cross-country, football, golf, tennis. *Women:* basketball, cheerleading, cross-country, softball, tennis, volleyball. **On-Campus Highlights:** Student Recreation Center, Game Room, Internet Cafe, The Loop, Palms Dining Center and quad. **Environmental Initiatives:** Recycling.

ADMISSIONS

Freshman Academic Profile: Average high school GPA 3.1. **Reported SAT (pre-2016 redesign) scores:** SAT Math middle 50% range 460-540. SAT Critical Reading middle 50% range 470-540. SAT Writing middle 50% range 450-530. **Concordant SAT scores:** SAT EBRW middle 50% 510–590. SAT Math middle 50% range 500–570. ACT middle 50% range 20-23. Minimum paper TOEFL 523. **Basis for Candidate Selection:** *Very important factors considered include:* academic GPA, standardized test scores. *Important factors considered include:* rigor of secondary school record, class rank, extracurricular activities, talent/ability, character/personal qualities. **Freshman Admission Requirements:** High school diploma is required and GED is not accepted. *Academic units required:* 4 English, 4 math, 3 science, 2 science labs, 2 foreign language, 3 social studies. **Freshman Admission Statistics:** 7,950 applied, 58.47% admitted, 48% enrolled. **Transfer Admission Requirements:** college transcript(s), Minimum college GPA of 2.0 required. Lowest grade transferable D. **General Admission Information:** Application fee $40. Regular application deadline 6/1. Nonfall registration accepted. Admission may be deferred for a maximum of 1 year.

COSTS AND FINANCIAL AID

Annual in-state tuition $3,644. Annual out-of-state tuition $13,224. Room and board $6,850. Required fees $1,910. Average book expense $1,200. **Required Forms and Deadlines:** FAFSA. **Notification of Awards:** Applicants will be notified of awards on a rolling basis beginning 4/15. **Types of Aid:** *Need-based scholarships/grants:* Federal Pell, FSEOG, State scholarships/grants, Private scholarships, College/university scholarship or grant aid from institutional funds, Federal Nursing Scholarships. *Loans:* Direct Subsidized Stafford Loans, Direct Unsubsidized Stafford Loans, Direct PLUS loans. *Student Employment:* Federal Work-Study Program available. Institutional employment available. **Financial Aid Statistics:** 89% needy freshmen, 82% needy undergrads receive need-based scholarship or grant aid. 6% freshmen, 5% undergrads receive non-need-based scholarship or grant aid. 87% freshmen, 77% undergrads receive need-based self-help aid. 1% freshmen, 0% undergrads receive athletic scholarships. 76% freshmen, 70% undergrads receive any aid. **Criteria for awarding aid:** *Need-based:* Art, Athletics, Minority status, Music/drama. *Non-need-based:* Academics, Art, Athletics, Minority status, Music/drama, State/district residency.

VALPARAISO UNIVERSITY

Duesenberg Welcome Center, Valparaiso, IN 46383
Phone: 219-464-5011 • **Financial Aid Phone:** 219-464-5015
E-mail: undergrad.admission@valpo.edu • **CEEB Code:** 1874
Fax: 219-464-6898 • **Website:** http://www.valpo.edu • **ACT Code:** 1256

This private school, affiliated with the Lutheran Church, was founded in 1859. It has a 320-acre campus.

RATINGS

Admissions Selectivity Rating: 84   **Fire Safety Rating:** 84   **Green Rating:** 75

STUDENTS AND FACULTY

Enrollment: 3,255. **Student Body:** 54% female, 46% male, 57% out-of-state, 5% international (33 countries represented). Asian 2%, African American 6%, Caucasian 72%, Hispanic 9%, Native American <1%, Pacific Islander <1%, Two or more races 3%, Race unknown 3%.
Retention and Graduation: 86% freshmen return for sophomore year. 54% freshmen graduate within 4 years. 66% freshmen graduate within 6 years. 17% grads go on to further study within 1 year. 14% grads pursue arts and sciences degrees. 1% grads pursue law degrees. 1% grads pursue business degrees. 1% grads pursue medical degrees. **Faculty:** Student/faculty ratio 13:1. 288 full-time faculty, 88% hold PhDs, 15% are are members of minority groups, 47% are women. 0% of classes are taught by teaching assistants.

ACADEMICS

Degrees: associate, bachelor's, certificate, doctoral/professional, master's, postbachelor's certificate, post-master's certificate, terminal. **Classes:** Most classes have 10-19 students. Most lab/discussion sessions have 10-19 students. **Most popular majors:** Registered Nursing/Registered Nurse; Mechanical Engineering; Biology/Biological Sciences. **Special Study Options:** Accelerated program, cooperative education program, cross-registration, distance learning, double major, English as a Second Language (ESL), exchange student program (domestic), honors program, independent study, internships, liberal arts/career combination, student-designed major, study abroad, teacher certification program. **Honors Programs:** Christ College, VU's honors college, provides an honors-level liberal arts curriculum dedicated to the study and practice of the basic arts of inquiry and committed to educational processes that enable students to achieve a measure of intellectual independence. Combined degree

programs: BA/JD, BA/MA, JD/MA, JD/MBA, JD/MALS, JD/MS, BSN/MSN, BA/EdS, BS/EdS, BS/MA, MEd/EdS, MSN/MHA, BS/MS, BS/MPH. **Disability Services:** Special programs offered to physically disabled students, including note-taking services, reader services, tape recorders, tutors. **Career Services:** Alumni network, Alumni services, Career/job search classes, Career assessment, Internships, Regional alumni.

FACILITIES

Housing: Coed dorms, women's dorms, fraternity/sorority housing, apartments for single students, ThemeHousingResidence hall for German language students. 59% of campus accessible to physically diasbled. **Special Academic Facilities/Equipment:** Art museum, galleries, language lab, planetarium, electron microscope, observatory, TV Studio, weather station, Virtual Nursing Learning Center, VisBox, non-linear video editing, Christopher Center for Learning and Information Resources, Doppler Radar facitiy **Computers:** 60% of classrooms, 100% of dorms, 100% of libraries, 100% of dining areas, 100% of student union, 15% of common outdoor areas have wireless network access. Students can register for classes online. Administrative functions (other than registration) can be performed online.

CAMPUS LIFE

Environment: Town. **Activities:** Choral groups, concert band, dance, drama/theater, jazz band, literary magazine, music ensembles, musical theater, pep band, radio station, student government, student newspaper, symphony orchestra, yearbook, Campus Ministries, Student Organization. 94 registered organizations, 33 honor societies, 7 religious organizations. 9 fraternities, 7 sororities. **Athletics (Intercollegiate):** *Men:* baseball, basketball, cross-country, diving, football, golf, soccer, swimming, tennis, track/field (outdoor), track/field (indoor). *Women:* basketball, bowling, cross-country, diving, golf, soccer, softball, swimming, tennis, track/field (outdoor), track/field (indoor), volleyball. **On-Campus Highlights:** Harre Union, Christopher Center for Library & Infor., VU Center for the Arts, Brauer Art Museum, Athletics-Recreation Center, Kallay-Christopher Hall Kade Duesenberg German House Grinder's Cafe.

ADMISSIONS

Freshman Academic Profile: Average high school GPA 3.7. 31% in top 10% of high school class, 62% in top 25% of high school class, 91% in top 50% of high school class. 80% from public high schools. **Reported SAT (pre-2016 redesign) scores:** SAT Math middle 50% range 490-600. SAT Critical Reading middle 50% range 500-600. SAT Writing middle 50% range 470-570. **Concordant SAT scores:** SAT EBRW middle 50% 540–640. SAT Math middle 50% range 520–620. ACT middle 50% range 23-29. Minimum internet-based TOEFL 80. Minimum paper TOEFL 550. **Basis for Candidate Selection:** *Very important factors considered include:* rigor of secondary school record, academic GPA, standardized test scores. *Important factors considered include:* class rank, extracurricular activities, talent/ability, character/personal qualities, alumni/ae relation. *Other factors considered include:* application essay, recommendation(s), interview, first generation, religious affiliation/commitment, racial/ethnic status, volunteer work, level of applicant's interest. **Freshman Admission Requirements:** High school diploma is required and GED is accepted. *Academic units required:* 4 English, 3 math, 2 science, 2 science labs, 2 foreign language, 2 history, 3 academic electives. *Academic units recommended:* 4 English, 4 math, 3 science, 3 science labs, 2 foreign language, 1 social studies, 2 history, 3 academic electives. **Freshman Admission Statistics:** 7,484 applied, 82.91% admitted, 14% enrolled. **Transfer Admission Requirements:** college transcript(s), essay or personal statement, statement of good standing from prior institution(s). Minimum college GPA of 2.0 required. Lowest grade transferable C-. **General Admission Information:** Priority deadline 12/1. Nonfall registration accepted. Admission may be deferred for a maximum of 1 year.

COSTS AND FINANCIAL AID

Annual tuition $37,550. Required fees $1,210. Average book expense $1,200. **Required Forms and Deadlines:** FAFSA. **Notification of Awards:** Applicants will be notified of awards on a rolling basis beginning 3/1. **Types of Aid:** *Need-based scholarships/grants:* Federal Pell, FSEOG, State scholarships/grants, Private scholarships, College/university scholarship or grant aid from institutional funds. *Loans:* Direct Subsidized Stafford Loans, Direct Unsubsidized Stafford Loans, Direct PLUS loans, Federal Perkins Loans, College/university loans from institutional funds. *Student Employment:* Federal Work-Study Program available. Institutional employment available. **Financial Aid Statistics:** 99% needy freshmen, 100% needy undergrads receive need-based scholarship or grant aid. 21% freshmen, 17% undergrads receive non-need-based scholarship or grant aid. 58% freshmen, 70% undergrads receive need-based self-help aid. 2% freshmen, 3% undergrads receive athletic scholarships. 94% freshmen, 92% undergrads receive any aid. Average cumulative indebtedness $37,294. **Criteria for awarding aid:** *Need-based:* Religious affiliation. *Non-need-based:* Academics, Alumni affiliation, Art, Athletics, Leadership, Music/drama, Religious affiliation, State/district residency.

VANDERBILT UNIVERSITY

2305 West End Avenue, Nashville, TN 37203
Phone: 615-322-2561 • **Financial Aid Phone:** 800-288-0204
E-mail: admissions@vanderbilt.edu • **CEEB Code:** 1871
Fax: 615-343-7765 • **Website:** www.vanderbilt.edu • **ACT Code:** 4036

This private school was founded in 1873. It has a 323-acre campus.

RATINGS
Admissions Selectivity Rating: 99   **Fire Safety Rating:** 91   **Green Rating:** 96

STUDENTS AND FACULTY
Enrollment: 6,844. **Student Body:** 50% female, 50% male, 90% out-of-state, 7% international (49 countries represented). Asian 12%, African American 9%, Caucasian 52%, Hispanic 9%, Native American <1%, Pacific Islander <1%, Two or more races 5%, Race unknown 5%.
Retention and Graduation: 97% freshmen return for sophomore year. 87% freshmen graduate within 4 years. 92 33% grads go on to further study within 1 year. 25% grads pursue arts and sciences degrees. 12% grads pursue law degrees. 3% grads pursue business degrees. 25% grads pursue medical degrees. **Faculty:** Student/faculty ratio 8:1. 956 full-time faculty, 96% hold PhDs, 17% are are members of minority groups, 39% are women.

ACADEMICS
Degrees: bachelor's, doctoral/professional, doctoral/research, doctoral, master's, post-master's certificate. **Classes:** Most classes have 10-19 students. Most lab/discussion sessions have 10-19 students. **Most popular majors:** Engineering Science; Social Sciences; Multi-/Interdisciplinary Studies. **Special Study Options:** Accelerated program, cooperative education program, cross-registration, distance learning, double major, dual enrollment, English as a Second Language (ESL), honors program, independent study, internships, liberal arts/career combination, student-designed major, study abroad, teacher certification program. **Honors Programs:** Psychology, Child Development, Cognitive Studies, and Child Studies, Biomedical Engineering, Biological Sciences Combined degree programs: BA/MA, BMUS/MBA, BA/MS Nursing, BS/MBA Eng.Sci.Mgmt. **Disability Services:** Special programs offered to physically disabled students, including note-taking services, reader services, tape recorders, tutors. **Career Services:** Alumni network, Career/job search classes, Career assessment, Internships. Parent / Student career education/networking event built around career clusters/industries that occurs during fall family weekend.

FACILITIES
Housing: Coed dorms, special housing for disabled students, men's dorms, special housing for international students, women's dorms, apartments for married students, apartments for single students, ThemeHousingThe Commons is a community of first-yar students, residential faculty, and professional staff. 95% of campus accessible to physically diasbled. **Special Academic Facilities/Equipment:** Art galleries, center for research on education and human development, multimedia classrooms, teaching center, observatories, free-electron laser, electron microscope. **Computers:** 100% of classrooms, 100% of dorms, 100% of libraries, 100% of dining areas, 100% of student union, 100% of common outdoor areas have wireless network access. Students can register for classes online. Administrative functions (other than registration) can be performed online.

CAMPUS LIFE
Environment: Metropolis. **Activities:** Choral groups, concert band, dance, drama/theater, jazz band, literary magazine, marching band, music ensembles, musical theater, opera, pep band, radio station, student government, student newspaper, student-run film society, symphony orchestra, television station, yearbook, Campus Ministries, Student Organization, Model UN. 329 registered organizations, 20 honor societies, 18 religious organizations. 19 fraternities, 12 sororities. **Athletics (Intercollegiate):** *Men:* baseball, basketball, cross-country, football, golf, tennis. *Women:* basketball, cross-country, golf, lacrosse, soccer, tennis, track/field (outdoor). **On-Campus Highlights:** The Commons, Jean and Alexander Heard Library, Student Recreation Center, Student Life Center, Sarratt Student Center. **Environmental Initiatives:** Greenhouse gas emissions reduction—Overall greenhouse gas emissions from Vanderbilt campus and medical center decreased by 12 percent from an all-time high reached in 2008'and by 7 percent from 2005 to 2011'even though Vanderbilt has seen significant growth in square footage, staff, students and research dollars over the last four years. GHG emissions per square foot have gone down 21 percent over the past seven years, which reflects a lot of hard work to improve

the energy efficiency of existing buildings, some that are very old, as well as new construction and renovation projects that have incorporated excellent energy efficiency. GHG emissions per person, per student, per research dollar, per inpatient day and per ambulatory visit also have trended significantly in a positive direction since 2005. Most university greenhouse gas inventory reports do not include research and/or patient care activity, making Vanderbilt's report more comprehensive than most and also more comprehensive than what is now required by the Environmental Protection Agency.

ADMISSIONS
Freshman Academic Profile: Average high school GPA 3.8. 87% in top 10% of high school class, 97% in top 25% of high school class, 99% in top 50% of high school class. 65% from public high schools. **Reported SAT (pre-2016 redesign) scores:** SAT Math middle 50% range 720-800. SAT Critical Reading middle 50% range 700-790. SAT Writing middle 50% range 690-770. **Concordant SAT scores:** SAT EBRW middle 50% 730–790. SAT Math middle 50% range 750–800. ACT middle 50% range 32-35. Minimum internet-based TOEFL 100. **Basis for Candidate Selection:** *Very important factors considered include:* rigor of secondary school record, class rank, academic GPA, standardized test scores, application essay, extracurricular activities, character/personal qualities. *Important factors considered include:* recommendation(s), talent/ability. *Other factors considered include:* interview, first generation, alumni/ae relation, geographical residence, state residency, racial/ethnic status, volunteer work, work experience. **Freshman Admission Requirements:** High school diploma is required and GED is accepted. *Academic units required:* 4 English, 3 math, 3 science, 2 science labs, 2 foreign language, 2 social studies, 1 history, 3 academic electives. *Academic units recommended:* 4 English, 4 math, 4 science, 3 science labs, 2 foreign language, 3 social studies, 1 history, 3 academic electives. **Freshman Admission Statistics:** 32,442 applied, 10.75% admitted, 46% enrolled. **Transfer Admission Requirements:** college transcript(s), essay or personal statement, statement of good standing from prior institution(s). Lowest grade transferable C. **General Admission Information:** Application fee $50. Priority deadline 1/1. Regular application deadline 1/1. Regular notification 4/1. Nonfall registration not accepted. Admission may be deferred for a maximum of 1 year.

COSTS AND FINANCIAL AID
Annual tuition $44,496. Room and board $14,962. Required fees $1,114. Average book expense $1,294. **Required Forms and Deadlines:** FAFSA, CSS/Financial Aid PROFILE. **Notification of Awards:** Applicants will be notified of awards on or about 4/1. *Types of Aid: Need-based scholarships/grants:* Federal Pell, FSEOG, State scholarships/grants, Private scholarships, College/university scholarship or grant aid from institutional funds. *Loans:* Direct Subsidized Stafford Loans, Direct Unsubsidized Stafford Loans, Direct PLUS loans, Federal Perkins Loans, Federal Nursing Loans, College/university loans from institutional funds. *Student Employment:* Federal Work-Study Program available. Institutional employment available. **Financial Aid Statistics:** 89% needy freshmen, 92% needy undergrads receive need-based scholarship or grant aid. 51% freshmen, 42% undergrads receive non-need-based scholarship or grant aid. 40% freshmen, 49% undergrads receive need-based self-help aid. 4% freshmen, 3% undergrads receive athletic scholarships. 69% freshmen, 65% undergrads receive any aid. Average cumulative indebtedness $24,122. **Criteria for awarding aid:** *Need-based:* Academics, Leadership, Music/drama. *Non-need-based:* Academics, Athletics, Leadership, Music/drama, State/district residency.

See page 1094.

VANDERCOOK COLLEGE OF MUSIC

3140 South Federal Street, Chicago, IL 60616-3731
Phone: 312-788-1120 • **Financial Aid Phone:** 312-788-1146
E-mail: admissions@vandercook.edu • **CEEB Code:** 1872
Fax: 312-225-5211 • **Website:** www.vandercook.edu • **ACT Code:** 1156

This private school was founded in 1909. It has a 1-acre campus.

RATINGS
Admissions Selectivity Rating: 73   **Fire Safety Rating:** 82   **Green Rating:** 60*

STUDENTS AND FACULTY
Enrollment: 103. **Student Body:** 49% female, 51% male, 24% out-of-state, 2% international (2 countries represented). Asian 1%, African American 7%, Caucasian 58%, Hispanic 22%, Native American 0%, Pacific Islander 0%, Two or more races 5%, Race unknown 5%.
Retention and Graduation: 89% freshmen return for sophomore year. 41% freshmen graduate within 4 years. 59% freshmen graduate within 6 years. **Faculty:** Student/faculty ratio 6:1. 13 full-time faculty, 38% hold PhDs, 23% are

are members of minority groups, 62% are women. 0% of classes are taught by teaching assistants.

ACADEMICS
Degrees: bachelor's, master's. **Special Study Options:** independent study, teacher certification program. **Career Services:** Alumni services, Career/job search classes, On-campus interviews. Our job listing bulletin board is updated weekly. Resume and credential development assistance is offered as well as mock interviews. On average, 90% of our graduates secure employment within their first year after graduation.

FACILITIES
Housing: Coed dorms, men's dorms, women's dorms, fraternity/sorority housing. 0% of campus accessible to physically diasbled.

CAMPUS LIFE
Environment: Metropolis. **Activities:** Choral groups, concert band, jazz band, music ensembles, musical theater, student newspaper. 5 registered organizations, 1 fraternity.

ADMISSIONS
Freshman Academic Profile: Average high school GPA 3.1. 29% in top 25% of high school class, 57% in top 50% of high school class. ACT middle 50% range 20-25. Minimum internet-based TOEFL 70. Minimum paper TOEFL 500. **Basis for Candidate Selection:** *Very important factors considered include:* application essay, talent/ability, character/personal qualities, level of applicant's interest. *Important factors considered include:* class rank, academic GPA, standardized test scores, recommendation(s), interview, alumni/ae relation. *Other factors considered include:* rigor of secondary school record, extracurricular activities, geographical residence, volunteer work, work experience. **Freshman Admission Requirements:** High school diploma is required and GED is accepted. *Academic units recommended:* 3 English, 2 math, 2 science, 2 foreign language, 3 social studies, and 3 units from above areas or other academic areas. **Freshman Admission Statistics:** 51 applied, 90.20% admitted, 43% enrolled. **Transfer Admission Requirements:** High school transcript, college transcript(s), essay or personal statement, interview, standardized test scores, Minimum college GPA of 2.5 required. Lowest grade transferable C. **General Admission Information:** Application fee $35. Priority deadline 4/1. Nonfall registration accepted. Admission may be deferred for a maximum of 1 year.

COSTS AND FINANCIAL AID
Annual tuition $25,440. Room and board $11,898. Required fees $1,740. Average book expense $1,900. **Required Forms and Deadlines:** FAFSA. **Notification of Awards:** Applicants will be notified of awards on a rolling basis beginning 5/1. **Types of Aid:** *Need-based scholarships/grants:* Federal Pell, FSEOG, State scholarships/grants, Private scholarships, College/university scholarship or grant aid from institutional funds. *Loans:* Direct Subsidized Stafford Loans, Direct Unsubsidized Stafford Loans, Direct PLUS loans. *Student Employment:* Federal Work-Study Program available. Institutional employment available. **Financial Aid Statistics:** 100% needy freshmen, 56% needy undergrads receive need-based scholarship or grant aid. 100% freshmen, 99% undergrads receive need-based self-help aid. 0% freshmen, 0% undergrads receive athletic scholarships. 100% freshmen, 95% undergrads receive any aid. 77% undergrads borrow to pay for school. Average cumulative indebtedness $47,042. **Criteria for awarding aid:** *Non-need-based:* Academics, Alumni affiliation, Music/drama.

VASSAR COLLEGE

Box 10, 124 Raymond Avenue, Poughkeepsie, NY 12604
Phone: 845-437-7300 • **Financial Aid Phone:** 845-437-5320
E-mail: admissions@vassar.edu • **CEEB Code:** 2956
Fax: 845-437-7063 • **Website:** www.vassar.edu • **ACT Code:** 2982

This private school was founded in 1861. It has a 1000-acre campus.

RATINGS
Admissions Selectivity Rating: 96　　**Fire Safety Rating:** 87　　**Green Rating:** 90

STUDENTS AND FACULTY
Enrollment: 2,414. **Student Body:** 56% female, 44% male, 74% out-of-state, 7% international (48 countries represented). Asian 11%, African American 5%, Caucasian 59%, Hispanic 11%, Native American <1%, Pacific Islander 0%, Two or more races 6%, Race unknown <1%.
Retention and Graduation: 94% freshmen return for sophomore year. 86% freshmen graduate within 4 years. 91% freshmen graduate within 6 years. 20% grads go on to further study within 1 year. 11% grads pursue arts and sciences degrees. 2% grads pursue law degrees. 1% grads pursue business degrees. 4% grads pursue medical degrees. **Faculty:** Student/faculty ratio 8:1. 275 full-time faculty, 87% hold PhDs, 24% are are members of minority groups, 47% are women. 0% of classes are taught by teaching assistants.

ACADEMICS
Degrees: bachelor's, master's. **Classes:** Most classes have 10-19 students. Most lab/discussion sessions have 10-19 students. **Most popular majors:** Psychology; Political Science and Government; Economics. **Special Study Options:** cooperative education program, cross-registration, double major, exchange student program (domestic), independent study, internships, liberal arts/career combination, student-designed major, study abroad, teacher certification program. Combined degree programs: BA/MA. **Disability Services:** Special programs offered to physically disabled students, including note-taking services, reader services, tape recorders. **Career Services:** Alumni network, Alumni services, Career/job search classes, Career assessment, Internships, Regional alumni.

FACILITIES
Housing: Coed dorms, special housing for disabled students, special housing for international students, women's dorms, apartments for married students, cooperative housing, apartments for single students, Wellness Housing, Quiet Housing. 75% of campus accessible to physically diasbled. **Special Academic Facilities/Equipment:** Art center, theatres, nursery school, environmental field station, geology museum, electron microscope, observatory, Skinner Music Hall, Fitness Center **Computers:** 100% of classrooms, 100% of dorms, 100% of libraries, 100% of dining areas, 100% of student union, 80% of common outdoor areas have wireless network access. Students can register for classes online. Administrative functions (other than registration) can be performed online.

CAMPUS LIFE
Environment: Town. **Activities:** Choral groups, concert band, dance, drama/theater, jazz band, literary magazine, marching band, music ensembles, musical theater, opera, radio station, student government, student newspaper, student-run film society, symphony orchestra, television station, yearbook, Campus Ministries, Student Organization, Model UN. 105 registered organizations, 2 honor societies, 11 religious organizations. **Athletics (Intercollegiate):** *Men:* baseball, basketball, crew/rowing, cross-country, diving, fencing, lacrosse, soccer, squash, swimming, tennis, track/field (outdoor), volleyball. *Women:* basketball, crew/rowing, cross-country, diving, fencing, field hockey, golf, lacrosse, soccer, squash, swimming, tennis, track/field (outdoor), volleyball.
On-Campus Highlights: Library, Shakespeare Garden, Class of 1951 Observatory, Frances Lehman Loeb Art Center, Center for Drama and Film. **Environmental Initiatives:** Tree Campus USA & Landscaping choices ?é?Çô in 2012/13 CCS and B&G worked together to phase out the use of harmful pesticides on campus to more environmentally friendly products. Concurrently, we have just been certified by Tree Campus USA, approved a formal tree care plan and seek to transition 3+ acres of lawn to naturalized habitat areas in spring 2013. During Winter 12/13 we have switched to a salt water brine solution, that has cut our total usage of salt on campus by 50%.

ADMISSIONS
Freshman Academic Profile: 72% in top 10% of high school class, 96% in top 25% of high school class, 99% in top 50% of high school class. **Reported SAT (pre-2016 redesign) scores:** SAT Math middle 50% range 660-740. SAT Critical Reading middle 50% range 670-750. SAT Writing middle 50% range 660-750. **Concordant SAT scores:** SAT EBRW middle 50% 710-770. SAT Math middle 50% range 690–760. ACT middle 50% range 30-33. Minimum internet-based TOEFL 100. Minimum paper TOEFL 600. **Basis for Candidate Selection:** *Very important factors considered include:* rigor of secondary school record. *Important factors considered include:* class rank, academic GPA, standardized test scores, application essay, recommendation(s), extracurricular activities, talent/ability, character/personal qualities. *Other factors considered include:* interview, first generation, alumni/ae relation, geographical residence, racial/ethnic status, volunteer work, work experience. **Freshman Admission Requirements:** High school diploma is required and GED is accepted. *Academic units recommended:* 4 English, 4 math, 4 science, 3 science labs, 4 foreign language, 2 social studies, 2 history. **Freshman Admission Statistics:** 7,556 applied, 25.77% admitted, 34% enrolled. **Transfer Admission Requirements:** High school transcript, college transcript(s), essay or personal statement, standardized test scores, statement of good standing from prior institution(s). Minimum college GPA of 3.0 required. Lowest grade transferable C. **General Admission Information:** Application fee $70. Regular application deadline 1/1. Regular notification 4/1. Nonfall registration not accepted. Admission may be deferred for a maximum of 12 months.

COSTS AND FINANCIAL AID

Annual tuition $50,550. Room and board $11,980. Required fees $750. Average book expense $900. **Required Forms and Deadlines:** FAFSA, CSS/Financial Aid PROFILE, Noncustodial PROFILE. **Notification of Awards:** Applicants will be notified of awards on or about 3/30. **Types of Aid:** *Need-based scholarships/grants:* Federal Pell, FSEOG, State scholarships/grants, Private scholarships, College/university scholarship or grant aid from institutional funds. *Loans:* Direct Subsidized Stafford Loans, Direct Unsubsidized Stafford Loans, Direct PLUS loans, Federal Perkins Loans, College/university loans from institutional funds. *Student Employment:* Federal Work-Study Program available. Institutional employment available. **Financial Aid Statistics:** 98% needy freshmen, 100% needy undergrads receive need-based scholarship or grant aid. 0% undergrads receive non-need-based scholarship or grant aid. 100% freshmen, 100% undergrads receive need-based self-help aid. 0% freshmen, 0% undergrads receive athletic scholarships. 61% freshmen, 58% undergrads receive any aid. 47% undergrads borrow to pay for school. Average cumulative indebtedness $17,847.

VAUGHN COLLEGE OF AERONAUTICS AND TECHNOLOGY

86-01 23rd Avenue, Flushing, NY 11369
Phone: 718-429-6600 • **Financial Aid Phone:** 718-429-6600
E-mail: admitme@vaughn.edu • **CEEB Code:** 2001
Fax: 718-779-2231 • **Website:** www.vaughn.edu

This private school was founded in 1932. It has a 6-acre campus.

RATINGS

Admissions Selectivity Rating: 73   **Fire Safety Rating:** 96   **Green Rating:** 60*

STUDENTS AND FACULTY

Enrollment: 1,605. **Student Body:** 13% female, 87% male, 11% out-of-state, 2% international. Asian 12%, African American 22%, Caucasian 13%, Hispanic 38%, Native American <1%, Pacific Islander 3%, Two or more races 5%, Race unknown 5%.
Retention and Graduation: 26% freshmen graduate within 4 years. **Faculty:** Student/faculty ratio 15:1. 41 full-time faculty, 49% hold PhDs, 37% are are members of minority groups, 20% are women. 0% of classes are taught by teaching assistants.

ACADEMICS

Degrees: associate, bachelor's, certificate, master's. **Classes:** Most classes have 20-29 students. Most lab/discussion sessions have 20-29 students. **Most popular majors:** Airframe Mechanics and Aircraft Maintenance Technology/Technician; Aeronautics/Aviation/Aerospace Science and Technology; Airline/Commercial/Professional Pilot and Flight Crew. **Special Study Options:** Accelerated program, distance learning, double major, independent study, internships, liberal arts/career combination. **Career Services:** Alumni network, Alumni services, Career/job search classes, Career assessment, Internships.

FACILITIES

Housing: Coed dorms. 100% of campus accessible to physically diasbled. **Computers:** 100% of classrooms, 100% of dorms, 100% of libraries, 100% of dining areas, 100% of common outdoor areas have wireless network access. Administrative functions (other than registration) can be performed online.

CAMPUS LIFE

Environment: City. **Activities:** dance, drama/theater, student government, yearbook, Student Organization. 21 registered organizations, 1 honor society. **Athletics (Intercollegiate):** *Men:* basketball, soccer. *Women:* tennis. **On-Campus Highlights:** Complex of six flight simulators, Laboratories, Observation Tower, Cafeteria, Library.

ADMISSIONS

Freshman Academic Profile: Average high school GPA 86.0. **Reported SAT (pre-2016 redesign) scores:** SAT Math middle 50% range 459-560. SAT Critical Reading middle 50% range 432-533. **Concordant SAT scores:** SAT Math middle 50% range 500–580. ACT middle 50% range 19-24. Minimum internet-based TOEFL 80. Minimum paper TOEFL 580. **Basis for Candidate Selection:** *Very important factors considered include:* rigor of secondary school record, academic GPA. *Important factors considered include:* standardized test scores, extracurricular activities, volunteer work, level of applicant's interest. *Other factors considered include:* application essay, recommendation(s), interview, talent/ability, character/personal qualities, work experience. **Freshman Admission Requirements:** High school diploma is required and GED is accepted. *Academic units required:* 4 English, 3 math, 2 science, 2 science labs, 1 social studies. *Academic units recommended:* 4 English, 4 math,

3 science, 3 science labs, 4 social studies. **Freshman Admission Statistics:** 813 applied, 74.78% admitted, 51% enrolled. **Transfer Admission Requirements:** college transcript(s), Minimum college GPA of 2.0 required. Lowest grade transferable C. **General Admission Information:** Application fee $40. Priority deadline 3/1. Nonfall registration accepted. Admission may be deferred for a maximum of 1 year.

COSTS AND FINANCIAL AID

Annual tuition $20,840. Room and board $12,365. Required fees $800. Average book expense $2,160. **Required Forms and Deadlines:** FAFSA, State aid form. **Notification of Awards:** Applicants will be notified of awards on a rolling basis beginning 4/15. **Types of Aid:** *Need-based scholarships/grants:* Federal Pell, FSEOG, State scholarships/grants, Private scholarships, College/university scholarship or grant aid from institutional funds. *Loans:* Direct Subsidized Stafford Loans, Direct Unsubsidized Stafford Loans, Direct PLUS loans. *Student Employment:* Federal Work-Study Program available. Institutional employment available. **Financial Aid Statistics:** 99% needy freshmen, 91% needy undergrads receive need-based scholarship or grant aid. 29% freshmen, 24% undergrads receive non-need-based scholarship or grant aid. 96% freshmen, 79% undergrads receive need-based self-help aid. 0% freshmen, 0% undergrads receive athletic scholarships. 94% freshmen, 95% undergrads receive any aid. **Criteria for awarding aid:** *Need-based:* Academics, Leadership. *Non-need-based:* Academics, Alumni affiliation, Leadership.

VERMONT TECHNICAL COLLEGE

PO Box 500, Randolph Center, VT 5061
Phone: 802-728-1242
E-mail: Admissions@vtc.edu
Fax: 802-728-1321 • **Website:** http://www.vtc.edu/

This is a public school.

RATINGS

Admissions Selectivity Rating: 79   **Fire Safety Rating:** 60*   **Green Rating:** 60*

STUDENTS AND FACULTY

Student Body: 40% female, 60% male, 21% out-of-state.
Retention and Graduation: 65% freshmen return for sophomore year.
Faculty: Student/faculty ratio 12:1. 79 full-time faculty, 80% hold PhDs, 0% are are members of minority groups, 47% are women.

ACADEMICS

Degrees: associate, bachelor's, certificate, diploma. **Classes:** Most classes have 10-19 students. Most lab/discussion sessions have 10-19 students. **Special Study Options:** distance learning, double major, dual enrollment, internships.

FACILITIES

Housing: Coed dorms.

CAMPUS LIFE

Activities: radio station, student government, television station, yearbook.

ADMISSIONS

Freshman Academic Profile: 8% in top 10% of high school class, 27% in top 25% of high school class, 60% in top 50% of high school class. **Reported SAT (pre-2016 redesign) scores:** SAT Math middle 50% range 450-560. SAT Critical Reading middle 50% range 410-520. SAT Writing middle 50% range 410-520. **Concordant SAT scores:** SAT EBRW middle 50% 460–580. SAT Math middle 50% range 490–580. **Basis for Candidate Selection:** *Very important factors considered include:* rigor of secondary school record, academic GPA. *Important factors considered include:* standardized test scores, recommendation(s), interview. *Other factors considered include:* application essay, extracurricular activities, character/personal qualities, first generation, alumni/ae relation, volunteer work, work experience. **Freshman Admission Requirements:** High school diploma is required and GED is accepted. *Academic units required:* 4 English, 3 math, 2 science, 1 science lab, 2 social studies, 2 history. *Academic units recommended:* 4 math, 3 science, 2 science labs, 2 foreign language. **Freshman Admission Statistics:** 920 applied, 57.50% admitted, 54% enrolled. **Transfer Admission Requirements:** college transcript(s), statement of good standing from prior institution(s). Lowest grade transferable C-. **General Admission Information:** Application fee $36. Nonfall registration accepted. Admission may be deferred.

COSTS AND FINANCIAL AID

Student Employment: Federal Work-Study Program available. Institutional employment available. **Financial Aid Statistics:** 80% needy freshmen, 74% needy undergrads receive need-based scholarship or grant aid. 3% freshmen, 5% undergrads receive non-need-based scholarship or grant aid. 85% freshmen, 84% undergrads receive need-based self-help aid. 0% freshmen, 0% undergrads receive athletic scholarships.

VILLA MARIA COLLEGE OF BUFFALO

240 Pine Ridge Road, Buffalo, NY 14225
Phone: 716-961-1805 • **Financial Aid Phone:** 716-961-1850
E-mail: admissions@villa.edu
Fax: 716-896-0705 • **ACT Code:** 2983

This private school, affiliated with the Roman Catholic Church, was founded in 1960. It has a 9-acre campus.

RATINGS
Admissions Selectivity Rating: 70   **Fire Safety Rating:** 60*   **Green Rating:** 60*

STUDENTS AND FACULTY
Enrollment: 469. **Student Body:** 68% female, 32% male, 3% out-of-state, 0% international (0 countries represented). Asian 1%, African American 26%, Caucasian 61%, Hispanic 6%, Native American <1%, Pacific Islander <1%, Two or more races 5%, Race unknown <1%.
Retention and Graduation: 59% freshmen return for sophomore year. 24% freshmen graduate within 4 years. 29% freshmen graduate within 6 years.
Faculty: Student/faculty ratio 8:1. 29 full-time faculty, 52% hold PhDs, 0% are are members of minority groups, 59% are women. 0% of classes are taught by teaching assistants.

ACADEMICS
Degrees: associate, bachelor's, certificate. **Classes:** Most classes have 10-19 students. Most lab/discussion sessions have 10-19 students. **Most popular majors:** Visual and Performing Arts; Physical Therapy Technician/Assistant. **Special Study Options:** cooperative education program, cross-registration, dual enrollment, internships, liberal arts/career combination, study abroad, Selected courses are offered in evening modules primarily with non-traditional students in mind. These offerings are limited. **Disability Services:** Special programs offered to physically disabled students, including tutors. **Career Services:** Alumni services, Career/job search classes, Career assessment, Internships.

FACILITIES
Housing: apartments for married students, apartments for single studentsHousing is available at Collegiate Village (college affiliated) which is a mile off-campus; however van service to campus is available. There is no on-campus housing. 80% of campus accessible to physically diasbled. **Special Academic Facilities/Equipment:** Art Gallery, Music Building, Recording Studio, Student Center, Athletic Center, Art Shop **Computers:** 100% of libraries, 100% of dining areas, have wireless network access. Students can register for classes online. Administrative functions (other than registration) can be performed online.

CAMPUS LIFE
Environment: City. **Activities:** Choral groups, jazz band, literary magazine, music ensembles, student government, student newspaper, Campus Ministries. 1 honor society. **On-Campus Highlights:** Athletic/Student Center, Recording Studio.

ADMISSIONS
Freshman Academic Profile: Average high school GPA 3.0. 28% in top 25% of high school class, 52% in top 50% of high school class. 93% from public high schools. Minimum internet-based TOEFL 133. Minimum paper TOEFL 450. **Basis for Candidate Selection:** *Very important factors considered include:* academic GPA, application essay, interview, talent/ability. *Important factors considered include:* level of applicant's interest. *Other factors considered include:* rigor of secondary school record, standardized test scores, recommendation(s), volunteer work, work experience. **Freshman Admission Requirements:** High school diploma is required and GED is accepted. *Academic units recommended:* 4 English, 3 math, 3 science, 4 social studies, 4 history. **Freshman Admission Statistics:** 248 applied, 79.84% admitted, 55% enrolled. **Transfer Admission Requirements:** college transcript(s), interview, Lowest grade transferable C. **General Admission Information:** Nonfall registration accepted. Admission may be deferred for a maximum of 2 semesters.

COSTS AND FINANCIAL AID
Annual tuition $18,520. Required fees $650. **Required Forms and Deadlines:** FAFSA. **Notification of Awards:** Applicants will be notified of awards on a rolling basis beginning 2/15. **Types of Aid:** *Need-based scholarships/grants:* Federal Pell, FSEOG, State scholarships/grants, Private scholarships, College/university scholarship or grant aid from institutional funds. *Student Employment:* Federal Work-Study Program available. **Financial Aid Statistics:** 98% needy freshmen, 99% needy undergrads receive need-based scholarship or grant aid. 49% freshmen, 48% undergrads receive non-need-based scholarship or grant aid. 19% freshmen, 15% undergrads receive need-based self-help aid. 0% freshmen, 0% undergrads receive athletic scholarships.

99% freshmen, 92% undergrads receive any aid. **Criteria for awarding aid:** *Need-based:* Academics, Alumni affiliation, Art, Leadership. *Non-need-based:* Academics, Alumni affiliation, Art, Leadership.

VILLANOVA UNIVERSITY

Austin Hall, 800 Lancaster Avenue, Villanova, PA 19085
Phone: 610-519-4000 • **Financial Aid Phone:** 610-519-4010
E-mail: gotovu@villanova.edu • **CEEB Code:** 2959
Fax: 610-519-6450 • **Website:** www.villanova.edu • **ACT Code:** 3744

This private school, affiliated with the Roman Catholic Church, was founded in 1842. It has a 254-acre campus.

RATINGS
Admissions Selectivity Rating: 93   **Fire Safety Rating:** 96   **Green Rating:** 96

STUDENTS AND FACULTY
Enrollment: 7,002. **Student Body:** 53% female, 47% male, 78% out-of-state, 2% international (49 countries represented). Asian 7%, African American 5%, Caucasian 75%, Hispanic 8%, Native American <1%, Pacific Islander <1%, Two or more races 2%, Race unknown 1%.
Retention and Graduation: 96% freshmen return for sophomore year. 87% freshmen graduate within 4 years. 90% freshmen graduate within 6 years. 23% grads go on to further study within 1 year. 7% grads pursue arts and sciences degrees. 5% grads pursue law degrees. 1% grads pursue business degrees. 2% grads pursue medical degrees. **Faculty:** Student/faculty ratio 12:1. 622 full-time faculty, 88% hold PhDs, 15% are are members of minority groups, 40% are women. 1% of classes are taught by teaching assistants.

ACADEMICS
Degrees: associate, bachelor's, doctoral/professional, doctoral/research, doctoral, master's, postbachelor's certificate, post-master's certificate. **Classes:** Most classes have 10-19 students. Most lab/discussion sessions have 10-19 students. **Most popular majors:** Finance; Registered Nursing/Registered Nurse; Mass Communication/Media Studies. **Special Study Options:** Accelerated program, cooperative education program, cross-registration, distance learning, double major, dual enrollment, English as a Second Language (ESL), exchange student program (domestic), honors program, independent study, internships, liberal arts/career combination, study abroad, teacher certification program. **Honors Programs:** Honors at Villanova is a comprehensive four-year program that offers challenging seminars, research opportunities, service projects, and cultural and social events designed to bring together superior students and dedicated faculty. Honors courses and co-curricular activities enrich and complement the academic experience inherent in a Villanova education. The Honors Program also works closely with the University's Center for Undergraduate Grants and Awards, which administers the Presidential Scholarship program for incoming students; Connelly-Delouvrier International Scholarships for study abroad; and Villanova's support for students pursuing prestigious national fellowships. The Villanova University Honors Program is an active member of both the National Collegiate Honors Council and the Northeast Region of the National Collegiate Honors Council. Combined degree programs: BA/MA, BS/MS, BS/MA. **Disability Services:** Special programs offered to physically disabled students, including note-taking services, reader services, tape recorders, tutors. **Career Services:** Alumni network, Alumni services, Career/job search classes, Career assessment, Internships, Regional alumni. Hundreds of companies recruit Villanova students for internships—either on campus or via job boards—each year. Many internships ultimately lead to full-time job offers.

FACILITIES
Housing: Coed dorms, men's dorms, women's dorms, apartments for single students, Wellness Housing, Theme Housing, Learning Communities. 95% of campus accessible to physically diasbled. **Special Academic Facilities/Equipment:** Driscoll Hall, home of the Villanova College of Nursing; the Villanova School of Business Applied Finance Lab; the Structural Engineering Teaching and Research Laboratory; the Augustinian Historical Museum, and the Villanova Observatory. **Computers:** 90% of classrooms, 90% of dorms, 100% of libraries, 100% of dining areas, 100% of student union, 10% of common outdoor areas have wireless network access. Students can register for classes online. Administrative functions (other than registration) can be performed online. Undergraduates are required to own a computer.

CAMPUS LIFE

Environment: Village. **Activities:** Choral groups, concert band, dance, drama/theater, jazz band, literary magazine, marching band, music ensembles, musical theater, pep band, radio station, student government, student newspaper, student-run film society, symphony orchestra, television station, yearbook, Campus Ministries, Student Organization, Model UN. 250 registered organizations, 34 honor societies, 15 religious organizations. 9 fraternities, 9 sororities. **Athletics (Intercollegiate):** *Men:* baseball, basketball, cheerleading, cross-country, diving, football, golf, lacrosse, soccer, swimming, tennis, track/field (outdoor), track/field (indoor). *Women:* basketball, cheerleading, crew/rowing, cross-country, diving, field hockey, lacrosse, soccer, softball, swimming, tennis, track/field (outdoor), track/field (indoor), volleyball, water polo. **On-Campus Highlights:** St. Thomas of Villanova Church, Davis Center for Athletics and Fitness, Villanova University Shop, Connelly Center and Cinema, Bartley Hall Exchange. **Environmental Initiatives:** Academic programs: The master degree in sustainable engineering; the first-year environmental leadership learning community; bachelor degrees in environmental science and environmental studies; an undergraduate minor in sustainability; a biology master degree, graduate certificate, and advanced graduate certificate with a concentration in ecology, evolution, and organismal biology; a master degree in water resources and environmental engineering, and a graduate certificate in urban water resources design.

ADMISSIONS

Freshman Academic Profile: Average high school GPA 4.0. 55% in top 10% of high school class, 87% in top 25% of high school class, 98% in top 50% of high school class. 52% from public high schools. **Reported SAT (pre-2016 redesign) scores:** SAT Math middle 50% range 610-710. SAT Critical Reading middle 50% range 590-690. SAT Writing middle 50% range 590-690. **Concordant SAT scores:** SAT EBRW middle 50% 650–730. SAT Math middle 50% range 630–740. ACT middle 50% range 29-32. Minimum paper TOEFL 550. **Basis for Candidate Selection:** *Very important factors considered include:* rigor of secondary school record, class rank, academic GPA, standardized test scores. *Important factors considered include:* application essay, recommendation(s), extracurricular activities, talent/ability, character/personal qualities, volunteer work, work experience. *Other factors considered include:* first generation, alumni/ae relation, geographical residence, state residency, racial/ethnic status, level of applicant's interest. **Freshman Admission Requirements:** High school diploma is required and GED is accepted. *Academic units required:* 4 English, 4 math, 4 science, 2 science labs, 2 foreign language, 2 academic electives, and 4 units from above areas or other academic areas. *Academic units recommended:* 4 English, 4 math, 4 science, 3 science labs, 4 foreign language, 2 academic electives, and 4 units from above areas or other academic areas. **Freshman Admission Statistics:** 16,206 applied, 47.89% admitted, 22% enrolled. **Transfer Admission Requirements:** High school transcript, college transcript(s), essay or personal statement, standardized test scores, statement of good standing from prior institution(s). Lowest grade transferable C. **General Admission Information:** Application fee $80. Priority deadline 12/15. Regular application deadline 1/15. Regular notification 4/1. Nonfall registration not accepted. Admission may be deferred for a maximum of 1 year.

COSTS AND FINANCIAL AID

Annual tuition $46,966. Room and board $12,720. Required fees $650. Average book expense $1,100. **Required Forms and Deadlines:** FAFSA, CSS/Financial Aid PROFILE, Noncustodial PROFILE. **Notification of Awards:** Applicants will be notified of awards on or about 4/1. **Types of Aid:** *Need-based scholarships/grants:* Federal Pell, FSEOG, State scholarships/grants, Private scholarships, College/university scholarship or grant aid from institutional funds. *Loans:* Direct Subsidized Stafford Loans, Direct Unsubsidized Stafford Loans, Direct PLUS loans, Federal Perkins Loans, Federal Nursing Loans. *Student Employment:* Federal Work-Study Program available. Institutional employment available. **Financial Aid Statistics:** 91% needy freshmen, 91% needy undergrads receive need-based scholarship or grant aid. 24% freshmen, 27% undergrads receive non-need-based scholarship or grant aid. 86% freshmen, 87% undergrads receive need-based self-help aid. 3% freshmen, 3% undergrads receive athletic scholarships. 67% freshmen, 68% undergrads receive any aid. 55% undergrads borrow to pay for school. Average cumulative indebtedness $33,588. **Criteria for awarding aid:** *Need-based:* Religious affiliation. *Non-need-based:* Academics, Alumni affiliation, Athletics, Leadership, Minority status, Religious affiliation.

VIRGINIA COMMONWEALTH UNIVERSITY

821 West Franklin Street, Richmond, VA 23284
Phone: 804-828-1222 • **Financial Aid Phone:** 804-828-6669
E-mail: upgrad@vcu.edu • **CEEB Code:** 5570
Fax: 804-828-1899 • **Website:** www.vcu.edu

This public school was founded in 1838. It has a 143-acre campus.

RATINGS

Admissions Selectivity Rating: 81   **Fire Safety Rating:** 94   **Green Rating:** 95

STUDENTS AND FACULTY

Enrollment: 22,758. **Student Body:** 59% female, 41% male, 7% out-of-state, 3% international (109 countries represented). Asian 13%, African American 19%, Caucasian 48%, Hispanic 9%, Native American <1%, Pacific Islander <1%, Two or more races 6%, Race unknown 3%. **Retention and Graduation:** 86% freshmen return for sophomore year. 36% freshmen graduate within 4 years. 62% freshmen graduate within 6 years. **Faculty:** Student/faculty ratio 18:1. 1,209 full-time faculty, 0% hold PhDs, 20% are are members of minority groups, 48% are women.

ACADEMICS

Degrees: bachelor's, certificate, doctoral/professional, doctoral/research, master's, postbachelor's certificate, post-master's certificate. **Classes:** Most classes have 10-19 students. Most lab/discussion sessions have 20-29 students. **Most popular majors:** Biology/Biological Sciences; Psychology; Health and Physical Education/Fitness. **Special Study Options:** Accelerated program, cooperative education program, distance learning, double major, dual enrollment, English as a Second Language (ESL), honors program, independent study, internships, liberal arts/career combination, student-designed major, study abroad, teacher certification program. **Honors Programs:** Mentorship Programs—All first year students are invited to participate in this program. In this program upper classmen volunteer to serve as mentors offering support and assistance to new honors students during their first semester. Combined degree programs: BA/MD, BA/DDS, Pharmacy (PharmD) as a part of Honors Program. **Disability Services:** Special programs offered to physically disabled students, including note-taking services, reader services, tape recorders, tutors. **Career Services:** Alumni network, Alumni services, Career/job search classes, Career assessment, Internships, Regional alumni.

FACILITIES

Housing: Coed dorms, special housing for disabled students, apartments for single students. 90% of campus accessible to physically diasbled. **Special Academic Facilities/Equipment:** Anderson Gallery, Student Art Gallery, Larrick Student Center, Shafer Ct. Dining Facilities, Student Commons, Siegel Center, Cabell Library, Biotech Research Bldgs., Tompkins McCaw Library and VCU Bookstores **Computers:** 75% of classrooms, 100% of dorms, 100% of libraries, 100% of dining areas, 100% of student union, 25% of common outdoor areas have wireless network access. Students can register for classes online. Administrative functions (other than registration) can be performed online. Undergraduates are required to own a computer.

CAMPUS LIFE

Environment: Metropolis. **Activities:** Choral groups, concert band, dance, drama/theater, jazz band, literary magazine, musical theater, pep band, radio station, student government, student newspaper, television station, yearbook, Campus Ministries, Student Organization. 377 registered organizations, 30 religious organizations. 22 fraternities, 13 sororities. **Athletics (Intercollegiate):** *Men:* baseball, basketball, cross-country, golf, soccer, tennis, track/field (outdoor). *Women:* basketball, cross-country, field hockey, soccer, tennis, track/field (outdoor), volleyball. **On-Campus Highlights:** Student Commons, Cabell Library, Siegel Center, Anderson Gallery, Shafer Court Dining Facility, Cary Street Recreation Complex.

ADMISSIONS

Freshman Academic Profile: Average high school GPA 3.6. 19% in top 10% of high school class, 47% in top 25% of high school class, 83% in top 50% of high school class. **Reported SAT (pre-2016 redesign) scores:** SAT Math middle 50% range 490-590. SAT Critical Reading middle 50% range 490-610. SAT Writing middle 50% range 470-580. **Concordant SAT scores:** SAT EBRW middle 50% 540–650. SAT Math middle 50% range 520–610. ACT middle 50% range 21-27. Minimum internet-based TOEFL 80. Minimum paper TOEFL 550. **Basis for Candidate Selection:** *Very important factors considered include:* rigor of secondary school record, academic GPA. *Important factors considered include:* application essay. *Other factors considered include:* class rank, standardized test scores, recommendation(s), extracurricular activities, talent/ability, character/personal qualities, first generation, volunteer work. **Freshman Admission Requirements:** High school diploma is required and GED is accepted. *Academic units required:* 4 English, 3 math, 3 science, 1 science lab, 2 foreign language, 1 social studies, 2 history. *Academic units recommended:* 4 English, 4 math, 4 science, 1 science lab, 3 foreign language, 1 social studies, 3 history, 1 visual/performing arts. **Freshman Admission Statistics:** 17,176 applied, 74.55% admitted, 33% enrolled. **Transfer Admission Requirements:** college transcript(s), Minimum college GPA of 2.25 required. Lowest grade transferable C. **General Admission Information:** Application fee $50. Priority deadline 1/15. Nonfall registration accepted. Admission may be deferred.

COSTS AND FINANCIAL AID
Required Forms and Deadlines: FAFSA. **Notification of Awards:** Applicants will be notified of awards on a rolling basis beginning 4/1. **Types of Aid:** *Need-based scholarships/grants:* Federal Pell, FSEOG, State scholarships/grants, Private scholarships, College/university scholarship or grant aid from institutional funds, United Negro College Fund. *Loans:* Direct Subsidized Stafford Loans, Direct Unsubsidized Stafford Loans, Direct PLUS loans, Federal Perkins Loans, Federal Nursing Loans. *Student Employment:* Federal Work-Study Program available. Institutional employment available. **Financial Aid Statistics:** 68% needy freshmen, 68% needy undergrads receive need-based scholarship or grant aid. 28% freshmen, 19% undergrads receive non-need-based scholarship or grant aid. 77% freshmen, 84% undergrads receive need-based self-help aid. 2% freshmen, 1% undergrads receive athletic scholarships. 77% freshmen, 65% undergrads receive any aid. 63% undergrads borrow to pay for school. Average cumulative indebtedness $31,512. **Criteria for awarding aid:** *Need-based:* Academics. *Non-need-based:* Academics, Alumni affiliation, Art, Athletics, Leadership, Music/drama.

VIRGINIA MILITARY INSTITUTE

VMI Office of Admissions, Lexington, VA 24450-0304
Phone: 540-464-7211 • **Financial Aid Phone:** 540-464-7208
E-mail: admissions@vmi.edu • **CEEB Code:** 5858
Fax: 540-464-7746 • **Website:** www.vmi.edu • **ACT Code:** 4418

This public school was founded in 1839. It has a 140-acre campus.

RATINGS
Admissions Selectivity Rating: 84   **Fire Safety Rating:** 79   **Green Rating:** 60*

STUDENTS AND FACULTY
Enrollment: 1,428. **Student Body:** 8% female, 92% male, 41% out-of-state, 2% international (9 countries represented). Asian 4%, African American 6%, Caucasian 84%, Hispanic 4%, Native American <1%, Pacific Islander 0%, Two or more races 0%, Race unknown 0%.
Retention and Graduation: 87% freshmen return for sophomore year. 8% grads go on to further study within 1 year. 3% grads pursue arts and sciences degrees. 2% grads pursue law degrees. 1% grads pursue business degrees. 1% grads pursue medical degrees. **Faculty:** Student/faculty ratio 10:1. 120 full-time faculty, 98% hold PhDs, 7% are are members of minority groups, 19% are women. 0% of classes are taught by teaching assistants.

ACADEMICS
Degrees: bachelor's. **Classes:** Most classes have 10-19 students. **Most popular majors:** Mechanical Engineering; Business/Managerial Economics; History. **Special Study Options:** Accelerated program, double major, exchange student program (domestic), honors program, independent study, internships, study abroad, teacher certification program, Summer Transition Program: Optional for incoming freshman. **Honors Programs:** Institute Honors Program, departmental honors programs. **Career Services:** Alumni network, Career/job search classes, Career assessment, Internships.

FACILITIES
Housing: Barracks (3-5 students/room). 50% of campus accessible to physically diasbled. **Special Academic Facilities/Equipment:** VMI Museum George C. Marshall Museum **Computers:** Students can register for classes online. Administrative functions (other than registration) can be performed online.

CAMPUS LIFE
Environment: Village. **Activities:** Choral groups, concert band, drama/theater, jazz band, literary magazine, marching band, music ensembles, musical theater, pep band, student government, student newspaper, yearbook. 50 registered organizations, 11 honor societies, 3 religious organizations. **Athletics (Intercollegiate):** *Men:* baseball, basketball, cross-country, football, golf, lacrosse, riflery, soccer, swimming, track/field (outdoor), track/field (indoor), wrestling. *Women:* cross-country, riflery, soccer, swimming, track/field (outdoor), track/field (indoor). **On-Campus Highlights:** VMI Museum, George C. Marshall Museum

ADMISSIONS
Freshman Academic Profile: Average high school GPA 3.4. 10% in top 10% of high school class, 40% in top 25% of high school class, 82% in top 50% of high school class. 84% from public high schools. **Reported SAT (pre-2016 redesign) scores:** SAT Math middle 50% range 530-620. SAT Critical Reading middle 50% range 510-620. SAT Writing middle 50% range 480-590. **Concordant SAT scores:** SAT EBRW middle 50% 550-660. SAT Math middle 50% range 560-640. ACT middle 50% range 21-26. Minimum paper TOEFL 500. **Basis for Candidate Selection:** *Very important factors considered include:* rigor of secondary school record, class rank, standardized test scores, character/personal qualities. *Important factors considered include:* interview, extracurricular activities, state residency, racial/ethnic status, volunteer work. *Other factors considered include:* recommendation(s), talent/ability, alumni/ae relation, geographical residence. **Freshman Admission Requirements:** High school diploma is required and GED is not accepted. *Academic units required:* 4 English, 3 math, 3 science, 3 science labs, 3 foreign language. *Academic units recommended:* 4 math, 4 foreign language. **Freshman Admission Statistics:** 1,600 applied, 53.63% admitted, 48% enrolled. **Transfer Admission Requirements:** High school transcript, college transcript(s), standardized test scores, Minimum college GPA of 2.0 required. Lowest grade transferable C. **General Admission Information:** Application fee $35. Regular application deadline 2/15. Nonfall registration not accepted.

COSTS AND FINANCIAL AID
Required Forms and Deadlines: FAFSA, Institution's own financial aid form. **Notification of Awards:** Applicants will be notified of awards on a rolling basis beginning 3/15. **Types of Aid:** *Need-based scholarships/grants:* Federal Pell, FSEOG, State scholarships/grants, Private scholarships, College/university scholarship or grant aid from institutional funds. *Loans:* Direct Subsidized Stafford Loans, Direct Unsubsidized Stafford Loans, Direct PLUS loans, Federal Perkins Loans. *Student Employment:* Federal Work-Study Program available. Institutional employment available. **Financial Aid Statistics:** 75% needy freshmen, 75% needy undergrads receive need-based scholarship or grant aid. 27% freshmen, 28% undergrads receive non-need-based scholarship or grant aid. 43% freshmen, 48% undergrads receive need-based self-help aid. 11% freshmen, 7% undergrads receive athletic scholarships. 85% freshmen, 82% undergrads receive any aid. **Criteria for awarding aid:** *Need-based:* Academics. *Non-need-based:* Academics, Alumni affiliation, Athletics, Leadership, Music/drama.

VIRGINIA STATE UNIVERSITY

One Hayden Drive, Petersburg, VA 23806
Phone: 804-524-5902 • **Financial Aid Phone:** 804-524-5990
E-mail: admiss@vsu.edu • **CEEB Code:** 5860
Fax: 804-524-5055 • **Website:** www.vsu.edu • **ACT Code:** 4424

This public school was founded in 1882. It has a 246-acre campus.

RATINGS
Admissions Selectivity Rating: 72   **Fire Safety Rating:** 60*   **Green Rating:** 60*

STUDENTS AND FACULTY
Enrollment: 4,481. **Student Body:** 60% female, 40% male, 32% out-of-state, <1% international (29 countries represented). Asian 0%, African American 85%, Caucasian 3%, Hispanic 2%, Native American <1%, Pacific Islander 0%, Two or more races 0%, Race unknown 9%.
Retention and Graduation: 61% freshmen return for sophomore year. 23% freshmen graduate within 4 years. 43% freshmen graduate within 6 years. **Faculty:** Student/faculty ratio 13:1. 296 full-time faculty, 0% hold PhDs, 0% are members of minority groups, 42% are women. 0% of classes are taught by teaching assistants.

ACADEMICS
Degrees: associate, bachelor's, doctoral/research, master's, postbachelor's certificate. **Most popular majors:** Physical Education Teaching and Coaching; Liberal Arts and Sciences/Liberal Studies; Sociology. **Special Study Options:** cooperative education program, double major, dual enrollment, exchange student program (domestic), honors program, independent study, internships, teacher certification program. **Disability Services:** Special programs offered to physically disabled students, including note-taking services, reader services, tutors. **Career Services:** Alumni network, Internships.

FACILITIES
Housing: Coed dorms, men's dorms, women's dorms, apartments for single studentsNote: Coed dorm—students required to have a 3.0 GPA and a record of leadership and service. (Honors Co-educational Residence Facility). 90% of campus accessible to physically diasbled. **Computers:** Administrative functions (other than registration) can be performed online.

CAMPUS LIFE

Environment: Town. **Activities:** Choral groups, concert band, dance, drama/theater, jazz band, literary magazine, marching band, music ensembles, pep band, radio station, student government, student newspaper, television station, yearbook, Campus Ministries. 70 registered organizations, 6 honor societies, 4 religious organizations. 5 fraternities, 4 sororities. **Athletics (Intercollegiate):** *Men:* baseball, basketball, cheerleading, cross-country, football, golf, tennis, track/field (outdoor), track/field (indoor). *Women:* basketball, bowling, cheerleading, cross-country, golf, softball, tennis, track/field (outdoor), track/field (indoor), volleyball.

ADMISSIONS

Freshman Academic Profile: Average high school GPA 2.9. 3% in top 10% of high school class, 17% in top 25% of high school class, 53% in top 50% of high school class. **Reported SAT (pre-2016 redesign) scores:** SAT Math middle 50% range 380-460. SAT Critical Reading middle 50% range 380-460. SAT Writing middle 50% range 370-440. **Concordant SAT scores:** SAT EBRW middle 50% 420–500. SAT Math middle 50% range 420–500. ACT middle 50% range 15-19. Minimum paper TOEFL 500. **Basis for Candidate Selection:** *Very important factors considered include:* rigor of secondary school record, academic GPA, standardized test scores. *Important factors considered include:* application essay, recommendation(s). *Other factors considered include:* extracurricular activities, talent/ability, character/personal qualities, first generation, alumni/ae relation, geographical residence, state residency, volunteer work, work experience. **Freshman Admission Requirements:** High school diploma is required and GED is accepted. *Academic units required:* 4 English, 3 math, 2 science, 1 science lab, 2 history. *Academic units recommended:* 2 foreign language, 2 social studies. **Freshman Admission Statistics:** 5,923 applied, 80.06% admitted, 19% enrolled. **Transfer Admission Requirements:** college transcript(s), essay or personal statement, statement of good standing from prior institution(s). Minimum college GPA of 2.0 required. Lowest grade transferable C. **General Admission Information:** Application fee $25. Priority deadline 3/31. Regular application deadline 5/1. Nonfall registration accepted.

COSTS AND FINANCIAL AID

Annual in-state tuition $4,876. Annual out-of-state tuition $14,132. Room and board $10,128. Required fees $3,126. Average book expense $1,300. **Required Forms and Deadlines:** FAFSA, Institution's own financial aid form. **Notification of Awards:** Applicants will be notified of awards on a rolling basis beginning 3/1. **Types of Aid:** *Need-based scholarships/grants:* Federal Pell, FSEOG, State scholarships/grants, Private scholarships, College/university scholarship or grant aid from institutional funds. *Loans:* Direct Subsidized Stafford Loans, Direct Unsubsidized Stafford Loans, Direct PLUS loans, Federal Perkins Loans, College/university loans from institutional funds. *Student Employment:* Federal Work-Study Program available. Institutional employment available. **Financial Aid Statistics:** 80% needy freshmen, 80% needy undergrads receive need-based scholarship or grant aid. 22% freshmen, 22% undergrads receive non-need-based scholarship or grant aid. 72% freshmen, 72% undergrads receive need-based self-help aid. 3% freshmen, 3% undergrads receive athletic scholarships. **Criteria for awarding aid:** *Need-based:* Academics, Alumni affiliation, Art, Athletics, Leadership, Minority status. *Non-need-based:* Academics, Alumni affiliation, Art, Athletics, Job skills, Leadership, Minority status, Music/drama, Religious affiliation.

VIRGINIA TECH

Undergraduate Admissions, Blacksburg, VA 24061
Phone: 540-231-6267 • **Financial Aid Phone:** 540-231-5179
E-mail: admissions@vt.edu • **CEEB Code:** 5859
Fax: 540-231-3242 • **Website:** www.vt.edu • **ACT Code:** 4420

This public school was founded in 1872. It has a 2600-acre campus.

RATINGS

Admissions Selectivity Rating: 88   **Fire Safety Rating:** 86   **Green Rating:** 96

STUDENTS AND FACULTY

Enrollment: 25,327. **Student Body:** 43% female, 57% male, 24% out-of-state, 6% international (116 countries represented). Asian 9%, African American 4%, Caucasian 68%, Hispanic 5%, Native American <1%, Pacific Islander <1%, Two or more races 4%, Race unknown 3%.

Retention and Graduation: 94% freshmen return for sophomore year. 83% freshmen graduate within 6 years. 31% grads go on to further study within 1 year. **Faculty:** Student/faculty ratio 14:1. 1,731 full-time faculty, 90% hold PhDs, 18% are are members of minority groups, 33% are women.

ACADEMICS

Degrees: associate, bachelor's, doctoral/professional, doctoral/research, master's, postbachelor's certificate, post-master's certificate. **Classes:** Most classes have 20-29 students. Most lab/discussion sessions have 20-29 students. **Most popular majors:** Engineering; Biology/Biological Sciences; Business Administration and Management. **Special Study Options:** Accelerated program, cooperative education program, distance learning, double major, dual enrollment, English as a Second Language (ESL), honors program, independent study, internships, study abroad, teacher certification program. Combined degree programs: BA/MA. **Disability Services:** Special programs offered to physically disabled students, including note-taking services, reader services, tape recorders, tutors. **Career Services:** Alumni network, Alumni services, Career/job search classes, Career assessment, Internships.

FACILITIES

Housing: Coed dorms, special housing for disabled students, men's dorms, special housing for international students, women's dorms, fraternity/sorority housing, Wellness Housing, Theme Housing, Housing for Corps of Cadets and athletes. The World–a cross cultural environment The W.E.L.L.–a personal health/development community. Foreign language hall and academic success hall available. The Wing–a transitional/orientation community for freshmen. Residential Leadership Community Biological and Life Sciences Learning Community Virginia Tech Design Collaborative. 60% of campus accessible to physically diasbled. **Special Academic Facilities/Equipment:** Art gallery, digital music facilities, multimedia labs, Black Cultural Center, television studio, anaerobic lab, CAD-CAM labs, observatory, wind tunnel, farms, Math Emporium, the CAVE (virtual reality learning facility). Virtual Reality Cave **Computers:** Students can register for classes online. Administrative functions (other than registration) can be performed online. Undergraduates are required to own a computer.

CAMPUS LIFE

Environment: Town. **Activities:** Choral groups, concert band, dance, drama/theater, jazz band, literary magazine, marching band, music ensembles, musical theater, pep band, radio station, student government, student newspaper, yearbook. 600 registered organizations, 32 honor societies, 53 religious organizations. 31 fraternities, 12 sororities. **Athletics (Intercollegiate):** *Men:* baseball, basketball, cheerleading, cross-country, diving, football, golf, soccer, swimming, tennis, track/field (outdoor), track/field (indoor), ultimate frisbee, water polo. *Women:* basketball, cheerleading, cross-country, diving, lacrosse, soccer, softball, swimming, tennis, track/field (outdoor), track/field (indoor), ultimate frisbee, volleyball, water polo. **Environmental Initiatives:** The Virginia Tech Climate Action Commitment and Sustainability Plan Implementation Virginia Tech is committed to being a Leader in Campus Sustainability. In April 2008 former Virginia Tech President Charles W. Steger charged the Energy and Sustainability Committee to develop a climate commitment and accompanying sustainability plan that was unique to our university. The Virginia Tech Climate Action Commitment & Sustainability Plan (VTCAC&SP) was developed as a comprehensive working document that addressed specific actions to be implemented in six broad sustainability categories to include: administrative structure and governance, facilities infrastructure, facilities operations, transportation, behavior and campus life, and academic programs. On June 1, 2009 the Virginia Tech Board of Visitors unanimously approved The Virginia Tech Climate Action Commitment and it became university policy (Presidential Policy Memorandum No. 262). The VTCAC contained 14 specific points and included the establishment of greenhouse gas emission reduction targets, the pursuit of USGBC LEED Silver ratings or higher for all future new construction and major renovations projects, and the creation of a sustainability office to oversee the implementation of our sustainability plan and to coordinate programs for campus sustainability and outreach. The Office of Energy and Sustainability established and maintained a comprehensive system to track our sustainability progress in over 100 specific areas of interest. During academic year 2012-13 the Energy and Sustainability Committee revised the VTCAC to take advantage of the many successes achieved and lessons learned in the initial three years of implementation. On May 6, 2013 University Council approved the Update to the Virginia Tech Climate Action Commitment (Presidential Policy Memorandum No. 262, Rev 1). See: http://www.it.vpas.vt.edu/docs/sust/op18/PPM262rev1.pdf Virginia Tech is a charter member of the AASHE Sustainability, Tracking, Assessment, and Rating System (STARS). STARS nationally recognized in higher education as the best management and reporting tool available to evaluate the effectiveness of your sustainability program. During academic year 2014-15, the Energy and Sustainability Committee reviewed and updated the VTCAC&SP. In the 2014 Update and Supplement to the 2009 VTCAC&SP the university has decided to have the AASHE STARS Program serve as our primary Sustainability Plan with additions based on initiatives that are unique to Virginia Tech. See: http://www.it.vpas.vt.edu/docs/sust/PA2/2014_SP_SupplementWithAppendices.pdf

On October 15, 2014 Virginia Tech received a STARS Gold Rating (version 1.2). Our overall score of 71.02 points placed the university in the top 10% of the nearly 300 colleges and universities having received a STARS rating as of that point in time. See: https://stars.aashe.org/institutions/virginia-tech-va/report/2014-10-15/ In addition to receiving recognition at the national level, Virginia Tech is the recipient of six Governor Environment Excellence Awards during the period 2008 through 2015 (two Gold and four Bronze), and this represents the most of any college or university in the Commonwealth of Virginia.

ADMISSIONS

Freshman Academic Profile: 39% in top 10% of high school class, 80% in top 25% of high school class, 98% in top 50% of high school class. **Reported SAT (pre-2016 redesign) scores:** SAT Math middle 50% range 560-680. SAT Critical Reading middle 50% range 540-640. SAT Writing middle 50% range 530-630. **Concordant SAT scores:** SAT EBRW middle 50% 590–680. SAT Math middle 50% range 580–710. Minimum paper TOEFL 550. **Basis for Candidate Selection:** *Very important factors considered include:* rigor of secondary school record, academic GPA, standardized test scores. *Other factors considered include:* recommendation(s), extracurricular activities, talent/ability, character/personal qualities, first generation, alumni/ae relation, geographical residence, state residency, racial/ethnic status, volunteer work, work experience, level of applicant's interest. **Freshman Admission Requirements:** High school diploma is required and GED is accepted. *Academic units required:* 4 English, 3 math, 2 science, 2 science labs, 1 social studies, 1 history, 4 academic electives. *Academic units recommended:* 4 math, 3 science, 3 foreign language. **Freshman Admission Statistics:** 22,280 applied, 73.41% admitted, 39% enrolled. **Transfer Admission Requirements:** High school transcript, college transcript(s), Minimum college GPA of 3.0 required. Lowest grade transferable C. **General Admission Information:** Application fee $60. Regular application deadline 1/15. Regular notification 4/1. Nonfall registration accepted. Admission may be deferred for a maximum of 1 year.

COSTS AND FINANCIAL AID

Annual in-state tuition $10,496. Annual out-of-state tuition $26,536. Room and board $8,266. Required fees $1,989. Average book expense $1,130. **Required Forms and Deadlines:** FAFSA. **Notification of Awards:** Applicants will be notified of awards on a rolling basis beginning 4/1. **Types of Aid:** *Need-based scholarships/grants:* Federal Pell, FSEOG, State scholarships/grants, Private scholarships, College/university scholarship or grant aid from institutional funds. *Loans:* Direct Subsidized Stafford Loans, Direct Unsubsidized Stafford Loans, Direct PLUS loans, Federal Perkins Loans, College/university loans from institutional funds. *Student Employment:* Federal Work-Study Program available. Institutional employment available. **Financial Aid Statistics:** 65% needy freshmen, 71% needy undergrads receive need-based scholarship or grant aid. 50% freshmen, 37% undergrads receive non-need-based scholarship or grant aid. 82% freshmen, 83% undergrads receive need-based self-help aid. 2% freshmen, 2% undergrads receive athletic scholarships. 75% undergrads receive any aid. 53% undergrads borrow to pay for school. Average cumulative indebtedness $28,873. **Criteria for awarding aid:** *Need-based:* Academics, Art, Leadership, Minority status, Music/drama. *Non-need-based:* Academics, Art, Athletics, Leadership, Minority status, Music/drama, State/district residency.

VIRGINIA WESLEYAN COLLEGE

1584 Wesleyan Drive, Norfolk/Virginia Beach, VA 23502-5599
Phone: 757-455-3208 • **Financial Aid Phone:** 757-455-3345
E-mail: admissions@vwc.edu • **CEEB Code:** 5867
Fax: 757-461-5238 • **Website:** www.vwc.edu • **ACT Code:** 4429

This private school, affiliated with the Methodist Church, was founded in 1961. It has a 300-acre campus.

RATINGS
Admissions Selectivity Rating: 76   **Fire Safety Rating:** 79   **Green Rating:** 85

STUDENTS AND FACULTY
Enrollment: 1,493. **Student Body:** 62% female, 38% male, 25% out-of-state, 1% international (7 countries represented). Asian 1%, African American 23%, Caucasian 56%, Hispanic 8%, Native American <1%, Pacific Islander <1%, Two or more races 6%, Race unknown 4%.

Retention and Graduation: 66% freshmen return for sophomore year. 42% freshmen graduate within 4 years. 48% freshmen graduate within 6 years. 32% grads go on to further study within 1 year. 1% grads pursue law degrees. 1% grads pursue business degrees. **Faculty:** Student/faculty ratio 13:1. 92 full-time faculty, 91% hold PhDs, 11% are are members of minority groups, 48% are women. 0% of classes are taught by teaching assistants.

ACADEMICS

Degrees: bachelor's. **Classes:** Most classes have 10-19 students. **Most popular majors:** Business Administration and Management; Criminal Justice/Safety Studies; Social Sciences. **Special Study Options:** double major, honors program, independent study, internships, liberal arts/career combination, student-designed major, study abroad, teacher certification program, Externships; PORTfolio, a 4-year competitive program designed to integrate liberal arts and experiential learning. **Honors Programs:** Wesleyan Scholars is an honors program which is designed for applicants with superior high school achievement records. The Honors and Scholars program, including Wesleyan Scholars, offers academically challenging honors courses and stimulating co-curricular experiences. Program enhancement is also offered through PORTfolio, a selective program designed to integrate the liberal arts with experiential learning opportunities available in Hampton Roads. **Disability Services:** Special programs offered to physically disabled students, including note-taking services, reader services, tape recorders, tutors. **Career Services:** Alumni network, Career/job search classes, Internships, Regional alumni.

FACILITIES

Housing: Coed dorms, special housing for disabled students, special housing for international students, women's dorms, fraternity/sorority housing, apartments for single students, Wellness Housing, Townhouses, Honors and Scholars Hall, Wellness Hall-a substance free hall which provides special programs focusing on social, physical, spiritual, emotional, and intellectual wellness. 90% of campus accessible to physically diasbled. **Special Academic Facilities/Equipment:** Greenhouse, language lab, teleconferencing facility, social science teach. and learn. lab, radio station, TV studio, Barclay Sheaks Art Gallery, computerized classrooms, Internet access all classrooms, 24-hr. computer lab, Lambuth M. Clarke Hall with state-of-the-art teaching technologies, three academic villages combining residences and campus offices and services. **Computers:** 20% of classrooms, 100% of libraries, 100% of student union, have wireless network access. Students can register for classes online. Administrative functions (other than registration) can be performed online.

CAMPUS LIFE

Environment: Metropolis. **Activities:** Choral groups, dance, drama/theater, literary magazine, music ensembles, musical theater, radio station, student government, student newspaper, yearbook, Campus Ministries, Student Organization, Model UN. 60 registered organizations, 19 honor societies, 4 religious organizations. 3 fraternities, 4 sororities. **Athletics (Intercollegiate):** *Men:* baseball, basketball, cross-country, golf, lacrosse, soccer, tennis, track/field (outdoor), track/field (indoor). *Women:* basketball, cheerleading, cross-country, field hockey, lacrosse, soccer, softball, tennis, track/field (outdoor), track/field (indoor), volleyball. **On-Campus Highlights:** The Marlin Restaurant, Jane P. Batten Student Center, Village III, Trinder Athletic Center **Environmental Initiatives:** Green Roof

ADMISSIONS

Freshman Academic Profile: Average high school GPA 3.3. 13% in top 10% of high school class, 38% in top 25% of high school class, 74% in top 50% of high school class. 86% from public high schools. **Reported SAT (pre-2016 redesign) scores:** SAT Math middle 50% range 430-550. SAT Critical Reading middle 50% range 440-550. SAT Writing middle 50% range 425-530. **Concordant SAT scores:** SAT EBRW middle 50% 490–600. SAT Math middle 50% range 470–570. ACT middle 50% range 18-25. Minimum paper TOEFL 550. **Basis for Candidate Selection:** *Very important factors considered include:* rigor of secondary school record, academic GPA, level of applicant's interest. *Important factors considered include:* standardized test scores, application essay, recommendation(s), extracurricular activities. *Other factors considered include:* interview, talent/ability, character/personal qualities, first generation, alumni/ae relation, volunteer work, work experience. **Freshman Admission Requirements:** High school diploma is required and GED is accepted. *Academic units required:* 4 English, 3 math, 2 science, 2 science labs, 2 foreign language, 1 history, 1 computer science. *Academic units recommended:* 4 English, 3 math, 2 science, 2 science labs, 2 foreign language, 1 history, 4 academic electives, 1 computer science. **Freshman Admission Statistics:** 2,072 applied, 89.04% admitted, 22% enrolled. **Transfer Admission Requirements:** High school transcript, college transcript(s), essay or personal statement, statement of good standing from prior institution(s). Minimum college GPA of 2.5 required. Lowest grade transferable C. **General Admission Information:** Application fee $40. Priority deadline 3/1. Nonfall registration accepted.

COSTS AND FINANCIAL AID

Annual tuition $32,636. Required fees $650. Average book expense $1,500. **Required Forms and Deadlines:** FAFSA, State aid form. **Notification of Awards:** Applicants will be notified of awards on a rolling basis beginning 2/15. **Types of Aid:** *Need-based scholarships/grants:* Federal Pell, FSEOG, State scholarships/grants, Private scholarships, College/university scholarship or grant aid from institutional funds. *Loans:* Direct Subsidized Stafford Loans, Direct Unsubsidized Stafford Loans, Direct PLUS loans, Federal Perkins Loans. *Student Employment:* Federal Work-Study Program available. Institutional employment available. **Financial Aid Statistics:** 100% needy freshmen, 100% needy undergrads receive need-based scholarship or grant aid. 19% freshmen, 17% undergrads receive non-need-based scholarship or grant aid. 78% freshmen, 78% undergrads receive need-based self-help aid. 0% freshmen, 0% undergrads receive athletic scholarships. 99% freshmen, 98% undergrads receive any aid. **Criteria for awarding aid:** *Need-based:* Art, Job skills, Music/drama. *Non-need-based:* Academics, Alumni affiliation, Leadership, Religious affiliation, State/district residency.

VITERBO UNIVERSITY

900 Viterbo Drive, La Crosse, WI 54601
Phone: 608-796-3010 • **Financial Aid Phone:** 608-496-3900
E-mail: admission@viterbo.edu • **CEEB Code:** 1878
Fax: 608-796-3020 • **ACT Code:** 4662

This private school, affiliated with the Roman Catholic Church, was founded in 1890. It has a 25-acre campus.

RATINGS

Admissions Selectivity Rating: 75   **Fire Safety Rating:** 73   **Green Rating:** 60*

STUDENTS AND FACULTY

Enrollment: 1,922. **Student Body:** 71% female, 29% male, 19% out-of-state, 1% international (15 countries represented). Asian 1%, African American 1%, Caucasian 93%, Hispanic 1%, Native American 1%, Pacific Islander 0%, Two or more races 0%, Race unknown 2%. **Retention and Graduation:** 74% freshmen return for sophomore year. 30% freshmen graduate within 4 years. 48% freshmen graduate within 6 years. 7% grads go on to further study within 1 year. 4% grads pursue arts and sciences degrees. 1% grads pursue law degrees. 2% grads pursue medical degrees. **Faculty:** Student/faculty ratio 13:1. 110 full-time faculty, 56% hold PhDs, 4% are are members of minority groups, 56% are women. 0% of classes are taught by teaching assistants.

ACADEMICS

Degrees: associate, bachelor's, master's, postbachelor's certificate, terminal, transfer. **Classes:** Most classes have 10-19 students. Most lab/discussion sessions have 10-19 students. **Most popular majors:** Elementary Education and Teaching Business Administration and Management. **Special Study Options:** Accelerated program, cross-registration, distance learning, double major, dual enrollment, honors program, independent study, internships, liberal arts/career combination, student-designed major, study abroad, teacher certification program, weekend college, Weekend college is basically for our Master's level programs. **Honors Programs:** The mission of the Viterbo University Honors Program is to provide a supportive, enriched learning environment responsive to the educational needs of highly able and exceptionally motivated undergraduate students who are committed to achieving academic excellence. The program provides honors sections of regular, general education courses, honors credit within regular sections, interdisciplinary Honors Capstone courses, oversight of senior honors projects, and increased opportunity for undergraduate research and creative activity. The program complements and enhances the Liberal Arts mission of the university. Together, honors students and faculty constitute a community of scholars. Combined degree programs: chiropractic. **Disability Services:** Special programs offered to physically disabled students, including note-taking services, reader services, tape recorders, tutors. **Career Services:** Alumni network, Alumni services, Career/job search classes, Career assessment, Internships, Regional alumni. We have been very successful placing our students in internships that have not only assisted the student but the larger La Crosse community.

FACILITIES

Housing: Coed dorms, apartments for single students, Theme floors in dorms and university owned theme houses. 90% of campus accessible to physically diasbled. **Special Academic Facilities/Equipment:** Fine Arts Center; Center for Ethics, Science and Technology with distance education labs and video conferencing; Nursing center with labs and simulated equipment; new recreation and education center co-sponsored by Viterbo University and the

Boys and Girls Club. **Computers:** Students can register for classes online. Administrative functions (other than registration) can be performed online.

CAMPUS LIFE

Environment: Town. **Activities:** Choral groups, dance, drama/theater, literary magazine, music ensembles, musical theater, opera, pep band, student government, student newspaper. 22 registered organizations, 2 honor societies, 2 religious organizations. **Athletics (Intercollegiate):** *Men:* baseball, basketball, golf, soccer. *Women:* basketball, golf, soccer, softball, volleyball. **On-Campus Highlights:** Reinhart Center for Ethics, Science and Technology, Fine Arts Center, Amie Mathy Center for Recreation and Education, Student Activity Center, Dancing Francis, Center for Ethics, Science and Technology opened the Fall of 2003. Center for Recreation and Wellness opens Fall 2005, co-sponsored by Viterbo and the Boys/Girls club. Dancing Francis is a bronze sculpture of Francis of Assisi by Paul Granland. Fine Arts Center is home of performing arts in the region. Student Activity Center is home to the V-Hawks as well as fitness center for all students.

ADMISSIONS

Freshman Academic Profile: Average high school GPA 3.3. 13% in top 10% of high school class, 39% in top 25% of high school class, 73% in top 50% of high school class. 97% from public high schools. ACT middle 50% range 20-24. Minimum paper TOEFL 550. **Basis for Candidate Selection:** *Very important factors considered include:* rigor of secondary school record, academic GPA, standardized test scores, character/personal qualities, level of applicant's interest. *Important factors considered include:* class rank, interview, talent/ability. *Other factors considered include:* application essay, recommendation(s), extracurricular activities, first generation, alumni/ae relation, volunteer work. **Freshman Admission Requirements:** High school diploma is required and GED is accepted. *Academic units required:* 3 English, 2 math, 2 science, 2 social studies, 5 academic electives. *Academic units recommended:* 4 English, 2 math, 2 science, 2 science labs, 2 foreign language, 2 social studies, 5 academic electives. **Freshman Admission Statistics:** 1,107 applied, 88.71% admitted, 37% enrolled. **Transfer Admission Requirements:** High school transcript, college transcript(s), statement of good standing from prior institution(s). Minimum college GPA of 2.0 required. Lowest grade transferable C-. **General Admission Information:** Application fee $25. Priority deadline 8/1. Nonfall registration accepted. Admission may be deferred.

COSTS AND FINANCIAL AID

Annual tuition $18,170. Room and board $6,140. Required fees $420. Average book expense $800. **Required Forms and Deadlines:** FAFSA, Institution's own financial aid form. **Notification of Awards:** Applicants will be notified of awards on a rolling basis beginning 4/1. **Types of Aid:** *Need-based scholarships/grants:* Federal Pell, FSEOG, State scholarships/grants, Private scholarships, College/university scholarship or grant aid from institutional funds. *Loans:* Federal Perkins Loans, Federal Nursing Loans, State Loans. *Student Employment:* Federal Work-Study Program available. Institutional employment available. **Financial Aid Statistics:** 98% needy freshmen, 97% needy undergrads receive need-based scholarship or grant aid. 6% freshmen, 6% undergrads receive non-need-based scholarship or grant aid. 94% freshmen, 93% undergrads receive need-based self-help aid. 0% freshmen, 1% undergrads receive athletic scholarships. 98% freshmen, 89% undergrads receive any aid. **Criteria for awarding aid:** *Need-based:* Academics, Alumni affiliation. *Non-need-based:* Academics, Alumni affiliation, Art, Athletics, Leadership, Minority status, Music/drama.

WABASH COLLEGE

PO Box 352, Crawfordsville, IN 47933
Phone: 765-361-6225 • **Financial Aid Phone:** 765-361-6370
E-mail: admissions@wabash.edu • **CEEB Code:** 1895
Fax: 765-361-6437 • **Website:** www.wabash.edu • **ACT Code:** 1260

This private school was founded in 1832. It has a 60-acre campus.

RATINGS

Admissions Selectivity Rating: 87   **Fire Safety Rating:** 92   **Green Rating:** 69

STUDENTS AND FACULTY

Enrollment: 867. **Student Body:** 0% female, 100% male, 23% out-of-state, 7% international (14 countries represented). Asian 1%, African American 6%, Caucasian 74%, Hispanic 7%, Native American <1%, Pacific Islander 0%, Two or more races 3%, Race unknown 2%.

Retention and Graduation: 85% freshmen return for sophomore year. 70% freshmen graduate within 4 years. 73% freshmen graduate within 6 years. 25% grads go on to further study within 1 year. 6% grads pursue arts and sciences degrees. 6% grads pursue law degrees. 1% grads pursue business degrees. 5% grads pursue medical degrees. **Faculty:** Student/faculty ratio 10:1. 80 full-time faculty, 99% hold PhDs, 10% are are members of minority groups, 35% are women. 0% of classes are taught by teaching assistants.

ACADEMICS

Degrees: bachelor's. **Classes:** Most classes have 10-19 students. Most lab/discussion sessions have 10-19 students. **Most popular majors:** History; Political Science and Government; Economics. **Special Study Options:** double major, independent study, internships, liberal arts/career combination, study abroad, teacher certification program, Student designed majors, minors, or areas of concentration. Immersion Learning courses are offered, which involve travel domestically and abroad. Combined degree programs: BA/MEng. **Disability Services:** Special programs offered to physically disabled students, including note-taking services, reader services, tape recorders, tutors. **Career Services:** Alumni network, Alumni services, Career/job search classes, Career assessment, Internships, Regional alumni. Our Entrepreneurial Support and Education programming, including an annual Entrepreneur Summit (250 participants last year, including students, alumni, community members, and participants from other colleges), SEED Grants, IdeaSpark Competition, The FORGE co-working space, Entrepreneur-In-Residence, and additional speakers, workshops, and seminars.

FACILITIES

Housing: special housing for disabled students, men's dorms, fraternity/sorority housing, College-owned houses and apartments. 70% of campus accessible to physically diasbled. **Special Academic Facilities/Equipment:** Malcolm X Institute of Black Studies, two art galleries, language lab, electron microscope, atomic absorption, nuclear and infrared spectrometers, Beowulf Supercomputer, Center of Inquiry in the Liberal Arts, Wabash Center for Teaching and Learning in Theology and Religion, Ramsey Archival Center **Computers:** 100% of classrooms, 100% of dorms, 100% of libraries, 100% of dining areas, 100% of student union, 100% of common outdoor areas have wireless network access. Administrative functions (other than registration) can be performed online.

CAMPUS LIFE

Environment: Village. **Activities:** Choral groups, concert band, drama/theater, jazz band, literary magazine, music ensembles, pep band, radio station, student government, student newspaper, student-run film society, symphony orchestra, yearbook, Campus Ministries, Student Organization, Model UN. 65 registered organizations, 7 honor societies, 5 religious organizations. 9 fraternities. **Athletics (Intercollegiate):** *Men:* baseball, basketball, cross-country, diving, football, golf, soccer, swimming, tennis, track/field (outdoor), track/field (indoor), wrestling. **On-Campus Highlights:** Allen Athletics and Recreation Center, Wabash Chapel, New Science Building, Hays Hall, Trippet Hall, Lilly Library, Malcolm X Institute of Black Studies. **Environmental Initiatives:** Printing Quota that saved 240,000 sheets of paper in the first semester (among 900 students)

ADMISSIONS

Freshman Academic Profile: Average high school GPA 3.7. 35% in top 10% of high school class, 71% in top 25% of high school class, 95% in top 50% of high school class. 92% from public high schools. **Reported SAT (pre-2016 redesign) scores:** SAT Math middle 50% range 530-640. SAT Critical Reading middle 50% range 510-610. SAT Writing middle 50% range 470-600. **Concordant SAT scores:** SAT EBRW middle 50% 550–660. SAT Math middle 50% range 560–660. ACT middle 50% range 22-28. Minimum internet-based TOEFL 80. Minimum paper TOEFL 550. **Basis for Candidate Selection:** *Very important factors considered include:* rigor of secondary school record, class rank, academic GPA, level of applicant's interest. *Important factors considered include:* standardized test scores, interview, extracurricular activities, talent/ability. *Other factors considered include:* application essay, recommendation(s), character/personal qualities, first generation, alumni/ae relation, geographical residence, racial/ethnic status, volunteer work, work experience. **Freshman Admission Requirements:** High school diploma is required and GED is accepted. *Academic units recommended:* 4 English, 4 math, 2 science, 2 science labs, 2 foreign language, 2 social studies, 2 history, 2 academic electives. **Freshman Admission Statistics:** 1,247 applied, 61.43% admitted, 31% enrolled. **Transfer Admission Requirements:** High school transcript, college transcript(s), essay or personal statement, standardized test scores, statement of good standing from prior institution(s). Lowest grade transferable C. **General Admission Information:** Application fee $40. Priority deadline 12/1. Nonfall registration accepted. Admission may be deferred for a maximum of 1 year.

COSTS AND FINANCIAL AID

Annual tuition $40,400. Room and board $9,600. Required fees $650. Average book expense $1,000. **Required Forms and Deadlines:** FAFSA. **Notification**

of Awards: Applicants will be notified of awards on or about 3/31. **Types of Aid:** *Need-based scholarships/grants:* Federal Pell, FSEOG, State scholarships/grants, Private scholarships, College/university scholarship or grant aid from institutional funds. *Loans:* Direct Subsidized Stafford Loans, Direct Unsubsidized Stafford Loans, Direct PLUS loans, College/university loans from institutional funds. *Student Employment:* Federal Work-Study Program available. Institutional employment available. **Financial Aid Statistics:** 99% needy freshmen, 98% needy undergrads receive need-based scholarship or grant aid. 20% freshmen, 15% undergrads receive non-need-based scholarship or grant aid. 79% freshmen, 83% undergrads receive need-based self-help aid. 0% freshmen, 0% undergrads receive athletic scholarships. 99% freshmen, 95% undergrads receive any aid. 91% undergrads borrow to pay for school. Average cumulative indebtedness $32,916. **Criteria for awarding aid:** *Need-based:* Academics. *Non-need-based:* Academics, Art, Leadership, Music/drama.

WAGNER COLLEGE

Staten Island, NY 10301
Phone: 718-390-3411 • **Financial Aid Phone:** 718-390-3183
E-mail: adm@wagner.edu • **CEEB Code:** 2966
Fax: 718-390-3105 • **Website:** www.wagner.edu • **ACT Code:** 2984

This private school was founded in 1883. It has a 110-acre campus.

RATINGS

Admissions Selectivity Rating: 83   **Fire Safety Rating:** 98   **Green Rating:** 60*

STUDENTS AND FACULTY

Enrollment: 1,797. **Student Body:** 64% female, 36% male, 52% out-of-state, 4% international (36 countries represented). Asian 3%, African American 8%, Caucasian 66%, Hispanic 11%, Native American <1%, Pacific Islander <1%, Two or more races 3%, Race unknown 5%.
Retention and Graduation: 85% freshmen return for sophomore year. 64% freshmen graduate within 4 years. 67 42% grads go on to further study within 1 year. 23% grads pursue arts and sciences degrees. 4% grads pursue law degrees. 26% grads pursue business degrees. 6% grads pursue medical degrees. **Faculty:** Student/faculty ratio 13:1. 110 full-time faculty, 87% hold PhDs, 10% are are members of minority groups, 50% are women. 0% of classes are taught by teaching assistants.

ACADEMICS

Degrees: bachelor's, doctoral/professional, master's, post-master's certificate. **Classes:** Most classes have 10-19 students. Most lab/discussion sessions have 10-19 students. **Most popular majors:** Business/Commerce; Visual and Performing Arts; Nursing Science. **Special Study Options:** double major, exchange student program (domestic), honors program, independent study, internships, study abroad, teacher certification program, Learning Communities. Combined degree programs: 7-year dental program with New York University; BS/MS in Accounting. **Disability Services:** Special programs offered to physically disabled students, including note-taking services, reader services, tape recorders, tutors. **Career Services:** Alumni network, Alumni services, Internships. Wagner College's curriculum unites deep learning and practical application. The Wagner Plan incorporates our longstanding commitment to the liberal arts, experiential learning and interdisciplinary education with our geographical location and enduring bond with New York City.

FACILITIES

Housing: Coed dorms, fraternity/sorority housing, apartments for single students, Theme Housing. 50% of campus accessible to physically diasbled. **Special Academic Facilities/Equipment:** Art gallery, early childhood center, nursing resource center, planetarium, two electron microscopes, solar energy project. **Computers:** 90% of classrooms, 100% of dorms, 100% of libraries, 100% of dining areas, 100% of student union, 50% of common outdoor areas have wireless network access. Students can register for classes online. Administrative functions (other than registration) can be performed online.

CAMPUS LIFE

Environment: Metropolis. **Activities:** Choral groups, dance, drama/theater, jazz band, literary magazine, music ensembles, musical theater, pep band, radio station, student government, student newspaper, yearbook, Campus Ministries, Student Organization, Model UN. 66 registered organizations, 11 honor societies, 4 religious organizations. 5 fraternities, 4 sororities. **Athletics**

(Intercollegiate): *Men:* baseball, basketball, cross-country, football, golf, lacrosse, tennis, track/field (outdoor), track/field (indoor). *Women:* basketball, cross-country, golf, lacrosse, soccer, softball, swimming, tennis, track/field (outdoor), track/field (indoor), water polo. **On-Campus Highlights:** Coffee House, Spiro Sports Center, Wagner Student Union, Main Hall Theatre, Foundation Hall, Hawk's Nest. **Environmental Initiatives:** competing in Recylemania, Spring 2009

ADMISSIONS

Freshman Academic Profile: Average high school GPA 3.6. 22% in top 10% of high school class, 53% in top 25% of high school class, 88% in top 50% of high school class. 67% from public high schools. **Reported SAT (pre-2016 redesign) scores:** SAT Math middle 50% range 500-600. SAT Critical Reading middle 50% range 500-600. SAT Writing middle 50% range 490-610. **Concordant SAT scores:** SAT EBRW middle 50% 550–660. SAT Math middle 50% range 530–620. ACT middle 50% range 22-27. Minimum internet-based TOEFL 79. Minimum paper TOEFL 550. **Basis for Candidate Selection:** *Very important factors considered include:* rigor of secondary school record, class rank, academic GPA. *Important factors considered include:* application essay, recommendation(s), interview, extracurricular activities, talent/ability, character/personal qualities. *Other factors considered include:* standardized test scores, volunteer work, work experience, level of applicant's interest. **Freshman Admission Requirements:** High school diploma is required and GED is accepted. *Academic units required:* 4 English, 3 math, 2 science, 1 science lab, 2 foreign language, 3 history, 7 academic electives. **Freshman Admission Statistics:** 2,790 applied, 72.94% admitted, 22% enrolled. **Transfer Admission Requirements:** college transcript(s), essay or personal statement, statement of good standing from prior institution(s). Minimum college GPA of 3.0 required. Lowest grade transferable C. **General Admission Information:** Application fee $60. Priority deadline 12/1. Regular application deadline 2/15. Nonfall registration accepted. Admission may be deferred for a maximum of 1 year.

COSTS AND FINANCIAL AID

Annual tuition $43,500. Room and board $13,260. Required fees $480. Average book expense $822. **Required Forms and Deadlines:** FAFSA, State aid form. **Notification of Awards:** Applicants will be notified of awards on a rolling basis beginning 3/1. **Types of Aid:** *Need-based scholarships/grants:* Federal Pell, FSEOG, State scholarships/grants, Private scholarships, College/university scholarship or grant aid from institutional funds. *Loans:* Direct Subsidized Stafford Loans, Direct Unsubsidized Stafford Loans, Direct PLUS loans, Federal Perkins Loans, Federal Nursing Loans. *Student Employment:* Federal Work-Study Program available. Institutional employment available. **Financial Aid Statistics:** 100% needy freshmen, 99% needy undergrads receive need-based scholarship or grant aid. 0% undergrads receive non-need-based scholarship or grant aid. 77% freshmen, 78% undergrads receive need-based self-help aid. 8% freshmen, 7% undergrads receive athletic scholarships. 98% freshmen, 93% undergrads receive any aid. **Criteria for awarding aid:** *Non-need-based:* Academics, Athletics, Leadership, Music/drama.

WAKE FOREST UNIVERSITY

P.O. Box 7305, Winston Salem, NC 27109
Phone: 336-758-5201 • **Financial Aid Phone:** 336-758-5154
E-mail: admissions@wfu.edu • **CEEB Code:** 5885
Fax: 336-758-4324 • **Website:** www.wfu.edu • **ACT Code:** 3168

This private school was founded in 1834. It has a 340-acre campus.

RATINGS

Admissions Selectivity Rating: 95   **Fire Safety Rating:** 95   **Green Rating:** 85

STUDENTS AND FACULTY

Enrollment: 4,866. **Student Body:** 53% female, 47% male, 78% out-of-state, 7% international (27 countries represented). Asian 5%, African American 6%, Caucasian 72%, Hispanic 7%, Native American <1%, Pacific Islander <1%, Two or more races 3%, Race unknown <1%.
Retention and Graduation: 93% freshmen return for sophomore year. 82% freshmen graduate within 4 years. 88 32% grads go on to further study within 1 year. 28% grads pursue arts and sciences degrees. 16% grads pursue law degrees. 36% grads pursue business degrees. 17% grads pursue medical degrees. **Faculty:** Student/faculty ratio 10:1. 573 full-time faculty, 93% hold PhDs, 16% are members of minority groups, 43% are women. 0% of classes are taught by teaching assistants.

ACADEMICS

Degrees: bachelor's, doctoral/professional, doctoral/research, master's.
Classes: Most classes have 10-19 students. Most lab/discussion sessions have 10-19 students. **Most popular majors:** Political Science and Government; Business/Commerce; Psychology. **Special Study Options:** cross-registration, double major, dual enrollment, honors program, independent study, internships, study abroad, teacher certification program. **Honors Programs:** For highly qualified students, a series of interdisciplinary honors courses are offered. Additionally, for students especially talented in individual areas of study, most departments in the College offer special studies leading to graduation with honors in a particular discipline. Combined degree programs: BS/MS in accountancy. **Disability Services:** Special programs offered to physically disabled students, including note-taking services, reader services, tape recorders, tutors. **Career Services:** Alumni network, Alumni services, Career/job search classes, Career assessment, Internships, Regional alumni.

FACILITIES

Housing: Coed dorms, fraternity/sorority housing, apartments for single students, Wellness Housing, Theme Housing, Wellness = Substance Free. **Special Academic Facilities/Equipment:** Museum of Anthropology; Charlotte and Philip Hanes Art Gallery; Scales Fine Arts Center; Reynolda House, Museum of American Art; Laser and Electron Microscope Labs. **Computers:** 100% of classrooms, 100% of dorms, 100% of libraries, 100% of dining areas, 100% of student union, 5% of common outdoor areas have wireless network access. Students can register for classes online. Administrative functions (other than registration) can be performed online. Undergraduates are required to own a computer.

CAMPUS LIFE

Environment: City. **Activities:** Choral groups, concert band, dance, drama/theater, jazz band, literary magazine, marching band, music ensembles, pep band, radio station, student government, student newspaper, student-run film society, symphony orchestra, television station, yearbook, Campus Ministries, Student Organization, Model UN. 168 registered organizations, 16 honor societies, 16 religious organizations. 14 fraternities, 9 sororities. **Athletics (Intercollegiate):** *Men:* baseball, basketball, cheerleading, cross-country, football, golf, soccer, tennis, track/field (outdoor), track/field (indoor). *Women:* basketball, cheerleading, cross-country, field hockey, golf, soccer, tennis, track/field (outdoor), track/field (indoor), volleyball. **On-Campus Highlights:** Charlotte and Philip Hanes Art Gallery, Museum of Anthropology, The Z. Smith Reynolds Library, Wait Chapel, Benson University Center. **Environmental Initiatives:** Campus Master Plan: Wake Forest has completed a new campus master plan that will guide development over the next 50 years. Heavily integrated into that plan are tenents for sustainable design (e.g. LEED) as well as stormwater management and biohabitat protection. This new master plan will guide the campus in integrating sustainability within the built and natural environments for the years ahead.

ADMISSIONS

Freshman Academic Profile: 77% in top 10% of high school class, 93% in top 25% of high school class, 98% in top 50% of high school class. 65% from public high schools. **Reported SAT (pre-2016 redesign) scores:** SAT Math middle 50% range 610-720. SAT Critical Reading middle 50% range 590-690. SAT Writing middle 50% range 600-700. **Concordant SAT scores:** SAT EBRW middle 50% 650–730. SAT Math middle 50% range 630–750. Minimum paper TOEFL 600. **Basis for Candidate Selection:** *Very important factors considered include:* rigor of secondary school record, class rank, academic GPA, application essay, character/personal qualities. *Important factors considered include:* recommendation(s), interview, extracurricular activities, talent/ability. *Other factors considered include:* standardized test scores, first generation, alumni/ae relation, geographical residence, state residency, religious affiliation/commitment, racial/ethnic status, volunteer work, level of applicant's interest. **Freshman Admission Requirements:** High school diploma is required and GED is accepted. *Academic units required:* 4 English, 3 math, 1 science, 2 foreign language, 2 social studies. *Academic units recommended:* 4 English, 4 math, 4 science, 4 foreign language, 4 social studies. **Freshman Admission Statistics:** 13,281 applied, 29.39% admitted, 33% enrolled. **Transfer Admission Requirements:** High school transcript, college transcript(s), essay or personal statement, statement of good standing from prior institution(s). Minimum college GPA of 2.0 required. Lowest grade transferable C. **General Admission Information:** Application fee $50. Regular application deadline 1/1. Nonfall registration not accepted.

COSTS AND FINANCIAL AID

Annual tuition $48,746. Room and board $14,748. Required fees $562. Average book expense $1,400. **Required Forms and Deadlines:** FAFSA, CSS/Financial Aid PROFILE, State aid form, Noncustodial PROFILE. **Notification of Awards:** Applicants will be notified of awards on a rolling basis beginning 4/1. **Types of Aid:** *Need-based scholarships/grants:* Federal Pell, FSEOG, State scholarships/grants, Private scholarships, College/university scholarship or grant aid from institutional funds. *Loans:* Direct Subsidized Stafford Loans, Direct Unsubsidized Stafford Loans, Direct PLUS loans, Federal Perkins Loans, State

Loans, College/university loans from institutional funds. *Student Employment:* Federal Work-Study Program available. Institutional employment available. **Financial Aid Statistics:** 93% needy freshmen, 95% needy undergrads receive need-based scholarship or grant aid. 55% freshmen, 54% undergrads receive non-need-based scholarship or grant aid. 90% freshmen, 93% undergrads receive need-based self-help aid. 3% freshmen, 3% undergrads receive athletic scholarships. 39% freshmen, 34% undergrads receive any aid. 39% undergrads borrow to pay for school. Average cumulative indebtedness $36,546. **Criteria for awarding aid:** *Non-need-based:* Academics, Alumni affiliation, Art, Athletics, Leadership, Music/drama, Religious affiliation, State/district residency.

WALLA WALLA UNIVERSITY

Office of Admissions, College Place, WA 99324-1198
Phone: 509-527-2615 • **Financial Aid Phone:** 509-527-2815
E-mail: info@wallawalla.edu • **CEEB Code:** 4940
Fax: 509-527-2253 • **Website:** www.wallawalla.edu • **ACT Code:** 4486

This private school, affiliated with the Seventh Day Adventist Church, was founded in 1892. It has a 77-acre campus.

RATINGS
Admissions Selectivity Rating: 70   **Fire Safety Rating:** 62   **Green Rating:** 60*

STUDENTS AND FACULTY
Enrollment: 1,250. **Student Body:** 50% female, 50% male, 59% out-of-state, 3% international (30 countries represented). Asian 0%, African American 3%, Caucasian 74%, Hispanic 10%, Native American 1%, Pacific Islander 7%, Two or more races 0%, Race unknown 1%.
Retention and Graduation: 78% freshmen return for sophomore year. 23% freshmen graduate within 4 years. **Faculty:** 112 full-time faculty, 69% hold PhDs, 6% are are members of minority groups, 39% are women. 0% of classes are taught by teaching assistants.

ACADEMICS
Degrees: associate, bachelor's, diploma, master's. **Classes:** Most classes have fewer than 10 students. Most lab/discussion sessions have fewer than 10 students. **Most popular majors:** Engineering; Social Work; Business/Commerce. **Special Study Options:** cooperative education program, distance learning, double major, honors program, independent study, internships, liberal arts/career combination, study abroad, teacher certification program. **Disability Services:** Special programs offered to physically disabled students, including note-taking services, reader services, tape recorders, tutors. **Career Services:** Alumni network, Career/job search classes, Career assessment, Internships. All of our accounting and management students participate in internships.

FACILITIES
Housing: special housing for disabled students, men's dorms, women's dorms, apartments for married students, apartments for single students, Wellness Housing. 75% of campus accessible to physically diasbled. **Special Academic Facilities/Equipment:** Marine station on the Rosario Strait of the Puget Sound in Washington state. **Computers:** Students can register for classes online.

CAMPUS LIFE
Environment: Town. **Activities:** Choral groups, concert band, drama/theater, literary magazine, music ensembles, radio station, student government, student newspaper, symphony orchestra, television station, yearbook, Campus Ministries, Student Organization. 33 registered organizations, 7 honor societies, 6 religious organizations. **Athletics (Intercollegiate):** *Men:* basketball, golf, soccer, volleyball. *Women:* basketball, softball, volleyball. **On-Campus Highlights:** The Dairy Express, Peterson Memorial Library, The Student Association Center, Winter Educational Complex: gym/climbing wall/pool, The College Store, Clyde and Mary Harris Gallery.

ADMISSIONS
Freshman Academic Profile: 9% from public high schools. Minimum paper TOEFL 550. **Basis for Candidate Selection:** *Very important factors considered include:* rigor of secondary school record, academic GPA, recommendation(s). *Important factors considered include:* character/personal qualities, level of applicant's interest. *Other factors considered include:* class rank, standardized test scores, extracurricular activities, talent/ability. **Freshman Admission Requirements:** High school diploma is required and GED is accepted. *Academic units required:* 4 English, 3 math, 2 science, 2 science labs, 2 history. *Academic units recommended:* 4 English, 4 math, 3 science, 2 science labs, 2 foreign language, 1 social studies, 2 history. **Freshman Admission Statistics:** 626 applied, 88.98% admitted, 54% enrolled. **Transfer Admission Requirements:** college transcript(s), Minimum college GPA of 2.0

required. Lowest grade transferable D-. **General Admission Information:** Application fee $40. Nonfall registration accepted. Admission may be deferred.

COSTS AND FINANCIAL AID
Annual tuition $23,670. Room and board $5,655. Required fees $528. Average book expense $1,068. **Required Forms and Deadlines:** FAFSA, Institution's own financial aid form. **Notification of Awards:** Applicants will be notified of awards on a rolling basis beginning 3/1. **Types of Aid:** *Need-based scholarships/grants:* Federal Pell, FSEOG, State scholarships/grants, Private scholarships, College/university scholarship or grant aid from institutional funds, Federal Nursing Scholarships. *Loans:* Direct Subsidized Stafford Loans, Direct Unsubsidized Stafford Loans, Direct PLUS loans, Federal Perkins Loans, Federal Nursing Loans, State Loans, College/university loans from institutional funds. *Student Employment:* Federal Work-Study Program available. Institutional employment available. **Financial Aid Statistics:** 79% needy freshmen, 79% needy undergrads receive need-based scholarship or grant aid. 99% freshmen, 80% undergrads receive non-need-based scholarship or grant aid. 89% freshmen, 93% undergrads receive need-based self-help aid. 0% freshmen, 0% undergrads receive athletic scholarships. 84% freshmen, 83% undergrads receive any aid. **Criteria for awarding aid:** *Need-based:* Academics, Alumni affiliation. *Non-need-based:* Academics, Leadership, Music/drama.

WALSH COLLEGE OF ACCOUNTANCY AND BUSINESS ADMINISTRATION

3838 Livernois Road, Troy, MI 48007-7006
Phone: 248-823-1610 • **Financial Aid Phone:** 248-823-1285
E-mail: admissions@walshcollege.edu
Fax: 248-823-1611 • **Website:** www.walshcollege.edu

This private school was founded in 1922. It has a 20-acre campus.

RATINGS
Admissions Selectivity Rating: 60*   **Fire Safety Rating:** 60*   **Green Rating:** 60*

STUDENTS AND FACULTY
Enrollment: 929. **Student Body:** 47% female, 53% male, 0% out-of-state, 2% international (46 countries represented). Asian 4%, African American 6%, Caucasian 84%, Hispanic 2%, Native American <1%, Pacific Islander <1%, Two or more races 1%, Race unknown 1%.
Faculty: Student/faculty ratio 13:1. 23 full-time faculty, 78% hold PhDs, 4% are are members of minority groups, 52% are women. 0% of classes are taught by teaching assistants.

ACADEMICS
Degrees: bachelor's, master's, postbachelor's certificate, post-master's certificate. **Classes:** Most classes have 20-29 students. **Most popular majors:** Pharmacy; Biology/Biological Sciences. **Special Study Options:** distance learning, double major, dual enrollment, independent study, internships. **Disability Services:** Special programs offered to physically disabled students, including note-taking services, reader services, tape recorders, tutors. **Career Services:** Alumni network, Alumni services, Career/job search classes, Career assessment, Internships.

FACILITIES
Housing: 100% of campus accessible to physically diasbled. **Computers:** 100% of classrooms, 100% of libraries, 100% of dining areas, have wireless network access. Students can register for classes online. Administrative functions (other than registration) can be performed online.

CAMPUS LIFE
Environment: City. **Activities:** student government, student newspaper, student-run film society 6 registered organizations, 1 honor society. **On-Campus Highlights:** Barry Center.

ADMISSIONS
Minimum internet-based TOEFL 79. Minimum paper TOEFL 550. **Transfer Admission Requirements:** college transcript(s), Minimum college GPA of 2.0 required. Lowest grade transferable C. **General Admission Information:** Application fee $25.

COSTS AND FINANCIAL AID
Annual tuition $9,850. **Required Forms and Deadlines:** FAFSA. **Types of Aid:** *Need-based scholarships/grants:* Federal Pell, FSEOG, State scholarships/grants, College/university scholarship or grant aid from institutional funds. *Loans:* State Loans. *Student Employment:* Federal Work-Study Program available. Institutional employment available. **Financial Aid Statistics:** 64% needy undergrads receive need-based scholarship or grant aid. 18% undergrads

receive non-need-based scholarship or grant aid. 100% undergrads receive need-based self-help aid. 0% undergrads receive athletic scholarships. **Criteria for awarding aid:** *Need-based:* Academics, Minority status. *Non-need-based:* Academics.

WALSH UNIVERSITY

2020 East Maple St, North Canton, OH 44720-3396
Phone: 330-490-7172 • **Financial Aid Phone:** 330-490-7367
E-mail: admissions@walsh.edu • **CEEB Code:** 1926
Fax: 330-490-7165 • **Website:** www.walsh.edu • **ACT Code:** 3349

This private school, affiliated with the Roman Catholic Church, was founded in 1958. It has a 140-acre campus.

RATINGS
Admissions Selectivity Rating: 78   **Fire Safety Rating:** 92   **Green Rating:** 61

STUDENTS AND FACULTY
Enrollment: 2,157. **Student Body:** 61% female, 39% male, 7% out-of-state, 4% international (30 countries represented). Asian 1%, African American 6%, Caucasian 75%, Hispanic 3%, Native American <1%, Pacific Islander <1%, Two or more races 2%, Race unknown 9%.
Retention and Graduation: 80% freshmen return for sophomore year. 16% grads go on to further study within 1 year. 9% grads pursue arts and sciences degrees. 1% grads pursue law degrees. 3% grads pursue business degrees. 2% grads pursue medical degrees. **Faculty:** Student/faculty ratio 13:1. 132 full-time faculty, 67% hold PhDs, 7% are are members of minority groups, 55% are women. 0% of classes are taught by teaching assistants.

ACADEMICS
Degrees: associate, bachelor's, certificate, doctoral/professional, master's. **Classes:** Most classes have 10-19 students. Most lab/discussion sessions have fewer than 10 students. **Most popular majors:** Business Administration and Management; Biology/Biological Sciences; Registered Nursing/Registered Nurse. **Special Study Options:** Accelerated program, double major, dual enrollment, English as a Second Language (ESL), exchange student program (domestic), external degree program, honors program, independent study, internships, liberal arts/career combination, study abroad, teacher certification program, Combined bachelor's/master's degree programs CCSA College Consortium for Study Abroad Rome Experience. **Honors Programs:** Honors Program students may pursue any major and have opportunity annually to attend the national honors conference, where Walsh students frequently present their research. Combined degree programs: BA/MA, 3-4 dentistry. **Disability Services:** Special programs offered to physically disabled students, including reader services, tape recorders, tutors. **Career Services:** Alumni network, Alumni services, Career assessment, Internships, Regional alumni. Shine while you dine (a dining etiquette and professional dress workshop).

FACILITIES
Housing: Coed dorms, special housing for disabled students, special housing for international students, apartments for single students, Wellness Housing, Apartment-style residence hall with kitchens. 100% of campus accessible to physically diasbled. **Special Academic Facilities/Equipment:** bioinformatics lab, Hoover Museum, human cadaver lab (prosection for undergrad), Gathering Garden for Education activities with schoolchildren, Religious Education Center **Computers:** 10% of classrooms, 12% of dorms, 100% of libraries, 100% of dining areas, 100% of student union, 5% of common outdoor areas have wireless network access. Students can register for classes online. Administrative functions (other than registration) can be performed online.

CAMPUS LIFE
Environment: City. **Activities:** Choral groups, dance, drama/theater, literary magazine, music ensembles, pep band, radio station, student government, student newspaper, Campus Ministries, Student Organization. 30 registered organizations, 10 honor societies, 3 religious organizations. **Athletics (Intercollegiate):** *Men:* baseball, basketball, cheerleading, cross-country, football, golf, soccer, tennis, track/field (outdoor), track/field (indoor). *Women:* basketball, cheerleading, cross-country, golf, soccer, softball, tennis, track/field (outdoor), track/field (indoor), volleyball. **On-Campus Highlights:** David Campus Center, Alumni Arena, University Apartments, Barrette Business and Community Center, Wellness Center. **Environmental Initiatives:** HVAC & electrical managament system

ADMISSIONS
Freshman Academic Profile: Average high school GPA 3.4. 17% in top 10% of high school class, 43% in top 25% of high school class, 76% in top 50% of high school class. 71% from public high schools. **Reported SAT (pre-2016 redesign) scores:** SAT Math middle 50% range 430-620. SAT Critical Reading middle 50% range 450-630. **Concordant SAT scores:** SAT Math middle 50% range 470–640. ACT middle 50% range 18-27. Minimum internet-based TOEFL 61. Minimum paper TOEFL 500. **Basis for Candidate Selection:** *Very important factors considered include:* rigor of secondary school record, academic GPA. *Important factors considered include:* recommendation(s). *Other factors considered include:* class rank, standardized test scores, application essay, interview, extracurricular activities, character/personal qualities, volunteer work, work experience. **Freshman Admission Requirements:** High school diploma is required and GED is accepted. *Academic units recommended:* 4 English, 3 math, 3 science, 2 foreign language, 3 social studies, 1 academic elective. **Freshman Admission Statistics:** 1,480 applied, 80.68% admitted, 37% enrolled. **Transfer Admission Requirements:** High school transcript, college transcript(s), Minimum college GPA of 2.0 required. Lowest grade transferable C. **General Admission Information:** Application fee $25. Regular application deadline 8/15. Nonfall registration accepted. Admission may be deferred for a maximum of 1 year.

COSTS AND FINANCIAL AID
Annual tuition $26,300. Room and board $9,920. Required fees $1,410. Average book expense $1,104. **Required Forms and Deadlines:** FAFSA. **Notification of Awards:** Applicants will be notified of awards on a rolling basis beginning 2/15. **Types of Aid:** *Need-based scholarships/grants:* Federal Pell, FSEOG, State scholarships/grants, Private scholarships, College/university scholarship or grant aid from institutional funds. *Loans:* Direct Subsidized Stafford Loans, Direct Unsubsidized Stafford Loans, Direct PLUS loans, Federal Perkins Loans, State Loans. *Student Employment:* Federal Work-Study Program available. Institutional employment available. **Financial Aid Statistics:** 80% needy freshmen, 79% needy undergrads receive need-based scholarship or grant aid. 100% freshmen, 87% undergrads receive non-need-based scholarship or grant aid. 81% freshmen, 78% undergrads receive need-based self-help aid. 18% freshmen, 19% undergrads receive athletic scholarships. 99% freshmen, 93% undergrads receive any aid. 85% undergrads borrow to pay for school. Average cumulative indebtedness $29,702. **Criteria for awarding aid:** *Non-need-based:* Academics, Alumni affiliation, Athletics, Music/drama, Religious affiliation, State/district residency.

WARNER PACIFIC COLLEGE

Office of Admissions, Portland, OR 97215
Phone: 503-517-1020 • **Financial Aid Phone:** 503-517-1091
E-mail: admissions@warnerpacific.edu • **CEEB Code:** 4595
Fax: 503-517-1540 • **Website:** http://www.warnerpacific.edu/

This private school, affiliated with the Church of God Church, was founded in 1937. It has a 15-acre campus.

RATINGS
Admissions Selectivity Rating: 79   **Fire Safety Rating:** 66   **Green Rating:** 60*

STUDENTS AND FACULTY
Enrollment: 360. **Student Body:** 56% female, 44% male, 35% out-of-state, 0% international (12 countries represented). Asian 4%, African American 7%, Caucasian 66%, Hispanic 9%, Native American <1%, Pacific Islander 2%, Two or more races 6%, Race unknown 5%.
Retention and Graduation: 32% freshmen return for sophomore year. 28% freshmen graduate within 4 years. 7% grads go on to further study within 1 year. 2% grads pursue arts and sciences degrees. 2% grads pursue business degrees. 1% grads pursue medical degrees. **Faculty:** Student/faculty ratio 11:1. 31 full-time faculty, 68% hold PhDs, 10% are are members of minority groups, 35% are women. 0% of classes are taught by teaching assistants.

ACADEMICS
Degrees: associate, bachelor's, certificate, master's. **Classes:** Most classes have 10-19 students. **Most popular majors:** Human Development and Family Studies; Business Administration, Management and Operations; Biology/Biological Sciences. **Special Study Options:** cooperative education program, double major, independent study, internships, student-designed major, study abroad, teacher certification program, weekend college, Adult Degree Program. **Disability Services:** Special programs offered to physically disabled students, including note-taking services, reader services, tape recorders, tutors. **Career Services:** Alumni network, Alumni services, Career assessment, Internships.

FACILITIES
Housing: men's dorms, women's dorms, apartments for married students, apartments for single students. 50% of campus accessible to physically diasbled. **Special Academic Facilities/Equipment:** Early learning center, electron microscopes. **Computers:** 100% of classrooms, 10% of dorms, 100% of libraries, 100% of dining areas, 100% of student union, 50% of common outdoor areas have wireless network access.

CAMPUS LIFE

Environment: Metropolis. **Activities:** Choral groups, concert band, dance, drama/theater, jazz band, literary magazine, music ensembles, musical theater, student government, student newspaper, yearbook, Campus Ministries, Student Organization. 20 registered organizations, 2 religious organizations. **Athletics (Intercollegiate):** *Men:* basketball, cross-country, golf, soccer, track/field (outdoor), track/field (indoor). *Women:* basketball, cross-country, golf, soccer, track/field (outdoor), track/field (indoor), volleyball. **On-Campus Highlights:** Tabor Grind Coffee Shop, Dining Hall, Student Union Building, Otto F. Linn Library, A.F. Gray lawn.

ADMISSIONS

Freshman Academic Profile: Average high school GPA 3.2. 8% in top 10% of high school class, 25% in top 25% of high school class, 77% in top 50% of high school class. **Reported SAT (pre-2016 redesign) scores:** SAT Math middle 50% range 410-550. SAT Critical Reading middle 50% range 420-550. SAT Writing middle 50% range 350-530. **Concordant SAT scores:** SAT EBRW middle 50% 430–600. SAT Math middle 50% range 450–570. ACT middle 50% range 16-22. Minimum internet-based TOEFL 71. Minimum paper TOEFL 525. **Basis for Candidate Selection:** *Very important factors considered include:* academic GPA, standardized test scores. *Other factors considered include:* application essay, recommendation(s), religious affiliation/commitment. **Freshman Admission Requirements:** High school diploma is required and GED is accepted. *Academic units recommended:* 4 English, 2 math, 2 science, 3 social studies. **Freshman Admission Statistics:** 948 applied, 52.74% admitted, 15% enrolled. **Transfer Admission Requirements:** college transcript(s), essay or personal statement, Minimum college GPA of 2.5 required. Lowest grade transferable d. **General Admission Information:** Nonfall registration accepted. Admission may be deferred for a maximum of 3 years.

COSTS AND FINANCIAL AID

Annual tuition $18,370. Room and board $7,690. Required fees $660. Average book expense $1,300. **Required Forms and Deadlines:** FAFSA. **Notification of Awards:** Applicants will be notified of awards on a rolling basis beginning 3/1. **Types of Aid:** *Need-based scholarships/grants:* Federal Pell, FSEOG, State scholarships/grants, Private scholarships, College/university scholarship or grant aid from institutional funds. *Loans:* Direct Subsidized Stafford Loans, Direct Unsubsidized Stafford Loans, Direct PLUS loans, Federal Perkins Loans. *Student Employment:* Federal Work-Study Program available. Institutional employment available. **Financial Aid Statistics:** 97% needy freshmen, 93% needy undergrads receive need-based scholarship or grant aid. 95% freshmen, 89% undergrads receive non-need-based scholarship or grant aid. 94% freshmen, 91% undergrads receive need-based self-help aid. 9% freshmen, 5% undergrads receive athletic scholarships. 99% freshmen, 99% undergrads receive any aid. **Criteria for awarding aid:** *Non-need-based:* Academics, Alumni affiliation, Athletics, Leadership, Music/drama, Religious affiliation, State/district residency.

WARREN WILSON COLLEGE

PO Box 9000, Asheville, NC 28815-9000
Phone: 828-771-2073 • **Financial Aid Phone:** 828-771-2082
E-mail: admit@warren-wilson.edu • **CEEB Code:** 5886
Fax: 828-298-1440 • **Website:** www.warren-wilson.edu • **ACT Code:** 3170

This private school, affiliated with the Presbyterian Church, was founded in 1894. It has a 1100-acre campus.

RATINGS

Admissions Selectivity Rating: 80   **Fire Safety Rating:** 69   **Green Rating:** 92

STUDENTS AND FACULTY

Enrollment: 749. **Student Body:** 60% female, 40% male, 74% out-of-state, 2% international (15 countries represented). Asian 1%, African American 4%, Caucasian 76%, Hispanic 9%, Native American 1%, Pacific Islander 0%, Two or more races 3%, Race unknown 4%.
Retention and Graduation: 63% freshmen return for sophomore year. 44% freshmen graduate within 4 years. 53% freshmen graduate within 6 years.
Faculty: Student/faculty ratio 10:1. 63 full-time faculty, 97% hold PhDs, 10% are are members of minority groups, 49% are women. 0% of classes are taught by teaching assistants.

ACADEMICS

Degrees: bachelor's, master's. **Classes:** Most classes have 10-19 students. **Most popular majors:** Environmental Studies; Psychology; Creative Writing. **Special Study Options:** cross-registration, double major, dual enrollment, English as a Second Language (ESL), exchange student program (domestic), honors program, independent study, internships, liberal arts/career combination, student-designed major, study abroad. **Disability Services:** Special programs offered to physically disabled students, including tape recorders. **Career Services:** Alumni network, Alumni services, Career/job search classes, Career assessment, Internships, Regional alumni.

FACILITIES

Housing: Coed dorms, men's dorms, women's dorms, apartments for married students, cooperative housing, apartments for single students. 90% of campus accessible to physically disabled. **Special Academic Facilities/Equipment:** 300-acre farm, 700-acre forest, community gardens, archaeological dig on campus, organically managed garden, GIS lab, photomicroscopy lab.

CAMPUS LIFE

Environment: Village. **Activities:** Choral groups, dance, drama/theater, jazz band, literary magazine, music ensembles, musical theater, student government, student newspaper, yearbook. 25 registered organizations, 5 religious organizations. **Athletics (Intercollegiate):** *Men:* basketball, cross-country, diving, kayaking, mountain biking, soccer, swimming, ultimate frisbee. *Women:* basketball, cross-country, diving, kayaking, mountain biking, soccer, swimming, ultimate frisbee. **On-Campus Highlights:** Sage Caf, Pond, Witherspoon/Morse Science Center, Dogwood-a short hike to this great view, Cow Pie Caf. **Environmental Initiatives:** Climate Action Plan to achieve 80% reduction in emissions campus wide by 2020 includes our formal climate change partnership with city of Asheville;quarterly emissions reports to support changes;college solar array KW's sold to NC Green Power for sustainability outreach to community to influence reduction in GHG's; 100% renewable energy wind credits purchased each year equal to total campus electric use; INSULATE! weatherization program in region for people in poverty where faculty/students and staff to do a house a weekend to provide assistance and reduce regional GHG emissions.

ADMISSIONS

Freshman Academic Profile: 17% in top 10% of high school class, 18% in top 25% of high school class, 77% in top 50% of high school class. 80% from public high schools. **Reported SAT (pre-2016 redesign) scores:** SAT Math middle 50% range 470-590. SAT Critical Reading middle 50% range 518-650. **Concordant SAT scores:** SAT Math middle 50% range 510–610. ACT middle 50% range 21-28. Minimum internet-based TOEFL 75. Minimum paper TOEFL 550. **Basis for Candidate Selection:** *Very important factors considered include:* academic GPA. *Important factors considered include:* rigor of secondary school record, application essay, recommendation(s). *Other factors considered include:* class rank, standardized test scores, interview, extracurricular activities, talent/ability, character/personal qualities, first generation, volunteer work, work experience. **Freshman Admission Requirements:** High school diploma is required and GED is accepted. *Academic units required:* 4 English, 3 math, 2 science, 2 science labs, 3 social studies. *Academic units recommended:* 2 foreign language. **Freshman Admission Statistics:** 809 applied, 83.81% admitted, 29% enrolled. **Transfer Admission Requirements:** High school transcript, college transcript(s), standardized test scores, Minimum college GPA of 3.0 required. Lowest grade transferable C. **General Admission Information:** Nonfall registration accepted. Admission may be deferred for a maximum of 1 year/2 sem.

COSTS AND FINANCIAL AID

Annual tuition $33,260. Room and board $10,250. Required fees $710. Average book expense $850. **Required Forms and Deadlines:** FAFSA, State aid form. **Notification of Awards:** Applicants will be notified of awards on a rolling basis beginning 3/1. **Types of Aid:** *Need-based scholarships/grants:* Federal Pell, FSEOG, State scholarships/grants, Private scholarships, College/university scholarship or grant aid from institutional funds. *Loans:* Direct Subsidized Stafford Loans, Direct Unsubsidized Stafford Loans, Direct PLUS loans, Federal Perkins Loans, College/university loans from institutional funds. *Student Employment:* Federal Work-Study Program available. Institutional employment available. **Financial Aid Statistics:** 100% needy freshmen, 100% needy undergrads receive need-based scholarship or grant aid. 28% freshmen, 27% undergrads receive non-need-based scholarship or grant aid. 100% freshmen, 100% undergrads receive need-based self-help aid. 0% freshmen, 0% undergrads receive athletic scholarships. 90% freshmen, 80% undergrads receive any aid. 71% undergrads borrow to pay for school. Average cumulative indebtedness $20,768. **Criteria for awarding aid:** *Need-based:* Academics. *Non-need-based:* Academics, Art, Leadership.

WARTBURG COLLEGE

100 Wartburg Blvd., Waverly, IA 50677-0903
Phone: 319-352-8264 • **Financial Aid Phone:** 319-352-8262
E-mail: admissions@wartburg.edu • **CEEB Code:** 6926
Fax: 319-352-8579 • **Website:** www.wartburg.edu • **ACT Code:** 1364

This private school, affiliated with the Lutheran Church, was founded in 1852. It has a 118-acre campus.

RATINGS
Admissions Selectivity Rating: 83   **Fire Safety Rating:** 82   **Green Rating:** 96

STUDENTS AND FACULTY
Enrollment: 1,447. **Student Body:** 52% female, 48% male, 29% out-of-state, 8% international (55 countries represented). Asian 1%, African American 5%, Caucasian 75%, Hispanic 4%, Native American 0%, Pacific Islander <1%, Two or more races 3%, Race unknown 3%.
Retention and Graduation: 80% freshmen return for sophomore year. 65% freshmen graduate within 4 years. 69% freshmen graduate within 6 years. 26% grads go on to further study within 1 year. 11% grads pursue arts and sciences degrees. 1% grads pursue law degrees. 2% grads pursue business degrees. 6% grads pursue medical degrees. **Faculty:** Student/faculty ratio 11:1. 96 full-time faculty, 93% hold PhDs, 5% are are members of minority groups, 45% are women. 0% of classes are taught by teaching assistants.

ACADEMICS
Degrees: bachelor's. **Classes:** Most classes have 20-29 students. Most lab/discussion sessions have 20-29 students. **Most popular majors:** Business, Management, Marketing, and Related Support Services; Biology/Biological Sciences; Mass Communication/Media Studies. **Special Study Options:** Accelerated program, double major, dual enrollment, honors program, independent study, internships, student-designed major, study abroad, teacher certification program. **Honors Programs:** Scholars Program—features small seminar classes, distinguished speaker series, sophomore-year program of lectures, concerts, and performances, student involvement in designing courses and activities, variety of social and travel opportunities, student-designed senior project Combined degree programs: BA/MEng, 3-1 nursing, 3-3 law, 3-1 occup. therapy, 3-2 phys therapy. **Disability Services:** Special programs offered to physically disabled students, including note-taking services, reader services, tutors. **Career Services:** Alumni network, Alumni services, Career/job search classes, Career assessment, Internships, Regional alumni.

FACILITIES
Housing: Coed dorms, men's dorms, women's dorms, apartments for single students, Theme Housing, Suite-style living. 85% of campus accessible to physically disabled. **Special Academic Facilities/Equipment:** Art gallery, fine arts center, institute for leadership education, planetarium, prairie preserve, state-of-the-art library, center for community engagement, wellness center. **Computers:** 30% of classrooms, 10% of dorms, 100% of libraries, 100% of dining areas, 100% of student union, 10% of common outdoor areas have wireless network access. Students can register for classes online. Administrative functions (other than registration) can be performed online.

CAMPUS LIFE
Environment: Village. **Activities:** Choral groups, concert band, dance, drama/theater, jazz band, literary magazine, music ensembles, musical theater, opera, pep band, radio station, student government, student newspaper, student-run film society, symphony orchestra, television station, yearbook, Campus Ministries, Student Organization. 90 registered organizations, 12 honor societies, 9 religious organizations. **Athletics (Intercollegiate):** *Men:* baseball, basketball, cross-country, football, golf, soccer, tennis, track/field (outdoor), track/field (indoor), wrestling. *Women:* basketball, cross-country, golf, soccer, softball, tennis, track/field (outdoor), track/field (indoor), volleyball. **On-Campus Highlights:** Konditorei Coffee Shop/Vogel Library, Sports and Wellness Center (new 2007), Saemann Student Center (renovated 2004), Walston-Hoover Stadium (new 2001), Old Main (on National Historic Registry), $31 million Sports and Wellness Center. **Environmental Initiatives:** LEED requirements for new Sports and Wellness Center.

ADMISSIONS
Freshman Academic Profile: Average high school GPA 3.5. 24% in top 10% of high school class, 50% in top 25% of high school class, 79% in top 50% of high school class. **Reported SAT (pre-2016 redesign) scores:** SAT Math middle 50% range 480-550. SAT Critical Reading middle 50% range 422-520. SAT Writing middle 50% range 420-550. **Concordant SAT scores:** SAT EBRW middle 50% 470–590. SAT Math middle 50% range 510–570. ACT middle 50% range 21-26. Minimum internet-based TOEFL 55. Minimum paper TOEFL 480. **Basis for Candidate Selection:** *Very important factors considered include:* rigor of secondary school record, class rank, academic GPA, standardized test scores, recommendation(s). *Important factors considered include:* interview, character/personal qualities. *Other factors considered include:* extracurricular activities, talent/ability, volunteer work, work experience, level of applicant's interest. **Freshman Admission Requirements:** High school diploma is required and GED is accepted. *Academic units required:* 4 English, 3 math, 3 science, 2 foreign language, 2 social studies. *Academic units recommended:* 1 computer science. **Freshman Admission Statistics:** 4,028 applied, 68.25% admitted, 16% enrolled. **Transfer Admission Requirements:** High school transcript, college transcript(s), standardized test scores, statement of good standing from prior institution(s). Minimum college GPA of 2.0 required. Lowest grade transferable C-. **General Admission Information:** Priority deadline 5/1. Nonfall registration accepted. Admission may be deferred.

COSTS AND FINANCIAL AID
Annual tuition $38,710. Room and board $9,748. Required fees $1,020. Average book expense $1,100. **Required Forms and Deadlines:** FAFSA. **Notification of Awards:** Applicants will be notified of awards on a rolling basis beginning 3/1. **Types of Aid:** *Need-based scholarships/grants:* Federal Pell, FSEOG, State scholarships/grants, Private scholarships, College/university scholarship or grant aid from institutional funds. *Loans:* Direct Subsidized Stafford Loans, Direct Unsubsidized Stafford Loans, Direct PLUS loans, Federal Perkins Loans, College/university loans from institutional funds. *Student Employment:* Federal Work-Study Program available. Institutional employment available. **Financial Aid Statistics:** 100% needy freshmen, 100% needy undergrads receive need-based scholarship or grant aid. 21% freshmen, 19% undergrads receive non-need-based scholarship or grant aid. 100% freshmen, 80% undergrads receive need-based self-help aid. 0% freshmen, 0% undergrads receive athletic scholarships. 100% freshmen, 99% undergrads receive any aid. 75% undergrads borrow to pay for school. Average cumulative indebtedness $39,794. **Criteria for awarding aid:** *Need-based:* Minority status. *Non-need-based:* Academics, Alumni affiliation, Leadership, Music/drama, Religious affiliation.

WASHBURN UNIVERSITY

1700 SW College Ave, Topeka, KS 66621
Phone: 785-670-1030
E-mail: admissions@washburn.edu
Fax: 785-670-1113 • **Website:** www.washburn.edu

This is a public school.

RATINGS
Admissions Selectivity Rating: 74   **Fire Safety Rating:** 60*   **Green Rating:** 60*

STUDENTS AND FACULTY
Student Body: 59% female, 41% male, 7% out-of-state.
Retention and Graduation: 68% freshmen return for sophomore year. 16% freshmen graduate within 4 years. 36% freshmen graduate within 6 years. **Faculty:** Student/faculty ratio 13:1. 286 full-time faculty, 84% hold PhDs, 14% are are members of minority groups, 55% are women.

ACADEMICS
Degrees: associate, bachelor's, certificate, doctoral/professional, master's, postbachelor's certifiate, post-master's certificate. **Classes:** Most classes have 20-29 students. Most lab/discussion sessions have 10-19 students. **Special Study Options:** cooperative education program, cross-registration, distance learning, double major, dual enrollment, English as a Second Language (ESL), honors program, independent study, internships, liberal arts/career combination, student-designed major, study abroad, teacher certification program, Transformational Experience.

FACILITIES
Housing: Coed dorms, fraternity/sorority housing, apartments for single students, Wellness Housing, Special interest housing.

CAMPUS LIFE
Activities: Choral groups, concert band, dance, drama/theater, jazz band, literary magazine, marching band, music ensembles, musical theater, pep band, student government, student newspaper, student-run film society, symphony orchestra, television station, yearbook, Campus Ministries, Student Organization, Model UN.

ADMISSIONS
Freshman Academic Profile: Average high school GPA 3.4. 13% in top 10% of high school class, 34% in top 25% of high school class, 67% in top 50% of high school class. 96% from public high schools. ACT middle 50% range 19-25. Minimum paper TOEFL 450. **Basis for Candidate Selection:** *Very important factors considered include:* rigor of secondary school record, academic GPA, standardized test scores. **Freshman Admission Requirements:** High school

diploma is required and GED is accepted. *Academic units recommended:* 4 English, 3 math, 3 science, 2 foreign language, 3 social studies, 1 history, 1 computer science. **Freshman Admission Statistics:** 1,458 applied, 98.77% admitted, 56% enrolled. **Transfer Admission Requirements:** college transcript(s), statement of good standing from prior institution(s). Minimum college GPA of 2.0 required. Lowest grade transferable 1. **General Admission Information:** Application fee $20. Regular application deadline 8/1. Nonfall registration accepted.

COSTS AND FINANCIAL AID
Annual in-state tuition $7,800. Annual out-of-state tuition $17,640. Room and board $6,830. Required fees $110. Average book expense $1,000. **Required Forms and Deadlines:** FAFSA. **Notification of Awards:** Applicants will be notified of awards on a rolling basis beginning 4/1. **Types of Aid:** *Need-based scholarships/grants:* Federal Pell, FSEOG, State scholarships/grants, Private scholarships, College/university scholarship or grant aid from institutional funds. *Loans:* Direct Subsidized Stafford Loans, Direct Unsubsidized Stafford Loans, Direct PLUS loans, Federal Perkins Loans, College/university loans from institutional funds. *Student Employment:* Federal Work-Study Program available. Institutional employment available. **Financial Aid Statistics:** 60% needy freshmen, 63% needy undergrads receive need-based scholarship or grant aid. 68% freshmen, 50% undergrads receive non-need-based scholarship or grant aid. 70% freshmen, 73% undergrads receive need-based self-help aid. 5% freshmen, 4% undergrads receive athletic scholarships. 68% undergrads borrow to pay for school. Average cumulative indebtedness $24,665. **Criteria for awarding aid:** *Non-need-based:* Academics, Alumni affiliation, Art, Athletics, Job skills, Leadership, Minority status, Music/drama, Religious affiliation, State/district residency.

WASHINGTON ADVENTIST UNIVERSITY

7600 Flower Avenue, Takoma Park, MD 20912
Phone: 301-891-4080 • **Financial Aid Phone:** 301-891-4005
E-mail: enroll@wau.edu • **CEEB Code:** 5890
Fax: 301-891-4230 • **ACT Code:** 1687

This private school, affiliated with the Seventh Day Adventist Church, was founded in 1904. It has a 19-acre campus.

RATINGS
Admissions Selectivity Rating: 71   **Fire Safety Rating:** 60*   **Green Rating:** 60*

STUDENTS AND FACULTY
Enrollment: 984. **Student Body:** 65% female, 35% male, 57% out-of-state, 0% international (47 countries represented). Asian 6%, African American 52%, Caucasian 11%, Hispanic 11%, Native American <1%, Pacific Islander 0%, Two or more races 0%, Race unknown 20%.
Retention and Graduation: 61% freshmen return for sophomore year. 13% freshmen graduate within 4 years. **Faculty:** Student/faculty ratio 14:1. 41 full-time faculty, 51% hold PhDs, 44% are are members of minority groups, 51% are women. 0% of classes are taught by teaching assistants.

ACADEMICS
Degrees: associate, bachelor's, certificate, master's. **Classes:** Most classes have fewer than 10 students. **Most popular majors:** Communication and Media Studies Business/Commerce. **Special Study Options:** Accelerated program, cooperative education program, cross-registration, distance learning, double major, dual enrollment, English as a Second Language (ESL), external degree program, honors program, independent study, internships, student-designed major, study abroad, teacher certification program, Co-Op Programs: Business, Biochemistry, Communication/Journalism, Computer Science, English. Other Special Programs: Adult education and external degree programs. **Honors Programs:** The Honors Program at CUC strives to provide academically talented students the opportunity to engage and explore subject material in greater depth. This does not mean more work, it means a different kind of work, with more individual attention. The honors classes are different in design as each class explores the topic from an interdisciplinary perspective, where areas of study are combined into one course. Combined degree programs: Liberal Studies—Combination of bachelors programs designed by students. **Disability Services:** Special programs offered to physically disabled students, including reader services, tutors. **Career Services:** Career assessment, Internships. Internships on Capitol Hill, NASA Cooperative Learning Experiences, White House Internships, NOAA Internships.

FACILITIES
Housing: men's dorms, women's dorms, apartments for married students, apartments for single students. 30% of campus accessible to physically disabled. **Special Academic Facilities/Equipment:** Hospital adjacent to campus for

students in health fields, performing arts at adfacent large church auditorium, learning center, radio station, playing fields and gymnasium. **Computers:** 100% of classrooms, 100% of dorms, 100% of libraries, 100% of dining areas, 100% of student union, 100% of common outdoor areas have wireless network access. Students can register for classes online. Administrative functions (other than registration) can be performed online.

CAMPUS LIFE
Environment: Metropolis. **Activities:** Choral groups, concert band, literary magazine, music ensembles, musical theater, radio station, student government, student newspaper, symphony orchestra, yearbook, Campus Ministries, Student Organization. 6 honor societies. **Athletics (Intercollegiate):** *Men:* baseball, basketball, cross-country, soccer, track/field (outdoor). *Women:* basketball, cross-country, soccer, softball, track/field (outdoor).

ADMISSIONS
Freshman Academic Profile: 53% from public high schools. Minimum paper TOEFL 550. **Basis for Candidate Selection:** *Very important factors considered include:* academic GPA, standardized test scores. *Important factors considered include:* recommendation(s), character/personal qualities. *Other factors considered include:* rigor of secondary school record, application essay, talent/ability, religious affiliation/commitment. **Freshman Admission Requirements:** High school diploma is required and GED is accepted. *Academic units required:* 4 English, 2 math, 2 science, 2 science labs, 4 history, 4 academic electives. *Academic units recommended:* 4 English, 4 math, 4 science, 4 science labs, 2 foreign language, 2 social studies, 4 history, 4 academic electives, 1 computer science. **Freshman Admission Statistics:** 1,293 applied, 41.07% admitted, 27% enrolled. **Transfer Admission Requirements:** college transcript(s), Minimum college GPA of 2.0 required. Lowest grade transferable C. **General Admission Information:** Application fee $25. Priority deadline 7/1. Regular application deadline 8/1. Nonfall registration accepted. Admission may be deferred for a maximum of 1 year.

COSTS AND FINANCIAL AID
Annual tuition $18,200. Room and board $7,200. Required fees $1,280. Average book expense $1,200. **Required Forms and Deadlines:** FAFSA, State aid form. **Notification of Awards:** Applicants will be notified of awards on a rolling basis beginning 5/1. **Types of Aid:** *Need-based scholarships/grants:* Federal Pell, FSEOG, State scholarships/grants, Private scholarships. *Loans:* Direct Subsidized Stafford Loans, Direct Unsubsidized Stafford Loans, Direct PLUS loans, Federal Perkins Loans. *Student Employment:* Federal Work-Study Program available. Institutional employment available. **Criteria for awarding aid:** *Non-need-based:* Academics, Athletics, Music/drama.

WASHINGTON & JEFFERSON COLLEGE

60 South Lincoln Street, Washington, PA 15301
Phone: 724-223-6025 • **Financial Aid Phone:** 724-223-6019
E-mail: admission@washjeff.edu • **CEEB Code:** 2967
Fax: 724-223-6534 • **Website:** www.washjeff.edu • **ACT Code:** 3746

This private school was founded in 1781. It has a 60-acre campus.

RATINGS
Admissions Selectivity Rating: 89   **Fire Safety Rating:** 94   **Green Rating:** 85

STUDENTS AND FACULTY
Enrollment: 1,369. **Student Body:** 49% female, 51% male, 22% out-of-state, 4% international (29 countries represented). Asian 2%, African American 5%, Caucasian 78%, Hispanic 3%, Native American <1%, Pacific Islander <1%, Two or more races 4%, Race unknown 5%.
Retention and Graduation: 70% freshmen graduate within 4 years. 76 36% grads go on to further study within 1 year. 20% grads pursue arts and sciences degrees. 11% grads pursue law degrees. 1% grads pursue business degrees. 11% grads pursue medical degrees. **Faculty:** Student/faculty ratio 11:1. 111 full-time faculty, 95% hold PhDs, 15% are are members of minority groups, 48% are women. 0% of classes are taught by teaching assistants.

ACADEMICS
Degrees: bachelor's. **Classes:** Most classes have 10-19 students. Most lab/discussion sessions have 10-19 students. **Most popular majors:** Psychology; Business/Commerce; Accounting. **Special Study Options:** Accelerated program, double major, dual enrollment, honors program, independent study, internships, student-designed major, study abroad, teacher certification

program, Advanced placement credit. Combined degree programs: BA/MD, BA/JD, BA/MEng, 3/3 law, podiatry, optometry. **Disability Services:** Special programs offered to physically disabled students, including tutors. **Career Services:** Alumni network, Alumni services, Career/job search classes, Career assessment, Internships, Regional alumni. While we are proud of many programs, we especially appreciate the support of our alumni, particularly with hosting interns. Many of these experiences result in full time employment.

FACILITIES

Housing: Coed dorms, special housing for disabled students, men's dorms, women's dorms, fraternity/sorority housing, apartments for single students, Wellness Housing, Theme Housing, On-campus suites. 90% of campus accessible to physically disabled. **Special Academic Facilities/Equipment:** Microplate Reader, Cell Culture Labs, Isolator Lab, X-Ray Diffraction Unit, Neuropsychology Lab, Atomic Absorption Unit, Nuclear Magnetic Resonance (NMR) Lab, Refrigerated Centrifuge, Global Learning Unit, Language Lab, Spectrometers, Laser Scanning Confocal Microscope Facility, Abernathy Field Station **Computers:** 100% of classrooms, 100% of dorms, 100% of libraries, 100% of dining areas, 100% of student union, 95% of common outdoor areas have wireless network access. Students can register for classes online. Administrative functions (other than registration) can be performed online.

CAMPUS LIFE

Environment: Village. **Activities:** Choral groups, concert band, dance, drama/theater, jazz band, literary magazine, music ensembles, musical theater, pep band, radio station, student government, student newspaper, student-run film society, symphony orchestra, yearbook, Campus Ministries, Student Organization, Model UN. 94 registered organizations, 21 honor societies, 4 religious organizations. 6 fraternities, 4 sororities. **Athletics (Intercollegiate):** *Men:* baseball, basketball, cheerleading, cross-country, diving, football, golf, lacrosse, soccer, swimming, tennis, track/field (outdoor), track/field (indoor), water polo, wrestling. *Women:* basketball, cheerleading, cross-country, diving, field hockey, golf, lacrosse, soccer, softball, swimming, tennis, track/field (outdoor), track/field (indoor), volleyball, water polo. **On-Campus Highlights:** The Hub (Student Center), Swanson Wellness Center, Monticellos Coffee House, Burnett (for meetings/studying), Ski Lodge/Barista in the Commons. **Environmental Initiatives:** Signed the ACUPCC, created the Sustainability Committee and a Climate Action Plan, which outlines many past accomplishments and current initiatives.

ADMISSIONS

Freshman Academic Profile: Average high school GPA 3.7. 24% in top 10% of high school class, 59% in top 25% of high school class, 90% in top 50% of high school class. 84% from public high schools. **Reported SAT (pre-2016 redesign) scores:** SAT Math middle 50% range 540-630. SAT Critical Reading middle 50% range 530-620. **Concordant SAT scores:** SAT Math middle 50% range 570–650. ACT middle 50% range 24-29. Minimum internet-based TOEFL 85. Minimum paper TOEFL 563. **Basis for Candidate Selection:** *Very important factors considered include:* rigor of secondary school record, class rank, academic GPA, application essay, recommendation(s), interview, character/personal qualities. *Important factors considered include:* extracurricular activities. *Other factors considered include:* standardized test scores, talent/ability, alumni/ae relation, geographical residence, state residency, racial/ethnic status, volunteer work, work experience, level of applicant's interest. **Freshman Admission Requirements:** High school diploma is required and GED is accepted. *Academic units required:* 3 English, 3 math, 1 science, 1 science lab, 2 foreign language, 6 academic electives. *Academic units recommended:* 4 English, 4 math, 2 science, 2 science labs, 3 foreign language, 6 academic electives. **Freshman Admission Statistics:** 7,155 applied, 45.53% admitted, 13% enrolled. **Transfer Admission Requirements:** High school transcript, college transcript(s), essay or personal statement, standardized test scores, statement of good standing from prior institution(s). Minimum college GPA of 2.50 required. Lowest grade transferable C. **General Admission Information:** Application fee $25. Priority deadline 1/15. Regular application deadline 3/1. Nonfall registration accepted. Admission may be deferred for a maximum of 1 Year.

COSTS AND FINANCIAL AID

Annual tuition $44,320. Room and board $11,854. Required fees $580. Average book expense $800. **Required Forms and Deadlines:** FAFSA. **Notification of Awards:** Applicants will be notified of awards on a rolling basis beginning 3/1. **Types of Aid:** *Need-based scholarships/grants:* Federal Pell, FSEOG, State scholarships/grants, Private scholarships, College/university scholarship or grant aid from institutional funds. *Loans:* Direct Subsidized Stafford Loans, Direct Unsubsidized Stafford Loans, Direct PLUS loans, Federal Perkins Loans, College/university loans from institutional funds. *Student Employment:* Federal Work-Study Program available. Institutional employment available. **Financial Aid Statistics:** 88% needy freshmen, 85% needy undergrads receive need-based scholarship or grant aid. 99% freshmen, 92% undergrads receive non-need-based scholarship or grant aid. 85% freshmen, 85% undergrads receive need-based self-help aid. 0% freshmen, 0% undergrads receive athletic scholarships. 100% freshmen, 99% undergrads receive any aid. **Criteria for**

awarding aid: *Need-based:* Academics. *Non-need-based:* Academics, Alumni affiliation, Leadership.

WASHINGTON AND LEE UNIVERSITY

204 W. Washington Street, Lexington, VA 24450-0303
Phone: 540-458-8710 • **Financial Aid Phone:** 540-458-8720
E-mail: admissions@wlu.edu • **CEEB Code:** 5887
Fax: 540-458-8062 • **Website:** www.wlu.edu • **ACT Code:** 4430

This private school was founded in 1749. It has a 322-acre campus.

RATINGS

Admissions Selectivity Rating: 97 **Fire Safety Rating:** 60* **Green Rating:** 86

STUDENTS AND FACULTY

Enrollment: 1,844. **Student Body:** 49% female, 51% male, 86% out-of-state, 4% international (32 countries represented). Asian 3%, African American 2%, Caucasian 82%, Hispanic 3%, Native American <1%, Pacific Islander 0%, Two or more races 3%, Race unknown 2%.
Retention and Graduation: 96% freshmen return for sophomore year. 88% freshmen graduate within 4 years. 91% freshmen graduate within 6 years. 26% grads go on to further study within 1 year. **Faculty:** Student/faculty ratio 8:1. 249 full-time faculty, 96% hold PhDs, 12% are are members of minority groups, 38% are women. 0% of classes are taught by teaching assistants.

ACADEMICS

Degrees: bachelor's, doctoral/professional, master's. **Classes:** Most classes have 10-19 students. Most lab/discussion sessions have fewer than 10 students. **Most popular majors:** Economics; Accounting and Business/Management; Business/Commerce. **Special Study Options:** double major, exchange student program (domestic), honors program, independent study, internships, liberal arts/career combination, student-designed major, study abroad, teacher certification program. **Honors Programs:** University Scholars, Bonner Scholars. **Career Services:** Alumni network, Career/job search classes, Career assessment, Internships, Regional alumni.

FACILITIES

Housing: Coed dorms, special housing for international students, fraternity/sorority housing, apartments for single students, Outing Club House, Spanish House, Chavis House. 80% of campus accessible to physically disabled. **Special Academic Facilities/Equipment:** History and porcelain museums performing arts center communications labs nuclear science lab scanning electron microscope **Computers:** Students can register for classes online. Administrative functions (other than registration) can be performed online.

CAMPUS LIFE

Environment: Village. **Activities:** Choral groups, dance, drama/theater, jazz band, literary magazine, music ensembles, radio station, student government, student newspaper, student-run film society, symphony orchestra, television station, yearbook. 90 registered organizations, 5 honor societies, 11 religious organizations. 14 fraternities, 5 sororities. **Athletics (Intercollegiate):** *Men:* baseball, basketball, cross-country, equestrian sports, football, golf, lacrosse, soccer, swimming, tennis, track/field (outdoor), track/field (indoor), wrestling. *Women:* basketball, cheerleading, cross-country, equestrian sports, field hockey, lacrosse, soccer, swimming, tennis, track/field (outdoor), track/field (indoor), volleyball. **On-Campus Highlights:** Lee Chapel, Elrod University Commons, Lenfest Center for the Arts, Doremus Fitness Center, Reeves Center and Watson Pavillion.

ADMISSIONS

Freshman Academic Profile: 85% in top 10% of high school class, 99% in top 25% of high school class, 100% in top 50% of high school class. 48% from public high schools. **Reported SAT (pre-2016 redesign) scores:** SAT Math middle 50% range 660-740. SAT Critical Reading middle 50% range 650-730. SAT Writing middle 50% range 650-730. **Concordant SAT scores:** SAT EBRW middle 50% 700–750. SAT Math middle 50% range 690–760. ACT middle 50% range 30-33. **Basis for Candidate Selection:** *Very important factors considered include:* rigor of secondary school record, class rank, extracurricular activities, character/personal qualities. *Important factors considered include:* academic GPA, standardized test scores, recommendation(s). *Other factors considered include:* application essay, interview, talent/ability, first generation, alumni/ae relation, geographical residence, state residency, racial/ethnic status, volunteer work, work experience, level of applicant's interest. **Freshman Admission Requirements:** High school diploma or equivalent is not required. *Academic units required:* 4 English, 3 math, 1 science, 1 science lab, 3 foreign language, 1 social studies, 1 history, 4 academic electives. *Academic units recommended:* 4 English, 4 math, 4 science, 4 foreign language, 2 social studies, 2 history, 4 academic electives. **Freshman Admission Statistics:** 5,377 applied, 23.88% admitted, 35% enrolled. **Transfer Admission Requirements:** High school transcript, college transcript(s), essay or personal statement, standardized test scores, statement of good standing from prior institution(s). Minimum college GPA of 2.0 required. Lowest grade transferable C. **General Admission Information:** Application fee $50. Regular application deadline 1/1. Regular notification 4/1. Nonfall registration not accepted. Admission may be deferred for a maximum of 1 year.

COSTS AND FINANCIAL AID

Annual tuition $45,460. Required fees $957. Average book expense $1,800. **Required Forms and Deadlines:** FAFSA, CSS/Financial Aid PROFILE, Noncustodial PROFILE. **Notification of Awards:** Applicants will be notified of awards on or about 4/1. **Types of Aid:** *Need-based scholarships/grants:* Federal Pell, FSEOG, State scholarships/grants, Private scholarships, College/university scholarship or grant aid from institutional funds. *Loans:* Direct Subsidized Stafford Loans, Direct Unsubsidized Stafford Loans, Direct PLUS loans, Federal Perkins Loans, College/university loans from institutional funds. *Student Employment:* Federal Work-Study Program available. Institutional employment available. **Financial Aid Statistics:** 100% needy freshmen, 100% needy undergrads receive need-based scholarship or grant aid. 30% freshmen, 25% undergrads receive non-need-based scholarship or grant aid. 63% freshmen, 63% undergrads receive need-based self-help aid. 0% freshmen, 0% undergrads receive athletic scholarships. 49% undergrads receive any aid. Average cumulative indebtedness $21,683. **Criteria for awarding aid:** *Need-based:* Academics. *Non-need-based:* Academics.

WASHINGTON COLLEGE

300 Washington Avenue, Chestertown, MD 21620
Phone: 410-778-7700 • **Financial Aid Phone:** 410-778-7214
E-mail: adm.off@washcoll.edu • **CEEB Code:** 5888
Fax: 410-778-7287 • **Website:** www.washcoll.edu • **ACT Code:** 1754

This private school was founded in 1782. It has a 144-acre campus.

RATINGS

Admissions Selectivity Rating: 88 **Fire Safety Rating:** 97 **Green Rating:** 67

STUDENTS AND FACULTY

Enrollment: 1,386. **Student Body:** 56% female, 44% male, 53% out-of-state, 10% international (32 countries represented). Asian 2%, African American 5%, Caucasian 73%, Hispanic 3%, Native American 1%, Pacific Islander 0%, Two or more races 2%, Race unknown 4%.
Retention and Graduation: 83% freshmen return for sophomore year. 71% freshmen graduate within 4 years. 75% freshmen graduate within 6 years. 50% grads go on to further study within 1 year. 12% grads pursue arts and sciences degrees. 4% grads pursue law degrees. 8% grads pursue business degrees. 3% grads pursue medical degrees. **Faculty:** Student/faculty ratio 11:1. 100 full-time faculty, 96% hold PhDs, 12% are are members of minority groups, 43% are women. 0% of classes are taught by teaching assistants.

ACADEMICS

Degrees: bachelor's, master's. **Classes:** Most classes have 10-19 students. Most lab/discussion sessions have 10-19 students. **Most popular majors:** Psychology; Business Administration and Management; Biology/Biological Sciences. **Special Study Options:** cross-registration, double major, dual enrollment, exchange student program (domestic), honors program, independent study, internships, liberal arts/career combination, student-designed major, study abroad, teacher certification program. **Honors Programs:** The Douglass Cater Society of Junior Fellows is the College's flagship academic enrichment program–one that rewards creativity, initiative and intellectual curiosity with competitive grants to support self-directed undergraduate research and scholarship anywhere in the world. The intent is to bring together the best and brightest in what founder Douglass Cater called "a companionship of learning." Combined degree programs: 3+2 nursing, 3+2 pharmacy. **Career Services:** Alumni network, Alumni services, Career/job search classes, Career assessment, Internships, Regional alumni. The Washington Center has over 35,000 alumni, many of whom are leaders in numerous professions and nations around the world. Based in the nation's capitol it offers exceptional experiential learning opportunities in various government and public service sectors.

FACILITIES

Housing: Coed dorms, special housing for disabled students, men's dorms, special housing for international students, women's dorms, fraternity/sorority housing, Wellness Housing, Theme Housing. 90% of campus accessible to physically diasbled. **Special Academic Facilities/Equipment:** Language lab, computer classroom, C.V. Starr Center for the Study of the American Experience, The Center for the Environment and Society, O'Neil Literary House. **Computers:** Administrative functions (other than registration) can be performed online.

CAMPUS LIFE

Environment: Rural. **Activities:** Choral groups, concert band, dance, drama/theater, jazz band, literary magazine, music ensembles, radio station, student government, student newspaper, yearbook, Campus Ministries, Student Organization, Model UN. 50 registered organizations, 13 honor societies, 4 religious organizations. 4 fraternities, 3 sororities. **Athletics (Intercollegiate):** *Men:* baseball, basketball, crew/rowing, lacrosse, sailing, soccer, swimming, tennis. *Women:* basketball, crew/rowing, field hockey, lacrosse, sailing, soccer, softball, swimming, tennis, volleyball. **On-Campus Highlights:** Miller Library, Johnson Lifetime Fitness Center, Gibson Center for the Arts, O'Neill Literary House, Hodson Commons Student Center, Hynson Pavillion and Washington College Boathouse providing water access and kayaks, sail boats, pantoons, canoes, motor boats, wakeboarding boats, etc. **Environmental Initiatives:** George Goes Green (G3) is Washington College's initiative for stewardship and sustainability. Situated on Maryland's Eastern Shore, the College is surrounded by the coastal and inland waters of the Chesapeake Bay, which informs our sense of history, our sense of self, and our sense of place. Our benefactor George Washington promoted sustainable economic cycles by advocating compost as a method to amend damaged soils. Today, Washington College is nationally renowned for promoting sustainability. Green at a Glance: Chesapeake Semester composting recycling environmentally-friendly products local foods native plant landscaping green facilities.

ADMISSIONS

Freshman Academic Profile: Average high school GPA 3.6. 65% from public high schools. **Reported SAT (pre-2016 redesign) scores:** SAT Math middle 50% range 540-640. SAT Critical Reading middle 50% range 530-650. SAT Writing middle 50% range 540-650. **Concordant SAT scores:** SAT EBRW middle 50% 590–700. SAT Math middle 50% range 570–660. ACT middle 50% range 25-30. **Basis for Candidate Selection:** *Very important factors considered include:* rigor of secondary school record, academic GPA, interview, level of applicant's interest. *Important factors considered include:* class rank, standardized test scores, application essay. *Other factors considered include:* recommendation(s), extracurricular activities, talent/ability, character/personal qualities, first generation, alumni/ae relation, geographical residence, state residency, racial/ethnic status, volunteer work, work experience. **Freshman Admission Requirements:** High school diploma is required and GED is accepted. *Academic units required:* 4 English, 3 math, 3 science, 2 science labs, 2 foreign language, 2 social studies, 2 history. *Academic units recommended:* 4 English, 4 math, 4 science, 3 science labs, 4 foreign language, 2 social studies, 2 history. **Freshman Admission Statistics:** 6,847 applied, 54.07% admitted, 11% enrolled. **Transfer Admission Requirements:** High school transcript, college transcript(s), essay or personal statement, statement of good standing from prior institution(s). **General Admission Information:** Application fee $50. Regular application deadline 2/15. Nonfall registration accepted. Admission may be deferred for a maximum of One year.

COSTS AND FINANCIAL AID

Annual tuition $42,844. Room and board $10,824. Required fees $998. Average book expense $850. **Required Forms and Deadlines:** FAFSA. **Notification of Awards:** Applicants will be notified of awards on a rolling basis beginning 1/5. **Types of Aid:** *Need-based scholarships/grants:* Federal Pell, FSEOG, State scholarships/grants, Private scholarships, College/university scholarship or grant aid from institutional funds. *Loans:* Direct Subsidized Stafford Loans, Direct Unsubsidized Stafford Loans, Direct PLUS loans. *Student Employment:* Federal Work-Study Program available. Institutional employment available. **Financial Aid Statistics:** 100% needy freshmen, 100% needy undergrads receive need-based scholarship or grant aid. 22% freshmen, 21% undergrads receive non-need-based scholarship or grant aid. 76% freshmen, 82% undergrads receive need-based self-help aid. 0% freshmen, 0% undergrads receive athletic scholarships. 95% freshmen, 92% undergrads receive any aid. 64% undergrads borrow to pay for school. Average cumulative indebtedness $36,991. **Criteria for awarding aid:** *Non-need-based:* Academics, Art, Music/drama.

See page 1096.

WASHINGTON STATE UNIVERSITY

PO Box 641067, Pullman, WA 99164-1067
Phone: 509-335-5586 • **Financial Aid Phone:** 509-335-9711
E-mail: admissions@wsu.edu • **CEEB Code:** 3800
Fax: 509-335-4902 • **Website:** www.wsu.edu • **ACT Code:** 4482

This public school was founded in 1890. It has a 1745-acre campus.

RATINGS
Admissions Selectivity Rating: 83   **Fire Safety Rating:** 92   **Green Rating:** 93

STUDENTS AND FACULTY
Enrollment: 24,362. **Student Body:** 52% female, 48% male, 11% out-of-state, 5% international (78 countries represented). Asian 6%, African American 3%, Caucasian 61%, Hispanic 14%, Native American 1%, Pacific Islander <1%, Two or more races 7%, Race unknown 2%.
Retention and Graduation: 79% freshmen return for sophomore year. 41% freshmen graduate within 4 years. 67% freshmen graduate within 6 years. **Faculty:** Student/faculty ratio 15:1. 1,353 full-time faculty, 88% hold PhDs, 15% are are members of minority groups, 43% are women. 14% of classes are taught by teaching assistants.

ACADEMICS
Degrees: bachelor's, certificate, doctoral/professional, doctoral/research, doctoral, master's, postbachelor's certifiate, post-master's certificate.
Classes: Most classes have 20-29 students. **Most popular majors:** Business Administration and Management; Education; Registered Nursing/Registered Nurse. **Special Study Options:** Accelerated program, cooperative education program, cross-registration, distance learning, double major, dual enrollment, English as a Second Language (ESL), exchange student program (domestic), external degree program, honors program, independent study, internships, liberal arts/career combination, student-designed major, study abroad, teacher certification program. **Honors Programs:** Now in its fiftieth year, the Honors College is one of the oldest and most highly regarded public university honors colleges in the country. It attracts top students in all majors from throughout the United States and around the world. The Honors College curriculum emphasizes global awareness and international impact. It immerses students in the study of international issues, builds their proficiency in a second language, and encourages them to study abroad. Instead of lecturing, professors teach courses interactively, inspiring discussions among students. Honors students conduct research as undergraduates, exploring an academic question of importance to them, documenting their analysis and conclusions, and orally presenting their work to faculty. The Honors College deepens students' intellectual curiosity and builds a lifelong love of learning, as well as skills in critical thinking, writing, public presentation, and information literacy. Graduates emerge with the tools required to become leaders in their fields.
Disability Services: Special programs offered to physically disabled students, including note-taking services, reader services, tape recorders, tutors. **Career Services:** Alumni network, Alumni services, Career/job search classes, Career assessment, Internships. Experiential Learning Opportunities and Internships and the Career Development Program. The Internship and Career Development Programs at The Center for Advising and Career Development work in partnership to provide comprehensive career counseling and services to help students integrate educational experiences with internships in the government, business, industry and non-profit sectors. Both programs are free for participants. The Internship Program is also a resource to WSU faculty, staff, and employers. It provides faculty/staff assistance regarding internship concerns and issues. The program assists employers with creating internship programs, recruiting for interns, and connecting with faculty/staff and students. On average, 1,600 students participate in internships per academic year.

FACILITIES
Housing: Coed dorms, special housing for disabled students, men's dorms, special housing for international students, women's dorms, fraternity/sorority housing, apartments for married students, apartments for single students, Wellness Housing, ThemeHousingfreshman focus-living/learning communities. 95% of campus accessible to physically diasbled. **Special Academic Facilities/Equipment:** Anthropology museum; arboretum; art museum; audio labs; bear research center; beef center; behavioral lab; cadaver anatomy laboratory; child development laboratory; composite materials and engineering center; creamery, culinary lab and teaching kitchen; dairy center; ecological reserve; electronic piano/music computer lab; electronic trading room; engineering and teaching research laboratory; feed preparation laboratory; food sensory evaluation laboratory; geological collections; greenhouses; historic textiles and costume collection; horticultural orchard and organic farm; entomological collection; natural history museum; observatory; oil and gas processing laboratory; planetarium; herbarium and mycological herbarium; soil monolith collection; veterinary anatomy teaching museum; laboratory for atmospheric research; laboratory for biotechnology and bioanalysis; electron microscopy center; environmental research center; geoanalytical laboratory; music listening library; music recording studio; nuclear radiation center; planetarium; public and student-run television stations; student-run radio stations; social and economic sciences research center; state of Washington water research center; center for spectroscopy; speech and hearing clinic; center for teaching, learning and technology; TV production studios and editing suites; vet teaching hospital; vertebrate zoology museum **Computers:** 100% of classrooms, 100% of dorms, 100% of libraries, 100% of dining areas, 100% of student union, 25% of common outdoor areas have wireless network access. Students can register for classes online. Administrative functions (other than registration) can be performed online.

CAMPUS LIFE
Environment: Town. **Activities:** Choral groups, concert band, dance, drama/theater, jazz band, literary magazine, marching band, music ensembles, musical theater, opera, pep band, radio station, student government, student newspaper, student-run film society, symphony orchestra, television station, yearbook, Campus Ministries, Student Organization, Model UN. 300 registered organizations, 36 honor societies, 19 religious organizations. 26 fraternities, 13 sororities. **Athletics (Intercollegiate):** *Men:* baseball, basketball, cross-country, football, golf, track/field (outdoor). *Women:* basketball, crew/rowing, cross-country, golf, soccer, swimming, tennis, track/field (outdoor), volleyball. **On-Campus Highlights:** Compton Union Building (CUB), Terrell Friendship Mall, Student Recreation Center, Beasley Performing Arts Coliseum, Martin Stadium, The newly renovated CUB stands at the heart of student leadership, engagement, and culture on campus. It is home to offices for student government and many student services. The building houses a selection of food vendors, the campus bookstore, banks, and a post office. Both wired and wireless Internet services serve students and faculty. Ballrooms, meeting rooms, and a surround-sound auditorium host a variety of events. A passage through the CUB gives students 24-hour access to the library. The whole student body comes together on Glenn Terrell Friendship Mall. Located at the heart of campus, the Mall is where culture, ideas, and lively dialogue are exchanged daily. It is the site of many outdoor events, including frequent live performances by student musicians. Students gather here as they walk to and from the library, the Compton Union Building (student union), and academic buildings, often staking out favorite spots to talk, relax, study, or catch a bite to eat. The 160,000-square-foot Student Recreation Center features the largest student weight and cardio center in the country, basketball and volleyball courts, indoor soccer, a four-lane indoor track, racquetball and squash courts, roller hockey, badminton, and much more. Swimmers enjoy the five-lane lap pool, leisure pool, and 53-person spa. Big crowds pack Beasley Performing Arts Coliseum for Pac-10 Cougar men's and women's basketball games and for big name entertainment for Dad's and Mom's Weekends. WSU students turn out for entertainment ranging from pop music concerts to ballet to wresting. Located in the center of campus, Martin Stadium is home to the Pac-10 Cougars. 2008 stadium renovations include a north-side concourse, additional concession and restroom areas, and a state-of-the-art scoreboard. Still to come are the addition of more seats and premium seating, slated for completion by fall of 2012. **Environmental Initiatives:** Sustainability & Environment Committee, established by the President of WSU. Meets monthly and has campus-wide representation.

ADMISSIONS
Freshman Academic Profile: Average high school GPA 3.4. **Reported SAT (pre-2016 redesign) scores:** SAT Math middle 50% range 470-585. SAT Critical Reading middle 50% range 460-580. SAT Writing middle 50% range 440-550. **Concordant SAT scores:** SAT EBRW middle 50% 500–620. SAT Math middle 50% range 510–610. ACT middle 50% range 20-26. Minimum internet-based TOEFL 79. Minimum paper TOEFL 550. **Basis for Candidate Selection:** *Very important factors considered include:* academic GPA, standardized test scores. *Important factors considered include:* rigor of secondary school record, class rank. *Other factors considered include:* application essay, recommendation(s), extracurricular activities, talent/ability, character/personal qualities, volunteer work, work experience. **Freshman Admission Requirements:** High school diploma is required and GED is accepted. *Academic units required:* 4 English, 3 math, 2 science, 2 foreign language, 3 social studies, 1 visual/performing arts, and 1 unit from above areas or other academic areas. *Academic units recommended:* 4 English, 4 math, 2 science, 2 foreign language, 3 social studies, 1 visual/performing arts, and 1 unit from above areas or other academic areas. **Freshman Admission Statistics:** 23,223 applied, 72.04% admitted, 27% enrolled. **Transfer Admission Requirements:** college transcript(s), Minimum college GPA of 2.5 required. Lowest grade transferable D. **General Admission Information:** Application fee $50. Priority deadline 1/31. Nonfall registration accepted.

COSTS AND FINANCIAL AID

Required Forms and Deadlines: FAFSA. **Notification of Awards:** Applicants will be notified of awards on a rolling basis beginning 4/15. **Types of Aid:** *Need-based scholarships/grants:* Federal Pell, FSEOG, State scholarships/grants, Private scholarships, College/university scholarship or grant aid from institutional funds, Federal Nursing Scholarships. *Loans:* Direct Subsidized Stafford Loans, Direct Unsubsidized Stafford Loans, Direct PLUS loans, Federal Perkins Loans, Federal Nursing Loans. *Student Employment:* Federal Work-Study Program available. Institutional employment available. **Financial Aid Statistics:** 87% needy freshmen, 86% needy undergrads receive need-based scholarship or grant aid. 72% freshmen, 46% undergrads receive non-need-based scholarship or grant aid. 63% freshmen, 69% undergrads receive need-based self-help aid. 2% freshmen, 1% undergrads receive athletic scholarships. 86% freshmen, 73% undergrads receive any aid. 58% undergrads borrow to pay for school. Average cumulative indebtedness $25,874. **Criteria for awarding aid:** *Need-based:* Academics. *Non-need-based:* Academics, Alumni affiliation, Art, Athletics, Job skills, Leadership, Minority status, Music/drama, Religious affiliation, State/district residency.

WASHINGTON UNIVERSITY IN ST. LOUIS

Campus Box 1089, St. Louis, MO 63130-4899
Phone: 314-935-6000 • **Financial Aid Phone:** 888-547-6670
E-mail: admissions@wustl.edu • **CEEB Code:** 6929
Fax: 314-935-4290 • **Website:** wustl.edu • **ACT Code:** 2386

This private school was founded in 1853. It has a 169-acre campus.

RATINGS

Admissions Selectivity Rating: 98   **Fire Safety Rating:** 97   **Green Rating:** 94

STUDENTS AND FACULTY

Enrollment: 7,116. **Student Body:** 53% female, 47% male, 92% out-of-state, 8% international (52 countries represented). Asian 18%, African American 7%, Caucasian 53%, Hispanic 8%, Native American <1%, Pacific Islander 0%, Two or more races 4%, Race unknown 2%.
Retention and Graduation: 96% freshmen return for sophomore year. 88% freshmen graduate within 4 years. 94% freshmen graduate within 6 years. 23% grads go on to further study within 1 year. **Faculty:** Student/faculty ratio 7:1. 930 full-time faculty, 94% hold PhDs, 24% are are members of minority groups, 37% are women.

ACADEMICS

Degrees: associate, bachelor's, certificate, doctoral/professional, doctoral/research, doctoral, master's, postbachelor's certificate, post-master's certificate. **Classes:** Most classes have 10-19 students. Most lab/discussion sessions have 10-19 students. **Most popular majors:** Social Sciences; Engineering; Business Administration and Management. **Special Study Options:** Accelerated program, cooperative education program, cross-registration, double major, dual enrollment, English as a Second Language (ESL), exchange student program (domestic), independent study, internships, liberal arts/career combination, student-designed major, study abroad, teacher certification program, The University Scholars Program at Washington University gives selected students the opportunity to be admitted to undergraduate study and a graduate program at the same time. Combined degree programs: BA/MA, BA/MEng, 5 year BA/BFA 3/2 AB/MSOT. **Disability Services:** Special programs offered to physically disabled students, including note-taking services, reader services, tape recorders, tutors. **Career Services:** Alumni network, Alumni services, Career/job search classes, Career assessment, Internships, Regional alumni. The Career Center annually sponsors multiple road shows focused on students' career aspirations. Typically over the course of two days small groups of students will visit organizational headquarters, experiencing first-hand what it is like to work in outstanding careers. Chicago, San Francisco, New York City, Silicon Valley, and Washington DC were this year's target cities, exploring careers in Advertising and Public Relations, Architecture, Art Direction + Design, Sustainability, Biotech + Biomedical, Entertainment, Fashion, Technology, and Government & Public Policy. Road shows illustrate the importance of networking and provide real world exposure to the industry. Reporting on engagements that were 'inspiring, informational, and fun', a short list of the many organizations visited include: Square, Tesla, Google, Stryker, Genentech, Abbott, Gensler, The Daily Show, The Brookings Institution, the CIA and NPR.

FACILITIES

Housing: Coed dorms, fraternity/sorority housing, apartments for married students, cooperative housing, apartments for single students, Wellness Housingspecial interest suites, upper-class housing, single sex floors in coed buildings, on-campus transfer-specific housing, and small-group housing for students who share common interests and goals. 95% of campus accessible to physically diasbled. **Special Academic Facilities/Equipment:** Art gallery, business/economics experimental lab, botanical garden, NASA planetary imaging facility, TAP reactor system, triple monochromator, Computer Automated Radioactive Particle Tracking and gamma ray Computed Tomography, Observatory, EADS learning center, Student Enterprise Zone, Edison Theatre, lab science building, outdoor Tyson Research Center. **Computers:** Students can register for classes online. Administrative functions (other than registration) can be performed online.

CAMPUS LIFE

Environment: City. **Activities:** Choral groups, concert band, dance, drama/theater, jazz band, literary magazine, music ensembles, musical theater, opera, pep band, radio station, student government, student newspaper, student-run film society, symphony orchestra, television station, Campus Ministries, Student Organization, Model UN. 200 registered organizations, 18 honor societies, 19 religious organizations. 12 fraternities, 6 sororities. **Athletics (Intercollegiate):** *Men:* baseball, basketball, cross-country, diving, football, soccer, swimming, tennis, track/field (outdoor), track/field (indoor). *Women:* basketball, cross-country, diving, golf, soccer, softball, swimming, tennis, track/field (outdoor), track/field (indoor), volleyball. **On-Campus Highlights:** Gallery of Art, Edison Theatre, Ursa's Cafe, Francis Gymnasium and Francis Field, Residence Halls.

ADMISSIONS

Freshman Academic Profile: 86% in top 10% of high school class, 98% in top 25% of high school class, 100% in top 50% of high school class. 57% from public high schools. **Reported SAT (pre-2016 redesign) scores:** SAT Math middle 50% range 710-800. SAT Critical Reading middle 50% range 690-770. SAT Writing middle 50% range 690-770. **Concordant SAT scores:** SAT EBRW middle 50% 730–780. SAT Math middle 50% range 740–800. ACT middle 50% range 32-34. **Basis for Candidate Selection:** *Very important factors considered include:* rigor of secondary school record, class rank, academic GPA, standardized test scores, application essay, recommendation(s), extracurricular activities, talent/ability, character/personal qualities, volunteer work, work experience. *Other factors considered include:* interview, first generation, alumni/ae relation, geographical residence, racial/ethnic status, level of applicant's interest. **Freshman Admission Requirements:** High school diploma is required and GED is accepted. *Academic units recommended:* 4 English, 4 math, 4 science, 4 science labs, 2 foreign language, 4 social studies, 4 history. **Freshman Admission Statistics:** 29,197 applied, 16.53% admitted, 37% enrolled. **Transfer Admission Requirements:** college transcript(s), essay or personal statement, statement of good standing from prior institution(s). Lowest grade transferable C. **General Admission Information:** Application fee $75. Regular application deadline 1/15. Regular notification 4/1. Nonfall registration not accepted. Admission may be deferred for a maximum of 2 years.

COSTS AND FINANCIAL AID

Annual tuition $50,650. Room and board $16,006. Required fees $883. Average book expense $992. **Required Forms and Deadlines:** FAFSA, Institution's own financial aid form, CSS/Financial Aid PROFILE, Noncustodial PROFILE. **Notification of Awards:** Applicants will be notified of awards on or about 4/1. **Types of Aid:** *Need-based scholarships/grants:* Federal Pell, FSEOG, State scholarships/grants, Private scholarships, College/university scholarship or grant aid from institutional funds. *Loans:* Direct Subsidized Stafford Loans, Direct Unsubsidized Stafford Loans, Direct PLUS loans, Federal Perkins Loans, State Loans, College/university loans from institutional funds. *Student Employment:* Federal Work-Study Program available. Institutional employment available. **Financial Aid Statistics:** 95% needy freshmen, 97% needy undergrads receive need-based scholarship or grant aid. 11% freshmen, 6% undergrads receive non-need-based scholarship or grant aid. 75% freshmen, 67% undergrads receive need-based self-help aid. 0% freshmen, 0% undergrads receive athletic scholarships. 50% freshmen, 53% undergrads receive any aid. 30% undergrads borrow to pay for school. Average cumulative indebtedness $23,577. **Criteria for awarding aid:** *Need-based:* Academics. *Non-need-based:* Academics, Art, Leadership.

WATKINS COLLEGE OF ART, DESIGN & FILM

2298 Rosa L Parks Blvd, Nashville, TN 37228
Phone: 615-277-7418 • **Financial Aid Phone:** 615-277-7421
E-mail: admissions@watkins.edu
Fax: 615-383-4849 • **Website:** www.watkins.edu • **ACT Code:** 4027

This private school was founded in 1895. It has a 13-acre campus.

RATINGS
Admissions Selectivity Rating: 73   Fire Safety Rating: 96   Green Rating: 60*

STUDENTS AND FACULTY
Student Body: 30% out-of-state, (4 countries represented).
Retention and Graduation: 53% freshmen return for sophomore year. 67% freshmen graduate within 6 years. 10% grads go on to further study within 1 year. 10% grads pursue arts and sciences degrees. **Faculty:** Student/faculty ratio 7:1. 20 full-time faculty, 60% hold PhDs, 0% are are members of minority groups, 50% are women. 0% of classes are taught by teaching assistants.

ACADEMICS
Degrees: bachelor's, postbachelor's certificate. **Classes:** Most classes have 10-19 students. **Most popular majors:** Film/Cinema/Video Studies; Graphic Design; Fine/Studio Arts. **Special Study Options:** dual enrollment, independent study, internships, study abroad. **Disability Services:** Special programs offered to physically disabled students, including note-taking services, reader services, tape recorders, tutors. **Career Services:** Alumni network, Alumni services, Career/job search classes, Career assessment, Internships available in all majors.

FACILITIES
Housing: Coed dorms, special housing for disabled students, women's dorms, apartments for single students. 100% of campus accessible to physically diasbled. **Special Academic Facilities/Equipment:** Brownlee O. Currey Gallery **Computers:** 100% of classrooms, 100% of dorms, 100% of libraries, 100% of dining areas, 100% of student union, 50% of common outdoor areas have wireless network access. Administrative functions (other than registration) can be performed online.

CAMPUS LIFE
Environment: Metropolis. **Activities:** student newspaper, student-run film society. **Environmental Initiatives:** Recycling Program.

ADMISSIONS
Freshman Academic Profile: 60% from public high schools. ACT middle 50% range 20-25. Minimum internet-based TOEFL 60. Minimum paper TOEFL 340. **Basis for Candidate Selection:** *Very important factors considered include:* application essay, talent/ability, level of applicant's interest. *Important factors considered include:* academic GPA, standardized test scores, recommendation(s), character/personal qualities. *Other factors considered include:* rigor of secondary school record, class rank, interview, extracurricular activities, volunteer work. **Freshman Admission Requirements:** *Academic units recommended:* 3 English, 2 math, 2 science, 1 foreign language, 3 social studies, 3 history, 3 computer science, 4 visual/performing arts. **Freshman Admission Statistics:** 113 applied, 83.19% admitted, 61% enrolled. **Transfer Admission Requirements:** college transcript(s), essay or personal statement, Minimum college GPA of 3.0 required. Lowest grade transferable C. **General Admission Information:** Application fee $50. Priority deadline 5/1. Regular application deadline 7/15. Nonfall registration accepted. Admission may be deferred for a maximum of 1 semester.

COSTS AND FINANCIAL AID
Annual tuition $18,900. Required fees $1,560. Average book expense $1,500. **Required Forms and Deadlines:** FAFSA, Institution's own financial aid form. **Notification of Awards:** Applicants will be notified of awards on a rolling basis beginning 5/1. **Types of Aid:** *Need-based scholarships/grants:* Federal Pell, FSEOG, State scholarships/grants, Private scholarships, College/university scholarship or grant aid from institutional funds. *Student Employment:* Federal Work-Study Program available. Institutional employment available. **Financial Aid Statistics:** 68% needy freshmen, 83% needy undergrads receive need-based scholarship or grant aid. 37% freshmen, 10% undergrads receive non-need-based scholarship or grant aid. 100% freshmen, 83% undergrads receive need-based self-help aid. 0% freshmen, 0% undergrads receive athletic scholarships. 50% freshmen, 40% undergrads receive any aid. **Criteria for awarding aid:** *Non-need-based:* Academics, Art.

WAYLAND BAPTIST UNIVERSITY

1900 West 7th Street, Plainview, TX 79072
Phone: 806-291-3500 • **Financial Aid Phone:** 806-291-3520
E-mail: admityou@wbu.edu
Fax: 806-291-1963 • **ACT Code:** 4246

This private school, affiliated with the Southern Baptist Church, was founded in 1908. It has a 80-acre campus.

RATINGS
Admissions Selectivity Rating: 74   Fire Safety Rating: 88   Green Rating: 60*

STUDENTS AND FACULTY
Enrollment: 3,715. **Student Body:** 48% female, 52% male, 31% out-of-state, 1% international (20 countries represented). Asian 2%, African American 16%, Caucasian 43%, Hispanic 28%, Native American 1%, Pacific Islander 1%, Two or more races 4%, Race unknown 4%.
Retention and Graduation: 45% freshmen return for sophomore year. 11% freshmen graduate within 4 years. 32% freshmen graduate within 6 years. **Faculty:** Student/faculty ratio 8:1. 174 full-time faculty, 78% hold PhDs, 14% are are members of minority groups, 34% are women. 0% of classes are taught by teaching assistants.

ACADEMICS
Degrees: associate, bachelor's, master's, transfer. **Classes:** Most classes have 10-19 students. **Most popular majors:** Business Administration and Management; Liberal Arts and Sciences Studies and Humanities; Criminal Justice/Law Enforcement Administration. **Special Study Options:** Accelerated program, distance learning, double major, dual enrollment, external degree program, honors program, internships, study abroad, teacher certification program. **Honors Programs:** The Honors Program offered by Wayland is designed to challenge the academically superior student to develop initiative and abilities beyond what is expected in a normal course of study. Electing an Honors program offers breadth and depth of content through independent study and research, aiding the student in preparation for entering a career upon graduation or attending graduate school in a field of choice. Honors work represents the highest level of academic work available at Wayland on the undergraduate level. **Disability Services:** Special programs offered to physically disabled students, including note-taking services, reader services, tutors. **Career Services:** Career assessment, On-campus interviews.

FACILITIES
Housing: men's dorms, women's dorms, apartments for married students. 100% of campus accessible to physically diasbled. **Special Academic Facilities/Equipment:** Llano Estacado Museum. **Computers:** 80% of classrooms, 80% of dorms, 100% of libraries, 100% of dining areas, have wireless network access. Students can register for classes online. Administrative functions (other than registration) can be performed online.

CAMPUS LIFE
Environment: Town. **Activities:** Choral groups, concert band, drama/ theater, marching band, music ensembles, musical theater, pep band, radio station, student government, student newspaper, television station, yearbook, Campus Ministries. 34 registered organizations, 4 honor societies, 7 religious organizations. **Athletics (Intercollegiate):** *Men:* baseball, basketball, cheerleading, cross-country, golf, soccer, track/field (outdoor), track/field (indoor). *Women:* basketball, cheerleading, cross-country, golf, soccer, track/ field (outdoor), track/field (indoor), volleyball. **On-Campus Highlights:** McClung University Center, Mabee Learning Resource Center, Gates Hall, Hutcherson Gymnasium, Harral Auditorium, Pete and Nelda Laney Activities Center. **Environmental Initiatives:** Installed energy efficient lighting campuswide.

ADMISSIONS
Freshman Academic Profile: Average high school GPA 3.3. 9% in top 10% of high school class, 29% in top 25% of high school class, 60% in top 50% of high school class. 86% from public high schools. **Reported SAT (pre-2016 redesign) scores:** SAT Math middle 50% range 420-530. SAT Critical Reading middle 50% range 390-520. SAT Writing middle 50% range 380-490. **Concordant SAT scores:** SAT EBRW middle 50% 430–560. SAT Math middle 50% range 460–560. ACT middle 50% range 17.5-23. Minimum internet-based TOEFL 61. Minimum paper TOEFL 500. **Basis for Candidate Selection:** *Very important factors considered include:* class rank, standardized test scores. *Important factors considered include:* rigor of secondary school record. **Freshman Admission Requirements:** High school diploma is required and GED is accepted. *Academic units required:* 3 English, 2 math, 2 science, 2 history. *Academic units recommended:* 3 math, 3 science. **Freshman Admission Statistics:** 548 applied, 97.26% admitted, 59% enrolled. **Transfer Admission Requirements:** college transcript(s), statement of good standing from prior institution(s). Minimum college GPA of 2.0 required. Lowest grade

transferable D. **General Admission Information:** Application fee $35. Priority deadline 8/1. Nonfall registration accepted.

COSTS AND FINANCIAL AID

Annual tuition $14,850. Room and board $6,072. Required fees $1,080. Average book expense $1,650. **Required Forms and Deadlines:** FAFSA, Institution's own financial aid form, State aid form. **Notification of Awards:** Applicants will be notified of awards on a rolling basis beginning 2/1. **Types of Aid:** *Need-based scholarships/grants:* Federal Pell, FSEOG, State scholarships/grants, Private scholarships, College/university scholarship or grant aid from institutional funds. *Loans:* Direct Subsidized Stafford Loans, Direct Unsubsidized Stafford Loans, Direct PLUS loans, Federal Perkins Loans, State Loans. *Student Employment:* Federal Work-Study Program available. Institutional employment available. **Financial Aid Statistics:** 99% needy freshmen, 97% needy undergrads receive need-based scholarship or grant aid. 11% freshmen, 9% undergrads receive non-need-based scholarship or grant aid. 68% freshmen, 77% undergrads receive need-based self-help aid. 13% freshmen, 8% undergrads receive athletic scholarships. 66% freshmen, 65% undergrads receive any aid. **Criteria for awarding aid:** *Need-based:* Academics. *Non-need-based:* Academics, Alumni affiliation, Art, Athletics, Leadership, Music/drama, Religious affiliation.

WAYNE STATE COLLEGE

1111 Main Street, Wayne, NE 68787
Phone: 402-375-7234 • **Financial Aid Phone:** 402-375-7230
E-mail: admit1@wsc.edu • **CEEB Code:** 6469
Fax: 402-375-7204 • **Website:** www.wsc.edu • **ACT Code:** 2472

This public school was founded in 1909. It has a 128-acre campus.

RATINGS

Admissions Selectivity Rating: 72   **Fire Safety Rating:** 60*   **Green Rating:** 60*

STUDENTS AND FACULTY

Enrollment: 2,641. **Student Body:** 56% female, 44% male, 15% out-of-state, <1% international (21 countries represented). Asian 1%, African American 3%, Caucasian 82%, Hispanic 8%, Native American 1%, Pacific Islander <1%, Two or more races 2%, Race unknown 2%.
Retention and Graduation: 67% freshmen return for sophomore year. **Faculty:** Student/faculty ratio 18:1. 121 full-time faculty, 85% hold PhDs, 7% are are members of minority groups, 50% are women.

ACADEMICS

Degrees: bachelor's, master's, post-master's certificate. **Classes:** Most classes have 20-29 students. Most lab/discussion sessions have 30-39 students. **Special Study Options:** cooperative education program, distance learning, double major, dual enrollment, honors program, independent study, internships, student-designed major, study abroad, teacher certification program, Learning Communities; First-Year Experience; Service Learning. **Disability Services:** Special programs offered to physically disabled students, including note-taking services, reader services, tape recorders, tutors. **Career Services:** Alumni network, Alumni services, Career/job search classes, Career assessment, Internships.

FACILITIES

Housing: Coed dorms. **Special Academic Facilities/Equipment:** Art gallery, fine arts center, planetarium, recreation center, telecommunications network. **Computers:** 100% of classrooms, 100% of dorms, 100% of libraries, 100% of dining areas, 100% of student union, 40% of common outdoor areas have wireless network access. Students can register for classes online. Administrative functions (other than registration) can be performed online.

CAMPUS LIFE

Environment: Rural. **Activities:** Choral groups, concert band, dance, drama/theater, jazz band, literary magazine, marching band, music ensembles, musical theater, pep band, radio station, student government, student newspaper, television station, Campus Ministries, Student Organization. 96 registered organizations, 18 honor societies, 7 religious organizations. 2 fraternities, 3 sororities. **Athletics (Intercollegiate):** *Men:* baseball, basketball, cross-country, football, golf, track/field (outdoor), track/field (indoor). *Women:* basketball, cross-country, golf, soccer, softball, track/field (outdoor), track/field (indoor), volleyball.

ADMISSIONS

Freshman Academic Profile: Average high school GPA 3.2. 12% in top 10% of high school class, 30% in top 25% of high school class, 60% in top 50% of high school class. ACT middle 50% range 18-25. Minimum paper TOEFL 550. **Freshman Admission Requirements:** High school diploma is required and GED is accepted. *Academic units recommended:* 4 English, 3 math, 2 science, 2 foreign language, 3 social studies, 2 computer science, 2 visual/performing

arts. **Freshman Admission Statistics:** 1,764 applied, 100.00% admitted, 33% enrolled. **Transfer Admission Requirements:** college transcript(s), Minimum college GPA of 2.0 required. Lowest grade transferable C-. **General Admission Information:** Priority deadline 12/1. Nonfall registration accepted. Admission may be deferred.

COSTS AND FINANCIAL AID

Required Forms and Deadlines: FAFSA. **Notification of Awards:** Applicants will be notified of awards on a rolling basis beginning 4/1. **Types of Aid:** *Need-based scholarships/grants:* Federal Pell, FSEOG, State scholarships/grants, Private scholarships, College/university scholarship or grant aid from institutional funds. *Loans:* Direct Subsidized Stafford Loans, Direct Unsubsidized Stafford Loans, Direct PLUS loans, Federal Perkins Loans. *Student Employment:* Federal Work-Study Program available. Institutional employment available. **Financial Aid Statistics:** 78% needy freshmen, 69% needy undergrads receive need-based scholarship or grant aid. 75% freshmen, 72% undergrads receive non-need-based scholarship or grant aid. 78% freshmen, 75% undergrads receive need-based self-help aid. 8% freshmen, 8% undergrads receive athletic scholarships. **Criteria for awarding aid:** *Non-need-based:* Academics, Art, Athletics, Leadership, Minority status, Music/drama, Religious affiliation, State/district residency.

WAYNE STATE UNIVERSITY

42 West Warren, Detroit, MI 48202
Phone: 313-577-2100 • **Financial Aid Phone:** 313-577-2100
E-mail: studentservice@wayne.edu • **CEEB Code:** 1898
Website: www.wayne.edu • **ACT Code:** 2064

This public school was founded in 1868. It has a 219-acre campus.

RATINGS

Admissions Selectivity Rating: 79   **Fire Safety Rating:** 82   **Green Rating:** 60*

STUDENTS AND FACULTY

Enrollment: 16,671. **Student Body:** 55% female, 45% male, 1% out-of-state, 2% international (38 countries represented). Asian 9%, African American 17%, Caucasian 58%, Hispanic 5%, Native American <1%, Pacific Islander <1%, Two or more races 4%, Race unknown 4%.
Retention and Graduation: 82% freshmen return for sophomore year. 13% freshmen graduate within 4 years. 39% freshmen graduate within 6 years. **Faculty:** Student/faculty ratio 15:1. 1,013 full-time faculty, 0% hold PhDs, 27% are are members of minority groups, 46% are women.

ACADEMICS

Degrees: bachelor's, certificate, doctoral/professional, doctoral/research, master's, postbachelor's certifiate, post-master's certificate. **Most popular majors:** Psychology; Biology/Biological Sciences; Health Professions and Related Clinical Sciences. **Special Study Options:** Accelerated program, cooperative education program, cross-registration, distance learning, double major, dual enrollment, English as a Second Language (ESL), external degree program, honors program, independent study, internships, liberal arts/career combination, study abroad, teacher certification program, weekend college. Combined degree programs: BA/MD, BA/MA, BA/MEng, 3+2 programs, accelerated prgorams (AGRADE), MedStart for BA/ or BS/MD. **Disability Services:** Special programs offered to physically disabled students, including note-taking services, reader services, tape recorders, tutors. **Career Services:** Career/job search classes, Career assessment, Internships.

FACILITIES

Housing: Coed dorms, special housing for disabled students, fraternity/sorority housing, apartments for married students, apartments for single students. 100% of campus accessible to physically diasbled. **Special Academic Facilities/Equipment:** Detroit Institute of Arts; Detroit Historical Museum; Detroit Science Museum; Charles H Wright Museum of African American History. **Computers:** Students can register for classes online. Administrative functions (other than registration) can be performed online.

CAMPUS LIFE

Environment: Metropolis. **Activities:** Choral groups, concert band, dance, drama/theater, jazz band, literary magazine, music ensembles, musical theater, opera, pep band, student government, student newspaper, student-run film society, symphony orchestra, yearbook. 166 registered organizations, 4 honor societies, 12 religious organizations. 7 fraternities, 8 sororities. **Athletics (Intercollegiate):** *Men:* baseball, basketball, cross-country, diving, fencing, football, golf, ice hockey, swimming, tennis. *Women:* basketball, cross-country, diving, fencing, ice hockey, softball, swimming, tennis, volleyball. **On-Campus Highlights:** Recreation and Fitness Center, Student Center Building, Subway,

Starbucks, Residence Halls. **Environmental Initiatives:** Past and ongoing LEED certified buildings being constructed.

ADMISSIONS

Freshman Academic Profile: Average high school GPA 3.4. 24% in top 10% of high school class, 51% in top 25% of high school class, 79% in top 50% of high school class. ACT middle 50% range 20-26. Minimum internet-based TOEFL 79. Minimum paper TOEFL 550. **Basis for Candidate Selection:** *Very important factors considered include:* academic GPA, standardized test scores. *Important factors considered include:* rigor of secondary school record. *Other factors considered include:* application essay, recommendation(s). **Freshman Admission Requirements:** High school diploma is required and GED is accepted. *Academic units recommended:* 4 English, 4 math, 3 science, 2 foreign language, 3 social studies, 2 visual/performing arts. **Freshman Admission Statistics:** 11,093 applied, 81.46% admitted, 29% enrolled. **Transfer Admission Requirements:** college transcript(s), Minimum college GPA of 2.0 required. Lowest grade transferable C. **General Admission Information:** Application fee $25. Priority deadline 8/1. Regular notification 9/15. Nonfall registration accepted. Admission may be deferred for a maximum of 1 year.

COSTS AND FINANCIAL AID

Annual in-state tuition $11,821. Annual out-of-state tuition $27,133. Room and board $9,747. Required fees $1,457. Average book expense $1,196. **Required Forms and Deadlines:** FAFSA. **Notification of Awards:** Applicants will be notified of awards on a rolling basis beginning 3/31. **Types of Aid:** *Need-based scholarships/grants:* Federal Pell, FSEOG, State scholarships/ grants, Private scholarships, College/university scholarship or grant aid from institutional funds, United Negro College Fund. *Loans:* Direct Subsidized Stafford Loans, Direct Unsubsidized Stafford Loans, Direct PLUS loans, Federal Perkins Loans, Federal Nursing Loans, College/university loans from institutional funds. *Student Employment:* Federal Work-Study Program available. Institutional employment available. **Financial Aid Statistics:** 79% needy freshmen, 75% needy undergrads receive need-based scholarship or grant aid. 71% freshmen, 54% undergrads receive non-need-based scholarship or grant aid. 63% freshmen, 73% undergrads receive need-based self-help aid. 2% freshmen, 1% undergrads receive athletic scholarships. 93% freshmen, 85% undergrads receive any aid. 73% undergrads borrow to pay for school. Average cumulative indebtedness $24,516. **Criteria for awarding aid:** *Need-based:* Academics, Art, Leadership. *Non-need-based:* Academics, Art, Athletics, Leadership, Music/drama.

WAYNESBURG UNIVERSITY

51 West College Street, Waynesburg, PA 15370
Phone: 724-852-3248 • **Financial Aid Phone:** 724-852-3208
E-mail: admissions@waynesburg.edu • **CEEB Code:** 2969
Fax: 724-627-8124 • **ACT Code:** 3748

This private school, affiliated with the Presbyterian Church, was founded in 1849. It has a 30-acre campus.

RATINGS

Admissions Selectivity Rating: 74 **Fire Safety Rating:** 95 **Green Rating:** 60*

STUDENTS AND FACULTY

Enrollment: 1,390. **Student Body:** 59% female, 41% male, 17% out-of-state, <1% international (1 countries represented). Asian 1%, African American 4%, Caucasian 91%, Hispanic 2%, Native American 0%, Pacific Islander 0%, Two or more races 3%, Race unknown 1%.
Retention and Graduation: 77% freshmen return for sophomore year. 53% freshmen graduate within 4 years. 62% freshmen graduate within 6 years.
Faculty: Student/faculty ratio 13:1. 79 full-time faculty, 67% hold PhDs, 8% are are members of minority groups, 49% are women. 0% of classes are taught by teaching assistants.

ACADEMICS

Degrees: bachelor's, doctoral/professional, doctoral/research, master's.
Classes: Most classes have 10-19 students. Most lab/discussion sessions have 10-19 students. **Most popular majors:** Registered Nursing/Registered Nurse; Criminal Justice/Law Enforcement Administration; Business Administration and Management. **Special Study Options:** Accelerated program, distance learning, double major, dual enrollment, English as a Second Language (ESL), honors program, independent study, internships, liberal arts/career combination, study abroad, teacher certification program, 3-2 program in engineering with Pennsylvania State University–University in State College, PA and Washington University in Saint Louis, MO, 3-1 program in marine

bioloy with Florida Institute of Technology; 3-3 law program with Duquesne University. Combined degree programs: BA/MA, 3/1 Marine Biology Florida Inst Tech; UNC-Wilmington. **Disability Services:** Special programs offered to physically disabled students, including tutors. **Career Services:** Alumni network, Alumni services, Career/job search classes, Career assessment, Internships, Regional alumni. Professional Development course for second semester juniors and seniors

FACILITIES

Housing: Coed dorms, men's dorms, women's dorms. 98% of campus accessible to physically diasbled. **Special Academic Facilities/Equipment:** Geology, biology, archaeology, and ceramics museum, arboretum, 174-acre farm, Center for Research and Economic Development. **Computers:** 95% of classrooms, 95% of libraries, 100% of dining areas, 100% of student union, 20% of common outdoor areas have wireless network access. Students can register for classes online. Administrative functions (other than registration) can be performed online.

CAMPUS LIFE

Environment: Village. **Activities:** Choral groups, concert band, dance, drama/ theater, literary magazine, marching band, music ensembles, musical theater, pep band, radio station, student government, student newspaper, television station, yearbook. 40 registered organizations, 16 honor societies, 7 religious organizations. **Athletics (Intercollegiate):** *Men:* baseball, basketball, cross-country, football, golf, soccer, tennis, track/field (outdoor), wrestling. *Women:* basketball, cross-country, golf, lacrosse, soccer, softball, tennis, track/field (outdoor), volleyball. **On-Campus Highlights:** Communication Department, Stover Campus Center, Museum, Alumni Hall/Chapel, New Residence Halls.

ADMISSIONS

Freshman Academic Profile: Average high school GPA 3.5. 12% in top 10% of high school class, 34% in top 25% of high school class, 74% in top 50% of high school class. 88% from public high schools. **Reported SAT (pre-2016 redesign) scores:** SAT Math middle 50% range 430-530. SAT Critical Reading middle 50% range 430-540. SAT Writing middle 50% range 410-508. **Concordant SAT scores:** SAT EBRW middle 50% 470–580. SAT Math middle 50% range 470–560. ACT middle 50% range 19-25. Minimum internet-based TOEFL 80. **Basis for Candidate Selection:** *Very important factors considered include:* rigor of secondary school record, class rank, academic GPA, standardized test scores, interview. *Important factors considered include:* extracurricular activities. *Other factors considered include:* application essay, recommendation(s), character/personal qualities, alumni/ae relation, volunteer work, work experience, level of applicant's interest. **Freshman Admission Requirements:** High school diploma is required and GED is accepted. *Academic units required:* 4 English, 3 math, 2 science, 2 social studies, 5 academic electives. *Academic units recommended:* 3 science, 2 foreign language. **Freshman Admission Statistics:** 1,478 applied, 93.71% admitted, 29% enrolled. **Transfer Admission Requirements:** High school transcript, college transcript(s), statement of good standing from prior institution(s). Minimum college GPA of 2.5 required. Lowest grade transferable C. **General Admission Information:** Application fee $20. Nonfall registration accepted.

COSTS AND FINANCIAL AID

Required Forms and Deadlines: FAFSA. **Notification of Awards:** Applicants will be notified of awards on a rolling basis beginning 2/15. **Types of Aid:** *Need-based scholarships/grants:* Federal Pell, FSEOG, State scholarships/grants, Private scholarships, College/university scholarship or grant aid from institutional funds. *Loans:* Direct Subsidized Stafford Loans, Direct Unsubsidized Stafford Loans, Direct PLUS loans, Federal Perkins Loans, Federal Nursing Loans. *Student Employment:* Federal Work-Study Program available. Institutional employment available. **Financial Aid Statistics:** 98% needy freshmen, 98% needy undergrads receive need-based scholarship or grant aid. 13% freshmen, 12% undergrads receive non-need-based scholarship or grant aid. 83% freshmen, 85% undergrads receive need-based self-help aid. 0% freshmen, 0% undergrads receive athletic scholarships. 94% freshmen, 87% undergrads receive any aid. 42% undergrads borrow to pay for school. Average cumulative indebtedness $25,615. **Criteria for awarding aid:** *Need-based:* Academics, Job skills, Leadership, Religious affiliation. *Non-need-based:* Academics, Alumni affiliation, Job skills, Leadership, Religious affiliation, State/ district residency.

WEBB INSTITUTE

298 Crescent Beach Road, Glen Cove, NY 11542
Phone: 516-671-8355 • **Financial Aid Phone:** 516-671-8355
E-mail: admissions@webb.edu • **CEEB Code:** 2970
Fax: 516-674-9838 • **Website:** www.webb.edu • **ACT Code:** 2987

This private school was founded in 1889. It has a 26-acre campus.

RATINGS
Admissions Selectivity Rating: 98   **Fire Safety Rating:** 98   **Green Rating:** 61

STUDENTS AND FACULTY
Enrollment: 92. **Student Body:** 17% female, 83% male, 79% out-of-state, 0% international (4 countries represented). Asian 12%, African American 0%, Caucasian 77%, Hispanic 0%, Native American 0%, Pacific Islander 0%, Two or more races 9%, Race unknown 2%.
Retention and Graduation: 81% freshmen return for sophomore year. 67% freshmen graduate within 4 years. 83% freshmen graduate within 6 years. 5% grads go on to further study within 1 year. **Faculty:** Student/faculty ratio 8:1. 9 full-time faculty, 56% hold PhDs, 0% are are members of minority groups, 11% are women. 0% of classes are taught by teaching assistants.

ACADEMICS
Degrees: bachelor's. **Classes:** Most classes have 20-29 students. **Most popular majors:** Naval Architecture and Marine Engineering. **Special Study Options:** double major, independent study, internships. **Career Services:** Alumni network, Alumni services, Career/job search classes, Internships, Regional alumni. Winter internship program. All students are required to work in the industry for 2 months of each academic year. Freshmen work in shipyards; Sophomore work onboard ships; Juniors and Seniors work in engineering design offices.

FACILITIES
Housing: Coed dorms, men's dorms, women's dorms. 70% of campus accessible to physically diasbled. **Special Academic Facilities/Equipment:** Towing tank for model testing, marine engineering lab. **Computers:** 100% of classrooms, 100% of dorms, 100% of libraries, 100% of dining areas, 100% of student union, 100% of common outdoor areas have wireless network access.

CAMPUS LIFE
Environment: Village. **Activities:** Choral groups, drama/theater, music ensembles, student government, yearbook. 2 registered organizations. **Athletics (Intercollegiate):** *Men:* basketball, cross-country, sailing, soccer, tennis, volleyball. *Women:* basketball, cross-country, sailing, soccer, tennis, volleyball. **On-Campus Highlights:** Stevenson Taylor Hall, Brockett Pub, Waterfront Facility.

ADMISSIONS
Freshman Academic Profile: Average high school GPA 4.0. 63% in top 10% of high school class, 37% in top 25% of high school class, 0% in top 50% of high school class. 64% from public high schools. **Reported SAT (pre-2016 redesign) scores:** SAT Math middle 50% range 730-770. SAT Critical Reading middle 50% range 680-720. SAT Writing middle 50% range 640-700. **Concordant SAT scores:** SAT EBRW middle 50% 700–740. SAT Math middle 50% range 760–780. ACT middle 50% range 34-35. **Basis for Candidate Selection:** *Very important factors considered include:* rigor of secondary school record, class rank, academic GPA, standardized test scores, recommendation(s), interview, character/personal qualities, level of applicant's interest. *Important factors considered include:* application essay, extracurricular activities. *Other factors considered include:* talent/ability, volunteer work, work experience. **Freshman Admission Requirements:** High school diploma is required and GED is not accepted. *Academic units required:* 4 English, 4 math, 2 science, 2 science labs, 2 social studies, 4 academic electives. **Freshman Admission Statistics:** 116 applied, 29.31% admitted, 82% enrolled. **Transfer Admission Requirements:** High school transcript, college transcript(s), interview, standardized test scores, Minimum college GPA of 3.5 required. **General Admission Information:** Application fee $25. Priority deadline 10/15. Regular application deadline 2/15. Nonfall registration not accepted.

COSTS AND FINANCIAL AID
Annual tuition $47,000. Room and board $14,400. Required fees $400. Average book expense $700. **Required Forms and Deadlines:** FAFSA, Institution's own financial aid form, Business/Farm Supplement. **Notification of Awards:** Applicants will be notified of awards on or about 8/1. **Types of Aid:** *Need-based*

scholarships/grants: Federal Pell, State scholarships/grants, Private scholarships, College/university scholarship or grant aid from institutional funds. *Loans:* Direct Subsidized Stafford Loans, Direct Unsubsidized Stafford Loans, Direct PLUS loans. **Financial Aid Statistics:** 100% needy freshmen, 100% needy undergrads receive need-based scholarship or grant aid. 33% freshmen, 53% undergrads receive non-need-based scholarship or grant aid. 100% freshmen, 100% undergrads receive need-based self-help aid. 0% freshmen, 0% undergrads receive athletic scholarships. 23% freshmen, 18% undergrads receive any aid. **Criteria for awarding aid:** *Non-need-based:* Academics.

WEBBER INTERNATIONAL UNIVERSITY

PO Box 96, Babson Park, FL 33827
Phone: 863-628-2910 • **Financial Aid Phone:** 863-638-2930
E-mail: admissions@webber.edu • **CEEB Code:** 5893
Fax: 863-638-1591 • **Website:** www.webber.edu • **ACT Code:** 773

This private school was founded in 1927. It has a 110-acre campus.

RATINGS
Admissions Selectivity Rating: 90   **Fire Safety Rating:** 91   **Green Rating:** 60*

STUDENTS AND FACULTY
Enrollment: 681. **Student Body:** 31% female, 69% male, 13% out-of-state, 24% international (45 countries represented). Asian 1%, African American 22%, Caucasian 39%, Hispanic 11%, Native American <1%, Pacific Islander 0%, Two or more races 2%, Race unknown 1%.
Retention and Graduation: 22% freshmen graduate within 4 years. 28% freshmen graduate within 6 years. 7% grads go on to further study within 1 year. 2% grads pursue law degrees. 5% grads pursue business degrees. **Faculty:** Student/faculty ratio 23:1. 21 full-time faculty, 71% hold PhDs, 10% are are members of minority groups, 33% are women. 0% of classes are taught by teaching assistants.

ACADEMICS
Degrees: associate, bachelor's, master's. **Classes:** Most classes have 20-29 students. **Most popular majors:** Parks, Recreation and Leisure Facilities Management; Business/Commerce; Business Administration and Management. **Special Study Options:** cooperative education program, cross-registration, distance learning, double major, dual enrollment, English as a Second Language (ESL), exchange student program (domestic), external degree program, independent study, internships, study abroad, weekend college. **Career Services:** Career/job search classes, Career assessment, Internships. As a Career Counselor I am most proud of the experiential learning in the classroom in classes like Career Development where we engage the learner at a more personal level by addressing the needs of the individual. In career development each student is treated as an individual and the learning process is individual not necessarily as a group. Students are given individual personality assessments and must demonstrate goal setting abilities while observing different occupations, in hands on setting and finally presenting the occupation they have chosen as a career. I am also very proud of our internship program which gives students a valuable learning tool and hands-on opportunity in the field they are most interested in.

FACILITIES
Housing: men's dorms, women's dorms. 90% of campus accessible to physically diasbled. **Computers:** Administrative functions (other than registration) can be performed online.

CAMPUS LIFE
Environment: Rural. **Activities:** marching band, pep band, student government, student newspaper, Student Organization. 6 registered organizations. **Athletics (Intercollegiate):** *Men:* baseball, basketball, bowling, cheerleading, cross-country, football, golf, soccer, tennis, track/field (outdoor). *Women:* basketball, bowling, cheerleading, cross-country, golf, soccer, softball, tennis, track/field (outdoor), volleyball. **On-Campus Highlights:** Student Union, Fitness Center, Computer Lab, Career Center.

ADMISSIONS
Freshman Academic Profile: Average high school GPA 3.1. 72% in top 10% of high school class, 100% in top 25% of high school class, 0% in top 50% of high school class. 75% from public high schools. **Reported SAT (pre-2016 redesign) scores:** SAT Math middle 50% range 430-530. SAT Critical Reading middle 50% range 430-510. **Concordant SAT scores:** SAT Math middle 50% range 470–560. ACT middle 50% range 17-23. Minimum paper TOEFL 500. **Basis for Candidate Selection:** *Very important factors considered include:* academic GPA, standardized test scores. *Important factors considered include:* rigor of secondary school record. *Other factors considered include:* class rank,

application essay, recommendation(s), interview, character/personal qualities, alumni/ae relation. **Freshman Admission Requirements:** High school diploma is required and GED is accepted. *Academic units required:* 4 English, 2 math, 1 science, 2 social studies, and 2 units from above areas or other academic areas. *Academic units recommended:* 3 math, 3 science, 1 foreign language, 2 history, 4 academic electives. **Freshman Admission Statistics:** 710 applied, 50.56% admitted, 42% enrolled. **Transfer Admission Requirements:** college transcript(s), statement of good standing from prior institution(s). Minimum college GPA of 2.0 required. Lowest grade transferable C. **General Admission Information:** Application fee $35.

COSTS AND FINANCIAL AID

Annual tuition $21,686. Average book expense $1,148. **Required Forms and Deadlines:** FAFSA, Institution's own financial aid form. **Types of Aid:** *Need-based scholarships/grants:* Federal Pell, FSEOG, State scholarships/grants, Private scholarships, College/university scholarship or grant aid from institutional funds. *Loans:* Direct Subsidized Stafford Loans, Direct Unsubsidized Stafford Loans, Direct PLUS loans, Federal Perkins Loans. *Student Employment:* Federal Work-Study Program available. Institutional employment available. **Financial Aid Statistics:** 98% needy freshmen, 97% needy undergrads receive need-based scholarship or grant aid. 5% freshmen, 6% undergrads receive non-need-based scholarship or grant aid. 83% freshmen, 81% undergrads receive need-based self-help aid. 10% freshmen, 16% undergrads receive athletic scholarships. 97% freshmen, 96% undergrads receive any aid. **Criteria for awarding aid:** *Need-based:* Academics, Athletics, Leadership. *Non-need-based:* Academics, Athletics, Leadership.

WEBER STATE UNIVERSITY

1137 University Circle, Ogden, UT 84408-1137
Phone: 801-626-6743 • **Financial Aid Phone:** 801-626-7569
E-mail: admissions@weber.edu • **CEEB Code:** 4941
Fax: 801-626-6747 • **Website:** weber.edu/ • **ACT Code:** 4282

This public school was founded in 1889. It has a 526-acre campus.

RATINGS

Admissions Selectivity Rating: 71   **Fire Safety Rating:** 87   **Green Rating:** 91

STUDENTS AND FACULTY

Enrollment: 18,062. **Student Body:** 54% female, 46% male, 11% out-of-state, 2% international (56 countries represented). Asian 2%, African American 2%, Caucasian 74%, Hispanic 11%, Native American 1%, Pacific Islander 1%, Two or more races 3%, Race unknown 6%.
Retention and Graduation: 62% freshmen return for sophomore year. 22% grads go on to further study within 1 year. **Faculty:** Student/faculty ratio 20:1. 504 full-time faculty, 87% hold PhDs, 12% are are members of minority groups, 44% are women. 0% of classes are taught by teaching assistants.

ACADEMICS

Degrees: associate, bachelor's, certificate, master's, postbachelor's certifiate, terminal, transfer. **Classes:** Most classes have 10-19 students. Most lab/discussion sessions have 10-19 students. **Most popular majors:** Registered Nursing/Registered Nurse; Computer Science; Business Administration and Management. **Special Study Options:** Accelerated program, cooperative education program, distance learning, double major, dual enrollment, English as a Second Language (ESL), exchange student program (domestic), external degree program, honors program, independent study, internships, student-designed major, study abroad, teacher certification program, First Year Experience. Combined degree programs: BA/MA. **Disability Services:** Special programs offered to physically disabled students, including note-taking services, reader services, tape recorders, tutors. **Career Services:** Alumni network, Alumni services, Career/job search classes, Career assessment, Internships, Regional alumni.

FACILITIES

Housing: special housing for disabled students, men's dorms, women's dorms, apartments for married students, apartments for single students. 99% of campus accessible to physically disabled. **Special Academic Facilities/Equipment:** Art gallery, language lab, TV studio, communication arts/technologies facilities, natural science museum, herbarium, planetarium, aerospace technology equipment for developing satellite projects, dental hygiene clinic. **Computers:** 50% of classrooms, 50% of dorms, 100% of libraries, 100% of dining areas, 100% of student union, 100% of common outdoor areas have wireless network access. Students can register for classes online. Administrative functions (other than registration) can be performed online.

CAMPUS LIFE

Environment: Town. **Activities:** Choral groups, concert band, dance, drama/theater, jazz band, literary magazine, marching band, music ensembles, musical theater, opera, pep band, radio station, student government, student newspaper, student-run film society, symphony orchestra, television station 100 registered organizations, 1 honor society, 4 religious organizations. 2 fraternities, 3 sororities. **Athletics (Intercollegiate):** *Men:* basketball, cheerleading, cross-country, football, golf, tennis, track/field (outdoor), track/field (indoor). *Women:* basketball, cheerleading, cross-country, golf, soccer, tennis, track/field (outdoor), track/field (indoor), volleyball. **On-Campus Highlights:** Health and Physical Education Center, Bowling Alley and Arcade, Student Union Building, Kimball Visual Arts Building, Val A. Browning Center, Student Union Building is under renovation, West side is completed, the East side will be compleded summer 2008. Pool tables and games have been moved to Promontory Tower for the time being. Bowling has been contracted out to a local alley. **Environmental Initiatives:** Weber State University is in the process of upgrading all interior and exterior campus lighting to high-efficiency flourescents, CLFs and LEDs in some applications. This project began last year and will continue for another 3 years.

ADMISSIONS

Freshman Academic Profile: Average high school GPA 3.3. 99% from public high schools. ACT middle 50% range 18-24. **Basis for Candidate Selection:** *Other factors considered include:* standardized test scores. **Freshman Admission Requirements:** High school diploma is required and GED is accepted. *Academic units recommended:* 4 English, 2 math, 2 science, 1 history, 4 academic electives. **Freshman Admission Statistics:** 6,199 applied, 100.00% admitted, 39% enrolled. **Transfer Admission Requirements:** college transcript(s), Minimum college GPA of 2.0 required. Lowest grade transferable C. **General Admission Information:** Application fee $30. Priority deadline 1/11. Regular application deadline 8/31. Nonfall registration accepted. Admission may be deferred for a maximum of 1 year.

COSTS AND FINANCIAL AID

Annual in-state tuition $4,611. Annual out-of-state tuition $13,837. Room and board $8,000. Required fees $912. Average book expense $1,200. **Required Forms and Deadlines:** FAFSA, Institution's own financial aid form. **Notification of Awards:** Applicants will be notified of awards on a rolling basis beginning 3/15. **Types of Aid:** *Need-based scholarships/grants:* Federal Pell, FSEOG, State scholarships/grants, Private scholarships, College/university scholarship or grant aid from institutional funds. *Loans:* Direct Subsidized Stafford Loans, Direct Unsubsidized Stafford Loans, Direct PLUS loans, Federal Perkins Loans. *Student Employment:* Federal Work-Study Program available. Institutional employment available. **Financial Aid Statistics:** 60% needy freshmen, 68% needy undergrads receive need-based scholarship or grant aid. 15% freshmen, 34% undergrads receive non-need-based scholarship or grant aid. 51% freshmen, 56% undergrads receive need-based self-help aid. 4% freshmen, 3% undergrads receive athletic scholarships. 82% freshmen, 63% undergrads receive any aid. 21% undergrads borrow to pay for school. Average cumulative indebtedness $22,029. **Criteria for awarding aid:** *Need-based:* Academics, Alumni affiliation, Art, Job skills, Minority status, Music/drama. *Non-need-based:* Academics, Alumni affiliation, Art, Athletics, Job skills, Leadership, Minority status, Music/drama, State/district residency.

WEBSTER UNIVERSITY

470 East Lockwood Avenue, Saint Louis, MO 63119-3194
Phone: 314-246-7800 • **Financial Aid Phone:** 314-968-6992
E-mail: admit@webster.edu • **CEEB Code:** 6933
Fax: 314-246-7116 • **Website:** www.webster.edu • **ACT Code:** 2388

This private school was founded in 1915. It has a 47-acre campus.

RATINGS

Admissions Selectivity Rating: 84   **Fire Safety Rating:** 89   **Green Rating:** 60*

STUDENTS AND FACULTY

Enrollment: 2,721. **Student Body:** 55% female, 45% male, 27% out-of-state, 5% international (56 countries represented). Asian 2%, African American 13%, Caucasian 64%, Hispanic 5%, Native American <1%, Pacific Islander <1%, Two or more races 3%, Race unknown 8%.
Retention and Graduation: 78% freshmen return for sophomore year. 43% freshmen graduate within 4 years. 62% freshmen graduate within 6 years. 14% grads go on to further study within 1 year. **Faculty:** Student/faculty ratio 9:1. 200 full-time faculty, 85% hold PhDs, 16% are are members of minority groups, 48% are women. 0% of classes are taught by teaching assistants.

ACADEMICS

Degrees: bachelor's, certificate, doctoral/research, master's, postbachelor's certificate, post-master's certificate. **Classes:** Most classes have 10-19 students. **Most popular majors:** Business Administration and Management; Psychology; Registered Nursing/Registered Nurse. **Special Study Options:** Accelerated program, cooperative education program, cross-registration, distance learning, double major, dual enrollment, English as a Second Language (ESL), exchange student program (domestic), independent study, internships, liberal arts/career combination, student-designed major, study abroad, teacher certification program, Certificate Programs, Combination bachelor's/master's degree in many subject areas, Independent study, Student Leadership Development Program. In addition to the programs offered at its four St. Louis area campuses, Webster University offers undergraduate degree completion programs at the following extended campus locations in the United States: Charleston, SC—**Website:** http://explore.webster.edu/admissions/undergraduate/worldwide/charleston.asp Columbia, SC—**Website:** http://explore.webster.edu/admissions/undergraduate/worldwide/columbia.asp Greenville, SC—**Website:** http://explore.webster.edu/admissions/undergraduate/worldwide/greenville.asp Kansas City, MO • **Website:** www.webster.edu/kc/ Orlando, FL • **Website:** http://explore.webster.edu/admissions/undergraduate/worldwide/orlando.asp Irvine, CA—**Website:** http://explore.webster.edu/admissions/undergraduate/worldwide/irvine.asp San Diego, CA • **Website:** http://explore.webster.edu/admissions/undergraduate/worldwide/sandiego.asp Undergraduate students may also study at Webster's international campuses, where they may complete their entire degree at the following locations: Geneva, Switzerland • **Website:** www.webster.ch Leiden, The Netherlands • **Website:** www.webster.nl London, UK, at Webster at Regent's College • **Website:** www.bacl.ac.uk Vienna, Austria • **Website:** www.webster.ac.at Cha-am, Thailand • **Website:** www.webster.ac.th. Combined degree programs: BA/MA, BS/MA, BS/MS, BSN/MSN, BM/MM. **Disability Services:** Special programs offered to physically disabled students, including note-taking services, reader services, tape recorders, tutors. **Career Services:** Alumni network, Alumni services, Career assessment, Internships, On-campus interviews. Walker EDGE and Webster University's Career Planning & Development Center have partnered with many multinational companies to develop internship opportunities for Walker students.

FACILITIES

Housing: Coed dorms, special housing for international students, women's dorms, apartments for married students, apartments for single students. 85% of campus accessible to physically diasbled. **Special Academic Facilities/Equipment:** Loretto-Hilton Center for Performing Arts (Houses St. Louis Repertory company, Opera Theatre of St. Louis, and Webster Symphony); Community Music School of Webster University. **Computers:** 10% of classrooms, 12% of dorms, 50% of libraries, 100% of dining areas, 100% of student union, 60% of common outdoor areas have wireless network access. Students can register for classes online. Administrative functions (other than registration) can be performed online.

CAMPUS LIFE

Environment: Metropolis. **Activities:** Choral groups, dance, drama/theater, jazz band, literary magazine, music ensembles, musical theater, opera, radio station, student government, student newspaper, student-run film society, symphony orchestra, television station, yearbook, Campus Ministries. 62 registered organizations, 1 honor society, 1 religious organization.1 fraternity. **Athletics (Intercollegiate):** *Men:* baseball, basketball, cross-country, golf, soccer, tennis, track/field (outdoor). *Women:* basketball, cross-country, soccer, softball, tennis, track/field (outdoor), volleyball. **On-Campus Highlights:** University Center, The Quadrangle, Emerson Library, Fitness Center, Marletto's Marketplace (dining hall).

ADMISSIONS

Freshman Academic Profile: Average high school GPA 3.5. 20% in top 10% of high school class, 47% in top 25% of high school class, 76% in top 50% of high school class. ACT middle 50% range 21-27. Minimum internet-based TOEFL 80. **Basis for Candidate Selection:** *Very important factors considered include:* academic GPA, standardized test scores. *Important factors considered include:* rigor of secondary school record, class rank, talent/ability. *Other factors considered include:* application essay, recommendation(s), interview, extracurricular activities, character/personal qualities, first generation, alumni/ae relation, geographical residence, volunteer work, work experience, level of applicant's interest. **Freshman Admission Requirements:** High school diploma is required and GED is accepted. *Academic units recommended:* 4 English, 3 math, 3 science, 2 science labs, 2 foreign language, 3 social studies, 3 academic electives, 1 visual/performing arts. **Freshman Admission Statistics:** 1,994 applied, 56.12% admitted, 37% enrolled. **Transfer Admission Requirements:** college transcript(s), essay or personal statement, Minimum college GPA of 2.5 required. Lowest grade transferable C. **General Admission Information:** Application fee $35. Priority deadline 3/1. Regular application deadline 8/1. Nonfall registration accepted. Admission may be deferred for a maximum of 12 months.

COSTS AND FINANCIAL AID

Annual tuition $25,300. Room and board $10,860. Required fees $200. Average book expense $1,000. **Required Forms and Deadlines:** FAFSA, Institution's own financial aid form. **Notification of Awards:** Applicants will be notified of awards on a rolling basis beginning 2/1. **Types of Aid:** *Need-based scholarships/grants:* Federal Pell, FSEOG, State scholarships/grants, Private scholarships, College/university scholarship or grant aid from institutional funds. *Loans:* Direct Subsidized Stafford Loans, Direct Unsubsidized Stafford Loans, Direct PLUS loans, Federal Perkins Loans. *Student Employment:* Federal Work-Study Program available. Institutional employment available. **Financial Aid Statistics:** 98% needy freshmen, 90% needy undergrads receive need-based scholarship or grant aid. 95% freshmen, 87% undergrads receive non-need-based scholarship or grant aid. 97% freshmen, 90% undergrads receive need-based self-help aid. 0% freshmen, 0% undergrads receive athletic scholarships. 78% undergrads borrow to pay for school. Average cumulative indebtedness $31,548. **Criteria for awarding aid:** *Need-based:* Minority status. *Non-need-based:* Academics, Art, Leadership, Music/drama.

WELLESLEY COLLEGE

Admission Office, Wellesley, MA 02481-8203
Phone: 781-283-2270 • **Financial Aid Phone:** 781-283-2360
E-mail: admission@wellesley.edu • **CEEB Code:** 3957
Fax: 781-283-3678 • **Website:** www.wellesley.edu • **ACT Code:** 1926

This private school was founded in 1870. It has a 500-acre campus.

RATINGS

Admissions Selectivity Rating: 96   **Fire Safety Rating:** 98   **Green Rating:** 65

STUDENTS AND FACULTY

Enrollment: 2,188. **Student Body:** 100% female, 0% male, 84% out-of-state, 12% international (93 countries represented). Asian 23%, African American 5%, Caucasian 39%, Hispanic 11%, Native American <1%, Pacific Islander 0%, Two or more races 6%, Race unknown 4%.
Retention and Graduation: 95% freshmen return for sophomore year. 86% freshmen graduate within 4 years. 93% freshmen graduate within 6 years. 34% grads go on to further study within 1 year. 31% grads pursue arts and sciences degrees. 5% grads pursue law degrees. 1% grads pursue business degrees. 9% grads pursue medical degrees. **Faculty:** Student/faculty ratio 7:1. 298 full-time faculty, 96% hold PhDs, 22% are are members of minority groups, 56% are women. 0% of classes are taught by teaching assistants.

ACADEMICS

Degrees: bachelor's. **Classes:** Most classes have 10-19 students. Most lab/discussion sessions have 10-19 students. **Most popular majors:** Economics; Psychology; Political Science and Government. **Special Study Options:** cross-registration, double major, dual enrollment, exchange student program (domestic), honors program, independent study, internships, student-designed major, study abroad, teacher certification program. Combined degree programs: BA/MA, Brandeis MA ief (International Economics and Finance). **Disability Services:** Special programs offered to physically disabled students, including note-taking services, reader services, tape recorders, tutors. **Career Services:** Alumni network, Alumni services, Career/job search classes, Career assessment, Internships, Regional alumni. Wellesley College funded at least one internship for more than half the class of 2016. This included grants of up $3,500 for what otherwise would have been unpaid internships over the summer.

FACILITIES

Housing: women's dorms, cooperative housing, apartments for single students, Wellness Housing, Theme Housing. 85% of campus accessible to physically diasbled. **Special Academic Facilities/Equipment:** Clapp Library Davis Museum and Cultural Center Harambee House Houghton Memorial Chapel Hunnewell Arboretum, Alexandra Botanic Gardens, and Ferguson Greenhouses Jewett Art Museum Keohane Sports Center Knapp Media and Technology Center Knapp Social Science Center Lake Waban Pforzheimer Learning and Teaching Center Ruth Nagel Jones Theatre Science Center, including NMR Spectrometers Slater International Center Wang Campus Center Wellesley Centers for Women Whitin Observatory, including 3 telescopes. **Computers:** 100% of classrooms, 100% of dorms, 100% of libraries, 100% of dining areas, 100% of student union, 5% of common outdoor areas have wireless network access. Students can register for classes online. Administrative functions (other than registration) can be performed online.

CAMPUS LIFE

Environment: Town. **Activities:** Choral groups, dance, drama/theater, jazz band, literary magazine, music ensembles, radio station, student government, student newspaper, student-run film society, symphony orchestra, yearbook, Campus Ministries, Student Organization. 160 registered organizations, 7 honor societies, 30 religious organizations. **Athletics (Intercollegiate):** *Women:* basketball, crew/rowing, cross-country, diving, fencing, field hockey, golf, lacrosse, soccer, softball, squash, swimming, tennis, track/field (outdoor), track/field (indoor), volleyball. **On-Campus Highlights:** Wang Campus Center, Davis Museum and Cultural Center, Clapp Library and Knapp Media Center, Science Center, Lake Waban.

ADMISSIONS

Freshman Academic Profile: 80% in top 10% of high school class, 95% in top 25% of high school class, 100% in top 50% of high school class. 65% from public high schools. **Reported SAT (pre-2016 redesign) scores:** SAT Math middle 50% range 650-750. SAT Critical Reading middle 50% range 640-740. SAT Writing middle 50% range 650-750. **Concordant SAT scores:** SAT EBRW middle 50% 690–760. SAT Math middle 50% range 670–770. ACT middle 50% range 29-33. **Basis for Candidate Selection:** *Very important factors considered include:* rigor of secondary school record, academic GPA, recommendation(s), character/personal qualities. *Important factors considered include:* class rank, standardized test scores, application essay, extracurricular activities, talent/ability. *Other factors considered include:* interview, first generation, alumni/ae relation, geographical residence, state residency, racial/ethnic status, volunteer work, work experience, level of applicant's interest. **Freshman Admission Requirements:** High school diploma or equivalent is not required. High school diploma is required and GED is not accepted. *Academic units recommended:* 4 English, 4 math, 3 science, 2 science labs, 4 foreign language, 4 social studies, 4 history. **Freshman Admission Statistics:** 4,555 applied, 30.30% admitted, 43% enrolled. **Transfer Admission Requirements:** High school transcript, college transcript(s), essay or personal statement, interview, standardized test scores, statement of good standing from prior institution(s). Lowest grade transferable C. **General Admission Information:** Application fee $50. Regular application deadline 1/15. Regular notification 4/1. Nonfall registration not accepted. Admission may be deferred for a maximum of 1 year.

COSTS AND FINANCIAL AID

Annual tuition $48,510. Required fees $292. Average book expense $800. **Required Forms and Deadlines:** FAFSA, CSS/Financial Aid PROFILE, Noncustodial PROFILE. **Notification of Awards:** Applicants will be notified of awards on or about 4/1. **Types of Aid:** *Need-based scholarships/grants:* Federal Pell, FSEOG, State scholarships/grants, Private scholarships, College/university scholarship or grant aid from institutional funds. *Loans:* Direct Subsidized Stafford Loans, Direct Unsubsidized Stafford Loans, Direct PLUS loans, Federal Perkins Loans, State Loans, College/university loans from institutional funds. *Student Employment:* Federal Work-Study Program available. Institutional employment available. **Financial Aid Statistics:** 96% needy freshmen, 100% needy undergrads receive need-based scholarship or grant aid. 0% undergrads receive non-need-based scholarship or grant aid. 89% freshmen, 91% undergrads receive need-based self-help aid. 0% freshmen, 0% undergrads receive athletic scholarships. 61% freshmen, 61% undergrads receive any aid. 49% undergrads borrow to pay for school. Average cumulative indebtedness $12,455.

WELLS COLLEGE

Route 90, Aurora, NY 13026
Phone: 315-364-3264 • **Financial Aid Phone:** 315-364-3289
E-mail: admissions@wells.edu • **CEEB Code:** 2971
Fax: 315-364-3227 • **Website:** www.wells.edu • **ACT Code:** 2971

This private school was founded in 1868. It has a 365-acre campus.

RATINGS

Admissions Selectivity Rating: 85   **Fire Safety Rating:** 90   **Green Rating:** 90

STUDENTS AND FACULTY

Enrollment: 552. **Student Body:** 71% female, 29% male, 32% out-of-state, 2% international (13 countries represented). Asian 2%, African American 6%, Caucasian 67%, Hispanic 4%, Native American 1%, Pacific Islander 0%, Two or more races 0%, Race unknown 18%.
Retention and Graduation: 76% freshmen return for sophomore year. 53% freshmen graduate within 4 years. 51% freshmen graduate within 6 years. 25% grads go on to further study within 1 year. 18% grads pursue arts and sciences degrees. 4% grads pursue law degrees. 1% grads pursue business degrees. 2% grads pursue medical degrees. **Faculty:** Student/faculty ratio 10:1. 39 full-time faculty, 95% hold PhDs, 18% are are members of minority groups, 54% are women. 0% of classes are taught by teaching assistants.

ACADEMICS

Degrees: bachelor's. **Classes:** Most classes have 10-19 students. **Most popular majors:** English Language and Literature; Psychology; Molecular Biology. **Special Study Options:** Accelerated program, cross-registration, double major, English as a Second Language (ESL), independent study, internships, student-designed major, study abroad, teacher certification program, Cross registration with Cornell University, Ithaca College, and Cayuga Community College. Combined degree programs: BA/MBA, BA/MPH, BA/DVM, BA/M.Ed. **Disability Services:** Special programs offered to physically disabled students, including tutors. **Career Services:** Alumni network, Alumni services, Career assessment, Internships, Regional alumni. Wells College's ability to connect our students to the real world, through the use of internships, study abroad and experiential learning makes us unlike any other.

FACILITIES

Housing: Coed dorms, women's dorms, Off campus college affiliated housing as well as an Environmental Science theme house. 58% of campus accessible to physically diasbled. **Special Academic Facilities/Equipment:** Two greenhouses, environmentally regulated animal room, the college theatre (Phillips Auditorium), recital hall, electronic music studio, 15 pianos, a Dowd harpsichord, an early instrument collection, a sculpture and ceramics studio, dark rooms, painting and drawing studio, a Book Arts Center, lithography presses, an extensive art library, art gallery, general and specialized clusters for the social sciences, foreign languages, and natural and mathematical sciences. **Computers:** 10% of classrooms, 90% of dorms, 100% of libraries, 100% of student union, have wireless network access. Students can register for classes online. Administrative functions (other than registration) can be performed online.

CAMPUS LIFE

Environment: Rural. **Activities:** Choral groups, dance, drama/theater, literary magazine, music ensembles, student government, student newspaper, yearbook, Model UN. 35 registered organizations, 2 honor societies, 2 religious organizations. **Athletics (Intercollegiate):** *Men:* basketball, cross-country, golf, lacrosse, soccer, swimming. *Women:* basketball, cross-country, field hockey, golf, lacrosse, soccer, softball, swimming, tennis. **On-Campus Highlights:** Sommer Center, Boat House, Schwartz Student Union, Macmillan Hall, Main Building.

ADMISSIONS

Freshman Academic Profile: Average high school GPA 3.5. 31% in top 10% of high school class, 65% in top 25% of high school class, 91% in top 50% of high school class. 88% from public high schools. **Reported SAT (pre-2016 redesign) scores:** SAT Math middle 50% range 480-600. SAT Critical Reading middle 50% range 500-630. SAT Writing middle 50% range 480-590. **Concordant SAT scores:** SAT EBRW middle 50% 550–660. SAT Math middle 50% range 510–620. ACT middle 50% range 22-27. Minimum paper TOEFL 550. **Basis for Candidate Selection:** *Very important factors considered include:* rigor of secondary school record, academic GPA, standardized test scores, recommendation(s), extracurricular activities. *Important factors considered include:* application essay, interview. *Other factors considered include:* class rank, talent/ability, character/personal qualities, alumni/ae relation, volunteer work, work experience, level of applicant's interest. **Freshman Admission Requirements:** High school diploma is required and GED is accepted. *Academic units required:* 4 English, 3 math, 2 science, 2 science labs, 1 social studies, 3 history, 2 academic electives. *Academic units recommended:* 4 math, 3 science, 3 science labs, 2 foreign language, 2 social studies, 2 history, 3 academic electives, and 2 units from above areas or other academic areas. **Freshman Admission Statistics:** 1,673 applied, 67.18% admitted, 13% enrolled. **Transfer Admission Requirements:** High school transcript, college transcript(s), essay or personal statement, standardized test scores, statement of good standing from prior institution(s). Minimum college GPA 2.0 required. Lowest grade transferable C-. **General Admission Information:** Application fee $40. Priority deadline 12/15. Regular application deadline 3/1. Regular notification 4/1. Nonfall registration accepted. Admission may be deferred for a maximum of 12 months.

COSTS AND FINANCIAL AID

Annual tuition $33,200. Room and board $11,900. Required fees $1,500. Average book expense $800. **Required Forms and Deadlines:** FAFSA. **Notification of Awards:** Applicants will be notified of awards on a rolling basis beginning 3/1. **Types of Aid:** *Need-based scholarships/grants:* Federal Pell, FSEOG, State scholarships/grants, Private scholarships, College/university scholarship or grant aid from institutional funds. *Loans:* Federal Perkins Loans. *Student Employment:* Federal Work-Study Program available. Institutional employment available. **Financial Aid Statistics:** 93% needy freshmen, 93% needy undergrads receive need-based scholarship or grant aid. 13% freshmen, 15% undergrads receive non-need-based scholarship or grant aid. 75% freshmen, 70% undergrads receive need-based self-help aid. 0% freshmen, 0% undergrads receive athletic scholarships. 96% freshmen, 95% undergrads receive any aid. **Criteria for awarding aid:** *Non-need-based:* Academics, Alumni affiliation, Leadership.

See page 1098.

WENTWORTH INSTITUTE OF TECHNOLOGY

550 Huntington Avenue, Boston, MA 02115-5998
Phone: 617-989-4000 • **Financial Aid Phone:** 617-989-4174
E-mail: admissions@wit.edu • **CEEB Code:** 3958
Fax: 617-989-4010 • **Website:** www.wit.edu

This private school was founded in 1904. It has a 35-acre campus.

RATINGS
Admissions Selectivity Rating: 74   **Fire Safety Rating:** 90   **Green Rating:** 86

STUDENTS AND FACULTY
Enrollment: 3,942. **Student Body:** 20% female, 80% male, 35% out-of-state, 9% international (53 countries represented). Asian 8%, African American 4%, Caucasian 63%, Hispanic 3%, Native American <1%, Pacific Islander <1%, Two or more races 6%, Race unknown 8%.
Retention and Graduation: 84% freshmen return for sophomore year. 46% freshmen graduate within 4 years. 68% freshmen graduate within 6 years. 17% grads go on to further study within 1 year. 11% grads pursue arts and sciences degrees. 2% grads pursue business degrees. **Faculty:** Student/faculty ratio 17:1. 157 full-time faculty, 59% hold PhDs, 18% are are members of minority groups, 31% are women. 0% of classes are taught by teaching assistants.

ACADEMICS
Degrees: associate, bachelor's, certificate, master's. **Classes:** Most classes have 20-29 students. Most lab/discussion sessions have 10-19 students. **Most popular majors:** Construction Management; Mechanical Engineering; Architecture. **Special Study Options:** cooperative education program, cross-registration, distance learning, study abroad, Cross registration available through the Colleges of the Fenway Consortium with member colleges: Simmons College, Emmanuel College, Wheelock College, Massachusetts College of Pharmacy and Health Sciences, Massachusetts College of Art, and Wentworth Institute of Technology. Combined degree programs: BARCH/MARCH. **Disability Services:** Special programs offered to physically disabled students, including note-taking services, reader services, tape recorders, tutors. **Career Services:** Alumni network, Alumni services, Career/job search classes, Career assessment, Internships. Active for over 30 years, WIT's co-op program is one of the largest and most comprehensive cooperative education programs of its kind in the nation. Co-op is a requirement for all majors. 100% of WIT's co-op placements are directly related to the student's field of study.

FACILITIES
Housing: Coed dorms. 75% of campus accessible to physically diasbled. **Computers:** 100% of classrooms, 100% of dorms, 100% of libraries, 100% of dining areas, have wireless network access. Students can register for classes online. Administrative functions (other than registration) can be performed online.

CAMPUS LIFE
Environment: Metropolis. **Activities:** Choral groups, dance, drama/theater, music ensembles, musical theater, radio station, student government, student newspaper, student-run film society, yearbook, Student Organization. 50 registered organizations, 3 honor societies, 1 religious organization. **Athletics (Intercollegiate):** *Men:* baseball, basketball, golf, ice hockey, lacrosse, riflery, soccer, tennis, volleyball. *Women:* basketball, golf, riflery, soccer, softball, tennis, volleyball. **On-Campus Highlights:** 550 Huntington Ave (newest residence hall), Beatty Hall (cafe, library, student activities), Computer Info Systems Networking Lab (, Tansey Gymnasium, Annex (architecture and design studios), Daily tours and info sessions, fall Open Houses, spring Special Events, see website www.wit.edu (under Prospective Students) for details.

ADMISSIONS
Freshman Academic Profile: Average high school GPA 3.1. **Reported SAT (pre-2016 redesign) scores:** SAT Math middle 50% range 530-630. SAT Critical Reading middle 50% range 480-590. **Concordant SAT scores:** SAT Math middle 50% range 560–650. ACT middle 50% range 21-28. Minimum internet-based TOEFL 79. Minimum paper TOEFL 550. **Basis for Candidate Selection:** *Important factors considered include:* rigor of secondary school record, academic GPA, standardized test scores, application essay, recommendation(s). *Other factors considered include:* extracurricular activities, talent/ability, character/personal qualities, first generation, alumni/ae relation, geographical residence, racial/ethnic status, volunteer work, work experience, level of applicant's interest. **Freshman Admission Requirements:** High

school diploma is required and GED is accepted. *Academic units required:* 4 English, 3 math, 2 science, 1 science lab. *Academic units recommended:* 4 math. **Freshman Admission Statistics:** 7,556 applied, 70.58% admitted, 18% enrolled. **Transfer Admission Requirements:** High school transcript, college transcript(s), essay or personal statement, Lowest grade transferable C. **General Admission Information:** Application fee $50. Priority deadline 2/15. Nonfall registration accepted. Admission may be deferred for a maximum of 12 months.

COSTS AND FINANCIAL AID
Annual tuition $31,840. Room and board $12,570. Average book expense $1,500. **Required Forms and Deadlines:** FAFSA. **Notification of Awards:** Applicants will be notified of awards on a rolling basis beginning 3/15. **Types of Aid:** *Need-based scholarships/grants:* Federal Pell, FSEOG, State scholarships/grants, Private scholarships, College/university scholarship or grant aid from institutional funds. *Loans:* Direct Subsidized Stafford Loans, Direct Unsubsidized Stafford Loans, Direct PLUS loans, Federal Perkins Loans, State Loans. *Student Employment:* Federal Work-Study Program available. Institutional employment available. **Financial Aid Statistics:** 87% needy freshmen, 77% needy undergrads receive need-based scholarship or grant aid. 99% freshmen, 89% undergrads receive non-need-based scholarship or grant aid. 90% freshmen, 86% undergrads receive need-based self-help aid. 0% freshmen, 0% undergrads receive athletic scholarships. 91% freshmen, 78% undergrads receive any aid. 81% undergrads borrow to pay for school. Average cumulative indebtedness $23,017,740. **Criteria for awarding aid:** *Non-need-based:* Academics, Leadership, State/district residency.

See page 1100.

WESLEYAN COLLEGE

4760 Forsyth Road, Macon, GA 31210-4462
Phone: 478-477-5206 • **Financial Aid Phone:** 478-757-5205
E-mail: admissions@wesleyancollege.edu • **CEEB Code:** 5895
Fax: 478-757-4030 • **Website:** www.wesleyancollege.edu • **ACT Code:** 876

This private school, affiliated with the Methodist Church, was founded in 1836. It has a 200-acre campus.

RATINGS
Admissions Selectivity Rating: 89   **Fire Safety Rating:** 96   **Green Rating:** 82

STUDENTS AND FACULTY
Enrollment: 613. **Student Body:** 100% female, 0% male, 11% out-of-state, 17% international (25 countries represented). Asian 3%, African American 27%, Caucasian 43%, Hispanic 6%, Native American 0%, Pacific Islander <1%, Two or more races 3%, Race unknown 1%.
Retention and Graduation: 71% freshmen return for sophomore year. 48% freshmen graduate within 4 years. 58% freshmen graduate within 6 years. 30% grads go on to further study within 1 year. 10% grads pursue arts and sciences degrees. 1% grads pursue law degrees. 15% grads pursue business degrees. 4% grads pursue medical degrees. **Faculty:** Student/faculty ratio 15:1. 27 full-time faculty, 15% are are members of minority groups, are women. 0% of classes are taught by teaching assistants.

ACADEMICS
Degrees: bachelor's, master's. **Classes:** Most classes have 10-19 students. Most lab/discussion sessions have fewer than 10 students. **Most popular majors:** Business Administration, Management and Operations; Registered Nursing/Registered Nurse; Accounting. **Special Study Options:** Accelerated program, cross-registration, double major, dual enrollment, exchange student program (domestic), honors program, independent study, internships, liberal arts/career combination, student-designed major, study abroad, teacher certification program, weekend college, Dual degree engineering(3/2) with Georgia Tech, Auburn University and Mercer University. **Honors Programs:** Honors Program. **Disability Services:** Special programs offered to physically disabled students, including note-taking services, tutors. **Career Services:** Alumni network, Career/job search classes, Career assessment, Internships, Regional alumni. Internships are required for most graduating seniors.

FACILITIES
Housing: special housing for disabled students, women's dorms, apartments for single studentsStudents required to live on campus unless married or living with family in the local area. 89% of campus accessible to physically diasbled. **Special Academic Facilities/Equipment:** Art and history museums, special collection of Georgiana and Americana, on-campus equestrian center. **Computers:** 80% of classrooms, 100% of libraries, 100% of dining areas, 100% of student union, 50% of common outdoor areas have wireless network access.

Students can register for classes online. Administrative functions (other than registration) can be performed online.

CAMPUS LIFE

Environment: City. **Activities:** Choral groups, dance, drama/theater, literary magazine, music ensembles, student government, student newspaper, yearbook, Campus Ministries, Student Organization, Model UN. 40 registered organizations, 10 honor societies, 5 religious organizations. **Athletics (Intercollegiate):** *Women:* basketball, cross-country, equestrian sports, soccer, softball, tennis, volleyball. **On-Campus Highlights:** Historic quad of buildings Georgian brick design, Equestrian and Fitness Centers, Lake, Residence Halls, Art Galleries. **Environmental Initiatives:** Plastic Bottle Policy.

ADMISSIONS

Freshman Academic Profile: Average high school GPA 3.4. 22% in top 10% of high school class, 49% in top 25% of high school class, 86% in top 50% of high school class. 80% from public high schools. **Reported SAT (pre-2016 redesign) scores:** SAT Math middle 50% range 450-530. SAT Critical Reading middle 50% range 480-588. SAT Writing middle 50% range 440-540. **Concordant SAT scores:** SAT EBRW middle 50% 510–620. SAT Math middle 50% range 490–560. ACT middle 50% range 19-26. Minimum internet-based TOEFL 80. Minimum paper TOEFL 550. **Basis for Candidate Selection:** *Very important factors considered include:* rigor of secondary school record. *Important factors considered include:* academic GPA, standardized test scores, recommendation(s), interview, extracurricular activities, talent/ability, alumni/ae relation. *Other factors considered include:* class rank, application essay, character/personal qualities, first generation, volunteer work, work experience, level of applicant's interest. **Freshman Admission Requirements:** High school diploma is required and GED is accepted. *Academic units required:* 4 English, 3 math, 3 science, 2 science labs, 2 foreign language, 3 social studies. *Academic units recommended:* 4 English, 4 math, 4 science, 3 science labs, 4 foreign language, 4 social studies, 2 academic electives. **Freshman Admission Statistics:** 842 applied, 37.65% admitted, 33% enrolled. **Transfer Admission Requirements:** college transcript(s), essay or personal statement, statement of good standing from prior institution(s). Minimum college GPA of 2.5 required. Lowest grade transferable C. **General Admission Information:** Application fee $30. Priority deadline 3/1. Regular application deadline 6/1. Nonfall registration accepted. Admission may be deferred for a maximum of 1 year.

COSTS AND FINANCIAL AID

Annual tuition $20,750. Room and board $9,290. Required fees $1,000. **Required Forms and Deadlines:** FAFSA, Institution's own financial aid form, State aid form. **Notification of Awards:** Applicants will be notified of awards on a rolling basis beginning 3/1. **Types of Aid:** *Need-based scholarships/grants:* Federal Pell, FSEOG, State scholarships/grants, Private scholarships, College/university scholarship or grant aid from institutional funds. *Loans:* Direct Subsidized Stafford Loans, Direct Unsubsidized Stafford Loans, Direct PLUS loans, Federal Perkins Loans, State Loans, College/university loans from institutional funds. *Student Employment:* Federal Work-Study Program available. Institutional employment available. **Financial Aid Statistics:** 100% needy freshmen, 99% needy undergrads receive need-based scholarship or grant aid. 18% freshmen, 17% undergrads receive non-need-based scholarship or grant aid. 69% freshmen, 76% undergrads receive need-based self-help aid. 0% freshmen, 0% undergrads receive athletic scholarships. 95% freshmen, 85% undergrads receive any aid. 57% undergrads borrow to pay for school. Average cumulative indebtedness $35,392. **Criteria for awarding aid:** *Need-based:* Academics, Alumni affiliation, Job skills, Religious affiliation. *Non-need-based:* Academics, Alumni affiliation, Art, Job skills, Leadership, Music/drama, Religious affiliation, State/district residency.

WESLEYAN UNIVERSITY

Best Colleges

70 Wyllys Avenue, Middletown, CT 6459
Phone: 860-685-3000 • **Financial Aid Phone:** 860-685-2800
E-mail: admission@wesleyan.edu • **CEEB Code:** 3959
Fax: 860-685-3001 • **Website:** www.wesleyan.edu • **ACT Code:** 614

This private school was founded in 1831. It has a 240-acre campus.

RATINGS

Admissions Selectivity Rating: 97 **Fire Safety Rating:** 92 **Green Rating:** 95

STUDENTS AND FACULTY

Enrollment: 2,913. **Student Body:** 54% female, 46% male, 92% out-of-state, 10% international (55 countries represented). Asian 7%, African American 7%, Caucasian 55%, Hispanic 10%, Native American <1%, Pacific Islander <1%, Two or more races 5%, Race unknown 5%.
Retention and Graduation: 94% freshmen return for sophomore year. 87% freshmen graduate within 4 years. 91% freshmen graduate within 6 years. 14% grads go on to further study within 1 year. 9% grads pursue arts and sciences degrees. 2% grads pursue law degrees. 1% grads pursue medical degrees.
Faculty: Student/faculty ratio 8:1. 372 full-time faculty, 92% hold PhDs, 21% are are members of minority groups, 47% are women. 0% of classes are taught by teaching assistants.

ACADEMICS

Degrees: bachelor's, doctoral/research, master's, post-master's certificate. **Classes:** Most classes have 10-19 students. Most lab/discussion sessions have 10-19 students. **Most popular majors:** Psychology; Economics. **Special Study Options:** cross-registration, double major, dual enrollment, exchange student program (domestic), honors program, independent study, student-designed major, study abroad. Combined degree programs: BA/MA. **Disability Services:** Special programs offered to physically disabled students, including note-taking services, reader services, tape recorders, tutors. **Career Services:** Alumni network, Alumni services, Career assessment, Internships, Regional alumni. "Winter on Wyllys" programs during our January term that include intensive career seminars, a job shadow program, and alumni speakers.

FACILITIES

Housing: Coed dorms, special housing for disabled students, fraternity/sorority housing, apartments for married students, apartments for single students, Wellness Housing, Theme Housing, 14 Residence halls, 32 program houses, 139 woodframe houses. 54% of campus accessible to physically disabled. **Special Academic Facilities/Equipment:** Art center, art galleries, Center for Afro-American studies, East Asian Studies Center, Cinema Archives, concert hall, public affairs center, language lab, electron microscope, observatory, nuclear magnetic resonance spectrometers. **Computers:** 90% of classrooms, 100% of dorms, 90% of libraries, 90% of dining areas, 100% of student union, 90% of common outdoor areas have wireless network access. Students can register for classes online. Administrative functions (other than registration) can be performed online.

CAMPUS LIFE

Environment: Town. **Activities:** Choral groups, concert band, dance, drama/theater, jazz band, literary magazine, music ensembles, musical theater, pep band, radio station, student government, student newspaper, student-run film society, symphony orchestra, yearbook, Campus Ministries. 220 registered organizations, 2 honor societies, 10 religious organizations. 9 fraternities, 4 sororities. **Athletics (Intercollegiate):** *Men:* baseball, basketball, crew/rowing, cross-country, diving, football, golf, ice hockey, lacrosse, soccer, squash, swimming, tennis, track/field (outdoor), track/field (indoor), wrestling. *Women:* basketball, crew/rowing, cross-country, diving, field hockey, ice hockey, lacrosse, soccer, softball, squash, swimming, tennis, track/field (outdoor), track/field (indoor), volleyball. **On-Campus Highlights:** Center for the Arts, Freeman Athletic Center, Center for Film Studies, Olin Memorial Library, Van Vleck Observatory, Freeman East Asian Studies Center. **Environmental Initiatives:** Energy conservation activities resulting in a 28% reduction of energy consumption campus wide and the construction of 3 PV solar system with a combined output of 215 kW.

ADMISSIONS

Freshman Academic Profile: 69% in top 10% of high school class, 98% in top 50% of high school class. 52% from public high schools. **Reported SAT (pre-2016 redesign) scores:** SAT Math middle 50% range 630-740. SAT Critical Reading middle 50% range 620-740. SAT Writing middle 50% range 640-750. **Concordant SAT scores:** SAT EBRW middle 50% 680–760. SAT Math middle 50% range 650–760. ACT middle 50% range 30-33. Minimum internet-based TOEFL 100. Minimum paper TOEFL 600. **Basis for Candidate Selection:** *Very important factors considered include:* rigor of secondary school record. *Important factors considered include:* class rank, academic GPA, application essay, recommendation(s), talent/ability, character/personal qualities, first generation, racial/ethnic status. *Other factors considered include:* standardized test scores, interview, extracurricular activities, alumni/ae relation, geographical residence, volunteer work, work experience. **Freshman Admission Requirements:** High school diploma is required and GED is accepted. *Academic units recommended:* 4 English, 4 math, 4 science, 3 science labs, 4 foreign language, 4 social studies, 4 history. **Freshman Admission Statistics:** 11,928 applied, 11.35% admitted, 57% enrolled. **Transfer Admission Requirements:** High school transcript, college transcript(s), essay or personal statement, standardized test scores, statement of good standing from prior institution(s). Lowest grade transferable C-. **General Admission Information:** Application fee $55. Regular application deadline 1/1. Regular notification 4/1. Nonfall registration not accepted. Admission may be deferred for a maximum of 1 year.

COSTS AND FINANCIAL AID

Annual tuition $50,312. Room and board $14,904. Required fees $300. Average book expense $1,200. **Required Forms and Deadlines:** FAFSA, CSS/Financial Aid PROFILE, Noncustodial PROFILE. **Notification of Awards:** Applicants will be notified of awards on or about 4/1. **Types of Aid:** *Need-based scholarships/grants:* Federal Pell, FSEOG, State scholarships/grants, Private scholarships, College/university scholarship or grant aid from institutional funds. *Loans:* Direct Subsidized Stafford Loans, Direct Unsubsidized Stafford Loans, Direct PLUS loans, Federal Perkins Loans, College/university loans from institutional funds. *Student Employment:* Federal Work-Study Program available. Institutional employment available. **Financial Aid Statistics:** 92% needy freshmen, 93% needy undergrads receive need-based scholarship or grant aid. 4% freshmen, 3% undergrads receive non-need-based scholarship or grant aid. 88% freshmen, 91% undergrads receive need-based self-help aid. 0% freshmen, 0% undergrads receive athletic scholarships. 53% freshmen, 48% undergrads receive any aid. 43% undergrads borrow to pay for school. Average cumulative indebtedness $22,495.

WEST CHESTER UNIVERSITY
OF PENNSYLVANIA

Messikomer Hall, West Chester, PA 19383
Phone: 610-436-3411 • **Financial Aid Phone:** 610-436-2627
E-mail: www.wcupa.edu/admissions • **CEEB Code:** 3328
Fax: 610-436-2907 • **Website:** www.wcupa.edu • **ACT Code:** 3750

This public school was founded in 1871. It has a 403.4-acre campus.

RATINGS
Admissions Selectivity Rating: 80 **Fire Safety Rating:** 98 **Green Rating:** 60*

STUDENTS AND FACULTY
Enrollment: 14,123. **Student Body:** 59% female, 41% male, 12% out-of-state, <1% international (71 countries represented). Asian 2%, African American 11%, Caucasian 76%, Hispanic 6%, Native American <1%, Pacific Islander <1%, Two or more races 3%, Race unknown 1%.
Retention and Graduation: 86% freshmen return for sophomore year. 46% freshmen graduate within 4 years. 70% freshmen graduate within 6 years. **Faculty:** 0% of classes are taught by teaching assistants.

ACADEMICS
Degrees: bachelor's, doctoral/professional, doctoral/research, master's, postbachelor's certificate, post-master's certificate. **Classes:** Most classes have 20-29 students. **Most popular majors:** Psychology; Early Childhood Education and Teaching; Criminal Justice/Safety Studies. **Special Study Options:** cooperative education program, cross-registration, distance learning, double major, dual enrollment, English as a Second Language (ESL), exchange student program (domestic), honors program, independent study, internships, liberal arts/career combination, student-designed major, study abroad, teacher certification program. **Honors Programs:** See the Honors College section of the WCU • **Website:** http://www.wcupa.edu/honors/. **Disability Services:** Special programs offered to physically disabled students, including note-taking services, reader services, tape recorders, tutors. **Career Services:** Alumni network, Alumni services, Career assessment, Internships, Regional alumni. WCU Shadows—job shadowing

FACILITIES
Housing: Coed dorms, special housing for disabled students, men's dorms, special housing for international students, women's dorms, fraternity/sorority housing, apartments for single students, Wellness Housing. 95% of campus accessible to physically disabled. **Special Academic Facilities/Equipment:** McKinney Gallery, Long Gallery, Emile K. Asplundh Concert Hall, Swope Auditorium, EO Bull Main Stage, Sykes Theater, Frances Harvey Green Library, Presser Music Library, Darlington Herbarium, Geology Museum, Speech and Hearing Clinic, Philips Autograph Library, Farrell Stadium, Hollinger Fieldhouse, Schmucker Science Center, The Center for Advanced Scientific Imaging and the Materials Research Center, WCU Planetarium, WCU Observatory, Robert B. Gordon Natural Area for Environmental Studies, The Children's Center, Southeastern PA Autism Resource Center, Geography and Planning Geographic Informatino Systems Lab, Philips Auditorium, Main Hall Auditorium, Schmucker Auditorium, Boucher Lecture Hall, Center for Government and Community Affairs, The Poetry Center **Computers:** 100% of classrooms, 20% of dorms, 100% of libraries, 100% of dining areas, 100% of student union, 100% of common outdoor areas have wireless network access.

Students can register for classes online. Administrative functions (other than registration) can be performed online.

CAMPUS LIFE
Environment: Village. **Activities:** Choral groups, concert band, dance, drama/theater, jazz band, literary magazine, marching band, music ensembles, musical theater, opera, pep band, radio station, student government, student newspaper, symphony orchestra, television station, yearbook, Campus Ministries, Student Organization. 233 registered organizations, 26 honor societies, 12 religious organizations. 12 fraternities, 13 sororities. **Athletics (Intercollegiate):** *Men:* baseball, basketball, cross-country, diving, football, golf, soccer, swimming, tennis, track/field (outdoor). *Women:* basketball, cheerleading, cross-country, diving, field hockey, golf, gymnastics, lacrosse, rugby, soccer, softball, swimming, tennis, track/field (outdoor), volleyball. **On-Campus Highlights:** Emilie K. Asplundh Concert Hall, E.O. Bull Main Stage, Farrell Stadium, Sykes Student Union Building, Educational Center for Earth Observation Systems. Please see our website for a campus events calendar: http://www.wcupa.edu/_INFORMATION/events/. **Environmental Initiatives:** More than half of all buildings on campus (55%) are now tied into our geothermal district exchange system for heating and cooling. The remaining buildings are heated and cooled with high-efficiency natural gas boilers. This allowed us to take our coal-fired boiler plant offline in 2014.

ADMISSIONS
Freshman Academic Profile: Average high school GPA 3.4. 10% in top 10% of high school class, 34% in top 25% of high school class, 72% in top 50% of high school class. 82% from public high schools. **Reported SAT (pre-2016 redesign) scores:** SAT Math middle 50% range 490-580. SAT Critical Reading middle 50% range 480-570. SAT Writing middle 50% range 460-560. **Concordant SAT scores:** SAT EBRW middle 50% 530–620. SAT Math middle 50% range 520–600. ACT middle 50% range 21-25. Minimum internet-based TOEFL 80. Minimum paper TOEFL 550. **Basis for Candidate Selection:** *Very important factors considered include:* rigor of secondary school record, class rank, academic GPA. *Important factors considered include:* standardized test scores. *Other factors considered include:* application essay, extracurricular activities, talent/ability, character/personal qualities, racial/ethnic status, volunteer work, work experience. **Freshman Admission Requirements:** High school diploma is required and GED is accepted. *Academic units required:* 4 English, 3 math, 3 science, 2 science labs, 2 social studies, 2 history, 2 academic electives. *Academic units recommended:* 4 English, 4 math, 3 science, 2 foreign language, 2 social studies, 2 history, 2 academic electives, 1 computer science, 1 visual/performing arts. **Freshman Admission Statistics:** 12,609 applied, 64.45% admitted, 30% enrolled. **Transfer Admission Requirements:** college transcript(s), essay or personal statement, Minimum college GPA of 2.0 required. Lowest grade transferable C. **General Admission Information:** Application fee $45. Priority deadline 2/1. Nonfall registration accepted.

COSTS AND FINANCIAL AID
Annual in-state tuition $7,238. Annual out-of-state tuition $18,096. Room and board $8,736. Required fees $2,482. Average book expense $1,200. **Required Forms and Deadlines:** FAFSA. **Notification of Awards:** Applicants will be notified of awards on a rolling basis beginning 4/1. **Types of Aid:** *Need-based scholarships/grants:* Federal Pell, FSEOG, State scholarships/grants, Private scholarships, College/university scholarship or grant aid from institutional funds. *Loans:* Direct Subsidized Stafford Loans, Direct Unsubsidized Stafford Loans, Direct PLUS loans, Federal Perkins Loans, Federal Nursing Loans. *Student Employment:* Federal Work-Study Program available. Institutional employment available. **Financial Aid Statistics:** 49% needy freshmen, 58% needy undergrads receive need-based scholarship or grant aid. 25% freshmen, 16% undergrads receive non-need-based scholarship or grant aid. 88% freshmen, 88% undergrads receive need-based self-help aid. 1% freshmen, 1% undergrads receive athletic scholarships. 79% freshmen, 73% undergrads receive any aid. 74% undergrads borrow to pay for school. Average cumulative indebtedness $33,814. **Criteria for awarding aid:** *Need-based:* Academics, Minority status. *Non-need-based:* Academics, Art, Athletics, Leadership, Music/drama.

WEST SUBURBAN COLLEGE OF NURSING

3 Erie Court, Oak Park, IL 60302
Phone: 708-763-6530 • **Financial Aid Phone:** 708-763-1426
E-mail: admission@wscn.edu
Fax: 708-763-1531 • **Website:** www.wscn.edu

This private school, affiliated with the Roman Catholic Church, was founded in 1914.

RATINGS
Admissions Selectivity Rating: 60* **Fire Safety Rating:** 60* **Green Rating:** 60*

STUDENTS AND FACULTY

Enrollment: 236. **Student Body:** 86% female, 14% male, 0% international. Asian 24%, African American 10%, Caucasian 40%, Hispanic 13%, Native American 0%, Pacific Islander 0%, Two or more races 0%, Race unknown 13%. **Retention and Graduation:** 0% grads go on to further study within 1 year. **Faculty:** Student/faculty ratio 10:1. 23 full-time faculty, 17% hold PhDs, 17% are are members of minority groups, 100% are women. 0% of classes are taught by teaching assistants.

ACADEMICS

Degrees: bachelor's, master's. **Classes:** Most classes have 10-19 students. Most lab/discussion sessions have fewer than 10 students. **Special Study Options:** Accelerated program, WSCN offers an Evening & Weekend program. There is also a Master of Science in Nursing program, which offers four separate majors. **Career Services:** Alumni services, Career assessment, On-campus interviews.

FACILITIES

Housing: 0% of campus accessible to physically diasbled. **Computers:** 100% of classrooms, 100% of libraries, 100% of dining areas, have wireless network access. Students can register for classes online. Administrative functions (other than registration) can be performed online. Undergraduates are required to own a computer.

CAMPUS LIFE

Environment: Metropolis. **Activities:** student government 2 registered organizations.

ADMISSIONS

Freshman Admission Requirements: High school diploma is required and GED is accepted. **Transfer Admission Requirements:** college transcript(s), essay or personal statement, standardized test scores, Minimum college GPA of 2.75 required. Lowest grade transferable C. **General Admission Information:** Application fee $30. Regular application deadline 4/1. Admission may be deferred for a maximum of 1 semester.

COSTS AND FINANCIAL AID

Types of Aid: *Need-based scholarships/grants:* Federal Pell, FSEOG, State scholarships/grants, Private scholarships, College/university scholarship or grant aid from institutional funds, Federal Nursing Scholarships. *Loans:* College/university loans from institutional funds. *Student Employment:* Federal Work-Study Program available. Institutional employment available. **Financial Aid Statistics:** 100% needy undergrads receive need-based scholarship or grant aid. 18% undergrads receive non-need-based scholarship or grant aid. 79% undergrads receive need-based self-help aid. 0% undergrads receive athletic scholarships. 86% undergrads receive any aid. **Criteria for awarding aid:** *Need-based:* Academics. *Non-need-based:* Academics.

WEST TEXAS A&M UNIVERSITY

PO Box 60907, Canyon, TX 79016-0001
Phone: 806-651-2020 • **Financial Aid Phone:** 806-651-2055
E-mail: admissions@mail.wtamu.edu • **CEEB Code:** 3665
Fax: 806-651-5268 • **Website:** www.wtamu.edu • **ACT Code:** 4250

This public school was founded in 1910. It has a 135-acre campus.

RATINGS

Admissions Selectivity Rating: 79   **Fire Safety Rating:** 91   **Green Rating:** 60*

STUDENTS AND FACULTY

Enrollment: 7,384. **Student Body:** 56% female, 44% male, 13% out-of-state, 2% international (37 countries represented). Asian 1%, African American 5%, Caucasian 60%, Hispanic 27%, Native American <1%, Pacific Islander <1%, Two or more races 2%, Race unknown 2%. **Retention and Graduation:** 66% freshmen return for sophomore year. 28% freshmen graduate within 4 years. 45% freshmen graduate within 6 years. 22% grads go on to further study within 1 year. **Faculty:** Student/faculty ratio 20:1. 329 full-time faculty, 65% hold PhDs, 14% are are members of minority groups, 47% are women. 4% of classes are taught by teaching assistants.

ACADEMICS

Degrees: bachelor's, doctoral/research, master's. **Classes:** Most classes have 20-29 students. Most lab/discussion sessions have 20-29 students. **Most popular majors:** Multi-/Interdisciplinary Studies; Business/Commerce; Registered Nursing/Registered Nurse. **Special Study Options:** cooperative education program, distance learning, double major, English as a Second Language (ESL), honors program, independent study, internships, liberal arts/career combination, study abroad, teacher certification program. **Honors**

Programs: The Honors Program at West Texas AandM University is committed to providing exceptional students with challenging academic studies, innovative approaches to instruction; increased opportunities for improving skills in critical thinking, research, developing creative works and writing; expanded cultural knowledge; and the opportunity to interact closely with faculty and similarly motivated students. Combined degree programs: BBA/MPA. **Disability Services:** Special programs offered to physically disabled students, including note-taking services, reader services, tape recorders, tutors. **Career Services:** Alumni network, Alumni services, Career/job search classes, Career assessment, Internships, Regional alumni.

FACILITIES

Housing: Coed dorms, special housing for disabled students, men's dorms, women's dorms, fraternity/sorority housing, Honors Program. 100% of campus accessible to physically diasbled. **Special Academic Facilities/Equipment:** Regional History Museum, Research Center, Panhandle Plains Historical Museum, Killgore Research Center. **Computers:** Students can register for classes online. Administrative functions (other than registration) can be performed online.

CAMPUS LIFE

Environment: Village. **Activities:** Choral groups, concert band, dance, drama/theater, jazz band, literary magazine, marching band, music ensembles, musical theater, opera, radio station, student government, student newspaper, symphony orchestra, Campus Ministries, Student Organization. 110 registered organizations, 15 honor societies, 13 religious organizations. 5 fraternities, 5 sororities. **Athletics (Intercollegiate):** *Men:* baseball, basketball, cross-country, football, golf, soccer. *Women:* basketball, cheerleading, cross-country, equestrian sports, golf, soccer, softball, volleyball. **On-Campus Highlights:** Panhandle-Plains Historical Museum, Jack B. Kelley Student Center, Virgil Henson Activities Center, Old Main (first building built on campus), WTAMU Horse Center, Panhandle-Plains Historical Museum is the largest historical museum in the State of Texas.

ADMISSIONS

Freshman Academic Profile: 14% in top 10% of high school class, 43% in top 25% of high school class, 77% in top 50% of high school class. 97% from public high schools. **Reported SAT (pre-2016 redesign) scores:** SAT Math middle 50% range 430-530. SAT Critical Reading middle 50% range 420-530. **Concordant SAT scores:** SAT Math middle 50% range 470–560. ACT middle 50% range 18-24. Minimum internet-based TOEFL 190. Minimum paper TOEFL 520. **Basis for Candidate Selection:** *Very important factors considered include:* class rank, academic GPA, standardized test scores. *Important factors considered include:* rigor of secondary school record. **Freshman Admission Requirements:** High school diploma is required and GED is accepted. *Academic units required:* 4 English, 4 math, 4 science, 2 foreign language, 4 social studies, 6 academic electives, 1 visual/performing arts. **Freshman Admission Statistics:** 6,163 applied, 59.81% admitted, 36% enrolled. **Transfer Admission Requirements:** college transcript(s), Minimum college GPA of 2.0 required. Lowest grade transferable C. **General Admission Information:** Application fee $40. Priority deadline 8/1. Nonfall registration accepted. Admission may be deferred for a maximum of 1 term.

COSTS AND FINANCIAL AID

Annual in-state tuition $5,289. Annual out-of-state tuition $6,279. Room and board $7,196. Required fees $2,392. Average book expense $1,000. **Required Forms and Deadlines:** FAFSA. **Notification of Awards:** Applicants will be notified of awards on a rolling basis beginning 3/1. **Types of Aid:** *Need-based scholarships/grants:* Federal Pell, FSEOG, State scholarships/grants, Private scholarships, College/university scholarship or grant aid from institutional funds. *Loans:* Direct Subsidized Stafford Loans, Direct Unsubsidized Stafford Loans, Direct PLUS loans, State Loans. *Student Employment:* Federal Work-Study Program available. Institutional employment available. **Financial Aid Statistics:** 80% needy freshmen, 78% needy undergrads receive need-based scholarship or grant aid. 49% freshmen, 36% undergrads receive non-need-based scholarship or grant aid. 75% freshmen, 80% undergrads receive need-based self-help aid. 2% freshmen, 3% undergrads receive athletic scholarships. 52% freshmen, 53% undergrads receive any aid. 62% undergrads borrow to pay for school. Average cumulative indebtedness $24,525. **Criteria for awarding aid:** *Need-based:* Academics. *Non-need-based:* Academics, Art, Athletics, Leadership, Music/drama.

WEST VIRGINIA STATE UNIVERSITY

106 Ferrell Hall, Institute, WV 25112
Phone: 304-766-3033 • **Financial Aid Phone:** 304-766-3131
E-mail: admissions@wvstateu.edu • **CEEB Code:** 5903
Fax: 304-766-5182 • **Website:** www.wvstateu.edu • **ACT Code:** 4538

This public school was founded in 1891. It has a 95-acre campus.

RATINGS
Admissions Selectivity Rating: 71   **Fire Safety Rating:** 60*   **Green Rating:** 60*

STUDENTS AND FACULTY
Enrollment: 2,033. **Student Body:** 54% female, 46% male, 8% out-of-state, 1% international (8 countries represented). Asian 0%, African American 14%, Caucasian 65%, Hispanic 1%, Native American <1%, Pacific Islander 0%, Two or more races 10%, Race unknown 9%.
Retention and Graduation: 6% grads go on to further study within 1 year. 3% grads pursue arts and sciences degrees. 1% grads pursue law degrees. 1% grads pursue business degrees. 1% grads pursue medical degrees.

ACADEMICS
Degrees: bachelor's, master's. **Most popular majors:** Elementary Education and Teaching; General Studies; Business Administration and Management. **Special Study Options:** cooperative education program, off-campus study: Washington, DC. **Disability Services:** Special programs offered to physically disabled students, including tutors.

FACILITIES
Housing: Coed dorms, men's dorms, women's dorms, apartments for married students. **Special Academic Facilities/Equipment:** On-campus day-care center, art gallery, ROTC Hall of Fame, Sports Hall of Fame.

CAMPUS LIFE
Environment: Village. **Activities:** Choral groups, concert band, jazz band, literary magazine, marching band, music ensembles, radio station, student government, student newspaper, television station, yearbook. 4 honor societies, 2 religious organizations. 6 fraternities, 3 sororities. **Athletics (Intercollegiate):** *Men:* baseball, basketball, cross-country, football, softball, tennis, track/field (outdoor), volleyball. *Women:* basketball, cross-country, softball, tennis, track/field (outdoor), volleyball.

ADMISSIONS
Freshman Academic Profile: 99% from public high schools. **Reported SAT (pre-2016 redesign) scores:** SAT Math middle 50% range 400-500. SAT Critical Reading middle 50% range 390-510. SAT Writing middle 50% range 373-480. **Concordant SAT scores:** SAT EBRW middle 50% 430–550. SAT Math middle 50% range 440–530. ACT middle 50% range 17-22. **Freshman Admission Requirements:** High school diploma is required and GED is accepted.High school diploma is required and GED is not accepted. *Academic units required:* 4 English, 2 math, 2 science, 2 foreign language, 3 social studies, 1 history. **Freshman Admission Statistics:** 1,439 applied, 94.09% admitted, 27% enrolled. **Transfer Admission Requirements:** college transcript(s), Minimum college GPA of 2.0 required. Lowest grade transferable D. **General Admission Information:** Application fee $20. Regular application deadline 8/22. Nonfall registration accepted.

COSTS AND FINANCIAL AID
Annual in-state tuition $2,116. Annual out-of-state tuition $5,150. Room and board $3,550. Required fees $125. Average book expense $500. **Required Forms and Deadlines:** FAFSA, Institution's own financial aid form. *Student Employment:* Federal Work-Study Program available. Institutional employment available.

WEST VIRGINIA UNIVERSITY

Admissions Office, Morgantown, WV 26506-6009
Phone: 304-293-2121 • **Financial Aid Phone:** 304-293-5242
E-mail: go2wvu@mail.wvu.edu • **CEEB Code:** 5904
Fax: 304-293-3080 • **Website:** www.wvu.edu • **ACT Code:** 4540

This public school was founded in 1867.

RATINGS
Admissions Selectivity Rating: 82   **Fire Safety Rating:** 98   **Green Rating:** 81

STUDENTS AND FACULTY
Enrollment: 21,428. **Student Body:** 46% female, 54% male, 48% out-of-state, 6% international (71 countries represented). Asian 2%, African American 5%, Caucasian 79%, Hispanic 4%, Native American <1%, Pacific Islander <1%, Two or more races 4%, Race unknown <1%.
Retention and Graduation: 79% freshmen return for sophomore year. 32% freshmen graduate within 4 years. 57% freshmen graduate within 6 years.
Faculty: Student/faculty ratio 19:1. 1,188 full-time faculty, 83% hold PhDs, 13% are are members of minority groups, 40% are women.

ACADEMICS
Degrees: bachelor's, doctoral/professional, doctoral/research, doctoral, master's. **Classes:** Most classes have 10-19 students. Most lab/discussion sessions have 20-29 students. **Most popular majors:** Journalism; Engineering; Business Administration and Management. **Special Study Options:** Accelerated program, cooperative education program, distance learning, double major, English as a Second Language (ESL), exchange student program (domestic), external degree program, honors program, independent study, internships, student-designed major, study abroad, teacher certification program, weekend college. **Honors Programs:** Honors Leadership Academy Combined degree programs: BA/MA, BA/MA in Ed., BA/MOT. **Disability Services:** Special programs offered to physically disabled students, including note-taking services, reader services, tape recorders, tutors. **Career Services:** Alumni network, Alumni services, Career/job search classes, Career assessment, Internships.

FACILITIES
Housing: Coed dorms, special housing for disabled students, men's dorms, special housing for international students, women's dorms, fraternity/sorority housing, apartments for married students, cooperative housing, apartments for single students, (Special interest "floors" available, Operation Jump Start places faculty residence hall leaders adjacent to residence halls allowing frequent opportunities for faculty-student interaction outside classroom. This program mandatory for freshmen). 99% of campus accessible to physically diasbled. **Special Academic Facilities/Equipment:** Art galleries, creative arts center, arboretum, herbarium, planetarium, concurrent engineering research center, discovery lab (for inventors), Appalachian hardwood center, small business development center, pharmacy museum, coal and energy museum, center for economic research, fluidization center, center for software development. **Computers:** 80% of classrooms, 75% of dorms, 100% of libraries, 40% of dining areas, 100% of student union, 10% of common outdoor areas have wireless network access. Students can register for classes online. Administrative functions (other than registration) can be performed online.

CAMPUS LIFE
Environment: Town. **Activities:** Choral groups, concert band, dance, drama/theater, jazz band, literary magazine, marching band, music ensembles, musical theater, pep band, radio station, student government, student newspaper, symphony orchestra, television station, yearbook, Campus Ministries, Student Organization. 370 registered organizations, 31 honor societies, 28 religious organizations. 14 fraternities, 9 sororities. **Athletics (Intercollegiate):** *Men:* baseball, basketball, diving, football, riflery, soccer, swimming, wrestling. *Women:* basketball, crew/rowing, cross-country, diving, gymnastics, riflery, soccer, swimming, tennis, track/field (outdoor), track/field (indoor), volleyball. **On-Campus Highlights:** New State of the Art Student Recreation Center, Mountainlair (Student Union), Personal Rapid Transit (PRT), Mountaineer Field, Historic Woodburn Circle, Core Arboretum. **Environmental Initiatives:** 1. Energy performance management and emissions reduction through a performance contract (approx. $30 million) between WVU and Siemens Inc. A behavior-based energy management program is currently being developed to educate and empower faculty, staff, and students to be better stewards of energy resources.

ADMISSIONS

Freshman Academic Profile: Average high school GPA 3.5. 20% in top 10% of high school class, 44% in top 25% of high school class, 76% in top 50% of high school class. **Reported SAT (pre-2016 redesign) scores:** SAT Math middle 50% range 470-580. SAT Critical Reading middle 50% range 460-560. **Concordant SAT scores:** SAT Math middle 50% range 510–600. ACT middle 50% range 21-26. Minimum internet-based TOEFL 61. Minimum paper TOEFL 550. **Basis for Candidate Selection:** *Very important factors considered include:* academic GPA, standardized test scores. *Important factors considered include:* rigor of secondary school record, state residency. *Other factors considered include:* extracurricular activities, talent/ability. **Freshman Admission Requirements:** High school diploma is required and GED is accepted. *Academic units required:* 4 English, 4 math, 3 science, 3 science labs, 2 foreign language, 3 social studies, 1 visual/performing arts. **Freshman Admission Statistics:** 21,558 applied, 76.12% admitted, 31% enrolled. **Transfer Admission Requirements:** college transcript(s), Minimum college GPA of 2.0 required. Lowest grade transferable D. **General Admission Information:** Priority deadline 3/1. Regular application deadline 8/1. Nonfall registration accepted. Admission may be deferred for a maximum of 1 year.

COSTS AND FINANCIAL AID

Annual in-state tuition $7,992. Annual out-of-state tuition $22,488. Average book expense $900. **Required Forms and Deadlines:** FAFSA, State aid form. **Notification of Awards:** Applicants will be notified of awards on a rolling basis beginning 3/15. **Types of Aid:** *Need-based scholarships/grants:* Federal Pell, FSEOG, State scholarships/grants, Private scholarships, College/university scholarship or grant aid from institutional funds, Federal Nursing Scholarships. *Loans:* Direct Subsidized Stafford Loans, Direct Unsubsidized Stafford Loans, Direct PLUS loans, Federal Perkins Loans, Federal Nursing Loans, College/university loans from institutional funds. *Student Employment:* Federal Work-Study Program available. Institutional employment available. **Financial Aid Statistics:** 70% needy freshmen, 70% needy undergrads receive need-based scholarship or grant aid. 94% freshmen, 86% undergrads receive non-need-based scholarship or grant aid. 92% freshmen, 92% undergrads receive need-based self-help aid. 1% freshmen, 2% undergrads receive athletic scholarships. 72% freshmen, 75% undergrads receive any aid. 64% undergrads borrow to pay for school. Average cumulative indebtedness $34,105. **Criteria for awarding aid:** *Need-based:* Academics. *Non-need-based:* Academics, Alumni affiliation, Art, Athletics, Job skills, Leadership, Minority status, Music/drama, Religious affiliation, State/district residency.

WEST VIRGINIA UNIVERSITY INSTITUTE OF TECHNOLOGY

Box 10 Old Main, Montgomery, WV 25136
Phone: 304-442-3167
E-mail: admissions@wvutech.edu
Fax: 304-442-3097 • **Website:** www.wvutech.edu

This is a public school.

RATINGS

Admissions Selectivity Rating: 75   **Fire Safety Rating:** 60*   **Green Rating:** 60*

STUDENTS AND FACULTY

Enrollment: 2,001. **Student Body:** 39% female, 61% male, 6% out-of-state, 4% international. Asian 1%, African American 8%, Caucasian 87%, Hispanic 1%, Native American <1%, Pacific Islander 0%, Two or more races 0%, Race unknown 0%.
Retention and Graduation: 62% freshmen return for sophomore year.
Faculty: Student/faculty ratio 16:1. 119 full-time faculty, 47% hold PhDs, 18% are are members of minority groups, 28% are women.

ACADEMICS

Degrees: associate, bachelor's, certificate, master's. **Classes:** Most classes have 10-19 students. Most lab/discussion sessions have 20-29 students. **Special Study Options:** cooperative education program, distance learning, double major, dual enrollment, internships, student-designed major.

FACILITIES

Housing: Coed dorms, men's dorms, women's dorms, fraternity/sorority housing.

CAMPUS LIFE

Activities: Choral groups, concert band, drama/theater, jazz band, marching band, music ensembles, pep band, student government, student newspaper.

ADMISSIONS

Freshman Academic Profile: Average high school GPA 3.2. 20% in top 10% of high school class, 21% in top 25% of high school class, 43% in top 50% of high school class. 88% from public high schools. **Reported SAT (pre-2016 redesign) scores:** SAT Math middle 50% range 400-580. SAT Critical Reading middle 50% range 380-530. **Concordant SAT scores:** SAT Math middle 50% range 440–600. ACT middle 50% range 17-23. Minimum paper TOEFL 500. **Basis for Candidate Selection:** *Very important factors considered include:* rigor of secondary school record, standardized test scores. *Other factors considered include:* class rank, recommendation(s), interview, extracurricular activities, talent/ability, character/personal qualities, alumni/ae relation, state residency, volunteer work. **Freshman Admission Requirements:** High school diploma is required and GED is accepted. *Academic units required:* 4 English, 2 math, 2 science, 2 science labs, 3 social studies. *Academic units recommended:* 4 English, 3 math, 2 science, 2 science labs, 2 foreign language, 3 social studies. **Freshman Admission Statistics:** 1,191 applied, 74.14% admitted, 47% enrolled. **Transfer Admission Requirements:** college transcript(s), Minimum college GPA of 1.7 required. Lowest grade transferable D. **General Admission Information:** Priority deadline 8/3. Nonfall registration accepted. Admission may be deferred for a maximum of 1 semester.

COSTS AND FINANCIAL AID

Annual in-state tuition $3,200. Annual out-of-state tuition $8,400. Room and board $4,896. Required fees $0. Average book expense $800. **Required Forms and Deadlines:** FAFSA, Institution's own financial aid form. **Notification of Awards:** Applicants will be notified of awards on a rolling basis beginning 3/3. **Types of Aid:** *Need-based scholarships/grants:* Federal Pell, FSEOG, State scholarships/grants, Private scholarships, College/university scholarship or grant aid from institutional funds. *Loans:* Direct Subsidized Stafford Loans, Direct Unsubsidized Stafford Loans, Direct PLUS loans, Federal Perkins Loans. *Student Employment:* Federal Work-Study Program available. Institutional employment available. **Financial Aid Statistics:** 78% needy freshmen, 78% needy undergrads receive need-based scholarship or grant aid. 70% freshmen, 48% undergrads receive non-need-based scholarship or grant aid. 59% freshmen, 70% undergrads receive need-based self-help aid. 2% freshmen, 6% undergrads receive athletic scholarships. **Criteria for awarding aid:** *Need-based:* Academics, Athletics, Music/drama. *Non-need-based:* Academics, Alumni affiliation, Art, Athletics, Music/drama.

WEST VIRGINIA WESLEYAN COLLEGE

59 College Avenue, Buckhannon, WV 26201
Phone: 304-473-8510 • **Financial Aid Phone:** 304-473-8080
E-mail: admission@wvwc.edu • **CEEB Code:** 5905
Fax: 304-473-8108 • **Website:** www.wvwc.edu • **ACT Code:** 4544

This private school, affiliated with the Methodist Church, was founded in 1890. It has a 120-acre campus.

RATINGS

Admissions Selectivity Rating: 81   **Fire Safety Rating:** 60*   **Green Rating:** 60*

STUDENTS AND FACULTY

Enrollment: 1,371. **Student Body:** 55% female, 45% male, 40% out-of-state, 5% international (22 countries represented). Asian 0%, African American 9%, Caucasian 79%, Hispanic 2%, Native American <1%, Pacific Islander <1%, Two or more races 3%, Race unknown 1%.
Retention and Graduation: 72% freshmen return for sophomore year. 38% freshmen graduate within 4 years. 50% freshmen graduate within 6 years. 35% grads go on to further study within 1 year. 57% grads pursue arts and sciences degrees. 11% grads pursue law degrees. 16% grads pursue business degrees. 6% grads pursue medical degrees. **Faculty:** Student/faculty ratio 13:1. 91 full-time faculty, 74% hold PhDs, 8% are are members of minority groups, 57% are women. 0% of classes are taught by teaching assistants.

ACADEMICS

Degrees: bachelor's, master's, postbachelor's certificate, post-master's certificate. **Classes:** Most classes have 10-19 students. Most lab/discussion sessions have 10-19 students. **Most popular majors:** Elementary Education and Teaching; Business Administration and Management; Kinesiology and Exercise Science. **Special Study Options:** double major, English as a Second Language (ESL), exchange student program (domestic), honors program, independent study, internships, liberal arts/career combination, student-designed major, study abroad, teacher certification program. **Honors Programs:** The Honors Program is offered to recognize and challenge the College's most academically talented students. Participation is voluntary for all qualified students. Combined degree programs: BA/MA. **Disability Services:** Special programs offered to physically disabled students, including note-taking services, reader services, tape recorders, tutors. **Career Services:** Alumni network, Alumni services, Career/job search classes, Internships.

FACILITIES

Housing: Coed dorms, special housing for disabled students, men's dorms, women's dorms, fraternity/sorority housing. **Computers:** Students can register for classes online. Undergraduates are required to own a computer.

CAMPUS LIFE

Environment: Village. **Activities:** Choral groups, dance, drama/theater, jazz band, literary magazine, music ensembles, musical theater, opera, radio station, student government, student newspaper, yearbook, Campus Ministries, Student Organization. 75 registered organizations, 31 honor societies, 6 religious organizations. 6 fraternities, 5 sororities. **Athletics (Intercollegiate):** *Men:* baseball, basketball, cross-country, football, golf, soccer, softball, swimming, tennis, track/field (outdoor), track/field (indoor). *Women:* basketball, cross-country, golf, lacrosse, soccer, swimming, tennis, track/field (outdoor), track/field (indoor), volleyball. **On-Campus Highlights:** Cat's Claw (alternate dining facility), Sunny Bucks (Convenience Store), Wesley Chapel, Sleeth Art Gallery, Atkinson Theatre.

ADMISSIONS

Freshman Academic Profile: Average high school GPA 3.5. 25% in top 10% of high school class, 53% in top 25% of high school class, 82% in top 50% of high school class. 88% from public high schools. **Reported SAT (pre-2016 redesign) scores:** SAT Math middle 50% range 420-550. SAT Critical Reading middle 50% range 420-540. SAT Writing middle 50% range 500-530. **Concordant SAT scores:** SAT EBRW middle 50% 510–590. SAT Math middle 50% range 460–570. ACT middle 50% range 20-25. Minimum paper TOEFL 500. **Basis for Candidate Selection:** *Very important factors considered include:* rigor of secondary school record, academic GPA, talent/ability. *Important factors considered include:* class rank, standardized test scores, extracurricular activities, character/personal qualities, volunteer work, work experience, level of applicant's interest. *Other factors considered include:* application essay, recommendation(s), interview. **Freshman Admission Requirements:** High school diploma is required and GED is accepted. *Academic units required:* 4 English, 3 math, 3 science, 1 science lab, 3 social studies. *Academic units recommended:* 2 foreign language. **Freshman Admission Statistics:** 1,782 applied, 77.22% admitted, 28% enrolled. **Transfer Admission Requirements:** High school transcript, college transcript(s), statement of good standing from prior institution(s). Minimum college GPA of 2.50 required. Lowest grade transferable C-. **General Admission Information:** Application fee $35. Priority deadline 2/1. Regular application deadline 8/15. Nonfall registration accepted. Admission may be deferred for a maximum of 1 yr.

COSTS AND FINANCIAL AID

Annual tuition $28,574. Room and board $8,248. Required fees $1,178. Average book expense $2,500. **Required Forms and Deadlines:** FAFSA. **Notification of Awards:** Applicants will be notified of awards on a rolling basis beginning 3/1. **Types of Aid:** *Need-based scholarships/grants:* Federal Pell, FSEOG, State scholarships/grants, Private scholarships, College/university scholarship or grant aid from institutional funds, Federal Nursing Scholarships. *Loans:* Direct Subsidized Stafford Loans, Direct Unsubsidized Stafford Loans, Direct PLUS loans, Federal Perkins Loans, Federal Nursing Loans. *Student Employment:* Federal Work-Study Program available. Institutional employment available. **Financial Aid Statistics:** 100% needy freshmen, 100% needy undergrads receive need-based scholarship or grant aid. 22% freshmen, 17% undergrads receive non-need-based scholarship or grant aid. 80% freshmen, 85% undergrads receive need-based self-help aid. 4% freshmen, 7% undergrads receive athletic scholarships. 99% freshmen, 98% undergrads receive any aid. 71% undergrads borrow to pay for school. Average cumulative indebtedness $29,296. **Criteria for awarding aid:** *Need-based:* Art, Leadership, Music/drama. *Non-need-based:* Academics, Alumni affiliation, Art, Athletics, Leadership, Music/drama, Religious affiliation.

See page 1102.

WESTERN CAROLINA UNIVERSITY

102 Camp Building, Cullowhee, NC 28723
Phone: 828-227-7317 • **Financial Aid Phone:** 828-227-7290
E-mail: admiss@email.wcu.edu • **CEEB Code:** 5897
Fax: 828-227-7319 • **Website:** www.wcu.edu • **ACT Code:** 3172

This public school was founded in 1889. It has a 682-acre campus.

RATINGS

Admissions Selectivity Rating: 84 **Fire Safety Rating:** 94 **Green Rating:** 82

STUDENTS AND FACULTY

Enrollment: 8,603. **Student Body:** 54% female, 46% male, 7% out-of-state, 2% international (28 countries represented). Asian 1%, African American 6%, Caucasian 80%, Hispanic 5%, Native American 1%, Pacific Islander <1%, Two or more races 3%, Race unknown 1%.
Retention and Graduation: 78% freshmen return for sophomore year. 39% freshmen graduate within 4 years. 58% freshmen graduate within 6 years.
Faculty: Student/faculty ratio 16:1. 493 full-time faculty, 76% hold PhDs, 5% are are members of minority groups, 48% are women. 1% of classes are taught by teaching assistants.

ACADEMICS

Degrees: bachelor's, doctoral/professional, doctoral/research, master's, postbachelor's certificate, post-master's certificate. **Classes:** Most classes have 20-29 students. Most lab/discussion sessions have 10-19 students. **Most popular majors:** Registered Nursing/Registered Nurse; Criminal Justice/Safety Studies; Junior High/Intermediate/Middle School Education and Teaching. **Special Study Options:** cooperative education program, distance learning, double major, dual enrollment, English as a Second Language (ESL), exchange student program (domestic), honors program, independent study, internships, student-designed major, study abroad, teacher certification program. **Honors Programs:** Western has a residential Honors College designed to enhance the academic and social university experience for high-achieving students. The college consists of honors courses throughout liberal studies with an emphasis on special projects and undergraduate research in the major. Also, special housing, academic, leadership and social programs are available for honors students. **Disability Services:** Special programs offered to physically disabled students, including note-taking services, reader services, tape recorders, tutors. **Career Services:** Alumni network, Alumni services, Career assessment, Internships. Co-op and internship experiences are very common among WCU students. Some departments require them for degree completion. Intern and co-op opportunities are available domestically and internationally.

FACILITIES

Housing: Coed dorms, special housing for disabled students, men's dorms, women's dorms, fraternity/sorority housing, apartments for married students, Wellness Housing, Theme Housing. 91% of campus accessible to physically diasbled. **Special Academic Facilities/Equipment:** Fine Arts Gallery, Mountain Heritage Center, Reading Center, North Carolina Center for the Advancement of Teaching, Speech/Hearing Center, Center for Applied Technology, CATA Lab (high technology computer lab), Fine and Performing Arts Center, Institute for the Economy and the Future, Public Policy Institute **Computers:** 90% of classrooms, 10% of dorms, 100% of libraries, 70% of dining areas, 100% of student union, 50% of common outdoor areas have wireless network access. Students can register for classes online. Administrative functions (other than registration) can be performed online. Undergraduates are required to own a computer.

CAMPUS LIFE

Environment: Rural. **Activities:** Choral groups, concert band, dance, drama/theater, jazz band, literary magazine, marching band, music ensembles, musical theater, pep band, radio station, student government, student newspaper, student-run film society, television station, Campus Ministries, Student Organization, Model UN. 103 registered organizations, 7 honor societies, 12 religious organizations. 11 fraternities, 8 sororities. **Athletics (Intercollegiate):** *Men:* baseball, basketball, cheerleading, cross-country, football, golf, track/field (outdoor), track/field (indoor). *Women:* basketball, cheerleading, cross-country, golf, soccer, softball, tennis, track/field (outdoor), track/field (indoor), volleyball. **On-Campus Highlights:** University Center, Campus Recreation Center, Hunter Library, Fine & Performing Arts Center, Ramsey Regional Activity Center, Courtyard Dining Hall is a new facility that opened in summer 2009. It provides students with the following options: All-you-can-eat, foodcourt with 4 restaurants, McAlisters Deli, Starbucks, and a C-store. **Environmental Initiatives:** Currently have two buildings under construction that will be LEED certified and completed in 2012.

ADMISSIONS

Freshman Academic Profile: Average high school GPA 3.8. 13% in top 10% of high school class, 39% in top 25% of high school class, 79% in top 50% of high school class. **Reported SAT (pre-2016 redesign) scores:** SAT Math middle 50% range 470-560. SAT Critical Reading middle 50% range 460-560. SAT Writing middle 50% range 430-530. **Concordant SAT scores:** SAT EBRW middle 50% 500–600. SAT Math middle 50% range 510–580. ACT middle 50% range 20-24. Minimum internet-based TOEFL 79. Minimum paper TOEFL 550. **Basis for Candidate Selection:** *Very important factors considered include:* rigor of secondary school record, class rank, academic GPA, standardized test scores, level of applicant's interest. *Important factors considered include:* application essay, recommendation(s), extracurricular activities, talent/ability, character/personal qualities, work experience. *Other factors considered include:* interview, first generation, geographical residence, state residency. **Freshman Admission Requirements:** High school diploma is required and GED is accepted. *Academic units required:* 4 English, 4 math, 3 science, 3 science labs, 2 foreign language, 2 social studies, 1 history, 4 academic electives. *Academic units recommended:* 4 English, 4 math, 3 science, 3 science labs, 2 foreign language, 1 history, 8 academic electives. **Freshman Admission Statistics:** 15,397 applied, 43.11% admitted, 26% enrolled. **Transfer Admission Requirements:** college transcript(s), statement of good standing from prior institution(s). Minimum college GPA of 2.0 required. Lowest grade transferable C. **General Admission Information:** Application fee $55. Priority deadline 11/15. Regular application deadline 3/1. Nonfall registration accepted.

COSTS AND FINANCIAL AID

Annual in-state tuition $3,669. Annual out-of-state tuition $14,062. Room and board $8,016. Required fees $2,826. Average book expense $708. **Required Forms and Deadlines:** FAFSA, Institution's own financial aid form. **Notification of Awards:** Applicants will be notified of awards on a rolling basis beginning 4/1. **Types of Aid:** *Need-based scholarships/grants:* Federal Pell, FSEOG, State scholarships/grants, Private scholarships, College/university scholarship or grant aid from institutional funds. *Loans:* Direct Subsidized Stafford Loans, Direct Unsubsidized Stafford Loans, Direct PLUS loans, Federal Perkins Loans. *Student Employment:* Federal Work-Study Program available. Institutional employment available. **Financial Aid Statistics:** 96% needy freshmen, 94% needy undergrads receive need-based scholarship or grant aid. 3% freshmen, 3% undergrads receive non-need-based scholarship or grant aid. 75% freshmen, 78% undergrads receive need-based self-help aid. 4% freshmen, 4% undergrads receive athletic scholarships. **Criteria for awarding aid:** *Need-based:* Academics, Minority status. *Non-need-based:* Academics, Art, Athletics, Leadership, Music/drama, State/district residency.

WESTERN CONNECTICUT STATE UNIVERSITY

Undergraduate Admissions Office, Danbury, CT 06810-6855
Phone: 203-837-9000 • **Financial Aid Phone:** 203-837-8588
E-mail: admissions@wcsu.edu • **CEEB Code:** 3350
Fax: 203-837-8338 • **Website:** www.wcsu.edu • **ACT Code:** 558

This public school was founded in 1903. It has a 364-acre campus.

RATINGS

Admissions Selectivity Rating: 75   **Fire Safety Rating:** 91   **Green Rating:** 60*

STUDENTS AND FACULTY

Enrollment: 5,001. **Student Body:** 52% female, 48% male, 6% out-of-state, <1% international (7 countries represented). Asian 4%, African American 11%, Caucasian 60%, Hispanic 18%, Native American <1%, Pacific Islander <1%, Two or more races 3%, Race unknown 3%.
Retention and Graduation: 73% freshmen return for sophomore year. 22% freshmen graduate within 4 years. 23% grads go on to further study within 1 year. 10% grads pursue arts and sciences degrees. 2% grads pursue law degrees. 3% grads pursue business degrees. 1% grads pursue medical degrees. **Faculty:** Student/faculty ratio 12:1. 222 full-time faculty, 86% hold PhDs, 20% are are members of minority groups, 54% are women. 0% of classes are taught by teaching assistants.

ACADEMICS

Degrees: associate, bachelor's, doctoral/professional, master's. **Classes:** Most classes have 20-29 students. Most lab/discussion sessions have 20-29 students. **Most popular majors:** Elementary Education and Teaching; Criminal Justice/ Police Science. **Special Study Options:** cooperative education program, cross-registration, distance learning, double major, dual enrollment, English as a Second Language (ESL), honors program, independent study, internships, student-designed major, study abroad, teacher certification program. **Honors Programs:** University Scholars Program. **Disability Services:** Special programs offered to physically disabled students, including note-taking services, reader services, tape recorders, tutors. **Career Services:** Career/job search classes, Career assessment, Internships. Career assessment utilizes career software, "SIG13", which assesses career interests; maintains an extensive career library which offers a large collection of literature on career fields, job search, company profiles, and graduate/professional school information; and hosts a major Career Fair each year.

FACILITIES

Housing: Coed dorms, women's dorms, apartments for single students, On campus housing assigned on a first-come, first-served basis. 100% of campus accessible to physically disabled. **Special Academic Facilities/Equipment:** Language lab, observatory, electron microscope, nature preserve, computer-enhanced classrooms, business library, Jane Goodall Institute. **Computers:** 50% of classrooms, 80% of dorms, 100% of libraries, 100% of dining areas, 100% of student union, have wireless network access. Students can register

for classes online. Administrative functions (other than registration) can be performed online.

CAMPUS LIFE

Environment: City. **Activities:** Choral groups, concert band, dance, drama/ theater, jazz band, literary magazine, music ensembles, musical theater, opera, pep band, radio station, student government, student newspaper, symphony orchestra, yearbook, Campus Ministries, Student Organization. 40 registered organizations, 8 honor societies, 3 religious organizations. 3 fraternities, 4 sororities. **Athletics (Intercollegiate):** *Men:* baseball, basketball, football, lacrosse, soccer, tennis. *Women:* basketball, field hockey, lacrosse, soccer, softball, swimming, tennis, volleyball. **On-Campus Highlights:** Student Centers (Midtown and Westside), O'Neill Center, Science Building, White Hall, Ancell Classroom Building. **Environmental Initiatives:** Think Green: Go Blue recycling efforts (with distribution campus wide of an instruction brochure).

ADMISSIONS

Freshman Academic Profile: 7% in top 10% of high school class, 25% in top 25% of high school class, 61% in top 50% of high school class. 91% from public high schools. **Reported SAT (pre-2016 redesign) scores:** SAT Math middle 50% range 440-540. SAT Critical Reading middle 50% range 440-550. SAT Writing middle 50% range 440-540. **Concordant SAT scores:** SAT EBRW middle 50% 490–600. SAT Math middle 50% range 480–570. Minimum internet-based TOEFL 79. Minimum paper TOEFL 550. **Basis for Candidate Selection:** *Very important factors considered include:* rigor of secondary school record, standardized test scores, talent/ability. *Important factors considered include:* class rank, extracurricular activities. *Other factors considered include:* application essay, recommendation(s), interview, character/personal qualities, alumni/ae relation, state residency, racial/ethnic status, volunteer work, work experience. **Freshman Admission Requirements:** High school diploma is required and GED is accepted. *Academic units required:* 4 English, 3 math, 2 science, 2 science labs, 2 foreign language, 1 social studies, 1 history. **Freshman Admission Statistics:** 5,484 applied, 66.83% admitted, 23% enrolled. **Transfer Admission Requirements:** college transcript(s), Minimum college GPA of 2.0 required. Lowest grade transferable C-. **General Admission Information:** Application fee $50. Nonfall registration accepted. Admission may be deferred for a maximum of 1 year.

COSTS AND FINANCIAL AID

Annual in-state tuition $5,216. Annual out-of-state tuition $16,882. Room and board $4,000. Required fees $4,801. Average book expense $1,300. **Required Forms and Deadlines:** FAFSA, Institution's own financial aid form. **Notification of Awards:** Applicants will be notified of awards on a rolling basis beginning 4/15. **Types of Aid:** *Need-based scholarships/grants:* Federal Pell, FSEOG, State scholarships/grants, Private scholarships, College/university scholarship or grant aid from institutional funds. *Loans:* Direct Subsidized Stafford Loans, Direct Unsubsidized Stafford Loans, Direct PLUS loans, Federal Perkins Loans, Federal Nursing Loans. **Financial Aid Statistics:** 95% needy freshmen, 83% needy undergrads receive need-based scholarship or grant aid. 2% freshmen, 1% undergrads receive non-need-based scholarship or grant aid. 75% freshmen, 81% undergrads receive need-based self-help aid. 0% freshmen, 0% undergrads receive athletic scholarships. 63% freshmen, 61% undergrads receive any aid. Average cumulative indebtedness $31,229. **Criteria for awarding aid:** *Need-based:* Academics, Art, Minority status, Music/drama. *Non-need-based:* Academics, Art, Minority status, Music/drama.

WESTERN ILLINOIS UNIVERSITY

1 University Circle, Sherman Hall 115, Macomb, IL 61455-1390
Phone: 309-298-3157 • **Financial Aid Phone:** 309-298-2446
E-mail: admissions@wiu.edu • **CEEB Code:** 1900
Fax: 309-298-3111 • **Website:** http://www.wiu.edu • **ACT Code:** 1158

This public school was founded in 1899. It has a 1050-acre campus.

RATINGS

Admissions Selectivity Rating: 77   **Fire Safety Rating:** 89   **Green Rating:** 69

STUDENTS AND FACULTY

Enrollment: 8,543. **Student Body:** 51% female, 49% male, 12% out-of-state, 2% international (54 countries represented). Asian 1%, African American 21%, Caucasian 60%, Hispanic 12%, Native American <1%, Pacific Islander <1%, Two or more races 3%, Race unknown 2%.
Retention and Graduation: 69% freshmen return for sophomore year. 31% freshmen graduate within 4 years. 53% freshmen graduate within 6 years. 24% grads go on to further study within 1 year. **Faculty:** Student/faculty ratio 15:1. 566 full-time faculty, 74% hold PhDs, 19% are are members of minority groups, 45% are women.

ACADEMICS

Degrees: bachelor's, doctoral/research, master's, postbachelor's certificate. **Classes:** Most classes have 20-29 students. Most lab/discussion sessions have 10-19 students. **Most popular majors:** Criminal Justice/Law Enforcement Administration; Biology/Biological Sciences; Agriculture. **Special Study Options:** distance learning, double major, dual enrollment, English as a Second Language (ESL), external degree program, honors program, independent study, internships, student-designed major, study abroad, teacher certification program, weekend college. **Honors Programs:** Illinois Centennial Honors College. **Disability Services:** Special programs offered to physically disabled students, including note-taking services, reader services, tape recorders, tutors. **Career Services:** Alumni network, Alumni services, Career/job search classes, Career assessment, Internships, On-campus interviews. Internships if required by an academic major, usually go through that department. However, we have numerous on-line internship resources. In addition at our 3 career fairs, many employers seek to hire interns.

FACILITIES

Housing: Coed dorms, men's dorms, special housing for international students, women's dorms, fraternity/sorority housing, apartments for married students, Wellness Housing. 95% of campus accessible to physically diasbled. **Special Academic Facilities/Equipment:** Art gallery, electron microscope **Computers:** 100% of classrooms, 100% of dorms, 100% of libraries, 100% of dining areas, 100% of student union, 100% of common outdoor areas have wireless network access. Students can register for classes online. Administrative functions (other than registration) can be performed online.

CAMPUS LIFE

Environment: Village. **Activities:** Choral groups, concert band, dance, drama/theater, jazz band, marching band, music ensembles, musical theater, pep band, radio station, student government, student newspaper, symphony orchestra, television station, yearbook, Campus Ministries, Student Organization. 200 registered organizations, 25 honor societies, 12 religious organizations. 14 fraternities, 11 sororities. **Athletics (Intercollegiate):** *Men:* baseball, basketball, cross-country, diving, football, golf, soccer, swimming, tennis, track/field (outdoor), track/field (indoor). *Women:* basketball, cheerleading, cross-country, diving, golf, soccer, softball, swimming, tennis, track/field (outdoor), track/field (indoor), volleyball. **On-Campus Highlights:** University Union, Student Recreation Center, Leslie Malpass Library **Environmental Initiatives:** In the last year Western has received two Illinois Clean Energy Community Foundation grants for energy efficient lighting upgrades. The most recent award of $59,262 is for an energy-efficient lighting upgrade in Morgan Hall consisting of retrofitting existing fluorescent lighting fixtures with high efficiency electronic ballasts and lamps that use 35 percent less energy than the original 35-year-old equipment.

ADMISSIONS

Freshman Academic Profile: Average high school GPA 3.2. 9% in top 10% of high school class, 30% in top 25% of high school class, 67% in top 50% of high school class. 91% from public high schools. ACT middle 50% range 18-23. Minimum internet-based TOEFL 79. Minimum paper TOEFL 550. **Basis for Candidate Selection:** *Very important factors considered include:* academic GPA, standardized test scores. *Other factors considered include:* rigor of secondary school record, level of applicant's interest. **Freshman Admission Requirements:** High school diploma is required and GED is accepted. *Academic units recommended:* 4 English, 3 math, 3 science, 3 social studies, 2 academic electives. **Freshman Admission Statistics:** 10,191 applied, 59.45% admitted, 25% enrolled. **Transfer Admission Requirements:** college transcript(s), Minimum college GPA of 2.0 required. Lowest grade transferable D. **General Admission Information:** Application fee $30. Regular notification 9/15. Nonfall registration accepted. Admission may be deferred.

COSTS AND FINANCIAL AID

Average book expense $900. **Required Forms and Deadlines:** FAFSA. **Notification of Awards:** Applicants will be notified of awards on a rolling basis beginning 1/15. **Types of Aid:** *Need-based scholarships/grants:* Federal Pell, FSEOG, State scholarships/grants, Private scholarships, College/university scholarship or grant aid from institutional funds. *Loans:* Direct Subsidized Stafford Loans, Direct Unsubsidized Stafford Loans, Direct PLUS loans, Federal Perkins Loans, College/university loans from institutional funds. *Student Employment:* Federal Work-Study Program available. Institutional employment available. **Financial Aid Statistics:** 74% needy freshmen, 68% needy undergrads receive need-based scholarship or grant aid. 57% freshmen, 45% undergrads receive non-need-based scholarship or grant aid. 91% freshmen, 92% undergrads receive need-based self-help aid. 3% freshmen, 4% undergrads receive athletic scholarships. 91% freshmen, 89% undergrads receive any aid. 83% undergrads borrow to pay for school. Average cumulative indebtedness $30,721. **Criteria for awarding aid:** *Non-need-based:* Academics, Alumni affiliation, Art, Athletics, Leadership, Minority status, Music/drama.

WESTERN KENTUCKY UNIVERSITY

Potter Hall 117, Bowling Green, KY 42101-1020
Phone: 270-745-2551 • **Financial Aid Phone:** 270-745-2755
E-mail: admission@wku.edu • **CEEB Code:** 1901
Fax: 270-745-6133 • **Website:** www.wku.edu • **ACT Code:** 1562

This public school was founded in 1906. It has a 235-acre campus.

RATINGS

Admissions Selectivity Rating: 77   **Fire Safety Rating:** 98   **Green Rating:** 87

STUDENTS AND FACULTY

Enrollment: 14,956. **Student Body:** 57% female, 43% male, 20% out-of-state, 5% international (69 countries represented). Asian 1%, African American 10%, Caucasian 77%, Hispanic 3%, Native American <1%, Pacific Islander <1%, Two or more races 3%, Race unknown 1%.
Retention and Graduation: 73% freshmen return for sophomore year. 30% freshmen graduate within 4 years. 52% freshmen graduate within 6 years. **Faculty:** Student/faculty ratio 18:1. 765 full-time faculty, 77% hold PhDs, 19% are are members of minority groups, 52% are women. 0% of classes are taught by teaching assistants.

ACADEMICS

Degrees: associate, bachelor's, certificate, doctoral/professional, master's, postbachelor's certificate, post-master's certificate. **Classes:** Most classes have 20-29 students. Most lab/discussion sessions have 10-19 students. **Most popular majors:** Registered Nursing/Registered Nurse; Business Administration and Management; Biology/Biological Sciences. **Special Study Options:** cooperative education program, distance learning, double major, dual enrollment, English as a Second Language (ESL), exchange student program (domestic), honors program, independent study, internships, study abroad, teacher certification program, Gatton Academy of Math and Science, Learning Communities/Block Scheduling, Honors College, American Democracy Project. **Honors Programs:** University Honors College Gatton Academy of Mathematics and Science Combined degree programs: Accountancy, Applied Economics, Biology, Chemistry, Computer Science, Engineering Technology Management, Geoscience, Kinesiology, Mathematics, Psychological Science, Sociology. **Disability Services:** Special programs offered to physically disabled students, including note-taking services, reader services, tape recorders, tutors. **Career Services:** Alumni network, Alumni services, Career/job search classes, Career assessment, Internships, Regional alumni.

FACILITIES

Housing: Coed dorms, men's dorms, special housing for international students, women's dorms, fraternity/sorority housing, ThemeHousingGatton Academy, Learning Communities, Themed Living options—Fit,Honors, Mosiac Communities. **Special Academic Facilities/Equipment:** Kentucky Museum, University Farm, Hardin Planetarium, Media and Technology Hall **Computers:** 100% of classrooms, 68% of dorms, 100% of libraries, 100% of dining areas, 100% of student union, have wireless network access. Students can register for classes online. Administrative functions (other than registration) can be performed online.

CAMPUS LIFE

Environment: Town. **Activities:** Choral groups, concert band, dance, drama/theater, jazz band, literary magazine, marching band, music ensembles, musical theater, opera, pep band, radio station, student government, student newspaper, student-run film society, symphony orchestra, television station, yearbook, Campus Ministries, Student Organization. 360 registered organizations, 28 honor societies, 23 religious organizations. 18 fraternities, 13 sororities. **Athletics (Intercollegiate):** *Men:* baseball, basketball, cross-country, diving, football, golf, riflery, swimming, tennis, track/field (outdoor), track/field (indoor). *Women:* basketball, cross-country, diving, golf, riflery, soccer, swimming, tennis, track/field (outdoor), track/field (indoor), volleyball. **On-Campus Highlights:** Downing University Center, Preston Health and Activities Center, E.A. Diddle Arena and L.T. Smith Stadium, Mass Media and Technology Hall, Guthrie Tower, Please visit www.wku.edu/tour.html for further information and an interactive tour of the university. **Environmental Initiatives:** Sustainability-oriented staff positions and Sustainability Committee, Education for Sustainability resolution adopted 2010, Sustainability in operations, services, and academics included in 2010-2012 University Strategic Plan.

ADMISSIONS

Freshman Academic Profile: Average high school GPA 3.3. 22% in top 10% of high school class, 44% in top 25% of high school class, 72% in top 50% of high school class. **Reported SAT (pre-2016 redesign) scores:** SAT Math middle 50% range 430-550. SAT Critical Reading middle 50% range 430-

540. **Concordant SAT scores:** SAT Math middle 50% range 470–570. ACT middle 50% range 19-26. Minimum internet-based TOEFL 71. Minimum paper TOEFL 525. **Basis for Candidate Selection:** *Very important factors considered include:* academic GPA, standardized test scores. **Freshman Admission Requirements:** High school diploma is required and GED is accepted. *Academic units required:* 4 English, 3 math, 3 science, 1 science lab, 2 foreign language, 3 social studies, 1 history, 5 academic electives, and 1 unit from above areas or other academic areas. **Freshman Admission Statistics:** 9,693 applied, 94.02% admitted, 35% enrolled. **Transfer Admission Requirements:** college transcript(s), statement of good standing from prior institution(s). Minimum college GPA of 2.0 required. Lowest grade transferable D°. **General Admission Information:** Application fee $45. Regular application deadline 8/1. Nonfall registration accepted. Admission may be deferred.

COSTS AND FINANCIAL AID

Annual in-state tuition $9,912. Annual out-of-state tuition $24,792. Room and board $7,713. Average book expense $1,000. **Required Forms and Deadlines:** FAFSA. **Notification of Awards:** Applicants will be notified of awards on a rolling basis beginning 3/1. **Types of Aid:** *Need-based scholarships/ grants:* Federal Pell, FSEOG, State scholarships/grants, Private scholarships, College/university scholarship or grant aid from institutional funds, United Negro College Fund. *Loans:* Direct Subsidized Stafford Loans, Direct Unsubsidized Stafford Loans, Direct PLUS loans. *Student Employment:* Federal Work-Study Program available. Institutional employment available. **Financial Aid Statistics:** 64% needy freshmen, 63% needy undergrads receive need-based scholarship or grant aid. 89% freshmen, 69% undergrads receive non-need-based scholarship or grant aid. 63% freshmen, 70% undergrads receive need-based self-help aid. 2% freshmen, 3% undergrads receive athletic scholarships. 93% freshmen, 87% undergrads receive any aid. 61% undergrads borrow to pay for school. Average cumulative indebtedness $28,081. **Criteria for awarding aid:** *Non-need-based:* Academics, Alumni affiliation, Art, Athletics, Job skills, Leadership, Minority status, Music/drama, Religious affiliation, State/district residency.

WESTERN MICHIGAN UNIVERSITY

1903 W Michigan Ave, Kalamazoo, MI 49008-5211
Phone: 269-387-2000 • **Financial Aid Phone:** 269-387-6000
E-mail: ask-wmu@wmich.edu • **CEEB Code:** 1902
Fax: 269-387-2096 • **Website:** https://wmich.edu/ • **ACT Code:** 2066

This public school was founded in 1903. It has a 1200-acre campus.

RATINGS

Admissions Selectivity Rating: 75   **Fire Safety Rating:** 88   **Green Rating:** 89

STUDENTS AND FACULTY

Enrollment: 17,984. **Student Body:** 49% female, 51% male, 8% out-of-state, 4% international (63 countries represented). Asian 2%, African American 13%, Caucasian 71%, Hispanic 6%, Native American <1%, Pacific Islander <1%, Two or more races 4%, Race unknown 1%.
Retention and Graduation: 79% freshmen return for sophomore year. 22% freshmen graduate within 4 years. 53% freshmen graduate within 6 years.
Faculty: Student/faculty ratio 17:1. 934 full-time faculty, 77% hold PhDs, 18% are are members of minority groups, 45% are women.

ACADEMICS

Degrees: bachelor's, doctoral/professional, doctoral/research, master's, postbachelor's certificate, post-master's certificate. **Classes:** Most classes have 20-29 students. Most lab/discussion sessions have 20-29 students. **Most popular majors:** Business Administration and Management; Health and Medical Administrative Services; Psychology. **Special Study Options:** Accelerated program, cross-registration, distance learning, double major, dual enrollment, English as a Second Language (ESL), exchange student program (domestic), honors program, independent study, internships, student-designed major, study abroad, teacher certification program. **Honors Programs:** The Lee Honors College The mission of the Carl and Winifred Lee Honors College is to provide a lively, rigorous undergraduate program for bright, highly motivated, and active students. Combined degree programs: BA/MA, BA/MEng, Audiology; Computer Science; Earth Science; Family&Consumer Sciences;Paper&Printing Science; Music; Orientation&Mobility; Vision Rehabilitation Therapy; Social Work; Communication; Spanish; Statistics. **Disability Services:** Special programs offered to physically disabled students, including note-taking services, reader services, tape recorders, tutors. **Career Services:** Alumni network, Career/job search classes, Career assessment, Internships.

FACILITIES

Housing: Coed dorms, special housing for disabled students, men's dorms, special housing for international students, women's dorms, fraternity/sorority housing, apartments for married students, apartments for single students, Wellness Housing, Theme Housing. Each hall has a special thematic concept that is developed through programming and student involvment. Examples are: Community Service, Honors, Arts and Athletics, First Year Initiative, Upper Class Students, Diversity. 85% of campus accessible to physically diasbled. **Special Academic Facilities/Equipment:** Pilot plant for manufacturing and printing of paper and for fiber recovery, behavior research and development center, nuclear accelerator, center for electron microscopy, particle accelerator lab, Library Department of Special Collections: Cistercian and Monastic Studies Collections, Medieval Studies Collections, Carol Ann Haenicke American Women's Poetry Collection, Nineteenth and Twentieth Century Literature and History Collection, Book Arts Collections: Paper and Fine Printing; Aviation **Computers:** 100% of classrooms, 25% of dorms, 100% of libraries, 100% of dining areas, 100% of student union, 100% of common outdoor areas have wireless network access. Students can register for classes online. Administrative functions (other than registration) can be performed online.

CAMPUS LIFE

Environment: City. **Activities:** Choral groups, concert band, dance, drama/ theater, jazz band, literary magazine, marching band, music ensembles, musical theater, opera, pep band, radio station, student government, student newspaper, student-run film society, symphony orchestra, Campus Ministries, Student Organization. 300 registered organizations, 7 honor societies, 21 religious organizations. 16 fraternities, 11 sororities. **Athletics (Intercollegiate):** *Men:* baseball, basketball, football, ice hockey, soccer, tennis. *Women:* basketball, cross-country, golf, gymnastics, soccer, softball, tennis, track/field (outdoor), track/field (indoor), volleyball. **On-Campus Highlights:** Bernhard Center, Waldo Library, University Recreation Center, Miller Auditorium, Gilmore Theatre Complex, Lawson Ice Arena and Gabel Natatorium provide swimming and skating facilities including lessons and family activities. **Environmental Initiatives:** Strategic Planning for Sustainability'Climate Action Plan (2012); University Strategic Plan Implementation utilizing the Sustainability Tracking, Assessment, and Rating System program as an overarching framework for evaluation; Sustainability Across Research & Teaching Survey, Luncheon Series, and Faculty Learning Community; Humanities Center Climate Change Study Group and lecture series; creation of a 7000 square foot Office for Sustainability building hosting several 2012 events; Office for Sustainability website upgrade www.wmich.edu/sustainability and http://www.youtube.com/user/WMUSustainability.

ADMISSIONS

Freshman Academic Profile: Average high school GPA 3.3. 12% in top 10% of high school class, 32% in top 25% of high school class, 69% in top 50% of high school class. ACT middle 50% range 19-25. Minimum internet-based TOEFL 80. Minimum paper TOEFL 550. **Basis for Candidate Selection:** *Very important factors considered include:* academic GPA, standardized test scores. *Important factors considered include:* rigor of secondary school record. *Other factors considered include:* application essay, recommendation(s), extracurricular activities. **Freshman Admission Requirements:** High school diploma is required and GED is accepted. *Academic units recommended:* 4 English, 3 math, 3 science, 3 social studies. **Freshman Admission Statistics:** 13,613 applied, 82.31% admitted, 27% enrolled. **Transfer Admission Requirements:** college transcript(s), Minimum college GPA of 2.0 required. Lowest grade transferable C. **General Admission Information:** Application fee $40. Nonfall registration accepted.

COSTS AND FINANCIAL AID

Annual in-state tuition $10,570. Annual out-of-state tuition $25,928. Room and board $9,561. Required fees $923. Average book expense $948. **Required Forms and Deadlines:** FAFSA. **Notification of Awards:** Applicants will be notified of awards on a rolling basis beginning 3/15. **Types of Aid:** *Need-based scholarships/grants:* Federal Pell, FSEOG, State scholarships/grants, Private scholarships, College/university scholarship or grant aid from institutional funds. *Loans:* Direct Subsidized Stafford Loans, Direct Unsubsidized Stafford Loans, Direct PLUS loans, Federal Perkins Loans. *Student Employment:* Federal Work-Study Program available. Institutional employment available. **Financial Aid Statistics:** 63% needy freshmen, 70% needy undergrads receive need-based scholarship or grant aid. 53% freshmen, 31% undergrads receive non-need-based scholarship or grant aid. 79% freshmen, 84% undergrads receive need-based self-help aid. 1% freshmen, 1% undergrads receive athletic scholarships. 83% freshmen, 83% undergrads receive any aid. 75% undergrads borrow to pay for school. Average cumulative indebtedness $35,454. **Criteria for awarding aid:** *Need-based:* Academics. *Non-need-based:* Academics, Alumni affiliation, Art, Athletics, Music/drama, State/district residency.

WESTERN NEW ENGLAND UNIVERSITY

Admissions Office, Springfield, MA 1119
Phone: 413-782-1321 • **Financial Aid Phone:** 413-796-2080
E-mail: learn@wne.edu • **CEEB Code:** 3962
Fax: 413-782-1777 • **ACT Code:** 1930

This private school was founded in 1919. It has a 215-acre campus.

RATINGS
Admissions Selectivity Rating: 79   **Fire Safety Rating:** 71   **Green Rating:** 65

STUDENTS AND FACULTY
Enrollment: 2,717. **Student Body:** 38% female, 62% male, 48% out-of-state, 3% international (22 countries represented). Asian 3%, African American 6%, Caucasian 73%, Hispanic 8%, Native American <1%, Pacific Islander <1%, Two or more races 2%, Race unknown 4%.
Retention and Graduation: 76% freshmen return for sophomore year. 51% freshmen graduate within 4 years. 57% freshmen graduate within 6 years. 22% grads go on to further study within 1 year. **Faculty:** Student/faculty ratio 12:1. 237 full-time faculty, 86% hold PhDs, 10% are are members of minority groups, 41% are women. 0% of classes are taught by teaching assistants.

ACADEMICS
Degrees: associate, bachelor's, certificate, doctoral/professional, doctoral/research, master's, postbachelor's certificate, terminal. **Classes:** Most classes have 20-29 students. Most lab/discussion sessions have 10-19 students. **Most popular majors:** Mechanical Engineering; Psychology; Accounting. **Special Study Options:** Accelerated program, cross-registration, distance learning, double major, dual enrollment, exchange student program (domestic), honors program, independent study, internships, liberal arts/career combination, student-designed major, study abroad, teacher certification program, 3+3 law program with Western New England College School of Law. Washington Semester Program. 5 Yr BSBS/MBA and Engr/MBA. 6 Yr BSBE/Law and 6 Yr BiomedEngr/Law. 5 yr BSEM/MSEM. **Honors Programs:** The Honors Program at Western New England College gives academically qualified and motivated students the opportunity to join a community of like students and participate in challenging courses taught by some of the College's best faculty. Honors students generally take one honors course per semester for their first three years and work on a senior honors project during their final year. Combined degree programs: BA/JD, BA/MEng, BS/MBA, BS/MSA. **Disability Services:** Special programs offered to physically disabled students, including note-taking services, reader services, tape recorders, tutors. **Career Services:** Alumni network, Career assessment, Internships.

FACILITIES
Housing: Coed dorms, special housing for disabled students, apartments for single students. **Special Academic Facilities/Equipment:** Art Gallery; Math, Writing Science Centers **Computers:** Students can register for classes online. Administrative functions (other than registration) can be performed online.

CAMPUS LIFE
Environment: City. **Activities:** Choral groups, concert band, dance, drama/theater, jazz band, literary magazine, music ensembles, pep band, radio station, student government, student newspaper, yearbook, Campus Ministries, Student Organization. 60 registered organizations, 8 honor societies. **Athletics (Intercollegiate): Men:** baseball, basketball, cross-country, football, golf, ice hockey, lacrosse, soccer, tennis, wrestling. *Women:* basketball, cross-country, field hockey, lacrosse, soccer, softball, swimming, tennis, volleyball. **On-Campus Highlights:** Alumni Healthful Living Center, St Germain Campus Center, D'Amour Library, Computer Labs, Rock Cafe.

ADMISSIONS
Freshman Academic Profile: Average high school GPA 3.4. 11% in top 10% of high school class, 39% in top 25% of high school class, 74% in top 50% of high school class. **Reported SAT (pre-2016 redesign) scores:** SAT Math middle 50% range 510-610. SAT Critical Reading middle 50% range 480-580. **Concordant SAT scores:** SAT Math middle 50% range 540–630. ACT middle 50% range 22-27. Minimum internet-based TOEFL 79. Minimum paper TOEFL 550. **Basis for Candidate Selection:** *Very important factors considered include:* academic GPA, standardized test scores. *Important factors considered include:* rigor of secondary school record. *Other factors considered include:* class rank, application essay, recommendation(s), interview, extracurricular activities, talent/ability, character/personal qualities, alumni/ae relation, volunteer work, work experience. **Freshman Admission Requirements:** High school diploma is required and GED is accepted. *Academic units required:* 4 English, 2 math, 1 science, 1 science lab, 1 social studies, 1 history. *Academic units recommended:* 4 English, 4 math, 2 science, 2 science labs, 2 foreign language, 2 social studies, 2 history. **Freshman Admission Statistics:** 6,399 applied, 79.61% admitted, 14% enrolled. **Transfer**

Admission Requirements: High school transcript, college transcript(s), Minimum college GPA of 2.3 required. Lowest grade transferable C-. **General Admission Information:** Application fee $40. Priority deadline 2/15. Nonfall registration accepted. Admission may be deferred for a maximum of 12 months.

COSTS AND FINANCIAL AID
Annual tuition $32,524. Room and board $13,214. Required fees $2,350. Average book expense $1,240. **Required Forms and Deadlines:** FAFSA. **Notification of Awards:** Applicants will be notified of awards on a rolling basis beginning 3/1. **Types of Aid:** *Need-based scholarships/grants:* Federal Pell, FSEOG, State scholarships/grants, Private scholarships, College/university scholarship or grant aid from institutional funds. *Loans:* Direct Subsidized Stafford Loans, Direct Unsubsidized Stafford Loans, Direct PLUS loans, Federal Perkins Loans. *Student Employment:* Federal Work-Study Program available. Institutional employment available. **Financial Aid Statistics:** 100% needy freshmen, 100% needy undergrads receive need-based scholarship or grant aid. 11% freshmen, 9% undergrads receive non-need-based scholarship or grant aid. 87% freshmen, 87% undergrads receive need-based self-help aid. 0% freshmen, 0% undergrads receive athletic scholarships. 96% freshmen, 93% undergrads receive any aid. 84% undergrads borrow to pay for school. Average cumulative indebtedness $44,013. **Criteria for awarding aid:** *Need-based:* Academics, Alumni affiliation, Leadership, Minority status. *Non-need-based:* Academics, Music/drama.

WESTERN OREGON UNIVERSITY

345 N Monmouth Avenue, Monmouth, OR 97361
Phone: 503-838-8211 • **Financial Aid Phone:** 877-877-1593
E-mail: wolfgram@wou.edu • **CEEB Code:** 4585
Fax: 503-838-8067 • **Website:** www.wou.edu • **ACT Code:** 3480

This public school was founded in 1856. It has a 157-acre campus.

RATINGS
Admissions Selectivity Rating: 72   **Fire Safety Rating:** 95   **Green Rating:** 60*

STUDENTS AND FACULTY
Enrollment: 4,809. **Student Body:** 61% female, 39% male, 19% out-of-state, 6% international (19 countries represented). Asian 4%, African American 4%, Caucasian 63%, Hispanic 14%, Native American 2%, Pacific Islander 3%, Two or more races <1%, Race unknown 4%.
Retention and Graduation: 74% freshmen return for sophomore year. 17% freshmen graduate within 4 years. 39% freshmen graduate within 6 years. **Faculty:** Student/faculty ratio 14:1. 291 full-time faculty, 70% hold PhDs, 15% are are members of minority groups, 53% are women. 0% of classes are taught by teaching assistants.

ACADEMICS
Degrees: bachelor's, master's, postbachelor's certificate. **Classes:** Most classes have 10-19 students. Most lab/discussion sessions have 20-29 students. **Most popular majors:** Teacher Education, Multiple Levels; Social Sciences; Business/Commerce. **Special Study Options:** distance learning, double major, dual enrollment, English as a Second Language (ESL), honors program, independent study, internships, study abroad, teacher certification program. **Honors Programs:** WOU Honors Program. **Disability Services:** Special programs offered to physically disabled students, including note-taking services, reader services, tape recorders, tutors. **Career Services:** Career/job search classes, Internships.

FACILITIES
Housing: Coed dorms, special housing for disabled students, apartments for married students, apartments for single students. 95% of campus accessible to physically disabled. **Special Academic Facilities/Equipment:** Jensen Arctic Museum **Computers:** 70% of classrooms, 90% of dorms, 100% of libraries, 90% of dining areas, 90% of student union, 20% of common outdoor areas have wireless network access. Students can register for classes online. Administrative functions (other than registration) can be performed online.

CAMPUS LIFE
Environment: Village. **Activities:** Choral groups, concert band, dance, drama/theater, jazz band, literary magazine, music ensembles, musical theater, student government, student newspaper, symphony orchestra, Campus Ministries, Student Organization. 50 registered organizations, 4 honor societies, 6 religious organizations. **Athletics (Intercollegiate): Men:** baseball, basketball, cheerleading, cross-country, football, track/field (outdoor). *Women:* basketball, cheerleading, cross-country, soccer, softball, track/field (outdoor), volleyball. **On-Campus Highlights:** Wayne and Lynn Hamersly Library, Neal Werner University Center, Paul Jensen Arctic Museum, Campbell Hall Art Gallery, Arbor Park Apartments. **Environmental Initiatives:** paper recyling.

ADMISSIONS

Freshman Academic Profile: Average high school GPA 3.3. 0% in top 10% of high school class, 3% in top 25% of high school class, 28% in top 50% of high school class. 95% from public high schools. **Reported SAT (pre-2016 redesign) scores:** SAT Math middle 50% range 420-530. SAT Critical Reading middle 50% range 420-540. SAT Writing middle 50% range 410-510. **Concordant SAT scores:** SAT EBRW middle 50% 460-580. SAT Math middle 50% range 460-560. ACT middle 50% range 17-23. Minimum paper TOEFL 500. **Basis for Candidate Selection:** *Very important factors considered include:* rigor of secondary school record, academic GPA, standardized test scores. *Important factors considered include:* class rank. *Other factors considered include:* recommendation(s), talent/ability, first generation, alumni/ae relation, racial/ethnic status. **Freshman Admission Requirements:** High school diploma is required and GED is accepted. *Academic units required:* 4 English, 3 math, 3 science, 1 science lab, 2 foreign language, 3 social studies. *Academic units recommended:* 4 English, 3 math, 3 science, 1 science lab, 2 foreign language, 3 social studies. **Freshman Admission Statistics:** 2,901 applied, 87.76% admitted, 32% enrolled. **Transfer Admission Requirements:** college transcript(s), Minimum college GPA of 2.0 required. Lowest grade transferable D-. **General Admission Information:** Application fee $60. Nonfall registration accepted. Admission may be deferred.

COSTS AND FINANCIAL AID

Annual in-state tuition $9,285. Annual out-of-state tuition $23,445. Room and board $9,798. **Required Forms and Deadlines:** FAFSA. **Notification of Awards:** Applicants will be notified of awards on a rolling basis beginning 3/15. **Types of Aid:** *Need-based scholarships/grants:* Federal Pell, FSEOG, State scholarships/grants, Private scholarships, College/university scholarship or grant aid from institutional funds, United Negro College Fund. *Loans:* Direct Subsidized Stafford Loans, Direct Unsubsidized Stafford Loans, Direct PLUS loans, Federal Perkins Loans, College/university loans from institutional funds. *Student Employment:* Federal Work-Study Program available. **Financial Aid Statistics:** 88% needy freshmen, 91% needy undergrads receive need-based scholarship or grant aid. 4% freshmen, 3% undergrads receive non-need-based scholarship or grant aid. 84% freshmen, 86% undergrads receive need-based self-help aid. 3% freshmen, 2% undergrads receive athletic scholarships. 65% freshmen, 58% undergrads receive any aid. 67% undergrads borrow to pay for school. Average cumulative indebtedness $30,586. **Criteria for awarding aid:** *Need-based:* Academics. *Non-need-based:* Academics, Athletics, Leadership, Music/drama.

WESTERN STATE COLORADO UNIVERSITY

600 N. Adams, Gunnison, CO 81231
Phone: 970-943-2119 • **Financial Aid Phone:** 970-943-3085
E-mail: admissions@western.edu • **CEEB Code:** 4946
Fax: 970-943-2363 • **Website:** www.western.edu • **ACT Code:** 536

This public school was founded in 1911. It has a 228-acre campus.

RATINGS

Admissions Selectivity Rating: 73   **Fire Safety Rating:** 90   **Green Rating:** 90

STUDENTS AND FACULTY

Enrollment: 1,988. **Student Body:** 40% female, 60% male, 30% out-of-state, <1% international (7 countries represented). Asian 1%, African American 3%, Caucasian 73%, Hispanic 11%, Native American 1%, Pacific Islander <1%, Two or more races 4%, Race unknown 7%.
Retention and Graduation: 69% freshmen return for sophomore year. 23% freshmen graduate within 4 years. 45% freshmen graduate within 6 years. 15% grads go on to further study within 1 year. **Faculty:** Student/faculty ratio 19:1. 117 full-time faculty, 83% hold PhDs, 3% are are members of minority groups, 39% are women. 0% of classes are taught by teaching assistants.

ACADEMICS

Degrees: bachelor's, master's, postbachelor's certificate. **Classes:** Most classes have 10-19 students. **Most popular majors:** Parks, Recreation and Leisure Studies; Business Administration and Management; Biology/Biological Sciences. **Special Study Options:** distance learning, double major, dual enrollment, honors program, independent study, internships, liberal arts/career combination, study abroad, teacher certification program. **Honors Programs:** Honors Program–based on the National Collegiate Honors Council–modeled City of Text explores urban environments, while the Partners in the Parks: Black Canyon of the Gunnison course immerses students in the ecosystems of one of America's most amazing national parks. **Disability Services:** Special programs offered to physically disabled students, including note-taking services, reader services, tape recorders, tutors. **Career Services:** Alumni network, Alumni services, Career/job search classes, Career assessment, Internships, Regional alumni.

College Directory

FACILITIES

Housing: Coed dorms, men's dorms, women's dorms, apartments for married students, apartments for single students, Theme Housing. 80% of campus accessible to physically diasbled. **Computers:** 100% of classrooms, 50% of dorms, 100% of libraries, 100% of dining areas, 100% of student union, have wireless network access. Students can register for classes online. Administrative functions (other than registration) can be performed online.

CAMPUS LIFE

Environment: Rural. **Activities:** Choral groups, concert band, dance, drama/theater, jazz band, literary magazine, music ensembles, pep band, radio station, student government, student newspaper, student-run film society, symphony orchestra, television station, Campus Ministries, Student Organization. 60 registered organizations, 8 honor societies, 5 religious organizations. **Athletics (Intercollegiate):** *Men:* basketball, cross-country, football, track/field (outdoor), track/field (indoor), wrestling. *Women:* basketball, cross-country, track/field (outdoor), track/field (indoor), volleyball. **On-Campus Highlights:** College Center–new student center, Hurst Hall—renovated science building, Kelley Hall–renovated social sciences, Gym—Highest Elevation NCAA basketball Court, Borick Business–new business building, College Center, Borick, Business Building and Kelley Hall are either LEED certified or seeking LEED certification. Kelley also features solar panels for energy efficiency. The new College Center features campus dining and a first-run movie theatre. **Environmental Initiatives:** President's Climate Committment–which is a significant challenge for one of the coldest locations in the nation and the isolated nature of Gunnison.

ADMISSIONS

Freshman Academic Profile: Average high school GPA 3.0. 6% in top 10% of high school class, 18% in top 25% of high school class, 50% in top 50% of high school class. **Reported SAT (pre-2016 redesign) scores:** SAT Math middle 50% range 440-550. SAT Critical Reading middle 50% range 450-570. **Concordant SAT scores:** SAT Math middle 50% range 480-570. ACT middle 50% range 19-25. Minimum paper TOEFL 550. **Basis for Candidate Selection:** *Very important factors considered include:* rigor of secondary school record, class rank, academic GPA, standardized test scores. *Important factors considered include:* application essay, recommendation(s). *Other factors considered include:* interview, extracurricular activities, talent/ability, character/personal qualities, first generation, alumni/ae relation, volunteer work. **Freshman Admission Requirements:** High school diploma is required and GED is accepted. *Academic units required:* 4 English, 4 math, 3 science, 2 science labs, 1 foreign language, 3 social studies, 1 history, 2 academic electives. *Academic units recommended:* 2 foreign language. **Freshman Admission Statistics:** 2,191 applied, 91.88% admitted, 23% enrolled. **Transfer Admission Requirements:** college transcript(s), Minimum college GPA of 2.0 required. Lowest grade transferable C. **General Admission Information:** Application fee $30. Priority deadline 5/1. Regular application deadline 8/1. Nonfall registration accepted. Admission may be deferred for a maximum of 1 year.

COSTS AND FINANCIAL AID

Required Forms and Deadlines: FAFSA. **Notification of Awards:** Applicants will be notified of awards on a rolling basis beginning 4/1. **Types of Aid:** *Need-based scholarships/grants:* Federal Pell, FSEOG, State scholarships/grants, College/university scholarship or grant aid from institutional funds. *Loans:* Direct Subsidized Stafford Loans, Direct Unsubsidized Stafford Loans, Direct PLUS loans, Federal Perkins Loans. *Student Employment:* Federal Work-Study Program available. Institutional employment available. **Financial Aid Statistics:** 92% needy freshmen, 90% needy undergrads receive need-based scholarship or grant aid. 90% freshmen, 47% undergrads receive non-need-based scholarship or grant aid. 72% freshmen, 75% undergrads receive need-based self-help aid. 5% freshmen, 6% undergrads receive athletic scholarships. 85% freshmen, 75% undergrads receive any aid. 66% undergrads borrow to pay for school. Average cumulative indebtedness $25,589. **Criteria for awarding aid:** *Non-need-based:* Academics, Art, Athletics, Leadership, Music/drama.

See page 1104.

WESTERN UNIVERSITY

Western Student Services Bldg., RM 3140, London, ON N6A 3K7
Phone: 519-661-2100 • **Financial Aid Phone:** 519-661-2100
E-mail: reg-admissions@uwo.ca
Fax: 519-661-3710 • **Website:** www.westernu.ca • **ACT Code:** 4837

This public school was founded in 1878. It has a 1178-acre campus.

RATINGS

Admissions Selectivity Rating: 70   **Fire Safety Rating:** 80   **Green Rating:** 86

STUDENTS AND FACULTY

Student Body: (76 countries represented).
Retention and Graduation: 93% freshmen return for sophomore year. 50% freshmen graduate within 4 years. 78% freshmen graduate within 6 years.
Faculty: 1,391 full-time faculty, 0% hold PhDs, 0% are are members of minority groups, 34% are women.

ACADEMICS

Degrees: bachelor's, certificate, diploma, doctoral/research, doctoral, master's, postbachelor's certificate. **Most popular majors:** Health Services/Allied Health/Health Sciences; Business Administration and Management; Biology/Biological Sciences. **Special Study Options:** Accelerated program, cooperative education program, cross-registration, distance learning, double major, dual enrollment, English as a Second Language (ESL), exchange student program (domestic), honors program, independent study, internships, liberal arts/career combination, student-designed major, study abroad, teacher certification program. **Honors Programs:** Scholar's Electives Combined degree programs: BA/JD. **Disability Services:** Special programs offered to physically disabled students, including note-taking services, reader services, tape recorders. **Career Services:** Alumni services, Career/job search classes, Career assessment, Internships. Western Scholars: The Western Scholars program is designed for exceptional student leaders interested in pursuing a unique and rewarding academic experience. The program provides opportunities for outstanding students to learn and grow as both students and global citizens in an engaging, enriching, and inspiring environment. Through this program, students are recognized as high achievers and are provided opportunities to participate in diverse activities to enhance their university experience.

FACILITIES

Housing: Coed dorms, special housing for disabled students, men's dorms, special housing for international students, women's dorms, apartments for married students, apartments for single students. **Special Academic Facilities/Equipment:** McIntosh Gallery, Hume Cronyn Memorial Observatory, Student Recreation Centre. **Computers:** 100% of libraries, 100% of student union, have wireless network access. Students can register for classes online. Administrative functions (other than registration) can be performed online.

CAMPUS LIFE

Environment: City. **Activities:** Choral groups, concert band, dance, drama/theater, jazz band, marching band, music ensembles, musical theater, opera, pep band, radio station, student government, student newspaper, student-run film society, symphony orchestra, television station, Campus Ministries, Student Organization, Model UN. 189 registered organizations, 14 fraternities, 5 sororities. **Athletics (Intercollegiate):** *Men:* badminton, baseball, basketball, crew/rowing, cross-country, curling, fencing, football, golf, ice hockey, rugby, soccer, squash, swimming, tennis, track/field (outdoor), track/field (indoor), volleyball, water polo, wrestling. *Women:* badminton, basketball, crew/rowing, cross-country, curling, fencing, field hockey, golf, ice hockey, lacrosse, rugby, soccer, squash, swimming, tennis, track/field (outdoor), track/field (indoor), volleyball, wrestling. **On-Campus Highlights:** University Community Centre, Student Recreation Centre, TD Waterhouse Stadium, Von Kuster Hall, McIntosh Gallery, McIntosh Gallery—Oldest university art gallery in Canada. **Environmental Initiatives:** Hiring an employee dedicated to sustainability initiatives on campus.

ADMISSIONS

Freshman Academic Profile: Average high school GPA 89.3. Minimum internet-based TOEFL 83. Minimum paper TOEFL 550. **Basis for Candidate Selection:** *Very important factors considered include:* rigor of secondary school record, academic GPA, standardized test scores. *Other factors considered include:* recommendation(s), extracurricular activities, talent/ability, first generation, volunteer work, work experience. **Freshman Admission Requirements:** High school diploma is required and GED is accepted. **Freshman Admission Statistics:** 33,924 applied, 57.59% admitted, 27% enrolled. **Transfer Admission Requirements:** High school transcript, college transcript(s), Lowest grade transferable C. **General Admission Information:** Application fee $155. Priority deadline 3/1. Regular application deadline 6/1. Nonfall registration not accepted. Admission may be deferred for a maximum of 1 year.

COSTS AND FINANCIAL AID

Annual in-state tuition $6,154. Required fees $1,373. Average book expense $1,500. **Required Forms and Deadlines:** FAFSA, Institution's own financial aid form, State aid form. **Types of Aid:** *Need-based scholarships/grants:* State scholarships/grants, Private scholarships, College/university scholarship or grant aid from institutional funds. *Student Employment:* Institutional employment available. **Criteria for awarding aid:** *Need-based:* Academics, Alumni affiliation, Art, Athletics, Leadership, Minority status, Music/drama. *Non-need-based:* Academics, Alumni affiliation, Art, Athletics, Leadership, Minority status, Music/drama, State/district residency.

WESTERN WASHINGTON UNIVERSITY

Mail Stop 9009, Bellingham, WA 98225-9009
Phone: 360-650-3440 • **Financial Aid Phone:** 360-650-3470
E-mail: admit@wwu.edu • **CEEB Code:** 4947
Fax: 360-650-7369 • **Website:** http://www.wwu.edu/ • **ACT Code:** 4490

This public school was founded in 1893. It has a 300-acre campus.

RATINGS

Admissions Selectivity Rating: 80   **Fire Safety Rating:** 92   **Green Rating:** 91

STUDENTS AND FACULTY

Enrollment: 14,483. **Student Body:** 56% female, 44% male, 10% out-of-state, 1% international (30 countries represented). Asian 7%, African American 2%, Caucasian 72%, Hispanic 9%, Native American <1%, Pacific Islander <1%, Two or more races 9%, Race unknown 1%.
Retention and Graduation: 82% freshmen return for sophomore year. 40% freshmen graduate within 4 years. 70% freshmen graduate within 6 years. 12% grads go on to further study within 1 year. **Faculty:** Student/faculty ratio 19:1. 619 full-time faculty, 87% hold PhDs, 15% are are members of minority groups, 46% are women. 2% of classes are taught by teaching assistants.

ACADEMICS

Degrees: bachelor's, certificate, master's, postbachelor's certificate, post-master's certificate. **Classes:** Most classes have 20-29 students. Most lab/discussion sessions have 10-19 students. **Most popular majors:** Business Administration, Management and Operations; Social Sciences; English Language and Literature. **Special Study Options:** distance learning, double major, English as a Second Language (ESL), exchange student program (domestic), honors program, independent study, internships, student-designed major, study abroad, teacher certification program. **Honors Programs:** Honors Program features small classes and interaction between students and faculty. It is an exciting opportunity for accomplished students who would like a more intimate college experience within the setting of a larger institution. Honors students are welcome to pursue any academic major, and all students complete a self-designed capstone senior project. Combined degree programs: BS/MS Mathematics & BS/MS Computer Science. **Disability Services:** Special programs offered to physically disabled students, including note-taking services, reader services, tape recorders, tutors. **Career Services:** Alumni network, Alumni services, Career/job search classes, Career assessment, Internships, Regional alumni. Our Career Services Center places a special point of emphasis on the power of internships. Based on a 2012 national survey by Intern Bridge, Western Washington University students are more likely to engage in internship opportunities (28.1%) than the national benchmark (23.9%). According to consistent findings in our own employment survey of recent graduates, students with internship experience get hired faster, have a higher starting salary, and are more likely to work within their field of study.

FACILITIES

Housing: Coed dorms, special housing for disabled students, apartments for married students, apartments for single students, ThemeHousingWellness floors, multicultural floors available. 100% of campus accessible to physically disabled. **Special Academic Facilities/Equipment:** Outdoor art museum, planetarium, electronic music studio, air pollution lab, motor vehicle research lab, marine lab, wind tunnel, electron microscope, neutron generator lab. **Computers:** 100% of classrooms, 100% of dorms, 100% of libraries, 100% of dining areas, 100% of student union, 100% of common outdoor areas have wireless network access. Students can register for classes online. Administrative functions (other than registration) can be performed online.

CAMPUS LIFE

Environment: City. **Activities:** concert band, dance, drama/theater, jazz band, literary magazine, marching band, music ensembles, musical theater, opera, pep band, radio station, student government, student newspaper, symphony orchestra, television station, Campus Ministries, Student Organization. 200 registered organizations, 4 honor societies, 18 religious organizations. **Athletics (Intercollegiate):** *Men:* basketball, cheerleading, crew/rowing, cross-country, golf, soccer, track/field (outdoor), track/field (indoor). *Women:* basketball, cheerleading, crew/rowing, cross-country, golf, soccer, softball, track/field (outdoor), track/field (indoor), volleyball. **On-Campus Highlights:** Viking Union Student Center, Red Square, Performing Arts Center, Sehome Arboretum, Student Recreation Center. **Environmental Initiatives:** WWU Green Energy Fee The GEF pays for purchase of Renewable Energy Credits to offset 100% of WWU's CO_2 emissions from electrical energy consumption, and pays for approximately $260,000 per year of on-campus sustainability projects. Due to our purchase of Renewable Energy Credits, WWU is ranked 17th by the EPA for largest higher ed. purchase of renewable energy in the US. This year's projects include a $167,000 solar array, high-speed hand driers, conversion of parking lot lights to high-efficiency LEDs, a paper towel composting system, and water bottle refilling stations.

ADMISSIONS

Freshman Academic Profile: Average high school GPA 3.4. 22% in top 10% of high school class, 56% in top 25% of high school class, 89% in top 50% of high school class. 89% from public high schools. **Reported SAT (pre-2016 redesign) scores:** SAT Math middle 50% range 490-600. SAT Critical Reading middle 50% range 500-620. SAT Writing middle 50% range 470-590. **Concordant SAT scores:** SAT EBRW middle 50% 540–660. SAT Math middle 50% range 520–620. ACT middle 50% range 23-28. Minimum internet-based TOEFL 80. Minimum paper TOEFL 550. **Basis for Candidate Selection:** *Very important factors considered include:* rigor of secondary school record. *Important factors considered include:* academic GPA, standardized test scores, application essay, level of applicant's interest. *Other factors considered include:* class rank, recommendation(s), extracurricular activities, talent/ability, character/personal qualities, first generation, alumni/ae relation, geographical residence, state residency, volunteer work, work experience. **Freshman Admission Requirements:** High school diploma is required and GED is accepted. *Academic units required:* 4 English, 3 math, 2 science, 1 science lab, 2 foreign language, 3 social studies. **Freshman Admission Statistics:** 10,519 applied, 83.12% admitted, 33% enrolled. **Transfer Admission Requirements:** college transcript(s), statement of good standing from prior institution(s). Minimum college GPA of 2.0 required. Lowest grade transferable D-. **General Admission Information:** Application fee $55. Regular application deadline 1/31. Nonfall registration accepted. Admission may be deferred for a maximum of 1 year.

COSTS AND FINANCIAL AID

Required Forms and Deadlines: FAFSA. **Notification of Awards:** Applicants will be notified of awards on a rolling basis beginning 3/20. **Types of Aid:** *Need-based scholarships/grants:* Federal Pell, FSEOG, State scholarships/grants, Private scholarships, College/university scholarship or grant aid from institutional funds. *Loans:* Direct Subsidized Stafford Loans, Direct Unsubsidized Stafford Loans, Direct PLUS loans, Federal Perkins Loans, State Loans, College/university loans from institutional funds. *Student Employment:* Institutional employment available. **Financial Aid Statistics:** 85% needy freshmen, 77% needy undergrads receive need-based scholarship or grant aid. 9% freshmen, 4% undergrads receive non-need-based scholarship or grant aid. 74% freshmen, 81% undergrads receive need-based self-help aid. 0% freshmen, 1% undergrads receive athletic scholarships. 54% freshmen, 49% undergrads receive any aid. 55% undergrads borrow to pay for school. Average cumulative indebtedness $19,727. **Criteria for awarding aid:** *Need-based:* Academics, Leadership. *Non-need-based:* Academics, Alumni affiliation, Art, Athletics, Job skills, Leadership, Minority status, Music/drama, State/district residency.

WESTFIELD STATE UNIVERSITY

Westfield State University, Westfield, MA 1086
Phone: 413-572-5218 • **Financial Aid Phone:** 413-572-5218
E-mail: admissions@westfield.ma.edu • **CEEB Code:** 3523
Fax: 413-572-0520 • **Website:** www.westfield.ma.edu • **ACT Code:** 1912

This public school was founded in 1838. It has a 227-acre campus.

RATINGS

Admissions Selectivity Rating: 74   **Fire Safety Rating:** 87   **Green Rating:** 79

STUDENTS AND FACULTY

Enrollment: 5,474. **Student Body:** 54% female, 46% male, 7% out-of-state, <1% international (17 countries represented). Asian 2%, African American 5%, Caucasian 76%, Hispanic 9%, Native American <1%, Pacific Islander <1%, Two or more races 5%, Race unknown 3%.
Retention and Graduation: 77% freshmen return for sophomore year. 53% freshmen graduate within 4 years. 66% freshmen graduate within 6 years.
Faculty: Student/faculty ratio 17:1. 234 full-time faculty, 90% hold PhDs, 16% are members of minority groups, 49% are women. 0% of classes are taught by teaching assistants.

ACADEMICS

Degrees: bachelor's, master's, postbachelor's certificate, post-master's certificate. **Classes:** Most classes have 20-29 students. Most lab/discussion sessions have 10-19 students. **Most popular majors:** Criminal Justice/Safety Studies; Business/Commerce; Liberal Arts and Sciences/Liberal Studies. **Special Study Options:** cooperative education program, cross-registration, distance learning, double major, dual enrollment, exchange student program (domestic), honors program, independent study, internships, student-designed major, study abroad, teacher certification program. **Disability Services:** Special programs offered

to physically disabled students, including note-taking services, reader services, tape recorders, tutors. **Career Services:** Alumni network, Alumni services, Career/job search classes, Career assessment, Internships, Career fairs, Career panels, Professional Networking Nights, GRE and LSAT workshops.

FACILITIES

Housing: Coed dorms, special housing for disabled students, apartments for single students, Living/Learning Unit (Honors/Academic Intensive), Quiet Living Section, All Women Section, Designated smoking Section (other housing smoke free), Movement Science, Student Section. 75% of campus accessible to physically diasbled. **Special Academic Facilities/Equipment:** Art gallery, language lab, electron microscope.

CAMPUS LIFE

Environment: Village. **Activities:** Choral groups, concert band, drama/theater, jazz band, literary magazine, music ensembles, musical theater, pep band, radio station, student government, student newspaper, television station, yearbook. **Athletics (Intercollegiate):** *Men:* baseball, basketball, cross-country, football, golf, soccer, track/field (outdoor). *Women:* basketball, cheerleading, cross-country, field hockey, soccer, softball, swimming, volleyball. **Environmental Initiatives:** RecycleMania: participated in the targeted paper competition in 2015.

ADMISSIONS

Freshman Academic Profile: Average high school GPA 3.1. 8% in top 10% of high school class, 27% in top 25% of high school class, 61% in top 50% of high school class. **Reported SAT (pre-2016 redesign) scores:** SAT Math middle 50% range 450-550. SAT Critical Reading middle 50% range 440-540. SAT Writing middle 50% range 430-530. **Concordant SAT scores:** SAT EBRW middle 50% 490–590. SAT Math middle 50% range 490–570. ACT middle 50% range 19-24. Minimum internet-based TOEFL 79. Minimum paper TOEFL 550. **Basis for Candidate Selection:** *Very important factors considered include:* rigor of secondary school record, academic GPA, standardized test scores. *Other factors considered include:* application essay, recommendation(s), extracurricular activities, talent/ability, character/personal qualities, volunteer work, work experience, level of applicant's interest. **Freshman Admission Requirements:** High school diploma is required and GED is accepted. *Academic units required:* 4 English, 4 math, 3 science, 2 science labs, 2 foreign language, 1 social studies, 1 history, 2 academic electives. **Freshman Admission Statistics:** 5,484 applied, 79.56% admitted, 24% enrolled. **Transfer Admission Requirements:** college transcript(s), Minimum college GPA of 2.0 required. Lowest grade transferable C-. **General Admission Information:** Application fee $50. Regular application deadline 3/1. Regular notification 3/15. Nonfall registration accepted. Admission may be deferred for a maximum of 1 semester.

COSTS AND FINANCIAL AID

Annual in-state tuition $970. Annual out-of-state tuition $7,050. Room and board $10,396. Required fees $8,305. Average book expense $1,006. **Required Forms and Deadlines:** FAFSA. **Notification of Awards:** Applicants will be notified of awards on a rolling basis beginning 4/1. **Types of Aid:** *Need-based scholarships/grants:* Federal Pell, FSEOG, State scholarships/grants, Private scholarships, College/university scholarship or grant aid from institutional funds. *Loans:* Direct Subsidized Stafford Loans, Direct Unsubsidized Stafford Loans, Direct PLUS loans, Federal Perkins Loans. *Student Employment:* Federal Work-Study Program available. Institutional employment available. **Financial Aid Statistics:** 70% needy freshmen, 69% needy undergrads receive need-based scholarship or grant aid. 33% freshmen, 25% undergrads receive non-need-based scholarship or grant aid. 87% freshmen, 97% undergrads receive need-based self-help aid. 0% freshmen, 0% undergrads receive athletic scholarships. 62% freshmen, 57% undergrads receive any aid. Average cumulative indebtedness $29,602. **Criteria for awarding aid:** *Non-need-based:* Academics.

WESTMINSTER COLLEGE

Best Colleges

1840 South 1300 East, Salt Lake City, UT 54105
Phone: 801-832-2200 • **Financial Aid Phone:** 801-832-2502
E-mail: admission@westminstercollege.edu • **CEEB Code:** 4948
Fax: 801-832-3101 • **Website:** www.westminstercollege.edu • **ACT Code:** 4284

This private school was founded in 1875. It has a 27-acre campus.

RATINGS

Admissions Selectivity Rating: 79   **Fire Safety Rating:** 95   **Green Rating:** 91

STUDENTS AND FACULTY

Enrollment: 2,095. **Student Body:** 57% female, 43% male, 40% out-of-state, 5% international (23 countries represented). Asian 3%, African American 2%, Caucasian 71%, Hispanic 10%, Native American 1%, Pacific Islander <1%, Two or more races 4%, Race unknown 4%.
Retention and Graduation: 79% freshmen return for sophomore year. 49% freshmen graduate within 4 years. 62% freshmen graduate within 6 years. 11% grads go on to further study within 1 year. 3% grads pursue arts and sciences degrees. 1% grads pursue law degrees. 2% grads pursue business degrees. 1% grads pursue medical degrees. **Faculty:** Student/faculty ratio 9:1. 154 full-time faculty, 94% hold PhDs, 11% are are members of minority groups, 51% are women. 0% of classes are taught by teaching assistants.

ACADEMICS

Degrees: bachelor's, master's, postbachelor's certificate. **Classes:** Most classes have 10-19 students. Most lab/discussion sessions have 10-19 students. **Most popular majors:** Health Services/Allied Health/Health Sciences; Business/Commerce; Social Sciences. **Special Study Options:** Accelerated program, cooperative education program, distance learning, double major, dual enrollment, English as a Second Language (ESL), honors program, independent study, internships, liberal arts/career combination, student-designed major, study abroad, teacher certification program, weekend college. **Honors Programs:** http://www.westminstercollege.edu/honors/. **Disability Services:** Special programs offered to physically disabled students, including note-taking services, reader services, tape recorders, tutors. **Career Services:** Alumni network, Alumni services, Career/job search classes, Career assessment, Internships. The Westminster College internship program provides students of all majors with a range of credit and experience opportunities. A limited number of internship stipends are also available for non-profit internship experiences.

FACILITIES

Housing: Coed dorms, men's dorms, women's dorms, apartments for single students. 98% of campus accessible to physically diasbled. **Special Academic Facilities/Equipment:** Emma Ecceles Jones Conservatory, Gore school of Business, Giovale Library, Dick Science Building, Climbing Wall, Converse Hall, Dolores Dore Eccles Health, Wellness, and Athletic Center **Computers:** 100% of classrooms, 100% of dorms, 100% of libraries, 100% of dining areas, 100% of student union, 25% of common outdoor areas have wireless network access. Students can register for classes online. Administrative functions (other than registration) can be performed online.

CAMPUS LIFE

Environment: Metropolis. **Activities:** Choral groups, dance, drama/theater, jazz band, literary magazine, music ensembles, musical theater, student government, student newspaper, student-run film society, symphony orchestra, Campus Ministries, Student Organization. 55 registered organizations, 4 honor societies, 4 religious organizations. **Athletics (Intercollegiate):** *Men:* basketball, cross-country, golf, lacrosse, skiing (downhill/alpine), snowboarding, soccer, track/field (outdoor), track/field (indoor). *Women:* basketball, cross-country, golf, lacrosse, skiing (downhill/alpine), snowboarding, soccer, track/field (outdoor), track/field (indoor), volleyball. **On-Campus Highlights:** Shaw Student Center, Giovale Library, Emma Eccles Jones Conservatory, Dolores Dore Eccles Health, Wellness, and Athletic, Residential Village. **Environmental Initiatives:** With guidance from the Environmental Center, students completed the STARS assessment in 2010, achieving a Silver rating. Westminster scored particularly well in co-curricular and curricular sustainability efforts.

ADMISSIONS

Freshman Academic Profile: Average high school GPA 3.5. 19% in top 10% of high school class, 52% in top 25% of high school class, 84% in top 50% of high school class. **Reported SAT (pre-2016 redesign) scores:** SAT Math middle 50% range 500-600. SAT Critical Reading middle 50% range 500-610. **Concordant SAT scores:** SAT Math middle 50% range 530–620. ACT middle 50% range 22-27. Minimum internet-based TOEFL 79. Minimum paper TOEFL 550. **Basis for Candidate Selection:** *Very important factors considered include:* rigor of secondary school record, academic GPA. *Important factors considered include:* class rank, standardized test scores, application essay, interview. *Other factors considered include:* recommendation(s), extracurricular activities, talent/ability, character/personal qualities, alumni/ae relation, geographical residence, volunteer work, work experience. **Freshman Admission Requirements:** High school diploma is required and GED is accepted. *Academic units required:* 4 English, 2 math, 3 science, 2 foreign language, 2 social studies, 1 history, 2 academic electives. *Academic units recommended:* 4 English, 3 math, 3 science, 3 foreign language, 2 social studies, 1 history, 3 academic electives. **Freshman Admission Statistics:** 1,938 applied, 93.91% admitted, 24% enrolled. **Transfer Admission Requirements:** High school transcript, college transcript(s), essay or personal statement, Minimum college GPA of 2.5 required. Lowest grade transferable C-. **General Admission Information:** Application fee $50. Priority deadline 2/1. Regular application deadline 8/16. Nonfall registration accepted. Admission may be deferred for a maximum of 2 years.

COSTS AND FINANCIAL AID

Annual tuition $31,584. Room and board $9,618. Required fees $520. Average book expense $1,000. **Required Forms and Deadlines:** FAFSA. **Notification of Awards:** Applicants will be notified of awards on a rolling basis beginning 3/1. **Types of Aid:** *Need-based scholarships/grants:* Federal Pell, FSEOG, State scholarships/grants, Private scholarships, College/university scholarship or grant aid from institutional funds. *Loans:* Direct Subsidized Stafford Loans, Direct Unsubsidized Stafford Loans, Direct PLUS loans, Federal Perkins Loans. *Student Employment:* Federal Work-Study Program available. Institutional employment available. **Financial Aid Statistics:** 100% needy freshmen, 99% needy undergrads receive need-based scholarship or grant aid. 15% freshmen, 13% undergrads receive non-need-based scholarship or grant aid. 86% freshmen, 86% undergrads receive need-based self-help aid. 3% freshmen, 4% undergrads receive athletic scholarships. 99% freshmen, 93% undergrads receive any aid. 59% undergrads borrow to pay for school. Average cumulative indebtedness $30,442. **Criteria for awarding aid:** *Need-based:* Academics, Alumni affiliation, Art, Leadership, Religious affiliation. *Non-need-based:* Academics, Alumni affiliation, Art, Athletics, Leadership, Minority status, Music/drama.

WESTMINSTER COLLEGE (MO)

Champ Auditorium, Westminster College, Fulton, MO 65251
Phone: 573-592-5251 • **Financial Aid Phone:** 800-475-3361
E-mail: admissions@westminster-mo.edu • **CEEB Code:** 6937
Fax: 573-592-5255 • **Website:** http://www.westminster-mo.edu/
ACT Code: 2392

This private school, affiliated with the Presbyterian Church, was founded in 1851. It has a 86-acre campus.

RATINGS

Admissions Selectivity Rating: 81   **Fire Safety Rating:** 87   **Green Rating:** 60*

STUDENTS AND FACULTY

Enrollment: 930. **Student Body:** 43% female, 57% male, 19% out-of-state, 15% international (69 countries represented). Asian 0%, African American 9%, Caucasian 65%, Hispanic 3%, Native American 2%, Pacific Islander 1%, Two or more races 1%, Race unknown 2%.
Retention and Graduation: 83% freshmen return for sophomore year. 48% freshmen graduate within 4 years. 66% freshmen graduate within 6 years. 30% grads go on to further study within 1 year. 10% grads pursue arts and sciences degrees. 4% grads pursue law degrees. 6% grads pursue business degrees. 3% grads pursue medical degrees. **Faculty:** Student/faculty ratio 14:1. 61 full-time faculty, 89% hold PhDs, 7% are are members of minority groups, 41% are women. 0% of classes are taught by teaching assistants.

ACADEMICS

Degrees: bachelor's. **Classes:** Most classes have 10-19 students. **Most popular majors:** Biology/Biological Sciences; Political Science and Government; Business/Commerce. **Special Study Options:** cooperative education program, cross-registration, double major, dual enrollment, exchange student program (domestic), honors program, independent study, internships, liberal arts/career combination, student-designed major, study abroad, teacher certification program, Urban Studies Program (Chicago). Other off-campus study opportunities supported through Office of International Programs. Coursework and certification are also available through the Center of Leadership and the Remley Women's Center. Combined degree programs: BA/MEng, BA/BSN Barnes Jewish College; BA/MEng—University of Missouri-Columbia; 3+3 with Logan University of Chiropractic. **Disability Services:** Special programs offered to physically disabled students, including note-taking services, reader services, tape recorders, tutors. **Career Services:** Alumni services, Career/job search classes, Career assessment, Internships, Regional alumni.

FACILITIES

Housing: Coed dorms, special housing for disabled students, men's dorms, women's dorms, fraternity/sorority housing, apartments for single students, Theme Housing. 70% of campus accessible to physically disabled. **Special Academic Facilities/Equipment:** Winston Churchill Memorial Museum, Coulter Science Center, language lab, NMR spectrometer, laser equipment. **Computers:** 100% of classrooms, 100% of libraries, 100% of dining areas, 100% of student union, 40% of common outdoor areas have wireless network access. Students can register for classes online. Administrative functions (other than registration) can be performed online.

CAMPUS LIFE

Environment: Village. **Activities:** Choral groups, dance, drama/theater, literary magazine, music ensembles, pep band, student government, student newspaper, yearbook, Campus Ministries, Student Organization, Model UN. 49 registered organizations, 15 honor societies, 2 religious organizations. 6 fraternities, 3 sororities. **Athletics (Intercollegiate):** *Men:* baseball, basketball, cheerleading, cross-country, football, golf, soccer, tennis, track/field (outdoor). *Women:* basketball, cheerleading, cross-country, golf, soccer, softball, tennis, track/field (outdoor), volleyball. **On-Campus Highlights:** Coulter Science Center, Johnson College Inn (student center), Hunter Activity Center, Library, Wetterau Athletic Facility.

ADMISSIONS

Freshman Academic Profile: Average high school GPA 3.4. 21% in top 10% of high school class, 40% in top 25% of high school class, 75% in top 50% of high school class. 70% from public high schools. **Reported SAT (pre-2016 redesign) scores:** SAT Math middle 50% range 530-615. SAT Critical Reading middle 50% range 428-535. SAT Writing middle 50% range 443-523. **Concordant SAT scores:** SAT EBRW middle 50% 490–590. SAT Math middle 50% range 560–640. ACT middle 50% range 21-26. Minimum paper TOEFL 550. **Basis for Candidate Selection:** *Very important factors considered include:* rigor of secondary school record, standardized test scores, character/personal qualities. *Important factors considered include:* class rank, academic GPA, recommendation(s), extracurricular activities, volunteer work. *Other factors considered include:* application essay, interview, talent/ability, alumni/ae relation, work experience. **Freshman Admission Requirements:** High school diploma is required and GED is accepted. *Academic units required:* 4 English, 3 math, 2 science, 2 science labs. *Academic units recommended:* 2 foreign language, 2 social studies, 2 academic electives. **Freshman Admission Statistics:** 1,789 applied, 63.67% admitted, 21% enrolled. **Transfer Admission Requirements:** college transcript(s), Lowest grade transferable C. **General Admission Information:** Nonfall registration accepted. Admission may be deferred.

COSTS AND FINANCIAL AID

Annual tuition $23,200. Room and board $9,480. Required fees $1,340. Average book expense $1,100. **Required Forms and Deadlines:** FAFSA. **Notification of Awards:** Applicants will be notified of awards on a rolling basis beginning 3/15. **Types of Aid:** *Need-based scholarships/grants:* Federal Pell, FSEOG, State scholarships/grants, Private scholarships, College/university scholarship or grant aid from institutional funds. *Loans:* Direct Subsidized Stafford Loans, Direct Unsubsidized Stafford Loans, Direct PLUS loans, Federal Perkins Loans. *Student Employment:* Federal Work-Study Program available. Institutional employment available. **Financial Aid Statistics:** 100% needy freshmen, 100% needy undergrads receive need-based scholarship or grant aid. 0% undergrads receive non-need-based scholarship or grant aid. 88% freshmen, 88% undergrads receive need-based self-help aid. 0% freshmen, 0% undergrads receive athletic scholarships. 100% freshmen, 98% undergrads receive any aid. 17% undergrads borrow to pay for school. Average cumulative indebtedness $29,573. **Criteria for awarding aid:** *Non-need-based:* Academics, Alumni affiliation, Leadership, Minority status, Music/drama, Religious affiliation.

WESTMINSTER COLLEGE (PA)

319 South Market Street, New Wilmington, PA 16172
Phone: 724-946-7100 • **Financial Aid Phone:** 724-946-6171
E-mail: admis@westminster.edu • **CEEB Code:** 2975
Fax: 724-946-7171 • **Website:** www.westminster.edu • **ACT Code:** 2975

This private school, affiliated with the Presbyterian Church, was founded in 1852. It has a 350-acre campus.

RATINGS

Admissions Selectivity Rating: 76   **Fire Safety Rating:** 97   **Green Rating:** 60*

STUDENTS AND FACULTY

Enrollment: 1,148. **Student Body:** 54% female, 46% male, 1% international (1 countries represented). Asian 1%, African American 5%, Caucasian 71%, Hispanic 1%, Native American <1%, Pacific Islander 0%, Two or more races 2%, Race unknown 18%.
Retention and Graduation: 83% freshmen return for sophomore year. 71% freshmen graduate within 6 years. 21% grads go on to further study within 1 year. 3% grads pursue law degrees. 2% grads pursue business degrees. 3% grads pursue medical degrees. **Faculty:** Student/faculty ratio 11:1. 90 full-time faculty, 93% hold PhDs, 3% are are members of minority groups, 48% are women. 0% of classes are taught by teaching assistants.

ACADEMICS

Degrees: bachelor's, master's. **Classes:** Most classes have 10-19 students. Most lab/discussion sessions have 10-19 students. **Most popular majors:** Education; Biology/Biological Sciences; Business Administration and Management. **Special Study Options:** double major, exchange student program (domestic), honors program, independent study, internships, liberal arts/career combination, student-designed major, study abroad, teacher certification program. Combined degree programs: BA/MA. **Disability Services:** Special programs offered to physically disabled students, including tutors. **Career Services:** Alumni network, Alumni services, Career/job search classes, Career assessment, Internships, Regional alumni. The College facilitate excellent internships in many settings and locations across the country, with particular strengths in Pittsburgh, Cleveland, and Washington, DC. Several academic majors require an internship.

FACILITIES

Housing: special housing for disabled students, men's dorms, women's dorms, fraternity/sorority housing. We offer townhouses for upperclass men and women. 90% of campus accessible to physically disabled. **Special Academic Facilities/Equipment:** On-campus preschool, Moeller pipe organs, planetarium, observatory, electron microscopes, X-ray diffractor, spectrometer. **Computers:** Administrative functions (other than registration) can be performed online.

CAMPUS LIFE

Environment: Village. **Activities:** Choral groups, concert band, dance, drama/theater, jazz band, literary magazine, marching band, music ensembles, musical theater, pep band, radio station, student government, student newspaper, television station, yearbook. 60 registered organizations, 21 honor societies, 3 religious organizations. 5 fraternities, 5 sororities. **Athletics (Intercollegiate):** *Men:* baseball, basketball, cheerleading, cross-country, football, golf, soccer, swimming, tennis, track/field (outdoor), track/field (indoor). *Women:* basketball, cheerleading, cross-country, golf, soccer, softball, swimming, tennis, track/field (outdoor), track/field (indoor), volleyball.

ADMISSIONS

Freshman Academic Profile: Average high school GPA 3.5. 22% in top 10% of high school class, 42% in top 25% of high school class, 75% in top 50% of high school class. 90% from public high schools. **Reported SAT (pre-2016 redesign) scores:** SAT Math middle 50% range 460-570. SAT Critical Reading middle 50% range 460-570. SAT Writing middle 50% range 430-550. **Concordant SAT scores:** SAT EBRW middle 50% 500–620. SAT Math middle 50% range 500–590. ACT middle 50% range 20-26. Minimum internet-based TOEFL 79. Minimum paper TOEFL 550. **Basis for Candidate Selection:** *Very important factors considered include:* rigor of secondary school record, standardized test scores, interview. *Important factors considered include:* class rank, application essay, recommendation(s), character/personal qualities. *Other factors considered include:* extracurricular activities, talent/ability, alumni/ae relation, racial/ethnic status, volunteer work, work experience. **Freshman Admission Requirements:** High school diploma is required and GED is accepted. *Academic units required:* 4 English, 3 math, 2 science, 2 science labs, 2 foreign language, 2 social studies, 1 history, 3 academic electives. **Freshman Admission Statistics:** 2,125 applied, 91.15% admitted, 19% enrolled. **Transfer Admission Requirements:** High school transcript, college transcript(s), essay or personal statement, interview, standardized test scores, Minimum college GPA of 2.5 required. Lowest grade transferable c. **General Admission Information:** Application fee $35. Regular application deadline 5/1. Nonfall registration not accepted. Admission may be deferred for a maximum of 1 year.

COSTS AND FINANCIAL AID

Annual tuition $34,830. Room and board $11,020. Required fees $1,400. Average book expense $1,700. **Required Forms and Deadlines:** FAFSA, Institution's own financial aid form. **Notification of Awards:** Applicants will be notified of awards on a rolling basis beginning 3/1. **Types of Aid:** *Need-based scholarships/grants:* Federal Pell, FSEOG, State scholarships/grants, Private scholarships, College/university scholarship or grant aid from institutional funds. *Loans:* Direct Subsidized Stafford Loans, Direct Unsubsidized Stafford Loans, Direct PLUS loans, Federal Perkins Loans. *Student Employment:* Federal Work-Study Program available. Institutional employment available. **Financial Aid Statistics:** 100% needy freshmen, 99% needy undergrads receive need-based scholarship or grant aid. 99% freshmen, 97% undergrads receive non-need-based scholarship or grant aid. 79% freshmen, 81% undergrads receive need-based self-help aid. 0% freshmen, 0% undergrads receive athletic scholarships. **Criteria for awarding aid:** *Need-based:* Academics. *Non-need-based:* Academics, Alumni affiliation, Leadership, Minority status, Music/drama, Religious affiliation, State/district residency.

WESTMONT COLLEGE

955 La Paz Road, Santa Barbara, CA 93108
Phone: 805-565-6200 • **Financial Aid Phone:** 888-963-4624
E-mail: admissions@westmont.edu • **CEEB Code:** 4950
Fax: 805-565-6234 • **Website:** www.westmont.edu • **ACT Code:** 478

This private school, affiliated with the Christian (Nondenominational) Church, was founded in 1937. It has a 133-acre campus.

RATINGS

Admissions Selectivity Rating: 85   **Fire Safety Rating:** 60*   **Green Rating:** 60*

STUDENTS AND FACULTY

Enrollment: 985. **Student Body:** 61% female, 39% male, 25% out-of-state, 1% international (8 countries represented). Asian 6%, African American 1%, Caucasian 67%, Hispanic 12%, Native American <1%, Pacific Islander 1%, Two or more races 8%, Race unknown 4%.
Retention and Graduation: 85% freshmen return for sophomore year. 72% freshmen graduate within 4 years. **Faculty:** Student/faculty ratio 11:1. 96 full-time faculty, 90% hold PhDs, 13% are are members of minority groups, 39% are women. 0% of classes are taught by teaching assistants.

ACADEMICS

Degrees: bachelor's, postbachelor's certificate. **Classes:** Most classes have 10-19 students. Most lab/discussion sessions have 10-19 students. **Most popular majors:** English/Language Arts Teacher Education; Cell/Cellular and Molecular Biology. **Special Study Options:** Accelerated program, double major, exchange student program (domestic), honors program, independent study, internships, student-designed major, study abroad, teacher certification program. **Honors Programs:** Some general education courses are designated as honors courses. Combined degree programs: 3/2 Engineering Program. **Disability Services:** Special programs offered to physically disabled students, including note-taking services, reader services, tape recorders, tutors. **Career Services:** Career/job search classes, Career assessment, Internships, On-campus interviews.

FACILITIES

Housing: Coed dorms, apartments for single students, The Coed dorms. are segregated by floors and/or suites. Men and women do not share hallways and bathrooms. There are selected visiting hours for members of the opposite sex. 65% of campus accessible to physically diasbled. **Special Academic Facilities/Equipment:** Reynolds Art Gallery features the gallery, art studios and classrooms; Carroll Observatory houses a 24-inch reflector telescope; Mericos Whittier Science facility includes state of the art technical equipment such as ultracentrifuge, Fouriertransform NMR spectrometer, etc., as well as the pre-med center; Voskuyl Library holds over 150,000 bound volumes; the physics department is developing advanced experiments for the lab; Ellen Porter Hall of Fine Arts showcases ten to twenty live musical and theatrical performances each year; Physiology Lab and Fithess Center for Kinesiology studies. **Computers:** Administrative functions (other than registration) can be performed online.

CAMPUS LIFE

Environment: City. **Activities:** Choral groups, dance, drama/theater, jazz band, literary magazine, music ensembles, musical theater, radio station, student government, student newspaper, student-run film society, symphony orchestra, yearbook, Campus Ministries. 50 registered organizations, 7 honor societies, 40 religious organizations. **Athletics (Intercollegiate):** *Men:* baseball, basketball, cross-country, soccer, tennis, track/field (outdoor). *Women:* basketball, cross-country, soccer, tennis, track/field (outdoor), volleyball.

ADMISSIONS

Freshman Academic Profile: Average high school GPA 3.8. 29% in top 10% of high school class, 66% in top 25% of high school class, 94% in top 50% of high school class. 70% from public high schools. **Reported SAT (pre-2016 redesign) scores:** SAT Math middle 50% range 540-660. SAT Critical Reading middle 50% range 520-650. SAT Writing middle 50% range 520-650. **Concordant SAT scores:** SAT EBRW middle 50% 580-700. SAT Math middle 50% range 570-690. ACT middle 50% range 24-29. Minimum paper TOEFL 560. **Basis for Candidate Selection:** *Very important factors considered include:* academic GPA, standardized test scores, character/personal qualities. *Important factors considered include:* rigor of secondary school record, application essay, recommendation(s), interview, extracurricular activities, talent/ability, religious affiliation/commitment, level of applicant's interest. *Other factors considered include:* class rank, first generation, alumni/ae relation, geographical residence, racial/ethnic status, volunteer work, work experience. **Freshman Admission Requirements:** High school diploma is required and GED is accepted. *Academic units required:* 4 English, 3 math, 3 science, 2 science labs, 2 foreign language, 1 social studies, 1 history, 2 academic electives. *Academic units recommended:* 3 foreign language, 4 academic electives. **Freshman Admission Statistics:** 2,145 applied, 70.16% admitted, 20% enrolled. **Transfer Admission Requirements:** High school transcript, college transcript(s), essay or personal statement, statement of good standing from prior institution(s). Lowest grade transferable C-. **General Admission Information:** Application fee $40. Priority deadline 2/15. Regular application deadline 8/15. Nonfall registration accepted.

COSTS AND FINANCIAL AID

Annual tuition $38,960. Room and board $12,580. Required fees $1,030. Average book expense $1,600. **Required Forms and Deadlines:** FAFSA, Institution's own financial aid form. **Notification of Awards:** Applicants will be notified of awards on a rolling basis beginning 4/1. **Types of Aid:** *Need-based scholarships/grants:* Federal Pell, FSEOG, State scholarships/grants, Private scholarships, College/university scholarship or grant aid from institutional funds. *Loans:* Direct Subsidized Stafford Loans, Direct Unsubsidized Stafford Loans, Direct PLUS loans, Federal Perkins Loans, College/university loans from institutional funds. *Student Employment:* Federal Work-Study Program available. Institutional employment available. **Financial Aid Statistics:** 99% needy freshmen, 99% needy undergrads receive need-based scholarship or grant aid. 11% freshmen, 12% undergrads receive non-need-based scholarship or grant aid. 98% freshmen, 88% undergrads receive need-based self-help aid. 6% undergrads receive athletic scholarships. 85% undergrads receive any aid. **Criteria for awarding aid:** *Non-need-based:* Academics, Art, Athletics, Music/drama.

WHEATON COLLEGE (IL)

501 College Avenue, Wheaton, IL 60187
Phone: 630-752-5011 • **Financial Aid Phone:** 630-752-5021
E-mail: admissions@wheaton.edu • **CEEB Code:** 1905
Fax: 630-752-5285 • **Website:** www.wheaton.edu • **ACT Code:** 1160

This private school was founded in 1860. It has a 80-acre campus.

RATINGS

Admissions Selectivity Rating: 89   **Fire Safety Rating:** 94   **Green Rating:** 70 ·

STUDENTS AND FACULTY

Enrollment: 2,432. **Student Body:** 53% female, 47% male, 73% out-of-state, 3% international (38 countries represented). Asian 9%, African American 3%, Caucasian 75%, Hispanic 6%, Native American <1%, Pacific Islander 0%, Two or more races 4%, Race unknown <1%.
Retention and Graduation: 95% freshmen return for sophomore year. 82% freshmen graduate within 4 years. 91 23% grads go on to further study within 1 year. 15% grads pursue arts and sciences degrees. 3% grads pursue law degrees. 1% grads pursue business degrees. 6% grads pursue medical degrees. **Faculty:** Student/faculty ratio 11:1. 215 full-time faculty, 95% hold PhDs, 14% are are members of minority groups, 35% are women. 0% of classes are taught by teaching assistants.

ACADEMICS

Degrees: bachelor's, doctoral/professional, doctoral/research, master's, postbachelor's certificate. **Classes:** Most classes have 10-19 students. Most lab/discussion sessions have 10-19 students. **Most popular majors:** English Language and Literature; Business/Managerial Economics; Biology/Biological Sciences. **Special Study Options:** cross-registration, double major, exchange student program (domestic), independent study, internships, liberal arts/career combination, student-designed major, study abroad, teacher certification program. **Honors Programs:** Some departments offer qualified students to submit an honors project. Combined degree programs: Liberal Arts/Engineering; Liberal Arts/Nursing. **Disability Services:** Special programs offered to physically disabled students, including note-taking services, reader services, tape recorders, tutors. **Career Services:** Alumni network, Alumni services, Career/job search classes, Career assessment, Internships, Regional alumni.

FACILITIES

Housing: Coed dorms, men's dorms, women's dorms, apartments for married students, cooperative housing, apartments for single students, Housing for disabled provided as needed. 97% of campus accessible to physically disabled. **Special Academic Facilities/Equipment:** World evangelism museum, language lab, observatory, Collection of works/papers of seven British authors, Billy Graham Center Museum **Computers:** 10% of classrooms, 100% of dorms, 100% of libraries, 100% of dining areas, 100% of student union, 75% of common outdoor areas have wireless network access. Students can register for classes online. Administrative functions (other than registration) can be performed online.

CAMPUS LIFE

Environment: Town. **Activities:** Choral groups, concert band, dance, drama/theater, jazz band, literary magazine, music ensembles, musical theater, opera, pep band, radio station, student government, student newspaper, student-run film society, symphony orchestra, television station, yearbook, Campus Ministries, Student Organization, Model UN. 85 registered organizations, 13 honor societies, 12 religious organizations. **Athletics (Intercollegiate):** *Men:* baseball, basketball, cross-country, football, golf, soccer, swimming, tennis, track/field (outdoor), track/field (indoor), wrestling. *Women:* basketball, cross-country, golf, soccer, softball, swimming, tennis, track/field (outdoor), track/field (indoor), volleyball, water polo. **On-Campus Highlights:** Billy Graham Center—archive, museum, Wade Center—collection of English auth, New Science Building opens Fall 2010, Todd M. Beamer Student Center, J. Dennis Hastert Center. **Environmental Initiatives:** Environmental Science Major.

ADMISSIONS

Freshman Academic Profile: Average high school GPA 3.7. 48% in top 10% of high school class, 76% in top 25% of high school class, 94% in top 50% of high school class. 45% from public high schools. **Reported SAT (pre-2016 redesign) scores:** SAT Math middle 50% range 580-690. SAT Critical Reading middle 50% range 590-710. SAT Writing middle 50% range 570-680. **Concordant SAT scores:** SAT EBRW middle 50% 640–730. SAT Math middle 50% range 600–720. ACT middle 50% range 27-32. Minimum internet-based TOEFL 95. Minimum paper TOEFL 587. **Basis for Candidate Selection:** *Very important factors considered include:* rigor of secondary school record, academic GPA, standardized test scores, application essay, recommendation(s), interview, character/personal qualities, religious affiliation/commitment. *Important factors considered include:* extracurricular activities, talent/ability, volunteer work, work experience. *Other factors considered include:* class rank, first generation, alumni/ae relation, geographical residence, state residency, racial/ethnic status, level of applicant's interest. **Freshman Admission Requirements:** High school diploma is required and GED is accepted. *Academic units required:* 4 English, 3 math, 3 science, 2 foreign language, 3 social studies. *Academic units recommended:* 4 English, 4 math, 4 science, 3 foreign language, 4 social studies. **Freshman Admission Statistics:** 1,850 applied, 78.65% admitted, 40% enrolled. **Transfer Admission Requirements:** High school transcript, college transcript(s), essay or personal statement, Minimum college GPA of 3.0 required. Lowest grade transferable C-. **General Admission Information:** Application fee $50. Regular application deadline 1/10. Regular notification 4/1. Nonfall registration accepted. Admission may be deferred for a maximum of 1 year.

COSTS AND FINANCIAL AID

Annual tuition $34,050. Room and board $9,560. Average book expense $800. **Required Forms and Deadlines:** FAFSA, Institution's own financial aid form. **Notification of Awards:** Applicants will be notified of awards on a rolling basis beginning 2/1. **Types of Aid:** *Need-based scholarships/grants:* Federal Pell, FSEOG, State scholarships/grants, Private scholarships, College/university scholarship or grant aid from institutional funds. *Loans:* Direct Subsidized Stafford Loans, Direct Unsubsidized Stafford Loans, Direct PLUS loans, Federal Perkins Loans. *Student Employment:* Federal Work-Study Program available. Institutional employment available. **Financial Aid Statistics:** 100% needy freshmen, 99% needy undergrads receive need-based scholarship or grant aid. 29% freshmen, 28% undergrads receive non-need-based scholarship

or grant aid. 77% freshmen, 77% undergrads receive need-based self-help aid. 0% freshmen, 0% undergrads receive athletic scholarships. 86% freshmen, 79% undergrads receive any aid. 54% undergrads borrow to pay for school. Average cumulative indebtedness $27,354. **Criteria for awarding aid:** *Non-need-based:* Academics, Alumni affiliation, Art, Minority status, Music/drama.

WHEATON COLLEGE (MA)

26 E Main Street, Norton, MA 2766
Phone: 508-286-8251 • **Financial Aid Phone:** 508-286-8232
E-mail: admission@wheatoncollege.edu • **CEEB Code:** 3963
Fax: 508-286-8271 • **Website:** www.wheatoncollege.edu • **ACT Code:** 1932

This private school was founded in 1834. It has a 400-acre campus.

RATINGS

Admissions Selectivity Rating: 87   **Fire Safety Rating:** 91   **Green Rating:** 73

STUDENTS AND FACULTY

Enrollment: 1,638. **Student Body:** 62% female, 38% male, 60% out-of-state, 12% international (72 countries represented). Asian 5%, African American 6%, Caucasian 65%, Hispanic 7%, Native American <1%, Pacific Islander <1%, Two or more races 3%, Race unknown 2%.
Retention and Graduation: 86% freshmen return for sophomore year. 76% freshmen graduate within 4 years. 79% freshmen graduate within 6 years.
Faculty: Student/faculty ratio 10:1. 137 full-time faculty, 91% hold PhDs, 20% are are members of minority groups, 53% are women. 0% of classes are taught by teaching assistants.

ACADEMICS

Degrees: bachelor's. **Classes:** Most classes have 10-19 students. Most lab/discussion sessions have 10-19 students. **Most popular majors:** Psychology; Business Administration and Management; Economics. **Special Study Options:** Accelerated program, cross-registration, double major, dual enrollment, exchange student program (domestic), honors program, independent study, internships, liberal arts/career combination, student-designed major, study abroad, teacher certification program. Combined degree programs: BA/MA, BA/MEng, BA/MBA;BA/BS;BA/OD. **Disability Services:** Special programs offered to physically disabled students, including note-taking services, reader services, tape recorders, tutors. **Career Services:** Alumni network, Alumni services, Career/job search classes, Career assessment, Internships, Regional alumni. The Wheaton Edge: We have sharpened the advantage that Wheaton College offers by guaranteeing funding for an internship, research position, or other experiential learning opportunity for every student before the start of their senior year.

FACILITIES

Housing: Coed dorms, special housing for disabled students, men's dorms, special housing for international students, women's dorms, Wellness Housing, Theme Housing, quiet house. **Special Academic Facilities/Equipment:** Art gallery,language lab, photography darkrooms,dance studio,on-campus nursery school, media center, observatory. **Computers:** 100% of classrooms, 100% of dorms, 100% of libraries, 100% of dining areas, 100% of student union, have wireless network access. Students can register for classes online. Administrative functions (other than registration) can be performed online.

CAMPUS LIFE

Environment: Village. **Activities:** Choral groups, dance, drama/theater, jazz band, literary magazine, music ensembles, musical theater, pep band, radio station, student government, student newspaper, student-run film society, symphony orchestra, yearbook, Student Organization, Model UN. 60 registered organizations, 8 honor societies, 4 religious organizations. **Athletics (Intercollegiate):** *Men:* baseball, basketball, cross-country, diving, lacrosse, soccer, swimming, tennis, track/field (outdoor), track/field (indoor). *Women:* basketball, cross-country, diving, field hockey, lacrosse, soccer, softball, swimming, synchronized swimming, tennis, track/field (outdoor), track/field (indoor), volleyball. **On-Campus Highlights:** Mars Arts and Humanities:a$20 million arts facility, Haas Athletic Center, Lyon's Den—coffee house, Mary Lyon Hall—college's oldest building, Balfour-Hood Student Center.

ADMISSIONS

Freshman Academic Profile: Average high school GPA 3.5. 27% in top 10% of high school class, 54% in top 25% of high school class, 85% in top 50% of high school class. 76% from public high schools. **Reported SAT (pre-**

2016 redesign) scores: SAT Math middle 50% range 530-630. SAT Critical Reading middle 50% range 520-640. SAT Writing middle 50% range 530-630. **Concordant SAT scores:** SAT EBRW middle 50% 580–680. SAT Math middle 50% range 560–650. ACT middle 50% range 24-30. Minimum internet-based TOEFL 90. **Basis for Candidate Selection:** *Very important factors considered include:* rigor of secondary school record, academic GPA, application essay, recommendation(s). *Important factors considered include:* character/personal qualities, alumni/ae relation. *Other factors considered include:* class rank, interview, extracurricular activities, talent/ability, geographical residence, state residency, religious affiliation/commitment, volunteer work, work experience, level of applicant's interest. **Freshman Admission Requirements:** High school diploma is required and GED is accepted. *Academic units required:* 4 English. *Academic units recommended:* 4 math, 4 science, 4 foreign language, 4 social studies, 4 history. **Freshman Admission Statistics:** 4,478 applied, 62.06% admitted, 19% enrolled. **Transfer Admission Requirements:** High school transcript, college transcript(s), essay or personal statement, statement of good standing from prior institution(s). Minimum college GPA of 3.0 required. Lowest grade transferable C. **General Admission Information:** Application fee $60. Priority deadline 1/1. Regular application deadline 1/15. Regular notification 4/1. Nonfall registration accepted. Admission may be deferred for a maximum of 1 year.

COSTS AND FINANCIAL AID

Annual tuition $48,694. Room and board $12,500. Required fees $318. Average book expense $940. **Required Forms and Deadlines:** FAFSA, CSS/Financial Aid PROFILE, Noncustodial PROFILE, Business/Farm Supplement. **Types of Aid:** *Need-based scholarships/grants:* Federal Pell, FSEOG, State scholarships/grants, Private scholarships, College/university scholarship or grant aid from institutional funds. *Loans:* Direct Subsidized Stafford Loans, Direct Unsubsidized Stafford Loans, Direct PLUS loans, Federal Perkins Loans. *Student Employment:* Federal Work-Study Program available. Institutional employment available. **Financial Aid Statistics:** 100% needy freshmen, 99% needy undergrads receive need-based scholarship or grant aid. 20% freshmen, 10% undergrads receive non-need-based scholarship or grant aid. 94% freshmen, 97% undergrads receive need-based self-help aid. 0% freshmen, 0% undergrads receive athletic scholarships. 92% freshmen, 85% undergrads receive any aid. Average cumulative indebtedness $33,040. **Criteria for awarding aid:** *Need-based:* Academics. *Non-need-based:* Academics.

WHEELING JESUIT UNIVERSITY

316 Washington Avenue, Wheeling, WV 26003
Phone: 304-243-2359 • **Financial Aid Phone:** 304-243–2304
E-mail: admiss@wju.edu • **CEEB Code:** 5906
Fax: 304-243-2397 • **Website:** www.wju.edu • **ACT Code:** 4546

This private school, affiliated with the Roman Catholic Church, was founded in 1954. It has a 70-acre campus.

RATINGS

Admissions Selectivity Rating: 76   **Fire Safety Rating:** 98   **Green Rating:** 76

STUDENTS AND FACULTY

Enrollment: 929. **Student Body:** 51% female, 49% male, 68% out-of-state, 5% international (27 countries represented). Asian 1%, African American 8%, Caucasian 75%, Hispanic 3%, Native American 1%, Pacific Islander 1%, Two or more races 2%, Race unknown 5%.
Retention and Graduation: 71% freshmen return for sophomore year. 48% freshmen graduate within 4 years. 58% freshmen graduate within 6 years. 22% grads go on to further study within 1 year. **Faculty:** Student/faculty ratio 10:1. 77 full-time faculty, 81% hold PhDs, 3% are are members of minority groups, 51% are women. 0% of classes are taught by teaching assistants.

ACADEMICS

Degrees: bachelor's, doctoral/professional, master's, postbachelor's certificate, post-master's certificate. **Classes:** Most classes have 10-19 students. Most lab/discussion sessions have 10-19 students. **Most popular majors:** Registered Nursing/Registered Nurse; Business Administration and Management; Psychology. **Special Study Options:** distance learning, double major, English as a Second Language (ESL), honors program, independent study, internships, liberal arts/career combination, student-designed major, study abroad, teacher certification program, Off-campus study: Washington, DC. **Honors Programs:** The Laut Honors program which is designed to introduces students to aspects of the arts and sciences that are not available in the regular curriculum in order to inspire and awaken curiosity through a variety of enriching experiences offered. Combined degree programs: 3-2 engineering program with Case Western Reserve, West Virginia University. **Disability Services:** Special programs offered to physically disabled students, including note-taking services,

reader services, tutors. **Career Services:** Alumni network, Alumni services, Career/job search classes, Internships, Regional alumni, On-campus interviews. A survey of the graduating class of 2014 revealed that 98 percent are either employed in a field requiring their diploma or in graduate school furthering their education. Outcomes showed 70 percent of the university's 2014 graduates were employed in fields requiring their diploma; 28 percent in graduate school.

FACILITIES

Housing: Coed dorms, special housing for disabled students, men's dorms, special housing for international students, women's dorms, apartments for married students. 85% of campus accessible to physically diasbled. **Special Academic Facilities/Equipment:** Center for Educational Technologies (NASA). **Computers:** 10% of classrooms, 100% of libraries, 100% of dining areas, 100% of student union, 10% of common outdoor areas have wireless network access. Students can register for classes online. Administrative functions (other than registration) can be performed online.

CAMPUS LIFE

Environment: Town. **Activities:** Choral groups, dance, drama/theater, literary magazine, musical theater, pep band, radio station, student government, student newspaper, television station, yearbook, Campus Ministries, Student Organization. 30 registered organizations, 9 honor societies, 6 religious organizations. **Athletics (Intercollegiate):** *Men:* baseball, basketball, cross-country, golf, lacrosse, soccer, swimming, track/field (outdoor), track/field (indoor). *Women:* basketball, cross-country, golf, soccer, softball, swimming, track/field (outdoor), track/field (indoor), volleyball. **On-Campus Highlights:** Coffee Shop- located in Swint Hall, McDonough Fitness Center, Creek Bank surrounding campus, Rathskeller- Pub on campus, McDonough indoor swimming pool and racqu. **Environmental Initiatives:** Faculty/student research related to environmental topics.

ADMISSIONS

Freshman Academic Profile: Average high school GPA 3.3. 17% in top 10% of high school class, 36% in top 25% of high school class, 69% in top 50% of high school class. 62% from public high schools. **Reported SAT (pre-2016 redesign) scores:** SAT Math middle 50% range 450-540. SAT Critical Reading middle 50% range 440-520. SAT Writing middle 50% range 380-470. **Concordant SAT scores:** SAT EBRW middle 50% 460–550. SAT Math middle 50% range 490–570. ACT middle 50% range 18-23. Minimum internet-based TOEFL 80. Minimum paper TOEFL 550. **Basis for Candidate Selection:** *Very important factors considered include:* academic GPA, standardized test scores. *Important factors considered include:* rigor of secondary school record. *Other factors considered include:* class rank, application essay, recommendation(s), interview, extracurricular activities, talent/ability, character/personal qualities, first generation, alumni/ae relation, volunteer work, work experience, level of applicant's interest. **Freshman Admission Requirements:** High school diploma is required and GED is accepted. *Academic units required:* 4 English, 2 math, 1 science, 1 science lab, 1 social studies, 1 history, 6 academic electives. *Academic units recommended:* 4 English, 2 math, 2 science, 2 science labs, 2 foreign language, 1 social studies, 1 history, 6 academic electives. **Freshman Admission Statistics:** 1,020 applied, 93.24% admitted, 23% enrolled. **Transfer Admission Requirements:** college transcript(s), Minimum college GPA of 2.3 required. Lowest grade transferable C. **General Admission Information:** Application fee $25. Nonfall registration accepted. Admission may be deferred for a maximum of one semester.

COSTS AND FINANCIAL AID

Annual tuition $27,000. Room and board $7,796. Required fees $1,110. Average book expense $1,300. **Required Forms and Deadlines:** FAFSA. **Notification of Awards:** Applicants will be notified of awards on a rolling basis beginning 3/10. **Types of Aid:** *Need-based scholarships/grants:* Federal Pell, FSEOG, State scholarships/grants, Private scholarships, College/university scholarship or grant aid from institutional funds. *Loans:* Direct Subsidized Stafford Loans, Direct Unsubsidized Stafford Loans, Direct PLUS loans, Federal Perkins Loans. *Student Employment:* Federal Work-Study Program available. Institutional employment available. **Financial Aid Statistics:** 88% needy freshmen, 69% needy undergrads receive need-based scholarship or grant aid. 100% freshmen, 96% undergrads receive non-need-based scholarship or grant aid. 78% freshmen, 74% undergrads receive need-based self-help aid. 8% freshmen, 10% undergrads receive athletic scholarships. 100% freshmen, 99% undergrads receive any aid. 71% undergrads borrow to pay for school. Average cumulative indebtedness $37,762. **Criteria for awarding aid:** *Non-need-based:* Academics, Alumni affiliation, Athletics, Music/drama, Religious affiliation.

WHEELOCK COLLEGE

200 Riverway, Boston, MA 2215
Phone: 617-879-2206 • **Financial Aid Phone:** 617-879-2443
E-mail: undergrad@wheelock.edu • **CEEB Code:** 3964
Fax: 617-879-2449 • **Website:** www.wheelock.edu • **ACT Code:** 1934

This private school was founded in 1888. It has a 6-acre campus.

RATINGS
Admissions Selectivity Rating: 73   **Fire Safety Rating:** 92   **Green Rating:** 60*

STUDENTS AND FACULTY
Enrollment: 809. **Student Body:** 84% female, 16% male, 39% out-of-state, 2% international (15 countries represented). Asian 4%, African American 13%, Caucasian 60%, Hispanic 11%, Native American 0%, Pacific Islander <1%, Two or more races 3%, Race unknown 7%.
Retention and Graduation: 68% freshmen return for sophomore year. 56% freshmen graduate within 4 years. 64% freshmen graduate within 6 years. 25% grads go on to further study within 1 year. **Faculty:** Student/faculty ratio 10:1. 75 full-time faculty, 85% hold PhDs, 25% are are members of minority groups, 73% are women. 0% of classes are taught by teaching assistants.

ACADEMICS
Degrees: bachelor's, master's, postbachelor's certificate. **Classes:** Most classes have 10-19 students. **Most popular majors:** Social Work; Counseling Psychology; Developmental and Child Psychology. **Special Study Options:** cross-registration, double major, honors program, independent study, internships, liberal arts/career combination, study abroad, teacher certification program. Combined degree programs: BA/MA, MSW/MS. **Disability Services:** Special programs offered to physically disabled students, including note-taking services, reader services, tape recorders, tutors. **Career Services:** Alumni network, Career/job search classes, Career assessment, Internships.

FACILITIES
Housing: Coed dorms, men's dorms, women's dorms, Wellness Floor First Year Floors. 85% of campus accessible to physically diasbled. **Special Academic Facilities/Equipment:** Art studio, resource center with fully equipped workshop for creating and developing original curriculum tools.

CAMPUS LIFE
Environment: Metropolis. **Activities:** Choral groups, dance, drama/theater, music ensembles, musical theater, student government, symphony orchestra 20 registered organizations, 1 honor society, 1 religious organization. **Athletics (Intercollegiate):** *Men:* basketball, tennis. *Women:* basketball, diving, field hockey, soccer, softball, swimming. **On-Campus Highlights:** The Wheelock Family Theater, The Student Center, The Library, Brookline Campus—Hawes Street, The Resource Center.

ADMISSIONS
Freshman Academic Profile: Average high school GPA 2.9. 11% in top 10% of high school class, 33% in top 25% of high school class, 57% in top 50% of high school class. 76% from public high schools. **Reported SAT (pre-2016 redesign) scores:** SAT Math middle 50% range 400-520. SAT Critical Reading middle 50% range 410-542. SAT Writing middle 50% range 410-530. **Concordant SAT scores:** SAT EBRW middle 50% 460-590. SAT Math middle 50% range 440-550. ACT middle 50% range 18-24. Minimum internet-based TOEFL 80. Minimum paper TOEFL 550. **Basis for Candidate Selection:** *Very important factors considered include:* rigor of secondary school record, academic GPA, application essay. *Important factors considered include:* standardized test scores, recommendation(s), extracurricular activities, volunteer work, work experience, level of applicant's interest. *Other factors considered include:* class rank, interview, talent/ability, character/personal qualities. **Freshman Admission Requirements:** High school diploma is required and GED is accepted. *Academic units required:* 4 English, 3 math, 2 science, 1 science lab, 1 social studies, 2 history, 3 academic electives. *Academic units recommended:* 4 English, 3 math, 2 science, 1 science lab, 1 social studies, 2 history, 3 academic electives. **Freshman Admission Statistics:** 1,331 applied, 95.42% admitted, 17% enrolled. **Transfer Admission Requirements:** High school transcript, college transcript(s), essay or personal statement, Minimum college GPA of 2.0 required. Lowest grade transferable C. **General Admission Information:** Priority deadline 3/1. Regular application deadline 5/1. Nonfall registration accepted. Admission may be deferred for a maximum of 1 year.

COSTS AND FINANCIAL AID
Annual tuition $33,600. Room and board $14,400. Required fees $1,125. **Required Forms and Deadlines:** FAFSA. **Notification of Awards:** Applicants will be notified of awards on a rolling basis beginning 3/1. **Types of Aid:** *Need-based scholarships/grants:* Federal Pell, FSEOG, State scholarships/grants, College/university scholarship or grant aid from institutional funds.

Loans: Direct Subsidized Stafford Loans, Direct Unsubsidized Stafford Loans, Direct PLUS loans, Federal Perkins Loans, College/university loans from institutional funds. *Student Employment:* Federal Work-Study Program available. Institutional employment available. **Financial Aid Statistics:** 0% freshmen, 0% undergrads receive athletic scholarships. **Criteria for awarding aid:** *Need-based:* Academics, Leadership. *Non-need-based:* Academics, Leadership, State/district residency.

WHITMAN COLLEGE

345 Boyer Ave, Walla Walla, WA 99362
Phone: 509-527-5176 • **Financial Aid Phone:** 509-527-5178
E-mail: admission@whitman.edu • **CEEB Code:** 4951
Fax: 509-527-4967 • **Website:** https://www.whitman.edu • **ACT Code:** 4492

This private school was founded in 1883. It has a 117-acre campus.

RATINGS
Admissions Selectivity Rating: 92   **Fire Safety Rating:** 81   **Green Rating:** 89

STUDENTS AND FACULTY
Enrollment: 1,463. **Student Body:** 57% female, 43% male, 65% out-of-state, 6% international (27 countries represented). Asian 5%, African American 1%, Caucasian 71%, Hispanic 7%, Native American <1%, Pacific Islander <1%, Two or more races 7%, Race unknown 2%.
Retention and Graduation: 94% freshmen return for sophomore year. 83% freshmen graduate within 4 years. 88% freshmen graduate within 6 years. **Faculty:** Student/faculty ratio 8:1. 140 full-time faculty, 93% hold PhDs, 9% are are members of minority groups, 50% are women. 0% of classes are taught by teaching assistants.

ACADEMICS
Degrees: bachelor's. **Classes:** Most classes have 10-19 students. Most lab/discussion sessions have 10-19 students. **Most popular majors:** Biology; Psychology; Biochemistry, Biophysics and Molecular Biology. **Special Study Options:** Accelerated program, cooperative education program, cross-registration, double major, dual enrollment, exchange student program (domestic), honors program, independent study, liberal arts/career combination, student-designed major, study abroad, Undergraduate research conference. Combined degree programs: BA/JD, BA/MA, Forestry or Environmental Management: 3-2 Duke University; Law: 3-3 Columbia University; Oceanography: 3-2 University of Washington. **Disability Services:** Special programs offered to physically disabled students, including note-taking services, reader services, tape recorders, tutors. **Career Services:** Alumni network, Alumni services, Career assessment, Internships, Regional alumni. The Whitman Internship Grant (WIG) provides funding for students to participate in unpaid summer internship experiences.

FACILITIES
Housing: Coed dorms, special housing for international students, women's dorms, fraternity/sorority housing, apartments for single students, Theme Housing, Interest houses. 96% of campus accessible to physically diasbled. **Special Academic Facilities/Equipment:** Art gallery, Asian art collection, anthropology museum, planetarium, outdoor observatory, two electron microscopes, outdoor sculpture walk, technology/video-conferencing center, indoor and outdoor rock-climbing walls, organic garden. **Computers:** 100% of classrooms, 100% of dorms, 100% of libraries, 100% of dining areas, 100% of student union, 40% of common outdoor areas have wireless network access. Students can register for classes online. Administrative functions (other than registration) can be performed online.

CAMPUS LIFE
Environment: Town. **Activities:** Choral groups, concert band, dance, drama/theater, jazz band, literary magazine, music ensembles, musical theater, radio station, student government, student newspaper, student-run film society, symphony orchestra, Campus Ministries, Student Organization, Model UN. 80 registered organizations, 3 honor societies, 7 religious organizations. 4 fraternities, 3 sororities. **Athletics (Intercollegiate):** *Men:* baseball, basketball, cross-country, golf, soccer, swimming, tennis. *Women:* basketball, cross-country, golf, soccer, swimming, tennis, volleyball. **On-Campus Highlights:** Reid Campus Center, Penrose Library, Baker Ferguson Fitness Center, Sheehan Art Gallery, Olin Hall, Harper Joy Theatre. **Environmental Initiatives:** Installed 21kW Solar Panels on roof of Bratton Tennis Center.

ADMISSIONS

Freshman Academic Profile: Average high school GPA 3.7. 55% in top 10% of high school class, 82% in top 25% of high school class, 96% in top 50% of high school class. **Reported SAT (pre-2016 redesign) scores:** SAT Math middle 50% range 600-700. SAT Critical Reading middle 50% range 600-720. SAT Writing middle 50% range 600-690. **Concordant SAT scores:** SAT EBRW middle 50% 650–740. SAT Math middle 50% range 620–730. ACT middle 50% range 28-32. Minimum internet-based TOEFL 85. Minimum paper TOEFL 560. **Basis for Candidate Selection:** *Very important factors considered include:* rigor of secondary school record, academic GPA, application essay, character/personal qualities. *Important factors considered include:* standardized test scores, recommendation(s), extracurricular activities, talent/ability. *Other factors considered include:* class rank, interview, first generation, alumni/ae relation, geographical residence, state residency, religious affiliation/commitment, racial/ethnic status, volunteer work, work experience, level of applicant's interest. **Freshman Admission Requirements:** High school diploma is required and GED is accepted. *Academic units recommended:* 4 English, 4 math, 3 science, 3 science labs, 2 foreign language, 2 social studies, 2 history. **Freshman Admission Statistics:** 3,749 applied, 51.08% admitted, 21% enrolled. **Transfer Admission Requirements:** High school transcript, college transcript(s), essay or personal statement, statement of good standing from prior institution(s). Lowest grade transferable C-. **General Admission Information:** Application fee $50. Priority deadline 11/15. Regular application deadline 1/15. Regular notification 4/1. Nonfall registration accepted. Admission may be deferred for a maximum of 1 year.

COSTS AND FINANCIAL AID

Annual tuition $47,490. Room and board $11,910. Required fees $372. Average book expense $1,400. **Required Forms and Deadlines:** FAFSA, CSS/Financial Aid PROFILE, Noncustodial PROFILE. **Notification of Awards:** Applicants will be notified of awards on or about 4/1. **Types of Aid:** *Need-based scholarships/grants:* Federal Pell, FSEOG, State scholarships/grants, Private scholarships, College/university scholarship or grant aid from institutional funds. *Loans:* Direct Subsidized Stafford Loans, Direct Unsubsidized Stafford Loans, Direct PLUS loans, Federal Perkins Loans. *Student Employment:* Federal Work-Study Program available. Institutional employment available. **Financial Aid Statistics:** 100% needy freshmen, 100% needy undergrads receive need-based scholarship or grant aid. 32% freshmen, 37% undergrads receive non-need-based scholarship or grant aid. 73% freshmen, 81% undergrads receive need-based self-help aid. 0% freshmen, 0% undergrads receive athletic scholarships. 80% freshmen, 77% undergrads receive any aid. 38% undergrads borrow to pay for school. Average cumulative indebtedness $18,089. **Criteria for awarding aid:** *Need-based:* Academics, Art, Minority status, Music/drama. *Non-need-based:* Academics, Art, Minority status, Music/drama.

WHITTIER COLLEGE

13406 Philadelphia Street, Whittier, CA 90608
Phone: 562-907-4238 • **Financial Aid Phone:** 562-907-4285
E-mail: admission@whittier.edu • **CEEB Code:** 4952
Fax: 562-907-4870 • **Website:** www.whittier.edu • **ACT Code:** 480

This private school was founded in 1887. It has a 75-acre campus.

RATINGS

Admissions Selectivity Rating: 84   **Fire Safety Rating:** 94   **Green Rating:** 60*

STUDENTS AND FACULTY

Enrollment: 1,645. **Student Body:** 56% female, 44% male, 16% out-of-state, 3% international (24 countries represented). Asian 10%, African American 5%, Caucasian 31%, Hispanic 44%, Native American <1%, Pacific Islander <1%, Two or more races 4%, Race unknown 1%. **Retention and Graduation:** 80% freshmen return for sophomore year. 60% freshmen graduate within 4 years. 66% freshmen graduate within 6 years. 18% grads go on to further study within 1 year. 7% grads pursue arts and sciences degrees. 2% grads pursue law degrees. 3% grads pursue business degrees. 1% grads pursue medical degrees. **Faculty:** Student/faculty ratio 12:1. 116 full-time faculty, 95% hold PhDs, 27% are members of minority groups, 50% are women. 0% of classes are taught by teaching assistants.

ACADEMICS

Degrees: bachelor's, doctoral/professional, master's. **Classes:** Most classes have 10-19 students. Most lab/discussion sessions have 10-19 students. **Most**

popular majors: Criminal Justice/Safety Studies; Business Administration and Management; Computer and Information Sciences. **Special Study Options:** double major, independent study, internships, liberal arts/career combination, student-designed major, study abroad, teacher certification program. Combined degree programs: BA/JD, 3-2 engineering programs. **Disability Services:** Special programs offered to physically disabled students, including note-taking services, reader services, tape recorders. **Career Services:** Alumni network, Alumni services, Career/job search classes, Career assessment, Internships, Regional alumni. Backpack to Briefcase: The Office of Career Services and the Office of Alumni Relations have teamed up to present a series of workshops throughout the school year to enable students to learn and develop practical career skills and explore diverse career paths, and at the same time showcase Whittier College alumni professionals, who serve as volunteer mentors and workshop leaders.

FACILITIES

Housing: Coed dorms, special housing for international students, living and learning community; special interest housing. 60% of campus accessible to physically diasbled. **Special Academic Facilities/Equipment:** Performing arts center, on-campus pre-school/ elementary school, image processing lab, state-of-the-art nightclub, on-air radio studio and production room, video production room **Computers:** 100% of classrooms, 100% of dorms, 100% of libraries, 100% of dining areas, 100% of student union, have wireless network access. Students can register for classes online. Administrative functions (other than registration) can be performed online.

CAMPUS LIFE

Environment: City. **Activities:** Choral groups, dance, drama/theater, jazz band, literary magazine, music ensembles, musical theater, radio station, student government, student newspaper, student-run film society, yearbook, Campus Ministries, Student Organization, Model UN. 60 registered organizations, 17 honor societies, 6 religious organizations. 4 fraternities, 5 sororities. **Athletics (Intercollegiate):** *Men:* baseball, basketball, cross-country, diving, football, golf, lacrosse, soccer, swimming, tennis, track/field (outdoor), water polo. *Women:* basketball, cross-country, diving, lacrosse, soccer, softball, swimming, tennis, track/field (outdoor), volleyball, water polo. **On-Campus Highlights:** The Campus Center, Bonnie Bell Wardman Library, Donald Graham Athletics Center, Ruth B. Shannon Center for the Performing Arts, the Rock (campus icon), The recently renovated Campus Center houses the student services division, campus dining, The Spot (campus cafe),student organization offices, KPOET radio, student newspaper. Quaker Campus, and an outdoor amphitheatre. **Environmental Initiatives:** Climate Commitment signatory.

ADMISSIONS

Freshman Academic Profile: Average high school GPA 3.5. 25% in top 10% of high school class, 1% in top 25% of high school class, 93% in top 50% of high school class. **Reported SAT (pre-2016 redesign) scores:** SAT Math middle 50% range 470-590. SAT Critical Reading middle 50% range 463-580. SAT Writing middle 50% range 450-560. **Concordant SAT scores:** SAT EBRW middle 50% 510–630. SAT Math middle 50% range 510–610. ACT middle 50% range 20-26. Minimum paper TOEFL 550. **Basis for Candidate Selection:** *Very important factors considered include:* rigor of secondary school record, academic GPA, application essay, recommendation(s), character/personal qualities. *Important factors considered include:* standardized test scores, interview, extracurricular activities, talent/ability, volunteer work. *Other factors considered include:* class rank, first generation, alumni/ae relation, geographical residence, state residency, racial/ethnic status, work experience. **Freshman Admission Requirements:** High school diploma is required and GED is accepted. *Academic units required:* 3 English, 2 math, 1 science, 1 science lab, 2 foreign language, 1 social studies. *Academic units recommended:* 4 English, 3 math, 2 science, 3 foreign language, 2 social studies. **Freshman Admission Statistics:** 5,192 applied, 62.62% admitted, 14% enrolled. **Transfer Admission Requirements:** High school transcript, college transcript(s), essay or personal statement, Lowest grade transferable C-. **General Admission Information:** Application fee $50. Priority deadline 2/1. Nonfall registration accepted. Admission may be deferred for a maximum of 1 year.

COSTS AND FINANCIAL AID

Required Forms and Deadlines: FAFSA. **Notification of Awards:** Applicants will be notified of awards on a rolling basis beginning 2/15. **Types of Aid:** *Need-based scholarships/grants:* Federal Pell, FSEOG, State scholarships/grants, Private scholarships, College/university scholarship or grant aid from institutional funds. *Loans:* Direct Subsidized Stafford Loans, Direct Unsubsidized Stafford Loans, Direct PLUS loans, Federal Perkins Loans. *Student Employment:* Federal Work-Study Program available. **Financial Aid Statistics:** 83% needy freshmen, 88% needy undergrads receive need-based scholarship or grant aid. 17% freshmen, 11% undergrads receive non-need-based scholarship or grant aid. 80% freshmen, 83% undergrads receive need-based self-help aid. 0% freshmen, 0% undergrads receive athletic scholarships. 92% freshmen, 89% undergrads receive any aid. 79% undergrads borrow to pay for school. Average cumulative indebtedness $33,323. **Criteria for awarding aid:** *Need-based:* Job skills, Leadership, Religious affiliation. *Non-need-based:* Academics, Alumni affiliation, Art, Minority status, Music/drama.

WHITWORTH UNIVERSITY

300 West Hawthorne Road, Spokane, WA 99251
Phone: 509-777-4786 • **Financial Aid Phone:** 509-777-4335
E-mail: admissions@whitworth.edu • **CEEB Code:** 4953
Fax: 509-777-3758 • **Website:** www.whitworth.edu • **ACT Code:** 4494

This private school, affiliated with the Presbyterian Church, was founded in 1890. It has a 200-acre campus.

RATINGS

Admissions Selectivity Rating: 82   **Fire Safety Rating:** 85   **Green Rating:** 60*

STUDENTS AND FACULTY

Enrollment: 2,280. **Student Body:** 60% female, 40% male, 29% out-of-state, 3% international (28 countries represented). Asian 5%, African American 2%, Caucasian 72%, Hispanic 9%, Native American 1%, Pacific Islander <1%, Two or more races 7%, Race unknown 1%.
Retention and Graduation: 85% freshmen return for sophomore year. 63% freshmen graduate within 4 years. 73% freshmen graduate within 6 years.
Faculty: Student/faculty ratio 11:1. 180 full-time faculty, 75% hold PhDs, 8% are are members of minority groups, 43% are women. 0% of classes are taught by teaching assistants.

ACADEMICS

Degrees: bachelor's, master's, postbachelor's certificate, post-master's certificate.
Classes: Most classes have 10-19 students. Most lab/discussion sessions have 10-19 students. **Most popular majors:** Multi-/Interdisciplinary Studies; Business Administration and Management; Social Sciences. **Special Study Options:** cooperative education program, cross-registration, double major, dual enrollment, English as a Second Language (ESL), exchange student program (domestic), honors program, independent study, internships, liberal arts/career combination, student-designed major, study abroad, teacher certification program. **Disability Services:** Special programs offered to physically disabled students, including note-taking services, reader services, tape recorders.
Career Services: Alumni network, Alumni services, Career/job search classes, Career assessment, Internships, Regional alumni.

FACILITIES

Housing: Coed dorms, men's dorms, women's dorms, Theme houses within walking distance to the campus. 80% of campus accessible to physically diasbled. **Special Academic Facilities/Equipment:** Language laboratory, art gallery, computer labs **Computers:** Students can register for classes online. Administrative functions (other than registration) can be performed online.

CAMPUS LIFE

Environment: City. **Activities:** Choral groups, concert band, dance, drama/theater, jazz band, music ensembles, musical theater, pep band, radio station, student government, student newspaper, symphony orchestra, yearbook. 50 registered organizations, 5 honor societies. **Athletics (Intercollegiate):** *Men:* baseball, basketball, cheerleading, cross-country, football, golf, soccer, swimming, tennis, track/field (outdoor). *Women:* basketball, cheerleading, cross-country, golf, soccer, softball, swimming, tennis, track/field (outdoor), volleyball. **On-Campus Highlights:** Hixon Union Building (Student Union)—cafe, Weyerhauser Hall (Teaching Theatre), Boppell Hall—new dormitory for upperclass man, Athletic Complex, Library.

ADMISSIONS

Freshman Academic Profile: Average high school GPA 3.8. 28% in top 10% of high school class, 60% in top 25% of high school class, 90% in top 50% of high school class. **Reported SAT (pre-2016 redesign) scores:** SAT Math middle 50% range 500-620. SAT Critical Reading middle 50% range 500-640. SAT Writing middle 50% range 480-620. **Concordant SAT scores:** SAT EBRW middle 50% 550-680. SAT Math middle 50% range 530-640. ACT middle 50% range 22-29. Minimum internet-based TOEFL 79. Minimum paper TOEFL 550. **Basis for Candidate Selection:** *Very important factors considered include:* academic GPA, application essay, recommendation(s). *Important factors considered include:* rigor of secondary school record, standardized test scores, interview, extracurricular activities, talent/ability, character/personal qualities, first generation, alumni/ae relation, geographical residence, state residency, racial/ethnic status, volunteer work, work experience. *Other factors considered include:* religious affiliation/commitment, level of applicant's interest. **Freshman Admission Requirements:** High school diploma is required and GED is accepted. *Academic units recommended:* 4 English, 3 math, 3 science, 2 science labs, 2 foreign language, 3 social studies, 3 history. **Freshman Admission Statistics:** 3,262 applied, 88.57% admitted, 21% enrolled. **Transfer Admission Requirements:** High school transcript, college transcript(s), essay or personal statement, standardized test scores, statement of good standing from prior institution(s). Minimum college GPA of 2.5 required. Lowest grade transferable C-. **General Admission Information:**

Priority deadline 3/1. Regular application deadline 8/1. Nonfall registration accepted. Admission may be deferred for a maximum of 1 year.

COSTS AND FINANCIAL AID

Annual tuition $41,086. Room and board $11,496. Required fees $1,100. Average book expense $840. **Required Forms and Deadlines:** FAFSA. **Notification of Awards:** Applicants will be notified of awards on a rolling basis beginning 3/15. **Types of Aid:** *Need-based scholarships/grants:* Federal Pell, FSEOG, State scholarships/grants, Private scholarships, College/university scholarship or grant aid from institutional funds. *Loans:* Direct Subsidized Stafford Loans, Direct Unsubsidized Stafford Loans, Direct PLUS loans, Federal Perkins Loans, College/university loans from institutional funds. *Student Employment:* Federal Work-Study Program available. Institutional employment available. **Financial Aid Statistics:** 99% needy freshmen, 99% needy undergrads receive need-based scholarship or grant aid. 12% freshmen, 10% undergrads receive non-need-based scholarship or grant aid. 86% freshmen, 84% undergrads receive need-based self-help aid. 0% freshmen, 0% undergrads receive athletic scholarships. 100% freshmen, 98% undergrads receive any aid. 61% undergrads borrow to pay for school. Average cumulative indebtedness $28,294. **Criteria for awarding aid:** *Need-based:* Academics, Music/drama. *Non-need-based:* Academics, Alumni affiliation, Art, Minority status, Music/drama.

WICHITA STATE UNIVERSITY

1845 Fairmount, Wichita, KS 67260
Phone: 316-978-3085 • **Financial Aid Phone:** 1-855-978-1787
E-mail: admissions@wichita.edu • **CEEB Code:** 6884
Fax: 316-978-3174 • **Website:** www.wichita.edu • **ACT Code:** 1472

This public school was founded in 1895. It has a 330-acre campus.

RATINGS

Admissions Selectivity Rating: 77   **Fire Safety Rating:** 72   **Green Rating:** 66

STUDENTS AND FACULTY

Enrollment: 11,037. **Student Body:** 53% female, 47% male, 8% out-of-state, 7% international (72 countries represented). Asian 7%, African American 6%, Caucasian 61%, Hispanic 11%, Native American 1%, Pacific Islander <1%, Two or more races 4%, Race unknown 2%.
Retention and Graduation: 72% freshmen return for sophomore year. 22% freshmen graduate within 4 years. 46% freshmen graduate within 6 years.
Faculty: Student/faculty ratio 19:1. 526 full-time faculty, 72% hold PhDs, 19% are are members of minority groups, 46% are women. 21% of classes are taught by teaching assistants.

ACADEMICS

Degrees: associate, bachelor's, certificate, doctoral/professional, doctoral/research, doctoral, master's, postbachelor's certificate, post-master's certificate, terminal, transfer. **Classes:** Most classes have 10-19 students. Most lab/discussion sessions have 20-29 students. **Most popular majors:** Liberal Arts and Sciences Studies and Humanities; Mechanical Engineering; Accounting. **Special Study Options:** Accelerated program, cooperative education program, cross-registration, distance learning, double major, dual enrollment, English as a Second Language (ESL), exchange student program (domestic), honors program, independent study, internships, study abroad, teacher certification program. **Honors Programs:** Emory Lindquist Honors Program. The Honors Program offers freshman/sophomore seminars, lower division regular classes, honors colloquia, and honors upper division sections of regular classes. Students can also choose to do independent study projects. The Honors Program also offers a Senior Project, which is an opportunity for students to earn special honors recognition in a student's academic major. **Disability Services:** Special programs offered to physically disabled students, including note-taking services, reader services, tape recorders, tutors. **Career Services:** Alumni network, Alumni services, Career/job search classes, Career assessment, Internships, Regional alumni.

FACILITIES

Housing: Coed dorms, fraternity/sorority housing, apartments for married students, apartments for single students, Some dorm floors are reserved for students majoring in Fine Arts, Health Professions, and for students in the Emory Lindquist Honors Program. 98% of campus accessible to physically diasbled. **Special Academic Facilities/Equipment:** Art museum, performance hall, media resource center, observatory, national institute of aviation research, supersonic wind tunnels,24-hour study room in library, outdoor sculpture collection. **Computers:** Students can register for classes online. Administrative functions (other than registration) can be performed online.

CAMPUS LIFE

Environment: Metropolis. **Activities:** Choral groups, concert band, dance, drama/theater, jazz band, literary magazine, music ensembles, musical theater, opera, pep band, radio station, student government, student newspaper, student-run film society, symphony orchestra, television station, Campus Ministries, Student Organization, Model UN. 140 registered organizations, 11 honor societies, 10 religious organizations. 11 fraternities, 10 sororities. **Athletics (Intercollegiate):** *Men:* baseball, basketball, bowling, cheerleading, cross-country, golf, rugby, swimming, tennis, track/field (outdoor). *Women:* basketball, bowling, cheerleading, cross-country, golf, softball, swimming, tennis, track/field (outdoor), volleyball. **On-Campus Highlights:** Rhatigan Student Center, Ulrich Museum of Art, Heskett Center, outdoor sculpture collection, Charles Koch arena, Wichita State University, founded in 1895 as a Congregational institution, is distinguished from other state supported schools in Kansas by its urban setting. Wichita State's location in the largest city in Kansas enhances the traditional classroom experience by providing students greater opportunities in resources, contacts with business and government leaders, employment, and internships. **Environmental Initiatives:** Recycle Program.

ADMISSIONS

Freshman Academic Profile: Average high school GPA 3.4. 19% in top 10% of high school class, 44% in top 25% of high school class, 80% in top 50% of high school class. **Reported SAT (pre-2016 redesign) scores:** SAT Math middle 50% range 500-625. SAT Critical Reading middle 50% range 440-600. **Concordant SAT scores:** SAT Math middle 50% range 530–650. ACT middle 50% range 21-26. Minimum internet-based TOEFL 72. Minimum paper TOEFL 530. **Basis for Candidate Selection:** *Very important factors considered include:* rigor of secondary school record, class rank, academic GPA, standardized test scores. *Other factors considered include:* extracurricular activities, talent/ability, volunteer work, work experience. **Freshman Admission Requirements:** High school diploma is required and GED is accepted. *Academic units required:* 4 English, 3 math, 3 science, 1 science lab, 3 social studies, 3 academic electives. *Academic units recommended:* 4 English, 3 math, 3 science, 1 science lab, 3 foreign language, 3 social studies, 3 academic electives, 3 computer science. **Freshman Admission Statistics:** 6,306 applied, 96.21% admitted, 24% enrolled. **Transfer Admission Requirements:** college transcript(s), Minimum college GPA of 2.0 required. Lowest grade transferable C. **General Admission Information:** Application fee $50. Nonfall registration accepted. Admission may be deferred for a maximum of 2 years.

COSTS AND FINANCIAL AID

Required Forms and Deadlines: FAFSA. **Notification of Awards:** Applicants will be notified of awards on a rolling basis beginning 10/15. **Types of Aid:** *Need-based scholarships/grants:* Federal Pell, FSEOG, State scholarships/grants, Private scholarships, College/university scholarship or grant aid from institutional funds. *Loans:* Direct Subsidized Stafford Loans, Direct Unsubsidized Stafford Loans, Direct PLUS loans, Federal Perkins Loans. *Student Employment:* Federal Work-Study Program available. Institutional employment available. **Financial Aid Statistics:** 65% needy freshmen, 74% needy undergrads receive need-based scholarship or grant aid. 64% freshmen, 32% undergrads receive non-need-based scholarship or grant aid. 70% freshmen, 78% undergrads receive need-based self-help aid. 5% freshmen, 3% undergrads receive athletic scholarships. 67% freshmen, 88% undergrads receive any aid. 61% undergrads borrow to pay for school. Average cumulative indebtedness $39,122. **Criteria for awarding aid:** *Need-based:* Leadership, Music/drama. *Non-need-based:* Academics, Alumni affiliation, Art, Athletics, Job skills.

WIDENER UNIVERSITY

One University Place, Chester, PA 19013
Phone: 610-499-4126 • **Financial Aid Phone:** 610-499-4152
E-mail: admissions.office@widener.edu • **CEEB Code:** 2642
Fax: 610-499-4676 • **Website:** www.widener.edu • **ACT Code:** 3652

This private school was founded in 1821. It has a 110-acre campus.

RATINGS

Admissions Selectivity Rating: 80   **Fire Safety Rating:** 60*   **Green Rating:** 60*

STUDENTS AND FACULTY

Enrollment: 3,293. **Student Body:** 55% female, 45% male, 40% out-of-state, 4% international (38 countries represented). Asian 4%, African American 13%, Caucasian 69%, Hispanic 5%, Native American <1%, Pacific Islander <1%, Two or more races 2%, Race unknown 2%.
Retention and Graduation: 78% freshmen return for sophomore year. 43% freshmen graduate within 4 years. 57% freshmen graduate within 6 years. 20%

grads go on to further study within 1 year. **Faculty:** Student/faculty ratio 12:1. 297 full-time faculty, 90% hold PhDs, 14% are are members of minority groups, 55% are women. 0% of classes are taught by teaching assistants.

ACADEMICS

Degrees: associate, bachelor's, certificate, doctoral/professional, doctoral/research, master's. **Classes:** Most classes have 10-19 students. Most lab/discussion sessions have fewer than 10 students. **Most popular majors:** Registered Nursing/Registered Nurse; Business/Commerce; Psychology. **Special Study Options:** Accelerated program, cooperative education program, distance learning, double major, English as a Second Language (ESL), honors program, independent study, internships, liberal arts/career combination, student-designed major, study abroad, teacher certification program, weekend college. **Honors Programs:** Honors Program in General Education Combined degree programs: BA/MD, BA/MA, BA/MEng. **Disability Services:** Special programs offered to physically disabled students, including note-taking services, reader services, tape recorders, tutors. **Career Services:** Alumni network, Alumni services, Career/job search classes, Career assessment, Regional alumni.

FACILITIES

Housing: Coed dorms, men's dorms, women's dorms, fraternity/sorority housing, cooperative housing, apartments for single students, Wellness Housing, Theme Housing. **Special Academic Facilities/Equipment:** Art gallery, restaurant lab, child development center education lab, recording studio, commercial graphics lab, physical therapy lab, science labs, engineering labs, nursing labs, multimedia classrooms, Media Center **Computers:** Students can register for classes online. Administrative functions (other than registration) can be performed online.

CAMPUS LIFE

Environment: Town. **Activities:** Choral groups, concert band, dance, drama/theater, jazz band, literary magazine, music ensembles, pep band, radio station, student government, student newspaper, student-run film society, television station, yearbook, Campus Ministries, Student Organization. 80 registered organizations, 29 honor societies, 3 religious organizations. 7 fraternities, 3 sororities. **Athletics (Intercollegiate):** *Men:* baseball, basketball, cross-country, football, golf, lacrosse, soccer, swimming, tennis, track/field (outdoor), track/field (indoor). *Women:* basketball, cheerleading, cross-country, field hockey, lacrosse, soccer, softball, swimming, tennis, track/field (outdoor), track/field (indoor), volleyball. **On-Campus Highlights:** University Center, Java City and Residential Restaurant, Schwartz Athletic Center, Greek Row, Art Gallery, PMC Museum, Media Center, Observatory.

ADMISSIONS

Freshman Academic Profile: Average high school GPA 3.5. 12% in top 10% of high school class, 41% in top 25% of high school class, 81% in top 50% of high school class. 55% from public high schools. **Reported SAT (pre-2016 redesign) scores:** SAT Math middle 50% range 470-570. SAT Critical Reading middle 50% range 460-550. **Concordant SAT scores:** SAT Math middle 50% range 510–590. ACT middle 50% range 21-25. Minimum paper TOEFL 500. **Basis for Candidate Selection:** *Very important factors considered include:* rigor of secondary school record, class rank, academic GPA, standardized test scores. *Other factors considered include:* application essay, recommendation(s), interview, extracurricular activities, talent/ability, character/personal qualities, alumni/ae relation, volunteer work, level of applicant's interest. **Freshman Admission Requirements:** High school diploma is required and GED is accepted. *Academic units required:* 4 English, 3 math, 3 science, 2 foreign language, 3 social studies, 3 academic electives. *Academic units recommended:* 4 English, 4 math, 4 science, 2 science labs, 2 foreign language, 4 social studies, 3 academic electives. **Freshman Admission Statistics:** 5,421 applied, 67.99% admitted, 23% enrolled. **Transfer Admission Requirements:** college transcript(s), Minimum college GPA of 2.0 required. Lowest grade transferable C. **General Admission Information:** Application fee $35. Priority deadline 2/15. Nonfall registration accepted. Admission may be deferred for a maximum of 1 academic year.

COSTS AND FINANCIAL AID

Annual tuition $40,418. Room and board $13,092. Required fees $806. Average book expense $1,300. **Required Forms and Deadlines:** FAFSA. **Notification of Awards:** Applicants will be notified of awards on a rolling basis beginning 3/15. **Types of Aid:** *Need-based scholarships/grants:* Federal Pell, FSEOG, State scholarships/grants, Private scholarships, College/university scholarship or grant aid from institutional funds, Federal Nursing Scholarships. *Loans:* Direct Subsidized Stafford Loans, Direct Unsubsidized Stafford Loans, Direct PLUS loans, Federal Perkins Loans. *Student Employment:* Federal Work-Study Program available. Institutional employment available. **Financial Aid Statistics:** 98% needy freshmen, 97% needy undergrads receive need-based scholarship or grant aid. 96% freshmen, 91% undergrads receive non-need-based scholarship or grant aid. 93% freshmen, 93% undergrads receive need-based self-help aid. 0% freshmen, 0% undergrads receive athletic scholarships. 99% freshmen, 90% undergrads receive any aid. **Criteria for awarding aid:** *Need-based:* Academics. *Non-need-based:* Academics, Leadership, Music/drama.

WILKES UNIVERSITY

84 W South St, Wilkes-Barre, PA 18766
Phone: 570-408-4400 • **Financial Aid Phone:** 570-408-2000
E-mail: admissions@wilkes.edu • **CEEB Code:** 2977
Fax: 570-408-4904 • **Website:** www.wilkes.edu • **ACT Code:** 3756

This private school was founded in 1933. It has a 27-acre campus.

RATINGS
Admissions Selectivity Rating: 80   **Fire Safety Rating:** 86   **Green Rating:** 60*

STUDENTS AND FACULTY
Enrollment: 2,418. **Student Body:** 47% female, 53% male, 19% out-of-state, 8% international (15 countries represented). Asian 3%, African American 5%, Caucasian 72%, Hispanic 7%, Native American <1%, Pacific Islander <1%, Two or more races 3%, Race unknown 2%.
Retention and Graduation: 76% freshmen return for sophomore year. 48% freshmen graduate within 4 years. 62% freshmen graduate within 6 years. **Faculty:** Student/faculty ratio 14:1. 182 full-time faculty, 90% hold PhDs, 13% are are members of minority groups, 45% are women. 0% of classes are taught by teaching assistants.

ACADEMICS
Degrees: bachelor's, doctoral/professional, doctoral/research, master's. **Classes:** Most classes have 10-19 students. Most lab/discussion sessions have 10-19 students. **Most popular majors:** Registered Nursing/Registered Nurse; Psychology; Mechanical Engineering. **Special Study Options:** cooperative education program, cross-registration, distance learning, double major, dual enrollment, English as a Second Language (ESL), external degree program, honors program, independent study, internships, student-designed major, study abroad, teacher certification program, weekend college. **Disability Services:** Special programs offered to physically disabled students, including note-taking services, reader services, tape recorders, tutors. **Career Services:** Alumni network, Alumni services, Career/job search classes, Career assessment, Internships, Regional alumni.

FACILITIES
Housing: Coed dorms, men's dorms, women's dorms, apartments for single students. **Special Academic Facilities/Equipment:** Art gallery, performing arts center, electron microscope, television studio. **Computers:** Students can register for classes online. Administrative functions (other than registration) can be performed online.

CAMPUS LIFE
Environment: City. **Activities:** Choral groups, dance, drama/theater, jazz band, literary magazine, music ensembles, musical theater, pep band, radio station, student government, student newspaper, television station, yearbook, Campus Ministries, Student Organization. 65 registered organizations, 19 honor societies. **Athletics (Intercollegiate):** *Men:* baseball, basketball, cross-country, football, golf, soccer, tennis, wrestling. *Women:* basketball, cross-country, field hockey, lacrosse, soccer, softball, tennis, volleyball.

ADMISSIONS
Freshman Academic Profile: Average high school GPA 3.5. 20% in top 10% of high school class, 51% in top 25% of high school class, 83% in top 50% of high school class. **Reported SAT (pre-2016 redesign) scores:** SAT Math middle 50% range 450-580. SAT Critical Reading middle 50% range 445-550. SAT Writing middle 50% range 420-540. **Concordant SAT scores:** SAT EBRW middle 50% range 490–600. SAT Math middle 50% range 490–600. ACT middle 50% range 20-25. Minimum internet-based TOEFL 61. Minimum paper TOEFL 500. **Basis for Candidate Selection:** *Very important factors considered include:* rigor of secondary school record, class rank. *Important factors considered include:* academic GPA, standardized test scores, extracurricular activities, character/personal qualities. *Other factors considered include:* recommendation(s), interview, talent/ability, alumni/ae relation, volunteer work, work experience. **Freshman Admission Requirements:** High school diploma is required and GED is accepted. *Academic units recommended:* 4 English, 3 math, 3 science, 2 science labs, 2 foreign language, 3 social studies, 1 computer science. **Freshman Admission Statistics:** 4,245 applied, 75.92% admitted, 21% enrolled. **Transfer Admission Requirements:** college transcript(s), statement of good standing from prior institution(s). Minimum college GPA of 2.0 required. Lowest grade transferable C. **General Admission Information:** Application fee $40. Nonfall registration accepted. Admission may be deferred for a maximum of 12 months.

COSTS AND FINANCIAL AID
Annual tuition $31,946. Room and board $13,746. Required fees $1,622. Average book expense $1,500. **Required Forms and Deadlines:** FAFSA. **Notification of Awards:** Applicants will be notified of awards on a rolling basis beginning 3/1. **Types of Aid:** *Need-based scholarships/grants:* Federal Pell, FSEOG, State scholarships/grants, Private scholarships, College/university scholarship or grant aid from institutional funds. *Loans:* Direct Subsidized Stafford Loans, Direct Unsubsidized Stafford Loans, Direct PLUS loans, Federal Perkins Loans, Federal Nursing Loans, State Loans, College/university loans from institutional funds. *Student Employment:* Federal Work-Study Program available. Institutional employment available. **Financial Aid Statistics:** 99% needy freshmen, 98% needy undergrads receive need-based scholarship or grant aid. 77% freshmen, 78% undergrads receive non-need-based scholarship or grant aid. 90% freshmen, 89% undergrads receive need-based self-help aid. 0% freshmen, 0% undergrads receive athletic scholarships. 97% freshmen, 90% undergrads receive any aid. 82% undergrads borrow to pay for school. Average cumulative indebtedness $43,241. **Criteria for awarding aid:** *Non-need-based:* Academics, Leadership, Minority status, Music/drama.

WILLAMETTE UNIVERSITY

900 State Street, Salem, OR 97301
Phone: 503-370-6303 • **Financial Aid Phone:** 503-370-6273
E-mail: libarts@willamette.edu • **CEEB Code:** 4954
Fax: 503-375-5363 • **Website:** www.willamette.edu • **ACT Code:** 3504

This private school, affiliated with the Methodist Church, was founded in 1842. It has a 72-acre campus.

RATINGS
Admissions Selectivity Rating: 87   **Fire Safety Rating:** 98   **Green Rating:** 92

STUDENTS AND FACULTY
Enrollment: 1,867. **Student Body:** 57% female, 43% male, 79% out-of-state, 1% international (14 countries represented). Asian 9%, African American 3%, Caucasian 62%, Hispanic 13%, Native American 1%, Pacific Islander <1%, Two or more races 9%, Race unknown 2%.
Retention and Graduation: 86% freshmen return for sophomore year. 70% freshmen graduate within 4 years. 78 20% grads go on to further study within 1 year. 5% grads pursue arts and sciences degrees. 3% grads pursue law degrees. 4% grads pursue business degrees. 2% grads pursue medical degrees. **Faculty:** Student/faculty ratio 10:1. 214 full-time faculty, 94% hold PhDs, 20% are are members of minority groups, 45% are women. 0% of classes are taught by teaching assistants.

ACADEMICS
Degrees: bachelor's, master's. **Classes:** Most classes have 10-19 students. Most lab/discussion sessions have 10-19 students. **Most popular majors:** Biology/Biological Sciences; Economics; Psychology. **Special Study Options:** Accelerated program, cross-registration, double major, dual enrollment, exchange student program (domestic), independent study, internships, student-designed major, study abroad, teacher certification program. **Honors Programs:** Our challenging curriculum includes a variety of opportunities for individualized honors study, for example: Presidential Scholars (senior year), Carson Undergraduate Research Program, Science Collaborative Research Program, various departmental honors programs. Combined degree programs: BA/JD, 5 year (BA/MBA); 4-2 program in Eng(BA/MS). **Disability Services:** Special programs offered to physically disabled students, including note-taking services, reader services, tape recorders, tutors. **Career Services:** Alumni network, Career/job search classes, Career assessment, Internships. Willamette University has a long tradition of academic internships. Three internship programs are in place: to explore career choices (Insight Internship), to gain deeper knowledge of a chosen field (Major Program Internship), or a program which places an emphasis on bridging the gap between liberal arts study and professional responsibilities (Professional Internship).

FACILITIES
Housing: Coed dorms, fraternity/sorority housing, apartments for single students, Substance-free Residence, Environmental Residence (Terra House), Intensive Study (24 hour quiet study) Residence. 95% of campus accessible to physically disabled. **Special Academic Facilities/Equipment:** Student Art purchased annually,and displayed in all public access buildings, Hallie Ford Museum of Art,Collections and papers of Congressional leaders from Oregon,Electron Microscope Lab (scanning and transmission), Herbarium, Japanese and Botanical Gardens, Carnegie Library(fully restored). **Computers:** 100% of classrooms, 100% of dorms, 100% of libraries, 100% of dining areas, 100% of student union, 50% of common outdoor areas have wireless network access. Students can register for classes online. Administrative functions (other than registration) can be performed online.

CAMPUS LIFE

Environment: City. **Activities:** Choral groups, concert band, dance, drama/theater, jazz band, literary magazine, music ensembles, musical theater, opera, student government, student newspaper, student-run film society, symphony orchestra, yearbook, Campus Ministries, Student Organization, Model UN. 107 registered organizations, 7 honor societies, 5 religious organizations. 4 fraternities, 3 sororities. **Athletics (Intercollegiate):** *Men:* baseball, basketball, crew/rowing, cross-country, football, golf, soccer, swimming, tennis, track/field (outdoor), track/field (indoor). *Women:* basketball, crew/rowing, cross-country, golf, soccer, softball, swimming, tennis, track/field (outdoor), track/field (indoor), volleyball. **On-Campus Highlights:** Hallie Ford Museum of Art, Montag Student Center, Sparks Sports and Recreation Center, Willamette Bistro, Mill Stream on campus. **Environmental Initiatives:** Kaneko Commons Residential Hall Ford Hall-Academic Building Purchased Zena Forest-nearby 308 Acre Sustainable forest for research and teaching New Construction Achieved LEED Gold status in 2007. Photo Voltaic panels, solar hot water heating, rainwater reclamation for flushing toilets, FSC wood products, Indoor Air Quality measures, low/no VOC materials and products, sustainability educational signage, high recycled content materials, energy efficient boilers, lighting control system, Energy Management System controls, 50% reduction in irrigation, low flow plumbing fixtures, use of plate to plate heat exchangers, sun shades, 95% recycle of construction waste, reflective roof coatings, use of local materials & labor, FSC cert furnishings, Fat Spaniel PV panel monitoring, electrical use monitoring, FLEX CAR program initiated, purchase of Green Power, energy star appliances, and more.

ADMISSIONS

Freshman Academic Profile: Average high school GPA 3.9. 41% in top 10% of high school class, 74% in top 25% of high school class, 96% in top 50% of high school class. 75% from public high schools. **Reported SAT (pre-2016 redesign) scores:** SAT Math middle 50% range 540-650. SAT Critical Reading middle 50% range 560-680. SAT Writing middle 50% range 540-660. **Concordant SAT scores:** SAT EBRW middle 50% 610–710. SAT Math middle 50% range 570–670. ACT middle 50% range 18-25. Minimum paper TOEFL 550. **Basis for Candidate Selection:** *Very important factors considered include:* rigor of secondary school record, class rank, academic GPA, standardized test scores, application essay. *Important factors considered include:* recommendation(s), interview. *Other factors considered include:* extracurricular activities, talent/ability, character/personal qualities, first generation, alumni/ae relation, geographical residence, racial/ethnic status. **Freshman Admission Requirements:** *Academic units recommended:* 4 English, 4 math, 4 science, 4 foreign language, 4 social studies, 4 academic electives, 4 visual/performing arts. **Freshman Admission Statistics:** 6,181 applied, 78.06% admitted, 10% enrolled. **Transfer Admission Requirements:** High school transcript, college transcript(s), essay or personal statement, statement of good standing from prior institution(s). Lowest grade transferable C. **General Admission Information:** Application fee $50. Priority deadline 1/15. Nonfall registration accepted. Admission may be deferred for a maximum of 1 year.

COSTS AND FINANCIAL AID

Annual tuition $46,900. Room and board $11,600. Required fees $317. Average book expense $950. **Required Forms and Deadlines:** FAFSA. **Notification of Awards:** Applicants will be notified of awards on a rolling basis beginning 4/1. **Types of Aid:** *Need-based scholarships/grants:* Federal Pell, FSEOG, State scholarships/grants, Private scholarships, College/university scholarship or grant aid from institutional funds. *Loans:* Direct Subsidized Stafford Loans, Direct Unsubsidized Stafford Loans, Direct PLUS loans, Federal Perkins Loans. *Student Employment:* Federal Work-Study Program available. Institutional employment available. **Financial Aid Statistics:** 99% needy freshmen, 99% needy undergrads receive need-based scholarship or grant aid. 30% freshmen, 17% undergrads receive non-need-based scholarship or grant aid. 79% freshmen, 78% undergrads receive need-based self-help aid. 0% freshmen, 0% undergrads receive athletic scholarships. 100% freshmen, 92% undergrads receive any aid. Average cumulative indebtedness $29,766. **Criteria for awarding aid:** *Need-based:* Academics, Alumni affiliation, Leadership, Minority status, Music/drama, Religious affiliation. *Non-need-based:* Academics, Alumni affiliation, Leadership, Minority status, Music/drama, Religious affiliation.

WILLIAM JEWELL COLLEGE

500 College Hill, Liberty, MO 64068
Phone: 816-415-7511 • **Financial Aid Phone:** 816-415-5974
E-mail: admission@william.jewell.edu • **CEEB Code:** 6941
Fax: 816-415-5040 • **Website:** www.jewell.edu • **ACT Code:** 2394

This private school was founded in 1849. It has a 200-acre campus.

RATINGS

Admissions Selectivity Rating: 88   **Fire Safety Rating:** 88   **Green Rating:** 60*

STUDENTS AND FACULTY

Enrollment: 992. **Student Body:** 58% female, 42% male, 39% out-of-state, 5% international (22 countries represented). Asian 1%, African American 4%, Caucasian 79%, Hispanic 4%, Native American <1%, Pacific Islander <1%, Two or more races 4%, Race unknown 3%.
Retention and Graduation: 79% freshmen return for sophomore year. 59% freshmen graduate within 4 years. 63% freshmen graduate within 6 years. 28% grads go on to further study within 1 year. 10% grads pursue arts and sciences degrees. 8% grads pursue law degrees. 1% grads pursue business degrees. 4% grads pursue medical degrees. **Faculty:** Student/faculty ratio 10:1. 81 full-time faculty, 83% hold PhDs, 2% are are members of minority groups, 47% are women. 0% of classes are taught by teaching assistants.

ACADEMICS

Degrees: bachelor's, master's, postbachelor's certificate. **Classes:** Most classes have 10-19 students. Most lab/discussion sessions have 10-19 students. **Most popular majors:** Biology/Biological Sciences; Business Administration and Management; Registered Nursing/Registered Nurse. **Special Study Options:** Accelerated program, double major, dual enrollment, honors program, independent study, internships, liberal arts/career combination, student-designed major, study abroad, teacher certification program, Pryor Leadership Studies. **Honors Programs:** The Oxbridge Honors Program combines British tutorial methods of instruction with opportunities for a year of study in Oxford or Cambridge. **Career Services:** Alumni network, Alumni services, Career/job search classes, Career assessment, Internships, Regional alumni. The Pryor Leadership Program requires 2 internships—one in service; one career-related. Over 50% of Jewell students participate in some form of internship or similar experiential learning opportunity.

FACILITIES

Housing: Coed dorms, men's dorms, women's dorms, fraternity/sorority housing, Off-campus housing utilized like residence halls. ADA compliant housing available for disabled students. 80% of campus accessible to physically diasbled. **Special Academic Facilities/Equipment:** Radio station, art gallery, observatory, language and computer labs, high-ropes course, Teleconferencing center. **Computers:** 80% of classrooms, 20% of dorms, 25% of libraries, 80% of dining areas, 90% of student union, have wireless network access. Students can register for classes online. Administrative functions (other than registration) can be performed online.

CAMPUS LIFE

Environment: Town. **Activities:** Choral groups, concert band, dance, drama/theater, jazz band, literary magazine, music ensembles, pep band, radio station, student government, student newspaper, symphony orchestra, Campus Ministries. 70 registered organizations, 13 honor societies, 7 religious organizations. 4 fraternities, 4 sororities. **Athletics (Intercollegiate):** *Men:* baseball, basketball, cheerleading, cross-country, football, golf, soccer, tennis, track/field (outdoor), track/field (indoor). *Women:* basketball, cheerleading, cross-country, golf, soccer, softball, tennis, track/field (outdoor), track/field (indoor), volleyball. **On-Campus Highlights:** The Perch–campus coffee shop, Mabee Center—athletic facility, The Quad—central campus quadrangle, Yates College Union—student union buil, Ely Triangle—first-year residence hall, Fitness Center. **Environmental Initiatives:** Campus recycling program.

ADMISSIONS

Freshman Academic Profile: Average high school GPA 3.7. 25% in top 10% of high school class, 55% in top 25% of high school class, 89% in top 50% of high school class. 90% from public high schools. **Reported SAT (pre-2016 redesign) scores:** SAT Math middle 50% range 500-620. SAT Critical Reading middle 50% range 480-665. **Concordant SAT scores:** SAT Math middle 50% range 530–640. ACT middle 50% range 22-28. Minimum internet-based TOEFL 80. Minimum paper TOEFL 550. **Basis for Candidate Selection:** *Very important factors considered include:* rigor of secondary school record, academic GPA. *Important factors considered include:* class rank, standardized test scores, recommendation(s), extracurricular activities, talent/ability, character/personal qualities, level of applicant's interest. *Other factors considered include:* application essay, interview, first generation, alumni/ae relation, volunteer work, work experience. **Freshman Admission Requirements:** High school diploma is required and GED is accepted. *Academic units required:* 4 English, 3 math, 3 science, 1 science lab, 2 foreign language, 3 social studies. *Academic units recommended:* 4 math, 3 foreign language, 2 academic electives. **Freshman Admission Statistics:** 2,081 applied, 51.08% admitted, 23% enrolled. **Transfer Admission Requirements:** college transcript(s), statement of good standing from prior institution(s). Minimum college GPA of 2.5 required. Lowest grade transferable C-. **General Admission Information:** Priority deadline 12/1. Nonfall registration accepted. Admission may be deferred for a maximum of 1 year, w/ a.

COSTS AND FINANCIAL AID

Annual tuition $32,850. Room and board $9,640. Required fees $770. Average book expense $800. **Required Forms and Deadlines:** FAFSA. **Notification of Awards:** Applicants will be notified of awards on a rolling basis beginning 3/1. **Types of Aid:** *Need-based scholarships/grants:* Federal Pell, FSEOG, State scholarships/grants, College/university scholarship or grant aid from institutional funds. *Loans:* Federal Perkins Loans, Federal Nursing Loans. *Student Employment:* Federal Work-Study Program available. Institutional employment available. **Financial Aid Statistics:** 100% needy freshmen, 91% needy undergrads receive need-based scholarship or grant aid. 100% freshmen, 94% undergrads receive non-need-based scholarship or grant aid. 72% freshmen, 74% undergrads receive need-based self-help aid. 7% freshmen, 14% undergrads receive athletic scholarships. 100% freshmen, 99% undergrads receive any aid. 69% undergrads borrow to pay for school. Average cumulative indebtedness $31,183. **Criteria for awarding aid:** *Need-based:* Leadership. *Non-need-based:* Academics, Alumni affiliation, Athletics, Music/drama.

WILLIAM PATERSON UNIVERSITY

Admissions Hall, Wayne, NJ 7470
Phone: 973-720-2125 • **Financial Aid Phone:** 973-720-2202
E-mail: admissions@wpunj.edu • **CEEB Code:** 2518
Fax: 973-720-2910 • **Website:** www.wpunj.edu • **ACT Code:** 2584

This public school was founded in 1855. It has a 370-acre campus.

RATINGS

Admissions Selectivity Rating: 75 **Fire Safety Rating:** 98 **Green Rating:** 68

STUDENTS AND FACULTY

Enrollment: 9,286. **Student Body:** 55% female, 45% male, 2% out-of-state, <1% international (33 countries represented). Asian 7%, African American 16%, Caucasian 43%, Hispanic 28%, Native American <1%, Pacific Islander 0%, Two or more races 3%, Race unknown 3%.
Retention and Graduation: 75% freshmen return for sophomore year. 20% freshmen graduate within 4 years. 48% freshmen graduate within 6 years. 14% grads go on to further study within 1 year. 53% grads pursue arts and sciences degrees. 4% grads pursue law degrees. 14% grads pursue business degrees. **Faculty:** Student/faculty ratio 14:1. 411 full-time faculty, 93% hold PhDs, 35% are are members of minority groups, 50% are women. 0% of classes are taught by teaching assistants.

ACADEMICS

Degrees: bachelor's, doctoral/professional, master's, postbachelor's certificate, post-master's certificate. **Classes:** Most classes have 10-19 students. **Most popular majors:** Speech Communication and Rhetoric; Psychology; Criminal Justice/Safety Studies. **Special Study Options:** Accelerated program, cross-registration, distance learning, double major, dual enrollment, English as a Second Language (ESL), exchange student program (domestic), honors program, independent study, internships, study abroad, teacher certification program, Cluster courses (a program that provides opportunities for students and faculty to study and learn together in courses grouped in interdisciplinary clusters of three. Three faculty members teach these courses that meet together once every week to help students see the interdisciplinary connections). University Honors Program (Honors major tracks are available, and "honors" general education courses are offered.) International exchange program. **Honors Programs:** University Honors Program offers honors major tracks as well as honors general education courses. For more information please visit our Honors College Homepage at: http://www.wpunj.edu/icip/honors/default.htm Combined degree programs: BA/MA. **Disability Services:** Special programs offered to physically disabled students, including note-taking services, reader services, tape recorders, tutors. **Career Services:** Alumni services, Career/

job search classes, Career assessment, Internships. Career Counseling, career coaching and job search assistance for all undergraduate and graduate students.

FACILITIES

Housing: Coed dorms, special housing for disabled students, apartments for single students. A floor for women is available in one of the residence halls. Apartment style housing is available in groups of single students who are 21 or older or are 20 with 58 or more credits. Academic interest housing is available; High Mountain East is freshmen scholars and High Mountain West houses upperclass students who maintain a 2.5 GPA or better. One residence hall is reserved for students who are 21 or older. 88% of campus accessible to physically disabled. **Special Academic Facilities/Equipment:** Art galleries; Collection of NJ State Documents; Collection of William Paterson's private papers; Interactive television classroom; Neurobiology facility; E-Trading Campus Network with ATM technology; Center for Computer Art and Animation; State-of-the-art electron microscopy facility; Teleconference Center with uplink and downlink capabilities; 44,000 square foot, state-of-the-art studio art facility; Center for Electro-Acoustic Music (CEM); E-Trade Financial Learning Center, a real-time simulated trading and financial educational facility; Russ Berrie Institute for Professional Sales including real-time Sales Laboratory. **Computers:** Students can register for classes online. Administrative functions (other than registration) can be performed online.

CAMPUS LIFE

Environment: Metropolis. **Activities:** Choral groups, concert band, dance, drama/theater, jazz band, literary magazine, music ensembles, student government, student newspaper, student-run film society, television station, yearbook, Campus Ministries, Student Organization, Model UN. 61 registered organizations, 21 honor societies, 4 religious organizations. 11 fraternities, 10 sororities. **Athletics (Intercollegiate):** *Men:* baseball, basketball, football, soccer, swimming. *Women:* basketball, cheerleading, field hockey, soccer, softball, swimming, volleyball. **On-Campus Highlights:** Student Center: Coffee Cafe (Starbucks), College of Business E-Trading Center, Power Art Gallery, Atrium Lobby, Library, New Student Center Facility, New Center for Student Services. **Environmental Initiatives:** ACUPCC.

ADMISSIONS

Freshman Academic Profile: Average high school GPA 3.1. 10% in top 10% of high school class, 31% in top 25% of high school class, 67% in top 50% of high school class. **Reported SAT (pre-2016 redesign) scores:** SAT Math middle 50% range 460-540. SAT Critical Reading middle 50% range 440-540. **Concordant SAT scores:** SAT Math middle 50% range 500–570. Minimum internet-based TOEFL 79. Minimum paper TOEFL 550. **Basis for Candidate Selection:** *Very important factors considered include:* rigor of secondary school record, academic GPA, standardized test scores. *Other factors considered include:* application essay, recommendation(s), interview, extracurricular activities, talent/ability, character/personal qualities, alumni/ae relation, volunteer work, level of applicant's interest. **Freshman Admission Requirements:** High school diploma is required and GED is accepted. *Academic units required:* 4 English, 3 math, 2 science, 2 science labs, 2 social studies, 5 academic electives. **Freshman Admission Statistics:** 9,848 applied, 74.28% admitted, 18% enrolled. **Transfer Admission Requirements:** college transcript(s), Minimum college GPA of 2.00 required. Lowest grade transferable C. **General Admission Information:** Application fee $50. Priority deadline 12/1. Regular application deadline 6/1. Nonfall registration accepted. Admission may be deferred for a maximum of 1 year.

COSTS AND FINANCIAL AID

Annual in-state tuition $6,967. Annual out-of-state tuition $14,131. Room and board $9,540. Required fees $8,832. Average book expense $1,600. **Required Forms and Deadlines:** FAFSA. **Notification of Awards:** Applicants will be notified of awards on or about 4/15. **Types of Aid:** *Need-based scholarships/grants:* Federal Pell, FSEOG, State scholarships/grants, Private scholarships, College/university scholarship or grant aid from institutional funds. *Loans:* Direct Subsidized Stafford Loans, Direct Unsubsidized Stafford Loans, Direct PLUS loans, Federal Nursing Loans, State Loans. *Student Employment:* Federal Work-Study Program available. Institutional employment available. **Financial Aid Statistics:** 69% needy freshmen, 68% needy undergrads receive need-based scholarship or grant aid. 33% freshmen, 25% undergrads receive non-need-based scholarship or grant aid. 77% freshmen, 80% undergrads receive need-based self-help aid. 0% freshmen, 0% undergrads receive athletic scholarships. 89% freshmen, 78% undergrads receive any aid. 76% undergrads borrow to pay for school. Average cumulative indebtedness $33,068. **Criteria for awarding aid:** *Need-based:* Academics. *Non-need-based:* Academics, Art, Music/drama.

WILLIAM PEACE UNIVERSITY

15 East Peace Street, Raleigh, NC 27604
Phone: 919-508-2214 • **Financial Aid Phone:** 919-508-2214
E-mail: admissions@peace.edu
Fax: 919-508-2306 • **Website:** www.peace.edu • **ACT Code:** 3136

RATINGS
Admissions Selectivity Rating: 72   **Fire Safety Rating:** 60*   **Green Rating:** 65

STUDENTS AND FACULTY
Enrollment: 1,076. **Student Body:** 72% female, 28% male, 6% out-of-state, <1% international. Asian 2%, African American 34%, Caucasian 43%, Hispanic 4%, Native American 1%, Pacific Islander 0%, Two or more races 5%, Race unknown 11%.
Retention and Graduation: 63% freshmen return for sophomore year. 28% freshmen graduate within 4 years. 41% freshmen graduate within 6 years.
Faculty: Student/faculty ratio 15:1. 24 full-time faculty, 79% hold PhDs, 4% are are members of minority groups, 58% are women. 0% of classes are taught by teaching assistants.

ACADEMICS
Degrees: bachelor's. **Classes:** Most classes have 10-19 students. **Career Services:** Alumni network, Career/job search classes, Career assessment, Internships. WPU is ranked #1 nationally when it comes to colleges with the highest rate of student internships, according to the 2013 U.S. News and World Report.

ADMISSIONS
Freshman Academic Profile: Average high school GPA 3.1. 6% in top 10% of high school class, 26% in top 25% of high school class, 57% in top 50% of high school class. **Reported SAT (pre-2016 redesign) scores:** SAT Math middle 50% range 400-510. SAT Critical Reading middle 50% range 410-520. **Concordant SAT scores:** SAT Math middle 50% range 440–540. ACT middle 50% range 16-21. Minimum internet-based TOEFL 80. Minimum paper TOEFL 550. **Basis for Candidate Selection:** *Very important factors considered include:* rigor of secondary school record, academic GPA, standardized test scores. *Important factors considered include:* application essay, recommendation(s), interview, extracurricular activities, volunteer work, level of applicant's interest. *Other factors considered include:* class rank, talent/ability, character/personal qualities, alumni/ae relation, geographical residence, work experience. **Freshman Admission Requirements:** *Academic units required:* 4 English, 3 math, 3 science, 2 science labs, 2 social studies. *Academic units recommended:* 4 math, 2 foreign language. **Freshman Admission Statistics:** 1,083 applied, 90.86% admitted, 33% enrolled. **General Admission Information:** Application fee $35. Nonfall registration accepted. Admission may be deferred for a maximum of 1 year.

COSTS AND FINANCIAL AID
Annual tuition $24,450. Room and board $9,450. Required fees $200. **Required Forms and Deadlines:** FAFSA. **Notification of Awards:** Applicants will be notified of awards on a rolling basis beginning 3/15. **Types of Aid:** *Need-based scholarships/grants:* Federal Pell, FSEOG, State scholarships/grants, Private scholarships, College/university scholarship or grant aid from institutional funds. *Loans:* Direct Subsidized Stafford Loans, Direct Unsubsidized Stafford Loans, Direct PLUS loans. *Student Employment:* Federal Work-Study Program available. Institutional employment available. **Financial Aid Statistics:** 84% needy freshmen, 85% needy undergrads receive need-based scholarship or grant aid. 76% freshmen, 88% undergrads receive non-need-based scholarship or grant aid. 94% freshmen, undergrads receive need-based self-help aid. 0% freshmen, 0% undergrads receive athletic scholarships. 91% freshmen, 91% undergrads receive any aid. **Criteria for awarding aid:** *Non-need-based:* Academics, Leadership, Music/drama.

WILLIAM PENN UNIVERSITY

201 Trueblood Avenue, Oskaloosa, IA 52577
Phone: 641-673-1012
E-mail: admissions@wmpenn.edu • **CEEB Code:** 6943
Fax: 641-673-2113 • **Website:** www.wmpenn.edu • **ACT Code:** 1372

This private school, affiliated with the Quaker Church, was founded in 1873. It has a 53-acre campus.

RATINGS
Admissions Selectivity Rating: 71   **Fire Safety Rating:** 60*   **Green Rating:** 60*

STUDENTS AND FACULTY
Enrollment: 1,489. **Student Body:** 48% female, 52% male, 28% out-of-state, 2% international. Asian 1%, African American 15%, Caucasian 68%, Hispanic 7%, Native American 1%, Pacific Islander <1%, Two or more races 1%, Race unknown 5%.
Faculty: Student/faculty ratio 14:1. 35 full-time faculty, 49% hold PhDs, 3% are are members of minority groups, 29% are women. 0% of classes are taught by teaching assistants.

ACADEMICS
Degrees: associate, bachelor's, master's, transfer. **Classes:** Most classes have fewer than 10 students. **Most popular majors:** Education; Business/Commerce; Psychology. **Special Study Options:** cooperative education program, double major, English as a Second Language (ESL), independent study, internships, study abroad, teacher certification program, College for Working Adults. **Disability Services:** Special programs offered to physically disabled students, including tape recorders, tutors. **Career Services:** Alumni services, Career/job search classes, Internships, On-campus interviews.

FACILITIES
Housing: Coed dorms, women's dorms, apartments for married students, apartments for single students. 75% of campus accessible to physically diasbled. **Special Academic Facilities/Equipment:** Foyer Gallery, Mid-East art and artifact collection.

CAMPUS LIFE
Environment: Rural. **Activities:** Choral groups, drama/theater, jazz band, literary magazine, music ensembles, musical theater, radio station, student government, student newspaper, yearbook. 34 registered organizations, 3 honor societies, 4 religious organizations. 3 fraternities, 3 sororities. **Athletics (Intercollegiate):** *Men:* baseball, basketball, cheerleading, cross-country, football, golf, soccer, track/field (outdoor), wrestling. *Women:* basketball, cheerleading, cross-country, soccer, softball, track/field (outdoor), volleyball.

ADMISSIONS
Freshman Academic Profile: 14% in top 25% of high school class, 47% in top 50% of high school class. 97% from public high schools. Minimum internet-based TOEFL 61. Minimum paper TOEFL 500. **Basis for Candidate Selection:** *Very important factors considered include:* rigor of secondary school record, academic GPA. *Important factors considered include:* class rank, standardized test scores, character/personal qualities. *Other factors considered include:* application essay, recommendation(s), interview, extracurricular activities, talent/ability, alumni/ae relation, volunteer work, work experience. **Freshman Admission Requirements:** High school diploma is required and GED is accepted. *Academic units recommended:* 4 English, 3 math, 3 science, 2 foreign language, 2 social studies, 2 history, 2 academic electives. **Freshman Admission Statistics:** 841 applied, 53.51% admitted, 53% enrolled. **Transfer Admission Requirements:** college transcript(s), Minimum college GPA of 2.0 required. Lowest grade transferable D. **General Admission Information:** Application fee $20. Priority deadline 7/1. Nonfall registration accepted.

COSTS AND FINANCIAL AID
Annual tuition $22,840. Room and board $5,472. Required fees $370. Average book expense $1,150. **Required Forms and Deadlines:** FAFSA. **Notification of Awards:** Applicants will be notified of awards on a rolling basis beginning 1/1. **Types of Aid:** *Need-based scholarships/grants:* Federal Pell, FSEOG, State scholarships/grants, Private scholarships, College/university scholarship or grant aid from institutional funds. *Loans:* Federal Perkins Loans. *Student Employment:* Federal Work-Study Program available. Institutional employment available. **Criteria for awarding aid:** *Need-based:* Academics, Alumni affiliation, Athletics, Leadership, Music/drama, Religious affiliation. *Non-need-based:* Academics, Alumni affiliation, Athletics, Leadership, Music/drama, Religious affiliation.

WILLIAMS COLLEGE

Best Colleges

995 Main St., Williamstown, MA 1267
Phone: 413-597-2211 • **Financial Aid Phone:** 413-597-4181
E-mail: admission@williams.edu • **CEEB Code:** 3965
Fax: 413-597-4052 • **Website:** www.williams.edu • **ACT Code:** 1936

This private school was founded in 1793. It has a 450-acre campus.

RATINGS

Admissions Selectivity Rating: 98   **Fire Safety Rating:** 60*   **Green Rating:** 90

STUDENTS AND FACULTY

Enrollment: 2,042. **Student Body:** 49% female, 51% male, 88% out-of-state, 8% international (54 countries represented). Asian 13%, African American 7%, Caucasian 53%, Hispanic 12%, Native American <1%, Pacific Islander 0%, Two or more races 6%, Race unknown 0%.
Retention and Graduation: 97% freshmen return for sophomore year. 86% freshmen graduate within 4 years. 94% freshmen graduate within 6 years.
Faculty: Student/faculty ratio 7:1. 278 full-time faculty, 97% hold PhDs, 22% are are members of minority groups, 46% are women. 0% of classes are taught by teaching assistants.

ACADEMICS

Degrees: bachelor's, master's. **Classes:** Most classes have fewer than 10 students. Most lab/discussion sessions have 10-19 students. **Most popular majors:** Economics; Psychology; English Language and Literature. **Special Study Options:** cross-registration, double major, independent study, internships, student-designed major, study abroad. Combined degree programs: Combined program in liberal arts and eng. **Disability Services:** Special programs offered to physically disabled students, including note-taking services, reader services, tape recorders, tutors. **Career Services:** Alumni network, Alumni services, Career/job search classes, Internships, Regional alumni.

FACILITIES

Housing: Coed dorms, cooperative housing **Special Academic Facilities/Equipment:** Hopkins Observatory; Williams College Museum of Art; Adams Memorial Theatre; Chapin Rare Books Library; Spencer Studio Art Building, '62 Center for Theatre and Dance, Hopkins Experimental Forest **Computers:** 100% of classrooms, 100% of dorms, 100% of libraries, 100% of dining areas, 100% of student union, 100% of common outdoor areas have wireless network access. Students can register for classes online. Administrative functions (other than registration) can be performed online.

CAMPUS LIFE

Environment: Village. **Activities:** Choral groups, dance, drama/theater, literary magazine, music ensembles, radio station, student government, student newspaper, student-run film society, symphony orchestra, yearbook, Student Organization. 110 registered organizations, 3 honor societies, 8 religious organizations. **Athletics (Intercollegiate):** *Men:* baseball, basketball, crew/rowing, cross-country, diving, football, golf, ice hockey, lacrosse, skiing (downhill/alpine), skiing (nordic/cross-country), soccer, squash, swimming, tennis, track/field (outdoor), track/field (indoor), wrestling. *Women:* basketball, crew/rowing, cross-country, diving, field hockey, golf, ice hockey, lacrosse, skiing (downhill/alpine), skiing (nordic/cross-country), soccer, softball, squash, swimming, tennis, track/field (outdoor), track/field (indoor), volleyball.
On-Campus Highlights: Paresky Student Center, Schow Science Library, Williams College Museum of Art, '62 Center for Theatre and Dance, Chandler Gymnasium.

ADMISSIONS

Freshman Academic Profile: 91% in top 10% of high school class, 98% in top 25% of high school class, 99% in top 50% of high school class. **Reported SAT (pre-2016 redesign) scores:** SAT Math middle 50% range 660-770. SAT Critical Reading middle 50% range 670-770. SAT Writing middle 50% range 670-770. **Concordant SAT scores:** SAT EBRW middle 50% range 710–780. SAT Math middle 50% range 690–780. ACT middle 50% range 31-34. **Basis for Candidate Selection:** *Very important factors considered include:* rigor of secondary school record, class rank, academic GPA, standardized test scores, recommendation(s), talent/ability. *Important factors considered include:* application essay, extracurricular activities, character/personal qualities, first generation, alumni/ae relation, racial/ethnic status. *Other factors considered include:* geographical residence, volunteer work, work experience. **Freshman Admission Requirements:** High school diploma or equivalent is not required. *Academic units recommended:* 4 English, 4 math, 4 science, 3 science labs,

4 foreign language, 4 social studies. **Freshman Admission Statistics:** 6,985 applied, 17.61% admitted, 45% enrolled. **Transfer Admission Requirements:** High school transcript, college transcript(s), essay or personal statement, standardized test scores, statement of good standing from prior institution(s). Minimum college GPA of 3.5 required. Lowest grade transferable C-. **General Admission Information:** Application fee $65. Regular application deadline 1/1. Nonfall registration not accepted. Admission may be deferred.

COSTS AND FINANCIAL AID

Required Forms and Deadlines: FAFSA, CSS/Financial Aid PROFILE, Noncustodial PROFILE. **Notification of Awards:** Applicants will be notified of awards on or about 4/1. **Types of Aid:** *Need-based scholarships/grants:* Federal Pell, FSEOG, State scholarships/grants, Private scholarships, College/university scholarship or grant aid from institutional funds. *Loans:* Direct Subsidized Stafford Loans, Direct Unsubsidized Stafford Loans, Direct PLUS loans, Federal Perkins Loans, College/university loans from institutional funds. *Student Employment:* Federal Work-Study Program available. Institutional employment available. **Financial Aid Statistics:** 99% needy freshmen, 99% needy undergrads receive need-based scholarship or grant aid. 0% undergrads receive non-need-based scholarship or grant aid. 100% freshmen, 100% undergrads receive need-based self-help aid. 0% freshmen, 0% undergrads receive athletic scholarships. 50% freshmen, 49% undergrads receive any aid. 43% undergrads borrow to pay for school. Average cumulative indebtedness $15,687.

WILMINGTON COLLEGE (DE)

320 Dupont Highway, New Castle, DE 19720
Phone: 302-328-9401
E-mail: mlee@wilmcoll.edu • **CEEB Code:** 5925
Fax: 302-328-5902 • **Website:** www.wilmcoll.edu • **ACT Code:** 635

This private school was founded in 1967. It has a 15-acre campus.

RATINGS

Admissions Selectivity Rating: 61   **Fire Safety Rating:** 60*   **Green Rating:** 60*

STUDENTS AND FACULTY

Enrollment: 4,399. **Student Body:** 53% female, 47% male, 3% out-of-state, 0% international. Asian 1%, African American 14%, Caucasian 64%, Hispanic 2%, Native American <1%, Pacific Islander 0%, Two or more races 0%, Race unknown 19%.
Retention and Graduation: 87% freshmen return for sophomore year. 50% grads go on to further study within 1 year. 9% grads pursue arts and sciences degrees. 10% grads pursue law degrees. 80% grads pursue business degrees. 1% grads pursue medical degrees. **Faculty:** Student/faculty ratio 18:1. 0% of classes are taught by teaching assistants.

ACADEMICS

Degrees: associate, bachelor's, certificate, master's, post-master's certificate. **Most popular majors:** Education; Business/Commerce. **Special Study Options:** Accelerated program, cooperative education program, distance learning, double major, independent study, internships, teacher certification program, weekend college. **Disability Services:** Special programs offered to physically disabled students, including tutors. **Career Services:** Alumni services, Career/job search classes, Career assessment, Internships.

FACILITIES

Housing: All housing is off campus.

CAMPUS LIFE

Environment: Village. **Activities:** student government 1 honor society. **Athletics (Intercollegiate):** *Men:* baseball, basketball, cross-country, soccer. *Women:* basketball, softball.

ADMISSIONS

Minimum paper TOEFL 500. **Basis for Candidate Selection:** *Important factors considered include:* rigor of secondary school record, recommendation(s). **Freshman Admission Requirements:** High school diploma is required and GED is accepted.High school diploma is required and GED is not accepted. **Transfer Admission Requirements:** college transcript(s), Minimum college GPA of 2.0 required. Lowest grade transferable C. **General Admission Information:** Application fee $25. Nonfall registration accepted. Admission may be deferred for a maximum of 12 months.

COSTS AND FINANCIAL AID

Annual tuition $6,060. Required fees $50. Average book expense $500. **Required Forms and Deadlines:** FAFSA. *Student Employment:* Federal Work-Study Program available.

WILMINGTON COLLEGE (OH)

Phone: 937-382-6661 • **CEEB Code:** 1909
Website: www.wilmington.edu • **ACT Code:** 3362

This private school, affiliated with the Quaker Church, was founded in 1870. It has a 65-acre campus.

RATINGS

Admissions Selectivity Rating: 85   **Fire Safety Rating:** 60*   **Green Rating:** 60*

STUDENTS AND FACULTY

Enrollment: 1,290. **Student Body:** 56% female, 44% male, 6% out-of-state, 1% international. Asian 0%, African American 11%, Caucasian 72%, Hispanic 1%, Native American 1%, Pacific Islander 0%, Two or more races 3%, Race unknown 11%. **Retention and Graduation:** 67% freshmen return for sophomore year. 46% freshmen graduate within 4 years. **Faculty:** Student/faculty ratio 14:1. 66 full-time faculty, 0% hold PhDs, 0% are are members of minority groups, 0% are women. 0% of classes are taught by teaching assistants.

ACADEMICS

Degrees: bachelor's, master's. **Classes:** Most classes have 10-19 students. **Most popular majors:** Psychology; Bible/Biblical Studies; Business Administration and Management. **Special Study Options:** cross-registration, double major, dual enrollment, honors program, independent study, internships, liberal arts/career combination, student-designed major, study abroad, teacher certification program, weekend college. **Disability Services:** Special programs offered to physically disabled students, including note-taking services, reader services, tape recorders, tutors. **Career Services:** Alumni services, Internships.

FACILITIES

Housing: Coed dorms, women's dorms, fraternity/sorority housing, apartments for single students. 100% of campus accessible to physically diasbled. **Special Academic Facilities/Equipment:** Hiroshima-Nagasaki memorial collection and peace resource center, education lab, language lab, three farms, observatory, electron microscope.

CAMPUS LIFE

Environment: Rural. **Activities:** Choral groups, drama/theater, literary magazine, music ensembles, musical theater, student government, student newspaper, yearbook, Campus Ministries, Student Organization. 48 registered organizations, 3 honor societies, 3 religious organizations. 6 fraternities, 5 sororities. **Athletics (Intercollegiate):** *Men:* baseball, basketball, cheerleading, cross-country, football, golf, soccer, swimming, tennis, track/field (outdoor), wrestling. *Women:* basketball, cheerleading, cross-country, golf, soccer, softball, swimming, tennis, track/field (outdoor), volleyball. **On-Campus Highlights:** Residence Hall room, Athletic Center, Student Center/Dining Hall, Computer labs, Class room.

ADMISSIONS

Freshman Academic Profile: Average high school GPA 3.2. 11% in top 10% of high school class, 36% in top 25% of high school class, 70% in top 50% of high school class. **Reported SAT (pre-2016 redesign) scores:** SAT Math middle 50% range 420-550. SAT Critical Reading middle 50% range 440-560. **Concordant SAT scores:** SAT Math middle 50% range 460–570. ACT middle 50% range 18-23. Minimum paper TOEFL 500. **Basis for Candidate Selection:** *Very important factors considered include:* academic GPA. *Important factors considered include:* rigor of secondary school record, class rank, standardized test scores, talent/ability, character/personal qualities, alumni/ae relation. *Other factors considered include:* recommendation(s), interview, extracurricular activities, volunteer work, level of applicant's interest. **Freshman Admission Requirements:** High school diploma is required and GED is accepted. *Academic units required:* 4 English, 2 math, 2 science, 2 science labs. *Academic units recommended:* 2 foreign language, 2 social studies. **Freshman Admission Statistics:** 1,651 applied, 28.29% admitted, 45% enrolled. **Transfer Admission Requirements:** college transcript(s), statement of good standing from prior institution(s). Minimum college GPA of 2.0 required. Lowest grade transferable C-. **General Admission Information:** Regular application deadline 8/1. Nonfall registration accepted.

COSTS AND FINANCIAL AID

Annual tuition $25,214. Room and board $8,520. Required fees $500. *Student Employment:* Federal Work-Study Program available. Institutional employment available.

WILSON COLLEGE

1015 Philadelphia Avenue, Chambersburg, PA 17201
Phone: 717-262-2002 • **Financial Aid Phone:** 717-262-2016
E-mail: admissions@wilson.edu • **CEEB Code:** 2979
Fax: 717-262-2546 • **ACT Code:** 3758

This private school, affiliated with the Presbyterian Church, was founded in 1869. It has a 300-acre campus.

RATINGS

Admissions Selectivity Rating: 85   **Fire Safety Rating:** 87   **Green Rating:** 60*

STUDENTS AND FACULTY

Enrollment: 510. **Student Body:** 92% female, 8% male, 24% out-of-state, 4% international (10 countries represented). Asian 0%, African American 5%, Caucasian 76%, Hispanic 3%, Native American 0%, Pacific Islander 0%, Two or more races 2%, Race unknown 10%. **Retention and Graduation:** 57% freshmen return for sophomore year. 43% freshmen graduate within 4 years. 56% freshmen graduate within 6 years. 30% grads go on to further study within 1 year. 6% grads pursue arts and sciences degrees. 9% grads pursue law degrees. 8% grads pursue business degrees. 8% grads pursue medical degrees. **Faculty:** Student/faculty ratio 10:1. 45 full-time faculty, 82% hold PhDs, 7% are are members of minority groups, 56% are women. 0% of classes are taught by teaching assistants.

ACADEMICS

Degrees: associate, bachelor's, master's. **Classes:** Most classes have 10-19 students. Most lab/discussion sessions have 10-19 students. **Most popular majors:** Veterinary/Animal Health Technology/Technician and Veterinary Assistant; Elementary Education and Teaching; Equestrian/Equine Studies. **Special Study Options:** cooperative education program, cross-registration, double major, English as a Second Language (ESL), honors program, independent study, internships, liberal arts/career combination, student-designed major, study abroad, teacher certification program. **Honors Programs:** Wilson Scholars Program. **Disability Services:** Special programs offered to physically disabled students, including note-taking services, reader services, tape recorders, tutors. **Career Services:** Alumni network, Alumni services, Career/job search classes, Career assessment, Internships. I am proudest of the variety of services we offer and the increased # of services. An alum commented last week on how much more we offer in the Career Development Center.

FACILITIES

Housing: women's dorms, Students of junior standing or above are guaranteed single residence hall room. We also offer women with children housing, maximum of 2 children. 49% of campus accessible to physically diasbled. **Special Academic Facilities/Equipment:** Archives, Bogigian Art gallery, Dance Studio, Helen M. Beach '24 Veterinary Medical Center, Penn Hall Equestrian Center, Natural History Museum, electron microscope, NMR spectrometer. **Computers:** 50% of classrooms, 100% of dining areas, 100% of student union, 15% of common outdoor areas have wireless network access. Students can register for classes online. Administrative functions (other than registration) can be performed online.

CAMPUS LIFE

Environment: Village. **Activities:** Choral groups, dance, drama/theater, literary magazine, music ensembles, radio station, student government, student newspaper, yearbook, Campus Ministries, Student Organization. 35 registered organizations, 1 honor society, 4 religious organizations. **Athletics (Intercollegiate):** *Women:* basketball, field hockey, gymnastics, lacrosse, soccer, softball, tennis. **On-Campus Highlights:** Penn Hall Equestrian Center, Helen M. Beach '24 Veterinary Medical Center, Complex for Science, Math & Technology, Prentis Hall Women with Children Residence, Lenfest Commons with Fitness Center and Coffee House. **Environmental Initiatives:** Organic farm.

ADMISSIONS

Freshman Academic Profile: Average high school GPA 3.4. 22% in top 10% of high school class, 50% in top 25% of high school class, 82% in top 50% of high school class. 84% from public high schools. **Reported SAT (pre-2016 redesign) scores:** SAT Math middle 50% range 430-550. SAT Critical Reading middle 50% range 450-570. SAT Writing middle 50% range 430-550. **Concordant SAT scores:** SAT EBRW middle 50% 490–620. SAT Math middle 50% range 470–570. ACT middle 50% range 21-23. Minimum internet-based TOEFL 61. Minimum paper TOEFL 500. **Basis for Candidate Selection:** *Very important factors considered include:* rigor of secondary school record. *Important factors considered include:* class rank, academic GPA, recommendation(s). *Other factors considered include:* standardized test scores, application essay, interview, extracurricular activities, talent/ability, character/

personal qualities, alumni/ae relation, volunteer work, work experience. **Freshman Admission Requirements:** High school diploma is required and GED is accepted. *Academic units required:* 4 English, 3 math, 2 science, 2 science labs, 2 foreign language, 4 social studies. **Freshman Admission Statistics:** 563 applied, 50.27% admitted, 33% enrolled. **Transfer Admission Requirements:** High school transcript, college transcript(s), essay or personal statement, Minimum college GPA of 2.0 required. Lowest grade transferable C. **General Admission Information:** Priority deadline 4/30. Nonfall registration accepted. Admission may be deferred for a maximum of 12 Months.

COSTS AND FINANCIAL AID

Annual tuition $28,745. Room and board $9,710. Required fees $595. Average book expense $1,000. **Required Forms and Deadlines:** FAFSA, Institution's own financial aid form, State aid form. **Notification of Awards:** Applicants will be notified of awards on a rolling basis beginning 2/15. **Types of Aid:** *Need-based scholarships/grants:* Federal Pell, FSEOG, State scholarships/grants, Private scholarships, College/university scholarship or grant aid from institutional funds. *Loans:* Federal Perkins Loans, College/university loans from institutional funds. *Student Employment:* Federal Work-Study Program available. Institutional employment available. **Financial Aid Statistics:** 100% needy freshmen, 99% needy undergrads receive need-based scholarship or grant aid. 11% freshmen, 9% undergrads receive non-need-based scholarship or grant aid. 83% freshmen, 81% undergrads receive need-based self-help aid. 0% freshmen, 0% undergrads receive athletic scholarships. 99% freshmen, 97% undergrads receive any aid. **Criteria for awarding aid:** *Need-based:* Academics, Art, Leadership, Music/drama, Religious affiliation. *Non-need-based:* Academics, Alumni affiliation, Religious affiliation, State/district residency.

WINGATE UNIVERSITY

Campus Box 3059, Wingate, NC 28174
Phone: 704-233-8200 • **Financial Aid Phone:** 704-233-8209
E-mail: admit@wingate.edu • **CEEB Code:** 5908
Fax: 704-233-8110 • **Website:** www.wingate.edu • **ACT Code:** 3176

This private school, affiliated with the Baptist Church, was founded in 1896. It has a 390-acre campus.

RATINGS

Admissions Selectivity Rating: 79 | **Fire Safety Rating:** 87 | **Green Rating:** 60*

STUDENTS AND FACULTY

Enrollment: 2,001. **Student Body:** 59% female, 41% male, 17% out-of-state, 4% international (21 countries represented). Asian 2%, African American 15%, Caucasian 64%, Hispanic 2%, Native American 1%, Pacific Islander <1%, Two or more races 4%, Race unknown 8%.
Retention and Graduation: 75% freshmen return for sophomore year. 43% freshmen graduate within 4 years. 53% freshmen graduate within 6 years. 20% grads go on to further study within 1 year. 9% grads pursue arts and sciences degrees. 2% grads pursue law degrees. 8% grads pursue business degrees. 1% grads pursue medical degrees. **Faculty:** Student/faculty ratio 16:1. 145 full-time faculty, 94% hold PhDs, 8% are are members of minority groups, 54% are women. 0% of classes are taught by teaching assistants.

ACADEMICS

Degrees: bachelor's, doctoral/professional, doctoral/research, master's, post-master's certificate. **Classes:** Most classes have 20-29 students. Most lab/discussion sessions have 10-19 students. **Most popular majors:** Biology/Biological Sciences; Business Administration and Management; Psychology. **Special Study Options:** cross-registration, double major, dual enrollment, honors program, independent study, internships, study abroad, teacher certification program, A Bachelor in Liberal Arts is offered to non-traditional students looking to complete a degree. This programs is offered at the Wingate Metro Center in Matthews, NC. **Honors Programs:** Our University Honors program offers students 18 hours of honors courses covering a spectrum of disciplines. Students may travel to New York City as part of the program. **Disability Services:** Special programs offered to physically disabled students, including note-taking services, tape recorders, tutors. **Career Services:** Alumni network, Career/job search classes, Career assessment, Internships. Undergraduate research is an integral component of the Wingate University experience. In 2006, Wingate developed a Quality Enhancement Plan (QEP) to enhance student learning through professional partnerships. One focus of the professional partnership initiative is to connect students with faculty mentors for collaboration on projects of creative and investigative significance. The goals of this program are to encourage faculty-student engagement by encouraging creative and investigative approaches to learning in the classroom, studio, and laboratory settings and by encouraging faculty and staff to actively mentor students in their learning pursuits. To accomplish these goals, Wingate promotes and facilitates student-faculty research initiatives and community events which showcase the partnership efforts.

FACILITIES

Housing: men's dorms, women's dorms, apartments for single students. 95% of campus accessible to physically disabled. **Special Academic Facilities/Equipment:** Douglas Helms Art Gallery, outdoor recreation lab, Batte Fine Arts Center. **Computers:** Administrative functions (other than registration) can be performed online.

CAMPUS LIFE

Environment: Village. **Activities:** Choral groups, drama/theater, jazz band, literary magazine, music ensembles, musical theater, student government, student newspaper, television station, yearbook. 45 registered organizations, 10 honor societies, 8 religious organizations. 4 fraternities, 4 sororities. **Athletics (Intercollegiate):** *Men:* baseball, basketball, cheerleading, cross-country, football, golf, lacrosse, soccer, swimming, tennis. *Women:* basketball, cheerleading, cross-country, golf, soccer, softball, swimming, tennis, volleyball. **On-Campus Highlights:** George A. Batte Jr. Fine Arts Center, Kondike Grill, Irwin Belk Football Stadium, Ethel's Cafe (in the Ethel K. Smith Library), Jefferson Clubhouse, Batte Fine Arts Center, a 44,000 sq. foot facility provides a venue foe musicians, singers, actors, and artists. The center features a 554 theatre, among other facilities. Ethel's Cafe provides a quiet environment to study while enjoying coffee, pastries, and other refreshments. Jefferson Clubhouse houses a convinience store, gym, swinmming pool, Health Services, and the offices of Greek Life.

ADMISSIONS

Freshman Academic Profile: Average high school GPA 3.3. 18% in top 10% of high school class, 50% in top 25% of high school class, 85% in top 50% of high school class. 85% from public high schools. **Reported SAT (pre-2016 redesign) scores:** SAT Math middle 50% range 470-570. SAT Critical Reading middle 50% range 440-550. SAT Writing middle 50% range 430-530. **Concordant SAT scores:** SAT EBRW middle 50% 490–600. SAT Math middle 50% range 510–590. ACT middle 50% range 19-24. Minimum paper TOEFL 550. **Basis for Candidate Selection:** *Very important factors considered include:* rigor of secondary school record, class rank. *Important factors considered include:* academic GPA, standardized test scores, recommendation(s). *Other factors considered include:* extracurricular activities, talent/ability, character/personal qualities. **Freshman Admission Requirements:** High school diploma is required and GED is accepted. *Academic units recommended:* 4 English, 3 math, 2 science, 1 science lab, 2 foreign language, 2 social studies. **Freshman Admission Statistics:** 5,323 applied, 79.30% admitted, 15% enrolled. **Transfer Admission Requirements:** High school transcript, college transcript(s), statement of good standing from prior institution(s). Minimum college GPA of 2.0 required. Lowest grade transferable C. **General Admission Information:** Application fee $30. Priority deadline 4/1. Nonfall registration accepted. Admission may be deferred for a maximum of 1 year.

COSTS AND FINANCIAL AID

Annual tuition $24,750. Room and board $10,400. Required fees $1,550. Average book expense $1,100. **Required Forms and Deadlines:** FAFSA, State aid form. **Notification of Awards:** Applicants will be notified of awards on a rolling basis beginning 3/15. **Types of Aid:** *Need-based scholarships/grants:* Federal Pell, FSEOG, State scholarships/grants, Private scholarships, College/university scholarship or grant aid from institutional funds. *Loans:* Direct Subsidized Stafford Loans, Direct Unsubsidized Stafford Loans, Direct PLUS loans. *Student Employment:* Federal Work-Study Program available. Institutional employment available. **Financial Aid Statistics:** 100% needy freshmen, 99% needy undergrads receive need-based scholarship or grant aid. 17% freshmen, 16% undergrads receive non-need-based scholarship or grant aid. 82% freshmen, 84% undergrads receive need-based self-help aid. 11% freshmen, 11% undergrads receive athletic scholarships. 97% freshmen, 96% undergrads receive any aid. **Criteria for awarding aid:** *Need-based:* Athletics. *Non-need-based:* Academics, Alumni affiliation, Art, Athletics, Leadership, Music/drama, Religious affiliation.

WINONA STATE UNIVERSITY

175 Mark Street, Winona, MN 55987
Phone: 507-457-5100 • **Financial Aid Phone:** 507-457-5090
E-mail: admissions@winona.edu • **CEEB Code:** 6680
Fax: 507-457-5620 • **Website:** www.winona.edu • **ACT Code:** 2162

This public school was founded in 1858. It has a 40-acre campus.

RATINGS
Admissions Selectivity Rating: 80   **Fire Safety Rating:** 92   **Green Rating:** 81

STUDENTS AND FACULTY
Enrollment: 7,486. **Student Body:** 63% female, 37% male, 29% out-of-state, 3% international (50 countries represented). Asian 2%, African American 3%, Caucasian 86%, Hispanic 3%, Native American <1%, Pacific Islander <1%, Two or more races 2%, Race unknown 1%.
Retention and Graduation: 77% freshmen return for sophomore year. 35% freshmen graduate within 4 years. 59% freshmen graduate within 6 years. 12% grads go on to further study within 1 year. **Faculty:** Student/faculty ratio 18:1. 340 full-time faculty, 77% hold PhDs, 14% are are members of minority groups, 51% are women. 0% of classes are taught by teaching assistants.

ACADEMICS
Degrees: associate, bachelor's, doctoral/professional, master's, postbachelor's certificate, post-master's certificate. **Classes:** Most classes have 20-29 students. Most lab/discussion sessions have 20-29 students. **Most popular majors:** Elementary Education and Teaching; Registered Nursing/Registered Nurse; Biology/Biological Sciences. **Special Study Options:** Accelerated program, cross-registration, distance learning, double major, dual enrollment, English as a Second Language (ESL), external degree program, independent study, internships, student-designed major, study abroad, teacher certification program. **Disability Services:** Special programs offered to physically disabled students, including note-taking services, reader services, tape recorders. **Career Services:** Alumni network, Alumni services, Career assessment, Internships, Regional alumni. While we do not offer career/job search 'classes,' we do provide nearly 150 workshops and presentations annually reaching an average of 5000 students; we also have podcasts on a variety of topics available online 24/7.

FACILITIES
Housing: Coed dorms, special housing for disabled students, men's dorms, women's dorms, apartments for single students, Residential College-Residence halls with classrooms and faculty offices. 100% of campus accessible to physically diasbled. **Special Academic Facilities/Equipment:** Paul Watkins Art Gallery **Computers:** 100% of classrooms, 50% of dorms, 100% of libraries, 100% of dining areas, 100% of student union, 85% of common outdoor areas have wireless network access. Students can register for classes online. Administrative functions (other than registration) can be performed online. Undergraduates are required to own a computer.

CAMPUS LIFE
Environment: Town. **Activities:** Choral groups, concert band, dance, drama/ theater, jazz band, literary magazine, music ensembles, musical theater, pep band, radio station, student government, student newspaper, student-run film society, symphony orchestra, television station, Campus Ministries, Student Organization, Model UN. 208 registered organizations, 14 honor societies, 10 religious organizations. 2 fraternities, 3 sororities. **Athletics (Intercollegiate):** *Men:* baseball, basketball, cross-country, football, golf. *Women:* basketball, cross-country, golf, gymnastics, soccer, softball, tennis, track/field (outdoor), track/field (indoor), volleyball. **On-Campus Highlights:** The Library, Lourdes Hall—Residential College, Central Courtyard and Clock Tower, The Smaug— Kryzsko Commons, Wabasha Hall Fitness Center. **Environmental Initiatives:** Recycling / Post Consumer Waste Reduction.

ADMISSIONS
Freshman Academic Profile: Average high school GPA 3.4. 10% in top 10% of high school class, 32% in top 25% of high school class, 70% in top 50% of high school class. ACT middle 50% range 20-25. Minimum internet-based TOEFL 68. Minimum paper TOEFL 520. **Basis for Candidate Selection:** *Very important factors considered include:* rigor of secondary school record, class rank, standardized test scores. *Important factors considered include:* academic GPA. *Other factors considered include:* recommendation(s). **Freshman Admission Requirements:** High school diploma is required and GED is accepted. *Academic units required:* 4 English, 3 math, 3 science, 3 science labs, 2 foreign language, 2 social studies, 1 history, 1 academic elective. **Freshman Admission Statistics:** 7,476 applied, 59.75% admitted, 36% enrolled. **Transfer Admission Requirements:** college transcript(s), Minimum college GPA of 2.4 required. Lowest grade transferable D. **General Admission Information:** Application fee $20. Regular application deadline 7/12. Nonfall registration accepted. Admission may be deferred for a maximum of 12 months.

COSTS AND FINANCIAL AID
Annual in-state tuition $7,103. Annual out-of-state tuition $12,800. Room and board $8,460. Required fees $1,972. Average book expense $1,200. **Required Forms and Deadlines:** FAFSA. **Types of Aid:** *Need-based scholarships/ grants:* Federal Pell, FSEOG, State scholarships/grants, Private scholarships, College/university scholarship or grant aid from institutional funds. *Loans:* Direct Subsidized Stafford Loans, Direct Unsubsidized Stafford Loans, Direct PLUS loans, Federal Perkins Loans, State Loans, College/university loans from institutional funds. *Student Employment:* Federal Work-Study Program available. Institutional employment available. **Financial Aid Statistics:** 74% needy freshmen, 69% needy undergrads receive need-based scholarship or grant aid. 18% freshmen, 10% undergrads receive non-need-based scholarship or grant aid. 84% freshmen, 88% undergrads receive need-based self-help aid. 33% freshmen, 19% undergrads receive athletic scholarships. 61% freshmen, 58% undergrads receive any aid. 76% undergrads borrow to pay for school. Average cumulative indebtedness $35,221. **Criteria for awarding aid:** *Non-need-based:* Academics, Alumni affiliation, Art, Athletics, Minority status, Music/drama.

WINTHROP UNIVERSITY

Admissions, Winthrop University, Rock Hill, SC 29733
Phone: 803-323-2191 • **Financial Aid Phone:** 803-323-2189
E-mail: admissions@winthrop.edu • **CEEB Code:** 5910
Fax: 803-323-2137 • **Website:** www.winthrop.edu • **ACT Code:** 3884

This public school was founded in 1886. It has a 418-acre campus.

RATINGS
Admissions Selectivity Rating: 83   **Fire Safety Rating:** 92   **Green Rating:** 80

STUDENTS AND FACULTY
Enrollment: 4,786. **Student Body:** 68% female, 32% male, 8% out-of-state, 2% international (39 countries represented). Asian 1%, African American 30%, Caucasian 58%, Hispanic 4%, Native American <1%, Pacific Islander <1%, Two or more races 4%, Race unknown <1%.
Retention and Graduation: 77% freshmen return for sophomore year. 36% freshmen graduate within 4 years. 56% freshmen graduate within 6 years. 25% grads go on to further study within 1 year. 6% grads pursue arts and sciences degrees. 4% grads pursue business degrees. 1% grads pursue medical degrees. **Faculty:** Student/faculty ratio 14:1. 282 full-time faculty, 89% hold PhDs, 14% are are members of minority groups, 54% are women. 0% of classes are taught by teaching assistants.

ACADEMICS
Degrees: bachelor's, certificate, master's, postbachelor's certificate, post-master's certificate. **Classes:** Most classes have 20-29 students. Most lab/ discussion sessions have 20-29 students. **Most popular majors:** Business/ Commerce; Design and Visual Communications; Biology/Biological Sciences. **Special Study Options:** cooperative education program, cross-registration, distance learning, double major, exchange student program (domestic), honors program, independent study, internships, study abroad, teacher certification program. **Disability Services:** Special programs offered to physically disabled students, including note-taking services, reader services, tape recorders. **Career Services:** Alumni network, Alumni services, Career/job search classes, Career assessment, Internships, Regional alumni. The Center for Career and Civic Engagement at Winthrop University combines Service Learning, Career Development, and Volunteer and Community Service functions in to one office. This allows us to provide very strong experiential learning activities including service work for our community partners and internships. It also allows us to share all opportunities (service or paid employment) on one database for easy student access. We have a high level of student engagement with our office through the combined opportunities.

FACILITIES
Housing: Coed dorms, men's dorms, women's dorms, fraternity/sorority housing, apartments for married students, apartments for single students. 90% of campus accessible to physically diasbled. **Special Academic Facilities/ Equipment:** Art gallery, on-campus nursery and kindergarten. **Computers:** 25% of classrooms, 10% of dorms, 100% of libraries, 100% of dining areas, 100% of student union, 10% of common outdoor areas have wireless network access. Students can register for classes online. Administrative functions (other than registration) can be performed online.

CAMPUS LIFE
Environment: Town. **Activities:** Choral groups, concert band, dance, drama/ theater, jazz band, literary magazine, music ensembles, musical theater, opera, pep band, radio station, student government, student newspaper, yearbook, Campus Ministries, Student Organization, Model UN. 184 registered

organizations, 23 honor societies, 10 religious organizations. 8 fraternities, 9 sororities. **Athletics (Intercollegiate):** *Men:* baseball, basketball, cross-country, golf, soccer, tennis, track/field (outdoor). *Women:* basketball, cross-country, golf, soccer, softball, tennis, track/field (outdoor), volleyball. **On-Campus Highlights:** Java City, Winthrop Coliseum, Frisbee-Golf Course. **Environmental Initiatives:** Very strong recycling program.

ADMISSIONS

Freshman Academic Profile: Average high school GPA 3.9. 22% in top 10% of high school class, 51% in top 25% of high school class, 87% in top 50% of high school class. **Reported SAT (pre-2016 redesign) scores:** SAT Math middle 50% range 450-560. SAT Critical Reading middle 50% range 460-570. **Concordant SAT scores:** SAT Math middle 50% range 490–580. ACT middle 50% range 20-26. Minimum internet-based TOEFL 68. Minimum paper TOEFL 520. **Basis for Candidate Selection:** *Very important factors considered include:* rigor of secondary school record, academic GPA, standardized test scores. *Other factors considered include:* application essay, recommendation(s), interview, extracurricular activities, talent/ability, volunteer work. **Freshman Admission Requirements:** High school diploma is required and GED is accepted. *Academic units required:* 4 English, 4 math, 3 science, 3 science labs, 2 foreign language, 2 social studies, 1 history, 1 academic elective, 1 visual/performing arts, and 1 unit from above areas or other academic areas. **Freshman Admission Statistics:** 4,876 applied, 67.10% admitted, 33% enrolled. **Transfer Admission Requirements:** college transcript(s), statement of good standing from prior institution(s). Minimum college GPA of 2.0 required. Lowest grade transferable C. **General Admission Information:** Application fee $40. Regular application deadline 5/1. Nonfall registration accepted. Admission may be deferred.

COSTS AND FINANCIAL AID

Annual in-state tuition $14,510. Annual out-of-state tuition $28,090. Room and board $8,572. Required fees $0. Average book expense $1,000. **Required Forms and Deadlines:** FAFSA. **Notification of Awards:** Applicants will be notified of awards on a rolling basis beginning 3/1. **Types of Aid:** *Need-based scholarships/grants:* Federal Pell, FSEOG, State scholarships/grants, Private scholarships, College/university scholarship or grant aid from institutional funds. *Loans:* Direct Subsidized Stafford Loans, Direct Unsubsidized Stafford Loans, Direct PLUS loans, Federal Perkins Loans. *Student Employment:* Federal Work-Study Program available. Institutional employment available. **Financial Aid Statistics:** 99% needy freshmen, 90% needy undergrads receive need-based scholarship or grant aid. 18% freshmen, 12% undergrads receive non-need-based scholarship or grant aid. 72% freshmen, 81% undergrads receive need-based self-help aid. 2% freshmen, 3% undergrads receive athletic scholarships. 70% freshmen, 83% undergrads receive any aid. **Criteria for awarding aid:** *Non-need-based:* Academics, Art, Athletics, Leadership, Music/drama.

WISCONSIN LUTHERAN COLLEGE

8800 West Bluemound Road, Milwaukee, WI 53226
Phone: 414-443-8811 • **Financial Aid Phone:** 414-443-8856
E-mail: admissions@wlc.edu • **CEEB Code:** 1513
Fax: 414-443-8514 • **Website:** www.wlc.edu • **ACT Code:** 4699

This private school, affiliated with the Lutheran Church, was founded in 1973. It has a 21-acre campus.

RATINGS

Admissions Selectivity Rating: 80   **Fire Safety Rating:** 75   **Green Rating:** 60*

STUDENTS AND FACULTY

Enrollment: 707. **Student Body:** 56% female, 44% male, 23% out-of-state, 2% international (9 countries represented). Asian 2%, African American 4%, Caucasian 89%, Hispanic 2%, Native American <1%, Pacific Islander 0%, Two or more races 0%, Race unknown 1%. **Retention and Graduation:** 76% freshmen return for sophomore year. 51% freshmen graduate within 4 years. 66% freshmen graduate within 6 years. **Faculty:** Student/faculty ratio 10:1. 60 full-time faculty, 67% hold PhDs, 0% are are members of minority groups, 33% are women. 0% of classes are taught by teaching assistants.

ACADEMICS

Degrees: bachelor's, master's. **Classes:** Most classes have 10-19 students. Most lab/discussion sessions have fewer than 10 students. **Most popular majors:** Speech Communication and Rhetoric; Psychology; Biology/Biological Sciences. **Special Study Options:** double major, dual enrollment, English as a Second Language (ESL), independent study, internships, student-designed major, study abroad, teacher certification program. **Disability Services:** Special programs offered to physically disabled students, including note-taking services, reader

services, tape recorders, tutors. **Career Services:** Alumni network, Career assessment, Internships.

FACILITIES

Housing: men's dorms, women's dorms, apartments for single students. 90% of campus accessible to physically disabled. **Special Academic Facilities/Equipment:** Center for Arts and Performance, Science Hall. **Computers:** Students can register for classes online.

CAMPUS LIFE

Environment: Metropolis. **Activities:** Choral groups, concert band, dance, jazz band, music ensembles, pep band, student government, student newspaper, Campus Ministries, Student Organization. 31 registered organizations. **Athletics (Intercollegiate):** *Men:* baseball, basketball, cross-country, football, golf, soccer, tennis, track/field (outdoor), track/field (indoor). *Women:* basketball, cross-country, golf, soccer, softball, tennis, track/field (outdoor), track/field (indoor), volleyball. **On-Campus Highlights:** Residence Halls, Center for Arts and Performance, Chapel, The Warrior Underground, The Recreation Complex, Science Hall, Warrior Fields.

ADMISSIONS

Freshman Academic Profile: Average high school GPA 3.3. 18% in top 10% of high school class, 43% in top 25% of high school class, 77% in top 50% of high school class. ACT middle 50% range 21-26. Minimum paper TOEFL 550. **Basis for Candidate Selection:** *Important factors considered include:* rigor of secondary school record, academic GPA, standardized test scores, recommendation(s), character/personal qualities, religious affiliation/commitment, level of applicant's interest. *Other factors considered include:* class rank, application essay, interview, extracurricular activities, talent/ability, first generation, alumni/ae relation, racial/ethnic status, volunteer work, work experience. **Freshman Admission Requirements:** High school diploma is required and GED is accepted. *Academic units required:* 4 English, 3 math, 2 science, 1 science lab, 2 foreign language, 2 history, 3 academic electives. *Academic units recommended:* 4 English, 4 math, 3 science, 2 science labs, 4 foreign language, 2 history, 3 academic electives. **Freshman Admission Statistics:** 646 applied, 76.32% admitted, 46% enrolled. **Transfer Admission Requirements:** college transcript(s), statement of good standing from prior institution(s). Minimum college GPA of 2.5 required. Lowest grade transferable CD. **General Admission Information:** Application fee $20. Priority deadline 3/1. Nonfall registration accepted. Admission may be deferred for a maximum of 1 semester.

COSTS AND FINANCIAL AID

Annual tuition $21,040. Room and board $7,700. Required fees $140. Average book expense $700. **Required Forms and Deadlines:** FAFSA, Institution's own financial aid form, Business/Farm Supplement. **Notification of Awards:** Applicants will be notified of awards on a rolling basis beginning 3/15. **Types of Aid:** *Need-based scholarships/grants:* Federal Pell, FSEOG, State scholarships/grants, Private scholarships, College/university scholarship or grant aid from institutional funds. *Loans:* State Loans. *Student Employment:* Federal Work-Study Program available. Institutional employment available. **Financial Aid Statistics:** 100% needy freshmen, 99% needy undergrads receive need-based scholarship or grant aid. 11% freshmen, 10% undergrads receive non-need-based scholarship or grant aid. 91% freshmen, 91% undergrads receive need-based self-help aid. 0% freshmen, 0% undergrads receive athletic scholarships. 100% freshmen, 98% undergrads receive any aid. **Criteria for awarding aid:** *Need-based:* Academics, Leadership, Minority status. *Non-need-based:* Academics, Art, Leadership, Music/drama.

WITTENBERG UNIVERSITY

PO Box 720, Springfield, OH 45501
Phone: 937-327-6314 • **Financial Aid Phone:** 937-327-7321
E-mail: admission@wittenberg.edu • **CEEB Code:** 1922
Fax: 937-327-6379 • **Website:** www.wittenberg.edu • **ACT Code:** 3364

This private school, affiliated with the Lutheran Church, was founded in 1845. It has a 71-acre campus.

RATINGS

Admissions Selectivity Rating: 80   **Fire Safety Rating:** 98   **Green Rating:** 79

STUDENTS AND FACULTY

Enrollment: 1,805. **Student Body:** 56% female, 44% male, 26% out-of-state, 1% international (26 countries represented). Asian 1%, African American 7%, Caucasian 81%, Hispanic 3%, Native American <1%, Pacific Islander 0%, Two or more races 6%, Race unknown 1%.
Retention and Graduation: 75% freshmen return for sophomore year. 59% freshmen graduate within 4 years. 64% freshmen graduate within 6 years.
Faculty: Student/faculty ratio 13:1. 122 full-time faculty, 97% hold PhDs, 13% are are members of minority groups, 43% are women. 0% of classes are taught by teaching assistants.

ACADEMICS

Degrees: bachelor's, master's. **Classes:** Most classes have 10-19 students. Most lab/discussion sessions have 10-19 students. **Most popular majors:** Business/Commerce; Biology/Biological Sciences; Education. **Special Study Options:** cross-registration, double major, dual enrollment, honors program, independent study, internships, liberal arts/career combination, student-designed major, study abroad, teacher certification program. **Honors Programs:** Honors Program, 3-2 Engineering Program, Pre-Health Programs. **Disability Services:** Special programs offered to physically disabled students, including note-taking services, reader services, tape recorders, tutors. **Career Services:** Alumni network, Alumni services, Career/job search classes, Career assessment, Internships, Regional alumni, Lutheran College Washington Semester.

FACILITIES

Housing: Coed dorms, special housing for international students, women's dorms, fraternity/sorority housing, apartments for married students, apartments for single students, University owned houses around campus. 81% of campus accessible to physically diasbled. **Special Academic Facilities/Equipment:** Language lab, electron microscope, observatory. **Computers:** 50% of classrooms, 100% of libraries, 100% of dining areas, 100% of student union, 100% of common outdoor areas have wireless network access. Students can register for classes online. Administrative functions (other than registration) can be performed online.

CAMPUS LIFE

Environment: Town. **Activities:** Choral groups, concert band, dance, drama/theater, jazz band, literary magazine, music ensembles, musical theater, opera, pep band, radio station, student government, student newspaper, student-run film society, symphony orchestra, yearbook, Campus Ministries, Student Organization. 126 registered organizations, 24 honor societies, 10 religious organizations. 6 fraternities, 5 sororities. **Athletics (Intercollegiate):** *Men:* baseball, basketball, cross-country, diving, football, golf, lacrosse, soccer, swimming, tennis, track/field (outdoor), track/field (indoor). *Women:* basketball, cheerleading, cross-country, diving, field hockey, golf, lacrosse, soccer, softball, swimming, tennis, track/field (outdoor), track/field (indoor), volleyball. **On-Campus Highlights:** HPERC Athletic Center, Benham Prince Student Center, Chakers Theatre, Weaver Observatory, Thomas Library.

ADMISSIONS

Freshman Academic Profile: Average high school GPA 3.4. 19% in top 10% of high school class, 45% in top 25% of high school class, 78% in top 50% of high school class. 83% from public high schools. **Reported SAT (pre-2016 redesign) scores:** SAT Math middle 50% range 490-610. SAT Critical Reading middle 50% range 490-610. SAT Writing middle 50% range 460-560. **Concordant SAT scores:** SAT EBRW middle 50% 530–640. SAT Math middle 50% range 520–630. ACT middle 50% range 22-28. Minimum paper TOEFL 550. **Basis for Candidate Selection:** *Very important factors considered include:* rigor of secondary school record, class rank, academic GPA. *Important factors considered include:* application essay, recommendation(s), extracurricular activities, talent/ability, character/personal qualities, volunteer work. *Other factors considered include:* standardized test scores, interview, first generation, alumni/ae relation, work experience. **Freshman Admission Requirements:** High school diploma is required and GED is accepted. *Academic units required:* 4 English, 3 math, 3 science, 2 science labs, 2 foreign language, 2 history. *Academic units recommended:* 4 English, 4 math, 5 science, 2 science labs, 3 foreign language, 3 history. **Freshman Admission Statistics:** 6,487 applied, 76.86% admitted, 10% enrolled. **Transfer Admission Requirements:** college transcript(s), Minimum college GPA of 2.0 required. Lowest grade transferable C. **General Admission Information:** Application fee $40. Priority deadline 3/15. Nonfall registration accepted. Admission may be deferred for a maximum of 12 months.

COSTS AND FINANCIAL AID

Annual tuition $37,230. Room and board $10,126. Required fees $860. Average book expense $1,000. **Required Forms and Deadlines:** FAFSA. **Notification of Awards:** Applicants will be notified of awards on a rolling basis beginning 3/1. **Types of Aid:** *Need-based scholarships/grants:* Federal Pell, FSEOG, State scholarships/grants, Private scholarships, College/university scholarship or grant aid from institutional funds, United Negro College Fund. *Loans:* Direct Subsidized Stafford Loans, Direct Unsubsidized Stafford Loans, Direct PLUS loans, Federal Perkins Loans, College/university loans from institutional funds.

Student Employment: Federal Work-Study Program available. Institutional employment available. **Financial Aid Statistics:** 100% needy freshmen, 100% needy undergrads receive need-based scholarship or grant aid. 0% undergrads receive non-need-based scholarship or grant aid. 82% freshmen, 80% undergrads receive need-based self-help aid. 0% freshmen, 0% undergrads receive athletic scholarships. 100% freshmen, 95% undergrads receive any aid. 73% undergrads borrow to pay for school. Average cumulative indebtedness $34,178. **Criteria for awarding aid:** *Need-based:* Academics, Alumni affiliation, Art, Leadership, Minority status, Music/drama, Religious affiliation. *Non-need-based:* Academics, Alumni affiliation, Art, Minority status, Music/drama, Religious affiliation, State/district residency.

WOFFORD COLLEGE

429 North Church Street, Spartanburg, SC 29303-3663
Phone: 864-597-4130 • **Financial Aid Phone:** 864-597-4160
E-mail: admission@wofford.edu • **CEEB Code:** 5912
Fax: 864-597-4147 • **Website:** www.wofford.edu • **ACT Code:** 3886

This private school, affiliated with the Methodist Church, was founded in 1854. It has a 170-acre campus.

RATINGS

Admissions Selectivity Rating: 87   **Fire Safety Rating:** 90   **Green Rating:** 60*

STUDENTS AND FACULTY

Enrollment: 1,606. **Student Body:** 51% female, 49% male, 45% out-of-state, 2% international (15 countries represented). Asian 2%, African American 8%, Caucasian 81%, Hispanic 4%, Native American <1%, Pacific Islander <1%, Two or more races 3%, Race unknown 1%.
Retention and Graduation: 87% freshmen return for sophomore year. 78% freshmen graduate within 4 years. 81% freshmen graduate within 6 years.
Faculty: Student/faculty ratio 11:1. 141 full-time faculty, 92% hold PhDs, 9% are are members of minority groups, 44% are women. 0% of classes are taught by teaching assistants.

ACADEMICS

Degrees: bachelor's. **Classes:** Most classes have 10-19 students. Most lab/discussion sessions have 20-29 students. **Most popular majors:** Biology/Biological Sciences; Finance; Business/Managerial Economics. **Special Study Options:** Accelerated program, cross-registration, double major, dual enrollment, independent study, internships, student-designed major, study abroad, teacher certification program, Presidential International Scholar program; "Success Initiative," Bonner Scholars, Community of Scholars, Learning Communities and Creative Writing Concentration. Combined degree programs: BA/MEng. **Disability Services:** Special programs offered to physically disabled students, including note-taking services, reader services, tape recorders, tutors. **Career Services:** Alumni network, Alumni services, Career/job search classes, Career assessment, Internships, Regional alumni, Institute for Professional Development.

FACILITIES

Housing: Coed dorms, apartments for single students, Wellness Housing. 85% of campus accessible to physically diasbled. **Special Academic Facilities/Equipment:** Campus is an Arboretum, Art galleries, Franklin W. Olin Building (teaching technology center), Milliken Science Center. **Computers:** 100% of classrooms, 10% of dorms, 100% of libraries, 100% of dining areas, 100% of student union, 40% of common outdoor areas have wireless network access. Students can register for classes online. Administrative functions (other than registration) can be performed online.

CAMPUS LIFE

Environment: City. **Activities:** Choral groups, concert band, dance, drama/theater, literary magazine, music ensembles, pep band, student government, student newspaper, yearbook, Campus Ministries. 105 registered organizations, 10 honor societies, 8 religious organizations. 8 fraternities, 4 sororities. **Athletics (Intercollegiate):** *Men:* baseball, basketball, cross-country, football, golf, riflery, soccer, tennis, track/field (outdoor), track/field (indoor). *Women:* basketball, cross-country, golf, riflery, soccer, tennis, track/field (outdoor), track/field (indoor), volleyball. **On-Campus Highlights:** The Roger Milliken Arboretum, Roger Milliken Science Center/Great Oaks, Main Building/Leonard Auditorium, Franklin W. Olin Building, Village Student Housing, Gibbs Stadium Richardson Physical Activities Building Russell C. King

Field and Switzer Stadium Joe E. Taylor Athletic Center. **Environmental Initiatives:** Establishment of an innovative and inter-disciplinary Environmental Studies program (a BS/BA major are offered through this program). Wofford "houses its Environmental Studies field studies, research, and community outreach programs in the state-of-the-art, LEED Platinum, historically significant Goodall Environmental Studies Center, situated eight miles from campus. The facility substantiates Wofford's commitment to real life, engaged learning. Wofford students, faculty, and staff, as well as area K-12 educators and community members all benefit from the Center's status as a living-learning laboratory for sustainability and environmental literacy." The college has a director for the environmental studies program.

ADMISSIONS

Freshman Academic Profile: Average high school GPA 3.6. 43% in top 10% of high school class, 74% in top 25% of high school class, 94% in top 50% of high school class. 65% from public high schools. **Reported SAT (pre-2016 redesign) scores:** SAT Math middle 50% range 530-640. SAT Critical Reading middle 50% range 520-630. SAT Writing middle 50% range 510-610. **Concordant SAT scores:** SAT EBRW middle 50% 570–670. SAT Math middle 50% range 560–660. ACT middle 50% range 24-29. Minimum internet-based TOEFL 80. Minimum paper TOEFL 550. **Basis for Candidate Selection:** *Very important factors considered include:* rigor of secondary school record, academic GPA. *Important factors considered include:* class rank, standardized test scores, application essay, extracurricular activities, talent/ability, character/personal qualities, volunteer work. *Other factors considered include:* recommendation(s), interview, first generation, alumni/ae relation, geographical residence, racial/ethnic status, work experience. **Freshman Admission Requirements:** High school diploma is required and GED is accepted. *Academic units required:* 4 English, 4 math, 3 science, 3 science labs, 3 foreign language, 3 social studies, 2 history. *Academic units recommended:* 4 English, 4 math, 3 science, 3 science labs, 3 foreign language, 3 social studies, 2 history, 1 academic elective, 1 computer science, 1 visual/performing arts. **Freshman Admission Statistics:** 2,937 applied, 70.11% admitted, 21% enrolled. **Transfer Admission Requirements:** High school transcript, college transcript(s), essay or personal statement, standardized test scores, statement of good standing from prior institution(s). Minimum college GPA of 2.5 required. Lowest grade transferable C. **General Admission Information:** Application fee $35. Regular application deadline 2/1. Regular notification 3/15. Nonfall registration accepted. Admission may be deferred for a maximum of 1 year.

COSTS AND FINANCIAL AID

Annual tuition $41,955. Room and board $12,140. Average book expense $1,200. **Required Forms and Deadlines:** FAFSA. **Notification of Awards:** Applicants will be notified of awards on or about 3/15. **Types of Aid:** *Need-based scholarships/grants:* Federal Pell, FSEOG, State scholarships/grants, Private scholarships, College/university scholarship or grant aid from institutional funds. *Loans:* Direct Subsidized Stafford Loans, Direct Unsubsidized Stafford Loans, Direct PLUS loans, Federal Perkins Loans. *Student Employment:* Federal Work-Study Program available. Institutional employment available. **Financial Aid Statistics:** 100% needy freshmen, 100% needy undergrads receive need-based scholarship or grant aid. 36% freshmen, 31% undergrads receive non-need-based scholarship or grant aid. 49% freshmen, 54% undergrads receive need-based self-help aid. 9% freshmen, 12% undergrads receive athletic scholarships. 96% freshmen, 94% undergrads receive any aid. Average cumulative indebtedness $31,102. **Criteria for awarding aid:** *Need-based:* Job skills. *Non-need-based:* Academics, Alumni affiliation, Art, Athletics, Job skills, Leadership, Minority status, Music/drama, Religious affiliation, State/district residency.

WOODBURY UNIVERSITY

7500 Glenoaks Boulevard, Burbank, CA 91510-7846
Phone: 818-767-0888 • **Financial Aid Phone:** 818-767-0888
E-mail: admissions@woodbury.edu • **CEEB Code:** 4955
Fax: 818-767-7520 • **ACT Code:** 481

This private school was founded in 1884. It has a 22-acre campus.

RATINGS

Admissions Selectivity Rating: 74   **Fire Safety Rating:** 63   **Green Rating:** 60*

STUDENTS AND FACULTY

Enrollment: 1,245. **Student Body:** 49% female, 51% male, 5% out-of-state, 25% international (41 countries represented). Asian 10%, African American 4%, Caucasian 33%, Hispanic 27%, Native American <1%, Pacific Islander 0%, Two or more races 0%, Race unknown 1%.
Retention and Graduation: 82% freshmen return for sophomore year. 20% freshmen graduate within 4 years. 46% freshmen graduate within 6 years.

Faculty: Student/faculty ratio 8:1. 86 full-time faculty, 74% hold PhDs, 16% are members of minority groups, 44% are women. 0% of classes are taught by teaching assistants.

ACADEMICS

Degrees: bachelor's, master's. **Classes:** Most classes have 10-19 students. **Most popular majors:** Business Administration and Management Fashion/Apparel Design. **Special Study Options:** Accelerated program, double major, dual enrollment, English as a Second Language (ESL), exchange student program (domestic), independent study, internships, liberal arts/career combination, student-designed major, study abroad, weekend college. **Disability Services:** Special programs offered to physically disabled students, including note-taking services, tape recorders, tutors. **Career Services:** Alumni services, Career assessment, Internships.

FACILITIES

Housing: Coed dorms, off-campus overflow apartments. 90% of campus accessible to physically diasbled. **Special Academic Facilities/Equipment:** Art Gallery; Architecture Gallery; **Computers:** 100% of classrooms, 100% of libraries, 100% of dining areas, have wireless network access. Students can register for classes online. Administrative functions (other than registration) can be performed online. Undergraduates are required to own a computer.

CAMPUS LIFE

Environment: City. **Activities:** student government 20 registered organizations, 3 honor societies, 2 fraternities, 2 sororities.

ADMISSIONS

Freshman Academic Profile: Average high school GPA 3.3. **Reported SAT (pre-2016 redesign) scores:** SAT Math middle 50% range 430-520. SAT Critical Reading middle 50% range 430-540. **Concordant SAT scores:** SAT Math middle 50% range 470–550. ACT middle 50% range 16-21. Minimum paper TOEFL 500. **Basis for Candidate Selection:** *Very important factors considered include:* academic GPA. *Important factors considered include:* rigor of secondary school record. *Other factors considered include:* class rank, standardized test scores, application essay, recommendation(s), interview, extracurricular activities, talent/ability, character/personal qualities, first generation, alumni/ae relation, geographical residence, state residency, volunteer work, work experience, level of applicant's interest. **Freshman Admission Requirements:** High school diploma is required and GED is accepted. *Academic units recommended:* 4 English, 4 math, 4 science, 1 science lab, 2 foreign language, 2 social studies, 2 history, 2 academic electives, 1 computer science, 1 visual/performing arts, and 1 unit from above areas or other academic areas. **Freshman Admission Statistics:** 1,342 applied, 57.60% admitted, 15% enrolled. **Transfer Admission Requirements:** college transcript(s), Minimum college GPA of 2.5 required. Lowest grade transferable C. **General Admission Information:** Application fee $50. Priority deadline 3/1. Nonfall registration accepted. Admission may be deferred for a maximum of 1 year.

COSTS AND FINANCIAL AID

Annual tuition $35,808. Room and board $10,668. Required fees $600. **Required Forms and Deadlines:** FAFSA, CSS/Financial Aid PROFILE. **Notification of Awards:** Applicants will be notified of awards on a rolling basis beginning 11/30. **Types of Aid:** *Need-based scholarships/grants:* Federal Pell, FSEOG, State scholarships/grants, Private scholarships, College/university scholarship or grant aid from institutional funds. *Loans:* Direct Subsidized Stafford Loans, Direct Unsubsidized Stafford Loans, Direct PLUS loans, Federal Perkins Loans. *Student Employment:* Federal Work-Study Program available. Institutional employment available. **Financial Aid Statistics:** 98% needy freshmen, 99% needy undergrads receive need-based scholarship or grant aid. 6% freshmen, 2% undergrads receive non-need-based scholarship or grant aid. 86% freshmen, 89% undergrads receive need-based self-help aid. 0% freshmen, 0% undergrads receive athletic scholarships. 79% freshmen, 86% undergrads receive any aid. 87% undergrads borrow to pay for school. Average cumulative indebtedness $40,626. **Criteria for awarding aid:** *Non-need-based:* Academics.

WORCESTER POLYTECHNIC INSTITUTE

Best Colleges

Admissions Office, Bartlett Center, Worcester, MA 1609
Phone: 508-831-5286 • **Financial Aid Phone:** 508-831-5469
E-mail: admissions@wpi.edu • **CEEB Code:** 3969
Fax: 508-831-5875 • **Website:** http://www.wpi.edu • **ACT Code:** 1942

This private school was founded in 1865. It has a 80-acre campus.

RATINGS

Admissions Selectivity Rating: 94   Fire Safety Rating: 91   Green Rating: 94

STUDENTS AND FACULTY

Enrollment: 4,177. **Student Body:** 33% female, 67% male, 57% out-of-state, 12% international (74 countries represented). Asian 5%, African American 2%, Caucasian 63%, Hispanic 8%, Native American <1%, Pacific Islander 0%, Two or more races 3%, Race unknown 6%.
Retention and Graduation: 96% freshmen return for sophomore year. 76% freshmen graduate within 4 years. 85% freshmen graduate within 6 years. 30% grads go on to further study within 1 year. 2% grads pursue law degrees. 2% grads pursue business degrees. 2% grads pursue medical degrees. **Faculty:** Student/faculty ratio 13:1. 359 full-time faculty, 94% hold PhDs, 18% are are members of minority groups, 28% are women. 0% of classes are taught by teaching assistants.

ACADEMICS

Degrees: bachelor's, doctoral/research, master's, post-master's certificate. **Classes:** Most classes have fewer than 10 students. **Most popular majors:** Computer Science; Electrical and Electronics Engineering; Mechanical Engineering. **Special Study Options:** Accelerated program, cooperative education program, cross-registration, distance learning, double major, dual enrollment, English as a Second Language (ESL), honors program, independent study, liberal arts/career combination, student-designed major, study abroad, teacher certification program, Completion of degree-required projects at off-campus locations (international and domestic) supervised by WPI faculty. This program requires the students to reside at the site for 2 months after having prepared for the experience for two months while on campus. **Honors Programs:** Chemistry and Biochemistry Scholars Program: Students selected for this highly competitive program will be given the opportunity to participate in faculty research within these departments beginning in the freshman year. In addition to the scholars program, each CBSP Scholar receives an academic merit scholarship. Scholarship amounts will vary, but typically range between $12,500 and $25,000, and are renewable for four years. Combined degree programs: BS/MS, BS/MBA, BS/MEng. **Disability Services:** Special programs offered to physically disabled students, including note-taking services, reader services, tape recorders, tutors. **Career Services:** Alumni network, Alumni services, Career/job search classes, Career assessment, Internships, Regional alumni. Two hands-on, professional-level projects that are the equivalent of three courses each are a requirement in our curriculum. They provide students with the opportunity to apply theory to practice through real-world problems and to find solutions that can be implemented by the project sponsors. As an example, one company implemented eight of nine student recommendations and saved $35,000 a day!

FACILITIES

Housing: Coed dorms, special housing for disabled students, special housing for international students, fraternity/sorority housing, apartments for single students, 4 co-ed residential houses/special interest housing. 90% of campus accessible to physically diasbled. **Special Academic Facilities/Equipment:** Several off-campus project centers, TV studio, robotics lab, CAD-CAM lab, laser labs, electron microscopes, wind tunnel, manufacturing engineering applications center, VLSI design lab, nuclear reactor. **Computers:** 100% of classrooms, 100% of dorms, 100% of libraries, 100% of dining areas, 100% of student union, 100% of common outdoor areas have wireless network access. Students can register for classes online. Administrative functions (other than registration) can be performed online.

CAMPUS LIFE

Environment: City. **Activities:** Choral groups, concert band, dance, drama/theater, jazz band, literary magazine, marching band, music ensembles, musical theater, pep band, radio station, student government, student newspaper, student-run film society, symphony orchestra, yearbook, Student Organization. 200 registered organizations, 20 honor societies, 4 religious organizations. 13 fraternities, 3 sororities. **Athletics (Intercollegiate):** *Men:* baseball, basketball, crew/rowing, cross-country, diving, football, soccer, swimming,

track/field (outdoor), track/field (indoor), wrestling. *Women:* basketball, crew/rowing, cross-country, diving, field hockey, soccer, softball, swimming, track/field (outdoor), track/field (indoor), volleyball. **On-Campus Highlights:** Student invented fountain, Campus Center, Robotics Lab, Wind Tunnels, Fire Protection Engineering Lab,—New biomedical and life sciences research center at Gateway Park—New pub-style restaurant on-campus—New apartment-style residence hall will open in summer 2008—New Sports and Recreation Center Opening in 2012. **Environmental Initiatives:** Creation of the President's Task Force on Sustainability, the creation of a Sustainability Coordinator position, and the creation of a Student Sustainability Coordination position.

ADMISSIONS

Freshman Academic Profile: Average high school GPA 3.8. 65% in top 10% of high school class, 91% in top 25% of high school class, 98% in top 50% of high school class. 66% from public high schools. **Reported SAT (pre-2016 redesign) scores:** SAT Math middle 50% range 640-740. SAT Critical Reading middle 50% range 570-680. SAT Writing middle 50% range 560-670. **Concordant SAT scores:** SAT EBRW middle 50% 620–710. SAT Math middle 50% range 660–760. ACT middle 50% range 27-32. Minimum internet-based TOEFL 79. Minimum paper TOEFL 550. **Basis for Candidate Selection:** *Very important factors considered include:* rigor of secondary school record, academic GPA. *Important factors considered include:* class rank, standardized test scores, recommendation(s), extracurricular activities, character/personal qualities. *Other factors considered include:* application essay, interview, talent/ability, first generation, alumni/ae relation, geographical residence, volunteer work, work experience, level of applicant's interest. **Freshman Admission Requirements:** High school diploma is required and GED is accepted. *Academic units required:* 4 English, 4 math, 2 science, 2 science labs. *Academic units recommended:* 4 science, 2 foreign language, 2 social studies, 1 history, 1 computer science. **Freshman Admission Statistics:** 10,172 applied, 48.55% admitted, 22% enrolled. **Transfer Admission Requirements:** college transcript(s), essay or personal statement, statement of good standing from prior institution(s). Minimum college GPA of 3.0 required. Lowest grade transferable C. **General Admission Information:** Application fee $65. Regular application deadline 2/1. Regular notification 4/1. Nonfall registration accepted. Admission may be deferred for a maximum of 1 year.

COSTS AND FINANCIAL AID

Annual tuition $46,364. Room and board $13,736. Required fees $630. Average book expense $1,000. **Required Forms and Deadlines:** FAFSA, CSS/Financial Aid PROFILE, Noncustodial PROFILE. **Notification of Awards:** Applicants will be notified of awards on or about 4/1. **Types of Aid:** *Need-based scholarships/grants:* Federal Pell, FSEOG, State scholarships/grants, Private scholarships, College/university scholarship or grant aid from institutional funds. *Loans:* Direct Subsidized Stafford Loans, Direct Unsubsidized Stafford Loans, Direct PLUS loans, Federal Perkins Loans, State Loans, College/university loans from institutional funds. *Student Employment:* Federal Work-Study Program available. Institutional employment available. **Financial Aid Statistics:** 100% needy freshmen, 96% needy undergrads receive need-based scholarship or grant aid. 32% freshmen, 34% undergrads receive non-need-based scholarship or grant aid. 53% freshmen, 54% undergrads receive need-based self-help aid. 0% freshmen, 0% undergrads receive athletic scholarships. 98% freshmen, 95% undergrads receive any aid. **Criteria for awarding aid:** *Need-based:* Academics, Minority status. *Non-need-based:* Academics, Leadership, Minority status.

See page 1106.

WORCESTER STATE UNIVERSITY

486 Chandler Street, Worcester, MA 01602-2597
Phone: 508-929-8040 • **Financial Aid Phone:** 508-929-8058
E-mail: admissions@worcester.edu • **CEEB Code:** 3524
Fax: 508-929-8183 • **Website:** www.worcester.edu • **ACT Code:** 1914

This public school was founded in 1874. It has a 58-acre campus.

RATINGS

Admissions Selectivity Rating: 73   Fire Safety Rating: 99   Green Rating: 84

STUDENTS AND FACULTY

Enrollment: 4,891. **Student Body:** 59% female, 41% male, 4% out-of-state, 1% international (20 countries represented). Asian 4%, African American 8%, Caucasian 68%, Hispanic 11%, Native American <1%, Pacific Islander <1%, Two or more races 3%, Race unknown 4%.
Retention and Graduation: 80% freshmen return for sophomore year. 56% freshmen graduate within 6 years. **Faculty:** Student/faculty ratio 18:1. 204 full-

time faculty, 80% hold PhDs, 13% are are members of minority groups, 56% are women. 0% of classes are taught by teaching assistants.

ACADEMICS

Degrees: bachelor's, master's, postbachelor's certificate, post-master's certificate. **Classes:** Most classes have 20-29 students. Most lab/discussion sessions have 10-19 students. **Most popular majors:** Business Administration and Management; Psychology; Criminal Justice/Safety Studies. **Special Study Options:** cross-registration, distance learning, double major, English as a Second Language (ESL), exchange student program (domestic), honors program, independent study, internships, liberal arts/career combination, study abroad, teacher certification program, Foreign Exchange Student Program. **Honors Programs:** Commonwealth Honors Program: The mission of the honors program at Worcester State College is to offer all qualified students an outstanding undergraduate experience through courses that emphasize innovative pedagogy and the values of liberal learning. Honors classes are small (often fewer than 20 students) and are designed to encourage active and lifelong learning. Small classes and extracurricular programs provide honors students with greater interaction between their peers and a select core of dedicated faculty members. In addition to stimulating classes, honors students also enjoy campus speakers, field trips to cultural centers, occasional luncheons with faculty members, and an annual dinner with the college president. Founded in 1996, the program currently enrolls 150 students and recently earned accreditation as a Commonwealth Honors Program from the Massachusetts Board of Higher Education. Combined degree programs: BA/MA, Occupational Therapy. **Disability Services:** Special programs offered to physically disabled students, including note-taking services, reader services, tape recorders, tutors. **Career Services:** Alumni network, Alumni services, Career/job search classes, Career assessment, Internships, Regional alumni. Sustainability Fair, Green Work.

FACILITIES

Housing: Coed dorms, special housing for disabled students, men's dorms, women's dorms. 100% of campus accessible to physically diasbled. **Special Academic Facilities/Equipment:** Art Studio **Computers:** 100% of classrooms, 100% of dorms, 100% of libraries, 100% of dining areas, 100% of student union, 100% of common outdoor areas have wireless network access. Students can register for classes online. Administrative functions (other than registration) can be performed online. Undergraduates are required to own a computer.

CAMPUS LIFE

Environment: City. **Activities:** Choral groups, concert band, dance, drama/theater, jazz band, music ensembles, radio station, student government, student newspaper, television station, yearbook, Campus Ministries, Student Organization. 39 registered organizations, 17 honor societies, 1 religious organization. **Athletics (Intercollegiate):** *Men:* baseball, basketball, cheerleading, cross-country, football, golf, ice hockey, soccer, track/field (outdoor), track/field (indoor). *Women:* basketball, cheerleading, cross-country, field hockey, lacrosse, soccer, softball, tennis, track/field (outdoor), track/field (indoor), volleyball. **On-Campus Highlights:** Wasylean Hall, Student Center Living Room, Science and Technology Building, Food Court, Campus Bookstore. **Environmental Initiatives:** 2015 was another exciting year for sustainability at WSU. I am most excited about the dual head EV chaging station that was installed in June. This is a big first step for us. At the Sustainability Fair in the fall, we had BMW here with their 100% EV for people to test drive and it was busy all day.

ADMISSIONS

Freshman Academic Profile: Average high school GPA 3.2. 91% from public high schools. **Reported SAT (pre-2016 redesign) scores:** SAT Math middle 50% range 460-560. SAT Critical Reading middle 50% range 430-540. SAT Writing middle 50% range 430-530. **Concordant SAT scores:** SAT EBRW middle 50% 480–590. SAT Math middle 50% range 500–580. ACT middle 50% range 20-26. Minimum internet-based TOEFL 79. Minimum paper TOEFL 550. **Basis for Candidate Selection:** *Very important factors considered include:* rigor of secondary school record, academic GPA, standardized test scores. *Important factors considered include:* class rank, character/personal qualities. *Other factors considered include:* application essay, recommendation(s), extracurricular activities, talent/ability, first generation, alumni/ae relation, geographical residence, state residency, racial/ethnic status, volunteer work. **Freshman Admission Requirements:** High school diploma is required and GED is accepted. *Academic units required:* 4 English, 4 math, 3 science, 2 science labs, 2 foreign language, 1 social studies, 1 history, 2 academic electives. **Freshman Admission Statistics:** 3,876 applied, 70.56% admitted, 29% enrolled. **Transfer Admission Requirements:** High school transcript, college transcript(s), statement of good standing from prior institution(s). Minimum college GPA of 2.5 required. Lowest grade transferable C-. **General Admission Information:** Application fee $50. Priority deadline 3/1. Regular application deadline 5/1. Nonfall registration accepted. Admission may be deferred for a maximum of 1 year.

COSTS AND FINANCIAL AID

Annual in-state tuition $970. Annual out-of-state tuition $7,050. Room and board $11,775. Required fees $8,232. Average book expense $1,368. **Required Forms and Deadlines:** FAFSA, Institution's own financial aid form. **Notification of Awards:** Applicants will be notified of awards on a rolling basis beginning 3/1. **Types of Aid:** *Need-based scholarships/grants:* Federal Pell, FSEOG, State scholarships/grants, Private scholarships, College/university scholarship or grant aid from institutional funds. *Loans:* Direct Subsidized Stafford Loans, Direct Unsubsidized Stafford Loans, Direct PLUS loans, Federal Perkins Loans, State Loans. *Student Employment:* Federal Work-Study Program available. Institutional employment available. **Financial Aid Statistics:** 86% needy freshmen, 81% needy undergrads receive need-based scholarship or grant aid. 52% freshmen, 36% undergrads receive non-need-based scholarship or grant aid. 98% freshmen, 94% undergrads receive need-based self-help aid. 0% freshmen, 0% undergrads receive athletic scholarships. 65% freshmen, 61% undergrads receive any aid. 78% undergrads borrow to pay for school. Average cumulative indebtedness $28,940. **Criteria for awarding aid:** *Non-need-based:* Academics.

WRIGHT STATE UNIVERSITY

3640 Colonel Glenn Highway, Dayton, OH 45435
Phone: 937-775-5700 • **Financial Aid Phone:** 937-775-4000
E-mail: admissions@wright.edu • **CEEB Code:** 1179
Fax: 937-775-4410 • **Website:** www.wright.edu • **ACT Code:** 3295

This public school was founded in 1964. It has a 557-acre campus.

RATINGS

Admissions Selectivity Rating: 75   **Fire Safety Rating:** 93   **Green Rating:** 73

STUDENTS AND FACULTY

Enrollment: 11,664. **Student Body:** 52% female, 48% male, 2% out-of-state, 4% international (65 countries represented). Asian 3%, African American 12%, Caucasian 73%, Hispanic 4%, Native American <1%, Pacific Islander <1%, Two or more races 4%, Race unknown <1%. **Retention and Graduation:** 66% freshmen return for sophomore year. 19% freshmen graduate within 4 years. 36% freshmen graduate within 6 years. **Faculty:** 2% of classes are taught by teaching assistants.

ACADEMICS

Degrees: associate, bachelor's, certificate, diploma, doctoral/professional, doctoral/research, doctoral, master's, postbachelor's certifiate, post-master's certificate. **Classes:** Most classes have 20-29 students. Most lab/discussion sessions have fewer than 10 students. **Most popular majors:** Registered Nursing/Registered Nurse; Mechanical Engineering; Biology/Biological Sciences. **Special Study Options:** cooperative education program, cross-registration, distance learning, double major, dual enrollment, English as a Second Language (ESL), honors program, independent study, internships, student-designed major, study abroad, teacher certification program, weekend college. **Honors Programs:** Honors Program. **Disability Services:** Special programs offered to physically disabled students, including note-taking services, reader services, tape recorders, tutors. **Career Services:** Alumni network, Alumni services, Career/job search classes, Career assessment, Internships. WSU has a very flexible set of programs that meet the needs of our students.

FACILITIES

Housing: Coed dorms, special housing for disabled students, apartments for married students, apartments for single students, Honors Dorm. 100% of campus accessible to physically diasbled. **Special Academic Facilities/Equipment:** Art gallery located in the Creative Arts Center **Computers:** 100% of classrooms, 100% of dorms, 100% of libraries, 100% of dining areas, 100% of student union, have wireless network access. Students can register for classes online. Administrative functions (other than registration) can be performed online.

CAMPUS LIFE

Environment: City. **Activities:** Choral groups, concert band, dance, drama/theater, jazz band, literary magazine, music ensembles, musical theater, opera, pep band, radio station, student government, student newspaper, symphony orchestra, television station, Campus Ministries, Model UN. 145 registered organizations, 22 honor societies, 9 religious organizations. 8 fraternities, 8 sororities. **Athletics (Intercollegiate):** *Men:* baseball, basketball, cheerleading, cross-country, diving, golf, soccer, swimming, tennis. *Women:* basketball, cheerleading, cross-country, diving, soccer, softball, swimming, tennis, track/field (outdoor), volleyball. **On-Campus Highlights:** Student Union, Garden of the Senses, Rec Center, Fitness Center, Nutter Center. **Environmental Initiatives:** Matthew O. Diggs III Laboratory for Life Sciences Research achieved LEED Gold status, the first laboratory in Ohio to achieve LEED-NC Gold status.

ADMISSIONS

Freshman Academic Profile: Average high school GPA 3.3. 18% in top 10% of high school class, 38% in top 25% of high school class, 68% in top 50% of high school class. **Reported SAT (pre-2016 redesign) scores:** SAT Math middle 50% range 470-610. SAT Critical Reading middle 50% range 460-600. SAT Writing middle 50% range 430-563. **Concordant SAT scores:** SAT EBRW middle 50% 500–640. SAT Math middle 50% range 510–630. ACT middle 50% range 18-25. Minimum internet-based TOEFL 61. **Basis for Candidate Selection:** *Very important factors considered include:* rigor of secondary school record, academic GPA, standardized test scores. *Important factors considered include:* class rank. *Other factors considered include:* recommendation(s), state residency. **Freshman Admission Requirements:** High school diploma is required and GED is accepted. *Academic units required:* 4 English, 3 math, 3 science, 3 science labs, 2 foreign language, 3 social studies, 1 visual/performing arts. **Freshman Admission Statistics:** 5,897 applied, 95.23% admitted, 41% enrolled. **Transfer Admission Requirements:** college transcript(s), Minimum college GPA of 2.0 required. Lowest grade transferable D. **General Admission Information:** Application fee $30. Nonfall registration accepted. Admission may be deferred for a maximum of One Year.

COSTS AND FINANCIAL AID

Annual in-state tuition $8,730. Annual out-of-state tuition $17,350. Room and board $9,436. Average book expense $1,248. **Required Forms and Deadlines:** FAFSA. **Notification of Awards:** Applicants will be notified of awards on a rolling basis beginning 3/15. **Types of Aid:** *Need-based scholarships/grants:* Federal Pell, FSEOG, State scholarships/grants, Private scholarships, College/university scholarship or grant aid from institutional funds, United Negro College Fund, Federal Nursing Scholarships. *Loans:* Direct Subsidized Stafford Loans, Direct Unsubsidized Stafford Loans, Direct PLUS loans, Federal Perkins Loans, Federal Nursing Loans, State Loans, College/university loans from institutional funds. *Student Employment:* Federal Work-Study Program available. Institutional employment available. **Financial Aid Statistics:** 87% needy freshmen, 80% needy undergrads receive need-based scholarship or grant aid. 12% freshmen, 8% undergrads receive non-need-based scholarship or grant aid. 91% freshmen, 93% undergrads receive need-based self-help aid. 2% freshmen, 2% undergrads receive athletic scholarships. 87% freshmen, 75% undergrads receive any aid. **Criteria for awarding aid:** *Need-based:* Academics, Art, Minority status, Music/drama. *Non-need-based:* Academics, Alumni affiliation, Art, Athletics, Leadership, Minority status, Music/drama, State/district residency.

XAVIER UNIVERSITY OF LOUISIANA

1 Drexel Drive, New Orleans, LA 70125
Phone: 504-520-7388 • **Financial Aid Phone:** 504-520-7835
E-mail: apply@xula.edu • **CEEB Code:** 6975
Fax: 504-520-7941 • **Website:** www.xula.edu • **ACT Code:** 1618

This private school, affiliated with the Roman Catholic Church, was founded in 1915. It has a 29-acre campus.

RATINGS

Admissions Selectivity Rating: 85   **Fire Safety Rating:** 92   **Green Rating:** 60*

STUDENTS AND FACULTY

Enrollment: 2,344. **Student Body:** 73% female, 27% male, 44% out-of-state. 2% international (8 countries represented). Asian 10%, African American 76%, Caucasian 4%, Hispanic 4%, Native American <1%, Pacific Islander <1%, Two or more races 3%, Race unknown 1%.
Retention and Graduation: 23% freshmen graduate within 4 years. 38 31% grads go on to further study within 1 year. **Faculty:** Student/faculty ratio 14:1. 221 full-time faculty, 97% hold PhDs, 43% are are members of minority groups, 48% are women. 0% of classes are taught by teaching assistants.

ACADEMICS

Degrees: bachelor's, doctoral/professional, master's. **Classes:** Most classes have 10-19 students. Most lab/discussion sessions have 20-29 students. **Most popular majors:** Psychology; Pre-Medicine/Pre-Medical Studies; Pre-Pharmacy Studies. **Special Study Options:** Accelerated program, cooperative education program, cross-registration, double major, dual enrollment, exchange student program (domestic), honors program, independent study, internships, study abroad, African American Studies Minor; Women Studies. Combined degree programs: BA/MEng. **Disability Services:** Special programs offered to physically disabled students, including note-taking services, reader services, tape recorders, tutors. **Career Services:** Career/job search classes, Career assessment, Internships.

FACILITIES

Housing: Coed dorms, special housing for disabled students, men's dorms, women's dorms. 99% of campus accessible to physically diasbled. **Computers:** 100% of classrooms, 100% of dorms, 100% of libraries, 100% of dining areas, 100% of student union, 100% of common outdoor areas have wireless network access. Students can register for classes online. Administrative functions (other than registration) can be performed online.

CAMPUS LIFE

Environment: Metropolis. **Activities:** Choral groups, concert band, dance, drama/theater, jazz band, literary magazine, music ensembles, opera, student government, student newspaper, symphony orchestra, television station, yearbook, Campus Ministries, Student Organization. 88 registered organizations, 8 honor societies, 1 religious organization. 4 fraternities, 4 sororities. **Athletics (Intercollegiate):** *Men:* basketball, cross-country, tennis, track/field (outdoor), track/field (indoor). *Women:* basketball, cross-country, tennis, track/field (outdoor), track/field (indoor), volleyball. **On-Campus Highlights:** New University Center, Gymnasium (The Barn), Library, University Quadrangle, Historic Administration Building.

ADMISSIONS

Freshman Academic Profile: Average high school GPA 3.4. 32% in top 10% of high school class, 58% in top 25% of high school class, 80% in top 50% of high school class. **Reported SAT (pre-2016 redesign) scores:** SAT Math middle 50% range 430-550. SAT Critical Reading middle 50% range 450-490. SAT Writing middle 50% range 410-530. **Concordant SAT scores:** SAT EBRW middle 50% 480–570. SAT Math middle 50% range 470–570. ACT middle 50% range 20-26. Minimum paper TOEFL 550. **Basis for Candidate Selection:** *Very important factors considered include:* rigor of secondary school record, academic GPA, standardized test scores, recommendation(s). *Important factors considered include:* class rank, application essay. *Other factors considered include:* interview, extracurricular activities, talent/ability, character/personal qualities, alumni/ae relation, volunteer work, work experience. **Freshman Admission Requirements:** High school diploma is required and GED is accepted. *Academic units required:* 4 English, 2 math, 2 science, 1 social studies, 7 academic electives. *Academic units recommended:* 4 math, 3 science, 1 foreign language, 1 history. **Freshman Admission Statistics:** 6,640 applied, 61.51% admitted, 19% enrolled. **Transfer Admission Requirements:** college transcript(s), Minimum college GPA of 2.00 required. Lowest grade transferable C. **General Admission Information:** Application fee $25. Priority deadline 3/1. Regular application deadline 7/1. Nonfall registration accepted. Admission may be deferred.

COSTS AND FINANCIAL AID

Annual tuition $19,800. Room and board $8,200. Required fees $2,549. Average book expense $1,220. **Required Forms and Deadlines:** FAFSA. **Notification of Awards:** Applicants will be notified of awards on a rolling basis beginning 4/1. **Types of Aid:** *Need-based scholarships/grants:* Federal Pell, FSEOG, State scholarships/grants, Private scholarships, College/university scholarship or grant aid from institutional funds, United Negro College Fund. *Loans:* Direct Subsidized Stafford Loans, Direct Unsubsidized Stafford Loans, Direct PLUS loans, Federal Perkins Loans. *Student Employment:* Federal Work-Study Program available. Institutional employment available. **Financial Aid Statistics:** 65% needy freshmen, 65% needy undergrads receive need-based scholarship or grant aid. 91% freshmen, 79% undergrads receive non-need-based scholarship or grant aid. 93% freshmen, 95% undergrads receive need-based self-help aid. 3% freshmen, 4% undergrads receive athletic scholarships. 94% freshmen, 24% undergrads receive any aid. **Criteria for awarding aid:** *Need-based:* Academics, Art, Athletics, Music/drama.

XAVIER UNIVERSITY (OH)

3800 Victory Parkway, Cincinnati, OH 45207-5311
Phone: 513-745-3301 • **Financial Aid Phone:** 513-745-3142
E-mail: xuadmit@xavier.edu • **CEEB Code:** 1965
Fax: 513-745-4319 • **Website:** www.xavier.edu • **ACT Code:** 3366

This private school, affiliated with the Roman Catholic-Jesuit Church, was founded in 1831. It has a 146-acre campus.

RATINGS

Admissions Selectivity Rating: 84   **Fire Safety Rating:** 88   **Green Rating:** 78

STUDENTS AND FACULTY

Enrollment: 4,503. **Student Body:** 54% female, 46% male, 52% out-of-state, 2% international (38 countries represented). Asian 3%, African American 9%, Caucasian 72%, Hispanic 5%, Native American <1%, Pacific Islander <1%, Two or more races 4%, Race unknown 4%.
Retention and Graduation: 87% freshmen return for sophomore year. 62% freshmen graduate within 4 years. 72% freshmen graduate within 6 years. 20% grads go on to further study within 1 year. 2% grads pursue arts and sciences degrees. 2% grads pursue law degrees. 3% grads pursue business degrees. 2% grads pursue medical degrees. **Faculty:** Student/faculty ratio 11:1. 355 full-time faculty, 78% hold PhDs, 15% are are members of minority groups, 54% are women. 0% of classes are taught by teaching assistants.

ACADEMICS

Degrees: associate, bachelor's, certificate, doctoral/professional, master's, postbachelor's certificate, post-master's certificate, terminal. **Classes:** Most classes have 20-29 students. Most lab/discussion sessions have 10-19 students. **Most popular majors:** Registered Nursing/Registered Nurse; Biology/Biological Sciences; Liberal Arts and Sciences/Liberal Studies. **Special Study Options:** cooperative education program, cross-registration, double major, dual enrollment, English as a Second Language (ESL), honors program, independent study, internships, study abroad, teacher certification program, weekend college, Service Learning Semester. **Honors Programs:** University Scholars Progam Philosophy, Politics and the Public Honors AB Combined degree programs: BSBA/MBA in Accounting. **Disability Services:** Special programs offered to physically disabled students, including note-taking services, reader services, tape recorders, tutors. **Career Services:** Alumni network, Alumni services, Career/job search classes, Career assessment, Internships, Regional alumni. Our premier programs include Xavier University Mentoring Program for all students that matches them with professionals across a wide variety of industries for personal and professional development. We also host the "Southwest Ohio, Northern Kentucky Education Career Fair," which is held at Xavier and attracts 60+ school districts and 450+ students. Additionally the Business Profession Program, an intentional four-year career development program for business undergraduates has received national attention.

FACILITIES

Housing: Coed dorms, special housing for disabled students, apartments for single students, Theme Housing. 99% of campus accessible to physically diasbled. **Special Academic Facilities/Equipment:** Student-run art gallery, Montessori lab school. **Computers:** 100% of classrooms, 100% of dorms, 100% of libraries, 100% of dining areas, 100% of student union, 100% of common outdoor areas have wireless network access. Students can register for classes online. Administrative functions (other than registration) can be performed online.

CAMPUS LIFE

Environment: Metropolis. **Activities:** Choral groups, concert band, dance, drama/theater, jazz band, literary magazine, music ensembles, musical theater, opera, pep band, radio station, student government, student newspaper, student-run film society, symphony orchestra, television station, Campus Ministries, Student Organization. 124 registered organizations, 10 honor societies, 11 religious organizations. **Athletics (Intercollegiate):** *Men:* baseball, basketball, cheerleading, cross-country, golf, soccer, swimming, tennis, track/field (outdoor), track/field (indoor). *Women:* basketball, cheerleading, cross-country, golf, soccer, swimming, tennis, track/field (outdoor), track/field (indoor), volleyball. **On-Campus Highlights:** Cintas Center basketball arena and conce, McDonald Library, The Gallagher Student Center, O'Conner Sports Center, Bellarmine Chapel. **Environmental Initiatives:** Growth and investment 'All-In': Linking the growth of new undergraduate and Masters programs with more students, regular field trips, social events, and lecture series—with the leadership team investment of time and talent participating on and leading local boards: Watershed Council, Economics of Compassion Board, Southwest Ohio sustainable farming board, and Green Business Council.

ADMISSIONS

Freshman Academic Profile: Average high school GPA 3.7. 19% in top 10% of high school class, 54% in top 25% of high school class, 82% in top 50% of high school class. 41% from public high schools. **Reported SAT (pre-2016 redesign) scores:** SAT Math middle 50% range 520-610. SAT Critical Reading middle 50% range 490-580. SAT Writing middle 50% range 480-590. **Concordant SAT scores:** SAT EBRW middle 50% 540–640. SAT Math middle 50% range 550–630. ACT middle 50% range 23-28. Minimum internet-based TOEFL 79. Minimum paper TOEFL 550. **Basis for Candidate Selection:** *Very important factors considered include:* rigor of secondary school record, academic GPA, standardized test scores. *Important factors considered include:* application essay, recommendation(s), extracurricular activities, character/personal qualities, volunteer work. *Other factors considered include:* class rank, talent/ability, first generation, alumni/ae relation, work experience, level of applicant's interest. **Freshman Admission Requirements:** High school diploma is required and GED is accepted. *Academic units recommended:* 4 English, 3 math, 3 science, 2 foreign language, 3 social studies, 5 academic electives, and 1 unit from above areas or other academic areas. **Freshman Admission Statistics:** 13,213 applied, 68.58% admitted, 12% enrolled. **Transfer Admission Requirements:** High school transcript, college transcript(s), statement of good standing from prior institution(s). Minimum college GPA of 2.0 required. Lowest grade transferable C-. **General Admission Information:** Application fee $35. Priority deadline 2/1. Nonfall registration accepted. Admission may be deferred for a maximum of 1 year.

COSTS AND FINANCIAL AID

Required Forms and Deadlines: FAFSA. **Notification of Awards:** Applicants will be notified of awards on a rolling basis beginning 3/1. **Types of Aid:** *Need-based scholarships/grants:* Federal Pell, FSEOG, State scholarships/grants, Private scholarships, College/university scholarship or grant aid from institutional funds. *Loans:* Direct Subsidized Stafford Loans, Direct Unsubsidized Stafford Loans, Direct PLUS loans, Federal Perkins Loans. *Student Employment:* Federal Work-Study Program available. Institutional employment available. **Financial Aid Statistics:** 97% needy freshmen, 67% needy undergrads receive need-based scholarship or grant aid. 32% freshmen, 30% undergrads receive non-need-based scholarship or grant aid. 61% freshmen, 62% undergrads receive need-based self-help aid. 3% freshmen, 3% undergrads receive athletic scholarships. 99% freshmen, 92% undergrads receive any aid. Average cumulative indebtedness $32,108. **Criteria for awarding aid:** *Need-based:* Job skills. *Non-need-based:* Academics, Alumni affiliation, Art, Athletics, Leadership, Music/drama, Religious affiliation.

YALE UNIVERSITY

PO Box 208234, New Haven, CT 06520-8234
Phone: 203-432-9300 • **Financial Aid Phone:** 203-432-2700
E-mail: student.questions@yale.edu • **CEEB Code:** 3987
Fax: 203-432-9392 • **Website:** www.yale.edu • **ACT Code:** 618

This private school was founded in 1701. It has a 320-acre campus.

RATINGS

Admissions Selectivity Rating: 99   **Fire Safety Rating:** 62   **Green Rating:** 92

STUDENTS AND FACULTY

Enrollment: 5,528. **Student Body:** 49% female, 51% male, 93% out-of-state, 11% international (118 countries represented). Asian 17%, African American 7%, Caucasian 47%, Hispanic 11%, Native American 1%, Pacific Islander <1%, Two or more races 6%, Race unknown 1%.
Retention and Graduation: 99% freshmen return for sophomore year. 88% freshmen graduate within 4 years. 97% freshmen graduate within 6 years. 21% grads go on to further study within 1 year. 7% grads pursue arts and sciences degrees. 4% grads pursue law degrees. 4% grads pursue medical degrees. **Faculty:** Student/faculty ratio 6:1. 1,159 full-time faculty, 93% hold PhDs, 28% are are members of minority groups, 36% are women.

ACADEMICS

Degrees: bachelor's, doctoral/professional, doctoral/research, master's, postmaster's certificate. **Classes:** Most classes have 10-19 students. **Most popular majors:** Economics; Political Science and Government; History. **Special Study**

Options: Accelerated program, distance learning, double major, English as a Second Language (ESL), honors program, independent study, internships, liberal arts/career combination, student-designed major, study abroad, teacher certification program. Combined degree programs: BA/MA, BA/MM in Music, BA/MA, BS/MS. **Disability Services:** Special programs offered to physically disabled students, including note-taking services, reader services, tape recorders, tutors. **Career Services:** Alumni network, Alumni services, Career/job search classes, Internships, Regional alumni. In coordination with the Yale Undergraduate Career Services department, the university helps place hundreds of students in (non-credit) internships across the country and around the world every year. UCS utilizes a vast array of resources, including alumni, private firms and research fellowships to place students in a wide variety of internships.

FACILITIES

Housing: Coed dorms, special housing for disabled students, Students are randomly assigned to 1 of 12 residential colleges where they live, eat, socialize, and pursue various academic and extracurricular activities. All undergraduate housing is provided through residential college system. **Special Academic Facilities/Equipment:** Art and history museums, observatory, electron microscopes, nuclear accelerators, center for international and areas studies, child study center, marsh botanical gardens, center for parallel supercomputing. **Computers:** 100% of classrooms, 100% of dorms, 100% of libraries, 100% of dining areas, 100% of student union, 100% of common outdoor areas have wireless network access. Students can register for classes online. Administrative functions (other than registration) can be performed online.

CAMPUS LIFE

Environment: City. **Activities:** Choral groups, concert band, dance, drama/theater, jazz band, literary magazine, marching band, music ensembles, musical theater, opera, pep band, radio station, student government, student newspaper, student-run film society, symphony orchestra, television station, yearbook, Campus Ministries, Student Organization, Model UN. 350 registered organizations. **Athletics (Intercollegiate):** *Men:* baseball, basketball, crew/rowing, cross-country, diving, fencing, football, golf, ice hockey, lacrosse, sailing, soccer, squash, swimming, tennis, track/field (outdoor), track/field (indoor). *Women:* basketball, crew/rowing, cross-country, diving, fencing, field hockey, golf, gymnastics, ice hockey, lacrosse, sailing, soccer, softball, squash, swimming, tennis, track/field (outdoor), track/field (indoor), volleyball. **On-Campus Highlights:** Old Campus, Sterling Memorial Library, Yale British Art Center, Beinecke Rare Book and Manuscript Library, Payne-Whitney Gymnasium, http://www.yale.edu/admit/visit/index.html. **Environmental Initiatives:** Greenhouse gas commitment of 43% below 2005 levels by 2020.

ADMISSIONS

Freshman Academic Profile: 97% in top 10% of high school class, 99% in top 25% of high school class, 100% in top 50% of high school class. 57% from public high schools. **Reported SAT (pre-2016 redesign) scores:** SAT Math middle 50% range 710-800. SAT Critical Reading middle 50% range 720-800. SAT Writing middle 50% range 710-790. **Concordant SAT scores:** SAT EBRW middle 50% 740–800. SAT Math middle 50% range 740–800. ACT middle 50% range 31-35. Minimum internet-based TOEFL 100. Minimum paper TOEFL 600. **Basis for Candidate Selection:** *Very important factors considered include:* rigor of secondary school record, class rank, academic GPA, standardized test scores, application essay, recommendation(s), extracurricular activities, talent/ability, character/personal qualities. *Other factors considered include:* interview, first generation, alumni/ae relation, geographical residence, state residency, racial/ethnic status, volunteer work, work experience. **Freshman Admission Requirements:** High school diploma or equivalent is not required. **Freshman Admission Statistics:** 30,236 applied, 6.73% admitted, 67% enrolled. **Transfer Admission Requirements:** High school transcript, college transcript(s), essay or personal statement, standardized test scores, statement of good standing from prior institution(s). Lowest grade transferable C. **General Admission Information:** Application fee $80. Regular application deadline 1/1. Regular notification 4/1. Nonfall registration not accepted. Admission may be deferred for a maximum of one year.

COSTS AND FINANCIAL AID

Annual tuition $49,480. Room and board $15,170. Required fees $0. Average book expense $3,580. **Required Forms and Deadlines:** FAFSA, CSS/Financial Aid PROFILE, Noncustodial PROFILE. **Notification of Awards:** Applicants will be notified of awards on or about 4/1. **Types of Aid:** *Need-based scholarships/grants:* Federal Pell, FSEOG, State scholarships/grants, Private scholarships, College/university scholarship or grant aid from institutional funds, United Negro College Fund. *Loans:* Direct Subsidized Stafford Loans, Direct Unsubsidized Stafford Loans, Direct PLUS loans, Federal Perkins Loans, State Loans. *Student Employment:* Federal Work-Study Program available. Institutional employment available. **Financial Aid Statistics:** 100% needy freshmen, 100% needy undergrads receive need-based scholarship or grant aid. 0% undergrads receive non-need-based scholarship or grant aid. 73% freshmen, 85% undergrads receive need-based self-help aid. 0% freshmen, 0% undergrads receive athletic scholarships. 51% freshmen, 52% undergrads

receive any aid. 17% undergrads borrow to pay for school. Average cumulative indebtedness $15,521.

YESHIVA UNIVERSITY

500 West 185th Street, New York, NY 10033-3299
Phone: 212-960-5277
E-mail: yuadmit@yu.edu • **CEEB Code:** 2990
Fax: 212-960-0086 • **Website:** www.yu.edu • **ACT Code:** 2992

This private school was founded in 1886. It has a 12-acre campus.

RATINGS

Admissions Selectivity Rating: 89　　**Fire Safety Rating:** 60*　　**Green Rating:** 60*

STUDENTS AND FACULTY

Enrollment: 2,871. **Student Body:** 46% female, 54% male, 35% out-of-state, 12% international (53 countries represented). Asian 0%, African American <1%, Caucasian 82%, Hispanic 2%, Native American <1%, Pacific Islander 0%, Two or more races 0%, Race unknown 4%. **Retention and Graduation:** 90% freshmen return for sophomore year. 49% freshmen graduate within 4 years. **Faculty:** Student/faculty ratio 7:1. 0% of classes are taught by teaching assistants.

ACADEMICS

Degrees: bachelor's, master's. **Classes:** Most classes have 10-19 students. Most lab/discussion sessions have 10-19 students. **Most popular majors:** Political Science and Government; Psychology; Jewish/Judaic Studies. **Special Study Options:** double major, honors program, independent study, internships, student-designed major, study abroad, teacher certification program. Combined degree programs: BA/MA, 3-2 and 4-2 engineering programs with Columbia U. **Career Services:** Career/job search classes, Career assessment, Internships.

FACILITIES

Housing: men's dorms, women's dorms, apartments for married students, apartments for single students. **Special Academic Facilities/Equipment:** Archives and rare book collection, museum of Jewish art, architecture, history, and culture.

CAMPUS LIFE

Activities: Choral groups, concert band, drama/theater, jazz band, literary magazine, music ensembles, musical theater, radio station, student government, student newspaper, yearbook. **Athletics (Intercollegiate):** *Men:* basketball, tennis, volleyball. *Women:* basketball, tennis.

ADMISSIONS

Freshman Academic Profile: Average high school GPA 3.5. 48% in top 10% of high school class, 77% in top 25% of high school class, 95% in top 50% of high school class. **Reported SAT (pre-2016 redesign) scores:** SAT Math middle 50% range 550-680. SAT Critical Reading middle 50% range 550-690. **Concordant SAT scores:** SAT Math middle 50% range 570–710. ACT middle 50% range 22-28. Minimum paper TOEFL 500. **Basis for Candidate Selection:** *Important factors considered include:* rigor of secondary school record, academic GPA, standardized test scores, application essay, interview, extracurricular activities, talent/ability. *Other factors considered include:* volunteer work, work experience. **Freshman Admission Requirements:** High school diploma is required and GED is accepted. *Academic units recommended:* 4 English, 2 math, 2 science, 2 foreign language, 2 social studies. **Freshman Admission Statistics:** 2,027 applied, 62.60% admitted, 65% enrolled. **Transfer Admission Requirements:** High school transcript, college transcript(s), essay or personal statement, interview, standardized test scores, Lowest grade transferable 75. **General Admission Information:** Application fee $40. Regular application deadline 2/15. Regular notification 4/1. Nonfall registration accepted. Admission may be deferred.

COSTS AND FINANCIAL AID

Annual tuition $31,594. Required fees $500. Average book expense $1,224. **Required Forms and Deadlines:** FAFSA, Institution's own financial aid form, CSS/Financial Aid PROFILE, State aid form, Noncustodial PROFILE, Business/Farm Supplement. **Types of Aid:** *Need-based scholarships/grants:* Federal Pell, FSEOG, State scholarships/grants, Private scholarships, College/university scholarship or grant aid from institutional funds. *Loans:* Federal Perkins Loans, College/university loans from institutional funds. *Student Employment:* Federal Work-Study Program available. Institutional employment available. **Financial Aid Statistics:** 89% needy freshmen, 85% needy undergrads receive need-based scholarship or grant aid. 14% freshmen, 10% undergrads receive non-need-based scholarship or grant aid. 80% freshmen, 77% undergrads receive need-based self-help aid. 0% freshmen, 0% undergrads receive athletic scholarships. **Criteria for awarding aid:** *Non-need-based:* Academics.

YORK COLLEGE

1125 E. 8th Street, York, NE 68467
Phone: 402-363-5627 • **Financial Aid Phone:** 402-363-5625
E-mail: enroll@york.edu
Fax: 402-363-5623 • **Website:** www.york.edu • **ACT Code:** 2484

This private school, affiliated with the Church of Christ Church, was founded in 1890. It has a 200-acre campus.

RATINGS
Admissions Selectivity Rating: 81   **Fire Safety Rating:** 97   **Green Rating:** 60*

STUDENTS AND FACULTY
Enrollment: 382. **Student Body:** 51% female, 49% male, 69% out-of-state, 1% international (6 countries represented). Asian 2%, African American 5%, Caucasian 73%, Hispanic 4%, Native American 0%, Pacific Islander 0%, Two or more races 0%, Race unknown 15%.
Retention and Graduation: 55% freshmen return for sophomore year.
Faculty: Student/faculty ratio 7:1. 33 full-time faculty, 36% hold PhDs, 3% are are members of minority groups, 27% are women. 0% of classes are taught by teaching assistants.

ACADEMICS
Degrees: associate, bachelor's, transfer. **Classes:** Most classes have fewer than 10 students. **Most popular majors:** Education; Psychology; Business Administration and Management. **Special Study Options:** double major, dual enrollment, internships, student-designed major, teacher certification program. **Career Services:** Alumni network, Career assessment, On-campus interviews. Most degrees require students to serve in some type of internship before graduation.

FACILITIES
Housing: special housing for disabled students, men's dorms, women's dorms, apartments for married students. 60% of campus accessible to physically diasbled. **Computers:** 100% of libraries, 100% of student union, have wireless network access.

CAMPUS LIFE
Environment: Village. **Activities:** Choral groups, drama/theater, literary magazine, music ensembles, musical theater, student government, student newspaper, yearbook, Campus Ministries. 12 registered organizations, 2 honor societies, 1 religious organization. 4 fraternities, 4 sororities. **Athletics (Intercollegiate):** *Men:* baseball, basketball, soccer, wrestling. *Women:* basketball, soccer, softball, volleyball. **On-Campus Highlights:** Mackey Center, Prayer Chapel, Spiritual Life Center/Coffee Shop, Gurganus Hall, Freeman Center.

ADMISSIONS
Freshman Academic Profile: Average high school GPA 3.4. 13% in top 10% of high school class, 25% in top 25% of high school class, 60% in top 50% of high school class. **Reported SAT (pre-2016 redesign) scores:** SAT Math middle 50% range 440-560. SAT Critical Reading middle 50% range 450-590. **Concordant SAT scores:** SAT Math middle 50% range 480–580. ACT middle 50% range 18-26. Minimum paper TOEFL 500. **Basis for Candidate Selection:** *Very important factors considered include:* rigor of secondary school record, class rank, academic GPA, standardized test scores. *Other factors considered include:* application essay, recommendation(s), extracurricular activities, talent/ability, character/personal qualities, first generation, alumni/ae relation, religious affiliation/commitment, volunteer work, level of applicant's interest. **Freshman Admission Requirements:** High school diploma is required and GED is accepted. *Academic units required:* 3 English, 2 math, 2 science, 1 social studies, 1 history. *Academic units recommended:* 4 English, 4 math, 4 science, 3 foreign language, 4 social studies, 4 history. **Freshman Admission Statistics:** 531 applied, 56.87% admitted, 30% enrolled. **Transfer Admission Requirements:** High school transcript, college transcript(s), Minimum college GPA of 2 required. Lowest grade transferable 1. **General Admission Information:** Application fee $20. Priority deadline 3/31. Regular application deadline 8/31. Nonfall registration accepted. Admission may be deferred.

COSTS AND FINANCIAL AID
Annual tuition $12,500. Room and board $4,500. Required fees $1,500. Average book expense $1,500. **Required Forms and Deadlines:** FAFSA. **Notification of Awards:** Applicants will be notified of awards on a rolling basis beginning 3/1. **Types of Aid:** *Need-based scholarships/grants:* Federal Pell, FSEOG,

State scholarships/grants, Private scholarships, College/university scholarship or grant aid from institutional funds. *Loans:* Direct Subsidized Stafford Loans, Direct Unsubsidized Stafford Loans, Direct PLUS loans, Federal Perkins Loans, Federal Nursing Loans, College/university loans from institutional funds. *Student Employment:* Federal Work-Study Program available. **Financial Aid Statistics:** 0% freshmen, 0% undergrads receive athletic scholarships. 89% freshmen, 89% undergrads receive any aid. **Criteria for awarding aid:** *Non-need-based:* Academics, Athletics, Leadership, Music/drama.

YORK COLLEGE OF PENNSYLVANIA

441 Country Club Road, York, PA 17403-3651
Phone: 717-849-1600 • **Financial Aid Phone:** 717-849-1682
E-mail: admissions@ycp.edu • **CEEB Code:** 2991
Fax: 717-849-1607 • **Website:** www.ycp.edu • **ACT Code:** 3762

This private school was founded in 1787. It has a 190-acre campus.

RATINGS
Admissions Selectivity Rating: 80   **Fire Safety Rating:** 96   **Green Rating:** 67

STUDENTS AND FACULTY
Enrollment: 4,847. **Student Body:** 55% female, 45% male, 42% out-of-state, <1% international (32 countries represented). Asian 1%, African American 5%, Caucasian 83%, Hispanic 5%, Native American <1%, Pacific Islander <1%, Two or more races 3%, Race unknown 2%.
Retention and Graduation: 75% freshmen return for sophomore year. 37% freshmen graduate within 4 years. 58% freshmen graduate within 6 years.
Faculty: Student/faculty ratio 16:1. 189 full-time faculty, 81% hold PhDs, 4% are are members of minority groups, 43% are women. 0% of classes are taught by teaching assistants.

ACADEMICS
Degrees: associate, bachelor's, doctoral/professional, master's, post-master's certificate. **Classes:** Most classes have 20-29 students. Most lab/discussion sessions have 10-19 students. **Most popular majors:** Biology/Biological Sciences; Business Administration and Management; Registered Nursing/Registered Nurse. **Special Study Options:** Accelerated program, cooperative education program, double major, dual enrollment, honors program, independent study, internships, liberal arts/career combination, student-designed major, study abroad, teacher certification program. **Honors Programs:** Honors Program includes coursework, special academic and career advising and extracurricular enrichment activities Combined degree programs: BS/MBA. **Disability Services:** Special programs offered to physically disabled students, including tape recorders, tutors. **Career Services:** Alumni network, Alumni services, Career/job search classes, Career assessment, Internships, Regional alumni. We are very proud of the experiential education opportunities that all of our students enjoy. Credit-based experiential learning is available in all academic programs and provides reflective learning and practical application of skills. Experiential education offerings vary based upon the academic program, and include internships, independent research, service-learning, course based projects, practica, student teaching, clinical rotations, and many other special learning opportunities. Co-ops are exclusive to our three engineering programs, and students are required to participate in 3 before graduating as well as a number of other hands-on experiences and projects.

FACILITIES
Housing: Coed dorms, men's dorms, women's dorms, fraternity/sorority housing, apartments for single students, Wellness Housing, Theme Housing. 98% of campus accessible to physically diasbled. **Special Academic Facilities/Equipment:** Museum, telecommunications center, science and foreign language labs. All of campus is wired to the computer network. **Computers:** 50% of classrooms, 35% of dorms, 100% of libraries, 100% of dining areas, 80% of student union, 65% of common outdoor areas have wireless network access. Students can register for classes online. Administrative functions (other than registration) can be performed online.

CAMPUS LIFE
Environment: City. **Activities:** Choral groups, concert band, drama/theater, jazz band, literary magazine, music ensembles, musical theater, radio station, student government, student newspaper, symphony orchestra, television station, Campus Ministries, Student Organization, Model UN. 80 registered organizations, 7 honor societies, 4 religious organizations. 9 fraternities, 7 sororities. **Athletics (Intercollegiate):** *Men:* baseball, basketball, cheerleading, cross-country, golf, lacrosse, soccer, swimming, tennis, track/field (outdoor), wrestling. *Women:* basketball, cheerleading, cross-country, field hockey, lacrosse, soccer, softball, swimming, tennis, track/field (outdoor), volleyball. **On-Campus Highlights:** Student Union Spart's Den, TV and Radio Studios, Bookstore, York College Art Galleries, Tyler Run Walking Path.

ADMISSIONS

Freshman Academic Profile: Average high school GPA 3.5. 12% in top 10% of high school class, 40% in top 25% of high school class, 77% in top 50% of high school class. **Reported SAT (pre-2016 redesign) scores:** SAT Math middle 50% range 480-578. SAT Critical Reading middle 50% range 470-560. SAT Writing middle 50% range 450-550. **Concordant SAT scores:** SAT EBRW middle 50% 510–610. SAT Math middle 50% range 510–600. ACT middle 50% range 20-25. Minimum internet-based TOEFL 72. Minimum paper TOEFL 530. **Basis for Candidate Selection:** *Very important factors considered include:* rigor of secondary school record, academic GPA. *Important factors considered include:* class rank, standardized test scores, character/personal qualities. *Other factors considered include:* application essay, recommendation(s), interview, extracurricular activities, talent/ability, alumni/ae relation, volunteer work, work experience, level of applicant's interest. **Freshman Admission Requirements:** High school diploma is required and GED is accepted. *Academic units required:* 4 English, 3 math, 3 science, 2 foreign language, 3 social studies. *Academic units recommended:* 4 English, 4 math, 3 science, 2 foreign language, 3 social studies. **Freshman Admission Statistics:** 9,934 applied, 73.51% admitted, 22% enrolled. **Transfer Admission Requirements:** college transcript(s), Minimum college GPA of 2.0 required. Lowest grade transferable C. **General Admission Information:** Nonfall registration accepted. Admission may be deferred for a maximum of 12 months.

COSTS AND FINANCIAL AID

Annual tuition $15,350. Room and board $9,580. Required fees $1,660. Average book expense $1,200. **Required Forms and Deadlines:** FAFSA. **Notification of Awards:** Applicants will be notified of awards on a rolling basis beginning 3/1. **Types of Aid:** *Need-based scholarships/grants:* Federal Pell, FSEOG, State scholarships/grants, Private scholarships, College/university scholarship or grant aid from institutional funds. *Loans:* Direct Subsidized Stafford Loans, Direct Unsubsidized Stafford Loans, Direct PLUS loans, Federal Perkins Loans, Federal Nursing Loans, College/university loans from institutional funds. *Student Employment:* Federal Work-Study Program available. Institutional employment available. **Financial Aid Statistics:** 61% needy freshmen, 67% needy undergrads receive need-based scholarship or grant aid. 99% freshmen, 78% undergrads receive non-need-based scholarship or grant aid. 85% freshmen, 89% undergrads receive need-based self-help aid. 0% freshmen, 0% undergrads receive athletic scholarships. 99% freshmen, 89% undergrads receive any aid. **Criteria for awarding aid:** *Need-based:* Minority status. *Non-need-based:* Academics, Alumni affiliation, Minority status, Music/drama.

YORK UNIVERSITY

Bennett Centre for Student Services, Toronto, ON M3J 1P3
Phone: 416-736-5000 • **Financial Aid Phone:** 416-872-9675
E-mail: intlenq@yorku.ca • **CEEB Code:** 894
Fax: 416-736-5536 • **Website:** www.yorku.ca

This public school was founded in 1959. It has a 550-acre campus.

RATINGS

Admissions Selectivity Rating: 60* **Fire Safety Rating:** 62 **Green Rating:** 95

STUDENTS AND FACULTY

Student Body: 59% female, 41% male, (170 countries represented).
Faculty: Student/faculty ratio 17:1. 1,480 full-time faculty, 0% hold PhDs, 0% are are members of minority groups, 46% are women.

ACADEMICS

Degrees: bachelor's, certificate, diploma, doctoral/research, doctoral, master's, postbachelor's certifiate. **Most popular majors:** Psychology. **Special Study Options:** Accelerated program, distance learning, double major, English as a Second Language (ESL), exchange student program (domestic), honors program, independent study, internships, student-designed major, study abroad, teacher certification program. Combined degree programs: MBA/LLB, BA/BEd, BSc/BEd, BFA/BEd, MES/LLB, MBA/MFA. **Disability Services:** Special programs offered to physically disabled students, including note-taking services, reader services, tape recorders, tutors. **Career Services:** Career/job search classes, Career assessment, Internships, On-campus interviews. The York University International Internship Program (YIIP) provides both York undergraduate and graduate students a non-credit opportunity to apply their academic knowledge to an international work environment and enhance their job-related skills in an international and intercultural setting.

FACILITIES

Housing: Coed dorms, special housing for disabled students, men's dorms, special housing for international students, women's dorms, apartments for married students, apartments for single students, Theme Housing. **Special Academic Facilities/Equipment:** 5 museums with more than 4.4 million items. Observatory with 2 telescopes. Robotics laboratory. 2 professionally staffed art galleries. 6 student-run art exhibition spaces. 3 theatres. 2 cinemas. 1 screening room. Wide-variety professional standard film and video production facilities. **Computers:** Students can register for classes online. Administrative functions (other than registration) can be performed online.

CAMPUS LIFE

Environment: Metropolis. **Activities:** Choral groups, concert band, dance, drama/theater, jazz band, music ensembles, pep band, radio station, student government, student newspaper, symphony orchestra, yearbook, Student Organization, Model UN. 259 registered organizations, 35 religious organizations. **Athletics (Intercollegiate):** *Men:* badminton, basketball, cross-country, fencing, football, ice hockey, soccer, swimming, tennis, track/field (outdoor), volleyball, water polo. *Women:* badminton, basketball, cross-country, fencing, field hockey, ice hockey, rugby, soccer, swimming, tennis, track/field (outdoor), volleyball, water polo. **On-Campus Highlights:** York Lanes: on-campus mall, Tait McKenzie Centre: sports complex, Student Centre: food court/lounge/club, Accolade East: theatre, art gallery, Central Square: Scott library, food court.

ADMISSIONS

Minimum internet-based TOEFL 83. Minimum paper TOEFL 560. **Basis for Candidate Selection:** *Very important factors considered include:* rigor of secondary school record, academic GPA. *Important factors considered include:* standardized test scores. *Other factors considered include:* class rank, interview. **Freshman Admission Requirements:** High school diploma is required and GED is not accepted. **Transfer Admission Requirements:** college transcript(s), Minimum college GPA of 2.5 required. Lowest grade transferable C. **General Admission Information:** Application fee $100. Nonfall registration accepted. Admission may be deferred for a maximum of 1 year.

COSTS AND FINANCIAL AID

Annual in-state tuition $6,712. Annual out-of-state tuition $6,712. Room and board $7,702. Average book expense $1,000. **Required Forms and Deadlines:** FAFSA. **Types of Aid:** *Loans:* Federal Perkins Loans. *Student Employment:* Institutional employment available. **Financial Aid Statistics:** freshmen, 0% undergrads receive athletic scholarships. **Criteria for awarding aid:** *Need-based:* Leadership. *Non-need-based:* Academics, Art, Music/drama.

YOUNGSTOWN STATE UNIVERSITY

One University Plaza, Youngstown, OH 44555
Phone: 330-941-2000 • **Financial Aid Phone:** 330-941-3505
E-mail: enroll@ysu.edu • **CEEB Code:** 1975
Fax: 330-941-3674 • **Website:** www.ysu.edu • **ACT Code:** 3368

RATINGS

Admissions Selectivity Rating: 78 **Fire Safety Rating:** 95 **Green Rating:** 60*

STUDENTS AND FACULTY

Enrollment: 10,188. **Student Body:** 52% female, 48% male, 14% out-of-state, 2% international (63 countries represented). Asian 1%, African American 10%, Caucasian 76%, Hispanic 4%, Native American <1%, Pacific Islander <1%, Two or more races 3%, Race unknown 4%.
Retention and Graduation: 75% freshmen return for sophomore year. 11% freshmen graduate within 4 years. 31% freshmen graduate within 6 years.
Faculty: Student/faculty ratio 17:1. 399 full-time faculty, 88% hold PhDs, 16% are are members of minority groups, 45% are women.

ACADEMICS

Degrees: associate, bachelor's, certificate, diploma, doctoral/professional, doctoral/research, doctoral, master's, postbachelor's certifiate, post-master's certificate, terminal, transfer. **Most popular majors:** Criminal Justice/Safety Studies; General Studies; Registered Nursing/Registered Nurse. Combined degree programs: BS/MS in Chemistry; Combined BS/MD Program, 4+1 Economics, 4+1 Mathematics. **Career Services:** Alumni network, Alumni services, Career/job search classes, Career assessment, Internships, Regional alumni. Pareparing students for the job market which includes: resume reviews, cover letter reviews, mock interviews, MyPlan Career Assessment, fall and spring career fairs.

FACILITIES

Housing: 98% of campus accessible to physically diasbled.

ADMISSIONS

Freshman Academic Profile: Average high school GPA 3.2. 13% in top 10% of high school class, 34% in top 25% of high school class, 65% in top 50% of high school class. **Reported SAT (pre-2016 redesign) scores:** SAT Math middle 50% range 430-550. SAT Critical Reading middle 50% range 420-540. SAT Writing middle 50% range 390-510. **Concordant SAT scores:** SAT EBRW middle 50% 450–580. SAT Math middle 50% range 470–570. ACT middle 50% range 18-25. Minimum internet-based TOEFL 61. Minimum paper TOEFL 500. **Basis for Candidate Selection:** *Very important factors considered include:* rigor of secondary school record, academic GPA, standardized test scores. *Important factors considered include:* class rank. **Freshman Admission Requirements:** *Academic units recommended:* 4 English, 4 math, 3 science, 1 science lab, 2 foreign language, 3 social studies, 1 visual/performing arts. **Freshman Admission Statistics:** 9,010 applied, 67.38% admitted, 34% enrolled. **General Admission Information:** Application fee $45. Priority deadline 2/15. Regular application deadline 8/1. Nonfall registration accepted. Admission may be deferred for a maximum of 12 months.

COSTS AND FINANCIAL AID

Required Forms and Deadlines: FAFSA, Institution's own financial aid form. **Notification of Awards:** Applicants will be notified of awards on a rolling basis beginning 4/1. **Types of Aid:** *Need-based scholarships/grants:* Federal Pell, FSEOG, State scholarships/grants, Private scholarships, College/university scholarship or grant aid from institutional funds. *Loans:* Direct Subsidized Stafford Loans, Direct Unsubsidized Stafford Loans, Direct PLUS loans, Federal Perkins Loans, State Loans. *Student Employment:* Federal Work-Study Program available. Institutional employment available. **Financial Aid Statistics:** 79% needy freshmen, 76% needy undergrads receive need-based scholarship or grant aid. 55% freshmen, 43% undergrads receive non-need-based scholarship or grant aid. 83% freshmen, 87% undergrads receive need-based self-help aid. 6% freshmen, 5% undergrads receive athletic scholarships. 94% freshmen, 90% undergrads receive any aid. **Criteria for awarding aid:** *Need-based:* Academics, Art, Athletics, Leadership, Minority status, Music/drama. *Non-need-based:* Academics, Alumni affiliation, Athletics, State/district residency.

SCHOOL SAYS . . .

In this section you'll find hundreds of colleges with extended listings describing admissions, curriculum, internships, and much more. This is your chance to get in-depth information on colleges that interest you. The Princeton Review charges each school a small fee to be listed, and the editorial responsibility is solely that of the college.

ALLEGHENY COLLEGE

AT A GLANCE

Recognized among Loren Pope's *40 Colleges That Change Lives*, Allegheny College is one of the nation's most prestigious and dynamic institutions of higher education—a place where students are encouraged to explore their unusual combinations of interests and talents. Allegheny is one of the only colleges in the country that requires its students to choose both a major and minor, ensuring they develop the skills needed to be analytical, creative, and innovative.

Allegheny is a leader in higher education innovation, having been recognized in 2016 as the nation's top baccalaureate college for undergraduate research by the Council on Undergraduate Research. Central to the college's focus on experiential learning is the Allegheny Gateway, which helps students connect classroom learning with real-world experience. Since its introduction in 2015, the Gateway has received national attention. It is a central location for collaboration and study in which students can access résumé and career services, pre-professional and graduate school advising, research funding and fellowships, internship opportunities, and more.

Allegheny students don't have to wait behind graduate students for research positions on faculty-led projects but instead are actively engaged as research collaborators. Students follow the guidance of faculty mentors through research, conference presentations, co-authored articles, and faculty-led study tours.

Our faculty members are people who pride themselves on being teachers first—they will advise and support you to move beyond what you can even imagine now. They will provide you with opportunities and challenges that will lead you from hard work and dedication to extraordinary outcomes.

LOCATION & ENVIRONMENT

Allegheny's beautiful 79-acre central campus includes historic architecture and cobblestone streets interspersed with advanced facilities bristling with the latest communications and research technology. Located on a hill overlooking the City of Meadville, Pa., the campus is a short walk to downtown and all the amenities you'll need to enjoy the Allegheny experience. Outdoor opportunities also abound on our 203-acre recreation area near campus and in the local community.

CAMPUS FACILITIES & EQUIPMENT

Campus Highlights

- The Allegheny Gateway, which brings together nine offices that help students connect classroom learning with real-world experience
- Nationally acclaimed science complex
- Multimillion-dollar center for communication arts and theatre
- Center for Business and Economics
- Environmental science center
- The Carrden, a hands-on learning and teaching garden
- Geographic Information System (GIS) Learning Laboratory
- Observatory and planetarium
- David V. Wise Sport & Fitness Center
- Olympic-style track and turf field
- 203-acre recreation area and 283-acre nature preserve
- North Village I and II offer townhouse-style student apartments and suite-style residences
- Tippie Alumni Center in historic Cochran Hall
- WARC radio and ACTV television stations
- Bowman, Penelec & Megahan art galleries
- Special-interest houses (past houses include an international theme and a jazz theme)
- Dance studios and performance spaces

TUITION, ROOM, BOARD, FEES

- Tuition and Fees: $45,470
- Room and Board: $12,150

FINANCIAL AID

The Princeton Review has featured Allegheny in their "Colleges That Pay You Back" rating, which measures 40 weighted data points including academics, cost, financial aid, student debt, graduation rates, alumni salaries, and job satisfaction.

Allegheny is committed to providing transformative education to ambitious, talented students independent of their financial or social means. Generous financial aid packages allow many students the opportunity to make a college choice based on value and fit, rather than financial constraints.

Allegheny's Trustee Scholarship is a merit-based award that any student who submits an admissions application will be evaluated to receive. The award is based on the same criteria that we value in the admission process: strength and rigor of academics, test scores (optional), essays and recommendations, and a student's contributions and achievements outside of the classroom. Based on those factors, students can receive up to $28,000 per year.

Because Allegheny encourages students to challenge themselves in the classroom, the Trustee Scholarship is guaranteed for eight semesters of full-time enrollment at Allegheny or for Allegheny-sponsored programs.

STUDENT ORGANIZATIONS & ACTIVITIES

Our Student Population

- 2,100 students
- 43 states represented
- 53 countries represented

It is our students who make Allegheny the vibrant, creative, and innovative place that it is. We invite students to explore all of their interests and talents. At Allegheny, opportunities to pursue one's passions are limited only by the imagination.

Allegheny has more than 120 clubs and organizations that are run and led by students spanning areas like activism and politics, performing arts and media, spiritual and religious life, and recreation and club sports. We are also home to 10 nationally affiliated social Greek organizations and were founding members of both the NCAA and North Coast Athletic Conference (NCAC).

These activities help develop students' leadership skills and make a lasting impact on Allegheny's campus culture. That's because Allegheny is all about active learning and fun—not just learning about foreign policy in class, but arguing for change. Not just writing papers on social activism, but working to educate others. Our students create, laugh, dance, play, explore, and serve together every day.

ADMISSIONS PROCESS

Allegheny's Admissions Committee values the hard work you do on a daily basis, and they give the greatest weight to the rigor of your high school courses and your performance. Also considered are your school/community activities, recommendations, personal character and qualities, essay, demonstrated interest, and special talents.

Allegheny embraces the concept that standardized test scores do not exclusively reflect a student's full range of abilities or potential to succeed in college. As a result, Allegheny is now test optional. SAT I or ACT scores are optional for U.S. citizens and permanent residents.

Apply today at allegheny.edu/apply. Allegheny is also a member of The Common Application.

ALVERNIA UNIVERSITY

AT A GLANCE

Alvernia's Franciscan heritage includes a rigorous intellectual tradition that recognizes and values the importance of diversity of thought, faiths and cultures. We challenge our students to shape the world and transform it as working professionals, concerned citizens and caring community members, consistent with the principles and teachings of Saint Francis of Assisi.

Alvernia Core Values

The mission statements of the Bernardine Franciscan Sisters and Alvernia University are the sources of the five core values from the Franciscan tradition. All members of the Alvernia community including trustees, administration, faculty, staff, and students embrace Alvernia's core Franciscan values which are:

- Service
- Humility
- Peacemaking
- Contemplation
- Collegiality

Our Franciscan Identity

"Knowledge Joined with Love"

"To Learn, To Love, To Serve"

LOCATION & ENVIRONMENT

Situated on a scenic 121-acre suburban campus, Alvernia is bordered by a park that features hiking trails, a picnic grove, and a nine-hole disk-golf course. When students want to explore big city life, Philadelphia (60 miles), New York, Baltimore, and Washington, D.C. are all just a short drive away.

CAMPUS FACILITIES & EQUIPMENT

Alvernia's fully networked campus is constantly investing in upgrades. Recent campus advancements include a new laser laboratory supporting science programs, state-of-the-art learning suites developed for our criminal justice and counseling programs, a theater and recital hall, with an art gallery, music studios and rehearsal spaces, an educational technology center and media suite, a healthcare science wing with multiple labs, an expanded library learning commons and a physical therapy center to support the Doctor of Physical Therapy program. On-campus housing includes traditional residence halls, apartments, suites, and town houses. Our award-winning residential facilities are clean, spacious and equipped with laundry, cable TV, and phones with voice mail.

A new student-designed Campus Commons building houses a two-story fitness center, a dance/aerobics studio, and a campus "living room," complete with a fireplace for leisure activities, study, and programs.

Alvernia recently announced plans to build an innovative Recreation, Wellness and Health Sciences Complex ("The PLEX"), as the highlight of a new East Campus at the university's Reading, Pa., location. This expansion is the largest, most ambitious in university history, adding more than 100,000 square feet of academic and recreation space and 15 acres to Alvernia's campus

Students have wireless access from their residence hall rooms, as well as from other campus locations including classrooms, the library, and labs. All students may connect personal computers through the university's secure system. Network access and Alvernia email accounts are available to all students.

OFF-CAMPUS OPPORTUNITIES

The Washington Center experience is a popular way for students to expand their education beyond the classroom. Earning college credit while spending a semester in Washington D.C., students serve as interns in a congressional office, government agency, major corporation, newspaper, news network, or nonprofit groups, or an agency devoted to legal affairs, international relations, or business and economics.

Global Study opportunities are constantly expanding at Alvernia. Global partnerships allow students to study in Austria, Belgium, China, Ecuador, England, Germany, Greece, India, Ireland, Mexico, New Zealand, Palestine and Spain!

ACADEMICS

Alvernia offers a range of academic programs with a learning approach grounded in the real world. With a foundation in the liberal arts tradition, the curriculum and instruction is designed to help students develop critical thinking skills and explore their own ideas. This approach produces well-rounded individuals who are ready to succeed no matter what path they choose.

Qualified students may participate in the Honors Program, which assists students of outstanding intellectual promise and high motivation that seek a more challenging program and are interested in pursuing future graduate or professional studies. The program encourages students to achieve, often letting them work at their own pace. It facilitates a stimulating exchange of ideas and information between students' varied interests and different disciplines.

In order to earn a bachelor's degree from Alvernia, students must complete a minimum of 123 credits, with 54 credits in the liberal arts. Additional requirements vary by major.

MAJORS & DEGREES OFFERED

Athletic Training

Behavioral Health

    Addiction Studies

    Child Welfare

    Mental Health

Biochemistry#

Biology #

Biology-Medical Laboratory Science

Business

    Accounting

    Finance

    Healthcare Administration

    Human Resource Management

    Management

    Marketing

    Sport Management

Chemistry

Communication

    Corporate

    Film, Culture and Creative Arts

    Journalism

    Media Design and Production

    Public Relations and Advertising

    Theatre Studies

Criminal Justice Administration°

Education

    Early Childhood (PreK-4)

    Early Childhood (PreK-4) & Special Education (PreK-8)

English

Environmental Biochemistry

Forensic Science°

General Science°

Healthcare Science#

History

Liberal Studies

Mathematics

Nursing

Occupational Therapy

Philosophy

Political Science

Psychology°#

Social Work

Theatre

Theology

° minor available

May be used to track toward application for Doctor of Physical Therapy Graduate Program (currently a candidate for accreditation status).

Additional Minors

Art

Community & Environmental Sustainability

Computer and Information Studies

Digital Media

Economics

Gerontology

Information Studies

Music

Physics

Sociology

Spanish

Women's & Gender Studies

Pre-professional Programs

Pre-Dental

Pre-Law

Pre-Medical

Pre-Pharmacy

Pre-Veterinary

Doctor of Nursing Practice (DNP) Program

Alvernia's Doctor of Nursing Practice (DNP) Program is a terminal degree program that paves the way for BSN graduates to seamlessly complete advance nursing practice clinical coursework and DNP requirements in one combined effort. The program of study emphasizes the knowledge and skills necessary to analyze and improve clinical environments; healthcare organizations and systems; translate evidence gained through nursing research to support improved practice; and meaningful use of clinical data to measure outcomes of patient groups, populations, and communities.

TUITION, ROOM, BOARD, FEES

Please visit this page for more information: http://www.alvernia.edu/financialaid/

FINANCIAL AID

Ninety-eight percent of students receive some form of financial aid. Financial aid is offered to students whose personal and family resources are insufficient to meet the full cost of an education. Aid usually comes in the form of scholarships, grants, loans, and work-study arrangements. Depending upon their academic record, incoming first-year students may be eligible for one of three merit-based scholarships: the Presidential Scholarship ($17,500), the Trustee's Scholarship ($15,500), and the Veronica Founder's Scholarship ($15,000). Applicants interested in financial aid should submit the FAFSA as soon as possible after January 1.

STUDENT ORGANIZATIONS & ACTIVITIES

More than 50 student organizations complement 24 men and women's athletics teams, including a new varsity football program, launching fall 2018. The university has made 33 appearances in NCAA Championships.

The Holleran Center for Community and Global Engagement at Alvernia helps students discover their passion through real world experiences, so that graduates can turn what they love into lifetimes of career success and personal fulfillment, while making a positive difference in the world. Alvernia's approach to real-world learning combines hands-on educational opportunities through internships, field experiences, co-ops, clinical assignments, research projects, community service and study/service abroad programs, roles in student organizations and other creative and relevant campus experiences.

Real-World Experience Awards are available to financially assist students for a variety of experiential opportunities, without reducing the amount of financial aid a student already has been awarded.

94% of our students are happy graduates

100% of our students receive real-world learning experiences

97% of our students are employed within six months of graduation

93% of our students are happy with Alvernia

98% of our students receive Financial Aid

100% of our students participate in some form of community service

Alvernia also has a 12:1 student to professor ratio, so they are able to receive the benefit of smaller class sizes.

ADMISSIONS PROCESS
Discover Alvernia!

We have many different ways to welcome you to our campus in Reading, Pennsylvania and you can choose what's important to you during your visit whether you wish to sit in on a class, meet students, spend the night or enjoy a sporting event. Get the full Alvernia experience!

Here are a few links to help you design your visit. You can also email us if you prefer.

- An Individual Visit experience allows us to tailor a one-on-one visit specifically to your needs. http://www.alvernia.edu/admissions/undergraduate/visit/individual.html

- Information Sessions and Open Houses are offered throughout the year and are opportunities to experience AU in a small group format. http://www.alvernia.edu/admissions/undergraduate/visit/info_sessions.html

- Students who have applied for Admission can spend even more time on campus by doing an Overnight Visit during the school year and experience a day (and night!) in the life of an Alvernia student. http://www.alvernia.edu/admissions/undergraduate/visit/overnights.html

- If you'd like to experience a day as an AU student, you can request a Shadow Visit, during which you'll be matched with someone already enrolled in the academic major that you're interested in…and you can go to class with them for the day. http://www.alvernia.edu/admissions/undergraduate/visit/overnights.html

ARKANSAS STATE UNIVERSITY

AT A GLANCE

Arkansas State's mission is to educate leaders, enhance intellectual growth and enrich lives. Founded in 1909, A-State is the second-largest university in the state and a leader within the Delta and Mid-South region. It hosts the first osteopathic medical school in the state of Arkansas, NYIT's College of Osteopathic Medicine, and is opening the first U.S.-style residential campus in Mexico in fall 2017.

Dedicated to teaching, research, and service, the university provides students with the broad educational foundations that help them develop critical thinking, decision-making, analytical, and communication skills. The university is the state's leading provider of nursing graduates, early childhood educators, and agricultural business graduates. In addition, A-State has top-ranked programs in creative media and speech communication. Degree programs in the nursing and health professions are in great demand nationwide, and A-State boasts clinical affiliations with more than 500 health care facilities, where both physical therapy and occupational therapy doctoral programs are emphasized, alongside a doctoral nurse practitioner program. A-State offers management education that includes international business, technology, entrepreneurship, and economic development through action-based learning. Arkansas State is also home to the state-of-the-art Arkansas Biosciences Institute, where graduate and undergraduate students conduct cutting-edge research.

The campus has seen more than $150 million in renovations and new facilities in the past six years, including the expansion of on-campus housing by 500 residents for fall 2017.

Incoming students will find more than 200 campus organizations, more than 20 men's and women's intramural sports, 17 national Greek organizations, and NCAA Football Bowl Subdivision intercollegiate athletic programs to enhance their university experience. Today, the institution has more than 80,000 alumni and meets the needs of individuals and communities at all points along the educational continuum.

LOCATION & ENVIRONMENT

Located in Jonesboro, Ark., and situated in the northeast corner of Arkansas, A-State is connected by interstate highways 55/555 to Memphis on the east and St. Louis to the north; and is less than two hours by four-lane highway to Little Rock.

Jonesboro is one of the fastest growing cities in Arkansas, and has seen remarkable growth in the medical sector with over $1 billion of new facilities completed or under construction related to health care. The town has one of the lowest unemployment rates in the state. As the commercial hub of the region, Jonesboro's business activity is considered one of the fastest expanding in the state and in the Delta region. The city serves an 18-county retail trade area of a half-million residents.

CAMPUS FACILITIES & EQUIPMENT

Home to the Arkansas Biosciences Institute, A-State is the location of the first osteopathic medical school in Arkansas with New York Institute of Technology's College of Osteopathic Medicine in historic Wilson Hall. One of the largest instructional buildings in higher education in Arkansas opened in 2015 at A-State: the 130,000 square foot Humanities and Social Sciences.

A pedestrian campus, A-State is also the first Bicycle Friendly University in Arkansas. A 2016 national survey ranked Arkansas State as one of the safest residential campuses, and another placed A-State's security in the top 10.

Campus life is currently at an all-time peak with record participation in on-campus activities and groups during the past five years. With residence hall occupancy at historic highs, space for 500 more graduate and undergraduate students were added for fall 2017.

A-State is the cultural hub of the region with the largest concert venue, the Convocation Center, as well as the largest concert hall and theatre located at Fowler Center. The Bradbury Art Museum is the region's leading facility. Arkansas State's Heritage Sites program operate four nationally or internationally known museum locations including the Johnny Cash Boyhood Home and the Hemingway-Pfeiffer Museum.

Annual events include the Agribusiness Conference hosted by the College of Agriculture, Engineering and Technology; the Delta Symposium hosted by the College of Liberal Arts and Communication; and the Women's Business Leadership Forum hosted by the College of Business. Among the major cultural events spanning multiple disciplines are the Delta Symposium and the Johnny Cash Heritage Festival.

ACADEMICS

Arkansas State University has been selected as one of the top-70 institutions of higher education in the Southern region by the editors of U.S. News & World Report magazine in the 2016 edition of "America's Best Colleges." Arkansas State is also ranked in the top Southern universities by Princeton Review. Among our individual academic programs, A-State has notable achievements, including the following:

- One of the nation's top-10 nursing programs according to NurseJournal.org;

- Back-to-back No. 10 rankings (2016 and 2017) in U.S. News & World Report's best online MBA programs;

- More international students enrolled than ever before, with more than 60 countries represented by 851 students;

- The largest online enrollment in the state of Arkansas with 34 programs delivered 100 percent online;

- A vibrant on-campus community that will grow by 500 to a residence hall capacity of 3,700 beginning in fall 2017;

- An incoming freshman class with an average ACT score of 23.6;

- Home to an Honors College with an enrollment of almost 1,000 students in the program;

- A veteran-friendly campus, recognized repeatedly by Military Times magazine, sponsors one of America's oldest ROTC units, and home to the Beck PRIDE Center for America's wounded veterans.

- Most A-State faculty members hold the highest possible degrees and are recognized leaders in their fields.

In addition, Arkansas State's First-Year Experience received the Apple Distinguished Program award.

A-State offers "Degree in 3" for accelerated undergraduate completion. Study Abroad is a major component of student experience at A-State. Students outside Arkansas should inquire about Beyond Boundaries scholarship opportunities.

MAJORS

As of fall 2016, Arkansas State had 45 degree programs with 161 major fields of study offered at the doctoral, specialist, master, bachelor, and associate degree levels. Master's degree programs were initiated in 1955, and A-State began offering its first doctoral degree program, educational leadership, in the fall of 1992. Arkansas State has seen continued growth in doctoral programs, adding Environmental Science in 1998, Heritage Studies in 2001, Molecular Biosciences in 2006, Physical Therapy in 2008, Nursing Practice in 2012, and, most recently, Occupational Therapy in 2016.

A-State is a leader in meeting Arkansas's need for educators and health care professionals. The College of Education and Behavioral Science graduates more teachers, counselors, and administrators than any other Arkansas institution, while the College of Nursing and Health Professions is among the state's leaders in graduating nurses with bachelor's degrees.

Arkansas State's commitment to excellence in higher education is demonstrated through its accreditation by The Higher Learning Commission of the North Central Association of Colleges and Schools, as well as more than 20 specialized accrediting organizations. A-State also holds membership in national and international organizations that support the highest educational standards.

TUITION, ROOM, BOARD, FEES

Based on a 15 hour schedule, resident students at Arkansas State University pay approximately $8,260 for tuition and fees for an academic year and an average of $8,240 in room and board costs. Non-resident students pay $14,480 in tuition and fees. Federal Title Four Programs are available to all eligible students through the FAFSA application process. A-State's awarding practices promote equity to all students keeping in mind the neediest populations.

FINANCIAL AID

Based on 16-17 reporting of finance data, 94% of the First-Time Full-Time students receive some financial aid. Approximately 46% receive PELL and 73% receive State / local governmental support to pursue education at Arkansas State University. A significantly higher number of students (84% of the FTFT degree seeking undergraduates) pay in-state tuition.

STUDENT ORGANIZATIONS & ACTIVITIES

Arkansas State's student body comes from all 50 states and over 60 countries. On-campus life is at record participation levels with new housing to expand residences to meet demand scheduled to open in Fall 2017.

ADMISSIONS PROCESS

Unconditional undergraduate admission is based on high school grade point average, official ACT score or comparable SAT, ASSET or Compass score taken within five years prior to the application date. The minimum grade point average accepted for unconditional admission is 2.75 and the minimum ACT or comparable score is 21.

ASSUMPTION COLLEGE

AT A GLANCE

Established in 1904 by the Augustinians of the Assumption, Assumption College is a Catholic coeducational institution known for its classic liberal arts curriculum and strong academic programs in business and professional studies. Our nearly 2,000 undergraduate students choose among 41 majors and 48 minors, gaining the depth and breadth of knowledge that is the foundation of lifelong success and personal fulfillment.

The educational experience is grounded in the rich Catholic intellectual tradition, which cultivates both the intellect and the personal values that students need to meet the demands of a constantly changing world. Undergraduates and graduate students closely interact with faculty members and staff in a thriving community that forms graduates known for critical intelligence, thoughtful citizenship and compassionate service.

At Assumption, 90 percent of undergraduates live on campus and housing is guaranteed for all four years. Ninety-eight percent of Assumption's 2015 graduates were employed or in graduate school within six months of graduation. The campus is lively seven days a week with academic programming, activities sponsored by student clubs and organizations, community service opportunities, campus ministry programs and intercollegiate, intramural and club sports.

The college also has its own campus in Rome, Italy, which has been ranked a top ten study abroad program.

LOCATION & ENVIRONMENT

Spanning 185 acres, the Assumption campus is situated in a beautiful, residential neighborhood just minutes from downtown Worcester, Massachusetts. Worcester, New England's second largest city, is a college town that is home to more than 35,000 students. Students enjoy a variety of local restaurants, cultural venues and programs, retail and entertainment options, and professional sports teams. The campus's location also provides students with an array of internship opportunities in virtually every field as well as a great network for career placements. Boston and Providence are only an hour's drive away, and there is regular rail service to Boston.

As a member of the Higher Education Consortium of Central Massachusetts (HEC-CMA), an association of 11 higher education institutions in the Worcester region, Assumption students can register for courses at other local colleges and participate in their social and cultural events.

CAMPUS FACILITIES & EQUIPMENT

Assumption offers first-rate facilities for learning and living.

A variety of housing options are available to accommodate the 90 percent of undergraduates who live on campus. Traditional residence halls, the Living/Learning Center, suites and apartments with full kitchens provide housing options for all four years. All resident students have individual hard-wired and wireless high speed Internet access in their rooms. Assumption's campus in Rome, the newly renovated Villino Dufault, accommodates up to 18 students a semester.

Scheduled to open in Fall 2017, the 62,000-square-foot Tsotsis Family Academic Center will integrate academics with the arts and features technology-equipped classrooms, a performance hall, the Business Studies Department and much more.

The Testa Science Center houses the Department of Natural Sciences and features multi-use classrooms, 10 teaching laboratories, seven laboratories dedicated for faculty and student research, a working greenhouse, conference rooms and student lounge areas.

The College's Information Technology Center has leading-edge software and computer systems as well as computer labs and classrooms available for collaborative projects, multimedia presentations, and foreign language study.

The Emmanuel d'Alzon Library is an ideal location to study and research. The professional library staff, collection of 140,000 print volumes, 150,000 e-books, 42,000 print and e-journal titles and extensive access to local, regional and national library networks and databases are vital resources for both students and faculty.

Assumption's Multi-Sport Stadium features a lighted, synthetic turf field with seating for 1,200 and is the home of Assumption's intercollegiate field hockey, football, men's and women's lacrosse and men's and women's soccer teams and the College's extensive outdoor intramural programs.

The Plourde Recreation Center offers a swimming pool, exercise and wellness classes, courts, and a fitness facility that is accessible to all students.

OFF-CAMPUS OPPORTUNITIES

Assumption encourages students to expand their horizons. In addition to the Rome campus, undergraduates can spend a semester or a year studying abroad—from France and England, to Japan, the Czech Republic and Australia, to name a few locations. Many students also augment their education and hone professional skills through local, regional, national and international internships. Assumption students have worked at diverse organizations around the globe, from the Department of Commerce, Central America Bureau and the Department of State (NAFTA Agreement), to Smith Barney, Fidelity, Morgan Stanley, ABC News, and the Alliance Francaise in Paris.

ACADEMICS

Assumption College's classic liberal arts curriculum promotes the lively discussion of the books, ideas, people and events that have shaped civilization. Faculty and students explore the rich Catholic intellectual tradition together as they seek "truth" and the nature of the world. In all areas of academic study, students learn not only how to find answers, but also how to ask important questions.

Undergraduates must take 120 credit hours and a minimum of 38 courses to complete their degree. The Assumption liberal arts core curriculum requires all students complete courses in English, philosophy, theology, humanities, history, social sciences, and select courses in art, music or theater, mathematics, laboratory science, and/or foreign language.

The College offers 41 different majors across a wide array of subject areas. Some of the most popular academic programs include English (concentrations in literature or writing and mass communications), history, political science, psychology and the natural sciences–biology, biotechnology and molecular biology, neuroscience, chemistry and environmental science. Other popular academic programs include education, human services and rehabilitation studies, business accounting, international business, management, marketing and organizational communication. Minors are offered in 48 areas.

Pre-professional preparation is available for careers in dentistry, medicine, and law. Additionally, Assumption has partnered with other colleges and universities of note to provide students with an array of additional academic options. Through these "partnership programs," eligible students can, for example, attend Assumption for three years and then go on to law school at Duquesne, Vermont or Western New England Law Schools. There is also a 3 + 2 engineering degree program with the University of Notre Dame and Washington University in St. Louis. There is guaranteed admission to specific graduate programs in the health and natural sciences fields for eligible students as well.

Assumption's special academic programs are specially designed to help students achieve their full potential. COMPASS, the College's first-year program, engages new students and helps them build the skills they'll need for success in college and beyond. The Honors Program encourages students to challenge themselves. SOPHIA offers crucial vocational guidance.

Assumption offers an array of academic resources designed to help students achieve their educational goals. The College's dedicated academic advisors, Academic Support Center and Disability Services office all play a role in supporting students' academic ambitions.

In addition to its undergraduate offerings, Assumption College offers seven premier graduate programs: Applied Behavior Analysis, Clinical Counseling Psychology, Health Advocacy, MBA, Rehabilitation Counseling, School Counseling and Special Education. Several of the College's graduate programs offer Assumption undergraduates the opportunity to pursue an accelerated master's degree by taking graduate-level courses in their senior year.

MAJORS

Area, Ethnic, Cultural, and Gender Studies: Italian Studies, Latin American Studies, Women's Studies

Biological and Biomedical Sciences: Biology/Biological Sciences, Biotechnology, Molecular Biology

Business, Management, Marketing, and Related Support Services: Accounting, Actuarial Science, Business Administration and Management, International Business/Trade/Commerce, Marketing/Marketing Management

Communication, Journalism, and Related Programs: Organizational Communication

Computer and Information Sciences and Support Services: Computer Science

Education: Teacher Education, Multiple Levels

English Language and Literature/Letters: English Language and Literature

Foreign languages, literatures, and Linguistics: Classics and Classical Languages, Literatures, and Linguistics, French Language and Literature, Linguistic, Comparative, and Related Language Studies and Services, Spanish Language and Literature

Health Professions and Related Clinical Sciences: Rehabilitation and Therapeutic Professions

History: History

Mathematics and Statistics: Mathematics

Multi/Interdisciplinary Studies: International/Global Studies

Natural Resources and Conservation: Environmental Science

Philosophy and Religious Studies: Psychology

Physical Sciences: Chemistry

Psychology: Psychology

Social Sciences: Criminology, Economics, International Economics, Political Science and Government, Sociology

Theology and Religious Vocations: Theology/Theological Studies

Visual and Performing Arts, Art History, Criticism and Conservation, Fine/Studio Arts, Graphic Design, Music

TUITION, ROOM, BOARD, FEES

Estimated costs for Fall 2017 are a tuition of $38,850; room and board for $12,000, required for all first-year residential students, and student fees of $750.

FINANCIAL AID

Assumption awards more than $34 million in scholarships and grants to students each year. The College offers both need-based financial aid and merit-based assistance. All students who apply for admission are considered for scholarships ranging to up to $20,000 annually and recipients are chosen based on their academic qualifications and demonstrated student leadership. To qualify for need-based financial aid, students must submit the Free Application for Federal Student Aid (FAFSA) by October 1.

Beginning with the class of 2021, Assumption College will award up to fifty $24,000/year Light the Way Scholarships, which are renewable for all four years. These scholarships are awarded to students who utilize their abilities to Light the Way for others. Whether it's through engaging in community service to help people in need, developing innovations that improve society, or volunteering to heal our planet, this scholarship recognizes and supports students who positively impact the world in their own meaningful way.

STUDENT ORGANIZATIONS & ACTIVITIES

Assumption's nearly 2,000 undergraduates come from 25 states and 36 countries. More than 90 percent of undergraduates live on campus.

Numerous social, athletic, recreational and cultural activities are offered both on and off campus, making Assumption a dynamic place to live. The College boasts more than 60 clubs and organizations that complement the educational process and offer opportunities for students to explore and develop their interests and talents. Students can participate in academic and professional development clubs, arts and entertainment groups, student publications, politics and student government organizations, service projects, special interest groups, or spiritual activities. In addition to providing a fun diversion, these groups also provide students opportunities to develop their leadership and team-building skills.

Extracurricular events range from large-scale annual programs such as Family Weekend, Siblings Weekend, Welcome Week, Midnight Madness and the Spring Concert to other smaller, more frequent events like comedian shows and film showings, as well as off-campus trips and outings.

Assumption fields 24 intercollegiate teams, as well as club and intramural sports. The College is a charter member of the Northeast-10 Conference and competes as an NCAA Division II institution. The intercollegiate sports for men include: baseball, basketball, cross country, football, golf, hockey, lacrosse, soccer, tennis and track & field (indoor and outdoor). Women's sports include: basketball, cross country, field hockey, lacrosse, rowing, soccer, softball, swimming, tennis, track & field (indoor and outdoor) and volleyball.

Established in 2013, Assumption College's Rome Campus takes full advantage of the "Eternal City's" position as a treasure of art, history and culture. Students who study at the Rome Campus are immersed in the very best of the classic liberal arts tradition, which is woven into the fabric of the city and Rome itself becomes a living classroom.

Assumption College's first year Program, Common Pursuit of Academic and Social Success (COMPASS), is specially designed to offer new students the tools and instruction they'll need for a successful college career and beyond. A semester-long program, COMPASS offers an environment where students can grow and challenge one another as they share their journey into college life.

Assumption's SOPHIA (SOPHomore Initiative at Assumption College) program is specially designed to help students discover a deeper connection between their spiritual, personal and professional lives. By combining residential, academic and travel opportunities, SOPHIA fosters a culture of vocational exploration that helps students pursue productive lives of meaning.

Assumption's Honors Program offers a demanding, intensive curriculum that helps students achieve their full potential within a supportive community of peers. The Honors Program aids students of all majors in challenging themselves and exploring their capabilities.

FACULTY

Assumption's professors are active scholars who are widely published in their respective fields. With a student/faculty ratio of just 12:1, they are able to mentor their students and challenge them to ask questions, find their own answers, and grow intellectually, socially and spiritually. They also regularly involve their pupils in invaluable collaborative research projects.

Assumption College's Career Development and Internship Center (CDIC) helps students build the skills and experience they'll need for a successful—and meaningful—career. The CDIC advisors aid students from the first year through graduation in choosing the career options that are right for them and ensuring that they have the professional development and networking tools to make those aspirations a reality.

ADMISSIONS PROCESS

Assumption College values students who demonstrate an active intellect and self-motivation. Applicants must compile a solid academic record and complete all prescribed high school requirements. The College encourages prospective students to schedule a campus visit prior to applying for admission. During the summer months, high school students are encouraged to attend group information sessions, tours and interviews Monday-Friday. In the fall semester, prospective students may attend group information sessions, held throughout the week and occasionally on Saturdays, or schedule a campus visit during the week.

To apply, students are required to submit the Common Application, a $50 application fee, their official high school transcripts, and a letter of recommendation. Assumption is test-score optional, so SAT or ACT scores are not required. Applications, including all supporting documents and recommendations, must be received in the Office of Admissions by February 15. Students wishing to be considered for Early Action must apply by November 1 and for Early Action II by December 15.

For more information, please contact:

Assumption College
Office of Admissions
500 Salisbury Street
Worcester, MA 01609
Telephone: 866-477-7776 (toll free) or 508-767-7285
Web: www.assumption.edu
E-mail: admiss@assumption.edu

BABSON COLLEGE

AT A GLANCE

Nationally recognized as No. 1 in entrepreneurship for 20 years and ranked the Best U.S. College for International Students and No. 1 private business school for ROI, Babson College provides a dynamic living and learning experience. Our students and faculty work together to address real-world problems and make a difference in the world through Entrepreneurial Thought and Action. This close-knit community gets involved, has fun, and builds lifelong relationships. Students discover their strengths, pursue their interests, and create their own path to success.

Babson College is the educator, convener, and thought leader for Entrepreneurship of All Kinds™. As the only school to teach Entrepreneurial Thought and Action®, Babson shapes the leaders our world needs most: those with strong functional knowledge and the skills and vision to navigate change, accommodate ambiguity, surmount complexity, and motivate teams in a common purpose. Every day, Babson students, faculty, alumni, and staff address real-world business and societal problems, creating sustainable economic and social value in today's fast-paced global economy.

LOCATION & ENVIRONMENT

This 370-acre suburban campus is located in Wellesley, Massachusetts. This is the ideal charming New England town, a classic setting for a college environment. Just 14 miles outside of Boston, students here are sure to experience the best of both worlds: the quaintness of small town life bordering the cultural and social excitement of the city of Boston.

CAMPUS FACILITIES & EQUIPMENT

Babson's contemporary facilities provide students with access to dynamic academic and social resources. Students frequent the Donald W. Reynolds Campus Center, the Richard W. Sorenson Family Visual Arts Center, the Richard W. Sorenson Center for the Arts, the Webster Athletic Center, the Glavin Family Chapel, the Innovation Center, and the Arthur M. Blank Center for Entrepreneurship. These centers offer students a state-of-the-art campus experience. Horn Library houses an extensive business collection of print, media, and computerized information resources. Students have campus-wide access to newspapers, journals, investment analyst reports, corporate records, directories, and international information. They also benefit from numerous electronic research and news services. The Stephen D. Cutler Center for Investments and Finance, exemplifies Babson College's innovative, real-world approach to business education and applied research. It is the hub for investment education programs, finance-related student organizations and a forum for thought leadership where industry practitioners, faculty and students collaborate, exchange ideas and learn from one another. Wireless access is available everywhere on campus. Every incoming Babson undergraduate student receives a leased laptop. After their sophomore year, Babson students return their laptops and receive brand new laptops, which are then returned at the end of their senior year. When students graduate, they have the option to purchase their current laptop at a very attractive price or a new laptop at Babson's discounted rate. Babson provides network accounts for student use complete with Internet access and a Babson Gmail account, including all Google Apps for Education.

OFF-CAMPUS OPPORTUNITIES

Babson is a living/learning laboratory in which entrepreneurship is infused throughout our curricular and cocurricular offerings-that means in and out of the classroom. With our student-centered, action-learning model, the Babson experience is a seamless blend of theory and practice, reflection and group activities, leadership and fellowship, and the freedom to make your own way, according to your particular goals, interests, and tastes. Maybe you hadn't thought that music and dance, sports and fitness, and clubs based on recreational interests or cultural backgrounds are part of the educational experience. But, being entrepreneurial means living entrepreneurially, and that's life at Babson: fun, eclectic, and innovative.

ACADEMICS

With an emphasis on hands-on experiential learning, our academic program is uniquely designed for students who want to study business with an entrepreneurial mindset. Our focus on Entrepreneurial Thought and Action® enables students to discover their strengths, pursue their interests, and take their own path to success. All students develop, launch, manage and liquidate their own businesses with money loaned by Babson during their first year as part of Foundations of Management and Entrepreneurship (FME). Students also have the opportunity to work as consultants to external organizations as part of the Management Consulting Field Experience (MCFE). Babson also offers experiential learning programs, a first-year seminar, semester and electives abroad, an honors program, a student-managed endowment fund, the Center for Women's Entrepreneurial Leadership and much more.

MAJORS & DEGREES OFFERED

At Babson College, concentrations are an optional way for you to organize your advanced studies, and certify that your focus of study is on your final transcript. Students may choose to plan their course of study around one (or two) of twenty-seven optional concentrations in both business and liberal arts disciplines.

TUITION, ROOM, BOARD, FEES

20017-18 Academic Year Tuition: $49,664, Room (average double): $10,222, Meal Plan $5,616

FINANCIAL AID

Babson is committed to educating students from diverse backgrounds, and we will do all we can to make it financially possible for qualified students to attend. Babson awards $43 million in undergraduate aid; $36 million comes directly from Babson in grants and scholarships. Federal and state grants, loans, and work-study are awarded based on financial need. Students who wish to apply for financial aid should submit the CSS/Financial Aid PROFILE and FAFSA by 11/15 for Early Decision and Early Actions candidates and 2/1 for Regular Decision candidates.

STUDENT ORGANIZATIONS & ACTIVITIES

Babson offers students an extensive variety of student activities. Over 100 student-run clubs and organizations are available across every interest spectrum. Some of these activities include: dance groups, theater, improv, literary magazine, cultural groups, music ensembles, radio station, student government, student news source, business focused, and service related. The school also has four fraternities, three sororities, and two gender inclusive business fraternities. Students also have a wide variety of leadership program opportunities across campus that allow them to develop as entrepreneurial leaders based on three concepts: learning, purpose, and network. Additionally, these co-curricular opportunities include 22 NCAA Division III (11 men's and 11 women's) intercollegiate athletic teams. Many Babson students also engage in a variety of intramural and club sports.

ADMISSIONS PROCESS

Babson College bases its acceptance of students on both academic and nonacademic factors. The academic factors include high school record, recommendations, standardized test scores, and essays. The nonacademic factors include extracurricular activities, demonstrated leadership, character/personal qualities, volunteer work, work experience, creativity and enthusiasm and a willingness to contribute to the Babson community in meaningful ways. Graduation from secondary school is required for admission. The most competitive students have taken approximately 5 solid academic courses per year at the highest available level (Honors, Advanced Placement or International Baccalaureate). The SAT I or ACT required for admission. The TOEFL or IELTS is required for students who are nonnative English speakers. Babson offers several application programs. Students may apply Early Decision (binding process), Early Action or Regular Decision. The deadline for Early Decision and Early Action is November 1. The Regular Decision Deadline is January 2. Transfer students may apply for September entrance by March 15 and for January entrance by October 15.

BARNARD COLLEGE

AT A GLANCE

Barnard is the most sought-after liberal arts college for women in the US. Barnard provides a cosmopolitan setting, dynamic academic programs, access to internships and a unique partnership with Columbia University.

Barnard is a small, highly selective liberal arts college for women located in New York City. Our student body of 2,500 are part of a diverse and close-knit community and study with leading scholars who serve as dedicated, accessible mentors and teachers in small, intimate classes. Founded in 1889, Barnard also engages in a unique partnership with Columbia University, situated directly across the street. Students have access to additional course offerings, extracurricular activities, NCAA Division I Ivy League athletic competition and a fully coed social life. Our location in New York City grants students access to thousands of internship opportunities in addition to unparalleled cultural, intellectual and social resources. Barnard's diverse student body includes residents from nearly every state and more than 50 countries worldwide. Over 40 percent of the 2017 incoming class identifies as students of color, and 15 percent of the class comes from non-college backgrounds.

LOCATION & ENVIRONMENT

Barnard is located north of Central Park on the upper west side of Manhattan, in the safe and student-friendly Morningside Heights neighborhood, directly across the street from Columbia University. The campus occupies 4 acres of urban property along Broadway between 116th and 120th streets and serves as an oasis from the hustle and bustle of New York City. The south end of the campus, referred to as the Quad, contains the Brooks, Reid, Hewitt, and Sulzberger residence halls; Additional residence halls (11 in total) provide those entering as first-years guaranteed housing for four years. The latest campus addition, the Diana Center, is a 70,000-square-foot student center, the hub of campus life. The College is in the midst of completing The Milstein Center.. The 128,000 square foot building scheduled to open in August 2018, will include a new kind of library, one that incorporates state-of-the art technologies and learning spaces in an interactive setting. It will act also as an academic core for the campus, linking departments and disciplines, both physically and philosophically.

CAMPUS FACILITIES & EQUIPMENT

The Quad is located at the south end of campus and includes four residence hall buildings: Brooks, Hewitt, Reid and Sulzberger. The Arthur Ross Courtyard is located in the Quad. The Jan R. and Marley Blue Lewis '05 Parlor is located on the 1st floor of Brooks Hall and is a reading room for quiet study.

The Diana Center opened in January 2010 and is located in the center of campus. Housed within are a coffee café called Liz's Place, the Diana Center café that serves lunch and dinner, and the Millicent Carey McIntosh Student Dining Room. The Louise Heublein McCagg '59 Gallery (McCagg Gallery), located in 400 Diana, 4th floor of The Diana Center. The space is for student exhibitions coordinated by the Art History and Architecture Departments. The Green Roof, located on the 6th floor of The Diana Center, has views of campus and the surrounding neighborhood. The Green Roof is used both as a classroom and as an event space.

The lawn is located in the center of the Barnard campus, in front of what will be The Milstein Center.

Under construction: The new 128,000 square foot Milstein Center. The new building will house:

- A library with a core collection of books, journals, special collections and archives that support a strong liberal arts education.

- A digital commons with five innovative teaching labs (movement lab, empirical reasoning center, digital humanities lab, creativity lab, and multimedia lab) and a range of flexible learning spaces that utilize new media and digital technologies.

- A computational science center equipped to support students and faculty in pioneering scientific, mathematical, and computational methods research, which physically connects to science classrooms and labs in neighboring Altschul Hall.

- Inviting student spaces that include a variety of active and quiet study areas for individuals and groups.

- Flexible, technologically current classrooms for seminars and large group instruction.

- Conferencing facilities connected to meeting and event spaces in The Diana Center.

- Departmental offices for economics, history, political science and urban studies.

- Homes for two signature programs: the Barnard Center for Research on Women and the Athena Center for Leadership Studies.

- A small café, serving coffee and grab-and-go items.

- Accessible outdoor terraces.

OFF-CAMPUS OPPORTUNITIES

Barnard's location offers its students a variety of work experiences through more than 2,500 internships. More than two thirds of Barnard students participate in internships throughout the academic year and/or summer. Furthermore, Barnard has a rich history and tradition of study abroad dating back to the 1930s. Today, qualified students are eligible to study in nearly 100 programs in more than fifty countries worldwide. Students may also participate in a domestic exchange with Spelman College in Atlanta, GA.

ACADEMICS

First-Year Experience: The First-Year Experience includes two semesters of seminar classes: First-Year Writing, focusing on reading literary texts critically and writing effectively, and First-Year Seminar, emphasizing disciplinary and interdisciplinary content that challenges students to write and speak persuasively. First-year students are also required to take one course in Physical Education.

Foundations Program

The Foundations Program designed to expose students to a variety of disciplines, approaches, and skills that, together, form the whole of a liberal arts education. The requirements are designed to be flexible; students choose from a wide spectrum of courses and take two courses each in languages, arts and humanities, social sciences, and sciences (one of which includes a lab). Furthermore, students follow Modes of Thinking that include one course each in of the following. Courses taken to satisfy Foundations can also be used to satisfy the Modes of Thinking requirement:

- Thinking Locally–New York City—where students examine the community and environment in which they find themselves as residents of New York City to better understand the significance of local context.

- Thinking through Global Inquiry—where students consider communities, places, and experiences beyond their immediate location, expanding their perspectives on the world and their place in it.

- Thinking about Social Difference—where students examine how difference is defined, lived, and challenged, and the disparities of power and resources in all their manifestations.

- Thinking with Historical Perspective—where students examine the ways in which historical context shapes and conditions the world, challenging them to see the past with fresh eyes.

- Thinking quantitatively and empirically—where students are exposed to numbers, data, graphs, and mathematical methods, in order to better understand quantitative and empirical approaches to thinking and problem solving.

- Thinking technologically and digitally—where students discover new ways of learning that open up innovative fields of study, including computational science and coding, digital arts and humanities, geographic information systems, and digital design.

MAJORS & DEGREES OFFERED

American Studies
Ancient Studies
Anthropology
Architecture
Art History
Asian and Middle Eastern Cultures
Biochemistry
Biological Sciences
Biopsychology
Chemistry
Comparative Literature
Computer Science
Dance
Economic History
Economics
Economics and Mathematics
English
Environmental Biology
Environmental Science
Foreign Area Studies
French
German
Greek (Classics)
Greek and Latin
History
Italian
Jewish Studies
Latin (Classics)
Linguistics
Mathematics
Medieval and Renaissance Studies
Music
Pan African Studies
Philosophy
Physics & Astronomy
Political Science
Psychology
Religion
Russian (Slavic)
Sociology
Spanish & Latin American Cultures
Statistics
Theatre
Urban Studies
Women's Studies

The College provides an excellent education program, leading to teaching certification with a specific urban studies track, and prepares students for programs in health and medicine, law, and business, as well as further study in a variety of graduate programs. Barnard College also offers double - and joint - degree programs in cooperation with other schools within the Columbia community. These include a five-year MPA/MIA program offered in conjunction with the School of International and Public Affairs. Through the School of Engineering and Applied Science, Barnard students can pursue a five-year (3-2) program in all branches of engineering, leading to both an A.B. and a B.S. degree. Through an agreement with List College of the Jewish Theological Seminary, students can simultaneously earn an A.B. degree from Barnard and a B.A. at JTS.

For a select group of scholars, the Arthur O. Eve Higher Education Opportunity Program (HEOP) and Barnard Opportunity Program (BOP) offers an additional pathway to admission to Barnard. A lending library, laptop computers, free tutoring, mentoring, and study skills workshops, and graduate school preparation and career guidance are available to all BOP and HEOP Scholars, in addition to the resources and support they receive as Barnard students. To be considered for HEOP, students

must be residents of New York State and meet other eligibility requirements. Additionally, a small number of students who are not New York State residents are identified by the office of admissions as BOP Scholars.

The Office of Academic Success and Enrichment Programs (ASEP) is committed to providing opportunities to enrich and complement the intellectual life of all students. Under the supervision of the Office of the Dean of Studies, ASEP works to engage students in rigorous academic experiences while providing the support needed to meet academic challenges and to discover their own capabilities.

TUITION, ROOM, BOARD, FEES

Full Time Tuition and fees (12-18 credits per semester) $50,794

On Campus Room Board $15,598

FINANCIAL AID

Barnard is need-blind for US citizens and permanent residents and meets full demonstrated need for all eligible students with a combination of grant, loan, and job opportunities. Students who are not U.S. citizens or U.S. permanent residents are considered international students. We are need-aware for international students and able to award a small number of need-based scholarships for international students in each first-year entering class. Barnard gives no merit scholarships.

STUDENT ORGANIZATIONS & ACTIVITIES

Barnard women have access to more than eighty clubs and organizations on the College campus alone. Add to this list the hundreds of additional dually recognized clubs with members from both Barnard and Columbia, provided for through Barnard's partnership with the University, and strong friendships develop among students from both sides of Broadway. Student groups include performance groups, academic and pre-professional, ethnic and cultural, language, community service, and publications. Social interaction and cooperation between Barnard and Columbia groups is virtually seamless, with Barnard women regularly joining and leading a variety of Columbia organizations. Students, faculty members, and administrators also serve on tripartite committees and share responsibility for policy on curriculum, housing, financial aid, orientation, and the library.

For students interested in Dance: https://dance.barnard.edu/faqs/prospective-students

For students interested in theater: https://theatre.barnard.edu/faq

ADMISSIONS PROCESS

The Committee on Admissions selects women of proven academic strength who exhibit the potential for further intellectual growth. Careful consideration is given to candidates' high school records, recommendations, writing skills, standardized test scores, special abilities and interests, and personal and educational context.

Admission to Barnard is highly selective and candidates for admission to the first-year class are expected to have taken a highly rigorous college-preparatory program. Barnard also requires first-year candidates to submit scores from the SAT Reasoning Test or the ACT. Students educated in a non-English-speaking setting or who have studied in English for less than four years must also take the TOEFL or IELTS exam. An interview is recommended for first-year students, but it is not required. Early decision applications must be submitted by November 1. Regular applications must be received by January 1. There is a non-refundable application fee of $75. Transfer applications must be submitted by November 1 for consideration for January enrollment and by March 15 for consideration for September enrollment.

BECKER COLLEGE

AT A GLANCE

Future-focused Becker College has an average placement rate of over 90% for employment or further study. Becker prepares over 2,000 students from across the globe to create value in the 21st century.

Becker College is a private, independent, co-educational, four-year institution with undergraduate (associate and bachelor) degrees; graduate degrees; adult education degrees (associate and bachelor's); certificate programs. The College is dedicated to its mission of providing students with a transformational learning experience that prepares them to thrive, contribute to, and lead in a global society.

The College prepares students—across all majors to navigate what experts have described as the greatest velocity of change in human history—through a foundation in learning agility known as The Agile Mindset. Becker believes The Agile Mindset is essential for success in the increasingly complex, automated, and hyper-connected world of the 21st century. It forms the foundation of the College's new core curricula.

The Agile Mindset merges learning agility and value-creation orientation with a focus on four uniquely human skillsets: empathy to understand the needs of others and inspire innovation; divergent thinking to explore possibilities and discover opportunities where they may not appear to exist; an entrepreneurial outlook to create new value regardless of job position; and social and emotional intelligence to collaborate effectively with others in interdisciplinary teams.

Becker College traces its history to 1784—one of the nation's top-25 oldest institutions of higher learning—with a founding charter signed by American Revolutionaries John Hancock and Samuel Adams.

LOCATION & ENVIRONMENT

Becker's Worcester campus is situated in the Elm Park section of Worcester, MA; a quiet area of tree-lined streets and historic homes—including 14 residence halls. The campus is a short walk from the downtown business district, which is also home to an additional apartment-style residence hall. An academic building and library, and a health science center stand on the Worcester campus quad, and a number of other college properties dot the neighborhood. The city of Worcester (pop. 182,544) is New England's second largest urban center.

On the Leicester campus, former homes dating from the 19th century, now student housing and faculty offices, surround a lush town common. There are eight residence halls, and additional facilities include a campus center which opened in 2012, academic buildings, an auditorium, library, gymnasium, athletic field, and the Lenfest Animal Health Center—a teaching facility which includes a veterinary clinic that is open to the public. The Becker College Equestrian Center is just a few scenic miles away, in Paxton, Mass.

Becker College maintains a shuttle schedule, from morning to evening, and on weekends, between the Worcester and Leicester campuses, and from the Worcester campus to Bancroft Hall, located in downtown Worcester.

CAMPUS FACILITIES & EQUIPMENT

In late 2017, Becker will open the Colleen C. Barrett Center for Global Innovation and Entrepreneurship—a 10,000 sq. ft. building— which will house several initiatives to spur global change through value creation and social impact. The Center will include meeting and co-work space, computer labs, and facilities dedicated to research, design, and new enterprise incubation.

The Lenfest Animal Health Center, a unique experience in higher education, is a teaching facility which includes a veterinary clinic that is open to the public and sees about 1,000 clients a year for wellness care and non-urgent medical and surgical care for dogs, cats, other small mammals, and birds.

A state of the art game design laboratory with the latest technologies including Augmented Reality, Virtual Reality, Audio Recording Studio, and 3D Printers.

Becker is home to the 1st Yunus Social Business Centre in the U.S. This Centre empowers individuals to identify real-world problems and create self-sustaining business solutions that have social impact while generating jobs and entrepreneurial opportunities that drive economic development regionally and around the world.

On Becker's Worcester campus, the Massachusetts Digital Games Institute (Mass-DiGI) operates as the statewide center for economic development, entrepreneurship, and academic cooperation in the Commonwealth's interactive media and game development ecosystem.

The Becker College Equestrian Center is situated on 30 acres of land and includes expansive turn-out pastures for the horses, an indoor riding arena, and a large outdoor ring. The center offers full board for horses and lessons to both Becker College students and the public.

The John J. Dorsey, Sr., Crime Scene Lab gives students the opportunity to assess a crime scene, understand the nature of physical evidence, learn the proper actions of the initial responding officer, perform evidence recognition and preservation tasks, and ultimately solve the crime.

OFF-CAMPUS OPPORTUNITIES

Worcester offers a wide array of social, cultural, and recreational opportunities, including entertainment and sports arenas, first-class museums, the Hanover Theatre, outdoor recreation areas, and a wide range of shopping and dining options.

Worcester features world-renowned museums and concert halls, theatres, galleries, as well as a wealth of performing groups, ethnic festivals, artists of every discipline, restaurants, specialty shops, and hotels. Becker students also have access to facilities, events, courses, and activities at the 10 other colleges in the Worcester area.

Just an hour's distance from Boston and Springfield, Mass., Providence, R.I., and Hartford, Conn., Worcester is at the crossroads of several major routes, including the Massachusetts Turnpike (I-90), Interstates 290 and 395, and Routes 146 and 20.

Becker College offers study abroad options through its partnerships with the Center for International Studies (CIS), CIEE, and Semester at Sea, as well as a wide range of service trips to such locations as Haiti, Jamaica, Boston, and more.

ACADEMICS

At Becker, preparing students appropriately for the future of work means cultivating adaptive learners with Agile Mindsets who can leverage the uniquely human skills of empathy, divergent thinking, an entrepreneurial outlook, and social and emotional intelligence to adapt and thrive in a world that is increasingly volatile, uncertain, complex, and ambiguous. The Agile Mindset is the academic foundation that equips students to navigate change and create new value in the hyper-connected, automated world of the 21st century.

While we believe that the Agile Mindset is the academic model to future-proof students, we also integrate the Agile Mindset outside of the classroom. By infusing the Agile Mindset into the fabric of our institutional culture, we engage and empower each and every member of the Becker community and thus create a compelling advantage that cannot be replicated in higher education.

MAJORS

Addictions Counseling
Animal Care
Applied Behavioral Analysis
Alcoholism/Drug Abuse Counseling (Certificate)
Applied Computer Science
Big Data Analytics
Biology
Business Administration
Business administration—3-year Program
Clinical Laboratory and Animal Medicine
Criminal Justice
Communications Design
Community Health and Wellness
Computer Information Systems
Data Science
Domestic Counter-Terrorism Studies: Policy, Research, and Management
Early Childhood and Youth Education
Early Childhood Education
Exercise Science—Community Health and Wellness
Exercise Science—Health and Fitness
Forensics/Crime Scene Processing
Forensic Psychology
Game Arts
Game Design
Game Development and Programming
Game Production and Management
Global Citizenship
Graphic Design
Human Resource Management (Certificate)
Interactive Media Design
Laboratory Animal Management
Liberal Arts
Management
Marketing
Mental Health Counseling
Nursing (AS, BS, MSN)
Policing/Law Enforcement
Pre-Law—Criminal Justice
Pre-Law Liberal Arts
Pre-PT/Health Science
Pre-Med/Health studies
Pre-Veterinary
Project Management (Certificate)
Psychology
Social Business (Certificate)
Sport Management
Terrorism Studies (Certificate)
Veterinary Science
Veterinary Technology
Women's Emergent Leadership Institute (Certificate)

TUITION, ROOM, BOARD, FEES

Full Time Tuition (12-18 credits per semester) $33,672

On Campus Room Board $12,850

Required Fees $3,600

FINANCIAL AID

Financial aid is available for all eligible students through federal, state, and Becker College programs.

STUDENT ORGANIZATIONS & ACTIVITIES

Becker College students participate in an active community through a variety of social, educational, and cultural programs. The Becker College student experience provides numerous opportunities to get involved and to follow your passion. Becker College empowers you to take initiative, get involved, and be a leader.

Becker College is home to more than 20 student organizations—from archery, music, cosplay, and pre-veterinary clubs, to P.R.I.D.E—People Respecting Identity Difference of Everyone, We are Global, Semester at Sea, and Young Americans for Liberty—and students are welcome to develop their interests and apply to establish new clubs. Campus events and programs for Becker College students are planned by Becker College students. The Campus Activities Board (CAB) is a student organization that works in conjunction with the Office of Campus Activities and Student Leadership. CAB provides student-led social, cultural, and educational events for Becker College students that align with the College's goals and mission. Any Becker College student can join CAB. Other opportunities include Becker's 16 Division III Varsity Sports and numerous intramural sports and activities.

ADMISSIONS PROCESS

To learn more about Becker College call 877.523.2537, email admissions@becker.edu, or visit www.becker.edu.

Complete applications must include:

- A completed application for admission, www.becker.edu/apply.

- An official copy of the secondary school transcript. Students who have received a General Equivalency Diploma (GED) must forward an official score report.

- SAT I or ACT scores. The Becker College CEEB code is 3079.

- Optional letter of recommendation. Becker College recognizes that all students are individuals and will consider each applicant's personal strengths and achievements. Any other supporting materials that are submitted will be considered.

- Optional essay on any topic, 250-500 words in length.

BELMONT UNIVERSITY

AT A GLANCE

Belmont University sits on 75 historic acres in the heart of Nashville, Tennessee, a thriving metropolis known worldwide as Music City. Belmont University is among the fastest growing Christian universities in the nation with approximately 7,700 students hailing from every state and 25 countries. Belmont University is accredited by the Commission on Colleges of the Southern Association of Colleges and Schools to award baccalaureate, master's, and doctoral degrees. Belmont offers over 90 areas of undergraduate study, over 20 master's programs and five doctoral degrees through its ten colleges: Jack C. Massey College of Business, Liberal Arts & Social Sciences, Mike Curb College of Entertainment and Music Business, Gordon E. Inman College of Health Sciences & Nursing, Law, Pharmacy, Theology & Christian Ministry, Science & Mathematics, University College, and Visual & Performing Arts.

LOCATION & ENVIRONMENT

Belmont University occupies a 75-acre campus in Nashville, Tennessee, just two miles from downtown and adjacent to the world famous Music Row. With more than 1.7 million residents, the metropolitan Nashville area is a cultural, educational, health-care, commercial, and financial center in the mid-South. Practical educational opportunities, offered through diverse curriculums, provide students with the hands-on experience they need in preparation for a meaningful career. The city's location, halfway between the northern and southern boundaries of the United States, with three intersecting interstate highways and an international airport, makes it accessible to students from across the country.

CAMPUS FACILITIES & EQUIPMENT

As Belmont's academic program offerings grow, so too does the physical campus. Additions in the last several years include the opening of an entertainment and student life complex which houses the Curb Event Center arena, the Beaman Student Life Center and the Maddox Grand Atrium. The Gordon E. Inman Center opened in 2006, a facility that houses Belmont's nursing, public health, social work, occupational therapy and physical therapy programs. The School of Nursing was recognized by Laerdal Medical Corporation as a Center of Educational Excellence in part due to the advanced training the school's multiple simulation models offer to its students.

More recent additions to the campus include the Baskin Center, home to Belmont's College of Law; McWhorter Hall (the 90,000 square foot, state-of-the-art academic building that houses the University's College of Pharmacy, Physical Therapy program, and Department of Psychological Science); and the wonderful McAfee Concert Hall, a large concert venue suitable for acoustic performances. Multiple new residence halls for freshmen through seniors have opened since 2010. Also the Janet Ayers Academic Center a new home to the liberal arts, social sciences, mathematics, natural sciences, religion and a 250-seat chapel opened in 2014. And finally the R. Milton and Denise Johnson Center, opened in fall 2015 which houses the Curb College of Entertainment and Music Business, the media studies program and Harrington Place Dining a vibrant new 950-seat cafeteria.

OFF-CAMPUS OPPORTUNITIES

A Christian Community of Learning and Service

Belmont is a student-focused, Christian community of learning and service where students hear from their first visit to campus until the day they graduate that they are created for a purpose in life. The Belmont faculty and staff dedicate themselves to preparing and empowering students to find their passion and use it to change the world. The university seeks to show every student how the love of Christ can compel them to lead lives of disciplined intelligence, compassion, courage and faith.

In fact, Belmont students, faculty and staff are consistently challenged to look at the hardest circumstances and ask, "What can we do?" Students are encouraged to engage and transform the world, locally and globally, by participation in disaster relief trips to everywhere from the tsunami-stricken areas of Southeast Asia to the Gulf Coast after Hurricane Katrina. Students serve locally at various relief and community organizations in Nashville throughout the year, and student-athletes take part annually in sports evangelism mission trips to South Africa, Ukraine and Brazil. Others have taken advantage of what they're learning at Belmont, incorporating their major studies into various service projects around the world, including working with orphans in India and assisting with physical therapy needs in Guatemala.

ACADEMICS

Intent on being a leader among teaching universities, Belmont brings together the best of liberal arts and professional education in a Christian community of learning and service. Belmont was ranked sixth on the U.S. News & World Report listing of "Best Universities" in the South and named a "Most Innovative" university for the 2017 edition of America's Best Colleges, making Belmont the highest ranked university in Tennessee in this category. Both Rolling Stone and Time magazines have hailed Belmont's Mike Curb College of Entertainment & Music Business as one of the best music business programs in the country. The Jack C. Massey Graduate School of Business has been named the best MBA program in the region, while Belmont's business administration and accounting programs have been accredited by AACSB International, the premier accrediting agency in that arena, placing Belmont amongst less than 1% of the world's business schools. Moreover, Belmont University's undergraduate School of Business consistently achieves a Top 100 national ranking in BusinessWeek's annual report on "The Best Undergrad B-Schools" in the U.S. Belmont's Enactus team has won multiple national championships and a World Cup.

Located in the heart of Music City, one of Belmont's consistent success stories is its world-renowned music and music business programs, including songwriting. Several big names in the music industry started their careers at Belmont including "American Idol" finalist Melinda Doolittle, Christian recording artists Ginny Owens and Steven Curtis Chapman, and country stars Trisha Yearwood, Lee Ann Womack, Brad Paisley, Josh Turner and Florida Georgia Line. The annual "Christmas at Belmont" concert showcases performing ensembles from many different genres and has been broadcast nationwide on PBS for several years.

Students who have passions outside of the music industry also have a home at Belmont. From international business and accounting to education, theology, nursing, journalism and the humanities, Belmont provides avenues of learning for almost any interest. Recent program additions include an undergraduate degree in public health, global leadership studies and sport administration, in addition to, a four-year dual PharmD/MBA degree, a Master of Arts in Mental Health Counseling and a Doctor of Nursing Practice program.

Belmont faculty members display a consistent commitment to excellence as well. Multiple professors have been awarded Fulbright awards, including a nursing professor who spent a year in Uganda as a guest lecturer while conducting research on how standards of nursing are adapted to austere conditions. Also, five Belmont professors (Finance, Psychology, Spanish, Philosophy and Mathematics) have been chosen as Tennessee Professor of the Year by CASE/Carnegie Foundation since 2000.

Belmont's boundaries extend beyond the Nashville campus through its Cool Springs campus and organized programs such as the Washington Center program and Belmont West in Los Angeles and Belmont East in New York City and Washington D.C. Study-abroad programs place students in China, Costa Rica, Great Britain, France, Germany, Italy, Russia, South Africa and Spain, among other foreign nations.

MAJORS

Belmont University is accredited by the Commission on Colleges of the Southern Association of Colleges and Schools to award baccalaureate, master's, and doctoral degrees. Belmont grants seven undergraduate degrees: the Bachelor of Arts, the Bachelor of Business Administration, the Bachelor of Fine Arts, the Bachelor of Music, the Bachelor of Science, the Bachelor of Science in Nursing, and the Bachelor of Social Work.

Undergraduate majors or concentrations are offered in:

Jack C. Massey College of Business: Accounting, Economics, Entrepreneurship, Finance, General Business, International Business, International Economics, Management, Management Information Systems, Marketing, Social Entrepreneurship

Mike Curb College of Entertainment & Music Business: Audio Engineering Technology, Entertainment Industry Studies, Motion Pictures, Music Business, Songwriting

Gordon E. Inman College of Health Sciences & Nursing: Nursing, Public Health, Social Work

College of Liberal Arts & Social Sciences:

School of Education: Early Childhood Education, Elementary Education, Exercise Science, Middle School Education, Secondary Education, Sport Administration

School of Humanities: English, French, German, Philosophy, Spanish

School of Social Sciences: Audio & Video Production, Communication Studies, Corporate Communication, History, International Politics, Journalism, Mass Communication, Multimedia Production, Political Science, Politics & Public Law, Public Relations, Publishing, Sociology, Video Production

College of Sciences & Mathematics: Applied Discrete Mathematics, Biochemistry & Molecular Biology, Biology, Chemistry, Computer Science, Engineering Physics, Environmental Science, Mathematics, Neuroscience, Pharmaceutical Studies, Physics, Physics—Pre Health, Psychology, Web Programming & Development

College of Theology & Christian Ministry: Biblical Languages, Biblical Studies, Christian Leadership, Church Leadership & Administration, Faith & Social Justice, Philosophy of Religion, Religion & the Arts, Religious Studies, Worship Leadership

College of Visual & Performing Arts:

Department of Art: Art, Art Education, Art History, Design Communications, Studio Art

Department of Theatre & Dance: Theatre, Theatre Directing, Theatre & Drama, Theatre Education, Theatre Performance, Theatre Production Design

School of Music: Church Music & Worship, Commercial Music, Music (Bachelor of Arts), Music Composition, Music Education, Music Performance, Music Theory, Music Therapy, Music with an Outside Minor, Musical Theatre, Piano Pedagogy

Interdisciplinary Programs: Asian Studies, Global Leadership Studies

Pre-Professional Programs Available In: Pre-Allied Health, Pre-Dental, Pre-Law, Pre-Medical, Pre-Occupational Therapy, Pre-Optometry, Pre-Pharmacy, Pre-Physical Therapy, Pre-Veterinary

TUITION, ROOM, BOARD, FEES

The total cost of attending Belmont is only 80 percent of the national average for a private college. For a full-time undergraduate student living on campus, the total cost for the 2017-18 academic year is approximately $44,500 which includes tuition, fees, room, and board.

FINANCIAL AID

The financial aid program at Belmont combines merit-based assistance with need-based assistance to make the university education affordable. Institutional merit awards range from highly selective full-tuition Presidential Scholarships to various levels of partial merit awards. Athletic and artistic scholarships are also available. Belmont also administers traditional state and federal financial aid programs. Campus employment is available. Parents may arrange monthly tuition payments through an outside vendor. To apply for need-based financial assistance, the student must complete the Free Application for Federal Student Aid (FAFSA). FAFSA Code: 003479

STUDENT ORGANIZATIONS & ACTIVITIES

Belmont's campus life offers 160+ clubs and organizations. The popular intramurals program includes everything from flag football and basketball to wiffleball and dodgeball. With more than half of Belmont's undergrads living on campus there's always something going on from socials, movie nights and concerts to the annual Fall Follies and Curb College Showcase Series.

And in terms of student activities, there's a club or group for nearly every interest. Belmont is home to five nationally recognized sororities and four nationally recognized fraternities representing NPC, IFC and NPHC. The Bruins are big on giving back, too, logging more than 200,000 hours of community service annually.

ATHLETICS

In addition to celebrating academic excellence and phenomenal growth, Belmont boasts 17 intercollegiate sports teams. The Belmont Bruins men's basketball team won the Ohio Valley Conference regular season championship in 2013, 2014 and 2015 and made its seventh appearance in the NCAA National Tournament in 2015 and competed in the NIT in 2014, 2016 and 2017. The Belmont Bruins women's basketball team made its first appearance in the NCAA National Tournament in 2016 and again in 2017. Baseball, both cross country teams, and the volleyball team have earned recent conference titles. Belmont student-athletes excel in the classroom, too, as Belmont has won the conference's All-Academic Trophy multiple times. The award is given annually to the conference school with the greatest percentage of student-athletes who earned a GPA of 3.0 or higher.

ADMISSIONS PROCESS

Belmont's Admissions Committee considers applications based on the total picture that a student's credentials present. High school students will be considered competitive for admission if they present a rigorous course of college-preparatory, academic studies. Students should have an above-average academic and cumulative grade point average and rank in the top half of their graduating class. Any college-level work is also expected to be at the above-average level. A strong correlation between high school grades and entrance examination scores is expected. The essays, list of activities, and recommendations are also strongly considered as indicators of success at Belmont. Additional requirements such as portfolios or auditions are considered in conjunction with the academic credentials for those programs that require them. Each application is considered on an individual basis. No two applicants will present the same credentials or the same "fit" with the university. Our desire is to work with each student to determine the likelihood of that student to enroll in, graduate from, and use the benefits of the Belmont educational experience.

For more information, contact:

Office of Admissions

Belmont University

1900 Belmont Boulevard

Nashville, TN 37212

615-460-6785

800-56ENROLL

Fax: 615-460-5434

admissions@belmont.edu

www.belmont.edu

CEEB Code: 1058

ACT Code: 3946

BENTLEY UNIVERSITY

AT A GLANCE

At Bentley University, we believe that business is everywhere and your education should prepare to learn how the world works; and how it thinks. To succeed in the modern world, you need an education that looks at business through a broader lens; one that embraces fusion and innovation, technological mastery and cultural literacy, practical expertise and the ability to share those skills with others. That's why at Bentley, our one-of-a-kind curriculum starts with a core business foundation, infused with the kind of critical thinking and cultural understanding that comes from the study of the arts and sciences. As a result, Bentley students are highly sought after by today's leading organizations because of their professionalism, exposure to state-of-the-art research tools, and diverse, real-world experience.

Located on a classic New England campus minutes from Boston, Bentley offers a wide variety of majors and minors, as well as optional liberal studies and business studies majors designed to create a modern intersection of the arts and sciences and business that's unique in higher education. Our career services office was recently ranked No. 1 in the country by the Princeton Review. The Miller Center for Career Services offers resources including an on-campus recruiting program involving 1,000 national and international companies; an online job and internship database; career fairs; workshops on topics such as interviewing and networking; and a Career Development Seminar (CDI 101) for first-year students.

In addition, students can develop a customized four-year plan, which will help build a framework for professional success. In 2016, more than 99 percent of students found employment or enrolled in graduate school within six months of graduation. Their median annual salary was $55,000.

LOCATION & ENVIRONMENT

Bentley's location in Waltham, Massachusetts-just minutes west of Boston—puts the city within easy reach. As the country's ultimate university town, Boston's options range from theater to art exhibits, dance clubs to concerts, and championship sports to world-class shopping. Bentley's free shuttle makes regular trips to Harvard Square in Cambridge, just a subway ride from Boston. Boston also offers many opportunities for internships and jobs after graduation.

CAMPUS FACILITIES & EQUIPMENT

Concepts taught in the classroom are put to use in several high-tech learning laboratories.

Bentley's financial Trading Room combines state-of-the-art technology and real-time data to offer first-hand exposure to financial concepts in simulated trading sessions. Resources include Bloomberg, Capital IQ, Datastream, FactSet, Thomson One Analytics, Portfolio Analysis, MATLAB, S&P Compustat, and Worldscope. The Center for Marketing Technology plays an integral role in marketing programs. Students gain a full grasp of software options, familiarity with research tools and techniques, and knowledge of new digital marketing frameworks.

The Accounting Center for Electronic Learning and Business Management (ACELAB) introduces cutting-edge technologies that are reshaping the accounting profession. Students have access to auditing and tax preparation software as well as other professional applications from industry leaders such as SAP and Oracle.

The Center for Languages and International Collaboration (CLIC) is a key resource for language courses, international studies majors, and students with an interest in global issues. The center promotes collaboration among Bentley students and their counterparts overseas. The Media and Culture Labs and Studio feature resources for video production and editing as well as digital photography. The lab provides students with industry-standard software programs for screenwriting, sound mixing, graphic design, and DVD authoring.

The User Experience Center (UXC) features labs ideal for usability testing. Students use the applications employed by technical communicators, Web developers, user-interface designers, and usability specialists. The brand-new CIS Learning and Technology Sandbox is a collaborative space for learning new technologies. Its resources include Google TVs, Xbox 360 with Kinect, study spaces, large-screen TVs, a smart board, specialized networking equipment, and tools such as Windows 8, Linux, and Android development software.

The Bentley Library is outfitted with computer workstations, group study rooms, and wireless network access. It also has an exceptional number of online database resources. In 2010, Bentley was ranked 14th on the Princeton Review's list of best college libraries.

OFF-CAMPUS OPPORTUNITIES

Hands-on experience is emphasized across the curriculum. Internships, study abroad, service-learning, and other opportunities allow students to apply classroom theory in the community. More than 90% of seniors complete one internship and 73% complete two or more, building valuable work experience and networking connections. Some of the top internship employers include Fidelity Investments, the TJX Companies, Liberty Mutual, Bain & Company, and all of the Big Four accounting firms.

Bentley students can gain insight into different cultures by studying abroad. Programs take place in more than 25 countries and vary in length from one week to a full academic year. Through Bentley's Service-Learning Center, students build skills in business, communication, and teamwork while assisting nonprofit and community-based organizations both locally and internationally.

ACADEMICS

The Bentley curriculum is a unique fusion of business and the liberal arts. The university's 4,200 undergraduates benefit from a breadth of programs and the ability to combine subjects to best fit their interests. A Bentley education also focuses on gaining hands-on experience in the classroom. Students benefit from classes where they partner with outside companies to solve current business problems and present their solutions directly to company executives. Bentley also offers top applicants a chance to enroll in the Honors Program. Participants select honors-level courses each semester that offer extra intellectual challenge in a seminar atmosphere.

MAJORS & DEGREES OFFERED

The Bentley curriculum is a groundbreaking integration of business and the arts and sciences that has been featured in the Wall Street Journal. "It's not about pitting lifelong learning skills against professional skills," President Gloria Larson told the paper. "A college degree should reflect both."

To that end, Bachelor of Science (B.S.) degree programs enable our students to gain in-depth knowledge and skills in specific business disciplines: accountancy, actuarial science, computer information systems, corporate finance and accounting, creative industries, economics–finance, finance, information design and corporate communication, information systems audit and control, management, managerial economics, marketing, mathematical sciences and professional sales.

Bentley also offers Bachelor of Arts (B.A.) degree programs with majors in global studies, health studies, history, liberal arts, media and culture, philosophy, public policy, Spanish studies, and sustainable science. All Bachelor of Arts students gain business experience through either the Business Studies Major (BSM) or minor. All students can also choose from minors such as entrepreneurial studies, law, and sports management. The Liberal Studies Major (LSM), an optional double major, can be combined with any business program. It provides students with a competitive edge by building meaningful connections across and within disciplines. To complete the LSM, students do not need to take any extra courses beyond those normally required. It allows students to add another credential to their degree, helping them stand out to employers. LSM concentrations include American studies; diversity and society; earth, environment, and global sustainability; ethics and social responsibility; global perspectives; health and industry; media arts and society; and quantitative perspectives.

FINANCIAL AID

Bentley's financial aid program includes both scholarships based on academic achievement, which are awarded through the admission process, as well as grants based on financial need. Bentley administered over $88 million in aid to undergraduate students last year. More than 75% of aid came as Bentley-funded grants and scholarships. Significant institutional resources are committed each year so that all academically qualified students have access to a Bentley education regardless of their financial resources. Currently, more than 75 percent of undergraduates receive some type of financial assistance-including grants, scholarships, loans and/or work study.

STUDENT ORGANIZATIONS & ACTIVITIES

Approximately 98 percent of freshmen live on campus. Twenty-three residence halls provide a range of housing options: dorms, suites, and apartments. Housing is provided for all four years; all residence halls are air-conditioned and typically include study lounges, exercise facilities, TV lounges, and game rooms.

Students live and learn in a multicultural environment that prepares them to thrive in today's diverse world. International students representing nearly 100 countries make up about 25% of the student body and bring valuable perspectives to the Bentley community.

Supporting Bentley's commitment to diversity are offices such as the Multicultural Center, Spiritual Life Center, Center for International Students and Scholars, Equity Center, Center for Women in Business, and the Women's Center.

The Student Center is the hub of campus activity and is home to 921 Dining Room and more than 100 student organizations. These groups represent academics, the arts, media, fraternity and sorority life, and cultural interests.

Athletic programs are a Bentley hallmark and include intramurals, recreational sports, and more than 20 varsity teams in NCAA Divisions I and II. The Dana Athletic Center houses a weight and fitness complex, food court, locker rooms, a gym, a basketball court, volleyball and racquetball courts, a competition-size pool with a diving tank, and saunas. Outdoor facilities include soccer and baseball fields, a track, and tennis courts.

ADMISSIONS PROCESS

Bentley University accepts the Common Application. Candidates for the fall semester are notified by April 1; spring semester candidates are notified on a rolling basis.

Prospective students can visit bentley.edu/undergraduate/applying for application information and deadlines. For more information, students should contact:

Office of Undergraduate Admission

Bentley University

175 Forest Street

Waltham, Massachusetts 02452-4705

Phone: 781.891.2244

800.523.2354 (toll-free)

Fax: 781.891.3414

E-mail: ugadmission@bentley.edu

Website: bentley.edu/undergraduate

facebook.com/bentleyadmission

twitter.com/bentleyu

BETHANY COLLEGE (WV)

AT A GLANCE

There was never a more glorious place to go to college. The rolling hillsides in the foothills of the Allegheny Mountains never lose their beauty throughout the seasons. For more than 175 years, Bethany has been a highly contemporary institution based in the tradition of the liberal arts. Once you visit our campus, you're ours, history is all around you.

CAMPUS FACILITIES & EQUIPMENT

The campus features a wide array of studies, in addition to beautiful architecture with a green academic mall. Facilities include beautiful historic landmarks, modern well-equipped classrooms, spacious sports/recreational areas, indoor and outdoor theaters, art galleries, an equestrian center, a teaching greenhouse and more.

More than 90 percent of students live in spacious on-campus apartments, residential halls or fraternity/sorority houses, which include Internet, cable TV and more. Computer labs with Internet and library access, e-mail, digital media labs, rehearsal halls, research and language labs, The McCann Learning Center for academic support, and other amenities are provided.

The Thomas Phillips Johnson Health and Recreation Center includes Hummel Fieldhouse (Nutting Gymnasium), three-court multi-use gymnasium (Sandwen Arena), Knight Natatorium (Olympic-size pool), two racquetball courts, a free-weight exercise fitness center with cardiovascular equipment, and an indoor jogging track. The Cummins Community Center is a state-of-the-art, 24-hour fitness center.

Outdoor Facilities: A multi-purpose stadium (Bison Stadium) with artificial turf and lights primarily serves football, lacrosse, and track and field. Hoag Soccer Field, John Cunningham Soccer Complex, equestrian center, 6 tennis courts, baseball and softball fields, football practice fields, and additional playing fields for intramural and club sports are at your convenience. The equestrian team trains at the Oglebay Stables.

OFF-CAMPUS OPPORTUNITIES

When you want to venture beyond our 1,300-acre campus, America's Most Livable City, Pittsburgh is only a 50 minute drive from campus and Wheeling, West Virginia; Washington, Pennsylvania; and Steubenville, Ohio are less than a half-hour away.

ACADEMICS

The College offers a wide array of studies, awarding Bachelor of Science, Bachelor of Arts, and Master of Arts in Teaching degrees. Students may choose from more than 25 departmental and 6 interdisciplinary majors, many with options for emphasis. Students also have the option of including one or more of 35 optional minors as part of their programs.

Accounting

Biology (options for emphasis on Biology, Biochemistry, and Biology Education)

Chemistry (options for emphasis on Professional Chemistry, Forensic Chemistry, Biochemistry, and Chemistry Education)

Communications and Media Arts (options for emphasis on Digital Media and Production, Graphics, Integrated Media and Marketing, and Sports Communication)

Computer Science

Computer Science and Accounting (Dual Major)

Cybersecurity

Cybersecurity—Information Assurance

Economics (options for emphasis on Managerial Economics and International Economics)

Economics and Mathematics (Dual Major)

Education (Elementary Education; Middle Childhood Education through individual department programs in the areas of English, General Science, Mathematics, Physical Education, Social Studies, and Spanish; Secondary Education through individual department programs in the areas of Art, Biology, Chemistry, English, Mathematics, Physical Education, Psychology, Social Studies, and Spanish)

English (options for emphasis on Creative Writing, Education, Literature, and Writing and Language)

Environmental Science (Interdisciplinary)

Finance

German Studies (Interdisciplinary)

History

International Business

International Economics with study abroad (Interdisciplinary)

International Relations (Interdisciplinary)

Management

Marketing

Mathematics (options for emphasis on Mathematics, Mathematics-Economics, Mathematics-Physics, Mathematics-Computer Science, Mathematics-Actuarial Science, and Mathematics Education)

Music

Music Technology (Interdisciplinary)

Physical Education and Sports Studies (options for emphasis on Sports Management, Recreational and Athletic Programming, and Teaching Physical Education)

Pre-Engineering/Physical Science

Political Science

Psychology (options for emphasis on Scientific Psychology, Human Services, Pre-Physical Therapy, and Pre-Occupational Therapy)

Psychology and Education (Interdisciplinary)

Psychology, Religion, and Culture (Interdisciplinary)

Psychology and Social Work (Dual Major)

Religious Studies

Social Work

Spanish

Theatre (options for emphasis on Performance and Technical Theatre)

Visual Art

Pre-Professional Studies

Pre-Dentistry

Pre-Engineering

Pre-Law

Pre-Medical

Pre-Ministry

Pre-Occupational Therapy

Pre-Physical Therapy

Pre-Veterinary

TUITION, ROOM, BOARD, FEES

The 2016-17 costs for resident students enrolled in the Fall 2016 semester or later are:

Tuition	$27,292
Fees	$1,209
Housing	$4,800 to $5,200
Meals	$5,268
Books	$1,000
Transportation	$1,000
Total	$40,769 (Total cost may vary depending on housing option.)

FINANCIAL AID

We are dedicated to making a financial commitment to our students. If your desire is to receive a Bethany education, our financial aid office will do everything we can to make it affordable for you and your family.

The College also awards scholarships based on academic performance, leadership capability and other academic factors. Additionally, need-based aid is awarded to all eligible students in accordance with FAFSA results. Financial aid packages generally consist of loans, grants, scholarships and student employment.

STUDENT ORGANIZATIONS & ACTIVITIES

Bethany offers more than 50 student organizations: scholastic and honorary, government, special interest and departmental.

Greek organizations include Phi Kappa Tau, Delta Tau Delta, Phi Mu, Alpha Xi Delta, Alpha Sigma Phi, Zeta Tau Alpha and Beta Theta Pi.

Bethany's 22 varsity athletic teams (11 women's and 11 men's) compete in the NCAA Division III Presidents Athletic Conference (PAC) and the Eastern College Athletic Association (ECAC). Bethany affords you the opportunity to become involved and find a home away from home. Whether it's the fraternity or sorority you join, the roommate you have, the team you play on, or the classes you take—you will have friends for life. You're in an historic college town, and you can study abroad. Earn yourself some bragging rights and become part of a long lineage of successful alumni, a big extended family—in all fields of work, and in all parts of the world.

ADMISSIONS PROCESS

Throughout our history, Bethany's alumni have achieved great success—become part of Bethany's tradition of academic excellence. You will learn, live and grow in an environment that encourages you to become involved in your education and your future.

Bethany College specializes in a personalized admission process for each student. At Bethany, our enrollment counselors evaluate each applicant individually and because of this, we are not limited by designated "cut-offs."

Application Deadline: Rolling

Apply Online: www.bethanywv.edu/apply

Interview Required: No, but strongly recommended

Enrollment Toll Free Number: (800) 922-7611

Enrollment E-mail: enrollment@bethanywv.edu

BOSTON UNIVERSITY

AT A GLANCE

Is Boston University the right place for you? At BU, you'll be taught by Pulitzer Prize winners, Nobel Laureates, Fulbright Scholars, or a MacArthur Fellow. With an average class size of 27 students and a faculty-to-student ratio of 12:1, your professors will want to hear what you have to say. They're looking for students who embrace academic challenges. If hands-on research is what interests you, the Undergraduate Research Opportunities Program (UROP) offers hundreds of research opportunities across all areas of study. And if you're not sure what your academic interests are yet, BU offers more than 250 programs of study to choose from, and you don't have to declare a major until the end of your sophomore year. So you can take classes in subjects as varied as biology, broadcast journalism, business, computer engineering, elementary education, film, international relations, physical therapy, psychology, and theatre, just to name a few. Offering thousands of extracurricular activities and social opportunities, and surrounded by the exciting city of Boston, you'll never experience a dull moment as a student.

LOCATION & ENVIRONMENT

No other city in the world can compete with Boston's remarkable concentration of history, higher education institutions, and culture. The city provides many opportunities for internship and research positions as well. In fact, 93% of undergraduates participate in at least one internship before graduating. The Undergraduate Research Opportunities Program (UROP) helps students locate research positions both within and beyond the university; BU's Center for Career Development works to provide students with the resources they need to get internships or part-time jobs in any number of fields. Boston is a world-class center for attractions including museums, libraries, baseball at Fenway Park, the Boston Symphony Orchestra, and a thriving theater district. Students make up 20 percent of Boston's population during the academic year.

Boston University has one of the world's most extensive study abroad programs. Among the University's 100+ programs are language and liberal arts programs; programs that combine studies with internships; fieldwork programs for students wishing to pursue academic or scientific research; and summer programs. Programs are available in Argentina, Australia, Belgium, China, Denmark, Ecuador, England, France, Germany, Guatemala, Ireland, Israel, Italy, Japan, Lebanon, Morocco, New Zealand, Singapore, South Korea, Spain, Switzerland, and Turkey. There are also programs available in Washington, D.C. and Los Angeles.

Types of Transportation Available to Campus

By the MBTA (The "T"): Take the Green Line train (Boston College, "B" line) to BU East. Exit and cross Commonwealth Avenue to Granby Street. Turn left on Bay State Road. The Admissions Reception Center is located on the right side, at 233 Bay State Road. For route and fare information, visit the "T" online at www.mbta.com. By Air: Taxis to Boston University from Boston's Logan International Airport may take approximately 30 minutes (fare: approximately $25). From the airport, the "T" may take an hour and requires a transfer from the Blue Line to the Green Line at Government Center Station (for directions to Boston University by MBTA, see above). For more information visit Logan International Airport online at www.massport.com. By Bus or Train: Amtrak service and major bus companies arrive at Boston's South Station. Taxis to Boston University take approximately 20 minutes (fare: approximately $20). The "T" may take 40 minutes and requires a transfer from the Red Line to the Green Line at Park Street Station (for directions to Boston University by MBTA, see above).

Driving Instructions to Campus

From West of Boston: Take Interstate 90 (Massachusetts Turnpike) to Exit 18 (Brighton/Cambridge). Pay toll, then follow signs for Cambridge down the ramp to the second set of lights. Turn right at the lights (do not cross over the bridge/Charles River) and travel on Soldiers Field Road/Storrow Drive to the second Boston University exit. Follow the Local Directions below. From North of Boston: Take Route 93 South to the Storrow Drive exit (Exit 26). Continue on Storrow Drive to the Kenmore Square exit (left exit). Follow signs for Kenmore Square. Follow the Local Directions below. From South of Boston: Take Interstate 93 North/Route 3 North to Storrow Drive exit (exit 26). Go west on Storrow Drive to Kenmore Square exit (left exit). Follow signs for Kenmore Square. Follow the local directions below. Local Directions: Turn right off the exit ramp at the traffic light (Beacon Street). Stay to the right to enter Bay State Road. The Admissions Reception Center will be on the right, 233 Bay State Road. Parking: Metered parking is available in front of the Reception Center on Bay State Road. Meters accept quarters only. A campus parking lot, which offers parking for a flat fee, is located off Commonwealth Avenue at the intersection of Granby Street.

CAMPUS FACILITIES & EQUIPMENT

Boston University's academic and athletic facilities are some of the best in the country. The Engineering Product Innovation Center (EPIC) is home to teaching space, a full carpentry and machine shop, a metals foundry, and laboratories; while the Photonics Center houses state-of-the-art laboratories devoted to developing new light-based technologies. The Student Village provides first-rate recreation, athletics, high-rise apartments, and dining. The Village includes the Fitness and Recreation Center and Agganis Arena, offering space for University sporting events as well as concerts and family shows. The University also offers the Yawkey Center for Student Services, which houses the Center for Career Development, Educational Resource Center, Pre-Professional Advising Offices, and Marciano Commons, a two-story dining hall.

OFF-CAMPUS OPPORTUNITIES

As an extension of the BU campus, the city of Boston is a hub for internship and research opportunities. Students can intern with top-tier financial services, biomedical, or engineering companies. The city is also home to world-class museums and art galleries, top-ranked hospitals and health services facilities, and more. The opportunities to learn outside the classroom are limitless thanks to BU's location in the heart of the city.

ACADEMICS

What does it mean to study at a world-class research university? You don't have to be science-minded to thrive in BU's culture of inquiry. As one of the country's top 25 funded research universities and a member of the prestigious Association of American Universities (AAU), BU expects students to formulate bold questions and seek out the answers. You'll have the rare opportunity to participate in research across the humanities, arts, and sciences as early as your freshman year. The academic flexibility offered by BU can maximize the value of your degree. Choose from more than 250 programs of study, Dual Degree programs, combined BA/MA programs, and chances to take coursework across schools and colleges. Think psychology and economics, or business and international relations.

TUITION, ROOM, BOARD, FEES

Tuition for the 2017-18 academic year is $50,980; standard room and board is $15,270. Additional mandatory fees are $1,102. Allowances for the cost of books, supplies, travel, and other incidental expenses brings the total cost of attendance for a student to $70,302.

FINANCIAL AID

Boston University Financial Assistance offers a wide variety of financial assistance programs and provides resources to help inform students and their families about payment strategies and financing options. Merit and scholarship awards, need-based scholarships, loans, student employment, and a payment plan are all offered.

Because Boston University believes scholars should be encouraged and recognized for their efforts, the University is committed to offering a variety of scholarships to selected freshmen. University need-based scholarships are offered based on several factors, including calculated financial eligibility, academic achievement, and the availability of funds for a student's program of study. While every effort is made to assist students with limited resources, the university does not have sufficient funds to offer a grant award to every admitted student who has calculated financial eligibility. Those who present the strongest academic credentials are most likely to be offered grant or scholarship aid. If aid is offered in your first year, the same amount is guaranteed for each of your undergraduate years through The BU Scholarship Assurance.

STUDENT ORGANIZATIONS & ACTIVITIES

Boston University students are extremely engaged, participating in academic clubs, cultural or religious organizations, and community service groups. There are more than 450 student organizations and more than 40 intramural and club sports that students can participate in. You can get involved with organizations such as Alianza Latina, Holistic Yoga Society, BU Habitat for Humanity, the Debate Society, or the Alpine Ski Team. A separate student government exists at each school and college to manage student affairs, and the Student Union includes members who represent all schools and colleges within the university.

ADMISSIONS PROCESS

The Board of Admissions evaluates each prospective student holistically. The Board's main focus centers on the rigor of a student's high school record, but required standardized test scores (SAT and ACT), personal qualities and integrity, interests, teacher and counselor references, and other relevant attributes are also considered carefully. All candidates must have graduated from high school or earned an equivalency diploma to be considered. For admission to the College of Fine Arts, most students are not required to submit the SAT or ACT but must either audition or submit a portfolio (some programs also require pre-screening). A few select programs require interviews for admission.

Students should visit www.bu.edu/admissions for additional information. Boston University also considers students with transferable credit from other institutions for admission. Boston University considers transfer applicants for September or January admission, depending on the program of interest.

Boston University offers early decision and early decision 2 (which are binding agreements), and regular decision programs. All applications for early decision must be submitted by November 1, applications for early decision 2 and regular decision must be submitted by January 2. Accelerated program applications must be submitted by November 15. Nominations and/or applications for admission to qualify for the Presidential or Trustee Scholarships must be submitted by December 1.

Transfer students seeking January admission must submit their application forms by November 1. Those seeking September admission must submit their application forms by March 1.

Transfer students cannot be admitted to the Accelerated Liberal Arts Medical or Dental Programs; or the nutrition or six-year, combined AT/DPT and DPT programs in the College of Health & Rehabilitation Sciences: Sargent College. Transfer students may not apply for January admission to the School of Theatre in the College of Fine Arts. They also cannot apply as "undeclared" to any school or college.

Boston University accepts qualified applicants regardless of age, color, disability, national origin, race, religion, sexual orientation, or gender to all of its activities and programs.

BRIAR CLIFF UNIVERSITY

AT A GLANCE

Perched on a scenic hilltop where three states meet, Briar Cliff University is a private, Catholic Franciscan institution that attracts students who dream about making a difference in the world.

As one of the country's most service and outreach-oriented universities, Briar Cliff was founded in 1930 by the Sisters of Saint Francis of Dubuque, with a mission to educate students in the Franciscan tradition of service, caring and openness to all.

More than three-quarters of classes at Briar Cliff are taught by full-time faculty—not adjunct instructors or graduate assistants—meaning students are able to form lasting relationships with their professors; working side-by-side on research, internship placements and networking opportunities. Briar Cliff faculty members are renowned and recognized in their field. They have published extensively, been recognized as Fulbright Scholars, worked on the global Human Genome Project and performed at Carnegie Hall. But more importantly, they take the most pride in the success of their students.

Briar Cliff's students find success after graduation, with 95% of 2015's graduates finding employment or continuing their education (74.2% finding employment and 20.7% pursuing graduate education). Of those finding employment, 78% found employment that was directly related to their major. Outside of the classroom, our students are also recognized for their efforts in giving back to the community, contributing over 10,000 hours of service to the region annually.

Beyond the classroom, Briar Cliff is nationally recognized for its community outreach as a member of the President's National Higher Education Community Service Honor Roll for six consecutive years. Briar Cliff students spend 10,000 hours annually spearheading service projects across the community, the region, the nation and the world. Often times, the service relates directly to the students' chosen field of study: Education majors tutor children in after-school programs; nursing students help with Red Cross disaster relief; accounting majors help low-income families file their taxes; kinesiology majors develop exercise workouts for local senior centers; and biology majors work to restore natural habitat at our local parks and nature centers.

The University has garnered national attention for its innovative "Learning Communities" initiative. The program places first-year students who have similar interests into academically themed learning groups which enroll in similar classes, team up on service projects and adjust to college life together. The result for the Fall 2015 incoming cohort was a retention rate of 78.9 percent.

Briar Cliff is also viewed as a forward-thinking institution when it comes to non-traditional college students. With its online degree completion offerings and highly respected night-and-weekend adult study program, the University provides convenient and high quality education to students in all stages of life. Briar Cliff is ranked among the nation's top 10 Catholic online institutions (onlinecolleges.com), its online Bachelor of Social Work program is ranked in the top 10 nationally (collegechoice.com) and BCU is listed as the second best online college in the state of Iowa (affordablecollegesonline.com).

Office of Admissions:

(800) 662-3303

briarcliff.edu/admissions

LOCATION & ENVIRONMENT

Perched on a beautiful, 70-acre hilltop overlooking the downtown Sioux City, Iowa skyline on one side and natural, rolling prairieland on the other, our campus provides safety, scenery and a strong sense of community. Briar Cliff is ranked among the safest college campuses in the United States, and from the moment you set foot on campus, you'll experience a genuine feeling of acceptance that will forever shape your life.

Ranked by Forbes Magazine as one of the Best Places for Business and Careers, and twice named an All-American City by the National Civic League, Sioux City is a dynamic, metropolitan area of 140,000 friendly people. It is located on the shores of the mighty Missouri River and nestled between the rolling Loess Hills where three states meet. Our vibrant community is a four-hour drive away from Minneapolis to the north and Kansas City to the south. It's the perfect blend of big city opportunity and small-town hospitality—and there's no place like it in the world.

CAMPUS FACILITIES & EQUIPMENT

BISHOP MUELLER LIBRARY

With more than 100,000 print and electronic resources available to students, along with mentoring services and the writing center for students who need academic help, the Bishop Mueller Library supports students and faculty at Briar Cliff. It also contains computer labs, conference small-group study rooms, and project collaboration spaces for students looking to study individually or with classmates.

CHAPEL OF OUR LADY OF GRACE

The resplendent Chapel of Our Lady of Grace is the place of worship for the Briar Cliff community; and home to music recitals and ceremonies throughout the academic year. The chapel was designed by Barry Byrne, a renowned church architect who was the first American to design a Catholic church outside of the U.S. Adjacent to the chapel is a small courtyard and prayer and reflection garden dedicated to the Sisters of Saint Francis, Briar Cliff's founding order.

HEELAN HALL

The home to the majority of Briar Cliff's academic departments and classrooms, Heelan Hall was recently renovated with the addition of cutting-edge classrooms, a revamped bookstore and state-of-the-art nursing, biology, chemistry and digital media laboratories. Its 8,150-square foot atrium and coffee shop have become a hub of student activity on campus. (or, a favorite stop for students between classes).

NEWMAN FLANAGAN CENTER

The Newman-Flanagan Center is Briar Cliff's main athletic complex. The 39,000-square foot facility, which was built literally into "The Cliff" (three-quarters of the complex is underground), is home of Ray Nacke Court, an athletic training facility, and coaching offices for most of Briar Cliff's 18 athletic programs. The building's 2,500-seat arena is also home to the "Blue Crew," the rowdy BCU student cheering section for the Chargers' home basketball and volleyball games.

RECREATION

Students at Briar Cliff can often be found grabbing a latte at Java City, catching a nap in the Roth Atrium, playing foosball in the Stark Student Center, or curbing late-night study cravings with a run to The Fire Pit. There are also sand volleyball courts, outdoor movies on Heffernan Mall, and a nine-hole disc golf course that has been built around campus.

RESIDENCE HALLS

The majority of undergraduate students (65-70%) live in one of the four campus residence halls, which are a quick, scenic walk from classrooms, labs and the library. Each of the university's residence halls comes with wireless networks, cable television service, dining services, study lounges, access to laundry and fitness facilities, and 24-hour, 7-day security and maintenance crews.

STARK STUDENT CENTER

The hub of student activity on campus, the multi-functional Stark Student Center houses Briar Cliff's cafeteria, conference and reception rooms, a pub and game area, student development offices, the university mail service, the Clausen Art Gallery, and is the site of a new, state-of-the-art fitness center.

OFF-CAMPUS OPPORTUNITIES

COMMUNITY SERVICE & OUTREACH

Every year, Briar Cliff students spend thousands of hours leading service projects close to home, and embarking on mission trips around the world. These high-impact opportunities not only make a difference for those they help; they also equip students with lifelong skills and values they will retain long after they graduate.

INTERNSHIPS

Advisors and faculty members at Briar Cliff work with students to find regional and national internships that provide hands-on experience in the field. Recently, Briar Cliff students have interned with the U.S. Congress, NASA, American Red Cross, Buzzfeed.com, Heritage Foundation, Mayo Foundation, Microsoft, the Iowa Department of Human Services and the Harlem Globetrotters.

STUDY ABROAD & TRAVEL OPPORTUNITIES

Briar Cliff is committed to increasing student participation in high-impact national and international travel experiences. These are chances for students to immerse themselves in different countries and cultures, and broaden their perspective as they see the world. Recent study abroad opportunities have included France, Italy, Tanzania, Costa Rica, Chile, Guatemala and Honduras.

ACADEMICS

RESEARCH OPPORTUNITIES

Students at Briar Cliff have the unique opportunity to perform undergraduate research, side-by-side with professors. As home to one of the region's only educational cadaver labs; state-of-the-art biology, chemistry, nursing and kinesiology laboratories; the Siouxland Research Center which helps area non-profits perform research; and the nation's largest urban tallgrass prairie, 150 acres of natural classroom in BCU's own backyard—students in the natural and social sciences have ample opportunities to boost their résumés and applications to graduate school.

PROFESSIONAL DEVELOPMENT SCHOOL

The Professional Development school is a collaboration with local elementary and high schools to give Briar Cliff education majors hands-on experience in local classrooms right away. The early exposure helps teaching candidates decide if they are choosing the right career field, and equips them with hundreds of hours of classroom experience before they ever start student-teaching.

THE BRIAR CLIFF REVIEW

Founded in 1989, the Briar Cliff Review is a nationally renowned literary and art magazine, published annually by students and faculty in the Department of Modern Languages at BCU. The Review is committed to nurturing emerging writers and artists and has helped cultivate the careers of several renowned authors, including New York Times and #1 international best-selling author Jenna Blum.

HONORS PROGRAM

Briar Cliff offers a selective honors program to provide motivated students with a platform to pursue their passion to the greatest extent possible. More than simply taking classes, the honors program provides for more active learning collaborations that transform Briar Cliff students, their community and our world. This is done through seminars, individual research projects, internships, community outreach, travel opportunities and even foreign study.

MENTORING PROGRAM

With the goal of giving all students a support system to be confident and successful, both inside and outside of the classroom, Briar Cliff has created a student mentor system—students helping other college students, on anything from honing study skills to dealing with homesickness to adjusting to college life in general. This support system includes peer mentors, course mentors, writing mentors, social mentors, tech mentors and research mentors.

MAJORS & DEGREES OFFERED

With more than 30 undergraduate degrees, several online degree completion programs for working adults and a host of graduate degrees, Briar Cliff supports students in all stages of higher education. To find available majors, visit briarcliff.edu/degrees.

TUITION, ROOM, BOARD, FEES

Annual undergraduate tuition and fees for 2017-18 is $29,606, while standard room and board is $8,640 at our private institution.

FINANCIAL AID

Each year, Briar Cliff awards over $20 million in financial aid to more than 1,300 students in the form of grants, scholarships, loans and work study employment. Briar Cliff believes in the value of a Catholic education, and it is our mission to make higher education accessible and affordable. As such, all first-year students are awarded financial aid based on merit, talent, leadership and financial need. Financial aid is awarded annually and FAFSA applications are available on Oct. 1. Briar Cliff's FAFSA code is 001846.

STUDENT ORGANIZATIONS & ACTIVITIES

Represented by a 46.7-percent diversity rate in its most recent incoming class, the Briar Cliff student body comes from all backgrounds, cultures and corners of the world. Nearly half (44.8%) of BCU freshmen are first-generation college students. At Briar Cliff, students, faculty and staff deeply value diversity and are committed to a culture of respect and support. Though BCU is a Catholic, Franciscan institution; the university invites all faiths and perspectives into its community.

From cheering on the Charger athletic teams in the Blue Crew, to participating on BCU's national-qualifying Enactus entrepreneurship team, to leading service projects with the social work club, Briar Cliff students place an emphasis on learning outside of the classroom. Students stay involved with more than 30 campus organizations—and the list is ever-evolving, because students launch several new clubs each year. Find more information at briarcliff.edu/clubs.

With 18 intercollegiate sports, Briar Cliff draws student-athletes with the drive to succeed both in competition and the classroom. Briar Cliff is an NAIA Champions of Character institution—so Charger student-athletes develop life-shaping qualities that stick with you long after competition has ended.

ADMISSIONS

ADMISSIONS PROCESS

1. Complete an application for admission (www.briarcliff.edu/apply)
2. Submit high school transcripts and test scores to Briar Cliff.
3. Schedule a visit to Briar Cliff's campus.
4. Complete a housing application, if you plan to live on campus.
5. Submit an enrollment deposit to save your housing spot.
6. Complete the Free Application for Federal Student Aid (FAFSA).
7. Sign up for a New Student Registration Day in Spring or Summer 2017.

BRYANT UNIVERSITY

AT A GLANCE

CONTINUOUS INNOVATION is woven into Bryant's DNA. The University is creating innovative leaders by cultivating curiosity, integrative thinking, and collaboration.

Preparing determined, visionary students with the knowledge, skills, and character to succeed in an interconnected world of unlimited global opportunity is at the core of Bryant's distinguished reputation.

Our world-class professors integrate theoretical and applied concepts in a broad range of majors from accounting to sociology, all complemented by rich co-curricular opportunities.

BRYANT'S PROVEN SUCCESS is highlighted by 99 percent of our students being employed or enrolled in graduate school within six months of Commencement. The median starting salary for a Bryant graduate is $57,000.

LOCATION & ENVIRONMENT

OUR STUNNING, 435-acre campus in Smithfield, Rhode Island has a small town feel with access to major cities. Bryant is just 15 minutes from downtown Providence, an hour from Boston, and three hours from New York City.

Our strategic location provides students with exciting internship and employment opportunities within driving distance, including the headquarters of multinational corporations, such as CVS and Hasbro, small businesses, and tech startups.

CAMPUS FACILITIES & EQUIPMENT

SINCE 1996, Bryant has invested $250 million in its facilities, which are purpose-built for student success. In the fall of 2016, we unveiled our groundbreaking Academic Innovation Center, where innovative learning is fostered in a creative environment designed for a new generation of pedagogy in both Bryant's College of Business and College of Arts and Sciences. The building's flexible, interactive environment is a living example of Bryant's entrepreneurial spirit and enthusiasm for real-world learning. The University also is a leader among academic institutions in its use of technology to provide more effective support and learning. All students receive a fully loaded laptop upon arrival.

OFF-CAMPUS OPPORTUNITIES

PREPARING VISIONARY CITIZENS of the world, Bryant's progressive international partnerships enable students to apply their energy, knowledge, and skills in ways that span academics, business, and culture.

With the University's first-of-its-kind campus in China, Bryant students learn and exchange ideas. Study-abroad opportunities range from the traditional semester abroad to our distinctive Sophomore International Experience, a three-credit course with a 10- to 12-day faculty-led travel component. Costa Rica, England, Malaysia, and Singapore are among some of the other destinations where Bryant scholars deepen their understanding of diverse cultures and the interconnected global economy.

ACADEMICS

FROM THE FIRST YEAR, Bryant delivers an integrated curriculum that is nationally recognized for innovation.

Incoming first-year students gain a competitive advantage through the First-Year Gateway Experience, designed to improve writing proficiency, critical thinking, cultural awareness, ethical reasoning, and information literacy—skills needed for success throughout college and beyond.

Students work with an industry expert in one class and gain experience through service learning in the next. Our world-class faculty integrates theoretical and applied concepts in a broad range of majors from accounting to sociology. They engage students with hands-on learning through: practicum experiences; social entrepreneurship; consulting opportunities; competitions; and business simulations.

Bryant's Archway Investment Fund provides professional training in an academic setting through a student-managed investment fund. Its portfolio exceeds $1 million and is managed entirely by students

MAJORS

COMBINE THE BEST of both worlds at Bryant. Our students graduate with a major in business and a complementary minor in the liberal arts or with a liberal arts major and a business minor. Bryant offers more than 100 courses of study ranging from Applied Analytics and Supply Chain Management to Environmental Science and Literary and Cultural Studies.

TUITION, ROOM, BOARD, FEES

Tuition°, 2017-2018: $41,700

°Includes a new laptop

Room and board: $15,095

Student activity fee: $409

FINANCIAL AID

THE VALUE of a Bryant education is measured in the academic, professional, cultural, and personal growth opportunities available to help students create their paths, expand their worlds, and achieve success.

However, the University understands that financing a student's education is a vital part of the decision about which college he or she will attend. To help ease that financial burden, Bryant awarded more than $16.6 million to incoming students in the fall of 2016.

STUDENT ORGANIZATIONS & ACTIVITIES

MORE THAN 100 student organizations - including academic clubs, community service groups, and cultural clubs - engage students in a wide variety of activities while developing leadership, collaboration, and other skills.

With 22 Division I athletic teams, the Bulldogs' team spirit inspires not only Bryant students and faculty but also the local community to turn out in force for football, basketball, and lacrosse games, among others.

ADMISSION PROCESS

Bryant offers several options to apply for admission. Early applications are accepted under Early Decision 1, Early Action, and Early Decision 2 programs.

To contact the Office of Admission, call 1-800-622-7001 or email admission@ bryant.edu.

Contact:

Bryant University

(800) 622-7002

admissions@bryant.edu admission.bryant.edu

BUCKNELL UNIVERSITY

AT A GLANCE

- 9:1 student-faculty ratio
- All classes are taught by faculty
- 92% of first-year students return as sophomores
- 84% of our students graduate within four years—well above the national average

Established in 1846, Bucknell University is highly selective, private, nonsectarian, coeducational, residential and undergraduate, with a small graduate program. Bucknell offers more than 50 majors and 65 minors in the arts, engineering, humanities, management, sciences and social sciences.

LOCATION & ENVIRONMENT

With its green spaces and striking vistas, Bucknell's 450-acre campus is a quintessential college environment in the heart of scenic central Pennsylvania. The restaurants and shops of downtown Lewisburg—including the Barnes & Noble at Bucknell University and the historic Campus Theatre—lie within walking distance of campus. The University is located within three to four-hours' driving distance of Baltimore, New York City, Philadelphia, Pittsburgh and Washington, D.C. For more information about Bucknell's location, see bucknell.edu/visit.

CAMPUS FACILITIES & EQUIPMENT

Bucknell's campus contains state-of-the-art facilities for performing arts, poetry, science, engineering, athletics and more, all accessible to undergraduates.

Bertrand Library holds nearly 860,000 volumes, providing access to books, maps, journals (both electronic and print) and nearly 300 databases, and offers a video-editing lab, thousands of audiovisual materials and multimedia equipment. Computer labs are available across campus, and there are more than 900 wireless access points to ensure almost complete wireless coverage no matter where you go.

Resources include a film/media production clinic, GIS lab, performing arts center, poetry center and more. Science and engineering programs offer sophisticated instrumentation available for student use, including a structural testing lab, an atomic force microscope and a nuclear magnetic resonance spectrometer.

Career Development—At Bucknell, you'll take advantage of career services such as advising, networking, mock interviews, internship support and employer fairs. You can explore your career options and network with alumni through summer internships with corporations, government organizations and non-profits locally, nationally and internationally. An externship program provides job-shadowing opportunities for sophomores. And all that work will pay off.

The career placement rate for recent Bucknell graduates is consistently high: 97% of the Class of 2016 was employed, in graduate school, both employed and in graduate school, preparing for graduate school or volunteering within nine months of graduation.

OFF-CAMPUS OPPORTUNITIES

Bucknell is a residential university, so most students live on campus, but learning, service, research and recreation extend off campus. You will have the opportunity to volunteer as close as the local nursing home, community center and sustainable farm and as far away as New Orleans and Nicaragua. Every year, students travel off campus to conduct research with faculty mentors. Destinations have included Alaska, Australia and Suriname.

More than 45 percent of students spend a summer, semester or year studying off campus through one of the university's own "in" programs or more than 400 other approved programs in Africa, Asia, Europe, Oceania and North and South America.

ACADEMICS

Bucknell's faculty includes about 350 full-time, tenure-line members. Our 9:1 student-faculty ratio means you will get to know your professors personally and they will provide help and advice—and not just in class. There are many opportunities to become involved in scholarly research and creative projects.

At Bucknell, your professors will challenge you to think critically, develop your ideas thoughtfully and apply what you learn. These skills will enrich your life and career whether you're working in business, education, research, medicine, law, the arts, service—or whichever path defines success for you.

Learn more at bucknell.edu/facultystories

Distinctive programs that complement the curriculum include, but are not limited to:

- Global & Off-campus Education—Gain global perspective as you take part in semester or summer off-campus experiences in University-approved programs around the world, plus our own "Bucknell in" off-campus study programs in France, Ghana and Spain, as well as Athens, London and Washington, D.C..

- Undergraduate research—Work side-by-side with faculty on intensive research projects during the semester or over the summer.

- Geisinger-Bucknell Autism & Developmental Medicine Center—Pursue clinical care, research and education in partnership with Geisinger Health System.

- Griot Institute for Africana Studies—Focus on intellectual and creative interdisciplinary investigation of the cultures, histories, narratives, peoples, geographies and arts of Africa and the African diaspora.

- Bucknell Institute for Public Policy—Investigate issues such as aging, labor, migration, health care, education, political polling and taxation.

- Institute for Leadership in Technology & Management—Participate in an intensive summer program that focuses on globalization, ethics, communication skills, critical thinking, teamwork and leadership.

- Bucknell Center for Sustainability & the Environment—Get involved in environmental and nature-related research or service.

- Bucknell Public Interest Program—Secure a stipend to cover your living expenses while you intern at a nonprofit organization.

- Residential Colleges—Theme-based living and learning program. Participating first-year students take a class together and join in programs and social activities that complement classroom learning. bucknell.edu/ResColleges

- Civic Engagement—You will have the opportunity to participate in academically-based service-learning and co-curricular community service locally, nationally and internationally..

MAJORS & DEGREES OFFERED

You can choose from more than 50 majors and 65 minors at Bucknell. Students build robots, write and perform in their own plays and debate solutions to global issues. Engineers can make art, artists can analyze DNA and philosophers can make music. You will choose your own path, but what unites everyone is a shared enthusiasm for learning and a desire to achieve deeper levels of understanding about life and the world.

The College of Arts & Sciences offers bachelor's degrees in arts, humanities, sciences and social sciences. Master's degrees are available in select disciplines.

The College of Management*, accredited by the Association to Advance Collegiate Schools of Business (AACSB), offers bachelor of science degrees in business administration with four majors: accounting & financial management; global management; managing for sustainability; and markets, innovation & design.

The College of Engineering offers a bachelor of science degree in eight majors, a five-year dual degree in engineering and management, a five-year dual degree in engineering and the liberal arts, and a five-year combined bachelor's and master's degree.

For details about academic programs, see bucknell.edu/majors.

*The School of Management will become the College of Management in July, 2017.

TUITION, ROOM, BOARD, FEES

For the 2016-17 academic year, tuition and fees are set at:

Tuition and fees: $51,960

Room and Board: $12,656

FINANCIAL AID

Bucknell's Office of Financial Aid is here to help you—through advice and through financial aid if you qualify. We offer a range of financial aid options, including need-based grants and scholarships, limited academic and arts merit scholarships, loans and student employment. We consider each family's financial circumstances on an individual basis and if your circumstances remain relatively constant from year to year, you apply by the deadline, and you maintain satisfactory academic progress, we will award you need-based aid at about the same level each year.

- The average total need-based financial aid package for a student in the Class of 2020 is $34,500, including scholarships, loans, and work-study.
- About 52 percent of students receive financial aid from Bucknell, and 62 percent receive financial aid of some form.
- The average loan total upon graduation is about $22,600.

Bucknell offers an education that provides lifelong personal and career benefits, and is ranked #3 among best-value liberal arts colleges for mid-career salary by PayScale 2016.

Important Note: If you are applying for Bucknell University financial aid, you must submit your CSS PROFILE by November 15 for Early Decision I and January 15 for Early Decision II and Regular Decision applications. To apply for federal financial aid, complete the Free Application for Federal Student Aid (FAFSA).

STUDENT ORGANIZATIONS & ACTIVITIES

Bucknell's undergraduate student body includes 3,600 students from most states and more than 45 countries. You'll join with active students whose voices are valued in the classroom, lab and creative spaces, in student government and throughout the University community.

Take advantage of speaker series, arts performances and scholarly lectures on campus. Become a member or leader of a student-run organization. From participating in undergraduate research, the arts, honor societies, cultural, political or religious organizations, to exploring the outdoors, you'll find your niche. You can compete in and support Division I athletics as well as intramural and club sports and be active in our state-of-the-art fitness center. About half of sophomores, juniors and seniors participate in fraternity and sorority life and students frequently volunteer in the local community or on one of our many national and international service opportunities.

Learn more at bucknell.edu/studentstories

ADMISSIONS PROCESS

Bucknell is looking for students with high academic achievement and leadership or creative skills, a sense of commitment to community and a desire to achieve broad learning throughout life. Grades, test scores and recommendations are extremely important, but we also look for students who are daring, who show us they'll cultivate their interests inside and outside the classroom and contribute to the world in thoughtful, bold and compassionate ways.

Apply for admission through the Common Application at www.commonapp.org. Early Decision students should also complete an Early Decision Form.

Deadlines

- Regular Decision applications should be filed by January 15 for notification by April 1.
- SAT and/or ACT results must be submitted before March 1.
- Early Decision candidates may apply for Early Decision I consideration by November 15 or Early Decision II consideration by January 15.
- Transfer student information is available at bucknell.edu/transfer. Applications for transfer students should be submitted by November 1 for spring enrollment and March 15 for fall enrollment.

For detailed information about admissions at Bucknell and to sign up for our mailing list, go to bucknell.edu/admissions.

We invite you to visit Bucknell's beautiful campus to learn more about our academic and co-curricular opportunities, meet faculty and students and see for yourself how Bucknell can help you reach your goals.

View visit options at bucknell.edu/visit

Take a virtual tour at bucknell.edu/virtualtour

Get in touch with us at admissions@bucknell.edu

CABRINI UNIVERSITY

AT A GLANCE

Cabrini University offers a supportive community that helps students discover who they are and what they can accomplish in their life, in their career, and in society. Students can choose from 35+ majors and enhance their experience with minors, dual degrees, advanced coursework for graduate school, and honors research.

With a 16:1 student-to-faculty ratio, students receive personalized attention from professors and staff who care about their success. And their success continues after graduation, with 93% of graduates employed or pursuing graduate work within six months of earning their degree.

We are a Catholic institution, founded in 1957 by the Missionary Sisters of the Sacred Heart of Jesus, with a mission to provide academic excellence, leadership development, and a commitment to social justice. Through international partnerships, community engagement, and hands-on experiences, students find their voice and how they can work for universal human rights and dignity.

Cabrini enrolls about 1,400 undergraduates and 900 students in graduate and doctoral programs.

LOCATION & ENVIRONMENT

Cabrini is a coeducational residential university located 12 miles from Philadelphia in Radnor, PA. Our campus is tucked onto 112-acres of peaceful woods, surrounded by a suburban setting with nearby shopping, restaurants, and recreation.

CAMPUS FACILITIES & EQUIPMENT

Cabrini has 12 residence halls comprised of single rooms, doubles, suites, and apartments. The remodeled Dixon House houses 75 upper-class students, and the renovated Woodcrest Hall provides a great central location for first-year students.

In 2016, a brand new Athletic and Recreation Pavilion added 38,000+ square feet to Cabrini's existing sports and recreation complex, including a state-of-the-art workout room, modern aerobic studios, lounge space, and a juice bar. This addition compliments our state-of-the-art science building, which includes facilities for our exercise-science laboratory.

OFF-CAMPUS OPPORTUNITIES

Cabrini is a short train ride to Philadelphia, and only two hours away from New York City and Washington, DC. The campus is also located 10 minutes from the King of Prussia Mall, the second largest mall in the country. A campus shuttle takes students to nearby locations, including the mall and train station.

ACADEMICS

A core part of Cabrini University's mission is to provide an excellent academic experience that will help students grow as individuals and as leaders. This experience starts with Cabrini's award-winning First Year Experience Program, which helps students transition to college and creates a supportive community where they can learn who they are and how they can succeed.

In the first year, students have the opportunity to live and/or study with classmates who share a common interest through Learning Communities and can begin to build strong connections with their faculty. Through the Engagements with the Common Good courses, students explore societal issues and consider possible solutions to inequity around the world. If students need additional support, Cabrini's Center for Student Success offers free peer tutoring, writing and math support, academic advising guidance, and counseling services.

Our Honors Program is dedicated to honing students' critical-thinking skills, developing creative and imaginative impulses, and pushing them to expand their intellectual horizons. The program strives to model lifelong learning, giving students the tools they need to succeed inside and outside the academic setting.

As early as the second semester of a student's first year, he or she has the opportunity to study abroad in semester, summer-, or year-long programs or to enroll in one of the short-term study abroad courses offered each spring semester. Students have studied science in Switzerland, the Spanish language and culture in Madrid, the European Union in Amsterdam, and theater in London.

MAJORS & DEGREES OFFERED

Cabrini offers more than 35 undergraduate programs, including biology, education (with teacher certification), English, criminology, communication, finance, psychology, and social work; and 10 pre-professional programs, including pre-dentistry, pre-pharmacy, pre-law, and pre-physician assistant studies. Students also can create their own major, minor, or concentration.

After graduating with a bachelor's degree, students can continue their academic career at Cabrini by pursuing graduate work in one of our six master's programs and our two doctoral programs.

TUITION, ROOM, BOARD, FEES

Full-time (12–18 credits) tuition and fees for the 2017–18 year is $31,350, which is below the national average for private institutions. Room and board, on average, cost $12,140 per year.

FINANCIAL AID

Cabrini is committed to providing an affordable, quality education, which is why 98% of our students receive financial aid and the average Cabrini financial award is $16,500. In addition, students may be eligible for PHEAA Grants (PA residents only), Pell Grants, and federal financial aid.

STUDENT ORGANIZATIONS & ACTIVITIES

Whether it's Cabrini Day or EPIC Week, Homecoming, or trips to Broadway, Cabrini's student-driven Center for Student Engagement and Leadership makes sure campus never slows down. With more than 300 student events each year and more than 50 student clubs and organizations—from intramural sports to honors societies to professional organizations—students have many opportunities to engage and get involved.

Cabrini has 19 Division III sports teams that compete in the Eastern Collegiate Athletic Conference and the Colonial States Athletic Conference and have won 106 CSAC Championships.

Our Nerney Leadership Institute offers leadership training and mentoring. Plus, students can make a difference with the Wolfington Center, which organizes service and social advocacy projects in the local community and around the world.

ADMISSIONS PROCESS

Cabrini University is test-optional and does not require students to submit their SAT or ACT scores. However, students may still choose to submit their scores; use SAT code 2071 and ACT code 3532.

To apply to Cabrini (undergraduate):

1. Complete the online application form at cabrini.edu/apply or commonapp.org.
2. Request that your high school send an official transcript to the Cabrini Admissions Office.
3. Submit a personal statement (250+ words, topic of your choice) in a Word document or PDF to essays@cabrini.edu.
4. Submit an application fee or fee waiver.

To apply to Cabrini (transfer):

1. Complete the online application form at cabrini.edu/apply
2. Send transcripts from your college or university (if you've already earned 24+ credits).
3. If you have fewer than 24 college credits, request your final official high school transcript to be sent to the Cabrini Admissions Office.
4. Submit a schedule of additional classes you'll finish before attending Cabrini (if applicable).
5. Provide a brief personal statement (250+ words, topic of your choice) in a Word document or PDF to essays@cabrini.edu.
6. Submit an application fee or fee waiver.

For more information about visiting or applying to Cabrini, email admit@cabrini.edu or visit cabrini.edu.

CENTRAL CONNECTICUT STATE UNIVERSITY

AT A GLANCE

One of Connecticut's premier comprehensive public universities, Central Connecticut State University is a vibrant learning centered community dedicated to teaching and scholarship.

Central Connecticut State University (CCSU) is a comprehensive public university. Dedicated to learning in the liberal arts and sciences the University comprises five schools: Carol Ammon College of Liberal Arts & Social Sciences; and the schools of Business; Education & Professional Studies; Engineering, Science & Technology; and Graduate Studies. CCSU offers full- and part-time undergraduate programs in more than 100 areas of study.

LOCATION & ENVIRONMENT

CCSU is located in suburban New Britain, conveniently located in the center of Connecticut, approximately 2 hours from Boston or New York. The campus has been recently renovated. The University is surrounded by a pleasant neighborhood, with shopping and dining facilities nearby.

OFF-CAMPUS OPPORTUNITIES

The School of Education has many connections to area schools, including several Professional Development Schools, which provide CCSU students nearly unique opportunities to perfect their teaching skills in a full range of elementary and secondary classrooms.

The School of Engineering, Science & Technology offers a wide array of internship opportunities in area engineering, manufacturing, and technology businesses.

The Center for International Education, nationally recognized for the quality of its Study Abroad programs, offers students a rich variety of study-abroad opportunities at more than 40 locations throughout the world and provides academic and cultural programs that promote a better understanding of peoples and cultures.

And the University and the New Britain Museum of American Art (an internationally acclaimed museum) have a partnership allowing students and faculty to visit the museum for free.

MAJORS & DEGREES OFFERED

CCSU is accredited by the New England Association of Schools and Colleges (NEASC). The University operates on a two-semester calendar and offers four summer sessions plus one winter session. Undergraduate programs include: Accounting; Anthropology; Art (Art History); Athletic Training; Biochemistry; Biology (Ecology; Biodiversity; Evolutionary; Environmental Science; General); Biomolecular Sciences; Chemistry; Civil Engineering; Civil Engineering Technology; Communication (Media Studies; Strategic Communications); Computer Engineering Technology; Computer Science; Construction Management; Criminology; Design (Graphic/Information); Earth Sciences; Economics (General; Operations Research); Education (Elementary; K-12; Secondary; Special Education); Electronics Technology; Engineering &Technology Education; Engineering Technology; English; Entrepreneurship; Exercise Science; Finance; French; Geography (Environmental; General Regional; Planning; Geographic Information Science; Tourism); German; History; Hospitality & Tourism; Industrial Technology (Electro-Mechanical Technology; Environmental & Occupational Safety; Graphics Technology; Manufacturing; Networking Technology; Technology Management); Interdisciplinary Science (Environmental Interpretation; Physical Sciences); International Business; International Studies; Italian; Journalism; Management (Entrepreneurship; Human Resource); Management Information Systems; Manufacturing Engineering Technology; Marketing; Mathematics (Actuarial; Statistics); Mechanical Engineering; Mechanical Engineering Technology; Music; Nursing (BSN & RN to BSN); Philosophy; Physical Education (Exercise Science & Health Promotion); Physics; Political Science (General; Public Administration); Psychology; Social Sciences; Social Work; Sociology; Spanish; Theatre.

Degrees: BA, BFA (Theatre); BS; BSN; BS-RN, Teacher Certification (elementary; secondary; k-12)

ACADEMIC PROGRAMS

CCSU also offers a number of interdisciplinary programs as well as independently designed majors. The Honors Program, a challenging interdisciplinary program of study for academically qualified students, offers half and full-tuition merit scholarships and a variety of other benefits and resources, including a new Honors Lab.

FACILITIES & EQUIPMENT

CCSU offers an attractive campus with new and renovated buildings adding to the classic collegiate style of its architecture. The academic buildings feature technologically state-of-the-art "smart classrooms" and seminar rooms, and the entire campus offers wireless access. The Student Center provides lounges, dining services, conference and game rooms, information services, and a range of other support services. Three theatres offer space for plays, concerts, and guest lectures. The S.T. Chen Art Gallery hosts shows by student, faculty, and visiting artists. The Student Technology Center features 250 computers plus printers and scanners for student use. Campus-based TV and radio stations provide exciting entertainment as well as opportunities to learn about the professions. The Elihu Burritt Library provides access to over 2 million books through an online catalog, a wide array of electronic databases and online resources, and special collections ranging from the unparalleled collection of Polish American materials to the Equity Archive. The University also offers many new athletic facilities, including an Olympic-sized swimming pool, modern exercise equipment, a state-of-the-art fitness center, a weight-training room, and an athletic training center. In the Kaiser Annex students can walk, jog, and play tennis or a pickup basketball game. CCSU recently opened new football, soccer, softball, and baseball fields to complement its basketball and volleyball arena. The residence halls and classrooms are fully networked. Approximately 26% of the students live on campus in nine residence halls.

TUITION, ROOM, BOARD AND FEES

TUITION & FEES (per year)

CT Resident

Tuition & fees $ 10,185

Housing (double occupancy) $ 6,820

Food (cost varies per meal plan) $ 4,826

Total $22,201

Out-of-State Resident

Tuition & fees $22,874

Housing (double occupancy) $6,820

Food (cost varies per meal plan) $4,996

Total $34,690

Annual costs for books, travel and personal expenses will vary and be about $2,500.

FINANCIAL AID

Approximately 75% of CCSU full-time students receive some form of financial aid. CCSU's office of Financial Aid works with students to help them meet educational expenses from their first year until graduation. To apply for financial aid students must complete the FAFSA form. For more information, call 860.832.2200, e-mail FinancialAid3@ccsu.edu, or on the Web at www.ccsu.edu/finaid.

STUDENT BODY

CCSU serves approximately 12,500 students—10,000 undergraduate and 2,500 graduate. Our distinguished alumni include successful business men and women, the first Latina state supreme court justice, CEOs in a wide range of industries and corporations, leading academics at national universities, award-winning educators and educational leaders, trainers and coaches at high schools and colleges as well as top NFL and MLB teams, journalists, novelists, and artists— each and all demonstrating that success begins with CCSU.

STUDENT ORGANIZATIONS & ACTIVITIES

There are 130 student clubs and organizations, which cover a broad range of interests: academic--such as the Anthropology or the Investment clubs; athletics--such as the crew or flying clubs; cultural--for example, the art club, the jazz band, and other musical organizations; ethnic--such as the Black Student Union, Latin American Students Organization, and the Muslim Student Association; religious--such as Hillel and the Newman Club; and such honors organizations as Delta Mu Delta, Lambda Delta, and Kappa Delta Pi. On-campus entertainment is wide and varied, including, most recently, "Devils Den@ 10"_student-run entertainment on Thursday evenings.

ADMISSIONS

CCSU is a learning community of students with a broad range of abilities, interests, and backgrounds. We value excellence and achievement in academic scholarship, community involvement, and extracurricular activities. Our admissions process evaluates the readiness of applicants to succeed based on past demonstrations of academic and personal successes.

CCSU has a "rolling" admissions policy, not a set admissions deadline, which gives students greater flexibility in applying. The University urges prospective students to apply as early as possible in their senior year. The University begins accepting students for the fall semester in mid-October and will continue to review applications until the class is filled.

First-year applicants are considered on the basis of performance in college preparatory classes, rank in class, SAT or ACT test scores, recommendations, and community and extracurricular involvement and leadership. A personal essay is required. For some applicants an interview with a representative of the Office of Recruitment & Admissions may be necessary. If the applicant ranks in the top 20% of his/her class, is an A-B student, and has SAT scores of 1100 or higher, the student should consider finding out about CCSU's Honors Program by calling 860-832-2938 for details. CCSU accepts most Advanced Placement (AP) courses for college credit, provided the minimum CCSU required score is achieved. Check with Admissions for the required scores.

Admission criteria include graduation from a regionally accredited secondary school. High school work should include college preparatory courses in: English (four years); Mathematics (covering algebra I, geometry, and algebra II); Science (two years including one-year lab science); Social sciences (two to three years including U.S. history). Coursework in foreign language is recommended (at least three consecutive years of the same foreign language up through the third level will satisfy the foreign language proficiency required of all CCSU-enrolled students). Students whose preparation does not follow this pattern may still qualify for admission if, in the judgment of the Director of Recruitment and Admissions, there is strong evidence that they have the potential to complete a degree program or if they meet other established criteria as authorized by the University President under authority delegated by the Board of Regents of the Connecticut State College & University System. Applicants who are not graduates of a secondary school should submit their secondary school transcript up to the time of withdrawal and a copy of their high school equivalency diploma and scores.

The most important thing for the applicant to remember is to provide as much information as possible achievements, awards, and examples of leadership when applying.

How to Apply

Students are encouraged to apply online at www.ccsu.edu/apply. For paper applications, please provide the Office of Recruitment & Admissions with 1) completed application for undergraduate admission 2) official high school transcript, SAT or ACT test scores, recommendations, and essay and 3) a non-refundable application fee of $50. All correspondence should be sent to the Office of Recruitment and Admissions, CCSU, P.O. Box 4010, 1615 Stanley Street, New Britain, CT 06050-4010.

Tours and information sessions may be arranged by calling 860.832.2289 or via e-mail at: admissions@ccsu.edu.

CHATHAM UNIVERSITY

AT A GLANCE

Founded in 1869, Chatham University in Pittsburgh, PA is a private institution with over 2,100 undergraduate and graduate students (on-campus and online).

Alma mater of environmental pioneer Rachel Carson '29, Chatham University offers over 40 majors in sustainability, the health sciences, business and communications, and the arts, sciences, and humanities.

LOCATION & ENVIRONMENT

With elements designed for the original Andrew Mellon estate by the renowned Olmsted Brothers, the Woodland Road location is one of the most beautiful places in the City of Pittsburgh. Designated a national arboretum, the 39-acre campus features renovated historic mansions now being used as residence halls, a labyrinth, pond, and 125 different varieties of flora. It is located minutes from the University of Pittsburgh and Carnegie Mellon University, the epicenter of a vibrant community with over 70,000 college students.

Chatham Eastside is a 250,000 square foot building located less than a mile from the University's Woodland Road location and just down the road from Bakery Square, home to Google's Pittsburgh office. It houses substantial skills labs and mock-up doctors' waiting rooms for classes and demonstrations for the physician assistant studies, physical therapy, and occupational therapy programs, as well as a mock-up apartment for working on specific tasks for daily living.

Located in Richland, PA, Chatham's Eden Hall Campus (EHC) is a 388-acre living laboratory and home to the Falk School of Sustainability & Environment. It produces more energy than it consumes, relies on geothermal energy for heating and cooling, and treats storm- and wastewater on site.

OFF-CAMPUS OPPORTUNITIES

Chatham's Shadyside campus is located between the leafy residential and commercial neighborhoods of Squirrel Hill and Shadyside—minutes from downtown Pittsburgh. According to the website payscale.com, the cost of living in Pittsburgh is about eight percent below the national average.

The Huffington Post has praised Pittsburgh as "a modern mecca of culture and education, [and] a hidden gem." According to national polls conducted by such organizations as Forbes and U.S. News and World Report, it is the safest mid-sized city and the most livable city in the country. It is one of the most affordable cities, and it boasts an unemployment rate significantly lower than the national average. With leading industries such as technology, finance, and medicine, as well as a booming arts community, Pittsburgh has a tremendous amount to offer.°

And not only that: in the Pittsburgh region within the next ten years, more than 290,000 Baby Boomers now in the workforce will be eligible to retire, and more than 50,000 new jobs are expected to be created here.°°

° Source: aboutpittsburgh.com

°° Inflection Point: Supply, Demand and the Future of Work in the Pittsburgh Region from the Allegheny Conference on Community Development, May 2016.

TUITION, ROOM, BOARD, FEES (2017-18)

- Full time (12-21° credits): $17,610 per term
- Part time (1-11 credits): $854 per credit

Undergraduate Housing

- Multiple Occupancy Room (Double, Triple or Quad): $2,635 - $2,910 per term
- Single Room: $2,635 - $3,195 per term
- Apartment (for Sophomores, Juniors & Seniors only): $2,415 per term
- Orchard Hall, Eden Hall Campus (for Sophomores, Juniors & Seniors only): $1,350 (single room) - $1,425 (single room, 2-peron suite) per term. Undergraduate residents are required to purchase the Chatham Eden Hall Meal Plan.
- Certain housing options are billed at a premium. Please refer to the Office of Residence Life for exact charges based on residence hall and room option selected.

Residence Hall Meal Plans

- Chatham Platinum: Unlimited meals, $35 Flex Dollars: $2,940 per term
- Chatham Gold: 19 meals/week, $65 Flex Dollars: $2,785 per term
- Chatham Silver: 14 meals/week, $120 Flex Dollars: $2,785 per term
- Chatham Bronze: 10 meals/week, $230 Flex Dollars: $2,785 per term
- Chatham Steel: 200 meals, $210 Flex Dollars: $2,255 per term

Apartment & Commuter Meal Plans

(Required for all students in Chatham and Chung Apartments)

- Cougar Platinum: 5 meals/week, $230 Flex Dollars: $1,215 per term
- Cougar Gold: 100 meals, $210 Flex Dollars: $1,215 per term
- Cougar Silver: 50 meals, $210 Flex Dollars: $760 per term
- Cougar Bronze: 25 meals, $210 Flex Dollars: $505 per term

Eden Hall Meal Plan

- Anytime Plan, unlimited meal accesses, $60 Flex Dollars; $2,125 per term

Eden Hall - Anytime access plans provide continuous access to the Eden Hall Dining Commons. Enter and exit the Dining Commons as frequently as you'd like and eat as many meals as you'd like. Flex dollars roll over fall semester to spring semester but not academic year to academic year. Flex dollars can be used at any Chatham dining facility; Shadyside, Eastside Café, Café Rachel, Eden Hall Dining Commons or The Dairy Barn Café.

Miscellaneous Fees

- College Fee: $240 per term
- Technology Fee: $405 per term
- Student Health Insurance: $1,400 per term

FINANCIAL AID

Chatham University is proud to offer both need-based financial aid and merit-based scholarships to incoming undergraduate students.

STUDENT ORGANIZATIONS & ACTIVITIES

From Amnesty International to the Outdoor Club, over 60 student organizations help students explore their passions and discover new ones. Activities include sports events, white-water rafting, bonfires, shopping excursions, plays, concerts, and camping. Clubs include Cougar spirit clubs, performance arts clubs, service organizations, religious organizations, and lots of special interest groups.

Chatham offers 16 NCAA Division III sports, allowing scholar-athletes to pursue excellence on the field while maintaining focus on their studies:

Women's: basketball, volleyball, softball, track & field, cross country, swimming & diving, ice hockey, soccer, lacrosse (Fall 2017)

Men's: basketball, baseball, track & field, cross country, swimming & diving, ice hockey (Fall 2017), and lacrosse (Fall 2017).

ADMISSIONS PROCESS

First-Year Students

First-year student admission is for applicants entering directly from high school, without enrolling in prior post-secondary course work (other than courses completed while attending high school).

The Office of Admission reviews each application in its entirety using a holistic review process to determine whether a student will thrive at Chatham. Since not all students showcase their abilities in the same way, each application is given careful consideration before an admission decision is reached.

- Official high school transcripts
- SAT (Chatham code: 2081) or ACT (Chatham Code: 3538) scores
- Essay or writing sample
- One or more letters of recommendation from guidance counselor or teachers.

Students may apply using our test optional policy and choose not to submit their standardized test scores at the time of application. If not submitting their scores, in additional to the required application materials, applicants must submit the following:

- Résumé
- Graded academic writing sample
- Complete an on-campus interview
- Portfolio (optional)

If applicants feel that these materials do not adequately represent their academic abilities or explain their academic history, they are encouraged to submit additional explanatory materials to strengthen their application.

Transfer Students

Chatham University welcomes applications from transfer candidates from junior and community colleges and other four-year institutions in the United States as well as other countries. More than one-third of Chatham students are transfer students.

Transfer student applicants must submit the following:

- Completed application for admission
- Official college transcripts from all former institutions attended
- Official high school transcripts (unless the student has over 24 transferable credits) (Form DOC)
- SAT (Chatham code: 2081) or ACT (Chatham Code: 3538) scores (unless the student has over 24 transferable credits)
- Personal essay or academic writing sample
- One or more letters of recommendation from a professor, community member, employer, etc.

Transfer students, with less than 24 transferrable credits, may apply using our test optional policy and choose not to submit their standardized test scores at the time of application. If not submitting their scores, in additional to the required application materials, they must also submit the following:

- Résumé
- Graded academic writing sample
- Complete an on-campus interview
- Portfolio (optional)

TRANSFER CREDITS

Students can transfer up to 90 credits previously earned from a two-year or four-year accredited college or university where the student has earned a C or higher. A preliminary evaluation of transfer credit is made at the time of admission to provide an indication of class standing.

All transfer credit must be submitted to the University prior to initial matriculation. Courses submitted for transfer after initial matriculation will not be accepted. This includes all AP credit, CLEP credit, and courses completed at previous institutions of higher education.

CHRISTOPHER NEWPORT UNIVERSITY

AT A GLANCE

Christopher Newport provides a liberal arts and sciences education that stimulates intellectual inquiry and fosters civic engagement. Students acquire qualities of mind and spirit that prepare them to lead lives of significance.

A four-year public university in Newport News, Virginia, Christopher Newport University enrolls 5,000 students in rigorous academic programs in the liberal arts and sciences through the College of Arts and Humanities, the College of Natural and Behavioral Sciences, the College of Social Sciences, and the Luter School of Business. CNU offers great teaching and small class sizes with an emphasis on leadership, civic engagement and honor.

At Christopher Newport, we want you to be successful in your studies. Even more importantly, we want you to lead a life of significance. With that in mind, we have designed an undergraduate experience to instruct and inspire great leaders for the 21st century. We want students who will make the world a better place—young women and men with a passion for engagement and a strong sense of civic responsibility.

CNU's outstanding curriculum shapes hearts and minds for a lifetime of service. From the moment you arrive on campus, you will enjoy countless opportunities to develop strong leadership traits. Your journey begins in the classroom, where you will study with distinguished faculty—accomplished scholars of outstanding quality. Outside the classroom—from athletics to clubs and student organizations—you will enhance your leadership skills by collaborating closely with your peers. You will work together on projects and initiatives that make a lasting impact on our campus, community and the world.

LOCATION & ENVIRONMENT

Located in Southeastern Virginia, CNU's picturesque, 260-acre campus is in the heart of one of the most historic—and beautiful—areas of the United States and conveniently located amid popular Virginia attractions including Williamsburg and Virginia Beach. When you venture off campus, you'll find unlimited activities for all interests as well as cultural and historical treasures within a short walk or drive.

CAMPUS FACILITIES & EQUIPMENT

Christopher Newport is committed to providing extraordinary buildings that support great learning and activities. We've completed nearly $1 billion in capital construction in recent years and have built a beautiful campus with world-class facilities that include dazzling and wildly popular residence halls. You'll enjoy our Freeman Sports and Convocation Center, Ferguson Center for the Arts, David Student Union, Trible Library—with more than 110,000 square feet of resources, Forbes Hall—an integrated science center with cutting-edge labs and technology, Luter Hall—home to the College of Social Sciences and the Luter School of Business, and Christopher Newport Hall—our new Student Success Center.

The Center for Career Planning directly assists students with academic major exploration, landing a first job or gaining admission to a top graduate school. Workshops, seminars, job fairs, on-campus interviews and career counseling—a full range of services—are available to students and alumni.

ACADEMICS

President's Leadership Program

Learn how to make an impact through the President's Leadership Program (PLP). Selected freshman applicants have excelled in their academic studies and demonstrated a passion for engagement. Through challenging courses, public service, foreign study and other targeted opportunities, PLP empowers leadership students to make a difference—to become caring, knowledgeable and effective leaders for America and the world. The President's Leadership Program offers priority registration, annual scholarships and study abroad stipends.

Honors Program

This unique program offers students more freedom to customize their academic experience for their personal and professional aspirations. The Honors Program allows more time for interdisciplinary seminar-style courses and challenges students by means of study abroad, independent research, internships, jobs and volunteer experience relevant to their passions. Each student receives an annual residential scholarship (including a study abroad stipend), as well as priority housing in an Honors Learning Community and priority course registration.

Undergraduate Research

Undergraduates engage in cutting-edge research at CNU. In all fields of study, our students collaborate with faculty mentors on key research, make conference presentations, and publish books and scholarly journal articles with faculty. Each spring the Paideia conference showcases outstanding student research, and the new Summer Scholars Program offers paid research assistantships for undergraduates.

Pre-Law Program

Interested in pursuing a career in law? The nation's top law schools seek applicants who have received a well-rounded undergraduate education—one like the liberal arts and sciences curriculum Christopher Newport offers. Many of our pre-law students pursue a philosophy of law minor or an American studies major with a constitutional studies concentration, but regardless of your undergraduate field of study, our Pre-Law Program is designed to help you gain admission to one of the nation's top 25 law schools.

Pre-Med and Pre-Health Program

Medical schools and other graduate programs seek applicants with a well-rounded undergraduate education. The Pre-Med and Pre-Health Program at Christopher Newport assists students pursuing any academic major to prepare for post-graduate study. In addition to the necessary prerequisite coursework, we offer several resources to help you gain admission to your professional school of choice—from academic and career advising to mentoring, clinical internships, workshops and seminars.

Study Abroad

We encourage you to study abroad, either accompanied by CNU faculty or independently. Learn about different cultures while falling in love with America. You may choose to study for an entire semester, year or more briefly between academic terms. These rich cultural experiences are as unique as the destinations. With scholarship opportunities available, the world is your classroom! CNU students have recently spent semesters or full academic years in Australia, Costa Rica, England, France, Germany, Greece, India, Italy, Japan, Mexico, Russia, Scotland, Spain and many other international locales.

Bachelor's to Master's Five-Year Degree Programs

Students can obtain a bachelor's and master's degree in the following five-year programs:

- Master of Arts in Teaching
- Master of Science in Applied Physics and Computer Science
- Master of Science in Environmental Science

Center for Academic Success

Throughout the CNU experience, the Center for Academic Success offers tutoring, workshops, seminars and one-on-one assistance to help students improve their academic performance with effective study strategies. Peer writing consultants available in the Writing Center offer specialized help with all stages of the writing process.

Service

Christopher Newport students contribute to the greater good by making a positive difference in the life of our campus, community and world. We offer countless opportunities—from service-learning initiatives and projects like Habitat for Humanity to the philanthropic work of our Greek organizations and student-athletes, among others. Through a partnership with the prestigious Bonner Foundation, CNU joins a national network of more than 75 colleges and universities who support four-year, service scholarships.

MAJORS & DEGREES OFFERED

We offer more than 90 areas of study in the liberal arts and sciences, providing a breadth and depth of knowledge that will prepare you to take advantage of any opportunity that presents itself in today's global marketplace. Through Christopher Newport's rigorous curriculum you will learn to think critically and communicate effectively while developing the tools and skills that will serve you for a lifetime.

Areas of Study:

Accounting , African-American Studies, American Studies, Constitutional Studies, Applied Physics , Asian Studies , Biochemistry, Biology, Biology—Cellular, Molecular and Physiological, Biology—Environmental , Biology—Integrative , Biology—Organismal , Business Administration, Chemistry, Childhood Studies , Civic Engagement and Social Entrepreneurship, Classical Studies, Classical Languages, Communication , Computer Engineering, Computer Science , Dance, Digital Humanities , Economics , Mathematical Economics, Electrical Engineering, English , Literature , Writing , Environmental Studies, Film Studies , Finance , Fine Arts , Art History, Studio Art, French , German, Greek Studies , History , Human Rights and Conflict Resolution, Information Science, Information Systems, Interdisciplinary Studies, International Culture and Business , Judeo-Christian Studies, Latin, Latin American Studies, Leadership Studies, Linguistics , Management , Marketing , Mathematics , Mathematics—Applied and Computational, Medieval and Renaissance Studies, Middle East and North Africa Studies, Military Science (ROTC), Museum Studies, Music , Choral Music Education, Composition, Instrumental Music Education, Jazz Studies, Performance, Neuroscience, Philosophy , Pre-Seminary Studies, Religious Studies, Philosophy and Religious Studies, Philosophy of Law, Photography and Video Art, Political Science, Psychology , Social Work , Sociology, Anthropology , Criminology , Spanish , Theater , Acting , Arts Administration, Design/Technology, Directing/Dramatic Literature, Music/Dance, Theater Studies, U.S. National Security Studies, Women's and Gender Studies

Advising Tracks:

Biotechnology and Management, Pre-Health, Pre-Law, Pre-Med

Bachelor's to Master's Five-Year Programs

Applied Physics and Computer Science, Environmental Science, Teaching (MAT)

TUITION, ROOM, BOARD, FEES

Christopher Newport offers exceptional academics, stunning facilities and a vibrant campus life. Yet we recognize paying for college can be a challenge. That's why we distribute nearly $50 million in aid to students each year. Most assistance comes in the form of federal and state grants, scholarships to reward merit and help students with financial need, educational loans, and college work-study programs.

2016-17 Costs per Year

In-State Tuition: $13,054

In-State Room and Board: $11,234

Total: $24,288

Out-of-State Tuition: $24,680

Out-of-State Room and Board: $11,234

Total: $35,914

FINANCIAL AID

Important New FAFSA Deadline:

To apply for financial aid or scholarships, submit your FAFSA by the December 15 preferred filing deadline or the March 1 priority filing deadline.

STUDENT ORGANIZATIONS & ACTIVITIES

Learning Communities

All freshmen are placed into a Learning Community based on their interests, which facilitates a successful transition from high school to college. Living together and sharing multiple classes with a small group of students and collaborating with faculty enables learning beyond the classroom while providing extra support.

Athletics

One of the nation's most successful NCAA Division III programs

23 Varsity Teams

600+ All-Americans

80 Individual and team championships

Top winning percentage nearly every year among all Virginia schools

ADMISSIONS PROCESS

We encourage students to apply to Christopher Newport as early as possible due to our selective admission standards. We anticipate receiving 8,000 applications for only 1,200 spaces in the fall freshman class. Students applying for Early Decision or Early Action will receive priority consideration for admission as well as academic scholarships.

Application Plan	Deadline to Apply	Notification Date
Early Decision	November 15	December 15
Early Action	December 1	January 15
Regular Decision	February 1 March 15	

We're a Common App School! Apply online at freshman.cnu.edu.

Application Review

When reviewing applications we consider each student's academic grades and curriculum, with special attention given to honors, Advanced Placement, International Baccalaureate or dual-enrollment courses. We also look for students who demonstrate leadership ability, a commitment to service and community involvement, exemplary talents, and diverse experiences. As part of the application review, CNU requires a personal statement or essay of no fewer than 250 words to learn more about you, your goals and ideas.

Admission Interviews

Any high school senior planning to apply is strongly encouraged to interview at Christopher Newport. This personal interaction is an important part of the application process. It is a great way to enhance your admission application and receive a personalized introduction to CNU. We want to meet you one-on-one to learn about you—your qualities, experiences and goals we can't discern from your test scores or GPA. An interview is required for Honors and PLP applicants.

CLEMSON UNIVERSITY

AT A GLANCE

One of the country's most selective public research universities, Clemson was founded in 1889 with a mission to be a "high seminary of learning" dedicated to teaching, research and service. Today, these three concepts remain at the heart of the University and provide the framework for an exceptional educational experience.

At Clemson professors take the time to get to know students and explore innovative ways of teaching. Exceptional teaching is one reason our retention and graduation rates rank among the highest in the country for public universities.

Exceptional teaching is also why Clemson continues to attract an increasingly talented student body. In 2016, more than half of the entering freshmen were ranked in the top 10 percent of their high school classes, and the freshman class averaged 1243 on the critical reading and math sections of the SAT.

The University is committed to the success of its students. For the fall 2015 class, Clemson's student retention rate was 92.6 percent. Much of this is due to the Academic Success Center (ASC), established in 2001 and recognized nationally and internationally for its programs in collegiate learning. The ASC is housed in a 35,000-square-foot facility where it offers free one-on-one tutoring services for more than 80 courses as well as for additional courses as the need arises. Peer-Assisted Learning, academic skills workshops and academic coaching are also available—free to all Clemson students. It is estimated that more than 75 percent of freshmen use ASC services during their first semester.

Clemson has also received national recognition for its innovative Communication Across the Curriculum (CAC) program, which makes writing across all curriculums a priority. At Clemson, CAC has become a standard teaching method used in nearly every department to provide real-life challenges that require students to think and communicate effectively.

From cheering on the Tigers at a football game to socializing at the Hendrix Student Center, Clemson students can participate in a wide variety of activities outside the classroom. The more than 400 campus clubs and organizations include fraternities and sororities, as well as honorary, international, military, performing arts, political, professional, religious, service, social interest, special interest, sports and fitness, and student media.

With 19 intercollegiate sports, Clemson offers exciting spectator sports year-round. Clemson is a charter member of the Atlantic Coast Conference and is an NCAA Division I school. Admission to regular-season home events is included in University fees for full-time students.

ADMISSIONS:

864-656-2287

clemson.edu/admissions/undergraduate

Campus Tours:

864-656-4789

clemson.edu/visitors

LOCATION & ENVIRONMENT

Clemson University is located in Clemson, S.C., a town of about 14,000 located in the middle of the I-85 corridor between Atlanta, Ga., and Charlotte, N.C. The 1,400-acre campus is next door to the S.C. Botanical Garden and borders the shores of Hartwell Lake and the foothills of the Blue Ridge Mountains.

OFF-CAMPUS OPPORTUNITIES

Study Abroad

Clemson students are strongly encouraged to incorporate a study-abroad experience in their overall Clemson journey. Programs are available on six continents for all disciplines and interests. These include faculty-led programs, exchange programs and programs available through Clemson's partnerships with study-abroad providers and institutions. Students in a variety of majors also have opportunities at Clemson campuses in South Carolina and around the world, including the Archbold Center in Dominica; the Daniel Center in Genoa, Italy; and the Brussels Center in Belgium.

Cooperative Education

The Cooperative Education program provides an opportunity for students to alternate periods of academic study with semesters of paid, career-related, engaged-learning experiences to bridge the gap between academic study and its application in professional practice. Clemson's career center pairs about 2,200 students annually with companies seeking interns or co-op students. Internships are also available on campus where students can work part- or full-time, with many in full-time positions having the option of earning credit. The Princeton Review ranks Clemson's career services program as the No. 5 career office in the nation.

Community Service

An important aspect of Clemson is its dedication to improving the world through public service. In a typical year, Clemson students contribute over 100,000 service hours, earning the University national recognition on the President's Higher Education Community Service Honor Roll. Opportunities to make a difference are available through student service organizations, ongoing service projects and one-time service events—on campus, in the community, across the nation or around the world. The 2015 National Survey on Student Engagement reports that 61 percent of first-year Clemson students and 94 percent of seniors said "at least some" of their courses included high-impact practices such as service-learning.

MAJORS & DEGREES

Students can select from more than 80 undergraduate and 119 graduate degree programs offered by seven colleges: Agriculture, Forestry and Life Sciences; Architecture, Arts and Humanities; Behavioral, Social and Health Sciences; Business; Education; Engineering, Computing and Applied Sciences; and Science. To find out what majors are available go to: clemson.edu/degrees.

Clemson University is accredited by the Commission on Colleges of the Southern Association of Colleges and Schools to award bachelor's, master's, specialist and doctoral degrees. Questions about the accreditation of Clemson University can be directed to the Commission on Colleges at 1866 Southern Lane, Decatur, Georgia 30033-4097; phone: 404-679-4500.

Honors College

Calhoun Honors College is a Universitywide program that combines the strengths of a public, land-grant university with those of a highly selective small college. Calhoun Scholars may choose to pursue departmental honors within their specific academic discipline. In addition, EUREKA! (Experiences in Undergraduate Research, Exploration and Knowledge Advancement) is a unique and exciting program that enables honors students to pursue research and scholarly activities with faculty members across all disciplines. The advantages of membership in the Honors College include priority registration, extended library loan privileges, honors research grants and a special living-learning community.

The National Scholars Program is a highly selective program for exceptional students who strive to meet their highest intellectual potential. One of its goals is to develop the interests and talents students need to compete for Rhodes, Marshall and Truman scholarships; Fulbright Grants; National Science Foundation Graduate Fellowships; and other prestigious international fellowships. In 2016, seven Clemson students received National Science Foundation Graduate Fellowships. Two recent Clemson graduates received Fulbright grants to conduct research or teach abroad, and one student was named a Goldwater Scholar.

Undergraduate Research

Clemson's Creative Inquiry (CI) program allows undergraduate students to engage in research about problems that spring from their own curiosity, from a professor's challenge or from the pressing needs of the world around them. Team-based investigations are led by a faculty mentor and typically span two to four semesters. Students take ownership of their projects and take the risks necessary to solve problems and get answers. This invaluable experience produces exceptional graduates, capable of thinking critically, solving problems as a team, and communicating and presenting their ideas to others. In 2015-16, 4,917 students participated in 421 CI teams.

Programs for Educational Enrichment and Retention

Clemson's nationally recognized Programs for Educational Enrichment and Retention (PEER) is committed to improving the academic performance of underrepresented students in engineering and science. According to a 2016 survey by the magazine Diverse: Issues In Higher Education, Clemson is the nation's 20th highest producer of African-American undergraduates receiving baccalaureate degrees.

Living-Learning Communities

Living-learning communities offer the chance for students to live and work with others who have similar interests and goals. There are living options for students interested in business, engineering and science, civics and service, honors courses, professional golf management and much more. Recognized as a national model, the communities are designed to help students be more successful by offering on-site advising and academic support, common course assignments, guest speakers, service opportunities and a variety of social activities.

CAMPUS FACILITIES

Fike Recreation Center

Fike is a 200,000-square-foot recreation center that features a fitness atrium complete with a suspended running track that overlooks the indoor courts. It's also equipped with indoor swimming facilities, fitness studios, racquetball courts, state-of-the-art cardio equipment, weights, locker rooms and a climbing wall.

Health Center

Redfern Health Center provides medical services, counseling and psychological services, and health-related programs like alcohol and drug education. It's one of the nation's few on-campus accredited health centers.

Hendrix Student Center

The Hendrix Student Center is the hub of campus activity and is located a step away from most housing. Here you can find people taking a yoga class or enjoying a meal at the food court. It's home to the University bookstore and offers plenty of quiet places to stop and study. It also has a movie theater, ice cream parlor and much more.

Housing

Located within a 10- to 15-minute walk to class, Clemson's 23 residence halls and four apartment communities offer a vast selection of living arrangements.

Information Technology

The University's wireless networking capability lets students communicate with professors and classmates, read online course materials, check email and conduct research—all from their own laptops.

Watt Family Innovation Center

The Watt Family Innovation Center offers a collaborative environment where students can engage with faculty and industry leaders to generate ideas and solve problems. Engineering and technology feature prominently in the 70,000-square-foot space for teaching and research, from the two-story media grid and moveable electronic walls to the lights that automatically sense when someone is in a room.

TUITION, ROOM, BOARD AND FEES

Estimated Costs for 2016-17 Academic Year

S.C Resident Full Time

Tuition and Fees°	$14,708
Room and Board (approximate)	$ 9,144
Books and Supplies (approximate)	$ 1,308
Total	$25,160

Nonresident Full Time

Tuition and Fees°	$34,590
Room and Board (approximate)	$ 9,144
Books and Supplies (approximate)	$ 1,308
Total	$45,042

Other Expenses

Estimated Personal and Transportation Expenses	$3,502
One-time computer cost°°	$1,800

°Assumes health and other mandatory fees (required for all full-time students) and average lab and loan fees.

°°All students are required to own a laptop computer. For details, go to clemson.edu/laptop.

FINANCIAL AID

Each year Clemson awards financial aid in the form of grants, scholarships, loans and part-time employment to more than 18,000 students. Overall, 84 percent of Clemson students receive awards ranging from $500 to all-inclusive cost coverage. Ninety-nine percent of first-time in-state students receive state scholarships. All financial aid is awarded annually, and FAFSA applications for the next year are available in January. Entering freshmen are evaluated on a competitive basis for scholarships using the admission application.

ADMISSIONS

Admission Requirements

In 2016, the University received about 23,506 applications for a fall freshman class of 3,685.

For freshman applicants, the following factors are considered: class standing, standardized test scores (SAT or ACT), high school curriculum, grades and choice of major. All entering freshmen must have completed 4 credits of English, 3 credits of mathematics, 3 credits of laboratory science, 3 credits of a foreign language (in the same language), 3 credits of social sciences, 1 credit of U.S. history, 1 credit of physical education or ROTC, and 1 credit of fine arts.

To be considered for transfer admission, candidates must have completed a full year of college study (a minimum of 30 semester hours or 45 quarter hours of transferable work), earned a cumulative GPA of at least 2.5 on a 4.0 scale (3.0 preferred) and completed freshman-level courses in English, science and mathematics for their intended major at Clemson.

Application deadlines for freshman admission are December 1 (priority date for fall semester), May 1 (fall semester) and December 15 (spring semester). For transfer admissions, the application deadlines are July 1 (fall semester) and December 15 (spring semester).

THE CLEVELAND INSTITUTE OF ART

AT A GLANCE

Cleveland Institute of Art is a premier college of art and design offering 15 BFA majors.

Cleveland Institute of Art is one of the nation's leading accredited independent colleges of art and design. For 135 years, the college has been an educational cornerstone in Cleveland, Ohio, producing competitive graduates who enter the workforce as studio artists, designers, photographers, contemporary craftsmen, and educators.

LOCATION & ENVIRONMENT

Cleveland Institute of Art is located in University Circle, recently named by Forbes Magazine as one of the most beautiful communities in the country. The neighborhood is home to world-renowned cultural, educational, and healthcare institutions and more than 8,000 students.

CAMPUS FACILITIES & EQUIPMENT

The state-of-the-art facilities at the Cleveland Institute of Art provide students with space designed specifically for studying, living, and exhibiting art and design.

CIA's campus is home to the Reinberger Gallery, a gallery space that presents exhibitions, events, and lectures; the Peter B. Lewis Theater, home of CIA's nationally acclaimed Cinematheque film program; the Jessica R. Gund Memorial Library, which has collections specifically developed for the visual artist, designer, and craftsperson; and individual studio spaces for all students once they enter their major during their sophomore year.

CIA's Uptown Residence Hall, home to first-year students, features suites with kitchenettes and two bedrooms connected by a shared workspace. Beyond the suite, students enjoy an onsite print center, free laundry facilities, workout machines, lounges, decks, street-level retail, and fabulous views of MOCA Cleveland, the downtown skyline, and Lake Erie.

Our campus is a creative, friendly environment that allows students to pursue their dreams. Visit our campus and see for yourself.

OFF-CAMPUS OPPORTUNITIES

Cleveland Institute of Art's campus is less than five miles from downtown Cleveland, where you can sample the city's hottest restaurants, take in a music or comedy show, tour independent galleries, take art walks, and visit community festivals. If you're a sports fan, plan on cheering on the Cleveland Indians, Cavaliers, or Browns at their downtown venues.

ACADEMICS

Cleveland Institute of Art offers 15 majors in art, design, craft, and digital media. You enter your major as a sophomore and spend three intense years building skills and mastering techniques. CIA faculty will encourage you to develop a wider perspective by experimenting with media outside your major through interdisciplinary study.

MAJORS & DEGREES OFFERED

At CIA, we've made an academic commitment to helping students build better futures by engaging them in community-based learning, real-world projects, and social practices. We call this commitment Cores + Connections, and it informs our curriculum across all 15 majors. At the core of CIA are academic and studio rigor and an energetic culture of world-class faculty mentorship. Add to that more than 600 connections to external partners and you have a set of collaborative, innovative, and imaginative educational opportunities that you will not find anywhere else.

TUITION, ROOM, BOARD, FEES

Estimated full-time tuition is US$37,980. Estimated fees are $2,681. Housing for incoming first-year students is $8,150 for our Uptown apartment-style Residence Hall, and $4,020 for meal plan.

FINANCIAL AID

Cleveland Institute of Art offers merit and need-based financial aid, as well as federal and state financial aid. 88% of incoming first-year students enrolling for 2015-16 received scholarships. Average financial aid package for 2015-16 was $36,833.

CIA's Office of Financial Aid is committed to helping students find ways to fund their education. Financial aid officers work with students to craft a personalized financial aid package that combines merit and need-based scholarships, federal loans and grants, scholarships, loans, and work study programs.

STUDENT ORGANIZATIONS & ACTIVITIES

With approximately 625 students from around the country and the world, CIA offers a personal educational experience with the benefits of a larger institution. Surrounded by creative-minded friends and mentors, CIA students find inspiration inside and outside of the studio. Students also experience a community full of cultural energy, ethnic neighborhoods, and an accessible downtown, all accessible by public transportation.

When not in the studio, CIA students can enjoy organized activities, annual campus traditions, and various student groups that specialize in topics from academics to religion. Some favorite traditions include late-night breakfasts during finals, the wildly creative Halloween costume party, and the year-end school-wide picnic.

ADMISSIONS PROCESS

To be considered for admission, you must follow the application procedures and criteria below.

1. Complete the application online at cia.edu

2. Submit the $40 application fee. Make checks payable to the Cleveland Institute of Art.

3. Complete a personal statement, in which you describe your purpose for attending a college of art and design, what led you to this decision, and why you have chosen to apply at CIA.

4. Arrange to have your high school transcript sent to the Office of Admissions. If you have successfully completed 24 college credits and attended a regionally accredited college or university full time for a year or more, you do not need to submit a high school transcript.

5. Have one letter of recommendation forwarded to CIA. We suggest this letter be from an art teacher. We also will accept this letter from a counselor or someone who understands your desire to pursue an arts education.

6. Request that SAT or ACT test results be sent to CIA. Our identification numbers are SAT-1152 and ACT-3243. International students whose first language is not English must submit the TOEFL with a minimum score of 550 PBT (paper-based test) or equivalent 213 CBT (computer-based test) or 79 IBT (Internet-based test). We also accept a band score of at least 6.0 on the IELTS or completion of Level 112 of ESL coursework.

7. Submit your portfolio of artwork. All work can be submitted online (cia.slideroom.com) or in CD or DVD form. Your portfolio should consist of no fewer than 12 and no more than 20 pieces of work. Please carefully follow all our portfolio guidelines.

Send all application materials to:

The Office of Admissions

Cleveland Institute of Art

11610 Euclid Avenue

Cleveland, Ohio 44106

Applications can be submitted at any time before the first day of classes and will be considered as long as space is available. However, candidates are encouraged to follow application deadlines to ensure admission to CIA and eligibility for merit scholarships and institutional financial aid. Dates and deadlines can be viewed at http://www.cia.edu/admissions/apply/dates--deadlines.

Applications are welcome from all qualified students. The admissions committee bases its decisions on a careful review of all credentials submitted by the applicant. Acceptance decisions are made without regard to race, color, sex, marital status, age, ethnic or national origin, religion, creed, veteran status, sexual orientation, or physical or mental disability in accordance with federal, state, and local laws.

Visit cia.edu/admissions for more info.

THE COLLEGE OF NEW JERSEY

AT A GLANCE

The College of New Jersey (TCNJ) has created a culture of constant questioning. In small classes, students and faculty members collaborate in a rewarding process. They seek to understand fundamental principles, apply key concepts, reveal new problems and pursue lines of inquiry to gain a fluency of thought in their disciplines. This transformative process is at the core of the educational experience at The College.

In order to enhance student development and empowerment, TCNJ's curriculum is built around Five Signature Experiences which permeate every major within seven academic schools. Small classes prioritizing discussion and inquiry create a Personalized, Rigorous, and Collaborative Learning Environment where students and faculty work side by side in developing skills and applying concepts. Undergraduate Research, Mentored Internships, and Field Experiences give TCNJ students opportunities to get out of the classroom, develop their professional skill sets, and discover exciting career paths and academic endeavors. Passion for civic responsibility and a commitment to Community-Engaged Learning ensures that TCNJ graduates enter the professional world as top-notch scholars and citizens. Opportunities for Global Engagement found on the TCNJ campus and facilitated through internationally recognized study-abroad programs allow students to expand their internal scope and frame their academic goals and achievements in a truly global context. Finally, academic and extracurricular programs designed to foster Leadership Development help students build confidence and decision-making skills that they will need to solve the problems of tomorrow and build a brighter future.

TCNJ admits a diverse class each year full of ambitious students, eager to build on their educational foundations and plunge into new topics. These students will ultimately find a home away from home on campus, and ninety-three percent of first year students will return for their second year. The most successful admits are prepared to steer their own academic pursuits toward post-graduation goals of graduate school, professional training, or satisfying careers.

Prestigious graduate schools, including the University of Pennsylvania, Georgetown Law School, Maxwell School at Syracuse University, NYU Law School, and Harvard, Yale, and Northwestern Universities, routinely welcome TCNJ alumni into their ranks. Eighty-four percent of TCNJ students who apply to medical school and other professional programs are accepted.

Many top corporations recruit TCNJ graduates, providing avenues into rewarding jobs directly after graduation. Other barometers of student success include the 100 percent pass rate of education majors taking the state teacher preparation test and the 96 percent three-year pass rate for nursing students going for their license. The numerous learning opportunities at The College prepare students to prosper in any arena after the conclusion of their undergraduate career.

LOCATION & ENVIRONMENT

Neoclassical Georgian Colonial architecture, meticulous landscaping and intentional design merge to meet the evolving needs of TCNJ students. Students enjoy a campus with 289 acres of trees, lakes, and open spaces within the suburban setting of Ewing Township, New Jersey. Two out of three undergraduate students take part in the on-campus residence hall experience. The residence halls vary in configuration from the communal-style freshman housing to suites and townhouse arrangements for upper class students. The College ensures that on-campus housing is available to all students in their first two years, with out-of-state students guaranteed to receive housing for all four years of study.

Nearby cities, such as Princeton, Trenton, Philadelphia, and New York, allow for abundant entertainment, employment, and social options. Many courses incorporate field trips to New York City or Washington DC.

In 2015, TCNJ completed the first phase of the Campus Town project. Adding an attractive downtown component to an already appealing campus, Campus Town offers students brand new residential opportunities, a pristine Barnes and Noble bookstore and café, and a comprehensive fitness center. Retail and dining establishments such as Panera Bread and Yummy Sushi have been incorporated as well, with additional businesses scheduled to open throughout 2017.

CAMPUS FACILITIES & EQUIPMENT

Learning, like everything else, is contextual. The surroundings in which students learn and the tools they use influence their experience. Not surprisingly, The College supports its educational aspirations with careful attention to the quality of its facilities. In the first decade of the 21st century, more than $250 million in ongoing and new facilities construction has ensured that TCNJ students can continue to thrive in an environment that not only meets their academic, athletic, social and living needs, but extends their reach resulting in higher scholarship, better health and fitness, closer community, and greater comfort.

OFF-CAMPUS OPPORTUNITIES

TCNJ fosters Global Engagement through an extensive international study program, featuring exchange programs in locations as diverse as Johannesburg, London and the University of Santiago. Some students choose to attend one of the 131 available institutions in the U.S., while others venture to one of the 50+ countries offering full-year or semester-long programs.

Mentored internships, both on and off campus, expose students to career options as they gain professional skills. With the college's location in the East Coast's center of corporate activity providing easy access to New York and Philadelphia, many internships are available either for pay or college credit.

Faculty mentors lend their advice and help students locate and procure appropriate opportunities including fellowships, research positions and internships. Students may also use resources at the Career Center to find positions in New York, Philadelphia, or with one of TCNJ's many corporate, government, or research partners located closer to campus.

ACADEMICS

A Liberal Learning Curriculum ensures that all students are grounded in the values of civic responsibility, intellectual and scholarly growth, and that they receive a well-rounded education in the liberal arts.

In 2004, the College completed a transformation of its curriculum requiring students to complete fewer courses, with each course providing a greater level of depth. Today, all courses feature a rigorous, engaging curriculum and contain a significant out-of-class requirement that provides for even more student and faculty interaction.

These small classes enable dialog between students and TCNJ's accomplished teaching staff. This staff is composed of professors with terminal degrees in exclusivity; no courses are taught by graduate students or Teacher's Assistants. The College shapes its curricula and educational experiences around the concept of Personalized, Collaborative, and Rigorous Intellectual Development.

The required First-Year Seminar, the cornerstone of The College's Liberal Learning program, introduces students to the habits of mind and the methodologies of research; it's seminar format of no more than 15 students reinforces the message that students are not to be passive recipients of knowledge but active contributors to their own learning. Liberal Learning requirements are grouped by diversity and community engagement goals that can be self-designed or designated as interdisciplinary concentrations.

Top students may enroll in TCNJ's Honors Program, designed to provide a core curriculum with additional challenges and opportunities for individualized work. Most honors classes take an interdisciplinary approach and encourage collaboration between faculty and students from multiple academic departments and disciplines. Independent study arrangements fall easily within the parameters of the Honors Program, as well.

MAJORS & DEGREES OFFERED

The College of New Jersey hosts seven schools: Arts and Communication; Business; Education; Engineering; Humanities and Social Sciences; Nursing, Health & Exercise Science; and Science. The College offers programs leading to the Bachelor of Arts, Bachelor of Fine Arts, Bachelor of Music, Bachelor of Science, and Bachelor of Science in Nursing degrees.

TCNJ grants degrees in the following majors: Accountancy, African American Studies, Art Education, Art History, Biomedical Engineering, Biology°, Business Administration (specializations in Finance, Interdisciplinary Business, Management, and Marketing), Chemistry°, Civil Engineering, Communication Studies, Computer Engineering, Computer Science, Criminology, Early Childhood Education, Economics° Education of the Deaf and Hard of Hearing, Electrical Engineering, Elementary Education, Engineering Science (students may specialize in Engineering Management or Policy and Society), English°, Health and Exercise Science, Health and Physical Education (teacher preparation K–12), History°, Interactive Multimedia, International Studies, i-STEM (Integrative Science, Technology, Engineering, and Mathematics), Journalism and Professional Writing, Mathematics°, Mechanical Engineering, Music (options in Education and Performance, Nursing, Philosophy, Physics°, Political Science, Psychology, Public Health, Sociology and Anthropology, Spanish°, Special Education, Technology Education/Pre-Engineering (K–12), Urban Education, Visual Arts (options in Fine Arts, Graphic Design, and Lens-Based Art), and Women, Gender, and Sexuality Studies.

°Programs in which students may prepare for teacher certification.

The College also offers a unique Self-Designed major option, catering to students who wish to forge their own academic path.

In addition to full degree programs, students may also choose to complete a minor, in one of the previously mentioned fields or another subject area, such as, Classical Studies, Comparative Literature, Religion, Public Administration, and Communication Disorders.

Specialized Programs:

TCNJ offers a number of 5-year combined Master of Arts in Teaching degrees with dual certification in Elementary Education, and either Special Education, Urban Education, or Deaf and Hard-of-Hearing Education. Students may also enroll in a 7-year B.S./M.D. degree program with the New Jersey Medical School (Newark, NJ) or a 7-year B.S./O.D. degree program with the State University of New York College of Optometry. The College also offers a Medical Careers Advisory Committee for premed students and a Pre-Law Advisement Committee for students planning a career in law. 64 percent of TCNJ undergraduates seeking Admission into Medical School and 88 percent of TCNJ undergraduates seeking Admission into Law School are accepted into their top choice programs. Both of these figures significantly exceed national averages.

TUITION, ROOM, BOARD, FEES

As a public institution with a smaller, intimate community, TCNJ's costs are lower than most equivalent private institutions. The tuition and fees for undergraduates in the 2016-2017 academic year are as follow:

In-state tuition and fees: $15,793

Out-of-state tuition and fees: $26,971

Room and board (all students): $12,881

FINANCIAL AID

Close to 50 percent of full-time undergraduates benefit from financial aid, whether from merit-based scholarships, work-study programs, loans, or government/institutional grants. All students seeking financial aid at the state or federal level must submit the Free Application for Federal Student Aid (FAFSA) form or renewal FAFSA to apply. The Title IV FAFSA Code for The College is 002642.

TCNJ also offers institutional need-based scholarships. Institutional need-based aid considerations are made based on information from the FAFSA.

Students may compete for the College's merit scholarships. These awards are offered to those applicants with top SAT/ACT scores and class rankings.

STUDENT ORGANIZATIONS & ACTIVITIES

Classroom learning at TCNJ is complemented by an extensive and acclaimed Leadership Development Program. Life outside the classroom is not something TCNJ students do on the side. It is an extension of the learning experience. At every turn from the first year on, students blur the boundary between living and learning, closing the gap between "scholar" and "citizen."

More than 250 student organizations flourish at The College of New Jersey. Anyone can find an intramural sports team, Greek organization, cultural club, or academic group to suit their interests. Many students build friendships and enrich their leisure time participating in these groups. In addition, the College Union Board-administered by TCNJ students-organizes events including concerts, performances, and comedy nights.

The College's highly successful Division III athletic programs also provide an opportunity to socialize and cheer on fellow classmates. TCNJ fields ten sports for men and ten for women. With more than 40 national titles, The College holds the record for the highest number of championship and runner-up titles since Division III was implemented in 1979. For those looking for something a little less competitive, intramural and club sports, including flag football, volleyball, softball, floor hockey, and basketball, have thriving coed leagues of their own. Intramural and club teams play in state, regional, and national tournaments.

ADMISSIONS PROCESS

The Admissions Committee at TCNJ accepts a class of motivated, ambitious, and highly talented students. Most successful applicants have taken at least 16 college-preparatory units in high school, demonstrating mastery of the core academic areas of Science, Math, Language Arts, Social Sciences, and Foreign Languages. They also show impressive class ranks and SAT/ACT scores. Most students admitted fall within the top 10 percent of their graduating class. The committee also considers extracurricular involvement, individual pursuits, and community participation. Standardized test scores are not required for students applying into the Art, Music or Interactive Multimedia disciplines.

The College of New Jersey is a member of the Common Application. The deadline for applications for Spring enrollment is November 1. The Regular Decision application deadline for Fall enrollment is February 1. There is a $75 application fee. Candidates who apply only to The College of New Jersey under the Early Decision agreement may apply before November 1 and will be notified on or before December 1. Early Decision applicants unable to complete and submit their application prior to November 1 may also choose to applyup until January 1 and receive notification on or before February 1. Students applying to the seven-year Accelerated Medical program must apply by December 1. For Fall enrollment, the College requires incoming students to pay an enrollment deposit of $600 no later than May 1.

For more information, students should contact:

Office of Admissions

The College of New Jersey

PO Box 7718

Ewing, NJ 08628-0718

Telephone: 609-771-2131

Website: http://www.tcnj.edu

DAEMEN COLLEGE

AT A GLANCE

Daemen is a private college located in suburban Amherst, NY. With over 50 majors, Daemen offers students a creative balance between programs providing career preparation and education in the liberal arts.

Daemen College is a private, non-sectarian, co-educational, comprehensive college located in Amherst, NY. Our suburban location offers convenient access to metropolitan Buffalo. Committed to an academic atmosphere that leads to open inquiry and debate, Daemen has achieved a creative balance between programs providing career preparation and education in the liberal arts. Programs in the major and the competency-based core curriculum encourage students to expand their horizons beyond the classroom through internships, service learning, clinical and field experiences, collaborative research with faculty, and study abroad. Daemen is distinguished by a low student/faculty ratio and consistently small class sizes, which encourage students to interact with professors and grow as individuals. Daemen has approximately 2,000 undergraduate and 1,000 graduate students.

LOCATION & ENVIRONMENT

Daemen's beautiful 39-acre campus is located in Amherst, NY, a peaceful suburb of Buffalo. Due to its proximity to Buffalo, Daemen's campus is close to many major rail, plane, and motor routes. While the campus setting is tranquil and residential, Buffalo is a vibrant cultural city, bustling with world-class entertainment, such as the Philharmonic Orchestra, the Albright-Knox Art Gallery, and Shea's Theater. The greater Buffalo area is rich with sports and recreational activities all year round, whether it be skiing and swimming, or watching our professional sports teams. Niagara Falls is only 30 minutes away and Toronto is just two hours by car. On campus, the numerous trees and open green spaces create a lovely environment to work and study.

CAMPUS FACILITIES & EQUIPMENT

Modern apartment-style residence halls provide separate housing for male and female students, in addition to our existing five-story residence hall. All residence halls have kitchens, laundry facilities, and lounges. Full-service meals are served in the main dining hall, with an a la carte selection in the snack bar. The recreation room and The Den are popular spots for socializing and relaxing during the day or evening.

The Research and Information Commons is a technological showcase that has become the hub of academic research, as well as the academic and social heart of the campus.

The Haberman Gacioch Center for Visual & Performing Arts is a dramatic space which features The Peter and Elizabeth C. Tower Gallery, studios for animation, illustration, figure drawing and painting, graphic design production area, computer labs, faculty offices and the Sr. Jeanne File Art History Resource Center. The building was designed with green technology and uses geothermal heating to contain energy costs.

Patricia E. Curtis Hall houses Physician Assistant, Psychology, and Social Work offices.

The Academic and Wellness Center, a multi-use building, is located across from Daemen's Main Street campus, providing 25,000 square feet of educational classrooms and lab areas primarily for the physical therapy, athletic training, and health promotion programs, as well as student lounges, office space, and indoor recreational and fitness space for the Daemen community.

OFF-CAMPUS OPPORTUNITIES

Daemen's Office of Community Engagement empowers students to engage in co-curricular activities in the real world to connect their education outside of the classroom.

The Career Services team offers a variety of services to assist students across all academic disciplines, as well as a lifetime resource to alumni in all phases of their career decision-making and job search. Career Services helps students find an internship so that they can gain real-world experience in their area of interest. Students often express how prepared they feel to have had the chance to experience what careers in their fields are really like. An added bonus, internship employers sometimes offer Daemen interns full-time positions after graduation. The opportunities are local, national, or international including opportunities with the Washington Internship Institute. Each year Career Services brings employers to campus for career and internship fairs.

Global Programs coordinates distinctive study abroad opportunities designed to facilitate students' professional aspirations. International study is a staple of the Daemen experience. In today's global economy, it makes sense to learn all you can about different cultures, political systems, and histories. An international experience is beneficial whether it's a week, semester, or even a year. Students have studied in Australia, China, Costa Rica, England, France, Greece, Italy, Mexico, and many other countries.

Daemen believes in "learning through service." Each academic year, nearly 500 Daemen students contribute over 30,000 volunteer hours to make a difference in the lives of youth, families, and communities. In the process, students serve, learn, and gain the leadership, cross-cultural, and communication skills necessary to become civic-minded individuals prepared to participate in a democratic society. Students can choose from a variety of service-learning courses and site placements in settings that include Boys & Girls Clubs, community centers, soup kitchens, housing rehabilitation and refugee resettlement agencies, shelters for the homeless, nursing homes, and many other health and human service agencies.

ACADEMICS

Daemen College is committed to complementing the depth of study in a major field with a well-rounded academic understanding in the liberal arts. The College's core curriculum ensures that every student graduates with the following seven core competencies: critical thinking and creative problem solving; communication skills; information and literacy; civic responsibility; contextual competency; affective awareness; and moral and ethical discernment. This innovative core curriculum competes with those of Ivy League Institutions and prepares the student in a holistic manner which not only makes them more marketable upon graduation but instructs them on alternative ways of approaching education and learning.

Daemen provides students with small classes and a caring and committed faculty, allowing for a personalized educational experience. Academics at Daemen will challenge you to test your knowledge, raise your expectations, and think critically and creatively. Daemen's core competencies, honors program, academic exchanges, global programs, and undergraduate research are just a few examples of what makes the College challenging and distinctive.

Daemen students are well-prepared for professional success. The vast majority obtain a professional position or admission to graduate study in less than a year after graduation. They are leaders in their communities, with a strong dedication to the improvement of the communities in which they live.

MAJORS & DEGREES OFFERED

Daemen College offers BA, BFA, BS, MS, MPH, MSW and DPT programs.

Majors offered at Daemen include: Accounting BS/MS, Animation, Art; Applied Theater, Drawing, Graphic Design, Illustration, Painting, Sculpture, Visual Arts Education K-12, Arts Administration BS/MS, Athletic Training BS/MS, Biology; Adolescence Education 7-12, Environmental Studies, Biology/Cytotechnology BS/MS, Biochemistry: Pre-Professional, Business Administration; Human Resource Management, International Business, Marketing, Sport Management, Business Administration/International Business BS/MS, Education; Adolescence Special Education 7-12, Childhood Education 1-6, Childhood Education/ Special Education1-6, Early Childhood Education/Special Education B-12, English; Adolescence Education 7-12, Professional Writing and Rhetoric Specialization, French; Adolescence Education 7-12, Health Promotion; Community Health, Complementary and Alternative Health Care Practices, Health and Fitness, Health Promotion/Public Health BS/MS, History, History and Political Science; Adolescence Education 7-12, Environmental Studies, Mathematics; Adolescence Education 7-12, Natural Sciences; Environmental Studies, Forensic Science, Health Science, Nursing, Paralegal, Physical Therapy BS,NS/DPT, Physician Assistant BS/MS, Political Science, Psychology, Religious Studies, Social Work, Spanish; Adolescence Education 7-12, Sustainability (Global and Local), Pre-Professional Programs; Pre-Dentistry, Pre-Law, Pre-Medicine, Pre-Pharmacy and Pre-Veterinary.

Graduate MS programs include Athletic Training, Arts Administration, Education: Special Education 1-6, Executive Leadership and Change, International Business, Nursing, Physical Therapy; OPMT Fellowship/MS, Physician Assistant, Public Health MPH, and Social Work MSW.

Doctorate programs include Doctor of Nursing Practice and Direct Entry Doctor of Physical Therapy.

TUITION, ROOM, BOARD, FEES

Tuition for the 2016-2017 academic year is $26,400, with additional fees of $540. Room and board are approximate $12,125. (Cost varies according to meal plan and residence facility.)

FINANCIAL AID

Daemen strives to create individualized financial aid packages for you and your family that will meet your needs and enable you to get the most out of your college education. Daemen offers merit-based scholarships and need-based financial assistance. More than 95% of current students receive some form of financial assistance. Daemen participates in all federal and state programs.

Learning to navigate the financial aid system can be a daunting task. That's why Daemen has trained professionals on hand to assist you every step of the way. The Admissions staff and Financial Aid counselors will assist you and your family with the process and will ensure you understand the necessary paperwork and deadlines required in order for you to receive the best financial aid package available.

STUDENT ORGANIZATIONS & ACTIVITIES

Student activities provide for the development of the whole person outside of the classroom. The Director of Student Activities on campus helps students participate in recognized organizations, form new ones, and plan events. With over 60 student organizations the possibilities for involvement at Daemen are limitless. Whether your interests are in art or skiing, there is bound to be something that grabs your interest and introduces you to students who share similar passions. Daemen believes that now is the time to discover exactly who you are; cultivating your hidden talents, taking new risks and challenging yourself to grow are all part of the Daemen experience. Daemen encourages all students to become actively engaged in the campus community.

Athletics

Daemen Athletics is an NCAA Division II member of the East Coast Conference. Wildcat Athletics sponsors 16 teams including: men's and women's basketball, soccer, tennis, cross country, track and field, men's golf, women's volleyball, bowling, and triathlon. Students have the opportunity to participate in recreation and intramural programs, and competitive club sports.

ADMISSIONS PROCESS

The average student enrolled has a 91 GPA and 1060 SAT. Daemen has a rolling admissions policy.

The admissions staff helps guide students through the process from start to finish.

Prospective students can apply for free online at daemen.edu/apply or commonapp.org.

Vist us on the web at daemen.edu or take a virtual tour at daemen.edu/virtualtour.

The best way to get to know Daemen is in person. On your visit, we'll take you on a campus tour, arrange for you to meet professors and current students, and plan a one-on-one meeting with an Admissions counselor. To schedule your appointment, contact the Office of Admissions at 800-462-7652 or 716-839-8225. You may make an individual visit Mon-Sat, attend our Fall and Spring Open Houses, or join us for many of our other special admissions events. We hope to see you on campus soon! If you have any questions you can email us at admissions@daemen.edu

DESALES UNIVERSITY

AT A GLANCE

DeSales University is a medium-sized, Catholic liberal arts university for men and women administered by the Oblates of St. Francis de Sales

Founded in 1964, DeSales University is a Catholic liberal arts university that offers courses in a wide range of disciplines. DeSales provides personal attention, small class size, and a feeling of community. The University uses a holistic approach to help students develop a "sense of self," enabling all students to reach their personal and academic potential. This student-centered philosophy is conveyed by an enthusiastic, accessible faculty.

LOCATION & ENVIRONMENT

DeSales University's suburban campus is located 15 minutes south of Bethlehem and Allentown, Pa., and only 1 hour from Philadelphia, 90 minutes from Scranton and Wilkes-Barre, Pa., less than 2 hours from New York City, and 3 hours from Baltimore. The campus is 500 acres with more than 16 major buildings.

CAMPUS FACILITIES & EQUIPMENT

Trexler Library has a collection of more than 500,000 items and there are electronic databases of newspapers, journal articles, and the Oxford Dictionary of National Biography. There are computer and multimedia labs and a staff who will help with any research topic. Trexler Library has wireless access both with personal laptops or laptops that can be borrowed to use in the building. The Library's resources can be accessed from anywhere on campus. There is online access to databases and full-text journal articles. Students can also instant message a librarian with a question.

The DeSales University Center features many menu choices—especially for healthy eaters—in a foodcourt setting. The University Center also has wireless laptop capability so you can eat and surf, as well as see panoramic views of campus.

The Priscilla Payne Hurd Science Center, a 37,500-square-foot facility, is equipped with up-to-date computers, labs, and medical equipment. The Hurd Science Center also features a sterile molecular/cell biology suite, complete with a freezer room, bench room, support room, dark room, and instrument room. An ecology/environmental lab with a growing chamber, an analytical/physical chemistry/inorganic laboratory, and a bioinformatics/physics lab also inhabit the two-story building.

The Gambet Center for Business and Health Care Education is a 77,000 square foot academic building that houses the school's business division and health care majors. It features a simulated trading room for business and finance majors, standardized patient areas, and a gross anatomy lab.

OFF-CAMPUS OPPORTUNITIES

Allentown and Bethlehem are a short 15-minute drive from campus and offer many dining, shopping, and outdoor activities, including the Promenade Shops at Saucon Valley, just minutes from campus. The Lehigh Valley, aka "College Valley," boasts beautiful hiking and biking trails, historic sites, museums, cultural festivals, and Dorney Park and Wildwater Kingdom. Skiing at nearby Blue Mountain and other Pocono resorts is just a short drive away. The Poconos also offer white water rafting trips down the Lehigh and Delaware Rivers.

ACADEMICS

DeSales University defines "global competence" as using an open, inquisitive mind to understand the norms and expectations of other cultures, and using this acquired knowledge to communicate and to work effectively outside of one's usual environment in the promotion of human solidarity. DeSales University presents opportunities for students to enlarge their world view, from activities and concerts to short and long-term study abroad programs.

Study abroad programs through DeSales present the opportunity for our students to live and work in this vibrantly interdependent world, and range from semester-long study to short-stay travel of 10 days. Our students can spend semesters in England, Greece, Italy, Ireland, Switzerland, France, Australia, and Monte Carlo. More importantly, DeSales uses a model of intense hands-on engagement through short-stay co-curricular trips of students, faculty, and staff. Trips to Ireland, Germany, Istanbul, South Africa, and Austria for short-stay intensive travel have been combined with academic courses, the activities of student organizations, or out-of-season competition for our athletic teams.

Freshman students are asked to participate in the Character U program, a self-assessment program based on the Golden Counsels of St. Francis de Sales. Each month, University programming addresses one of these Golden Counsels or traits including patience, trust and cooperation, and perseverance. The DeSales Experience offers opportunities to learn and lead outside the classroom.

The University's Academic Resource Center can offer assistance in reading comprehension, study skills, time management, and effective writing techniques. Additionally, they can help find a tutor if you need it or provide you with the opportunity to become a peer tutor.

CAREER SERVICES & PLACEMENT

The Career Development Center can help students strategically showcase skills and stand out from a sea of competitors. The Center starts early by helping students define goals and make the right major and career choices. Job shadowing, learning to network, practice for interviews, and preparing resumes are all part of the process.

MAJORS

DeSales University offers more than 35 bachelor's degrees including 8 pre-professional programs, and 8 graduate programs through the divisions of business, liberal arts and social sciences, performing arts, natural sciences, and health care. Our more popular majors include criminal justice, theatre, medical studies, and business administration.

The newest majors are economics, health communication, healthcare administration, homeland security, and supply chain management. New tracks within the business department include financial planning and supply chain management.

Special Programs

At DeSales, qualified business, nursing, criminal justice, and computer science majors have an option to earn both a bachelor's degree and a master's degree in five years. Qualified health science or medical studies majors are guaranteed an interview into the doctor of physical therapy program or the graduate physician assistant program respectively. Criminal Justice majors have an opportunity to receive Pennsylvania Act 120 training, which is required to become a police officer or state trooper in the state of Pennsylvania. The Act 120 training is included in the student's undergraduate tuition.

DeSales also has an Exploratory Studies Program, a structured program that helps students determine his or her major. This program includes a 3-credit course called Major Decision Making that will introduce different majors while fulfilling an elective requirement for graduation. Another exploratory course—Career Development and Planning—is available in the spring semester.

TUITION, ROOM, BOARD, FEES

Tuition and Fees (2017-18): $34,500

Room and Board: $12,592

Student & Technology Fee: $1,600

Total: $48,692

FINANCIAL AID

Nine out of 10 DeSales University students receive financial aid in the form of grants, scholarships, work study, and loans. About 85% of the students receive grants directly from DeSales University, and funds are also available from federal and state programs to those who qualify. The amount of aid received and the composition of an aid package will depend on financial need and on academic achievement and potential.

Academic scholarships are also available through DeSales University. All applicants for admission are automatically considered for each of the scholarships offered by the University.

Students can also compete for one of six full-tuition Leadership Scholarships by writing an essay about leadership and service experience and, if selected, participating in an interview.

STUDENT ORGANIZATIONS & ACTIVITIES

There are approximately 1,600 full-time undergraduate students and about 65% live on campus. The male to female ratio is 43% to 57%. More than 11% of our undergraduate students are Hispanic and 8.6% are American minorities. Our students come to DeSales from 28 states and 5 other countries with many coming from Pennsylvania.

DeSales University has more than 30 campus organizations, including the Student Activities crew, which helps plan student events, bus trips, and on-campus performances. The McShea Student Union includes a student activities lounge open to students for entertainment and socializing and a café that offers another dining option in the form of a Sandella's Cafe. The McShea Student Union has been renovated to accommodate increased special events such as independent movie nights, comedians, music acts, and expanded space for programs sponsored by various student organizations.

DeSales University has 19 intercollegiate varsity sports teams and all are members of the NCAA Division III, Middle Atlantic States Collegiate Athletic Corporation (MAC) Freedom Conference, and the Eastern College Athletic Conference (ECAC).

The University's men's sports are baseball, basketball, cross-country, golf, lacrosse, soccer, tennis, and indoor and outdoor track and field. Women's sports are basketball, cross-country, field hockey, lacrosse, soccer, softball, indoor and outdoor track and field, tennis, and volleyball. The University also has club sports, including cheerleading, cycling, disc golf, equestrian, ice hockey, and men's volleyball.

There are intramural sports for all seasons, or student can visit the Billera Hall fitness center, which offers aerobic, Nautilus, and free-weight training.

ADMISSIONS PROCESS

To Apply for Admission you need to:

Complete a DeSales University application and submit it to our Admissions Office.

Have your high school guidance department send your official high school transcript to our Admissions Office.

Have your standardized test scores (SAT or ACT) sent to our Admissions Office. Our code number for SAT scores is 2021. Submitting SAT or ACT test scores is strongly encouraged but not required for the following majors: dance, early childhood education, exploratory studies (undeclared), marriage & family studies, philosophy, psychology, Spanish, sport management, and theology. Students who don't submit test scores will need to have a personal interview with the admissions office.

Have a guidance counselor and teacher complete the recommendation forms and send to our Admissions Office.

DIGIPEN INSTITUTE OF TECHNOLOGY

AT A GLANCE

DigiPen Institute of Technology is an educational leader in the teaching and advancement of the arts and computer sciences as applied to the world of game and software development. As the first school in the world to offer a bachelor's degree in game simulation technology, DigiPen has advanced the digital entertainment industry by preparing students to become skilled artists, designers, and engineers.

Through a combined academic focus on both theory and application, students graduate with a deep foundational knowledge of their chosen field and a portfolio of work that is demonstrative of their practical and creative capabilities. DigiPen alumni have proven to be among the most sought-after employees in the games industry and beyond. In addition to being credited on well over 1,000 popular game titles over the last 20 years, they continue to advance the boundaries of what technology can accomplish.

LOCATION & ENVIRONMENT

DigiPen's campus is located in Redmond, Washington, a global hub for game and software development. The region is home to more than 350 interactive media companies, including tech industry giants like Microsoft, Nintendo, Amazon, and several more.

Situated about 15 miles east of Seattle, the Redmond area is home to much more than a wide range of successful economic enterprises. It's a renowned center of artistic excellence, cultural diversity, and beautiful outdoor surroundings.

DigiPen also operates at two international campuses in Singapore and Bilbao, Spain.

CAMPUS FACILITIES & EQUIPMENT

Students at DigiPen go beyond the textbook—putting knowledge and theory into daily practice through extensive project coursework that brings together multiple areas of study including art, music, design, and computer science. As such, the DigiPen campus features several dedicated lab spaces, including:

- Two large-scale production labs dedicated to game project teams.

- Two music and sound labs, complete with recording studio, instrument practice rooms, and digital audio workstations.

- A Nintendo console development lab with special access to licensed software development kits.

- A computer engineering lab.

- An MFA computer lab.

- Numerous game lab spaces for prototyping and play testing projects, from board games to video games.

As a testing ground for new ideas, DigiPen students regularly work and experiment with emerging technologies, such as virtual and augmented reality devices. Thanks to industry connections with local technology companies, DigiPen students have been among the first to get their hands on software development kits for products like the HTC Vive, Microsoft HoloLens, and more. Compared to most institutions, DigiPen provides its students with an unparalleled depth of hands-on experience that—combined with their solid knowledge base—gives them a competitive edge when beginning their careers.

In addition to DigiPen's lab and classroom spaces, the DigiPen campus library houses a vast collection of print and digital materials, including books, periodicals, films, and a growing catalogue of over 500 video games and game console equipment—an exceptional resource both for study and amusement.

OFF-CAMPUS OPPORTUNITIES

DigiPen's close proximity to hundreds of game and technology companies doesn't just benefit students after they graduate. It allows them to tap into a deep well of industry experience and begin building their professional network even before they graduate, thanks to a wealth of local off-campus events and internship opportunities.

DigiPen's internship program is a carefully monitored work experience in which students learn about their discipline in a professional development studio under the supervision of an industry veteran. DigiPen interns have earned their names in the credits of published AAA game titles, taken part in Microsoft research projects, and even assisted in the development of the Nintendo Wii controller.

Outside of the classroom, students can take advantage of a mix of fun activities throughout Redmond and the greater Seattle area. At the annual PAX West, a gaming expo that draws tens of thousands of visitors each year, DigiPen students plan, set up, and operate a student game arcade booth where they demo their academic projects to attendees—in the same venue as some of the largest game publishers in the world. The region is also home to other annual events, such as the Emerald City Comicon, Bumbershoot, GeekGirlCon, and more.

ACADEMICS

DigiPen's degree programs give students a comprehensive understanding of the academic fundamentals of their field while preparing them with the skills that will allow them to thrive in a professional environment.

While many schools tout their programs as being "interdisciplinary," the concept of an integrated curriculum is more than a buzzword at DigiPen—it's a central component of what students experience every day on campus. Beginning with a strong focus on foundational theory, each program at DigiPen challenges students to apply what they learn in the classroom toward intensive, sometimes year-long projects. Whether working on games, animations, or computer hardware devices, students put their knowledge into practice in a results-driven studio environment where they quickly learn the value of teamwork and communications. By working alongside their peers from other degree programs, students begin to think beyond the boundaries of their individual areas of study and to "speak the language" of the other disciplines. This cooperative method allows them to achieve the kind of standout student work that would be impossible to accomplish alone and prepares them for the challenges and realities of working in the professional industries after they graduate.

By the time they complete their degrees, students are equipped with a portfolio of work that can help them stand out to prospective employers, as well as the industry connections needed to jump-start their job search. More importantly, they leave with a depth of knowledge and experience that allows them to meaningfully contribute to their team from day one on the job.

FACULTY EXPERTISE

DigiPen faculty instructors come from a wide range of academic and professional backgrounds. From Ph.D. professors who have worked on Nobel-prize winning physics projects to instructors who cut their teeth on classic video games and blockbuster films, these faculty members bring to the classroom a unique blend of both scholarly and commercial expertise. Instructors at DigiPen are dedicated teachers whose primary motivation is to impart their years of knowledge to a new generation of creators and innovators. And with an impressive student-to-faculty ratio of 11:1, DigiPen students are able to receive individual mentorship and guidance.

MAJORS & DEGREES OFFERED

DigiPen offers eight bachelor's programs and two master's degree programs in fields relating to computer science and engineering, as well as art, music, and design.

Computer Science

BS in Computer Science in Real-Time Interactive Simulation

BS in Computer Science and Game Design

BS in Computer Science and Digital Audio

BS in Computer Science

MS in Computer Science

Art, Music, and Design

BFA in Digital Art and Animation

BA in Game Design

BA in Music and Sound Design

MFA in Digital Arts

Engineering

BS in Computer Engineering (an ABET-accredited program)

TUITION, ROOM, BOARD, FEES

Tuition for the 2017-18 academic year is $29,800, which covers the cost of 32-44 course credits per year and access to all of DigiPen's on-campus facilities and support services. There is no additional tuition cost for out-of-state students. Housing and meals, for students living in a DigiPen Housing apartment, costs an estimated $11,375. Administrative fees are $200 per year.

FINANCIAL AID

There are several types of financial aid available for students who qualify. DigiPen's Office of Financial Aid is ready to help by connecting students with a range of financial resources, including:

- Scholarships
- Grants
- Loans
- Federal Work Study
- Veterans Benefits

For the 2015-16 academic year, approximately 67% of DigiPen students received financial assistance in the form of scholarships, state grants, and federal grants and loans. The average scholarship awarded that year was $8,430.

DigiPen is committed to helping all students make the most of their financial investment by providing the resources needed to succeed, including one-on-one financial aid counseling, to help make the costs of attendance affordable.

ON-CAMPUS EMPLOYMENT

In addition to offering Federal Work Study for students who qualify, DigiPen also provides a number of on-campus employment opportunities. Students can earn income and work experience by applying to student job openings in several academic and administrative departments on campus. Each summer, DigiPen employs hundreds of current students to work as teachers and teaching assistants for DigiPen's ProjectFUN youth education programs for students in grades 1-12.

STUDENT ORGANIZATIONS & ACTIVITIES

The student body at DigiPen is a tight-knit community of people who share a passion for games, art, and technology. Students thrive on teamwork, creativity, and a spirit of learning—both in and out of the classroom.

Despite being a small school, DigiPen has attracted an amazing community of students who have come to campus from nearly 50 countries. DigiPen is committed to fostering a diverse campus culture that is welcoming and supportive to students of all backgrounds.

A Lasting Network

The shared experience among students doesn't end at graduation. It's not uncommon for DigiPen alumni to be working together as professionals as well, either at major technology companies or at small, entrepreneurial startups. Some DigiPen graduates have also continued to give back to their alma mater by participating in the DigiPen Alumni Mentorship Program, helping current students to effectively prepare for the transition from college to career.

Campus Support Systems

At any time during their education, DigiPen students do not have to look far to receive the support they need. Students have access to a wealth of on-campus services, such as:

- Professional mental health counseling
- Disability support services
- Peer tutors and advisors
- Academic and faculty advisors

While the demands of DigiPen's curriculum can be intense, students also have plenty of ways to relax, unwind, and explore new interests and activities. From organizing clubs and social events to participating in the Student Senate leadership group, students join together to create a vibrant and inclusive campus community.

Speaking of student clubs, there are several to choose from, with brand new groups springing up each year. For those drawn to the friendly competition of Pokémon Club or for anyone looking to become educated on LGBTQ issues through DigiPen's PRISM (People Respecting Individuals and Sexual Minorities) club, these and other campus groups provide a great way to connect with fellow students outside the classroom.

ADMISSIONS PROCESS

DigiPen works on a rolling-admissions basis. Applications for admission are accepted year-round, and those who apply can typically expect to be notified of the college's decision within two to four weeks of submitting their application. You can learn more about DigiPen's specific admissions requirements, which vary by degree program, on the college's website.

Because applicants must select their degree program prior to enrolling, DigiPen encourages all of its prospective students to do as much research as possible before applying. Prospective students can learn more by visiting the website, requesting information, or participating in an on-campus or online informational event.

DigiPen Pre-College Program

DigiPen's Pre-College Program is an intensive college preparatory experience for students who have completed their sophomore, junior, or senior year of high school. Designed for students with strong academic aspirations, this program provides a glimpse into the DigiPen college experience and is an ideal introduction for students who may be interested in attending the Institute. Taught by DigiPen faculty over a four-week period during the summer, the Pre-College Program not only exposes students to DigiPen's academic coursework but also requires students to work together on multidisciplinary project teams.

DRAKE UNIVERSITY

AT A GLANCE

Drake University's unique size creates a distinctive learning environment that offers a broad-based liberal arts education, while its location in the state's center for business, publishing, government, and culture allows for unmatched professional preparation.

Drake University is widely regarded as one of the top ranking master's institutions, both in the Midwest and nationally, for academic quality and value. Drake enrolls a heterogeneous group of nearly 5300 students, from 49 states and more than 50 foreign countries. Drake's unique size creates a distinctive learning environment that offers a broad-based liberal arts education, while its location in the state's center for business, publishing, government, and culture allows for unmatched professional preparation. Students thrive within an intellectual environment offering more than 70 majors, covering subjects from the liberal arts to professional and pre-professional programs. Drake prides itself on alumni success, noting that 99% percent of 2016 Drake graduates embarked on careers or started graduate programs during their first six months out of school. Drake University is ranked #1 on the Federal College Scorecard for an average alumni salary of $55,700 within 10 years of enrollment.

The Drake Commitment

Drake provides the life-defining opportunities that a student needs to launch into a career, service, or graduate school through the Drake Commitment, which provides students with personal mentorship with professors, learning through service on a local, national, and global scale, an academic flexibility to explore interests, and the development of an exceptional resume through high-caliber internships.

LOCATION & ENVIRONMENT

Students take advantage of Drake's location in Des Moines, Iowa, the state capital and a thriving business center. Internships are available in fields such as government, banking, insurance, publishing, nonprofit organizations, and health care, and nearly over 90 percent of students participate in at least one internship during their four years at the University..

CAMPUS FACILITIES & EQUIPMENT

Students have access to the Cowles Library and its more than more than 600,000 books and journals, 100,000 federal and state government documents, 777,000 microform records, 118 electronic databases, and approximately 22,000 scholarly online journals. The collections also include DVDs and music CDs, as well as a digital repository of scholarship and historical material unique to Drake. In addition, many classes utilize the resources in specialized collections in the Law School, College of Pharmacy and Health Sciences, Center for Teacher Education, and School of Fine Arts. Between the Dwight D. Opperman Hall and Law Library, there are 330,000 volumes, along with computer labs and study facilities. The Studio Theater, the Monroe Recital Hall, and the Hall of the Performing Arts are housed in the Harmon Fine Arts Center. Another performance hall, Sheslow Auditorium with a capacity of 755 seats, is located in Old Main. The Bell Center offers a gym, pool, aerobic dance room, fitness room, basketball, volleyball, and badminton courts. A student-only fitness facility is also located in the student union. Additional athletic facilities are available in the Knapp Center, such as racquetball, volleyball and basketball courts, a jogging track, and a weight room. More than 7,000 people can congregate in Knapp for major events. Basketball courts and a track are available at the Fieldhouse, while the Tennis Center provides six indoor and six outdoor tennis courts. In 2015, Drake University is breaking ground on a $65 million dollar STEM complex.

OFF-CAMPUS OPPORTUNITIES

Many students take advantage of overseas studies options offered through the Center for International Programs and Services, which includes semester and yearlong programs offered in more than 60 countries. In addition, Drake students are encouraged, through the Drake Commitment, to explore interests through a January Term (three week) course— with no added tuition cost. January Term courses often have travel seminar components.

VISITING CAMPUS

Drake University welcomes prospective students to Drake Monday-Friday for individual visits, which include a campus tour led by a current student and a counselor appointment. Opportunities to meet with faculty in your field or dine on campus may be requested, limited to availability of schedules. In addition, Drake University offers a variety of campus visit programs each fall, spring, and summer. Check upcoming visit options and register for a visit at www.drake.edu/visit.

ACADEMICS

From their first classes on the Drake campus, students have the chance to learn in an individualized, challenging, and supportive environment. Research opportunities abound; students work closely with their professors and often publish their findings. With more than 160 student-run organizations on campus, there is an outlet for students to investigate career paths and network with professionals in their field.

Students benefit from a combination of liberal arts training and professional preparation. Through the Drake Curriculum, all students take interactive classes that develop their critical thinking and expressive skills. Students also receive personalized academic advising. At the end of their four years, students undertake the Senior Capstone, which is a research project, thesis, or other major work that shows the concepts and skills the student has acquired at Drake. Drake's Honors Program is open to top students who wish to undertake a rigorous, interdisciplinary course of study.

MAJORS & DEGREES OFFERED

College of Arts and Sciences:

Those studying in the College of Arts and Sciences receive a classic liberal arts education, preparing them for futures in science, mathematics, politics, and the arts, among many other areas. Students may earn their Bachelor of Arts and Bachelor of Science degrees in the following areas: anthropology and sociology; astronomy; biochemistry, cell and molecular biology; biology; chemistry; computer science; data analytics; English;; environmental science; history; international relations; kinesiology, law, politics, and society; mathematics; mathematics education (secondary); neuroscience; philosophy; physics; politics; psychology; religion; rhetoric and communication studies; sociology; study of culture and society; sustainability and resilience; and writing. Some students design their own majors, while others opt for open enrollment and do not immediately declare a major. The University also administers pre-professional study in dentistry, engineering, law, medicine and veterinary medicine. Concentrations are available in anthropology, geography, Latin American studies, animal behavior, women's and gender studies, zoo and conservation science, and most fields that offer majors.

Students who attend the School of Fine Arts pursue their Bachelor of Arts, Bachelor of Fine Arts, Bachelor of Music, and Bachelor of Music Education degrees. The available fields include art, music, and theatre arts with a dual focus on teaching excellence and artistic creativity. Holding accreditation from by the National Association of Schools of Art and Design, Drake's Department of Art and Design offers instruction in art history, graphic design, and studio art (drawing, painting, printmaking, and sculpture). Students in the Department of Music select from degrees in applied music (instrumental, piano or vocal music performance) and music education. Other alternatives exist, such as a Bachelor of Arts degree with a music major, a Bachelor of Music degree with elective studies in business, and a Bachelor of Music with a jazz studies concentration. Those who wish to study theatre, acting, directing, theatre design, musical theatre, and theatre education enroll in the Department of Theatre Arts.

College of Business and Public Administration:

Students enrolled in the Drake University College of Business and Public Administration complete their undergraduate degree of Bachelor of Science in Business Administration in four years. Available majors include accounting, actuarial science, data analytics, economics, entrepreneurial management, finance, general business, information systems, international business, management, and marketing. Concentrations in insurance and law and business are also available. The College allows interdisciplinary majors, combinations of majors, and open business (undeclared) status. The College is a member of The International Association to Advance Collegiate Schools of Business.

College of Pharmacy and Health Sciences:

The College of Pharmacy and Health Sciences offers pre-professional and professional programs in athletic training (3+2 master's in athletic training), Occupational Therapy (pre-OT/Doctor of Occupational Therapy with options for either a six or seven year track), and Pharmacy (pre-pharmacy/PharmD in six years). First-year students admitted directly to the pre-AT, pre-OT, or pre-pharmacy programs in the College of Pharmacy and Health Sciences complete are guaranteed consideration for admission into their professional programs, after completing the pre-professional requirements at Drake. A health sciences major with two tracks clinical and applied sciences and health services management— is also available. The College is accredited by the Accreditation Council for Pharmacy Education and belongs to the American Association of Colleges of Pharmacy.

School of Journalism and Mass Communication:

The School of Journalism and Mass Communications offers a Bachelor of Arts majors in advertising, digital media production, news journalism, magazines, strategic political communication, or public relations. The School allows an open enrolled (undeclared) option and holds accreditation from the Accrediting Council on Education in Journalism and Mass Communication.

Programs at the School of Education lead to degrees in elementary or secondary education. Students may earn a Bachelor of Science or Bachelor of Arts degree that is tailored to prepare graduates for employment in elementary or secondary schools. Other options include adding middle school and coaching endorsements to teaching credentials. Drake University has belonged to the American Association of Colleges for Teacher Education since the association's founding.

Interdisciplinary Concentrations:

Interdisciplinary concentrations are offered in behavior analysis of developmental disabilities, global public health and comparative studies and human resources management.

Law School/3+3 Law:

The Drake Law School boasts the only first-year (1L) Trial Practicum in the United States. Undergraduate students in the College of Arts and Sciences, the College of Business and Public Administration, the College of Pharmacy and Health Sciences, and the School of Journalism offer combined 3+3 programs with the Drake University Law School. Students in this program can obtain their undergraduate degrees in three years in one of the aforementioned colleges or schools, then pursue a law degree for the next three years at the Law School.

Graduate Programs:

Drake grants master's degrees in: accounting, athletic training (starting in 2017), business administration, communication leadership, education, financial management, jurisprudence, and public administration. Students may also pursue their Doctor of Pharmacy, Doctor of Occupational Therapy, Doctor of Jurisprudence, and Doctor of Education degrees. Joint degrees are also available in MBA/JD, MPA/JD, MBA/PharmD, MPA/PharmD, and PharmD/JD.

TUITION, ROOM, BOARD, FEES

Students entering Drake University in the fall of 2017 will participate in Drake's Tuition Guarantee. The Tuition Guarantee is a straightforward model of tuition pricing gives students and their family's peace of mind in knowing that the cost of their tuition will not change in their four years at Drake. Tuition for these students will be $38,916 annually. Locking in tuition also means that a student's scholarship from Drake will not lose value—as a percentage of tuition—during your college career. For more information about the Tuition Guarantee, please visit our website: drake.edu/tuition-gaurantee.com.

http://www.drake.edu/admission/undergraduate/costsfinancialaid/tuitionfees/

FINANCIAL AID

More than 98 percent of full-time students at Drake have their education financed to some degree with the help of financial aid. Students enrolling directly from high school received on average $19,090 in grants and scholarships from Drake University. More than 5,000 awards, worth $48 million, are given annually, in the form of need or merit-based grants and scholarships.

STUDENT ORGANIZATIONS & ACTIVITIES

With more than 160 organizations operating on campus, students can always find activities that suit their interests. Elected student representatives run the Student Senate. Students also hold seats on some committees in the Faculty Senate. The Student Activities Board is charged with putting on special events, including cultural celebrations, social functions, guest speakers, and concerts. Drake also maintains the Residence Hall Association, composed of students who manage the logistics and activities surrounding residential life.

FACULTY

The University employs professors who demonstrate a dedication to students along with academic prowess. Students benefit from the low 12:1 student-faculty ratio, and they never take classes from graduate students or teaching assistants.

ADMISSIONS PROCESS

While admission is selective, Drake University considers the full record of each candidate for admission. Since the University prefers students with varied talents and interests, there is no single and inflexible set of admission standards applied to all candidates for admission. The admission process involves a comprehensive review of a students academic background (courses and grades), standardized test scores (ACT or SAT), personal essay, recommendations, and activities both in high school and the community. Drake also offers the opportunity for most students to apply via our test flexible admission process which allows them to substitute their ACT or SAT score with an interview as a part of the process. Eligible students must have a cumulative high school grade point average of 3.0 or higher (weighted or unweighted). Depending on the intended program of study or scholarship application, some students will be required to follow the standard path and submit either the ACT or SAT. Drake University does not discriminate on the basis of age, sex, sexual orientation, race, religion, color, national or ethnic origin, or disability.

A completed application for first-year admission contains the following items: a completed application form an official high school transcript, and ACT or SAT scores and a personal essay. A recommendation, while not required, is strongly encouraged. Letters of recommendation can be submitted on your behalf by a teacher or high school counselor. Students may also have a counselor complete the High School Report & Counselor Recommendation supplement form. Students applying to transfer to Drake are required to submit official transcripts for all previous college-level coursework. Students applying via the test flexible path will be contacted by their admission counselor to participate in an interview.

Application for admission to undergraduate degree programs, except pre-pharmacy, may be made for any fall, spring, or summer term. Beginning October 15, students are notified of the admission decision within four to six weeks of the date that all materials are received. December 1 is the Early Action Priority Deadline priority deadline for consideration for admission and merit and need-based financial aid. Early Action Priority Applicants will be eligible for the following benefits:

- Priority consideration and notification for admission and the Presidential Scholarship.
- Priority for housing preferences.
- Early notification of financial aid package by February 1.
- Pre-Pharmacy notification in December. (Please note Test-Flexible admission is not offered to pre-pharmacy students.)
- Regular Decision Deadline is March 1.

Freshman applicants to the pre-pharmacy program in the College of Pharmacy and Health Sciences must submit a completed application by the December 1 deadline. Transfer students are only admitted to the professional PharmD program.

Candidates should contact:
Drake University
Office of Admission
2507 University Avenue
Des Moines, IA 50311
800-44-DRAKE, x3181 or 1-800-443-7253 x 3181
515-271-3181 (locally and outside the U.S)
Fax: 515-271-2831
www.drake.edu
admission@drake.edu

School Says . . .

953

EMERSON COLLEGE

AT A GLANCE

Emerson College in Boston has exceptional programs in communications, visual and media arts, performing arts, journalism, marketing, political communication, and writing, literature and publishing.

Emerson College is the only college in America dedicated exclusively to communication and the arts in a liberal arts context. Established in 1880 as a small regional school of oratory, Emerson has evolved into a diverse, coeducational, and multifaceted institution that educates students to assume positions of leadership in communication and the arts. Emerson is forward thinking, grounded in academic excellence, and committed to advancing the scholarship and creative work that brings innovation, depth, and diversity to those disciplines. Emerson has always been at the forefront of instruction in communications and the arts. Students are taking classes taught by industry professionals while engaging in hands-on projects to put what they learn in the classroom into practice.

LOCATION & ENVIRONMENT

Emerson's campus is located across from historic Boston Common in the heart of the city's thriving Theatre District, and offers multiple theaters, television and film studios, and cutting-edge technical facilities for students. Emerson's connection with Boston's media, theater, and arts industries, as well as government, hospitals, and businesses, provides many opportunities for student internships and professional growth.

Emerson is home to 14 varsity sport teams, and over 80 student organizations including performance groups, student publications, and honor societies. More than half of the students are housed on-campus, some in learning communities such as the Writers' Block, Film Immersion Community, and Digital Culture Floor.

CAMPUS FACILITIES & EQUIPMENT

Emerson has the highest quality equipment, including sound-treated television studios, digital editing labs, audio post-production suites, industry standard software, a professional marketing research suite, and an integrated digital newsroom for aspiring journalists. Additionally, an 11-story performance and production center houses a theatre design/technology center, makeup lab, and costume shop. The College's Paramount Center opened in 2010 and includes a 560-seat theater, black box, scene shop, film screening room, and sound stage. Emerson is also home to the Robbins Speech, Language and Hearing Center, which provides evaluation and treatment for children and adults with communication challenges and serves as the primary clinical training facility for the Department of Communication Sciences and Disorders.

OFF-CAMPUS OPPORTUNITIES

Internships are popular with Emerson students and hundreds of opportunities exist throughout Boston and in major cities across the country, including exclusive placements at in Los Angeles, home to Emerson's residential study and internship program.

Emerson's relationship with Los Angeles is long-standing, but Emerson Los Angeles (ELA) is a brand new, state-of-the-art facility that houses classrooms, residential space, faculty offices, an auditorium, screening room, event spaces, studios and more. It solidifies Emerson's commitment to their Los Angeles program and to creating opportunities for students and alumni on the west coast. The internship program enrolls approximately 200 students, mostly seniors, during both the fall and spring semesters. Emerson students who participate in the ELA program gain the knowledge, skills, and confidence to pursue their chosen fields before launching their post-graduate lives on the west coast.

In addition to ELA, Emerson owns a restored 14th-century medieval castle, Kasteel Well, which is home to their semester abroad program in The Netherlands. The castle is a national historical monument that provides living accommodations, classrooms, a resource center, and related facilities. Emerson also sponsors a semester in Washington, D.C. and, Beijing (at Communication University of China University), along with our Global Pathways Summer Programs in more than 14 locations including London, Prague, and Greece.

ACADEMICS

Emerson offers a wide range of undergraduate, graduate, and professional studies programs in communications and the arts. All undergraduate students take part in a robust curriculum including general education and liberal arts courses with advanced, specialized classes that are specific to individual departments and academic programs. Internships for academic credit are available to juniors and seniors, and the College's Institute for Liberal Arts and Interdisciplinary Studies offers first-year seminars, independent study options, and innovative courses that cut across academic disciplines. In addition, students can cross-register for courses with the six-member ProArts Consortium (Berklee College of Music, Boston Architectural College, Boston Conservatory, Emerson, Massachusetts College of Art, and the School of the Museum of Fine Arts).

MAJORS & DEGREES OFFERED

Undergraduate students can earn a Bachelor of Arts, Bachelor of Science, or Bachelor of Fine Arts degree, depending on which major they select. More than 20 majors are available throughout the departments of Communication Sciences & Disorders, Communication Studies, Journalism, Marketing Communication, Performing Arts, Visual & Media Arts, Writing, Literature & Publishing and Liberal Arts & Interdisciplinary Studies. Students can also minor in several areas, including business, comedy, dance, entrepreneurship, fiction, hearing and deafness, history, literature, music appreciation, philosophy, photography, poetry, political science, publishing, psychology, radio, sociology, and women's and gender studies.

Emerson is accredited by the New England Association of Schools and Colleges and operates on a two-semester calendar.

FASHION INSTITUTE OF TECHNOLOGY

TUITION, ROOM, BOARD, FEES

Basic expenses related to attending Emerson for the 2016-2017 academic year are $42,144 (tuition), $16,320 (double room and board), and $764 (Student Services Fee).

FINANCIAL AID

Emerson is committed to offering its students an excellent education at an affordable price. They have consistently set their tuition below their nearest competitors and are seen as a superb value in higher education. Students have all of the benefits of living in a world-class city, working with state-of-the-art equipment and in beautiful facilities, and learning from faculty who are top in their fields. The Office of Financial Aid will makes every effort to help students finance the cost of their education. Emerson offers several types of financial assistance programs: need-based grants, employment, low-interest loans, merit scholarships, and alternative payment plans to help make an Emerson education possible. Each year, approximately two-thirds of the students receive some form of financial assistance. The College makes every effort to help students finance their education and provides need-based support packaged in awards that typically combine grant and scholarship, loan, and college work-study aid.

To apply for financial aid, students must complete the Free Application for Federal Student Assistance (FAFSA) and CSS PROFILE forms. More information can be found online at http://www.emerson.edu/financial_services or by contacting the Office of Student Financial Services at 617-824-8655 or finaid@emerson.edu.

STUDENT ORGANIZATIONS & ACTIVITIES

In addition to the myriad of activities and events in Boston, student life at Emerson revolves around the more than 80 student-run organizations. These include radio stations, TV networks, publications, performance groups, service clubs, spiritual and cultural organizations, non-residential fraternities and sororities, professional societies, and intercollegiate and recreational athletics. Information about the specific organizations on campus can be found at http://www.emerson.edu/student-life/activities-organizations.

ADMISSIONS PROCESS

Emerson College accepts the Common Application or our Emerson Application and requires an application supplement. Admission is competitive. The college looks for students who present academic promise in their secondary school record, recommendations, and writing competency, as well as personal qualities as seen in extracurricular activities, community involvement, and demonstrated leadership. Beginning in 2018, Emerson will become a test optional institution. Applicants may choose not to submit SAT and/or ACT scores unless they feel as though it assists in the review of their application.

Successful candidates typically have four years of English and three years each of mathematics, science, social science, and three years of a single foreign language. The application deadline for September admission is January 15 (Early Action, November 1), and for January admission it is November 1. Transfer applicants should apply by March 15 for September admission, or by November 1 for January admission.

Prospective students are encouraged to visit campus. Tours and information sessions may be scheduled online at www.emerson.edu/ugvisit or by contacting the Admission Office at 617-824-8600 or admission@emerson.edu.

FASHION INSTITUTE OF TECHNOLOGY

AT A GLANCE

The Fashion Institute of Technology (FIT), a leader in career-oriented education, is a college of art and design, business and technology of the State University of New York (SUNY).

Founded in 1944, FIT is a State University of New York (SUNY) college granting both undergraduate and graduate degrees. FIT's schools include Art and Design, the Jay and Patty Baker School of Business and Technology, Liberal Arts, and Graduate Studies. FIT is accredited by the Middle States Commission on Higher Education, the National Association of Schools of Art and Design, The Council for Interior Design Accreditation and the American Alliance of Museums.

FIT provides it's over 9,500 students with an unmatched combination of specialized curricula, an in-depth liberal arts education, affordable tuition, and an extraordinary campus located in the center of New York City, the world capital of the arts, business, and communications industries. Students may also study at FIT's campuses in Florence and Milan or at select study abroad sites across the globe.

Undergraduates choose from among 29 distinctive majors and 26 minors leading to an AAS, BFA or BS degree. Our seven graduate programs lead to either a MA, MFA or MPS degree. The Center for Continuing and Professional Studies offers non-credit courses and credit/noncredit certificates designed for the non-traditional learner. FIT offers two fully online degrees including an AAS in Fashion Business Management and a BS in International Trade and Marketing. Students in middle school and high school may enroll in FIT's Pre-College Program offering a diverse curriculum of courses and workshops.

One of New York City's premier public institutions, FIT is an internationally recognized college for design, fashion, art, communications, and business. We are known for our rigorous, unique, and adaptable academic programming, experiential learning opportunities, academic and industry partnerships, and commitment to research, innovation, and entrepreneurship.

LOCATION & ENVIRONMENT

Occupying an entire tree-lined block in Manhattan's dynamic Chelsea neighborhood, FIT's campus places students at the heart of the fashion, advertising, visual arts, design, business, and communications industries. Approximately 2,300 undergraduate students live on campus, in accommodations ranging from traditional dorm-style rooms with meal plans to apartment-style suites with kitchens, and from single to quad occupancy. FIT students studying abroad for a semester, year or summer term will also find suitable accommodations in major global centers.

CAMPUS FACILITIES & EQUIPMENT

The FIT campus is home to a creative community with diverse interests, talents, and backgrounds. With four undergraduate residence halls, two fitness centers, an intercollegiate athletics program, more than 60 clubs, and hundreds of on-campus activities, students find a wide range of resources for study, exploration, and fun. The David Dubinsky Student Center houses lounges, a game room, a dining hall, Barnes and Noble, Starbucks, a student radio station, a student-run boutique, student government and club offices, health services, disability support services (FIT-ABLE), Educational Opportunity Program (EOP), gyms, a dance studio, a fitness center, a counseling center, studios, and laboratories. The FIT Career and Internship Center provides an array of services to current students, alumni and employers.

Students have access to state-of-the-art technology and equipment in FIT's studios and labs. Facilities include art, printmaking, display design, and photography studios, a model-making workshop, a graphics printing service bureau, a toy design lab, and a textile testing lab. A computer-aided design and communications facility allows students to explore the latest advancements in technology and their integration in design, photography, and computer graphics and animation. The Annette Green Fragrance Foundation Studio, a professionally equipped fragrance development lab, is the only one of its kind on a U.S. college campus. Cutting and sewing labs offer the most advanced apparel production machinery among educational facilities in the nation. Other facilities include a lighting laboratory, broadcast studio, knitting and weaving labs, and a multimedia foreign language lab.

The Museum at FIT is New York City's only museum dedicated to fashion. Students, designers, and historians use the museum for research and inspiration. The museum, which is accredited by the American Alliance of Museums, operates year-round, and its exhibitions are free and open to the public. The Gladys Marcus Library provides more than 300,000 volumes of print, non-print, and electronic materials. The newspaper and periodicals collection includes 500 current subscriptions. On-line resources include more than 90 searchable databases. The library also offers specialized resources, such as clipping files, fashion and trend forecasting services, and sketch collections. Also on campus are three multimedia venues-the Katie Murphy Amphitheatre, the Morris W. and Fannie B. Haft Auditorium, and the John E. Reeves Great Hall-used for fashion shows, exhibitions, student presentations, industry panels, conferences, and special events.

OFF-CAMPUS OPPORTUNITIES

FIT draws on its New York City location to provide a vibrant, creative environment for our college community. Students enjoy a wealth of opportunities to learn, to play, and to explore the city's abundant resources. A wide range of cultural and entertainment options-from museums to dining to theater are available within walking distance of the campus, which also offers convenient access to subway and bus lines and major rail and bus transportation hubs. One of New York's most dynamic neighborhoods, Chelsea boasts a lively gallery scene, exotic restaurants, a wide variety of retail outlets, and historic landmarks. FIT students also benefit from the campuses close proximity to industries, corporations, and organizations that offer our students internships and jobs.

ACADEMICS

FIT prepares students for professional excellence in design and business through rigorous and adaptable academic programs, experiential learning, and innovative partnerships. FIT fosters creativity, career focus, and a global perspective and educates its students to embrace inclusiveness, sustainability, and a sense of community. Our innovative approach to education-experiential learning through professional critiques, industry competitions, internships and case studies---is the key to our students' future success.

FIT's liberal arts courses are creatively adapted to the needs of particular majors, and liberal arts minors are designed to balance each major's specialty skill. Presidential Scholars, FIT's honors program, offers a select group of high-achieving students specially designed liberal arts courses to stimulate their intellectual curiosity and creativity. Scholars receive a stipend and participate in a monthly colloquia series, annual retreats, and extracurricular and community service activities.

MAJORS & DEGREES OFFERED

School of Art and Design

Accessories Design, Advertising Design, Communication Design Foundation, Computer Animation and Interactive Media, Fabric Styling, Fashion Design, Fine Arts, Graphic Design, Illustration, Interior Design, Jewelry Design, Menswear, Packaging Design, Photography, Textile/Surface Design, Toy Design, and Visual Presentation and Exhibition Design.

Jay and Patty Baker School of Business and Technology

Advertising and Marketing Communications, Cosmetics and Fragrance Marketing, Direct and Interactive Marketing, Entrepreneurship for the Fashion and Design Industries, Fashion Business Management, Home Products Development, International Trade and Marketing for the Fashion Industries, Production Management: Fashion and Related Industries, Technical Design, and Textile Development and Marketing.

School of Liberal Arts

Art History and Museum Professions, Film and Media, and liberal arts minors including both subject-based and interdisciplinary.

School of Graduate Studies

Art Market, Cosmetics and Fragrance Marketing and Management, Fashion Design, Exhibition and Experience Design, Fashion and Textile Studies: History, Theory, Museum Practice, Global Fashion Management, and Illustration.

TUITION, ROOM, BOARD, FEES

Fall 2016-Spring 2017 Tuition per Semester

	NY State Residents	Non-NY State Residents
Associate-Level	$2,295	$6,885
Baccalaureate-Level	$3,235	$9,796
Graduate-Level	$5,435	$11,105

Undergraduate room and board rates vary based on the number of residents per traditional halls/apartment-style housing. Rates depending on the housing selection and with/without meal plans range from $6,175 to $7,038 per semester for double rooms or quads.

FINANCIAL AID

FIT attempts to remove financial barriers to college entrance by providing scholarships, grants, loans, and part-time employment based on available funds for students with financial need. The FIT is committed to providing a superior education at an affordable cost and to helping students find a way to pay for it. Financial aid is available to citizen of the United States from a variety of sources including scholarships, grants, federal loans, and work-study. Endowed scholarships are donated to the FIT Foundation by many companies, organizations, and individuals to support our students. Students must file the Free Application for Federal Student Aid (FAFSA) to be considered for need-based financial aid. International students are not eligible to be considered for federal, state or need-based financial aid at FIT.

STUDENT ORGANIZATIONS & ACTIVITIES

FIT's over 9,500 students hail from across the country and around the world. They join a dynamic student body that includes full and part-time undergraduates, graduate students, non-traditional and on-line learners. Thirty percent of our full-time undergraduates live on campus in one of FIT's four residence halls located on 27th Street across from all major campus facilities. Upperclassmen live on 33rd Street in an apartment-style residence hall just a few blocks from campus. Students also commute from home or live in off-campus housing in and around New York City.

ADMISSIONS PROCESS

Undergraduate Admission

Admission to FIT's undergraduate degree programs is based on a holistic review of the applicant's academic profile, essay and personal characteristics including extracurricular activities and achievements. Applicants to the School of Art and Design must also submit a portfolio that demonstrates their artistic and creative ability. Detailed information on the portfolio requirements for each major offered in the School of Art and Design can be found at fitnyc.edu/admissions

http://fitnyc.edu/admissions

First-year applicants must submit an official high school transcript and essay. Results of the SAT or ACT are not required for admission unless the applicant is interested in being considered for the Presidential Scholars honors program. FIT requires its first-year enrolled students to take English and math placement examinations unless they have submitted SAT or ACT scores. International applicants must submit the results of either the TOEFL, ILETS or PTE exam if English is not their first language. Transfer applicants must also submit official transcripts of all post-secondary coursework.

First-year applicants are considered only for admission to the two-year, AAS degree and must indicate their intended major on the application. Upon successful completion of the AAS degree, students are considered for admission into a two-year, BFA or BS program. Transfer applicants may be admitted either to a one-year or two-year AAS program or directly into the BFA or BS program based on their post-secondary coursework.

Graduate Admission

Applicants to the School of Graduate Studies will be considered for admission based on their academic profile, essay, recommendations and an interview. In addition, there are major-specific criteria which may include a portfolio, work experience and standardized test scores. Prospective students interested in learning about the graduate programs and admission criteria should contact the admissions office at fitnyc.edu/graduate-studies.

Continuing and Professional Studies

Prospective students should visit fitnyc.edu/ccps for detailed information on available courses and registration.

Deadlines and Important Dates

Undergraduate Admission

Prospective undergraduate students must submit their application and $50 non-refundable fee to www.suny.edu/applysuny and indicate their interest in being considered for admission to FIT for either the spring or fall semesters.

	Fall Semester	Spring Semester
Application Deadlines	January 1	October 1
Application Complete Date	February 1	November 1
Notification Dates	April 1	December 1
Tuition Deposit Deadlines	May 1	Two weeks from notification date

Prospective undergraduate students are encouraged to visit the campus for an information session and student-led tour. The admissions office also hosts weekend information sessions, open houses and portfolio preview days during select times throughout the academic year. For more information and to make a reservation please visit fitnyc.edu/admissions.

Please visit fitnyc.edu/graduate-studies for graduate application deadlines and fitnyc.edu/ccps for detailed information on credit, non-credit, certificates and Pre-College programs.

THE GEORGE WASHINGTON UNIVERSITY

AT A GLANCE

The George Washington University, located in downtown Washington, D.C., provides students with invaluable learning experiences on campus, throughout the city and around the world.

Founded in 1821 by an Act of Congress, the George Washington University (GW) offers more than 70 majors and over 2,000 courses across seven undergraduate schools.

We go beyond the typical university experience with an education that is deeply connected to our location in the center of Washington, D.C. Our nearly 10,000 undergraduates actively engage the city and the world through hands-on learning experiences, where they study alongside faculty experts, policy leaders and extraordinary individuals in every discipline to shape global progress and define the issues that will shape the present and future.

LOCATION & ENVIRONMENT

GW maintains two fully integrated campuses in Washington, D.C., with residence halls and classrooms located on both and free shuttle service provided. Through these two different learning environments, students have the ability to create a college experience that is uniquely their own.

Our Foggy Bottom campus is blocks from the major landmarks that make Washington one of the most recognizable cities in the world. Our students can study on the steps of the Lincoln Memorial, jog to the Washington Monument or take a stroll to the White House and Kennedy Center.

Our Mount Vernon campus, just a few miles from the hustle and bustle of downtown, offers a residential liberal arts campus experience while still providing all the opportunities of D.C. Our Women's Leadership Program and GW Athletic fields are located on this campus.

Explore both campuses in our virtual tour at http://virtualtour.gwu.edu.

CAMPUS FACILITIES & EQUIPMENT

GW is full of world-class facilities, such as Gelman Library, at the heart of campus, the Smith Center, home of GW Athletics, Lisner Auditorium, which hosts performances and lectures to enrich our community, and the Science and Engineering Hall, full of highly specialized lab facilities. Learn more about our facilities at http://virtualtour.gwu.edu.

OFF-CAMPUS OPPORTUNITIES

What distinguishes a GW education is the way we consistently put knowledge into action through research, internship and service opportunities for students in all academic areas.

Our students have access to innovative facilities and faculty to support their research in all subjects. Students and faculty have worked together on topics including food waste in D.C. public schools, cholesterol transport in HIV and Tangier disease, and how personality affects purchasing.

As the top-ranked school for internships, we excel at helping students land internships in the nation's capital and beyond. GW students gain invaluable professional experience and often even security clearance during internships at the White House, U.S. Department of State, Folger Shakespeare Library and NPR, just to name a few.

In addition, we encourage students to give back on the local, national and international levels through university-wide community service, including Freshman Day of Service and Alternative Spring Breaks. That dedication to service continues after graduation, as GW is the top-ranked Peace Corps feeder among medium-sized schools.

ACADEMICS

Learn more about these programs at https://undergraduate.admissions.gwu.edu/special-interest-programs.

Civic House
Politics & Values Program
Scholars in Quantitative and Natural Sciences
Seven-Year B.A./M.D. Program
University Honors Program
Women's Leadership Program

MAJORS & DEGREES OFFERED

With more than 2,000 courses in over 70 majors for undergraduate students, GW offers a wide range of academic opportunities, including business, engineering, fine art, international affairs, journalism, liberal arts and public health. Our average class size is 28, and 70 percent of classes have fewer than 30 students. Browse all of our majors at http://go.gwu.edu/gwmajors.

Columbian College of Arts & Sciences

- Africana Studies
- American Studies
- Anthropology
- Arabic Studies
- Archaeology
- Astronomy and Astrophysics
- Biological Anthropology
- Biology
- Biophysics
- Chemistry
- Chinese Language and Literature
- Classical Studies
- Communication
- Criminal Justice
- Dramatic Literature
- Economics
- English
- English and Creative Writing
- Environmental Studies
- French Language and Literature
- Geography
- Geological Sciences
- German Language and Literature
- History
- Human Services and Social Justice
- Japanese Language and Literature
- Judaic Studies
- Mathematics
- Organizational Sciences
- Peace Studies
- Philosophy
- Physics
- Political Science
- Pre-law option
- Pre-medicine option
- Psychology
- Religion
- Russian Language and Literature
- Sociology
- Spanish and Latin American Languages, Literature and Culture
- Speech and Hearing Sciences

- Statistics
- Women's Studies

Corcoran School of the Arts & Design

- Art History
- Art History and Fine Arts
- Dance
- Fine Art
- Fine Art Photography
- Graphic Design
- Interior Architecture and Design
- Music
- Photojournalism
- Theatre

Elliott School of International Affairs

- Asian Studies
- International Affairs
- Latin American and Hemispheric Studies
- Middle East Studies

School of Media & Public Affairs

- Journalism and Mass Communication
- Political Communication

Milken Institute School of Public Health

- Exercise Science
- Public Health

School of Business

- Accountancy
- Business Administration
- Finance

School of Engineering & Applied Science

- Applied Science and Technology
- Biomedical Engineering
- Civil Engineering
- Computer Engineering
- Computer Science
- Electrical Engineering
- Mechanical Engineering
- Systems Engineering

TUITION, ROOM, BOARD, FEES

Earning a GW degree is invaluable, but it takes an investment of time, effort and money. We believe that investment is within reach for every admitted student, and we leverage our resources to make it worthwhile.

GW guarantees students fixed tuition for up to five years of study, meaning the tuition you pay your first semester will be the tuition you pay for your final semester. No surprises here.

GW also invests more than $185 million in financial aid, which is awarded to 70 percent of the incoming freshman class.

We believe that your investment in GW will pay dividends for the rest of your life.

Tuition $51,875

Room and Board $12,500

Student Association Fee $75

FINANCIAL AID

All applicants for admission are automatically considered for scholarships (with the exception of special programs which may require a separate application). Need-based aid is determined by the Office of Student Financial Assistance. For more information, visit http://financialaid.gwu.edu.

STUDENT ORGANIZATIONS & ACTIVITIES

Our nearly 10,000 undergraduate students come from all across the U.S. and more than 130 countries. While at GW, they participate in student organizations and community groups. GW's student body is regularly ranked as the most politically active, which should be no surprise given our close proximity to the White House and the nation's top policy makers. Students have an open dining plan, which offers options on and off campus, and are required to live on campus for their first 3 years.

450 student clubs and organizations

50 club sports and intramural teams

27 NCAA Division I sports teams

35 Greek life chapters

ADMISSIONS PROCESS

GW strives to recruit a diverse and inclusive class each and every year. We do this through our holistic review process, which takes into account not just overall grades, but also course rigor, essays, recommendation letters and extracurricular activities. This allows us to admit students who have the academic preparation, personal qualities and motivation to thrive in GW's dynamic environment.

GW is test-optional, allowing students to choose whether or not to submit SAT/ACT scores, because we believe that a student's performance throughout high school is the best indication of college readiness.

GEORGIAN COURT UNIVERSITY

AT A GLANCE

Georgian Court University is a coeducational, diverse, forward-thinking institution that encourages intellectual inquiry, moral analysis, and social dialogue. At GCU, you will experience a comprehensive liberal arts education in the Mercy Roman Catholic tradition. GCU students learn to expand possibility while fostering their unique gifts and becoming more engaged citizens of the world. The university, which maintains a historic special concern for women, welcomes students of all faiths and backgrounds and offers a curriculum that is broad enough to be truly liberal, yet specialized enough to prepare you for graduate study or an exceptional career.

Georgian Court University is a place where you will learn the Mercy core values of integrity, respect, compassion, justice and service. Upon graduation, you will leave armed with unimaginable knowledge, a powerful sense of purpose, and a determination to change our world.

Georgian Court University is set on a magnificent 156-acre estate, rich with an amazing history, which once belonged to financier George Jay Gould. We are conveniently located one hour from New York City and Philadelphia and only 15 minutes from the Jersey Shore. The campus borders Lake Carasaljo, and is both a National Historic Landmark and a National Arboretum.

POINTS OF PRIDE

2016 Washington Monthly

"Best Bang for the Buck"

2016 US News & World Report

"Best Colleges & Universities"

2016 Catholic College of Distinction

2016 College of Distinction

2017 Military-Friendly School

LOCATION & ENVIRONMENT

With over 2,100 students of diverse faiths and backgrounds and a 13:1 student/teacher ratio, Georgian Court University also offers seven lush garden spaces, including a Japanese Garden, a marble pool, a bowling alley, four residence halls and GCU is the only American University with a court tennis court.

Georgian Court University cares about its students and the environment. 1,639 solar panels help heat and cool Jeffries Hall; and, there are low-mow natural zones and recycling initiatives throughout campus.

CAMPUS FACILITIES & EQUIPMENT

GCU's 67,000-square-foot Wellness Center is a state-of-the-art centerpiece on a campus fully equipped for physical fitness, athletic excellence, and environmental awareness. The LEED®-gold certified center features recycled materials, water and energy-saving design, and an Earth-friendly roof. The Wellness Center Complex features:

A 1,200-seat arena, five athletics fields (including new synthetic turf), a six-court outdoor tennis center, and an abundance of training space for GCU's conference-winning NCAA Division II student-athletes; An advanced exercise science lab and two professional dance studios; A state-of-the-art fitness center; and a rich, diverse range of fitness and wellness programs.

Jeffries Hall is Georgian Court's largest academic building, providing classrooms, seminar rooms, offices, art studios, and computer labs. The state-of-the-art Audrey Birish George Science Center offers the latest laboratory and instruction space for scientific study.

Other campus buildings include the Sister Mary Joseph Cunningham Library, the Raymond Hall Complex, which houses the School of Education, the Raymond Hall Computer Center, and the GCU Dining Hall. The School of Business and the Department of Psychology reside in Farley Center, which includes a computer lab, student lounge, and an International Collaboration Center.

OFF-CAMPUS OPPORTUNITIES

Georgian Court University is conveniently located one hour from the Big Apple (New York City) and historic Philadelphia, and only 15 minutes from the beautiful beaches at the Jersey Shore. GCU is conveniently accessible from Rte. 9, the garden state parkway and I95 allowing students to venture out and enjoy all the local amenities the Jersey Shore has to offer.

ACADEMICS

Academic Programs:

- Undergraduate Programs
- Graduate Programs
- Evening Programs
- Online / Off Campus Programs
- Nursing Program

Coming Fall 2018—RN to BSN and MBA Programs

GCU works to help students develop their academic skills in a supportive, caring environment. The Academic Development & Support Center (ADSC) offers tutoring and other academic support services so students can get the most out of their education. Disabilities Services, Peer Tutoring, and a fee-based support program for students with learning differences are also available.

Georgian Court University's Honors Program allows students to pursue academic honors and collaborate with faculty members in a variety of special courses. Honors students can benefit from courses that emphasize primary texts and sources, rigorous scholarly writing assignments and oral presentations, belonging to a committed community of scholars, preference in academic advisement and course registration, assistance with funding to present at regional and national conferences, and special advising regarding graduate and professional school applications and prestigious fellowship opportunities.

The Office of Career Services, Corporate Engagement and Continuing Education helps bridge the gap from being a student to becoming a professional and progressing through a career. The office has a wide array of tools and resources to help students find jobs and internships, identify and market their skill set, network, compile a resume, and prepare for interviews. These life-long, free services are available to both students and alumni.

MAJORS & DEGREES OFFERED

The Schools of GCU

GCU is comprised of three schools that serve our undergraduate and graduate students:

- The School of Arts and Sciences
- The School of Business & Digital Media
- The School of Education/

GCU boasts more than 30 undergraduate degrees, 10 graduate degrees, and a variety of certificate programs for existing professionals looking to advance their careers. In fact, GCU is ranked by U.S. News & World Report as one of the best regional universities—and one of the best colleges for veterans.

Degrees Offered

- Bachelor's Degree
- Master's Degree
- Certificate
- Post-Bachelor's certificate
- Post-Master's certificate

Georgian Court University offers degree programs in the following disciplines:

Accounting; Applied Arts & Sciences; Art & Visual Studies; Biochemistry; Biology; Business Administration; Chemistry; Clinical Laboratory Sciences; Criminal Justice; Dance; Digital Communication; Digital Design; Education; English; Exercise Science, Wellness & Sports; Finance; Graphic Design & Multimedia; Health Information Management; History; Interdisciplinary Studies; Latino Business Studies; Management; Marketing; Mathematics; Medical Imaging Sciences; Natural Sciences; Nursing; Pre-Professional Career Preparation (preparation for medical careers); Psychiatric Rehabilitation & Psychology; Psychology; Religious Studies; Social Work; Spanish; and Visual Art.

Minors are offered in: Accounting; American Studies; Anthropology; Biology; Business Administration; Chemistry; Coaching; Computer Information Systems; Dance; Dance Therapy; Digital Communication; Economics; English; Exercise Science, Wellness, & Sports; Finance; Gerontology; Global Justice & Society; Graphic Design; History; Homeland Security; Integrative Health; International Area Studies; Latino/a and Caribbean Studies; Law Enforcement & Corrections; Management; Marketing; Mathematics; Politics, Law and History; Psychology; Religious Studies; Social Media Marketing; Social Work; Sociology; Spanish; Sports Management; Studio Art; Sustainability; The USA and the World; Women's Studies; and Writing.

TUITION, ROOM, BOARD, FEES

For the 2016-17 academic year, tuition was $15,079 per semester for full-time students (12–18 credits); the nursing program tuition was $16,147. Part-time tuition (11 credits or fewer) was $690. Room and board was $5,404 per semester, with a $1,293 single room supplement. Fees included a full-time comprehensive fee of $730, a part-time comprehensive fee of $365, and a full-year parking fee of $193 (plus $13.51 New Jersey sales tax). Other small miscellaneous fees may be applicable.

A deposit of $250 is required for resident and commuter students. This is applied to the semester bill and is nonrefundable.

*All tuition charges are for full time and based on full-time attendance.

The charges listed are in effect for the 2016-2017 academic year. The university reserves the right to change its schedule of tuition, fees, and refunds policies at any time.

FINANCIAL AID

Being able to pay for attending college is no easy task. Located in the Lake House, the Office of Financial Aid offers assistance to you and your parents to ensure that you have the financial resources to focus on your education.

Whether you are an incoming freshman, a returning undergraduate, a transfer student or a graduate student, we offer a wide range of financial aid options such as loans, grants, and scholarships to make your education at GCU possible.

Georgian Court University is proud to meet the financial aid needs of its students with an annual budget of $20,000,000 in institutional aid. The University believes that a good education is a right—not a privilege. Through internal scholarships and outside scholarships, Georgian Court strives to make education attainable for all students.

In addition, there are GCU institutional, Federal, and State grants available for students who meet specific criteria. Students can also take advantage of the loan programs that are explained in further detail in the student loan section of the University's website.

STUDENT ORGANIZATIONS & ACTIVITIES

Georgian Court University is a proud member of the National Collegiate Athletic Association (NCAA) Division II. We also belong to the Central Atlantic Collegiate Conference (CACC). Division II reflects our own philosophy. It's an ideal balance between athletic excellence and academic achievement. GCU student-athletes maintain an above-average GPA, participate regularly in community service projects, and make their mark on college athletics. Many qualify for athletic scholarships.

The Student Government Association (SGA) of Georgian Court University is the official representative voice of the GCU student body. The SGA advocates on behalf of the students' interests and concerns. Through representation on University committees and other special meetings, the Student Government Association continues to play a vital role in fostering community and providing a direct link between students, faculty, and administration. The University also boasts several programs to help engage and develop students' leadership abilities, as well as a plethora of other clubs and organizations catering to a broad range of interests and lifestyles.

The Office of Campus Ministry at Georgian Court University exists to support the spiritual growth of all members of the GCU community. Campus ministry's mission includes: Gathering a vibrant community for worship, prayer, and reflection; Celebrating the Catholic Christian faith of our sponsors, the Sisters of Mercy; Cultivating faith-filled leaders who can have a positive impact on our world; and Animating the GCU community for compassionate service and advocacy for justice.

ADMISSIONS PROCESS

Georgian Court University welcomes applications from qualified students of all faiths and backgrounds who desire a liberal arts education. The University strives to enroll students who can benefit most from its academic program. In 2016, 45% of GCU's student population were first-generation college students. Entrance is based on individual merit. The high school record of achievement is of primary importance and must reflect solid performance. The majority of students at Georgian Court ranked in the upper half of their senior high school class. Transfer students are accepted into the freshman, sophomore, and junior classes for fall and spring semesters. All transfer applicants must be in good standing at their previous college. Applicants with fewer than 24 credits must fulfill all requirements for admission to the freshman class.

Further consideration is given to the applicant's extracurricular activities and the letters of recommendation submitted by teachers, counselors, employers, or similarly qualified people.

Applicants must submit their completed application (online via the Common Application or print and complete a paper application), a $40 application fee, their official high school transcript, SAT (GCU code: 2274) or ACT (GCU code: 2562) scores, two letters of recommendation, and an optional essay. Georgian Court has rolling deadlines for first-year students, so applications can be accepted throughout the year.

A campus interview is encouraged but not necessary. A guided tour of the campus is available at the interview.

Undergraduate Student Profile (update as of Fall 2016)

- 1591 undergraduate students (711 graduate students)
- 72% female, 28% male
- 21 states and 12 foreign countries represented
- 74% of first-year applicants are accepted

Faculty (update as of Fall 2016)

- 13:1 student-faculty ratio
- 96 full-time instructional faculty members
- 140 industry professionals serving as adjunct Faculty
- 90% of full-time faculty members have doctoral degrees

GONZAGA UNIVERSITY

AT A GLANCE

Gonzaga University, founded in 1887, is an independent, comprehensive university with a distinguished background in the Catholic, Jesuit, and humanistic tradition. Gonzaga emphasizes the moral and ethical implications of learning, living, and working in today's global society. Through the University Core Curriculum, each student develops a strong liberal arts foundation, which many alumni cite as a most valuable asset. In addition, students specialize in any of more than 75 academic programs and majors. Gonzaga enrolls approximately 5,000 undergraduates and 2,500 graduate and law students.

Gonzaga's 131-acre campus combines the old and new: College Hall, the original administration building, and DeSmet Residence Hall with the modern architectural structures of the John J. Hemmingson Center, Foley Library, Hughes Life Sciences Building, Jundt Art Center and Museum, and the PACCAR Center for Applied Science. The campus is characterized by sprawling green lawns and majestic evergreen trees. Towering above the campus are the stately spires of St. Aloysius Church, the well-recognized landmark featured in the University logo.

Gonzaga encompasses five undergraduate schools: Arts and Sciences, Business Administration, Education, Engineering and Applied Science, and Nursing and Human Physiology. The University offers the BA, BBA, BEd, BS, BSCE, BSCpE, BSCS, BSEE, BSEM, BSME, and BSN degrees.

Gonzaga offers several unique options for students. The Honors Program provides a rigorous liberal arts curriculum for intellectually curious students who thrive in a competitive academic environment. Business leaders mentor the Hogan Entrepreneurial Leadership Program students, and internships are an integral part of the program. The award-winning Gonzaga Alumni Mentor Program (GAMP) connects current students and recent graduates with alumni in their professional areas of interest. Students in the Comprehensive Leadership Program take a leadership minor curriculum that may be combined with any major, and they participate in valuable, interactive leadership experiences. The Army ROTC unit prepares select women and men as leaders in service for their communities and their country. Gonzaga's nationally ranked debate team includes all skill levels. The Mock Trial Team competes nationally and involves students majoring in many different areas of study. Internships, research with faculty, and community service learning enhance class time while providing students first-hand experience.

LOCATION & ENVIRONMENT

As the hub of the Inland Northwest, Spokane plays a vital role in shaping the University's character. While offering urban advantages such as museum exhibits, shopping, symphony, Broadway and ballet performances, Spokane still maintains an intimate, friendly, and community atmosphere. Used for running and cycling, part of the 37-mile Centennial Trail, runs through campus and to Coeur d' Alene, Idaho. Within a short distance of campus, students snow and water ski, hike, cycle, rock climb, swim, camp, and golf. With an average rainfall of only 16.7 inches per year, outdoor activities are easily accessible.

The 24 residence halls and apartments on campus, both single-sex and coed, house 40 to 360 students each. Freshmen and sophomores are required to live on campus. TheZagweb network provides students round-the-clock electronic access to email, Internet, campus intranet, and library holdings, all directly from residence hall rooms. Additionally, the whole campus is wireless. Resident Directors and Assistants, along with a Resident Chaplain, provide a fun, secure, and nurturing environment.

CAMPUS FACILITIES & EQUIPMENT

The Foley Library contains more than 800,000 volumes and microform titles, with two special collections of material especially rich in the areas of philosophy and classical civilization, as well as the nation's most extensive collection of works concerning the famous Jesuit poet Gerard Manley Hopkins. The historic College Hall houses the recently-renovated Harry & Colleen Magnuson Theatre, a 24-hour computer lab, a Florentine-style University Chapel, and numerous classrooms and faculty offices.

Students are able to produce sophisticated multimedia presentations and research hundreds of libraries across the country from their own residence hall rooms, by accessing campus-wide wireless, or from one of the 10 labs on campus. The Communications Building offers an arts lab for the Bulletin (the weekly student-published newspaper), KAGU, the University's radio station, and GUTV, a state-of-the-art TV production station where students learn all aspects of broadcast studies. The Herak Center for Engineering offers state-of-the-art CAD/CAM, electronic, digital, microwave, and calibration labs, and the PACCAR Center for Applied Science, which received a "Gold" certification rating from the Leadership in Energy and Environmental Design (LEED), adds more classroom space, a robotics lab, a computer science lab with a high-speed cluster computer array, and the rapidly growing Electric Utility Transmission & Distribution program.

The Martin Athletic Centre boasts a 13,000 sq. ft. state-of-the-art fitness center, and next door, the 6000-seat McCarthey Athletic Center houses the men's and women's basketball games as well as concerts and events throughout the year. Washington Trust Field at Patterson Baseball Complex hosts the Gonzaga baseball program.

Gonzaga has committed that any new buildings on campus (including the recent addition of the 167,726 square-foot John J. Hemmingson Center which was certified "Gold") will seek at least "Silver" LEED certification. Additionally, as a signatory of the Presidents' Climate Commitment, Gonzaga has created a Climate Action Plan to reduce its carbon footprint by 20% by 2020 and 50% by 2035 (from 2009 levels).

OFF-CAMPUS OPPORTUNITIES

Recognizing the importance of an international perspective for learning, Gonzaga offers study abroad programs in over 35 countries, including Argentina, Australia, Austria, Belgium, Benin, China, Costa Rica, El Salvador, England, Finland, France, Ireland, Italy, Japan, Jordan, Mexico, the Netherlands, Northern Ireland, Panama, Scotland (Honors Program students), South Africa, Spain, Taiwan, Tanzania, Thailand, Turkey, Turks and Caicos, and Zambia. Gonzaga's campus in Florence, Italy is the most popular option.

ACADEMICS

The core curriculum (an intentionally-designed set of courses bookended by the first-year and final year core integration seminars), encourages students to embrace an interdisciplinary mindset. All students take classes in writing, reasoning, scientific inquiry, mathematics, communication & speech, philosophy, religious studies, and English literature, and they further broaden their education with classes in the arts, humanities, social/behavior sciences, social justice, and global studies designated courses. The College of Arts & Sciences adds a requirement in modern or classical language proficiency that complements the core. Often, classes at Gonzaga require oral presentations or use of the written and discussion-based communication skills emphasized in the core curriculum.

MAJORS & DEGREES OFFERED

Gonzaga offers the following areas of study in the five undergraduate schools. The College of Arts and Sciences offers art, biochemistry, biology (research), broadcast studies, chemistry, classical civilizations, communication studies, computer science and computational thinking, criminal justice, economics, English (writing concentration), environmental studies, French, history, international studies (including international relations and Asian, European, and Latin American studies), Italian studies, journalism, mathematics, mathematics/computer science, music (including emphases in composition, general studies, and performance), music education, philosophy (Kossel concentration option), physics, political science, psychology, public relations, religious studies (Christian theology and religious pluralism concentrations), sociology, Spanish, and theatre arts (performance and technical concentrations). Additionally, the School offers minors in Catholic studies, conducting, dance, German, Italian, jazz performance, leadership studies, Native American studies, solidarity and social justice, Women's & Gender studies, and writing. Students interested in the following areas take tracks of classes respectively in pre-dentistry, pre-law, pre-medicine, pre-physical therapy, and pre-veterinary studies. The School of Business Administration offers majors in accounting or business administration (with concentrations in economics, entrepreneurship and innovation, finance, human resource management, individualized study, international business, law and public policy, management information systems, marketing, and operations and supply chain management). As well as granting teacher certification on both the elementary and secondary levels, the School of Education offers degrees in kinesiology and physical education, special education, and sport management. The School of Engineering and Applied Science offers computer science and civil, computer, electrical, and mechanical engineering degrees, as well as an engineering management degree and a 5-year BSEM/MBA option. Also, The School of Nursing and Human Physiology offers human physiology and nursing degrees at the undergraduate level. Advanced degrees in accounting, business, communication and leadership, education, educational leadership, engineering, law, leadership studies, nursing, organizational leadership, philosophy, teaching English as a second language, and theology and leadership are also offered.

TUITION, ROOM, BOARD, FEES

Tuition for the 2017-2018 academic year is $40,540; room and board is estimated at $11,560. Including tuition, room and board, books, fees, transportation, and living expenses, Gonzaga estimates $57,436 as the total cost of attendance for the 2017-2018 year.

FINANCIAL AID

99.6% percent of students receive financial aid. The average package for 2016-2017 was $26,757 awarded in the form of grants, scholarships, loans, and campus employment. A number of merit-based, merit/need-based, athletic, music, debate, and other program scholarships are awarded to students each year. The Free Application for Federal Student Aid (FAFSA) is available on October 1, and Gonzaga encourages students to apply as close to October 1 as they can and up to February 1 to be eligible for Gonzaga's Priority Awarding Pool. Also, check the website for scholarship information and online applications. Gonzaga is committed to working with students and families to finance their investment in a quality education.

STUDENT ORGANIZATIONS & ACTIVITIES

GU students enjoy a wide variety of activities on and off campus. The Gonzaga Student Body Association (GSBA) oversees over one hundred academic, social, and cultural clubs and provides the structure of student government. Some of the most popular clubs include the Outdoors Club, THIRST (a non-denominational worship group), GUTS (an improvisational comedy team), and the Hawaii Pacific Islanders Club. GSBA organizes service and conservation projects, dances, and countless other activities to channel and challenge the talents and passions of motivated men and women who seek to make a difference.

As the leading provider of service hours in the entire city of Spokane, Gonzaga University encourages students to volunteer their services at any of the area nonprofit organizations. University Ministry, the Gonzaga Student Body Association, Unity Multicultural Education Center, and the Center for Community Action and Service Learning (CCASL) provide organized projects through which students become involved in the greater Spokane community and other cities.

Division I, West Coast Conference sports include baseball (men), basketball, crew, cross-country/track, golf, soccer, tennis, and volleyball (women). Approximately 60% of students participate in intramural and club sports such as ultimate frisbee and rugby. The Harry & Colleen Magnuson Theatre hosts main-stage plays (including musicals), dance recitals, GUTS, sketch comedy, numerous one-acts and student directed scenes. Gonzaga's musical groups include a nationally recognized University Choir, a Chorale, the GU Symphony, the Jazz Ensemble, the Gonzaga Bulldog Band, The Big Bing Theory-an a cappella group, the Boone Street Band, and numerous other ensembles. GU's students also host programs on Gonzaga's TV and radio stations. Additionally, many students participate in University Ministry events, such as retreats, the annual Pilgrimage hike, THIRST, Masses, Christian Life Communities, and interdenominational and/or interfaith services.

ADMISSIONS PROCESS

The University seeks diligent, inquisitive applicants with diverse backgrounds who will benefit from the rigorous Jesuit instruction at Gonzaga as well as enhance the University environment. A Common Application (www.commonapp.org) and the Gonzaga member page, SAT I (Essay Section not required) or ACT scores (Writing Section not required), a transcript, a teacher recommendation, a school report, an activities list or resume, and an essay are required. Transfer students and students with any college credit must submit official transcripts from all colleges. Transfer students must also complete the Common Application for Transfers, including the Transfer College Report and Academic Evaluation. International students must also submit official transcripts from all colleges attended. Additionally, international students must submit official results of their TOEFL examination. The Non-binding Early Action application deadline for freshmen is November 15, and decisions are mailed by January 15. The main advantages of the Early Action Program are early communication of admission and financial aid packages. Nursing and Engineering applicants are highly encouraged to apply under Early Action as those programs have direct entry admissions, and the limited spaces available make the majors the most competitive. The Regular Decision application date for freshmen is February 1. Students applying Regular Decision by this date will receive an admission decision by the beginning of April. After February 1, applications will be accepted only if space is available.

For more information on Gonzaga, please see: www.gonzaga.edu.

GRACELAND UNIVERSITY

AT A GLANCE

Founded in 1895 and sponsored by Community of Christ, Graceland University is much more than a school. Graceland is a community of passionate, caring and dedicated individuals who make up a worldwide community network that reaches far beyond the two campuses, located in Lamoni, Iowa, and Independence, Missouri.

Graceland University creates and maintains high academic standards of excellence by prioritizing a close student/faculty learning environment, providing nurturing communities that foster intellectual engagement and curiosity, and embracing the philosophy that learning is not confined to the classroom. Graceland integrates a strong tradition in the liberal arts with targeted professional learning.

LOCATION & ENVIRONMENT

Situated on 170 acres of southern Iowa's rolling hills, our main campus in Lamoni, is home to about 1,000 students and provides a beautiful, safe, residential campus where diversity of thought and culture are celebrated.

Graceland University integrates learning inside and outside of the classroom and provides limitless opportunities for involvement in educational service, leadership, and entertainment activities.

Graceland's Independence, Missouri Campus offers online learning opportunities--both graduate and undergraduate--in nursing, religion, and education.

Life at Graceland includes forums and guest speakers on the current issues of the day; community service projects; poetry readings at a downtown coffee house; new opportunities in an active Sustainability group or 50 other club organizations, as well as quiet time in a relaxed, countryside setting.

CAMPUS FACILITIES & EQUIPMENT

In 2012, Graceland's Lamoni campus finished construction of the $1.6 million Fitzgerald Fitness Center, a new student wellness center with a group exercise area and a variety of weight and cardio equipment.

Graceland also re-introduced the Shaw Center in the fall of 2012 after the $16 million expansion and renovation project. The Shaw Center features JR Theatre, a state-of-the-art black box facility; Carol Hall, an acoustically perfect recital hall; the Shaw Family Auditorium, with over 500 seating capacity; the outdoor Amphitheatre for spring jazz concerts and more. The Shaw Center is one of the most remarkable performing arts venues in Iowa.

The Resch Science and Technology Hall was dedicated in 2009. It provides state-of-the-art sciences and math facilities. Nearly everything, including the computer science equipment, is new and industry-standard in Resch Hall. The Helene Center for the Visual Arts (2004) includes 29,000 square feet of classrooms, studios and exhibit space, and a large Mac lab with industry standard programs. It is regarded by artists as "the perfect place to be creative."

Campus computer facilities include three microcomputer labs and industry-standard equipment for desktop publishing and graphic design. Graceland's Internet Cafe provides 24-hour computer and printing access in a cozy atmosphere.

Our Closson Athletic Center boasts an indoor track and field facility with a beautiful hardwood basketball and volleyball court. We have a FieldTurf (an artificial turf football field), a wonderful outdoor track facility with a Rekortan track installed in 2016, and a top soccer complex with multiple practice fields. The new Baughman Athletic Center boasts a large wrestling practice room, new locker facilities, and an indoor pitching practice area for the baseball and softball teams.

The Frederick Madison Smith Library uses the latest technologies to provide information services to accommodate student needs. Fully networked computer workstations offer access to the Internet and many research databases, including seven reference databases and more than 45 periodical databases, many providing access to full-text articles. Access to LIBBIE, the library's online catalog, and to the online reference sources, is available to all patrons. Articles and books may be ordered from a worldwide network of research libraries.

OFF-CAMPUS OPPORTUNITIES

Lamoni is a small, friendly town with a big heart. There's an old-fashioned pizza place, a bustling coffee house, and a university-owned movie theatre, called the Coliseum, all just a five-minute walk from campus. It's easy to venture into the Lamoni community. Hike around a beautiful nearby lake or use new, city bike trails by checking out one of the GU Sustainability bicycles available. Popular lakes at Slip Bluff County Park and Nine Eagles State Park offer swimming, boating, fishing, and camping, and both are only a few miles away. There are close bonds between Graceland and the small, but vibrant town of Lamoni, home to 2,500 residents. Des Moines is just a little over an hour north providing all the amenities of a large city

ACADEMICS

Students learn in an individualized, challenging, yet supportive environment, with a 15:1 student/faculty ratio. Graceland helps students shape a new vision for their lives. It is a transformative education where each student can explore their interests and passions. The Graceland community will help them understand their strengths and values. And along the way, they will discover something invaluable: themselves. The University offers over 40 academic programs. Students will work closely with professors who are both teachers and scholars. Most of Graceland's professors hold a doctorate or the highest degree in their field. The Honors Program, highly acclaimed by participants, is designed for motivated students who want to expand their learning beyond the regular curriculum. The program takes annual cultural trips to Chicago and Minneapolis and gives students the opportunity to present at regional Honors conferences.

Graceland has a nationally competitive Enactus team with nearly 10 percent of all Lamoni campus students participating. Enactus is a worldwide program where students collaborate and compete on entrepreneurial-based projects that help develop the skills needed to become highly capable and socially responsible leaders. Graceland's Enactus team has won regional championships 12 out of the last 13 years. Our 80-strong Enactus team placed first in the U.S. and second in the world (at the competition in Paris) in 2006.

Graceland has a unique and strong sense of community that helps each student to succeed. It is The Power of Together. Graceland graduates go on to stellar careers in the sciences, the arts, nursing, education, business, athletics and human services. The GU alumni network is worldwide, and alumni state that their time at Graceland helped focus their passions and shape their futures. A new mentoring program, GU4U, infused with student energy, pairs successful alumni with current students for career tips, internship opportunities, and guidance.

In addition to traditional programs, Graceland offers many options for distance learners. Programs offered by our renowned School of Nursing include the Bachelor of Arts with a major in Healthcare Management, B.S.N. to R.N., R.N. to B.S.N., R.N. to M.S.N., and the Doctor of Nurse Practitioner program. The Master of Science in Nursing program has two tracks: Family Nurse Practitioner and Adult Gerontology Acute Care Nurse Practitioner. Post graduate Certificates include Family Nurse practitioner, Nurse Educator, and Adult Gerontology Acute Care Nurse Practitioner. The nationally ranked Gleazer School of Education offers a Master of Education with five different emphases and three certificate programs. The Master of Education program is offered in Independence, Missouri; and online. The Community of Christ Seminary through Graceland offers a Master of Arts in Religion in a blended delivery system of classes offered online and face-to-face.

MAJORS & DEGREES OFFERED

Bachelor's Degrees

Accounting
Agricultural Business
Allied Health
Art: Studio°
Art: Graphic Design
Biology°
Business Administration
Chemistry°
Communications°
Computer Science and Information Technology
Criminal Justice
Economics
Elementary Education
English°
Health and Movement Science:
- Coaching
- Health
- Health Education°
- Physical Education°
- Recreation
Health Care Management
History°
International Studies
Liberal Studies
Mathematics°
Music°
Nursing
Organizational Leadership
Psychology
Social Media Marketing
Sociology:
- Criminology Concentration
- Human Services Concentration
Sport Management
Theatre°
Web Design
°Secondary teacher education program offered.
Pre-Professional Programs
Pre-Chiropractic
Pre-Dentistry
Pre-Forensic Science
Pre-Law
Pre-Medicine
Pre-Optometry
Pre-Pharmacy
Pre-Physical Therapy
Pre-Veterinary Medicine

Masters Programs

Master of Arts in Religion
Master of Education
Master of Science in Nursing
Doctorate Program
Doctor of Nursing Practice

TUITION, ROOM, BOARD, FEES

Graceland University has been named a "Best College in the Midwest" by The Princeton Review. We are committed to managing our costs, now and in the future, while maintaining the quality of education we provide every student. Costs for traditional students for the 2015-2016 academic year are listed below. Online program costs vary.

	Annual	Semester
Tuition	$27,500	$13,750
Room	$3,300	$1,650
Board	$5,180	$2,590
Activity Fee	$370	$185
Total Direct Costs	$36,590	$18,295

FINANCIAL AID

Student Financial Aid is available for those students who qualify. All aid is based upon financial need, academic achievement, and/or meritorious performance. Financial aid is viewed as a supplement to the effort of the family to finance their student's college education. In order to receive federal or state financial aid, students must file a Free Application for Federal Student Aid (FAFSA) each year (add Graceland's code: 001866), and maintain satisfactory academic progress. Institutional Scholarships and Grants may be awarded to full-time students for academics, athletics, performing arts, and for Community of Christ students. When Graceland University receives all documents needed to complete a Financial Aid Package, an award notice will be sent to the student for review. More than 98 percent of Graceland residential students receive some form of financial aid.

STUDENT ORGANIZATIONS & ACTIVITIES

Graceland sponsors more than 50 student clubs and organizations. GU boasts 18 varsity and numerous junior varsity teams and a variety of performing arts groups including a new drumline. Anyone who wants to play or perform at Graceland has ample opportunity to do so.

The basic residential and social unit of student life is known as a "House." The house system at Graceland on the Lamoni campus is a unique program that started in the 1960s and is based on the principle of inclusion. The importance of each student is recognized. Unlike fraternities and sororities, every student is involved in the house system. Members of each house elect a leadership council that plans social events and represents students in Student Government. By cooperative effort, the house organizes its own social, religious and intramural programs. Each student determines the extent of his/her participation in all house activities. Graceland students love this community approach to residential life with a built-in social system where all students are welcomed and made to feel at home.

Students hail from more than 40 states and 21 countries. Graceland's International Club is a hub of constant activity. GU is committed to providing an environment that is free of alcohol and tobacco. Graceland cares about spiritual life as well. Whatever faith tradition, GU students' spiritual lives will be nurtured through a wide range of worship experiences, service projects, and religion classes in an environment that is accepting with opportunities to learn and grow.

ADMISSIONS PROCESS

To be considered for acceptance at Graceland, students must meet two of the three following criteria: rank in the upper 50 percent of high school class, have a 2.5 grade point average (based on a 4.0 system) and a minimum composite ACT score of 21, or a minimum combined SAT score of 960. International students also need to score at or above 550 on TOEFL and prove ability to cover expenses while enrolled. Transfer students need a minimum 2.0 GPA on previous college coursework.

GROVE CITY COLLEGE

AT A GLANCE

Grove City College is a private, Christian liberal arts and sciences college that develops leaders of the highest proficiency, purpose, and principles ready to advance the common good.

Founded in 1876, the College is known as a bastion of educational independence and academic freedom that is grounded in conservative values.

Grove City College equips students to pursue their unique callings through an academically excellent and Christ-centered learning and living experience distinguished by a commitment to affordability and its promotion of the Christian worldview, the foundations of free society, and the love of neighbor.

Unique in the higher education landscape, Grove City College is defined by its foundational values of faithfulness, excellence, community, stewardship, and independence.

Students are challenged academically and nourished spiritually by a unique curriculum that aims to both educate and enlighten. The College is more than just a school, it's a community dedicated to faith and learning that cares about students and challenges them to excel in the classroom and the world at large.

Students gain the knowledge and skills they'll need to compete in the marketplace and a strong spiritual foundation that will enable them not only to do well, but to do good.

The connection between faith and learning is central at Grove City College. Christian truth and inspired wisdom form the foundation on which the faculty teach and the worldview that the institution embraces. That is not a limiting principle, but a liberating one. Faith illuminates knowledge, puts education into an immutable context, and enriches the human condition.

Graduates see not only higher than average starting and mid-career salaries, but also high levels of job satisfaction and community involvement.

While the quality of education at Grove City College is unsurpassed, the price tag is most decidedly not. Tuition is less than half the cost of competitive, private liberal arts colleges. Considered a "Best Value" college by Forbes based on low tuition, a high four-year graduation rate and a healthy return on investment, Grove City College offers students a range of opportunities for academic and personal development.

LOCATION & ENVIRONMENT

Grove City College is located north of Pittsburgh in western Pennsylvania in a classic small town setting. The picturesque 180-acre campus was designed by the same architects that designed New York's Central Park. Neo-gothic buildings are set on wide lawns, surrounded by century-old trees.

CAMPUS FACILITIES & EQUIPMENT

Campus encompasses academic buildings, including the state-of-the-art STEM Hall; 10 residence halls; the Henry Buhl Library; the Physical Learning Center, which features a competition pool, indoor track, basketball arena, fitness rooms, and a bowling alley; Breen Student Union, home to the GeDunk café and campus bookstore; the Pew Fine Arts Center, featuring three theaters, practice rooms, studio space, and an art gallery; a Christian activities building; varsity sports facilities, including Robert E. Thorne Field, soccer, baseball and softball fields, as well as expansive intramural playing fields; a technical learning center that is home to WSAJ studios; and Harbison Chapel, a beautiful neo-gothic cathedral that anchors the campus' central quad.

ACADEMICS
Special programs

The Center for Entrepreneurship & Innovation at Grove City College is making its mark in the business world, fostering the startup ambitions of students through a variety of programs, including the VentureLab business incubator. The College's Center for Vision & Values promotes faith and freedom in the public square and holds an annual conference that draws leading thinkers and speakers. The Trustee Scholar program supports some of the country's best students and future leaders. Red Box and Inner-City Outreach missions provide students with opportunities to serve here and abroad, exercise leadership and expand their horizons.

CAREER SERVICES & PLACEMENT

Grove City College's nationally-ranked Career Services Office works with students throughout their college career to help determine and pursue their professional calling. Along the way, students have access to exclusive internships and amazing opportunities through the office, which sponsors hundreds of on-campus job interviews and recruiting visits and coordinates an annual career fair that brings together students and recruiters from manufacturing, business, education, government agencies and ministry organizations. Within six months, 96 percent of Grove City College graduates are at work or continuing their education.

FACULTY

Our extraordinary faculty are dedicated to educating hearts and minds. They are Christian scholars who understand their disciplines as deeply and as well as they understand humankind's place in God's creation. They are teachers, mentors and friends to students ready to be challenged and informed. Grove City College is a place where high academic standards produce outstanding outcomes for graduates well-prepared to pursue their life's calling. It's a transformational experience in more ways than you can imagine.

ADDITIONAL INFORMATION

Check www.gcc.edu for more on Grove City College, including detailed information on programs and majors, student success, faculty perspectives and the latest news.

MAJORS & DEGREES OFFERED

Grove City College is dedicated to the liberal arts and sciences. Through courses that form the humanities core, all students are exposed to the leading thinkers, books and ideas in religion, philosophy, history, political science, economics, literature, art and music that represent our common heritage and encompass the wisdom of civilization. The College is known as a top undergraduate engineering school and one of the few Christian colleges to offer fully-accredited mechanical, electrical and computer engineering courses. Biology, education, communications studies are among the other strong programs that produce graduates prepared to enter the working world or continue their education at graduate or professional schools.

TUITION, ROOM, BOARD, FEES

Grove City College is committed to keeping college affordable for students and families. Tuition and room and board for a year is less than $26,000 before scholarships and financial aid. That's about half the cost of competitive private colleges and the lowest cost among Pennsylvania's private schools. The College does not accept any federal aid, including student loans and Pell Grants, but provides access to private loans, aid and scholarship opportunities. The College offers no discounts to attract students, since those discounts only result in higher costs for other students. Many students are able to graduate with little or no debt. For more about financial aid at Grove City College, visit www.gcc.edu/futurestudents/financialaid/Pages/Financial%20Aid.aspx

STUDENT ORGANIZATIONS & ACTIVITIES

Grove City College attracts students from a national pool, with the 2,500-member student body hailing from 40 states and a dozen foreign countries. Known as "Grovers," they reflect the institution's Christian character and commitment to faith and learning. They are very involved in campus organizations—of which there are more than 130—intramural sports, service-learning, campus and community service and entrepreneurship, along with their academic pursuits.

ADMISSIONS PROCESS

Average GPA: 3.68 (high school GPA)

Average ACT: 26 composite

Average SAT: 1195 (writing score not factored in)

Essay: Required

Interview: Not required, but strongly recommended

Application deadline: Early Decision: November 15; Regular Decision—February 1

Application fee: $50

Website: www.gcc.edu/futurestudents

HILLSDALE COLLEGE

AT A GLANCE

Convinced that it is the best preparation for meeting the challenges of modern life, Hillsdale offers a traditional, classically based, liberal arts education with teaching faculty and a strong core curriculum.

Hillsdale College is a private, independent, nonsectarian institution of higher learning founded in 1844 by men and women who described themselves as "grateful to God for the inestimable blessings" resulting from civil and religious liberty and as "believing that the diffusion of learning is essential to the perpetuity of those blessings." The College has maintained institutional independence since its founding by refusing to accept aid from or control by federal authorities. Far-reaching private support from a national constituency has enabled Hillsdale to continue its trusteeship of the intellectual and spiritual inheritance tracing to Athens and Jerusalem. The undergraduate enrollment for Fall 2016 was 1,486, 50 percent men and 50 percent women, from 48 states and 13 foreign countries. Approximately 35% of students are from Michigan. The entering freshman class in Fall 2016 had an average GPA of 3.8, ACT of 30, and SAT of 1983. Hillsdale students are housed in dormitories, fraternity and sorority houses, and various off-campus dwellings. Single and double rooms are available on campus; there are no coed dormitories. Each College-owned residence hall is supervised by a resident director and resident advisers. All freshmen (except commuters) are required to live on campus; upperclass students seeking to live off campus must apply to the dean of men or dean of women for this privilege. Hillsdale's Charger athletes compete in 14 intercollegiate NCAA Division II varsity sports as part of the Great Midwest Athletic Conference (GMAC). An active intramural program is also available.

LOCATION & ENVIRONMENT

Hillsdale College is located amidst the hills, dales, and lakes of south-central Michigan. The Indiana and Ohio turnpikes are each 30 minutes away, and the College is within close reach of such metropolitan areas as Detroit, Chicago, Cleveland, Toledo, Ft. Wayne, and Indianapolis. The town of Hillsdale is a county seat with a population of 10,000. Stores, churches, restaurants, and coffee shops are all within walking distance of the campus, and a movie theater within a 5-minute drive.

CAMPUS FACILITIES & EQUIPMENT

The Hillsdale College Mossey Library is a three-floor facility with a collection of more than 2,000,000 volumes. In addition to the main study and research collections, the Library also contains a number of rare and special holdings, including the Ludwig von Mises, Russell Kirk, Richardson Heritage, and Richard Weaver collections. Connected to other Michigan libraries through MelCat, and with college libraries nationwide via interlibrary loan, students have access to almost any material necessary for on-campus research. Numerous individual study areas and group study rooms are available for students, as well as computer research terminals. Lane and Kendall Halls at the front of campus serve as the primary academic facilities in the humanities and social sciences and contain classroom space and faculty offices, as well as a special laboratory for experimental psychology. The Strosacker Science Center houses the departments of biology, chemistry, and physics. The Joseph H. Moss Family Laboratory Wing, completed in 2008, is a 17,000-square-foot addition that includes a microbiology/cell biology lab, anatomy/physiology lab with human cadaver access, conservation genetics lab, water lab, greenhouse, and organic/general chemistry labs. The 32,000-square-foot Herbert Henry Dow Science Building provides additional classrooms, research laboratories, animal rooms, and a computer lab. The Mary Randall Preschool is a circular laboratory school in which nursery school children are taught by students specializing in early childhood education and psychology. Experts in the field have called this building "a model for the nation." The Hillsdale Academy, a K–12 private model school, provides additional opportunities for classroom observation. The Roche Sports Complex is a facility available to varsity athletes and the general student body alike. The building houses the 60,000-square-foot Dawn Tibbetts Potter Arena, which features a student fitness center and basketball/volleyball courts. The building also houses the John "Jack" McAvoy Natatorium for swimming and diving, an exercise physiology and sports medicine facility, four racquetball courts, extensive locker room space, and a weight/fitness room. Adjacent is the 7,000-seat capacity Frank "Muddy" Waters Stadium, which features an artificial surface football field; all-weather, Olympic-quality eight-lane running track; outdoor tennis courts; and fields for soccer, baseball, and women's softball. The new Margot V. Biermann Athletic Center houses a six-lane track and four tennis courts. The Sage Center for the Arts is home to the departments of art, theatre, and rhetoric and public address. This 47,000-square-foot facility contains studios, classroom space, an exhibition gallery, a prop and scene-construction shop, a sound studio, graphics lab, black box theatre, and the Markel Auditorium, a 353-seat performance hall (with orchestra pit). Completed in 2003, the 32,809-square-foot Howard Music Hall houses office, studio, classroom, rehearsal, and performance space for the John E. N. and Dede Howard Department of Music. Notable features include the McNamara Rehearsal Hall, Conrad Recital Hall, and studio space for percussion and jazz studies. Lower-level practice rooms are available to students during business hours without reservation. Dedicated in January 2008, the 53,000-square-foot Grewcock Student Union is the center of student life. The two-story structure houses the cafeteria, bookstore, student mail center, offices for student activities and publications, a lounge with a 100-inch flat screen television, a formal lounge and conference room, AJ's Café, and a game area.

OFF-CAMPUS OPPORTUNITIES

For forty years, the Washington Hillsdale Internship Program (WHIP) has provided students the opportunity to participate in full-time, academically intensive internships in the nation's capital. The program has been significantly bolstered with the 2008 establishment of the Hillsdale College Allan P. Kirby, Jr. Center for Constitutional Studies and Citizenship in Washington, D.C. Past interns and fellows have been placed in locations as challenging and rewarding as the U.S. House of Representatives, the U.S. Senate, the White House, various think tanks including the Heritage Foundation, news and media outlets, national security agencies, lobbying firms, international trade and relations organizations, and private sector companies. Through the College's affiliations with the Center for Medieval and Renaissance Studies and the Oxford Study Abroad Program, Hillsdale students are able to study abroad for a summer or a year at one of the more than thirty colleges of Oxford University. Hillsdale offers a summer business program in cooperation with Regent's College in London, England, and the opportunity to study at the University of St. Andrews in St. Andrews, Scotland. Science students benefit from Hillsdale's 685-acre field research laboratory in northern Michigan, as well as from a marine biology program in the Florida Keys, and internship opportunities with the Omaha Zoo. Foreign language students frequently study abroad in Argentina, France, Germany, and Spain. Qualified individual students who wish to study in another country for a semester or a year are assisted by their faculty adviser and the registrar in planning a program that enables them to gain academic credit as well as take full advantage of their experience.

ACADEMICS

Hillsdale operates on a two-semester schedule, with the fall term beginning in late August and ending in mid-December and the spring term beginning in mid-January and ending in mid-May. Two 3-week summer sessions are also offered. The College believes that a sound classical liberal arts education includes study in the humanities, natural sciences, and social sciences, and each student is required to complete a structured core of courses in these areas. All students declare a major by the end of the junior year. To graduate, students must complete a minimum 124 hours of course work and fulfill the requirements of at least one major field. The B.A. program includes a foreign language proficiency requirement. The B.S. program requires additional studies in mathematics and the natural sciences. The Collegiate Scholars Program enriches the academic experience of high-performing students by providing opportunities to become broadly and deeply versed in the contents and methods of inquiry of the liberal arts, preeminently of the Western intellectual tradition of humanistic and scientific learning in a manner consonant with the aims of the College's Core Curriculum. A combination of special seminars, campus lectures and discussions, retreats, subsidized foreign travel to a destination relevant to the Program's purpose, and the completion of an interdisciplinary senior thesis help to meet this goal. The Center for Constructive Alternatives conducts four weeklong symposia during the academic year and is one of the largest college lecture series in America. These programs, with themes ranging from historical to political, business, science, and the arts, bring to the campus distinguished scholars and public figures of national and international renown. All students are required to enroll in one seminar for credit.

MAJORS & DEGREES OFFERED

Hillsdale awards Bachelor of Arts and Bachelor of Science degrees in accounting, art, biochemistry, biology, chemistry, classics, economics, English, exercise science, financial management, French, German, Greek, history, Latin, marketing/management, mathematics, music, philosophy, philosophy and religion, physical education, physics, politics, psychology, religion, rhetoric, Spanish, sport management, sport psychology, and theatre. Interdisciplinary majors are also available in American studies, Christian studies, comparative literature, European studies, international business and foreign language, political economy, and sociology and social thought. Pre-professional programs are offered in allied health sciences, engineering, environmental sciences, law, medicine, ministry, pharmacy, and veterinary medicine.

TUITION, ROOM, BOARD, FEES

Annual tuition for the 2016-17 academic year was $24,670, room was $5,040, board was $5,160, and general fees were $852. Books, supplies, and personal expenses (including travel, recreation, and clothing) are estimated at $3,200 per year.

FINANCIAL AID

Financial aid at Hillsdale is available in many forms. Academic scholarships are awarded on a competitive basis, regardless of financial need, to students who rank in the top 10 percent of their high school class and have standardized test scores in the top 10 percent according to national test norms. The priority deadline for academic scholarship consideration is January 1. The application for admission also serves as the Hillsdale application for merit-based aid. Athletic scholarships are available on a competitive basis in men's baseball, football, and golf; men's and women's basketball, tennis, track, and cross-country; and women's swimming, softball, and volleyball. The departments of art and music also award a select number of scholarships based on strength of portfolio/audition. To apply for aid on the basis of financial need, students are required to file Hillsdale's Confidential Family Financial Statement (CFFS) in January or February of the year of prospective enrollment at Hillsdale. Grants and loans are available from the College.

STUDENT ORGANIZATIONS & ACTIVITIES

Four national fraternities, three national sororities, and more than 100 other social, academic, spiritual, and service organizations provide Hillsdale students with a diverse array of cocurricular opportunities. A resident drama troupe and dance company, a concert choir and chamber chorale, a jazz program with big band and combos, instrumental chamber ensembles from string quartets to percussion ensemble, and a symphony orchestra and band constitute the College's performing arts organizations. Special student services provided by the College include career planning and placement counseling, academic advising and tutoring, and a health service staffed by a physician and a resident nurse.

ADMISSIONS PROCESS

Admission is a privilege extended to students who will benefit from, and contribute to, the academic, social, and spiritual environments of the College. Important determinants for admission are intellectual curiosity, ambition, leadership, and volunteerism. Accordingly, grade-point average, test scores, class rank, strength of curriculum, extracurricular activities, interviews, self-evaluations, writing samples, and recommendations are all reviewed carefully and are important in the evaluation process. An admissions interview is strongly encouraged. Although some factors are necessarily more important than others, seldom is any single criterion, however important, decisive. Transfer students must submit the standard application, including the high school record, SAT, ACT or CLT (Classic Learning Test) scores, transcripts from all colleges previously attended, and a transfer form from the dean of students of the most recent college attended. Applications by transfers are evaluated similarly to non-transfers. Candidates for admission from other countries follow the regular entrance procedures. Students who come from a non-English-speaking country must complete the ACT or SAT to demonstrate proficiency in English as well as academic preparedness. The Test of English as a Foreign Language (TOEFL) or the Michigan Test of English Proficiency are recommended to help further demonstrate English proficiency. Students may apply to Hillsdale College any time after the completion of the junior year of high school. A formal application includes a completed application form accompanied by a nonrefundable fee of $35 (free if submitted online) and all required credentials. Students may apply under one of two plans. Early Decision is a binding application deadline, where students are asked to withdraw applications from other institutions should their application be accepted by Hillsdale. The due date for Early Decision candidates is November 1. All other students may apply under Regular Decision. The deadline for Regular Decision is April 1, and students are notified of a decision within four weeks of finalizing their application (beginning December 15). Students wishing to be considered for priority scholarship should apply no later than January 1. Hillsdale College has been distinguished since its founding in 1844 by voluntarily adhering to a nondiscriminatory policy regarding race, religion, sex, and national or ethnic origin—long before the government began regulating such matters.

HOFSTRA UNIVERSITY

AT A GLANCE
Discover Your Pride and Purpose at Hofstra University

Hofstra University is one of the largest private colleges on Long Island, New York, and one of only three universities in the New York metropolitan area with schools of medicine, law, and engineering. Since its founding in 1935, Hofstra has evolved into an internationally renowned university that continues to achieve recognition as an institution of academic excellence. Hofstra is consistently recognized on the Best College lists of U.S. News & World Report, The Princeton Review, Fiske Guide to Colleges, Washington Monthly, and Forbes.

Our students roll up their sleeves, and make things happen. You will be encouraged to grow academically, as well as personally, through community service, leadership development, cultural and social exploration, study abroad and internships on Long Island and in New York City.

At Hofstra, Pride & Purpose means celebrating our history and traditions, and challenging ourselves, individually and collectively, to use our talents to make our campus, our community and our world a better place.

LOCATION & ENVIRONMENT
The Best of Both Worlds

At Hofstra University, students live, work and study on a beautiful, state-of-the-art campus that's only 25 miles east of Manhattan. Our 244-acre campus is lush, green and spacious, with ivy-covered buildings and cutting edge facilities, just minutes from all the adventure and opportunity that New York City has to offer. Hofstra University's 115 buildings include state-of-the-art teaching facilities, six theaters, a museum, newly renovated Fitness Center, and libraries containing 1.2 million print volumes and providing 24/7 electronic access to more than 95,000 journals and electronic books.

With top-notch resources and wide-ranging programs of a large university, and the sense of community and personal attention of a small college, Hofstra is a great place for students who are looking for a traditional campus experience without sacrificing the networking opportunities, internship experiences, and cultural offerings of a bustling metropolis. Students can also explore Long Island, which offers world-class beaches and parks, the Hamptons, sport fishing and boating, and conveniently located shopping malls.

CAMPUS FACILITIES & EQUIPMENT

As a Hofstra student, you can chose to live in one of our 35 residence halls, each with a unique flair, community and life of its own. We also offer eight living/learning communities, which give students the opportunity to live with many of the same students they are in classes with, as well as students who share the same passion for leadership, health professions, or the visual or performing arts.

Hofstra students have endless opportunities for experiential learning, on and off-campus. Opportunities are available to conduct research with a distinguished professor; and intern with top-tier companies in finance or media, in the state Legislature or Congress.

Students live and learn on a campus that is home to state-of-the-art facilities. C. V. Starr Hall, home to the Frank G. Zarb School of Business, features the Martin B. Greenberg Trading Room, which has 34 Bloomberg terminals and is among the largest academic training facilities in the world. Hofstra has invested $12 million to open a cell and tissue engineering lab, a big data lab, and a mechatronics lab at the Fred DeMatteis School of Engineering and Applied Science.

The Lawrence Herbert School of Communication contains one of the largest broadcast facilities in the northeastern United States, as well as a converged newsroom and multimedia classroom. Plus, Hofstra students benefit from real-world experience at the award-winning on-campus radio station, WRHU 88.7 FM (Radio Hofstra University), which was ranked the top college radio station in the country by The Princeton Review (2015 and 2016) and is the only college radio station in the nation that is the flagship for a professional sports franchise, the NHL's New York Islanders.

The David S. Mack Sports and Exhibition Complex, a 93,000-square-foot facility, is home to the Hofstra Pride men's and women's basketball teams and wrestling, and is also the site for events such as commencements, exhibitions, trade shows, televised political events, and concerts. Other recreational and athletic facilities include an indoor, Olympic-sized swimming pool, and various athletic fields.

OFF-CAMPUS OPPORTUNITIES
Hofstra extends learning beyond the classroom through active internship programs and dynamic and varied study abroad opportunities. The internship program takes advantage of the proximity of New York City, allowing students to gain on-the-job experience in areas such as finance, business, media, advertising, and entertainment. Through study abroad programs in Europe, Asia, South America, etc., students can explore the world while earning college credits. Visit hofstra.edu/studyabroad for more information.

ACADEMICS
A Program Meant for You

Hofstra's faculty members are knowledgeable and insightful thinkers, dedicated to providing the foundation and tools students need to succeed. With an average undergraduate class size of 21 and a student-faculty ratio of 14-to-1, students are challenged and encouraged to debate, question, do research, discuss and think critically in an open, collaborative learning environment. And, 93 percent of our full-time faculty hold the highest degree in their respective fields.

Requirements for graduation vary among schools and majors. A liberal arts core curriculum is an integral part of all areas of concentration. The University calendar is organized on a traditional fall and spring semester system, and offers an optional January session and three optional Summer sessions (between May and August).

Hofstra offers innovative programs designed to meet the needs of its diverse student body. These include Hofstra University Honors College, Legal Education Accelerated Program (LEAP), Hofstra 4+4 Program, First-Year Connections, and living/learning communities.

Hofstra University Honors College students can elect to study in any of the University's undergraduate programs and are involved in all fields of advanced study.

MAJORS & DEGREES OFFERED

Change to: Hofstra holds 25 academic and 28 total accreditations. The university offers six undergraduate degrees—BA, BBA, BE, BFA, BS and BSED—and 160 undergraduate program options. In addition, they offer more than 100 dual degree programs, which allows students to earn both an undergraduate and graduate degree in less time than if each degree was pursued separately, saving them the cost of one or more semesters of tuition.

The University comprises the following schools: Hofstra College of Liberal Arts and Sciences, which includes The School of Education, The School of Humanities, Fine and Performing Arts, The School of Natural Sciences and Mathematics, and The Peter S. Kalikow School of Government, Public Policy and International Affairs; Hofstra University Honors College; The Frank G. Zarb School of Business; The Lawrence Herbert School of Communication; The Fred DeMatteis School of Engineering and Applied Science; The School of Health Professions and Human Services; The Maurice A. Deane School of Law at Hofstra University; The Hofstra Northwell School of Graduate Nursing and Physician Assistant Studies; and The Hofstra Northwell School of Medicine at Hofstra University.

TUITION, ROOM, BOARD, FEES

The 2016-17 annual tuition and fees for a full-time undergraduate student were $42,160. The cost of a housing and dining plan was approximately $14,460. Books and supplies cost approximately $1,000; personal expenses and transportation generally amount to $3,245. For the full tuition and fees schedule, visit hofstra.edu/tuition.

FINANCIAL AID

Hofstra University works hard to make a private college education affordable for students and families, and offers several financial aid options for new undergraduates, including interest-free payment plans and a money-saving four-year locked-in rate for tuition and fees (hofstra.edu/lockedintuitionrate) that can help students manage costs from admission through graduation. For detailed information, students should visit hofstra.edu/FinancialAid.

STUDENT ORGANIZATIONS & ACTIVITIES

Hofstra offers 17 intercollegiate athletic programs that compete at the NCAA Division I level and more than 200 academic, fraternal/sororal, media, multicultural, performance, pre-professional, religious, social, social/political, and sports clubs and organizations.

Hofstra also recognizes the value of bringing experiential learning opportunities to our campus, most notably by hosting three US presidential debates in 2008, 2012 and 2016, as well as the New York State gubernatorial debate in 2010, allowing our students to observe the democratic process firsthand.

The Student Government Association (SGA) is Hofstra University's student-run governing body and is comprised of full-time undergraduate students that act as a liaison between Hofstra students and the University's faculty, administration, and Board of Trustees. In addition, SGA plans and executes multiple programs and initiatives throughout the academic year, and oversees and finances of over 180 clubs and organizations.

ADMISSIONS
Applying to Hofstra

Hofstra University seeks to enroll talented first-year and transfer students from diverse backgrounds and locations, with varied interests. Applications are accepted for fall and spring admission. The Admission Committee reviews each application individually to assess academic achievement, curricular rigor, leadership potential, and depth of extracurricular activities, standardized test scores and overall interest in attending Hofstra University. The application process provides an opportunity for the applicant to share information that may not be apparent on a transcript or through a test score. For more information about the admission process, go to hofstra.edu/admission or go to hofstra.edu/visit and schedule a campus visit, today!

JOHNS HOPKINS UNIVERSITY

AT A GLANCE

As America's first research institution, Johns Hopkins University emphasizes the importance of exploration and discovery in the undergraduate experience.

Johns Hopkins is a place where ambitious, talented, and creative students thrive. Learning occurs through hands-on experiences across all academic disciplines and within every subject imaginable. Academic freedom allows students to create their own unique interdisciplinary schedules. They choose classes they are genuinely interested in, not just required to take, so there's a real sense of curiosity around learning that extends beyond the classroom setting.

Students can make an impact as soon as they arrive on campus. They get to know their professors and classmates the way they would at a small liberal arts college but have all of the opportunities of a major research institution with a global reach. With the nation's most research funding for 37 consecutive years, Johns Hopkins is well known for ground-breaking advances in everything from technology to history. As a part of this community, undergraduates run with projects of their own design and work alongside experts who share their passions.

The Homewood campus brings together students with diverse passions. Diversity of thought, culture, and interests cultivates a dynamic, open-minded environment. With over 300 student-run organizations, students find leadership opportunities and the chance to get involved on campus and beyond.

The admissions committee approaches applications from a holistic perspective, evaluating the 'whole student.' In addition to looking at a student's academic achievement and intellectual curiosity, we seek students who are excited about learning and living at Johns Hopkins. We look for students who will contribute to the campus community while taking advantage of all Johns Hopkins has to offer.

LOCATION & ENVIRONMENT

Johns Hopkins is an active and supportive community, filled with students of different viewpoints, cultures, and backgrounds. The thing that brings them all together is their desire to be here and to celebrate everything this place has to offer.

There's always something going on--and freshmen are encouraged to get involved. Every week offers lectures, concerts, art and photography exhibitions, theater, movies, volunteer opportunities, and whatever else anybody has an idea to do. You'll never run out of things to try.

OFF-CAMPUS OPPORTUNITIES

Baltimore's resources make it an extension of the classroom and an integral part of a Hopkins education. Off campus, the city provides unique academic, cultural, and pre-professional experiences. Some classes partner with local organizations to give students practical experiences that complement classroom lectures—like engineering a "fish ladder" at Maryland's Bloede Dam or replicating ancient Greek pottery work at Baltimore Clayworks. Due to the vast network of Hopkins schools and facilities that extends throughout Baltimore (and abroad), undergraduates have the chance to take courses and participate in research at the other divisions of Johns Hopkins University, including the Peabody Conservatory, the School of Nursing, the Bloomberg School of Public Health, the Nitze School of Advanced International Studies, the School of Education, the Carey Business School, and the School of Medicine.

Hopkins students also embrace the university's long-standing commitment to Baltimore and use their skills to make an impact on the city that becomes their second home. The pre-professional, volunteer, and just-for-fun experiences Hopkins students encounter create lasting memories and offer preparation for future success in a wide variety of industries.

ACADEMICS

The academic landscape at Hopkins is interdisciplinary by nature. Students from various backgrounds bring different perspectives to class discussions, creating a more dynamic, engaging learning environment. Collaboration is encouraged—between students and across disciplines. Virtually all programs combine different areas of study to help students think more comprehensively about issues. More than 60 percent of Hopkins students double major or minor, often creating unique combinations like electrical engineering and romance languages, mathematics and philosophy, or biomedical engineering and entrepreneurship and management.

Undergraduates in all programs within the Krieger School of Arts & Sciences and Whiting School of Engineering gain practical experiences through research conducted both on and off campus. Several funded programs, such as the Provost's Undergraduate Research Awards and the Woodrow Wilson Undergraduate Research Fellowship, are available to give participants the chance to complete projects of their own design. Students also encounter real-world experiences—like implementing marketing plans for local companies and heading startup businesses on campus—through the Center for Leadership Education, which houses the popular entrepreneurship and management minor. Students can pursue their creative interests through the Center for Visual Arts, which offers an array of programs and almost 40 studio courses.

Several combined programs are available for undergraduates looking to broaden their educational experience. The Peabody Double Degree Program allows qualified students to simultaneously earn a bachelor of music from The Johns Hopkins Peabody Institute and a B.A or B.S. from Johns Hopkins University. The Direct Matriculation Program: Master's in International Studies allows qualified students displaying a strong interest in international studies to pursue a combined bachelor's/master's degree with the Johns Hopkins School of Advanced International Studies (SAIS) in Washington, DC. Similarly, the Direct Matriculation Program: Master's in Global Health Studies offers qualified students displaying a strong interest in public health to pursue a combined bachelor's/master's degree with the Johns Hopkins Bloomberg School of Public Health.

Johns Hopkins has schools, centers, and affiliates all over the Baltimore area—and they are often linked by free shuttle bus—in Washington, D.C., across the country, and around the world. The larger Hopkins network offers opportunities for cross registration, independent projects, and internships.

MAJORS

Students interested in pursuing law or medicine choose any of the 52 majors and 47 minors but follow a pre-law or pre-med advising track offered through the Office of Pre-Professional Advising. The biomedical engineering (BME) program at Johns Hopkins is widely regarded as one of the best in the world.

CAMPUS FACILITIES & EQUIPMENT

Collaborative learning is fundamental to the academic environment and many of the newest buildings were designed to foster collaboration across disciplines. The Brody Learning Commons (BLC) is one of the most popular places for students to gather, study, and work together. Designed with student input, the building is directly connected to the library and contains the latest learning technology to support collaborative work—like interactive projectors that allow students to write on walls and video teleconferencing capabilities. The Undergraduate Teaching Labs (UTL) is another recently constructed building, a 105,000-square-foot facility equipped with the latest lab technology that enables synergistic, cross-disciplinary partnerships and research opportunities. Malone Hall was built less than two years ago and is a hub for the computer science department, where faculty and students work on innovative projects.

The Milton S. Eisenhower Library on the Homewood campus is part of the university's Sheridan Libraries, which comprise the Milton S. Eisenhower Library, the John Work Garrett Library, the Albert D. Hutzler Undergraduate Reading Room, and the George Peabody Library. Together, these libraries provide one of the most comprehensive learning resources in the world. Two on-campus creative centers provide resources for students in the arts: The Mattin Student Arts Center contains theaters, a dance studio, music practice rooms, film and digital labs, darkrooms, and art studios; the Brown Foundation Digital Media Center offers digital tools like high-end computers and cameras that enable digital and audio composition and editing, animation, virtual painting, 3-D modeling, and workshops for programs like Adobe After Effects. Off campus, just a short shuttle ride away, the Johns Hopkins–MICA Film Center gives students access to state-of-the-art production facilities.

The Ralph S. O'Connor Recreation Center, open for use by all students, houses basketball and volleyball courts, a rock-climbing wall, a weight room, and fitness training and aerobics areas, as well as access to the Athletic Center's swimming facilities. Popular fitness classes include yoga, Pilates, kickboxing, step aerobics, spinning, West African dance, and sports conditioning.

TUITION, ROOM, BOARD, FEES

Costs for 2016-2017 are $50,410 for tuition and $14,976 for room and board, plus personal expenses like book and travel. (Expenses such as travel and room and board vary based on choices.)

FINANCIAL AID

Johns Hopkins is dedicated to enrolling the strongest students each year regardless of financial need and does so by offering a variety of financial support programs for all types of families as well as personalized guidance through the process of finding the right path for them. The university will meet 100% of calculated need and also offers a broad range of grants and support. Last year, students received over $80 million in grant money towards their Hopkins education, with an average need-based grant for first-year students of over $38,000.

STUDENT ORGANIZATIONS & ACTIVITIES

Homewood is an active, engaged campus where students are members of over 300 student groups and organizations. All Johns Hopkins student groups are governed and managed by students, and there is something for everybody with organizations dedicated to—theater and performing arts, politics, investments, service work, publications, student government, and even fire juggling. Athletics fuel school spirit, often found in full force at the Nest, a student seating section of Homewood Field. One out of six Johns Hopkins students participates in one of our twenty Division III teams or club athletics, and more than half participate in the popular intramural program.

The 140-acre undergraduate campus featuring grassy quads and brick buildings is surrounded by residential areas and neighborhoods that boast one-of-a-kind boutiques, restaurants ranging from fancy to funky, historic theaters, museums, and an arts and entertainment district. The nearby Charles Village community located just beyond the Homewood campus front gates is home to many shops, restaurants, some student housing, and the Barnes and Noble bookstore. Students can grab lunch or coffee at chains and local mom-and-pop spots and have access to banks, dry cleaners, and grocery stores.

ADMISSIONS PROCESS

The university looks for students who are eager to take advantage of the resources and opportunities at Johns Hopkins, and who will contribute to the campus community. The student's academic character, intellectual curiosity, impact and initiative, and extracurricular involvement play a significant role in application review. A student's intellectual interests and accomplishments are of primary importance, and the admissions committee considers each applicant's scholastic record, standardized test results, essays, and recommendations from secondary school officials. In addition to the application and the Hopkins supplemental essay, other required documents include: Two teacher recommendations, secondary school report, and the SAT Reasoning Test or the ACT. The university enrolls a first-year class of approximately 1,300 men and women from across the globe. In addition, transfer students from other colleges and universities are admitted to the sophomore and junior classes.

KETTERING UNIVERSITY

AT A GLANCE

Kettering University is a national leader in experiential STEM education, integrating an intense academic curriculum in science, technology, engineering, mathematics and business with applied professional and cooperative learning experiences. Through this proven approach, Kettering University inspires students to realize their potential and advance their ideas.

During study terms, students learn in small classes taught by professors, not teaching assistants. During work terms, they gain professional experience at corporations related to their studies. Students in all degree programs alternate between study terms and work terms.

Kettering students graduate with up to 2 1/2 years of real world experience and envy-worthy resumes. Our students have done everything from testing ballistic systems and re-engineering crowd management to designing biomedical tools.

All of this experience pays off. Research shows that students who participate in co-op and experiential learning programs are more mature, better problem solvers, and more technically knowledgeable. Employers know that Kettering students are the cream of the crop 98% of Kettering University students graduate with job offers within their fields or are attending graduate school within six months of graduating. The average yearly starting salary of a Kettering student is $64,000. Kettering ranks among the top 1% of private institutions in the U.S. to offer $1 million plus return on investment to its graduates according to Affordable Colleges Online.

LOCATION & ENVIRONMENT

Kettering University is located in Flint, MI, roughly 60 miles north of Detroit and a short drive from Lake Huron. Flint has approximately 100,000 residents. The Flint Cultural Center -located just one-and-a-half miles from campus houses the Sloan Museum, Whiting Auditorium, Longway Planetarium, the Flint Institute of Music, and the Flint Institute of Arts. The nearby DTE Energy Music Center is one of the nation's top-ranked amphitheater venues and hosts more than 70 events each summer. While a sizable city, Flint also has 11,000 acres of woods, water and trails to offer all part of Michigan's largest country park system. Students can enjoy golfing, hiking, kayaking, hunting, skiing and snowmobiling, and more. All freshmen live on campus while 36% percent of students live on campus the remainder of their college experience.

CAMPUS FACILITIES & EQUIPMENT

The unique structure of Kettering's program allows students to fulfill the academic requirements of 160 credit hours throughout a four and a half year period. This is completed over nine academic semesters and up to 11 co-op work semesters. Students also complete a culminating undergraduate experience during their senior year for credit toward the 160 required hours. These capstone experiences come in the form of a thesis project on behalf of their co-op employer, a research thesis project, a professional practice thesis project or an entrepreneurship thesis project. The academic year consists of two 11-week academic terms on-campus in Flint and two 12-week co-op terms working for the corporate employer; students alternate their time between Flint and the employer's site.

OFF-CAMPUS OPPORTUNITIES

More than half of a Kettering student's time is spent off campus, fulfilling professional co-op and experiential work requirements at a corporation that relates to their degree or interests. On average, students spend 11 academic semesters working for their employer and nine academic semesters in the classroom. Students work at one of Kettering's more than 500 employer partners located throughout North America and the globe. On average, students earn up to $65,000 over their entire college career.

Undergrads living on campus 36%

Registered Student Organizations: 50+

Number of Honor Societies: 13

ACADEMICS

The unique structure of Kettering's program allows students to fulfill the academic requirements of 160 credit hours throughout a four and a half year period. This is completed over nine academic semesters and up to 11 co-op work semesters. Students also complete a capstone thesis project on behalf of their co-op employer during their senior year for credit toward the 160 required hours. The academic year consists of two 11-week academic terms on-campus in Flint and two 12-week academic terms working for the corporate employer; students alternate their time between Flint and the employer's site. On average, a freshman student who spends 24 weeks during the academic year working for the professional co-op employer earns $11,000.

MAJORS

Kettering University's four and a half year cooperative and experiential learning program allows students to earn designated Bachelor of Science degrees in:

Applied Biology

Applied Mathematics

Applied Physics

Biochemistry

Business Administration

Chemical Engineering

Chemistry

Computer Engineering

Computer Science

Electrical Engineering

Engineering Physics

Industrial Engineering

Mechanical Engineering

Kettering also offers more than 50 minors, concentrations, specialties, courses of study and dual degrees, in areas such as Applied Optics, Pre-Law, Computer Gaming, System and Data Security, and Pre-Med. Additionally, the school offers 12 Master's Degrees, including an accredited MBA program. Please visit kettering.edu for more information.

TUITION, ROOM, BOARD, FEES

Tuition for the 2016-17 academic year is $19,895* per term. Kettering is proud to offer students a Fixed Tuition Guarantee. Students making normal progress towards their degree will pay the same tuition rates for their entire college career. Kettering has also eliminated all academically-related fees in its all-inclusive tuition package.

Room and Board for the 2016-17 academic year is $3,890 per term.

*Please remember that tuition and fees are subject to change at any time.

FINANCIAL AID

Kettering University offers traditional need and merit-based financial aid, including a generous merit scholarship program. In fact, more than 99% of Kettering students receive some level of financial assistance. Factor in co-op earnings the average hourly wage of a Kettering student is $14.40 for freshmen and $17.70 for seniors—and our fixed-rate tuition guarantee, and students are looking at one of the best values in education today. Aid is given as grants, scholarships, loans, and work-study awards. Students should fill out the Free Application for Federal Student Aid (FAFSA) and request a copy of the analysis be sent to Kettering University. The University works to create a financial package based on those results.

STUDENT ORGANIZATIONS & ACTIVITIES

College life should offer students more than just learning opportunities. To this end, Kettering offers more than 50+ student organizations, such as SAE, DECA and Engineers without Borders, and numerous social activities and intramural sports. Approximately a third of Kettering students join the 12 national fraternities and 7 sororities that are represented on campus. The school's active student government produces programs to develop peers' leadership skills, self-confidence, interpersonal relations, and organizational operations. Students come from approximately 48 states and 18 countries, so they also benefit from learning and sharing with this diverse community.

ADMISSIONS PROCESS

Admission to Kettering University is competitive and based on scholastic achievement and extracurricular interests, activities, and achievements. Applicants are required to have completed the following courses (one credit represents two semesters or one year of study): Two credits algebra, one credit geometry, a half credit trigonometry, two credits laboratory science (one of these credits must be from physics or chemistry, and both are strongly recommended), and three credits English. Applicants must submit SAT or ACT scores. Most Kettering University students rank at or near the top 10 percent of their high school class.

Kettering University also accepts transfer students. A minimum of 14 credits is required, but 16-20 credits are strongly encouraged. Admission decisions for transfer applicants are based on college records for those who have completed at least 30 credits.

Although applications are accepted all year long, prospective students are encouraged to file their application early in their senior year. Early application significantly improves students' chances for early co-op employment. Interested students can apply online at www.kettering.edu/apply.

KEYSTONE COLLEGE

AT A GLANCE

Keystone College is a small, private college that educates students in the liberal arts tradition. Keystone College has a long history of serving students. What began as Keystone Academy in 1868 has now become one of the most popular and most diverse institutions in northeastern Pennsylvania. Keystone College is consistently recognized for its small class sizes and exceptional reputation by organizations like U.S. News and World Report.

Keystone College aspires to transform lives by inspiring and empowering a community where learning flourishes. By offering students a personalized, hands-on learning atmosphere combined with a guarantee of success, Keystone College has quickly become a leader in quality education.

Also included in the Keystone College story is a personalized educational experience. With an 11:1 student-to-faculty ratio the college is able to ensure the individual attention that students deserve. Keystone offers a variety of opportunities for experiential learning. Students have completed internships for such places as Good Morning America (ABC TV), the Philadelphia Eagles, the U.S. Secret Service, Walt Disney World, and the United States Olympic Committee. Students may also choose to take their studies or internships abroad. Recently, Keystone students have studied or worked recently in England, the Czech Republic, India, Australia, Ireland, Spain, and Costa Rica. Hands-on learning is also available without setting foot off campus through access to unique offerings like the Oppenheim Family Children's Center, a daycare and preschool where education students can train, and the campus's woodlands, streams, and ponds, which provide a natural classroom for students in environmental programs.

In addition to its commitment to its student body, Keystone College is fully dedicated to the protection of our environment. Through several green initiatives, the College has greatly reduced the size of the carbon footprint left behind by the campus. These initiatives include: the purchase of four electric vans which replaced three gas powered vehicles, the purchase of Energy Star rated appliances throughout campus, special parking for carpoolers; and Trayless Tuesdays and the utilization of biomass packaging in dining areas. The strength of The Keystone Family makes the picturesque campus a source of intellectual growth, cultural awareness, environmental stewardship, and service opportunities.

Keystone has a diverse student body of approximately 1400 students from across the United States and the globe. With an 11:1 student-to-faculty ratio and an average class size of about 13 students, Keystone is able to ensure the individual attention that students deserve.

LOCATION & ENVIRONMENT

Nestled in the heart of the Endless Mountains in Northeastern Pennsylvania, Keystone College's rural 276-acre campus is truly special. Located only 15 minutes from Downtown Scranton and a short road trip away from New York City and Philadelphia, Keystone is near some of the best entertainment, cultural, and sporting venues in the Northeast. The large campus includes 170 woodland acres with 7 miles of nature trails.

CAMPUS FACILITIES & EQUIPMENT

At Keystone you will find the Regional 3-D Design Center (KC3D), an additive manufacturing and 3-D printing center for students to gain visual arts and workforce experience; the Oppenheim Family Children's Center, a daycare and preschool where education students can train; and the Thomas Cupillari '60 Astronomical Observatory, an educational and research facility for the Keystone community and general public. The campus's woodlands campus boasts facilities for Field Biology coursework, such as a maple sugar shack, apple orchard, nature trails, vernal pool, and apiary. Visual arts students also benefit from having access to sculpture, printmaking, painting and photography studios, a foundry, and the region's only hot glass studio.

OFF-CAMPUS OPPORTUNITIES

An off-campus shuttle is available for trips to Scranton and the Dickson City shopping areas. Students also have opportunities every semester for bus trips to Philadelphia and New York City.

ACADEMICS

In its effort to transform lives by inspiring and empowering a community where learning flourishes, Keystone has designed the Stairs to Success program, a four-year plan for undergraduates to get the most of their college experience and be prepared for the real world as Keystone graduate. Keystone enhances every student's experience through its unique pledge to graduates: "The Keystone Promise." This guarantee of success includes a promise in writing that within six months of graduating from Keystone College students will have received at least one job offer, or where appropriate, be accepted into a graduate or transfer program. In the unlikely event this does not occur, we will provide you with additional courses and career counseling at no additional charge. Keystone offers a variety of opportunities for experiential learning in all of our programs which prepares our graduates for successful careers. Some of the recent graduates have gained placement at successful companies such as ABC News, UPS, NBA, ESPN, and Time Warner; and with government agencies including Federal Homeland Security, Department of Defense, IRS, FDA, and National Park Service. Keystone alumni are also enrolled at prestigious graduate schools across the U.S.

FACULTY

The dedicated faculty at Keystone College support the students through advising, academics, and undergraduate research. Faculty members serve as mentors to students in both student-and faculty-initiated research, and they provide students with opportunities to connect with professionals in their field and gain experience.

MAJORS

Keystone offers over 40 degree options for every interest, including Business, Education, Arts, Criminal Justice, and the Natural Sciences.

TUITION, ROOM, BOARD, FEES

Tuition, fees, room, and board for a new student living on campus for the 2017-2018 academic year is $36,200. Tuition and fees for a commuter student is $25,648.

Textbooks and course materials are included in the price of tuition, through the IncludeED program. This eliminates the difficulty many college students face in being able to afford the additional cost of textbooks after paying for tuition, room, and board, and ensures that no student goes without the materials they need in order to succeed. Students will have access to all texts, whether electronic or traditional hard-copy format, as well as other materials such lab coats and art supplies. As an added benefit, full-time students will be given a free table to access online texts and coursework.

FINANCIAL AID

Keystone College is committed to making a college education affordable. 96% of Keystone students receive financial aid. Generous merit scholarships are awarded at the time of admission, and range from $6,500 per year to full tuition. Students are automatically considered for merit scholarships, but should file a FAFSA to be considered for additional institutional aid, as well as federal and state financial aid. Keystone's FAFSA code is 003280.

Keystone College recognizes that many students and parents have concerns about student loans. Keystone College wants students to be free to pursue the career of their choice without the worry of student loans standing in the way. The Keystone Commitment Loan Repayment Assistance Program is a pledge offered to first-time, full-time freshmen pursuing a bachelor's degree. If a student graduates within six years with their baccalaureate degree and does not earn $40,000 per year, Keystone will help repay their student (and parent PLUS) loans until they do. This is an added benefit and there is no charge to students.

STUDENT ORGANIZATIONS & ACTIVITIES

Keystone College offers a variety of diverse activities for all areas of interest including academic, social, spiritual, recreational, or athletic. The College boasts over 30 student-run clubs and organizations, 10 instrumental and voice ensembles, intramural sports, and plenty of leadership opportunities. Most activities, including music lessons and instrument rentals, are at no cost.

Keystone students also have a reputation for being involved in the community. Through our Office of Civic Engagement and Service Learning, Keystone students have recorded over 24,000 hours of community service in one year, gaining them status on the President's Honor Roll for Community Service with Distinction. In addition, Keystone College is a military friendly school with a very active Armed Forces Club.

Keystone College has 21 NCAA Division III varsity sports.

SPECIAL PROGRAMS

Among other unique programs to Keystone College, Stairs to Success is a four-year developmental program designed for students to get the most out of their education and be fully prepared to step into the world beyond college. The plan describes events, academic curriculum, and career development opportunities that, if followed, will make the most of your college years and help you success with your academic goals and career dreams.

ADMISSIONS PROCESS

Keystone reviews applications on a rolling basis; meaning that students will receive an admissions decision once the office receives their application materials. Starting for Fall 2017 applicants, Keystone is now test optional, which allows students to receive an admissions decision without submitting SAT or ACT scores. Test scores will be considered if submitted, and Keystone reserves the right to require them in some instances. Students should submit scores if they feel they are a positive reflection of their ability, but they will not be at a disadvantage if scores are withheld. By simply sending an application and transcripts from all institutions attended (high school and college/university), a student will receive a quick admissions decision and merit scholarship review. Additional requirements may be requested from international students or those applying to one of Keystone's visual arts programs.

KING'S COLLEGE (PA)

AT A GLANCE

King's is a Catholic, comprehensive college in the liberal arts tradition founded by the Congregation of Holy Cross offering 36 majors in business and 25 NCAA Division III athletic programs for men and women.

King's is a Catholic, comprehensive college in the liberal arts tradition founded in 1946 by the Congregation of Holy Cross from the University of Notre Dame. King's is located on a small urban campus in Wilkes-Barre, Pennsylvania. King's offers 36 majors in business, the humanities, engineering, social sciences, education, sciences and allied health programs, as well as seven pre-professional programs and 11 special concentrations. With over 50 clubs and activities and 25 NCAA Division III athletic programs for men and women, there is plenty to do outside the classroom.

Small classes and labs allow for meaningful interaction between professors and students. The average class size is 18 students, average lab size is 13 students, and the student/faculty ratio is 12:1. The favorable student-teacher ration means more opportunities for personal attention, which in turn accounts for King's superior graduation rates.

King's academic programs are accredited by highly respected accrediting agencies, including the following:

- The Association to Advance Collegiate Schools of Business (AACSB) (The William G. McGowan School of Business is one of only 42 undergraduate schools of business nationwide accredited by the AACSB.)

- The National Council for the Accreditation of Teacher Education (King's is one of only 19 colleges in Pennsylvania with this accreditation.)

- The Accreditation Review Commission on Education for Physician Assistants

- The Commission on Accreditation of Athletic Training Education

- The American Chemical Society

LOCATION & ENVIRONMENT

King's College is located in the City of Wilkes-Barre in northeastern Pennsylvania, within driving distance of New York City, Philadelphia, Washington, D.C. and other east coast attractions. The atmosphere is friendly and inviting, with a strong sense of community. The King's campus is easy to navigate and has impressive facilities, equal to those at much larger institutions. Located near to campus are malls, theatres and restaurants. The region hosts a busy schedule of cultural events, ethnic celebrations and festivals.

CAMPUS FACILITIES & EQUIPMENT

The new King's on the Square facility, located in the heart of Wilkes-Barre, is home to King's allied health programs. The College features a state-of-the-art sports medicine clinic for its athletic training program. New science labs and equipment enable students to conduct hands-on research. On campus radio and television studios offer audio and video editing equipment for students involved in communications or media. The D. Leonard Corgan Library offers a comprehensive collection of books, periodicals and catalogs, providing students with the informational resources they need to enhance their skills. The College's new food services partner maintains outstanding dining facilities, including a full-service Chick-Fil-A restaurant, located at King's on the Square.

Residence halls offer a variety of living arrangements from single rooms to apartments. Amenities include 24-hour computer labs in several residence halls; each room is equipped with cable TV access. These facilities are all secure, accessible either by student ID card or by the desk attendant on staff 24-hours a day. A state-of-the-art Wi-Fi network is accessible across the entire King's campus.

Athletics Facilities

The 33-acre Robert L. Betzler Fields at McCarthy Stadium is one of the finest facilities in the MAC for football, field hockey, baseball, softball, soccer, lacrosse and track and field. The William S. Scandlon Physical Education Center features the Robert McGrane Basketball Arena. The center also includes a sports medicine clinic, swimming pool, handball and racquetball courts, wrestling room, and new locker rooms. In addition, the recently completed gym expansion project has added a new facility to the Scandlon Center, including three multi-purpose courts as well as new offices, meeting rooms, and additional sports medicine facilities.

OFF-CAMPUS OPPORTUNITIES

It's not all limited to campus, we've got malls, theatres and restaurants minutes away as well as specialty shops, cultural events, ethnic celebrations and festivals. Our bookstore is located in a Barnes & Noble/Starbucks Cafe and is the centerpiece of a bustling downtown.

ACADEMICS

Special Concentrations

Chemistry of Materials
Ethics
Forensic Studies
Geography
International Studies
Latin American Studies
Physics
Political Economy
Statistics
Women's Studies

Core Curriculum

All King's College students, regardless of their majors, participate in the Core Curriculum. Core courses are broadly based so that fundamental aspects of human experience are approached from diverse viewpoints represented by a variety of disciplines. The Core Curriculum is designed to help students achieve competence in writing, speaking, critical reading and thinking, problem solving using mathematics, and making effective use of library and information resources. The Core also ensures students achieve a critical understanding of history, civilization, art, and literature, an awareness of global issues, an understanding of the scientific method and the ability to reason ethically.

MAJORS & DEGREES OFFERED

Athletic Training
Biology
Biochemistry/Molecular Biology
Business
- Accounting
- Finance
- Human Resources Management
- International Business Management
- Marketing
Chemistry
Clinical Laboratory Science/
- Medical Technology
Computers and Information Systems
Computer Science
Criminal Justice
Economics
Education
- Preschool-Grade 4
- Middle Level - Math/Science (Grade 4-8)
- Secondary Level
- Foreign Language (Grades K-12)
- Special Education
Engineering
- Civil
- Mechanical
Engineering (dual degree with University of Notre Dame)
- Chemistry
- Computer Science
- Environmental Science
- Physics
English—Literature
English—Professional Writing

Environmental Science
Environmental Studies
Exercise Science
French
General Science
History
Mass Communications
Mathematics
Neuroscience
Nursing (beginning Fall 2018)
Philosophy
Physician Assistant (five-year master's)
Physics
Political Science
Pre-Health
- Pre-Chiropractic
- Pre-Dental
- Pre-Medical
- Pre-Pharmaceutical
- Pre-Veterinarian

Pre-Law
Pre-Theological
Psychology
Sociology
Spanish
Theatre
Theology

TUITION, ROOM, BOARD, FEES

2017/2018 Costs:

Cost	RESIDENT	COMMUTER
Tuition and Fees (full-time)	$35,830	$35,830
Average Room and Board	$12,408	N/A
Total	$48,238	$35,830

The College encourages every student to apply for financial aid no matter what their family circumstances are. Only after you have applied and been considered for all available assistance will you have a true idea of what your costs will be.

FINANCIAL AID

Ninety-nine percent of King's first-year students receive financial assistance. The College offers numerous scholarship, grant, loan and work-study programs, because we believe college is an investment in the future-both yours and ours. In 2016-2017, our average gift aid was $20,783, with average first year Financial Aid awards at $26,283. The King's College Office of Financial Aid takes the guesswork out of the application process. For more information, call 1-888-KINGS PA or email finaid@kings.edu.

STUDENT ORGANIZATIONS & ACTIVITIES

At King's, we're proud of our diverse student body that includes individuals from many ethnic and religious traditions from across the country and around the world. Recognizing that involvement in student clubs and organizations is an important part of the educational experience, King's offers more than 50 student organizations to meet virtually any interest.

More than 82 percent of the King's College faculty has a Ph.D. or equivalent degrees. Faculty members have been entrepreneurs and practitioners, are authors, scientists, and researchers. They engage in scholarly research and ongoing professional development to support and strengthen their primary role of teaching.

The American Association of Colleges and Universities (AACU) Greater Expectations Initiative named King's as one of only 16 Leadership Institutions nationwide as part of an organized effort to influence the future of liberal arts higher education. The Center for Excellence in Learning and Teaching (CELT) gives King's faculty members a wealth of teaching resources. At King's, faculty members take the time to explain the lesson one more time, answer the question you just couldn't bring yourself to ask in class, and listen intently to your theories and opinions. Professors are interested in their students' success as individuals and therefore make themselves available whether it's during scheduled office hours, e-mail or even over coffee.

The Office of Career Planning offers a broad range of services from credit-bearing academic courses, individualized career counseling, and a variety of professional development activities, programs, and events. The Career Resource Center offers up-to date job search information by field and graduate school resources. The Center also sponsors and provides information about recruiting events, including company visits and information about job fairs and professional development seminars.

King's offer a number of special programs to enhance your learning experience. The First-Year Experience helps new students adjust to campus life. Special honors programs give exceptional students additional challenges. King's study abroad programs offer the chance to travel and study different cultures first hand. ROTC programs provide students an opportunity to serve their country. Other programs, such as the McGowan Center for Ethics and Social Responsibility, prepare you intellectually, morally, and spiritually for a satisfying and purposeful life. Guided internships enable you to experience and earn credit while working within your field of study, and the Experiencing the Arts program is designed to help you explore your artistic side.

ADMISSIONS PROCESS

Information about the King's College application process and downloadable (.pdf) versions of the application form can be found here: https://www.kings.edu/admissions/application-forms-and-links. Online versions of the King's application can be found here: https://www.kings.edu/admissions/applying_to_kings. (Note: The application fee is waived if you apply online.)

HIGH SCHOOL STUDENTS must complete the application form in its entirety. You must also complete the top section of the school report form and submit it to your guidance counselor. Be sure to forward your SAT or ACT scores. (We accept either direct reports from the testing services or test scores included on an official high school transcript.) If you are choosing the Test Optional application decision, you must select that option on the application for it to be processed. If applicable, please submit any college/university transcript indicating course work completed.

PARENTS should complete the Free Application for Federal Student Aid (FAFSA) after October 1, 2016. The King's College Federal School Code is 003282 (this code must be entered correctly on the FAFSA in order for King's College to receive access to your federal record). Be sure to accurately report your social security number on the application for admission, financial aid application, and the FAFSA forms. To help, the College has assembled a number resources to help you navigate the application process, which can be downloaded here: https://www.kings.edu/admissions/application-forms-and-links.

TRANSFER STUDENTS may enroll at King's in the fall or spring semester after completing at least one semester or 12 transferable credits at another school. To apply, submit a completed application and the $30 fee. (Note: The application fee is waived if you apply online at www.kings.edu/admissions/applying_to_kings.) You must also submit official transcript(s) from all post-secondary institutions (including two - and four-year colleges), an official transcript from a secondary school or a G.E.D., SAT or ACT scores (if available), and a personal essay.

INTERNATIONAL STUDENTS must complete the International Application for Admission, available here: https://www.kings.edu/non_cms/pdf/international_application.pdf. Be sure to enclose the $50 non-refundable application fee when mailing. Checks should be made payable to King's College. (NOTE: There is no application fee if you apply online at https://www.kings.edu/admissions/applying_to_kings.) You must also submit your official high school transcript. Your official SAT, TOEFL or IELTS scores must also be submitted to the Office of Admission. If you have any questions about the application, please contact the Office of International Student Recruitment at 001-570-208-5834. In special cases we may choose to waive requirements and will process the application with available information.

For all students, we value the opportunity to meet our applicants in person and therefore strongly recommend scheduling a personal interview at your earliest convenience. For more information, contact the Office of Admission at 1-888-KINGS PA or email admissions@kings.edu.

KNOX COLLEGE

AT A GLANCE

We believe that beauty and sweat go together, that hard work is a beautiful thing, that every experience is an education, that every new venture, every fantastic idea, every great journey, is human-powered. We also believe you learn the most from the people least like you. Knox is one of the 50 most diverse campuses in America, with a campus community of 1,400 students from nearly every state and 51 countries, including a wide array of races, ethnicities, ages, cultures, backgrounds, genders and gender identities, sexual orientations, and beliefs.

A Knox education is not something you sit and watch—it's something you do. Our students test their knowledge by applying theory to practice both in and out of the classroom. That can take the form of advanced research and creative work, internships, off-campus (sometimes way off-campus) programs, community service, or some combination of your own devising. We help make these experiences possible with a $2,000 Power of Experience Grant available to all incoming students during their junior and senior years.

These experiences, combined with opportunities to live and learn with students from different backgrounds, empower students to find success after Knox. Our students become engaged, innovative, and productive global citizens, ready to lead lives of purpose. They run Fortune 500 companies and grassroots nonprofits, they conduct major research at sites around the world, they found startups and music festivals, they see a human need and they meet it.

Our future is also rooted in our past. The commitment to put learning to use to accomplish both personal and social goals dates back to the founding of the College in 1837. We take particular pride in the College's early commitment to increase access to all qualified students of varied backgrounds, races, and conditions, regardless of financial means.

Today, we continue to expand that historic mission and the tradition of active liberal arts learning. We provide an environment where students and dedicated faculty work closely together and where teaching is characterized by inviting and expecting students to pursue fundamental questions in order to reach their own reflective but independent judgments. Our aim is to foster a lifelong love of learning and a sense of competence, confidence, and proportion that will enable us to live with purpose and to contribute to the well-being of others.

LOCATION & ENVIRONMENT

Knox is located in Galesburg, Illinois (pop. 33,000), full of enterprising, big-hearted people. Galesburg was founded alongside Knox, surrounded by prairie and farmland. We are at the heart of a national rail network; there's an Amtrak station a few blocks from campus; Chicago (home to many Knox alumni) is three hours away. And two regional airports are less than an hour away.

The Knox campus consists of 90 acres located in the heart of Galesburg. While our campus is home to academic and administrative buildings, both historic and modern, residence halls, and athletic facilities, it also features wide-open spaces that provide beautiful prairie vistas and provides plenty of room for our Ultimate Frisbee team to practice alongside students studying on the lawn. Our own 700-acre Green Oaks Biological Field Station—one of the country's oldest prairie restoration sites—is 20 miles from campus.

And one last slightly esoteric note about this exact place: The land around us is fairly flat. No one lives high on a mountaintop or deep in a valley. There's something deeply democratic about this. We all have power. We all have a voice. We all stand on equal ground.

CAMPUS FACILITIES & EQUIPMENT

Libraries: Knox College maintains two libraries: Seymour Library and the Science-Mathematics Library, housing more than 350,000 volumes, as well as Special Collections & Archives, which contains primary source materials used by students, faculty, and researchers from around the world.

Arts: The Ford Center for the Fine Arts houses theatre, dance, and music and features the 600-seat Harbach theatre (with a 360-degree rotating stage), the 325-seat Kresge Recital Hall, the Studio Theatre, as well as dance and music studios. Our newly constructed Whitcomb Art Center provides a state-of-the-art facility for students to study, create, and share their art.

Science: Knox continues to expand an equipment roster that includes electron microscopes, NMR, ESR, GC-MS, other spectrometers and chromatographs, X-ray, laser labs, 3-D printers, experimental psychology labs, four computer labs, a rooftop observatory, and a greenhouse. Green Oaks Biological Field Station, about 20 miles east of Knox, encompasses 700 acres of tallgrass prairie, old-growth oaks, second-growth oak-hickory forest, lakes, and streams.

Athletics: Fleming Fieldhouse provides an indoor six-lane 200-meter track and court space for numerous activities. Andrew Fitness Center offers separate cardio/weight machine and free-weight floors. Knosher Bowl, a true bowl stadium, features artificial turf and one of the best playing surfaces in Division III football. Blodgett Field is a pro-level baseball diamond, with special soil composition. Knox also maintains a main gym and basketball court, a six-lane outdoor track, softball and soccer fields, tennis courts, and natatorium. Golf is played at a nearby private 18-hole course.

OFF-CAMPUS OPPORTUNITIES
A few of the many reasons to like Galesburg:

It knows what it is: It is not Chicago; it is not a tiny farm town. It is a small city (pop. 33,000) that was founded alongside a great liberal arts college, surrounded by prairie and farmland, with 23 city parks, a public beach, and wooded biking/walking trails.

It runs on collective ingenuity: If you have a great idea, it's easy to bring people together to bring it to life. Example: A Knox alumnus wanted to turn Seminary Street into a classic independent shopping district. Now it's home to locally owned cafes, restaurants, a natural foods store, and an antique mall.

People make art here: At the Prairie Players Civic Theatre or in the Knox-Rootabaga Jazz Festival. Plus: The Galesburg Civic Art Center hosts exhibits by local artists. The Knox-Galesburg Symphony Orchestra—featuring many Knox students—performs at the historic Orpheum Theatre.

You can make a difference here: Our students contribute thousands of hours of service in Galesburg every year, through long-standing programs like the Knox Prairie Community Kitchen, our Days of Service, and the groundbreaking Knox-Corps program, which places current students and recent graduates in long-term positions with local organizations.

ACADEMICS

We believe that every experience is a kind of education. Everything you learn gains value when you apply it. That's why every Knox student will participate in some form of experiential learning before they graduate. All students receive a $2,000 Power of Experience Grant during their junior or senior year to support a qualifying experiential learning opportunity, including research or creative work, an internship, community service, or study abroad.

Our immersive terms allow students to focus on one topic (entrepreneurship, studio art, Japanese language and history, clinical psychology) for an entire term. They all provide hands-on experience—internships, research, travel, creative work. Two examples: In Green Oaks Term, students live at our biological field station, take interdisciplinary coursework in science, anthropology, and the arts, conduct research, and build a community. In Repertory Theatre Term, students research, design, produce, and perform two full-length plays—the most comprehensive undergraduate theatre experience in the country.

Knox has a longstanding (and pioneering) commitment to supporting advanced student research—intensive, long-term projects that go beyond coursework. The vast majority of our students (89%) produce research, independent studies, or creative work.

Half of our students study abroad, and our off-campus study programs—nearly 90 in total—are designed to work with the Knox experience. You take what you've studied at Knox out into the world; you gather new information, new ideas, new experiences; and you come back with a new way of seeing yourself, your education, and your future.

Our career center helps students find meaningful professional experience by making the most of their education, resources, and connections to secure internships and postgraduate opportunities across the country and around the world.

MAJORS & DEGREES OFFERED

Knox's program provides a balanced curriculum in the arts, humanities, sciences, and social sciences. Our 3-3 academic calendar—three terms (fall, winter, and spring), three courses per term—allows students to fully explore course subject matter and fulfill research expectations.

With five new minors—arts management, astronomy, design, health studies, and statistics—we offer more than 60 courses of study. Many students double major; you can also design your own major. Choosing a major, and thinking broadly about the work you'll do in college and beyond, is in many ways a collaborative process, involving intensive conversations with peers, professors, counselors, and advisors (who are, in fact, professors).

TUITION, ROOM, BOARD, FEES

Expenses per academic year:

Tuition: $44,191

Room: $4,854

Board: $4,842

Fees: $767

Total: $54,654

Average cost for books and supplies: $900

FINANCIAL AID

Knox was founded on the idea that college should be accessible to people regardless of their financial means. We offer more than $40 million in financial aid every year. We're proud to offer a range of scholarships that recognize students' achievements in academics, arts, service and leadership.

For more information on scholarships or financial aid, visit knox.edu, or contact us at 800-678-KNOX.

STUDENT ORGANIZATIONS & ACTIVITIES

Clubs and Organizations: The one quality that binds our 100+ student clubs and organizations is that they are all student-driven. Students create and run organizations in response to interests and needs. Some clubs focus on academic disciplines such as chemistry or physics. Others, such as Common Ground, Model United Nations, and Allied Blacks for Liberty and Equality focus on identity, culture, and politics. And, our successful club-level Ultimate Frisbee team and our music, dance, and performance ensembles provide an athletic and creative energy that characterizes Knox.

Intramural Clubs: More than half of our students participate in some kind of organized athletic activity, from club sports (water polo, fencing, women's lacrosse); to intramurals (basketball, indoor soccer, softball, volleyball); to fitness classes organized and taught by students (a few recent examples: Balinese dancing, yoga).

Student Governance: Our student government actually governs. The Student Senate helps determine how funds from student activity fees are spent, makes student appointments to faculty committees, and serves as a forum for the debate of important issues on campus. Our students shape the future of Knox; their work is a lasting legacy.

Civic Engagement: We pride ourselves on being deeply engaged in the life of a strong, sustainable community—whether that community is local or global. Our students contribute tens of thousands of hours of service every year through established partnerships, special programs, and our KnoxCorps program. Knox was the first college or university in the country to offer an official Peace Corps Preparatory Program; we rank among the top producers of Peace Corps volunteers.

ADMISSIONS PROCESS

Knox seeks students who are active, engaged learners. We value students who demonstrate their appreciation for a variety of educational experiences, both in and out of the classroom. Our admission counselors consider you as an individual when making our admission decisions.

You can apply to Knox online via the Common Application. Deadlines for first-year admission are November 1 for Early Decision and Early Action I, December 1 for Early Action II, and January 15 for Regular Decision. We also accept transfer applications for fall, winter, and spring terms.

For more information, please visit admission online or contact us directly.

Office of Admission

Knox College

2 East South Street

Galesburg, Illinois 61401-4999

United States

Phone: 800-678-KNOX or 309-341-7100

Fax: 309-341-7070

E-mail: admission@knox.edu

Web: knox.edu

LAKE FOREST COLLEGE

AT A GLANCE

Lake Forest offers students a rare combination: an exceptionally beautiful residential campus offering a rigorous curriculum, and the opportunity to tap into the many academic, cultural, and social resources of nearby Chicago.

Founded in 1857, Lake Forest College has a long tradition of academic excellence and is known for its innovative curriculum. In addition to majors in the humanities, social sciences, and natural sciences, the College features programs of study in pre-law, pre-health, communication, business, finance, computer science, and still other practical areas. Lake Forest prepares students to lead successful lives, and many go on to competitive graduate programs and top jobs. Abundant internships, research opportunities, personal guidance from professors, and connections to nearby Chicago also set the Lake Forest apart. Students learn in a rigorous academic environment in small class settings where professors do all the teaching and also serve as advisors and mentors. Professors are accomplished scholars, published authors, and recipients of prestigious grants. Many have come from some of the top PhD programs in the country.

Students represent nearly every state and 71 countries around the world and international and ethnic minorities make up more than 25 percent of the student body. Together they comprise a learning community that prepares them to succeed in a global society. More than eighty student groups provide a host of extracurricular opportunities that develop leadership skills and enhance students' campus experience and post-college prospects. Lake Forest College offers recreational music, art, and theater programs, as well as 19 varsity sports and intramural and club sports. It competes in NCAA Division III.

LOCATION & ENVIRONMENT

Just an hour's train ride to Chicago, the College is located in the town of Lake Forest, Illinois, 30 miles north of the city along the shores of Lake Michigan. The 107-acre residential campus is a safe academic home in a beautiful wooded suburban setting within walking distance to the train to downtown Chicago, historic Lake Forest, and the beaches of Lake Michigan.

The College is only 25 miles from O'Hare International Airport and is also served by Midway Airport and Mitchell International Airport in Milwaukee.

The campus is surrounded by lush wooded neighborhoods, ravines, natural prairies, the beautiful beaches along Lake Michigan, and an extensive network of bike and running trails. Nearby Chicago boasts nearly 70 world-class museums, more than 200 theaters, seven major league sports teams, and one of the nation's top opera companies. Chicago is known for its cleanliness, abundant green space, good transportation system, and friendly people.

CAMPUS FACILITIES & EQUIPMENT

A $40 million renovation and expansion project of the Johnson Science Center will be completed by 18-19 academic year.

A new 230-bed residence hall opened in August 2013 and features doubles, suites, and super suites with living rooms, lounges, kitchen, and a multipurpose room for group events.

The Sports and Recreation Center is a popular facility on campus and includes multipurpose courts, a suspended running track, an aerobic and dance studio, a batting/golf cage, strength, cardio, and fitness spaces, a pool, and an indoor ice rink just next door.

The Mohr Student Center is a student-centered social space that is the hub of social activity on campus. It features pool tables and other games, stage and performance space, large-screen TVs, lounges, deli/snack bar, grocery store, and an outdoor terrace with seating.

Center for Chicago Programs

Chicago provides a hands-on resource for student learning through research, internships, study, and fun. It is the hub for all Chicago-related programming. At the Center, students can plan visits to the city and professors can get help incorporating Chicago resources into their classrooms. The Center also brings well-known Chicagoans to the College for lectures and performances.

OFF-CAMPUS OPPORTUNITIES

Lake Forest encourages students to take advantage of study, internship, and research opportunities in Chicago, around the United States, and abroad. Internship opportunities are plentiful in the Chicago area and students have interned at places such as the Art Institute of Chicago, Chicago Blackhawks, Chicago Board of Trade, Chicago Council on Global Affairs, Edelman Public Relations Worldwide, Morgan Stanley, NBC Chicago, Second City, and the John G. Shedd Aquarium, among others. Students can choose to spend a semester living an interning in Chicago through the College's In The Loop program.

In addition to a well-established internship program, Lake Forest College students gain international experience through access to over 200 study abroad and internship options in more than 70 countries. There are international and/or domestic programs suited for every major, minor, or program, at Lake Forest. Students can choose a program based on major, minor, language ability, and desired semester. Most students' financial aid packages can be applied to the program of choice.

ACADEMICS

The First-Year Studies Program (FIYS)

First-year studies classes are small in size to encourage interaction and discussion. The FIYS professors also serve as the students' primary academic advisors and help them navigate the College's academic offerings during their first year. With many topics to choose from, first-year studies courses cover a wide range of academic interests from music, art, and politics to neuroscience, terrorism and religion, many with a focus on Chicago or directly utilizing the resources available there. Chicago plays an integral role in the FIYS program. Students travel to the city with their class during orientation week, providing a first-hand introduction to how the educational, cultural, and social resources of Chicago will influence their coursework and experiences during their four years at Lake Forest.

The Richter Scholars Program This program provides students, early in their academic careers, with the opportunity to conduct independent, individual research with Lake Forest faculty. In the summer after their first year, each student in the Richter Program is employed for a ten-week period and does independent research one-on-one with a faculty member.

Self-Designed Major

This program allows students to develop an academic major of their own, working closely with a faculty advisor, culminating in a thesis or a creative project.

MAJORS & DEGREES OFFERED

The academic calendar is based on two 15-week semesters, beginning in August and January. Students normally take four four-credit courses per semester (the equivalent of 16 credits).

There are no teaching assistants at the College. Courses are taught in small classroom settings by professors who are experts in their fields and who also serve students as one-on-one advisors. In addition to classroom studies, students are encouraged to complete an internship, conduct original research, and study abroad for a semester.

A Lake Forest graduate will have studied a broad range of ideas; developed real competence in writing, speaking, and quantitative skills; and gained significant experience in humanities, natural sciences and mathematics, and social sciences while completing requirements for a major in an academic department or interdisciplinary program. The College's General Education Curriculum, advising system, and major requirements are designed to support these educational ideals.

Lake Forest awards the Bachelor of Arts (BA) degree in both traditional academic departments and interdisciplinary programs. Areas of study include: African American studies, American studies, anthropology, area studies, studio art, art history, art education, Asian studies, biology, border studies, business (concentrations in accounting and marketing available), chemistry, cinema studies, classical studies, communication, computer science, digital media design, economics, education (elementary and secondary), engineering (dual degree), English (literature and writing), environmental studies, finance, history, international relations, Islamic world studies, Latin American studies, legal studies, mathematics, media design and technology, metropolitan studies, modern languages and literatures (Arabic, Chinese, French, German, Italian, Japanese, and Spanish), music, music education, neuroscience, philosophy, physics, politics, psychology, religion, rhetoric, social justice, sociology, theater, women's and gender studies. Lake Forest also offers pre-professional programs in law, medicine, dentistry, and veterinary medicine.

Accelerated and dual-degree programs are offered. Three-year degree programs are available in communication and philosophy. Dual-degree programs are available in law, international studies, pharmacy, and engineering. Lake Forest is affiliated with several competitive law schools that allow students to complete a bachelor's degree and a law degree in a total of six years, rather than the usual seven. Qualified Lake Forest College students may be admitted to the Monterey Institute of International Studies with accelerated status, and can complete their master's degrees with 48 credits as opposed to the 60 normally required. A dual-degree program has been arranged, leading to a bachelor of arts Degree in biology from Lake Forest College and a doctor of pharmacy from the Rosalind Franklin University of Medicine and Science. The engineering program is in cooperation with the Sever Institute of Technology at Washington University (St. Louis).

TUITION, ROOM, BOARD, FEES

2016 -2017 Tuition: $43,392.00

Room: $4,684.00

Board: $5,126.00

Fees: $724.00

FINANCIAL AID

Lake Forest College provides an affordable, high-quality education through maintaining a strong commitment to supporting each student's demonstrated financial need.

The College offers academic scholarships up to $30,000 and talent-based scholarships in music, studio art, and theater.

STUDENT ORGANIZATIONS & ACTIVITIES

Lake Forest College is a place to study, work, and live. With the diversity of the student body there is an eclectic mix of activities and opportunities outside the classroom.

Student organizations include student government, international interest groups, Greek Life, academic honor societies, community service, publications and media, music and performance, spiritual and religious groups, and many others.

Students have a voice in how the College is run and are actively involved in governance committees such as the College Council and have representation on the Board of Trustees. Student writers and performers can showcase their talents on stage with the Garrick Players, by hosting a show on "WMXM," the College's FM radio station, or through the student newspaper, literary magazines, chorus and instrumental ensembles. Academic honor societies enjoy active student participation as do the community service groups and many special-interest clubs. The College provides and maintains a comprehensive intramural and intercollegiate athletic program. There are two national fraternities and five national sororities, all housed within the residence halls. All students have equal opportunity to take advantage of the richness of the College's programs.

Lake Forest College competes in the NCAA Division III fielding twelve women's and eleven men's intercollegiate varsity teams. Women's teams include basketball, cross-country, golf, handball, ice hockey, soccer, softball, swimming and diving, tennis, volleyball, and track (indoor and outdoor). Men's teams include basketball, cross-country, football, golf, handball, ice hockey, soccer, swimming and diving, tennis, and track (indoor and outdoor). The College also offers an extensive roster of intramural and club sports.

The College's Center for Chicago Programs facilitates engagement with the resources of Chicago which often complements programs for student organizations as well as provides students with information on cultural and social activities happening downtown. The train to Chicago is a short walk from campus and students enjoy traveling to the city for fun and entertainment. The College shuttle provides service seven days a week to popular shopping areas and destinations around campus.

ADMISSIONS PROCESS

The criteria used for selection include assessment of a student's program of study, academic achievement, aptitude, intellectual curiosity, qualities of character and personality, and activities.

Standardized test scores (ACT/SAT) are optional, except for international or home-schooled candidates, and those applying for some academic scholarships. A personal interview is required for students who do not submit scores.https://admission.utulsa.edu/

LAWRENCE TECHNOLOGICAL UNIVERSITY

AT A GLANCE

Lawrence Technological University is a private, personally focused university providing students a rigorous, high-quality education—an education that pays off. The Brookings Institution ranks Lawrence Technological University fifth among U.S. colleges and universities for boosting graduates' earning potential. Payscale.com reports that salaries of LTU bachelor's graduates are in the top 10 percent nationally. Some 88 percent of students are employed or registered for graduate school by the date of their graduation, greater than the national average.

The University, including its graduate programs, is accredited by the Higher Learning Commission and is a member of the North Central Association of Colleges and Schools. In addition to its ranking by the Princeton Review, LTU placed in the top tier of Best University-Masters-Midwest in the U.S. News and World Report's 2017 America's Best Colleges rankings. Other distinctions include designation as a Military Friendly School by G.I. Jobs.

Lawrence Tech's honors program is available for highly motivated and qualified students, as well as Quest, which encourages students to go above and beyond their studies and explore their interests on a deeper level. A scholars program is also available, designed to ease the transition from high school to college by providing support services. LTU's unique Leadership Program, integrated into all bachelor's degrees, helps students gain critical thinking, teamwork, and communication skills.

LTU's student-faculty ratio is 12:1. Most undergraduate classes have 19 or fewer students, and less than 1 percent of the classes enroll more than 50. Nearly 700 students live in University Housing. Women make up 23 percent of the student body, and 36 states and 45 nations are represented on campus.

LOCATION & ENVIRONMENT

The University is situated in Southfield, a dynamic suburb in Oakland County, Michigan. Hundreds of Fortune 500 and international companies are located nearby, and the region has one of the largest concentrations of engineering, architecture, and technology jobs in the world. Southeastern Michigan also offers a rich variety of recreational and cultural activities, with public transportation making most areas accessible to students. Hundreds of major research, manufacturing, scientific, and business enterprises are located nearby, aiding students who work full or part-time while attending classes, as well as those in co-ops and internships, and participating in professional societies. The campus is close to major freeways and about a 30-minute drive north of downtown Detroit and Detroit Metro Airport.

CAMPUS FACILITIES & EQUIPMENT

Lawrence Tech's modern 107-acre campus includes a variety of academic, recreational, and housing facilities. Students use advanced, leading-edge facilities, including LTU's acclaimed Center for Innovative Materials Research; an environmental scanning microscope; architectural and design studios; a structural testing lab; a wind tunnel; wood, metal, and model shops; a 4 x 4 chassis dynamometer; and labs for alternative energy, robotics, biomedical research, graphics, and LTU's Taubman Engineering, Architecture, and Life Sciences Complex.

High-end personal laptops, , customized with all the professional software students need, are provided through the LTuZone. This unique benefit, with an average retail value of $75,000, is the only one of its kind in the nation.

The University's three residence halls feature community living and one and two-bedroom apartment-style suites that accommodate two to four students. All utilities, wifi, basic cable TV, and parking are included.

LTU's library offers a wide selection of print and electronic materials, including numerous online databases, visual resources, digital images, and full-text periodical titles accessible on and off campus. Librarians provide research guidance and instruction. As a key part of the research community in Michigan, LTU's library participates in the reciprocal borrowing and sharing of resources with many other institutions.

The A. Alfred Taubman Student Services Center consolidates all student support services—from admissions through career services—into a convenient one-stop center. This innovative 42,000-square-foot building, which utilizes many energy-efficient and environmentally friendly features and technologies, serves as a "living laboratory" of sustainability, and is part of a regional stormwater management effort.

LTU's Johnson Controls Vehicle Engineering Systems Laboratory provides students opportunities to conduct sponsored research on a unique 4 x 4 vehicle chassis dynamometer.

OFF-CAMPUS OPPORTUNITIES

Students can participate in applied research partnerships that offer remarkable hands-on experience. Professional organizations provide additional opportunities to network with industry leaders.

Lawrence Tech's Detroit design programs are housed under one roof at the Detroit Center for Design + Technology, allowing students to explore community-based architectural, urban design, and community development projects. Architecture students regularly build homes for Habitat for Humanity.

LTU's Study-Abroad Program is open to all students. The University has partnerships with universities in China, India, Canada, Brazil, Mexico, Europe, and the Middle East. The Global Engineering Program arranges for engineering students to work and study abroad.

ACADEMICS
Theory and Practice

LTU provides students the tools they need to compete and succeed within their chosen profession. Whether inside or outside of the classroom, the University's theory and practice approach to learning provides opportunities to combine practical knowledge with real-world applications.

Lawrence Tech is the recipient of numerous grants and awards for the development and implementation of innovative materials and practices that are expected to double the lifespan of concrete bridges and highways, and provide armor protection for soldiers.

Student engineering teams design, build, and race hybrid, Supermileage, Baja, and Formula-style vehicles. Students also compete in bridge building and assembling and designing zero energy homes, airplanes, robots, and concrete canoes and toboggans.

MAJORS

LTU is a 4,500-student university offering over 100 undergraduate, master's, and doctoral programs in Colleges of Architecture and Design, Arts and Sciences, Engineering, and Management. Most programs are available days or evenings; many are offered on weekends and online. Dual majors and customized degree programs combining either associate and bachelor's programs or bachelor's and master's programs also are available. Pre-professional preparation includes pre-dental, pre-law, and pre-medical programs, as well as a post-baccalaureate certificate in premedical studies.

LTU's College of Architecture and Design offers bachelor's degrees in architecture, architectural studies, game art, graphic design, industrial design, interaction design, interior architecture, and transportation design. Lawrence Tech enrolls more architectural students than any other school in Michigan, and is one of the top 10 largest architecture schools in the nation.

LTU's College of Arts and Sciences offers bachelor's degrees in chemical biology, chemistry, computer science (business software development, game software development, scientific software development, and software engineering), English and communication arts, environmental chemistry, humanities, mathematical sciences, mathematics and computer science, media communication, molecular and cell biology, nursing, physics, physics and computer science, and psychology (clinical, general and applied, industrial/organizational, and pre-medical/biobehavioral).

Bachelor's degrees offered by LTU's College of Engineering are audio engineering technology, biomedical engineering, civil engineering, computer engineering, construction engineering technology and management, electrical engineering (computer engineering, electronics engineering, and power engineering), embedded software engineering, industrial engineering, mechanical and manufacturing engineering technology, mechanical engineering (aeronautical, alternative energy, automotive, manufacturing, nanoscience and nanotechnology, solid mechanics, and thermal fluids), and robotics engineering. A direct-entry master's degree in architectural engineering, combining bachelor's and master's programs, is also offered.

The College of Management offers undergraduate degrees in business administration (accounting, finance, general business, information technology, and marketing) and information technology.

Minors include aeronautical engineering, biology, business, chemistry, computer science, economics, energy engineering, English, general sciences, history, mathematics, media communication, military sciences and leadership (ROTC), nanoscience and nanotechnology, philosophy, physics, psychology, and technical and professional communication.

Associate degrees are offered in chemical technology, general studies, and radio and television broadcasting.

Undergraduate certificates can be earned in building information modeling and computer visualization, computer science, electrical power systems, embedded systems, entrepreneurial skills, industrial/organizational psychology, technical and professional communication, and television and video production.

TUITION, ROOM, BOARD, FEES

Tuition for all undergrads includes being provided a laptop with all required software. The 2016-17 tuition for students majoring in arts and sciences is $825 per credit hour for basic studies courses. Sophomores, juniors, and seniors in arts and sciences, and management pay $1045 per credit hour. In architecture and design, tuition for freshmen and sophomores is $975; for juniors and seniors, it is $1045 per credit hour. Tuition for engineering majors is $1045 per credit hour for all four years.

A normal course load is 12–17 credit hours per semester. The undergraduate registration fee is $135 each semester. International students on temporary visas must have sufficient funds to pay for an entire year of tuition, room and board, and books at the time of first registration. Additional fees for specific labs and studio courses vary.

Room costs vary, but average $6,500 per year. Meal plans are $2,702, per year, with a variety of options.

FINANCIAL AID

Nearly 71 percent of students receive financial assistance and the University awards more than $42 million in scholarships, grants, loans, and work-study funds each academic year. The average annual, need-based financial aid package is $24,483. Many privately funded scholarships are awarded to qualified students, based on need and/or scholastic performance. Part-time employment is available at the University on a first-come, first-served basis for full-time students. Student loans are also available from a variety of sources—state, federal, and private. Prospective students are urged to contact the Office of Financial Aid for information on deadlines and requirements for eligibility (www.ltu.edu/financial_aid).

STUDENT ORGANIZATIONS & ACTIVITIES

More than 60 student clubs and organizations, including fraternities, sororities, honor societies, and student chapters of professional groups are active on campus and sponsor a variety of activities during the year. The Student Government sponsors and supports a variety of campus activities.

LTU features NAIA, ACHA, MCLA, NWLL, and USBC varsity and junior varsity athletics in men's and women's basketball, soccer, cross-country, lacrosse, bowling, ice hockey, golf, volleyball, and tennis; as well as women's softball, and men's baseball and football. Students can also show their Blue Devil spirit on LTU's pep band and dance team. Intramural leagues and tournaments are active in 18 sports. Club sports include lacrosse, mixed martial arts, and biking. LTU's Don Ridler Field House is open to all students and features a fitness track, gymnasium, racquetball courts, game room, saunas, and weight and conditioning room.

ADMISSIONS PROCESS

Admissions decisions are based on a student's recalculated GPA, ACT/SAT scores, essay, and letters of recommendation. Strong emphasis is placed on grade trends as well as the strength of the curriculum and rigor of a student's senior schedule. A portfolio is required for art and design majors.

Lawrence Tech's ACT code is 2020 and SAT is 1399. Required high school courses vary with the curriculum, and LTU offers a number of basic studies courses designed to augment incoming students' backgrounds if deficiencies exist.

Programs start in August and January, and an optional summer semester begins in May. Entry in the fall semester is advised but not required. Students must submit transcripts from all schools attended, along with a nonrefundable $30 application fee. Students may also fill out a brief survey and apply free at ltu.edu/applyfree. See our campus video at ltu.edu/StudentStories. To learn more, visit ltu.edu or contact:

Lawrence Technological University

Office of Admissions

21000 West Ten Mile Road

Southfield, MI 48075-1058

800.225.5588 or 248.204.3160

admissions@ltu.edu

ltu.edu

LE MOYNE COLLEGE

AT A GLANCE

Le Moyne College is a four-year, coeducational Jesuit college of approximately 2,800 full-time undergraduate students that uniquely balances a comprehensive liberal arts education with preparation for specific career paths or graduate study.

Founded in 1946, Le Moyne is the second youngest of the twenty-eight Jesuit colleges and universities in the United States. Its emphasis is on the education of the whole person and on the search for meaning and value as integral parts of an intellectual life. Learning, leadership and service are the hallmarks of a Le Moyne College education. Those values are evident in the College's undergraduate majors in more than 30 areas of study, as well as in its pre-professional studies and graduate programs in business administration, arts administration, education, nursing, occupational therapy, information systems and physician assistant studies.

Le Moyne's personal approach to education is reflected in the quality of contact between students and faculty members. With approximately 150 full-time faculty members, Le Moyne has a student-faculty ratio of 13:1 and an average class size of 20.

LOCATION & ENVIRONMENT

Le Moyne's 160-plus acre, tree-lined campus is located in a residential setting 10 minutes from downtown Syracuse, the heart of New York state, whose metropolitan population is about 700,000. Just a few miles outside the city are the rolling hills, picturesque lakes, and miles of open country for which central New York is renowned.

CAMPUS FACILITIES & EQUIPMENT

Le Moyne students benefit from an ongoing commitment to technological excellence. The College's 42 buildings are equipped with accounting, biological sciences, chemistry, computer science, physics, psychology, and statistics laboratories. The W. Carroll Coyne Center for the Performing Arts houses generous production, performance, and classroom space; the latest light and sound technology; scene and costume shops; an aerobics and dance studio; and rehearsal rooms for instrumental and choral music. Academic facilities also include an extensively renovated color television studio; a radio/recording studio; a receiver-antenna satellite dish; transmission and scanning electron microscopes; a nuclear magnetic resonance spectrometer; a gas chromatograph/mass spectrophotometer; a 240,000-volume, open-stack library; and extensive on-site computer facilities. A wireless network allows students easy access to the campus network and Internet. All classrooms are smart classrooms, with multimedia capabilities that expand and enrich the learning process. Le Moyne students have access to other libraries through the Central New York Library Resources Council, and the campus Academic Support Center is available to students for instructional support. In addition, Le Moyne recently opened a 48,000 square foot addition to its existing science complex, as well as the new Madden School of Business featuring a state-of-the-art live trading floor and analytics lab. Athletic facilities include a new soccer and lacrosse turf field, a new softball field; baseball field, tennis, basketball, and wellness studios; a weight-training and fitness center; practice fields; and two gymnasiums. A recreation center houses an Olympic-size indoor swimming pool, jogging track, indoor tennis and volleyball courts, and additional basketball, racquetball, and fitness areas. The College also has a plaza, which houses its bookstore, a cafe, and a pizzeria. The Dolphin Den, which features a food court and a convenience store, is a popular space for students to meet, have a bite to eat, or just spend a quiet moment relaxing by the fireplace.

OFF-CAMPUS OPPORTUNITIES

Syracuse is convenient to most major cities throughout the Northeast, New England, and Canada and offers a wide array of shopping centers and restaurants, many near Le Moyne. Syracuse offers year-round entertainment in the form of rock concerts at the Landmark Theatre, professional baseball and hockey, the Bristol Omni-theatre, Syracuse Stage, the Everson Museum of Art, and the Armory Square district downtown, which offers one-of-a-kind eateries, pubs, and coffeehouses in addition to a wide variety of social and cultural events. Central New York is home to an extensive network of state and county parks, recreational areas, and other facilities that offer an abundance of recreational opportunities, including swimming, boating, hiking, downhill and cross-country skiing, snowboarding, and golf.

ACADEMICS

While each major department has its own sequence requirements for the minimum 120 credit hours needed for the Le Moyne degree, the College is convinced that there is a fundamental intellectual discipline that should characterize the graduate of a superior liberal arts college. Le Moyne's interdisciplinary core curriculum provides the foundation by including studies of English language and literature, mathematics, philosophy, history, theology and religion, natural science, and social science to reflect international trends within a liberal arts education. For exceptional students, Le Moyne offers an integral honors program that includes an interdisciplinary humanities sequence as well as departmental honors courses. The study-abroad program allows qualified students to spend a semester or year in numerous countries around the world. Le Moyne College has study-abroad programs or affiliations in Czech Republic, Dominican Republic, England, Germany, Ireland, Scotland, and Spain. Students can also use partner programs to study in locations such as Australia, Costa Rica, Egypt, France, Italy, Japan, and South Africa. Le Moyne is a participant in the sixty-member New York State Visiting Student Program. As part of the mission of preparing future leaders, Le Moyne College places a strong emphasis on career preparation through internships and other forms of experiential education. Academic departments and the Office of Career Advising and Development both provide programs and services for students interning part time and full time, both locally and in major cities such as New York and Washington, D.C. The Offices of Service Learning and the Academic Deans are also involved in experiential education to promote learning outside the classroom. In the sciences, students take part in campus research with faculty mentors. Others receive assistance in pursuing outstanding opportunities off campus in leading research laboratories and health-care settings. Through the College's long-standing relationship with The Washington Center for Internships and Academic Seminars, students from all majors complete full-time semester-long internships in Washington, D.C., with government, business, or major nonprofit organizations. Faculty members in the Department of Political Science assist students interested in opportunities in Albany, N.Y., the state's seat of government, with either the State Senate or Assembly. Finally, the education programs at Le Moyne put students into school classrooms starting immediately as freshmen and continuing each year until graduation. Le Moyne students may enroll in Army and Air Force ROTC programs in conjunction with Syracuse University.

MAJORS & DEGREES OFFERED

Le Moyne College awards the Bachelor of Arts degree in biological sciences, communication and film studies, computer science, criminology, economics, english (creative writing, literature), French, history, mathematics (actuarial science, applied mathematics, pure mathematics, statistics), peace and global studies, philosophy, physics, political science, psychology, religious studies, sociology (anthropology, criminology, human services, research and theory), software application and system development, Spanish, and theatre arts. The Bachelor of Science degree is awarded in biochemistry, biological sciences (health professions, molecular biology, neurobiology), chemistry, economics, environmental science systems, environmental studies, physics, and psychology. The Bachelor of Science in business is awarded in accounting, business analytics, finance, human resource management, information systems, management and leadership, and marketing. A Bachelor of Science in nursing is also offered. Students may minor in advanced writing, arts administration, Catholic studies, classical humanities, film, gender and women's studies, health information systems, Irish literature, Italian, Latin, legal studies, medieval studies, music, or visual arts as well as most of the major fields of study offered. Pre-professional programs are offered in dentistry, law, medicine, optometry, physical therapy, direct entry physician assistant studies, podiatry, dental medicine, occupational therapy, and veterinary science. Students may prepare for teaching careers through certification programs in adolescent education, dual adolescent/special education, dual childhood/special education, and TESOL.

Le Moyne College and the L. C. Smith College of Engineering and Computer Science at Syracuse University have a dual-degree program in which students may earn a bachelor's degree from Le Moyne and a master's degree in engineering from Syracuse University in as few as five and a half years. Concentrations include aerospace, bioengineering, chemical, civil/structural, computer, electrical, environmental, geotechnical, and mechanical engineering.

Formal accelerated 3+3 and 3+4 programs are offered in physical therapy, dentistry, law, optometry, communication, public administration, forensic science, library science, and podiatry in cooperation with the State University of New York at Buffalo School of Dentistry, New York College of Podiatric Medicine, School of Information Studies at Syracuse University, Forensic and National Security Sciences Institute at Syracuse University, S.I. Newhouse School of Public Communication at Syracuse University, Maxwell School of Citizenship and Public Affairs at Syracuse University, and Syracuse University College of Law.

TUITION, ROOM, BOARD, FEES

For 2017-18, Le Moyne's tuition is $32,840. Room costs are $8,360 and board charges (19-meal plan) is $5,040. Additional fees amount to approximately $1,065.

FINANCIAL AID

Financial aid is offered to a large percentage of Le Moyne's students through scholarships, grants, loans, and work-study assignments. Le Moyne offers a generous program of merit-based academic and athletic scholarships as well as financial aid based on a student's need and academic promise. Federal funds are available through the Federal Pell Grant, Federal Work-Study, Federal Supplemental Educational Opportunity Grant, and Federal Perkins Loan programs. A student's eligibility for need-based financial aid is determined from both the Free Application for Federal Student Aid (FAFSA) and the Le Moyne Financial Aid Application Form. It is recommended that these forms be mailed by February 1.

STUDENT ORGANIZATIONS & ACTIVITIES

A wide range of student-directed activities, athletics, clubs, and service organizations complement the academic experience. Intramural sports are very popular with Le Moyne students; nearly 85 percent of the students participate. Le Moyne also has twenty-one NCAA intercollegiate teams (ten for men and eleven for women). Between 80 and 85 percent of students live in residence halls, apartments, and town houses on campus. The Residence Hall Councils and the Le Moyne Student Programming Board organize a variety of campus activities, including concerts, dances, a weekly film series, student talent programs, and special lectures as well as off-campus trips and skiing excursions.

The College encourages student leadership in all activities with positions open to students in all class years. Students are represented by a Student Government Association and have formal representation through the senate on most College-wide committees involved in decision making and policy formation.

ADMISSIONS PROCESS

Le Moyne seeks qualified students who are well prepared for serious academic study. Secondary school preparation must have included at least 17 college-preparatory high school units, 4 of which must be in English, 4 in social studies, 3–4 in mathematics, 3–4 in foreign language, and 3–4 in science. It is also recommended that prospective science and mathematics majors complete 4 units of mathematics and science. Le Moyne is test optional, which means SAT and/or ACT scores are not required for admission. However, test scores must be submitted to be considered for top academic scholarships, for certain programs of study, for students who have been Home Schooled, and for international students for whom English is not a first language. SAT and/or ACT exams should be taken no later than December or January of the senior year in high school for test scores to be submitted as part of the application. Campus visits are strongly recommended, as the admission process is a personal one. As bases for selection, academic achievement and secondary school recommendations are of primary importance. Out-of-state students are encouraged to apply.

Le Moyne offers students the opportunity to apply in two ways: early action or regular admission. The early action program is nonbinding and provides high school students the opportunity to receive an admission decision starting December 15 of their senior year. The early action application deadline is November 15. Regular admission applications are reviewed and admission decisions are made on a rolling basis beginning January 1. The priority deadline for applications is February 1; all students who wish to be considered for academic merit scholarships should have a completed application on file in the Office of Admission before this date. Transfer students are encouraged to apply before August 1 for the fall semester and December 1 for the spring semester. Orientation programs for incoming freshmen take place in June and early July. Transfer student orientation programs are offered throughout the summer.

LEWIS & CLARK COLLEGE

AT A GLANCE

On a stunning campus in one of the most exciting and progressive cities anywhere, the next generation of global thinkers gathers to discard conventional thinking, civic complacency, and outmoded preconceptions. Leaders, visionaries, and problem-solvers, we come together to explore new ways of knowing through classic liberal learning and innovative collaboration.

At Lewis & Clark College in Portland, Oregon, we welcome all who are alive to inquiry, open to diversity, and eager to shape the new global century. Through our undergraduate programs in the arts, humanities, and sciences, and through our graduate and professional studies in education, counseling, and law, we undertake original research, interdisciplinary studies, and community service. We push beyond what is known in order to discover something new every day.

Reflecting the College's national and global reach, approximately 90 percent of Lewis & Clark's 2,033 undergraduate students come from outside Oregon, representing 46 states plus the District of Columbia and 75 countries.

LOCATION & ENVIRONMENT

Founded in 1867, Lewis & Clark College moved to its present location in Portland's southwest hills in 1942. The 137-acre campus sits on a wooded hilltop just six miles from Portland's dynamic downtown, offering stunning views of snow-covered Mount Hood.

Portland is a very livable city with an excellent public transportation system that includes buses, light-rail, and the Portland streetcar. In addition, a free Lewis & Clark shuttle runs frequently into the heart of the city and back to campus. The scenic Willamette River bisects metropolitan Portland, which is home to approximately 2.3 million people. There are endless things to do in Portland: 10,477 acres of parks; diverse galleries, museums, music groups, and theater and dance companies; and a nationally recognized food scene. The city also offers professional hockey, soccer, and the NBA's Portland Trail Blazers. Our students take advantage of the many internship and service opportunities available in the Portland metro area.

Just 50 miles east of campus rises Mount Hood with its 10-month-a-year skiing and snow-boarding. The rugged Oregon coastline is just 90 miles to the west. Throughout the state lie innumerable hiking, climbing, and backpacking opportunities.

CAMPUS FACILITIES & EQUIPMENT

Located on Palatine Hill on a former estate, Lewis & Clark offers students a campus of unmatched physical beauty, along with academic and residential buildings designed to support a rigorous academic environment and strong sense of community.

Academic buildings include the Aubrey R. Watzek library, which is open 24 hours on weekdays during the school year and houses over 740,000 items including books, documents, audiovisual materials, microforms, and periodicals. The library is a member of the Summit consortium, allowing access to approximately 28 million items from the 39 member institutions in the Pacific Northwest. Watzek library also houses the most extensive collection of printed materials known to exist on the Lewis and Clark Expedition. Evans Music Center includes a 410-seat recital hall equipped with an orchestra pit and stage elevator, 22 practice rooms, 43 pianos, 2 harpsichords, a Javanese gamelan, a Baroque organ, and an electronic music studio with digitally-based music production capability. An 85-rank Casavant organ is housed in the college chapel. Fir Acres Theatre houses a 225-seat Main Stage performance/teaching theatre and a black-box experimental theatre (also used as dance studio) along with a scene shop, costume room, green room and design lab. The Olin Center (physics and chemistry), the Biology-Psychology building, and BoDine (mathematical sciences) all house well-equipped classrooms and extensive laboratory spaces for our natural sciences. Our notable science facilities include a scanning electron microscope, a time-lapse deconvolution microscope, a gas chromatograph/mass spectrometer, a high-pressure liquid chromatograph, a 300 MHz nuclear magnetic resonance spectrometer, an observatory with Newtonian and solar telescopes, an astrophysics lab, an electrical instrumentation lab, a molecular modeling lab, a lab for studying the biomechanics of animal locomotion, and a lab for studying parallel computing. Nearby Tryon Creek State Park and the Columbia River Gorge are frequently used as laboratories for field courses in biology and geology.

Other academic buildings include the Fields Center, which houses studio facilities for drawing, painting, sculpture, ceramics, graphic design, and photography. The Miller Center and Howard Hall are home to the humanities and social sciences and offer state-of-the-art classrooms, small auditoriums, and the Keck Interactive Learning Center, a digital language lab.

Computer facilities include several computer labs around campus available for student use. These labs house more than 130 computers, along with peripherals such as scanners, laser printers, and digital video editing equipment. Other equipment including digital still and video cameras, digital audio recorders, and more are available for checkout. All residence halls have wireless capability. The institution has an 1000 Mbps connection to the internet.

OFF-CAMPUS OPPORTUNITIES

Overseas and off-campus study programs have been a big part of Lewis & Clark for more than 50 years. Each year, about 300 students participate in approximately 30 programs abroad and in selected areas of the United States. During the next few years, programs will be offered in the Arizona borderlands, Australia, Chile, China, Cuba, Dominican Republic, East Africa, Ecuador, England, France, Germany, Greece, India, Ireland, Italy, Japan, Morocco, New York City, New Zealand, Russia, Senegal, South Korea, Spain, Vietnam and Washington, D.C.

Whether their off-campus study is domestic or abroad, students earn credit (equivalent to a full semester or year) for their academic work. Depending on the specific program content, it is possible to earn General Education and/or major credit during these programs. 60% of students participate in one of these programs prior to graduating from Lewis & Clark. Students can use Lewis & Clark's financial aid and scholarships for assistance in these programs.

ACADEMICS

A liberal arts education at Lewis & Clark connects classical learning with fresh inquiry and exciting research that pushes the frontiers of knowledge. Lewis & Clark considers the following elements essential to a liberal arts education:

1. Mastery of the fundamental techniques of intellectual inquiry: effective writing and speaking, active reading, and critical and imaginative thinking.

2. Exposure to the major assumptions, knowledge, and approaches in the fine arts, humanities, natural sciences and social sciences.

3. Critical understanding of important contemporary and historical issues.

4. Awareness of international and cross-cultural issues and gender relations.

5. Application of theory and knowledge to the search for informed, thoughtful and responsible solutions to important human problems.

The curriculum combines structure and freedom. Depth and breadth of subject matter are highly valued, but equally important are creativity and critical thinking. There are many opportunities for students to take their learning to a higher level, such as honors projects within academic departments, independent research, and internships. Our fast-growing Center for Entrepreneurship offers academic and cocurricular opportunities to translate knowledge and experiences into skills for success beyond college.

Two 15-week semesters make up the academic year, and each semester students normally take four 4-semester-credit courses, and one or more activity courses. The average student course load is 16 credits per semester. The requirement for graduation is 128 semester credits, approximately eight classes each year.

MAJORS

Lewis & Clark offers one degree: the Bachelor of Arts. Students have a wide selection of majors from which to choose: art (studio), art history, Asian studies, biochemistry and molecular biology, biology, chemistry, classics, computer science, computer science and mathematics, economics (international, public policy, and theory), English, environmental studies, French, German, Hispanic studies, history, international affairs, mathematics, music, philosophy, physics, political science, psychology, religious studies, rhetoric and media studies, sociology/anthropology, theater, and world languages and literature. Students may also design their own major, pursue a double major, or select from 28 minors. Pre-professional preparation is available in the fields of law, business, education, entrepreneurship, and medicine. Dual degree (3-2 or 4-2) programs in engineering are offered in cooperation with Columbia University, Washington University in St. Louis, and the University of Southern California. A dual degree, 4-2 B.A/M.B.A. program is available in conjunction with the Simon Graduate School of Business at the University of Rochester. A dual degree, 4-1 B.A/M.A.T program is offered through Lewis & Clark's Graduate School of Education and Counseling. In addition, there is a guaranteed admission agreement with Lewis & Clark's Law School for students meeting certain criteria.

TUITION, ROOM, BOARD, FEES

2017-18 tuition and fees are $48,988, and room and board are $11,996.

FINANCIAL AID

During the 2015-16 academic year approximately 91 percent of Lewis & Clark students received some form of financial assistance. Individual aid packages ranged from $1,000 to $61,000. Institutional, state, and federal resources including grants, loans and work-study may be part of an aid package. Eligibility for need-based funds is based primarily on an analysis of the income and asset information submitted on the Free Application for Federal Student Aid (FAFSA) and the College Board's CSS/Financial Aid PROFILE. To receive priority consideration for all sources of need-based financial aid, students must meet appropriate deadlines for admission and should submit the FAFSA and PROFILE by the date appropriate for their admissions plan as noted at go.lclark.edu/fao.

STUDENT ORGANIZATIONS & ACTIVITIES

With over 120 student-run organizations, there's never a lack of things to do at Lewis & Clark. Cultural events include lectures, symposia, art exhibits, plays, musical events, and dance performances. Athletics play an important role on campus, where 19 varsity teams, 7 club teams, and numerous intramural sports keep students physically active. Nature-lovers will enjoy the College Outdoors program, which offers activities such as hiking, backpacking, rafting, skiing, and kayaking in the wilderness of the Pacific Northwest. There are also plenty of opportunities for volunteering in and around the Portland area.

Lewis & Clark is committed to residential education, to creating a community dedicated to the exploration of ideas, values, beliefs and backgrounds, to the discovery of lifelong friendships; and to collaboration, both formal and informal, with peers, faculty, and staff. There is no Greek system at Lewis & Clark.

About 69 percent of undergraduates live on campus in residence halls; most of our residential space is co-ed. Along with personal living space (usually shared by two to four students) are several community venues within the residence halls, including coffee houses, convenience stores, art centers, outdoor basketball courts, recreation and fitness centers, lounges, and game rooms. A variety of themed communities within the residence halls are also available (visual and performing arts, multicultural engagement, outdoor pursuits, environmental action, holistic wellness, and more).

ADMISSIONS PROCESS

Commitment to academic excellence and personal and intellectual growth is imperative for successful Lewis & Clark applicants. Lewis & Clark is very selective, and every part of the application matters: academic records, essays, involvement in activities at school and in the community, leadership, and the strength of recommendations. Students are encouraged to visit our campus. Interviews are available but not required. The best-prepared applicants will have had four years of English, four years of mathematics, three to four years of history or social sciences, three years of laboratory sciences, two to three years of a foreign language, and one year of fine arts. Required credentials include: an essay; an official transcript including senior grades from first semester; a counselor recommendation; and one academic teacher recommendation. Lewis & Clark requires the SAT or ACT, unless the student is applying via the Test-Optional Portfolio Path (see lclark.edu for details). Students apply using the online Common Application. There is no application fee. Keep in mind these deadlines for first-year applicants: November 1 for binding Early Decision (notification, December 15), November 1 for non-binding Early Action (notification, January 1) and January 15 for Regular Decision (notification, April 1). Transfer applicants are reviewed on a rolling basis beginning January 1.

LIM COLLEGE

AT A GLANCE

Situated in the center of the fashion capital of the world, LIM College has been a major force in fashion and business education for nearly 80 years. Its graduates can be found throughout all areas of the fashion and related industries, and its high quality of education has earned LIM College accreditation from the Middle States Association of Colleges and Schools. The College's, BBA, BPS, and associate degrees are also accredited by the Accreditation Council of Business Schools and Programs (ACBSP).

A 2015 study measuring colleges' contributions to undergraduate student outcomes identified LIM as being among the top 10% of four-year colleges in the nation. The report from the Brookings Institution was titled, "Using earnings data to rank colleges: A value-added approach updated with College Scorecard data." And according to the College Scorecard, the median salary of LIM students 10 years after entering college is 42% higher than the national average.

LIM College offers a highly personal environment where students learn about the business of fashion, with an emphasis on academic and professional study. Lifelong friends are made at LIM, while long-lasting careers are launched. Although most students come to the College directly from high school or transfer from other colleges, there are also those of nontraditional college age. Students come to LIM College from many parts of the country and the world. As of Fall 2016, undergraduate enrollment was just about 1,500 students.

The Department of Experiential Education & Career Management is one of LIM College's chief assets. Every student receives extensive career advising throughout their time at the College, beginning in the first semester. This helps direct students to career opportunities within their field of study. A student's relationship with EECM is intended to strengthen throughout the college years and extend beyond graduation, as the department offers lifetime services.

The unique nature of LIM College's curriculum provides students with a foundation of core courses in liberal arts and business while offering diverse and intensive real-world preparation for the fashion and related industries. This affords graduates the opportunity to accept executive training, merchandising, management, marketing, visual, and communications positions in a wide variety of areas within the fashion and business worlds.

Support services are important at LIM College. In addition to academic and career advising, personal counseling is available. Because of the College's small size and the close relationships between students and staff members, faculty members and administrators are readily accessible to help and advise all students.

Support services are important at LIM College. In addition to academic and career advising, personal counseling is available. Faculty members and administrators are readily accessible to help and advise all students.

Student life at LIM College is also very dynamic. Active clubs include the Fashion Show Production Club, the Student Life Activities Board, the Student Leadership Council, The Lexington Line student magazine (online and print), the Dance Team, and many more.

Located on the Upper East Side of Manhattan, LIM's residence hall offers a host of attractive amenities. All rooms have private bathrooms, complimentary wireless Internet access, phone service, and over 100 cable channels. Rooms are also equipped with refrigerators and 25-inch flat-screen televisions. In addition, the residence hall contains a private gym, game room, computer lab, and a brand-new communal kitchen.

LIM College's Open House program offers students and their families the opportunity to tour the campus and learn not only about LIM College's unique academic programs, but also about the vast array of career options in the fashion industry. The day also includes presentations on financial aid, study abroad, and student activities. Current LIM students assist in hosting the event and are available to answer questions. There are also many other opportunities to visit, including weekly information sessions, Transfer Services Days, mock classes for accepted students, and other special events.

LOCATION & ENVIRONMENT

LIM College is situated in three buildings—on East 53rd Street, East 45th Street, and on Fifth Avenue, one of the most fashionable locales in the world. A whole world of fashion is at the College's doorstep and includes such famous stores as Saks Fifth Avenue, Henri Bendel, Armani, and Ralph Lauren. New York City offers unparalleled resources, many of which are directly incorporated into the LIM College curriculum. New York is the headquarters for the garment, cosmetics, advertising, publishing, and textile industries, all of which are essential to the fashion industry and are visited regularly by LIM College students.

CAMPUS FACILITIES & EQUIPMENT

Facilities include the 5,000-square-foot Adrian G. Marcuse Library, with over 14,700 books, 1,118 librarian-selected e-books, 164 scholarly journals and print magazines, 855 bound volumes of magazine back issues, 1,161 DVDs, an archive of historic materials, and a large collection of fashion, business, and marketing books to assist students in their research. The library also has 42 CAD-enabled computers. The 54 subscription databases located on the library-run web page are available 24/7, on or off-campus, and can be accessed by computer, tablet, smart phone, or any other Internet-ready device. The Math Center and Writing Center offer one-on-one tutoring for all students.

LIM College's Fifth Avenue location is equipped with two fashion merchandising studios, two 1,100-square-foot visual merchandising studios, as well as a Color and Materials Lab.

OFF-CAMPUS OPPORTUNITIES

From two-week immersion programs to semester-long study abroad experiences, LIM College offers students the opportunity to see the world and experience fashion on an international stage. With programs in Australia, Canada, China, England, France, Italy, the Netherlands, Spain, and Taiwan, students are given a global education for a global industry.

ACADEMICS

LIM College offers a combination of classroom education and supervised internships designed to prepare students for executive training programs and other entry-level executive positions in various areas of the fashion industry.

Experiential education is an integral component of the LIM College curriculum. Students are required to complete three internships in order to earn their bachelor's degree. Each internship has a prerequisite seminar attached to it that includes activities such as field trips, guest speakers, and portfolio-building activities that help students network with industry professionals and develop into dynamic business leaders.

Courses are sequential, each built upon the knowledge and experience a student gains through the process of learning. The experiential education program begins with a course designed to increase a student's knowledge of the industry, building a foundation upon which to launch a career in fashion. The program culminates with a nearly full-time Senior Co-op internship during which students also work closely with instructors and advisers.

LIM College accepts qualified students as transfers throughout the four years. The maximum number of credits that LIM will accept is 65. Transfer students must complete the last consecutive 46 credits at LIM College, including the Senior Co-op semester.

The College calendar runs on a traditional semester format, offering both fall and spring start dates. Summer and Saturday Fashion Lab programs for high school students are also available. Fashion Lab courses, such as Fashion Buying and Fashion Magazines, blend academics with hands-on experience and are a great way to explore the fashion industry.

MAJORS

LIM College offers four-year programs in Fashion Media, Fashion Merchandising, Management, Marketing, and Visual Merchandising, leading to the Bachelor of Business Administration (BBA) degree, as well as programs in Fashion Media and International Business leading to the Bachelor of Science (BS) degree. Also offered is a four-year Bachelor of Professional Studies (BPS) program in Fashion Merchandising as well as two-year programs in Fashion Merchandising leading to the Associate in Applied Science (AAS) and the Associate in Occupational Studies (AOS) degrees. The Fashion Merchandising program has a track in Retail Buying and Planning. The College also has a broad variety of concentrations, such as Home Fashions and Event Planning, which allow students to pursue a focused area of study that complements their major. At the graduate level, LIM offers four Master of Professional Studies (MPS) degree programs—two of which are also available online.

TUITION, ROOM, BOARD, FEES

Undergraduate tuition for the 2017–18 school year is $25,725 with additional mandatory fees of $575. Housing charges for the 2017–18 year are $16,350. Books and supplies average approximately $900 per academic year and students living on campus may spend up to $4,000 a year on meal expenses. Students who commute spend from $1,200 to $2,000 for transportation, depending on distance, and personal expenses are approximately $1,500 per academic year. For students who do not have their own accident and health insurance, the mandatory insurance offered by LIM College is $1,736.

FINANCIAL AID

LIM College believes that lack of funds should not keep students from attaining a degree. Therefore, admissions decisions and financial aid are totally separate, and a request for aid has no effect on admission. Approximately 82 percent of LIM College's students received some form of financial aid during the 2014–15 academic year. Institutional scholarships, Federal Pell Grants, Federal Supplemental Educational Opportunity Grants, and New York State TAP grants are all available for eligible students. In addition, the College participates in the Federal Stafford Loan program for students and Federal PLUS Loan program for parents. The College also works with several private lenders to offer alternative education loans for students to supplement their federal loans. International students are eligible to apply for alternative loans with a credit-worthy U.S.-based co-signer. The Free Application for Federal Student Aid (FAFSA) should be filed by all applicants by March 1 for priority consideration. Aid is granted on the basis of financial need and scholarships are merit-based, although some awards take need into consideration. Details of the financial aid programs are available on the LIM College website or are available directly from the Office of Student Financial Services.

LIM College offers a merit scholarship program for incoming freshmen and transfer students. These scholarship monies are awarded for academic achievement in high school or college. Students can remain eligible for their scholarship throughout their stay at the College by maintaining a GPA of 3.0 or above.

STUDENT ORGANIZATIONS & ACTIVITIES

The Office of Student Life is the center of student activities and clubs at LIM College. This department supports student government, approves student organizations, and establishes operating budgets. One of LIM's most popular clubs is the Fashion Show Production Club, which produces an annual fashion show attended by an audience of more than 1,000. Another popular activity is the student-run The Lexington Line magazine (online and print). LIM's Office of Student Life plans many other activities including diversity programming, philanthropic service opportunities, New York City outings, and holiday celebrations.

ADMISSIONS PROCESS

LIM College's Admissions Committee recognizes that many intangibles go into the making of a successful student, and it evaluates each applicant individually and holistically. The College uses a rolling admission policy. Applicants are informed of the admission decision within approximately four to six weeks after all admission requirements have been fulfilled. An application may be obtained from the LIM College website or by contacting the Office of Admissions.

All undergraduate applicants are required to submit high school transcripts, SAT or ACT scores, two letters of recommendation, an essay, and the completed application with the application fee. Transfer students must also submit all college transcripts. The standardized test requirement will be waived if the applicant for undergraduate admission has satisfactorily earned 15 credit hours (21 on a quarter or trimester system) at the time of application. International students should review the LIM College website and contact the Office of Admissions for specific requirements. It is also strongly suggested that all applicants create an activity sheet or resume highlighting their experience, with an emphasis on business and fashion activities.

LOYOLA UNIVERSITY CHICAGO

AT A GLANCE

Ranked a Top 100 university by U.S. News & World Report, Loyola University Chicago will help you prepare for a career with 80+ programs in business, sciences, and other disciplines.

Consistently ranked a "Top National University" by U.S. News & World Report, Loyola University Chicago continues to advance the 450-year-old Jesuit tradition of rigorous academic study firmly grounded in the liberal arts.

Loyola is the largest Jesuit Catholic university in the United States, enrolling 16,422 students. Incoming freshmen come from 43 states and 57 countries. Loyola offers more than 80 undergraduate majors and more than 140 graduate, professional, and graduate-level certificate programs as well as three professional programs in law, medicine, and nursing.

Loyola helps students prepare for meaningful careers with top academic programs in business, the sciences, and numerous other disciplines, along with opportunities for internships throughout the city of Chicago and beyond. Loyola's well-rounded, transformative education will help students develop as a whole person-intellectually, socially, physically, and spiritually.

LOCATION & ENVIRONMENT

Loyola gives students the best of campus and city life with diverse living and learning opportunities in the world-class city of Chicago. Loyola's Lake Shore Campus, home to the College of Arts and Sciences, the Graduate School, and the Marcella Niehoff School of Nursing, is located on the picturesque shore of Lake Michigan and offers students the comforts of a traditional residential campus. Located off North Michigan Avenue, Chicago's Magnificent Mile, Loyola's dynamic Water Tower Campus is home to the Quinlan School of Business as well as the Schools of Communication, Continuing and Professional Studies, Education, Law, and Social Work and connects students to myriad internship, job, and service opportunities. The Stritch School of Medicine is housed at the Medical Sciences Campus in west suburban Maywood, Illinois.

Exposure to Loyola's three Chicago campuses gives students three diverse experiences: a vibrant urban environment, the comfort of a more traditional collegiate setting, and the bustle of a professional medical environment. At each campus, students have access to computers, study areas, and dining halls, as well as a network of student groups and activities. A free intercampus shuttle is available between the Lake Shore and Water Tower Campuses.

Students may also study abroad at the John Felice Rome Center in Italy; or they may attend The Beijing Center for Chinese Studies or choose from one of 150 other study abroad programs in 70 countries.

CAMPUS FACILITIES & EQUIPMENT

The recently completed, 100,000+ sq. ft. Damen Student Center is a LEED Silver certified building. Named after the founder of Loyola University Chicago, the Arnold J. Damen, S.J. Student Center provides students a dedicated space to build community and encourage co-curricular engagement. Damen is the place to relax, study, play pool, watch TV, grab a snack, or hang out with friends.

Not only is the recently completed Cuneo Hall a state-of-the-art building with a cutting-edge academic center—but it also uses sustainable technologies to reduce its ecological footprint. Cuneo is LEED Gold certified and will use approximately 60% less energy than comparable academic buildings.

The renovated Mundelein Center offers new options for fine arts programming. For plays and theatre are the new Newhart Family Theatre and the Underground Laboratory Theatre. Mundelein Music Hall has been completely renovated as well. These new spaces give students an opportunity to hone their craft in contemporary surroundings.

The School of Communication is in the heart of Chicago's creative and business communities. Located at the Water Tower Campus, the building features generously equipped computer labs, state-of-the-art classrooms and offices, and on-site production facilities, including street-side lab with a TV studio and radio interview sets.

The Information Commons is a four-story lakeside research facility that provides individual and group study space for students, as well as state-of-the-art technology with more than 200 computers, wireless internet connections, and a lakefront café.

Loyola's Michael R. and Marilyn C. Quinlan Life Sciences Education and Research Center provides numerous opportunities for undergraduates to engage in the latest scientific research alongside their professors in modern labs for biology, bioinformatics, chemistry, ecology, and other life sciences.

The Loyola University Museum of Art (LUMA) showcases permanent and rotating exhibitions of professional and student work. The Sullivan Center for Student Services consolidates a dozen student services offices into one convenient location.

For information about campus facilities, visit http://www.luc.edu/campus_community.shtml.

ACADEMICS

The Core Curriculum is the foundation of Loyola's liberal arts education. Core courses are aimed at increasing students' understanding of themselves and the world while they explore diverse subjects and cultivate new interests. Courses provide a strong base of knowledge, skills, and values that will help students achieve academic, professional, and personal success throughout their lives.

Exceptionally well-qualified students may apply to the Interdisciplinary Honors Program.

Other special academic opportunities include pre-professional programs for law and health professions; U.S./Europe Double Degree in Business; 33 five-year (bachelor's/master's) degree programs; 19 interdisciplinary programs; a six-year, early admission to Loyola's School of Law; early assurance to Loyola's Stritch School of Medicine; and the Loyola/Midwestern University Dual-Acceptance Pharmacy Program.

MAJORS

The College of Arts and Sciences offers undergraduate majors in African Studies and the African Diaspora, anthropology, art history, biochemistry, bioinformatics, biology, biophysics, chemistry, classical civilization, communications networks and security, computer science, criminal justice and criminology, dance, economics, English, forensic science, French, Greek (ancient), history, human services, information technology, international studies, Italian, Latin, mathematics, mathematics and computer science, music, neuroscience, philosophy, physics, physics and computer science, physics and engineering, political science, psychology, religious studies, sociology, sociology and anthropology, software engineering, Spanish, statistics, studio art, theater, theology, theoretical physics and applied mathematics, visual communication, and women's studies and gender studies.

The Department of Engineering Science offers an undergraduate major in engineering science, with specializations in biomedical, computer, and environmental engineering.

The Institute of Environmental Sustainability offers majors in Environmental Policy, Environmental Science, and Environmental Studies.

The Quinlan School of Business offers majors in accounting, economics, entrepreneurship, finance, human resource management, information systems, international business, management, marketing, operations management, and sport management.

The School of Communication offers majors in advertising and public relations, communication studies, film and digital media, and journalism.

The School of Education offers majors in bilingual/bicultural education, early childhood/special education, elementary education, middle grade education, secondary education and foreign language, and special education.

The Marcella Niehoff School of Nursing offers the Bachelor of Science in Exercise Science, Bachelor of Science in Nursing, a Bachelor of Science in Health Systems Management, a Bachelor of Science in Exercise Science, an RN to BSN, and an Accelerated BSN program, which is available to students who have already completed a baccalaureate degree.

The School of Social Work offers an undergraduate major in social work and a combined bachelor's and master's degree in social work, which can be completed in five years.

Learn more at LUC.edu/majors.

TUITION, ROOM, BOARD, FEES

Tuition for 2016-2017 entering students (per year): $40,700

Room and board (per year): Room and board cost is dependent on students' selection of residence hall and meal plan (average is $14,110).

Tuition part-time (per credit hour): $751

FINANCIAL AID

Loyola, we're committed to making a high-quality education affordable. Our Financial Aid Office works with students and families to address each student's specific situation and needs. Our expert staff evaluates financial aid eligibility for resources such as grants, scholarships, and loans to help make a Loyola education a possibility for students.

Approximately 97% of Loyola freshmen receive grants or scholarships. Students are encouraged to file the Free Application for Federal Student Aid (FAFSA) by Loyola's March 1 priority processing date.

In addition to the many scholarships awarded with admission, students may also explore more than 75 types of additional scholarships. For more information, visit LUC.edu/scholarships.

STUDENT ORGANIZATIONS & ACTIVITIES

Loyola offers students the chance to develop leadership and social skills by participating in any of its more than 200 academic, athletic, cultural, hobby, media, political, social, and spiritual student-run organizations.

The Institute of Environmental Sustainability at Loyola provides practical experiences that will translate to your future workplace, such as working on the student-run farm or in the ecosystem research labs, as well as through degree options in environmental studies and environmental science. Our student--run biodiesel program is the first and only school operation licensed to sell reclaimed biodiesel fuel in the U.S.

Our Engineering Science degree offers students a change to build hands-on skills and prepare for a career in engineering. Students can choose one of three concentrations—biomedical, computer, and environmental engineering. Learn more at LUC.edu/engineeringscience.

Loyola faculty are committed to being engaged with students. Approximately 93% of faculty hold the highest degrees in their field—that, along with Loyola's 14:1 student faculty ratio means that you will enjoy frequent interaction and collaboration with accomplished professors.

ADMISSIONS PROCESS

Students seeking admission to Loyola are evaluated on their overall academic record, including ACT or SAT scores. The freshman class entering in Fall 2016 had middle 50% ACT score ranges between 24 and 29, middle 50% range on the SAT Verbal between 520 and 630, middle 50% range on the SAT Math between 510 and 630, and an average GPA of 3.74. Most Loyola students rank in the upper quarter of their graduating class, but consideration is given to students in the upper half.

Transfer students with 20 credit hours or more are evaluated on the basis of their college work only. The minimum acceptable GPA varies from 2.0 to 2.5, depending upon academic interest. Candidates must also be in good standing at the last college attended.

Loyola notifies applicants four to six weeks after the application, supporting credentials, and secondary school counselor or teacher recommendation are received. The application is only available online and there is no application fee at LUC.edu/apply.

Prospective students are encouraged to visit campus by arranging individual appointments and campus tours up to two weeks in advance. Arrange a visit at LUC.edu/visit.

To obtain an application, get more information, or arrange a visit, contact:

Undergraduate Admission Office

Loyola University Chicago

820 North Michigan Avenue

Chicago, IL 60611

Telephone: 312.915.6500 or 800.262.2373 (toll-free)

E-mail: admission@luc.edu

Website: LUC.edu/undergrad

MANHATTAN COLLEGE

AT A GLANCE

Manhattan College is a Lasallian Catholic college in Riverdale, NY, which offers more than 100 majors and programs in liberal arts, business, education and health, engineering and science.

Manhattan College was founded in 1853 by the Brothers of the Christian Schools, a teaching order started by Saint John Baptist de La Salle, patron saint of teachers. The Lasallian mission drives everything we do. It's an integral part of who we are and how we live.

There are more than 100 majors and programs guided by an internationally recognized faculty, sought-after leaders and real-world consultants in their fields, 93 percent of whom hold doctoral degrees. Students have opportunities to study abroad in more than 30 countries.

Manhattan College participates in Division I sports as part of the MAAC, with 19 teams. The College is known for its student-athletes, with many ranking on the MAAC All-Academic teams, while also contributing to winning teams.

LOCATION & ENVIRONMENT

At Manhattan College, we offer a truly unique location within the boundaries of New York City right next door to a subway stop. Unlike many other New York City schools, we have a true college campus—22 acres centered around a quad, where students play Frisbee, study under the sun and hang out with friends. Manhattan's professors use NYC as a classroom with field trips to Wall Street, museums and other world-famous locations.

The student body of 3,576 hails from 41 states and 39 countries. With a four-year guarantee of resident housing, 82 percent of freshmen live on campus in both traditional style dorms and suite style living. Common interest communities bring students with a particular interest under one roof to live and learn throughout the year.

CAMPUS FACILITIES & EQUIPMENT

The Raymond W. Kelly ('63) Student Commons opened in fall 2014. The 70,000-square-foot building significantly enhances the College's ability to integrate academics and student life, and provides space for fitness and wellness programming, cultural and community events, dining, student activities, and student collaboration.

O'Malley Library is home to a number of new features and services, including more than 100 computer workstations, a round-the-clock Internet Café, a media center equipped with teleconferencing capabilities, and many group study rooms scattered throughout the five-story layout.

Both commuters and residents can take advantage of the Fitness Center and newly renovated cafeterias. There are a variety of dining options, as well as spaces to relax and study.

OFF-CAMPUS OPPORTUNITIES

Students actively define their commitment toward community around the city, country and world. Each year, Campus Ministry and Social Action (CMSA) runs several L.O.V.E. programs (Lasallian Outreach Volunteer Experience) giving students service experiences in areas such as New Orleans, Kenya, Ecuador, the Dominican Republic and West Virginia.

Many students also participate in local community service projects. These include Habitat for Humanity, working with the elderly in nearby nursing homes, volunteering in soup kitchens and tutoring at local schools.

Students are provided with internship opportunities in their field of study throughout the metropolitan area often networking with alumni.

ACADEMICS

Manhattan College is one of the few American colleges to have chapters of all five of these distinguished national honor societies: Beta Gamma Sigma, Kappa Delta Pi, Phi Beta Kappa, Sigma Xi and Tau Beta Pi. Manhattan College is one of 276 institutions in the U.S. with a chapter of Phi Beta Kappa, the nation's oldest and most widely known academic honor society, which celebrates and advocates excellence in the liberal arts and sciences.

Other programs at Manhattan College:

1. The National Model United Nations: a unique opportunity to better understand the inner workings of the United Nations and other international organizations while building skills in diplomacy and compromise.

2. The Branigan Fellowships Program: undergraduate research in the humanities for student-initiated projects (grants over $3,000).

3. The Fellowships Committee; encourage graduate study and helps work through sometimes challenging application processes (students and alumni).

4. The Pre-Law Advisory Committee

5. Study Abroad Program: programs run for a semester, an academic year, a month-long summer program or a seven-week summer program.

6. Manhattan's Mentorship Program: opportunities to gain insight into intended careers by being paired with professionals, generally Manhattan alumni in those careers.

7. College Internship Program: complete at the minimum of one internship within their four years of study.

8. Manhattan's Finance and Economics Club: student preparation and participation in the Volunteer Income Tax Assistance Program (VITA) and other service activities.

9. Jasper Summer Research Scholars: a fellowship that will offer a stipend to scholars to pursue on campus summer research. It is managed though the Center for Graduate School and Fellowship Advisement and supports up to three students from each of the undergraduate schools.

MAJORS & DEGREES OFFERED

Manhattan College offers more than 40 major fields of study on the undergraduate level and graduate degrees in education, engineering and business. The College's professional schools are externally accredited by the following accrediting organizations: school of business, Association to Advance Collegiate Schools of Business (AACSB); school of education, Teacher Education Accrediting Council (TEAC); and individual school of engineering programs are accredited by the Engineering Accreditation Commission (EAC) of ABET, Inc.

Programs include:

Liberal Arts: Art History, Communication, Economics, English, Environmental Studies, French, Government, History, International Studies, Labor Studies, Peace Studies, Philosophy, Psychology, Religious Studies, Sociology, Spanish, Urban Studies.

Business: Accounting, Business Analytics, Computer Information Systems, Economics, Finance, Global Business Studies, Management and Marketing. Graduate programs: Bachelor of Science in Professional Accounting / Master of Business Administration Program and the Bachelor of Science in Business / Master of Business Administration Program (five-year multiple award program).

Education: Early Childhood Education, Childhood Education, Dual: Childhood/Special Education and Adolescent Education; and two undergraduate majors in the department of Physical Education and Human Performance in Physical Education Teaching (grades K-12) or Exercise Science. Graduate: Five-Year Childhood/Special Education Program, which combines baccalaureate and graduate work, allowing the student to receive a bachelor's and master's degree with eligibility to pursue certification for grades 1-6 in regular and special education; master's degrees and professional diplomas in school counseling, mental health counseling, special education and school building leadership.

Radiological and Health Professions Program: Nuclear Medicine Technology, Radiation Therapy Technology, Radiologic Technology (X-ray) or Allied Health.

Engineering: Chemical Engineering, Civil Engineering, Computer Engineering, Electrical Engineering and Mechanical Engineering. Graduate: Chemical Engineering, Civil Engineering, Computer Engineering, Electrical Engineering, Environmental Engineering and Mechanical Engineering. Graduate Certificate programs: Engineering Management, Environmental Management, Engineering Law, Engineering Mathematics, Biochemical Engineering, Manufacturing/Systems,

HVAC (Heating, Ventilation and Air Conditioning), Construction Management, Electrical Power Engineering, Computer Engineering and Energy Management.

Science: Biology, Biochemistry, Chemistry, Computer Science, Mathematics and Physics.

Another option is the Five-Year Childhood/Special Education Program, which combines baccalaureate and graduate work, allowing the student to receive a bachelor's and master's degree with eligibility to pursue certification for grades 1-6 in regular and special education. The school of education also offers master's degrees and professional diplomas in school counseling, mental health counseling, special education and school building leadership.

The Radiological and Health Professions Program is also part of the school of education and health and is available to students pursuing a Bachelor of Science with three major selections: Nuclear Medicine Technology, Radiation Therapy Technology, Radiologic Technology (X-ray) or Allied Health. The Engineering program offers programs leading to the baccalaureate degree in five disciplines: Chemical Engineering, Civil Engineering, Computer Engineering, Electrical Engineering and Mechanical Engineering. Graduate study at the master's level is also available in: Chemical Engineering, Civil Engineering, Computer Engineering, Electrical Engineering, Environmental Engineering and Mechanical Engineering.

Graduate Certificate programs currently available to engineering students are: Engineering Management, Environmental Management, Engineering Law, Engineering Mathematics, Biochemical Engineering, Manufacturing/Systems, HVAC (Heating, Ventilation and Air Conditioning), Construction Management, Electrical Power Engineering, Computer Engineering and Energy Management.

The Science program offers students the chance to major in the following areas: Biology, Biochemistry, Chemistry, Computer Science, Mathematics and Physics.

TUITION, ROOM, BOARD, FEES
Full Time Students, 2017-2018
New Students entering 2017-18: $19,100 (per semester)
Continuing students: $18,450 (per semester)

FINANCIAL AID
Manhattan College provides the maximum financial aid available to qualified students to make their attendance at Manhattan financially possible.

New Students: Students admitted to the College and demonstrating financial need will receive a financial aid assistance offer in the form of a financial aid award letter from the Office of Admissions and Financial Aid, which is based on an assessment of your financial need.

Continuing Eligibility: All financial aid is renewable on a yearly basis provided the student remains eligible.

Presidential Scholarships: Non-need based scholarships awarded to extraordinary applicants. Eligibility is based on exceptional SAT or ACT scores, secondary school grade point average, and rank in class.

Dean's Award: Dean's Awards are offered to academically gifted students who fall slightly below Presidential Scholarship requirements.

Manhattan College Grant-in-Aid: Manhattan College awards grants-in-aid to accepted students who demonstrate financial need.

Manhattan College Campus Employment Program: Manhattan offers its own campus work program to students who need employment to meet college expenses but are not eligible for Federal Work Study

Athletic Grants: The Manhattan College Athletics department may fund athletic grants to students who, by the possession of certain athletic skills, can add to the community spirit and morale of the campus.

Resident Assistant Grants: These grants are awarded to students selected to serve as Resident Assistants in the dormitories.

Dollars for Scholars: As a collegiate partner, Manhattan College matches Scholarship of America awards up to $500 a year.

Other programs: Veterans Administration Educational Benefits, Post-9/11 GI Bill Participant, Tuition Remission, Tuition Exchange Scholarship

The school also awards endowed and special category scholarships as part of the existing financial aid package.

STUDENT ORGANIZATIONS & ACTIVITIES
Manhattan College offers many events and activities for students to participate in with more than 60 clubs and organizations on campus.

Cultural Groups: Asian Culture Club, Association for Black Culture, Gaelic Society, International Student Association and the Multicultural Student Union

Special Interest Groups: Christ in Your Life, Lasallian Outreach Volunteer Experience (L.O.V.E.), Electronics Club, Fashion Student Association, Just Peace, LaSallian Collegians (service group), New York Water Environmental Association, Relay for Life and Student Government.

Club Sports: Cheerleading & Crew

Social Leisure Clubs: Games Club, Outdoors Club, Steppers

Performing Arts: Bagpipers, Jasper Dancers, Jasper Band, Jazz Band, Orchestra, Players, Scatterbomb and Singers.

Communication: Manhattanite (yearbook), MCTV, Quadrangle (college newspaper), WRCM radio station

Social Fraternities & Sororities

Alpha Sigma Beta, Fraternity

Alpha Upsilon Pi, Sorority

Gamma Alpha Sigma, Fraternity

Crimson & Cream Delta Sigma Theta Sorority

Co-curricular clubs: Accounting Society, American Advertising Federation, American Chemistry Society, American Institute of Biological Science, American Institute of Chemical Engineers, American Society of Mechanical Engineers, Amnesty International, Association for Supervision and Curriculum Development, Biological Engineering Student Society, Communications Club, Economics and Finance Society, Italian Club, Information Technology Club, Institute of Electronic and Electrical Engineers, French Club, Manhattan Magazine, Mini Baja, National Society of Black Engineers, Phi Delta Epsilon, Psychology Club, Radiological Science Society, Society of Civil Engineers, Society of Hispanic Professional Engineers, Society of Mechanical Engineers, Society of Women Engineers, St. Thomas More Law Society.

ADMISSIONS PROCESS
1) Course Selection and Performance: Most emphasis is placed upon student course selection on the secondary level and grades earned in those subjects.

2) SAT and/or ACT Scores

3) 1 Letter of Recommendation

4) Personal Statement

Students who are transferring without an associate degree or with an A.A.S. degree must submit:

- High school transcript
- Official college transcripts
- List of courses presently being taken
- College catalogs from all institutions previously attended

Financial aid transcripts from all collegiate institutions previously attended (even if you only took one or two courses while in high school)

MARLBORO COLLEGE

AT A GLANCE

Marlboro College is an intentionally small, intellectually demanding liberal arts school located in southern Vermont. Home to 300 students, Marlboro empowers students with the freedom and responsibility to create an individualized course of study in collaboration with faculty members and to participate in a self-governing community. Instead of traditional majors, students pursue a self-designed Plan of Concentration based on their academic interests, culminating in a major work of scholarship. Students graduate having completed a profound intellectual journey, and go out into the world with greater self-reliance and the skills needed to forge their own career path or pursue graduate-level study.

LOCATION & ENVIRONMENT

Marlboro College's setting in rural southern Vermont provides students with space for quiet contemplation as well as myriad opportunities for outdoor recreation. With 40 miles of trails on or near our 300-acre campus, and the Green Mountain National Forest nearby, students have easy access to hiking, mountain biking, skiing, caving, climbing and kayaking (among other activities). Each season includes Marlboro traditions such as Apple Days in the fall and the broomball tournament in winter.

Tucked on its own Potash Hill, the college is an integral part of the town of Marlboro, a community of less than 1,000 where many staff, faculty and students are active citizens. Some of the many benefits shared by both the college and the town include a volunteer fire company, a community newsletter called the Marlboro Mixer, cross-country ski trails, the Marlboro Historical Society, the Southern Vermont Natural History Museum, the Marlboro Community Fair and the January Book Swap. Marlboro is also the site of the world famous Marlboro Music Festival which occupies the campus during the summer.

CAMPUS FACILITIES & EQUIPMENT

The core of campus buildings is made up of historic farmhouses and barns, renovated into classrooms and dorms by the first students who attended Marlboro. These include Dalrymple Hall, the main classroom building; the dining hall; the admissions building; and Mather, the administrative building. Over many years the college has added more buildings, including residence halls, student cabins and cottages, Persons Auditorium/gymnasium, Whittemore Theater, Rice-Aron Library, the Campus Center and Total Health Center, and the Serkin Center for Performing Arts. The new Snyder Visual Arts Center adds exciting new gallery, studio and classroom space for the integration of visual arts with other disciplines. Other facilities include an integrated science lab, a DNA lab, a computer lab, and a digital media lab.

OFF-CAMPUS OPPORTUNITIES

With the vibrant town of Brattleboro just 10 miles away, Marlboro students have easy access to many resources and activities. Brattleboro is an eclectic community located in the Connecticut River Valley and a regional center for art, commerce and technology. It was listed as one of the "20 Best Small Towns in America" by Smithsonian magazine, one of the "10 Best Small Towns in America" by Fodor's, and in the top 10 in the book The 100 Best Art Towns in America, with many galleries, music venues, bookstores and performance spaces to experience. Among the blocks of historic red-brick buildings one can find cozy cafes and four-star restaurants featuring local fare and international cuisines including Thai, Korean, Greek and Italian. Mother Earth News named Brattleboro one of "Eight Great Places You've Never Heard Of", and it's college-town feel was recently highlighted on Vermont Public Radio. Vans run from the college into Brattleboro multiple times a day and trips to Northeastern cities such as Northampton, Boston, New York and Montreal occur several weekends each semester.

ACADEMICS

Rather than follow a prescribed academic program, Marlboro students work closely with faculty advisors to map out an individualized course of study based on their intellectual interests. This approach allows students to study broadly and creatively across disciplines before embarking on their self-designed Plan of Concentration, an in-depth examination of a focused academic area that culminates in a major work of scholarship. By taking ownership of and responsibility for the scope and topography of their intellectual exploration, Marlboro students learn how to define a set of goals, develop a comprehensive plan to meet them, and work through the obstacles that inevitably arise along the way. They employ initiative and grit throughout the process and emerge at the end with a joyful sense of accomplishment, heightened confidence, and invaluable experience.

Marlboro's faculty members bring an extraordinary degree of commitment, passion and academic mentoring to their teaching endeavors. Beyond the traditional classroom setting, faculty members interact with students through one-on-one tutorials, Plan advising sessions, service-learning trips and collaborative projects ranging from scholarly papers to films. Whether participating in Town Meeting or composing original music for a promotional video, faculty members make significant contributions to the vitality and spirit of Marlboro's learning community on a regular basis.

Whether their academic interests lean toward Russian literature or contemporary dance, students write prodigiously over the course of their time at Marlboro. Within their first three semesters, students must fulfill the Clear Writing Requirement, which involves submitting a portfolio of clear, concise and grammatically correct writing samples for approval by the faculty. Marlboro's focus on helping students develop their command of the written word speaks to the college's underlying focus on clear thinking, which is both a product and reflection of clear writing. Whatever career paths Marlboro students forge, they all benefit from the ability to process complex information and effectively communicate their ideas to others.

MAJORS & DEGREES OFFERED

Marlboro College empowers undergraduate students to create an individualized course of study in collaboration with faculty members. Based on their personal academic interests and goals, students study broadly across disciplines before embarking on a self-designed Plan of Concentration that culminates in a major work of scholarship. This approach allows students to take ownership of and responsibility for the scope and structure of their intellectual exploration. Degrees offered include Bachelor of Arts, Bachelor of Science and, through the World Studies Program, Bachelor of Arts or Science in International Studies. Our degree fields are:

American Studies
Anthropology
Art History
Asian Studies
Astronomy
Biochemistry
Biology
Ceramics
Chemistry
Computer Science
Cultural History
Dance
Economics
Environmental Studies
Film/Video Studies
Gender Studies
History
Languages
Liberal Studies
Literature
Mathematics
Music
Painting, Drawing, and Mixed Media
Philosophy
Photography

Physics
Politics
Psychology
Religion
Sculpture
Sociology
Theater
Visual Arts
World Studies
Writing

TUITION, ROOM, BOARD, FEES

For the 2016-2017 academic year, the fees are as follows:

Tuition: $39,086

Fees: $944

Room: $5,948

Board: $4,854

Total: $50,832

FINANCIAL AID

As a very small, private liberal arts college, Marlboro makes a conscious and continuous effort to keep tuition and fees as affordable as possible. In recent years, we've increased the amount of need-based grant aid provided to students and increased other awards for financial aid. Today more than 90 percent of full-time Marlboro students receive some form of financial assistance. Applicants should contact the Financial Aid Office directly to request a financial aid packet, which includes step-by-step instructions. The priority deadline for completing the Free Application for Federal Student Aid (FAFSA) is March 1. The financial aid office can be reached at 802-258-9312 or finaid@marlboro.edu.

STUDENT ORGANIZATIONS & ACTIVITIES

Marlboro College operates based on a model of community governance. Students, faculty, and staff play an integral role in shaping campus life through their participation in Town Meeting, a monthly assembly during which college-wide issues are discussed and brought to vote. Students also serve on committees in areas ranging from curriculum development and faculty hiring to public art and food services.

Campus life at Marlboro College correlates directly with student interests. Extracurricular groups and activities evolve yearly with each incoming class. Through this ongoing collective creation of community, Marlboro students develop valuable skills in teamwork and community organizing as well as a strong sense of civic investment.

One of the most popular resources for student activities is the Outdoor Program, OP for short. The OP offers a variety of activities from week-long orientation trips for new students to weekend mini trips, to winter-and spring-break trips in tropical climates. Some of the popular activities have been rock climbing, hiking, rafting, kayaking, camping, yoga, intramural soccer, broomball, and Ultimate Frisbee. The college also has an indoor climbing wall and regular intramural activities.

For a small campus, students enjoy a wide range of social, artistic, and cultural activities. A sampling of student activities in one semester would include performances by rock, folk, jazz, and ethnic bands; dances; lectures; poetry readings; recitals; plays; and concerts. Annual events that are considered traditions include midnight breakfast, Wendell-Judd Cup cross country ski event, Work Day, President's Fall Ball, Trails Day, broomball tournament, community and international dinners, Gender Bender Ball, and Apple Days.

ADMISSIONS PROCESS

If you are looking for an intentionally small, intellectually demanding liberal arts school where students are seen, heard, known and valued, Marlboro College would be a great college choice for you. Marlboro assesses student potential in the unique context of each applicant's experience, without the confines of GPAs or standardized test scores. There is no formula for what makes a student a "good fit" for Marlboro, but applicants are reviewed with an eye towards intellectual promise, self-motivation, self-discipline and ability to positively contribute to our community.

Students may apply to Marlboro under three different application plans.

Early Decision: Deadline-November 15; Notification-December 1

Early Action: Deadline-January 15; Notification-February 1

Regular Admission: Rolling

Please note that if you are applying for financial aid it is important to file the FAFSA by March 1.

In order to be considered for admission, please submit the following: a completed Common Application and Marlboro College Supplement with the "Why Marlboro?" personal statement (or the optional Marlboro College Application, if you are not already filling out the Common Application), the $50 nonrefundable application fee, all high school and college transcript(s), an expository writing sample, and two letters of recommendation (teacher and general). An interview is required for all students. Submission of SAT or ACT scores is optional.

MICHIGAN TECHNOLOGICAL UNIVERSITY

AT A GLANCE

Michigan Technological University (www.mtu.edu) is a leading public research university developing new technologies and preparing students to create the future for a prosperous and sustainable world. Ninety-three percent of graduates find jobs in their fields.

Michigan Tech was established in 1885 as a school for mining engineers, to support the copper mines that flourished here. As the mines closed and the economy changed, Michigan Tech changed too, developing recognized expertise in automotive, civil, environmental and chemical engineering, as well as more recently, health sciences, biomedical engineering, environmental science and computer science.

Michigan Tech faculty are known for their innovative concepts and entrepreneurial spirit. In fact, so many faculty and alumni have turned ideas developed at Michigan Tech into marketable products and thriving high-tech businesses that the north shore of Lake Superior is coming to be known as Innovation Shore.

Michigan Tech stresses learning by doing. Undergraduate participation in research is the norm. In our Enterprise Program and other special programs, students can try their hand at solving real-world problems, using the skills they've learned in class. They invest real money in the stock market; build satellites, snowboards, and video games; and journey to foreign nations to help the less-fortunate improve their access to clean water, sanitation, schools and other human needs.

Ninety-four percent of graduates find jobs in their field.

LOCATION & ENVIRONMENT

Our rural setting on the Upper Peninsula of Michigan enables us to provide an excellent education in a spectacular location. Recreational opportunities abound, including a university-owned ski hill, a golf course, and 600 acres of on-campus recreational forest and trails for cross-country running, skiing, hiking, and biking.

The 925-acre campus is on the banks of the Keweenaw Waterway, just a few miles from Lake Superior. The air and water are clean, and the North Woods that surround us, pristine.

Ford Forest, in nearby Alberta, Michigan, is a 4,000-acre research forest managed by our School of Forest Resources and Environmental Science, with educational, recreational and conference facilities.

OFF-CAMPUS OPPORTUNITIES

The entire local area is made for outdoor enthusiasts, with easy access to rivers, lakes, woods, downhill and cross-country skiing, and hiking/biking trails. There is an extensive system of snowmobile and ATV trails. Downtown Houghton and its sister city, Hancock (combined population 14,000) offer coffee shops, theaters, stores, and restaurants, as well as many kinds of specialty shops. Major retailers are a short drive or bus ride from campus. There is local bus service. Theatre, concerts, plays, ballet and other performances provide cultural experiences. Houghton and Hancock are safe communities with little traffic. It's said that in Houghton and Hancock, "rush hours" are "rush minutes." All in all, it's a great combination: a world-class education in a beautiful, liveable location.

MAJORS & DEGREES OFFERED

Michigan Tech offers more than 120 undergraduate and graduate degree and certificate programs in engineering; forest resources; computing; technology; business; economics; natural, physical and environmental sciences; arts; humanities; and social sciences. Degrees include Bachelor of Arts, Bachelor of Science, Master of Arts, Master of Science, Master of Business Administration, Master of Engineering, Master of Forestry, and 27 PhDs in a variety of fields.

ACADEMIC PROGRAM

Our Physics Department awards one of the highest percentages nationally of PhDs to women. Our scientific and technical communication program is among the nation's largest. Our newest academic programs include a Bachelor of Science in Natural Resources Management, a Bachelor of Science in Statistics and a Master of Science in Applied Physics, as well as a graduate certificate in post-secondary STEM education. Many academic programs cross traditional disciplinary lines, as students and faculty work together on complex problems requiring input from diverse fields.

The Enterprise Program involves more than 1,000 students on 25 teams from all across campus, putting their classroom learning to work solving real problems for industry. Enterprise students are working on projects related to energy, the environment, robotics, video games, and homeland security, to name just a few.

The Pavlis Honors College draws together students and faculty from several honors programs throughout the university. The Honors College embraces any student with a sincere desire to become a scholar and a leader. There is no minimum GPA requirement.

The Applied Portfolio Management Program has won global investment competitions several years in a row. They control the investment of $1 million in actual money. The student investors also have their own "stock exchange," the LSGI Trading Room.

FACILITIES & EQUIPMENT

State-of-the-art laboratories and classrooms are found across campus, and wireless internet service is everywhere. On the waterfront, our Great Lakes Research Center (GLRC) is advancing knowledge in environmental studies, particularly winter-related research, across multiple academic fields. The GLRC houses a supercomputer called Superior, used by the entire campus.

Nineteen research centers and institutes enable Michigan Tech faculty, staff, and students to focus on a broad range of inquiry, from climate change to transportation, from power and energy to computational science. The newest institute is doing pioneering work on pressing issues of cybersecurity. The Keweenaw Research Center hosts the annual Clean Snowmobile Challenge, and the Michigan Tech Research Institute in Ann Arbor focuses on remote sensing technologies, including the use of drones for road and bridge maintenance.

Tech's MacInnes Student Ice Arena features skyboxes, a new ice plant, and a high-tech video scoreboard.

COST & AID

1. Tuition, Room, Board and Fees

Undergraduate (in-state): $14,334 per academic year (2 semesters)

Room and Board: $9.558 to 14,054 per academic year (2 semesters)

Graduate Tuition: $1,026.50/credit hour

*Undergraduate tuition is based on 12-18 credit hours per semester. Out-of-state students pay $30,668 tuition per academic year (2 semesters).

2. Financial Aid

Scholarships are the most familiar and sought-after type of financial aid. All admitted students are automatically considered for most merit-based scholarships. A special application form is not required, except for the Michigan Tech Leading Scholars Award and career-interest scholarships.

Grants are aid based on financial need and are available to US citizens and permanent residents. Accepted students are automatically considered for grants if their FAFSA results are released to Michigan Tech. Students must apply for grant renewal each year.

Loans consist of borrowed funds that must be repaid. They are available to most US citizens and permanent residents. Each loan program has certain maximum limits for borrowing. Students may not borrow more than the cost of attendance, less any other financial aid received. Accepted students are automatically considered for loans if their FAFSA results are released to Michigan Tech and they have indicated on the FAFSA an interest in receiving loans. Students must apply for loan renewal each year and make progress toward obtaining their degree according to the Satisfactory Progress Policy.

Part-time employment on campus is available through government-funded and university-funded programs. Students who complete the FAFSA and indicate they would like to work on campus are automatically considered for work-study employment.

Federal Work-Study

Federal Work-Study programs provide funds to employ students who are US citizens or permanent residents and who have financial need. Students must reapply for work-study each year and meet the Satisfactory Progress Policy requirements.

Specific departmental work-study assignments are made by the Financial Aid Office. Students normally work eight to ten hours per week. The hourly rate paid is equivalent to at least minimum wage.

University-Funded Student Employment

University-funded, on-campus employment is available to students regardless of need. Students may apply directly to the desired departments. On average, 2,000 to 2,500 students are employed on campus each year. Nearly every department employs students.

FULL & PART-TIME FACULTY

There are 473 faculty members at Michigan Tech, including all tenured, tenure-track, non-tenure-track, instructional and research faculty. The student-to-faculty ratio is 12:1 and the average class size is 23.

STUDENT BODY

More than 200 student organizations offer individual and group activities and leadership opportunities in many categories, including Academic/Honors, Arts and Culture, Club Sports, Governance, Greeks, Programming/Social, Religious, and Service. There are active Undergraduate and Graduate Student Governments.

More than 27 percent of the student body is female, and 17 percent is international, coming to study at Michigan Tech from more than 60 countries. A majority of undergraduates live in campus residence halls. Many graduate students with families live in University-owned Daniell Heights Apartments.

Our traditions include Winter Carnival, featuring massive snow statues built by students, stage shows, and wacky winter competitions like snow volleyball, ice bowling, and broomball. The annual Parade of Nations and Multicultural Festival celebrates the international flavor and heritage of the Keweenaw and Michigan Tech. Other traditional events include K-Day on Lake Superior's shore and Spring Fling on campus.

ADMISSION PROCESSES & REQUIREMENTS

Applying to college doesn't have to be stressful. In fact, Michigan Tech makes it pretty easy. You don't need to get teacher recommendations or even apply for scholarships with a separate form. Just submit your application for admission, official high school and/or college transcripts, and official ACT or SAT test scores.

Additional application materials are required for students applying for admission to the following degree programs: Audio Production and Technology, Sound Design, Theatre and Electronic Media Performance, and Theatre and Entertainment Technology.

Apply by January 15 of the year you plan to enroll for priority consideration for admission, financial aid, and scholarships.

We'll review your high school transcript (including your freshman year) and evaluate the courses you took in high school and the grades you received. The cumulative GPA provided by your high school is used in the admissions process. We do not recalculate your GPA.

MOLLOY COLLEGE

AT A GLANCE

Where can you get a great education with small classes, wonderful internships, community service projects and international trips, plus an amazing campus life program to round out your college experience? Welcome to Molloy College.

Molloy, an independent Catholic college based in Rockville Centre, was founded in 1955 by the Sisters of Saint Dominic in Amityville, NY. The College serves a student population of more than 4,900 undergraduate and graduate students. Molloy students can earn degrees in a variety of outstanding academic programs, including nursing, business, education, computer studies, social work, music therapy and many more.

1 All-Star Value

Prospective students are always looking for an academic environment that offers the best fit for the student and the best value for their tuition dollar. Look no further than Molloy, recently named the # 1 Value All-Star in the nation by MONEY® magazine. This recognition was part of the magazine's annual college rankings, which acknowledge the best of the country's institutions in a variety of categories. Molloy's top ranking was based on a variety of factors, including graduation rates and earnings of graduates.

Molloy continues to earn recognition in many areas. College Factual recently named Molloy the #1 college for health professions, as well as naming Molloy's undergraduate nursing program the best in the nation. Additionally, the College's residence halls were voted Best in New York by Niche.com, and these rankings also referenced Molloy's freshmen retention rate, which is among the highest in the country (85%). Also of note, Molloy graduates' starting salaries have ranked among the highest in the U.S. in surveys conducted by Georgetown University and PayScale.com.

LOCATION & ENVIRONMENT

Molloy is located on the South Shore of Long Island in Rockville Centre. Our proximity to New York City allows for our students to benefit from the cultural and social opportunities that Manhattan has to offer - and it's just a short train ride away from our 30-acre campus.

Molloy College also offers off campus locations for study at the Suffolk Center in East Farmingdale, just off of the Rt. 110 corridor. In addition, the College offers courses at area hospitals and schools - all designed to provide convenience for our graduate and continuing education students.

CAMPUS FACILITIES & EQUIPMENT
What's New

The College continues to find new ways to help its students grow. In recent years Molloy has added a number of new facilities, including two residence halls, a student center and a performing arts theatre, all of which enhance the student experience. Additionally, Molloy recently opened the Barbara H. Hagan School of Nursing to support its nationally ranked nursing programs.

Molloy is a wireless campus and our computer labs house more than 325 PCs. Also, many departments have their own computer labs with state-of-the-art equipment.

The James E. Tobin (JET) Library is the center of academic research on the Molloy College campus. Beyond the library's physical collection of books, media and periodicals, it also provides 24x7 access to over 250,000 ebooks as well as full text to over 170 million articles contained within its 80+ subscription databases. The facility itself contains reference computers, three classrooms, a media center and designated areas for both group and private study. The Information Commons, located in the Public Square, offers an additional 40 computers as well as four study rooms that can be reserved in advance. Reference services are available to both on campus and remote researchers in a variety of ways, including a chat service that is available all of the hours the library is open.

The Wilbur Arts Center features numerous art and music studios, a cable television studio, and the Lucille B. Hays Theatre. The school also has six science labs, a language lab, the education resource center, new state-of-the-art nursing labs, and a behavioral sciences research facility.

OFF-CAMPUS OPPORTUNITIES

Molloy students are also instilled with the belief that they can make a difference beyond the classroom. As part of Molloy's tradition of service, students become involved in projects that help underserved populations in New York City, New Orleans, Puerto Rico and Haiti, to name but a few locations. Through the College's international education program, students seek enrichment and greater understanding of the world by participating in trips to Europe, Japan, South America and other locales around the globe.

ACADEMICS

At Molloy, small class size, engaging and experienced faculty and renowned academic programs will help ensure your success, both in the classroom and in your professional life. Our vibrant student life program will help you make a smooth transition to our campus.

We also make it easy for you to take classes when it is convenient for YOU. We offer evening and weekend classes, many in online and hybrid formats, with accelerated schedules designed to accommodate your busy schedule.

A minimum of 128 credit hours is required for a baccalaureate degree; these courses include a strong liberal arts general education curriculum for every major field of study. Students may choose a double major, and many minors are available. Molloy has a 4-1-4 academic calendar.

Students may earn CLEP and CPE credit, and advanced placement credit is granted for a score of 3 or better on the AP exam. Qualified full-time students may participate in the Army ROTC program at Hofstra University or St. John's University on a cross enrolled basis. Molloy students may also elect Air Force ROTC on a cross enrolled basis with New York Institute of Technology.

The vast majority of students at Molloy enjoy an internship at some point in their academic careers. These real-world experiences are a crucial part of the learning process and ensure that students enter their chosen field ready to make strong contributions.

MAJORS

Molloy offers the AA degree in liberal arts; the AAS degree in cardiovascular technology and respiratory care; and the BA or BS degree in accounting, art, biology, business management, communications, computer science, computer information systems, criminal justice, education, English, earth and environmental studies, finance, history, interdisciplinary studies, marketing, mathematics, modern languages, music, music therapy, new media, nuclear medicine technology, nursing, philosophy, political science, psychology, sociology, speech language pathology/audiology, theatre arts and theology; the BSW degree in Social Work; and the BFA in art, music and theatre arts. Teacher certification programs are available in childhood (1-6), adolescence (7-12), special education and birth—grade 2 childhood special education.

On the graduate level, Molloy offers a Master of Science degree as well as post-master's certification in nursing and education. M.B.A. programs are available in business, accounting, healthcare, marketing and personal financial planning; a master's program in clinical mental health counseling was recently launched as well. A master's in social work is offered through Molloy's partnership with Fordham University. Molloy also offers graduate degrees in criminal justice, music therapy, and speech-language pathology. The College offers three doctoral programs, a Ph.D. in nursing and a Doctor of Nursing Practice (D.N.P.), as well as an Ed.D. in Education.

Students interested in pre-dental, pre-law, pre-medical, or pre-veterinary programs are offered special advisement.

Experienced admissions counselors will evaluate your credits and put you on the path towards completing your degree. Articulation agreements with community colleges and established transfer credit policies ensure ease of transferability.

TUITION, ROOM, BOARD, FEES

For 2016–17, tuition was $28,000 and required fees were $1,190. Students can expect to spend about $1,400 on books.

FINANCIAL AID

Financial aid, which is based on academic achievement and financial need, is awarded to more than 85 percent of the student body. Aid is awarded in the form of scholarships, grants, loans, and Federal Work-Study Program employment. Merit-based scholarships and grants are also available. Students are required to complete the FAFSA application every year. Full and partial tuition scholarships are available through the following: Molloy Scholars, Dominican Scholarships, Fine Arts Scholarships, Community Service Awards, and other funded scholarships. The Transfer Scholarship Program awards partial tuition scholarships to students transferring into Molloy College with at least a 3.0 cumulative GPA. Nursing transfers are required to have a 3.3 GPA to be eligible for a transfer scholarship. Athletic grants (Division II only) are awarded to full-time students who show superior athletic ability in baseball, basketball, cross-country, equestrian, lacrosse, soccer, softball, tennis, or volleyball.

STUDENT ORGANIZATIONS & ACTIVITIES

With more than 4,900 undergraduate and graduate students, Molloy has something for everyone.

There are more than 50 academic programs, approximately 60 clubs and honor societies, various service opportunities and NCAA Division II athletics, providing abundant opportunities for each student to not only strive for academic excellence, but also explore new interests, pursue athletics and enrich our community.

ADMISSIONS PROCESS

Molloy College's admissions committee recommends that applicants meet the following admission qualifications: graduation from a four-year public or private high school or equivalent (GED test) with a minimum of 20.5 units, including 4 in English, 4 in social studies, 3 in a foreign language, 3 in mathematics, and 3 in science. Nursing applicants must have completed biology and chemistry courses. Mathematics applicants must have taken 4 units of math and 2 of science (including chemistry or physics). Biology applicants must have credits in biology, chemistry, and physics and 4 units in math. Art applicants must submit a portfolio; music students must audition. The committee selects candidates based on the following: high school record, SAT I or ACT scores, class rank, and the school's recommendation. Personality and character are considered in admissions decisions, as are talent or ability in a non-curricular field, as well as alumni relationships.

A select group of freshmen are invited to participate in the Molloy College Honors Program. This program offers challenging coursework and encourages reflection and personal growth. Honors students are provided with several special participation incentives such as a laptop computer, and priority registration.

The HEOP and the Albertus Magnus programs may be options for students not normally eligible for admission.

Early admission is available. Molloy admits students on a rolling basis and students are advised of the admission decision within a few weeks of completion of the application filing process.

Prospective students should submit the following to the admissions office to be considered for enrollment: a completed application for admission (the Common Application is accepted), a nonrefundable $40 application fee, an official high school transcript or GED score report, official SAT I or ACT score, and official college transcripts (transfer students only).

MONMOUTH UNIVERSITY

AT A GLANCE

Monmouth University is a first-tier, private university that empowers students to reach their full potential as leaders able to make significant contributions to their community and society.

Monmouth offers a comprehensive array of baccalaureate degree programs in areas that are in demand in the workplace. Through small classes geared toward individual attention and led by an innovative faculty, students are afforded a challenging learning environment on a campus that blends classic beauty with the latest technology.

A comprehensive selection of baccalaureate and graduate degree programs in subject areas that are in demand in the workplace are offered. Small classes geared toward individual attention, and led by an innovative faculty, provide a transformative learning environment where students are active participants in their education.

Monmouth's academics—including majors like political science, communications, homeland security, business, and more-can easily be linked with world-class learning experiences in New York City and other nearby major urban areas. Students interested in coastal environmental studies can focus on biological, chemical, and physical sciences, together with environmental policy and natural resource conservation and management.

The University is also close to many technology firms, financial institutions, and a business-industrial sector that provides both employment possibilities for graduates and opportunities for undergraduates to gain experience.

Our location and network provide tremendous academic opportunities to students. For example, students in Monmouth's music industry program interface with industry professionals in and beyond the classroom, managing their own record label, Blue Hawk Records. There is a real spirit of entrepreneurship on campus that comes to life through student activities like the student-managed investment fund Hawk Capital. Marine and environmental biology and policy students benefit from the University's proximity to coastal waterways.

While preparing students for successful careers in leadership roles, Monmouth University believes that a major goal of higher education is to help students develop values. These include senses of citizenship and social responsibility that enable graduates to contribute actively to the societies in which they live. Academic programs and personal development opportunities at Monmouth prepare students to take the lead in an increasingly complex, multicultural world. These opportunities--combined with the myriad of art exhibits, concerts, lectures, and sightseeing trips planned each year--provide students with shared experiences outside the classroom to match the ones they receive inside.

LOCATION & ENVIRONMENT

Located in the town of West Long Branch, New Jersey, Monmouth is situated on a beautiful, coastal campus that is one mile from the beaches of the Atlantic Ocean and also about one hour from New York City and Philadelphia. The 156-acre campus is home to a diverse student body comprising some 6,400 undergraduate and graduate students. Students come to Monmouth from 32 states and 34 countries to participate in the University's academic programs.

A fully wireless campus and a wide array of digital resources along with new academic facilities allows students to actively participate in learning opportunities with innovative faculty members. A ratio of 14 students to each professor enables a personalized learning environment along with mentoring opportunities.

CAMPUS FACILITIES & EQUIPMENT

The Monmouth University Library holds approximately 360,000 print and electronic monographs, 74,000 print and electronic periodicals, 180 databases, and 1,200 media assets including CDs and DVDs. All academic programs are amply supported by state-of-the-art computer hardware and software and classroom/laboratory facilities. The major components supporting Monmouth academic programs include Windows, Mac OS, and Unix systems connected via an expansive wired and wireless network, which spans all campus buildings and encompasses more than 2,400 workstations in general and specialty labs and classrooms.

OFF-CAMPUS OPPORTUNITIES

Putting learning into action is what makes education come alive. Experiential education, which includes internships, study abroad, select service learning projects, dedicated experiential coursework, or cooperative learning experiences, is a required part of the undergraduate curriculum. By their senior year, seventy-seven percent of Monmouth undergraduate students have completed a practicum, internship, co-op, or similar real world experience; only forty-nine percent of graduating students at comparable institutions have done this according to the latest National Survey of Student Engagement.

At Monmouth, professional-quality experience comes in many forms, from collaborating on original research with faculty that can be presented at national and international conferences to traveling with the mock trial team and engaging in a wide-variety of academic field experiences. Students study abroad in Australia, England, Italy, Spain, and more. Additionally, Monmouth's alternative break allows students to take part in service projects and community building activities in locales around the globe including Guatemala, Haiti, and Nicaragua.

ACADEMICS

Undergraduate students interested in the sciences, if qualified, can be involved in hands-on original research projects with faculty. These students are presenting award-winning research at regional, national, and international conferences along with earning faculty co-authorship in peer-reviewed publications.

At Monmouth, about ten percent of first-year students enroll in one of the University's five-year baccalaureate/master's programs. Subject areas for five-year programs are offered in computer science, business, criminal justice, education (select programs), English, history, social work, and software engineering.

Additionally, Graduate Studies at Monmouth University provides high-quality master's degree and certificate programs to students seeking to increase their professional skills and enhance their intellectual development. Monmouth also offers a Doctor of Nursing Practice (DNP). Every program curriculum aims to improve students' leadership qualities and prepare them for career advancement, career changes, or further study.

Graduate students have chances to advance their knowledge and engage in scholarly research with faculty members who are not only impassioned teachers and mentors, but also leaders in their chosen fields. Those enrolled benefit from Monmouth's commitment to personalized attention and a strong bond between students and faculty members.

MAJORS & DEGREES OFFERED

Majors

Anthropology°
Art°: optional concentration in Photography°
Biology°: optional concentration in Molecular Cell Physiology
Business Administration°: concentrations in Accounting°, Economics°, Economics and Finance, Finance°, Finance and Real Estate, International Business, Management and Decision Sciences, Marketing°, Marketing, Management, and Decision Sciences, or Real Estate
Chemistry°: optional concentrations in Advanced Chemistry, Biochemistry, or Chemical Physics
Clinical Laboratory Sciences: concentration in Medical Laboratory Science
Communication°: Communication Studies, Public Relations/Journalism, or Radio/TV
Computer Science°: concentrations in Advanced Computing or Applied Computing
Criminal Justice°
Education: Early Childhood, Elementary, Middle School, Secondary, English as a Second Language, Teacher of Students with Disabilities
English°: optional concentration in Creative Writing°
Fine Arts: concentrations in Animation or Graphic and Interactive Design
Foreign Language: concentrations in Spanish, Spanish and Communication/Journalism, or Spanish and Communication/Radio and TV
Health and Physical Education (teaching and non-teaching options)
Health Studies°
History°
History and Political Science Homeland Security°
Marine and Environmental Biology and Policy
Mathematics°: optional concentration in Statistics°
Medical Laboratory Science

Music: optional concentration in Music Industry
Nursing (BSN) (direct admit program, freshmen only)
Nursing (RN to BSN) (transfer students with RN license only)
Political Science°: optional concentration in International Relations or Legal Studies°
Psychology°
Social Work
Sociology°
Software Engineering
Spanish and International Business

Minors

Archaeology
Art History
Asian Studies
Business of Healthcare
Communication Sciences and Disorders
Forensic Investigation
Gender Studies
General Management
Geographic Information Systems
Geography
Global Sustainability
Graphic Design/Computer Graphics
Information Technology
Interactive Media
Irish Studies
Italian
Journalism
Leadership Communication
Media Production
Musical Theatre
Philosophy
Philosophy and Religious Studies
Physics
Popular Music
Professional Writing
Public Policy
Public Relations
Religious Studies
Screen Studies
Social Justice
Social Services
Spanish
Spanish for Business
Sports Communication
Theatre

FIVE-YEAR BACCALAUREATE/ MASTER'S DEGREE PROGRAMS

Business Administration
Computer Science
Criminal Justice
Education (certain programs)
English
History
Social Work
Software Engineering

PRE-PROFESSIONAL ADVISING

Pre-Dentistry
Pre-Law
Pre-Medicine
Pre-Veterinary

°Major and minor available

TUITION, ROOM, BOARD, FEES

$36,733 (Commuter)

$50,184 (Resident)

FINANCIAL AID

Approximately 99% of our incoming students receive some form of financial aid. Those packages typically include scholarships, grants, student loans, and work-study that may be applied toward tuition and fees, room and board or living expenses, books, and other personal expenses.

Here are some facts to consider about the financial aid packages created for Monmouth's undergraduates last year:

99% received some form of financial aid.

The average scholarship/grant package was $22,521.

The average financial aid package, including student loans and work-study, was approximately $26,900.

More than $59 million in University grants and scholarships was awarded; this places Monmouth among the more affordable private universities in New Jersey.

STUDENT ORGANIZATIONS & ACTIVITIES

The University is proud to host a successful NCAA Division I intercollegiate athletics program that fields 23 teams for men and women. The University's basketball and track and field teams compete in the 153,200-square-foot OceanFirst Bank Center—a 4,200-seat venue that opened in 2009. All Monmouth students have access to the arena, which also houses a 200-meter, six-lane indoor track; fitness center; conference space; the University Store; and luxury suites. The University's football, men's/women's lacrosse and outdoor track and field programs open their new home in Fall 2017, with the debut of Monmouth Stadium. The new stadium, adjacent to the OceanFirst Bank Center, will accommodate 4,200 fans and feature state-of-the-art media facilities and end zone to end zone seating

Beyond athletics, students have an assortment of extracurricular activities to choose from, including more than 110 student-run clubs and organizations, as well as sororities and fraternities that engage in service work on behalf of the University and the community. Students can also get involved with the Student Government Association, the campus newspaper (The Outlook), the student-run online news portal (The Verge), the FM radio station (WMCX), the television station (Hawk TV), the yearbook (Shadows), and the literary magazine (Monmouth Review).

ADMISSIONS PROCESS

The early action deadline for first-time, full-time students is December 1, and for regular decision it is March 1.

Students applying to the spring semester must do so by December 1.

If you're applying as a part-time student, applications for the fall semester are due by July 15, and for the spring semester they are due by December 1.

Applicants to the Bachelor of Science in Nursing (BSN) program should submit their applications by December 1 for the fall start term only.

A complete application includes the application form, a non-refundable $50 application fee, all official transcripts, standardized test scores, at least one letter of recommendation, and a personal essay of 250 to 500 words.

NAZARETH COLLEGE

AT A GLANCE

Nazareth seeks students who are ready for academic rigor and excited by the chance to learn, grow, and make their mark on the world. That's why the College recommends that applicants complete a rigorous college-preparatory curriculum in high school that includes English, mathematics, social studies, science, and foreign language. Admissions decisions are primarily based on academic achievement. In addition, there are audition requirements for the dance, music, and theatre programs and portfolio requirements for art and technical production majors. Co-curricular activities are also considered. A campus tour and interview are highly recommended but not required. Information sessions and campus tours are available Mondays through Saturdays. For more: naz.edu/visit

Nazareth is a test optional college. Approximately 75 percent of Nazareth applicants submit test scores, but there is no disadvantage for those who do not. The scores are helpful, but the College also realizes there are inequities in students' resources and high school offerings to prepare for the exams. Full admissions details: naz.edu/admissions, or email admissions@naz.edu, or call (585) 389-2860 or toll-free (800) 462-3944.

LOCATION & ENVIRONMENT

Nazareth has a cozy setting, situated on more than 150 acres of expansive lawns, shady woodland groves, and landscaped gardens. Climate-controlled tunnels make it easy to get around in the winter. Cultural opportunities abound on campus. Students get free tickets to world-class theatre, music, dance, and international entertainment at the Nazareth College Arts Center. Cross-cultural events on campus include gourmet cooking classes and Italian meals in our Casa Italiana, frequent foreign films, Black History Month celebrations, foreign language conversation clubs, professional conferences, and talks by visiting overseas scholars.

Nazareth College is in the charming town of Pittsford, a short walk from specialty shops and restaurants in the village center as well as bike trails and boat rides along the Erie Canal. The campus is seven miles from Rochester, New York state's third-largest city, known for its universities, important inventions, and innovations in consumer products. Rochester is rich in culture and entertainment, including the internationally renowned George Eastman House/International Museum of Photography and Film and Strong National Museum of Play. Ski and snowboarding resorts are within an hour's drive. For more: naz.edu/campus-life

Types of Transportation Available to Campus

Rochester International Airport is 10 miles from Nazareth College. The Syracuse Hancock International Airport is approximately an hour and a half from campus with the Buffalo Niagara International Airport about an hour from campus. Students and families also have access to Amtrak train station, as well as NYS Trailways and Greyhound Bus terminals, all located in downtown. Services from rental car companies, taxi's and limousine companies are available at any of these stations or terminals.

Local Accommodations

The Hampton Inn (Victor and Rochester locations), Hilton Garden Inn, The Lodge at Woodcliff, and the Microtel Inn-Victor are within 6 miles of campus. The Delmonte Lodge is approximately a quarter of a mile from campus, along the Erie Canal. For more, see: go.naz.edu/lodging.

CAMPUS FACILITIES & EQUIPMENT

The new $15.6 million Music Performance Center, an extension of the renowned Arts Center planned for 2018, will provide the highest caliber performance space for professional and student musicians alike. Engineered for a premier acoustic experience, the stage is designed for large stage and instrumental groups while the 550-seating capacity will offer an intimate audience experience.

The Golisano Athletic Training Center, a $15.5 million campus improvement scheduled for 2018, will complement Nazareth's existing athletic facilities while providing a venue for regional Special Olympics initiatives and creating a new model of inclusion, fitness, and wellness. Its indoor track, field, courts, and training facilities will offer unique opportunities for collaborative learning and training.

Nazareth's expanded and completely renovated York Wellness and Rehabilitation Institute, which opened in 2015, doubled the clinic and collaboration space for health and human services and brought all those fields under one roof. The building's design promotes interdisciplinary work among nursing, speech-language pathology, occupational therapy, physical therapy, art and music therapy, speech and hearing services, and social work. The proximity and new meeting spaces facilitate important student-faculty research to improve health outcomes and clinical practice. For more: naz.edu/yorkwri

The College's Integrated Center for Math and Science in Peckham Hall, built in 2012, features state-of-the-art labs for instruction and research as well as classrooms and space for student-faculty collaboration. For more: www.naz.edu/icms

A $10.5 million renovation to the Nazareth College Arts Center provided state-of-the-art sound, lighting, and other upgrades for our 1,000-seat theater with a proscenium-thrust stage and modified fly system. In addition to student theatre productions, the Arts Center presents internationally renowned performers and Nazareth students receive a free ticket to each production. For more: artscenter.naz.edu

Three foreign-language houses on campus attract students who want to be immersed in French, Spanish, or Italian language and customs; Nazareth also has a German Cultural Center.

Athletics

One in four students participate in organized athletics in addition to focusing on academics. Nazareth's NCAA Division III teams include men's and women's basketball, cross-country, equestrian, golf, lacrosse, soccer, swimming and diving, tennis, volleyball, track and field; as well as women's field hockey and softball and men's ice hockey. For more: athletics.naz.edu

ACADEMICS

Through rigorous academic programs, global and cross-cultural experiences, and hands-on career experience, Nazareth College prepares students not just for one job, but for their life's work.

Liberal arts courses comprise about a third of a college student's investment in time and money, and Nazareth's approach is to make that part as valuable and rewarding as the classes in a student's major. The College's uncommon core curriculum gives students the tools, experience, guidance, and support to be the architect of their education, career, and future. Nazareth's core curriculum is also ideal for students who are still exploring which major they'll select, providing a foundation of engaging classes and experiential learning while students also get help from professors, academic advisors, and tools such as assessments to find their path.

All students choose courses across a liberal arts menu to build knowledge, pursue interests, and develop the skills most sought by employers problem solving, critical thinking, and exceptional communication. Along the way, students learn how to analyze deep questions in different disciplines and then explore a question of their choosing through three courses they select. Nazareth's general education curriculum requires experiential learning in the form of credit-based internships, co-curricular service, fieldwork, research, leadership roles, and more. These hands-on experiences directly challenge and reinforce coursework, connect students with career contacts and employers, and/or help students better understand themselves, the broader world, and current issues.

Nazareth's Center for Civic Engagement, Center for Entrepreneurship and Innovation, Center for International Education, and Center for Spirituality support students in this work. Nazareth College was named one of just five Presidential Awardees in the 2013 President's Higher Education Community Service Honor Roll and was a finalist for the 2014 award. The distinction is the highest honor a college or university can receive for its commitment to volunteering, service learning, and civic engagement.

Professors help students integrate the full experience, so that you leave college with the knowledge, adaptable skills, and comfort with complexity that you'll need to be successful in today's constantly changing world. More about the core: naz.edu/core

MAJORS

Nazareth offers Bachelor of Arts, Bachelor of Fine Arts, Bachelor of Music, and Bachelor of Science degrees in the following areas: accounting, acting, American studies, anthropology, art (studio), art education (B.S./M.S.), art history, biochemistry, biology, biomedical sciences, business management, chemistry, Chinese, clinical laboratory sciences, communication and media, communication sciences and disorders (speech pathology), community youth development, dance studies, economics, education (adolescence, inclusive childhood), English, environmental science and sustainability, finance, French, German, history, international and global studies, Italian, law (3+3 with Syracuse University), legal studies, marketing, mathematics, modern foreign languages, museums, archives, and public history, music education, music performance, music therapy, musical theatre, nursing, nursing accelerated weekend R.N. to B.S., occupational therapy (5-year master's), peace and justice, philosophy, physical therapy (6-year D.P.T. program), political science, psychology, public health, religious studies, social science, social work, sociology, Spanish, technical production, theatre arts, toxicology, visual communication design, and women and gender studies.

Nazareth offers pre-professional programs in audiology, dentistry, law, medicine, and veterinary science. Students may combine education certification with their declared major to earn certification in secondary education (grades 7-12) or double major in inclusive education (elementary and special education with a liberal arts major). Nazareth offers certification in art (5-year B.S./M.S.), music, and speech and hearing (birth-grade 12).

Most majors are also available as academic minors. Other minors include American studies; bioethics; cognitive neuropsychology; credentialed alcoholism and substance abuse counselor; digital marketing and design; entertainment and recording industry; entrepreneurship; environmental science; environmental studies; ethics; foreign language for business; gerontology; horticultural therapy; information technology; information systems; interfaith studies; international business; jazz; middle eastern studies; multicultural studies; music history (concentration for B.A. music); music theory (concentration for B.A. music); pre-audiology; pre-dental; pre-law; pre-medical; pre-veterinary; religious studies: Christian studies; religious studies: religion in contemporary culture; religious studies: sacred texts; social welfare; social research; Spanish; and sport management.

Graduate degrees include Master of Science in the following areas: American studies, art education, arts therapy, business organization and management, higher education student affairs administration, human resource development, human resource management, inclusive education (early childhood, childhood, adolescence), integrated marketing and communications, law (3+3 program with Syracuse University), literacy specialist, management, music education, music performance & pedagogy, music therapy, social work, speech-language pathology, TESOL, TESOL for international educators; and a doctoral program in physical therapy. Details about each program: naz.edu/academics

TUITION, ROOM, BOARD, FEES

The College offers merit-based awards for excellence in academics, art, music, and drama, as well as need-based aid.

FINANCIAL AID

Students seeking aid complete the Free Application for Federal Student Aid (FAFSA). Full cost and financial aid details: go.naz.edu/tuition-aid

STUDENT ORGANIZATIONS & ACTIVITIES

All campus clubs are initiated and led by students. Current campus clubs and organizations include Art Club; Art Therapy Club; ASL Club; Association of Social Work Students; Campus Activities Board; Center for Spirituality Council; Chinese Club; Communications, Sciences and Disorders Association; Club Italianissimo; Colleges Against Cancer; Collegiate QuizBowl Team; Community Youth Development Collective; Dare2Dance; Diversity Council; Finance Society; French Club; German Club; Gerontology Club; Golden Gazette; Habitat for Humanity, Inc.; International Club; Jazz Club; Lambda Association; LASMA-Spanish Club; Math Club; Music Business Club; Music Therapy Club; National Association for Music Education; Nazareth Commuter Association; Nazareth Dance Organization; Naz Ultimate; Nursing Club; Philosophy Club; Physical Therapy Club; Pre-Health Professionals Club; Psychology; Quidditch Club; Residence Hall Council; Science Club; Ski and Snowboard Club; Student Athlete Mentors; Student Occupational Therapy Association; Take Note; Theatre League; Wishing Well; Women's Health Club; and WNAZCampus Radio Station. The Undergraduate Association provides student advocacy. For more: naz.edu/student-activities

ADMISSIONS PROCESS

Nazareth seeks students who are ready for academic rigor and excited by the chance to learn, grow, and make their mark on the world. That's why the College recommends that applicants complete a rigorous college-preparatory curriculum in high school that includes English, mathematics, social studies, science, and foreign language. Admissions decisions are primarily based on academic achievement. In addition, there are audition requirements for the dance, music, and theatre programs and portfolio requirements for art and technical production majors. Co-curricular activities are also considered. A campus tour and interview are highly recommended but not required. Information sessions and campus tours are available Mondays through Saturdays.

Nazareth is a test optional college. Approximately 75 percent of Nazareth applicants submit test scores, but there is no disadvantage for those who do not. The scores are helpful, but the College also realizes there are inequities in students' resources and high school offerings to prepare for the exams. Full admissions details: naz.edu/admissions, or email admissions@naz.edu, or call (585) 389-2860 or toll-free (800) 462-3944. The College offers merit-based awards for excellence in academics, art, music, and drama, as well as need-based aid. Students seeking aid complete the Free Application for Federal Student Aid (FAFSA). Full cost and financial aid details: go.naz.edu/tuition-aid

NEW YORK UNIVERSITY

AT A GLANCE

New York University is the largest independent research university in the United States, and is unlike any other institution of higher education. NYU has degree-granting campuses in New York, Abu Dhabi, and Shanghai, and 11 global academic centers around the world.

NYU's more than 20,000 undergraduates come from all 50 states and over 130 countries. NYU is both the No. 1 sender and receiver of students studying internationally, and we believe our global network raises the level of discourse in the classroom and provides a modern education for our global society. NYU's global sites are fully owned, operated, and staffed by NYU, creating a seamless experience for students.

The energy and resources within New York City, Abu Dhabi, and Shanghai serve as extensions of our campuses which, by design, are in and of their cities, providing unique opportunities for research, internships, and job placement. Within our New York campus, NYU has 10 undergraduate schools and colleges nine of which surround Washington Square and one, our school of engineering, in downtown Brooklyn.

Students choose from thousands of courses in over 230 areas of study. Despite our size, we have a remarkably intimate academic environment on our campuses. In fact, our student to faculty ratio in New York is 10:1 and our average class size is fewer than 30 students.

A faculty of renowned scholars, researchers, and artists teach our students who take courses both inside and outside a chosen major, providing breadth across different disciplines and depth in a chosen area of concentration. NYU's urban locations enables us to attract stunning diversity in academia talent, with faculty who have won awards ranging from the Pulitzer Prize and Abel Prize in Mathematics to the Grammys and Tony's.

Being in cities at the crossroads of the world enables us to offer students thousands of internship opportunities and comprehensive career preparation during their undergraduate studies. For the class of 2016, over 95% of our students were employed or enrolled in graduate school within six months of graduation. NYU is also ranked #1 for graduate employability by Times Higher Education.

LOCATION & ENVIRONMENT

The energy and resources within New York City, Abu Dhabi, and Shanghai serve as extensions of our campuses which, by design, are in and of their cities, providing unique opportunities for research, internships, and job placement. Within our New York campus, NYU has 10 undergraduate schools and colleges nine of which surround Washington Square and one, our school of engineering, in downtown Brooklyn.

CAMPUS FACILITIES & EQUIPMENT

NYU offers an exceptional range of facilities and student services, including a range of residence halls, meal plans, and dining locations on each campus. Academic facilities include nine libraries and institutes renowned for their research in applied mathematics, physics, neural science, and fine arts. Foreign language and cultural centers offer lectures, films, and concerts. Students may also access NYU's Wasserman Center for Career Development, and student support offices addressing almost every student need, from health and wellness to academic support and enrichment. The Kimmel Center for Student Life houses dining facilities, student lounges, computers, club spaces, and the Skirball Center for the Performing Arts, lower Manhattan's largest performance space.

OFF-CAMPUS OPPORTUNITIES

Students have access to NYU's extensive global network, within which they can pursue their studies and explore new cultures and perspectives while remaining connected to all of the University's academic resources. They may choose from 11 global academic centers—in Accra, Ghana; Berlin, Germany; Buenos Aires, Argentina; Florence, Italy; London, England; Madrid, Spain; Paris, France; Prague, Czech Republic; Sydney, Australia; Tel Aviv, Israel; and Washington, DC—or in one of many exchange programs NYU has with outstanding research universities around the world. Each location provides a rich curriculum in which students—whose financial aid will travel with them—can complete some of their general degree requirements and, in many fields, take courses in their major. In fact, a number of NYU's schools, colleges, and programs (like the Global Liberal Studies program and the major in Business and Political Economy) offer specific curricula and majors with an international focus. With all of these opportunities, it's no surprise that NYU is #1 for the number of students who study abroad (per the most recent IIE Open Doors report).

ACADEMICS

At NYU in New York City, students enroll into one of the University's undergraduate schools, colleges, or programs: The College of Arts and Science; the Core Program in Liberal Studies; the Global Liberal Studies Program; the Leonard N. Stern School of Business; the Steinhardt School of Culture, Education, and Human Development; the Tisch School of the Arts; the Gallatin School of Individualized Study; the Silver School of Social Work; the Meyers College of Nursing; the School of Professional Studies; and the Tandon School of Engineering.

NYU Abu Dhabi is NYU's second degree-granting campus and a major research center. Located in the United Arab Emirates, it draws students from around the world, preparing them for the challenges and opportunities of our interconnected world. It offers degrees in the liberal arts and sciences as well as engineering, and is the first comprehensive liberal arts college in the Middle East to be operated by and integrated into an American private research university.

NYU Shanghai is NYU's third and newest degree-granting campus in China. NYU Shanghai offers students an immensely cross-cultural, close-knit learning community, along with a strong foundation in the liberal arts and sciences with emphasis in science, technology, engineering, and mathematics, as well as Chinese language and culture. It supports world-class academic research and graduate and professional education.

NYU faculty are among the world's leading scholars, and have received Nobel, Crafoord, and Pulitzer Prizes; MacArthur, Guggenheim, and Fulbright Fellowships; and Oscar and Emmy Awards. Faculty members teach undergraduate and graduate courses, allowing undergraduate students to become directly involved in research projects with internationally renowned professors and experts in their fields.

MAJORS & DEGREES OFFERED

NYU students begin their studies at one of NYU's three dynamic urban locations: in New York City; in Abu Dhabi, UAE; or in Shanghai, China. No matter where their home campus is, all students graduate with an NYU degree, and may travel throughout the NYU global network as they complete their majors.

In New York, students enroll directly into one of the aforementioned undergraduate schools, colleges, or programs, all of which have earned national recognition in their respective fields.

Among the more than 230 areas of study offered by NYU's three campuses are: Anthropology, Arab Crossroads Studies, Biochemistry, Economics, Dance, Education, Engineering, Environmental Science, Film and Television, Finance, Global Public Health, Hospitality and Tourism Management, Individualized Study, Integrated Digital Media, Marketing, Metropolitan Studies, Nursing, Real Estate, Social Work, Theatre, and Recorded Music.

TUITION, ROOM, BOARD, FEES

On average, tuition and fees are approximately $49,000 for two semesters; room and board cost approximately $24,000 per year. Most NYU students receive one or more forms of financial aid to support contributions made by them and their families. (Financial aid information is subject to change; please visit admissions.nyu.edu for the most up-to-date information.)

FINANCIAL AID

The vast majority of financial aid awarded at NYU is need-based. Low-interest education loans are available for both students and parents. NYU also offers or participates in a variety of payment plans, ranging from interest-free prepayment plans to extensive loan programs that allow families to finance the cost of a college education over many years. A financial aid package might include any combination of scholarships, loans, or work-study programs. The average scholarship/grant for incoming freshmen in New York is approximately $30,000.

Students wishing to be considered for financial aid must submit the Free Application for Federal Student Aid (FAFSA)° and the CSS/Financial Aid PROFILE (and CSS Noncustodial Parent PROFILE, if applicable), administered by the College Board.

Financial aid information is subject to change; visit admissions.nyu.edu for the latest deadlines and more specific details pertaining to financial aid for each NYU campus.

°NYU Abu Dhabi applicants, and any non-US citizens or US permanent residents are not required to complete the FAFSA.

STUDENT ORGANIZATIONS & ACTIVITIES

NYU's more than 20,000 undergraduates come from all 50 states and over 130 countries.

With 21 varsity sports teams that compete at the NCAA Division III level, as well as intramural sports, club athletics, over 400 student clubs, and numerous volunteer activities, NYU students are actively involved both on and off campus.

Student-run clubs are as varied as the student body. Whether their interests lie in world languages, politics, ballroom dancing, writing for the Washington Square News or working at NYU's radio station, students will find something (or more likely, a dozen things!) they love to do.

Hundreds of students annually serve communities across the city, country and world through the Office of Student Activities' C-Team, Alternative Breaks Program, student OutReach Program, fraternities and sororities, and student grassroots organizations. Students deliver meals to the needy and homebound, tutor children, paint public schools, clean up parks, rebuild areas devastated by natural disasters, provide healthcare services in underdeveloped areas, and more.

NYU is anything but cookie-cutter—that's one of the best things about being a part of a larger, global university. The culture of openness, opportunity, and inclusion that is cultivated here allows NYU students to thrive. There are so many choices here about what to do that no two students make the same selection.

ADMISSIONS PROCESS

When choosing a new entering class, the Admissions Committee conducts a holistic review, carefully considering many significant factors, including a comprehensive review of the applicant's academic background, standardized test scores, extracurricular activities, an essay, personal statements, and recommendation letters. Several programs also require the applicant to audition or submit creative materials. Applicants who have successfully completed a broad range of challenging course work throughout high school are the most desirable candidates. Also considered are your unique talents, personal attributes, and future goals.

Applicants are expected to demonstrate their talents and mastery of subject matter to support their applications and to make their best case for admission. As a result, NYU accepts a wide range of national examinations in addition to the SAT, ACT, SAT Subject Tests, AP exams, and IB scores. International students may be required to submit TOEFL, iELTS, or PTE Academic results as proof of English language proficiency. More information about NYU's complete standardized testing requirements can be found online at admissions.nyu.edu

NYU accepts applications in three separate rounds: Early Decision I, Early Decision II, and Regular Decision.

Certain programs at NYU conduct interviews, which are by invitation only. Prospective students are strongly encouraged to visit campus and attend an information session. The admissions staff also visits high schools and hosts receptions worldwide. For dates and times, and for reserving a space at our information sessions and campus tours, go to admissions.nyu.edu/visit.

NIAGARA UNIVERSITY

AT A GLANCE

Founded by the Vincentian community in 1856, Niagara University is a comprehensive institution, blending the best of a liberal arts and professional education, grounded in a values-based, Catholic tradition. With more than 80 majors, nearly 60 minors, six preprofessional options, combined master's programs, and a Ph.D. program, NU students are immersed in meaningful real-world learning opportunities from the moment they step foot on the university's beautiful campus.

Niagara's colleges of Arts and Sciences, Business Administration, Education, and Hospitality and Tourism Management offer programs at the baccalaureate, master's and doctoral level. All four of the university's academic colleges have received the highest rankings from the top accreditation boards in their fields. In addition, the university offers an award-winning Academic Exploration program for students who are undecided about their academic major.

A student-to-faculty ratio of 13:1 and an average class size of approximately 19 allow for personal attention and classroom interaction. The faculty members at Niagara are internationally renowned for their abilities as researchers and teachers, helping students to accomplish things they never thought possible. A recent survey indicated that 96 percent of Niagara's graduating class was employed or enrolled in graduate school within one year of graduation.

Niagara offers a wide variety of entertainment options on and off-campus, including trips to professional sporting events, local landmarks, concerts, malls, restaurants and cultural festivals in the U.S. and nearby Ontario, Canada. And with 18 Division I athletics programs, there are numerous chances for NU students to put their "Purple Pride" on full display.

LOCATION & ENVIRONMENT

Niagara University's picturesque 160-acre campus is located in the town of Lewiston, New York, two minutes off the I-190 on Route 104. The campus is situated on Monteagle Ridge overlooking the lower Niagara River, which connects the two Great Lakes of Erie and Ontario. The University's suburban campus setting is just a few miles from the world-famous Niagara Falls, 20 minutes from Buffalo, which offers a variety of cultural events, sports, and entertainment opportunities, and just 90 minutes from Rochester and Toronto, Canada's largest metropolitan area. In addition, the University is minutes away from the quaint village of Lewiston, New York, and the city of Niagara Falls, New York.

CAMPUS FACILITIES & EQUIPMENT

Niagara University's housing accommodations include five residence halls, a grouping of five small cottages, and a student apartment complex.

The university's library supports student learning and knowledge creation by providing assistance and access to online and print information resources, technology, and individual and collaborative work and study space. Assistance is available in person and via online chat, text, email, and phone. The library's main floor is open 24 hours a day during the school year.

The B. Thomas Golisano Center for Integrated Sciences, the newest structural addition to Niagara's campus, offers 50,000-square-feet of learning space and cutting-edge equipment that encourages collaboration among scientific disciplines. The Academic Complex, the home to the College of Education and the College of Business Administration (Bisgrove Hall), is a state-of-the-art learning facility, with a simulated trading floor in the Glynn Atrium. Dunleavy Hall, outstanding both educationally and architecturally, includes a computerized lecture hall and TV production rooms. The university's facilities also include the Computer Center; St. Vincent's Hall; the Kiernan Center, NU's athletic and recreation center; the Elizabeth Ann Clune Center for Theatre; the Castellani Art Museum; Dwyer Arena, a dual-rink ice hockey complex; and a renovated and expanded Dining Commons in Clet Hall.

ACADEMICS

Niagara University's curricula enable students to pursue their academic preferences and to complete courses that lead to proficiency in other academic areas. Courses that have been considered upper-division courses are available to all students. This provides students with the opportunity to avoid introductory and survey courses and permits motivated students to take advantage of more challenging courses early in their collegiate career. The honors program provides special academic opportunities that stimulate, encourage and challenge participants. In addition, an accelerated three-year degree program is offered to qualified students. Students pursuing a bachelor's degree must complete a total of 40 or 42 course units (120 or 126 credit hours) to meet graduation requirements. Niagara grants credit for successful scores on the Advanced Placement and the College-Level Examination Program and the International Baccalaureate tests. Internships, research, independent study, study abroad and cooperative education are available in many academic programs. An Army-ROTC program is also offered. NU is fully accredited by the Middle States Association of Colleges and Schools. Its programs in the respective areas are accredited by the National Council for Accreditation of Teacher Education, AACSB International–The Association to Advance Collegiate Schools of Business, and the Council on Social Work Education, and the chemistry department has the approval of the American Chemical Society. The travel, hotel and restaurant administration program is accredited by the Commission for Programs in Hospitality Administration.

MAJORS & DEGREES OFFERED

The College of Arts and Sciences offers the bachelor of arts degree in art history with museum studies, chemistry (with a concentration in environmental studies), communication studies, English, French, gerontology, history, international studies, liberal arts, life sciences, mathematics, philosophy, political science (with a concentration in environmental studies), psychology, religious studies, social sciences, sociology, and Spanish. The Bachelor of Science degree is awarded in actuarial science, biochemistry (with a concentration in bioinformatics), biology (with concentrations in bioinformatics, biotechnology, and environmental studies), chemistry (with concentrations in computational chemistry and environmental studies), computer and information sciences, criminology and criminal justice, mathematics, nursing, psychology and social work. This division also offers the bachelor of fine arts degree in theatre studies (with concentrations in performance, design & production, and theatre specializations). Preprofessional programs are offered in dentistry, law, medicine, pharmacy, veterinary medicine, and Army ROTC. An associate of arts degree is available in general studies. Enrichment courses in fine arts and languages are also available. A combination five-year B.S./M.S. program is available to students in the criminal justice administration program; psychology majors can engage in a six-year B.A. or B.S./M.S. program in clinical educational mental health counseling; an accelerated nursing program, and an R.N.-to-B.S. program is offered for students who already have their R.N.

Preprofessional Partnerships: In addition to the programs listed above, NU offers a number of preprofessional partnerships. These include a 3+4 partnership in pharmacy with the State University of New York at Buffalo (SUNY), a 2+3 partnership in pharmacy with Lake Erie College of Osteopathic Medicine (LECOM), a 3+4 partnership in medicine with LECOM, and a 3+4 partnership in dentistry with SUNY at Buffalo. Qualified premedical Niagara students are eligible to apply for the early assurance program sponsored by the SUNY at Buffalo.

Niagara University's College of Business Administration is accredited by AACSB International—The Association to Advance Collegiate Schools of Business and offers a B.B.A. and a combination B.B.A./M.B.A. degree (five-year program) in accounting. This division offers B.S. degrees in economics, finance, management (with concentrations in human resources, international business, and supply chain management), and marketing (with a concentration in food marketing), as well as a B.A. in economics. In addition, an A.A.S. degree can be earned in business. Students gain real-world experiences through internships, study abroad, and via cooperative education programs as well as research being conducted in several business-focused campus centers. These centers include the Family Business Center, the Center for Supply Chain Management, the Center for International Accounting and Research, and the Technology Transfer Center.

Holding the highest accreditations possible in both the United States and Canada—the United States Council for the Accreditation of Educator Preparation (CAEP) and Canada's Ontario College of Teachers—Niagara University's College of Education provides students with an option of earning dual certification to teach in both countries. The College of Education offers bachelor's degree programs leading to New York State initial certification in early childhood (birth–grade 6), childhood (grades 1–6), childhood and middle childhood (grades 1–9), middle childhood and adolescence (grades 5–12), adolescence (grades 7–12), certification for teaching students with disabilities (grades 1–6 childhood and grades 7–12 adolescence), and in Teaching English to Speakers of Other Languages (TESOL). All education majors pursue an academic concentration to establish expertise in one of the following subject areas: business & marketing, English, French, liberal arts, mathematics, social studies, and Spanish. Business education is offered only for grades 5–12. The academic concentration in liberal arts can only be pursued in the early childhood and childhood (birth–grade 6), and special education and childhood (grades 1–6). Most other states, and Puerto Rico, have reciprocity agreements with New York, so an NU education would qualify education majors to teach in those states as well.

The College of Hospitality and Tourism Management provides a career-oriented curriculum leading to a B.S. degree in three specific areas: hotel and restaurant management (with concentrations in food and beverage management; luxury hospitality operations; and hotel planning, development, and operations), sport management (with concentrations in sport operations and revenue management), and tourism and recreation management (with concentrations in event and meeting management and tourism destination management). The College of Hospitality and Tourism Management offered the world's first bachelor's degree in tourism. NU's hotel and restaurant program, the second oldest in New York state, has the distinction of being the seventh program nationally to be accredited by the Accreditation Commission for Programs in Hospitality Administration by the Council of Hotel, Restaurant, and Institutional Education. The College introduces students to a comprehensive body of knowledge about the hotel, restaurant, tourism, and recreational areas and applies this knowledge to current industry challenges. The College requires that its students accumulate 800 hours of industry-related experience. These and other practical experiences offer NU students the knowledge necessary to advance in the field. Students work with industry leaders in classroom projects, join academic clubs and professional organizations, and participate in special trips to trade shows and conventions and specially designed study-abroad experiences, making NU a national leader in the area.

For students who are undecided about which major to choose, Niagara University offers its award-winning Academic Exploration Program (AEP). AEP provides a structured opportunity for students to participate in a thorough, organized process of selecting a major that meets their academic talents and career goals while fulfilling requirements to graduate with classmates on time.

TUITION, ROOM, BOARD, FEES

Tuition for 2016–17 was $29,500. Room and board (with a choice of meal plans) cost an additional $12,700 per year. Fees were estimated at $1,450 per year.

FINANCIAL AID

The highest in quality, Niagara is also an exceptional value—a prestigious private university education at a reasonable cost when financial aid packages are taken into account.

Ninety-nine percent of entering freshmen and transfers receive financial aid. This aid may come in the form of merit scholarships, loans, grants, or campus employment. Students seeking financial assistance should file the Free Application for Federal Student Aid (FAFSA). New York State residents should also file a Tuition Assistance Program (TAP) application.

Niagara University offers a program (NUOP) that provides institutional admittance as well as financial and intensive academic assistance to students who otherwise would not meet admission criteria.

Additionally, the Level Tuition Program allows first semester freshmen to "lock in" one tuition rate for four consecutive years. This makes it much easier for students and families to budget the cost of their education.

Finally, Niagara's NUSTEP program reduces the overall cost of attendance by providing high school students with opportunities to obtain college credits.

STUDENT ORGANIZATIONS & ACTIVITIES

There are approximately 3,200 undergraduate and 825 graduate students enrolled at Niagara. A large percentage of these students take advantage of the more than 100 extracurricular and cocurricular activities offered, including student government, NU Honors, WNIA (student radio), Club Managers Association of America and Brothers and Sisters in Christ.

ADMISSIONS PROCESS

The university welcomes men and women who have demonstrated aptitude and academic achievement at the high school level. Either SAT or ACT test scores are required. International students are required to submit the results of their TOEFL examination and, if transcripts are not in English, these transcripts must be sent to Niagara University via the World Education Services (WES) for a "Course by Course Report" evaluation. Interviews are recommended. Transfer students are accepted in any semester. (Transfer credit is evaluated individually by the dean of each division.) Students who complete high school in less than four years are eligible for early admission. Students may also apply under an early action program. Economically and educationally disadvantaged students from New York State are eligible to apply for admission through the Higher Educational Opportunity Program (HEOP).

Niagara operates on a rolling admission basis and adheres to the College Board Candidates Reply Date. Nursing and theatre applicants are encouraged to apply by mid-December of their senior year. A visit to the campus is recommended, and overnight accommodations in a residence hall are available through the Niagara Nights program.

NORTHEASTERN UNIVERSITY

AT A GLANCE

A world leader in experiential-learning education, Northeastern emphasizes educational programs that link course work with a variety of practical experiences, including global opportunities, service-learning, research and our signature co-op program.

There's a certain energy about Northeastern University. It comes from the bright, ambitious students, exhibiting a strong sense of purpose in the classroom and while working or studying abroad. In the city of Boston—the ultimate college town—and across the globe, Northeastern students challenge themselves intellectually, investigate career options, participate in community service, and graduate both personally and professionally prepared for their future careers and graduate school.

Founded in 1898, Northeastern is a leader in interdisciplinary research, urban engagement, and the seamless integration of classroom learning with real-world experiences. The academic curriculum is enhanced by experiential learning through research, professional, global, and service experiences. Anchored by the world's largest, most innovative cooperative education program, Northeastern prepares students for a lifetime of achievement, and allows them to make an impact on the world before they graduate.

The current undergraduate enrollment of 17,923 is made up of students of all backgrounds and interests, giving Northeastern its distinctive culture. Students can participate in any of Northeastern's 400 student organizations, join a cultural club, participate in cutting-edge research with faculty from various disciplines, or perform with an award-winning a cappella group. They can travel to nearby New Hampshire for a ski club trip, play varsity or club basketball, tutor local children, and more. Students have countless opportunities to make lifelong friendships, to try something brand new—a class, a sport, or a career path—to hone their leadership skills, and have fun. Quiet corners of the campus feel far from city streets and give students a secluded haven to read, write, or relax. The 73-acre campus is dynamic and welcoming, a beautiful stretch of leafy green in the heart of Boston.

LOCATION & ENVIRONMENT

Northeastern's residential campus is located in the heart of Boston, where the distinctive neighborhoods of the Back Bay, the South End, the Fenway, and Roxbury meet. Over half of the student body lives on campus and many of the residence halls have amazing views of the Boston skyline.

The Back Bay area, known for its many cultural and educational institutions, is just steps away from Symphony Hall, the New England Conservatory of Music, the Museum of Fine Arts, and the Isabella Stewart Gardner Museum. The South End is home to elegant Victorian row houses, a vibrant arts scene, hidden gardens, and some of the finest dining in Boston. The Fenway area, with its beautiful rose garden, bicycle and jogging paths, and Fenway Park (home of the Boston Red Sox) is also just a few blocks away.

CAMPUS FACILITIES & EQUIPMENT

Northeastern is home to more than fifty research centers and undergraduates have ample opportunities to work alongside their professors to aid and conduct research on a variety of topics. The university library system is comprised of Snell Library, a 240,000-square-foot central library on the Boston campus, the School of Law Library, and a small supplemental collection at the Nahant Marine Science Center. Snell Library houses 780,669 print volumes, 548,806 e-books, 1,163,735 microfilms, and access to 83,511 licensed electronic journals, as well as 23,437 audio, video, and computer software items, and 5,712 linear feet of archival material as of June 2014.

Northeastern University provides a broad range of academic and administrative computer resources to students, faculty, and staff members. Many computing resources are available, including an extensive wireless network, Internet connections for all offices and university-owned residence halls, technology-assisted classrooms, computer labs, and the myNEU Admitted Student Portal, which allows students to access many administrative and academic functions online.

ACADEMICS

At the heart of a Northeastern education are award-winning faculty mentors, a rigorous and innovative curriculum, and undergraduate research and global experiences that challenge and transform. Northeastern's innovative programs encompass a wide range of majors, concentrations, and interdisciplinary studies along with honors, pre-professional, and study-abroad programs.

Northeastern's approach to educating its students integrates a challenging academic curriculum with a variety of experiential learning opportunities including research, global experiences, service learning, and the university's signature cooperative education program (co-op), enabling students to make deep connections between their field of study and the world around them. After completing their freshman year, Northeastern students integrate classroom learning with six-month periods of full-time, immersive professional work, global study, or research experiences related to their major or interests. Northeastern's flexibility enables students to choose a four or five-year path with up to eighteen months of experience, strengthening their professional network and giving them confidence-and a significant edge in the job market. Students learn what career is a good fit for them—and what careers are not—all before graduating. In addition, over half of the students are offered full-time jobs from co-op employers. Northeastern partners with over 3,350 co-op employers around the globe, including some of the world's largest and most reputable companies: Pfizer, John Hancock, Yahoo, Fidelity Investments, IBM, General Electric, Massachusetts General Hospital, Microsoft, and the Boston Globe, just to name a few.

Experiential learning opportunities-including U.S. and international professional co-op, service learning, research, and study abroad-are currently available in 134 countries around the world.

The University Honors Program allows students to participate in enriched educational experiences and offers opportunities that include honors sections of required academic courses, honors seminars, independent research, and specialized study abroad.

The university has more than 1,260 full and part-time faculty members with a wide variety of research and teaching interests and specialties. Academic counselors in each college work closely with students to assist them in developing programs suited to their interests and abilities. Co-op advisors assist students in resume-building, honing interview skills and tactics, and in developing contacts with businesses and employers to support networking and professional opportunities.

MAJORS & DEGREES OFFERED

Northeastern's academic programs are divided among eight colleges. The College of Arts, Media and Design awards undergraduate degrees in architecture, art, media arts and design, communication studies, game design, journalism; media and screen studies, music/music industry, music composition and technology, studio art, and theater (including concentrations in performance and production).

The D'Amore-McKim School of Business offers two degree options: the Bachelor of Science in Business Administration (B.S.B.A.) and the Bachelor of Science in International Business (B.S.I.B.). The B.S.I.B. program includes language instruction and international study and work. The college offers concentrations in accounting, entrepreneurship and innovation, finance, management, management information systems, marketing, and supply chain management.

The College of Computer and Information Science awards degrees in computer science and information science and also offers combined majors that pair computer science with biology, business, cognitive psychology, communication studies, computer engineering, cyber operations, digital art, environmental science, game design, interactive media, journalism, mathematics, music, music composition and technology.

The College of Engineering offers degrees in bioengineering, chemical, civil, computer, electrical, industrial, and mechanical engineering.

The Bouvé College of Health Sciences awards degrees in health sciences, nursing, pharmacy and physical therapy. The college also offers a six-year Doctor of Pharmacy degree and a six-year program leading to a Doctor of Physical Therapy.

The College of Science awards undergraduate degrees in applied physics, behavioral neuroscience, biochemistry, biology, biomedical physics, chemistry, environmental science, environmental studies, linguistics, marine biology, mathematics, physics, and psychology.

The College of Social Sciences and Humanities awards undergraduate degrees in African American studies, American Sign Language, Asian studies, criminal justice, cultural anthropology, economics, English, history, human services, international affairs, Jewish studies (combined major only), philosophy, political science, religious studies, sociology, and Spanish.

The Explore Program for undeclared students offers a wide array of academic opportunities designed to help students who feel strongly about exploring their options before making a commitment to a major. The program provides the support and guidance students need to explore and eventually choose one of Northeastern's undergraduate programs.

TUITION, ROOM, BOARD, FEES

For 2016-17, tuition was $46,720, and room and board fees were $15,050. Regardless of time to degree, tuition is charged only while students are earning course credits.

FINANCIAL AID

The university operates a substantial aid program designed to make attendance feasible for all qualified students. By coordinating the resources of the university and various public and private scholarship programs, the Office of Student Financial Services was able to provide more than $253.8 million in grant and scholarship assistance. More than 75 percent of students receive some form of financial aid. Northeastern participates in all federal aid programs. Financial aid is based on need and academic merit and may consist of grants, loans, work-study employment, or any combination of the three. To apply, students must file the Free Application for Federal Student Aid (FAFSA) and a CSS PROFILE form with the College Scholarship Service by the priority filing date of February 15.

STUDENT ORGANIZATIONS & ACTIVITIES

Students have access to over 400 clubs and organizations and an extensive network of advisement and counseling services. Approximately 16,500 students participate in student organizations. Programs and services sponsored by the African American Institute, the Latino/a Student Cultural Center, the Asian American Center, the International Student & Scholar Institute, and many other organizations enrich Northeastern's social life and cultural fabric. In athletics, Northeastern competes in NCAA Division I and maintains varsity teams in 8 men's and 10 women's sports.

ADMISSIONS PROCESS

Students may enter the university with advanced credit on the basis of test scores on Advanced Placement (AP) examinations, the International Baccalaureate (I.B.) examinations, or with successful completion of accredited college-level courses. In addition to the application for admission, prospective freshmen must submit official high school transcript(s) (or official GED score reports); official transcripts for any college-level course work taken while a secondary-school student; written recommendations from their secondary school counselor and a teacher; and scores on the SAT (Northeastern's College Board code is 3667) or ACT, including the writing section. Please visit the university's website for additional admission details for specific student populations and transfer admissions requirements (northeastern. edu/admissions).

Application and Information

Admission to Northeastern is selective and competitive. For the freshman class entering in Fall 2016, the university received more than 51,000 applications for 2,800 seats in the freshman class. Students are reviewed in the context of their environment, with attention paid to their academic course selections and rigor, academic achievement, extracurricular involvement and impact, and their potential fit with Northeastern, including the demonstration of personal traits like leadership, adaptability, a global perspective, or an entrepreneurial spirit.

November 1 is the deadline for the early action admission program. Northeastern will also offer a binding early decision program for which the deadline will be November 1. Students who have carefully explored their college options and have decided that Northeastern is where they want to enroll may choose to apply under the early decision program. The deadline for the regular admission program is January 1. Admitted early action and regular decision students are required to pay a deposit by May 1 to secure a place in the class. Early decision students are required to pay a deposit by January 15. For transfer students, the admissions deadlines are April 1 for fall and October 1 for spring admission. Fall transfer and spring admission decisions are made on a space-available, rolling basis.

Northeastern offers a variety of visit options including information sessions and campus tours. For more information, or to register, visit northeastern.edu/admissions/connect/visit. For more information, students should contact:

Office of Undergraduate Admissions

240 West Village F

Northeastern University

360 Huntington Avenue

Boston, Massachusetts 02115

Phone: 617-373-2200

E-mail: admissions@northeastern.edu

Website: northeastern.edu/admissions

ORAL ROBERTS UNIVERSITY

AT A GLANCE

Oral Roberts University was founded to educate the whole person—spirit, mind and body. With over 80 bachelor's, 12 master's and 2 doctoral degree programs, ORU is the world's leading interdenominational, Spirit-empowered University. Learn more at oru.edu.

WHOLE PERSON EDUCATION

Oral Roberts University was founded to educate the whole person—spirit, mind and body, and after five decades of being the first university of its kind, ORU is still the world's leading interdenominational, Spirit-empowered University. Its vibrant Christ-centered community and unique Whole Person Education equips students to reach and exceed their academic and professional goals… all while empowering them on their quest for wholeness through an environment that challenges them to be spiritually alive, intellectually alert, physically disciplined, socially adept and professionally competent.

ORU is accredited by the Higher Learning Commission of the North Central Association of Colleges and Schools (HLC), and a member of the Council for Christian Colleges and Universities (CCCU), the Oklahoma Independent Colleges and Universities (OICU) and the Council of Independent Colleges (CIC).

"MAKE NO LITTLE PLANS HERE"

This powerful challenge from OUR's Founder has inspired more than 40,000 ORU alumni to take God's healing power to over 145 nations around the globe, permeating every area of society—business, education, medicine, politics, media, science, engineering, ministry and much more.

ORU has been recognized annually by US News and World Report and Princeton Review as one of the best regional universities in the U.S. In addition to housing one of the world's most respected colleges for theology and ministry, it is also one of the leading liberal arts universities in the U.S., with educational opportunities spanning every interest and stage of learning.

- Six unique colleges with bachelor's, master's and doctoral degree programs
- 135+ undergraduate majors and minors
- 12 master's programs
- Two doctoral programs
- 100% online bachelor's, graduate, diploma and certificate programs
- On-campus and online dual-enrollment programs for high school students

ACTIVE STUDENT LIFE

Aside from enjoying all that Tulsa has to offer, ORU's campus experience is like none other:

- A cutting-edge student center that houses one of Oklahoma's largest TV's, gaming areas, a coffee shop, Moe's Southwest grill and much, much more.
- 14 NCAA Division I sports programs.
- Exciting dorm life with each dorm having a brother/sister floor or "wing" to hang-out with and enjoy fun activities on-campus and around Tulsa.
- Competitive intramural sports between wings
- On-campus eating options, from unlimited food options in ORU's dining hall to delicious alternatives like Chick-fil-A, Moe's Southwest Grill, and many more.
- Over 35 academic and co-curricular clubs
- An on-campus aerobics center with cardio and exercise machines, racquetball courts, an Olympic size pool, full-sized basketball courts, an indoor track, a weight room and more.

DYNAMIC SPIRITUAL ATMOSPHERE

Faith and the pursuit of a stronger, Spirit-empowered relationship with the Lord are central to the ORU experience. Weekly chapel services are fused with powerful student-led worship, life-changing messages and multi-media packed experiences. Events like student-led worship events and The Prayer Movement group are just a sample of the spiritual opportunities on campus. ORU students are making a difference in Tulsa and around the world every year through local outreach and mission trip opportunities.

LOCATION & ENVIRONMENT
TAKE A VIRTUAL TOUR

ORU's beautiful 263-acre campus can now be experienced on your phone, tablet or computer. Visit oru.edu/virtual_tour to experience it today.

TULSA, OKLAHOMA

ORU's campus is located in the vibrant and opportune city of Tulsa, Oklahoma. If a future ORU student were to describe a perfect college town, it might go something like this: growing city, great job opportunities, entertainment options and plenty of places of worship. That describes Tulsa perfectly!

This flourishing city, settled in the heartland of the U.S., has the friendliness and close-knit attitude of a much smaller town, but with almost 1 million residents in the metropolitan area, it's the second largest city in the state of Oklahoma.

PROGRAMS AND RESOURCES

ORU has built a network of programs and resources to prepare every student for success in the classroom and after graduation. The following are key programs and services that ORU offers:

- Advantage Program: online and on-campus dual enrollment courses for high school students (advantage.oru.edu).
- Bridges for Success Program: assists students who do not fully meet admissions criteria to successfully adjust to the University.
- Career Services: helps students and graduates to find and secure a career.
- Chaplain Program: consists of student chaplains who oversee and encourage spiritual community in the dorms.
- Comprehensive Advisement Center: helps all new students develop their first semester schedules.
- Disability Service Center: assures that no qualified individual with a disability will be denied reasonable accommodations in modification of policies, practices, and procedure.
- Eli Center: provides services and resources for student athletes.
- Freshman Leadership Program: allows freshman students opportunities for leadership development.
- Graduate Quest Fellows and Scholarship Program: opportunities for incoming graduate students to receive full-tuition coverage or annual scholarships up to $5,000 (quest.oru.edu/grad).
- Honors Program: provides exceptional opportunities and scholarships up to $20,000 per year for students with extraordinary intellectual talents.
- International Student Center: helps ORU's growing international community adjust to student life at ORU and navigate Tulsa.
- Intramural Sports: recreational and competitive sports leagues for students
- Missions and Outreach: provides opportunities for students to serve alongside partner ministries and organizations on a weekly basis or on short-term mission trips across the globe.
- One-2-One Tutoring Program: caters to the individual academic and tutoring needs of each student at ORU.
- ORU Worship Center: an artistic community of ORU students who lead the student body during times of worship.
- Prayer Movement: teams of students who work with prayer and worship leaders to arrange and facilitate times of prayer throughout the week.
- Quest Whole Person Scholarship Program: opportunities for incoming undergraduate students to receive additional scholarships worth up to $20,000 per year (quest.oru.edu).

- Resident Advisor Program: student leaders who assist with the development of the residents on a wing by providing daily support, accountability and helping with maintenance or emergency situations.

- Residual ACT: offers multiple on-campus ACT testing dates throughout the year.

- Student Association: students elected and assigned by ORU students who represents the student body and facilitates events and activities throughout the year.

- Study-abroad Trips: semester or summer-long opportunities for students who want to be immersed in a new culture and language, or combine the adventure of traveling with the benefits of taking classes in a new place.

In addition to personable 16:1 classroom sizes, ORU professors are leaders within their respective fields; and with a deep conviction to equip the next generation of Spirit-empowered leaders, they invest one-on-one with students through mentoring relationships.

ORU faculty members want their students to succeed and change the world. This reflects in their commitment to excellence in the classroom; their guidance and friendship outside the classroom; and their continued advice, networking and counsel even after students graduate.

MAJORS & DEGREES OFFERED

ORU is committed to providing excellent academics through its matchless Whole Person Education, whether that's to students on ORU's Tulsa campus or to online students around the globe. Grounded in a conviction to send Spirit-empowered leaders into every person's world, ORU houses six unique colleges offering over 80 bachelor degrees, 12 master's programs and 2 doctoral degree programs that span every interest, dream and calling:

The following list covers degree programs according to their respective college, then department. For details about specific degree programs, visit oru.edu/academics.

COLLEGE OF ARTS AND CULTURAL STUDIES

COMMUNICATION, ARTS AND MEDIA

Advertising/Art Education/Cinema, TV, Digital Media/Communication (on-campus or online)/Communication Arts Education/Convergence Journalism/Dance Performance/Drama, TV, Film Performance/Graphic Design/Musical Theatre/Public Relations/Studio Art/Theatre Arts

ENGLISH AND MODERN LANGUAGES

English Education/English Literature/French/Modern Foreign Language Education/Spanish/Translation and Interpreting/Writing

HISTORY, HUMANITIES AND GOVERNMENT

Global Studies /Government (on-campus or online)/History/International Community Development/International Relations/Leadership Studies (on-campus or online)/Liberal Arts, Liberal Studies/Social Studies Education

MUSIC

Music Arts/Music Composition/Music Education/Music Performance/Music Production/Music Therapy/Worship Arts

COLLEGE OF BUSINESS

BUSINESS

Accounting/Business Administration (on-campus or online)/Finance/International Business/International Business and Ministry (on-campus or online)/Management (on-campus or online)/Marketing/Quantitative Business Administration

COLLEGE OF EDUCATION

EDUCATION

Early Childhood Education/Elementary Education/English Language Teaching in the Global Classroom/Special Education, Mild-Moderate Disabilities

COLLEGE OF NURSING

NURSING

Bachelor of Science in Nursing/RN to BSN Program (online)

COLLEGE OF SCIENCE AND ENGINEERING

BEHAVIORAL SCIENCES

Psychology (on-campus or online)/Social Justice /Social Work

BIOLOGY AND CHEMISTRY

Biology/Biomedical Chemistry /Chemistry/Global Environmental Sustainability/Medical Technology/Science Education with Biology Emphasis

COMPUTING AND MATHEMATICS

Computer Information Technology /Math Education/Mathematical Finance/Mathematics /Mathematics Physics /Mathematics Preactuary

ENGINEERING

Biomedical Engineering/Engineering /Engineering Physics

HEALTH, LEISURE AND SPORT SCIENCES

Health and Exercise Science /Health, Physical Education/Leisure Science/Sports Management

COLLEGE OF THEOLOGY AND MINISTRY

THEOLOGY AND MINISTRY

Biblical Literature (on-campus or online)/Christian Caregiving and Counseling (on-campus or online)/Church Ministries (online)/Global Ministry and the Marketplace/Ministry and Leadership/Theological, Historical Studies

TUITION, ROOM, BOARD, FEES

Visit http://www.oru.edu/financial-assistance/ for the most up-to-date cost of education.

FINANCIAL AID

Visit http://www.oru.edu/financial-assistance/ for the most up-to-date scholarships and financial aid offerings.

STUDENT ORGANIZATIONS & ACTIVITIES

ORU is a diverse yet unified community with students from more than 90 nations and every corner of the U.S. Students create lasting relationships with peers and professors who have a rich variety of backgrounds and experiences. In fact, Huffington Post recently ranked ORU for being one of the top friendliest universities.

ORU students are known in Tulsa and across the globe for being at the top-of-their-game. Companies pursue ORU graduates because they embody the Whole Person lifestyle, carrying integrity, skill and excellence into every area of life, especially their careers.

ADMISSIONS PROCESS

ORU operates with a rolling admission policy for most programs. For specific questions, please visit oru.edu/admissions, or contact ORU's Office of Admissions at 918.495.6518 or admissions@oru.edu.

Note: ORU's $35 application fee is waived if applications are completed online at apply.oru.edu.

PRINCETON UNIVERSITY

AT A GLANCE

Princeton combines the strengths of a major research university with the qualities of an outstanding liberal arts college. The University prepares its 5,200 undergraduates for lives of leadership and service.

Chartered in 1746, Princeton is the fourth-oldest college in the nation. It is a private, non-sectarian university.

LOCATION & ENVIRONMENT

Princeton is a residential campus set on 500 park-like acres located in the town of Princeton (pop: 30,000) in central New Jersey. Known for its beauty and architectural variety, including the famed "Collegiate Gothic" style of architecture, the campus is home to historic landmarks such as Nassau Hall, which was built in 1756 and played an important role during the American Revolution.

Princeton students enjoy convenient transportation options to New York City and Philadelphia, both only about an hour away by car. Other nearby attractions include numerous parks, cultural venues, and commercial hubs. For arts lovers, the Mc-Carter Theatre is a campus treasure within easy walking distance.

CAMPUS FACILITIES & EQUIPMENT

Academic support services include academic advising centered in each of the six residential colleges; the McGraw Center, which offers workshops and individual consultations with students as they evolve as scholars; and the Writing Program, which strengthens students' writing skills through a required seminar. Ongoing tutoring sessions also are available at the program's Writing Center.

Throughout their undergraduate careers, Princeton students are supported by a range of first-rate academic resources, including libraries, laboratories, and one of the leading university art museums in the country. The largest library on campus, Firestone Library, contains more than 70 miles of shelving and a vast range of electronic resources. The Peter B. Lewis Library, designed by renowned architect Frank Gehry, offers impressive print and digital collections in the sciences. In the past several years, new initiatives in African American studies and neuroscience have resulted in expanded activities.

A new state-of-art and environmentally sustainable science facility houses the chemistry department and provides laboratory space for research and teaching. A new neuroscience and psychology building recently opened, and the new Andlinger Center for Energy and the Environment opened in 2015.

Numerous venues for the arts as well as a range of athletic facilities also are available.

ACADEMICS

Students are encouraged to bring a multidisciplinary approach to their studies, synthesizing what they discover in different classes and through their own research. This approach may be informal, based on a student's particular avenue of study, or it may be more formally structured, such as with the integrated science curriculum that combines the study of physics, mathematics, computer science, and molecular biology.

A global perspective is emphasized across the curriculum, with special opportunities such as the Study Abroad Program and the Princeton Institute for International and Regional Studies. Global summer internships are available through the International Internship Program and the Princeton Environmental Institute Summer Internship Program. The Bridge Year Program allows selected students to delay the start of their first year to engage in nine months of University-sponsored service abroad.

MAJORS & DEGREES OFFERED

Princeton undergraduates pursue either the bachelor of arts (A.B.) or the bachelor of science in engineering (B.S.E.) degree. Students in the A.B. degree program choose a concentration (major) in one of 31 departments in the arts, humanities, social sciences, and natural sciences, including undergraduate programs in the Woodrow Wilson School of Public and International Affairs and the School of Architecture. The B.S.E. degree is granted by the School of Engineering and Applied Science, which has six engineering departments.

Princeton offers doctoral programs in a range of subjects in the humanities, natural sciences, social sciences, School of Architecture, School of Engineering and Applied Science, and within the Woodrow Wilson School of Public and International Affairs.

In addition to their major course of study, students are encouraged to enroll in one or more of the University's 53 interdisciplinary certificate programs, which offer diverse fields of study. For example, a student may wish to concentrate in ecology and evolutionary biology while pursuing a certificate in musical performance.

Undergraduates benefit from small class sizes, a 5-to-1 student-to-faculty ratio, and one-on-one advising with faculty, particularly while working on independent projects such as the junior paper and senior thesis. The university's 1,278 faculty members are leaders in their disciplines, and it is not uncommon for students to receive classroom instruction from a Nobel laureate, Pulitzer Prize winner, or MacArthur fellow. During their first year, students are introduced to many of Princeton's notable faculty through the freshman seminars program, which offers small discussion-focused classes on a variety of topics. One such freshman seminar may cover the art and science of motorcycle design; another may explore the qualities that make a poem endure.

TUITION, ROOM, BOARD, FEES

Estimated cost of attendance for 2017-18

Tuition: $47,500

Room charge: $8,860

Board rate: $6,635

Estimated miscellaneous expenses (books, supplies, laundry, telephone, recreation, etc.): $3,650

Total: $66,645

FINANCIAL AID

Princeton offers one of the strongest need-based financial aid programs in the country, ensuring that all qualified students, regardless of financial need, can afford to attend. There is no income cutoff on Princeton's aid application; any family who feels the need for financial assistance is welcome to apply for aid.

Since 2001, when Princeton initiated its landmark no-loan financial aid program, the university has been a leader in changing the face of financial aid policy. The university offers every aid recipient a financial aid package that replaces loans with grant aid that students do not pay back.

If admitted, applicants can be confident that their financial need, as determined by Princeton's aid office, will be met. Today, about 60 percent of undergraduates receive aid, compared with 38 percent more than a decade ago. As a result, Princeton has been able to enroll growing numbers of students from low and middle-income backgrounds. About 84% of students graduate without debt, and those who choose to borrow for additional expenses, such as a laptop computer, graduate with an average debt of $8,500. The average aid package for the Class of 2020 was $48,000, which exceeds the cost of tuition.

STUDENT ORGANIZATIONS & ACTIVITIES

Princeton is a residential campus that provides a close-knit living environment for its undergraduates. Through its six residential colleges, students pursue a host of recreational and academic activities. The residential colleges also serve as home base for academic advising for students, who learn about all that the university has to offer from faculty and staff advisers, peer mentors, and fellow students.

With more than 300 student organizations, as well as an extensive calendar of cultural and athletic events, students find it easy to pursue their interests or explore new ones. The Frist Campus Center serves as the hub of campus life, and is home to the Women's Center, the LGBT Center, the Pace Center for Civic Engagement, and the Undergraduate Student Government, as well as many other student clubs and organizations.

For many students, social life at Princeton includes becoming a member of an eating club. The 11 historic eating clubs are open to juniors and seniors and are run independently of the university. Fraternities and sororities are not recognized as official student organizations on campus.

Princeton is an NCAA Division I school. The university offers 37 varsity sports and 38 club teams. Each year more than 1,000 students participate in intercollegiate varsity and junior varsity sports. In any given year, more than half of Princeton's varsity athletic teams compete in national championships. In recent years, Princeton teams have won national titles in lacrosse, rowing, fencing, track and field, and squash. The women's basketball team finished its 2014-15 regular season with an unprecedented 30-0 record.

ADMISSIONS PROCESS

Princeton's admission process goes beyond simply looking for academically accomplished students. For each first-year class, Princeton brings together a varied mix of high-achieving, intellectually gifted students from diverse backgrounds to create an exceptional learning community. American minorities comprise about 43% of the undergraduate student body, and students from more than 110 countries are represented.

Princeton cares about what students have accomplished in and out of the classroom. The admission process is highly selective. In 2016, the university offered admission to 6.5 percent of applicants for the class of 2020.

Students applying to Princeton are asked to describe their talents, academic accomplishments, and personal achievements. A transcript and recommendations also are required. To be considered for admission to Princeton, students must submit the results of the SAT Reasoning Test with Essay or ACT with Writing, Two SAT Subject Tests are recommended but not required. Students may apply to the university online, or submit a paper application, if needed.

Under Princeton's admission policy, need for financial aid is not in any way a disadvantage. Princeton welcomes applications from talented students of diverse economic backgrounds. An application fee waiver is available to students from low-income backgrounds or if the application fee presents a financial hardship.

QUINNIPIAC UNIVERSITY

AT A GLANCE

A survey of recent graduates indicated that close to 95 percent were either employed or in graduate school within six months of graduation.

Quinnipiac, founded in 1929, is a private, co-educational, non-sectarian university located in a uniquely attractive New England setting in Hamden, Connecticut and nearby North Haven. Quinnipiac's mission is to provide a supportive and stimulating environment for the intellectual and personal growth of its 7100 undergraduate and 2800 graduate, law and medical students.

The university offers broadly-based undergraduate programs together with graduate programs in selected professional fields. At the undergraduate level, through integrated liberal arts and professional curricula, programs in the Schools of Business, Engineering, Communications, Education, Health Sciences, Nursing, and the College of Arts and Sciences prepare students for career entry or advanced studies. Graduate programs are designed to provide professional qualifications for success in business, education, health sciences, nursing, communications, social work, medicine and law.

An education at Quinnipiac embodies the university's commitment to three important values: excellence in education, a student-centered campus, and a spirit of community. The entire university shares a service orientation toward students and their needs. Its collegial atmosphere fosters a strong sense of community, identity and purpose among faculty, staff and students.

LOCATION & ENVIRONMENT

Hamden, Connecticut: 8 miles north of New Haven, midway between Boston and New York City. Quinnipiac is a suburban campus with 600 acres on three sites. The Mount Carmel Campus is adjacent to Sleeping Giant State Park, with 1,700 acres of trails for hiking and walking. A picturesque setting provides an enjoyable academic and residential campus experience for students. Ninety-five percent of freshmen choose to live on campus. A campus shuttle system provides easy access to theaters, shopping, museums, sports, recreation and a variety of area dining and entertainment options. The nearby York Hill Campus is home to the TD Bank Sports Center with 3500-seat twin arenas for basketball and ice hockey, a lodge-like student/recreation center, plus suite-style residence halls with single and double rooms, kitchens and common living areas. The North Haven Campus, about 5 miles away, provides upper-level and graduate students in Health Sciences, Nursing, Education, Medicine, and Law with a state-of-the-art setting on 100 acres.

Driving time to Quinnipiac from Boston or New York City is about two hours. Metro-North and Amtrak provide train service to New Haven's Union Station, which is 15 minutes from campus. Airline service is available through Bradley International Airport, about 40 minutes from campus, and through John F. Kennedy and LaGuardia airports serving the New York City area. Ground transportation is available from all airports to New Haven.

CAMPUS FACILITIES & EQUIPMENT

Academic life focuses on the Bernhard Library, open 24/7 during the fall and spring semesters. Automated library systems, wireless technology, 60 public computers and 600 power/data connections are located throughout the library, along with individual study carrels and team study rooms.

The Learning Commons offers free academic tutoring as well as sessions to improve study techniques, writing skills and research methods. Quinnipiac's Writing Across the Curriculum program is designed to help students develop strong critical thinking and communication skills through writing. Essential Learning Outcomes (ELOs) have been identified that broaden students' knowledge and engage them in the educational process.

The University Honors Program fosters the needs and interests of our most academically talented and committed students. Service Learning courses integrate meaningful community service with instruction and reflection to enrich the learning experience, teach civic responsibility and strengthen communities

OFF-CAMPUS OPPORTUNITIES

Quinnipiac is a suburban campus with easy access to nearby shopping, restaurants and activities offered in Hamden, New Haven and North Haven. Students, faculty and staff are involved in community service through the "Big Event" held each April. Local community service opportunities also include Habitat for Humanity and tutoring in the elementary schools.

ACADEMICS

School of Business majors include: accounting, biomedical marketing, computer information systems, entrepreneurship, finance, international business, management and marketing. The Lender School of Business Center has case method classrooms, a financial technology center, center for innovation and entrepreneurship, software application development classroom and team study rooms for project work. An innovative 3+1 BS/MBA invites academically strong students to complete two degrees in four years. (AACSB accredited)

The School of Engineering, with programs in civil, industrial, mechanical and software engineering, and computer science, offers state-of-the-art labs including: a thermodynamics and heat workshop, environmental and hydraulics workshop, geotechnical lab, and an advanced automation and production lab.

The Schools of Health Sciences and Nursing majors include: athletic training, biomedical sciences, diagnostic medical sonography, health science studies, microbiology and immunology, nursing, occupational therapy (5½-year BS/MOT Master's program), physician assistant (6-year BS/MHS Master's program), physical therapy (6- or 7-year BS/DPT Doctorate) and radiologic sciences. The North Haven facility offers cutting-edge labs including a diagnostic imaging suite, orthopedics lab, adaptive model apartment, clinical skills labs, intensive care unit, clinical simulation labs and biomechanics lab.

College of Arts and Sciences majors include: behavioral neuroscience, biochemistry, biology, chemistry, criminal justice, economics, English, game design and development, gerontology, history, independent majors, interdisciplinary studies, law in society, mathematics, philosophy, political science, psychology, sociology, Spanish language and literature, and theater.

School of Communications majors include: advertising and integrated communications, communications /media studies, film, television & media arts, interactive digital design, journalism, and public relations. The Ed McMahon Center for Mass Communications provides a high-tech facility with a digital high-definition television production studio, media innovation classroom, audio production studio, 4k editing room, and more. An innovative 3+1 4-year BA/MS degree offers academically talented students the opportunity to complete two degrees in four years. Students also may study for a semester in Los Angeles, combining classes with an internship in the fall, spring or summer.

For those interested in teaching, completion of an undergraduate major in a liberal arts or natural sciences discipline, combined with junior and senior year courses in the School of Education and ending with a fifth year full-time graduate education program, culminates in the Master of Arts in Teaching degree.

A pre-med program is designed to provide the undergraduate student interested in a career as a health professional the appropriate background necessary to meet the entrance requirements of a variety of medical schools.

All programs at Quinnipiac offer an ideal combination of classroom learning with internships or clinical experiences. Students in business, engineering, communications, and liberal arts and sciences intern at nearby corporations, health care agencies, or media outlets. Students in health sciences and nursing are placed in a wide variety of clinical settings as part of their learning experience.

Students can take advantage of study abroad opportunities during the academic year or summer months (3.0 cumulative GPA required.) Program sites include: Ireland, Australia, Austria, Czech Republic, England, France, Spain, Italy, Netherlands and South Africa and through affiliates such as AIFS, API, and Semester at Sea.

Quinnipiac is where professors who want to know students by name come to teach, and where students who want a personal, challenging education come to learn. Quinnipiac's approximately 400 full-time faculty members are experts in their respective fields and include published authors, health care practitioners and researchers. Generous with their time and eager to share their knowledge with students, Quinnipiac faculty also lend their expertise to the public forum through op-ed pieces, newspaper articles and television discussions.

Students can take advantage of Career Development services within each academic division provide students with assistance with résumé writing, interview skills and job placement. A survey of recent graduates indicated that close to 95 percent were either employed or in graduate school within six months of graduation. Each year about half of students in internships are offered permanent jobs as a result of their work.

MAJORS

Undergraduate students can choose from almost 60 majors through the College of Arts and Sciences and the Schools of Business, Engineering, Education, Communications, Health Sciences and Nursing. About 30% of all entering freshmen remain at Quinnipiac through their graduate degree program.

Graduate students specialize in law, business, organizational leadership, health management, computer information systems, journalism, interactive media, public relations, education, social work, and health science programs for physician assistant, pathologists' assistant, medical laboratory sciences, molecular and cell biology, cardiovascular perfusion, radiologist assistant and nursing. Several programs are offered online.

TUITION, ROOM, BOARD, FEES

Costs for 2017-18: Tuition & Fees $46,100; Technology Fee $680, Room and Board $14,190

FINANCIAL AID

The Office of Financial Aid works with all applicants to ensure they receive the maximum state and federal aid for which they are eligible. Families are encouraged to file the FAFSA for federal student aid (code: 001402) after Oct. 1. The university also offers merit-based scholarships to incoming freshmen (fall semester). No additional application is necessary for scholarship consideration; recipients are notified by the admissions office. If you have any questions, please contact the Office of Financial Aid at (203) 582-8750 or (800) 462-1944, or e-mail: finaid@qu.edu.

STUDENT ORGANIZATIONS & ACTIVITIES

Quinnipiac University offers more than 110 student clubs and organizations including student government, newspaper, yearbook, radio station, service organizations, community activities, religious fellowships, diversity awareness (Black Student Union, Latino Cultural Society, Asian and Pacific Islander Association), dance and drama productions, and Greek life, along with numerous recreation activities, providing a balanced college experience. An active intramural program has team competition in more than 30 sports and activities.

Quinnipiac's 9400 undergraduate, graduate, law and medical students hail from 46 states and 61 countries. Housing options include traditional residence halls, suites, and suites with kitchens. Freshmen and sophomores generally live on the Mt. Carmel campus; juniors and seniors live on the York Hill campus and in university-owned houses.

Quinnipiac Bobcats: www.quinnipiacbobcats.com

The NCAA Division I athletic program in 21 sports includes Men: basketball, baseball, cross country, lacrosse, ice hockey, tennis, and soccer. Women: acrobatics & tumbling, basketball, softball, cross country and track (indoor and outdoor), field hockey, golf, ice hockey, lacrosse, rugby, soccer, tennis and volleyball. Quinnipiac competes in the MAAC in most sports, the ECAC (ice hockey, acrobatics & tumbling), Rugby Northeast (rugby) and the Big East (field hockey.)

Athletic facilities include a multi-purpose gymnasium, two fully-equipped fitness centers, a Spinning® studio, dance/yoga studios, tennis courts, a 24,000-square-foot recreation center with an indoor track, and a sports center with twin 3500-seat arenas for ice hockey and basketball.

ADMISSIONS PROCESS

High school students should begin applying for admission early in their senior year. Visit www.qu.edu/apply for application information. Quinnipiac is a member of the Common Application. A completed application consists of the application form, followed by official high school transcript, first-quarter senior grades, essay and one letter of recommendation. Students applying to the Schools of Health Sciences or Nursing must submit official SAT (QU code—3712) and/or ACT (QU code—0582) test scores. International and homeschooled students, as well as athletes playing a Division I sport (per NCAA rules) also must submit official test scores. For all other majors, files will be reviewed for an admission decision as well as consideration for scholarships based on overall academic work. If test scores are received, the highest critical reading and math scores (from the 'new' SAT) or the highest ACT composite score will be chosen.

Quinnipiac reviews applications on a 'rolling admissions' basis and also offers an Early Decision option for freshmen applicants. Early Decision students must file their application by November 1. The admissions office begins reviewing applications as soon as they are complete, and begins notifying students of admission decisions in November. Students applying for the 6-year BS/Physician Assistant program should submit the application by Oct 15, those applying for the BS/DPT in physical therapy, BS/MOT occupational therapy and BS nursing programs should apply by November 15. For all other applicants, February 1 is the recommended deadline.

All programs subscribe to the nationally recognized candidate reply date of May 1. Waitlisted students who indicate an interest in being considered if spaces become available will be notified as soon after May 1 as possible. In general, Quinnipiac admits between 60-64% of its applicants.

Transfer students who have or will receive an associate's degree prior to entrance are not required to provide high school transcripts and SAT results. We must receive transcripts of all courses taken at other colleges. The physician assistant and physical therapy programs are not available to transfer students.

To schedule an interview, campus tour, group information session or register for a spring or fall open house, go to www.qu.edu/visit . For questions, email admissions@qu.edu or call 800-462-1944 or 203-582-8600. www.qu.edu.

RAMAPO COLLEGE OF NEW JERSEY

AT A GLANCE

Established in 1969, Ramapo College is New Jersey's Public Liberal Arts College, dedicated to providing students a strong foundation for a lifetime of achievement and preparing them to be successful leaders for a changing world.

Ramapo College offers bachelor's degrees in the arts, business, humanities, social sciences and the sciences, as well as in professional studies, which include nursing, social work, and teacher certification at the elementary and secondary levels. Ramapo College also offers graduate programs, as well as, articulated programs with other reputable institutions.

Ramapo College of New Jersey is sometimes viewed as a private college. This is, in part, due to its unique interdisciplinary academic structure, its size of approximately 6,000 students and its pastoral setting in the foothills of the Ramapo Mountains on the New Jersey/New York border. Ramapo College students receive an elite education at the cost of a public college.

The College is committed to academic excellence through interdisciplinary and experiential learning, and international and intercultural understanding. The international mission is accomplished through a wide range of study abroad and student exchange links with institutions all over the world. Additional experiential programs include internships, co-op and service learning.

The College's interdisciplinary commitment helps students push intellectual boundaries; our commitment to experiential, hands-on learning allows them to push personal and professional boundaries as well. The commitment of our faculty to attentive teaching and mentoring empowers students to learn actively and attain the skills they will need to succeed professionally and become lifelong learners.

Ramapo College is committed to maintaining strength and opportunity through diversity of age, race, gender, sexual orientation, ethnicity, and economic background among faculty, staff, and students. Ramapo College is a selective institution committed to providing equal access to under-represented populations. Barrier-free, the College maintains a continuing commitment to persons with disabilities.

LOCATION & ENVIRONMENT

Ramapo College is spread across 300 acres, resting within the foothills of the Ramapo mountains in Mahwah, New Jersey. Enhancing these tranquil surroundings is the knowledge that the campus is approximately 30 miles from the nation's cultural mecca, New York City.

Campus is located just five minutes from major highways such as I-287, the New York State Thruway, and Route 17, making it very easy to bring you right to Ramapo's doorstep.

CAMPUS FACILITIES

A campus-wide building program during recent years has resulted in the completion of the Anisfield School of Business academic facility, featuring a real-time Global Financial Market trading laboratory; the Bill Bradley Sports and Recreation Center, with its 2,200-seat arena, fitness center, climbing wall, 25-meter pool, jogging track, dance/ aerobics studio and locker room facilities; the Overlook and Laurel residence halls and the Village apartment complex.

Construction projects completed in May 2015 include the Adler Center for Nursing Excellence and the renovation of the G-Wing building. The renovations include expanded classrooms, a research and simulation laboratory space, a student lounge, and study areas. This 36,000-square-foot facility is connected by an overhead walkway to the College's science/social science building.

The Sharp Sustainability Education Center and the Salameno Spiritual Center were completed in 2009.

The Angelica and Russ Berrie Center for Performing and Visual Arts, completed in 1999, houses performance theaters, art galleries and specialized spaces devoted to fine arts, computer art, photography, theater, dance and music.

CAMPUS EQUIPMENT

The campus features new and upgraded facilities that enhance all areas of campus life, including a library with electronic research facilities; a student life building with FM radio station, student offices, cafeteria, and entertainment and meeting rooms; housing for more than 3,000 students; and modern academic buildings with 24-hour computer labs.

OFF-CAMPUS OPPORTUNITIES

Ramapo College encourages students to take advantage of experiences outside of the classroom, such as internships, co-op, and study abroad opportunities.

Ramapo College has developed a diverse selection of more than 400 individual study-abroad program options in more than 60 countries. Opportunities exist for ALL majors and range from one week to a full year.

Being only 32 miles away from New York City makes it easy for Ramapo College students to take advantage of internship opportunities with over 200 NYC companies and even more in New Jersey. Ramapo students have completed a co-op or internship at companies like Google, Madison Square Garden, Yahoo!, BMW of North America, Deloitte, etc.

Students are able to purchase discounted bus tickets from Roadrunner Central and take a bus service that leaves from campus and takes them to The Port Authority of NY & NJ station in Manhattan.

ACADEMICS

Undergraduate students can choose from 36 different academic programs. Ramapo College boasts an average student/faculty ratio of 18:1 and average class size of 23, affording students the opportunity to develop close ties to the College's exceptional faculty.

At Ramapo College, 95 percent of our faculty hold terminal degrees in their field, allowing them to be excellent mentors to students inside and outside the classroom.

Undergraduate students have the opportunity to engage in faculty-guided research, present papers at national conferences, and take advantage of internship and co-op opportunities with 250 nearby New York City companies.

To strengthen the students' college background before concentrating on major courses for a degree, students are required to complete an all-college general education program consisting of courses in English, mathematics, the humanities, social sciences, and natural sciences.

All students are assigned an academic advisor during their first semester, allowing the choice of major to be made by the end of the sophomore year (with the exception of Nursing and Biology). There is ample time to explore several fields of interest before selecting a major.

MAJORS & DEGREES OFFERED

The College offers the following degrees:

- Bachelor of Arts
- Bachelor of Science
- Bachelor of Social Work
- Bachelor of Science in Nursing
- Bachelor of Science in Biology/Doctor of Physical Therapy (joint degree program with Rutgers Biomedical and Health Sciences)
- Bachelor of Science in Biology/Master of Science in Physician Assistant (joint degree program with Rutgers Biomedical and Health Sciences)

- Bachelor of Science/Doctor of Chiropractic (joint degree program with New York Chiropractic College)

- Bachelor of Science/Doctor of Optometry (join degree program with SUNY College of Optometry)

- Bachelor of Science in Biology/Doctor of Osteopathic Medicine (joint degree program with Lake Erie College of Osteopathic Medicine)

- Bachelor of Science in Biology/Doctor of Dental Medicine (joint degree program with Lake Erie College of Osteopathic Medicine)

- Bachelor of Science in Biology/Doctor of Pharmacy (joint degree program with Lake Erie College of Osteopathic Medicine)

- Bachelor of Arts in Visual Arts/Master of Arts in Mental Health Counseling with Art Therapy Specialization (joint degree program with Caldwell University)

- Bachelor of Arts in Political Science/Juris Doctorate (joint law program with Seton Hall Law School)

- Bachelor of Arts in Law and Society/Juris Doctorate (joint law program with Seton Hall Law School)

TUITION, ROOM, BOARD, FEES

The approximate tuition and fees for undergraduates in the 2016-2017 academic year are as follows:

In-state tuition and fees: $13,870.40

Out-of-state tuition and fees: $22,870.40

Room and board (all students): $11,900

FINANCIAL AID

Because Ramapo College is a state-assisted college, the cost of attending is affordable compared to many other institutions. About 82 percent of Ramapo's students receive some form of financial assistance. This aid includes grants—funds which the students are awarded but don't have to pay back—and loans, which must be repaid. Students also can receive a work-study job to earn money to help pay for school.

To apply for aid at Ramapo, students should complete the Free Application for Federal Student Aid (FAFSA) by March 1. No other application forms are required. By complying with this priority deadline, students will be notified by April 1 about their expected aid package. The FAFSA is available after October 1 at www.fafsa. ed.gov. Applicants should use Ramapo's school code (009344) when filing.

Transfer students must initiate a school code change on the Student Aid Report (SAR) to ensure that their account will be appropriately credited. Students should begin this process at the time of application. Contact Ramapo's Financial Aid Office at 201-684-7549.

STUDENT ORGANIZATIONS & ACTIVITIES

At Ramapo College, student clubs and organizations are recognized as important parts of the total learning experience. Students are urged to take advantage of the many opportunities available, since not all their time is spet in class.

There are more than 100 groups including cultural, academic, religious, recreational, entertainment, political, social and special interest groups. Joining clubs helps students establish lasting friendships, and gives them lifelong memories of their college years.

Ramapo College also offers 18 different NCAA Division III sports.

ADMISSIONS PROCESS

Every year, Ramapo College welcomes more than 900 freshmen primarily from New Jersey, the Mid-Atlantic and Northeast regions of the United States and from many foreign countries. In addition, Ramapo College receives over 6,000 applications from all 21 counties in New Jersey, 21 different states and 31 foreign countries.

A complete application to Ramapo College includes:

- Application (Apply at ramapo.edu/apply or at commonapp.org)
- $60 application fee
- Official high school transcripts
- One letter of recommendation (two preferred)
- Essay
- Official SAT or ACT scores

The Test of English as a Foreign Language (TOEFL) is required of all international students and is recommended for all students who have resided in the United States fewer than four years.

Ramapo College practices a holistic review process. Each application is evaluated individually with emphasis placed on academic achievement in high school and standardized test scores, however, successful applicants also present a record of extracurricular activities that reflect maturity, responsibility and commitment.

Ramapo College seeks the very best students for its Educational Opportunity Fund (EOF) Program. If you qualify, you will join a community of achievers who are supported by a partnership between the college and EOF that is outstanding not only in financial assistance to cover your college cost, but also in personal and academic counseling, career planning, and leadership training. Your admission to the Ramapo College EOF program depends upon meeting our financial eligibility requirements and academic standards.

Fall application deadlines:

Ramapo College offers binding Early Decision for students who know Ramapo College is their number one choice. Early Decision applicants must apply by November 1 and will receive their decision by December 5.

Students who are applying to the Nursing or Biology program must apply by December 15. The priority deadline for merit scholarship consideration for all majors is also December 15. The supporting documents and credential deadline (date by which Ramapo College must receive your documents, including transcript, test scores, recommendation letters, and EOF financial documentation, if applicable) is January 15.

The final deadline for all other majors outside of the Nursing and Biology program is March 1.

All decisions for completed applications will be sent by April 1.

Scholarships:

Ramapo College scholarships are merit-based opportunities, meaning they are offered to students based on their academic and personal achievements, not financial need. Students who apply by December 15 and submit all required credentials by January 15 and are in the top 10 percent of their high school class with new SAT scores of at least a 1270 total OR 27 ACT composite will be considered for a merit-based scholarship.

Unfortunately, due to an increase in applications and limited funding, the college may be unable to offer every student that fits the above criteria a merit-based scholarship.

Awards are continued for four years provided that students maintain the required number of credits and grade point average. No separate application for a potential award is necessary.

REED COLLEGE

AT A GLANCE

Intellectual. Free-thinking. Classical. Iconoclastic. Paradoxical. This constellation of features only begins to describe Reed: one of the most distinctive colleges in the nation.

Reed attracts serious scholars. Always engaged and often engrossed in a demanding, exhilarating educational adventure, "Reedies" thrive on a mix of classical study, critical analysis, and guided inquiry that rewards creativity, independence, and reflection. Classes are small, faculty members are highly accessible, and students adhere to an honor principle both inside and outside the classroom.

Reed recruits nationally, with strong representation from California, the Pacific Northwest, and the East Coast. The student body is also composed of 11 percent international students. Reed ranks second among U.S. liberal arts colleges in the percentage of graduates going on to earn doctoral degrees and fourth among all institutions of higher education. The breadth, depth, and rigor of the curriculum provide great preparation for nearly any career. Many Reed alumni found or lead companies and organizations, earn medical or law degrees, write books or create works of art, and work to make life on the planet better for all.

LOCATION & ENVIRONMENT

Located in a quiet residential neighborhood is a 116-acre campus of verdant lawns, winding paths, statuesque trees, a wooded natural wetland preserve, and a spring-fed lake frequented by migratory birds and other wildlife. Reed is a short bicycle, bus, and light rail ride from the energy and excitement of downtown Portland, which is widely cited as the nation's most livable urban center. Portland boasts a wealth of diverse cultural, entertainment, shopping, and dining opportunities in an environment characterized by a combination of youthful exuberance and Pacific Northwest nonchalance. The Oregon Coast is 90 minutes to the west and Mt. Hood 90 minutes to the east where Reed has its own ski cabin.

On the campus itself, century-old brick Tudor gothic buildings are interspersed with newer traditionally designed and remodeled facilities. The library, classrooms, and laboratories resonate with the history of decades of inquiry and discovery, supported with modern technology.

CAMPUS FACILITIES & EQUIPMENT

The Reed College campus was established on a tract of land known in 1910 as Crystal Springs Farm. In a park-like setting near the heart of the city, the rolling lawns and open spaces of Reed's 116-acre campus include some of the largest and finest specimen trees in the Portland area.

The social center of the college is the Gray Campus Center. It includes a commons building, student union, kitchen, dining room, private meeting rooms, student activities offices, bookstore, and mail services.

At the physical center of campus is the canyon, a beautiful wooded upland surrounding a spring-fed lake and emergent marsh. A walking trail around the lake provides numerous opportunities to observe migratory birds and other woodland wildlife. The college recently built a fish passageway that creates a link from the upper Reed Lake area to the Crystal Springs stream below.

In fall 2013, Reed opened a new Performing Arts Building, representing a major step forward in the College's commitment to the important role the arts have played throughout Reed's first 100 years. For the first time in Reed's history, the departments of music, dance, and theatre are housed in one building that includes rehearsal and performance space, offices, scene and costume studios, collaborative spaces, and a multimedia lab.

Housing at Reed includes traditional residence halls, as well as theme dorms, co-ops, and language houses.

OFF-CAMPUS OPPORTUNITIES

Reed undergraduates may participate in a number of domestic exchange and study abroad opportunities. Domestic programs include: Howard University in Washington, D.C.; Sarah Lawrence College in New York; and Sea Education Association in Massachusetts. In addition, Reed provides study-abroad opportunities for students in Australia, Argentina, China, Costa Rica, Cuba, Ecuador, Egypt, France, Germany, Greece, Hungary, Ireland, Israel, Italy, Morocco, Kenya, Lebanon, Palestine, Russia, South Africa, Spain, Turks and Caicos, and the United Kingdom. Students may also arrange independent study plans in consultation with appropriate faculty members.

ACADEMICS

The curriculum at Reed is both demanding and wide-ranging. Through required studies, Reed students receive a solid grounding in the liberal arts and sciences.

All freshmen must complete Humanities 110, an immersive examination of the Ancient Greek, Roman, North African, and Mesopotamian canons from multiple analytic perspectives. Distribution requirements set a substantial portion of a student's curriculum for the first two years at Reed. Freshmen and sophomores must complete two courses in each of the four major divisions of the college. Beyond Humanities 110, no specific courses are required; students are free to pursue their interests within the boundaries of the requirements.

Reed juniors take a comprehensive qualifying exam in their major to allow faculty members the chance to evaluate and assist in the student's readiness for his or her senior thesis project. The required senior thesis is the capstone experience of a Reed education. Every senior produces an original independent research project over the course of the final year.

Reed strongly believes that learning should be undertaken for its own sake, not for the sake of letter grades. Accordingly, students do not receive grade reports unless they wish to. A student's transcript does include letter grades for all courses taken, but students can better gauge their progress through professors' written evaluations of their work and one-on-one meetings with faculty. Most prefer this system, which greatly reduces competition among students and allows them to focus on the content of their academic work.

MAJORS & DEGREES OFFERED

Reed confers the bachelor of arts degree in 38 traditional academic departments and interdisciplinary combinations across a wide selection of fields. Approval of an interdisciplinary program (linking two or more disciplines) is reviewed by the student's adviser and the departments concerned.

Reed offers a number of 3-2 (dual degree) programs; these allow undergraduates to earn a three-year bachelor's degree from Reed, then earn a professional degree in engineering, computer science, or forestry from a cooperating institution (Caltech, Columbia, Duke, RPI) in two additional years.

TUITION, ROOM, BOARD, FEES

Tuition for the 2016-2017 academic year is $51,850. A $300 student body fee is added. Room and board is an additional $13.150, bringing the yearly total cost to $65,300.

FINANCIAL AID

Reed College meets 100% of the demonstrated need for its incoming students and continuing students who maintain good academic standing and who meet all other requirements of the aid process (such as application deadlines). The college maintains a need-based assistance program that allows students of all economic backgrounds to attend the college. For the incoming class of 2020, the average financial aid package including grants, loans, and work opportunities was approximately $40,290. Reed students' average graduating loan debt for all four years is $19,528, well below the national average. The college is the primary source of grant money for its students. Reed also administers federal grants and a number of other awards. Campus employment and work-study programs also figure into many aid packages. Roughly 50% of Reed undergraduates receive financial aid.

STUDENT ORGANIZATIONS & ACTIVITIES

Reed maintains inclusivity in all organizations and activities, so the college has no fraternities or sororities and no NCAA or NAIA athletic teams (more about sports below). All campus organizations are student-created and student-run. Student organizations must lobby the Student Senate for funding annually, after which the Senate oversees a vote in which the entire student body decides what organizations should be funded. Thus, the number and nature of campus organizations at Reed changes every year to meet current student interests. Instead of NCAA or NAIA competition, students participate in sports on an informal basis. Intramural sports and club sports proliferate in basketball, fencing, rugby, sailing, soccer, squash and ultimate Frisbee. A three-semester physical education requirement underscores the importance of physical fitness and the balance of healthy mind and body.

ADMISSIONS

Reed seeks students who demonstrate a commitment to learning and to the ideals embodied by a rigorous and stimulating liberal arts education. Freshman and transfer applications are welcome. The ideal incoming class is diverse in its range of talents, interests, ethnic and socioeconomic backgrounds, and perspectives, and comprised of students who share a common passion for academic inquiry. Successful applicants have pursued a rigorous secondary school curriculum that includes honors and advanced courses and typically includes 4 years of English, at least 3 years of a foreign or classical language, 3 to 4 years of mathematics, 3 to 4 years of science, and 3 to 4 years of history or social studies. Because secondary school curricula vary widely in quality and content, Reed sets no fixed requirements in this area. With rare exceptions, incoming students have obtained a secondary school diploma prior to enrollment. The admissions committee sets no "cutoff points" for high school grades, college grades (for transfer students), or standardized test scores. Reed seeks candidates who demonstrate excellence of character, motivation, intellectual curiosity, individual responsibility, and social consciousness. The admission committee recognizes the importance of creating a diverse community in which individual differences contribute to the vitality of the campus. Reed recommends a personal interview but an interview is not required. Early Decision applications should arrive at Reed by November 15 (Option 1) or December 20 (Option 2). Early Decision at Reed is binding: students who are admitted under Early Decision are expected to matriculate. Early Action applications should arrive at Reed by November 15. The deadline for regular freshman admission applications is January 1. Transfer candidates should apply no later than March 1.

REGIS COLLEGE

AT A GLANCE

Regis is a leading Catholic, co-ed university that prepares students to succeed in an evolving, global world. Founded by the Sisters of Saint Joseph, Regis students benefit from the unique perspective of a values-based education that is integrated with cutting-edge technology and opportunities.

Regis offers a full range of innovative degrees from bachelor's to master's and doctorate level programs. Its close proximity to Boston provides students with access to internships and clinicals at world-class hospitals and research centers, leading corporations, and non-profit organizations.

LOCATION & ENVIRONMENT

Regis is a suburban university located on a beautiful 132-acre campus in Weston, Massachusetts, just 12 miles from downtown Boston.

Regis guarantees four-year, on-campus housing for undergraduates, with approximately 70 percent of students living on campus. Students are able to take classes at several other nearby universities as part of our cross-registration program.

A complimentary shuttle transports students to surrounding areas and public transportation for easy access to work, internships, and social engagements.

The Campus Experience

Regis' campus features modern suite-style residences, beautiful green spaces, and a recently renovated learning commons. Academic facilities include state-of-the-art medical imaging labs, nursing simulation centers, and occupational therapy labs.

Regis' Athletic Facility features an indoor and outdoor complex. Indoor facilities include three fitness rooms, a six-lane swimming pool, gymnasium, athletic training room, and team room. Outdoor facilities consist of a turf field surface for field hockey, lacrosse, and soccer; an eight-lane track around the field; six tennis courts; and a softball diamond with a dirt infield and grass outfield.

OFF-CAMPUS OPPORTUNITIES

Regis is located just 12 miles from Boston, the nation's ultimate college town. Students have direct access to exciting events and attractions such as Fenway Park, home of the Boston Red Sox; the TD Garden, home of the Boston Bruins; the Museum of Fine Arts; and Prudential and Copley shopping districts. Regis is also located 4 miles from Waltham and only minutes away from restaurants, shops, and businesses.

The Center for Internships and Career Placement provides a variety of career-development and job-search services for Regis students and alumni. Career Center staff assists students and graduates in planning careers, securing internships, developing resumes, implementing effective job-search strategies, identifying employers in various industries, and exploring graduate-school options. In addition, the office maintains listings of internship opportunities, as well as full-time, part-time, and summer jobs for both on and off-campus positions. Internships have proven invaluable in the careers and academic development of Regis students.

Regis believes that internships allow students to apply classroom learning to the world of work and enable students to explore various careers while developing marketable skills. Regis requires students to participate in at least one internship before graduating. 97% of the class of 2015 had secured professional employment and/or attended graduate school six months after graduation.

ACADEMICS

Regis empowers students to take leadership roles in their education. Majors at Regis are uniquely designed to offer students academic support and flexibility as they complete their studies.

Regis offers several special academic opportunities that allow students to explore subjects that they are interested in, customizing their learning experience. Students can extend their learning beyond the classroom through various methods, including seminars, off-campus study, global experiences, individualized study, pre-professional programs, special cooperative degree programs, and academic honors programs.

A Classroom Without Walls

Regis is committed to providing an academic experience that is increasingly enriched by technological resources. Through the iPad initiative, all students are provided iPads to facilitate collaboration and enhance learning.

The campus network provides access to campus apps and the internet through 24/7 wireless and wired connectivity, spanning across campus in all classrooms, learning spaces, residential halls, and exterior spaces.

A Global Perspective

Whether students are interested in a semester-, academic year-, or week-long trip, the Office of Global Connections provides personalized support to ensure that students have an enriching global experience.

Regis is directly affiliated with Regent's College in London, England; University College Cork in Cork, Ireland; Assumption College Rome in Rome, Italy; and Kyoto Notre Dame University in Kyoto, Japan.

Students can also participate in faculty-led programs that supplement coursework. Trips range from one to three weeks and have taken place in Italy, England, Cuba, and Belize.

Regis faculty members are exceptionally accomplished and actively engaged in their disciplines, conducting research, publishing books and articles, and serving as leaders in in their areas of expertise. Interaction between faculty and students is a hallmark of the Regis educational experience. With an 11:1 student-to-faculty ratio, faculty members get to know each student and are instrumental in advising them with everything from research and graduate school programs to internships and job opportunities.

MAJORS

Regis is a comprehensive university offering a wide selection of majors across three schools: Arts & Sciences, Health Sciences, and Nursing. Majors include: Biology, Biomedical Engineering, Communication, Criminal Justice Studies, Security, Diagnostic Medical Sonography, Education, English, Environmental Sustainability, Exercise Science, Global Business Management, Interdisciplinary Studies in the Humanities, Neuroscience, Nuclear Medicine, Nursing, Nutrition, Psychology, Public Health, Social Work, and Sports Management.

Pre-professional and special programs include 3+3 Law Degree, Pre-Dental, Pre-Healthcare Advising with Occupational Therapy, Physical Therapy, and Physician Assistant Tracks, Pre-Law, Pre-Medical, and Pre-Veterinary.

Fast Track to Master's 4+1 Program

Regis offers a five-year combined bachelor's and master's track for certain areas of study, including Communication, Education, Heritage Studies, Health Administration, and Regulatory and Clinical Research Management.

° Some restrictions apply

Articulation Agreements

Regis has a variety of articulation agreements for undergraduate students wishing to transfer in for a bachelor's degree and for students wishing to earn a graduate degree after finishing a bachelor's degree at their home school.

Regis has agreements for direct entry into select graduate programs once a student completes the bachelor's degree at Regis. Graduate schools include Saint George's University in Grenada School of Medicine and School of Veterinary Medicine; Salve Regina University; and Western New England University School of Law.

Honors Program

The honors program at Regis provides qualified students with an intellectually stimulating and challenging academic experience that extends beyond the classroom, as leaders in both campus activities and community service. Students in the honors program complete a total of six honors courses, including a required honors seminar and five other courses. With prior approval, upper-division honors students may also enroll in designated graduate courses. Honors program students provide tutoring for other Regis students, accompanied by a seminar in tutoring techniques and instruction methods. They also provide a substantial number of hours of voluntary service to the organization of their choice.

Writing Program

The Regis Writing Program offers students the opportunity to practice writing for learning and thinking, to communicate their ideas in a thorough, clear way, to affect their audiences through persuasive writing, and to give creative expression to various levels of thinking. The fundamental goal of the Writing Program is to help students develop and clearly communicate their ideas in writing for a variety of audiences and purposes using proper format, grammar, punctuation, and mechanics.

Academic Support

The Academic Center for Excellence (ACE) offers comprehensive support services to empower Regis students of all abilities to enhance their academic development, achieve degree completion, and maximize their full potential. Services include academic coaching; writing assistance, tutoring support for courses with quantitative components, peer tutoring, and access to live online tutoring.

First-Year Seminar

First-Year Seminar (FYS) is an essential part of all incoming students' fall semester. FYS introduces new students to the Regis history and heritage, build their academic and social skills, engage in a variety of co-curricular experiences, and participate in a challenge-based learning project. FYS is taught by faculty members from across Regis who also serve as the student's academic advisor during his or her entire first year. During the spring semester, students stay with their FYS classmates and are enrolled in a linked-course that meets one of the Regis Core Curriculum requirements.

STUDENT ORGANIZATIONS & ACTIVITIES

Students have many different opportunities to become involved on campus, from joining one of the many active clubs and organizations to playing intramural sports such as volleyball, flag football, and dodgeball.

Regis's student body represents a diverse mixture of backgrounds and heritages. 30 percent of the population consists of minority and international students, and 40 percent are first-generation college students.

The Office of Student Programming and Leadership sponsors many events throughout the semester, including musical and comedy performances, cultural and sporting events, a monthly "Pizza with the President," and other social get-togethers. Additionally, the office coordinates a number of Regis's traditional events, including Welcome Week, Regis Fest Family Weekend, Halloween, Senior Week, Spring Weekend, and the annual Christmas Tree Lighting.

Health and Wellness

Regis has a comprehensive Health Center on campus which provides students with medical care, including counseling services. Health Services also offers health education programs and events throughout the year.

Athletics

Regis in a member of the NCAA: Division III New England Commonwealth Conference (NECC), and is transitioning to Great Northeast Athletics Conference (GNAC) beginning with the 2017-18 academic year. The Regis Pride compete in 18 varsity sports (10 women's: basketball, cross country, field hockey, lacrosse, soccer, softball, swimming & diving, tennis, track & field, volleyball. 8 men's: basketball, cross country, lacrosse, soccer, swimming & diving, tennis, track & field; and volleyball). In the 2015-2016 season, six teams won conference championships. Student athletes at Regis are involved in community service and have an active Student Athlete Advisory Council (SAAC).

TUITION, ROOM, BOARD, FEES

2017-2018 Academic Year:

Tuition: $39,820

Room and Board: $14,740

Student Health Insurance: $2,123

At Regis, we are committed to making an investment in a student's potential. More than 90 percent of our full-time, incoming first-year students receive some type of financial aid. The average award not including federal and state funding is $20,000.

We offer educational opportunities to students regardless of their ability to pay. The decision to accept a student is made regardless of financial circumstances, and only after acceptance are financial aid applications considered. Students are only required to complete the FAFSA.

FINANCIAL AID

Merit scholarships are awarded upon acceptance to the university and federal aid eligibility is evaluated using the FAFSA. Additional scholarship opportunities are available to students who graduate from select parochial schools, students with siblings at the university, and students who receive the Alumni Sponsor Award.

The Financial Aid team at Regis works with students on payment plan opportunities through Tuition Management Systems. Additionally, Regis students have the opportunity to use SALT program, a free and interactive money-management tool to help students with their financial planning.

ADMISSIONS PROCESS

Students seeking acceptance to Regis submit the online Common Application. In addition to the application, first-year applicants are required to submit:

- Official secondary school transcript
- One signed letter of recommendation on official letterhead from a secondary school counselor/college counselor or teacher
- Application fee of $50
- Regis is a Test Optional institution and only requires SAT/ACT scores for those students seeking admission into the Nursing program, or homeschooled students. The SAT CEEB code is 3723; the ACT code is 1886.

RIPON COLLEGE

AT A GLANCE

Established in 1851, Ripon College is Wisconsin's best-value private college and a national leader in liberal arts education, devoted to ensuring every student realizes their unique potential. Ripon's five-course Catalyst curriculum rigorously develops the 21st-century skills employers seek while streamlining the path to graduation. Students enjoy extensive freedom to pursue their passions and craft their own academic program of study. Students are overwhelmingly satisfied with the amount of personalized attention they receive from devoted faculty and staff throughout their time on campus. Within six months of graduation, 96 percent of alumni are employed, in graduate school or student-teaching.

Ripon is a member of the prestigious Associated Colleges of the Midwest (ACM). We compete athletically as part of the Midwest Conference and offer 21 NCAA Division III varsity teams.

Ripon has a student to faculty ratio of 11 to 1, and the average class size is fewer than 20 students. As a matter of fact, 76 percent of classes at Ripon have fewer than 20 students, and 92 percent of classes have fewer than 30 students.

LOCATION & ENVIRONMENT

The College is located in the historic city of Ripon, Wisconsin—a friendly, safe community of just under 8,000 people, 80 miles northwest of Milwaukee, 70 miles southwest of Green Bay, 73 miles northeast of Madison, 180 miles northwest of Chicago and 255 miles southeast of the Twin Cities in Minnesota. The nearest airport is 40 minutes away in Appleton, Wisconsin.

The campus spans 250 tree-lined acres and includes 27 buildings—10 of which are listed on the National Register of Historic Places. A sustainable campus, Ripon is home to the Ceresco Prairie Conservancy with 130 acres of native prairie, oak savanna and wetland habitat in the making.

CAMPUS FACILITIES & EQUIPMENT

The Ripon campus is adjacent to downtown Ripon and includes tree-lined walkways and 27 buildings—10 of which are listed on the National Register of Historic Places. Historic limestone buildings are complemented with more modern structures and continual updates, such as an apartment-style residence hall, a $22.5 million renovation and expansion of athletics, health and wellness facilities, and upgrades to the student union, dining facilities, and student activity spaces.

The athletics, health and wellness facilities are undergoing a $22 million renovation and expansion that will feature new classrooms, an atrium and state-of-the-art fitness center, and an NCAA indoor track, performance courts, fitness studios, athletic training center, and other upgrades that are set to be completed in August 2017.

Ripon College provides a secure, high-speed (802.11ac) WiFi network in every building on campus. In addition, a state of the art fiber optic network (10 Gb/s) connects all academic buildings, administrative buildings and residence halls. Connectivity to the Internet and Internet2 is provided by WiscNet at a speed of 1 Gb/s.

Student, faculty, and staff are issued a G Suite account that offers a variety of productivity tools (Gmail, Calendar, Drive, Docs, Hangouts…) to enhance campus collaboration and communication. Multi-functional devices (MFDs) are located in every academic and administrative building to service the campus printing, copying and scanning needs. The College also has a 3D printer that several faculty have incorporated into their course curricula.

Open-use computer labs are located across campus, offering both Windows and Mac OS devices, projectors, and MFDs.

Ripon College has partnered with Apogee to provide a cutting-edge cable TV/video solution. With the revolutionary IPTV service, Stream2, students can view HD content live, on-demand, or recorded (20 hours of DVR storage per user) on their laptops, tablets, and smartphones.

Library staff provide friendly, efficient circulation, reference, instruction and interlibrary loan services that aid in research. The library also houses the College archives, a computer lab, digital media stations and more than a 25 online databases. Library holdings include access to over 300,000 physical and electronic books, and 55,000 periodicals.

C.J. Rodman Center for the Arts is home to a theater with a state-of-the-art computerized lighting system, a recital hall with one of only 50 existing Bedient organs, an art gallery, a high-tech lab and a sculpture garden.

Bovay's Study Bar & Mercantile opened in March 2017 in a historic building in downtown Ripon. This unique venue features a 30-student high-tech classroom, office space, a study bar with barista coffee service, a mercantile with official Ripon College apparel and gifts, and flexible meeting space. Bovay's is open late into the evening and features barista coffee service during peak study hours. Student interns working in the space will benefit from hands-on experiential training in marketing, merchandising and small business management.

OFF-CAMPUS OPPORTUNITIES

U.S. or abroad? Three weeks, one semester, two semesters? Choose from more than 40 programs, each officially sanctioned by and affiliated with Ripon. Although most programs are connected with a major or minor program, all are open to every Ripon student, regardless of major. Scholarships are available to pursue off-campus study.

U.S. Programs: Chicago, Illinois - Chicago: Arts (ACM), Chicago, Illinois - Chicago: Business, Entrepreneurship and Society (ACM), Chicago, Illinois - Chicago: Urban Studies (ACM), Chicago, Illinois - Newberry Seminar in the Humanities (ACM), Chicago, Illinois - Teach Chicago! Program, Chicago, Illinois - Urban Education: Student Teaching (ACM), Knoxville, Tennessee - Oak Ridge Science Semester (ACM), Nashville, Tennessee - Fisk-Ripon Exchange Program, Southwest, USA - American Indian Reservation Project, Washington, D.C. - Washington Semester, Woods Hole, Massachusetts - SEA: Sea Education Association, Woods Hole, Massachusetts - SES: Semester in Environmental Science, Marine Biology Laboratory.

International Programs: Argentina - Córdoba, Botswana - Development in Southern Africa (ACM), Brazil - Semester Exchange Program (ACM), Costa Rica - Community Engagement in Public Health, Education & the Environment (ACM), Costa Rica - Field Research in the Environment, Social Sciences & Humanities (ACM), England/Italy - London & Florence: Arts in Context (ACM), France -Montpellier, France - Paris, Germany - Bonn Program, Hungary - Budapest, India - Pune: Culture, Traditions & Globalization (ACM), India - Pune & Jaipur: Development Studies & Hindi Language (ACM), International Education - Indiana University Global Gateway Program, Italy - Coldigioco: Earth and Environment, Italy - Florence: Arts, Humanities & Culture (ACM), Japan - Tokyo (ACM), Jordan - Amman (ACM-AMIDEAST), Russia - St. Petersburg, Scotland - University of St. Andrews, Spain - Alicante, Spain - Madrid, Spain - Seville, Spain - Toledo, Tanzania - Ecology & Human Origins (ACM), Wales - Bangor, Bangor University, Wales - Swansea University Program.

Ripon College offers three-week Liberal Arts In Focus courses in May and August. Taught in short, intensive blocks, In Focus courses are designed as immersion experiences to provide a bridge between the theory and content of disciplines. Recent courses have included history lessons in Italy, intensive biology field studies in Costa Rica and the Wilderness Field Station near Ely, Minnesota, and a unique English course in Great Britain covering children's fantasy literature from Beatrix Potter to Harry Potter.

ACADEMICS

Our innovative new curriculum, Catalyst, began rolling out to the first-year class during the fall semester of 2016. The five-course curriculum rigorously develops the 21st-century skills that employers seek while streamlining the path to graduation. Catalyst ensures students have extensive freedom and are able to complete multiple majors and minors, study abroad and hold internships in four years.

Ripon's liberal arts curriculum introduces students to a wide variety of disciplines. About 40 percent of our students complete double or triple majors, while some create special self-designed majors. Hallmarks of a Ripon education are excellent communications skills, both written and oral; critical-thinking and problem-solving skills; and the opportunity to explore serious research pursuits alongside faculty as an undergraduate, no matter what your major.

A Ripon education will take you anywhere! You could study psychology and play basketball at Ripon, and then become a seven-time Grammy winner like jazz singer Al Jarreau (1962). You could become a Nobel Prize winner in economics like Oliver Williamson (1954). You could guide the space shuttle into orbit like Jeff Bantle (1980), a chief flight director with NASA, or become an international opera star like Gail Dobish (1976). Perhaps you'll set records in medical science like neonatologist Dr. John Muraskas (1978), who is on record for saving the world's smallest premature baby, or cover world events, like Richard Threlkeld (1959), former Moscow correspondent for CBS News. You could make your mark in the world of entertainment like Harrison Ford (1964), Spencer Tracy (1924) or Justin Neibank (1978). Or perhaps you'll end up studying at Oxford University as a Rhodes Scholar like Zach Morris (2002), who also found time to play touch football with former President Bill Clinton and spent an evening at Buckingham Palace with the Queen.

MAJORS

Ripon College offers a four-year graduation guarantee with 31 majors and 42 minors, including a variety of fast-track pre-professional programs. Every student graduates with a concentration in Applied Innovation upon completing the five-course Catalyst curriculum.

Majors include Anthropology, Art History, Biology, Business Management, Chemistry, Chemistry-Biology, Communication, Economics, Educational Studies, English, Environmental Studies, Exercise Science/Athletic Training Track, Foreign Languages, Global Studies, History, Latin American & Caribbean Studies, Mathematics, Music, Philosophy, Physical Education, Physical Science, Politics and Government, Psychobiology, Psychology, Recreation Physical Education, Religion, Sociology, Spanish, Sport Management, Studio Art, and Theatre.

Minors include American Studies, Anthropology, Applied Communication, ARMS (Ancient, Renaissance & Medieval Studies), Art History, Astronomy, Biology, Business Management, Chemistry, Classical Studies, Coaching, Communication, Criminal Justice, Dramatic Literature, Economics, Educational Studies, English, Entrepreneurship, Environmental Biology, Francophone Studies, French, Health, History, Latin, Latin American & Caribbean Studies, Law and Society, Mathematics, Military Leadership, Music, National Security Studies, Nonprofit Management, Philosophy, Physics, Politics and Government, Psychology, Religion, Socially Responsible Leadership, Sociology, Spanish, Studio Art, Theatre Production, Women's and Gender Studies

Pre-professional programs include Government Service, Journalism, Library and Information Science, Military Leadership, Ministry, Pre-Engineering, Pre-Law, Pre-Med & Health Sciences

(medicine, dentistry, veterinary medicine, optometry, podiatry, physical therapy, pharmacy, nursing, chiropractic medicine, sports medicine), and Social Work.

Teacher certification is offered in Early Childhood, Elementary, Middle/Junior High, Secondary, and Bilingual/ESL. In addition, Ripon offers licensure in 21 subject areas. Teacher certification programs approved by the Wisconsin Department of Public Instruction prepare students for licensure at the early childhood/middle childhood level (grades PK through 5), the middle childhood/early adolescence level (grades 1 through 8), and the early adolescence/adolescence level (grades 6 through 12). The educational studies department also offers PK-12 certification programs in art, foreign language (French and Spanish), music, physical education, physical education and health, and theatre (pending program approval).

TUITION, ROOM, BOARD, FEES

Pursuing a college degree is an important investment in your future. That's why at Ripon College your family's financial circumstances will never affect our admission decision. We provide 100 percent of our students with the financial assistance necessary to graduate and make it our mission to ensure a great economic value per every dollar spent. Tuition is $41,535, room and board is $8,156, and fees are $300, for a total cost of $49,991.

FINANCIAL AID

We are proud to offer our students competitive packages with funding from many sources: merit-based scholarships, need-based grants, educational loans, work study and scholarships from outside organizations. Academic scholarships range from $16,000 to $32,000 per year.

STUDENT ORGANIZATIONS & ACTIVITIES

The faculty committee on academic standards establishes the criteria for admission. The school considers a variety of factors. An admission application and secondary school record are required for admission while standardized test scores (SAT or ACT), recommendations, a written essay, and extracurricular or community service activities may also be considered. Ripon's admission process reflects the personal attention students can expect to receive during their college careers, and applicants are encouraged to provide any additional information that they consider helpful.

From pre-professional programs to paintballing, Ripon College hosts more than 60 student-run clubs and organizations. Students at Ripon are encouraged to lead the programs, supported by the Student Senate's activity fee. This allows students to collaborate together in conceiving, organizing, marketing and developing unique activities.

In addition, Ripon offers a variety of intramural sports throughout the year, including: kickball, dodgeball, flag football, indoor soccer, inner tube water polo, basketball, bowling, volleyball and aerobics.

Ripon's NCAA Division III Intercollegiate Teams compete in the Midwest Conference:

Men's varsity sports: baseball, basketball, cross-country, cycling, football, soccer, swimming and diving, tennis, and indoor and outdoor track and field.

Women's varsity sports: basketball, dance, cross-country, cycling, soccer, softball, swimming and diving, tennis, indoor and outdoor track and field.

ADMISSIONS PROCESS

Ripon encourages applications from those students who are best prepared to benefit from and contribute to the academic and extracurricular programs that it offers. In evaluating applications, attention is paid to evidence of academic achievement, as indicated both by the distribution of courses taken in secondary school and by performance in those courses.

The faculty committee on academic standards establishes the criteria for admission. Ripon is now test optional. We will consider test scores if you elect to submit them.

For more information contact:

Admission Office

Ripon College

300 Seward Street

PO Box 248

Ripon, WI 54971

Telephone: 800-947-4766

E-mail: adminfo@ripon.edu

ROCHESTER INSTITUTE OF TECHNOLOGY

AT A GLANCE

As one of the world's leading career-oriented, technological universities, RIT's goal is to prepare students for 21st century career success.

RIT is a place where brilliant minds assemble and collaborate, where they pool together their individual talents across disciplines in service of creative projects and innovative solutions. It is a vibrant community teeming with students collaborating with experts and specialists; a hub of innovation and creativity. As one of the nation's largest private universities, RIT has an unmatched array of specialized, career-oriented academic programs that attracts designers, artists, photographers, journalists, and filmmakers on the one hand, and scientists, engineers, computing scientists, social scientists, and entrepreneurs on the other. It is a launching pad for a brilliant career, and a highly unique state of mind.

LOCATION & ENVIRONMENT

RIT's 1,300-acre campus is located in the suburbs, about six miles from downtown Rochester, NY. More than 7,100 diverse, creative, ambitious students live on campus in residence halls or apartments, and the self-contained, suburban location gives the campus a safe, residential atmosphere. RIT also maintains locations in China, Croatia, Dubai, and Kosovo.

CAMPUS FACILITIES & EQUIPMENT

The campus is filled with the latest equipment, software, laboratories, and conveniences to give students the tools they need to excel. RIT offers academic facilities that are rarely matched on other university campuses.

OFF-CAMPUS OPPORTUNITIES

Rochester provides a perfect setting--it's large enough to provide the dining, shopping, and night life opportunities found in a bigger city, yet small and friendly enough to be inviting and accessible. In fact, Rochester was ranked 10th best among large cities in the Northeast in a recent Money magazine Best Places to Live in America survey. The greater Rochester area is home to more than 1 million people, making it the third-largest metropolitan area in New York State. Rochester's reputation as an active and inventive community is supported by extensive cultural and intellectual opportunities.

ACADEMICS

At RIT, some of the world's most talented, ambitious, and creative students find a remarkable array of academic programs; diverse, talented and accessible faculty; sophisticated facilities; an unusual emphasis on experiential learning; and a vibrant, connected community that is home to students from more than 100 countries. Excelling in teaching and research, RIT's faculty are passionate about their role in the classroom and in their field. RIT's faculty are diverse, innovative and resourceful, and engage students in the process of personal and professional discovery. RIT's nine colleges offer more than 90 undergraduate programs. To complement their specialized field of study, students select from more than 80 minors available at RIT. Students can also complete a master's degree in five years through one of the university's accelerated BS/MS or 4+1 MBA programs.

Since 1912, the hallmark of an RIT has been experiential education. RIT was among the first universities in the world to offer cooperative education, and its co-op program is now one of the largest in the world. Last year more than 4,400 students completed nearly 6,000 co-op work assignments by alternating periods of study on campus with paid employment in more than 2,200 firms across the United States and overseas. Experiential learning also includes internships, study abroad, and undergraduate research.

Regardless of background or academic interest, students find that RIT offers a stimulating environment for intellectual and personal growth.

MAJORS

Few universities provide RIT's variety of career-oriented programs. RIT's nine colleges offer more than 90 undergraduate programs in areas such as engineering, computing, information technology, engineering technology, business, hospitality, art, design, science, psychology, public policy, game design, photography, film and animation, health sciences, and biomedical sciences.

TUITION, ROOM, BOARD, FEES

For 2016-17, tuition and fees cost $38,568; room and board averaged $12,274; and books, transportation, and other expenses averaged $2,026.

FINANCIAL AID

RIT's Office of Financial Aid and Scholarships assists students and their families in identifying sources of financial aid to help meet the cost of a quality education. Currently, more than 12,000 RIT undergraduate and graduate students receive over $300 million dollars in financial assistance from federal, state, and institutional resources, in the form of scholarships, grants, loans, and part-time employment.

STUDENT ORGANIZATIONS & ACTIVITIES

The backgrounds and interests of RIT students contribute in many ways to the quality of campus life. With students from all 50 states and more than 100 countries, RIT is a living-learning environment rich in diversity in classrooms, residence halls, and everywhere else on campus. RIT attracts students from every state and approximately 2,700 international students from more than 100 countries. Embodying our commitment to diversity, nearly 3,200 students of color have elected to study at RIT. Adding a social and educational dynamic not found at any other university are more than 1,100 deaf and hard-of-hearing students supported by RIT's National Technical Institute for the Deaf.

Students take their academic pursuits seriously, but they'll be the first to tell you that they are passionate about life outside of the lectures, labs and studios. RIT is alive with energy and excitement-24/7. A number of campus organizations and student services focus on the unique needs and interests of minority, deaf, and international students at RIT. You'll have plenty of opportunity to interact with a mind expanding mix of people. More than 7,100 full-time students live on campus in residence halls or apartments, and our self-contained, suburban location creates a safe and secure atmosphere. Clubs and organizations exist to bring students of similar interest together and provide them with opportunities to become effective leaders. These groups enhance the quality of student life by fostering social interaction, leadership development, school spirit and an affinity to RIT. Clubs and Organizations promote activities, diversity, service and learning outside of the classroom. Currently there are approximately 300 active clubs, 10 Major Student Organizations, and 30 Greek Organizations on campus. Last year, clubs and organizations held nearly 1,300 events on campus.

RIT's intercollegiate teams have a history of excellence, recording many impressive seasons and capturing a number of conference and national championships. The men's and women's hockey teams are Division I. The remainder of the intercollegiate teams competes at Division III. RIT teams are members of the National Collegiate Athletic Association (NCAA), the Eastern College Athletic Conference (ECAC), the Atlantic Hockey Association, the College Hockey America, the Liberty League, and the New York State Women's Collegiate Athletic Association.

ADMISSIONS PROCESS

RIT seeks a diverse and multicultural student body. Entering students come from a variety of geographic, social, cultural, economic, and ethnic backgrounds. Admission to RIT is competitive, but the admission process is a personal one. The university is interested in learning about students' interests, abilities, and goals in order to provide the best information and guidance as they select the college that is right for them. Factors considered in our admission decisions include, but are not limited to, past high school and/or college performance (particularly in required academic subjects), admission test scores, competitiveness of high school or previous college, and academic program selected.

Students applying for freshman admission for the fall semester (September) may apply through an Early Decision Plan or Regular Decision Plan. The Early Decision Plan is designed for students who consider RIT their first-choice college and wish to make an early commitment regarding admission. Early Decision requires that candidates file their applications and supporting documents by November 15. Regular Decision applicants should file the required application materials by January 15.

SAINT ANSELM COLLEGE

AT A GLANCE

Saint Anselm College encourages you not only to challenge yourself academically, but also to lead a life that is both creative and generous. Saint Anselm students are active both in and out of the classroom.

Saint Anselm College prepares students for life. With a liberal arts education, they're ready for real career experience, for the challenges that lie ahead. They take their Saint Anselm experience with them to think critically, communicate effectively, and solve problems creatively.

Saint Anselm graduates are CEOs, doctors, engineers, teachers, marketers, and researchers. They are humanitarians, healers, and philanthropists. They graduate Saint Anselm with the drive to achieve, empowered to make the world a better place.

In fact, 99% of the class of 2016 was employed, in graduate school, or engaged in service within 6 months of graduation.

The Princeton Review ranks Saint Anselm as one of the country's best institutions for an undergraduate education and number 8 out of 3,000 national colleges for its food.

LOCATION & ENVIRONMENT

Saint Anselm College is located on 380 acres in Manchester, N.H., the largest city in the state. Just minutes from downtown Manchester, students can find great restaurants and coffee shops and all the venues a small city has to offer, a theatre, museum, minor league baseball and hockey teams, and the Verizon Arena to name a few. The Manchester-Boston Regional Airport is also just minutes from campus. The college is an hour drive from Boston, the seacoast, and the White Mountains.

CAMPUS FACILITIES & EQUIPMENT

There's much to see and do on campus from open skate nights at Sullivan Arena to spring concerts on the quad. Academic buildings including the Goulet Science Center and Gadbois Hall house innovative labs where remarkable research happens every day. There are cell culture labs, climate controlled environmental chambers, a green house, a sleep lab, SimMan labs in Nursing, and more. In the library, students have access to a range of workspaces for individuals and groups in addition to technological advances.

Recreational facilities include the Carr Center with basketball courts and the recently renovated 9,000-square-foot, three-level fitness center. Saint Anselm College boasts some of the top athletic facilities in the Northeast-10 Conference. The college's 20 intercollegiate athletic teams play all of their home contests on campus (with the exception of the golf and alpine ski teams) whether at Grappone Stadium, Sullivan Arena, or Melucci Field.

Ninety-one percent of Saint Anselm students live on campus in traditional residence halls, suites, townhouses, or apartments. A new 47,000-square-foot, 150-bed residence hall opened in August 2014 offering students an innovative, living-learning community. Whether students live on campus or commute, everyone has access to Saint Anselm College's amazing food, named 8th in the nation by the Princeton Review.

Saint Anselm is home to the New Hampshire Institute of Politics & Political Library (NHIOP), which offers unparalleled opportunities for students to be in the front row of the democratic process. It's auditorium, West Wing, TV-studio, and classrooms are where students meet today's most prominent political policy thinkers and researchers, journalists and authors, scientists, industry executives, global leaders and presidential candidates. Have we mentioned all the U.S. presidents in the last 50 years have visited Saint Anselm?

OFF-CAMPUS OPPORTUNITIES

At Saint Anselm College, a liberal arts education gives students a solid foundation for any career but opportunities out-of-the-classroom give students a competitive edge and real job experience.

Students find all kinds of experiential learning opportunities at Saint Anselm College including internships, research, study abroad, and volunteering. Students of all majors and interests can find opportunities for internships through the Office of Career Services, which also brings employers to campus and advises students throughout their job search.

Internships are offered in Boston, M.A., New York City, N.Y., Washington, D.C. and Manchester, N.H. Recent internships opportunities include: The White House, The Boston Bruins, United States Secret Service, Fidelity Investments, The United States Senate, Fox News, and the American Cancer Society.

Many students work closely on research projects with faculty on campus to gain valuable lab skills but there are also opportunities at local hospitals and businesses.

Students interested in study abroad can travel the world visiting such places as Thailand, Morocco, and South Africa. In recent years, students have studied marine biology on Australia's Great Barrier Reef, art history in the museums of Florence, finance in London, language in Spain and France, the culture of peace in Peru, and political history in Ireland.

If studying abroad for an entire semester seems too long, Saint Anselm students have traveled with faculty members on week-long trips to places such as China, Panama, Vietnam, and Belize.

Saint Anselm students have gained essential leadership and organizational skills through volunteering. Last year, students volunteered more than 51,907 hours through the Meelia Center for Community Engagement doing everything from teaching English to new Americans to working the crisis hotline at the YWCA.

In addition, every winter and spring break, Saint Anselm students travel to organizations around the country to volunteer at service sites through Service & Solidarity Mission Trips. These service trips challenge students, giving them valuable perspectives and changing their views on the world.

ACADEMICS

The core curriculum focuses on humanities, college writing, and learning outcomes. It is a balance between common courses that foster academic community and elective courses that allow for individual choice.

At Saint Anselm College's New Hampshire Institute of Politics & Political Library, students hear major policy speeches and meet today's most prominent political policy thinkers, journalists, scientists, industry executives, and global leaders. The Institute, nationally known to political scholars and strategists, is an essential campaign stop for presidential candidates offering unparalleled opportunities for students to be in the front row of the democratic process. In fact, every United States president in the last 50 years has visited Saint Anselm College.

MAJORS & DEGREES OFFERED

At Saint Anselm College, students may pursue the Bachelor of Arts degree in the following academic programs and majors: accounting, American studies, archaeology, biochemistry, biology, business, chemistry, classics, communication, computer science, computer science with business, computer science with mathematics, criminal justice, economics, education (secondary and elementary), engineering (3-2 program), English, environmental studies, environmental science, finance, fine arts, forensic science, French, German studies, great books, history, international business, international relations, mathematics, mathematics with economics, natural science, peace and justice studies, philosophy, physics (applied), physics, politics, psychology, social work, sociology, Spanish, and theology. The college also offers a Bachelor of Science in Nursing (BSN) through a traditional, undergraduate nursing program and a hybrid RN to BSN Program.

Saint Anselm students may pursue pre-professional programs in dentistry, law, medicine, theology, and veterinary medicine.

The engineering physics (3-2 program) partners with the University of Notre Dame, University of Massachusetts-Lowell, Catholic University of America, and Manhattan College. Learn more at www.anselm.edu/engineering.

TUITION, ROOM, BOARD, FEES

The 2017-2018 school year tuition is $38,960 and room and board costs are $14,146. Total cost is $54,136.

FINANCIAL AID

Saint Anselm provides students with financial aid opportunities through both private and federal aid programs. The college provides financial aid to offset the reasonable monetary investment that the student and family are expected to contribute.

Ninety-seven percent of the college's undergraduates receive some degree of financial aid. Saint Anselm's financial aid opportunities include grants, loans, scholarships, and employment positions. Outstanding students may also be eligible for merit scholarships through the Office of Admission.

Merit awards are awarded to outstanding students. Two forms are required in applying for institutional need-based aid; the student must submit the CSS/Financial Aid PROFILE and the Free Application for Federal Student Aid (FAFSA) by March 15.

Average Freshman Total Need-Based Gift Aid= $23,638

STUDENT ORGANIZATIONS & ACTIVITIES

With more than 60 clubs and organizations, 20 varsity athletic teams, a performing arts center, and an art gallery, Saint Anselm students have plenty of activities to explore. From the soccer club to the mock trial team to the Muslim Student Association, there is a club for every interest, cultural to academic.

Students interested in service will be right at home volunteering through the Meelia Center for Community Engagement or through Campus Ministry. Saint Anselm students volunteered more than 51,907 hours last year doing everything from teaching English to new Americans to working the crisis hotline at the YWCA. Every winter and spring break, Saint Anselm students travel to organizations around the country to volunteer at service sites through Service & Solidarity Mission Trips.

Saint Anselm College with 1,900 enrolled students, is part of the Division II Northeast-10 and ECAC Conferences with 20 varsity teams: men's intercollegiate sports in baseball, basketball, cross-country, football, golf, ice hockey, lacrosse, skiing, soccer, and tennis and women's sports in basketball, cross-country, field hockey, ice hockey, lacrosse, skiing, soccer, softball, tennis, and volleyball. For students interested in club or intramurals, Saint Anselm has a variety of club, recreational, and intramural sports teams.

ADMISSIONS PROCESS

In reviewing applicants for the first-year class, admission considers each prospective student carefully. Counselors assess each applicant's secondary school performance, SAT I or ACT scores (optional for non-nursing majors, nursing majors must submit scores and should apply Early Action or Early Decision), recommendation letters, extracurricular involvement, and the written essay. Of highest priority is the applicant's secondary school transcript, with a specific focus on both the rigor of course study and the marks received. Saint Anselm invites transfer and international students to apply.

Saint Anselm College has the following admission deadlines:

Early Action, November 15

Nursing Majors, November 15 or December 1

Early Decision, December 1

Regular Decision, February 1

Saint Anselm College invites students and families to visit campus for a tour, information session and/or interview.

For more information, students should contact:

Office of Admission

Saint Anselm College

100 Saint Anselm Drive

Manchester, NH 03102-1310

Telephone: 603-641-7500 or 888-426-7356 (toll-free)

Fax: 603-641-7550

Email: admission@anselm.edu

website: www.anselm.edu

SAINT FRANCIS UNIVERSITY (PA)

AT A GLANCE

Saint Francis is a private, Catholic, co-educational liberal arts university. Established in 1847, the University is among America's first Franciscan institutions and is the nation's 12th-oldest Catholic institution of higher education. Saint Francis operates under the conventions of the Franciscan Friars of the Third Order Regular. The University is dedicated to providing each student with top-rated academics, a vibrant student life, opportunities for leadership, and unflagging attention from a distinguished faculty. For the past century and a half, Saint Francis University's commitment to academics and student life has embodied two important values: high-quality education and respecting students as individuals.

LOCATION & ENVIRONMENT

Saint Francis University is located on a 600-acre mountaintop campus in the town of Loretto, Pennsylvania. Just 80 miles east of Pittsburgh and 60 miles west of State College, the campus has its own lake, nature trails, ski tubing park and championship golf course. Near to campus are three state parks, four biking/ walking trails and four ski resorts. The beautiful campus has an impressive suite of academic and research facilities as well as 19 residence halls to offer students a comprehensive experience.

CAMPUS FACILITIES & EQUIPMENT

Saint Francis offers a totally wireless campus, computer labs, a Macintosh-based computer lab, and numerous Smart Classrooms. The cost of attendance at Saint Francis includes a laptop computer as well as technical support. Other facilities that complement student learning include well-equipped science labs, on-campus radio and television stations, and the Southern Alleghenies Museum of Art.

A recently completed state-of-the-art Science Center sits at the center of campus. The facility houses highly competitive science, technology, engineering and mathematics programs. The DiSepio Institute for Rural Health and Wellness education and research center features the DiSepio Center for Rehabilitation, Student Health Services, Fitness Center, Spiritual Wellness Center, Human Performance Laboratory, and Ernest J. Scharpf Family Conference Center. A complete renovation of Schwab Hall was just completed in an effort to house the Shields School of Business.

OFF-CAMPUS OPPORTUNITIES

Saint Francis University's Office for Study Abroad offers a truly unique semester abroad program in the beautiful village of Ambialet, in southern France. Students can experience the adventure, beauty, and history of Europe in the halls of a centuries-old Franciscan monastery. Travel and research abroad are components of many academic programs at Saint Francis University.

ACADEMICS

Bachelor degrees are typically earned within eight semesters. To graduate, each student is required to complete a course of study that meets with approval from the University Provost. The University operates on a two-semester academic calendar, with three sessions in the summer. The University offers students over forty academic programs of study and a wide variety of minors and concentrations to choose. Among the most competitive academic offerings are 2 entry-level Masters health science majors (Occupational Therapy and Physician Assistant Science) and an entry-level Doctoral program in Physical Therapy. The institution is well known for the cooperative student-faculty research that occurs within the School of Science. Petroleum & Natural Gas Engineering and Environmental Engineering are among the most recent program additions to the School of Science. In the School of Arts & Letters Early Childhood Education students may complete dual certification in Special Education in four years. Saint Francis University also has an extensive list of minors and concentrations available for students to complement their academic program of study.

MAJORS

SCHOOL OF ARTS & LETTERS

American Studies

Arts & Letters

Criminal Justice

Digital Media

Strategic Communications

Education

-Early Childhood (PreK-4)

-Education/Special Education Certification

-Middle Childhood (Grades 4-8)

-Education/Special Education Certification

-Secondary Education Certification

English

-Literature (C)

-Media Studies (C)

-Secondary Education (C)

Environmental Studies

Fermentation Arts

-Fermentation Administration (C)

-Fermentation Culture (C)

History

-Pre-Law (C)

-Secondary Education (C)

International Business French

International Business Spanish

International Studies

Philosophy

Philosophy and Religious Studies

Political Science

-Political Communications (C)

-Pre-Law (C)

Psychology

-Secondary Education (C)

Public Administration/Government Service

Religious Studies

Social Work

Sociology

Spanish

-Secondary Education (C)

SCHOOL OF BUSINESS

Accounting

Economics

Finance

Management

-Healthcare Management (C)

Management Information Systems

Marketing

-Entrepreneurship (C)

SCHOOL OF HEALTH SCIENCES

Exercise Physiology

-Fitness Professionals (C)

-Pre-Allied Health (C)

-Pre-Professional (C)

-Research/Graduate (C)

Health Care Studies

-Pre-Allied Health (C)

-Pre-Occupational Therapy (C)

-Pre-Physician Assistant (C)

Nursing

Occupational Therapy (MOT)

Physical Therapy (DPT)

-B.S. Health Science

-B.S. Exercise Physiology

Physician Assistant Sciences (MPAS)

Public Health

-Pre-Professional (C)

SCHOOL OF SCIENCES

Aquarium and Zoo Science

Biology

-Biochemistry (C)

-Environmental Science (C)

-Marine Biology (C)

-Molecular Biology (C)

-Pre-Pharmacy (C)

-Pre-Professional (C)

-Secondary Education (C)

Biochemistry

Chemistry

-Biochemistry (C)

-Environmental Chemistry (C)

-Forensic Science (C)

-Pre-Pharmacy (C)

-Pre-Professional (C)

-Secondary Education (C)

Computer Science

-Gaming/New Media Design and Production (C)

-Information Technology and Security (C)

-Software Development (C)

Engineering (3-2)

Environmental Engineering

-Ecological Engineering (C)

-Renewable Energies (C)

General Engineering

Petroleum and Natural Gas Engineering

Medical Laboratory Science/Med Tech

Mathematics

-Actuarial Science (C)

-Applied Mathematics (C)

-Secondary Education (C)

Pharmacy

-Pharm.D. Affiliate Program with Lake Erie College of Osteopathic Medicine

-Pharm.D. Affiliate Program with Mylan School of Pharmacy at Duquesne University

(C) denotes concentration

TUITION, ROOM, BOARD, FEES

2015-2016 Tuition and Fees:

Tuition $31,078

Technology Fee $1,050

Room/Board $11,082

FINANCIAL AID

Saint Francis University awards financial aid to greater than 90 percent of its student body. Aside from offering aid through federal and state programs, the University's ample grant and scholarship programs provide awards ranging from $1,000 to $16,500 scholarships to students who have demonstrated their academic potential through strong high-school grade point averages and impressive ACT or SAT I (math and critical reading) scores. As a member of the NCAA Division I, scholarships may be granted to athletes in all 22 sports. Students can also receive scholarship money in all sports, Pep Band, Marching Band, Cheerleading, and Dance.

STUDENT ORGANIZATIONS & ACTIVITIES

The University provides students many opportunities to exercise their interests and talents. For instance, 60-plus on-campus clubs and organizations are active. These range from departmental clubs to volunteer organizations, and include social and service sorority and social, service, and business fraternities. Student-run activities on campus include the Bell Tower yearbook, Red Radio, theatre, SFU singers, and the Troubadour newspaper. Each year, the Student Activities Organization brings a lively docket of comedians, concerts, films, and lectures to campus. The University is a NCAA Division I member institution and maintains a comprehensive program that consists of men's and women's teams. Extensive club sports teams and intramurals provide students varied recreational outlets. Students may also participate in cheerleading, pep band, and marching band.

ADMISSIONS PROCESS

Admission to Saint Francis University is granted on rolling basis. All applicants must submit a completed admissions application including essay, an official high-school transcript, ACT or SAT I (critical reading and math) scores, and a minimum of one recommendation letter. A November 15 application deadlines applies to the physician assistant program. The physical therapy and occupational therapy programs have a Priority Application Deadline of January 15. To learn more about Saint Francis University, students and families are encouraged to call the Office of Admissions at 1-866-DIAL-SFU (toll free).

SAINT LOUIS UNIVERSITY

AT A GLANCE

Since 1818, Saint Louis University has been a home to innovators and pioneers, a community of scholars who push intellectual boundaries and seek creative, meaningful ways to impact the world.

WORLD-CLASS: SLU is a Jesuit, Catholic research university, highly ranked by the Princeton Review and by U.S. News & World Report.

SLU boasts 17 academic programs in the top 50 in their fields and several in the top 10, along with accolades for campus sustainability efforts, military-friendliness and as a "best value" in private education. SLU is also the first Jesuit university to receive the Higher Education Excellence in Diversity Award.

URBAN AND INTERNATIONAL: With two dynamic, urban campuses—in St. Louis, Missouri, and Madrid, Spain—the university is home to nearly 13,000 students from 50 states and 78 countries. SLU's international focus and 45+ study abroad programs invite students to engage with and learn from the global community. The St. Louis campus is a welcoming residential oasis located steps from some of the region's top art and culture venues, while SLU-Madrid puts students in the heart of one of Europe's most vibrant, history-rich cities.

HANDS-ON: One of only nine Catholic universities with a "higher" or "highest" research activity designation, SLU empowers students to collaborate with faculty mentors on groundbreaking research and gain hands-on experience. From developing systems to filter arsenic pollution out of water to exploring innovative ways to get fresh produce into low-income neighborhoods, students don't just contemplate solutions to the day's most challenging problems—they actively work to make those solutions reality.

SERVICE-MINDED: Jesuit tradition inspires the SLU community's commitment to service and social justice. Designated a "character-building college," SLU was also the first institution named to the President's Higher Education Community Service Honor Roll for nine consecutive years. Students cook meals in the Campus Kitchen, volunteer at student-run medical and law clinics, and work alongside dozens of community organizations to serve their neighbors.

A SLU education gives graduates not only the skills to succeed in their careers but also the wisdom to lead lives of meaning and purpose. SLU alumni have become mayors of major cities, helped put men on the moon, directed Hollywood blockbusters and worked side-by-side with Mother Theresa.

LOCATION & ENVIRONMENT

At Saint Louis University, students are in the center of everything, whether studying at SLU's Midtown St. Louis campus or SLU's international campus in Madrid, Spain.

ST. LOUIS: SLU's beautiful urban campus in Midtown St. Louis stretches across more than 230 acres of lush greenery, flowers and fountains. Students and visitors alike appreciate the unique vibe of a close-knit community nestled in the middle of a dynamic city.

The St. Louis metro region boasts nearly 3 million people. The city's mix of Midwestern friendliness and large-city amenities has helped St. Louis garner its ranking as one of the best cities for young professionals. In 2015, St. Louis grabbed the No. 1 spot on Popular Mechanics' "Best Startup Cities in America" list. The city also is home to the iconic Gateway Arch and a variety of cultural, historical and sporting attractions.

Students love cheering on the SLU Billikens. The only NCAA Division I school in town, SLU fields teams in 11 different sports, and the Billikens have earned many accolades, including 10 NCAA men's soccer championships—more than any other team in the United States.

MADRID: In 1969, SLU became one of first American universities to establish a foreign campus. Each semester, 670+ students from 49 countries pursue their studies at SLU-Madrid. Southern Europe's greenest city, Madrid offers refreshing parks and a beautiful riverside promenade. The historic central district is easy to cross on foot, and the barrios popular among students are only a few metro stops away—Madrid's mass transit system is among the best in the world.

CAMPUS FACILITIES & EQUIPMENT

During the past three decades, Saint Louis University improvements and expansions have totaled approximately $850 million. In recent years, the University completed some of the most significant building projects in its history, including the $82 million Edward A. Doisy Research Center, which offers SLU's innovative researchers a world-class facility.

In 2016, SLU's newest residence hall, a $43.8 million, eight-story, 153,000-square-foot facility opened to students. A second new residence hall is scheduled to open in the fall of 2017.

Also on campus is the 10,600-seat Chaifetz Arena, which is the home of Billiken basketball and also hosts many of the country's top entertainment acts, and SLU's 70,000-square-foot Center for Global Citizenship. Students can enjoy countless recreational activities at the university's 120,000-square-foot Simon Recreation Center, which features indoor basketball and handball courts, a bouldering wall and an indoor pool.

OFF-CAMPUS OPPORTUNITIES

ST. LOUIS: Midtown St. Louis offers access to affordable living as well as the excitement of the Grand Center arts district, the cultural heart of St. Louis. The booming performing arts neighborhood features opportunities to experience world-class art, theater, dance and music just steps away from SLU's campus.

Minutes away by car, bus or light rail train, students can explore Forest Park, the 1904 World's Fair site that's larger than even New York City's Central Park and home to the city's world-class art museum, zoo, science center and history museum—all free to the public. Check out the Delmar Loop, one of the "10 Great Streets in America," or head to "The Hill," a nationally noted neighborhood for authentic Italian cuisine, including St. Louis' famous toasted ravioli. Then go downtown to catch a game. St. Louis is noted for being one of the nation's best sports cities, and residents root for the St. Louis Cardinals baseball team, St. Louis Blues hockey team, and a bevy of independent sports teams.

MADRID: The city of Madrid is home to 230,000 university students. It's a cosmopolitan capital, a metropolis alive with learning and all that Spanish life has to offer, from flamenco shows to late-night tapas.

Madrid offers cultural experiences to rival any city in Europe, including a Royal Palace, a train station designed by Eiffel, countless theaters, museums and glorious churches. Gorgeous fountains with splashing waters can be found at the intersections of the city's grand, tree-lined avenues, and the city's beautiful parks are ideal for weekend picnics or morning runs.

ACADEMICS

High-achieving young men and women come from around the globe to pursue a world-class education at Saint Louis University. SLU offers nearly 90 undergraduate programs of study and more than 100 graduate and professional programs, with many ranked among the nation's top 50 programs in their respective disciplines.

For the most up-to-date selection of majors and programs offered, visit slu.edu/majors-and-programs.

UNDERGRADUATE PROGRAMS

Accounting °
Aeronautics/Flight Science ^
Aerospace Engineering
African American Studies
American Studies °
Analytics and Enterprise Systems
Anthropology
Art History
Athletic Training °
Aviation Management
Biochemistry
Biology ° ^
Biomedical Engineering

Biostatistics
Chemistry °
Civil Engineering
Classical Humanities
Communication ° ^
Communication Sciences and Disorders °
Computer Engineering
Computer Information Systems ^
Computer Science
Criminology and Criminal Justice °
Economics
Education ^
Electrical Engineering ° ^
Engineering Physics
English ° ^
Entrepreneurship
Environmental Science ^
Environmental Studies ^
Finance
Forensic Science
French °
General Studies
Geology
Geophysics
German Studies
Greek and Latin Languages and Literature
Health Information Management
Health Management
Health Sciences
History °
Information Technology Management
Interdisciplinary Engineering
International Business °
International Studies
Investigative and Medical Sciences
Italian Studies
Latin American Studies
Leadership and Human Resource Management
Magnetic Resonance Imaging
Marketing
Mathematics °
Mechanical Engineering
Medical Laboratory Science
Medieval Studies
Meteorology °
Music ^
Neuroscience
Nuclear Medicine Technology
Nursing ° ^ »
Nutrition and Dietetics ° ^
Occupational Science
Organizational Studies
Organizational Leadership and Technology
Philosophy ° ^
Physics
Physical Therapy (direct-entry doctoral program)
Political Science °
Psychology »
Public Health °
Radiation Therapy
Russian Studies
Security and Strategic Intelligence
Social Work °
Sociology ° ^

Spanish °
Sports Business
Studio Art ^
Theatre
Theological Studies ° ^
Women's and Gender Studies °

° Indicates graduate program offered

^ Indicates undergraduate concentrations offered

» Indicates graduate concentrations offered

TUITION, ROOM, BOARD, FEES

Annual tuition for full-time undergraduate students is $40,100. Room and board amounts to approximately $10,640 per student (depending on specific residence hall and board plan). Fees average $625 per year.

FINANCIAL AID

Saint Louis University remains committed to keeping its one-of-a-kind education within reach and understands the sacrifices students and families make for quality education. SLU is dedicated to serving others, in part, by providing financial access to an unparalleled and life-changing educational experience.

In 2016, 98 percent of SLU's first-time freshmen received some sort of scholarship or financial assistance.

Scholarships are awarded based on academic merit, talents, service, leadership and financial need. In addition to SLU's financial aid programs, the state of Missouri and the federal government also provide assistance.

Contact SLU's office of student financial services at 314-977-2350, 800-SLU-FOR-U or sfs@slu.edu.

STUDENT ORGANIZATIONS & ACTIVITIES

Students participate in more than 200 clubs, honor societies and service organizations; 18 NCAA Division I teams; intramural sports; and community service efforts that see 80 percent of SLU students volunteering at least once during the academic year.

Talent and commitment matter at SLU, and high levels of energy and dedication exist in everything Saint Louis University students pursue: academic societies, athletics, performing arts and media groups, student government, cultural and political organizations, and fraternities and sororities. SLU's multicultural organizations highlight and celebrate the diversity of the University community, and a variety of faith-based organizations support and challenge students as they explore their own faith traditions.

ADMISSIONS PROCESS

For information about the admission process at Saint Louis University or to schedule a campus visit, call the office of admission at 800-SLU-FOR-U, email admission@slu.edu, or check out visit.slu.edu.

SAN DIEGO STATE UNIVERSITY

AT A GLANCE

San Diego State University is a major public research institution providing transformative experiences and a rich campus life, both inside and outside of the classroom, for its 36,000 undergraduate, graduate and doctoral students.

SDSU is a major public research institution with a community of people committed to student success and life-changing opportunities for students, such as study abroad, undergraduate research, internships and entrepreneurial experiences. SDSU is the oldest higher education institution in the San Diego region, and these deep community roots provide access to internships, mentoring relationships, and volunteer opportunities that complement and enhance the classroom experience

LOCATION & ENVIRONMENT

SDSU's campus is within a 15-minute drive of downtown San Diego and the Pacific Ocean and only two hours south of Los Angeles. The second largest city in California, San Diego is a thriving cultural, scientific and educational center. Bordering the Pacific Rim and Mexico, San Diego is recognized globally as a dynamic international hub. SDSU's Spanish revival architecture reflects the diversity and history of the region, with bell towers, beautiful arched walkways and ornamental ironwork.

CAMPUS FACILITIES & EQUIPMENT

SDSU's campus is a unique blend of old and new, classic and modern. The exterior of the Conrad Preys Aztec Student Union, for example, draws inspiration from historic Spanish revival architecture. But its interior is an ultramodern Double LEED Platinum certified hub for student organizations, events and activity. The soon-to-open Engineering and Interdisciplinary Sciences Complex also embraces the Spanish style architecture with an interior that will feature state-of-the-art labs and collaborative teaching space necessary for trans-formative innovation and exploration.

ACADEMICS

SDSU ranks in the top 10 in the number of students who study abroad to gain new perspectives and to grow personally and intellectually. More than 2,400 SDSU students study abroad each year in 65 countries, including the United Kingdom, China, Italy, Mexico and Spain.

The campus-based academic programs reinforce this global perspective. They include the Center for International Business Education and Research; the Center for Latin American Studies; the International Security and Conflict Resolution degree program; and the International Business major, which ranks No. 14 in the nation.

Additionally, SDSU is dedicated to entrepreneurship and innovation with the belief that these skills encourage students to turn their ideas into tangible products that will benefit the student, SDSU and the San Diego community. Entrepreneurship at SDSU involves a unique blend of coursework and experiential learning opportunities. This combination enables students to adopt innovative thinking and develop the competencies they will need to succeed in today's society, regardless of their educational field.

MAJORS & DEGREES OFFERED

SDSU is an academically comprehensive university that provides endless possibilities for students: bachelor's degrees in 91 areas, master's degrees in 78 fields, and 22 doctoral degrees (Ph.D., Ed.D., Au.D., DNP, and DPT). SDSU is a place for the best and brightest to study disciplines from biology and viromics to international business, and from entrepreneurship to musical theater.

TUITION, ROOM, BOARD, FEES

SDSU is consistently ranked among the best value universities in the nation and for the number of students graduating with the least amount of debt.

California resident students are charged flat rate tuition and fees depending on enrollment. Full time fees are charged for students who enroll in more than 6 units; part time fees are charged for students enrolling in 6 or fewer units. In addition to basic tuition and fees, nonresident and international students pay non-resident tuition. SDSU has a wide variety of on-campus housing and dining options. Costs vary depending on location, number of roommates, and meal plan chosen.

To apply for all federal, state, and institutional aid, file a Free Application for Federal Student Aid (FAFSA) as soon as possible after October 1. Be sure to check Aid-Link, SDSU's online financial aid system, regularly to see if additional documentation is needed.

SDSU offers a large number of scholarships based on need, academic merit, and other criteria. Applications are submitted online, and the largest scholarship cycle runs from August through February.

MAJORS & DEGREES OFFERED

SDSU is an academically comprehensive university that provides endless possibilities for students: bachelor's degrees in 91 areas, master's degrees in 78 fields, and 22 doctoral degrees (Ph.D., Ed.D., Au.D., DNP, and DPT). SDSU is a place for the best and brightest to study disciplines from biology and viromics to international business. And from entrepreneurship to musical theater.

STUDENT ORGANIZATIONS & ACTIVITIES

Diversity is a hallmark of the SDSU's community of 36,000 students. Upon becoming Aztecs, students embrace the 120-year history of SDSU and its mission of education, research and service. They are active in more than 300 different student clubs and organizations, many of which participate in community service and philanthropic projects. Our students are enthusiastic supporters of Aztec Athletics; in fact, The Show, a legion of men's basketball fans, has created a game-day atmosphere rivaled by few in the nation.

Faculty in SDSU's eight colleges are equally committed to ensuring student success and advancing research in their fields. Our faculty members have authored (widely used) textbooks, chaired national academic organizations, published research in peer-reviewed journals, and received research funding from the National Institutes of Health and the National Science Foundation. At the same time, they are skilled teachers and mentors, drawing on knowledge of the latest developments in their fields to enrich the classroom experience.

Through partnerships, education and programming, SDSU's Career Services Department provides current Aztecs and Aztec alumni with many opportunities to define, develop and realize their career potential. We work closely with employers and community partners to fill important staffing and internship positions from within the diverse and talented Aztec student body. Career Services oversees two important programs – The Aztec Mentor Program, which pairs more than 1,200 students with alumni mentors in their chosen fields, and Aztecs Hiring Aztecs, which works with alumni-owned and -operated businesses to transition recent graduates into the workplace.

ADMISSIONS PROCESS

SDSU attracts highly qualified students each year. The average high school GPA for fall 2017 admitted freshmen was 3.88 with an average SAT Reasoning (critical reading and math) score of 1229 or ACT score of 27. Prospective students can apply as a freshman for fall 2018 as long as they haven't graduated from high school and are on track to graduate with a high school diploma by spring 2018, or they haven't taken any college-level classes beyond the summer after high school graduation.

Students can apply online at CSUMentor.edu between October 1 and November 30, 2017 for fall 2018 admission.

The following criteria is used to evaluate applications:

1. Eligibility Index (a calculation of GPA and SAT/ACT scores)

2. Completion of the "a-g" college prep curriculum

3. Intended major

For more information about applying to SDSU for fall 2018 admission, visit sdsu.edu/admissions.

SCHOOL OF VISUAL ARTS

AT A GLANCE

School of Visual Arts, located in the heart of New York City, has been a leader in the education of artists, designers and creative professionals for more than six decades. With a faculty of more than 1,000 distinguished working professionals, a dynamic curriculum and an emphasis on critical thinking, SVA is a catalyst for innovation and social responsibility. Comprising more than 6,000 students at its Manhattan campus and 35,000 alumni in 100 countries, SVA also represents one of the most influential artistic communities in the world.

Bachelor of Fine Arts degrees are offered in Advertising, Animation, Cartooning, Computer Art, Computer Animation and Visual Effects; Design, Film & Video, Fine Arts, Illustration, Interior Design, Photography, and Visual & Critical Studies.

Master of Arts degrees are offered in Critical Theory and the Arts, Curatorial Practice; and Design Research, Writing and Criticism.

Master of Fine Arts degrees are offered in Art Practice, Art Writing, Computer Art, Design, Design for Social Innovation, Fine Arts, Illustration as Visual Essay, Interaction Design, Photography, Video and Related Media; Products of Design, Social Documentary Film, and Visual Narrative.

Master of Professional Studies degrees are offered in Art Therapy, Branding, Digital Photography, Directing, and Fashion Photography.

A Master of Arts in Teaching degree is offered in Art Education.

SVA also offers workshops, continuing education classes, studio residencies, international student programs, summer programs abroad, and a pre-college program for high school students.

For more information on the College and its offerings, visit sva.edu.

LOCATION & ENVIRONMENT

SVA's urban-style campus comprises 15 buildings with state-of-the-art studio facilities, workshops, residence halls and gallery spaces. As the creative capital of the world, New York City is home to more artists than any other U.S. city, with a creative workforce of 300,000. It is also home to over 14,000 creative businesses and non-profits. Students come here to be immersed in real-world experience, not the insulated experience of other schools. Surrounded by a thriving and artistic urban environment during their years at SVA, students are able to transition to the working world with ease, finding unique opportunities for internships and mentorships.

TUITION, ROOM, BOARD, FEES

Expenses for 2016-2017

Application fee: $50

Tuition: $36,500 per year for undergraduate programs; for Graduate program tuition, please visit http://www.sva.edu/students/student-accounts/tuition-and-fees

Departmental fees: $640 to $1,340 per semester depending on undergraduate major

Estimated Supplies: $1,050 to $3,150

Housing Charges: range from $14,000 to $18,500 per year

FINANCIAL AID

Currently, 43% of SVA first-time freshmen receive some form of financial aid. Undergraduate merit scholarships are also available through Admissions. A payment plan is available.

STUDENT ORGANIZATIONS & ACTIVITIES

The Student Engagement and Leadership Office provides a diverse range of programming designed to enrich the SVA student's experience. Students are offered the opportunity to tap into a multitude of social, cultural, educational and recreational activities. Students are encouraged to take advantage of all New York City has to offer.

The Visual Arts Student Association (VASA), the student government, represents the students' point of view at SVA. Participating in VASA gives students the opportunity to develop leadership skills by coordinating events and activities. VASA funds and supports a number of clubs and activities that are organized by students.

ADMISSIONS PROCESS

Undergraduate Application Deadlines:

Deadline for freshman and transfers: rolling

Deadline for Early Action: December 1

Deadline for all application materials to be submitted for the Silas H. Rhodes Scholarship Program: February 1 for first-time freshman applicants and March 1 for transfer applicants. There is no separate application for the Silas H. Rhodes Scholarship Program.

Requirements:

-Application for Undergraduate Admission

-A nonrefundable $50 application fee

-Official transcripts from all high schools and colleges attended

-Results of the SAT or ACT

-Statement of intent

-Portfolio

-Interview (optional)

-Demonstration of English proficiency (required of all international applicants whose primary language is not English)

SEATTLE UNIVERSITY

AT A GLANCE

Students who are adventurous, forward-thinking, creative and have an interest in social justice are drawn to Seattle University, located in the heart of a city with unparalleled access to innovation and culture.

Seattle has produced some of the world's most prestigious and influential companies such as Microsoft, Starbucks, Amazon and Costco. This urban setting is where all walks converge to find a better way forward. Seattle University is a school of action with an ever-growing impact on the city, the community and throughout the world.

The greatest successes at Seattle University are the result of people coming together and standing united to bring about great change. A good example: The Seattle University Youth Initiative, the university's largest-ever community engagement project, which continues to grow as it transforms academic achievement at the city's most underperforming public elementary school. The lure of the Youth Initiative is compelling-so much so that an increasing number of incoming students say it's the top reason they choose to come to SU. Worldwide, other universities-20 and counting -see the Youth Initiative as a successful prototype. The White House took notice, too, and honored the Youth Initiative with several awards for community service in each of the last three years.

In a state like Washington, where dozens of different languages are spoken and every race, religion and perspective is represented, Seattle University's 4,700 undergraduate students from 53 states and 89 nations fit right in.

A transformation happens when you're a student here. A Seattle University education instills in you a lifelong capacity to create a more just and humane world.

LOCATION & ENVIRONMENT

Centrally located in the beautiful Emerald City—just up the hill from downtown and Pike Place Market—Seattle University's 50-acre campus is located in a forward-thinking hub of innovation.

CAMPUS FACILITIES & EQUIPMENT

The university is considered an "urban oasis" between the First Hill and Capitol Hill neighborhoods in the center of Seattle. The campus has 28 buildings enhanced by $200 million in additions, renovations or new construction in the past 15 years.

A major expansion of the campus library, now the Lemieux Library and McGoldrick Learning Commons, provides state-of-the-art digital learning opportunities. The library's media production center features a recording studio, control room, audio/video editing facilities and a theater-style screening room.

The College of Nursing's 20,000-square-foot Clinical Performance Lab is among the most technically advanced in the nation, with two clinical practice rooms and a suite of laboratories. The state-of-the-art William F. Eisiminger Fitness Center, tennis courts, track and both natural and synthetic turf playing fields draw students in their off hours. School spirit gets a big boost from Division I athletics, and the university completed a renovation of the Connolly Complex in 2016 to improve the experience of athletes and spectators alike

OFF-CAMPUS OPPORTUNITIES

As the Pacific Northwest's largest city, Seattle is a cultural center known for its first-run entertainment. The Seattle International Film Festival is the largest and most highly attended of its kind in the United States. With more than 250 feature and 150 short films from 70-plus countries, this 25-day festival takes place here every spring.

You can catch a professional sporting event such as Sounders FC soccer or Mariners baseball. And what about those Seattle Seahawks? You, too, can become part of the 12th Man crowd and cheer them on with the loudest fans in the NFL.

Just a quick walk from Seattle University, you'll find music, coffee houses and restaurants galore in the Capitol Hill neighborhood. People watch at a cafe, experience an author reading in a quirky bookstore or browse through one of the area's many thrift shops. Feeling hungry? Consider a night out at one of the city's ethnic eateries and restaurants nearby. Additionally, over 120 coffee shops within a mile radius of campus (no joke!) will make you feel like a true Seattleite.

Take in the breathtaking skyline at the top of the iconic Space Needle or on the Seattle Great Wheel, a 175-foot Ferris wheel on Seattle's waterfront alongside Puget Sound. Catch a sightseeing ferry ride across Puget Sound or wander through Pike Place Market, the Olympic Sculpture Park or the Museum of History and Industry, all a short distance from campus.

Even in the city, you're not far from wooded hiking trails and challenging ski slopes. Experience mountain views of the Cascades to the East and the Olympics to the West.

Numerous lakes, the largest of which are Lake Washington and Lake Union, also are part of the territory. With the blast of a cannon and a parade of boats, Seattle rings in Opening Day of boating season. There's also Seafair featuring a flight demonstration by the Blue Angels.

In the summer, there's the famous Fremont Solstice Parade and Festival. Northwest Folklife and Bumbershoot are a pair of music festivals that take place over Memorial Day and Labor Day weekends that draw national acts to Seattle Center under the Space Needle. There's plenty more to grab your attention in this dynamic and diverse city. Seattle Center also hosts more than 20 ethnic festivals that range from the Seattle Cherry Blossom and Japanese Cultural Festival to French Fest, from a Vietnamese Lunar New Year celebration to an Irish Festival around St. Patrick's Day.

ACADEMICS

Central to the academic excellence of SU is the Core curriculum, which enriches academic rigor and engages new students quickly, deeply and thoughtfully. The Core offers a glimpse at how SU inspires insightful and creative thinkers and serves as an important foundation for studies in the various majors and minors.

Designed to help students develop intellectual abilities, there's a strong liberal arts focus with broad exposure to the humanities, social sciences, natural sciences and arts. Instead of broad survey courses, Core courses focus on specific questions. The study of those questions gives students a closer look at a discipline and how knowledge is pursued. Theology and philosophy play critical roles. There's also a focus on global engagement so students can examine their roles in local, regional, national and transnational cultures and communities.

Seattle University continues its long-term relationship with the University of Central America in Nicaragua for exchange programs. In addition, students are in educational or service programs abroad in more than 40 countries. Among them, the senior economics major who spent a quarter in Chiang Mai, Thailand, at a sanctuary that's home to more than 30 rescued elephants, and the junior political science major on a yearlong study in Santiago, Chile, where he wrote for the Santiago Times.

MAJORS & DEGREES OFFERED

The university offers 64 majors and 31 minors in five colleges and schools: Albers School of Business and Economics, College of Arts and Sciences, College of Nursing, College of Science and Engineering and Matteo Ricci College. Undergraduate degrees include Bachelor of Arts, of Science, of Science in Nursing, of Social Work, of Criminal Justice and of Arts in Business Administration. For specifics on majors and minors, visit the Seattle University website at seattleu.edu.

TUITION, ROOM, BOARD, FEES

For the 2017-2018 academic year, full-time tuition is $42,120; room and meals are $12,072. The estimate for books, supplies, fees and personal expenses is an additional $5,415. Travel costs vary. Costs are subject to change. Seattle University operates on a quarter calendar with fall term beginning in late September. Students are required to live on campus for their first two years, and six on-campus residence halls house more than 2,000 students.

FINANCIAL AID

More than 87% of undergraduates in 2015-16 received financial aid; the average award was $26,717. These awards usually include scholarships, grants, loans and Federal Work-Study. Last year, Seattle University awarded more than $110 million in aid to undergraduates. Over $73 million of that came from the university's own funds. Students are required to apply for financial aid by Feb. 1, as awards are made early each spring for the following fall quarter. Applications that are received after this deadline will be evaluated in the order received for any remaining aid. Students must submit the Free Application for Federal Student Aid (FAFSA) and be accepted for admission to be considered for financial assistance. A number of freshman scholarships are awarded on the basis of academic achievement, extracurricular involvement and community service. Transfer scholarships also are available.

STUDENT ORGANIZATIONS & ACTIVITIES

Student Government of Seattle University promotes opportunities for student leadership and involvement and assists in the development of a cohesive undergraduate community. You also can take your pick from more than 130 extracurricular clubs and organizations.

ADMISSIONS PROCESS

Seattle University is committed to qualitative decision making based on evaluations of students as a whole. Decisions are based primarily on individual course selection, performance and trends. The expected academic program comprises 16 units of coursework, including four years of English, three years of social studies or history, two years of a foreign language, three years of college-preparatory mathematics and two units of lab science (three are preferred). Laboratory physics and chemistry, as well as four units of college-preparatory mathematics are required for engineering; the university also requires laboratory chemistry and biology for admission to the nursing program. Also required for all programs are official scores from either the ACT or the SAT. The middle 50 percent of enrolling freshmen have secondary school averages of 3.4-3.9 (on a 4.0 scale).

Essays or personal statements are required for admission and are carefully considered during application review. College credit is awarded to those who have successfully earned minimum scores on Advanced Placement or International Baccalaureate examinations.

Applications and information can be obtained by contacting the Admissions Office. Secondary school students who have completed at least six semesters are encouraged to complete the application process no later than Jan. 15 of their senior year, the deadline for regular admission. For those who wish to apply via Early Action, the deadline is Nov. 15. Transfer students must submit official transcripts from all post-secondary institutions attended, regardless of whether course work was completed. The recommended financial aid/admission deadline for transfers is March 1, however transfer applications are welcomed until Aug. 15.

Campus visits are scheduled Monday through Friday and many Saturdays. Guests can attend a class, meet with faculty, participate in a campus tour and speak individually with representatives from admissions.

Students can apply directly or online at seattleu.edu. Seattle University is a member of The Common Application.

SETON HALL UNIVERSITY

AT A GLANCE

As one of the nation's leading Catholic universities, Seton Hall provides over 90 rigorous academic programs that are highly ranked by The Princeton Review, U.S.News & World Report and Bloomberg Businessweek. We offer all the advantages of a large research university national reputation; challenging academic programs; notable alumni; state-of-the-art facilities; renowned faculty; and extensive opportunities for internships, research and scholarship with all the benefits of a small, supportive and nurturing environment. Our 14:1 student-to-faculty ratio and average class size of 21 students means faculty know more than just your name.

Our accomplished faculty include Fulbright Scholars, prominent researchers, authors, artists, filmmakers, former school superintendents and principals, leaders in nursing, former ambassadors, analysts and lawmakers-all of whom are dedicated to their fields and their students. They have graduated from some of the nation's leading institutions, including Seton Hall, Harvard, Columbia, Yale, Princeton and Dartmouth. Each day, our faculty members shine in the lecture halls and on the national stage. They meet regularly with students outside the classroom and help them learn to think critically.

Seton Hall offers more than 17,000 internship opportunities, and over 80 percent of our students have an internship or two on their resume before graduation, this is just one of the reasons our students have a 90% employment rate after graduation and mid-career earnings 50% higher than the national average. In fact, Seton Hall was recently ranked top 5 in the nation for providing internship opportunities. Our national reputation and stellar academic programs draw over 550 employers to campus each year just to recruit our graduates.

Seton Hall is a Catholic university with over a 160-year tradition of educational excellence. A welcoming community, Seton Hall embraces students of all faiths and inspires students to become servant leaders who make a difference in the world. That's why our community performs over 40,000 hours of community service annually. You'll feel at home on our campus, where it's easy to make friends and get involved.

LOCATION & ENVIRONMENT

Nestled in the suburban village of South Orange, New Jersey, Seton Hall provides small-town charm combined with big-city opportunities. The University's suburban, 58-acre park-like campus sits proudly within this picturesque town with tree-lined streets; historic, gracious homes; and quaint shops just 14 miles from New York City close to all the action, yet not engulfed by it.

Just a five-minute walk from campus lands you in the middle of a bustling town center where you'll find diners and pizzerias, banks, pharmacies, Starbucks, Cold Stone Creamery, a gourmet marketplace, South Orange Performing Arts Center, a movie Theatre, and so much more. You might not ever want to leave this quiet suburbia, but if you do, the train station, right in the center of town, is your direct link to NYC's Penn Station just 30 minutes away.

We take full advantage of all the Big Apple has to offer-where the worlds of entertainment, art, publishing, global finance, international diplomacy and fashion collide. NYC is also one of the world's largest job markets, brimming with internship and job placement opportunities in a variety of companies. Over 80% of Seton Hall students have an internship or two on their resume before graduation at leading companies like Goldman Sacs, American Express, CNN, the Secret Service, Merck, Lincoln Center, The New York Mets, the United Nations, The New York Times, NBC, Prudential, Sony Music, JP Morgan Chase and more.

And if all the advantage and opportunity of the Big Apple aren't enough, New Jersey's got you covered. One of the wealthiest states in the nation, New Jersey is brimming with opportunity. Seton Hall's backyard boasts a powerhouse corporate corridor of more than 50 Fortune 500 companies, pharmaceutical giants and major corporations. For you this means networking, internships and career opportunities.

CAMPUS FACILITIES & EQUIPMENT

Seton Hall places a strong emphasis on the use of state-of-the-art technology, facilities and support services to aid in its students' development. Many investments have been made to the campus infrastructure, including the recent construction of a new academic classroom building, new residence hall space, a new parking deck, a Dunkin Donuts and a new state of the art recreation and fitness center. In addition the campus boasts a state-of-the-art research library complete with a computerized catalog and 200 computer terminals. The Science and Technology Center, is home to state-of-the-future biology and chemistry labs, an atrium and auditorium, as well as an observatory and greenhouse. The campus also offers man unique learning labs like our Mock Trading Room, Patient Simulation Laboratory, Market Research Center, student-run radio station, Sport Polling Center. Plus all incoming students are provided new, fully loaded laptop.

ACADEMICS

Seton Hall offers over 90 rigorous academic programs in seven undergraduate colleges. They have excellent programs in business, education, communication, diplomacy and International relations, nursing, humanities, social sciences, biology, chemistry, physics as well as direct admission joint degree programs in physical therapy, athletic training, occupational therapy, physician assistant and speech language pathology. In 2018 they are slated to open a new medical school in partnership with NJ's leading Hospital Hackensack University Medical center. The University plans to offer direct admission BS/MD programs in the near future. The New School of Medicine will be located in Clifton & Nutley, NJ on the former site of Roche Pharmaceuticals. The site will also house our School of Health and Medical Sciences as well as our College of Nursing which is ranked in the top 5% of Nursing programs nationwide.

Seton Hall's Stillman School of Business has the number one rated leadership program in the country and has AACSB accreditation, the most rigorous accreditation a business school can hold, putting them in the top 10% of business schools in the world and their accounting program in the top 1% in the world. Graduates of the business school, along with graduates of the College of Communication and the Arts, The College or Education and the School of Diplomacy and International Relations have 100% admit rates into graduate school and nearly a 100% employment rate for students within six months of graduation. Seton Hall also has a 93% admit rate into medical school for its pre-med students.

MAJORS

Accounting•
Accounting (5-year B.S./M.S. dual-degree∞)
Africana Studies•
American Humanics√
Ancient Greek†
Anthropology•
Applied Scientific Mathematics†
Arabic†
Archaeology†
Art (Art History•, Fine Arts•, Graphic Interactive and Advertising Design•)
Art (BA/MA in Museum Professions)§
Asian Studies•
Athletic Training (5-year B.S./M.S. or B.A./M.S. dual-degree)∞
Biochemistry
Biology (B.A. or B.S.)
Broadcasting and Visual Media•
Business Administration•‡
Catholic Studies•‡
Catholic Theology•
Chemistry•
Classical Culture†
Classical Languages†
Classical Studies•
Communication Studies (B.A./M.A. in Communication or Public Relations)∞
Computer Graphics√
Computer Science•
Creative Writing
Criminal Justice•
Data Visualization and Analysis√
Digital Media and Video√
Digital Media Production for the Web√
Diplomacy and International Relations•
Early Childhood Education (integrated with elementary and special education)
Elementary Education (integrated with early childhood and special education)

Education with Speech Language Pathology (6-year B.S.E./M.S. dual degree)∞
Economics (B.A. or B.S.)
Engineering (Biomedical, Chemical, Civil, Computer, Electrical, Industrial, Mechanical)§
English•
Entrepreneurial Studies√
Environmental Sciences†
Environmental Studies•
Ethics and Applied Ethics†
Finance
French•
Gerontology√
History•
Information Technologies√
Information Technology Management‡
International Business†
International Relations
Italian•
Italian Studies†
Journalism•
Latin†
Latin America and Latino/Latina Studies•
Law (3+3 with Seton Hall Law)∞
Legal Studies in Business†
Liberal Studies
Management
Marketing
Mathematical Finance
Mathematics•
M.B.A. (5-year B.S./M.B.A. or B.A./ M.B.A. dual-degree)∞
Modern Languages
Music (Comprehensive Music/Music Education, Music Performance•)
Musical Theatre†
Nonprofit Studies†
Nursing
Occupational Therapy (6-year B.A./M.S. dual-degree)∞
Online Course Development and Management√
Philosophical Theology√
Philosophy•
Physical Therapy (6-year B.S./D.P.T. dual-degree)∞
Physician Assistant (6-year B.S./M.S. dual-degree)∞
Physics (B.A. or B.S.)•
Political Science•
Pre-Dental°
Pre-Law°
Pre-Medical°
Pre-Optometry°
Pre-Veterinary°
Psychology (B.A. or B.S.)•
Religion•
Russian†
Russian and East European Studies†√
Secondary Education (optional integration with special education)
Social and Behavioral Sciences
Social Work•
Sociology•
Spanish•
Special Education (integrated with early childhood, elementary, and secondary education)
Speech Language Pathology (6-year B.S.E./M.S. dual degree)∞
Sport Management•
Supply Chain Management√
Theatre•
Web Design√

Women and Gender Studies†
Writing†
Undecided

• Minor also available

† Minor only

√ Certificate program only

‡ Certificate program also available

§ Dual-degree Program with NJIT

∞ Seton Hall dual-degree program (please contact the Office of Admissions for details)

° Pre-professional programs (you must also select a major)

TUITION, ROOM, BOARD, FEES

Seton Hall offers a flat-tuition rate for students taking between 12-18 credit hours. The 2016-17 tuition and fees are $39,558. Room and Board fees range depending on meal plans; however, an average cost is $13,108.

FINANCIAL AID

Paying for college is a major investment. Seton Hall University is committed to providing students with the resources needed to make your dreams a reality. The University gives over $90 million in aid each year and 98 percent of our students receive some form of financial aid with 97 percent receiving scholarships or grants directly from the University. Seton Hall University has been rated as one of the best schools in the nation for a return on your investment. Most scholarships are automatically awarded upon admission and do not require a separate applications. However there are also several special scholarships for which students can apply learn more at shu.edu/go/scholarships. Seton Hall also provides ned-based aid to eligible students who complete the Free Application for Federal Student Aid (FAFSA) form by December 1.

STUDENT ORGANIZATIONS & ACTIVITIES

On campus, Seton Hall leaders learn to put their ideas into action; discover something new; become part of a community; and build trust, spirit and lasting friendships. Here, you'll find activities galore, over 130 clubs and organizations and 22 Greek societies. You can audition for one of the nearly dozen theatre performances cast each year or broadcast at the #1 ranked college radio station in the nation, WSOU-FM, which attracts more than 120,000 listeners a week from the NYC area. Join the Brownson Speech and Debate Team, ranked in the Top 20 college and university forensics teams for years or write for one of our three student newspapers. You'll not only make lots of new friends and have fun, you'll also learn about your leadership style. More than two-thirds of our students participate in clubs and organizations.

You don't have to be a superstar athlete to be part of the game at Seton Hall. Our athletic programs include competition on varsity, intramural and club levels. In fact, almost 50 percent of our students participate in club or intramural sports. Even if you don't know a handball from a handoff, you'll be decked out in blue and cheering your heart out when you attend any one of Seton Hall's 14 NCAA division I Big East athletic events. So grab your friends and catch some Pirate fever!

ADMISSIONS PROCESS

At Seton Hall, we take a holistic approach to reviewing your application. When we receive your application, we start by considering your academic performance in high school, your grades and the rigor of your curriculum, as well as your standardized SAT and/or ACT scores. These are essential indicators of your ability to succeed at Seton Hall. We also will consider your personal essay, recommendations and extracurricular activities.

The typical student who enter Seton hall last year had an average GPA of 3.5 (B+) and an average SAT score of 1150 (old) 1220 (new) (25 on the ACT).

For more information, contact the Office of Undergraduate Admission:

Website: admissions.shu.edu
Telephone: 1-800-THE-HALL (843-4255)
E-mail: thehall@shu.edu
#halladmissions
Text: 973-996-8181

SKIDMORE COLLEGE

AT A GLANCE

The world doesn't need more silent observers and passive assessors; it needs creative thinkers and passionate doers. Creative thought matters because it is creating the future. And that's what Skidmore is all about.

Founded in 1903, Skidmore College is an independent, coeducational, liberal arts college in Saratoga Springs, N.Y., that prides itself on its creative approaches to just about everything. Hence the college's core belief that Creative Thought Matters. With a diverse student body of 2,500 students from 44 states and 59 countries and a faculty of 304 dedicated teacher-scholars, Skidmore offers 43 majors in the humanities, sciences, and social sciences, as well as in pre-professional fields.

Skidmore is known for its interdisciplinary approach to learning, faculty-student collaborative research, funded research opportunities, off-campus study, and the prominence of the performing and visual arts. Students enjoy close relationships with faculty members who have earned recognition through Guggenheim, Pulitzer, and Emmy awards, and fellowships and grants from Fulbright, MacArthur, the National Science Foundation, and others. Half of our students carry two majors or add a related minor to their major, and nearly 60% are attending graduate or professional school or have completed advanced degrees within five years of graduation.

LOCATION & ENVIRONMENT

Skidmore truly offers the best of both worlds—a beautiful, safe, and expansive campus and an active, thriving hometown in Saratoga Springs, one of the most interesting and vibrant small cities in the US. Famed for its "health, history, and horses," Saratoga Springs is a popular year-round cultural and tourist destination. The Saratoga Performing Arts Center is summer home to the New York City Ballet, Philadelphia Orchestra, and Opera Saratoga, and is a performing venue for top rock and jazz musicians. And downtown Saratoga is brimming with galleries, museums, shops, coffeehouses, bistros, and restaurants. No wonder Travel & Leisure named it the sixth-best college town in the nation. The city's location near the foothills of the Adirondack Mountains puts an abundance of outdoor recreational opportunities within an hour's drive, including great downhill and Nordic skiing. Boston, New York City, and Montreal are each approximately 180 miles from campus.

CAMPUS FACILITIES & EQUIPMENT

Skidmore's 1,000-acre campus offers buildings that are designed and arranged to blend with the natural surroundings and to foster intellectual and social interaction. The newest academic building, the Arthur Zankel Music Center, features a spectacular 600-seat recital hall and a state-of-the-art recording studio. The beautifully renovated Murray-Aikins Dining Hall boasts a variety of food stations and intimate seating arrangements. On the residential side, the Sussman Village Apartments were completed in 2013, enabling 90% of Skidmore's student body to reside on campus. And field hockey, lacrosse, soccer, and softball venues have all been recently outfitted with the latest turf fields.

Several years ago, Skidmore installed a solar array that meets 12% of Skidmore's electricity needs. In addition, Skidmore began receiving 18% of its electricity needs through a micro-hydro facility. Forty-five percent of Skidmore's heating and cooling needs come through geothermal energy, the most of any organization in the region. Soon more than half of campus building space will be heated and cooled through geothermal energy, with a goal of 60% by 2025.

ACADEMICS

Skidmore offers numerous pre-professional and cooperative programs: prelaw advising; premedical/health professions advising; 4+1 M.B.A. programs (Clarkson, RIT); Whitman M.B.A. Advantage Program, 4+1 M.S.A., and 4+1 M.S.F. (Syracuse); dual-degree engineering programs (Clarkson, Dartmouth, RPI); B.S.N. (NYU School of Nursing); dual-degree programs in occupational therapy and physical therapy (Sage Graduate School); M.S. in Accountancy (Wake Forest); M.S. in Teaching (Clarkson– 12 months); internships (academic credit, funded summer programs); applied civic-engagement courses; Periclean Honors Forum; faculty-student collaborative research (academic year and summer program); international and domestic off-campus study options; and the Moore Documentary Studies Collaborative.

Off-campus study: With more than 60% of students studying abroad at some point during their college years, Skidmore was recently ranked in the top 10 on the list of top 40 baccalaureate institutions for number of students studying abroad for a semester. Students can choose from 120 approved programs in more than 40 countries, including Skidmore-run programs in England, France, and Spain.

MAJORS & DEGREES OFFERED

Skidmore offers bachelor degrees in the following 43 majors: American studies, anthropology, art (studio), art history, Asian studies, biology, business (business-French, business-German, business-Spanish, and business-political science), chemistry, classics, computer science, dance, economics, education studies, English, environmental science, environmental studies, exercise science, French, gender studies, geosciences, German, history, international affairs, mathematics, music, neuroscience, philosophy, physics, political science (political science-French, political science-German, and political science-Spanish), psychology, religious studies, a self-determined major, social work, sociology, Spanish, and theater.

Most majors have minors. Others include arts administration, Chinese, intergroup relations, Italian, Japanese, Latin American studies, and media and film studies.

TUITION, ROOM, BOARD, FEES

Skidmore 2016–17 costs were as follows: tuition/fees: $50,684; room: $7,998 (dorm double); and board: $5,532.

FINANCIAL AID

Skidmore annually provides $44 million in financial aid on the basis of demonstrated financial need. The most recent first-year aid package was $39,900, ranging from $2,000 to $65,000; 42% of students received need-based grants; 50% received some form of financial aid; and 50% took advantage of the opportunity to work on campus. Average post-college student debt (just under $23,000) is well below the national average.

Aid is provided in the form of a student-aid package that usually includes a grant, campus job, and loan. We encourage any student interested in applying for admission to do so regardless of his or her intention to seek financial aid. A great place to start is our Skidmore student aid calculator, which will give you an idea for where you stand. A Free Application for Federal Student Aid (FAFSA), a copy of the federal income tax form, and the CSS Profile must be filed each year.

Skidmore also hosts an annual Filene Music Scholarship Competition to award four to six $48,000 ($12,000 per year) scholarships on the basis of musical ability without regard to financial need. Five to seven $15,000 Porter Presidential Scholarships in Science and Mathematics scholarships are also awarded annually ($60,000 over four years).

STUDENT ORGANIZATIONS & ACTIVITIES

Students: Skidmore's 2,500 students come from 44 states and 59 countries; 40% are men, 60% women; 22% are domestic students of color and 11% international students; 6% of students carry dual passports; and 13% are first-generation college students.

Additional Information Varsity sports: A founding member of the highly competitive NCAA, Division III Liberty League, Skidmore offers 19 varsity sports: baseball, basketball (men and women), field hockey, golf, ice hockey, lacrosse (men and women), riding, rowing (men and women), soccer (men and women), softball, swimming/diving (men and women), tennis (men and women), and volleyball. Liberty League members are Bard, Clarkson, Hobart & William Smith, RPI, RIT, Rochester, St. Lawrence, Skidmore, Vassar, and Union.

Student clubs/organizations/leadership: Whether you engage in one of Skidmore's 130 student clubs or serve as a residential advisor, a varsity athlete or intramural participant, a student gardener, or a volunteer in a local school, you will find opportunities to use your creativity and round yourself out while giving back to the larger community.

Student Academic Services (SAS) serves all Skidmore students interested in strengthening their academic performance or skills by organizing peer tutoring, study groups, and drop-in tutoring and by offering professional one-on-one and small-group academic support. SAS collaborates with other campus offices and faculty to support Skidmore students with specific responsibility for international students, English Language Learners, students of color, student-athletes, and students with disabilities.

ADMISSIONS PROCESS

In 2016–17, Skidmore received more than 10,000 applications for a first-year class targeted at about 660 (including 25 students spending their first semester in London); fewer than 30% were offered admission; nearly half enrolled through Early Decision.

Those seeking admission to Skidmore's first-year class should complete a secondary-school curriculum that includes at least 16 credits in college-preparatory courses. The Admissions Committee also considers applications from qualified high school juniors who plan to accelerate and enter college early. Applicants typically have completed four years of English, a foreign language, mathematics, and social studies, and three to four years of laboratory science. Applicants must provide a secondary school transcript, letters of recommendation from two teachers of academic subjects, and a report from their guidance counselor. Skidmore encourages a campus visit and interview.

Skidmore is test-optional when it comes to standardized testing (SAT, ACT), though the college does require standardized test results from international students other than those who have attended an English language–based school for at least three years, homeschooled students, and students attending secondary schools offering written evaluations without accompanying grades. Applicants for the Porter Presidential Scholarships in Science and Mathematics are encouraged to submit SAT/ACT and any SAT subject tests in math and science. Of course, students may submit either the SAT or ACT if they feel their standardized testing results best represent their academic potential.

Through its participation in the Higher Education Opportunity Program (HEOP), Skidmore enrolls capable and ambitious New Yorkers who, because of their academic and financial situations, would not otherwise gain admission to the college under traditional requirements. Skidmore's Academic Opportunity Program (AOP) enrolls similar students who reside out of state and/or whose family income slightly exceeds HEOP guidelines. Together, HEOP and AOP are referred to as the Opportunity Program (OP). About 180 OP students are enrolled at Skidmore.

An applicant for admission must complete the Common Application and submit it with a $65 fee. All information for Regular Decision applicants should be postmarked by January 15. Applications from Early Decision applicants should be submitted by November 15 for the Round I Early Decision plan or by January 15 for the Round II Early Decision plan. Regular Decision applicants can convert their applications to Early Decision until February 1. Transfer applicants must submit their applications by November 1 for January admission or by April 1 for September admission.

International students are given special attention throughout the admissions process. Applicants whose first language is not English are encouraged to submit the results of the Test of English as a Foreign Language (TOEFL). There are a limited number of need-based financial-aid awards available for outstanding international students.

Career Services & Placement

Thanks in part to the college's strong internship, student-faculty summer research, and off-campus study programming, some 80% of Skidmore students report being employed one year after graduating. Close to 60% complete or are enrolled in advanced-degree programs within five years of graduation. Career Development offers one-on-one career counseling (in person and virtual) for life; job fairs in NYC, Boston, Washington, D.C., and Los Angeles; off-campus job and internship interviewing fairs in New York, Boston, Washington, D.C., and Los Angeles; internship openings reserved for Skidmore students; graduate and professional school expo (nearly 50 institutions); several summer funded internship awards programs; and networking events such as Career Jam and Creative Thought (Net)Works.

FACULTY

277 full-time (304 FTE), 87% with doctoral or highest degree in their field. National and international recognitions include Guggenheim, MacArthur, Pulitzer, and Emmy awards and major fellowships and grants from Fulbright, Getty, NEH, NIH, NSF, and the Andy Warhol Foundation.

SOUTHERN ILLINOIS UNIVERSITY CARBONDALE

AT A GLANCE

Southern Illinois University Carbondale (SIU), chartered in 1869, is a comprehensive, state-supported institution with nationally and internationally recognized instructional, research and service programs. SIU is fully accredited by the North Central Association of Colleges and Schools. SIU offers more than 200 undergraduate majors, minors and specializations; three associate degree programs; 95 baccalaureate degree programs; 80 master's degree programs; 34 doctoral programs; and professional degrees in law and medicine. SIU is a multi-campus university that includes the Carbondale campus as well as the SIU School of Medicine at Springfield.

During the 2016 academic year, SIU's enrollment was 15,987, which included 12,182 undergraduate students, 3,183 graduate students and 622 professional students. The average age of undergraduates is 23.2. International students account for 8.5 percent of SIU's total enrollment. Of U.S. undergraduate students, 17.19 percent are African-American, 0.2 percent are American Indian/Alaskan, 1.8 percent are Asian or Pacific Islander and 8.8 percent are Hispanic.

Students who are ready to start college but not ready to commit to a specific major can enroll in SIU's Exploratory Student-Undeclared (EXPU) program. Advisers and career counselors help these students plan their education and careers.

LOCATION & ENVIRONMENT

Carbondale is a city of 26,000 located six hours south of Chicago, two hours southeast of St. Louis and three hours north of Nashville, Tennessee. Four large recreational lakes, two great rivers (the Mississippi and the Ohio) and the 270,000-acre Shawnee National Forest are within reach of the campus. The mid-South climate is ideal for year-round outdoor activities.

CAMPUS FACILITIES & EQUIPMENT

In addition to the 2.6 million volumes, 3.6 million microfilms and more than 43,000 current periodicals and serials available in Morris Library, students and faculty members have access to more than 200,000 e-books. More details are available online at lib.siu.edu.

Students learn and practice in the Transportation Education Center based at the Southern Illinois Airport, outdoor laboratories, the student-run Daily Egyptian newspaper, WSIU-TV, WSIU-FM, art and natural history museums, a literary magazine, McLeod Theater, Memorial Hospital, a vivarium, plant biology greenhouses, University Farms and Touch of Nature Environmental Center.

All single students under the age of 21 not residing with their parents or legal guardians, and with fewer than 26 credit hours earned after high school, are required to live in university-owned and operated residence halls. SIU offers four on-campus residential areas for single students, each with a dining hall, post office and laundry facilities. Learning Resource Centers, available on both sides of campus, offer writing centers, computer labs and student lounges. University Housing Residence Hall Dining provides all-you-care-to-eat meals and late-night dining. Residence Hall Dining offers a variety of menus, vegetarian and light entrees, display cooking and a full-time dietitian to help students with special dietary needs. Apartment housing is available for sophomore-, junior- and senior-level undergraduates, graduate students and students with families.

OFF-CAMPUS OPPORTUNITIES

Southern Illinois University Carbondale is committed to serving statewide, national and international needs. This commitment is reflected in SIU Extended Campus, which offers educational opportunities located off campus. SIU Extended Campus is present at 20 military installations and 17 nonmilitary locations across 14 states, offering 12 online degree programs, 12 off-campus programs and five military programs.

Off-campus credit programs are designed to meet the educational needs of adults wishing to pursue a degree but who are unable to travel to the Carbondale campus. Faculty members who teach off-campus courses travel to distant sites to teach SIU courses.

All credit courses offered through these programs carry full SIU academic credit and are taught by faculty members appointed by the academic departments of the university. Additional information can be found online at extendedcampus.siu.edu.

ACADEMICS

SIU's Continuing Education and Outreach auxiliary service provides nonacademic support services for SIU's Carbondale campus. Its noncredit classes, workshops and conference, as well as its contractual services program, offers the university's resources to a variety of groups and individuals both on and off campus. Continuing Education and Outreach provides specialized educational services to groups, organizations, governmental agencies and businesses on a cost-recovery basis. These services are provided regionally, nationally and internationally. Additional information can be found online at continuinged.siu.edu.

Faculty members are dedicated to excellence in teaching and to their advancement of knowledge in a wide variety of disciplines and professions. Many faculty members are well-known nationally and internationally for their varied research contributions. The student-faculty ratio is 14.52:1. There are 1,130 full-time and 224 part-time instructional faculty members.

MAJORS & DEGREES OFFERED

The university offers two Associate in Applied Science degree programs—aviation flight and physical therapist assistant—at the College of Applied Sciences and Arts.

The College of Applied Sciences and Arts offers bachelor's degree programs in architectural studies; automotive technology; aviation management; aviation technologies; dental hygiene; electronic systems technologies; fashion design and merchandising; public safety management (off-campus only); health care management; information systems technologies; interior design; mortuary science and funeral service; radiologic sciences; and technical resource management.

The College of Agricultural Sciences offers bachelor's degree programs in agribusiness economics; agricultural systems; animal science; crop, soil and environmental management; forestry; horticulture; hospitality and tourism administration; and human nutrition and dietetics.

The College of Business offers bachelor's degree programs in accounting; business and administration; business economics; finance; management; and marketing.

The College of Education and Human Services offers bachelor's degree programs in almost two dozen undergraduate programs, many in conjunction with other colleges on campus. The programs include (° denotes educator licensure required through the university's Teacher Education Program): °agricultural education; °art education; behavior analysis and therapy; °biological science education; communication disorders and sciences; °early childhood; °elementary education; °English teacher education; exercise science; °foreign languages; °history teacher education; leisure services management; °mathematics education; °physical education teacher education; public health; organizational training and development; outdoor recreation leadership and management; rehabilitation services; social work; °special education; sport administration; and therapeutic recreation.

The College of Engineering offers bachelor's degree programs in civil engineering; computer engineering; electrical engineering; engineering technology; industrial management and applied engineering; mechanical engineering; and mining engineering.

The College of Liberal Arts offers bachelor's degrees in Africana studies; anthropology; art; classics; communication studies; criminology and criminal justice; design; economics; English; foreign language and international trade; French; geography and environmental resources; German; history; international studies; linguistics; music; musical theater; paralegal studies; philosophy; political science; psychology; sociology; Spanish; theater; and university studies.

The College of Mass Communication and Media Arts offers bachelor's degrees in cinema and photography; journalism; and radio, television and digital media.

The College of Science offers bachelor's degree programs in biological sciences; chemistry and biochemistry; computer science; geology; mathematics; microbiology; physics; physiology; plant biology; zoology; and pre-professional programs and advisement in the following areas: chiropractic; dental; medical; nursing; occupational therapy; optometry; osteopathic medicine; pharmacy; physical therapy; physician assistant; podiatry; public health; and veterinary medicine.

In addition to the many majors offered at SIU, specializations are offered in all colleges in many areas.

TUITION, ROOM, BOARD, FEES

Tuition and fee charges for the 2016-17 academic year (fall and spring) for students enrolled in 15 or more semester hours were $13,481 for Illinois residents and $27,130 for out-of-state residents, including international students. Room and board totaled $10,186. (All costs are subject to change.) Starting in fall 2017, domestic, nonresident undergraduate students will be assessed tuition at a resident ("in-state") rate. The cost of books and school supplies varies among programs. The average cost is $1,100 per academic year.

FINANCIAL AID

More than $293 million in financial aid was distributed to 17,453 SIU students in fiscal year 2015-16 through federal, state and institutionally funded financial aid programs.

To apply for financial aid at SIU, students should complete the Free Application for Federal Student Aid (FAFSA). Applications that are filed before April 1 receive priority consideration for campus-based aid. The FAFSA can be completed electronically at the U.S. Department of Education's website (fafsa.ed.gov). When completing the FAFSA, students should list Southern Illinois University Carbondale (Federal School Code 001758) as a school of choice.

SIU has one of the largest student employment programs in the country, with about 4,000 students employed each year in a wide variety of job classifications.

STUDENT ORGANIZATIONS & ACTIVITIES

SIU intercollegiate sports teams compete at the NCAA Division I level (football is Division I-FCS). Conference affiliations include the Missouri Valley Conference and the Missouri Valley Football Conference. Intercollegiate sports teams include men's and women's basketball, cross-country, diving, golf, swimming, and track and field; men's baseball and football; and women's softball and volleyball. The campus has various playing fields, several tennis courts, and a campus lake with a beach and boat dock. SIU's Student Recreation Center offers an Olympic-size pool; indoor tracks; handball/racquetball and squash courts; a climbing wall; weight rooms; basketball, volleyball and tennis courts; outdoor equipment rental; an aerobic area; wallyball; martial arts; and dance and cardio studios.

The Student Center is one of the largest in the United States without a hotel. It holds a bookstore, several restaurants, a craft shop, facilities for bowling and billiards, headquarters for more than 275 student organizations and the student government office, four ballrooms and an auditorium.

ADMISSIONS PROCESS

Freshman applicants whose ACT composite score is at or above 23 (SAT score at or above 1070) and whose high school grade point average at or above 2.0 (on a 4.0 scale) are admitted to the university. Applicants also can be admitted with an ACT composite score at or above 18 (SAT score at or above 870) and a high school GPA at or above 3.0 (on a 4.0 scale). All other applicants who meet the course subject pattern requirements will undergo a holistic review to determine potential admissibility. Admission of students who do not meet automatic admission requirements may be subject to conditions. Freshman applicants must meet course pattern requirements: four years of English, three years of mathematics, three years of laboratory science, three years of social science and two years of electives.

Transfer applicants must have an overall grade point average of at least 2.0 on a 4.0 scale, based on work attempted at all institutions and calculated by SIU grading policies. Transfer applicants must also be eligible to continue at the last institution attended. Some programs have higher admission requirements or require additional screening for admission. Undergraduates can apply online at admissions.siu.edu.

http://admissions.siu.edu/

Admission is granted on a rolling basis. Application priority deadlines for freshmen and transfer students are May 1 for the summer term and fall semester, and Dec. 1 for the spring semester. The application fee is $40. For more information, prospective students should contact:

Undergraduate Admissions

Mail Code 4710

1263 Lincoln Drive

Southern Illinois University Carbondale

Carbondale, IL 62901

Phone: 618/536-4405

Email: admissions@siu.edu

Website: www.siu.edu

Facebook:http://www.facebook.com/SouthernIllinoisUniversityCarbondale

Twitter: twitter.com/siuc

SOUTHWESTERN UNIVERSITY

AT A GLANCE

Southwestern has been committed to "Fostering a liberal arts community whose values and actions encourage contributions toward the well-being of humanity" for more than 175 years.

Committed to "Fostering a liberal arts community whose values and actions encourage contributions toward the well-being of humanity," Southwestern is unique in many ways.

Southwestern is located in the heart of Central Texas. Its 1,515 students enjoy warm and sunny weather. The University is within walking distance to downtown Georgetown where students enjoy iconic restaurants, coffee shops, and exploring nearby parks and trails. The campus is also less than 30 minutes north of Austin, the "Live Music Capital of the World"—a booming city filled with year-round festivals and events that attract visitors from all over the world.

Southwestern's residential campus offers a true liberal arts education with small classes and numerous collaborative undergraduate research opportunities. Outside the classroom, students are civically engaged and volunteer in the community at more than twice the national average! One-third of students study abroad and most take advantage of leadership, service and activism opportunities in Southwestern's 90+ student organizations. Our scholar-athletes compete on one of 20 NCAA Division III varsity teams. Go Pirates!

Two-thirds of all Southwestern students complete at least one internship experience and 92 percent have found employment or have been accepted to graduate/professional school within 10 months of graduation. All of this (and more!) combined creates a lifelong Southwestern Experience.

"Southwestern is a place and time of personal growth and joint endeavor. The first moment I walked onto this campus as a prospective student, I knew Southwestern was home. It was so real, so genuine." Katherine Tanner '13

Office of Admissions

Southwestern University

1001 E. University Street

Georgetown, TX 78626

Telephone: 1-800-252-3166

E-mail: admissions@southwestern.edu

Website: go.southwestern.edu

LOCATION & ENVIRONMENT

Southwestern's 700-acre, residential campus is everything you imagine when you dream about college. Grand buildings radiate from the heart of campus our lush, open air academic mall offering a spacious sports/recreational center, pedestrian access to classrooms, the library, research laboratories, an observatory, a teaching greenhouse, renovated residence halls and apartments, and numerous athletic fields.

Southwestern is located in historic Georgetown, just a short drive north of Austin-the social cultural and political center of Texas. With an average temperature of 79 degrees, it's an excellent location for a number of year-round outdoor activities (boating, camping, fishing, skiing, hiking, biking and . . . studying), cultural events, and of course, great food.

Forbes magazine found the Austin area to be one of the most desirable places for recent college graduates to live and work. Our close proximity to Austin puts internships, community and volunteer engagement, and an abundance of employment opportunities at your fingertips.

ACADEMICS

Southwestern's unique academic offerings include Paideia, an innovative and nationally-respected program promoting interdisciplinary study and close faculty-student collaboration; The King Creativity Fund, a grant program supporting innovative and visionary student projects; the Research and Creative Works Symposium, an opportunity for students to present original research and creative work in an academic conference setting; and unique opportunities for study abroad and civic engagement.

Paideia helps students to connect different classes and departments in ways they never knew possible. Students will collaborate with other students, faculty and staff on projects centered on a particular theme. They will also have the opportunity to participate in civic engagement and intercultural learning experiences that allow them to apply their new-found knowledge beyond the classroom.

Three interconnected courses (a "cluster"), followed by a team-taught interdisciplinary Paideia Seminar, will further help to connect the dots. The seminars provide the opportunity for students and their "cohort" to reflect on their clustered courses and explore how their interdisciplinary experiences relate to their major.

The King Creativity Fund annually supports innovative and visionary projects of student projects and grant awards. Creative projects may be carried out on or off-campus. The purpose of this fund is to encourage students to be creative and to think outside of the box. The most recent winning King Creativity project, title "Finding Inspiration in Formula: Mathematical Invention in Painting," united principles of mathematics and computer science in the form of four large-scale oil paintings.

The Research and Creative Works Symposium is a day-long celebration of the work of our students, faculty, and staff. Southwestern aims for diversity in the presentations to provide an opportunity for everyone to engage in conversations on thought-provoking topics, to question our own perspectives, and to see the world from a multi-faceted view.

About one-third of Southwestern University students study abroad at some point during their academic career at Southwestern. The Office of Intercultural Learning works with students to help them integrate intercultural experiences into their liberal arts education, and to reflect on their position and responsibilities in the world. We take a holistic approach to off-campus study by preparing and supporting students to live and learn in a new cultural setting and then helping students continue the learning process as they return to campus. Study abroad also works closely with Paideia, helping to weave an intercultural experience into the student's liberal arts education.

Consistent with Southwestern's core values, we encourage students to develop and act upon a heightened sense of responsibility to one's communities. At Southwestern, 66 percent of students volunteer and contribute nearly 14,000 hours of service each year. Through civic engagement, individuals —as citizens of their communities, their nations, and the world— are empowered as agents of positive social change for a more democratic world.

The faculty of Southwestern are undoubtedly our most valuable resource.

As persons of learning, our faculty stand among the best in their profession (ninety-nine percent of tenured or tenure-track faculty hold a doctorate or the highest degree in their respective fields). As educators, Southwestern faculty excel at teaching in an intimate and engaged environment (student-to-faculty ratio is 12:1, with an average class size of 15 students). As citizens of our community, Southwestern faculty bring a collaborative and personal approach to their work: our classes are taught by professors, not teaching assistants, and collaborative research and publication with students is common.

MAJORS

Southwestern professors balance the highest level of scholarship with a serious dedication to teaching and collaboration with students. Our 26 academic departments offer 36 majors and seven pre-professional programs that prepare students for success in any professional (or personal) endeavor.

MAJORS & MINORS

- Anthropology
- Applied Physics
- Architecture & Design Studies°
- Art (Studio)
- Art History
- Biochemistry
- Biology
- Business
- Chemistry
- Chinese°
- Classics
- Communications Studies
- Computational Mathematics
- Computer Science
- Dance°
- Economics
- Education
- English
- Environmental Studies
- Exercise & Sports Studies°
- Feminist Studies
- French
- German
- Greek
- History
- Independent Major
- International Studies
- Kinesiology
- Latin
- Latin American & Border Studies
- Mathematics
- Music
- Philosophy
- Physics
- Political Science
- Psychology
- Race & Ethnicity Studies°
- Religion
- Sociology
- Spanish
- Theatre
- ° Indicates Minor Only

PRE-PROFESSIONAL PROGRAMS

- Pre-Dentistry
- Pre-Engineering
- Pre-Law
- Pre-Medicine
- Pre-Ministry
- Pre-Physical Therapy
- Pre-Veterinary Medicine

TUITION, ROOM, BOARD, FEES

Costs for 2017-18 Academic Year

Tuition (Full-time, 12-19 hours per semester): $40,560

Room and Board (approximate): $12,041

Other Fees:

- Part-Time Tuition-per credit: $1,690

- Fine Arts Music Fee/ Applied Music Lessons-per credit: $180

- Vehicle Registration Fee-per semester: $100

- Lab fee-per applicable class: $75

FINANCIAL AID

For a world-class liberal arts education at one of the best schools in the country, Southwestern is a great value. When comparing college costs, make sure you're looking at the bottom line: Tuition at public universities may seem lower at first glance, but when you factor in scholarship and financial aid and graduation rates, it can be quite a different story.

Each year Southwestern awards over $30 million in merit scholarships and need-based grants. In addition, SU awards over $2 million in federal and state grants and over $4 million in student loans. First-year merit scholarship amounts start at $16,000. Entering freshmen and transfers are evaluated on a holistic review basis for merit scholarships using information from the admission application. All financial aid is awarded annually, and FAFSA applications will be available in October of 2017.

STUDENT ORGANIZATIONS & ACTIVITIES

Southwestern's Career Services ranks #4 nationally by The Princeton Review. Career Services offers 50 programs per year, students gain skills they will need to obtain a job or continue their education upon graduation. They teach career-management skills needed throughout a lifetime including resume writing, interviewing, job search strategies. They provide opportunities to explore a variety of occupations and gain experience through internships. They also make connections to employers, graduate schools, and other resources.

With the help of Career Services, at least two-thirds of all students complete at least one internship program and 92 percent of graduates are employed or in graduate school within ten months.

This year, Southwestern introduced The Alumni Network Mentoring Program. This program provides Southwestern students the opportunity to be mentored by Southwestern alumni. Students are matched with alumni based on their professional interests and activities.

ADMISSIONS PROCESS

In looking for engaged learners, we consider academic performance, both grades earned and challenging courses in areas of interest, above all else. Additionally, strength and depth of writing samples, SAT and/or ACT score, participation and demonstrated leadership in extracurricular activities, cogency and content of recommendations, a visit to campus, legacy connections, United Methodist Church membership, and recognition/achievement in national programs allow us to determine how a student will fit within our community. We value the opportunity to get to know students better through an optional interview.

Our mission is to treat all applicants fairly and with respect. In all cases, our decisions are reached by multiple individuals reviewing the application and voting in a manner s/he believe is in the best interest of both the student and the University. We take this responsibility seriously and realize we are dealing with the lives and future directions of our applicants.

Beginning August 1, 2017, students may choose to apply Early Decision (binding), Early Action or Regular Decision, based on the time frame that works best for the student. Students may apply by submitting a Common Application, an Apply Texas application or by submitting Southwestern's own application.

Transfer students, students who have completed at least one semester (12 hours or more) following high school graduation, are welcomed during the Fall and Spring semesters and may apply using either the Common Application or Apply Texas. Students should submit an essay, an official high school transcript, an official college transcripts from all schools attended, official SAT/ACT scores and a college official's report. An individual interview allows transfer students to ask question regarding course transferability.

To learn more, visit southwestern.edu/admission

ST. JOSEPH'S COLLEGE

AT A GLANCE

Since 1916, St. Joseph's College (SJC) has helped students achieve their highest personal and academic goals. Through our three campuses—SJC Long Island in Patchogue, SJC Brooklyn in Clinton Hill and SJC Online—the College offers degrees in more than 50 majors, special course offerings and certificates, and affiliated and pre-professional programs. A St. Joseph's education, regardless of major or field of study, is rooted in a liberal arts foundation—an essential component for success in any profession. As one of the most affordable private colleges in New York, SJC is the top choice for students seeking a quality return on their investment.

In small, hands-on classes with a 14:1 student-to-faculty ratio, students receive individual attention from dedicated professors. SJC's academic and career counselors will guide students through all aspects of their college career, from coursework preparation to job applications. Faculty and staff value commitment to personal growth and are mentors and valued advisers.

SJC is consistently recognized for its commitment to academic excellence and its status as an outstanding college. For more than a decade, SJC has been selected as one of the nation's top colleges by U.S. News & World Report. SJC is also one of the nation's most affordable private colleges. In 2016, Washington Monthly ranked SJC 7th out of 386 as a "Best Bang for the Buck" college in the Northeast, making it the highest ranked college in New York.

Celebrating its centennial in 2016, SJC honors its deep-rooted past of providing excellence in higher education, while continually introducing new areas of study and incorporating contemporary trends into its curriculum. In recent years, SJC has developed programs in studio art, forensic computing, journalism and new media studies, hospitality and tourism management and nursing to meet growing demands. The launch of SJC Online has also provided the best in education—all on your schedule.

STUDENT BODY

SJC students have an abundance of extracurricular opportunities within reach through the Office of Student Involvement and Leadership. Students can join clubs, athletic teams, organizations and committees that emphasize leadership, community service and effective communication.

CAMPUS LIFE

SJC Brooklyn

Architecturally stunning halls in the historic Clinton Hill neighborhood of Brooklyn, an outdoor theater, The Hill Center and the nationally recognized Dillon Child Study Center combine to make SJC Brooklyn a unique community. The recently opened Hill Center is home to SJC Brooklyn's NCAA Division III athletic teams. It features a regulation-size gymnasium, a state-of-the-art fitness facility and many multipurpose areas. Career opportunities and extensive cultural attractions in Manhattan are within reach via public transportation.

SJC Long Island

SJC Long Island features the Business Technology Center, the John A. Danzi Athletic Center, the Clare Rose Playhouse, the Callahan Library and the state-of-the-art outdoor athletic field complex for soccer, lacrosse, baseball, softball and tennis.

SERVICE

Service is at the heart of a St. Joseph's education. Students volunteer at numerous organizations throughout the year and often participate in service-based trips, where they help rebuild communities that have been affected by hurricanes, earthquakes and other natural disasters. Service-based destinations have included Colorado, South Carolina, Missouri, New Jersey and Nicaragua. SJC provides a strong academic and value-oriented education at the undergraduate and graduate levels, and prepares students for a life characterized by integrity, intellectual and spiritual values, social responsibility and service.

ADMISSIONS

What are the admissions requirements?

St. Joseph's College is a selective institution. Applicants are evaluated on an individual basis. The College enrolls students who are academically talented and diverse. Successful admissions candidates typically have:

- A high school diploma or its equivalent, or postsecondary transcripts.
- A personal statement or essay of recommendation.
- Standardized test scores that demonstrate the promise of success in college-level courses.
- Two letters of recommendation and a personal essay.

Students can obtain a copy of our application or also apply online, by visiting sjcny.edu/applynow.

When should I apply? When is the application deadline?

SJC admits students on a rolling basis, but there are scholarship priority dates. For the fall semester, the scholarship priority date is March 15 for freshmen and August 1 for transfer students. For the spring semester, the priority date is January 1 for both freshmen and transfer students.

What do I need to submit as a transfer student?

Applications can be submitted by mail or online. Transfer students should request that official transcripts from all former colleges, and a listing of courses in progress, be sent to our Office of Admissions. You are not required to submit a high school transcript if you have an A.A. degree or have successfully completed 24 or more credits from an accredited college. You may transfer a maximum of 64 credits if you have an A.A. degree; certain A.A.S. degrees are also transferable.

UNDERGRADUATE MAJORS

Accounting

Biology

Biology—secondary education

Business Administration

Chemistry

Chemistry—secondary education

Child Study

Criminal Justice

Computer Information Technology

English

English—secondary education

History

History, Social Studies—secondary education

Hospitality Tourism Management

Human Relations

Journalism and New Media Studies

Leisure Services Management

Marketing

Mathematics

Mathematics—secondary education

Medical Technology

Nursing

Philosophy and Religious Studies

Political Science

Psychology

Spanish

Spanish—secondary education

Speech

Social Sciences

Sociology

Studio Art

Therapeutic Recreation

MINORS

Accounting

Art history

Fine Arts (LI)

Studio Art

Biology

Chemistry

Computer Information Technology

Computer Science

Criminal Justice

Economics

English

Film/Media

History

Human Relations

Human Resources

Journalism New Media Studies

Labor, Class, Ethics

Latino Studies

Marketing

Mathematics

Music (LI)

Music History

Peace and Justice Studies

Philosophy

Political Science

Psychology

Religious Studies

Sociology

Speech

Spanish

Therapeutic Recreation

GRADUATE PROGRAMS

Accounting

Adult-Gerontology Primary Care Nurse Practitioner

Computer Information Technology

Criminal Justice

Forensic Computing

General Studies

Health Administration

Hospitality Tourism Management

Human Services

Medical Technology

Nursing

Organizational Management

CERTIFICATE PROGRAMS

In addition to our undergraduate programs, SJC offers credit-bearing certificates that part-time students can complete in less than a year. These certificates may be earned individually or as part of an undergraduate degree. Certificate programs enable you to delve deeper into your specific interests, help you focus on your career goals and give you a head start when entering the work world.

We offer certificate programs in:

- Business Administration Marketing (Brooklyn and LI)
- Criminal Justice (Brooklyn and LI)
- Human Services (Brooklyn and LI)
- Industrial Organizational Psychology
- Mathematics and Computer Science (Brooklyn and LI)
- Psychology (LI)
- Religious Studies (Brooklyn and LI)
- Social Sciences (LI)

A SERVICE MEMBERS OPPORTUNITY COLLEGE

As a core member of the Servicemembers Opportunity College Degree Network System, SJC is committed to the transfer of relevant course credits, flexible academic residence requirements and credit learning from appropriate military training and work experience. SJC also offers online, on- and off-site class schedules for its military and veteran students, including class offerings at Fort Hamilton in Brooklyn and Fort Wadsworth in Staten Island, New York. In addition, SJC is an active participant in the Post-9/11 GI Bill Yellow Ribbon Program, offering veteran students financial support, a monthly housing allowance and an annual stipend for books and school supplies.

TUITION AND AID

SJC is committed to providing quality education while maintaining one of the lowest private college tuition rates in New York. To supplement the cost of education, scholarships, loans and work-study programs are some of the financial aid options available. Currently, more than 80 percent of SJC students receive some form of financial aid.

SJC offers generous scholarships and financial aid packages to students who qualify. For a listing of scholarships available at SJC Long Island, visit sjcny.edu/long-island/admissions/financial-aid/sjc-scholarships. For a listing of scholarships available at SJC Brooklyn, visit sjcny.edu/brooklyn/admissions/financial/sjc-scholarships.

ST. LAWRENCE UNIVERSITY

AT A GLANCE

Nestled in the small upstate New York town of Canton that's closer to Canada than it is to Manhattan, St. Lawrence is a liberal arts school with a strong sense of community and a dedication to academics. For one history major, St. Lawrence is "a university that pushes me to pursue my dreams," a place where "it felt like I was coming home, not leaving home." With roughly 2,400 students and a student to faculty ratio of 12:1, St. Lawrence prides itself on small classes and a tight knit environment where students and professors know their fellow Laurentians by name. With interdisciplinary studies encouraged, the most popular majors at St. Lawrence include economics, biology, government, psychology, and mathematics. Even though its location might be considered remote, the school's proximity to the Adirondacks is a huge draw and, as one anthropology major jokes, "St. Lawrence manages to be a place with countless opportunities and things going on despite being in the middle of nowhere."

LOCATION & ENVIRONMENT

St. Lawrence University provides a distinctive learning environment, offering 63 majors, 40 minors, and three graduate programs in education. Its First-Year Program has become a national model as a living-learning environment that transitions students successfully out of high school and into college life. Just 80 miles from Ottawa, St. Lawrence is the closest American university to a foreign capital and is only 100 miles from Montréal. St. Lawrence celebrates diversity in the widest sense, welcoming students from more than 60 countries. It also boasts the Collegiate Science and Technology Entry Program, the Ronald E. McNair Scholars Program, and is a partner with the New York State Higher Education Opportunity Program.

CAMPUS FACILITIES & EQUIPMENT

St. Lawrence University has two libraries, the Owen D. Young Library and Launders Science Library, containing more than 630,000 print volumes as well as a number of electronic resources, a writing center, and ample space for reading and research.

Students also enjoy a performing arts center with recital hall and two theaters as well as an art gallery containing a 7,000-piece art collection and Newell Center for Arts Technology.

With a commitment to sustainability, St. Lawrence opened in 2007 the Johnson Hall of Science, which was the first LEED-gold certified science building in New York State. And in 2014, the University opened Kirk Douglas Hall, a 155-bed residence hall that features 24 geothermal heating/cooling wells and was built to LEED gold standards. There's also the 15,000-square-foot Sullivan Student Center, which is available for student activities and meetings, studying, staff offices, and a popular dining facility.

Recreational facilities include a network of trails available for running and cross-country skiing; a 133-station fitness center; a three-story climbing wall; indoor and outdoor tennis courts; and two gymnasium/fieldhouse complexes, one with a 9-lane/400-meter track and five tennis/basketball courts and the other with a 200-meter track, three tennis courts, and ten squash courts. There's also a pool, equestrian center, golf course, indoor golf facility, AstroTurf field, baseball, soccer and softball fields, and a boathouse for rowing teams located on the St. Lawrence River, Appleton Arena is home to St. Lawrence's only NCAA Division I sport teams, men's and women's hockey teams.

OFF-CAMPUS OPPORTUNITIES

St. Lawrence University offers 24 off-campus program sites in 19 countries, including Australia, Austria, Canada, China, Costa Rica, Czech Republic, Denmark, England, France, India, Italy, Japan, Kenya, New Zealand, Spain, Thailand, and Trinidad and Tobago. Students can also direct-enroll at foreign universities through the International Student Exchange Program (ISEP).

The University also offers four off-campus study programs within the United States at American University, Washington, D.C.; an exchange program with Fisk University, Nashville, Tennessee; the Liberal Arts in New York City, the Adirondack Semester, and a Sustainability Program located just 5 miles from campus.

ACADEMICS

The University offers the following degrees: Bachelor of Arts, Bachelor of Science, Master of Education, Master of Science in Mental Health Counseling, and a Certificate of Advanced Studies in Education.

There are 63 majors, which include a number of combined major programs in areas such as environmental studies, economics and biology. Students can even design their own major with faculty approval. The University also offers 40 minors and 53 interdisciplinary programs (see Majors & Degrees Offered.)

St. Lawrence has a number of affiliations, giving students the opportunity to pursue a five-year program in business administration (this program leads to the MBA) and engineering, combining coursework at St. Lawrence with work at other institutions.

Students can also enter a number of affiliate programs leading to degrees in pharmacy, nursing, physician assistant, and physical therapy. There are also tracks for pre-med and pre-law.

The St. Lawrence distribution requirements involve coursework in six areas. All students are expected to demonstrate writing competence before graduating. The University provides extensive opportunities for honors projects and independent work.

MAJORS & DEGREES OFFERED

Students have the following major/minors to choose from:

African Studies, African-American Studies, Anthropology, Applied Statistics, Arabic Studies, Art & Art History, Asian Studies, Biochemistry, Biology, Biology-Physics, Business in the Liberal Arts, Canadian Studies, Caribbean and Latin American Studies, Chemistry, Chinese Studies, Communications, Computer Science, Conservation Biology, Creative Writing, Dance, Economics, Economics-Mathematics, Education Studies, English, Environmental Studies, Estudios Hispanicos (Spanish), European Studies, Exercise Science, Film and Representation Studies, Francophone Studies (French), Gender and Sexuality Studies, Geology, Geology-Physics, German Studies, Global Studies, Government, History, International Economics, International Studies, Italian Studies, Latin American Studies, Mathematics, Multi-Languages, Multifield (self-designed), Music, Native American Studies, Neuroscience, Outdoor Studies, Peace Studies, Performance and Communication Arts, Philosophy, Physics, Political Science, Psychology, Religious Studies, Sociology, Sports Studies and Exercise Science, Statistics.

TUITION, ROOM, BOARD, FEES
2017-2018

Tuition:	$ 52,610
Room:	$ 7,356
Board:	$ 6,300
Fees:	$ 380
Total:	$ 66,646

FINANCIAL AID

St. Lawrence University offers merit scholarships, as well as need-based financial assistance. The school grants aid in some form to more than 97 percent of its students. Aid packages typically consist of grants, student loans, and campus jobs.

Aid applicants must submit the Free Application for Federal Student Aid (FAFSA) between October 1 and February 1; the financial aid award will be included in the decision package if all required documentation is received by the deadline.

STUDENT ORGANIZATIONS & ACTIVITIES

All first-year undergraduate students are enrolled in St. Lawrence University's nationally-recognized First-Year Program, which places approximately 30 first-year students in small communities that live and learn together.

Once they achieve upper-class status, students may choose to live in traditional residence halls, interest-based theme suites, theme cottages, Greek houses, or senior townhouses.

St. Lawrence provides a full range of services to students, including comprehensive career planning as well as graduate and professional school guidance.

Students seeking co-curricular activities can choose from over 100 organizations, including everything from student government to interest groups, to arts and culture.

St. Lawrence boasts 34 intercollegiate teams including NCAA Division I teams in men's and women's ice hockey. All other teams compete in the NCAA's Division III. Club sports are also available, as is participation in a broad range of popular intramural sports.

ADMISSIONS PROCESS

St. Lawrence seeks undergraduates with the capacity to manage a demanding academic regimen successfully. In addition, the ideal student contributes substantially to the quality of community life. The University strives to enroll students who represent the broadest possible range of economic, ethnic, geographic, and social backgrounds. The admissions committee values academic achievement, but ability in athletics, community service, leadership, or the creative arts is also considered a strong indicator of a student's capacity to benefit from her or his time at St. Lawrence. The University is test optional for all domestic students, so students may choose to submit the results of their SAT, ACT, both SAT and ACT, or none. Any submitted tests will be used during the evaluation process. Students are strongly encouraged to plan a campus visit; interviews may be scheduled to occur on campus. In certain areas, off-campus interviews are also an option.

The University makes no requirement of applicants' high school curricula; however, successful applicants generally demonstrate extensive preparation in the humanities, mathematics, the natural sciences, and the social sciences. Advanced Placement, IB and honors work are looked upon favorably, as they demonstrate the applicants' intellectual curiosity and maturity. These are qualities that are highly sought by the admissions committee.

St. Lawrence uses the Common Application exclusively. The application processing fee is $60, which is waived with an official campus visit. Applicants pursuing regular decision should submit all materials by February 1 and will be notified in mid-March of the University's decision. Students whose first choice is St. Lawrence may apply for early decision: the priority deadline for early decision applications begins on November 1 and goes until February 1. Notification of the early decision is sent approximately two weeks after the application folder is complete.

To request additional information, students should contact:

Office of Admissions and Financial Aid

St. Lawrence University

Canton, NY 13617

Visit www.stlawu.edu/admissions

ST. NORBERT COLLEGE

AT A GLANCE

With a liberal arts foundation that teaches critical-thinking, problem-solving, communication and leadership skills, St. Norbert College offers academic excellence, individual attention and faculty members focused on student success.

St. Norbert is a private, coeducational institution with more than 40 fields of study, including several pre-professional programs, all of which can be enhanced by our honors program, student-faculty collaborative research (as early as your first year), professional internships and our study-abroad program. With a four-year graduation guarantee, St. Norbert offers students a true value when considering the personal attention that a St. Norbert education offers, and the high graduate-school and career placement that our graduates achieve.

Founded in 1898, St. Norbert has become one of the top 10 Catholic liberal arts colleges in the nation. St. Norbert is open to students of all faiths and committed to a well-rounded education fueled by the Norbertine tradition of communio (a deep-rooted, heartfelt sense of community). At St. Norbert, our goal is to help students pursue their passions and become engaged, informed global citizens.

CAMPUS FACILITIES & EQUIPMENT

Located on the banks of the Fox River in De Pere (a residential community of 23,000) in northeastern Wisconsin, the St. Norbert campus comprises 40+ buildings on 111 beautifully landscaped acres. Students also have easy access to the neighboring all-American city of Green Bay and its suburbs, with a metropolitan population of about 300,000. With a safe, supportive atmosphere on campus and a thriving corporate, cultural and entertainment industry close at hand, St. Norbert is a place that students love so much that they often refer to it as "home."

St. Norbert continues to experience great momentum with record high enrollment in recent years, as well as increasingly high-achieving students. And as the students come, so do the facilities to support them. New is St. Norbert's $40 million Gehl-Mulva Science Center, also home to the Medical College of Wisconsin's northeast Wisconsin campus. Integrated facilities for hands-on learning, collaborative research and interdisciplinary study abound in this LEED-certified, state-of-the-art science center. Also new is the $26 million Mulva Family Fitness and Sports Center.

The past several years have also seen the opening of the Cassandra Voss Center, for women's and gender studies, and Dudley Birder Hall, a performing-arts space, both in renovated, historic buildings. In 2011, a remodeled visitor and welcome center, and a $7.7 million completely renovated student dining facility Michels Commons were added to the campus.

Built in 2010, an outdoor athletics complex serves as the practice and competition venue for Green Knights football, soccer, and track and field. The Miriam B. and James J Mulva library was dedicated in 2009, and in 2013 its lower level became home to a high-tech collaborative workspace for students.

Among other facilities, a campus center and marina located on the Fox River offer students a relaxing environment to grab a bite to eat, sit out on the deck or in the gazebo, work out in the fitness center or gym, or gather for a concert or movie. The campus coffee shop Ed's is another favorite student hangout.

Only a five-minute drive from campus, Green Bay and all its restaurants, shopping malls, museums and performing arts opportunities can be easily accessed by students when they've exhausted the shops and boutiques of charming De Pere. Metro bus services offer free transportation throughout the metropolitan area with a student ID.

ACADEMICS

Experiential learning is the norm at St. Norbert. Research fellowships, as early as freshman year, give students hands-on opportunities to experience graduate-level research from Day One. Those opportunities for collaborating with St. Norbert faculty continue throughout students' four years, and they often have the opportunity to present their work at local, regional or national conferences.

Students are also privileged to experience one of the more prolific study-abroad programs in the country spanning six continents, 29 countries and more than 75 program sites for St. Norbert students to experience a global perspective. In fact, an average of 30 percent of St. Norbert students study abroad each year—well above the national average.

And that international perspective is part of the fabric at St. Norbert. Our Center for International Education on campus encourages a diverse student body, typically including more than 100 students, representing more than 20 countries.

All students are assigned an adviser, who helps them chart their academic career and ensure they can graduate in four years. Students have the option of designing a personal major to help them achieve their academic objectives.

For high-achieving students, a challenging honors program provides plenty of opportunity for academic engagement. Honors students have been particularly fond of participating in their own living-learning community of intellectually curious and creative students.

The metropolitan Green Bay area offers students nearly unlimited opportunities for internships. The region boasts Fortune 500 companies, hospitals, schools and service organizations that play host to many student internships. Of course, students also regularly intern for the 13-time world champion Green Bay Packers, who hold their summer training camp on campus.

For those students more interested in volunteering, the Norbertine philosophy of self-emptying service is a perfect fit. Local, national and international service opportunities are hallmarks of a St. Norbert education.

MAJORS & DEGREES OFFERED

We offer Bachelor of Arts (BA), Bachelor of Science (BS), Bachelor of Music (BM) and Bachelor of Business Administration (BBA) undergraduate degrees.

Undergraduate Programs:

Accounting

American Studies

Art

Art Education

Biochemistry

Biology

Business Administration

Business Information Systems

Chemistry

Classical Studies

Communication and Media Studies

Computer Science

Economics

Education

English and Creative Writing

Environmental Science

French

Geography

Geology

German

Graphic Design

Graphic Design and Implementation

History

Humanities and Fine Arts

Human Services

International Business and Language Area Studies

International Studies

Japanese

Leadership Studies

Mathematics

Military Science

Modern Languages and Literatures

Music

Music Education

Natural Sciences

Nursing

Peace and Justice

Philosophy

Physics

Political Science

Pre-Dental

Pre-Engineering

Pre-Law

Pre-Medical

Pre-Veterinary

Psychology

Sociology

Spanish

Special Education

Theatre Studies

Theology and Religious Studies

Women's and Gender Studies

Graduate Programs:

Master of Business Administration

Master of Arts in Liberal Studies

Master of Science in Education

Master of Theological Studies

TUITION, ROOM, BOARD, FEES

Full-time undergraduate students (3 or more full courses/12-18 credits):

$35,878 Tuition

$ 9,860 Average room and board

$ 715 Fees

FINANCIAL AID

More than 96 percent of St. Norbert students receive some form of financial aid, with the average award being more than $24,500. To achieve our goal of helping students obtain an affordable and quality college education, St. Norbert allocates funds each year for distribution to students whose families lack necessary funds. More than $50 million in financial aid is available annually at St. Norbert College in the form of scholarships, grants, student employment and loans. We encourage students to submit the Free Application for Federal Student Aid (FAFSA) as early as possible, and preferably by January 1. The St. Norbert FAFSA code is 003892. Financial aid awards typically go out in mid to late January.

STUDENT ORGANIZATIONS & ACTIVITIES

Students quickly adjust to campus with a welcoming community of faculty, students and staff. First Year Experience (FYE) programming helps students acclimate to campus and to college life in general. The Norbertine principle of radical hospitality is immediately evident when arriving on campus.

Students at St. Norbert tend to be very involved. Because it's a residential campus, activities and opportunities are close at hand. The college offers 90 student organizations and clubs that provide a rich co-curricular campus environment. Students can find opportunities in academic, diversity, ethnic and cultural, Greek, social, special interest, governing, programming and media, recreation, and service and faith organizations. And if students are looking for a particular interest that hasn't found its place on campus yet, they can create a new student organization.

A Division III school, we offer 10 men's and 10 women's varsity sports, and our athletes have been named Academic All-Americans more times than any other school in the Midwest Conference. Additionally, our men's and women's hockey teams compete in the Northern Collegiate Hockey Association. The Green Knights are frequent conference champions, averaging about four per year. Nearly one quarter of our students are involved in varsity sports, with many others participating in intramurals.

ADMISSIONS PROCESS

Students can apply using either the St. Norbert College online application or the Common Application.

Because St. Norbert reviews applications on a rolling basis and gives preference to students according to the date of admission and enrollment deposit, it benefits students to apply as early as possible during their senior year.

Notification of the admission decision is made on a rolling basis beginning in late September. After St. Norbert receives all of the required admission information, students receive notification via mail of their admission status within 2-4 weeks. A nonrefundable $350 deposit is required to confirm enrollment.

First-year domestic student important dates:

August 15 admission office begins reviewing applications

September 1 admission office begins notifying students of their application status

October 1 apply for financial aid at www.fafsa.ed.gov; St. Norbert's FAFSA school code is 003892

January 1 financial aid priority deadline

May 1 priority date for enrollment deposit

June summer orientation

For more information, prospective students are encouraged to contact:

St. Norbert College

Office of Admission

100 Grant Street

De Pere, WI 54115-2099

Phone: 920-403-3005 or 800-236-4878

Fax: 920-403-4072

Email: admit@snc.edu

Web: snc.edu

STATE UNIVERSITY OF NEW YORK—
COLLEGE OF ENVIRONMENTAL SCIENCE AND FORESTRY

AT A GLANCE

Founded in 1911, the College of Environmental Science and Forestry is a premier environmental college focused on building a sustainable future through research and degree programs in the environmental sciences, engineering, design and management.

In 2016, ESF was listed among the nation's top "Cool Schools" by Sierra magazine and ranked No. 2 among the nation's "green colleges" by the Princeton Review. It is the oldest and largest college in the United States focused solely on the environment. ESF inspires tomorrow's environmental leaders, creates knowledge and options for innovative solutions, and seeks societal consensus on the great environmental challenges of our time.

ESF is a doctoral degree (Ph.D.)-granting institution in Syracuse, New York. In addition to the College's main campus in Syracuse, New York, ESF operates 25,000 acres of field stations, experimental forests and study sites across New York state. These natural environments include stunningly beautiful and ecologically rich locations in the Thousand Islands and the Adirondacks.

ESF's status as a doctoral degree-granting institution tells you a lot about the academic quality you'll find here. Colleges with doctoral programs typically attract top-notch faculty who want to push the boundaries of knowledge in their academic specialties, and they accomplish that by working with outstanding students on cutting-edge research and real-world problems.

At some colleges (most often the bigger ones), the best faculty members work primarily with graduate students, but at ESF our small-college environment ensures undergraduates also get the personal attention they deserve. You'll find ESF faculty members want to help you succeed in your academic program and prepare for a rewarding career, and that process begins in the smaller classes ESF often provides. When U.S. News & World Report ranked the nation's 100 "Best National Universities" based on percentage of classes with fewer than 20 students (2015 edition), ESF was ranked 18th in the nation, with 66 percent of our classes at that size.

The outstanding students who choose ESF also make a difference in the learning environment. They are well prepared for the focused and challenging academic programs offered at the College, and they come to ESF with a strong commitment to solving environmental problems. This results in a close-knit community of faculty and students who share many interests and work together to improve the world around them.

The faculty at ESF come from impressive backgrounds and work on research aimed at solving many of the world's environmental problems. Students work side by side with faculty members on current research ranging from restoring polluted lakes to developing new sources of biofuels. ESF has more faculty and students in academic programs focused on the environment than any other college in the United States, but our faculty get to know students on a first-name basis. Outstanding teaching is the top priority of our faculty.

Students participate in classroom, laboratory, and field work at our main campus in Syracuse and in the forest and wetlands at ESF's regional campuses and field stations. ESF faculty and students are also conducting environmental research all around the globe, and our study-abroad programs can take you to exotic locations.

Career-related internships provide invaluable work experience and often pave the way to a permanent position after graduation. The College has an extensive internship program to help students with the internship process. Every ESF major requires some type of experiential learning to enhance your education.

Next door to ESF's Syracuse campus is Syracuse University, and ESF students can take advantage of a wide variety of programs and services at both institutions. ESF students are able to take selected courses at SU and participate in academic and cultural events.

SU also provides ESF students with a greater choice of options for on-campus recreation, activities, clubs, dining and religious services. You can attend exciting Division I sports events in the Carrier Dome and join more than 350 student organizations and clubs on both campuses.

ESF has earned top rankings from U.S. News & World Report in its annual survey of "America's Best Colleges," which placed ESF among the top 50 "best value" colleges in the nation and among the top 100 national universities for quality and reputation. Forbes magazine has ranked ESF 20th in its list of "best college buys" and third in its list of the nation's best colleges for women studying science and engineering.

LOCATION & ENVIRONMENT

ESF's main campus is in Syracuse, New York, immediately adjacent to the Syracuse University campus. This offers students a unique "small and large school" environment, where students benefit from small classes and personal attention from faculty on the ESF campus while also having access to the academic facilities, diverse student population, and active social life offered by Syracuse University.

CAMPUS FACILITIES & EQUIPMENT

Students participate in classroom, laboratory and fieldwork at ESF's Syracuse campus and in more than 25,000 acres of forest and wetlands at seven regional campus and field stations throughout the state. In 2016, ESF was listed among the nation's top "Cool Schools" by Sierra magazine and was ranked No. 2 among the nation's green colleges by the Princeton Review. The College features a number of sustainability demonstration projects and a LEED platinum-rated student center. Computing, library, dining and sports facilities are available at ESF and at neighboring Syracuse University.

OFF-CAMPUS OPPORTUNITIES

Syracuse is a medium-size city and a "college town" featuring many cultural and entertainment options. Students often attend Division I sports events at the Syracuse University Carrier Dome. The downtown area is a five-minute shuttle bus ride from campus, and the city culture is student-friendly. The largest shopping mall in the northeast (Destiny USA) is in Syracuse.

ACADEMIC PROGRAMS

ESF's long-standing partnership with Syracuse University (SU) provides students with the opportunity to take classes at SU as part of their ESF degree program, providing access to hundreds of elective courses in the liberal arts, management and other areas that are offered by SU. ESF offers a highly selective Honors Program focused on undergraduate research opportunities. Study-abroad opportunities take students to many countries and provide options to conduct research in a range of ecosystems.

MAJORS & DEGREES OFFERED

ESF offers more than 50 associate's, bachelor's, master's and doctoral degree programs focused on sustainability and the science, design, engineering and management of our environment and natural resources. All degree programs offer research and experiential learning opportunities. Popular programs include wildlife science, environmental engineering, landscape architecture, forestry and natural resources management, biochemistry, environmental studies, bioprocess engineering, environmental science, biotechnology, environmental health, conservation biology and several others.

TUITION, ROOM, BOARD AND FEES

Tuition, room, board and fees for the 2016-17 academic year total $23,143 for New York state residents and $32,993 for out-of-state residents.

FINANCIAL AID

ESF has been ranked among the top 50 "Best Buy" colleges in the nation. Special scholarships offset out-of-state costs. The College awards approximately half of its scholarships based on academic potential and half based on financial need. Students file the Free Application for Federal Student Aid (FAFSA) for financial aid consideration, with a priority deadline of Feb. 1. Admissions applications must be submitted by Feb. 1 for academic (merit) scholarship consideration.

STUDENT ORGANIZATIONS & ACTIVITIES

Students participate in approximately 30 clubs and organizations sponsored by ESF's student government and may join more than 300 student organizations at Syracuse University. ESF offers intercollegiate athletics teams in basketball, soccer, golf, cross country, track and timber sports. Community service is an important part of the student culture at ESF, and many student activities focus on outdoor recreation and travel.

ADMISSIONS

Admission is selective and the College attracts a diverse and academically qualified entering class. An Early Decision (first choice) application plan is offered. See www.esf.edu/admissions. Students apply to the specific major that interests them and most programs require strong grades in high school mathematics and science. SAT/ACT scores are also important, along with a demonstrated interest in sustainability and the environment.

ESF attracts a large number of transfer students (more than 250 per year) in addition to the entering first-year class, and a minimum college GPA of 2.80 or higher is generally required for transfer admission.

Students most often use the Common Application when applying, and a campus visit is strongly encouraged.

STEPHENS COLLEGE

AT A GLANCE

Founded in 1833, Stephens College believes in providing bold, ambitious young women with the tools, knowledge and experiences they need to chase down their dreams. The College focuses on the creative arts and health sciences and emphasizes experiential learning, career preparation and leadership. The growing college town location provides a wealth of recreational and social opportunities while the tradition of the Ten Ideals encourages a culture of respect and responsibility.

LOCATION & ENVIRONMENT

Ranked (over and over and over again) as one of the best college towns in America, Columbia, Mo. is home to 36,000+ college students. Columbia has it all: big time college sports; film, music and arts festivals; amazing recreation; and a great downtown with lots of places to eat, shop, snack and check out the latest bands. Stephens College is just steps from downtown yet the campus itself is known for historic charm with red brick buildings and lovely green spaces.

CAMPUS FACILITIES & EQUIPMENT

From Pillsbury Science Center to Catharine Webb Studios (home to the School of Design), Stephens features carefully renovated spaces with the latest equipment and technologies for collaborative and hands-on learning. The School of Performing Arts features two theatres for public performances and a range of studios and rehearsal spaces (as well as a summer stock theatre located in Iowa). Education students benefit from an on-site lab school (pre-school and K-5) while students majoring in Equestrian Studies enjoy an Equestrian Center that is just steps from campus.

Most students live right on campus—steps away from friends, professors, classrooms, labs, dining and free laundry facilities. Students also have access to facility crews when needed and 24-hour, 7-day security. Halls have wifi throughout. Stephens offers traditional residential halls, special housing communities and apartment-style suites and options —all with residential advisers and programming. The pet-friendly campus includes pet-friendly housing and halls where pets are not allowed.

OFF-CAMPUS OPPORTUNITIES

The pursuit of international opportunities (study abroad, service abroad) is encouraged and students have travelled from South Africa to Soeul, Korea. A Student Success Center provides a comprehensive list of services to ensure students are well prepared and excited by the academic experience. A Stephens Scholars program provides additional academic challenge and service opportunities.

ACADEMICS

Stephens College is committed to helping students and alumnae prepare for success in the workforce and life. We take a holistic approach to career and life planning and understand the importance of connecting the right graduate with the right opportunity. Stephens' College-to-Career curriculum includes a non-academic graduation requirement that focuses on career exploration, counseling and assessment. A step-by-step approach begins at student orientation and builds to a student's final year.

Academic advising is a form of teaching and an integral part of each student's education. Quality, thoughtful advising is taken seriously at Stephens. A first-year advising program helps students get started on their college journey. Subsequent years of advising focus on career planning. Advisers take the time to listen and are committed to helping students navigate their way. Stephens believes that small class sizes and individual attention are essential to success and promotes a 10-to-1 student-to-teacher ratio.

MAJORS & DEGREES OFFERED

Stephens is a leader in the creative arts and health sciences and all programs empha-size hands-on experiential learning, leadership cultivation and career experiences. Students benefit from a wide range of offerings in the performing arts, health sciences and fashion. Popular majors also include equestrian studies, education, film, English and creative writing, marketing, design, event and convention management, and psychology. Self-directed majors and minors offer more options.

Many majors can be completed in 3 years including several in the School of Performing Arts. The school applies a 3-year/2-summer approach that includes summer intensives to ensure students graduate on time with an impressive body of experiences, well prepared for their next career step.

TUITION, ROOM, BOARD, FEES

Annual tuition for 2016-17 is $29,554 with room/board ranging from $8,187 to $12,268 at the private institution.

FINANCIAL AID

Ninety-eight percent of Stephens students receive some form of financial aid. The College Office of Financial Aid is always available to help families understand their options and works hard to help all families afford a quality education.

STUDENT ORGANIZATIONS & ACTIVITIES

Stephens College is proud to be the second-oldest women's college in the country yet part of a large co-educational college town. Students (as well as faculty, staff and alumnae) deeply value diversity in all its forms, commit to a culture of respect and support, and empower women's leadership and creativity.

As a women's college, Stephens recognize and celebrates the skills and talents of student-athletes. Athletics programs provide opportunities for students to challenge themselves physically, to experience teamwork in action and to simply a life of sport. We are committed to the philosophy of developing student-athletes whose first priority is education. We're affiliated with the National Association of Inter-collegiate Athletics (NAIA) and a member of the American Midwest Conference. Athletics programs include Basketball, Competitive Dance, Cross Country, Golf, Soccer, Tennis and Volleyball.

Stephens College has been consistently recognized as the most pet-friendly campus in the country and welcomes dogs, cats, birds, gerbils, guinea pigs, hamsters, lizards, mice, rabbits, rats, sugar gliders, turtles and hedgehogs, and includes scholarships for pet fostering, pet parades and activities, and even Doggy Daycare. Stephens also offers pet-free zones too including residence halls with no pets allowed, providing options for everyone.

ADMISSIONS PROCESS

Stephens uses a rolling admissions review process, which means it is never too early or late to apply. However, the date of a student's deposit is taken into consideration for housing and class registration so early applications are strongly encouraged. The information provided during the application process will be automatically reviewed for scholarship eligibility.

STEVENS INSTITUTE OF TECHNOLOGY

AT A GLANCE

Located in Hoboken, NJ on the Hudson River overlooking the Manhattan skyline, Stevens is a high-energy, highly engaged campus community in which hands-on learning complements academic experiences. The combination of a rigorous curriculum, a focus on innovation and entrepreneurship, and tremendous opportunities for experiential learning aligned with industry needs has proven to be a winning formula for Stevens graduates over the years.

Recognized for putting the "hire" in higher education, a Stevens degree is a passport to a successful and stimulating career. Exceptional opportunities for internships, undergraduate research and cooperative education prepare students with skills that are in demand by the world's most influential employers, because they are skills that impact industries and innovations that drive our economy.

Students choose from 35 undergraduate majors in Business, Humanities, Arts, Computer Science, Engineering and the Sciences; many students double major or choose to pursue both bachelor's and master's degrees. Graduates are highly skilled in creating solutions at the intersections of disciplines and can lead in today's complex, cross-functional and highly technical environments, and have always fared exceptionally well in career and graduate school placement. Stevens is consistently ranked among the nation's elite for total return on investment and mid-career salaries of graduates—#17 and #12 in the nation respectively, according to reports by PayScale. Our graduates are recruited into highly competitive positions and accepted into top graduate programs: 96% of the Class of 2016 secured outcomes within six months of graduation. Stevens' 3,115 undergraduate students come from more than 45 states and 68 countries, creating a diverse, dynamic environment. Stevens also boasts an outstanding campus life—students will find more than 75 student clubs and organizations and 26 NCAA Division III athletics teams.

LOCATION & ENVIRONMENT

Stevens is located in one of the most exciting, cosmopolitan towns in the United States. Hoboken, NJ, is a quaint one-mile-square city with old Victorian brownstones and tree-lined streets dotted with great restaurants and trendy shops. Located on the Hudson River, the 55-acre campus is home to stretches of green lawns, majestic trees, and historic classroom buildings that have been updated with the most current teaching and learning technologies. With the heart of New York City a mere 10-minute commute away, Stevens students take advantage of being close to top companies with exciting internships and career placements as well as unlimited cultural experiences and events throughout the year.

In addition to the robust on-campus student life, Stevens' location provides for exciting off-campus activities. Dining, entertainment, and major attractions offer numerous artistic, cultural, athletic and recreational opportunities.

Stevens students enjoy a safe and dynamic living environment. Eighty-eight percent of Stevens undergraduate students live on campus, and housing is guaranteed for undergraduates. There are seven on-campus residence halls in addition to various on-and off-campus apartments for upperclassmen. Sixteen fraternities and sororities have chapters on campus and most maintain houses where members may live. Stevens also features "affinity housing" for students interested in community service and civic engagement, as well as a women's center. The dining program features late night hours to meet students' busy schedules, and many establishments in Hoboken also accept Stevens' Duck Bills, reloadable on student ID cards.

CAMPUS FACILITIES & EQUIPMENT

Stevens operates within a technology-centric environment to meet the needs of a technologically fluent campus, offering a variety of centralized, departmental, and individual resources. Facilities include "smart" classrooms, computer-aided design and manufacturing labs, graphics labs, robotic sites, a media arts center, green screen, sound synthesis lab, a computer-aided education lab, a new motion capture lab, and a financial systems center with a Wall Street trading room. Stevens offers its community an extensive wireless networking system. Two pioneering projects underway, the Unified Communications and Collaboration Environment and the Virtual Learning Environment, will have transformative impact on our graphic-and computing-intensive technology applications for learning.

Our research enterprise focuses on key areas that address major interdisciplinary topics of national significance: healthcare and medicine, sustainable energy, financial systems, security, coastal sustainability, and STEM education. Supporting these areas are many specialized laboratory facilities on campus used for academic and research functions, applied research, and educational programs in systems integration that meet and support the needs of government and industry. The Office of Innovation and Entrepreneurship fosters an entrepreneurial culture across the university, advances the outcomes of the research, and engages in the technology transfer that brings new ideas to the marketplace.

OFF-CAMPUS OPPORTUNITIES

Stevens cultivates the value of being a world citizen, giving back to the community and building bridges across cultures. In addition to the popular internship, research, and cooperative education opportunities offered at Stevens, students take their educational experience across the globe through study abroad, service-oriented organizations, and department-sponsored trips.

Community service has a prominent place in campus life. From tutoring local school children to assisting the elderly and participating in neighborhood community projects, Stevens students are very much a part of our hometown. This service orientation extends beyond Hoboken to the global community, with opportunities to bring the benefits of Stevens innovation to countries and areas of need.

ACADEMICS

Stevens offers unique and challenging educational opportunities that foster innovation and lead students to success. Research projects and summer internships are available for all major fields of study. Stevens blends humanities and technology subjects, and is distinctive in the encouragement of students to bridge disciplines and interests. Our technology orientation, combined with humanities and business offerings, provides an optimal blend for developing leadership qualities. Considering these fields together helps students gain perspective not only about the ways in which things work, but also why they matter, what the societal impact might be, and how we can influence progress. Students in different majors collaborate on high-impact projects, like the U.S. Department of Energy's Solar Decathlon competition.

The Cooperative Education (co-op) program is also distinctive. Co-op students alternate semesters of on-campus study with semesters of paid, professional work experiences. Co-op students graduate with a competitive edge in the job market, having gained a higher level of confidence through development of significant workplace skills. Our co-op program is one of the reasons Stevens ranks 3rd in the nation for career placement (Princeton Review's Colleges That Pay You Back, 2015) and was named among the top 50 "Colleges That Create Futures" (Princeton Review, 2015)..

The Pinnacle Scholars Program allows exceptional students to participate in honors seminars and summer research. Many take advantage of the 4+1 Master's Program to graduate with a bachelor's and master's degree in five years, receiving a scholarship equal to 20 percent of graduate tuition in the fifth year.

The annual Stevens Innovation Expo is one of many programs aimed at promoting entrepreneurial thinking at Stevens. In addition to the design project showcase, student inventors present their technologies in a fast-paced and exciting venture-style pitch competition, where students propose business ideas for their new technologies to a panel of five experts, who evaluate and award the most viable projects with the greatest potential for market realization.

Stevens Technical Enrichment Program (STEP) helps broaden the access of minority and economically disadvantaged students to careers in engineering, science, and technology through pre-college and in-college programs and support services.

MAJORS & DEGREES OFFERED

Stevens students are committed to exploring the frontiers of engineering, computer science, sciences, business, the humanities and arts. Undergraduate degrees awarded include the Bachelor of Engineering (BE), Bachelor of Science (BS), and Bachelor of Art (BA) degrees.

Business Majors: Business and Technology; Economics; Finance; Information Systems; Management; Marketing; Quantitative Finance

Humanities & Arts Majors: History; Literature; Music and Technology; Philosophy; Science Communication; Science, Technology and Society; Social Sciences; Visual Arts and Technology

Computer Science Majors: Computer Science; Cybersecurity

Engineering Majors: Biomedical Engineering; Chemical Engineering; Civil Engineering; Computer Engineering; Electrical Engineering; Engineering Management; Environmental Engineering; Mechanical Engineering; Naval Engineering; Software Engineering.

Science Majors: Biology; Chemical Biology; Chemistry; Computational Science; Engineering Physics; Mathematics; Physics.

Many students pursue dual degree options or opt to complete requirements for both bachelor's and master's degrees during their four or five years on campus.

Stevens offers a 6-year Accelerated Law program (Bachelor's/J.D.) and a 7-year Accelerated Medicine (B.S./M.D.) program with partner universities; a 5-year Master's program; a competitive Pinnacle Scholars program; and the unique Innovation and Entrepreneurship Summer Research Program.

TUITION, ROOM, BOARD, FEES

Stevens tuition and fees for 2016-2017 are $47,366. Room and board total $15,200 (typical on-campus, double occupancy/typical meal plan; other plans vary). Student fees consist of a student activity fee, health service fee and technology fee.

FINANCIAL AID

Stevens is committed to assisting, investing in, and ensuring the highest quality of service to its students. The university offers a wide range of institutional merit scholarships and need-based grants, federal and state grants, loans, and work opportunity programs for eligible students. Stevens requires new students file the College Scholarship Service (CSS) Profile for consideration for all institutional scholarships and grants. The Free Application for Federal Student Aid (FAFSA) is required of all students for consideration for all federal and state financial aid programs. The deadline to submit both the FAFSA and CSS Profile is February 15. Early Decision I and Early Decision II applicants must submit the CSS Profile by December 1 or January 15 respectively.

STUDENT ORGANIZATIONS & ACTIVITIES

The energy at Stevens extends well beyond the classroom activities and career orientation of our students into a robust student life. Nearly 100 student organizations and 26 NCAA Division III athletics teams add to an enriching student experience and prepare students for a healthy and energizing balance of hard work and fun.

Clubs and organizations include sororities and fraternities, performing arts and athletic groups, student government, ethnic organizations, professional societies, and more. The Alpha Phi Omega service fraternity, Engineers Without Borders, and Habitat for Humanity are service-oriented groups with active student engagement. Campus traditions like Boken and TechFest (campus-wide festivals), the Unity Show, and Midnight Breakfast during finals study periods are among students' favorites.

The Schaefer Athletic and Recreation Center features a NCAA competition-size pool with jacuzzi, four-court basketball gymnasium, racquetball courts, and a fitness center. DeBaun Field has been surfaced in a state-of the-art, durable, year-round playing surface for varsity and intramural competition. Walker Gym has an elevated indoor track plus a weightlifting facility and dance studios. There are also six outdoor tennis courts with spectacular Manhattan skyline views and a sand volleyball court. In 2013, Stevens was the recipient of the ECAC/Jostens "Institution of the Year" award, from among more than 320 Division I, II, and III schools, for excellence in academics and athletics—one of only three schools to have received this honor more than once.

Stevens competes in NCAA Division III sports. For men: baseball, basketball, cross-country, fencing, golf, indoor/outdoor track and field, lacrosse, soccer, swimming, tennis, volleyball and wrestling. For women: basketball, cross-country, equestrian, fencing, field hockey, indoor/outdoor track and field, lacrosse, soccer, swimming, tennis, softball and volleyball. Students may also join a club team or play intramural sports, take health and wellness or fitness classes, or participate in outdoor adventure trips.

ADMISSIONS PROCESS

Stevens is highly competitive. Undergraduate applicants must submit (detailed requirements by program or type of applicant can be found on our website: stevens. edu/admissions/undergraduate-admissions/how-apply

- An application for admission
- Official transcripts
- Standardized test scores
- Two letters of recommendation
- Essay (as a part of the application)

Admission Statistics (incoming Fall 2016)

Applicants: 7,409

Acceptance rate: 39.1%

New students enrolling: 737

SAT Range°: 1260-1440, combined math/reading (°middle 50%)

Average GPA: 3.80

The freshman application deadline for the fall semester is February 1 (Early Decision I and II deadlines are November 15 and January 15, respectively). For additional deadlines for different programs and transfer students, please refer to our website: https://www.stevens.edu/admissions/undergraduate-admissions/how-apply/admission-timeline

SWARTHMORE COLLEGE

AT A GLANCE

Swarthmore College has supported thinkers and doers for more than 150 years. Swarthmore students are creators, inventors, debaters, and problem solvers. If that appeals to you, we invite you to join us. As you help shape this place, it shapes you; your way of looking at the world, your way of interacting with it, your way of making it a better place. After four years on our campus—described as equal parts "challenging and busy" and "idyllic and enchanting"—you'll emerge prepared to work with others to make things happen. Whether that means advancing sustainability research, starting a microfinance incubator, founding a dance-based youth empowerment program, or making adaptations for blind students in engineering curriculum, as a Swattie you'll have what it takes to apply your knowledge with meaning and purpose.

One of our students said, "It doesn't ultimately matter what courses you take here. What matters is that you took them here." Swarthmore students immerse themselves in a world of intellect and action, collaboration and connection. Every course is designed to make you think, which means that you and your classmates will struggle together, laugh together, and end up discovering more than you thought possible.

What lies at the heart of our community? It's passion. We don't trade in the type of motivation that's extrinsically imposed on you. That's coercion. We don't value a superficial reward: that's a pat on the head. We believe that it's hard to motivate in a vacuum, and that's why the quality of the people around you makes such a difference. Everyone at Swarthmore is on an intellectual journey. The students are compelled to find their calling—undauntingly and unceasingly. The faculty is inspired to work with students on joint research projects, which helps students realize themselves as scholars and leaders and doers. That leads to even greater involvement, which leads to the kind of discussions you can't stop thinking about, which leads to even deeper levels of collaboration. Before long, you're asking questions your professor can't answer. You're thinking of ways to apply your ideas, to make them more relevant to the world.

LOCATION & ENVIRONMENT

The path from the beauty and tranquility of Swarthmore's 425-acre arboretum campus to the adventure and opportunity of the wider world is far shorter than you might think. Each fall, the College's seniors screen The Graduate on the lawn in front of Parrish Hall, and each fall, the film reminds students to contemplate life beyond campus, and the rest of their lives. With Philadelphia less than 30 minutes away, and New York City and Washington, D.C. within a 90-minute train ride, life-shaping experiences are within easy reach. And even on campus, incredible opportunities present themselves in surprising ways, such as the student who, partly on the strength of helping to build a database of Crum Woods ecological data, was offered a position at Google. The bottom line: Swarthmore's sense of place prepares you for anything and everything. Our alumni are equipped to make the most of where they've been—and make sense of what they haven't yet seen.

CAMPUS FACILITIES & EQUIPMENT

Swarthmore has a dynamic array of arts spaces to enjoy—or stage—a performance. Avenues of exploration abound, whether it's immersing yourself in Language Resource Center technology to learn a new dialect, getting lost in the stars in the observatory, or studying or sharing samosas with friends in the Kohlberg coffee bar. The forthcoming biology, engineering, psychology (BEP) building will open new doors of discovery for students. The new, gleaming Matchbox facility offers a multifaceted, modern approach to wellness, recreation, and the performing arts, imbuing creativity, fitness, and community.

OFF-CAMPUS OPPORTUNITIES

Swarthmore belong to the Tri-College consortium, which links to nearby Bryn Mawr and Haverford Colleges both academically and socially. In addition, students can take courses at the University of Pennsylvania, a short train ride away. These extensions of the Swarthmore experience allow students to expand their intellectual and social capital, whether it's watching a play at Haverford, connecting with a Penn professor about an internship reference, or sharing a meal at Bryn Mawr. The College offers shuttles to the other Tri-Co schools, community service sites, local restaurants and shops, and more. There's also a train station adjacent to campus, inviting students to the rich cultural tapestry of center city Philadelphia (less than 30 minutes away).

ACADEMICS

The College offers more than 600 courses a year; an exceptional Honors Program; individual special majors; a program in education that leads to Pennsylvania secondary school certification; and significant undergraduate research opportunities in the sciences, social sciences, humanities, and engineering.

If you're like most Swatties, you've worked really hard to prepare for college and paid a lot of attention to grades. So in your first semester at Swarthmore, we want you to focus on learning without worrying about your GPA. Our distinctive freshman pass/fail semester has obvious benefits: You'll explore topics that interest you, expose yourself to new disciplines, challenge yourself, and discover potentially life-changing passions—without being paralyzed by the stultifying fear of failure. In addition, you'll have a chance to adjust to college life and achieve a balance between coursework and everything else.

Some of our students prefer to take a deep dive into their area of passion. Those students find their intellectual home in Swarthmore's Honors Program, which represents intellectual inquiry at its highest levels. Modeled on the Oxford tutorial system, it features small groups of students working collaboratively with faculty to explore topics through spirited debate and thoughtful exploration of ideas. At the close of their senior year, Honors Program candidates are evaluated by visiting examiners, such as Federal Reserve economists and directors of world-class theater companies. You know you've truly mastered a topic when it's time to discuss your ideas with brilliant strangers.

MAJORS

Swarthmore College awards two degrees, the Bachelor of Arts and the Bachelor of Science. The College offers the following courses of study:

Art and Art History

Asian Studies

Astronomy

Biology

Black Studies

Chemistry and Biochemistry

Classics

Cognitive Science

Comparative Literature

Computer Science

Dance

Design Your Own Major

Economics

Educational Studies

Engineering

English Literature

Environmental Studies

Film and Media Studies

Gender and Sexuality Studies

History

Interpretation Theory

Islamic Studies

Latin American and Latino Studies

Linguistics

Mathematics and Statistics

Medieval Studies

Modern Languages and Literatures (including Arabic, Chinese, French, German, Japanese, Russian, and Spanish)

Music

Peace and Conflict Studies

Philosophy

Physics

Political Science

Psychology

Religion

Sociology and Anthropology

Theater

TUITION, ROOM, BOARD, FEES

For 2016–2017, the College charges, including tuition, room, board, and student activity fee, amount to $63,550. The activity fee covers not only the usual student services—health, library, laboratory fees, for example—but admission to all social, cultural, and athletic events on campus. In addition, the College's Quaker roots manifest themselves in a cash-free campus, as the annual activity fee covers everything from digital printing and laundry to sporting events, campus movie screenings, and dance performances.

FINANCIAL AID

Swarthmore's robust financial aid program is a hallmark of affordability for admitted students. Last year, Swarthmore awarded over $31 million in loan-free financial aid. The average award for the Class of 2020 was $46,931. Swarthmore does not consider a family's ability to pay when it makes its admissions decisions for U.S. citizens, permanent residents, and undocumented/DACA students graduating from U.S. high schools. If you are admitted, Swarthmore will carefully consider many factors to assess your family's ability to pay tuition, and then offer an aid award to meet up to 100 percent of demonstrated need. Almost 60% of the Class of 2020 received financial aid in 2015-2016. Swarthmore also provides assistance to some international students. This comprehensive program reflects our commitment to maximizing access to an outstanding educational experience.

STUDENT ORGANIZATIONS & ACTIVITIES

With more than 100 student clubs and organizations on campus, dozens of community service groups, 22 Division III varsity athletic teams, free lectures and performances occurring daily on campus, and full course loads, Swarthmore students are in perpetual motion.

ADMISSIONS PROCESS

Striving for a diverse, well-rounded class, the admissions staff carefully considers a number of criteria without a rigid emphasis on any one factor. Applicants are evaluated holistically, based on the following criteria:

• High school record (as well as strength of curriculum)

• Rank in class (if high school ranks)

• Standardized tests (SAT or ACT)

• Extracurricular commitments

• Essays (included in application)

• Recommendations (two from academic teachers, one from counselor)

• Interview (highly recommended but not required)

TEMPLE UNIVERSITY

AT A GLANCE

Temple University attracts some of the most diverse, driven and motivated minds from across the nation and around the world. These students and faculty bring the university to life and fuel its palpable momentum in academics, athletics, research and the arts. Powering Temple's ascent are innovative approaches in admissions and affordability; a campus transformation; plentiful creative and research opportunities; rigorous academic programs; an indelible bond with the city of Philadelphia; and groundbreaking work in science, research and technology.

Temple is home to nearly 40,000 students, is the fifth-largest provider of professional education in the U.S., and offers 153 undergraduate degree programs in 17 schools and colleges, on eight campuses, including locations in Japan and Italy.

Nearly 3,800 distinguished faculty; top art, business, dental, law and medical schools; five professional schools; and dozens of renowned programs make Temple an academic powerhouse. Students enjoy the advantages and atmosphere of a large urban, public research university with the individualized attention that comes from a 15:1 student-to-faculty ratio.

The majority of freshmen students live on campus, where they are steps away from class, the TECH Center, the library, fitness and recreation facilities, dining options from cafés and dining halls to food trucks, and the many arts, cultural, sports and scholarly events that happen daily university-wide and throughout the city.

One of Temple's newest living and learning residences is the 27-story Morgan Hall, which offers unparalleled views of the Philadelphia skyline. Because Temple is in the midst of a transformation, Morgan Hall is only one of several state-of-the-art facilities rising on the university's main campus. The 250,000-square foot Science Education and Research Center boosts student and faculty opportunities for discovery and innovation. And a new, state-of-the-art library that will feature a robotic book retrieval system and spaces devoted to traditional library activities, as well as to technology-enhanced activities, such as data visualization and 3-D printing, is now under construction.

Temple's influence also extends around the globe, with long-standing campuses in Tokyo and Rome; programs in London, Beijing and other locations worldwide; nearly 160 cooperations in 48 countries; and more than 310,000 alumni. Nearly 3,700 international students at Temple's Main Campus hail from more than 110 countries.

No matter their background, Temple students—nicknamed Owls—are drawn to the university's vibrant location in the heart of Philadelphia. The professional world is right outside their doors, where thousands of possibilities exist for hands-on learning and internships in business, healthcare, education, the arts and beyond.

By living and learning in an urban environment, Temple students are well prepared for the real world. Employers laud Owls for their tenacity, teamwork and talent. Students also have access to an immense alumni network for mentoring, guidance, connections and job opportunities.

LOCATION & ENVIRONMENT

Temple students enjoy an electric campus in one of the country's liveliest urban centers. Philadelphia—named the No. 1 place to visit in the U.S. by Lonely Planet in 2016—is home to history, arts and culture, government, technology and innovation, healthcare, and many other fields and interests. Opportunities for learning, whether through a class, an internship or a research project, abound.

More than 14,000 students now live on or near campus. They take tree-canopied walks to class, relax on the grass outside the library, meet friends at the skate park, get lunch at one of the many food trucks, and can work out at several different fitness facilities.

Temple's campus has seven residence halls and students can choose a living and learning community tailored to their major or interest.

CAMPUS FACILITIES & EQUIPMENT

Whether in the glass-blowing studio or the virtual balance lab, Temple students are immersed in world-class facilities. The Science Education and Research Center is one of the university's newest buildings and home to 68 research and teaching labs and leading-edge technologies such as clean rooms, powerful supercomputers and a scanning tunneling microscope that allows scientists to study matter at the nanoscale.

In the TECH Center—one of the largest student computing lab in the country—students can collaborate in breakout rooms, edit video in specialized labs, get assistance from the 24-hour help desk or work on one of 700 computers. There are also more than 100 other computer labs on campus, 3,600 student workstations and 450 technology-enabled classrooms.

Temple's libraries host intrepid, curious students and scholars. With the equivalent of more than four million bound volumes and an extensive special collection of rare books and archives, Temple's libraries rank among the top research libraries in North America.

OFF-CAMPUS OPPORTUNITIES

Temple's Main Campus is located 1.5 miles from the center of Philadelphia. For Temple students, the city blends seamlessly with their studies. Those studying stormwater management work hands-on with the water department, art students restore fading historical signs on older buildings, and political science majors learn from civic leaders.

As much as the city is a classroom, it's also a place of adventure. Students can explore nearly 200 museums, a thriving restaurant scene, numerous sports teams and the largest landscaped urban park in the nation.

Owls interested in experiencing different languages and cultures by studying abroad have dozens of options. They can study at Temple campuses in Tokyo or Rome or join summer programs in Brazil, South Africa, Spain and beyond. Many of the programs tie in to areas of study, like business students studying real markets in hubs such as Paris and Mumbai, or art and architecture students studying among the masterpieces in Rome.

ACADEMICS

Temple has a long tradition of self-made success. It started in 1884 as a night school so students who worked during the day could keep their jobs. Though a lot has changed, Temple's heritage still drives the work ethic of its students. Owls turn opportunities into accomplishments. World-class labs are the proving grounds for world-changing ideas. A classroom doubles as a tech startup's boardroom. Professors mentor students through graduate school and beyond. And it's all because of the uncommon drive Temple students and faculty share.

Students customize their college life in numerous ways: living and learning communities; an immersive Honors program; interdisciplinary majors; creative and research grants; internships; and career preparation and placement.

Temple encourages the spirit of entrepreneurship university-wide, so Owls know how to thrive no matter their course in life. To help foster such skills, annual innovation and business-idea competitions are open to the entire Temple community, and all students have access to mentors, resources and guidance to develop their business ideas and plans.

Temple also propels students into top graduate programs through challenging academic work, research opportunities and close partnerships with professors.

MAJORS & DEGREES OFFERED

Students passionate about learning are attracted to Temple because of its variety of academic programs: 540 are offered, including 153 bachelor's degree programs. Students who need time to decide on a major work with advisors and professors to discover their strengths and options.

TUITION, ROOM, BOARD, FEES

Tuition and fees for the 2016–2017 academic year were approximately $15,384 for Pennsylvania residents and $26,376 for out-of-state residents (tuition rates vary by major). Room and board for the same period was $11,298.

FINANCIAL AID

Temple is known for its innovation in student-loan debt reduction and college affordability. Each year, the university awards more than $100 million in scholarships. A variety of programs are available and 71 percent of first-year students receive need-based financial aid. No separate application is necessary.

Applicants for need-based aid must file the Free Application for Federal Student Aid, also called FAFSA. Transfer students must file a financial aid transcript, even if they have received no aid from their previous school.

In the fall of 2016, 93 percent of incoming freshman signed up for Temple's Fly in 4 program, which helps students limit their debt by graduating in four years. As a part of Fly in 4, Temple awards four-year grants to 500 eligible students to reduce their need to work for pay. Temple also helps Owls take charge of their finances through courses, workshops and a money-management website.

STUDENT ORGANIZATIONS & ACTIVITIES

No matter their interests, likes or passions, students find a place at Temple, thanks to hundreds of student organizations, clubs, events and activities. From political and cultural groups to scientific and scholarly pursuits, there's no shortage of ways to express one's individuality.

Throughout the year, all over campus, students can attend music and dance performances, theater productions, academic talks and panels, films, art exhibits, and sports and cultural events.

There are several large venues for concerts and shows, including the historic Temple Performing Arts Center and the university's 10,200-seat entertainment complex, which also hosts its NCAA Division I basketball games.

To keep students healthy and strong, Temple offers multiple indoor and outdoor sports, recreation and fitness facilities, including an outdoor volleyball court, a rock-climbing wall, running tracks, pools and several locations for weightlifting and classes.

ADMISSIONS PROCESS

The Temple Option is a new admissions path for talented students who may not perform well on standardized tests. If students choose the Temple Option, they answer brief essay questions instead of submitting SAT or ACT scores. The Temple Option reflects the university's commitment to provide talented, motivated students of all backgrounds opportunities for high-quality college experiences.

For freshman admissions, high-school grades, standardized test scores (sent directly from the appropriate testing agencies) or the Temple Option responses, and other factors (such as a required essay, recommendations, extracurricular activities, work or leadership experience and other personal circumstances) are considered.

Temple has rolling admissions and early-action plans for the fall semester. The early-action deadline is November 1, with notifications scheduled for mid-January (or before). The rolling admissions deadline is February 1.

Temple's admissions process is holistic: Every aspect of a student's academic history is considered. Typically, students with B+ averages or better in strong, college-preparatory curricula in grades 9 through 12 and in the top 30 percent of their graduating classes are accepted. For students submitting test scores, admitted students in 2016 averaged a 27 composite on the ACT, and an 1170 SAT (on a 1600 scale); this concords to a 1240 on the new SAT.

Students who apply as freshmen are automatically considered for merit-based scholarships and honors.

The application fee is $55, and most students apply online through Temple or the Common Application.

Temple University welcomes transfer applicants who make up almost half of each entering class. Applicants are considered transfer students if they have attempted 15 or more college-level credits after high school.

Apply to Temple at admissions.temple.edu/apply or via the Common Application. If you have questions, visit admissions.temple.edu, email askanowl@temple.edu or find Temple Admissions on Twitter, Instagram or Snapchat: @admissionsTU

TROY UNIVERSITY

AT A GLANCE

Troy University, based in Alabama, is a public university founded in 1887. Through a network of locations and a robust online offering, TROY serves both traditional students and adult learners.

TROY operates four campuses in Alabama—Troy, Dothan, Montgomery and Phenix City -and locations in 7 states, in both Japan and Korea and partnerships with universities in China, Vietnam and Malaysia.

TROY is accredited by the Southern Association of Colleges and Schools Commission on Colleges, and offers degree programs at the Associate's, Bachelor's, Master's and Doctoral level.

Founded as a college to train teachers, Troy University has today grown into a thriving international university that enrolls nearly 1,200 international students, representing more than 65 countries. Each day on the residential campus in Troy, as many as 85 different languages can be heard. Also highlighting the University's international focus, TROY is home to Alabama's only Confucius Institute that maintains a statewide mission of educating about the Chinese language, culture and history and forging economic development ties between the state and China.

Troy University offers degree programs in high-demand fields across its five colleges—the College of Arts and Sciences; the Sorrell College of Business; the College of Communication and Fine Arts; the College of Education; and, the College of Health and Human Services.

Troy University has more than 150,000 alumni worldwide and the University's Alumni Association has 63 local alumni chapters throughout the United States and international chapters in China, Russia and Vietnam.

LOCATION & ENVIRONMENT

The complete university experience may be found at Troy University's beautiful, historic campus in Troy, Ala. The Troy, Ala. campus provides top-notch academic programs as well as experiences that shape careers and lives. Students on the Troy Campus enjoy more than 150 clubs, Greek organizations and philanthropic groups, as well study abroad programs, Division I athletics, an honors program and more.

The Troy Campus also offers a wide variety of residence halls, including apartment style units. The surrounding city of Troy is a charming Southern city with a picturesque town square featuring unique boutiques and food options.

Troy's Dothan Campus is located between Dothan and Fort Rucker and serves primarily adult learners through day, evening and weekend classes. The campus is home to R. Terry Everett Hall, named in honor of the longtime Alabama Congressman from the state's Wiregrass region, and includes in its library collection Everett's Congressional papers. The Wiregrass Archives, featuring historical photos and documents from the region, is also located at the campus.

The University's Montgomery Campus is located in the heart of the state's capital city, and has been a catalyst to revitalization within the downtown area. The campus' administrative offices are located in the former Whitley Hotel, which was renovated to include office and classroom space in what is now known as Whitley Hall. Another revitalization project that is a centerpiece of the campus is the Davis Theatre for the Performing Arts, a 1,200-seat theatre and performing arts venue which features performing groups from throughout the region. The campus is also home to the Rosa Parks Library and Museum, which is located on the site of Mrs. Parks' 1955 arrest that sparked the Montgomery Bus Boycott. The museum pays tribute to Mrs. Parks' legacy of courage and celebrates the people and events of the 381-day boycott, which led to the integration of the city's public transportation system.

The Phenix City Campus, includes a location on the banks of the Chattahoochee River, which has served as a catalyst for development along the East Alabama city's riverfront. The Phenix City campus serves primarily adult learners from East Alabama and neighboring Columbus, Georgia.

CAMPUS FACILITIES & EQUIPMENT

The Troy Campus offers a full complement of facilities for students, including numerous on-campus computer labs and study facilities, a dining hall complete with numerous dining options; the Trojan Student Center, which includes activity space for events, bookstore, food court, fitness center and game room area; a comprehensive library; numerous residence halls that provide a variety of living options; fraternity and sorority houses; athletic facilities, including the 30,000-seat Veterans Memorial Stadium and Trojan Arena, which is home to men's and women's basketball.

Students also can take advantage of opportunities that will help them hone their skills and enhance their academic success. The John W. Schmidt Center for Student Success provides programs and services that enhance students' academic achievement, personal and social growth, campus and civic engagement and persistence to graduation.

ACADEMICS

With a student-first philosophy, Troy University continues to serve both traditional college-aged students and adult learners with quality academic programs, in high-demand fields, through its five colleges—the Sorrell College of Business, the College of Communication and Fine Arts, Arts and Sciences, Education and Health and Human Services.

Academic programs include a range of options in business, management and accounting, human resource management, criminal justice, education, psychology and counseling, social work, nursing, public administration and political science, athletic training, theatre and dance, art and design, and sport, tourism and hospitality management, among many others.

MAJORS & DEGREES OFFERED

Troy University offers more than 225 undergraduate and graduate academic programs and concentrations, and is accredited by the Southern Association of Colleges and Schools Commission on Colleges to award associate, baccalaureate, master's, education specialist and doctoral degrees.

TUITION, ROOM, BOARD, FEES

Undergraduate tuition for the 2016-2017 academic year is $301 per credit hour for in-state students, and $602 per credit hour for out-of-state students. Graduate tuition for the 2016-2017 academic year is $397 per credit hour for in-state students and $794 per credit hour for out-of-state students.

Fees charged each semester include:

- General University fee -$39 per credit hour
- Registration fee -$50 per semester
- Student Facility fee (Troy Campus only) -$100 per semester in fall and spring semesters and $50 in summer semester.

The Troy Campus features a variety of residential living options that vary in pricing. On campus residents are also required to purchase a meal plan that can be used in Trojan Dining or the food court located in the Trojan Student Center.

FINANCIAL AID

Troy University is committed to providing exceptional service to students and their families who apply for financial assistance. The Office of Financial Aid offers a variety of services and programs designed to help you find ways to meet the costs of education. Additional information on the various types of financial aid and their requirements can be found at www.troy.edu/financialaid.

A number of scholarship opportunities are also available through the University that can help students finance their education. For more information on available scholarships and their requirements, visit www.troy.edu/scholarships.

STUDENT ORGANIZATIONS & ACTIVITIES

The University's Troy Campus is home to a diverse student population, including students from across the United States and nearly 1,200 international students representing more than 65 countries. Each day on the residential campus, as many as 85 different languages can be heard.

Students on the Troy Campus have a variety of opportunities to enrich their college experience. Troy students have nearly 200 student organizations from which to choose, including fraternities and sororities, academic/professional clubs, honor societies, leadership and service groups, political and special interest organizations, religious groups, performing groups and campus publications.

One of the campus' largest student organizations is the Sound of the South Marching Band, which includes students from each of the University's five colleges. A variety of performing ensembles are also available through the John M. Long School of Music.

Leadership opportunities are available through participation in the Student Government Association, the Freshman Forum, Trojan Ambassadors, and IMPACT orientation leaders, among others.

In addition, the Office of Service Learning and Civic Engagement, a part of the John W. Schmidt Center for Student Success, connects Troy University students to applied learning opportunities where students can develop skills in leadership, project management and civic action, while making a difference in the local community. Current student Service Learning and Civic Engagement initiatives include: poverty and hunger, sustainability, healthy futures and community action and outreach.

ADMISSIONS

Undergraduate Admission: High School graduates may be admitted as Freshmen to Troy University on the basis of acceptable high school records (a 2.0 Grade Point Average) and scores achieved on the American College Testing Program (minimum composite of 20 on the ACT) or the Scholastic Aptitude Test (minimum composite of 950 or 1030 if taken since March 2016). Applicants who are 25 years of age or older are not required to submit ACT/SAT scores for admission to the university. All applicants who are graduates of accredited high schools must submit an official transcript showing graduation and a minimum of fifteen Carnegie units, with three or more units in English. Of the units presented, eleven must be in academic courses. Applicants who are graduates of non-accredited secondary schools may be admitted provided they meet the same requirements as students from accredited schools. Pending judgment of the Admissions Committee, these students are expected to complete satisfactory academic work.

Undergraduate students applying to Troy University will be charged a $30 application fee.

Graduate Admission: Those students wishing to apply to Troy University to pursue graduate degrees must submit a letter of recommendation and final official transcripts from all colleges/universities attended, including the degree granted and award date. Graduate students must submit official test score results for the GRE, the MAT or the GMAT.

Graduate students applying to Troy University will be charged a $50 application fee.

Apply online today at www.troy.edu/admissions.

TRUMAN STATE UNIVERSITY

AT A GLANCE

Truman State University is Missouri's premier liberal arts and sciences university and the only highly selective public institution in the state. As one of the very few publicly funded liberal arts schools in the nation, Truman successfully combines affordability with the type of education and personal attention typically only offered at a private institution.

Truman has established an impeccable reputation in the Midwest and throughout the nation for the high-quality undergraduate programs offered. In fact, for the nineteenth consecutive year, U.S. News & World Report has ranked Truman State University as the number one master's level public institution in the Midwest. A commitment to student achievement and learning is the focus of the University.

LOCATION & ENVIRONMENT

The Truman campus is beautifully situated on 140 acres in Kirksville, a town of approximately 17,000 located in the northeast corner of Missouri. The historic downtown area is within walking distance of the Truman campus and provides a connection to the Kirksville community with local restaurants, shops, and entertainment.

CAMPUS FACILITIES & EQUIPMENT

Students take advantage of numerous academic resources and facilities available to them. Improvements to campus facilities have included the expansion of Truman's Science facility, Magruder Hall. Renovations to Barnett Hall include a new Student Media Center encompassing facilities for the student-produced newspaper, Midwest travel magazine, radio station, and TV studio. Students also enjoy dining, socializing, and relaxing in the newly renovated Student Union Building.

The Health Sciences Building houses a speech and hearing clinic for Communication Disorders students, an independent learning center for Nursing students, a Human Performance lab, and the Fontaine C. Piper Movement Analysis lab. Additional facilities include a biofeedback laboratory, an organic chemistry lab, an observatory, a 400-acre university farm, a multicultural affairs center, student health center, and a career center. Athletic facilities include a 5,000-seat football stadium, a 3,000-seat arena with three basketball courts, an Olympic-size swimming pool, soccer and rugby fields, baseball and softball fields, tennis courts, a dance studio, and a Student Recreation Center.

Truman has been measuring its energy consumption and is implementing appropriate measures to lower it. Solar panels are located on five different buildings across campus. During the 2014-15 academic year, Truman saw a reduction of 113.5 tons of CO2 emissions producing 108 kW of useable energy from these panels. Efforts to manage the consumption of our natural resources are also a priority. We are proud of our beautiful campus, which has been named a Tree Campus USA site by the Arbor Day Foundation.

Residence halls also provide comfortable and enriching living environments for students. Most of the halls have been renovated within the last five years. All residence halls offer lounges, kitchenettes, laundry facilities, high-speed internet (including wireless), cable TV, and many other amenities. Students can eat in dining halls or in the food court style dining in the Student Union Building.

ACADEMICS

Truman also offers a challenging Honors Scholar Program. Students have the opportunity to select the most rigorous honors courses to satisfy the liberal arts component of their respective programs. Those who successfully complete this program benefit from an even richer academic experience at Truman and receive special recognition at graduation. Departmental honors are also available in several disciplines.

Students at Truman are active both inside and outside of the classroom. More than 400 Truman students participate in enriching and life-changing study abroad experiences each year. Students can participate in programs ranging from a couple weeks to a year in duration, and can choose from numerous destinations worldwide. The Chronicle for Higher Education recognized Truman as a top producer of Fulbright students for the 2014-15 school year. This federal grant provides funds for studying or working abroad after graduation.

Truman offers a wide variety of experiential internships, a required component of some academic programs. The "Truman in Washington" program provides work-experience opportunities in the nation's capital in such areas as foreign affairs/diplomacy, government affairs, criminal justice, international relations, health and human services, and communications as well as other areas. Truman also offers internship opportunities with the Missouri State Legislature. In recent years, students have completed internships with United States senators, the United States Supreme Court, the governor of Missouri, business and industry managers, advertising agencies, physical therapists, and artists. For the fall 2015 semester, Truman had three interns at the White House.

MAJORS & DEGREES OFFERED

Undergraduate degrees offered by Truman include the Bachelor of Arts (B.A.), Bachelor of Science (B.S.), Bachelor of Music (B.M.), Bachelor of Fine Arts (B.F.A.), and Bachelor of Science in Nursing (B.S.N.). Truman offers more than forty areas of study in the following disciplines: Accounting, Agricultural Science, Art, Art History, Athletic Training, Biology, Business Administration, Chemistry, Classics, Communication, Communication Disorders, Computer Science, Creative Writing, Economics, English, Exercise Science, French, German, Health Science, History, Interdisciplinary Studies, Justice Systems, Linguistics, Mathematics, Music, Nursing, Philosophy and Religion, Physics, Political Science, Psychology, Romance Languages, Russian, Sociology/Anthropology, Spanish, and Theatre.

Professional paths include but are not limited to dentistry, engineering, law, medicine, optometry, pharmacy, physical therapy, occupational therapy and veterinary medicine.

The teaching degree at Truman is the Master of Arts in Education. Students wishing to pursue a teaching career first complete a bachelor's degree in an academic discipline and then apply for admission into professional study at the master's level. Master's programs in special education, elementary education, middle school education, and secondary education are available.

Truman also offers Master's level degrees in Accountancy (MAc), Biology (MS), Communication Disorders (MA), Counseling (MA), English (MA), Leadership (MA) and Music (MA).

The Liberal Studies Program is the heart of Truman's curriculum and is intended to serve as a foundation for all major programs of study. The philosophy behind the Liberal Studies Program is based upon a commitment that Truman has made to provide students with essential skills needed for lifelong learning, breadth across the traditional liberal arts and sciences through exposure to various discipline-based modes of inquiry, and interconnecting perspectives that stress interdisciplinary thinking and integration as well as linkage to other cultures and experiences.

Students at Truman complete a "capstone," or culminating experience their senior year. This experience prompts seniors to reflect on the knowledge they have gained throughout their learning experience and to integrate the knowledge, skills, and attitudes of liberal learning with an in-depth understanding of the major.

TUITION, ROOM, BOARD, FEES

Tuition for Missouri residents for the 2015-16 academic year is $7,152; out-of-state tuition is $13,376. The average room and board rate for both Missouri residents and nonresidents is $8,480. Additional fees include a one-time freshman orientation fee, and annual fees including an activities fee, an athletic fee, a Student Health Center fee, a sustainability fee, a technology fee, and a parking fee for those with a vehicle, plus costs of books and personal expenses.

FINANCIAL AID

Truman offers automatic scholarships ranging from $500 to $5,000. Competitive scholarship awards vary from $500 up to full tuition, room and board, plus a $4,000 study-abroad stipend. The application for admission also serves as the application for the automatic and competitive scholarship programs, and it is free to apply.

A limited number of scholarships are awarded to students for excellence in fine arts, debate or foreign language. These scholarships are available for instrumental or vocal music; acting or dramatic production; studio art or art history; speech or debate; and foreign languages offered at Truman. Of special interest to piano students is the Truman Piano Fellowship Competition, a February competition offering scholarships to top pianists.

Truman, a National Collegiate Athletic Association Division II member, offers 20 men's and women's sports. The NCAA and the University authorize a limited number of grants to outstanding athletes. The value of this aid may vary with each individual recipient.

Truman accepts the Free Application for Federal Student Aid (FASFA) and participates in all Federal Title IV financial aid programs. Financial aid estimates are available upon request.

STUDENT ORGANIZATIONS & ACTIVITIES

With approximately 250 student organizations to choose from, encompassing service, Greek, honorary, professional, religious, social, political and recreational influences, Truman students have tremendous opportunities to become involved on campus and in the Kirksville community. Truman student organizations sponsor a number of events throughout the year, such as Truman Live, International Idol, guest speakers, poetry slams, musical performances, dance recitals, volunteering events, and ever-popular food nights.

The Kohlenberg Lyceum Series also provides a variety of cultural programs that interest students throughout the year. Past programs have included brilliant performances by the Peking Acrobats, American Shakespeare Center, Vocalosity, and the Russian Festival Ballet.

Truman's Student Activity Board sponsors a variety of entertainment events. Recent SAB concerts include Phillip Phillips, Andy Grammer, and Todrick Hall. Comedic acts like Vanessa Bayer and Pete Davidson have also come to Truman's campus in recent years.

ADMISSIONS PROCESS

Each applicant is evaluated for admission based upon academic and co-curricular record, ACT or SAT results, and the admission essay. Truman requires the following high school core: 4 units of English, 3 units of mathematics (4 recommended), 3 units of social studies/history, 3 units of natural science, 1 unit of fine arts and 2 units of the same foreign language.

Candidates are considered for admission on a rolling basis, although those interested in scholarship and financial aid programs are strongly encouraged to apply for admission and submit a resume/activity list by December 1. There is no application fee. Students may apply online at the website listed below or through the Common Application. For further information or to schedule a campus visit, students should contact:

Office of Admission

Truman State University

100 East Normal

Kirksville, Missouri 63501

Telephone: 660.785.4114 or 800.892.7792

Fax: 660.785.7456

E-mail: admissions@truman.edu

http://admissions.truman.edu

UNION COLLEGE (NY)

AT A GLANCE

Union College, chartered by the state of New York in 1795, is one of the nation's oldest and most distinguished liberal arts colleges. Union is a leader in educating students to be engaged, innovative and ethical contributors to a diverse, global and technologically complex society. The Union curriculum emphasizes collaboration with students and faculty through small classes and undergraduate research, interdisciplinary and international study, and service learning. The approximately 2,200 full-time undergraduates come from 39 U.S. states and territories and 37 other countries. Some 20 percent of students identify themselves as members of a multicultural group.

LOCATION & ENVIRONMENT

The first planned campus in America, Union was designed by noted French architect Joseph Ramée and includes the 16-sided Nott Memorial, a historic landmark, and Jackson's Garden, a certified natural wildlife habitat. Union is located on 130 acres in the revitalized city of Schenectady, part of Upstate New York's Capital Region. Steps from campus, the city has a mix of shops, restaurants, the Sunday greenmarket, movies and professional theater. The region's rich cultural heritage and thriving high-tech industry offer opportunities for student/faculty research, internships and jobs. A 20-minute drive from Albany International Airport, Union is within easy reach of New York City and Boston (three hours), Montreal (four hours), and rural and wilderness areas, including the Adirondack Mountains (one-to-two hours).

CAMPUS FACILITIES & EQUIPMENT

Union recently announced plans for a $100 million makeover and expansion of the Science and Engineering Center, the largest and most ambitious project in the College's history. A centerpiece of the revamped complex will be an arc-shaped building featuring floor-to-ceiling glass walls and a four-story lightwell that allows individuals to glimpse the work of other disciplines. The reconstruction is designed to revolutionize teaching, learning and research across engineering, science and the liberal arts.

The Peter Irving Wold Center, an interdisciplinary hub, offers leading-edge programs in biochemistry, environmental studies, electrical engineering and music research. The Center for Neuroscience in Butterfield Hall brings together computer and research labs, classrooms and collaborative spaces. The F.W. Olin Center houses high-tech classrooms and laboratories.

The Nott Memorial is used for study, exhibits and special events, including the annual Study Abroad Fair, the Lothridge Festival of Dance, and guest lectures by such noted figures as U.S. Sen. Kirsten Gillibrand, architect Maya Lin, environmentalist Bill McKibben, activist Cornel West and journalist Bob Woodward.

Schaffer Library has over 1 million print and electronic volumes and more than 11,000 current print and electronic serial titles. Union also participates in the ConnectNY consortium, giving users access to the holdings of 14 other member libraries. The College Archives, Language Lab, Special Collections and Writing Center are also housed at Schaffer Library.

Karp Hall houses the departments of English, and Modern Languages and Literature. Lippman Hall is home to the Social Sciences, including Economics, History, Political Science and Sociology. Lamont House is home to Anthropology, Classics and Philosophy, and the Religious Studies program.

The new Feigenbaum Center for Visual Arts includes studios for drawing, painting, sculpture, printmaking, 2D and 3D design, and metal-working, as well as a media lab, traditional dark rooms, public galleries and classrooms. Other arts facilities include the Mandeville Gallery and Wikoff Student Gallery, both in the Nott Memorial; the all-Steinway Taylor Music Center; the Yulman Theater, home to Mountebanks, the nation's oldest student performing group; and the Henle Dance Pavilion. The Kelly Adirondack Center in nearby Niskayuna houses one of the largest research collections on the Adirondack region.

Residential options for students include traditional dorms, apartment-style housing, theme houses, Minerva Houses, Greek houses, College Park Hall and Garnet Commons, fully furnished apartments for upper class students. Reamer Campus Center includes dining facilities, the bookstore and offices for student activities.

Among the athletic facilities are Alumni Gymnasium, which features the Breazzano Fitness Center, a swimming/diving pool, and exercise and yoga studios. Other recreational and sports facilities include the 3,000-seat Messa Rink at Achilles Center, home of Union's Div. I hockey teams; the Viniar Athletic Center for basketball and volleyball; and the Travis J. Clark '00 Strength Training Facility for varsity athletes. The men's and women's crew teams train at the College's boathouse on the Mohawk River. The Wicker Wellness Center offers health, wellness and counseling services and is the home of Jenna, the campus therapy dog.

The Becker Career Center works with employers and alumni to guide students in competing effectively in today's job market. Students can connect with alumni in all fields through the Union Career Advisory Network (UCAN). HireU, the center's internship and job database, contains opportunities from alumni and employers who are seeking Union students.

Union's new Cogeneration Plant, a combined heat and power plant, is designed to ease demand on current systems, result in significant energy saving costs and move the College closer to its goal of carbon neutrality.

OFF-CAMPUS OPPORTUNITIES

Union offers 44 terms and mini-term programs in 29 countries. Sixty percent of Union students go on terms abroad, one of the highest percentages among colleges and universities. Most programs are led by Union faculty. Students also may design their own program of study abroad, and participate in non-Union and exchange programs. Three-week mini-terms are offered during winter and summer breaks in various U.S. cities and countries.

ACADEMICS

Union's interdisciplinary approach to the liberal arts combines the humanities and social sciences with science and engineering, emphasizing the practical application of ideas through experience. Students gain deep knowledge within their majors and also experience ideas and insights from multiple disciplines.

Students must complete a minimum of 36 courses (up to 40 for engineering degrees) and satisfy departmental and Common Curriculum requirements, including the First-Year Preceptorial and Sophomore Research Seminar, which promote reading, writing, research and critical thinking skills. Distribution requirements in the humanities, literature, social sciences, linguistic and cultural competency, quantitative mathematical reasoning and the sciences promote a breadth of knowledge about the social and natural world, and key skills in analysis, literacy and numeracy.

Union encourages student research in all disciplines. Three-quarters of students actively engage in research. They work one-on-one with professors and have access to sophisticated instrumentation often reserved for graduate students at large universities. At Steinmetz Symposium each spring, some 500 students present their research, scholarship and creative work. Approximately 140 students participate in summer research. Many students co-author publications with faculty and present at major conferences. Union consistently ranks among the top of its peer institutions in National Science Foundation awards.

Academic advisers help students select the right coursework, develop research topics, and pursue internships and service. Union's innovative custom advising tool, Notice-Choose-Tell, embraces a process of self-reflection and communication, encouraging students to make meaningful, informed academic decisions consistent with their goals and aspirations.

Students participate in businesses, health care, government and social service internships. Writing Across the Curriculum requires students to take five designated courses from at least two divisions and one Senior Writing Experience.

MAJORS

Union offers more than 40 majors and 58 minors. Students may choose double majors; combine majors and minors; pursue interdepartmental and multidisciplinary concentrations; or opt for area, ethnic and cultural studies. Many students design their own Organizing Theme major. Most students take three courses in each of the three 10-week terms that comprise Union's academic calendar. The average introductory class has 22 students; the average upper level class, 14.

Union offers Bachelor of Arts (B.A.) and Bachelor of Science (B.S.) degrees. Union also offers a 3+3 Accelerated Law Program with Albany Law School (B.A. and J.D.); and the following programs with Clarkson University (Capital Region Campus): five-year Business/Management program (B.A. or B.S., and M.B.A.) and eight-year Leadership in Medicine program, in conjunction with Albany Medical College (B.S., M.S. or M.B.A., and M.D.).

TUITION, ROOM, BOARD, FEES

Union's comprehensive fee, which includes tuition, room, board, and mandatory fees, is $66,609 for the 2017-18 academic year. The estimated cost for books and personal expenses is approximately $2,000.

FINANCIAL AID

Union is committed to admitting an economically diverse student body and to meeting the full demonstrated need of all admitted students. The College offers $43.6 million annually in scholarships. Scholarship awards are based on academic performance and financial need. The average Union scholarship is $34,000; the average need-based financial aid package is $42,100; and the average merit award is $10,500. Families who are unable to pay full tuition and fees are typically covered by a financial aid package consisting of a grant, loan and work opportunity. More than 60 percent of students receive assistance from the College; 15 percent of College resources are in the form of merit awards.

Candidates for aid should complete the Free Application for Federal Student Aid (FAFSA) and the College Scholarship Service's PROFILE form and mail them directly to the appropriate agencies by Feb. 1.

STUDENT ORGANIZATIONS & ACTIVITIES

Union has more than 100 campus clubs, including arts and cultural groups; the student newspaper, Concordiensis, and radio station, WRUC; sports clubs; academic societies; service and political interest groups; 10 residential Greek organizations; and 13 theme houses (such as Culinary, Iris, Ozone and Technology houses). Cultural events include concerts, theater, dance, film and exhibits. Union's comprehensive athletics program offers 26 varsity intercollegiate sports, organized intramurals, club sports, and recreational and fitness activities. Union is a member of the NCAA, Liberty League and ECAC Hockey. Men's and women's ice hockey compete in NCAA Division I programs; other teams are Division III. Union triumphed in the Frozen Four to capture the national men's hockey title in 2014.

The Minerva House system is a vibrant community and launch pad for an array of college experiences. All students and faculty members belong to one of seven on-campus houses, where they contribute in distinct ways to Union's social, cultural, academic and intellectual life. Student-run Minerva programs range from book clubs and barbecues to language tables, current events discussions and cooking dinner with professors. The Kenney Community Center connects students with Big Brothers Big Sisters, Habitat for Humanity, tutoring programs and many civic projects. Some 1,200 students each year are involved more than 30 service programs and other opportunities for service and leadership.

ADMISSIONS PROCESS

More than 6,000 applicants typically seek first-year class positions; roughly 70 percent are in the top 10 percent of their secondary school class. Admissions counselors look at grades, rigor of courses taken, class rank, teacher recommendations and extracurricular involvement. Typically, 16 units of secondary school preparation are required for admission. These should include credits in such fundamental subjects as English, foreign language, mathematics, social studies and science. It is strongly recommended that students visit Union for an interview and student-guided tour. Alumni interviews may be requested online. A student can choose not to submit his or her SAT or ACT scores for review, except for accelerated programs, which require applicants to submit the SAT and two SAT Subject Tests.

Early decision (ED) candidates have two options. The application deadline (including all supporting credentials) for Option I is Nov. 15, with notification by Dec. 15. Option II has a Jan. 15 deadline (including all supporting credentials) and Feb. 15 notification. Applications for regular decision (RD) admission must be filed by Jan.15; decisions are mailed by April 1. Applications to the Leadership in Medicine program are due no later than Dec. 15, and for Law and Public Policy, by Jan. 1. Those deferred under ED and all regular applicants are given a final decision by April 1. Accepted students have until May 1 to commit.

THE UNIVERSITY OF CENTRAL FLORIDA

AT A GLANCE

The University of Central Florida is a comprehensive research university with over 64,000 students. As one of the nation's fastest growing and largest universities UCF enrolls a diverse student body representing all 50 states and over 120 countries. The University offers educational and research programs that complement the economy, with strong components in aerospace engineering, business, education, film, health, nursing, social sciences, and hospitality management. UCF's programs in communication and the fine arts help to meet the cultural and recreational needs of a growing metropolitan area. The University also offers many graduate programs leading to masters and doctoral degrees.

UCF has established extensive partnerships with businesses and industry in the central Florida area and beyond that provide students with exceptional research and learning experiences. These partnerships bring practical learning environments to UCF students through co-op and internship programs. Joint curriculum development strategies are used throughout the university.

The on-campus and campus-affiliated housing facilities include traditional residence halls, apartment-style options, and Greek housing that accommodates approximately 11,500 students. Several thousand students live in apartments located within walking distance of the campus.

LOCATION & ENVIRONMENT

The University of Central Florida: Competitive Advantages

A Focus on Undergraduate Education: We're committed to teaching and providing advising and academic support services for all students. Our undergraduates have access to state-of-the-art wireless buildings, high-tech classrooms and research labs, Web-based classes and an undergraduate Research and Mentoring program.

A Talented Student Body: As one of the fastest growing universities, total enrollment has reached over 64,000; 55,783 are undergraduates. Our emphasis on excellence in undergraduate education has produced many rewarding results: a Goldwater Scholarship awardee, a Rhodes Scholarship finalist, a Clarion awardee in Radio/Television, a Zonta International Amelia Earhart fellowship awardee, and a nationally ranked Computer Science programming and Cyber Defense teams.

Career Opportunities: Our Career Services professionals help students gain practical experiences at NASA, schools, hospitals, high-tech companies, local municipalities, and the entertainment industry. UCF faculty sit on boards and planning committees, and our graduates make their mark in engineering, business, computer science, education, health care, science, tourism, film and public service.

An International Presence: With an international focus to our curricula and research programs, we currently enroll international students from over 120 nations. Our study abroad programs and other study and research opportunities include agreements with 98 institutions and 36 countries, including Australia, France, Germany, Holland, Italy, Russia, South Africa, Spain and Wales.

A Spacious, Modern Campus, plus Orlando: UCF's 1,415-acre campus provides a safe and serene setting for learning, with natural lakes and woodlands. The university provides housing for approximately 11,500 students on campus and through affiliated housing. The bustle of Orlando lies a short distance away: the Orlando Magic, the Orlando City Soccer Club, the Kennedy Space Center, major film studios, Walt Disney World, Universal Orlando, Sea World, and sandy beaches are all nearby.

CAMPUS FACILITIES & EQUIPMENT

In addition to the academic programs offered on the Orlando campus, upper division students can work toward a degree at 10 locations around the central Florida area. These regional campuses work cooperatively with local state colleges to provide all four years of course work in many academic areas. The library houses over 1.8 million print volumes and subscribes to more than

50,600 periodicals and journals (49,000 in electronic format). Students have access to an online computer catalog that provides information on the collections of the State University System libraries. An extensive online network of more than 600 computer terminals (both PC and Mac) cover the campus. The Institute for Simulation and Training gives students the opportunity to pursue undergraduate research. The College of Optics and Photonics allows faculty members and students to work directly with industrial personnel in conducting basic and applied research at the regional and national level. The Central Florida Research Park, located next to the UCF campus, houses more than 125 high-technology firms and agencies. This proximity fosters relationships between industry and the University, which strengthens the academic programs at UCF.

OFF-CAMPUS OPPORTUNITIES

Career Services and Experiential Learning provides comprehensive and coordinated career development, enhances academic study, and builds ongoing partnerships with employers and the community. The Department of Modern Languages offers summer study-abroad programs. Courses are available in the subject areas of language (all levels), art, and civilization. UCF is also a participant in the National Student Exchange Consortium.

ACADEMICS

The University offers the degrees of Bachelor of Applied Science, Bachelor of Arts, Bachelor of Design, Bachelor of Fine Arts, Bachelor of Music, Bachelor of Music Education, Bachelor of Science, Bachelor of Science in Business Administration, Bachelor of Science in Education, Bachelor of Science in Engineering, Bachelor of Science in Nursing, Bachelor of Social Work, and Bachelor of Science in Social Sciences.

MAJORS & DEGREES OFFERED

These degrees are available in the colleges listed below, with majors or areas of specialization as indicated.

The College of Arts and Humanities offers degrees in art, Architecture, digital media, English, film, French, history, humanities and cultural studies, Latin American Studies, music, Music Education, philosophy, Photography, Religion and Cultural Studies, Spanish, Theatre Studies, and Writing and Rhetoric.

The College of Business Administration offers degrees in accounting, Business Economics, economics, finance, Integrated Business, management, real estate and marketing.

The College of Education and Human Performance offers degrees in art education, early childhood development and education, elementary education, English language arts education, world languages education, mathematics education, science education, sport and exercise science, social science education, and technical education and industry training.

The College of Engineering and Computer Science offers degrees in aerospace engineering, civil engineering, computer engineering, computer science, construction engineering, electrical engineering, environmental engineering, industrial engineering, Information Technology and mechanical engineering.

The College of Health and Public Affairs offers degrees in athletic training, Communication Sciences and Disorders, criminal justice, Health Informatics and information management, health services administration, health sciences, legal studies, public administration, and social work.

The College of Nursing offers degrees in nursing.

The College of Optics and Photonics offers degrees in Photonic Science and Engineering.

The College of Sciences offers degrees in advertising/public relations, anthropology, biology, chemistry, Communication and Conflict, forensic science, International and Global Studies, Human Communication, journalism, mathematics, physics, political science, psychology, radio/television, social sciences, sociology, and statistics.

The Rosen College of Hospitality Management offers degrees in Hospitality Management, Event Management, Entertainment Management, and Restaurant and Foodservice Management.

The College of Medicine and the Burnett School of Biomedical Sciences offers degrees in Biotechnology, Medical Laboratory Sciences, and biomedical sciences.

The College of Undergraduate Studies offers degrees in Interdisciplinary Studies.

Pre-professional programs are offered in chiropractic, medicine, optometry, osteopathy, pharmacy, podiatry, dentistry, veterinary medicine and law.

TUITION, ROOM, BOARD, FEES

Approximate Tuition, Health Fee, Room and Board Annual Rates 2016-17:

	Florida Resident	Florida Non-Resident
Tuition and Fees	$6,368	$22,466
Room and Board	$9,764	$9,764
Books (estimate)	1,152	$1,152
Approximate Total / Annual Cost	$17,284	$33,382

Based on 15 credit hours per semester, double room and meal plan.

FINANCIAL AID

Financial aid is awarded according to each student's demonstrated need in relation to college costs and may include grants, loans, scholarships and part-time employment. Programs based on need include the Federal Perkins Loan, Federal Pell Grant, Florida Student Assistance Grant, Federal Work-Study, Florida College Career Work-Study Program, and Federal Stafford Student Loan. To qualify for these programs, students must complete the Free Application for Federal Student Aid (FAFSA). The priority application deadline is December 1. Approximately 76 percent of UCF students receive some form of financial aid.

STUDENT ORGANIZATIONS & ACTIVITIES

Students participate in over 600 organizations, including special interest clubs, multicultural associations, fraternities and sororities, honor societies, and academic and pre-professional organizations. The Office of Student Involvement schedules a wide array of extracurricular programs, including concerts, movies, and guest speakers. The innovative LEAD Scholars Academy fosters leadership and service commitment through a comprehensive student development program for freshman. The Major Exploration Program (MEP) helps entering freshmen define their career goals and develop an academic strategy to reach their goals. UCF offers Air Force and Army ROTC programs.

The University of Central Florida is a member of the NCAA and the American Athletic Conference. All teams compete on the NCAA Division 1 Level. UCF's men's teams compete in intercollegiate baseball, basketball, football, golf, soccer, and tennis. Women's teams compete in basketball, cross-country, golf, rowing, soccer, softball, tennis, track and field, and volleyball. Intercollegiate coed club activities include championship cheerleading, crew, and waterskiing teams. The university offers an extensive intramural sports program.

ADMISSIONS PROCESS

A freshman applicant is a student with fewer than 12 hours of college coursework after high school graduation. The most important criteria in the admission decision for these applicants is the high school academic record, rigor of course work, grade point average, grade trends, and SAT I or ACT test scores. UCF operates on a rolling admission basis. Students are generally notified of their initial admission decision within two to three weeks after receipt of the application and all supporting documents. If the number of qualified applicants exceeds the number that the university is permitted to enroll, a waiting list will be established.

All applicants must have earned a minimum of 18 high school academic units (yearlong courses that are not remedial in nature). These include 4 units of English (3 must include substantial writing), 4 units of mathematics at or above algebra I, 3 units of natural science (2 must include a laboratory), 3 units of social science, 2 units of one world language, and 2 units of academic electives. Grades in honors courses, International Baccalaureate, Advanced Placement, AICE and dual enrollment courses are given additional weight in the GPA computation. Students must meet the Department of Education minimum eligibility to be considered for admission. Applicants should understand that the satisfaction of minimum requirements does not automatically guarantee admission to UCF.

Admission requirements for Transfer applicants vary by the number of college credit hours the student has successfully completed prior to enrolling at UCF. For complete details, go to http://admissions.ucf.edu/apply/transfer/. A transfer credit summary evaluation is provided to students once they are offered admission to UCF.

Students are encouraged to apply several months in advance. Transfers can apply online at http://admissions.ucf.edu/ and Freshmen can apply online at http://admissions.ucf.edu/ or through the Common Application. It is recommended that freshman students apply early during the fall semester of their senior year. Applications are accepted up to one year prior to the start of the term for which entry is desired. Priority application deadlines are May 1 for the fall term (July 1 for transfers), November 1 for the spring term, and March 1 for the summer term.

THE UNIVERSITY OF DELAWARE

AT A GLANCE

The University of Delaware, chartered in 1743, located in Newark, Delaware and situated halfway between New York City and Washington, D.C. is home to more than 17,000 undergraduate students from nearly all 50 states and 100 countries.

Students choose Delaware for our Honors Program, Study Abroad opportunities, 150+ majors, and discovery learning experiences that ensure they will graduate with impressive resumes and meaningful degrees. Our distinguished faculty includes internationally known authors, scientists and artists. State-of-the-art facilities support UD's academic, research and service activities. You'll find campus life is welcoming, enriched by distinguished guest speakers, NCAA Division I intercollegiate athletics, 350-plus engaged student organizations, concerts and other arts and cultural activities.

LOCATION & ENVIRONMENT

The University of Delaware is located in the suburban community of Newark, Delaware -halfway between New York City and Washington, D.C. with easy access to Baltimore and Philadelphia.

CAMPUS FACILITIES & EQUIPMENT

The University of Delaware's Science, Technology and Advanced Research (STAR) Campus provides educational and professional opportunities to students for research and collaboration. STAR campus is home to four cutting-edge, research-driven clinics as well as multiple laboratories providing undergraduates with opportunities to participate in research. Here you will find the Speech Language Hearing Clinic, Physical Therapy Clinic, Nurse-Managed Primary Health Care Center and Human Anatomy Lab.

The Patrick T. Harker Interdisciplinary Science and Engineering Laboratory (Harker ISE Lab) brings together students and faculty from various disciplines to teach, learn and conduct research in a collaborative environment. ISE Lab's four problem-based learning instructional laboratories feature lab spaces adjoining classrooms so students can discuss a problem and then immediately test a solution. UD faculty have designed curricula to optimally utilize these rooms.

The Venture Development Center (VDC) is home to the entrepreneurial community on campus and an applied learning laboratory for students that has meeting and co-working space, computer and printing resources, in-house media production, and an extensive network of community connections.

JP Morgan Chase Innovation Center engages faculty, students and JPMorgan Chase employees in joint applied research projects. The Innovation Center, built as part of a strategic JPMorgan Chase-University of Delaware collaboration, creates a pipeline of technology talent through University curriculum, enriching internships and joint research projects to drive innovation.

OFF-CAMPUS OPPORTUNITIES

Downtown Newark is located just blocks from the University of Delaware campus and features a multitude of restaurants, shops and businesses. A nearby Amtrak station offers easy day trips to Philadelphia, New York and Washington, D.C. good for exploring, internship opportunities and job hunting.

ACADEMICS

Students can apply to be considered for the UD Honors Program. They can also choose to supplement their major with over 100 minors or choose to enhance their degree as part of our Scholars and Fellows programs centered around Cybersecurity, Community Engagement, Global Studies, Engineering or Entrepreneurship.

MAJORS & DEGREES OFFERED

The University of Delaware offers more than 150 major fields of study across seven different colleges: Agriculture and Natural Resources, Arts & Sciences, Business & Economics, Earth, Ocean and Environment, Education and Human Development, Engineering and Health Sciences. Find your passion at www.udel.edu/majorfinder

http://www.udel.edu/majorfinder/

- Accounting
- Actuarial Sciences

- Agriculture and Natural Resources
- Ancient Greek and Roman Studies
- Animal Science
- Anthropology
- Anthropology Education
- Apparel Design
- Applied Mathematics
- Applied Nutrition
- Art
- Art Conservation
- Art History
- Asian Studies
- Athletic Training
- Biochemistry
- Biological Sciences
- Biological Sciences Education
- Biomedical Engineering
- Black American Studies
- Business Undeclared
- Chemical Engineering
- Chemistry
- Chemistry Education
- Chinese Studies
- Civil Engineering
- Classics and History
- Cognitive Science
- Communication
- Comparative Literature
- Computer Engineering
- Computer Science
- Criminal Justice
- Dietetics
- Early Childhood Education/Early Childhood Special Education
- Earth Science Education
- Economics
- Electrical Engineering
- Elementary Teacher Education
- Energy and Environmental Policy
- Engineering Undecided
- English
- English Education
- Entrepreneurship & Technology Innovation
- Environmental Engineering
- Environmental Science
- Environmental Studies
- Environmental and Resource Economics
- European Studies
- Exercise Science
- Fashion Merchandising
- Finance
- Financial Planning
- Fine Arts
- Food Science
- Food and Agribusiness Marketing and Management
- French Education
- French Studies
- French and History
- French and Political Science
- Geography
- Geography Education
- Geological Sciences
- German Education
- German Studies
- German and History

- German and Political Science
- Health Behavior Science
- History
- History Education
- History and Foreign Language
- Hospitality Industry Management
- Hotel, Restaurant and Institutional Management
- Human Services
- Information Systems
- Insect Ecology and Conservation
- International Business Studies
- International Relations
- Italian Education
- Italian Studies
- Japanese Studies
- Landscape Architecture
- Landscape Horticulture and Design
- Languages, Literatures and Cultures
- Latin American and Iberian Studies
- Latin Education
- Linguistics
- Linguistics and French
- Management
- Management Information Systems
- Marine Science
- Marketing
- Mathematics
- Mathematics Education
- Mathematics and Economics
- Mechanical Engineering
- Medical Diagnostics
- Medical Diagnostics-Pre Physician Assistant
- Medical Laboratory Science
- Meteorology and Climatology
- Music
- Music Applied
- Music Composition
- Music Education
- Music History and Literature
- Music Management
- Music Theory
- Natural Resource Management
- Neuroscience
- Nursing
- Nutritional Science
- Occupational Therapy
- Operations Management
- Organizational and Community Leadership
- Pharmaceutical Sciences
- Philosophy
- Physics
- Physics Education
- Plant Science
- Political Science
- Political Science Education
- Pre-Veterinary Medicine and Animal Biosciences
- Psychology
- Psychology Education
- Public Policy
- Quantitative Biology
- Russian Studies
- Russian and History
- Sociology
- Sociology Education

- Spanish Education
- Spanish Studies
- Spanish and History
- Spanish and Political Science
- Sport Management
- Statistics
- Three Foreign Languages
- University Studies
- Visual Communications
- Wildlife Ecology and Conservation
- Women and Gender Studies

TUITION, ROOM, BOARD, FEES

Resident Tuition & Fees:

- Tuition: $11,540
- Room: $7,316
- Board: $4,752
- Fees: $1,290
- Total: $24,898

Non-Resident:

- Tuition: $30,960
- Room: $7,316
- Board: $4,752
- Fees: $1,290
- Total: $44,318

FINANCIAL AID

The University of Delaware awards more than 250 million dollars annually in financial aid, over 100 million dollars of this funding is in the form of grants and scholarships. To apply for need-based aid, complete the Free Application for Federal Student Aid (FAFSA) at www.fafsa.ed.gov as soon as possible after October 1. If you wish to be considered for merit scholarships, apply by January 15. No additional application is necessary for consideration.

STUDENT ORGANIZATIONS & ACTIVITIES

UD is a medium sized University that attracts students from nearly all 50 states and 100 countries, with approximately 70 percent of the student population coming from out-of-state. You'll feel right at home with our welcoming community and endless opportunities to get involved including social, cultural and co-curricular activities. Students have plenty of ways to explore their interests with more than 350 campus organizations ranging from community service, cultural and religious programming, leadership organizations, fraternity and sorority life and athletics.

ADMISSIONS PROCESS

Students applying to UD should have a strong background in core academic courses. High school honors, advanced placement, and International Baccalaureate coursework is encouraged. Applicants are required to have 18 core high school units including four years of English, 3 years of Mathematics, three years of science (two with a lab) and two years of the same Foreign Language. The Admissions Commit - tee takes a holistic approach to the admissions process and will consider academic performance, standardized test scores, letters of recommendation and essays when making a decision.

UNIVERSITY OF FINDLAY

AT A GLANCE

Findlay cultivates the potential within each student through academic excellence, transformative experiences and a supportive community that is grounded in Christian faith.

Established in 1882 through a joint partnership between the Churches of God, General Conference and the city of Findlay, the University is known not only for science, health professions, animal science and equestrian studies programs, but also for cultivating the next generation of business leaders, educators and innovative thinkers through a dedication to experiential learning, both in and outside of the classroom.

University of Findlay has nearly 60 undergraduate programs of study leading to baccalaureate degrees and offers 10 master's degrees and four doctorate degrees including: Doctor of Pharmacy, a Doctor of Education, a Doctor of Physical Therapy and a Doctor of Occupational Therapy.

Nearly 4,200 students from approximately than 40 countries are enrolled at Findlay. Approximately 1,250 students live on campus in University housing. With an international student population of nearly 600, Findlay's campus offers global experiences to students from all over the world. In addition, our faculty and staff strive to create a supportive community in which our students grow and find their path to a meaningful life and productive career.

University of Findlay encompasses more than 388 acres, including a 72-acre main campus and six off-campus facilities.

LOCATION & ENVIRONMENT

University of Findlay is located in Findlay, Ohio, a small city that is pleasant and progressive. Findlay has been designated a "dream town" by Demographics Daily, and it has been repeatedly named one of the top 10 "micropolitan" areas (small cities) in the U.S. by Site Selection magazine three years in a row. Findlay is the only city in Ohio to have been named one of the 100 Best Communities for Young People by America's Promise Alliance, an organization founded by Colin Powell.

University of Findlay encompasses more than 388 acres, including a 72-acre main campus and six off-campus facilities. Students may participate in any of more than 100 organizations, including special interest clubs, student media, student government, music and theater groups, service clubs, academic honorary organizations, spiritual life groups, and Greek sororities and fraternities.

Findlay also has an intramural program with 25 activities, including flag football, basketball, co-ed volleyball, billiards, bowling and more.

CAMPUS FACILITIES & EQUIPMENT

University of Findlay participates in 24 NCAA Division II intercollegiate sports: 10 men's (baseball, basketball, cross country, football, golf, indoor and outdoor track, soccer, swimming and diving, tennis and wrestling); 10 women's (basketball, cheerleading, cross country, dance team, golf, lacrosse, softball, soccer, swimming and diving, tennis, indoor and outdoor track and volleyball); and two men's and women's Intercollegiate Horse Show Association (IHSA) sports, western and English equestrian riding teams.

The Findlay campus has been expanded dramatically in the last two decades with the inclusion of five significant new buildings and the acquisition of the former Owens Community College Findlay-branch campus. A significant 42,000 square-foot addition to the Davis Street Building greatly enhancing the environment for science education at Findlay.

In addition to the main campus resources, the University operates a 42-acre facility on the east side of town, the James L. Child, Jr. Equestrian Complex, containing the English equestrian studies program and University Equine Veterinary Services, Inc. Just south of campus is a University-owned 72-acre farm housing the western riding and pre-veterinary medicine programs. In 2009, the University dedicated the Dr. C. Richard Beckett Animal Science Building on this site, an impressive $3.7 million facility that has allowed room for growth of its premier animal science programs.

The five-acre All Hazards Training Center provides hands-on simulations for students, industry and government agencies involving emergency planning and response. The 30-acre Olive Street Wilderness Area is a well-utilized nature preserve, and the 54-acre Rieck Center for Habitat Studies serves as a biology field station.

Findlay's newest build is an $18 million 72,000 square foot multi-purpose Center For Student Life and College of Business building. Plans are to open this new building in August 2017. In addition, the University plans to renovate the first floor of Old Main and make some other facility improvements.

OFF-CAMPUS OPPORTUNITIES

Opportunities abound for learning leadership and interpersonal skills outside the classroom. Students may participate in any of nearly 100 student organizations, including special interest clubs, student media, student government, performing arts groups, service clubs, academic honorary organizations, spiritual life groups and Greek sororities and fraternities. Club sports and 18 intramural sports keep the competitive spirit alive.

ACADEMICS

Undergraduate Programs

- Majors/Bachelor's Degrees
- Associate Degrees and Minors
- Undergraduate-Level Certificates and Endorsements
- Online Degree Completion Program

Graduate and Professional Programs

- Master's Degree Programs
- Doctoral/Professional Programs
- Graduate-Level Certificates, Endorsements and Professional Development Programs

Professional Development Programs

- Teacher Education
- All Hazards Training Center Courses

MAJORS & DEGREES OFFERED

University of Findlay has nearly 60 undergraduate programs of study leading to baccalaureate degrees and offers 10 master's degrees and four doctorate degrees including: Doctor of Pharmacy, a Doctor of Education, a Doctor of Physical Therapy and a Doctor of Occupational Therapy.

TUITION, ROOM, BOARD, FEES

Regular Academic Program 2016-2017

Tuition	$16,165
Room (Residence Hall, double occupancy)	$2,425
Board	$2,425
Student Activity Fee (non-refundable)	$100
General Service Fee (non-refundable)	$395
Total per semester	$21,520

FINANCIAL AID

At Findlay, our college investment plan is designed to make investing in your future more affordable. The Office of Financial Aid is here to help you and your family determine the best approach to cover the cost of your education. We work with each student every step of the way to develop a customized, financial aid plan that meets your financial needs to help you reach your educational goals.

STUDENT ORGANIZATIONS & ACTIVITIES

Approximately 1,250 students live on campus in University housing. With an international student population of nearly 600, Findlay's campus offers global experiences to students from all over the world. In addition, our faculty and staff strive to create a supportive community in which our students grow and find their path to a meaningful life and productive career.

Opportunities abound for learning leadership and interpersonal skills outside the classroom. Students may participate in any of nearly 100 student organizations, including special interest clubs, student media, student government, performing arts groups, service clubs, academic honorary organizations, spiritual life groups and Greek sororities and fraternities. Club sports and 18 intramural sports keep the competitive spirit alive on campus.

The fine arts flourish on campus with a variety of theatre productions, art exhibits and vocal and instrumental music concerts that offer creative outlets and training for students, as well as serve as a source of cultural enrichment for the community.

University of Findlay participates in 24 NCAA Division II intercollegiate sports: 10 men's (baseball, basketball, cross country, football, golf, indoor and outdoor track, soccer, swimming and diving, tennis and wrestling); 10 women's (basketball, cheerleading, cross country, dance team, golf, lacrosse, softball, soccer, swimming and diving, tennis, indoor and outdoor track and volleyball); and two men's and women's Intercollegiate Horse Show Association (IHSA) sports, western and English equestrian riding teams.

ADMISSIONS PROCESS

Many kinds of students come to the University of Findlay to earn their bachelor's degree. Some come directly from high school, but others have started their education at other colleges and universities. Others come to earn a few credits over the summer or even while still in high school to get ahead before officially entering college.

Regardless of where our students come from, they all find an education based on science, arts and technology. It may seem challenging, but everything you need is here. Start with our free application, submit your requirements, and make sure you pay attention to your deadlines!

We look forward to learning about your achievements, talents and goals. We approach the admission process with genuine respect for you. We will give your application serious consideration. Thank you for your interest in University of Findlay. We wish you all the best!

UNIVERSITY OF MAINE

AT A GLANCE

UMaine: Define Tomorrow

The University of Maine (UMaine) offers extensive academic opportunities expected from a major research university, with the close-knit feel of a small college. The University of Maine is Maine's Flagship University offering the most comprehensive academic experience in the state. There are nearly 100 majors and academic programs, 75 graduate degree programs and 30 doctoral programs. All majors benefit from a strong foundation in the liberal arts. Top students are invited to join the Honors College, one of the oldest and most prestigious honors college in the nation. UMaine is also the state's only public research university housing facilities with international reputations for excellence. UMaine students have extraordinary opportunities to gain real-world experience through research and experiential learning. Our undergraduates have the opportunity to collaborate with faculty, conduct fieldwork, and participate in internships around the world. Wildlife ecology studies learn about animal behavior by working with wildlife biologists and baby black bears. Many engineering students secure co-ops that typically lead to employment immediately upon graduation and are global leaders in deepwater offshore wind energy research. Education majors have the opportunity to take advantage of urban, rural, and international student teaching opportunities, and our marine science students have the opportunity to spend a semester by the sea at out world renowned Darling Marine Center. There are over 200 student organizations such as SPIFFY, the student investment club that manages a $2.3 million real money portfolio, Greek Life, Division I athletics, and many more.

LOCATION & ENVIRONMENT

There's no place like Maine. Located in Orono, Maine, students are surrounded by the great outdoors and ample opportunity to explore everything that Maine has to offer. Orono is nestled between the Stillwater and Penobscot rivers, providing a truly beautiful and unique campus feel. The campus has a traditional New England feel with ivy-covered brick buildings, towering pines, and beautiful fall foliage that is second to none. Some of the best skiing in the northeast is within easy driving distance. Beautiful tourist attractions such as Bar Harbor, Acadia National Park, Baxter State Park, and the northern terminus of the Appalachian Trail are just a short drive from campus. The University of Maine is also only 10 minutes from the city of Bangor, Maine's third largest city, which contains its own international airport.

CAMPUS FACILITIES & EQUIPMENT

The University of Maine is home to state-of-the-art research facilities, classrooms and teaching laboratories.

Fogler Library is the state's largest library and located right in the center of campus. It houses more than 1.4 million volumes, 2.38 million microforms, 2.3 million U.S. and Canadian government publications, and papers written by famous UMaine Alumni, Stephen King. BR>

Students will also have access to the Capital Markets Training Laboratory with state-of-the-art technology and 12 Bloomberg Terminals that allow for hands-on learning in financial education.

Engineering students get the opportunity to work alongside professors and research scientists in the internationally recognized, Advanced Structures and Composite Center. Students have assisted on projects for NASA, off shore wind resources, the United States Military and "Bridge in a Backpack." The Advanced Structures and Composite Center has partnered with more than 500 national and international companies.

The Virtual Environment and Multimodal Interaction Laboratory (VEMI) is a research facility that combines fully immersive virtual reality with augmented reality technologies in an integrated research and development environment. Students from all interest and majors collaborate in projects in the VEMI Lab on the latest research in areas such as aging research, vision impairment research and virtual realities.

OFF-CAMPUS OPPORTUNITIES

There are also many ways to explore Maine off campus as well. There is outdoor recreation, music and food festivals, museums and much more. Bangor, is a 10-minute drive from campus. Bangor hosts Summer Concerts in the Park, the American Folk Festival, and the State Fair. Take a trip to Maine's famous Lobster Festival in Rockport or to Acadia National Park in Bar Harbor. There are over 120 miles of hiking trails to explore. There is also 15 miles of hiking right behind UMaine's campus!

Students at the University of Maine also have many opportunities to travel abroad. Through our study abroad programs, students will be able to explore globally while enhancing their education by taking courses, volunteering, or researching. Students have traveled to China to study emerging financial markets, to Italy to learn about Renaissance art history, to Turkey to study film, and to Brazil to look at our world's diverse ecosystem. Students will have the opportunity to enhance their education and experience at UMaine with fun, enriching, on and off-campus activities.

ACADEMICS

UMaine offers nearly 100 majors and programs across six colleges at the undergraduate level: The College of Education and Human Development, College of Engineering, College of Liberals Arts & Sciences, College of Natural Sciences, Forestry & Agriculture, the Maine Business School, and the School of Engineering Technology. In addition to these programs, UMaine also offers the Explorations program which is designed to help undecided students identify a major best fit for a degree program to pursue. The Division of Lifelong Learning offers online classes, Summer University session, and distance-learning opportunities for students who need a flexible class schedule.

Students at the University of Maine benefit from a solid liberal arts foundation in addition to their major or concentration within their degree program. Students develop and refine the qualities needed in order to fully engage with the world around them, regardless of the discipline being studied.

Undergraduate research is a major component of the learning atmosphere. The University of Maine offers students true hands on research experience, as early as their first year on campus. UMaine is the state's largest research university providing rich and diverse opportunities to publish findings, travel around the globe, and work alongside UMaine's world-class scholars and researchers. The Center of Undergraduate Research connects students with faculty projects applicable to their academic interests and future careers. The abundance of research opportunities also provides students with great mentoring connections between faculty and students that carry benefits beyond the classroom. The skills students develop through research creates applicants who are much more competitive for the workplace and graduate school placement.

The University of Maine is also host to one of the country's oldest and most prestigious Honors College. The Honors College provides an in-depth, academically challenging curriculum for qualified students across all majors. Honors College student take part in unique research, academic and cultural opportunities, and have the option for exclusive housing.

STUDENT ORGANIZATIONS & ACTIVITIES

Students get will get a full and enriching college experience at UMaine. The University of Maine hosts many on-campus programs and opportunities for students to explore and meet new people. Students can kayak, ski, snowshoe, canoe, hike, and much more. 15 miles of walking, biking, and cross county ski trails surround UMaine's beautiful campus. There are also over 200 clubs and organizations for students to get involved in, such as Greek Life, The Woodsmen's Club, Robotics Club, Spanish Club and countless more. The Campus Activities Board also puts on free events during the school year including movies, karaoke, game nights, and astronomy shows. You can join an athletic team or cheer on the UMaine Black Bears Division I teams to victory for free during the year. In fact, the Wall Street Journal names UMaine's Alfond Arena the best atmosphere in college hockey.

ADMISSIONS PROCESS

Admission to the University of Maine is a highly competitive and selective process. Successful applicants are those whose scholastic achievement, intellectual curiosity, and established study habits promise success in a comprehensive university environment. Applicants may apply using the University of Maine System application or the Common Application. The University of Maine also uses a holistic process. This process looks at the strength of high school curriculums, grades achieved, class rank, counselor recommendation, SAT or ACT score, student essay, and extracurricular involvement to evaluate for admission consideration. The University of Maine also recognizes Advance Placement tests, honors, and higher education courses. Student who pass examinations may be exempt from certain courses at UMaine.

The University of Maine has an Early Action deadline of December 1st. Complete applications that are postmarked by December 1st are considered for Early Action. Early Action candidates are given first consideration for the Honors College and merit scholarships awarded by the Admissions Office.

Select programs also have a December 1st application deadline. Students interested in Nursing, Bioengineering, Construction Engineering Technology, Mechanical Engineering and Mechanical Engineering Technology need to apply by December 1st for admission consideration into these specific programs.

All other applicants are encouraged to submit their applications and all supporting documents by February 1st, and are notified by rolling admission.

Students should also submit their Free Application for Federal Student Aid (FAFSA) by March 1st to be considered for the maximum possible financial aid eligibility. UMaine's School Code for the FAFSA is 002053.

Overview: Applicants

15,000   Acceptance Rate

80% Average GPA

3.22 (on 4.0 scale)

Testing Policies: Superscore ACT

YES   Superscore SAT

YES ACT Writing Policy:

ACT with or without Writing accepted

SAT Writing Policy: SAT with or without Writing accepted

Deadlines: Early Action:

December 1st

Bioengineering:

December 1st   Construction Engineering Technology:

 December 1st

Mechanical Engineering:

December 1st   Mechanical Engineering Technology:

December 1st

Nursing:

December 1st

THE UNIVERSITY OF MARYLAND, BALTIMORE COUNTY

AT A GLANCE

An Honors University with the teaching and student support traditions of a small liberal arts college. UMBC is also among the most rapidly developing and diverse research universities in the nation.

UMBC attracts creative and motivated students and rewards them with the resources and attention they need to succeed. We're a place where it's cool to be smart, and where students can be confident investing in their education.

UMBC is nationally recognized for professors who regularly involve students in research and creative collaboration. Cross-collaboration between fields of study (with both peers and faculty) results in active, interdisciplinary learning, which prepares students for multi-dimensional opportunities.

With an ideal proximity to Baltimore and Washington, D.C. students are interning, studying and working with industry leaders-and UMBC has built a reputation for getting students into jobs and graduate programs. In fact, 83% of UMBC class of 2015 is employed and/or in graduate school!

The on campus climate is friendly and energetic; undergraduates have enough ideas and interests to support more than 250 groups, including Greek organizations, recreational sports clubs, community outreach efforts, and campus events. Students enthusiastically follow UMBC NCAA Division I athletic teams and attend games in the UMBC Stadium and Retriever Activities Center.

UMBC President Freeman A. Hrabowski, III, has been named "one of the 10 best college presidents" and "one of the 100 most influential people in the world" by Time Magazine.

Theatre students rank third nationally in invitations to perform at the Kennedy Center American College Theatre Festival. A new Performing Arts and Humanities building opened in 2014, providing state-of-the-art facilities for several arts and humanities departments and programs.

Approximately 75% of freshman students live on campus, with 14% from out of state. The undergraduate student population is 45% female, 24% Asian American, 12% African American, 4% Hispanic American and Native American. UMBC houses nearly 4,000 students, 1,600 live in UMBC's three new residence suites and apartment communities. Residential communities feature ten living-learning programs, including the Center for Women in Technology; Intercultural Living Exchange; Shriver Living Learning Center.

LOCATION & ENVIRONMENT

Located a few miles south of Baltimore, UMBC is 15 minutes from downtown Baltimore and 30 minutes from Washington, D.C. The Baltimore-Washington area is known for its music, sports, museums, restaurants, and historical traditions. UMBC's 530-acre campus with housing and dining facilities on one side and core facilities (classroom/lab buildings, performing arts center, a library, galleries, a student union, a bookstore, a gymnasium, an Olympic-size pool, and tennis courts) surrounding a central walkway. bwtech@UMBC Research and Technology Park, adjacent to the campus, attracts firms in the high-technology fields, including engineering, information technology, and the life sciences.

CAMPUS FACILITIES & EQUIPMENT

UMBC's landmark building, the Albin O. Kuhn Library and Gallery, contains over 1 million books and bound volumes of journals, an extensive reference collection, 4,200 journal and database subscriptions, more than 200 computers, wireless and wired connections for laptops, and more than 3 million other items, including slides, photographs, maps, musical scores, recordings, and microforms. The Commons, UMBC's state-of-the-art student center, the hub of campus life includes a food court, general lounges, the University bookstore, meeting spaces, a student recreation center, a full-service bank, student organization offices, retail-type spaces, wireless computer connectivity, and web-accessible kiosks. UMBC students have access to research opportunities and equipment such as conducting AIDS research on one of the world's largest nuclear magnetic resonance spectrometers in the only Howard Hughes Medical Institute lab at a public university in Maryland. Newer facilities include a Public Policy Building and a state-of-the-art Information Technology/Engineering Building. UMBC's a new Performing Arts and Humanities Building houses seven departments and new performance space that showcase the University's strong arts and humanities programs and creates a regional and national appreciation of UMBC as a cultural attraction.

OFF-CAMPUS OPPORTUNITIES

Surrounded by business, government, and metropolitan centers, UMBC places students in over 1,200 co-ops and internships in more than 500 organizations each year in the Baltimore-Washington area. UMBC matches students with such employers as the federal Centers for Medicare and Medicaid, Bank of America, Silicon Graphics, MBNA, the Smithsonian Institution, NASA, and the National Aquarium. The university encourages students to participate in study abroad experiences during the semester or travel-study opportunities during winter and summer breaks. The Shriver Center links the resources of the campus to urgent social problems, places students in co-ops and internships at hundreds of businesses and organizations, organizes and manages community service projects that bring the resources of the university to people in need, and connects students to a wide range of social service projects.

THE UNIVERSITY OF MASSACHUSETTS LOWELL

ACADEMICS

UMBC's academic calendar consists of fall and spring semesters, a four-week mini session in January, and summer sessions from six to eight weeks. To receive a UMBC degree, students complete 120 to 128 credits plus two physical education courses. In addition to the requirements for the chosen major, the general education program (GEP), provides a solid basis for a lifetime of learning. GEP courses encompass humanities and fine arts, mathematics and natural sciences, social sciences, and languages and culture. The Honors College at UMBC is a special option for students seeking a community of like-minded people for whom the quest for knowledge is its own reward. All Honors College students must take at least one honors course per semester. Students choose from honors versions of core courses, special honors seminars, and plenty of other honors courses.

MAJORS

Programs leading to Bachelor of Arts, Bachelor of Fine Arts, and Bachelor of Science degrees: acting, Africana studies, American studies, aging services, ancient studies, Asian studies, biochemistry and molecular biology, bioinformatics and computational biology, biological sciences, business technology administration, chemical engineering, chemistry and biochemistry, chemistry education, computer engineering and computer science, cultural anthropology, dance, economics and financial economics, emergency health services, English, environmental science and environmental studies, gender and women's studies, geography, health administration and policy, history, information systems, innovation and entrepreneurship, interdisciplinary studies, mathematics and statistics, mechanical engineering, media and communication studies, modern languages, linguistics and intercultural communication, music, philosophy, physics education, physics, political science, psychology, social work, sociology, theater, and visual arts. New programs include computer gaming, media and communication studies, Asian studies, global studies and physics education. An interdisciplinary studies program allows students to design their own course of study according to their specific educational and career goals. UMBC offers pre-professional studies programs, including two-and four-year advisement programs to prepare students for clinical training in dental hygiene, medical and research technology, medicine, nursing, pharmacy, physical therapy, and veterinary medicine. Minors include Africana studies, American studies, ancient studies, anthropology, applied politics, art history and theory, astronomy, biological sciences, chemistry, computer science, dance, East Asian history, economics, emergency health services, environmental geography, gender and women's studies, geography, history, international affairs, international economics, Judaic studies, legal policy, literature, mathematics, modern languages and linguistics, music, philosophy, physics, political science, political thought, psychology, public administration, religious studies, social welfare, sociology, statistics, theater, writing, and media and communication studies.

TUITION, ROOM, BOARD, FEES

Tuition and fees for 2015-2016 are $11,006 for Maryland residents and $23,790 for out-of-state students. Room and board averaged $13,310 . Miscellaneous expenses, books, and transportation cost about $1,500 per year.

FINANCIAL AID

More than 45% of undergraduates receive some financial aid. UMBC uses the Free Application for Federal Student Aid (FAFSA) to help determine a student's financial need. Aid is awarded to qualified applicants on a first-come, first-served basis. Since aid is awarded only to admitted students, early application for admission is also important. Well-qualified freshmen are automatically considered for general merit scholarships once they are admitted to the University. The Scholars Programs at UMBC provide special opportunities for outstanding entering freshmen who want to focus their education through intense study in their major. Scholars participate in a wide range of academic and cultural enrichment activities, extracurricular travel, or summer study. The selection process for specialty scholarships includes application, an interview, and, in some cases, nomination from a high school official.

STUDENT ORGANIZATIONS & ACTIVITIES

The campus climate is friendly and energetic. UMBC's more than 11,379 undergraduates have enough ideas and interests to support more than 250 student groups, including Greek organizations and recreational sports clubs, such as fencing and sailing; community outreach efforts, such as Habitat for Humanity; and campus events, including lectures, films, concerts, and plays. Students enthusiastically follow UMBC NCAA Division I athletic teams, such as basketball, lacrosse, and soccer and attend games in the UMBC Stadium and Retriever Activities Center, which includes a multipurpose gym, auxiliary gym, weight room, and classrooms. Elections are held each year for officers in UMBC's Student Government Association (SGA). The SGA represents the student body on a number of administrative committees, including the Undergraduate Council, the Library Committee, and the Student Health Advisory Committee.

ADMISSIONS PROCESS

In fall 2015, the average incoming freshman had a 3.73 cumulative GPA, 53% ranked in the top quarter of his or her senior class, and had a combined SAT I score of 1214. Approximately 59% of freshman applicants are admitted each year. Academic performance and curriculum strength play an important part in the decision. An essay is required, and a letter of recommendation is strongly encouraged. Transfer students with at least 30 semester hours of college-level work are admitted based on the strength of college success. A minimum 2.5 GPA is recommended for full consideration. Prospective freshmen are encouraged to submit applications by the early action deadline of November 1. The final deadline is February 1 for full consideration for admission, campus housing, financial aid, and scholarships. The priority deadline for transfer students is March 15 for fall admission and November 1 for spring admission for students seeking admission to special programs or wishing to be considered for campus housing, financial aid, or scholarships.

CEEB Code: 1058

ACT Code: 3946

THE UNIVERSITY OF MASSACHUSETTS LOWELL

AT A GLANCE

The University of Massachusetts Lowell (UMass Lowell) is a doctoral-level public research university ranked in the top tier of U.S. News & World Report's national universities. Founded in 1894, the university is built on a tradition of innovation and entrepreneurship. Extensive partnerships with industry and community advance research, provide public service, and enrich the student experience. UMass Lowell graduates are ready to contribute meaningfully in the workplace, build lives around the principles and passions they develop in college, and make a difference in the world.

The university is part of the University of Massachusetts system and comprises the Francis College of Engineering; the College of Fine Arts, Humanities and Social Sciences (includes the School of Criminology and Justice Studies); the College of Health Sciences (includes the School of Nursing); the Kennedy College of Sciences; the Graduate School of Education; the Manning School of Business; and the Honors College. Together, the colleges offer more than 120 bachelor's, 40 master's and 30 doctoral degrees, and a number of certificate programs. All programs are accredited at the highest levels and incorporate vigorous hands-on learning and personalized attention. Students in all undergraduate disciplines who participate in the Honors College and complete the program requirements graduate with a Commonwealth Honors designation on their degrees.

UMass Lowell maintains a student-faculty ratio of 18:1 and focuses on putting the lessons of the classroom into practice in real-world settings through co-ops, internships, service learning, and research. Approximately 50 percent of undergraduate classes have fewer than 20 students. A growing number of interdisciplinary programs, such as the biomedical engineering and technology minor offered jointly by the colleges of Engineering, Sciences, and Health Sciences, reflect emerging fields in the global economy. Dozens of accelerated bachelor's-to-master's programs allow students to earn two degrees in as few as five years. All academic programs are accredited and meet the most rigorous board standards in higher education.

All first-year students belong to academic learning communities. Optional Living-Learning Communities in the residence halls include: honors, art, music, women in science and engineering, pre-med, business innovation, health professions, DifferenceMakers, criminal justice, creative arts, veterans, and more. The Centers for Learning offer tutoring and academic support programs. The Career Services and Cooperative Education Center helps students prepare for the transition to the working world. The DifferenceMaker program encourages student teams to address real-world problems through entrepreneurial action and sponsors the annual $25,000 Idea Challenge pitch contest.

To be considered for admission to undergraduate day programs, applicants must have a high school or a general equivalency diploma. Applicants have two application choices: the first is to apply with ACT and/or SAT scores; the second is to apply test-optional. Test-optional applicants need to answer additional supplemental application questions. Admissions standards vary by program. Last year's incoming freshmen had an average GPA of 3.59 and SAT scores of 1171 (reading and math).

Transfer students are considered for fall or spring semester admissions. Transcripts of completed work must be on file prior to acceptance. Depending on the number of transfer credits and college GPA, transfer students who seek admission as matriculating day students may be asked to provide a high school record and SAT scores.

Special-entrance programs that provide nontraditional admissions pathways for international students are available.

UMass Lowell admits students through early action, regular admission, and transfer admission. Entering freshmen are admitted for the fall or spring semesters. The early action deadline for freshmen is November 1; the regular admission deadline is February 1. Applicants to the School of Nursing must apply by the early action deadline. The preferred deadline for transfer applications is August 15 for the fall and January 7 for the spring. Applicants can apply using the Common Application or the UMass Lowell application; both require an essay and a letter of recommendation. Both applications are available online at www.uml.edu/apply.

ACADEMICS AND MAJORS

The university calendar includes two semesters, a three-week intersession in January, and a summer term with two sessions. Full-time undergraduates generally take five courses each semester. A minimum of 120 credits is required for baccalaureate degrees; the minimum credits required for professional degree programs are generally higher. Qualified students in all majors are invited to join the Honors College. The academic climate is serious, competitive, and requires self-motivation.

Dual majors are permitted. Dual B.A./B.S. degrees and bachelor's-to-master's degree programs (indicated with an asterisk in the lists below) are available in all fields. Pre-medical, pre-law and other pre-professional advising is available to interested students in all majors. Many of the majors offered have additional program options available, as noted in parentheses below.

The College of Fine Arts, Humanities and Social Sciences offers baccalaureate programs in: American studies; criminal justice and criminology° (corrections, homeland security, information technology, police, violence), economics°, English (creative writing, journalism and professional writing, literature, theatre arts), fine arts (animation, painting, printmaking, sculpture, photography, graphic design, web design, interactive media), history, legal studies, liberal arts (art history, Asian studies, comparative arts, cultural studies, economics, education, English/literature, environment and society, environmental studies, gender studies, history, languages, legal studies, music, philosophy, political science, psychology, sociology, theatre arts, writing), modern languages (French, Spanish, French/Spanish, Italian/Spanish), music business, music performance (instrumental, vocal), music studies (instrumental, vocal), peace and conflict studies°, philosophy (communication and critical thinking), political science, psychology°, sociology, and sound recording technology°.

The Kennedy College of Sciences offers baccalaureate programs in: biology° (bioinformatics, biotechnology, ecology), chemistry (cheminformatics, forensics), computer science° (bioinformatics/cheminformatics), environmental science (atmospheric science [meteorology], environmental studies, geoscience), mathematics° (applied computational mathematics, bioinformatics, business applications, computer science, probability and statistics, teaching), and physics° (general, optics, radiological health).

The James B. Francis College of Engineering offers baccalaureate programs in: biomedical engineering, chemical engineering° (biological engineering, computer-aided process design and controls, engineered materials, nanomaterials engineering, nuclear engineering, paper engineering), civil and environmental engineering°, electrical and computer engineering°, mechanical engineering°, and plastics engineering°. Engineering programs are accredited by the Accreditation Board for Engineering and Technology, Inc.

The College of Health Sciences and School of Nursing offer baccalaureate programs in: clinical laboratory and nutritional sciences (clinical laboratory sciences, clinical science, medical laboratory science, nutritional science), community health and sustainability (community health, environmental health), exercise physiology, nursing, and public health. A B.S. degree-completion program for RNs is offered through the Division of Online and Continuing Education. Accreditation is by the National Accrediting Agency for Clinical Laboratory Sciences and the National League for Nursing Accrediting Commission.

The Manning School of Business offers baccalaureate programs in: business administration° (accounting, corporate finance, entrepreneurship, financial markets, general finance, international business, management, management information systems, marketing, and supply chain/operations management). A one-year M.B.A. is available as a bachelor's-to-master's program. All programs are accredited by the Association to Advance Collegiate Schools of Business (AACSB) International.

The university's Graduate School of Education offers widely respected master's and doctoral programs as well as a range of initial certification courses. Undergraduates in STEM majors who are considering teaching can get classroom experience and a teaching minor through UTeach, a national teacher-training program whose only Northeast chapter is at UMass Lowell. Bachelor's-to-master's programs with initial Massachusetts teacher licensure are also available through the Fast Track to Teaching program.

The Princeton Review's Complete Book of Colleges

The Division of Online and Continuing Education offers a wide range of programs that are delivered online and on campus in the evening. Intercollegiate programs in aerospace studies, robotics, and joint military studies are available

Tuition, Room, Board, and Fees

The annual costs for 2016–17 for full-time undergraduate residents of Massachusetts were $14,307 per year; for nonresidents of Massachusetts, they were $30,875 per year. Room and board charges were $12,073 per year. Books and supplies are estimated at $400 to $800, depending on program. Quoted rates are subject to change.

The majority of freshmen choose to live in university housing, which includes traditional residence halls, apartments, suites, townhomes, and a combined conference center/residence hall located downtown. Housing is guaranteed for freshmen and available to most returning and transfer students who want it.

The campus features nearly twenty eateries, including Crossroads Café, Sal's Pizza, Starbucks, Subway, Red Mango, and traditional dining halls. The vibrant campus life includes supporting eighteen Division I athletics teams, which compete in the America East and Hockey East Conferences. The Campus Recreation Center runs intramural sports, fitness classes, and an outdoor adventure program. The 7,800-seat Tsongas Center is a popular venue for national acts.

FINANCIAL AID

UMass Lowell is committed to making higher education accessible to all qualified students. The university participates in federal and state programs, assisting students through grants-in-aid, loans, employment opportunities, and scholarships. The amount of a financial aid award is determined by need, as indicated by the Free Application for Federal Student Aid (FAFSA), which should be filed by March 1. The university awards a growing number of merit-based scholarships. More than $160 million in financial aid was awarded to students in the 2015–16 academic year, meeting approximately 90 percent of need.

STUDENT BODY

The campus community is ethnically, culturally, and economically diverse; students come from 50 states and over 100 countries. Thirty-two percent of undergraduates identify as students of color. More than 200 active student organizations include a marching band, a weekly newspaper, and an FM radio station. Leadership opportunities are provided through the Student Government Association, the Residence Hall Association and a variety of other student-run organizations. Students also participate in the disciplinary system and in most university committees.

ADMISSIONS

All undergraduate day applicants must have a high school diploma or a general equivalency diploma and satisfactory SAT scores. The incoming freshman class for fall 2016 had an average GPA of 3.59 and the average SAT score (combined reading and math) was 1171. Students whose high school average is below the required minimum may be considered for admission if they present SAT verbal and mathematics scores that are higher than those specified for the admission of degree candidates by the college or program to which they wish to apply.

Transfer students are considered for fall or spring semester admissions. Transcripts of completed work must be on file prior to acceptance. Depending on the number of transfer credits and college GPA, transfer students who seek admission as matriculating day students may be asked to provide a high school record and SAT scores.

For day programs, the university admits students through early action, regular admission and transfer admission. Entering freshmen are admitted for the fall or spring semester. The early action deadline for freshman applications is November 1; the deadline for regular admission is February 1. Applicants to the nursing program must apply by the early action deadline. The preferred deadline for transfer applications is August 15 for the fall semester and January 7 for the spring semester.

For further information, contact:

Office of Undergraduate Admissions

University of Massachusetts Lowell

University Crossing

Suite 420, 220 Pawtucket Street

Lowell, Massachusetts 01854

United States

Phone: 978-934-3931

admissions@uml.edu

LOCATION

The university is clustered along the Merrimack River in Lowell, a city of 110,000 that has gained national attention by successfully leveraging its history, ethnic diversity, and entrepreneurial spirit to create a vital urban center. The site of a unique, urban National Historical Park, Lowell is home to an acclaimed professional theater company, literary and folk festivals, and numerous restaurants and museums. Lowell is located 25 miles from Boston and Cambridge and within the region's major business corridors, which provide internship and co-op opportunities for students. It is also within easy reach of major outdoor recreational areas via major highways and regional train and bus service.

CAMPUS FACILITIES & EQUIPMENT

The campus is in the midst of a bold expansion. Twelve new facilities have opened in the last six years, including the Mark and Elisia Saab Emerging Technologies and Innovation Center, the Health and Social Sciences Building, the Pulichino Tong Business Center, two suite-style residence halls, the McGauvran Student Center, and the Perkins Complex townhomes. A new writing center, a television studio, and a 14,500-square-foot anatomy and physiology lab opened three years ago. University Crossing, the hub of student services and activities, opened in summer 2014 and connects the university's three campuses to the downtown business and cultural district. Both libraries feature new learning commons with areas for quiet and group study as well as Starbucks cafés.

OFF-CAMPUS OPPORTUNITIES

Extensive opportunities for study abroad with credit include faculty-led courses, affiliate programs, exchanges, and more than 120 partnerships with prestigious institutions in 40 countries. Recent faculty-led courses include seminars on health care in Peru; Cuban culture and history in Havana; crime, law, and asset protection in Hong Kong and Macau; migration in Prague; and innovation and entrepreneurship in India. Numerous service-learning and research opportunities as well as co-ops and internships occur with our partners located throughout the region and worldwide.

Office of Undergraduate Admissions

University of Massachusetts Lowell

University Crossing, Suite 420

200 Pawtucket St.

Lowell, Massachusetts 01854

Phone: 978-934-3931

Website: http://www.uml.edu

http://www.facebook.com/umlowell

http://www.twitter.com/umasslowell

http://www.youtube.com/user/umasslowell

http://instagram.com/umasslowell

THE UNIVERSITY OF NEW ENGLAND

AT A GLANCE

The University of New England is a private, top-ranked university offering flagship programs in the health and life sciences, as well as degrees in business, education, the social sciences and the liberal arts. UNE's three beautiful campuses in Biddeford and Portland, Maine, and Tangier, Morocco, are home to an active and close-knit student community engaged in rigorous academic experiences.

Innovation drives the University each day. In state-of-the-art facilities in Maine, Morocco and beyond, hands-on learning, interdisciplinary engagement and global awareness empower the next generation of leaders for New England and the world.

LOCATION & ENVIRONMENT
BIDDEFORD CAMPUS

UNE's waterfront campus in Biddeford, Maine, offers more than 4,000 feet of scenic shoreline where the Saco River flows into the Atlantic Ocean. The local area has a long history as a coastal vacation destination. Within its 540 acres, the Biddeford Campus is the hub of undergraduate student life from its vibrant campus clubs and athletics teams, to its innovative study and living spaces.

PORTLAND CAMPUS

A rustic brick port sets the stage for a thriving buy-local economy and hip cultural scene —with outdoor adventure all around. UNE's Portland Campus, a classic, century-old New England quad just a short drive from the waterfront, anchors UNE's tight-knit, engaged community within this exciting city.

TANGIER CAMPUS

UNE set a new study abroad standard with its Tangier, Morocco campus, which features state-of-the-art labs and modern accommodations, as well as easy access to beaches, downtown and cultural attractions. Students can enjoy a semester abroad at our Morocco campus or with partner universities in Spain, France and Iceland for about the same cost as a semester in Maine.

CAMPUS FACILITIES & EQUIPMENT

Both the Biddeford and Portland Campuses feature buildings with a variety of uses to support the needs of the University community. On the Biddeford Campus, several research facilities are on campus, including the Arthur P. Girard Marine Science Center; the Harold Alfond Center for Health Sciences, with biology and chemistry labs as well as lecture halls, classrooms, a gross anatomy lab, and UNE's medical school facilities; the Pickus Center for Biomedical Research; and the Peter and Cécile Morgane Hall, a science center providing additional classrooms and an undergraduate teaching laboratory. The Department of Creative and Fine Arts offers a dedicated building that provides faculty offices and studio space for drawing, painting, printmaking, sculpting and photography. The Biddeford Campus includes undergraduate student housing, graduate and undergraduate classrooms, labs and a makerspace; cafés and innovative study and gathering spaces in the new Danielle N. Ripich Commons; and various athletic facilities and fields, including an NHL-size hockey arena, blue turf field, basketball arena, and much more.

The Portland Campus houses Maine's only College of Dental Medicine, the College of Pharmacy, and the Westbrook College of Health Professions, which offers undergraduate and graduate programs in several allied health fields. The 41-acre campus also includes the Center for Global Humanities, Art Gallery and Maine Women Writers Collection. The Blewett Science Center, home to UNE's nursing program, consists of science labs and classrooms. UNE's Interprofessional Simulation and Innovation Center, which provides customized training and education for students and health professionals, is also on the Portland Campus.

OFF-CAMPUS OPPORTUNITIES

On any given weekend at UNE, thrilling adventures await. Students can ride countless miles of mountain bike trails and scenic rural roads, kayak and sail on Casco Bay, camp and hike at hundreds of great parks, or just take in some sun at UNE's own Freddy Beach. With more than 90 clubs and organizations on UNE's campuses, students discover many opportunities to get involved. Whether an academic club, an arts club, student government, a cultural organization or an outdoor recreation group, like-minded people are ready to welcome new students aboard.

ACADEMICS

Academic programs ensure that students have plenty of opportunities for extensive fieldwork, clinical experiences, research, internships and global experiences at both the undergraduate and graduate levels.

Bachelor's degrees are offered in animal behavior, applied exercise science, applied mathematics, applied social and cultural studies, aquaculture and aquarium science, art and design media, art education, athletic training, biochemistry, biological sciences, business, chemistry, communications, dental hygiene, elementary/middle education, English, environmental science, environmental studies, global studies, sustainability and business, health, wellness and occupational studies, history, laboratory science, interdisciplinary studies in the humanities (including pre-law), marine entrepreneurship, marine sciences, medical biology (pre-dental medicine, pre-medicine, pre-optometry, pre–physician assistant, and pre-veterinary medicine), neuroscience, nursing, nutrition, marine affairs, political science, pre-pharmacy, pre-physical therapy, psychology, public health, secondary education, social work, sociology, and sport and recreation management..

Master's degrees are offered in applied nutrition, biological sciences, education, health informatics, marine sciences, nurse anesthesia, occupational therapy, physician assistant, public health, and social work.

Doctorates offered include dental medicine (D.M.D.), education leadership (Ed.D.), osteopathic medicine (D.O.), pharmacy (Pharm.D.), and physical therapy (D.P.T.).

MAJORS & DEGREES OFFERED

An education at UNE goes beyond training and beyond the traditional. Professors include world-class researchers, authors and scholars who help students reach further, working side-by-side with them in the lab, in the field or across the globe.

UNE offers more than 40 undergraduate and 32 graduate/professional academic programs in needed, fascinating fields. UNE is home to Maine's only medical school and the only college of dental medicine in Northern New England. UNE is one of a handful of private universities with a comprehensive health education mission including medicine, pharmacy, dental medicine, nursing and an array of allied health professions. In addition to health sciences disciplines, the full range of liberal arts classes and majors makes UNE a unique participatory, educational environment.

TUITION, ROOM, BOARD, FEES

The costs for undergraduate students per academic year for 2016–17:

Tuition: $34,380;

Room and board: $13,250;

Fees:$1,250.

FINANCIAL AID

In 2015–16, 98 percent of all full-time students received some form of financial assistance. The average package was $27,000, including scholarships, grants, loans and employment. The University of New England has an extensive academic scholarship program. Merit awards range from $4,000 to $20,000 per year.

STUDENT ORGANIZATIONS & ACTIVITIES

UNE offers a variety of cultural and social events and encourages students to become involved in activities, clubs and sports. Popular interests include scuba diving, skiing, hiking, biking, varsity and intramural sports, swimming, surfing, music, theater, community service and student leadership development programs.

UNE athletes—called Nor'easters after one of the nastiest storms in Mother Nature's arsenal —strive for success on and off the field. With 11 conference championships in the last five years, student athletes at UNE have a cumulative grade point average of 3.37. Our intercollegiate teams compete at the Division III level in men's basketball, cross country, golf, ice hockey, lacrosse and soccer. Football will see its first varsity action beginning in 2018. Varsity women's sports include basketball, cross country, field hockey, ice hockey, lacrosse, rugby, soccer, softball, swimming and volleyball.

The personal attention students receive from faculty both in and out of class, and the quality of faculty as experts in their fields are key strengths of the UNE experience. Students appreciate their faculty members as mentors and trust them as accomplished scholars who impact their fields. From designing coastal trails and restoring wetlands on campus to caring for patients in need, UNE faculty members work side-by-side with their students and are recognized by their peers and other leaders for their expertise. UNE faculty members are national award recipients, Fulbright scholars, authors and world-class researchers, and they share their knowledge unselfishly with their students.

ADMISSIONS PROCESS

Students applying for admission should submit a completed application, a $40 nonrefundable application fee, transcripts of all academic work (high school and college), and scores on either the ACT or SAT. Students who do not use English as their primary language must submit TOEFL scores. Students applying for admission should have completed a curriculum that includes English, mathematics, science, and social sciences. International students must also complete the International Student Supplemental Application.

The undergraduate admission application deadline is February 15. Applications received after that date are reviewed on a space-available basis. There is a nonbinding December 1 early action application deadline with a December 31 notification date. Applications for the spring term are accepted through December 1.

All prospective students are strongly encouraged to visit the University of New England at an open house or for an information session and tour. Information sessions and tours are held daily Monday through Friday; Saturday tours are also available on select weekends throughout the year. Prospective students can register for a tour at www.une.edu/visit.

UNIVERSITY OF NEW HAVEN

AT A GLANCE

Founded in 1920, the University of New Haven is a private, co-educational institution that offers a wide range of majors in a small, intimate college environment. The university attracts students who are interested in a Liberal Arts education with an emphasis on career preparation through internships, co-operative education, research, community service, study abroad and more! With over 100 different programs of study for 4,600 full-time undergraduate students, the University of New Haven offers a personalized experience that focuses on "experiential learning" reflecting the belief that students learn best if they are actively engaged in real-world applications of what they learn.

LOCATION & ENVIRONMENT

The University of New Haven is located in suburban West Haven, Connecticut. The campus is conveniently situated 75 miles from New York City and 135 miles from Boston. Only minutes away from the beautiful beaches along Long Island Sound, the university offers a shuttle to downtown New Haven and other local areas.

CAMPUS FACILITIES & EQUIPMENT

Some of the finest anywhere in the United States. Over $200 million has been invested in facilities and academic programs in just the past five years. Some of these include a brand new freshman residence hall (Westside Hall) and new student dining area (Food on Demand), opened in Fall 2014, the 58,000 square-foot David A. Beckerman Recreation Center, the $48 million Celentano Residence Hall for upperclassmen, the Henry C. Lee Institute of Forensic Science, National Crime Scene Training & Technology Center, Laurel Vlock Center for Convergent Media, Samuel Bergami Learning Center for Finance & Technology, TV and Film Production Studio, Digital and Analog Recording Studios, MIDI and Sound Synthesis Lab, Music Practice Rooms, 300-seat addition to our main dining hall, Ralph A. DellaCamera Stadium featuring our Blue & Gold turf field, Solar Testing & Training Laboratory, Hazel Nut Café (student-run coffee shop), and the planned 2018 opening of a new Center for Marine Sciences right on the water in the greater New Haven area.

ACADEMICS

The University of New Haven mixes traditional degrees along with many unique programs in five academic colleges. The university also offers 30 graduate degree programs.

MAJORS & DEGREES OFFERED

College of Arts and Sciences

The College of Arts and Sciences offers traditional majors such as Art, Biology, Communication, English, History, Mathematics, Psychology, and Political Science as well as unique majors in the areas of Dental Hygiene, Environmental Science, Genetics & Biotechnology, Forensic Psychology Health Sciences, Global Studies, Graphic Design, Digital Art and Design, Interior Design, Interior Design—Pre-Architecture, Marine Biology, Music, Music Industry, Music & Sound Recording, Nutrition & Dietetics, and Theater Arts. The university also offers minors in languages such as Arabic, Chinese, Russian, Farsi, Portuguese and Spanish.

College of Business

The College of Business offers degrees in Business Management, Accounting, Economics, Finance, International Business, Marketing, Sport Management, and Hospitality and Tourism Management with concentrations in Hotel & Resort Management, Foodservice Management, and Event & Tourism Management.

Tagliatela College of Engineering

The Tagliatela College of Engineering offers degrees in Chemistry, General Engineering, Chemical Engineering, Civil Engineering, Computer Engineering, Electrical Engineering, Industrial and Systems Engineering, Mechanical Engineering, Computer Science, and Cyber Systems with focus areas of study in Cyber Forensics and Cybersecurity, and Wireless Networking.

Henry C. Lee College of Criminal Justice and Forensic Sciences

The Henry C. Lee College of Criminal Justice and Forensic Sciences offers degrees in Criminal Justice, Forensic Science, Fire Science, Legal Studies, Paramedicine and National Security Studies. The university offers six eight separate Criminal Justice concentrations in Investigative Services, Crime Analysis, Law Enforcement Administration, Juvenile and Family Justice, Victim Services and Corrections. The Henry C. Lee College of Criminal Justice and Forensic Sciences also contains three distinct degrees in the area of Fire Science: Arson Investigation, Fire Science Administration, and Fire Protection Engineering. Legal Studies programs are offered in Paralegal Studies, Public Affairs, and Dispute Resolution.

Lyme Academy College of Fine Arts

The Lyme Academy College of Fine Arts is located in Old Lyme, Connecticut. Lyme offers four BFA degrees in Drawing, Illustration, Painting, and Sculpture.

Accreditations and Recognitions

Many of our academic programs have earned further distinction through high-level private accrediting bodies in the respective fields:

AACSB (The Association to Advance Collegiate Schools of Business) accredits five of our undergraduate business degree programs: Accounting, Business Management, Finance, Marketing, and Sport Management.

ABA (American Bar Association) approves our undergraduate degree in Legal Studies, one of only a few such programs at the undergraduate level in the entire country.

ABET (Accreditation Board of Engineering and Technology) accredits six of our undergraduate academic degree programs in the Tagliatela College of Engineering: Civil Engineering, Chemical Engineering, Computer Engineering, Computer Science, Electrical Engineering, and Mechanical Engineering.

ACEND (Accreditation Council for Education in Nutrition and Dietetics) of the American Academy of Nutrition and Dietetics accredits our very popular undergraduate degree in Nutrition and Dietetics, leading many of our students to become Registered Dietitians (R.D.).

ACS (American Chemical Society) accredits our Chemistry program. FEPAC (Forensic Science Education Programs Accreditation Commission) accredits our nationally renowned Forensic Science program. Only a select number of programs have earned this level of distinction through the American Academy of Forensic Science (A.A.F.S.).

ADA (American Dental Association) accredits our Dental Hygiene program.

NASAD (National Association of Schools of Art and Design) accredits our programs in Drawing, Painting, Illustration, and Sculpture at the Lyme Academy College of Fine Arts.

Marvin K. Peterson Library

The Marvin K. Peterson Library offers over 240,000 volumes, 1,400 print journal and newspaper subscriptions, and electronic access to over 19,000 full-text journal and newspaper titles, approximately 550,000 pieces of microfiche, 12,000 volumes of microfilm, e-books, 33,000 e-journals and 162,000 paper U.S. Government documents. Students have access to numerous Internet stations and ports throughout the library and a coffee shop and lounge area for students to study and take a break.

TUITION, ROOM, BOARD, FEES

Cost for the 2017-2018 Academic year is: Tuition & Fees—$38,110 and Room & Board—$15,030.

FINANCIAL AID

Students are automatically considered for merit-based academic scholarships by simply applying for admission to the University of New Haven. Students must complete their admission application by May 1 for the fall semester or by January 2 for the spring semester in order to be eligible for merit-based awards. Merit-based scholarships range from $10,000 to $24,000 per academic year for students who qualify.

To file for need-based aid, the priority deadline for Financial Aid is March 1 for the fall semester and December 1 for the spring semester. Students must fill out the Free Application for Federal Student Aid (FAFSA), which is available online at http://www.fafsa.gov in order to be considered for need-based aid at the University of New Haven.

STUDENT ORGANIZATIONS & ACTIVITIES

Study Abroad

The University of New Haven opened its satellite campus in Prato, Italy (Tuscany Region) in the fall of 2012. The course offerings at the Tuscany campus change from semester to semester. Students can take a total of 15 credits (5 courses) during the semester including one mandatory Italian language course. Each semester the university sends full-time faculty to teach courses alongside Italian faculty. Students can study abroad at our Prato, Italy campus as early as first-semester freshman year. UNH is also a leading provider of study abroad education, offering students over 300 options worldwide. We also offer an intensive study abroad program which offers 2-week abroad sessions with a University of New Haven faculty member during intersession for six credits at a number of locations such as London, Dubai, Rome and more.

Athletics

As a member of the Northeast 10 Conference, UNH competes in 17 Division II varsity sports (7 men's and 10 women's) baseball, basketball, cross-country, field hockey, football, lacrosse, soccer, softball, tennis, track, and volleyball. The university also has a number of club sports, which compete at the intercollegiate level including: baseball, cheerleading, field hockey, gymnastics, ice hockey, lacrosse (men's), rugby (men's and women's), soccer (men's), tennis, volleyball (men's) and wrestling. The 58,000-square-foot David A. Beckerman Recreation Center adds another dimension to athletic opportunities at UNH. It features a fitness center with aerobic equipment, weights, and televisions; multi-purpose rooms for yoga, aerobics, Pilates, spinning, and other wellness activities; two basketball/volleyball courts; a multi-sport court for rollerblading, floor hockey, indoor soccer, and other activities; an elevated indoor running track; and lounge areas including a juice bar/café.

Residential Life

The university has 12 on-campus and 6 off-campus housing options which offers a variety for students to choose from ranging from a traditional residence hall to apartment-style housing with suites of two or more bedrooms. In 2005, the university started a Living Learning Community (LLC) program where students combine their residence hall and academic experience by interacting with faculty members outside of the classroom and living with students in the same academic area of interest as theirs. Participants also enjoy special trips and opportunities geared towards their major of interest. Currently, LLC's are offered in Business, Criminal Justice, Community of the Arts, Engineering, Fire Science, Forensic Science, Forensic Psychology, Health Sciences, Health and Wellness, Marine Biology, Music/Music Industry/Music & Sound Recording, Honors Program, and ROTC.

STUDENT ORGANIZATIONS & ACTIVITIES

The Undergraduate Student Government Association (USGA) oversees all aspects of undergraduate life, organizing campus social and cultural activities, supporting the student-run radio station and student-produced publications, and overseeing the budget for all undergraduate organizations.

There are more than 170 campus clubs and organizations, including chapters of several professional societies, religious groups, social clubs, student councils, cultural clubs, and national fraternities and sororities.

ADMISSIONS PROCESS

The University of New Haven has an Early Decision and Early Action Admissions Policy; we begin to review applications on September 1st and continue until programs are filled. The university offers one binding and three non-binding admission programs for fall admission. To be considered for certain programs applicants must follow the established timelines and important dates. Early Decision Applications are due by December 1, Early Action Applications are due by December 15, Early Action 2 Applications are due by February 15, Regular Decision Applications are due after December 15, and Spring Admission Applications are due no later than January 15.

Students may apply using the Common Application. To be considered for admission, candidates must complete the application form and submit it along with a non-refundable $50 application fee. An application is considered complete once we receive the application, personal essay (250-600 words), transcript(s), standardized test scores (SAT I or ACT), and one letter of recommendation (from an academic source).

Visiting Campus

We encourage all prospective students and their families to visit us and see what the University of New Haven has to offer. The university offers a variety of campus visits for students and their families to choose from seven days a week! Visits to choose from include daily campus information sessions and tours, Open Houses, Enhanced Visits, Accepted Student Days and much more! To view our campus visit calendar and register for an event, visit our website at www.newhaven.edu/visitUNH.

For further information about the University of New Haven and to schedule a campus visit or personal interview, students may contact:

Office of Undergraduate Admissions

Phone: 203-932-7319

Fax: 203-931-6093

Email: admissions@newhaven.edu

Visit our website: www.newhaven.edu

THE UNIVERSITY OF SAN FRANCISCO

AT A GLANCE

The University of San Francisco—a premier, private Jesuit university—reflects the diverse and dynamic city that surrounds it. USF provides students from all backgrounds an education that is intensely personalized, intellectually inspiring, and designed expressly to help them change the world for the better. USF enrolls 6,682 undergraduate and 3,988 graduate students.

USF offers over 100 undergraduate and graduate degree programs and boasts an ever-expanding network of 103,756 alumni who live in all 50 states, six US territories, and 129 countries. The school's 55-acre campus, in the geographic heart of San Francisco, overlooks downtown to the east and the Pacific Ocean to the west.

As one of the most diverse universities in the United States, USF delivers the world on a campus. Students from 47 states and 87 countries create a rich environment, and in the best Jesuit tradition, USF welcomes students from all backgrounds—and from all religious faiths or no faith—and invites input from every perspective. The combination of academic rigor and open-minded inquiry creates an atmosphere in which students grow and thrive. USF has produced 270 U.S. judges (including four California Supreme Courts justices); a former United States senator; a California lieutenant governor; two Pulitzer Prize winners; an Olympic medalist; countless priests, nuns, and other religious leaders; educators; police chiefs; corporate CEOs and entrepreneurs; three NBA Hall of Famers; three NFL Hall of Famers; and Alejandro Toledo, the former president of Peru.

LOCATION & ENVIRONMENT

USF's 55-acre campus is a small and supportive community in the heart of a large city. Located in the geographic center of San Francisco, the main campus is just minutes from the Financial District, Golden Gate Park, and the Pacific Ocean. More than 90 percent of incoming freshmen live on campus, and all USF students take advantage of all the city has to offer—music, museums, theater, dining, the ballet, major sporting events—plus a wide range of research, internship, and employment opportunities. Also, students can connect with an ever-expanding network of 103,756 alumni who live in all 50 states, six US territories, and 129 countries.

CAMPUS FACILITIES & EQUIPMENT

USF students have access to Gleeson Library's 1.8 million holdings and to Lo Schiavo Center for Science and Innovation, which houses a digital lecture hall, ample space for collaborative learning, and labs for chemistry, toxicology, advanced biotechnology, and mathematics. Cowell Hall, the base for nursing classes and the Nursing Skills Laboratory, also includes the Instructional Media Center. Malloy Hall, headquarters for the School of Management, houses an additional computer laboratory and special seminar rooms. Kalmanovitz Hall houses all programs in the humanities and social sciences and features state-of-the-art classrooms, a rooftop sculpture garden, and seventeen laboratories for language, writing, media, and psychology.

The Koret Health and Recreation Center provides facilities for exercise, racquetball, court games, weight training, massage, personal training, and various aquatic activities in an Olympic-size pool. Fitness interval training, spin, yoga, pilates mat, and Zumba are just some of the free classes offered at Koret. Outdoor adventures include horseback riding, sailing, skiing/snowboarding, and sea kayaking. Intramural and club sports include basketball, soccer, flag football, sailing, table tennis, karate, lacrosse, rugby, water polo, ultimate frisbee, and volleyball. NCAA Division I sports include baseball, basketball, cross-country, golf, soccer, tennis, track and field, and women's volleyball and sand volleyball.

OFF-CAMPUS OPPORTUNITIES

USF students have many opportunities for university-sponsored study abroad programs, such as ones to Sophia University (Tokyo), Oxford (England) through USF's St. Ignatius Institute, a program at Universidad Iberoamericana in Mexico City. USF is connected to Gonzaga University's study abroad program in Florence (Italy) and to Loyola University of Chicago's program in Rome. The Institute of European and Asian Studies, of which USF is an associate member, offers programs in Durham and London, England; Paris, Dijon, and Nantes, France; Berlin and Freiburg, Germany; Vienna, Austria; Madrid and Salamanca, Spain; Milan, Italy; Tokyo and Nagoya, Japan; Moscow, Russia; Adelaide and Canberra, Australia; Beijing, China; and Singapore. There are many other study abroad opportunities as well. Students receive assistance from USF in all aspects of the program: choosing a location, completing applications, arranging financial matters, registering for academic credit, obtaining a passport and visa, and organizing travel plans.

ACADEMICS

The University of San Francisco delivers a well-rounded education that prepares students not only for successful careers but also for fulfilling lives. A baccalaureate degree is issued upon the successful completion of a 128-unit curriculum. The curriculum consists of 44 units of core courses chosen from six specified categories in addition to 80–85 units that are divided among departmental major requirements and electives. An honors program is available for select students seeking a strong academic challenge. The academic year is based on the two-semester system with summer sessions and a winter intersession also available.

USF honors advanced placement credits, as certified by the College Board's Advanced Placement Program exams and the International Baccalaureate program. The University also cooperates with the College-Level Examination Program (CLEP). Students in the College of Arts and Sciences can also accelerate the traditional undergraduate process and earn a bachelor's degree in three years with a combination of advanced placement credits and an academically rigorous schedule.

The St. Ignatius Institute offers a core curriculum based on the great books of Western civilization and an emphasis on critical analysis to promote the common good. Any undergraduate student at the University, regardless of major, may take courses through the Institute to meet core curriculum requirements. The University also offers Army ROTC. ROTC scholarships are available for qualified applicants and continuing students.

USF's Center for Global Education has numerous study-abroad programs available to academically eligible undergraduate students. Exchanges with Jesuit universities include locations in Japan, Mexico, China, Spain, Philippines, El Salvador, and Chile. USF's St. Ignatius Institute program includes an exchange with Oxford University in England. USF is also an associate member of the Institute of European and Asian Studies, which offers programs in Durham and London, England; Paris, Dijon, and Nantes, France; Berlin and Freiburg, Germany; Vienna, Austria; Madrid and Salamanca, Spain; Milan, Italy; Tokyo and Nagoya, Japan; Moscow, Russia; Adelaide and Canberra, Australia; Beijing, China; and Singapore. Numerous other study-abroad opportunities are also available. USF assists students in selecting a location, applying to programs, making financial arrangements, registering for academic credit, securing a passport and visa, and making travel plans.

CAREER SERVICES & PLACEMENT

USF leverages its location, alumni base, and relationships with industry leaders to help connect students to internship and career opportunities in the Bay Area and beyond. Top employers regularly visit campus. Students visit the Career Services Center to research potential employers, get help with their resumes, and take part in practice interviews. USF alumni report an average mid-career salary of $92,400 and can be found working for organizations like Apple, Teach for America, Google, Salesforce, and the San Francisco Unified School District.

MAJORS

The College of Arts and Sciences offers both B.A. and B.S. degrees. The School of Management offers B.S. degrees. The School of Nursing and Health Professions offers a direct-entry, four-year B.S. in Nursing for qualified high school and transfer applicants. Majors: Accounting, Advertising, Architecture and Community Design, Art History/Arts Management, Asian Studies, Biology, Business Administration, Chemistry, Communication Studies, Comparative Literature and Culture, Computer Science, Critical Diversity Studies, Data Science, Design, Economics, English, Entrepreneurship and Innovation, Environmental Science, Environmental Studies, Finance, Fine Arts, French Studies, Health Studies, History, Hospitality Management, International Business, International Studies, Japanese Studies, Kinesiology, Latin American Studies, Marketing, Management, Mathematics, Media Studies, Nursing, Organizational Behavior and Leadership, Performing Arts & Social Justice, Philosophy, Physics, Politics, Psychology, Sociology, Spanish, Theology and Religious Studies, Urban Studies.

USF has 77 minors and offers special programs that enhance the learning experience at USF. Special programs include astronomy; African history; African-American studies; Asia Pacific studies; Catholic studies and social thought; ethnic studies; film studies; honors program in the humanities; journalism; Judaic studies; Latino/a and Chicano/a Studies; Middle Eastern studies; neuroscience; 4+3 dual degrees in law, premedical, and other pre-professional health studies; public relations; a five-year dual-degree teacher preparation program that results in teacher certification at the elementary or secondary level; and the School of Management honors cohort program.

TUITION, ROOM, BOARD, FEES

Tuition for the 2016–17 academic year is $44,040. Room and board are $13,990.

FINANCIAL AID

A variety of financial aid programs are available at the University, including scholarships, grants, loans, and campus employment opportunities. Domestic students who wish to be considered for financial aid must file the Free Application for Federal Student Aid (FAFSA) and College Scholarship Service Profile (CSS) by February 15. More than two thirds of all USF students receive some type of financial aid.

In addition to need-based financial aid, the University has a generous academic scholarship program based on the applicant's high school record and test scores. Eligible students are identified during the admission process and can apply as early action, early decision, or regular action applicants.

STUDENT ORGANIZATIONS & ACTIVITIES

USF is one of the most diverse campuses in the United States. Living and learning in a community that comprises students from 47 states and 87 countries is a unique opportunity. All undergraduates, freshmen, and transfer students who enter with 40 or fewer college credits must live on campus for their first two semesters at USF, unless they live within a 40-mile radius of campus. More than 90 percent of the incoming freshmen live on campus.

It's hard to be bored at USF. Students participate in over 100 student-run organizations, including fraternities, sororities, honor societies, and clubs. Students also participate in a whole host of Campus Activities Board sponsored events including Spring Carnival, Campus Movie Fest, and Late Nights@Crossroads.

At USF, all students are encouraged to give back to the community and to change the world in ways both small and large. The Leo T. McCarthy Center for Public Service and the Common Good maintains relationships with more than 250 community service organizations, and students participate in service-learning projects that include socially just urban design, outreach to underprivileged children in local schools, and habitat restoration.

ADMISSIONS PROCESS

The University seeks students who are sincerely interested in pursuing a well-rounded education and who hope to make a positive difference in the world. The admission process is selective, and each application is reviewed individually. To enhance the quality and diversity of its student body, USF welcomes men and women of all races, nationalities, and religious beliefs—or no religious belief—to apply. Eligibility is based on high school course work and GPA, the application essay, an academic recommendation, extracurricular involvement, and test scores. Domestic applicants are required to submit SAT or ACT test scores. International applicants are required to submit TOEFL or IELTS test scores; however, if an international applicant submits sufficient SAT or ACT test scores, the TOEFL or IELTS may be waived.

SPECIAL PROGRAMS

The USF Pre-Professional Health Committee serves to guide and recommend students to medical and dental professional schools as well as to schools for pharmacy, optometry, veterinary medicine, and podiatry. A student may complete the premedical or other pre–health science requirements as part of, or in addition to, the requirements of an academic major. The Pre-Professional Health Committee assists students with the application process, collects and mails recommendations to professional schools, conducts interviews in preparation for application, and endorses approved candidates via a committee letter of recommendation sent to all professional schools selected by the student.

THE UNIVERSITY OF TAMPA

AT A GLANCE

The University of Tampa is a private, medium-sized, comprehensive university in the heart of Tampa. UT offers students an exciting combination of challenging coursework and real-world learning experience in more than 200 areas of study. Situated on a beautiful 110-acre campus, the University is adjacent to the Hillsborough River and downtown Tampa. Students enjoy a traditional, self-contained campus only steps away from the professional and cultural opportunities of a bustling city. At the center of campus lies Plant Hall, once a luxurious hotel for the rich and famous. This historical landmark is complemented by modern surroundings and excellent facilities including a student union, art studios and gallery, theaters, computer resource centers, athletic facilities, science labs and new residence halls. Approximately 8,310 students (7,000 full-time undergraduates) are enrolled at UT. With students from all 50 states and 140 countries, UT provides diverse and dynamic environment. Students may choose from 230 clubs and organizations, including honor societies, student media, fraternities and sororities, community service groups and intramural sports. The University of Tampa has one of the top NCAA Division II sports programs in the nation, winning 15 national championships, including recent championships in baseball (2015, 2013, 2007, 2006), women's volleyball (2014, 2006) and women's soccer (2007).

LOCATION & ENVIRONMENT

Located on the west central coast of Florida, Tampa has far more to offer than beautiful beaches and a pleasant climate. The Tampa Bay area is one of the fastest growing regions in the United States and is a leading center for the arts, international business, law, education, media and health and scientific research. Forbes and Newsweek consistently pick Tampa Bay as one of the nation's best places to live.

CAMPUS FACILITIES & EQUIPMENT

UT has invested approximately $530 million in new academic facilities, technology and residence halls since 2000, making this national historic landmark the model of a modern university. Ninety-three% of residence halls are new within the past 15 years and most others have been renovated recently. (For residence hall video tours, visit www.ut.edu/residencelife/videos.) The Vaughn Center and residence hall complex serves as the hub of student life. Here students find food courts, recreational areas, a theater, student office space, the Barnes & Noble campus store and a ninth-floor conference center with incredible views of Tampa Bay. Morsani Hall offers state-of-the-art amenities and eight separate dining venues. Other outstanding facilities and resources include the Sykes College of Business, a waterfront Marine Science Field Station and research vessels, Ferman Music Center, Reeves Theater, the 1,000-seat Falk Theatre, R.K. Bailey Art Studios and Sykes Chapel and Center for Faith and Values. The newly renovated Martinez Athletics Center, Naimoli Family Softball Complex and Naimoli Family Athletics and Intramural Complex represent some of the best athletic facilities in the country. Students also enjoy a new 21st-century fitness center, completed in fall 2016.

OFF-CAMPUS OPPORTUNITIES

Across the river in downtown is the Tampa Museum of Art, Straz Center for the Performing Arts, Florida Aquarium, Amalie Arena and an outstanding public library. Busch Gardens is several miles from campus, and Walt Disney World and Universal Studios are only 90 minutes away. Tampa International Airport is 5 miles from campus.

ACADEMICS

The University of Tampa's undergraduate curriculum is designed to give students a broad academic and cultural background as well as a concentrated study in a major. Students complete a comprehensive core curriculum known as the Baccalaureate Experience, which is highlighted by the unique and innovative First-Year Experience—an extensive orientation program that encourages student development via exploration of global issues, career possibilities and critical thinking and communication skills. International experience is an important focus at The University of Tampa. Through globally oriented courses and study abroad opportunities, students are prepared to live and work internationally. In 2016 there were more than 20 faculty-led travel courses to countries such as Costa Rica, Ghana, Cuba, Morocco and France. For qualifying students, UT offers a rigorous and rewarding Honors Program of expanded instruction, student research, internships and the opportunity to study at Oxford University.

MAJORS

The University of Tampa offers bachelor's degrees in accounting, advertising and public relations, allied health, applied dance, art, athletic training, biochemistry, biology, business information technology, chemistry, communication, criminology and criminal justice, cybersecurity, digital arts, economics, education (elementary and secondary certification), English, entrepreneurship, environmental science, film and media arts, finance, financial enterprise systems, forensic science, graphic design, history, human performance, international business, international studies, journalism, liberal studies, management, management information systems, marine science (biology and chemistry), marketing, mathematical programming, mathematics, music, music education, music performance, musical theatre, new media production, nursing, philosophy, physical education, physics, political science, psychology, public health, sociology, Spanish, sport management, theatre and writing. Minors and concentrations are offered in advertising, aerospace studies, applied sociology, art history, art therapy, Asian studies, biology/business, biology/molecular, biology/organismal and evolutionary, business administration, business analytics, criminal investigation, exercise physiology, French, international studies, law, justice and advocacy, leadership studies, military science, naval science, professional and technical writing, recreation, speech/theatre and women's and gender studies. Pre-professional programs offered include pre-dentistry, pre-law, pre-medicine, pre-veterinary science, allied health and chemistry. Certificate programs include Chinese, European studies, French, German, Italian, Japanese, Portuguese and Spanish. An undergraduate School of Continuing Studies offers 30 degree programs designed for adults who want to study part-time. Four summer sessions also offer excellent learning and professional advancement opportunities. At the graduate level, the business school offers an MBA (full time and part time), 4+1 MBA and M.S. degrees in accounting, entrepreneurship, finance and marketing. An M.S. in Nursing, M.S. in Exercise and Nutrition Science, M.S. in Criminology and Criminal Justice, MFA in Creative Writing, M.Ed. in Curriculum and Instruction, M.Ed. in Educational Leadership, 4+1 M.Ed. and M.S. in Instructional Design and Technology are also offered. For a full list of programs, visit www.ut.edu/degrees.

TUITION, ROOM, BOARD, FEES

The average cost for the 2017-2018 academic year is $28,390 for tuition and fees and $10,502 for room and board. The average financial aid award for students in 2016 is $18,088, with 94% of students receiving financial assistance.

FINANCIAL AID

The high-quality, private education offered by The University of Tampa is not as difficult to finance as some students may think. Each family's situation is evaluated individually for need-based assistance. Academic achievements, leadership potential, athletic skills and other special talents are also recognized, regardless of need. Academic scholarships are awarded to most entering first-year students with a 3.0 unweighted GPA or above. Transfer, leadership, departmental, Phi Theta Kappa, International Baccalaureate and ROTC scholarships are also available. Learn more at www.ut.edu/financialaid.

STUDENT ORGANIZATIONS & ACTIVITIES

UT offers 230 clubs, organizations and teams, making it easy for students to get involved in campus life. Options include academic and social clubs, leadership groups and student government, amongst many others. For a full list, visit www.ut.edu/studentorgs.

ADMISSIONS PROCESS

The University of Tampa is an academically competitive institution that offers several non-binding early action admission dates. Visit www.ut.edu/admissions for more details.

UNIVERSITY OF TULSA

AT A GLANCE

The University of Tulsa (TU) is a private, comprehensive doctoral-degree-granting university that provides education of the highest quality in the arts, humanities, sciences, engineering, business, education, applied health sciences and law. TU features four undergraduate colleges: the Kendall College of Arts and Sciences, the Collins College of Business, the College of Engineering and Natural Sciences and the Oxley College of Health Sciences, as well as the College of Law and Graduate School.

TU's 11:1 student/faculty ratio, average class size of 21, and emphasis on individual attention anchor an educational culture where students are rigorously challenged and comprehensively supported.

The university is fully accredited by the North Central Association of Colleges and Universities, and is an NCAA Division IA participant in the American Athletic Conference. TU maintains a covenant relationship with the Presbyterian Church (USA).

Extracurricular opportunities include intramural sports, special-interest clubs, pre-professional organizations, national fraternities and sororities, community service organizations, an active student government, departmental honorary organizations and campus ministry groups.

Total fall 2016 enrollment was 4,563, with 3,406 undergraduates and 1,157 graduate and law students. The ratio of men to women is 57:43 and 18% are multicultural students. Over half the students are from out of state and international students make up 23% of the student population, with 72 countries represented. U.S. News & World Report's 2017 Best Colleges

LOCATION & ENVIRONMENT

TU's 216-acre residential campus is in Tulsa, Oklahoma (961,561 MSA). The city's prominent industries include energy, telecommunications, high technology, manufacturing, health care, aerospace and education which present opportunities for internships and employment after graduation. Tulsans enjoy Broadway shows in the Performing Arts Center and pop concerts in the BOK Center (arena) as well as acclaimed ballet and opera companies, symphony, Philbrook Museum, Gilcrease Museum, Brady Arts District and cultural festivals. Local professional sports include minor league baseball, hockey and arena football. The popular River Parks area features jogging and bicycling trails, while Guthrie Green is a popular arts, music, and food truck destination.

CAMPUS FACILITIES & EQUIPMENT

Since 2002, The University of Tulsa has added one million square feet of building space and a stunning entrance.

Hardesty Hall, TU's newest building, houses 300 residents and houses the offices of Career Services, Center for Global Education, Multicultural Affairs, Greek Life and the English Institute for international students.

The Lorton Performance Center, which houses the School of Music and the Department of Film Studies, features a 700-seat concert hall, specialized rehearsal and practice rooms and a film production suite with post-production editing and scoring capabilities.

In 2012, the College of Engineering & Natural Sciences added two new buildings: J. Newton Rayzor Hall, which features 24 integrated classroom and state-of-the-art teaching/research laboratories. Razor houses the Tandy School of Computer Science and the Department of Electrical and Computer Engineering. Stephenson Hall is home for the McDougall School of Petroleum Engineering and the Department of Mechanical Engineering. Additional research facilities are located at TU's North Campus where government and industry-funded research consortia foster student learning while exploring innovations and solving petroleum industry problems.

The historic McFarlin Library and the Mabee Legal Information Center house more than 5 million items. McFarlin holdings include 991,000 volumes, more than 680,000 titles, 54,000 electronic journals, 450,000 electronic books, and more than 1,000 collections of electronic reference sources and databases as well as print resources. McFarlin's Department of Special Collections and University Archives' rare book holdings are internationally recognized, particularly in Native American history and law. The department includes one of the five largest collections in the world on James Joyce, the life archive of Nobel Laureate Sir V.S. Naipaul, and holdings in nineteenth and twentieth century Irish, British and American Literature. The library's Academic Technology Center annex includes computer labs, a coffee shop and reading rooms.

Helmerich Hall, which houses the Collins College of Business, was renovated to include innovative learning spaces such as the Williams Student Services Center and Studio Blue. Academic centers include the Schools of Accounting and CIS; Energy Economics, Policy and Commerce and Finance, Operations Management and International Business; as well as the Departments of Economics and Management and Marketing.

The Mary K. Chapman Center for Communicative Disorders, part of the university's new Oxley College of Health Sciences, serves the community in its clinical facility and is the learning center for the Department of Communication Disorders. The department has the latest equipment for research, diagnostic, and therapy activities.

Kendall Hall is home to the Departments of Theatre and Musical Theatre and features two fully equipped theatres, a scene shop, costume shop and computer design lab.

Renovated in 2014, the Allen Chapman Student Union includes a food court with nine eateries and a convenience store. It also houses an ATM, offices for student organizations, lecture and meeting rooms, the Faculty Club, post office and the Hurricane Hut sports bar.

The Donald W. Reynolds Center is TU's arena and convocation center. This facility, home for the intercollegiate basketball and volleyball programs, has cutting-edge facilities for video editing and training.

The university's sports and recreation complex features the Collins Fitness Center, Michael Case Tennis Center (which has hosted NCAA Finals), track, intramural and NCAA-grade soccer fields, and softball fields.

In partnership with the city of Tulsa, the university manages Gilcrease Museum as well as the Zarrow Center for Art and Education, which provides gallery space, classes and studio space in the city's Brady Arts District.

TU students have the option of hundreds of attractive and convenient on-campus apartments and residence halls.

OFF-CAMPUS OPPORTUNITIES

The university strongly supports studying abroad, and the Office of Global Education helps students locate the perfect program, whether it is for TU credit or as an intern/volunteer. Students have hundreds of options through direct exchange with an international university, through an affiliate-sponsored program, or as part of a faculty-led course.

Many students take advantage of the of internship opportunities afforded by the city of Tulsa's business and industry community, as well as in the arts, social services and government agencies.

ACADEMICS

The Tulsa Curriculum links a broad, humanities-based core and writing for all students across all disciplines. TU students can receive a personalized education that is well-rounded. Candidates for graduation must complete at least 124 semester hours of course work.

The Honors Program engages students in a critical examination of the major epochs and ideas of Western thought and culture through careful study of primary texts. A separate application is required. The Tulsa Undergraduate Research Challenge (TURC) program combines advanced research, scholarship, and community service.

TU's Global Scholars Program engages students in global issues from the perspective of their particular major. Students take a set of classes that explore the big questions affecting the world today and participate in monthly programming on campus and an international study, research, or intern experience.

The TU Center for Information Security is developing defenses against cyber-terrorist attacks and information warfare. The center supports TU's National Security Agency (NSA)-accredited certificate program in information assurance and a curriculum that integrates information security with computer law and policy issues. TU has been designated a Center of Excellence in Information Assurance by the NSA and is one of six pioneer institutions selected by the National Science Foundation for the Federal Cyber Service Initiative (Cyber Corps).

Air Force ROTC is available through a satellite program.

Students may receive credit through Advanced Placement testing. Depending on their test scores, students who complete the International Baccalaureate diploma can receive up to 30 college credits.

The University of Tulsa operates on a semester calendar. The fall term begins in late August, the spring term in mid-January, and the summer session in late May.

MAJORS & DEGREES OFFERED

The Kendall College of Arts and Sciences grants the Bachelor of Arts or Bachelor of Science degree in anthropology, art, art history, arts management, Chinese studies, classics, communication, creative writing, deaf education, economics, education, English, environmental policy, film studies, French, German, history, music, musical theatre, organizational studies, philosophy, political science, psychology, religion, Russian studies, sociology, Spanish, theatre, women's and gender studies, and a self-designed major. Minors include most disciplines as well as advertising, Chinese, dance, early childhood intervention, film scoring, Greek, Latin and Russian. Secondary teacher certification is available in designated disciplines. Through interdisciplinary certificate programs, students can focus their interests in advertising, African American studies, classics, creative writing, international studies, journalism studies, Judaic studies, museum studies, political philosophy and visual studies.

The Collins College of Business awards the Bachelor of Science in Business Administration degree in accounting, computer information systems (CIS), economics, energy management, finance, management, and marketing and a Bachelor of Science in International Business and Language. Minors are available in most disciplines plus business administration (for non-majors), coaching, healthcare informatics, and international business. Certificate programs are available in accounting, CIS, finance, not-for-profit administration and sport administration. Management majors may choose specializations in business law, entrepreneurship and family business management, or human resource management. The college is home to several specialized centers, including the Energy Management Program, the Family Owned Business Institute, the Genave King Rogers Center for Business Law, the Williams Risk Management Center, and Studio Blue.

The College of Engineering and Natural Sciences offers the Bachelor of Science degree in applied mathematics, biochemistry, biogeosciences, biological science (options in Pre-Medicine, Pre-Dentistry, and Pre-Veterinary), chemical engineering, chemistry, computer science, computer simulation and gaming, earth and environmental science, electrical engineering, electrical and computer engineering, engineering physics, geology, geophysics, information technology, mathematics, mechanical engineering, petroleum engineering and physics. Minors are available in the science and computational science disciplines. The college features state-of-the-art research facilities, including the Center for Information Security and the Williams Communications Fiber Optic Networking Laboratory. Since 1995, more than 50 TU engineering students have received the prestigious Barry M. Goldwater Scholarship, the nation's premier award for undergraduate students studying engineering, math, or science.

The Oxley College of Health Sciences, TU's newest college, offers the Bachelor of Science degree in athletic training, exercise and sports science, nursing and speech-language pathology. The college, which includes a physician assistant program and houses TU's faculty of Community Medicine, will advance the university's strong partnership with the Laureate Institute for Brain Research. The Early Careers in Community Medicine Program offers qualified students provisional acceptance into the University of Oklahoma's School of Medicine after completing an undergraduate degree at TU. A separate application is required.

Master of Arts, Master of Science, Master of Business Administration and Ph.D. degrees are offered in each college through the Graduate School. The College of Law awards the J.D. and L.L.M degrees.

TUITION, ROOM, BOARD, FEES

Estimated costs for the 2017-18 academic year are as follows: the typical cost for students living on campus is $51,600 including $40,484 for tuition, $11,116 for room and board, and $1,025 fees. Expenses for books average about $1,200 per year.

TU invested over $20,000,000 via scholarships to the freshman class of 2016. The average combined financial aid and scholarship package offered to Tulsa students is approximately $29,500.

FINANCIAL AID

In 2016, 93 percent of entering students received some form of financial aid (including grants, scholarships, work-study, and loans). TU offers a limited number of highly competitive Presidential Scholarships that cover full tuition, room, and board. All applicants may be considered for a range of university scholarships based on academic merit. Performance scholarships are available in music and theater by audition. The University of Tulsa participates in National Merit and National Achievement Scholarship Corporation's Finalist program, and the National Hispanic Scholar Program. Applicants for aid should submit the Free Application for Federal Student Aid (FAFSA) as soon as possible after October 1 for priority consideration.

DATES—Notification Date—February 1

BOTTOM LINE Tuition at Tulsa runs at $40,484 annually, with an additional $11,116 approximately for room and board, books, and fees. Forty-two percent of Tulsa students have borrowed through one of the various loan programs, while the average need-based gift award for freshmen is roughly $8,400 (and $6,900 for other undergraduates). The average financial aid package offered to Tulsa students is approximately $24,900, and on average, Tulsa graduates leave school with around $29,161 of debt.

EXPENSES PER ACADEMIC YEAR—Tuition $40,484; Required Fees $1,025

STUDENT ORGANIZATIONS & ACTIVITIES

TU hosts more than 200 student organizations and societies that appeal to a wide range of student interests—from professional to recreational. (For the complete listing, see https://utulsa.edu/campus-life/student-activities/student-organizations/.) Students can participate in a variety of activities on and off campus including intramural sports, special interest clubs, trips to Tulsa's museums, parks, shopping malls, cultural events, etc.

ADMISSIONS PROCESS

The University of Tulsa seeks students whose academic background indicates potential for success in the university's rigorous academic environment. Performance in high school college-preparatory subjects and scores on the SAT or ACT are key factors in the admission evaluation, but each applicant is reviewed holistically. The counselor recommendation, extracurricular activities, and indicators of leadership, creativity, and focus are all taken into consideration. Campus visits and interviews are highly recommended.

TU has a non-binding, Early Action freshman admission plan with an application deadline of November 1. Decisions are mailed within three weeks. Applications received after November 1 are reviewed under a Rolling Admission process with notifications made on an ongoing basis after mid-December.

An application with a $50 application fee, official high school transcript, ACT or SAT score results, and a guidance counselor recommendation are required of freshman applicants. TU accepts the Common Application or TU's application online, or paper application form. TU adheres to the national Candidate's Reply Date of May 1.

For additional information, students should contact:

The University of Tulsa

Office of Admission

800 South Tucker Drive

Tulsa, Oklahoma 74104-3189

Telephone: 918-631-2307 (in Tulsa), 800-331-3050 (toll-free)

Fax: 918-631-5008

E-mail: admission@utulsa.edu

Web: www.utulsa.edu/admission

UNIVERSITY OF WEST FLORIDA

AT A GLANCE

Founded in 1963, the University of West Florida is a vibrant, distinctive institute of higher learning with undergraduate, graduate and targeted research programs serving multiple locations in Northwest Florida.

LOCATION & ENVIRONMENT

The UWF Pensacola Campus spans 1,600 acres and is located just minutes away from historic Pensacola and some of the world's most beautiful beaches. It features state-of-the-art facilities comfortable residence halls, and a beautiful landscape that offers a variety of recreational activities.

CAMPUS FACILITIES & EQUIPMENT

Center for Cybersecurity: Our state-of-the-art lab is the only one of its kind in Florida. Student learn how to launch, detect, and defeat hackers' attacks.

Skylab: A non-traditional computer lab, information literacy classroom, multimedia studio and media conversion center.

Center for Entrepreneurship: Supports and encourages initiatives related to entrepreneurship and entrepreneurial thinking and serves as a comprehensive resource for economic innovation for students, faculty, industry, and community partners.

Academic Center for Excellence: An academic facility that provides free academic support services to all students including individual tutoring, group tutoring, and quiet study spaces.

Recreation and Sports Services: Aquatic Center, Massage Therapy Studios, Tennis/ Beach Volleyball Court(s), and an Olympic size swimming pool.

OFF-CAMPUS OPPORTUNITIES

Pensacola's waters provide a wealth of opportunities for activities including swimming, surfing, kayaking, canoeing, fishing and diving. The white sands and warm waters along the Gulf of Mexico attract thousands of locals and vacationing visitors to the beach throughout the year.

STUDENT ORGANIZATIONS & ACTIVITIES

Fall 2015 Profile:

Age Range—14-90

Median Age—23

Males—5,287

Females—7,511

Part Time % 40%

Full Time % 60%

Population >12,000

Professor to Student Ratio—34:1

Averages—3.67 GPA, 24 ACT, and 1150 SAT

Student organizations play a vital role in the campus life at the University of West Florida, engaging thousands of students in a variety of valuable experiences and relationships. University Commons & Student Involvement's role is to promote student involvement, create a vibrant campus life and support our student leaders in achieving organizational and personal goals.

ADMISSIONS PROCESS

Our incoming freshmen typically have an average high school GPA of 3.61, ACT of 24, and SAT of 1550 (M+CR+W). We understand that our prospective students their families have questions. An Admissions Counselor works with each applicant. Please don't hesitate to contact them if you have questions.

Academic Requirements

Those who successfully gain acceptance typically have engaged in a rigorous college preparatory curriculum (listed below), hold a competitive grade point average, and possess strong SAT or ACT scores.

- High School Academic Courses: Eligible candidates will have the following courses completed in these subject areas at the time of high school graduation:

4 units—English

4 units—Math (Algebra I and above)

3 units—Natural Science

3 units—Social Science

2 units—Foreign Language Level 1 & 2 (same language)

2 units—Electives from areas above

- Official SAT or ACT scores are required for an admission decision. We superscore, which means, we will take the best sub sectional scores from each ACT or SAT you submit. Therefore, you should submit all SAT or ACT scores for consideration.

- Optional Items:

Letters of recommendation

Personal Essay

Resume summary of involvement & leadership

ZeeMee Share your story and how you could add to our Argonaut community. We have partnered with ZeeMee.com, a free social media service for prospective college students that helps promote your individuality to Universities through videos, pictures, and documents. Create your ZeeMee page & then copy/paste your link in your Splash Portal so that we can get to know you better.

VANDERBILT UNIVERSITY

AT A GLANCE

In 1873, on the heels of the Civil War, "Commodore" Cornelius Vanderbilt gave $1 million to the university that now bears his name, with the hope that it would "contribute to strengthening the ties which should exist between all sections of our common country." Since then, Vanderbilt has consistently enrolled intelligent and talented students and challenged them daily to expand their intellectual horizons in an inclusive environment based on open inquiry and respect. Vanderbilt's comprehensive interdisciplinary approach to education allows students to pursue a wide array of academic and curricular interests outside of their main focus of study, and the university's Opportunity Vanderbilt financial aid program ensures that it is often cited among the country's best values. Consistently ranked among the top 20 universities in the country by U.S. News & World Report, Vanderbilt is a private research university that features four undergraduate schools and six graduate and professional schools. Each year, 1,600 first-year students join the university, bringing the total undergraduate population to approximately 6,900 students, more than half of whom collaborate with professors on research across disciplines. The university's 8:1 student-faculty ratio gives students access to faculty members of prominence in every area of academic study. Faculty members provide a challenging, comprehensive education that encourages broad perspectives and critical thinking.

LOCATION & ENVIRONMENT

Vanderbilt is located in the heart of Nashville, home to a diverse population of 1.7 million and marked by its unique blend of cosmopolitan flair and small-town charm. A thriving center of entertainment, publishing, health care, and technology, Nashville is consistently ranked as one of America's friendliest cities and was honored as one of the Best Places to Go in 2017 by Frommer's Travel Guide. Nashville sits at the intersection of three major interstates, and Nashville International Airport provides nonstop service to more than 50 markets.

CAMPUS FACILITIES & EQUIPMENT

Vanderbilt University is located 1.5 miles southwest of downtown Nashville on a 330-acre, park-like campus that was designated an official arboretum in 1988. The university comprises over 200 buildings, including a world-class medical center and the Jean and Alexander Heard Library, home to over 8 million items. Recent additions to campus include The Martha Rivers Ingram Commons, a living-learning community for first-year students; Warren and Moore residential colleges, living-learning communities for upperclass students; a 230,000-square-foot state-of-the-art Engineering and Science Building; and a cross-disciplinary creative and makerspace called the Wond'ry, the new campus epicenter for innovation and entrepreneurship.

OFF-CAMPUS OPPORTUNITIES

Study abroad programs allow students to immerse themselves in languages and cultures around the world. More than 120 programs are offered in Argentina, Australia, Austria, Chile, China, Cuba, the Czech Republic, Denmark, the Dominican Republic, Egypt, England, France, Israel, Italy, Japan, Russia, Singapore, South Africa, and Spain, among others. Students receive direct credit for courses, and the cost of tuition is usually the same as for study on campus in Nashville. In addition, any scholarships, grants, or loans a student has been awarded apply to Vanderbilt study abroad programs. Students may also participate in programs sponsored by other universities by working with an adviser.

Students also take advantage of internships in many industries located in Nashville, including entertainment, business, health care, government, publishing, and education.

ACADEMICS

Students apply directly to one of Vanderbilt's four undergraduate schools: the College of Arts and Science, School of Engineering, Peabody College of Education and Human Development, or Blair School of Music. In all four schools, honors programs and opportunities for research, independent study, and internships are available. About 30 percent of undergraduate students pursue double majors within or across the four undergraduate schools, and about half add an optional minor.

The College of Arts and Science (A&S) offers a wide spectrum of courses in the humanities, social sciences, and natural sciences along with majors in 50 departments and interdisciplinary areas. The core curriculum, AXLE (Achieving eXcellence in Liberal Education), fosters critical thinking, analytical expertise from diverse perspectives, and effective written and oral communication skills.

The Blair School of Music offers the Bachelor of Music degree in composition, musical arts, musical arts/teacher education, and performance. Instruction is available in every instrument of the orchestra as well as piano, organ, euphonium, multiple woodwinds, saxophone, and voice. Unlike many schools of music, Blair has no graduate students. The curriculum combines intensive musical training with liberal arts studies. The Blair School also offers music minors and a wide variety of courses, private instruction, and performing organizations for non-majors.

For more than 125 years, the School of Engineering has educated engineers for careers in industry, government, consulting, teaching, and research. In addition to technical courses, each student's program includes a complement of course work in the humanities and social sciences, resulting in a balanced foundation for future achievement. All programs leading to a Bachelor of Engineering degree are ABET-accredited, and students can earn the Bachelor of Science degree while majoring in Computer Science or Engineering Science.

Ranked one of the top seven graduate school of education (according to U.S. News & World Report) for fifteen consecutive years, Peabody College offers degree programs leading to teacher certification and to careers in other areas of education and human development, including child development, child studies, cognitive studies, and human and organizational development. The degree reflects a strong liberal arts foundation combined with a solid program of pre-professional courses and a multitude of internship and practicum opportunities. All undergraduates must complete requirements in communications, the humanities, mathematics, the natural sciences, and the social sciences. Students gain an abundance of field experiences throughout their four years.

Across all four undergraduate schools, students engage in hands-on learning that complements and furthers their academic experience at Vanderbilt. Immersion Vanderbilt calls for each undergraduate student to participate in an intensive learning experience that takes place in and beyond the classroom and culminates in the creation of a final project. Students will engage in a civic and professional, creative expression, international, or research immersion experience.

MAJORS

Degrees are offered in African American and Diaspora studies; American studies; anthropology; art; Asian studies; biochemistry and chemical biology; biological sciences; biomedical engineering; chemical engineering; chemistry; child development; child studies; cinema and media arts; civil engineering; classical civilization; classical languages; classics; cognitive studies; communication of science and technology; communication studies; computer engineering; computer science; earth and environmental sciences; ecology, evolution, and organismal biology; economics; economics and history; education (early childhood and elementary, secondary, and special education); electrical engineering; engineering science; English; environmental sociology; European studies; French; French and European studies; German; German and European studies; history; history of art; human and organizational development; Italian and European studies; Jewish studies; Latin American studies; Latina and Latino studies; mathematics; mechanical engineering; medicine, health, and society; molecular and cellular biology; musical arts; musical arts and teacher education; music composition; music performance; neuroscience; philosophy; physics; political science; psychology; public policy studies; religious studies; Russian; Russian and European studies; sociology; Spanish, Spanish and European studies; Spanish and Portuguese; Spanish, Portuguese, and European studies; theatre; women's and gender studies.

TUITION, ROOM, BOARD, FEES

The estimated costs for 2017-2018 include: tuition, $46,498; housing, $10,114; meals, $5,372; books and supplies, $1,294; student activities and recreation fee, $1,164; personal expenses allowance, $2,850; travel allowance varies; first-year experience fee, $765; new student transcript fee, $30; engineering lab fee°, $650; and engineering laptop allowance°, $1,500 °The engineering laptop allowance and laboratory fee are for engineering students only. First-year engineering students are required to provide their own computer that meets published requirements.

FINANCIAL AID

Through Opportunity Vanderbilt, the university makes three important commitments to ensure that students from many different economic circumstances can enroll as undergraduates at Vanderbilt: the admissions process is need-blind for all U.S. citizens and eligible non-citizens; Vanderbilt meets 100 percent of demonstrated need for all admitted students; and Vanderbilt's financial aid packages do not include loans. This initiative does not involve income bands or income cutoffs that limit eligibility. Need-based aid is awarded according to the evaluation of the FAFSA and the CSS/Financial Aid PROFILE.

Vanderbilt also awards approximately 250 merit-based scholarships to select first-year applicants who demonstrate exceptional accomplishment and intellectual promise. Three signature scholarship programs comprise the majority of these merit scholarships: the Ingram Scholarship Program, the Cornelius Vanderbilt Scholarship Program, and the Chancellor's Scholarship Program. All three programs require a separate application in addition to the application for admission.

In the 2016/2017 school year, 65 percent of the University's undergraduate students received some type of financial assistance.

STUDENT ORGANIZATIONS & ACTIVITIES

Vanderbilt undergraduates come from all 50 states and 48 countries, 51% are female, 49% are male, 36.3% are minority students and 7.2% are international students. Vanderbilt is recognized for an active campus life, where students balance their academic lives with enriching experiences outside the classroom. Students can select from among 420+ student-run organizations, including pre-professional, cultural, religious, political, recreational, and social clubs. Elected representatives of Vanderbilt Student Government work in conjunction with other student leaders and faculty to bring noted speakers, events, and musicians to campus. Vanderbilt also has a thriving college athletics program. A founding member of the SEC, Vanderbilt has 16 Division I teams that have won three national championships and 26 individual and team league championships since 2000.

ADMISSIONS PROCESS

Vanderbilt seeks students with high standards of scholarship and character. Admission is based on a holistic review of academic and personal credentials. The typical applicant will have completed 20 or more units in a challenging high school curriculum, including at least two years of a foreign language. School of Engineering applicants should complete at least four units of mathematics; calculus and physics are strongly recommended.

Generally, applicants who are admitted to Vanderbilt have exceptional academic credentials and are highly engaged in their communities, often serving in leadership roles. Admissions decisions are based on strength of high school transcript, standardized test results (either the SAT Reasoning Test or ACT), personal essays, official recommendations, and extracurricular activities. SAT Subject Tests are not required.

Students may apply to Vanderbilt through Early Decision I or II, or Regular Decision. Early Decision I and II are binding decision plans, and may be appropriate for students who are committed to attending Vanderbilt if they are admitted. The application deadline is November 1 for Early Decision I and January 1 for Early Decision II; admissions decisions are available by December 15 for Early Decision I and by February 15 for Early Decision II. Regular Decision applications are due January 1 and admissions decisions are available by April 1.

To apply, applicants must submit official standardized test scores and all required parts of the Common Application, Coalition Application, QuestBridge Application, or Universal College Application, including two academic teacher letters of recommendation, a counselor letter of recommendation, an official high school transcript, and a $50 application fee, or fee waiver for qualified students. In addition to completing standard application materials, applicants to the Blair School of Music must submit a Blair DecisionDesk Application, which includes a prescreening video. Selected applicants will be invited to audition in person.

Campus visits are encouraged, although a student's demonstrated interest in Vanderbilt is not considered in admissions decisions. Students should visit vu.edu/visit to learn about group information sessions, campus tours, and half-and full-day visit programs. To visit Vanderbilt without traveling, take the virtual tour at vu.edu/virtualtour. Vanderbilt does not conduct on-campus interviews, but optional alumni interviews are available to first-year applicants in many locations.

WASHINGTON COLLEGE

AT A GLANCE

Washington College, one of the nation's leading liberal arts institutions, is passionate about providing students a truly personalized education.

The first college chartered in the new nation, Washington College was founded in 1782 to cultivate responsible, educated citizen-leaders who could nurture the new democracy. Today, the ideals of that founding purpose hold true. The College's rich history helps distinguish it among the nation's selective liberal arts colleges: General George Washington lent his name, donated 50 guineas to our founding, and served on our first Board of Visitors and Governors. His examples of citizenship and leadership continue to shape our traditions and our high expectations for our students.

We believe that a broad, general education in the liberal arts—one shaped by personal relationships with professors and classmates in a supportive residential community—is not only mentally liberating but also the most effective way to prepare for a successful career and a meaningful life. In your first two years on campus, we will encourage you to explore many interests, examine different perspectives, and challenge old ways of thinking. We also will invite you to pursue creative endeavors, athletic competition, recreational activities, and leadership roles.

LOCATION & ENVIRONMENT

Located in Chestertown, Md., our 120-acre campus breathes history, natural beauty, and rural charm, yet it's only 75 miles from the urban hubs of Washington, D.C., Baltimore, and Philadelphia. This proximity brings our students a wealth of distinguished speakers, intern opportunities, institutional partnerships, and other occasions for academic and cultural enrichment. That said, we also take full advantage of our setting in a historic river town close by the Chesapeake Bay. The Eastern Shore becomes an extension of the campus-a learning laboratory for intellectual, social, and personal growth.

Historic Chestertown is rooted in a strong sense of self and a diverse and creative local character. You'll experience this through events like First Fridays, when downtown reverts once a month to one big street party; the Farmers' Market on Saturdays, loaded with goods showcasing the region's rich agrarian culture; and at venues like the Garfield Center for the Arts in the beautifully restored Prince Theatre.

The Chester River meets the town at the foot of High Street. At its riverfront facility, just blocks from the main campus, the College maintains a variety of vessels that support coursework in underwater archaeology, marine and estuarine biology, environmental chemistry, and environmental studies. The College also supports nationally ranked programs in rowing and sailing.

CAMPUS FACILITIES & EQUIPMENT

Our beautiful campus is a collection of historic redbrick, Georgian-style structures, large shade trees, and brick walkways, seamlessly combined with new and renovated buildings featuring expanses of glass that create modern spaces flooded with light. The oldest buildings, the Hill Dorms, were built in the mid-nineteenth century; the newest, the $2.1 million Johnson Fitness Center, opened in 2013.

The Gibson Center for the Arts, opened in August 2009, is a glittering showcase where students can learn, rehearse, practice, perform, and exhibit their work. The $24 million facility encompasses a main stage, an experimental theater, a music recital hall, and an art gallery, as well as all the latest tools and technology to support professional theater, concerts, and exhibitions.

Opened in fall 2009, Hodson Hall Commons includes the main dining hall, a student lounge, an intimate space for meetings and performances, and several specialty eateries.

The Chester and Sassafras residence halls, completed in Summer 2008, were the first buildings on campus to incorporate geothermal heating and cooling. A major renovation of the campus library in 2012 included a geothermal system along with a new coffee shop and popular group-study rooms.

According to Lacrosse Magazine, our Roy Kirby, Jr. Stadium is among the top ten venues for collegiate lacrosse in the nation. The stadium, completed in 2008, is the only Division III venue to make the cut. In 2009, Athey Park, the College's baseball park, was built to mirror Kirby Stadium.

Advances in technology are incorporated throughout the curriculum, from sequencing DNA in the lab to accessing primary sources for a Shakespeare project via the library's Early English Books Online database. Other examples include the new mass spectrometry lab, used for environmental chemistry, geology, and biology research; side-scan sonar, sub-bottom profilers, remotely operated vehicles (ROVs), and marine magnetometers to explore below the surface of the Chester River; and eye-scanning and brain-mapping technology the psychology department uses to test cognitive function.

OFF-CAMPUS OPPORTUNITIES

Small Campus, Big Opportunities

With a student body of 1,500 undergraduates, the College remains defiantly, confidently small and celebrates the interaction between student and professor. The average class size is 17 students; only one class in seven will have more than 25 students enrolled. Faculty members reach beyond the classroom to challenge and nurture a student's maturing intellect and creativity with collaborative research, independent and self-directed study, and a rigorous senior "capstone" project.

Washington College offers a growing array of internships and field experiences, including fellowships for the study of American history, internships with theaters and museums and model diplomacy programs. Students can participate in a summer archaeology field school, make investment decisions for the $500,000 Alex. Brown Fund, and work at the College-run research center that studies migrating birds and sustainable land management.

Writing Across the Curriculum

Washington College is recognized for its rich literary arts environment-the Rose O'Neill Literary House hosts a steady stream of significant writers and editors supported by the Sophie Kerr Program, and each year, one graduating senior is awarded the Sophie Kerr Prize, the largest undergraduate literary award in the world. (The 2013 winner took home $61,000.) The College is committed to helping all students become better writers, no matter what major they pursue. Writing-intensive courses help students cultivate proficiency in the language arts, as well as stay up-to-date with ever-evolving information technologies

ACADEMICS

With a student body of 1,500 undergraduates, the College's deliberately small size celebrates the interaction between student and professor. The average class size is 17 students; only one class in seven will have more than 25 students enrolled. Faculty members challenge and nurture a student's maturing intellect and creativity with collaborative research, independent and self-directed study, and a rigorous senior "capstone" project.

Washington College is recognized for its rich literary arts environment. The Rose O'Neill Literary House hosts a steady stream of significant writers and editors supported by the Sophie Kerr Program, and each year, one graduating senior is awarded the Sophie Kerr Prize, the largest undergraduate literary award in the world (the 2013 winner took home $61,000). The College is committed to helping all students become stronger writers. Writing-intensive courses across disciplines and majors help students cultivate proficiency in the language arts.

Two centers of special research and programming, The C.V. Starr Center for the Study of the American Experience and the Center for Environment & Society, take advantage of the region's history, rural and maritime cultures, and natural resources. The Chesapeake Semester, offered through the Center for Environment & Society, uses the nation's largest estuary as a classroom and then connects those studies globally with a trip to Peru. Based on the Chesapeake Semester's successful model, the CES in 2014 initiated the Puget Sound Summer Program.

The Douglass Cater Society of Junior Fellows is our flagship academic enrichment program, rewarding initiative and intellectual curiosity with competitive grants to support self-directed undergraduate research, internships, and scholarship anywhere in the world. Another important academic opportunity, the Presidential Fellows program, puts high-achieving freshmen on the fast track to academic distinction, including the chance to work with full Cater Fellows as an apprentice.

Washington College offers a growing array of internships and field experiences, as we believe that hands-on education outside of the classroom best prepares students for their careers. Among them are: The Comegys Bight Fellowships, which place students in paid summer internships at prestigious institutions including the Library of Congress, National Constitution Center, and the Smithsonian American Art Museum; the Alex. Brown Fund, which enables students to manage an equities portfolio of $500,000; the Washington to Wall Street Program, which uses the College's strong alumni network to offer internships to students pursuing careers in business or the financial sector (100 percent of those who participated in 2013's inaugural program are in graduate school or employed in the field); the John S. Toll Science Fellows and Hodson Science Fellows programs, which enable students to conduct in-depth research with faculty while earning a stipend and a housing allowance; the Summer Archaeology Field School, in which students conduct digs at area sites, bringing artifacts back to the school's Archaeology Lab for further study; the celebrated Kiplin Hall Program offered through the English department, which takes students to England, Ireland, and Scotland to study Romantic poets and writers while hiking and traveling through the world that inspired them; and the biology department's Maine Summer Program, in which students spend two weeks earning four credits while studying the diverse ecology of Acadia National Park in Mt. Desert Island, Maine.

Washington College also offers an extensive study abroad program. With 28 partner institutions for semester and academic-year study abroad, and up to ten short-term programs led by College faculty, the programs traverse 24 countries, including South Africa, Australia, Ecuador, and the United Kingdom.

MAJORS & DEGREES OFFERED

We believe that a liberal arts education gives students the strongest set of lifelong skills to never stop exploring the world. More than 40 areas of study allow you to investigate a wide variety of possibilities and combinations that will lead to a bachelor of arts or a bachelor of science. You will choose a major (or two) at the end of sophomore year.

American Studies, Anthropology, Art and Art History, Business Management, Communication & Media Studies, Economics, English, Environmental Studies, French Studies, German Studies, Hispanic Studies, History, Human Development, Humanities, International Literature and Culture, International Studies, Mathematical Science, Music, Psychology-Clinical/Counseling, Sociology, Theatre **Bachelor of Science degrees are awarded in the following:**

Biology, Chemistry, Physics, Psychology-Behavioral Neuroscience , The College offers interdisciplinary programs of study, minors and/or concentrations in the following:, Accounting and Finance, African Studies, Archaeology, Art History, Asian Studies, Behavioral Neuroscience, Biochemistry, Biophysics and Biological Chemistry, Black Studies, Cell/Molecular Biology & Infectious Diseases, Chesapeake Regional Studies, Clinical Counseling, Creative Writing, Dance, Earth and Planetary Science, Ecology and Evolution, Elementary Education, Engineering, Ethnomusicology, European Studies, Gender Studies, Geographic Information Systems, Global Business Studies, Greener Materials Science, Information Systems, Justice, Law, and Society , Latin American Studies, Marketing, Near Eastern Studies, Nursing 3+2, Organic and Medicinal Chemistry, Peace and Conflict Studies, Pharmacy 3+4, Physical and Instrumental Chemistry, Physiology and Organismal Biology, Pre-Law Preparation, Premedical Program, Secondary Education, Social Welfare, Studio Art

TUITION, ROOM, BOARD, FEES

Basic educational fees for 2017-2018

Tuition (full-time) $43,702

Student Service Fee $748

Student Health Fee $250

Campus Housing $5,608

Meal Plans per year 19/week $5,432

FINANCIAL AID

Washington College is committed to providing educational excellence and equity for all students; 90% of our students receive need-based financial aid and/or merit-based scholarships. We develop financial packages that include tuition scholarships, tuition grants, work/study, and low-interest loans, in addition to federal, state, and independent aid programs for eligible students. With the investment of funds for scholarships and grants from donors and benefactors, the College provides more than $20 million annually in scholarships and grants to help make it possible for students to get an education here. More than 50% of all Washington College students qualify for merit-based tuition scholarships averaging from $13,000 to $23,000 per year. In 2016, Washington College announced a fixed-rate tuition policy, FixedFor4, that will enable families to plan for college costs.

STUDENT ORGANIZATIONS & ACTIVITIES

We cherish our residential tradition because it brings constant opportunities for academic, social, and personal growth. We may be a small campus, but Washington College supports more than 80 clubs, from the nationally recognized Habitat for Humanity Club to wakeboarding, sailing, and entrepreneurial activism through Enactus.

A Division III member of the NCAA, the College fields 17 intercollegiate teams that compete in the Centennial Conference. About 25% of students are varsity athletes, while 60% of students participate in sports including clubs and intramurals. The Student Events Board creates a variety of activities that everyone on campus can enjoy, from festivals and quiz nights to the semi-formal George Washington's Birthday Ball. While students reap the benefits of living in one of the best small college towns on the East Coast and the relaxed informality characteristic of the Chesapeake Bay region, they also take advantage of the campus's proximity to Washington, D.C, Baltimore, and Philadelphia.

ADMISSIONS PROCESS

Washington College is a selective institution. In order to assess an applicant's "fit" with the College, the Admission Committee requires the submission of all relevant academic records and test scores, an activity profile, an essay/personal statement, and a letter of recommendation. In some cases, an on-campus interview may also be required.

Prospective applicants are strongly encouraged to come to campus for an information session and tour. These visits should be scheduled in advance by calling 410-778-7700 or visiting washcoll.edu/admissions.

Prospective students may apply online using the Common Application or via washcoll.edu/apply. Application deadlines are: November 15 for early decision; December 1 for early action; February 15 for regular decision. Admitted applicants must pay a $700.00 enrollment deposit by May 1. For details, visit www.washcoll.edu/admissions.

WELLS COLLEGE

AT A GLANCE

Wells College is a private, liberal arts coeducational college located in Aurora, New York. The College's modern liberal arts curriculum combines theory with real-world practice, cultivating not just lifelong scholars but citizens of the world with a clear understanding of social responsibility. The College boasts a highly collaborative learning environment with a 10:1 student-to-faculty ratio. The majority of Wells faculty holds doctoral or terminal degrees in their fields. Wells' students contribute valuable depth to the campus dialogue through their diverse backgrounds. Wells seeks to foster a connected community in which free speech, openness, acceptance, and inclusion of all beliefs are appreciated and considered in their appropriate settings. The College's living-learning philosophy also means our students benefit from required internships and an array of study abroad opportunities that provide hands-on experiences. Wells students not only take a direct role in shaping their education, they are prepared to pursue advanced and professional studies as well as meaningful careers.

LOCATION & ENVIRONMENT

The beautiful 300-acre lakeside campus is located in the historical village of Aurora on Cayuga Lake, in the heart of the Finger Lakes Region of New York State. Students enjoy phenomenal views and access to our campus boathouse. The campus is 30 minutes from Ithaca, one hour from Syracuse and Rochester, and approximately five hours from New York City.

CAMPUS FACILITIES & EQUIPMENT

Wells College provides state-of-the-art facilities for all students and student-athletes. Indoor facilities include a field house, fitness center, swimming pool, locker rooms, tennis courts, a renovated gymnasium, and athletic administration offices. Outdoor facilities include dedicated fields for men's and women's soccer, men's and women's lacrosse, and field hockey, along with four outdoor tennis courts. Completed in 2016, the new artificial turf field will serve as the primary site of competition for field hockey, baseball, softball, men's and women's soccer, and men's and women's lacrosse.

OFF-CAMPUS OPPORTUNITIES

During their four years at Wells, students may also participate in study abroad or affiliated programs in the following countries: Australia; Belize, Chile; China; Costa Rica; Germany; Ireland; Italy; Japan; New Zealand; South Africa; Spain; and the United Kingdom. Students may also pursue global study through the School for Field Studies in Australia, Cambodia, Costa Rica, Panama, Peru, Tanzania, and Turks and Caicos. The Albany Internship Experience at Marist University in Albany, N.Y. is another popular option. Wells students may also take courses at nearby Cornell University or Ithaca College through a unique exchange program.

ACADEMICS

The Wells experience is deeply personal and intensely focused on superior academic achievement. Wells offers 25 majors and nearly 50 minors. With one professor for every TEN students, professors really get to know each student. The average class size has THIRTEEN students and is taught seminar-style, with discussions taking precedence over lectures. Fundamental to the Wells curriculum is an interdisciplinary approach to the liberal arts with the opportunity to experience hands-on work and innovative teaching methods. Through the Wells experiential learning program, students have opportunities to participate in quality internships, off campus study programs around the world, and academic research projects tailored to individual interests and goals. Experiential learning in the curriculum enables students to apply principles learned in the classroom to real-life situations in professional organizations.

MAJORS

Wells College offers a Bachelor's degree with majors in the following areas: Biochemistry and Molecular Biology, Biological and Chemical Sciences, Biology, Business, Chemistry, Computer Science, Criminal Justice, Economics and Management (Economics, Management), Inclusive Childhood Education, English (Literature, Creative Writing), Environmental Science, Film and Media Studies, Health Sciences Individualized Major, History, International Studies, Individualized Major, Mathematics, Philosophy, Physics, Political Science, Psychology, Sociology and Anthropology, Spanish, Sustainability, Theatre and Dance, Visual Arts (Art History, Studio Art, Book Arts), Women's and Gender Studies.

TUITION, ROOM, BOARD, FEES

For the 2016-2017 year: Tuition and fees: $38,530; Room and board: $13,360

FINANCIAL AID

Wells College offers both merit-based and need-based financial aid. Merit-based scholarships are awarded to students who demonstrate outstanding academic achievement, leadership skills, and have a strong record of service in their schools and communities. Nearly 100% of students at Wells College receive aid to fund their education. To receive need-based financial aid from Wells College, students must submit the Free Application for Federal Student Aid (FAFSA). Wells recommends families submit their completed FAFSA by December 1st. Students eligible to receive need-based financial aid may receive grants, scholarships, student loans, and campus work study, additional to merit scholarships.

STUDENT ORGANIZATIONS & ACTIVITIES

Wells students enjoy all of the advantages of living in a closely-knit community. A well-respected Honor Code shapes the educational and social atmosphere of the campus. Wells supports more than 30 clubs and organizations including a literary journal and social issues magazine, music and drama groups, and political and cultural organizations, in addition to student-sponsored events, lectures, and performances. Wells is also a member of Division III NCAA. Wells women compete in nine intercollegiate sports: cross country, field hockey, tennis, lacrosse, soccer, softball, basketball, volleyball and swimming. Wells men compete in seven intercollegiate sports: baseball, basketball, cross country, lacrosse, soccer, volleyball and swimming. Wells campus also has a nine-hole golf course and canoes, kayaks, and sailboats available for seasonal student use.

ADMISSIONS PROCESS

Wells students are intellectually curious, open-minded, and creative. They are comfortable expressing themselves, listening to others and sharing ideas. They are caring citizens of the world, eager to travel beyond the campus. Wells students love to learn. If you love learning, you will love the Wells experience.

Candidates for admission are expected to complete a solid college preparatory program throughout their four years in secondary school. The college recommends a program which provides the best background for study at Wells, including four years of English grammar, composition, and literature; four years of history; three years of mathematics; two years of laboratory science; and coursework in a foreign language. Student records are enhanced by the addition of courses such as computer science, art, and music, when appropriate curricular choices are offered. To apply for admission to Wells College candidates must submit a completed application through the Wells application or Common Application by March 1 of the year of entrance.

In addition, the following credentials are required: A transcript of all secondary school work and at least one letter of recommendation from teachers in academic subject areas. A personal on-campus connection with your admissions counselor and your personal Zeemee profile are recommended.

Wells College is committed to reviewing applications holistically and considering all facets of a student's potential. To honor that commitment, admission to Wells is now test optional. As of Fall 2016, we no longer require SAT or ACT scores in the application evaluation process. International students must prove English language proficiency. (TOEFL, IELTS, SAT or ACT scores accepted).

Admissions Deadline Options

Early Decision. December 15: Students whose first choice is Wells College are encouraged to apply under the early decision option. This is a binding admissions option; if admitted; early decision applicants agree to accept Wells offer of admission and agree to withdraw their applications from all other colleges.

Early Action. December 15: Students who would like to receive an early review of their application files are encouraged to apply under the early action option. This is a non-binding admissions option.

Regular Admission. March 1: All other applications to the college should be received by the regular admission deadline.

WENTWORTH INSTITUTE OF TECHNOLOGY

AT A GLANCE

Founded in 1904, Wentworth Institute of Technology is an independent, co-educational, nationally-ranked institution offering career-focused education through 17 bachelor's degree programs in areas such as applied mathematics, architecture, business management, computer science and networking, construction management, design, and engineering. The Institute also offers master's degrees in applied computer science, architecture, civil engineering, construction management, facility management, and technology management.

A leader in engineering, technology, design and management education, Wentworth's unique three-part experiential learning model combines class work, laboratory/studio work, and cooperative education (co-op) experience to provide students with a hands-on approach to learning. The co-op program, one of the largest and most comprehensive of its kind in the nation, has been active for 40 years and provides Wentworth students the ability to gain the professional work experience needed to succeed in their field. Wentworth is well-known for its academic excellence, community service, and support for the economic growth of the region.

Wentworth offers exciting opportunities for students looking to build a framework for success in the innovation economy. Wentworth's unique interdisciplinary curriculum combines technical studies, opportunities to collaborate and innovate, meaningful career training experiences, and an environment focused on developing practical solutions to real-world challenges. The result: Excellent preparation for a successful career. Additionally, Wentworth is a member of one of Boston's largest academic collaborations, the Colleges of the Fenway consortium, which is an association of six Fenway area institutions including Emmanuel College, Massachusetts College of Art and Design, Massachusetts College of Pharmacy and Health Sciences University, Simmons College, Wentworth, and Wheelock College.

For more information, please visit www.wit.edu.

LOCATION & ENVIRONMENT
Small school benefits, big city resources.

This private, coeducational college is located on 31 acres in the heart of Boston. With over 4,000 students, it provides the friendliness of a small school, alongside the resources and excitement of the ultimate college town.

When it comes to college towns, there is no place more exciting or full of more opportunities than Boston. The original center of higher education in the U.S., it hosts 50 colleges and universities and draws a quarter of a million students every year, with nearly 20,000 of those students coming from outside the country. Boston is a city with exceptional character. In addition to its rich history, it's also a hub for technology, business and medicine giving Wentworth students access to educational and career opportunities they would not find elsewhere.

CAMPUS FACILITIES & EQUIPMENT

The Wentworth campus is well-appointed to deliver the top-notch education and living conditions demanded by today's students. Our modernized laboratories are at the vanguard of technology; the equipment mirrors that found in the leading employers in industry. The Institute has spent millions of dollars to upgrade its information technology infrastructure. And the facilities for sleeping are just as impressive as the ones for studying. The Institute operates seven residence halls: Evans Way/Tudbury Hall, Edwards/Rodgers Hall, Baker Hall, Louis Prang Apartments, 610 Huntington Avenue, 555 Huntington Avenue and the Apartments at 525 Huntington.

Whether you're looking for state-of-the-art computing resources, healthcare you can rely on, or one of any of a number of other services that make campus life better, you can rest assured that Wentworth is working hard to meet your needs.

The Flanagan Campus Center is the hub of student life at Wentworth. The campus center is home to the bookstore, the cafeteria, the Schuman Fitness Center. The Intercultural Center, Wentworth Internet Radio Experience (WIRE), a recreation room, study areas, and the Office of Campus Life.

The Learning Center and The Writing Center provide students with academic support services such as peer and faculty tutoring, computer-based tutorials, and subject study groups. We are dedicated to preparing students for academic success.

Wentworth is committed to helping you make the best use of computers. We offer a range of computing resources including: a wireless campus; labs equipped with the latest hardware and software; and a full-time Office of Information Technology. The result is a highly connected academic and social community where advanced computing is accessible and convenient.

Wentworth subscribes to the policies set forth in the Americans with Disabilities Act and in Section 504 of the Federal Rehabilitation Act of 1973, which mandate equal opportunity in educational programs and activities for students with disabilities.

At Wentworth, we work hard to provide the very best health services. In addition to expert primary medical care, we also offer specialized services including counseling, disability services and comprehensive health education.

In order to make the transition for international students as smooth as possible, Wentworth employs a full-time international student advisor who has extensive experience with international students, and assists them in their personal, social and academic adjustment to Wentworth and the U.S.

Conveniently located at the center of campus, the Douglas D. Schumann Library & Learning Commons is a valuable resource. The online catalogue includes the holdings of nine other libraries all available for use by Wentworth students. And, membership in the 14-institution Fenway Library Consortium provides access to more than 2,900,000 volumes and 13,000 periodical titles. Various services are also available through the Alumni Library.

OFF-CAMPUS OPPORTUNITIES

At Wentworth, building professional, paid work experience into the academic program is a priority. Co-op has been a fundamental part of our curriculum for 40 years, and ours is one of the largest and most comprehensive programs of its kind in the nation. All full-time day bachelor's degree candidates must complete two semesters of co-op, beginning after the first two years of study.

Wentworth's Office of Career Services assists students every step of the way, as they take advantage of opportunities in Boston, in other areas of the US, and abroad.

ACADEMICS

A leader in technology education for over a century, Wentworth offers bachelor's degrees in 17 practical, career-oriented majors. All programs center on Wentworth's distinctive three part experiential learning model, which incorporates classes, labs and studios, and co-op.

As Wentworth is a member of the Colleges of the Fenway, students can cross-register for one course each semester at the participating colleges (Emmanuel, Simmons, and Wheelock Colleges, the Massachusetts College of Art and Design, and the Massachusetts College of Pharmacy and Health Sciences University).

MAJORS & DEGREES OFFERED

Applied Mathematics (three-year program with a four-year option); Architecture Biological Engineering; Biomedical Engineering; Business Management; Civil Engineering; Computer Engineering; Computer Information Systems; Computer Networking; Computer Science; Construction Management; Electrical Engineering; Electromechanical Engineering (five-year program); Engineering-Interdisciplinary; Industrial Design; Interior Design; Mechanical Engineering

TUITION, ROOM, BOARD, FEES

Tuition for full-time students (12-20 credits) for 2016-2017 is $31,840 per year. Tuition includes the cost of a laptop computer. Laptops are provided to each student along with the specific software required for their major.

The per credit charge (less than 12 and over 20) is $995 per credit.

Room and Board is approximately $13,530 per year.

Health Insurance, required by Commonwealth of Massachusetts is $1,884 per year (can be waived if student is covered by parent's health insurance).

FINANCIAL AID

We are dedicated to helping you to create a financial plan that allows you and your family to afford a Wentworth education. In cooperation with financial aid specialists, financial services specialists can help discern how best to combine a student's financial aid package with alternative parent or student loans, as well as with Wentworth's monthly payment plan.

Approximately 85 percent of our students receive financial aid. For the fall of 2015, the average financial aid package for a first-time full time student was $16,657. A typical package is made up of a combination of grants, loans, and work-study earnings. To be considered for financial aid you must complete the Free Application for Federal Student Aid (FAFSA) as early as possible after October 1. You do not have to be an applicant for admission to complete the FAFSA. However, you must be accepted to Wentworth to receive notification of your actual financial aid award.

STUDENT ORGANIZATIONS & ACTIVITIES

Wentworth participates in 17 NCAA-sponsored varsity sports. More than twenty professional organizations operate on campus, offering unbeatable networking opportunities to students in every field. In addition, there are more than a forty-five clubs and organizations to help students make productive and fun use of their hours outside the classroom. And if students can't find what they're looking for on the Wentworth campus, they simply visit one of the five neighboring Colleges of the Fenway institutions with which the Institute is affiliated. In addition to Wentworth, the Colleges of the Fenway consist of the Massachusetts College of Art, Massachusetts College of Pharmacy, and Emmanuel, Simmons, and Wheelock Colleges.

Here's the makeup of the student body of Wentworth Institute of Technology during the 2015-2016 academic year:

4,324 students (3,902 day, 354 evening & weekend, 157 Graduate)

738 women (18.6%)

Students from Massachusetts 62%

Students from other New England states 21%

Students from New York, New Jersey, Pennsylvania 6%

Students from 29 other states and territories 3%

Students from 52 other countries 8%

1110: mean SAT score of entering class

77% of new students live in on-campus housing

NCAA Sports

Baseball (M)
Basketball (M, W)
Cross Country (M)
Golf (M)
Hockey (M)
Indoor Track (M)
Lacrosse (M, W)
Rowing (M)
Soccer (M, W)
Softball (W)
Tennis (M, W)
Volleyball (M, W)

Academic and Professional Organizations

American Institute of Architecture Students (AIAS)
American Society of Civil Engineers (ASCE)
American Society of Mechanical Engineers
American Society of Professional Estimators
Association of IT Professional Construction Management Association
Industrial Design Society of America Institute of Electrical and Electronics Engineers (IEEE)
Mechanical Contractors Association (MCA)
National Society of Black Engineers Phi Sigma Pi (Honor Society)

Society of Automotive Engineers (SAE)
Society of Hispanic Professional Engineers
Society of Manufacturing Engineers
Society of Women Engineers
Solar-Powered Vehicle Club
Student Association of Facilities Management (SAFM)
Student Association of Interior Designers (SAID)
Wentworth Architecture Club (WAC)
Wentworth Robotics Association

Student Life Organizations (partial list)

Competitive Video Gaming Club
Dance Team
Game Design Club
Longboard Club
Louise Stokes Alliance for Minority Participation (LSAMP)
Mini Baja Club
Mountain Biking Club
Multicultural Student Association (MSA)
Note-oriety (A Cappella Club)
Outdoors Club
Parkour Club
PEAK (Peer Empowerment Advocacy Krew)
Real Life (Christian Organization)
Road Cycling Club
Rugby (M,F)
Self Defense Club
Ski & Adventure Club
The Green Team (Environmental Club)
Ultimate Frisbee Club
Wentworth Events Board (WEB)
Wentworth Improvisational Theater Club (WITC)
Wentworth International Students Club (WISC)
Wentworth Internet Radio Experience (WIRE)
Wentworth Student Government (WSG)
WIT Alliance (GBLT Organization)
And many more!

ADMISSIONS PROCESS

At Wentworth, we look for students who are qualified and motivated to succeed in engineering, design, technology, and management programs. We make our admissions decisions based on: Academic achievement

Measured by official transcripts

Performance on standardized tests (SAT I or ACT)

Personal qualities, such as leadership or creativity, indicated by information in the completed application form

At Wentworth, it's our goal to assist students and their parents as much as possible as they move through the admissions process. In fact, every applicant has a regional admissions counselor they can contact directly with questions.

To apply to Wentworth, you must submit the following materials: A completed Wentworth application ($50 application fee)

Official high school transcripts

SAT I or ACT scores

A written personal statement

At least one letter of recommendation from a guidance counselor or teacher

TOEFL score, if your native language is not English

Wentworth practices rolling admissions, which means we review each completed application as soon as we receive it -so you can apply early and get a decision early.

WEST VIRGINIA WESLEYAN COLLEGE

AT A GLANCE

Find Your Voice. West Virginia Wesleyan is a private four-year co-educational residential college that is affiliated with The United Methodist Church. West Virginia Wesleyan creates a unique learning environment enabling our students to develop the skills, values, relationships, and perspective needed for them to obtain employment, enhance their careers, and demonstrate leadership throughout their lives. Wesleyan graduates are well prepared to be successful and respected citizens in a rapidly changing world. Of those reporting, 95% of Wesleyan graduates either find employment in their respective field or attend graduate school within 6 months of graduation.

Over 80 percent of Wesleyan's faculty hold the highest degree in their respective teaching field and the student faculty ratio is 14:1. The College offers over 40 majors and over 40 minors of study, and several additional Master's programs spanning Athletic Training, Business Administration, English (Creative Writing), and Nursing.

West Virginia Wesleyan is accredited by the Commission on Institutions of Higher Education of the North Central Association of Colleges and Schools, and approved by the University Senate of The United Methodist Church. It is a member of the National Association of Schools of Music and is approved by the West Virginia Department of Education and the National Council for the Accreditation of Teacher Education. The College participates in the Interstate Certification Project whereby a number of states certify teachers graduating from Wesleyan's Department of Education. The athletic training program is accredited by the Commission on Accreditation of Allied Health Education Programs. Degree programs offered in business and economics, including the Master of Business Administration program, are accredited by the International Assembly for Collegiate Business Education.

All academic programs either require or strongly encourage the completion of an internship experience. Wesleyan's academic calendar is 4-4-1 that includes an optional May Term in which students pursue unique study abroad courses or intensive study curricular offerings. The Advising and Career Center assists students with course scheduling, academic advising, internships and study abroad, resume writing, job searches, and graduate and professional school placement. The Learning Center provides tutoring services as well as comprehensive services for students with diagnosed learning disabilities.

Of the more than 1,375 undergraduate students, 53 percent are from West Virginia, while the other 47 percent originate from 39 states and 19 countries. 16 percent of Wesleyan's American students are minority students. Over 90 percent of Wesleyan's students live on-campus and the College guarantees four years of on-campus housing for all undergraduate students. Housing options include double and single rooms, suites, and apartments. Campus dining is provided and prepared by a contracted professional catering service.

LOCATION & ENVIRONMENT

Situated in the foothills of the Allegheny Mountains, Wesleyan's beautiful 100-acre campus is located in the quaint, residential town of Buckhannon, West Virginia. Buckhannon has been included in Norman Crampton's book, The Top 100 Best Small Towns in America, a Random House Publication. Many students are drawn to this personal and picturesque setting and the numerous outdoor opportunities located in close proximity to campus. The local community offers movie theatres, coffee houses, department stores, and a wide selection of local and chain restaurants. Wesleyan is a short two-hour drive from Pittsburgh, Pennsylvania, and 90 minutes from Charleston, West Virginia, the state capital.

CAMPUS FACILITIES & EQUIPMENT

Wesleyan's 23 buildings include 10 modern residence hall units, including two suite style halls renovated or newly built in the last eight years. Located in the center of campus is Wesley Chapel, which chapel serves as a focal point of campus and houses many campus events, both religious and cultural. The hub of the campus, Benedum Campus and Community Center, houses a convenience store, bookstore, swimming pool, campus radio station, student development offices, study lounges, and a cabaret-style restaurant, The Cat's Claw. The Rockefeller Physical Education Center includes a main arena that seats 3,700 spectators, an intramural gymnasium, training rooms, and an indoor astro-turf training area. The multimillion dollar Reemsnyder Research Center was opened in 2009 and boasts state of the art laboratory space for the sciences. Other vital buildings on campus include Christopher Hall of Science; Middleton Hall, which houses the Nursing Department and region-renowned simulation faciltiies; and the Lynch-Raine Administration Building. In addition, the multimillion dollar Virginia Thomas Law Center for the Performing Arts, opened in 2009, offers the most advanced performing arts facility of its kind in the region. Most recently, a brand new student wellness center was opened in 2012 along with a new multi-sport stadium project in phase one in 2015. Since 2015 more than 20 classroom spaces have been completely updated and renovated with 20+ more planned for 2016 and 2017.

Wesleyan's Annie Merner Pfeiffer Library is committed to providing high quality resources and services that empower students for advanced learning. Currently, the number of print and electronic books is nearly equal at 150,000 each, and the nearly 20,000 electronic journal titles far exceed the 300 received in print. In addition to its collections and research services, the Library offers media viewing facilities, areas for group study, and a quiet place for reading and reflection.

The entire campus has been outfitted with a ubiquitous campus-wide wireless network ensuring access to all students, faculty, and staff from all major campus buildings and every residence hall room. Network speeds are improved yearly and rival any private college in the region.

OFF-CAMPUS OPPORTUNITIES

Wesleyan encourages all students to expand their education beyond the traditional classroom. Many students have studied abroad in such places as England, Ireland, Wales, Germany, Spain, Kenya, Scotland, and Australia. Professional internships are available in the Buckhannon area, Charleston, WV, Washington, D.C.; New York, NY; Pittsburgh, PA; and other states and countries.

ACADEMICS

Wesleyan's liberal arts curriculum begins with a broad base view in a variety of core courses designed to enrich the student's whole view. The classes range from the humanities to contemporary issues and can be intermingled with the courses in the individual's major throughout the four-year program.

Wesleyan's Honors Program is offered for superior students who meet the specific requirements and demonstrate a high quality of academic excellence. Challenging, yet rewarding, classes, along with culturally enriching outings, offer Honors students a diverse and unique educational experience.

MAJORS

West Virginia Wesleyan offers four undergraduate degrees: the Bachelor of Arts; the Bachelor of Music Education; the Bachelor of Science; and the Bachelor of Science in Nursing. The most popular programs of study are in the sciences (biology, physics / engineering, pre-professional studies, etc.); education; business; athletic training; and nursing. Wesleyan also offers a number of master's degree programs.

TUITION, ROOM, BOARD, FEES

The 2016-2017 total direct costs at Wesleyan are $29, 574 for tuition, $8,436 for standard room and board, and $1,178 for student fees, which includes a student activity fee, facilities fee, and a technology fee. These costs do not include books, travel, clothing, the laptop computer, medical insurance, or other personal expenses. Wesleyan offers an interest-free monthly payment plan during the academic year.

FINANCIAL AID

The College offers financial aid on the basis of a variety of criteria: scholastic achievements, special talents and abilities, and financial need. A number of scholarships are available including awards for academics, athletics, performing arts, leadership, community service, and visual arts. Student employment is available in most areas of the College community, financed through a blend of institutional and federal funds. Students may apply for low-cost federal loans. All students should file the Free Application for Federal Student Aid. Currently, more than 95 percent of all students receive grants or scholarships from Wesleyan.

STUDENT ORGANIZATIONS & ACTIVITIES

Wesleyan has a balanced and diverse student life program that includes more than 70 campus organizations. Included among these are a campus radio station, newspaper, student government, departmental clubs, national fraternities and sororities, and religious organizations. Over 84 percent of Wesleyan students of those reporting in the NSSE survey participate in community service activities that include the complete administration of a youth basketball program to Special Olympics, to tutoring, mentoring, and educational activities to senior citizens programs to more global programs such as hurricane relief and international service trips.

Wesleyan features 21 varsity programs in NCAA Division II. Wesleyan competes in the Mountain East Conference. Our newest sports include Women's Lacrosse and Acrobatics and Tumbling.

While Wesleyan is affiliated with The United Methodist Church, students of all faiths are welcome and active. The College holds an optional weekly ecumenical worship service every Tuesday morning and a Catholic Mass each Saturday evening.

ADMISSIONS PROCESS

Students are selected by the Office of Admission on the basis of ability, interests, academic preparation, character, and promise, as indicated by their own statements on the application, as well as by high school or college records, recommendations, and standardized test results. Open without discrimination to all qualified students, the College reserves the right to refuse to admit any applicant who, because of low scholarship or citizenship record, is deemed by the Admission and Academic Standing Council to be unlikely to succeed within the standards the College seeks to maintain.

Persons wishing to be admitted directly from high school should present an application for admission with $35 fee (waived for online applications); a transcript of record from an accredited high school; and a record of either SAT or ACT scores. Applicants from non-accredited high schools or completing General Educational Development may be considered for admission if satisfactory ability and achievement are demonstrated. Students are encouraged to apply for free online (www. wvwc.edu) or via the Common Application (www.commonapp.org). Neither of these applications require a fee.

Persons seeking to transfer from another accredited college or university may be admitted to advanced standing upon presentation of an application for admission with $35 fee (waived for on-line applications); an official transcript showing all credits attempted at all post-secondary institutions previously attended; a high school transcript certifying graduation and showing courses pursued and grades earned and, if the cumulative grade point average is less than 2.5, either SAT I or ACT scores. Wesleyan will accept transfer credit courses compatible with its academic program. Grades and hours so earned shall count toward graduation. The College accepts no more than 60 semester hours of credit from a junior or community college.

Students who transfer to Wesleyan with an associate degree from a regionally accredited community or junior college may be admitted with the degree credited as fulfilling Wesleyan's general studies requirements when the total educational background, including high school record, shows compatibility with Wesleyan's general studies requirements. Deficiencies in general studies requirements, as determined by the Admission and Academic Standing Council, must be satisfied after enrollment at Wesleyan.

Wesleyan participates in the Advanced Placement Program of the College Entrance Examination Board and the International Baccalaureate Diploma Program. Students who have successfully completed AP or IB programs should contact the Office of Admission for credit transfer policies.

WESTERN STATE COLORADO UNIVERSITY

AT A GLANCE

Western State Colorado University is one of the best higher education values in the entire country. It offers world-class academics and a wide variety of programs at a very modest cost. This may be why enrollment has been up for five years in a row and why Western has been ranked one of Forbes' America's Top Colleges four years in a row.

The benefit of Western's location, academic excellence and value combine to offer students a private college experience at a public school cost. And with a student-faculty ratio of just 17 students, professors will handcraft your education to fit your interests.

LOCATION & ENVIRONMENT

Setting: rural

Campus size: 2,908 students

Geographic location: Deep in the heart of the Rocky Mountains, 200 miles west of Denver

Area facts:

Elevation: 7,700 feet

Days of sun per year: 300+

30 minutes from Crested Butte Mountain Resort

45 minutes from Monarch Mountain

10 minutes from Blue Mesa Reservoir, Colorado's largest body of water

4 miles from Hartman Rocks, a world-class mountain biking destination

Gunnison population: 5,854

- We have a backyard laboratory for fields such as Exercise Sport Science, Outdoor Recreation, Geology, Environmental Science, Biology and more.

- The location lends itself to programs like Western's Mountain Sports—trail running, mountain biking, skiing and snowboarding—run by Hall-Of-Fame mountain biker Dave Wiens. Western also has the only collegiate Mountain Rescue Team in the country.

CAMPUS FACILITIES & EQUIPMENT

University Center—As the hub of student life on campus, the recently renovated University Center houses several eating options, including Rare Air Café and Mad Jack snack and coffee shop; the university theater; Wilderness Pursuits; the Multicultural Center and the offices of several other student organizations. It also includes the mailroom and lounge space for students.

Mountaineer Field House—This 65,000 square-foot, state-of-the-art facility includes an athletic strength and conditioning room, athletic training room, batting cage, golf cage, climbing and bouldering walls, fitness center, High Altitude Performance Lab, indoor 200-meter track, in-ground trampoline and foam pit, three multi-purpose courts, a throwing cage and jump pit for field events, and more.

Quigley Hall—The building that houses our Art and Music departments, Quigley Hall just underwent renovations, including a second story addition, improved soundproofing for music rooms, new professional gallery space, and a wraparound balcony and expanded stage in the recital hall.

Wilderness Pursuits—A fully-stocked, low-cost gear rental shop and guide services available to students.

ICE Lab—A brand-new space on campus dedicated to Innovation, Creativity and Entrepreneurship (ICE). The ICE Lab contains a coffee and beer bar, fully modular workspaces, 3D printers, gigabit Internet, Colorado Small Business Development Center (CSBDC) consulting, and specialty workshops and trainings.

Housing options—married, single, co-ed, male, female, theme housing, and accessible housing for disabled students

OFF-CAMPUS OPPORTUNITIES

Career Services helps Western students and alumni create and review career-related documents: resumes, cover letters and personal statements. Additionally, the office guides students as they develop, evaluate, and implement career plans, including experiential learning opportunities, internships, volunteer experience and jobs. Career services helps students polish their interviewing skills and career-search techniques.

Career Services offers:

On-campus job interviews

Alumni network

Alumni services

Classes

Mock interviews

Graduate school preparation

Internships

Professional Development Dinner and Etiquette Seminar

ACADEMICS

Western offers more than 75 academic programs.

MAJORS

Psychology

Sociology

History

Politics & Government

Education

Business Administration

Accounting

Economics

Computer Science

Mathematics

Chemistry

Biology

Geology

Anthropology

Exercise & Sport Science

Recreation & Outdoor Education

Environment & Sustainability

Music

Art (BA/BFA)

Spanish

English

Communication Arts

Including programs in:

Criminal Justice

Resort Management

Energy Management

Wildlife Biology

Pre-Med and Pre-Nursing

Petroleum Geology

Philosophy

And many others.

TUITION, ROOM, BOARD, FEES

Value is perhaps the single biggest concern of parents and students with regard to higher education today. Western is difficult to beat in this category.

Forbes ranked Western one of the Top 100 Colleges in the West for the last four years in a row.

Both Best Value Schools and Washington Monthly ranked Western as one of their top value schools.

Western's tuition is the 3rd lowest of any four-year school in Colorado, with an in-state tuition of around six thousand dollars and out of state of just over eighteen thousand.

This often amounts to tens of thousands of dollars of savings for a bachelor's degree as compared with the vast majority of competitors.

All of this is why Western students graduate with dramatically lower student loan debt than our competitors—53% less than national average for students who borrow.

Western is truly a private school experience at a public school cost.

Tuition in-state: $6,624

Tuition out-of-state: $18,096

Room: $5,030

Board: $4,516

Fees $3,178

FINANCIAL AID

Scholarships—Merit scholarships are automatically awarded to incoming freshmen based on high school GPA and SAT/ACT scores. Additional merit based scholarships are available through private donors within the university and by students' majors.

Tuition Discount Programs—Western Undergraduate Exchange and Central Plains Program are for out-of-state students who do not qualify for a merit scholarship; they will be charged 150% of in-state tuition. States eligible are: Alaska, Arizona, California, Hawaii, Idaho, Montana, Nevada, New Mexico, North Dakota, Oregon, South Dakota, Utah, Washington, Wyoming, Illinois, Indiana, Iowa, Kansas, Michigan, Minnesota, Missouri, Nebraska, Oklahoma, Texas, Wisconsin. The Neighboring States Program allows students with a permanent address in Arizona, Kansas, Nebraska, New Mexico, Oklahoma, Utah, or Wyoming to be automatically considered for a $1,000 per-year grant. The College Opportunity Fund is for full-time undergraduate, in-state students. It provides a per-credit hour stipend to reduce the cost of tuition. The stipend varies every year; for 2015-16 it was $75 per credit hour.

STUDENT ORGANIZATIONS & ACTIVITIES

With about 98% of undergraduate students living in residence halls or nearby in Gunnison, campus is a bustling center of student life. Whether students become involved in growing local food in one of the campus greenhouses, join the only collegiate mountain rescue team in the country or take part in any of the other 50+ clubs and organizations on campus, there's always something to do.

Men's NCAA sports: basketball, cross country, football, track & field, wrestling

Women's NCAA sports: basketball, cross country, soccer, swimming & diving, track & field, volleyball

Mountain Sports: nordic skiing, alpine ski racing, freeride skiing & snowboarding, freestyle skiing & snowboarding, ski mountaineering, mountain biking, trail running

Club sports: baseball, boxing, ice hockey, lacrosse, rugby, soccer, swimming

Intramural sports: slow-pitch softball, flag football, ultimate frisbee, kickball, bubble ball soccer, indoor soccer, floor hockey, pickleball, inner-tube water polo, dodgeball, volleyball, basketball, ping-pong and billiards

Student organizations: (59)

Clubs: Active Minds, Anthropology Club, Archery, Art League, Association for Students of Exercise & Sport Science, Chemistry Club, Christian Challenge, Circle K International (Student Service Club), Frisbee Golf (18-hole course), Geology Club, Ignite (Campus Crusades for Christ), KWSB Radio, Mana Nigame Video Game Club, Mountain Rescue Team, Mountaineers Disc Golf Club, Moutaineer Media, Music—Ensemble, Music—Instrumentals, National Association for Music Education, Newman Club, Organics Guild, Pathfinder Magazine, Peak Productions, Politics Club, Pre-Health Club, Program Council, Psychology Club, Republican Party Club, Sexual Assault Prevention Advocates, Sociology Club, Spectrum (Gay & Straight Alliance), Student Government Association, Sustainability Coalition, Top 'o the World (Weekly Newspaper) Urban Gaming, Western Association of Professional Landmen, Westerners—West Elk Wranglers, Whitewater Club, Wildlife Society, WordHorde (English Club)

Honor Societies: Omicron Delta Kappa—Leadership, Alpha Kappa Delta—Sociology, Gamma Chapter of Tri Beta—Biology; Lambda Alpha—Anthropology; Phi Alpha Theta—History; Pi Sigma Alpha—Political Science; Psi Chi—Psychology; Sigma Tau Delta—English

Multicultural organizations: Amigos, Asian Pacific Islanders Club, Black Student Alliance, Native American Student Council

Demographics:

Total undergraduate enrollment—2,419

Out of State: 31%

Full time: 78%

Part time: 22%

Female: 45%

Male: 55%

ADMISSIONS PROCESS

of Applicants: 2246

Acceptance rate: 92%

Average HS GPA: 3.20

Deadline: June 1 for scholarship consideration, rolling-deadline application process

Other admission factors: Academic rigor of secondary school record, class rank, academic GPA, standardized test scores, non-academic extracurricular activities, talent and ability, character and personal qualities, first-generation status, alumni relation

Additional information:

Campus-wide Internet network

Email and web access available

100% of classrooms equipped with wireless Internet

19 computer labs/classrooms, including one 24-hour computer lab

Average number of computers per lab: 15

Online class registration available

No requirement for undergraduates to own a personal computer

75% of undergraduates own a personal computer

Webcasting, digital audio or video-streaming of campus radio

WORCESTER POLYTECHNIC INSTITUTE

AT A GLANCE

Here, you don't just learn—you do. Everything about WPI is designed to stimulate your curiosity, challenge you, and support you so that you can imagine anything and innovate everything.

Worcester Polytechnic Institute (WPI) is a nationally renowned, private research university college focused on science, technology, engineering, and math. WPI's founding motto of "Theory and Practice" provides a distinctive approach to education by balancing rigorous academics with hands-on learning. At WPI, students go above and beyond traditional classroom education. Here, you don't just learn—you do. Everything about WPI is designed to stimulate your curiosity, challenge you, and support you so that you can imagine anything and innovate everything.

WPI's unique project-based education converts classroom concepts into real-world impact. The WPI Plan (wpi.edu/wpi-plan) will set you apart in the world first as a student, then as a sought-after young professional, and ultimately across your career and life. In 1970, the WPI Plan was a bold experiment. Today, it's a proven and highly effective model for undergraduate learning that's both adaptable and rigorous.

All WPI students complete two projects that allow them to tackle issues they feel passionate about and make a lasting difference on the world around us from improving access to clean water in rural communities to developing robots for underwater research. Through the Plan, you learn how to learn by applying your classroom experiences to projects that challenge you from a proficiency, social, and global perspective.

WPI was recently ranked No. 1 by the Wall Street Journal for "The Top Faculties; Schools that do the Best in Combining Scholarly Research with Classroom Instruction" and consistently receives high rankings as one of America's Best Colleges, according to the U.S. News & World Report. The university has earned praise and attention for its project-based curriculum, small class sizes, robust career services, study-abroad opportunities, return on investment, and ability to create futures. These results are typical at WPI. The education you get here is anything but. Find out more at wpi.edu/+formula.

LOCATION & ENVIRONMENT

Founded in 1865, WPI's 95-acre campus is located in a residential area of Worcester (Wus-tah), Massachusetts, the second largest city in New England behind only Boston. With its beautiful architecture, green spaces and ivy-covered walls, WPI has a classic New England feel. Ranked ninth on Forbes' "America's Most Livable Cities," the up-and-coming city offers the charm and ease of a college town with the convenience of urban living.

ACADEMICS

WPI's academic program is built to be flexible. Students take the equivalent of three courses (as courses or project work) during each of four 7-week terms (two in the fall and two in the spring). As part of the WPI Plan, you have the freedom and the responsibility to choose the courses and experiences that best suit your goals and interests.

In addition, WPI does not have failing grades, in order for the focus to be on learning, teamwork, and collaboration, not on competing. You earn A, B, C, or NR (No Record). This unique grading system encourages you to branch out, experiment, and cross disciplines- that's where amazing things happen at WPI, and ultimately, in your career.

Ranked No. 1 as the best study abroad program by Princeton Review in 2016 and referred to as "life changing," over 65 percent of WPI students travel to more than 40 off-campus locations. Students make a difference to communities and organizations around the globe by bringing ingenious approaches to an astounding array of societal and technological challenges. Past projects have included the creation of an ambulance dispatch system for the city of Venice and improvements on earthquake mitigation and recovery efforts in Taipei.

MAJORS & DEGREES OFFERED

WPI offers over 50 areas of study in engineering, science, management, and the liberal arts leading to the Bachelor of Science (B.S.) or Bachelor of Arts (B.A.) degree. Exciting interdisciplinary programs, driven by real-world demand, include interactive media and game development, environmental engineering, architectural engineering, and the nation's first undergraduate program in robotics engineering.

WPI offers pre-professional programs (law, medicine, dentistry, and veterinary) and a fourplus five-year BS/MS program. You can even create your own major or minor program and go out on co-op. A comprehensive academic advising program and a wide array of academic support services help students make the right choices and reach their goals.

TUITION, ROOM, BOARD, FEES

A great education costs a lot of money—so you should make sure to attend a university that delivers the return on your investment. WPI graduates have 32% higher starting salaries than the national average, and graduates are able to move quickly up the ranks to positions of influence as a result of WPI's real-world training.

Top-tier employers seek out WPI graduates for their real-world experience and ability to work collaboratively. With more than 92 percent of graduates in jobs or attending graduate school within several months of graduation, students are recruited by leading organizations such as Pfizer, General Electric, Fidelity Investments, Tesla, and Google. Each year, WPI graduates are accepted at many prestigious graduate schools, including MIT, Yale University, Princeton University, Johns Hopkins University and Tufts University Medical School.

FINANCIAL AID

All admitted applicants are considered for merit-based scholarships based upon academic performance, leadership, extracurricular involvement and community service—and there is no separate application required. Students can also indicate they wish to be considered for need-based aid. Around 97 percent of WPI students receive merit or need-based aid to attend the university, not including federal aid. Most applicants will receive a financial aid package within two weeks of their acceptance.

Scholarships vary in amounts, but typically range between $10,000 and $25,000, and are renewable for four years. Valedictorians and Salutatorians are guaranteed a minimum scholarship of $20,000.

Students are required to file the FAFSA and CSS Profile no later than February 1. It is best to file on or near the application deadline. By filing early, you will receive notification of your aid much sooner, allowing you to make informed decisions.

WPI boasts a 98.1% loan repayment rate, far above the national average of 88.7%—showing that WPI graduates earn strong salaries and are able to pay off their loans and live the life they want.

STUDENT ORGANIZATIONS & ACTIVITIES

The WPI community is welcoming, close-knit, with a robust support system ready to help academically, emotionally, physically, and culturally. The university prioritizes inclusiveness and acceptance.

The student community of innovators and explorers that thrive here make their own decisions and set their own course, want to be leaders and not followers, are eager to tackle the issues that will make the world a better place, work in teams to get things done and love math and science but feel just as passionate about other subjects.

There's lots to do here at WPI and in the surrounding Worcester area to complement the skills you gain from the classroom with many different academic, professional, social, and athletic organizations. You can volunteer your time at a number of local nonprofit organizations, join a fraternity or sorority, offer your talents to over 200 student life groups, such as an a cappella group or theatre production, or channel your inner Saturday Night Live performer and participate in a sketch comedy group, and that's just the beginning.

Twenty varsity sports, and 44 club sports and intramural teams are sponsored by WPI, supporting a wide range of athletic interests and abilities. In addition, WPI's Sports & Recreation Center, opened in 2013, is one of the finest higher education athletic facilities in the Northeast, as well as one of the greenest sports centers in the nation.

ADMISSIONS PROCESS

WPI is a member of the Common Application, the exclusive method by which to apply to WPI. A $65 application fee is required for all applicants. (WPI endorses the fee waiver policy of the College Board, as well as accepts fee waivers from guidance or college counselors.) Seniors in high school should interview before December 15th of their senior year. Interviews are optional but are highly encouraged.

WPI is test-optional; SAT/ACT scores are accepted, but not required. Academic requirements include four years of math (including pre-calculus), four years of English, and two years of lab science.

Other requirements include:

- High school transcript including most recent senior grades
- Teacher recommendation (preferably in math or science)
- Guidance counselor recommendation
- Personal essay
- TOEFL, IELTS, or Pearson Exam scores for international students whose first language is not English

INDEXES

ALPHABETICAL INDEX

The Princeton Review's Complete Book of Colleges

The Princeton Review's Complete Book of Colleges

INDEX BY LOCATION

INTERNATIONAL

INDEX BY SIZE

1,000—2,000 STUDENTS

2,000—5,000 STUDENTS

5,000—10,000 STUDENTS

The University of Memphis	746
University of Mississippi	752
University of Nebraska—Lincoln	759
University of Nevada, Las Vegas	760
University of New Mexico	763
The University of North Carolina at Chapel Hill	766
University of North Carolina at Charlotte	767
The University of North Carolina at Greensboro	767
University of North Georgia	771
University of Oklahoma	775
University of Oregon	776
University of Pittsburgh— Pittsburgh Campus	782
University of Southern California	798
University of Tennessee, Knoxville	805
The University of Texas at Dallas	807
The University of Texas at San Antonio	808
University of Texas—El Paso	809
University of Utah	812
University of Virginia	814
University of Wisconsin—Milwaukee	822
Utah State University	830
Virginia Commonwealth University	837
Washington State University	851
Wayne State University	854
Weber State University	857
Western Michigan University	869
West Virginia University	864

OVER 25,000 STUDENTS

American Public University System	25
Arizona State University at the Tempe campus	35
Brigham Young University (UT)	91
California State University, Fullerton	107
California State University, Long Beach	108
California State University, Northridge	110
California State University, Sacramento	111
Excelsior College	238
Florida International University	249
Florida State University	250
Indiana University Bloomington	319
Iowa State University	327
Kennesaw State University	343
Michigan State University	418
New York University	462, 1006
Northern Arizona University	471
The Ohio State University—Columbus	487
Pennsylvania State University University Park	513
Purdue University—West Lafayette	530

Rutgers, The State University of New Jersey— New Brunswick	560
San Diego State University	579, 1034
San Jose State University	581
Temple University	659, 1062
Texas A&M University at Galveston	661
Texas A&M University—College Station	662
Texas State University	665
Texas Tech University	666
The University of Alabama—Tuscaloosa	691
University of Arizona	693
University of California, Berkeley	698
University of California, Davis	698
University of California, Irvine	699
University of California, Los Angeles	700
University of California, San Diego	702
University of Central Florida	705, 1070
University of Colorado Boulder	711
University of Florida	718
University of Georgia	719
University of Houston	723
University of Illinois at Urbana-Champaign	727
University of Maryland, College Park	742
University of Michigan—Ann Arbor	747
University of Minnesota— Twin Cities Campus	751
University of Missouri	753
University of North Texas	772
University of Phoenix	779
University of South Carolina—Columbia	796
University of South Florida	797
The University of Texas at Arlington	806
The University of Texas at Austin	806
University of Washington	815
University of Wisconsin—Madison	821
Virginia Tech	839

Notes

Notes